The HAMMOND ALMANAC

of a million facts records forecasts

1981

Martin A. Bacheller, Editor in Chief

Hammond Almanac, Inc.

Maplewood, N. J. 07040

CONTENTS

THE FUTURE

A special report prepared for the Hammond Almanac by the staff of the World Future Society.

Focus on what's been happening in the Communications Revolution and what the future holds for —

- **Television**
- **Videotapes and Videodiscs**
- **Microcomputers**
- **New Ways to Play Post Office**
- **Telephones**
- **The Electronic Newspaper and Instant Information**
- **Robots and the Automated Factory**
- **Work and Careers**
- **The Automated Office**
- **Home of the Future**
- **The Information Society in the Early 21st Century**

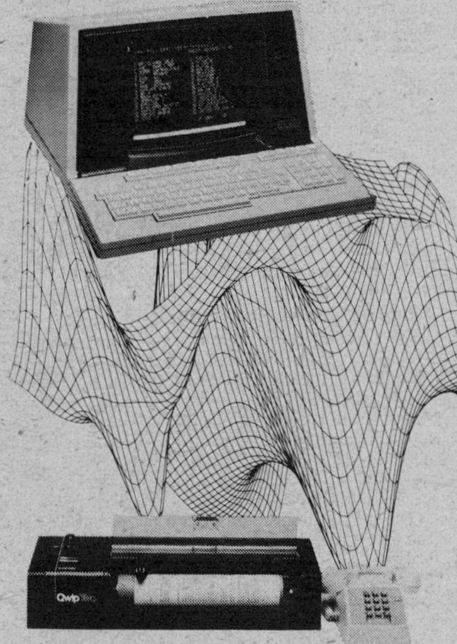

Above: *NCR computer terminal and Qwip desk facsimile unit; computer graphics design from* Computer Graphics: 118 Computer-Generated Designs, *Dover Publications.*

The World Future Society is a nonprofit, nonpartisan association of scholars, scientists and others interested in forecasts of what may happen in technology, society, human values and other fields during the coming years. The Society's headquarters are at 4916 St. Elmo Avenue, Washington, D.C. 20014.

The Information Society:
Communications and Computers

by **Edward Cornish**

President of the
World Future Society
Washington, D.C.

Of all the flood of new technological developments destined to impinge on human life during the 1980s, those in communications and computers promise to be the most revolutionary in their consequences. We must anticipate a genuine transformation in the nature of human work, play, education and other aspects of society.

Over the past century and a half, inventions in telecommunications — starting with the telegraph in the 1830s — have, of course, changed our lives in many, many ways. What is remarkable about the 1980s is that during a short 10-year period a staggering amount of new equipment is expected to move into homes, offices and factories.

What is Information?

Computers as well as communications have a long history, at least if the computer is defined broadly as a device for storing and processing information. Nature developed computers — that is, protoplasmic brains — billions of years ago. The human brain, which appeared approximately two million years ago, represented a major advance in the development of the "wet computers." Almost unquestionably the development of the human brain was accompanied by the rapid development of human languages — a major breakthrough in communications. Thanks to his powerful computer and communications abilities, man became the dominant animal on the earth.

The next really great advance in communications did not occur until about 5,000 years ago with the invention of writing. Writing made it possible to encapsulate information and transmit it great distances in both time and space. It was now possible to store information outside of the human brain. In addition, information could be carried thousands of miles and be absorbed by another brain in some distant location. To be sure, the method of transmitting the message was slow: a messenger proceeding on foot, horseback, or boat. Still, the communications system — primitive as it seems by modern standards — enabled the Roman emperors to govern vast territories extending from Britain to Egypt. Down through the ages, stupendous efforts were exerted to develop rapid communications. In the 1400s, the Incas had a system which employed messengers who ran relays of about a mile each, enabling a message to travel across the Inca kingdom at the rate of about 150 miles per day. There was no really significant improvement on this method until the 19th century, when the first electronic method of communication — the telegraph — made its appearance. The last gasp of pre-electronic telecommunications systems was the Pony Express, organized by the U.S. Government to carry the mail swiftly on horseback from St. Joseph, Missouri, to the Pacific Coast. Started in 1860, it lasted only 16 months but made an indelible impression on American consciousness. The "ponies" — actually fleet American horses — were stationed at "stages" from 10 to 15 miles apart along the 1,966-mile route. Each rider rode three animals successively, covering at least 33 miles before passing the pouch to the next rider. The fastest trip took seven days and 17 hours, but the regular schedule was 10 days — hardly better than the Incas' system.

The telegraph, soon to be followed by the telephone, made communications virtually instantaneous over hundreds, even thousands of miles. Until 1866 the new communication stopped at the water's edge. Though the news of Lincoln's assassination could be transmitted by telegraph instantaneously to California 3,000 miles away, it could not cover a similar distance across the Atlantic. As a result, news of Lincoln's assassination took 12 days to reach London.

By the late 19th century, transoceanic cables were playing an important role in world communications. In 1895 Marconi invented the wireless telegraph and by 1907 Lee De Forest had perfected the vacuum tube that made it possible to transmit the human voice through the air electronically. However, it was not until the 1920s that radio became the mass communications medium that broadcasting is today. President Hoover made use of radio. Roosevelt became famous for his "fireside chats," heard all over the country by people clustering around their radios. Motion pictures, which had evolved from the nickelodeon into the great silent pictures of the 1920s, began to talk in the early 1930s and were acquiring color by the end of the decade. Television, demonstrated experimentally as early as 1929, did not enter U.S. homes until after World War II. During the 1950s, television swept into homes at a stupendous rate: In 1950 less than 10 percent of American homes had television; by 1960 more than 90 percent of the nation's households had television.

The First Computers

While radio and television were moving into modern consciousness, there were developments elsewhere that seemed initially to have little bearing on mass communications. Large businesses and governments had vast amounts of information that they needed to handle more economically and more swiftly. One approach led to the development of punched cards which could be manipulated mechanically by machines operating at great speed. Such devices made it possible to retrieve information more economically and at a faster rate. But perhaps the biggest impetus to the development of rapid data-handling systems came from the U.S. military, which was trying to do such things as aim missiles over long distances. For many military applications, human mathematicians operating with paper, pencil and a mechanical desk calculator could not perform

the necessary calculations quickly enough. The military allocated funds for the development of electronic calculators, which eventually became known as computers.

The experimental computers of the late 1940s and early 1950s were very large, often occupying a good-sized room, and were monstrously expensive. Furthermore they were extremely stupid by the standards of today's computers. However, these early electronic calculating devices demonstrated in a crude fashion their great potential. The capability of computers to manipulate data increased dramatically; equally dramatic was the decrease in the cost of their doing so. At first it seemed that only a few organizations could use computers — large government agencies such as the Census Bureau, for example. It also seemed as if computer technology could be used for only a relatively few purposes, such as solving certain types of mathematical equations rapidly. But as people gained more and more experience with the new technology, the electronic "brains" showed they could be made to perform a fantastic number of tasks. Furthermore, researchers found ways to shrink the size of computers; eventually the power of one of the room-sized computers could be placed in a small silicon wafer, or "chip," no bigger than a fingernail!

And a funny thing began to happen: The computers began to "talk" to each other and to human beings by means of telephone lines. At the same time the telephone companies began to find computers increasingly useful for keeping track of long-distance communications. So the barriers that once seemed to separate communications and computers into two entirely separate fields began to break down. By the early 1970s U.S. officials were in a serious quandary because the Communications Act of 1934 authorized the Federal Communications Commission to regulate electronic communications, but the Commission found it virtually impossible to find a legal formula that clearly distinguished between communications and data processing. Technology had made obsolete the laws that were designed to regulate it.

Reducing Information to Bits

One reason for the convergence of communication and computer technologies is that both have tended more toward "digital" processes. Any kind of information — a telephone conversation, a book, a television program — can be coded and transmitted in the form of binary digits, or "yes-no" signals. It may take very large numbers of such bits, transmitted at very high speeds, to do the job.

A "bit" is the smallest amount of information that can be transmitted. It offers a single unit of information, such as a "yes" or "no" answer. A bit may be likened to a light bulb which can transmit a signal to an observer by being either on or off at a particular moment. It cannot be partly on and partly off to show gradations of an answer. The human body also operates on a binary basis; that is, a neuron may be either conducting an electrical impulse or not conducting it. The neuron is either "on" or "off." The great advantage of the binary system is that the "bits" can be manipulated easily, because each is a discrete item and errors are less likely to creep in. It is much easier to tell if a light is on or off than to tell just how bright it is. Yet the tiny "bits" of information can be made to convey any amount of information. For example, the picture we see reproduced in a newspaper is composed of tiny areas of light and dark. Similarly a television screen image is composed of tiny dots of glowing phosphor light. The most complex picture can be broken down into small segments either lighted or not lighted which then can be transcribed into a series of simple yes-no electronic signals.

With digitalization, almost any sort of communication can be translated into common form and put into almost any type of information storage or system of transmission, switching, processing and display. A medieval manuscript, a map of the United States, an episode of "Mork and Mindy," a scientific journal or a tape recording of a poet reading his works could all be transmitted on the same wavelength or cable and stored on the same magnetic tape until needed.

The convergence of communications and computers may be viewed as natural in that both are dealing with information. Computers store and manipulate information; communication systems transmit the information from one point to another.

The telecommunications field took a giant step with the development of orbiting satellites and sophisticated space-race electronic gear. Suddenly it was economically feasible to send signals anywhere in the world — to the remotest island, jungle or desert outpost. Though the telecommunications field may not be moving quite so rapidly as microcomputers, the total size of the industry is awesome. Hugh Collins, Director of Communications Studies and Planning Ltd., in London, says the worldwide telecommunications network "is already arguably the largest machine in the world," consisting of a network of some 440 million telephones, 1.2 million telex terminals, data networks and other special-purpose transmission systems. And that is only where things stood in 1980; during the next few years the telecommunications network is expected to expand enormously.

The importance of information is hard to overstate; we use information as the basis for all our actions. If we have the correct information, we can reach our goals quickly and easily. Information can literally move mountains; a radio signal is often used to touch off explosives. Better communications offer the hope of solving problems in energy, food, water, politics and in many other areas.

The Computer Revolution

Since the invention of the telegraph, communications have improved at a steadily increasing pace. The escalating improvement in communications is now awesome — especially in the area of computers. Musing on microcomputers, Stanford University economist Edward Steinmuller has been quoted as saying: "If the airlines had progressed as rapidly as this technology, the Concorde would be carrying half a million passengers at 20 million miles an hour for less than a penny apiece!"

A writer in the *Washington Star* went even further:

Had the automobile developed at a pace equivalent to that of the computer during the past 20 years, today a Rolls Royce would cost less than $3, get three million miles to the gallon, deliver enough power to drive the *Queen Elizabeth II* and six of them would fit on the head of a pin!

Such statements may seem to be mere hyperbole, but the microcomputer revolution has awed even its proponents. One writer, Adam Osborne, titled his book *Running Wild*, since, he says, that is what microcomputers are doing. Neither government nor big business has the power to halt the racing advance of the silicon chip.

Impact

The impact of the communications revolution is and will continue to be pervasive, unsettling, subtle and mysterious. The new technologies in communications and computers — sometimes abbreviated to *compunications* — are expected to change the way we do our shopping, work, learn, amuse ourselves, and even the way we practice our religion. The new technologies will help us to save energy, prevent crime, drive more safely, do more of our work at home and take the agony — at least a lot of it — out of preparing our income tax returns. On the other hand, the compunications revolution may make obsolete a lot of jobs, lead to a lot of white-collar computer crimes and electronic cheating, and perhaps take away a lot of our privacy.

The information revolution may also change our present views of mankind. Down through the centuries man has taken pride in his knowledge, even giving himself the name *Homo sapiens*, or "knowing man." But already some computers are smarter than human beings — at least in some respects. In 1980 human and computer chess players squared off at a the National Conference on Artificial Intelligence, held at Stanford University in Palo Alto, California. Paul Benjamin, an expert-ranked chess player from New York City, won one game from a computer but lost a second. An exhausted Benjamin congratulated his opponent for its "brilliant tactical" play. "I was definitely inferior."

Television: Good News for Viewers
Plus Some Lingering Questions

Coming up on television screens everywhere is a lot of good news: viewers will have a much wider range of choice than they had during the 1970s. In addition, more and more viewers will have an opportunity to "talk back" to their sets — expressing their views on public issues, ordering merchandise they see in commercials or simply expressing their approval (or disapproval) of the program they have just watched.

Making it all possible is a proliferating technology which, combined with more permissive governmental regulations and strong economic incentives, makes possible increasingly powerful satellites, the steady growth and spread of cable television networks and interactive television.

Cable TV

Cable television, which grew slowly during the 1960s and 70s, is now taking a major leap forward. According to some projections it could reach as many as 30 percent of U.S. households by the end of 1981. Cable is proving to be something that people are willing to pay for today even though the offerings are still far below the potential. And as more viewers hook into the networks, more and more material becomes available.

Cable TV began in 1949, when a local radio dealer in an Appalachian Mountain village recognized that the mountains were spoiling the reception of TV signals from Philadelphia. To improve sales of sets, he set up a tall antenna on a mountain where reception was good and ran cable from the antenna into the homes of people willing to pay a small fee; cable television was born.

Every year since its inception, the number of cable TV subscribers has steadily increased, despite government regulations and lobbying by the networks during the 1950s and 60s. By 1978, cable television had reached about 10 million homes. By the end of the 1980s, probably a majority of all U.S. homes will be on the cable.

The significance of cable television is not just that it improves reception in areas where it might otherwise be poor. The same cable that brings in broadcast signals from afar can also be used to send into the home other programs that are not broadcast to the public at large but created solely for the cable subscriber.

Cable television also provides an opportunity for viewers to pay directly for what they are watching and therefore see programs unavailable on commercial broadcasts. One pay-television service, Home Box Office, now delivers first-run motion pictures, sports events, children's films, etc., to subscribers who pay a fee for the service. Similar subscriber television fare can now be delivered by satellite to remote areas where cable or microwave towers cannot easily be built.

The use of satellites to send programs to cable television networks has provided an opportunity for a new type of piracy. Some people now buy a microwave antenna, which can now be purchased for a few hundred dollars, to capture the signal sent out by the satellites and watch the program on their own television sets without paying the cable television company anything. The cable television networks and producers are,

understandably, upset at the loss of revenues. The Subscription Television Association has already taken some "pirates" to court, but the legal issues remain unresolved. Possibly technology will solve the dilemma: signals can be coded so they require a decoding device to receive them.

Participatory TV

Cable television has the potential to convert into interactive television, making it possible for the subscriber to communicate with the cable TV station. For instance, if a local cable TV station were to broadcast a city council meeting, it would be possible through the cable for the citizenry to express its views on various issues that the council was deliberating.

So far, the possibilities of interactive television — that is, television that allows the viewer to respond in a wide variety of ways to things seen on his television set — is more of a possibility than an actuality. But experiments are underway in many countries now, and the early results are extremely promising. The possibilities of the new interactive technology seem to be limited only by one's imagination. The television set has the capacity of changing, at the user's will, into an electronic school, a post office, a bank, a stockbroker's office, a supermarket or a library with practically unlimited resources. To get the services provided by these institutions, a user would simply have to press a few buttons on a keyboard. For instance, if he wanted to know what the local supermarket was offering as specials that week, he could request that information, and after it appeared on his television screen, proceed to order his groceries by pushing some buttons. In addition it will be possible soon for funds to be transferred electronically from his

Harris Corp.

Dish antenna used to pick up television signals sent to earth from orbiting satellites.

bank account to the store along with the purchase. (Paying bills by telephone is already gaining in acceptance.)

In Columbus, Ohio, the Warner Cable Corporation, a division of Warner Communications, introduced a two-way television system in 1977. The system now has thousands of subscribers who can order a wide variety of goods and services merely by pushing a button after they have viewed the products on their television screens. A Columbus book store chain is already taking orders with this system. A magazine is using the system to find out what covers are most attractive to readers. Viewers of the system, known as QUBE (pronounced cube), are already using it to express their opinions of political candidates or questions of national importance. For subscribers who own a home computer terminal, the cable service will provide daily newspaper columns, detailed stock and bond information, computer games; the cost — $5 an hour.

Cable television — connected to homes because residents want more entertainment, opens the way for a variety of services. Reaching beyond the television set, Warner is now offering subscribers a security system, consisting of a burglar alarm, a fire alarm and a medical alert system. The burglar and fire alarm systems are connected to touch and infrared sensors and smoke and heat detectors. The medical alert system consists either of buttons placed strategically around the home or of small transmitting devices the size of a silver dollar which a person can carry. When a signal comes from one of these devices, the computer will send out an alert along with pertinent medical data.

The menu for potential services is almost limitless, but unsolved is the question of how many "extras" will people pay money for. Also to be resolved is who will deliver the new TV services which are still in experimental stage. Both the cable TV people and AT&T's new "communication service" division will be competing for subscribers.

"Narrow-casting"

As cable television and other new technologies increase the diversity of programs available to viewers, broadcasters may turn to "narrow-casting." The rapidly increasing diversity of offerings may result in more and more people deserting the mass-audience networks. Specialized television programs will come into their own, and anyone who wants comedy or ethnic programming or classical drama will be able to choose among a far greater variety of programs than is possible today. It will be possible for an opera lover to watch operas every evening; a basketball fan to have plenty of basketball fare, including many games that today would never appear on television; and a physician to receive medical programs all day. The time may come when broadcasters no longer can count on reaching huge audiences that gather around their sets to watch special network programs.

Large Screens, Stereo and 3-D TV

During the 1970s, television projectors which produce life-size images on a screen measuring 12 feet across began to penetrate U.S. markets. Some restaurants and bars found them useful to insure patronage on Monday evenings when customers would gather around to watch football games. Hospitals and medical schools found the same equipment useful for demonstrating operations to students. But perhaps the biggest market of all proved to be well-to-do citizens who wanted the "large-screen experience." As prices drop, large-screen television is expected to become more and more popular.

The addition of a second television audio channel makes it possible for home viewers to receive stereophonic or bilingual broadcasts. High-fi stereo TV is expected to be entering U.S. homes during the early 1980s. Stereo TV systems are already in about one half of the television homes in Japan and are selling at about a rate of 100,000 per month. The additional channel adds about $150 to $300 to the

Viewdata Corp. of America, Inc.

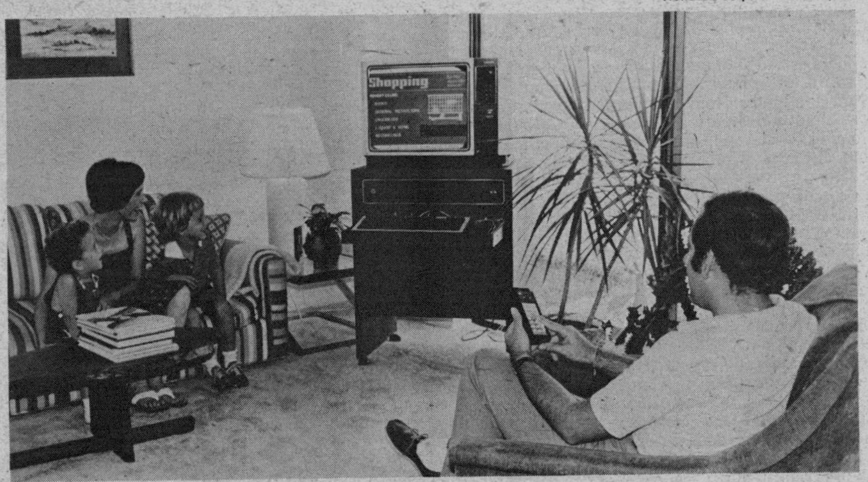

Family looking at advertising on a TV computer terminal in their home. Viewers will be able to order goods they see on the screen by typing messages into the terminal.

price of a receiver; so far the industry has not moved rapidly to upgrade audio reproduction because it would substantially raise the cost of program production and transmission. However, the industry is beginning to respond to the competitive threat of such new technologies as the videodisc as well as the need for a fuller sound in the new large-screen receivers.

Experiments with three-dimensional television have been going on for decades, but a commercially viable system seems unlikely to appear during the early 1980s. However, experiments seem to suggest that 3-D TV will eventually be realized, perhaps within the next 20 years. Current experiments include the use of holography, which is a way of taking a 3-dimensional picture. Making holographic images of moving scenes is difficult, but some short holographic movies have already been made. Engineers are continuing to explore the possibilities, and it seems likely that they will eventually succeed.

Another new wrinkle in television is a set with an advanced microcomputer built in, making it possible for the viewer to see nine channels at once on a single screen. This means that he can scan the other channels during a commercial break and decide whether to switch channels or not.

For better or worse, television is continuing to expand its way across the world. In February 1980, Libya temporarily replaced the United States as the largest overseas market for Japan's color television sets, according to the Electronics Industries Association of Japan. The Association also reports that Japan's total color exports during 1980 have been running about one third higher than the year before. All over the world, people are rushing to get color television sets as fast as their budgets allow. In Israel many people have bought color television sets even though there was nothing in color for them to watch. The color TV set had become a status symbol and a way to escape inflation.

The Influence of Television

No one doubts that television has had pervasive and intense influence on America. The "boob tube" or "one-eyed monster" directly influences the average child for many more hours than do the schools. A typical American schoolchild graduates from high school having spent about 11,000 hours in school and 15,000 in front of a television set. Some physicians report that children who are heavy television viewers are aggressive, easily distracted and lacking in imagination and reading ability. Heavy viewers are the pupils who can't sit still and listen to a story without squirming but calm down immediately and sit motionless when a television screen is placed before them.

Many educators believe that people who watch television habitually seem to lose the ability to remain engaged in one subject or to pay attention to a single topic for any length of time. Television's quick cuts and fast action "condition the brain to change but not to continuity of thought," says Kate Moody, author of *Growing Up On Television*. "If there is not enough flash-and-dash on one station, the viewer flips to another and further interrupts any continuity of thinking."

The hundreds of thousands of commercials broadcast to the American people each year provide an advertising world of fantasies, dreams, myths — and products that offer immediate solutions to all of life's dull and frustrating realities. Since Americans now are conditioned to believe that relief from all of life's agonies is only a purchase away, Americans will spend three to ten times more for a heavily advertised brand name than for an identical but less well-known brand. The television commercial is the stuff of dreams. It offers viewers youth, vibrancy, attractiveness, headache-free days, shiny floors, family happiness, parties, picnics, successful sporting events, intimate moments and enough smiles to last a dozen lifetimes. The entire myth comes beautifully wrapped in wrinkle-free plastic from a tropical island where worry and reality never intrude. By the time the average child in America reaches graduation he has seen more than 350,000 commercials — enough to thoroughly offset any sermons heard from the pulpit or lectures from parents and teachers.

Many educators have hoped to "tame" television by converting it into "educational television." The largest use of educational television is perhaps Britain's Open University, where thousands of students receive lectures at home via television (and radio). The students are mailed reading matter and homework assignments, which they return later by mail. Elsewhere television has been used successfully to teach all kinds of courses both to the general public and in university or school classrooms. At its best, television can be a superb teacher, as even its severest critics concede. The Alistair Cooke *America* series brought history to life in an extraordinarily vivid way, as have many of the Masterpiece Theatre dramas. At the other extreme are many programs that observers feel are likely to "turn a viewer's mind into oatmeal" or into a hypnotically controlled robot capable of making no decision more complicated than selecting the sponsor's product at the supermarket. In the broadest sense, as notes Nicholas Johnson, a former member of the Federal Communications Commission, "All television is educational television. The question is: What is it teaching?"

Telepornography

Subscribers to the British Electronic information system, Prestel, were recently given the possibility of accessing a "Dirty Books Guide" which was, by all accounts rather complete. The incident upset Sir William Barlow, (Chairman of the British Post Office, which operates Prestel) and led a member of Parliament to sponsor a special Act covering "indecent displays" on viewdata systems.

Too much #%$?A$ on citizens band radio?

The sudden slump of CB radio sales in the late seventies is attributed in some quarters to the language of some CB users. Perhaps an answer to the bad-language problem has been found by the makers of CB Simulator, an electronic game that allows players to talk to each other as if they were on CB radio. The game has a "PornoTrap," which detects the use of obscenities, admonishes an offending player and posts a warning on the electronic bulletin board.

Videotapes and Videodiscs

Sales of videocassette recorders (VCRs) were expected to reach a new record in 1980 — something approaching 800,000 units, according to one industry estimate. This would represent a continuation of the sharply rising sales recorded during the 1970s; in 1979, 475,000 units were sold. Starting in 1981, sales of VCRs may go over the million mark. Despite the upsurge in sales, only about 1 percent or 2 percent of U.S. homes now have videocassette recorders. But that situation is expected to change drastically during the next few years. By 1990 a majority of U.S. homes may have a videocassette recorder and/or a videodisc player, and this new technology may be exerting an impact as great as that of television when it entered U.S. homes in the 1950s.

Videotape Recorders

The rapidly growing popularity of videotape recorders stems from improvements in the quality of the systems and falling prices. In addition, video stores have sprung up to supply a wide variety of material on tape. Highly popular motion pictures like *Patton* or *The Sting* are now readily available in cassettes, enabling a viewer to watch a favorite film over and over again. Most viewers do not, however, buy their material. Instead, they record it from broadcast television. The tape recorder allows viewers to record material even when they are not physically present, thanks to a timer which turns on the videotape recorder at any desired time. The VCR also solves the problem posed when a a viewer wants to watch two TV programs being broadcast at the same time. While the viewer watches one program, the VCR can record the other for later viewing.

A viewer who is watching a program being recorded can leave out the commercials so that they will not appear on the tape when it is seen later. In this way, a viewer can acquire a commercial-free recording of a film and then watch it to his heart's content. Some viewers build up large collections of videotapes of their favorite films such as Humphrey Bogart movies. Whenever one grows tired of whatever is recorded on a tape, it can simply be reused to record something else.

People with VCRs find that their habits of viewing gradually change. Hollis Vail, a management consultant in Washington, D.C., says that before he bought his VCR he hardly ever watched anything other than the six o'clock news and a few programs between 8:00 and 11:00 P.M.

"My viewing habits did not change instantly after I bought the recorder," Vail reports, "but I did begin to let my eyes wander over the entire TV schedule. Somewhat to my surprise, I found that there *are* some interesting programs in the morning between 5:00 and 8:00 A.M.; college courses and other public service programs are often broadcast during these hours. So I began setting my VCR to pick up these programs while I was asleep or getting off to work. I later watched the programs at a more favorable time.

"I also began to take more of an interest in daytime TV. Many people see daytime TV as a video wasteland. Soap operas, kid's cartoons and

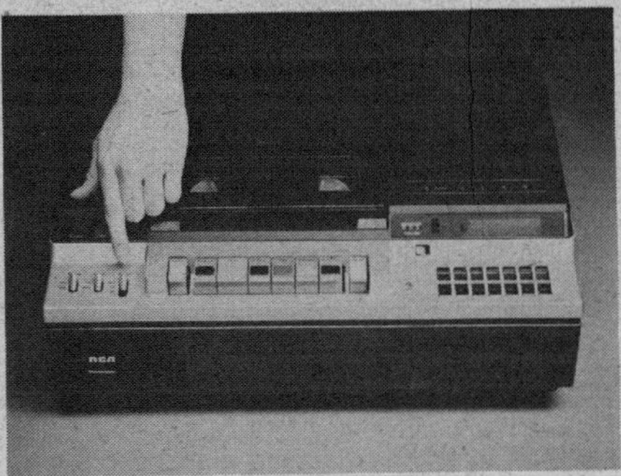

The growing popularity of videocassette recorders will push sales in U.S. over the million mark in 1981.

an assortment of generally inane game shows seemed to populate this time period. But actually, the daytime has a number of shows worth seeing. Some programs dealing with issues of public interest are broadcast live during the day. My VCR lets me see the entire event at my convenience rather than just the excerpts on the evening news."

No longer a prisoner of prime-time television, Vail began enjoying a new freedom. "I was no longer bound to the evening TV schedules. Nor did I have to miss episodes of two-, three- or four-part programs because I could not stay home to watch TV on all those nights. I now can plan and accept evening engagements without the slight pang I used to feel when I knew that a night out, as enjoyable as it might be, meant that I would have to miss a TV program that I really did want to see."

Furthermore, Vail found that if friends or family happened to drop by while he was watching TV, he could turn on the recorder, turn off the TV set and join the gathering. "With a few exceptions, I have stopped letting my favorite program govern my evenings and have scheduled instead, other activities. In a way, VCRs put TV in its place."

So far, videocassette recorders have been bought mainly by a minority of high-income households who use the equipment mainly for time-shifting of program schedules to fit the viewers' own hours and life-style. One survey indicated that 75 percent of those who bought VCRs used them for that purpose; the other 25 percent bought them for a variety of reasons, but primarily to record and keep specific programs such as movies.

One major reason for people buying VCRs is to see things that cannot be seen on regular television, such as hard-core pornography. X-rated movies are possibly the hottest selling items in the fledgling videotape market, and advertisements for videotape porn now appear in a number of sex-oriented magazines. Many people who are afraid to go to a theatre to see X-rated movies are perfectly willing to do so in their homes. Some couples use video cameras so they can make their own pornography.

Curiously, video storekeepers report that the same people who buy X-rated material themselves may also buy cassettes for their children because they want the youngsters to see something that is better than the normal children's fare offered by the commercial stations.

The price of video cameras has fallen to as little as a few hundred dollars, which enables increasing numbers of people to make their own video "movies." In general, video cameras are much easier to use than movie cameras and the results may be seen immediately, since the film does not have to be sent away to be processed. Thus more and more people will be seeing themselves on their television sets.

Videocassette Piracy

Videocassette tapes have led to a substantial black market in such popular American movies as *Star Wars* and *Jaws*. While moviegoers stand patiently in line at theatres, some VCR owners are watching pirated versions on their home screens. Before the VCR appeared, a movie pirate needed a laboratory to copy films, but now anyone can set up a piracy business in his own home with nothing more than two videocassette recorders. Video piracy is estimated to cost the industry at least $100 million in lost revenues. Such piracy has been called "one of the fastest growing white-collar crimes in the world."

Pirated U.S. films are extremely popular in Saudi Arabia and other Middle Eastern countries, where the are few movie theatres, as well as South Africa, where strict censorship prohibits most U.S. movies from being shown without major cuts. In Colombia, pirated versions of some major movies are so valuable they can be traded for heroin!

Another problem plaguing the industry is incompatibility. Most VCRs appearing in the U.S. are made by two Japanese electronics giants — Sony and Matsushita. Unfortunately, Sony's Betamax, possibly the best known of the brands, is incompatible with the Matsushita, marketed in America by RCA, Magnavox, Sylvania and other firms. The battle of the Japanese giants goes on in stores everywhere.

Videotape recorders are finding a wide variety of uses in industry. For example major corporations now prepare corporate newscasts as a supplement to employee magazines. In this way a top manager of Exxon or General Mills can speak directly and intimately with thousands of employees at many different locations. At the same time, a company can provide training videotapes explaining corporate procedures, new technology and whatever else the corporation wishes to get across to its employees.

Videotapes also are being used to enable people in the field to give first-person reports on their activities to a variety of people in the home office, who can watch the videotape at their convenience. Lawyers now are recording wills on videotape. A videotaped will may help to insure that the deceased's estate goes to the desired persons or organizations. A videotaped will has an authenticity lacking in a simple signature on a typewritten document. Lawyers videotaping wills may use two cameras; one is focused at all times on the client, his attorney, and the witnesses; the other can show the will as it is being read. The testator must be sure to state the actual date, making sure to say that the will

being made on that date takes precedence over all other wills previously made.

Another growing use of videotapes is in "videodating." Already there are a dozen or so videodating services around the United States, which offer people a chance to see a potential date on videotape before actually going out for an evening's entertainment. A videodating service in Washington, D.C., allows participants to see the tapes of six other persons each month. If a participant likes what he or she sees on the tape, the viewee gets to see the tape of the viewer. As soon as both parties have indicated an interest, both receive the full name and telephone number of the other party and either can initiate a call.

Videodiscs

The videocassette's rival — the videodisc — is only beginning to enter U.S. homes but is expected to have significant impact by about 1982. Unlike videotapes and cassettes, videodiscs cannot be used by amateurs at home to record "off-the-air." In addition they cannot be used by amateurs at home to make home movies — at least with current technology. But videodiscs have major advantages such as the low cost of the discs themselves. A disc may cost only a tenth as much as a cassette. Furthermore the discs are easier to store and ship, and information on the discs can be accessed much more easily than information on videotapes.

In many respects, the videodisc may be likened to the phonograph record, which it strongly resembles in appearance. (A casual observer might think that the videodisc was simply an aluminum-plated phonograph record.) Videotapes may be likened to audiotapes in that they can be erased and used to record other material. Americans have found it useful to have both audiotapes and phonograph records because of the inherent advantages that each technology has over the other. In the same way, industry experts anticipate that both videocassettes and videodiscs will coexist in American homes during the 1980s and perhaps much longer, or until there are major changes in the technology.

As with videocassettes, manufacturers are providing a choice of videodisc systems, each with significant differences from the others. In one system, developed by Philips, the Dutch electronics giant, and MCA, Inc., a thin beam of laser light shines on the discs and reads the signals encoded on the surface of the videodisc in the form of tiny hills and depressions. The disc rotates 30 times a second, and each rotation results in one full frame — a complete scan of the television screen. Each side of the disc can hold up to 54,000 frames — the equivalent of one-half hour of broadcast television. Besides the picture signal, there is room for two separate sound tracks. A different system developed by RCA is scheduled to move strongly into the market in late 1980 and 1981. The RCA product is not compatible with the Philips/MCA equipment.

"The videodisc is expected to become a multi-billion-dollar industry in the 1980s, achieving a 30 to 50 percent penetration of all homes with color TV sets in its first 10 years," says RCA in its annual report. The RCA player, which is expected to sell for less than $500, uses a grooved disc played with a diamond stylus. The disc revolves at 450 revolutions per minute and has up to one hour of programming per side. The player attaches to any color or black and white TV set. This videodisc, says RCA, will represent the company's "largest single investment in a new consumer electronics product — including color television, which the company pioneered in 1954."

One major competitive breakthrough in the videodisc market was an agreement by CBS Incorporated, RCA's hotly competitive rival, to manufacture and distribute videodiscs compatible with the RCA system. "It's the first time I can remember that we've ever cooperated on anything!" an RCA official was reported as saying. The compatibility of the RCA/CBS systems will make it much easier for videodiscs to become popular.

RCA expects to manufacture and sell about 200,000 players in 1981. At a meeting of the National Association of Broadcasters, Herbert S. Schlosser, executive vice president of RCA, discussed "TV's fragmented future" — a future in which the viewer will have many more choices than ever before, thanks to videodiscs, cable TV, pay TV and videotape.

"The total impact of the new media will be to reduce commercial television's audience somewhat, to knock the corners off that audience," Schlosser said. "But those are big corners, and new businesses can thrive in them.

"The reservoir of hours of television watching is so huge — over 230,000 hours per home per year — that even with some audience loss, commercial broadcasting will remain a strong and vital business and will continue to be a necessity to advertisers."

Since videodiscs will be very inexpensive to manufacture, they open fantastic new possibilities for education, information, entertainment and other applications. It will be possible to have videodisc magazines which can be sent through the mail. Such video magazines might contain advertisements as well as articles, pictures and so on. A videodisc magazine could go beyond the material presented in an ordinary magazine, because it could have motion sequences. A viewer reading an article on Australia might be given some text and still pictures to begin with and then be shown a motion sequence of a kangaroo roundup in the outback. A videodisc magazine might also offer a stupendous number of full-color still pictures — far more than could be accommodated even in a very thick art book. Imagine an art book with 50,000 full-color pictures each the size of a television screen.

Thanks to its enormous storage capabilities, the new videodisc technology is expected to lead to a growing number of videodisc libraries in schools, offices and homes.

The videodisc may revolutionize education — especially when it is linked up to a small computer. The combination of the two technologies constitutes a teaching system of incredible power. Students can see on their screens the material they are to learn, and the computer can test them to make sure they are mastering the material.

Videocassettes and videodiscs are expected to end the need for programs that appeal to mass audiences. Groups as small as a few thousand might support a videodisc production and the product could be sold over a number of years. In this way it should be possible to have a growing number of programs of much higher quality and more specific information. Furthermore, the viewer can have material free of commercials. But advertisers may not be easily beaten; it may be that videotape manufacturers will include commercial announcements as a way of reducing the cost of the finished product — just as they do with printed magazines.

Philips/MCA, Inc.

The first videodisc player system to reach the U.S. market was produced by Philips Corporation of the Netherlands and MCA, Inc. It operates by shining a thin beam of laser light onto a 12-inch disc that can play a half hour of TV programming per side.

RCA

RCA developed SelectaVision, its own video player system (shown here with J. J. Brandinger, division vice president). It uses a diamond-tipped stylus and has one hour of programming per side of the grooved conductive plastic disc.

Microcomputers: Intelligence on a Chip

Experts all agree that microcomputers — while still unfamiliar to a vast majority of people — have been transforming our society. They are everywhere at work, in business, factories, laboratories and libraries. The next area of widespread impact will be personal computers for ordinary people. However, like those earlier marvels of technology, the telephone and television, the microcomputer must overcome a Catch-22 dilemma: people have to buy microcomputers in order to discover how useful they are, but until they know how useful they are, they won't buy them.

In its early days, the telephone was not a practical investment for most people because so few others had phones. Years later television faced the same sort of dilemma: since so few people had sets, viewing was limited to only a few hours of sports and newsreels per week, and since viewing was limited, most families felt that buying a set was not worthwhile. Eventually, however, almost every home acquired a telephone and a TV set. Wealthy people, who bought telephones and TV sets as status symbols, provided a small market that gradually grew into a mass market as prices declined and the usefulness of the equipment increased.

The microcomputer is now overcoming its Catch-22 obstacles and is spreading like wildfire. About 278,000 units were sold in 1978, and over 1.2 million will be sold in 1982, according to one marketing firm's forecast. This would be a growth of well over 400 percent. The market for microcomputers, which is presently around $100 million per year, could swell as high as $3 billion within a few years. Jim Eldin, director of Micro-Marketing Consultants, sums up this growth: "The microcomputer is a watershed technology — like the electric light, the automobile, and the telephone it stands to change our everyday lives more than we can know."

How Microcomputers Developed

The basis of all computers is the constant switching on and off of "yes-no," or binary, signals. Anything a computer is working with — letters, numbers or symbols — can be coded in this binary language. The first electronic digital computer, ENIAC (Electronic Numerical Integrator and Computer), built in 1945, contained thousands of such switching devices in the form of electronic vacuum tubes, filled a large room and was slow and clumsy by today's standards.

A major breakthrough in reducing the size and increasing the speed of computers was made in 1947, when Bell Laboratories developed the transistor, a simple switching device made of semiconductive material such as germanium and silicon. The transistor uses much less power, lasts longer and is smaller and much more dependable than the vacuum tube it replaced. Batch processing of many transistors at once brought the cost down to pennies. A more sophisticated transistor, the MOS (Metal Oxide Semiconductor), appeared in 1959, opening the way for microelectronics and the development of the minicomputer industry, beginning in 1962.

In 1971, researchers at Intel, a California firm, developed the microprocessor-on-a-chip or, more simply, microprocessor. The microprocessor is the nerve center, or brain, of the microcomputer and serves as the central arithmetic and logic unit. "The microprocessor, more than any other microelectronics invention is responsible for the microelectronic industrial revolution," says Adam Osborne in his book *Running Wild*, widely hailed as the "bible" of microcomputer buffs. The microprocessor is small enough to fit on the tip of your finger and costs less than ten dollars yet it is equal to the large computers of twenty years ago that cost half a million dollars.

The microprocessor was incorporated in the first microcomputer in 1975. The microcomputer consisted basically of three integrated silicon chips: a central processing unit (CPU) to control the functions of the other parts of the computers; a direct memory chip; and input/output (I/O) interfaces, which allow control of peripheral devices such as a display screen or electronic printer. Although terminology varies, a microcomputer is generally considered to be a silicon chip that incorporates these three functions.

Sperry-Univac

IBM

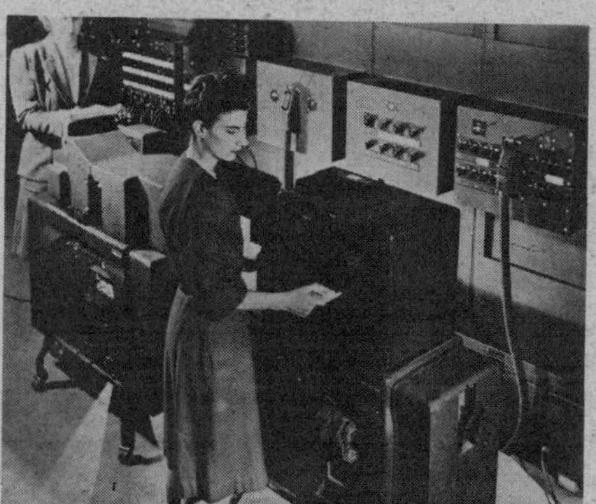

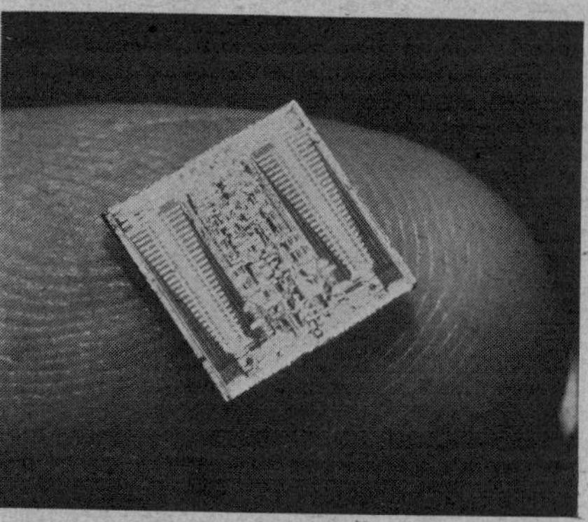

ENIAC, the world's first fully electronic computer (left), contained 18,000 vacuum tubes. The new 65,000-memory-bit chip (right) fits on a fingertip and contains the logic that once filled an entire room.

Microcomputers do the same thing with large-scale integrated circuit chips as larger computers formerly did with simple transistors, and before that with vacuum tubes. Each silicon chip contains thousands of minute circuits which are capable of storing or processing data and which enable the microcomputer to handle its computations. A single integrated circuit chip can contain the electronic capability of a hundred thousand vacuum tubes. Each year the storage capacity of specialized "miracle" chips goes ever higher. (Currently the most advanced commercially available random access memory (RAM) chip has a storage capacity of 65,536 bits of computer data.)

Direct Applications

Microcomputers can be put into virtually any instrument, machine or appliance which can benefit from a memory, calculations, or automatic controls. The microcomputer gives the device some "smarts," making it a better servant. For instance, a smart microwave oven can thaw a roast, then cook the roast, then turn itself off. The oven needs no reminders from the human cook.

The microcomputer has made it possible for ordinary people and small businesses to own computers, whereas a few years ago only the largest corporations, government agencies or public utilities could afford them.

Today microcomputers have become commonplace in businesses; schools are experimenting with them, and an increasing number of computers is being sold to consumers for home use. According to a recent article in the *Wall Street Journal,* sales of personal computers practically double every year.

In business, microcomputers have greatly expedited such tasks as inventory control, budget allocation, text processing, payroll design and transaction processing, just to name a few of the thousands of applications.

In schools, microcomputers are used for teaching such traditional courses as mathematics, English and history. A classroom computer can be used to drill students individually, praising them for correct answers and preventing them from continuing when they make a mistake. Classroom computers are also capable of "branching": the computer assesses a student's strengths and weaknesses and adjusts its questioning to a

Microprocessor display terminal with keyboard and 12-inch green phosphor screen is used for entering or retrieving data from computer systems.

The personal computer system below includes a microcomputer keyboard, a monitor and disk memory storage system with two floppy disks at right.

The heart of a computer is to be found in the silicon chips mounted on a circuit board.

A mainframe computer with a video-display (CRT) terminal and an electronic printer.

ComputerSpeak—A Glossary

Access time — that interval between the instant in which a computer calls for the transfer of data from storage and the instant in which it is received.

Address — an identification, key name or number, for a storage register or other location of data or information. All stored information must have an address.

ALGOL (ALGOrithmic Language) — a procedure-oriented language used to express a formula for computer use in solving a problem.

Analog computer — a machine designed to work with continuously variable physical quantities of data (cf., digital computer).

Bar-code scanner — a device that reads thin and thick lines or bars by means of reflected light, such as the Universal Product Code that is printed on most supermarket products and is read by a scanner at the check-out line.

Bit — (a contraction of binary digit) the smallest amount of information that can be known. A binary digit is the choice of only one of two alternatives, generally thought of as 0 or 1, yes/no, or on/off (see page 341). Computers use long series of bits to communicate, store, and compute all their information.

Branch — to alter slightly the normal or expected sequence of instructions in a computer program, due to conditions or results. For instance, a computer can be programmed with a series of ten mathematical operations. Step 4 may say: "If the total is over 100, go to step 8." Thus the computer branches past steps 5–7.

Bug — a programming error or equipment fault.

Byte — a group of bits (usually eight) acting as a unit.

Cathode ray tube (CRT) — a tube that provides a viewing screen, as in a television set. Video display terminals employ CRTs.

Central processing unit (CPU) — the control center of a computer. The CPU decodes instructions and controls the circuits of a computer.

COBOL (COmmon Business Oriented Language) — a computer language whose statements closely resemble business English.

Cursor — a spot of light that appears on a video display screen to show where the next character will appear. Cursors are generally used to show where corrections, additions, or deletions should go.

Data base — those items of information held in storage for use in various programming processes.

Digital computer — a machine designed to perform logical and/or mathematical operations on discrete or discontinuous data.

Direct access — a type of storage device which enables information at various locations to be retrieved with little time loss.

Floppy disk — thin, flexible plastic disk, similar to a phonograph record that stores information electromagnetically. Also called diskette.

FORTRAN (FORmula TRANslation) — a computer language which uses algebraic notation-type instructions.

Friendly computer — a self-programming or very easily programmable computer that allows inexperienced humans to operate it easily.

Hard copy — information printed on paper so that it may be saved. Much computer information appears only briefly on video display screens.

Hardware — the physical equipment of a computer, as opposed to the program or instructions that the computer may be given. (See software)

Integrated circuit — a complete electronic circuit which cannot be interrupted or disassembled without destroying it.

Language — an established set of conventions or commands used for programming.

Mainframe — a large computer.

MICR (Magnetic Ink Character Recognition) — the machine reading of information printed with magnetic ink.

Modem — a contraction of modulator - demodulator. A device that allows computers to "talk" to each other over telephone lines or other communication systems. This is accomplished by changing digital information into tones (modulating) and changing tones into digital information (demodulating).

Online — relating to devices in direct communication with the CPU which are controlled by the computer.

Optical character recognition (OCR) — the process involving a computer's reading printed characters by using light-sensitive devices.

Peripheral — a device capable of communicating with a computer. Examples: printers, keyboards, video display screens.

Program — an explicit series of instructions designed for a particular function of a computer. A program must be in a language the computer can understand. Used as a verb, program means to design and/or execute such a series of instructions.

PROM — Programmable read-only memory storage.

RAM — Random-access memory storage.

ROM — Read-only memory storage.

Semiconductor — a solid material that conducts electricity under certain conditions but not others. Semiconductors act as gates in microelectronic circuits.

Silicon Valley — the area of San Jose, California, characterized by a concentration of companies that make silicon chips for use in computers and other devices.

Software — programmer-written directions. Software can refer to anything that instructs a computer, a floppy disk, magnetic tape, etc.

Speech compression — the method of speeding up recorded messages while maintaining the original pitch, thus avoiding the "Donald Duck" sound commonly heard when a recorded tape or phonograph is played too fast. Though people speak at about 150 words per minute, a speech compressor can play at 300–400 words per minute.

Terminal — the equipment that allows a person to communicate with the computer. Typically, a terminal will consist of a keyboard console and a video display unit.

Voice print — the pattern of a person's voice is highly distinctive and can be used as a means of identification like fingerprints. In the future a person may be able to unlock a door simply by speaking to it.

Word processing — the automated storage, manipulation and printing of text.

level difficult enough to be challenging to the student but not so difficult as to be frustrating. Classroom computers can also be used for unit review, self-testing and analysis of laboratory data.

In the next few years, microcomputers will become still more powerful and easy to use. Increasingly, computers will become self-programming and therefore require very little if any technical training for operation. Microcomputing expert Jim Eldin points out that computers simply won't be economically viable unless they can be "commanded" rather than programmed. He compares the situation to automobiles: if cars were still made with highly complicated gears, manual steering and double clutch, few people would buy them.

A prototype of the self-programming computer has just come on the market. Proteus, developed at Massachusetts Institute of Technology and marketed by Solid State Technologies, requires no codes or special languages, so users need not be familiar with computer programming. Proteus works by letting the user design the symbols which tell the computer what to do.

The advances which may follow, possibly within five years, are mind-boggling. Though industry specialists don't agree about how quickly the advances will come or how far the technology can ultimately go, even the most conservative forecasts are startling.

Today, a pocket calculator that costs about ten dollars, weighs under a pound and is only a few inches long is more powerful than a bulky calculator that could easily have cost a thousand dollars a decade ago. By 1985, say some industry enthusiasts, a programmable hand-held computer will have the power of today's most powerful computer, which now costs $9 million. The nanoprocessor, which is a thousand times more powerful than the microprocessor, is expected to be available within a decade. The next step after that will be the picoprocessor, one million times more powerful and based on molecule-sized circuits. Lewis M. Branscomb, vice president and chief scientist of IBM, has speculated that the picoprocessor might be patterned on DNA (deoxyribonucleic acid) the molecule that

Supercomputer, the Cray-1 system, is designed for highly complex tasks, as in this installation at the European Centre for Medium Range Weather Forecasts (ECMWF) in Reading, England.

controls heredity, might be grown in a petri dish, and might rival the human brain in the compactness of its intelligence.

During the past five years, the number of components that can be put on a chip has increased by a factor of 100. As technological and economic limits of miniaturization and integration are reached, this rate of growth may slow somewhat, but it is likely that microelectronic complexity will increase 10,000-fold by 1990. Just how society will use all the mechanical intelligence is a fascinating subject for speculation.

How many computer experts does it take to change a light bulb?

1,111. One to push the button that activates the computerized light bulb-changing system, ten to decide where to place the system to change the light bulb, one hundred to write the special program for the system and one thousand to provide explanations as to why the system failed to work.

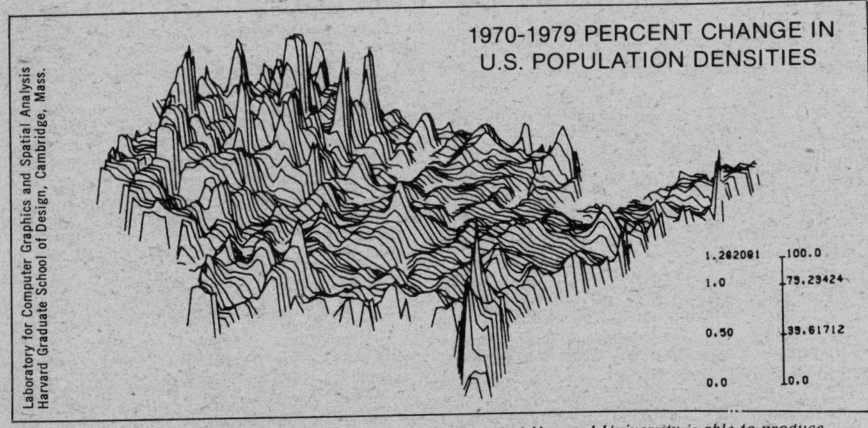

Aspex, a computer graphics mapping program developed at Harvard University is able to produce a variety of perspective maps such as this one on changes in U.S. population.

New Ways To Play Post Office

Mail service, which had begun in the British Colonies in North America in the 1600s, met its initial significant challenge in the telegraph — the first system of electronic communications. Later came the telephone, invented in 1876 by Alexander Graham Bell, providing a far easier and more satisfactory means for most interpersonal communications, especially within a city.

Despite the new competition, the U.S. Post Office continued to grow strongly in response to increased customer demand. Businesses discovered that they could sell goods by sending out catalogs and brochures describing their offers. Companies whose business had heretofore been confined to their local areas could now expand, some even nationwide. (Sears, Roebuck is a prime example: many people, who had once been dependent on itinerant peddlers and occasional trips to the nearest large town for their purchases, now could explore the great world of merchandise through the Sears catalog.) The expansion of the professions meant that more bills were rendered through the mails and, thanks to the expanding banking system, more and more people found it easier to mail a check for payment rather than to deliver it in person. As literacy spread, there was a growing demand for newspapers, magazines and books. These could all be delivered by the mail service.

But the postal system, now known as the U.S. Postal Service, today faces perhaps the sharpest challenge in its history. Within 20 years the system as we know it could become little more than a memory. New technologies have made it possible for nonpostal organizations to offer better and/or cheaper alternatives to traditional mail delivery in many areas, and the Service must change greatly if it is to compete successfully. The U.S. Postal Service is well aware of the dangers it faces and is fighting back hard.

In August 1980 the postal board of governors gave a go-ahead for the nation's first electronic mail system. Dubbed ECOM for Electronic Computer Originated Mail, the new electronic mail system is scheduled to begin operating in January 1982. Postal officials have determined that the Service will have difficulty surviving without electronic mail, which can cut down on labor costs, now accounting for about 85 percent of the Postal Service budget.

ECOM will enable businesses that have large volumes of computerized mail — such as bills — to send a communication quickly to its destination. Under the current plan, a company would authorize a communications carrier such as Western Union or a telephone company to send the bill or other communication to 25 post offices especially equipped to receive such messages.

The messages will be printed out at the designated post offices and placed in envelopes for delivery as first-class mail. In this way the Postal Service may gain additional revenue because it will be helping substantially in the preparation of the bill rather than acting simply as a carrier for a previously prepared and stamped bill.

In announcing their decision to proceed with electronic mail, the board of governors said: "Electronic mail holds out the promise of significantly improved postal service for citizens of this nation, and it will, in important respects, determine the course of the Postal Service's future operations."

Under the present plan, the Postal Service is, in effect, giving private carriers a piece of the action. However, the Service has indicated it will ask the Postal Rate Commission to hold further hearings on the question of whether the Service can accept messages directly from a firm without going through another communications carrier. The Commission had rejected in 1979 the Postal Service's request for monopoly control over the transmission of electronic mail. The Commission said the service should be competitive, with more than one company being allowed to transmit the messages from a company's computer to the post office.

The enthusiasm of the Postal Service for electronic mail stems in large measure from the fact that it has no alternative. All kinds of messages which might travel by mail are already moving through a growing number of private networks employing telephone lines and/or broadcast signals flashed between satellites and ground stations. These systems represent an end-run around the entire postal system. In 1979 some 40 million messages were transmitted by computerized systems — and the number could exceed 275 million in 1982.

Electronic mail systems come in three basic configurations — facsimile, communicating word processors and computer-based message systems.

Facsimile

Developed more than 100 years ago, facsimile remains the most prevalent electronic-mail system in existence. Furthermore, it has grown rapidly over the past decade. In 1970 an estimated 15,000 units were installed in North America. Today there may be more than 200,000 in North America plus another 100,000 abroad. Facsimile transmission permits exact copies of written, printed and pictorial information to be sent and received over conventional lines. A facsimile transceiver works by means of a scanning device which converts visual images into electronic signals. These signals are coded for transmission to a receiving unit, which decodes the information and prints out a copy (facsimile) of the original. Facsimile machines are easy to operate and currently cost less than other electronic mail systems. They can handle both intercompany and intracompany communications. Growth in facsimile devices averages about 12 percent a year. In ten years' time facsimile machines will be able to transmit in full color.

The principles of the facsimile process were first demonstrated in 1842 by the Scottish inventor, Alexander Bain. In the early 1900s the process was improved upon and facsimile came into wide use transmitting photographs for newspapers. Newspapers have continued to be strong users of facsimile. Such newspapers as the *Wall Street Journal* and the *Christian Science Monitor* pioneered in the use of facsimile processes to transmit — via telephone circuits and, in some cases, satellites — full pages of newspaper texts to distant printing plants. In 1978 *U.S. News and World Report* became the first magazine to send full pages via satellite to other locations for simultaneous printing.

Facsimile machine sends and receives pictures and letters over ordinary telephone lines.

Facsimile is today widely used to send such things as high-priority mail, legal documents, hospital records, press releases, etc. Facsimile offers powerful advantages over other electronic mail systems. For one thing, it can send graphic information such as charts, advertising layouts, and engineering drawings as well as written or printed material. The material is transmitted just as it is; there is no possibility for operator input error. A facsimile machine can be located anywhere a telephone and electric outlet are available, and no special training is required.

Communicating Word Processors

A very different approach to electronic mail is offered by the word processors that are moving into offices everywhere. The word processor is essentially a microcomputer with a keyboard and video screen. A letter or other text can be typed into the word processor and then edited until it is in final draft. Word processors can be connected together within a firm so that a message typed on one word processor can be transmitted instantaneously to other word processors as interoffice mail or for further editing. In addition, the message can be sent by telephone lines to a word processor at its ultimate destination. Communicating word processors, while well adapted to many office purposes tend to be expensive when used as an electronic mail system.

Computer-based Message Systems

The possibility of using a computer as a postman was obvious as soon as it became possible for people at different locations to tap into the same computer. At that point, all that was necessary was for the different users to be able to read each others' messages. Computers were programmed to receive messages from one user to another, and users soon developed the habit of asking the computer "Any messages for me?" In some instances, the computer may not even wait to be asked, but displays messages as soon as the user signs on.

One type of computer-based electronic mail is the message-switching system. In effect, it is a way to speed up computer mail by collecting regularly from all terminals and transmitting it to the terminal addressed, where it is typed out on the computer printer. In one system, consisting of terminals installed at various locations and a "host" computer that controls the network, operators keyboard messages and the host computer picks up the mail by calling the terminal every 30 minutes.

Electronic mail is expected to be far cheaper over the long run than regular mail. The Office of Telecommunications Policy, a branch of the White House's Executive Office, reviewed electronic message service systems and reported that three selected by the Postal Service for consideration all showed "the potential to reduce costs-per-message to as low as 25 to 50 percent of the current first-class letter postage rates."

James Martin, in his book *The Wired Society*, says, "If sufficiently large volumes were sent, electronic mail would be much cheaper than manual mail. The cost of electronic mail will drop substantially whereas the costs of typing, addressing, delivering, receiving, opening, distributing and filing paper mail are rising."

Another advantage of electronic mail over ordinary mail is that it allows a person to send a message to a large audience. In effect it is the electronic equivalent of a bulletin board. People are already using these electronic bulletin boards to send out all kinds of messages addressed "To Whom It May Concern." In 1979, *Intelligent Machines Journal* printed samples of actual items appearing on a computerized bulletin board at the Massachusetts Institute of Technology. The messages included items from people who wanted to sell cars, rent apartments, locate jobs, etc. One person inquired if anybody had seen a missing overhead projector; somebody else wanted to borrow a 1,000-watt voltage converter and several others just wanted to share jokes they had enjoyed.

Electronic mail could take a major step forward with the availability of very inexpensive terminals. Low-price desk units would enable almost everyone to begin sending electronic mail. Already there is talk of portable terminals which could be used for electronic messages. Nixdorf Computer Products in Burlington, Massachusetts, has a language translator comprised of a hand-held keyboard and calculator-style display complete with language-translation software. The device can be viewed as a hand-held computer, and there are rumors that a variation of the device could be equipped to be connected to a standard telephone and might sell for less than $500.

The U.S. Postal Service's competition in the electronic mail industry is rather formidable; companies such as AT&T, ITT, IBM and Xerox are vigorously pursuing all forms of electronic information transmission. Despite its planned move, the Postal Service is likely to wind up with only about one quarter of the market. In its fight to survive, the Postal Service is attempting to change its image. The swift couriers completing their daily rounds in the post office motto will soon be receiving some much needed help from even speedier electrons. Improvements in traditional delivery systems are also being made, and postal authorities have even backed off from proposals to cut Saturday deliveries. Certainly the Postal Service is trying hard to meet the challenge of an electronic age.

Telephones

Instantaneous, Interactive and Individual

The telephone is now so much a part of everyday life that it seems difficult to imagine how life was before the invention of the telephone over a century ago. Yet when it first appeared, few people realized how important the telephone would become. In 1876 when Alexander Graham Bell offered Western Union exclusive rights to his new invention, the Western Union president, William Orton, responded by asking, "What use could this company make of an electrical toy?" After it had rejected the offer, the company's managers watched helplessly as the "electrical toy" gobbled up most of their market.

Even more than the telegraph, the telephone revolutionized communications because it posesses several important advantages:

— The telephone provides instantaneous communication between people in their homes and at their work in contrast to the telegraph, which offers instantaneous communication from station to station, but with messages usually being carried to their final destination.

— The telephone is interactive. For the first time, people could get an immediate response. They could ask and answer questions and agree or disagree — a real conversation was possible.

— The telephone carries the individual's voice. This allows people to hear intonations, which may mean more than the words themselves. The telephone can communicate emotions far better than the written word ever could.

At first telephones were a luxury most individuals could not afford, but businesses, government agencies and wealthy persons bought so many telephones that the cost dropped and service improved. Within two years of the invention of the telephone, there were 2,600 in operation. By the turn of the century, there were 1.5 million. At the end of World War II, there were 28 million telephones in the U.S. Today there are 135 million, and AT&T expects to install another 100 million phones by the year 2000. Long-distance phone calls are expected to show the greatest growth as their cost drops and the increasing cost of travel causes people to replace visits in person with telephone calls.

Competition in telecommunications has intensified. In the past, the capital needed to create a long-distance network was too great to allow many companies to enter the market, even if legally permitted to do so. But the new microwave and satellite long-distance networks have proven cheaper than the traditional service offered through AT&T and its affiliates, and companies like MCI Communications Corp., International Telephone & Telegraph Corp., Western Union and the Southern Pacific Co. have moved into telephone communications. The new systems work as follows: A caller dials a local access number which connects him to a computer. Then he dials his personal access number, followed by the area code and number he is calling. A microwave signal is sent to a receiving tower in the metropolitan area of the recipient; the call is then relayed through the local telephone network. Industry sources claim their alternatives to "Ma Bell" save customers from 20 to 40 percent on their long-distance phone bills.

Despite a long-term drop in the cost of making a telephone call, increased usage will cause home telephone bills to more than double by 1990, according to one market research firm, International Resource Development. A part of the increased expenditures will be in payment for a variety of new services: "Customer Calling Service" will allow automatic connection with some frequently used numbers. A number can be called by simply pressing a button. "Store and Forward Voice," also called "Voice Mail," will allow everyone using a telephone to leave and receive recorded messages; no special answering machine will be needed. The telephone company's computer will record a message and ring the number periodically until it is answered. If you are away from your home, you will be able to call your own telephone number and hear any messages left for you. In May 1980 the 3M Company of St. Paul, Minnesota, installed an in-house system that allows one executive to record a voice message and leave it in an absent executive's computer "mail box." On return, the second executive calls the computer to see if there are any messages, then receives the recorded "mail," in the voice of the person who sent it. The system can be instructed to deliver the message immediately or to wait a few days. Some executives leave themselves messages to be delivered later as reminders.

Bell Telephone Company, a subsidiary of AT&T, announced plans to put voice mail technology in its switching offices. This will allow homeowners or small businessmen who can't afford a full-scale voice mail system to enjoy many of the same benefits. The estimated cost is about $15 a month.

"Text telephones" that print the text of a conversation are already available in some places. Sweden's estimated 7,000 hard-of-hearing citi-

Motorola, Inc.

Lightweight portable radiotelephone allows people to stay in contact.

zens will soon have text telephones. Developed by Televeket, a communications equipment firm and financed primarily by the Swedish government, these text telephones have a keyboard that resembles a regular typewriter and a nine-inch display screen. A light indicates that the phone is ringing or is off the hook.

The Bell System is also considering a variety of other new services, such as automatic wake-up calls, transmission of company memos over the phone to receiving devices throughout an organization, voting by phone, cordless phones, and a national telephone number for each individual, to enable calls to be easily forwarded.

One important engineering change coming is the conversion of telephone transmission from analog to the digital system. An analog transmission mirrors changes in tone and volume of sound by intensifying and diminishing the electrical current. Thus the signal is analogous to the information transmitted. Digital transmission codes the sound into binary digits and leads to systems that are more reliable, more versatile and less expensive. Furthermore, this change can be implemented with a minimum of inconvenience to the customer.

"It is only a matter of time before the largely analog telephone system becomes all-digital," says Sam G. Pitroda, vice president and general manager of Wescom Switching. Digital equipment for voice transmission is now no more expensive than analog devices and functions more reliably. Digital switching networks are easier to install and maintain, take up less space and dissipate less power. They can also handle more traffic and provide clearer transmission. Video, audio and facsimile signals can all be transmitted in digital form. Computers, which function in digital mode, can communicate directly through digital equipment.

Although the changeover from analog to digital transmission has been gradual, the pace is quickening. The expense of converting to universal digital transmission immediately would be prohibitively expensive, but digital equipment can be installed piecemeal with very little interruption to customer service.

One customer service innovation, the video telephone, has been around for some time but has yet to catch fire. In 1970 a Pittsburgh company became the first to have Picturephone® service, an innovation of Bell Telephone. The growth so far has been far below industry estimates. Part of the reason for the slow acceptance of Picturephone® is the difficulty of establishing a network of lines to carry the video as well as the audio signal; as a result, video telephones cost too much for most potential users. Picturephone® service requires transmission capacity 1,000 times as great as voice telephone service. But the cost may drop significantly in the future, thanks to new technologies such as fiber optical transmission cables. One approach to cutting costs would be to utilize conventional mass-produced television sets, but there remains the lack of adequate cables and switching facilities at the present time.

Despite the problems, videophones are being used by many organizations, primarily for teleconferencing, which has become increasingly popular. In the long run, household videophones will become as commonplace as the "talking heads" of the evening TV newscast.

Talking Chips

More and more people are talking to machines, and the machines are talking back. All the microelectronic circuitry necessary to simulate human speech can be contained on one to three silicon chips, though a tradeoff must be made between the quality of the sound produced and the size of the vocabulary of the "talking chips."

The most renowned product is the single-circuit voice synthesizer patented by Texas Instruments and utilized in TI's educational toy, Speak and Spell™. The product can store over 200 words in its memory and pronounce them quite clearly. The machine speaks a word, and the child tries to spell it by typing it on a keyboard. If the child fails to spell the word correctly, the machine says, "That is incorrect" and spells it correctly.

Microchips "talk" in several different ways. One method of speech synthesis involves storing the sound waveform and volume of a word on a microchip. When the word needs to be spoken, the memory converts it to voltages, which are fed to an amplifier.

A second method, called *formant synthesis* or phoneme coding, stores the phonemes (building-block sounds of language) necessary for words to be spoken. The computer then assembles the phonemes in the necessary order. This system requires a lower number of bits per word for storage, but the quality of sound is poorer.

A third method, similar to phoneme coding, produces a higher quality of speech but also requires more bits per word. As with phoneme coding, the microchip stores the basic utterances of human speech, but it also employs a mathematical model of the human vocal tract in order to provide a more realistic transition from one sound to the next and to alter intonation.

Recognizing human speech is far more complex than synthesizing it. The acoustic features of words vary from speaker to speaker and will even vary at different times with the same speaker. Furthermore, the computer has difficulty determining where one word ends and another begins. For instance the computer can't tell the difference between "a head" and "ahead" or between homonyms like "right" and "write."

But speech-recognition technology is already available in limited form. Generally speaking, computers understand only a few specific command words and must be "trained" to recognize the voice of a specific person. The IBM Corporation is trying to perfect an automatic dictation machine which would accept voice dictation and return a typed manuscript.

Voice-recognition technology can be used for security devices. Locks of all kinds can be equipped with a voice-recognition system that allows only specific persons to open the lock. This "lock" will likely be far more difficult to "pick" than today's tumbler-based locks. Another voice-security system could be employed in the electronic transfer of funds or in the use of credit cards over the phone.

Instant Information About Everything
The Electronic Challenge to Newspapers, Magazines, Book Publishers and Libraries

As early as the 1950s the rapid increase in the ability of computers to hold vast amounts of information and produce it instantaneously upon command led to speculation that they might someday move into the information area, replacing the traditional paper-using information media. Why couldn't the information that we now find in our daily newspaper be put into a computer and sent electronically into people's homes without the present cumbersome system involving the cutting down of vast forests for paper, fleets of trucks and battalions of newsboys? And why couldn't the contents of libraries be stored in computers so that the information could be accessed by users almost anywhere?

During the 1960s, many studies were made by the Library of Congress and numerous other institutions to determine what role computers might play in storing and disseminating information. Many of the studies could be summarized as follows: yes, it was technically feasible to do most of the things suggested by the computer enthusiasts, but the current computer technology was insufficiently advanced to make most projects economically desirable. There were exceptions; for example, the Library of Congress decided to computerize its card catalogs, and during the 1970s, libraries in the United States and elsewhere adopted computers for many of their book-handling procedures. Libraries computerized "information about information" — titles and authors of books, reference numbers so books could be located, etc. — but the information itself remained in the form of books and other materials on paper.

Newspapers also began to introduce computers into their newsrooms and composing rooms, and by 1980 major papers all over the United States were thoroughly computerized. In the new system a reporter types his article on a computer console and the information is stored in the computer while editors work on it. The editors edit copy on a video display tube, a device looking much like a television screen but showing written text instead of pictures. The system allows an editor to carry out all normal editing functions; words can be changed or deleted, material can be inserted and paragraphs can be shifted about. Once an article has been edited and typesetting instructions given, the computer system generates the electronic signals needed to control the typesetting operation. But the final product of a newspaper in 1980 is still a collection of large paper sheets on which articles and advertisements have been printed in ink.

The truly electronic newspaper — a contradiction in terms, since it is a paperless "newspaper" — made its appearance in the late 1970s. The leading country in this area appears to have been Britain, although a number of other countries, including the U.S., are now moving rapidly in that direction. As happens so often in technological innovation, the breakthroughs did not come from the traditional provider of the service. The British post office and the BBC established services that could be described as electronic newspapers; news could be called up on a video screen and read whenever one wished.

In Britain's BBC version of the electronic newspaper, subscribers can call up news and other information on their television screens. For instance, a subscriber may select "headlines" and then press the appropriate buttons on the mechanism (which is the size of a pocket calculator). The headlines then appear on the screen. After reading them, the viewer can turn to other subjects that can be selected such as "foreign news," "consumer news," "people," "weather," etc. An electronic newspaper may have hundreds of pages of information in its memory.

The broadcast versions of electronic newspapers such as the BBC's allow the viewer to call up a wide variety of information that is being broadcast simultaneously. The viewer has the feeling of being able to interact with the system, but the interaction is really limited to the electronic equivalent of looking at different pages in a printed newspaper. There is no direct communication with the producer of the paper. By contrast, the British post office's electronic newspaper, Prestel, has the technical feasibility of allowing direct contact between the reader and the editors of the paper since Prestel is transmitted by telephone lines. Being two-way, the system allows a viewer to ask for any information in the post office memory bank. Many thousands of pages of information can be made available because the system is not limited by the constraints of the airwaves.

Because of its enormous information capacity, the post office system provides a potential bridge from the electronic newspaper to the electronic library. It is now possible to put the contents of hundreds of thousands of books onto computer tape and allow people to call up the contents on their home viewing screens.

The terminology of the new electronic information systems is unsettled, but *teletext* is often used to suggest a system employing a television signal for transmission while *viewdata* (or *videotext*) is often used in cases where the information is transmitted by cable or telephone lines. However, these terms are still used rather inter-

Columbus Dispatch Photo

Columbus, Ohio, subscribers can select newspaper articles for viewing on their home screens.

changeably. But it is important to bear in mind the distinctively different technologies that are used.

No one knows how rapidly the new electronic information systems will catch on. So far the British systems have not proved outstandingly popular, in part because of the substantial costs involved. If more people acquire home computing equipment (for whatever reason) the way will be open for the electronic information systems to move in more strongly.

A French system known as Antiope is currently being introduced in the United States. The terminal required to receive Antiope's information is small enough to be built into an ordinary television set and will raise the price to only about 10 or 20 percent above the price of a normal color TV. Antiope employs a simple hand-held key pad about the size of a pocket calculator to call up the latest news, sports, stock market prices, weather, traffic reports or other information on television programs. The Antiope organization is planning to add airline and rail schedules, theatre and movie listings, listings of educational courses and a wide variety of other information.

In France the telephone company is already planning to abolish the traditional telephone directory and in its place give every phone subscriber an Antiope terminal. Providing millions of terminals free of charge is believed to be cheaper in the long run than providing all those directories.

The use of the French electronic information system to provide a substitute for printed telephone books is running parallel with efforts by AT&T to provide subscribers with electronic "yellow pages." The widely known slogan, "Let Your Fingers do the Walking," might thus be changed to "Let Your Terminal do the Shopping."

AT&T has already run a "concept trial" in Albany, New York, to test reactions from residential and business participants to the idea of a handy electronic directory. Today's yellow pages have a serious limitation; they are difficult to update, and are therefore revised only once a year, and have ad rates too costly for many potential listings. For the average person who has a house to rent or an automobile to sell, the yellow pages are impractical. But if telephone companies make their yellow pages electronic, it will be possible for them to invade the classified ad market, which is one of the richest sources of newspaper revenue. Unfortunately for the newspapers, the electronic systems appear to be inherently cheaper and faster. It is at least theoretically possible for someone to advertise a sofa for sale on an electronic system and have it sold in the time required to dictate a classified ad over the telephone to a newspaper!

Conceding probable defeat, newspapers are now actively trying to get into the electronic act themselves. Eleven major newspapers, including the *New York Times, Los Angeles Times* and the *Washington Post,* have been selected to join a national computer data network and will supply their entire editorial material every evening to a service based in Columbus, Ohio. The service, CompuServe Information Service, is available at $5 an hour as a time-sharing fee to anyone with a home or office computer.

The electronic newspaper system got under way when the *Columbus Dispatch* began trans-

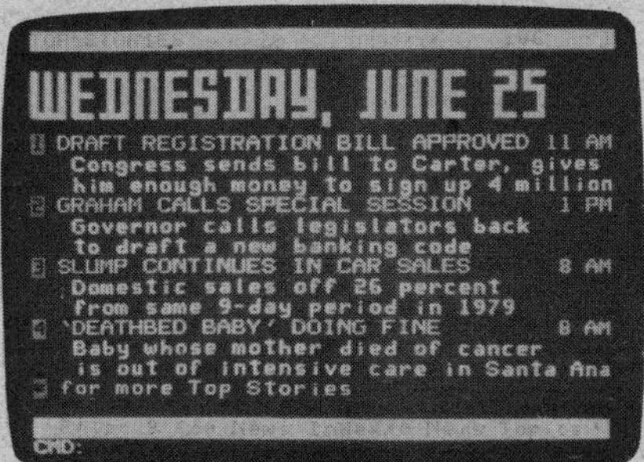

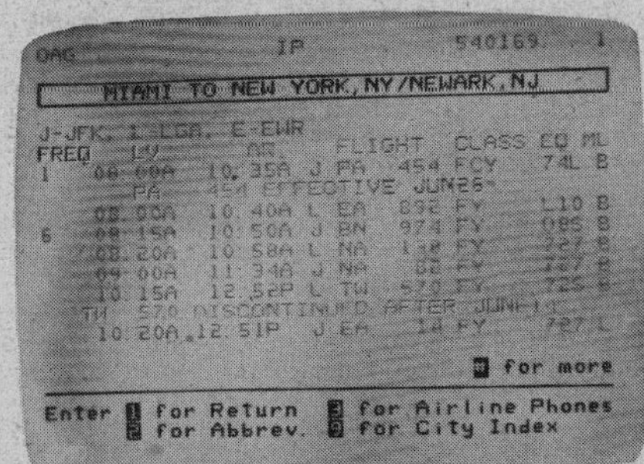

Some of the viewdata services available in Knight-Ridder Newspapers trial in Florida.

mitting its entire editorial content in July, 1980 to 3,000 home terminals. The subscribers, whose numbers are expected to swell to 100,000 by the end of 1981, can call up any of the articles in the newspapers, and the newspapers will receive 20 percent of the time-sharing charge levied on the subscriber. Initially, only editorial copy will be supplied, but the newspapers are expected to sell national ads on the computer media beginning sometime in 1982.

Another experiment is under way in Coral Gables, Florida, where the Knight-Ridder newspapers are supplying news, advertising and consumer services via 200 personal computers installed at no cost in selected homes. If viewers want to order goods they see advertised, they can type messages on their terminals, charging their purchases to their credit cards.

The growing use of computer terminals may greatly speed up the arrival of the electronic newspaper. The Source Telecomputing Corporation of America, based in McLean, Virginia, allows its subscribers (who pay as little as $2.75 an hour in the evening) to access all kinds of information, including the United Press International dispatches from around the world and the *New York Times* Information Bank. In addition, Source subscribers can post messages on an electronic bulletin board or send messages to each other, and they can play electronic games. The availability of these other services means that people have a variety of reasons for acquiring a computer terminal, which once acquired can be used for additional kinds of information.

The advent of electronic information systems means that people will be able to get more up-to-date information in their areas of interest than is possible with present publishing methods. Book publishers recognize the challenge of electronic publishing and are moving into the field themselves. According to one industry estimate, U.S. elementary and high schools presently spend about $2 billion a year on instructional materials. About 3.5 percent of the total goes for computer-based equipment. By 1985, according to one forecast, computer spending may jump to 14 percent — four times greater. Textbook publishers are adapting their products to meet the computer challenge.

Computers and telecommunications are making a strong impact on the academic world. For instance, two scholars thousands of miles apart may use a computer as a communications link while they are collaborating on a "paper." Each suggests ideas, paragraphs, clarifications, etc., and watches for misspellings by the other. Eventually the "paper" is completed and the question then becomes what to do with it. One approach would be to put it into a traditional journal printed on paper. Another approach, however, would be to keep the article in the computer and let other scholars access it by means of their computer terminals. In this way the paper would go only to those really interested in it, and a large amount of paper and mailing costs would be saved.

Networking

The concept of "networking" has emerged as one of the most exciting ideas in the information area. In a sense, the concept is so natural that one might wonder what the excitement is all about. Networking really implies little more than a shift in the way we view the general storage of information. It can be stored in a central location such as a huge computer. However, the same information might be stored in smaller computers at a wide variety of locations. The arrival of microcomputers, which can be bought by ordinary people, means that it is possible for a person to develop a computer program that can be used by many other people. When his computer or computer terminal is connected into a network linking other computer equipment in a wide variety of locations, the individual computer user suddenly has access to enormous resources and he himself becomes a resource for other people on the network. Questions can be asked and answered. Contacts can be established. An individual in the network can be both a user and a supplier of information.

Hundreds of computer networks are now springing up all over the United States. In some instances these networks may consist of nothing more than a few individuals who share an interest in something. In other cases the networks have thousands of individual and organizational members and have easy access to vast stores of information. The networks make it possible for ordinary people to access huge data banks such as the Index Medicus (medical index) maintained by the National Library of Medicine in Bethesda, Maryland. As these networks grow, each individual will have easier access to more and more information. To an increasing degree, we will all be able to find almost everything we want to know about anything whenever we want it.

Microcomputer being used in an elementary grade.

Computer typing system allows easy editing of text.

Critical Issues of the Information Society

Information Overload

The amount of information available to people is enormous and rapidly increasing, but one's ability to make use of it seems to be declining. The very massiveness of the available information seems to make it harder to cope with. As James Thurber once commented, "So much has been written about everything that you can't find out anything about it." Obtaining the right information at the right time for good decision making will challenge us all in the years ahead.

Infringement of Copyrights

Photocopying machines, audiotape recorders and videotape recorders have made it easy for people to copy works that cost a lot of money and creative effort to produce. The new technology makes everyone a potential publisher. And it is impractical to station a police officer at every machine. Such piracy deprives authors, actors, directors and others from the revenue they have earned and which keeps them in business. Literary piracy threatens the volume and even the existence of high-quality books, magazines and motion pictures. Just how the piracy can be effectively curbed is another question.

Privacy

There is a basic conflict between the desirability of making information freely available to people who need it for worthwhile purposes and the desire of individuals not to have their private affairs poked into. In the area of public health, for instance, it is important for medical authorities to know if someone has a contagious disease and to make that information available so that the disease can be properly controlled. At the same time, the individual who has contracted the disease does not want the fact to become public information. The computerization of medical records could make it easy for unauthorized persons to gain access to confidential information.

Security

The new electronic information systems could make it much easier for people to tap into information that could be highly dangerous. Today much information may be kept out of the hands of potential wrongdoers simply because it is difficult to obtain. (Diligent university students have reportedly found in their college libraries most of the information required to manufacture an atom bomb.) The issue of censoring potentially dangerous information is not, of course, new; but the vast improvement in information systems makes the issue more critical.

Depersonalization

Many people feel they are losing their individuality when a computer treats them as a series of mathematical symbols. And as we know from experience, the victim of a computer error feels anger toward the impersonal machine. However, in recent years some changes have taken place which tend to modify our perceptions of computers. The objections that people have to being "depersonalized" by a computer seem to be diminishing as computers are made more "friendly" — simpler and more responsive to human wishes and feelings. For one thing, they have become more sophisticated and are talking to people in a language that people find more "human." Curiously, many schoolchildren who are working on computer terminals in various subject areas find that their computer teachers are often more sympathetic than their human teachers. The children appreciate the enormous patience of the computer teacher, which allows them to take a long time in composing an answer. In addition, students like the fact that the machine cannot criticize or reject them.

Computer Errors

When a computer makes an error that causes serious damage to someone, who should be thrown in jail or fined? The computer programmer? The computer operator? The computer owner? The computer manufacturer? In medieval times, dogs and cats were put on trial for their offenses and duly punished! The responsibility for computer errors is no small matter. Millions of dollars may be misallocated by an errant computer. U.S. defense systems have been "spooked" on several occasions, and conceivably a computer might launch a major attack on some nation due to a spurious warning signal.

International Data Flow

Nations have traditionally regulated the flow of goods into and out of their territories, but have not worried much about letters or telephone calls. Today, however, information concerning one nation may be stored in another. For example, much data concerning Canadian residents is stored in computers located in the United States. Some nations today worry that information vital to their national interests might be stored in a foreign computer that could be seized by an unfriendly government. Other governments do not want their citizens to be exposed to propaganda and misinformation. In the past, governments could seize the relatively few printing presses and thus silence dissent; but it is hard to silence a satellite beaming a foreign news broadcast or control all copiers and tape recorders.

Loss of Cultures

Modern communications have increased pressures for common standards and a common language throughout the world. This has led, for example, to the nearly universal adoption of the metric system and the widespread use of the English language. However, the move toward standardization is causing a significant loss of cultural richness and results in occasional bloodshed, as when French-Canadians, Basque-speakers in Spain, or Flemish-speakers in Belgium battle to preserve their mother tongues.

Factory of the Future: Robots and Automation

Despite all the talk about robots, U.S. manufacturers have "hired" only about 5,000 so far, mainly for the automobile industry. But during the next ten years, the industrial robots are expected to take over more and more assembly line jobs. In Japan, which discovered the economical advantages of robots before most other industrial nations, the goal is to have whole factories without any human workers at all by 1985. Robots are a manager's dream; they never take coffee breaks or lunch hours; they willingly work three eight-hour shifts a day; they don't complain about doing unpleasant work, and they never take time off for union meetings. Robots now can do many tasks faster, cheaper and better than human beings.

Just what is a robot? Generally speaking, a robot is any machine that performs jobs previously assigned to a human being, is self-operating and is "intelligent"—that is, it contains electronic logic in the form of a microcomputer. A robot must be versatile, a characteristic provided for by microprocessors. Versatility makes robots economically feasible, because robots can be used in production tasks that frequently change. Manufacturing tasks such as yarn spinning that are highly standardized will continue to be done with highly automated machinery rather than by robots. However, when a particular function may be performed only 50 or 100 times in a manufacturing process, the robot's capacity to be programmed will allow the task to be automated. The robot can be repeatedly reprogrammed to perform different functions, depending on the needs of the factory. Since automobile models, for example, change each year, often drastically, the versatility of the robot will make further automation of the motor vehicle industry feasible.

Most industrial robots in use today and in the near future are and will be hardly recognizable as robots. They do not look like mechanical men but more like parts of automatic machinery. Usually a robot is simply a mechanical "arm," with two to six joints and a control system. The robot's "hand," called an "end effector," can be switched, depending on the job. The "hand" may be a welder, a riveter, a paint spray gun or a claw.

Modern industrial robots are quite easily programmable. All the programmer need do is guide it through the motions of a task, step by step, and press a program memory button. The robot remembers the process and can repeat it any number of times. A computerized robot does not have to be taught by leading the arm-gripper through a routine. It receives instructions electronically. Such "smart" robots may improve their own work-routine efficiency.

Robots can handle uncomfortable, dangerous jobs. Unlike their human counterparts, robots frequently handle loads up to 500 pounds or work in temperatures from 40 to 120 degrees. The die-casting industry, for instance, uses robots because of the danger of working near molten plastic. And because a robot can't daydream or be distracted, it is less likely to leave its arm in the way of other machinery. Even if an accident occurs a damaged robot can generally be repaired.

Despite recent advances, robots are still extremely limited in their usefulness because they must be programmed to perform one function at a time in a very precise manner and the materials they are working with must be precisely coordinated. For instance a spot-welding robot on an automobile assembly line will weld the exact same place time and time again until it is turned off or reprogrammed. If the auto parts moving down the assembly line move just a fraction of an inch out of place, the robot will miss the spot to be welded.

To deal with this and other problems, designers are developing sensory capabilities for robots. Some robots used by Texas Instruments to manu-

Unimation Inc.

Automobile assembly line utilizes robots to spot-weld auto bodies.

Industrial robot easily handles glowing iron billets in this drop forge operation.

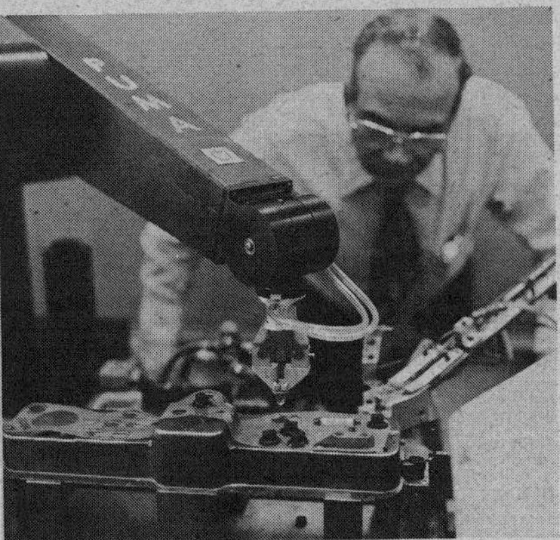

This industrial robot was designed to assemble small automotive components.

facture calculators are now able to "see." Seeing robots are still crude, clumsy and costly, but their skill is expected to improve and their price is expected to fall in the next few years.

Draper Labs has developed a robot with a rudimentary sense of touch. The robot can tell when a part doesn't "feel" right in its "hand," and can alert its foreman. The robot is also able to jiggle a part until it fits properly into place.

Robots that can hear would also be a boon to the factory of the future. With a microphone for an eardrum, robots can convert sound waves into number sequences and then compare these with various number sequences stored in their memories to determine the meaning. Hearing is still a difficult task for robots, but robot capabilities are expected to improve rapidly in this area, too, during the 1980s.

The next step in creating the sophisticated robot of the future is the combining of the three senses — sight, touch and hearing — with more sophisticated electronic logic that will enable robots to make many very limited decisions. A robot would be able to decide such things as whether a damaged part is repairable or should be discarded. If the robot itself is slightly damaged, it would be able to decide whether to turn itself off and alert a human or wait to end of its "shift."

The long-term impact of robots and computers on the factory of the future will almost certainly be profound. To keep tabs on the situation, The United Auto Workers have an official robot watcher, but labor unions do not now view robots as a threat to workers because they must constantly be maintained and fed parts to work with — and they must first be manufactured. So far robots have been used mainly for dangerous or extremely unpleasant jobs. But in the future robots may take away jobs that humans want, although opinions vary widely on just how many occupations are likely to be eliminated because of increased automation in the factory. Furthermore, unions realize that if robots can cause increased economic growth (as automation generally does), more jobs will be created than lost.

But there remains the possibility of a totally unmanned factory. The Italian automobile company, FIAT, believes sensory robots could slash manpower requirements by 90 percent over the next ten years; computer programmers and technicians might comprise most of its workforce by 1990. In his book *Running Wild*, Adam Osborne says, "Given the tasks that robots will be able to perform, their impact on the blue-collar force will be profound. Most assembly line jobs will be eliminated. Automobiles, washing machines, and television sets will all be assembled by robots. Robots will even assemble themselves."

Besides controlling robots, computers will work harder and harder in the factory of the future. Computer-Aided Design (CAD) and Computer-Aided Manufacture (CAM) are automating warehousing, packaging, inspecting and product testing and inventory control. Computers are controlling a wide variety of manufacturing equipment. Computers are even automating management, helping company executives make decisions about advertising, marketing and purchasing. Computers are also involved in rating and improving factory efficiency.

Computers have also begun automating order handling for factories. A computer can contain all the records of invoices, purchase orders and payments — records that traditionally take up rows and rows of filing cabinets. If a clerk wishes to apply payment to an outstanding invoice, he can use a light pen to pick out the invoice number from a masterlist on a computer terminal's display screen. The computer can then produce the full invoice and the account can be updated. The procedure has reduced the cost of handling transactions by 30 percent. At the same time, computerized credit checks have reduced losses due to bad debt.

The factory of the future will almost certainly be vastly more automated than today's factory. Just as the Industrial Revolution took many workers out of agriculture and employed them in industry, so the information revolution may take many workers out of industry and employ them in information and other services.

Work and Careers

The new computers and communications technology will radically change the world of work. No one seems to doubt that. But there is curiously little agreement on just what the overall impact will be or even whether it will be good or bad.

Millions of jobs are likely to be eliminated. But it is at least possible that even more jobs will be created! Will the final result be more jobs or fewer jobs? The jury is still out. Pessimists raise the specter of massive unemployment, while optimists talk of a new leisure society in which all the dull routine jobs are done by machines.

The displacement of workers by machines is an old story but one that has intensified during the past two centuries. In the 1700s, weavers in France were threatened by the invention of the jacquard loom; in the mid-20th century, farmworkers in the southern United States were displaced by mechanical equipment.

In recent years, newspapers and other publishing establishments have switched steadily from machines that set hot metal type to computerized "cold-type" equipment. The new equipment greatly reduces the cost of typesetting but has meant that many typesetters who had spent years on the older machines were suddenly deprived of their livelihood.

The experience of these typesetters may be duplicated on a massive scale during the 1980s as the new electronic technology sweeps through offices and factories. Postal workers are threatened by the development of electronic mail which may never go near a post office, and bank tellers will compete with automatic tellers for jobs. Jon Roland, a microcomputer expert writing in *The Futurist*, says:

"It is a useful exercise in forecasting to assume the general use within the next few years of personal computers as terminals, and then systematically to survey the businesses and occupations listed in the yellow pages of the telephone directory of any large metropolitan area, considering the likely impact of the microprocessor revolution on each. The result of such a survey is staggering: More than half of the occupations represented in such listings will cease to exist! Most of the others will be radically affected. Most businesses and industries will have to be extensively restructured and many will not survive the change."

Many labor experts have thought that jobs lost in manufacturing could be replaced by jobs appearing in the service area. However, there are signs that here also occupations are being substantially automated. Computers can be used to answer routine office letters. A computer, with some slight coaching from human beings, can select pre-written paragraphs on specified topics, and after typing a letter, put the address on the envelope. Other equipment can add the signature, stuff the letter in the envelope, seal it, apply postage and have it ready for the robot mail cart pick-up.

Virtually any service can be automated, to a considerable degree, with astute application of electronic equipment that is either available now or soon will be. Computers will, for example, be available to teach a foreign language, help people to do their income tax and act as their stockbroker.

New Technology Creates New Jobs

The evidence seems clear that the new communications and computer technology will, in fact, displace millions of workers from their jobs. But it does not necessarily follow that the overall employment situation will be horrendous.

One reason for thinking that employment may actually *increase* as a result of the new technology is that the number of jobs in industrialized countries has, in fact, tended to increase as labor-saving equipment was introduced. One reason for that contradictory-seeming circumstance is that the labor-saving equipment reduces the cost of labor and therefore the cost of the goods and services it renders. More people are then able to buy the lower-priced goods or services.

A second important reason why new technology does not necessarily cause unemployment over the long term is that it often results in new services that people want. The telephone, for example, was a new way of communicating which created whole new fields of employment.

Another instance of the new electronics enlarging the market for a product is the development of the hand-held calculator. The calculator replaced bulky mechanical calculators and slide rules. But outside of a few professions, those devices were rarely used and production was limited. By contrast, the hand-held calculator has entered homes, offices and schools everywhere. The upshot is that there are probably far more people making electronic calculators today than were making the earlier devices.

People are needed to manufacture the new equipment, and they are needed to sell, service and operate it. The first computer store in the United States opened in 1975. By the end of 1978 there were 700 stores. Today they probably number in the thousands. Toy stores are now selling a wide variety of electronic TV games and children's teaching aids. These video games provide jobs for the manufacturers and sales people involved.

Even if automation does not destroy more jobs than it creates, many observers worry that certain groups of people will lose disproportionately. For instance, in a study of textile industries the International Labour Organization found that when a new machine was installed the tendency as a whole was to substitute male workers for female workers, and in a study of the postal and telecommunications services, the ILO discovered that the introduction of new technical equipment often eliminated posts traditionally held by women — clerks, bookkeepers, switchboard operators, etc. By contrast, the introduction of phototypesetting into the publishing field has resulted in a large displacement of male workers by female workers.

Robots introduced into factories generally take away more blue-collar positions — jobs often held by members of minority groups or handicapped people — but recent reports suggest that middle managers and even top managers are not immune to the impact of the new technology. For one thing the new computers and communications devices probably make it easier for a single manager to handle a larger enterprise. Just as a security guard can monitor a dozen entrances

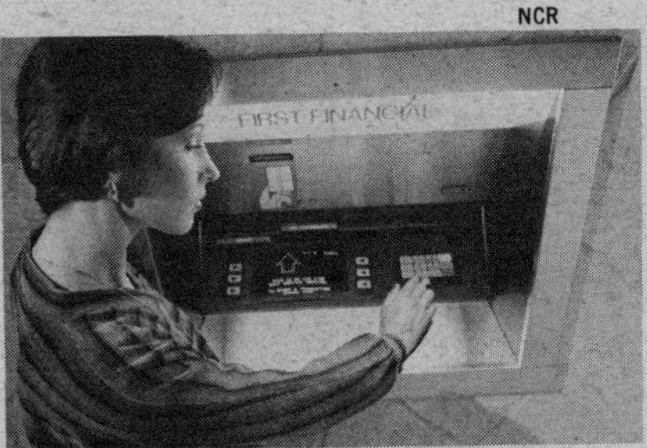

Self-service banking terminal eliminates jobs.

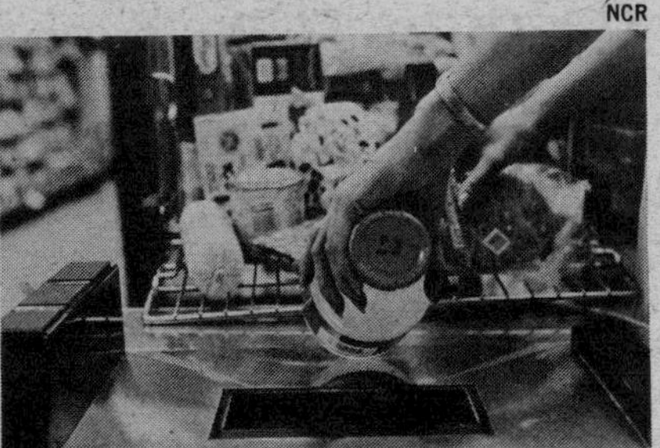

Electronic scanning speeds supermarket checkouts.

by means of closed-circuit television, a sales manager may be able to keep tabs on a very large sales force by means of computerized record keeping and teleconferencing.

Meanwhile, professional people face the same possibility of displacement — at least as far as some of their functions go. Programs are being developed to substitute computers for medical and psychiatric interviews. Studies indicate, incidentally, that computers are more accurate in diagnosing a patient's problems than are human physicians! Engineers using computers can design equipment much more rapidly than others who do not have the computer's aid, suggesting that fewer engineers may be needed for a given task in the future. Architects, lawyers, accountants and many other professionals can also do their work more efficiently with the new technology. The reduction in costs will make it possible for more people to avail themselves of the services of these professionals. There might be just as many jobs in those fields as previously, but the possibility exists for major displacement in some professions. Certainly, displacement is already a major problem for engineers. New engineers fresh out of the universities are often in high demand because they have been educated in the latest technology and have lower salary requirements. As a result, many older engineers, trained in technologies that are no longer in demand, find themselves without jobs. Older workers in many occupations are facing similar displacement.

The Increase of Leisure

A decline in the number of jobs can be slowed or even halted by reducing the number of hours of work. At the beginning of the 20th century the normal work week in factories was 60 hours. The impetus behind the adoption of the 40-hour week was, in large measure the desire to spread work so as to provide jobs for more people.

The increasing efficiency of the information technology should mean a great deal more leisure for the average person in the years ahead, according to many scholars. The prospect of unemployment arouses fear, but most people would welcome three-day work weeks. Probably few would object to having two months of vacation rather than two weeks. The main problem of the future, says science-fiction writer Arthur C. Clarke, is the development of social systems based on full *un*employment policies. Clarke believes that ultra-intelligent machines will eventually take over all work now done by human beings.

Kurt Vonnegut, in his novel *Player Piano,* foresaw a society in which a small group of engineers runs the productive machinery and the majority of the citizens are reduced to menial chores like repairing the streets and cleaning up the litter. Alvin Toffler in his 1980 *The Third Wave,* offers a more optimistic view. In the future, Toffler suggests, "Most boring jobs can be done by machines; lengthy commuting can be avoided; we can have enough leisure to follow interesting pursuits outside our work; environmental destruction can be avoided; and the opportunities for personal creativity will be unlimited."

More Work at Home?

The new communications technology clearly makes it more feasible for many people to work at home — or wherever else they like. It is easy to imagine a future businessman snorkling in Pago Pago, pausing only occasionally to dictate memos to a secretary in New York City and receiving a response in only 20 minutes.

With the installation of computer terminals or other forms of electronic equipment, the ability to work at home either full or part time should open many jobs to many homemakers and to handicapped people. Working at home may boost productivity. Some studies have shown that people working at home usually put in 20 percent more time than people working at the office.

As machines take over more and more jobs, what human skills will be prized in workers during the coming years? It seems likely that human workers will be prized for those things that machines, for some reason, cannot be made to do — or at least cannot do very well. What are these special skills that human beings have that machines lack?

One skill seems to be versatility. Although robots are becoming increasingly versatile — that is, capable of performing a very wide variety of tasks — even the best robots lack the very wide range of perceptions, mechanical skills and talents that even a very ordinary human being has. Human workers will also be valued for their ability to deal with other human beings and make judgments based on human values and the subtleties of human language.

Adaptability is perhaps the major weapon that the average human being has in confronting the machine. People who cannot easily adapt are likely to be the ones who will suffer most during the information transformation. The people who will make out best will be those who are constantly developing new skills.

The Office of the Future

New communications technologies will make it possible for people to do so much work at home that the first question one might ask about the office of the future is: Will there really be one? That is, will there continue to be places outside the home where people will go to perform management and other office work?

Future executives, whether they work for large companies or small, will be able to take the essential part of their offices with them and will be reachable at all times by fellow workers. For many small businesses, the office of the future may be nothing more than a small, portable package of computer and communications equipment (complete with video display screen) that contains the records of the business. The "office" will be wherever that little package is — right next to the executive as he sits talking to a client or at home with him at night. Periodically, the executive might link his portable office to the telephone system so that his bank, clients and suppliers could receive bank deposits, bills, payments and other business correspondence.

A big business will almost certainly find it desirable to have something more than a portable office because of such important limitations as size. For one thing, the display screen of a portable office will necessarily be small and cannot have the dramatic impact of a large one. Clearly there will be a need for much larger screens that can give executives a richer, more exciting picture of what is happening in their organizations. This suggests the need for *situation rooms* — environments like the Pentagon's "war rooms" equipped with all kinds of maps, charts, televison screens, and even three-dimensional models showing the current disposition of units.

At times, the executives of a corporation may wish to meet with the executives of different divisions all around the world, united electronically by microwave and satellites in a teleconference, held in a designated conference room.

Such situation and conference rooms may be highly useful for certain business operations, but other administrative functions may be carried out better in a somewhat different habitat. For example, people may want a quieter, less distracting environment in which to hold private conversations. In fact, the influx of electronic gadgets and the confidential nature of such business discussion may make it desirable to have "safe rooms" — that is, rooms which are carefully constructed and monitored to make sure that there are no listening devices to destroy the confidentiality of conversations.

In large companies, some executives may spend the better part of their work time in the fully equipped central control areas or situation rooms. Others will use smaller conference rooms because their work will require face-to-face conversations — or they will simply prefer such settings for more reflective endeavor. Most executives will probably have to spend considerable time dictating their thoughts to their portable office equipment for transmission to fellow workers and for storage in the firm's computer memory.

Current trends suggest that the office of the

Computers are changing the "office look."

future will be different from the standard office of today with its knee-hole desk, chair, telephone and filing cabinet. The typewriter will have given way to word processing equipment. The telephone, chair and desk may survive in some form. However, that old standby of the office — the four-drawer filing cabinet — will probably be gone. Paper may become almost as rare in offices of the future as nib pens and blotting paper are in today's offices. Most experts seem agreed that one of the principal keys to office efficiency will be the switch from putting information on paper to putting it into computers.

The recorded voice transmission system will make it far easier for all employees of an organization to share information or make known their needs and capabilities. The voice recordings can be stored permanently in the archives of the firm, giving future historians a wealth of oral documentation. Since computers will keep track of production, people will be able to work wherever as well as whenever they like — at least within certain limits. Flex-*place* will join flex*time*, since the computer will monitor output, automatically alerting a supervisor when production falls below minimum standards.

Many features of the office of the future will strike people today as sinister, suggestive of Orwell's *1984.* In addition to the increasing volume of permanent records of people's conversations, there may be electronic sensors almost everywhere. People may never be quite sure whether the video screens are there to give information or to collect it — or perhaps both. On the other hand, it may become easier to ascertain the truth of a situation because of the availability of ample electronic documentation.

Today the office is mainly a place where information is transmitted, stored and processed. But as electronic technology takes over the simple information-processing tasks, office workers will face a new challenge — creating visions of the future and deciding which ones to try to realize.

The Home of the Future

The new electronic technology will change home life in thousands of subtle ways. One development already occurring is the appearance of the "media room," in which one can while away countless hours drenched in visual and auditory sensations.

A large color television set or projection (large-screen) TV system customarily remains in one place, since it cannot easily be moved around the house. If a video recorder is added along with its library of cassettes or discs, more space is required. An additional reason to house electronic entertainment equipment in one room arises from coming improvements in TV sound and a step-up in the number of speakers needed. Hence the seemingly inevitable development of the media room — the eighties' answer to the recreation room of the TV-and-tots fifties and sixties.

It is worth noting that even modest versions of the different types of equipment that would go into a completely furnished media center can easily run $5,000 to $10,000. Once a videotape recorder is acquired, people begin building up a library of cassettes of broadcast television programs (costing about $20 per cassette of raw tape) and also prerecorded cassettes, costing $50 and up.

Interior designers are beginning to orient their decor around the new media. Many people are installing their electronics behind wood-panel doors, partly to protect the equipment and partly because owners often find the wooden panels more decorative than the equipment itself.

Based on current projections and the experience of people who already have media rooms, a typical media room in the mid-1980s may contain a large-screen television set (possibly of the projection variety which allows a bigger-than-life picture), a videotape recorder and/or a videodisc player connected to the television equipment, a stereophonic system with speakers at several locations in the room, shelves for storing videocassettes, videodiscs, audiotapes and phonograph records, etc. Facing the screen will be a number of comfortable chairs and/or sofas, and cushions for people who like to lie on the rug while enjoying their entertainment.

The home computer system may well be kept separate from the video equipment, especially in multiperson households. For one thing, the computer is more likely to be used for serious work, typically involving only one member of the household. However, in the single-person household, where work and entertainment are unlikely to conflict with each other, all of the equipment may be concentrated in a single room.

As more electronic entertainment and information features become available, there will probably be a strong tendency in households with two or more members to duplicate some of the equipment. Possibly there may be one media room where the best entertainment equipment is kept, but there will also be one or more computer terminals and/or video centers at other locations. If youngsters are using computers increasingly in their homework, as now seems probable, the adults in the home will want separate terminals so they can carry on their own work. As computer prices continue to decline, the number of terminals will increase just as the number of television sets in U.S. households increased when prices dropped. It is now quite common to find households with three or more televison sets, and by 1990 a household with three computer terminals may be totally unremarkable.

The new technology will mean that youngsters can learn about as effectively at home as in a classroom — perhaps more so for the motivated student. Educators and communications specialists are beginning to develop courses that link the capabilities of video and computers. It is possible to envision extraordinarily effective teaching systems that will be even better in some regards than a student having a private tutor. For instance, a course in the French language and culture could include videotapes showing a wide variety of full-color scenes of life in France with a variety of scenes involving French people talking in common situations. The computer would be used to test and reinforce the student's proficiency after viewing the tapes.

While Johnny is learning different subjects on electronic equipment, one parent may be using the computer to figure out the family income tax and the other may be using the interactive advertising system to find out what is currently on sale at local stores and may even be making purchases by transferring funds through the electronic system.

The new technology may make it possible for many people to live in what has been called an "electronic cocoon" — that is an environment virtually sealed off from the outside world. There may be far less need for household members to leave the house. The new technology will make it possible for much work to be done at home. The professional consultant can both provide information and do his billing and collecting electronically. And someone who has become an expert in, say the Dr. Dolittle series, may be able to earn a modest living by serving as consultant to people around the world who happen to want to know something about Dr. Dolittle and his creator, Hugh Lofting.

The home computer and its sisters — the small microprocessors that will inhabit most household appliances — will convert the home into a totally controlled environment. Computer systems will monitor the temperature, humidity and other features of the house and signal for appropriate corrections if the readings are not within acceptable limits. There will also be sensors to alert the computer to any suspicion of illegal entry or fire and warn the proper authorities automatically.

We may also have a system which will remind us to do things. When we wake up in the morning, a computer may automatically inform us of the date, weather and things we are supposed to do that day. The computer may also have our breakfast ready and waiting by the time we finish our showers. And when we sit down to eat, we may find ourselves surrounded by sculpture and paintings that have been created with the help of a computer. Even the music we hear may have a computer as its creator.

The Information Society in the Early 21st Century

Alexander Jones reports on his visit to the Chicago headquarters of Intergalactic Widgets, Limited, in the year 2002.

The main headquarters of Intergalactic Widgets, Ltd., lies under Lake Michigan, two miles from central Chicago. The complex was built with government subsidies because it was thought desirable to have a number of shelters for use in case of war. Intergalactic Widgets leases space in the sublake environment for its headquarters and as a place to condition employees for work in space stations, where workers are cut off from the normal earth environment.

I arrived at Intergalactic Widgets on the special subway train that runs from O'Hare International Airport directly to the underlake complex, making only one stop in downtown Chicago. The underground train trip lasts only six minutes, including the two-minute stop in the downtown section.

On my arrival, I boarded an unmanned autocar that moves along a track system to the various parts of the complex. To get to Intergalactic, I touched the desired destination on the car's control panel; the unseen computer did the rest. In a few moments, the autocar spoke: "You have arrived at Intergalactic Widgets. Please make sure you do not leave anything in the car when you get off."

At the gateway a speaking robot addressed me: "Good morning. Welcome to Intergalactic Widgets. Please tell me your name and the name of the person you wish to see." After I complied, the robot said, "Thank you. Please enter and board the transporter on your right."

Once I was seated, the unmanned computerized car took me quickly on my way without further instructions. Part of the time, it traveled vertically through the building in what looked like an elevator shaft; the rest of the time it moved horizontally. In a few moments I was at my destination — the office of my contact, Toby Smith.

"How are you, Alex?" asked Toby. "I'm delighted to have a chance to show you my office. It's nothing special, but it's my home away from home."

Toby's office had a few vids (video display screens), a bed-chair (which serves both for sleeping and sitting), a number of shelves with souvenirs and a table, on which rested Toby's portable office, resembling one of the attaché cases that were common in times past. The room was soundproof; by closing the door, Toby could isolate himself from almost all sounds in the building.

"Before starting our tour, let's listen to the office news." Toby touched the controls on his portable office and a moment later one of the vids lit up with the picture of a young man wearing a large bow tie.

"Good afternoon, fellow employees. The company has had a good day so far. An order for 2,000 widgets has just been received by our branch in Sumatra and another for 1,400 by our branch in Afghanistan. Congratulations to them both. . . . The legal department says it is making headway in its battle to sell widgets through the new United Nations agency in Mongolia. . . . And now for the office news:

Marilyn Pierce in Purchasing has a new baby girl. . . . Janet Minelli has just returned from her wedding trip to the moon. She and her husband stayed at the new Lunar Hilton, located near the monument marking the spot where the astronauts first landed."

Toby turned off the broadcast.

"The gossip is just junk," he said in disgust. "For the real gossip, you have to go to the Relaxatory."

"What's that?"

"Our recreation center. Come on, we'll start our tour there."

The Relaxatory turned out to be a series of very large rooms, each with its own distinctive character but designed to provide a pleasant, carefree environment for the employees of Intergalactic Widgets.

We chose the Waikiki Room, which simulates the Hawaiian environment and life-style. In addition to the soft Hawaiian music there were the sound of breaking surf and a stretch of sandy beach leading down to a swimming pool. A videotape system flashed exotic Oahu beach scenes on multiple screens covering the walls, so that if the Waikiki Room was not the real thing, it was close to it. An artificial ocean breeze, complete with a smack of salt, blew gently across the room. Most people were lying on the sand; some in groups and some alone. Others bathed in the pool.

"We spend a lot of time in the Relaxatory," Toby explained. "In fact, I would say that we do our best work here. And we get the *real* gossip—the juicy bits about who's knifing whom. There are other rooms that simulate a mountain environment, a farm with real cows and ducks, a Parisian boulevard, a Western ranch and a 19th-century New England village. But come along. I want you to see one of our situation rooms."

The situation room he showed me was large, and its walls were completely covered with video screens, charts and control panels. In the center, a small group of executives occupied bed-chairs. They alternately contemplated the video screens and discussed business matters with each other. Occasionally one would manipulate the control panel of his portable office, sending out new instructions to Intergalactic Widgets' far-flung branch offices in response to an executive decision or an inquiry from the field.

"This is the heart of Intergalactic Widgets," said Toby. "Those are our top executives. It's unusual to see so many of them together in the Big Situation Room. Generally they're in the Relaxatory. But come along. My wife is expecting you for dinner."

Toby and I boarded a nearby autocar, which whisked us to the subway. A short time later we transferred to a driverless bus, which took us out across the countryside on a superspeed highway.

"Remember when people were scared to ride in these driverless buses?" asked Toby. "They couldn't quite get used to the idea that computers are better drivers than people. When did you ever hear of a computer drinking too much or falling asleep at the wheel?"

At Toby's house, his wife, Ann, welcomed us warmly. The exterior of the home was executed in the environmental style favored in the late 1980s; the interior was decorated by the usual vids projecting a preselected decor designed to fit a certain mood. Ann Smith appeared to favor tranquil pastoral scenes with sunsets and dramatic cloud patterns drifting across the screen.

"What would you like for dinner?" asked Ann. "Our autokitchen is pretty good on soufflés, and its veal scallopini is quite tasty."

"That sounds fine to me."

"I'll order dinner for 20 minutes from now, unless you are so hungry you can't wait."

Ann Smith touched the panel of the remote control unit beside the sofa on which she was sitting and began chatting about some new videotapes she had received from the 1,000-inhabitant space station currently under construction in orbit. Mrs. Smith works for a real estate agency specializing in space station residential properties; her clients are mainly high-income people buying sites as tax shelters; but some are young couples who want to experience life on the High Frontier. To illustrate one point in her talk, she touched her control panel, and, a moment later, scenes of the space station appeared on the screen. While we were discussing life in space, a robot appeared at the doorway of the living room; the robot looked like a mobile cabinet with metal arms and control panels. The body was painted red, white and blue and bore the name JEEVES on his name plate.

"Your dinner is ready," said Jeeves. "Shall I bring it into the dining room now?"

"Yes, Jeeves," said Ann.

We moved from the living room to the dining room, where the robot butler was setting the plates out on the table. After completing the job, Jeeves stood motionless, awaiting further instructions.

"Thank you, Jeeves," said Ann. Jeeves moved silently back to the kitchen, traveling on a cushion of air.

"We call him Jeeves because he's a British robot," said Ann. "We used to have a Japanese robot whom we called Mr. Moto, but we traded him in when the new generation of robots came out."

"We had a slight problem with Mr. Moto," added Toby. "We'd be in the midst of a conversation and something we said would set him off; he'd suddenly start cooking supper or emptying the garbage for no reason that we could figure out. Our new robot, Jeeves, is programmed so that he only responds to commands that include his name. If his name isn't part of the command, he won't do anything at all."

"It's a good security device," added Mrs. Smith. "You remember reading about the burglar who ordered a robot to attack the people in the house he was robbing? That can't happen to us. Jeeves has been programmed to respond only to Toby and me — and only when we use his name. Otherwise he won't do anything."

We continued to chat about the robot problem, which has been a burning issue since the 1990s, when household robots became common. Everyone had a new robot joke and there were the usual anecdotes suggesting that robots might eventually turn the tables and make human beings do the work. It was nonsense, of course. Still, the stories sometimes make you wonder. But all in all, people are really quite happy with their robots — certainly nobody is ready to give them up. In fact, it is hard to imagine what life was like before there were robots to do most of the chores of everyday life.

Dwight Dobbins

NEWS MAPS

NORWEGIAN
SEA
ICELAND
Floating oil-rig platform collapses in storm, killing 123 workers (Mar. 27, 1980).
British commandos storm Iranian embassy in London to rescue 19 hostages (May 5, 1980); 5 terrorists killed and 1 hostage dead.
SWEDEN
FINLAND
Helsinki
NORWAY
Prime Minister Jack Lynch resigns (Dec. 7, 1979) and is succeeded by Charles Haughey.
Oil
Stockholm
BALTIC SEA
Polish government grants workers right to form independent trade unions following wave of strikes idling 350,000 workers (Aug.-Sept. 1980). Stanislaw Konia replaces Edward Gierek as party chief (Sept. 6, 1980).
Oil
UNITED
No. Ire.
NORTH SEA
DENMARK
IRELAND
KINGDOM
Gdańsk
U.S.S.R.
Princess Beatrix becomes monarch of the Netherlands (Apr. 30, 1980), succeeding her mother, Queen Juliana, 71, who announced her abdication in January.
NETHERLANDS
London
EAST
WEST
Berlin
POLAND
Josip Broz Tito, president of Yugoslavia, dies at age 87 (May 4, 1980) after four-month illness.
BELGIUM
Rhine
GERMANY
GERMANY
Paris
LUX.
GERMANY
CZECHOSLOVAKIA
NATO ministers approve the deployment of 572 medium-range nuclear missiles (Dec. 12, 1979).
SWITZERLAND
AUSTRIA
HUNGARY
FRANCE
ROMANIA
Venice
Belgrade
Danube
BLACK SEA
PORTUGAL
YUGOSLAVIA
BULGARIA
ITALY
Madrid
Leaders of U.S., Japan, West Germany, U.K., Canada, France and Italy meet and pledge to end reliance on OPEC oil (June 22-23, 1980).
Rome
ALBANIA
Lisbon
SPAIN
TURKEY
GREECE
MEDITERRANEAN
Athens
Autonomous regional governments established (March 1980) in Basque region (Euzkadi) and Catalonia. Basque terrorist activity continues.
MALTA
SEA
MOROCCO
Greece to become full member of European Community Jan. 1, 1981.
TUNISIA
ALGERIA
EGYPT
LIBYA
European Community members are underlined
© Copyright HAMMOND INCORPORATED, Maplewood, N.J.
EUROPE

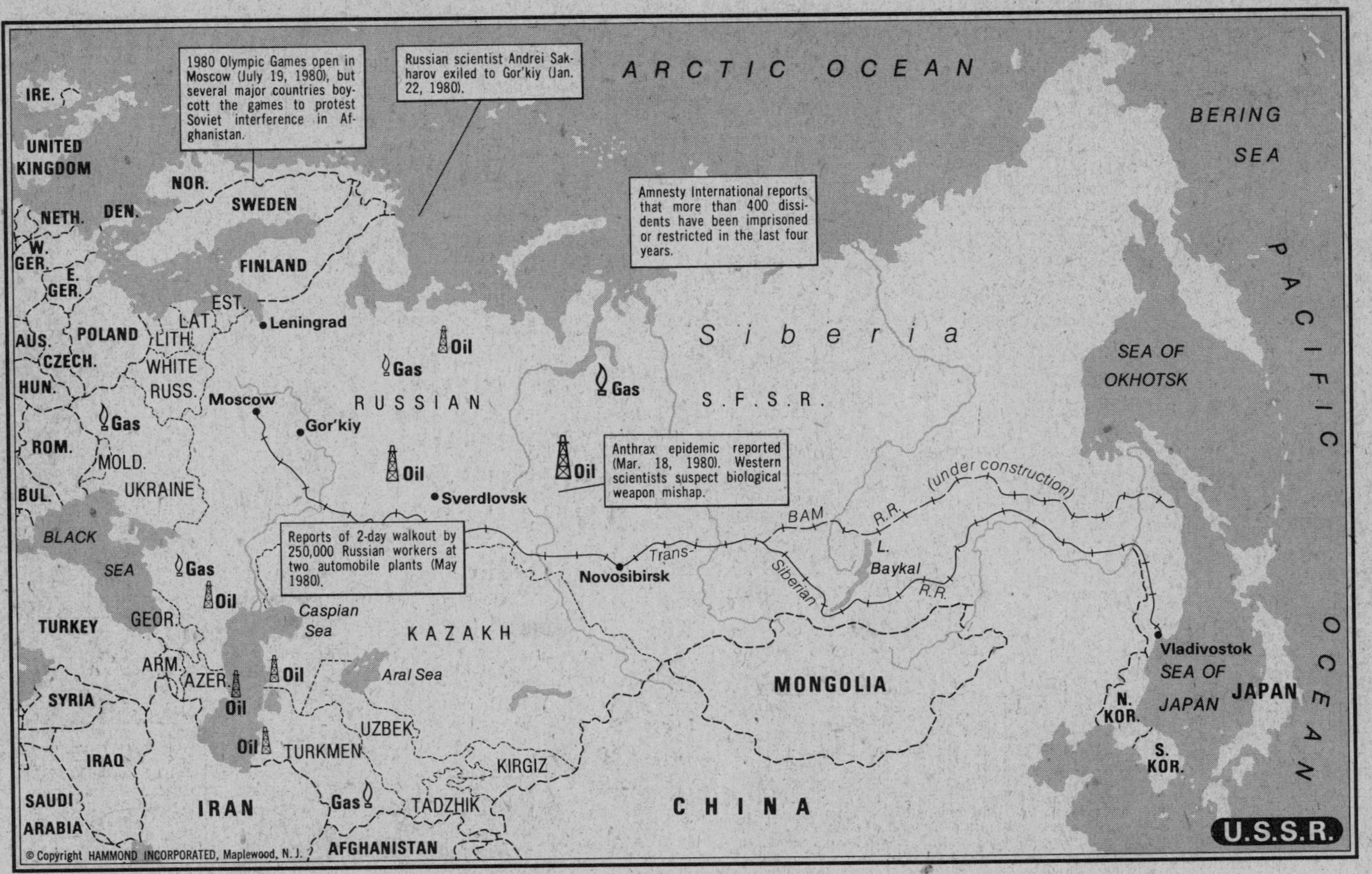
U.S.S.R.
ARCTIC OCEAN
BERING SEA
PACIFIC OCEAN
SEA OF OKHOTSK
SEA OF JAPAN
JAPAN
N. KOR.
S. KOR.
Vladivostok
Siberia
S.F.S.R.
BAM
R.R.
(under construction)
Trans Siberian
R.R.
L. Baykal
MONGOLIA
CHINA
KAZAKH
Aral Sea
KIRGIZ
UZBEK
TADZHIK
TURKMEN
Gas
AFGHANISTAN
IRAN
IRAQ
SYRIA
SAUDI ARABIA
TURKEY
GEOR.
ARM.
AZER.
Oil
Oil
Oil
Oil
BLACK SEA
Gas
Caspian Sea
Novosibirsk
Oil
Gas
Sverdlovsk
Oil
Gas
Gor'kiy
Moscow
RUSSIAN
Oil
Gas
Leningrad
EST.
LAT.
LITH.
WHITE RUSS.
MOLD.
UKRAINE
ROM.
BUL.
Gas
FINLAND
SWEDEN
NOR.
DEN.
NETH.
W. GER.
E. GER.
POLAND
CZECH.
AUS.
HUN.
UNITED KINGDOM
IRE.
1980 Olympic Games open in Moscow (July 19, 1980), but several major countries boycott the games to protest Soviet interference in Afghanistan.
Russian scientist Andrei Sakharov exiled to Gor'kiy (Jan. 22, 1980).
Amnesty International reports that more than 400 dissidents have been imprisoned or restricted in the last four years.
Anthrax epidemic reported (Mar. 18, 1980). Western scientists suspect biological weapon mishap.
Reports of 2-day walkout by 250,000 Russian workers at two automobile plants (May 1980).

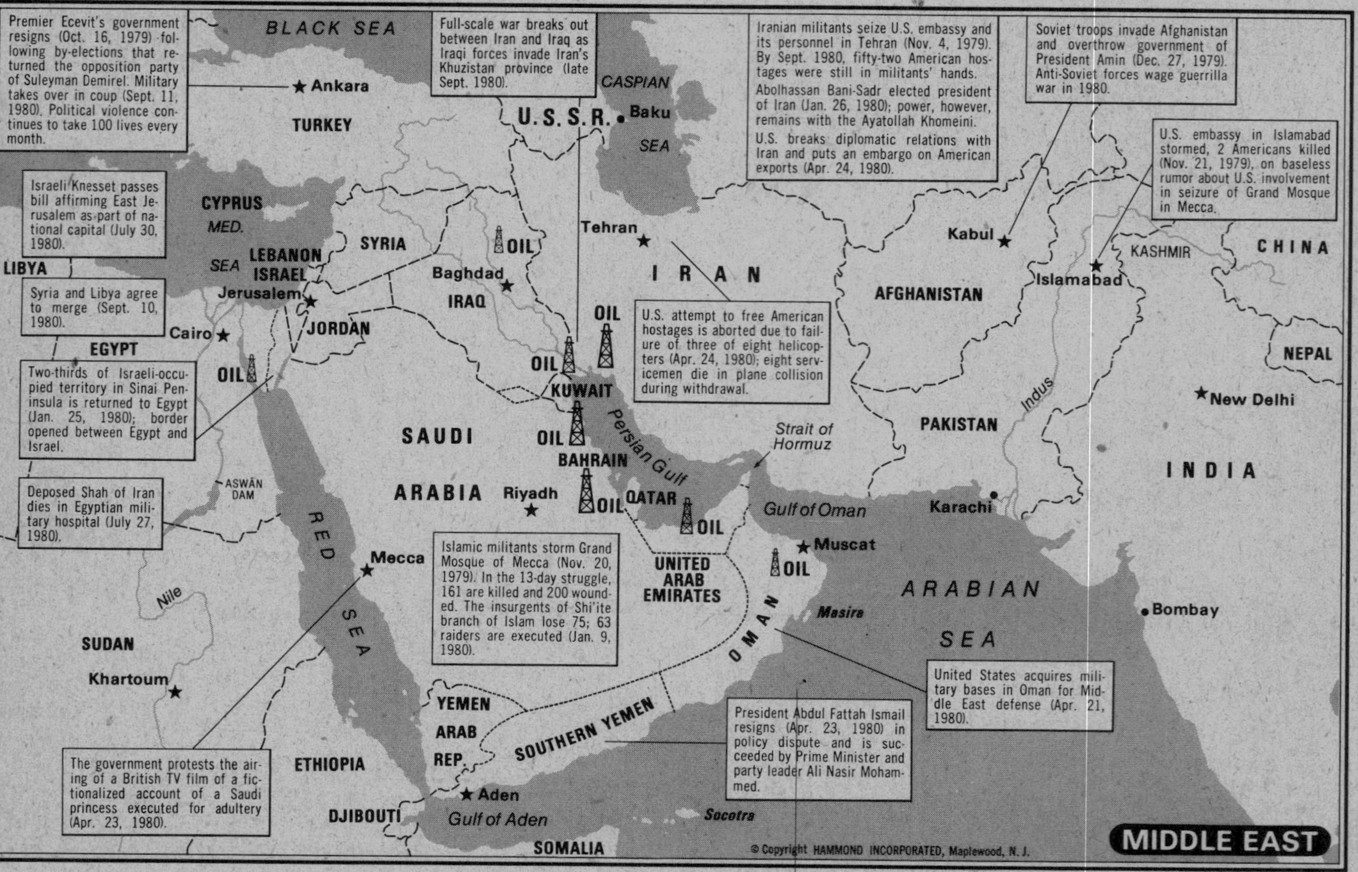
Premier Ecevit's government resigns (Oct. 16, 1979) following by-elections that returned the opposition party of Suleyman Demirel. Military takes over in coup (Sept. 11, 1980). Political violence continues to take 100 lives every month.

Israeli Knesset passes bill affirming East Jerusalem as part of national capital (July 30, 1980).

Syria and Libya agree to merge (Sept. 10, 1980).

Two-thirds of Israeli-occupied territory in Sinai Peninsula is returned to Egypt (Jan. 25, 1980); border opened between Egypt and Israel.

Deposed Shah of Iran dies in Egyptian military hospital (July 27, 1980).

Full-scale war breaks out between Iran and Iraq as Iraqi forces invade Iran's Khuzistan province (late Sept. 1980).

Iranian militants seize U.S. embassy and its personnel in Tehran (Nov. 4, 1979). By Sept. 1980, fifty-two American hostages were still in militants' hands.
Abolhassan Bani-Sadr elected president of Iran (Jan. 26, 1980); power, however, remains with the Ayatollah Khomeini.
U.S. breaks diplomatic relations with Iran and puts an embargo on American exports (Apr. 24, 1980).

U.S. attempt to free American hostages is aborted due to failure of three of eight helicopters (Apr. 24, 1980); eight servicemen die in plane collision during withdrawal.

Soviet troops invade Afghanistan and overthrow government of President Amin (Dec. 27, 1979). Anti-Soviet forces wage guerrilla war in 1980.

U.S. embassy in Islamabad stormed, 2 Americans killed (Nov. 21, 1979), on baseless rumor about U.S. involvement in seizure of Grand Mosque in Mecca.

Islamic militants storm Grand Mosque of Mecca (Nov. 20, 1979). In the 13-day struggle, 161 are killed and 200 wounded. The insurgents of Shi'ite branch of Islam lose 75; 63 raiders are executed (Jan. 9, 1980).

President Abdul Fattah Ismail resigns (Apr. 23, 1980) in policy dispute and is succeeded by Prime Minister and party leader Ali Nasir Mohammed.

United States acquires military bases in Oman for Middle East defense (Apr. 21, 1980).

The government protests the airing of a British TV film of a fictionalized account of a Saudi princess executed for adultery (Apr. 23, 1980).

BLACK SEA
Ankara
TURKEY
U.S.S.R.
Baku
CASPIAN SEA
CYPRUS
MED. SEA
LEBANON
ISRAEL
Jerusalem
SYRIA
JORDAN
Cairo
EGYPT
LIBYA
OIL
Baghdad
IRAQ
OIL
Tehran
IRAN
OIL
OIL
KUWAIT
OIL
Persian Gulf
BAHRAIN
OIL
QATAR
OIL
SAUDI ARABIA
Riyadh
ASWAN DAM
Nile
RED SEA
Mecca
SUDAN
Khartoum
ETHIOPIA
YEMEN ARAB REP.
SOUTHERN YEMEN
Aden
DJIBOUTI
Gulf of Aden
SOMALIA
UNITED ARAB EMIRATES
OMAN
OIL
Muscat
Gulf of Oman
Strait of Hormuz
Masira
Socotra
Kabul
AFGHANISTAN
Islamabad
KASHMIR
CHINA
PAKISTAN
Indus
NEPAL
New Delhi
INDIA
Karachi
Bombay
ARABIAN SEA

© Copyright HAMMOND INCORPORATED, Maplewood, N.J.

MIDDLE EAST

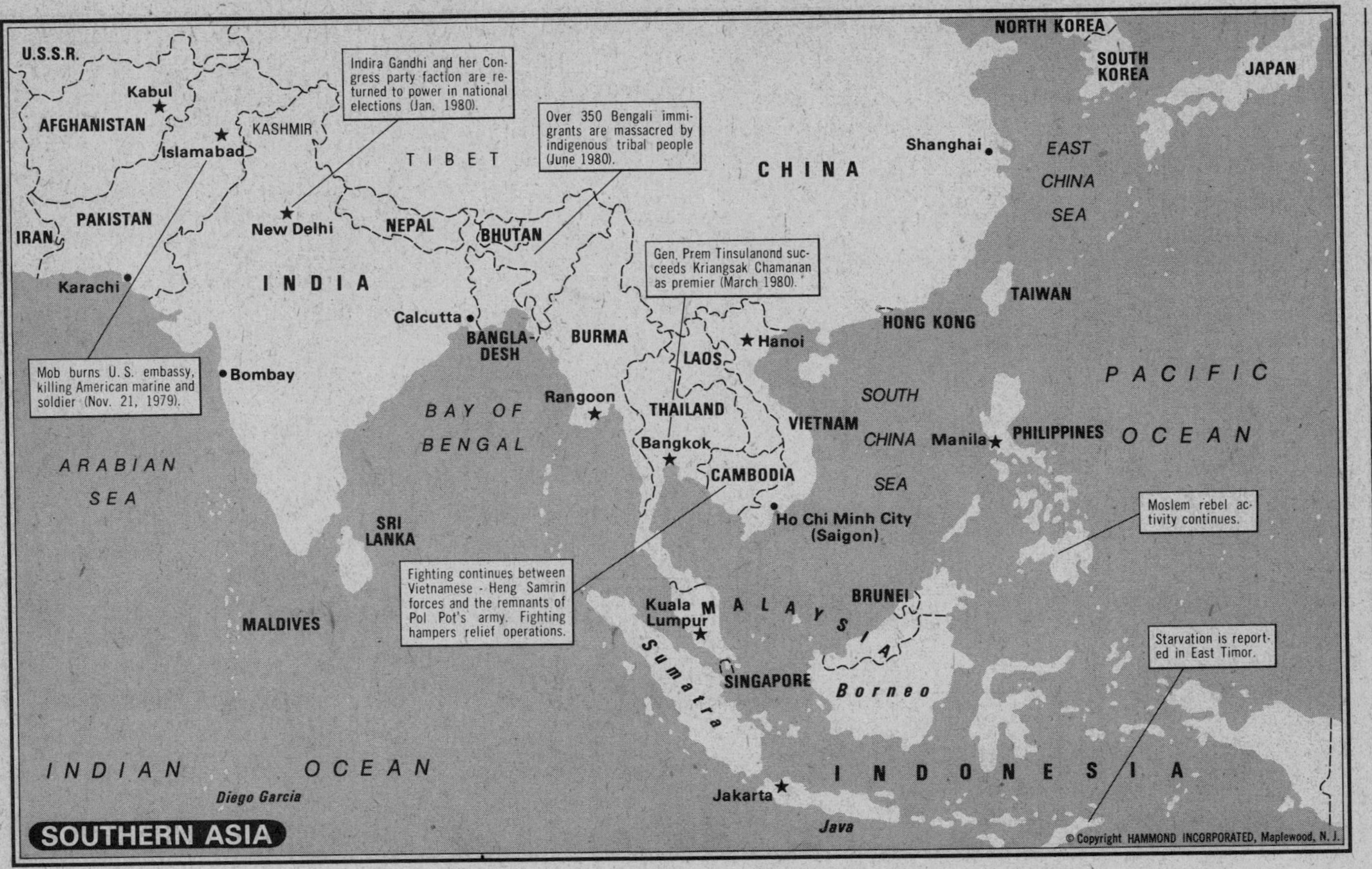

U.S.S.R.
Indira Gandhi and her Congress party faction are returned to power in national elections (Jan. 1980).
Over 350 Bengali immigrants are massacred by indigenous tribal people (June 1980).
NORTH KOREA
SOUTH KOREA
JAPAN
Kabul
AFGHANISTAN
KASHMIR
Islamabad
TIBET
Shanghai
CHINA
EAST CHINA SEA
IRAN
PAKISTAN
New Delhi
NEPAL
BHUTAN
Gen. Prem Tinsulanond succeeds Kriangsak Chamanan as premier (March 1980).
TAIWAN
Karachi
INDIA
Calcutta
BANGLA-DESH
BURMA
HONG KONG
Mob burns U.S. embassy, killing American marine and soldier (Nov. 21, 1979).
Bombay
Rangoon
LAOS
Hanoi
SOUTH CHINA SEA
PACIFIC OCEAN
BAY OF BENGAL
THAILAND
VIETNAM
Bangkok
CHINA
Manila
PHILIPPINES
ARABIAN SEA
CAMBODIA
Ho Chi Minh City (Saigon)
Moslem rebel activity continues.
SRI LANKA
Fighting continues between Vietnamese - Heng Samrin forces and the remnants of Pol Pot's army. Fighting hampers relief operations.
BRUNEI
Kuala Lumpur
MALAYSIA
MALDIVES
Starvation is reported in East Timor.
Sumatra
SINGAPORE
Borneo
INDIAN OCEAN
INDONESIA
Diego Garcia
Jakarta
Java
SOUTHERN ASIA
© Copyright HAMMOND INCORPORATED, Maplewood, N. J.

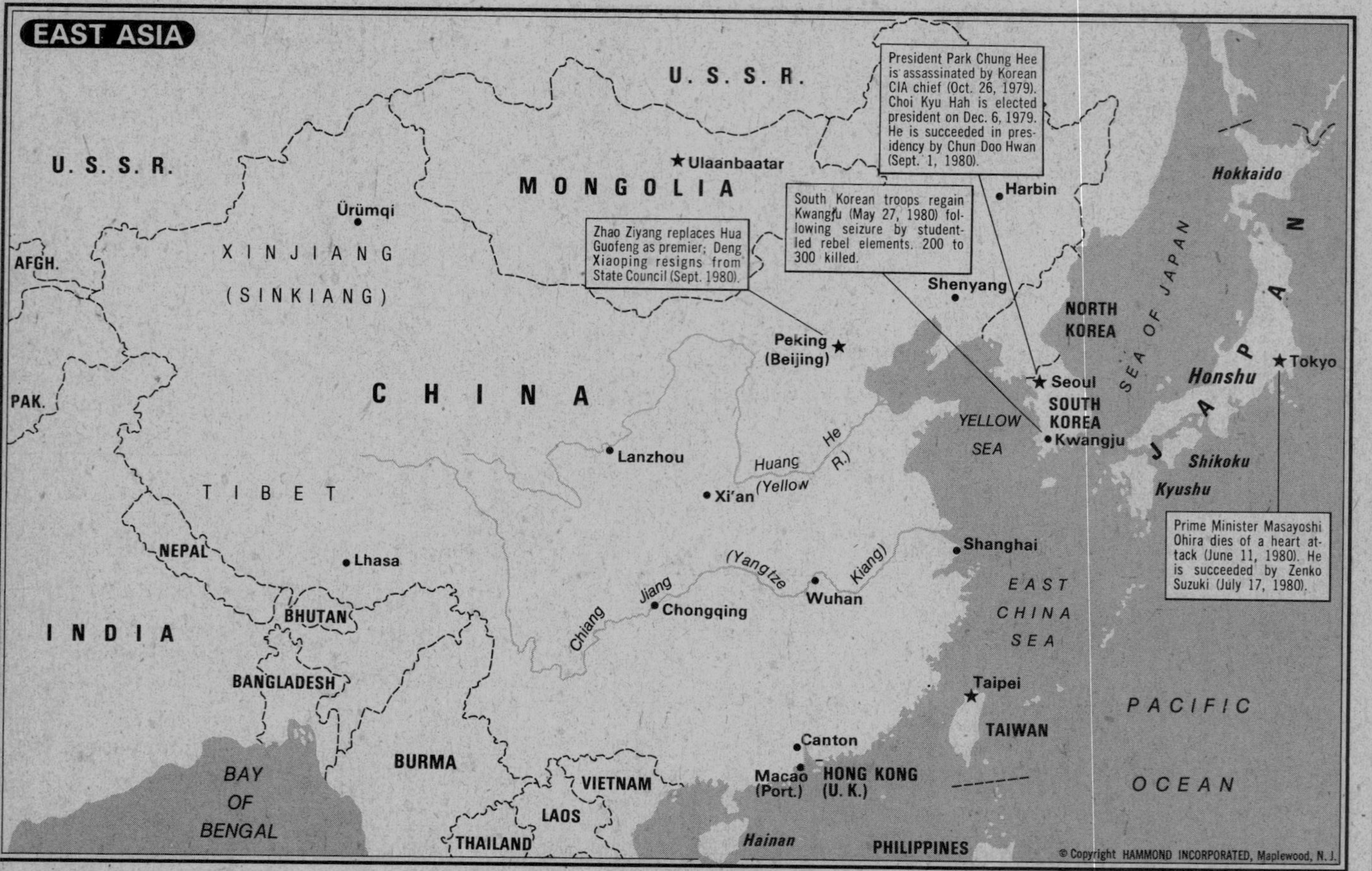

EAST ASIA
U.S.S.R.
U.S.S.R.
MONGOLIA
★ Ulaanbaatar
Ürümqi
AFGH.
PAK.
XINJIANG
(SINKIANG)
CHINA
TIBET
Lhasa
NEPAL
BHUTAN
BANGLADESH
INDIA
BURMA
VIETNAM
LAOS
THAILAND
BAY OF BENGAL
Lanzhou
Xi'an
Huang (Yellow)
He R.
Peking (Beijing) ★
Harbin
Shenyang
NORTH KOREA
★ Seoul
SOUTH KOREA
Kwangju
YELLOW SEA
Chiang
Jiang
Chongqing
(Yangtze)
Kiang)
Wuhan
Shanghai
Canton
Macao (Port.)
HONG KONG (U.K.)
Hainan
PHILIPPINES
TAIPEI
Taipei ★
TAIWAN
EAST CHINA SEA
SEA OF JAPAN
Hokkaido
Honshu
JAPAN
★ Tokyo
Shikoku
Kyushu
PACIFIC OCEAN
President Park Chung Hee is assassinated by Korean CIA chief (Oct. 26, 1979). Choi Kyu Hah is elected president on Dec. 6, 1979. He is succeeded in presidency by Chun Doo Hwan (Sept. 1, 1980).
South Korean troops regain Kwangju (May 27, 1980) following seizure by student-led rebel elements. 200 to 300 killed.
Zhao Ziyang replaces Hua Guofeng as premier; Deng Xiaoping resigns from State Council (Sept. 1980).
Prime Minister Masayoshi Ohira dies of a heart attack (June 11, 1980). He is succeeded by Zenko Suzuki (July 17, 1980).
© Copyright HAMMOND INCORPORATED, Maplewood, N.J.

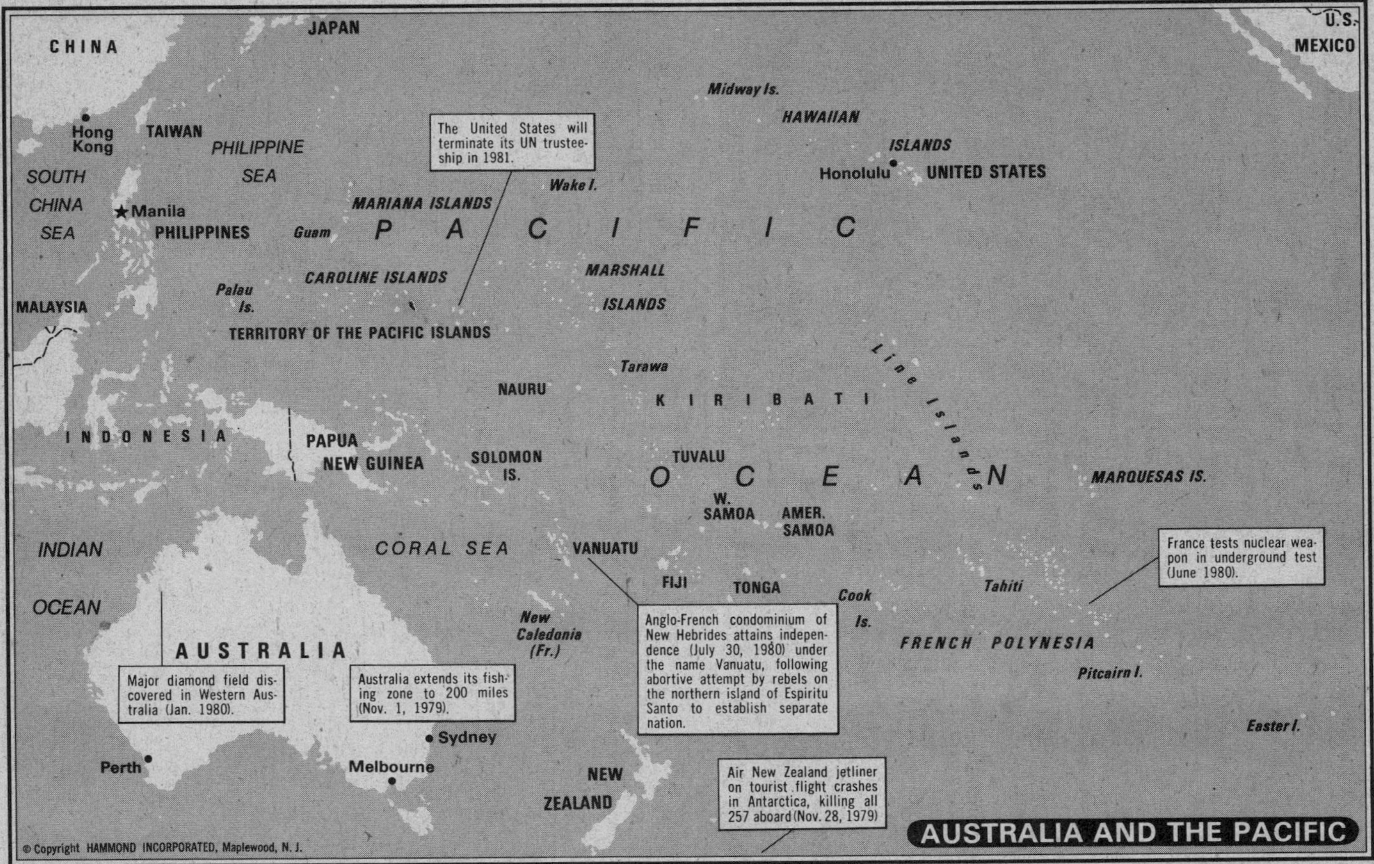
CHINA
JAPAN
U.S.
MEXICO
Hong Kong
TAIWAN
PHILIPPINE
SEA
SOUTH CHINA SEA
Midway Is.
HAWAIIAN
ISLANDS
Honolulu
UNITED STATES
Manila
MARIANA ISLANDS
Wake I.
PACIFIC
PHILIPPINES
Guam
CAROLINE ISLANDS
MARSHALL
ISLANDS
MALAYSIA
Palau Is.
TERRITORY OF THE PACIFIC ISLANDS
Tarawa
NAURU
KIRIBATI
Line Islands
INDONESIA
PAPUA NEW GUINEA
SOLOMON IS.
TUVALU
OCEAN
MARQUESAS IS.
W. SAMOA
AMER. SAMOA
INDIAN
OCEAN
CORAL SEA
VANUATU
FIJI
TONGA
Cook Is.
Tahiti
AUSTRALIA
New Caledonia (Fr.)
FRENCH POLYNESIA
Pitcairn I.
Perth
Melbourne
Sydney
NEW ZEALAND
Easter I.
The United States will terminate its UN trusteeship in 1981.
Major diamond field discovered in Western Australia (Jan. 1980).
Australia extends its fishing zone to 200 miles (Nov. 1, 1979).
Anglo-French condominium of New Hebrides attains independence (July 30, 1980) under the name Vanuatu, following abortive attempt by rebels on the northern island of Espiritu Santo to establish separate nation.
France tests nuclear weapon in underground test (June 1980).
Air New Zealand jetliner on tourist flight crashes in Antarctica, killing all 257 aboard (Nov. 28, 1979)
AUSTRALIA AND THE PACIFIC

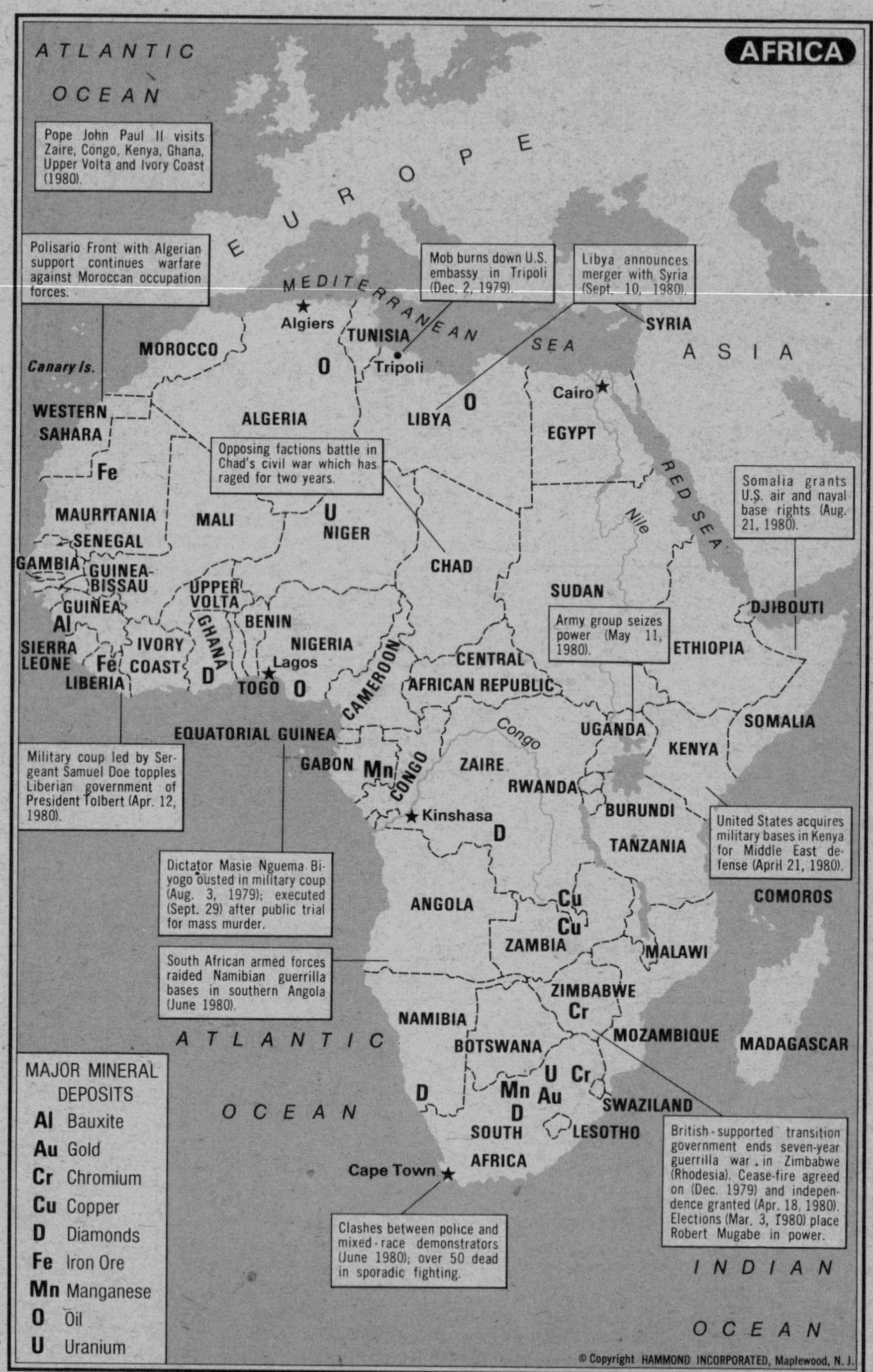
AFRICA
ATLANTIC OCEAN
Pope John Paul II visits Zaire, Congo, Kenya, Ghana, Upper Volta and Ivory Coast (1980).
Polisario Front with Algerian support continues warfare against Moroccan occupation forces.
EUROPE
MEDITERRANEAN SEA
Mob burns down U.S. embassy in Tripoli (Dec. 2, 1979).
Libya announces merger with Syria (Sept. 10, 1980).
SYRIA
ASIA
Algiers
TUNISIA
MOROCCO
Canary Is.
O
Tripoli
Cairo
WESTERN SAHARA
Fe
ALGERIA
LIBYA
O
EGYPT
Opposing factions battle in Chad's civil war which has raged for two years.
Somalia grants U.S. air and naval base rights (Aug. 21, 1980).
MAURITANIA
MALI
U
NIGER
CHAD
RED SEA
Nile
SENEGAL
GAMBIA
GUINEA-BISSAU
GUINEA
Al
SIERRA LEONE
Fe
IVORY COAST
D
UPPER VOLTA
GHANA
BENIN
TOGO
O
NIGERIA
Lagos
CAMEROON
CENTRAL AFRICAN REPUBLIC
SUDAN
Army group seizes power (May 11, 1980).
ETHIOPIA
DJIBOUTI
LIBERIA
EQUATORIAL GUINEA
Congo
UGANDA
KENYA
SOMALIA
Military coup led by Sergeant Samuel Doe topples Liberian government of President Tolbert (Apr. 12, 1980).
GABON
Mn
CONGO
ZAIRE
RWANDA
BURUNDI
United States acquires military bases in Kenya for Middle East defense (April 21, 1980).
Dictator Masie Nguema Biyogo ousted in military coup (Aug. 3, 1979); executed (Sept. 29) after public trial for mass murder.
Kinshasa
D
TANZANIA
ANGOLA
Cu
Cu
ZAMBIA
MALAWI
COMOROS
South African armed forces raided Namibian guerrilla bases in southern Angola (June 1980).
ZIMBABWE
Cr
MOZAMBIQUE
MADAGASCAR
NAMIBIA
BOTSWANA
ATLANTIC OCEAN
U
Cr
Mn
Au
D
SWAZILAND
D
SOUTH AFRICA
LESOTHO
British-supported transition government ends seven-year guerrilla war . in Zimbabwe (Rhodesia). Cease-fire agreed on (Dec. 1979) and independence granted (Apr. 18, 1980). Elections (Mar. 3, 1980) place Robert Mugabe in power.
Cape Town
Clashes between police and mixed-race demonstrators (June 1980); over 50 dead in sporadic fighting.
INDIAN OCEAN
MAJOR MINERAL DEPOSITS
Al Bauxite
Au Gold
Cr Chromium
Cu Copper
D Diamonds
Fe Iron Ore
Mn Manganese
O Oil
U Uranium

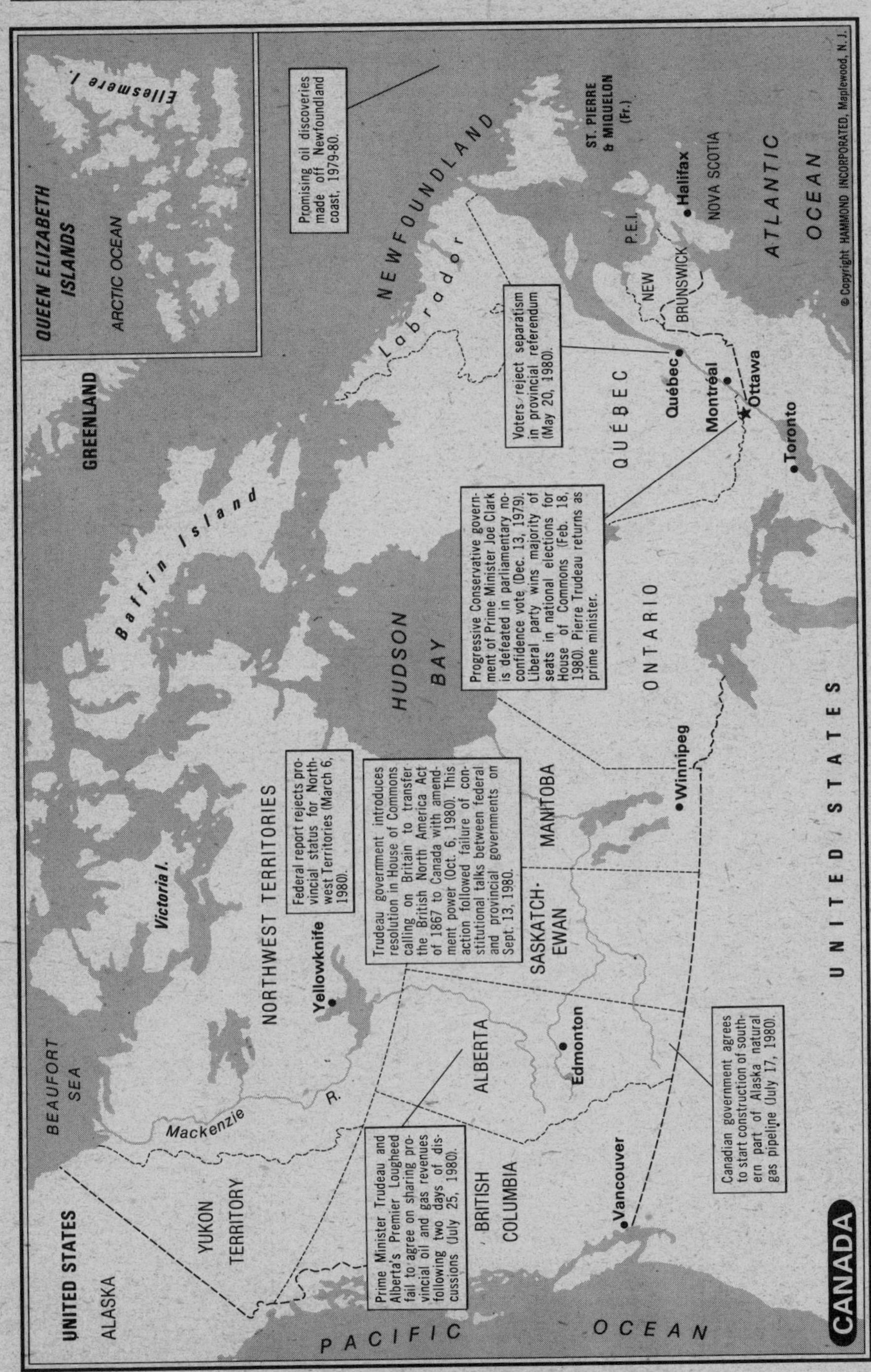
CANADA
UNITED STATES
ALASKA
BEAUFORT SEA
YUKON TERRITORY
Mackenzie R.
BRITISH COLUMBIA
Vancouver
ALBERTA
Edmonton
NORTHWEST TERRITORIES
Yellowknife
Victoria I.
SASKATCH-EWAN
MANITOBA
Winnipeg
Baffin Island
GREENLAND
QUEEN ELIZABETH ISLANDS
ARCTIC OCEAN
Ellesmere I.
HUDSON BAY
Labrador
NEWFOUNDLAND
ONTARIO
QUÉBEC
Québec
Montréal
Ottawa
Toronto
NEW BRUNSWICK
P.E.I.
NOVA SCOTIA
Halifax
ST. PIERRE & MIQUELON (Fr.)
ATLANTIC OCEAN
UNITED STATES
PACIFIC OCEAN
Promising oil discoveries made off Newfoundland coast, 1979-80.
Voters reject separatism in provincial referendum (May 20, 1980).
Progressive Conservative government of Prime Minister Joe Clark is defeated in parliamentary no-confidence vote (Dec. 13, 1979). Liberal party wins majority of seats in national elections for House of Commons (Feb. 18, 1980). Pierre Trudeau returns as prime minister.
Federal report rejects pro-vincial status for North-west Territories (March 6, 1980).
Trudeau government introduces resolution in House of Commons calling on Britain to transfer the British North America Act of 1867 to Canada with amend-ment power (Oct. 6, 1980). This action followed failure of con-stitutional talks between federal and provincial governments on Sept. 13, 1980.
Prime Minister Trudeau and Alberta's Premier Lougheed fail to agree on sharing pro-vincial oil and gas revenues following two days of dis-cussions (July 25, 1980).
Canadian government agrees to start construction of south-ern part of Alaska natural gas pipeline (July 17, 1980).
© Copyright HAMMOND INCORPORATED, Maplewood, N.J.

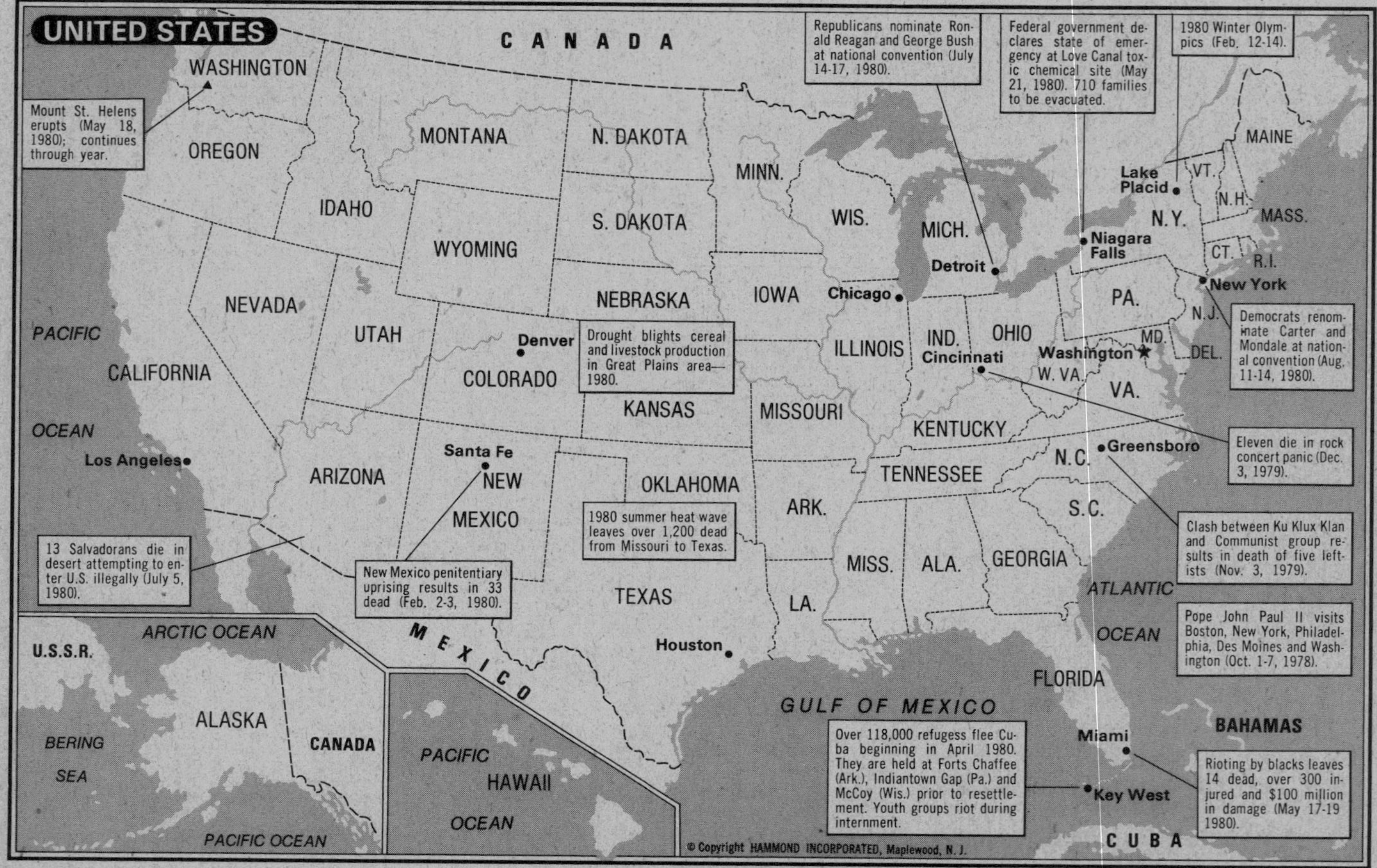
UNITED STATES
CANADA
Republicans nominate Ronald Reagan and George Bush at national convention (July 14-17, 1980).
Federal government declares state of emergency at Love Canal toxic chemical site (May 21, 1980). 710 families to be evacuated.
1980 Winter Olympics (Feb. 12-14).
Mount St. Helens erupts (May 18, 1980); continues through year.
WASHINGTON
OREGON
MONTANA
N. DAKOTA
MINN.
MAINE
Lake Placid
VT.
N.H.
IDAHO
WYOMING
S. DAKOTA
WIS.
MICH.
N.Y.
MASS.
CT.
R.I.
Niagara Falls
Detroit
New York
NEVADA
IOWA
Chicago
PA.
N.J.
PACIFIC
UTAH
Denver
ILLINOIS
IND.
OHIO
Cincinnati
Washington
MD.
DEL.
CALIFORNIA
COLORADO
Drought blights cereal and livestock production in Great Plains area—1980.
KANSAS
MISSOURI
W. VA.
VA.
Democrats renominate Carter and Mondale at national convention (Aug. 11-14, 1980).
OCEAN
KENTUCKY
Los Angeles
Santa Fe
NEW
MEXICO
ARIZONA
OKLAHOMA
1980 summer heat wave leaves over 1,200 dead from Missouri to Texas.
ARK.
TENNESSEE
N.C.
Greensboro
Eleven die in rock concert panic (Dec. 3, 1979).
S.C.
13 Salvadorans die in desert attempting to enter U.S. illegally (July 5, 1980).
New Mexico penitentiary uprising results in 33 dead (Feb. 2-3, 1980).
TEXAS
MISS.
ALA.
GEORGIA
Clash between Ku Klux Klan and Communist group results in death of five leftists (Nov. 3, 1979).
LA.
ATLANTIC
OCEAN
Pope John Paul II visits Boston, New York, Philadelphia, Des Moines and Washington (Oct. 1-7, 1978).
ARCTIC OCEAN
U.S.S.R.
Houston
MEXICO
FLORIDA
GULF OF MEXICO
BAHAMAS
Miami
BERING
SEA
ALASKA
CANADA
PACIFIC
HAWAII
OCEAN
Over 118,000 refugess flee Cuba beginning in April 1980. They are held at Forts Chaffee (Ark.), Indiantown Gap (Pa.) and McCoy (Wis.) prior to resettlement. Youth groups riot during internment.
Key West
Rioting by blacks leaves 14 dead, over 300 injured and $100 million in damage (May 17-19 1980).
PACIFIC OCEAN
CUBA
© Copyright HAMMOND INCORPORATED, Maplewood, N.J.

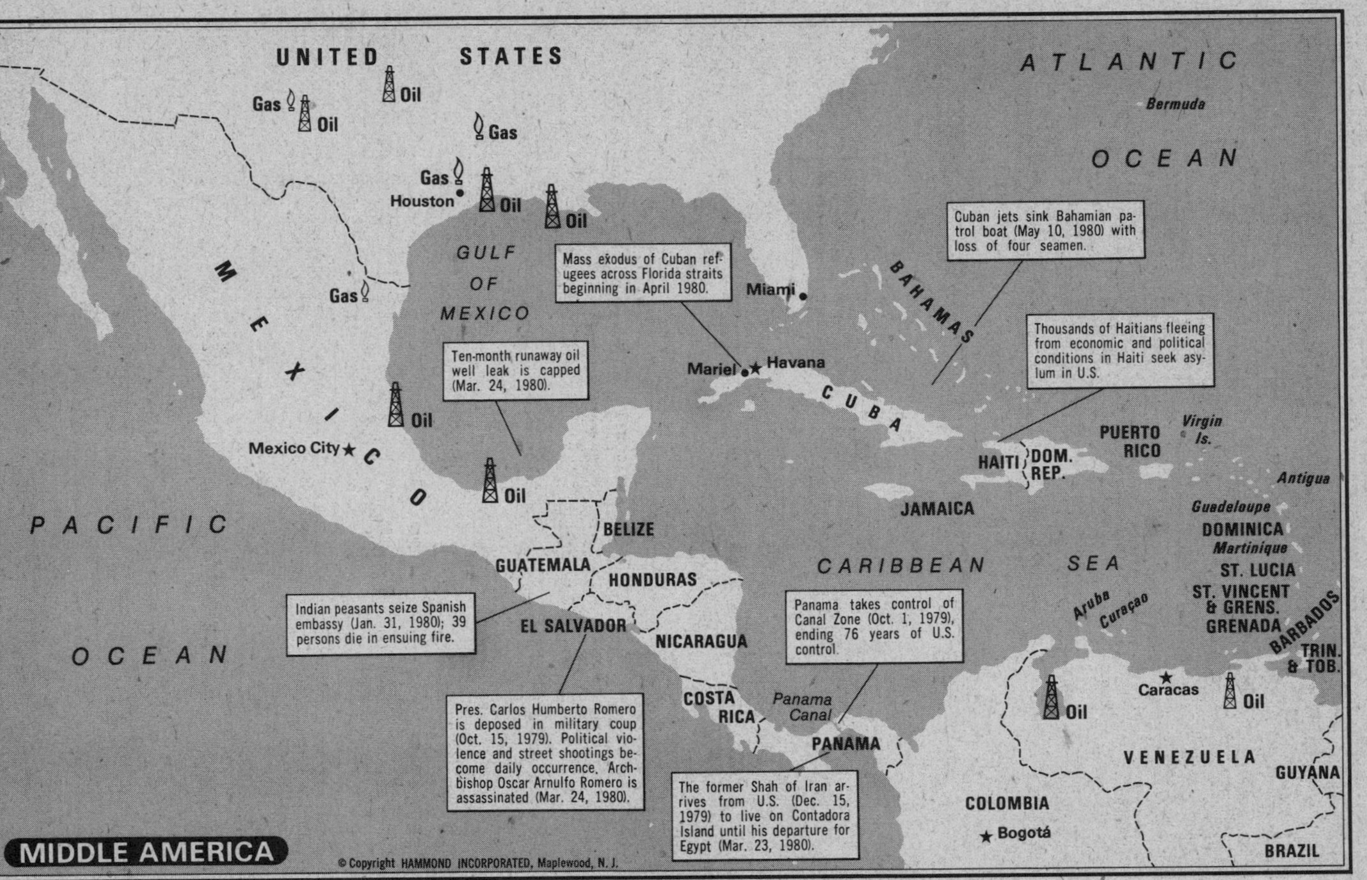

UNITED STATES
Gas Oil
Oil
Gas
Gas
Houston
Oil
Oil
MEXICO
GULF OF MEXICO
Gas
Oil
Mexico City
Oil
PACIFIC OCEAN
GUATEMALA
BELIZE
HONDURAS
EL SALVADOR
NICARAGUA
COSTA RICA
Panama Canal
PANAMA
ATLANTIC OCEAN
Bermuda
BAHAMAS
Miami
Mariel Havana
CUBA
JAMAICA
CARIBBEAN SEA
HAITI DOM. REP.
PUERTO RICO
Virgin Is.
Antigua
Guadeloupe
DOMINICA
Martinique
ST. LUCIA
ST. VINCENT & GRENS.
GRENADA
BARBADOS
TRIN. & TOB.
Aruba Curaçao
Oil
Caracas
Oil
VENEZUELA
GUYANA
COLOMBIA
Bogotá
BRAZIL
Cuban jets sink Bahamian patrol boat (May 10, 1980) with loss of four seamen.
Mass exodus of Cuban refugees across Florida straits beginning in April 1980.
Thousands of Haitians fleeing from economic and political conditions in Haiti seek asylum in U.S.
Ten-month runaway oil well leak is capped (Mar. 24, 1980).
Indian peasants seize Spanish embassy (Jan. 31, 1980); 39 persons die in ensuing fire.
Panama takes control of Canal Zone (Oct. 1, 1979), ending 76 years of U.S. control.
Pres. Carlos Humberto Romero is deposed in military coup (Oct. 15, 1979). Political violence and street shootings become daily occurrence. Archbishop Oscar Arnulfo Romero is assassinated (Mar. 24, 1980).
The former Shah of Iran arrives from U.S. (Dec. 15, 1979) to live on Contadora Island until his departure for Egypt (Mar. 23, 1980).
MIDDLE AMERICA
© Copyright HAMMOND INCORPORATED, Maplewood, N.J.

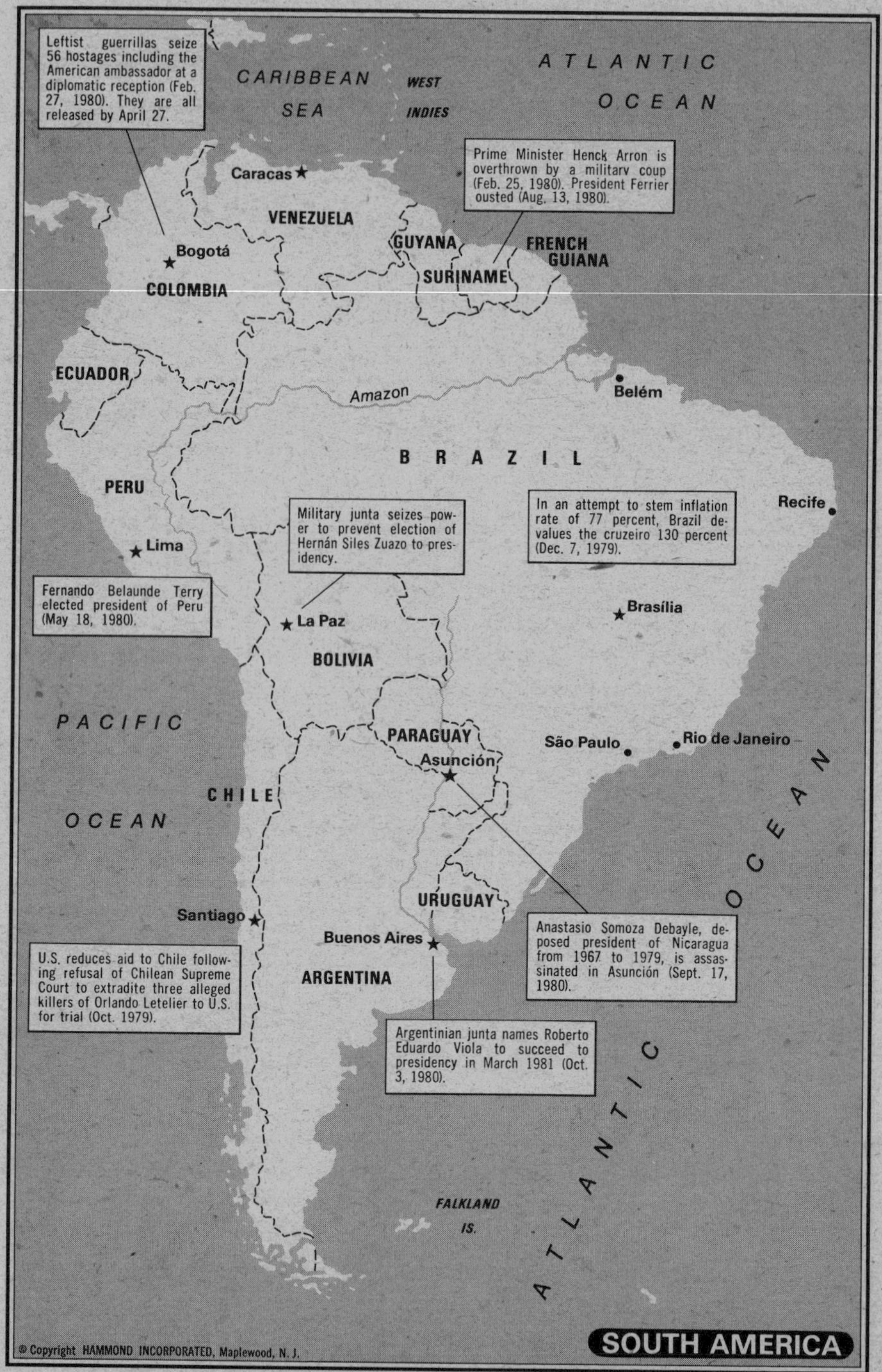

Leftist guerrillas seize 56 hostages including the American ambassador at a diplomatic reception (Feb. 27, 1980). They are all released by April 27.
CARIBBEAN SEA
WEST INDIES
ATLANTIC OCEAN
Caracas
VENEZUELA
Prime Minister Henck Arron is overthrown by a military coup (Feb. 25, 1980). President Ferrier ousted (Aug. 13, 1980).
Bogotá
COLOMBIA
GUYANA
SURINAME
FRENCH GUIANA
ECUADOR
Amazon
Belém
BRAZIL
PERU
Recife
Military junta seizes power to prevent election of Hernán Siles Zuazo to presidency.
In an attempt to stem inflation rate of 77 percent, Brazil devalues the cruzeiro 130 percent (Dec. 7, 1979).
Lima
Fernando Belaunde Terry elected president of Peru (May 18, 1980).
Brasília
La Paz
BOLIVIA
PACIFIC
PARAGUAY
São Paulo
Rio de Janeiro
Asunción
CHILE
OCEAN
URUGUAY
Santiago
Anastasio Somoza Debayle, deposed president of Nicaragua from 1967 to 1979, is assassinated in Asunción (Sept. 17, 1980).
Buenos Aires
U.S. reduces aid to Chile following refusal of Chilean Supreme Court to extradite three alleged killers of Orlando Letelier to U.S. for trial (Oct. 1979).
ARGENTINA
Argentinian junta names Roberto Eduardo Viola to succeed to presidency in March 1981 (Oct. 3, 1980).
ATLANTIC
OCEAN
FALKLAND IS.
Copyright HAMMOND INCORPORATED, Maplewood, N.J.
SOUTH AMERICA

'79/'80 MONTH-BY-MONTH CHRONOLOGY

OCTOBER 1979

NATIONAL

1 / Pope John Paul II arrives in Boston, beginning seven-day tour of the United States that includes visits to New York, Philadelphia, Des Moines, Chicago and Washington, D.C.

3 / Juanita Kreps announces that she will step down as Secretary of Commerce at the end of October, citing "personal reasons" for her resignation.

4 / Federal appeals court rules three Houston police officers were illegally granted probation following 1978 conviction for violating civil rights of Jose Compos Torres, an Hispanic youth who died in their custody; but judge in original case resentences them to time served plus a token one-day in jail.

6 / Chairman Paul A. Volcker announces Federal Reserve Board will raise its discount lending rate to a record 12 percent — up one percentage point — as part of a series of anti-inflation measures.

9 / House ends budget deadlock by passing two separate appropriations bills; one includes strict controls on abortion, the other grants Congress and top Federal employees a 5.5 percent pay hike.

11 / Senate votes 81-15 to "denounce" Georgia Democrat Herman E. Talmadge for mishandling his financial affairs; Talmadge claims vindication because he was not found guilty of any willful misconduct.

13 / President Carter wins majority of 520 delegates in Democratic caucuses in Florida, beating slate for Sen. Edward Kennedy by a 2-to-1 margin.

16 / Special Federal investigator Paul J. Curran clears Carter family business of wrongdoing, citing "no evidence" that loans made to President Carter's peanut warehouse were illegally diverted into his 1976 Presidential campaign.

17 / House votes 217-to-198 to strictly limit campaign contributions to Congressional races by special interest groups and "political committees."

19 / Presidential commission on Three Mile Island mishap recommends freeze on building new reactors until the atomic power industry adopts its proposals for improving plant safety.

22 / Federal government brings suit against Sears Roebuck, charging world's largest retailer with discrimination against women and minorities.

Nevada authorities execute convicted killer Jesse Walter Bishop, resuming capital punishment after 18 years; Bishop had confessed to 18 murders for hire, and resisted attempts to stay his sentence.

23 / House votes by 301-112 final legislative approval authorizing President Carter to ready an emergency standby gasoline rationing plan.

25 / Chrysler and UAW reach accord on a three-year contract that will save the financially strapped automaker $203 million by 1981; company will also nominate union president Douglas A. Fraser to the Chrysler board of directors.

30 / Senate votes 70-23 to narrow President's authority to limit oil imports, allowing Congress to block any import quotas set by the White House.

Federal judge in Philadelphia backs Mayor Frank L. Rizzo, dismissing major part of Federal suit accusing mayor and other city officials of condoning systematic police brutality against minorities.

31 / House-Senate conferees agree to a compromise $547.6 billion budget for 1980, including a $29.9-billion deficit.

Western Airlines DC-10 flight from Los Angeles crashes upon landing in Mexico City, killing 71 of 90 persons aboard and three persons on the ground.

INTERNATIONAL

1 / President Carter announces measures to offset Soviet troops in Cuba, including increased surveillance and creation of a U.S. Navy Caribbean task force based in Key West.

Panama takes control of Canal Zone in accordance with 1977 treaty; but U.S. will continue to operate and guard the canal—and occupy 40 percent of the Zone's 533 square miles — until 1999.

Chile's Supreme Court rejects U.S. appeal to extradite three intelligence officers indicted for the 1976 slaying of exile leader Orlando Letelier.

3 / Britain submits "final draft" of new constitution for Zimbabwe at London conference; talks had stalled between Salisbury and Patriotic Front guerrillas.

5 / Washington recalls U.S. Ambassador to Seoul after government expels Kim Young Sam, leader of South Korea's political opposition, from National Assembly.

Zimbabwe's Prime Minister Abel T. Muzorewa tentatively accepts British proposal for pre-independence constitution, in return for London's lifting of economic sanctions against Salisbury.

6 / Soviet Pres. Leonid I. Brezhnev says in East Berlin speech that USSR will withdraw 20,000 troops and 1,000 tanks from the GDR by 1981; Brezhnev also hints Moscow may reduce its medium-range missiles aimed at Western Europe if no new comparable weapons are deployed by NATO.

7 / Japan's ruling Liberal Democrats win 248 of 511 seats in parliamentary elections; short of a majority, party remains in power when 10 independents elected to lower house join the government.

8 / Johannesburg court convicts Eschel M. Rhoodie, head of South Africa's covert propaganda campaign to gain Western support for apartheid, of diverting $90,000 in government funds to his personal use; Rhoodie is sentenced to a six-year jail term.

11 / Pres. Fidel Castro arrives in New York to address UN General Assembly as leader of the non-aligned bloc; addressing the UN Oct. 12, Castro proposes that U.S. and other industrialized nations give $300 billion over the next decade to an international fund to aid developing nations.

14 / Turkey's ruling left-center Republican People's party is defeated in crucial by-elections; right-wing Justice party wins five contested seats, short a majority in the 450-member National Assembly, but enough to topple Premier Bulent Ecevit's government.

15 / El Salvador's Pres. Carlos Humberto Romero is deposed in bloodless military coup; acting to halt rising political violence, junta seeks to form a moderate government with civilian participation.

16 / Chinese dissident Wei Jingsheng, leader of underground movement for more democracy, is convicted and sentenced in Peking to 15 years for espionage and "counterrevolutionary" activities.

17 / Martial law imposed in South Korea after anti-government demonstrations erupt in port city of Pusan.

Federal judge rules President Carter's cancelling of the mutual defense treaty with Taiwan is unconstitutional without Congressional assent.

19 / Accord is reached in London between Patriotic Front leaders and Britain, affirming that future government in Zimbabwe will not be responsible for compensating white farmers for expropriated lands.

21 / Moshe Dayan resigns as Israel's Foreign Minister, citing disagreements with Prime Minister Menachem Begin over status of the occupied territories; Dayan had urged a more moderate position toward Arab self-rule.

The *Times* of London resumes publication after an 11-month absence, as management concludes contract with last of striking print-trades unions.

22 / President Carter, in major policy shift, approves U.S. military aid to Morocco; aid will help Rabat combat Algerian-supplied Polisario guerrillas seeking independence for Western Sahara.

Israel's Supreme Court orders dismantling of controversial West Bank outposts established on seized Arab lands, a setback for Begin government's settlement policies.

Mohammed Reza Pahlavi, the deposed Shah of Iran, arrives in New York from Mexico for treatment of a gall bladder ailment and cancer.

23 / Six Czechoslovak dissidents are convicted of "subversion" in Prague trial; playwright Vaclav Havel, economist Peter Uhl and Charter 77 spokesman Vaclav Benda are sentenced to 4-to-5 years in prison.

24 / President Carter pledges $70 million in U.S. food aid to Cambodia in international relief effort; political conflicts with Vietnamese-backed regime over aid delivery had caused widespread famine.

26 / South Korea's Pres. Park Chung Hee is killed by Kim Jae Kyu, chief of Korea's CIA; termed an "accident," shooting emerges as part of a plot by Kim to seize power. Prime Minister Choi Kyu Hah becomes acting Chief of State.

29 / Violence erupts in El Salvador's capital as soldiers fire on anti-government demonstrators in San Salvador, killing 24.

NOVEMBER 1979

NATIONAL

1 / Carter Administration proposes record $1.5 billion in loan guarantees to Chrysler Corp.

Senate Minority leader Howard H. Baker of Tennessee announces his candidacy for the 1980 Republican Presidential nomination.

House approves creation of an Energy Mobilization Board, the first White House energy bill to pass Congress; agency will have wide powers to spur development of synthetic fuel and conservation projects.

3 / Four persons are killed in Greensboro, N.C., as twelve men fire on anti-Ku Klux Klan demonstrators; later identified as Klan members, all are arrested and charged with murder.

6 / Local elections nationwide see Democrats winning gubernatorial races in Kentucky and Mississippi, checking predicted GOP resurgence. Republican Lt. Gov. George V. Voinovich defeats controversial incumbent Democrat Dennis C. Kucinich in Cleveland's mayoral race; Democrat William J. Green defeats GOP challenger, former prosecutor David Marston, for Mayor of Philadelphia.

7 / Senator Edward M. Kennedy announces he will run for President in 1980, saying he is "compelled by events and my commitment to public life" to oppose President Carter for the Democratic nomination.

8 / Gov. Edmund G. ("Jerry") Brown, Jr., citing the nation's "need for increased leadership," formally declares his candidacy for the 1980 Democratic Presidential nomination.

13 / Ronald Reagan officially opens his campaign for President in New York, calling for a new economic and military partnership with Mexico and Canada; polls show Reagan leading a crowded field for the 1980 GOP nomination.

14 / House approves 301-to-99 bill providing $5.9 billion in assistance to businesses in economically distressed areas; $2 billion is also earmarked for local public works programs if unemployment hits a quarterly rate of 6.5 percent.

15 / House rejects by 234-to-166 mandatory controls on hospital costs, a major setback for President Carter's anti-inflation policies.

George Meany steps down as president of the AFL-CIO, which he founded and led since 1955; labor convention elects Meany aide Lane Kirkland (Nov. 19) to succeed the ailing 85-year-old labor leader.

16 / Emergency funding bill is passed by Congress before a 10-day recess, breaking budget deadlock in compromise on use of Federal funds for abortions.

American Airlines pays $500,000 fine — largest ever imposed by the Federal Aviation Administration — for improper maintenance of its DC-10 jumbo jets, including the plane that crashed in Chicago May 23, killing 273 persons.

17 / Ronald Reagan defeats John Connolly in straw poll conducted by Florida's Republican convention; former CIA director George Bush runs third.

President Carter nominates Chicago businessman Philip M. Klutznick as Secretary of Commerce, replacing Juanita Kreps, who resigned Oct. 3.

21-22 / Record November blizzard with 70 mph winds virtually paralyzes parts of Colorado, Wyoming and Nebraska under snowdrifts up to eight feet deep; eight people perish in the storm.

27 / U.S. Steel announces closing of some 15 plants nationwide in a major retrenchment move affecting 13,000 workers.

29 / House rejects freeze on new nuclear reactors by 254-135 vote; bill would halt new construction for six months while the NRC worked to upgrade existing facilities.

Federal court panel appoints Arthur M. Christy, former U.S. Attorney in New York, as special prosecutor in Justice Department inquiry into allegations of cocaine use against White House Chief of Staff Hamilton Jordan.

INTERNATIONAL

1 / Bolivia's new elected civilian government is overthrown in coup led by army Col. Alberto Natusch Busch; military faces opposition by Congress and a general strike that paralyzes most of the country.

4 / U.S. Embassy in Tehran is seized by radical Iranian students; militants hold over 60 Americans hostage, demanding that the deposed Shah — in New York since Oct. 22 — be returned to stand trial.

5 / Washington rejects Iranian student demands that the Shah be returned; government in Tehran pledges to seek Americans' release, but seizure is backed by the Ayatollah Khomeini.

6 / Prime Minister Mehdi Bazargan's government falls in face of embassy seizure in Tehran; militants holding hostages say Americans will be killed if Washington attempts to use force to rescue them.

7 / Moscow attacks NATO's planned deployment of new medium-range missiles, claiming Atlantic alliance seeks military superiority over Warsaw Pact forces.

9 / UN Security Council urges release of Americans held by Iranian students in Tehran "without delay."

Senate Foreign Relations Committee approves SALT-II treaty in 9-to-6 vote; but support is too narrow to ensure its passage by the Senate.

10 / Tehran's new government supports students holding U.S. hostages, demanding Shah be returned for trial. President Carter orders deportation proceedings against Iranian students in the U.S. illegally; over 50,000 Iranians are ordered to report to Immigration authorities by Dec. 14.

11 / Israeli authorities arrest Bassam al-Shaka, mayor of the West Bank town of Nablus, pending his deportation to Jordan for alleged sympathies with Palestinian terrorists.

12 / President Carter orders halt to all oil imports from Iran, urging Americans to "redouble" efforts to conserve energy.

13 / Palestinian mayors in Israeli-occupied West Bank territories resign *en masse* to protest arrest and possible deportation of Nablus mayor Bassam al-Shaka.

14 / Washington freezes all Iranian assets after Tehran announces it will liquidate its U.S. accounts; Tehran asserts that American banking interests aided the Shah's admission to the U.S.

UN General Assembly votes 91-to-21 to demand the Vietnamese evacuation of Cambodia.

15 / President Carter denounces Iran for "an act of terrorism totally outside the bounds of international law," warning Tehran it will be held accountable for the safety of the 60 U.S. hostages.

Accord on new constitution and transition to independence for Zimbabwe Rhodesia is reached by all sides in London conference; parley will now discuss truce terms to end seven-year war between Salisbury and Patriotic Front guerrillas.

Spy scandal surfaces in Britain; Tory government concedes in Parliament that Sir Anthony Blunt, former art curator to Queen Elizabeth II, had been a Soviet spy, the long-sought "fourth man" in the Maclean-Burgess espionage case of the 1950s; Blunt's deeds had apparently been known since 1964, when he was granted immunity from prosecution.

16 / Bolivia's Congress forces military junta led by Col. Natusch Busch to step down; legislators appoint Lidia Gueilar Tejada as interim president until elections are held in May 1980.

Civil liberties groups and the Socialist Workers party file suit in Washington Federal court to halt Justice Department's deportation proceedings against Iranian students in the U.S.

17 / Ayatollah Khomeini orders the release of 13 black and female American hostages in Tehran, who are all freed by November 19. Students holding U.S. Embassy say remaining hostages will stand trial as "spies."

20 / Armed Islamic fanatics storm the Grand Mosque in Mecca—the holiest shrine in Islam—and resist attempts by Saudi Arabian troops to retake holy sites.

President Carter orders task force headed by aircraft carrier *Kitty Hawk* to Indian Ocean for possible action in the Persian Gulf; White House says military force may be used if remaining 49 American hostages are not released by Iran.

21 / Angry mobs in Pakistan, responding to Iranian claims that America was behind the storming of the Grand Mosque, sack U.S. consulates in Rawalpindi and Lahore, and burn U.S. Embassy in Islamabad; two Americans and two Pakistani employees are killed.

23 / Saudi troops retake most of Grand Mosque in Mecca; rebels are identified as fundamentalist Sunnis seeking overthrow of Saudi Arabia's monarchy. Last rebel stronghold surrenders Dec. 4.

Accused IRA terrorist Thomas McMahon, 31, is convicted in Dublin, Ireland, trial for the August 27 bombing death of Lord Mountbatten; he is sentenced to life imprisonment with no provision for appeal.

25 / Rep. George Hansen (R.-Idaho) visits the U.S. hostages in Tehran and says they are "healthy"; Hansen also says he may seek a Congressional inquiry into Iran's charges against the Shah.

26 / State Department announces partial evacuation of Americans from ten Muslim nations, following the Nov. 21 attack on U.S. Embassy in Pakistan.

27 / Seven top officials are indicted in South Korea for planning the death of Pres. Park Chung Hee; they are scheduled to face a military trial in December.

28 / All 257 people aboard a DC-10 tourist flight bound from New Zealand die as airliner crashes into the side of a volcano in Antarctica.

Iran's Foreign Minister Abolhassan Bani-Sadr is dismissed by Ayatollah Khomeini after saying he would negotiate with militant students for release of their American hostages.

29 / Shah Mohammed Pahlavi's departure from U.S. is stalled as Mexico refuses to readmit the deposed monarch. Washington asks the International Court of Justice at The Hague to order the release of the American hostages in Iran.

30 / U.S. Court of Appeals upholds President Carter's right to abrogate the mutual defense treaty with Taiwan without Congressional consent, overturning lower court's ruling that approval by the Senate is required.

Pope John Paul II visits Ecumenical Patriarch Dimitrios I of the Eastern Orthodox Church in Istanbul; both pledge to work toward healing the 1,000-year schism between the two churches.

DECEMBER 1979

NATIONAL

3 / Two U.S. enlisted men die as busload of Navy base employees is ambushed outside San Juan, Puerto Rico; Nationalist groups claim responsibility.

Eleven persons die in Cincinnati as fans pushing to get seats at sold-out concert by "The Who" at Riverfront Stadium cause crowd to panic, trampling several people.

4 / President Carter officially announces he will seek reelection to a second term.

5 / Sonia Johnson, 43, is excommunicated from the Mormon Church after a religious trial finds her guilty of "spreading false doctrines" because of her support for the Equal Rights Amendment.

7 / President Carter appoints John Ahearne to replace Joseph M. Hendrie as chairman of the Nuclear Regulatory Commission; saying U.S. "cannot shut the door" on nuclear energy, Carter announces changes in Federal regulations to improve nuclear plant safety.

8 / Republican David C. Treen is elected the first GOP governor of Louisiana since Reconstruction, defeating Democrat Louis Lambert in a close race.

10 / National Organization for Women announces it will not support President Carter for reelection, citing his lackluster support for ERA and restriction of abortion rights under his Administration.

11 / Federal judge overrules as unconstitutional Justice Department order that Iranian students in U.S. must submit to special immigration checks or face possible deportation.

San Francisco's Diane Feinstein wins election as city's first woman mayor—she was appointed to post in November 1978—as voters fail to return most city officials to office.

12 / President Carter pledges to increase defense spending by 4.5 percent annually and to seek a $157-billion military budget for 1981, in effort to win Senate backing for SALT-II.

13 / Women's groups meet with President Carter to discuss the Equal Rights Amendment; NOW members protest their exclusion, after group announced it would not back Carter's reelection bid.

14 / President Carter issues back-to-work order for striking employees of the Long Island Railroad, ending week-long walkout for 60 days while arbitration board seeks to end contract dispute.

17 / Senate approves "windfall" profits tax on oil industry by 74-to-24 vote; levy will increase Federal revenues by $178 billion within the next ten years.

Chicago transit workers walk out over city threats to cut cost-of-living provisions in current contract; strike affecting over a million commuters ends Dec. 20 as court orders union back to work, with dispute to be submitted to binding arbitration.

18 / House approves $1.5 billion Federal loan guarantees for fiscally ailing Chrysler company by a 271-236 vote.

19 / Senate votes 55-44 to approve Chrysler aid package passed by House; joint Congressional assent for financial bailout of the nation's third-largest automaker is achieved Dec. 20.

21 / National Transportation Safety Board cites faulty maintenance by American Airlines and design flaws in key DC-10 components as causes of May 23 crash in Chicago that claimed 273 lives.

26 / NRC draft report on Three Mile Island calls for closing any nuclear reactor if residents within a 30-mile radius of plant cannot be evacuated in case of an accident, and recommends ban on new reactors until sweeping changes in Federal regulation of nuclear facilities are made.

27 / Federal court of appeals upholds Justice Dept. special checks on Iranian students in the U.S., with authorities to expel those failing to report.

31 / Labor Department reports composite index of leading economic indicators fell 1.3 percent in November after a 1.4 percent drop in October, the worst decline since the 1974-75 recession.

INTERNATIONAL

2 / Shah Mohammed Reza Pahlavi leaves New York after treatment for cancer, and flies to San Antonio, Tex., where he is granted refuge at Lackland Air Force Base.

Right-wing Democratic Alliance is victor in Portugal's general elections, winning 46.6 percent of the vote and an absolute majority in Parliament.

3 / Constitution codifying power of the clergy and affirming Ayatollah Khomeini's leadership for life is ratified by landslide vote in Iran; but referendum is boycotted in Kurdistan and Azerbaijan, where opposition to control from Tehran is strong.

4 / UN Security Council votes unanimously to demand the immediate release of U.S. hostages in Iran.

5 / Bassam al-Shaka, mayor of West Bank town of Nablus, is released from jail after Israeli court reverses a previous decision to deport him.

6 / Revolt erupts in Iran's Azerbaijan province as supporters of Ayatollah Kazem Shariat-Madari clash with pro-government forces in demonstrations for regional autonomy; Madari had opposed the new Islamic constitution for giving too much power to Ayatollah Khomeini and the clergy.

7 / Ireland's ruling Fianna Fail party picks Charles J. Haughey as party chief and head of government, after Prime Minister Jack Lynch resigns both posts.

8 / South Korea's newly appointed President Choi Kyu Hah frees dissident leader Kim Jae Dung, imprisoned since 1976; Kim calls on Choi to honor his promise to hold early presidential elections.

9 / Iran's Foreign Minister Sadegh Ghotbzadeh says American hostages will not be released until U.S. "crimes" are investigated by a Tehran-approved tribunal.

12 / NATO ministers' conference approves deployment of 572 medium-range nuclear missiles, and proposes new arms talks with Moscow to limit both Soviet and American missiles in Europe.

Washington orders most Iranian diplomats to leave the U.S. in retaliation for Tehran's holding of 50 American hostages.

13 / Prime Minister Joe Clark's Conservative government loses no-confidence vote in Canada's House of Commons over high energy prices and austerity budget; Clark dissolves Parliament, and sets Feb. 18 as date for new elections.

Four leading oil producers — Saudi Arabia, Venezuela, Qatar and the U.A.E. — raise prices on crude oil production by one third; Saudis will keep current output at 9.6 million barrels daily through April 1980 to prevent a new oil shortage.

14 / Moscow denounces NATO plans to deploy new U.S. nuclear missiles, saying move "kills" possible talks on limiting strategic weapons in Western Europe.

Four American employees of NATO are slain by gunmen in Turkey; leftists claim responsibility.

15 / Shah of Iran leaves United States for Panama, responding to what White House calls "a long-standing invitation." International Court of Justice at

The Hague orders Tehran to release 50 Americans held in Iran.

17 / Patriotic Front leaders accept British cease-fire plan, ending talks on future of Zimbabwe Rhodesia; in previous agreement, country reverted to a British colony Dec. 11, with a 1,300-strong Commonwealth force to enforce truce. Accords for new constitution and early elections are signed in London Dec. 21.

18 / Vatican censures Rev. Hans Kung, liberal Swiss theologian and professor at West Germany's Tubingen University, barring him from teaching because his works "deviate" from traditional Church doctrines.

19 / Military court in Seoul convicts seven officers of conspiracy in the assassination of Pres. Park; all are sentenced to death, including former KCIA director Kim Jae Kyu.

20 / OPEC nations fail to agree on price structure at Caracas, Venezuela, conference. The "hawks," Libya and Iran, had pressed Saudi Arabia to raise its $25-a-barrel price, which had stabilized world prices.

21 / President Carter announces he will ask the UN Security Council to impose economic sanctions against Iran.

Security Council votes to lift UN economic sanctions against Zimbabwe imposed in 1967.

22 / Tehran declares state of emergency in Baluchistan province, as ethnic tensions flare into clashes causing several deaths.

Somalia offers U.S. use of former Soviet naval base at Berbera on the Gulf of Aden; Washington seeks new bases in region to strengthen options for possible military action against Iran.

23 / Frontline African states of Tanzania, Zambia, Botswana, Mozambique and Angola — who backed the Patriotic Front guerrillas in war against Salisbury — lift economic sanctions against Zimbabwe.

25 / Christmas services are held for the American hostages in Iran; three U.S. clergymen are allowed to see 43 captives in U.S. Embassy and report they seem well. Washington and Tehran trade charges on exactly how many captives are being held in the U.S. Embassy, but eventually agree that 50 hostages remain captives there.

Moscow airlifts over 5,000 troops to Afghanistan in major escalation of its aid to pro-Soviet regime in Kabul in putting down growing Muslim insurgency.

27 / Heavy fighting in Afghan capital of Kabul follows coup toppling Pres. Hafizullah Amin, who is executed; former deputy Premier Babrak Karmal becomes President with Soviet backing.

28 / President Carter brands Soviet invasion of Afghanistan "a grave threat to peace"; U.S. will seek cooperation from NATO allies on a possible united response to Soviet actions.

United States asks UN Secretary General Kurt Waldheim to negotiate the release of the 50 American hostages; Waldheim announces Jan. 30 that Tehran has agreed to such a mission.

30 / Soviets contend that its troops in Afghanistan are a "limited military contingent" sent to repel foreign aggression, in Moscow's first acknowledgement of its intervention.

31 / UN Security Council votes 11-0 to give Iran one remaining week to free American hostages or face economic sanctions.

JANUARY 1980

NATIONAL

1 / Republican National Chairman Bill Brock blasts President Carter's call for national unity on Iran crisis as "policy of deception" that diverts attention

from Administration weaknesses which led to take-over of U.S. Embassy in Tehran and Moscow's invasion of Afghanistan.

3 / Cleveland's teachers return to work after an 11-week strike, ratifying new contract providing an immediate 10 percent pay raise and a further 14 percent increase through 1981.

9 / Officials of the International Longshoremen's Association (ILA) announce boycott of Soviet ships and cargoes in all East Coast and Gulf ports.

10 / George Meany, organized labor's principal leader and spokesman since he founded the AFL-CIO in 1955, dies at the age of 85.

14 / U.S. Surgeon General report finds incidence of of lung cancer in women has risen sharply; linked to increased cigarette smoking, it may soon surpass breast tumors as leading cancer killer among females.

18 / Washington reports moderate 1.4 percent growth rate for the nation's economy in last quarter of 1979, with inflation pegged at 8.8 percent annually.

21 / President Carter tells Congress he will not seek a tax cut in his 1981 budget, saying in detailed State of the Union message that "restraining inflation is my highest domestic priority."

Iowa caucus results show President Carter out-polling Sen. Kennedy by a 2-to-1 margin; former UN Ambassador George Bush beats front-runner Ronald Reagan in a close Republican race.

22 / Christopher J. Boyce, convicted in 1977 of selling defense secrets to the Soviet Union, escapes from maximum security Federal prison in Lompoc, Calif., where he was serving a 20-year sentence.

23 / President Carter, in televised State of the Union address to Congress, calls for reinstitution of the peacetime draft, asking for authorization to begin registration; Carter calls volunteer army adequate for current needs; but says draft will be reimposed if national defense requires it.

25 / Washington reports consumer prices rose 13.3 percent in 1979, the largest increase in 33 years, with rises in food, fuel and housing costs seen as major reasons for record fourth-quarter increases.

Exxon reports record profits of $4.3 billion in 1979, an increase of 55.8 percent in year that major gasoline shortages caused higher prices; record gross revenues of $84.35 billion is highest any business has ever reported for one year.

28 / President Carter presents $615.8-billion budget — including a $16-billion deficit — for 1981 to Congress; budget would increase military spending by 3.3 percent to $142.7 billion, stressing inflation as the nation's major long-term economic problem.

Senator Edward Kennedy criticizes "Carter doctrine," on Afghan crisis, saying a "measured response" is needed rather than unilateral U.S. action in the Persian Gulf; Kennedy also calls for immediate gas rationing and a six-month freeze on wages and prices to combat inflation.

30 / Carter Administration, in its annual Economic Report to Congress, predicts recession and increased unemployment for 1980, with continued inflation and declining economic growth for the next two years.

31 / Treasury Secretary G. William Miller is accused by the Securities and Exchange Commission of making "erroneous and misleading" statements to stockholders of Textron Inc., by denying that while he was chairman of the board the company had made improper or illegal payments abroad.

INTERNATIONAL

1 / UN Secretary-General Kurt Waldheim arrives in Tehran to negotiate the release of 50 U.S. hostages, but militants holding U.S. hostages reject his attempts at mediation.

2 / White House proposes delay in consideration of SALT-II arms pact in response to Soviet intervention in Afghanistan; President Carter recalls U.S. Ambassador Thomas J. Watson, Jr., from Moscow.

3 / Kurt Waldheim meets with Revolutionary Council in Tehran, but is rebuffed in attempt to obtain release of the American hostages; denied an audience by Ayatollah Khomeini, he returns to New York Jan. 4.

4 / President Carter orders a halt to U.S. sales of high technology and cutbacks in grain shipments to the Soviet Union in retaliation for Soviet invasion of Afghanistan.

6 / U.S. Defense Secretary Harold Brown, in first trip by top Defense official to China, asks Peking to join Washington in "complementary" actions to stem Soviet expansion in the Near East; talks end Jan. 9 as Peking agrees to seek greater cooperation with Washington, but with no Chinese pledge on any joint response to Soviet action in Afghanistan.

7 / Soviet Union vetoes UN Security Council resolution calling for withdrawal of all foreign troops in Afghanistan.

Prime Minister Menachem Begin and Pres. Anwar Sadat meet in Aswan, Egypt, for summit conference on establishing trade and diplomatic relations; both leaders offer United States use of military bases to cope with crisis in Iran and Afghanistan.

8 / Returns from India's parliamentary elections show landslide victory for Indira Gandhi's Congress party faction, which wins 350-seat majority in the 542-member lower house; Gandhi is sworn in as Prime Minister Jan. 14, three years after electorate in world's largest democracy voted her out of office.

11 / UN Secretary-General Kurt Waldheim asks Security Council to delay sanctions against Iran after receiving new Iranian proposal for release of the American hostages; Tehran demands UN recognize "legitimacy" of demand for extradition of the Shah and convene a commission of inquiry into grievances against the deposed monarch and the U.S.

12 / Soviet chief Leonid I. Brezhnev accuses the Carter Administration of seeking to "poison" U.S.-Soviet relations, in his first public statement on Moscow's intervention into Afghanistan.

13 / Soviet Union vetoes U.S.-backed resolution in the United Nations Security Council to impose economic sanctions upon Iran.

Washington offers Pakistan a tentative $400-million military aid package for defensive purposes against possible Soviet aggression; Administration will also seek European participation in aid program.

14 / UN General Assembly votes 104-to-18 to demand "the immediate, unconditional and total withdrawal" of all foreign troops in Afghanistan, in a major diplomatic setback for the USSR.

Revolutionary Council orders the expulsion of all American journalists from Iran, claiming that U.S. news organizations are guilty of bias.

17 / Pro-Soviet regime in Kabul orders expulsion of all U.S. reporters from Afghanistan, accusing them of bias and "interference" in country's internal affairs.

Pakistani Pres. Mohammed Zia ul-Haq dismisses $400-million U.S. military aid offer as "peanuts"; Zia had criticized Washington for imposing 1979 aid ban against Pakistan, claiming it encouraged Soviet expansionism in the region.

20 / President Carter proposes that the 1980 Moscow Olympics be cancelled or moved if the Soviet Union does not withdraw its troops from Afghanistan by Feb. 20; he also urges athletes to boycott games even if the International Olympics Committee does not.

Washington offers Egypt $1.1 billion in arms aid over the next two years in the form of military credits, underlining closer U.S. military cooperation with Cairo since signing of Camp David accords.

Surgeons in Belgrade amputate left leg of Yugoslavia's President Josip Broz Tito, 86, to prevent spread of gangrene that had "jeopardized" his life, following an unsuccessful operation Jan. 12 to relieve a vascular blockage.

22 / Soviet dissident Andrei D. Sakharov is arrested in Moscow, and is later exiled to the scientific community of Gorkiy for allegedly passing military secrets to foreigners, in apparent retaliation for his denunciation of Soviet invasion of Afghanistan.

23 / President Carter warns in annual State of the Union address that the U.S. will "use any means necessary, including military force," to repel any threat to Western oil supplies in the Persian Gulf region; seen as an "ultimatum" to Moscow.

24 / Pentagon officials announce sale of U.S. military equipment to China in major policy shift; a response to Soviet presence in Afghanistan, sales will be limited to non-offensive support equipment.

U.S. House of Representatives votes 386-to-12 to back President Carter's move to cancel or move the Moscow Olympics.

25 / Finance Minister Abolhassan Bani-Sadr is elected Iran's new president by a landslide vote; a moderate member of the ruling Revolutionary Council, he pledges his first act as chief executive will be to seek the release of the American hostages still held in Tehran.

Israel relinquishes 5,500 square miles of Sinai territory to Egypt, completing first phase of two-stage withdrawal from the peninsula set by the Camp David peace accords; border between Egypt and Israel is opened Jan. 26 as normal relations are formally established.

27 / Iran's president-elect Bani-Sadr says U.S. must take responsibility for ending the hostage crisis, with release of 50 Americans in Tehran dependent on Washington ceasing "its policy of expansionism and violating the sovereignty of other nations."

28 / Meeting of Islamic foreign ministers in Islamabad, Pakistan, unanimously condemns Moscow's intervention in Afghanistan, demanding "immediate and unconditional" withdrawal of Soviet troops; conference also rebukes Iran Jan. 29 for continuing to hold 50 American hostages.

29 / U.S. and Canadian officials announce that six Americans in Iran had successfuly escaped the country; all had hidden in the Canadian Embassy in Tehran and fled posing as Canadian diplomats.

U.S. Senate approves boycott of Olympics by 88-4 vote; resolution would bar American participation even if Moscow withdraws its forces from Afghanistan.

31 / Over 39 people die in Guatemala as peasants storm the Spanish Embassy in Guatemala City; fire breaks out after they attempt to occupy Embassy, with peasants accusing the police of responsibility for blaze.

FEBRUARY 1980

NATIONAL

1 / Labor Department reports the nation's jobless rate rose sharply in January to 6.2 percent of the total work force, after unemployment had remained relatively stable for the last 17 months.

2 / News reports disclose Justice Department "Abscam" investigation of Congressmen accused of accepting bribes from F.B.I. agents who posed as Arab sheiks; those implicated are said to include Senator Harrison A. Williams (D.-N.J.) and seven House members.

Inmates seize the New Mexico state prison near Santa Fe, taking 11 guards hostage; prisoners demand an end to overcrowded living conditions.

3 / Justice Department says several Congressmen implicated in the "Abscam" bribery scandal have agreed to cooperate with prosecutors; House and Senate ethics panels pledge "full" inquiry into charges against their members.

State police and National Guard retake New Mexico's state prison seized by prisoners Feb. 2; takeover had unleashed 36-hour rampage of arson and violence, leaving at least 35 inmates dead.

5 / Federal bribery inquiry widens as new allegations link Sen. Harrison A. Williams to a proposed casino gambling project in Atlantic City, N.J.

7 / Chrysler Corporation reports fourth-quarter loss of $375.8 million in 1979, bringing auto maker's total deficit for year to a record $1.1 billion.

8 / President Carter announces his plan to reinstate the draft will require women to register along with men for military service, but that they would only be called up for noncombat duty.

Treasury Secretary G. William Miller admits to Senate Banking Committee he failed to prevent improper overseas payments while chairman of Textron Inc., but denies he knew about payments when he testified at 1978 Senate hearings to confirm his nomination as head of the Federal Reserve Board.

10 / President Carter defeats Senator Edward Kennedy in Maine's Democratic party caucuses; California Gov. Jerry Brown runs third.

Chicago's striking teachers approve compromise agreement to end six-day walkout begun Feb. 4; pact restores 300 teaching jobs and 200 teacher-aide positions cut by the city's Board of Education.

14 / Fire fighters in Chicago walk off the job after talks with the city collapse over disputed issues, including a proposed no-strike pledge.

15 / Federal Reserve Board raises discount lending rate by one point to a record 13 percent, responding to rising prices and continued inflation.

17 / Former Ambassador George Bush wins in Puerto Rico's Republican primary, defeating Senator Howard H. Baker, Jr., and six other GOP hopefuls.

18 / Justice Department documents obtained by the *New York Times* reveal F.B.I. director J. Edgar Hoover blocked prosecution of four Ku Klux Klansmen responsible for church bombing in Birmingham, Ala. that killed four black children in 1963; Federal agents also covered up involvement in attacks on blacks and civil rights activists by Gary Thomas Rowe, Jr., the Bureau's chief informant inside the Ku Klux Klan in the 1960s.

19 / Supreme Court rules that 1978 book by former CIA employee Frank W. Snepp III on the fall of Saigon, *Decent Interval,* violated the agreement he signed not to publish any material on the Agency without prior approval, though it contains no classified material; Court directs Snepp to forfeit all earnings from his book to the Government.

21 / Rep. Richard Kelly (R.-Fla.), who admitted taking $25,000 from undercover agents during the "Abscam" probe, resigns from the House Republican Conference in the face of possible expulsion from the GOP.

26 / Ronald Reagan defeats challenger George Bush in New Hampshire's Republican primary by a wide margin, as President Carter wins the Democratic contest against Senator Kennedy.

Former Rep. Daniel J. Flood (D.-Pa.) pleads guilty to conspiracy in influence-buying trial, and receives a one-year probationary sentence; Flood had resigned from Congress Jan. 31, after previous trial on the same charges ended in a hung jury in 1979.

INTERNATIONAL

1 / Israel and Egypt agree to interim steps toward Palestinian self-rule in the West Bank and Gaza territories, in talks in Israel with U.S. special envoy Sol Linowitz.

4 / Syria announces it will withdraw its peacekeeping forces from Beirut, raising fears of renewed civil war; but Damascus postpones immediate pullout Feb. 5 after Lebanon's Premier Selim al-Hoss protests move.

Ayatollah Khomeini condemns Soviet invasion of of Afghanistan, pledging "unconditional" support to Muslim rebels fighting Soviet-backed Kabul regime.

5 / France and West Germany demand Moscow withdraw from Afghanistan "without delay"; statement by Chancellor Helmut Schmidt and Pres. Valéry Giscard d'Estaing brands Soviet presence an "unacceptable" threat to peace.

10 / Israel's Cabinet approves Jewish settlements in Hebron, an Arab city on the West Bank; step breaks with past policy of limiting Israeli settlements on the West Bank to vacant rural lands.

A group of 49 private American citizens meet with student captors of Americans in Tehran, but are not allowed to see the hostages at the U.S. embassy.

11 / Washington announces that it has gained tentative permission to use naval and air bases on the Arabian Sea by Oman, Kenya and Somalia in return for U.S. military aid.

Iran's Pres. Bani-Sadr suggests formula for release of the American hostages, with Washington to acknowledge its "crimes" over the past 25 years and pledge to stay out of Iran's internal affairs; but U.S. responds that it will not "profess guilt" to win release of 50 captive Americans.

Three former Nazi SS officers are convicted by West German court in Strasbourg of complicity in the deportation and murder of 50,000 Jews from occupied France; they are sentenced to prison terms of from six to twelve years, in what is likely the last war crimes trial of Nazi atrocities committed in World War II.

12 / International Olympics Committee unanimously approves Moscow site for the 1980 Summer Games.

International panel on North-South relations calls for more aid to underdeveloped nations from the industrial world; commission headed by Willy Brandt calls for emergency $30-billion in annual increase in aid by 1985.

13 / President Carter, noting "some positive signs" from Iran, signals his acceptance of a "carefully defined" international commission of inquiry into Iranian grievances to gain release of 50 Americans held in Tehran.

The Winter Olympics opens formally at Lake Placid, N.Y., with athletes from 37 countries participating; but Taiwan, barred from competing as the Republic of China, does not participate.

17 / UN Secretary-General Kurt Waldheim chooses Harry W. Jayewardene, noted Sri Lankan attorney and human rights activist, to head commission of inquiry to Iran to seek release of the American hostages.

India's Pres. Sanjiva Reddy dissolves nine state assemblies controlled by opposition parties, ordering new elections in an action strengthening Indira Gandhi's Congress party at the local level.

18 / Canada's Liberal party returns to power after winning a majority in parliamentary elections; led by Pierre Trudeau, Liberals defeat Prime Minister Joe Clark's Progressive Conservative government — in office a scant six months — as polling displays displeasure with Clark's proposed sharp increases in domestic energy prices.

19 / Conference of West European foreign ministers calls for the neutrality of Afghanistan under international guarantees, in return for withdrawal of Soviet troops.

20 / White House declares U.S. boycott of Moscow Olympics "final and irrevocable" as deadline for withdrawal of Soviet troops from Afghanistan expires.

21 / Anti-Soviet protests by Afghan merchants close nearly all businesses in capital of Kabul; pro-Moscow regime institutes martial law Feb. 22 as anti-Russian rioting breaks out, with hundreds reported killed. Soviet troops are said to assume control of the city Feb. 25.

22 / Soviet Pres. Leonid I. Brezhnev says Moscow will agree to pull its troops out of Afghanistan in return for "guarantee" by Washington and Pakistan not to interfere in Kabul's internal affairs.

23 / UN Commission arrives in Tehran to begin inquiry aimed at resolving Iranian grievances against U.S.; but Ayatollah Khomeini rules out release of American hostages before elections for a new congress in April.

25 / Winter Olympic games end, as American speedskater Eric Heiden wins an unprecedented five gold medals, and U.S. ice hockey team wins against favored Soviet team, leading to final victory over Finland for a gold medal. But in White House ceremony honoring the athletes, Heiden tells President Carter that most on U.S. team oppose his call for a boycott of the Moscow Summer Olympics.

26 / Egypt and Israel exchange ambassadors for the first time, at Cairo and Jerusalem ceremonies that mark beginning of formal diplomatic relations; both nations pledge to seek a lasting Middle East peace.

27 / Leftist guerrillas in Bogotá, Colombia, seize 80 hostages — including the U.S. Ambassador — after shooting their way into a diplomatic reception at the Dominican embassy compound; guerrillas demand release of 300 political prisoners and $500-million ransom, threatening to "execute" captives unless the Colombian government accedes to their demands.

28 / Urban guerrillas release 13 hostages from embassy in Bogotá, but continue to hold 67 diplomats and aides; Colombian government says it will "examine" guerrillas' demands.

29 / Soviet and pro-government troops begin major spring offensive against Muslim insurgents in Afghanistan; rebel sources in Islamabad report attacks on five towns along the Pakistani border.

MARCH 1980

NATIONAL

1 / Former President Gerald R. Ford invites draft effort for the Republican nomination in 1980, saying that Ronald Reagan could not be elected in November.

3 / Supreme Court, in 5-to-2 ruling, backs Henry A. Kissinger by preventing disclosure of telephone conversations he made as National Security advisor and Secretary of State under Nixon; court holds that once Kissinger removed transcripts from his office, they were exempt from the Freedom of Information Act.

4 / Senator Edward Kennedy defeats President Carter in Democratic primary in his home state of Massachusetts; George Bush wins the GOP primary, followed by Rep. John Anderson of Illinois and Ronald Reagan.

5 / Senator Howard Baker of Tennessee withdraws from the GOP Presidential race after a disappointing fourth-place finish in Massachusetts.

6 / House Armed Services subcommittee vote rejects President Carter's plan to register women for the draft by an 8-to-1 vote.

8 / Ronald Reagan defeats John B. Connolly in South Carolina's Republican primary by a 2-to-1 margin; George Bush runs third. Connolly, former governor of Texas and Treasury Secretary, quits GOP race March 9, and endorses Ronald Reagan.

Chicago's fire fighters end 23-day strike — the first in city's history — accepting interim pact granting partial amnesty to strikers; fact-finding panel will arbitrate unresolved issues.

11 / President Carter and Ronald Reagan are winners in primaries in Florida, Alabama and Georgia; Carter swamps rival Edward Kennedy in his native region, with Reagan beating Bush by 2-to-1.

13 / Ford *Pinto* trial in Winamac, Ind., ends as jury exonerates auto maker of reckless homicide charges in the 1978 deaths of three young women killed when subcompact they were driving burst into flames after being hit from behind by another vehicle.

John W. Gacy is convicted in Chicago of murdering 33 boys and young men whom he then buried under his suburban home; 37-year-old contractor is sentenced to death in one of the most bizarre murder trials in the annals of American jurisprudence.

14 / President Carter announces he will cut Federal spending by $13 billion to balance the budget by 1981, and will seek immediately to place a levy on imported oil that would raise gasoline prices by 10 cents a gallon.

15 / Gerald R. Ford announces that he will not seek the GOP nomination for President in 1980, saying entering race would only "further divide my party."

16 / President Carter defeats Ted Kennedy by a slim margin in Puerto Rico's Democratic primary.

18 / President Carter wins Illinois primary by a 2-to-1 margin over Senator Kennedy, who had support of Chicago's Mayor Jane Byrne; Ronald Reagan defeats liberal Rep. John Anderson in his home state.

21 / United States Steel Corporation files suit against seven West European steel-producing nations, accusing foreign firms of "dumping" steel products at uncompetitive prices on the American market; Washington then suspends Federal "trigger" price protection for domestic steel makers.

22 / Over 30,000 demonstrators march in Washington, D.C. to protest President Carter's proposal to reinstate the draft.

25 / Senator Edward Kennedy defeats President Carter decisively in the Democratic primaries in New York and Connecticut; George Bush wins Republican contest in his home state of Connecticut, while Ronald Reagan wins GOP polling in New York.

26 / Governors of both Utah and Nevada blast MX missile system at Congressional hearings; both say Pentagon's plans to install 200 mobile ICBMs at cost of $34 billion would cause huge environmental and economic problems in those two western states.

27 / President Carter's "windfall" profits tax wins final Senate approval by a 66-to-31 vote; tax on domestic oil industry profits is expected to raise $227.3 billion by 1990.

31 / President Carter sends revised budget for 1981 to Congress; fiscal package includes $611.5 billion in expenditures and a $16.5-billion surplus, mandating across-the-board cuts in Federal spending to cure inflation without a new recession.

INTERNATIONAL

1 / United States votes with majority in United Nations Security Council to condemn Israel for increasing Jewish settlements in the territories occupied following the 1967 Mideast war.

3 / Returns in elections for majority rule in Rhodesia (Zimbabwe) show Robert Mugabe's Patriotic Front with an absolute majority in the new 100-member assembly; Mugabe's party wins 55 of the 80 seats reserved for blacks, defeating Bishop Abel T. Muzorewa, former Prime Minister.

President Carter acknowledges that U.S. vote against Israel at the UN March 1 was "a mistake" resulting from failure in communication within his Administration. Israel assails U.S. "apology," rejecting the resolution itself as "repugnant."

5 / Pakistan declines $400 million in U.S. arms aid; Foreign Minister Agha Shahi calls offer insufficient to safeguard Pakistan against Soviet threat, and says Islamabad will instead rely on ties with Islamic nations and the non-aligned bloc. Washington suspends aid plan March 6.

6 / Militants in Tehran, bowing to pressure from Iran's new civilian government, announce they will surrender their 50 American hostages to the Revolutionary Council.

Col. Pak Hung Ju, convicted of conspiracy to kill Pres. Park Chung Hee last October, is executed in Seoul, South Korea.

7 / Syrian peacekeeping troops pull out of Christian suburbs of Beirut, turning over positions to Lebanese army authority without incident.

8 / Plans to transfer custody of U.S. hostages in Tehran from student captors to the Revolutionary Council collapse when militants balk at turning over hostages to Foreign Minister Ghotbzadeh.

9 / Prime Minister Menachem Begin appoints Speaker of the Knesset Yitzhak Shamir to succeed Moshe Dayan as Foreign Minister; a conservative, Shamir abstained on vote approving Camp David peace accord with Egypt.

10 / UN Commission prepares to leave Tehran after failing to gain release of 50 Americans; Ayatollah Khomeini had backed student captors in refusing to yield hostages to government or to allow UN party to see them.

Israel expropriates 1,000 acres of Arab land on the outskirts of Jerusalem for a new Jewish housing development; area is part of the West Bank territory seized from Jordan in the 1967 war.

11 / Accord on composition of new government in Zimbabwe is reached in Salisbury; Robert Mugabe appoints Joshua Nkomo, co-leader of the Patriotic Front and his political rival, as Minister of Home Affairs, with control over national police. Mugabe later appoints two whites to economic posts, and is officially named Prime Minister.

14 / Eighty-seven people aboard a Polish LOT jetliner are killed when the plane crashes prior to landing in Warsaw; passengers include 14 members of the U.S. Amateur Athletic Union boxing team and eight AAU officials, and seven other Americans.

15 / Iranians turn out by the millions to elect new Parliament, the first since overthrow of the Shah; early returns indicate pro-Khomeini Islamic Republican party will win a majority in the legislature.

18 / Washington reports that the Soviet Union has apparently continued building up its germ-warfare arsenal despite 1975 accord banning toxic agents, but reports that contamination of Siberian city of Sverdlovsk in 1979 was caused by a "lethal biological agent" is denied by Moscow, claiming outbreak was anthrax caused by tainted meat.

19 / Italy's Prime Minister Francesco Cossiga resigns after Socialists announce they will oppose government on key issues; Cossiga later forms new center-left coalition of Christian Democrats, Socialists and Republicans April 4.

23 / Reza Mohammed Pahlavi leaves Panama for Cairo, as Iran formally seeks his extradition; deposed Shah accepts Pres. Anwar Sadat's long-standing offer to settle in Egypt.

Sweden's voters approve limited expansion of nuclear energy by 52-48 percent margin in non-binding referendum; nation's reactors could be doubled from the present six to 12, with moratorium on further construction.

24 / El Salvador's Archbishop Oscar Arnulfo Romero, that nation's most respected cleric and an outspoken opponent of the ruling junta, is assassinated in San Salvador while officiating at a memorial mass.

25 / Britain's Olympic committee approves participation in the Moscow summer games, rejecting appeals by Prime Minister Margaret Thatcher to support U.S. boycott of the Olympics.

26 / Iran's Revolutionary Council postpones second round of parliamentary elections amid charges of voting fraud, delaying decision on fate of 53 U.S. hostages now counted as held in Tehran by the new Parliament.

27 / Disaster strikes in the North Sea as heavy storms cause a floating oil-rig platform to collapse, hurling over 200 men into the raging sea; 91 are rescued by March 28, but death toll is put at 137.

28 / The former Shah of Iran undergoes surgery in Cairo; Dr. Michael E. DeBakey reports the Shah's enlarged spleen has been removed successfully, with the deposed monarch in "satisfactory" condition following complications from cancer therapy.

29 / Turkey and U.S. sign mutual aid treaty in Ankara allowing continued American use of an air base, intelligence listening posts along Soviet border, and seven communications outposts in return for military and economic assistance.

30 / Pres. Bani-Sadr announces he has received a letter from President Carter he terms an "ultimatum"; Washington confirms March 31 it has given Iran until April 1 to announce steps freeing the hostages from their student captors, or face economic and political retaliations.

APRIL 1980

NATIONAL

1 / President Carter wins landslide victory over Senator Kennedy in Wisconsin's Democratic primary, with Ronald Reagan winning GOP contest against George Bush; Gov. Edmund G. Brown of California announces his withdrawal from Democratic race.

New York City grinds to a halt as 33,000 workers strike the nation's largest mass-transit system, after talks between Transit Workers Union and the Metropolitan Transit Authority break down. Long Island Railroad employees also stage a walkout as unions and the MTA reject Federal wage settlement; but LIRR union members return to work April 2.

4 / Hearings in Congress brand Agent Orange as a probable cause of cancer; studies presented by Rep. Thomas A. Daschie (S. Dak.) and Rep. David E. Bonior (Mich.), contradict Veterans Administration claims that chemical defoliant used near U.S. troops in Vietnam was non-carcinogenic.

5 / President Carter and Ronald Reagan are victors in Louisiana's Democratic and Republican primaries over rivals Senator Edward Kennedy and George Bush.

7 / President Carter announces restrictions on the entry of Iranians into the U.S., in new sanctions against Iran for holding American hostages.

11 / TWU leaders in New York accept tentative contract for two-year, 20 percent wage hike, union members return to work April 12, later ratifying pact with MTA. LIRR unions also reach accord with MTA after 15 months; new contract provides a three-year, 24 percent wage increase retroactive to January 1979.

15 / Ford Motor Co. announces it will close three assembly plants and dismiss at least 9,000 workers permanently, due to slump in car and truck sales.

16 / House Ethics Committee finds Rep. Charles H. Wilson (D.-Calif.) violated House rules by diverting campaign funds to his personal use and improperly accepting cash from businessmen; panel later votes April 24 to recommend his censure by the House.

17 / President Carter cites slowdown in economy as evidence that expected recession has begun, but says "any recession will be mild and short" in duration.

22 / George Bush scores upset victory over Ronald Reagan in Pennsylvania's GOP primary, as Edward Kennedy beats President Carter in Democratic contest.

Supreme Court, in 6-3 decision, overturns lower court ruling that an at-large city electoral system in Mobile, Ala., unconstitutionally dilutes the voting strength of blacks.

23 / House passes proposed $611.8-billion balanced budget for 1981 by a 261-143 vote.

24 / Rep. John B. Anderson announces he will quit the GOP primaries and enter the race for President as an independent, pledging to attract a "new coalition" of voters and raise issues the other candidates will avoid, injecting an unpredictable element into 1980 elections.

26 / Senator Kennedy wins the Michigan Democratic party caucuses, narrowly defeating President Carter.

28 / Cyrus R. Vance announces his resignation as Secretary of State; Vance had refused to back President Carter's decision to attempt a rescue of the 53 American hostages in Iran.

Ford Motor Co. records a first-quarter loss of $164 million for 1980; decline is blamed on rising fuel costs and high interest rates on auto loans.

29 / President Carter announces he will appoint Democratic Senator Edmund S. Muskie of Maine to succeed Cyrus Vance as Secretary of State.

House votes 244-173 to increase spending in current budget by $24 billion, raising the Federal deficit by $13 billion.

30 / President Carter announces he will resume campaigning to explain his policies, saying problems that led to his self-imposed Rose Garden exile six months ago had "become more manageable."

Bert Lance is acquitted on nine bank fraud charges as jury fails to return a verdict on three other counts against former Federal budget director and two co-defendants in three-month trial; other charges are dropped June 7.

INTERNATIONAL

1 / President Carter defers new sanctions against Iran in expectation of transfer of 53 U.S. hostages from militant captors to government jurisdiction pledged by Pres. Bani-Sadr; but Revolutionary Council April 3 fails to reach accord over American assurances of non-interference in transfer process.

5 / Hundreds seeking asylum in Peru's embassy in Havana since April 4 are told they can leave Cuba if they obtain visas from their country of destination; crowd swells to over 10,000 by April 6.

6 / Ruling Council in Tehran gives final say on transfer of American hostages to government custody to Ayatollah Khomeini, who rules students should retain control over Americans until parliament meets to decide their fate.

7 / Washington retaliates against Iran for holding American hostages, severing diplomatic relations and imposing an embargo on U.S. exports; President Carter warns 156-day crisis will incur "increasingly heavy costs" for Iran unless captives are freed.

8 / Egypt's Pres. Anwar Sadat meets President Carter in Washington to discuss agreement with Israel on Palestinian self-rule; Sadat on April 10 assails Tel Aviv's establishing civilian settlements on occupied Arab lands as "an invitation to further violence and unrest."

9 / Israeli forces cross into Lebanon, advancing over five miles and digging in for a long stay; Tel Aviv calls action precautionary "patrols" against P.L.O. activity, after guerrilla attack on kibbutz in northern Israel April 7, which resulted in the deaths of three Israelis and five Arabs. Troops are later withdrawn April 14.

11 / President Carter reiterates his opposition to the Moscow Olympics, threatening "legal actions" to halt American participation; U.S. Olympic Committee votes April 12 to back White House on boycott.

12 / Liberia's President William R. Tolbert, Jr., is killed in a military *coup d'etat* by enlisted men, as 28-year-old Master Sergeant Samuel K. Doe becomes head of state; thirteen former high officials are later executed in Monrovia April 22.

14 / White House announces U.S. will admit up to 3,500 Cuban refugees, urging other countries to give asylum to thousands crowding Peru's embassy in Havana.

15 / Prime Minister Menachem Begin of Israel ends two-day meeting with President Carter in Washington, with proposal that negotiations with Egypt be "accelerated and intensified" in order to reach accord on Palestinian autonomy by proposed May 26 deadline.

16 / Washington announces both Egypt and Israel have pledged to redouble efforts to achieve agreement on pact for Palestinian autonomy in the West Bank by May 26.

17 / President Carter indicates military action might be the only alternative in Iranian crisis if sanctions fail to gain release of U.S. hostages; White House also announces ban on Iranian exports and bars travel to Iran by all Americans except journalists.

Rhodesia gains independence as the new nation of Zimbabwe, after a decade of struggle for majority rule; Britain's Prince Charles delivers documents conferring independence in Salisbury ceremony.

18 / Inter-American Human Rights Commission accuses Argentina's military regime of torturing and killing political prisoners; panel charges that thousands of "missing" persons there "can be presumed dead."

20 / Costa Rica tells Havana it will grant asylum to all 10,000 Cubans who had sought refuge at the Peruvian embassy.

21 / Prime Minister Masayoshi Ohira says Japan is ready to "make some sacrifices" to help gain the release of the American hostages in Tehran; Tokyo formally imposes sanctions April 27.

Barbara Timms and her son, Marine Sgt. Kevin Hermening—held hostage at U.S. embassy in Tehran—are reunited in tearful meeting; Washington urges other hostage families not to violate ban on travel to Iran, but excepts Timms and her husband because current ban was not published until after their April 18 departure for Tehran from Paris.

22 / Foreign Ministers of the Common Market nations vote unanimously to impose full economic sanctions against Iran by May 17 unless "decisive progress" is made toward the release of 53 American hostages.

23 / Iran signs new trade agreement with Soviet Union, East Germany and Romania, announcing that Moscow has agreed to supply Iran by land in the event of a U.S. naval blockade.

Hundreds of Cuban exiles begin arriving in Florida aboard flotilla of fishing boats and pleasure craft as Cuba challenges Washington to accept all the dissidents who wish to emigrate.

24 / An attempted U.S. effort to rescue hostages in Iran fails, resulting in the deaths of eight American servicemen; President Carter April 25 cancels any further rescue operations now under way or planned for immediate future. Special air-borne task force had to scrub mission within striking distance of Tehran, after mechanical failure hobbled several back-up helicopters, threatening success of the rescue attempt. During withdrawal, a transport plane and an Army helicopter collided, killing the eight Americans and injuring several others.

25 / A chartered Boeing 727 carrying 146 British passengers and crew members crashes just prior to arrival at Santa Cruz de Tenerife, in the Canary Islands; search finds no trace of survivors.

26 / Militants holding 53 Americans in Tehran say hostages will now be dispersed from U.S. embassy to cities throughout Iran to foil future rescue attempts.

27 / Guerrillas in Bogotá, Colombia, release six more captives at the Dominican embassy—which they had seized Feb. 27—for a total of 68; guerrillas, carrying an undisclosed ransom and accompanied by 12 remaining hostages, including U.S. Ambassador Diego C. Ascencio, are then flown to Havana, Cuba, where the last of the hostages are released.

30 / Iran's embassy in London is seized by three armed men demanding autonomy for Iran's Arab minority in Khuzestan province; gunmen hold 20 persons hostage, threatening to blow up building if Tehran does not meet their demands, including immediate release of 91 prisoners from Iranian jails.

Queen Beatrix, 42, is invested as the new sovereign of the Netherlands in Amsterdam ceremony marking the abdication of 71-year-old Queen Juliana, announced Jan. 31.

MAY 1980

NATIONAL

2 / Labor Department reports record jump in unemployment to 7 percent in April, an eight-tenths increase over March, the biggest monthly rise since 1975.

3 / Texas voters hand President Carter and Ronald Reagan new primary victories against Edward Kennedy and George Bush, respectively.

5 / Rep. Robert F. Drinan (D.-Mass.), liberal five-term Congressman and a Jesuit priest, announces he will not seek reelection because of directive from Pope John Paul II barring all Roman Catholic clergy from political office and activity.

6 / Carter and Reagan score major victories in Indiana, Tennessee and North Carolina primaries.

7 / House votes 275-193 to adopt strict budget in 1981, approving spending of $611.8 billion with a $2 billion surplus.

8 / Edmund S. Muskie assumes new post as Secretary of State; in talk to State Department staffers, Muskie infers he will become President Carter's "principal" foreign policy advisor in place of National Security chief Zbigniew Brzezinski.

9 / Ship strikes the 15-mile-long Sunshine Skyway Bridge, shearing off a 1,000-foot section and hurling a bus and three cars 140 feet into Tampa Bay, Florida; over 32 persons are killed.

10 / Chrysler loan guarantee board declares ailing auto maker is eligible for $1.5 billion in Federal loan assurances, rescuing company from bankruptcy.

12 / Senate votes 68-28 to approve $613.1-billion Federal budget for 1981, which is balanced with funds previously earmarked for a tax cut.

13 / Carter and Reagan win Democratic and Republican primaries in Maryland and Nebraska.

Federal judge strikes down President Carter's 10 cents per gallon tax on gasoline, holding that White House lacks legal authority to impose a gas surcharge.

14 / President Carter calls for controls on flow of Cuban exiles to the U.S., in attempt to halt influx of refugees from Cuba to south Florida.

17 / Environmental Protection Agency officials say 710 families in the Love Canal area of Niagara Falls, N.Y., may be evacuated due to possible toxic effects of chemical wastes dumped there by Hooker Chemical Corp.; tests link high incidence of cancer, birth defects and miscarriages to chromosome damage from pollution, which forced evacuation of 239 families in 1978.

Fourteen die in riots in Miami, Fla., as black community explodes following acquittal by all-white jury of four white police officers accused of killing a black businessman; two-day rampage is worst racial outbreak since 1967.

18 / Mount St. Helens, long-dormant volcano in south Washington state which had displayed active signs for nearly a month, erupts in a violent explosion, blanketing much of the Pacific Northwest with clouds of volcanic ash and steam; though most residents had evacuated the area, estimates place death toll at 32 killed, with over 88 still missing by May 24.

19 / Federal Court orders the Los Angeles, Calif., school system to implement comprehensive cross-district busing to promote integration by this fall.

20 / George Bush defeats GOP frontrunner Ronald Reagan in Michigan's Republican primary, with Edward Kennedy beating Jimmy Carter in Democratic polling.

22 / Federal grand jury indicts three members of Philadelphia's city council and a local attorney for accepting bribes in "Abscam" investigation.

26 / George Bush announces he will bow out of campaign for the GOP presidential nomination, as primaries show Ronald Reagan has the convention locked up.

27 / Federal grand jury in Brooklyn, N.Y., indicts Rep. Michael O. Meyers (D.-Pa.) and Camden, N.J., Mayor Angelo J. Errichetti for accepting bribes in Abscam probe.

28 / Special prosecutor Arthur M. Christie tells Federal panel there is "insufficient evidence" to indict White House chief of staff Hamilton Jordan on charges he used cocaine at Manhattan's Studio 54 discotheque in 1978.

Federal grand jury indicts Rep. Raymond F. Lederer (D.-Pa.) on charges stemming from the Abscam undercover inquiry.

29 / Vernon Jordan, head of the National Urban League, is shot and critically wounded outside his motel in Fort Wayne, Ind.; FBI announces it will investigate possible civil rights violations in attack against the prominent black leader.

30 / Justice Department says it will not prosecute Senator Herman E. Talmadge (D.-Ga.) for mishandling office and campaign finances, as Federal grand jury finds it lacks evidence to bring charges in case.

INTERNATIONAL

1 / Strike wave sweeps Sweden, with all industries and nearly one million workers affected; but strike ends May 11 following lockout by employers after workers win a seven percent wage hike.

2/ Palestinian terrorists attack Jewish settlers in occupied West Bank city of Hebron; six Israelis are killed and 17 more wounded.

Pope John Paul II begins 10-day pilgrimage to Africa; Pontiff visits Congo, Zaire, Kenya, Ghana, Upper Volta and Ivory Coast.

3 / Israel expels three West Bank Arab leaders from occupied territories in retaliation for terrorist raid May 2.

4 / Josip Broz Tito, 87, President of Yugoslavia and that nation's undisputed leader since the Second World War, dies in Ljubljana after a long illness.

5 / British commandos and police storm Iran's embassy in London, freeing 19 hostages and killing three of five armed kidnappers; security forces acted after Arab gunmen who seized embassy April 30 killed two hostages to emphasize demands for regional autonomy.

8 / UN Security Council votes 14-0 to demand Israel rescind "illegal" deportation of three West Bank Arab leaders; U.S. abstains because resolution omits reference to terrorist raid that provoked action.

11 / Ugandan soldiers overthrow government of Pres. Godfrey Binaisa in Kampala following dismissal of army chief of staff Gen. David Oyite Ojok; six-man military commission assumes power May 14.

13 / French Olympic Committee votes to send team to Moscow Summer Games, rejecting U.S. appeal to boycott the Olympics.

14 / Thirteen NATO allies agree to military measures strengthening Western defenses, a rebuke to Moscow's invasion of Afghanistan; Brussels summit also urges Iran "to release immediately" 53 U.S. hostages.

Nearly 50,000 student demonstrators clash with police in Seoul, South Korea, in demonstrations for a return to democracy and the end of martial law.

15 / West Germany's Olympic Committee votes 59-40 not to participate in the Moscow Games.

16 / U.S. Secretary of State Edmund S. Muskie meets with Soviet Foreign Minister Andrei A. Gromyko in first U.S.-Soviet talks in eight months; meeting reviews major Soviet-American differences since Moscow's invasion of Afghanistan.

Japan's Prime Minister Masayoshi Ohira calls for new general elections in June, following defeat in no-confidence vote in Parliament.

18 / NATO foreign ministers in Naples announce substance of economic sanctions to be imposed against Iran by May 22; but ban applies only to contracts signed since Nov. 4, 1979, taking of U.S. hostages.

Seoul government closes all universities, and bans political gatherings and strikes, in extension of martial law to all South Korea.

19 / French Pres. Valéry Giscard d'Estaing and Soviet chief Leonid Brezhnev meet in Warsaw for conference on Afghanistan; summit reaches no real solution, but Giscard says progress has been made toward resolving conflicts in the Near East.

20 / Voters in Canada's Quebec province reject "sovereignty-association" to renegotiate its status as part of Canada; referendum shows most of the mainly French-speaking populace oppose plan of Premier René Lévesque.

Unrest continues in South Korea as over 30,000 demonstrators clash with army in provincial capital of Kwangju, amid reports that national intelligence chief Chun Doo Hwan has taken control of the government.

21 / South Korean student protesters take over Kwangju, demanding ouster of military strongman Chun Doo Hwan and the release of opposition leader Kim Dae Jung, a native of the city.

22 / Tokyo approves freeze on exports to Iran, which has been Japan's leading trade partner, but new sanctions will only affect contracts signed after the Nov. 4 seizure of the U.S. hostages. Tokyo joins Olympic boycott May 24.

23 / Australia's Olympic Federation votes to attend Summer Games in Moscow, rebuffing Canberra's early support to U.S.-backed boycott of the Olympics.

24 / International Court of Justice at The Hague orders immediate release of U.S. hostages in Iran, warning Tehran not to try the captives.

Kim Jae Kyu, convicted of killing South Korea's Pres. Park Chung Hee, is executed in Seoul along with four others found guilty in the plot.

25 / Ezer Weizman resigns as Israel's Defense Minister after long dispute with Prime Minister Begin's hard-line policy in the occupied Arab territories.

European Socialist leaders embark on fact-finding mission to Iran to resolve hostage crisis; group is led by Austrian Chancellor Bruno Kreisky, the first head of state to visit Tehran since the Revolution.

26 / Deadline arrives for completion of talks on Palestinian autonomy between Israel and Egypt with no resolution in sight; little progress is expected until after U.S. presidential elections in November.

27 / South Korean troops retake Kwangju from student-led rebels, after a six-day seige.

Prime Minister Menachem Begin appoints Yitzhak Shamir, Israel's Foreign Minister, to succeed Ezer Weizman as Defense Minister.

28 / Iran's parliament convenes for the first time; body empowered to resolve the question of American hostages held in Tehran will first organize itself and choose a prime minister.

29 / Pentagon approves U.S. sale of defense-related military hardware to China, and the building of support facilities by American companies there, though weapons sales to Peking are still forbidden.

30 / Italy's Premier Francesco Cossiga is accused in Parliament of protecting son of the vice-president of his Christian Democratic party from arrest as a terrorist; opposition deputies led by Communists call for impeachment hearings.

31 / Government in South Korea announces formation of military-dominated Special Committee for National Security to make government policy, placing military on a par with civilian authorities.

JUNE 1980

NATIONAL

1 / Cuban refugees riot at Fort Chaffee, Ark., relocation center over delays in their resettlement; 200 flee compound, but are forced to return.

3 / President Carter wins majority of delegates at stake in eight Democratic primaries; Sen. Edward Kennedy wins in New Jersey and California, but Carter takes Ohio and West Virginia.

Full Senate approves intelligence oversight bill requiring prior Congressional notification of covert intelligence operations, except in extreme cases.

Rep. Charles C. Diggs, Jr. (D.-Mich.), senior black member of Congress, resigns after Supreme Court declines to review his 1978 conviction on mail fraud and payroll kickback charges.

4 / President Carter's oil-import fee—imposed in March to conserve energy and balance the budget—is rejected by Congress; Carter vetoes action June 5, but is overridden in 335-34 House vote.

6 / Senate kills oil-import fee by 68-10 vote, overriding veto by President Carter; measure would have raised gasoline prices by 10 cents a gallon.

7 / President Carter orders Justice Department to expel refugees who committed serious crimes in Cuba, and orders prosecution of those responsible for June 1 rioting at Fort Chaffee, Ark.

10 / House of Representatives votes to censure Rep. Charles H. Wilson of California—defeated for re-election in state's Democratic primary—for converting campaign funds to his own use.

11 / House-Senate conferees adopt $613.6-billion budget for fiscal 1981; opposed by President Carter for excessive military funding, Senate approves measure, which passes the House June 12.

President Carter names Jack H. Watson, Jr.—special assistant on Cuban refugees—as White House chief of staff, replacing Hamilton Jordan, who will now head Carter's reelection effort.

12 / Senate approves draft registration by 58-34 vote; conscription sign-up wins final approval in the House by 234-168 vote June 25.

Federal grand jury in Houston indicts speaker of Texas House of Representatives Billy Wayne Clayton and three others on fraud, conspiracy and racketeering charges stemming from an undercover FBI probe.

13 / Rep. John W. Jenrette, Jr. (D.-S.C.), is indicted in Abscam inquiry; Jenrette is accused of sharing in $50,000 payment from Federal agents and soliciting an additional $125,000 bribe.

16 / Supreme Court upholds right of companies to patent living organisms in controversial "genetic engineering" case; 5-4 decision allows company to patent "oil-eating" bacteria it developed, but Court urges Congress to prohibit patents on living things.

18 / Equal Rights Amendment loses critical test in Illinois, as state House of Representatives fails to approve measure, the seventh time legislature has failed to pass ERA in eight years.

20 / Carter Administration affirms that majority of the 129,000 Cuban and Haitian refugees just arrived in the U.S. will be allowed to remain for at least six months; most could become permanent residents within two years, if Congress assents.

21 / GOP chairman Bill Brock authorizes investigation of possible bugging of Republican National Committee headquarters in Washington, after deputy chairwoman, Mary Crisp, hired a security consultant who confirmed her suspicions that office was under electronic surveillance. But District of Columbia police report June 22 that GOP offices had not been bugged.

25 / Ronald Reagan calls for a $36-billion cut in Federal taxes, to take effect by Nov. 1; Reagan proposes 10 percent reduction in personal income taxes, and simplified process for business deductions on new investments.

27 / House kills President Carter's Energy Mobilization Board in 232-131 vote; proposal enabling White House to cut oil imports had passed House in 1979.

Heat wave strikes Texas and the Southwest; temperatures hit a record 113° in Dallas-Ft. Worth June 26 as heat is blamed for at least seven deaths.

28 / Operators of Three Mile Island nuclear plant in Pennsylvania begin venting of radioactive krypton-85 gas from reactor containment housing, but venting is halted as monitors erroneously record excessive levels of radiation. Venting is resumed June 29.

30 / Supreme Court upholds curbs on Federal funding of abortions; 5-4 ruling holds Hyde Amendment by Congress banning Medicaid financing of abortions does not violate equal protection provisions of the Constitution.

INTERNATIONAL

1 / Israel's Cabinet backs Menachem Begin in dual role as Prime Minister and Defense Minister, after Deputy Premier Yigael Yadin vetoes appointment of Foreign Minister Yitzhak Shamir to key post.

2 / Three West Bank Arab mayors are targets of bomb attacks in occupied Arab territory; two victims are seriously injured in apparent terrorist campaign by Israeli extremists.

Former U.S. Attorney General Ramsey Clark leads 10-member American delegation to Tehran to attend "U.S. Intervention in Iran" conference, in defiance of White House travel ban.

Indira Gandhi's Congress party wins elections in eight of nine states where New Delhi had dissolved local assemblies; but half of India's 22 states remain in opposition hands.

3 / Ramsey Clark urges Iranians to free all 53 American hostages, volunteering to take the place of any of them to help end the crisis; Clark later pledges to undertake an inquiry into U.S. policies in Iran during Shah's reign.

4 / Sources in Seoul report that strongman Lt. Gen. Chun Doo Hwan has imposed firm military control over South Korea; new regime is dominated by generals, with Chun appointing most high-ranking officials.

5 / UN Security Council rebukes Israel for failing to protect Arab lives in the occupied West Bank in 14-0 vote—with the U.S. abstaining.

7 / Attorney General Benjamin Civiletti orders inquiry into Ramsey Clark's trip to Iran to determine whether Clark and nine other Americans violated the law in defying White House travel ban.

9 / Al Fatah, the largest guerrilla group in the Palestine Liberation Organization, says it will begin launching new attacks against Israel from bases in Jordan.

11 / Four OPEC nations raise oil prices by nearly $2 a barrel following oil ministers meeting in Algiers; Kuwait, Venezuela, Iraq and Qatar take immediate raises, as Saudi Arabia and the United Arab Emirates defer increases until September meeting.

12 / Japan's Prime Minister Masayoshi Ohira, 70, dies of a heart attack in Tokyo, 10 days before ruling Liberal Democrats face crucial elections.

13 / Common Market leaders conclude two-day summit in Venice urging full self-determination for the Palestinians, calling for the PLO to be "associated with" present Mideast peace talks; Western leaders also call on Israel to end occupation of the West Bank and Gaza Strip, denouncing its settlement policy as "a serious obstacle to peace."

South African forces launch major attack against guerrillas of the South-West African Peoples Organization in Angola, with several major SWAPO bases "destroyed"; Angola accuses Pretoria of aggression June 26.

15 / Over 350 Bengalis are massacred by tribal inhabitants in India's northeast border state of Tripura; tensions had grown due to influx of refugees from neighboring Bangladesh.

16 / Washington announces request from Saudi Arabia for long-range missiles and other hardware increasing range and firepower of 60 F-15 jet fighters already sold to Riyadh; upgrading would enable Saudi air forces to strike at Israel.

17 / At least eight people are killed in Cape Town, South Africa, as police fire on crowds in mixed-race neighborhoods protesting apartheid in schools; death toll in worst racial outburst since the 1976 Soweto rebellion rises to 42 by June 18.

Jordan's King Hussein meets with President Carter in Washington to discuss Mideast peace negotiations; Hussein insists he will not join in autonomy talks while Israel continues to occupy captured West Bank of the Jordan River, but assures U.S. that Amman will not allow PLO to use Jordan as a base for attacks against Israel.

18 / White House announces President Carter will allow India to purchase 38 tons of nuclear fuel banned by the NRC; order is opposed by Congress because New Delhi never signed nuclear non-proliferation treaty.

19 / Washington approves U.S. sale of 100 M-60 tanks with advanced armament to Jordan; deal with Amman is expected to draw Congressional fire on its possible threat to Israel.

20 / Iraq holds its first national elections since its 1958 revolution, but polling for 250-member National Assembly is expected to rubberstamp Pres. Saddam Hussein's Arab socialist Ba'ath party rule.

21 / President Carter confers with West Germany's Chancellor Helmut Schmidt prior to economic summit in Venice; both agree on plans to modernize NATO's nuclear deterrent force in Western Europe.

22 / Allied leaders in Venice respond cautiously to Soviet offer to withdraw some of its troops from Afghanistan, saying move will not end East-West tensions unless USSR signals start of a complete pullout.

Japan's ruling Liberal Democrats score victory in general elections, winning a 272-seat majority in 465-member lower house of Parliament.

23 / Western leaders in Venice pledge commitment to develop alternative energy sources to save 15-20 million barrels of oil daily by 1990; leaders of seven major industrial nations also endorse policies to fight inflation and insure economic growth.

Sanjay Gandhi, 33, son and heir apparent of Prime Minister Indira Gandhi, is killed in a small-plane crash in New Delhi, India.

Vietnamese troops attack guerrillas across the Cambodia-Thailand border, leading to clash with Thai forces in which 16 are killed; Vietnamese later withdraw, as Bangkok protests incursion to Hanoi.

26 / France has the neutron bomb; Pres. Valéry Giscard d'Estaing announces Paris has tested a prototype of weapon in the Pacific, and will decide within two to three years whether or not to produce it.

28 / The Shah of Iran suffers a relapse in Egypt, after a recent bout with pneumonia; but monarch is said to rally following surgery June 30.

30 / Soviet leader Leonid Brezhnev meets West German Chancellor Helmut Schmidt in first round of summit talks; Schmidt reportedly urges Moscow to withdraw from Afghanistan and negotiate deployment of medium-range missiles in Europe "without preconditions."

JULY 1980

NATIONAL

2 / Supreme Court rules 6-3 to uphold affirmative action in Federal public works programs earmarking 10 percent of bids to minority contractors.

Federal judge in Miami finds U.S. Immigration authorities violated the rights of Haitian refugees seeking asylum; ruling in class-action suit orders INS to halt further deportations until it develops court-approved plan to reconsider claims for asylum.

6 / Thirteen illegal aliens die in the Arizona desert; group of El Salvadoreans were smuggled over Mexican border but then stranded, with only 13 survivors, including one of the smugglers.

7 / Republicans split over support to Equal Rights Amendment in Detroit meeting to draft national platform; compromise plank is approved July 9 which repeals GOP support to the ERA, but affirms as "legitimate" efforts to ban sex discrimination by constitutional means.

8 / President Carter announces Federal aid to auto industry in visit to Detroit; program will ease emissions and safety standards, speed depreciation tax write-offs and seek to lessen competition from foreign imports.

11 / Operators of Three Mile Island nuclear power plant complete venting of radioactive krypton gas after 13 days; NRC reports radiation levels in area are within safety standards.

14 / Billy Carter registers as an agent of Libya; the President's brother is silent on Justice Department charges of impropriety, but admits to receiving more than $220,000 in payments from Libyan government in 1980, promising not to engage in further activities without filing a "complete" registration statement.

15 / Rep. Richard Kelly (R.-Fla.) is indicted by a Federal grand jury on charges he accepted a $25,000 bribe from an undercover FBI agent; Kelly is first Republican charged in Abscam inquiry.

16 / "Killer" heat wave continues to ravage the Southwest; month-long 100°-plus temperatures and drought continue for most of the summer, claiming over 1,200 lives by the end of July.

16-17 / Republicans at Detroit Convention nominate Ronald Reagan for President by acclamation July 16, with George Bush picked as his running mate. In July 17 acceptance speech, Reagan asks Americans to "recapture our destiny" by embracing a new compact that returns Federal controls to the state and local levels, promising to limit growth of government and ease the tax burden on the average citizen.

18 / Draft registration is enjoined by court order; Federal judge in Philadelphia rules in ACLU suit that registration is unconstitutional because it excludes women.

Government reports a 9.1 percent decline in the economy for the second quarter of 1981, the worst three-month downturn since the 1974-75 recession.

19 / Associate Justice William F. Brennan rules draft registration may begin July 21 as scheduled, overturning a lower court injunction.

21 / Draft registration for 19- and 20-year-old males begins; thousands demonstrate outside post offices around the nation in mostly low-keyed protests.

Federal judge in Texas rules unconstitutional a 1975 state law barring children of illegal aliens from attending the state's public schools.

22 / White House discloses National Security advisor Zbigniew Brzezinski asked Billy Carter to arrange meeting with a Libyan representative last November to seek Libyan help in freeing the American hostages in Iran; in March, Billy tried to help a U.S. firm obtain Libyan oil, after a White House official told him not to engage in activities that might embarrass Jimmy Carter or his Administration.

24 / Both Democratic and Republican leaders agree to begin Senate inquiry into Billy Carter's Libyan connection, and the Administration's handling of his activities as a paid foreign agent.

25 / Attorney General Benjamin R. Civiletti says he discussed Billy Carter's Libyan involvement with President Carter on June 17, calling Billy "foolish" for not registering as a Libyan agent, but did not mention Justice Department's investigations to him; Civiletti had said he never spoke about Billy's troubles to the President.

27 / Iranian protest march in Washington, D.C., erupts into violent clashes between pro- and anti-Tehran factions, resulting in arrest of 200 pro-Khomeini students; Federal officials later release Iranians Aug. 5 after determining they are in the country legally, following threats by Tehran regime that it would retaliate against American hostages for "mistreatment" of jailed students.

28 / An ex-policeman is indicted by Federal grand jury in Miami on charges of violating the civil rights of Arthur McDuffie, a black insurance executive fatally beaten by police Dec. 17, 1979; Charles R. Veverka, 29, had testified under state immunity against four other officers charged in beating, whose acquittal May 17 touched off major racial violence in Miami.

30 / White House discloses President Carter discussed classified State Department cables dealing with September 1978 trip to Libya with his brother Billy; text of cables are released July 31, but Billy Carter denies he ever had copies of those cables, saying that Jimmy never showed them to him.

Senator Howard Cannon (D.-Nev.) is cleared by the Senate Ethics Committee; unanimous vote comes after Cannon had been accused of financial improprieties.

31 / Ronald Reagan releases data on his earnings, showing the GOP presidential nominee had an adjusted gross income of $515,878 in 1979, in major shift on personal financial disclosures.

Chrysler reports a $536.1-million loss in second quarter of 1980, the largest 3-month loss by an American auto maker; total deficit for 1980 is reported at $984.9 million.

INTERNATIONAL

1 / West German Chancellor Helmut Schmidt ends two-day summit with Soviet Pres. Leonid Brezhnev on limiting deployment of medium-range missiles in Europe. Washington confirms July 2 report from Bonn that Brezhnev changed his stance on arms control talks, dropping Soviet demands that NATO must first abandon planned missile deployment, with Moscow now ready to begin discussions with Washington on limiting short-range nuclear missiles prior to ratification of SALT-II by the U.S.

2 / Pope John Paul II deplores poverty he finds on tour of slum neighborhoods in Rio de Janeiro, Brazil; Pontiff denounces inequities and calls for peaceful social change during 12-day visit that ends July 11.

3 / Polish workers stage work stoppages in major factories across the country to protest government meat-price increases; similar protests forced Communist regime to rescind price hikes in 1976.

Martial Law Command announces 37 South Koreans will face trial on charges of trying to overthrow Seoul government last May; accused includes jailed opposition leader Kim Dae Jung.

10 / President Carter meets with China's Premier Hua Guofeng in Tokyo; Carter praises U.S.-Peking ties, saying they will "minimize" Soviet military threat.

11 / Richard Queen, 28, U.S. diplomat held captive in American embassy in Tehran since Nov. 4, is released on humanitarian grounds after 250-day ordeal; flown to Zurich, Switzerland, he is hospitalized for multiple sclerosis, and returns to U.S. July 18.

Iran announces arrest of 17 air force officers allegedly involved in abortive coup attempt July 10; several officers and others involved are reported executed.

13 / Egypt and Isarel resume talks on Palestinian autonomy in Egypt; talks are expected to produce schedule for full conference with U.S. participation in Alexandria next month.

15 / Washington announces it will sell the Trident I missile system—the most advanced submarine-launched system deployed by U.S.—to Britain.

Zenko Suzuki is chosen Liberal Democratic party president, and is elected Japan's prime minister by Parliament July 17.

17 / Armed forces stage *coup d'etat* in Bolivia, in move to block expected victory of leftist candidate Herman Siles Zuaso in selection as President by Congress; rebels seize capital of La Paz, taking Pres. Lidia Gueiler and Cabinet prisoners. Army sets up three-man junta, which appoints army chief of staff Gen. Luis Garcia Meza President July 19.

18 / Shahpur Bakhtiar, the Shah of Iran's last prime minister and leader of anti-Khomeini Iranian exiles, narrowly escapes assassination in Paris.

19 / The 1980 Summer Olympics open in Moscow, with ceremonies led by Soviet Pres. Leonid I. Brezhnev; 81 nations participate in Games, though U.S. and 64 other countries boycott Olympics to protest Soviet invasion of Afghanistan. Games end Aug. 3.

Terrorists in Turkey assassinate Nihat Erim, premier during military crackdown on leftists and intellectuals in 1971-72; leftist terrorists later claim responsibility.

20 / Iran's Parliament takes over legislative power from the Revolutionary Council, and elects Ayatollah Hashemi Rafsanjani as speaker; head of hard-line Islamic Republican party, Rafsanjani favors putting the U.S. hostages on trial as spies.

21 / Former Syrian premier Salah el-Bitar—a foe of Pres. Hafez al-Assad—is assassinated in Paris; Damascus denies any connection to his death.

22 / A former Iranian official is slain at his home in Bethesda, Md.; Ali Akbar Tabatabai was press attaché at Tehran's Washington embassy under the Shah, and had been an outspoken critic of Ayatollah Khomeini.

25 / Canada faces potential political crisis as Prime Minister Pierre Trudeau and Alberta's Premier Peter Lougheed break off talks in Ottawa on sharing the benefits from provincial oil and natural gas deposits.

Secretary of State Edmund Muskie announces sanctions against Bolivia to protest July 17 coup; military and economic aid will be cancelled, and U.S. embassy staff in La Paz "substantially reduced."

27 / The deposed Shah of Iran, 60, dies of advanced lymphatic cancer, near Cairo, Egypt. Mohammed Reza Pahlavi ruled Iran for nearly 40 years, until he was overthrown in 1979 by rebellion led by Ayatollah Khomeini. Cairo funeral July 28 is marked by the absence of most world leaders, except Egypt's Pres. Anwar Sadat and Richard M. Nixon.

Italy's Premier Francesco Cossiga is cleared of charges he divulged government secrets to colleague whose son is a suspected terrorist; Parliament votes to dismiss charges and end impeachment inquiry.

29 / UN General Assembly votes 112-7 in favor of creating a Palestinian state; Washington votes against resolution, but 24 Western nations abstain on motion calling for Israeli withdrawal from East Jerusalem and other occupied territories.

30 / Jerusalem, including East Jerusalem, formally becomes Israel's capital city, as Knesset passes bill in 69-15 vote; both U.S. and Egypt criticize move for increasing difficulties in renewing Palestinian autonomy talks.

AUGUST 1980

NATIONAL

1 / White House confirms that Billy Carter received a copy of State Department cable sent to President Carter following Billy's 1978 trip to Libya, along with complimentary note from Jimmy on his having done a "good job."

4 / President Carter gives deposition to Senate panel, claiming his brother had no influence on Administration policy toward Libya.

13 / Senate panel on Libyan influence in Washington is reported investigating purported Libyan plan to pay $15 million to American officials to influence the sale of eight military transport planes to Tripoli.

14 / Democrats at National Convention in New York City renominate Jimmy Carter and Walter Mondale for President and Vice-President. Carter forces beat back Kennedy challenge by defeating "open convention" rule changes on Aug. 11. Delegates vote to deny funds to any candidate not supporting the ERA, and later back Kennedy policies by adding $12-billion jobs program to platform. In acceptance speech, Carter attacks Republicans for offering a "fantasy America" of "simple and wrong solutions."

NRC calls for reopening of Three Mile Island nuclear plant near Harrisburg, Pa., saying plant could be decontaminated with no significant risk.

16 / Two airliners are hijacked to Cuba on the same day; a Republic Airlines DC-9 bound from Miami to Orlando, Fla., is seized in mid-flight, with a Delta Air Lines flight from Puerto Rico to Miami diverted 30 minutes later, the fifth and sixth in less than a week.

19 / Senate votes 78-14 approving Alaska lands bill, designed to limit development of over 100 million acres of wilderness area in that state.

20 / Republican Vice-Presidential candidate George Bush meets with Chinese leaders in Peking, who had blasted Reagan for recent statements inferring that a Reagan administration would pursue a "two-China" policy. Bush reassures Chinese that Reagan's call for "official" U.S. ties with Taiwan actually mean "unofficial" liaison. Reagan, Aug. 25, retreats on upgrading U.S. liaison office with Taiwan to official status, saying he made misstatements.

N.Y. Times reports that Pentagon is developing new type of jet aircraft that is virtually invisible to radar; new "stealth aircraft" was developed secretly by Defense Department for past two years.

21 / Billy Carter testifies before Senate that he was never asked by Libyans to influence U.S. foreign policy; Carter also says he never asked anything of brother Jimmy Carter on Libya's behalf.

25 / Independent Presidential candidate John Anderson announces that Patrick J. Lucey, former governor of Wisconsin and deputy manager of Edward Kennedy's Presidential campaign, has accepted offer to be Anderson's running mate in "national unity" campaign.

Senator Herman E. Talmadge (D.-Ga.) wins runoff election for a fifth term; Talmadge was censured by Senate for mishandling office and campaign funds.

27 / Senator Mike Gravel is defeated in Alaska's Democratic primary by Clark Gruening, in campaign centering on source of Gravel's campaign funds.

28 / President Carter outlines his "economic revitalization" plan to speed recovery from recession while avoiding inflation; program extends unemployment benefits to 52 weeks and increases revenue-sharing aid to cities by $1 billion, but defers any income tax reduction beyond next year.

29 / President Carter approves 9.1 percent pay hike for 1.4 million Federal employees, to take effect Oct. 1 unless vetoed by Congress.

30 / Independent Anderson-Lucey ticket presents its platform for 1980 elections; program bars a tax cut until Federal budget is balanced, and calls for voluntary wage and price controls to hold down inflation.

Jury in Brooklyn, N.Y. Abscam trial convicts Rep. Michael J. Myers, Mayor Angelo J. Errichetti of Camden, N.J., and two other defendants on Federal bribery and conspiracy charges.

INTERNATIONAL

2 / Egypt's Pres. Anwar Sadat formally protests Israeli annexation of East Jerusalem to Prime Minister Menachem Begin; Cairo asks postponement of Palestinian autonomy talks set to begin in Alexandria August 3.

Explosion at main train station in Bologna, Italy kills 76 persons and injures 200 more; bombing, suspected to be work of neo-fascist group, is worst act of terrorism in nation's history.

5 / Washington announces Carter Administration has adopted new U.S. strategy for nuclear war, giving priority to striking military targets in the Soviet Union rather than major cities and industrial areas, as in past policy which relied on threat of mutual destruction as a deterrent to war.

6 / Scandal threatens Patriotic Front regime in Zimbabwe, as Manpower Minister Edgar Z. Tekere is charged with murder in the killing of a 68-year-old white farm manager outside Salisbury.

Hurricane Allen strikes Jamaica; 100 mph winds and torrential rains batter the island and threaten western Cuba, claiming 272 lives by Aug. 11.

11 / Education minister Mohammed Ali Rajai is confirmed by Parliament as Iran's new Prime Minister; Rajai was nominated by Pres. Bani-Sadr as compromise with Islamic fundamentalists who dominate legislature.

13 / Violence between Muslims and Hindus claims 86 lives in India's northern state of Uttar Pradesh, as riots erupt in city of Moradabad after rumors spread that police let pigs roam near a local mosque. Death toll reaches 142 by Aug. 16, with unrest spreading to Kashmir Aug. 17.

14 / Labor unrest in Poland spreads as 17,000 workers at the Lenin Shipyard in port city of Gdańsk strike, taking over facility to back up their demands, which include establishment of independent trade unions.

15 / Strike wave in Poland spreads as bus drivers join nearly 60,000 shipyard workers in Gdańsk to demand lower food prices and free trade unions; Premier Edward Babiuch asks workers to return to their jobs, warning that Warsaw will not rescind increases in meat prices, which had caused unrest.

South Korea's President Choi Kyu Hah resigns in Seoul; military *shogun* Gen. Chun Doo Hwan is named Aug. 18 to succeed him, and is elected President by the National Conference of Unification, Aug. 27.

17 / Strikers in Poland unite to strengthen their position with the government; committee representing 50,000 workers in the Baltic ports draws up list of demands putting them on a collision course with Communist regime.

Trial of opposition leader Kim Dae Jung and 23 associates on sedition charges opens in Seoul, South Korea. Jung, 56, denies charges he violated National Security Law, testifying Aug. 19 that he was confined and interrogated continuously for 60 days following his May 17 arrest.

18 / Polish Communist party chief Edward Gierek promises Baltic port workers a general pay increase in effort to end strike paralyzing industry and port facilities, where 100,000 workers are now on strike.

19 / Saudi jetliner lands in flames at Riyadh, Saudi Arabia, with all 301 persons aboard reported killed.

Israeli forces strike into southern Lebanon in "preemptive" raid against Palestinian bases, with 60 terrorists reported killed.

20 / Secretary of State Edmund Muskie votes in UN Security Council to abstain on resolution censuring Israel for annexing East Jerusalem, which urges UN members not to recognize city as Israel's capital.

Defense Secretary Harold Brown says U.S. missiles may be vulnerable to attack by the Soviet Union; in defending new Washington strategy on nuclear war, Brown says American nuclear strike force is threatened by military programs developed by Moscow.

Authorities in Poland arrest 14 leaders of dissident Committee of Social Self-Defense (KOR) in attempt to quell strike wave in Baltic region.

21 / Striking fishing trawlers blockade Mediterranean port of Fos, France, in strike over crew cutbacks and refusal by government to increase fuel subsidies.

22 / Roman Catholic Church expresses sympathy for Polish strikers; statement from Polish church "understands" strikers' demands but implicitly criticizes their methods.

West German Chancellor Helmut Schmidt cancels scheduled upcoming visit to East Germany, saying current labor unrest in Poland makes visit ill-timed.

23 / Polish strikers win a major concession from the Communist regime, as Warsaw officials agree to negotiate with strikers' elected representatives.

24 / Poland's Premier Edward Babiuch resigns, along with three members of the ruling Politburo, in shakeup by Communist party secretary Edward Gierek to stem crisis caused by Baltic strikers.

26 / Crippling strikes spread from the northern Baltic to other cities throughout Poland, as workers resume negotiations broken off Aug. 24; labor leaders later threaten general strike if their demands are not met, prompting Warsaw and Church leaders to warn against provoking possible Soviet intervention.

27 / French Navy tugs smash blockade by fishermen at country's largest oil-tanker terminal at Fos outside Marseille.

28 / Washington assails South Korea; in testimony before Congress, officials accuse authorities in Seoul of manipulating news media to distort American criticisms of new regime to give a false impression of U.S. support.

Amnesty International calls on Iran to halt executions and imprisonment of citizens for their beliefs or origins; appeal claims at least 1,200 have been executed within first 18 months of the Islamic revolution.

29 / Polish strike wave spreads to coal miners in southern industrial region of Silesia. Secretary of State Edmund Muskie says Washington will "refrain from words or actions" that could exacerbate crisis.

Cuban refugees in Lima, Peru hijack a California-bound DC-8, seizing 14 hostages and demanding they be flown to United States; Washington says 185 Cubans on board plane will be arrested if they force entry to the U.S.

30 / Polish workers win right to strike and organize trade unions free of Communist party control, in tentative agreement between Warsaw and strikers at the Lenin shipyard in Gdańsk.

China's National People's Congress opens in Peking; China's highest legislative body announces sweeping changes in the economy August 31, with government controls loosened and emphasis placed on local accountability and profit incentive.

31 / Strikes in Poland are called off by labor leaders after winning further concessions from Warsaw, which pledges to restrain censorship and open government-controlled press to a wide variety of opinions, in addition to major victory, the right to free and independent trade unions elected by the workers.

SEPTEMBER 1980

NATIONAL

1 / Presidential campaigning starts in earnest, as Jimmy Carter blasts Ku Klux Klan at Labor Day rally in Tuscumbia, Ala., but Ronald Reagan criticizes Carter for starting campaign in "the birthplace of the Klan."

2 / President Carter assails Ronald Reagan for Labor Day "slurs and innuendos" about the South; Carter says GOP nominee seeks to start "a massive arms race" with Moscow that would endanger world peace.

3 / St. Louis schools are desegregated peacefully after eight-year struggle; over 16,000 pupils are bused to classes on first day of court-ordered program, with no violence reported.

Trial of Rep. John J. Jenrette (D.-S.C.) for bribery in Abscam "sting," opens in Federal District Court in Washington, D.C.

4 / House presses fiscal restraint as bipartisan coalition approves $9.1 billion package of budget cuts and revenue increases.

Federal Elections Commission rules John Anderson will be eligible for retroactive Federal matching funds if he receives 5 percent of the popular vote for President, allowing his independent campaign to borrow against these funds.

AFL-CIO endorses Jimmy Carter for reelection, calling Ronald Reagan unfit to be President. Reagan charges Administration with "abuse of public trust" in disclosures on secret "stealth" aircraft.

5 / Unemployment for August is 7.6 percent, down from 7.8 percent in July, indicating possible easing of the current recession.

8 / Six Army divisions were not ready for combat in December 1979; Pentagon says preparedness ratings for all 10 divisions in continental U.S. are below par, with other services sharing lack of readiness.

9 / John B. Anderson accepts invitation from League of Women Voters to take part in first televised Presidential debates; Reagan accepts, but President Carter refuses, insisting first round include only the two major party contenders.

Senator Jacob K. Javits, 79, loses New York's GOP primary, defeated by conservative Alfonse D'Amato; Brooklyn Rep. Elizabeth Holtzman wins Democratic race against consumer activist Bess Myerson, former mayor John V. Lindsay, and Brooklyn D.A. John Santucci. Javits will continue to seek reelection on the Liberal party line.

11 / A Cuban diplomat is slain in New York; Felix Garcia Rodriguez, an attaché at Cuba's UN mission, is shot dead in Queens, with anti-Castro terrorist group Omega 7 taking credit.

13 / Allegations of cocaine use are made against Timothy Kraft, President Carter's national campaign manager, as Washington announces charges will be investigated by an independent prosecutor; Kraft steps down as Carter campaign manager Sept. 14.

New York's Liberal party endorses John Anderson for President, marking first time party has rejected Democratic nominee.

14 / Abortion issue is raised in Massachusetts, as Archbishop Humberto Cardinal Medeiros of Boston warns Catholics not to support candidates who favor abortion in upcoming primary. But two Democrats who support liberal abortion policies win nomination to Congress in Sept. 17 polling.

Consumer Price Index is reported up by seventenths of a percent in August, for a projected 8.6 percent annual rate of inflation.

Voters in Maine approve continued use of nuclear power by a 3-2 margin; referendum to shut down Maine Yankee, the state's only nuclear power plant which provides one-third of its electricity, would also have banned construction of new plants.

24 / House ethics committee votes 10-2 to recommend expulsion of Rep. Michael J. Myers (D.-Pa.), for his conviction in New York Abscam bribery trial.

American Motors sets $200-million accord with Renault, making France's state-owned company principal owner of fourth-largest U.S. car maker.

25 / Federal District judge in Detroit invalidates 1980 Census for undercounting black and Hispanic Americans, ordering Census Bureau to adjust its figures upward for those groups around the country.

Senate rejects in 54-38 vote Republican-backed bill for $40 billion in individual and business tax cuts for 1981, dooming measure until after elections.

26 / Carter Administration moves to increase plutonium output for nuclear weapons, in policy shift after Pentagon report disclosed Sept. 16 warns current U.S. supplies might not meet the needs of nuclear-weapons production in the 1980s.

27 / *New York Times*/CBS Poll shows Ronald Reagan's standing with voters improved after Sept. 21 debate with John Anderson.

29 / Senate Judiciary panel's draft report on Billy Carter is disclosed; report says Carter's business relationships with Libya "merits condemnation," but finds he committed no crime, with no evidence he received special treatment from the Justice Department. Report criticizes White House National Security advisor Zbigniew Brzezinski and Attorney General Benjamin Civiletti for their handling of the matter, and concludes that President Carter should have more explicitly disassociated himself from his brother's dealings with Libya.

30 / Joint House-Senate finance committe authorizes New York City to issue $300-million in federally guaranteed municipal bonds, a major part of city's budgetary plan for fiscal solvency.

White House unveils aid package for ailing steel industry; program delays pollution control deadlines and increases tariffs to protect domestic producers from "dumping" of foreign steel on U.S. markets.

INTERNATIONAL

1 / Polish strikers return to work, ending 18-day protest that wrung major political and economic concessions from the Communist regime; demands granted include release of dissident KOR leaders who supported the strike, and establishment of country's first independent trade unions since the Communists seized power.

Secretary of State Muskie asks that hostages be freed in letter to Iran's Premier Ali Rajai, in first direct contact between Washington and Tehran since failed April 24 attempted rescue.

2 / Strikes in Poland's coal mining region of Silesia continue as government officials meet with strikers' representatives, with Warsaw agreeing in principle with their demands for higher wages and safe working conditions, as well as their own free unions.

3 / Polish coal miners return to work after settling their grievances with Government, as turmoil that gripped country for nearly three weeks draws to a close. AFL-CIO announces it will aid new Polish trade unions financially, but Secretary of State Muskie urges labor leaders to shelve plan, which Soviets might use as pretext to intervene against labor-government accords.

Sol M. Linowitz, U.S. Mideast envoy, announces that Egypt and Israel have agreed to resume Palestinian autonomy talks, ending a six-day mission to Cairo and Tel Aviv.

6 / Edward Gierek is dismissed as Polish Communist party secretary — a post he has held since 1970 — after reportedly suffering a heart attack; he is replaced by Stanislaw Kania, 53-year-old Politburo member and former head of the national police, who pledges to honor concessions to strikers.

7 / Hua Guofeng resigns as China's Prime Minister, with National People's Congress naming deputy premier Zhao Ziyang to replace him; Hua will remain party chairman, but resignation is seen as victory for Deng Xiaoping, China's paramount leader.

8 / Canada's constitutional conference opens in Ottawa, but talks called by Prime Minister Pierre Trudeau seeking to replace the 1867 British North America Act with a new constitution end Sept. 13, with Federal and provincial leaders unable to agree on major issues. Trudeau says he will take unilateral steps toward constitutional reform without the required unanimous consent of provinces.

9 / Iran's Prime Minister Ali Rajai rejects new appeal by Secretary of State Muskie to free U.S. hostages, saying Washington must first "repent."

Britain closes its embassy in Tehran, withdrawing four remaining diplomats after Iranian officials had issued threats against consulate.

10 / Libya and Syria announce they will merge two countries to bolster "Arab unity" and the "anti-Zionist struggle," after negotiations in Tripoli between Syrian Pres. Hafez al-Assad and Libya's Col. Muammar el-Qaddafi.

11 / Voters in Chile approve new constitution by 2-1 margin; plebiscite allows Pres. Augusto Pinochet — who overthrew Salvador Allende's Marxist regime in 1973 — to remain in office until 1989, and continues ban on parties and political activity.

12 / Military overthrows Premier Suleyman Demirel's government in Turkey; six-member National Security Council headed by Gen. Kenan Evren in Ankara calls for all-out war against terrorism, and promises quick return to civilian rule.

Ayatollah Khomeini softens his stand on hostages, setting four conditions for release of Americans in Tehran speech — including U.S. noninterference in Iran's affairs, unfreezing Iranian assets in U.S., returning the Shah's wealth, and dropping American claims against Tehran — which omits previous demand for apology from Washington.

14 / Iran's *Majlis* begins discussing U.S. hostage issue; parliament puts off debate on captives Sept. 16, but agrees to set up special commission to weigh their fate.

15 / Hopes for quick resolution of hostage crisis fade as speaker of Iran's parliament Hashemi Rafsanjani indicates Tehran still demands a U.S. apology before hostages can be released.

A Russian soldier seeks asylum in the U.S. embassy in Kabul, Afghanistan, but U.S. returns him to Soviet custody Sept. 21, after Moscow promises he will not be prosecuted, and American officials are satisfied he is returning of his own accord.

17 / Anastasio Somoza Debayle is assassinated in Paraguayan capital of Asunción; 56-year-old ousted dictator of Nicaragua dies as hail of machine-gun and bazooka fire rakes his car, also killing his driver and a bodyguard. Authorities claim assassins are Nicaraguan, though Managua government denies any connection to killing.

Clashes between Iran and Iraq are reported along frontier; simmering border conflict prompts Baghdad to announce it has terminated five-year accord — signed by the Shah of Iran in 1975 — providing for joint administration of the disputed Shatt al Arab waterway at the mouth of the Persian Gulf, and setting the nations' common border as running through its middle and deepest channel.

Military court in Seoul convicts South Korean dissident leader Kim Dae Jung of treason, sentencing him to death; 23 co-defendants are found guilty and sentenced from 3 to 20 years in prison.

18 / President Carter rules out an apology to Iran, saying American honor precludes such action.

Saudi Arabia agrees to increase oil prices by $2 a barrel — to $30 — in accord reached at three-day OPEC conference in Vienna; Riyadh ends policy of producing more oil to hold down prices, as other members pledge to gradually reduce their prices.

U.S. House votes 298-98 to ban proposed shipment of 38 tons of enriched uranium to India, which has rejected international inspections and prohibitions on nuclear weapons.

19 / Heavy border fighting is reported by both Iran and Iraq; Baghdad has reportedly deployed 10,000 troops to seize 90 square miles of Iranian territory it claims rightfully belongs to Iraq.

20 / Iran calls up reservists to "defend integrity of the country" in conflict with Iraq, as Pres. Bani-Sadr takes direct command of military operations.

21 / Border war between Iran and Iraq heats up, with heavy fighting in oil-rich region over disputed Shatt al Arab waterway. *Majlis* in Tehran freezes action on U.S. hostage issue, but agrees Sept. 30 to hear regular reports on special panel's findings.

22 / Iraqi jets attack 10 Iranian air bases — including Tehran's Mehrabad Airport—as border war escalates.

23 / Fighting between Iran and Iraq continues; Iraqi attacks center on oil-refining center of Abadan, as Iran's jets bomb Baghdad. President Carter pledges U.S. noninterference in conflict, and hints that release of American hostages might lead to resumption of military aid to Tehran. UN Security Council calls for a cease-fire in border war.

India's Prime Minister Indira Gandhi issues executive order allowing regime to jail opponents for one year without trial, seen by many as reviving the "state of emergency" measures imposed in 1977.

24 / Iraqi troops push deeper into Iran, reportedly seizing 10-mile deep strip of territory; fighting rages around strategic oil facilities, with Iran's major oil terminal at Kharg Island reported bombed. Three Americans are killed in Iranian attacks on Iraqi oil fields. Fighting halts all oil exports from both nations.

U.S. Senate votes 48-46 to approve sale of 38 tons of uranium fuel to India; House had blocked shipments, but rejection by majority in both chambers is necessary to halt sale.

25 / Secretary of State Edmund Muskie and Foreign Minister Andrei Gromyko meet in New York, and later pledge both U.S. and Soviet Union will stay neutral in Persian Gulf conflict.

26 / Muslim nations meet at UN in New York to mediate an end to Iranian-Iraqi war; Baghdad claims its terms for peace include recognition of its sovereignty over Shatt al Arab waterway and Tehran's pledge not to interfere in its internal affairs. Iraq suspends all oil exports, withdrawing 3.3 million barrels daily from world market.

Cuba ends boatlift which brought over 125,000 refugees to U.S., expelling some 100 U.S. vessels still waiting in Mariel Harbor to pick up refugees.

Bomb explodes at Munich's *Oktoberfest,* killing 13; West German authorities arrest six members of a neo-Nazi party Sept. 28, after evidence suggests one of that illegal group killed in blast had set the bomb.

27 / Iraq gains in fighting in Iran's Khuzistan province, claiming capture of capital of Ahwaz, as its troops advance on major southern oil port of Khurramshahr. Pakistan's Pres. Zia ul-Haq arrives in Tehran as "goodwill" emmissary of Islamic Conference to mediate conflict.

Italy's center-left coalition government resigns, following defeat by a one-vote margin in parliament on government's economic proposals.

Authorities in Peking say China's disgraced Gang of Four, including Mao Zedong's widow, Jiang Qing, will be put on trial with six others on charges of sedition, facing a possible death sentence.

28 / Iraqi Pres. Hussein says he welcomes a cease-fire with Iran and is prepared to negotiate, but only if Tehran agrees to Baghdad's territorial demands. UN Security Council urges speedy end to crisis, calling on both sides to accept mediation of border disputes.

29 / Tehran vows to carry on war with Iraq regardless of its losses, as Iraq continues offensive against strategic oil installations in Khuzistan; Baghdad says it will accept UN call to end fighting if Iran will also halt hostilities. Washington discloses it is conferring with allies on forming a task force to protect Western interests in the Persian Gulf.

30 / Iran rejects calls for peace with Iraq, as Iraqi advance stalls in Khuzistan; Iranian jets attack targets in Baghdad, including a nuclear power plant, with 11 Iraqis reported killed. Iraqi Foreign Minister Saadun Hamadi meets with Secretary of State Muskie in New York, assuring Washington that Baghdad seeks only "limited objectives" in war.

Washington sends four U.S. radar command aircraft and support personnel to Saudi Arabia, granting request for help in protecting Riyadh's oilfields.

THE UNITED STATES

OUTLINE OF UNITED STATES HISTORY

16TH CENTURY

1564 French Huguenots failed in attempts to establish settlements in present-day South Carolina and Florida.

1565 Spaniards built fort at St. Augustine, Florida, first permanent white colony in present-day United States.

1585 Sir Walter Raleigh dispatched expedition to Roanoke Island, Virginia; settlement abandoned (1586).

1590 No traces found of second Roanoke settlement—the Lost Colony (established 1587)—and birthplace of Virginia Dare, first English child born (1587) in America.

1598 Juan de Oñate began settlement in New Mexico.

17TH CENTURY

1607 Colony established at Jamestown, Virginia; Captain John Smith elected (1608) head of group. Pocahontas, daughter of Powhatan, head of an Indian confederacy in that region, rescued John Smith after Indian capture.

1612 John Rolfe developed effective method of curing tobacco; later (1614) married Pocahontas.

1614 Dutch established trading post in what is now New York State.

1619 House of Burgesses, first representative assembly in America, met at Jamestown.
The first 20 blacks arrived in Virginia as indentured servants.

1620 Pilgrims arrived from England in *Mayflower* and founded colony at Plymouth, Massachusetts; signed Mayflower Compact, first written constitution in colonies.

1626 Peter Minuit bought Manhattan Island from Indians for the equivalent of $24 and named it New Amsterdam.

1629 Massachusetts Bay Company formed; John Winthrop elected governor.

1630 Settlement established at Boston, Massachusetts.

1630–1640 "Great Migration" of Puritans from England settled Massachusetts and Connecticut.

1632 Cecilius Calvert, 2d Lord Baltimore, established Roman Catholic colony in Maryland.

1636 Banished (1635) from Massachusetts Bay colony, Roger Williams founded Providence, Rhode Island, first English colony to grant religious freedom.
Harvard College founded.

1638 First printing press established in Cambridge, Massachusetts; printed (1640) *Bay Psalm Book*.

1647 Peter Stuyvesant became head of New Netherlands; his dictatorial rule was resented.

1655 Stuyvesant seized Swedish forts on Delaware, ending Swedish rule in North America.

1662 Virginia became the first colony to declare slavery hereditary.

1664 English took New Amsterdam, changing name to New York.

1676 Nathaniel Bacon led Virginia frontiersmen against raiding Indians and then against Governor Berkeley; Bacon's death virtually ended rebellion.

1677 William Penn framed first charter separating church and state at the Quaker colony of West Jersey.

1680 New Hampshire became separate province.

1682 La Salle reached mouth of Mississippi and claimed area from Quebec to Gulf Coast—Louisiana—for France.
William Penn founded Philadelphia for Quakers.

1686 New England made a royal dominion; tyrannical rule of Edmund Andros ended in 1689 when England's "Glorious Revolution" spread to the colonies.

1689 King William's War between French and English began as part of greater European war; Treaty of Ryswick (1697) restored prewar positions.

1690 Benjamin Harris published first newspaper, in Boston, that was suppressed after one issue for criticizing conduct of war.

1692 Witch trials began in Salem, Massachusetts; 20 "witches" executed before hunt ended (1693).

1693 William and Mary College founded in Williamsburg, Virginia.

1699 Sieur d'Iberville founded Old Biloxi (now Ocean Springs) on Biloxi Bay, first permanent settlement in Louisiana Territory.

18TH CENTURY

1700 By this date, shipbuilding and whaling industries had developed in New England; plantation system in Virginia, Maryland, and Carolina fully established.

1704 Boston *News-Letter*, first continuous colonial newspaper, was started.

1716 First American theater built, in Williamsburg.

1724 English established Fort Dummer near site of Brattleboro, considered first permanent Vermont settlement.

1732–1757 Benjamin Franklin annually published *Poor Richard's Almanack*.

1733 James Oglethorpe founded colony in Savannah, Georgia, last of the original 13 colonies to be settled.

1734–1735 John Peter Zenger, editor and publisher of *New-York Weekly Journal*, tried for sedition; acquittal was landmark in assuring freedom of press in America.

1734–1750 Jonathan Edwards, in New England, and George Whitefield, in Georgia, led Great Awakening, a series of religious revivals.

1741 Captain Vitus Bering discovered Alaska and claimed it for Russia.

1744 King George's War, extension in America of War of the Austrian Succession in Europe, began; Treaty of Aix-la-Chapelle (1748) restored prewar position.

1754 French erected Fort Duquesne, on site of Pittsburgh, Pennsylvania.
George Washington's fight with French in Ohio territory became first skirmish of French and Indian War, which spread (1756) to Europe and became known as the Seven Years War.

1763 Treaty of Paris ended French control east of Mississippi; Spain ceded Florida to England in return for Cuba.

1764 Parliament passed the Sugar Act, first law to raise money for crown in the colonies, and Currency Act, which forbade all colonies to issue paper money.
James Otis denounced acts in pamphlet, noting British offense of taxation without representation.

1765 College of Philadelphia (later part of University of Pennsylvania) offered first professional medical training in colonies.
Parliament issued Stamp Act, first direct tax levied by crown on American colonies.
Colonials convoked Stamp Act Congress; organized Sons of Liberty.

1766 Stamp Act repealed, but Parliament passed Declaratory Act, affirming its right to legislate for colonies.

1767 Townshend Acts passed by Parliament, imposing import duties; many colonies enacted nonimportation agreements.

1769–1782 Fray Junípero Serra founded nine Franciscan missions in California.

1770 In Boston, several colonists were killed by English soldiers in a melee, later known as the Boston Massacre.
Townshend Acts repealed, except for tea tax; colonial merchants worked for conciliation.

1773 Parliament passed Tea Act granting East India Company full remission of all tea duties.
Boston Tea Party occurred, when patriots dressed

as Indians dumped tea shipment into Boston Harbor.

1774 First Continental Congress met in Philadelphia, with representatives from all colonies except Georgia.

1775 Patrick Henry made his "Liberty or Death" speech before Virginia Assembly.

Parliament passed New England Restraining Act, forbidding colonies to trade with any nation except Britain and British West Indies.

Minutemen fought British at Lexington and Concord, signaling start of American Revolution's military phase.

Second Continental Congress met in Philadelphia and appointed Washington chief of Continental forces.

The first abolitionist society in America was established in Philadelphia.

British defeated Americans at Bunker Hill and attacked Boston; city under siege until March 1776.

1776 Thomas Paine's *Common Sense* published, calling for American independence.

Declaration of Independence adopted by Congress.

Nathan Hale ("I only regret that I have but one life to lose for my country") executed by British as American spy.

Washington, leading troops across Delaware River, made surprise attack on British at Trenton, New Jersey.

1777 General Burgoyne's defeat at Saratoga was major American victory.

Articles of Confederation adopted by Congress (ratified by all colonies by 1781).

Congress recommended that colonial governments appropriate Loyalist property.

Washington and troops took up winter quarters at Valley Forge, Pennsylvania.

1778 Americans and French signed Treaty of Alliance. British took Savannah, Georgia.

1779 John Paul Jones ("I have not yet begun to fight"), commanding *Bon Homme Richard*, defeated British frigate *Serapis*, off coast of England.

1780 Washington's troops mutinied at Morristown, New Jersey, because of sparse supplies and delayed salaries.

Benedict Arnold's treason exposed.

1781 Washington and Rochambeau planned joint Franco-American Yorktown (Va.) campaign, which brought surrender of Cornwallis and virtually ended hostilities.

Congress chartered Bank of North America to supply government with money.

1782 John Adams, Benjamin Franklin, and John Jay negotiated peace treaty with British in Paris.

1783 Treaty of Paris acknowledged independence of the United States.

Almost the entire American army disbanded without authority and Congress fled Philadelphia to escape discontented soldiers.

Last of 100,000 Loyalists fled country.

General Washington bade farewell to his officers at Fraunces Tavern, New York City.

1786 Daniel Shays led discontented Massachusetts farmers in armed rebellion; insurrection crushed (1787) and later Massachusetts enacted more liberal legislation.

1787 Constitutional Convention held in Philadelphia.

Congress adopted the Northwest Ordinance creating and providing a government for the Northwest Territory; slavery in region was prohibited.

Alexander Hamilton, James Madison, and John Jay began writing *The Federalist Papers,* which urged acceptance of Constitution.

Delaware was first state to ratify Constitution.

1788 New Hampshire ratified the Constitution, thereby achieving the necessary nine-state acceptance.

1789 George Washington elected nation's first President and John Adams became Vice-President.

First Congress met in New York, nation's first capital.

Federal Judiciary Act provided for organization of Supreme Court, 13 district courts, and three circuit courts; John Jay became first Chief Justice.

1790 Hamilton organized national fiscal program.

First census recorded American population as 3,929,214.

Capital temporarily moved to Philadelphia.

1791 Bill of Rights became part of Constitution.

Bank of the United States established.

1793 Washington declared American neutrality vis-à-vis France and Britain.

Citizen Genêt, Minister of French Republic to the United States, asked to leave because of his conduct; later became American citizen.

The Fugitive Slave Act was passed, making it illegal to give comfort to or prevent the arrest of a runaway slave.

Eli Whitney invented cotton gin.

1794 Federal troops put down Whisky Rebellion in western Pennsylvania.

Jay's treaty with Britain concluded; provision included British agreement to withdraw from Northwest posts; ratified (1795).

1795 11th Constitutional Amendment is ratified: a state cannot be sued by citizen of another state.

1796 In his Farewell Address, Washington warned of permanent foreign alliances and encouraged temporary ones in times of emergency.

John Adams (Federalist) elected President; Thomas Jefferson (Democratic-Republican) elected Vice-President.

1797 Affairs with France deteriorated, especially after the XYZ Affair: Talleyrand's agents tried to extort bribes from American commissioners in Paris.

1798–1800 Americans fought undeclared naval war with France; Convention of 1800 released United States from alliance with France.

1798 Alien and Sedition Acts passed by Federalists to repress political opposition.

Kentucky and Virginia Resolutions maintained unconstitutionality of Alien and Sedition Acts; expressed early states rights theory.

1799 Washington died at Mount Vernon.

19TH CENTURY

1800 Washington, D.C., became nation's capital.

1801 House of Representatives chose Jefferson for President and Aaron Burr Vice-President after electoral tie; Jefferson was first President inaugurated in new capital.

1802 Congress established U.S. Military Academy at West Point, New York.

1803 In *Marbury* v. *Madison*, Chief Justice Marshall established principle of judicial review.

United States purchased Louisiana from France for about $15 million, doubling nation's area.

Meriwether Lewis and William Clark began their westward expedition.

1804 Hamilton killed in duel with Aaron Burr.

1807 Congress enacted law prohibiting importation of slaves after January 1, 1808.

Embargo enacted because of British harassment on seas; repealed (1809), but trade with France and Great Britain still prohibited.

1808 Congress prohibited the admission of any new slaves into the United States.

1809 James Madison sworn in as President with George Clinton as Vice-President.

1811 General William Henry Harrison defeated Tecumseh's forces at Battle of Tippecanoe.

1812 War declared on Great Britain for impressing U.S. seamen, blockading, and violating neutrality; Americans suffered setbacks on land, but naval successes boosted low morale.

1813 British blockaded coast, but Captain Oliver Hazard Perry's naval victory secured Lake Erie for United States.

1814 British took offensive, capturing and burning Washington, but suffered losses in attempt to invade New York from Canada.

Francis Scott Key wrote lyrics of "Star-spangled Banner."

At Hartford Convention, New England delegates met to revise Constitution and oppose war.

Treaty of Ghent ended war.

1815 Andrew Jackson defeated British at New Orleans before news of peace arrived.

Fleet under Stephen Decatur ended Barbary states' imposition of tribute on American merchant vessels.

1816 James Monroe elected President and Daniel D. Tompkins, Vice-President.

First protective tariff enacted.

1817 New York State legislature authorized construction of Erie Canal; it opened in 1825.

1818 U.S.-Canadian boundary to Rockies fixed; United States and Britain agreed to occupy Oregon Territory jointly.

1819 Financial panic seized nation.

Adams-Onís Treaty, ceding Spain's Florida holding to the United States, signed; Andrew Jackson became (1821) Florida's first governor.

1820 Missouri Compromise prohibited slavery in Louisiana Territory north of Missouri's southern border; Missouri admitted to Union as slave state and Maine as free state.

First American missionaries arrived in Hawaii.

1821 Spain granted Moses Austin land in Texas for settlement.

1822–1826 U.S. government recognized newly independent Latin American republics.

1823 Monroe Doctrine promulgated: any further European effort to colonize the Americas or interfere in their affairs would be considered a hostile act.

1824–1825 Presidential election resulted in no candidate having a majority; House chose John Quincy Adams President after much bargaining between candidates.

1828 Congress passed protectionist "Tariff of Abominations."

Andrew Jackson elected first Democratic President; introduced spoils system on national level; Calhoun reelected Vice-President.

1829 David Walker, a free black, published his famous "Appeal," one of the most militant antislavery documents.

1830 Senators Daniel Webster (Mass.) and Robert Y. Hayne (S.C.) engaged in historic states' rights debate.

1831 William Lloyd Garrison began to publish *The Liberator*.

Nat Turner led major slave insurrection in Virginia.

1832 President Jackson vetoed renewal of National Bank.

South Carolina nullified U.S. tariff laws; Jackson declared action was rebellion and ordered Forts Moultrie and Sumter reinforced.

1833 Jackson began second term; ordered public deposits withdrawn from Bank of the United States and put into state banks; Secretary of the Treasury Taney deposited funds in "pet banks."

American Anti-Slavery Society founded at Philadelphia as abolitionist movement grew more vocal.

1834 Whig party had come into being; Henry Clay led group formed by National Republicans, states' righters, and dissident Democrats.

1835 Seminoles in Florida resisted forced transportation West; despite capture (1837) of their leader Osceola, resistance continued until 1842.

1836 Mexican leader Santa Anna captured fort of Alamo at San Antonio, Texas; Sam Houston later led American victory at Battle of San Jacinto.

Texas declared its independence from Mexico; Houston became president of independent republic.

1837 Martin Van Buren inaugurated as President.

Panic of 1837 depressed economy.

1840 By this time, Underground Railroad was fully organized to rescue fugitive slaves.

1841 President William Henry Harrison died a month after inauguration; John Tyler became first Vice-President to succeed to Presidency as a result of incumbent's death.

Horace Greeley founded the New York *Tribune*.

1842 Webster-Ashburton Treaty with Britain settled northeastern U.S. boundary.

1843 United States recognized independence of Hawaii.

1844 James K. Polk elected President; George M. Dallas elected Vice-President.

1845 Texas agreed to join Union and was annexed.

Mexico broke off diplomatic relations with United States.

U.S. Naval Academy established at Annapolis, Maryland.

1846 Mexican War broke out after Mexican troops crossed Rio Grande; Zachary Taylor led American victory at Battles of Palo Alto, Resaca de la Palma, Monterrey, and Buena Vista.

Oregon boundary established by treaty with Great Britain.

Wilmot Proviso, banning slavery in territory acquired from Mexican War, failed to pass (1846, 1847) Congress.

1847 General Winfield Scott captured Mexico City.

Led by Brigham Young, the Mormons settled at Salt Lake City, Utah.

1848 Treaty of Guadalupe Hidalgo signed by the United States and Mexico; established Rio Grande as boundary; Mexico recognized U.S. claim to Texas and ceded New Mexico and California in return for $15 million.

First Women's Rights Convention, led by Lucretia Mott and Elizabeth Cady Stanton, held at Seneca Falls, New York.

Discovery of gold in California touched off "Gold Rush."

1849 Zachary Taylor (Whig) was inaugurated.

The first school integration lawsuit was filed by Benjamin Roberts against the City of Boston. The Massachusetts Supreme Court rejected the suit, setting the groundwork for the "separate but equal" doctrine.

1850 Vice-President Millard Fillmore (Whig) succeeded to the Presidency after Taylor died of cholera.

Congress passed Henry Clay's Compromise of 1850: California admitted as free state; remainder of Mexican territory divided into New Mexico and Utah, without prior decision on slavery; more effective Fugitive Slave Law enacted; slave trade abolished in capital.

Clayton-Bulwer Treaty, concerning freedom of future canal zone, signed with Britain; abrogated (1901).

1852 Harriet Beecher Stowe's *Uncle Tom's Cabin* published.

1853 Commodore Matthew C. Perry visited Japan and obtained (1854) trade agreement.

Gadsden Purchase: land now included in New Mexico and Arizona purchased from Mexico.

1854 Congress enacted Kansas and Nebraska Act, sponsored by Stephen A. Douglas: repealed Missouri Compromise and provided that people in states would decide slavery issue.

1854–1856 Settlement of Kansas brought bloody fighting; U.S. Senate engaged in violent debates.

1856 Republican party, formed in large part by Northern Whigs, held its first convention.

1857 Supreme Court's Dred Scott decision ruled Missouri Compromise unconstitutional, holding that a slave's residence in free territory did not make him free and denying citizenship rights to descendants of slaves.

1858 Abraham Lincoln debated Senator Douglas on slavery issue and became national figure.

1859 John Brown, Kansas abolitionist, unsuccessfully tried to seize federal arsenal at Harpers Ferry, Virginia, to start slave insurrection; captured, he was hanged for treason.

First oil well drilled at Titusville, Pa., by Col. Edwin L. Drake.

1860 Lincoln elected President; South Carolina passed ordinance of secession.

1861 Mississippi, Florida, Alabama, Georgia, Louisiana, and Texas seceded from Union; Confederate States of America formed with Jefferson Davis (Miss.) as president; constitution based on states' rights doctrine.

South Carolina troops fired on Fort Sumter (April 12), forcing Union troops to evacuate; signaled start of Civil War.

Lincoln proclaimed blockade of Confederate states.

Virginia, Arkansas, Tennessee, and North Carolina joined Confederacy.

Robert E. Lee and Joseph E. Johnston resigned from U.S. Army.

West Virginia broke away from Virginia; admitted to Union in 1863.

1862 Lincoln issued Emancipation Proclamation to take effect January 1863.

Major Civil War battles of Shiloh, *Monitor* and *Merrimack*, Peninsular Campaign, Second Bull Run, Antietam, and Fredericksburg occurred.

1863 First national conscription act enacted; draft riots exploded in New York City.

General George Meade's Union forces defeated General Lee's army at Gettysburg; Lincoln delivered famous address at dedication of Gettysburg Cemetery.

1864 General Ulysses S. Grant became commander of Union armies.

General William Tecumseh Sherman marched through Georgia to the sea; captured Atlanta and Savannah.

1865 13th Amendment abolishing slavery was ratified.

Lee surrendered (April 9) at Appomattox (Va.) Courthouse.

Lincoln assassinated (April 14) by John Wilkes Booth at Ford's Theater, Washington, D.C.; Vice-President Andrew Johnson became President.

1866 Ku Klux Klan formed in Tennessee.

Civil Rights Act, bestowing citizenship on blacks passed over Johnson's veto.

Congress adopted the 14th Amendment containing "due process" and "equal protection" clauses guaranteeing civil rights of blacks.

1867 Three Reconstruction Acts passed over Johnson's vetoes; divided South into military districts and abolished qualifications for Confederate States' readmission to Union.

Secretary of State William H. Seward purchased Alaska from Russia for $7.2 million.

Northerners, called "carpetbaggers," participated in Southern Reconstruction; Southern whites allying themselves with Radicals were called "scalawags."

1868 Andrew Johnson was impeached by House and tried by Senate; two-thirds vote required for conviction failed by one vote.

Seven former Confederate states readmitted to Union.

14th Amendment was ratified.

The transcontinental railroad was completed.

1869 15th Amendment, giving blacks right to vote, proposed; ratified (1870).

1870 *New York Times* began exposé of Tammany Hall corruption; led to eventual imprisonment of Boss Tweed.

Joseph H. Rainey of South Carolina became the first black to sit in the House of Representatives after election to the 41st Congress; he subsequently was reelected four times.

General Robert E. Lee died.

The 15th Amendment was adopted, guaranteeing the right to vote to all U.S. citizens.

1871 Civil service reform began with establishment of first Civil Service Commission.

Disastrous fire destroyed most of Chicago.

1872 New York *Sun* charged prominent Republicans with taking bribes in Crédit Mobilier scandal (corruption in building Union Pacific railroad); resulted (1873) in Congressional investigation.

1873 Financial panic developed into five-year depression, worst to date.

1875 Civil Rights Act was passed forbidding discrimination against blacks in public facilities.

1876 General Custer and his troops were massacred by Sitting Bull's Sioux Indians at the Little Bighorn.

Presidential election contest between Samuel Tilden and Rutherford B. Hayes disputed; special electoral commission declared (1877) Hayes President.

1877 Reconstruction Era officially ended.

Federal troops put down a series of railroad strikes.

1878 Bland-Allison Act, passed over Hayes's veto, required government to purchase silver.

1881 President James A. Garfield was shot; succeeded by Chester A. Arthur.

1882 Chinese Exclusion Act barred immigration of Chinese laborers for 10 years; later legislation continued policy until 1943.

1883 Pendleton Act established civil service system.

Supreme Court ruled antidiscrimination portions of 1875 Civil Rights Act invalid, opening the way for repassage of Jim Crow laws.

1886 American Federation of Labor organized with Samuel Gompers as first president.

Statue of Liberty unveiled in New York harbor.

Capture of Apache chief Geronimo ended Southwest Indian warfare.

Anarchists convicted of Haymarket Massacre.

1889 Oklahoma "land rush" opened all but panhandle of Oklahoma Territory for settlement.

U.S.-Latin American conference established (1890) body later called Pan American Union.

1890 Sherman Anti-Trust Act became law.

Highly protective McKinley Tariff adopted.

1891 Populist party formed as part of agrarian protest movement.

1893 Financial panic caused partly by severe gold drain began; thousands of banks and commercial institutions failed before economy recovered (1897).

World's Columbian Exposition held in Chicago.

1894 Unemployment became widespread; "Coxey's Army" of the jobless marched on Washington to demand public works program.

Pullman strike brought federal intervention.

1895 Southern states inaugurated "grandfather" clauses as part of program (including literacy tests and poll taxes) to disfranchise blacks.

U.S. involvement in British-Venezuelan dispute led to broad construction of Monroe Doctrine, stressing right of the United States to intercede in hemispheric disputes.

1896 Supreme Court in *Plessy* v. *Ferguson* upheld Louisiana law requiring segregated railroad facilities, under "separate but equal" doctrine.

1897 Gold rush in Klondike began.

1898 Spanish-American War broke out after battleship *Maine* exploded in harbor of Havana, Cuba; in Treaty of Paris Spain granted Cuba independence, ceded Puerto Rico, Guam, and Philippines to United States in return for payment of $20 million; Cuba came under U.S. military control, headed by General Leonard Wood.

United States annexed Hawaii.

1899 United States participated in first Hague Conference, which established Permanent Court of Arbitration.

20TH CENTURY

1900 United States expressed its commitment to Chinese Open Door policy.

U.S. troops helped relieve Peking during Boxer Rebellion.

Samoan Islands were divided between the United States and Germany.

1901 U.S. military rule of Philippines ended and civil government organized; islands became territory (1902).

Platt amendment, which Cubans had to incorporate (1902) in their constitution and recognize (1903) in treaty, made island virtual American protectorate; abrogated (1934).

Second Hay-Pauncefote Treaty gave Americans free hand in Isthmian canal.

President McKinley was shot in Buffalo; Theodore Roosevelt became President.

1902 Roosevelt pledged "Square Deal" for both labor and industry; began "trust-busting" with prosecution of the Northern Securities Company.

1903 Wright brothers flew first successful heavier-than-air machine.

1904 Roosevelt's annual message contained his "Corollary" to the Monroe Doctrine: United States' obligation to maintain order in Latin America.

1905 Russo-Japanese peace treaty signed at Portsmouth, New Hampshire; Roosevelt's role of mediator brought him (1906) Nobel Peace Prize.

Industrial Workers of the World, radical labor organization, founded in Chicago.

1906 Earthquake and fire destroyed San Francisco.

Pure Food and Drug and Meat Inspection Acts signed.

1907 "Gentlemen's Agreement": Japan agreed not to allow laborers to migrate to America.

1908 William Howard Taft elected President.

1909 Payne-Aldrich Tariff set high protective rates.

Robert E. Peary discovered North Pole.

1912 Roosevelt bolted Republican party and was Progressive (Bull Moose) party's candidate for President.

Woodrow Wilson won three-way Presidential race.

U.S. marines landed in Nicaragua to protect American interests during revolt.

1913 The 16th (income tax) and 17th (popular election of U.S. Senators) Amendments ratified.

Federal Reserve System established national banking and currency system.

United States began intervention in Mexican Revolution.

1914 Federal Trade Commission established.

Clayton Anti-Trust Act supplemented and strengthened Sherman Anti-Trust Act.

United States proclaimed its neutrality in World War I.

U.S. naval forces bombarded and occupied Vera Cruz, Mexico.

Panama Canal opened.

1915 *Lusitania* and *Arabic* sinkings brought strong protest notes from Wilson and modification of German submarine warfare.

1916 General John J. Pershing's troops pursued Pancho Villa 200 miles into Mexico without success.

1916–1924 U.S. troops occupied Santo Domingo.

1917 United States severed relations with Germany.

Publication of secret Zimmermann note, proposing German-Mexican alliance, helped Wilson gain House approval for arming merchantmen.

Congress declared war on Germany (April 6); General Pershing appointed head of American Expeditionary Force (AEF).

Congress passed Selective Service Act; Espionage Act; and Trading with the Enemy Act, forbidding commerce with enemy nations.

United States purchased Virgin Islands from Denmark.

1918 Wilson announced his "Fourteen Points" for peace.

Germany surrendered and armistice signed (November 11); U.S. war deaths, 112,432, many from disease.

Sedition Act passed; many Socialist and pacifist leaders imprisoned during next few years.

1919 Wilson toured country on behalf of League of Nations; awarded Nobel Peace Prize; suffered stroke.

18th Amendment (Prohibition) ratified.

1920 19th Amendment (women's suffrage) ratified.

Socialist Presidential candidate Eugene Debs, in prison, polled almost a million votes.

A. Mitchell Palmer ordered mass arrests of agitators during "Red scare" period.

Senate refused to ratify Versailles Treaty, ending World War I.

Warren G. Harding (Republican) and Calvin Coolidge elected President and Vice-President.

1922 Leading powers agreed to limit naval forces at Washington Arms Conference.

1923 Harding died; Coolidge became President.

1923–1924 Knowledge that Secretary of the Interior Albert B. Fall had secretly leased Teapot Dome oil reserves to Harry F. Sinclair was one of many Harding administration scandals made public.

1924 Soldiers Bonus Act compensated veterans for overseas duty.

1925 John Scopes, Tennessee schoolteacher, was defended by Clarence Darrow and prosecuted by William Jennings Bryan; Bryan secured the conviction of Scopes for teaching evolution.

1926 Richard Byrd and Floyd Bennett became first men to fly over North Pole.

U.S. troops landed in Nicaragua to quell rebellion; troops finally withdrawn in 1933.

1927 Charles A. Lindbergh made first nonstop solo flight from New York to Paris, becoming an international hero overnight.

1928 Kellogg-Briand Pact, outlawing war, signed by the United States; ratified by Senate (1929).

Al Smith, a Roman Catholic, ran as Democratic Presidential candidate.

Herbert C. Hoover and Charles Curtis elected President and Vice-President.

1929 Stock Market crash grew into worldwide Great Depression; low point came 1932–1933.

St. Valentine's Day massacre in Chicago marked peak of gangster wars.

1930 United States, Great Britain, and Japan agreed to limit navies at London Naval Conference.

Hawley-Smoot Tariff brought duty level to an all-time high.

1931 Hoover proposed one-year moratorium on inter-allied debts and reparations because of worldwide economic crisis.

1932 Reconstruction Finance Corporation established.

Lindbergh's son kidnapped and slain.

"Bonus Army," camped in Washington seeking early payment of veterans' benefits, was dispersed by Army troops led by Douglas MacArthur.

Franklin Delano Roosevelt and John Nance Garner were elected President and Vice-President.

1933 Roosevelt's "New Deal" began with bank holiday to lessen severe economic crisis; later he took nation off gold standard and delivered his radio "fireside chats."

"Hundred Days" session of Congress produced Emergency Banking Relief Act, Agricultural Adjustment Act, Federal Emergency Relief Act, and established Civilian Conservation Corps, Civil Works Administration, and Federal Bank Deposit Insurance Corporation. Supreme Court later declared several New Deal Acts unconstitutional.

Congress created Tennessee Valley Authority and established Commodity Credit Corporation.

21st Amendment repealed Prohibition.

Roosevelt's "Good Neighbor Policy" included opposition to armed intervention in Latin America.

1933–1936 Severe drought converted Great Plains into "Dust Bowl."

1934 Export-Import Bank established.

Congress passed Securities Exchange Act and established Federal Communications Commission and Federal Housing Administration.

John Dillinger slain by FBI agents in Chicago.

1935 Additional New Deal agencies created included Works Progress Administration, with Harry L. Hopkins as head; Resettlement Administration, directed by Rexford G. Tugwell; Rural Electrification Administration; and a new National Labor Relations Board.

Social Security Act created federal-state system of unemployment and old-age compensation.

1937 Supreme Court upheld New Deal legislation such as N.L.R.A. and Social Security; Roosevelt allowed "Court packing" plan to drop.

Relations with Japan started to deteriorate after sinking of U.S. gunboat *Panay*.

1938 Congress voted billion-dollar naval building program.

Fair Labor Standards Act (Wages and Hours Law) set up minimum wage and maximum hours for companies connected with interstate commerce.

Mexican expropriation of U.S. oil property caused long controversy.

1939 American neutrality pledged after war broke out in Europe; but "cash and carry" policy allowed for exports of arms to belligerent powers.

Albert Einstein and other scientists told Roosevelt of possibilities of developing atomic bomb.

1940 Smith Act (Alien Registration Act) included provisions that made it unlawful to advocate or teach the overthrow or destruction of any government in the United States by force and to be a member of any group dedicated to such a policy.

Selective Training and Service Act (Burke-Wadsworth Bill), nation's first peacetime program of compulsory military service was enacted.

1941 Roosevelt delivered Four Freedom's speech.

Lend-Lease Act allowed friendly nations to secure arms without cash.

Atlantic Charter, joint statement of postwar aims, issued by Roosevelt and Prime Minister Churchill.

Japanese attacked (December 7) Pearl Harbor; Congress declared war on Japan.

Germany and Italy declared war (December 11) on United States.

1942 Pacific Coast Japanese-Americans were relocated to Western detention camps; released in 1944; action upheld by Supreme Court.

In Pacific, Bataan and Corregidor fell to Japanese; U.S. Marines won major victory at Guadalcanal; U.S. planes, led by Major General James H. Doolittle, raided Tokyo.

First self-sustaining nuclear reaction achieved at the University of Chicago.

United Nations Pact signed by 26 nations at Washington.

1943 American forces helped drive Germans from North Africa and invaded Italy, which surrendered to Allies.

U.S. troops in the Pacific began island-hopping operations and combined with ANZAC troops to force retreat of Japanese in New Guinea.

Roosevelt attended conferences in Casablanca, Quebec, Cairo, and Teheran.

1944 Dwight D. Eisenhower became Supreme Commander of American Expeditionary Forces.

Allies invaded Europe and liberated France, Belgium, and Luxembourg.

Bretton Woods Conference set up International Monetary Fund and International Bank for Reconstruction and Development.

Roosevelt defeated Thomas E. Dewey and won fourth term; Harry S. Truman elected Vice-President.

1945 U.S. troops recaptured Philippines from Japanese.

Churchill, Roosevelt, and Stalin met at Yalta.

Roosevelt died (April 12); succeeded by Truman.

United Nations established in San Francisco.

Germany surrendered (May 7) unconditionally.

United States dropped atomic bombs on Japanese cities of Hiroshima and Nagasaki; Japan surrendered (August 14).

Potsdam Conference, to plan occupation and settlement of Europe, attended by Truman, Churchill (succeeded by Clement Attlee), and Stalin.

1946 Philippines gained independence from U.S.

United States set up Atomic Energy Commission for civilian control of atomic energy.

United Nations established permanent headquarters in New York City.

Churchill delivered his "Iron Curtain" speech at Fulton, Missouri; marked beginning of Cold War.

1947 "Truman Doctrine," economic and military assistance, began with aid to Greece and Turkey; doctrine was part of policy to contain Communism.

General George C. Marshall proposed plan for European recovery.

Taft-Hartley Act, limiting power of labor, passed over Truman's veto.

1948 Whittaker Chambers accused Alger Hiss of transmitting documents to Russians; Hiss denied charges, was indicted for perjury, and convicted (1950).

Truman issued Executive Order ending segregation in the armed forces.

U.S. airlift frustrated Soviet blockade of Berlin.

Truman defeated Dewey in upset election.

1949 Truman outlined his Point Four program of technical assistance to aid world peace.

North Atlantic Treaty Organization approved.

1950 South Korea invaded by North Korean troops; Truman ordered U.S. forces into area.

Senator Joseph McCarthy charged that the State Department was infiltrated by Communists.

1951 22d Amendment, limiting President to two terms, ratified.

Truman recalled General MacArthur from Korea for insubordination.

1952 Supreme Court declared Truman's seizure of steel mills during strike unconstitutional.

McCarran-Walter Bill restricted immigration.

General Dwight D. Eisenhower became first Republican to win Presidency since 1928.

1953 Korean armistice signed.

1954 *Brown* v. *Board of Education of Topeka:* Supreme Court outlawed racial segregation in public schools, as "inherently unequal."

United States commitment in Southeast Asia began with formation of SEATO and financial aid to Indo-China (Vietnam, Laos, and Cambodia).

1955 Supreme Court ordered school desegregation to proceed "with all deliberate speed."

AFL and CIO merged into one labor organization.

1956 Arrest of seamstress Rosa Parks for refusing to give her seat to a white man on a bus in Montgomery, Alabama, resulted in a bus boycott led by Martin Luther King, Jr.

1957 Eisenhower extended Truman Doctrine to Middle East with aid to Jordan.

Governor Orval Faubus called out Arkansas National Guard to prevent integration of Little Rock schools; Eisenhower sent federal troops to protect rights of black students.

Civil Rights Act was passed—the first such legislation since Reconstruction.

1958 First U.S. Earth satellite was launched.

Eisenhower sent marines to Lebanon during civil insurrection.

1959 Alaska and Hawaii admitted to Union.

Soviet Premier Khrushchev met with Eisenhower at Camp David, Maryland.

1960 American U-2 reconnaissance plane shot down over Soviet territory; Francis Gary Powers, pilot, exchanged for Rudolf Abel in 1962.

John F. Kennedy elected President with Lyndon B. Johnson as Vice-President.

1961 Anti-Castro invasion at Bay of Pigs failed.

Kennedy established Peace Corps and proposed Alliance for Progress.

Alan B. Shepard, Jr.; first American in space.

1962 After bloody campus clashes, James H. Meredith became the first black to enter the University of Mississippi.

John H. Glenn, Jr.; first American to orbit Earth.

Kennedy protested presence of Russian missiles on Cuba; danger of nuclear war ended with Soviet dismantling of weapons.

1963 Racial violence broke out in Birmingham, Ala.

United States, Britain, and Soviet Union signed treaty barring atmospheric nuclear testing.

Washington and Moscow opened "hot line" phone connection to reduce risk of accidental war.

Martin Luther King led "March on Washington."

Kennedy assassinated in Dallas; Lyndon B. Johnson became President.

1964 Civil Rights Act strengthened voting guarantee, prohibited segregation in public facilities.

24th Amendment, abolishing poll tax, ratified.

Johnson won landslide victory over Barry Goldwater in Presidential election.

1965 Large-scale antiwar demonstrations developed after Johnson announced Vietnam troop build-up.

Race riot erupted in Watts section of Los Angeles.

Johnson sent troops to Dominican Republic.

1966 Medicare program went into effect.

Chicago, Cleveland, and other Northern cities experienced major race riots.

1967 Antiwar, antidraft, and race riots increased.

Johnson and Premier Kosygin met at Glassboro, New Jersey.

25th Amendment, providing continuity in case of Presidential disability, ratified.

Treaty pledging peaceful uses of outer space signed with Soviet Union and Great Britain.

1968 North Korea seized U.S. Navy intelligence ship *Pueblo;* men released 11 months later.

Reverend Martin Luther King, Jr. and Senator Robert F. Kennedy assassinated.

Delegates from Washington and Hanoi met in Paris for preliminary Vietnam peace talks.

Richard M. Nixon won Presidential election; Spiro Agnew became Vice-President.

1969 Americans Neil A. Armstrong and Edwin E. Aldrin, Jr., were first men to land on Moon.

1970 U.S. and South Vietnamese troops enter Cambodia.

1971 26th Amendment grants voting rights to 18-year-olds. Nixon froze wages and prices; devalued dollar by 8.57%.

1972 Nixon visited Russia and China.

"Watergate Burglars" caught inside Democratic party's national headquarters.

Richard M. Nixon and Spiro T. Agnew reelected President and Vice-President.

1973 "Watergate" dominated American political scene.

Spiro T. Agnew resigned vice-presidency; Gerald R. Ford replaced him.

1974 President Nixon resigned and Gerald Ford became the 38th president.

1975 The Vietnam war ended. Unemployment reached 9.2%, highest since 1941.

1976 Jimmy Carter defeated Ford in Presidential election; Walter F. Mondale elected Vice-President.

1977 Carter established "human rights" as a key element in U.S. foreign policy.

1978 U.S. dollar fell in value against Western European and Japanese currencies.

1979 U.S. recognized the People's Republic of China.

Gasoline and fuel oil prices rose sharply.

Canal Zone ceded to Panama.

U.S. Embassy personnel taken hostage in Iran.

1980 Over 125,000 refugees fled Cuba for U.S.

In CONGRESS, July 4, 1776

A DECLARATION

By the REPRESENTATIVES of the UNITED STATES OF AMERICA,

In GENERAL CONGRESS assembled.

WHEN in the Course of human Events, it becomes necessary for one People to dissolve the Political Bands which have connected them with another, and to assume among the Powers of the Earth, the separate and equal Station to which the Laws of Nature and of Nature's God entitle them, a decent Respect to the Opinions of Mankind requires that they should declare the causes which impel them to the Separation.

We hold these Truths to be self-evident, that all Men are created equal, that they are endowed by their Creator with certain unalienable Rights, that among these are Life, Liberty, and the Pursuit of Happiness—That to secure these Rights, Governments are instituted among Men, deriving their just Powers from the Consent of the Governed, that whenever any Form of Government becomes destructive of these Ends, it is the Right of the People to alter or to abolish it, and to institute new Government, laying its Foundation on such Principles, and organizing its Powers in such Form, as to them shall seem most likely to effect their Safety and Happiness. Prudence, indeed, will dictate that Governments long established should not be changed for light and transient Causes; and accordingly all Experience hath shewn, that Mankind are more disposed to suffer, while Evils are sufferable, than to right themselves by abolishing the Forms to which they are accustomed. But when a long Train of Abuses and Usurpations, pursuing invariably the same Object, evinces a Design to reduce them under absolute Despotism, it is their Right, it is their Duty, to throw off such Government, and to provide new Guards for their future Security. Such has been the patient Sufferance of these Colonies; and such is now the Necessity which constrains them to alter their former Systems of Government. The History of the present King of Great-Britain is a History of repeated Injuries and Usurpations, all having in direct Object the Establishment of an absolute Tyranny over these States. To prove this, let Facts be submitted to a candid World.

He has refused his Assent to Laws, the most wholesome and necessary for the public Good.

He has forbidden his Governors to pass Laws of immediate and pressing Importance, unless suspended in their Operation till his Assent should be obtained; and when so suspended, he has utterly neglected to attend to them.

He has refused to pass other Laws for the Accommodation of large Districts of People, unless those People would relinquish the Right of Representation in the Legislature, a Right inestimable to them, and formidable to Tyrants only.

He has called together Legislative Bodies at Places unusual, uncomfortable, and distant from the Depository of their public Records, for the sole Purpose of fatiguing them into Compliance with his Measures.

He has dissolved Representative Houses repeatedly, for opposing with manly Firmness his Invasions on the Rights of the People.

He has refused for a long Time, after such Dissolutions, to cause others to be elected; whereby the Legislative Powers, incapable of Annihilation, have returned to the People at large for their exercise; the State remaining in the mean time exposed to all the Dangers of Invasion from without, and Convulsions within.

He has endeavoured to prevent the Population of these States; for that Purpose obstructing the Laws for Naturalization of Foreigners; refusing to pass others to encourage their Migrations hither, and raising the Conditions of new Appropriations of Lands.

He has obstructed the Administration of Justice, by refusing his Assent to Laws for establishing Judiciary Powers.

He has made Judges dependent on his Will alone, for the Tenure of their Offices, and the Amount and Payment of their Salaries.

He has erected a Multitude of new Offices, and sent hither Swarms of Officers to harass our People, and eat out their Substance.

He has kept among us, in Times of Peace, Standing Armies, without the consent of our Legislatures.

He has affected to render the Military independent of and superior to the Civil Power.

He has combined with others to subject us to a Jurisdiction foreign to our Constitution, and unacknowledged by our Laws; giving his Assent to their Acts of pretended Legislation:

For quartering large Bodies of Armed Troops among us:

For protecting them, by a mock Trial, from Punishment for any Murders which they should commit on the Inhabitants of these States:

For cutting off our Trade with all Parts of the World:

For imposing Taxes on us without our Consent:

For depriving us, in many Cases, of the Benefits of Trial by Jury:

For transporting us beyond Seas to be tried for pretended Offences:

For abolishing the free System of English Laws in a neighbouring Province, establishing therein an arbitrary Government, and enlarging its Boundaries, so as to render it at once an Example and fit Instrument for introducing the same absolute Rule into these Colonies:

For taking away our Charters, abolishing our most valuable Laws, and altering fundamentally the Forms of our Governments:

For suspending our own Legislatures, and declaring themselves invested with Power to legislate for us in all Cases whatsoever.

He has abdicated Government here, by declaring us out of his Protection and waging War against us.

He has plundered our Seas, ravaged our Coasts, burnt our Towns, and destroyed the Lives of our People.

He is, at this Time, transporting large Armies of foreign Mercenaries to compleat the Works of Death, Desolation, and Tyranny, already begun with circumstances of Cruelty and Perfidy, scarcely paralleled in the most barbarous Ages, and totally unworthy the Head of a civilized Nation.

He has constrained our fellow Citizens taken Captive on the high Seas to bear Arms against their Country, to become the Executioners of their Friends and Brethren, or to fall themselves by their Hands.

He has excited domestic Insurrections amongst us, and has endeavoured to bring on the Inhabitants of our Frontiers, the merciless Indian Savages, whose known Rule of Warfare, is an undistinguished Destruction of all Ages, Sexes and Conditions.

In every stage of these Oppressions we have Petitioned for Redress in the most humble Terms: Our repeated Petitions have been answered only by repeated Injury. A Prince, whose Character is thus marked by every act which may define a Tyrant, is unfit to be the Ruler of a free People.

Nor have we been wanting in Attentions to our British Brethren. We have warned them from Time to Time of Attempts by their Legislature to extend an unwarrantable Jurisdiction over us. We have reminded them of the Circumstances of our Emigration and Settlement here. We have appealed to their native Justice and Magnanimity, and we have conjured them by the Ties of our common Kindred to disavow these Usurpations, which, would inevitably interrupt our Connections and Correspondence. They too have been deaf to the Voice of Justice and of Consanguinity. We must, therefore, acquiesce in the Necessity, which denounces our Separation, and hold them, as we hold the rest of Mankind, Enemies in War, in Peace, Friends.

We, therefore, the Representatives of the UNITED STATES OF AMERICA, in General Congress, Assembled, appealing to the Supreme Judge of the World for the Rectitude of our Intentions, do, in the Name, and by Authority of the good People of these Colonies, solemnly Publish and Declare, That these United Colonies are, and of Right ought to be, Free and Independent States; that they are absolved from all Allegiance to the British Crown, and that all political Connection between them and the State of Great-Britain, is and ought to be totally dissolved; and that as Free and Independent States, they have full Power to levy War, conclude Peace, contract Alliances, establish Commerce, and to do all other Acts and Things which Independent States may of right do. And for the support of this Declaration, with a firm Reliance on the Protection of divine Providence, we mutually pledge to each other our Lives, our Fortunes, and our sacred Honor.

Signed by Order *and in* Behalf *of the* Congress,

JOHN HANCOCK, President

Attest.

CHARLES THOMSON, Secretary.

SIGNERS OF THE DECLARATION OF INDEPENDENCE: 1776

Name	Age	Occupation	Education	Representing	Birthplace	Born	Died
John Adams	40	Lawyer	Harvard	Massachusetts	Braintree, Mass.	1735	1826
Samuel Adams	53	Politician	Harvard	Massachusetts	Boston, Mass.	1722	1803
Josiah Bartlett	46	Physician	Private tutors	New Hampshire	Amesbury, Mass.	1729	1795
Carter Braxton	39	Planter	William & Mary	Virginia	Newington, Va.	1736	1797
Charles Carroll	38	Planter	Educated in Europe	Maryland	Annapolis, Md.	1737	1832
Samuel Chase	35	Lawyer	Private tutors	Maryland	Somerset Co., Md.	1741	1811
Abraham Clark	40	Lawyer-Farmer	Self-educated	New Jersey	Elizabethtown, N.J.	1726	1794
George Clymer	37	Merchant	Self-educated	Pennsylvania	Philadelphia, Pa.	1739	1813
William Ellery	48	Lawyer	Harvard	Rhode Island	Newport, R.I.	1727	1820
William Floyd	41	Farmer	Private tutors	New York	Brookhaven, N.Y.	1734	1821
Benjamin Franklin	71	Public servant	Grammar school	Pennsylvania	Boston, Mass.	1706	1790
Elbridge Gerry	31	Merchant	Harvard	Massachusetts	Marblehead, Mass.	1744	1814
Button Gwinnett	c. 41	Planter	Preparatory studies	Georgia	Gloucestershire, England	c. 1735	1777
Lyman Hall	52	Physician	Yale	Georgia	Wallingford, Conn.	1724	1790
John Hancock	39	Merchant	Harvard	Massachusetts	Braintree, Mass.	1737	1793
Benjamin Harrison	c. 50	Planter	Attended William & Mary	Virginia	Charles City Co., Va.	c. 1726	1791
John Hart	c. 65	Farmer	Self-educated	New Jersey	Stonington, Conn.	c. 1711	1779
Joseph Hewes	46	Merchant	Grammar school	North Carolina	Kingston, N.J.	1730	1779
Thomas Heyward	29	Lawyer	Studied law in England	South Carolina	St. Helena's Parish, S.C.	1746	1809
William Hooper	34	Lawyer	Harvard	North Carolina	Boston, Mass.	1742	1790
Stephen Hopkins	70	Public servant	Self-educated	Rhode Island	Providence, R.I.	1707	1785
Francis Hopkinson	38	Lawyer	College of Philadelphia[1]	New Jersey	Philadelphia, Pa.	1737	1791
Samuel Huntington	45	Lawyer	Self-educated	Connecticut	Windham, Conn.	1731	1796
Thomas Jefferson	33	Lawyer-Planter	William & Mary	Virginia	Goochland Co., Va.	1743	1826
Richard Henry Lee	44	Planter	Private tutors	Virginia	Westmoreland Co., Va.	1732	1794
Francis Lightfoot Lee	41	Planter	Private tutors	Virginia	Westmoreland Co., Va.	1734	1797
Francis Lewis	63	Merchant	Grammar school	New York	Llandaff, Wales	1713	c. 1802
Philip Livingston	60	Merchant	Yale	New York	Albany, N.Y.	1716	1778
Thomas Lynch	26	Planter	Studied law in England	South Carolina	Prince George's Parish, S.C.	1749	1779
Thomas McKean	42	Lawyer	Preparatory studies	Delaware	New London Township, Pa.	1734	1817
Arthur Middleton	34	Planter	Studied law in England	South Carolina	near Charlestown, S.C.	1742	1787
Lewis Morris	50	Landowner	Yale	New York	Morrisania, N.Y.	1726	1798
Robert Morris	42	Merchant	Self-educated	Pennsylvania	Liverpool, England	1734	1806
John Morton	c. 42	Surveyor	Private tutors	Pennsylvania	Ridely, Pa.	c. 1724	1777

Name	Age	Occupation	Education	Representing	Birthplace	Born	Died
Thomas Nelson	41	Planter	Educated in England	Virginia	Yorktown, Va.	1738	1789
William Paca	37	Lawyer	College of Philadelphia;[1] attended schools in England	Maryland	near Abingdon, Md.	1740	1799
Robert Treat Paine	45	Lawyer	Harvard	Massachusetts	Boston, Mass.	1731	1814
John Penn	c. 36	Lawyer	Self-educated	North Carolina	Caroline Co., Va.	c. 1740	1788
George Read	42	Lawyer	Preparatory studies	Delaware	near Northeast, Cecil Co., Md.	1733	1798
Caesar Rodney	48	Landowner	Private tutors	Delaware	near Dover, Del.	1728	1784
George Ross	46	Lawyer	Preparatory studies	Pennsylvania	New Castle, Del.	1730	1779
Benjamin Rush	30	Physician	College of New Jersey;[2] medical education, Univ. of Edinburgh	Pennsylvania	Byberry, Pa.	1745	1813
Edward Rutledge	26	Lawyer	Studied law in England	South Carolina	Charleston, S.C.	1749	1800
Roger Sherman	55	Merchant	Self-educated	Connecticut	Newton, Mass.	1721	1793
James Smith	c. 57	Lawyer-Iron master	Preparatory studies	Pennsylvania	Ireland	c. 1719	1806
Richard Stockton	46	Lawyer	College of New Jersey[2]	New Jersey	Princeton, N.J.	1730	1781
Thomas Stone	c. 33	Lawyer-Planter	Private tutors	Maryland	Charles Co., Md.	1743	1787
George Taylor	c. 60	Iron master	Preparatory studies	Pennsylvania	Ireland	1716	1781
Matthew Thornton	c. 62	Physician	Preparatory studies	New Hampshire	Ireland	c. 1714	1803
George Walton	c. 35	Lawyer	Self-educated	Georgia	Prince Edward Co., Va.	c. 1741	1804
William Whipple	46	Merchant	Grammar school	New Hampshire	Kittery, Me.	1730	1785
William Williams	45	Public servant-Merchant	Harvard	Connecticut	Lebanon, Conn.	1731	1811
James Wilson	33	Lawyer	Educated in Scotland	Pennsylvania	near St. Andrews, Scotland	1742	1798
John Witherspoon	53	College president-Clergyman	Univ. of Edinburgh	New Jersey	Gifford, Haddingtonshire, Scotland	1723	1794
Oliver Wolcott	49	Lawyer	Yale	Connecticut	Windsor, Conn.	1726	1797
George Wythe	c. 50	Lawyer	Attended William & Mary	Virginia	Elizabeth City Co., Va.	1726	1806

[1] now University of Pennsylvania. [2] now Princeton University.

THE CONSTITUTION

WE, the People of the United States, in order to form a more perfect union, establish justice, insure domestic tranquility, provide for the common defence, promote the general welfare, and secure the blessings of liberty to ourselves and our posterity, do ordain and establish this Constitution for the United States of America.

ARTICLE I.

Sect. 1. ALL legislative powers herein granted shall be vested in a Congress of the United States, which shall consist of a Senate and House of Representatives.

Sect. 2. The House of Representatives shall be composed of members chosen every second year by the people of the several states, and the electors in each state shall have the qualifications requisite for electors of the most numerous branch of the state legislature.

No person shall be a representative who shall not have attained to the age of twenty-five years, and been seven years a citizen of the United States, and who shall not, when elected, be an inhabitant of that state in which he shall be chosen.

[1][Representatives and direct taxes shall be apportioned among the several states which may be included within this Union, according to their respective numbers, which shall be determined by adding to the whole number of free persons, including those bound to service for a term of years, and excluding Indians not taxed, three-fifths of all other persons.] The actual enumeration shall be made within three years after the first meeting of the Congress of the United States, and within every subsequent term of ten years, in such manner as they shall by law direct. The number of representatives shall not exceed one for every thirty thousand, but each state shall have at least one representative; and until such enumeration shall be made, the state of New-Hampshire shall be entitled to chuse three, Massachusetts eight, Rhode-Island and Providence Plantations one, Connecticut five, New-York six, New-Jersey four, Pennsylvania eight, Delaware one, Maryland six, Virginia ten, North-Carolina five, South-Carolina five, and Georgia three.

When vacancies happen in the representation from any state, the Executive authority thereof shall issue writs of election to fill such vacancies.

The House of Representatives shall chuse their Speaker and other officers; and shall have the sole power of impeachment.

Sect. 3. The Senate of the United States shall be composed of two senators from each state, [2][chosen by the legislature thereof,] for six years; and each senator shall have one vote.

Immediately after they shall be assembled in consequence of the first election, they shall be divided as equally as may be into three classes. The seats of the senators of the first class shall be vacated at the expiration of the second year, of the second class at the expiration of the fourth year, and of the third class at the expiration of the sixth year, so that one-third may be chosen every second year; [3][and if vacancies happen by resignation, or otherwise, during the recess of the

[1] The part enclosed by brackets was changed by section 2 of Amendment XIV. [2] The clause enclosed by brackets was changed by clause 1 of Amendment XVII. [3] The part enclosed by brackets was changed by clause 2 of Amendment XVII.

Legislature of any state, the Executive thereof may make temporary appointments until the next meeting of the Legislature, which shall then fill such vacancies.]

No person shall be a senator who shall not have attained to the age of thirty years, and been nine years a citizen of the United States, and who shall not, when elected, be an inhabitant of that state for which he shall be chosen.

The Vice-President of the United States shall be President of the Senate, but shall have no vote, unless they be equally divided.

The Senate shall chuse their other officers, and also a President pro tempore, in the absence of the Vice-President, or when he shall exercise the office of President of the United States.

The Senate shall have the sole power to try all impeachments. When sitting for that purpose, they shall be on oath or affirmation. When the President of the United States is tried, the Chief Justice shall preside: And no person shall be convicted without the concurrence of two-thirds of the members present.

Judgment in cases of impeachment shall not extend further than to removal from office and disqualification to hold and enjoy any office of honor, trust or profit under the United States; but the party convicted shall nevertheless be liable and subject to indictment, trial, judgment and punishment, according to law.

Sect. 4. The times, places and manner of holding elections for senators and representatives, shall be prescribed in each state by the legislature thereof; but the Congress may at any time by law make or alter such regulations, except as to the places of chusing Senators.

The Congress shall assemble at least once in every year, and such meeting shall ⁴[be on the first Monday in December,] unless they shall by law appoint a different day.

Sect. 5. Each house shall be the judge of the elections, returns and qualifications of its own members, and a majority of each shall constitute a quorum to do business; but a smaller number may adjourn from day to day, and may be authorized to compel the attendance of absent members, in such manner, and under such penalties as each house may provide.

Each house may determine the rules of its proceedings, punish its members for disorderly behaviour, and, with the concurrence of two-thirds, expel a member.

Each house shall keep a journal of its proceedings, and from time to time publish the same, excepting such parts as may in their judgment require secrecy; and the yeas and nays of the members of either house on any question shall, at the desire of one-fifth of those present, be entered on the journal.

Neither house, during the session of Congress shall, without the consent of the other, adjourn for more than three days, nor to any other place than that in which the two houses shall be sitting.

Sect. 6. The senators and representatives shall receive a compensation for their services, to be ascertained by law, and paid out of the treasury of the United States. They shall in all cases, except treason, felony and breach of the peace, be privileged from arrest during their attendance at the session of their respective houses, and in going to and returning from the same; and for any speech or debate in either house, they shall not be questioned in any other place.

No senator or representative shall, during the time for which he was elected, be appointed to any civil office under the authority of the United States, which shall have been created, or the emoluments whereof shall have been encreased during such time; and no person holding any office under the United States, shall be a member of either house during his continuance in office.

Sect. 7. All bills for raising revenue shall originate in the house of representatives; but the senate may propose or concur with amendments as on other bills.

Every bill which shall have passed the house of representatives and the senate, shall, before it become a law, be presented to the president of the United States; if he approve he shall sign it, but if not he shall return it, with his objections to that house in which it shall have originated, who shall enter the objections at large on their journal, and proceed to reconsider it. If after such reconsideration two-thirds of that house shall agree to pass the bill, it shall be sent, together with the objections, to the other house, by which it shall likewise be reconsidered, and if approved by two-thirds of that house, it shall become a law. But in all such cases the votes of both houses shall be determined by yeas and nays, and the names of the persons voting for and against the bill shall be entered on the journal of each house respectively. If any bill shall not be returned by the President within ten days (Sundays excepted) after it shall have been presented to him, the same shall be a law, in like manner as if he had signed it, unless the Congress by their adjournment prevent its return, in which case it shall not be a law.

Every order, resolution, or vote to which the concurrence of the Senate and House of Representatives may be necessary (except on a question of adjournment) shall be presented to the President of the United States; and before the same shall take effect, shall be approved by him, or, being disapproved by him, shall be repassed by two-thirds of the Senate and House of Representatives, according to the rules and limitations prescribed in the case of a bill.

Sect. 8. The Congress shall have power

To lay and collect taxes, duties, imposts and excises, to pay the debts and provide for the common defence and general welfare of the United States; but all duties, imposts and excises shall be uniform throughout the United States;

To borrow money on the credit of the United States;

To regulate commerce with foreign nations, and among the several states, and with the Indian tribes;

To establish an uniform rule of naturalization, and uniform laws on the subject of bankruptcies throughout the United States;

To coin money, regulate the value thereof, and of foreign coin, and fix the standard of weights and measures;

To provide for the punishment of counterfeiting the securities and current coin of the United States;

To establish post offices and post roads;

To promote the progress of science and useful arts, by securing for limited times to authors and inventors the exclusive right to their respective writings and discoveries;

---

⁴ The clause enclosed by brackets was changed by section 2 of Amendment XX.

To constitute tribunals inferior to the supreme court;

To define and punish piracies and felonies committed on the high seas, and offences against the law of nations;

To declare war, grant letters of marque and reprisal, and make rules concerning captures on land and water;

To raise and support armies, but no appropriation of money to that use shall be for a longer term than two years;

To provide and maintain a navy;

To make rules for the government and regulation of the land and naval forces;

To provide for calling forth the militia to execute the laws of the union, suppress insurrections and repel invasions;

To provide for organizing, arming, and disciplining, the militia, and for governing such part of them as may be employed in the service of the United States, reserving to the States respectively, the appointment of the officers, and the authority of training the militia according to the discipline prescribed by Congress;

To exercise exclusive legislation in all cases whatsoever, over such district (not exceeding ten miles square) as may, by cession of particular States, and the acceptance of Congress, become the seat of the government of the United States, and to exercise like authority over all places purchased by the consent of the legislature of the states in which the same shall be, for the erection of forts, magazines, arsenals, dock-yards, and other needful buildings;—And

To make all laws which shall be necessary and proper for carrying into execution the foregoing powers, and all other powers vested by this constitution in the government of the United States, or in any department or officer thereof.

Sect. 9. The migration or importation of such persons as any of the states now existing shall think proper to admit, shall not be prohibited by the Congress prior to the year one thousand eight hundred and eight, but a tax or duty may be imposed on such importation, not exceeding ten dollars for each person.

The privilege of the writ of habeas corpus shall not be suspended, unless when in cases of rebellion or invasion the public safety may require it.

No bill of attainder or ex post facto law shall be passed.

No capitation, or other direct, tax shall be laid, unless in proportion to the census or enumeration herein before directed to be taken.[5]

No tax or duty shall be laid on articles exported from any state. No preference shall be given by any regulation of commerce or revenue to the ports of one state over those of another: nor shall vessels bound to, or from, one state, be obliged to enter, clear, or pay duties in another.

No money shall be drawn from the treasury, but in consequence of appropriations made by law; and a regular statement and account of the receipts and expenditures of all public money shall be published from time to time.

No title of nobility shall be granted by the United States:—And no person holding any office of profit or trust under them, shall, without the consent of the Congress, accept of any present, emolument, office, or title, of any kind whatever, from any king, prince, or foreign state.

Sect. 10. No state shall enter into any treaty, alliance, or confederation; grant letters of marque and reprisal; coin money; emit bills of credit; make any thing but gold and silver coin a tender in payment of debts; pass any bill of attainder, ex post facto law, or law impairing the obligation of contracts, or grant any title of nobility.

No state shall, without the consent of the Congress, lay any imposts or duties on imports or exports, except what may be absolutely necessary for executing its inspection laws; and the net produce of all duties and imposts, laid by any state on imports or exports, shall be for the use of the Treasury of the United States; and all such laws shall be subject to the revision and controul of the Congress. No state shall, without the consent of Congress, lay any duty of tonnage, keep troops, or ships of war in time of peace, enter into any agreement or compact with another state, or with a foreign power, or engage in war, unless actually invaded, or in such imminent danger as will not admit of delay.

I I .

Sect. 1. The executive power shall be vested in a president of the United States of America. He shall hold his office during the term of four years, and, together with the vice-president, chosen for the same term, be elected as follows.

Each state shall appoint, in such manner as the legislature thereof may direct, a number of electors, equal to the whole number of senators and representatives to which the state may be entitled in the Congress: but no senator or representative, or person holding an office of trust or profit under the United States, shall be appointed an elector.

[6][The electors shall meet in their respective states, and vote by ballot for two persons, of whom one at least shall not be an inhabitant of the same state with themselves. And they shall make a list of all the persons voted for, and of the number of votes for each; which list they shall sign and certify, and transmit sealed to the seat of the government of the United States, directed to the president of the senate. The president of the senate shall, in the presence of the senate and house of representatives, open all the certificates, and the votes shall then be counted. The person having the greatest number of votes shall be the president, if such number be a majority of the whole number of electors appointed; and if there be more than one who have such majority, and have an equal number of votes, then the house of representatives shall immediately chuse by ballot one of them for president; and if no person have a majority, then from the five highest on the list the said house shall in like manner chuse the president. But in chusing the president, the votes shall be taken by states, the representation from each state having one vote; a quorum for this purpose shall consist of a member or members from two-thirds of the states, and a majority of all the states shall be necessary to a choice. In every case, after the choice of the president, the person having the greatest number of votes of the electors shall be the vice-president. But if there should remain two or more who have equal votes, the senate shall chuse from them by ballot the vice-president.]

The Congress may determine the time of chusing the electors, and the day on which they shall give their votes; which day shall be the same throughout the United States.

---

[5] See also Amendment XVI. [6] This paragraph has been superseded by Amendment XII.

No person except a natural born citizen, or a citizen of the United States, at the time of the adoption of this constitution, shall be eligible to the office of president; neither shall any person be eligible to that office who shall not have attained to the age of thirty-five years, and been fourteen years a resident within the United States.

[7]In case of the removal of the president from office, or of his death, resignation, or inability to discharge the powers and duties of the said office, the same shall devolve on the vice-president, and the Congress may by law provide for the case of removal, death, resignation or inability, both of the president and vice-president, declaring what officer shall then act as president, and such officer shall act accordingly, until the disability be removed, or a president be elected.

The president shall, at stated times, receive for his services, a compensation, which shall neither be encreased nor diminished during the period for which he shall have been elected, and he shall not receive within that period any other emolument from the United States, or any of them.

Before he enter on the execution of his office, he shall take the following oath or affirmation:

"I do solemnly swear (or affirm) that I will faithfully execute the office of president of the United States, and will to the best of my ability, preserve, protect and defend the constitution of the United States."

Sect. 2. The president shall be commander in chief of the army and navy of the United States, and of the militia of the several States, when called into the actual service of the United States; he may require the opinion, in writing, of the principal officer in each of the executive departments, upon any subject relating to the duties of their respective offices, and he shall have power to grant reprieves and pardons for offences against the United States, except in cases of impeachment.

He shall have power, by and with the advice and consent of the senate, to make treaties, provided two-thirds of the senators present concur; and he shall nominate, and by and with the advice and consent of the senate, shall appoint ambassadors, other public ministers and consuls, judges of the supreme court, and all other officers of the United States, whose appointments are not herein otherwise provided for, and which shall be established by law. But the Congress may by law vest the appointment of such inferior officers, as they think proper, in the president alone, in the courts of law, or in the heads of departments.

The president shall have power to fill up all vacancies that may happen during the recess of the senate, by granting commissions which shall expire at the end of their session.

Sect. 3. He shall from time to time give to the Congress information of the state of the union, and recommend to their consideration such measures as he shall judge necessary and expedient; he may, on extraordinary occasions, convene both houses, or either of them, and in case of disagreement between them, with respect to the time of adjournment, he may adjourn them to such time as he shall think proper; he shall receive ambassadors and other public ministers; he shall take care that the laws be faithfully executed, and shall commission all the officers of the United States.

Sect. 4. The president, vice-president and all civil officers of the United States, shall be removed from office on impeachment for, and conviction of, treason, bribery, or other high crimes and misdemeanors.

III.

Sect. 1. The judicial power of the United States, shall be vested in one supreme court, and in such inferior courts as the Congress may from time to time ordain and establish. The judges, both of the supreme and inferior courts, shall hold their offices during good behaviour, and shall, at stated times, receive for their services, a compensation, which shall not be diminished during their continuance in office.

Sect. 2. The judicial power shall extend to all cases, in law and equity, arising under this constitution, the laws of the United States, and treaties made, or which shall be made, under their authority; to all cases of admiralty and maritime jurisdiction; to controversies to which the United States shall be a party; to controversies between two or more States, between a state and citizens of another state,[8] between citizens of different States, between citizens of the same state claiming lands under grants of different States, and between a state, or the citizens thereof, and foreign States, citizens or subjects.

In all cases affecting ambassadors, other public ministers and consuls, and those in which a state shall be party, the supreme court shall have original jurisdiction. In all the other cases before mentioned, the supreme court shall have appellate jurisdiction, both as to law and fact, with such exceptions, and under such regulations as the Congress shall make.

The trial of all crimes, except in cases of impeachment, shall be by jury; and such trial shall be held in the state where the said crimes shall have been committed; but when not committed within any state, the trial shall be at such place or places as the Congress may by law have directed.

Sect. 3. Treason against the United States, shall consist only in levying war against them, or in adhering to their enemies, giving them aid and comfort. No person shall be convicted of treason unless on the testimony of two witnesses to the same overt act, or on confession in open court.

The Congress shall have power to declare the punishment of treason, but no attainder of treason shall work corruption of blood, or forfeiture except during the life of the person attainted.

IV.

Sect. 1. Full faith and credit shall be given in each state to the public acts, records, and judicial proceedings of every other state. And the Congress may by general laws prescribe the manner in which such acts, records and proceedings shall be proved, and the effect thereof.

Sect. 2. The citizens of each state shall be entitled to all privileges and immunities of citizens in the several states.

A person charged in any state with treason, felony, or other crime, who shall flee from justice, and be found in another state, shall, on demand of the executive authority of the state from which he fled, be delivered up, to be removed to the state having jurisdiction of the crime.

[9][No person held to service or labour in one state, under the laws thereof, escaping into another, shall, in consequence of any law or regulation therein, be discharged from such service or labour, but shall be delivered up on claim of

<hr>

[7] Affected by Amendment XXV. [8] Affected by Amendment XI. [9] Superseded by Amendment XIII.

the party to whom such service or labour may be due.]

Sect. 3. New states may be admitted by the Congress into this union; but no new state shall be formed or erected within the jurisdiction of any other state; nor any state be formed by the junction of two or more states, or parts of states, without the consent of the legislatures of the states concerned as well as of the Congress.

The Congress shall have power to dispose of and make all needful rules and regulations respecting the territory or other property belonging to the United States; and nothing in this Constitution shall be so construed as to prejudice any claims of the United States, or of any particular state.

Sect. 4. The United States shall guarantee to every state in this union a Republican form of government, and shall protect each of them against invasion; and on application of the legislature, or of the executive (when the legislature cannot be convened) against domestic violence.

V.

The Congress, whenever two-thirds of both houses shall deem it necessary, shall propose amendments to this constitution, or, on the application of the legislatures of two-thirds of the several states, shall call a convention for proposing amendments, which, in either case, shall be valid to all intents and purposes, as part of this constitution, when ratified by the legislatures of three-fourths of the several states, or by conventions in three-fourths thereof, as the one or the other mode of ratification may be proposed by Congress; Provided, that no amendment which may be made prior to the year one thousand eight hundred and eight shall in any manner affect the first and fourth clauses in the ninth section of the first article; and that no state, without its consent, shall be deprived of its equal suffrage in the senate.

VI.

All debts contracted and engagements entered into, before the adoption of this Constitution, shall be as valid against the United States under this Constitution, as under the confederation.

This constitution, and the laws of the United States which shall be made in pursuance thereof; and all treaties made, or which shall be made, under the authority of the United States, shall be the supreme law of the land; and the judges in every state shall be bound thereby, any thing in the constitution or laws of any state to the contrary notwithstanding.

The senators and representatives beforementioned, and the members of the several state legislatures, and all executive and judicial officers, both of the United States and of the several States, shall be bound by oath or affirmation, to support this constitution; but no religious test shall ever be required as a qualification to any office or public trust under the United States.

VII.

The ratification of the conventions of nine States, shall be sufficient for the establishment of this constitution between the States so ratifying the same.

[Done in Convention, by the unanimous consent of the States present, the seventeenth day of September, in the year of our Lord one thousand seven hundred and eighty-seven, and of the Independence of the United States of America the twelfth. In witness whereof we have hereunto subscribed our Names.]

SIGNERS OF THE CONSTITUTION: 1787

Name	Age	Occupation	Education	Representing	Birthplace	Born	Died
Abraham Baldwin	32	Lawyer	Yale	Georgia	Guilford, Conn.	1754	1807
Richard Bassett	42	Lawyer	Private tutors	Delaware	Cecil Co., Md.	1745	1815
Gunning Bedford	c. 40	Lawyer	College of New Jersey[1]	Delaware	Philadelphia, Pa.	1747	1812
John Blair	c. 55	Jurist	Studied law in England	Virginia	Williamsburg, Va.	1732	1800
William Blount	38	Public servant	Private tutors	North Carolina	Bertie Co., N.C.	1749	1800
David Brearley	42	Jurist	Private tutors	New Jersey	Spring Grove, N.J.	1745	1790
Jacob Broom	35	Businessman	Preparatory studies	Delaware	Wilmington, Del.	1752	1810
Pierce Butler	43	Planter	Private tutors	South Carolina	Co. Carlow, Ireland	1744	1822
Daniel Carroll	57	Planter-Businessman	Educated at Jesuit schools in Maryland and France	Maryland	Upper Marlboro, Md.	1730	1796
George Clymer	48	Merchant	Self-educated	Pennsylvania	Philadelphia, Pa.	1739	1813
Jonathan Dayton	26	Lawyer	College of New Jersey[1]	New Jersey	Elizabeth-Town, N.J.	1760	1824
John Dickinson	55	Public servant	Studied law in England	Delaware	Talbot Co., Md.	1732	1808
William Few	39	Lawyer	Self-educated	Georgia	near Baltimore, Md.	1748	1828
Thomas Fitzsimons	c. 46	Businessman	Self-educated	Pennsylvania	Ireland	1741	1811
Benjamin Franklin	81	Public servant	Grammar school	Pennsylvania	Boston, Mass.	1706	1790
Nicholas Gilman	32	Public servant	Grammar school	New Hampshire	Exeter, N.H.	1755	1814
Nathaniel Gorham	49	Businessman	Private tutors	Massachusetts	Charlestown, Mass.	1738	1796
Alexander Hamilton	32	Lawyer	King's College[2]	New York	West Indies	1755	1804
Jared Ingersoll	37	Lawyer	Yale; studied law in England	Pennsylvania	New Haven, Conn.	1749	1822
Daniel of St. Thomas Jenifer	c. 64	Planter-Public servant	Preparatory studies	Maryland	Charles Co., Md.	1723	1790
William Samuel Johnson	59	Lawyer-College president	Yale; A.M., Harvard	Connecticut	Stratford, Conn.	1727	1819
Rufus King	32	Lawyer	Harvard	Massachusetts	Scarboro, Mass.	1755	1827
John Langdon	46	Businessman	Grammar School	New Hampshire	Portsmouth, N.H.	1741	1819
William Livingston	53	Public servant	Yale	New Jersey	Albany, N.Y.	1723	1790
James Madison	36	Lawyer	College of New Jersey[1]	Virginia	Port Conway, Va.	1751	1836
James McHenry	c. 34	Businessman	Educated in Ireland and Delaware; studied medicine under Benjamin Rush	Maryland	Ireland	c. 1753	1816
Thomas Mifflin	33	Merchant	College of Philadelphia[3]	Pennsylvania	Philadelphia, Pa.	1744	1800
Gouverneur Morris	35	Lawyer	King's College[2]	Pennsylvania	Morrisania, N.Y.	1752	1816
Robert Morris	53	Merchant	Self-educated	Pennsylvania	Liverpool, England	1734	1806
William Paterson	31	Lawyer	College of New Jersey[1]	Maryland	Co. Antrim, Ireland	1745	1806

Name	Age	Occupation	Education	Representing	Birthplace	Born	Died
Charles Pinckney	29	Lawyer	Preparatory studies	South Carolina	Charleston, S.C.	1757	1824
Charles Cotesworth Pinckney	41	Lawyer	Oxford	South Carolina	Charleston, S.C.	1746	1825
George Read	53	Lawyer	Preparatory studies	Delaware	near Northeast, Cecil Co., Md.	1733	1798
John Rutledge	c. 58	Public servant	Studied law in England	South Carolina	Charleston, S.C.	1739	1800
Roger Sherman	66	Businessman	Self-educated	Connecticut	Newton, Mass.	1721	1793
Richard Dobbs Spaight	29	Planter	Educated in Ireland and Scotland	North Carolina	New Bern, N.C.	1758	1802
George Washington ...	55	Planter	Private tutors	Virginia	Westmoreland Co., Va.	1732	1799
Hugh Williamson	41	Businessman-Physician	College of Philadelphia;[3] M.D., Univ. of Utrecht	North Carolina	West Nottingham, Pa.	1735	1819
James Wilson	44	Lawyer	Educated in Scotland	Pennsylvania	Scotland	1742	1798

[1] now Princeton University. [2] now Columbia University. [3] now University of Pennsylvania.

THE CONSTITUTIONAL AMENDMENTS

The first ten amendments* to the original Constitution are known as the Bill of Rights.

AMENDMENT [I]

Congress shall make no law respecting an establishment of religion, or prohibiting the free exercise thereof; or abridging the freedom of speech, or of the press; or the right of the people peaceably to assemble, and to petition the Government for a redress of grievances.

AMENDMENT [II]

A well regulated Militia, being necessary to the security of a free State, the right of the people to keep and bear Arms, shall not be infringed.

AMENDMENT [III]

No Soldier shall, in time of peace be quartered in any house, without the consent of the Owner, nor in time of war, but in a manner to be prescribed by law.

AMENDMENT [IV]

The right of the people to be secure in their persons, houses, papers, and effects, against unreasonable searches and seizures, shall not be violated, and no Warrants shall issue, but upon probable cause, supported by Oath or affirmation, and particularly describing the place to be searched, and the persons or things to be seized.

AMENDMENT [V]

No person shall be held to answer for a capital, or otherwise infamous crime, unless on a presentment or indictment of a Grand Jury, except in cases arising in the land or naval forces, or in the Militia, when in actual service in time of War or public danger; nor shall any person be subject for the same offence to be twice put in jeopardy of life or limb; nor shall be compelled in any criminal case to be a witness against himself, nor be deprived of life, liberty, or property, without due process of law; nor shall private property be taken for public use, without just compensation.

AMENDMENT [VI]

In all criminal prosecutions, the accused shall enjoy the right to a speedy and public trial, by an impartial jury of the State and district wherein the crime shall have been committed, which district shall have been previously ascertained by law, and to be informed of the nature and cause of the accusation; to be confronted with the witnesses against him; to have compulsory process for obtaining witnesses in his favor, and to have the Assistance of Counsel for his defence.

AMENDMENT [VII]

In Suits at common law, where the value in controversy shall exceed twenty dollars, the right of trial by jury shall be preserved, and no fact tried by a jury, shall be otherwise re-examined in any Court of the United States, than according to the rules of the common law.

AMENDMENT [VIII]

Excessive bail shall not be required, nor excessive fines imposed, nor cruel and unusual punishments inflicted.

AMENDMENT [IX]

The enumeration in the Constitution, of certain rights, shall not be construed to deny or disparage others retained by the people.

AMENDMENT [X]

The powers not delegated to the United States by the Constitution, nor prohibited by it to the States, are reserved to the States respectively, or to the people.

AMENDMENT [XI][1]

The Judicial power of the United States shall not be construed to extend to any suit in law or equity, commenced or prosecuted against one of the United States by Citizens of another State, or by Citizens or Subjects of any Foreign State.

AMENDMENT [XII][2]

The Electors shall meet in their respective states, and vote by ballot for President and Vice-President, one of whom, at least, shall not be an inhabitant of the same state with themselves; they shall name in their ballots the person voted for as President, and in distinct ballots the person voted for as Vice-President, and they shall make distinct lists of all persons voted for as President, and

* The first 10 amendments, together with 2 others that failed of ratification, were proposed to the several States by resolution of Congress on September 25, 1789. The ratifications were transmitted by the Governors to the President and by him communicated to Congress from time to time. The first 10 amendments were ratified by 11 of the 14 States. Virginia completed the required three fourths by ratification on December 15, 1791, and its action was communicated to Congress by the President on December 30, 1791. The legislatures of Massachusetts, Georgia, and Connecticut ratified them on March 2, 1939, March 18, 1939, and April 19, 1939, respectively.

[1] The Eleventh Amendment was proposed by resolution of Congress on March 4, 1794. It was declared by the President, in a message to Congress dated January 8, 1798, to have been ratified by three fourths of the several States. Records of the National Archives show that the 11th Amendment was ratified by 13 of the 16 States. It was not ratified by New Jersey or Pennsylvania.

[2] The Twelfth Amendment was proposed in lieu of the original third paragraph of section 1 of article II, by resolution of Congress on December 9, 1803. It was declared in a proclamation of the Secretary of State, dated September 25, 1804, to have been ratified by three fourths of the States. Records of the National Archives show that it was ratified by 14 States and rejected by Connecticut and Delaware.

of all persons voted for as Vice-President, and of the number of votes for each, which lists they shall sign and certify, and transmit sealed to the seat of the government of the United States, directed to the President of the Senate;—The President of the Senate shall, in the presence of the Senate and House of Representatives, open all the certificates and the votes shall then be counted;—The person having the greatest number of votes for President, shall be the President, if such number be a majority of the whole number of Electors appointed; and if no person have such majority, then from the persons having the highest numbers not exceeding three on the list of those voted for as President, the House of Representatives shall choose immediately, by ballot, the President. But in choosing the President, the votes shall be taken by states, the representation from each state having one vote; a quorum for this purpose shall consist of a member or members from two-thirds of the states, and a majority of all the states shall be necessary to a choice. **³[And if the House of Representatives shall not choose a President whenever the right of choice shall devolve upon them, before the fourth day of March next following, then the Vice-President shall act as President, as in the case of the death or other constitutional disability of the President.]**—The person having the greatest number of votes as Vice-President, shall be the Vice-President, if such number be a majority of the whole number of Electors appointed, and if no person have a majority, then from the two highest numbers on the list, the Senate shall choose the Vice-President; a quorum for the purpose shall consist of two-thirds of the whole number of Senators, and a majority of the whole number shall be necessary to a choice. But no person constitutionally ineligible to the office of President shall be eligible to that of Vice-President of the United States.

AMENDMENT [XIII]⁴

Section 1. Neither slavery nor involuntary servitude, except as a punishment for crime whereof the party shall have been duly convicted, shall exist within the United States, or any place subject to their jurisdiction.

Section 2. Congress shall have power to enforce this article by appropriate legislation.

AMENDMENT [XIV]⁵

Section 1. All persons born or naturalized in the United States, and subject to the jurisdiction thereof, are citizens of the United States and of the State wherein they reside. No State shall make or enforce any law which shall abridge the privileges or immunities of citizens of the United States; nor shall any State deprive any person of life, liberty, or property, without due process of law; nor deny to any person within its jurisdiction the equal protection of the laws.

Section 2. Representatives shall be apportioned among the several States according to their respective numbers, counting the whole number of persons in each State, excluding Indians not taxed. But when the right to vote at any election for the choice of electors for President and Vice President of the United States, Representatives in Congree, the Executive and Judicial officers of a State, or the members of the Legislature thereof, is denied to any of the male inhabitants of such State, being twenty-one years of age, and citizens of the United States, or in any way abridged, except for participation in rebellion, or other crime, the basis of representation therein shall be reduced in the proportion which the number of such male citizens shall bear to the whole number of male citizens twenty-one years of age in such State.

Section 3. No person shall be a Senator or Representative in Congress, or elector of President and Vice President, or hold any office, civil or military, under the United States, or under any State, who, having previously taken an oath, as a member of Congress, or as an officer of the United States, or as a member of any State legislature, or as an executive or judicial officer of any State, to support the Constitution of the United States, shall have engaged in insurrection or rebellion against the same, or given aid or comfort to the enemies thereof. But Congress may by a vote of two-thirds of each House, remove such disability.

Section 4. The validity of the public debt of the United States, authorized by law, including debts incurred for payment of pensions and bounties for services in suppressing insurrection or rebellion, shall not be questioned. But neither the United States nor any State shall assume or pay any debt or obligation incurred in aid of insurrection or rebellion against the United States, or any claim for the loss or emancipation of any slave; but all such debts, obligations and claims shall be held illegal and void.

Section 5. The Congress shall have power to enforce, by appropriate legislation, the provisions of this article.

AMENDMENT [XV]⁶

Section 1. The right of citizens of the United States to vote shall not be denied or abridged by the United States or by any State on account of race, color, or previous condition of servitude.

Section 2. The Congress shall have power to enforce this article by appropriate legislation.

AMENDMENT [XVI]⁷

The Congress shall have power to lay and collect taxes on incomes, from whatever source de-

---

³ The part enclosed by brackets has been superseded by section 3 of Amendment XX.

⁴ The Thirteenth Amendment was proposed by resolution of Congress on January 31, 1865. It was declared in a proclamation of the Secretary of State, dated December 18, 1865, to have been ratified by 27 States. Subsequent records of the National Archives show that the 13th Amendment was ratified by 7 additional States. It was rejected by Kentucky and Mississippi.

⁵ The Fourteenth Amendment was proposed by resolution of Congress on June 13, 1866. By a concurrent resolution of Congress adopted July 21, 1868, it was declared to have been ratified by "three fourths and more of the several States of the Union," and the Secretary of State was required duly to promulgate the amendment as a part of the Constitution. He accordingly issued a proclamation, dated July 28, 1868, declaring the amendment to have been ratified by 30 States, "being more than three fourths." Records of the National Archives show that the 14th Amendment was subsequently ratified by 8 additional States. It was rejected by Kentucky.

⁶ The Fifteenth Amendment was proposed by resolution of Congress on February 26, 1869. It was declared in a proclamation of the Secretary of State, dated March 30, 1870, to have been ratified by 29 States, which "constitute three fourths." Records of the National Archives show that the 15th Amendment was subsequently ratified by 6 more of the States. It was rejected by Kentucky, Maryland, and Tennessee.

⁷ The Sixteenth Amendment was proposed by resolution of Congress on July 12, 1909. It was declared in a proclamation of the Secretary of State, dated February 25, 1913, to have been ratified by 38 States, which "constitute three fourths." Subsequent records of the National Archives show that the 16th Amendment was ratified by 4 additional States. It was rejected by Connecticut, Florida, Rhode Island, and Utah.

rived, without apportionment among the several States, and without regard to any census or enumeration.

AMENDMENT [XVII][8]

The Senate of the United States shall be composed of two Senators from each State, elected by the people thereof, for six years; and each Senator shall have one vote. The electors in each State shall have the qualifications requisite for electors of the most numerous branch of the State legislatures.

When vacancies happen in the representation of any State in the Senate, the executive authority of such State shall issue writs of election to fill such vacancies: *Provided,* That the legislature of any State may empower the executive thereof to make temporary appointments until the people fill the vacancies by election as the legislature may direct.

This amendment shall not be so construed as to affect the election or term of any Senator chosen before it becomes valid as part of the Constitution.

AMENDMENT [XVIII][9]

[Section 1. After one year from the ratification of this article the manufacture, sale, or transportation of intoxicating liquors within, the importation thereof into, or the exportation thereof from the United States and all territory subject to the jurisdiction thereof for beverage purposes is hereby prohibited.

[Sec. 2. The Congress and the several States shall have concurrent power to enforce this article by appropriate legislation.

[Sec. 3. This article shall be inoperative unless it shall have been ratified as an amendment to the Constitution by the legislatures of the several States, as provided in the Constitution, within seven years from the date of the submission hereof to the States by the Congress.]

AMENDMENT [XIX][10]

The right of citizens of the United States to vote shall not be denied or abridged by the United States or by any State on account of sex.

Congress shall have power to enforce this article by appropriate legislation.

AMENDMENT [XX][11]

Section 1. The terms of the President and Vice President shall end at noon on the 20th day of January, and the terms of Senators and Representatives at noon on the 3d day of January, of the years in which such terms would have ended if this article had not been ratified; and the terms of their successors shall then begin.

Sec. 2. The Congress shall assemble at least once in every year, and such meeting shall begin at noon on the 3d day of January, unless they shall by law appoint a different day.

Sec. 3. If, at the time fixed for the beginning of the term of the President, the President elect shall have died, the Vice President elect shall become President. If a President shall not have been chosen before the time fixed for the beginning of his term, or if the President elect shall have failed to qualify, then the Vice President elect shall act as President until a President shall have qualified; and the Congress may by law provide for the case wherein neither a President elect nor a Vice President elect shall have qualified, declaring who shall then act as President, or the manner in which one who is to act shall be selected, and such person shall act accordingly until a President or Vice President shall have qualified.

Sec. 4. The Congress may by law provide for the case of the death of any of the persons from whom the House of Representatives may choose a President whenever the right of choice shall have devolved upon them, and for the case of the death of any of the persons from whom the Senate may choose a Vice President whenever the right of choice shall have devolved upon them.

Sec. 5. Sections 1 and 2 shall take effect on the 15th day of October following the ratification of this article.

Sec. 6. This article shall be inoperative unless it shall have been ratified as an amendment to the Constitution by the legislatures of three-fourths of the several States within seven years from the date of its submission.

AMENDMENT [XXI][12]

Section 1. The eighteenth article of amendment to the Constitution of the United States is hereby repealed.

Sec. 2. The transportation or importation into any State, Territory, or possession of the United States for delivery or use therein of intoxicating liquors, in violation of the laws thereof, is hereby prohibited.

Sec. 3. This article shall be inoperative unless it shall have been ratified as an amendment to the Constitution by conventions in the several States, as provided in the Constitution, within seven

---

[8] The Seventeenth Amendment was proposed by resolution of Congress on May 13, 1912. It was declared in a proclamation of the Secretary of State, dated May 31, 1913, to have been ratified by 36 States, which "constitute three fourths." Records of the National Archives show that the 17th Amendment was subsequently ratified by 1 additional State. It was rejected by Utah and Delaware.

[9] The Eighteenth Amendment was proposed by resolution of Congress on December 18, 1917. It was declared in a proclamation of the Acting Secretary of State, dated January 29, 1919, to have been ratified by 36 States, which "constitute three fourths." Subsequent records of the National Archives show that the 18th Amendment was ratified by 10 additional States. It was rejected by Rhode Island. By its own terms the 18th Amendment became effective one year after its ratification, which was consummated on January 16, 1919, and therefore went into effect on January 16, 1920.

Repeal of the 18th Amendment on December 5, 1933, was proclaimed by the President in his proclamation of that date, when the ratification of the 21st Amendment was certified by the Acting Secretary of State.

[10] The Nineteenth Amendment was proposed by resolution of Congress on June 4, 1919. It was declared in a proclamation of the Secretary of State, dated August 26, 1920, to have been ratified by 36 States, which "constitute three fourths." Subsequent records of the National Archives show that the 19th Amendment was ratified by 5 additional States. It was rejected by Georgia, South Carolina, Mississippi, Delaware, and Louisiana.

[11] The Twentieth Amendment was proposed by resolution of Congress on March 2, 1932. It was declared in a proclamation of the Secretary of State, dated February 6, 1933, to have been ratified by 39 States, which "constitute more than the requisite three fourths." Subsequent records of the National Archives show that the 20th Amendment was ratified by all 48 States before sections 1 and 2 became effective on October 15, 1933. The other sections of the amendment became effective on January 23, 1933, when its ratification was consummated by three fourths of the States.

[12] The Twenty-first Amendment was proposed by resolution of Congress on February 20, 1933. It was certified in a proclamation of the Acting Secretary of State dated December 5, 1933, to have been ratified by conventions of 36 States, which "constitute the requisite three fourths of the whole number of States." Subsequent records of the National Archives show that the 21st Amendment was ratified by 2 additional States. It was rejected by the convention of South Carolina. North Carolina voted against holding a convention.

years from the date of the submission hereof to the States by the Congress.

AMENDMENT [XXII][13]

Section 1. No person shall be elected to the office of the President more than twice, and no person who has held the office of President, or acted as President, for more than two years of a term to which some other person was elected President shall be elected to the office of the President more than once. But this Article shall not apply to any person holding the office of President when this Article was proposed by the Congress, and shall not prevent any person who may be holding the office of President, or acting as President, during the term within which this Article becomes operative from holding the office of President or acting as President during the remainder of such term.

Sec. 2. This article shall be inoperative unless it shall have been ratified as an amendment to the Constitution by the legislatures of three-fourths of the several States within seven years from the date of its submission to the States by the Congress.

AMENDMENT [XXIII][14]

Section 1. The District constituting the seat of Government of the United States shall appoint in such manner as the Congress may direct:

A number of electors of President and Vice President equal to the whole number of Senators and Representatives in Congress to which the District would be entitled if it were a State, but in no event more than the least populous State; they shall be in addition to those appointed by the States, but they shall be considered, for the purposes of the election of President and Vice President, to be electors appointed by a State; and they shall meet in the District and perform such duties as provided by the twelfth article of amendment.

Section 2. The Congress shall have power to enforce this article by appropriate legislation.

AMENDMENT [XXIV][15]

Section 1. The right of citizens of the United States to vote in any primary or other election for President or Vice President, for electors for President or Vice President, or for Senator or Representative in Congress, shall not be denied or abridged by the United States or any State by reason of failure to pay any poll tax or other tax.

Section 2. The Congress shall have power to enforce this article by appropriate legislation.

AMENDMENT [XXV][16]

Section 1. In case of removal of the President from office or of his death or resignation, the Vice President shall become President.

Sec. 2. Whenever there is a vacancy in the office of the Vice President, the President shall nominate a Vice President who shall take office upon confirmation by a majority vote of both Houses of Congress.

Sec. 3. Whenever the President transmits to the President pro tempore of the Senate and the Speaker of the House of Representatives his written declaration that he is unable to discharge the powers and duties of his office, and until he transmits to them a written declaration to the contrary, such powers and duties shall be discharged by the Vice President as Acting President.

Sec. 4. Whenever the Vice President and a majority of either the principal officers of the executive departments or of such other body as Congress may by law provide, transmit to the President pro tempore of the Senate and the Speaker of the House of Representatives their written declaration that the President is unable to discharge the powers and duties of his office, the Vice President shall immediately assume the powers and duties of the office as Acting President.

Thereafter, when the President transmits to the President pro tempore of the Senate and the Speaker of the House of Representatives his written declaration that no inability exists, he shall resume the powers and duties of his office unless the Vice President and a majority of either the principal officers of the executive department or of such other body as Congress may by law provide, transmit within four days to the President pro tempore of the Senate and the Speaker of the House of Representatives their written declaration that the President is unable to discharge the powers and duties of his office. Thereupon Congress shall decide the issue, assembling within forty-eight hours for that purpose if not in session. If the Congress, within twenty-one days after receipt of the latter written declaration, or, if Congress is not in session, within twenty-one days after Congress is required to assemble, determines by two-thirds vote of both Houses that the President is unable to discharge the powers and duties of his office, the Vice President shall continue to discharge the same as Acting President; otherwise, the President shall resume the powers and duties of his office.

AMENDMENT [XXVI][17]

Section 1. The right of citizens of the United States, who are eighteen years of age or older, to vote shall not be denied or abridged by the United States or by any State on account of age.

Sec. 2. The Congress shall have power to enforce this article by appropriate legislation.

---

[13] The Twenty-second Amendment was proposed by resolution of Congress on March 24, 1947. Ratification was completed on February 27, 1951, when the thirty-sixth State (Minnesota) approved the amendment. On March 1, 1951, the Administrator of General Services certified that "the States whose Legislatures have so ratified the said proposed Amendment constitute the requisite three-fourths of the whole number of States in the United States." Records of the National Archives show that the 22d Amendment was subsequently ratified by 5 additional States.

[14] The Twenty-third Amendment was proposed by resolution of Congress on June 16, 1960. The Administrator of General Services certified the ratification and adoption of the amendment by three-fourths of the States on April 3, 1961. It was rejected by Arkansas.

[15] The Twenty-fourth Amendment was proposed by resolution of Congress on August 27, 1962. It was declared in a Proclamation of the Administrator of General Services dated February 4, 1964, to have been ratified by three-fourths of the States. It was rejected by the legislature of Mississippi on December 20, 1962.

[16] The Twenty-fifth Amendment to the Constitution was proposed by the Congress on July 6, 1965. It was declared in a certificate of the Administrator of General Services, dated February 23, 1967, to have been ratified by the legislatures of 39 of the 50 States. Ratification was completed on February 10, 1967.

[17] The Twenty-sixth Amendment was proposed by resolution of Congress on March 23, 1971. On July 5, 1971, the Administrator of General Services certified the ratification and adoption of the amendment by three fourths of the states.

ADMINISTRATIONS, CABINETS, AND CONGRESSES

SOURCE: *Biographical Directory of the American Congress and other sources*

A cabinet officer is not appointed for a fixed term and does not necessarily go out of office with the President who appointed him; while it is customary to tender his resignation at the time a change of administration takes place, he remains formally at the head of his department until a successor is appointed. Subordinates acting temporarily as heads of departments are not considered cabinet officers; in the earlier period of the nation's history, not all cabinet officers were heads of departments.

The dates immediately following the names of executive officers are those upon which commissions were issued, unless otherwise specifically noted. Where periods of time are indicated by dates as, for instance, March 4, 1793–March 3, 1797, both such dates are included as portions of the time period.

The National Security Act of 1947 (Pub. Law 253, 80th Cong., 1st sess.), approved July 26, 1947, created the office of Secretary of Defense and merged the War and Navy Departments into the National Military Establishment. The act was subsequently amended (Pub. Law 216, 81st Cong., 1st sess.): Section 201. (a) There is hereby established, as an executive department of the Government, the **Department of Defense.**

The Reorganization Plan Number 1 of 1953 (Pub. Law 13, 83d Cong., 1st sess.), approved April 1, 1953, abolished the Federal Security Agency and created the **Department of Health, Education, and Welfare,** which was renamed the **Department of Health and Human Services** in 1979.

The **Department of Housing and Urban Development** was established by the Department of Housing and Urban Development Act of September 9, 1965 (79 Stat. 667; 5 U.S.C. 642).

The **Department of Transportation** was established by the Department of Transportation Act of October 15, 1966 (80 Stat. 931; 49 U.S.C. 1681).

As of July 1, 1971, the Post Office Department became **The U.S. Postal Service,** a quasi-independent nonprofit corporation. The Postmaster General ceased to be a member of the cabinet.

The **Department of Energy** was established by Public Law 95-91, August 4, 1977.

The **Department of Education** was established by Public Law 96-88, October 17, 1979.

Congressional vacancies are not noted below.

First Administration of GEORGE WASHINGTON
APRIL 30, 1789, TO MARCH 3, 1793

PRESIDENT—George Washington, of Virginia (No party). VICE-PRESIDENT—John Adams, of Massachusetts. SECRETARY OF STATE—John Jay, of New York, was Secretary for Foreign Affairs under the Confederation, and continued to act, at the request of Washington, until Jefferson took office. Thomas Jefferson, of Virginia, September 26, 1789; entered upon duties March 22, 1790. SECRETARY OF THE TREASURY—Alexander Hamilton, of New York, September 11, 1789. SECRETARY OF WAR—Henry Knox, of Massachusetts, September 12, 1789. ATTORNEY GENERAL—Edmund Randolph, of Virginia, September 26, 1789; entered upon duties February 2, 1790. POSTMASTER GENERAL—Samuel Osgood, of Massachusetts, September 26, 1789. Timothy Pickering, of Pennsylvania, August 12, 1791; entered upon duties August 19, 1791.

1st Congress

1st Session: Mar. 4, 1789–Sept. 29, 1789[1]; 2d Session: Jan. 4, 1790–Aug. 12, 1790; 3d Session: Dec. 6, 1790–Mar. 3, 1791.

President pro tempore of the Senate: John Langdon, of New Hampshire (elected Apr. 6, 1789). Speaker of the House: Frederick A. C. Muhlenberg, of Pennsylvania (elected Apr. 1, 1789).

Senate: 17 pro-administration; 9 opposition
House: 38 pro-administration; 26 opposition

2d Congress

1st Session: Oct. 24, 1791–May 8, 1792; 2d Session: Nov. 5, 1792–Mar. 2, 1793; Special Session of the Senate: Mar. 4, 1791.

President pro tempore of the Senate: Richard H. Lee, of Virginia (elected Apr. 18, 1792); John Langdon, of New Hampshire (elected Nov. 5, 1792 and Mar. 1, 1793). Speaker of the House: Jonathan Trumbull, of Connecticut (elected Oct. 24, 1791).

Senate: 16 Federalist; 13 Democratic-Republican
House: 37 Federalist; 33 Democratic-Republican

Second Administration of GEORGE WASHINGTON
MARCH 4, 1793, TO MARCH 3, 1797

PRESIDENT—George Washington, of Virginia (No party). VICE-PRESIDENT—John Adams, of Massachusetts. SECRETARY OF STATE—Thomas Jefferson, of Virginia, continued from preceding administration. Edmund Randolph, of Virginia, January 2, 1794. Timothy Pickering, of Pennsylvania (Secretary of War), ad interim, August 20, 1795. Timothy Pickering, of Pennsylvania, December 10, 1795. SECRETARY OF THE TREASURY—Alexander Hamilton, of New York, continued from preceding administration. Oliver Wolcott, Jr., of Connecticut, February 2, 1795. SECRETARY OF WAR—Henry Knox, of Massachusetts, continued from preceding administration. Timothy Pickering, of Pennsylvania, January 2, 1795. Timothy Pickering, of Pennsylvania (Secretary of State), ad interim, December 10, 1795, to February 5, 1796. James McHenry, of Maryland, January 27, 1796; entered upon duties February 6, 1796. ATTORNEY GENERAL—Edmund Randolph, of Virginia, continued from preceding administration. William Bradford, of Pennsylvania, January 27, 1794; entered upon duties January 29, 1794. Charles Lee, of Virginia, December 10, 1795. POSTMASTER GENERAL—Timothy Pickering, of Pennsylvania, continued from preceding administration. Timothy Pickering, of Pennsylvania, recommissioned June 1, 1794. Joseph Habersham, of Georgia, February 25, 1795.

3d Congress

1st Session: Dec. 2, 1793–June 9, 1794; 2d Session: Nov. 3, 1794–Mar. 3, 1795; Special Session of the Senate: Mar. 4, 1793.

President pro tempore of the Senate: Ralph Izard, of South Carolina (elected May 31, 1794); Henry Tazewell, of Virginia (elected Feb. 20, 1795). Speaker of the House: Frederick A. C. Muhlenberg, of Pennsylvania (elected Dec. 2, 1793).

Senate: 17 Federalist; 13 Democratic-Republican
House: 57 Democratic-Republican; 48 Federalist

4th Congress

1st Session: Dec. 7, 1795–June 1, 1796; 2d Session: Dec. 5, 1796–Mar. 3, 1797; Special Session of the Senate: June 8, 1795–June 26, 1795.

President pro tempore of the Senate: Henry Tazewell, of Virginia (elected Dec. 7, 1795), Samuel Livermore, of New Hampshire (elected May 6, 1796), William Bingham, of Pennsylvania (Feb. 16, 1797). Speaker of the House: Jonathan Dayton, of New Jersey (elected Dec. 7, 1795).

Senate: 19 Federalist; 13 Democratic-Republican
House: 54 Federalist; 52 Democratic-Republican

Administration of JOHN ADAMS
MARCH 4, 1797, TO MARCH 3, 1801

PRESIDENT—John Adams, of Massachusetts (Federalist). VICE-PRESIDENT—Thomas Jefferson, of Virginia. SECRETARY OF STATE—Timothy Pickering, of Pennsylvania, continued from preceding administration; resignation requested May 10, 1800, but declining to resign, he was dismissed May 12, 1800. Charles Lee, of Virginia (Attorney General), ad interim, May 13, 1800. John Marshall, of Virginia, May 13, 1800; entered upon duties June 6, 1800. John Marshall, of Virginia (Chief Justice of the United States), ad interim, February 4, 1801, to March 3, 1801. SECRETARY OF THE TREASURY—Oliver Wolcott, Jr., of Connecticut, continued from preceding administration. Samuel Dexter, of Massachusetts, January 1, 1801. SECRETARY OF WAR—James McHenry, of Maryland, continued from preceding administration. Benjamin Stoddert, of Maryland (Secretary of the Navy), ad interim, June 1, 1800, to June 12, 1800. Samuel Dexter, of Massachusetts, May 13, 1800; entered upon duties June 12, 1800. Samuel Dexter, of Massachusetts (Secretary of the Treasury), ad interim, January 1, 1801. ATTORNEY GENERAL—Charles Lee, of Virginia, continued from preceding administration. POSTMASTER GENERAL—Joseph Habersham, of Georgia, continued from preceding administration. SECRETARY OF THE NAVY—Benjamin Stoddert, of Maryland, May 21, 1798; entered upon duties June 18, 1798.

5th Congress

1st Session: May 15, 1797–July 10, 1797; 2d Session: Nov. 13, 1797–July 16, 1798; 3d Session: Dec. 3, 1798–Mar. 3, 1799; Special Sessions of the Senate: Mar. 4, 1797; July 17, 1798–July 19, 1798.

President pro tempore of the Senate: William Bradford, of Rhode Island (elected July 6, 1797); Jacob Read, of South Carolina (elected Nov. 22, 1797); Theodore Sedgwick, of Massachusetts (elected June 27, 1798); John Laurence, of New York (elected Dec. 6, 1798); James Ross of Pennsylvania (elected Mar. 1, 1799). Speaker of the House: Jonathan Dayton, of New Jersey (reelected May 15, 1797); George Dent, of Maryland served as Speaker pro tempore Apr. 20, 1798, and May 28, 1798.

Senate: 20 Federalist; 12 Democratic-Republican
House: 58 Federalist; 48 Democratic-Republican

---

[1] Both houses met for the first time on Mar. 4, 1789, but each lacked a quorum. They met from day to day until the House attained a quorum on Apr. 1, 1789, and the Senate on Apr. 6, 1789.

6th Congress

1st Session: Dec. 2, 1799–May 14, 1800; 2d Session: Nov. 17, 1800–Mar. 3, 1801.

President pro tempore of the Senate: Samuel Livermore, of New Hampshire (elected Dec. 2, 1799); Uriah Tracy, of Connecticut (elected May 14, 1800); John E. Howard, of Maryland (elected Nov. 21, 1800); James Hillhouse, of Connecticut (elected Feb. 28, 1801). Speaker of the House: Theodore Sedgwick, of Massachusetts (elected Dec. 2, 1799).

Senate: 19 Federalist; 13 Democratic-Republican
House: 64 Federalist; 42 Democratic-Republican

First Administration of THOMAS JEFFERSON
MARCH 4, 1801, TO MARCH 3, 1805

PRESIDENT—Thomas Jefferson, of Virginia (Democratic-Republican). VICE-PRESIDENT—Aaron Burr, of New York. SECRETARY OF STATE—John Marshall, of Virginia (Chief Justice of the United States), for one day (March 4, 1801), and for a special purpose. Levi Lincoln, of Massachusetts (Attorney General), ad interim, March 5, 1801. James Madison, of Virginia, March 5, 1801; entered upon duties May 2, 1801. SECRETARY OF THE TREASURY—Samuel Dexter, of Massachusetts, continued from preceding administration to May 6, 1801. Albert Gallatin, of Pennsylvania, May 14, 1801. SECRETARY OF WAR—Henry Dearborn, of Massachusetts, March 5, 1801. ATTORNEY GENERAL—Levi Lincoln, of Massachusetts, March 5, 1801, to December 31, 1804. POSTMASTER GENERAL—Joseph Habersham, of Georgia, continued from preceding administration. Gideon Granger, of Connecticut, November 28, 1801. SECRETARY OF THE NAVY—Benjamin Stoddert, of Maryland, continued from preceding administration. Henry Dearborn, of Massachusetts (Secretary of War), ad interim, April 1, 1801. Robert Smith, of Maryland, July 15, 1801; entered upon duties July 27, 1801.

7th Congress

1st Session: Dec. 7, 1801–May 3, 1802; 2d Session: Dec. 6, 1802–March 3, 1803; Special Session of the Senate: Mar. 4, 1801–Mar. 5, 1801.

President pro tempore of the Senate: Abraham Baldwin, of Georgia (elected Dec. 7, 1801; Apr. 17, 1802); Stephen R. Bradley, of Vermont (elected Dec. 14, 1802; Feb. 25, 1803; Mar. 2, 1803). Speaker of the House: Nathaniel Macon, of North Carolina (elected Dec. 7, 1801).

Senate: 18 Democratic-Republican; 14 Federalist
House: 69 Democratic-Republican; 36 Federalist

8th Congress

1st Session: Oct. 17, 1803–Mar. 27, 1804; 2d Session: Nov. 5, 1804–Mar. 3, 1805.

President pro tempore of the Senate: John Brown, of Kentucky (elected Oct. 17, 1803; Jan. 23, 1804); Jesse Franklin, of North Carolina (elected Mar. 10, 1804); Joseph Anderson, of Tennessee (elected Jan. 15, 1805; Feb. 28, 1805; Mar. 2, 1805). Speaker of the House: Nathaniel Macon, of North Carolina (reelected Oct. 17, 1803).

Senate: 25 Democratic-Republican; 9 Federalist
House: 102 Democratic-Republican; 39 Federalist

Second Administration of THOMAS JEFFERSON
MARCH 4, 1805, TO MARCH 3, 1809

PRESIDENT—Thomas Jefferson, of Virginia (Democratic-Republican). VICE-PRESIDENT—George Clinton, of New York. SECRETARY OF STATE—James Madison, of Virginia, continued from preceding administration. SECRETARY OF THE TREASURY—Albert Gallatin, of Pennsylvania, continued from preceding administration. SECRETARY OF WAR—Henry Dearborn, of Massachusetts, continued from preceding administration. John Smith (chief clerk), ad interim, February 17, 1809. ATTORNEY GENERAL—John Breckinridge, of Kentucky, August 7, 1805 (died December 14, 1806). Caesar A. Rodney, of Delaware, January 20, 1807. POSTMASTER GENERAL—Gideon Granger, of Connecticut, continued from preceding administration. SECRETARY OF THE NAVY—Robert Smith, of Maryland, continued from preceding administration.

9th Congress

1st Session: Dec. 2, 1805–Apr. 21, 1806; 2d Session: Dec. 1, 1806–Mar. 3, 1807; Special Session of the Senate: Mar. 4, 1805.

President pro tempore of the Senate: Samuel Smith, of Maryland (elected Dec. 2, 1805; Mar. 18, 1806; Mar. 2, 1807). Speaker of the House: Nathaniel Macon, of North Carolina (reelected Dec. 2, 1805).

Senate: 27 Democratic-Republican; 7 Federalist
House: 116 Democratic-Republican; 25 Federalist

10th Congress

1st Session: Oct. 26, 1807–Apr. 25, 1808; 2d Session: Nov. 7, 1808–Mar. 3, 1809.

President pro tempore of the Senate: Samuel Smith, of Maryland (elected Apr. 16, 1808); Stephen R. Bradley, of Vermont (elected Dec. 28, 1808); John Milledge, of Georgia (elected Jan. 30, 1809). Speaker of the House: Joseph B. Varnum, of Massachusetts (elected Oct. 26, 1807).

Senate: 28 Democratic-Republican; 6 Federalist
House: 118 Democratic-Republican; 24 Federalist

First Administration of JAMES MADISON
MARCH 4, 1809, TO MARCH 3, 1813

PRESIDENT—James Madison, of Virginia (Democratic-Republican). VICE-PRESIDENT—George Clinton, of New York. (Died April 20, 1812.) SECRETARY OF STATE—Robert Smith, of Maryland, March 6, 1809. James Monroe, of Virginia, April 2, 1811; entered upon duties April 6, 1811. SECRETARY OF THE TREASURY—Albert Gallatin, of Pennsylvania, continued from preceding administration. SECRETARY OF WAR—John Smith (chief clerk), ad interim, continued from preceding administration. William Eustis, of Massachusetts, March 7, 1809; entered upon duties April 8, 1809; served to December 31, 1812. James Monroe, of Virginia (Secretary of State), ad interim, January 1, 1813. John Armstrong, of New York, January 13, 1813; entered upon duties February 5, 1813. ATTORNEY GENERAL—Caesar A. Rodney, of Delaware, continued from preceding administration; resigned December 5, 1811. William Pinkney, of Maryland, December 11, 1811; entered upon duties January 6, 1812. POSTMASTER GENERAL—Gideon Granger, of Connecticut, continued from preceding administration. SECRETARY OF THE NAVY—Robert Smith, of Maryland, continued from preceding administration. Charles W. Goldsborough (chief clerk), ad interim, March 8, 1809. Paul Hamilton, of South Carolina, March 7, 1809; entered upon duties May 15, 1809; served to December 31, 1812. Charles W. Goldsborough (chief clerk), ad interim, January 7, 1813, to January 18, 1813. William Jones, of Pennsylvania, January 12, 1813; entered upon duties January 19, 1813.

11th Congress

1st Session: May 22, 1809–June 28, 1809; 2d Session: Nov. 27, 1809–May 1, 1810; 3d Session: Dec. 3, 1810–Mar. 3, 1811; Special Session of the Senate: Mar. 4, 1809–Mar. 7, 1809.

President pro tempore of the Senate: Andrew Gregg, of Pennsylvania (elected June 26, 1809); John Gaillard, of South Carolina (elected Feb. 28, 1810; Apr. 17, 1810); John Pope, of Kentucky (elected Feb. 23, 1811). Speaker of the House: Joseph B. Varnum, of Massachusetts (reelected May 22, 1809).

Senate: 28 Democratic-Republican; 6 Federalist
House: 94 Democratic-Republican; 48 Federalist

12th Congress

1st Session: Nov. 4, 1811 to July 6, 1812; 2d Session: Nov. 2, 1812–Mar. 3, 1813.

President pro tempore of the Senate: William H. Crawford, of Georgia (elected Mar. 24, 1812). Speaker of the House: Henry Clay, of Kentucky (elected Nov. 4, 1811).

Senate: 30 Democratic-Republican; 6 Federalist
House: 108 Democratic-Republican; 36 Federalist

Second Administration of JAMES MADISON
MARCH 4, 1813, TO MARCH 3, 1817

PRESIDENT—James Madison, of Virginia (Democratic-Republican). VICE-PRESIDENT—Elbridge Gerry, of Massachusetts (died November 23, 1814). SECRETARY OF STATE—James Monroe, of Virginia, continued from preceding administration. James Monroe, of Virginia (Secretary of War), ad interim, October 1, 1814. James Monroe, of Virginia, February 28, 1815. SECRETARY OF THE TREASURY—Albert Gallatin, of Pennsylvania, continued from preceding administration. William Jones, of Pennsylvania (Secretary of the Navy), performed the duties of the Secretary of the Treasury during the absence of Mr. Gallatin in Europe (April 21, 1813, to February 9, 1814). George W. Campbell, of Tennessee, February 9, 1814. Alexander J. Dallas, of Pennsylvania, October 6, 1814; entered upon duties October 14, 1814. William H. Crawford, of Georgia, October 22, 1816. SECRETARY OF WAR—John Armstrong, of New York, continued from preceding administration. James Monroe, of Virginia (Secretary of State), ad interim, August 30, 1814. James Monroe, of Virginia, September 27, 1814; entered upon duties October 1, 1814. James Monroe, of Virginia (Secretary of State), ad interim, March 1, 1815. Alexander J. Dallas, of Pennsylvania (Secretary of the Treasury), ad interim, March 14, 1815, to August 8, 1815. William H. Crawford, of Georgia, August 1, 1815; entered upon duties August 8, 1815. George Graham (chief clerk), ad interim, October 22, 1816, to close of administration. ATTORNEY GENERAL—William Pinkney, of Maryland, continued from preceding administration. Richard Rush, of Pennsylvania, February 10, 1814; entered upon duties the day following. POSTMASTER

GENERAL—Gideon Granger, of Connecticut, continued from preceding administration. Return J. Meigs, Jr., of Ohio, March 17, 1814; entered upon duties April 11, 1814. SECRETARY OF THE NAVY—William Jones, of Pennsylvania, continued from preceding administration. Benjamin Homans (chief clerk), ad interim, December 2, 1814. Benjamin W. Crowninshield, of Massachusetts, December 19, 1814; entered upon duties January 16, 1815.

13th Congress
1st Session: May 24, 1813–Aug. 2, 1813; 2d Session: Dec. 6, 1813–Apr. 18, 1814; 3d Session: Sept. 19, 1814–Mar. 3, 1815.
President pro tempore of the Senate: Joseph B. Varnum, of Massachusetts (elected Dec. 6, 1813); John Gaillard, of South Carolina (elected Apr. 18, 1814; Nov. 25, 1814). Speaker of the House: Henry Clay, of Kentucky (reelected May 24, 1813); Langdon Cheves, of South Carolina (elected Jan. 19, 1814).
Senate: 27 Democratic-Republican; 9 Federalist
House: 112 Democratic-Republican; 68 Federalist

14th Congress
1st Session: Dec. 4, 1815–Apr. 30, 1816; 2d Session: Dec. 2, 1816–Mar. 3, 1817.
President pro tempore of the Senate: John Gaillard, of South Carolina (continued from preceding Congress). Speaker of the House: Henry Clay, of Kentucky (reelected Dec. 4, 1815).
Senate: 25 Democratic-Republican; 11 Federalist
House: 117 Democratic-Republican; 65 Federalist

First Administration of JAMES MONROE
MARCH 4, 1817, TO MARCH 3, 1821

PRESIDENT—James Monroe, of Virginia (Democratic-Republican). VICE-PRESIDENT—Daniel D. Tompkins, of New York. SECRETARY OF STATE—John Graham (chief clerk), ad interim, March 4, 1817. Richard Rush, of Pennsylvania (Attorney General), ad interim, March 10, 1817. John Quincy Adams, of Massachusetts, March 5, 1817; entered upon duties September 22, 1817. SECRETARY OF THE TREASURY—William H. Crawford, of Georgia, continued from preceding administration. William H. Crawford, of Georgia, recommissioned March 5, 1817. SECRETARY OF WAR—George Graham (chief clerk), ad interim, March 4, 1817. John C. Calhoun, of South Carolina, October 8, 1817; entered upon duties December 10, 1817. ATTORNEY GENERAL—Richard Rush, of Pennsylvania, continued from preceding administration to October 30, 1817. William Wirt, of Virginia, November 13, 1817; entered upon duties November 15, 1817. POSTMASTER GENERAL—Return J. Meigs, Jr., of Ohio, continued from preceding administration. SECRETARY OF THE NAVY—Benjamin W. Crowninshield, of Massachusetts, continued from preceding administration. John C. Calhoun, of South Carolina (Secretary of War), ad interim, October 1, 1818. Smith Thompson, of New York, November 9, 1818; entered upon duties January 1, 1819.

15th Congress
1st Session: Dec. 1, 1817–Apr. 20, 1818; 2d Session: Nov. 16, 1818–Mar. 3, 1819; Special Session of the Senate: Mar. 4, 1817–Mar. 6, 1817.
President pro tempore of the Senate: John Gaillard, of South Carolina (continued from preceding Congress; elected Mar. 6, 1817; Mar. 31, 1818). James Barbour, of Virginia (elected Feb. 15, 1819). Speaker of the House: Henry Clay, of Kentucky (reelected Dec. 1, 1817).
Senate: 34 Democratic-Republican; 10 Federalist
House: 141 Democratic-Republican; 42 Federalist

16th Congress
1st Session: Dec. 6, 1819–May 15, 1820; 2d Session: Nov. 13, 1820–Mar. 3, 1821.
President pro tempore of the Senate: James Barbour, of Virginia (continued from preceding Congress); John Gaillard, of South Carolina (elected Jan. 25, 1820). Speaker of the House: Henry Clay, of Kentucky (reelected Dec. 6, 1819), John W. Taylor, of New York (elected Nov. 15, 1820).
Senate: 35 Democratic-Republican; 7 Federalist
House: 156 Democratic-Republican; 27 Federalist

Second Administration of JAMES MONROE
MARCH 4, 1821, TO MARCH 3, 1825

PRESIDENT—James Monroe, of Virginia (Democratic-Republican). VICE-PRESIDENT—Daniel D. Tompkins, of New York. SECRETARY OF STATE—John Quincy Adams, of Massachusetts, continued from preceding administration. SECRETARY OF THE TREASURY—William H. Crawford, of Georgia, continued from preceding administration. SECRETARY OF WAR—John C. Calhoun, of South Carolina, continued from preceding administration. ATTORNEY GENERAL—William Wirt, of Virginia, continued from preceding administration. POSTMASTER GENERAL—Return J. Meigs, Jr., of Ohio, continued from preceding administration. John McLean, of Ohio, commissioned June 26, 1823, to take effect July 1, 1823. SECRETARY OF THE NAVY—Smith Thompson, of New York, continued from preceding administration. John Rodgers (commodore, United States Navy, and President of the Board of Navy Commissioners), ad interim, September 1, 1823. Samuel L. Southard, of New Jersey, September 16, 1823.

17th Congress
1st Session: Dec. 3, 1821–May 8, 1822; 2d Session: Dec. 2, 1822–Mar. 3, 1823.
President pro tempore of the Senate: John Gaillard, of South Carolina (elected Feb. 1, 1822; Feb. 19, 1823). Speaker of the House: Philip P. Barbour, of Virginia (elected Dec. 4, 1821).
Senate: 44 Democratic-Republican; 4 Federalist
House: 158 Democratic-Republican; 25 Federalist

18th Congress
1st Session: Dec. 1, 1823–May 27, 1824; 2d Session: Dec. 6, 1824–Mar. 3, 1825.
President pro tempore of the Senate: John Gaillard, of South Carolina (elected May 21, 1824). Speaker of the House: Henry Clay, of Kentucky (elected Dec. 1, 1823).
Senate: 44 Democratic-Republican; 4 Federalist
House: 187 Democratic-Republican; 26 Federalist

Administration of JOHN QUINCY ADAMS
MARCH 4, 1825, TO MARCH 3, 1829

PRESIDENT—John Quincy Adams, of Massachusetts (Democratic-Republican). VICE-PRESIDENT—John C. Calhoun, of South Carolina. SECRETARY OF STATE—Daniel Brent (chief clerk), ad interim, March 4, 1825. Henry Clay, of Kentucky, March 7, 1825. SECRETARY OF THE TREASURY—Samuel L. Southard, of New Jersey (Secretary of the Navy), ad interim, March 7, 1825. Richard Rush, of Pennsylvania, March 7, 1825; entered upon duties August 1, 1825. SECRETARY OF WAR—James Barbour, of Virginia, March 7, 1825. Samuel L. Southard, of New Jersey (Secretary of the Navy), ad interim, May 26, 1828. Peter B. Porter, of New York, May 26, 1828; entered upon duties June 21, 1828. ATTORNEY GENERAL—William Wirt, of Virginia, continued from preceding administration. POSTMASTER GENERAL—John McLean, of Ohio, continued from preceding administration. SECRETARY OF THE NAVY—Samuel L. Southard, of New Jersey, continued from preceding administration.

19th Congress
1st Session: Dec. 5, 1825–May 22, 1826; 2d Session: Dec. 4, 1826–Mar. 3, 1827; Special Session of the Senate: Mar. 4, 1825–Mar. 9, 1825.
President pro tempore of the Senate: John Gaillard, of South Carolina (elected Mar. 9, 1825). Nathaniel Macon, of North Carolina (elected May 20, 1826; Jan. 2, 1827; Mar. 2, 1827). Speaker of the House: John W. Taylor, of New York (elected Dec. 5, 1825).
Senate: 26 pro-administration; 20 opposition
House: 105 pro-administration; 97 opposition

20th Congress
1st Session: Dec. 3, 1827–May 26, 1828; 2d Session: Dec. 1, 1828–Mar. 3, 1829.
President pro tempore of the Senate: Samuel Smith, of Maryland (elected May 15, 1828). Speaker of the House: Andrew Stevenson, of Virginia (elected Dec. 3, 1827).
Senate: 20 pro-administration; 26 opposition
House: 94 pro-administration; 119 opposition

First Administration of ANDREW JACKSON
MARCH 4, 1829, TO MARCH 3, 1833

PRESIDENT—Andrew Jackson, of Tennessee (Democratic). VICE-PRESIDENT—John C. Calhoun, of South Carolina (resigned December 28, 1832). SECRETARY OF STATE—James A. Hamilton, of New York, ad interim, March 4, 1829. Martin Van Buren, of New York, March 6, 1829; entered upon duties March 28, 1829. Edward Livingston, of Louisiana, May 24, 1831. SECRETARY OF THE TREASURY—Samuel D. Ingham, of Pennsylvania, March 6, 1829. Asbury Dickins (chief clerk), ad interim, June 21, 1831. Louis McLane, of Delaware, August 8, 1831. SECRETARY OF WAR—John H. Eaton, of Tennessee, March 9, 1829. Philip G. Randolph (chief clerk), ad interim, June 20, 1831. Roger B. Taney, of Maryland (Attorney General), ad interim, July 21, 1831. Lewis Cass, of Ohio, August 1, 1831; entered upon duties August 8, 1831. ATTORNEY GENERAL—John M. Berrien, of Georgia, March 9, 1829, to June 22, 1831. Roger B. Taney, of Maryland, July 20, 1831. POSTMASTER GENERAL—John McLean, of Ohio, continued from preceding administration. William T. Barry, of Kentucky, March 9, 1829; entered upon duties April 6, 1829. SECRETARY OF THE NAVY—Charles Hay (chief clerk), ad interim, March 4, 1829. John Branch, of North Carolina, March 9, 1829. John Boyle (chief clerk), ad interim, May 12, 1831. Levi Woodbury, of New Hampshire, May 23, 1831.

21st Congress

1st Session: Dec. 7, 1829–May 31, 1830; 2d Session: Dec. 6, 1830–Mar. 3, 1831; Special Session of the Senate: Mar. 4, 1829–Mar. 17, 1829.

President pro tempore of the Senate: Samuel Smith, of Maryland (elected Mar. 13, 1829; May 29, 1830; Mar. 1, 1831). Speaker of the House: Andrew Stevenson, of Virginia (reelected Dec. 7, 1829).

Senate: 26 Democratic; 22 National Republican

House: 139 Democratic; 74 National Republican

22d Congress

1st Session: Dec. 5, 1831–July 16, 1832; 2d Session: Dec. 3, 1832–Mar. 2, 1833.

President pro tempore of the Senate: Littleton W. Tazewell, of Virginia (elected July 9, 1832); Hugh L. White, of Tennessee (elected Dec. 3, 1832). Speaker of the House: Andrew Stevenson of Virginia (reelected Dec. 5, 1831).

Senate: 25 Democratic; 21 National Republican

House: 141 Democratic; 58 National Republican

Second Administration of ANDREW JACKSON
MARCH 4, 1833, TO MARCH 3, 1837

PRESIDENT—Andrew Jackson, of Tennessee (Democratic). VICE-PRESIDENT—Martin Van Buren, of New York. SECRETARY OF STATE—Edward Livingston, of Louisiana, continued from preceding administration. Louis McLane of Delaware, May 29, 1833. John Forsyth, of Georgia, June 27, 1834; entered upon duties July 1, 1834. SECRETARY OF THE TREASURY—Louis McLane, of Delaware, continued from preceding administration. William J. Duane, of Pennsylvania, May 29, 1833; entered upon duties June 1, 1833. Roger B. Taney, of Maryland, September 23, 1833. McClintock Young (chief clerk), ad interim, June 25, 1834. Levi Woodbury, of New Hampshire, June 27, 1834; entered upon duties July 1, 1834. SECRETARY OF WAR—Lewis Cass, of Ohio, continued from preceding administration. Carey A. Harris, of Tennessee (Commissioner of Indian Affairs), ad interim, October 5, 1836. Benjamin F. Butler, of New York (Attorney General), ad interim, October 26, 1836. Benjamin F. Butler, of New York, commissioned March 3, 1837, ad interim, "during the pleasure of the President, until a successor, duly appointed, shall accept such office and enter upon the duties thereof." ATTORNEY GENERAL—Roger B. Taney, of Maryland, continued from preceding administration to September 23, 1833. Benjamin F. Butler, of New York, November 15, 1833; entered upon duties November 18, 1833. POSTMASTER GENERAL—William T. Barry, of Kentucky, continued from preceding administration. Amos Kendall, of Kentucky, May 1, 1835. SECRETARY OF THE NAVY —Levi Woodbury, of New Hampshire, continued from preceding administration. Mahlon Dickerson, of New Jersey, June 30, 1834.

23d Congress

1st Session: Dec. 2, 1833–June 30, 1834; 2d Session: Dec. 1, 1834–Mar. 3, 1835.

President pro tempore of the Senate: Hugh L. White, of Tennessee (continued from the previous Congress); George Poindexter, of Mississippi (elected June 28, 1834); John Tyler, of Virginia (elected Mar. 3, 1835). Speaker of the House: Andrew Stevenson, of Virginia (reelected Dec. 2, 1835); John Bell, of Tennessee (elected June 2, 1834); Henry Hubbard, of New Hampshire served as Speaker pro tem May 16, 1834.

Senate: 20 Democratic; 20 National Republican

House: 147 Democratic; 113 various parties

24th Congress

1st Session: Dec. 7, 1835–July 4, 1836; 2d Session: Dec. 5, 1836–Mar. 3, 1837.

President pro tempore of the Senate: William R. King, of Alabama (elected July 1, 1836; Jan. 28, 1837). Speaker of the House: James K. Polk, of Tennessee (elected Dec. 7, 1835).

Senate: 27 Democratic; 25 Whig

House: 145 Democratic; 98 Whig

Administration of MARTIN VAN BUREN
MARCH 4, 1837, TO MARCH 3, 1841

PRESIDENT—Martin Van Buren, of New York (Democratic). VICE-PRESIDENT—Richard M. Johnson, of Kentucky. SECRETARY OF STATE—John Forsyth, of Georgia, continued from preceding administration. SECRETARY OF THE TREASURY—Levi Woodbury, of New Hampshire, continued from preceding administration. SECRETARY OF WAR—Benjamin F. Butler, of New York, ad interim, continued from preceding administration. Joel R. Poinsett, of South Carolina, March 7, 1837; entered upon

duties March 14, 1837. ATTORNEY GENERAL—Benjamin F. Butler, of New York, continued from preceding administration. Felix Grundy, of Tennessee, July 5, 1838, to take effect September 1, 1838. Henry D. Gilpin, of Pennsylvania, January 11, 1840. POSTMASTER GENERAL—Amos Kendall, of Kentucky, continued from preceding administration. John M. Niles, of Connecticut, May 19, 1840, to take effect May 25, 1840; entered upon duties May 26, 1840. SECRETARY OF THE NAVY—Mahlon Dickerson, of New Jersey, continued from preceding administration. James K. Paulding, of New York, June 25, 1838, to take effect "after the 30th instant"; entered upon duties July 1, 1838.

25th Congress

1st Session: Sept. 4, 1837–Oct. 16, 1837; 2d Session: Dec. 4, 1837–July 9, 1838; 3d Session: Dec. 3, 1838–Mar. 3, 1839; Special Session of the Senate: Mar. 4, 1837–Mar. 10, 1837.

President pro tempore of the Senate: William R. King, of Alabama (elected Mar. 7, 1837; Oct. 13, 1837; July 2, 1838; Feb. 25, 1839). Speaker of the House: James K. Polk, of Tennessee (reelected Sept. 4, 1837).

Senate: 30 Democratic; 18 Whig; 4 other

House: 108 Democratic; 107 Whig; 24 other

26th Congress

1st Session: Dec. 2, 1839–July 21, 1840; 2d Session: Dec. 7, 1840–Mar. 3, 1841.

President pro tempore of the Senate: William R. King, of Alabama (continued from the preceding Congress; reelected July 3, 1840; Mar. 3, 1841). Speaker of the House: Robert M. T. Hunter, of Virginia (elected Dec. 16, 1839).

Senate: 28 Democratic; 22 Whig

House: 124 Democratic; 118 Whig

Administration of WILLIAM HENRY HARRISON
MARCH 4, 1841, TO APRIL 4, 1841

PRESIDENT—William Henry Harrison, of Ohio (Whig) (died April 4, 1841). VICE-PRESIDENT—John Tyler, of Virginia. SECRETARY OF STATE—J. L. Martin (chief clerk), ad interim, March 4, 1841. Daniel Webster, of Massachusetts, March 5, 1841. SECRETARY OF THE TREASURY—McClintock Young (chief clerk), ad interim, March 4, 1841. Thomas Ewing, of Ohio, March 5, 1841. SECRETARY OF WAR—John Bell, of Tennessee, March 5, 1841. ATTORNEY GENERAL—John J. Crittenden, of Kentucky, March 5, 1841. POSTMASTER GENERAL—Selah R. Hobbie, of New York (First Assistant Postmaster General), ad interim, March 4, 1841. Francis Granger, of New York, March 6, 1841; entered upon duties March 8, 1841. SECRETARY OF THE NAVY —John D. Simms (chief clerk), ad interim, March 4, 1841. George E. Badger, of North Carolina, March 5, 1841.

Administration of JOHN TYLER
APRIL 6, 1841, TO MARCH 3, 1845

PRESIDENT—John Tyler, of Virginia (Whig). SECRETARY OF STATE—Daniel Webster, of Massachusetts, continued from preceding administration. Hugh S. Legaré, of South Carolina (Attorney General), ad interim, May 9, 1843. William S. Derrick (chief clerk), ad interim, June 21, 1843. Abel P. Upshur, of Virginia (Secretary of the Navy), ad interim, June 24, 1843. Abel P. Upshur, of Virginia, July 24, 1843 (killed by the explosion of a gun on the U.S.S. Princeton February 28, 1844). John Nelson, of Maryland (Attorney General), ad interim, February 29, 1844. John C. Calhoun, of South Carolina, March 6, 1844; entered upon duties April 1, 1844. SECRETARY OF THE TREASURY —Thomas Ewing, of Ohio, continued from preceding administration. McClintock Young (chief clerk), ad interim, September 13, 1841. Walter Forward, of Pennsylvania, September 13, 1841. McClintock Young (chief clerk), ad interim, March 1, 1843. John C. Spencer, of New York, March 3, 1843; entered upon duties March 8, 1843. McClintock Young (chief clerk), ad interim, May 2, 1844. George M. Bibb, of Kentucky, June 15, 1844; entered upon duties July 4, 1844. SECRETARY OF WAR—John Bell, of Tennessee, continued from preceding administration. Albert M. Lea, of Maryland (chief clerk), ad interim, September 12, 1841. John C. Spencer, of New York, October 12, 1841. James M. Porter, of Pennsylvania, March 8, 1843. William Wilkins, of Pennsylvania, February 15, 1844; entered upon duties February 20, 1844. ATTORNEY GENERAL—John J. Crittenden, of Kentucky, continued from preceding administration. Hugh S. Legaré, of South Carolina, September 13, 1841; entered upon duties September 20, 1841 (died June 20, 1843). John Nelson, of Maryland, July 1, 1843. POSTMASTER GENERAL— Francis Granger, of New York, continued from preceding administration. Selah R. Hobbie, of New York (First Assistant Postmaster General) ad interim, September 14, 1841. Charles A. Wickliffe, of Kentucky, September 13, 1841; entered upon duties October 13, 1841. SECRETARY OF THE NAVY—George E. Badger, of North Carolina, continued from preceding administration. John D. Simms (chief clerk), ad interim, September 11, 1841. Abel P. Upshur, of Virginia, September 13, 1841; entered upon duties October 11, 1841. David Henshaw, of Massachusetts, July 24, 1843. Thomas W. Gilmer, of Virginia, February 15, 1844; entered upon duties February 19, 1844 (killed by the explosion of a gun on the U.S.S. **Princeton** February 28, 1844). Lewis Warrington (captain, United States Navy), ad interim, February 29, 1844. John Y. Mason, of Virginia, March 14, 1844, entered upon duties March 26, 1844.

27th Congress

1st Session: May 31, 1841–Sept. 13, 1841; 2d Session: Dec. 6, 1841–Aug. 31, 1842; 3d Session: Dec. 5, 1842–Mar. 3, 1843; Special Session of the Senate: Mar. 4, 1841–Mar. 15, 1841.

President pro tempore of the Senate: William R. King, of Alabama (elected Mar. 4, 1841); Samuel L. Southard, of New Jersey (elected Mar. 11, 1841); Willie P. Mangum, of North Carolina (elected May 31, 1842). Speaker of the House: John White, of Kentucky (elected May 31, 1841).

Senate: 28 Whig; 22 Democratic; 2 other
House: 133 Whig; 102 Democratic; 6 other

28th Congress

1st Session: Dec. 4, 1843–June 17, 1844; 2d Session: Dec. 2, 1844–Mar. 3, 1845.

President pro tempore of the Senate: Willie P. Mangum, of North Carolina (continued from the preceding Congress). Speaker of the House: John W. Jones, of Virginia (elected Dec. 4, 1843); George Hopkins acted as Speaker for part of the day Feb. 28, 1845.

Senate: 28 Whig; 25 Democratic; 1 other
House: 115 Whig; 108 Democratic; 4 other

Administration of JAMES K. POLK
MARCH 4, 1845, TO MARCH 3, 1849

PRESIDENT—James K. Polk, of Tennessee (Democratic). VICE-PRESIDENT—George M. Dallas, of Pennsylvania. SECRETARY OF STATE—John C. Calhoun, of South Carolina, continued from preceding administration. James Buchanan, of Pennsylvania, March 6, 1845; entered upon duties March 10, 1845. SECRETARY OF THE TREASURY—George M. Bibb, of Kentucky, continued from preceding administration. Robert J. Walker, of Mississippi, March 6, 1845; entered upon duties March 8, 1845. SECRETARY OF WAR—William Wilkins, of Pennsylvania, continued from preceding administration. William L. Marcy, of New York, March 6, 1845; entered upon duties March 8, 1845. ATTORNEY GENERAL—John Nelson, of Maryland, continued from preceding administration. John Y. Mason, of Virginia, March 6, 1845; entered upon duties March 11, 1845. Nathan Clifford, of Maine, October 17, 1846, to March 18, 1848, when he resigned. Isaac Toucey, of Connecticut, June 21, 1848; entered upon duties June 29, 1848. POSTMASTER GENERAL—Charles A. Wickliffe, of Kentucky, continued from preceding administration. Cave Johnson, of Tennessee, March 6, 1845. SECRETARY OF THE NAVY—John Y. Mason, of Virginia, continued from preceding administration. George Bancroft, of Massachusetts, March 10, 1845. John Y. Mason, of Virginia, September 9, 1846.

29th Congress

1st Session: Dec. 1, 1845–Aug. 10, 1846; 2d Session: Dec. 7, 1846–Mar. 3, 1847; Special Session of the Senate: Mar. 4, 1845–Mar. 20, 1845.

President pro tempore of the Senate: Ambrose H. Sevier, of Arkansas (under designation of the Vice-President served Dec. 27, 1845); David R. Atchison, of Missouri (elected Aug. 8, 1846; Jan. 11, 1847; Mar. 3, 1847). Speaker of the House: John W. Davis, of Indiana (elected Dec. 1, 1845).

Senate: 31 Democratic; 25 Whig
House: 143 Democratic; 77 Whig; 6 other

30th Congress

1st Session: Dec. 6, 1847–Aug. 14, 1848; 2d Session: Dec. 4, 1848–Mar. 3, 1849.

President pro tempore of the Senate: David R. Atchison, of Missouri (elected Feb. 2, 1848; June 1, 1848; June 26, 1848; July 29, 1848; Dec. 26, 1848; Mar. 2, 1849). Speaker of the House: Robert C. Winthrop, of Massachusetts (elected Dec. 6, 1847); Armistead Burt served as Speaker pro tem June 19–22, 1848.

Senate: 36 Democratic; 21 Whig; 1 other
House: 115 Whig; 108 Democratic; 4 other

Administration of ZACHARY TAYLOR
MARCH 4, 1849, TO JULY 9, 1850

PRESIDENT—Zachary Taylor, of Louisiana (Whig). (Oath administered March 5, 1849. Died July 9, 1850.) VICE-PRESIDENT

—Millard Fillmore, of New York. SECRETARY OF STATE—James Buchanan, of Pennsylvania, continued from preceding administration. John M. Clayton, of Delaware, March 7, 1849. SECRETARY OF THE TREASURY—Robert J. Walker, of Mississippi, continued from preceding administration. McClintock Young (chief clerk), ad interim, March 6, 1849. William M. Meredith, of Pennsylvania, March 8, 1849. SECRETARY OF WAR—William L. Marcy, of New York, continued from preceding administration. Reverdy Johnson, of Maryland (Attorney General), ad interim, March 8, 1849. George W. Crawford, of Georgia, March 8, 1849, entered upon duties March 14, 1849. ATTORNEY GENERAL—Isaac Toucey, of Connecticut, continued from preceding administration. Reverdy Johnson, of Maryland, March 8, 1849. POSTMASTER GENERAL—Cave Johnson, of Tennessee, continued from preceding administration. Selah R. Hobbie, of New York (First Assistant Postmaster General), ad interim, March 6, 1849. Jacob Collamer, of Vermont, March 8, 1849. SECRETARY OF THE NAVY—John Y. Mason, of Virginia, continued from preceding administration. William B. Preston, of Virginia, March 8, 1849. SECRETARY OF THE INTERIOR—Thomas Ewing, of Ohio, March 8, 1849.

Administration of MILLARD FILLMORE
JULY 10, 1850, TO MARCH 3, 1853

PRESIDENT—Millard Fillmore, of New York (Whig). SECRETARY OF STATE—John M. Clayton, of Delaware, continued from preceding administration. Daniel Webster, of Massachusetts, July 22, 1850 (died October 24, 1852). Charles M. Conrad, of Louisiana (Secretary of War), ad interim, October 25, 1852. Edward Everett, of Massachusetts, November 6, 1852. SECRETARY OF THE TREASURY—William M. Meredith, of Pennsylvania, continued from preceding administration. Thomas Corwin, of Ohio, July 23, 1850. SECRETARY OF WAR—George W. Crawford, of Georgia, continued from preceding administration. Samuel J. Anderson (chief clerk), ad interim, July 23, 1850. Winfield Scott (major general, U.S. Army), ad interim, July 24, 1850. Charles M. Conrad, of Louisiana, August 15, 1850. ATTORNEY GENERAL—Reverdy Johnson, of Maryland, continued from preceding administration, served to July 22, 1850. John J. Crittenden, of Kentucky, July 22, 1850; entered upon duties August 14, 1850. POSTMASTER GENERAL—Jacob Collamer, of Vermont, continued from preceding administration. Nathan K. Hall, of New York, July 23, 1850. Samuel D. Hubbard, of Connecticut, August 31, 1852; entered upon duties September 14, 1852. SECRETARY OF THE NAVY—William B. Preston, of Virginia, continued from preceding administration. Lewis Warrington (captain, U.S. Navy), ad interim, July 23, 1850. William A. Graham, of North Carolina, July 22, 1850; entered upon duties August 2, 1850. John P. Kennedy, of Maryland, July 22, 1852; entered upon duties July 26, 1852. SECRETARY OF THE INTERIOR—Thomas Ewing, of Ohio, continued from preceding administration. Daniel C. Goddard (chief clerk), ad interim, July 23, 1850. Thomas M. T. McKennan, of Pennsylvania, August 15, 1850. Daniel C. Goddard (chief clerk), ad interim, August 27, 1850. Alexander H. H. Stuart, of Virginia, September 12, 1850; entered upon duties September 16, 1850.

31st Congress

1st Session: Dec. 3, 1849–Sept. 30, 1850; 2d Session: Dec. 2, 1850–Mar. 3, 1851; Special Session of the Senate: Mar. 5, 1849–Mar. 23, 1849.

President pro tempore of the Senate: David R. Atchison, of Missouri (elected Mar. 5, 1849; Mar. 16, 1849). William R. King, of Alabama (elected May 6, 1850, July 11, 1850). Speaker of the House: Howell Cobb, of Georgia (elected Dec. 22, 1849), Robert C. Winthrop, of Massachusetts, served as Speaker pro tem April 19, 1850.

Senate: 35 Democratic; 25 Whig; 2 other
House: 112 Democratic; 109 Whig; 9 other

32d Congress

1st Session: Dec. 1, 1851–Aug. 31, 1852; 2d Session: Dec. 6, 1852–Mar. 3, 1853; Special Session of the Senate: Mar. 4, 1851–Mar. 13, 1851.

President pro tempore of the Senate: William R. King, of Alabama (continued from preceding Congress); David R. Atchison, of Missouri (elected Dec. 20, 1852). Speaker of the House: Linn Boyd, of Kentucky (elected Dec. 1, 1851).

Senate: 35 Democratic; 24 Whig; 3 other
House: 140 Democratic; 88 Whig; 5 other

Administration of FRANKLIN PIERCE
MARCH 4, 1853, TO MARCH 3, 1857

PRESIDENT—Franklin Pierce, of New Hampshire (Democratic). VICE-PRESIDENT—William R. King, of Alabama (died April 18, 1853). SECRETARY OF STATE—William Hunter (chief clerk), ad interim, March 4, 1853. William L. Marcy, of New York,

March 7, 1853. SECRETARY OF THE TREASURY—Thomas Corwin, of Ohio, continued from preceding administration. James Guthrie, of Kentucky, March 7, 1853. SECRETARY OF WAR—Charles M. Conrad, of Louisiana, continued from preceding administration. Jefferson Davis, of Mississippi, March 7, 1853. Samuel Cooper (Adjutant General, U.S. Army), ad interim, March 3, 1857. ATTORNEY GENERAL—John J. Crittenden, of Kentucky, continued from preceding administration. Caleb Cushing, of Massachusetts, March 7, 1853. POSTMASTER GENERAL—Samuel D. Hubbard, of Connecticut, continued from preceding administration. James Campbell, of Pennsylvania, March 7, 1853. SECRETARY OF THE NAVY—John P. Kennedy, of Maryland, continued from preceding administration. James C. Dobbin, of North Carolina, March 7, 1853. SECRETARY OF THE INTERIOR—Alexander H. H. Stuart, of Virginia, continued from preceding administration. Robert McClelland, of Michigan, March 7, 1853.

33d Congress

1st Session: Dec. 5, 1853–Aug. 7, 1854; 2d Session: Dec. 4, 1854–Mar. 3, 1855; Special Session of the Senate: Mar. 4, 1853–Apr. 11, 1853.

President pro tempore of the Senate: David R. Atchison, of Missouri (elected Mar. 4, 1853); Lewis Cass, of Michigan (elected Dec. 4, 1854); Jesse D. Bright, of Indiana (elected Dec. 5, 1854). Speaker of the House: Linn Boyd, of Kentucky (reelected Dec. 5, 1853).

Senate: 38 Democratic; 22 Whig; 2 other
House: 159 Democratic; 71 Whig; 4 other

34th Congress

1st Session: Dec. 3, 1855–Aug. 18, 1856; 2d Session: Aug. 21, 1856–Aug. 30, 1856; 3d Session: Dec. 1, 1856–Mar. 3, 1857.

President pro tempore of the Senate: Jesse D. Bright, of Indiana (continued from preceding Congress; elected June 11, 1856); Charles E. Stuart, of Michigan (served June 5, 1856; elected June 9, 1856); James M. Mason, of Virginia (served Jan. 5, 1857; elected Jan. 6, 1857). Speaker of the House: Nathaniel P. Banks, of Massachusetts (elected Feb. 2, 1856).

Senate: 40 Democratic; 15 Republican; 5 other
House: 108 Republican; 83 Democratic; 43 other

Administration of JAMES BUCHANAN
MARCH 4, 1857, TO MARCH 3, 1861

PRESIDENT—James Buchanan, of Pennsylvania (Democratic). VICE-PRESIDENT—John C. Breckinridge, of Kentucky. SECRETARY OF STATE—William L. Marcy, of New York, continued from preceding administration. Lewis Cass, of Michigan, March 6, 1857. William Hunter (chief clerk), ad interim, December 15, 1860. Jeremiah S. Black, of Pennsylvania, December 17, 1860. SECRETARY OF THE TREASURY—James Guthrie, of Kentucky, continued from preceding administration. Howell Cobb, of Georgia, March 6, 1857. Isaac Toucey, of Connecticut (Secretary of the Navy), ad interim, December 10, 1860. Philip F. Thomas, of Maryland, December 12, 1860. John A. Dix, of New York, January 11, 1861; entered upon duties January 15, 1861. SECRETARY OF WAR—Samuel Cooper (Adjutant General, U.S. Army), ad interim, March 4, 1857. John B. Floyd, of Virginia, March 6, 1857. Joseph Holt, of Kentucky (Postmaster General), ad interim, January 1, 1861. Joseph Holt, of Kentucky, January 18, 1861. ATTORNEY GENERAL—Caleb Cushing, of Massachusetts, continued from preceding administration. Jeremiah S. Black, of Pennsylvania, March 6, 1857; entered upon duties March 11, 1857. Edwin M. Stanton, of Pennsylvania, December 20, 1860; entered upon duties December 22, 1860. POSTMASTER GENERAL—James Campbell, of Pennsylvania, continued from preceding administration. Aaron V. Brown, of Tennessee, March 6, 1857 (died March 8, 1859). Horatio King, of Maine (First Assistant Postmaster General), ad interim, March 9, 1859. Joseph Holt, of Kentucky, March 14, 1859. Horatio King, of Maine (First Assistant Postmaster General), ad interim, January 1, 1861. Horatio King, of Maine, February 12, 1861. SECRETARY OF NAVY—James C. Dobbin, of North Carolina, continued from preceding administration. Isaac Toucey, of Connecticut, March 6, 1857. SECRETARY OF THE INTERIOR—Robert McClelland, of Michigan, continued from preceding administration. Jacob Thompson, of Mississippi, March 6, 1857; entered upon duties March 10, 1857. Moses Kelly (chief clerk), ad interim, January 10, 1861.

35th Congress

1st Session: Dec. 7, 1857–June 14, 1858; 2d Session: Dec. 6, 1858–Mar. 3, 1859; Special Sessions of the Senate: Mar. 4, 1857–Mar. 14, 1857; June 15, 1858–June 16, 1858.

President pro tempore of the Senate: James M. Mason, of Virginia (elected Mar. 4, 1857); Thomas J. Rusk, of Texas (elected Mar. 14, 1857); Benjamin Fitzpatrick, of Alabama (elected Dec. 7, 1857; Mar. 29, 1858; June 14, 1858; Jan. 25, 1859). Speaker of the House: James L. Orr, of South Carolina (elected Dec. 7, 1857).

Senate: 36 Democratic; 20 Republican; 8 other
House: 118 Democratic; 92 Republican; 26 other

36th Congress

1st Session: Dec. 5, 1859–June 25, 1860; 2d Session: Dec. 3, 1860–Mar. 3, 1861: Special Sessions of the Senate: Mar. 4, 1859–Mar. 10, 1859; June 26, 1860–June 28, 1860.

President pro tempore of the Senate: Benjamin Fitzpatrick, of Alabama (elected Mar. 9, 1859; Dec. 19, 1859; Feb. 20, 1860; June 26, 1860); Jesse D. Bright, of Indiana (June 12, 1860); Solomon Foot, of Vermont (elected Feb. 16, 1861). Speaker of the House: William Pennington, of New Jersey (elected Feb. 1, 1860).

Senate: 36 Democratic; 26 Republican; 4 other
House: 114 Republican; 92 Democratic; 31 other

First Administration of ABRAHAM LINCOLN
MARCH 4, 1861, TO MARCH 3, 1865

PRESIDENT—Abraham Lincoln, of Illinois (Republican). VICE-PRESIDENT—Hannibal Hamlin, of Maine. SECRETARY OF STATE—Jeremiah S. Black, of Pennsylvania, continued from preceding administration. William H. Seward, of New York, March 5, 1861. SECRETARY OF THE TREASURY—John A. Dix, of New York, continued from preceding administration. Salmon P. Chase, of Ohio, March 5, 1861; entered upon duties March 7, 1861. George Harrington, of the District of Columbia (Assistant Secretary), ad interim, July 1, 1864. William P. Fessenden, of Maine, July 1, 1864; entered upon duties July 5, 1864. SECRETARY OF WAR—Joseph Holt, of Kentucky, continued from preceding administration. Simon Cameron, of Pennsylvania, March 5, 1861; entered upon duties March 11, 1861. Edwin M. Stanton, of Pennsylvania, January 15, 1862; entered upon duties January 20, 1862. ATTORNEY GENERAL—Edwin M. Stanton, of Pennsylvania, continued from preceding administration. Edward Bates, of Missouri, March 5, 1861. James Speed, of Kentucky, December 2, 1864; entered upon duties December 5, 1864. POSTMASTER GENERAL—Horatio King, of Maine, continued from preceding administration. Montgomery Blair, of the District of Columbia, March 5, 1861; entered upon duties March 9, 1861. William Dennison, of Ohio, September 24, 1864; entered upon duties October 1, 1864. SECRETARY OF THE NAVY—Isaac Toucey, of Connecticut, continued from preceding administration. Gideon Welles, of Connecticut, March 5, 1861; entered upon duties March 7, 1861. SECRETARY OF THE INTERIOR—Moses Kelly (chief clerk), ad interim, March 4, 1861. Caleb B. Smith, of Indiana, March 5, 1861. John P. Usher, of Indiana (Assistant Secretary), ad interim, January 1, 1863. John P. Usher, of Indiana, January 8, 1863.

37th Congress

1st Session: July 4, 1861–Aug. 6, 1861; 2d Session: Dec. 2, 1861–July 17, 1862; 3d Session: Dec. 1, 1862–Mar. 3, 1863; Special Session of the Senate: Mar. 4, 1861–Mar. 28, 1861.

President pro tempore of the Senate: Solomon Foot, of Vermont (elected Mar. 23, 1861; July 18, 1861; Jan. 15, 1862; Mar. 31, 1862; June 19, 1862; Feb. 18, 1863). Speaker of the House: Galusha A. Grow, of Pennsylvania (elected July 4, 1861).

Senate: 31 Republican; 10 Democratic; 8 other
House: 105 Republican; 43 Democratic; 30 other

38th Congress

1st Session: Dec. 7, 1863–July 4, 1864; 2d Session: Dec. 5, 1864–Mar. 3, 1865; Special Session of the Senate: Mar. 4, 1863–Mar. 14, 1863.

President pro tempore of the Senate: Solomon Foot, of Vermont (elected Mar. 4, 1863; Dec. 18, 1863; Feb. 23, 1864; Mar. 11, 1864; Apr. 11, 1864); Daniel Clark, of New Hampshire (elected Apr. 26, 1864; Feb. 9, 1865). Speaker of the House: Schuyler Colfax, of Indiana (elected Dec. 7, 1863).

Senate: 36 Republican; 9 Democratic; 5 other
House: 102 Republican; 75 Democratic; 9 other

Second Administration of ABRAHAM LINCOLN
MARCH 4, 1865, TO APRIL 15, 1865

PRESIDENT—Abraham Lincoln, of Illinois (Republican) (died April 15, 1865). VICE-PRESIDENT—Andrew Johnson, of Tennessee. SECRETARY OF STATE—William H. Seward, of New York, continued from preceding administration. SECRETARY OF THE TREASURY—George Harrington, of the District of Columbia (Assistant Secretary), ad interim, March 4, 1865. Hugh McCulloch, of Indiana, March 7, 1865; entered upon duties March 9, 1865. SECRETARY OF WAR—Edwin M. Stanton, of Pennsylvania, continued from preceding administration. ATTORNEY GENERAL—James Speed, of Kentucky, continued from preceding administration. POSTMASTER GENERAL—William Dennison, of Ohio, continued from preceding administration. SECRETARY OF THE NAVY—Gideon Welles, of Connecticut, continued from preceding administration. SECRETARY OF THE INTERIOR—John P. Usher, of Indiana, continued from preceding administration.

Administration of ANDREW JOHNSON
APRIL 15, 1865, TO MARCH 3, 1869

PRESIDENT—Andrew Johnson, of Tennessee (Republican). SECRETARY OF STATE—William H. Seward, of New York, continued from preceding administration. SECRETARY OF THE TREASURY—Hugh McCulloch, of Indiana, continued from preceding administration. SECRETARY OF WAR—Edwin M. Stanton, of Pennsylvania, continued from preceding administration; suspended August 12, 1867. Ulysses S. Grant (General of the Army), ad interim, August 12, 1867. Edwin M. Stanton, of Pennsylvania, reinstated January 13, 1868, to May 26, 1868. John M. Schofield, of Illinois, May 28, 1868; entered upon duties June 1, 1868. ATTORNEY GENERAL—James Speed, of Kentucky, continued from preceding administration. J. Hubley Ashton, of Pennsylvania (Assistant Attorney General), acting, July 17, 1866. Henry Stanbery, of Ohio, July 23, 1866. Orville H. Browning, of Illinois (Secretary of the Interior), ad interim, March 13, 1868. William M. Evarts, of New York, July 15, 1868; entered upon duties July 20, 1868. POSTMASTER GENERAL—William Dennison, of Ohio, continued from preceding administration. Alexander W. Randall, of Wisconsin (First Assistant Postmaster General), ad interim, July 17, 1866. Alexander W. Randall, of Wisconsin, July 25, 1866. SECRETARY OF THE NAVY—Gideon Welles, of Connecticut, continued from preceding administration. SECRETARY OF THE INTERIOR—John P. Usher, of Indiana, continued from preceding administration. James Harlan, of Iowa, May 15, 1865. Orville H. Browning, of Illinois, July 27, 1866, to take effect September 1, 1866.

39th Congress
1st Session: Dec. 4, 1865–July 28, 1866; 2d Session: Dec. 3, 1866–Mar. 3, 1867; Special Session of the Senate: Mar. 4, 1865–Mar. 11, 1865.

President pro tempore of the Senate: Lafayette S. Foster, of Connecticut (elected Mar. 7, 1865); Benjamin F. Wade, of Ohio (elected Mar. 2, 1867). Speaker of the House: Schuyler Colfax, of Indiana (reelected Dec. 4, 1865).

Senate: 42 Union; 10 Democratic
House: 149 Union; 42 Democratic

40th Congress
1st Session: Mar. 4, 1867–Mar. 30, 1867; July 3, 1867–July 20, 1867; Nov. 21, 1867–Dec. 1, 1867; 2d Session: Dec. 2, 1867–July 27, 1868; Sept. 21, 1868; Oct. 16, 1868; Nov. 10, 1868; 3d Session: Dec. 7, 1868–Mar. 3, 1869; Special Session of the Senate: Apr. 1, 1867–Apr. 20, 1867.

President pro tempore of the Senate: Benjamin F. Wade, of Ohio (continued from the preceding Congress). Speaker of the House: Schuyler Colfax, of Indiana (reelected Mar. 4, 1867); Theodore M. Pomeroy, of New York (elected Mar. 3, 1869).

Senate: 42 Republican; 11 Democratic
House: 143 Republican; 49 Democratic

First Administration of ULYSSES S. GRANT
MARCH 4, 1869, TO MARCH 3, 1873

PRESIDENT—Ulysses S. Grant, of Illinois (Republican). VICE-PRESIDENT—Schuyler Colfax, of Indiana. SECRETARY OF STATE—William H. Seward, of New York, continued from preceding administration. Elihu B. Washburne, of Illinois, March 5, 1869. Hamilton Fish, of New York, March 11, 1869; entered upon duties March 17, 1869. SECRETARY OF THE TREASURY—Hugh McCulloch, of Indiana, continued from preceding administration. John F. Hartley, of Maine (Assistant Secretary), ad interim, March 5, 1869. George S. Boutwell, of Massachusetts, March 11, 1869. SECRETARY OF WAR—John M. Schofield, of Illinois, continued from preceding administration. John A. Rawlins, of Illinois, March 11, 1869. William T. Sherman, of Ohio, September 9, 1869; entered upon duties September 11, 1869. William W. Belknap, of Iowa, October 25, 1869; entered upon duties November 1, 1869. ATTORNEY GENERAL—William M. Evarts, of New York, continued from preceding administration. J. Hubley Ashton, of Pennsylvania (Assistant Attorney General), acting, March 5, 1869. Ebenezer R. Hoar, of Massachusetts, March 5, 1869; entered upon duties March 11, 1869. Amos T. Akerman, of Georgia, June 23, 1870; entered upon duties July 8, 1870. George H. Williams, of Oregon, December 14, 1871, to take effect January 10, 1872. POSTMASTER GENERAL—St. John B. L. Skinner, of New York (First Assistant Postmaster General), ad interim, March 4, 1869. John A. J. Creswell, of Maryland, March 5, 1869. SECRETARY OF THE NAVY—William Faxon, of Connecticut (Assistant Secretary), ad interim, March 4, 1869. Adolph E. Borie, of Pennsylvania, March 5, 1869; entered upon duties March 9, 1869. George M. Robeson, of New Jersey, June 25, 1869. SECRETARY OF THE INTERIOR—William T. Otto, of Indiana (Assistant Secretary), ad interim, March 4, 1869. Jacob D. Cox, of Ohio, March 5, 1869; entered upon duties March 9, 1869. Columbus Delano, of Ohio, November 1, 1870.

41st Congress
1st Session: Mar. 4, 1869–Apr. 10, 1869; 2d Session: Dec. 6, 1869–July 15, 1870; 3d Session: Dec. 5, 1870–Mar. 3, 1871; Special Session of the Senate: Apr. 12, 1869–Apr. 22, 1869.

President pro tempore of the Senate: Henry B. Anthony, of Rhode Island (elected Mar. 23, 1869; Apr. 9, 1869; May 28, 1870; July 1, 1870; July 14, 1870). Speaker of the House: James G. Blaine, of Maine (elected Mar. 4, 1869).

Senate: 56 Republican; 11 Democratic
House: 149 Republican; 63 Democratic

42d Congress
1st Session: Mar. 4, 1871–Apr. 20, 1871; 2d Session: Dec. 4, 1871–June 10, 1872; 3d Session: Dec. 2, 1872–Mar. 3, 1873; Special Session of the Senate: May 10, 1871–May 27, 1871.

President pro tempore of the Senate: Henry B. Anthony, of Rhode Island (elected Mar. 10, 1871; April 17, 1871; May 23, 1871; Dec. 21, 1871; Feb. 23, 1872; June 8, 1872; Dec. 4, 1872; Dec. 13, 1872; Dec. 20, 1872; Jan. 24, 1873). Speaker of the House: James G. Blaine, of Maine (reelected Mar. 4, 1871).

Senate: 52 Republican; 17 Democratic; 5 other
House: 134 Democratic; 104 Republican; 5 other

Second Administration of ULYSSES S. GRANT
MARCH 4, 1873, TO MARCH 3, 1877

PRESIDENT—Ulysses S. Grant, of Illinois (Republican). VICE-PRESIDENT—Henry Wilson, of Massachusetts (died November 22, 1875). SECRETARY OF STATE—Hamilton Fish, of New York, continued from preceding administration. Hamilton Fish, of New York, recommissioned March 17, 1873. SECRETARY OF THE TREASURY—George S. Boutwell, of Massachusetts, continued from preceding administration. William A. Richardson, of Massachusetts, March 17, 1873. Benjamin H. Bristow, of Kentucky, June 2, 1874; entered upon duties June 4, 1874. Charles F. Conant, of New Hampshire (Assistant Secretary), ad interim, June 21, 1876, to June 30, 1876. Lot M. Morrill, of Maine, June 21, 1876; entered upon duties July 7, 1876. SECRETARY OF WAR—William W. Belknap, of Iowa, continued from preceding administration. William W. Belknap, of Iowa, recommissioned March 17, 1873. George M. Robeson, of New Jersey (Secretary of the Navy), ad interim, March 2, 1876. Alphonso Taft, of Ohio, March 8, 1876; entered upon duties March 11, 1876. James D. Cameron, of Pennsylvania, May 22, 1876; entered upon duties June 1, 1876. ATTORNEY GENERAL—George H. Williams, of Oregon, continued from preceding administration. George H. Williams, of Oregon, recommissioned March 17, 1873. Edwards Pierrepont, of New York, April 26, 1875, to take effect May 15, 1875. Alphonso Taft, of Ohio, May 22, 1876; entered upon duties June 1, 1876. POSTMASTER GENERAL—John A. J. Creswell, of Maryland, continued from preceding administration. John A. J. Creswell, of Maryland, recommissioned March 17, 1873. James W. Marshall, of Virginia, July 3, 1874; entered upon duties July 7, 1874. Marshall Jewell, of Connecticut, August 24, 1874; entered upon duties September 1, 1874. James N. Tyner, of Indiana, July 12, 1876. SECRETARY OF THE NAVY—George M. Robeson, of New Jersey, continued from preceding administration. George M. Robeson, of New Jersey, recommissioned March 17, 1873. SECRETARY OF THE INTERIOR—Columbus Delano, of Ohio, continued from preceding administration. Columbus Delano, of Ohio, recommissioned March 17, 1873. Benjamin R. Cowen, of Ohio (Assistant Secretary), ad interim, October 1, 1875. Zachariah Chandler, of Michigan, October 19, 1875.

43d Congress
1st Session: Dec. 1, 1873–June 23, 1874; 2d Session: Dec. 7, 1874–Mar. 3, 1875; Special Session of the Senate: Mar. 4, 1873–Mar. 26, 1873.

President pro tempore of the Senate: Mathew H. Carpenter, of Wisconsin (elected Mar. 12, 1873; Mar. 26, 1873; Dec. 11, 1873; Dec. 23, 1874); Henry B. Anthony, of Rhode Island (elected Jan. 25, 1875; Feb. 15, 1875). Speaker of the House: James G. Blaine (reelected Dec. 1, 1873).

Senate: 49 Republican; 19 Democratic; 5 other
House: 194 Republican; 92 Democratic; 14 other

44th Congress
1st Session: Dec. 6, 1875–Aug. 15, 1876; 2d Session: Dec. 4, 1876–Mar. 3, 1877; Special Session of the Senate: Mar. 5, 1875–Mar. 24, 1875.

President pro tempore of the Senate: Thomas W. Ferry, of Michigan (elected Mar. 9, 1875; Mar. 19, 1875; Dec. 20, 1875). Speaker of the House: Michael C. Kerr, of Indiana (elected Dec. 6, 1875); Samuel J. Randall, of Pennsylvania (elected Dec. 4, 1876).

Senate: 45 Republican; 29 Democratic; 2 other
House: 169 Democratic; 109 Republican; 14 other

Administration of RUTHERFORD B. HAYES
MARCH 4, 1877, TO MARCH 3, 1881

PRESIDENT—Rutherford B. Hayes, of Ohio (Republican) (oath administered March 5, 1877). VICE-PRESIDENT—William A. Wheeler, of New York. SECRETARY OF STATE—Hamilton Fish, of

New York, continued from preceding administration. William M. Evarts, of New York, March 12, 1877. SECRETARY OF THE TREASURY—Lot M. Morrill, of Maine, continued from preceding administration. John Sherman, of Ohio, March 8, 1877; entered upon duties March 10, 1877. SECRETARY OF WAR—James D. Cameron, of Pennsylvania, continued from preceding administration. George W. McCrary, of Iowa, March 12, 1877. Alexander Ramsey, of Minnesota, December 10, 1879; entered upon duties December 12, 1879. ATTORNEY GENERAL—Alphonso Taft, of Ohio, continued from preceding administration. Charles Devens, of Massachusetts, March 12, 1877. POSTMASTER GENERAL— James N. Tyner, of Indiana, continued from preceding administration. David M. Key, of Tennessee, March 12, 1877; resigned June 1, 1880; served to August 24, 1880. Horace Maynard, of Tennessee, June 2, 1880; entered upon duties August 25, 1880. SECRETARY OF THE NAVY—George M. Robeson, of New Jersey, continued from preceding administration. Richard W. Thompson, of Indiana, March 12, 1877. Alexander Ramsey, of Minnesota (Secretary of War), ad interim, December 20, 1880. Nathan Goff, Jr., of West Virginia, January 6, 1881. SECRETARY OF THE INTERIOR—Zachariah Chandler, of Michigan, continued from preceding administration. Carl Schurz, of Missouri, March 12, 1877.

45th Congress

1st Session: Oct. 15, 1877–Dec. 3, 1877; 2d Session: Dec. 3, 1877–June 20, 1878; 3d Session: Dec. 2, 1878–Mar. 3, 1879; Special Session of the Senate: Mar. 5, 1877–Mar. 17, 1877.

President pro tempore of the Senate: Thomas W. Ferry of Michigan (elected Mar. 5, 1877; Feb. 26, 1878; Apr. 17, 1878; Mar. 3, 1879). Speaker of the House: Samuel J. Randall, of Pennsylvania (reelected Oct. 15, 1877).

Senate: 39 Republican; 36 Democratic; 1 other
House: 153 Democratic; 140 Republican

46th Congress

1st Session: Mar. 18, 1879–July 1, 1879; 2d Session: Dec. 1, 1879–June 16, 1880; 3d Session: Dec. 6, 1880–Mar. 3, 1881.

President pro tempore of the Senate: Allen G. Thurman, of Ohio (elected Apr. 15, 1879; Apr. 7, 1880, May 6, 1880). Speaker of the House: Samuel J. Randall, of Pennsylvania (reelected Mar. 18, 1879).

Senate: 42 Democratic; 33 Republican; 1 other
House: 149 Democratic; 130 Republican; 14 other

Administration of JAMES A. GARFIELD
MARCH 4, 1881, TO SEPTEMBER 19, 1881

PRESIDENT—James A. Garfield, of Ohio (Republican) (died September 19, 1881). VICE-PRESIDENT—Chester A. Arthur, of New York. SECRETARY OF STATE—William M. Evarts, of New York, continued from preceding administration. James G. Blaine, of Maine, March 5, 1881; entered upon duties March 7, 1881. SECRETARY OF THE TREASURY—Henry F. French, of Massachusetts (Assistant Secretary), ad interim, March 4, 1881. William Windom, of Minnesota, March 5, 1881; entered upon duties March 8, 1881. SECRETARY OF WAR—Alexander Ramsey, of Minnesota, continued from preceding administration. Robert T. Lincoln, of Illinois, March 5, 1881; entered upon duties March 11, 1881. ATTORNEY GENERAL—Charles Devens, of Massachusetts, continued from preceding administration. Wayne MacVeagh, of Pennsylvania, March 5, 1881; entered upon duties March 7, 1881. POSTMASTER GENERAL—Horace Maynard, of Tennessee, continued from preceding administration. Thomas L. James, of New York, March 5, 1881; entered upon duties March 8, 1881. SECRETARY OF THE NAVY—Nathan Goff, Jr., of West Virginia, continued from preceding administration. William H. Hunt, of Louisiana, March 5, 1881; entered upon duties March 7, 1881. SECRETARY OF THE INTERIOR—Carl Schurz, of Missouri, continued from preceding administration. Samuel J. Kirkwood, of Iowa, March 5, 1881; entered upon duties March 8, 1881.

Administration of CHESTER A. ARTHUR
SEPTEMBER 20, 1881, TO MARCH 3, 1885

PRESIDENT—Chester A. Arthur, of New York. SECRETARY OF STATE—James G. Blaine, of Maine, continued from preceding administration. Frederick T. Frelinghuysen, of New Jersey, December 12, 1881; entered upon duties December 19, 1881. SECRETARY OF THE TREASURY—William Windom, of Minnesota, continued from preceding administration. Charles J. Folger, of New York, October 27, 1881; entered upon duties November 14, 1881 (died September 4, 1884). Charles E. Coon, of New York (Assistant Secretary), ad interim, September 4, 1884. Henry F. French, of Massachusetts (Assistant Secretary), ad interim, September 8, 1884. Charles E. Coon, of New York (Assistant Secretary), ad interim, September 15, 1884. Walter Q. Gresham, of Indiana, September 24, 1884. Henry F. French, of Massachusetts (Assistant Secretary), ad interim, October 29, 1884. Hugh McCulloch, of Indiana, October 28, 1884; entered upon duties

October 31, 1884. SECRETARY OF WAR—Robert T. Lincoln, of Illinois, continued from preceding administration. ATTORNEY GENERAL—Wayne MacVeagh, of Pennsylvania, continued from preceding administration. Samuel F. Phillips, of North Carolina (Solicitor General), ad interim, November 14, 1881. Benjamin H. Brewster, of Pennsylvania, December 19, 1881; entered upon duties January 3, 1882. POSTMASTER GENERAL—Thomas L. James, of New York, continued from preceding administration. Thomas L. James, of New York, recommissioned October 27, 1881. Timothy O. Howe, of Wisconsin, December 20, 1881; entered upon duties January 5, 1882 (died March 25, 1883). Frank Hatton, of Iowa (First Assistant Postmaster General), ad interim, March 26, 1883. Walter Q. Gresham, of Indiana, April 3, 1883; entered upon duties April 11, 1883. Frank Hatton, of Iowa (First Assistant Postmaster General), ad interim, September 25, 1884. Frank Hatton, of Iowa, October 14, 1884. SECRETARY OF THE NAVY—William H. Hunt, of Louisiana, continued from preceding administration. William E. Chandler, of New Hampshire, April 12, 1882; entered upon duties April 17, 1882. SECRETARY OF THE INTERIOR—Samuel J. Kirkwood, of Iowa, continued from preceding administration. Henry M. Teller, of Colorado, April 6, 1882; entered upon duties April 17, 1882.

47th Congress

1st Session: Dec. 5, 1881–Aug. 9, 1882; 2d Session: Dec. 4, 1882–Mar. 3, 1883; Special Sessions of the Senate: Mar. 4, 1881–May 20, 1881; Oct. 10, 1881–Oct. 29, 1881.

President pro tempore of the Senate: Thomas F. Bayard, of Delaware (elected Oct. 10, 1881); David Davis, of Illinois (elected Oct. 13, 1881); George F. Edmunds, of Vermont (elected Mar. 3, 1883). Speaker of the House: J. Warren Keifer, of Ohio (elected Dec. 5, 1881).

Senate: 37 Republican; 37 Democratic; 1 other
House: 147 Republican; 135 Democratic; 11 other

48th Congress

1st Session: Dec. 3, 1883–July 7, 1884; 2d Session: Dec. 1, 1884–Mar. 3, 1885.

President pro tempore of the Senate: George F. Edmunds, of Vermont (reelected Jan. 14, 1884). Speaker of the House: John G. Carlisle, of Kentucky (elected Dec. 3, 1883).

Senate: 38 Republican; 36 Democratic; 2 other
House: 197 Democratic; 118 Republican; 10 other

First Administration of GROVER CLEVELAND
MARCH 4, 1885, TO MARCH 3, 1889

PRESIDENT—Grover Cleveland, of New York (Democratic). VICE-PRESIDENT—Thomas A. Hendricks, of Indiana (died November 25, 1885). SECRETARY OF STATE—Frederick T. Frelinghuysen, of New Jersey, continued from preceding administration. Thomas F. Bayard, of Delaware, March 6, 1885. SECRETARY OF THE TREASURY—Hugh McCulloch, of Indiana, continued from preceding administration. Daniel Manning, of New York, March 6, 1885; entered upon duties March 8, 1885. Charles S. Fairchild, of New York, April 1, 1887. SECRETARY OF WAR—Robert T. Lincoln, of Illinois, continued from preceding administration. William C. Endicott, of Massachusetts, March 6, 1885. ATTORNEY GENERAL—Benjamin H. Brewster, of Pennsylvania, continued from preceding administration. Augustus H. Garland, of Arkansas, March 6, 1885; entered upon duties March 9, 1885. POSTMASTER GENERAL—Frank Hatton, of Iowa, continued from preceding administration. William F. Vilas, of Wisconsin, March 6, 1885. Don M. Dickinson, of Michigan, January 16, 1888. SECRETARY OF THE NAVY—William E. Chandler, of New Hampshire, continued from preceding administration. William C. Whitney, of New York, March 6, 1885. SECRETARY OF THE INTERIOR—Merritt L. Joslyn, of Illinois (Assistant Secretary), ad interim, March 4, 1885. Lucius Q. C. Lamar, of Mississippi, March 6, 1885. Henry L. Muldrow, of Mississippi (First Assistant Secretary), ad interim, January 11, 1888. William F. Vilas, of Wisconsin, January 16, 1888. SECRETARY OF AGRICULTURE— Norman J. Colman, of Missouri, February 13, 1889.

49th Congress

1st Session: Dec. 7, 1885–Aug. 5, 1886; 2d Session: Dec. 6, 1886–Mar 3, 1887; Special Session of the Senate: Mar. 4, 1885–Apr. 2, 1885.

President pro tempore of the Senate: John Sherman, of Ohio (elected Dec. 7, 1885); John J. Ingalls, of Kansas (elected Feb. 25, 1887). Speaker of the House: John G. Carlisle, of Kentucky (reelected Dec. 7, 1885).

Senate: 43 Republican; 34 Democratic
House: 183 Democratic; 140 Republican; 2 other

50th Congress

1st Session: Dec. 5, 1887–Oct. 20, 1888; 2d Session: Dec. 3, 1888–Mar. 3, 1889.

President pro tempore of the Senate: John J. Ingalls, of Kansas (continued from the preceding Congress). Speaker of the House: John G. Carlisle, of Kentucky (reelected Dec. 5, 1887).

Senate: 39 Republican; 37 Democratic
House: 169 Democratic; 152 Republican; 4 other

Administration of BENJAMIN HARRISON
MARCH 4, 1889, TO MARCH 3, 1893

PRESIDENT—Benjamin Harrison, of Indiana (Republican). VICE-PRESIDENT—Levi P. Morton, of New York. SECRETARY OF STATE—Thomas F. Bayard, of Delaware, continued from preceding administration. James G. Blaine, of Maine, March 5, 1889; entered upon duties March 7, 1889. William F. Wharton, of Massachusetts (Assistant Secretary), ad interim, June 4, 1892. John W. Foster, of Indiana, June 29, 1892. William F. Wharton, of Massachusetts (Assistant Secretary), ad interim, February 23, 1893. SECRETARY OF THE TREASURY—Charles S. Fairchild, of New York, continued from preceding administration. William Windom, of Minnesota, March 5, 1889; entered upon duties March 7, 1889 (died January 29, 1891). Allured B. Nettleton, of Minnesota (Assistant Secretary), ad interim, January 30, 1891. Charles Foster, of Ohio, February 24, 1891. SECRETARY OF WAR—William C. Endicott, of Massachusetts, continued from preceding administration. Redfield Proctor, of Vermont, March 5, 1889. Lewis A. Grant, of Minnesota (Assistant Secretary), ad interim, December 6, 1891. Stephen B. Elkins, of West Virginia, December 22, 1891; entered upon duties December 24, 1891. ATTORNEY GENERAL—Augustus H. Garland, of Arkansas, continued from preceding administration. William H. H. Miller, of Indiana, March 5, 1889. POSTMASTER GENERAL—Don M. Dickinson, of Michigan, continued from preceding administration. John Wanamaker, of Pennsylvania, March 5, 1889. SECRETARY OF THE NAVY—William C. Whitney, of New York, continued from preceding administration. Benjamin F. Tracy, of New York, March 5, 1889. SECRETARY OF THE INTERIOR—William F. Vilas, of Wisconsin, continued from preceding administration. John W. Noble, of Missouri, March 5, 1889; entered upon duties March 7, 1889. SECRETARY OF AGRICULTURE—Norman J. Colman, of Missouri, continued from preceding administration, Jeremiah M. Rusk, of Wisconsin, March 5, 1889; entered upon duties March 7, 1889.

51st Congress

1st Session: Dec. 2, 1889–Oct. 1, 1890; 2d Session: Dec. 1, 1890–Mar. 2, 1891; Special Session of the Senate: Mar. 4, 1889–Apr. 2, 1889.

President pro tempore of the Senate: John J. Ingalls, of Kansas (reelected Mar. 7, 1889; Apr. 2, 1889; Feb. 28, 1890; Apr. 3, 1890); Charles F. Manderson, of Nebraska (elected Mar. 2, 1891). Speaker of the House: Thomas B. Reed, of Maine (elected Dec. 2, 1889).

Senate: 39 Republican; 37 Democratic
House: 166 Republican; 159 Democratic

52d Congress

1st Session: Dec. 7, 1891–Aug. 5, 1892; 2d Session: Dec. 5, 1892–Mar. 3, 1893.

President pro tempore of the Senate: Charles F. Manderson, of Nebraska (continued from preceding Congress). Speaker of the House: Charles F. Crisp, of Georgia (elected Dec. 8, 1891).

Senate: 47 Republican; 39 Democratic; 2 other
House: 235 Democratic; 88 Republican; 9 other

Second Administration of GROVER CLEVELAND
March 4, 1893, TO MARCH 3, 1897

PRESIDENT—Grover Cleveland, of New York (Democratic). VICE-PRESIDENT—Adlai E. Stevenson, of Illinois. SECRETARY OF STATE—William F. Wharton, of Massachusetts (Assistant Secretary), ad interim, continued from preceding administration. Walter Q. Gresham, of Illinois, March 6, 1893 (died May 28, 1895). Edwin F. Uhl, of Michigan (Assistant Secretary), ad interim, May 28, 1895. Alvey A. Adee, of the District of Columbia (Second Assistant Secretary), ad interim, May 31, 1895. Edwin F. Uhl, of Michigan (Assistant Secretary), ad interim, June 1, 1895. Richard Olney, of Massachusetts, June 8, 1895; entered upon duties June 10, 1895. SECRETARY OF THE TREASURY—Charles Foster, of Ohio, continued from preceding administration. John G. Carlisle, of Kentucky, March 6, 1893. SECRETARY OF WAR—Stephen B. Elkins, of West Virginia, continued from preceding administration. Daniel S. Lamont, of New York, March 6, 1893. ATTORNEY GENERAL—William H. H. Miller, of Indiana, continued from preceding administration. Richard Olney, of Massachusetts, March 6, 1893. Judson Harmon, of Ohio, June 8, 1895; entered upon duties June 11, 1895. POSTMASTER GENERAL—John Wanamaker, of Pennsylvania, continued from preceding administration. Wilson S. Bissell, of New York, March 6, 1893. William L. Wilson, of West Virginia, March 1, 1895; entered upon duties April 4, 1895. SECRETARY OF THE NAVY—Benjamin F. Tracy, of New York, continued from preceding administration. Hilary A. Herbert, of Alabama, March 6, 1893. SECRETARY OF THE INTERIOR—John W. Noble, of Missouri, continued from preceding administration. Hoke Smith, of Georgia, March 6, 1893. John M. Reynolds, of Pennsylvania (Assistant Secretary), ad interim, September 1, 1896. David R. Francis, of Missouri, September 1, 1896; entered upon duties September 4, 1896. SECRETARY OF AGRICULTURE—

Jeremiah M. Rusk, of Wisconsin, continued from preceding administration. Julius Sterling Morton, of Nebraska, March 6, 1893.

53d Congress

1st Session: Aug. 7, 1893–Nov. 3, 1893; 2d Session: Dec. 4, 1893–Aug. 28, 1894; 3d Session: Dec. 3, 1894–Mar. 3, 1895; Special Session of the Senate: Mar. 4, 1893–Apr. 15, 1893.

President pro tempore of the Senate: Charles F. Manderson, of Nebraska (continued from preceding Congress); Isham G. Harris, of Tennessee (elected Mar. 22, 1893; Jan. 10, 1895); Matt W. Ransom, of North Carolina (elected Jan. 7, 1895). Speaker of the House: Charles F. Crisp, of Georgia (reelected Aug. 7, 1893).

Senate: 44 Democratic; 38 Republican; 3 other
House: 218 Democratic; 127 Republican; 11 other

54th Congress

1st Session: Dec. 2, 1895–June 11, 1896; 2d Session: Dec. 7, 1896–Mar. 3, 1897.

President pro tempore of the Senate: William P. Frye, of Maine (elected Feb. 7, 1896). Speaker of the House: Thomas B. Reed, of Maine (elected Dec. 2, 1895).

Senate: 43 Republican; 39 Democratic; 6 other
House: 244 Republican; 105 Democratic; 7 other

First Administration of WILLIAM McKINLEY
MARCH 4, 1897, TO MARCH 3, 1901

PRESIDENT—William McKinley, of Ohio (Republican). VICE-PRESIDENT—Garret A. Hobart, of New Jersey (died November 21, 1899). SECRETARY OF STATE—Richard Olney, of Massachusetts, continued from preceding administration. John Sherman, of Ohio, March 5, 1897. William R. Day, of Ohio, April 26, 1898; entered upon duties April 28, 1898. Alvey A. Adee (Second Assistant Secretary), ad interim, September 17, 1898. John Hay, of the District of Columbia, September 20, 1898; entered upon duties September 30, 1898. SECRETARY OF THE TREASURY—John G. Carlisle, of Kentucky, continued from preceding administration. Lyman J. Gage, of Illinois, March 5, 1897. SECRETARY OF WAR—Daniel S. Lamont, of New York, continued from preceding administration. Russell A. Alger, of Michigan, March 5, 1897. Elihu Root, of New York, August 1, 1899. ATTORNEY GENERAL—Judson Harmon, of Ohio, continued from preceding administration. Joseph McKenna, of California, March 5, 1897; entered upon duties March 7, 1897. John K. Richards, of Ohio (Solicitor General), ad interim, January 26, 1898. John W. Griggs, of New Jersey, January 25, 1898; entered upon duties February 1, 1898. POSTMASTER GENERAL—William L. Wilson, of West Virginia, continued from preceding administration. James A. Gary, of Maryland, March 5, 1897. Charles Emory Smith, of Pennsylvania, April 21, 1898. SECRETARY OF THE NAVY—Hilary A. Herbert, of Alabama, continued from preceding administration. John D. Long, of Massachusetts, March 5, 1897. SECRETARY OF THE INTERIOR—David R. Francis, of Missouri, continued from preceding administration. Cornelius N. Bliss, of New York, March 5, 1897. Ethan A. Hitchcock, of Missouri, December 21, 1898; entered upon duties February 20, 1899. SECRETARY OF AGRICULTURE—Julius Sterling Morton, of Nebraska, continued from preceding administration. James Wilson, of Iowa, March 5, 1897.

55th Congress

1st Session: Mar. 15, 1897–July 24, 1897; 2d Session: Dec. 6, 1897–July 8, 1898; 3d Session: Dec. 5, 1898–Mar. 3, 1899; Special Session of the Senate: Mar. 4, 1897–Mar. 10, 1897.

President pro tempore of the Senate: William P. Frye, of Maine (continued from preceding Congress). Speaker of the House: Thomas B. Reed, of Maine (reelected Mar. 15, 1897).

Senate: 47 Republican; 34 Democratic; 7 other
House: 204 Republican; 113 Democratic; 40 other

56th Congress

1st Session: Dec. 4, 1899–June 7, 1900; 2d Session: Dec. 3, 1900–Mar. 3, 1901.

President pro tempore of the Senate: William P. Frye, of Maine (continued from preceding Congress). Speaker of the House: David B. Henderson, of Iowa (elected Dec. 4, 1899).

Senate: 53 Republican; 26 Democratic; 8 other
House: 185 Republican; 163 Democratic; 9 other

Second Administration of WILLIAM McKINLEY
MARCH 4, 1901, TO SEPTEMBER 14, 1901

PRESIDENT—William McKinley, of Ohio (Republican) (died September 14, 1901). VICE-PRESIDENT—Theodore Roosevelt, of New York. SECRETARY OF STATE—John Hay, of the District of Columbia, continued from preceding administration. John Hay, of the District of Columbia, recommissioned March 5, 1901. SECRETARY OF THE TREASURY—Lyman J. Gage, of Illinois, continued from preceding administration. Lyman J. Gage, of

Illinois, recommissioned March 5, 1901. SECRETARY OF WAR—Elihu Root, of New York, continued from preceding administration. Elihu Root, of New York, recommissioned March 5, 1901. ATTORNEY GENERAL—John W. Griggs, of New Jersey, continued from preceding administration. John W. Griggs, of New Jersey, recommissioned March 5, 1901. John K. Richards, of Ohio (Solicitor General), ad interim, April 1, 1901. Philander C. Knox, of Pennsylvania, April 5, 1901; entered upon duties April 10, 1901. POSTMASTER GENERAL—Charles Emory Smith, of Pennsylvania, continued from preceding administration. Charles Emory Smith, of Pennsylvania, recommissioned March 5, 1901. SECRETARY OF THE NAVY—John D. Long, of Massachusetts, continued from preceding administration. John D. Long, of Massachusetts, recommissioned March 5, 1901. SECRETARY OF THE INTERIOR—Ethan A. Hitchcock, of Missouri, continued from preceding administration. Ethan A. Hitchcock, of Missouri, recommissioned March 5, 1901. SECRETARY OF AGRICULTURE—James Wilson, of Iowa, continued from preceding administration. James Wilson, of Iowa, recommissioned March 5, 1901.

First Administration of THEODORE ROOSEVELT
SEPTEMBER 14, 1901, TO MARCH 3, 1905

PRESIDENT—Theodore Roosevelt, of New York (Republican). SECRETARY OF STATE—John Hay, of the District of Columbia, continued from preceding administration. SECRETARY OF THE TREASURY—Lyman J. Gage, of Illinois, continued from preceding administration. Leslie M. Shaw, of Iowa, January 9, 1902; entered upon duties February 1, 1902. SECRETARY OF WAR—Elihu Root, of New York, continued from preceding administration. William H. Taft, of Ohio, January 11, 1904, to take effect February 1, 1904. ATTORNEY GENERAL—Philander C. Knox, of Pennsylvania, continued from preceding administration. Philander C. Knox, of Pennsylvania, recommissioned December 16, 1901. William H. Moody, of Massachusetts, July 1, 1904. POSTMASTER GENERAL—Charles Emory Smith, of Pennsylvania, continued from preceding administration. Henry C. Payne, of Wisconsin, January 9, 1902. Robert J. Wynne, of Pennsylvania, October 10, 1904. SECRETARY OF THE NAVY—John D. Long, of Massachusetts, continued from preceding administration. William H. Moody, of Massachusetts, April 29, 1902; entered upon duties May 1, 1902. Paul Morton, of Illinois, July 1, 1904. SECRETARY OF THE INTERIOR—Ethan A. Hitchcock, of Missouri, continued from preceding administration. SECRETARY OF AGRICULTURE—James Wilson, of Iowa, continued from preceding administration. SECRETARY OF COMMERCE AND LABOR—George B. Cortelyou, of New York, February 16, 1903. Victor H. Metcalf, of California, July 1, 1904.

57th Congress

1st Session: Dec. 2, 1901–July 1, 1902; 2d Session: Dec. 1, 1902–Mar. 3, 1903; Special Session of the Senate: Mar. 4, 1901–Mar. 9, 1901.

President pro tempore of the Senate: William P. Frye, of Maine (reelected Mar. 7, 1901). Speaker of the House: David B. Henderson, of Iowa (reelected Dec. 2, 1901).

Senate: 55 Republican; 35 Democratic; 4 other
House: 197 Republican; 151 Democratic; 9 other

58th Congress

1st Session: Nov. 9, 1903–Dec. 7, 1903; 2d Session: Dec. 7, 1903–Apr. 28, 1904; 3d Session: Dec. 5, 1904–Mar. 3, 1905; Special Session of the Senate: Mar. 5, 1903–Mar. 19, 1903.

President pro tempore of the Senate: William P. Frye, of Maine (continued from preceding Congress). Speaker of the House: Joseph G. Cannon, of Illinois (elected Nov. 9, 1903).

Senate: 57 Republican; 33 Democratic
House: 208 Republican; 178 Democratic

Second Administration of THEODORE ROOSEVELT
MARCH 4, 1905, TO MARCH 3, 1909

PRESIDENT—Theodore Roosevelt, of New York (Republican). VICE-PRESIDENT—Charles Warren Fairbanks, of Indiana. SECRETARY OF STATE—John Hay, of the District of Columbia, continued from preceding administration. John Hay, of the District of Columbia, recommissioned March 6, 1905 (died July 1, 1905). Francis B. Loomis, of Ohio (Assistant Secretary), ad interim, July 1, 1905, to July 18, 1905. Elihu Root, of New York, July 7, 1905; entered upon duties July 19, 1905. Robert Bacon, of New York, January 27, 1909. SECRETARY OF THE TREASURY—Leslie M. Shaw, of Iowa, continued from preceding administration. Leslie M. Shaw, of Iowa, recommissioned March 6, 1905. George B. Cortelyou, of New York, January 15, 1907, to take effect March 4, 1907. SECRETARY OF WAR—William H. Taft, of Ohio, continued from preceding administration. William H. Taft, of Ohio, recommissioned March 6, 1905. Luke E. Wright, of Tennessee, June 29, 1908; entered upon duties July 1, 1908. ATTORNEY GENERAL—William H. Moody, of Massachusetts, continued from preceding administration. William H. Moody, of Massachusetts, recommissioned March 6, 1905. Charles J. Bonaparte, of Maryland, December 12, 1906; entered upon duties December 17, 1906. POSTMASTER GENERAL—Robert J.

Wynne, of Pennsylvania, continued from preceding administration. George B. Cortelyou, of New York, March 6, 1905. George von L. Meyer, of Massachusetts, January 15, 1907, to take effect March 4, 1907. SECRETARY OF THE NAVY—Paul Morton, of Illinois, continued from preceding administration. Paul Morton, of Illinois, recommissioned March 6, 1905. Charles J. Bonaparte, of Maryland, July 1, 1905. Victor H. Metcalf, of California, December 12, 1906; entered upon duties December 17, 1906. Truman H. Newberry, of Michigan, December 1, 1908. SECRETARY OF THE INTERIOR—Ethan A. Hitchcock, of Missouri, continued from preceding administration. Ethan A. Hitchcock, of Missouri, recommissioned March 6, 1905. James R. Garfield, of Ohio, January 15, 1907, to take effect March 4, 1907. SECRETARY OF AGRICULTURE—James Wilson, of Iowa, continued from preceding administration. James Wilson, of Iowa, recommissioned March 6, 1905. SECRETARY OF COMMERCE AND LABOR—Victor H. Metcalf, of California, continued from preceding administration. Victor H. Metcalf, of California, recommissioned March 6, 1905. Oscar S. Straus, of New York, December 12, 1906; entered upon duties December 17, 1906.

59th Congress

1st Session: Dec. 4, 1905–June 30, 1906; 2d Session: Dec. 3, 1906–Mar. 3, 1907; Special Session of the Senate: Mar. 4, 1905–Mar. 18, 1905.

President pro tempore of the Senate: William P. Frye, of Maine (continued from preceding Congress). Speaker of the House: Joseph G. Cannon, of Illinois (reelected Dec. 4, 1905).

Senate: 57 Republican; 33 Democratic
House: 250 Republican; 136 Democratic

60th Congress

1st Session: Dec. 2, 1907–May 30, 1908; 2d Session: Dec. 7, 1908–Mar. 3, 1909.

President pro tempore of the Senate: William P. Frye, of Maine (reelected Dec. 5, 1907). Speaker of the House: Joseph G. Cannon, of Illinois (reelected Dec. 2, 1907).

Senate: 61 Republican; 31 Democratic
House: 222 Republican; 164 Democratic

Administration of WILLIAM H. TAFT
March 4, 1909, TO MARCH 3, 1913

PRESIDENT—William H. Taft, of Ohio (Republican). VICE-PRESIDENT—James S. Sherman, of New York (died October 30, 1912). SECRETARY OF STATE—Robert Bacon, of New York, continued from preceding administration. Philander C. Knox, of Pennsylvania, March 5, 1909. SECRETARY OF THE TREASURY—George B. Cortelyou, of New York, continued from preceding administration. Franklin MacVeagh, of Illinois, March 5, 1909; entered upon duties March 8, 1909. SECRETARY OF WAR—Luke E. Wright, of Tennessee, continued from preceding administration. Jacob M. Dickinson, of Tennessee, March 5, 1909; entered upon duties March 12, 1909. Henry L. Stimson, of New York, May 16, 1911; entered upon duties May 22, 1911. ATTORNEY GENERAL—Charles J. Bonaparte, of Maryland, continued from preceding administration. George W. Wickersham, of New York, March 5, 1909. POSTMASTER GENERAL—George von L. Meyer, of Massachusetts, continued from preceding administration. Frank H. Hitchcock, of Massachusetts, March 5, 1909. SECRETARY OF THE NAVY—Truman H. Newberry, of Michigan, continued from preceding administration. George von L. Meyer, of Massachusetts, March 5, 1909. SECRETARY OF THE INTERIOR—James R. Garfield, of Ohio, continued from preceding administration. Richard A. Ballinger, of Washington, March 5, 1909. Walter Lowrie Fisher, of Illinois, March 7, 1911. SECRETARY OF AGRICULTURE—James Wilson, of Iowa, continued from preceding administration. James Wilson, of Iowa, recommissioned March 5, 1909. SECRETARY OF COMMERCE AND LABOR—Oscar S. Straus, of New York, continued from preceding administration. Charles Nagel, of Missouri, March 5, 1909.

61st Congress

1st Session: Mar. 15, 1909–Aug. 5, 1909; 2d Session: Dec. 6, 1909–June 25, 1910; 3d Session: Dec. 5, 1910–Mar. 3, 1911; Special Session of the Senate: Mar. 4, 1909–Mar. 6, 1909.

President pro tempore of the Senate: William P. Frye, of Maine (continued from preceding Congress). Speaker of the House: Joseph G. Cannon, of Illinois (reelected Mar. 15, 1909).

Senate: 61 Republican; 32 Democratic
House: 219 Republican; 172 Democratic

62d Congress

1st Session: Apr. 4, 1911–Aug. 22, 1911; 2d Session: Dec. 4, 1911–Aug. 26, 1912; 3d Session: Dec. 2, 1912–Mar. 3, 1913.

President pro tempore of the Senate: William P. Frye, of Maine (continued from preceding Congress). Charles Curtis, of Kansas (elected to serve Dec. 4–12, 1911). Augustus O. Bacon, of Georgia (elected to serve Jan. 15–17, 1912; Mar. 11–12, 1912; Apr. 8, 1912; May 10, 1912; May 30–June 3, 1912; June 13–July 5, 1912; Aug. 1–10, 1912; Aug. 27–Dec. 15, 1912; Jan. 5–18, 1913; Feb. 2–15, 1913). Jacob H. Gallinger, of New

Hampshire (elected to serve Feb. 12–14, 1912; April 26–27, 1912; May 7, 1912; July 6–31, 1912; Aug. 12–26, 1912; Dec. 16, 1912–Jan. 4, 1913; Jan. 19–Feb. 1, 1913; Feb. 16–Mar. 3, 1913). Henry C. Lodge, of Massachusetts (elected to serve Mar. 25–26, 1912). Frank B. Brandegee, of Connecticut (elected to serve May 25, 1912). Speaker of the House: James B. Clark, of Missouri (elected Apr. 4, 1911).

Senate: 51 Republican; 41 Democratic
House: 228 Democratic; 161 Republican; 1 other

First Administration of WOODROW WILSON
MARCH 4, 1913, TO MARCH 3, 1917

PRESIDENT—Woodrow Wilson, of New Jersey (Democratic). VICE-PRESIDENT—Thomas R. Marshall, of Indiana. SECRETARY OF STATE—Philander C. Knox, of Pennsylvania, continued from preceding administration. William Jennings Bryan, of Nebraska, March 5, 1913. Robert Lansing, of New York (counselor), ad interim, June 9, 1915. Robert Lansing, of New York, June 23, 1915. SECRETARY OF THE TREASURY—Franklin MacVeagh, of Illinois, continued from preceding administration. William Gibbs McAdoo, of New York, March 5, 1913; entered upon duties March 6, 1913. SECRETARY OF WAR—Henry L. Stimson, of New York, continued from preceding administration. Lindley M. Garrison, of New Jersey, March 5, 1913. Hugh L. Scott (United States Army), ad interim, February 12, 1916; served from February 11 to March 8, 1916. Newton D. Baker, of Ohio, March 7, 1916; entered upon duties March 9, 1916. ATTORNEY GENERAL—George W. Wickersham, of New York, continued from preceding administration. James Clark McReynolds, of Tennessee, March 5, 1913; entered upon duties March 6, 1913. Thomas Watt Gregory, of Texas, August 29, 1914; entered upon duties September 3, 1914. POSTMASTER GENERAL—Frank H. Hitchcock, of Massachusetts, continued from preceding administration. Albert Sidney Burleson, of Texas, March 5, 1913. SECRETARY OF THE NAVY—George von L. Meyer, of Massachusetts, continued from preceding administration. Josephus Daniels, of North Carolina, March 5, 1913. SECRETARY OF THE INTERIOR—Walter Lowrie Fisher, of Illinois, continued from preceding administration. Franklin Knight Lane, of California, March 5, 1913. SECRETARY OF AGRICULTURE—James Wilson, of Iowa, continued from preceding administration. David Franklin Houston, of Missouri, March 5, 1913; entered upon duties March 6, 1913. SECRETARY OF COMMERCE—Charles Nagel, of Missouri (Secretary of Commerce and Labor), continued from preceding administration. William C. Redfield, of New York, March 5, 1913. SECRETARY OF LABOR—Charles Nagel, of Missouri (Secretary of Commerce and Labor), continued from preceding administration. William Bauchop Wilson, of Pennsylvania, March 5, 1913.

63d Congress
1st Session: Apr. 7, 1913–Dec. 1, 1913; 2d Session: Dec. 1, 1913–Oct. 24, 1914; 3d Session: Dec. 7, 1914–Mar. 3, 1915; Special Session of the Senate: Mar. 4, 1913–Mar. 17, 1913.

President pro tempore of the Senate: James P. Clarke, of Arkansas (elected Mar. 13, 1913). Speaker of the House: James B. Clark, of Missouri (reelected Apr. 7, 1913).

Senate: 51 Democratic; 44 Republican; 1 other
House: 291 Democratic; 127 Republican; 17 other

64th Congress
1st Session: Dec. 6, 1915–Sept. 8, 1916; 2d Session: Dec. 4, 1916–Mar. 3, 1917.

President pro tempore of the Senate: James P. Clarke, of Arkansas (reelected Dec. 6, 1915); Willard Saulsbury, of Delaware (elected Dec. 14, 1916). Speaker of the House: James B. Clark, of Missouri (reelected Dec. 6, 1915).

Senate: 56 Democratic; 40 Republican
House: 230 Democratic; 196 Republican; 9 other

Second Administration of WOODROW WILSON
MARCH 4, 1917, TO MARCH 3, 1921

PRESIDENT—Woodrow Wilson, of New Jersey (Democratic). (Oath administered March 5, 1917.) VICE-PRESIDENT—Thomas R. Marshall, of Indiana. SECRETARY OF STATE—Robert Lansing, of New York, continued from preceding administration. Frank L. Polk, of New York (Under Secretary), ad interim, February 14, 1920, to March 13, 1920. Bainbridge Colby, of New York, March 22, 1920; entered upon duties March 23, 1920. SECRETARY OF THE TREASURY—William Gibbs McAdoo, of New York, continued from preceding administration. Carter Glass, of Virginia, December 6, 1918; entered upon duties December 16, 1918. David F. Houston, of Missouri, January 31, 1920; entered upon duties February 2, 1920. SECRETARY OF WAR—Newton D. Baker, of Ohio, continued from preceding administration. ATTORNEY GENERAL—Thomas Watt Gregory, of Texas, continued from preceding administration. A. Mitchell Palmer, of Pennsylvania, March 5, 1919. POSTMASTER GENERAL—Albert Sidney Burleson, of Texas, continued from preceding administration. Albert Sidney Burleson, of Texas, recommissioned January 24, 1918. SECRETARY OF THE NAVY—Josephus Daniels, of North Carolina, con-

tinued from preceding administration. SECRETARY OF THE INTERIOR—Franklin Knight Lane, of California, continued from preceding administration. John Barton Payne, of Illinois, February 28, 1920; entered upon duties March 13, 1920. SECRETARY OF AGRICULTURE—David Franklin Houston, of Missouri, continued from preceding administration. Edwin T. Meredith, of Iowa, January 31, 1920; entered upon duties February 2, 1920. SECRETARY OF COMMERCE—William C. Redfield, of New York, continued from preceding administration. Joshua Willis Alexander, of Missouri, December 11, 1919; entered upon duties December 16, 1919. SECRETARY OF LABOR—William Bauchop Wilson, of Pennsylvania, continued from preceding administration.

65th Congress
1st Session: Apr. 2, 1917–Oct. 6, 1917; 2d Session: Dec. 3, 1917–Nov. 21, 1918; 3d Session: Dec. 2, 1918–Mar. 3, 1919; Special Session of the Senate: Mar. 5, 1917–Mar. 16, 1917.

President pro tempore of the Senate: Willard Saulsbury, of Delaware (continued from preceding Congress). Speaker of the House: James B. Clark, of Missouri (reelected Apr. 2, 1917).

Senate: 53 Democratic; 42 Republican
House: 216 Democratic; 210 Republican; 6 other

66th Congress
1st Session: May 19, 1919–Nov. 19, 1919; 2d Session: Dec. 1, 1919–June 5, 1920; 3d Session: Dec. 6, 1920–Mar. 3, 1921.

President pro tempore of the Senate: Albert B. Cummins, of Iowa (elected May 19, 1919). Speaker of the House: Frederick H. Gillett, of Massachusetts (elected May 19, 1919).

Senate: 49 Republican; 47 Democratic
House: 240 Republican; 190 Democratic; 3 other

Administration of WARREN G. HARDING
MARCH 4, 1921, TO AUGUST 2, 1923

PRESIDENT—Warren G. Harding, of Ohio (Republican) (died August 2, 1923). VICE-PRESIDENT—Calvin Coolidge, of Massachusetts. SECRETARY OF STATE—Bainbridge Colby, of New York, continued from preceding administration. Charles Evans Hughes, of New York, March 4, 1921; entered upon duties March 5, 1921. SECRETARY OF THE TREASURY—David F. Houston, of Missouri, continued from preceding administration. Andrew W. Mellon, of Pennsylvania, March 4, 1921; entered upon duties March 5, 1921. SECRETARY OF WAR—Newton D. Baker, of Ohio, continued from preceding administration. John W. Weeks, of Massachusetts, March 5, 1921. ATTORNEY GENERAL—A. Mitchell Palmer, of Pennsylvania, continued from preceding administration. Harry M. Daugherty, of Ohio, March 5, 1921. POSTMASTER GENERAL—Albert Sidney Burleson, of Texas, continued from preceding administration. Will H. Hays, of Indiana, March 5, 1921. Hubert Work, of Colorado, March 4, 1922. Harry S. New, of Indiana, February 27, 1923; entered upon duties March 5, 1923. SECRETARY OF THE NAVY—Josephus Daniels, of North Carolina, continued from preceding administration. Edwin Denby, of Michigan, March 5, 1921. SECRETARY OF THE INTERIOR—John Barton Payne, of Illinois, continued from preceding administration. Albert B. Fall, of New Mexico, March 5, 1921. Hubert Work, of Colorado, February 27, 1923; entered upon duties March 5, 1923. SECRETARY OF AGRICULTURE—Edwin T. Meredith, of Iowa, continued from preceding administration. Henry C. Wallace, of Iowa, March 5, 1921. SECRETARY OF COMMERCE—Joshua Willis Alexander, of Missouri, continued from preceding administration. Herbert C. Hoover, of California, March 5, 1921. SECRETARY OF LABOR—William Bauchop Wilson, of Pennsylvania, continued from preceding administration. James J. Davis, of Pennsylvania, March 5, 1921.

First Administration of CALVIN COOLIDGE
AUGUST 3, 1923, TO MARCH 3, 1925

PRESIDENT—Calvin Coolidge, of Massachusetts (Republican). SECRETARY OF STATE—Charles Evans Hughes, of New York, continued from preceding administration. SECRETARY OF THE TREASURY—Andrew W. Mellon, of Pennsylvania, continued from preceding administration. SECRETARY OF WAR—John W. Weeks, of Massachusetts, continued from preceding administration. ATTORNEY GENERAL—Harry M. Daugherty, of Ohio, continued from preceding administration. Harlan F. Stone, of New York, April 7, 1924; entered upon duties April 9, 1924. POSTMASTER GENERAL—Harry S. New, of Indiana, continued from preceding administration. SECRETARY OF THE NAVY—Edwin Denby, of Michigan, continued from preceding administration. Curtis D. Wilbur, of California, March 18, 1924. SECRETARY OF THE INTERIOR—Hubert Work, of Colorado, continued from preceding administration. SECRETARY OF AGRICULTURE—Henry C. Wallace, of Iowa, continued from preceding administration (died October 25, 1924). Howard M. Gore, of West Virginia (Assistant Secretary), ad interim, October 26, 1924, to November 22, 1924. Howard M. Gore, of West Virginia, November 21, 1924; entered upon duties November 22, 1924. SECRETARY OF COMMERCE—

Herbert C. Hoover, of California, continued from preceding administration. SECRETARY OF LABOR—James J. Davis, of Pennsylvania, continued from preceding administration.

67th Congress

1st Session: Apr. 11, 1921–Nov. 23, 1921; 2d Session: Dec. 5, 1921–Sept. 22, 1922; 3d Session: Nov. 20, 1922–Dec. 4, 1922; 4th Session: Dec. 4, 1922–March 3, 1923; Special Session of the Senate: Mar. 4, 1921–Mar. 15, 1921.

President pro tempore of the Senate: Albert B. Cummins, of Iowa (reelected Mar. 7, 1921). Speaker of the House: Frederick H. Gillett, of Massachusetts (reelected Apr. 11, 1921).

Senate: 59 Republican; 37 Democratic

House: 303 Republican; 131 Democratic; 1 other

68th Congress

1st Session: Dec. 3, 1923–June 7, 1924; 2d Session: Dec. 1, 1924–Mar. 3, 1925.

President pro tempore of the Senate: Albert B. Cummins, of Iowa (continued from preceding Congress). Speaker of the House: Frederick H. Gillett, of Massachusetts (reelected Dec. 3, 1923).

Senate: 51 Republican; 43 Democratic; 2 other

House: 225 Republican; 205 Democratic; 5 other

Second Administration of CALVIN COOLIDGE

MARCH 4, 1925, TO MARCH 3, 1929

PRESIDENT—Calvin Coolidge, of Massachusetts (Republican). VICE-PRESIDENT—Charles G. Dawes, of Illinois. SECRETARY OF STATE—Charles Evans Hughes, of New York, continued from preceding administration. Frank B. Kellogg, of Minnesota, February 16, 1925; entered upon duties March 5, 1925. SECRETARY OF THE TREASURY—Andrew W. Mellon, of Pennsylvania, continued from preceding administration. SECRETARY OF WAR—John W. Weeks, of Massachusetts, continued from preceding administration. Dwight F. Davis, of Missouri, October 13, 1925; entered upon duties October 14, 1925. ATTORNEY GENERAL—James M. Beck, of Pennsylvania (Solicitor General), ad interim, March 4, 1925, to March 16, 1925. John G. Sargent, of Vermont, March 17, 1925; entered upon duties March 18, 1925. POSTMASTER GENERAL—Harry S. New, of Indiana, continued from preceding administration. Harry S. New, of Indiana, recommissioned March 5, 1925. SECRETARY OF THE NAVY—Curtis D. Wilbur, of California, continued from preceding administration. SECRETARY OF THE INTERIOR—Hubert Work, of Colorado, continued from preceding administration. Roy O. West, of Illinois, ad interim, July 25, 1928, to January 21, 1929. Roy O. West, January 21, 1929. SECRETARY OF AGRICULTURE—Howard M. Gore, of West Virginia, continued from preceding administration. William M. Jardine, of Kansas, February 18, 1925; entered upon duties March 5, 1925. SECRETARY OF COMMERCE—Herbert C. Hoover, of California, continued from preceding administration. William F. Whiting, of Massachusetts, ad interim, August 21, 1928, to December 11, 1928. William F. Whiting, December 11, 1928. SECRETARY OF LABOR—James J. Davis, of Pennsylvania, continued from preceding administration.

69th Congress

1st Session: Dec. 7, 1925–July 3, 1926; Nov. 10, 1926; 2d Session: Dec. 6, 1926–Mar. 3, 1927; Special Session of the Senate: Mar. 4, 1925–Mar. 18, 1925.

President pro tempore of the Senate: Albert B. Cummins, of Iowa (continued from preceding Congress); George H. Moses, of New Hampshire (elected Mar. 6, 1925). Speaker of the House: Nicholas Longworth, of Ohio (elected Dec. 7, 1925).

Senate: 56 Republican; 39 Democratic; 1 other

House: 247 Republican; 183 Democratic; 4 other

70th Congress

1st Session: Dec. 5, 1927–May 29, 1928; 2d Session: Dec. 3, 1928–Mar. 3, 1929.

President pro tempore of the Senate: George H. Moses, of New Hampshire (reelected Dec. 15, 1927). Speaker of the House: Nicholas Longworth, of Ohio (reelected Dec. 15, 1927).

Senate: 49 Republican; 46 Democratic; 1 other

House: 237 Republican; 195 Democratic; 3 other

Administration of HERBERT C. HOOVER

MARCH 4, 1929, TO MARCH 3, 1933

PRESIDENT—Herbert C. Hoover, of California (Republican). VICE-PRESIDENT—Charles Curtis, of Kansas. SECRETARY OF STATE—Frank B. Kellogg, of Minnesota, continued from preceding administration. Henry L. Stimson, of New York, March 4, 1929; entered upon duties March 29, 1929. SECRETARY OF THE TREASURY—Andrew W. Mellon, of Pennsylvania, continued from preceding administration. Ogden L. Mills, of New York, February 10, 1932; entered upon duties February 13, 1932. SECRETARY OF WAR—Dwight F. Davis, of Missouri, continued from preceding administration. James W. Good, of Illinois, March 5, 1929; entered upon duties March 6, 1929. Patrick J. Hurley, of Oklahoma, December 9, 1929. ATTORNEY GENERAL—John G. Sar-

gent, of Vermont, continued from preceding administration. James DeWitt Mitchell, of Minnesota, March 5, 1929; entered upon duties March 6, 1929. POSTMASTER GENERAL—Harry S. New, of Indiana, continued from preceding administration. Walter F. Brown, of Ohio, March 5, 1929; entered upon duties March 6, 1929. SECRETARY OF THE NAVY—Curtis D. Wilbur, of California, continued from preceding administration. Charles F. Adams, of Massachusetts, March 5, 1929. SECRETARY OF THE INTERIOR—Roy O. West, of Illinois, continued from preceding administration. Ray L. Wilbur, of California, March 5, 1929. SECRETARY OF AGRICULTURE—William M. Jardine, of Kansas, continued from preceding administration. Arthur M. Hyde, of Missouri, March 5, 1929; entered upon duties March 6, 1929. SECRETARY OF COMMERCE—William F. Whiting, of Massachusetts, continued from preceding administration. Robert P. Lamont, of Illinois, March 5, 1929. Roy D. Chapin, of Michigan, ad interim, August 8, 1932, to December 14, 1932. Roy D. Chapin, of Michigan, December 14, 1932. SECRETARY OF LABOR—James J. Davis, of Pennsylvania, continued from preceding administration. William N. Doak, of Virginia, December 8, 1930; entered upon duties December 9, 1930.

71st Congress

1st Session: Apr. 15, 1929–Nov. 22, 1929; 2d Session: Dec. 2, 1929–July 3, 1930; 3d Session: Dec. 1, 1930–Mar. 3, 1931; Special Sessions of the Senate: Mar. 4, 1929–Mar. 5, 1929; July 7, 1930–July 21, 1930.

President pro tempore of the Senate: George H. Moses, of New Hampshire (continued from preceding Congress). Speaker of the House: Nicholas Longworth, of Ohio (reelected Apr. 15, 1929).

Senate: 56 Republican; 39 Democratic; 1 other

House: 267 Republican; 167 Democratic; 1 other

72d Congress

1st Session: Dec. 7, 1931–July 16, 1932; 2d Session: Dec. 15, 1932–Mar. 3, 1933.

President pro tempore of the Senate: George H. Moses, of New Hampshire (continued from preceding Congress). Speaker of the House: John N. Garner, of Texas (elected Dec. 7, 1931).

Senate: 48 Republican; 47 Democratic; 1 other

House: 220 Democratic; 214 Republican; 1 other

First Administration of FRANKLIN DELANO ROOSEVELT

MARCH 4, 1933, TO JANUARY 20, 1937

PRESIDENT—Franklin Delano Roosevelt, of New York (Democratic). VICE-PRESIDENT—John N. Garner, of Texas. SECRETARY OF STATE—Cordell Hull, of Tennessee, March 4, 1933. SECRETARY OF THE TREASURY—William H. Woodin, of New York, March 4, 1933. Henry Morgenthau, Jr., of New York (Under Secretary), ad interim, January 1, 1934, to January 8, 1934. Henry Morgenthau, Jr., of New York, January 8, 1934. SECRETARY OF WAR—George H. Dern, of Utah, March 4, 1933. ATTORNEY GENERAL—Homer S. Cummings, of Connecticut, March 4, 1933. POSTMASTER GENERAL—James A. Farley, of New York, March 4, 1933. SECRETARY OF THE NAVY—Claude A. Swanson, of Virginia, March 4, 1933. SECRETARY OF THE INTERIOR—Harold L. Ickes, of Illinois, March 4, 1933. SECRETARY OF AGRICULTURE—Henry A. Wallace, of Iowa, March 4, 1933. SECRETARY OF COMMERCE—Daniel C. Roper, of South Carolina, March 4, 1933. SECRETARY OF LABOR—Frances Perkins, of New York, March 4, 1933.

73d Congress

1st Session: March 9, 1933–June 15, 1933; 2d Session: Jan. 3, 1934–June 18, 1934; Special Session of the Senate: Mar. 4, 1933–Mar. 6, 1933.

President pro tempore of the Senate: Key Pittman, of Nevada (elected Mar. 9, 1933). Speaker of the House: Henry T. Rainey, of Illinois (elected Mar. 9, 1933).

Senate: 60 Democratic; 35 Republican; 1 other

House: 310 Democratic; 117 Republican; 5 other

74th Congress

1st Session: Jan. 3, 1935–Aug. 26, 1935; 2d Session: Jan. 3, 1936–June 20, 1936.

President pro tempore of the Senate: Key Pittman, of Nevada (reelected Jan. 7, 1935). Speaker of the House: Joseph W. Byrnes, of Tennessee (elected Jan. 3, 1935); William Bankhead, of Alabama (elected June 4, 1936).

Senate: 69 Democratic; 25 Republican; 2 other

House: 319 Democratic; 103 Republican; 10 other

Second Administration of FRANKLIN DELANO ROOSEVELT

JANUARY 20, 1937, TO JANUARY 20, 1941

PRESIDENT—Franklin Delano Roosevelt, of New York (Democratic). VICE-PRESIDENT—John N. Garner, of Texas. SECRETARY OF STATE—Cordell Hull, of Tennessee, continued from preceding administration. SECRETARY OF THE TREASURY—Henry Morgenthau, Jr., of New York, continued from preceding administration. SECRETARY OF WAR—George H. Dern, of Utah, continued from preceding administration (died August 27, 1936). Harry H. Woodring, of Kansas (Assistant Secretary), ad interim, September 25, 1936, to May 6, 1937. Harry H. Woodring, of Kansas, May 6, 1937. Henry L. Stimson, of New York, July 10, 1940. ATTORNEY GENERAL—Homer S. Cummings, of Connecticut, continued from preceding administration. Frank Murphy, of Michigan, ad interim, January 2, 1939, to January 17, 1939. Frank Murphy, of Michigan, January 17, 1939. Robert H. Jackson, of New York, January 18, 1940. POSTMASTER GENERAL—James A. Farley, of New York, continued from preceding administration. James A. Farley, of New York, recommissioned January 22, 1937. Frank C. Walker, of Pennsylvania, September 10, 1940. SECRETARY OF THE NAVY—Claude A. Swanson, of Virginia, continued from preceding administration (died July 7, 1939). Charles Edison, of New Jersey, Acting Secretary from August 5, 1939, to December 30, 1939. Charles Edison, of New Jersey (Assistant Secretary), ad interim, December 30, 1939, to January 11, 1940. Charles Edison, of New Jersey, January 11, 1940. Frank Knox, of Illinois, July 10, 1940. SECRETARY OF THE INTERIOR—Harold L. Ickes, of Illinois, continued from preceding administration. SECRETARY OF AGRICULTURE—Henry A. Wallace, of Iowa, continued from preceding administration. Claude R. Wickard, of Indiana, August 27, 1940; entered upon duties September 5, 1940. SECRETARY OF COMMERCE—Daniel C. Roper, of South Carolina, continued from preceding administration. Harry L. Hopkins, of New York, ad interim, December 24, 1938, to January 23, 1939. Harry L. Hopkins, of New York, January 23, 1939. Jesse H. Jones, of Texas, September 16, 1940; entered upon duties September 19, 1940. SECRETARY OF LABOR—Frances Perkins, of New York, continued from preceding administration.

75th Congress
1st Session: Jan. 5, 1937–Aug. 21, 1937; 2d Session: Nov. 15, 1937–Dec. 21, 1937; 3d Session: Jan. 3, 1938–June 16, 1938.

President pro tempore of the Senate: Key Pittman, of Nevada (continued from preceding Congress). Speaker of the House: William B. Bankhead, of Alabama (reelected Jan. 5, 1937).

Senate: 76 Democratic; 16 Republican; 4 other
House: 331 Democratic; 89 Republican; 13 other

76th Congress
Jan. 3, 1939–Aug. 5, 1939; 2d Session: Sept. 21, 1939–Nov. 3, 1939; 3d Session: Jan. 3, 1940–Jan. 3, 1941.

President pro tempore of the Senate: Key Pittman, of Nevada (continued from preceding Congress); William H. King, of Utah (elected Nov. 19, 1940). Speaker of the House: William B. Bankhead, of Alabama (reelected Jan. 3, 1940); Sam Rayburn, of Texas (elected Sept. 16, 1940).

Senate: 69 Democratic; 23 Republican; 4 other
House: 261 Democratic; 164 Republican; 4 other

Third Administration of FRANKLIN DELANO ROOSEVELT
JANUARY 20, 1941, TO JANUARY 20, 1945

PRESIDENT—Franklin Delano Roosevelt, of New York (Democratic). VICE-PRESIDENT—Henry A. Wallace, of Iowa. SECRETARY OF STATE—Cordell Hull, of Tennessee, continued from preceding administration. Edward R. Stettinius, of Virginia, November 30, 1944; entered upon duties December 1, 1944. SECRETARY OF THE TREASURY—Henry Morgenthau, Jr., of New York, continued from preceding administration. SECRETARY OF WAR—Henry L. Stimson, of New York, continued from preceding administration. ATTORNEY GENERAL—Robert H. Jackson, of New York, continued from preceding administration. Francis Biddle, of Pennsylvania, September 5, 1941. POSTMASTER GENERAL—Frank C. Walker, of Pennsylvania, continued from preceding administration. Frank C. Walker, of Pennsylvania, recommissioned January 27, 1941. SECRETARY OF THE NAVY—Frank Knox, of Illinois, continued from preceding administration (died April 28, 1944). James V. Forrestal, of New York, May 18, 1944. SECRETARY OF THE INTERIOR—Harold L. Ickes, of Illinois, continued from preceding administration. SECRETARY OF AGRICULTURE—Claude R. Wickard, of Indiana, continued from preceding administration. SECRETARY OF COMMERCE—Jesse H. Jones, of Texas, continued from preceding administration. SECRETARY OF LABOR—Frances Perkins, of New York, continued from preceding administration.

77th Congress
1st Session: Jan. 3, 1941–Jan. 2, 1942; 2d Session: Jan. 5, 1942–Dec. 16, 1942.
President pro tempore of the Senate: Pat Harrison, of Mississippi (elected Jan. 6, 1941); Carter Glass, of Virginia (elected July 10, 1941). Speaker of the House: Sam Rayburn, of Texas (reelected Jan. 3, 1941).
Senate: 66 Democratic; 28 Republican; 2 other
House: 268 Democratic; 162 Republican; 5 other

78th Congress
1st Session: Jan. 6, 1943–Dec. 21, 1943; 2d Session: Jan. 10, 1944–Dec. 19, 1944.

President pro tempore of the Senate: Carter Glass, of Virginia (continued from preceding Congress). Speaker of the House: Sam Rayburn, of Texas (reelected Jan. 6, 1943).

Senate: 57 Democratic; 38 Republican; 1 other
House: 222 Democratic; 208 Republican; 5 other

Fourth Administration of FRANKLIN DELANO ROOSEVELT
JANUARY 20, 1945, TO APRIL 12, 1945

PRESIDENT—Franklin Delano Roosevelt, of New York (Democratic) (died April 12, 1945). VICE-PRESIDENT—Harry S. Truman, of Missouri. SECRETARY OF STATE—Edward R. Stettinius, of Virginia, continued from preceding administration. SECRETARY OF THE TREASURY—Henry Morgenthau, Jr., of New York, continued from preceding administration. SECRETARY OF WAR—Henry L. Stimson, of New York, continued from preceding administration. ATTORNEY GENERAL—Francis Biddle, of Pennsylvania, continued from preceding administration. POSTMASTER GENERAL—Frank C. Walker, of Pennsylvania, continued from preceding administration. Frank C. Walker, of Pennsylvania, recommissioned February 6, 1945. SECRETARY OF THE NAVY—James V. Forrestal, of New York, continued from preceding administration. SECRETARY OF THE INTERIOR—Harold L. Ickes, of Illinois, continued from preceding administration. SECRETARY OF AGRICULTURE—Claude R. Wickard, of Indiana, continued from preceding administration. SECRETARY OF COMMERCE—Jesse H. Jones, of Texas, continued from preceding administration. Henry A. Wallace, of Iowa, March 1, 1945; entered upon duties March 2, 1945. SECRETARY OF LABOR—Frances Perkins, of New York, continued from preceding administration.

First Administration of HARRY S TRUMAN
APRIL 12, 1945, TO JANUARY 20, 1949

PRESIDENT—Harry S Truman, of Missouri (Democratic). SECRETARY OF STATE—Edward R. Stettinius, of Virginia, continued from preceding administration. James F. Byrnes, of South Carolina, July 2, 1945; entered upon duties July 3, 1945. George C. Marshall, of Pennsylvania, January 8, 1947; entered upon duties January 21, 1947. SECRETARY OF THE TREASURY—Henry Morgenthau, Jr., of New York, continued from preceding administration. Fred M. Vinson, of Kentucky, July 18, 1945; entered upon duties July 23, 1945. John W. Snyder, of Missouri, June 12, 1946; entered upon duties June 25, 1946. SECRETARY OF DEFENSE—James Forrestal, of New York, July 26, 1947; entered upon duties September 17, 1947. SECRETARY OF WAR—Henry L. Stimson, of New York, continued from preceding administration. Robert Porter Patterson, of New York, September 26, 1945; entered upon duties September 27, 1945. Kenneth C. Royall, of North Carolina, July 21, 1947; entered upon duties July 25, 1947, and served until September 17, 1947. ATTORNEY GENERAL—Francis Biddle, of Pennsylvania, continued from preceding administration. Tom C. Clark, of Texas, June 15, 1945; entered upon duties September 27, 1945. POSTMASTER GENERAL—Frank Walker, of Pennsylvania, from preceding administration. Robert E. Hannegan, of Missouri, May 8, 1945; entered upon duties July 1, 1945. Jesse M. Donaldson, of Missouri, December 16, 1947. SECRETARY OF THE NAVY—James V. Forrestal, of New York, continued from preceding administration; served until September 17, 1947. SECRETARY OF THE INTERIOR—Harold L. Ickes, of Illinois, continued from preceding administration. Julius A. Krug, of Wisconsin, March 6, 1946; entered upon duties March 18, 1946. SECRETARY OF AGRICULTURE—Claude R. Wickard, of Indiana, continued from preceding administration. Clinton P. Anderson, of New Mexico, June 2, 1945; entered upon duties June 30, 1945. Charles F. Brannan, of Colorado, May 29, 1948; entered upon duties June 2, 1948. SECRETARY OF COMMERCE—Henry A. Wallace, of Iowa, continued from preceding administration. William Averell Harriman, of New York, ad interim, September 28, 1946, to January 28, 1947. William Averell Harriman, of New York, January 28, 1947. Charles Sawyer, of Ohio, May 6, 1948. SECRETARY OF LABOR—Frances Perkins, of New York, continued from preceding administration. Lewis B. Schwellenbach, of Washington, June 1, 1945; entered upon duties July 1, 1945 (died June 10, 1948). Maurice J. Tobin, of Massachusetts, ad interim, August 13, 1948.

79th Congress
1st Session: Jan. 3, 1945–Dec. 21, 1945; 2d Session: Jan. 14, 1946–Aug. 2, 1946.

President pro tempore of the Senate: Kenneth McKellar, of Tennessee (elected Jan. 6, 1945). Speaker of the House: Sam Rayburn, of Texas (reelected Jan. 3, 1945).

Senate: 56 Democratic; 38 Republican; 1 other
House: 242 Democratic; 190 Republican; 2 other

80th Congress
1st Session: Jan. 3, 1947–Dec. 19, 1947; 2d Session: Jan. 6, 1948–Dec. 31, 1948.

President pro tempore of the Senate: Arthur H. Vandenberg, of Michigan (elected Jan. 4, 1947). Speaker of the House: Joseph W. Martin, Jr., of Massachusetts (elected Jan. 3, 1947).

Senate: 51 Republican; 45 Democratic

House: 245 Republican; 188 Democratic; 1 other

Second Administration of HARRY S TRUMAN

JANUARY 20, 1949, TO JANUARY 20, 1953

PRESIDENT—Harry S Truman, of Missouri (Democratic). VICE-PRESIDENT—Alben W. Barkley, of Kentucky. SECRETARY OF STATE—Dean G. Acheson, of Connecticut, January 19, 1949; entered upon duties January 21, 1949. SECRETARY OF THE TREASURY—John W. Snyder, of Missouri, continued from preceding administration. SECRETARY OF DEFENSE—James V. Forrestal, of New York, continued from preceding administration. Louis A. Johnson, of West Virginia, March 23, 1949; entered upon duties March 28, 1949. George C. Marshall, of Pennsylvania, September 20, 1950; entered upon duties September 21, 1950. Robert A. Lovett, of New York, September 14, 1951; entered upon duties September 17, 1951. ATTORNEY GENERAL—Tom C. Clark, of Texas, continued from preceding administration. J. Howard McGrath, of Rhode Island, August 19, 1949; entered upon duties August 24, 1949. James P. McGranery, of Pennsylvania, May 21, 1952; entered upon duties May 27, 1952. POSTMASTER GENERAL—Jesse M. Donaldson, of Missouri, continued from preceding administration. Jesse M. Donaldson, of Missouri, recommissioned February 8, 1949. SECRETARY OF THE INTERIOR—Julius A. Krug, of Wisconsin, continued from preceding administration. Oscar L. Chapman, of Colorado (Under Secretary), ad interim, December 1, 1949, to January 19, 1950. Oscar L. Chapman, of Colorado, January 19, 1950. SECRETARY OF AGRICULTURE—Charles F. Brannan, of Colorado, continued from preceding administration. SECRETARY OF COMMERCE—Charles Sawyer, of Ohio, continued from preceding administration. SECRETARY OF LABOR—Maurice J. Tobin, of Massachusetts, ad interim, continued from preceding administration. Maurice J. Tobin, of Massachusetts, recommissioned February 1, 1949.

81st Congress

1st Session: Jan. 3, 1949–Oct. 19, 1949; 2d Session: Jan. 3, 1950–Jan. 2, 1951.

President pro tempore of the Senate: Kenneth D. McKellar, of Tennessee (elected Jan. 3, 1949). Speaker of the House: Sam Rayburn, of Texas (elected Jan. 3, 1949).

Senate: 54 Democratic; 42 Republican

House: 263 Democratic; 171 Republican; 1 other

82d Congress

1st Session: Jan. 3, 1951–Oct. 20, 1951; 2d Session: Jan. 8, 1952—July 7, 1952.

President pro tempore of the Senate: Kenneth D. McKellar, of Tennessee (continued from preceding Congress). Speaker of the House: Sam Rayburn, of Texas (reelected Jan. 3, 1951).

Senate: 49 Democratic; 47 Republican

House: 234 Democratic; 199 Republican; 1 other

First Administration of DWIGHT D. EISENHOWER

JANUARY 20, 1953, TO JANUARY 20, 1957

PRESIDENT—Dwight D. Eisenhower, of New York (Republican). VICE-PRESIDENT—Richard M. Nixon, of California. SECRETARY OF STATE—John Foster Dulles, of New York, January 21, 1953. SECRETARY OF THE TREASURY—George M. Humphrey, of Ohio, January 21, 1953. SECRETARY OF DEFENSE—Charles E. Wilson, of Michigan, January 26, 1953; entered upon duties January 28, 1953. ATTORNEY GENERAL—Herbert Brownell, Jr., of New York, January 21, 1953. POSTMASTER GENERAL—Arthur E. Summerfield, of Michigan, January 21, 1953. SECRETARY OF THE INTERIOR—Douglas McKay, of Oregon, January 21, 1953. Frederick A. Seaton, of Nebraska, June 6, 1956; entered upon duties June 8, 1956. SECRETARY OF AGRICULTURE—Ezra Taft Benson, of Utah, January 21, 1953. SECRETARY OF COMMERCE—Sinclair Weeks, of Massachusetts, January 21, 1953. SECRETARY OF LABOR—Martin P. Durkin, of Maryland, January 21, 1953. James P. Mitchell, of New Jersey, ad interim, October 9, 1953, to January 19, 1954. James P. Mitchell, of New Jersey, January 19, 1954. SECRETARY OF HEALTH, EDUCATION, AND WELFARE—Oveta Culp Hobby, of Texas, April 10, 1953; entered upon duties April 11, 1953. Marion B. Folsom, of New York, July 20, 1955; entered upon duties August 1, 1955.

83d Congress

1st Session: Jan. 3, 1953—Aug. 3, 1953; 2d Session: Jan. 6, 1954–Dec. 2, 1954.

President pro tempore of the Senate: Styles Bridges, of New Hampshire (elected Jan. 3, 1953). Speaker of the House: Joseph W. Martin, Jr., of Massachusetts (elected Jan. 3, 1953).

Senate: 48 Republican; 47 Democratic; 1 other

House: 221 Republican; 211 Democratic; 1 other

84th Congress

1st Session: Jan. 5, 1955–Aug. 2, 1955; 2d Session: Jan. 3, 1956–July 27, 1956.

President pro tempore of the Senate: Walter F. George, of Georgia (elected Jan. 5, 1955). Speaker of the House: Sam Rayburn, of Texas (elected Jan. 5, 1955).

Senate: 48 Democratic; 47 Republican; 1 other

House: 232 Democratic; 203 Republican

Second Administration of DWIGHT D. EISENHOWER

JANUARY 20, 1957, TO JANUARY 20, 1961

PRESIDENT—Dwight D. Eisenhower, of Pennsylvania (Republican). VICE-PRESIDENT—Richard M. Nixon, of California. SECRETARY OF STATE—John Foster Dulles, of New York, continued from preceding administration. Christian A. Herter, of Massachusetts, April 21, 1959; entered upon duties April 22, 1959. SECRETARY OF THE TREASURY—George M. Humphrey, of Ohio, continued from preceding administration. Robert Bernerd Anderson, of Connecticut, July 2, 1957; entered upon duties July 29, 1957. SECRETARY OF DEFENSE—Charles E. Wilson, of Michigan, continued from preceding administration. Neil H. McElroy, of Ohio, August 19, 1957; entered upon duties October 9, 1957. Thomas S. Gates, Jr., of Pennsylvania, ad interim, December 1, 1959, to January 26, 1960. Thomas S. Gates, Jr., of Pennsylvania, January 26, 1960. ATTORNEY GENERAL—Herbert Brownell, Jr., of New York, continued from preceding administration. William P. Rogers, of Maryland, ad interim, November 8, 1957, to January 27, 1958. William P. Rogers, of Maryland, January 27, 1958. POSTMASTER GENERAL—Arthur E. Summerfield, of Michigan, continued from preceding administration. Arthur E. Summerfield, of Michigan, recommissioned February 4, 1957. SECRETARY OF THE INTERIOR—Frederick A. Seaton, of Nebraska, continued from preceding administration. SECRETARY OF AGRICULTURE—Ezra Taft Benson, of Utah, continued from preceding administration. SECRETARY OF COMMERCE—Sinclair Weeks, of Massachusetts, continued from preceding administration. Lewis L. Strauss, of New York, ad interim, November 13, 1958, to June 27, 1959. Frederick H. Mueller, of Michigan (Under Secretary), ad interim, July 21, 1959, to August 6, 1959. Frederick H. Mueller, of Michigan, August 6, 1959. SECRETARY OF LABOR—James P. Mitchell, of New Jersey, continued from preceding administration. SECRETARY OF HEALTH, EDUCATION, AND WELFARE—Marion B. Folsom, of New York, continued from preceding administration. Arthur S. Flemming, of Ohio, July 9, 1958; entered upon duties August 1, 1958.

85th Congress

1st Session: Jan. 3, 1957–Aug. 30, 1957; 2d Session: Jan. 7, 1958–Aug. 24, 1958.

President pro tempore of the Senate: Carl Hayden, of Arizona (elected Jan. 3, 1957). Speaker of the House: Sam Rayburn, of Texas (reelected Jan. 3, 1957).

Senate: 49 Democratic; 47 Republican

House: 233 Democratic; 200 Republican

86th Congress

1st Session: Jan. 7, 1959–Sept. 15, 1959; 2d Session: Jan. 6, 1960–Sept. 1, 1960.

President pro tempore of the Senate: Carl Hayden, of Arizona (continued from preceding Congress). Speaker of the House: Sam Rayburn, of Texas (reelected Jan. 7, 1959).

Senate: 64 Democratic; 34 Republican

House: 283 Democratic; 153 Republican

Administration of JOHN F. KENNEDY

JANUARY 20, 1961, TO NOVEMBER 22, 1963

PRESIDENT—John F. Kennedy, of Massachusetts (Democratic) (died November 22, 1963). VICE-PRESIDENT—Lyndon B. Johnson, of Texas. SECRETARY OF STATE—Dean Rusk, of New York, January 20, 1961. SECRETARY OF THE TREASURY—C. Douglas Dillon, of Washington, D.C., January 20, 1961. SECRETARY OF DEFENSE—Robert S. McNamara, of Michigan, January 20, 1961. ATTORNEY GENERAL—Robert F. Kennedy, of Massachusetts, January 20, 1961. POSTMASTER GENERAL—J. Edward Day, of California, January 20, 1961, to August 9, 1963. John A. Gronouski of Wisconsin, September 10, 1963. SECRETARY OF THE INTERIOR—Stewart L. Udall, of Arizona, January 20, 1961. SECRETARY OF AGRICULTURE—Orville L. Freeman, of Minnesota, January 20, 1961. SECRETARY OF COMMERCE—Luther H. Hodges, of North Carolina, January 20, 1961. SECRETARY OF LABOR—Arthur J. Goldberg, of Washington, D.C., January 20, 1961. W. Willard Wirtz, of Illinois, September 25, 1962. SECRETARY OF HEALTH, EDUCATION, AND WELFARE—Abraham A. Ribicoff, of Connecticut, January 21, 1961, to July 13, 1962. Anthony J. Celebrezze, of Ohio, July 31, 1962.

First Administration of LYNDON B. JOHNSON
NOVEMBER 22, 1963, TO JANUARY 20, 1965

PRESIDENT—Lyndon B. Johnson, of Texas (Democratic). SECRETARY OF STATE—Dean Rusk, of New York, continued from preceding administration. SECRETARY OF THE TREASURY—C. Douglas Dillon, of Washington, D.C., continued from preceding administration. SECRETARY OF DEFENSE—Robert S. McNamara, of Michigan, continued from preceding administration. ATTORNEY GENERAL—Robert F. Kennedy, of Massachusetts, continued from preceding administration. Nicholas Katzenbach, of Illinois, ad interim, Sept. 4, 1964. POSTMASTER GENERAL—John S. Gronouski, of Wisconsin, continued from preceding administration. SECRETARY OF THE INTERIOR—Stewart L. Udall, of Arizona, continued from preceding administration. SECRETARY OF AGRICULTURE—Orville L. Freeman of Minnesota, continued from preceding administration. SECRETARY OF COMMERCE—Luther H. Hodges, of North Carolina, continued from preceding administration to January 15, 1965. John T. O'Connor, of New Jersey, January 15, 1965. SECRETARY OF LABOR—W. Willard Wirtz, of Illinois, continued from preceding administration. SECRETARY OF HEALTH, EDUCATION, AND WELFARE—Anthony J. Celebrezze, of Ohio, continued from preceding administration.

87th Congress

1st Session: Jan. 3, 1961–Sept. 27, 1961; 2d Session: Jan. 10, 1962–Oct. 13, 1962.

President pro tempore of the Senate: Carl Hayden, of Arizona (continued from preceding Congress). Speaker of the House: Sam Rayburn, of Texas (reelected Jan. 3, 1961); John W. McCormack, of Massachusetts (elected Jan. 10, 1962).

Senate: 65 Democratic; 35 Republican
House: 263 Democratic; 174 Republican

88th Congress

1st Session: Jan. 9, 1963–Dec. 30, 1963; 2d Session: Jan. 7, 1964–Oct. 3, 1964.

President pro tempore of the Senate: Carl Hayden, of Arizona (continued from preceding Congress). Speaker of the House: John W. McCormack (reelected Jan. 9, 1963).

Senate: 67 Democratic; 33 Republican
House: 258 Democratic; 177 Republican

Second Administration of LYNDON B. JOHNSON
JANUARY 20, 1965 TO JANUARY 20, 1969

PRESIDENT—Lyndon B. Johnson, of Texas (Democratic). VICE-PRESIDENT—Hubert H. Humphrey, of Minnesota. SECRETARY OF STATE—Dean Rusk, of New York, continued from preceding administration. SECRETARY OF THE TREASURY—C. Douglas Dillon, of Washington, D.C., continued from preceding administration to March 31, 1965. Henry H. Fowler, of Virginia, April 1, 1965 to December 20, 1968. Joseph W. Barr, of Indiana, December 23, 1968. SECRETARY OF DEFENSE—Robert S. McNamara, continued from preceding administration. Clark Clifford, of Maryland, January 19, 1968. ATTORNEY GENERAL—Nicholas Katzenbach, of Illinois, ad interim, continued from preceding administration, confirmed on Feb. 10, 1965. Ramsey Clark, of Texas, March 2, 1967. POSTMASTER GENERAL—John A. Gronouski, of Wisconsin, continued from preceding administration. Lawrence O'Brien, of Massachusetts, August 29, 1965, to April 10, 1968. Marvin Watson, of Texas, April 10, 1968. SECRETARY OF THE INTERIOR—Stewart L. Udall, of Arizona, continued from preceding administration. SECRETARY OF AGRICULTURE—Orville L. Freeman, of Minnesota, continued from preceding administration. SECRETARY OF COMMERCE—John T. O'Connor, of New Jersey, continued from preceding administration to January 18, 1967. Alexander B. Trowbridge, of New York, May 23, 1967, to February 16, 1968. C. R. Smith, of New York, March 1, 1968. SECRETARY OF LABOR—W. Willard Wirtz, of Illinois, continued from preceding administration. SECRETARY OF HEALTH, EDUCATION, AND WELFARE—Anthony J. Celebrezze, of Ohio, continued from preceding administration. John W. Gardner, of New York, July 27, 1965. Wilbur J. Cohen, of Michigan, May 16, 1968. SECRETARY OF HOUSING AND URBAN DEVELOPMENT—Robert C. Weaver, of Washington, D.C., January 18, 1966 to January 1, 1969. Robert C. Wood, of Massachusetts, January 2, 1969. SECRETARY OF TRANSPORTATION—Alan S. Boyd, of Florida, January 16, 1967.

89th Congress

1st Session: Jan. 4, 1965–Oct. 23, 1965; 2d Session: Jan. 10, 1966–Oct. 22, 1966.

President pro tempore of the Senate: Carl Hayden, of Arizona (continued from preceding Congress). Speaker of the House: John W. McCormack, of Massachusetts (reelected Jan. 4, 1965).

Senate: 68 Democratic; 32 Republican
House: 295 Democratic; 140 Republican

90th Congress

1st Session: Jan. 10, 1967–Dec. 15, 1967; 2d Session: Jan. 15, 1968–Oct. 14, 1968.

President pro tempore of the Senate: Carl Hayden, of Arizona (continued from preceding Congress). Speaker of the House: John W. McCormack, of Massachusetts (reelected Jan. 10, 1967).

Senate: 64 Democratic; 36 Republican
House: 248 Democratic; 187 Republican

First Administration of RICHARD M. NIXON
JANUARY 20, 1969, TO JANUARY 20, 1973

PRESIDENT—Richard M. Nixon, of California (Republican). VICE-PRESIDENT—Spiro T. Agnew, of Maryland. SECRETARY OF STATE—William P. Rogers, of New York, January 22, 1969. SECRETARY OF THE TREASURY—David M. Kennedy, of Illinois, January 22, 1969 to February 10, 1971. John B. Connally, of Texas, February 11, 1971. George P. Shultz of Illinois, June 12, 1972. SECRETARY OF DEFENSE—Melvin R. Laird, of Wisconsin, January 22, 1969. ATTORNEY GENERAL—John N. Mitchell, of New York, January 22, 1969. Richard G. Kleindienst, of Arizona, ad interim, Feb. 15, 1972; took office June 12, 1972. POSTMASTER GENERAL—Winton M. Blount, of Alabama, January 22, 1969 to July 1, 1971. This office was then abolished as a cabinet post. SECRETARY OF THE INTERIOR—Walter J. Hickel, of Alaska, January 23, 1969. Fred J. Russell, of California, ad interim, Nov. 26, 1970. Rogers C. B. Morton, of Maryland, Jan. 29, 1971. SECRETARY OF AGRICULTURE—Clifford M. Hardin, of Nebraska, Jan. 22, 1969. Earl L. Butz, of Indiana, Dec. 2, 1971. SECRETARY OF COMMERCE—Maurice H. Stans, of New York, Jan. 22, 1969. Peter G. Peterson, of Illinois, Feb. 21, 1972. SECRETARY OF LABOR—George P. Shultz, of New York, Jan. 22, 1969. James D. Hodgson, of California, July 2, 1970. SECRETARY OF HEALTH, EDUCATION, AND WELFARE—Robert H. Finch, of California, Jan. 22, 1969. Elliot L. Richardson, of Massachusetts, June 15, 1970. SECRETARY OF HOUSING AND URBAN DEVELOPMENT—George W. Romney, of Michigan, Jan. 22, 1969. SECRETARY OF TRANSPORTATION—John A. Volpe, of Massachusetts, Jan. 22, 1969.

91st Congress

1st Session: Jan. 3, 1969–Dec. 23, 1969; 2d Session: Jan. 19, 1970–Jan. 2, 1971.

President pro tempore of the Senate: Richard B. Russell, of Georgia (elected Jan. 3, 1969). Speaker of the House: John W. McCormack, of Massachusetts (reelected Jan. 3, 1969).

Senate: 57 Democratic; 43 Republican
House: 244 Democratic; 191 Republican

92d Congress

1st Session: Jan. 21, 1971–Dec. 17, 1971; 2d Session: Jan. 18, 1972–Oct. 18, 1972

President pro tempore of the Senate: James O. Eastland of Mississippi (elected July 28, 1972). (Richard B. Russell, continued from preceding Congress, died in office. Allen J. Ellender of Louisiana, who was elected Jan. 22, 1971, died in office.) Speaker of the House: Carl Albert, of Oklahoma (elected Jan. 21, 1971). Senate: 54 Democratic; 44 Republican; 1 Independent-Democratic; 1 Conservative-Republican.
House: 255 Democratic; 180 Republican

Second Administration of RICHARD M. NIXON
JANUARY 20, 1973, TO AUGUST 9, 1974

PRESIDENT—Richard M. Nixon, of California (Republican). Resigned August 9, 1974. VICE PRESIDENT—Spiro T. Agnew, of Maryland. Resigned October 10, 1973. Gerald R. Ford, Jr., of Michigan, December 6, 1973. SECRETARY OF STATE—William P. Rogers, of Maryland, continued from preceding administration. Kenneth Rush, of New York (Deputy Secretary of State), ad interim, September 4, 1973. Henry A. Kissinger, of the District of Columbia, September 21, 1973. SECRETARY OF THE TREASURY—George P. Shultz, of Illinois, continued from preceding administration. William E. Simon, of New Jersey, April 30, 1974. SECRETARY OF DEFENSE—Melvin R. Laird, of Wisconsin, continued from preceding administration. Elliot L. Richardson, of Massachusetts, January 29, 1973. William P. Clements, Jr., of Texas, ad interim, May 26, 1973. James R. Schlesinger, of Virginia, June 28, 1973. ATTORNEY GENERAL—Richard G. Kleindienst, of Arizona, continued from preceding administration. Elliot L. Richardson, of Massachusetts, May 23, 1973. Robert H. Bork, of Pennsylvania (Solicitor General), ad interim, October 20, 1973. William B. Saxbe, of Ohio, Feb. 4, 1974. SECRETARY OF THE INTERIOR—Rogers C. B. Morton, of Maryland, continued from preceding administration. SECRETARY OF AGRICULTURE—Earl L. Butz, of Indiana, continued from preceding administration. SECRETARY OF COMMERCE—Frederick B. Dent, of South Carolina, ad interim, Jan. 18, 1973; took office Feb. 2, 1973. SECRETARY OF LABOR—James D. Hodgson, of California, continued from preceding administration. Peter J. Brennan, of New York, January 31, 1973. SECRETARY OF HEALTH, EDUCATION, AND WELFARE—Elliot L. Richardson, of Massachusetts, continued from preceding administration. Caspar W. Weinberger, of California, February 8, 1973. SECRETARY OF HOUSING AND URBAN DEVELOPMENT—George Romney, of Michigan, continued from preceding administration. James T. Lynn, of Ohio, January 31, 1973. SECRETARY OF TRANSPORTATION—John A. Volpe, of Massachusetts, continued from preceding administration.

Claude S. Brinegar, of California, January 18, 1973.

93rd Congress

1st Session: Jan. 3, 1973-Dec. 22, 1973; 2nd Session: Jan. 21, 1974-Dec. 20, 1974.

President pro tempore of the Senate: James O. Eastland of Mississippi (continued from preceding Congress). Speaker of the House: Carl Albert, of Oklahoma (continued from preceding Congress).

Senate: 56 Democratic; 42 Republican; 1 Conservative-Republican; 1 Independent

House: 244 Democratic; 191 Republican; 1 Independent

Administration of GERALD R. FORD, JR.
AUGUST 9, 1974 TO JANUARY 20, 1977

PRESIDENT—Gerald R. Ford, Jr., of Michigan. VICE PRESIDENT—Nelson A. Rockefeller, of New York, December 19, 1974. SECRETARY OF STATE—Henry A. Kissinger, of the District of Columbia, continued from preceding administration. SECRETARY OF THE TREASURY—William E. Simon, of New Jersey, continued from preceding administration. SECRETARY OF DEFENSE—James R. Schlesinger, of Virginia, continued from preceding administration. Donald H. Rumsfeld, of Illinois, November 18, 1975. ATTORNEY GENERAL—William B. Saxbe, of Ohio, continued from preceding administration. Edward H. Levi, of Illinois, February 5, 1975. SECRETARY OF THE INTERIOR—Rogers C.B. Morton, of Maryland, continued from preceding administration. D. Kent Frizzell, of Kansas (Solicitor), ad interim, May 1, 1975. Stanley K. Hathaway of Wyoming, June 11, 1975. D. Kent Frizzell, of Kansas (Solicitor), ad interim, July 25, 1975. Thomas S. Kleppe, of North Dakota, October 9, 1975. SECRETARY OF AGRICULTURE—Earl L. Butz, of Indiana, continued from preceding administration. John A. Knebel, of Oklahoma, ad interim, October 4, 1976. John A. Knebel, November 5, 1976. SECRETARY OF COMMERCE—Frederick B. Dent, of South Carolina, continued from preceding administration. John K. Tabor, of Pennsylvania (Under Secretary), ad interim, March 12, 1975. Rogers C.B. Morton, of Maryland, April 25, 1975. Elliot L. Richardson, of Massachusetts, December 11, 1975. SECRETARY OF LABOR—Peter J. Brennan, of New York, continued from preceding administration. John T. Dunlop, of Massachusetts, March 6, 1975. Willie J. Usery, Jr., of Georgia, February 4, 1976. SECRETARY OF HEALTH, EDUCATION, AND WELFARE—Caspar W. Weinberger, of California, continued from preceding administration. Forrest David Mathews, of Alabama, June 26, 1975. SECRETARY OF HOUSING AND URBAN DEVELOPMENT—James T. Lynn, of Ohio, continued from preceding administration. Carla A. Hills, of California, March 5, 1975. SECRETARY OF TRANSPORTATION—Claude S. Brinegar, of California, continued from preceding administration. William T. Coleman, Jr., of Pennsylvania, March 3, 1975.

94th Congress

1st Session: Jan. 14, 1975-Dec. 19, 1975; 2nd Session: Jan. 19, 1976-Oct. 1, 1976.
President pro tempore of the Senate: James O. Eastland, of Mississippi (continued from preceding Congress). Speaker of the House: Carl Albert, of Oklahoma (continued from preceding Congress).

Senate: 61 Democratic; 37 Republican; 1 Conservative-Republican; 1 Independent

House: 291 Democratic; 144 Republican

Administration of JIMMY CARTER
FROM JANUARY 20, 1977

PRESIDENT—Jimmy (James E.) Carter, of Georgia, VICE PRESIDENT—Walter F. Mondale, of Minnesota. SECRETARY OF STATE—Cyrus R. Vance, of New York, January 23, 1977. Edmund S. Muskie, of Maine, May 8, 1980. SECRETARY OF THE TREASURY—W. Michael Blumenthal, of Michigan, January 23, 1977. G. William Miller, of Oklahoma, August 6, 1979. SECRETARY OF DEFENSE—Harold Brown, of California, January 21, 1977. ATTORNEY GENERAL—Griffin B. Bell, of Georgia, January 26, 1977. Benjamin R. Civiletti, of Maryland, August 16, 1979. SECRETARY OF THE INTERIOR—Cecil R. Andrus, of Idaho, January 23, 1977. SECRETARY OF AGRICULTURE—Robert S. Bergland, of Minnesota, January 23, 1977. SECRETARY OF COMMERCE—Juanita M. Kreps, of North Carolina, January 23, 1977. Philip M. Klutznick, of Illinois, January 2, 1980. SECRETARY OF LABOR—F. Ray Marshall, of Texas, January 27, 1977. SECRETARY OF HEALTH AND HUMAN SERVICES—Joseph A. Califano, Jr., of the District of Columbia, January 25, 1977. Patricia R. Harris, of the District of Columbia, August 3, 1979. (On Sept. 27, 1979 Congress gave final approval to a bill establishing a cabinet-level Department of Education; the Department of Health, Education and Welfare is to be renamed the Department of Health and Human Resources) SECRETARY OF HOUSING AND URBAN DEVELOPMENT—Patricia R. Harris, of the District of Columbia, January 23, 1977. Moon Landrieu, of Louisiana, September 24, 1979. SECRETARY OF TRANSPORTATION—Brockman Adams, of Washington, January 23, 1977. Neil E. Goldschmidt, of Oregon, August 15, 1979. SECRETARY OF ENERGY—James R. Schlesinger, of Virginia, August 5, 1977. Charles W. Duncan, of Texas, August 24, 1979. SECRETARY OF EDUCATION—Shirley M. Hufstedler, of California, December 6, 1979.

95th Congress

1st Session: Jan. 4, 1977-Dec. 15, 1977; 2nd Session: Jan. 19, 1978-Oct. 15, 1978
President pro tempore of the Senate: James O. Eastland, of Mississippi (continued from preceding Congress). Deputy President pro tempore of the Senate: Hubert H. Humphrey,[1] of Minnesota. Speaker of the House: Thomas P. O'Neill, Jr., of Massachusetts.
Senate: 61 Democratic; 38 Republican; 1 Independent
House: 290 Democratic; 145 Republican

96th Congress

1st Session: Jan. 3, 1979-Jan. 3, 1980[2];
2nd Session: Jan. 3, 1980
President pro tempore of the Senate: Warren G. Magnuson, of Washington. Speaker of the House: Thomas P. O'Neill, Jr., of Massachusetts. (continued from preceding Congress) Senate: 58 Democratic; 41 Republican; 1 Independent. House: 276 Democratic; 159 Republican.

[1]Office of Deputy President pro tempore was established January 5, 1977, pursuant to Senate Resolution 17, Ninety-fifth Congress. This office no longer exists since the death of Hubert H. Humphrey, Jan. 13, 1978. [2]The Senate adjourned sine die Dec. 20, 1979.

LINCOLN'S GETTYSBURG ADDRESS

Four score and seven years ago our fathers brought forth on this continent, a new nation, conceived in Liberty, and dedicated to the proposition that all men are created equal.

Now we are engaged in a great civil war, testing whether that nation, or any nation so conceived and so dedicated, can long endure. We are met on a great battle-field of that war. We have come to dedicate a portion of that field, as a final resting place for those who here gave their lives that that nation might live. It is altogether fitting and proper that we should do this.

But, in a larger sense, we can not dedicate—we can not consecrate—we can not hallow—this ground. The brave men, living and dead, who struggled here, have consecrated it, far above our poor power to add or detract. The world will little note, nor long remember what we say here, but it can never forget what they did here. It is for us the living, rather, to be dedicated here to the unfinished work which they who fought here have thus far so nobly advanced. It is rather for us to be here dedicated to the great task remaining before us—that from these honored dead we take increased devotion to that cause for which they gave the last full measure of devotion—that we here highly resolve that these dead shall not have died in vain—that this nation, under God, shall have a new birth of freedom—and that government of the people, by the people, for the people, shall not perish from the earth.

THE PRESIDENTIAL BIOGRAPHIES

George Washington

George Washington, 1st President (1789–1797), son of Augustine and Mary (Ball) Washington, was born on February 22, 1732, in Westmoreland County, Virginia. Of a family that migrated from England in 1658, George's father was a moderately well-to-do planter. He died when George was 11, and young Washington was brought up by his half-brother, Lawrence, whom he idolized and who took over the estate and functioned as a surrogate father.

George received a simple education at the parish church and at 16 entered the employ of Lord Thomas Fairfax as a land surveyor. Adept at mathematics and athletics, Washington in surveying Fairfax's vast holdings in mountainous western Virginia, learned to live in the wilderness, govern his helpers, and maintain accurate survey records on which land titles were based. In 1752, Lawrence Washington died. George inherited a share of Lawrence's lands, and he was commissioned (1753) a major and put in charge of training militia in southern Virginia. He immediately began to study histories of wars and books on military tactics.

Soon after, Washington emerged into public view when he volunteered for a hazardous and vital mission. Governor Robert Dinwiddie of Virginia was eager to warn the French that they must withdraw their troops from the Ohio River Valley, which the British hoped to settle. Bearing Dinwiddie's message, Washington, prudent and an excellent horseman, led a small party through the snow-covered wilderness to the successful completion of the mission.

At 22, Washington was promoted to lieutenant colonel as the French and Indian Wars commenced and was assigned as aide to British General Edward Braddock, a respected professional soldier, who led a disastrous expedition against the French at Fort Duquesne. Washington's personal skill in the battle was widely praised, and he was appointed (1755) colonel and entrusted with the defense of Virginia's 350-mile western frontier. At his urging, a new attack was made upon Fort Duquesne, and he again distinguished himself by capturing the French stronghold. With the French retreating into Canada, the fighting ceased, and Washington, now the most famous American-born soldier, retired to private life.

At Mount Vernon, which initially he leased from Lawrence's widow, he became at the age of 26, a country gentleman and successful businessman. He also commenced his political career by serving from 1759 to 1774 as a member of Virginia's House of Burgesses. This legislative background stood him well. A leader in opposition to British policy, Washington was a delegate to the First Continental Congress (1774-75) and, with the outbreak of the Revolutionary War, he was named commander-in-chief of the Continental forces.

Beset with obstacles seldom faced by military commanders, Washington described his troops as "raw militia, badly officered, and with no government." Since his troops preferred short-term enlistments and summer fighting to winter, he seldom commanded 10,000 men at one time. Weak in power, Congress supported Washington poorly, sometimes leaving him without adequate funds to pay his troops. Many subordinate officers were preoccupied with jealousies and intrigues.

Yet by ingenious retreats and thrusts, Washington kept his army afield, survived defeat at Germantown, a cruel winter at Valley Forge, and built up an able force that entrapped Cornwallis's army at Yorktown and forced its surrender. Washington emerged from the Revolution as the unrivaled hero and symbol of the new nation.

In 1783, he again retired to Mount Vernon, where life was pleasantly calm. However, by 1786, he like other leaders was distressed by the weaknesses of American government under the Articles of Confederation. When the Constitutional Convention gathered at Philadelphia in 1787, Washington received a hero's welcome as head of the Virginia delegation, and he was promptly elected president of the convention. In fashioning a strong Presidency, the convention, Pierce Butler wrote, "cast their eyes toward General Washington . . ."

After the Constitution was ratified, the first Electoral College met on February 4, 1789, and unanimously elected Washington President. On April 30, he was inaugurated at Federal Hall, in New York City, the capital. "I walk on untrodden ground," Washington said soon after beginning his new responsibilities. "There is scarcely any part of my conduct that may not hereafter be drawn into precedent."

Facing times that overflowed with crises, Washington left the republic far stronger and more confident than when he took office. An output of measures, highly impressive by today's standards, flowed from his administration. The Revolutionary debts of the states were assumed by the national government, a national currency was issued, and a Bank of the United States established to provide credit. Manufacture and trade were promoted by tariffs and bounties; inventions were protected by patent and copyright laws. A postal system was established; national security was improved by the reorganization of the army and the navy, the founding of West Point, and the construction of fortifications on the eastern seaboard and in the West. In the development of many of these measures, Washington was aided by his brilliant Secretary of the Treasury, Alexander Hamilton.

Hamilton's advocacy of a Bank of the United States touched off a dispute with Secretary of State Thomas Jefferson and Attorney General Edmund Randolph, who considered the bank unconstitutional because express authorization was not provided in the fundamental law. Washington sided with Hamilton, who argued that the national government could use all powers, except those denied by the Constitution. Time and again, where the Constitution was unclear, Washington exercised executive authority.

The President truly dominated the executive branch. With few exceptions, he prescribed the duties of his department heads and kept abreast of daily detail. So confident was he of his mastery that he brought together two of the most gifted and assertive department heads the nation has ever known—Jefferson and Hamilton. Washington succeeded outstandingly, where many of his successors have failed, in relations with Congress. He converted his popularity into major laws without tarnishing his prestige in political struggles. He prized the intrinsic dignity of the Presidency and gave the office a regal quality.

In 1793, Washington was reelected again by a unanimous electoral vote; his second term was to be more difficult than the first. War now raged between England and France, growing out of the French Revolution. Hamilton and Jefferson, in conflict over domestic questions, were also bitterly divided over the war. Each led a party reflecting his views: Hamilton—the Federalists, Jefferson—the Anti-Federalists (Democratic-Republicans). Hamilton's party sympathized with Britain and Jefferson's with France. As usual, Washington tried to be a moderating influence between his two strong secretaries. In weighing policy toward the war, he found convenience in meeting with all his secretaries simultaneously: and the institution known as the Cabinet was born.

On April 22, 1793, Washington issued a neutrality proclamation calling for "conduct friendly and impartial" to the warring nations. American vessels were barred from carrying war supplies to the belligerents. When the French minister to the United States, Citizen Genêt, attempted to outfit warships in American ports and to send them against the British, Washington requested that France recall its representative, because of his threat to American neutrality.

American relations with Britain also were badly deteriorating. British warships intercepted United States' vessels bearing food supplies to France, seizing their cargoes and impressing their seamen into the British navy. The British also refused to give up western frontier forts as they were obligated to under the treaty ending the Revolutionary War; instead, they stirred up the Indians in the surrounding area. To resolve these prickly questions, Washington dispatched Chief Justice John Jay to Britain. The resulting Jay Treaty dealt with trade and the frontier forts, but not with Britain's halting of American ships and seizure of seamen. Senate consideration of the treaty occasioned a bitter fight between the Federalists who supported it and the Anti-Federalists. Hostile newspapers called for Washington's impeachment. And some denounced him as an aristocrat and an enemy of true democracy. The Senate eventually approved the treaty.

In 1794, Washington demonstrated that he could enforce federal laws in the states when he put down the Whisky Rebellion by dispatching troops against farmers in western Pennsylvania who refused to pay federal taxes on whisky.

Declining to serve a third term, Washington issued his Farewell Address in 1796, announcing his retirement and warning against "permanent alliances" with foreign powers. Washington had gotten the U.S. Presidency off to a strong start, perhaps most fundamentally because of the bold, enterprising view he took of his office and his inspiring personal qualities. Washington retired to Mount Vernon, where he died on December 14, 1799.

John Adams

John Adams, 2d President (1797–1801), was born October 30, 1735, in Braintree (now Quincy), Massachusetts. The son of a Puritan farmer, Adams was graduated (1755) from Harvard College. After teaching briefly, he read law, was admitted (1758) to the bar.

An opponent of the Stamp Act, he was elected (1771) to the Massachusetts colonial legislature. There he steadily resisted British colonial policies and in 1774, just prior to the American Revolution, he was chosen a delegate to the First Continental Congress. At the Second Continental Congress (1775), he pressed for American independence and persuaded Congress to organize the Continental Army and to appoint George Washington as commander-in-chief. Adams helped draft and defend the Declaration of Independence amid turbulent Congressional debates.

In 1778 Adams was dispatched to Paris to build ties between France and the struggling new nation, but his impatience, ready candor, and pride served him ill in diplomacy, and he returned home. A year later, he was elected to the convention that prepared the important Massachusetts state constitution. He returned (1780) to diplomacy as minister to the Netherlands, where he won recognition for the United States and, more important, negotiated a loan. With John Jay and Benjamin Franklin, Adams negotiated (1782) the Treaty of Paris with Great Britain that ended the American Revolution. Three years later, Congress named him the first United States minister to Britain. He was rebuffed by the British, and in 1788 he asked to be recalled.

Soon after his return to America, he was elected Vice-President under George Washington. Despite his characterization of his new post as "the most insignificant office that ever the invention of man contrived or his imagination conceived," Adams was a constructive influence in filling his duties in the Senate.

When Washington declined (1796) to serve a third Presidential term, the Federalists, led by Alexander Hamilton, supported Adams for the Presidency, while the Democratic-Republicans turned to Thomas Jefferson. Adams won by three votes.

At the outset, Adams stressed that his Presidency would be an extension of Washington's. He retained his predecessor's entire cabinet and, in his inaugural address, promised to continue the Washington policies. Despite these reassurances, Federalists became distrustful when Adams, deeming it necessary to improve relations with France, offered the ministry to that country to Jefferson.

When Jefferson declined, Adams was on the point of conferring the post upon another Democratic-Republican leader, James Madison. However, a cabinet upheaval loomed over the step, and Adams reconsidered. Although President, Adams was not leader of his party. Alexander Hamilton, who held no government post was the Federalist leader, and the loyalties of some cabinet members ran to him rather than to Adams.

The central problems and policies of the Adams administration derived from the French Revolution and the ensuing war between France and Britain. Both countries claimed the right to seize American vessels, and the French Directory went so far as to declare that all Americans serving on British vessels were pirates. Adams sought to steer a middle course between Hamilton and his strong partiality toward Britain and Jefferson's similar disposition toward France.

The President called Congress into special session to consider ways of keeping peace. To his cabinet he distributed a series of questions on the Franco-British situation, seeking advice before framing his message to Congress. The questions were leaked to Hamilton, who prepared replies that were submitted through the cabinet to Adams, who accepted their substance, proposing that defenses be strengthened.

Simultaneously, the President dispatched ministers to France to arrange a treaty. The French representatives demanded a bribe and a loan, touching off the sensational episode that became known as the XYZ Affair. Adams again asked his cabinet for advice, and again Hamilton surreptitiously supplied it, proposing a more vigorous policy toward France and closer ties with Britain. Adams accepted the former, but not the latter. Congress responded with actions just short of war, by declaring all treaties with France null and void, creating a Navy Department, and increasing the army and authorizing new ships.

Eager to keep peace, Adams moved to restore diplomatic relations with France. (Adams first nominated W. Vans Murray to become minister to France. The President acted without consulting the cabinet, which enraged the Hamiltonians in it. Federalists in the Senate raised various objections as a prelude to rejecting it. In a bold move, Adams replaced the Murray nomination with the proposal of a three-member peace commission. The step brought press and public opinion so strongly to the President's side that the commission was approved.) Fearful of an Anglo-American alliance, the French this time were cooperative and war was averted. Adams achieved his supreme goal of maintaining peace, but at the high price of alienating his ardently pro-British Federalist party.

In 1798, smarting under criticism of their opposition to France, the Federalists passed the repressive Alien and Sedition laws that were designed to limit and punish criticism of the government and its officers. Adams neither supported the laws' passage nor applied them. Nevertheless, anti-Federalist journalists were arrested and sentiment turned against the administration.

His successful avoidance of war with France alienated Federalist leaders who deemed Adams a traitor to his party. Jefferson, leader of the Democratic-Republicans, observed that the followers of Hamilton were only "a little less hostile" to Adams than to himself. After long, calculated delay, Adams dealt with his cabinet secretaries who, in effect, were Hamilton's spies. One, James McHenry, resigned after a stormy confrontation with Adams, and another, Timothy Pickering, was dismissed.

Without a party behind him, Adams made a poor showing in seeking reelection in 1800. Both Jefferson and Aaron Burr exceeded him in electoral votes (73 each), while Adams received 65. The election was ultimately decided by the House of Representatives.

So aggrieved was Adams by his defeat that he refused to remain in Washington for Jefferson's inauguration and returned home to Quincy. Subsequently the two Presidents—Jefferson and Adams—renewed their friendship. Adams lived longer than any other President, dying on July 4, 1826, a few months before his 91st birthday.

Thomas Jefferson

Thomas Jefferson, 3d President (1801–1809), was born at Shadwell in Goochland County, Virginia, on April 13, 1743. His father was a planter, scholar, militia colonel, and a member of the House of Burgesses; his mother was a Virginia Randolph. Something of Jefferson's democratic impulse doubtless derived from the frontier influences of the Blue Ridge region in which he was reared. Educated by tutors and in local schools, Jefferson studied at William and Mary College, from which he was graduated (1762).

After leaving college, Jefferson studied law under George Wythe and was admitted (1767) to the bar. His practice was soon very successful, and in 1769, his political career began with his election to the House of Burgesses, in which he served until 1774. Not a brilliant speaker (later, as President, he abandoned the practice of delivering Congressional messages in person), Jefferson was brilliant at drafting laws and resolutions. As relations with the British deteriorated, Jefferson on the eve of the Revolution was a busy draftsman of protest documents. A triumph of revolutionary logic was his pamphlet "A Summary View of the Rights of British America," printed in 1774.

A year later, Jefferson was sent as a delegate to the Continental Congress. Always standing with those who were resolved to resist Great Britain, he was deputed to draft the Declaration of Independence, which with few changes Congress adopted on July 4, 1776.

Two months later, Jefferson resigned from Congress and returned to the Virginia House of Delegates, in which he served until 1779 when he was elected governor of Virginia, succeeding Patrick Henry. Disinclined toward the military life, he did not fight in the Revolutionary War. As a Virginia lawmaker, Jefferson was a powerful democratizing influence who moved his state away from virtual control by a few wealthy slaveholders. By amendment of the Virginia land laws, he effected a more equitable land distribution, which was the key to voting rights and educational opportunity. Even more important were his bills to assure religious freedom. Although he failed in his attempt to pass laws that would have gradually abolished slavery in Virginia, he remained opposed to that institution.

Jefferson resigned (1781) as governor, believing that the British army's threat to his state necessitated a military man to serve as chief executive. During a brief interval of private life, Jefferson began writing his *Notes on Virginia*, an extended statement of his beliefs.

He served (1784–89) in several diplomatic assignments and replaced Benjamin Franklin as minister to France. Jefferson sympathized openly with the French Revolution, believing it similar in essence to the American rebellion. His wide travel in Europe broadened his interests, particularly in architecture and agriculture.

Jefferson was abroad and did not participate in the Constitutional Convention of 1787, but his influence was felt in the quick preparation of the Bill of Rights; its omission from the original Constitution he had considered intolerable. He served as Secretary of State in Washington's first administration.

Jefferson was soon sharply at odds with the Secretary of the Treasury, Alexander Hamilton. After supporting several of Hamilton's early financial measures for the sake of unity, Jefferson, preferring an agricultural society, opposed Hamilton's plans to encourage manufacturing and trade and to found a national bank. In resisting Hamilton's broad interpretation of the Constitution to justify these measures, Jefferson advocated states' rights and "strict construction" of the Constitution, limiting the federal government's powers to those that the document specifically granted. Jefferson and Hamilton fought bitterly over foreign policy. Jefferson and the "Democratic-Republicans" who gathered as a party around him (and who were precursors of today's Democratic party) favored France, while Hamilton and the Federalists favored England. Late in 1793 their differences became so acute that Jefferson resigned.

He was elected (1796) Vice-President, with the Federalist John Adams as President. After four years of bitter party strife, Jefferson was elected (1800) President. His Vice-Presidential running mate, Aaron Burr, received the same number of electoral votes, and the election was referred to the House of Representatives. Thanks to the intervention of Hamilton, who advised Federalists to support Jefferson, the sage of Monticello won.

The first President to be inaugurated in Washington, Jefferson quickly set an example of simplicity. His inaugural address was an appeal for bipartisan cooperation—"We are all Republicans —we are all Federalists"—and his conception of government was largely negative, in the sense that he believed the federal government should deal chiefly with foreign affairs, leaving local matters to the states. Jefferson's view was that government should restrain men from harming one another, but otherwise leave them to their own concerns. Federal expenditures should be curtailed and excise taxes repealed.

Although Jefferson appointed followers such as James Madison as Secretary of State and Albert Gallatin as Secretary of the Treasury, he found the lesser offices, the infant bureaucracy, filled with Federalists. Noting that vacancies "by death are few; by resignations none," Jefferson foreshadowed the spoils system by replacing some Federalists in lesser offices with Democratic-Republicans. He refused to honor the Federalist appointment of "midnight judges" in the outgoing Adams' administration. Near the close of his Presidential tenure, Republicans held a majority of executive-branch appointments.

Through his party, Jefferson exerted strong control over Congress and accomplished the repeal of major Federalist statutes, including the Judiciary Act of 1801. His action was rebuked in *Marbury* v. *Madison*, the principle of which was that the Supreme Court may invalidate an act of Congress; Jefferson never accepted this principle. In pardoning those convicted of violating the Alien and Sedition laws, he asserted Presidential power over Congressional law. Heartily approving the use of the impeachment power against partisan Federalist judges, he was regretful of its failure when it was directed against Justice Samuel Chase, who had been impeached (1804) for discrimination against Jeffersonians.

The extraordinary diplomatic achievement of Jefferson's Presidency was the Louisiana Purchase (1803), which was negotiated by Robert Livingston and James Monroe. The temptation of acquiring a vast territory under favorable terms and of protecting the Mississippi's freedom of navigation overwhelmed Jefferson's devotion to strict Constitutional construction. Observing later that he "stretched the Constitution till it cracked," Jefferson submitted the purchase treaty to the Senate which readily approved it.

Jefferson was unsuccessful in seeking to acquire West Florida, chiefly because his lack of candor offended Congress. His reliance on diplomacy collapsed against the depredations of the Barbary pirates off North Africa. Ultimately, he dispatched a naval force and blockaded ports, and later he ordered frigates into action against the sultan of Morocco.

Aided by economic prosperity as well as political achievement, Jefferson was reelected in 1804 by an overwhelming majority. A major event in the second term was the trial of former Vice-President Aaron Burr, who was suspected by Jefferson of having politicked for the Presidency and now was accused of treasonable plottings. Burr's trial became a contest of wits between Jefferson and Chief Justice John Marshall. The latter's definition of treason made Burr's conviction impossible, to Jefferson's disgust.

Jefferson's diplomatic skill at peace-keeping was severely tested by the pressures of European war upon American neutrality. The Napoleonic decrees, British impressment of American seamen, and the audacity of a British frigate in firing on the United States' *Chesapeake*, combined to drive Jefferson to issue a proclamation denying British armed vessels the hospitality of United States waters.

In December 1807, Jefferson forced the Embargo Act through Congress; it prohibited exporting any produce from an American port or sailing any American ship to a foreign port. Enforcement of the act cast the administration in the role of exercising arbitrary power against key rights of the individual. Ironically, the exigencies of the Presidency brought Jefferson to violate the very values with which he was so long and so thoroughly identified—the sanctity of individual rights against governmental encroachment.

The embargo fell more heavily and injuriously upon the United States than upon France and England. Idle ships, unsold goods, and commercial unemployment fired opposition in New England, embittered the sections most loyal to Jefferson, and brought Congress to rebel against the President. Ultimately, Jefferson retreated by approving the Non-Intercourse Act of 1809 under which the embargo was partially raised.

Despite the rocky conclusion of his tenure, Jefferson handpicked his successor, Madison. He retired to Monticello, pursued scientific farming, counseled Presidents Madison and Monroe, and kept in touch with public affairs through a large correspondence. He died on July 4, 1826, on the same day as John Adams and on the 50th anniversary of the adoption of the Declaration of Independence.

James Madison

James Madison, 4th President (1809–1817), was born on March 16, 1751, in Port Conway, Virginia, the son of a planter and justice of the peace, whose forebears had settled in Virginia in the 1600s. A frail and sickly child, Madison was educated by private tutors and graduated (1771) from the College of New Jersey (now Princeton). A year of postgraduate study there was devoted to Hebrew, history, and law.

Torn between the ministry and politics, he chose the latter and was elected (1774) to the Committee of Safety in Orange County, Virginia, an important organ of local government in the twilight of the colonial period. In 1776, Madison was a delegate to the Williamsburg convention that declared for independence and established a state government. Serving in Virginia's first legislative assembly, Madison met Thomas Jefferson and began a lifelong friendship. In 1778, Madison was a member of the executive council, and in 1779 the state legislature elected him to the Continental Congress.

Until 1788, Madison served either in the Virginia legislature or in Congress, where he quickly became convinced that the Continental Congress needed more power, particularly in financial affairs. Although only 36 years old, Madison represented (1787) Virginia at the Constitutional Convention in Philadelphia and took a leading part in the deliberations. Champion of a strong central government, he drafted the "Virginia Plan" on which the Constitution was based. Known as the "Father of the Constitution," Madison kept a journal of the convention—the most complete record available of the proceedings—and his knowledge of past governments and the inherent problems of federalism was invaluable. Madison was a member of the Virginia ratifying convention and, with John Jay and Alexander Hamilton, wrote *The Federalist,* a series of newspaper essays that are regarded as the best explanation of the American constitutional system.

In 1789, Madison defeated James Monroe for election to the new U.S. House of Representatives. One of its most able members, Madison drafted key legislation and played a leading part in preparing the first 10 amendments to the Constitution, known as the Bill of Rights. Soon convinced that Hamilton's policies were hurtful to farmers in the South and West, Madison joined Jefferson in founding the Democratic-Republican party. In 1797, Madison retired, briefly, from politics; however, outraged by the repressive Alien and Sedition Acts (1798), he drafted the Virginia Resolutions, condemning the acts and holding that the states could declare them unconstitutional.

Upon becoming President in 1801, Jefferson appointed Madison Secretary of State. He passed a busy apprenticeship in an administration that, like his own would be, was preoccupied with foreign affairs and the problems of European war. In 1808, after two Presidential terms, Jefferson, following the tradition of George Washington, declined a third term. He chose Madison to be his successor. Madison received 122 electoral votes to 47 for Federalist C. C. Pinckney.

Small and unimpressive in person, Madison at his inaugural, wrote Washington Irving, looked like "a withered little apple-John."

In its early months, Madison's administration was largely an inherited Presidency. He made no changes in Jefferson's cabinet, except to move Robert Smith from the Navy to the State Department. The cabinet, however, had an additional heritage, an old feud between Smith and Treasury Secretary Albert Gallatin. Eventually, Madison dismissed Smith and made Monroe his Secretary of State.

The war between Britain and France was continuing as were their depredations upon American shipping, despite Jefferson's policy of neutrality. In 1810, an act of Congress called for the resumption of trade with both France and Britain, but warned of American withdrawal if either power resumed shipping violations. France soon began such violations, and Britain stirred up the Indians in the West. In the House of Representatives, "hawks" such as Henry Clay and John Calhoun clamored for a war which, they believed would result in the annexation of Canada and Spanish Florida. New England was opposed to war; the rest of the nation demanded it; ultimately Madison called for war against Great Britain, and Congress declared it on June 18, 1812.

Later that year Madison was reelected President by 128 electoral votes to 89 for Mayor De Witt Clinton of New York City.

Both by his contemporaries and by historians, Madison is not rated as a good war President. Calhoun wrote of him, "Our President though a man of amiable manners and great talents has not I fear those commanding talents, which are necessary to control those about him." Madison was handicapped by poor field commanders and by acute sectional and factional differences. Northern Republicans hobbled his efforts to seize the remainder of the Floridas, and Southern Republicans were unenthusiastic about conquering Canada. Each party faction feared that out of conquered territory might come new states favoring the other. Federalists generally opposed "Mr. Madison's War."

In its early stage the war went badly for the United States. For two years, every thrust into Canada was foiled. Britain clamped a tight blockade upon the eastern coast. On August 24, 1814, British forces occupied and burned Washington, and the Madisons fled the White House. But then American fortunes brightened. A British thrust down Lake Champlain was repulsed, and Andrew Jackson won a thrilling victory at New Orleans. In the Treaty of Ghent, however, signed December 24, 1814, not a single U.S. war aim was achieved. At Madison's direction, the demand upon Britain to renounce impressments was dropped. The only demand imposed was that Britain leave occupied American territory.

The war's close saw the decline of the Federalist party, a decline speeded by Madison's adopting its key principles. He approved a new bank of the United States, a tariff act of 1816 to protect "infant industries," and the establishment of substantial military and naval forces on a permanent basis. However, Madison did not accept the Federalist plank of internal domestic improvements to be undertaken by the national government. Such ventures, he thought, necessitated a constitutional amendment.

After leaving the Presidency, Madison lived in retirement on his estate at Montpelier, Virginia. He was a member of the Virginia Constitutional Convention of 1829 and occasionally offered counsel to his successor, James Monroe. Madison died at Montpelier on June 28, 1836, and is buried nearby.

James Monroe

James Monroe, 5th President (1817–1825), was born April 28, 1758, in Westmoreland County, Virginia, the eldest of five children of a circuit judge and planter. A student at William and Mary College when the Revolution broke out, Monroe joined the army, fought in major battles, and was wounded at Harlem Heights in New York and at the Battle of Trenton.

After the Revolution, Monroe studied law under Thomas Jefferson, then the governor of Virginia, and an important friendship between the two began. Monroe's political career commenced with his election (1780) to the Virginia legislature. Three years later he was elected to the Continental Congress, in which he opposed a highly centralized government but supported tariff-making by Congress. In 1786, he returned from Congress to serve in the Virginia Assembly.

Monroe was a state delegate to the Virginia convention that was called to ratify the new U.S. Constitution. So strong was his admiration for Jefferson that he moved to Charlottesville, Virginia, where he built Ash Lawn, not far from Jefferson's estate, Monticello.

Monroe ran unsuccessfully against James Madison for the first U.S. House of Representatives; however, the Virginia legislature elected him (1790) to the U.S. Senate. Allied with Jefferson and Madison, Monroe opposed the centralizing policies of Alexander Hamilton and, aided by Albert Gallatin and Aaron Burr, shared in the founding of the Democratic-Republican party. In 1794, Washington appointed Monroe minister to France, a country he deeply admired. He criticized Jay's (Anglo-American) Treaty so severely, however, that Washington, with whom he had previously clashed, recalled him in 1796.

From 1799 to 1802, Monroe was governor of Virginia. During Jefferson's Presidency, he was dispatched (1802) to Paris to help Robert R. Livingston arrange the Louisiana Purchase; the next year in Spain he aided in the unsuccessful negotiations for the purchase of the Floridas. In 1803 Jefferson named Monroe minister to Britain. From 1811 to 1816, he was Madison's Secretary of State.

In 1816, Monroe was elected President, winning easily over his Federalist opponent, Senator Rufus King of New York. He was reelected in 1820, with only one electoral vote cast against him.

Monroe's Presidency coincided with "the era of good feeling." After the election of 1816, the Federalist party disappeared and the Democratic-Republicans flourished as the country's only party. Thanks to fast developing industry and western settlement, the country prospered. Not even the depression of 1818 dampened the good feeling.

Few disturbing domestic political issues troubled Monroe's first Presidential years. He opposed "the American System" of House Speaker Henry Clay, who demanded internal domestic improvements and a protective tariff. A strict constructionist, Monroe in his first annual message declared that Congress lacked the constitutional power to establish a system of internal improvements. Subsequently, however, he modified his position by granting an appropriation to repair the Cumberland Road and approving the first harbor act. He also approved the 1824 tariff act and moved to a middle-of-the-road position on tariffs and domestic improvements.

In 1819, Missouri applied for admission to the Union as a slave state. A bitter legislative struggle followed on the questions of limiting slavery in Missouri and in the remainder of the Louisiana Purchase. Although sympathetic to the South, Monroe, in keeping with his view of the Presidency, did not involve himself in the struggle until a bill reached him. It provided for the admission of Missouri as a slave state, while banning slavery from much of the rest of the Louisiana Purchase.

Monroe doubted that Congress could constitutionally impose such a ban. His cabinet also had doubts but, ultimately, he decided to leave the question unresolved, signing the act that became known as the Missouri Compromise of 1820.

Attentive to the public's attitude toward his administration, Monroe traveled through the Northeast—a venture that increased his popularity—and later toured the South and Southwest. Monroe demonstrated unusual personal growth in the Presidency by moving away from the evident sectionalism of his first years toward national perspectives. With breadth of vision and a talent for conciliation, Monroe led a cabinet of strong personalities drawn from the country's major regions: John Quincy Adams (Secretary of State), John Calhoun (War), William Wirt (Attorney General), and William H. Crawford (Treasury).

In foreign affairs, the Monroe administration arranged with Great Britain to limit armaments on the Great Lakes and resolved a long-standing dispute with Newfoundland and Labrador over fishing rights. Monroe acquired (1819) Florida from Spain by the Adams-Onís Treaty, even though midway in the negotiations Andrew Jackson had invaded Florida (1818). Monroe also approved of the American Colonization Society settling Liberia; Monrovia was named for him.

A triumph of skillful Presidential leadership, the Monroe Doctrine began its evolution with the clamors for recognition by Spain's former Latin American colonies. Monroe dispatched special agents to those emerging countries and sought to associate Congress with his eventual policy. He recognized the former colonies and, on learning that European powers contemplated a reconquest of them, he and his cabinet developed the message to Congress of December 2, 1823, that set forth the doctrine. In effect, it threatened war against European powers that attempted to "extend their system to any portion of this hemisphere." Although Secretary of State Adams played an important part in the formulation of the doctrine, Monroe conceived the idea of a legislative message to convey it and drafted its central paragraphs.

After leaving office, Monroe retired to his estate near Leesburg, Virginia. He served as regent of the University of Virginia and was presiding officer of the Virginia Constitutional Convention in 1829. Financial distress, stemming from long years of public service, forced Monroe to move (1830) to New York City to live with his married daughter. He died there on July 4, 1831. Subsequently his remains were moved to Richmond, Virginia.

John Quincy Adams

John Quincy Adams, 6th President (1825–1829), was born July 11, 1767, in Braintree (now Quincy), Massachusetts, the eldest son of the 2d President of the United States. Because his father had served as American diplomatic representative to several European countries during the Revolution, Adams received his early schooling abroad. His advanced learning enabled him to enter Harvard College as a junior and graduate in 1787. After reading law for three years, he was admitted to the bar.

But having few clients, Adams took up political journalism. He wrote articles replying to Tom Paine's *The Rights of Man*, which he considered too radical, and attacked the French Minister Edmond Genêt, who during the Washington administration urged the United States to join France in her war with Great Britain. In 1794, George Washington appointed the 27-year-old Adams minister to the Netherlands and, two years later, to Portugal. He served as minister to Prussia after his father became (1797) President.

With the advent (1801) of the Jefferson administration, Adams abandoned diplomacy and turned to politics as a Federalist; he was elected (1802) to the Massachusetts Senate but the Federalist leader there soon considered Adams "too unmanageable." A year later he was elected to the U.S. Senate from Massachusetts. In the Senate, he often voted with the Democratic-Republicans, although a Federalist, and he supported Jefferson's embargo policy to which other New England Federalists were bitterly opposed. When the end of Adams' term approached, the Federalists, feeling betrayed, elected (1808) another man to his place, and Adams immediately resigned.

He returned (1809) to diplomacy under James Madison, who appointed him minister to Russia. Near the end of his service there (1814), he became one of the U.S. commissioners who negotiated the Treaty of Ghent ending the War of 1812. In 1815 Madison appointed Adams minister to Britain; in 1817 James Monroe named him Secretary of State. Adams was a leading influence in the formulation of the Monroe Doctrine.

Just as Madison and Monroe had risen to the Presidency from the post of Secretary of State, Adams considered himself qualified for a similar ascent in the election of 1824. Proud, highminded, and an independent in politics (which made party men look askance at him), Adams made little effort to obtain votes. Moreover, he faced formidable opponents: John Calhoun, Henry Clay, Andrew Jackson, and William Crawford. Calhoun soon withdrew from the Presidential race and was elected Vice-President. For President, Jackson received 99 electoral votes; Adams, 84; Crawford, 41; and Clay, 37. Since none of the candidates had won a majority, the House of Representatives had to choose among the three leading candidates.

Before the House voted, however, Jackson's followers charged that Adams had promised Clay a cabinet post in exchange for his support. Following his election, Adams appointed Clay Secretary of State, prompting Jacksonians in Congress to cry that Adams and Clay had made "a corrupt bargain." These circumstances assured Adams of unrelenting Jacksonian hostility.

In his inaugural address, Adams advocated an ambitious program of domestic improvements and, in his first annual message, he called for federal promotion of the arts and sciences, establishment of a national university and astronomical observatories, and support for scientific enterprises. Strict Northern constructionists were distressed by Adams' liberal interpretations of the Constitution, while Southerners were fearful that the logic of these Constitutional views might lead to federal abolition of slavery.

Neither by personality nor by circumstance was Adams sufficiently endowed to excel in two critical Presidential roles: as party leader and as legislative leader. Although his party controlled the House, the opposition ruled the Senate. Adams himself had little faith in his ability to command success in Congress. A simple proposal, such as his request for authority to dispatch a mission to the Panama Congress of Latin American states, encountered rough trouble in the legislature. A master of diatribe, John Randolph, launched a pointed attack on the supposed Adams-Clay "deal." Worse than Randolph's attack was the failure of anyone in the President's own party to defend him.

Adams made no attempt to soften Congressional opposition by the adroit use of patronage. Seemingly self-obstructive, his principles took precedence over party claims. His administration made only 12 removals from office, a degree of restraint that alienated friends and encouraged enemies. In other ways, too, Adams demonstrated that he was very little of a politician. His cabinet contained no one who had openly supported him for President. He even countenanced the aid openly given by one cabinet secretary to the future Presidential candidacy of Jackson.

The midterm Congressional elections went against Adams' interests, and for the first time in the history of the Presidency a large majority of Congress opposed the administration.

Adams' chief legislative success was the enactment (1828) of the "tariff of abominations," the high rates of which favored New England manufacturers and hurt Southern farmers, who had to pay more for imports. Southern resentment endangered Adams' chances for reelection.

The 1828 Presidential campaign was one of unparalleled bitterness. Adams did not answer—although his supporters did—the attacks of Jackson and his followers. Adams believed it beneath the dignity of the President to engage in political debate. Adams had no party of his own to cope with the well-organized opposition, and Jackson won an overwhelming victory: 178 electoral votes to 83 for Adams. But Adams did not regret leaving the Presidency.

After his Presidential term, Adams briefly enjoyed political retirement, until his election to the House of Representatives. Taking his seat in 1831, he served there for 17 years. He was the first Congressman to argue that slaves could be freed in time of war, an argument that Lincoln was to utilize in the Emancipation Proclamation.

Adams died of a paralytic stroke in the Speaker's Room of the House of Representatives on February 23, 1848. He is buried in Quincy, Massachusetts.

Andrew Jackson

Andrew Jackson, 7th President (1829–1837), was born on March 15, 1767, in Waxhaw, South Carolina, the son of a linen weaver who, upon migrating to the United States from Ireland, became a farmer. Jackson's mother, too, was born in Ireland. In the frontier wilderness of the Carolinas, Jackson grew up with little education or refinement, and with a combative nature. But he was also energetic, self-confident, honest, and straightforward. He was genuinely the first of the "log-cabin" Presidents.

In the American Revolution, Jackson at 13 joined the South Carolina militia and was captured (1781) by the British. After the war, he read law and was admitted (1787) to the bar at the age of 20. In 1788, he became solicitor of the western district of North Carolina (now Tennessee) and soon excelled at sending law violators and debtors to jail. His success in public office rapidly enlarged his private law practice. Through successful land speculation, Jackson also increased his fortune, and he acquired the Hermitage, a plantation near Nashville.

Later that year, he was elected to the U.S. House of Representatives. His rough frontier manners won him attention and popularity, and he was appointed (1797) to the U.S. Senate at the age of 30. But impatient of the slow pace of life in Philadelphia (then the capital) and eager to care for his private affairs, Jackson resigned from the Senate the following year. The Tennessee legislature made his political retirement short lived by making him justice of the state supreme court (July 1798), and he served in that capacity until 1804. The pressures of creditors forced him to resign and devote himself to private affairs. By selling off land and winning steadily on his horses, Jackson withstood his creditors.

His already substantial public service had not compensated for his scanty formal education. A critic said that "his letters, with their crudities in spelling and grammar, would make the better educated angels weep." Nor did his temper diminish; he was party to many duels.

His service in the War of 1812 established him as a national military hero and a popular idol of the West. His best-known victory, at New Orleans, was gained after the treaty of peace had been signed, but before he had learned of it. In 1817 Jackson led a military expedition to Florida to guard the border, but he engaged and defeated the Seminole Indians in battle, pursuing them into northwest Florida. He ordered two British subjects, accused of inciting the Seminoles, hanged, thus precipitating diplomatic crises with Britain and Spain.

As a war hero, Jackson was attractive to politicians, and they began to talk of electing him President. In 1822 the Tennessee legislature nominated him to run for President in 1824 and, as a step in that direction, the legislature elected him to the U.S. Senate in 1823. Jackson again favorably impressed the Washington political community.

In the bitterly fought Presidential election of 1824, Jackson was one of five major candidates. Although he received more electoral votes than any of his rivals, he lacked a majority and the choice went to the House of Representatives. Supporters of Henry Clay in the House gave their votes to John Quincy Adams, who was elected. When Adams appointed Clay as Secretary of State, Jackson was convinced that he had been cheated out of the Presidency by "a corrupt bargain" between his two rivals.

The Presidential election of 1828 was even more bitter. It was the first election in which each Presidential nomination was made by state legislatures and mass meetings, instead of the traditional Congressional caucuses. Seeking reelection, Adams was the "National Republican" or Whig candidate. Jackson won easily, with 178 electoral votes to 83 for Adams.

His inaugural address was a true harbinger of Jackson's future policies. "The Federal Constitution," he said, "must be obeyed, state rights preserved, our national debts must be paid, direct taxes and loans avoided, and the Federal Union preserved." Jackson, who expressed and believed in the phrase "Let the people rule," invited the inaugural crowd into the White House. The results were disastrous: people grabbed up food and punch, stood on chairs, tore draperies, and broke china. The crowd's pressure endangered Jackson, who gladly escaped through a window.

Consistent with his desire for popular rule, Jackson became the first President to use the spoils system on a substantial scale. To Jackson's friend, Senator William L. Marcy of New York, is credited the slogan, "to the victor belong the spoils." Under the Jacksonian conception of spoils, experts were unnecessary for the conduct of government. The people could do its tasks and, best of all, members of the victorious party.

Although Jackson extolled popular rule, he also maximized his own personal rule as President, sometimes to the point of arbitrary power. He developed what became known as the "kitchen cabinet," a small group of personal advisers who were not in the cabinet but, in some cases, occupied subcabinet positions. The kitchen cabinet advised on policies and helped implement them; it tended to supplant the regular cabinet with which Jackson was chronically dissatisfied.

Jackson's revulsion to anything smacking of class privilege led him to attack the Bank of the United States. Although privately owned and managed, the bank, as chartered by Congress, had control over the nation's currency system. Jackson considered the act of Congress that had created the bank unconstitutional. On economic grounds, also, he opposed the bank. Jackson criticized it for failing to establish a "uniform and sound" currency, since he favored a "hard money" policy—one in which paper money would be based on specie (gold and silver).

In 1832 when Congress passed a bill rechartering the bank, Jackson vetoed it. Hitherto Presidents had restricted their use of the veto to constitutional grounds, but Jackson broke new ground by elaborating on the policy considerations prompting his action.

The election of 1832 was a landmark in Presidential history. For the first time, Presidential nominees were chosen by national conventions. The Democratic-Republican party broke into two parties. Jackson's opponents, who called themselves "National Republicans," nominated Henry Clay, while Jackson's followers continued to style themselves as "Republicans" or "Democratic-Republicans." The election was fought on the issue "Jackson or the Bank," and Jackson again won easily, with 219 electoral votes to 49 for Clay.

Spurred by his victory, Jackson continued to move against the Bank of the United States. He directed that government funds deposited with it be removed and placed in state banks, which opponents called "pet banks." "The dying monster," as Jackson called the Bank of the United States, was defeated after a savage fight and transformed itself into a state bank of Pennsylvania.

Meanwhile, banks having the use of government funds issued paper money in enormous quantities, prompting wild speculation. In 1836, Jackson suddenly issued his "specie circular," declaring that the government would accept only gold or silver in payment for public lands. He also required these banks to give up the money deposited with them, so that he might lend it to the states. The result was a disastrous panic that reached full force in the administration of his successor, Martin Van Buren.

Jackson also enhanced Presidential influence by his firm handling of the nullification crisis. In November 1832, South Carolina declared the high tariff acts of 1828 and 1832 null and void and threatened to secede. By proclamation, Jackson warned South Carolina that the law would be enforced and ordered troops and warships concentrated near Charleston. Congress passed a force bill, authorizing the President to employ the armed forces to collect tariffs. Eventually a new compromise tariff law was passed, and South Carolina withdrew its nullification of the tariff laws.

Jackson took a different course when Georgia disregarded the authority of the United States, as expressed by the Supreme Court. The Court had held unconstitutional a Georgia law concerning lands which by treaties had been given to the Indians. When Georgian authorities imprisoned a violator of the state law, Jackson refused to use the executive power to uphold the decision of the Supreme Court, and merely remarked, "John Marshall has made the decision; now let him enforce it." Some explain Jackson's position as one motivated by his long-standing distaste for Indians and for Marshall.

The audacious, enterprising, politically skillful Jackson remade the Presidency. His unprecedented use of spoils and the national nominating convention made it a party office. As a popular President and effective party leader, he became the first President to appeal to the people over the heads of their legislative representatives.

After leaving the Presidency, Jackson retired to the Hermitage and supported the Presidencies of his protégés—Van Buren and Polk. He died on June 8, 1845, and is buried at the Hermitage.

Martin Van Buren

Martin Van Buren, 8th President 1837–1841), was born on December 5, 1782, in Kinderhook, New York, the son of a truck-farmer who was also tavern keeper. As a child, Van Buren enjoyed listening to his father's patrons discuss politics. At the age of 14, he left school to serve an apprenticeship in law offices at Kinderhook and Albany and was admitted to the bar in 1803.

While practicing in Kinderhook, he gained (1808) his first public office, being appointed surrogate of Columbia County by Gov. Daniel D. Tompkins. Van Buren rose rapidly in his New York political career, serving as state senator, attorney general, U.S. Senator, and delegate to the New York constitutional convention of 1821. An admirer of the ideas of Thomas Jefferson, Van Buren was a Democratic-Republican. As U.S. Senator (1821–28), he led in the fight against imprisonment for debt and the extension of the slave trade.

In 1828, Van Buren was elected governor of New York and gave invaluable support to the Presidential race of Andrew Jackson. A grateful Jackson named him Secretary of State but, more important, Van Buren rose to primacy among Jackson's advisers. Completely in accord with Jackson's policies, Van Buren in 1832 ran successfully for Vice-President, Jackson being reelected. As Jackson's chosen successor, Van Buren received the Democratic Presidential nomination in 1836 and won the election virtually unopposed.

Van Buren entered office pledged to follow the footsteps of his predecessor. The new President inherited not only policies but a legacy of problems as well. The worst of these was the feverish speculation in public lands that had developed in the latter days of the Jackson administration. Rich and poor alike, banks and their branches had all indulged in speculation. To check it, Jackson had issued the Specie Circular of July 1, 1836, that stipulated the government need only accept gold and silver in payment for public lands. Despite this restraint and others, a financial crash occurred (May 10, 1837) on Van Buren's 36th day in office. Bank closings and failures spread like plague, the nation having begun its first great depression.

Van Buren perceived neither the power nor the duty of the Presidency to help the people in their economic plight. Despite loud clamors of opposition, Van Buren held to Jackson's Specie Circular. His financial policies alienated conservative (or "bank") Democrats, especially in the politically important states of Virginia and New York. The rival Whig party denounced Van Buren for indifference and "heartlessness," pointing to his failure to issue paper money and resort to other relief measures that might have benefited the people and the economy. Van Buren, whose talents lay more in political manipulation than in persuasive public leadership, followed the practice of ignoring his critics. At this time, as throughout his political career, he was confident that "the sober second thought" of the people would support him.

Another Jacksonian inheritance was America's fiercest and costliest Indian war, the Seminole War in Florida. The great treasure of lives and money required to prosecute the eight-year war further diminished Van Buren's popularity. Even more costly, politically, was his policy toward Canada, since Americans sympathized with the Canadian rebellion of 1837. When British authorities seized an insurgent vessel in American waters, Van Buren resisted vociferous opinion that the country go to war with Great Britain. The President and his administration were derided as "tools of Victoria." In 1839, a border dispute between Maine and New Brunswick erupted, threatening war again, but Van Buren prevailed for peace with patience and tact.

Foreign policy, however, damaged his standing with the Southern base of his party. Facing pressures to annex the now independent Texas, he resisted because he did not want war with Mexico. He also opposed the extension of slavery, which the acquisition of Texas augured.

Dignified, courtly, and given to dandified dress and expensive tastes, Van Buren was a cartoonist's delight. But he was a leader with principles and convictions that he held to at the price of unpopularity and failure of reelection. His party bravely renominated him in 1840. In the boisterous "hard-cider" campaign of 1840, the Whigs delighted to chant that "Little Van" was "a used-up man." In his overwhelming defeat, Van Buren even lost his own state of New York.

Although driven from the Presidency, Van Buren remained active in politics for the next two decades. He continued to oppose annexation of Texas and approved the Wilmot Proviso, which barred slavery in territory acquired from Mexico. In 1848, he was the Presidential nominee of the Free-Soil party. Although defeated, he took so many votes in New York from the Democratic nominee, Lewis Cass, that the Whigs' Zachary Taylor was elected. Van Buren supported Democratic Presidents Pierce and Buchanan, as well as the prosecution of the Civil War. He died at his country estate of Lindenwald, near his birthplace, July 24, 1862.

William Henry Harrison

William Henry Harrison, 9th President (March 4–April 4, 1841), was born at Berkeley, Charles City County, Virginia, on February 9, 1773. His father, a plantation owner and member of the Virginia aristocracy, was a signer of the Declaration of Independence.

Harrison attended Hampden-Sydney College and studied medicine in Philadelphia. Unattracted by the medical profession, he accepted an appointment by President Washington to the army as ensign in 1791.

Harrison served with distinction in the Indian campaigns of the Northwest Territory, rose to a captaincy, and in 1798 resigned his commission to settle at North Bend, Ohio, near Cincinnati. President John Adams appointed him secretary of the Northwest Territory. In 1799, he became the first territorial delegate to Congress.

For 12 years Harrison was territorial governor of Indiana and superintendent of Indian affairs. By negotiating vast land cessions from the Indians, he opened Ohio and Indiana to American settlement. When Tecumseh, a chieftain of the Shawnee Indians, and his brother the Shawnee Prophet objected to the land cessions, Harrison in November 1811 defeated the Indians in a formidable battle at Tippecanoe on the Wabash River. The battle made Harrison a national hero, admiringly called "Old Tippecanoe."

In the War of 1812, Harrison was commissioned a major general in command of forces in the Northwest. He took Detroit in September 1813, and in early October he established American hegemony in the West, when he defeated the combined Indian and British forces at the Thames River in Ontario, where Tecumseh was finally killed.

Harrison resigned his commission and as a war hero was elected in 1816 to the U.S. House of Representatives. He subsequently served in the Ohio Senate and in the U.S. Senate. Appointed minister to Colombia by President John Quincy Adams, Harrison was recalled when Andrew Jackson came to power. He retired to his farm at North Bend, and, to supplement his income, served as county recorder and clerk of the county court.

In 1836, Harrison's political fortunes recovered dramatically when the Whigs nominated him for President. Although defeated by Martin Van Buren, the Democratic candidate, Harrison ran an impressive race, carrying seven states. In 1840, the Whigs, including Daniel Webster and Henry Clay, nominated Harrison for President and John Tyler for Vice-President.

The 1840 Presidential campaign, famous for its slogan "Tippecanoe and Tyler too," is a classic of political demagoguery. Harrison's standing as a war hero, the absence of a platform, and diversionary political propaganda, enabled the Whigs to avoid the emerging issue of slavery. Van Buren, the incumbent, was portrayed drinking champagne from a crystal goblet at a table laden with costly viands and dinnerware. Harrison was seen content with a log cabin and hard cider. Aided also by the suffering of the Panic of 1837, Harrison scored an overwhelming victory.

His inaugural stirred enormous enthusiasm. His address, partly the work of Webster, prolix and abounding in classical allusions, was an extended statement of the Whig doctrine of the Presidency. Deferential to Congress, it viewed the legislators as the center of decision.

Harrison appointed a cabinet of high quality, headed by Daniel Webster as Secretary of State. On March 17, the President called a special session of Congress to meet on May 31 to act on the country's continuing financial distress. A week later, he took ill, developed pneumonia, and died, a month after his inauguration. Harrison was the first of our Presidents to die in office.

John Tyler

John Tyler, 10th President (1841–1845), was born on March 29, 1790, in Charles City County, Virginia, the son of Judge John Tyler, a distinguished lawyer and governor of Virginia. Young Tyler graduated from William and Mary College at 17, was admitted to the bar at 19, and at 21 his public career began with his election to the Virginia House of Delegates.

Tyler moved steadily through a political career of remarkable breadth, as U.S. Congressman, Senator, governor of Virginia, and delegate to the important Virginia constitutional conventions of 1829 and 1830. In 1836, he was an unsuccessful candidate for the Vice-Presidency, but in the "Tippecanoe and Tyler too" campaign of 1840, with William Henry Harrison heading the Whig ticket, he ran again, this time successfully. Harrison died a month after his inauguration, and on April 4, 1841, Tyler became the first Vice-President to succeed to the Presidency.

Some chose to interpret the succession provision of the Constitution to mean that Tyler was only "Acting President," but he insisted upon the office's full title and powers. The reluctance to grant Tyler recognition was partly rooted in the unusual circumstances of his nomination. Tyler was an ex-Democrat who, as a legislator, had been a stubborn advocate of states' rights and consequently opposed to nationalistic Whig policies. The Whigs had nonetheless nominated him for the Vice-Presidency to attract Southern votes. They reasoned that, as Vice-President, Tyler would command no influence in the Harrison administration.

After Tyler became President, his ambiguous situation was further complicated by the presence in the Senate of Henry Clay, the heavy-handed but powerful leader of the Whig party. Clay was soon scornfully speaking of Tyler as "a President without a party." Tyler was also an obstacle to Clay's driving ambition to become President; if Tyler could be discredited to the point of being denied renomination, Clay might himself seize the prize.

Tyler, in a conciliatory step, retained the entire Harrison cabinet, which presumably should have satisfied the Whigs and Clay, but they were irreconcilable. A rift quickly developed over the Whig measure to reestablish a national bank. Twice Tyler vetoed the national bank bill. As a strict constitutionalist, he argued that a national bank must not be permitted to establish branches in the states without their prior consent. After the second bank veto, Tyler's entire cabinet resigned, with the exception of Daniel Webster, the Secretary of State. Webster remained only long enough to complete a treaty with Canada setting the northeast boundary of the United States.

With Clay now openly saying of the President that "I'll drive him before me," Tyler's own measures encountered rough treatment in Congress and his nominations to office were usually blocked.

Despite the deadlock with his own party, Tyler brought off some substantial achievements. He was adept at seizing upon issues that by their merit or popularity transcended partisanship. He was not unskilled at political maneuver and when a favorite project to annex Texas by treaty was lost—with every Whig but one voting against it—Tyler outmaneuvered his opponents and arranged for annexation by joint resolution.

A cultivated Southern gentleman, master of the good story and easy conversation, Tyler was attractive to Congressmen and, as a veteran legislator, experienced in dealing with them. Under his evident influence Congress passed a number of constructive laws. The Navy was thoroughly reorganized. A bureau was established for nautical charts and instruments, which later developed into the Naval Observatory. An act opening the way to initiating a national telegraphic system was passed, a step leading to the development of the Weather Bureau.

As President, Tyler excelled as an administrator and in employing his powers in foreign affairs. He conducted the government with a minimum of waste, although Congress provided no system for controlling public funds. Tyler brought the Seminole War to an end, entered into a treaty with China opening the doors of the Orient for the first time, and applied the Monroe Doctrine to Texas and Hawaii.

Despite his achievements, Tyler could muster only minor factional support for renomination in 1844. Withdrawing from the Presidential race, he retired to his estate, Sherwood Forest, in Virginia on the James River. There he lived in virtual retirement for 14 years, except for service as chancellor of the College of William and Mary from 1859 to 1861. In 1861, he proposed and presided over the secret North-South Conference held at Washington in an eleventh-hour effort to prevent the Civil War. When this failed, he advocated immediate secession and was elected a member of the congress of the Confederacy, but he died on January 18, 1862, before he could take his seat in that body.

James Knox Polk

James Knox Polk, 11th President (1845–1849) was born on November 2, 1795, near Pineville in Mecklenburg County, North Carolina. Polk was of Scots-Irish stock, and his father soldiered in the Revolution. In 1806, the large and growing Polk family moved to central Tennessee, and Polk's schooling in that frontier district was fragmentary. Nevertheless, he entered the University of North Carolina at the age of 20, compiled an impressive record, and graduated in 1818. He studied law under Felix Grundy, the politician and noted criminal lawyer, was admitted to the bar, and practiced in Columbia, Tennessee.

An able orator in demand at political meetings, Polk became known as "the Napoleon of the Stump." This talent, as well as his friendship with Andrew Jackson, propelled him into a political career. In 1823 he was elected to the Tennessee House of Representatives, and in 1825 to the U.S. Congress, where he served seven consecutive terms, the last two as Speaker.

In 1839, he was elected governor of Tennessee. Although an ardent Jacksonian Democrat, he was defeated for reelection in 1841 and again in 1843.

Polk then turned to national politics, and when the Democratic national convention gathered in Baltimore in 1844, he was considered a serious candidate for the Vice-Presidency, but was unthought of for the Presidency. Circumstances, however, brought him an unexpected Presidential nomination: the first successful "dark horse" candidate in the history of the office.

Just before the convention met, former President Martin Van Buren issued a statement opposing the annexation of Texas, which offended both Western and Southern interests. This position eliminated Van Buren, the leading contender for the Democratic nomination. Polk's stand on Texas and the disputed territory of Oregon—"Reannexation of Texas and Reoccupation of Oregon"—won him the nomination and the election. Since Polk lacked national prominence, the rival Whig party's campaign slogan was, "Who is James Polk?" The Democrats countered with "54–40 or Fight!", a reference to the entire Oregon territory, which the United States, it was felt, should possess even at the price of war with Great Britain. In the election Polk narrowly defeated Henry Clay, the Whig candidate, by winning New York State.

His inaugural address exalted the Union and deplored sectional discord. More specifically, he opposed a tariff "for protection merely" and asserted uncompromisingly that the United States' title to Oregon was "clear and unquestionable."

The independent treasury bill of 1846, which he adroitly shepherded through Congress, reestablished a financial system that endured, with only minor modification, until the Federal Reserve System was established during Woodrow Wilson's administration.

The Walker Tariff Act of 1846, true to Polk's purpose, put most tariff duties on a revenue basis and used ad valorem in place of specific duties. Polk prevailed against political foes who foresaw only ruination for manufacturing and the public treasury.

Oregon proved a more difficult issue. Aided by Secretary of State James Buchanan and after long negotiations with Great Britain, Polk won a settlement that was something less than his campaign slogan had demanded. Buchanan proposed that the Oregon Territory be divided by extending to the Pacific coast the boundary provided by the 49th parallel. When Britain rejected the compromise, Polk boldly reasserted his claim to the entire Oregon Territory. Britain then acquiesced to the 49th parallel line, except for Vancouver Island, and the treaty that was signed (1846) incorporated this division.

The acquisition of California was a severe test of Polk's political skills. Aiming to secure the territory by purchases, he reasserted some longstanding damage claims against Mexico. Certain that Mexico could not pay her debt, he expected her to cede the territory. Mexico rejected any kind of bargain, and American troops under Gen. Zachary Taylor provoked hostilities along the Rio Grande. Polk asked Congress on May 9, 1846, for a declaration of war because of the unpaid claims and because Mexico had invaded American soil. The treaty at the end of the Mexican War ceded California and New Mexico to the United States, for which Mexico was paid $15 million, and the old damage claims were assumed by the United States. Polk's opponents charged that he had forced the war upon Mexico to extend slavery.

To induce Mexico to accept the treaty, Polk had asked Congress for $2 million to be used for "diplomatic purposes." The sum was to be devoted to paying the Mexican army, a step that was indispensable to acceptance of the treaty. David Wilmot offered a proviso to the appropriation, directing that slavery be excluded from any territory acquired through use of the funds made available to the President. Polk angrily termed Wilmot's proviso "a mischievous and foolish amendment," aimed at diplomatic embarrassment. After Polk threatened to veto it, the proviso was defeated, but it brought the building conflict between North and South into the open.

In foreign affairs, Polk extended the reach of the Monroe Doctrine from a prohibition of forcible foreign interference to any kind of interference in American affairs. He effectively opposed an invitation by the people of Yucatán in Mexico for Britain or Spain to exert sovereignty over their territory.

Polk was an exacting administrator who closely supervised the affairs of his departments. He bore ungladly the less palatable aspects of politics. He was contemptuous of the spoils system and, in a rare act for a President, vetoed two river-and-harbor bills, Congress's traditional and politically sacred pork-barrel method of legislation.

Serious and diligent almost to a fault, Polk had little time for pleasure and small talk. Secretive, particularly in dealing with Congress, he offended many by his reticence and sly maneuvers. He was lacking in personal magnetism and had few intimate friends, although Bancroft deemed him "generous and benevolent."

Just before taking office, Polk declared he would not be a candidate for reelection. He died on June 15, 1849, shortly after leaving office.

Zachary Taylor

Zachary Taylor, 12th President (March 4, 1849–July 9, 1850) was born November 24, 1784, at Montebello, Orange County, Virginia. His father was a farmer and a colonel in the Revolution. When he was less than a year old, Taylor and his family migrated to Kentucky. There on the frontier, schools were little known, and Taylor absorbed a sketchy education from tutoring.

In 1808, he obtained a commission as first lieutenant in the army. During 40 years of military service, which ended when he was nominated for President, Taylor fought in the War of 1812, against the Indians in the Northwest and in Florida, and in the Mexican War. In the Seminole Indian War in Florida, the muscular, stocky Taylor became known as "Old Rough and Ready" to troops who admired his valor and candor. His dis-

tinction at the battle of Okeechobee against the Seminoles won him the rank of brevet brigadier general.

Taylor commanded the army in Texas, and a Mexican attack upon his forces in 1846 was used by Congress as justification for declaring war. After Taylor's victory at Monterrey, Mexico, President James K. Polk, distrustful of Taylor's independent spirit and his potential as a political rival, turned over most of Taylor's troops to a new commander. Santa Anna, the Mexican commander, learning of Taylor's weakened forces, attacked him at Buena Vista with troops that were numerically far superior. A stunning victory in an all-day battle made Taylor a national hero and immediately inspired both leading parties, the Democrats and the Whigs, to consider him as a candidate for the Presidential election of 1848.

As a lifelong soldier, Taylor had never voted, and his political views, if any existed, were unknown. Mindful of their victory with another military hero, W. H. Harrison in 1840, the Whigs in 1848 chose Taylor as their nominee over such other formidable contenders as Henry Clay and Daniel Webster.

Stressing that his administration would be nonpartisan and free from party pledges, Taylor defeated his Democratic opponent, Lewis Cass, and the Free-Soil nominee, Martin Van Buren, in the first election to be held simultaneously in all the states.

As President, Taylor was a potential force to check the widening breach between the North and South over slavery. He was a slave owner, but numbered among his closest counselors the antislavery Whig, Senator William H. Seward of New York. In addition, his electoral victory was fashioned by substantial support from both sections; he carried seven Northern and eight Southern states. His inaugural address urged Congress to work for conciliation of sectional controversies and offered a program no one could criticize: friendly relations in foreign affairs, an efficient army and navy, and encouragement of agriculture, commerce, and manufacture.

For all of this political insulation, Taylor had to face the fiery issue of the admission of new states to the Union on a free or slave basis. Thanks largely to his overriding nationalistic sentiment, Taylor quickly took an antislavery position, for above all he wanted to annex the territories won in the Mexican War. He wrote to Jefferson Davis that nature had excluded slavery from the new Southwest, and, in a Pennsylvania address, he assured Northerners they "need have no apprehension of the further extension of slavery."

Taylor dispatched a special emissary, Thomas Butler King, to counsel Californians in forming a constitution and applying for statehood. Similar assistance was given New Mexico. In special messages to Congress in 1850, he urged unconditional admission for California and statehood for New Mexico.

In a counterthrust, Southern legislators filibustered against the admission of California and insisted that all measures concerning territories ceded by Mexico be taken up in a single bill. Southern Whigs withdrew their support of Taylor, and such Southern leaders as Alexander Stephens and Robert Tombs threatened the President with secession.

In Congress, Henry Clay framed a series of bills known collectively as the Compromise of 1850 in an effort to placate both the North and the South. Taylor would doubtless have opposed the compromise, but following ceremonies connected with building the Washington Monument, he was stricken with cholera and died after a Presidential tenure of only 16 months.

In foreign affairs, Taylor's Secretary of State, John M. Clayton, negotiated the Clayton-Bulwer Treaty with Great Britain which guaranteed the neutrality of an isthmian canal. (The previous Polk administration had secured rights to build a canal across Nicaragua.)

Millard Fillmore

Millard Fillmore, 13th President (July 10, 1850–March 3, 1853), was born in Locke (now Summerhill) in Cayuga County, New York, on January 7, 1800. The son of a frontier farmer who had migrated from Vermont, young Fillmore had scant schooling and was apprenticed to a wool carder. Intent upon studying law, he migrated to Buffalo, where he worked in a lawyer's office for room and board. In 1823, he was admitted to the bar and began practice in East Aurora, New York.

Fillmore's political career began with his election in 1828 to the New York State Assembly on an Anti-Mason ticket. He secured the passage of a law that abolished imprisonment for debt and formed a friendship with the Albany publisher and political leader, Thurlow Weed. In 1830, Fillmore moved back to Buffalo and a year later was elected to the first of four terms in the U.S. Congress. He supported the emerging Whig party and the nationalistic policies of Henry Clay. As chairman of the powerful Ways and Means Committee, he oversaw the 1842 tariff act that raised duties on manufactured goods. On the burning issue of slavery, he was a moderate.

In 1844, Fillmore ran as the Whig candidate for governor of New York but was unsuccessful and returned to his law practice. In 1846, he became the first chancellor of the University of Buffalo. A year later, he was elected comptroller of New York.

Fillmore's acceptability to both Northern and Southern Whigs and his backing by Henry Clay resulted in his election as Vice-President with Zachary Taylor in 1848. As Vice-President, he presided over the bitter Senate debates on the slavery compromise measures of 1850 with notable fairness. Midway in this political turbulence President Taylor died, and Fillmore became the second "accidental President."

The Taylor Cabinet promptly resigned. Fillmore's nomination of Daniel Webster of New Hampshire as Secretary of State and John Crittenden of Kentucky as Attorney General was indicative of the new President's preference for a moderate Whig position and his readiness to compromise in the growing conflict between North and South. In his message to Congress of August 6, 1850, Fillmore made a compelling plea for settlement by compromise. An opponent, Salmon Chase, credited the Presidential message with winning over six New England votes in the Senate and moving Congress down the compromise road.

Clay's "omnibus" compromise bill, unable to be passed as a whole, was separated into its several parts. These sections were soon enacted, and the President approved them believing that only through them could the Union be saved. Fillmore and Clay led not a united party, but rather one that represented a bipartisan coalition of Northern Democrats and Southern Whigs. To Southerners, a key element of the compromise was the new Fugitive Slave Law; Fillmore's approval of it cost him the support of Northern Whigs. Since the Presidency was Whig and Congress Democratic, little important legislation was passed, other than the Compromise of 1850.

In seeking renomination as the Whig standard-bearer in 1852, Fillmore enjoyed support from Southern Whigs. His rival, Webster, was backed by New Englanders, and another rival, General Winfield Scott, by an extreme antislavery group. When the Fillmore-Webster factions failed to unite, the nomination passed to Scott. Like other Presidents from Jackson to Lincoln, Fillmore was limited to one Presidential term by the slavery dispute, which prevented the Chief Executive from satisfying both the Northern and Southern wings of his party.

As President, Fillmore presented an image of cool-headedness and caution. His paramount political value was preservation of the Union, a goal to which he subordinated any specific interest or issue in the slavery controversy. From his deathbed, Henry Clay urged Fillmore's renomination, while Webster hailed his administration as one of the ablest.

Fillmore's advent to politics coincided with the emergence of the Whig party, and his departure with its demise. The 1852 elections were the last national campaign in which the Whigs were active. In 1856, Fillmore was the Presidential nominee of the American, or Know-Nothing, party. Stressing the value of unity and the dangers of sectionalism, he ran last in a three-way race. Always preferring conciliation to coercion, Fillmore opposed Lincoln's policies in the Civil War and supported Andrew Johnson's stand against radical reconstruction.

For all his lack of early advantages, Fillmore, according to a contemporary, possessed "a grace and polish of manner which fitted him for the most refined circles of the metropolis." Fillmore's political activities ended with the Reconstruction. He died on March 8, 1874. In 1969, a substantial body of Fillmore papers was discovered.

Franklin Pierce

Franklin Pierce, 14th President (1853–1857), was born on November 23, 1804, in Hillsboro, New Hampshire. His father, Benjamin Pierce, served in the Revolution and later was a brigadier general in the state militia. He was also a two-term governor of New Hampshire and left a valuable heritage of political connections for his son, who, after study at nearby academies and at Phillips Exeter, entered Bowdoin College in Maine.

After graduating from Bowdoin in 1824, Pierce read law and was admitted to the bar in 1827. He began practice in Hillsboro and two years later commenced his political career by winning election as a Jacksonian Democrat to the New Hampshire House of Representatives. Reelected two years later, he also became Speaker. In 1833, he began a term in the U.S. House of Representatives and after a second term was elected to the U.S. Senate. He was the youngest member of that body, which then included such giants as Webster, Clay, and Calhoun. Because of his wife's poor health, Pierce resigned from the Senate in 1842 and resumed law practice in Concord, New Hampshire.

When the Mexican War broke out, Pierce, a staunch nationalist, inspired by his father's record in the Revolution, enlisted as a private. He advanced rapidly to brigadier general and served in key battles. In 1848, he resigned from the army, and two years later he became president of New Hampshire's Fifth State Constitutional Convention.

In 1852, Pierce became the Democratic Presidential nominee, a classic instance of a successful "dark horse" candidate. He received no votes until the 35th ballot and won on the 49th, as an acceptable compromise candidate in the deepening North-South split over slavery. An advocate of the Compromise of 1850, Pierce was regarded as a Northerner with Southern sympathies. Pierce was victorious over his Whig opponent, General Winfield Scott, by carrying every state but four, although with less than a 50,000 plurality.

By having avoided issues in his campaign, Pierce hoped to make his administration one of harmony. His cabinet was a perfect political balance of two conservative Southerners, two conservative Northerners, an antislavery Northerner, a states' rights Southerner, and a New England Whig. His inaugural address and early actions stressed objectives of general appeal. He promised a vigorous foreign policy and an economical and efficient administration. He called for a larger and better army and navy and reduction of the debt through use of the Treasury surplus. But Pierce's strategy of harmony was bedeviled by rising Northern sentiment against slavery and its expansion.

In foreign affairs, Pierce was an expansionist. His policies reflected his nationalism and, presumably, were designed to divert attention from domestic issues and gratify Southern hopes of introducing the slave economy into new territories. Accordingly, Pierce sought to convince Great Britain that under the Clayton-Bulwer Treaty she ought to withdraw from Nicaragua and Honduras. When negotiations failed, he tacitly supported a proslavery "filibustering" expedition against Nicaragua.

Pierce negotiated to acquire Hawaii, but the venture failed when the king of the islands died. Pierce's overtures to the Russians for the purchase of Alaska were unavailing. His administration's most brazen move was the Ostend Manifesto, a declaration by three proslavery American ministers calling for the annexation of Cuba. The public, the Senate, and the President's own party reacted indignantly to this move.

Pierce's foreign policies were not altogether blanketed with failure. A treaty was made with Japan in 1854, opening that country to American trading interests. James Gadsden, a special Presidential emissary, negotiated the purchase of land from Mexico that settled a boundary dispute and secured right-of-way for a southern railroad to the Pacific.

The President's preoccupation with foreign policy could not forestall a sudden, unexpected upsurge of the slavery issue. Leading Democratic Senators brought up a bill to organize Kansas and Nebraska as new territories out of the Indian lands, thus threatening the slender slavery truce. When the Kansas-Nebraska Bill became law in 1854, both proslavery and antislavery settlers poured into the territory, and trouble quickly developed as both factions vied for control. Civil war erupted in Kansas when a free-soil group organized a government independent of the President's. Ultimately, Pierce ordered the free-soil government to cease and put federal troops at the disposal of the governor of Kansas. The Kansas experience served to reinforce the Democratic party's identification with slavery and to spur the rise of the new Republican party and the Know-Nothing party.

Pierce strove energetically to restore his crumbling popularity and win renomination. He launched an anti-British drive and demanded the recall of the British Minister Crampton for illegally recruiting troops in the United States for the Crimean War. But the Democratic national convention of 1856, apprehensive of rising Republican strength, looked for a "safer" man; it found him in James Buchanan, who, by having been abroad, had been untouched by the controversies of the Pierce era.

Although humiliated by his rejection for renomination, Pierce labored diligently to reduce and master problems before leaving office. He established a regular (proslavery) government in Kansas and, thanks to the continued presence of troops, he could proclaim that "peace now reigns in Kansas." A treaty was negotiated under which Britain agreed to abandon its interests in Central America except those in Honduras. The Senate, however, withheld its approval. Upon leaving office, Pierce at least had the satisfaction of seeing his party retain control of the Presidency and regain Congress.

After leaving the Presidency, Pierce traveled abroad to aid his wife's health. In the Civil War, having returned to Concord, he was an outspoken critic of Lincoln's, holding that war could have been averted by better leadership. The increasing unpopularity of his views relegated him to obscurity. His death on October 8, 1869, was almost unnoticed.

James Buchanan

James Buchanan, 15th President (1857–1861), was born April 23, 1791, in Cove Gap, Pennsylvania, the second of 11 children and the son of a merchant-farmer. After graduation (1809) from Dickinson College in Carlisle, Pennsylvania, Buchanan studied law in Lancaster and began practice there in 1812. He volunteered for duty in the War of 1812 and helped defend the city of Baltimore.

Originally a Federalist, Buchanan was elected (1814) to the Pennsylvania House of Representatives. In 1816 he ran unsuccessfully for the U.S. Congress but, four years later, he won and began 10 years of service in that body. Joining the Democratic party, he supported the Presidential race of Andrew Jackson in 1824 and again in 1828, when Jackson won. Grateful for Buchanan's continued support, President Jackson appointed him (1831) minister to Russia. After negotiating America's first trade treaty with Russia, Buchanan returned to the United States, and in 1834 he was elected U.S. Senator.

Buchanan was a favorite-son candidate for the Democratic Presidential nomination of 1844, but he withdrew his name before the convention met. James K. Polk, who was elected, made Buchanan his Secretary of State in 1845. In this post,

Buchanan oversaw the negotiations that secured the southern half of the Oregon country and the vast territory in the Southwest from Mexico. His support of the annexation of Texas and the acquisition of Cuba led to the charge that he was a proslavery politician.

When the Whigs recaptured the Presidency in 1849, Buchanan retired to Wheatland, his estate near Lancaster. He was an unsuccessful aspirant for the Presidency in 1852. Franklin Pierce, who was nominated and elected, appointed Buchanan minister to Great Britain. By serving abroad, Buchanan avoided the fierce domestic political struggle over the Kansas-Nebraska Act and was, therefore, highly available in 1856 for the Democratic Presidential nomination. As the eventual nominee, Buchanan stressed the necessity of preserving the Union and avoided taking a stand on the slavery question. In a three-cornered race, Buchanan won only a popular plurality, although he secured a large majority of the electoral vote. He was a bachelor and the only Pennsylvanian to have become President.

Buchanan's plan for halting the worsening schism over slavery was revealed in his inaugural address and in the formation of his cabinet. In choosing his department heads, he preserved "the sacred balance," giving equal representation to slaveholding and nonslaveholding states. In his inaugural address, he declared that the question of slavery in the territories was a matter for the courts to determine, a view that he asserted confidently after learning how the pending Dred Scott case would be decided.

Buchanan hoped to deflect national attention from grievous domestic problems by fostering a dynamic foreign policy. He moved to acquire Cuba, but Congress failed to provide the necessary appropriations to begin negotiations. To avoid European intervention, he proposed to bolster the Benito Juarez government in Mexico, but Congress again would not lend financial support to the scheme.

Buchanan's image as a Northern man with Southern sympathies was affirmed by his accepting the Dred Scott decision as final and by his support of the proslavery Kansas constitution. Buchanan stressed that this constitution was republican in form and properly left the question of slavery up to popular determination once Kansas became a state. The President's stand divided the Democratic party into two great factions. It identified the administration with the Southern wing and ignited a revolt by the followers of Stephen A. Douglas.

The growing crisis of disunion was magnified when South Carolina moved toward secession. Buchanan rejected the advice of his military commanders to garrison Southern ports. (In his annual legislative message, however, he had emphatically denied the right of secession.) Simultaneously, he admitted an inability to deal with actual secession, since federal officers in South Carolina, through whom he enforced the law, had resigned. In a close construction of Presidential authority, Buchanan held that except for defending U.S. property in South Carolina and collecting customs, the Chief Executive lacked authority to act. Congress alone could decide whether existing laws were amendable for carrying out the Constitution.

Buchanan dispatched a personal agent, Caleb Cushing, to dissuade the South Carolinians from secession and again rejected military advice to reinforce the forts in Charleston harbor. A South Carolina convention, nevertheless, voted to secede and Major Robert Anderson moved his Federal troops from indefensible Fort Moultrie to Fort Sumter, a step that South Carolina spokesmen said violated a Presidential commitment to keep the status quo.

In the quickening tension, Buchanan's cabinet collapsed, with both Northern and Southern members resigning. The President filled the vacancies with Northern and border-state members, a harbinger of firmer policies. Buchanan sent reinforcements to Fort Sumter and announced his intent to hold it and keep peace until "the question shall have been settled by competent authority." Buchanan proposed new legislation to deal with the crisis, but Congress was unresponsive.

Buchanan retired into obscurity at Wheatland and died on June 1, 1868.

Abraham Lincoln

Abraham Lincoln, 16th President (March 4, 1861–April 14, 1865), was born in a dirt-floor log cabin in Hardin (now Larue) County, Kentucky, on February 12, 1809. His father, Thomas, was a migratory frontier farmer and carpenter, who was nearly always poor and moved from Kentucky to Indiana and, eventually, to Illinois. Of Lincoln's mother, Nancy Hanks of Rockingham County, Virginia, little is known. She died when young Lincoln was nine, and his home seemed empty and lonely after her death, until his father married Sarah (Bush) Johnston, a widow, who brought affection to the family. Lincoln may have spoken of her when he said: "God bless my mother; all that I am or ever hope to be I owe to her."

Lincoln absorbed a scanty frontier education (his formal education probably totaled less than one year). Books were scarce, but Lincoln taught himself to read and was a close student of the family Bible. His boyhood readings in it provided the store of Biblical quotations and references that later abounded, with great effect, in his addresses and writings.

As a strong, large-boned youth of 6 feet, 4 inches, Lincoln was admirably suited for hard work, which he experienced in the full. He split logs for fence rails, plowed fields, cut corn, threshed wheat, and took a flat boat loaded with farm produce to New Orleans. As a boy, he showed talent as a speaker; his knack for telling stories and imitating local personalities made people gather to hear him, often at a store in which he was a clerk. His homely face and black coarse hair added fascination to what he said.

From 1831 to 1837, Lincoln was settled in New Salem, Illinois, a log-cabin community near Springfield. For a time he clerked in a store (which soon failed). As unemployment threatened, the Black Hawk War commenced, and Lincoln volunteered for service. His company elected him captain, but he saw no fighting except, he said, "with the mosquitoes."

Returning (1832) from the war, Lincoln groped for a way to make a livelihood. With a partner, he bought a grocery store in New Salem on credit. When the store failed and the partner died, Lincoln paid off the debts, an accomplishment that won him the nickname "Honest Abe." In 1833, Lincoln was appointed postmaster of New Salem, and eked out a living as a deputy to the county surveyor and from other odd-job fees.

Trying for the state legislature in 1834, Lincoln won as a Whig and served four successive two-year terms. His ready stories and sharp wit enabled him to excel in debate, and his leadership gifts were recognized in his selection as the Whig's floor leader. Simultaneous with his young political career, Lincoln read law and won (1836) his license to practice. In Springfield, he experienced a succession of partnerships, including one with William H. Herndon, who later became his biographer.

Lincoln "traveled the circuit," accompanying judges and fellow lawyers through the counties to try cases. The cases were heard in inns, which permitted Lincoln to indulge his talent for strong, effective argument when he thought his client was right.

Lincoln emerged in national politics when he was elected as a Whig to the U.S. House of Representatives and on December 6, 1847, took his seat in Congress where, to the displeasure of his constituents, he opposed President Polk and his conduct of the Mexican War. When his term ended on March 4, 1849, Lincoln did not dare run again because of the general unpopularity of his war views among his constituency. Convinced that his political career was ended, he returned to Springfield where, through hard work and a fast-growing practice, he became one of the best-known lawyers in Illinois in the 1850s.

In 1855, agitated by the national political issue of slavery, Lincoln again turned to politics. Opposed to slavery, although he was never an abolitionist, Lincoln spoke against the principal author of the Kansas-Nebraska Act, Illinois Senator Stephen A. Douglas, and supported the candidacies of legislators opposed to the act. In that same year, Lincoln ran unsuccessfully for the U.S. Senate. Believing that slavery was the negation of the nation's commitment to freedom and equality, he left the Whigs and joined the antislavery Republican party.

In 1858, Lincoln was nominated to run against Douglas for the U.S. Senate. In his speech at the Illinois Republican convention, Lincoln said that "I believe this government cannot endure permanently half slave and half free." The Senatorial contest included a series of debates between Lincoln and Douglas centered on the extension of slavery into free territory. Holding that he was not an abolitionist, Lincoln condemned slavery "as a moral, social, and political evil." Douglas won the election, but the debates gained Lincoln national attention.

In May 1860, the Republican national convention nominated Lincoln for President on the third ballot, after William H. Seward of New York had led on the first two ballots. Considered a moderate on the slavery question, Lincoln received 180 electoral votes to 72 for Breckinridge, 39 for Bell, and 12 for Douglas. Lincoln, elected President, was pledged not to abolish slavery, but to preserve the Union and to prevent the spread of slavery.

However, Southern secession began as soon as Lincoln's election was assured. On December 20, 1860, South Carolina passed a secession ordinance. By the time Lincoln was inaugurated (March 4, 1861), seven states had seceded and formed the Confederate government. Denying in his inaugural address that the federal government would interfere with slavery in states in which the Constitution protected it, he warned that he would use the full power of the nation to "hold, occupy, and possess" the "property and places belonging to the Federal government."

With the coming of war, Lincoln acted boldly and energetically. He called out the militia to suppress the "insurrection," expanded the regular army and navy, raised a volunteer army, closed the post office to "treasonable correspondence," imposed a blockade on Southern ports, and suspended the writ of habeas corpus in areas where Southern sympathizers were active. He also ordered the spending of unappropriated funds for purposes unauthorized by Congress.

For Lincoln's wartime Presidency, the Civil War was a severe test of the human spirit. A succession of battlefield defeats afflicted the North, and a substantial body of Northern opinion demanded peace. Many were willing to fight to preserve the Union, but not to destroy slavery. Others urged the destruction of slavery as the war's supreme goal. Lincoln had to keep the antislavery extremists in check to prevent the secession of the border states. Jealousies and frictions unsettled his cabinet. He appointed and removed a succession of field commanders in the vain hope of securing a major military victory.

In mid-1862, Lincoln decided to drop his reserve on the slavery question and issue a proclamation of emancipation. On the advice of Secretary of State Seward, he awaited a Northern victory. Seizing upon the dubious success of Union forces at Antietam (September 1862), Lincoln issued the proclamation on September 22. He declared that slaves in states in rebellion on January 1, 1863, would be free. Lincoln's action gave a clear-cut moral purpose to the war, setting the stage for the 13th Amendment to the Constitution (adopted in December 1865) that ended slavery throughout the United States.

The tide of the war ran strongly in the Union's favor in 1863 and 1864. Lincoln was renominated (1864), and easily defeated his Democratic opponent, General George B. McClellan, by an electoral vote of 212 to 21 and a popular majority that exceeded 400,000 votes. When Lincoln again took the oath of office (March 4, 1865), the end of the war was in sight, and his inaugural address outlined a postwar policy. He urged that, instead of vengeance, there be "malice toward none" and "charity for all." Pressed to decide if seceded states were in or out of the Union, Lincoln, in his last public address (April 11, 1865), said that the question was unimportant: the Southern states "finding themselves safely at home, it would be utterly immaterial whether they had ever been abroad."

On April 14, five days after Lee's surrender, Lincoln was mortally shot by John Wilkes Booth—an actor and fanatical supporter of the Confederacy—at Ford's Theater in Washington and died the next morning.

Lincoln as President withstood the trials of war with a granitic self-confidence. Yet he was a man of the purest humility, extraordinary wisdom, and shrewd judgment—a master politician in understanding and shaping public opinion. His lean, beautiful, moving prose brought to his Presidency an eloquence that no other incumbent has matched.

Andrew Johnson

Andrew Johnson, 17th President (April 15, 1865–March 3, 1869), was born on December 29, 1808, at Raleigh, North Carolina. His father, who was a sexton, porter, and constable, died when Johnson was four, and at 10 he was apprenticed to a tailor. Thanks to the tailor's practice of employing someone to read aloud as his workmen stitched, and to the local newspaper and a few books, Johnson became familiar with American history and politics.

In 1826, Johnson moved to Greeneville, Tennessee, where he set up his own tailor shop. His efforts in organizing a workingman's party led to his election as alderman in opposition to the local slave-holding aristocracy's candidate. In 1830, he became mayor of Greeneville, and five years later he was elected to the Tennessee legislature and served continuously until 1843. Although formally unschooled, Johnson continued his political rise when elected (1843) to the U.S. House of Representatives in which he served for 10 years.

In Congress Johnson staunchly represented the interests of the "common people" and, in 1845, he introduced the first homestead bill for providing farms for landless citizens from public lands. Johnson's political beliefs were influenced by his fellow Tennessean, Andrew Jackson. Johnson's powerful voice and quick mind enhanced his popularity while provoking concern among Southern aristocrats who opposed his homestead policy. Johnson was elected (1853) Tennessee governor and U.S. Senator (1857), thus becoming one of the few major Southern officeholders of the time who had supported himself by manual labor. Although a slaveholder and a Democrat, Johnson defended the Union. In fact, he was the only Southern Senator not to resign and secede with his state. When Union armies won back (1862) control of western Tennessee, Lincoln appointed Johnson military governor of the state and, by 1864, he had organized a loyal government. This achievement won Johnson the Vice-Presidential nomination on Lincoln's Republican ticket in 1864.

Upon Lincoln's assassination, Johnson assumed the office of President in an atmosphere of grief and rage. Quickly moving to restore conditions of peace after the Civil War, Johnson disbanded most of the Federal army, revoked the blockade of the South, and restored trade. For the difficult problem of reestablishing local government in the seven states of the former Confederacy, Johnson faced rival Presidential and Congressional plans that had been formulated under Lincoln.

Although claiming to assert Lincoln's plan, Johnson actually altered it in some particulars. Unlike Lincoln, who had offered a general amnesty, Johnson required that 14 classes of persons —particularly the well-to-do—apply for pardon. But in judging the loyalty of a state government, Johnson required neither that there be a stipulated proportion of loyal voters nor that state legislatures or conventions take specific steps.

Under Johnson's stimulation, new state governments were organized, secession ordinances were repealed, and slavery abolished. The 13th Amendment was ratified (1865) by all Southern states, except Mississippi. The new governments, however, failed to extend suffrage to qualified blacks, as Johnson suggested. The President did not curb Southern police regulations that were aimed, presumably, at keeping order among blacks but quickened Northern suspicions of an attempt to restore slavery.

Congress, which had not been in session, met in December 1865. The Radical Republicans, who favored harsh reconstruction terms for the South, realized that they would be outnumbered if Southern legislators were seated. As a result, the Radicals refused to seat the Southerners, arguing that they had been illegally elected. Led by Congressman Thaddeus Stevens of Pennsylvania, the Radicals further contended that the Southern states had to come in as new states or continue to be regarded as conquered territory. However, in his message to Congress, Johnson viewed the states and the Constitution as intertwined: since the act of secession was null and void under the Constitution to begin with, Southern state functions had been in his view simply suspended, not destroyed.

In the conflict that developed, Congress' lawmaking powers were pitted against the President's veto power. Congress passed an act extending the Freedman's Bureau, but Johnson vetoed it. His veto of the Civil Rights Act, however, failed. The act aimed to guarantee the rights of freedmen against violation by state law. Congress also passed (1868) the 14th Amendment, which was designed to incorporate the substance of the act into the Constitution.

With the Congressional elections of 1866 in prospect, Johnson decided to present his case to the people and made his "swing around the circle," as it was known, through the East and Midwest in August and September. Although the venture began well, Johnson was provoked into making some ill-tempered remarks when goaded by Radical hecklers, and a hostile press ran biased accounts of his conduct. The election results imperiled Johnson: Congressional foes increased and, consequently, his veto power deteriorated.

Emboldened by its ability to overwhelm the President's veto power, Congress now began to encroach seriously on his domain. It circumvented the Presidential pardoning power, which Johnson had used on behalf of prominent Confederates, by excluding Confederates from office until Congress granted amnesty. The Tenure of Office Act (1867), which was passed despite Presidential veto, prohibited the Chief Executive from removing, without Senate consent, any officer appointed with the Senate's consent. The Supreme Court declined to review the act.

On August 12, 1867, Johnson suspended Secretary of War Edwin M. Stanton, a Radical informer, and appointed General Ulysses S. Grant as temporary secretary. But Grant was also a Radical sympathizer and, in January 1868, he returned his office to Stanton. On February 21, Johnson, formally removing Stanton, made General Lorenzo Thomas Secretary ad interim. Stanton, however, locked himself in his office to prevent Thomas from taking over, and the Senate refused to confirm Thomas' nomination.

A few days later, the House of Representatives voted 128 to 47 to impeach Johnson on 11 counts. A garish extravaganza of 11½ weeks' duration, the trial was presided over by Chief Justice Salmon P. Chase who, although wanting to be President with an intensity that Lincoln had once likened to insanity, proved to be a model of fairness. If the President was convicted, the new President was to be one of the Senate's own, Ben Wade of Ohio, its president pro tempore, who stood first in the line of succession under a law that dated back to 1792.

As the proceedings moved on, the case against Johnson proved thin and revealed that some Senators were more intent upon punishing him than seeing justice done. Fierce pressure was brought to bear on undecided Senators to build up the two-thirds vote required for conviction.

On May 16, the Senate voted on the eleventh charge, the one that Johnson's opponents believed the most likely to pass. As the vote proceeded, it became clear that the outcome would depend on the vote of Senator Edmund G. Ross of Kansas, who said "not guilty" and saved Johnson by a single vote. Votes were taken on only two other articles with identical results, and the trial ended.

In foreign affairs, Johnson and Secretary of State Seward achieved (1867) the purchase of Alaska from Russia and in 1865, by threat of force, they induced Napoleon III to withdraw his troops from Mexico. Maximilian, who was installed (1864) by Napoleon III as Mexico's emperor while the United States was distracted by the Civil War, was overthrown by Juarez.

For all of his travail, Johnson nonetheless aspired to be the Democratic nominee for President in 1868, but the party chose Governor Horatio Seymour of New York.

After leaving the White House, Johnson ran unsuccessfully for Congress in 1869 and 1872. In 1874, however, he was elected to the U.S. Senate, the only former President to become a Senator. Johnson served only in a special short session in March 1875. After returning to Tennessee, he suffered a paralytic stroke and died on July 31, 1875.

Ulysses Simpson Grant

Ulysses Simpson Grant, 18th President (1869–1877), was born on April 27, 1822, in Point Pleasant, Ohio, the eldest son of a farmer and tanner. An excellent horseman but disinclined toward farm work, Grant applied to West Point.

An average student at West Point, Grant impressed his classmates as academically lazy and careless in dress. Graduating in 1843, he served with distinction in the Mexican War and attained the rank of first lieutenant.

After the war, Grant served in western posts and drank excessively, until his commanding officer ordered him either to reform or to resign. In 1854 he did resign and took up farming near St. Louis. Handicapped by poor land, Grant sold the farm in 1859 and became employed in a real estate office, but performed his main duty—collecting rents—poorly. He next worked, briefly, in the U.S. Customhouse, and in 1860 joined his father's hardware store in Galena, Illinois. As a storekeeper, he was unsuccessful, too.

At the outbreak of the Civil War, Grant, now 40 years old and unsettled, drilled a company of volunteers in Galena and then went to Springfield to work for the Illinois adjutant general. His request to the War Department for a colonelcy was ignored; however, in May 1861 the governor of Illinois appointed him colonel of the 21st Illinois Volunteers. By August, he was a brigadier general of volunteers and was given command of southwestern Missouri. An aggressive field commander, he swept through victories in Missouri, Kentucky, and Tennessee. In 1862, he gave

the Union its first major victory when he captured Forts Henry and Donelson. At the latter fort he specified, "No terms other than an unconditional and immediate surrender can be accepted." This earned him the nickname "Unconditional Surrender Grant."

Grant moved on to larger commands and greater victories at Shiloh, Vicksburg, and Chattanooga. In March 1864, Lincoln made him a lieutenant-general, placed him in command of all the Union armies, and said of Grant that "he makes things git." Grant took personal command of the Army of the Potomac to confront the Confederates under General Robert E. Lee. Relentlessly applying superior manpower and force, Grant wore down the enemy and brought Lee to surrender at Appomattox, April 9, 1865. Generous in victory, Grant permitted the vanquished Confederates to keep their horses "for the spring plowing." Lavishly hailed in the victorious Union, Grant was made a full general in 1866, the first such designation since George Washington.

In 1868, Grant the military hero won the Republican nomination for President and triumphed easily over his Democratic opponent, Governor Horatio Seymour of New York. A newcomer to politics, Grant accepted the nomination in a note the brevity of which was unheard of for Presidential candidates, but it did contain the apt sentiment, "Let us have peace." Always a man of opinions, Grant declined to ride in the inaugural with the outgoing President, Andrew Johnson, owing to an estrangement that stemmed from Johnson's imbroglio with the War Department.

Unfamiliar and uneasy with politics, Grant conducted business in the executive mansion in a military style. Military aides did much of the work of the administration and Grant, upon issuing orders, expected battle-command compliance. To his misfortune, he did not readily perceive the subtle resistances and manipulations of civilian administrators.

Cabinet appointments, often used by a President to build support within his party, were devoted by Grant to the indulgence of his personal preferences. As Secretary of State he named his close friend Elihu Washburne. His military aide, John A. Rawlins, became Secretary of War. Grant sought to implant in the Treasury his friend, the merchant Alexander T. Stewart, who proved legally ineligible. Grant also made appointments with little regard to actual job fitness and soon had to redesign his Cabinet to recognize both party considerations and competence.

Aided by a distinguished Secretary of State, Hamilton Fish (Washburne's successor), Grant cleared up the serious controversies with Great Britain over the *Alabama* claims (when the United States claimed damages for British-supported Confederate cruisers) and carefully preserved the neutrality of the United States in Spain's suppression of Cuban insurrection. Grant made a bold, but embarrassingly futile, attempt to annex Santo Domingo, and when Charles Sumner, a powerful Republican leader, denounced Grant, he was removed as chairman of the Foreign Relations Committee; this break with Sumner was perhaps Grant's worst disaster in foreign affairs.

The Civil War left a heritage of bonds and other securities that were easy prey to manipulation by speculators. To foil them, Grant approved legislation establishing the policy of ultimate redemption of legal tender notes in coin. But the speculators and gamblers—especially Jim Fisk and Jay Gould—struck back by cornering gold on the market and by "buying" cronies and administrative associates of the President with favors. Grant, to whom defeat and submission were alien, released a flood of gold from the Treasury to overwhelm the corner. The victory was costly, resulting in the "Black Friday" of 1869, when thousands were ruined.

Never vindictive toward the South, Grant declined to enforce the 14th amendment, which had granted Negro rights. His detachment coincided with the beginnings of intimidation in the old Confederacy of Negro voters.

In 1872, Grant was unanimously renominated and won reelection against Horace Greeley, nominee of the Democrats as well as the Liberal Republicans, who were seeking both a more radical Reconstruction policy and a more competent administration.

Grant's second term was dominated by scandals. His private secretary, Orville Babcock, was implicated in the notorious Whisky Ring and suspected of wrongdoing in the Santo Domingo negotiations. Secretary of War William Belknap was revealed to have accepted bribes from a trader at an Indian post. Through the loyalty of Grant, both escaped punishment. Grant himself was criticized for coarse tastes, excessive appetite for material enjoyment, and low associations. He was seen in public with the "robber baron" Jim Fisk and offered the post of Chief Justice to the notorious political boss Roscoe Conkling.

Although Grant is rated as one of the worst Presidents, he nevertheless piloted the country and the Presidency through the difficult aftermath of Andrew Johnson's confrontation with Congress. He also overcame a severe financial crisis and brought Anglo-American relations into a new era of harmony and mutual respect.

In 1880 Grant was the candidate of Roscoe Conkling and the powerful Stalwart faction for the Republican Presidential nomination, but he was defeated on a late ballot by Garfield.

After leaving office, Grant settled in New York City and lost (1884) his savings in a fraudulent banking firm. A merciful Congress appointed him general at full pay and subsequently added retirement pay. While suffering from throat cancer, Grant wrote his memoirs. Published (2 vols., 1885–86) by Mark Twain, they were a remarkable financial success and rank among the great military narratives of history. Grant soon died, on July 23, 1885, but his courage and indomitable spirit in the face of grave illness had restored his family's security.

Rutherford Birchard Hayes

Rutherford Birchard Hayes, 19th President (1877–1881), was born on October 4, 1822, in Delaware, Ohio. His father, a storekeeper from Vermont, died the year he was born. Raised by an uncle, Hayes graduated from Kenyon College (Ohio) as valedictorian. After study at Harvard Law School, he began the practice of law at Lower Sandusky (now Fremont), Ohio, and in 1849 he moved to Cincinnati.

Upon the outbreak of the Civil War, Hayes volunteered and was commissioned a major. Wounded four times, he advanced to the rank of major general. While on the battlefield, he was nominated for the U.S. House of Representatives and elected. A staunch Republican, he supported the Radical postwar reconstruction program and was reelected. However, he resigned from Congress to become governor of Ohio. Reelected twice, he ran on a platform in 1875 calling for "sound money" in opposition to Democratic monetary policy.

Hayes's hard-money position helped win him the Republican Presidential nomination in 1876 over the better-known James G. Blaine. Hayes defeated the Democratic nominee, Samuel J. Tilden, in a fiercely disputed election that threatened the country with civil war. Although Hayes received only a minority of the popular votes, a partisan election commission awarded him the office.

Hayes became President under a cloud of resentment over the dubious legitimacy of his incumbency. So restive was the country's mood that he took the oath of office privately, and the inaugural parade and ball were omitted. His shadowed Presidency coincided with a critical juncture in the nation's affairs. Wise statesmanship was needed to bring the stormy Reconstruction Period to an end.

Despite his electoral handicap, Hayes bravely faced problems and justified the boast of a forebear that "the name of Hayes began by valor." Days after his inauguration, Hayes removed federal troops from the South, thereby ending the period of Reconstruction. Wade, Blaine, and other leading Republicans angrily protested the step which imperiled the Republican "carpetbag" governments. These had made Hayes's election possible and could not exist without military protection. The wisdom of Hayes's policy was demonstrated by the end of violence and by the emergence of normalcy in the South.

Like other Presidents of his era, Hayes grappled with the problem of civil service reform. He offended the Stalwarts, the spoils-minded faction of his party, by declaring that appointments to office must be made on the basis of ability and tenure must be protected. Beginning with Secretary of the Interior Carl Schurz, Hayes's department heads applied these principles widely.

Hayes won admiration from "sound money" advocates for his devotion to the resumption of specie payments. The farmers of the Midwest and city workingmen, beset by the severe economic depression of 1876–77, widely favored soft money—"an irredeemable paper currency," and the "free coinage of silver." The House of Representatives passed bills for both in 1877. In a vigorous message of opposition to Congress, Hayes insisted upon resumption and payment of the public debt in gold. Hayes's action forestalled the Senate from passing a bill to postpone resumption. His veto, however, could not defeat the Bland-Allison bill calling upon the government to coin each month from $2 million to $4 million in silver dollars to be full legal tender.

Despite the business depression and political opposition, Hayes continued to accumulate a gold reserve, and on January 1, 1879, for the first time since the Civil War, the government declared that it would pay out gold, or "specie," in exchange for paper money.

Just as he showed little sympathy for the economically embattled farmer, Hayes was insensitive to the plight of labor in the economic depression. In 1877, with a railroad strike raging in 10 states, Hayes furnished state authorities with arms from national arsenals and, as commander-in-chief, transferred Federal troops from remote posts to the scenes of trouble.

Assertive toward Congress, Hayes vetoed a Chinese exclusion bill because it violated a treaty with China. He fought Congress successfully on "riders" to two appropriation bills. In an uncommon achievement for a President, he brought Congress to remove the riders.

Convinced that a President performed better if he served for only one term, Hayes in accepting the nomination in 1876 expressed his resolve to be a single-term President. Party leaders, dismayed by his bursts of independence, encouraged him to keep that resolve.

Hayes left office with the satisfaction of seeing the resentment over his flawed Presidential victory evaporate. His hard work, efficiency, and tough moral fiber impressed the public. After leaving office, he devoted his final years to education and philanthropy. He died in Fremont, Ohio, on January 17, 1893.

James Abram Garfield

James Abram Garfield, 20th President (March 4, 1881–September 19, 1881), was born on November 19, 1831, in Orange, Ohio, the son of a frontier farmer. Fatherless at two, Garfield became "a self-made man," who supported his widowed mother by working on farms and as a carpenter.

At 18, Garfield began study at Hiram (Ohio) College and later transferred to Williams College, Williamstown, Massachusetts. Graduating in 1856, Garfield returned to Ohio and rose to a professorship of ancient languages and literature at Hiram College and served as president from 1857 to 1861.

With the outbreak of the Civil War, Garfield was commissioned a lieutenant colonel of an Ohio volunteer regiment. Serving at Chickamauga and as chief of staff to General Rosecrans, he rose to the rank of major general. In 1863 when he was elected to the U.S. House of Representatives, Garfield resigned from the army.

Serving for 17 years in the House, Garfield was a regular Republican of antislavery convictions and a firm advocate of Radical reconstruction. He was an influential member of key House committees on finance and military affairs and in 1876 was minority leader. Garfield was also a member of the Electoral Commission created by Congress to decide state contests in the disputed election of 1876.

In the Republican National Convention of 1880, Garfield, a compromise candidate, was nominated for President on the 36th ballot. A "dark horse," he had defeated ex-President Grant, whom the Stalwarts, a party faction, were promoting for a third term. Because Garfield was a member of a rival Republican faction, Chester A. Arthur, a Stalwart, was nominated for Vice-President.

The Stalwarts, headed by Senator Roscoe Conkling of New York, remained unappeased. Upon becoming President, Garfield became embroiled with Conkling in a war over patronage. Garfield sent to the Senate the nominations of men of his own choice for minor posts in the New York Custom House. Conkling felt the step violated pledges given in return for his acceptance of Garfield as Presidential nominee and invoked Senatorial courtesy to defeat the nominations.

Garfield's conflict with leading Republican personalities spread to the Post Office, where the "star route" frauds were uncovered. The Post Office scandalously overpaid certain persons operating these mail routes, including the chairman of the Republican National Committee. Despite intimidation, Garfield had prosecutions launched against offenders. He also withdrew all nominations for New York appointments, except for the Custom House, to stress Presidential independence and integrity in the appointive process.

Since Republican control of the Senate was insecure, the Republican caucus chose not to break with the President and supported his New York Custom House appointments. An outraged Conkling resigned from the Senate and invited the New York legislature to vindicate him.

Garfield approved the proposal of his Secretary of State James G. Blaine to call a conference of Latin-American nations to review the Clayton-Bulwer Treaty with Great Britain, entered into in 1850. Garfield and Blaine were eager to advance a proposed isthmian canal and to shake off the treaty's provision that called for Anglo-American control of the waterway.

Before the conference could take place, Garfield was shot on July 2, 1881, by Charles Guiteau, a Stalwart and an office-seeker disappointed by the deadlock over patronage. Garfield lingered on until September 19, 1881, when he died.

Chester Alan Arthur

Chester Alan Arthur, 21st President (1881–1885), was born on October 5, 1830, at Fairfield, Vermont, the son of a Baptist clergyman. Arthur graduated from Union College, Schenectady, in 1848, where he was elected to Phi Beta Kappa. After teaching school in Vermont and serving as school principal in Cohoes, New York, Arthur moved to New York City to study law, and in 1854 was admitted to the bar.

A brilliant lawyer, Arthur won fame in two civil liberties lawsuits. One, a pre-Civil War case, held that a slave brought into New York became free. The other established that Negroes enjoyed the same rights on New York streetcars as whites.

Arthur, a staunch Republican, was rewarded in 1861 with the post of engineer-in-chief of New York State, and in the Civil War, he held further political positions as inspector general of New York troops and quartermaster of New York State. As such he helped organize the New York militia. After the war, in 1871, President Grant appointed him to the well-paid office of collector of the Port of New York, one of the choicest of political plums.

Competent and honest as the collector, Arthur, in the fashion of the day, ran the Custom House as an adjunct of Roscoe Conkling's New York Republican machine. Patronage was openly distributed, clerks freely attended party caucuses and conventions, got out the vote, and slacked on the job. Eventually, Arthur was removed by his fellow Republican, reform-minded President Rutherford Hayes.

At the Republican national convention of 1880, James Garfield was nominated for the Presidency, after the Conkling clique of New York Republicans, the Stalwarts, failed to nominate Grant for a third term. To sweeten the defeat, the convention chose Arthur, a leading Stalwart, for the Vice-Presidency.

Garfield's assassination soon after his inauguration made Arthur President.

Arthur is a classic instance of a man who became a better President than was generally expected. Forebodings of the day saw Arthur running the Presidency as a machine politician and spoilsman, and opening the hospitality of the White House to the Custom House loafers. Many ridiculed Arthur as a "dude" and "Gentleman Boss," owing to his courtly manners and dandified dress. But Arthur proved otherwise. His bearing as President was dignified, honorable, and constructive. His devotion to principle in the manner of his younger days as a civil liberties attorney quickly transformed his image into that of a man well capable of being President.

In addressing himself to the emerging problems of the day, especially the shabby morality of post-Civil War politics, Arthur suffered imposing handicaps; his cabinet was inherited from the rival Garfield faction, and he lacked a working majority in Congress. Matters worsened after the 1882 elections, when the Democrats won control of the House of Representatives.

Nevertheless, Arthur built a commendable record of effort and achievement. When he recommended the Civil Service Reform Act of 1883—the basis of the present-day personnel system—his former friends and colleagues felt betrayed because it drastically limited patronage.

He demonstrated courage and conscience in vetoing a Chinese exclusion bill that violated a treaty with China. Congress, however, overrode his veto. He also vetoed a river and harbor appropriation bill of 1882, contending that it wastefully committed public funds for improper local purposes. Congress again defeated his veto. His several defeats weakened his standing with professional politicians.

Arthur extracted from Congress laws to build a modern navy to replace the obsolete fleet dating back to the Civil War. He worked for tariff reform, and secured a new protective tariff act, with little reform. The Alaska Territory was organized. A treaty of friendship, commerce, and navigation was signed with Korea; a treaty for the construction of a canal with Nicaragua; and an agreement for a coaling and repair station at Pearl Harbor with Hawaii. Although lacking in drama, Arthur's administration was marked by growing prosperity in the country.

Arthur aspired to renomination for the Presidency in 1884, but his candidacy withered at an early stage. Professional politicians, bitter over his support of the civil service law, widely opposed him and reformers failed to support him.

At the end of his Presidential term, he returned to New York City where he resumed his law practice. He died on November 18, 1886, a little more than a year after leaving office, and was buried in Albany, New York.

Grover Cleveland

Grover Cleveland, 22d (1885–1889) and 24th President (1893–1897), was born in Caldwell, New Jersey, on March 18, 1837. He was the fifth of nine children of a Presbyterian country minister and a relative of Moses Cleaveland, founder of Cleveland, Ohio. While a child, his family moved to Fayetteville and then to Clinton, in upstate New York. His father's death barred Cleveland from a college education. Heading west to seek his fortune, he proceeded no farther than Buffalo, where an uncle secured him a clerkship in a law office. In 1859, at the age of 22, he was admitted to the bar. When the Civil War erupted, Cleveland could not enlist because of the necessity of supporting his mother and sisters, and he borrowed money to hire a conscription substitute.

The industrious Cleveland entered politics as a ward worker for the Democratic party in Buffalo. In 1862, he was elected ward supervisor, and a year later he was appointed assistant district attorney of Erie County. His political career remained uneventful until 1871, when he was elected sheriff of Erie County, and in 1882, he was elected mayor of Buffalo. His efficiency and rigorous honesty ("Public office is public trust," he once said) won him rapid fame. After one year as mayor, he was chosen governor of New York.

In their national convention of 1884, the Democrats nominated Cleveland for President. His Republican opponent was the glamorous James G. Blaine and, in the ensuing campaign, the character of the candidates was viciously assailed. The Democratic party was described by the opposition as the party of "Rum, Romanism, and Rebellion." Offended Catholic voters supported Cleveland, and the "mugwumps," a reform wing of the Republican party, backed him, impressed by his reform record. Winning in a close race, Cleveland became the first Democratic President since the Civil War.

An awaiting question for his Presidency was whether Cleveland could transfer to the larger, more complex arena of national politics the atmosphere of probity and reform he so successfully cultivated in state and local officeholding. He was quickly tested by the new Civil Service Reform Law passed in the twilight of the previous administration. His "mugwump" supporters pressed for civil service reform, but from Cleveland's own party came a long line of Democratic office seekers, hungry for reward after 24 years of exclusion from Presidential patronage.

Pledged to "practical reform," Cleveland gave slow and reserved recognition to partisan demands. Simultaneously, he lent steady support to the new Civil Service Commission and induced Congress to repeal the Tenure of Office Act, a shadow upon the Presidency since 1867. He skillfully preserved Presidential independence in appointments, but his sturdy middle course served to offend both the politicians and the reformers.

Cleveland also championed the cause of tariff reform. Embarrassed by the substantial surplus in the Treasury, and convinced that it was fostered by excessive tariff rates, Cleveland called for tariff revision to diminish what he regarded as improper favoritism to protected industries.

Cleveland was renominated in 1888, and although he won a larger popular vote than his Republican opponent, Benjamin Harrison, the latter mustered a majority of the electoral vote to win the election.

In 1892, Cleveland regained the Presidency, a popular figure in the face of wide disgruntlement over the McKinley Tariff Act of 1890 and its high-rate structure. But the pleasure of victory was quickly displaced by the storms of economic crisis. From the Harrison administration, Cleveland inherited the forces that produced the Panic of 1893; bank failures, bankruptcies, and massive unemployment seized the economy. Cleveland resisted demands for inflation by Western and Southern Democrats and Populists and, instead, chose to combat the crisis through sound money policies and orthodox economic measures. Cleveland won a long, bitter fight only by receiving substantial Republican support, since the Democratic party was characterized by a cleavage between sound money and inflationary factions.

The animosities raised by the fight crippled Cleveland's chances for tariff reform. The Wilson-Gorman bill that finally passed so reflected the views of protectionist Democrats that Cleveland termed the legislation "party perfidy and party dishonor." Unwilling to sign the Wilson bill, Cleveland permitted it to become law without his signature.

Cleveland's sound money policy was beset by sharp declines in Treasury holdings of gold, and he was forced to replenish the reserves through large bond issues arranged with a syndicate of Eastern financiers. His vocal Democratic opponents charged the President with being in alliance with Wall Street.

In the wake of the Panic of 1893, strikes were widespread, and in 1894 striking employees of the Pullman Company and Eugene V. Debs' American Railway Union halted trains across the country. Violence erupted in Chicago, the center of the strike. In a historic intervention, the President declared that the strikers had interfered with the free flow of the mails, and regular army troops were dispatched to Chicago to enforce the laws. Governor J. P. Altgeld of Illinois, who did not want the troops, demanded their recall in vain.

In foreign affairs, Cleveland rejected the imperialist tendencies of recent American policy. He refused to deal with a new government in Hawaii, established by a revolution managed by American residents. Cleveland rejected domestic pressures to intervene in behalf of Cuban insurrectionists and make war with Spain; he ignored a Congressional resolution recognizing Cuba.

Cleveland was assertive in foreign affairs when what he regarded as legitimate American interests were at stake. In Venezuela's boundary dispute with Britain, he gave new precision to the Monroe Doctrine by articulating the hegemony of the United States in the Americas and our specific interest in the boundary dispute.

By the end of Cleveland's term, the "silver" or inflationary Democrats dominated his party and, at the national convention of 1896, they nominated—to Cleveland's great distress—William Jennings Bryan, the silver orator. Cleveland preferred the Republican nominee, William McKinley, and his sound-money policies, but he took no part in the campaign.

After leaving the Presidency, Cleveland lived in Princeton, New Jersey. He lectured at the University, served as a trustee, and in 1904 published *Presidential Problems,* one of the most penetrating books by a former President about the office. He died June 24, 1908, and fittingly, his last words were: "I have tried so hard to do right."

Benjamin Harrison

Benjamin Harrison, 23d President (1889–1893), was born on August 20, 1833, at North Bend, Ohio. Of distinguished ancestry, he was the great-grandson of a signer of the Declaration of Independence, a grandson of President William Henry Harrison, and the son of a congressman. He studied at Miami University (Ohio), graduating in 1852, and was admitted to the bar the following year. In 1854 he moved to Indianapolis, where he practiced law and politics.

During the Civil War Harrison served with distinction on the battlefield and was brevetted brigadier general. A prosperous corporation lawyer in Indianapolis after the war, he was active in Republican politics and held various local and party offices. In 1876 he ran unsuccessfully for governor, but five years later he won a seat in the United States Senate.

His distinguished background, war record, and the importance of Indiana to Republican electoral strategy gained him the Presidential nomination in 1888. He received a majority of the electoral vote, although Grover Cleveland, running for reelection, won a plurality of the popular vote.

In the White House, Harrison and his Secretary of State, James G. Blaine, conducted an assertive foreign policy as the United States moved toward a posture of imperialism. A Pan-American Congress was highly successful. The United States established its claims in Samoa and checked German expansion there. Harrison was less successful, however, in a controversy with Great Britain over the killing of fur seals in the Bering Sea. Aggressive efforts to establish American rights to Mole St. Nicholas in Haiti failed. The Harrison administration also engaged in bitter negotiations with Chile following an attack on American sailors in Valparaiso; the United States demanded an apology and ultimately received it.

One of Harrison's fondest projects was the annexation of Hawaii. In his administration's closing days, he sent a treaty for that purpose to the Senate. His successor, Grover Cleveland, however, withdrew the treaty before the Senate voted.

In domestic affairs, Harrison was torn between the demands of the Civil Service Reform Act of 1883 and the more traditional spoils system. He followed a moderate course that displeased both the reformers and the organization politicians. On balance, his civil service record was statesman-like. He appointed and retained Theodore Roosevelt as civil service commissioner, and angered the spoilsmen by adding 11,000 civil service positions to the classified list.

In legislation, Harrison was disinclined to oppose policies his party advocated in Congress. Since the party was in the hands of leaders he could not control, his impact upon the laws of the day was minor. Congress passed the McKinley Tariff Act, imposing the highest duties up to that time. Harrison, however, secured the insertion of a reciprocity provision, the act's only popular feature.

Harrison approved the Sherman Silver Purchase Act to help the silver industry. He signed a rivers and harbors act, a giant pork-barrel measure, and an act markedly increasing pension expenditures. He supported a federal elections bill, embodying several reforms, but it failed. Harrison also aided the Sherman Anti-Trust Act, passed to counteract popular feeling that the Republicans were the party of big business. However, this was insufficient to forestall the Democrats from winning control of the House in 1890, which further diminished Harrison's influence on legislation.

Opposed by party leaders and bosses, such as Quay, Platt, and "Czar" Reed, Harrison secured renomination in 1892 only with difficulty. They and other politicians were offended by his limited patronage policy and cold personality. His reserve, a frigid look darting from steel-gray eyes, and his brevity of response wore badly with politicians. Despite his manner, Harrison was a remarkably effective public speaker, bringing one observer to note: "Harrison can make a speech to 10,000 men, and every man of them will go away his friend. Let him meet the same 10,000 men in private, and every one will go away his enemy."

Party apathy, labor hostility to an administration heavily partial to business, and other factors caused Harrison's defeat in his race for reelection in 1892 against Cleveland.

After leaving the Presidency, Harrison continued to gain distinction as a lawyer, and in 1898 he represented Venezuela in her boundary dispute with Great Britain. He died in Indianapolis on March 13, 1901.

William McKinley

William McKinley, 25th President (March 4, 1897–September 14, 1901), was born on January 29, 1843, at Niles, Ohio, the son of an iron-founder. After attending Poland Seminary (Ohio) and Allegheny College (Pennsylvania), McKinley taught school.

Following service in the Union Army in the Civil War, where he rose to the rank of major, McKinley studied at Albany (New York) Law School and was admitted to the bar in 1867; he soon moved to Canton, Ohio, where he began practice.

McKinley began his political career in 1869 by election as prosecuting attorney for Stark County, Ohio. In 1876, he was elected as a Republican to the U.S. House of Representatives, where he remained, except for one term, until 1891. As Congressman, McKinley sponsored the McKinley Tariff Act, which set record-high protective duties, and voted for the Bland-Allison (silver purchase) act.

Defeated for reelection in 1890, McKinley attracted the friendship and support of Mark Hanna, a powerful, wealthy Ohio Republican. Their lasting political partnership helped McKinley win election as governor in 1891 and reelection in 1893.

In 1896, McKinley's popularity and Hanna's shrewd management brought the Republican Presidential nomination to the governor. Pitted against him as the Democratic nominee was the colorful William Jennings Bryan whose free silver doctrines and Populist ties alarmed the business community and alienated many Democratic conservatives. Bryan, a superb orator, made a record number of speaking appearances. McKinley and Hanna, in contrast, perfected the "front porch" campaign; instead of the candidate going to the people, the people came to the candidate. Cooperating railroads gave excursion rates so low that one newspaper said that visiting McKinley was "cheaper than staying home."

McKinley's election was interpreted as a mandate for a high protective tariff and for a gold monetary standard, as opposed to a silver standard. Promptly after his inauguration, McKinley called a special session of Congress to act on the tariff; the Dingley Tariff Act resulted, the high duties of which delighted business. Not until 1900 was a monetary law enacted. It established the gold dollar as the United States standard and strictly limited the coinage of silver.

The monetary law was delayed by the Spanish-American War. When McKinley was inaugurated, Cuba was in revolt against Spain. The United States battleship *Maine* was blown up in Havana harbor, and McKinley was pressed to intervene. He did not want to go to war, nor fight legislators who were demanding war. Ultimately, he referred the problem to Congress, knowing that it favored war; Congress directed the President to intervene in Cuba to establish Cuban independence.

As a war President, McKinley was handicapped by an inadequate war department and army. Disease was more deadly and inefficiency more harassing than the Spanish enemy. Although the navy performed creditably, McKinley was fortunate in facing a weak enemy.

McKinley did not want to annex territory, but as in the coming of the war, his political style prevailed over his political ends. As a politician, he eschewed conflict. His natural kindliness and his background as a tariff negotiator adept at conciliating everyone ruled his approach to foreign affairs. As a public leader, famous for "keeping his ear close to the ground," he was seldom more than a half-step ahead of his constituents. Convinced from a tour of the Midwest that the people favored annexation, he instructed his peace negotiators accordingly. The Philippines, Guam, and Puerto Rico were ceded to the United States. Cuba was placed under American control until it could establish a government of its own. During the war, the Hawaiian Islands were annexed by joint resolution of Congress.

McKinley guided the country through its initial experiences as an imperial nation. A law to govern the new insular possessions was passed. The war department was reorganized. Rebellious Filipinos, seeking independence, were fought, and a commission headed by William Howard Taft was dispatched to the islands to set up the government of the United States there. In 1899 Secretary of State John Hay negotiated the Open Door policy with European nations with interests in China. But the Boxer Rebellion in China soon prompted intervention by many powers, including the United States.

In 1900, McKinley was reelected, upon defeating Bryan, this time to the cry of "a full dinner-pail for four years more." The war had turned the McKinley era into one of booming prosperity, and the election returns showed that the benign McKinley had the support of the people. The electorate also approved the new imperialism.

McKinley was at the crest of popularity and political vindication when he was shot by an anarchist, Leon Czolgosz, on September 6, 1901, at Buffalo, New York. He died on September 14.

McKinley's term, divided between the 19th century and the 20th, aptly symbolizes his contribution as a bridge between the old and the modern Presidency. With him ended the line of Presidents who had fought in the Civil War, and his popularity throughout the country signified that the breach between the North and South had been healed and was no longer a preoccupation of the Chief Executive. Likewise, he presided over the advent of a new era, in which the United States, through war with Spain, first took rank as a world power.

Theodore Roosevelt

Theodore Roosevelt, 26th President (September 14, 1901–March 3, 1909), was born on October 27, 1858, in New York City, the son of a wealthy merchant of Dutch ancestry and of a mother of distinguished Georgian family whose brother served in the Confederate navy. Endowed with great energy, curiosity, and grit, Roosevelt was handicapped by frail health; however, by careful exercise, he built up unusual strength. He traveled widely and was educated by tutors until he entered Harvard (1876). After graduating (1880), he enrolled in Columbia Law School but, legal studies not proving of interest, turned to politics.

In 1881, at the age of 23, Roosevelt, as a Republican, was elected to the New York State Assembly. At first his fellow legislators looked askance at his expensive dress and pronounced sideburns, but his vitality and intelligence won their respect to the point that they elected (1882) him Republican minority leader. His disinclination to follow orders, however, prompted the party bosses to remove him. Roosevelt, nevertheless, remained highly influential in the assembly, working closely with Democratic Governor Grover Cleveland for the advancement of civil service reform.

In 1884, Roosevelt abandoned his political career in remorse over the deaths of his wife and mother, passing the next two years on his ranches in the Dakota Territory. There he developed his skills at riding and hunting and acquired Western flairs. In 1886, he remarried and returned to his home at Sagamore Hill (Oyster Bay) on Long Island. That year he also returned to politics, running unsuccessfully for mayor of New York City against overwhelming Democratic strength.

Roosevelt's speech-making for the Presidential candidacy of Benjamin Harrison was rewarded by Harrison's appointing him (1889) a member of the U.S. Civil Service Commission. Shrewd in cultivating publicity, Roosevelt brought the commission out of the shadows, interested the public in its work, and accomplished remarkable gains against the spoils system. As police commissioner of New York City (1895–97), he again used the power of publicity to restore discipline and stamp out police dishonesty.

In 1897 President William McKinley, for whom Roosevelt had campaigned the year before, appointed him Assistant Secretary of the Navy. Roosevelt worked to strengthen the navy but, when the United States and Spain went to war in 1898, Roosevelt resigned at once and organized the spectacular volunteer cavalry regiment that won fame as the "Rough Riders."

Roosevelt returned from Cuba a military hero and, with the Republican party in New York State besmirched by scandal, his nomination for governor was supported even by Boss Tom Platt, who was personally averse to the reform-minded Roosevelt. Elected, Roosevelt promoted reform legislation and forced through a law taxing the franchises of public service corporations. Large business interests were angered, and "Boss" Platt and other Republican leaders resolved to rid New York of Roosevelt by moving him into the 1900 national election as McKinley's running mate for the Vice-Presidency, presuming that in that office Roosevelt would be harmless and forgotten. Against his own inclinations, the governor accepted.

Ten months after the Republican victory that ensued, McKinley was assassinated, and Roosevelt became President at the early age of 42. Although he kept all members of McKinley's cabinet and said reassuringly that he would continue the late President's policies "absolutely unbroken," Roosevelt's zest and political skill soon broke the confines of this heritage, and business leaders, recalling his state reform policies, quavered.

In his first message to Congress (December 1901), Roosevelt addressed himself to the growing problem of business trusts, proposing not their prohibition, but regulation. His policy was illustrated by the government's suit (1902) against the Northern Securities Company, which J. P. Morgan interests had formed to control major railroads in the West. The company was charged with reducing competition, and the Supreme Court, upholding the government, ordered its dissolution. In all, the administration filed suits against 43 other corporations and achieved triumphs against the tobacco and oil trusts.

Roosevelt was the first President conspicuously friendly to labor. In 1902, facing a widespread anthracite coal strike and lacking express legal authority, Roosevelt nonetheless intervened, urging the disputants to arbitrate. When the miners agreed, but the mine-owners balked, Roosevelt threatened to have the army seize and operate the pits. Eventually a settlement was reached favorable to the miners, to whom public opinion was sympathetic. At Roosevelt's recommendation, Congress established (1903) a Department of Commerce and Labor.

In the foreign policy of his first term, Roosevelt used "the big stick"—the threat of force to advance his purposes. In 1902, he had applied the Monroe Doctrine when German and British naval forces threatened Venezuelan ports, trying to force payments of debts. Roosevelt warned Germany that the United States might use force if any Venezuelan territory was occupied. As a result, Germany withdrew her vessels, and a settlement was negotiated. In 1904, when Santo Domingo was staggering under European debts, the "Roosevelt Corollary" of the Monroe Doctrine was born. Under it, the United States announced that it was prepared to exercise "an international police power" in instances "of wrongdoing or impotence."

While negotiating (1903) to secure a strip of land across Panama—a prelude to the eventual construction of the canal—Roosevelt supported and recognized a revolutionary Panamanian government that signed the necessary treaty, and American troops protected this new government from Colombian forces.

Roosevelt was reelected (1904) by a record popular majority over the Democratic nominee, Judge Alton B. Parker. At the President's initiative, his often reluctant Congress passed a pure food law, a meat inspection law, and the Hepburn law that conferred on the Interstate Commerce Commission the power of railroad rate-making. Roosevelt promoted an aggressive conservation policy, which added enormous acreage to the national forests, and also promoted the reclamation and irrigation of arid lands.

Foreign affairs continued to be demanding during Roosevelt's second term. His mediation and strong personal influence brought the Russo-Japanese War to an end in 1905, an achievement that brought him the Nobel Peace Prize. Roosevelt, however, retained faith in the efficacy and value of a show of force. When relations with Japan deteriorated and possible attack on the Philippines was feared, he dispatched (1908) the fleet to the Far East and around the world. This step prompted several diplomatic agreements with Japan.

Roosevelt was the first President whose administration was continuously involved in major foreign policy, and his Square Deal program of social justice—he called his office "a bully pulpit" —was also the first of its kind. He was extraordinarily skillful at rallying public opinion; however, a contemporary cartoon that depicted him with large clenched teeth, a thick spiked club, and a belt full of pistols also tells much of his style. Audacious and innovative in legislative relations, he began the practice of supplementing his messages with actual drafts of bills, and he was the first of modern Presidents to appeal to public opinion to advance his measures in Congress.

After his election in 1904, Roosevelt declared that "under no circumstances" would he run again for President. He chose his Secretary of War, William Howard Taft, as his successor, and Taft was both nominated and elected.

After leaving office, Roosevelt went big-game hunting in Africa and, when he returned (1910) to the United States, he was approached by disgruntled progressive Republicans who felt that Taft had betrayed them. Failing to bring Taft around to his own progressive ways, Roosevelt broke with his protégé and, in 1912, he ran for a Presidential third term. After winning in Republican primaries, he was denied the nomination in the Taft-controlled convention. Roosevelt and his supporters bolted and formed the Bull Moose party. In the tumultuous campaign, Roosevelt survived an attempted assassination to run second in the three-way race that was easily won by the Democratic candidate: Woodrow Wilson.

In 1913 and 1914, Roosevelt made pioneering explorations in the Brazilian jungle. After the outbreak of World War I, he was an early advocate of preparedness against Germany and critical of Wilson's caution. When America entered the war, Roosevelt wanted to raise and lead an army division, but Wilson refused. Roosevelt opposed American entry into the League of Nations, which he considered an excessive limitation on national sovereignty. He would probably have been a leading contender for the Republican Presidential nomination in 1920 but for his unexpected death on January 6, 1919. He is buried at Sagamore Hill.

William Howard Taft

William Howard Taft, 27th President (1909–1913), was born on September 15, 1857, in Cincinnati. His father, Alphonso Taft, had served as a judge in Ohio, as a cabinet officer under President Grant, and as U.S. minister to Austria and Russia. A huge, studious youth, William graduated (1878) with honors from Yale and (1880) from the Cincinnati Law School.

Admitted to the bar, he promptly moved into public service. He served (1881–82) as assistant prosecuting attorney for Hamilton County, Ohio. In 1882, President Chester Arthur appointed Taft, a Republican, collector of internal revenue for the first district, with headquarters in Cincinnati. Within a year he resigned, because he could not in good conscience discharge competent employees to open up jobs for Republicans.

After a brief return to private law practice, Taft resumed (1885) his public career as assistant solicitor for Hamilton County. He filled out a vacancy on the Superior Court in 1887, and the following year was elected for a five-year term. Except for the Presidency, this was the only office to which he was ever elected. He moved on to national prominence in 1890 when President Benjamin Harrison appointed him U.S. Solicitor General. Two years later, he became a United States Circuit Court judge, and his rulings occasionally displeased labor unions.

In 1900, Taft was thrust into a totally new endeavor—both for himself and for the nation—when President McKinley appointed him chairman of a commission to govern the Philippine Islands, which had been acquired in the Spanish-American War. Designated governor the following year, Taft was a model administrator, building roads and harbors, establishing civil courts, and installing organs of self-government. In 1904, President Theodore Roosevelt appointed Taft Secretary of War. In addition to presiding with marked competence over a complex department, he also became a kind of trouble-shooter, assisting in Roosevelt's Panamanian policies and in negotiations for concluding the Russo-Japanese War.

When Roosevelt declined (1908) to run, he recommended that Taft become his successor. Preferring appointment to the Supreme Court, Taft acquiesced after some hesitation. He easily defeated the Democratic Presidential nominee, William Jennings Bryan. The ponderous, good-humored Taft, cautious in action and conservative in temperament, illustrates the type of public figure who diminishes his exceptional record as administrator and judge in the Presidency.

At a disadvantage by being the heir to the scintillating Roosevelt, Taft suffered in the inevitable comparison. Almost immediately, he was confronted with a profound struggle in the House of Representatives, in which progressive Republicans, led by George Norris of Nebraska, overthrew "Cannonism"—the almost unlimited power wielded by House Speaker "Uncle Joe" Cannon. Taft declined to support the Norris forces, and they, after their victory, declined to cooperate with the President.

Taft had been elected on a platform pledged to revise the tariff. A believer in protection, he felt that somewhat reduced duties would help control the trusts. Summoning Congress into special session to deal with the tariff, he seemed highly restrained in promoting his views on Capitol Hill. Although the House enacted a bill with big tariff reductions, the Senate, led by the devoted protectionist Nelson W. Aldrich of Rhode Island worked to keep duties high. Although the eventual Payne-Aldrich Tariff Act lowered some rates slightly, the general rate level was undisturbed. Taft disapproved of the bill, but he signed it, deeming it the best that could be then secured.

Taft further damaged his standing with progressive Republicans in the dispute between Chief Forester Gifford Pinchot and Secretary of the Interior Richard Ballinger. Pinchot charged that Roosevelt's conservation policies were being desecrated by the Interior Department, which he accused of selling land concessions too cheaply to water and power companies, as well as of illegal transactions in the sale of Alaskan coal lands. Taft backed Ballinger, whose conduct was investigated and upheld by a Congressional committee. Taft then dismissed Pinchot, and angered progressive Republicans moved back toward Theodore Roosevelt.

Despite its political troubles, the Taft administration made solid accomplishments. The 16th Amendment (income tax) and the 17th (direct election of Senators) were added to the Constitution—the first new amendments since the aftermath of the Civil War. At Taft's initiative, Congress enlarged the powers of the Interstate Commerce Commission and created a commerce court, a children's bureau, the Postal Savings system, and a parcel post. The Department of Labor was also established, and Alaska achieved full territorial government. Taft took the first steps toward establishing a federal budget, by requesting his department heads to submit detailed reports of their financial needs.

Although the Theodore Roosevelt administration tends to be identified with an aggressive antitrust policy, Taft well outdid his predecessor. In four years, the Taft administration launched almost twice as many "trust-busting" prosecutions for violations of the Sherman Anti-Trust Act than Roosevelt had in almost eight years.

In foreign affairs, Secretary of State Philander Knox played a large part in promoting "dollar diplomacy," by which trade, finance, and commerce were used to increase America's diplomatic influence. The U.S. government negotiated loans with China, Honduras, Nicaragua, and other countries, as a step toward encouraging private bankers to make additional loans to these nations.

In 1910, Roosevelt returned from a hunting trip to Africa and hustled into the political arena. His speeches advocating a "new nationalism" attracted Republican progressives, while Republican conservatives moved behind Taft to win him renomination. The conservatives, or "Stand-Patters," proved too strong for the progressives, or insurgents, and the President defeated Roosevelt in 1912 by being renominated on the first ballot. Roosevelt and his followers then left the convention and organized the new Progressive, or "Bull Moose," party, with Roosevelt as its Presidential nominee. With the Republican vote so divided, the Democratic nominee, Woodrow Wilson, was elected. Taft received only 8 electoral votes, Roosevelt 88, and Wilson 435.

Upon leaving the Presidency, Taft became a Yale law professor in 1913, and that year he was also elected president of the American Bar Association. In World War I, he was joint chairman of the National War Labor Board. President Harding appointed him (1921) Chief Justice of the United States, which he deemed his greatest public honor. Taft served with distinction until 1930, when declining health forced his retirement. He died on March 8, 1930, and is buried in Arlington National Cemetery.

Woodrow Wilson

Woodrow Wilson, 28th President (1913–1921), was born on December 28, 1856, at Staunton, Virginia. The son of a Presbyterian minister, Thomas Woodrow Wilson (his full name) was reared in an atmosphere of religious piety and respect for scholarship. Wilson entered Davidson College in North Carolina at the age of 17, transferring after a year to Princeton University, from which he was graduated (1879). He studied law at the University of Virginia, but withdrew (1881) from the school because of poor health.

In 1882, Wilson began to practice law in Atlanta; however, after a year of few clients and a discovered distaste for the commercial world, he returned to academic life and studied political science at Johns Hopkins University, where his thesis, *Congressional Government*, earned wide acclaim. After taking his Ph.D., he taught at Bryn Mawr College and Wesleyan University. In 1890, he became professor of jurisprudence and political economy at Princeton University. His reputation as a teacher and scholar having grown steadily, Wilson was named (1902) president of Princeton. Highly innovative as an administrator and tenacious in purpose against the most formidable odds, Wilson reorganized the curriculum, but suffered defeats in attempting to reform the eating clubs and revamp the graduate school.

Wilson's Princeton controversies resulted in his resignation as president, but the attendant publicity cast him as a fighter for democracy against the snobbery of privilege. New Jersey Democratic boss James Smith, Jr., and Colonel George Harvey, a party leader and publisher of *Harper's Weekly*, were both impressed with Wilson's political potential and secured (1910) his nomination for governor of New Jersey.

Once elected, Wilson fought Smith and his conservative organization and pushed through a primary election law, a corrupt practices act, an employer's liability law, an improved education law, and other legislation that suddenly placed New Jersey in the vanguard of progressivism.

Wilson's gubernatorial achievements also won national attention and established him in the confidence of William Jennings Bryan, who, despite three defeats for the Presidency, was still a dominant force in the Democratic party. At the 1912 national convention in Baltimore, Wilson won the Presidential nomination on the 46th ballot. Bryan's support was invaluable, and Wilson proved acceptable to the party's large progressive wing. With Republicans divided between Taft and Theodore Roosevelt, Wilson won the election easily.

His inaugural address (March 4, 1913) sounded progressive themes: "Here muster not the forces of party, but the forces of humanity." He immediately set a swift pace of initiative and activity, calling Congress into special session and addressing the two houses in person, thus breaking a century-long precedent. Wilson moved through Congress an extraordinary body of legislation that comprised his "New Freedom" program. A new tariff law lowered duties and removed them altogether on such commodities as wool, sugar, and iron ore. The Clayton Anti-Trust Act was passed (1914), and the Federal Trade Commission was established (also 1914) to regulate trusts and interstate trade. The Federal Reserve System was created (1913)—in effect, a central banking system empowered to provide a new currency and to facilitate the flow of capital through 12 reserve banks.

Wilson promoted this extraordinary legislative output with a generous investment of his own energies and skills. He worked closely with Democratic legislative leaders and the powerful committee chairmen. Adroit in using patronage, he was indefatigable in employing his own impressive powers of personal persuasion. He encouraged the revival of the long-dormant Congressional caucus as a forum in which his program might be presented to legislators for the purpose of organizing support. His exceptional gifts of articulation rallied attention to his program.

Wilson's early Presidential years were also preoccupied with foreign policy. He made amends for the recently assertive, if not highhanded, policies of the United States toward its Latin-American neighbors, assuring them (Mobile, Alabama, in 1913) that "the United States would never again seek one additional foot of territory by conquest." When the reform government of Francisco Madero in Mexico was overthrown, Wilson declined to recognize the new master, Victoriano Huerta, who had caused Madero's murder. Against raging turmoil within Mexico and intense pressure at home to intervene because of endangered American interests, Wilson nonetheless held to a policy of "watchful waiting" to permit the Mexican people to choose a government for themselves.

In August 1914, foreign policy compounded its demands on Wilson when World War I exploded. The President echoed the dominant sentiment of the nation when he proclaimed its neutrality. He was continuously buffeted in seeking to hold to this policy by the ravages of German submarines, by Britain's close administration of her blockade that often proved detrimental to American shipping interests, and by the solidifying of different segments of domestic opinion toward the belligerents. In 1915, neutrality was severely tested by the heavy loss of American life suffered when a German submarine sank the British passenger vessel *Lusitania*. Secretary of State William Jennings Bryan resigned, deeming Wilson's protest notes to Germany too strong; other Americans considered Wilson too detached and neutral by stating that there was such a thing as being "too proud to fight."

With Democrats promoting the slogan: "He kept us out of war," Wilson won reelection in 1916. However, he had declined to use neutrality as a campaign promise, and the defeat of Wilson's Republican opponent, Charles Evans Hughes, was a close race. Weeks before Wilson's second inauguration, Germany resumed unrestricted submarine warfare against all shipping, including American vessels. On April 2, 1917, Wilson went before Congress to request a declaration of war, averring that "the world must be made safe for democracy."

Wilson was an impressive war leader. Both for the United States and the world, he more than anyone articulated the purposes and the issues of the war. He infused the conflict with moral aspiration and harmonized its goals with his previous progressive domestic program. In a speech (January 8, 1918), he set forth the Fourteen Points that were his framework for a peace settlement. Among other things, he called for "a general association of nations," "open covenants of peace openly arrived at," freedom of the seas,

arms reduction, and independence for various territories and countries. Wilson's guidelines afforded Germany a basis on which to appeal for peace.

Wilson personally headed the American delegation to the peace conference at Paris. Eager to make his Fourteen Points the center of the settlement, he believed that the United States should be represented by its head of government as the other major allies were. In the hard bargaining at the conference table, Wilson, to win acceptance of his plan for the League of Nations, and other of the Fourteen Points, had to make concessions and compromises.

He encountered more difficulty on his return to the United States, where he faced the task of securing Senate approval of the peace treaty and the League of Nations, for not only had Wilson been under criticism for excluding senators in the United States' delegation to the peace conference, but his general political position in the nation had weakened. He had asked for the election of Democrats to Congress in 1918 as a demonstration of popular confidence, but the voters responded by increasing Republican strength.

In the Senate, the peace treaty met fierce resistance from isolationists, such as Senators Hiram W. Johnson, James A. Reed, and William E. Borah as well as from many others, led by Henry Cabot Lodge, who were ready to approve the treaty but with important changes.

Deciding to take his fight for the league to the people, Wilson began (September 4, 1919) an ambitious speaking tour of the Midwest and Far West. Always frail in health, he had been weakened by the recent demands of office, and his doctors had advised against the trip. On September 25, following a speech at Pueblo, Colorado, Wilson collapsed from fatigue and tension aboard his train. The remainder of his tour was abandoned, and he returned to Washington. On October 3, he suffered a paralytic stroke.

The Presidency now sustained its longest and most difficult experience with an invalided Chief Executive. Seldom leaving his bed, Wilson did not call a cabinet meeting for more than six months, until April 13, 1920. The President's second wife, Mrs. Edith Bolling Wilson, not only guided his hand as he signed documents, but selected and digested the matters that were submitted for his personal attention.

From his sickbed, the President waged a losing fight for the peace treaty. The Senate Foreign Relations Committee, led by its chairman Senator Lodge, added 14 reservations, including one that declared the United States undertook no obligation to support the League of Nations. Wilson requested his Senate supporters to vote against the decimated treaty, but his term of office closed without its approval.

Repudiated at home, Wilson nevertheless was honored abroad as the recipient of the Nobel Peace Prize in 1920. He died in Washington on February 3, 1924, and is buried in the National Cathedral.

Warren Gamaliel Harding

Warren Gamaliel Harding, 29th President (1921–1923), was born on November 2, 1865, in Blooming Grove, Ohio; he was the son of a homeopathic doctor and descended from an English family that had landed at Plymouth and migrated (1820) to Ohio. After study at local schools, Harding entered Ohio Central College, when he was only 14 years old and graduated three years later.

Harding moved (1882) with his parents to Marion, Ohio, where he taught briefly in a one-room schoolhouse; he also read law, sold insurance, and eventually turned to journalism. He soon became editor and part owner of the Marion *Star*. As editor, he was drawn into local political life and gained prominence as an orator. He was elected to the Ohio senate in 1900 and to the lieutenant governorship in 1904. He was the unsuccessful Republican candidate for governor in 1910, but five years later he was elected to the U.S. Senate. In Ohio politics, Harding became the close friend of Harry M. Daugherty, an astute political manager who desired to make Harding President, just as Mark Hanna in an earlier day had charted the course to the White House of his fellow Ohioan, William McKinley.

As Senator, Harding was a member of the Foreign Relations Committee and supported approval of the peace treaty of World War I, with reservations "sufficient to safeguard" American interests. Genial and good-looking, Harding enjoyed the fellowship of the Senate, but introduced no important legislation.

His emergence as a dark-horse, compromise nominee for the Presidency in 1920 was the outcome of deliberations by leading Republican Senators and party bosses in what Harry Daugherty called a "smoke-filled room" in Chicago's Blackstone Hotel. Conducting a "front-porch" campaign, Harding took no clear-cut stand on the leading issue: the League of Nations. He attacked it, but at the same time promised support for an "association of nations." He sidestepped domestic issues by promising a restoration of "normalcy." Harding easily defeated the Democratic nominee, James M. Cox.

Few Presidents have come into office facing more difficult tasks than Harding. The Versailles peace treaty was suspended uncertainly in the political air, having failed to win the Senate's approval under President Wilson. Powerful Republican Senators wanted to scrap the league; other legislators, who were eager to avoid future war, sought to salvage it. Substantial unemployment attended the changeover from a wartime to a peacetime economy. Harding approached these problems with a Presidential theory that looked to Congress and the cabinet for leadership; he rejected Wilson's performance as representing an encroachment on the powers of Congress.

Aided by a strong Secretary of State, Charles Evans Hughes, Harding was assertive in foreign affairs. The President moved quickly and energetically to break the impasse on the League of Nations. He made peace treaties with Germany and other enemy powers that omitted the league covenant. Harding's most conspicuous achievement in foreign policy was the Washington Disarmament Conference (1921), which resulted in treaties among the United States, Britain, France, Japan, and Italy that limited naval armament, restricted submarine use, and banned the use of poison gas in warfare.

The Harding era was marked by a surge of isolation; legislation was passed that for the first time placed quotas on immigration, and the Fordney-McCumber tariff act (1922) raised duties to record highs. Remaining aloof from European politics, the administration declined to take part in conferences at Geneva and The Hague. Unofficial American representatives on the Reparations Commission were withdrawn, and American troops stationed on the Rhine were gradually reduced. Harding himself, however, was a non-isolationist, and he repeatedly urged the promotion of peace through international friendship, as well as advocating American participation in the Permanent Court of International Justice at The Hague.

In domestic affairs, Harding largely acquiesced to what cabinet officers, Congress, and assertive group interests put forward for public policy. The excess profits tax was repealed, to the delight of business. The "farm bloc"—legislators of both parties devoted to agricultural interests—put through measures responsive to their needs.

Harding's cabinet included such strong and highly regarded public personalities as Secretary of State Hughes and Secretary of Commerce Herbert Hoover, as well as appointees who brought the administration into deep discredit. In addition, Harding had about him what became known as "the Ohio gang," whom he enjoyed as social companions and favored with responsible appointments.

Corruption set in and spread widely. Harding suffered a drastic shrinkage of political popularity not only because of betrayal by friends, but also due to deepening agricultural depression that brought heavy losses to Republicans in the 1922 Congressional elections, in which the Republican House majority fell from 165 to 15 and the Senate from 24 to 10.

In June 1923, Harding moved to restore his administration to public approval by embarking on a speaking tour through the West and Alaska. En route he received distressing news concerning the Senate investigation of oil leases, or what soon fanned out as the Teapot Dome scandal. Secretary of the Interior Albert B. Fall was subsequently convicted of accepting a bribe for leasing naval oil reserves to private oil interests. Harding's political manager, Attorney General Harry M. Daugherty, was implicated (but not convicted) in malfeasance in the Alien Property Custodian's Office. A friend and aide of Daugherty, Jesse W. Smith, committed suicide following revelations of settlements that Smith had arranged between the justice department and law violators.

In Seattle, Harding developed an illness that was attributed to food poisoning. His tour was suspended in San Francisco, where doctors said he was suffering from pneumonia. After a brief gain, Harding died there on August 2, 1923. There was no autopsy, and the precise cause of his death remains unknown. He was spared the humiliation of experiencing the trials of his two cabinet officials, Fall and Daugherty.

Historians generally rank Harding as one of the weakest of Presidents. But the qualities that made him weak also made him appealing to the bosses in the "smoke-filled room" and to a nation weary of Wilsonian zeal.

Calvin Coolidge

Calvin Coolidge, 30th President (1923–1929), was born John Calvin Coolidge on July 4, 1872, in Plymouth Notch, Vermont. He was the son of John Calvin Coolidge, a farmer and shrewd, experienced politician who served in the Vermont legislature and held local offices. The son was graduated (1895) from Amherst College. He read law with a firm in Northampton, Massachusetts, was admitted (1897) to the bar, and soon opened his own office in Northampton.

In the tradition of the young smalltown lawyer, Coolidge entered politics as a Republican campaign worker in 1896. Three years later, he was elected a member of the Northampton City Council and, over the next five years, served as city solicitor and clerk of county courts. He was elected (1906) to the Massachusetts House of Representatives and reelected (1907).

Remarkable for his taciturnity—the very opposite of the stereotype extrovert politician—Coolidge moved up a career line of city and state politics with electoral invincibility. He was elected (1909) mayor of Northampton and reelected (1910). From 1912 to 1915, he served in the Massachusetts Senate, of which he was president for two terms. He was elected (1915) lieutenant governor and twice reelected. In 1918, he v as elected governor.

In that office, Coolidge became a national figure by his resolute handling of the 1919 Boston police strike, declaring with cryptic force, "There is no right to strike against the public safety by anybody, anywhere, any time." By his firm action of calling in the militia, Coolidge suppressed the strike and won reelection overwhelmingly. The strike also helped boost him into the 1920 Vice-Presidential nomination. The Harding-Coolidge ticket won easily.

Upon Harding's death in 1923, Coolidge became President and the following year was elected to a full term. He commenced his tenure under extraordinarily difficult political circumstances. Scarcely had he declared his intention to carry out policies begun by Harding, when the Teapot Dome and other scandals of the previous administration were exposed. In this test, too, Coolidge was resolute, acting with fearless probity. He eluded the political temptation to shield the Harding administration against scandalous disclosure by bringing about the resignations of Harding's Attorney General, Harry Daugherty, and other important officials. Only three members of the Harding cabinet continued in office throughout the Coolidge administration.

Coolidge continued Harding's policy of responsiveness to the needs and interests of business. Declaring that "the business of America is business," Coolidge promoted a program of what he called "constructive economy." His principal policies were high tariffs, reduced income taxes, lowering the national debt, and strict governmental economy. So devoted was Coolidge to public thrift that he committed the rare political act of vetoing a (World War I) veterans' bonus bill, although Congress overrode him.

Paradoxically, Coolidge's bent for economy in government was enormously popular at a time when society, thanks to a soaring economy, was spendthrift. It was the era of rampant stock market speculation, freely countenanced Prohibition violations, "flaming youth," and the "jazz age." Champion of a rejected code of thrift and propriety, the President was a beloved figure—a reminder of old values that, although discarded, were still respected. In public addresses, Coolidge's pithy, apt expression of the old philosophy was widely appreciated. For example: "Let men in public office substitute the light that comes from the midnight oil for the limelight."

Distrustful of progressivism and opposed to legislation favoring any interest but business, Coolidge employed the veto in important instances where Congress transgressed his principles. For example, he vetoed legislation authorizing government operation of Muscle Shoals (Tennessee River rapids) for the production of electric power. Agriculture did not share in the booming prosperity, but suffered from falling prices and declining exports. Coolidge nonetheless twice vetoed legislation affording relief for farmers through government purchase of surplus products and sale abroad.

In foreign affairs, Coolidge, aided by Secretary of State Frank B. Kellogg, moved the country away from its isolationist tendencies. The secretary negotiated the Kellogg-Briand Pact, to which many nations subscribed, that sought to outlaw war. Although Coolidge opposed United States membership in the League of Nations, he favored joining the World Court. But when the Senate imposed unacceptable conditions, Coolidge dropped the project. A plan worked out by Vice-President Dawes and an international committee provided a new basis on which Germany might pay her World War I reparations.

Under Coolidge, relations with Mexico improved when Ambassador Dwight Morrow negotiated the settlement of old issues and obtained important concessions for American oil interests. With Japan, however, relations declined following Congress's passage of an immigration law that completely excluded Japanese; the President signed it under protest.

As the expected Republican Presidential nominee in 1928, Coolidge astounded the nation on August 2, 1927, by handing the press a slip of paper on which was written: "I do not choose to run for President in 1928." In his autobiography, he stated his conviction that "the chances of having wise and faithful public service are increased by a change in the Presidential office after a moderate length of time."

After leaving the Presidency, Coolidge returned to Northampton, where he wrote an autobiography and a series of daily newspaper articles that dealt mainly with political and economic topics. He was distressed by the coming of the depression in 1929, and it was reported that he felt he should have used the Presidency more assertively to have prevented it. He died on January 5, 1933.

Herbert Clark Hoover

Herbert Clark Hoover, 31st President (1929–1933) and the first President from west of the Mississippi River, was born in West Branch, Iowa, on August 10, 1874. His father was a farmer and village blacksmith, and the family was strong in the Quaker faith. Orphaned at eight years of age, Hoover was raised by relatives in the West.

After graduation (1895) from Stanford University, Hoover became a successful mining engineer and businessman, with offices in New York, San Francisco, and London. His work took him all over the world and won him a fortune, as well as an international engineering and administrative reputation. In World War I, driven by his Quaker principles, he put aside his business affairs and administered to human suffering as chairman of the American Relief Commission with exceptional success that made him an international public figure.

In 1919, both the Republican and Democratic parties pressed Hoover to become their candidate for President the following year. Hoover clarified the question of his party affiliation by announcing that he was a Republican and that he would not be a candidate. In 1921, President Harding appointed him Secretary of Commerce, a post that Hoover continued in under President Coolidge.

As secretary, Hoover again functioned as a dynamic administrator with wide-ranging concerns. Under his hand, the Department of Commerce dramatically expanded its activities, and he oversaw conferences on foreign trade, industrial production, labor affairs, child welfare, and housing. The new industries of radio communication and aviation also came under his regulation.

When President Coolidge declined to run for reelection in 1928, Hoover easily won the Republican Presidential nomination. In a hard-fought campaign against his Democratic opponent, Governor Alfred E. Smith of New York, Hoover envisaged the day when poverty would be eliminated, and Americans would have "two chickens in every pot and a car in every garage." Impressed with Republican prosperity, voters expected even more of it from Hoover because of his genius for economic success. Elected overwhelmingly, he won 40 of the 48 states, with 444 electoral votes to Smith's 87.

Hoover's inaugural address sounded the notes of optimism. "In no nation," he said, "are the fruits of accomplishment more secure." He moved to help depression-ridden farmers by calling Congress into special session (April 1929) and bringing it to create a Federal Farm Board to encourage the growth of farm cooperatives and to absorb agricultural surpluses. Hoover also proposed an increase of tariff duties on farm imports to protect domestic markets. The resulting Hawley-Smoot Tariff Act not only incorporated Hoover's recommendations, but raised duties on many nonagricultural items. As a result, American foreign trade dropped, a contributing factor to the oncoming depression.

Seven months after Hoover's inaugural, the stock market crashed, and the upheaval of the Great Depression, which had long been building in the Harding-Coolidge era, exploded with devastating fury. Stocks collapsed in value, thousands became unemployed, fortunes evaporated overnight. The depression's root cause, in Hoover's view, was not material or political, but psychological: an erosion of confidence. Consequently, Hoover organized conferences with businessmen and labor leaders to spread reassurance and to secure their help in keeping wages and prices stable and avoiding strikes. The President aimed to improve confidence both by paring back federal expenditure and balancing the budget.

But the depression not only persisted but deepened. Unemployment reached a peak of one-fourth of the labor force. Bank failures rocketed, and mortgage foreclosures became commonplace. Reflecting his political philosophy, Hoover stressed the initiation of public works by states and localities to aid the unemployed. The Federal government, he believed, could help indirectly and, in 1932 at Hoover's request, Congress established the Reconstruction Finance Corporation (RFC), which made loans to banks to save them from bankruptcy and supported state relief programs.

Hoover also promoted conservation and federally administered public works programs to reduce unemployment. Federal flood control and navigation improvement projects were undertaken, and construction of Boulder (now Hoover) Dam on the Colorado River was begun. The Hoover administration substantially increased the acreage of national parks and forests, and it also launched major programs of public buildings and major highway construction.

In June 1932, some 15,000 veterans marched on Washington to pressure Congress into passing a bonus law. Opposing the bonus as financially unsound, Hoover eventually employed troops to drive the veterans out of the capital.

Under Hoover, American foreign policy tended toward forbearance and cooperation. He brought Congress to agree to a moratorium on war debt and reparation payments and also stressed goodwill in relations with Latin America. Following his election, he toured Latin America and as President removed the marines from an extended presence in Nicaragua. Hoover also concluded an agreement with Haiti that looked to the withdrawal of American troops in 1934.

Eager to promote disarmament, Hoover proposed that the principles of the London Naval Treaty of 1930 be extended to reduce land weapons; however, the proposal was declined by other nations. In 1931, when the Japanese invaded Manchuria and the League of Nations condemned Japan as an aggressor, Hoover announced that the United States would not recognize territorial aggrandizement that violated the Kellogg-Briand Pact.

A man whose motto was "Work is life," Hoover put in long hours at his desk and drove his staff hard. "He has the greatest capacity for assimilating and organizing information of any man I ever knew," said his Secretary of State, Henry L. Stimson. Yet a solution to the depression eluded this brilliant administrator. Hoover's critics contended that he overrelied on state, local, and private action, and was handicapped by a philosophical indisposition to exploit federal opportunities and resources.

With the nation still deep in depression, the Republicans dutifully renominated Hoover in 1932; however, his Democratic opponent, Franklin D. Roosevelt, promising a "new deal," defeated him by carrying 42 of the 48 states and by collecting 472 electoral votes to Hoover's 59.

After leaving the Presidency, Hoover was a vigorous critic of Roosevelt's New Deal, and later President Truman named Hoover chairman of the Famine Emergency Commission to report on the needs of many nations suffering from the ravages of World War II. Hoover made a similar study of Germany and Austria. In 1947, Truman appointed Hoover chairman of the Commission on Organization of the Executive Branch of the Government. Better known as "the Hoover Commission," the group proposed important changes in governmental organization and management. A second Hoover Commission was created in 1953. Hoover died on October 20, 1964, at age 90.

Franklin Delano Roosevelt

Franklin Delano Roosevelt, 32d President (March 4, 1933–April 12, 1945), was born on January 30, 1882, at Hyde Park, New York, into a wealthy family which in the 1640s had migrated from Holland to New Amsterdam (later New York City). He was a fifth cousin of Theodore Roosevelt.

After studying at Groton and graduating from Harvard, Franklin extended his studies for another year and entered (1904) Columbia Law School. Admitted to the bar in 1907, Roosevelt evidenced little interest in the practice of law, but he soon discovered a keen taste for politics and won election (1910) as a Democrat to the New York Senate against great odds. As state senator, he demonstrated extraordinary adroitness as a political leader by thwarting party bosses who were bent on boosting a Tammany nominee into the U.S. Senate.

Following his vigorous campaign for Presidential aspirant Woodrow Wilson in 1912, Roosevelt was appointed Assistant Secretary of the Navy. Tammany secured its revenge two years later by helping defeat his quest in a primary for nomination to the U.S. Senate. Roosevelt's full emergence into national prominence was betokened by his nomination for the Vice-Presidency in 1920, with James M. Cox heading the ticket in an unsuccessful race.

Roosevelt returned to private life as vice-president of the Fidelity and Deposit Company of Maryland. A year later, he succumbed to poliomyelitis, which paralyzed him from the waist down. By great courage and effort, Roosevelt in time managed to walk a little by wearing braces on his legs and using crutches. In 1924, he surged back into national politics by nominating Alfred E. Smith for the Presidency, as a thrilled convention watched him master his crippling illness by walking slowly to the podium.

At Smith's insistence, Roosevelt ran (1928) for governor of New York and was barely elected. Reelected in 1930, Roosevelt won acclaim for his broad attack on the Great Depression with measures that were to find their counterparts in his subsequent program as President.

He received the Democratic Presidential nomination in 1932 and became the first nominee to make an acceptance speech at a national convention. Promising a "new deal" to bring the nation out of the depression, he easily defeated his Republican opponent, President Herbert Hoover.

At the moment of Roosevelt's inaugural, the depression was at its worst: breadlines of unemployed, mounting mortgage foreclosures, closed banks, and the widespread, gray despair that the country's complex paralyzing economic forces might never be fathomed and overcome.

Roosevelt created an immediate impression of action and initiative. He declared a "bank holiday," closing down the banks for federal inspection; those in good financial condition were permitted to reopen. The confidence of depositors, which had been shaken by rampant bank failures, was restored. He summoned Congress into special session, and between March 9 and June 16, 1933, the famous "100 Days," more legislation of major impact was passed than ever before.

The New Deal, as these accumulated economic and social measures became known, included relief for the unemployed, aid for farm mortgages, a civilian conservation corps, a Tennessee Valley Authority, a National Industrial Recovery Act, and an Agricultural Adjustment Act under which a price subsidy was provided to farmers who agreed to limit their output. Roosevelt's measures were directed to the unemployed, the farmer, labor, the young, the aged, and the Negro, all of whom suffered most acutely from the depression.

In advancing his program, Roosevelt gave a bravura performance as Presidential leader and politician. In "fireside chats," as his national radio addresses were called, he explained his purposes, actions, and plans. His press conferences were remarkably newsworthy and conducted with a skill and charm that left many reporters warmly disposed toward his administration. As legislative leader, Roosevelt was adept at attracting bipartisan support, at timing his measures well, and at exploiting his political opportunities. To the country, he appeared a confident leader whose easy humor and ready laughter were marks of self-possession in the face of national crisis.

In 1936, Roosevelt was overwhelmingly reelected, defeating the Republican nominee, Governor Alfred M. Landon of Kansas. Roosevelt's political fortunes now went into something of a tailspin, to the delight of his many foes and detractors, who considered him a "traitor to his class." The Supreme Court held such key measures as the National Industrial Recovery Act, the Agricultural Adjustment Act, and other laws unconstitutional. Roosevelt moved in 1937 to "pack the court." Although rebuffed, he did slow the pace of hostile court decisions.

Foreign policy was largely preoccupied with the war clouds gathering over Europe and the Pacific, culminating in Germany's invasion of Poland on September 1, 1939. Although restricted by neutrality legislation, Roosevelt sought to give "all aid short of war" to nations fighting the Axis. The neutrality laws were modified in the directions that Roosevelt urged. Isolationists, who believed the United States should remain uninvolved, attacked Roosevelt as bent upon bringing the United States into the struggle. When he shattered precedent by running for the Presidency for a third time, he was severely attacked and was driven to promise to try to keep the nation out of war. He prevailed over his Republican opponent, Wendell Willkie, but with reduced majorities.

Following France's surrender to Germany in June 1940, Roosevelt undertook bold initiatives to aid embattled Britain. He exchanged old American destroyers for American assumption of leases on several British bases in the Western Hemisphere. He promoted the Lend-Lease Act that authorized the provision of war supplies to any nation fighting the Axis. In a meeting with Winston Churchill in August 1941 on the high seas, the two leaders adopted the Atlantic Charter that attested to the ideals of freedom of the seas, the territorial integrity of nations, peaceful trade, freedom of choice of governmental form. Earlier in a speech on January 6, 1941, Roosevelt had declared that all men are entitled to at least four freedoms: freedom from want, freedom of worship, freedom of speech, and freedom from fear. The two documents provided a foundation of ideals and aims for the war.

With America's deepening commitment to the Allies, relations with Germany, Italy, and Japan deteriorated rapidly. On December 7, 1941, Japan attacked the United States fleet at Pearl Harbor and the nation found itself quickly at war with the Axis. Decisions of the utmost magnitude faced the President. After conferring with Churchill in Washington, for example, Roosevelt chose to concentrate on the defeat of Germany first, after which the full force of war was to be directed against Japan.

As commander-in-chief, Roosevelt was the chief architect of the North African invasion, which commenced on November 7, 1942. This was followed by invasions of Sicily and Italy, and finally the cross-channel, D-Day invasion of Normandy. In the latter enterprise, Roosevelt was under pressure from Joseph Stalin to create a second front quickly to relieve German pressure on the Russians. Stalin wanted the Normandy venture to begin before the President was convinced the Allies were prepared for it. Churchill preferred a thrust up through the Balkans to check the western surge of the Russians. Roosevelt remained the master of the decision.

The President furthered war diplomacy in a 1943 meeting with Churchill at Casablanca, where they agreed to accept only unconditional surrender by the Axis.

With the war at its peak, Roosevelt reluctantly ran (1944) for a fourth Presidential term, and he easily defeated his Republican opponent, Thomas E. Dewey. Roosevelt began his new term in obviously failing health, yet journeyed to Yalta in the Crimea to confer with Churchill and Stalin. The Crimea Declaration, which emerged from the conference, affirmed the principles of the Atlantic Charter and the objectives of the Casablanca conference. Plans for the defeat and occupation of Germany were drawn, and a future meeting at San Francisco was agreed on at which the United Nations would be organized as an enduring international structure. In return for Far East concessions, Russia agreed to enter the war against Japan.

In the weeks following the Yalta meeting, Roosevelt, whose wartime policies had assumed the continued goodwill and cooperation of the Soviet Union, grew restive with doubts over Soviet attitudes.

On April 12, 1945, about a month before Germany surrendered, Roosevelt suddenly died at Warm Springs, Georgia. He was buried at Hyde Park.

As President, Roosevelt employed the resources of his office with boldness and initiative. He delighted to break precedents and embark on new ways. His cabinet appointees were lively and resourceful, and he was given to employing both "Brain Trusters," who were usually academicians fertile in ideas, and wide-ranging White House assistants. Adroit in political controversy, he impressed fellow politicians with his canny sense of timing. Although given to deviousness, he unfailingly projected an air of rectitude. In the age of radio, he excelled at stirring public opinion, and as party leader he solidified the loyalties of such groups as labor and blacks to the Democratic party. These groups, joined with the South, city party organizations, and farmers constituted "the Roosevelt coalition," which endured for decades after its creator's death.

Harry S Truman

Harry S Truman, 33d President (April 12, 1945–January 20, 1953), was born on May 8, 1884, in Lamar, Missouri. The oldest of three children of a farmer and livestock dealer, Truman was raised on a farm near Independence. A voracious reader of military history, he hoped to attend West Point, but was rejected because of unsatisfactory vision. After finishing high school, he worked as a timekeeper for a railroad construction gang, as a mail clerk for a Kansas City newspaper, and as a bookkeeper in Kansas City banks. In World War I, Truman helped recruit a field artillery regiment. He saw action in France, was discharged (1919) as a major, and later rose to a colonelcy in the reserves.

After the war, Truman invested in a men's clothing store, in Kansas City, but it failed in the farm depression of 1921. At this bleak moment, Truman turned to politics and secured an introduction to "Big Tom" Pendergast, Democratic boss of Kansas City. Impressed with Truman's political promise, Pendergast supported (1922) Truman's successful campaign for administrator of Jackson County; however, after a two-year term, Truman was defeated for reelection because of factional strife within his party. In his free time, Truman studied law at Kansas City Law School, and in 1926, he was elected presiding judge, serving in that capacity until 1934. Overseeing large projects of public works construction, he earned a reputation for probity and efficiency.

With Pendergast's backing, Truman was elected (1934) to the U.S. Senate. During a decade in the Senate, Truman strongly supported the New Deal, and during World War II he achieved national renown as chairman of the Senate's Special Committee to investigate the National Defense Program. The Truman Committee, as it was known, excelled at uncovering waste and inefficiency in war production.

In 1944, Truman won the Democratic Vice-Presidential nomination as a compromise choice in a spirited contest between several contenders. When President Roosevelt suddenly died, Truman became President at a critical moment in the nation's history. Within his first weeks as President, Germany surrendered and the United Nations was launched at the San Francisco conference as a postwar international organization. He met with the British and Soviet leaders at Potsdam, and made the grave decision to employ the atomic bomb against Japan to bring World War II to a quick conclusion.

Truman now had to lead the nation's reconversion from its wartime mobilization to a peacetime footing. In a message to Congress (September 6, 1945), he proposed a sweeping program (the "Fair Deal,") that was an extension of the New Deal. His proposals included an expanded social security system, a higher minimum wage, a permanent fair employment practices commission to protect minority rights, comprehensive housing legislation, government aid for scientific research, and public power projects on the Missouri, Columbia, and Arkansas rivers.

Few of Truman's proposals were enacted. In 1946, the Republicans gained control of both houses of Congress, and the President's program was blocked by a coalition of conservative Republicans and Democrats. His chief success was legislation for public housing that was passed with substantial help from the Senate Republican leader, Robert A. Taft. In 1947, Congress approved Truman's plan to unify the armed forces by creating the U.S. Department of Defense. In that same year, Congress passed the Taft-Hartley Labor Act, a far-ranging measure for regulating labor unions and labor-management relations. In a bitterly worded message, Truman vetoed the act but was overridden by Congress.

In foreign affairs, United States relations with the Soviet Union swiftly deteriorated as the Communists gained control in the nations of Eastern Europe. To check the Communist tide, Truman advanced a doctrine of American aid to nations that resisted either direct or indirect Communist aggression. The Truman Doctrine, as it became known, was prompted by Britain's inability to continue her aid to Greece and Turkey in their struggle against Communist actions, and American aid checked a Communist-supported civil war in Greece and bolstered Turkey's military strength.

In 1947, the Marshall Plan (European Recovery Program) extended the Truman Doctrine to speed the recovery of Western European economies from the devastation resulting from World War II. The Marshall Plan was a combination of European self-help supported by massive American outlays. The Soviet Union was invited to join the plan, but declined.

The continuing decline in American-USSR relations became known as "The Cold War," and the Truman administration's policy of applying counterforce—political, economic, or military— corresponding to the shifts and maneuvers of the Soviet Union was spoken of as the policy of "containment." Congress generously supported the President through appropriations and statutory authority.

While coping with the Cold War, Truman faced sharp political strife at home in the 1948 election. A segment of liberal Democrats formed the Progressive party and nominated Henry A. Wallace for President. Other liberal Democrats sought unsuccessfully to deny Truman the Democratic nomination. Conservative Southern Democrats formed the Dixiecrat party and nominated J. Strom Thurmond. Against mountainous odds and almost miraculously, Truman defeated the Republican nominee, Governor Thomas E. Dewey. Truman relied upon a "whistle-stop" campaign and rousing oratory that was directed at the Republican 80th Congress, which he characterized as "do-nothing" and "the worst in memory."

Foreign affairs dominated Truman's new term. A 1948 Communist coup in Czechoslovakia prompted Western European nations to draw together in their defenses and led to the creation of the North Atlantic Treaty Organization (NATO) under which the United States and other pact nations agreed that an attack on one member would be regarded as an attack on all member nations. An Anglo-American airlift thwarted the Communist blockade of Berlin in 1948.

In his inaugural address, Truman proposed "a bold new program" by which American technical and production skills could help "underdeveloped" areas. Implementation of the proposal began (1950) when Congress established the Point Four Program. In 1951, Truman initiated a foreign-aid program for Southeast Asian countries threatened by Communism. A Mutual Security program was also instituted to improve military defenses in many countries worldwide.

The Cold War became hot (June 25, 1950), when Communist North Korea invaded South Korea. Truman quickly responded by committing United States forces to South Korea's defense under UN auspices. Commanded by General Douglas MacArthur, UN forces overran most of North Korea, only to have Communist China enter the war. MacArthur proposed to bomb Communist bases in Manchuria, but Truman, who did not wish to extend the war, rejected the plan. When MacArthur publicly criticized the administration, Truman removed him from his command, igniting a furor of debate and criticism.

In domestic affairs, Truman fared little better with the new Democratic Congress than he had with the former Republican one. The Truman administration faced charges of Communist infiltration into the U.S. Department of State that were lodged by Senator Joseph McCarthy of Wisconsin. A House investigating committee made similar accusations about other agencies. As a result, Truman set up a federal loyalty board to deal with the problem, and the justice department launched prosecutions of American Communist leaders. The administration was hobbled by exposures of corruption among subordinates, who were generously defended by the President for reasons of friendship or party necessity.

On March 29, 1952, Truman announced that he would not seek reelection. Nevertheless, he campaigned strenuously for the unsuccessful Democratic nominee, Adlai E. Stevenson. After leaving office, Truman wrote his memoirs, which were published in two volumes, commented occasionally on national issues, and remained interested in the Democratic party. He died on December 26, 1972, and is buried at Independence, Missouri.

Winston Churchill credited President Truman with making "great and valiant decisions." Other admirers of his administration cited his courage and his gift of seeing issues divested of complication and of stating them in plain, blunt terms. His critics felt that his candor and affinity for strong language were undignified. Others considered him a man of the people, and Truman acknowledged these differences of opinion by once saying that he expected to be "cussed and discussed" for years to come.

Dwight David Eisenhower

Dwight David Eisenhower, 34th President (1953–1961), was born in Denison, Texas, on October 14, 1890 as David Dwight Eisenhower. Of Swiss and German ancestry, Eisenhower's parents belonged to the River Brethren religious sect, which was opposed to war and violence. While young, Eisenhower moved to Abilene, Kansas; after graduating from high school, he worked in the local creamery where his father was engineer.

To the disappointment of his parents, Eisenhower entered West Point at the age of 21 and graduated in the 1915 class that included Omar Bradley and James Van Fleet. In World War I, he was commander of a tank training center near Gettysburg, Pennsylvania. His postwar career included service in the Canal Zone; study at the General Staff School at Fort Leavenworth, Kansas, and at the U.S. Army War College. Eisenhower became (1933) an aide of General Douglas MacArthur in the Philippines. Brilliance in field maneuvers won him assignment to the war plans division of the war department, and he became (1942) head of the operations division. At midyear, Eisenhower was named U.S. commander of the European Theater of Operations.

Eisenhower oversaw the North African invasion (November 1942) and directed the invasions of Sicily and Italy. He was named (1943) supreme commander of the Allied Expeditionary Force (AEF) that was organized for the Normandy invasion. He excelled at bringing proud, independent generals of various nations into working harmony and directing the military operations of an unprecedented scale that achieved (1945) the unconditional surrender of Germany. Made a five-star general (1944) and chief of staff of the U.S. Army (1945), Eisenhower played a leading part in the "unification" of the armed services under the newly established U.S. Department of Defense. He retired (1948) from active duty to become president of Columbia University.

After soundings made by both Democratic and Republican sources, Eisenhower announced (1948) his unavailability as a Presidential candidate. After 30 months he left his Columbia post to serve as NATO commander and to organize the forces of that alliance.

The approaching 1952 elections brought new pressures on Eisenhower to run for the Presidency, and he responded. He retired from the army to campaign successfully for the Republican nomination against Senator Robert A. Taft. Promising to "clean up the mess in Washington" and that "I shall go to Korea" to help end the war, the enormously popular "Ike" Eisenhower easily defeated his Democratic opponent, Adlai E. Stevenson. Eisenhower also helped his party win control of both houses of Congress. Soon after the election, he journeyed to Korea to observe the war firsthand.

From long observation of the Presidency during his military career, Eisenhower considered that the office was administered with excessive informality. As a result, he installed a staff system comparable to the military's and designated Sherman Adams, former governor of New Hampshire, as his chief White House aide. For the first time, the cabinet worked regularly according to a prearranged agenda, records of cabinet proceedings were kept, and each cabinet officer was responsible for monitoring problems and taking initiatives in his area of affairs.

Eisenhower was an apostle of what he termed Modern Republicanism, which, in its most ambitious projection, looked for major policy changes in his party. It called for the strengthening of federal social programs, and the President secured an expanded coverage of the social security system—its largest extension since its beginning under FDR. The minimum wage was also increased. Eisenhower was watchful that new measures did not encroach on state jurisdictions.

The President's domestic program included a 13-year highway building program that was urgently needed, because of a construction backlog that had accumulated during World War II. Eisenhower also succeeded in bringing Congress to modify the traditional rigid price supports of certain staple farm products.

In national security, the Eisenhower administration introduced "the new look" that shifted the emphasis of military expenditure from conventional forces and weapons to atomic weapons, which were regarded as more economical. In foreign affairs, an agreement was reached between the United States and Canada for joint development of the St. Lawrence Seaway.

More than most Presidents, Eisenhower faced substantial encroachment (or its threat) on his office and the functioning of the executive branch. Senator John Bricker of Ohio sponsored an amendment to curb the President's power to make treaties and executive agreements. After a strenuous fight, the President and his Secretary of State, John Foster Dulles, defeated the amendment.

Another Republican Senator, Joseph R. McCarthy of Wisconsin, steadily confronted the administration with accusations of subversion and Communist infiltration of the executive branch. Eisenhower, who declined to deal "in terms of personality," refrained from directly attacking McCarthy, a stand that prompted criticism. But when McCarthy charged that the United States Information Agency had Communist books in its European libraries, Eisenhower counseled students in an address at Dartmouth College: "Don't join the bookburners. . . . Don't be afraid to go to the library and read every book."

In foreign affairs, Eisenhower made important gains for peace and guided the Korean war to a close. He advanced (1953) the "Atoms for Peace" program, under which the world nations were to pool atomic energy information and output for peaceful purposes. The proposal led to the creation (1957) of the International Atomic Agency. The President proposed (1955) that the United States and the Soviet Union permit air inspection of each other's military installations, but the USSR declined.

On September 24, 1955, Eisenhower suffered a heart attack, the first of several illnesses with which he was afflicted during his years in office. His good recovery enabled him to run for a second term in 1956, when he again easily defeated Adlai Stevenson.

In his second term, Eisenhower sent (1957) Federal troops to Little Rock, Arkansas, to enforce school desegregation that was being resisted by Governor Orval Faubus. The nation suffered an economic recession in 1957 and 1958, but business improved markedly during the latter half of 1958. Eisenhower lost his chief assistant, Sherman Adams, in 1958, when Congressional investigations revealed that he had accepted gifts from a businessman who was under scrutiny by government agencies. Adams denied any wrongdoing, but resigned his White House post.

Eisenhower's hopes to develop a more peaceful international climate were defeated by repeated difficulties with the Communist world. The Soviet's launching (1957) of Sputnik I—the first manmade satellite—emboldened the Russians. Crisis in the Middle East evoked the "Eisenhower Doctrine," pledging American military aid to any Middle East nation that requested it to repel Communist aggression, and Eisenhower applied (1958) the doctrine to Lebanon. When Chinese Communists shelled Nationalist-held Quemoy island in 1958, the President committed American naval aid to protect Chinese Nationalist convoys.

Eisenhower met (1959) with Soviet Premier Nikita Khrushchev in a summit conference in the United States; however, a further summit conference at Paris (1960) was broken up by Khrushchev, because of an American U-2 reconnaissance aircraft that had been shot down over Russian territory. Following many provocations by Fidel Castro, Eisenhower broke off diplomatic relations with Cuba in 1961.

Eisenhower was the first President to be limited to two terms by the 22d Constitutional Amendment. Retiring to his farm in Gettysburg, Pennsylvania, Eisenhower wrote memoirs of his Presidential years and other books, supported Richard Nixon's Presidential campaigns, and discussed various political questions. He died on March 28, 1969, and is buried at Abilene, Kansas.

John Fitzgerald Kennedy

John Fitzgerald Kennedy, 35th President (January 20, 1961–November 22, 1963) was born into a political family on May 29, 1917, in Brookline, Massachusetts. His paternal grandfather was a state senator and Boston ward boss, and his maternal grandfather was John F. ("Honey Fitz") Fitzgerald—Boston mayor, state senator, and U.S. Representative. Kennedy's father, Joseph P. Kennedy, was a self-made millionaire and ambassador to Great Britain during World War II.

After studies at the London School of Economics and Princeton, Kennedy graduated (1940) from Harvard, where he majored in political science and international relations. His senior thesis, *Why England Slept,* became a best-selling book.

At the outbreak of World War II, Kennedy enlisted in the Navy and served as commander of a PT boat in the South Pacific. In action off the Solomon Islands, a Japanese destroyer sank his boat. Kennedy heroically saved an injured member of his crew. After release from the Navy, Kennedy worked briefly as a reporter for the Hearst newspapers.

The World War II death of his older brother Joe, who had been expected to become the family politician, devolved that function on John Kennedy. He was elected (1946) to the U.S. House of Representatives, defeating eight opponents in the Democratic primary of the Massachusetts 11th district and easily overcoming his Republican opponent. As Congressman, Kennedy voted regularly for Truman's Fair Deal program. Reelected twice, Kennedy became (1952) Senator in an upset defeat of the popular Henry Cabot Lodge. Kennedy underwent (1954–55) operations to correct a spinal injury that he had sustained in the war; while recovering, he wrote *Profiles in Courage,* for which he won the Pulitzer Prize.

In 1956, Kennedy was a strong contender for the Vice-Presidential nomination, losing to Estes Kefauver in a close race. Kennedy was easily reelected (1958) to the Senate. From 1956 onward, however, he was busily preparing to make a Presidential race and eventually won the 1960 Democratic nomination, after scoring several crucial primary victories. In a hard-fought contest with his Republican opponent, Richard M. Nixon, Kennedy—a youthful, handsome, and wealthy figure with an attractive wife and a highly persuasive television style—won the election in the closest race of the century. Vital to his success were his televised debates with Nixon. At the age of 43, Kennedy became the youngest man ever elected President, and he was also the first Roman Catholic to occupy the office.

Kennedy's Presidential campaign had been geared largely to the industrial and urban states. On attaining office, he promoted legislative measures that he had promised to support if elected. Included in his recommendations to Congress were major educational legislation, medical aid for the aged, the creation of a Department of Urban Affairs, and an increase in the minimum wage.

He suffered severe resistance in the House of Representatives, where a conservative coalition of Republicans and Democrats thwarted much of his program. Because of this opposition, he long held back the promotion of major civil rights legislation. He sustained defeats on his farm bill, the urban department, health care for the aged, and education. His chief legislative triumph was the passage (1962) of the Trade Expansion Act, which gave the President broad powers to reduce tariffs to enable the United States to trade freely with the European Common Market.

In a rare step, President Kennedy sought to break the legislative logjam by seeking, with Speaker Sam Rayburn's help, to enlarge the House Rules Committee, at which point much legislation was stopped. The administration's position in the committee became somewhat improved following the fight, but not sufficiently to push key measures through.

Although blocked on Capitol Hill on civil rights legislation, Kennedy was diligent and ingenious in advancing civil rights policies through executive initiatives and actions. The Kennedy administration, with Robert Kennedy as Attorney General, was aggressive in prosecuting violations of the Supreme Court's school desegregation decisions; it directed U.S. marshals, the regular army, and the federalized National Guard to quell (1961) rioting against black and white "freedom riders" in Montgomery, Alabama; it employed the government contract to improve the civil rights standards of private employers; and it demanded that the civil service improve black recruitment and promotion. In televised appeals, the President promoted understanding of civil rights problems.

More than most modern Presidents, Kennedy was preoccupied with crisis, both foreign and domestic. In 1962, certain steel companies raised their prices, after Kennedy had induced labor to scale down its demands to check inflation. Outraged by management's action, the President moved forcefully against the companies involved and denounced them publicly. The companies withdrew the price rises, but the stock market soon underwent its sharpest drop since 1929. Within weeks, Kennedy faced a civil rights crisis in Mississippi, when the governor refused to obey a federal court order requiring that James Meredith, a black, be enrolled at the University. The President dispatched Federal troops and marshals, and Meredith was enrolled.

In foreign affairs, the President seemed never without crisis. Prepared and outfitted under American auspices, Cuban rebels invaded their homeland to overthrow the Communist-backed leader (1961), Fidel Castro. The assault was savagely repulsed, and Kennedy publicly took responsibility for the disaster. Berlin was a constant concern of the President. Aiming to end the Allied participation in control of the city, the Soviet Union and East Germany engaged in a series of maneuvers that culminated in the erection of the Berlin Wall, which sealed off escape from East to West Berlin. The President called up army reserves and dispatched military units to the border until the tense situation eased.

Kennedy faced (1961–62) spreading Communist penetration in Southeast Asia and made substantial commitments of American troops and matériel to the defense of South Vietnam and Thailand. Military advisers were sent to Laos.

Late in 1962, Kennedy became the first President to engage in a confrontation with another nuclear power. The Soviet Union built missile sites in Cuba from which it would have been possible to launch attacks on American cities. Kennedy imposed a blockade or "quarantine," barring the introduction of any offensive missiles to Cuba. The President also made clear that the United States would respond to any nuclear attack from Cuba on a Western Hemisphere nation by retaliating against the Soviet Union. After 14 days of intense deliberations by the President and his counselors and exchanges of messages with Russia, the crisis was resolved by Premier Khrushchev's ordering that the Cuban bases be dismantled and the missiles returned to Russia. In world eyes, Kennedy emerged from this crisis as a well-poised, rational, and resolute leader who had thoroughly excelled his Soviet opponent.

The Kennedy years were an era when young men were in charge of Presidential institutions. In his inaugural address, the President noted that a new generation was coming into power. Himself the first President born in the 20th century, Kennedy filled his chief posts with men in their 30s and early 40s. His administration he described as the "New Frontier." In foreign affairs, its chief innovations were establishment of the Peace Corps and the Latin-American Alliance for Progress and the nuclear test-ban treaty. In domestic affairs, he demonstrated new "vigor" in attacking urban problems. The Kennedy administration was also marked by new attention to American culture. Not since the days of Theodore Roosevelt did so many musicians, artists, writers, and scientists visit the White House.

For all of the power and majesty of his office, Kennedy displayed a remarkable gift for self-depreciation. A master of irony, both keen and gentle, he directed it at himself as well as at others. A capacity for self-criticism helped Kennedy maintain exceptional composure in crisis, to keep his assessments of problems and people in balance, and to question the well-settled responses of the past.

On November 22, 1963, the Kennedy era was suddenly ended in Dallas, Texas, where Lee Harvey Oswald murdered the President. An appalled nation and world mourned his death. He is buried at a simple site in Arlington National Cemetery.

Lyndon Baines Johnson

Lyndon Baines Johnson, 36th President (November 22, 1963–January 20, 1969), was born on a farm near Stonewall, Texas, on August 27, 1908, the son of a state legislator and school teacher. The family moved (1913) to Johnson City, Texas, where young Johnson was educated in the local public schools. He taught (1928) grade school in Cotulla, Texas, and graduated (1930) from Southwest Texas State Teachers College. For the next two years, he taught public school in Houston.

Johnson began his political career in 1932 as secretary to a Texas Congressman and attended Georgetown University Law School in Washington. An enthusiastic supporter of the New Deal, Johnson became (1935) state director of the National Youth Administration in Texas. His first attempt at elective office was successful, when voters chose him to fill a vacancy in 1937 in the U.S. House of Representatives, and he was continuously reelected until 1948.

Immediately after the Japanese attack on Pearl Harbor, Johnson became the first member of Congress to go into uniform, entering active service in the U.S. Navy. He rose to lieutenant commander before being called back to Congress.

Johnson was elected (1948) to the U.S. Senate after winning the Democratic primary election by a hairline margin of 87 votes. Proving himself well-endowed with the gifts for legislative leadership and steeped in knowledge of Congressional procedures, Johnson rose rapidly in the Senate. He became (1951) Democratic whip, and he was elected (1953) Democratic leader, serving until 1960. He was reelected (1954) to the Senate and suffered a serious heart attack a year later. As Senate leader, Johnson was moderate in policy, extraordinarily persuasive, and skillful in effecting compromise. He was a top contender for the Democratic Presidential nomination in 1960, but it was won by John F. Kennedy, who chose him to be his Vice-President.

Kennedy's assassination on November 22, 1963, suddenly brought Johnson into the Presidency. Under these tragic circumstances, he quickly administered the office with a skill and self-possession that reassured the nation and the world. He guided through Congress the Civil Rights Act of 1964, a major education bill, a new tax law, and an economic opportunity act that declared "war on poverty."

In the 1964 Presidential elections, Johnson won an overwhelming victory over his Republican opponent, Barry M. Goldwater. Johnson received the largest percentage of popular votes ever accorded a President and perhaps, more important, he won lop-sided Democratic majorities in Congress.

Against this extraordinarily favorable legislative background, Johnson, with shrewd strategy and relentless drive, pushed legislation through Congress in 1965 and 1966 that instituted more innovations in domestic affairs than any other President in any other single session of Congress in this century. The "Great Society" program, as his platform became known, included medical care for the aged under social security, the first comprehensive aid-to-education law, a voting rights bill, a broad housing program, immigration reform, programs for highway beautification and for combating heart disease and cancer, and water and air pollution measures. After the 1966 Congressional elections that resulted in a loss of Democratic strength, the legislative output fell significantly.

The Presidential Succession Constitutional Amendment (25th) was adopted (1967) with Johnson's strong backing, and Congress passed (1968) a strong civil rights bill that included guarantees of open housing.

Crisis flared (1965) in the Dominican Republic, when the President dispatched U.S. marines to thwart a take-over by what he termed "a band of Communist conspirators."

The dominant preoccupation, however, of the Johnson administration was the Vietnamese war, which was already large in scale by the time that Johnson took office. When U.S. warships were alleged to have been attacked (1964) in the Gulf of Tonkin, Johnson ordered a bombing of North Vietnamese PT-boat bases, and Congress expressed approval in a broadly stated resolution. The President increased (1965) the numbers of American fighting men in Vietnam, although he encouraged the North Vietnamese to begin "unconditional negotiations."

In late 1967, additional U.S. troops were committed to the conflict. In the face of heavy Vietcong offensives in 1968 against South Vietnam cities, the President was criticized by "hawks" for restricting bombing in North Vietnam and by "doves" for not ending the bombing altogether. On March 31, the President announced a partial end to the bombing of North Vietnam and simultaneously appointed representatives to negotiate with the North Vietnamese in Paris. On October 31, Johnson ordered a complete halt to the bombing and shelling of North Vietnam.

Johnson pursued policies aiming toward improved relations with Eastern Europe and the Soviet Union, proposed treaties barring military activity in outer space and the proliferation of nations producing nuclear weapons, conducted a summit conference with Soviet Premier Kosygin at Glassboro, New Jersey, in 1967, and sought to prevent and terminate the Arab-Israeli war of 1967. In 1968, North Korea seized the U.S.S. *Pueblo*, precipitating a potentially major crisis that Johnson contained with diplomacy.

In a televised address (March 31, 1968), announcing a partial halt to the bombing of North Vietnam, Johnson also disclosed that he would "not accept the nomination of my party as your President."

Johnson's forte in the Presidency was clearly in the area of legislative relations, toward which his previous career was so strongly directed. "I am a compromiser and a manipulator," he once described himself. His perceptions of the nature of power moved him more to the backstage than to the frontstage of politics. "In every town," he once said, "there's some guy on top of the hill in a big white house who can get things done. I want to get that man on my side." As a public leader, he was handicapped by the unfriendliness toward him of many academics, the press, and American youth. Johnson did not have the great strength in the national party organization that Franklin D. Roosevelt enjoyed, nor did he have the personal organization for party affairs of John F. Kennedy. These deficiencies undoubtedly added to the troubles involved in his possible renomination in 1968. With roots in Populism and the Southwest, Johnson had difficulty winning national acceptance, particularly in the East. He died Jan. 22, 1973 and is buried near Johnson City, Texas.

Richard Milhous Nixon

Richard Milhous Nixon, 37th President (January 20, 1969–August 9, 1974), was born of Quaker parentage in Yorba Linda, California, on January 9, 1913. When he was nine years old, the Nixon family moved to Whittier, California, where his father ran a combination grocery store and gas station. After graduating from Whittier College (1934) and Duke University Law School (1937), he practiced law in Whittier and worked briefly as an attorney for the Office of Price Administration in Washington, D. C. Following United States entry into World War II, he served (1942–46) as a naval officer.

Nixon's political career began in 1946, when a group of California Republicans urged him to run for Congress. He won a hard-fought contest (during which he accused his opponent, a New Deal Democrat, of being soft on Communism) and was reelected in 1948. In the House of Representatives, he contributed importantly to the development of the Marshall Plan and the Taft-Hartley act. He gained national prominence in 1948–49 by pressing an investigation by the House Un-American Activities Committee into charges that Alger Hiss, a former State Department official, had passed government information to Russian agents in the 1930s. In 1950, a federal district court convicted Hiss of perjury.

On the crest of the prominence attained by the Hiss case, Nixon was elected (1950) to the Senate from California. Two years later, Republicans nominated Nixon as the Vice-Presidential running mate of Dwight D. Eisenhower.

In 1960 Nixon was defeated by John F. Kennedy in a close race for the Presidency. The campaign witnessed the first televised debate between Presidential candidates. Turning to authorship, Nixon published (1962) *Six Crises,* a personal account of major interludes in his career. That year he also ran unsuccessfully against incumbent Edmund (Pat) Brown for governor of California.

He entered a crowded field of contestants for the 1968 Republican Presidential nomination, excelled in the primaries, and by forestalling defection of Southern delegates to his rival, Governor Ronald Reagan of California, won a first-ballot nomination. His selection of Governor Spiro T. Agnew of Maryland as a running mate and the firm adherence of Southern delegates, led by Strom Thurmond of South Carolina, to his nomination, prompted discussion that Nixon was pursuing a "Southern strategy."

Projecting a "New Nixon" image, he appealed to the nation's discontent with the Vietnam War and its concern for preserving law and order. In a close race, he defeated Hubert H. Humphrey, who led a divided Democratic party, and George C. Wallace, nominee of the American Independent party.

Nixon was engrossed, during his first term, in the Indo-China war. He sought a negotiated settlement, but despite both private and public talks in Paris, the war continued to drag on. In August, 1972, the American ground combat role ended in Vietnam as the last combat infantry unit was returned to the U.S. To replace the departing forces, the President depended on a policy of "Vietnamization," and American warplanes based throughout Southeast Asia.

To offset criticism that the United States was absorbed in Vietnam to the neglect of other parts of the world, the President visited several West European capitals in 1969, and he became the first President in nearly 25 years to visit a

Communist nation (Romania). His 1972 visits to Russia and China were hailed as historic moments in American diplomacy.

In domestic affairs Nixon was less successful in combating inflation. In August 1971, he instituted price and wage controls. It was the first time such constraints had been applied to the U.S. economy during peacetime, but by the time he left office in 1974, the economy was in a recession.

The President was reelected in 1972 by one of the greatest margins in U.S. history. He was helped by a disorganized Democratic party that was deeply split when old-line party leaders were routed in their effort to block the nomination of Sen. George McGovern of South Dakota.

Allegations of major scandals broke before the election, but apparently had little effect on the outcome. Not until the following year, when the bugging of Democratic headquarters in the Watergate Hotel was fully understood, did public opinion turn sharply downward.

In 1973 peace negotiations in Paris finally bore fruit, at least for the United States. Peace accords were signed in January which called for the end of all fighting and the withdrawal of American and other foreign troops from Vietnam and the rest of Indochina. What the President called "peace with honor" did not bring a halt in the fighting between North and South Vietnam or between Communist insurgents and government forces in Cambodia. U.S. bombing was halted with the peace treaty in Vietnam but continued in Cambodia until August when Nixon halted the bombing under heavy congressional pressure.

For the first time in years, Vietnam and other foreign crises were completely eclipsed by events in Washington. Although the White House initially wrote off the Watergate incident as of no major significance, the combined forces of the press, a Senate investigating committee, and a special prosecutor, eventually forced Nixon to resign in disgrace and left many of his former top assistants accused of obstruction of justice.

Gerald R. Ford

Gerald Rudolph Ford, 38th President (August 9, 1974-January 20, 1977), is unique in American history. He was neither elected president nor vice president, but rather, was first appointed vice president under a new Constitutional amendment, when Vice President Agnew resigned in disgrace, and then became President when Nixon resigned.

Prior to becoming vice president, Ford had spent his entire political career in the U.S. House of Representatives, where he was the respected Republican House Minority Leader. After assuming the Presidency, Ford's popularity was initially very high, but continuing inflation, the pardon of former President Nixon, and the granting of limited amnesty to Vietnam-era draft evaders and deserters, quickly brought this "honeymoon" to an end.

President Ford was born in Omaha, Neb., on July 14, 1913. His mother and father were divorced shortly after his birth, and when his mother remarried, her second husband adopted the future president, renaming Leslie Lynch King, Jr., Gerald R. Ford, Jr.

Ford was raised in Grand Rapids, Mich.; was graduated from the University of Michigan, where he was captain of the football team; and received his law degree from Yale University.

In 1942 he entered the U.S. Navy, serving 47 months and participating for two years in 3d and 5th Fleet Carrier operations with the U.S.S. *Monterey*. After discharge, in 1946, Ford resumed his law practice briefly in Grand Rapids before being elected, in 1948, to the U.S. House of Representatives, a seat he retained for 25 years, through the election of 1972. In 1963, Ford was appointed by President Lyndon Johnson as a member of the Warren Commission to investigate the assassination of President Kennedy.

From the time of his entry into Congress, Gerald Ford's views tended toward the conservative. He voted against most social welfare legislation, in favor of weakened minimum wage bills, and he opposed forced school busing. He supported, however, key civil rights bills at the time of their final passage.

By 1959, Ford was gaining increasing party support for leadership of the House Republicans. In 1960, he was endorsed by Michigan Republicans as the state's favorite son for the G.O.P. vice-presidential nomination. By 1964, he had gained sufficient support to challenge successfully Rep. Charles R. Halleck for the post of House Minority Leader. Generally content with Ford's noncombative, middle-of-the-road approach to issues in his years as Minority Leader, his contituency continued to return him to Congress with majorities of over 60 per cent.

When, on October 12, 1973, Ford was nominated to succeed Spiro T. Agnew as Vice President, he willingly offered to make public any personal information or documentation asked for, including a full statement of net worth, as a way of removing any stigma attached to the office by the departed Vice President.

Richard M. Nixon resigned as President of the United States on August 9, 1974, and Gerald R. Ford was sworn in as his successor on the same day. Ford immediately moved to assure a stable transition of power, retaining Henry Kissinger as Secretary of State, meeting with foreign envoys to reaffirm the Nixon Administration's foreign policies, and conferring with members of the Cabinet, the National Security Council, and the government's economic advisors.

In 1975 President Ford twice escaped death at the hands of would-be assassins. In May when a U.S. merchant ship, the "Mayaguez", was fired on, boarded and seized by Cambodians, Ford reminded the world of his enormous power by ordering a swift attack by Marines which resulted in the rescue of the ship and its crew.

The nomination of an incumbent president by his own party is traditionally assured, but Ford had to meet a strong challenge from former Governor of California, Ronald Reagan. In August 1976, Ford was nominated on the first ballot as the Republican presidential candidate at the Republican National Convention in Kansas City, Missouri. In the November election, he was defeated by his Democratic opponent, Jimmy Carter.

Jimmy Carter

Jimmy Carter, 39th President (January 20, 1977-   ) was born in the small farming town of Plains, Georgia, on October 1, 1924. His father, James Earl Carter, had managed a dry goods store and brokered in peanuts; his mother, Lillian, was a registered nurse. The Carter family roots in Georgia go back 150 years for eight generations.

The first member of his family to be graduated from high school, Jimmy Carter attended Georgia Southwestern College and Georgia Institute of Technology prior to his entrance into the U.S. Naval Academy at Annapolis. He graduated 59th in a class of 820 and for six years had a series of assignments which took him from battleships to submarines. In 1952 he was selected by Adm. Hyman G. Rickover to be a part of the Navy's nuclear submarine program. When his father died in 1953, Carter left the Navy and returned to Plains, where he took over the family's peanut warehousing business and built it into a thriving operation.

A deacon in the Plains Baptist Church and member of the local school board, Carter entered politics in 1962. He won a seat in the Georgia Senate that year, but it took a court suit to reverse irregularities that at first gave the primary to his opponent. He easily won a second term in 1964. In his bid for the governorship in 1966, he was third in a six-man primary contest. Encouraged by his showing, he campaigned again in 1970, winning the primary nomination and the election by a comfortable margin.

As governor, Carter reorganized that state's government, consolidating agencies and introducing a system of zero-based budgeting. He extended state hospital services and was a strong advocate of environmental protection. His stand on equal rights for "the poor, rural, black or not influential" brought Carter his first nationwide attention.

Barred by state law from a second term as governor, he announced in December 1974, one month before the end of his term, that he would run for President. For over a year, almost unnoticed by the press, politicians and the public, Jimmy Carter was on the road. A good showing in the Iowa caucus in mid-January brought media attention; and his win in the New Hampshire primary launched the series of victories which ended in June with the Ohio and New Jersey wins that clinched his nomination more than a month before the Democratic convention. Carter won the close election against President Gerald Ford by holding together enough of the basic old Democratic coalition, namely labor, blacks and liberals.

One of Carter's first acts as President was to grant a pardon to almost all Vietnam draft evaders. A reorganization of the complex structure of departments and agencies was begun, and a new, Cabinet-level Department of Energy was created. Late in 1978, Carter's proposals for civil service reform, designed to promote greater efficiency in government, were approved by Congress.

Carter's program on energy, announced in April 1977, called for a reduction of the annual energy-demand growth rate to 2 percent from the mid-1977 rate of 4.6 percent. To reduce gasoline and oil consumption, Carter asked for a tax on "gas guzzlers" and incentives for the purchase of small cars. Increases in coal production, greater use of solar energy and effective insulation were other key elements in the package. After an 18-month legislative stalemate, a substantially modified version of the program was enacted by Congress in October 1978. Missing from the final bill were penalties on heavy energy consumption.

In the area of foreign affairs, the effect of President Carter's policies and methods was immediate. Carter set his own course, acting boldly and speaking with fervor, giving a moral content to American foreign policy that had been missing in earlier years. He won respect if not total admiration for concluding treaties that would turn the Panama Canal over to Panama by the year 2000 and for the restraint shown in coping with troubles in Iran, Afghanistan and Nicaragua. Carter scored a diplomatic coup in December 1978 when he surprised the world by announcing that, after a lapse of almost 30 years, the U.S. and Mainland China would resume full diplomatic relations.

The President's forthright championing of human rights and his outspoken defense of Soviet dissidents caused an immediate negative reaction in Moscow, which showed its displeasure by cracking down on dissidents and Western correspondents. Relations became increasingly strained by Western suspicions concerning a Soviet arms buildup and moves by Moscow in Africa. Long, arduous sessions of the Strategic Arms Limitations Talks (SALT II) produced an agreement signed on June 15, 1980, but not yet ratified.

In defense matters, Carter served notice on the Pentagon that he was in charge. He scrapped the B-1 bomber program, used his veto to block construction of a new nuclear aircraft carrier, and deferred production of the neutron bomb, although Soviet unwillingness to show similar restraint in deploying new weapons led him to keep open the option to produce it later. The President approved the development of the MX mobile ICBM in June 1979.

In the Middle East, the Carter Administration gained much in bringing Israel and Egypt to the 1978 Camp David peace negotiations. Some of the bloom came off Carter's Middle East success with the seizure of the American hostages in Tehran in November 1979 and the Soviet takeover of Afghanistan two months later. Carter called for a boycott of the Moscow Olympics and a cutback of exports to the USSR, thus cooling off U.S.-Soviet relations, but neither diplomatic pressure nor an aborted military rescue mission could free the U.S. hostages.

The events of late 1979 were working against Carter's chances of securing a second term. Part of the erosion of Carter's popularity came from the nation's sagging economy. Inflation was running in double-digit figures, interest rates were at an all-time high and the predictions were for a long-term recession. However, the President was able to defeat his Democratic challenger, Senator Edward Kennedy, in the primaries and win renomination.

In the three-man contest in November, Carter lost to his Republican opponent, former Governor Ronald Reagan. John Anderson, running as an independent, finished third.

U.S. PRESIDENTIAL INDEX

(F) = Federal Party; (D-R) = Democratic-Republican Party; (W) = Whig Party; (D) = Democratic Party; (R) = Republican Party.

President and Political Party	Place and Date of Birth	Parents	Ancestry	Religious Affiliation
1. George Washington (F)	Westmoreland Co., Va.; Feb. 22, 1732	Augustine and Mary (Ball) Washington	English	Episcopalian
2. John Adams (F)	Braintree, Mass.; Oct. 19, 1735	John and Susanna (Boylston) Adams	English	Unitarian
3. Thomas Jefferson (D-R)	Goochland Co., Va.; Apr. 13, 1743	Peter and Jane (Randolph) Jefferson	Welsh	No formal affiliation
4. James Madison (D-R)	Port Conway, Va.; Mar. 16, 1751	James and Eleanor (Conway) Madison	English	Episcopalian
5. James Monroe (D-R)	Westmoreland Co., Va.; Apr. 28, 1758	Spence and Elizabeth (Jones) Monroe	Scottish, Welsh	Episcopalian
6. John Quincy Adams (D-R)	Braintree, Mass.; July 11, 1767	John and Abigail (Smith) Adams	English	Unitarian
7. Andrew Jackson (D)	Waxhaw, S.C.; Mar. 15, 1767	Andrew and Elizabeth (Hutchinson) Jackson	Scots-Irish	Presbyterian
8. Martin Van Buren (D)	Kinderhook, N.Y.; Dec. 5, 1782	Abraham and Maria (Hoes) Van Buren	Dutch	Dutch Reformed
9. William H. Harrison (W)	Charles City Co., Va.; Feb. 9, 1773	Benjamin and Elizabeth (Bassett) Harrison	English	Episcopalian
10. John Tyler (W)	Charles City Co., Va.; Mar 29, 1790	John and Mary (Armistead) Tyler	English	Episcopalian
11. James Knox Polk (D)	Mecklenburg Co., N.C.; Nov. 2, 1795	Samuel and Jane (Knox) Polk	Scots-Irish	Presbyterian
12. Zachary Taylor (W)	Orange Co., Va.; Nov. 24, 1784	Richard and Sarah (Strother) Taylor	English	Episcopalian
13. Millard Fillmore (W)	Locke, N.Y.; Jan. 7, 1800	Nathaniel and Phoebe (Millard) Fillmore	English	Unitarian
14. Franklin Pierce (D)	Hillsboro, N.H.; Nov. 23, 1804	Benjamin and Anna (Kendrick) Pierce	English	Episcopalian
15. James Buchanan (D)	Cove Gap, Pa.; Apr. 23, 1791	James and Elizabeth (Speer) Buchanan	Scots-Irish	Presbyterian
16. Abraham Lincoln (R)	Hardin Co., Ky.; Feb. 12, 1809	Thomas and Nancy (Hanks) Lincoln	English	No formal affiliation
17. Andrew Johnson (D)	Raleigh, N.C.; Dec. 29, 1808	Jacob and Mary (McDonough) Johnson	Scottish, Irish, English	No formal affiliation
18. Ulysses Simpson Grant (R)	Point Pleasant, Ohio; Apr. 27, 1822	Jesse and Hannah (Simpson) Grant	Scottish, English	Methodist
19. Rutherford B. Hayes (R)	Delaware, Ohio; Oct. 4, 1822	Rutherford and Sophia (Birchard) Hayes	English, Scottish	No formal affiliation
20. James Abram Garfield (R)	Orange, Ohio; Nov. 19, 1831	Abram and Eliza (Ballou) Garfield	English, Huguenot	Disciples of Christ
21. Chester Alan Arthur (R)	Fairfield, Vt.; Oct. 5, 1830	William and Malvina (Stone) Arthur	Scots-Irish, English	Episcopalian
22., 24. Grover Cleveland (D)	Caldwell, N.J.; Mar. 18, 1837	Richard and Ann (Neal) Cleveland	English, Scots-Irish	Presbyterian
23. Benjamin Harrison (R)	North Bend, Ohio; Aug. 20, 1833	John and Elizabeth (Irwin) Harrison	English	Presbyterian
25. William McKinley (R)	Niles, Ohio; Jan. 29, 1843	William and Nancy (Allison) McKinley	Scots-Irish, English	Methodist
26. Theodore Roosevelt (R)	New York, N.Y.; Oct. 27, 1858	Theodore and Martha (Bulloch) Roosevelt	Dutch, Scottish, English, Huguenot	Dutch Reformed
27. William Howard Taft (R)	Cincinnati, Ohio; Sept. 15, 1857	Alphonso and Louise (Torrey) Taft	English, Scots-Irish	Unitarian
28. Woodrow Wilson (D)	Staunton, Va.; Dec. 28, 1856	Joseph and Jessie (Woodrow) Wilson	Scots-Irish, Scottish	Presbyterian
29. Warren G. Harding (R)	Blooming Grove, Ohio; Nov. 2, 1865	George and Phoebe (Dickerson) Harding	English, Scots-Irish	Baptist
30. Calvin Coolidge (R)	Plymouth Notch, Vt.; July 4, 1872	John and Victoria (Moor) Coolidge	English	Congregationalist
31. Herbert Clark Hoover (R)	West Branch, Iowa; Aug. 10, 1874	Jesse and Huldah (Minthorn) Hoover	German-Swiss, English	Quaker
32. Franklin D. Roosevelt (D)	Hyde Park, N.Y.; Jan. 30, 1882	James and Sara (Delano) Roosevelt	Dutch, Huguenot, English	Episcopalian
33. Harry S Truman (D)	Lamar, Mo.; May 8, 1884	John and Martha (Young) Truman	English, Scots-Irish	Baptist
34. Dwight D. Eisenhower (R)	Denison, Tex.; Oct. 14, 1890	David and Ida (Stover) Eisenhower	German	Presbyterian
35. John F. Kennedy (D)	Brookline, Mass.; May 29, 1917	Joseph and Rose (Fitzgerald) Kennedy	Irish	Roman Catholic
36. Lyndon Baines Johnson (D)	Near Stonewall, Tex.; Aug. 27, 1908	Samuel and Rebekah (Baines) Johnson	English	Disciples of Christ
37. Richard Milhous Nixon (R)	Yorba Linda, Calif.; Jan. 9, 1913	Frank and Hannah (Milhous) Nixon	English, Scots-Irish	Quaker
38. Gerald R. Ford (R)	Omaha, Neb.; July 14, 1913	Gerald R. and Dorothy (Gardner) Ford	English	Episcopalian
39. Jimmy Carter (D)	Plains, Ga.; Oct. 1, 1924	James Earl and Lillian (Gordy) Carter	English	Baptist

Occupation Prior to Politics	Elected From	Age at Inauguration	Date of Death and Place of Burial	Presidential Terms	Vice-President
Surveyor, Soldier, Planter	Virginia	57	Dec. 14, 1799; "Mount Vernon," near Alexandria, Va.	Apr. 30, 1789–Mar. 3, 1793 Mar. 4, 1793–Mar. 3, 1797	John Adams John Adams
Teacher, Lawyer	Massachusetts	61	July 4, 1826; Quincy, Mass.	Mar. 4, 1797–Mar. 3, 1801	Thomas Jefferson
Planter, Lawyer	Virginia	57	July 4, 1826; "Monticello," near Charlottesville, Va.	Mar. 4, 1801–Mar. 3, 1805 Mar. 4, 1805–Mar. 3, 1809	Aaron Burr George Clinton
Planter	Virginia	57	June 28, 1836; "Montpelier," near Orange, Va.	Mar. 4, 1809–Mar. 3, 1813 Mar. 4, 1813–Mar. 3, 1817	George Clinton Elbridge Gerry
Lawyer	Virginia	58	July 4, 1831; Richmond, Va.	Mar. 4, 1817–Mar. 3, 1821 Mar. 4, 1821–Mar. 3, 1825	Daniel Tompkins Daniel Tompkins
Lawyer	Massachusetts	57	Feb. 23, 1848; Quincy, Mass.	Mar. 4, 1825–Mar. 3, 1829	John Calhoun
Planter, Lawyer, Soldier	Tennessee	61	June 8, 1845; "Hermitage," near Nashville, Tenn.	Mar. 4, 1829–Mar. 3, 1833 Mar. 4, 1833–Mar. 3, 1837	John Calhoun Martin Van Buren
Lawyer	New York	54	July 24, 1862; Kinderhook, N.Y.	Mar. 4, 1837–Mar. 3, 1841	Richard Johnson
Soldier, Planter	Ohio	68	Apr. 4, 1841; North Bend, Ohio	Mar. 4, 1841–Apr. 4, 1841	John Tyler
Lawyer	Virginia	51	Jan. 18, 1862; Richmond, Va.	Apr. 6, 1841–Mar. 3, 1845	—
Lawyer	Tennessee	49	June 15, 1849; Nashville, Tenn.	Mar. 4, 1845–Mar. 3, 1849	George Dallas
Soldier, Planter	Louisiana	64	July 9, 1850; near Louisville, Ky.	Mar. 4, 1849–July 9, 1850	Millard Fillmore
Lawyer	New York	50	Mar. 8, 1874; Buffalo, N.Y.	July 10, 1850–Mar. 3, 1853	—
Lawyer	New Hampshire	48	Oct. 8, 1869; Concord, N.H.	Mar. 4, 1853–Mar. 3, 1857	William King
Lawyer	Pennsylvania	65	June 1, 1868; Lancaster, Pa.	Mar. 4, 1857–Mar. 3, 1861	John Breckinridge
Lawyer	Illinois	52	Apr. 15, 1865; Springfield, Ill.	Mar. 4, 1861–Mar. 3, 1865 Mar. 4, 1865–Apr. 15, 1865	Hannibal Hamlin Andrew Johnson
Tailor	Tennessee	56	July 31, 1875; Greeneville, Tenn.	Apr. 15, 1865–Mar. 3, 1869	—
Soldier, Farmer, Clerk	Illinois	46	July 23, 1885; New York, N.Y.	Mar. 4, 1869–Mar. 3, 1873 Mar. 4, 1873–Mar. 3, 1877	Schuyler Colfax Henry Wilson
Lawyer	Ohio	54	Jan. 17, 1893; Fremont, Ohio	Mar. 4, 1877–Mar. 3, 1881	William Wheeler
Laborer, Professor	Ohio	49	Sept. 19, 1881; Cleveland, Ohio	Mar. 4, 1881–Sept. 19, 1881	Chester Arthur
School Teacher, Lawyer	New York	50	Nov. 18, 1886; Albany, N.Y.	Sept. 19, 1881–Mar. 3, 1885	—
Lawyer	New York	47, 55	June 24, 1908; Princeton, N.J.	Mar. 4, 1885–Mar. 3, 1889 Mar. 4, 1893–Mar. 3, 1897	Thomas Hendricks Adlai Stevenson
Lawyer	Indiana	55	Mar. 13, 1901; Indianapolis, Ind.	Mar. 4, 1889–Mar. 3, 1893	Levi Morton
School Teacher, Clerk, Lawyer	Ohio	54	Sept. 14, 1901; Canton, Ohio	Mar. 4, 1897–Mar. 3, 1901 Mar. 4, 1901–Sept. 14, 1901	Garret Hobart Theodore Roosevelt
Historian, Rancher	New York	42	Jan. 6, 1919; Oyster Bay, N.Y.	Sept. 14, 1901–Mar. 3, 1905 Mar. 4, 1905–Mar. 3, 1909	— Charles Fairbanks
Lawyer	Ohio	51	Mar. 8, 1930; Arlington, Va.	Mar. 4, 1909–Mar. 3, 1913	James Sherman
Lawyer, University President	New Jersey	56	Feb. 3, 1924; Washington, D.C.	Mar. 4, 1913–Mar. 3, 1917 Mar. 4, 1917–Mar. 3, 1921	Thomas Marshall Thomas Marshall
Newspaper Editor and Publisher	Ohio	55	Aug. 2, 1923; Marion, Ohio	Mar. 4, 1921–Aug. 2, 1923	Calvin Coolidge
Lawyer	Massachusetts	51	Jan. 5, 1933; Plymouth, Vt.	Aug. 3, 1923–Mar. 3, 1925 Mar. 4, 1925–Mar. 3, 1929	— Charles Dawes
Engineer, Relief Administrator	California	54	Oct. 20, 1964; West Branch, Iowa	Mar. 4, 1929–Mar. 3, 1933	Charles Curtis
Lawyer	New York	51	April 12, 1945; Hyde Park, N.Y.	Mar. 4, 1933–Jan. 20, 1937 Jan. 20, 1937–Jan. 20, 1941 Jan. 20, 1941–Jan. 20, 1945 Jan. 20, 1945–Apr. 12, 1945	John Garner John Garner Henry Wallace Harry Truman
Clerk, Haberdasher, Farmer	Missouri	60	Dec. 26, 1972; Independence, Mo.	Apr. 12, 1945–Jan. 20, 1949 Jan. 20, 1949–Jan. 20, 1953	— Alben Barkley
Soldier	New York	62	Mar. 28, 1969; Abilene, Kan.	Jan. 20, 1953–Jan. 20, 1957 Jan. 20, 1957–Jan. 20, 1961	Richard Nixon Richard Nixon
Author, Reporter	Massachusetts	43	Nov. 22, 1963; Arlington, Va.	Jan. 20, 1961–Nov. 22, 1963	Lyndon Johnson
School Teacher	Texas	55	Jan. 22, 1973; near Johnson City, Texas	Nov. 22, 1963–Jan. 20, 1965 Jan. 20, 1965–Jan. 20, 1969	— Hubert Humphrey
Lawyer	New York	55	—	Jan. 20, 1969–Jan. 20, 1973 Jan. 20, 1973–Aug. 9, 1974	Spiro Agnew Gerald R. Ford
Lawyer	—	61	—	Aug. 9, 1974–Jan. 20, 1977	Nelson Rockefeller
Businessman, Farmer	Georgia	52	—	Jan. 20, 1977	Walter Mondale

THE VICE-PRESIDENTS

For those Vice-Presidents who became Presidents—John Adams, Thomas Jefferson, Martin Van Buren, John Tyler, Millard Fillmore, Andrew Johnson, Chester A. Arthur, Theodore Roosevelt, Calvin Coolidge, Harry S. Truman, Lyndon B. Johnson, Richard M. Nixon, and Gerald R. Ford—see the Presidential biographies.

Aaron Burr

Vice-President (1801–1805) to Thomas Jefferson *Political Party:* Democratic-Republican *Born:* Newark, New Jersey, February 6, 1756 *Ancestry:* English *Religious Affiliation:* Presbyterian *Education:* College of New Jersey (now Princeton University), 1772; thereafter briefly studied theology *Wives:* Married Mrs. Theodosia Prevost in 1782; she died in 1794. Married Mrs. Stephen Jumel in 1833; she petitioned for divorce a year later *Children:* Two by first wife *Home:* New York *Occupations before Vice-Presidency:* Revolutionary soldier, lawyer, politician, U.S. Senator (1791–1797) *Age at Inauguration:* 44 *Outstanding Facts:* In the Presidential election of 1800, an electoral vote tie between Aaron Burr and Thomas Jefferson threw the election into the House of Representatives, where, mainly through the efforts of Alexander Hamilton, the Presidency was finally won by Jefferson, with the Vice-Presidency going to Burr. In 1804, after Burr had been nominated for the governorship of New York, Hamilton again contributed to his defeat. Burr challenged Hamilton to a duel and killed him. This, as well as President Jefferson's suspicions that Burr had intrigued for the Presidency, effectively ended his political career. As Vice-President, Burr presided over the Senate with impartiality *Occupation after Vice-Presidency:* He became involved in a political conspiracy, the aims of which still remain unclear, and was tried for treason but acquitted. He left the country and schemed abroad but, frustrated in his plans, returned to the United States, where he again took up the practice of law *Died:* Sept. 14, 1836 *Place of Burial:* Princeton, N.J.

George Clinton

Vice-President (1805–1812) to Thomas Jefferson and James Madison *Political Party:* Democratic-Republican *Born:* Little Britain (now Ulster County), New York, July 26, 1739 *Ancestry:* English, Scots-Irish *Religious Affiliation:* Presbyterian *Education:* Private tutoring *Wife:* Married Cornelia Tappen in 1770 *Children:* Six *Home:* New York *Occupations before Vice-Presidency:* Lawyer, Revolutionary soldier, politician, governor of New York (1777–1795, 1801–1804) *Age at Inauguration:* 65 *Outstanding Facts:* An advocate of state sovereignty, Clinton was one of the chief opponents of the Constitution. He hoped to be President but lost out to James Madison, to whom he was openly hostile. He spent much time in New York and was a poor presiding officer of the Senate. Clinton was the first Vice-President to die in office *Died:* April 20, 1812 *Place of Burial:* Washington, D.C.; reinterred (1908) in Kingston, Ulster County, N.Y.

Elbridge Gerry

Vice-President (1813–1814) to James Madison *Political Party:* Democratic-Republican *Born:* Marblehead, Massachusetts, July 17, 1744 *Ancestry:* English *Religious Affiliation:* Episcopalian *Education:* Harvard College, 1762 *Wife:*
Married Ann Thompson in 1786 *Children:* Nine *Home:* Massachusetts *Occupations before Vice-Presidency:* Merchant, politician, signer of the Declaration of Independence, governor of Massachusetts (1810–1812) *Age at Inauguration:* 63 *Outstanding Facts:* He socialized a great deal during his brief tenure and is now chiefly remembered for *gerrymander*, the term given to his attempt while governor of Massachusetts to redistrict the state in his party's favor *Died:* November 23, 1814 *Place of Burial:* Washington, D.C.

Daniel D. Tompkins

Vice-President (1817–1825) to James Monroe *Political Party:* Democratic-Republican *Born:* Fox Meadow (now Scarsdale), New York, June 21, 1774 *Ancestry:* Scottish, English *Religious Affiliation:* Presbyterian *Education:* Columbia College, 1795 *Wife:* Married Hannah Minthorne in 1798 *Children:* Eight *Home:* New York *Occupations before Vice-Presidency:* Lawyer, politician, governor of New York (1807–1817) *Age at Inauguration:* 42 *Outstanding Facts:* He spent much time contesting court cases arising out of actions he took over expenditures made while he was governor of New York during the War of 1812 *Occupation after Vice-Presidency:* He continued contesting various court actions *Died:* June 11, 1825 *Place of Burial:* New York City

John Caldwell Calhoun

Vice-President (1825–1832) to John Quincy Adams and Andrew Jackson *Political Party:* Democratic *Born:* Abbeville, South Carolina, March 18, 1782 *Ancestry:* Scots-Irish *Religious Affiliation:* Presbyterian *Education:* Yale College, 1804, studied (1805–1806) at Litchfield (Conn.) Law School *Wife:* Married Floride Calhoun in 1811 *Children:* Nine *Home:* South Carolina *Occupations before Vice-Presidency:* Lawyer, planter, U.S. Congressman (1811–1817), Secretary of War (1817–1825) *Age at Inauguration:* 42 *Outstanding Facts:* A strong supporter of Jackson, he opposed Adams throughout the latter's administration. In 1828 in his *South Carolina Exposition,* he set forth the principles of states' rights and nullification. Originally thought of as Jackson's successor, he broke with the President over a variety of issues, including the very nature of the federal union. Calhoun resigned as Vice-President upon being elected to the Senate in 1832. In the Senate he eloquently defended his states' rights principles and proslavery viewpoint in dramatic debates with Daniel Webster *Occupations after Vice-Presidency:* Senator (1832–1844, 1845–1850), Cabinet officer (Secretary of State, 1844–1845) *Died:* March 31, 1850 *Place of Burial:* Charleston, South Carolina

Richard Mentor Johnson

Vice-President (1837–1841) to Martin Van Buren *Political Party:* Democratic *Born:* Beargrass Creek (a frontier settlement on the present location of Louisville), Kentucky, autumn of 1780 *Ancestry:* English *Religious Affiliation:* Baptist *Education:* Preparatory school and private instruction *Wife:* Johnson was a bachelor *Home:* Kentucky *Occupations before Vice-Presidency:* Lawyer, soldier, educator, politician, U.S. Congressman (1814–1819, 1829–1837), Senator (1819–1829) *Age at Inauguration:* 56 *Outstanding Facts:* A hero of the War of 1812, Johnson was said to be the slayer of Chief Tecumseh at the Battle of the Thames. Johnson has been the only Vice-President ever elected by the Senate; he failed to get enough electoral votes. *Occupations after Vice-Presidency:* Businessman, state legislator (1841-1842, 1850) *Died:* Nov. 19, 1850 *Place of Burial:* Frankfort, Ky.

George Mifflin Dallas

Vice-President (1845–1849) to James K. Polk *Political Party:* Democratic *Born:* Philadelphia, July 10, 1792 *Ancestry:* Scottish, English *Religious Affiliation:* Presbyterian *Education:* Princeton College, 1810 *Wife:* Married Sophia Chew in 1816 *Children:* Eight *Home:* Pennsylvania *Occupations before Vice-Presidency:* Lawyer, politician, diplomat *Age at Inauguration:* 52 *Outstanding Facts:* Although nominated as a protectionist, he cast (1846) the deciding vote for a lower tariff *Occupations after Vice-Presidency:* Lawyer, diplomat, writer *Died:* December 31, 1864 *Place of Burial:* Philadelphia

William Rufus Devane King

Vice-President (1853) to Franklin Pierce *Political Party:* Democratic *Born:* Sampson County, North Carolina, April 7, 1786 *Ancestry:* Scots-Irish, Huguenot *Religious Affiliation:* Presbyterian *Education:* University of North Carolina, 1803 *Wife:* King was a bachelor *Home:* Alabama *Occupations before Vice-Presidency:* Lawyer, politician, U.S. Congressman (1811–1816), Senator (1819–1844; 1848–1852), diplomat *Age at Inauguration:* 66 *Outstanding Facts:* Elected while recovering from tuberculosis in Cuba, he died shortly after his return. *Died:* April 18, 1853 *Place of Burial:* "Kings Bend," Ala.; reinterred in Selma, Ala.

John Cabell Breckinridge

Vice-President (1857–1861) to James Buchanan *Political Party:* Democratic *Born:* "Cabell's Dale" (near Lexington), Kentucky, January 21, 1821 *Ancestry:* English, Scots-Irish *Religious Affiliation:* Presbyterian *Education:* Centre College (Ky.), 1838; thereafter he studied law at Transylvania University *Wife:* Married Mary Cyrene Burch in 1843 *Children:* Five *Home:* Kentucky *Occupations before Vice-Presidency:* Lawyer, soldier, politician, U.S. Congressman (1851–1855) *Age at Inauguration:* 36 *Outstanding Facts:* The youngest man ever to become Vice-President, he was dignified beyond his years and ably presided over the Senate. Breckinridge tried to achieve some kind of compromise during the years prior to the Civil War. *Occupations after Vice-Presidency:* U.S. Senator (1861), Confederate soldier, Confederate Secretary of War (1865), lawyer, businessman *Died:* May 17, 1875 *Place of Burial:* Lexington, Kentucky

Hannibal Hamlin

Vice-President (1861–1865) to Abraham Lincoln *Political Party:* Republican *Born:* Paris, Maine, August 27, 1809 *Ancestry:* English *Religious Affiliation:* Unitarian *Education:* Preparatory studies *Wives:* Married Sarah Jane Emery in 1833; she died in 1855. Married her half-sister Ellen Vesta Emery in 1856 *Children:* Five by first wife, two by second wife *Home:* Maine *Occupations before Vice-Presidency:* Farmer, printer, lawyer, politician, U.S. Senator (1857–1861) *Age at Inauguration:* 51 *Outstanding Facts:* Hamlin was a staunch advocate of emancipation *Occupations after Vice Presidency:* Political appointee, lawyer, businessman, U.S. Senator (1869–1881), diplomat *Died:* July 4, 1891 *Place of Burial:* Bangor, Maine

Schuyler Colfax

Vice-President (1869–1873) to Ulysses S. Grant *Political Party:* Republican *Born:* New York City, March 23, 1823 *Ancestry:* English, Huguenot *Religious Affiliation:* Dutch Reformed *Education:* Grade school *Wives:* Married Evelyn Clark in 1844; she died in 1862. Married Ellen Wade in 1868 *Children:* One by second wife *Home:* Indiana *Occupations before Vice-Presidency:* Political appointee, journalist, U.S. Congressman (1855–1869), speaker of the House (1863–1869) *Age at Inauguration:* 45 *Outstanding Facts:* In 1870, midway through his term, he announced his retirement from political life, hoping that the public would demand that he remain. No such clamor developed, and Colfax rescinded his decision. Colfax failed of renomination. Later it was revealed that Colfax had been involved in the Credit Mobilier railroad scandal, which effectively ended his public career *Occupation after Vice-Presidency:* Lecturer *Died:* January 13, 1885 *Place of Burial:* South Bend, Indiana

Henry Wilson

Vice-President (1873–1875) to Ulysses S. Grant *Political Party:* Republican *Born:* Farmington, New Hampshire, February 16, 1812 *Ancestry:* Scots-Irish *Religious Affiliation:* Congregationalist *Education:* Little formal schooling *Wife:* Married Harriet Malvina Howe in 1840 *Children:* One *Home:* Massachusetts *Occupations before Vice-Presidency:* Indentured worker, school teacher, cobbler, businessman, newspaperman, politician, U.S. Senator (1855–1873) *Age at Inauguration:* 61 *Outstanding Facts:* As Vice-President ill health made his attendance in presiding over the Senate irregular, and he died in office *Died:* November 22, 1875 *Place of Burial:* Natick, Massachusetts

William Almon Wheeler

Vice-President (1877–1881) to Rutherford B. Hayes *Political Party:* Republican *Born:* Malone, New York, June 30, 1819 *Ancestry:* English *Religious Affiliation:* Presbyterian *Education:* Attended (1838–1840) the University of Vermont *Wife:* Married Mary King in 1845 *Children:* None *Home:* New York *Occupations before Vice-Presidency:* Lawyer, banker, businessman, politician, U.S. Congressman (1861–1863, 1869–1877) *Age at Inauguration:* 57 *Outstanding Facts:* Little known nationally when nominated for the office, he performed its major function, presiding over the Senate, with faithfulness *Occupation after Vice-Presidency:* Poor health resulted in general inactivity; unsuccessfully nominated for U.S. Senator in 1881 *Died:* June 4, 1887 *Place of Burial:* Malone, N.Y.

Thomas Andrews Hendricks

Vice-President (1885) to Grover Cleveland *Political Party:* Democratic *Born:* Zanesville, Ohio, September 7, 1819 *Ancestry:* Scottish, English, Huguenot *Religious Affiliation:* Episcopalian *Education:* Hanover College (Indiana), 1841 *Wife:* Married Eliza Morgan in 1845

Children: One *Home:* Indiana *Occupations before Vice-Presidency:* Lawyer, politician, defeated candidate for Vice-President in 1876 *Age at Inauguration:* 65 *Outstanding Fact:* He died 8 months after taking office. *Died:* Nov. 25, 1885 *Place of Burial:* Indianapolis, Ind.

Levi Parsons Morton

Vice-President (1889–1893) to Benjamin Harrison *Political Party:* Republican *Born:* Shoreham, Vermont, May 16, 1824 *Ancestry:* English *Religious Affiliation:* Episcopalian *Education:* Preparatory schools *Wives:* Married Lucy Young Kimball in 1856; she died in 1871 Married Anna Livingston Read Street in 1873 *Children:* One by first wife; six by second wife *Home:* New York *Occupations before Vice-Presidency:* Clerk, school teacher, businessman, U.S. Congressman (1879–1881), diplomat *Age at Inauguration:* 64 *Outstanding Fact:* He was passed over for renomination as Vice-President *Occupations after Vice-Presidency:* Real estate investor, banker, Governor of New York (1895–1897) *Died:* May 16, 1920 *Place of Burial:* Rhinebeck, N.Y.

Adlai Ewing Stevenson

Vice-President (1893–1897) to Grover Cleveland *Political Party:* Democratic *Born:* Christian County, Kentucky, October 23, 1835 *Ancestry:* Scots-Irish *Religious Affiliation:* Presbyterian *Education:* Attended Centre College (Kentucky) two years *Wife:* Married Letitia Green in 1866 *Children:* Four *Home:* Illinois *Occupations before Vice-Presidency:* Lawyer, politician, U.S. Congressman (1875–1877, 1879–1881) *Age at Inauguration:* 57 *Outstanding Facts:* He presided with fairness over a Senate that had recently turned him down for a District of Columbia judicial post. A "soft money" advocate, he was unsympathetic to President Cleveland's monetary views but never embarrassed the administration with open disagreement *Occupations after Vice-Presidency:* Lawyer and politician *Died:* June 14, 1914 *Place of Burial:* Bloomington, Illinois

Garret Augustus Hobart

Vice-President (1897–1899) to William McKinley *Political Party:* Republican *Born:* Long Branch, New Jersey, June 3, 1844 *Ancestry:* English, Dutch, Huguenot *Religious Affiliation:* Presbyterian *Education:* Rutgers College, 1863 *Wife:* Married Jennie Tuttle in 1869 *Children:* Two *Home:* New Jersey *Occupations before Vice-Presidency:* Lawyer, businessman, banker, politician *Age at Inauguration:* 52 *Outstanding Facts:* He presided over the Senate with ability. Hobart cast the deciding vote against granting the Philippine Is. independence *Died:* In office, Nov. 21, 1899 *Place of Burial:* Paterson, N.J.

Charles Warren Fairbanks

Vice-President (1905–1909) to Theodore Roosevelt *Political Party:* Republican *Born:* Near Unionville Center, Ohio, May 11, 1852 *Ancestry:* English *Religious Affiliation:* Methodist *Education:* Ohio Wesleyan, 1872 *Wife:* Married Cornelia Cole in 1874 *Children:* Five *Home:* Indiana *Occupations before Vice-Presidency:* Newspaperman, railroad lawyer, politician, U.S. Senator (1897–1905) *Age at Inauguration:* 52 *Outstanding Facts:* Although Fairbanks and President Roosevelt represented opposite wings of the Republican Party, they maintained cordial relations *Occupations after Vice-Presidency:* Lawyer, unsuccessful candidate for Vice-Pres. in 1916 *Died:* June 4, 1918 *Place of Burial:* Inlianapolis, Ind.

James Schoolcraft Sherman

Vice-President (1909–1912) to William Howard Taft *Political Party:* Republican *Born:* Utica, New York, October 24, 1855 *Ancestry:* English *Religious Affiliation:* Dutch Reformed *Education:* Hamilton College, 1878 *Wife:* Married Carrie Babcock in 1881 *Children:* Three *Home:* New York *Occupations before Vice-Presidency:* Lawyer, banker, politician, U.S. Congressman (1887–1891, 1893–1909) *Age at Inauguration:* 53 *Outstanding Facts:* An affable man known as "Sunny Jim," he presided well over the Senate. Renominated but died before the election *Died:* October 30, 1912 *Place of Burial:* Utica, N.Y.

Thomas Riley Marshall

Vice-President (1913–1921) to Woodrow Wilson *Political Party:* Democratic *Born:* North Manchester, Indiana, March 14, 1854 *Ancestry:* English *Religious Affiliation:* Presbyterian *Education:* Wabash College, 1873 *Wife:* Married Lois Irene Kimsey in 1895 *Children:* None *Home:* Indiana *Occupations before Vice-Presidency:* Lawyer, politician, governor of Indiana (1909–1913) *Age at Inauguration:* 58 *Outstanding Facts:* Marshall was the first Vice-President in nearly a century to succeed himself. While President Wilson was ill, Marshall acted as ceremonial head of state, but he refused to accept any of the President's powers. He was well known for his quip, "What this country needs is a good five-cent cigar" *Occupations after Vice-Presidency:* Lawyer, lecturer, political appointee *Died:* June 1, 1925 *Place of Burial:* Indianapolis, Ind.

Charles Gates Dawes

Vice-President (1925–1929) to Calvin Coolidge *Political Party:* Republican *Born:* Marietta, Ohio, August 27, 1865 *Ancestry:* English *Religious Affiliation:* Congregationalist *Education:* Marietta College, 1884; Cincinnati Law School, 1886 *Wife:* Married Caro D. Blymer in 1889 *Children:* Four (two adopted) *Home:* Illinois *Occupations before Vice-Presidency:* Lawyer, banker, businessman, soldier, politician *Age at Inauguration:* 59 *Outstanding Facts:* Dawes shared the Nobel Peace Prize in 1925 for his work in attempting to settle through the Dawes Plan the problem of German reparations. A short-tempered man, he infuriated the Senate by telling that body it was time to change its antiquated rules *Occupations after Vice-Presidency:* Diplomat, public servant, banker, businessman *Died:* April 23, 1951 *Place of Burial:* Chicago

Charles Curtis

Vice-President (1929–1933) to Herbert Hoover *Political Party:* Republican *Born:* Topeka, Kansas, January 25, 1860 *Ancestry:* American Indian, English, French *Religious Affiliation:* Episcopalian *Education:* High school *Wife:* Married Annie E. Baird in 1884 *Children:* Three *Home:* Kansas *Occupations before Vice-Presidency:* Lawyer, politician, U.S. Congressman (1893–1907), Senator (1907–1913, 1915–1929) *Age at Inauguration:* 69 *Outstanding Facts:*

Lacking a close relationship with President Hoover, Curtis had little to say or do *Occupations after Vice-Presidency:* Lawyer, businessman *Died:* February 8, 1936 *Place of Burial:* Topeka, Kansas

John Nance Garner

Vice-President (1933–1941) to Franklin D. Roosevelt *Political Party:* Democratic *Born:* Blossom Prairie, Texas, November 22, 1868 *Ancestry:* English, Welsh, Scottish *Religious Affiliation:* Methodist *Education:* High school *Wife:* Married Elizabeth Rheiner in 1895 *Children:* One *Home:* Texas *Occupations before Vice-Presidency:* Lawyer, businessman, banker, politician, U.S. Congressman (1903–1933), Speaker of the House of Representatives (1931–1933) *Age at Inauguration:* 63 *Outstanding Facts:* Garner retained much of his influence with Congress while Vice-President and during his first term helped to obtain passage of much New Deal legislation. During his second term, he increasingly found himself out of sympathy with President Roosevelt's programs, and he was not renominated *Occupations after Vice-Presidency:* Businessman, banker, cattle rancher *Died:* November 7, 1967 *Place of Burial:* Uvalde, Texas

Henry Agard Wallace

Vice-President (1941–1945) to Franklin D. Roosevelt *Political Party:* Democratic *Born:* Near Orient, Iowa, October 7, 1888 *Ancestry:* Scots-Irish *Religious Affiliation:* Episcopalian *Education:* Iowa State College, 1910 *Wife:* Married Ilo Browne in 1914 *Children:* Three *Home:* Iowa *Occupations before Vice-Presidency:* Editor, farmer, Secretary of Agriculture (1933–1940) *Age at Inauguration:* 52 *Outstanding Facts:* President Roosevelt cast the Vice-Presidency under Wallace into its most active role up to that time. Wallace served as good-will ambassador to Latin America, the Soviet Union, and the Far East. He also undertook various defense duties. However, his political and social views caused him to be viewed suspiciously by the Democratic Party and he failed of renomination *Occupations after Vice-Presidency:* Secretary of Commerce (1945–1946), author, farmer, defeated candidate for President in 1948 *Died:* November 18, 1965 *Place of Burial:* Des Moines, Iowa

Alben William Barkley

Vice-President (1949–1953) to Harry S Truman *Political Party:* Democratic *Born:* Near Lowes, Kentucky, November 24, 1877 *Ancestry:* Scots-Irish *Religious Affiliation:* Methodist *Education:* Marvin College (Kentucky), 1897; attended University of Virginia Law School *Wives:* Married Dorothy Brower in 1903; she died in 1947. Married Mrs. Carleton S. Hadley in 1949 *Children:* Three by first wife *Home:* Kentucky *Occupations before Vice-Presidency:* Lawyer, politician, U.S. Senator (1927–1949) *Age at Inauguration:* 71 *Outstanding Facts:* Very popular, he was nicknamed "Veep" during his tenure. He was the only Vice-President to marry while in office. After President Truman announced he would not run again, Barkley attempted to win the Presidential nomination but failed *Occupations after Vice-Presidency:* Lawyer, U.S. Senator (1955–1956) *Died:* April 30, 1956 *Place of Burial:* Paducah, Kentucky

Hubert Horatio Humphrey

Vice-President (1965–1969) to Lyndon B. Johnson *Political Party:* Democratic *Born:* Wallace, South Dakota, May 27, 1911 *Ancestry:* Welsh, Norwegian *Religious Affiliation:* Congregationalist *Education:* University of Minnesota, 1939; M.A., Louisiana State, 1940; began work for a Ph.D. *Wife:* Married Muriel Fay Buck in 1936 *Children:* Four *Home:* Minnesota *Occupations before Vice-Presidency:* Pharmacist, teacher, politician, U.S. Senator (1949–1965) *Age at Inauguration:* 53 *Outstanding Facts:* Humphrey was an energetic Vice-President and traveled widely as a spokesman of the United States. He was a vigorous defender of the Johnson administration. Humphrey ran unsuccessfully for the Presidency in 1968. *Occupations after Vice-Presidency:* College teaching, U.S. Senator (1971-1978) *Died:* January 13, 1978 *Place of Burial:* Minneapolis, Minnesota

Spiro Theodore Agnew

Vice-President (1969–1973) to Richard M. Nixon *Political Party:* Republican *Born:* Baltimore, Maryland, November 9, 1918 *Ancestry:* Greek, English *Religious Affiliation:* Episcopalian *Education:* University of Baltimore Law School, 1947 *Wife:* Married Eleanor Isabel Judefind in 1942 *Children:* Four *Home:* Maryland *Occupations before Vice-Presidency:* Lawyer, politician, governor of Maryland (1967–1969) *Age at Inauguration:* 50 *Outstanding Facts:* Agnew resigned his office and pleaded "no contest" to one charge of income tax evasion after being implicated in a kickback scheme. He was the first Vice-President in history to resign under duress.

Nelson Aldrich Rockefeller

Vice-President (1974-1977) to Gerald R. Ford *Political Party:* Republican *Born:* Bar Harbor, Maine, July 8, 1908 *Ancestry:* English, Scottish, German *Religious Affilation:* Baptist *Education:* Dartmouth College, 1930 *Wives:* Mary Todhunter Clark, June 23, 1930 (div. 1962), Margaretta Fitler Murphy, May 1963 *Home:* New York and Bar Harbor, Maine *Occupation before Vice-Presidency:* various government posts, four-term governor of New York *Age at Inauguration:* 66 *Outstanding Facts:* Nominated under the 25th Amendment by President Ford following resignation of Richard M. Nixon as President and Ford's assumption of the presidency *Occupations after Vice Presidency:* Art interests *Died:* January 26, 1979 *Place of Burial:* Pocantico Hills, New York

Walter Frederick Mondale

Vice-President (1977-   ) to Jimmy Carter *Political Party:* Democratic *Born:* Ceylon, Minnesota, January 5, 1928 *Ancestry:* Norwegian *Religious Affiliation:* Methodist *Education:* University of Minnesota Law School, 1956 *Wife:* Married Joan Adams in 1955 *Children:* Three *Home:* Minnesota *Occupation before Vice-Presidency:* Lawyer, state attorney general, U.S. Senator (1965-1977) *Age at Inauguration:* 49 *Outstanding Facts:* His untraditional role as the President's personal international emissary has added new responsibility and power to the previously passive, ceremonial role of the Vice-President.

THE FIRST LADIES

Mrs. George Washington—Born Martha Dandridge, daughter of a planter, in New Kent County, Virginia, on June 21, 1731. At 18, she married Daniel Parke Custis, heir to a large estate, and she bore him four children, two of whom died in infancy. After Custis died on July 8, 1757, leaving her reputedly the richest widow in Virginia, she married Colonel George Washington on January 6, 1759; at 27, she was eight months older than her second husband.

Besides adding substantially to his property (she provided 17,000 acres and 300 slaves, compared with his own estate of 5,000 acres and 49 slaves), she also gave him a happy domestic life. Small, plump, and cheerful, she was amply blessed with common sense, if not brilliance. When Washington became President, many contemporaries thought she humanized her austere husband—"Mrs. Washington is one of those unassuming characters which create love and esteem," Mrs. John Adams wrote to a sister.

In New York, then Philadelphia, where "Lady" Washington held sway in makeshift mansions while the new capital of Washington was being planned, she made an amiable hostess at the formal receptions and dinners her husband instituted as the social side of his official duties.

There were no children of her second marriage, but she was a doting mother to the offspring of her first husband, who were treated as his own by Washington. Although her daughter, Martha (Patsy) Parke Custis, died at 17, her son, John Parke Custis, married and had three daughters and a son. Mrs. Washington survived her husband two years, dying on May 22, 1802, at Mount Vernon, where she was buried.

Mrs. John Adams—Born Abigail Smith on November 11, 1744, in Weymouth, Massachusetts, the daughter of a Congregational minister. Although she had no formal schooling, she read much more widely than most girls, and first attracted the notice of her future husband by the breadth of her intellectual interests. But before they married on October 25, 1764, they were deeply in love, and theirs was a devoted union.

Shrewd, witty, and warm-hearted, Mrs. Adams was of inestimable help in furthering the careers of both her husband and her son, John Quincy Adams, the nation's sixth President: she is the only woman in American history to have been the wife of one President and the mother of another. She also won celebrity in her own right as a gifted letter-writer with a keen political instinct.

Mrs. Adams was the first First Lady to live in the Executive Mansion in Washington, moving there in November 1800 when most of the rooms were still unfinished; she gained lasting fame in American folklore by having her laundry set out to dry before the fire in the East Room, one of the few chambers where some warmth could be obtained. During the brief period before her husband's term expired on March 3, 1801, she had the distinction, too, of holding the first formal gathering in the Mansion—a reception on New Year's Day of 1801, when 135 callers were greeted in the crimson-hung Oval Room. Besides John Quincy, she had two other sons and a daughter; another daughter died in infancy. Mrs. Adams died at the Adams home in Quincy, Massachusetts, on October 28, 1818, and was buried there.

Mrs. Thomas Jefferson—Born Martha Wayles on October 30, 1748, in Charles City County, Virginia, the daughter of a wealthy lawyer and planter. At 18, she married a young Virginian, Bathurst Skelton, who died on September 30, 1768, leaving her with an infant son. No portrait or reliable facts about her have survived, but she was said to be musically inclined and well-off when she married Thomas Jefferson on January 1, 1772. Her firstborn child, and four of the six children she bore her second husband, died in early childhood. After just 10 years as Mrs. Jefferson, she died on September 6, 1782, and was buried at Monticello; so Jefferson had been a widower for 18 years when he became President.

Being opposed to elaborate state entertaining, he held such functions to a minimum, but when he did receive guests, often his hostess was Mrs. James (Dolley) Madison, the wife of his Secretary of State, or one of his two surviving daughters—Mrs. John Wayles Eppes and Mrs. Thomas Mann Randolph, whose eighth child, James Madison Randolph, was the first baby born in the Executive Mansion (on January 17, 1806).

Mrs. James Madison—Born Dolley Paine on May 20, 1768, the daughter of Virginia Quakers temporarily settled in North Carolina. When she was 15, her family moved to Philadelphia, and on January 7, 1790, she married John Todd, a Quaker lawyer who died three years later, leaving her with one son; another had already died. Strikingly handsome despite her plain garb, the young widow quickly attracted new suitors, among them "the great little Madison," as she described him in a letter. They were married on September 15, 1794, when he was 43 and she 26.

She soon blossomed forth in elegant dress, but with a warmth and simplicity of manner that made her one of the best loved figures of her day. As White House hostess during the Jefferson administration, then as First Lady, she reigned socially supreme in Washington from 1801 to 1817. The first Inaugural Ball, on March 4, 1809, marked her husband's assumption of the Presidency, and she appeared there in queenly yellow velvet, set off by a plumed satin headdress.

Dolley Madison put much effort into furnishing the Executive Mansion suitably, but her fine draperies were destroyed when the British burned the building on August 24, 1814. Mrs. Madison is supposed to have saved the famous Gilbert Stuart portrait of Washington from the flames and also her husband's invaluable notes describing the Constitutional Convention of 1787.

While the White House was being rebuilt, the Madisons lived in Octagon House, a private mansion. They had no children, and her one son grew up a ne'er-do-well. Upon leaving Washington, Mrs. Madison continued entertaining on a grand scale at Montpelier, her husband's Virginia plantation. She returned to Washington following his death, and took up residence in 1837 in a small house across Lafayette Square from the White House. Here she received homage till she died on July 12, 1849, and was buried at Montpelier.

Mrs. James Monroe—Born Elizabeth Kortright in New York City on June 30, 1768, the daughter of a former British Army captain. At 17, on February 16, 1786, she married James Monroe, 10 years her senior. Succeeding the popular Dolley Madison as First Lady, Mrs. Monroe precipitated a social storm.

Reserved and regal in manner, she refused to follow Mrs. Madison's custom of paying calls on capital hostesses, and she added to the outrage felt by much of Washington society by declining to make the White House's first wedding into an elaborate official ceremony; only relatives and close friends were invited to the marriage of the younger of the Monroes' two daughters, Maria, to Samuel L. Gouverneur on March 9, 1820. But during her husband's second term, Mrs. Monroe's policy of restricting the social obligations of the Presidential family to the receiving of guests, without any ritual paying of calls, won general approval, and it has been followed ever since. Mrs. Monroe died on September 23, 1830, at Oak Hill, her husband's Virginia plantation, and she was buried in Richmond.

Mrs. John Quincy Adams—Born Louisa Catherine Johnson in London on February 12, 1775, the daughter of a Marylander serving as a financial agent in England. In London, on July 27, 1797, she became the wife of John Quincy Adams, then serving his first diplomatic tour of duty abroad. The mother of three sons—the youngest, Charles Francis Adams, was the highly regarded American Minister to Great Britain during the Civil War—Mrs. Adams was plagued by ill health but made a gracious First Lady.

Much less stiff in manner than her husband, she was noted for her ornate headdresses and fashionable gowns when she received at the fortnightly levees held in the White House during her regime there. Besides her own sons and one daughter, her family during her years in the Executive Mansion also included the three orphaned children of one of her sisters, and many nieces and nephews paid frequent visits. Mrs. Adams died in the family's private residence in Washington on May 15, 1852, and was buried in Quincy, Massachusetts.

Mrs. Andrew Jackson—Born Rachel Donelson in 1767, the daughter of Colonel John Donelson of Virginia. When she was 13, her family moved to Kentucky, where she married Captain Lewis Robards in 1785. He proved a suspicious husband, and five years later he sought permission from the legislature to divorce her.

Mistakenly believing a divorce had been granted, she and Andrew Jackson were married near Natchez in 1791; then on discovering two years afterward that Robards had just obtained the divorce, they were remarried on January 17, 1794. As Jackson's fame spread, gossip about this unfortunate episode hurt his wife increasingly. He fought at least one duel to defend her honor (killing Charles Dickinson in Kentucky in 1806), but when the slander was revived in the scurrilous Presidential campaign of 1828, he could not protect her. Her death of a heart attack on December 22, 1828, just as he was preparing to leave for Washington, was widely blamed on scandalmongers. She was buried at The Hermitage, Jackson's home near Nashville.

A kindly woman fond of smoking a corncob pipe, though by no means illiterate as often charged, Mrs. Jackson had no children, but she and her husband adopted a nephew. During Jackson's administration, Mrs. Andrew Jackson Donelson, wife of his nephew, often served as his hostess.

Mrs. Martin Van Buren—Born Hannah Hoes on March 8, 1783, in Kinderhook, New York, where she knew her future husband from early childhood. Distant relatives on his mother's side, they were married February 21, 1807, and had four sons before she died in Albany on February 5, 1819; she was buried at Kinderhook. A widower for 18 years when he entered the Executive Mansion, Van Buren had as his official hostess Mrs. Abraham Van Buren, the South Carolina-born wife of his oldest son.

Mrs. William Henry Harrison—Born Anna Tuthill Symmes on July 25, 1775, near Morristown, New Jersey, the daughter of Colonel John Cleves Symmes, who later became a judge and large landholder in the Northwest Territory. When Lieutenant William Henry Harrison asked Colonel Symmes for his daughter's hand, the application was rejected on the ground that an Army officer could not support a wife. As a result, the couple ran off to be married by a justice of the peace on November 25, 1795.

While her husband advanced militarily and politically, Mrs. Harrison brought up 10 children. Because she had only recently recovered from an illness, she did not attend her husband's inauguration on March 4, 1841. She remained at the Harrison home in North Bend, Ohio, to complete her convalescence, expecting to be well enough by May to assume her duties as First Lady in Washington. But her husband took cold and died exactly one month after assuming office, and Mrs. Harrison never did move into the Executive Mansion. Surviving until February 25, 1864, when she died and was buried at North Bend, she outlived all but one of her children—John Scott Harrison, whose son Benjamin became President in 1889.

Mrs. John Tyler—The first Mrs. Tyler was born Letitia Christian in New Kent County, Virginia, on November 12, 1790. Married on March 29, 1813, she had eight children, one of whom died in infancy. Partially paralyzed by a stroke in 1839, she was unable to assume any social duties when her husband became President two years later. Her only appearance downstairs at the Executive Mansion came at the wedding of her daughter, Elizabeth, to William Nevison Waller on January 31, 1842. Mrs. Tyler died on September 10, 1842, in the White House and was buried at Cedar Grove, Virginia.

The role of official hostess during most of Tyler's administration was taken by his daughter-in-law, Mrs. Robert Tyler, a former actress born Priscilla Cooper in Bristol, Pennsylvania. But on June 26, 1844, the 54-year-old President married the 24-year-old Julia Gardiner, who in the nine months remaining to his term established herself as one of the nation's most flamboyant First Ladies. Born May 4, 1820, on Gardiner's Island, New York, she belonged to a wealthy society family, and she surrounded herself with a "court" of elegant young ladies when she began entertaining lavishly in Washington. The mother of seven children, she survived her husband 27 years; she died on July 10, 1889, in Richmond and was buried there beside him.

Mrs. James Knox Polk—Born Sarah Childress on September 4, 1803, in Murfreesboro, Tennessee, the daughter of a wealthy merchant. After attending the Female Academy in Salem, North Carolina, considered then to be the South's outstanding school for girls, she married James Polk on January 1, 1824.

A shrewd and ambitious woman, she had no children and devoted herself to advancing her husband's political career. As First Lady, she opened the Executive Mansion to the public two evenings a week, besides holding formal receptions and dinners frequently. Under her direction, the building received its first complete redecorating since Monroe's administration. Though a strict Presbyterian who frowned on dancing and Sunday visiting, she allowed wine to be served and was fond of showy clothes. Mrs. Polk survived her husband 42 years, dying on August 14, 1891, in Nashville, where she was buried.

Mrs. Zachary Taylor—Born Margaret Mackall Smith on September 21, 1788, in Calvert County, Maryland, the daughter of a planter. On June 21, 1810, she married Lieutenant Zachary Taylor and spent most of the next 35 years at frontier Army posts. She had six children, two of whom died in infancy. By the time her husband was elected President, ill health prevented her taking an active role as First Lady, and her youngest daughter, Mrs. William Wallace Bliss, acted as her father's official hostess. Mrs. Taylor died on August 18, 1852, near Pascagoula, Louisiana, and was buried beside her husband in Springfield, Kentucky.

Mrs. Millard Fillmore—The first Mrs. Fillmore was born Abigail Powers on March 13, 1798, in Stillwater, New York. The daughter of a Baptist minister, she met her future husband at a nearby academy when he appeared as a fellow pupil. Two years older than he, and much more cultivated, she helped him with his studies. They were married on February 5, 1826, and had two children.

In poor health when she became First Lady, she assigned her official duties to her daughter, Mary Abigail, her own contribution being her successful effort to secure funds from Congress for setting up a small library in the White House. At the inauguration ceremonies for her husband's successor, she caught a cold which developed into pneumonia, and she died in Washington on March 30, 1853. She was buried in Buffalo.

Five years later, on February 10, 1858, former President Fillmore married Mrs. Caroline C. McIntosh, the 44-year-old widow of a Troy, New York, merchant. The second Mrs. Fillmore, who had no children, survived her husband seven years, dying in Buffalo on August 11, 1881.

Mrs. Franklin Pierce—Born Jane Means Appleton on March 12, 1806, in Hampton, New Hampshire, the daughter of Jesse Appleton, who later became president of Bowdoin College. After the death of her father, she married Franklin Pierce on November 10, 1834. Frail and shy but with strict ideas of propriety, she had a tragic life. Two of her three sons died of infant ailments, and eight weeks before her husband's inauguration as President, their only remaining child—an 11-year-old boy whom she idolized—was killed in a train accident. She never recovered from this blow and spent her years in the White House secluded in her own room, pitifully writing pencil notes to her lost son.

For the limited official entertaining carried on during her husband's administration, her girlhood friend, Mrs. Abby L. Means, who had come to Washington as her companion, served as hostess. Mrs. Pierce died on December 2, 1863, in Andover, Massachusetts, and was buried in Concord, New Hampshire.

Buchanan Administration—James Buchanan, the nation's only bachelor President, had as his official hostess his orphaned niece, Miss Harriet Lane. A charming young woman with a taste for splendor, she entertained elaborately during her uncle's administration. Five years after leaving the White House, in 1866, she married Henry E. Johnson, a Baltimore banker.

Mrs. Abraham Lincoln—Born Mary Ann Todd on December 13, 1818, in Lexington, Kentucky, the daughter of a prosperous merchant. At 22, while visiting a married sister, Mrs. Ninian Edwards, in Springfield, Illinois, she became engaged to one of her brother-in-law's fellow legislators, the backwoods lawyer Abraham Lincoln. Under controversial circumstances—some say Lincoln failed to appear the first time the wedding was scheduled—the engagement was broken; but the marriage finally took place on November 4, 1842.

Lively and intelligent, Mrs. Lincoln was also quick-tempered to the point of emotional instability. In the White House, she aroused widespread criticism for her grasping attitude toward money and her poor judgment in choosing friends. She was so shocked by her husband's assassination that her behavior became increasingly erratic.

After leaving Washington, she brought about a new wave of newspaper abuse by attempting to sell her old clothes and jewelry. On May 19, 1875, a Chicago court adjudged her insane, and she was confined in a private sanitorium at Batavia, Illinois, for four months. Thereafter, she lived quietly abroad or with relatives until she died on July 16, 1882, in Springfield, where she was buried beside her husband. Of their four sons, only the oldest, Robert Todd Lincoln, survived her.

Mrs. Andrew Johnson—Born Eliza McCardle on October 4, 1810, in Leesburg, Tennessee, the daughter of a shoemaker. She was a 16-year-old schoolgirl living with her widowed mother in the Tennessee town of Greeneville when Andrew Johnson arrived to take up tailoring there; a few months later, on May 5, 1827, they were married. Finding he could hardly read and not write at all, she taught him these skills during the next several years. Mrs. Johnson had five children, one of whom died in infancy.

When her husband unexpectedly became President, she was a frail grandmother who told a White House visitor: "We are plain people from Tennessee temporarily in a high place, and you must not expect too much of us in a social way." During her husband's administration, the role of official hostess was shared by their two daughters, Mrs. David Patterson and Mrs. Daniel Stover. Mrs. Johnson died on January 15, 1876, in Greene County, Tennessee and was buried beside her husband in Greeneville.

Mrs. Ulysses S. Grant—Born Julia Boggs Dent on January 26, 1826, in St. Louis, Missouri, the daughter of Colonel Frederick Dent. She met her future husband while he was stationed at the nearby Jefferson Barracks, and they were married on August 22, 1848. The mother of three sons and a daughter, she took the hardships of being an Army wife cheerfully, even living in a tent at times when she joined her husband in the field during the Civil War, but she also enjoyed the glitter of capital society and entertained elaborately as First Lady. Her daughter, Nellie, became Mrs. Algernon Sartoris in a splendid White House wedding on May 21, 1874. Mrs. Grant died on December 14, 1902, in Washington and was buried beside her husband in Grant's Tomb in New York City.

Mrs. Rutherford Birchard Hayes—Born Lucy Ware Webb on August 28, 1831, in Chillicothe, Ohio, the daughter of a physician. A sweet-tempered and devout Methodist, she met her future husband while attending Wesleyan Female College in Cincinnati. He was a lawyer, eight years her senior, who called on her at the urging of his mother, who had already chosen Lucy Webb as the ideal candidate for her son's wife. Rutherford Hayes agreed, the marriage took place on December 30, 1852, and he gained a devoted companion who bore him one daughter and seven sons (three died in infancy). He also gave his country its first First Lady with a college diploma.

But for all her gentle submissiveness, Mrs. Hayes had strong temperance convictions. To please her, President Hayes banished wine from the White House during his administration, thereby inadvertently subjecting her to widespread ridicule as "Lemonade Lucy." Yet Mrs. Hayes was no hard-eyed reformer. She was a warm, friendly woman whose most lasting contribution in the White House was her initiation of annual Easter egg-rolling contests in 1878. She died of a stroke on June 25, 1889, at the Hayes home in Fremont, Ohio, and she was buried there.

Mrs. James Abram Garfield—Born Lucretia Rudolph on April 19, 1832, the daughter of the leading merchant in Hiram, Ohio. She met her future husband while attending a local academy her father had helped to found; after teaching a few years, she married James Garfield on November 11, 1858. They had seven children, two of whom died in infancy. Her tenure as First Lady was brief, but made memorable by tragedy. "The wife of the President is the bravest woman in the Universe," the New York *Herald* said of her. For she had only just recovered from a near-fatal attack of malaria and was convalescing at a seaside cottage in Elberon, New Jersey, when she received word on July 2, 1881, that her husband had been shot.

She immediately returned to Washington and displayed remarkable composure during the 80 days that he lingered on the brink of death. She traveled back to Elberon with him when he was moved there on September 6, and she was at his bedside when he died on September 19, 1881. Mrs. Garfield survived her husband 36 years. She died on March 14, 1918, in Pasadena, California, and was buried beside her husband in Cleveland.

Mrs. Chester Alan Arthur—Born Ellen Lewis Herndon on August 30, 1837, in Fredericksburg, Virginia, the daughter of Captain William Lewis Herndon of the U.S. Navy and explorer of the Amazon. Brought up in gracious Southern style, she was taken on a European tour at 16 and, while visiting New York City a few years later, met Chester Arthur; they were married on October 25, 1859. She had three children, one dying in infancy.

Beautiful and cultivated, she helped her Vermont-born husband develop a taste for elegance but did not live to reign as First Lady. She died of pneumonia in New York on January 12, 1880, ten months before her husband's nomination to the Vice-Presidency, and she was buried in Albany. Arthur's widowed sister, Mrs. John McElroy, served as his hostess while he was in the White House.

Mrs. Grover Cleveland—Born Frances Folsom on July 21, 1864, in Buffalo, New York, the daughter of Oscar Folsom, a lawyer who was killed in a buggy accident in 1875. Her father's partner, Grover Cleveland, then assumed responsibility for her. A tall, attractive young woman, she was attending Wells College when he became President in 1885. He was 48 years old and a bachelor. On June 2, 1886, they were married in the Blue Room of the White House, and this first Presidential wedding in the Executive Mansion was celebrated by the pealing of every church bell in Washington. (John Tyler, the only other President to marry while in office, had been wed at the Church of the Ascension in New York City.)

The 22-year-old Mrs. Cleveland won immediate popularity and was considered the most charming First Lady since Dolley Madison. Her friendliness drew large crowds to her public receptions. She had five children, the second—Esther, who later became Mrs. William Bosanquet—being the only Presidential child to be born in the White House (on September 9, 1893). Mrs. Cleveland survived her husband 39 years and, five years after his death, on February 10, 1913, she became the first Presidential widow to remarry. Her second husband was Thomas J. Preston, a Princeton professor of archaeology. She died on October 29, 1947, in Baltimore and was buried in Princeton.

Mrs. Benjamin Harrison—The first Mrs. Harrison was born Caroline (Carrie) Scott, on October 1, 1832, in Oxford, Ohio. She was the daughter of a Presbyterian minister who also conducted a school for girls. After teaching briefly, she married Benjamin Harrison on October 20, 1853; they had two children. As First Lady, she became the first President General of the National Society of the Daughters of the American Revolution. Prevented by ill health from taking an active social role, she died in the White House on October 25, 1892, and was buried in Indianapolis. The duties of official hostess during much of the Harrison administration were assumed by Mrs. Mary Scott Dimmick, a widowed niece of Mrs. Harrison's.

After leaving office, former President Harrison married Mrs. Dimmick in New York City on April 6, 1896; she was 37, and he was then 62. They had one child. The second Mrs. Harrison, a native of Honesdale, Pennsylvania, survived her husband 46 years, dying in New York on January 5, 1948.

Mrs. William McKinley—Born Ida Saxton on June 8, 1847, the daughter of a leading banker in Canton, Ohio. Charming but high-strung, she was, unconventionally, working as a cashier in her father's bank when she met a handsome newcomer to town, Major William McKinley; they were married on January 25, 1871. A year later, she gave birth to a daughter, then became pregnant again soon afterward. Before the birth of her second baby, her mother died, and Mrs. McKinley became severely depressed. The subsequent death of both her infant daughters left her a nervous invalid subject to frequent epileptic fits. Nevertheless, as her husband rose politically, she insisted on appearing with him at all social functions, and he became adept at shielding her when she suffered a seizure.

The nature of her illness was not generally known when she became First Lady, and her delicate health required many innovations in official entertaining. Despite protocol, she was seated beside the President at state dinners, and Mrs. Garret Hobart, wife of McKinley's Vice-

President during his first term, assisted her in many ceremonial duties. Mrs. McKinley survived her slain husband five years, dying on May 26, 1907, in Canton, where she was buried beside him.

Mrs. Theodore Roosevelt—The first Mrs. Roosevelt was born Alice Hathaway Lee on July 29, 1861, in Chestnut Hill, Massachusetts. As a charming girl of 17, she met her future husband while he was attending Harvard. They were married on October 27, 1880, soon after his graduation, when he was 22 and she 19. But two days after the birth of their first child—a daughter, also named Alice—she died (on February 14, 1884) of a previously unsuspected case of Bright's disease. Roosevelt lost his beloved young wife on the same day his mother died of typhoid fever.

He gradually recovered from the shock of this double tragedy after renewing his childhood friendship with Edith Kermit Carow. They were married in London, where she was temporarily living, on December 2, 1886. The daughter of a New York merchant, she had been born in Connecticut on August 6, 1861. The second Mrs. Roosevelt, who gave her husband four sons and another daughter, made an unusually poised and capable First Lady.

Besides coping with the antics of her high-spirited youngsters, she supervised an extensive remodeling of the White House which changed the mansion, her husband said, from "a shabby likeness of the ground floor of the Astor House into a simple and dignified dwelling for the head of a republic." In addition, she arranged an elegant East Room wedding when "Princess Alice" married Congressman Nicholas Longworth of Ohio on February 17, 1906. Mrs. Roosevelt died on September 30, 1948, at the family's summer home in Oyster Bay, New York, and she was buried there.

Mrs. William Howard Taft—Born Helen Herron on June 2, 1861, in Cincinnati, but always called Nellie. The daughter of Judge John Williamson Herron, she visited the White House at 17 as the guest of her father's former law partner, President Rutherford B. Hayes, and decided then that she would like to be First Lady. Studious as well as ambitious, she taught a few years before marrying William Howard Taft on June 19, 1886.

Two months after she did move into the White House, she suffered a stroke which prevented her from taking part in social activities for more than a year; then after her recovery, she and her husband celebrated their 25th wedding anniversary with an evening garden party for which the grounds of the Executive Mansion were spectacularly illuminated. Mrs. Taft left a lasting physical impression on Washington by sponsoring the planting of the capital's famous Japanese cherry trees, which she admired from the time of a diplomatic trip to Japan with her husband. The eldest of her three children, Robert A. Taft, became the distinguished Senator from Ohio. Mrs. Taft died on May 22, 1943, in Washington and was buried beside her husband in Arlington National Cemetery.

Mrs. Woodrow Wilson—The first Mrs. Wilson was born Ellen Louise Axson in Rome, Georgia, on May 15, 1860. Daughter of a Presbyterian minister, she married Wilson on June 24, 1885. An art student with a fondness for music and literature, she had a great influence on her husband; from their marriage to her death, they were never separated a day. They had three daughters, two of whom were married in the White House—Jessie, who became Mrs. Francis Bowes Sayre in an elaborate East Room ceremony on November 25, 1913, and Eleanor, who became Mrs. William Gibbs McAdoo at a smaller wedding in the Blue Room on May 7, 1914. The latter occasion was marred by the increasing weakness of Mrs. Wilson, who died in the White House on August 6, 1914.

Her death left the President so depressed by grief and loneliness that his physician, Dr. Cary T. Grayson, became alarmed until he, perhaps inadvertently, provided a cure. Dr. Grayson introduced Mrs. Edith Bolling Galt, an attractive 42-year-old widow, to Wilson's cousin, Miss Helen Woodrow Bones, who was temporarily serving as White House hostess. Miss Bones invited Mrs. Galt to tea in March of 1915. Just two months later, the President proposed marriage to Mrs. Galt, and they were married at her Washington home on December 18, 1915.

Born in Wytheville, Virginia, on October 15, 1872, the second Mrs. Wilson had been married to Norman Galt, a Washington jeweler, in 1896, then widowed twelve years later. As First Lady during World War I, she kept official entertaining to a minimum. After her husband was partly paralyzed by a stroke on October 2, 1919, she shielded him from visitors to the extent that she was called "the nation's first Lady President." She survived him 36 years, dying in Washington on December 28, 1961.

Mrs. Warren Gamaliel Harding—Born Florence Kling on August 15, 1860, the daughter of a banker who was the richest man in the small Ohio city of Marion. At 19, she eloped with Henry De-Wolfe, the black sheep in an old local family. A year later, he abandoned her and an infant son, and she was forced to return to her stern father whose rule she had sought to escape.

After being divorced, she married Warren Harding on July 8, 1891; she was five years his senior. Then she took over the business side of the Marion *Star*, which Harding had recently acquired. Mrs. Harding was sometimes credited with inspiring her husband's political career, and in Ohio political circles she was known as "The Duchess." In the White House, failing health limited her social activities, but she survived her husband by a year, dying on November 21, 1924, in Marion, where she was buried.

Mrs. Calvin Coolidge—Born Grace Goodhue in Burlington, Vermont, on January 3, 1879, the daughter of a mechanical engineer. After graduating from the University of Vermont in 1902, she became a teacher at the Clarke Institute for the Deaf in Northampton, Massachusetts. An exceptionally warm person, she married the silent Calvin Coolidge on October 4, 1905, and was sometimes described as his most important asset.

In the White House, despite her husband's frugal management of menu planning, her charm won her wide popularity. She had two sons, but the younger, Calvin Jr., died at 16 of blood poisoning on July 7, 1924, less than a year after his father succeeded to the Presidency. Mrs. Coolidge died on July 8, 1957, in Northampton, and she was buried in Plymouth, Vermont.

Mrs. Herbert Clark Hoover—Born Lou Henry in Waterloo, Iowa, on March 29, 1874, the daughter of a banker who subsequently moved his family to Monterey, California. She entered Stanford University in 1894, planning to become a geology teacher, but she married Hoover, a fellow student, on February 10, 1899, and went to China with him. After living in many foreign lands, while her husband pursued his career, and raising two sons, Mrs. Hoover enjoyed settling in Washington in 1921, when her husband entered President Harding's Cabinet.

By the time she moved into the White House on March 4, 1929, she had a large circle of friends in the capital, and she entertained extensively as First Lady. But on January 1, 1930, she held what proved to be the last of the annual New Year's Day receptions in the Executive Mansion. When Mrs. John Adams had started the custom in 1801, 135 guests appeared to be greeted by the President and his wife; in 1930, more than 9,000 people sought admission, causing Mr. and Mrs. Hoover to make a point of being out of Washington over New Year's during the rest of his term. (His successor, President Franklin Roosevelt, formally discontinued these gatherings which had grown so unwieldy.) Mrs. Hoover died in New York City on January 7, 1944. The gravesite is located at West Branch, Iowa.

Mrs. Franklin Delano Roosevelt—Born Anna Eleanor Roosevelt on October 11, 1884, in New York City, the daughter of Theodore Roosevelt's younger brother, Elliott. Owing to the early death of both her parents, she was brought up by her maternal grandmother, Mrs. V. G. Hall. A shy and solitary child, she was educated in Europe; then on March 17, 1905, she married her fifth cousin, Franklin Roosevelt. They had six children, one son dying in infancy. After her husband's crippling attack of infantile paralysis in 1921, she took an increasingly active part in politics, serving as his eyes and ears at meetings he could not attend.

In the White House, she continued this role on a much broader scale, traveling thousands of miles to inspect coal mines and prisons and American military installations everywhere. A controversial figure as First Lady because of her outspoken support for humanitarian and civil rights causes, Mrs. Roosevelt broke with tradition by holding regular press conferences, lecturing widely, and writing a syndicated newspaper column, "My Day."

She won worldwide esteem as one of the century's outstanding women. President Truman, after her husband's death, appointed her to the United States delegation to the United Nations. She also served the world organization as chairman of its Commission for Human Rights. She died on November 7, 1962, in New York City, and was buried beside her husband at Hyde Park, New York.

Mrs. Harry S Truman—Born Elizabeth Virginia Wallace in Independence, Missouri, on February 13, 1885, but always called Bess. Her maternal grandparents owned a flour mill. As a little girl with blond curls, she captivated her future husband at Sunday school in the First Presbyterian Church. Married on June 28, 1919, she had one daughter.

Unassuming and not fond of ceremony, Mrs. Truman tried to avoid personal publicity as First Lady. She was helped in her effort to live quietly by the fact that serious structural weaknesses were discovered in the White House during her residence there; and from November 1948 until March 1952, the Trumans lived across Pennsyl-

vania Avenue in Blair House. After her husband left office, Mrs. Truman was happy to retire with him to the family home in Independence.

Mrs. Dwight David Eisenhower—Born Mamie Geneva Doud on November 14, 1896, the daughter of a prosperous meat packer in Boone, Iowa. When she was 10, her family moved to Denver, but usually spent the colder months visiting San Antonio. Early in the winter of 1915, while at San Antonio, a young second lieutenant stationed at nearby Fort Sam Houston was introduced to the pretty and popular Miss Doud; on Valentine's Day, they became engaged, and they were married on July 1, 1916. For the next several decades, she lived at Army posts all over the world. She had two sons, but the older died at three.

A warm and friendly woman, Mrs. Eisenhower became accustomed to official entertaining during her Army years. But she described herself as "nonpolitical." After leaving the White House, she enjoyed retirement at the Gettysburg farm that was their first home.

After a massive stroke in late September 1979, she was hospitalized at Walter Reed Army Medical Center in Washington, D.C., where she died in her sleep on November 11, 1979. She was buried beside her husband in Abilene, Kansas.

Mrs. John Fitzgerald Kennedy—Born Jacqueline Lee Bouvier on July 28, 1929, in Southampton, New York, the daughter of John Vernon Bouvier 3d, a wealthy stockbroker. With generations of social prominence on both sides of her family, she attended private schools, had her own pony, and made a glittering début at Newport in 1947. (After the divorce of her parents in 1940, her mother married Hugh D. Auchincloss of Washington and Newport.) Then she went on to further study at Vassar, the Sorbonne, and George Washington University, from which she graduated in 1951. As the "Inquiring Camera Girl" for the Washington *Times-Herald*, she interviewed a young senator whom she had recently met at a dinner party; they were married on September 12, 1953, in St. Mary's Roman Catholic Church at Newport.

The nation's third youngest First Lady, she was 31 on moving into the White House. She won admiration everywhere for her tasteful redecoration of the White House and the glamorous receptions she arranged; this "Kennedy style" to which she contributed so much was a major ingredient in her husband's popularity.

With her two children, she lived in New York City after leaving the White House until her marriage on October 20, 1968, to Aristotle Socrates Onassis, the Greek shipping multimillionaire who died on March 15, 1975.

Mrs. Lyndon Baines Johnson—Born Claudia Alta Taylor on December 22, 1912, in Karnack, Texas, the daughter of Thomas Jefferson Taylor, a prosperous landowner and merchant. When she was two, a nursemaid called her Lady Bird—because she was "as purty as a lady bird"—and the nickname stuck. Brought up by an aunt after her mother died when she was five, she grew into a shy and nature-loving girl with an interest in studying.

Shortly after receiving a journalism degree from the University of Texas, she met the tall secretary to a Texas Congressman; and Lyndon Johnson proposed to her the next day. They were married two months later, on November 17, 1934. Mrs.

Johnson helped her husband along every step of his career. She provided the money for his first Congressional campaign (by borrowing against the $67,000 she was due to inherit from her mother), and she ran his Washington office while he took military leave during World War II.

In the White House, Mrs. Johnson's personal warmth was often credited with smoothing over difficulties caused by her husband's more abrasive personality. She showed a broader concern about public questions than any First Lady with the exception of Mrs. Franklin Roosevelt. Mrs. Johnson was particularly interested in promoting efforts to beautify the nation's cities and towns.

Mrs. Richard Milhous Nixon—Born Thelma Ryan on March 16, 1912, in Ely, Nevada, the daughter of a miner who took up farming a year later, and moved his family to Artesia, California. Her father always called her Pat, and the nickname stayed with her.

After graduating with honors from the University of Southern California in 1937, she taught commercial subjects at Whittier High School in Whittier, California, where she met her future husband in a local amateur theater group; they were married on June 21, 1940. Throughout his career, she has tirelessly supported him at every step. She gained valuable experience toward meeting her responsibilities while her husband was Vice-President under President Eisenhower.

Poised and imperturbable, she has brought up two daughters, the younger of whom, Julie, married David Eisenhower, grandson of the former President, in December 1968. Although she fulfilled her role of official hostess with grace, she generally shunned the limelight while in the White House. In 1976 she suffered a partial stroke.

Mrs. Gerald R. Ford—Born Elizabeth Anne Bloomer on April 8, 1918, in Chicago, Illinois, but moved to Grand Rapids, Michigan at the age of three. Mrs. Ford attended the Bennington School of Dance in Vermont and studied modern dance with Martha Graham. She spent two years in New York as a dancer in the Martha Graham Concert Group. In 1942, she returned to Grand Rapids and married William Warren. They were divorced in 1947. While in Grand Rapids she organized her own dance group and, in addition, became a model and fashion coordinator for a Grand Rapids department store. On October 15, 1948, she married Gerald R. Ford. The Fords have four children.

In Washington, Betty Ford was active in the Republican Wives Club, on the Board of Directors of the League of Republican Women in the District of Columbia, and as President of the Senate Red Cross Club. Mrs. Ford is noted for her candor in expressing her opinions and beliefs and is concerned with promoting equal opportunities for women.

Mrs. Jimmy Carter—Born Eleanor Rosalynn Smith on August 18, 1927, on her maternal grandfather's farm in Plains, Georgia, the daughter of town garage mechanic, Edgar Smith. While attending Georgia Southwestern College, Rosalynn studied interior decorating. She lived at home and helped her family from age 15 when she first went to work in a local beauty parlor. When 18-year-old Rosalynn married Jimmy Carter on July 7, 1946, she had known the U.S. Naval Academy midshipman for five years as her best friend's brother. The Carters have four children. Rosalynn enjoyed travelling from base to base until the death of Carter's father caused the couple's return to Plains in 1953 and catalyzed their first team effort in the family peanut business. Rosalynn deftly managed bookkeeping, office work, tax returns and helped to create a thriving business. Rosalynn profoundly influenced Carter's key presidential campaign strategy: to run in all possible primaries.

In the White House, Rosalynn has demonstrated extraordinary determination and drive. She has gone along on presidential junkets both at home and abroad. On her own, she has toured the U.S. in support of her favorite causes, campaigning and acting as observer for her husband; abroad she has represented him at a presidential inauguration and a papal funeral. But more importantly, Rosalynn has maintained her position as advisor to the President, a position which has both grown in importance and become increasingly evident.

MINORITY PRESIDENTS

Source: U.S. Library of Congress and other sources

Under the Electoral College System, 15 Presidents have been elected who did not receive a majority of the popular votes cast. Three of them—John Quincy Adams, Rutherford B. Hayes, and Benjamin Harrison—actually trailed their opponents in the popular vote. The table shows the percentage of the popular vote received by the candidates.

Year	Elected	Opponents		
1824	Adams 30.54	Jackson 43.13	Clay 13.24	Crawford 13.09
1844	Polk 49.56	Clay 48.13	Birney 2.30	——
1848	Taylor 47.35	Cass 42.52	Van Buren 10.13	——
1856	Buchanan 45.63	Frémont 33.27	Fillmore 21.08	Smith .01
1860	Lincoln 39.79	Douglas 29.40	Breckinridge 18.20	Bell 12.60
1876	Hayes 48.04	Tilden 50.99	Cooper .97	——
1880	Garfield 48.32	Hancock 48.21	Weaver 3.35	Others .12
1884	Cleveland 48.53	Blaine 48.24	Butler 1.74	St. John 1.49
1888	Harrison 47.86	Cleveland 48.66	Fisk 2.19	Streeter 1.29
1892	Cleveland 46.04	Harrison 43.01	Weaver 8.53	Others 2.42
1912	Wilson 41.85	Roosevelt 27.42	Taft 23.15	Others 7.58
1916	Wilson 49.26	Hughes 46.12	Benson 3.16	Others 1.46
1948	Truman 49.51	Dewey 45.13	Thurmond 2.40	H. Wallace 2.38
1960	Kennedy 49.71	Nixon 49.55	Unpledged .92	Others .27
1968	Nixon 43.16	Humphrey 42.73	G. Wallace 13.63	Others .48

U.S. PRESIDENTIAL ELECTIONS: 1789—1972

The first four Presidential elections (1789, 1792, 1796, and 1800) were held under Article II, Section 1, of the Constitution, which provided for the College of Electors to vote for two candidates —the one with the majority of votes was elected President, and the next highest became Vice-President. A tie in the Electoral College in 1800 led to the passage of the Twelfth Amendment, which provides for separate ballots for President and Vice-President.

Prior to the election of 1824, records of popular vote are scanty and inaccurate.

ELECTION OF 1789

The Political Scene: The struggle over the ratification of the Constitution had led to the emergence of two political factions, the Federalists, who supported the new Constitution, and the Anti-Federalists, who opposed it.

Nominations and Campaign: George Washington, although identified with the Federalists, was unopposed for the Presidential nomination and received a unanimous vote from the 69 electors.

Results of 1789 Election:

Presidential Candidate	Party	Electoral Votes
George Washington	None	69
John Adams	None	34
Other candidates	None	35
Votes not cast	—	4

Comments: Rhode Island and North Carolina had not yet ratified the Constitution when the electors cast their ballots, and a deadlock between the Federalist Senate and the Anti-Federalist Assembly in New York prevented the choosing of any electors.

ELECTION OF 1792

The Political Scene: Thomas Jefferson and James Madison in Virginia and George Clinton and Aaron Burr in New York provided the leadership of the Democratic-Republican party, which emerged in opposition to Alexander Hamilton's financial policy, to the Federalist emphasis on a strong central government, and to a loose or flexible interpretation of the Constitution.

Nominations: Both parties urged that Washington accept another term, but the Jeffersonians opposed Adams' re-election with Clinton's candidacy.

The Campaign: Adams was accused of being antidemocratic and a secret monarchist, but the real target of the Democratic-Republicans was Hamilton.

Results of 1792 Election:

Presidential Candidate	Party	Electoral Votes
George Washington	Federalist	132
John Adams	Federalist	77
George Clinton	Democratic-Republican	50
Other candidates	—	5
Votes not cast	—	3

ELECTION OF 1796

The Political Scene: Washington, who deplored partisan politics, refused to consider another term, thus insuring the first real contest for the Presidency.

Nominations: Jefferson was the logical candidate for the Democratic-Republicans, but Hamilton was less than happy about the candidacy of John Adams of Massachusetts for the Federalists and hoped that Thomas Pinckney, the ostensible Federalist Vice-Presidential candidate, might win if Federalist electors in the South withheld their votes from Adams.

The Campaign: Adams electors in New England countered Hamilton's scheme by omitting Pinckney from their ballots. The unexpected result of the Federalist bickering was the election of Jefferson to the Vice-Presidency.

Results of 1796 Election

Presidential Candidate	Party	Electoral Votes
John Adams	Federalist	71
Thomas Jefferson	Democratic-Republican	68
Thomas Pinckney	Federalist	59
Aaron Burr	Democratic-Republican	30
Other candidates	—	48

ELECTION OF 1800

The Political Scene: The wars of the French Revolution had created another area of disagreement between the Federalists, who favored Great Britain, and the Democratic-Republicans, who tended to support France. The apparent desire of some Federalist leaders for a war with France alarmed the nation.

Nominations: Congressional caucuses of each party chose the candidates: Adams and Pinckney for the Federalists and Jefferson and Burr for the Democratic-Republicans.

The Campaign: The Federalists gave their opponents a powerful campaign issue in the repressive Alien and Sedition Acts that Jefferson and Madison eloquently denounced in the Virginia and Kentucky Resolutions.

Results of 1800 Election:

Presidential Candidate	Party	Electoral Votes
Thomas Jefferson	Democratic-Republican	73
Aaron Burr	Democratic-Republican	73
John Adams	Federalist	65
Charles C. Pinckney	Federalist	64
John Jay	Federalist	1

Comments: Because the candidates for President and Vice-President were not separately nominated, Jefferson and Burr ended in a tie. The House of Representatives elected Jefferson on the 36th ballot after seven days of balloting. To prevent the situation from arising again, the Twelfth Amendment, ratified in 1804, provided for separate balloting for President and Vice-President. Jefferson's triumph ended the Federalist era and ushered in a quarter century of Democratic-Republican control of the Presidency.

ELECTION OF 1804

The Political Scene: Jefferson's efficient administration and the acquisition of the vast Louisiana Territory gained his party almost universal support and led the more extreme Federalist leaders into the Essex Junto, an abortive scheme to separate the northeastern states from the Union.

Nominations: The Congressional caucuses of each party chose the candidates. A falling-out between Jefferson and Burr led to the latter's replacement as Vice-Presidential candidate by George Clinton of New York. Charles C. Pinckney of South Carolina and Rufus King of New York comprised the Federalist ticket.

The Campaign: The machinations of the Essex Junto all but destroyed the Federalist party; the only question remaining was the size of Jefferson's victory.

Results of 1804 Election:

Presidential Candidate	Party	Electoral Votes	Vice-Presidential Candidate	Party	Electoral Votes
Thomas Jefferson	Democratic-Republican	162	George Clinton	Democratic-Republican	162
Charles C. Pinckney	Federalist	14	Rufus King	Federalist	14

Comments: Jefferson won every electoral vote but those of Connecticut and Delaware and two in Maryland.

ELECTION OF 1808

The Political Scene: The disastrous effects of the Embargo of 1808 on American commerce revived the Federalist party in New England and caused dissension among the Jeffersonians.

Nominations: It took considerable pressure by Jefferson to get the rebellious factions within his party to accept his choice of James Madison of Virginia to succeed him. Clinton of New York was again the Vice-Presidential candidate. Federalist leaders engineered the renomination of the 1804 ticket of Pinckney and King.

The Campaign: Running primarily on the Embargo issue, the Federalists considerably improved their showing over the previous election, but could not overcome the solid Democratic-Republican majority that had been created.

Results of 1808 Election:

Presidential Candidate	Party	Electoral Votes	Vice-Presidential Candidate	Party	Electoral Votes
James Madison	Democratic-Republican	122	George Clinton	Democratic-Republican	113
Charles C. Pinckney	Federalist	47	Rufus King	Federalist	47
George Clinton	Democratic-Republican	6	Other candidates	—	15
Votes not cast	—	1	Votes not cast	—	1

ELECTION OF 1812

The Political Scene: Conflict with Great Britain over maritime rights and alleged incitement of Indian rebellion caused Madison to request a declaration of war in June 1812.

Nominations: The Republican congressional caucus, dominated by young "War Hawk" representatives from the frontier states, renominated Madison, a month before the war message. Elbridge Gerry of Massachusetts received the Vice-Presidential nomination. Insurgent Republicans in New York put up DeWitt Clinton, who thereupon received Federalist support but not an official endorsement. Jared Ingersoll of Pennsylvania ran with him.

The Campaign: Although Clinton tried to avoid running as a Peace-Federalist candidate, his strength clearly lay in the Northeast, the section most unenthusiastic about the war.

Results of 1812 Election:

Presidential Candidate	Party	Electoral Votes	Vice-Presidential Candidate	Party	Electoral Votes
James Madison	Democratic-Republican	128	Elbridge Gerry	Democratic-Republican	131
DeWitt Clinton	Federalist	89	Jared Ingersoll	Federalist	86
Votes not cast	—	1	Votes not cast	—	1

Comments: The vote of Pennsylvania together with the solid backing of the South and West elected Madison.

ELECTION OF 1816

The Political Scene: The end of the War of 1812 and an economic boom assured the continued ascendancy of the Democratic-Republicans.

Nominations: The congressional caucus chose James Monroe of Virginia over William H. Crawford of Georgia in a close contest. The choice of Daniel D. Tompkins for the Vice-Presidency renewed the Virginia-New York alliance. Rufus King of New York, although not selected by any formal process, was considered the Federalist nominee.

The Campaign: King, the last Federalist candidate, received only the votes of Massachusetts, Connecticut, and Delaware in a campaign he hardly contested at all.

Results of 1816 Election:

Presidential Candidate	Party	Electoral Votes	Vice-Presidential Candidate	Party	Electoral Votes
James Monroe	Democratic-Republican	183	Daniel D. Tompkins	Democratic-Republican	183
Rufus King	Federalist	34	John E. Howard	Federalist	22
Votes not cast	—	4	Other candidates	—	12
			Votes not cast	—	4

Comments: Following Washington, Jefferson, and Madison, Monroe was the last of the Virginia dynasty and the last of the men of the revolutionary era to hold the Presidency.

ELECTION OF 1820

The Political Scene: No great national issue disturbed the country enough for anyone to oppose Monroe's reelection.

Nomination and Campaign: Monroe received every electoral vote except that of William Plumer of New Hampshire.

Results of 1820 Election:

Presidential Candidate	Party	Electoral Votes	Vice-Presidential Candidate	Party	Electoral Votes
James Monroe	Democratic-Republican	231	Daniel D. Tompkins	Democratic-Republican	218
John Quincy Adams	Independent	1	Other candidates	—	14
Votes not cast	—	3	Votes not cast	—	3

Comments: The tradition that Plumer voted for John Quincy Adams in order to preserve for Washington alone the honor of a unanimous selection is of dubious validity; Plumer simply disliked Monroe and his policies.

ELECTION OF 1824

The Political Scene: The "Era of Good Feelings" ended as the Democratic-Republican organization dissolved into sectional groupings.

Nominations: A poorly attended congressional caucus selected William H. Crawford of Georgia, while various state legislatures nominated Henry Clay of Kentucky, Andrew Jackson of Tennessee, John Quincy Adams of Massachusetts, and John C. Calhoun of South Carolina. Calhoun subsequently withdrew to run for the Vice-Presidency on Jackson's ticket.

The Campaign: Clay put forward his celebrated plan calling for a strong protective tariff, domestic improvements, and a national bank—policies that Adams also endorsed. Jackson relied on his popular appeal as a military hero.

Results of 1824 Election:

Presidential Candidate	Party	Electoral Votes	Popular Vote Total	Popular Vote Percentage	Vice-Presidential Candidate and Electoral Votes		Party
John Quincy Adams	None	84	115,696	31.9	John C. Calhoun	182	None
Andrew Jackson	None	99	152,933	42.2	Nathan Sanford	30	None
William H. Crawford	None	41	46,979	12.9	Nathaniel Macon	24	None
Henry Clay	None	37	47,136	13.0	Other candidates	25	—

Comments: Since no candidate had gained a majority of the electoral vote, the House of Representatives, voting by states and with each state having one vote, chose Adams on the first ballot.

ELECTION OF 1828

The Political Scene: More than two-thirds of the electorate had voted against Adams in 1824. This circumstance negated his hopes for a successful administration, and the Jacksonians commenced their plans to unseat him.

Nominations: The Tennessee legislature renominated Jackson in 1825, and the incumbent Vice-President Calhoun once again agreed to be his running mate. This is considered the first ticket of the modern Democratic party. Adams ran for reelection as a National Republican.

The Campaign: Although important differences on national questions divided Adams and Jackson, these issues disappeared in a welter of vituperative personal attacks against each standard-bearer.

Results of 1828 Election:

Presidential Candidate	Party	Electoral Votes	Popular Vote Total	Percentage	Vice-Presidential Candidate and Electoral Votes		Party
Andrew Jackson	Democratic	178	647,292	56.0	John C. Calhoun	171	Democratic
John Quincy Adams	National Republican	83	507,730	44.0	Richard Rush	83	National Republican
					William Smith	7	Democratic

Comments: The election of Jackson, the frontier hero, represented a triumph for the West and the South. It also symbolized the arrival of the common people to political power.

ELECTION OF 1832

The Political Scene: Internal disputes within Jackson's cabinet and the President's strong stand against nullification caused a break between Jackson and Calhoun. Jackson's veto of a bill rechartering the Bank of the United States, however, created the major issue in the campaign.

Conventions and Nominees: For the first time the national nominating convention was employed by the three parties in the field. All met at Baltimore, with the Anti-Masonic party holding the first convention (September 26, 1831) and choosing William Wirt of Maryland. The National Republicans nominated the legislative champion of the Bank of the United States—Henry Clay of Kentucky, while the Democrats unanimously endorsed Jackson and replaced Calhoun for the Vice-Presidency with Martin Van Buren of New York. The Democratic convention adopted a rule requiring a two-thirds vote of the whole convention for nomination. This remained in effect until 1936.

The Campaign: Clay attacked Jackson's veto of the bank bill and his opposition to internal improvements. He misjudged the popular temper; to the average voter, Jackson's bank policy was a blow against monopoly and privilege.

Results of 1832 Election:

Presidential Candidate	Party	Electoral Votes	Popular Vote Total	Percentage	Vice-Presidential Candidate and Electoral Votes		Party
Andrew Jackson	Democratic	219	688,242	54.5	Martin Van Buren	189	Democratic
Henry Clay	National Republican	49	473,462	37.5	John Sergeant	49	National Republican
John Floyd	Independent	11	—	—	Henry Lee	11	Independent
William Wirt	Anti-Masonic	7	101,051	8.0	Amos Ellmaker	7	Anti-Masonic
Votes not cast	—	2	—	—	William Wilkins	30	Independent
					Votes not cast	2	—

Comments: The Anti-Masonic party, opposed to the Masons and other secret societies, was the first third party in American history. On December 28, 1832, following the election, Vice-President Calhoun resigned his office.

ELECTION OF 1836

The Political Scene: Opponents of "King Andrew" Jackson formed the Whig party, taking the name of the antimonarchial English political party to emphasize Jackson's alleged autocratic tendencies.

Conventions and Nominees: Jackson desired his Vice-President Martin Van Buren of New York to succeed him, and the Democratic convention at Baltimore (May 20–22, 1835) unanimously ratified his choice. Richard M. Johnson of Kentucky was the Vice-Presidential candidate. The Whigs, lacking a leader with national appeal, nominated three sectional candidates (Daniel Webster of Massachusetts, Hugh L. White of Tennessee, and William Henry Harrison of Ohio) in an effort to throw the election into the House of Representatives.

The Campaign: Jackson's personality and the record of his administration provided the issues for the campaign. The influence of "Old Hickory" was probably decisive, since Van Buren received a bare majority of the popular vote. The Senate, for the only time in history, elected the Vice-President with 33 votes for Johnson, 16 for Granger.

Results of 1836 Election:

Presidential Candidate	Party	Electoral Votes	Popular Vote Total	Percentage	Vice-Presidential Candidate and Electoral Votes		Party
Martin Van Buren	Democratic	170	764,198	50.9	Richard M. Johnson	147	Democratic
William H. Harrison	Whig	73	549,508	36.6	Francis Granger	77	Whig
Hugh L. White	Whig	26	145,352	9.7	John Tyler	47	Democratic
Daniel Webster	Whig	14	41,287	2.7	William Smith	23	Independent
W. P. Mangum	Independent	11	—	—			

ELECTION OF 1840

The Political Scene: The Panic of 1837, which had been caused mainly by Jackson's erratic financial policies, fell with full force during Van Buren's administration, hurting his prospects for reelection.

Conventions and Nominees: The Whigs in Pennsylvania met at Harrisburg (May 4–5, 1840) to name William Henry Harrison of Ohio and John Tyler of Virginia as their ticket, while the Democrats convening at Baltimore (May 5–7) unanimously renominated Van Buren. The antislavery Liberty party in a convention at Albany, New York, nominated James G. Birney of New York and Thomas Earle of Pennsylvania.

The Campaign: The Whigs avoided any divisive issues and conducted a campaign of parades and ballyhoo, complete with the first memorable political slogan, "Tippecanoe and Tyler too."

Results of 1840 Election:

Presidential Candidate	Party	Electoral Votes	Popular Vote Total	Percentage	Vice-Presidential Candidate and Electoral Votes		Party
William H. Harrison	Whig	234	1,275,612	52.9	John Tyler	234	Whig
Martin Van Buren	Democratic	60	1,130,033	46.8	Richard Johnson	48	Democratic
James G. Birney	Liberty	—	7,053	.3	Thomas Earle	—	Liberty
					L. W. Tazewell	11	Independent
					James K. Polk	1	Democratic

Comments: Barely a month after his inauguration, Harrison became the first President to die in office and was succeeded by Tyler on April 6, 1841.

ELECTION OF 1844

The Political Scene: In his one term Tyler managed to disrupt the Whig party and to secure the annexation of Texas, but he failed to settle the Oregon question.

Conventions and Nominees: The Whigs convened at Baltimore (May 1) to nominate Henry Clay for President and Senator Theodore Frelinghuysen of New Jersey for Vice-President. Later in the month at the same city, the Democrats chose the first "dark horse" nominee for the Presidency. Ex-President Van Buren had a clear majority on the early ballots but could not reach the required two-thirds vote. On the ninth ballot, the convention chose James K. Polk of Tennessee with George M. Dallas of Pennsylvania as the Vice-Presidential candidate. The Liberty party meeting at Buffalo, New York (August 1843), again named James G. Birney with Thomas Morris of Ohio as his running mate.

The Campaign: Polk, an ardent expansionist, favored the Texas annexation and the acquisition of Oregon with the slogan "Fifty-four forty or fight." Clay was hurt in the South by his wavering on Texas, and in the North by the defection of antislavery Whigs to the Liberty party.

Results of 1844 Election:

Presidential Candidate	Party	Electoral Votes	Popular Vote Total	Percentage	Vice-Presidential Candidate
James K. Polk	Democratic	170	1,339,368	49.6	George M. Dallas
Henry Clay	Whig	105	1,300,687	48.1	Theodore Frelinghuysen
James G. Birney	Liberty	—	62,197	2.3	Thomas Morris

Comments: Although far from conclusive, Polk's victory was regarded as a popular endorsement of a vigorous policy of expansion.

ELECTION OF 1848

The Political Scene: Polk settled the Oregon dispute with Great Britain, led the nation through a successful war with Mexico, and secured a vast accretion of territory. Yet he left office immensely unpopular and with the question of the extension of slavery into the new territories threatening to divide the country.

Conventions and Nominees: Polk had renounced a second term and the Democratic convention meeting at Baltimore (May 1848) picked a ticket of Lewis Cass of Michigan and William O. Butler of Kentucky. Although most Whigs had opposed the Mexican War, it provided them with their party's two leading Presidential candidates, Generals Zachary Taylor and Winfield Scott. The convention at Philadelphia named Taylor of Louisiana with Millard Fillmore of New York. Antislavery dissidents from both parties formed the Free Soil party and, meeting at Buffalo (August 1848), nominated ex-President Martin Van Buren with Charles Francis Adams of Massachusetts as his running mate.

The Campaign: On the paramount issue, the Free Soilers opposed extension of slavery into the newly acquired territories, while Cass endorsed the concept of popular sovereignty, or letting the settlers decide. Taylor refused to take any stand at all, correctly counting on his war popularity to carry him to victory.

Results of 1848 Election:

Presidential Candidate	Party	Electoral Votes	Popular Vote Total	Percentage	Vice-Presidential Candidate
Zachary Taylor	Whig	163	1,362,101	47.3	Millard Fillmore
Lewis Cass	Democratic	127	1,222,674	42.4	William O. Butler
Martin Van Buren	Free Soil	—	291,616	10.1	Charles Francis Adams

Comments: Taylor died on July 9, 1850. The succession of Fillmore to the Presidency made possible the Compromise of 1850.

ELECTION OF 1852

The Political Scene: Moderates in both parties had been alarmed by threats of disunion and vainly hoped the Compromise of 1850 would stifle the slavery agitation.

Conventions and Nominees: President Fillmore desired another term, but the Whigs again turned to a military hero, selecting General Winfield Scott of Virginia on the 53d ballot. The convention then named William A. Graham of North Carolina for the Vice-Presidency. The Democrats, who like the Whigs met at Baltimore in June, had a number of potential nominees, but none of the leaders could gain the necessary two-thirds majority. On the 99th ballot, "dark horse" Franklin Pierce of New Hampshire was named with William R. King of Alabama as the party's Vice-Presidential candidate. The remnants of the Free Soil party met in Pittsburgh in August to choose a ticket of John P. Hale of New Hampshire and George W. Julian of Indiana.

The Campaign: Both sides avoided the slavery question, and personalities dominated a rather listless campaign.

Results of 1852 Election:

Presidential Candidate	Party	Electoral Votes	Popular Vote Total	Percentage	Vice-Presidential Candidate
Franklin Pierce	Democratic	254	1,609,038	50.8	William R. King
Winfield Scott	Whig	42	1,386,629	43.8	William A. Graham
John P. Hale	Free Soil	—	156,297	4.9	George Julian

Comments: Scott was the last Presidential candidate of the Whig party.

ELECTION OF 1856

The Political Scene: Despite their overwhelming victory in 1852, the Democrats found it more and more difficult to reconcile their Northern and Southern wings, while the Whigs disintegrated entirely. The passage of the Kansas-Nebraska Act led to the founding of the Republican party.

Conventions and Nominees: In their first national convention at Philadelphia in June, the Republicans nominated John C. Frémont of California and William L. Dayton of New Jersey. Although widely considered to be the ablest leader in the party, Stephen A. Douglas' sponsorship of the Kansas-Nebraska Act prevented his nomination by the Democratic convention at Cincinnati in June. On the 17th ballot a Northerner acceptable to the South, James Buchanan of Pennsylvania, was named with John C. Breckinridge of Kentucky as his running mate. The anti-immigrant, anti-Catholic, American (or Know-Nothing) party had nominated ex-President Fillmore and Andrew J. Donelson at its convention in Philadelphia in February.

The Campaign: The Republicans endorsed a protective tariff and condemned the extension of slavery into the territories. The Democratic platform supported the Kansas-Nebraska Act and the principle of popular sovereignty for the territories.

Results of 1856 Election:

Presidential Candidate	Party	Electoral Votes	Popular Vote Total	Percentage	Vice-Presidential Candidate
James Buchanan	Democratic	174	1,839,237	45.6	John C. Breckinridge
John C. Frémont	Republican	114	1,341,028	33.3	William L. Dayton
Millard Fillmore	American	8	849,872	21.1	Andrew J. Donelson

Comments: Frémont's 114 electoral votes—all from free states—demonstrated the sectional nature of the new Republican party.

ELECTION OF 1860

The Political Scene: The Dred Scott decision, bloody fighting between sectional partisans in Kansas, and John Brown's raid on Harpers Ferry had widened the gulf between the free and slave states. Politicians in the states of the Deep South openly threatened secession if a Republican President was elected.

Conventions and Nominations: The Democrats meeting at Charleston (April 23–May 3, 1860) failed to nominate a candidate after 57 ballots, because the delegations of eight southern states withdrew in protest against the platform statement on slavery in the territories. Reassembling in Baltimore (June 18–23) the party nominated Stephen A. Douglas of Illinois and Benjamin Fitzpatrick of Alabama after further Southern defections. When Fitzpatrick declined to run, the national committee chose Herschel V. Johnson of Georgia. The Southern seceders, calling themselves the National Democratic party, convened in Baltimore on June 28 and nominated John Breckinridge of Kentucky and Joseph Lane of Oregon on a platform that endorsed slavery in the territories. The Constitutional Union party, which was composed mainly of former Whigs and was strongest in the border states, had met in Baltimore (May 9) to choose John Bell of Tennessee and Edward Everett of Massachusetts. Abraham Lincoln of Illinois required only three ballots to defeat preconvention favorite William H. Seward at the Republican convention in Chicago (May 18–20).

The Campaign: The Republicans promised congressional action to preserve freedom in the territories. Slavery and the sectional issues dominated the scene.

Results of 1860 Election:

Presidential Candidate	Party	Electoral Votes	Popular Vote Total	Percentage	Vice-Presidential Candidate
Abraham Lincoln	Republican	180	1,867,198	39.8	Hannibal Hamlin
Stephen A. Douglas	Democratic	12	1,379,434	29.4	Herschel V. Johnson
John C. Breckinridge	National Democratic	72	854,248	18.2	Joseph Lane
John Bell	Constitutional Union	39	591,658	12.6	Edward Everett

Comments: The division among his opponents seemed to insure Lincoln's election. Curiously, however, if all the popular votes cast for his opponents had been given to one man, Lincoln still would have won the electoral vote, because of the heavy distribution of his vote among the more populous states. A little more than a month after the election, South Carolina seceded from the Union.

ELECTION OF 1864

The Political Scene: The apparent inability of the Union armies to end Confederate resistance increased the sentiment for peace, causing many leading Republicans to oppose Lincoln's renomination.

Conventions and Nominees: The Republicans (styling themselves the National Union party) met at Baltimore in June and renominated Lincoln. War-Democrat Andrew Johnson of Tennessee became the Vice-Presidential candidate. The Democrats meeting at Chicago in August nominated a ticket of General George B. McClellan of New Jersey and George H. Pendleton of Ohio.

The Campaign: The Democratic platform pronounced the war a failure and demanded a cessation of hostilities and the restoration of peace on the basis of the Federal Union of States. But spectacular Union victories at Mobile Bay, Atlanta, and in the Shenandoah Valley destroyed this peace platform, and insured Lincoln's victory.

Results of 1864 Election:

Presidential Candidate	Party	Electoral Votes	Popular Vote Total	Percentage	Vice-Presidential Candidate
Abraham Lincoln	Republican	212	2,219,362	55.1	Andrew Johnson
George McClellan	Democratic	21	1,805,063	44.9	George Pendleton
Votes not cast	—	1	—	—	Votes not cast

Comments: John Wilkes Booth assassinated Lincoln, who was succeeded on April 15, 1865, by Andrew Johnson.

ELECTION OF 1868

The Political Scene: President Johnson and the Republican leadership fell out over Reconstruction policies. The Senate failed by one vote of removing the President by impeachment in May 1868.

Conventions and Nominees: The Republicans met (as the Union Republican party) at Chicago in May and selected General Ulysses S. Grant of Illinois with Schuyler Colfax of Indiana as his running mate. The Democrats meeting in Tammany Hall, New York City, in July drafted Horatio Seymour of New York after 21 ballots and complex maneuverings had failed to produce a candidate. The Vice-Presidential nod went to Francis P. Blair of Missouri.

The Campaign: In 1868 and for a generation thereafter, the Republicans used the "bloody shirt" tactic, attempting to label the Democrats as the party of secession and treason.

Results of 1868 Election:

Presidential Candidate	Party	Electoral Votes	Popular Vote Total	Percentage	Vice-Presidential Candidate
Ulysses S. Grant	Republican	214	3,013,313	52.7	Schuyler Colfax
Horatio Seymour	Democratic	80	2,703,933	47.3	Francis P. Blair, Jr.

Comments: Texas, Virginia, and Mississippi were not readmitted to the Union until 1870, therefore they cast no votes in this election. Grant greatly benefited from black votes in the South.

ELECTION OF 1872

The Political Scene: Evidence of corruption within his administration and disagreement with his Southern policy led many Republicans to oppose Grant's renomination.

Conventions and Nominees: When it became apparent, however, that Grant would be renominated, a group of dissenters calling themselves the Liberal Republican party met at Cincinnati in May and nominated a ticket of Horace Greeley of New York and B. Gratz Brown of Missouri. Greeley's nomination provided a dilemma for the Democrats. Greeley had consistently criticized their party, but to nominate someone else would serve only to reelect Grant. Accordingly, the Democrats in convention at Baltimore in July accepted Greeley and Brown. The Republicans at Philadelphia in June had unanimously renominated Grant.

The Campaign: Although tariff and currency questions were debated to some extent, the Republicans relied on Grant's war record to overcome the scandals. Most Democratic voters reacted unenthusiastically to Greeley.

Results of 1872 Election:

Presidential Candidate	Party	Electoral Votes	Popular Vote Total	Percentage	Vice-Presidential Candidate	Electoral Votes
Ulysses S. Grant	Republican	286	3,597,375	55.6	Henry Wilson	286
Horace Greeley	Democratic, Liberal Republican	—	2,833,711	43.8	B. Gratz Brown	47
Thomas A. Hendricks	Democratic	42	—	—	Other candidates	19
B. Gratz Brown	Democratic, Liberal Republican	18	—	—	Votes not cast	14
Other candidates		3	—	—		—
Votes not cast		17	—	—		—

Comments: Greeley died after the election and his electoral votes went to other candidates.

ELECTION OF 1876

The Political Scene: Growing national indignation at the scandals of Grant's second administration caused both parties to seek Presidential candidates associated with reform government.

Conventions and Nominees: The Republicans met at Cincinnati in June to select Rutherford B. Hayes of Ohio on the seventh ballot after the reform element had blocked the nomination of James G. Blaine. William A. Wheeler of New York was the Vice-Presidential candidate. Samuel J. Tilden of New York, who was acclaimed for his part in breaking up the notorious Tweed Ring, received a first-ballot nomination from the Democrats at St. Louis in June. Thomas A. Hendricks of Indiana was named for the Vice-Presidency. The inflationary Greenback party named Peter Cooper of New York and Samuel F. Carey of Ohio.

The Campaign: Hayes's good record as governor of Ohio somewhat blunted Democratic efforts to capitalize on the corruption of the Grant regime. Tilden waged a very cautious campaign and probably did not pay enough attention to the "solid South."

Results of 1876 Election:

Presidential Candidate	Party	Electoral Votes	Popular Vote Total	Percentage	Vice-Presidential Candidate
Rutherford B. Hayes	Republican	185	4,035,924	47.9	William A. Wheeler
Samuel J. Tilden	Democratic	184	4,287,670	50.9	Thomas A. Hendricks
Peter Cooper	Greenback	—	82,797	1.0	Samuel F. Carey

Comments: When the returns came in, the 19 electoral votes of South Carolina, Florida, and Louisiana were in dispute. After months of controversy over rival sets of returns, Congress established an electoral commission composed of five senators, five representatives, and five members of the Supreme Court to determine the valid returns. The commissioners—eight Republicans and seven Democrats—voted along strict party lines to award the 19 votes and the Presidency to Hayes.

ELECTION OF 1880

The Political Scene: Throughout the entire period of the "Gilded Age," few significant issues divided the two parties. This was particularly true in 1880 when, appealing to the veteran vote, both Republicans and Democrats nominated former generals.

Conventions and Nominees: The Republicans met in Chicago in June to choose "dark horse" James A. Garfield of Ohio on the 36th ballot, after reform or "Mugwump" delegates had blocked a proposed third term for Grant and a drive for James G. Blaine had collapsed. Chester A. Arthur of New York was named for the Vice-Presidency. Winfield S. Hancock of Pennsylvania and William H. English of Indiana comprised the ticket selected by the Democrats at Cincinnati in June. The Greenback party nominated a third general, James B. Weaver of Iowa, with B. J. Chambers of Texas named for the Vice-Presidency.

The Campaign: Personal attacks on the candidates characterized the campaign. The Democrats emphasized Garfield's involvement in the Crédit Mobilier Scandal, while the Republicans harped on Hancock's inexperience and naiveté.

Results of 1880 Election:

Presidential Candidate	Party	Electoral Votes	Popular Vote Total	Percentage	Vice-Presidential Candidate
James A. Garfield	Republican	214	4,454,433	48.3	Chester A. Arthur
Winfield S. Hancock	Democratic	155	4,444,976	48.2	William English
James B. Weaver	Greenback	—	308,649	3.3	B. J. Chambers

Comments: In July 1881 Charles J. Guiteau, a deranged and disappointed office-seeker, shot Garfield, who died on September 19, 1881. Arthur succeeded to the Presidency the following day.

ELECTION OF 1884

The Political Scene: Although President by accident, Arthur made a respectable record in the office. He failed, however, to build up enough support for a nomination in his own right.

Conventions and Nominees: Despite a challenge from Arthur, James G. Blaine of Maine succeeded in this his third try for the Republican nomination. The Chicago convention meeting in June then picked John A. Logan of Illinois as his running mate. The Democrats convening in Chicago on July 8 nominated Grover Cleveland of New York and Thomas A. Hendricks of Indiana.

The Campaign: In what has been remembered as the dirtiest campaign in American history, Cleveland was charged with fathering an illegitimate child, and Blaine was abused for alleged shady practices while Speaker of the House. Many prominent "Mugwump" Republicans refused to support Blaine and endorsed Cleveland.

Results of 1884 Election:

Presidential Candidate	Party	Electoral Votes	Popular Vote Total	Percentage	Vice-Presidential Candidate
Grover Cleveland	Democratic	219	4,875,971	48.5	Thomas A. Hendricks
James G. Blaine	Republican	182	4,852,234	48.3	John A. Logan
Benjamin F. Butler	Greenback	—	175,066	1.7	A. M. West
John P. St. John	Prohibition	—	150,957	1.5	William Daniel

Comments: Just prior to election day, one of Blaine's supporters referred to the Democrats as the party of "Rum, Romanism and Rebellion," a slur on Irish Catholic voters that probably caused Blaine to lose New York State and, hence, the election.

ELECTION OF 1888

The Political Scene: Cleveland's firm, honest, and conservative administration gained him a great deal of respect, but at the same time offended powerful pressure groups such as the Grand Army of the Republic and the tariff protectionists.

Conventions and Nominees: The Democrats renominated Cleveland by acclamation in St. Louis in June. Allen G. Thurman of Ohio joined him on the ticket. In a convention marked with much intrigues and bargaining, the Republicans named Benjamin Harrison of Indiana and Levi P. Morton of New York at Chicago in June.

The Campaign: The Democrats condemned the inequities of the high protective tariff. The Republicans replied that the system of protection served the interests of America over those of Europe.

Results of 1888 Election:

Presidential Candidate	Party	Electoral Votes	Popular Vote Total	Percentage	Vice-Presidential Candidate
Benjamin Harrison	Republican	233	5,445,269	47.8	Levi P. Morton
Grover Cleveland	Democratic	168	5,540,365	48.6	Allen G. Thurman
Clinton B. Fisk	Prohibition	—	250,122	2.2	John A. Brooks
Aaron J. Streeter	Union Labor	—	147,606	1.3	C. E. Cunningham

Comments: The Republicans managed to turn part of the Irish vote against Cleveland, when, on a pretext, a foolish letter favoring Cleveland over Harrison was obtained from the British Minister in Washington.

ELECTION OF 1892

The Political Scene: Popular anger with veteran and tariff legislation combined with a growing militancy among farmers to hand the Republicans a stunning defeat in the midterm elections of 1890 and brighten Democratic prospects for regaining the Presidency.

Conventions and Nominees: Both parties met in June, the Democrats at Chicago and the Republicans at Minneapolis, to renominate their standard-bearers of 1888—Cleveland and Harrison. For the Vice-Presidency, the Democrats chose Adlai E. Stevenson of Illinois; the Republicans, Whitelaw Reid of New York. The Populist or People's party held its first national nominating convention at Omaha in July, endorsing James B. Weaver of Iowa and James G. Field of Virginia.

Campaign Issues: Debate centered on controversial measures of the Harrison administration together with the demand for the free and unlimited coinage of silver and the general agrarian unrest.

Results of 1892 Election:

Presidential Candidate	Party	Electoral Votes	Popular Vote Total	Percentage	Vice-Presidential Candidate
Grover Cleveland	Democratic	277	5,556,982	46.0	Adlai E. Stevenson
Benjamin Harrison	Republican	145	5,191,466	43.0	Whitelaw Reid
James B. Weaver	Populist	22	1,029,960	8.5	James G. Field
John Bidwell	Prohibition	—	271,111	2.2	James B. Cranfill

Comments: The Populists became the first third party since 1860 to win any electoral votes.

ELECTION OF 1896

The Political Scene: The Panic of 1893 struck with full force after Cleveland's inauguration, and the subsequent "hard times" were blamed on the Democrats. It appeared possible that the Populists could replace the Democrats as the second major party.

Conventions and Nominees: The Republican convention at St. Louis in June nominated William McKinley of Ohio on the first ballot and Garrett Hobart of New Jersey as his running mate. The Democrats meeting at Chicago in July named William Jennings Bryan of Nebraska on the fifth ballot. Arthur Sewall of Maine was selected for the Vice-Presidential nomination. The Populists at their St. Louis convention in July accepted Bryan, but named Thomas E. Watson of Georgia for the Vice-Presidency.

The Campaign: Bryan's stand for the "free and unlimited coinage of silver" brought down on him the fury of the country's conservative interests. McKinley conducted a "front porch" campaign, but a strenuous and expensive effort was carried on in his behalf under the direction of Mark Hanna.

Results of 1896 Election:

Presidential Candidate	Party	Electoral Votes	Popular Vote Total	Percentage	Vice-Presidential Candidate
William McKinley	Republican	271	7,113,734	51.0	Garret Hobart
William J. Bryan	Democratic-Populist	176	6,516,722	46.7	Arthur Sewall / Thomas E. Watson
John M. Palmer	National Democratic	—	135,456	.97	Simon Buckner
Joshua Levering	Prohibition	—	131,285	.94	Hale Johnson

Comments: Bryan, whose "Cross of Gold" speech is perhaps the most famous ever made at a convention, failed to win any of the nation's industrial states, indicating the limited appeal of the free-silver issue.

ELECTION OF 1900

The Political Scene: The successful conclusion of the Spanish-American War and returning prosperity buoyed Republican hopes for another Presidential victory.

Conventions and Nominees: At the Republicans' Philadelphia convention in June, McKinley was unanimously renominated and war hero Theodore Roosevelt of New York was selected for the Vice-Presidency. The Democrats met at Kansas City, Missouri, in July to choose Bryan again. Adlai E. Stevenson of Illinois was named for Vice-President. This year Eugene V. Debs of Indiana received the first of his five Presidential nominations by the Socialist party.

The Campaign: Theodore Roosevelt did most of the campaigning for the Republican ticket, stressing the "full dinner pail" of McKinley prosperity and the national pride in territories acquired from Spain. Bryan once more endorsed free silver, but called imperialism the paramount issue. He also criticized the growth of the giant trusts.

Results of 1900 Election:

Presidential Candidate	Party	Electoral Votes	Popular Vote Total	Percentage	Vice-Presidential Candidate
William McKinley	Republican	292	7,219,828	51.7	Theodore Roosevelt
William J. Bryan	Democratic	155	6,358,160	45.5	Adlai E. Stevenson
John C. Wolley	Prohibition	—	210,200	1.5	Henry B. Metcalf
Eugene V. Debs	Socialist	—	95,744	.7	Job Harriman

Comments: McKinley, who was shot by anarchist Leon Czolgosz at the Pan-American Exposition in Buffalo, died on September 14, 1901. At the age of 42, Roosevelt became the youngest President in history.

ELECTION OF 1904

The Political Scene: Roosevelt's moderately progressive policies, his energetic regimen, and his obvious relish of the Presidency made him the most popular President since Lincoln.

Conventions and Nominees: Mark Hanna's death early in 1904 removed the only man capable of challenging Roosevelt for the Presidential nomination. The Republican convention meeting at Chicago in June gave "T.R." its unanimous vote and chose Charles W. Fairbanks of Indiana to run with him. Having lost twice with the progressive Bryan, the Democrats turned to a more conservative candidate, Judge Alton B. Parker of New York. The convention, which met at St. Louis in July, then named Henry G. Davis of West Virginia for Vice-President.

The Campaign: Parker, who endorsed the gold standard, was portrayed by the Democrats as a safe, conservative candidate. A colorless figure, he could not hope to match Roosevelt's popular appeal.

Results of 1904 Election:

Presidential Candidate	Party	Electoral Votes	Popular Vote Total	Percentage	Vice-Presidential Candidate
Theodore Roosevelt	Republican	336	7,628,831	56.4	Charles W. Fairbanks
Alton B. Parker	Democratic	140	5,084,533	37.6	Henry G. Davis
Eugene V. Debs	Socialist	—	402,714	3.0	Benjamin Hanford
Silas C. Swallow	Prohibition	—	259,163	1.9	George W. Carroll

Comments: After his great victory, Roosevelt announced that he would not be a candidate for a third term, a pledge that was to haunt him in 1912.

ELECTION OF 1908

The Political Scene: Roosevelt, the unchallenged leader of his party, determined to pick his successor. Following Parker's decisive defeat, the Democrats were ready to return to Bryan.

Conventions and Nominees: The Republican conclave at Chicago in June ratified Roosevelt's choice of his Secretary of War William Howard Taft of Ohio and named James S. Sherman of New York to run with him. The Democrats meeting at Denver in July picked a ticket of Bryan and John W. Kern of Indiana.

The Campaign: In a dull campaign, Bryan promised to revise the tariff downward; Taft replied that he also intended to work for a downward revision.

Results of 1908 Election:

Presidential Candidate	Party	Electoral Votes	Popular Vote Total	Percentage	Vice-Presidential Candidate
William H. Taft	Republican	321	7,679,114	51.6	James S. Sherman
William J. Bryan	Democratic	162	6,410,665	43.0	John W. Kern
Eugene V. Debs	Socialist	—	420,858	2.8	Benjamin Hanford
Eugene W. Chafin	Prohibition	—	252,704	1.7	Aaron S. Watkins

Comments: Bryan was the only major party candidate in American history to run three unsuccessful races for the Presidency.

ELECTION OF 1912

The Political Scene: The opposition of progressive Republicans to Taft's policies led to an open rupture of the party, with Theodore Roosevelt leading the insurgents.

Conventions and Nominees: When the Republican convention meeting at Chicago in June decided a contest for disputed delegate seats in favor of Taft, Roosevelt ordered his delegates to abstain from voting. Taft and Sherman were renominated on the first ballot, but Roosevelt's delegates became the nucleus of the Progressive or "Bull Moose" party, which met in Chicago in August to nominate Roosevelt and Hiram Johnson of California. The Democrats convening in Baltimore (June 25–July 2) produced a drawn-out but exciting contest. Champ Clark of Missouri obtained a majority on the 10th ballot but could not reach the necessary two thirds. On the 46th ballot, the delegates chose Woodrow Wilson of New Jersey. Thomas R. Marshall of Indiana was selected for the Vice-Presidency.

The Campaign: With Wilson, Roosevelt, and Socialist nominee Eugene V. Debs all campaigning as reform candidates, the voters were asked to decide which man could best implement progressive policies. Wilson's New Freedom program emphasized dissolution of the great trusts and the return to free competition. Roosevelt's New Nationalism stressed regulation of big business by the federal government.

Results of 1912 Election:

Presidential Candidate	Party	Electoral Votes	Popular Vote Total	Percentage	Vice-Presidential Candidate
Woodrow Wilson	Democratic	435	6,301,254	41.8	Thomas R. Marshall
Theodore Roosevelt	Progressive	88	4,127,788	27.4	Hiram Johnson
William H. Taft	Republican	8	3,485,831	23.1	{ James S. Sherman / Nicholas M. Butler
Eugene V. Debs	Socialist	—	901,255	6.0	Emil Seidel
Eugene Chafin	Prohibition	—	209,644	1.4	Aaron S. Watkins

Comments: Three-quarters of the popular vote went to the reform candidates, indicating the strength of the progressive movement in the country. The Republican split insured Wilson's election.

ELECTION OF 1916

The Political Scene: The question of possible American involvement in World War I overshadowed the domestic controversies of the Wilson administration.

Conventions and Nominees: The Republicans nominated Charles Evans Hughes of New York and Charles W. Fairbanks of Indiana at their convention at Chicago in June. The Progressive party disintegrated when Theodore Roosevelt refused to be its candidate again. The Democrats at St. Louis in June renominated Wilson and Marshall.

The Campaign: The Democrats went before the electorate as the party of peace, using the slogan "Wilson and Peace with Honor, or Hughes with Roosevelt and War." Hughes had the difficult task of reconciling the belligerent Theodore Roosevelt with his antiwar supporters among German-Americans and other groups.

Results of 1916 Election:

Presidential Candidate	Party	Electoral Votes	Popular Vote Total	Percentage	Vice-Presidential Candidate
Woodrow Wilson	Democratic	277	9,131,511	49.3	Thomas R. Marshall
Charles E. Hughes	Republican	254	8,548,935	46.1	Charles W. Fairbanks
Allan L. Benson	Socialist	—	585,974	3.2	George R. Kirkpatrick
J. Frank Hanly	Prohibition	—	220,505	1.2	Ira Landrith

Comments: Wilson's carrying of California's electoral vote proved decisive.

ELECTION OF 1920

The Political Scene: An immense reaction against the idealism of the Wilson years and the sacrifices entailed by World War I characterized the mood of the American people, who were anxious to return to normalcy.

Conventions and Nominees: The Republican choice fell upon "dark horse" Warren G. Harding, an Ohio editor, whose selection on the 10th ballot at Chicago on June 12, came after a meeting of party leaders in the famous "smoke-filled room" of the Blackstone Hotel. Calvin Coolidge of Massachusetts, who had won popular acclaim for his opposition to the Boston police strike, received the Vice-Presidential nod.

For the Democrats, Wilson probably desired a third nomination, but his physical incapacity and political unpopularity made this impossible. The San Francisco convention chose a relative unknown in James M. Cox of Ohio on the 44th ballot on July 6th and Franklin D. Roosevelt of New York, the possessor of a magnetic name, as his running mate.

The Campaign: The League of Nations was the most debated campaign topic, with Cox supporting American entry into the world body and Harding straddling the issue.

Results of 1920 Election:

Presidential Candidate	Party	Electoral Votes	Popular Vote Total	Percentage	Vice-Presidential Candidate
Warren G. Harding	Republican	404	16,153,115	60.3	Calvin Coolidge
James M. Cox	Democratic	127	9,133,092	34.1	Franklin D. Roosevelt
Eugene V. Debs	Socialist	—	915,490	3.4	Seymour Stedman
Parley P. Christensen	Farmer-Labor	—	265,229	1.0	Max S. Hayes

Comments: The massive Republican victory represented more of a rejection of Wilson and the Democrats than a personal mandate for Harding, who died in office after a scandal-marred administration and was succeeded by Calvin Coolidge on August 3, 1923.

ELECTION OF 1924

The Political Scene: The cautious conservatism and New England frugality of Calvin Coolidge reduced the political capital the Democrats hoped to make out of the Harding administration's scandals.
Conventions and Nominees: The Republican convention at Cleveland in June chose Coolidge with Charles G. Dawes of Illinois. The Democratic convention in New York City lasted from June 24 until July 29, and the resulting contest between Alfred E. Smith and William Gibbs McAdoo led to the most ballots ever taken in a Presidential nominating convention. Finally after Smith and McAdoo had withdrawn, the delegates nominated John W. Davis of West Virginia on the 103d ballot. Charles W. Bryan of Nebraska was the Vice-Presidential selection. Dissident farm and labor elements in both parties formed the Progressive party, which named a ticket of Robert M. LaFollette of Wisconsin and Burton K. Wheeler of Montana at a convention held in Cleveland in July.
The Campaign: The bitter Democratic convention destroyed what little chance the party had of unseating Coolidge. Both major candidates concentrated their fire on LaFollette rather than each other.

Results of 1924 Election:

Presidential Candidate	Party	Electoral Votes	Popular Vote		Vice-Presidential Candidate
			Total	Percentage	
Calvin Coolidge	Republican	382	15,719,921	54.0	Charles G. Dawes
John W. Davis	Democratic	136	8,386,704	28.8	Charles W. Bryan
Robert M. LaFollette	Progressive	13	4,832,532	16.6	Burton K. Wheeler

Comments: LaFollette won the electoral vote of Wisconsin.

ELECTION OF 1928

The Political Scene: In the summer of 1927, Coolidge announced "I do not choose to run for President . . ." Despite the efforts of a "draft Coolidge" movement, most Republicans were willing to turn to another candidate.
Conventions and Nominees: The Republicans met at Kansas City, Missouri, in June and nominated a ticket of Herbert Hoover of California and Charles Curtis of Kansas. The Democrats meeting at Houston in June needed only one ballot to name Alfred E. Smith of New York for the Presidency and Joseph T. Robinson of Arkansas for the Vice-Presidency.
The Campaign: Smith, who differed with Hoover on the issues of prohibition, public power, and agriculture, found it difficult to make a dent in the public satisfaction with Republican prosperity.

Results of 1928 Election:

Presidential Candidate	Party	Electoral Votes	Popular Vote		Vice-Presidential Candidate
			Total	Percentage	
Herbert C. Hoover	Republican	444	21,437,277	58.22	Charles Curtis
Alfred E. Smith	Democratic	87	15,007,698	40.8	Joseph T. Robinson
Norman M. Thomas	Socialist	—	265,583	.7	James Maurer

Comments: Smith, the first Roman Catholic candidate nominated by a major party, lost many votes particularly in the South because of his religion, but gained many others for the same reason in the Northeast and Midwest.

ELECTION OF 1932

The Political Scene: The Wall Street crash of 1929 and the subsequent economic depression made a Democratic victory almost certain and quickened the race for the party's nomination.
Conventions and Nominees: The Republicans meeting at Chicago in June renominated Hoover and Curtis. The Democrats held their convention during the same month in the same city. Franklin D. Roosevelt of New York, who had outdistanced a large field of contenders in the preconvention maneuvering, was nominated on the fourth ballot with John N. Garner of Texas as his running mate.
The Campaign: Roosevelt promised the country a New Deal and a willingness to experiment with different approaches in an effort to end the economic crisis. Hoover warned of even greater difficulties if the Democrats won.

Results of 1932 Election:

Presidential Candidate	Party	Electoral Votes	Popular Vote		Vice-Presidential Candidate
			Total	Percentage	
Franklin D. Roosevelt	Democratic	472	22,829,501	57.4	John Nance Garner
Herbert C. Hoover	Republican	59	15,760,684	39.6	Charles Curtis
Norman M. Thomas	Socialist	—	884,649	2.2	James Maurer

Comments: Roosevelt's landslide victory carried into office many Democratic Congressmen who were to help implement his program.

ELECTION OF 1936

The Political Scene: New Deal policies enraged political conservatives, but gained the Democrats many new supporters.
Conventions and Nominees: Delegates convening in Cleveland in June named a Republican ticket of Alfred M. Landon of Kansas and Frank Knox of Illinois. The Democrats met later in the month at Philadelphia to renominate Roosevelt and Garner by acclamation. The convention also abolished the two-thirds rule for choosing candidates, making a simple majority sufficient. Father Charles E. Coughlin, Dr. Francis Townsend, and Gerald L. K. Smith, all radical critics of the New Deal, formed the Union party at Cleveland in August and nominated William Lemke of North Dakota and Thomas C. O'Brien of Massachusetts.
The Campaign: The Republicans attacked Roosevelt and the New Deal for allegedly building a giant and wasteful bureaucracy. Roosevelt was content to run on his record.

Results of 1936 Election:

Presidential Candidate	Party	Electoral Votes	Popular Vote		Vice-Presidential Candidate
			Total	Percentage	
Franklin D. Roosevelt	Democratic	523	27,757,333	60.8	John Nance Garner
Alfred M. Landon	Republican	8	16,684,231	36.5	Frank Knox
William Lemke	Union	—	892,267	2.0	Thomas C. O'Brien

Comments: Roosevelt won the most sweeping electoral victory in modern history, carrying every state but Maine and Vermont.

ELECTION OF 1940

The Political Scene: With the outbreak of World War II in 1939, American neutrality once again became the dominant political issue in an election year.
Conventions and Nominees: The Republicans convened in Philadelphia in June. A tremendous groundswell of public opinion for Wendell L. Willkie of New York enabled him to overcome the early lead of Thomas E. Dewey and Robert A. Taft and win the nomination on the sixth ballot. His running mate was Charles L. McNary of Oregon. Roosevelt won his third nomination from the Democratic convention held in Chicago in July. At his insistence, Henry Wallace of Iowa replaced Garner for the Vice-Presidency.
The Campaign: The Democratic platform and Roosevelt were pledged against participation in foreign wars, except in

case of attack. Willkie endorsed most New Deal measures and did not differ substantially from Roosevelt on foreign policy, but he stressed that Roosevelt's attempt to win a third term threatened democratic government.

Results of 1940 Election:

Presidential Candidate	Party	Electoral Votes	Popular Vote Total	Percentage	Vice-Presidential Candidate
Franklin D. Roosevelt	Democratic	449	27,313,041	54.7	Henry A. Wallace
Wendell L. Willkie	Republican	82	22,348,480	44.8	Charles L. McNary

Comments: Roosevelt, destined to win a fourth term as well, was the only man to win more than two elections or to serve more than eight years as President.

ELECTION OF 1944

The Political Scene: In the nation's third wartime election, Roosevelt benefited from the general reluctance "to change horses in midstream."

Conventions and Nominees: The Republicans held their convention at Chicago in June. Thomas E. Dewey of New York received all but one vote on the first ballot, and John W. Bricker of Ohio was the unanimous choice as his running mate. The Democrats convening at Chicago in July once again chose Roosevelt, but Wallace had earned the enmity of many party leaders, and the delegates turned to Harry S Truman of Missouri for the Vice-Presidency.

The Campaign: The Republicans called for new political leadership for the work of peace and reconstruction, but agreed with the Democrats in the necessity of American participation in a postwar international organization.

Results of 1944 Election:

Presidential Candidate	Party	Electoral Votes	Popular Vote Total	Percentage	Vice-Presidential Candidate
Franklin D. Roosevelt	Democratic	432	25,612,610	53.3	Harry S Truman
Thomas E. Dewey	Republican	99	22,017,617	45.9	John W. Bricker

Comments: On April 12, 1945, Roosevelt died and was succeeded on the same day by Truman.

ELECTION OF 1948

The Political Scene: Deep splits within the Democratic party and an apparent public desire for a change portended a Republican victory.

Conventions and Nominees: The Republicans meeting at Philadelphia in June again nominated Thomas E. Dewey. Earl Warren of California was the Vice-Presidential choice. The Democrats met in the same city the following month and unenthusiastically nominated a ticket of Truman and Alben W. Barkley of Kentucky. Several Southern delegations that were opposed to the party's civil rights platform bolted the convention and named a States' Rights or "Dixiecrat" ticket of Strom Thurmond of South Carolina for President and Fielding L. Wright of Mississippi for Vice-President. A fourth party, the Progressive, which was composed largely of liberal and left-wing Democrats critical of Truman's foreign policy, ran Henry A. Wallace of Iowa and Glenn Taylor of Idaho.

The Campaign: A distinct underdog because of the Dixiecrat and Progressive tickets, Truman undertook a vigorous campaign in which he castigated the Republican-controlled 80th Congress as a "do nothing" one. Dewey, who was indicated the certain winner in the public opinion polls, conducted a very cool and careful campaign.

Results of 1948 Election:

Presidential Candidate	Party	Electoral Votes	Popular Vote Total	Percentage	Vice-Presidential Candidate
Harry S Truman	Democratic	303	24,179,345	49.6	Alben W. Barkley
Thomas E. Dewey	Republican	189	21,991,291	45.1	Earl Warren
J. Strom Thurmond	States' Rights	39	1,176,125	2.4	Fielding L. Wright
Henry A. Wallace	Progressive	—	1,157,326	2.4	Glenn Taylor

Comments: Truman's upset victory reflected his ability to hold almost the entire labor and Negro vote and to carry the key Midwestern farm states of Ohio, Iowa, and Wisconsin.

ELECTION OF 1952

The Political Scene: Truman announced early in the year that he would not be a candidate for a third term. In any case, the Korean War had dimmed his prospects of reelection.

Conventions and Nominees: General Dwight D. Eisenhower beat off the strong challenge of Robert A. Taft to win the nomination of the Republican convention that was held in Chicago in July. Richard M. Nixon of California received the Vice-Presidential designation. The Democrats convened in Chicago later in the same month and named a ticket of Adlai E. Stevenson of Illinois and John J. Sparkman of Alabama.

The Campaign: The Republicans used the slogan "Communism, Korea, and corruption," and Eisenhower promised a personal visit to Korea. Stevenson, a first-rate campaigner, was nonetheless forced on the defensive.

Results of 1952 Election:

Presidential Candidate	Party	Electoral Votes	Popular Vote Total	Percentage	Vice-Presidential Candidate
Dwight D. Eisenhower	Republican	442	33,936,234	55.1	Richard M. Nixon
Adlai E. Stevenson	Democratic	89	27,314,992	44.4	John J. Sparkman

Comments: Eisenhower carried the Republicans to victory in both houses of Congress, marking the only time since 1931 or after that the party has controlled the executive and legislative branches of government at the same time.

ELECTION OF 1956

The Political Scene: Suffering a serious heart attack in September 1955, Eisenhower waited until the end of February 1956 before announcing that he would run for a second term.

Conventions and Nominees: Senator Estes Kefauver of Tennessee conducted an extensive primary campaign; however, he withdrew in favor of Stevenson a week before the Democrats met in Chicago in August. Kefauver then won a spirited contest with John F. Kennedy for the Vice-Presidency. The Republicans meeting in San Francisco in August renominated Eisenhower and Nixon.

The Campaign: Stevenson proposed the possibility of ending the draft system and an agreement with the Soviet Union on Cold War issues. In addition, the Democrats referred to Eisenhower's health and the possibility of Nixon's succession to the Presidency. The Republicans emphasized the "peace and prosperity" of the Eisenhower years.

Results of 1956 Election:

Presidential Candidate	Party	Electoral Votes	Popular Vote Total	Percentage	Vice-Presidential Candidate
Dwight D. Eisenhower	Republican	457	35,590,472	57.4	Richard M. Nixon
Adlai E. Stevenson	Democratic	73	26,022,752	42.0	Estes Kefauver
Walter B. Jones	No party	1	—	—	

Comments: Eisenhower became the first winning Presidential candidate since Zachary Taylor in 1848 to fail to carry his party to victory in either the House of Representatives or the Senate.

ELECTION OF 1960

The Political Scene: The mood of the country was somewhat restive, primarily because of economic recessions in 1953, 1957, and 1960, but also because of increasing disquiet over issues relating to civil rights and race relations.

Conventions and Nominations: John F. Kennedy of Massachusetts entered several Presidential primaries to disprove alleged liabilities of his youth and his Roman Catholic religion; victories in key contests in Wisconsin and West Virginia assured his first ballot victory at the Democratic Convention in Los Angeles (July 11–15), where he chose Lyndon B. Johnson of Texas as his running mate. Vice-President Richard Nixon of California easily overcame a challenge from Nelson Rockefeller of New York to win a first ballot endorsement from the Republican National Convention at Chicago (July 25–28).

The Campaign: Nixon emphasized the unity, strength, and stability that he claimed the Republicans had given the country during the previous eight years. Kennedy complained of stagnation and apathy in Washington and decline of American prestige abroad, promising to get the country moving again and, particularly, to revitalize the economy.

Results of 1960 Election:

Presidential Candidate	Party	Electoral Votes	Popular Vote Total	Percentage	Vice-Presidential Candidate
John F. Kennedy	Democratic	303	34,226,731	49.7	Lyndon B. Johnson
Richard M. Nixon	Republican	219	34,108,157	49.5	Henry Cabot Lodge
Harry F. Byrd	No party	15	440,298	.6	—

Comments: Kennedy built his victory on the large industrial states of the Northeast and key states in the South, where Johnson's candidacy helped. Kennedy was assassinated on November 22, 1963, in Dallas by Lee Harvey Oswald.

ELECTION OF 1964

The Political Scene: In less than a year in office, Lyndon Johnson had compiled a record of legislative achievements that put him in excellent position for the campaign.

Conventions and Nominees: The Republican convention meeting at San Francisco in July witnessed the first victory for the conservative wing of the party in over a generation with the nomination of Barry M. Goldwater of Arizona. William Miller of New York was selected as his running mate. The Democrats convened at Atlantic City in August to nominate Johnson and Hubert H. Humphrey of Minnesota, both of whom were named by acclamation.

The Campaign: The Democrats were happy to run on the record of the Kennedy-Johnson administration, while depicting Goldwater as a dangerous reactionary, Goldwater assailed the Johnson administration for permitting a decline in government morality and efficiency and a deterioration of national prestige abroad.

Results of 1964 Election:

Presidential Candidate	Party	Electoral Votes	Popular Vote Total	Percentage	Vice-Presidential Candidate
Lyndon B. Johnson	Democratic	486	43,129,484	61.1	Hubert H. Humphrey
Barry M. Goldwater	Republican	52	27,178,188	38.5	W. E. Miller

Comments: Johnson gained a larger percentage of the popular vote than any candidate in modern times. Only Franklin Roosevelt in 1936 received more electoral votes.

ELECTION OF 1968

The Political Scene: On March 31, Johnson announced he would not seek reelection following repeated attacks on his Vietnam war policy. Sen. Robert F. Kennedy was assassinated in June following his victory in the California primary. Ronald Reagan and Nelson Rockefeller challenged Richard Nixon for the Republican nomination.

Conventions and Nominees: The Republicans met in Miami in August and nominated Richard Nixon on the first ballot. Spiro T. Agnew was chosen for the Vice-Presidency. At a Chicago convention marred by much turbulence, the Democrats chose Hubert H. Humphrey of Minnesota; Edmund S. Muskie of Maine was the Vice-Presidential nominee. George C. Wallace of Alabama ran as Presidential candidate of the American Independent Party among other designations.

The Campaign: Nixon promised an honorable conclusion of the Vietnam war and the restoration of law and order throughout the country. Humphrey pledged to seek a political solution to the struggle in Vietnam and promised to work toward ending divisiveness in American life. Wallace, an extreme conservative, appeared to hope to force the election into the House of Representatives, where his electors might hold the balance of power.

Results of 1968 Election:

Presidential Candidate	Party	Electoral Votes	Popular Vote Total	Percentage	Vice-Presidential Candidate
Richard M. Nixon	Republican	301	31,785,480	43.4	Spiro T. Agnew
Hubert H. Humphrey	Democratic	191	31,275,165	42.7	Edmund S. Muskie
George C. Wallace	American Independent	46	9,906,473	13.5	Curtis E. LeMay

Comments: Nixon received the lowest percentage of the popular vote for a successful candidate since 1912.

ELECTION OF 1972

The Political Scene: The first Nixon administration reveled in its diplomatic gains abroad, while attempting to diminish the domestic problems of unemployment and inflation. The Democrats attacked Nixon's record on domestic affairs, along with hurling charges against the Committee to Reelect the President, accused of masterminding a break-in at the Democratic headquarters in the Watergate complex.

Conventions and Nominees: The Democrats met in Miami, Florida, in July and nominated Sen. George McGovern on the first ballot. His choice for Vice-President, Sen. Thomas F. Eagleton of Missouri, was endorsed by the convention's acclamation. Eagleton resigned from the ticket in late August, however, and was replaced by R. Sargent Shriver of Maryland. The Republicans met in Miami in August, and the incumbents were nominated without opposition.

The Campaign: Nixon did little active campaigning, using his spectacular trips to Moscow and Peking to give him exposure. McGovern had come from behind to win the Democratic nomination, but his campaign never regained its momentum when his first running mate, Sen. Thomas Eagleton, withdrew following disclosures that he had undergone shock treatment for depression. The Democrats were defeated in a near-record landslide.

Results of 1972 Election:

Presidential Candidates	Party	Electoral Votes	Popular Vote Total	Percentage	Vice-Presidential Candidate
Richard M. Nixon	Republican	520	47,167,319	60.7	Spiro T. Agnew
George S. McGovern	Democratic	17	29,169,504	37.5	R. Sargent Shriver
John G. Schmitz	American	—	1,102,963	1.4	Thomas J. Anderson
John Hospers	Libertarian	1	2,691	—	Theodora Nathan

Comments: Division among the Democrats, with many party conservatives turning to Nixon, contributed to the Republican victory, along with apparent voter apathy regarding the Watergate issue.

FINAL 1976 PRESIDENTIAL ELECTION RESULTS

State	Electoral Vote	Popular Vote				Percentages			
		Carter	Ford	McCarthy	Other	Carter	Ford	McCarthy	Other
Alabama	9	659,170	504,070	—	19,610	56	43	—	1
Alaska	3	44,058	71,555	—	7,961	36	58	—	6
Arizona	6	295,602	418,642	19,229	9,246	40	56	3	1
Arkansas	6	498,604	267,903	639	389	65	35	—	—
California	45	3,742,284	3,882,244	—	179,242	48	50	—	2
Colorado	7	460,801	584,278	26,047	10,314	43	54	2	1
Connecticut	8	647,895	719,261	—	19,199	47	52	—	1
Delaware	3	122,461	109,780	2,432	969	52	47	1	—
Dist. Columbia	3	137,818	27,873	—	3,139	82	17	—	1
Florida	17	1,636,000	1,469,531	23,643	21,457	52	47	1	—
Georgia	12	979,409	483,743	—	—	67	33	—	—
Hawaii	4	147,375	140,003	—	3,923	51	48	—	1
Idaho	4	126,549	204,151	—	10,232	37	60	—	3
Illinois	26	2,271,295	2,364,269	55,939	29,779	48	50	1	1
Indiana	13	1,014,714	1,185,958	—	21,690	46	53	—	1
Iowa	8	619,931	632,863	20,051	6,461	48	49	2	1
Kansas	7	430,421	502,752	13,185	11,487	45	53	1	1
Kentucky	9	615,717	531,852	6,837	12,736	53	46	—	1
Louisiana	10	661,365	587,446	6,490	22,082	52	46	—	2
Maine	4	232,279	236,320	10,874	3,495	48	49	2	1
Maryland	10	759,612	672,661	—	—	53	47	—	—
Massachusetts	14	1,429,475	1,030,276	65,637	22,170	56	40	3	1
Michigan	21	1,696,714	1,893,742	47,905	13,229	47	52	1	—
Minnesota	10	1,070,440	819,395	35,490	24,606	55	42	2	1
Mississippi	7	381,329	366,846	4,074	16,141	50	48	—	2
Missouri	12	998,387	927,443	24,029	3,741	51	48	1	—
Montana	4	149,259	173,703	—	5,772	45	53	—	2
Nebraska	5	233,293	359,219	9,383	4,854	38	59	2	1
Nevada	3	92,479	101,273	—	8,124	46	50	—	4
New Hampshire	4	147,645	185,935	4,095	1,952	43	55	1	1
New Jersey	17	1,444,653	1,509,688	32,717	27,414	48	50	1	1
New Mexico	4	201,148	211,419	—	4,023	48	51	—	1
New York	41	3,389,558	3,100,791	—	177,913	51	46	—	3
North Carolina	13	927,365	741,960	—	8,581	55	44	—	1
North Dakota	3	136,078	153,684	2,952	4,594	46	52	—	2
Ohio	25	2,009,959	2,000,626	58,267	41,604	49	49	1	1
Oklahoma	8	532,442	545,708	14,101	—	49	50	1	—
Oregon	6	490,407	492,120	40,207	7,142	48	48	4	—
Pennsylvania	27	2,328,677	2,205,604	50,584	35,922	50	48	1	1
Rhode Island	4	227,636	181,249	—	1,699	55	44	—	1
South Carolina	8	450,807	346,149	—	5,627	56	43	—	1
South Dakota	4	147,068	151,505	—	2,105	49	50	—	1
Tennessee	10	825,879	633,969	5,004	11,494	56	43	—	1
Texas	26	2,082,319	1,953,300	20,118	16,147	51	48	1	—
Utah	4	182,110	337,908	3,907	17,293	34	62	1	3
Vermont	3	77,798	100,387	4,001	1,716	42	55	2	1
Virginia	12	813,896	836,554	—	46,644	48	49	—	3
Washington	9	717,323	777,732	36,986	23,493	46	50	2	2
West Virginia	6	435,864	314,726	—	—	58	42	—	—
Wisconsin	11	1,040,232	1,004,987	34,943	21,174	49	48	2	1
Wyoming	3	62,239	92,717	624	763	40	59	—	1
Total Popular Votes		**40,825,839**	**39,147,770**	**680,390**	**949,348**				
Total Popular Votes, all candidates		**81,603,346**							

Minor candidates: Roger McBride (Libertarian Party), 171,627; Lester G. Maddox (American Independent Party), 168,264; Thomas Anderson (American Party), 152,513; Peter Camejo (Socialist Workers Party), 90,287; Gus Hall (Communist Party), 58,692; Margaret Wright (People's Party), 49,014; Lyndon H. LaRouche (U.S. Labor Party), 40,043; Benjamin C. Bubar (Prohibition Party), 15,902; Jules Levin (Socialist Labor Party), 9,322; Frank P. Zeidler (Socialist Party), 5,991; Others, 187,693.

ELECTION OF 1976

The Political Scene: Following the turmoil of the second Nixon administration, with the resignation of Spiro T. Agnew and then Nixon himself, Gerald R. Ford hoped to retain the Presidency, a position to which he had never been elected. The Democrats saw an opportunity to regain the White House by stressing the need for a return to "moral" government, while Eugene J. McCarthy of Minnesota, an independent, campaigned on a platform which called for the abolition of the two-party system, one which he felt made the government less responsive to the will of the people.

Conventions and Nominees: In July the Democrats met in New York City, with Jimmy Carter of Georgia virtually assured a first-ballot nomination after a string of primary victories. Walter F. Mondale of Minnesota was chosen the Vice-Presidential nominee. Incumbent Gerald R. Ford of Michigan successfully fought off a conservative challenge by Ronald W. Reagan of California in the Republicans' August convention in Kansas City, Missouri. Robert J. Dole of Kansas was selected by Ford to be his running mate. McCarthy picked Willam Clay Ford of Michigan to share his independent ticket.

RESULTS OF 1976 ELECTION

Presidential Candidate	Party	Electoral Votes	Popular Vote		Vice-Presidential Candidates
			Total	Percentage	
Jimmy Carter	Democratic	297	40,825,839	50.0+	Walter F. Mondale
Gerald R. Ford	Republican	240	39,147,770	47.9	Robert J. Dole
Ronald Reagan	No Party	1	—	—	—

Comments: Carter was the first President elected from a southern state since Zachary Taylor in 1848.

1980 PRESIDENTIAL ELECTION RESULTS BY STATE

SOURCE: The Associated Press

(Preliminary results as of 11/5/80, subject to official canvass)

STATE	CARTER (DEMOCRAT) VOTES			REAGAN (REPUBLICAN) VOTES			ANDERSON (INDEPENDENT) VOTES		
	Popular	%	Electoral	Popular	%	Electoral	Popular	%	Electoral
ALABAMA	624,752	48		636,426	49	9	15,669	1	
ALASKA	31,408	26		66,874	55	3	8,091	7	
ARIZONA	243,498	28		523,124	61	6	75,805	9	
ARKANSAS	397,919	48		402,946	48	6	21,057	3	
CALIFORNIA	3,040,680	36		4,447,266	53	45	727,871	9	
COLORADO	367,895	31		649,389	55	7	130,360	11	
CONNECTICUT	537,407	39		672,648	48	8	168,260	12	
DELAWARE	106,650	45		111,631	47	3	16,344	7	
DISTRICT OF COLUMBIA	124,376	76	3	21,765	13		14,971	9	
FLORIDA	1,358,758	39		1,923,543	55	17	177,328	5	
GEORGIA	868,809	56	12	629,462	41		33,727	2	
HAWAII	135,879	45	4	130,112	43		32,021	11	
IDAHO	109,410	25		290,087	67	4	27,096	6	
ILLINOIS	1,933,545	42		2,325,304	50	26	343,188	7	
INDIANA	834,787	38		1,229,129	56	13	106,773	5	
IOWA	507,825	39		675,199	51	8	114,295	9	
KANSAS	321,729	34		556,146	58	7	66,826	7	
KENTUCKY	605,876	48		626,072	49	9	29,428	2	
LOUISIANA	707,981	46		796,240	52	10	26,198	2	
MAINE	220,387	42		238,156	46	4	53,450	10	
MARYLAND	706,327	47	10	656,255	44		113,452	8	
MASSACHUSETTS	1,048,391	42		1,054,390	42	14	382,044	15	
MICHIGAN	1,659,208	43		1,914,559	49	21	272,948	7	
MINNESOTA	891,569	47	10	820,512	43		165,162	9	
MISSISSIPPI	429,115	48		440,712	50	7	11,811	1	
MISSOURI	916,201	44		1,053,401	51	12	76,336	4	
MONTANA	107,754	32		187,958	57	4	27,035	8	
NEBRASKA	164,270	26		413,338	66	5	44,024	7	
NEVADA	66,468	27		154,570	64	3	17,580	7	
NEW HAMPSHIRE	108,859	28		221,198	58	4	49,295	13	
NEW JERSEY	1,111,980	39		1,495,022	52	17	221,884	8	
NEW MEXICO	164,913	37		245,537	55	4	28,403	6	
NEW YORK	2,627,959	44		2,790,498	47	41	441,863	7	
NORTH CAROLINA	876,102	47		914,974	49	13	52,366	3	
NORTH DAKOTA	76,533	26		187,483	65	3	22,390	8	
OHIO	1,744,040	41		2,202,129	52	25	255,535	6	
OKLAHOMA	392,564	35		666,532	60	8	36,645	3	
OREGON	445,627	39		554,545	48	6	109,253	10	
PENNSYLVANIA	1,929,873	43		2,248,354	50	27	284,090	6	
RHODE ISLAND	185,126	48	4	145,423	37		56,091	14	
SOUTH CAROLINA	422,029	48		445,364	50	8	14,876	2	
SOUTH DAKOTA	103,909	32		198,102	61	4	21,342	7	
TENNESSEE	782,624	48		787,962	49	10	35,892	2	
TEXAS	1,770,138	41		2,418,999	56	26	102,941	2	
UTAH	123,447	21		435,839	73	4	30,191	5	
VERMONT	80,304	39		92,555	44	3	31,242	15	
VIRGINIA	743,241	40		974,880	53	12	91,553	5	
WASHINGTON	582,105	38		761,614	49	9	164,983	11	
WEST VIRGINIA	353,508	49	6	326,645	46		30,499	4	
WISCONSIN	988,255	43		1,089,750	48	11	159,793	7	
WYOMING	49,102	28		110,707	63	3	12,072	7	
TOTAL	34,731,139	41	49	42,968,326	51	489	5,552,349	7	0

U.S. CONGRESSIONAL REPRESENTATIVES UNDER EACH APPORTIONMENT: 1790-1970

State	1790	1800	1810	1820	1830	1840	1850	1860	1870	1880	1890	1900	1910[1]	1930	1940	1950	1960	1970
Alabama	..	..	[2]1	3	5	7	7	6	8	8	9	9	10	9	9	9	8	7
Alaska	..	..	..	..	..	..	..	..	..	..	..	..	..	..	..	..	[2]1	1
Arizona	..	..	..	..	..	..	..	..	..	..	..	..	[2]1	1	2	2	3	4
Arkansas	..	..	..	..	[2]1	1	2	3	4	5	6	7	7	7	7	6	4	4
California	..	..	..	..	..	[2]2	2	3	4	6	7	8	11	20	23	30	38	43
Colorado	..	..	..	..	..	..	..	..	[2]1	1	2	3	4	4	4	4	4	5
Connecticut	5	7	7	7	6	6	4	4	4	4	4	4	5	5	6	6	6	6
Delaware	1	1	1	2	1	1	1	1	1	1	1	1	1	1	1	1	1	1
Florida	..	..	..	..	..	[2]1	1	1	2	2	2	3	4	5	6	8	12	15
Georgia	3	2	4	6	7	9	8	8	7	9	10	11	11	12	10	10	10	10
Hawaii	..	..	..	..	..	..	..	..	..	..	..	..	..	..	..	..	[2]1	2
Idaho	..	..	..	..	..	..	..	..	..	[2]1	1	1	2	2	2	2	2	2
Illinois	..	..	[2]1	1	3	7	9	14	19	20	22	25	27	27	26	25	24	24
Indiana	..	..	[2]1	3	7	10	11	11	13	13	13	13	13	12	11	11	11	11
Iowa	..	..	..	..	..	[2]2	2	6	9	11	11	11	11	9	8	8	7	6
Kansas	..	..	..	..	..	..	..	1	3	7	8	8	8	7	6	6	5	5
Kentucky	2	6	10	12	13	10	10	9	10	11	11	11	11	9	9	8	7	7
Louisiana	..	..	[2]1	3	3	4	4	5	6	6	6	7	8	8	8	8	8	8
Maine	..	..	[3]7	7	8	7	6	5	5	4	4	4	4	3	3	3	2	2
Maryland	6	8	9	9	9	8	6	6	5	6	6	6	6	6	6	6	7	8
Massachusetts	8	14	17	[3]13	13	12	10	11	10	11	12	13	14	16	15	14	14	12
Michigan	..	..	..	..	[2]1	3	4	6	9	11	12	12	13	17	17	18	19	19
Minnesota	..	..	..	..	..	..	[2]2	2	3	5	7	9	10	9	9	9	8	8
Mississippi	..	..	[2]1	1	2	4	5	5	6	7	7	8	8	7	7	6	5	5
Missouri	..	..	..	1	2	5	7	9	13	14	15	16	16	13	13	11	10	10
Montana	..	..	..	..	..	..	..	..	..	[2]1	1	1	2	2	2	2	2	2
Nebraska	..	..	..	..	..	..	..	[2]1	1	3	6	6	6	5	4	4	3	3
Nevada	..	..	..	..	..	..	..	[2]1	1	1	1	1	1	1	1	1	1	1
New Hampshire	3	4	5	6	6	5	4	3	3	3	2	2	2	2	2	2	2	2
New Jersey	4	5	6	6	6	6	5	5	5	7	7	8	10	12	14	14	15	15
New Mexico	..	..	..	..	..	..	..	..	..	..	..	..	[2]1	1	2	2	2	2
New York	6	10	17	27	34	40	34	33	31	33	34	37	43	45	45	43	41	39
North Carolina	5	10	12	13	13	13	9	8	7	8	9	10	10	11	12	12	11	11
North Dakota	..	..	..	..	..	..	..	..	..	[2]1	1	2	3	2	2	2	2	1
Ohio	..	[2]1	6	14	19	21	21	19	20	21	21	21	22	24	23	23	24	23
Oklahoma	..	..	..	..	..	..	..	..	..	..	..	[2]5	8	9	8	6	6	6
Oregon	..	..	..	..	..	..	[2]1	1	1	1	2	2	3	3	4	4	4	4
Pennsylvania	8	13	18	23	26	28	24	25	27	28	30	32	36	34	33	30	27	25
Rhode Island	1	2	2	2	2	2	2	2	2	2	2	2	3	2	2	2	2	2
South Carolina	5	6	8	9	9	9	7	6	4	5	7	7	7	7	6	6	6	6
South Dakota	..	..	..	..	..	..	..	..	..	[2]2	2	2	3	2	2	2	2	2
Tennessee	[2]1	3	6	9	13	11	10	8	10	10	10	10	10	9	10	9	9	8
Texas	..	..	..	..	..	[2]2	2	4	6	11	13	16	18	21	21	22	23	24
Utah	..	..	..	..	..	..	..	..	..	..	[2]1	1	2	2	2	2	2	2
Vermont	..	2	4	6	5	5	4	3	3	3	2	2	2	2	1	1	1	1
Virginia	10	19	22	23	22	21	15	13	11	9	10	10	10	10	9	9	10	10
Washington	..	..	..	..	..	..	..	..	..	[2]1	2	3	5	6	6	7	7	7
West Virginia	..	..	..	..	..	..	..	..	3	4	4	5	6	6	6	6	5	4
Wisconsin	..	..	..	..	..	[2]2	3	6	8	9	10	11	11	10	10	10	10	9
Wyoming	..	..	..	..	..	..	..	..	..	[2]1	1	1	1	1	1	1	1	1
Total	65	106	142	186	213	242	232	237	243	293	332	357	391	435	435	435	437	435

[1] No apportionment was made in 1920. [2] The following representation was added after the several census apportionments indicated when new States were admitted and is included in the above table: First. Tennessee, 1. Second. Ohio, 1. Third. Alabama, 1; Illinois, 1; Indiana, 1; Louisiana, 1; Mississippi, 1. Fifth. Arkansas, 1; Michigan, 1. Sixth. California, 2; Florida, 1; Iowa, 2; Texas, 2; Wisconsin, 2. Seventh. Minnesota, 2; Oregon, 1. Eighth. Nebraska, 1; Nevada, 1. Ninth. Colorado, 1. Tenth. Idaho, 1; Montana, 1; North Dakota, 1; South Dakota, 2; Washington, 1; Wyoming, 1. Eleventh. Utah, 1. Twelfth. Oklahoma, 5. Thirteenth. Arizona, 1; New Mexico, 1. Seventeenth. Alaska, 1; Hawaii, 1. [3] Twenty Members were assigned to Massachusetts, but 7 of these were credited to Maine when that area became a State.

96th CONGRESS: January 3, 1979 —

Democratic members are in roman. Republicans in *italics*.

THE HOUSE OF REPRESENTATIVES

Democrats 276; *Republicans* 159; Total: 435

Speaker: Thomas P. O'Neill, Jr., Mass.
Majority Leader: James C. Wright, Jr., Texas
Majority Whip: John Brademas, Ind.
Minority Leader: *John J. Rhodes, Ariz.*
Minority Whip: *Robert H. Michel, Ill.*
Clerk: Edmund L. Henshaw, Jr.
Sergeant at Arms: Benjamin J. Guthrie
Parliamentarian: William Holmes Brown
Doorkeeper: James T. Molloy
Postmaster: Robert V. Rota
Press Gallery Superintendent: Benjamin C. West
Chaplain: Rev. James David Ford, B.D.

THE SENATE

Democrats 58; *Republicans* 41; Independents 1

President: Walter F. Mondale
President Pro Tempore: Warren G. Magnuson, Wash.
Majority Leader: Robert C. Byrd, W.Va.
Majority Whip: Alan Cranston, Calif.
Minority Leader: *Howard H. Baker, Jr., Tenn.*
Assistant Minority Leader: *Ted Stevens, Alaska*
Secretary: Joseph S. Kimmitt
Assistant Secretary: William A. Ridgely
Sergeant at Arms: Frank N. Hoffmann
Secretary for the Majority: Walter J. Stewart
Secretary for the Minority: William F. Hildenbrand
Chaplain: The Rev. Edward L. R. Elson, S.T.D.

UNITED STATES HOUSE OF REPRESENTATIVES — 1980 ELECTION RESULTS
(as of November 5, 1980)

Source: The Associated Press

COMPOSITION BY PARTY

	Pre-election	Post-election
Democrats	276	242
Republicans	159	192
Independents		1

* = Incumbent   R = Republican   L = Liberal   C = Conservative   I = Independent
+ = Winner   D = Democrat   Lib = Libertarian   RTL = Right to Life

---

ALABAMA (D 4, R 3)

1st District
Edwards (R)* .... ---

2nd District
Wyatt (D) 62,867
Dickinson (R)* ..... 103,556+

3rd District
Nichols (D)* .... ---

4th District
Bevill (D)* .... ---

5th District
Flippo (D)* .... ---

6th District
Clifford (D) 80,738
Smith, A.L. (R) .... 89,613+

7th District
Shelby (D)* .... 119,612+
Bacon (R) 42,676

ALASKA (D 0, R 1)

At Large
Parnell (D) 30,428
Young (R) .... 87,403+

ARIZONA (D 2, R 2)

1st District
Jancek (D) 40,000
Rhodes (R)* .... 136,781+

2nd District
Udall (D)* .... 122,710+
Huff (R) 84,364

3rd District
Stump (D)* .... 141,280+
Croft (R) 66,311

4th District
Miller (D).......... 84,637
Rudd (R)*........... 141,920+

ARKANSAS (D 2, R 2)

1st District
Alexander (D)* ..... ---

2nd District
Reid (D) 39,456
Bethune (R) .... 159,477+

3rd District
Hammerschmidt (R)* . ---

4th District
Anthony, Jr. (D)* .. ---

CALIFORNIA (D 22, R 21)

1st District
Johnson (D)* ...., 107,388
Chappie (R) .... 144,702+

2nd District
Bork (D) 108,423
Clausen (R)* .... 139,835+

3rd District
Matsui (D)* .... 168,682+
Murphy (R) 63,359

4th District
Fazio (D)* .... 132,420+
Dehr (R) 59,983

5th District
Burton, J.L. (D)* .. 100,066+
McQuaid (R) 88,287

6th District
Burton, P. (D)* ..... 91,810+

Spinosa (R) 33,423

7th District
Miller (D)* .... 141,565+
St. Clair (R) 70,203

8th District
Dellums (D)* .... 107,554+
Hughes (R) 75,972

9th District
Stark (D)* .... 89,589+
Kennedy (R) 66,580

10th District
Edwards (D)* .... 100,901+
Lutton (R) 45,234

11th District
Lantos (D) .... 85,203+
Royer (R)* 79,586

12th District
Olsen (D) 36,163
McCloskey (R)* ...... 139,737+

13th District
Mineta (D)* .... 129,188+
Gagne (R) 77,576

14th District
Cerney (D) 79,260
Shumway (R)* .... 132,516+

15th District
Coelho (D)* .... 106,793+
Schwartz (R) 37,423

16th District
Panetta (D)* .... 157,230+
Roth (R) 54,192

17th District
Johnson (D) 53,320
Pashayan (R)* .... 127,939+

18th District
Timmermans (D) 50,029
Thomas (R)* .... 122,639+

19th District
Lodise (D) 36,601
Lagomarsino (R)* .... 160,893+

20th District
Miller, M. (D) 42,275
Goldwater, Jr. (R)* . 195,789+

21st District
Corman (D)* 72,288
Fiedler (R) .... 73,152+

22nd District
O'Donnell (D) 56,407
Moorhead (R)* .... 112,533+

23rd District
Beilenson (D)* ...... 123,038+
Winckler (R) 61,009

24th District
Waxman (D)* .... 91,568+
Cayard (R) 38,631

25th District
Roybal (D)* .... 48,283+
Ferraro (R) 20,665

26th District
Lisoni (D) 39,375
Rousselot (R)* ..... 113,991+

27th District
Peck (D) 97,663
Dornan (R)* .... 106,342+

28th District
Dixon (D)* .... 106,975+
Reid (R) 22,638

29th District
Hawkins (D)* .... 79,100+
Hirt (R) 10,094

30th District
Danielson (D)* ...... 72,995+
Platten (R) 23,683

31st District
Dymally (D) .... 68,160+
Grimshaw (R) 37,447

32nd District
Anderson, G.M. (D)* . 82,436+
Adler (R) 38,250

33rd District
Anderson, F.L. (D) .. 49,664
Grisham (R)* .... 120,421+

34th District
Simone (D) 45,386
Lungren (R)* .... 135,253+

35th District
Lloyd (D)* 86,728
Dreier (R) .... 99,134+

36th District
Brown (D)* .... 87,895+
Stark (R) 73,096

37th District
Rusk (D) 57,815
Lewis (R)* .... 164,663+

38th District
Patterson (D)* ...... 90,647+
Jacobson (R) 65,340

39th District
Lahtinen (D) 53,738
Dannemeyer (R)* ..... 172,029+

40th District
Dow (D) 65,388
Badham (R)* .... 209,775+

41st District
Wilson (D) 99,102
Lowery (R) .... 120,617+

42nd District
Van Deerlin (D)* 68,354
Hunter (R) .... 77,819+

43rd District
Metzger (D) 45,623
Burgener (R)* .... 292,039+

COLORADO (D 3, R 2)

1st District
Schroeder (D)* ..... 107,332+
Bradford (R) 67,811

2nd District
Wirth (D)* .... 153,568+
McElderry (R) 111,792

3rd District
Kogovsek (D)* ...... 105,814+
McCormick (R) 84,399

4th District
Barragan (D) 76,987
Brown (R) .... 178,275+

5th District
Schreiber (D) 62,003
Kramer (R)* .... 177,304+

CONNECTICUT (D 4, R 2)

1st District
Cotter (D)* .... 137,477+
Anderson (R) 80,873

2nd District
Gejdenson (D) ...... 118,893+
Guglielmo (R) 102,859

3rd District
Lieberman (D) 97,119
DeNardis (R) .... 108,213+

4th District
Phillips (D) 73,820
McKinney (R)* ...... 122,540+

5th District
Ratchford (D)* ..... 116,938+
Donahue (R) 115,059

6th District
Moffett (D)* .... 142,980+
Schaus (R) 98,349

DELAWARE (D 0, R 1)

At Large
Maxwell (D) 81,805
Evans (R)* .... 133,557+

FLORIDA (D 11, R 4)

1st District
Hutto (D)* .... 110,415+
Briggs (R) 67,609

2nd District
Fuqua (D)* .... 131,434+
LaCapra (R) 53,753

3rd District
Bennett (D)* .... 98,382+
Radcliffe (R) 28,837

4th District
Chappell (D)* ...... 136,301+
Dillard (R) 71,308

5th District
Best (D) 137,136
McCollum (R) .... 172,107+

6th District
Young (R)* .... ---

7th District
Gibbons (D)* .... 126,686+
Jones (R) 48,982

8th District
Ireland (D)* .... 146,008+
Nicholson (R) 57,833

9th District
Nelson (D)* .... 130,498+
Dowiat (R) 53,330

10th District
Sparkman (D) 70,066
Bafalis (R)* .... 262,425+

11th District
Mica (D)* .... 198,477+
Coogler (R) 134,433

12th District
Becker (D) 103,090
Shaw (R) .... 121,465+

13th District
Lehman (D)* .... 122,555+
Entin (R) 40,825

14th District
Pepper (D)* .... 91,096+
Estrella (R) 30,675

15th District
Fascell (D)* .... 125,208+
Hoodwin 65,122

GEORGIA (D 9, R 1)

1st District
Ginn (D)* .... ---

2nd District
Hatcher (D) .... 91,678+
Harrell (R) 32,937

3rd District
Brinkley (D)* ..... ---

4th District
Levitas (D)* .... 106,298+
Billington (R) 45,773

5th District
Fowler (D)* .... 101,613+
Dowda (R) 35,664

6th District
Davis (D) 66,496
Gingrich (R)* ...... 95,599+

7th District
McDonald (D)* ...... 114,363+
Castellucis (R) 53,936

8th District
Evans (D)* .... 87,444+
Carter, D. (R) 31,007

9th District
Jenkins (D)* .... 115,351+
Ashworth (R) 55,802

10th District
Barnard (D)* .... 102,010+
Neubauer (R) 25,172

HAWAII (D 2, R 0)

1st District
Heftel (D)* .... 98,256+
Nobel (R) 19,819

2nd District
Akaka (D)* .... 141,477+
Smith (Lib) 15,903

IDAHO (D 0, R 2)

1st District
Nichols (D) 100,870
Craig (R) .... 116,976+

2nd District
Bilyeu (D) 81,364
Hansen (R)* .... 116,125+

ILLINOIS (D 10, R 14)

1st District
Washington (D) ..... 115,617+
Williams (R) 6,471

2nd District
Savage (D) .... 118,148+
Harris (R) 16,305

3rd District
Russo (D)* .... 131,683+
Sarsoun (R) 58,888

4th District
Jalovec (D) 70,022
Derwinski (R)* ..... 146,299+

5th District
Fary (D)* .... 99,704+
Kotowski (R) 26,242

6th District
Reda (D) 58,378
Hyde (R)* .... 116,782+

7th District
Collins (D)* .... 75,135+
Hooper (R) 13,233

8th District
Rostenkowski (D)* .. 91,719+
Zilke (R) 17,067

9th District
Yates (D)* .... 98,098+
Andrica (R) 36,025

10th District
Weinberger (D) 85,716
Porter (R)* .... 132,032+

11th District
Annunzio (D)* ...... 116,317+
Zanillo (R) 51,226

12th District
McCartney (D) 61,859
Crane, P.M. (R)* ... 177,594+

13th District
Reese (D) 52,086
McClory (R)* .... 131,751+

14th District
Kennel (D) 60,702
Erlenborn (R)* ..... 200,934+

15th District
Quillin (D) 45,722
Corcoran (R)* ...... 150,897+

16th District
Aurand (D) 64,337
Martin (R) .... 133,412+

17th District
Murer (D) 64,869
O'Brien (R)* .... 131,719+

18th District
Knuppel (D) 76,689
Michel (R)* .... 125,644+

19th District
Hand (D) 51,248
Railsback (R)* ..... 143,260+

20th District
Robinson (D) 96,590
Findley (R)* .... 122,977+

21st District
Severns (D) 63,473
Madigan (R)* .... 132,174+

22nd District
Voelz (D) 65,483
Crane, D.B. (R)* ... 144,586+

23rd District
Price (D)* .... 107,106+
Davinroy (R) 59,617

24th District
Simon (D)* .... 111,838+
Anderson, J.T. (R) .. 109,801

INDIANA (D 6, R 5)

1st District
Benjamin (D)* ...... 112,016+
Harkin (R) 43,537

2nd District
Fithian (D)* .... 122,325+
Niemeyer (R) 106,110

3rd District
Brademas (D)* 83,791
Hiler (R) .... 102,055+

4th District
Walda (D) 75,123
Coats (R) .... 115,381+

5th District
Ackerson (D) 79,988
Hillis (R)* .... 128,864+

6th District
Evans (D)* .... 95,955+
Crane, D.G. (R) 95,037

7th District
Carroll (D) 67,508
Myers (R)* .... 134,119+

8th District
Snider (D) 97,228
Deckard (R)* .... 119,810+

9th District
Hamilton (D)* ...... 136,537+
Meyer (R) 75,609

10th District
Sharp (D)* .... 102,996+
Frazier (R) 91,980

11th District
Jacobs (D)* .... 96,225+
Suess (R) 71,771

IOWA (D 3, R 3)

1st District
Larew (D) 72,438
Leach (R)* .... 134,248+

2nd District
Sovern (D) 87,223
Tauke (R)* .... 116,829+

3rd District
Cutler (D) 101,639
Evans (R) .... 107,830+

4th District
Smith (D)* .... 117,716+
Young (R) 100,162

5th District
Harkin (D)* .... 128,687+
Hultman (R) 84,968

6th District
Bedell (D)* .... 128,009+
Carney (R) 72,049

KANSAS (D 1, R 4)

1st District
Martin (D) 73,402
Roberts (R) .... 119,688+

2nd District
Keys (D) 77,464
Jeffries (R)* .... 90,452+

3rd District
Watkins (D) 82,000
Winn (R)* .... 109,277+

4th District
Glickman (D)* .... 123,940+
Hunter (R) 56,189

5th District
Miller (D) 45,285
Whittaker (R)* .... 140,501+

KENTUCKY (D 4, R 3)

1st District
Hubbard (D)* ....   ---

2nd District
Natcher (D)* .... 99,682+
Watson (R) 52,123

3rd District
Mazzoli (D)* .... 84,091+
Cesler (R) 45,676

4th District
McGary (D) 60,831
Snyder (R)* .... 122,794+

5th District
Marcum (D) 53,716
Rogers (R) .... 111,779+

6th District
Easterly (D) 70,999
Hopkins (R)* .... 103,271+

7th District
Perkins (D)* ....   ---

LOUISIANA (D 6, R 2)

1st District
Livingston (R)* ....   ---

2nd District
Boggs (D)* ....   ---

3rd District
Tauzin (D)* ....   ---

4th District
Leach (D)* 58,641
Roemer (D) .... 103,511+

5th District
Huckaby (D)* ....   ---

6th District
Moore (R)* ....   ---

7th District
Breaux (D)* ....   ---

8th District
Long (D)* ....   ---

MAINE (D 0, R 2)

1st District
Pachios (D) 87,367
Emery (R)* .... 186,663+

2nd District
Silverman (D) 50,228
Snowe (R)* .... 186,083+

MARYLAND (D 7, R 1)

1st District
Dyson (D) .... 96,394+
Bauman (R)* 88,736

2nd District
Long (D)* .... 115,846+
Bentley (R) 88,490

3rd District
Mikulski (D)* .... 100,677+
Schaffer (R) 31,346

4th District
Riley (D) 45,869
Holt (R)* .... 116,162+

5th District
Spellman (D)* .... 103,150+
Igoe (R) 24,728

6th District
Byron (D)* .... 140,142+
Beck (R) 60,419

7th District
Mitchell (D)* .... 96,014+
Clark (R) 12,257

8th District
Barnes (D)* .... 140,214+
Steers (R) 94,714

MASSACHUSETTS (D 10, R 2)

1st District
Doyle (D) 52,438
Conte (R)* .... 156,167+

2nd District
Boland (D)* .... 120,511+
Swank (R) 38,675

3rd District
Early (D)* .... 140,632+
Skehan (R) 54,409

4th District
Frank (D) .... 103,461+
Jones (R) 95,895

5th District
Shannon (D)* .... 136,711+
Sawyer (R) 70,578

6th District
Mavroules (D)* ...... 111,344+
Trimarco (R) 103,120

7th District
Markey (D)* ....   ---

8th District
O'Neill (D)* .... 126,425+
Barnstead (R) 35,802

9th District
Moakley (D)* ....   ---

10th District
McCarthy (D) 83,557
Heckler (R)* .... 131,600+

11th District
Donnelly (D)* ....   ---

12th District
Studds (D)* .... 195,294+
Doane (R) 71,468

MICHIGAN (D 12, R 7)

1st District
Conyers (D)* .... 122,912+
Bell (R) 6,265

2nd District
O'Reilly (D) 84,441
Pursell (R)* .... 115,562+

3rd District
Wolpe (D)* .... 112,547+
Gilmore (R) 101,988

4th District
Furst (D) 47,801
Stockman (R)* .... 136,407+

5th District
Sprik (D) 101,664
Sawyer (R)* .... 117,855+

6th District
Carr (D)* 109,563
Dunn (R) .... 113,316+

7th District
Kildee (D)* ....   ---

8th District
Traxler (D)* .... 123,803+
Hughes (R) 77,066

9th District
Vander Jagt (R)* ....   ---

10th District
Albosta (D)* .... 125,252+
Allen (R) 110,027

11th District
Dorrity (D) 74,630
Davis (R)* .... 144,931+

12th District
Bonior (D)* .... 113,608+
Walsh (R) 91,559

13th District
Crockett (D) .... 79,148+
Hurd (R) 6,496

14th District
Hertel (D) .... 89,609+
Caputo (R) 77,961

15th District
Ford (D)* .... 114,484+
Carlson (R) 53,570

16th District
Dingell (D)* .... 105,478+
Seay (R) 42,657

17th District
Brodhead (D)* .... 126,754+
Patterson (R) 44,277

18th District
Blanchard (D)* ...... 135,587+
Suida (R) 68,356

19th District
Daniels (D) 60,125
Broomfield (R)* ..... 165,040+

MINNESOTA (D 3, R 5)

1st District
Smith (D) 66,682
Erdahl (R)* .... 170,170+

2nd District
Bergquist (D) 102,561
Hagedorn (R)* .... 157,547+

3rd District
Saliterman (D) 47,431
Frenzel (R)* .... 145,265+

4th District
Vento (D)* .... 119,172+
Berg (R) 82,784

5th District
Sabo (D)* .... 121,201+
Doherty (R) 46,060

6th District
Baumann (D) 119,097
Weber (R) .... 139,548+

7th District
Wenstrom (D) 123,317
Strangeland (R)* .... 133,784+

8th District
Oberstar (D)* .... 180,069+
Fiore (R) 70,417

MISSISSIPPI (D 3, R 2)

1st District
Whitten (D)* .... 103,904+
Moffett (R) 61,088

2nd District
Bowen (D)* .... 93,898+
Drake (R) 41,937

3rd District
Montgomery (D)* .... ---

4th District
Singletary (D) 52,832
Hinson (R)* .... 69,808+

5th District
McVeay (D) 46,363
Lott (R)* .... 130,422+

MISSOURI (D 6, R 4)

1st District
Clay (D)* .... 89,890+
White (R) 38,463

2nd District
Young, R.A. (D)* ... 148,620+
Shields (R) 82,563

3rd District
Gephardt (D)* ...... 141,221+
Cedarburg (R) 40,714

4th District
Skelton (D)* .... 151,455+
Baker, Bill (R) 71,868

5th District
Bolling (D)* .... 110,952+
Baker, V.E. (R) 47,309

6th District
King (D) 61,955
Coleman (R)* .... 149,821+

7th District
Young, Ken (D) 65,651
Taylor (R)* .... 140,943+

8th District
Gardner (D) 95,744
Bailey (R) .... 127,668+

9th District
Volkmer (D)* .... 135,618+
Turner (R) 107,818

10th District
Burlison (D)* 95,198
Emerson (R) .... 116,715+

MONTANA (D 1, R 1)

1st District
Williams (D)* ...... 107,312+
McDonald (R) 67,103

2nd District
Monahan (D) 59,904
Marlenee (R)* ...... 85,181+

NEBRASKA (D 0, R 3)

1st District
Story (D) 43,131
Bereuter (R)* ...... 158,746+

2nd District
Fellman (D) 87,674
Daub (R) .... 105,783+

3rd District
Ditus (D) 34,693
Smith (R)* .... 180,537+

NEVADA (D 1, R 0)

At Large
Santini (D)* .... 164,714+
Saunders (R) 62,920

NEW HAMPSHIRE (D 1, R 1)

1st District
D'Amours (D)* ...... 114,061+
Cobleigh (R) 73,555

2nd District
Arel (D) 63,182
Gregg (R) .... 113,091+

NEW JERSEY (D 8, R 7)

1st District
Florio (D)* .... 145,717+
Sibert (R) 41,493

2nd District
Hughes (D)* .... 131,527+
Fox (R) 93,835

3rd District
Howard (D)* .... 106,140+

Muhler (R) 104,119

4th District
Thompson (D)* 68,881
Smith (R) .... 89,334+

5th District
Pillion (D) 40,910
Fenwick (R)* .... 154,858+

6th District
Weinstein (D) 90,233
Forsythe (R)* .... 120,930+

7th District
Maguire (D)* 95,089
Roukema (R) .... 104,033+

8th District
Roe (D)* .... 96,351+
Cleveland (R) 44,666

9th District
Ambrosio (D) 72,647
Hollenbeck (R)* .... 110,864+

10th District
Rodino (D)* .... 72,472+
Jennings (R) 11,310

11th District
Minish (D)* .... 100,990+
Davis (R) 55,162

12th District
Monyek (D) 33,193
Rinaldo (R)* .... 117,840+

13th District
Stickle (D) 55,553
Courter (R)* .... 152,019+

14th District
Guarini (D)* .... 75,707+
Teti (R) 38,464

15th District
Dwyer (D) .... 91,349+
O'Sullivan (R) 74,989

NEW MEXICO (D 0, R 2)

1st District
Richardson (D) 117,402
Lujan (R)* .... 123,288+

2nd District
King (D) 54,791
Skeen (R) .... 60,055+
Runnels, D. (I) 45,027

NEW YORK (D 22, R 17)

1st District
Twomey (D) 81,695
Carney (R,C,RTL)* ..... 107,661+
Cummings (L) 3,326

2nd District
Downey (D)* .... 78,651+
Modica (R,RTL) 62,681

3rd District
Ambro (D,RTL)* 73,385
Carman (R,C) .... 86,842+
Meehan (L) 4,151

4th District
Brennan (D,L) 58,146
Lent (R,C,RTL)* .... 116,931+

5th District
Burstein (D,L) 76,927
McGrath (R,C,RTL) ..... 104,668+

6th District
Wolff (D,L)* 79,701
LeBoutillier (R,C,RTL) . 90,008+

7th District
Addabbo (D,R,L)* ...... 94,025+
Lees (C,RTL) 4,700

8th District
Rosenthal (D,L)* ...... 83,445+
Lemishow (R,C,RTL) 26,979

9th District
Ferraro (D)* .... 63,015+
Battista (R,C,RTL) 44,086
Geniale (L) 1,080

10th District
Biaggi (D,R,L)* ...... 93,451+
Cavanna (C) 3,989
Mari (RTL) 1,519

11th District
Scheuer (D,L)* .... 70,703+
Carlan (R,RTL) 25,173

12th District
Chisholm (D,L)* ...... 34,431+
Gibbs (R) 3,540
Carrano (C) 1,457
Caesar (RTL) 745

13th District
Solarz (D,L)* .... 80,379+
DeMell (R,C) 19,582
Connolly (RTL) 1,677

14th District
Richmond (D,L)* ...... 44,469+
Lovell (R,C) 8,423
McKenzie (RTL) 668

15th District
Zeferetti (D)* .... 48,303+
Atanasio (R,C) 46,107
McNeill (L) 2,839

16th District
Schumer (D,L) .... 66,841+
Silverman (R,C) 16,840
Spaulding (RTL) 2,522

17th District
Murphy (D, RTL)* 49,164
Molinari (R,C) .... 67,663+
Codd (L) 23,179

18th District
Green, M.J. (D,L) 67,724
Green, S.W. (R)* ..... 87,540+
Washburn (RTL) 1,063

19th District
Rangel (D,R,L)* ...... 83,507+
Garvey (C,RTL) 2,915

20th District
Weiss (D,L)* .... 84,661+
Greene, J.E. (R) 15,147
Caplan (C) 2,217

21st District
Garcia (D,R,L)* ...... 31,839+
Aceto (C) 275
Cordero (RTL) 319

22nd District
Bingham (D,L)* .... 64,914+
Black (R) 9,919
Whalen (C) 2,719

23rd District
Peyser (D)* .... 67,847+
Albanese (R,C) 56,110

24th District
Ottinger (D)* .... 77,803+
Christiana (R,C,RTL) . 53,234
Reyes (L) 1,671

25th District
Ozols (D) 37,429
Fish (R,C)* .... 149,666+

26th District
Victor (D,L) 38,712
Gilman (R)* .... 134,896+
Farrell (RTL) 8,838

27th District
McHugh (D)* .... 100,099+
Wallace (R,C) 80,126
Muenkel (RTL) 1,776

28th District
Stratton (D)* .... 163,453+
Wicks (R) 38,873
Bradt (C,RTL) 6,609

29th District
Hurley (D) 68,261
Solomon (R,C,RTL)* ... 136,680+

30th District
Krupsak (D,L) 53,667
Martin (R,C) .... 106,675+
Zagame (RTL) 7,416

31st District
Schwartz (D,L) 36,884
Mitchell (R, RTL)* . 127,318+

32nd District
Brooks (D) 53,557
Wortley (R,C) ...... 102,983+
Del Giorno (RTL) ... 11,279

33rd District
Reed (D,L) 39,245
Lee (R,C)* .... 129,122+
Jones (RTL) 2,777

34th District
Toole (D) 35,351
Horton (R)* .... 125,198+
Benoy (C) 5,579
Bastuk (RTL) 3,472

35th District
Owens (D,C) 40,055
Conable (R)* .... 112,819+
O'Connor (RTL) 3,287

36th District
LaFalce (D,L)* ..... 118,961+
Feder (R,C,RTL) 47,626

37th District
Nowak (D,L)* .... 91,033+
Heymanowski (R,C) .. 16,245
O'Connor (RTL) 2,807

38th District
Denn (D,L) 37,932
Kemp (R,C,RTL)* .... 161,899+

39th District
Lundine (D)* .... 93,123+
Abdella (R,C) 74,173
Ronan (RTL) 2,434

NORTH CAROLINA (D 7, R 4)

1st District
Jones (D)* .... ---

2nd District
Fountain (D)* ...... 89,878+
Gardner (R) 36,286

3rd District
Whitley (D)* .... 84,873+
Parker (R) 40,043

4th District
Andrews (D)* .... 103,047+
Hogan (R) 84,685

5th District
Neal (D)* .... 99,006+
Bagnal (R) 94,593

6th District
Preyer (D)* 76,916
Johnston (R) .... 80,263+

7th District
Rose (D)* .... 88,167+
Wright (R) 40,103

8th District
Hefner (D)* .... 94,041+
Harris (R) 66,356

9th District
Kincaid (D) 70,479
Martin (R)* .... 98,288+

10th District
Icenhour (D) 52,518
Broyhill (R)* ...... 120,748+

11th District
Gudger (D)* 90,597
Hendon (R) .... 104,214+

NORTH DAKOTA (D 1, R 0)

At Large
Dorgan (D) .... 161,441+
Smykowski (R) 120,669

OHIO (D 10, R 13)

1st District
Zwick (D) 38,451
Gradison (R)* ...... 123,806+

2nd District
Luken (D)* .... 103,366+

Atkins (R) 72,721

3rd District
Hall (D)* .... 95,426+
Sealy (R) 66,590

4th District
Tebben (D) 51,329
Guyer (R)* .... 133,781+

5th District
Sherck (D) 57,790
Latta (R)* .... 136,859+

6th District
Strickland (D) 84,231
McEwen (R) .... 101,230+

7th District
Hollister (D) 38,964
Brown (R)* .... 123,917+

8th District
Griffin (D) 44,049
Kindness (R)* ...... 139,355+

9th District
Ashley (D)* 68,753
Weber (R) .... 96,900+

10th District
Stecher (D) 49,350
Miller (R)* .... 143,092+

11th District
Donlin (D) 50,553
Stanton (R)* .... 125,972+

12th District
Shamansky (D) ...... 108,598+
Devine (R)* 97,618

13th District
Pease (D)* .... 111,968+
Armstrong (R) 63,310

14th District
Seiberling (D)* .... 103,015+
Mangels (R) 55,794

15th District
Freeman (D) 48,361
Wylie (R)* .... 128,333+

16th District
Slagle (D) 39,194
Regula (R)* .... 149,799+

17th District
Yunker (D) 48,486
Ashbrook (R)* ...... 128,974+

18th District
Applegate (D)* ..... 134,650+
Hammersley (R) 42,301

19th District
Meshel (D) 76,944
Williams (R)* ...... 103,866+

20th District
Oakar (D)* .... ---

21st District
Stokes (D)* .... 82,288+
Woodhall (R) 11,136

22nd District
Eckart (D) .... 102,383+
Nahra (R) 80,408

23rd District
Mottl (D)* .... ---

OKLAHOMA (D 5, R 1)

1st District
Jones (D)* .... 115,381+
Freeman (R) 82,293

2nd District
Synar (D)* .... 100,341+
Richardson (R) 86,105

3rd District
Watkins (D)* .... ---

4th District
McCurdy (D) .... 74,707+
Rutledge (R) 73,363

5th District
Hood (D) 35,500
Edwards (R)* .... 86,518+
Rushing (Lib) 4,810

6th District
English (D)* .... 110,180+
McCurley (R) 59,592

OREGON (D 3, R 1)

1st District
AuCoin (D)* .... 197,042+
Engdahl (R) 100,824

2nd District
Ullman (D)* 136,923
Smith (R) .... 140,310+

3rd District
Wyden (D) .... 149,323+
Conger (R) 57,246

4th District
Weaver (D)* .... 158,172+
Fitzgerald (R) 130,287

PENNSYLVANIA (D 12, R 12, I 1)

1st District
Myers (D)* 51,770
Burke (R) 36,919
Foglietta (I) ...... 56,529+

2nd District
Gray (D)* .... ---

3rd District
Lederer (D)* .... 67,660+
Phillips (R) 40,294

4th District
Magrann (D) 73,892
Dougherty (R)* ..... 124,904+

5th District
Brickhouse (D) 45,958
Schulze (R)* .... 146,411+

6th District
Yatron (D)* .... 117,559+
Hulshart (R) 58,038

7th District
Edgar (D)* .... 98,083+
Rochford (R) 87,618

8th District
Kostmayer (D)* 99,588
Coyne, J. (R) ...... 103,557+

9th District
Shuster (R)* .... ---

10th District
Basalyga (D) 42,881
McDade (R)* .... 144,312+

11th District
Musto (D)* 86,386
Nelligan (R) .... 93,439+

12th District
Murtha (D)* .... 107,927+
Getty (R) 72,903

13th District
Slawek (D) 57,558
Coughlin (R)* ...... 137,563+

14th District
Coyne, W. (D) ...... 101,308+
Thomas (R) 43,429

15th District
Reibman (D) 68,324
Ritter (R)* .... 99,062+

16th District
Woodcock (D) 37,330
Walker (R)* .... 125,847+

17th District
Ertel (D)* .... 96,950+
Seiverling (R) 63,278

18th District
Walgren (D)* .... 127,154+
Snyder (R) 58,965

19th District
Noll (D) 41,577
Goodling (R)* ...... 136,539+

20th District
Gaydos (D)* .... 121,260+
Meyer (R) 46,659

21st District
Bailey (D)* .... 112,144+
Matson (R) 51,834

22nd District
Murphy (D)* .... 114,501+
Ecoff (R) 49,579

23rd District
Atigan (D) 41,079
Clinger (R)* .... 123,171+

24th District
DiCarlo (D) 86,293
Marks (R)* .... 86,578+

25th District
Atkinson (D)* ...... 119,338+
Morris (R) 58,708

RHODE ISLAND (D 1, R 1)

1st District
St. Germain (D)* ... 116,149+
Montgomery (R) 55,559

2nd District
Beard (D)* 88,158
Schneider (R) ...... 110,175+

SOUTH CAROLINA (D 2, R 4)

1st District
Ravenel (D) 71,908
Hartnett (R) .... 74,034+

2nd District
Turnipseed (D) 73,143
Spence (R)* .... 92,285+

3rd District
Derrick (D)* .... 86,589+
Parker (R) 53,428

4th District
Campbell (R)* ..... ---

5th District
Holland (D)* .... ---

6th District
Jenrette (D)* 71,232
Napier (R) .... 76,141+

SOUTH DAKOTA (D 1, R 1)

1st District
Daschle (D)* .... 109,918+
Kull (R) 57,140

2nd District
Stofferahn (D) 63,415
Roberts (R) .... 87,932+

TENNESSEE (D 5, R 3)

1st District
Quillen (R)* .... ---

2nd District
Dunaway (D) 46,383
Duncan (R)* .... 146,983+

3rd District
Bouquard (D)* ...... 117,323+
Byers (R) 75,168

4th District
Gore (D)* .... 137,004+
Seigneur (R) 35,722

5th District
Boner (D)* .... 118,627+
Adams (R) 62,715

6th District
Beard (R)* .... ---

7th District
Jones (D)* .... 133,162+
Campbell (R) 39,470

8th District
Ford (D)* .... ---

TEXAS (D 19, R 5)

1st District
Hall, S.B. (D)* .... ---

2nd District
Wilson (D)* .... 139,536+
Pannill (R) 59,756

3rd District
Porter (D) 49,918
Collins (R)* .... 216,096+

4th District
Hall, R.M. (D) .... 101,407+
Wright, Jon (R) 93,260

5th District
Mattox (D)* .... 69,523+
Pauken (R) 66,739

6th District
Gramm (D)* .... 142,514+
Haskins (R) 59,913

7th District
Hutchings (D) 48,600
Archer (R)* .... 242,551+

8th District
Eckhardt (D)* 67,921
Fields (R) .... 72,020+

9th District
Brooks (D)* .... ---

10th District
Pickle (D)* .... 134,713+
Biggar (R) 88,460

11th District
Leath (D)* .... ---

12th District
Wright, James C. (D)* . 99,104+
Bradshaw (R) 65,005

13th District
Hightower (D)* .... 98,564+
Slover (R) 80,789

14th District
Patman (D) .... 91,546+
Concklin (R) 67,993

15th District
de la Garza (D)* ..... 103,772+
McDonald (R) 44,699

16th District
White (D)* .... ---

17th District
Stenholm (D)* .... ---

18th District
Leland (D)* .... 71,986+
Kennedy (R) 16,128

19th District
Hance (D)* .... ---

20th District
Gonzalez (D)* .... 84,113+
Nash (R) 17,725

21st District
Sullivan (D) 57,800
Loeffler (R)* .... 185,821+

22nd District
Andrews (D) 101,121
Paul (R)* .... 106,766+

23rd District
Kazen (D)* .... 103,341+
Locke (R) 44,746

24th District
Frost (D)* .... 91,933+
Smothers (R) 57,623

UTAH (D 0, R 2)

1st District
McKay (D)* 143,049
Hansen (R) .... 156,211+

2nd District
Monson (D) 87,459

Marriott (R)* .... 193,120+

VERMONT (D 0, R 1)

At Large
Jeffords (R)* .... ---

VIRGINIA (D 1, R 9)

1st District
Trible (R)* .... ---

2nd District
Whitehurst (R)* ..... ---

3rd District
Mapp (D) 60,978
Bliley (R) .... 96,619+

4th District
Jenkins (D) 59,727
Daniel, R.W. (R)* ... 92,671+

5th District
Daniel, Dan (D)* .... ---

6th District
Butler (R)* .... ---

7th District
Robinson (R)* .... ---

8th District
Harris (D)* 94,391
Parris (R) .... 95,556+

9th District
Ferguson (D) 51,521
Wampler (R)* .... 116,619+

10th District
Fisher (D)* 106,193
Wolf (R) .... 110,821+

WASHINGTON (D 5, R 2)

1st District
Drake (D) 38,542
Pritchard (R)* ...... 162,298+

2nd District
Swift (D)* .... 147,465+
Snider (R) 74,054

3rd District
Bonker (D)* .... 136,744+
Culp (R) 80,122

4th District
McCormack (D)* 90,308
Morrison (R) .... 120,191+

5th District
Foley (D)* .... 108,520+
Sonneland (R) 101,106

6th District
Dicks (D)* .... 101,214+
Beaver (R) 86,653

7th District
Lowry (D)* .... 101,439+
Dunlap (R) 74,650

WEST VIRGINIA (D 2, R 2)

1st District
Mollohan (D)* .... 107,119+
Bartlett (R) 61,273

2nd District
Hamilton (D) 69,377
Benedict (R) .... 96,479+

3rd District
Hutchinson (D)* 84,076
Staton (R) .... 94,084+

4th District
Rahall (D)* .... 115,938+
Covey (R) 35,405

WISCONSIN (D 5, R 4)

1st District
Aspin (D)* .... 126,331+
Canary (R) 95,960

2nd District
Kastenmeier (D)* .... 142,031+
Wright (R) 119,435

continued on bottom of next page

UNITED STATES SENATE — 1980 ELECTION RESULTS   (as of November 5, 1980)

SOURCE: The Associated Press

	Pre-election	Offices Contested	Offices Won	Gain or Loss	97th Congress
Democrats	58	24	12	-12	46
Republicans	41	10	22	+12	53
Independents	1	0	--	--	1

* = Incumbent	R = Republican	Lib = Libertarian
+ = Winner	D = Democrat	I = Independent
	L = Liberal	Unc = Uncontested

ALABAMA
- Folsom (D) 600,610
- Denton (R) .... 633,982+

ALASKA
- Gruening (D) 53,674
- Murkowski (R) ...... 65,924+

ARIZONA
- Schulz (D) 418,371
- Goldwater (R)* ..... 426,171+

ARKANSAS
- Bumpers (D)* .... 461,952+
- Clark (R) 318,072

CALIFORNIA
- Cranston (D)* .... 4,638,448+
- Gann (R) 3,038,180

COLORADO
- Hart (D)* .... 585,047+
- Buchanan (R) 563,752

CONNECTICUT
- Dodd (D) .... 765,126+
- Buckley (R) 575,644

FLORIDA
- Gunter (D) 1,634,089
- Hawkins (R) ...... 1,721,172+

GEORGIA
- Talmadge (D)* 767,911
- Mattingly (R) ...... 792,107+

HAWAII
- Inouye (D)* .... 224,485+
- Brown (R) 53,068

IDAHO
- Church (D)* 214,351
- Symms (R) .... 218,793+

ILLINOIS
- Dixon (D) .... 2,472,861+

- O'Neal (R) 1,909,372

INDIANA
- Bayh (D)* 998,772
- Quayle (R) .... 1,162,509+

IOWA
- Culver (D)* 580,301
- Grassley (R) .... 683,747+

KANSAS
- Simpson (D) 334,006
- Dole (R)* .... 588,546+

KENTUCKY
- Ford (D)* .... 719,679+
- Foust (R) 382,434

LOUISIANA
- Long (D)* .... Unc

MARYLAND
- Conroy (D) 423,879
- Mathias, Jr. (R)* .. 811,925+

MISSOURI
- Eagleton (D)* .... 1,055,981+
- McNary (R) 965,271

NEVADA
- Gojack (D) 92,203
- Laxalt (R)* .... 143,781+

NEW HAMPSHIRE
- Durkin (D)* 178,943
- Rudman (R) .... 195,053+

NEW YORK
- Holtzman (D) 2,538,921
- D'Amato (R) ...... 2,627,458+
- Javits (L)* 629,468

NORTH CAROLINA
- Morgan (D)* 884,572
- East (R) .... 891,209+

NORTH DAKOTA
- Johanneson (D) 83,591
- Andrews (R) .... 203,856+

OHIO
- Glenn (D)* .... 2,731,088+
- Betts (R) 1,129,003

OKLAHOMA
- Coats (D) 463,369
- Nickles (R) .... 557,539+
- Murphy (Lib)........ 10,091
- Nesbett (I) 31,905

OREGON
- Kulongoski (D) 490,511
- Packwood (R)* ...... 575,515+

PENNSYLVANIA
- Flaherty (D) 2,100,507
- Specter (R) ...... 2,235,807+

SOUTH CAROLINA
- Hollings (D)* ...... 595,210+
- Mays (R) 233,052

SOUTH DAKOTA
- McGovern (D)* 128,956
- Abdnor (R) .... 190,726+

UTAH
- Berman (D) 150,495
- Garn (R)* .... 433,943+

VERMONT
- Leahy (D)* .... 101,721+
- Ledbetter (R) 99,455

WASHINGTON
- Magnuson (D)* 700,637
- Gorton (R) .... 830,666+

WISCONSIN
- Nelson (D)* 1,061,899
- Kasten, Jr. (R) .. 1,101,669+

---

continued from page 170

3rd District
- Baldus (D)* 126,797
- Gunderson (R) ...... 131,581+

4th District
- Zablocki (D)* ...... 144,572+
- Honadel (R) 60,578

5th District
- Reuss (D)* .... 129,509+
- Bathke (R) 37,366

6th District
- Goyke (D) 98,616
- Petri (R)* .... 143,992+

7th District
- Obey (D)* .... 162,010+
- Vesta (R) 89,134

8th District
- Monfils (D) 81,474
- Roth (R)* .... 169,296+

9th District
- Benedict (D) 56,040
- Sensenbrenner (R)* .. 204,972+

WYOMING (D 0, R 1)

At Large
- Rogers (D) 53,309
- Cheney (R)* .... 116,344+

U.S. SENATORS WHOSE TERMS END IN 1983 OR 1985

R = Republican   D = Democrat   L = Liberal   I = Independent

State	Senator	State	Senator	State	Senator
ALABAMA	Heflin (D) 1985	MASSACHUSETTS	Kennedy (D).........1983	OHIO	Metzenbaum (D)......1983
ALASKA	Stevens (R).........1985		Tsongas (R).........1985	OKLAHOMA	Boren (D)...........1985
ARIZONA	DeConcini (D)......1983	MICHIGAN	Riegle, Jr. (D)....1983	OREGON	Hatfield (R).......1985
ARKANSAS	Pryor (D)...........1985		Levin (D)...........1985	PENNSYLVANIA	Heinz III (R)......1983
CALIFORNIA	Hayakawa (R).......1983	MINNESOTA	Durenberger (R).....1983	RHODE ISLAND	Pell (D)...........1985
COLORADO	Armstrong (R)......1985		Boschwitz (R).......1985		Chafee (R).........1983
CONNECTICUT	Weicker, Jr. (R)....1983	MISSISSIPPI	Stennis (D).........1983	SOUTH CAROLINA	Thurmond (R).......1985
DELAWARE	Roth, Jr. (R).......1983		Cochran (R).........1985	SOUTH DAKOTA	Pressler (R).......1985
	Biden, Jr. (D).....1985	MISSOURI	Danforth (R)........1983	TENNESSEE	Baker, Jr. (R).....1985
FLORIDA	Chiles, Jr. (D)....1983	MONTANA	Melcher (D).........1983		Sasser (D).........1983
GEORGIA	Nunn (D)............1985		Baucus (D)..........1985	TEXAS	Tower (R)..........1985
HAWAII	Matsunaga (D).......1983	NEBRASKA	Zorinsky (D)........1983		Bentsen (D)........1983
IDAHO	McClure (R).........1985		Exon, Jr. (D)......1985	UTAH	Hatch (R)..........1983
ILLINOIS	Percy (R)...........1985	NEVADA	Cannon (D)..........1983	VERMONT	Stafford (R).......1983
INDIANA	Lugar (R)...........1983	NEW HAMPSHIRE	Humphrey (R)........1985	VIRGINIA	Byrd, Jr., H.F. (I).1983
IOWA	Jepsen (R)..........1985	NEW JERSEY	Williams, Jr. (D)...1983		Warner (R).........1985
KANSAS	Kassebaum (R).......1985		Bradley (D).........1985	WASHINGTON	Jackson (D)........1983
KENTUCKY	Huddleston (D)......1985	NEW MEXICO	Domenici (R)........1985	WEST VIRGINIA	Randolph (D).......1985
LOUISIANA	Johnston, Jr. (D)...1985		Schmitt (R).........1983		Byrd, R.C. (D).....1983
MAINE	Mitchell (D)........1983	NEW YORK	Moynihan (D, L)....1983	WISCONSIN	Proxmire (D).......1983
	Cohen (R)...........1985	NORTH CAROLINA	Helms (R)...........1985	WYOMING	Wallop (R)......... 1983
MARYLAND	Sarbanes (D)........1983	NORTH DAKOTA	Burdick (D).........1983		Simpson (R)........1985

GOVERNORS — 1980 ELECTION RESULTS (as of November 5, 1980)

SOURCE: The Associated Press

	Pre-election	Offices Contested	Offices Won	Gain or Loss	Post-election
Democrats	31	10	6	-4	27
Republicans	19	3	7	+4	23

* = Incumbent   + = Winner   D = Democrat   R = Republican

ARKANSAS

Clinton (D)* 391,030
White (R) .... 420,542+

DELAWARE

Gordy (D) 64,903
Du Pont (R)* .... 159,773+

INDIANA

Hillenbrand II (D) 900,428
Orr (R) .... 1,231,213+

MISSOURI

Teasdale (D)* 967,757
Bond (R) .... 1,079,454+

MONTANA

Schwinden (D) ...... 182,419+
Ramirez (R) 146,271

NEW HAMPSHIRE

Gallen (D)* .... 226,506+
Thomson (R) 156,290

NORTH CAROLINA

Hunt, Jr. (D)* ..... 1,127,970+
Lake, Jr. (R) 687,096

NORTH DAKOTA

Link (D)* 135,269
Olson (R) .... 157,067+

RHODE ISLAND

Garrahy (D)* .... 283,995+
Cianci (R) 99,379

UTAH

Matheson (D)* .... 327,806+
Wright (R) 264,523

VERMONT

Diamond (D) 75,456
Snelling (R)* .... 120,437+

WASHINGTON

McDermott (D) 668,852
Spellman (R) .... 867,848+

WEST VIRGINIA

Rockefeller IV (D)* ... 387,269+
Moore (R) 328,911

STANDING CONGRESSIONAL COMMITTEES

HOUSE OF REPRESENTATIVES

Agriculture: Agriculture and forestry in general, including price stabilization, farm credit and security, crop insurance, meat and livestock inspections, soil conservation, and rural electrification.

Appropriations: Appropriation of money for the support of the government, examination of operations of any executive department or agency (including agencies of which the majority stock is government owned).

Armed Services: Matters relating to the national military establishment, including military space activities; conservation of naval petroleum resources; strategic materials; scientific research and development for military purposes; Selective Service.

Banking, Finance and Urban Affairs: Financial matters other than taxes and appropriations, including price, commodity, rent, or services controls; deposit insurance, the Federal Reserve System; the valuation of the dollar; public and private housing.

Budget: To set ceilings for overall government spending, giving Congress a coordinated approach to the federal budget for the first time; to study effects of legislation on budget outlays and tax expenditures.

District of Columbia: Municipal affairs (except appropriations) of the District.

Education and Labor: Measures relating to education and labor, including child labor and convict labor; wages and hours; arbitration of labor disputes; the school-lunch program.

Foreign Affaris: U.S. relations with other governments; the UN and international monetary organizations; the diplomatic service, foreign loans, protection of American citizens abroad; interventions and declarations of war.

Government Operations: Budget and accounting measures other than appropriations; relationships of federal government with states and municipalities; reorganizations of executive branch; studies of all levels of government operations; reports of Comptroller General.

House Administration: General administration of the House, including employment of clerks and reporters; federal elections; corrupt practices; contested elections; and the Library of Congress.

Interior and Insular Affairs: Public lands in general; forest reserves and national parks created from the public domain; the Geological Survey; public mineral resources; irrigation; insular possessions; and American Indian affairs.

Interstate and Foreign Commerce: Commerce, communications, and transportation (except water transportation that is not subject to the Interstate Commerce Commission); interstate power transmission (except installation of connections between government waterpower projects); railroad commerce and labor; civil aeronautics; inland waterways; interstate oil compacts; petroleum and natural gas (except on public lands); securities and exchanges; public health; and the Weather Bureau.

Judiciary: Judicial proceedings in general; federal courts and judges; Constitutuional amendments; civil rights; interstate compacts; immigration and naturalization; apportionment of representatives; meetings of Congress and attendance of members; Presidential succession; the Patent Office; claims against the United States;

bankruptcy, mutiny, espionage, and counterfeiting; protection of trade and commerce.

Merchant Marine and Fisheries: The merchant marine in general; navigation and pilotage laws; regulation of common carriers by water (except matters falling under the jurisdiction of the Interstate Commerce Commission); the Coast Guard; the National Ocean Survey; oversees the activities of the Panama Canal Commission; and fisheries and wildlife, including research and conservation.

Post Office and Civil Service: Postal service and federal civil service; the census and collection of statistics; and the National Archives.

Public Works and Transportation: Public buildings and roads; flood control; improvement of rivers and harbors; public works for navigation, including bridges and dams (other than international); water power; and pollution of navigable waters.

Rules: Rules and order of business of the House; recesses and final adjournments of Congress; creation of committees.

Science and Technology: Scientific and astronautical research and development in general; the National Aeronautics and Space Administration; the National Aeronautics and Space Council; the National Science Foundation; the Bureau of Standards; science scholarships.

Small Business: Assistance to and protection of small businesses; participation of small business enterprises in federal procurement and government contracts.

Standards of Official Conduct: Regulations and standards for members, officers, and employees of the House.

Veterans' Affairs: Veterans' measures in general; pensions, armed forces life insurance, rehabilitation and education; and veterans' hospitals.

Ways and Means: Revenue and tax measures in general; customs; transportation of dutiable goods; federal Social Security; reciprocal trade agreements; U.S. bonded debt; and deposit of public moneys.

SENATE

Agriculture, Nutrition, and Forestry: Agriculture in general, including meat and livestock inspection, farm credit and security, sold conservation, crop insurances, and rural electrification; domestic and foreign matters relating to food, nutrition and hunger; forestry and forest reserves (excluding those created from the public domain) in general.

Appropriations: Appropriation of money for the support of the government.

Armed Services: Matters relating to the national military establishment, including military space activities; oversees activities of the Panama Canal Commission; conservation of naval petroleum resources; and strategic materials.

Banking, Housing, and Urban Affairs: Financial matters other than appropriations and taxes; deposit insurance; Federal Reserve System; valuation of the dollar; price control; public and private housing; and financial aid to industry on matters assigned to other committees.

Budget: To set ceilings for overall government spending, giving Congress a coordinated approach to the federal budget for the first time; to study effects of legislation on budget outlays and tax expenditures.

Commerce, Science, and Transportation: Interstate and foreign commerce; interstate railroads, buses, trucks, and pipelines; communications; civil aeronautics; non-military aeronautical and space sciences; merchant marine and navigation, both inland and oceanic; Coast Guard; oceans, weather, and atmospheric activities; fish and wildlife conservation; consumer product regulation; Bureau of Standards; science, engineering, and technology research and development.

Energy and Natural Resources: Energy policy, regulation, conservation, research and development; nuclear and solar energy; production, distribution and utilization of energy sources; public lands and forests; national parks; territorial possessions.

Environment and Public Works: Environmental policy, research and development; water resources; flood control; public works; pollution control; regional economic development; highway construction and maintenance; public buildings and their grounds.

Finance: Revenue and tax matters in general; deposit of public moneys; U.S. bonded debt; customs; transportaion of dutiable goods; reciprocal trade agreements; tariffs; import quotas; Social Security.

Foreign Relations: Relations with foreign nations, as well as treaties; protection of American citizens abroad; interventions and declarations of war; diplomatic service; American business interests abroad; the U.N. and international monetary organizations; foreign loans.

Governmental Affairs: Budget and accounting measures other than appropriations; executive branch reorganizations; Comptroller General reports; studies of all levels of government operations; study of relations between the U.S. and states, municipalities, and international organizations of which the U.S. is a member; postal service; census.

Judiciary: Judicial proceedings; federal courts and judges; Constitutional amendments; the Patent Office; claims against the U.S.; civil liberties; protection of trade and commerce; meetings of Congress and attendance of members; immigration and naturalization; bankruptcy, mutiny, espionage, counterfeiting; apportionment of representatives; interstate compacts.

Labor and Human Resources: Education, health, and public welfare; labor, including foreign laborers; private pension plans; aging; arts and humanities.

Rules and Administration: General administration of the Senate; federal elections; corrupt practices; contested elections; management of Library of Congress; reorganization acts; creation of new standing committees.

Veterans' Affairs: Veterans' hospitals, education, compensation, and welfare.

CONGRESSIONAL JOINT COMMITTEES, COMMISSIONS AND BOARDS

Joint Committees on:
  Library, Printing, Taxation
Joint Economic Committee
Commission on Art and Antiquities of U.S. Senate
Commission on Security and Cooperation in Europe
Commission on the West Central Front of the U.S. Capitol
Consumer Product Safety Commission
District of Columbia Law Revision Commission
Franklin Delano Roosevelt Memorial Commission
House Commission on Congressional Mailing Standards
House Office Building Commission
Japan-United States Friendship Commission
Migratory Bird Conservation Commission
National Alcohol Fuels Commission
National Commission for Employment Policy
National Commission on Air Quality
National Transportation Policy Study Commission

Permanent Committee for the Oliver Wendell Holmes Devise Fund
President's Commission on the Coal Industry
President's Commission on Mental Retardation
Senate Office Building Commission
Temporary Commission on Financial Oversight of the District
  of Columbia
Environmental Study Conference
Members of Congress for Peace Through Law
North Atlantic Assembly
The Interparliamentary Union
Board for International Broadcasting
Board of Visitors to the Air Force Academy
Board of Visitors to the Coast Guard Academy
Board of Visitors to the Merchant Marine Academy
Board of Visitors to the Military Academy
Board of Visitors to the Naval Academy

THE WHITE HOUSE OFFICE—1980

Assistant to the President
and Chief of Staff . . . . Jack H. Watson, Jr.

Assistant to the President for
National Security Affairs . . . . Zbigniew Brzezinski

Counsel to the President . . . . Lloyd N. Cutler

Staff Director for the First Lady . . . . . . Edith J. Dobelle

Secretary to the Cabinet and Assistant
to the President for
Intergovernmental Affairs . . . . Eugene Eidenberg

Assistant to the President for
Domestic Affairs and Policy . . . . Stuart E. Eizenstat

Advisor to the President on Inflation . . Alfred E. Kahn

Assistant to the President and Staff
Director . . . . Alonzo L. McDonald, Jr.

Assistant to the President for
Congressional Liaison . . . . Frank B. Moore

Press Secretary to the President . . . . . Joseph L. Powell

Assistant to the President . . . . Sarah C. Weddington

Assistant to the President . . . . Anne Wexler

Special Assistant to the President for
Ethnic Affairs . . . . Stephen R. Aiello

Special Assistant to the President
for Administration . . . . Hugh A. Carter, Jr.

Special Assistant to the President
for Information Management . . . . . . Richard M. Harden

Special Assistant to the
President . . . . C. Ray Jenkins

Special Assistant to the
President . . . . Louis E. Martin

Special Advisor to the President . . . . . Alfred H. Moses

Special Assistant to the President
for Consumer Affairs . . . . Esther Peterson

Counselor to the President on Aging . . Harold L. Sheppard

Special Assistant to the
President for Hispanic Affairs . . . . . Esteban E. Torres

Appointments Secretary to the
President . . . . Phillip J. Wise, Jr.

Deputy Assistant for National
Security Affairs . . . . David L. Aaron

Deputy Press Secretary . . . . Patricia Y. Bario

Deputy Assistant to the
President . . . . Landon Butler

Deputy Assistant for Congressional
Liaison (House) . . . . William H. Cable

Deputy Counsel . . . . Michael H. Cardozo V

Deputy Assistant for Domestic Affairs
and Policy . . . . Bertram W. Carp

Deputy Assistant to the
President . . . . Michael H. Chanin

Deputy Assistant for
Congressional Liaison . . . . James M. Copeland Jr.

Deputy Appointments Secretary . . . . . Robert H. Dunn

Deputy Press Secretary . . . . Rex L. Granum

Deputy Assistant to the President for
Intergovernmental Affairs and
Deputy Secretary to the
Cabinet . . . . Bruce Kirschenbaum

Deputy Counsel . . . . Joseph N. Onek

Deputy Assistant for Congressional
Liaison (Senate) . . . . Danny C. Tate

Deputy Assistant . . . . William E. Albers

Special Assistant for
Congressional Liaison . . . . Robert G. Beckel

Personal Assistant/Secretary
to the President . . . . Susan S. Clough

Special Assistant for
Congressional Liaison (House) . . . . James C. Free

Deputy Assistant . . . . Richard Hernandez

Chief Speechwriter . . . . Hendrik Hertzberg

Press Secretary to the First Lady . . . . . Mary Finch Hoyt

Senior Associate Counsel . . . . Douglas B. Huron

Staff Secretary . . . . Richard G. Hutcheson III

Special Assistant for
Congressional Liaison (House) . . . . Robert Maher

Director of the Presidential Personnel
Office . . . . Arnie Miller

Special Assistant for
Congressional Liaison (House) . . . . Valerie F. Pinson

Deputy Assistant for Research . . . . Elizabeth A. Rainwater

Deputy to the Staff Director . . . . Michael J. Rowny

Special Assistant for
Congressional Liaison . . . . Robert K. Russell, Jr.

Associate Assistant (Wexler) . . . . John Ryor

Deputy Assistant . . . . William G. Simpson

Special Assistant for
Congressional Liaison (House) . . . . Terrence D. Straub

Deputy Assistant . . . . Linda Tarr-Whelan

Special Assistant for
Congressional Liaison . . . . Robert Thomson

Deputy Appointments Secretary . . . . . Frances M. Voorde

Deputy Special Assistant—
Military Office . . . . Marvin L. Beaman, Jr.

Deputy Special Assistant for
White House Operations . . . . Daniel Malachuk, Jr.

Personal Assistant to the
First Lady . . . . Madeline F. MacBean

Social Secretary . . . . Gretchen Poston

Special Assistant for Congressional
Liaison . . . . Robert M. Schule

Deputy Director of the
Presidential Personnel Office . . . . . . Harley M. Frankel

Deputy Assistant for Labor Liaison . . . Bernard Aronson

Special Assistant for Congressional
Liaison . . . . Ronna Freiberg

Associate Assistant . . . . Jane D. Hartley

Special Assistant to the Staff Director . Robert S. Meyers

Deputy Chief Speechwriter . . . . Gordon C. Stewart

Counsel to the Intelligence Oversight
Board . . . . James V. Dick

Associate Press Secretary . . . . Claudia M. Townsend

Associate Director, Presidential
Personnel Office . . . . Peggy E. Rainwater

Director of Projects for the First Lady . Kathryn E. Cade

Associate Counsel . . . . Patrick Apodaca

Director, Visitor's Office . . . . Nancy A. Willing

Editor, News Summary . . . . Janet E. McMahon

Physician to the President . . . . Rear Adm. William M.
Lukash, MC USN

Chief Usher . . . . Rex W. Scouten

U.S. GOVERNMENT OFFICIALS: ANNUAL SALARIES SOURCE: Office of Personnel Management

Executive Branch		Legislative Branch		Judicial Branch	
President	$200,000	Speaker of the House	$79,125	Chief Justice	$79,125[2]
Vice-President	79,125	President Pro Tem (Senate)	68,575	Associate Justices	75,960[2]
Top Executive Positions[1]		Majority and Minority Leaders	68,575	Judges of the U.S. Court of Appeals	60,662.50[2]
I	69,630	Members of Congress	60,662.50	Judges of the U.S. District Court	57,497.50[2]
II	60,662.50	Comptroller General	60,662.50	Director of the Administrative Office of the	
III	55,387.50	Heads of Other Legislative Agencies	52,750	United States Courts	57,497.50[2]
IV	52,750				
V	50,112.50				

[1]Top Executive positions are in levels I-V, ranging from Secretaries of Executive departments at level I to heads of major bureaus at level V; for a listing, see Sections 5312-5316 of Title 5, United States Code. [2]Reflects a pay increase of only 5.5%, although executive order of October 1979 approved a 12.2% increase, to be decided by pending court action.

THE U.S. CABINET: 1980

Secretary of State: Edmund S. Muskie, b. Mar. 28, 1914, Rumford, Maine; ed., Bates College (B.A., 1936), Cornell University Law School (LL.B., 1939). U.S. Navy during World War II. Maine House of Representatives (1946-1952); Governor of Maine (1954-1958); U.S. Senator (1959-1980). Democratic vice presidential nominee 1968. Assumed his cabinet post on May 8, 1980.

Secretary of the Treasury: G. William Miller, b. Mar. 9, 1925, Sapulpa, Okla.; ed., U.S. Coast Guard Academy (B.S., 1945), University of California at Berkeley (J.D., 1952). Line officer in the U.S. Navy (1945-1949), private law practice (1952-1956). He joined a business firm in 1956 and later became chairman of the board of a large U.S. conglomerate. Chairman of the Federal Reserve Board (1978-1979). He assumed his cabinet post on August 6, 1979.

Secretary of Defense: Dr. Harold Brown, b. Sept. 19, 1927, New York, N.Y.; ed., Columbia University (A.B., 1945; A.M., 1946; Ph.D., 1949). Taught physics at Columbia University and Stevens Institute (1947-1952); research scientist at various laboratories (1952-1961), held several special government appointments (1956-1965); Secretary of the Air Force (1965-1969); president of California Institute of Technology (1969-1977). He assumed his cabinet post on January 21, 1977.

Attorney General: Benjamin R. Civiletti, b. July 17, 1935, Peekskill, N.Y.; ed., Johns Hopkins University (B.A., 1950), University of Maryland Law School (LL.B., 1961). Assistant U.S. Attorney in Maryland (1962-1964), private law practice (1964-1977); Assistant Attorney General in charge of the Criminal Division in the Justice Department (Mar. 1977-Jan. 1978); Deputy U.S. Attorney General (May 1978). He assumed his position as Attorney General on August 16, 1979.

Secretary of the Interior: Cecil D. Andrus[1], b. Aug. 25, 1931, Hood River, Oreg.; ed., attended Oregon State University. U.S. Navy during the Korean conflict, Idaho State Senator (1960-1970); Governor of Idaho (1970-1977). He assumed his cabinet post on January 23, 1977.

Secretary of Agriculture: Bob S. Bergland, b. July 22, 1928, Roseau, Minn.; ed., School of Agriculture, University of Minnesota. Farmer (1950-1961); served the state and federal governments (1961-1968); U.S. Congressman (1970-1976). He assumed his cabinet post on January 23, 1977.

Secretary of Commerce: Philip M. Klutznick, b. July 9, 1907, Kansas City, Mo.; ed., attended universities of Kansas and Nebraska, Creighton University (LL.B., 1929). Attorney and businessman, primarily associated with real estate development in Chicago. He served as a member of several state organizations and federal commissions, including Federal Public Housing Authority (1944-1946), President's Advisory Committee on Indo-Chinese Refugees, several U.S. delegations to the United Nations, and as a deputy to the UN ambassador (1961-1963). He assumed his cabinet post on January 9, 1980.

Secretary of Labor: Dr. F. Ray Marshall, b. Aug. 22, 1928, Oak Grove, La.; ed., Millsaps College (B.A., 1949), Louisiana State University (M.A., 1950), University of California at Berkeley (Ph.D., 1954). Professor at Mississippi, Louisiana State, Kentucky, and Texas universities (1953-1976); author of several books on labor economics. He assumed his cabinet post on January 27, 1977.

Secretary of Health and Human Services: Patricia Roberts Harris, b. 1924, Mattoon, Ill.; ed., Howard University (A.B., 1945), George Washington University (J.D., 1960). Private law practice and professor at Howard University (1960-1965, and 1970-1976); Ambassador to Luxembourg (1965-1967). Active in civil rights movement for more than 30 years. Secretary of Housing and Urban Development (1977-1979). She assumed her cabinet post as Secretary of HHS on August 3, 1979.

Secretary of Housing and Urban Development: Moon Landrieu, b. July 23, 1930, New Orleans, La.; ed., Loyola University New Orleans (B.B.A., 1952) and (LL.B., 1954). Judge Advocate General Corps, U.S. Army (1954-1957). Private law practice (1957-1969); Louisiana House of Representatives (1960-1965); Councilman-at-large City of New Orleans (1966-1970); Mayor of New Orleans (1970-1978); president of a commercial real estate firm (1978-1979). He assumed office on September 24, 1979.

Department of Transportation: Neil E. Goldschmidt, b. June 16, 1940, Eugene, Ore.; ed., University of Oregon (A.B. in Political Science 1963), University of California Law School at Berkeley (LL.B., 1967). Interned in the Washington office of U.S. Senator Maurine Newberger (1964-1965). Attorney with Legal Aid Society of Oregon (1967-1970); Portland, Oregon, councilman (1970-1972); Mayor of Portland (1972-1979). He assumed office on August 15, 1979.

Secretary of Energy: Charles W. Duncan, Jr., b. Sept. 9, 1926, Houston, Texas; ed., Rice University (B.S., 1947), graduate study at University of Texas. U.S. Army Air Corps in World War II; chemical engineer with oil company before entering food business, then became president of large soft drink company; became Deputy Secretary of Defense on Jan. 31, 1977, then Secretary of Energy on August 24, 1979.

Secretary of Education: Shirley M. Hufstedler, b. Aug. 24, 1925, Denver, Colo.; ed. University of New Mexico (B.S., 1945); Stanford University (LL.B. 1949). Attorney in Los Angeles (1950-1960); Judge of Los Angeles Superior Court (1961-1966); Judge California State Court of Appeals (1966-1968); Judge U.S. Court of Appeals, 9th District (1968-1979). She assumed her cabinet post Dec. 6, 1979, although department was not officially opened until May 4, 1980.

CABINET LEVEL POSTS:

Counsel to the President: Lloyd N. Cutler

Special Representative of the United States Trade Office: Reubin O'D. Askew

Director of the Office of Management and Budget: James T. McIntyre, Jr.

U.S. Ambassador to the United Nations: Donald F. McHenry

Assistant to the President and Chief of Staff: Jack H. Watson, Jr.

---

[1]Andrus plans to resign before the end of 1980.

FEDERAL EMPLOYMENT†   SOURCE: Office of Personnel Management

	Employees
Total, All Agencies	**3,001,307**
LEGISLATIVE BRANCH	39,739
Congress	19,023
Architect of the Capitol	2,195
General Accounting Office	5,530
Government Printing Office	6,900
Library of Congress	5,450
JUDICIAL BRANCH	14,318
EXECUTIVE BRANCH	2,947,250
Executive Office of the President	1,878
White House Office	405
Office of the Vice-President	28
Office of Management and Budget	615
Council of Economic Advisors	35
Executive Departments:	
State (Includes AID)	23,832
Treasury	138,146
Defense:	
Military, Total	966,266
Department of the Army	346,858
Department of the Navy	310,241
Department of the Air Force	232,898
Civilian, Total	76,269
Justice	56,261
Interior	80,290
Agriculture	120,150
Commerce	148,002
Labor	23,901
Health, Education, and Welfare	166,971*
Housing and Urban Development	17,581
Transportation	73,075
Energy	21,189
ACTION	1,997
Environmental Protection Agency	14,300
Equal Employment Opportunity Commission	3,694
Federal Communications Commission	2,228
Federal Deposit Insurance Corporation	3,459
Federal Trade Commission	1,874
General Services Adminstration	37,997
International Communication Agency	8,122
Interstate Commerce Commission	2,079
National Aeronautics and Space Administration	23,341
National Labor Relations Board	2,987
Nuclear Regulatory Commission	3,171
Office of Personnel Management	8,416
Securities and Exchange Commission	2,073
Small Business Adminstration	5,723
Smithsonian Institution	4,463
Tennessee Valley Authority	50,407
U.S. Postal Service	658,494
Veterans Administration	238,726

†List includes selected federal agencies with 1,500 or more employees. The total, however, represents all paid civilian employees of the U.S. government. Employees of the CIA, National Security Agency, and Special Youth Programs are not included. Data as of March 1980. *Includes employment figures for the new Department of Education which was formally established on May 3, 1980. The Department of Health, Education, and Welfare was renamed the Department of Health and Human Services.

HEADS OF FEDERAL DEPARTMENTS AND AGENCIES*

Departments and Agencies	Head
ACTION	Samuel W. Brown, Jr.
806 Connecticut Avenue N.W. 20525	Director
Central Intelligence Agency	Adm. Stansfield Turner
Washington, D.C. 20505	Director
Civil Aeronautics Board	Marvin S. Cohen
1825 Connecticut Ave. N.W. 20428	Chairman
Commission on Civil Rights	Dr. Arthur S. Flemming
1121 Vermont Ave. N.W. 20425	Chairman
Community Services Admin.	Richard J. Rios
1200 19th St. N.W. 20506	Director
Consumer Product Safety Commission	Susan B. King
1111 18th St. N.W. 20207	Chairwoman
Council of Economic Advisors	Charles L. Schultze
Executive Office Bldg. 20506	Director
Council on Environmental Quality	Gus Speth
722 Jackson Pl. N.W. 20006	Chairman
Council on Wage and Price Stability	R. Robert Russel
726 Jackson Pl. N.W. 20506	Director
Department of Agriculture	Bob S. Bergland
14th St. and Independence Ave. S.W. 20250	Secretary of Agriculture
Deputy Secretary	Jim Williams
Department of Commerce	Philip M. Klutznick
14th St. between Constitution Ave. and E St. N.W. 20230	Secretary of Commerce
Under Secretary	Luther H. Hodges, Jr.
Patent & Trademark Office Crystal Plaza, Arlington, Va.	Sidney Diamond Commissioner
Bureau of Economic Analysis 1401 K St. N.W. 20230	George Jaszi Director
Bureau of the Census Suitland, Md. 20233	Vincent P. Barabba Director
National Bureau of Standards I-270 & Quince Orchard Rd., Gaithersburg, Md. 20234	Ernest Ambler Director
National Oceanic and Atmospheric Administration 6001 Executive Blvd., Rockville, Md. 20852	Richard A. Frank Administrator
Department of Defense	Dr. Harold R. Brown
The Pentagon 20301	Secretary of Defense
Deputy Secretary of Defense	W. Graham Claytor, Jr.
Joint Chiefs of Staff	Gen. David C. Jones USAF Chairman
Department of the Air Force The Pentagon 20330	Dr. Hans M. Mark Secretary of the Air Force
Department of the Army The Pentagon 20310	Clifford L. Alexander, Jr. Secretary of the Army
Department of the Navy The Pentagon 20350	Edward Hidalgo Secretary of the Navy
Commandant of the Marine Corps	Gen. Robert H. Barrow
Department of Education	Shirley M. Hufstedler
400 Maryland Ave. S.W. 20202	Secretary of Education
Under Secretary	Steven A. Minter
Department of Energy	Charles W. Duncan, Jr.
1110 Independence Ave. S.W. 20314	Secretary of Energy
Deputy Secretary	Vacant
Federal Energy Regulatory Commission	Charles B. Curtis Chairman
Department of Health and Human Services	Patricia R. Harris
200 Independence Ave. S.W. 20201	Secretary of Health and Human Services
Under Secretary	Hale Champion
Office of Human Development Services	Cesar A. Perales Ass't Sec. for Human Development Services
Food and Drug Administrations 5600 Fishers Lane, Rockville, Md. 20857	Jere E. Goyan Commissioner
National Institutes of Health 9000 Rockville Pike, Bethesda, Md. 20205	Donald S. Fredrickson Director
Public Health Service 5600 Fishers Lane, Rockville, Md. 20857	Julius B. Richmond Ass't Sec. for Health
Social Security Administration 330 Indiana Ave. S.W. 20201	William J. Driver Commissioner
Department of Housing and Urban Development	Moon Landrieu Secretary of Housing and Urban Development
451 7th St. S.W. 20410	
Under Secretary	Victor Marrero
Department of the Interior	Cecil D. Andrus[1]
C St. between 18th and 19th Sts. N.W. 20240	Secretary of the Interior
Under Secretary	James A. Joseph
Bureau of Indian Affairs	William E. Hallett Commissioner
Bureau of Mines	Lindsay D. Norman Director
Geological Survey	H. William Menard Director
National Park Service	Russell E. Dickenson Director
Department of Justice	Benjamin R. Civiletti
Constitution Ave. and 10th St. N.W. 20530	Attorney General
Deputy Attorney General	Charles B. Renfrew
Solicitor General	Sana F. Shtasel
F.B.I.	William H. Webster Director
Immigration and Naturalization Service	Matt W. Garcia[2] Commissioner
Drug Enforcement Administration	Peter B. Bensinger
1405 I St. N.W. 20537	Administrator
Department of Labor	F. Ray Marshall
200 Constitution Ave. N.W. 20210	Secretary of Labor
Under Secretary	John N. Gentry
Department of State	Edmund S. Muskie
2201 C St. N.W. 20520	Secretary of State
Deputy Secretary of State	Warren M. Christopher
Chief of Protocol	Abelardo L. Valdez
Department of Transportation	Neil E. Goldschmidt
400 7th St. S.W. 20590	Secretary of Transportation
Deputy Secretary	William J. Beckham, Jr.
U.S. Coast Guard	Adm. John B. Hayes, USCG Commandant
Federal Aviation Administration	Langhorne M. Bond Administrator
Federal Highway Administration	John S. Hassell, Jr. Administrator
Federal Railroad Administration	John M. Sullivan Administrator
Department of the Treasury	G. William Miller
15th St. and Pennsylvania Ave. N.W. 20220	Secretary of the Treasury
Deputy Secretary	Robert Carswell
Commissioner of Customs	Robert E Chasen
Bureau of Engraving and Printing	Harry R. Clements Director
Bureau of the Mint	Stella B. Hackel Director
Internal Revenue Service	Jerome Kurtz[1] Commissioner
Comptroller of the Currency	John G. Heimann
Treasurer of the U.S.	Azie T. Morton
U.S. Secret Service	H. Stuart Knight Director
Bureau of Alcohol, Tobacco & Firearms	George R. Dickerson Director

*All addresses are Washington, D.C., unless otherwise noted. [1]Plans to resign in late 1980. [2]Nominated.

District of Columbia . . . . Marion Barry
District Building, 14th &   Mayor of the District
E Sts. N.W. 20004   of Columbia

Domestic Policy Staff . . . . Stuart Eizenstat
1600 Pennsylvania Ave. N.W.   Ass't to the Pres. for
20500   Domestic Affairs and Policy

Environmental Protection . . . . Douglas M. Costle
Agency   Administrator
401 M St. S.W. 20460

Equal Employment . . . . Eleanor Holmes Norton
Opportunity Commission   Chairperson
2401 E St. N.W. 20506

Export-Import Bank of the . . . . John L. Moore, Jr.
United States   President & Chairman
811 Vermont Ave. N.W. 20571

Farm Credit Administration . . . . Donald E. Wilkinson
490 L'Enfant Plaza East S.W.   Governor
20578

Federal Communications . . . . Charles D. Ferris
Commission   Chairman
1919 M St. N.W. 20554

Federal Deposit . . . . Irvine Sprague
Insurance Corporation   Chairman
550 17th St. N.W. 20429

Federal Election Commission . . . . Robert O. Tiernan
1325 K St. N.W. 20463   Chairman

Federal Maritime Commission . . . . . . Richard J. Daschbach
1100 L St. 20573   Chairman

Federal Mediation and . . . . Wayne L. Horvitz
Conciliation Service   Director
2100 K St. N.W. 20427

Federal Reserve System, ... Paul A. Volcker
Board of Governors of the   Chairman
Constitution Ave. and 20th
St. N.W. 20551

Federal Trade Commission . . . . Michael Pertschuk
Pennsylvania Ave. and 6th   Chairman
St. N.W. 20580

Foreign Claims Settlement . . . . Richard W. Yarborough
Commission of the U.S.   Chairman
1111 20th St. N.W. 20579

General Accounting Office . . . . Elmer B. Staats
441 G St. N.W. 20548   Comptroller General

General Services Administration . . . . Rowland G. Freeman III
18th and F Sts. N.W. 20405   Administrator
Archivist of the U.S. . . . . Robert M. Warner

Government Printing Office . . . . Gerald R. Dillon[1]
North Capitol and H Sts. N.W.   Public Printer
20401

International Communication . . . . John E. Reinhardt
Agency   Director
1750 Pennsylvania Ave. N.W.
20547

Interstate Commerce Commission . . . Darius W. Gaskins, Jr.
12th St. and Constitution   Chairman
Ave. N.W. 20423

Library of Congress . . . . Daniel J. Boorstin
10 First St. S.E. 20540   Librarian of Congress
Copyright Office . . . . David L. Ladd
Crystal Mall Annex,   Register of Copyrights
Arlington, Va. 20559

National Aeronautics and . . . . Robert A. Frosch
Space Administration   Administrator
400 Maryland Ave. S.W. 20546

National Credit Union . . . . Lawrence Connell
Administration   Administrator
1776 G St. N.W. 20456

**National Foundation on
the Arts and the Humanities**
National Endowment . . . . Livingston L. Biddle, Jr.
for the Arts   Chairman
2401 E St. N.W. 20520
National Endowment . . . . Joseph D. Duffey
for the Humanities   Chairman
806 15th St. N.W. 20506

National Labor Relations Board . . . . . John H. Fanning
1717 Pennsylvania Ave. N.W.   Chairman
20570

National Mediation Board . . . . Robert O. Harris
1425 K St. N.W. 20572   Chairman

National Science Foundation . . . . John B. Slaughter
1800 G St. N.W. 20550   Director

National Security Council . . . . Christine Dodson
Executive Off. Bldg. 20506   Staff Secretary

National Transportation Safety . . . . . . James B. King
Board   Chairman
800 Independence Ave. S.W.
20594

Nuclear Regulatory Commission . . . . Albert Carnesale
1717 H St. N.W. 20555   Chairman

Occupational Safety and Health . . . . . Timothy F. Cleary
Review Commission   Chairman
1825 K St. 20006

Office of Management and . . . . James T. McIntyre, Jr.
Budget   Director
Executive Office Building 20503

Office of Personnel Management . . . . Alan K. Campbell
1900 E. St. N.W. 20415   Director

Office of Technology Assessment . . . . John H. Gibbons
600 Pennsylvania Ave. S.E.   Director
20510

Office of the United States . . . . Reubin O'D. Askew
Trade Representative   United States Trade
1800 G St. N.W. 20506   Representative

Panama Canal Commission . . . . Thomas M. Constant
425 13th St. N.W. 20004   Secretary

Postal Rate Commission . . . . A. Lee Fritschler
2000 L St. N.W. 20268   Chairman

Securities and Exchange . . . . Harold M. Williams
Commission   Chairman
500 N. Capitol St. N.W.
20549

Selective Service System . . . . Bernard D. Rostker
600 E St. N.W. 20435   Director

Small Business Administration . . . . . . A. Vernon Weaver, Jr.
1441 L St. N.W. 20416   Administrator

Smithsonian Institution . . . . S. Dillon Ripley
1000 Jefferson Drive S.W.   Secretary
20560

Synthetic Fuels Corporation[2] . . . . . . John C. Sawhill
     Chairman

Tennessee Valley Authority . . . . S. David Freeman
400 Commerce Ave.   Chairman
Knoxville, Tenn. 37902

United States Arms Control . . . . Ralph Earle II
and Disarmament Agency   Director
320 21st St. N.W. 20451

United States International Develop- . Thomas Ehrlich
ment Cooperation Agency   Director
320 21st St. N.W. 205234

United States International Trade . . . . Bill Alberger
Commission   Chairman
701 E St. N.W. 20436

United States Postal Service . . . . William F. Bolger
475 L'Enfant Plaza West S.W.   Postmaster General
20260

Veterans Administration . . . . Max Cleland
810 Vermont Ave. N.W. 20420   Administrator

---

[1]Nominated 9/9/80. [2]Newly created organization; chairman and officers need Senate confirmation.

MEMBERS OF THE U.S. SUPREME COURT

Source: Supreme Court of the United States and other sources

Name	Place of Birth	Year of Birth	Education	Appointed by President	Date Oath Taken	Age at Oath	Date Service Ended	Service Ended By	Years of Service	Age at End of Term	Date of Death
CHIEF JUSTICES											
Jay, John	New York	1745	King's College (now Columbia University), grad. 1764	Washington	Oct. 1789	44	June 1795	resigned	5	49	May 1829
Rutledge, John*	South Carolina	1739	Studied law at Middle Temple, London	Washington				rejected	0	56	June 1800
Ellsworth, Oliver	Connecticut	1745	Attended Yale College; College of New Jersey (now Princeton University), grad. 1766	Washington	Mar. 1796	50	Dec. 1800	resigned	4	55	Nov. 1807
Marshall, John	Virginia	1755	Attended College of William and Mary	Adams	Feb. 1801	45	July 1835	death	34	79	July 1835
Taney, Roger Brooke	Maryland	1777	Dickinson College, Penn., grad. 1795	Jackson	Mar. 1836	59	Oct. 1864	death	28	87	Oct. 1864
Chase, Salmon Portland	New Hampshire	1808	Attended Cincinnati College; Dartmouth College, grad. 1826	Lincoln	Dec. 1864	56	May 1873	death	8	65	May 1873
Waite, Morrison Remick	Connecticut	1816	Yale College, grad. 1837	Grant	Mar. 1874	57	Mar. 1888	death	14	71	Mar. 1888
Fuller, Melville Weston	Maine	1833	Bowdoin College, grad. 1853; attended Harvard Law School	Cleveland	Oct. 1888	55	July 1910	death	21	77	July 1910
White, Edward Douglass*	Louisiana	1845	Attended Mount St. Mary's College, Md.; Jesuit College in New Orleans, La.; and Georgetown College, Washington, D.C.	Taft	Dec. 1910	65	May 1921	death	10	75	May 1921
Taft, William Howard	Ohio	1857	Yale College, grad. 1878; Cincinnati Law School, LL.B. 1880	Harding	July 1921	63	Feb. 1930	retired	8	72	Mar. 1930
Hughes, Charles Evans*	New York	1862	Attended Colgate University; Brown University, Rhode Island, grad. 1881; M.A. 1884; Columbia Law School, LL.B. 1884	Hoover	Feb. 1930	67	June 1941	retired	11	79	Aug. 1948
Stone, Harlan Fiske*	New Hampshire	1872	Amherst College, Mass., grad. 1894; M.A. 1897; Columbia Law School, LL.B. 1898	Roosevelt, F.	July 1941	68	Apr. 1946	death	4	73	Apr. 1946
Vinson, Frederick Moore	Kentucky	1890	Kentucky Normal College, grad.; Centre College, Ky., grad. 1909; LL.B. 1911	Truman	June 1946	56	Sept. 1953	death	7	63	Sept. 1953
Warren, Earl	California	1891	University of California, LL.B. 1912; J.D. 1914	Eisenhower	Oct. 1953	62	June 1969	retired	16	78	July 1974
Burger, Warren Earl	Minnesota	1907	Attended University of Minnesota; St. Paul College of Law, LL.B. 1931	Nixon	June 1969	61	—	—	—	—	—
ASSOCIATE JUSTICES											
Cushing, William	Massachusetts	1732	Harvard College, grad. 1751	Washington	Sept. 1789	57	Sept. 1810	death	20	77	Sept. 1810
Wilson, James	Scotland	1742	Attended University of St. Andrews (Scotland)	Washington	Sept. 1789	47	Aug. 1798	death	8	56	Aug. 1798
Blair, John Jr.	Virginia	1732	College of William and Mary, grad. 1754; studied law at Middle Temple, London	Washington	Sept. 1789	57	Jan. 1796	resigned	6	63	Aug. 1800
Iredell, James	England	1751	Private tutoring	Washington	Feb. 1790	39	Oct. 1799	death	8	48	Oct. 1799
Johnson, Thomas	Maryland	1732	No formal education	Washington	Nov. 1791	59	Sept. 1793	resigned	1	61	Oct. 1819
Paterson, William	Ireland	1745	College of New Jersey (now Princeton University), grad. 1763; M.A. 1766	Washington	Feb. 1793	47	Sept. 1806	death	13	61	Sept. 1806
Chase, Samuel	Maryland	1741	Private tutoring	Washington	Jan. 1796	55	June 1811	death	15	70	June 1811
Washington, Bushrod	Virginia	1762	College of William and Mary, grad. 1778	Adams, J.	Dec. 1798	36	Nov. 1829	death	31	67	Nov. 1829
Moore, Alfred	North Carolina	1755	Attended private schools	Adams, J.	Oct. 1799	44	Feb. 1804	resigned	4	48	Oct. 1810
Johnson, William	South Carolina	1771	College of New Jersey (now Princeton University), grad. 1778	Jefferson	Apr. 1804	32	Aug. 1834	death	30	63	Aug. 1834
Livingston, Brockholst	New York	1757	College of New Jersey (now Princeton University), grad. 1774	Jefferson	Sept. 1806	49	Mar. 1823	death	16	65	Mar. 1823
Todd, Thomas	Virginia	1765	Private tutoring	Jefferson	Mar. 1807	42	Feb. 1826	death	18	60	Feb. 1826
Duvall, Gabriel	Maryland	1752	Dartmouth College, graduation date unknown	Madison	Feb. 1812		? 1835	resigned	22	81	Mar. 1844
Story, Joseph	Massachusetts	1779	Harvard College, grad. 1798	Madison	Nov. 1811	32	Sept. 1845	death	33	65	Sept. 1845
Thompson, Smith	New York	1768	College of New Jersey (now Princeton University), grad. 1798	Monroe	Dec. 1823	55	Dec. 1843	death	20	75	Dec. 1843
Trimble, Robert	Virginia	1776	Attended Kentucky Academy (now Transylvania College	Adams, J. Q.	Apr. 1826	49	Aug. 1828	death	2	51	Aug. 1828
McLean, John	New Jersey	1784	Private tutoring	Jackson	? 1829	44	Apr. 1861	death	32	76	Apr. 1861

* Also served as associate justice: Rutledge (1789–91); White (1894–1910); Hughes (1910–16); Stone (1925–41).

Associate Justices	Place of Birth	Year of Birth	Education	Appointed by President	Date Oath Taken	Age at Oath	Date Service Ended	Service Ended By	Years of Service	Age at End of Term	Date of Death
Baldwin, Henry	Connecticut	1780	Yale College, grad. 1797	Jackson	? 1830	50	Apr. 1844	death	14	64	Apr. 1844
Wayne, James M.	Georgia	1790	College of New Jersey (now Princeton University), grad. 1808	Jackson	Jan. 1835	45	July 1867	death	32	77	July 1867
Barbour, Philip P.	Virginia	1783	No record of formal education	Jackson	Mar. 1836	53	Feb. 1841	death	5	58	Feb. 1841
Catron, John	Pennsylvania	1786	No record of formal education	Jackson	Mar. 1837	51	May 1865	death	28	79	May 1865
McKinley, John	Virginia	1780	No record of formal education	Van Buren	? 1837	57	July 1852	death	15	72	July 1852
Daniel, Peter V.	Virginia	1784	Attended College of New Jersey (now Princeton Univ.)	Van Buren	Feb. 1841	57	May 1860	death	19	76	May 1860
Nelson, Samuel	New York	1792	Middlebury College, grad. 1813	Tyler	Mar. 1845	53	Nov. 1872	resigned	27	80	Dec. 1873
Woodbury, Levi	New Hampshire	1789	Dartmouth College, grad. 1809	Polk	May 1845	56	Sept. 1851	death	5	61	Sept. 1851
Grier, Robert C.	Pennsylvania	1794	Dickinson College, grad. 1812	Polk	Aug. 1846	52	Feb. 1870	resigned	23	75	Aug. 1870
Curtis, Benjamin	Massachusetts	1809	Harvard College, grad. 1829	Fillmore	Dec. 1851	42	Sept. 1857	resigned	6	48	Sept. 1874
Campbell, John A.	Georgia	1811	University of Georgia, grad. 1826; Attended West Point, 1826–28	Pierce	Mar. 1853	42	Apr. 1861	resigned	8	50	Mar. 1889
Clifford, Nathan	New Hampshire	1803	Attended private schools	Buchanan	Jan. 1858	55	July 1881	death	23	78	July 1881
Swayne, Noah Haynes	Virginia	1804	No record of formal education	Lincoln	Jan. 1862	57	Jan. 1881	retired	18	76	June 1884
Miller, Samuel Freeman	Kentucky	1816	Transylvania University, Ky., grad. 1838	Lincoln	July 1862	46	Oct. 1890	death	28	74	Oct. 1890
Davis, David	Maryland	1815	Kenyon College, Ohio, grad. 1832; Yale Law School, LL.B. 1835	Lincoln	Dec. 1862	47	Mar. 1877	resigned	14	61	June 1886
Field, Stephen Johnson	Connecticut	1816	Williams College, Mass., grad. 1837	Lincoln	May 1863	46	Dec. 1897	retired	34	81	Apr. 1899
Strong, William	Connecticut	1808	Yale College, grad. 1828; M.A. 1831; attended Yale Law School	Grant	Mar. 1870	61	Dec. 1880	retired	10	72	Aug. 1895
Bradley, Joseph P.	New York	1813	Rutgers College, grad. 1836	Grant	Mar. 1870	57	Jan. 1892	death	21	78	Jan. 1892
Hunt, Ward	New York	1810	Union College, N.Y., grad. 1828	Grant	Jan. 1873	62	Jan. 1882	disabled	9	71	Mar. 1886
Harlan, John Marshall	Kentucky	1833	Centre College, Ky., grad. 1850; studied law at Transylvania College, Ky.	Hayes	Dec. 1877	44	Oct. 1911	death	33	78	Oct. 1911
Woods, William Burnham	Ohio	1824	Yale College, grad. 1845	Hayes	Jan. 1881	56	May 1887	death	6	62	May 1887
Matthews, Stanley	Ohio	1824	Kenyon College, Ohio, grad. 1840	Garfield	May 1881	56	Mar. 1889	death	7	64	Mar. 1889
Gray, Horace	Massachusetts	1828	Harvard College, grad. 1845; Harvard Law School, LL.B. 1849	Arthur	Jan. 1882	53	Sept. 1902	death	20	74	Sept. 1902
Blatchford, Samuel	New York	1820	Columbia College, grad. 1837	Arthur	Apr. 1882	62	July 1893	death	11	73	July 1893
Lamar, Lucius Quintus C.	Georgia	1825	Emory College, Ga., grad. 1845	Cleveland	Jan. 1888	62	Jan. 1893	death	5	67	Jan. 1893
Brewer, David Josiah	Asia Minor	1837	Yale College, grad. 1856; M.A. 1859; Albany (N.Y.) Law School, LL.B. 1858	Harrison	Jan. 1890	52	Mar. 1910	death	20	72	Mar. 1910
Brown, Henry Billings	Massachusetts	1836	Yale College, grad. 1856	Harrison	Jan. 1891	54	May 1906	retired	15	70	Sept. 1913
Shiras, George, Jr.	Pennsylvania	1832	Yale College, grad. 1853; Yale Law School, LL.B. 1854	Harrison	Oct. 1892	60	Feb. 1903	retired	10	71	Aug. 1924
Jackson, Howell Edmunds	Tennessee	1832	West Tennessee College, grad. 1849; attended University of Virginia; Cumberland University, Tenn., LL.B. 1856	Harrison	Mar. 1893	60	Aug. 1895	death	2	63	Aug. 1895
Peckham, Rufus Wheeler	New York	1838	Attended Albany (N.Y.) Academy	Cleveland	Jan. 1896	57	Oct. 1909	death	13	70	Oct. 1909
McKenna, Joseph	Pennsylvania	1843	Benicia Collegiate Institute, Calif., grad. 1865	McKinley	Jan. 1898	54	Jan. 1925	retired	26	81	Nov. 1926
Holmes, Oliver Wendell	Massachusetts	1841	Harvard College, grad. 1861; LL.B. 1866	Roosevelt, T.	Dec. 1902	61	Jan. 1932	retired	29	90	Mar. 1935
Day, William Rufus	Ohio	1849	University of Michigan, grad. 1870	Roosevelt, T.	Mar. 1903	53	Nov. 1922	retired	19	73	July 1923
Moody, William Henry	Massachusetts	1853	Harvard College, grad. 1876; att. Harvard Law School	Roosevelt, T.	Dec. 1906	52	Nov. 1910	disabled	3	56	July 1917
Lurton, Horace Harmon	Kentucky	1844	Attended Douglas University, Chicago (now University of Chicago); Cumberland University, Tenn., LL.B. 1867	Taft	Jan. 1910	65	July 1914	death	4	70	July 1914
Van Devanter, Willis	Indiana	1859	Attended Indiana Asbury (now De Pauw) University; Cincinnati Law School, LL.B. 1881	Taft	Jan. 1911	51	June 1937	retired	26	78	Feb. 1941
Lamar, Joseph Rucker	Georgia	1857	Bethany College, W. Va., grad. 1877; studied law, Washington and Lee University, Va.	Taft	Jan. 1911	53	Jan. 1916	death	5	58	Jan. 1916
Pitney, Mahlon	New Jersey	1858	College of New Jersey (now Princeton University), grad. 1879	Taft	Mar. 1912	54	Dec. 1922	resigned	10	64	Dec. 1924

Associate Justices (cont.)	Place of Birth	Year of Birth	Education	Appointed by President	Date Oath Taken	Age at Oath	Date Service Ended	Service Ended By	Years of Service	Age at End of Term	Date of Death
McReynolds, James Clark	Kentucky	1862	Vanderbilt University, Tenn., grad. 1882; University of Virginia Law School, LL.B. 1884								
Brandeis, Louis Dembitz	Kentucky	1856	Harvard Law School, LL.B. 1877	Wilson	Oct. 1914	52	Jan. 1941	retired	26	78	Aug. 1946
Clarke, John Hessin	Ohio	1857	Western Reserve University, Ohio, grad. 1877	Wilson	June 1916	59	Feb. 1939	retired	22	82	Oct. 1941
Sutherland, George	England	1862	Studied law at the University of Michigan	Wilson	Oct. 1916	59	Sept. 1922	resigned	5	65	Mar. 1945
Butler, Pierce	Minnesota	1866	Carleton College, Minn., grad. 1887	Harding	Oct. 1922	60	Jan. 1938	retired	15	75	July 1942
Sanford, Edward Terry	Tennessee	1865	University of Tennessee, grad. 1883; Harvard University, M.A. 1889; Harvard Law School, LL.B. 1889	Harding	Jan. 1923	56	Nov. 1939	death	16	73	Nov. 1939
Roberts, Owen Josephus	Pennsylvania	1875	University of Pennsylvania, grad. 1895; LL.B. 1898	Harding	Feb. 1923	57	Mar. 1930	death	7	64	Mar. 1930
Cardozo, Benjamin Nathan	New York	1870	Columbia University, grad. 1889; M.A. 1890; attended Columbia Law School	Hoover	June 1930	55	July 1945	resigned	15	70	May 1955
Black, Hugo Lafayette	Alabama	1886	University of Alabama, Law School, LL.B. 1906	Hoover	Mar. 1932	61	July 1938	death	6	68	July 1938
Reed, Stanley Forman	Kentucky	1884	Kentucky Wesleyan College, grad. 1902; also Yale University, grad. 1906; studied law at Columbia University	Roosevelt, F.	Aug. 1937	51	Sept. 1971	retired	34	85	Sept. 1971
Frankfurter, Felix	Austria	1882	City College of New York, grad. 1902; Harvard Law School, LL.B. 1906	Roosevelt, F.	Jan. 1938	53	Feb. 1957	retired	19	72	Apr. 1980
Douglas, William Orville	Minnesota	1898	Whitman College, Wash., grad. 1920; Columbia Law School, LL.B. 1925	Roosevelt, F.	Jan. 1939	56	Aug. 1962	retired	23	79	Feb. 1965
Murphy, Frank	Michigan	1890	University of Michigan, LL.B. 1914; studied law at Lincoln's Inn, London, and Trinity College, Dublin	Roosevelt, F.	Apr. 1939	40	Nov. 1975	retired	36	77	Jan. 1980
Byrnes, James Francis	South Carolina	1879	No record of formal education	Roosevelt, F.	Feb. 1940	49	July 1949	death	9	59	July 1949
Jackson, Robert Houghwout	New York	1892	Attended Albany (N.Y.) Law School	Roosevelt, F.	July 1941	62	Oct. 1942	resigned	1	63	Apr. 1972
Rutledge, Wiley Blount	Kentucky	1894	University of Wisconsin, grad. 1914; University of Colorado, LL.B. 1922	Roosevelt, F.	July 1941	49	Oct. 1954	death	13	62	Oct. 1954
Burton, Harold Hitz	Massachusetts	1888	Bowdoin College, Me., grad. 1909; Harvard Law School, LL.B. 1912	Roosevelt, F.	Feb. 1943	48	Sept. 1949	death	6	55	Sept. 1949
Clark, Thomas Campbell	Texas	1899	University of Texas, grad. 1921; LL.B. 1922	Truman	Oct. 1945	57	Oct. 1958	retired	13	70	Oct. 1964
Minton, Sherman	Indiana	1890	Indiana University, LL.B. 1915	Truman	Aug. 1949	49	June 1967	retired	18	67	June 1977
Harlan, John Marshall	Illinois	1899	Princeton University, grad. 1920; Rhodes Scholar to Oxford University, 1921–23; New York Law School, LL.B. 1924	Truman	Oct. 1949	58	Oct. 1956	retired	7	65	Apr. 1965
Brennan, William Joseph, Jr.	New Jersey	1906	University of Pennsylvania, grad. 1928; Harvard Law School, LL.B. 1931	Eisenhower	Mar. 1955	55	Sept. 1971	retired	16	72	Dec. 1971
Whittaker, Charles Evans	Kansas	1901	University of Kansas City, LL.B. 1924	Eisenhower	Oct. 1956	50	—	—	—	—	—
Stewart, Potter	Michigan	1915	Yale University, grad. 1937; attended Cambridge University, England; Yale Law School, LL.B. 1941	Eisenhower	Mar. 1957	56	Apr. 1962	retired	5	61	Nov. 1973
White, Byron Raymond	Colorado	1917	University of Colorado, grad. 1938; Rhodes Scholar, Oxford, England, 1939; Yale Law School, LL.B. 1946	Eisenhower	Oct. 1958	43	—	—	—	—	—
Goldberg, Arthur Joseph	Illinois	1908	Northwestern University, grad. 1929; J.D. 1930	Kennedy	Apr. 1962	44	—	—	—	—	—
Fortas, Abe	Tennessee	1910	Southwestern College, grad. 1930; Yale Law School, LL.B. 1933	Kennedy	Oct. 1962	54	July 1965	resigned	3	56	—
Marshall, Thurgood	Maryland	1908	Lincoln University, grad. 1929; Howard University, LL.B. 1933	Johnson	Oct. 1965	55	May 1969	resigned	4	58	—
Blackmun, Harry Andrew	Minnesota	1908	Harvard College, grad. 1929; Harvard Law School, LL.B. 1932	Johnson	Oct. 1967	59	—	—	—	—	—
Powell, Lewis Franklin, Jr.	Virginia	1907	Washington and Lee University, grad. 1929, LL.B., 1931; Harvard University, LL.M., 1932	Nixon	June 1970	61	—	—	—	—	—
Rehnquist, William Hubbs	Wisconsin	1924	Stanford University, grad. 1948; M.A. Harvard University 1950; LL.B., Stanford 1952	Nixon	Jan. 1972	64	—	—	—	—	—
Stevens, John Paul	Illinois	1920	Univ. of Chicago, grad. 1941; Northwestern Univ. School of Law, J.D. 1947	Nixon	Jan. 1972	47	—	—	—	—	—
				Ford	Dec. 1975	55	—	—	—	—	—

THE U.S. COURTS SOURCE: Administrative Office of the U.S. Courts

SUPREME COURT OF THE UNITED STATES
Washington, D.C.

Chief Justice (Salary: $79,125[1]): Warren E. Burger of Virginia.

Associate Justices (Salaries: $75,960[1]): William J. Brennan, Jr., of New Jersey; Potter Stewart of Ohio; Byron R. White of Colorado; Thurgood Marshall of New York; Harry A. Blackmun of Minnesota; Lewis F. Powell, Jr., of Virginia; William H. Rehnquist of Arizona; John P. Stevens of Illinois.

U.S. COURT OF APPEALS

(Salaries: $60,662.50[1])

District of Columbia Circuit: J. Skelly Wright, Chief Judge; Carl McGowan, Edward Allen Tamm, Spottswood W. Robinson III, Roger Robb, George E. MacKinnon, Malcolm Richard Wilkey, Patricia M. Wald, Abner J. Mikva, Harry T. Edwards.

First Circuit (Maine, Massachusetts, New Hampshire, Rhode Island, Puerto Rico): Frank M. Coffin, Chief Judge, Portland, Maine; Levin H. Campbell, Boston, Mass.; Hugh H. Bownes, Concord, N.H.

Second Circuit (Connecticut, New York, Vermont): Irving R. Kaufman, Chief Judge, New York, N.Y.; James L. Oakes, Brattleboro, Vt.; William H. Timbers, Bridgeport, Ct.; Thomas J. Meskill, New Britain, Ct.; Wilfred Feinberg, Walter R. Mansfield, William H. Mulligan, Amalya L. Kearse, all of New York, N.Y.; Ellsworth Van Graafeiland, Rochester, N.Y.; Jon O. Newman, Hartford, Ct.

Third Circuit (Delaware, New Jersey, Pennsylvania, Virgin Islands): Collins J. Seitz, Chief Judge, Wilmington, Del.; James Hunter III, Camden, N.J.; A. Leon Higginbotham, Arlin M. Adams, Dolores Korman Sloviter, all of Philadelphia, Pa.; Ruggero J. Aldisert, Joseph F. Weis, Jr., both of Pittsburgh, Pa.; John J. Gibbons, Leonard I. Garth, both of Newark, N.J.; Max Rosenn, Wilkes-Barre, Pa.

Fourth Circuit (Maryland, North Carolina, South Carolina, Virginia, West Virginia): Clement F. Haynsworth, Jr., Chief Judge, Greenville, S.C.; Harrison L. Winter, Baltimore, Md.; John D. Butzner, Jr., Richmond, Va.; Donald Stuart Russell, Spartanburg, S.C.; H. Emory Widener, Jr., Abingdon, Va.; Kenneth K. Hall, James M. Sprouse, both of Charleston, W. Va.; James Dickson Phillips, Jr., Durham, N.C.; Francis D. Murnaghan, Jr., Baltimore, Md.; Samuel J. Ervin III, Asheville, N.C.

Fifth Circuit[2] (Alabama, Florida, Georgia, Louisiana, Mississippi, Texas, Canal Zone[3]): James P. Coleman, Chief Judge, Ackerman, Miss.; Alvin B. Rubin, Baton Rouge, La.; Robert A. Ainsworth, Jr., Albert Tate, Jr., both of New Orleans, La.; John C. Godbold, Frank M. Johnson, Jr., both of Montgomery, Ala.; Gerald B. Tjoflat, Jacksonville, Fla.; Phyllis A. Kravitch, Albert J. Henderson, James C. Hill, all of Atlanta, Ga.; Charles Clark, Jackson, Miss.; Paul H. Roney, St. Peterburg, Fla.; Thomas G. Gee, Thomas M. Reavley, Samuel D. Johnson, Jr., Jerre S. Williams, all of Austin, Tex.; Peter T. Fay, Miami, Fla.; Robert S. Vance, Birmingham, Ala.; Henry A. Politz, Shreveport, La.; Joseph W. Hatchett, Tallahassee, Fla.; R. Lanier Anderson III, Macon, Ga.; John R. Brown and Carolyn D. Randall, both of Houston, Tex.; Reynaldo G. Garza, Brownsville, Tex.; Thomas A. Clark, Tampa, Fla.

Sixth Circuit (Kentucky, Michigan, Ohio, Tennessee): George Clifton Edwards, Jr., Chief Judge, Cincinnati, Ohio; Paul C. Weick, Akron, Ohio; Anthony J. Celebrezze, Cleveland, Ohio; Pierce Lively, Danville, Ky.; Albert J. Engel, Grand Rapids, Mich.; Gilbert S. Merritt, Nashville, Tenn.; Damon J. Keith, Cornelia Kennedy, both of Detroit, Mich.; Bailey Brown, Memphis, Tenn.; Boyce F. Martin, Jr., Louisville, Ky.; Nathaniel R. Jones, Cincinnati, Ohio.

Seventh Circuit (Illinois, Indiana, Wisconsin): Thomas E. Fairchild, Chief Judge, Chicago, Ill.; Luther M. Swygert, Walter J. Cummings, Richard D. Cudahy, Wilbur F. Pell, Jr., Robert A. Sprecher, William J. Bauer, Harlington Wood, Jr., all of Chicago, Ill.

Eighth Circuit (Arkansas, Iowa, Minnesota, Missouri, Nebraska, North Dakota, South Dakota): Donald Lay, Chief Judge, Omaha, Nebr.; Gerald W. Heaney, Duluth, Minn.; Myron H. Bright, Fargo, N. Dak.; Donald R. Ross, Omaha, Nebr.; Roy L. Stephenson, Des Moines, Iowa; J. Smith Henley, Richard S. Arnold, both of Little Rock, Ark.; Theodore McMillian, St. Louis, Mo.

Ninth Circuit (Arizona, California, Idaho, Montana, Nevada, Oregon, Washington, Alaska, Hawaii, Guam): James R. Browning, Chief Judge, San Francisco, Calif.; Euguene A. Wright, Betty B. Fletcher, Jerome J. Farris, all of Seattle, Wash.; Thomas Tang, Mary M. Schroeder, William C. Canby, Jr., all of Phoenix, Ariz.; Herbert Y.C. Choy, Honolulu, Hawaii; Alfred T. Goodwin, Otto R. Skopil, Jr., both of Portland, Oregon; J. Clifford Wallace, San Diego, Calif.; Joseph T. Sneed, Cecil F. Poole, both of San Francisco, Calif.; Anthony M. Kennedy, Sacramento, Calif.; J. Blaine Anderson, Boise, Idaho; Procter Hug, Jr., Reno, Nevada; Harry Pregerson, Arthur L. Alarcon, Warren J. Ferguson, Dorothy W. Nelson, William A. Norris, Stephen R. Reinhardt, all of Los Angeles, Calif.; Robert Boochever, Juneau, Alaska.

Tenth Circuit (Colorado, Kansas, New Mexico, Oklahoma, Utah, Wyoming): Oliver Seth, Chief Judge, Santa Fe, N. Mex.; William J. Holloway, Jr., Oklahoma City, Okla.; James E. Barrett, Cheyenne, Wyo.; William E. Doyle and Robert H. McWilliams, both of Denver, Colo.; Monroe McKay, Salt Lake City, Utah; James K. Logan, Olathe, Kansas; Stephanie K. Seymour, Tulsa, Okla.

U.S. DISTRICT COURTS

Judges of U.S. District Courts and the Chief Judge of the District of Columbia receive annual salaries of $57,497.50[1].

U.S. TERRITORIAL JUDGES

The 4 District Judges earn annual salaries of $56,970[1].

U.S. COURT OF CLAIMS

717 Madison Place, N.W., Washington, D.C.
(Salaries: $60,135[1])

Chief Judge: Daniel M. Friedman, **Associate Judges:** Oscar H. Davis, Philip Nichols, Jr., Shiro Kashiwa, Robert L. Kunzig, Marion T. Bennett and Edward S. Smith.

U.S. COURT OF CUSTOMS AND PATENT APPEALS

717 Madison Place, N.W., Washington, D.C.
(Salaries: $60,662.50[1])

Chief Judge: Howard T. Markey, **Associate Judges:** Giles S. Rich, Jack R. Miller, Philip B. Baldwin, Helen W. Nies.

U.S. CUSTOMS COURT

1 Federal Plaza, New York, N.Y.
(Salaries: $57,497.50[1])

Chief Judge: Edward D. Re, **Judges:** Paul P. Rao, Morgan Ford, Scovel Richardson, Frederick Landis, James L. Watson, Herbert N. Maletz, Bernard Newman, Nils A. Boe.

[1]Reflects a pay increase of only 5.5%, although executive order of October 1979 approved a 12.2% increase, to be decided by pending court action. [2]At the end of September 1980, Congress passed legislation to split the Fifth Circuit judicial district, which becomes effective October 1, 1981. The new Fifth Circuit will consist of Alabama, Florida, and Georgia, with its seat in Atlanta, Ga. The new Eleventh Circuit will consist of Louisiana, Mississippi, Texas, and the Canal Zone, with its seat in New Orleans, La. [3]In accordance with the Panama Canal Treaty between the United States and Panama, which became effective October 1, 1979, 40% of the former Panama Canal Zone remains in the control of the U.S. Panama Canal Commission until December 31, 1999. The present Fifth Circuit continues its jurisdiction for this area.

1980 CENSUS — EARLY RESULTS

PRELIMINARY WORKING FIGURES

(as of October 29, 1980)

The editors of THE HAMMOND ALMANAC had hoped to present in this edition the full preliminary results of the 1980 Census of the United States for all states, metropolitan areas and incorporated places of more than 6,500 inhabitants. The Bureau of the Census had originally projected that the preliminary population figures would be issued between August and October 1980. However, delays in completing the enumeration process and litigation by many municipalities have prevented the publication of the preliminary population counts as of this time (October 1980).

Listed below are the 1980 *preliminary working population figures* for certain cities of the United States. These figures were obtained from press reports and from various nation-wide municipal government authorities as provided to them by the Bureau of the Census. All are subject to revision and many are being contested in the courts by the city governments concerned. They are also subject to transcription errors due to the indirect manner in which they were gathered.

City	1980 Population	1970 Population	Percent Change
Albany, N.Y.	101,767	115,781	— 12.1
Albuquerque, N. Mex.	326,000	243,751	+ 33.7
Allentown, Pa.	102,263	109,871	— 6.9
Atlanta, Ga.	402,000	497,421	— 19.2
Atlantic City, N.J.	36,000	47,859	— 24.8
Baltimore, Md.	737,000	905,787	— 18.6
Bayonne, N.J.	64,982	72,743	— 10.7
Binghamton, N.Y.	51,000	64,123	— 20.5
Birmingham, Ala.	265,000	300,910	— 11.9
Boston, Mass.	505,000	641,071	— 21.2
Bridgeport, Conn.	134,500	156,542	— 14.1
Buffalo, N.Y.	347,670	462,768	— 24.9
Cambridge, Mass.	95,350	100,361	— 5.0
Camden, N.J.	84,763	102,551	— 17.3
Charleston, S.C.	64,266	66,945	— 4.0
Chicago, Ill.	2,725,295	3,369,357	— 19.1
Cleveland, Ohio	535,000	750,879	— 28.8
Clifton, N.J.	74,477	82,437	— 9.7
Columbus, Ohio	545,934	540,025	+ 1.0
Dallas, Tex.	845,060	844,401	+ 0.1
Danbury, Conn.	59,000	50,781	+ 16.2
Denver, Colo.	455,000	514,678	— 11.6
Detroit, Mich.	1,180,000	1,513,601	— 22.0
East Orange, N.J.	73,455	75,471	— 2.7
Elizabeth, N.J.	102,818	112,654	— 8.7
Erie, Pa.	116,656	129,231	— 9.7
Fort Worth, Tex.	366,200	393,476	— 6.9
Hartford, Conn.	130,000	158,017	— 17.7
Houston, Tex.	1,420,000	1,232,802	+ 15.2

City	1980 Population	1970 Population	Percent Change
Indianapolis, Ind.	677,498	746,302	— 9.2
Jacksonville, Fla.	541,269	528,865	+ 2.3
Jersey City, N.J.	222,764	260,350	— 14.4
Kansas City, Mo.	429,177	507,330	— 15.4
Los Angeles, Calif.	2,878,039	2,809,813	+ 2.4
Louisville, Ky.	289,272	361,706	— 20.0
Memphis, Tenn.	636,000	623,530	+ 2.0
Miami, Fla.	347,600	334,859	+ 3.8
Milwaukee, Wis.	632,989	717,372	— 11.8
Minneapolis, Minn.	351,000	434,400	— 19.2
Mount Vernon, N.Y.	64,818	72,778	— 10.9
Nashville, Tenn.	423,291	447,877	— 5.5
Newark, N.J.	308,960	381,930	— 19.1
New Haven, Conn.	116,000	137,707	— 15.8
New Orleans, La.	556,913	593,471	— 6.2
New Rochelle, N.Y.	69,528	75,385	— 7.8
New York, N.Y.	6,808,370	7,895,563	— 13.8
Bronx Borough	1,124,806	1,472,216	— 23.6
Manhattan Borough	1,323,333	1,524,541	— 13.2
Niagara Falls, N.Y.	70,000	85,615	— 18.2
Oakland, Calif.	338,721	361,561	— 6.3
Omaha, Nebr.	314,000	346,929	— 9.5
Parsippany-Troy Hills, N.J.	49,432	55,112	— 10.3
Passaic, N.J.	50,500	55,124	— 8.4
Paterson, N.J.	133,504	144,824	— 7.8
Philadelphia, Pa.	1,607,070	1,949,996	— 17.6
Phoenix, Ariz.	761,745	582,500	+ 30.8
Pittsburgh, Pa.	410,000	520,117	— 21.2
Portland, Oreg.	343,950	379,967	— 9.5
Providence, R.I.	152,000	179,116	— 15.1
Rochester, N.Y.	227,007	296,233	— 23.4
Rome, N.Y.	39,000	50,148	— 22.2
Sacramento, Calif.	274,488	257,105	+ 6.8
St. Louis, Mo.	425,000	622,236	— 31.7
St. Paul, Minn.	258,746	309,714	— 16.5
Salt Lake City, Utah	162,960	175,885	— 7.3
San Antonio, Tex.	747,800	654,153	+ 14.3
San Diego, Calif.	857,035	697,027	+ 23.0
San Francisco, Calif.	674,063	715,674	— 5.8
San Jose, Calif.	598,000	445,779	+ 34.1
Schenectady, N.Y.	67,877	77,958	— 12.9
Scranton, Pa.	84,942	103,564	— 18.0
Seattle, Wash.	475,000	530,831	— 10.5
Springfield, Mass.	152,212	163,905	— 7.1
Stamford, Conn.	98,300	108,798	— 9.6
Syracuse, N.Y.	163,500	197,297	— 17.1
Tampa, Fla.	253,666	277,753	— 8.7
Trenton, N.J.	95,000	104,786	— 9.3
Troy, N.Y.	56,614	62,918	— 10.0
Union City, N.J.	48,760	57,305	— 14.9
Utica, N.Y.	72,000	91,340	— 21.2
Washington, D.C.	635,185	756,510	— 16.0
White Plains, N.Y.	46,089	50,346	— 8.5
Wilmington, Del.	70,363	80,386	— 12.5
Worcester, Mass.	156,286	176,572	— 11.5
Yonkers, N.Y.	191,913	204,297	— 6.1

STATE AND LOCAL GOVERNMENT EXPENDITURES: PER CAPITA   SOURCE: U.S. Bureau of the Census

Year	Total general	Education	Highways	Public welfare	Health and hospitals	Police and fire
1902	$ 12.80	$ 3.22	$ 2.21	$ .47	$ .75	$ 1.14
1913	21.23	5.93	4.31	.53	1.11	1.70
1922	47.41	15.49	11.76	1.08	2.35	3.17
1932	62.15	18.50	13.93	3.55	3.65	4.23
1936	59.63	16.98	11.12	6.45	3.64	4.05
1940	69.85	19.97	11.91	8.75	4.61	4.54
1944	64.04	20.18	8.67	8.19	4.74	4.80
1946	78.00	23.74	11.83	9.97	5.79	5.47
1948	120.60	36.68	20.71	14.31	8.38	7.16
1950	150.22	47.31	25.07	19.38	11.52	8.34
1952	166.29	53.00	29.63	17.76	13.92	9.71
1954	189.06	65.01	34.04	18.84	14.83	10.98
1956	219.42	79.02	41.56	18.76	16.57	12.35
1958	258.76	91.84	49.43	22.03	19.97	14.33
1959	276.96	97.91	54.34	23.43	21.10	14.87
1960	288.21	104.00	52.38	24.47	21.08	15.85
1961	307.01	112.39	53.78	25.78	22.32	16.96
1962	324.00	119.56	55.74	27.36	23.37	17.51
1963	339.19	125.81	59.11	28.74	24.59	17.99
1964	362.20	137.38	60.96	30.13	25.66	18.74
1965	385.30	147.37	63.05	32.58	27.66	19.89
1966	422.97	169.95	65.20	34.50	30.17	21.19
1967	471.79	191.64	70.41	41.53	33.56	22.99
1968	512.41	205.93	72.46	49.32	37.76	25.18
1969	578.14	233.94	76.35	59.97	42.19	28.19
1970	646.20	259.39	80.83	72.23	47.57	32.07
1971	730.52	288.05	87.73	88.36	54.32	36.50
1972	801.38	311.60	91.29	101.18	61.79	41.07
1973	863.60	332.21	88.70	112.37	65.97	45.18
1974	941.19	358.74	94.36	118.67	75.43	48.85
1975	1082.58	412.24	105.71	132.11	88.43	56.54
1976	1195.99	452.89	111.37	151.89	96.37	62.56
1977	1268.37	475.22	106.80	166.14	104.20	67.82
1978	1361.90	507.91	112.85	179.49	114.41	73.87

U.S. — BUDGET: 1789-1981   SOURCE: U.S. Office of Management and Budget (in millions of dollars)

Fiscal Year	Receipts	Outlays	Surplus or Deficit (—)	Fiscal Year	Receipts	Outlays	Surplus or Deficit (—)
1789–1849	1,160	1,090	+70	1941	8,621	13,634	—5,013
1850–1900	14,462	15,453	—991	1942	14,350	35,114	—20,764
1901	588	525	+63	1943	23,649	78,533	—54,884
1902	562	485	+77	1944	44,276	91,280	—47,004
1903	562	517	+45	1945	45,216	92,690	—47,474
1904	541	584	—43	1946	39,327	55,183	—15,856
1905	544	567	—23	1947	38,394	34,532	+3,862
1906	595	570	+25	1948	41,774	29,773	+12,001
1907	666	579	+87	1949	39,437	38,834	+603
1908	602	659	—57	1950	39,485	42,597	—3,112
1909	604	694	—89	1951	51,646	45,546	+6,100
1910	676	694	—18	1952	66,204	67,721	—1,517
1911	702	691	+11	1953	69,574	76,107	—6,533
1912	693	690	+3	1954	69,719	70,890	—1,170
1913	714	715	—*	1955	65,469	68,509	—3,041
1914	725	726	—*	1956	74,547	70,460	+4,087
1915	683	746	—63	1957	79,990	76,741	+3,249
1916	761	713	+48	1958	79,636	82,575	—2,939
1917	1,101	1,954	—853	1959	79,249	92,104	—12,855
1918	3,645	12,677	—9,032	1960	92,492	92,223	+269
1919	5,130	18,493	—13,363	1961	94,389	97,795	—3,406
1920	6,649	6,358	+291	1962	99,676	106,813	—7,137
1921	5,571	5,062	+509	1963	106,560	111,311	—4,751
1922	4,026	3,289	+736	1964	112,662	118,584	—5,922
1923	3,853	3,140	+713	1965	116,833	118,430	—1,596
1924	3,871	2,908	+963	1966	130,856	134,652	—3,796
1925	3,641	2,924	+717	1967	149,552	158,254	—8,702
1926	3,795	2,930	+865	1968	153,671	178,833	—25,161
1927	4,013	2,857	+1,155	1969	187,784	184,548	+3,236
1928	3,900	2,961	+939	1970	193,743	196,588	—2,845
1929	3,862	3,127	+734	1971	188,392	211,425	—23,033
1930	4,058	3,320	+738	1972	208,649	232,021	—23,373
1931	3,116	3,577	—462	1973	232,225	247,074	—14,849
1932	1,924	4,659	—2,735	1974	264,932	269,620	—4,688
1933	1,997	4,598	—2,602	1975	280,997	326,185	—45,188
1934	3,015	6,645	—3,630	1976	300,005	366,439	—66,434
1935	3,706	6,497	—2,791	TQ	81,773	94,729	—12,956
1936	3,997	8,422	—4,425	1977	357,762	402,725	—44,963
1937	4,956	7,733	—2,777	1978	401,997	450,836	—48,839
1938	5,588	6,765	—1,177	1979	465,940	493,673	—27,733
1939	4,979	8,841	—3,862	1980 est.	517,900	578,800	—60,900
1940	6,361	9,456	—3,095	1981 est.[1]	604,000	633,800	—29,800

* Less than $500,000. [1] Based on the 1981 budget from the Mid-Session Review in July 1980. [2] Fiscal years through 1976 began on July 1 and ended the following June 30. Beginning with fiscal year 1977, each fiscal year begins on October 1 and ends on the following September 30. The Transition Quarter (TQ) refers to the 3-month period from the end of fiscal year 1976 on June 30, 1976, to the beginning of fiscal year 1977 on October 1, 1976.
Note: Data for 1789–1939 are for the administrative budget; 1940 and thereafter are for the unified budget.

THE BUDGET DOLLAR
SOURCE: Office of Management and Budget
Fiscal Year 1981

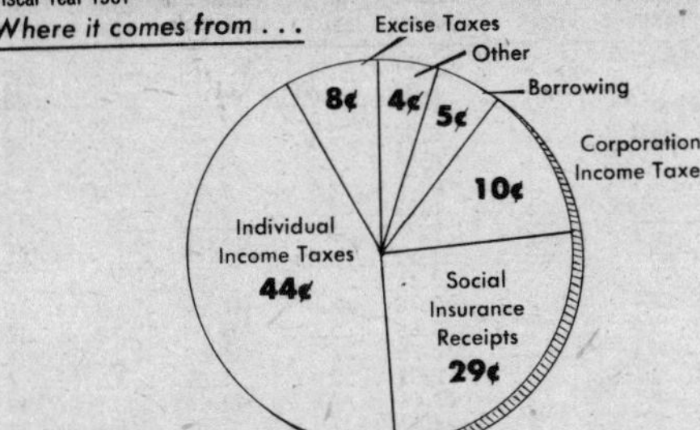

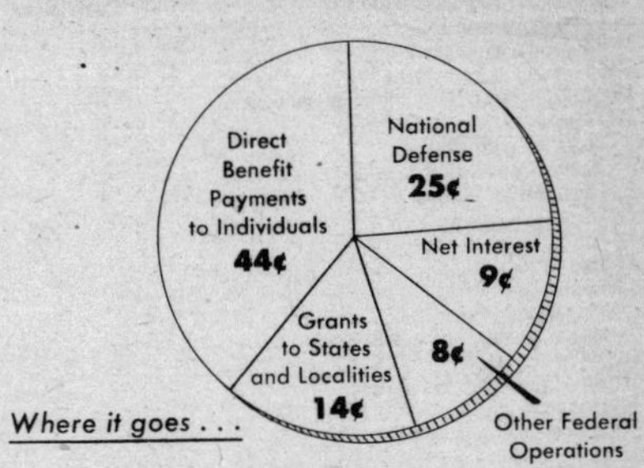

FEDERAL GRANTS TO STATES[1]
SOURCE: Tax Foundation, Inc.

These comparisons of Federal tax burdens for aid payments per $1.00 of assistance do not actually indicate the entire costs which state and local governments incur for obtaining Federal grants. The comparisons, with few exceptions, do not take into account the costs to these governments of administering the programs for which the aid is granted, nor the amounts of matching funds which the state and local governments must make available out of their own revenue in order to qualify as recipients of these grants. In the last few years, it is estimated that state and local governments provided approximately $1.00 of matching funds for each $3.00 of Federal aid.

"PAYING STATES"[1]

Twenty-three states paid more in U.S. taxes to support grant programs than they received in aid in fiscal year 1979.

State	Grants (millions)	Estimated tax burden for grants (millions)	Tax Burden for $1 of Aid	
			All Grants	Rev. Sharing
Ind.	$1,390.8	$1,955.2	$1.41	$1.22
Texas	3,588.2	4,883.9	1.36	1.30
Ohio	3,070.1	4,022.1	1.31	1.25
Conn.	1,074.6	1,396.5	1.30	1.47
Ill.	3,781.5	4,915.8	1.30	1.26
Fla.	2,392.9	3,056.4	1.28	1.36
Iowa	877.1	1,053.4	1.20	1.10
Nev.	263.7	311.2	1.18	1.61
Kansas	720.7	853.9	1.18	1.22
N.J.	2,715.4	3,144.2	1.16	1.21
Neb.	473.3	542.7	1.15	1.13
Wash.	1,381.3	1,556.2	1.13	1.38
Calif.	8,165.4	9,265.1	1.13	1.01
Wy.	163.5	183.6	1.12	1.25
Colo.	915.3	1,013.5	1.11	1.18
Mo.	1,509.1	1,643.9	1.09	1.09
Oregon	877.1	949.7	1.08	1.06
Va.	1,715.6	1,843.4	1.07	1.12
N.H.	291.6	311.2	1.07	1.15
Md.	1,600.1	1,699.8	1.06	1.08
Mich.	3,565.4	3,726.8	1.05	1.12
Penn.	4,096.5	4,205.6	1.03	1.07
Del.	232.4	239.4	1.03	1.03

"RECEIVING STATES"

Twenty-seven states and the District of Columbia paid less in taxes to support grant programs than they received in aid.

State	Grants (millions)	Estimated tax burden for grants (millions)	Tax Burden for $1 of Aid	
			All Grants	Rev. Sharing
Ariz.	$ 795.5	$ 790.1	$.99	$ .85
Okla.	945.7	933.7	.99	1.09
Minn.	1,512.0	1,484.3	.98	.87
Wisc.	1,723.4	1,588.1	.92	.83
N.C.	1,785.7	1,604.0	.90	.77
Tenn.	1,442.3	1,292.8	.90	.84
Utah.	433.0	383.1	.88	.77
Hawaii	407.7	351.1	.86	.88
Idaho	315.4	263.4	.83	.87
La.	1,509.3	1,229.0	.81	.71
S.C.	983.9	798.0	.81	.69
Ala.	1,341.9	1,037.4	.77	.77
Mass.	2,725.5	2,090.8	.77	.83
R.I.	412.2	319.2	.77	.91
Ky.	1,340.9	1,021.5	.76	.77
N.Y.	8,870.3	6,703.4	.76	.76
W. Va.	770.1	550.6	.72	.74
N.D.	292.5	207.5	.71	1.02
Ga.	2,176.2	1,508.3	.69	.82
Ark.	839.4	550.6	.66	.66
N.M.	535.4	351.1	.66	.66
Mont.	406.4	255.4	.63	.82
S.D.	311.4	191.5	.62	.70
Alaska	379.9	231.4	.61	.90
Maine	503.1	295.3	.59	.53
Vt.	241.3	135.7	.56	.57
Miss.	1,035.5	550.6	.53	.43
D.C.	905.1	311.2	.34	.91

[1]Excludes shared revenues; includes general revenue sharing and trust fund aids.

EXPENDITURE OF FEDERAL TAX DOLLARS (FISCAL YEAR 1981)
SOURCE: Tax Foundation, Inc.; Budget Revisions, Fiscal Year 1981 (March 1980)

Item	Federal Tax Burden Per Household
Total	$7,516
Income security	2,704
National defense	1,849
Interest	840
Health	761
Education, training, employment and social services	376
Veterans' benefits	263
Transportation	234
Natural resources and environment	153
International affairs	124
Community and regional development	104

Item	Federal Tax Burden Per Household
General purpose fiscal assistance	$ 91
Energy	85
General science, space, & technology	76
General government	59
Administration of justice	56
Agriculture	25
Allowances for contingencies and pay raises	17
Commerce and housing credit	5
Undistributed offsetting receipts	−306
Intragovernmental adjustments	−238
Rents and royalties in the Outer Continental Shelf	− 68

THE U.S. BUDGET: RECEIPTS AND OUTLAYS (in billions of dollars)

SOURCE: U.S. Office of Management and Budget

Description	1976 Actual	TQ[1] Actual	1977 Actual	1978 Actual	1979 Actual	1980[2] Est	1981[2] Est
Receipts by source:							
Individual income taxes	131.6	38.8	157.6	181.0	217.8	240.7	278.2
Corporation income taxes	41.4	8.5	54.9	60.0	65.7	65.5	66.4
Social insurance taxes and contributions	92.7	25.8	108.7	123.4	141.6	160.5	184.5
Excise taxes	17.0	4.5	17.5	18.4	18.7	25.4	48.7
Estate and gift taxes	5.2	1.5	7.3	5.3	5.4	6.1	6.3
Customs duties	4.1	1.2	5.2	6.6	7.4	7.0	7.5
Miscellaneous receipts	8.0	1.6	6.5	7.4	9.2	12.7	12.5
Total receipts:	**300.0**	**81.8**	**357.8**	**402.0**	**465.9**	**517.9**	**604.0**
Outlays by function:							
National defense[3]	89.4	22.3	97.5	105.2	117.7	135.6	157.5
International affairs	5.6	2.2	4.8	5.9	6.1	10.9	10.3
General science, space, and technology	4.4	1.2	4.7	4.7	5.0	5.7	6.2
Energy	3.1	.8	4.2	5.9	6.9	6.5	7.2
Natural resources and environment	8.1	2.5	10.0	10.9	12.1	13.7	13.1
Agriculture	2.5	.6	5.5	7.7	6.2	5.8	2.2
Commerce and housing credit	3.8	1.4	—*	3.3	2.6	8.3	0.7
Transportation	13.4	3.3	14.6	15.4	17.5	20.8	19.2
Community and regional development	4.8	1.3	6.3	11.0	9.5	9.5	9.3
Education, training, employment, and social services	18.7	5.2	21.0	26.5	29.7	29.9	30.9
Health	33.4	8.7	38.8	43.7	49.6	56.9	63.4
Income security	127.4	32.8	137.9	146.2	160.2	193.5	230.4
Veterans benefits and services	18.4	4.0	18.0	19.0	19.9	20.9	21.8
Administration of justice	3.3	.9	3.6	3.8	4.2	4.6	4.6
General government	2.9	.9	3.3	3.7	4.2	5.0	4.7
General purpose fiscal assistance	7.2	2.1	9.5	9.6	8.4	8.6	7.3
Interest	34.5	7.2	38.0	44.0	52.6	64.3	67.6
Allowances[4]	—	—	—	—	—	—*	1.4
Undistributed offsetting receipts	−14.7	−2.6	−15.1	−15.8	−18.5	−21.9	−24.0
Total outlays:	**366.4**	**94.7**	**402.7**	**450.8**	**493.7**	**578.8**	**633.8**
Budget deficit:	**−66.4**	**−12.9**	**−44.9**	**−48.8**	**−27.8**	**−60.9**	**−29.8**

* $50 million or less. [1]See footnote 2, page 184. [2]Based on estimates of the 1981 Budget of the Mid-Session Review in July 1980. [3]Includes civilian and military pay raises for Department of Defense. [4]Includes allowances for civilian agency pay raises. The current 1980 and 1981 estimates include an allowance for the government-wide rescission of furniture purchases as provided in the 1980 Supplemental Appropriations and Rescission Act. The current 1981 estimate also includes an allowance for the care, maintenance, and resettlement of recent Cuban/Haitian entrants.

FEDERAL, STATE & LOCAL GOVERNMENT FINANCES: 1929—1979

SOURCE: U.S. Department of Commerce, Bureau of Economic Analysis

	(Billions of Dollars)						
	1929	1939	1949	1959	1977	1978	1979*
Total Government**							
Receipts	11.3	15.4	55.9	129.4	606.6	685.7	771.7
Expenditures	10.3	17.6	59.3	131.0	626.1	686.0	758.6
Federal Government							
Receipts	3.8	6.7	38.7	89.8	375.4	432.1	497.6
Expenditures	2.6	8.9	41.3	91.0	421.7	459.8	509.0
State and Local Government							
Receipts	7.6	9.6	19.5	46.4	298.8	331.0	354.6
Expenditures	7.8	9.6	20.2	46.9	271.9	303.6	330.0

*Preliminary. **Total government is after subtraction of Federal grants-in-aid to state and local governments.

STATE PER CAPITA INCOME: 1978 and 1979

SOURCE: U.S. DEPARTMENT OF Commerce, Bureau of Economic Analysis

Rank	State	1978 Income	1979 Income	Percent of National Average 1979
	United States	$ 7,840	$ 8,706	100
	States			
1.	Alaska	10,849	11,252	129
—	District of Columbia	9,598	10,911	125
2.	Nevada	9,377	10,204	117
3.	Connecticut	8,915	9,959	114
4.	California	8,916	9,913	114
5.	Illinois	8,870	9,823	113
6.	New Jersey	8,775	9,702	111
7.	Wyoming	8,687	9,657	111
8.	Delaware	8,531	9,537	110
9.	Washington	8,553	9,435	108
10.	Hawaii	8,465	9,353	107
11.	Michigan	8,487	9,269	106
12.	Maryland	8,348	9,150	105
13.	New York	8,230	9,098	105
14.	Kansas	7,846	9,055	104
15.	Colorado	8,116	8,945	103
16.	Massachusetts	7,926	8,844	102
17.	Oregon	8,076	8,842	102
18.	Ohio	7,857	8,775	101
19.	Minnesota	7,904	8,760	101
20.	Indiana	7,703	8,686	100
21.	Texas	7,746	8,649	99
22.	Virginia	7,721	8,605	99
23.	Iowa	7,856	8,589	99
24.	Pennsylvania	$7,744	$8,559	98
25.	Florida	7,578	8,532	98
26.	Wisconsin	7,532	8,419	97
27.	Nebraska	7,544	8,341	96
28.	Arizona	7,385	8,305	95
29.	Rhode Island	7,447	8,266	95
30.	New Hampshire	7,378	8,231	95
31.	Oklahoma	7,127	8,226	94
32.	Missouri	7,287	8,132	93
33.	North Dakota	7,432	7,774	89
34.	Georgia	6,779	7,515	86
35.	Louisiana	6,738	7,477	86
36.	West Virginia	6,629	7,470	86
37.	Idaho	7,074	7,446	86
38.	Montana	6,915	7,412	85
39.	North Carolina	6,640	7,359	85
40.	Kentucky	6,605	7,342	84
41.	South Dakota	6,585	7,334	84
42.	Tennessee	6,561	7,299	84
43.	New Mexico	6,599	7,294	84
44.	Vermont	6,601	7,280	84
45.	Utah	6,594	7,185	83
46.	Maine	6,308	7,057	81
47.	South Carolina	6,292	7,027	81
48.	Alabama	6,325	6,976	80
49.	Arkansas	6,121	6,785	78
50.	Mississippi	5,582	6,167	71

INTERNAL REVENUE TAXES

SOURCE: U.S. Internal Revenue Service

Year	Collections	Cost of Collecting $100	Tax per Capita
1866	$310,120,448	$2.47	$8.49
1868	190,374,926	4.90	4.98
1870	184,302,828	4.47	4.62
1873	113,504,013	5.83	2.64
1875	110,071,515	4.83	2.44
1876	116,768,096	4.09	2.53
1878	110,654,163	3.67	2.30
1880	123,981,916	3.63	2.47
1881	135,229,912	3.74	2.62
1883	144,553,345	3.53	2.67
1885	112,421,121	3.96	1.98
1886	116,902,896	3.68	2.02
1888	124,326,475	3.20	2.05
1890	142,594,697	2.87	2.26
1891	146,035,416	2.88	2.27
1893	161,004,990	2.62	2.40
1895	143,246,078	2.88	2.06
1896	146,830,616	2.78	2.07
1898	170,866,819	2.29	2.32
1900	295,316,108	1.58	3.88
1901	306,871,669	1.55	3.95
1903	230,740,925	2.07	2.86
1905	234,187,976	2.01	2.79
1906	249,102,738	1.90	2.92
1908	251,665,950	1.92	2.84
1910	289,957,220	1.74	3.14
1911	322,526,300	1.68	3.44
1913	344,424,454	1.59	3.54
1915	415,681,024	1.64	4.13
1916	512,723,288	1.40	5.03
1917	809,393,640	0.95	7.83
1918	3,698,955,821	0.33	35.38
1919	3,850,150,079	0.53	36.65
1921	4,595,357,062	0.72	42.34
1925	2,584,140,268	1.44	22.31
1926	2,835,999,892	1.23	24.16
1928	2,790,535,538	1.17	23.16
1929	2,939,054,375	1.17	24.14
1930	3,040,145,733	1.13	24.68
1932	$1,557,729,043	$2.17	$12.47
1934	2,672,239,195	1.08	21.13
1935	3,299,435,572	1.29	25.91
1937	4,653,195,315	1.12	36.08
1939	5,181,573,953	1.13	39.55
1941	7,370,108,378	0.89	55.04
1942	13,047,868,518	0.58	96.39
1943	22,371,385,497	0.44	163.00
1944	40,121,760,233	0.32	288.82
1945	43,800,387,576	0.33	311.82
1946	40,672,096,998	0.43	286.55
1948	41,864,542,295	0.44	284.39
1950	38,957,131,768	0.59	255.84
1951	50,445,686,315	0.49	325.71
1952	65,009,585,560	0.42	412.62
1954	69,919,990,791	0.38	428.89
1955	66,288,692,000	0.42	399.50
1957	80,171,971,000	0.38	466.16
1958	79,978,476,484	0.42	457.33
1959	79,797,972,806	0.44	448.73
1960	91,774,802,823	0.40	507.96
1961	94,401,086,398	0.44	513.91
1962	99,440,839,245	0.45	533.09
1963	105,925,395,281	0.47	559.74
1964	112,260,257,115	0.49	585.03
1965	114,434,633,721	0.52	588.95
1966	128,879,961,342	0.48	655.68
1967	148,374,814,552	0.45	746.68
1968	153,636,837,665	0.46	765.48
1969	187,919,559,668	0.40	927.19
1970	195,722,096,497	0.45	955.31
1971	191,647,198,138	0.51	925.63
1972	209,855,736,878	0.54	1,004.83
1973	237,787,204,058	0.49	1,130.11
1974	268,952,253,663	0.49	1,269.24
1975	293,822,725,772	0.54	1,375.96
1976	302,519,791,922	0.56	1,406.30
1977	358,139,416,730	0.50	1,647.91
1978	399,776,389,362	0.49	1,826.61
1979	460,412,185,013	0.46	2,083.82

ADDRESSES OF U.S. INTERNAL REVENUE OFFICES

If you are located in:	Send your return to:
Alabama, Florida, Georgia, Mississippi, South Carolina	Internal Revenue Service Center Atlanta, Georgia 31101
Delaware, District of Columbia, Maryland, Pennsylvania	Internal Revenue Service Center Philadelphia, Pennsylvania 19255
Michigan, Ohio	Internal Revenue Service Center Cincinnati, Ohio 45999
Arkansas, Kansas, Louisiana, New Mexico, Oklahoma, Texas	Internal Revenue Service Center Austin, Texas 73301
Illinois, Iowa, Missouri, Wisconsin	Internal Revenue Service Center Kansas City, Missouri 64999
Connecticut, Maine, Massachusetts, New Hampshire, New York (except N.Y.C., and Nassau, Rockland, Suffolk, and Westchester counties), Rhode Island, Vermont	Internal Revenue Service Center Andover, Massachusetts 05501
Indiana, Kentucky, North Carolina, Tennessee, Virginia, West Virginia	Internal Revenue Service Center Memphis, Tennessee 37501

U.S. citizens with foreign addresses (except A.P.O. and F.P.O.) and those excluding income under sec. 911 or 931: file with Internal Revenue Service, Philadelphia, Pa. 19255
U.S. citizens with A.P.O. or F.P.O. address; file with center for home state.

If you are located in:	Send your return to:
Alaska, Arizona, Colorado, Idaho, Minnesota, Montana, Nebraska, Nevada, North Dakota, Oregon, South Dakota, Utah, Washington, Wyoming	Internal Revenue Service Center Ogden, Utah 84201
California, Hawaii	Internal Revenue Service Center Fresno, California 93888
New York City and N.Y. counties of Nassau, Rockland, Suffolk, and Westchester; New Jersey	Internal Revenue Service Center Holtsville, New York 00501
American Samoa	Internal Revenue Service Center Philadelphia, Pennsylvania 19255
Guam	Commissioner of Revenue and Taxation Agana, Guam 96910
Puerto Rico (or if excluding income under section 933), Virgin Islands: Non permanent residents	Internal Revenue Service Center Philadelphia, Pennsylvania 19255
Virgin Islands: Permanent residents	Department of Finance, Tax Division Charlotte Amalie, St. Thomas Virgin Islands 00801

TAX TIPS

Prepared by H & R Block, Inc.
America's Largest Tax Service

Early tax planning is helpful in keeping your income tax as low as is possible within the law. The tax tips discussed here are based on current tax law as of July 1, 1980. New tax legislation could result in changes.

KEEP RECORDS AND RECEIPTS!

The federal tax code requires that all deductions be substantiated. Good record-keeping is an important part of minimizing tax liability.

INVESTMENTS, CAPITAL GAINS

U.S. series EE bonds may be a worthwhile investment. Interest earned is not taxable until the bonds mature (plus extensions) or are cashed. Or, you may elect to report the interest each year as it accrues. If the latter choice is made, all such interest in all future years is taxable as it accrues. This election may be wise when it is expected that gross income will be greater in the year(s) the bonds will be cashed than in the intervening years (such as bonds purchased for a child which will be used for his or her future). The first year the election is made, a return must be filed with a statement on the option chosen. Thereafter a return is filed or not based on the usual filing requirements.

You may open a savings account or purchase stock to save for your child's college education or future without paying tax on the earnings.

The security or savings must be in the child's name and neither the principal nor earnings can be used for the child's support or in any way used by you. You may be custodian of the investment. The child is not required to file a return for any year that his or her investment income is less than $1000 and gross income is less than $3300. And if the child is required to file, his or her tax on this income would most likely be less than the adult would have paid.

Sales of capital assets should be planned to gain the greatest possible tax advantage without sacrificing economic results. Try to avoid sales at a loss in the same year in which you will have a long-term gain. Only 40% of a net long-term capital gain is taxable, but gains and losses must be combined to determine the net gain or loss. To realize 100% of a long-term loss, sell short-term assets at a gain. (Only 50% of a net long-term loss is deductible against ordinary income.) Generally, property owned over one year is long term. Commodity futures are long term if held over 6 months.

SELLING YOUR PRINCIPAL RESIDENCE

If you sell your home, any gain will not be taxed immediately if, within 18 months, you buy and occupy another home that costs as much or more than the adjusted sales price of the old home. The deferred gain reduces the basis of the new home. Gain on each succeeding sale is deferred as long as a new home of equal or greater value is purchased. A taxpayer age 55 or over on the date of sale may exclude up to $100,000 gain from sale of his or her principal residence. To qualify, you must have owned and lived in the home three of the five years ending on the date of sale. This election may be made only once in a lifetime.

INSTALLMENT METHOD

If you sell your home on contract and cannot defer all or part of the gain, you may be able to use the installment method. Gain is reported over the years that payments are received instead of all in the year of sale. This method can also be used to report gain from the sale of other real property and certain personal property if qualifications are met.

END-OF-YEAR TAX PLANNING

Before the end of the year, you should estimate whether the total of your itemized deductions will exceed your zero bracket amount. If it will, it may be beneficial to pay any outstanding obligations that are deductible before the end of the year. If the total itemized deductions will not exceed the zero bracket amount, it will be better to postpone (wherever possible) payment of deductible obligations until the beginning of the new tax year. Payment of various items, such as charitable contributions, medical expenses, and the fourth installment of estimated state and local income tax, can be timed to derive the greatest tax benefit.

Special attention should be paid to medical expenses, since they are deductible only in excess of 3 percent of adjusted gross income. If medical expenses approach this level and deductions will be itemized, you may reduce your tax liability by paying outstanding medical bills before the end of the year. Also have necessary optical and dental work done and paid for before the end of the year.

CHARITABLE CONTRIBUTIONS

You may deduct actual transportation expenses incurred in performing volunteer work for a charitable organization. In lieu of actual costs, you may deduct eight cents a mile plus parking fees and tolls. Also deductible are the cost and upkeep of uniforms required to be worn and equipment or supplies purchased to perform volunteer work. All items must be used solely for the charitable work.

You may deduct up to 50 percent of adjusted gross income for cash contributions made to churches, educational organizations, certain medical organizations, public organizations such as libraries and symphony orchestras, and other charities that receive most of their support from the general public or government.

CASUALTY LOSS

Loss or damage to your property resulting from a sudden or unusual event such as severe weather, fire, accident or theft may be deductible. If you sustained such a loss in an area determined by the President to warrant federal disaster assistance, the loss may be claimed on your tax return for the year of the loss or the preceding year, whichever is more advantageous.

AGE 65 BRINGS TAX BENEFITS

You are allowed an additional personal exemption if you are 65 or older on the last day of the year. For tax purposes, you are considered 65 on the day before your 65th birthday.

You may be eligible for a tax credit if you are age 65 or older or are under age 65 and receive a pension or annuity from a public retirement system. The maximum credit is $375 for single individuals, $562.50 for married individuals filing a joint return, and $281.25 for married individuals filing a separate return. Married individuals must file a joint return to claim the credit unless they lived apart during the entire year. Nonresident aliens are generally not eligible for the credit.

CLAIMING DEPENDENTS

It is not always necessary to provide more than half of the support for a relative to claim him or her as a dependent. If you and one or more persons could claim the relative as a dependent, except for the support test and together contribute more than 50 percent of the support, you can agree to let any one who individually furnishes more than 10 percent of the support claim the dependent. The other contributors must sign Multiple Support Declarations (Form 2120) which are to be attached to the return of the individual who claims the exemption.

Parents who provide over half the total support of their working child (who is under 19 or is a student) may claim a dependent exemption regardless of the amount the child earns. A double benefit — the child claims his or her own personal exemption.

DIVORCED TAXPAYERS

Generally, the parent who has custody of the child for the greater part of the year is entitled to claim the exemption. There are two exceptions to this rule. The noncustody parent is entitled to the exemption if he or she:

1) contributed at least $600 toward each child's support during the year and the divorce decree or other agreement specifies that this parent is entitled to the exemption. Any agreement must be in writing. OR

2) provided $1,200 or more of support for each child during the year and the parent having custody cannot prove that he or she provided more support.

These rules do not apply if a third party has custody for more than half the year and/or provides more than 50% of the support.

Child support payments are neither deductible by the payer nor taxable to the recipient. If the decree does not specify an amount as child support, the entire payment is alimony. Alimony payments, generally, are deductible by the payer and taxable to the recipient. Deductible alimony is claimed as an adjustment, deductible regardless of whether deductions are itemized.

EARNED INCOME CREDIT

Some individuals will qualify for the earned income credit. If both your adjusted gross income and your earned income are less than $10,000 and you maintain your home for a qualifying child you may be eligible for this credit. Maximum credit is $500.

OTHER CREDITS

An investment credit is available when qualified business property is purchased. Employees may be able to claim this credit if required to use their own vehicles, tools, etc. in their work.

Residential energy credit is available for insulation, storm or thermal windows and certain energy saving devices installed in your home. Also for solar, wind or geothermal equipment. Energy investment credit is available to businesses for energy-conserving expenditures.

You may be able to claim a credit if you pay for the care of your child or disabled dependent that enables you to be gainfully employed.

These credits range from 10% to 30% of the qualified costs.

INDIVIDUAL RETIREMENT ACCOUNTS

An employee who is not covered by a pension, profit-sharing, or other qualified plan may establish an Individual Retirement Account (IRA). If eligible, you may contribute and deduct up to the lesser of 15 percent of your compensation or $1,500 each year. In addition, the amount earned on the contributions is not taxable until it is withdrawn. Generally, no amount may be withdrawn until you reach age 59 1/2.

If you and your spouse are eligible to establish an IRA and your spouse received no earned income during the year, you may contribute to spousal IRAs. The maximum deduction and contribution for spousal IRAs is the lesser of 15% of compensation or $1,750, one-half to each account. You have until the due date of your tax return to establish and contribute to an IRA for that year.

DECEASED SPOUSE

A taxpayer whose spouse died during the current year is considered to be married for the entire year if he or she does not remarry before the end of the year. A joint return, generally, may be filed.

A person meeting the following requirements may file as a qualifying widow or widower for the two tax years immediately succeeding the one in which the spouse died: (1) you must have been entitled to file a joint return with your spouse in the year of death. (2) You must not have remarried before the close of the tax year. (3) You must have a child or stepchild who qualifies as your dependent. (4) You must furnish over half the cost of maintaining a home, which is the principal residence of the dependent child for the entire year, except for temporary absences. A qualifying widow or widower cannot claim an exemption for the deceased spouse, but can use the zero bracket amount and tax rates for married persons filing a joint return.

After two years the surviving spouse may file as head of household if those qualifications are met.

Life insurance proceeds paid because of the death of the insured, whether received in a lump sum or installments, generally are not taxable. If a surviving spouse elects to receive the proceeds in installments up to $1,000 per year of the interest may be excluded from income. If you elect to receive interest only, it is fully taxable.

The first $5,000 of payments to beneficiaries of deceased employees made by or for an employer because of an employee's death is excludable from the income of the beneficiaries. The excludable amount may not exceed $5,000, regardless of the number of employers or the number of beneficiaries.

FEDERAL TAX COLLECTIONS

SOURCE: Tax Foundation, Inc. Based on official U.S. Government figures.

SELECTED FISCAL YEARS 1959-1981

(Figures in millions)

SOURCE	1959	1969	1978	1979	1980*	1981*
Total	$77,520	$182,575	$389,164	$450,817	$506,288	$580,852
Income and profits taxes	54,028	123,927	240,940	283,518	311,020	345,941
Individual income	36,719	87,249	180,988	217,841	238,717	274,367
Corporate income and profits	17,309	36,678	59,952	65,677	72,303	71,574
Excise taxes	10,675	15,222	18,376	18,745	26,333	40,209
Alcoholic beverages	2,979	4,482	5,492	5,531	5,598	5,624
Tobacco products	1,793	2,136	2,446	2,492	2,523	2,738
Manufacturers' excises	3,928	6,243	6,328	5,901	6,307	6,723
Gasoline	1,687	3,053	4,296	4,383	4,078	4,097
Passenger automobiles[1]	1,031	1,858	—	—	—	—
Tires and tubes	277	582	803	852	821	818
Automobile and truck parts and accessories	165	90	183	221	247	269
Trucks and buses	214	516	834	927	934	1,054
Lubricating oils	73	93	104	107	103	105
Other manufacturers' excises	481	51	108	117	124	380
Retailers' excises	353	—[2]	526[3]	552[3]	580[3]	590[3]
Miscellaneous excises	1,624	2,361	3,584	3,563	11,325	24,534
Telephone and telegraph	685	1,304	1,642	1,340	1,077	732
Transportation of persons	225	222	1,107	1,282	1,455	1,995
Other miscellaneous excises	714	835	835[4]	941[4]	8,793[4,5]	21,807[4,5]
Estate and gift taxes	1,333	3,491	5,285	5,411	5,777	5,938
Employment taxes	8,526	34,236	103,893	120,074	138,609	161,608
Unemployment taxes[6]	2,024	3,328	13,850	15,387	16,847	18,645
Customs	925	2,319	6,573	7,439	7,600	8,403
Miscellaneous	9	52	247	243	102	108

*Data for 1980 and 1981 are estimated.   [1]Repealed as of July 15, 1971.   [2]Repealed as of June 22, 1965.   [3]Includes taxes on noncommercial aviation fuels and diesel fuels used on highways.   [4]Includes Black Lung disability fund taxes and undistributed tax deposits and unapplied collections.   [5]Includes inland waterway trust fund taxes and windfall profits taxes.   [6]Includes state unemployment taxes deposited with the Treasury.

PER CAPITA PROPERTY TAX COLLECTIONS

SOURCE: Bureau of the Census and the Tax Foundation

State	Amount 1968	Amount 1978	Percent Increase	State	Amount 1968	Amount 1978	Percent Increase	State	Amount 1968	Amount 1978	Percent Increase
U.S. Avg.	$139	$305	119.4	Ky.	$ 60	$121	101.7	Ohio	$136	$247	81.6
Ala.	34	69	102.9	La.	55	98	78.2	Okla.	85	134	57.6
Alaska	91	808	787.9	Maine	129	290	124.8	Oreg.	152	362	138.2
Ariz.	151	341	125.8	Md.	137	281	105.1	Pa.	94	223	137.2
Ark.	52	118	126.9	Mass.	204	522	155.9	R.I.	146	361	147.3
Calif.	226	494	118.6	Mich.	151	348	130.5	S.C.	45	139	208.9
Colo.	159	315	98.1	Minn.	173	301	74.0	S.D.	182	322	76.9
Conn.	186	436	134.4	Miss.	55	128	132.7	Tenn.	64	147	129.7
Del.	73	146	100.0	Mo.	108	195	80.6	Texas	111	253	127.9
Fla.	115	228	98.3	Mont.	192	393	104.7	Utah	124	206	66.1
Ga.	76	194	155.3	Nebr.	186	350	88.2	Vt.	138	353	155.8
Hawaii	82	173	111.0	Nev.	180	315	75.0	Va.	80	212	165.0
Idaho	119	215	80.7	N.H.	165	394	138.8	Wash.	121	287	137.2
Ill.	151	325	115.2	N.J.	200	477	138.5	W.Va.	63	120	90.5
Ind.	146	245	67.8	N.M.	62	123	98.4	Wisc.	160	326	103.8
Iowa	172	303	76.2	N.Y.	192	471	145.3	Wy.	208	466	124.0
Kansas	166	334	101.2	N.C.	63	150	138.1	D.C.	137	291	112.4
				N.D.	152	240	57.9				

TAX BURDEN: SELECTED COUNTRIES

SOURCE: Tax Foundation, Inc. Based on OECD data.

Country	TAXES AS % OF GROSS DOMESTIC PRODUCT 1968	1973	1978 (prelim.)	Country	TAXES AS % OF GROSS DOMESTIC PRODUCT 1968	1973	1978 (prelim.)
Australia	24.77	26.84	29.68[a]	Japan	17.86	22.35	22.22[a]
Austria	35.29	37.84	41.30	Luxembourg	31.42	35.60	41.30
Belgium	34.32	37.40	44.40	Netherlands	38.81	43.73	46.70
Canada	29.61	31.41	32.30	New Zealand	25.93	29.05	32.30
Denmark	36.14	42.33	43.20	Norway	37.69	45.29	47.30
Finland	33.66	36.12	38.90	Portugal	19.94	22.04	27.15[a]
France	35.38	35.66	39.40	Spain	18.46	19.03	22.52[a]
Germany, West	32.06	36.27	38.00	Sweden	39.81	43.20	53.10
Greece	24.32	22.71	28.07[a]	Switzerland	22.58	26.33	31.50
Ireland	29.13	31.42	33.70	Turkey	17.06	21.40	24.77[a]
Italy	31.08	28.55	34.50	United Kingdom	35.15	32.36	35.20
				United States	27.51	29.70	30.40

[a]1977

STATE INCOME TAX RATES AND EXEMPTIONS: 1981

SOURCE: Reprinted with permission from the *State Tax Guide*, published by Commerce Clearing House, Inc.

Five states have neither personal nor corporate income tax; they are Nevada, South Dakota, Texas, Washington, and Wyoming. Under personal exemptions, additional exemptions for aged and/or blind are not included. All figures are as of May 1980

State	Personal Exemptions	Individual Rates	Corporation Rates
ALABAMA	Single .... $1,500 Married .... 3,000 Dependent 300	1st $1,000 .... 1.5% Next 2,000 .... 3 Next $2,000 .... 4.5% Over 5,000 5	5%. Financial institutions 6%
ALASKA	Single .... $1,000 Married ...... 2,000 Dependent 1,000	The Alaska personal income tax was repealed by the state legislature and signed into law in late September 1980. Refunds are due all persons who paid taxes for the year 1979 and during 1980.	5.4% plus 4% surtax.
ARIZONA	Single .... $1,000 Married ...... 2,000 Dependent 600	1st $1,000 .... 2% Next 1,000 .... 3 Next 1,000 .... 4 Next 1,000 .... 5 Next $1,000 .... 6% Next 1,000 .... 7 Over 6,000 .... 8 Joint returns may split their income.	1st $1,000 2.5% 2nd 1,000 4 3rd 1,000 5 4th 1,000 6.5 5th 1,000 8 6th 1,000 9 Over 6,000 10.5
ARKANSAS	From tax: Single .... $17.50 Married .... 35.00 Dependent 6.00	1st $2,999 .... 1% Next 3,000 .... 2.5 Next 3,000 .... 3.5 Next $6,000 .... 4.5% Next 10,000 .... 6 $25,000 and over 7	1st $3,000 1% 2nd 3,000 2 Next 5,000 3 Next 14,000 5 Over 25,000 6
CALIFORNIA	From tax: Single .... $25.00 Married ...... 50.00 Dependent 8.00	1st $2,000 .... 1% Next 1,500 .... 2 Next 1,500 .... 3 Next 1,500 .... 4 Next 1,500 .... 5 Next 1,500 .... 6 Next $1,500 .... 7% Next 1,500 .... 8 Next 1,500 .... 9 Next 1,500 .... 10 Over 15,500 .... 11 Tax rates for heads of households range from 1% of taxable income not over $4,000 to 11% of taxable income over $18,000.	9.6%. Financial institutions, other than banks, are allowed limited offset for personal property taxes and license fees.
COLORADO	Single .... $ 850 Married ...... 1,700 Dependent 850	1st $1,000 .... 3% Next 1,000 .... 3.5 Next 1,000 .... 4 Next 1,000 .... 4.5 Next 1,000 .... 5 Next $1,000 .... 5.5% Next 1,000 .... 6 Next 1,000 .... 6.5 Next 1,000 .... 7 Next 1,000 .... 7.5 Over 10,000 .... 8 Surtax on intangible income over $5,000 .... 2% Tax reduction credit applies to reduce the effective rate of tax ½ of 1% in each bracket up to $9,000.	5%.
CONNECTICUT	Single .... $100 Married, filing jointly ...... 200 Married, filing separately .. 100	Rates ranging from 1% on the net capital gains and dividends of at least $20,000, up to 9% on $100,000 and over.	10%, $50 min., or .31 of 1 mill per dollar of net income, whichever is greatest. $100,000 maximum.
DELAWARE	Single .... $ 600 Married ...... 1,200 Dependent 600	1st $1,000 .... 1.5% Next 1,000 .... 2.1 Next 1,000 .... 3.15 Next 1,000 .... 4.3 Next 1,000 .... 5.35 Next 1,000 .... 6.4 Next 2,000 .... 7.45 Next 2,000 .... 8.4 Next 5,000 .... 8.5 Next $5,000 .... 8.6% Next 5,000 .... 9.05 Next 5,000 .... 9.65 Next 10,000 .... 11.55 Next 10,000 .... 12.8 Next 25,000 .... 14.45 Next 25,000 .... 15 Over 100,000 .... 16.65	8.7%.
D. OF COLUMBIA	Single .... $1,000 Married ...... 2,000 Dependent 1,000	1st $1,000 .... 2% Next 1,000 .... 3 Next 1,000 .... 4 Next 1,000 .... 5 Next 1,000 .... 6 Next $5,000 .... 7% Next 3,000 .... 8 Next 4,000 .... 9 Next 8,000 .... 10 Over 25,000 11	9% plus 10% surtax. Minimum $25.
FLORIDA	No personal income tax.		5%.
GEORGIA	Single .... $1,500 Married ...... 3,000 Dependent 700	1st $1,000 .... 1% Next 2,000 .... 2 Next 2,000 .... 3 Next $2,000 .... 4% Next 3,000 .... 5 Over 10,000 6	6%.
HAWAII	Single .... $1,000 Married ...... 2,000 Dependent 1,000	1st $ 500 .... 2.25% Next 500 .... 3.25 Next 500 .... 4.5 Next 500 .... 5 Next 1,000 .... 6.5 Next 2,000 .... 7.5 Next $5,000 .... 8.5% Next 4,000 .... 9.5 Next 6,000 .... 10 Next 10,000 .... 10.5 Over 30,000 11	1st $25,000 5.85% Over 25,000 6.435
IDAHO	Single .... $1,000 Married ...... 2,000 Dependent 1,000	1st $1,000 .... 2% Next 1,000 .... 4 Next 1,000 .... 4.5 Next $1,000 .... 5.5% Next 1,000 .... 6.5 Over 5,000 .... 7.5 Additional $10 due from each person (joint returns deemed one person) filing return. Joint returns may split their income.	6.5%. Additional tax $10.
ILLINOIS	Single .... $1,000 Married ...... 2,000 Dependent 1,000	2½% of federal adjusted income.	4%.
INDIANA	Single .... $1,000 Married ...... 2,000 Dependent. 500	1.9% of federal adjusted gross income.	3% + 3% supplemental income tax.
IOWA	From tax: Single .... $16.00 Married ...... 32.00 Dependent 11.00	1st $1,000 .... .5% 2nd 1,000 .... 1.25 3rd 1,000 .... 2.75 4th 1,000 .... 3.5 5th, 6th and 7th $1,000 .. 5% 8th and 9th 1,000 .. 6 10th through 15th 1,000 .. 7 16th through 20th 1,000 .. 8	1st $ 25,000 6% Next 75,000 8 Over 100,000 10

State	Personal Exemptions	Individual Rates	Corporation Rates
IOWA (cont'd)		21st through 25th $ 1,000 .... 9% 26th through 30th 1,000 .... 10 31st through 40th 1,000 .... 11 41st through 75th 1,000 .... 12 Over 75,000 13	Financial institutions: 1st $ 25,000 5% Next 50,000 6 Next 25,000 7 Over 100,000 8
KANSAS	Single .... $1,000 Married ...... 2,000 Dependent 1,000	1st $2,000 .... 2% Next $ 3,000 .... 6.5% Next 1,000 .... 3.5 Next 10,000 .... 7.5 Next 2,000 .... 4 Next 5,000 .... 8.5 Next 2,000 .... 5 Over 25,000 .... 9.0	4.5% + 2¼% surtax over $25,000.
KENTUCKY	From tax: Single .... $20 Married ...... 40 Dependent 20	1st $3,000 .... 2%. Next $3,000 .... 5% Next 1,000 .... 3 Over 8,000 .... 6 Next 1,000 4	1st $25,000 3% Next 25,000 4 Next 50,000 5 Over 100,000 10
LOUISIANA	Single .... $2,500 Married ...... 5,000 Dependent .... 400 (Personal exemptions are deductible from 2% tax bracket only.)	1st $10,000 .... 2% Next 40,000 .... 4 Over 50,000 .... 6 Joint returns may split their income.	Up to $ 25,000 4% Next 25,000 5 Next 50,000 6 Next 100,000 7 Over 200,000 8
MAINE	Single .... $1,000 Married ...... 2,000 Dependent 1,000	1% on the first $2,000 to 10% of taxable income over $25,000.	1st $25,000 4.95% Over 25,000 6.93
MARYLAND	Single .... $ 800 Married ...... 1,600 Dependent 800	1st $1,000 .... 2% Next $1,000 .... 4% Next 1,000 .... 3 Over 3,000 5	7%.
MASSACHUSETTS	From earned income: Single .... $2,000 Married (joint return) ..... 2,000 plus up to $2,000 for spouse with lower income plus $700 if that spouse's income was under $2,000. Dependent 700	Interest, dividends, net capital gains .... 10% Earned income, annuities .... 5 (Plus 7.5% surtax)	8.33% of net income plus $2.60 per $1,000 of tangible property, or $200 (whichever is greater), plus 14% surtax.
MICHIGAN	Single .... $1,500 Married ...... 3,000 Dependent 1,500	4.6% of adjusted gross income.	2.35%.
MINNESOTA	From tax: Single .... $ 60 Married ...... 120 Dependemt ... 60	1st 500 .... 1.6% Next $ 2,000 .... 10.2% Next 500 .... 2.2 Next 2,000 .... 11.5 Next 1,000 .... 3.5 Next 3,500 .... 12.8 Next 1,000 .... 5.8 Next 7,500 .... 14 Next 1,000 .... 7.3 Next 7,500 .... 15 Next 1,000 .... 8.8 Over 27,500 16	12%. Minimum, $100.
MISSISSIPPI	Single .... $4,500 Married ...... 6,500 Dependent 750	1st $5,000 .... 3% Over 5,000 4	1st $5,000 3% Over 5,000 4
MISSOURI	Single .... $1,200 Married ...... 2,400 Dependent 400	1st $1,000 .... 1.5% 6th $1,000 .... 4% 2nd 1,000 .... 2 7th 1,000 .... 4.5 3rd 1,000 .... 2.5 8th 1,000 .... 5 4th 1,000 .... 3 9th 1,000 .... 5.5 5th 1,000 .... 3.5 Over 9,000 6	5%.
MONTANA	Single .... $ 800 Married ...... 1,600 Dependent 800	1st $1,000 .... 2% Next $ 4,000 .... 8% Next 1,000 .... 3 Next 6,000 .... 9 Next 2,000 .... 4 Next 15,000 .... 10 Next 2,000 .... 5 Over 35,000 .... 11 Next 2,000 .... 6 (Plus 10% surtax.) Next 2,000 7	6¾%. Minimum tax for corporations, $50, except $10 for small business corporations.
NEBRASKA	Single .... $1,000 Married ...... 2,000 Dependent 1,000	17% of adjusted federal income tax liability.	1st $25,000 4.25% Over 25,000 4.675
NEW HAMPSHIRE	$600	(Interest and dividend tax). 5% on income from interest and dividends.	8%.
NEW JERSEY	Single .... $1,000 Married ...... 2,000 Dependent 1,000	1st $20,000 .... 2% Over $20,000 .... 2.5% New York and Pennsylvania residents working in New Jersey are taxed at the same respective rate of their state of residence.	7¼% on allocated net income of interstate corporations, plus additional tax on net worth.
NEW MEXICO	Single .... $1,000 Married ...... 2,000 Dependent 1,000	Rates range from 0.8% of net income for 1st $2,000 to 9% of net income over $100,000.	5%. Banks and financial corps., 6%.

State	Personal Exemptions	Individual Rates	Corporation Rates
NEW YORK	Single .... $ 600 Married ...... 1,200 Dependent 600	1st $1,000 .... 2% Next 2,000 .... 3 Next 2,000 .... 4 Next 2,000 .... 5 Next 2,000 .... 6 Next 2,000 .... 7 Next 2,000 .... 8 Next $ 2,000 .... 9% Next 2,000 .... 10 Next 2,000 .... 11 Next 2,000 .... 12 Next 2,000 .... 13 Over 23,000 14	10% of net income, min. $250 or a tax on three alternative bases, whichever produces the greatest tax.
NORTH CAROLINA	Single .... $1,000 Married ...... 2,000 Dependent 600	1st $2,000 .... 3% Next 2,000 .... 4 Next 2,000 .... 5 Next $ 1,000 .... 6% Over 10,000 7	6%.
NORTH DAKOTA	Single .... $1,000 Married ...... 2,000 Dependent 1,000	1st $3,000 .... 1% Next 2,000 .... 2 Next 3,000 .... 3 Next $ 4,000 .... 4% Next 18,000 .... 5 Over 30,000 .... 7.5	1st $ 3,000 3% Next 5,000 4 Next 7,000 5 Next 10,000 6 Over 25,000 8.5
OHIO	Single .... $ 650 Married ...... 1,300 Dependent 650	1st $5,000 .... 0.5% Next 5,000 .... 1 Next 5,000 .... 2 Next $ 5,000 .... 2.5% Next 20,000 .... 3 Over 40,000 .... 3.5	4% of first $25,000 of net value; 8% of value over $25,000; or 5 mills per dollar of value, whichever is greater. Min., $50.
OKLAHOMA	Single .... $1,000 Married ...... 2,000 Dependent 1,000	1st $2,000 .... 0.5% Next 3,000 .... 1 Next 2,500 .... 2 Next 2,500 .... 3 Next $2,500 .... 4% Next 2,500 .... 5 Remainder 2,500 6	
OREGON	Single .... $1,000 Married ...... 2,000 Dependent 1 000	1st $ 500 .... 4% Next 500 .... 5 Next 1,000 .... 6 Next 1,000 .... 7 Next $1,000 .... 8% Next 1,000 .... 9 Over 5,000 10	7½%.
PENNSYLVANIA	None	No personal income tax. 2.2% of specified classes of income.	10.5%.
RHODE ISLAND	Single .... $1,000 Married ...... 2,000 Dependent 1 000	19% of modified federal income tax liability.	8% of net income or 40¢ per $100 of corporate net worth, whichever is the greater.
SOUTH CAROLINA	Single .... $ 800 Married ...... 1,600 Dependent 800	1st $2,000 .... 2% Next 2,000 .... 3 Next 2,000 .... 4 Next $ 2,000 .... 5% Next 2,000 .... 6 Over 10,000 7	6%; banks 4.5%.
TENNESSEE	None	6% on dividends and interest.	6%.
UTAH	Single .... $1,000 Married ...... 2,000 Dependent 1,000	Rates for single taxpayers range from 2¼% of taxable income not over $750 to $214 plus 7.75% of taxable income over $4,500. Married couples filing jointly pay rates ranging from 2.75% if taxable income not over $1,500 to $356 plus 7.75% of taxable income over $7,500.	4%. Minimum $25.
VERMONT	Single .... $1,000 Married ...... 2,000 Dependent 1,000	23% of federal income tax liability.	1st $ 10,000 5% Next 15,000 6 Next 225,000 7 Next 250,000 7.5 Min. $50.
VIRGINIA	Single .... $ 600 Married ...... 1,200 Dependent 600	1st $3,000 .... 2% Next 2,000 .... 3 Next 7,000 .... 5 Over $12,000 .... 5¾%	6%.
WEST VIRGINIA	Single .... $ 600 Married ...... 1,200 Dependent 600	1st $2,000 .... 2.1% 2nd 2,000 .... 2.3 3rd 2,000 .... 2.8 4th 2,000 .... 3.2 5th 2,000 .... 3.5 6th 2,000 .... 4.0 7th 2,000 .... 4.6 8th 2,000 .... 4.9 9th 2,000 .... 5.3 10th 2,000 .... 5.4 11th 2,000 .... 6.0 Next 4,000 .... 6.1 Next $ 6,000 .... 6.5% Next 6,000 .... 6.8 Next 6,000 .... 7.2 Next 6,000 .... 7.5 Next 10,000 .... 7.9 Next 10,000 .... 8.2 Next 10,000 .... 8.6 Next 10,000 .... 8.8 Next 10,000 .... 9.1 Next 50,000 .... 9.3 Next 50,000 .... 9.5 Next 200,000 .... 9.6	6%.
WISCONSIN	From tax: Single .... $20 Married ...... 40 Dependent 20	1st $3,000 .... 3.4% Next 3,000 .... 5.2 Next 3,000 .... 7.0 Next 3,000 .... 8.2 Next $ 3,000 .... 8.7% Next 5,000 .... 9.1 Next 20,000 .... 9.5 Over 40,000 .... 10.0	1st $1,000 2.3% Next 1,000 2.8 Next 1,000 3.4 Next 1,000 4.5 Next 1,000 5.6 Next 1,000 6.8 Over 6,000 7.9

STATE SALES AND USE TAX RATES

SOURCE: *State Tax Guide,* Commerce Clearing House, Inc.

State	Sales*	Use*	State	Sales*	Use*	State	Sales*	Use*
Alabama[1]	4%	4%	Kentucky[1]	5%	5%	Ohio[1]	4%	4%
Arizona[1]	4%	4%	Louisiana[1]	3%	3%	Oklahoma[1]	2%	2%
Arkansas[1]	3%	3%	Maine	5%	5%	Pennsylvania[1]	6%	6%
California[1]	4¾%	4¾%	Maryland	5%	5%	Rhode Island	6%	6%
Colorado[1]	3%	3%	Massachusetts	5%	5%	South Carolina	4%	4%
Connecticut	7½%[2]	7½%[2]	Michigan	4%	4%	South Dakota[1,2]	5%	5%
D.C.	5%	5%	Minnesota[1]	4%	4%	Tennessee[1]	3%	3%
Florida	4%	4%	Mississippi	5%	5%	Texas[1]	4%	4%
Georgia[1]	3%	3%	Missouri[1]	3⅛%	3⅛%	Utah[1]	4%	4%
Hawaii	4%	4%	Nebraska[1]	3%	3%	Vermont	3%	3%
Idaho	3%	3%	Nevada[1]	3%	3%	Virginia[1]	3%	3%
Illinois[1]	4%	4%	New Jersey	5%	5%	Washington [1]	4½%	4½%
Indiana	4%	4%	New Mexico[1]	3¾%	3¾%	West Virginia[1]	3%	3%
Iowa	3%	3%	New York[1]	4%	4%	Wisconsin[1]	4%	4%
Kansas[1]	3%	3%	North Carolina[1]	3%	3%	Wyoming[1]	3%	3%
			North Dakota	3%	3%			

*As of May 1980. The list of states imposing sales and use taxes does not include Alaska and Delaware. Alaska imposes a business license (gross receipts) tax, and Delaware imposes a merchants' and manufacturers' license tax and a use tax on leases. Other states impose occupation, admission, license, or gross receipts taxes in addition to sales and use taxes. [1]Local tax rates are additional. [2]Manufacturing production machinery is taxed at 2.5% and enumerated business services are taxed at 3.5%.

CITY SALES TAX RATES

SOURCE: *All-State Sales Tax Reports,* published by Commerce Clearing House, Inc.

For these selected U.S. cities, the first rate given is the state sales tax applicable in the city. The second is the city or county rate. The third is the additional sales and use tax. The rates added together give total city sales tax rate.

City	Sales Tax Rate
Atlanta	3% + 1%
Birmingham	4% + 1%
Buffalo	4% + 3%
Chicago	4% + 1%
Cincinnati	4% + ½%
Cleveland	4% + ½%
Dallas	4% + 1%
Denver	3% + 3%
Greensboro, N.C.	3% + 1%
Houston	4% + 1%
Kansas City, Mo.	3⅛% + ½%
Los Angeles	4¾% + 1¼% + 1%
Memphis	3% + 1½%
New Orleans	3% + 2% + 2%
New York City	4% + 4%
Norfolk	4% + 1%
Oklahoma City	2% + 2%
Omaha	3% + 1½%
Phoenix	4% + 1%
Richmond	3% + 1%
St. Louis	3⅛% + 1%
Salt Lake City	4% + ¾% + ¼%
San Antonio	4% + 1%
San Diego	4¾% + 1¼% + 1%
San Francisco	4¾% + 1¼% + 1%
Seattle	4½% + ½%

CITY INCOME TAXES

SOURCE: Commerce Clearing House, Inc.

CITIES (500,000 OR MORE)

	Present rate	Date of Introduction
Alabama		
Birmingham	1.0	1970
Maryland		
Baltimore	50% of state income tax[1]	1966
Michigan		
Detroit	2.0	1962
Missouri		
St. Louis	1.0	1948
New York		
New York	0.9 to 4.3	1966
Ohio		
Cleveland	1.5	1967
Columbus	1.5	1947
Pennsylvania		
Philadelphia	4⁵⁄₁₆	1939
Pittsburgh	1.25	1976

[1]Individual income tax only.

CITIES (125,000 TO 499,000)

	Present rate	Date of Introduction
Kentucky		
Louisville	2.2	1948
Missouri		
Kansas City	1.0	1964
Michigan		
Flint	1.0	1965
Grand Rapids	1.0	1967
Lansing	2.2	1968
Ohio		
Akron	1.5	1962
Canton	1.5	1954
Cincinnati	2.0	1954
Dayton	1.75	1949
Toledo	1.5	1967
Youngstown	1.5	1948
Pennsylvania		
Erie	1.0	1948

FINANCE/INDUSTRY/LABOR

FACTS ABOUT U.S. MONEY
SOURCE: U.S. Treasury Department

In the early days of our nation, before United States money was issued, there were in circulation English shillings, French louis d'ors, and Spanish doubloons, along with other units of those nations' money. This caused confusion and slowed up trade. The dollar was adopted (1785) by the Congress existing under the Articles of Confederation as the unit of our money, and the decimal system as the method of reckoning. In 1792 the United States monetary system was established, and the U.S. Mint began coining money at Philadelphia in 1793.

Many changes in the laws governing coinage and the denominations themselves have been made since the original 1792 act. Coins no longer in use include the half-cent, two-cent, three-cent, and 20-cent pieces, as well as the silver half dime. The five-cent nickel coin was introduced in 1866. Gold coins were struck from 1795 through 1933, in denominations ranging from $1 to $20. The minting and isssuance of gold coins were terminated by Section 5 of the Gold Reserve Act of 1934.

President Johnson signed (July 23, 1965) an historic bill providing for the first major change in U.S. coinage in more than a century. Silver was eliminated altogether from the dime and quarter and substanially reduced in the half dollar.

On Dec. 31, 1970, President Nixon signed the Bank Holding Company Act calling for the removal of all silver from silver dollars and half dollars. This legislation also authorized a silver dollar with a design emblematic of the symbolic eagle of the Apollo 11 landing on the Moon. Once adopted, a coin design may not be changed more often than once in 25 years without specific legislation.

The selection of coin designs is usually made by the Director of the Mint, with the approval of the Secretary of the Treasury. However, Congress has, in a few instances, prescribed them. For example, as a part of the bicentennial celebration of Washington's birth in 1932, Congress declared that the likeness of our first President should appear on the quarter dollar.

The Lincoln penny was the first portrait coin of a regular series minted by the United States. The 100th anniversary of Lincoln's birth aroused sentiment sufficiently strong to overcome a long-prevailing popular prejudice against the use of portraits on coins. A new reverse design was adopted in 1959, when the sesquicentennial of Lincoln's birth was observed. The familiar likeness on the obverse remains unchanged. Others which followed are the 25-cent coin, with Washington's profile, first minted in 1932; the five-cent piece honoring Jefferson, adopted in 1938; the FDR dime, introduced in 1946, and in 1971 the Eisenhower silver dollar, manufacture of which was discontinued in December 1978.

In July 1979, a new, smaller dollar coin was introduced whose size is between the half dollar and the quarter; its smaller size will save in the cost of dollar bill production and help the circulation of the little-used dollar coin. This coin bears the likeness of women's suffrage leader Susan B. Anthony.

Portraits of living persons on American coins are extremely rare and confined to a few commemorative issues of limited minting.

The year 1976 marked the 200th anniversary of American Independence. One of the most far-reaching Government observances was the issuance of specially designed dollars, half dollars, and quarters. Circulation commenced on July 4, 1975, and production ended on December 31, 1976.

The design selection used for American paper currency, including the selection of portraits, is a responsibility of the Secretary of the Treasury, who acts with the advice of the Director of the Bureau of Engraving and Printing, the Treasurer of the United States, and others. By tradition, portraits used on present paper money are those of deceased statesmen of assured historical significance.

The first regular issue of United States currency, the Demand notes that were issued in 1861, carried the portraits of Alexander Hamilton (first Secretary of the Treasury) on the $5 denomination and of Abraham Lincoln on the $10 denomination.

Those design features of U.S. paper currency that have historical or idealistic significance, as distinct from purely ornamental or security implications, include the following:

(1) The New Treasury Seal: Approved on January 29, 1968, the seal of the Department of the Treasury is found on the face of each note. Balance scales, a key, and a chevron with 13 stars appear on the seal, along with the date "1789," the year the Department was created.

(2) The obverse and reverse of the Great Seal of the United States are reproduced on the backs of $1 bills.

(3) Portraits of great Americans used on the face of currency.

(4) Pictures of famous buildings, monuments or events used on the back of currency.

All notes of the same denomination bear the same portrait. Designs on U.S. currency (Federal Reserve Notes) now in circulation are as follows:

Denomination and Class	Portrait	Back
$1 Fed. Reserve Note	Washington	Obverse and reverse of Great Seal of U.S.
$2 Fed. Reserve Note	Jefferson	John Trumbull's "Declaration of Independence"
$5 Fed. Reserve Note	Lincoln	Lincoln Memorial
$10 Fed. Reserve Note	Hamilton	U.S. Treasury Building
$20 Fed. Reserve Note	Jackson	White House
$50 Fed. Reserve Note	Grant	U.S. Capitol
$100 Fed. Reserve Note	Franklin	Independence Hall

Notes of the higher denominations ($500, $1,000, $5,000, and $10,000) have not been printed for many years. As they are returned to Federal Reserve banks, they are removed from circulation and destroyed. The portraits selected for these small-sized notes were McKinley for the $500, Cleveland for the $1,000, Madison for the $5,000, and Chase for the $10,000.

The motto "In God We Trust" owes its presence on U.S. coins largely to the increased religious sentiment existing during the Civil War. Salmon P. Chase, then Secretary of the Treasury, received a number of appeals from devout persons throughout the country urging that the Deity be suitably recognized on our coins as it was on the coins of other nations.

The approved motto first made its appearance on the two-cent coin, authorized by Act of Congress (April 22, 1864), but its use has not been uninterrupted. In 1866 the motto was introduced on the double eagle, eagle, and half eagle gold coins and on the silver dollar, half dollar, and the quarter dollar pieces. It was included in the nickel five-cent design from 1866 to 1883, when it was dropped and not restored until the introduction of the Jefferson nickel in 1938. The motto has been in continuous use on the penny since 1909 and on the dime since 1916.

A law passed by the 84th Congress and approved by the President on July 11, 1955, provides that "In God We Trust" shall appear on all United States paper currency and coins.

By a joint resolution of the 84th Congress, approved by the President on July 30, 1956, "In God We Trust" was declared to be the official motto of the United States.

COMPOUND INTEREST TABLE

What a $1 deposit, compounded monthly, grows to over a thirty-year period.

Interest Rates

Years	5%	5¼%	5½%	5¾%	6%	6¼%	6½%	6¾%	7%	7¼%	7½%	7¾%	8%
1	1.0512	1.0538	1.0564	1.0590	1.0617	1.0643	1.0670	1.0696	1.0723	1.0750	1.0776	1.0803	1.0830
1½	1.0778	1.0812	1.0858	1.0899	1.0939	1.0980	1.1021	1.1062	1.1104	1.1145	1.1187	1.1229	1.1270
2	1.1049	1.1105	1.1160	1.1216	1.1272	1.1328	1.1384	1.1441	1.1498	1.1555	1.1613	1.1671	1.1729
2½	1.1329	1.1399	1.1470	1.1542	1.1614	1.1686	1.1759	1.1833	1.1906	1.1981	1.2055	1.2130	1.2206
3	1.1615	1.1702	1.1789	1.1878	1.1967	1.2056	1.2147	1.2238	1.2329	1.2422	1.2514	1.2608	1.2702
3½	1.1908	1.2012	1.2117	1.2223	1.2330	1.2438	1.2547	1.2657	1.2767	1.2879	1.2991	1.3105	1.3219
4	1.2209	1.2331	1.2455	1.2579	1.2705	1.2832	1.2960	1.3090	1.3221	1.3353	1.3486	1.3621	1.3757
4½	1.2517	1.2658	1.2801	1.2945	1.3091	1.3238	1.3387	1.3538	1.3690	1.3844	1.4000	1.4157	1.4316
5	1.2834	1.2994	1.3157	1.3322	1.3489	1.3657	1.3828	1.4001	1.4176	1.4354	1.4533	1.4715	1.4898
5½	1.3158	1.3339	1.3523	1.3709	1.3898	1.4090	1.4284	1.4480	1.4680	1.4882	1.5087	1.5214	1.5504
6	1.3490	1.3693	1.3899	1.4108	1.4320	1.4536	1.4754	1.4976	1.5201	1.5429	1.5661	1.5896	1.6135
6½	1.3831	1.4057	1.4286	1.4519	1.4755	1.4996	1.5240	1.5489	1.5741	1.5997	1.6258	1.6522	1.6791
7	1.4180	1.4430	1.4683	1.4941	1.5204	1.5471	1.5742	1.6019	1.6300	1.6586	1.6877	1.7173	1.7474
7½	1.4539	1.4813	1.5092	1.5376	1.5666	1.5961	1.6261	1.6567	1.6879	1.7196	1.7520	1.7849	1.8185
8	1.4906	1.5206	1.5511	1.5823	1.6141	1.6466	1.6797	1.7134	1.7478	1.7829	1.8187	1.8552	1.8925
8½	1.5282	1.5609	1.5943	1.6284	1.6631	1.6987	1.7350	1.7721	1.8099	1.8485	1.8880	1.9283	1.9694
9	1.5668	1.6023	1.6386	1.6758	1.7137	1.7525	1.7922	1.8327	1.8742	1.9166	1.9599	2.0042	2.0495
9½	1.6064	1.6449	1.6842	1.7245	1.7658	1.8080	1.8512	1.8954	1.9407	1.9871	2.0346	2.0832	2.1329
10	1.6470	1.6885	1.7311	1.7747	1.8194	1.8652	1.9122	1.9603	2.0097	2.0602	2.1121	2.1652	2.2196
10½	1.6886	1.7333	1.7792	1.8263	1.8747	1.9243	1.9752	2.0274	2.0810	2.1361	2.1925	2.2505	2.3099
11	1.7313	1.7793	1.8287	1.8795	1.9316	1.9852	2.0402	2.0968	2.1549	2.2147	2.2760	2.3391	2.4039
11½	1.7750	1.8266	1.8796	1.9342	1.9903	2.0480	2.1075	2.1686	2.2315	2.2962	2.3627	2.4312	2.5016
12	1.8198	1.8750	1.9319	1.9904	2.0508	2.1129	2.1769	2.2428	2.3107	2.3807	2.4527	2.5269	2.6034
12½	1.8658	1.9248	1.9856	2.0483	2.1130	2.1798	2.2486	2.3196	2.3928	2.4683	2.5462	2.6265	2.7093
13	1.9130	1.9759	2.0408	2.1079	2.1772	2.2488	2.3227	2.3990	2.4778	2.5591	2.6431	2.7299	2.8195
13½	1.9613	2.0283	2.0976	2.1693	2.2434	2.3200	2.3992	2.4811	2.5658	2.6533	2.7438	2.8374	2.9341
14	2.0108	2.0821	2.1560	2.2324	2.3115	2.3934	2.4782	2.5660	2.6569	2.7509	2.8483	2.9491	3.0535
14½	2.0616	2.1374	2.2159	2.2974	2.3817	2.4692	2.5599	2.6538	2.7512	2.8522	2.9568	3.0653	3.1777
15	2.1137	2.1941	2.2776	2.3642	2.4541	2.5474	2.6442	2.7447	2.8489	2.9572	3.0695	3.1860	3.3069
15½	2.1671	2.2524	2.3409	2.4330	2.5286	2.6280	2.7313	2.8386	2.9501	3.0660	3.1864	3.3115	3.4414
16	2.2218	2.3121	2.4061	2.5038	2.6055	2.7112	2.8213	2.9358	3.0549	3.1788	3.3077	3.4419	3.5814
16½	2.2780	2.3735	2.4730	2.5766	2.6846	2.7971	2.9142	3.0363	3.1634	3.2958	3.4337	3.5774	3.7271
17	2.3355	2.4365	2.5418	2.6516	2.7662	2.8856	3.0102	3.1402	3.2757	3.4171	3.5645	3.7183	3.8786
17½	2.3945	2.5011	2.6125	2.7288	2.8502	2.9770	3.1094	3.2477	3.3921	3.5429	3.7003	3.8647	4.0364
18	2.4550	2.5675	2.6852	2.8082	2.9368	3.0712	3.2118	3.3588	3.5125	3.6732	3.8413	4.0169	4.2006
18½	2.5170	2.6357	2.7598	2.8899	3.0260	3.1685	3.3176	3.4738	3.6373	3.8084	3.9876	4.1751	4.3714
19	2.5806	2.7056	2.8366	2.9739	3.1179	3.2688	3.4269	3.5927	3.7665	3.9486	4.1395	4.3395	4.5492
19½	2.6458	2.7774	2.9155	3.0605	3.2126	3.3723	3.5398	3.7157	3.9002	4.0939	4.2971	4.5104	4.7342
20	2.7126	2.8511	2.9966	3.1495	3.3102	3.4790	3.6564	3.8429	4.0387	4.2446	4.4608	4.6880	4.9268
20½	2.7812	2.9268	3.0800	3.2412	3.4108	3.5892	3.7769	3.9744	4.1822	4.4008	4.6037	4.8727	5.1272
21	2.8514	3.0045	3.1657	3.3355	3.5144	3.7028	3.9013	4.1104	4.3307	4.5627	4.8071	5.0646	5.3357
21½	2.9235	3.0842	3.2537	3.4325	3.6211	3.8200	4.0298	4.2511	4.4845	4.7306	4.9902	5.2640	5.5527
22	2.9973	3.1660	3.3442	3.5324	3.7311	3.9410	4.1626	4.3966	4.6438	4.9047	5.1803	5.4173	5.7786
22½	3.0730	3.2501	3.4373	3.6352	3.8445	4.0658	4.2997	4.5471	4.8087	5.0852	5.3776	5.6868	6.0136
23	3.1507	3.3663	3.5329	3.7410	3.9613	4.1945	4.4134	4.7028	4.9795	5.2724	5.5825	5.9017	6.2582
23½	3.2302	3.4249	3.6311	3.8498	4.0816	4.3273	4.5877	4.8637	5.1563	5.4664	5.7951	6.1435	6.5127
24	3.3118	3.5157	3.7321	3.9618	4.2056	4.4643	4.7388	5.0302	5.3394	5.6676	6.0159	6.3854	6.7776
24½	3.3955	3.6090	3.8360	4.0771	4.3333	4.6056	4.8949	5.2024	5.5291	5.8762	6.2450	6.6369	7.0533
25	3.4813	3.7048	3.9427	4.1957	4.4650	4.7514	5.0562	5.3804	5.7254	6.0924	6.4829	6.8983	7.3402
25½	3.5692	3.8031	4.0523	4.3178	4.6006	4.9019	5.2228	5.5646	5.9288	6.3166	6.7928	7.1699	7.6387
26	3.6594	3.9041	4.1651	4.4434	4.7404	5.0570	5.3948	5.7551	6.1393	6.5491	6.9862	7.4523	7.9494
26½	3.7518	4.0077	4.2809	4.5727	4.8844	5.2172	5.5725	5.9521	6.3573	6.7901	7.2523	7.7458	8.2727
27	3.8466	4.1141	4.4000	4.7058	5.0327	5.3823	5.7561	6.1558	6.5831	7.0400	7.5285	8.0508	8.6092
27½	3.9438	4.2232	4.5224	4.8427	5.1856	5.5527	5.9457	6.3665	6.8169	7.2991	7.8153	8.3679	8.9594
28	4.0434	4.3353	4.6482	4.9836	5.3431	5.7285	6.1416	6.5844	7.0590	7.5677	8.1130	8.6974	9.3238
28½	4.1456	4.4504	4.7775	5.1286	5.5055	5.9099	6.3439	6.8098	7.3097	7.8462	8.4220	9.0399	9.7030
29	4.2503	4.5685	4.9104	5.2778	5.6727	6.0970	6.5529	7.0429	7.5693	8.1350	8.7428	9.3959	10.0976
29½	4.3577	4.6897	5.0467	5.4314	5.8450	6.2900	6.7688	7.2839	7.8381	8.4344	9.0758	9.7659	10.5083
30	4.4677	4.8192	5.1874	5.5894	6.0226	6.4872	6.9918	7.5332	8.1165	8.7448	9.4215	10.1505	10.9357

GOLD PRODUCTION

SOURCE: U.S. Bureau of Mines (figures in millions of dollars at $35 per fine ounce through 1971, $38 per fine ounce in 1972 and 1973, and $42.22 per fine ounce beginning in 1974)

	1960	1965	1970	1972	1974	1975	1976	1977	1978	1979[1]
South Africa	784.4	1,069.0	1,128.0	1,109.7	1,029.7	968.4	968.4	950.0	956.3	955.4
Canada	162.0	125.6	84.3	77.2	71.7	69.8	71.2	72.5	71.8	71.8
United States	58.8	58.6	63.5	55.1	47.6	44.4	44.2	46.5	42.2	38.4
Other Africa	67.7	55.4	51.1	53.8	69.1	63.7	63.9	51.3	47.2	47.6
Ghana	30.8	26.7	24.6	27.5	25.9	22.1	22.5	20.3	17.0	17.3
Zimbabwe	19.7	—	17.5	19.1	33.8	33.8	33.8	25.3	25.3	25.3
Zaire	11.1	2.3	6.2	5.4	5.5	4.4	4.3	3.4	3.2	3.4
Latin America	50.2	39.8	32.4	34.1	42.4	52.4	61.0	57.3	57.2	61.3
Colombia	15.2	11.2	7.1	7.1	11.2	13.0	12.6	10.9	10.4	12.2
Mexico	10.5	7.6	6.9	5.5	5.7	6.1	6.9	9.0	8.5	9.7
Nicaragua	6.9	5.4	4.0	4.3	3.5	3.0	3.2	2.8	2.8	2.5
Peru	4.9	3.7	3.3	3.0	4.2	3.3	3.4	4.1	4.4	4.9
Asia	35.6	41.8	44.2	47.3	47.3	44.8	45.7	49.4	50.5	53.3
Philippines	14.4	15.4	21.1	23.0	22.7	21.2	21.2	23.6	25.7	27.4
Japan	11.8	18.1	24.8	32.2	5.9	6.1	5.8	7.2	3.5	3.6
India	5.6	4.6	3.6	4.0	4.3	3.8	4.3	3.9	3.7	3.6
Europe*	12.2	—	10.4	13.3	25.2	21.5	28.3	27.2	23.0	23.7
Oceania	43.3	36.1	26.7	47.8	53.0	51.1	76.1	59.7	60.8	58.5
Australia	38.0	30.7	21.9	28.7	21.6	22.2	21.0	26.2	27.4	27.4
World Total	1,178	1,440	1,450	1,442	1,386	1,386	1,359	1,314	1,309	1,310

[1]Estimated   *Data exclude USSR

COMPANIES WITH THE LARGEST NUMBER OF COMMON STOCKHOLDERS

SOURCE: New York Stock Exchange

(Figures rounded to nearest thousand)

EARLY 1980

Company	Stockholders	Company	Stockholders
American Tel. & Tel.	2,978,000	Niagara Mohawk Power	209,000
General Motors	1,219,000	DuPont (EI) Denemours	209,000
International Business Machines	697,000	Chrysler Corporation	207,000
Exxon Corporation	686,000	Northeast Utilities	200,000
General Electric	527,000	Atlantic Richfield	193,000
General Tel. & Electronics	462,000	Southern California Edison	181,000
Texaco Incorporated	415,000	Westinghouse Electric	181,000
Gulf Oil	343,000	Standard Oil (Indiana)	176,000
Southern Company	341,000	BankAmerica	174,000
Ford Motor	337,000	Ohio Edison	173,000
Sears, Roebuck	334,000	Union Carbide Corporation	171,000
American Electric Power	295,000	Virginia Electric & Power	170,000
Mobil Corporation	274,000	General Public Utilities	169,000
Philadelphia Electric	260,000	Consumers Power	165,000
U.S. Steel	259,000	Union Electric	158,000
Standard Oil of California	256,000	Occidental Petroleum	156,000
Pacific Gas & Electric	255,000	Pennsylvania Power	155,000
Consolidated Edison	248,000	Columbia Gas System	152,000
Commonwealth Edison	245,000	Long Island Lighting	152,000
Eastman Kodak	242,000	Bethlehem Steel	151,000
RCA	239,000	Middle South Utilities	147,000
Tenneco Incorporated	232,000	Transamerica Corporation	146,000
Detroit Edison	232,000	Greyhound Corporation	146,000
Public Service Electric & Gas	227,000	Pan American World Airways	145,000
International Tel. & Tel.	220,000	American Motors	145,000

U.S. CORPORATE PROFITS (In billions of dollars)

SOURCE: U.S. Department of Commerce, Bureau of Economic Analysis

	Total pre-tax profits	Tax liability	After-tax profits	Dividends	Undistributed profits
1929	10.0	1.4	8.6	5.8	2.8
1930	3.7	.8	2.9	5.5	-2.6
1931	- .4	.5	- .9	4.1	-4.9
1932	-2.3	.4	-2.7	2.5	-5.2
1933	1.0	.5	.4	2.0	-1.6
1935	3.6	1.0	2.6	2.8	- .2
1940	10.0	2.8	7.2	4.0	3.2
1945	19.7	10.7	9.0	4.6	4.4
1950	42.6	17.9	24.7	8.8	15.9
1955	48.4	22.0	26.4	10.3	16.1
1960	48.5	22.7	25.8	12.9	13.0
1965	75.2	30.9	44.3	19.1	25.2
1968	85.6	39.4	46.2	21.9	24.2
1969	83.4	39.7	43.8	22.6	21.2
1970	71.5	34.5	37.0	22.9	14.1
1971	82.0	37.7	44.3	23.0	21.3
1972	96.2	41.5	54.6	24.6	30.0
1973	115.8	48.7	67.1	27.8	39.3
1974	126.9	52.4	74.5	31.0	43.6
1975	120.4	49.8	70.6	31.9	38.7
1976	155.9	63.8	92.2	37.5	54.7
1977	177.1	72.6	104.5	42.1	54.7
1978	195.8	84.5	111.3	42.1	69.2
1979	224.0	92.7	131.3	47.6	83.6

FOREIGN EXCHANGE RATES: 1949-1980

SOURCE: Federal Reserve Bulletin (in U.S. cents)

Year	United Kingdom (pound)	Canada (dollar)	Netherlands (guilder)	West Germany* (deutsche mark)	Switzerland (franc)	France† (franc)	Belgium (franc)	Japan‡ (yen)	Italy (lira)
1949	368.72	92.88	34.53	NA	23.31	.3017	2.20	NA	.1699
1950	280.07	91.47	26.25	23.84	23.14	.2858	1.99	NA	.1601
1951	279.96	94.94	26.26	23.84	23.06	.2856	1.99	NA	.1600
1953	281.27	101.65	26.34	23.84	23.32	.2856	2.00	NA	.1600
1956	279.57	101.60	26.11	23.79	23.33	.2855	2.00	.2779	.1600
1958	280.98	103.03	26.42	23.85	23.33	.2858	2.00	.2779	.1601
1960	280.76	103.12	26.51	23.98	23.15	20.39	2.00	.2778	.1610
1962	280.78	93.56	27.76	25.01	23.12	20.41	2.01	.2771	.1611
1964	279.21	92.69	27.72	25.16	23.15	20.40	2.01	.2763	.1601
1966	279.30	92.81	27.63	25.01	23.11	20.35	2.01	.2760	.1601
1968	239.35	92.80	27.63	25.05	23.17	20.19	2.00	.2774	.1604
1970	239.59	95.80	27.65	27.42	23.20	18.09	2.01	.2792	.1595
1972	250.08	100.94	31.15	31.36	26.19	19.83	2.27	.3300	.1713
1974	234.03	102.26	37.27	38.72	33.69	20.81	2.57	.3430	.1537
1975	222.16	98.30	39.63	40.73	38.74	23.35	2.73	.3371	.1533
1976	180.48	101.41	37.85	39.74	40.01	20.94	2.59	.3374	.1204
1977	174.49	94.11	40.75	43.08	41.71	20.34	2.79	.3734	.1133
1978	191.84	87.73	46.28	49.87	56.28	22.22	3.18	.4798	.1178
1979	212.24	85.39	49.84	54.56	60.12	23.50	3.41	.4583	.1204
1980 (April)	220.94	84.31	48.57	53.31	56.86	22.99	3.32	.3998	.1142

*Beginning with June 1950.   †Beginning with 1960, 100 old francs = 1 new franc.   ‡Beginning with November 1956.   NA = Not available.

MONEY DEPRECIATION: ANNUAL RATES

SOURCE: International Monetary Fund and Citibank

The value of money is here measured by reciprocals of official cost-of-living or consumer price indexes. (1970 = 100)

	INDEXES: VALUE OF MONEY 1978	1979	RATE OF DEPRECIATION 1970-79
Germany, West	67	64	5.0
Switzerland	66	64	5.1
Egypt	69	63	5.3
Austria	60	58	6.3
United States	60	53	7.2
Belgium	55	53	7.4
Netherlands	58	53	7.4
Canada	56	51	7.7
Norway	52	50	8.1
Sweden	50	47	8.7
Netherlands Antilles	52	47	8.7
Japan	47	46	9.1
Bahamas	51	46	9.2
France	50	45	9.2
Guatemala	50	44	9.4
Denmark	48	44	9.6
Dominican Republic	47	43	9.7
Syria	45	43	9.8
South Africa	47	42	10.2
Australia	45	41	10.4
Finland	41	39	11.2
Jordan	44	38	11.3
New Zealand	41	36	12.0
Ecuador	38	35	12.5
Trinidad & Tobago	40	34	12.5
Italy	38	33	13.0
Greece	39	33	13.1
United Kingdom	37	33	13.2
Saudi Arabia	33	33	13.2
Ireland	37	33	13.2
Bahrain	33	32	13.5
Spain	33	29	14.9
Mexico	32	27	15.6
Jamaica	32	25	16.9
Yugoslavia	29	24	17.4
Indonesia	28	23	17.8
Portugal	27	22	18.5
Colombia	23	19	20.3
Turkey	22	14	24.4
Peru	19	11	27.3
Brazil	14	9	30.8
Israel	13	7	34.1
Uruguay	2	1	62.6
Argentina	*	*	121.5
Chile	*	*	144.3

*Less than 1.

CENTRAL BANK DISCOUNT RATES

SOURCE: International Monetary Fund (end of period quotations in percent per annum)

	1961	1963	1965	1967	1969	1971	1973	1975	1977	1978	1979	1980[1]
United States	3.00	3.50	4.50	4.50	6.00	4.50	7.50	6.00	6.00	9.50	12.00	12.00
United Kingdom	6.00	4.00	6.00	8.00	8.00	5.00	13.00	11.25	7.00	12.50	17.00	17.00
Industrial Europe												
Austria	5.00	4.50	4.50	3.75	4.75	5.00	7.75	6.00	5.50	4.50	3.75	5.25
Belgium	4.50	4.25	4.75	4.00	7.50	5.50	9.00	6.00	9.00	6.00	10.50	10.50
France	3.50	4.00	3.50	3.50	8.00	6.50	11.00	8.00	9.50	9.50	9.50	9.50
Germany	3.00	3.00	4.00	3.00	6.00	4.00	7.00	3.50	3.00	3.00	6.00	6.00
Italy	3.50	3.50	3.50	3.50	3.50	3.50	6.50	6.00	11.50	10.50	15.00	15.00
Netherlands	3.50	3.50	4.50	4.50	6.00	5.00	8.00	4.50	4.50	6.50	9.50	9.50
Norway	3.50	3.50	3.50	3.50	4.50	4.50	4.50	5.00	6.00	7.00	9.00	9.00
Sweden	5.00	4.00	5.50	6.00	7.00	5.00	5.00	6.00	8.00	6.50	9.00	10.00
Switzerland	2.00	2.00	2.50	3.00	3.75	3.75	4.50	3.00	1.50	1.00	2.00	2.00
Canada	3.24	4.00	4.75	6.00	8.00	4.75	7.25	9.00	7.50	10.75	14.00	14.00
Japan	7.30	5.84	5.48	5.84	6.25	4.75	9.00	6.50	4.25	3.50	6.25	6.25

[1] January.

MONETARY TERMS

Balance of Payment—A nation's transactions with other nations, for trade, investment, tourism, foreign aid, and the like. A deficit occurs when more is paid out than a nation earns.

Balance of Trade—That part of the balance of payments covering exports and imports of goods.

Devalue or Devaluation—The act of changing a currency's par value downward.

Exchange Control—Government controls on purchase of foreign currencies for various purposes, aimed at protecting a nation's reserves.

Foreign Exchange—The term applied to foreign currencies.

Foreign Exchange Market—The market in which foreign currencies are bought and sold and the daily trading price in terms of dollars is set. It is not a specific place but rather a series of trading "desks," mainly at banks.

Par Value—The international value of a currency, expressed as so many ounces of gold or so many U.S. dollars and cents.

Reserves—A nation's holdings of gold plus certain foreign currencies.

Reserve Currency—A currency in which other nations hold part of their reserves.

"Run" or "Attack"—A mass wave of selling of a particular currency on the foreign exchange markets.

Support—Official intervention in the foreign exchange market by a nation's central bank to hold up the price of the nation's currency.

U.S. GROSS NATIONAL PRODUCT† SOURCE: U.S. Department of Commerce, Bureau of Economic Analysis

	1929	1933	1945	1955	1965	1975	1978	1979
Gross National Product	103.4	55.8	212.3	399.3	688.1	1528.8	2127.6	2369.4
GNP in Constant (1972) Dollars	314.7	222.1	559.0	654.8	925.9	1202.1	1399.2	1431.7
Personal Consumption Expenditures	77.3	45.8	119.5	253.7	430.2	980.4	1350.8	1510.0
Durable goods	9.2	3.5	8.0	38.6	62.8	132.9	200.3	213.1
Nondurable goods	37.7	22.3	71.9	122.9	188.6	409.3	530.6	596.9
Services	30.3	20.1	39.6	92.1	178.7	438.2	619.8	700.0
Gross Private Domestic Investment	16.2	1.4	10.6	68.4	112.0	189.1	351.5	387.2
Fixed Investment	14.5	3.0	11.7	62.4	102.5	200.6	329.1	368.8
Nonresidential	10.5	2.4	10.1	38.3	71.3	49.1	221.1	254.6
Structures	5.0	0.9	2.8	14.4	26.1	52.9	76.5	92.7
Producers' durable equipment	5.5	1.4	7.3	23.9	45.1	96.3	144.6	161.9
Residential	4.0	0.6	1.6	24.1	31.2	51.5	108.0	114.2
Nonfarm structures	3.8	0.5	1.4	23.0	29.9	49.5	104.4	110.3
Farm structures	0.2	*	0.1	0.6	0.6	0.9	1.8	1.9
Producers' durable equipment	*	*	*	0.4	0.7	1.1	1.9	2.0
Change in business inventories	1.7	−1.6	−1.0	6.0	9.5	−11.5	22.3	18.5
Net exports of goods and services	1.1	0.4	−0.6	2.2	7.6	20.4	−10.3	−4.2
Government purchases	8.8	8.2	82.8	75.0	138.4	338.9	435.6	476.4
Federal	1.4	2.1	74.6	44.5	67.3	123.3	152.6	166.6
National defense	—	—	73.5	38.4	49.4	83.9	99.0	108.3
Non-defense	—	—	1.1	6.0	17.8	39.4	53.6	58.4
State and local	7.4	6.1	8.2	30.6	71.1	215.6	283.0	309.8

†In billions of dollars. *Less than $0.1 billion.

GROSS NATIONAL PRODUCT: SELECTED NATIONS 1979

SOURCE: Dr. Herbert Block, *The Planetary Product*

	GNP Total ($ Millions)	GNP Per Capita (Dollars)	Population Mid-1979 (Millions)
Western Europe			
Austria	47,374	6,311	7.51
Belgium	78,575	7,978	9.85
Denmark	43,347	8,470	5.12
Finland	27,738	5,814	4.77
France	460,953	8,619	53.48
Germany, West	582,776	9,507	61.30
Greece	27,206	2,881	9.44
Iceland	1,472	6,542	0.23
Ireland	11,543	3,533	3.27
Italy	238,390	4,191	56.88
Luxembourg	2,768	7,754	0.36
Netherlands	99,003	7,057	14.03
Norway	35,723	8,762	4.08
Portugal	17,258	1,754	9.84
Spain	104,910	2,830	37.08
Sweden	83,548	10,071	8.30
Switzerland	59,873	9,439	6.34
United Kingdom	277,933	4,972	55.90
Africa (Excluding Egypt)			
Algeria	27,100	1,485	18.25
Ethiopia	3,699	116	31.78
Gabon	2,730	4,707	0.58
Ghana	5,484	467	11.74
Ivory Coast	6,630	812	7.76
Kenya	4,476	284	15.78
Libya	20,200	7,031	2.87
Morocco	11,415	560	20.37
Nigeria	38,412	515	74.59
South Africa	41,900	1,507	27.80
Sudan	5,780	318	18.17
Tanzania	3,152	182	17.36
Tunisia	6,750	1,071	6.31
Uganda	3,280	248	13.23
Zaire	3,796	135	28.09
Zimbabwe	3,338	460	7.25
South Asia			
Afghanistan	2,858	197	14.54
Bangladesh	9,578	109	88.09
Burma	5,552	165	33.59
India	121,180	182	667.33
Pakistan	17,960	214	84.08
Sri Lanka	4,141	284	14.59
Near East			
Egypt	14,270	348	40.99
Iran	56,070	1,492	37.58
Iraq	32,020	2,481	12.91
Israel	16,926	4,621	3.66
Jordan	2,223	988	2.25
Kuwait	15,990	12,520	1.28
Qatar	6,470	38,743	0.17
Saudi Arabia	71,230	10,958	6.50
Syria	8,350	983	8.51
Turkey	36,910	828	44.56
United Arab Emirates	12,584	13,980	0.90
East Asia			
China, Rep. of (Taiwan)	27,690	1,586	17.46
Hong Kong	15,771	3,360	4.69
Indonesia	56,550	382	148.09
Japan	839,427	7,244	115.88
Korea, South	40,950	1,036	39.54
Malaysia	16,380	1,198	13.67
Philippines	25,190	528	47.68
Singapore	9,120	3,863	2.36
Thailand	24,670	528	46.69
Oceania			
Australia	110,249	7,647	14.42
New Zealand	17,427	5,587	3.12
Latin America			
Argentina	52,000	2,291	27.21
Bolivia	3,364	645	5.21
Brazil	214,850	1,803	119.18
Chile	17,836	1,644	10.85
Colombia	22,760	869	26.21
Dominican Republic	5,367	967	5.55
Ecuador	7,680	987	7.78
Guatemala	6,673	974	6.85
Jamaica	3,422	1,532	2.23
Mexico	117,446	1,786	65.77
Panama	2,673	1,436	1.86
Peru	18,436	1,074	17.16
Uruguay	4,402	1,513	2.91
Venezuela	45,180	3,108	14.54
North America			
Canada	219,450	2,264	23.67
UNITED STATES	2,369,400	10,765	220.10
Communist Countries			
Albania	1,940	720	2.70
Bulgaria	26,700	3,034	8.80
China, People's Rep.	375,000	370	1,012.20
Cuba	12,700	1,297	9.80
Czechoslovakia	76,600	5,039	15.20
Germany, East	89,100	5,335	16.70
Hungary	35,700	3,336	10.70
Korea, North	14,100	753	18.72
Mongolia	1,280	800	1.60
Poland	119,100	3,384	35.20
Romania	78,900	3,586	22.00
USSR	1,155,593	4,387	263.40
Vietnam	7,450	143	52.10
Yugoslavia	64,400	2,905	22.17
WORLD	**9,291,400**	**2,110**	**4,404.45**

OIL IMPORTS: 1978-1979   SOURCE: Social and Economic Statistics Administration, U.S. Dept. of Commerce

(Quantity in barrels, value in dollars.)

Country of Origin	General Imports Calendar Year 1979		Country of Origin	General Imports Calendar Year 1978	
	Net Quantity	F.a.s. Value		Net Quantity	F.a.s. Value
Canada	104,674,468	$ 1,887,827,000	Canada	63,668,088	$ 892,553,098
Mexico	162,740,395	3,040,753,000	Mexico	112,152,740	1,490,148,711
Trinidad	45,204,148	884,336,000	Trinidad	50,864,009	736,312,271
Venezuela	133,032,215	2,127,676,000	Venezuela	26,253,303	336,284,017
Colombia	219,911	2,570,000	Ecuador	16,721,195	213,566,711
Ecuador	12,927,052	281,385,000	Peru	8,892,552	117,215,881
Peru	16,193,100	399,973,000	Bolivia	610,306	9,095,943
Norway	34,274,840	713,127,000	Chile	281,443	4,013,377
United Kingdom	68,442,200	1,391,133,000	Brazil	127,974	1,597,116
Italy	180,616	8,610,000	Norway	48,085,211	670,694,430
Syria	5,763,620	152,883,000	United Kingdom	52,209,175	719,361,759
Iran	119,928,183	2,565,097,000	Union of Soviet Socialist Republics	276,389	3,482,530
Kuwait	2,485,385	55,351,000	Syria	1,016,049	11,829,189
Iraq	33,745,076	612,941,000	Iraq	18,627,040	231,712,015
Saudi Arabia	490,353,252	7,855,478,000	Iran	211,521,682	2,689,847,062
Qatar	13,104,486	278,896,000	Kuwait	1,718,182	21,075,148
United Arab Emirates	109,991,603	1,963,047,000	Saudi Arabia	406,528,669	5,211,041,303
Oman	14,030,808	248,768,000	Qatar	24,445,200	317,729,173
Malaysia	18,705,323	393,327,000	United Arab Emirates	139,006,647	1,851,988,617
Indonesia	136,981,450	2,404,511,000	Oman	23,699,584	308,699,011
Brunei	2,279,941	40,335,000	Malaysia	15,684,994	222,658,752
China	4,109,411	71,789,000	Indonesia	196,768,102	2,676,624,618
Australia	424,949	8,170,000	Brunei	2,435,246	34,131,751
Algeria	218,292,361	4,282,415,000	Algeria	232,993,709	3,300,865,263
Egypt	17,209,337	344,633,000	Tunisia	1,093,498	15,912,443
Gabon	16,775,758	313,649,000	Libya	268,731,319	3,706,082,141
Congo (Brazzaville)	3,774,570	67,596,000	Egypt	6,002,106	76,408,329
Tunisia	4,243,416	90,318,000	Cameroon	2,204,841	28,158,843
Libya	251,780,242	5,162,444,000	Nigeria	321,975,860	4,546,457,056
Cameroon	7,059,179	150,652,000	Gabon	12,676,516	162,735,154
Ghana	461,211	7,406,000	Angola	10,290,837	137,417,434
Nigeria	401,659,051	7,973,608,000	Congo (Brazzaville)	5,354,671	70,946,776
Angola	14,660,865	288,529,000	Zaire	263,369	3,529,145
Zaire	1,606,361	30,743,000	Other Countries	5	669
Other Countries	259	7,000			
Total	**2,467,315,042**	**$46,099,983,000**	**Total**	**2,283,180,511**	**$30,820,175,736**

LARGEST U.S. COMMERCIAL BANKS   SOURCE: *Fortune* Magazine

Bank	Assets[1] ($000)	Rank '79	Rank '78	Deposits ($000)	Rank	Loans[2] ($000)	Rank
BankAmerica Corp. (San Francisco)	108,389,318	1	1	84,984,746	1	57,096,295	2
Citicorp (New York)	106,370,619	2	2	70,290,725	2	62,536,389	1
Chase Manhattan Corp. (New York)	64,708,018	3	3	48,456,210	3	39,749,569	3
Manufacturers Hanover Corp. (New York)	47,675,446	4	4	38,156,078	4	25,230,815	4
J.P. Morgan & Co. (New York)	43,487,679	5	5	30,278,552	5	22,158,171	6
Chemical New York Corp.	39,375,293	6	6	28,986,820	6	20,337,991	7
Continental Illinois Corp. (Chicago)	35,790,119	7	7	24,007,200	7	22,861,532	5
Bankers Trust New York Corp.	30,952,922	8	9	22,436,852	9	15,975,911	10
First Chicago Corp.	30,181,800	9	10	21,106,060	10	15,563,358	11
Western Bancorp. (Los Angeles)	29,687,134	10	8	23,631,073	8	16,813,824	8
Security Pacific Corp. (Los Angeles)	24,923,382	11	11	18,450,827	11	16,145,246	9
Wells Fargo & Co. (San Francisco)	20,593,124	12	12	15,831,015	12	14,735,678	12
Irving Bank Corp. (New York)	16,702,433	13	14	13,525,148	13	7,275,544	16
Crocker National Corp. (San Francisco)	16,138,650	14	15	12,516,820	14	10,433,489	13
Marine Midland Banks (Buffalo)	15,728,156	15	13	12,509,007	15	9,007,151	14

[1]As of December 31, 1979.   [2]Net of unearned discount and loan loss reserve.

LARGEST DIVERSIFIED FINANCIAL COMPANIES   SOURCE: *Fortune* Magazine

Company	Assets[1] ($000)	Rank '79	Rank '78	Revenues ($000)	Rank	Net Income ($000)	Rank
Aetna Life & Casualty (Hartford)	30,228,463	1	1	11,446,880	1	585,418	1
Travelers Corp. (Hartford)	19,159,864	2	2	7,888,901	2	395,046	2
American Express (New York)	17,108,200	3	3	4,666,500	3	345,300	3
H.F. Ahmanson (Los Angeles)	12,137,253	4	5	1,211,220	18	117,137	21
Merrill Lynch & Co. (New York)	10,556,100	5	6	2,051,996	11	118,743	20
First Charter Financial (Beverly Hills)	9,548,833	6	8	846,313	24	90,848	24
Great Western Financial (Beverly Hills)	9,453,989	7	7	878,354	23	93,071	23
INA (Philadelphia)	8,987,035	8	4	4,551,372	4	261,637	5
Loews (New York)	8,842,683	9	9	4,065,475	5	208,580	11
Transamerica (San Francisco)	7,983,535	10	12	4,044,647	6	240,202	7
Lincoln National (Fort Wayne, Ind.)	7,770,900	11	11	2,445,099	8	165,009	12
Continental (New York)	7,458,312	12	10	3,252,707	7	273,585	4
American General Insurance (Houston)	6,548,192	13	13	1,886,052	13	218,650	9
Imperial Corp. of America (San Diego)	6,520,823	14	14	583,152	33	74,180	29
Beneficial (Wilmington)	6,031,300	15	21	982,900	22	101,100	22

[1]As of December 31, 1979.

LARGEST INDUSTRIAL CORPORATIONS

SOURCE: *Fortune* Magazine

Company	Sales ($000)	Rank '79	Rank '78	Assets ($000)	Rank	Net Income ($000)	Rank
Exxon (New York)	79,106,471*	1	2	49,489,964	1	4,295,243	1
General Motors (Detroit)	66,311,200	2	1	32,215,800	2	2,892,700	3
Mobil (New York)	44,720,908	3	4	27,505,756	3	2,007,158	4
Ford Motor (Dearborn, Mich.)	43,513,700	4	3	23,524,600	5	1,169,300	11
Texaco (Harrison, N.Y.)	38,350,370	5	5	22,991,955	6	1,759,069	6
Standard Oil of California (San Francisco)	29,947,554	6	6	18,102,632	7	1,784,694	5
Gulf Oil (Pittsburgh)	23,910,000*	7	9	17,265,000	8	1,322,000	9
International Business Machines (Armonk, N.Y.)	22,862,776	8	7	24,529,974	4	3,011,259	2
General Electric (Fairfield, Conn.)	22,460,600	9	8	16,644,500	10	1,408,800	8
Standard Oil (Ind.) (Chicago)	18,610,347*	10	12	17,149,899	9	1,506,618	7
International Telephone & Telegraph (New York)	17,197,423	11	11	15,091,321	12	380,685	42
Atlantic Richfield (Los Angeles)	16,233,959	12	13	13,833,387	13	1,165,894	12
Shell Oil (Houston)	14,431,211*	13	14	16,127,016	11	1,125,561	13
U.S. Steel (Pittsburgh)	12,929,100	14	15	11,029,900	15	(293,000)	492
Conoco (Stamford, Conn.)	12,647,998	15	18	9,311,171	17	815,360	17

*Does not include excise taxes.

LARGEST UTILITIES

SOURCE: *Fortune* Magazine

Company	Assets[1] ($000)	Rank '79	Rank '78	Operating Revenues ($000)	Rank	Net Income[2] ($000)	Rank
American Telephone & Telegraph (New York)	113,768,836	1	1	45,408,078	1	5,674,248	1
General Telephone & Electronics (Stamford, Conn.)	18,405,965	2	2	9,957,817	2	645,070	2
Southern Company (Atlanta)	10,552,095	3	3	3,128,169	5	219,127	10
Pacific Gas & Electric (San Francisco)	10,310,763	4	4	4,372,220	3	458,234	3
Commonwealth Edison (Chicago)	9,172,615	5	6	2,720,922	10	296,678	6
American Electric Power (New York)	8,780,368	6	5	2,813,691	9	260,635	8
Consolidated Edison (New York)	7,133,210	7	7	3,332,786	4	323,912	5
Southern California Edison (Rosemead, Calif.)	6,977,237	8	8	2,563,974	11	346,219	4
Middle South Utilities (New Orleans)	6,503,068	9	10	1,823,059	22	182,058	19
Public Service Electric & Gas (Newark)	6,104,183	10	9	2,416,707	15	233,329	9
Virginia Electric & Power (Richmond)	5,960,584	11	11	1,703,309	25	196,467	14
Texas Utilities (Dallas)	5,821,933	12	12	1,756,289	24	211,151	11
Duke Power (Charlotte)	5,626,075	13	13	1,492,557	30	274,760	7
Consumers Power (Jackson, Mich.)	5,579,087	14	14	2,003,374	18	203,787	13
Philadelphia Electric	5,241,260	15	15	1,578,505	27	194,471	15

[1]As of December 31, 1979. [2]After extraordinary items.

LARGEST RETAILING COMPANIES

SOURCE: *Fortune* Magazine

Company	Sales ($000)	Rank '79	Rank '78	Assets ($000)	Rank	Net Income ($000)	Rank
Sears Roebuck (Chicago)	17,514,252	1	1	16,421,972	1	810.082	1
Safeway Stores (Oakland)	13,717,861	2	2	3,100,768	6	143,323	8
K mart (Troy, Mich.)	12,858,585	3	3	5,642,439	2	357,999	2
J.C. Penney (New York)	11,274,000	4	4	5,077,000	3	244,000	3
Kroger (Cincinnati)	9,029,315	5	5	1,776,111	11	85,721	14
Great Atlantic & Pacific Tea (Montvale, N.J.)	7,469,659	6	6	1,281,226	16	(52,186)	49
F.W. Woolworth (New York)	6,785,000	7	7	2,927,000	7	180,000	7
Lucky Stores (Dublin, Calif.)	5,815,927	8	10	1,221,547	17	98,094	11
Federated Department Stores (Cincinnati)	5,806,442	9	8	3,295,344	5	203,228	4
Montgomery Ward (Chicago)	5,251,085	10	9	3,598,715	4	73,383	18
Winn-Dixie Stores (Jacksonville)	4,930,538	11	11	857,239	27	94,462	12
City Products (Des Plaines, Ill.)	3,918,800	12	14	1,214,600	18	57,100	22
Southland (Dallas)	3,856,222	13	15	1,367,575	15	83,141	16
American Stores (Wilmington)	3,786,332	14	39	1,201,934	19	44,434	25
Jewel Companies (Chicago)	3,764,266	15	13	1,012,367	23	50,686	24

LARGEST LIFE INSURANCE COMPANIES

SOURCE: *Fortune* Magazine

Company	Assets[1] ($000)	Rank '79	Rank '78	Premium & Annuity Receipts ($000)	Rank	Life Insurance in Force ($000)	Rank
Prudential (Newark)*	54,734,107	1	1	8,007,951	1	367,283,576	1
Metropolitan (New York)*	44,967,563	2	2	5,934,722	2	323,588,876	2
Equitable Life Assurance (New York)*	30,839,211	3	3	4,576,910	4	183,491,377	3
Aetna Life (Hartford)	18,548,768	4	6	4,729,187	3	127,618,848	4
New York Life*	18,479,224	5	4	2,598,658	6	111,892,459	6
John Hancock Mutual (Boston)*	17,318,502	6	5	2,170,657	8	125,594,445	5
Connecticut General Life (Bloomfield)	12,240,721	7	7	2,434,535	7	73,574,843	8
Travelers (Hartford)	11,816,987	8	8	3,642,396	5	95,652,561	7
Northwestern Mutual (Milwaukee)*	10,553,947	9	9	1,246,917	11	51,667,387	10
Massachusetts Mutual (Springfield)*	8,340,825	10	10	1,222,180	12	44,526,715	13
Teachers Insurance & Annuity (New York)	8,297,558	11	11	1,135,270	13	6,195,971	44
Mutual of New York*	7,412,472	12	12	1,024,812	15	33,936,777	16
Bankers Life (Des Moines)*	6,764,447	13	14	1,441,554	9	31,150,903	17
New England Mutual (Boston)*	6,314,187	14	13	940,021	17	28,194,982	19
Mutual Benefit (Newark)*	5,181,444	15	15	791,509	18	34,698,250	14

[1]As of December 31, 1979.   *Mutual company.

LEADING U.S. FARM CROPS

SOURCE: U.S. Department of Agriculture, Crop Reporting Board, ESCS

Crop	Unit	PRODUCTION 1978	PRODUCTION 1979	YIELD PER ACRE[4] 1978	YIELD PER ACRE[4] 1979
Corn,grain	Bushels	7,081,849,000	7,763,771,000	101.2	109.4
Sorghum, grain	Bushels	748,410,000	814,308,000	55.1	62.9
Oats	Bushels	601,477,000	534,386,000	52.2	54.4
Barley	Bushels	447,008,000	378,067,000	48.4	50.6
Wheat, total	Bushels	1,798,712,000	2,141,732,000	31.6	34.2
Winter	Bushels	1,248,272,000	1,608,897,000	32.1	36.9
Durum	Bushels	133,328,000	106,654,000	33.1	27.1
Other spring	Bushels	417,112,000	426,181,000	30.0	28.2
Rice	Cwt	137,805,000	136,667,000	4,505.0[3]	4,588.0[3]
Rye	Bushels	26,160,000	24,549,000	26.3	25.9
Soybeans for beans	Bushels	1,842,647,000	2,267,647,000	29.2	32.2
Flaxseed	Bushels	10,921,000	13,539,000	12.7	13.3
Peanuts for nuts	Pounds	3,977,465,000	3,976,140,000	2,632.0	2,607.0
Sunflower	Pounds	3,748,370,000	7,305,590,000	1,362.0	1,350.0
Popcorn	Pounds	398,027,000	537,980,000	2,827.0	3,012.0
Cotton, lint	Bales	10,841,000	14,872,900	421.0[3]	551.0[3]
Hay	Tons	142,264,000	145,878,000	2.31	2.39
Beans, dry edible	Cwt	19,117,000	20,665,000	1,279.0[3]	1,457.0[3]
Peas, dry edible	Cwt	3,601,000	2,039,000	1,783.0[3]	1,499.0[3]
Potatoes	Cwt	360,467,000	347,648,000	263.0	272.0
Sweet Potatoes	Cwt	13,862,000	14,421,000	116.0	115.0
Tobacco	Pounds	2,015,695,000	1,547,355,000	2,124.0	1,864.0
Sugar beets	Tons	25,868,000	21,996,000	20.3	19.6
Sugarcane	Tons	27,022,000	27,681,000	35.9	37.8
Coffee	Pounds	1,780,000	1,800,000	940.0	1,000.0
Hops	Pounds	55,071,000	54,929,000	1,782.0	1,727.0
Cranberries	Barrels	2,466,500	2,474,500	106.5	106.7
Apples, Com'l	Pounds	7,552,600,000	7,766,700,000		
Peaches	Pounds	2,701,000,000	2,977,500,000		
Pears	Tons	727,200	846,800		
Grapes	Tons	4,428,700	4,924,000		
Oranges	Boxes	219,620,000[1]	210,500,000[2]		
Grapefruit	Boxes	73,700,000[1]	67,020,000[2]		
Lemons	Boxes	26,100,000[1]	19,400,000[2]		
Limes	Boxes	460,000[1]	720,000[2]		

[1]1977-78 production figures.   [2]1978-79 production figures.   [3]Yield in pounds.   [4]Yield per acre figures not available for fruit.

INCLUSIVE STATE—FARM PAYMENT TOTALS: 1979

SOURCE: U.S. Department of Agriculture, Agricultural Stabilization & Conservation Service

State	Amount	State	Amount	State	Amount
Alabama	$ 12,072,213	Maine	$ 5,540,063	Oregon	$ 8,471,636
Alaska	269,714	Maryland	2,126,785	Pennsylvania	6,036,038
Arizona	9,071,704	Massachusetts	592,254	Rhode Island	78,403
Arkansas	32,563,952	Michigan	15,593,153	South Carolina	6,457,201
California	61,327,807	Minnesota	78,435,636	South Dakota	53,681,312
Colorado	35,520,373	Mississippi	12,887,133	Tennessee	8,432,453
Connecticut	418,562	Missouri	31,340,338	Texas	312,911,902
Delaware	366,963	Montana	32,058,192	Utah	5,231,686
Florida	5,776,948	Nebraska	142,322,862	Vermont	1,215,189
Georgia	17,944,672	Nevada	1,337,193	Virginia	5,947,437
Hawaii	741,020	New Hampshire	617,268	Washington	16,672,722
Idaho	21,058,744	New Jersey	806,495	West Virginia	2,038,585
Illinois	33,210,416	New Mexico	20,611,375	Wisconsin	28,472,901
Indiana	18,586,692	New York	9,035,767	Wyoming	7,520,269
Iowa	79,189,296	North Carolina	8,306,290	Puerto Rico	589,605
Kansas	124,530,452	North Dakota	45,808,955	Virgin Islands	14,723
Kentucky	6,658,833	Ohio	10,601,719	Undistributed	2,729,198
Louisiana	20,189,195	Oklahoma	40,198,962	Total	$1,404,219,266

LIVESTOCK POPULATION ON U.S. FARMS AND RANCHES (as of January 1)

SOURCE: Federal Aviation Administration.

Year	CATTLE AND CALVES	SHEEP AND LAMBS	HOGS AND PIGS	CHICKENS[2]
1959	92,322,000	32,606,000	58,045,000	387,002,000
1961[3]	97,700,000	32,725,000	55,560,000	366,082,000
1963	104,488,000	29,176,000	62,726,000[1]	375,575,000
1965	109,000,000	25,127,000	56,106,000	394,118,000
1967	108,783,000	23,953,000	57,125,000	428,746,000
1969	110,015,000	21,350,000	60,829,000	413,287,000
1971	114,578,000	19,731,000	67,285,000	433,280,000[1]
1973	121,539,000	17,641,000	59,017,000	404,191,000
1975	132,028,000	14,515,000	54,693,000	384,101,000
1976	127,980,000	14,311,000	49,267,000	379,754,000
1977	122,810,000	12,766,000	54,934,000	378,238,000
1978	116,375,000	12,348,000	56,539,000	386,429,000
1979	110,864,000	12,224,000	59,860,000	394,505,000
1980	110,961,000	12,513,000	66,950,000	399,767,000

[1]Begins inventory as of December 1 preceding year.   [2] Excludes commercial broilers.   [3]Includes Alaska and Hawaii beginning 1961.

U.S. PASSENGER CAR PRODUCTION: 1979

SOURCE: Motor Vehicle Manufacturers Association of the United States, Inc.

Company	Automobile Production
AMERICAN MOTORS CORP.	184,636
Spirit/AMX (Gremlin)	64,363
Concord	88,580
Pacer	5,729
Eagle	25,964
CHRYSLER CORP.	936,146
Horizon	169,981
Voyager	6,312
Volaré	183,486
Gran Fury	5,412
Caravelle	9,213
Total Plymouth	374,404
LeBaron	103,678
Chrysler	77,749
Total Chrysler-Plymouth	555,831
Omni	148,125
Sportsman	23,124
Aspen	132,610
Diplomat	50,610
St. Regis	25,846
Total Dodge	380,315
FORD MOTOR CO.	2,043,014
LTD	167,170
LTD II	22,667
Thunderbird	264,451
Club Wagon	36,177
Granada	139,402
Fairmont	213,761
Pinto	172,619
Mustang	365,357
Total Ford	1,381,604
Marquis	100,937
Cougar	1,919
Cougar XR 7	133,479
Monarch	59,810
Zephyr	62,837
Bobcat	43,374
Capri	107,094
Lincoln	71,783
Mark VI/V	68,313
Versailles	11,864
Total Lincoln-Mercury	661,410
GENERAL MOTORS CORP.	5,091,908
Chevrolet	447,343
Corvette	48,568
Monte Carlo	227,043
Malibu	322,764
Camaro	257,872
Citation/Nova	343,821
Monza	157,979
Chevette	413,648
Acadian	17,133
Total Chevrolet	2,236,171
Pontiac	144,486
Grand Prix	93,158
LeMans	88,652
Firebird	194,033
Phoenix	88,184
Sunbird	105,998
Total Pontiac	714,511
Oldsmobile	365,327
Toronado	53,552
Cutlass	509,726
Omega	58,032
Starfire	21,609
Total Oldsmobile	1,008,246
Buick	252,220
Riviera	58,029
Century/Regal	330,560
Skylark	121,625
Skyhawk	24,715
Total Buick	787,149
Cadillac	230,958
Eldorado	66,565
Seville	48,308
Total Cadillac	345,831
CHECKERS MOTORS CORP.	4,766
VOLKSWAGEN OF AMERICA	173,192
TOTAL PASSENGER CARS	8,433,662

WORLD MOTOR VEHICLE PRODUCTION: 1979

SOURCE: *U.N. Monthly Bulletin of Statistics,* © United Nations, July 1980

Country	Passenger Cars	Commercial Vehicles	Total
United States	8,562,000	3,080,000	11,642,000
Japan	6,176,000	3,470,000	9,646,000
Germany, West	3,943,000	314,000	4,257,000
France	3,731,000	462,000	4,193,000
USSR	1,314,000	780,000[2]	2,081,000
Italy[1]	1,512,000	146,400	1,658,400
Canada	987,900	644,000	1,631,900
United Kingdom	1,069,000	406,000	1,475,000
Spain	973,100	165,900	1,139,000
Brazil	553,400	574,300	1,127,700
Australia[3]	403,200	55,200	458,400
Mexico[3]	296,700	121,700	418,400
Poland	350,300	63,800	414,100
Sweden[1]	258,000	40,800	298,800
Yugoslavia	206,200	64,300	270,500
Czechoslovakia	182,400	87,900	270,300
Argentina[3]	190,600	62,600	253,200
Germany, East[1]	170,400	37,200	207,600
Netherlands	88,900	16,100	105,000
India	42,300	58,900	101,200
Romania	67,200	33,600	100,800
Hungary	—	15,200	15,200
Austria	2,700	6,400	9,100

[1]1978 figures.   [2]Excluding wheeled tractors.   [3]Including assembly.

NEW PASSENGER CARS, TRUCKS AND BUSES IMPORTED INTO THE UNITED STATES: 1978

SOURCE: Motor Vehicle Manufacturers Association of the United States, Inc.

Country	Number
Japan	1,891,537
Canada	1,197,363
Germany, West	413,340
Italy	72,245
Sweden	63,719
United Kingdom	55,232
France	31,822
Belgium	17
TOTAL	3,725,275

LARGEST PASSENGER CAR PRODUCER FOR EACH COUNTRY: 1978†

SOURCE: Motor Vehicle Manufacturers Association of the United States, Inc.

Country	Producer	1978 Production
Argentina	Ford Motor Argentina S.A.	34,951
Australia	Ford	108,000
Belgium	Ford-Werke A.G. Genk	326,191
Brazil	Volkswagen	284,286
Canada	General Motors	571,683
France	Renault	1,240,941
West Germany	Volkswagen	1,177,106
India	Hindustan Motors	20,987
Italy	Fiat	1,193,462
Japan	Toyota Motor	2,039,115
Mexico	Volkswagen de Mexico	86,306
Netherlands	Daf & Volvo	62,412
Peru	Volkswagen	2,783
Poland	Fabryka Samochodow Malolitrazowych	224,617
Spain	S.E.A.T.	284,480
Sweden	Volvo	181,740
Turkey	Oyak (Renault)	33,668
United Kingdom	British Leyland	611,625
Venezuela	Chrysler de Venezuela	19,626
Yugoslavia	Zavodi Crvena Zastava	197,404

†Excluding United States.

THE U.S. LABOR FORCE

SOURCE: U.S. Department of Labor, Bureau of Labor Statistics

TOTAL LABOR FORCE*

Year	Number	% of population	Total Civilian Employed
1948	62,080,000	60.4	60,254,000
1950	63,858,000	59.4	58,344,000
1952	65,730,000	59.9	58,920,000
1954	66,993,000	60.0	60,110,000
1956	69,409,000	61.0	63,802,000
1957	69,729,000	60.6	64,071,000
1958	70,275,000	60.4	63,036,000
1959	70,921,000	60.2	64,630,000
1960	72,142,000	60.2	65,778,000
1961	73,031,000	60.2	65,746,000
1962	73,442,000	59.7	66,702,000
1963	74,571,000	59.6	67,762,000
1964	75,830,000	59.6	69,305,000
1965	77,178,000	59.7	71,088,000
1966	78,893,000	60.1	72,895,000
1967	80,793,000	60.6	74,372,000
1968	82,272,000	60.7	75,920,000
1969	84,239,000	61.1	77,902,000
1970	85,903,000	61.3	78,627,000
1971	86,929,000	61.0	79,120,000
1972	88,991,000	61.0	81,702,000
1973	91,040,000	61.4	84,409,000
1974	93,240,000	61.8	85,936,000
1975	94,793,000	61.8	84,783,000
1976	96,917,000	62.1	87,485,000
1977	99,534,000	62.8	90,546,000
1978	102,537,000	63.7	94,373,000
1979	104,996,000	64.2	96,945,000

*Persons 16 years of age and over; includes members of the armed forces.

UNEMPLOYMENT RATES: BY SEX AND RACE

SOURCE: U.S. Department of Labor, Bureau of Labor Statistics

Year	Unemployment Rate Total	Male	Female	White Total	Male	Female	Black and other Total	Male	Female
1948	3.8	3.6	4.1	3.5	3.4	3.8	5.9	5.8	6.1
1950	5.3	5.1	5.7	4.9	4.7	5.3	9.0	9.4	8.4
1952	3.0	2.8	3.6	2.8	2.5	3.3	5.4	5.2	5.7
1954	5.5	5.3	6.0	5.0	4.8	5.6	9.9	10.3	9.3
1956	4.1	3.8	4.8	3.6	3.4	4.2	8.3	7.9	8.9
1957	4.3	4.1	4.7	3.8	3.6	4.3	7.9	8.3	7.3
1958	6.8	6.8	6.8	6.1	6.1	6.2	12.6	13.8	10.8
1959	5.5	5.3	5.9	4.8	4.6	5.3	10.7	11.5	9.4
1960	5.5	5.4	5.9	4.9	4.8	5.3	10.2	10.7	9.4
1961	6.7	6.4	7.2	6.0	5.7	6.5	12.4	12.8	11.8
1962	5.5	5.2	6.2	4.9	4.6	5.5	10.9	10.9	11.0
1963	5.7	5.2	6.5	5.0	4.7	5.8	10.8	10.5	11.2
1964	5.2	4.6	6.2	4.6	4.1	5.5	9.6	8.9	10.6
1965	4.5	4.0	5.5	4.1	3.6	5.0	8.1	7.4	9.2
1966	3.8	3.2	4.8	3.3	2.8	4.3	7.3	6.3	8.6
1967	3.8	3.1	5.2	3.4	2.7	4.6	7.4	6.0	9.1
1968	3.6	2.9	4.8	3.2	2.6	4.3	6.7	5.6	8.3
1969	3.5	2.8	4.7	3.1	2.5	4.2	6.4	5.3	7.8
1970	4.9	4.4	5.9	4.5	4.0	5.4	8.2	7.3	9.3
1971	5.9	5.3	6.9	5.4	4.9	6.3	9.9	9.1	10.8
1972	5.6	4.9	6.6	5.0	4.5	5.9	10.0	8.9	11.3
1973	4.9	4.1	6.0	4.3	3.7	5.3	8.9	7.6	10.5
1974	5.6	4.8	6.7	5.0	4.3	6.1	8.9	9.1	10.7
1975	8.5	7.9	9.3	7.8	7.2	8.6	13.9	13.7	14.0
1976	7.7	7.0	8.6	7.0	6.4	7.9	13.1	12.7	13.6
1977	7.0	6.2	8.2	6.2	5.5	7.3	13.1	12.4	14.0
1978	6.0	5.2	7.2	5.2	4.5	6.2	11.9	10.9	13.9
1979	5.8	5.1	6.8	5.1	4.4	5.9	11.3	10.3	12.3

MINORITY GROUP PARTICIPATION IN THE U.S. LABOR MARKET: 1978 Preliminary

SOURCE: Equal Employment Opportunity Commission

% OF MINORITY WORKERS IN PARTICULAR CATEGORY[1]

	Total	White Collar Total	Professional	Technical	Clerical	Blue Collar	Service Workers
Black, Total[1]	11.2%	6.8%	4.0%	8.2%	10.1%	14.3%	21.5%
Male	6.1	2.4	1.9	3.5	1.9	9.9	9.8
Female	5.1	4.4	2.1	4.7	8.2	4.4	11.7
Hispanic, Total	5.0	3.1	1.8	3.3	4.1	6.9	7.0
Male	3.1	1.4	1.2	2.1	0.9	4.9	4.1
Female	1.9	1.7	0.6	1.2	3.2	2.0	2.9
Asian or Pacific Islander, Total	1.3	1.6	3.2	2.0	1.5	0.8	1.7
Male	0.7	0.8	2.0	1.2	0.4	0.4	0.8
Female	0.6	0.8	1.2	0.8	1.1	0.3	0.9
American Indian or Alaskan Native, Total	0.4	0.3	0.2	0.4	0.4	0.5	0.4
Male	0.3	0.2	0.2	0.2	0.1	0.4	0.2
Female	0.1	0.2	0.1	0.1	0.3	0.1	0.2
All Minorities, Total	17.9	11.8	9.2	13.8	16.0	22.5	30.6
Male	10.1	4.7	5.2	7.1	3.2	15.6	15.0
Female	7.8	7.0	4.0	6.7	12.8	6.9	15.6

[1]Percent of total employment in given occupational category.

MINORITY GROUP EMPLOYEES IN U.S. LABOR MARKET: 1978 Preliminary

SOURCE: Equal Employment Opportunity Commission

Figures are in thousands

	Total	White Collar Total	Professional	Technical	Clerical	Blue Collar	Service Workers
All U.S. Employees	36,029	17,952	2,963	1,729	5,659	14,716	3,360
Male	21,634	9,121	1,960	1,081	1,008	10,986	1,526
Female	14,395	8,831	1,003	648	4,651	3,730	1,834
All Black Employees	4,051	1,224	117	142	569	2,105	722
Male	2,209	427	55	61	105	1,452	330
Female	1,842	797	62	81	464	653	392
All Hispanics	1,798	548	53	56	233	1,014	236
Male	1,106	243	35	36	51	724	139
Female	692	305	18	20	182	290	97
All Asian or Pacific Islander	453	278	95	34	84	117	57
Male	236	142	59	21	20	66	28
Female	217	136	36	13	64	51	29
All American Indian or Alaskan Native	146	60	7	6	21	72	14
Male	93	33	5	4	6	54	6
Female	53	27	2	2	15	18	8
All Minority Employees	6,449	2,110	273	239	907	3,308	1,029
Male	3,645	845	155	123	182	2,296	503
Female	2,804	1,265	118	116	725	1,012	526

PRINCIPAL U.S. LABOR UNIONS AND EMPLOYEE ASSOCIATIONS, 1978

SOURCE: Bureau of Labor Statistics

The following is a list of selected labor unions with a 1978 membership of more than 100,000.

International Brotherhood of Teamsters, Chauffeurs, Warehousemen, and Helpers of America, * 25 Louisiana Avenue, N.W., Washington, D.C. 20001; **Membership:** 1,924,000

National Education Association, * 1201 16th St., N.W., Washington, D.C. 20036; **Membership:** 1,696,000

International Union, United Automobile, Aerospace and Agricultural Implement Workers of America, * 8000 East Jefferson Ave., Detroit, Mich. 48214; **Membership:** 1,499,000

United Steelworkers of America, Five Gateway Center, Pittsburgh, Pa. 15222; **Membership:** 1,286,000

United Food and Commercial Workers Union, 1775 K St., N.W., Washington, D.C. 20006; **Membership:** 1,236,000

American Federation of State, County and Municipal Employees, 1625 L Street, N.W., Washington, D.C. 20005; **Membership:** 1,020,000

International Brotherhood of Electrical Workers, 1125 15th St., N.W., Washington, D.C. 20005; **Membership:** 1,012,000

International Association of Machinists and Aerospace Workers, 1300 Connecticut Ave., N.W., Washington, D.C. 20036; **Membership:** 921,000

United Brotherhood of Carpenters and Joiners of America, 101 Constitution Ave., N.W., Washington, D.C. 20001; **Membership:** 769,000

Communications Workers of America, 1925 K St., N.W., Washington, D.C. 20006; **Membership:** 625,000

Laborers' International Union of North America, 905 16th St., N.W., Washington, D.C. 20006; **Membership:** 610,000

Service Employees' International Union, 2020 K St., N.W., Washington, D.C. 20006; **Membership:** 575,000

Amalgamated Clothing and Textile Workers of America, 15 Union Square, New York, N.Y. 10003; **Membership:** 500,000

American Federation of Teachers, 11 Dupont Circle, Washington, D.C. 20036; **Membership:** 500,000

International Union of Operating Engineers, 1125 17th St., N.W., Washington, D.C. 20036; **Membership:** 412,000

Hotel and Restaurant Employees and Bartenders International Union, 120 E. Fourth St., Cincinnati, Oh. 45202; **Membership:** 404,000

International Ladies' Garment Workers Union, 1710 Broadway, New York, N.Y. 10019; **Membership:** 348,000

United Association of Journeymen and Apprentices of the Plumbing and Pipefitting Industry of the United States and Canada, 901 Massachusetts Ave., N.W., Washington, D.C. 20001; **Membership:** 337,000

American Federation of Musicians, 1500 Broadway, New York, N.Y. 10036; **Membership:** 330,000

United Mine Workers of America, * 900 15th Street, N.W., Washington, D.C. 20005; **Membership:** 308,000

United Paperworkers International Union, 163—03 Horace Harding Expressway, Flushing, N.Y. 11365; **Membership:** 284,000

American Federation of Government Employees, 1325 Massachusetts Avenue, N.W., Washington, D.C. 20005; **Membership:** 266,000

International Union of Electrical, Radio, and Machine Workers, 1126 16th St., N.W., Washington, D.C. 20036; **Membership:** 255,000

American Postal Workers Union, 817 Fourteenth Street, N.W., Washington, D.C. 20005; **Membership:** 246,000

*Independent—not members of AFL-CIO

National Association of Letter Carriers, 100 Indiana Ave., N.W., Washington, D.C. 20001; **Membership:** 227,000

Brotherhood of Railway, Airline, and Steamship Clerks, Freight Handlers, Express and Station Employees, 6300 River Rd., Rosemont, Illinois 60018; **Membership:** 200,000

United Rubber, Cork, Linoleum, and Plastic Workers of America, 87 South High St., Akron, Ohio 44308; **Membership:** 200,000

National Association of Government Employees, * 285 Dorchester Ave., Boston, Mass. 02127; **Membership:** 200,000

Retail, Wholesale, and Department Store Union, 101 West 31st St., New York, N.Y. 10001; **Membership:** 198,000

International Brotherhood of Painters and Allied Trades of the United States and Canada, 1750 New York Avenue, N.W., Washington, D.C. 20006; **Membership:** 190,000

American Nurses Association, * 2420 Pershing Rd., Kansas City, Mo. 64108; **Membership:** 187,000

Oil, Chemical, and Atomic Workers International Union, P.O. Box 2812, 1636 Champa St., Denver, Colo. 80201; **Membership:** 180,000

International Association of Firefighters, 1750 New York Avenue, N.W., Washington, D.C. 20006; **Membership:** 176,000

United Transportation Union, 14600 Detroit Avenue, Cleveland, Ohio, 44107; **Membership:** 175,500

International Association of Bridge and Structural Iron Workers, 1750 New York Ave., N.W., Suite 400, Washington, D.C. 20006; **Membership:** 175,000

Bakery, Confectionary, and Tobacco Workers' International Union of America, 1828 L St., N.W., Washington, D.C. 20036; **Membership:** 167,000

United Electrical, Radio, and Machine Workers of America, * 11 East 51st St., New York, N.Y. 10022; **Membership:** 166,000

Sheet Metal Workers' International Association, United Unions Building, New York Ave., N.W., Washington, D.C. 20006; **Membership:** 159,000

Amalgamated Transit Union, 5025 Wisconsin Ave., N.W., Washington, D.C. 20016; **Membership:** 154,000

International Brotherhood of Boilermakers, Iron Ship Builders, Blacksmiths, Forgers, and Helpers, New Brotherhood Bldg., 8th St. at State Ave., Kansas City, Kansas 66101; **Membership:** 146,000

Fraternal Order of Police, * G—3136 Pasadena Ave., Flint, Mich. 48504; **Membership:** 140,000

International Union of Bricklayers and Allied Craftsmen, 815 15th St., N.W., Washington, D.C. 20005; **Membership:** 134,744

Transport Workers Union of America, 1980 Broadway, New York, New York 10023; **Membership:** 130,000

International Printing and Graphic Communications Union, 1730 Rhode Island Avenue, N.W., Washington, D.C. 20036; **Membership:** 120,000

Brotherhood of Maintenance of Way Employees, 12050 Woodward Ave., Detroit, Mich. 48203; **Membership:** 119,000

International Woodworkers of America, 1622 North Lombard St., Portland, Oregon 97217; **Membership:** 118,000

California State Employees Association, * 1108 0 Street, Sacramento, Calif. 95814; **Membership:** 105,000

International Typographical Union, P.O. Box 157, Colorado Springs, Colorado 80901; **Membership:** 100,449

AVERAGE UNION HOURLY SCALE

SOURCE: U.S. Department of Labor—Bureau of Labor Statistics

	Building		Printing		Local trucking		
Year	Journeymen	Helpers and laborers	Book and job	Newspapers	Drivers	Helpers	Local transit workers
1960	$3.86	$2.88	$3.08	$3.48	$2.68	$2.38	$2.37
1965	4.64	3.54	3.58	3.94	3.26	2.90	2.88
1970	6.54	4.86	4.65	5.13	4.41	3.91	4.03
1972	7.69	5.68	5.49	6.09	5.49	4.90	4.68
1973	8.02	6.06	5.91	6.43	5.90	5.30	5.04
1974	$ 8.55	$6.53	$6.34	$7.01	$6.39	$5.84	$5.62
1975 ...	9.32	7.06	6.86	7.57	6.87	6.27	6.25
1976 ...	9.92	7.54	7.41	8.17	7.42	6.67	6.63
1977	0.44	8.03	7.91	8.74	8.09	7.28	7.12
1978	11.05	8.54	8.51	9.23	—	—	7.53

UNION CONTRACTS OF 1979

SOURCE: U.S. Department of Labor, Bureau of Labor Statistics

Major collective bargaining settlements reached during 1979 generally provided for smaller wage adjustments than settlements reached in 1978. Wage-rate adjustments achieved during 1979 averaged 7.4 percent for the first year and 6.0 percent annually (when averaged over the agreement term) compared with 7.6 percent in the first year and 6.4 percent over the term in 1978.

Wages and benefits combined (package settlements) larger in 1979 than in the previous year. Package gains in major contracts reached in 1979 averaged 9.0 percent for the first year and 6.6 percent annually over the contract life compared with 8.3 and 6.3 percent, respectively, in 1978. Both wage-rate and package measures exclude automatic cost-of-living gains.

In manufacturing, wage-rate adjustments in new settlements averaged 6.9 percent in the first year and 5.4 percent annually over the contract life, compared with 8.3 percent and 6.6 percent in 1978. In non-manufacturing, adjustments averaged 8.0 percent in the first year and 6.8 percent annually over the contract life, compared with 7.4 percent and 6.4 percent in 1978. In construction, wage adjustments averaged 8.8 percent in the first year and 8.3 percent annually over the contract life, compared with 6.5 and 6.3 percent in 1978.

UNEMPLOYMENT INSURANCE BENEFITS (1979 Calendar year)

SOURCE: U.S. Department of Labor

State unemployment insurance benefits for the totally unemployed are listed below. Where two figures are given for legal minimum and maximum benefits, the larger figures include dependents' allowances.

State	Weekly Benefit Amounts — Average Unemployment Benefit[1]	Legal Minimum[2]	Legal Maximum[2]	Duration of Benefits, Weeks — Actual Average[1]	Legal Range[2]
U.S. Avg...	$ 89.67†	—	—	13.1†	—
Ala.	73.38	$15	$ 90	10.8	11-26
Alaska	82.52	18-28	90-120	16.8	14-28
Ariz.	76.44	25	90	10.8	12-26
Ark.	77.53	15	124	11.5	10-26
Calif.	77.82	30	120	13.6	12-26*
Colo.	102.65	25	142	10.5	7-26*
Conn.	94.50	15-20	134-201	11.1	26-26*
Del.	100.25	20	150	12.3	11-26
D.C.	114.49	13-14	181*	19.7	17-34
Fla.	66.53	10	95	12.1	10-26
Ga.	76.26	27	90	9.2	4-26
Hawaii	95.38	5	144	13.3	26-26*
Idaho	90.07	17	121	10.8	10-26
Ill.	106.12	15	133-177	16.1	26-26
Ind.	79.41	35	74-124	9.6	3-26
Iowa	110.71	17-18	131-148	12.7	15-26
Kans.	94.91	30	123	11.2	10-26
Ky.	92.31	12	120	12.4	15-26
La.	98.64	10	149	13.9	12-28
Maine	77.98	12-17	96-144	10.3	13-26*
Md.	84.84	10-13	106*	11.8	26-26
Mass.	89.47	12-18	131-197	15.1	9-30*
Mich.	99.03	16-18*	97-136	11.4	11-26
Minn.	105.38	30	150	13.1	13-26
Miss.	63.81	10	90	11.5	12-26
Mo.	77.82	15	105	10.8	10-26*
Mont.	88.29	30	119	13.0	12-26
Nebr.	83.93	12	106	10.6	17-26
Nev.	90.87	16	115	11.7	11-26
N.H.	78.76	21	114	7.1	26-26
N.J.	93.39	20	123	16.1	15-26
N.M.	75.49	22	106	14.7	18-30
N.Y.	89.19	25	125	19.2	26-26
N.C.	76.45	15	130	8.4	13-26
N.D.	94.65	36	131	14.2	12-26
Ohio	114.59	10	128-202	11.8	20-26
Okla.	88.30	16	132	11.4	20-26
Oreg.	88.05	35	127	12.5	6-26
Pa.	102.78	13-18	162-170	13.5	30-30
P.R.	50.06	7	72	9.7	20-20*
R.I.	83.62	30-35	120-140	13.8	12-26
S.C.	74.85	10	111	11.2	10-26
S.D.	85.63†	28	109	10.9†	13-26
Tenn.	70.45	14	100	11.4	12-26
Texas	75.23	18	105	12.1	9-26
Utah	95.28	10	137	12.5	10-36*
Vt.	82.30	18	115	13.4	26-26
Va.	87.32	38	122	11.5	12-26
Wash.	98.05	17	137	12.4	8-30*
W.Va.	92.08	18	166	10.3	28-28
Wis.	103.39	29	155	11.5	1-34*
Wyo.	95.30	24	131	9.7	12-26*

†Preliminary. *Provisional. [1] 1979 Calendar year. [2] 1980 Calendar year.

EMPLOYMENT OUTLOOK TO 1990

Occupation	Average Annual Openings 1978 through 1990
Accountants	61,000
Actors and actresses	850
Airplane pilots	3,800
All-round mechanics	22,500
Anthropologists	350
Architects	4,000
Astronomers	40
Bank clerks	45,000
Bank officers and managers	28,000
Bank tellers	17,000
Barbers	9,700
Blacksmiths	300
Bookkeeping workers	96,000
Bricklayers, stonemasons, etc.	6,200
Local transit busdrivers	3,100
Carpenters	58,000
Chemists	6,100
Chiropractors	1,500
Computer operating personnel	12,500
Construction laborers	49,000
Cooks and chefs	86,000
Cosmetologists	28,500
Dentists	5,500
Dietitians	3,300
Drafters	11,000
Economists	7,800
Electricians (construction)	12,900
Engineers	46,500
Firefighters	7,500
Furniture upholsterers	1,100
Gasoline station attendants	5,200
Geographers	500
Geologists	1,700
Geophysicists	600
Health services administrators	18,000
Historians	700
Hotel managers and assistants	8,900
Industrial designers	550
Insurance agents, brokers, and underwriters	30,000
Interior designers	3,600
Landscape architects	1,100
Lawyers	37,000
Librarians	8,000
Locomotive engineers	2,000
Mail carriers	7,000
Mathematicians	1,000
Mechanics and repairers— Central office craft occupations	1,000
Line installers and cable splicers	600
Telephone and PBX installers and repairers	3,000
Airconditioning, refrigeration and heating	8,200
Appliance repairers	6,900
Automobile body repairers	7,800
Automobile mechanics	37,000
Business machine repairers	4,200
Computer service technicians	5,400
Farm equipment mechanics	3,500
Industrial machinery repairers	58,000
Maintenance electricians	15,500
Piano and organ tuners and repairers	700
Shoe repairers	1,600
Television and radio service technicians	6,100
Truck and bus mechanics	6,800
Medical laboratory workers	14,800
Meteorologists	300
Newspaper reporters	2,400
Licensed practical nurses	60,000
Registered nurses	85,000
Oceanographers	150
Office machine operators	9,700
Optometrists	1,600
Painters and paperhangers	27,500
Personnel and labor relations workers	17,000
Pharmacists	7,800
Photographers	3,800
Physicians and osteopathic physicians	19,000
Physicists	1,000
Plasterers	1,100
Plumbers and pipefitters	20,000
Podiatrists	600
Police officers	16,500
Political scientists	500
Postal clerks	2,000
Printing occupations Bookbinders and bindery workers	2,600
Compositors	3,900
Lithographers	2,300
Photoengravers	150
Printing press operators and assistants	5,000
Private household workers	45,000
Programmers	9,200
Psychologists	6,700
Public relations workers	7,500
Purchasing agents	13,400
Radiologic (X-ray) technologists	9,000
Radio and Television announcers	850
Real estate agents and brokers	50,000
Retail trade sales workers	226,000
Wholesale trade sales workers	40,000
School counselors	1,700
Secretaries and stenographers	305,000
Social workers	22,000
Sociologists	600
Statisticians	1,500
Surveyors	2,300
Systems analysts	7,900
College and university teachers	11,000
Kindergarten and elementary school teachers	86,000
Secondary school teachers	7,200
Telephone operators	9,900
Occupational therapists	1,300
Physical therapists	2,700
Local truck drivers	64,000
Long distance truck drivers	21,500
Typists	59,000
Urban planners	800
Veterinarians	1,700
Welders	35,000

U.S. LICENSED COMMERCIAL NUCLEAR POWER PLANTS AS OF MARCH 1, 1980

SOURCE: Nuclear Regulatory Commission

State	Name of Facility	Operating Company	Authorized Power Level (MWe)	Type*
Alabama	Farley 1	Alabama Power Company	829	PWR
Alabama	Browns Ferry 1	TVA	1,065	BWR
Alabama	Browns Ferry 2	TVA	1,065	PWR
Alabama	Browns Ferry 3	TVA	1,065	BWR
Arkansas	Arkansas 1	Arkansas Power & Light Company	850	PWR
Arkansas	Arkansas 2	Arkansas Power & Light Company	912	PWR
California	Rancho Seco	Sacramento Municipal Utility District	918	PWR
California	San Onofre 1	Southern California Edison Company	430	PWR
Colorado	Ft. St. Vrain	Public Service Company of Colorado	330	HTGR
Connecticut	Connecticut. Yankee	Connecticut Yankee Atomic Power Company	575	PWR
Connecticut	Millstone 1	Northeast Nuclear Energy Company	660	BWR
Connecticut	Millstone 2	Northeast Nuclear Energy Company	830	PWR
Florida	Crystal River 3	Florida Power Corporation	825	PWR
Florida	St. Lucie 1	Florida Power & Light Company	802	PWR
Florida	Turkey Point 3	Florida Power & Light Company	693	PWR
Florida	Turkey Point 4	Florida Power & Light Company	693	PWR
Georgia	Edwin I. Hatch 1	Georgia Power Company	786	BWR
Georgia	Edwin I. Hatch 2	Georgia Power Company	795	BWR
Illinois	Dresden 1	Commonwealth Edison Company	200	BWR
Illinois	Dresden 2	Commonwealth Edison Company	794	BWR
Illinois	Dresden 3	Commonwealth Edison Company	794	BWR
Illinois	Quad-Cities 1	Commonwealth Edison Company	789	BWR
Illinois	Quad-Cities 2	Commonwealth Edison Company	789	BWR
Illinois	Zion 1	Commonwealth Edison Company	1,040	PWR
Illinois	Zion 2	Commonwealth Edison Company	1,040	PWR
Iowa	Duane Arnold	Iowa Electric Light & Power Company	538	BWR
Maine	Maine Yankee	Maine Yankee Atomic Power Company	790	PWR
Maryland	Calvert Cliffs 1	Baltimore Gas & Electric Company	845	PWR
Maryland	Calvert Cliffs 2	Baltimore Gas & Electric Company	845	PWR
Massachusetts	Pilgrim 1	Boston Edison Company	655	BWR
Massachusetts	Yankee-Rowe	Yankee Atomic Electric Company	175	PWR
Michigan	Big Rock Point	Consumers Power Company	72	BWR
Michigan	Palisades	Consumers Power Company	805	PWR
Michigan	D.C. Cook 1	Indiana & Michigan Electric Company	1,054	PWR
Michigan	D.C. Cook 2	Indiana & Michigan Electric Company	1,060	PWR
Minnesota	Monticello	Northern States Power Company	545	BWR
Minnesota	Prairie Island 1	Northern States Power Company	530	PWR
Minnesota	Prairie Island 2	Northern States Power Company	530	PWR
Nebraska	Cooper Station	Nebraska Public Power District	778	BWR
Nebraska	Ft. Calhoun	Omaha Public Power District	457	PWR
New Jersey	Oyster Creek 1	Jersey Central Power & Light Company	650	BWR
New Jersey	Salem	Public Service Electric & Gas Company	1,090	PWR
New York	Indian Point 2	Consolidated Edison Company of New York	873	PWR
New York	Nine Mile Point 1	Niagara Mohawk Power Corporation	610	BWR
New York	Indian Point 3	Power Authority of the State of New York	873	PWR
New York	Fitzpatrick	Power Authority of the State of New York	821	PWR
New York	R.E. Ginna 1	Rochester Gas & Electric. Corporation	490	PWR
North Carolina	Brunswick 1	Carolina Power & Light Comnpany	821	BWR
North Carolina	Brunswick 2	Carolina Power & Light Company	821	BWR
Ohio	Davis-Besse 1	Toledo Edison Company	906	PWR
Oregon	Trojan	Portland General Electric Company	1,130	PWR
Pennsylvania	Beaver Valley 1	Duquesne Light Company	852	PWR
Pennsylvania	Three Mile I. 1*	Metropolitan Edison Company	819	PWR
Pennsylvania	Peach Bottom 2	Philadelphia Electric Company	1,065	BWR
Pennsylvania	Peach Bottom 3	Philadelphia Electric Company	1,065	BWR
South Carolina	H.E. Robinson 2	Carolina Power & Light Company	700	PWR
South Carolina	Oconee 1	Duke Power Company	887	PWR
South Carolina	Oconee 2	Duke Power Company	887	PWR
South Carolina	Oconee 3	Duke Power Company	887	PWR
Vermont	Vermont Yankee	Vermont Yankee Nuclear Power Corporation	514	BWR
Virginia	North Anna 1	Virginia Electric & Power Company	Fuel Loading	PWR
Virginia	Surry 1	Virginia Electric & Power Company	822	PWR
Virginia	Surry 2	Virginia Electric & Power Company	822	PWR
Wisconsin	Lacrosse	Dairyland Power Cooperative	50	BWR
Wisconsin	Point Beach 1	Wisconsin-Michigan Power Company & Wisconsin Electric Power Company	497	PWR
Wisconsin	Point Beach 2	Wisconsin-Michigan Power Company	497	PWR
Wisconsin	Kewaunee	Wisconsin Public Service Corporation	535	PWR

* PWR—Pressurized Water Reactor; BWR—Boiling Water Reactor; HTGR—High Temperature Gas Cooled Reactor

U.S. PRODUCTION OF ENERGY BY TYPE

SOURCE: Energy Information Administration

Fuel	Unit	1976	1977	1978	1979[1]
Coal[2]	million short tons	684.2	697.2	670.2	775.8
	quadrillion Btu	15.85	15.83	15.04	17.41
Natural gas[3]	trillion cubic feet	19.10	19.16	19.12	18.83
	quadrillion Btu	19.48	19.57	19.49	19.19
Petroleum[4]	million barrels	2,976	3,009	3,178	3,108
	quadrillion Btu	17.26	17.45	18.43	18.02
Natural Gas	million barrels	587	590	572	607
Plant Liquids	quadrillion Btu	2.33	2.33	2.25	2.38
Hydropower[5]	billion kilowatt hours	286.9	224.0	283.8	283.4
	quadrillion Btu	2.98	2.34	2.96	2.96
Nuclear Power	billion kilowatt hours	191.1	250.9	276.4	255.4
	quadrillion Btu	2.11	2.70	2.98	2.75
Geothermal	billion kilowatt hours	3.6	3.6	3.0	3.9
	quadrillion Btu	0.08	0.08	0.06	0.08
Wood & Waste[6]	billion kilowatt hours	0.3	0.5	0.3	0.5
	quadrillion Btu	[7]	0.01	[7]	0.01
Total Energy Production	quadrillion Btu	60.09	60.30	61.21	62.80

[1]Preliminary. [2]Bituminous coal, lignite, and anthracite. [3]Marketed production. [4]Crude oil and lease condensate. [5]Electric utility and industrial generation of hydropower. [6]Wood, refuse, and other vegetal fuels consumed by electric utilities. [7]Less than 0.005 quadrillion Btu.

NUCLEAR POWER

SOURCE: International Atomic Energy Agency

During the 24 years which have lapsed since the 1955 Geneva Conference, a tremendous development effort has taken place in the nuclear power field. Roughly speaking, the first decade from 1955-1965 was marked by the emergence of several promising nuclear power systems which bridged the gap between prototypes and industrial plants. The second period from 1965 to the present witnessed the rapid introduction of large nuclear stations in the electric systems of industrial countries and the commissioning of a few nuclear power plants in some developing countries.

In 1956 there were in the world two power reactors with a total capacity of 0.6 MWe in two countries. By 1965, these members had risen to 44 reactors operating in 9 countries and with a total capacity of 4.9 MWe. By 1980, we find 238 stations with a capacity of over 124,493 MWe operating in 21 countries, and by 1994, 549 plants with close to 407,289 MWe in 33 states.

ESTIMATED WORLD NUCLEAR POWER GROWTH*

Country	1980 No. Reactors	1980 Capacity (1000 MWe)	1994 est. No. Reactors	1994 est. Capacity (1000 MWe)
Argentina	1	0.3	4	2.2
Belgium	3	1.7	7	5.5
Brazil	—	—	3	3.1
Bulgaria	2	0.8	4	1.6
Canada	10	5.2	25	15.2
Cuba	—	—	2	0.8
Czechoslovakia	2	0.8	14	6.8
Egypt	—	—	1	0.6
Finland	3	1.7	5	3.2
France	18	10.0	53	45.7
Germany, East	5	1.7	9	3.3
Germany, West	14	8.6	31	27.5
Hungary	—	—	4	1.6
India	3	0.6	8	1.7
Israel	—	—	1	0.6
Italy	4	1.4	9	5.3
Japan	22	14.3	38	27.2
Korea, South	1	0.6	7	5.5
Mexico	—	—	2	1.3
Netherlands	2	0.5	2	0.5
Pakistan	1	0.1	2	0.7
Philippines	—	—	1	0.6
Poland	—	—	2	0.8
Romania	—	—	1	0.4
South Africa	—	—	2	1.8
Spain	3	1.1	18	15.1
Sweden	6	3.7	12	9.4
Switzerland	4	1.9	5	2.9
Turkey	—	—	1	0.7
USSR	32	11.6	54	31.7
U.K.	32	6.9	44	14.4
United States	70	50.9	176	167.8
Yugoslavia	—	—	2	1.6
Total*	238	124.5	549	407.3

* Does not include People's Republic of China, for which no information is available.

ENERGY CONSUMPTION PER CAPITA IN 1976 (Kg of coal equivalent per capita)

SOURCE: United Nations *Statistical Yearbook 1978;* © United Nations

Country	1976	Country	1976	Country	1976
World	2,069	Greece	2,250	Poland	5,253
Algeria	729	Hungary	3,553	Portugal	1,050
Argentina	1,804	Iceland	4,556	Romania	4,036
Australia	6,657	India	218	Saudi Arabia	1,901
Austria	4,013	Iran	1,490	South Africa	2,985
Belgium	6,049	Ireland	3,170	Spain	2,399
Brazil	731	Israel	2,541	Sweden	6,036
Bulgaria	4,710	Italy	3,284	Switzerland	3,340
Canada	9,950	Japan	3,679	Thailand	308
China	706	Korea, North	3,072	Tunisia	456
Cuba	1,225	Korea, South	1,020	Turkey	743
Czechoslovakia	7,397	Libya	1,589	United Kingdom	5,268
Denmark	5,320	Mexico	1,227	UNITED STATES	11,554
Egypt	473	Netherlands	6,224	USSR	5,259
Finland	5,177	New Zealand	3,617	Uruguay	1,000
France	4,380	Nigeria	94	Venezuela	2,838
Germany, East	6,789	Norway	5,263	Yugoslavia	2,016
Germany, West	5,992	Philippines	329	Zimbabwe	634

LARGEST FOREIGN INDUSTRIAL COMPANIES: 1979 SOURCE: *Fortune* magazine, August 11, 1980

Rank '79	Rank '78	Company	Country	Industry	Sales ($000)
1	1	Royal Dutch Shell Group	Netherlands-Britain	Petroleum	59,416,560
2	2	British Petroleum	Britain	Petroleum	38,713,496
3	4	Unilever	Britain-Netherlands	Food products	21,748,583
4	10	ENI	Italy	Petroleum	18,984,960
5	46	Fiat	Italy	Motor vehicles	18,300,000
6	11	Française des Pétroles	France	Petroleum	17,305,220
7	17	Peugeot-Citroën	France	Motor vehicles	17,270,104
8	7	Volkswagenwerk	Germany	Motor vehicles	16,765,6833
9	5	Phillips' Gloeilampenfabrieken	Netherlands	Electronics, appliances	16,576,123
10	9	Renault	France	Motor vehicles	16,117,376
11	6	Siemens	Germany	Electronics, appliances	15,069,575
12	12	Daimler-Benz	Germany	Motor vehicles	14,942,324
13	13	Hoechst	Germany	Chemicals	14,785,464
14	14	Bayer	Germany	Chemicals	14,196,027
15	16	BASF	Germany	Chemicals	14,138,872
16	24	Petróleos de Venezuela	Venezuela	Petroleum	14,115,899
17	8	Toyota Motor	Japan	Motor vehicles	14,012 345
18	22	Thyssen	Germany	Steel and industrial products	13,636,918
19	26	Elf-Aquitaine	France	Petroleum	13,385,876
20	15	Nestlé	Switzerland	Food products, beverages	13,016,940
21	19	Nissan Motor	Japan	Motor vehicles	12,652,060
22	23	Hitachi	Japan	Electronics, appliances	12,632,844
23	20	Nippon Steel	Japan	Metal refining — steel	12,595,259
24	21	Mitsubishi Heavy Industries	Japan	Motor vehicles, industrial equipment	11,959,912
25	27	Imperial Chemical Industries	Britain	Chemicals	11,391,003
26	18	Matsushita Electric Industrial	Japan	Electronics, appliances	11,127,658
27	25	Petrobrás (Petróleo Brasileiro)	Brazil	Petroleum	10,278,517
28	28	B.A.T. Industries	Britain	Tobacco	9,478,860
29	34	Ruhrkohle	Germany	Mining—coal	8,856,975
30	29	Saint-Gobain-Pont-à-Mousson	France	Building materials, metal products	8,354,964

WORLD CRUDE PETROLEUM PRODUCERS

SOURCE: United Nations *Monthly Bulletin of Statistics*, © United Nations, May 1980

The list below is a compilation of the latest available figures on the oil production of selected countries. The figures for Communist countries are generally estimates. All figures are given in thousands of metric tons per average calendar month.

Region and Country	1973	1978	1979
North America:			
Canada	7,336	5,356	6,067[1]
Mexico	1,938	5,069	6,035[1]
Trinidad and Tobago	734	988	921[1]
United States	37,849	35,766	34,988
South America:			
Argentina	1,790	1,936	2,019
Bolivia	183	126	113
Brazil	690*	643*	691*
Chile	106	78	N.A.
Colombia	791	563	528[2]
Ecuador	885	849	914
Peru	290	642	780
Venezuela	14,648	9,456	10,240[1]
Europe:			
Austria	215	149	146
Czechoslovakia	14	10	9
Denmark	6	36	38
France	105	93	100
Germany, West	553	422	398
Hungary	166	183	169
Italy	87	118	139
Netherlands	124	117	106
Norway	132	1,440	1,524
Romania	1,191	1,144	N.A.
Spain	64	73	75
United Kingdom	31*	4,448	6,483
USSR	35,753*	47,705*	48,410*
Yugoslavia	278	340	345

Region and Country	1973	1978	1979
Africa			
Algeria	4,229	4,783	4,176
Angola	680	683	558
Congo	174	134	217
Egypt	707	2,032	2,165
Gabon	633	949	899
Libya	8,740	7,980	8,273
Nigeria	8,480	7,908	9,626
Tunisia	324	408	459
Zaire	N.A.	95	86
Asia:			
Bahrain	284	221	208
Burma	81	118	128[1]
India	600	939	1,069
Indonesia	5,579	6,704	6,511
Iran	24,403	21,814	12,411
Iraq	8,295	10,756	14,048
Japan	58	45	40
Kuwait	12,702	8,765	10,500
Malaysia	362	860	N.A.
Oman	1,219	1,309	1,228
Pakistan	36	40	43
Qatar	2,292	1,935	2,037
Saudi Arabia	31,482	34,194	39,692
Syria	462	834	745
Turkey	293	238	242[2]
United Arab Emirates	6,813	7,502	7,486
Oceania:			
Australia	1,595	1,772	1,805

*Includes natural gas liquids. N.A.: Data insufficient or not available. [1]Average of 10 months of 1979. [2]Average for 9 months of 1979.

U.S. METALS PRODUCTION

SOURCE: American Iron & Steel Institute; U.S. Bureau of Mines; Zinc Institute Inc. (figures in short tons)

Year	Pig Ion and Ferroalloys	Steel Ingots[2]	Rolled Iron and Steel Products	Aluminum[2]	Copper[3]	Zinc[4]	Lead[3]
1961	66,565,063	98,104,492	73,411,563	1,903,200	1,165,155	896,900	261,921
1965	90,918,000	131,461,601	99,304,221	2,754,500	1,351,734	1,078,300	301,147
1970	93,851,000	131,514,000	N.A.	3,976,148	1,719,657	961,153	571,767
1971	83,468,000	120,443,000	N.A.	3,925,223	1,522,183	840,178	578,550
1972	91,338,000	133,241,000	N.A.	4,122,452	1,664,840	706,898	618,915
1973	103,089,000	150,799,000	N.A.	4,529,116	1,717,940	687,861	603,024
1974	98,332,000	145,720,000	N.A.	4,903,000	1,597,000	590,181	663,870
1975	81,850,000	116,642,000	N.A.	3,879,000	1,413,000	445,916	621,000
1976	88,874,000	128,000,000	N.A.	4,251,000	1,606,000	535,953	610,000
1977	82,968,000	125,330,000	N.A.	4,539,000	1,503,000	434,054	592,000
1978	87,679,000	137,031,000	N.A.	4,804,000	1,496,000	445,879	584,000
1979	87,003,000[2]	136,341,000[2]	N.A.	5,015,000	1,576,000	537,427	562,000

[1]Plus castings. [2]Primary. [3]Primary output from domestic ore. [4]Primary slab smelter output.

WORLD MINERAL-PRODUCTION LEADERS: 1979

SOURCE: *UN Monthly Bulletin of Statistics*, July 1980, © United Nations (data in thousands of metric tons per calendar month.)

ITEM	COUNTRY AND PRODUCTION			
Bauxite	Australia (2,137)	Guinea (1,005)	Jamaica (977.7)[1]	Suriname (440.7)[1]
Coal	USSR (59,900)	U.S. (58,646)	Poland (16,760)	U.K. (10,234)
Coal, Lignite & Brown	E. Germany (21,106)[1]	USSR (13,628)[1]	W. Germany (10,882)	Czechoslovakia (8,017)
Copper Ore	U.S. (120.1)	Chile (88.9)	Zambia (60.3)	Canada (52.9)
Crude Oil	USSR (48,410)	Saudi Arabia (39,692)	U.S. (35,038)	Iraq (14,048)
Iron Ore	USSR (19,976)[2]	U.S. (7,207)	Australia (7,015)	Canada (4,976)
Lead Ore	U.S. (43.3)	Australia (34.9)	Canada (28.5)	Mexico (14.5)
Natural Gas[3]	U.S. (403,843)	USSR (282,526)	Canada (59,730)[4]	Romania (25,933)[1]
Tin Concentrates	Malaysia (5,250)	Thailand (2,681)[5]	Bolivia (2,445)[6]	Indonesia (2,311)
Zinc Ore	Canada (100.4)	Australia (40.3)	U.S. (22.0)	Japan (20.3)

[1]1978 figures; [2]1977 figures; [3]In teracalories; [4]Average for first 11 months of 1979; [5]Average for first 9 months of 1979; [6]Average for first 8 months of 1979.

U.S. EXPORTS AND IMPORTS: GEOGRAPHIC AREAS

SOURCE: U.S. Dept. of Commerce, International Trade Administration

Area	Exports (millions of $)			Imports (millions of $)			Trade Balance
	1977	1978	1979	1977	1978	1979	1979
Total	121,212	143,663	181,802	147,685	183,093	218,927	−37,125
Developed Countries	74,891	85,585	110,566	78,620	104,807	117,529	− 6,963
Developing Countries	43,307	52,895	62,982	67,703	76,301	98,739	−35,757
Communist Areas in Europe	2,715	4,503	7,408	1,436	1,977	2,652	+ 4,756
Canada	25,788	28,374	33,096	29,599	34,644	39,021	− 5,925
Latin American Republics	16,371	20,185	26,257	16,450	19,523	26,085	+ 172
Other Western Hemisphere	1,592	1,835	2,200	4,648	4,627	5,984	− 3,784
Western Europe	34,760	39,929	54,331	27,669	38,897	44,448	+ 9,883
Japan	10,529	12,885	17,579	18,550	26,461	28,163	−10,584
Near East	11,021	12,412	11,030	13,019	12,899	16,253	− 5,223
East and South Asia	10,698	13,509	18,438	17,709	23,553	26,898	− 8,460
Australia and Oceania	2,877	3,464	4,319	1,185	2,644	3,402	+ 917
Africa	4,564	5,887	6,299	16,950	17,859	26,014	− 9,715

U.S. EPORTS AND IMPORTS: PRINCIPAL COMMODITIES

SOURCE: U.S. Dept. of Commerce, International Trade Administration

Area	Exports (millions of $)			Imports (millions of $)			Trade Balance
	1977	1978	1979	1977	1978	1979	1979
Total	$117,966	$141,065	$178,525	$147,848	$173,276	$206,456	$ − 27,931
Excluding military grant aid	117,899	140,212	178,360	—	—	—	—
Crude foods	9,438	12,723	15,788	7,065	7,240	7,689	+ 8,099
Manufactured foods	5.356	6.648	7,581	6,755	8,128	9,624	− 2,043
Crude materials	13,976	15,654	20,088	40,822	40,123	56,001	−35,913
Agricultural	8,804	10,470	11,894	1,732	1,971	2,339	+ 9,555
Semimanufactures	14,107	18,908	30,984	24,182	29,171	34,263	− 3,279
Finished manufactures	75,084	87,133	103,920	69,025	88,614	98,879	+ 5,041
Excluding military grant aid	75,022	86,280	103,755	—	—	—	—

U.S. EXPORTS AND IMPORTS: SELECTED MERCHANDISE

SOURCE: U.S. Dept. of Commerce, International Trade Administration

Exports (millions of $)	1977	1978	1979
Food and live animals	14,116	18,333	22,245
Grains and preparations	8,755	11,634	14,451
Wheat	2,699	4,335	5,264
Corn	4,139	5,301	7,022
Beverages and Tobacco	1,847	2,293	2,337
Crude Inedible Materials (nonfuel)	13,086	15,553	20,755
Mineral Fuels	4,184	3,878	5,616
Animal and Vegetable Oils	1,309	1,521	1,845
Chemicals	10,812	12,618	17,306
Machinery and Transport Equipment	50,248	59,270	70,491
Electronic Computers	3,264	4,359	3,604
Electrical Apparatus	9,805	11,001	8,635
Transport Equipment	17,619	21,161	25,750
Road Motor Vehicles & Parts	10,887	12,148	15,077
Aircraft, Parts and Accessories	5,874	8,203	9,719

Imports (millions of $)	1977	1978	1979
Food and live animals	12,558	13,521	15,171
Meat	1,276	1,856	2,539
Fish	2,056	2,212	2,639
Coffee	3,910	3,728	3,820
Beverages and Tobacco	1,669	2,221	2,566
Crude Inedible Materials (nonfuel)	8,464	9,294	10,651
Mineral Fuels	44,537	42,096	60,061
Chemicals	4,970	6,430	7,485
Machinery and Transport Equipment	36,407	47,590	53,678
Electrical Apparatus	8,432	6,136	6,175
Automobiles and Parts	15,844	20,631	22,075
Other Manufactured Goods	35,176	46,296	51,131
Paper	2,402	2,923	3,357
Metals	12,278	15,712	17,457
Textiles & Clothing	5,836	7,856	8,082
Footware	1,806	2,585	2,859

LEADING U.S. TRADING PARTNERS: 1979

SOURCE: U.S. Department of Commerce, International Trade Administration (figures in millions of dollars)

Export Trade

COUNTRY	VALUE	COUNTRY	VALUE
Canada	$33,096	West Germany	$8,482
Japan	17,579	Netherlands	6,907
United Kingdom	10,635	France	5,587
Mexico	9,847	Saudi Arabia	4,875

Import Trade

COUNTRY	VALUE	COUNTRY	VALUE
Canada	$39,021	Saudi Arabia	$8,730
Japan	28,163	Nigeria	8,650
West Germany	11,610	United Kingdom	8,504
Mexico	8,996	Republic of China	6,426

VALUE OF U.S. EXPORTS AND IMPORTS

SOURCE: U.S. Department of Commerce, International Trade Administration (figures in millions of dollars)

Year	Total Exports*	Total Imports	Trade Balance	Year	Total Exports*	Total Imports	Trade Balance	Year	Total Exports*	Total Imports	Trade Balance
1979	181,802	218,927	− 7,125	1970	42,659	39,952	+2,707	1961	20,226	14,761	+5,465
1978	143,663	183,093	−39,430	1969	37,332	36,043	1,289	1960	19,659	15,073	4,586
1977	121,212	147,685	−26,473	1968	34,063	33,226	837	1959	16,426	15,690	736
1976	115,150	121,009	− 5,859	1967	31,030	26,889	4,141	1958	16,375	13,392	2,983
1975	107,130	96,116	+11,014	1966	29,490	25,618	3,872	1957	19,516	13,418	6,098
1974	97,908	100,997	−13,089	1965	26,742	21,427	5,315	1956	17,343	12,905	4,438
1973	70,823	69,476	+ 1,347	1964	25,832	18,749	7,083	1955	14,298	11,566	2,732
1972	49,199	55,583	− 6,384	1963	22,467	17,207	5,260	1954	12,857	10,371	2,486
1971	43,549	45,563	− 2,014	1962	20,986	16,464	4,522				

*Excluding aid in the form of military grants.

U.S. SHARE OF WORLD TRADE: 1938-1979

SOURCE: United Nations *Monthly Bulletin of Statistics*, June 1980, © United Nations (figures in millions of dollars)

Year	Total World Exports*	U.S. Exports	Year	Total World Imports*	U.S. Imports
1979	1,471,500	178,578	1979	1,489,200	217,664
1978	1,175,100	141,154	1978	1,211,600	182,787
1977	1,017,700	119,042	1977	1,044,900	156,758
1976	897,400	113,323	1976	911,300	128,872
1975	788,000	106,157	1975	801,700	102,984
1974	768,700	97,144	1974	774,700	107,112
1973	517,800	70,223	1973	529,100	68,656
1972	372,300	48,968	1972	384,200	55,282
1971	314,100	43,492	1971	328,300	45,516
1970	280,000	42,590	1970	294,100	39,756
1969	243,500	37,462	1969	256,400	35,863
1968	212,500	34,199	1968	224,700	33,066
1967	189,900	31,243	1967	201,500	26,813
1966	180,600	29,998	1966	192,000	25,439
1965	164,800	27,189	1965	174,800	21,348
1964	152,200	26,300	1964	161,000	18,666
1963	135,400	23,104	1963	143,500	17,072
1962	141,400	21,446	1962	149,800	16,317
1960	128,000	20,412	1960	135,500	15,071
1958	108,100	17,755	1958	114,100	13,298
1953	82,700	15,661	1953	84,200	10,915
1948	57,500	12,545	1948	63,600	7,183
1938	23,500	3,064	1938	25,400	2,180
it0,0					

*Excluding trade of the Centrally Planned Economies.

WORLD ECONOMIC SUMMARY: 1975-1979

SOURCE: United Nations *Monthly Bulletin of Statistics*, June 1980, © United Nations

Item	Unit*	1975	1979
Agricultural production:			
Barley	Mil. tons	153	173
Coffee	1,000 tons	4,644	4,855
Corn	Mil. tons	326	383
Cotton (lint)	1,000 tons	12,294	14,119
Eggs	Mil. tons	23.6	26.5
Meat	Mil. tons	122.8	136.8
Milk	Mil. tons	430	461
Potatoes	Mil. tons	285	281
Rice	Mil. tons	360	376
Tea	1,000 tons	1,546	1,785
Tobacco	1,000 tons	5,441	5,492
Wheat	Mil. tons	356	420
Wool, greasy	1,000 tons	2,637	2,687
Rubber (natural)	1,000 tons	3,315	3,805
Fish catches	Mil. tons	68.6	72.4†
Industrial Production:			
Coal[2]	Mil. tons	1,889	2,141
Crude petroleum[2]	Mil. tons	2,575	2,999
Wheat flour[2]	Mil. tons	125.7	130.1‡
Sugar	Mil. tons	81.6	88.9
Sawnwood	1,000 cu.m.	404	443‡
Woodpulp	Mil. tons	81.1	90.8‡
Newsprint	Mil. tons	20.9	22.7‡
Cement[2]	Mil. tons	703	705
Pig iron and ferroalloys[2]	Mil. tons	456	495
Crude steel[2]	Mil. tons	615	683
Tin[2 3 4 5]	1,000 tons	176	178
Merchant vessels, launched[2 3 4]	Mil. gr.tons	34.20	11.46
Motor vehicles (passenger)[2]	Millions	25.22	31.34
Electric energy[2]	Bil. kw.-hr.	6,331	7,519
External trade:[1 2 4]			
Imports, c.i.f.	Bil. U.S. dol.	801.7	1,489.2
Exports, f.o.b.	Bil. U.S. dol.	788.0	1,471.5
Transport:			
Railway freight	Bil. tons-km	5,958	6,408†
Merchant shipping, loaded	Mil. tons	3,072	3,461†
Civil aviation, km flown[4 6]	Millions	7,510	9,000

*Data are in metric units. †Latest available figures are from 1978. ‡Latest available figures are from 1977. [1]Excludes Eastern Europe. [2]Excludes China. [3]Excludes East Germany. [4]Excludes USSR. [5]Excludes North Korea. [6]Includes ICAO members.

WALL STREET GLOSSARY

SOURCE: New York Stock Exchange

Assets: Everything a corporation owns or has outstanding: cash, investments, money due it, materials and inventories (current assets); buildings and machinery (fixed assets); and patents and good will (intangible assets).

Averages: Various ways of measuring the trend of securities prices, the most popular of which is the Dow-Jones average of 30 industrial stocks listed on the New York Stock Exchange. The numbers are not true numerical averages, but take into account such factors as past splits, etc.

Balance Sheet: A condensed statement showing the nature and amount of a company's assets, liabilities, and capital on a given date. In dollar amounts, the balance sheet shows what the company owned, what it owed, and the ownership interest in the company of its stockholders.

Bear: Someone who believes the market will decline.

Blue Chip: Common stock in a company known nationally for the quality and wide acceptance of its products or services and its ability to make money and pay dividends. Usually such stocks are relatively high priced and offer relatively low yields.

Bond: Basically an IOU or promissory note of a corporation, usually issued in multiples of $1,000 or $5,000. A bond is evidence of a debt on which the issuing company usually promises to pay the bondholders a specified amount of interest for a specified length of time, and to repay the loan on the expiration date. In every case a bond represents debt—its holder is a creditor of the corporation and not a part owner as is the shareholder.

Book Value: An accounting term. Book value of a stock is determined from the company's records, by adding all assets (generally excluding intangibles), then deducting all debts and other liabilities, plus the liquidation price of any preferred issues. The sum arrived at is divided by the number of common shares outstanding and the result is book value per common share. Book value may have little or no significant relationship to market value.

Bull: One who believes the market will rise.

Capital Gain or Capital Loss: Profit or loss from the sale of a capital asset. Under current federal income tax laws, a capital gain may be either short-term (12 months or less) or long-term (more than 12 months). A short-term capital gain is taxed at the reporting individual's full income tax rate. A long-term capital gain is subject to a lower tax.

Capitalization: Total amount of the various securities issued by a corporation. Capitalization may include bonds, debentures, preferred and common stock. Bonds and debentures are usually carried on the books of the issuing company in terms of their par or face value. Preferred and common shares may be carried in terms of par or stated value. Stated value may be either an arbitrary figure decided upon by the directors, or may represent the amount received by the company from the sale of the securities at the time of issuance.

Cash Flow: Reported net income of a corporation *plus* amounts charged off for depreciation, depletion, amortization, extraordinary charges to reserves, which are bookkeeping deductions and not paid out in actual dollars and cents.

Common Stock: Securities that represent an ownership interest in a corporation. If the company has also issued preferred stock, both common and preferred have ownership rights, but the preferred normally has prior claim on dividends and, in the event of liquidation, assets. Claims of both common and preferred stockholders are junior to claims of bondholders or other creditors of the company. Common-stock holders assume greater risk than preferred-stock holders, but generally exercise greater control and may gain greater reward.

Conglomerate: A corporation that has diversified its operations usually by acquiring enterprises in widely varied industries.

Convertible: A bond, debenture, or preferred share that may be exchanged by the owner for common stock or another security, usually of the same company, in accordance with the terms of the issue.

Dealer: An individual or firm in the securities business acting as a principal rather than as an agent. Typically, a dealer buys for his own account and sells to a customer from his own inventory. The dealer's profit or loss is the difference between the price he pays and the price he receives for the same security.

Discretionary Account: An account in which the customer gives the broker or someone else discretion, which may be complete or within specific limits, as to the purchase and sales of securities or commodities including selection, timing, amount and price to be paid or received.

Dollar Cost Averaging: A system of buying securities at regular intervals with a fixed dollar amount. Under this system the investor buys by the dollars' worth rather than by the number of shares. If each investment is of the same number of dollars, payments buy more when the price is low and fewer when it rises. Thus temporary downswings in price benefit the investor if he continues periodic purchases in both good times and bad and the price at which the shares are sold is more than their average cost.

Dow Theory: A theory of market analysis based upon the performance of the Dow-Jones industrial and transportation stock price averages. The Theory says that the market is in a basic upward trend if these averages advance above a previous important high. When the averages dip, there is said to be a downward trend.

Fiscal Year: A corporation's accounting year. Due to the nature of their particular business, some companies do not use the calendar year for their bookkeeping.

Growth Stock: Stock of a company with prospects for future growth—a company whose earnings are expected to increase at a relatively rapid rate.

Investment Banker: Also known as an underwriter. He is the middleman between the corporation issuing new securities and the public. One or more investment bankers buy outright from a corporation a new issue of stocks or bonds. The group forms a syndicate to sell the securities to individuals and institutions. Investment bankers also distribute very large blocks of stocks or bonds.

Investment Company: A company or trust which uses its capital to invest in other companies. There are two principal types: the closed-end and the open-end, or mutual fund. Closed-end shares are readily transferable in the open market and are bought and sold like other shares. Open-end funds sell their own new shares to investors, stand ready to buy back their old shares, and are not listed.

Legal List: A list of investments selected by various states in which certain institutions and fiduciaries, such as insurance companies and banks, may invest.

Liquidity: The ability of the market in a particular security to absorb a reasonable amount of buying or selling at reasonable price changes. Liquidity is one of the most important characteristics of a good market.

Listed Stock: The stock of a company that is traded on a securities exchange and for which a listing application and a registration statement, giving detailed information about the company and its operations, have been filed with the Securities & Exchange Commission (SEC), unless otherwise exempted, and the exchange itself. The various stock exchanges have different standards for listing.

Load: The portion of the offering price of shares of open-end investment companies that covers sales commissions and all other costs of distribution. The load is incurred only on purchase, there being, in most cases, no charge when the shares are sold (redeemed).

Margin: The amount paid by the customer when he uses his broker's credit to buy a security. Under Federal Reserve regulations, the initial margin required in the past 20 years has ranged from 50 percent of the purchase price all the way to 100 percent.

NASD: The National Association of Securities Dealers, Inc., an association of brokers and dealers in the over-the-counter securities business.

NYSE Common Stock Index: A composite index covering price movements of all common stocks listed on the "Big Board." It is based on the close of the market December 31, 1965, as 50.00 and is weighted according to the number of shares listed for each issue. The index is computed continuously by the Exchange's Market Data System and printed on the ticker tape each half hour. Point changes in the index are converted to dollars and cents so as to provide a meaningful measure of changes in the average price of listed stocks. The composite index is supplemented by separate indexes for four industry groups: industrials, transportation, utilities, and finances.

Option: A right to buy (call) or sell (put) a fixed amount of a given stock at a specified price within a limited period of time. The purchaser hopes that the stock's price will go up (if he bought a call) or down (if he bought a put) by an amount sufficient to provide a profit greater than the cost of the contract and the commission and other fees required to exercise the contract. If the stock price holds steady or moves in the opposite direction, the price paid for the option is lost entirely.

Over-the-Counter: A market for securities made up of securities dealers who may or may not be members of a securities exchange. Thousands of companies have insufficient shares outstanding, stockholders, or earnings to warrant application for listing on a stock exchange. Securities of these companies are traded in the over-the-counter market between dealers who act either as principals or as brokers for customers. The over-the-counter market is the principal market for U.S. Government bonds and municipals.

Par: In the case of a common share, a dollar amount assigned to the share by the company's charter. Par value may also be used to compute the dollar amount of the common shares on the balance sheet. Par value has little significance so far as market value of common stock is concerned. Many companies today issue no-par stock, but give a stated per share value on the balance sheet. In the case of preferred shares and bonds, however, par is important. It often signifies the dollar value upon which dividends on preferred stocks and interest on bonds are figured. The issuer of a 3% bond promises to pay that percentage of the bond's par value annually.

Point: In the case of shares of stock, a point means $1. In the case of bonds, a point means $10.

Portfolio: Holdings of securites by an individual or institution. A portfolio may contain bonds, preferred stocks and common stocks of various types of enterprises.

Preferred Stock: A class of stock with a claim on the company's earnings before payment may be made on the common stock, usually also entitled to priority over common stock if the company liquidates. It is usually entitled to dividends at a specified rate before payment of a dividend on the common stock.

Price-Earnings Ratio: The price of a share of stock divided by earnings per share for a twelve-month period.

Principal: The person for whom a broker executes an order, or a dealer buying or selling for his own account. The term "principal" may also refer to a person's capital or to the face amount of a bond.

Puts and Calls: see **Option**

Quotation: Often shortened to "quote." The highest bid to buy and the lowest offer to sell a security in a given market at a given time. A "quote" on a stock might be "45¼ to 45½." This means that $45.25 is the highest price any buyer would pay at the time the quote was given on the floor of the Exchange, and that $45.50 was the lowest price that any seller would take at the same time.

REIT: Real Estate Investment Trust, an organization similar to an investment company but concentrating its holdings in real estate. The yield is generally liberal since REIT's are required to distribute as much as 90% of their income.

Registration: Before a public offering may be made of new securities by a company, or of outstanding securities by controlling stockholders—through the mails or in interstate commerce—the securities must be registered under the Securities Act of 1933. Registration statement is filed with the SEC by the issuer. It must disclose pertinent information relating to the company's operations, securities, management, and purpose of the public offering. Securities of railroads under jurisdiction of the Interstate Commerce Commission (ICC), and certain other types of securities, are exempted.

Round Lot: A unit of trading or a multiple thereof. On the New York Stock Exchange, the unit of trading is generally 100 shares in stocks and $1,000 par value in the case of bonds. In some inactive stocks, the unit of trading is 10 shares.

Short Sale: A person who believes a stock will decline and and sells it though he does not own any has made a short sale. Your broker borrows the stock so he can deliver the 100 shares to the buyer. The money value of the shares borrowed is deposited by your broker with the lender. Sooner or later you must cover your short sale by buying the same amount of stock you borrowed for return to the lender. If you are able to buy at a lower price than you sold it for, your profit is the difference between the two prices—not counting commissions and taxes. Stock exchange and federal regulations govern and limit the conditions under which a short sale may be made on a national securities exchange.

Specialist: A member of the New York Stock Exchange who has two functions: First, to maintain an orderly market in the stocks in which he is registered as a specialist. The Exchange expects the specialist to buy or sell for his own account, to a reasonable degree, when there is a temporary disparity between supply and demand. Second, the specialist acts as a broker's broker. When a commission broker on the exchange floor receives a limit order, he cannot wait at the particular post where the stock is traded until the price reaches the specified level. He leaves the order with the specialist, who will try to execute it in the market if and when the stock declines to the specified price. The specialist must always put his customers' interests first.

Split: The division of the outstanding shares of a corporation into a larger number of shares. A 3-for-1 split by a company with 1 million shares outstanding would result in 3 million shares outstanding. After the 3-for-1 split, each holder of 100 shares would have 300 shares.

Take-Over: The acquiring of one corporation by another — usually in a friendly merger but sometimes marked by a "proxy fight."

Yield: Also known as return. The dividends or interest paid by a company expressed as a percentage of the current price. A stock with a current market value of $40 a share paying dividends at the rate of $2.00 is said to return 5% ($2.00 − $40.00).

WALL STREET INDEXES

Dow Jones Industrial Average: The addition of closing prices for 30 stocks divided by the current divisor. The divisor is never the number of stocks listed, but by reflecting splits, mergers, and bankruptcies, it is constantly revised.

NASDAQ Composite Index: The measure of all domestic common issues traded over-the-counter included in the NASDAQ System, exclusive of those listed on an exchange and those with only one market maker. The index is market value-weighted, in that the importance of each stock is proportional to its price times the number of shares outstanding.

New York Stock Exchange Common Stock Index: The current aggregate market value (sum of all shares times the price per share) divided by the adjusted base market value and multiplied by 50. The adjusted value reflects additions or deletions of listings, but remains unaffected by stock splits and dividends.

Standard and Poor's Index: The aggregate market value (price of each share times the number of shares) for 425 industrial stocks, expressed as one-tenth the percentage of the average market value relative to the average market value during the years 1941-43.

THE AMERICAN SHAREHOLDER

The latest NYSE shareownership survey, conducted during 1975, revealed that almost 1 out of 5 shareowners had left the stock market since early 1970. U.S. shareowners numbered 25.3 million and included 1 out of 6 adult Americans in mid-1975. In this five-and-one-half-year period, the median age of shareowners increased by 5 years, from 48 to 53. For the first time since the Exchange began conducting shareownership surveys in 1952, the number of shareowners in the U.S. did not increase.

These 25 million shareowners held shares in some 11,000 publicly owned corporations and investment companies, which had 40.7 billion shares of stock outstanding at a total market value of $800 billion. While the number of shares of stock outstanding increased 12.6% from 36.2 billion in 1970, depressed economic conditions reduced the total market value of stocks outstanding, which declined 21.3% from $1.1 trillion in 1970.

Although the total number of U.S. shareowners declined 18.1%, the number of shareowners of NYSE-listed stocks declined only 1.9% to 18.0 million. Adult female shareowners slightly outnumbered adult males.

The average shareowner's income rose from $13,500 in early 1970 to $19,000 in mid-1975, paralleling changes in purchasing power. The incidence of shareowners with household incomes below $10,000 declined from 28.8% of all U.S. shareowners in 1970 to 14.6% in mid-1975.

Year	Number of Shareowners (millions)	Percent of U.S. Population
1952	6.5	4%
1959	12.5	7
1962	17.0	9
1965	20.1	10
1971	31.9	17
1972	32.5	17
1973	31.7	15
1974	30.9	14
1975	25.3	12

INSTITUTIONAL FAVORITES

SOURCE: Standard & Poor's Corporation

The Standard & Poor's Corporation issues most favored by institutional investors are ranked here by the number of companies owning them.

Issue	Ind. Div. Rate $	% Yld. on Div.	P-E Ratio
Int'l Bus. Mach.	3.44	6.4	10
American Tel & Tel	5.00	9.6	6
Exxon Corp.	4.80	8.1	5
General Electric	2.80	6.0	7
Eastman Kodak	2.90	5.9	8
General Motors	4.95	11.7	7
Xerox Corp.	2.80	5.3	8
Atlantic Richfield	3.40	3.9	9
Texaco Inc.	2.40	6.9	5
Merck & Co.	2.30	3.4	13
Mobil Corp.	3.00	4.2	7
Standard Oil (Ind.)	1.80	3.6	9
Minnesota Mng./Mfg.	2.80	5.5	9
Schlumberger, Ltd.	1.32	1.3	18
Standard Oil of Cal.	3.20	4.7	6
Sears, Roebuck & Co.	1.36	8.5	6
Amer. Home Prods.	1.70	6.8	10
Dow Chemical	1.60	5.1	7
Phillips Petroleum	1.80	4.2	7
Halliburton Co.	2.00	2.2	14
K Mart	.92	4.5	7
Caterpillar Tractor	2.40	5.1	8
Philip Morris Inc.	1.60	4.3	9
Citicorp	1.42	7.4	5
duPont (E.I.) deNem.	2.75	7.7	6
General Tel. & Elect.	2.72	10.0	7
Gulf Oil	2.25	5.7	6
Procter & Gamble	3.40	4.9	9
Union Carbide	3.00	7.6	4
Coca-Cola Co.	2.16	6.5	10
Burroughs Corp.	2.60	3.9	9
Tenneco, Inc.	2.40	6.9	6
Conoco Inc.	2.20	4.9	5
Pfizer, Inc.	1.44	3.6	12
Johnson & Johnson	2.30	3.1	12
Ford Motor	4.00	16.5	2
Bristol-Myers	1.60	4.6	10
Texas Utilities	1.76	9.1	8
Avon Products	2.80	7.9	8
Pepsico Inc.	1.14	4.8	8
Int'l Tel. & Tel.	2.40	9.1	5
Warner-Lambert	1.32	7.2	8
Union Pacific	1.40	3.8	9
Reynolds (R.J.) Indus.	2.10	6.3	6
Union Oil of Calif.	1.30	2.7	8
Eli Lilly & Co.	2.10	4.1	11
Abbott Laboratories	1.20	3.0	13
Penney (J.C.)	1.84	7.6	7
Standard Oil Ohio	2.80	3.2	7
Commonwealth Edison	2.60	12.2	8
Alcan Aluminum Ltd.	1.20	4.8	4
Int'l Paper	2.40	7.0	6
Monsanto Co.	3.40	7.6	5
Central & So. West.	1.50	10.5	7
Weyerhaeuser Co.	1.30	4.4	7
American Express	2.00	6.0	7
BankAmerica Corp.	1.44	5.8	6
Digital Equipment	—	—	13
Morgan (J.P.) & Co.	2.80	6.1	7
Marathon Oil	1.80	3.4	11
Dresser Industries	1.10	2.1	9
General Foods	2.00	7.5	5
Emerson Electric	1.60	5.1	9
Raytheon Co.	2.00	2.9	11
Houston Industries	2.68	9.2	6
INCO Ltd.	.82	3.7	8
Georgia-Pacific	1.20	4.9	8
Schering-Plough	1.60	4.6	8
Boeing Co.	1.87	5.1	7
McDonald's Corp.	.56	1.3	9
Aetna Life & Casual.	2.12	6.0	5
Goodyear Tire & Rub.	1.30	10.9	5
Smithkline Corp.	1.66	3.1	13
RCA Corp.	1.80	8.6	6
Florida Pwr. & Light	2.72	9.9	7

THE 50 LEADING STOCKS IN MARKET VALUE (AS OF DEC. 31, 1979)

SOURCE: New York Stock Exchange

Issue	Listed Shares (in millions)	Market Value (in millions)
Int'l Business Machines	583.9	$ 37,734
American Tel. & Tel.	700.8	36,529
Exxon Corp.	453.2	24,983
General Motors	291.4	14,605
Schlumberger, N.V.	133.6	12,524
Standard Oil Co. (Ind.)	152.2	12,002
General Electric	231.5	11,747
Mobil Corp.	212.2	11,726
Standard Oil Co. of Calif.	171.0	9,638
Atlantic Richfield	114.6	9,208
Shell Oil	154.4	8,376
Texaco Inc.	274.3	7,920
Eastman Kodak	161.6	7,796
Phillips Petroleum	154.4	7,414
Gulf Oil	211.9	7,311
Getty Oil	88.5	6,529
Dow Chemical	200.4	6,436
Procter & Gamble	82.7	6,140
Minnesota Mining & Mfg.	118.0	5,944
duPont deNemours	145.8	5,886
Sears, Roebuck & Co.	324.6	5,844
Merck & Co.	75.9	5,501
Conoco	113.3	5,353
Standard Oil (Ohio)	60.3	5,327
Xerox Corp.	82.1	5,098
Halliburton Co.	58.9	$ 5,009
Johnson & Johnson	61.3	4,857
Caterpillar Tractor	86.4	4,667
American Home Products	168.3	4,585
Philip Morris Inc.	124.5	4,484
Eli Lilly & Co.	73.3	4,380
Teledyne, Inc.	32.3	4,325
Coca-Cola Co.	124.0	4,292
Sun Company, Inc.	60.0	4,194
Tenneco Inc.	106.1	4,110
Weyerhaeuser Co.	128.6	4,084
General Tel. & Electronics	144.5	4,081
BankAmerica Corp.	147.5	4,074
Union Oil Co. of California	86.6	3,877
Smithkline Corp.	60.9	3,827
Hewlett-Packard Co.	59.2	3,500
Reynolds (R.J.) Industries	101.5	3,478
Union Pacific Corp.	47.7	3,449
Ford Motor Co.	106.2	3,398
Superior Oil Co.	25.5	3,366
Boeing Co.	65.1	3,294
Burroughs Corp.	41.1	3,223
Marathon Oil Co.	61.4	3,072
Citicorp	128.6	3,038
Int'l Tel & Tel.	115.9	2,971
TOTAL	**7,508.0**	**$375,206**

REGULAR DIVIDEND PAYERS

SOURCE: Standard & Poor's Corporation

The following companies have paid quarterly, semi-annual, or annual dividends for 60 years or more. Dividends are for 1979.

Company	Dividends Began	Dividend	Company	Dividends Began	Dividend	Company	Dividends Began	Dividend
Allied Chemical	1887	2.000	Equimark Corporation	1872	.960	Norfolk & Western Ry	1901	2.200
American Brands	1905	5.500	Exxon Corporation	1882	4.800	Northern States Power	1910	2.280
American District Teleg	1903	1.160	Fairmont Foods	1904	.760	Oklahoma Gas & Electric	1908	1.600
American Electric Power	1909	2.220	Fidelity Union Banc	1893	2.800	Orange/Rockland Util	1908	1.560
American Express	1870	2.000	Fst Intrnatl. Bancshares	1875	1.500	Owens-Illinois	1907	1.400
American Home Products	1919	1.700	First National Boston	1784	2.200	Pacific Gas & Electric	1919	2.600
American Natural Res	1904	3.440	First Natl. St. Bancorp	1812	2.200	Pacific Lighting	1909	2.240
American Sterilizer	1914	.320	First Pennsylvania	1828	.440	Pennwalt Corporation	1863	2.200
American Tel. & Tel	1881	5.000	Fisher Scientific	1907	.520	Pfizer, Incorporated	1901	1.440
Amfac, Incorporated	1898	1.320	Foxboro Company	1916	1.300	Philadelphia Electric	1902	1.800
Anchor Hocking	1914	1.280	Gatx Corporation	1919	2.200	Potomac Electric Power	1904	1.400
Arizona Public Service	1920	2.000	General Bancshares	1913	.800	PPG Industries	1899	2.160
Atlantic City Electric	1919	1.840	General Electric	1899	2.800	Proctor & Gamble	1891	3.400
Avon Products	1919	2.800	General Mills	1898	1.320	Pub. Service of Colorado	1907	1.600
Baltimore Gas & Electric	1910	2.440	General Motors	1915	4.950	Pub. Serv. Elec. & Gas	1907	2.320
Bancal Tri-State	1875	1.120	Gillette Company	1906	1.720	Pullman Incorporated	1867	1.000
Bank of N.Y. Company	1785	2.720	Great Lakes Internatl	1920	1.510	Quaker Oats	1906	1.400
Bankers Trust N.Y.	1904	3.300	Great Northern Nekoosa	1910	1.600	Raybestos-Manhattan	1895	1.600
Bay State Gas	1853	2.200	Hackensack Water	1886	2.000	Reece Corporation	1882	.600
Bell & Howell	1915	.960	Handy & Harman	1905	.700	Republic Financial Serv	1920	1.000
Bell Telephone of Canada	1881	1.640	Harris Bank Corporation	1908	2.000	Republic of Texas	1920	1.160
Borden, Incorporated	1899	1.820	Hawaiian Electric	1901	2.440	Rexnord, Incorporated	1894	1.040
Boston Edison	1890	2.720	Heinz (H.J.)	1911	2.200	Reynolds (RJ) Industries	1900	2.100
Bristol-Myers	1900	1.600	Hercules, Incorporated	1913	1.200	San Diego Gas & Electric	1909	1.520
British Petroleum	1917	1.529	Hobart Corporation	1906	1.200	Scott Paper	1915	1.000
Burroughs Corporation	1895	2.600	Houghton Mifflin	1908	1.600	Scoville Incorporated	1856	1.520
Campbell Soup	1902	1.900	Household Finance	1917	1.550	Security Pacific	1881	2.000
Cannon Mills	1890	1.200	Huyck Corporation	1907	.720	Shell Transport/Trade	1898	1.908
Carpenter Technology	1907	1.900	Idaho Power	1917	2.400	Sierra Pacific Power	1916	1.460
Carter-Wallace	1883	.400	Ideal Basic Industries	1911	1.600	Southeast Banking	1908	.880
Castle & Cooke	1896	.800	INA Corporation	1874	2.200	Southern Calif. Edison	1909	2.720
Caterpiller Tractor	1914	2.400	Industrial National	1791	1.600	Southern New Eng. Tel	1891	3.600
CBS, Incorporated	1931	2.800	Ingersoll-Rand	1910	3.320	Springs Mills	1898	1.200
Central Hudson G. & E	1903	2.160	Interco, Incorporated	1913	2.640	Squibb Corporation	1902	1.140
Champion Spark Plug	1919	.800	IBM	1916	3.440	Standard Brands	1899	1.640
Chase Manhattan	1848	2.800	International Harvester	1910	2.500	Standard Oil of Calif	1912	3.200
Chemical New York	1827	3.480	Iowa Resources	1909	2.520	Standard Oil, Indiana	1894	1.800
Chesebrough-Pond's	1883	1.280	Irving Bank Corporation	1865	2.720	Stanley Works	1877	1.240
Cincinnati Bell	1879	2.520	Jefferson-Pilot	1913	1.200	Stauffer Chemical	1915	1.200
Cincinnati Gas & Elec	1853	2.040	Johnson Controls	1901	1.200	Sterling Drug	1902	.920
Citicorp	1813	1.420	Johnson & Johnson	1905	2.300	Sun Company, Inc	1904	3.600
Cleveland Elec. Illinois	1901	2.000	K Mart	1913	.920	Tampa Electric	1900	1.560
Coca-Cola, Company	1893	2.160	Kroger Company	1902	1.360	Texaco Incorporated	1903	2.400
Colgate-Palmolive	1895	1.080	Liggett Group	1912	2.500	Texas Commerce Bankshare	1920	1.600
Combustion Engineer	1911	2.600	Lilly (Eli) & Company	1885	2.100	Texas Utilities	1917	1.760
Commonwealth Edison	1890	2.600	Lincoln National	1920	2.800	Thompson (J Walter)	1917	2.160
Cone Mills	1914	2.000	Louisville Gas & Elec	1913	2.060	Times Mirror	1892	1.440
Conn General Insurance	1867	1.520	Ludlow Corporation	1872	.800	Tokheim Corporation	1920	.700
Connecticut Natural Gas	1851	1.600	Manhattan Life Corp	1851	.320	Trans Union	1914	2.360
Consolidated Edison	1885	2.680	Manufacturers Hanover	1852	2.520	Travelers Corporation	1864	2.480
Consumers Power	1913	2.360	May Department Stores	1911	1.540	Tucson Electric Power	1918	1.520
Continental Corporation	1854	2.200	Melville Corporation	1916	1.600	UGI Corporation	1885	1.760
Conwood Corporation	1903	1.800	Minn. Mining/Mfg	1916	2.800	Union Carbide	1918	3.000
Corning Glass Works	1881	2.120	Mirro Corporation	1902	.960	Union Electric	1906	1.440
CPC International	1920	3.400	Mobil Corporation	1902	3.000	Union Oil of California	1916	1.300
Dayton Power & Light	1919	1.740	Monarch Machine Tool, Co.	1913	1.300	Union Pacific	1900	1.400
Dentsply International	1900	.880	Morgan (J.P.) & Company	1892	2.800	United Illuminating	1900	2.680
Detroit Edison	1909	1.600	Mountain Sts. Tel. & Tel	1911	2.320	U.S. Gypsum	1919	2.400
Diamond International	1882	2.200	Murphy (G.C.)	1913	1.280	U.S. Tobacco	1912	2.080
Dome Mines, LTD	1920	.700	Nabisco, Incorporated	1899	1.620	UpJohn Company	1909	1.720
Donnelley (RR) & Sons	1911	1.140	National Fuel Gas	1903	2.540	Walker (H) Cons Hm	1848	1.400
Dow Chemical	1911	1.600	National-Standard	1916	1.240	Washington Gas Light	1852	2.520
Dow Jones & Company	1906	1.600	National Steel	1907	2.700	Washington Water Power	1899	2.160
DuPont (EI) Denemours	1904	2.750	NCNB Corporation	1903	.720	West Pt.-Pepperell	1888	2.800
Duquesne Light	1913	1.800	New England Tel. & Tel	1886	3.400	Westvaco Corporation	1892	1.500
Eastman Kodak	1902	2.900	New York St. Elec. & Gas	1910	1.760	Wickes Corporation	1895	1.040
Emhart Corporation	1902	2.400	NL Industries	1906	1.200	Woolworth, (F.W.)	1912	1.800
Equifax Incorporated	1913	2.200	NLT Corporation	1920	1.320	Wrigley, (Wm) Jr	1913	2.490

ENERGY: THE NATION'S FUTURE

DWINDLING U.S. PETROLEUM AND NATURAL GAS RESERVES
SOURCE: Geological Survey, Circular 725

Area	Cumulative Production	Reserves — Demonstrated		Inferred[4]	Undiscovered Recoverable Resources Range[5] (95%–5%)
		Measured[2]	Indicated[3]		
Crude Oil[1] (billions of barrels)					
Lower 48 Onshore	99.892	21.086	4.315	14.3	20–64
Alaska Onshore	0.154	9.944	0.013	6.1	6–19
Total Onshore	100.046	31.030	4.328	20.4	37–81
Lower 48 Offshore	5.634	3.070	0.308	2.6	5–18
Alaska Offshore	0.456	0.150	Negligible	0.1	3–31
Total Offshore	6.090	3.220	0.308	2.7	10–49
Total Onshore and Offshore	106.136	34.250	4.636	23.1	50–127
Natural Gas[1] (trillions of cubic feet)					
Lower 48 Onshore	446.366	169.454		119.4	246–453
Alaska Onshore	0.482	31.722		14.7	16–57
Total Onshore	446.848	201.176		134.1	264–506
Lower 48 Offshore	33.553	35.811	Not Applicable	67.4	26–111
Alaska Offshore	0.423	0.145		0.1	8–80
Total Offshore	33.976	35.956		67.5	42–181
Total Onshore and Offshore	480.824	237.132		201.6	322–655
Natural Gas Liquids (billions of barrels)					
Total Onshore and Offshore	15.730	6.350	Not Applicable	6	11–22[6]

[1] Cumulative production and estimates of reserves and resources reflect assumed recovery of about 32% of oil and 80% of gas-in-place. Some portion of remaining oil-in-place is recoverable through application of improved recovery techniques. Estimates based on figures released by the American Petroleum Institute (API) and the American Gas Association (AGA) in April 1975. [2] Identified resources that can be economically extracted with existing technology. Estimates are the "proved reserves" of the API and AGA. [3] Identified resources, economically recoverable by known fluid injection technology. Estimates from the API. [4] Resources estimated recoverable in the future from extensions, revisions of estimates, and new pays in known fields beyond "indicated reserves." [5] Low value of the range is quantity associated with a 95% probability that there is at least this amount. High value is quantity with a 5% probability that there is at least this amount. Totals for the low and high values are derived by statistical methods. [6] Calculated estimates of undiscovered recoverable resources are derived from natural gas estimates by applying historical NGL/Natural Gas ratios. These figures suggest that if added to crude oil estimates, natural gas liquids would increase estimates of petroleum liquids by approximately 20%.

U.S. ENERGY DEMAND AND SUPPLY PROJECTIONS FOR 1985
SOURCE: Congressional Research Service

	Scenario I: Planning base		Scenario II: Possible supply	
	Conventional units	Million barrels per day oil equivalent	Conventional units	Million barrels per day oil equivalent
Total primary energy demand (desired demand):				
CRS, Project Interdependence, base case[1]		44.8		44.8
National energy plan		46.4		46.4
Domestic energy supply:				
Oil and NGL[2]	9.5 million barrels per day	9.5	10.9 million barrels per day[3]	10.9
Natural gas (dry gas to domestic use)[4]	16.9 trillion cubic feet	8.1	17.6 trillion cubic feet[5]	8.5
Coal (domestic use only)[6]	855 million short tons	8.9	965 million short tons[7]	10.0
Nuclear power[8]	113 gigawatts	3.0	126 gigawatts[9]	3.4
Hydro/geo/solar		1.9		1.9
Total domestic supply		31.6		34.8
Oil and natural gas imports:				
Natural gas	2.1 trillion cubic feet	1.0	2.5 trillion cubic feet[10]	1.2
Oil (including 0.3 million barrels per day for storage).	12.7 to 14.3 million barrels per day.	12.7–14.3	9.2 to 10.8 million barrels per day	9.2–10.8

[1] Assumes 3.5 percent average annual GNP growth rates and 2.9 percent energy growth rates; 50 percent increase of oil price through 1990; doubling of natural gas price through 1990. [2] CRS, Project Interdependence, low supply case. Requires a 50-percent increase of finding rates through 1985 (compared with finding rates of past decade). [3] Assumes that oil reserve additions will almost double between 1977 and 1986 compared with the previous decade. Based on CRS Project Interdependence, base case under optimistic economic and political assumptions. [4] CRS, Project Interdependence, base case (based on mean figure of production estimates under favorable political and economic criteria by 12 of the largest oil and gas producing companies in the U.S.) [5] Assumes slightly higher natural gas finding rates than projected in scenario I. Based on CRS Project Interdependence, high natural gas supply case. [6] CRS, Project Interdependence, base case (700,000,000 tons for utilities, which is comparable to FEA's National Energy Outlook of 1976 for 1985; assumes industrial use by 1985 of only 160,000,000 tons, which would mean virtually no cost conversion in that sector). [7] Assumes considerable exemptions of provisions in the Clean Air Act, and that several other constraints and demand and supply of coal will be removed. [8] July 1977 estimate of probable 1985 capacity by FEA/ERDA/NRC. [9] Assumes speeding up of construction of nuclear powerplants. [10] Assumes approval of additional LNG projects over and above those that have already been approved by the FPC.

MAJOR U.S. VEHICULAR TUNNELS

SOURCE: Federal Highway Administration

UNDERWATER TUNNELS

State or City	Name and Location	Length Portal to Portal (Feet)
Alabama	Bankhead Tunnel at Mobile, Mobile River	3,109
Alabama	George C. Wallace Tunnel, Interstate 10, Mobile River	3,000
California	Posey Tube, Oakland Estuary	3,500
California	Webster St. Tube, Oakland Estuary	3,350
Louisiana	Harvey Tunnel Intracoastal Canal	1,080
Maryland	Baltimore Harbor Tunnel	7,650
Massachusetts	Sumner Tunnel, Boston Harbor	5,650
Massachusetts	Lt. Wm. F. Callahan, Jr. Tunnel, Boston Harbor	5,047
Michigan	Detroit-Windsor Tunnel	5,160
New York City	Holland Tunnel, Hudson River	8,557
New York City	Lincoln Tunnel, Hudson River	8,215
New York City	Lincoln Tunnel (3d Tube), Hudson River	8,013
New York City	Queens Midtown Tunnel, East River	6,414
New York City	Brooklyn-Battery Tunnel, Upper New York Bay	9,117*
Texas	Baytown Tunnel, Houston Ship Channel	3,009
Texas	Washburn Tunnel, Houston Ship Channel	2,936
Virginia	Elizabeth River, near Norfolk	3,920
Virginia	2d Elizabeth River, near Norfolk	4,194
Virginia	Hampton Roads, near Norfolk, I-64	7,479
Virginia	2d Hampton Roads Tunnel near Norfolk, Interstate 64	7,500
Virginia	Chesapeake Bay Crossing (Cape Charles to Cape Henry):	
Virginia	Baltimore Channel Tunnel	5,450
Virginia	Thimble Shoal Tunnel	5,738

LAND TUNNELS

State or City	Name and Location	Length Portal to Portal (Feet)
Arizona	Mule Pass, Benson Douglas Highway	1,400
Arizona	Queen Creek Tunnel, Superior-Miami	1,200
California	Wawona, Yosemite Nat'l Park	4,233
California	Big Oak Flat, Yosemite Nat'l Park	2,083
California	Broadway, Low Level Twin Bore, Oakland	2,944
California	Caldecott (New) Tunnel No. 3, Oakland	3,371
California	Broadway, San Francisco	1,616
California	Park Presidio, San Francisco	1,300
California	Waldo Tunnel, Marin County	1,000
California	Elephant Butte, Plumas	1,187
California	International Airport Underpass, Los Angeles	1,910
Colorado	SN-WPH 81 G(1), near Idaho Springs—U.S. 6	1,036
Colorado	1-F Entrance Road, Mesa Verde Nat'l Park	1,470
Colorado	Eisenhower Memorial Tunnel, I-70 (2 bores)	8,950†
Colorado	Interstate 70, near Glenwood Springs	1,045
Connecticut	West Rock Tunnel, near New Haven	1,200
D. C.	9th Street Expressway	1,600
D. C.	Center Leg Mall Tunnel, I-95	3,400
Hawaii	Kalihi Tunnel, Honolulu	2,780

LAND TUNNELS (Cont.)

State or City	Name and Location	Length Portal to Portal (Feet)
Hawaii	Nuuanu-Pali Tunnel No. 1	1,000
Massachusetts	John F. Fitzgerald Expressway, Boston	2,335
Massachusetts	Prudential Passageway, Boston	1,980
Minnesota	Lowry Hill Tunnel at Minneapolis—Interstate 94	1,500
Nevada	Carlin Canyon Tunnel, near Elko on Interstate 80	1,400
New York City	Battery Park	2,300
New York City	First Avenue	1,377
New York City	F.D.R. Drive (42–48 Sts.)	1,600
New York City	F.D.R. Drive (81–89 Sts.)	2,400
New York City	Park Avenue	1,400
New York City	178–179 Sts., Cross-Town	2,414
North Carolina	Beaucatcher Tunnel, Asheville	1,100
North Carolina	Along Pigeon River, Haywood County	1,035
North Carolina	Along Pigeon River, Haywood County	1,122
North Carolina	Blue Ridge Parkway, near Waynesville	820
Ohio	Lytle Park Tunnel in Cincinnati—Interstate 71	850
Oregon	Arch Cape, U.S. 101	1,228
Oregon	Elk Creek Umpqua Highway, State Rt. 58	1,102
Oregon	U.S. Route 26, Vista Ridge, Portland	1,100
Oregon	Sunset Tunnel	779
Oregon	Tooth Park, Route 30	837
Pennsylvania	Squirrel Hill Tunnel, Pittsburgh	4,225
Pennsylvania	Armstrong Hill Tunnel, Pittsburgh	1,325
Pennsylvania	Liberty Tubes, Pittsburgh	6,336
Pennsylvania	Fort Pitt, Pittsburgh	3,550
Pa. Turnpike	Allegheny Tunnel	6,070
—	Tuscarora Tunnel	5,326
—	Kittatinny Tunnel	4,727
—	Blue Mountain	4,339
—	Evans Tunnel, NE Extensions	4,379
Rhode Island	Providence Reconverted Streetcar Tunnel	1,793
Tennessee	Bachman Tunnel, U.S. Route 41, Chattanooga	1,027
Tennessee	Wilcox Tunnel, Chattanooga	1,312
Utah	Copperfield Tunnel, Copperfield	6,989
Utah	Zion Nat'l Park Tunnel, Rt. 1, State Rt. 15	5,766
Virginia	Colonial Parkway, Project 1D3	1,200
Virginia	Route I-77, Big Walker Mountain	4,200
Washington	State Rt. 1-AW-3, Battery Street Tunnel, Seattle	2,140
Washington	State Rt. 2-639, U.S. 10—approach to Lake Washington, Seattle	1,466
Washington	Cayuse Pass Tunnel, Mt. Rainier	510
West Virginia	West Virginia Turnpike	2,669
West Virginia	I-70, Wheeling	1,485
West Virginia	East River Mountain Tunnel, near Bluefield—Interstate 77	5,700
Wyoming	I-80, Green River	1,137

VEHICULAR TUNNELS UNDER CONSTRUCTION

State or City	Name and Location	Length Portal to Portal (Feet)
D. C.	Center Leg Air Rights Tunnel, I-95	1,200
Pennsylvania	Society Hill, Philadelphia, I-95	1,800

* Longest underwater U.S. vehicular tunnel. † Longest U.S. land vehicular tunnel.

RAILROAD PASSENGER SERVICE

SOURCE: Interstate Commerce Commission

Year ended Dec. 31[1]	Average miles of road operated	Passengers carried (Thousands)	Total passenger-miles (Millions)	Revenues per passenger per mile* (Cents)	Revenues per passenger per mile† (Cents)	Passenger train-miles (Thousands)	Train-miles per train-hour	Percent passenger cars unserviceable
1960	94,117	325,872	21,258	3.01	3.03	209,367	40.7	8.7
1965	76,993	298,877	17,389	3.18	3.14	172,344	41.3	7.9
1968	59,259	295,618	15,201	3.19	3.13	149,820	41.7	8.2
1969	56,484	295,880	13,120	3.38	3.33	122,591	41.0	8.3
1970	49,533	283,970	12,169	3.60	3.63	107,106	41.0	7.8
1971[2]	40,261	272,401	8,833	4.27	4.64	69,127	37.1	9.6
1972[2]	29,398	261,099	8,560	4.76	5.31	60,993	38.3	15.3
1973[2]	28,286	254,506	9,298	4.76	5.19	60,768	37.6	17.4
1974[2]	31,344	274,298	10,337	5.22	5.85	64,368	38.2	17.1
1975[2]	31,576	269,394	9,735	5.50	6.31	65,766	39.2	17.9
1976[2]	34,474	271,581	10,307	5.72	6.30	66,487	31.2	16.9
1977[2]	31,903	275,322	10,295	5.91	6.64	66,237	33.0	20.4
1978[2]	30,369	281,069	10,223	5.95	6.62	64,190	32.3	19.6
1979[3]	28,200	301,300	11,306	5.65	6.50	61,679	34.3	N.A.

[1]Effective Jan. 1, 1965, the revenue qualification of a Class I railroad was increased from average annual operating revenues of $3 million or more to $5 million or more; effective Jan. 1, 1976, this was again raised to $10 million or more. [2]Includes National Railroad Passenger Corp. (AMTRAK). [3]Preliminary. *Includes commutation. †Excludes commutation.

INTERCITY BUS LINES

SOURCE: American Bus Association

Summary of Operations

	1960	1964	1968	1972	1978	1979[5]
Operating companies	1,150	1,100	1,050	1,000	1,100	1,150
Buses	20,974	20,500	21,000	21,400	20,200	20,500
Miles of highway served[1]	265,000	260,000	260,000	270,000	279,000	280,000
Employees[2]	45,000	46,800	47,300	49,100	43,700	45,000
Total bus miles (millions)	1,092	1,183	1,190	1,182	1,081	1,132
Fare-paying passengers (millions)	366	360	398	393	338	360
Fare-paying passenger-miles (millions)	19,300	23,300	24,500	25,600	25,400	27,200
Operating revenue, all serv ices ($ millions)	556.2	686.7	797.6	974.4	1,388.4	1,627.0
Operating expenses ($ millions)	494.8	594.9	708.7	882.1	1,334.2	1,539.1
Net operating revenue before income taxes ($ millions)	61.4	91.8	88.9	92.3	54.2	87.9
Operating ratio[4]	89.0	86.6	88.9	90.5	96.1	94.6
Taxes assigned to operations ($ millions)[3]	53.2	63.5	67.9	84.1	100.7	N/A

[1]Includes duplication between carriers. [2]Operating companies only. [3]Excludes income taxes. [4]Operating expenses divided by operating revenues. [5]Preliminary.

AMTRAK

On May 1, 1971, Amtrak was established as the National Railroad Passenger Corporation. Amtrak had several basic objectives: to reverse the downward trend in passenger ridership, to provide modern, efficient intercity rail passenger service and to develop fully the potential of modern intercity rail service.

The Corporation operates trains through contractual agreements with existing railroads outside of the Northeast. In 1976, Amtrak assumed full ownership and operating control of the Boston-Washington Northeast Corridor.

In Fiscal Year 1979, Amtrak operated an average of 250 trains daily, serving 524 stations, and carried 21.4 million passengers while grossing $382 million. During the fiscal year, the Corporation placed 51 new bi-level cars in service, built or rehabilitated 61 stations and continued its rebuilding program for hundreds of its older steam-equipped cars. It completed the year's Northeast Corridor rebuilding program on schedule. The program will result in New York to Washington trip times of two hours and 40 minutes.

CONRAIL

A private, for-profit corporation created by an Act of Congress, the Consolidated Rail Corporation (Conrail) began operations on April 1, 1976. It was conveyed most of the rail properties of the Central of New Jersey, Erie Lackawanna, Lehigh and Hudson River, Lehigh Valley, Penn Central, and Reading lines. Operating over a 17,000-mile system in 16 eastern and midwestern states, the District of Columbia and two provinces of Canada, Conrail is the largest railroad in the United States in traffic carried and freight revenues.

Conrail is primarily a freight railroad, operating more than 1,300 trains a day. In addition, Conrail operates certain rail commuter services under contract with local, regional or state authorities, and some intercity passenger trains under contract with Amtrak.

Conrail's purpose is to create a viable, private-sector rail freight system in the Northeast quadrant, providing efficient and essential rail service to customers.

LONGEST RAILWAY TUNNELS

SOURCE: *Railway Directory and Yearbook*

There are considerable discrepancies in figues given by various authorities on precise tunnel lengths.

Tunnel	Date of Opening	Length Miles	Length Yards	Operating Railway	Country
Seikan	U.C.	33	810	Japanese National	Japan
Dai-shimizu	U.C.	13	1,403	Japanese National	Japan
Simplon No. II	Oct. 16, 1922	12	559	Swiss Federal & Italian State	Switzerland-Italy
Simplon No. I	June 1, 1906	12	537	Swiss Federal & Italian State	Switzeralnd-Italy
New Kanmon	March 10, 1975	11	1,059	Japanese National	Japan
Appenine	Apr. 22, 1934	11	892	Italian State	Italy
Rokko	March 15, 1972	10	132	Japanese National	Japan
Gotthard	Jan. 1, 1882(a)	9	562	Swiss Federal	Switzerland
Lötschberg	July 15, 1913	9	140	Bern-Lötschberg-Simplon	Switzerland
Hokuriku	June 10, 1962	8	1,055	Japanese National	Japan
Mont Cenis (Fréjus)	Sept. 17, 1871	8	855	Italian State	France-Italy
New Shimizu	Oct. 1, 1967	8	651	Japanese National	Japan
Aki	March 10, 1975	8	141	Japanese National	Japan
Cascade	Jan. 12, 1929	7	1,397	Great Northern	United States
Kita-Kyushu	March 10, 1975	7	493	Japanese National	Japan
Kubiki	Oct. 1, 1969	7	70	Japanese National	Japan
Flathead	November 1970	6	5,275	Great Northern	United States
Arlberg	Sept. 20, 1884	6	650	Austrian Federal	Austria
Moffat	Feb. 27, 1928	6	373	Denver & Rio Grande Western	United States
Shimizu	Sept. 1, 1981	6	35	Japanese National	Japan
Kvineshei	Dec. 17, 1943(b)	5	1,112	Norwegian State	Norway
Bingo	March 10, 1975	5	915	Japanese National	Japan
Rimutaka	Nov. 3, 1955	5	821	New Zealand Government	New Zealand
Ricken	Oct. 1, 1910	5	608	Swiss Federal	Switzerland
Grenchenberg	Oct. 1, 1915	5	581	Swiss Federal(c)	Switzerland
Otira	Aug. 4, 1923	5	564	New Zealand Government	New Zealand
Tauern	July 7, 1909	5	551	Austrian Federal	Austria
Haegebostad	Dec. 17, 1943(b)	5	467	Norwegian State	Norway
Fukuoka	March 10, 1975	5	458	Japanese National	Japan
Ronco	Apr. 4, 1889	5	277	Italian State	Italy
Hauenstein (Lower)	Jan. 8, 1916	5	95	Swiss Federal	Switzerland
Connaught	Dec. 6, 1916	5	39	Canadian Pacific	Canada
Karawanken	Oct. 1, 1906	4	1,683	Austrian Federal	Austria-Yugoslavia
New Tanna	Oct. 1, 1964	4	1,663	Japanese National	Japan
Somport	July 18, 1928	4	1,572	French National	France-Spain
Tanna	Dec. 1, 1934	4	1,493	Japanese National	Japan
Ulrikken	Aug. 1, 1964	4	1,338	Norwegian State	Norway
Hoosac	Feb. 9, 1875	4	1,230	Boston & Maine	United States
Monte Orso	Oct. 28, 1927	4	1,230	Italian State	Italy
Lupacino	Sept. 24, 1958	4	1,178	Italian State	Italy
Vivola	Oct. 28, 1927	4	1,004	Italian State	Italy
Monte Adone	Apr. 22, 1934	4	760	Italian State	Italy
Jungfrau	Aug. 1, 1912	4	750	Jungfrau	Switzerland
Borgallo	Aug. 1, 1894	4	700	Italian State	Italy
Severn	Sept. 1, 1886	4	628	Western Region	Great Britain
Lusse (Vosges)	Aug. 9, 1937	4	474	French National	France
Marianopoli	Aug. 1, 1885	4	42	Italian State	Italy

(a) For goods traffic; passengers: June 1, 1882. (b) These were wartime openings under German Occupation. Full traffic began March 1, 1944. (c) The Gronchenberg tunnel is owned but not worked by the Bern-Lötschberg-Simplon Railway.

ESTIMATED AUTOMOBILE REGISTRATIONS: 1979 (in thousands)

SOURCE: U.S. Federal Highway Administration

State	Registrations	State	Registrations	State	Registrations	State	Registrations
Alabama	2,105	Illinois	6,080	Montana	563	Rhode Island	590
Alaska	168	Indiana	2,910	Nebraska	858	South Carolina	1,541
Arizona	1,261	Iowa	1,786	Nevada	465	South Dakota	369
Arkansas	999	Kansas	1,377	New Hampshire	583	Tennessee	2,401
California	12,343	Kentucky	1,834	New Jersey	4,284	Texas	7,720
Colorado	2,021	Louisiana	1,899	New Mexico	661	Utah	684
Connecticut	2,051	Maine	544	New York	7,335	Vermont	305
Delaware	322	Maryland	2,331	North Carolina	3,386	Virginia	2,996
Dist. of Col.	212	Massachusettts	3,295	North Dakota	360	Washington	2,254
Florida	5,939	Michigan	5,300	Ohio	6,441	West Virginia	863
Georgia	2,975	Minnesota	2,012	Oklahoma	1,715	Wisconsin	2,284
Hawaii	460	Mississippi	1,178	Oregon	1,486	Wyoming	255
Idaho	485	Missouri	2,406	Pennsylvania	5,793	**Total**	**120,485**

ESTIMATED LICENSED DRIVERS, BY SEX: 1978 (in thousands)

SOURCE: Federal Highway Administration

STATE	MALE DRIVERS	FEMALE DRIVERS	TOTAL DRIVERS	STATE	MALE DRIVERS	FEMALE DRIVERS	TOTAL DRIVERS
Alabama	1,150	1,010	2,160	Montana	323	257	580
Alaska	1294	92	221	Nebraska	555	506	1,061
Arizona	893	720	1,613	Nevada	282	245	527
Arkansas	732	635	1,367	New Hampshire	324	289	613
California	7,990	7,030	15,020	New Jersey	2,291	2,206	4,497
Colorado	1,043	954	1,997	New Mexico	412	391	803
Connecticut	1,020	1,041	2,061	New York	5,129	3,997	9,126
Delaware	208	195	403	North Carolina	1,887	1,712	3,599
Dist. of Col.	192	157	349	North Dakota	214	189	403
Florida	3,714	3,154	6,868	Ohio	4,942	3,236	8,178
Georgia	1,689	1,525	3,214	Oklahoma	959	915	1,874
Hawaii	298	236	534	Oregon	987	840	1,827
Idaho	312	275	587	Pennsylvania	3,940	3,131	7,071
Illinois	3,671	3,183	6,854	Rhode Island	305	276	581
Indiana	1,841	1,689	3,530	South Carolina	962	852	1,814
Iowa	1,072	949	2,021	South Dakota	248	222	470
Kansas	927	851	1,778	Tennessee	1,420	1,275	2,695
Kentucky	1,117	921	2,038	Texas	4,520	4,049	8,569
Louisiana	1,212	1,047	2,259	Utah	401	372	773
Maine	362	321	683	Vermont	173	155	328
Maryland	1,343	1,207	2,550	Virginia	1,659	1,600	3,25)
Masachusetts	1,893	1,833	3,726	Washington	1,321	1,164	2,485
Michigan	3,291	2,959	6,250	West Virginia	814	609	1,423
Minnesota	1,175	1,060	2,235	Wisconsin	1,533	1,366	2,899
Mississippi	881	707	1,588	Wyoming	173	146	319
Missouri	1,665	1,499	3,164	**Total**	**75,594**	**65,250**	**140,844**

WORLD MOTOR VEHICLE FATALITY RATES

(per 100,000 population)

SOURCE: *U.N. Demographic Yearbook* 1978, © United Nations

Nation	Rate
Kuwait (1977)	36.0
Venezuela (1977)	34.2
Austria (1976)	28.8
Australia (1977)	27.2
Italy (1972)	25.9
Belgium (1976)	25.1
France (1970)	23.5
Germany, West (1976)	23.5
Canada (1976)	22.5
UNITED STATES (1976)	21.9
Costa Rica (1977)	21.3
new Zealand (1976)	21.1
Switzerland (1977)	20.2
Czechoslovakia (1976)	19.5
Netherlands (1977)	18.6
Greece (1976)	17.9
Hungary (1977)	17.6
Iceland (1977)	17.6
Denmark (1976)	17.1
Germany, East (1976)	16.4
Mexico (1975)	16.4
Argentina (1977)	16.1
Israel (1977)	15.7
Spain (1975)	15.1
Sweden (1975)	15.1
Jordan (1976)	14.1
Bulgaria (1976)	12.6
England & Wales (1976)	12.3
Norway (1977)	11.6
Singapore (1977)	11.4
Japan (1977)	10.6

AUTO CASUALTY RATES

SOURCE: International Road Federation

	Vehicle per 1,000 pop.	Rate per 100-million vehicle-kilometers Injuries	Rate per 100-million vehicle-kilometers Deaths
Australia (1978)	402	87[2]	3.5[2]
Belgium (1978)	302	208[1]	2.9[1]
Canada (1977)	408	109[2]	2.9[2]
Denmark (1978)	295	69	3.0
Finland (1978)	234	51[1]	3.0[1]
France (1978)	332	130	4.7
Iceland (1977)	316	51	3.3
Italy (1978)	289	87[1]	3.9[1]
Japan (1978)	184	176[1]	2.7[1]
Netherlands (1978)	293	109[1]	4.4[1]
New Zealand (1978)	392	NA	NA
Norway (1978)	282	71[1]	2.6[1]
United Kingdom (1978)	258	130[1]	2.5[1]
United States (1978)	682	115[1]	1.9[1]
West Germany (1978)	354	163	4.7

[1] 1977. [2] 1976.

U.S. DEATHS AND DEATH RATES FROM MOTOR VEHICLE ACCIDENTS

SOURCE: National Center for Health Statistics

Year	Number	Rate per 100,000 population
1977	49,510	22.9
1976	47,038	21.9
1975	45,853	21.5
1974	46,402	22.0
1973	55,511	26.5
1972	56,278	27.0
1970	54,633	26.9

U.S. ROAD MILEAGE

	Atlanta	Baltimore	Birmingham	Boston	Buffalo	Chicago	Cincinnati	Cleveland	Dallas	Denver
Akron	672	331	702	653	207	366	230	33	1173	1385
Albuquerque	1396	1889	1266	2194	1767	1289	1378	1581	639	422
Atlanta		669	152	1068	877	695	461	686	805	1401
Baltimore	669		787	399	345	687	494	351	1458	1701
Birmingham	152	787		1185	902	636	476	716	653	1282
Boston	1068	399	1185		449	975	876	632	1819	1989
Buffalo	877	345	902	449		529	430	186	1373	1543
Chicago	695	687	656	975	529		295	343	936	1016
Cincinnati	461	494	476	876	430	295		244	943	1169
Cleveland	686	351	716	632	186	343	244		1187	1357
Columbus	549	408	579	769	323	359	107	137	1050	1233
Dallas	805	1458	653	1819	1373	936	943	1187		784
Denver	1401	1701	1282	1989	1543	1016	1169	1357	784	
Des Moines	894	1025	808	1311	865	338	571	679	604	679
Detroit	726	511	741	*699	*252	275	265	167	1188	1284
El Paso	1427	2034	1275	2391	1945	1434	1524	1759	622	654
Hartford	972	303	1090	102	380	903	752	562	1690	1883
Houston	814	1449	662	1916	1470	1085	1040	1284	242	1026
Indianapolis	508	580	480	941	495	187	108	309	882	1061
Jacksonville	314	793	426	1191	1067	1009	775	952	994	1708
Kansas City, Mo.	810	1099	706	1456	1010	499	590	824	499	604
Little Rock	505	1086	386	1494	1048	644	618	862	325	957
Los Angeles	2197	2695	2056	3052	2606	2095	2186	2420	1403	1134
Louisville	394	604	366	986	540	301	110	354	833	1120
Memphis	366	947	247	1355	909	544	479	723	464	1035
Mexico City	1800	2435	1648	2902	2456	2071	2026	2270	1149	1754
Miami	665	1144	765	1542	1418	1360	1126	1303	1309	2046
Milwaukee	784	776	745	1064	618	91	384	432	1015	1040
Minneapolis/St. Paul	1105	1097	1066	1385	939	412	705	753	956	841
Montgomery	169	838	92	1236	979	748	568	793	650	1374
Montreal	1230	562	1289	324	393	*848	820	576	1763	*1862
Nashville	256	725	205	1165	719	451	290	533	686	1158
New Orleans	493	1138	351	1536	1253	925	820	1063	498	1282
New York City	855	187	974	216	445	843	659	507	1607	1851
Oklahoma City	845	1321	726	1684	1308	797	844	1052	215	615
Omaha	1012	1163	911	1449	1003	476	691	817	656	540
Philadelphia	766	97	884	304	365	762	578	426	1526	1770
Phoenix	1810	2325	1658	2682	2236	1722	1816	2050	1005	818
Pittsburgh	697	230	742	598	217	461	284	125	1232	1482
Portland, Ore.	2654	2816	2552	3085	2639	2112	2405	2453	2043	1278
Providence	1033	364	1151	45	444	967	813	626	1751	1944
Reno	2408	2613	2288	2919	2482	1956	2173	2290	1677	1041
St. Louis	558	817	476	1178	802	291	338	546	645	856
Salt Lake City	1900	2118	1781	2405	1958	1431	1644	1772	1241	512
San Francisco	2523	2876	2393	3163	2716	2189	2402	2530	1806	1270
Seattle	2756	2748	2575	3036	2590	2063	2356	2404	2112	1347
Toledo	668	454	683	742	296	241	207	110	1154	1250
Topeka	873	1162	764	1519	1073	562	653	887	505	541
Tulsa	783	1219	664	1650	1204	693	740	948	271	693
Washington, D.C.	630	39	748	437	359	687	492	351	1372	1696

	Des Moines	Detroit	Houston	Indianapolis	Kansas City, Mo.	Los Angeles	Memphis	Milwaukee	Minneapolis	Montreal
Akron	707	190	1270	295	779	2368	709	455	776	597
Albuquerque	994	1538	829	1272	790	806	1030	1370	1247	*2111
Atlanta	894	726	814	508	810	2197	366	784	1105	1230
Baltimore	1025	511	1449	580	1099	2695	947	776	1097	562
Birmingham	808	741	662	480	706	2056	247	745	1066	1289
Boston	1311	*699	1916	941	1456	3052	1355	1064	1385	324
Buffalo	865	*252	1470	495	1010	2606	909	618	939	393
Chicago	338	275	1085	187	499	2095	544	91	412	*848
Cincinnati	571	265	1040	108	590	2186	479	384	705	820
Cleveland	679	167	1284	309	824	2420	723	432	753	576
Columbus	695	189	1147	172	656	2245	586	448	769	713
Dallas	704	1188	242	882	499	1403	464	1015	956	1763
Denver	679	1284	1026	1061	604	1134	1035	1040	841	*1862
Des Moines		606	946	483	213	1801	608	361	252	*1184
Detroit	606		1337	277	751	2347	713	364	685	*573
El Paso	1139	1686	755	1423	935	798	1086	1513	1339	*2280
Hartford	1232	731	1752	822	1306	2895	1226	992	1317	317
Houston	946	1337		997	741	1553	561	1174	1198	1860
Indianapolis	483	277	997		484	2080	436	276	597	885
Jacksonville	1208	996	911	822	1123	2397	673	1098	1419	1355
Kansas City, Mo.	213	751	741	484		1596	459	580	457	*1324
Little Rock	573	896	441	562	405	1701	139	723	825	1438
Los Angeles	1801	2347	1553	2080	1596		1831	2176	1940	*2920
Louisville	569	375	930	114	516	2107	369	390	711	930
Memphis	608	713	561	436	459	1831		624	840	1299
Mexico City	1852	2337	986	1983	1647	2017	1547	2164	2104	2846
Miami	1559	1347	1216	1173	1470	2712	1011	1449	1770	1705
Milwaukee	361	364	1174	276	580	2176	624		326	*937
Minneapolis/St. Paul	252	685	1198	597	457	1940	840	326		*1258
Montgomery	900	833	659	572	798	2053	339	837	1158	1369
Montreal	*1184	*573	1860	885	*1324	*2920	1299	*937	*1258	
Nashville	638	555	783	294	554	2058	222	540	861	1109
New Orleans	989	1085	359	805	821	1901	401	1013	1241	1640
New York City	1173	667	1636	729	1319	2915	1138	932	1253	388
Oklahoma City	560	1049	457	743	347	1357	479	876	813	1671
Omaha	139	744	898	583	205	1662	664	500	358	*1317
Philadelphia	1092	586	1546	648	1238	2721	1057	851	1172	467
Phoenix	1430	1977	1155	1710	1226	398	1466	1806	1630	*2550
Pittsburgh	804	285	1319	354	937	2533	758	550	871	611
Portland, Ore.	1819	2385	2233	2297	1846	970	2305	2026	1690	*2746
Providence	1296	795	1813	883	1367	2956	1287	1056	1381	342
Reno	1623	2218	1867	2065	1639	477	2041	1979	1773	2803
St. Louis	336	543	794	237	252	1848	294	370	546	*1116
Salt Lake City	1094	1700	1431	1536	1116	734	1534	1455	1239	*2273
San Francisco	1852	2458	1955	2294	1874	403	2157	2213	1997	*3031
Seattle	1773	2336	2302	2248	1872	1145	2331	1977	1641	*2697
Toledo	572	58	1247	221	717	2313	686	330	651	*631
Topeka	276	814	745	547	63	1537	522	643	520	*1387
Tulsa	471	945	513	641	258	1461	417	772	715	*1518
Washington, D.C.	1018	511	1410	564	1048	2644	908	776	1097	600

	Nashville	New Orleans	New York City	Philadelphia	Phoenix	Pittsburgh	St. Louis	Salt Lake City	San Francisco	Seattle	Washington, D.C.
Akron	519	1049	487	406	2003	105	532	1800	2541	2427	331
Albuquerque	1289	1137	2001	1918	454	1626	1040	611	1127	1482	1838
Atlanta	256	493	855	766	1810	697	558	1900	2523	2756	630
Baltimore	725	1138	187	97	2325	230	817	2118	2876	2748	39
Birmingham	205	351	974	884	1658	742	476	1781	2393	2575	748
Boston	1165	1536	216	304	2682	598	1178	2405	3163	3036	437
Buffalo	719	1253	445	365	2236	217	802	1958	2716	2590	359
Chicago	451	929	843	762	1722	461	291	1431	2189	2063	687
Cincinnati	290	820	659	578	1816	284	338	1644	2402	2356	492
Cleveland	533	1063	507	426	2050	125	546	1772	2530	2404	351
Columbus	396	926	557	476	1882	182	409	1701	2459	2420	392
Dallas	686	498	1607	1526	1005	1232	645	1241	1806	2112	1372
Denver	1158	1282	1851	1770	818	1482	856	512	1270	1347	1696
Des Moines	638	989	1173	1092	1430	804	336	1094	1852	1773	1018
Detroit	555	1085	667	586	1977	285	543	1700	2458	2336	511
El Paso	1308	1114	2254	2173	400	1872	1180	869	1200	1740	1983
Hartford	1027	1445	121	207	2530	477	1059	2326	3076	2955	342
Houston	783	359	1636	1546	1153	1319	794	1431	1955	2302	1410
Indianapolis	294	805	729	648	1710	354	237	1536	2294	2245	564
Jacksonville	570	572	980	890	1999	865	872	2207	2799	3070	754
Kansas City, Mo.	554	821	1319	1238	1226	937	252	1116	1874	1872	1048
Little Rock	361	416	1282	1201	1330	897	353	1456	2027	2277	1047
Los Angeles	2058	1901	2915	2721	398	2533	1848	734	403	1145	2644
Louisville	180	710	769	688	1757	394	264	1632	2390	2362	596
Memphis	222	401	1138	1057	1466	758	294	1534	2157	2331	908
Mexico City	1769	1345	2622	2532	1625	2305	1794	2100	2419	2948	2396
Miami	921	875	1330	1241	2314	1216	1223	2545	3075	3421	1105
Milwaukee	540	1013	932	851	1806	550	370	1455	2213	1977	776
Minneapolis/St. Paul	861	1241	1253	1172	1630	871	546	1239	1997	1641	1097
Montgomery	297	324	1024	935	1655	819	572	1873	2456	2667	799
Montreal	1109	1640	388	467	*2550	611	*1116	*2273	*3031	*2697	600
Nashville		530	949	868	1725	559	302	1670	2410	2512	686
New Orleans	530		1325	1235	1503	1093	695	1739	2303	2610	1099
New York City	949	1325		92	2459	386	966	2267	3025	2904	225
Oklahoma City	738	678	1472	1391	987	1097	506	1108	1678	1962	1307
Omaha	756	1026	1312	1230	1335	942	454	955	1713	1667	1156
Philadelphia	868	1235	92		2464	305	885	2186	2944	2823	136
Phoenix	1725	1503	2459	2464		2163	1478	653	800	1541	2274
Pittsburgh	559	1093	386	305	2163		591	1890	2648	2522	230
Portland, Ore.	2398	2541	2953	2872	1366	2571	2096	802	652	175	2797
Providence	1088	1506	182	268	2591	538	1120	2390	3140	3019	403
Reno	2192	2175	2765	2685	736	2394	1890	530	221	742	2618
St. Louis	302	695	966	885	1478	591		1368	2126	2109	801
Salt Lake City	1670	1739	2267	2186	653	1890	1368		759	871	2111
San Francisco	2410	2303	3025	2944	800	2648	2126	759		827	2869
Seattle	2512	2610	2904	2823	1541	2522	2109	871	827		2748
Toledo	497	1027	610	529	1943	228	509	1670	2428	2302	454
Topeka	617	884	1382	1301	1171	1000	315	1053	1811	1831	1111
Tulsa	634	689	1370	1289	1091	995	404	1191	1776	2038	1205
Washington, D.C.	686	1099	225	136	2274	230	801	2111	2869	2748	

* via Canadian routes.

U.S. AIR DISTANCES

(See also, AIR DISTANCES BETWEEN MAJOR WORLD CITIES, pp. 234–235)

	Atlanta	Birmingham	Boston	Buffalo	Charleston, S.C.	Chicago	Cincinnati	Cleveland	Dallas	Denver	Des Moines	Detroit	Houston	Indianapolis	Jacksonville	Kansas City, Mo.	Los Angeles	Louisville	Miami	Minneapolis	Nashville	New Orleans	New York City	Omaha	Philadelphia	Phoenix	Pittsburgh	Portland, Ore.	St. Louis	Salt Lake City	San Francisco	Seattle	Tulsa	Washington, D.C.
Albuquerque	1272	1138	1972	1580	1539	1129	1251	1421	588	334	837	1364	754	1169	1488	720	664	1178	1698	983	1119	1029	1815	721	1753	330	1499	1107	942	484	896	1184	604	1653
Amarillo	999	866	1722	1338	1266	894	992	1173	334	358	626	1124	533	915	1219	481	937	915	1441	812	848	776	1560	526	1494	598	1244	1304	685	668	1157	1359	335	1391
Atlanta		140	937	697	267	587	369	554	721	1212	739	596	701	426	285	676	1936	319	604	907	214	424	748	817	666	1592	521	2172	467	1583	2139	2182	678	543
Billings	1519	1425	1861	1473	1761	1073	1304	1369	1092	453	798	1283	1315	1204	1796	846	959	1275	2085	742	1309	1479	1760	703	1727	872	1479	686	1057	387	904	668	930	1669
Birmingham	140		1052	776	402	578	406	618	581	1095	670	641	567	433	374	579	1802	331	665	862	182	312	864	732	783	1456	608	2066	400	1466	2013	2082	552	661
Boston	937	1052		400	820	851	740	551	1551	1769	1159	613	1605	807	1017	1251	2596	826	1255	1123	943	1359	188	1282	271	2300	483	2540	1038	2099	2699	2493	1398	393
Buffalo	697	776	400		699	454	393	173	1198	1370	760	216	1286	435	879	861	2198	483	1181	731	627	1086	292	883	279	1906	178	2156	662	1699	2300	2117	1023	292
Burlington, Vt.	951	1049	182	304	884	749	690	476	1501	1654	1049	516	1580	739	1079	1161	2485	780	1347	985	916	1361	260	1171	328	2202	445	2385	704	1845	2405	2428	945	453
Charleston, S.C.	267	402	820	699		757	506	609	981	1474	967	681	936	594	197	928	2203	500	482	1104	455	630	641	1058	562	1857	528	2425	704	1845	2405	2428	945	453
Charlotte	227	361	721	538	177	587	335	435	930	1358	819	504	927	428	341	803	2119	343	652	939	340	649	533	918	451	1783	362	2290	[illegible]	[illegible]	[illegible]	[illegible]	[illegible]	[illegible]
Cheyenne	1229	1119	1735	1335	1486	891	1082	1199	726	96	583	1125	947	986	1493	560	882	1033	1763	642	1032	1131	1604	463	1556	663	1298	947	795	371	967	973	588	1477
Chicago	587	578	851	454	757		252	308	803	920	309	238	940	165	863	414	1745	269	1188	355	397	833	713	432	666	1453	410	1758	262	1260	1858	1737	598	597
Cincinnati	369	406	740	393	506	252		222	814	1094	510	235	892	100	626	541	1897	90	952	605	238	706	570	622	503	1581	257	1985	309	1453	2043	1972	661	404
Cleveland	554	618	551	173	609	308	222		1025	1227	617	90	1114	263	770	700	2049	311	1087	630	459	924	405	739	360	1749	115	2055	492	1568	2166	2026	853	306
Dallas	721	581	1551	1198	981	803	814	1025		663	632	999	225	763	908	451	1240	726	1111	862	617	443	1374	586	1299	887	1070	1633	547	999	1483	1681	236	1185
Denver	1212	1095	1769	1370	1474	920	1094	1227	663		610	1156	879	1000	1467	558	831	1038	1726	700	1023	1082	1631	488	1579	586	1320	982	796	371	949	1021	550	1494
Des Moines	739	670	1159	760	967	309	510	617	632	610		546	821	411	1023	180	1438	476	1333	235	525	827	1022	123	973	1155	715	1475	273	953	1550	1467	396	896
Detroit	596	641	613	216	681	238	235	90	999	1156	546		1105	240	831	645	1983	316	1152	543	470	939	482	669	443	1690	205	1969	455	1492	2091	1938	813	396
El Paso	1291	1152	2072	1692	1552	1252	1335	1525	572	557	983	1479	676	1264	1473	839	701	1254	1643	1157	1169	983	1905	878	1836	346	1590	1286	1034	689	995	1376	674	1728
Fargo	1114	1060	1300	919	1317	569	820	835	972	642	397	745	1183	725	1399	549	1427	818	1716	214	902	1222	1210	390	1184	1225	949	1239	679	1200	1645	1891	442	1220
Houston	701	567	1605	1286	936	940	892	1114	225	879	821	1105		865	821	644	1374	803	968	1056	665	318	1420	794	1341	1017	1137	1836	679	1200	1645	1891	442	1220
Indianapolis	426	433	807	435	594	165	100	263	763	1000	411	240	865		699	453	1809	107	1024	511	251	712	646	525	585	1499	330	1885	231	1356	1949	1872	591	494
Jacksonville	285	374	1017	879	197	863	626	770	908	1467	1023	831	821	699		950	2147	594	326	1191	499	504	838	1098	758	1794	703	2439	751	1837	2374	2455	921	647
Kansas City, Mo.	676	579	1251	861	928	414	541	700	451	558	180	645	644	453	950		1356	480	1241	413	473	680	1097	166	1038	1049	781	1497	238	925	1506	1506	216	945
Knoxville	155	235	818	548	316	454	219	400	767	1178	651	442	790	290	410	624	1941	188	736	792	161	547	632	745	492	1007	1137	779	291	1148	1688	1785	231	892
Little Rock	456	325	1259	913	723	552	524	740	293	780	478	723	388	483	690	325	1480	435	949	708	325	355	1081	492	1007	1137	779	1759	347	[illegible]	[illegible]	[illegible]	[illegible]	[illegible]
Los Angeles	1936	1802	2596	2198	2203	1745	1897	2049	1240	831	1438	1983	1374	1809	2147	1356		1829	2339	1524	1780	1673	2451	1315	2394	357	2136	825	1589	579	347	959	1266	2300
Louisville	319	331	826	483	500	269	90	311	726	1038	476	316	803	107	594	480	1829		919	605	154	623	652	580	582	1508	344	1950	242	1402	1986	1943	582	476
Memphis	337	217	1137	803	604	482	410	630	420	879	485	623	484	384	590	369	1603	320	872	699	197	358	957	529	881	1263	660	1849	240	1250	1802	1867	341	765
Miami	604	665	1255	1181	482	1188	952	1087	1111	1726	1333	1152	968	1024	326	1241	2339	919		1511	815	669	1092	1397	1019	1982	1010	2708	1061	2089	2594	2734	1176	923
Minneapolis	907	862	1123	731	1104	355	605	630	862	700	235	543	1056	511	1191	413	1524	605	1511		697	1051	1018	290	985	1280	743	1427	466	987	1584	1395	626	934
Nashville	214	182	943	627	455	397	238	459	617	1023	525	470	665	251	499	473	1780	154	815	697		469	761	607	685	1446	472	1969	254	1393	1963	1975	515	569
New Orleans	424	312	1359	1086	630	833	706	924	443	1082	827	939	318	712	504	680	1673	623	669	1051	469		1171	847	1089	1316	919	2063	598	1434	1926	2101	548	966
New York City	748	864	188	292	641	713	570	405	1374	1631	1022	482	1420	646	838	1097	2451	652	1092	1018	761	1171		1094	83	2145	317	2445	875	1972	2571	2408	1231	205
Omaha	817	732	1282	883	1058	432	622	739	586	488	123	669	794	525	1098	166	1315	580	1397	290	607	847	1094		1094	1036	836	1371	354	833	1429	1369	352	1014
Philadelphia	666	783	271	279	562	666	503	360	1299	1579	973	443	1341	585	758	1038	2394	582	1019	985	685	1089	83	1094		2083	259	2412	811	1925	2523	2380	1163	123
Phoenix	1592	1456	2300	1906	1857	1453	1581	1749	887	586	1155	1690	1017	1499	1794	1049	357	1508	1982	1280	1446	1316	2145	1036	2083		1828	1005	1272	504	653	1114	932	1983
Pittsburgh	521	608	483	178	528	410	257	115	1070	1320	715	205	1137	330	703	781	2136	344	1010	743	472	919	317	836	259	1828		2165	559	1668	2264	2138	917	192
Portland, Ore.	2172	2066	2540	2156	2425	1758	1985	2055	1633	982	1475	1969	1836	1885	2439	1497	825	1950	2708	1427	1969	2063	2445	1371	2412	1005	2165		1723	636	534	145	1531	2354
Raleigh	356	491	609	490	220	642	396	428	1057	1463	902	510	1056	495	414	905	2237	429	695	996	457	776	426	1008	345	1903	330	2377	667	1829	2410	2367	972	233
St. Louis	467	400	1038	662	704	262	309	492	547	796	273	455	679	231	751	238	1589	242	1061	466	254	598	875	354	811	1272	559	1723		1162	1744	1724	361	712
Salt Lake City	1583	1466	2099	1699	1845	1260	1453	1568	999	371	953	1492	1200	1356	1837	925	579	1402	2089	987	1393	1434	1972	833	1925	504	1668	636	1162		600	701	917	1848
San Antonio	882	744	1766	1430	1122	1051	1039	1256	252	802	882	1238	189	999	1011	702	1204	949	1148	1110	823	507	1584	828	1507	849	1291	1720	792	1087	1490	1787	486	1388
San Francisco	2139	2013	2699	2300	2405	1858	2043	2166	1483	949	1550	2091	1645	1949	2374	1506	347	1986	2594	1584	1963	1926	2571	1429	2523	653	2264	534	1744	600		678	1461	2442
Seattle	2182	2082	2493	2117	2428	1737	1972	2026	1681	1021	1467	1938	1891	1872	2455	1506	959	1943	2734	1395	1975	2101	2408	1369	2380	1114	2138	145	1724	701	678		1560	2329
Spokane	1961	1865	2266	1888	2204	1508	1744	1796	1489	826	1240	1709	1704	1644	2237	1287	940	1717	2520	1166	1752	1898	2179	1146	2151	1019	1908	290	1500	550	727	229	1353	2100
Syracuse	781	875	264	138	738	592	514	303	1326	1508	898	354	1403	567	928	998	2336	603	1212	861	739	1187	194	1021	220	2044	268	2281	796	1835	2435	2238	1157	290
Tulsa	678	552	1398	1023	945	598	661	853	236	550	396	813	442	591	921	216	1266	582	1176	626	515	548	1231	352	1163	932	917	1531	361	917	1461	1560		1058
Washington, D.C.	543	661	393	292	453	597	404	306	1185	1494	896	396	1220	494	647	945	2300	476	923	934	569	966	205	1014	123	1983	192	2354	712	1848	2442	2329	1058	
Wichita	776	658	1424	1036	1039	591	702	873	340	437	334	821	559	620	1031	177	1197	633	1297	546	594	677	1266	257	1204	879	950	1411	394	808	1369	1437	130	1106

U.S. RAILROAD DISTANCES

	Albuquerque	Atlanta	Baltimore	Birmingham	Boston	Buffalo	Chicago	Cincinnati	Cleveland	Dallas	Denver	Des Moines	Detroit	El Paso	Houston	Indianapolis	Jacksonville	Kansas City, Mo.	Los Angeles	Memphis	Miami	Mobile	New Orleans	New York City	Oklahoma City	Philadelphia	Pittsburgh	Portland, Ore.	St. Louis	St. Paul	Salt Lake City	San Francisco	Seattle	Washington, D.C.
Albuquerque		1554	2102	1388	2356	1862	1338	1528	1678	723	477	1108	1610	253	925	1430	1819	887	889	1135	2185	1369	1229	2216	648	2124	1776	1849	1190	1363	985	1209	2031	2047
Amarillo	374	1181	1728	1014	2028	1534	1010	1154	1339	370	465	780	1282	444	634	1056	1466	559	1216	761	1832	1016	876	1866	274	1775	1427	1837	816	1039	973	1537	2019	1690
Altanta	1554		676	167	1091	934	734	490	750	825	1526	952	748	1471	856	585	350	890	2285	420	716	353	493	862	907	771	806	2798	612	1130	2051	2718	2824	638
Baltimore	2102	676		799	416	395	796	582	459	1448	1822	1154	624	2095	1517	691	794	1198	2908	967	1160	1029	1154	187	1454	95	328	3030	920	1193	2310	3059	2937	38
Billings	1133	1921	2085	1788	2296	1802	1278	1559	1618	1491	656	1041	1550	1386	1755	1462	2226	1051	1452	1535	2592	1958	1924	2186	1394	2094	1747	961	1310	882	669	1418	903	2043
Birmingham	1388	167	799		1215	925	651	481	741	658	1373	819	739	1304	718	503	438	737	2118	253	804	266	355	986	740	894	797	2665	479	1047	1906	2551	2691	761
Boston	2356	1091	416	1215		494	1018	938	678	1864	2044	1376	746	2414	1933	962	1210	1469	3244	1382	1576	1444	1569	229	1743	321	668	3217	1202	1414	2532	3281	3159	454
Buffalo	1862	934	395	925	494		524	444	184	1418	1550	882	252	1920	1554	468	1190	975	2750	938	1556	1191	1280	396	1249	415	260	2723	708	920	2038	2787	2665	434
Butte	1369	2157	2305	2024	2526	2032	1514	1795	1854	1727	892	1377	1780	1622	1991	1692	2462	1287	1216	1771	2828	2194	2160	2416	1631	2330	1983	725	1546	1112	433	1182	667	2273
Cheyenne	583	1532	1791	1399	2013	1519	995	1259	1335	941	106	652	1267	836	1205	1161	1877	702	1302	1186	2243	1569	1447	1903	845	1811	1463	1266	921	855	519	1268	1448	1759
Chicago	1338	734	796	651	1018	524		281	340	968	1026	358	272	1396	1205	184	1083	451	2227	527	1449	917	921	908	794	816	468	2199	284	396	1514	2263	2141	764
Cincinnati	1528	490	582	481	938	444	281		260	975	1252	639	258	1561	1110	109	840	616	2370	494	1206	747	836	755	880	664	316	2470	338	677	1778	2527	2422	544
Cleveland	1678	750	459	741	678	184	340	260		1234	1366	698	164	1736	1370	283	1100	791	2555	754	1466	1007	1096	571	1065	479	131	2539	523	736	1854	2603	2481	427
Columbia, S.C.	1801	254	515	420	930	910	867	586	846	1078	1747	1173	844	1724	1110	681	280	1111	2538	673	646	607	747	701	1160	610	772	3019	833	1263	2272	2971	3045	476
Dallas	723	825	1448	658	1864	1418	968	975	1234		835	738	1200	646	264	951	1096	517	1460	481	1462	646	506	1635	236	1543	1291	2227	711	997	1343	1930	2394	1410
Denver	477	1526	1822	1373	2044	1550	1026	1252	1366	835		683	1298	730	1099	1154	1811	636	1353	1120	2177	1481	1341	1934	739	1842	1494	1372	914	886	570	1374	1554	1790
Des Moines	1108	952	1154	819	1376	882	358	639	698	738	683		630	1166	1002	542	1301	221	1954	645	1667	988	1039	1266	565	1174	826	1918	340	259	1171	1920	1944	1122
Detroit	1610	748	624	739	746	252	272	258	164	1200	1298	630		1668	1368	303	1098	723	2499	752	1464	1005	1094	648	1031	644	296	2505	489	668	1786	2535	2413	592
Duluth	1515	1202	1265	1119	1486	992	468	749	808	1149	1038	411	740	1577	1413	652	1551	632	2309	1031	1917	1374	1425	1376	976	1285	937	1820	726	152	1526	2275	1762	1233
El Paso	253	1471	2095	1304	2414	1920	1396	1561	1736	646	730	1166	1668		827	1500	1764	945	814	1128	2130	1292	1152	2310	718	2190	1834	2002	1223	1425	1238	1284	2184	2056
Fargo	1605	1372	1435	1289	1656	1162	638	919	978	1239	1128	501	910	1667	1503	822	1721	722	2092	1121	2087	1464	1515	1546	1066	1454	1107	1601	816	242	1309	2058	1503	1403
Houston	925	856	1517	718	1933	1554	1205	1110	1370	264	1099	1002	1368	827		1107	975	781	1641	616	1341	503	363	1703	500	1612	1426	2491	921	1261	1607	2111	2656	1478
Indianapolis	1430	585	691	503	962	468	184	109	283	951	1154	542	303	1500	1107		935	518	2272	491	1301	769	858	811	782	719	371	2427	241	580	1680	2429	2325	653
Jacksonville	1819	350	794	438	1210	1190	1083	840	1100	1096	1811	1301	1098	1764	975	935		1175	2578	691	366	472	612	981	1178	890	1052	3148	917	1479	2344	2989	3129	756
Kansas City, Mo.	887	890	1198	737	1469	975	451	616	791	517	636	221	723	945	781	518	1175		1776	484	1541	926	873	1329	343	1237	889	1968	278	480	1206	1970	1954	1160
Knoxville	1556	197	545	254	961	737	574	296	553	903	1454	880	551	1549	972	388	547	818	2363	422	913	520	609	732	909	640	609	2726	540	970	2001	2720	2715	507
Los Angeles	889	2285	2908	2118	3244	2750	2227	2370	2555	1460	1353	1954	2499	814	1641	2272	2578	1776		1942	2944	2106	1966	3082	1490	2991	2643	1188	2032	2157	783	470	1370	2906
Louisville	1463	474	696	392	1052	558	295	114	374	861	1188	614	372	1508	996	111	824	552	2306	380	1190	658	747	869	867	778	430	2460	274	691	1713	2462	2486	658
Memphis	1135	420	967	253	1382	938	527	494	754	481	1120	645	752	1128	616	491	691	484	1942		1057	394	394	1153	487	1062	810	2496	305	879	1653	2298	2438	929
Miami	2185	716	1160	804	1576	1556	1449	1206	1466	1462	2177	1667	1464	2130	1341	1301	366	1541	2944	1057		838	978	1347	1544	1256	1418	3514	1283	1845	2710	3355	3495	1122
Mobile	1369	353	1029	266	1444	1191	917	747	1007	646	1481	988	1005	1292	503	769	472	926	2106	394	838		140	1215	871	1124	1063	2872	648	1222	1988	2553	2861	991
Nashville	1374	288	761	205	1177	745	446	301	561	720	1238	664	559	1367	855	298	637	602	2181	239	1003	471	560	948	726	856	617	2511	324	842	1892	2537	2537	723
New Orleans	1229	493	1154	355	1569	1280	921	836	1096	506	1341	1039	1094	1152	363	858	612	873	1966	394	978	140		1355	742	1264	1152	2732	699	1273	1848	2436	2900	1115
New York City	2216	862	187	986	229	396	908	755	571	1635	1934	1266	648	2310	1703	811	981	1329	3082	1153	1347	1215	1355		1592	91	439	3107	1051	1304	2422	3171	3049	225
Oklahoma City	648	907	1454	740	1743	1249	794	880	1065	236	739	565	1031	718	500	782	1178	343	1490	487	1544	871	742	1592		1501	1153	2131	542	824	1247	1811	2293	1424
Omaha	1015	1025	1284	892	1506	1012	488	752	828	712	538	145	760	1140	976	654	1330	195	1809	679	1696	1062	1068	1396	538	1304	956	1773	414	348	1026	1775	1799	1252
Philadelphia	2124	771	95	894	321	415	816	664	479	1543	1842	1174	644	2190	1612	719	890	1237	2991	1062	1256	1124	1264	91	1501		348	3015	959	1212	2330	3079	2957	133
Pittsburgh	1776	806	328	797	668	260	468	316	131	1291	1494	826	296	1834	1426	371	1052	889	2643	810	1418	1063	1152	439	1153	348		2668	611	865	1982	2731	2610	296
Portland, Ore.	1849	2798	3030	2665	3217	2723	2199	2470	2539	2227	1372	1918	2505	2002	2491	2427	3148	1968	1188	2496	3514	2872	2732	3107	2131	3015	2668		2187	1803	884	718	182	3025
Richmond	2038	579	155	735	570	550	862	581	544	1385	1833	1220	708	2031	1435	690	640	1197	2845	903	1006	932	1072	341	1390	250	413	3095	919	1258	2359	3108	3003	117
St. Louis	1190	612	920	479	1202	708	284	338	523	711	914	340	489	1223	921	240	917	278	2032	305	1283	648	699	1051	542	959	611	2187		574	1440	2189	2213	882
St. Paul	1363	1130	1193	1047	1414	920	396	677	736	997	886	259	668	1425	1261	580	1479	480	2157	879	1845	1222	1273	1304	824	1212	865	1803	574		1374	2123	1745	1161
Salt Lake City	985	2051	2310	1906	2532	2038	1514	1778	1854	1343	570	1171	1786	1238	1607	1680	2344	1206	783	1653	2710	1988	1848	2422	1247	2330	1982	884	1440	1374		821	1066	2278
San Antonio	870	1066	1720	928	2125	1631	1208	1247	1447	271	1083	1009	1413	617	210	1164	1185	788	1431	753	1551	713	573	1906	507	1815	1535	2498	924	1268	1614	1901	2666	1681
San Francisco	1209	2718	3059	2551	3281	2787	2263	2527	2603	1930	1374	1920	2535	1284	2111	2429	2989	1970	470	2298	3355	2553	2436	3171	1811	3079	2731	718	2189	2123	821		900	3028
Seattle	2031	2824	2937	2691	3159	2665	2141	2422	2481	2394	1554	1944	2413	2184	2656	2325	3129	1954	1370	2438	3495	2861	2900	3049	2293	2957	2610	182	2213	1745	1066	900		2906
Spokane	1726	2514	2628	2381	2849	2355	1831	2112	2171	2084	1249	1634	2103	1979	2348	2015	2819	1644	1556	2128	3185	2551	2590	2739	1987	2647	2300	368	1903	1435	790	1086	310	2596
Tucson	565	1783	2407	1616	2726	2232	1708	1873	2048	958	1042	1478	1980	312	1139	1775	2076	1257	502	1440	2442	1604	1464	2586	1030	2494	2146	1690	1572	1737	1285	972	1872	2368
Washington, D.C.	2047	638	38	761	454	434	764	544	427	1410	1790	1122	592	2056	1478	653	756	1160	2906	929	1122	991	1115	225	1424	133	296	3025	882	1161	2278	3028	2906	

TOLL-FREE TELEPHONE NUMBERS

The following lists contain the toll-free telephone numbers for airlines, hotels, motels, and car rental companies. Airline companies often have local telephone numbers for reservations and information. If no local number is listed, dial 800 followed by the number given in the first column. In Atlanta and Boston, precede all 800 numbers with "1." EN (Enterprise) numbers require operator assistance.

AIRLINES	800 Toll-Free Number	ATLANTA	CHICAGO	LOS ANGELES	NEW YORK	WASHINGTON, D.C.
Aer Lingus Irish	223-6292			800 223-6537	212 557-1110	800 223-6270
Aerocondor	327-0743		312 341-9570		212 697-9303	
Aeroflot					212 661-4050	202 296-8060
Aerolineas Argentinas	223-5450		312 922-0707	213 683-1633	212 757-6400	202 296-2863
Aeromexico	223-9780	404 321-4534		213 380-6030	212 391-2900	
Aero Perú			800 327-4363	800 327-4363	800 327-4363	202 457-0857
Air Canada		800 621-6464	312 527-3900	213 776-7000	212 421-8000	202 638-2132
Air Florida		800 327-2971	800 327-2971		800 327-2971	800 327-2971
Air France		800 221-2110	312 782-6181	213 625-7171	212 247-0100	202 337-8711
Air India	223-7776			800 223-7776	212 751-6200	
Air Jamaica		800 523-5585	312 527-3923	800 523-5618	212 421-9750	
Air New Zealand	421-0066			213 776-8790		
Air Panama Internacional	327-2417			213-488-1065		
Alaska Airlines	426-0333					
Alitalia		800 223-9770	312 427-4720	800 223-5730	212 582-8900	202 393-2829
American		404 521-2655	312 372-8000	213 937-6811	212 661-4242	202 393-2345
Avianca		800 327-9899	312 346-8252	800 221-2200	212 586-6040	
Aviateca International			312 236-6941			
Bahamasair	327-8080					
Braniff International		404 577-7700	312 372-8900	213 680-2202	212 687-8200	202 296-2400
British Airways	327-9722		312 332-7744	800 252-0045	800 421-0611	800 221-7150
B.W.I.A. International	327-7401				212 581-3200	800 221-6874
CP Air	426-7000	404 767-1214		213 625-0131		
Capitol International		404 261-5477	312 263-0244	213 986-8445	212 883-0740	202 544-1300
Cathay Pacific			312 782-8191	213 627-3253	212 541-9750	202 833-9393
China Airlines		0-WX-6935	312 263-0244	213 624-6160	212 581-6500	202 833-1760
Commuter Airlines			800 252-1490	800 252-1490	800 252-1490	800 847-1462
Continental	525-0280		312 686-6500	213 772-6000	212 974-0028	202 628-6666
Czechoslovak Air Lines			312 372-1551	800 621-1140	212 682-5833	202 577-4300
Delta Air Lines		404 765-5000	312 346-5300	213 386-5510	212 239-0700	202 920-5500
Eastern Air Lines		404 435-1111	312 467-2900	213 380-2070	212 986-5000	202 393-4000
Ecuatoriana Airlines	327-1337					
El Al Israel Airlines	223-6280			800 223-6700	212 486-2600	
Ethiopian Airlines			312 663-4100	213 462-7291	212 867-0095	202 659-2915
Finnair	223-5308			800 223-5700	212 889-7070	800 223-5260
Frontier Airlines		404 523-5487	312 236-3790			
Gulf Air			312 861-0117	213 879-3645	212 986-4500	202 296-2910
Hawaiian Airlines	367-5320	404 237-2885	312 236-5196		212 355-4843	
Iberia Air Lines of Spain	221-9640			800 221-9741	212 793-3300	
Icelandair	223-5390			800 223-5500	212 757-8585	800 223-5190
Japan Air Lines	223-5405		312 263-1384	213 620-9580	212 759-9100	
KLM Royal Dutch Airlines	223-5322		312 346-3635	213 776-6300	212 759-3600	
Korean Airlines		404 522-7461	312 558-9300	800 252-0128	212 244-8330	202 785-3644
Kuwait Airlines			312 263-3858	213 627-1485	212 581-9412	202 296-4644
Lacsa				213 385-2272	212 245-6370	
Laker Skytrain			800 221-0374	213 646-9600	212 459-6092	800 221-0374
Lan-Chile Airlines	327-3614			213 627-4293		
Lot Polish Airlines			312 236-3388		212 869-1074	
Lufthansa German Airlines	645-3880				212 357-8400	
Mexicana Airlines	421-2150	404 237-8661	800 421-8301	213 646-9500		
National Airlines		800 327-2330		213 381-5777	212 697-9000	202 549-7633
Northwest Airlines	328-7747	404 577-3271	312 346-4900	213 380-1511	212 564-2300	
Olympic Airways	424-9231		312 329-0200	213 624-6441	212 838-3600	202 659-2511
Ozark Air Lines		404 688 9565	312 726-4680		212 586-3612	202 347-4744

AIRLINES	800 Toll-Free Number	ATLANTA	CHICAGO	LOS ANGELES	NEW YORK	WASHINGTON, D.C.
Pakistan International			312 263-3082	213 626-0245	212 949-0477	202 296-1755
Pan Am		404 688-9830	312 236-4494	213 776-0710 800 652-1555	212 973-4000	202 833-1000
Philippine Airlines	227-4600					
Piedmont Airlines		404 681-3100	312 263-3656		212 489-1460	202 347-1800
Qantas Airways	227-4500			800 622-0850		
Republic Airlines		404 762-5561	312 346-9860		212 581-8851	202 347-0448
Sabena Belgian World Airlines	645-3790			800 645-1382	212 961-6200	800 645-3933
SAS Scandinavian Airlines	221-2350			213 655-8600	212 657-7700	
Singapore Airlines	227-3314	404 577-5644		800 792-2962	800 227-3314	202 466-3747
South African Airways		0-WX-6477	312 467-1186	800 223-9870	212 826-1245	
Swissair	221-4750				212 995-8400	800 221-6030
TAN-SAHSA Honduras Airlines			312 236-3246	213 485-0261	212 730-0800	800 327-1225
TAP The Airline of Portugal	221-2061			800 221-7370	212 944-2100	
Thai Airways International			312 855-3930	800 426-5030	800 426-5204	800 426-5204
Trans Australian Airlines			312 329-1266	213 849-2151	800 227-4500	
Trans World Airlines		404 522-5738	312 332-7600	213 483-1100	212 290-2121	202 659-1000
Transamerica Airlines	228-5800					
UTA French Airlines		0-WX-7250	312 782-6181	213 625-7171	212 247-0100	202 337-8711
United Airlines		404 394-2234	312 569-3000	213 772-2121	212 867-3000	202 893-3400
U.S. Air		800 245-1640	312 726-1201		212 736-3200	202 783-4500
Varig Brazilian Airlines	223-5720				212 682-3100	
Vasp Brazilian Airlines				800 327-4361	800 327-4361	
Viasa Venezuelan International Airways	327-5454				212 421-7722	800 221-2492
Western Airlines	328-4990		312 782-8296	213 776-2311	212 966-1646	202 737-4825
World Airways		404 233-6705	312 663-5433	213 646-9404	212 267-7111	202 298-7155
Yugoslav (JAT) Airlines			312 782-1322	213 388-0379	212 757-9676	

HOTELS and MOTELS	Telephone Number
Americana Hotels	800 228-3278
Best Western Motels	800 528-1234
Club Mediterranee	800 528-3131
Days Inns	800 241-7111
Holiday Inns	800 238-8000
Howard Johnson Motor Lodges	800 654-2000
Hyatt Hotels	800 228-9000
Marriott Hotels	800 228-9290
Omni International Hotels	800 241-5500
Pick Hotels	800 621-4404
Playboy Club-Hotels	800 621-1116
Princess Hotels	800 223-1818
Quality Inns	800 228-5151
Ramada Inns	800 228-2828
Rockresorts	
In Atlanta:	404 939-4896
In Chicago:	312 266-0609
In Los Angeles:	213 843-3070
In New York:	212 586-4459
In Washington:	202 737-6787

HOTELS and MOTELS	Telephone Number
Sheraton Hotels	800 325-3535
Sonesta Hotels	800 343-7170
Stouffer Hotels	800 321-6888
Travelodge Motels	800 255-3050
Treadway Inns	800 631-0182
Trust Houses Forte Hotels	800 223-5672
Western International Hotels	800 228-3000

CAR RENTAL COMPANIES

Agency Rent-a-Car	800 321-1972
Ajax Rent-A-Car	800 421-0896
Avis Rent a Car	800 331-1212
Budget Rent A Car	800 228-9650
Dollar Rent-a-Car	800 421-6868
Econo-Car	800 228-1000
Greyhound Rent-a-Car	800 327-2501
Hertz Rent A Car	800 654-3131
National Car Rental	800 328-4567
Sears Rent a Car	800 228-2800
Thrifty Rent A Car	800 331-4200

THE NATIONAL PARK SYSTEM

SOURCE: National Park Service, U.S. Department of the Interior

Park Service Areas	Number	Park Service Areas	Number	Park Service Areas	Number	Park Service Areas	Number
National Parks	40	National Battlefield Parks	3	National Capital Parks	1	National Scenic Trail	1
National Historical Parks	23	National Battlefield Sites	1	White House	1	National Preserves	2
National Monuments	91			National Recreation Areas	17	"Other" Parks	10
National Military Parks	11	National Historic Sites	59	National Lakeshores	4	National Mall	1
National Battlefields	9	National Memorials	22	National Rivers (wild and scenic)	10	National Visitor Center	1
National Seashores	10	National Parkways	4				

Total 321

OUR NATIONAL PARKS

Acadia National Park, Maine; (gross acreage, 38,631.86). Rugged coastal area on Mount Desert Island, highest elevation on eastern seaboard; picturesque Schoodic peninsula on mainland. Includes Isle au Haut. Sieur de Monts National Monument est. July 8, 1916; est. as Lafayette National Park Feb. 26, 1919; changed to Acadia National Park Jan. 19, 1929. Visits (1979): 3,183,300

Arches National Park, Utah; (gross acreage, 73,378.98). Extraordinary products of erosion in the form of giant arches, windows, pinnacles, and pedestals. Proclaimed as a national monument April 12, 1929; est. as a national park November 12, 1971. Visits (1979): 269,800

Badlands National Park, South Dakota; (gross acreage, 243,302.33). Carved by erosion, this scenic landscape contains animal fossils of 40 million years ago, and supports bison, bighorn sheep, deer, and antelope. Authorized Mar. 4, 1929; wilderness designated Oct. 20, 1976; renamed national park Oct. 10, 1978. Visits (1979): 870,100

Big Bend National Park, Texas; (gross acreage, 708,118.40). Spectacular mountain and desert scenery; variety of unusual geological formations; enclosed in the great bend of the Rio Grande. Authorized June 20, 1935; est. June 12, 1944. Visits (1979): 340,700

Bryce Canyon National Park, Utah; (gross acreage, 35,835.08). Contains perhaps the most colorful and unique erosional forms in the world. In horseshoe-shaped amphitheaters along the edge of the Paunsaugunt Plateau of southern Utah stand innumerable highly colored and grotesque pinnacles, walls, and spires. Bryce Canyon National Monument est. June 8, 1923; Utah National Park authorized June 7, 1924; changed to Bryce Canyon National Park Feb. 25, 1928. Est. Sept. 15, 1928. Visits (1979): 559,100

Canyonlands National Park, Utah; (gross acreage, 337,570.43). Geological wonderland of rock, spires, and mesas rising more than 7,800 feet. Extensive and sometimes large petroglyphs (stone carvings) chipped by prehistoric Indians about 1,000 years ago. Est. Sept. 12, 1964. Visits (1979): 75,100

Capitol Reef National Park, Utah; (gross acreage, 241,904.26). Sixty-mile uplift of sandstone cliffs, with highly colored sedimentary formations dissected by narrow high-walled gorges. Dome-shaped white rock along the Fremont River accounts for the name. Proclaimed as a national monument Aug. 2, 1937; est. as a national park Dec. 18, 1971. Visits (1979): 317,100

Carlsbad Caverns National Park, New Mexico; (gross acreage, 46,755.33). Largest underground chambers yet discovered; a series of connected caverns with countless magnificent and curious formations. Carlsbad Cave National Monument est. Oct. 25, 1923; Carlsbad Caverns National Park est. May 14, 1930. Visits (1979): 721,600

Channel Islands National Park, California; (est. gross acreage, 190,000). Channel Islands National Monument was est. as a national park March 5, 1980, and is 12 to 45 miles off Los Angeles. It is rich in marine life and aquatic recreation, and has the only northern fur seal breeding colony south of Alaska. Proclaimed Apr. 26, 1938; boundary changes 1939, 1978. Visits (1979): 103,500

Crater Lake National Park, Oregon; (gross acreage, 160,290.33). Lake of deepest blue in heart of once-active volcano, Mt. Mazama; encircled by multicolored lava walls 500 to 2,000 feet high. Est. May 22, 1902. Visits (1979): 446,400

Everglades National Park, Florida; (gross acreage, 1,398,800.00). Largest remaining subtropical wilderness in conterminous United States; extensive fresh- and salt-water areas, open Everglades prairies, mangrove forests; abundant wildlife, including rare birds. Authorized May 30, 1934. Est. June 20, 1947. Visits (1979): 838,600

Glacier National Park, Montana; (gross acreage, 1,013,594.67). Superb Rocky Mountain scenery, with numerous glaciers and lakes nestling among the highest peaks; forms part of Waterton-Glacier International Peace Park, est. May 2, 1932. Est. May 11, 1910. Visits (1979): 1,446,200

Grand Canyon National Park, Arizona; (gross acreage, 1,218,375.24). Most spectacular part of the Colorado River's greatest canyon, which is 217 miles long and 4 to 18 miles wide; exposure of rocks representing vast geologic time. First Grand Canyon National Monument est. Jan. 11, 1908; national park est. Feb. 26, 1919. Marble Canyon and second Grand Canyon National Monuments and other lands absorbed Jan. 3, 1975. Visits (1979): 2,310,300

Grand Teton National Park, Wyoming; (gross acreage, 310,515.89). Series of peaks comprising the most impressive part of the Teton range; once a noted landmark of Indians and "Mountain Men." Includes part of Jackson Hole; winter feeding ground of largest American elk herd. Est. Feb. 26, 1929. Visits (1979): 3,466,400

Great Smoky Mts. National Park, N.C.-Tenn.; (gross acreage, 517,378.61). Loftiest range east of the Black Hills and one of the oldest uplands on earth. Diversified and luxuriant plant life, often of extraordinary size. Federal acreage: in N.C., 273,550.70; in Tenn., 241,206.83. Authorized May 22, 1926; est. for administration and protection only Feb. 6, 1930; est. for full development June 15, 1934. Visits (1979): 11,186,900

Guadalupe Mts. National Park, Texas; (gross acreage, 76,293.06). Mountain mass rising from desert contains portions of the world's most extensive and significant Permian limestone fossil reef. Also features a tremendous earth fault, lofty peaks, unusual flora and fauna. Authorized Oct. 15, 1966. Visits (1979): 110,500

Haleakala National Park, Hawaii; (gross acreage, 28,655.25). World-famous 10,023-foot Haleakala volcano (dormant), with one of the largest and most colorful craters known, in which grows a species of the rare silversword; native and migratory birdlife. Authorized Sept. 13, 1960; est. July 1, 1961. Visits (1979): 686,500

Hawaii Volcanoes National Park, Hawaii; (gross acreage, 229,177.03). Scene of impressive active volcanism on the island of Hawaii; luxuriant vegetation at lower elevations; rare plants and animals. Est. as Hawaii National Park Aug. 1, 1916; changed to Hawaii Volcanoes National Park Sept. 22, 1961. Visits (1979): 2,266,400

Hot Springs National Park, Arkansas; (gross acreage, 5,826.26). Mineral hot springs (47), used in the treatment of certain ailments. Set aside as Hot Springs Reservation by federal government Apr. 20, 1832; national park est. Mar. 4, 1921. Visits (1979): 5,148,900

Isle Royale National Park, Michigan; (gross acreage, 571,796.18). Forested island, the largest in Lake Superior, distinguished for its wilderness character; moose and wolves; pre-Columbian copper mines. Authorized Mar. 3, 1931; est. Apr. 3, 1940. Visits (1979): 14,800

Kings Canyon National Park, California; (gross acreage, 460,136.20). Mountain wilderness dominated by two enormous canyons of the Kings River and by the summit peaks of the High Sierra. The former General Grant National Park, with its giant sequoias, is a detached section of the park. General Grant National Park est. Oct. 1, 1890, abolished Mar. 4, 1940, and its lands made part of Kings Canyon National Park; est. Mar. 4, 1940. Visits (1979): 809,300

Lassen Volcanic National Park, California; (gross acreage, 106,372.36). Lassen Peak, which erupted between 1914 and 1921, exhibits volcanic phenomena. Lassen Peak and Cinder Cone National Monuments est. May 6, 1907; made part of Lassen Volcanic National Park Aug. 9, 1916, when it was est. Visits (1979): 380,000

Mammoth Cave National Park, Kentucky; (gross acreage, 52,452.22). Series of underground passages, 146 miles explored; beautiful limestone, gypsum and cave onyx formations; deep pits and high domes; river 360 feet below surface. Authorized May 25, 1926; provided for minimum park area May 14, 1934; minimum area accepted for administration May 22, 1936; fully est. July 1, 1941. Visits (1979): 1,558,000

Mesa Verde National Park, Colorado; (gross acreage, 52,085.14). Best preserved prehistoric cliff dwellings in the United States. Est. June 29, 1906. Visits (1979): 474,500

Mount McKinley National Park, Alaska; (gross acreage, 1,939,492.80). Mount McKinley, highest mountain (20,320 feet) in North America; large glaciers of the Alaska Range; caribou, Dall sheep, moose, grizzly bears, wolves, and other spectacular wildlife. Est. Feb. 26, 1917. Visits (1979): 538,400

Mount Rainier National Park, Washington; (gross acreage, 235,404.00). Greatest single-peak glacial system in the conterminous United States, radiating from the summit and slopes of an ancient volcano; dense forests, flowered meadows. Est. Mar. 2, 1899. Visits (1979): 1,981,500.

North Cascades National Park, Washington; (gross acreage, 504,780.94). Wild alpine region of jagged peaks, mountain lakes, and numerous glaciers. Est. Oct. 2, 1968. Visits (1979): 800,300*

Olympic National Park, Washington; (gross acreage, 908,781.42). Mountain wilderness containing finest remnant of Pacific Northwest rain forest; active glaciers; rare Roosevelt elk. Mount Olympus National Monument est. Mar. 2, 1909; transferred from U.S. Dept. of Agriculture Aug. 10, 1933; Olympic National Park est. June 29, 1938. Visits (1979): 2,589,400

Petrified Forest National Park, Arizona; (gross acreage, 93,492.57). Extensive natural exhibit of petrified wood; Indian ruins and petroglyphs; portion of colorful Painted Desert. Est. as a national monument Dec. 8, 1906; changed to national park Dec. 9, 1962. Visits (1979): 675,200

Redwood National Park, California; (gross acreage, 109,027.04). Coastal redwood forests contain virgin groves of ancient trees, including the world's tallest (369.2 feet). Park includes 40 miles of scenic Pacific coastline. Est. Oct. 2, 1968. Visits (1979): 480,400

Rocky Mountain National Park, Colorado; (gross acreage, 263,808.71). One of the most diversified sections of the Front Range of the Rocky Mountains with 107 named peaks in excess of 11,000 feet. Est. Jan. 26, 1915. Visits (1979): 2,580,000

Sequoia National Park, California; (gross acreage, 403,023.00). Great groves of giant sequoias, world's largest and among the oldest living things; magnificent High Sierra scenery, including Mount Whitney, highest mountain (14,494 feet) in conterminous United States. Est. Sept. 25, 1890. Visits (1979): 800,000

Shenandoah National Park, Virginia; (gross acreage, 194,825.10). Outstanding portion of Blue Ridge with Skyline Drive traversing crest; magnificent vistas of historic Shenandoah Valley, Piedmont; hardwood forests; wealth of wildflowers. Authorized May 22, 1926; est. Dec. 26, 1935. Visits (1979): 1,625,700

Theodore Roosevelt National Park, North Dakota; (gross acreage, 70,416.39). The park includes scenic badlands along the Little Missouri River, some original prairie grasslands, and part of Theodore Roosevelt's Elkhorn Ranch. Memorial park est. Apr. 25, 1947; renamed Oct. 10, 1978. Visits (1979): 599,100

Virgin Islands National Park, V.I.; (gross acreage, 14,696.90). St. John, an island of lush green hills and white sandy beaches; rich in tropical plant and animal life; pre-historic Carib Indian relics; remains of Danish colonial sugar plantations. Authorized Aug. 2, 1956; est. Dec. 1, 1956. Visits (1979): 734,900

Voyageurs National Park, Minnesota; (gross acreage, 219,128.00). Beautiful northern lakes and forests; interesting geology; historically used as passage between Great Lakes and Northwest Territory by French fur traders. Land area, 144,891.16 acres. Authorized January 8, 1971. Visits (1979): 201,400

Wind Cave National Park, South Dakota; (gross acreage, 28,292.08). Limestone caverns in scenic Black Hills, decorated by beautiful boxwork and calcite crystal formations; elk, deer, pronghorn, prairie dog towns and bison herd. Est. Jan. 9, 1903. Visits (1979): 951,800

Yellowstone National Park, Wyo.-Mont.-Idaho; (gross acreage, 2,219,822.70). World's greatest geyser area, with about 10,000 geysers and hot springs; spectacular falls and canyons of the Yellowstone River; one of the world's greatest wildlife sanctuaries. First and largest national park. By far the greatest portion of the park is situated in Wyoming. Est. Mar. 1, 1872. Visits (1979): 1,874,500

Yosemite National Park, California; (gross acreage, 760,917.18). Mountainous region of unusual beauty; Yosemite and other inspiring gorges with sheer granite cliffs; spectacular waterfalls; three groves of giant sequoias. Est. Oct. 1, 1890. El Portal administrative site, 991.19 acres of federal land adjacent to the park, authorized Sept. 2, 1958. Visits (1979): 2,441,400

Zion National Park, Utah; (gross acreage, 146,551.10). Outstanding colorful canyon and mesa scenery; erosion and faulting patterns that create phenomenal shapes and landscapes; former volcanic activity. Zion Canyon, a vertical-walled chasm, readily accessible. Est. as Munkuntuweap National Monument July 31, 1909; changed to Zion National Monument Mar. 18, 1918; est. as a national park (including the National Monument to 1937) Nov. 19, 1919. Visits (1979): 1,145,500

*Acreage and visitor figures include those for Lake Chelan and Ross Lake National Recreation Areas

LARGE FOREIGN PARKS (over 3,000 sq. mi.)

SOURCE: United Nations—I.U.C.N. (1975)

NATIONAL PARKS

Name (Country)	Area (sq. mi.)
Northeast Greenland (Denmark)	270,270
Wood Buffalo (Canada)	17,300
Salonga (Zaire)	14,116
Gemsbok (Botswana)	9,575
Kafue (Zambia)	8,649
Etosha (Namibia)	8,598
Kluane (Canada)	8,500
Baffin Island (Canada)	8,290
Tsavo (Kenya)	8,031
Southern (Sudan)	7,710
Kruger (South Africa)	7,523
Bernardo O'Higgins (Chile)	6,800
Iona (Angola)	6,178
Northeast Svalbard (Norway)	c. 6,000
Manu (Peru)	5,918
Wankie (Zimbabwe)	5,645
Namib Desert (Namibia)	5,442
Laguna San Rafael (Chile)	5,213
Serengeti (Tanzania)	5,000
Fiordland (New Zealand)	4,725
Upemba (Zaire)	4,529
Comoé (Ivory Coast)	4,440
Ruah (Tanzania)	4,440
Jasper (Canada)	4,200
Maiko (Zaire)	4,181
Chobe (Botswana)	4,000
Bamingui-Bangoran (Central African Republic)	3,861
Canaima (Venesuela)	3,861
Quiçama (Angola)	3,846
Kalahari Gemsbok (S. Africa)	3,703
South Luangwa (Zambia)	3,494
Gorongosa (Mozambique)	3,359
Niokolo Koba (Senegal)	3,189
Virunga (Zaire)	3,124
Alberto M. de Agostini (Chile)	3,089
Hernando de Magallanes (Chile)	3,089
Skeleton Coast (Namibia)	3.089

THE U.S. PASSPORT

SOURCE: Department of State, Passport Services

A passport is your official identification as a citizen of the United States. Application for a passport should be made, in person, before a passport agent at one of the passport agencies located in Boston; Chicago; Detroit; Honolulu; Houston; Los Angeles; Miami; New Orleans; New York; Philadelphia; San Francisco; Seattle; Stamford, Conn.; and Washington, D.C.; or a clerk of any federal court or state court of record or a judge or clerk of any probate court accepting applications; or a postal employee designated by the postmaster at a post office which has been selected to accept passport applications.

When you apply for a passport you must present the following items: proof of U.S. citizenship (a previously issued passport, birth certificate, or naturalization papers); two identical photographs taken within six months of the date of your application (have them taken by a professional photographer who knows the requirements concerning pose and size of prints); identification—a document such as a driver's license with your signature and your photograph or physical description on it. The fee for a passport is $10, plus a $4 execution fee. Allow about two to three weeks for processing of your application, longer if you apply during peak travel periods.

A passport is valid for five years from the date of issue unless specifically limited to a shorter period by the Secretary of State. A new passport will be required for travel after expiration of the five-year period.

Application for a new passport must be made in person at the places listed above, or—under certain circumstances—a person who is the bearer of a passport issued within eight years prior to the date of his or her new application may apply for a subsequent passport by mail.

The applicant must submit completed form DSP-82 (Application for Passport by Mail), which is available from travel agents and the places listed above, the previous passport, two new signed passport photographs, and a fee of $10. The applicant should carefully read the instructions on the application to determine his or her eligibility to use this form.

Loss or theft of a valid passport is a serious matter and should be reported in writing immediately to Passport Services, Department of State, Washington, D.C. 20524 or the nearest Passport Agency. If the passport holder is abroad when the loss occurs, he or she should notify the nearest U.S. consulate. Theft of a passport should also be reported to local police authorities.

Visas

A visa is official permission to visit a country granted by the government of that country. An American who plans to go abroad can check the general visa requirements for each country he or she plans to visit in a booklet entitled "Visa Requirements of Foreign Governments," which is available at any office accepting passport applications. Specific details should be obtained from the nearest embassy or consulate of the country in which you wish to do any traveling.

FOREIGN GOVERNMENT TOURIST OFFICES

Australian Tourist Commission
1270 Ave. of the Americas, Rm. 2908
New York, NY 10020

Austrian National Tourist Office
545 Fifth Avenue
New York, NY 10017

Bahamas Tourist Office
30 Rockefeller Plaza
New York, NY 10020

Belgian National Tourist Office
745 Fifth Avenue
New York, NY 10022

Bermuda Government Official Travel Information Office
630 Fifth Avenue
New York, NY 10020

British Tourist Authority
680 Fifth Avenue
New York, NY 10019

Canadian Government Office of Tourism
1251 Ave. of the Americas
New York, NY 10020

(Cedok) Czechoslovak Travel Bureau
10 East 40th Street
New York, NY 10016

Dominican Tourist Information Center, Inc.
485 Madison Avenue
New York, NY 10022

Egyptian Government Tourist Office
630 Fifth Avenue
New York, NY 10020

Finland National Tourist Office
75 Rockefeller Plaza
New York, NY 10020

French Government Tourist Office
610 Fifth Avenue
New York, NY 10020

German National Tourist Office
630 Fifth Avenue
New York, NY 10022

Greek National Tourist Organization
645 Fifth Avenue
New York, NY 10022

Haiti Government Tourist Bureau
30 Rockefeller Plaza
New York, NY 10020

India Government Tourist Office
30 Rockefeller Plaza
New York, NY 10020

Irish Tourist Board
590 Fifth Avenue
New York, NY 10036

Israel Government Tourist Office
350 Fifth Avenue
New York, NY 10016

Italian Government Travel Office
630 Fifth Avenue
New York, NY 10020

Jamaica Tourist Board
2 Hammarskjöld Plaza
New York, NY 10017

Japan National Tourist Organization
45 Rockefeller Plaza
New York, NY 10020

Kenya Tourist Office
60 East 56th Street
New York, NY 10022

Korea National Tourism Corp.
Suite 323 510 Building
510 West 6th Street
Los Angeles, Ca 90014

Malaysian Tourist Center
420 Lexington Avenue
New York, NY 10017

Mexican National Tourist Council
405 Park Avenue
New York, NY 10022

Moroccan National Tourist Office
521 Fifth Avenue
New York, NY 10017

Panama Government Tourist Bureau
630 Fifth Avenue
New York, NY 10020

Polish National Tourist Office
500 Fifth Avenue
New York, NY 10036

Romanian National Tourist Office
573 Third Avenue
New York, NY 10016

Scandinavian National Tourist Office
75 Rockefeller Plaza
New York, NY 10020

South African Tourist Corporation
610 Fifth Avenue
New York, NY 10020

Spanish National Tourist Office
665 Fifth Avenue
New York, NY 10022

Sri Lanka Ceylon Tourist Board
609 Fifth Avenue
New York, NY 10017

Suriname Tourist Bureau
1 Rockefeller Plaza
New York, NY 10020

Swiss National Tourist Office
608 Fifth Avenue
New York, NY 10020

Thailand Tourist Organization
20 East 82nd Street
New York, NY 10028

Turkish Government Tourism Office
821 United Nations Plaza
New York, NY 10017

Yugoslav State Tourist Office
630 Fifth Avenue
New York, NY 10020

Zambia National Tourist Bureau
150 East 58th Street
New York, NY 10022

FOREIGN CITY WEATHER

Two figures are given for each of the months, thus 88/73. The first figure is the average daily high temperature (°F) and the second is the average daily low temperature (°F) for the month. The boldface figures indicate the average number of days with rain for each month.

City	January	February	March	April	May	June	July	August	September	October	November	December
ABIDJAN, Ivory Coast	88/73 3	90/75 4	90/75 6	90/75 9	88/75 16	85/73 18	83/73 8	82/71 7	83/73 8	85/74 13	87/74 13	88/74 6
ACAPULCO, Mexico	85/70 0	87/70 0	87/70 0	87/71 1	89/74 4	89/76 15	89/75 11	89/75 14	88/75 18	88/74 12	88/72 4	87/70 1
ACCRA, Ghana	87/73 1	88/75 2	88/76 4	88/76 6	87/75 9	84/74 10	81/73 4	80/71 3	81/73 4	85/74 6	87/75 3	88/75 2
ADDIS ABABA, Ethiopia	75/43 2	76/47 5	77/49 8	77/50 10	77/50 10	74/49 20	69/50 28	69/50 27	72/49 21	75/45 3	73/43 2	73/41 2
ALGIERS, Algeria	59/49 11	61/49 9	63/52 9	68/55 5	73/59 5	78/65 2	83/70 1	85/71 1	81/69 4	74/63 7	66/56 11	60/51 12
AMSTERDAM, Netherlands	40/34 19	41/34 15	46/37 13	52/43 14	60/50 12	65/55 12	69/59 14	68/59 14	64/56 15	56/48 18	47/41 19	41/35 19
ANKARA, Turkey	39/24 8	42/26 8	51/31 7	63/40 7	73/49 7	78/53 5	86/59 2	87/59 1	78/52 3	69/44 5	57/37 6	43/29 9
APIA, Western Samoa	86/75 22	85/76 19	86/74 19	86/75 14	85/74 12	85/74 7	85/74 9	84/75 9	84/74 11	85/75 14	86/74 16	85/74 19
ATHENS, Greece	54/42 7	55/43 6	60/46 5	67/52 3	77/60 3	85/67 2	90/72 1	90/72 1	83/66 2	74/60 4	64/52 6	57/46 7
BAGHDAD, Iraq	60/39 4	64/42 3	71/48 4	85/57 3	97/67 1	105/73 0	110/76 0	110/76 0	104/70 0	92/61 1	77/51 3	64/42 5
BALI, Indonesia	88/74 19	88/74 14	88/74 13	88/74 7	88/73 5	87/71 3	87/70 1	87/70 1	89/71 1	90/73 2	90/75 6	88/74 14
BANGKOK, Thailand	89/68 1	91/72 1	93/75 3	95/77 3	93/77 9	91/76 10	90/76 13	90/76 13	89/76 15	88/75 14	87/72 5	87/68 1
BARCELONA, Spain	56/42 5	57/44 7	61/47 7	64/51 8	71/57 8	77/63 5	81/69 4	82/69 5	78/65 7	71/58 8	62/50 7	57/44 6
BEIRUT, Lebanon	62/51 15	63/51 12	66/54 9	72/58 5	78/64 2	84/74 12	83/73 11	84/74 11	84/74 9	85/74 9	85/73 12	85/73 15
BELFAST, Northern Ireland	45/34 22	47/34 18	49/35 20	53/39 18	59/43 17	64/49 10	66/51 18	65/51 20	62/48 17	55/42 19	50/37 21	46/35 25
BELGRADE, Yugoslavia	37/27 8	41/27 6	53/35 7	64/45 9	74/53 9	79/58 9	84/61 6	83/60 7	76/55 6	65/47 8	52/39 7	40/30 9
BERLIN, Germany	35/26 10	38/27 8	46/32 9	55/38 9	65/46 8	70/51 9	74/55 10	72/54 10	66/48 8	55/41 8	43/33 8	37/29 11
BIARRITZ, France	54/40 10	52/38 11	63/43 11	63/44 11	69/53 11	72/56 10	80/66 7	77/61 7	77/58 9	74/55 11	58/44 12	53/41 14
BOGOTÁ, Colombia	67/48 6	68/49 7	67/50 13	67/51 20	66/51 17	65/51 16	64/50 18	65/50 16	66/49 13	66/50 20	66/50 16	66/49 15
BOMBAY, India	83/67 1	83/67 1	86/72 1	89/76 1	91/80 1	89/79 14	85/77 21	85/76 19	85/76 13	89/76 3	89/73 1	87/69 1
BONN, West Germany	39/30 7	37/26 6	50/35 7	58/39 14	67/46 13	69/52 19	73/56 16	72/55 17	67/50 16	58/45 16	47/37 15	44/36 15
BRASÍLIA, Brazil	80/65 17	81/64 20	82/64 7	82/62 10	79/56 5	77/52 0	78/51 2	82/55 0	87/60 2	82/64 16	82/66 17	78/64 16
BRINDISI, Italy	55/43 10	57/43 6	60/45 5	65/50 5	73/57 5	80/64 2	84/68 1	84/69 3	80/65 4	70/58 8	64/52 10	58/46 8
BUCHAREST, Romania	33/20 6	38/24 5	51/33 6	63/41 6	74/51 8	81/58 9	86/61 7	86/60 5	76/53 5	65/44 5	49/35 6	37/26 6
BUDAPEST, Hungary	35/26 7	40/28 6	51/36 7	62/44 8	72/52 9	78/57 8	82/61 7	81/59 6	74/53 7	61/45 8	47/37 8	38/31 9
BUENOS AIRES, Argentina	85/63 7	83/63 6	79/60 7	72/53 8	64/47 7	57/41 7	57/42 8	60/43 9	64/46 8	69/50 9	76/56 9	82/61 8
CAIRO, Egypt	65/47 1	69/48 1	75/52 1	83/57 1	91/63 1	95/68 0	96/70 0	95/71 0	90/68 0	86/65 1	78/58 1	68/50 1
CALCUTTA, India	80/55 1	84/59 2	93/69 2	97/75 3	96/77 7	92/79 13	89/79 18	89/78 18	90/78 13	89/74 6	84/64 1	79/55 1
CAPE TOWN, South Africa	78/60 3	79/60 2	77/58 3	72/53 6	67/49 9	65/46 9	63/45 10	64/46 9	65/49 7	70/52 5	73/55 3	76/58 3
CARACAS, Venezuela	75/56 6	77/56 2	79/58 3	81/60 4	80/62 9	78/62 14	78/61 15	79/61 15	80/61 13	79/61 12	77/60 13	78/58 10
CHARLOTTE AMALIE, Virgin Islands	82/73 18	81/72 13	82/73 12	83/74 13	85/76 15	86/77 15	87/78 16	88/78 19	87/78 17	87/77 18	85/76 19	83/74 18
COLOMBO, Sri Lanka	86/72 7	87/72 6	88/74 8	88/76 14	87/78 19	85/77 18	85/77 12	85/77 11	85/77 13	85/75 19	85/73 16	85/72 10
COPENHAGEN, Denmark	36/29 9	36/28 7	41/31 8	50/37 9	61/44 8	67/51 8	72/55 9	69/54 12	63/49 8	53/42 9	43/35 10	38/32 11
DARWIN, Australia	90/77 20	90/77 18	91/77 17	92/76 6	91/73 1	88/69 1	87/67 0	89/70 0	91/74 2	93/77 5	94/78 10	92/78 15
DJAKARTA, Indonesia	84/74 18	84/74 17	86/74 15	87/75 11	87/75 9	87/74 7	87/73 5	87/73 4	88/74 5	87/74 8	86/74 12	85/74 14
DUBLIN, Ireland	47/35 13	47/35 11	51/36 10	54/38 11	59/42 11	65/48 11	67/51 13	67/51 13	63/47 12	57/43 12	51/38 12	47/36 13
EDINBURGH, Scotland	43/35 18	43/35 15	47/36 15	50/39 16	55/43 15	62/48 15	65/52 17	64/52 17	60/48 16	53/44 18	47/39 18	44/36 17
FLORENCE, Italy	49/35 9	53/36 9	60/40 7	68/46 7	75/53 9	84/58 5	89/63 4	88/62 4	81/58 6	69/51 9	58/42 10	50/37 9
GENEVA, Switzerland	39/29 10	43/30 9	51/35 10	58/41 11	66/48 12	73/55 11	77/58 9	76/57 10	69/52 10	58/44 11	47/37 11	40/31 10
GUAYAQUIL, Ecuador	88/70 20	87/71 25	88/72 24	89/71 14	88/68 9	87/68 4	84/67 2	86/65 0	87/66 2	86/68 3	88/68 4	88/70 10
HAMBURG, West Germany	35/28 12	37/30 10	42/33 10	51/39 11	60/47 9	67/53 10	69/56 12	67/55 13	63/51 10	53/44 11	44/36 11	38/31 12
HAMILTON, Bermuda	68/58 14	68/57 13	68/57 12	71/59 9	76/64 9	81/69 9	85/73 10	86/74 13	84/72 10	79/69 12	74/63 13	70/60 15
HAVANA, Cuba	79/65 6	79/65 4	81/67 4	84/69 4	86/72 7	88/74 10	89/75 9	89/75 10	88/75 11	85/73 11	81/69 7	79/67 6
HELSINKI, Finland	27/17 11	26/15 8	32/22 8	43/31 8	55/41 8	63/49 9	71/57 8	66/55 12	57/46 11	45/37 12	37/30 11	31/22 11
HONG KONG	64/56 4	63/55 5	67/60 7	75/67 8	82/74 13	85/78 18	87/78 17	87/78 15	85/77 12	81/73 6	74/65 2	68/59 3
JERUSALEM, Israel	55/41 9	56/42 11	65/46 3	73/50 3	81/57 1	85/60 1	87/63 0	87/64 0	85/62 1	81/59 1	70/53 4	59/45 7
JOHANNESBURG, South Africa	78/58 12	77/58 9	75/55 9	72/50 4	66/43 3	62/39 1	63/39 1	68/43 1	73/48 2	77/53 7	77/55 10	78/57 11
KARACHI, Pakistan	77/55 1	79/58 1	85/67 1	90/73 1	93/79 1	93/82 1	91/81 2	88/79 2	88/77 1	91/72 1	87/64 1	80/57 1
KINGSTON, Jamaica	86/67 3	86/67 3	86/68 2	87/70 3	87/72 4	89/74 5	90/73 4	90/73 7	89/73 6	88/73 9	87/71 5	87/69 4
LAGOS, Nigeria	88/74 2	89/77 3	89/78 7	89/77 10	87/76 16	85/74 20	83/74 16	82/73 10	83/74 14	85/74 16	88/75 7	88/75 2
LA PAZ, Bolivia	63/43 21	63/43 18	64/42 16	65/40 9	64/37 5	62/34 2	62/33 2	63/35 4	64/38 9	66/40 9	67/42 11	65/42 18

City	January	February	March	April	May	June	July	August	September	October	November	December
LAS PALMAS, Canary Is.	70/58 8	71/58 5	71/59 5	71/61 3	73/62 1	75/65 1	77/67 1	79/70 1	79/69 1	79/67 5	76/64 7	72/60 8
LENINGRAD, USSR	23/12 17	24/12 15	33/18 13	45/31 11	58/42 12	66/51 12	71/57 13	66/53 15	57/45 14	45/37 15	34/27 17	26/18 18
LIMA, Peru	82/66 1	83/67 1	83/66 1	80/63 1	74/60 1	68/58 1	67/57 1	66/56 2	68/57 1	71/58 1	74/60 1	78/62 1
LISBON, Portugal	56/46 9	58/47 8	61/49 10	64/52 7	69/56 6	75/60 2	79/63 1	80/64 1	76/62 4	69/57 7	62/52 10	57/47 10
LIVERPOOL, England	44/36 18	44/36 13	48/38 13	52/41 14	58/46 14	63/51 13	66/55 15	65/55 16	61/51 15	55/46 17	48/41 17	45/37 18
LONDON, England	44/35 17	45/35 13	51/47 11	56/40 14	63/45 13	69/51 11	73/55 13	72/54 13	67/51 13	58/44 14	49/39 16	45/36 16
MADRID, Spain	47/33 9	51/35 9	57/40 11	64/44 9	71/50 9	80/57 6	87/62 3	86/62 2	77/56 6	66/48 8	54/40 10	48/35 9
MANILA, Philippines	86/69 6	88/69 3	91/71 4	93/73 4	93/75 12	91/75 17	88/75 24	87/75 23	88/75 22	88/74 19	88/72 14	86/70 11
MARACAIBO, Venezuela	90/73 1	90/73 1	91/74 1	92/76 1	92/77 6	93/77 6	94/76 5	94/77 7	94/77 7	92/76 9	91/76 8	91/75 2
MARSEILLE, France	53/38 10	52/37 9	55/38 8	59/41 10	65/46 10	72/52 9	78/58 6	83/61 4	82/61 5	76/57 7	67/50 10	59/43 11
MELBOURNE, Australia	78/57 9	78/57 8	75/55 9	68/51 13	62/47 14	57/44 16	56/42 17	59/43 17	63/46 15	67/48 14	71/51 13	75/54 11
MEXICO CITY, Mexico	66/42 4	69/43 5	75/47 9	77/51 14	78/54 17	76/55 21	73/53 27	73/54 27	74/53 23	70/50 13	68/46 6	66/43 4
MILAN, Italy	40/29 7	47/33 6	56/38 6	66/46 6	72/54 9	80/61 6	84/64 6	82/63 6	76/58 6	64/49 7	51/39 7	42/33 7
MONTEVIDEO, Uruguay	83/62 6	82/61 5	78/59 5	71/53 6	64/48 6	59/43 5	58/43 6	59/43 7	63/46 6	68/49 6	74/54 6	79/59 7
MOSCOW, USSR	21/9 11	23/10 9	32/17 8	47/31 9	65/44 9	73/51 10	76/55 12	72/52 12	61/43 9	46/34 11	31/23 10	23/13 9
MUNICH, West Germany	33/23 10	37/25 9	45/31 10	54/37 13	63/45 13	69/51 14	72/54 14	71/53 13	64/48 11	53/40 10	42/31 9	36/26 11
NAIROBI, Kenya	77/54 5	79/55 6	77/57 11	75/58 16	72/56 17	70/53 9	69/51 6	70/52 7	75/52 6	76/55 8	74/56 15	74/55 11
NAPLES, Italy	54/42 11	55/43 11	60/46 6	67/50 6	73/56 6	81/62 3	86/67 1	86/67 3	81/63 6	72/56 9	63/49 11	57/45 11
NASSAU, Bahamas	77/65 6	77/64 5	79/66 5	81/69 6	84/71 9	87/74 12	88/75 14	89/76 14	88/75 15	85/73 13	81/70 9	79/67 6
NEW DELHI, India	70/44 2	75/49 2	87/58 1	97/68 1	105/79 2	102/83 4	96/81 8	93/79 8	93/75 4	93/65 1	84/52 1	73/46 1
NICE, France	56/40 8	56/41 8	59/45 8	64/49 7	69/56 8	76/62 5	81/66 2	81/66 5	77/62 6	70/55 9	62/48 7	58/43 8
NOUMEA, New Caledonia	86/72 10	85/73 12	85/72 16	83/70 13	79/66 15	77/64 13	76/62 13	76/61 12	78/63 8	80/65 7	83/68 7	86/70 6
ODESSA, USSR	28/22 7	31/26 4	39/32 5	52/41 6	67/55 6	74/62 7	79/65 6	78/65 5	68/56 4	57/47 5	43/35 5	33/27 6
OSLO, Norway	30/20 8	32/20 7	40/25 7	50/34 7	62/43 7	69/51 8	73/56 10	69/53 11	60/45 8	49/37 10	37/29 9	31/24 10
PALERMO, Sicily, Italy	58/47 14	60/47 10	62/49 7	67/53 5	83/59 5	82/66 1	86/71 1	87/72 1	83/69 4	75/62 10	67/55 9	61/50 11
PALMA, Majorca, Spain	57/42 8	59/43 8	62/45 8	66/49 5	73/55 5	80/61 3	84/66 1	86/67 2	81/64 6	74/57 8	65/50 9	59/44 10
PAPEETE, Tahiti	89/72 16	89/72 16	89/72 17	89/72 10	87/70 10	86/69 8	86/68 5	86/68 6	86/69 6	87/70 4	88/71 13	88/72 14
PARIS, France	42/32 15	45/33 13	52/36 15	60/41 14	67/47 13	73/52 11	76/55 12	75/55 12	69/50 11	59/44 14	49/38 15	43/33 17
PEKING, China	35/15 3	41/20 3	53/30 3	68/44 4	80/56 6	88/65 9	89/71 13	87/69 11	80/58 7	69/44 4	50/30 2	37/19 2
PHNOM PENH, Cambodia	87/70 1	90/72 1	93/74 3	94/76 6	92/76 14	91/76 15	89/75 16	89/76 17	88/76 19	87/76 17	86/74 9	86/71 4
PORT-AU-PRINCE, Haiti	87/68 3	88/68 5	89/69 7	89/71 11	90/72 13	92/73 8	94/74 7	93/73 11	91/73 12	90/72 12	88/71 7	87/69 3
PORT OF SPAIN, Trinidad	85/67 14	86/67 8	87/67 8	88/69 7	89/70 10	87/71 17	87/70 20	87/71 21	88/71 18	88/71 16	87/70 17	86/69 16
PRAGUE, Czechoslovakia	34/25 12	38/28 11	45/33 13	55/40 12	65/49 13	72/55 14	74/58 14	73/57 12	65/52 11	54/44 11	41/35 12	34/29 13
RANGOON, Burma	89/65 1	92/67 1	96/71 1	97/76 2	92/77 14	86/76 23	85/76 26	85/76 25	86/76 20	88/76 10	88/73 3	88/67 1
RIO DE JANEIRO, Brazil	84/73 13	85/73 11	83/72 12	80/69 10	77/66 10	76/64 7	75/63 7	76/64 7	75/65 11	77/66 13	79/68 13	82/71 14
ROME, Italy	54/39 8	56/39 11	62/42 5	68/46 6	74/55 6	82/60 3	88/64 2	88/64 3	83/61 6	73/53 9	63/46 9	56/41 9
SAIGON (HO CHI MINH CITY), Vietnam	89/70 2	91/71 1	93/74 2	95/76 4	92/76 16	89/75 21	88/75 23	88/75 21	88/74 21	88/74 20	87/73 11	87/71 7
SAN JUAN, Puerto Rico	80/70 20	80/70 15	81/70 15	82/72 14	84/74 16	85/75 17	85/75 19	85/76 20	86/75 18	85/75 18	84/73 19	81/72 21
SANTIAGO, Chile	85/53 0	84/52 0	80/49 1	74/45 1	65/41 5	58/37 6	59/37 6	62/39 5	66/42 3	72/45 3	78/48 1	83/51 0
SÃO PAULO, Brazil	81/63 19	82/64 17	81/62 15	78/58 10	73/54 10	71/51 8	71/49 6	73/51 8	74/54 11	76/57 13	79/59 14	80/61 13
SEOUL, South Korea	32/15 8	37/20 6	47/29 7	62/41 8	72/51 10	80/61 10	84/70 16	87/71 13	82/66 11	67/45 7	51/32 9	37/20 9
SEVILLE, Spain	59/41 8	62/44 9	67/48 9	73/51 8	80/57 9	89/63 7	96/67 1	97/68 1	89/64 1	78/57 5	67/49 9	60/44 8
SHANGHAI, China	46/33 6	47/34 9	55/40 9	66/50 9	77/59 9	76/63 12	90/74 9	90/74 9	86/66 11	74/57 4	63/45 8	53/36 6
SINGAPORE, Singapore	86/73 17	88/73 11	88/75 14	88/75 15	89/75 15	89/75 13	88/75 13	87/75 14	87/75 14	87/74 16	87/74 18	87/74 19
SOFIA, Bulgaria	34/22 6	39/25 6	51/32 8	62/41 8	70/49 11	84/65 9	82/57 7	82/56 6	74/50 6	63/42 7	50/35 7	37/26 7
STOCKHOLM, Sweden	31/23 8	31/22 7	37/26 7	45/32 6	57/41 8	65/49 7	70/55 9	66/53 10	58/46 8	48/39 9	38/31 9	33/26 9
SYDNEY, Australia	78/65 14	78/65 13	76/63 14	71/58 14	66/52 13	61/48 12	60/46 12	63/48 11	67/51 12	71/56 12	74/60 12	77/63 13
TAIPEI, Taiwan, China	66/54 9	65/53 13	70/57 12	77/63 14	83/69 12	89/73 13	92/76 10	91/75 12	88/73 10	81/67 9	75/62 7	69/57 8
TEHRAN, Iran	45/27 4	50/32 4	59/39 5	71/49 3	82/58 2	93/66 1	99/72 1	97/71 1	90/64 1	76/53 1	63/43 3	51/33 4
TEL AVIV, Israel	63/48 10	65/48 8	67/50 9	74/54 2	81/60 1	84/65 0	87/69 0	87/70 0	86/68 1	84/64 2	77/59 7	66/52 11
TOKYO, Japan	47/29 5	48/31 6	54/36 10	63/46 10	71/54 10	76/63 12	83/70 10	86/72 9	79/66 12	69/55 11	60/43 7	52/33 5
VALPARAISO, Chile	72/56 1	72/56 1	70/54 1	67/52 1	63/50 5	60/48 7	60/47 7	61/47 5	62/48 2	65/50 2	69/52 1	71/54 1
VENICE, Italy	43/33 6	46/35 5	54/41 6	63/49 5	71/57 8	78/64 8	82/67 8	82/67 5	78/62 5	65/52 7	54/43 7	46/37 7
VIENNA, Austria	34/26 8	38/28 7	47/34 7	57/41 9	66/50 9	71/56 9	75/59 9	73/58 10	66/52 7	55/44 8	44/36 8	37/30 9
WELLINGTON, New Zealand	69/56 10	69/56 9	67/54 11	63/51 13	58/47 16	55/44 17	53/42 18	54/43 17	57/46 15	60/48 14	63/50 13	67/54 12
ZURICH, Switzerland	48/14 11	52/15 11	62/22 14	70/32 14	77/39 14	83/47 15	86/51 15	84/49 14	78/42 11	68/32 14	57/25 12	49/16 13

CUSTOMS HINTS

SOURCE: U.S. Customs Service

Customs exemptions: These apply only to articles brought back at the time of your return to the United States. You have a $300 exemption (subject to limitations on cigars, cigarettes, and liquor), if you are returning from a stay abroad of at least 48 hours (no minimum time limit for Mexico and American Virgin Islands), and you have not used the $300 exemption or any part of it within the preceding 30 days. Articles in excess of the $300 exemption up to $600 in value, based on the fair retail price of each item in the country of purchase, may be entered at a flat rate of 10% , if accompanying you at the time of your return, if acquired as an incident to your trip, if for personal or household use, and if properly declared to customs.

Cigars and Cigarettes—Not more than 100 cigars and 200 cigarettes (one carton) may be included in your exemption. Your cigarettes, however, may be subject to a tax imposed by state and local authorities.

Liquor—One liter of alcoholic beverages may be included in the exemption if you are 21 years old or older.

Articles imported in excess of your customs exemption: Will be subject to duty unless the items are entitled to free entry or prohibited. After deducting your exemption and the value of any articles duty free, a flat rate of duty will be applied to the next $600 worth (fair retail value) of merchandise. Any dollar amount of an article over $600 will be dutiable at various rates of duty based on wholesale value. The flat rate of duty is 10% of fair retail value in the country of acquisition; 5% for articles purchased in certain U.S. Territories.

Traveling back and forth across border: If you cross the border at one point and then swing back into the United States to enter the foreign country at another point, you might lose your exemption unless certain requirements are met. Ask a customs officer about these.

American Virgin Islands, American Samoa, Guam: If you return either directly or indirectly from these places, you have a $600 customs exemption provided that not more than $300 of it is applied to merchandise obtained elsewhere than these insular possessions. (The American Virgin Islands are exempt from the 48-hour-minimum time requirement.) Articles whole value exceeds $600 and were acquired in the insular possessions will be assessed at a rate of 5%, and they may accompany you or be shipped home. These articles must be for your own use or for gifts. Four liters of alcoholic beverages may be included in this exemption provided that not more than one liter is acquired elsewhere than in these islands.

Customs declarations: All articles acquired abroad and in your possession at the time of your return must be declared to U.S. customs, either orally or in writing. Declaration lists are distributed on planes and ships and should be prepared well in advance. Your declaration must include items that you are bringing back for another person at his request, any article that you intend to use or sell in your business, alterations or repairs of articles taken abroad, and gifts given to you while abroad. Wearing or using an article acquired abroad does not exempt it from duty, and it must be declared at the price you paid for it. The customs officer may make a reduction in value for wear and use.

Necessary written declarations: All articles acquired abroad must be declared in writing when their total value (including alterations and repairs) exceeds $300, when more than one liter of alcoholic beverages or more than 100 cigars are included, when some of the items are intended for other than personal or household use, or when a customs duty or internal revenue tax is collectible on any article in your possession, or unaccompanied tourist purchases are being sent from U.S. insular possessions.

Family declarations: A family head may make a joint declaration for all members residing in the same household and returning with him as a group. A family may bring in articles free of duty valued up to $300 for each member (e.g., a family of seven: $2,100), even if the articles acquired by some members exceed their $300 exemptions. Returning infants and children are entitled to the same exemptions as adults (except for alcoholic beverages). Children born abroad who have never resided in the United States are not eligible for the exemption, but may claim Customs exemption as a nonresident.

Value of articles: You must declare the price actually paid for each article. If you do not know the price, say so. If an article was not purchased, state its fair value in the country where it was acquired. If you understate the value of an article or misrepresent an article, you may have to pay a penalty in addition to payment of duty.

Preparation for customs: It is helpful to make a list of items obtained abroad before reaching the port of entry. Retain sales slips and have these readily available for examination. Pack articles acquired abroad separately.

Foreign-made articles taken abroad: These are dutiable each time they are brought into our country unless you have acceptable proof of prior possession. Documents which fully describe the article, such as a bill of sale or an insurance policy may be considered. Items which may be readily identified by serial number or permanently affixed markings may be taken to the Customs office nearest you and registered before your departure to expedite free entry of these items when you return.

Gifts: These are considered to be for your personal use and may be included in your exemption. This proviso includes both gifts given to you while abroad and those you intend to give to others after your return. Gifts intended for business or pomotional purposes may not be included. While abroad you may send gifts totaling $25 ($40 from U.S. insular possessions) retail value to people in the United States without duty or tax, provided that the addressee does not receive in a single day (at the customs processing station) gift parcels exceeding the $25 limitation. Write "unsolicited gift–Value under $25" in large letters on the outside of package as well as the retail value of the contents. Alcoholic beverages and tobacco products may not be sent, nor alcoholic perfumes valued at more than $5.

Personal belongings sent home: Personal belongings of U.S. origin taken abroad may be sent back by mail duty free if, on the outside wrapper or enclosed in the package, it is stated that the articles were taken out of the U.S. as personal effects and are being returned without having been repaired or altered while abroad.

Automobiles, boats, airplanes: Vehicles taken abroad for noncommercial use may be returned duty free by proving they were taken out of this country. Proof may be the state registration for an automobile, the Federal Aviation Agency certificate of registration for an airplane, a yacht license or motorboat identification, or a customs registration certificate for any vehicle. Dutiable repairs or accessories acquired abroad must be declared. A leaflet entitled "Importing a Car" is available from any customs office for those considering purchase abroad of a foreign car.

Household effects: If you plan to reside overseas for more than one year, household effects may be sometimes duty free. Check with a customs office or U.S. consulate.

$25 exemption: If you are not entitled to the $300 exemption because of the 30-day or 48-hour limitations, you may bring in free of duty or tax articles that were acquired abroad for your personal or household use, if their total retail value does not exceed $25. This is an individual exemption that cannot be grouped on a family declaration. You may include any of the following in this exemption: 50 cigarettes, 10 cigars, four ounces of alcoholic beverages, or four ounces of alcoholic perfume. If the value of any article (or articles) exceeds $25, no article may be exempted from duty or tax.

GSP: Generalized System of Preferences (GSP) is designed to help improve the economy of 107 developing nations and 32 dependent territories by exempting certain items from import duty when brought into the U.S. from these areas. The brochure "GSP & The Traveler" or a customs office can provide further information.

PROHIBITED AND RESTRICTED ARTICLES

Articles considered injurious to the general welfare are prohibited entry. Among these items are obscene publications, lottery tickets, wild birds, their eggs and feathers, endangered wildlife and items made from them, protected marine mammals, liquor-filled candies, switchblade knives.

Narcotics are also prohibited. If your medical condition requires drugs containing narcotics, you should carry a prescription or written statement from your doctor.

Trademarked articles: Foreign-made TM articles may be limited as to the quantity which may be brought into the U.S. if the registered TM has been recorded by an American trademark owner with U.S. Customs. Persons arriving in the U.S. with a TM article are allowed an exemption, usually one article, unless the TM owner allows a quantity over this amount.

Fruits, plants, vegetables: These, with cuttings, seeds, and unprocessed plant products, are either prohibited from entry or require an import license. Address applications to: Quarantines, U.S.D.A., Federal Center Bldg., Hyattsville, Md. 20782.

Meats, livestock, poultry: These items and their by-products (such as sausage, paté), are prohibited or restricted from entering the U.S., depending on the animal disease condition in the country of origin. Fresh meat is generally prohibited; canned meat is permited if the inspector can determine that it is commercially canned, hermetically sealed, and can be kept without refrigeration. Other canned, cured, and dried meat is severely restricted from most countries. Cheese, except cottage cheese, may be brought into the country.

Money or all types of negotiable instruments: Any amount may be brought into or taken out of the United States. Persons importing or exporting an amount of more than $5,000 are required to file a report of the transaction with U.S. Customs. Ask a customs officer for the form at the time you arrive or depart with such amounts.

Pets: There are controls, restrictions and prohibitions on the entry if animals, birds, turtles, wildlife and all endangered species. Cats and dogs must be free of evidence of diseases communicable to man. Vaccination against rabies is not required for cats or dogs arriving from rabies-free countries. Personally owned pet birds may be entered (limit of two if of the Psittacine family), but APHIS and Public Health Service requirements must be met. This includes quarantine at any APHIS facility at specified locations, at the owner's expense. Advance reservations are required. For more information write: Veterinary Services, APHIS, U.S.D.A., Hyattsville, Md. 20782.

Monkeys—Live monkeys and other non-human primates may not be imported into the United States except by a registered importer for scientific, educational, or exhibition purposes.

Biological materials: Disease organisms and vectors for research and educational purposes require a permit. Write the Foreign Quarantine Program, Center for Disease Control, Atlanta, Ga. 30333.

Prohibited merchandise: Tourists may import items for their personal use up to a value of $100 from the following countries: Cuba, North Korea, Vietnam, and Cambodia. This allowance may only be used once every six months, and the articles must accompany the visitor upon his return.

Firearms and ammunition: Up to three nonautomatic firearms may be taken out of the country and returned if they are registered with customs or field office of the Bureau of Alcohol, Tobacco and Firearms. Firearms and ammunition are subject to import restrictions. Contact the Bureau of Alcohol, Tobacco and Firearms, Department of the Treasury, Washington, D.C. 20226.

HEALTH HINTS FOR TRAVELERS

SOURCE: U.S. Public Health Service

Under the International Health Regulations adopted by the World Health Organization a country, under certain conditions, may require International Certificates of Vaccination against Smallpox, Cholera, or Yellow Fever. Some countries in Africa and Asia require vaccination against smallpox. Most countries do not require vaccination. **No vaccinations are required to return to the U.S. from any country.**

Those immunizations required by governments must be recorded in the International Certificates of Vaccination, form PHS-731—the only acceptable immunization document for international travel. You can obtain this form with your passport application, from your local health department, or from the Superintendent of Documents, Government Printing Office, Washington, D.C. 20402, for 50 cents.

The Certificates must be signed by you and your physician or by a person under his supervision and be validated with an approved stamp. Validation of Smallpox and Cholera Certificates can be obtained at most health departments or from vaccinating physicians who possess a validation stamp. Yellow Fever vaccinations must be given at an officially designated Yellow Fever Vaccination Center and the Certificate validated by the Center that administers the vaccine. Information on the location of Yellow Fever Vaccination Centers is available from state and local health departments.

The Smallpox Certificate is valid for three years, beginning eight days after the date of successful primary vaccination or on the date of revaccination.

The Cholera Certificate is valid for 6 months beginning 6 days after 1 injection of vaccine or on the date of revaccination if within 6 months of the first injection.

The Yellow Fever Certificate is valid for 10 years beginning 10 days after primary vaccination or on the date of revaccination if within 10 years of the first injection.

Military personnel and their dependents, as well as other persons traveling under the auspices of the Department of Defense, are required to receive the immunizations as set forth by current service regulations.

RECOMMENDED VACCINATIONS

The risk of acquiring illness in international travel depends on the areas visited. In most developed countries such as Canada, Australia, New Zealand, and Europe, the risk to the health of the traveler will be no greater than that incurred while traveling throughout the United States. In the countries of Africa, Asia, South America, and in the countries of southern North America, the South Pacific, Middle East and Far East, living conditions and standards of sanitation and hygiene vary greatly. For travel to primarily tourist areas on itineraries which do not include travel in rural areas and consequently less risk of exposure to food or water of questionable quality, the risk of disease remains quite small. Travelers to smaller cities off the usual tourist routes and those who visit small villages or rural areas for extended periods are at greater risk of acquiring infectious diseases because of exposure to water and food of uncertain quality and closer contact with local residents who may harbor the organisms that cause such diseases. The risk of contacting hepatitis-A varies with living conditions, the prevalence of hepatitis in the areas visited, and particularly the length of stay. Vaccination against plague is not indicated for most travelers to countries reporting cases, particularly if their travel is limited to urban areas with modern lodgings.

There is a risk of acquiring malaria when traveling to parts of the Caribbean, Central and South America, Africa, the Middle East, the Indian subcontinent, and the Far East. You are strongly advised to seek information from your health department or private physician concerning the need for protection against malaria and for instructions on how the prophylactic drugs should be taken.

You are advised to contact your local health department, physician or agency two weeks prior to departure to obtain current information on vaccinations required by and recommended for the countries to be visited.

Unvaccinated Travelers: A traveler who does not have the required vaccinations upon entering a country may be subject to vaccination, medical follow-up, and/or isolation.

Exemption from Vaccination: If a physician thinks vaccination should not be performed on medical grounds, the traveler should be given a signed, dated statement of the reasons on the physician's letterhead stationery.

HEALTH PROTECTION HINTS

If you wear glasses, take along your lens prescription.

If you need medications regularly, take an adequate supply with you. Because of possible serious consequences to your health, do not buy medications "over the counter" unless you are familiar with the product.

If you have diabetes, are allergic to penicillin, or have any physical condition that may require emergency care, have some identification—a tag or bracelet or card—on your person at all times indicating this. Diabetics should take along an extra supply of medication. Drugs or medicines which must be taken should be accompanied by a letter from the traveler's physician.

Water can be considered safe only if it is obtained from adequately chlorinated sources, if boiled for ten minutes, or if treated with liquid chlorine laundry bleach or tincture of iodine.

Do not swim in unchlorinated pools.

Take it easy in unaccustomed conditions of heat and high altitudes.

It is wise to check with the local American Embassy or consulate for a list of acceptable doctors and dentists, and hospitals, if needed.

WORLD CITIES: COST-OF-LIVING INDEX: 1979

SOURCE: *UN Monthly Bulletin of Statistics* (Special Table I), March 1980, © United Nations

Note: This table shows the relative cost-of-living comparison, based on prices for goods, services and housing for international UN officials stationed in various cities of the world. In the following table, the cost-of-living is based on New York City = 100.

City	Index	City	Index	City	Index
Afghanistan, Kabul	89	Greece, Athens	112	Nicaragua, Managua	75
Argentina, Buenos Aires	143	Guatemala, Guatemala	99	Pakistan, Islamabad	86
Australia, Sydney	100	Guinea, Conakry	139	Panama, Panama City	88
Austria, Vienna	141	Guyana, Georgetown	86	Paraguay, Asunción	104
Bangladesh, Dacca	89	Haiti, Port-au-Prince	96	Peru, Lima	80
Barbados, Bridgetown	102	Hungary, Budapest	96	Philippines, Manila	95
Belgium, Brussels	151	India, New Delhi	83	Poland, Warsaw	72
Benin, Cotonou	97	Indonesia, Jakarta	104	Romania, Bucharest	85
Brazil, Rio de Janeiro	80	Iran, Tehran	110	Senegal, Dakar	130
Bulgaria, Sofia	101	Iraq, Baghdad	88	Singapore, Singapore	94
Burma, Rangoon	88	Italy, Rome	102	Spain, Madrid	123
Canada, Montréal	79	Jamaica, Kingston	60	Sri Lanka, Colombo	57
Chile, Santiago	111	Japan, Tokyo	153	Sudan, Khartoum	120
Colombia, Bogotá	96	Kenya, Nairobi	101	Swaziland, Mbabane	80
Cuba, Havana	89	Korea, South, Seoul	117	Switzerland, Geneva	166
Cyprus, Nicosia	83	Kuwait, Kuwait	93	Syria, Damascus	125
Czechoslovakia, Bratislava	74	Liberia, Monrovia	113	Thailand, Bangkok	83
Denmark, Copenhagen	147	Libya, Tripoli	133	Togo, Lomé	108
Dominican Rep., Santo Domingo	86	Madagascar, Antananarivo	114	Tunisia, Tunis	126
Ecuador, Quito	85	Malaysia, Kuala Lumpur	92	Turkey, Ankara	89
Egypt, Cairo	87	Malta, Valletta	76	United Kingdom, London	125
El Salvador, San Salvador	99	Mauritius, Port Louis	83	United States, Washington, DC	93
Ethiopia, Addis Ababa	90	Mexico, Mexico City	86	Uruguay, Montevideo	101
Fiji, Suva	87	Morocco, Rabat	119	Venezuela, Caracas	140
France, Paris	146	Nepal, Kathamandu	83	Yemen, San'a	137
Germany, West, Bonn	154	Netherlands, The Hague	147	Yugoslavia, Belgrade	108

RATES OF CUSTOMS DUTY: 1980   SOURCE: U.S. Customs Service

This abbreviated list of popular items imported by tourists is intended to be used as an advisory guide only. The customs officer examining baggage at the point of entry determines the rates of duty on dutiable articles. Rates are often higher for items imported from certain Communist-controlled countries. These rates apply to those articles brought in after the $600 maximum has been reached and the 10% flat rate (5% for insular possessions) no longer applies.

Item	Rate
Antiques: produced prior to 100 years before the date of entry	Free
Automobiles, passenger	2.9%
Beads:	
imitation precious, and semi-precious stones	4.7 to 13%
ivory	9.3%
Binoculars, prism	18.5%
Books, foreign author or foreign language	Free
Cameras:	
motion picture, over $50 each	5.8%
still, over $10 each	6.9%
cases, leather	8.1 to 10%
lenses	11.6%
China:	
bone	16.3%
nonbone, other than tableware	20.8 to 26%
China tableware, nonbone, available in 77-piece sets:	
valued not over $56 per set	37%
valued over $56 per set	17.1%
Cigarette lighters:	
pocket, valued at over 42 cents each	20.8%
table	11.1%
Clocks, valued over $5 but not over $10	69¢ + 14.8% + 5.7¢ for each jewel
valued over $10 each	$1.03 + 14.6% + 5.7¢ for each jewel
Drawings (done all by hand)	Free
Earthenware tableware, household available in 77-piece sets:	
valued not over $38 per set	10¢ doz. + 21%
valued over $38 per set	10.5%
Figurines, china	11.8 to 20.8%
Fur: wearing apparel	8.1 to 17.1%
other manufactures of	8.5 to 15.5%
Furniture:	
wood, chairs	8.1%
wood, other than chairs	4.7%
Gloves:	
wool, over $4 per dozen	37.5¢ lb. + 18.5%
horsehide or cowhide	15%
Handkerchiefs, cotton, plain	25% to 5¢ lb. + 35%
Ivory, manufactures of	5.8%
Jade, cut but not set	2.5%
other articles of jade	21%
Jewelry, precious metal or stone:	
silver chief value, valued not over $18 per doz.	27.5%
other	11.3%
Leather:	
pocketbooks, bags	8.1 to 10%
other manufactures of	3.5 to 11%
Motorcycles	4.8%
Musical Instruments:	
music boxes, wood	7.4%
woodwind, except bagpipes	7.2%
Paintings (done all by hand)	Free
Pearls, loose or temporarily strung and without clasp:	
genuine	Free
cultured	2.5%
imitation	18.5%
permanently or temporarily strung with clasp attached or separate)	11.3 to 27.5%
Perfume	7¢ lb. + 7.2%
Postage stamps	Free
Radios:	
transistors	9.9 to 10.1%
other	6%
Rattan:	
furniture	16%
other manufactures of	11.8%
Records, phonograph	4.8%
Shaver, electric	6.2%
Shell, manufactures of	5.5%
Shoes, leather	2.5 to 20%
Sterling flatware and tableware:	
knives and forks	3.5¢ each + 8.1%
spoons and tableware	11.8%
Stereo equipment	5.3 to 10.1%
Stones, cut but not set:	
diamonds not over one-half carat	4%
diamonds over one-half carat	5%
other	Free to 4.4%
Sweaters, of wool, over $5 per pound	37.5¢ lb. + 20%
Tape recorders	5.3 to 7.2%
Toys	16.2%
Watches, on $100 watch, duty varies from $6 to $13	
Wearing apparel:	
embroidered or ornamented	21 to 42.5%
not embroidered, not ornamented cotton, knit	21%
cotton, not knit	8 to 21%
linen, not knit	7.5%
manmade fiber, knit	25¢ lb. + 32.5%
manmade fiber, not knit	25¢ lb. + 27.5%
silk, knit	10%
silk, other	16%
wool, knit	37.5¢ lb. + 15.5 to 32%
Wood, manufactures of	7.6%

ALCOHOLIC BEVERAGES IMPORT RESTRICTIONS

State laws: Liquor may not be imported in violation of state law.

Mail importations: United States postal laws prohibit the shipment of alcoholic beverages by mail.

Gift packages: Alcoholic beverages may not be included in gift parcels sent to persons in the U.S.A. and are not entitled to free entry under the $25 gift exemption.

Customs Exemption: A returning resident 21 years or older may include in his $300 customs exemption one liter of alcoholic beverages free of duty and internal revenue tax. The importation must be for his own use or for a gift and not in violation of the laws of the state of arrival.

MAJOR COMMERCIAL PASSENGER PLANES

Country Company and Type	Maximum Number of Passengers	Maximum Speed (MPH)	Wingspan (Feet)	Length (Feet)	Height (Feet)
International Europe					
Airbus Industrie A300	345	576	147.1	175.1	54.2
France					
Dassault Mercure	134	575	100.3	114.3	37.3
Aerospatiale Caravelle IIR	50	498	112.5	107.3	28.6
Aerospatiale Caravelle III	99	500	112.5	105.0	28.6
Aerospatiale Super Caravelle	118	498	112.5	108.3	28.6
Aerospatiale Concorde	140	1300	84.0	203.9	37.1
United Kingdom					
BAC 111-475	89	541	93.6	93.6	24.6
BAC 111-500	119	541	93.6	107.0	24.6
British Aerospace 1150 Super VC 10	163	600	146.2	171.8	39.5
British Aerospace Trident 1E	139	605	95.0	115.8	27.0
British Aerospace Comet 4	83	530	115.0	111.5	29.5
British Aerospace Avro 748	60	281	98.6	67.0	24.1
British Aerospace Concorde	140	1300	84.0	203.9	37.1
Handley Page HPR 7-200	56	275	94.8	75.5	24.1
Hawker Siddeley Comet 4	81	530	115.0	111.5	29.5
Hawker Siddeley Trident 1E	139	605	95.0	114.8	27.0
Japan					
Nihon YS-11	60	297	105.0	86.3	29.5
Netherlands					
Fokker F27 MK500	60	298	95.2	82.2	28.6
Fokker F27 MK600	48	298	95.2	77.3	27.9
Fokker F28 MK3000	65	524	82.25	89.9	27.8
Fokker F28 MK4000	85	524	82.25	97.1	27.8
Fokker F28 MK6000	85	524	82.25	97.1	27.8
USSR					
Ilyushin IL-18V	110	425	122.7	117.8	—
Ilyushin IL-62	186	560	142.0	174.2	40.5
Tupolev TU-134	72	621	95.2	114.5	29.7
Tupolev TU-144	130	M.2.3	81.0	180.0	—
Tupolev TU-154	164	559	123.3	157.2	37.5
United States					
Boeing 707-120	181	600	130.9	144.5	42.0
Boeing 707-320	219	600 plus	145.7	152.9	42.5
Boeing 707-420RWL	189	593	142.7	152.9	42.5
Boeing 720	167	600	130.9	136.2	41.8
Boeing 727-200	189	600 plus	108.0	153.2	34.0
Boeing 737-100	103	580 plus	93.0	94.0	37.0
Boeing 737-200	130	573	93.0	100.0	37.0
Boeing 747	550	640	195.6	231.3	63.4
Boeing 757	233	600	124.5	155.25	44.5
Boeing 767	289	600	155.07	159.1	52.0
Fairchild Hiller F-27	48	275	95.2	77.2	27.5
Fairchild Hiller FH-227	52	300	95.2	83.1	27.5
General Dynamics 240	40	304†	91.8	74.8	26.9
General Dynamics Metropolitan 440	44	310	105.3	81.5	28.2
General Dynamics Convair 580	53	342†	105.3	81.5	29.1
General Dynamics 600	46	317	91.8	74.8	26.9
General Dynamics Convair 880	107	600	120.0	129.0	42.0
General Dynamics Convair 990	130	500	131.0	141.0	42.0
Lockheed TriStar L-1011	400	620	155.4	178.7	55.4
McDonnell Douglas DC-9 Series 10	90	586	89.3	104.3	27.5
McDonnell Douglas DC-9 Series 20	90	586	93.3	104.3	27.5
McDonnell Douglas DC-9 Series 30	139	586	93.3	119.25	27.5
McDonnell Douglas DC-9 Series 40	139	576	93.3	125.5	28.0
McDonnell Douglas DC-9 Series 50	139	576	93.3	133.5	28.0
McDonnell Douglas DC-9 Super 80	172	576	107.8	147.9	29.3
McDonnell Douglas DC-10 Series 10	380	600 plus	155.3	182.25	58.1
McDonnell Douglas DC-10 Series 30	380	600 plus	165.3	181.6	58.1
McDonnell Douglas DC-10 Series 40	380	600 plus	165.3	182.25	58.1

† Best cruising speed.

OPERATIONS AT 30 TOP-RANKING U.S. AIRPORTS: FISCAL YEAR 1979
Source: Federal Aviation Administration

Tower	Rank	1979 Operations†	Tower	Rank	1979 Operations†
Chicago O'Hare Int'l, Ill.	1	735,524	Torrance Municipal, Calif.	16	408,506
Long Beach, Calif.	2	646,401	Phoenix Sky Harbor Int'l, Ariz.	17	394,731
Santa Ana, Claif.	3	616,870	Fort Worth Meacham, Tex.	18	383,184
Atlanta International, Ga.	4	594,410	Miami International, Fla.	19	378,939
Van Nuys, Calif.	5	586,037	San Jose Reid Hillview, Calif.	20	372,389
Los Angeles Int'l, Calif.	6	547,960	Las Vegas McCarran Int'l, Nev.	21	369,211
Opa Locka, Fla.	7	527,579	Memphis International, Tenn.	22	369,069
Oakland International, Calif.	8	523,453	San Francisco, Calif.	23	363,791
Denver Stapleton Int'l, Colo.	9	482,389	Boston Logan, Mass.	24	355,959
Tamiami, Fla.	10	456,101	La Guardia, N.Y.	25	353,968
San Jose Municipal, Calif.	11	452,102	Washington National, D.C.	26	351,485
Dallas Ft. Worth Regional, Tex.	12	436,362	Pittsburgh Greater Int'l, Pa.	27	346,838
Denver Arapahoe County, Colo.	13	428,649	Philadelphia Int'l, Pa.	28	344,630
Seattle Boeing, Wash.	14	426,711	St. Louis Int'l, Mo.	29	341,854
Honolulu, Hawaii	15	411,376	Fort Lauderdale, Fla.	30	338,780

†Takeoffs and landings.

AIR DISTANCES BETWEEN MAJOR WORLD CITIES (See also, U.S. AIR DISTANCES, p. 221)

SOURCE: USAF Aeronautical Chart and Information Center (in statute miles)

	Bangkok	Berlin	Cairo	Cape Town	Caracas	Chicago	Hong Kong	Honolulu	Istanbul	Lima	London	Madrid	Melbourne
Accra	6,850	3,330	2,672	2,974	4,576	5,837	7,615	10,052	3,039	5,421	3,169	2,412	9,325
Amsterdam	5,707	360	2,015	5,997	4,883	4,118	5,772	7,254	1,372	6,538	222	921	10,286
Anchorage	6,022	4,545	6,116	10,478	5,353	2,858	5,073	2,778	5,388	6,385	4,491	5,181	7,729
Athens	4,930	1,121	671	4,957	5,815	5,447	5,316	8,353	352	7,312	1,488	1,474	9,297
Auckland	4,645	9,995	8,825	6,574	9,620	9,507	4,625	5,346	9,203	7,989	10,570	10,884	1,610
Baghdad	3,756	2,029	798	4,924	7,020	6,430	4,260	8,399	1,006	8,487	2,547	2,675	8,105
Bangkok	—	5,351	4,521	6,301	10,558	8,569	1,076	6,610	4,648	12,241	5,929	6,334	4,579
Beirut	4,272	1,689	341	4,794	6,520	6,097	4,756	8,536	614	7,972	2,151	2,190	8,579
Belgrade	5,073	623	1,147	5,419	5,587	5,000	5,327	7,882	500	7,169	1,053	1,263	9,578
Berlin	5,351	—	1,768	5,958	5,242	4,415	5,443	7,323	1,075	6,893	580	1,162	9,929
Bombay	1,870	3,915	2,717	5,103	9,034	8,066	2,679	8,036	3,000	10,389	4,478	4,689	6,101
Buenos Aires	10,490	7,395	7,360	4,285	3,155	5,582	11,478	7,554	7,608	1,945	6,907	6,236	7,219
Cairo	4,521	1,768	—	4,510	6,337	6,116	5,057	8,818	741	7,725	2,158	2,069	8,700
Cape Town	6,301	5,958	4,510	—	6,361	8,489	7,377	11,534	5,204	6,074	5,988	5,306	6,428
Caracas	10,558	5,242	6,337	6,361	—	2,500	10,171	6,024	6,050	1,699	4,662	4,351	9,703
Chicago	8,569	4,415	6,116	8,489	2,500	—	7,797	4,256	5,485	3,772	3,960	4,192	9,667
Copenhagen	5,361	222	1,964	6,179	5,215	4,263	5,392	7,101	1,252	6,886	595	1,289	9,936
Denver	8,409	5,092	6,846	9,331	3,078	920	7,476	3,346	6,164	3,986	4,701	5,028	8,755
Frankfurt (W. Germany)	5,581	270	1,817	5,815	5,022	4,344	5,709	7,450	1,160	6,660	408	885	10,133
Helsinki	4,903	689	2,069	6,490	5,658	4,442	4,867	6,818	1,330	7,349	1,135	1,835	9,448
Hong Kong	1,076	5,443	5,057	7,377	10,171	7,797	—	5,557	4,989	11,415	5,986	6,556	4,605
Honolulu	6,610	7,323	8,818	11,534	6,024	4,256	5,557	—	8,118	5,944	7,241	7,874	5,501
Houston	9,261	5,337	7,005	8,608	2,262	942	8,349	3,902	6,400	3,123	4,860	5,014	8,979
Istanbul	4,648	1,075	741	5,204	6,050	5,485	4,989	8,118	—	7,593	1,551	1,701	9,100
Karachi	2,305	3,365	2,222	5,153	8,502	7,564	2,977	8,059	2,457	9,943	3,928	4,152	6,646
Keflavik	6,300	1,505	3,267	7,107	4,269	2,942	6,044	6,085	2,578	5,965	1,188	1,802	10,552
Kinshasa	5,974	3,916	2,618	2,047	5,752	7,085	6,904	11,178	3,241	6,322	3,951	3,305	8,112
Leningrad	4,718	826	2,034	6,500	5,843	4,589	4,687	6,816	1,306	7,534	1,307	1,985	9,263
Lima	12,241	6,893	7,725	6,074	1,699	3,772	11,415	5,944	7,593	—	6,316	5,907	8,052
Lisbon	6,651	1,442	2,352	5,301	4,040	4,001	6,862	7,835	2,015	5,591	989	317	11,049
London	5,929	580	2,158	5,988	4,662	3,960	5,986	7,241	1,551	6,316	—	786	10,508
Madrid	6,334	1,162	2,069	5,306	4,351	4,192	6,556	7,874	1,701	5,907	786	—	10,766
Melbourne	4,579	9,929	8,700	6,428	9,703	9,667	4,605	5,501	9,100	8,052	10,508	10,766	—
Mexico City	9,793	6,054	7,677	8,516	2,234	1,688	8,789	3,791	7,106	2,635	5,558	5,642	8,420
Montreal	8,337	3,740	5,403	7,920	2,443	746	7,736	4,919	4,798	3,967	3,256	3,449	10,390
Moscow	4,394	1,001	1,770	6,277	6,176	4,984	4,443	7,049	1,087	7,855	1,556	2,140	8,965
Nairobi	4,481	3,947	2,217	2,543	7,179	8,012	5,447	10,740	2,957	7,821	4,229	3,840	7,159
New Delhi	1,812	3,598	2,752	5,769	8,837	7,486	2,339	7,413	2,837	10,430	4,178	4,528	6,340
New York City	8,669	3,980	5,598	7,801	2,124	714	8,061	4,969	5,022	3,635	3,473	3,596	10,352
Oslo	5,395	523	2,243	6,477	5,167	4,050	5,342	6,801	1,518	6,857	718	1,485	9,934
Panama City	10,871	5,856	7,118	7,021	867	2,321	10,089	5,254	6,756	1,454	5,285	5,081	9,027
Paris	5,877	549	1,973	5,782	4,735	4,145	5,992	7,452	1,400	6,367	215	652	10,442
Peking	2,027	4,600	4,687	8,034	8,978	6,625	1,195	5,084	4,407	10,365	5,089	5,759	5,632
Rabat	6,652	1,623	2,230	4,954	4,111	4,282	6,954	8,177	2,008	5,590	1,254	474	10,856
Rio de Janeiro	9,987	6,207	6,153	3,773	2,805	5,288	11,002	8,295	6,378	2,351	5,751	5,045	8,218
Rome	5,493	735	1,305	5,231	5,198	4,823	5,773	8,040	853	6,748	892	849	9,940
Saigon (Ho Chi Minh City)	467	5,771	4,987	6,534	10,905	8,695	938	6,302	5,102	12,180	6,345	6,779	4,168
San Francisco	7,930	5,673	7,436	10,248	3,908	1,860	6,904	2,397	6,711	4,516	5,369	5,806	7,850
Santiago	10,967	7,772	7,967	4,947	3,033	5,295	11,615	6,861	8,135	1,528	7,241	6,639	7,017
Seattle	7,455	5,060	6,809	10,205	4,096	1,737	6,481	2,681	6,077	4,961	4,799	5,303	8,176
Shanghai	1,797	5,231	5,188	8,062	9,508	7,071	760	4,947	4,975	10,665	5,728	6,386	4,991
Shannon	6,256	940	2,534	6,188	4,320	3,583	6,246	7,006	1,938	5,992	387	884	10,826
Singapore	887	6,167	5,143	6,007	11,408	9,376	1,608	6,728	5,379	11,689	6,747	7,079	3,767
St. Louis	8,763	4,676	6,370	8,549	2,414	265	7,949	4,134	5,744	3,589	4,215	4,426	9,476
Stockholm	5,141	505	2,084	6,422	5,422	4,288	5,115	6,873	1,347	7,109	892	1,613	9,693
Tehran	3,392	2,184	1,220	5,240	7,322	6,502	3,844	8,072	1,274	8,850	2,739	2,974	7,838
Tokyo	2,865	5,557	5,937	9,155	8,813	6,313	1,792	3,860	5,574	9,628	5,956	6,704	5,070
Vienna	5,252	323	1,455	5,656	5,374	4,696	5,432	7,632	791	6,990	767	1,124	9,802
Warsaw	5,032	322	1,588	5,934	5,563	4,679	5,147	7,368	858	7,212	901	1,425	9,609
Washington D.C.	8,807	4,182	5,800	7,892	2,051	2,598	8,157	4,839	5,225	3,504	3,676	3,794	10,174

Mexico City	Montreal	Moscow	Nairobi	New Delhi	New York	Paris	Peking	Rio de Janeiro	Rome	San Francisco	Singapore	Stockholm	Tehran	Tokyo	Vienna	Warsaw
6,677	5,146	4,038	2,603	5,279	5,126	2,988	7,359	3,501	2,624	7,688	7,183	3,835	3,874	8,594	3,100	3,440
5,735	3,426	1,337	4,136	3,958	3,654	271	4,890	5,938	807	5,465	6,526	701	2,533	5,788	581	681
3,776	3,133	4,364	8,287	5,709	3,373	4,697	3,997	8,145	5,263	2,005	6,678	4,102	5,654	3,463	4,856	4,601
7,021	4,737	1,387	2,827	3,120	4,938	1,305	4,757	6,030	654	6,792	5,629	1,498	1,539	5,924	801	996
8,274	10,231	9,018	7,315	6,420	10,194	10,519	5,626	8,259	10,048	7,692	3,848	9,732	7,935	5,017	9,886	9,676
8,082	5,768	1,583	2,431	1,966	6,007	2,405	3,925	6,938	1,836	7,466	4,427	2,164	431	5,199	1,781	1,752
9,793	8,337	4,394	4,481	1,812	8,669	5,877	2,027	9,987	5,493	7,930	887	5,141	3,392	2,865	5,252	5,032
7,707	5,405	1,514	2,420	2,479	5,622	1,987	4,352	6,478	1,368	7,302	4,935	1,931	913	5,598	1,401	1,459
6,610	4,305	1,066	3,328	3,270	4,526	902	4,634	6,145	449	6,296	5,833	1,010	1,741	5,720	309	516
6,054	3,740	1,001	3,947	3,598	3,980	549	4,600	6,207	735	5,673	6,167	505	2,184	5,557	323	322
9,739	7,524	3,132	2,811	722	7,811	4,367	2,953	8,334	3,846	8,406	2,427	3,880	1,743	4,196	3,725	3,601
4,580	5,597	8,369	6,479	9,823	5,279	6,857	11,994	1,231	6,925	6,455	9,870	7,799	8,565	11,411	7,334	7,656
7,677	5,403	1,770	2,217	2,752	5,598	1,973	4,687	6,153	1,305	7,436	5,143	2,084	1,220	5,937	1,455	1,588
8,516	7,920	6,277	2,543	5,769	7,801	5,782	8,034	3,773	5,231	10,248	6,007	6,422	5,240	9,155	5,656	5,934
2,234	2,443	6,176	7,179	8,837	2,124	4,735	8,978	2,805	5,198	3,908	11,408	5,422	7,322	8,813	5,374	5,563
1,688	746	4,984	8,012	7,486	714	4,145	6,625	5,288	4,823	1,860	9,376	4,288	6,502	6,313	4,696	4,679
5,918	3,605	971	4,156	3,640	3,857	642	4,503	6,321	953	5,473	6,195	325	2,287	5,415	540	417
1,438	1,639	5,501	8,867	7,730	1,631	4,900	6,385	5,866	5,887	953	9,079	4,879	7,033	5,815	5,395	5,322
5,945	3,650	1,261	3,865	3,811	3,857	295	4,853	5,932	595	5,700	6,386	745	2,346	5,831	388	559
6,101	3,845	554	4,282	3,247	4,126	1,192	3,956	6,872	1,370	5,435	5,759	248	2,062	4,872	895	569
8,789	7,736	4,443	5,447	2,339	8,061	5,992	1,195	11,002	5,773	6,904	1,608	5,115	3,844	1,792	5,432	5,147
3,791	4,919	7,049	10,740	7,413	4,969	7,452	5,084	8,295	8,040	2,397	6,728	6,873	8,072	3,860	7,632	7,368
749	1,605	5,925	8,746	8,388	1,419	5,035	7,244	5,015	5,702	1,648	9,954	5,227	7,442	6,685	5,609	5,609
7,106	4,798	1,087	2,957	2,837	5,022	1,400	4,407	6,378	853	6,711	5,379	1,347	1,274	5,574	791	858
9,249	6,997	2,600	2,708	678	7,277	3,817	3,020	8,082	3,306	8,078	2,942	3,340	1,194	4,313	3,175	3,052
4,614	2,317	2,083	5,404	4,749	2,597	1,402	4,951	6,090	2,068	4,196	7,181	1,352	3,568	5,497	1,813	1,745
7,915	6,378	4,328	4,234	4,692	6,378	3,742	7,002	4,105	3,186	8,920	6,132	4,388	3,612	8,307	3,619	3,910
6,276	4,005	396	4,230	3,069	4,291	1,350	3,789	7,028	1,460	5,523	5,575	431	1,926	4,733	986	642
2,635	3,967	7,855	7,821	10,430	3,635	6,367	10,365	2,351	6,748	4,516	11,689	7,109	8,850	9,628	6,990	7,212
5,396	3,255	2,433	4,013	4,844	3,377	904	6,040	4,777	1,163	5,679	7,393	1,862	3,288	6,943	1,432	1,720
5,558	3,256	1,556	4,229	4,178	3,473	215	5,089	5,751	892	5,369	6,747	892	2,739	5,956	767	901
5,642	3,449	2,140	3,840	4,528	3,596	652	5,759	5,045	849	5,806	7,079	1,613	2,974	6,704	1,124	1,425
8,420	10,390	8,965	7,159	6,340	10,352	10,442	5,632	8,218	9,940	7,850	3,767	9,693	7,838	5,070	9,802	9,609
—	2,315	6,671	9,218	9,119	2,086	5,723	7,772	4,769	6,374	1,889	10,331	5,965	8,182	7,036	6,316	6,335
2,315	—	4,397	7,267	7,012	333	3,432	6,541	5,082	4,102	2,544	9,207	3,667	5,879	6,470	4,007	4,021
6,671	4,397	—	3,928	2,703	4,680	1,550	3,627	7,162	1,477	5,884	5,236	764	1,534	4,663	1,039	716
9,218	7,267	3,928	—	3,371	7,365	4,020	5,720	5,556	3,340	9,598	4,636	4,299	2,709	6,996	3,625	3,800
9,119	7,012	2,703	3,317	—	7,319	4,103	2,350	8,747	3,684	7,691	2,574	3,466	1,584	3,638	3,467	3,277
2,086	333	4,680	7,365	7,319	—	3,638	6,867	4,805	4,293	2,574	9,539	3,939	6,141	6,757	4,233	4,271
5,722	3,418	1,024	4,446	3,726	3,686	838	4,395	6,462	1,248	5,196	6,249	260	2,462	5,238	839	661
1,496	2,542	6,720	8,043	9,422	2,213	5,388	8,939	3,296	5,916	3,326	11,692	5,956	8,011	8,441	6,031	6,175
5,723	3,432	1,550	4,020	4,103	3,638	—	5,138	5,681	688	5,579	6,676	964	2,624	6,054	643	853
7,772	6,541	3,627	5,720	2,350	6,867	5,138	—	10,778	5,076	5,934	2,754	4,197	3,496	1,305	4,664	4,340
5,612	3,537	2,579	3,733	4,841	3,636	1,125	6,206	4,589	1,184	5,995	7,348	2,084	3,263	7,174	1,546	1,866
4,769	5,082	7,162	5,556	8,747	4,805	5,681	10,778	—	5,704	6,621	9,776	6,638	7,368	11,535	6,124	6,453
6,374	4,102	1,477	3,340	3,684	4,293	688	5,076	5,704	—	6,259	6,231	1,229	2,126	6,140	476	819
9,718	8,558	4,798	4,874	2,268	8,889	6,303	2,072	10,290	5,943	7,829	682	5,534	3,851	2,689	5,687	5,454
1,889	2,544	5,884	9,598	7,691	2,574	5,579	5,934	6,621	6,259	—	8,449	5,372	7,362	5,148	5,992	5,854
4,094	5,436	8,770	7,180	10,518	5,106	7,224	11,859	1,820	7,391	5,926	10,190	8,120	9,185	10,711	7,760	8,059
2,340	2,289	5,217	9,006	7,046	2,409	5,012	5,432	6,890	5,680	679	8,074	4,731	6,686	4,793	5,381	5,222
8,033	7,067	4,248	5,951	2,646	7,384	5,772	645	11,339	5,679	6,150	2,363	4,837	3,974	1,097	5,281	4,963
5,172	2,873	1,863	4,563	4,529	3,086	563	5,288	5,597	1,247	5,040	7,089	1,135	3,117	6,064	1,153	1,258
10,331	9,207	5,236	4,636	2,574	9,539	6,676	2,754	9,776	6,231	8,449	—	5,993	4,106	3,304	6,039	5,846
1,425	978	5,248	8,231	7,736	878	4,398	6,792	5,218	5,073	1,744	9,544	4,552	6,766	6,407	4,955	4,942
5,965	3,667	764	4,299	3,466	3,939	964	4,197	6,638	1,229	5,372	5,993	—	2,217	5,091	771	504
8,182	5,879	1,534	2,709	1,584	6,141	2,624	3,496	7,386	2,126	7,362	4,106	2,217	—	4,775	1,983	1,878
7,036	6,479	4,663	6,996	3,638	6,757	6,054	1,305	11,535	6,140	5,148	3,304	5,091	4,775	—	5,689	5,346
6,316	4,007	1,039	3,625	3,467	4,233	643	4,664	6,124	476	5,992	6,039	771	1,983	5,689	—	347
6,335	4,021	716	3,800	3,277	4,271	853	4,340	6,453	819	5,854	5,846	504	1,878	5,346	347	—
1,883	490	4,873	7,550	7,500	203	3,841	6,965	4,783	4,496	2,444	9,667	4,135	6,340	6,792	4,436	4,471

WORLD AVIATION RECORDS

SOURCE: National Aeronautic Association

JET AND ROCKET AIRPLANES

Date   Record

1/10-11/62   Distance in a Straight Line
U.S.: 12,532.28 miles
Major Clyde P. Evely, USAF
Boeing B52-H
Kadena, Okinawa, to Madrid, Spain

6/6-7/62   Distance over a Closed Circuit
U.S.: 11,336.92 miles
Captain William Stevenson, USAF
Boeing B52-H
Seymour-Johnson, North Carolina; Kindley, Bermuda; Sondrestrom, Greenland; Anchorage, Alaska; March AFB, California; Key West, Florida; Seymour-Johnson, N.C.

8/31/77   Altitude
USSR: 123,523.58 feet
Alexander Fedotov
E-226M Airplane
Podmoskovnoye, USSR

7/17/62   Altitude (Rocket Powered)
U.S.: 314,750 feet
Major Robert M. White, USAF
North American X-15-1 (NASA Aircraft)
Edwards Air Force Base, California

7/28/76   Altitude in Horizontal Flight
U.S.: 85,068,997 feet
Capt. Robert C. Helt, USAF
Lockheed SR-71

7/28/76   Speed over a Straight Course
U.S.: 2,913.16 miles per hour
Capt. Eldon W. Joersz, USAF
Lockheed SR-71
Beale Air Force Base, California

7/27/76   Speed over a Closed Circuit
U.S.: 2,092.294 miles per hour
Major Adolphus H. Bledsoe, Jr., USAF
Lockheed SR-71
Beale Air Force Base, California

PROPELLER-DRIVEN AIRPLANES

Date   Record

9/29/46   Distance in a Straight Line
U.S.: 11,235.6 miles
Commander T. D. Davies, USN
Lockheed P2V-1 Monoplane
Perth, Australia to Columbus, Ohio

11/7-9/69   Distance in a Closed Circuit
U.S.: 8,974.0 miles
James R. Bede
BD-2 Airplane
Columbus, Ohio, to Kansas City Course

10/22/38   Altitude
ITALY: 56,046 feet
Mario Pezzi
Caproni 161 Biplane
Montecelio, Italy

8/14/79   Speed over a 3-Km. Course
U.S.: 499.04 miles per hour
Steve Hinton
P-51D
Tonopah, Nevada

4/9/51   Speed over a 15/25-Km. Course
U.S.: 464.374 miles per hour
Jacqueline Cochran
North American P-51
Indio, California

7/20-25/75   Speed around the World
AUSTRALIA: 203.64 miles per hour
Pilot: D. N. Dalton; Copilot: T. Gwynne-Jones
Beechcraft Duke
Brisbane, Tarawa, Honolulu, San Jose, Toronto, Gander, Gatwick, Damascus, Dubai, Madras, Singapore, Darwin, Brisbane
Elapsed Time: 5 days, 2 hours, 19 minutes, 57 seconds

Date   Record

TURBOPROP AIRPLANES

Date   Record

2/20/72   Distance in a Straight Line
U.S.: 8,732.09 miles
Lt. Col. Edgar L. Allison, Jr., USAF
Lockheed HC-130 Hercules
Ching-Chuan Kang, Taiwan to Scott AFB, Ill.

11/4/72   Distance in a Closed Circuit
U.S.: 6,278.05 miles
Cdr. Philip R. Hite, U.S. Navy
Lockheed RP-3D
NAS Patuxent River, Md.

1/27/71   Speed over a 15/25-Km. Course
U.S.: 501.44 miles per hour
Commander D. H. Lilienthal, USN
Lockheed P3C Orion
NAS Patuxent River, Md.

3/27/72   Altitude
U.S.: 51,014 feet
Donald R. Wilson
LTV-L450F Airplane
Greenville, Texas

WORLD COMMERCIAL AIRCRAFT SPEEDS

Date   Record

11/2/77   Barbados/London
ENGLAND: 1,134.85 miles per hour
Captain Norman Todd
Concorde
Elapsed time: 3 h, 42 m, 5 s

9/6/62   Chicago/Mexico City
U.S.: 534.15 miles per hour
Captain D. W. Ledbetter
Boeing 720B
Elapsed time: 3 h, 10 m, 06.3 s

4/30/60   London/Athens
GREECE: 506.29 miles per hour
Captain P. Ioanides (Olympic Airways)
Comet DH-106-4B (SXDAK)
Elapsed time: 3 h, 13 m, 42 s

6/5/62   London/Miami
ENGLAND: 321.02 miles per hour
Captain G. N. Henderson (Cunard Eagle Airways); Captain P. Wilson
Boeing 707/465
Elapsed time: 13 h, 46 m, 38 s

12/1/66   Los Angeles/Mexico City
MEXICO: 597.88 miles per hour
Captain Rafael T. Zapata (Mexicana de Aviacion)
Boeing 727-64
Elapsed time 2 h, 36 m

12/8/61   Los Angeles/New York
U.S.: 636.8 miles per hour
Captain William Miller (American Airlines, Inc.)
Boeing 707B-123
Elapsed time: 3 h, 52 m, 43 s

9/6/62   Mexico City/Chicago
U.S.: 558.28 miles per hour
Captain E. Schlanser (American Airlines, Inc.)
Boeing 720B
Elapsed time: 3 h, 1 m, 53.2 s

5/6/62   Miami/London
ENGLAND: 419.94 miles per hour
Captain P. Wilson (Cunard Eagle Airways)
Captain M. Gudmundsson
Boeing 707/465
Elapsed time: 10 h, 31 m, 55 s

5/28/60   Montreal/London
CANADA: 565.29 miles per hour
Captain R. M. Smith (Trans-Canada Air Lines)
Douglas DC 8-40
Elapsed time: 5 h, 44 m, 42 s

6/2/63   New York/Bergen
NORWAY: 533.13 miles per hour
Captain B. Bjornstad (Scandinavian Airlines Systems)
Douglas DC-8
Elapsed time: 6 h, 32 m, 20 s

Date   Record

11/26/54   New York/Madrid
SPAIN: 379.624 miles per hour
Captain C. I. Batida (Iberian Airlines)
Lockheed Super Constellation L-1049E
Elapsed time: 9 h, 29 m

2/19/74   New York/Rio de Janeiro
U.S.: 594.28 miles per hour
Capt. Theodore C. Patecell (Pan American World Airways)
Boeing 707 300 B/A
Elapsed time: 8 h, 5 m, 30 s

6/3/60   New York/San Francisco
AUSTRALIA: 510.092 miles per hour
Captain A. Yates (Quantas Empire Airways)
Boeing 707-138 VH-EBE
Elapsed time: 5 h, 3 m, 48.35 s

8/18/78   Paris/Washington, D.C.
FRANCE: 1,071.86 miles per hour
Captain Pierre Chanoine (Air France)
Concorde
Elapsed time: 3 h, 35 m, 15 s

12/8/61   San Francisco/New York
U.S.: 658 miles per hour
Captain T. E. Jonson (American Airlines, Inc.)
Boeing 707B-123
Elapsed time: 3 h, 55 m, 50 s

NATIONAL COMMERCIAL AIRCRAFT SPEEDS

Date   Record

4/10/63   West to East Transcontinental: 680.90 miles per hour
Captain Wylie H. Drummond (American Airlines, Inc.)
Boeing 707-123
Los Angeles International Airport/Idlewild Airport
Distance: 2,474 statute miles
Elapsed time: 3 h, 38 m

8/15/62   East to West Transcontinental: 575.52 miles per hour
Captain Gene Kruse (American Airlines, Inc.)
Boeing 707-720B
Idlewild Airport/Los Angeles International Airport
Distance: 2,474 statute miles
Elapsed time: 4 h, 19 m, 15 s

8/5/47   Atlanta/Chicago: 290.501 miles per hour
Captain H. T. Merrill (Eastern Air Lines)
Lockheed Constellation
Atlanta Municipal Airport/Chicago Municipal Airport
Distance: 590 miles; 2 hours, 1 minute, 55 seconds

7/19/63   Atlanta/Los Angeles: 566.82 miles per hour
Captain L. L. Caruthers (Delta Air Lines)
Douglas DC-8
Atlanta Municipal Airport/Los Angeles International Airport
Distance: 1,946 miles; 3 hours, 25 minutes, 59 seconds

1/21/63   Atlanta/New York: 589.64 miles per hour
Captain Michael Winicki (Delta Air Lines)
Douglas DC-8-51
Atlanta Municipal Airport/Idlewild Int'l Airport
Distance: 760 miles; 1 hour, 17 minutes, 20 seconds

10/30/62   Baltimore/Los Angeles: 563.46 miles per hour
Captain Howard U. Morton (American Airlines)
Boeing 707
Friendship Int'l Airport/Los Angeles Int'l Airport

Date	Record
4/29/65	**Boston/Los Angeles:** 562.57 miles per hour Captain George C. Dent (American Airlines) Boeing 707 Logan Int'l Airport/Los Angeles Int'l Airport Distance: 2,610 miles; 4 hours, 38 minutes, 21 seconds
7/20/63	**Boston/New York:** 414.61 miles per hour Captain Peter C. Bals (American Airlines) Convair 990 Logan Int'l Airport/Idlewild Int'l Airport Distance: 186 miles; 00 hours, 26 minutes, 55 seconds
8/5/47	**Chicago/Atlanta:** 326.925 miles per hour Captain H. T. Merrill (Eastern Air Lines) Lockheed Constellation Chicago Municipal Airport/Atlanta Municipal Airport Distance: 590 miles; 1 hour, 48 minutes, 20 seconds
2/16/65	**Chicago/Boston:** 692.28 miles per hour Captain Alden Young (American Airlines) Convair 990 Chicago O'Hare Airport/Logan Int'l Airport Distance: 865 miles; 1 hour, 14 minutes, 58 seconds
4/20/65	**Chicago/Fort Worth:** 548.85 miles per hour Captain Glen L. Stockwell (American Airlines) Boeing 727 O'Hare Int'l Airport/Greater Southwest Int'l Airport Distance: 809 miles; 1 hour, 28 minutes, 26 seconds
4/9/65	**Chicago/Indianapolis:** 494.93 miles per hour Captain P. G. Cook (American Airlines) Boeing 707 O'Hare Int'l Airport/WEIR Cook Int'l Airport Distance: 179 miles; 00 hours, 21 minutes, 42 seconds
1/2–3/62	**Chicago/Miami:** 588 miles per hour Captain Dean Clifton (Delta Air Lines) Convair 880 Chicago O'Hare Airport/Miami Int'l Airport Distance: 1,184 miles; 2 hours, 1 minute
10/28/65	**Chicago/New York:** 644.36 miles per hour Captain W. J. Callahan (American Airlines) Boeing 727 O'Hare Int'l Airport/LaGuardia Airport Distance: 733 miles; 1 hour, 8 minutes, 15 seconds
2/3/65	**Chicago/Washington, D.C.** 510.58 miles per hour Captain A. B. Perriello (American Airlines) Lockheed Electra L-188 O'Hare Int'l Airport/Washington National Airport Distance: 612 miles; 1 hour, 11 minutes, 5 seconds
3/12/65	**Dallas/New York:** 686.73 miles per hour Captain William F. Bonnell (American Airlines) Boeing 707/720 Love Field/John F. Kennedy Int'l Airport Distance: 1,384 miles; 2 hours, 6 minutes

Date	Record
2/18/65	**Dallas/San Francisco:** 580.46 miles per hour Captain W. R. Swain (American Airlines) Boeing 707/720 Love Field/San Francisco Int'l Airport Distance: 1,477 miles; 2 hours, 32 minutes, 40 seconds
3/12/65	**Dallas/Washington, D.C.:** 643.06 miles per hour Captain W. T. Fleming (American Airlines) Boeing 707/720 Love Field/Dulles Int'l Airport Distance: 1,162 miles; 1 hour, 48 minutes, 25 seconds
12/7/61	**Los Angeles/Baltimore:** 657.68 miles per hour Captain Stan Smith (American Airlines) Boeing 707/123B Los Angeles Int'l Airport/Friendship Airport Distance: 2,329 miles; 3 hours, 32 minutes, 28 seconds
11/26/65	**Los Angeles/Boston:** 666.61 miles per hour Captain Simon P. Bittner (American Airlines) Boeing 707 Los Angeles Int'l Airport/Logan Int'l Airport Distance: 2,610 miles; 3 hours, 54 minutes, 55 seconds
4/9/63	**Los Angeles/Chicago:** 672.80 miles per hour Captain George R. Russon (American Airlines) Boeing 707/123 Los Angeles Int'l Airport/O'Hare Int'l Airport Distance: 1,746 miles; 2 hours, 35 minutes, 42 seconds
3/9/65	**Los Angeles/Dallas:** 689.00 miles per hour Captain W. R. Hunt (American Airlines) Boeing 707/123 Los Angeles Int'l Airport/Love Field Distance: 1,245 miles; 1 hour, 48 minutes, 25 seconds
7/16/47	**Miami/Chicago:** 300.390 miles per hour Captain H. T. Merrill (Eastern Air Lines) Lockheed Constellation 36th Street Airport/Chicago Municipal Airport Distance: 1,183 miles; 3 hours, 56 minutes, 22 seconds
5/28/47	**Miami/New York:** 314.477 miles per hour Captain E. R. Brown (Eastern Air Lines) Lockheed Constellation 36th Street Airport/LaGuardia Airport Distance: 1,096 miles; 3 hours, 29 minutes, 11.4 seconds

MAN-POWERED AIRCRAFT

Date	Record
6/12/79	**Duration, Distance** U.S.: 2 hours, 49 minutes; 25 miles Bryan Allen Gossamer Albatross Folkestone, England to Cap Gris-Nez, France

BALLOONS (LARGE)

Date	Record
8/12-17/78	**Duration, Distance** U.S.: 137 hrs., 5 min., 50 secs.; 3,107.61 miles Ben L. Abruzzo, Maxie L. Anderson, Larry M. Newman; Double Eagle II Presque Isle, Maine to Miserey, France

Date	Record
5/4/61	**Altitude** U.S.: 113,739.9 feet Commander Malcolm D. Ross, USNR "Lee Lewis Memorial" Gulf of Mexico

GLIDERS

Date	Record
4/25/72	**Distance in a Straight Line** W. GERMANY: 907.7 miles Hans Werner Grosse ASK 12 Sailplane Luebeck, W. Ger. to Biarritz, France.
1/14/78	**Distance to a Goal** NEW ZEALAND: Group Flight; David Wapier Speight, S. H. Georgeson, Bruce Lindsay Drake Nimbus 2
5/9/77	**Distance to a Goal and Return** U.S.: 1,015.81 miles Karl Striedieck ASW 17 Sailplane Lock Haven, Pennsylvania
2/25/61	**Altitude above Sea Level** U.S.: 46,267 feet Paul F. Bikle Schweizer SCG 123 E. Sailplane Mojave, Lancaster, California
2/25/61	**Altitude Gained** U.S.: 42,303 feet Paul F. Bikle Schweizer SGA 123 E. Sailplane Mojave, Lancaster, California

HELICOPTERS

Date	Record
4/6–7/66	**Distance in a Straight Line** U.S.: 2,213.04 miles Robert G. Ferry Hughes YOH 6A helicopter Culver City, California to Daytona Beach, Florida
3/26/66	**Distance in a Closed Circuit** U.S.: 1,739.96 miles Jack Schweibold Hughes YOH-6A helicopter Edwards AFB, California
6/21/72	**Altitude** FRANCE: 40,820 feet Jean Boulet Alouette SA 315-001 "Lama" Helicopter Istres, France
11/4/71	**Altitude in Horizontal Flight** U.S.: 36,122 feet CWO James K. Church, USA Sikorsky CH-54B Helicopter Stratford, Connecticut
12/14/70	**Speed over a 3 Km Course** U.S.: 216.839 miles per hour Byron Graham Sikorsky S-67 Helicopter Windsor Locks, Connecticut
9/21/78	**Speed over a 15/25 Km Course** USSR: 228.91 Miles per hour Gourguen Karapetyan Helicopter A-10 Podmoskovnoye Aerodrome

HANG GLIDING

Date	Record
7/7/79	**Distance in a straight line** U.S.: 64.77 miles Alan Reeter UP Mosquito Bishop, California
7/22/78	**Gain in Altitude** U.S.: 11,700 feet George D. Worthington Seagull 10 Meter Cerro Gordo Peak, California
7/21/77	**Straight Distance to Goal** U.S.: 95.44 miles George D. Worthington ASG-21 Albatross Sails Cerro Gordo Peak, Calif. to Benton Station, Calif.

BUSIEST WORLD AIRPORTS Source: International Civil Aviation Organization

Airports are ranked here according to their total passenger traffic (embarked plus disembarked) for 1978. USSR airports opened to domestic traffic exclusively are not included.

Airport	Passengers (in millions)	Airport	Passengers (in millions)	Airport	Passengers (in millions)	Airport	Passengers (in millions)
Chicago (O'Hare)	49.2	Miami	16.5	Pittsburgh	9.7	Minneapolis	8.4
Atlanta	36.5	Frankfurt	14.9	Houston	9.7	Saint Louis	8.2
Los Angeles	32.9	Osaka	14.7	Philadelphia	9.5	Palma de Mallorca	7.9
London (Heathrow)	26.5	Washington (Nat'l)	14.2	Amsterdam	9.1	London (Gatwick)	7.8
New York (Kennedy)	24.8	Honolulu	13.8	Las Vegas	9.1	Zürich	7.3
San Francisco	21.5	Paris (Orly)	13.7	Mexico City	9.1	Sydney	7.3
Tokyo Int'l	20.6	Boston (Logan)	13.5	Paris (De Gaulle)	9.0	Cleveland	7.1
Dallas/Fort Worth	19.9	Toronto	12.4	Copenhagen	8.7	Tampa	7.0
Denver	18.9	Madrid	10.6	New York (Newark)	8.5	Taipei	6.4
New York (La Guardia)	17.1	Rome (Fiumicino)	10.3	Athens	8.4	Düsseldorf	6.2
		Detroit	9.6	Seattle	8.4	San Diego	6.2

MAJOR INTERNATIONAL AIRPORTS Source: International Civil Aviation Organization

Airports on the list are ranked according to the total international passenger traffic for 1978. *Estimated data.

Airport	City	PASSENGERS (000)			COMM'L OPERATIONS (000)		
		International	Domestic	Total	International	Domestic	Total
Heathrow	London	22,782	3,709	26,491	210.4	58.4	268.8
J.F. Kennedy	New York	12,521	12,318	24,839	94.1	163.7	257.8
Frankfurt-Main	Frankfurt	10,304	4,558	14,862	131.9	71.3	203.2
Schiphol	Amsterdam	8,986	129	9,115	137.6	5.6	143.2
Orly	Paris	8,263	5,430	13,693	98.2	73.1	171.3
De Gaulle	Paris	8,054	995	9,049	87.3	16.1	103.4
Zürich	Zürich	6,979	341	7,320	103.5	7.6	111.1
Gatwick	London	6,966	793	7,759	74.5	24.5	99.0
Kastrup	Copenhagen	6,908	1,766	8,674	118.6	32.9	151.5
Fiumicino	Rome	6,200*	4,083*	10,283	—	—	143.0
Miami Int'l	Miami	5,939	10,562	16,501	—	—	281.5
Palm de Mallorca	Palma de Mallorca	5,920	1,961	7,881	54.4	24.6	79.0
Toronto Int'l	Toronto	5,873	6,499	12,372	66.7	101.3	168.0
Hong Kong Int'l	Hong Kong	5,590	—	5,590	52.6	.3	52.9
Athinai	Athens	4,865*	3,546*	8,411*	68.7*	41.1*	109.8*
Bruxelles Nat'l	Brussels	4,824	5	4,829	80.6	.2	80.8
Singapore	Singapore	4,814	—	4,814	63.4	—	63.4
Düsseldorf	Düsseldorf	4,403	1,795	6,198	47.2	34.2	81.4
Los Angeles Int'l	Los Angeles	4,155	28,711	32,866	36.7	343.8	380.5
Barajas	Madrid	3,861	6,718	10,579	48.8	75.5	124.3
Cairo Int'L	Cairo	3,653	319	3,972	43.6	8.0	51.6
New Tokyo Int'l	Tokyo	3,600*	343	3,943	—	—	35.6
Arlanda	Stockholm	3,387	986	4,373	51.2	17.8	69.0
Cointrin	Geneva	3,275	638	3,913	56.8	14.7	71.5
Linate	Milan	3,200*	1,647*	4,847	—	—	78.0
Bangkok	Bangkok	3,181	350	3,531	42.1	6.7	48.8
München	Munich	3,031	2,252	5,283	42.1	37.7	79.8
Benito Juarez	Mexico City	3,028	6,030	9,058	37.0	72.7	109.7
O'Hare Int'l	Chicago	2,823	46,362	49,185	29.5	708.2	737.7
Tokyo Int'l	Tokyo	2,686	17,937	20,623	22.6	119.0	141.6
Sheremetievo	Moscow	2,642	1,029	3,671	43.5	16.2	59.7
Schwechat	Vienna	2,577	3	2,580	49.0	.2	49.2
Ben Gurion	Tel Aviv	2,516	—	2,516	20.8	—	20.8

AIRLINE TRAFFIC VOLUME Source: International Civil Aviation Organization

According to estimates released in March 1980 by the International Civil Aviation Organization for its 145 member states,* in 1979 the airlines carried 640 million passengers for a total of 794,000 million kilometers (553,000 million passenger miles on scheduled services), representing increases of 14.9 percent over 1978.

Year	Miles Flown	Hours Flown	Passengers Carried	Passenger-Miles	Average Number of Passengers per Aircraft	Average Number of Miles Flown per Passenger	Average Number of Miles Flown per hr.
	(In Millions)						
1979	5,590	14.2	640	553,000	99	864	394
1978	5,780	14.0	580	495,000	94	853	377
1977	5,030	13.4	517	429,000	85	830	377
1976	4,870	13.0	475	393,000	81	828	374
1975	4,670	12.6	436	356,000	76	817	371
1974	4,580	12.5	424	340,000	74	802	366
1973	4,660	12.7	405	323,000	69	798	367
1972	4,480	12.2	368	288,500	64	784	367
1971	4,390	12.2	333	253,500	58	771	360
1970	4,355	12.1	311	237,500	55	762	360
1969	4,170	11.8	293	218,000	52	744	354
1968	3,730	11.0	262	192,500	52	736	339
1967	3,290	10.2	233	169,500	52	727	320
1966	2,790	9.3	200	142,000	51	711	301
1965	2,550	8.7	177	123,000	48	696	292
1964	2,300	8.2	155	106,000	46	687	280
1963	2,130	7.9	135	91,500	43	674	270
1962	2,015	7.8	121	80,500	40	668	261
1961	1,940	8.0	111	72,500	38	656	242
1960	1,930	8.6	106	67,500	35	640	224
1959	1,920	9.0	99	61,000	32	615	214
1958	1,820	8.8	88	53,000	29	603	208
1957	1,765	8.7	86	51,000	29	590	202
1956	1,580	8.0	77	44,000	28	570	199
1955	1,425	7.3	68	38,000	27	562	196

*Except USSR

SAFETY RECORD: U.S. CERTIFICATED AND SUPPLEMENTAL AIR CARRIERS*

SOURCE: National Transportation Safety Board

Year	Number of Accidents		Fatalities				Aircraft Miles Flown	Accident Rate per Million Aircraft Miles Flown	
	Total	Fatal	Passg.	Crew	Others	Total		Total Accidents	Fatal Accidents
1960	90	17	429	57	13	499	1,130,069,000	.078	.011
1965	83	9	226	35	0	261	1,536,395,000**	.054	.006
1967	70	12	229	39	18	286	2,179,739,000**	.032	.006
1968	71	15	306	37	6	349	2,498,848,000**	.028	.005
1969	63	10	132	22	4	158	2,736,596,000**	.023	.003
1970	55	8	118	24	4	146	2,684,552,000**	.020	.003
1971	48	8	174	23	6	203	2,660,731,000**	.018	.002
1972	50	8	160	17	13	190	2,619,043,000**	.019	.003
1973	43	9	200	26	1	227	2,646,669,000**	.016	.003
1974	47	9	421	46	0	467	2,464,295,000**	.019	.003
1975	45	3	113	11	0	124	2,477,764,000**	.018	.001
1976	28	4	39	6	0	45	2,568,113,000**	.011	.002
1977	26	5	381	17	257	655	2,684,072,000**	.010	.002
1978	24	6	141	12	10	163	2,742,860,000	.009	.002
1979[1]	33	6	321	29	3	353	2,928,950,000	.011	.002

*Beginning in 1975, accidents involving commercial operators of large aircraft are included. Beginning in 1979, accidents of deregulated all-cargo carriers are included.

**Nonrevenue miles of the supplemental air carriers are not reported.

[1]Preliminary.

SAFETY RECORD: WORLD SCHEDULED AIRLINES[1]

SOURCE: International Civil Aviation Organization

Year	Number of Accidents: Passenger-carrying Aircraft	Number of Passengers Killed	Fatality Rate (per 100 million Pass.-mi.)	Fatal Accidents (per 100 million Mi. Flown)	Fatal Accidents[†]	Year	Number of Accidents: Passenger-carrying Aircraft	Number of Passengers Killed	Fatality Rate (per 100 million Pass.-mi.)	Fatal Accidents (per 100 million Mi. Flown)	Fatal Accidents[†]
1950	27	581	3.15	3.02	0.54	1969	32	946	0.43	0.77	0.27
1952	21	386	1.54	1.90	0.34	1970	28	687	0.29	0.64	0.23
1954	28	443	1.36	2.19	0.42	1971	31	867	0.34	0.71	0.26
1956	27	552	1.25	1.71	0.34	1972	42	1,210	0.42	0.94	0.34
1958	30	609	1.15	1.65	0.34	1973	36	862	0.27	0.77	0.28
1960	34	873	1.29	1.71	0.38	1974	29	1,299	0.38	0.62	0.23
1962	29	778	1.97	1.44	0.37	1975	20	443	0.13	0.43	0.16
1964	25	616	0.58	1.09	0.30	1976	20	734	0.19	0.41	0.15
1966	31	1,001	0.70	1.12	0.33	1977	24	516	0.11	0.48	0.18
1968	35	912	0.47	0.94	0.32	1978	25	755	0.15	0.47	0.18
						1979*	31	871	0.16	0.57	0.22

[†]Per 100,000 aircraft hours.   [1]Excluding USSR.   *Preliminary figures.

WORLD'S FASTEST TRAINS[1]

SOURCE: Donald M. Steffee

Railroad	Train	From	To	Miles	Time (min.)	Speed (mph)
Passenger						
Japanese National	Hikari Train	Nagoya	Shizuoka	108.4	59	110.2
British Rail	High Speed Trains (2 runs)	Stevenage	Peterborough	48.8	271/2	106.5
French National	Etendard	St. Pierre des Corps	Poitiers	62.7	37	101.5
German Federal	Two Trains	Uelzen	Celle	32.5	21	92.9
VIA (Canada)	Turbotrain	Kingston	Guildwood	145.1	101	86.2
Amtrak	Chesapeake	Perryville	Elkton	14.6	10	87.6
Swedish State	No. 142	Skvode	Laza	52.2	41	77.4
Italian State	Rapido	Rome	Chiusi	91.9	72	76.6
Freight						
British Rail	Freightliner	Carlisle	Wigan	105.3	951/2	66.2
Union Pacific	BASV	North Platte	Cheyenne	225.4	205	66.0
French National	Freight Express	Orange	St. Rambert de Albon	87.6	81	64.9

[1]Fastest run in each country.

FASTEST AMERICAN PASSENGER TRAINS

SOURCE: Donald M. Steffee

Railroad	Train	From	To	Miles	Time (min.)	Speed (mph)
Amtrak	Chesapeake	Perryville	Elkton	14.6	10	87.6
Amtrak	Southwest Limited	Garden City	Lamar	99.9	73	82.1
Amtrak	Southwest Limited	Dodge City	Hutchinson	120.1	90	80.1
Amtrak	Chesapeake	Elkton	Perryville	14.6	11	79.7
Conrail	Jersey Arrow	Princeton Jct.	Newark	38.4	29	79.4
Amtrak	Southwest Limited	Lamar	Garden City	99.9	77	77.8
Amtrak	San Francisco Zephyr	Akron	McCook	142.9	112	76.5
Amtrak	Chesapeake	Edmondson	Odenton	15.3	12	76.5
Amtrak	Metroliners (9 runs)	Wilmington	Baltimore	68.4	54	76.0
Amtrak	Southwest Limited	Marceline	Carrollton	39.1	31	75.7

SELECTED MERCHANT FLEETS OF THE WORLD SOURCE: U.S. Maritime Administration

Country of Registry	Number	Gross Tons	Dead-weight Tons	Country of Registry	Number	Gross Tons	Dead-weight Tons
TOTAL—ALL COUNTRIES	24,641	380,312	647,378	Italy	609	11,007	18,606
United States	879	14,681	21,926	Ivory Coast	21	192	250
Privately Owned	584	12,158	18,981	Japan	1,781	35,126	59,947
Government Owned	295	2,523	2,945	Korea, North*	14	58	85
Reserve Fleet	260	2,197	2,561	Korea, South	301	2,856	4,7788
Other	35	326	384	Kuwait	88	2,174	3,677
Algeria	69	1,133	1,774	Lebanon	66	197	264
Argentina	188	1,842	2,710	Liberia	2,439	79,389	154,180
Australia	80	1,401	2,173	Libya	26	835	1,531
Austria	11	75	115	Malaysia	54	519	782
Bangladesh	27	236	342	Maldives	30	86	110
Belgium	68	1,547	2,421	Mexico	52	550	850
Brazil	285	3,679	6,071	Morocco	46	320	521
British Colonies	175	2,865	4,483	Netherlands	443	4,777	7,701
Bulgaria*	112	1,058	1,530	New Zealand	26	210	256
Canada	130	1,119	1,676	Nigeria	23	302	492
Chile	48	529	837	Norway	884	27,889	49,875
China (People's Rep.)*	559	5,385	8,078	Pakistan	48	424	570
China (Republic of)	149	1,744	2,813	Panama	2,170	19,895	32,605
Colombia	41	271	352	Peru	43	427	655
Cuba*	86	658	871	Philippines	178	1,060	1,564
Cyprus	483	2,136	3,088	Poland	310	3,121	4,917
Czechoslovakia	15	151	226	Portugal	85	1,086	1,767
Denmark	340	5,061	8,472	Romania*	163	1,546	2,324
Ecuador	24	195	271	Saudi Arabia	61	1,197	2,115
Egypt	82	428	585	Singapore	634	7,342	12,051
Finland	181	2,081	3,309	Somalia	16	91	130
France	383	11,220	19,704	South Africa	35	575	746
Germany, East*	155	1,288	1,798	Spain	495	7,175	12,733
Germany, West	592	8,759	14,289	Sweden	265	6,245	10,819
Ghana	23	137	186	Switzerland	27	235	354
Greece	2,693	33,744	57,146	Thailand	48	265	405
Honduras	24	123	128	Tunisia	19	105	144
Hungary*	23	78	110	Turkey	154	1,179	1,801
Iceland	33	63	93	USSR[1]*	2,501	16,209	21,411
India	364	5,570	9,044	United Arab Emirates	14	112	201
Indonesia	219	900	1,234	United Kingdom	1,228	28,122	46,921
Iran	57	1,053	1,734	Venezuela	74	727	1,045
Iraq	36	1,228	2,257	Vietnam	34	170	258
Ireland	25	156	241	Yugoslavia	245	2,279	3,475
Israel	37	406	542	Zaire	9	86	129

†Oceangoing ships (1,000 gross tons and more) as of December 31, 1978. Tonnage in thousands. *Source material limited [1]Includes 2 U.S. Government-owned ships transferred to USSR under lend-lease agreements.

FOREIGN COMMERCE AT SELECTED U.S. PORTS: 1977

SOURCE: U.S. Corps of Engineers (figures in thousands of short tons of cargo)

Port	Imports	Exports	Port	Imports	Exports
ATLANTIC COAST PORTS			New Orleans, La.	25,214	39,074
New Haven Harbor, Conn.	1,963	209	Pascagoula Harbor, Miss.	8,965	2,228
New Castle and vicinity, Del.	3,407	1	Beaumont, Texas	23,870	2,934
Wilmington Harbor, Del.	1,248	200	Brownsville, Texas	848	284
Canaveral Harbor, Fla.	1,328	52	Corpus Christi, Texas	19,926	4,282
Jacksonville Harbor, Fla.	3,994	1,815	Freeport Harbor, Texas	10,140	1,277
Miami Harbor, Fla.	957	1,118	Galveston Channel, Texas	1,653	5,922
Port Everglades Harbor, Fla.	1,705	145	Harbor Island, Texas	7,392	10
Savannah Harbor, Ga.	4,130	2,074	Houston Ship Channel, Texas	35,514	15,527
Portland Harbor, Maine	13,288	30	Matagorda Ship Channel, Texas	2,958	261
Baltimore Harbor and Channels, Md.	14,101	14,040	Port Arthur, Texas	14,009	2,601
Fall River Harbor, Mass.	5,285	1,947	Texas City Channel, Texas	12,314	740
Port of Boston, Mass.	7,547	502			
Salem Harbor, Mass.	1,649	932	**PACIFIC COAST PORTS**		
Portsmouth Harbor, N.H.	1,977	—	Skagway Harbor, Alaska	374	630
Camden-Gloucester, N.J.	1,899	328	Long Beach Harbor, Calif.	17,545	4,988
Paulsboro and vicinity, N.J.	12,805	66	Los Angeles Harbor, Calif.	13,661	3,165
Port of Albany, N.Y.	1,765	685	Oakland Harbor, Calif.	1,737	1,991
Port of New York, N.Y. and N.J.	60,921	5,687	Richmond Harbor, Calif.	10,738	439
Port of Wilmington, N.C.	3,405	300	San Francisco Harbor, Calif.	660	745
Marcus Hook and vicinity, Pa.	15,348	108	Stockton, Calif.	327	805
Penn Manor and vicinity, Pa.	4,613	22	Barbers Point Harbor, Hawaii	4,795	—
Philadelphia Harbor, Pa.	26,592	3,477	Honolulu Harbor, Hawaii	1,059	89
Providence River and Harbor, R.I.	1,246	408	Coos Bay, Oreg.	45	4,816
Charleston Harbor, S.C.	3,460	1,553	Port of Astoria, Oreg.	32	1,258
Norfolk Harbor, Va.	6,394	26,114	Port of Portland, Oreg.	1,736	6,848
Port of Newport News, Va.	801	5,618	Anacortes Harbor, Wash.	6,161	60
San Juan Harbor, P.R.	3,312	295	Everett Harbor & Snowhomish R., Wash.	665	1,305
			Grays Harbor & Chehalis R., Wash.	1	2,138
GULF COAST PORTS			Port Angeles Harbor, Wash.	746	1,539
Mobile Harbor, Ala.	8,167	5,521	Port of Longview, Wash.	684	4,256
Tampa Harbor, Fla.	4,585	16,472	Port of Vancouver, Wash.	1,072	310
Baton Rouge, La.	16,826	8,679	Seattle Harbor, Wash.	4,630	1,990
Lake Charles (Calcasieu R. & Pass), La.	8,130	1,530	Tacoma Harbor, Wash.	2,678	4,579

MAJOR WORLD SHIP CANALS

Name	Location	Year Opened	Length (Miles)	Minimum Depth (Feet)	Minimum Width (Feet)
Baltic-White Sea	USSR: Povenets on Lake Onega to Belmorsk on White Sea	1933	140	16	NA
Cape Cod	U.S.: Buzzards Bay to Cape Cod Bay, Mass.	1914	17.4	32	450
Chesapeake and Delaware	U.S.: Delaware River to Chesapeake Bay	1927	19	35	450
Chicago Sanitary and Ship	U.S.: Lake Michigan to Des Plaines River, Ill.	1900	33.8	20	160
Corinth	Greece: Gulf of Athens to Gulf of Corinth	1893	3.5	26.25	69
Houston Ship	U.S.: Houston, Texas, to Gulf of Mexico	1914	50	36	300
Kiel (Nord-Ostsee)	Germany: North Sea to Baltic Sea	1895	53.2	38	144
Manchester Ship	England: Manchester to Mersey River	1894	35.5	28	90
Moscow	USSR: Moscow to Volga River	1937	80	18	280
North Sea	Netherlands: Amsterdam to IJmuiden	1876	17.5	45	443
Panama	Panama: Cristóbal on Atlantic Ocean to Balboa on Pacific Ocean	1914	50.72	41.6	300
St. Lawrence Seaway	U.S.-Canada: Atlantic Ocean to Great Lakes system	1959	2,347*	27	450
Sault Sainte Marie (Canadian)	U.S.-Canada: Lake Huron to Lake Superior	1895	1.38	27	150
Sault Sainte Marie (American)	U.S.-Canada: Lake Huron to Lake Superior	1855	1.8	27	80
Suez	Egypt: Port Said on Mediterranean Sea to Suez on Gulf of Suez	1869	100.76	42	196
Terneuzen-Ghent	Belgium-Netherlands: Ghent to Scheldt Estuary at Terneuzen	1827	11	29	164
Volga-Baltic	USSR: Caspian Sea to Leningrad on Baltic Sea	1964	225	NA	NA
Volga-Don	USSR: Volga River to Don River, as linking waterway for Baltic-Black Sea route	1952	62	NA	NA
Welland	Canada: Lake Erie to Lake Ontario	1932	27.6	27	80

* Distance from Strait of Belle Isle to Duluth, Minnesota. NA = Not Available.

PANAMA CANAL USERS: 1978

SOURCE: *Statistical Abstract of the U.S.,* 1979

Commercial Ocean Traffic

Nationality of vessel	Transits	Net tons (1,000)	Cargo (1,000 long tons)
UNITED STATES	1,633	27,000	25,200
Germany, West	525	5,200	3,800
United Kingdom	1,093	12,500	10,200
Greece	1,316	15,300	17,900
Japan	912	13,100	8,300
Liberia	1,847	28,200	29,400
Netherlands	177	1,600	1,200
Norway	523	8,900	7,400
Panama	975	8,700	7,500
Sweden	247	3,900	2,400
All Others	3,429	32,500	29,200

PANAMA CANAL TRAFFIC, 1950-1978

SOURCE: *Statistical Abstract of the U.S.,* 1979

Commercial Ocean Traffic

	Total Transits	Transits	Cargo (long tons)
1950	5,900	5,400	28,900,000
1955	8,300	8,000	40,600,000
1960	12,100	10,800	59,300,000
1965	12,900	11,800	76,600,000
1970	15,500	13,700	114,300,000
1972	15,200	13,800	109,200,000
1973	15,100	13,800	126,100,000
1974	15,300	14,000	147,900,000
1975	14,700	13,600	140,100,000
1976	13,200	12,200	117,200,000
1977	13,100	11,900	123,000,000
1978	13,800	12,700	142,500,000

WORLD CITIES: STANDARD TIME DIFFERENCES

When it is 12 noon in New York (Eastern Standard Time), the standard time in other cities is as follows:

City	Time	City	Time	City	Time	City	Time
Alexandria	7:00 p.m.	Delhi	10:30 p.m.	Ketchikan	9:00 a.m.	Rome	6:00 p.m.
Amsterdam	6:00 p.m.	Denver	10:00 a.m.	Kinshasa	6:00 p.m.	Salt Lake City	10:00 a.m.
Anchorage	7:00 a.m.	Djakarta	12:00 Midnight	Lima	12:00 Noon	San Francisco	9:00 a.m.
Athens	7:00 p.m.			Lisbon	6:00 p.m.		
Auckland	5:00 a.m.*	Dublin	5:00 p.m.	London (Greenwich)	5:00 p.m.	San Juan	1:00 p.m.
Baghdad	8:00 p.m.	Fairbanks	7:00 a.m.	Los Angeles	9:00 a.m.	Santiago	1:00 p.m.
Bangkok	12:00 Midnight	Frankfurt	6:00 p.m.	Madrid	6:00 p.m.	Seattle	9:00 a.m.
Barcelona	6:00 p.m.	Frobisher Bay	1:00 p.m.	Manila	1:00 a.m.*	Seoul	2:00 a.m.*
Basra	8:00 p.m.	Gander	1:30 p.m.	Melbourne	3:00 a.m.*	Shanghai	1:00 a.m.*
Beirut	7:00 p.m.	Geneva	6:00 p.m.	Miami	12:00 Noon	Singapore	12:30 a.m.*
Berlin	6:00 p.m.	Glasgow	5:00 p.m.	Monrovia	4:15 p.m.	Stockholm	6:00 p.m.
Bogotá	12:00 Noon	Halifax	1:00 p.m.	Montevideo	2:00 p.m.	Suva	5:00 a.m.*
Bombay	10:30 p.m.	Hamilton (Bermuda)	1:00 p.m.	Moscow	8:00 p.m.	Sydney	3:00 a.m.*
Boston	12:00 Noon	Havana	12:00 Noon	New Orleans	11:00 a.m.	Tehran	8:30 p.m.
Brussels	6:00 p.m.	Helsinki	7:00 p.m.	Nome	6:00 a.m.	Tel Aviv	7:00 p.m.
Bucharest	7:00 p.m.	Ho Chi Minh City (Saigon)	1:00 a.m.*	Nouméa	4:00 a.m.*	Tokyo	2:00 a.m.*
Budapest	6:00 p.m.			Oslo	6:00 p.m.	Tucson	10:00 a.m.
Buenos Aires	2:00 p.m.			Papeete	7:00 a.m.	Valparaíso	1:00 p.m.
Cairo	7:00 p.m.	Hong Kong	1:00 a.m.*	Paris	6:00 p.m.	Vancouver	9:00 a.m.
Calcutta	10:30 p.m.	Honolulu	7:00 a.m.	Peking	1:00 a.m.*	Vienna	6:00 p.m.
Cape Town	7:00 p.m.	Istanbul	7:00 p.m.	Phoenix	10:00 a.m.	Vladivostok	2:00 a.m.*
Caracas	1:00 p.m.	Jerusalem	7:00 p.m.	Portland	9:00 a.m.	Warsaw	6:00 p.m.
Chicago	11:00 a.m.	Johannesburg	7:00 p.m.	Rangoon	11:30 p.m.	Washington, D.C.	12:00 Noon
Copenhagen	6:00 p.m.	Juneau	8:00 a.m.	Recife	2:00 p.m.	Whitehorse	9:00 a.m.
Dakar	5:00 p.m.	Karachi	10:00 p.m.	Reykjavík	5:00 p.m.	Yokohama	2:00 a.m.*
Damascus	7:00 p.m.			Rio de Janeiro	2:00 p.m.	Zürich	6:00 p.m.

* = following day.

PASSENGER LINERS

SOURCE: Cruise Lines International Association

Ship Name	Line	Flag	Length, ft.	Tonnage	Max. No. Passengers
Norway	Norwegian Caribbean Lines	Norwegian	1,035	66,348	2,000
Queen Elizabeth 2	Cunard Line, Ltd.	British	963	67,139	1,815
Canberra	P & O Cruises, Ltd.	British	820	45,000	1,800
Oriana	P & O Cruises, Ltd.	British	804	42,000	1,800
Oceanic	Home Lines Cruises	Panamanian	774	39,241	1,034
Festivale	Carnival Cruise Lines	Panamanian	760	38,175	1,400
Rotterdam	Holland America Cruises	Netherlands	748	38,000	1,050
Italis	Chandris, Inc.	Panamanian	723	34,449	2,258
Arcadia	P & O Cruises, Ltd.	British	721	30,000	1,275
Eugenio C.	Costa Cruises	Italian	713	30,000	1,637
Sea Princess	P & O Cruises, Ltd.	British	660	27,000	844
Mardi Gras	Carnival Cruise Lines	Panamanian	650	27,250	1,240
Britanis	Chandris, Inc.	Greek	642	24,351	1,600
Ellinis	Chandris, Inc.	Greek	642	24,351	1,642
Statendam	Holland America Cruises	Netherlands	642	24,500	800
Carnivale	Carnival Cruise Lines	Panamanian	640	27,250	1,350
Maxim Gorki	Black Sea Shipping Co.	USSR	639	25,002	650
Song of Norway	Royal Caribbean Cruise Line	Norwegian	635	23,005	1,040
Nordic Prince	Royal Caribbean Cruise Line	Norwegian	635	23,000	1,038
Navarino	Karageorgis Cruises	Greek	631	23,000	772
Doric	Home Lines Cruises	Panamanian	629	25,300	720
Vistafjord	Norwegian American Cruises	Norwegian	628	25,000	660
Emerald Seas	Eastern Steamship Lines	Panamanian	622	24,458	920
Sagafjord	Norwegian American Cruises	Norwegian	620	24,000	475
Veendam	Holland America Cruises	Panamanian	617	23,500	666
Volendam	Holland America Cruises	Panamanian	617	23,500	679
Fairsea	Sitmar Cruises	Liberian	608	25,000	830
Fairwind	Sitmar Cruises	Liberian	608	25,000	830
Federico C.	Costa Cruises	Italian	606	20,416	800
Calypso	Paquet Cruises	Panamanian	603	20,000	734

WORLD'S LEADING BRIDGES

SOURCE: American Society of Civil Engineers

Bridges listed here are grouped by type of construction and ranked by the length of their spans.

SUSPENSION BRIDGES (Steel)

Bridge	Main Span Meters	Feet	Completion Date	Location
Humber	1,410	4,626	*	Hull, England
Verrazano-Narrows	1,298	4,260	1964	New York City
Golden Gate	1,280	4,200	1937	San Francisco
Mackinac Straits	1,158	3,800	1957	Mackinaw City, Michigan
Bosporus	1,074	3,524	1973	Istanbul, Turkey
George Washington	1,067	3,500	1931	New York City
Tagus	1,013	3,323	1966	Lisbon, Portugal
Forth Road	1,006	3,300	1964	Scotland
Severn	988	3,240	1966	England/Wales
Tacoma Narrows	853	2,800	1950	Washington
Angostura	712	2,336	1967	Ciudad Bolívar, Venezuela
Kanmon Strait	712	2,336	1973	Honshu, Japan
San Francisco-Oakland	704	2,310	1936	San Francisco
Bronx-Whitestone	701	2,300	1939	New York City
Quebec	668	2,190	1970	Quebec, Canada
Delaware Memorial I & II	655	2,150	1951, 1968	Wilmington, Delaware
Melville Gas Pipe	610	2,000	1951	Louisiana
Walt Whitman	610	2,000	1957	Philadelphia
Tancarville	608	1,995	1959	Le Havre, France
Lillebaelt	600	1,968	1970	Lillebaelt Strait, Denmark
Ambassador	564	1,850	1929	Detroit, Michigan
Throgs Neck	549	1,800	1961	New York City
Benjamin Franklin	533	1,750	1926	Philadelphia
Skojmen	525	1,722	1972	Narvik, Norway
Kvalsund	525	1,722	1976	Kvalsund, Norway
Kleve-Emmerich	500	1,640	1965	Emmerich, West Germany
Bear Mountain	497	1,632	1924	New York
Newport	487	1,600	1969	Rhode Island
Chesapeake	487	1,600	1952	Maryland
Williamsburg	487	1,600	1903	New York City
Brooklyn	486	1,595	1883	New York City
Lion's Gate	472	1,550	1938	British Columbia, Canada
Hirado	465		1977	Nagasaki, Japan
Mid-Hudson	457	1,500	1930	New York
Manhattan	448	1,470	1909	New York City
Triborough	420	1,380	1937	New York City

CABLE-STAYED BRIDGES

Orthotropic Steel Deck

Bridge	Main Span Meters	Feet	Completion Date	Location
Hooghly River	457	1,500	*	Calcutta, India
Saint Nazaire	404	1,325	1975	Brittany, France
Stretto di Rande	400	1,312	*	Vigo, Spain
Luling	376	1,235	*	Louisiana
Yamatogawa	355		*	Osaka, Japan
Duisburg-Neuenkamp	350	1,148	1970	West Germany
West Gate	336	1,102	1974	Melbourne, Australia
Brazo Largo	330	1,083	1977	Guazu, Argentina
Zarate	330	1,083	1977	Palmas, Argentina
Kohlbrand	325	1,066	1974	Hamburg, West Germany
Knee	320	1,050	1969	Dusseldorf, West Germany

Prestressed Concrete Deck

Bridge	Main Span Meters	Feet	Completion Date	Location
Brotonne	320	1,050	1976	Caudebec, France
Pasco, Kennewick	299	981	1979	Washington
Wadi-Kuf	282	925	1972	Beida, Libya
Tiel	267	876	1975	Waal, Netherlands
Manuel Belgrano	245	804	1973	Corrientes, Argentina
Rafael Urdaneta	235	771	1962	Maracaibo, Venezuela
Poleevera	208	682	1967	Genoa, Italy

*Under construction.

STEEL TRUSS BRIDGES

Bridge	Main Span (Meters)	Main Span (Feet)	Completion Date	Location
Cantilever				
Quebec	549	1,800	1918	St. Lawrence River, Canada
Forth	521	1,710	1889	Scotland
Minato	510	1,673	1974	Osaka, Japan
Commodore J.J. Barry	501	1,644	1974	Pennsylvania
Greater New Orleans	480	1,575	1958	Louisiana
Howrah	457	1,500	1943	Calcutta, India
East Bay	427	1,400	1936	Oakland, Calif.
Baton Rouge	376	1,235	1968	Louisiana
Astoria	376	1,235	1966	Oregon
Tappan Zee	369	1,212	1956	New York
Longview	366	1,200	1930	Washington
Baltimore	366	1,200	1976	Maryland
Queensboro	360	1,182	1908	New York City
Continuous				
Astoria	376	1,235	1966	Oregon
Oshima	325	1,066	1976	Japan
Tenmon	300	984	1966	Japan
Kuronoseto	300	984	1974	Japan
Dubuque	258	945	1943	Iowa
Braga Memorial	256	840	1966	Massachusetts
Earle	252	825	1956	Kentucky
Lincoln Trail	252	825	1966	Indiana
Cairo	250	820	1975	Illinois
Simple Span				
Metropolis	219	720	1917	Illinois
Municipal	204	668	1910	St. Louis, Missouri
Elizabethtown	179	586	1906	Ohio

LONGEST ARCHES

Bridge	Main Span (Meters)	Main Span (Feet)	Completion Date	Location
Steel				
New River Gorge	518	1,700	1977	West Virginia
Bayonne	510	1,675	1931	New Jersey
Sydney Harbor	509	1,670	1932	Sydney, Australia
Fremont	383	1,255	1971	Oregon
Zdakov	380	1,244	1967	Orlik, Czechoslovakia
Port Mann	366	1,200	1964	B.C., Canada
Runcorn	330	1,082	1961	Mersey, England
Birchenough	329	1,080	1935	Sabi, Zimbabwe
Glen Canyon	313	1,028	1959	Arizona
Lewiston-Queenston	305	1,000	1962	Niagara River, U.S.A.-Canada
Hellgate	298	978	1916	New York City
Concrete				
KRK	390	1,280	1974	Zagreb, Yugoslavia
Gladesville	305	1,000	1964	Sydney, Australia
Amizade	290	951	1964	Foz do Ignacu, Brazil
Arrabida	270	885	1963	Oporto, Portugal
Sando	264	866	1943	Kramfors, Sweden

LONGEST BRIDGES IN THE WORLD

SOURCE: American Society of Civil Engineers

Measurements that determine the longest bridges in the world include the bridge span or spans, as well as its approach roads.

Name of Bridge	Length In Feet	Completed	Location
Lake Pontchartrain Causeway II	126,055	1969	New Orleans-Lewisburg, La.
Lake Pontchartrain Causeway I	125,827	1956	New Orleans-Lewisburg, La.
Chesapeake Bay Bridge-Tunnel	93,203	1964	Cape Henry-Cape Charles, Va.
Presidente Costa e Silva Bridge	45,866	1974	Rio de Janeiro—Niteroi, Brazil
Marathon Key-Bahia Honda Key Bridge	38,915	1910	Florida Keys
San Mateo-Hayward Bridge I	37,183	1929	San Francisco Bay
San Mateo-Hayward Bridge II	35,708	1967	San Francisco Bay
Lake Maracaibo Bridge	28,473	1962	Punta Piedras-Punta Iguana, Venezuela
Transbay Bridge	27,286	1936	San Francisco-Oakland
Lake Pontchartrain Trestle	24,927	1927	Blind Bayou-Slidell, La.
Mackinac Straits Bridge	23,390	1957	Mackinaw City-St. Ignace, Mich.
James River Bridge	23,177	1928	Chuckatuck Creek-Newport News, Va.
Huey P. Long Bridge	22,996	1935	New Orleans
Sunshine Skyway (Structure C)	22,373	1954	St. Petersburg-Palmetto, Fla.
Richmond-San Rafael Bridge	21,965	1957	San Pablo Bay, Calif.
Astoria Bridge	21,697	1966	Pt. Ellice, Wash.-Astoria, Ore.
Chesapeake Bay Bridge	21,286	1952	Sandy Point-Kent Island, Md.
Öland Island Bridge	19,882	1972	Svinö-Möllstorp, Sweden
Oosterschelde Bridge	16,475	1965	Middelburg-Zierikzee, Netherlands
Tappan Zee Bridge	16,013	1955	South Nyack—Tarrytown, N.Y.

U.S. POPULATION AND AREA: 1790–1979

SOURCE: Bureau of the Census (Series P–25)

Year	Number (1,000)	Percent Increase	Per Square Mile[1]	AREA (1,000 sq. mi.) Land	AREA (1,000 sq. mi.) Water
1790	3,929	(X)	4.5	865	24
1800	5,308	35.1	6.1	865	24
1810	7,240	36.4	4.3	1,682	34
1820	9,638	33.1	5.6	1,749	39
1830	12,866	33.5	7.4	1,749	39
1840	17,069	32.7	9.8	1,749	39
1850	23,192	35.9	7.9	2,940	53
1860	31,443	35.6	10.6	2,970	53
1870	39,818	26.6	13.4	2,970	53
1880	50,156	26.0	16.9	2,970	53
1890	62,948	25.5	21.2	2,970	53
1900	75,995	20.7	25.6	2,970	53
1910	91,972	21.0	31.0	2,970	53
1920	105,711	14.9	35.6	2,969	53
1930	122,775	16.1	41.2	2,977	45
1940	131,669	7.2	44.2	2,977	45
1950	150,697	14.5	50.7	2,975	48
1960	179,323	18.5	50.5	3,541	74
1970	203,235	13.3	57.5	3,537	78
1971*	206,219	1.5	58.3	3,537	78
1972*	208,234	1.0	58.9	3,537	78
1973*	209,860	0.8	59.3	3,537	78
1975*	213,121	0.8	60.3	3,537	78
1976*	214,659	0.7	60.7	3,537	78
1978*	218,228	1.7	61.7	3,537	78
1979*	220,099	0.9	62.2	3,537	78

(X) Not applicable. [1] Land area only. * As of July 1.

U.S. POPULATION BY AGE GROUP

SOURCE: Bureau of the Census (Series P–25)

PROJECTIONS (figures in thousands)

Age Group	1978	1980	1990	2000
All Ages	218,059	222,159	243,513	260,378
Under 5 years	15,361	16,020	19,437	17,852
5 to 9 years	16,885	16,096	19,040	19,000
10 to 14 years	18,577	17,800	16,718	20,153
15 to 19 years	20,996	20,609	16,777	19,727
20 to 24 years	20,243	20,918	17,953	16,898
25 to 29 years	17,944	18,930	20,169	16,469
30 to 34 years	15,833	17,242	20,917	17,981
35 to 39 years	13,020	14,033	19,261	20,435
40 to 44 years	11,300	11,688	17,331	20,909
45 to 49 years	11,353	11,030	13,889	18,990
50 to 54 years	11,824	11,668	11,422	16,885
55 to 59 years	11,236	11,401	10,416	13,106
60 to 64 years	9,432	9,797	10,360	10,151
65 to 69 years	8,575	8,700	10,022	9,192
69 to 74 years	6,359	6,793	7,782	8,244
75 to 79 years	4,168	4,324	5,501	6,394
80 to 84 years	2,746	2,816	3,639	4,236
85 years and over	2,206	2,294	2,881	3,756

RESIDENT U.S. POPULATION BY STATE AND RANK, JULY 1, 1979

SOURCE: U.S. Bureau of the Census (Series P–25)   (Population in thousands)

Rank	State	Population	Rank	State	Population	Rank	State	Population
1	California	22,694	18	Maryland	4,148	35	Nebraska	1,574
2	New York	17,648	19	Minnesota	4,060	36	Utah	1,367
3	Texas	13,380	20	Louisiana	4,018	37	New Mexico	1,241
4	Pennsylvania	11,731	21	Washington	3,926	38	Maine	1,097
5	Illinois	11,229	22	Alabama	3,769	39	Rhode Island	929
6	Ohio	10,731	23	Kentucky	3,527	40	Hawaii	915
7	Michigan	9,207	24	Connecticut	3,115	41	Idaho	905
8	Florida	8,860	25	South Carolina	2,932	42	New Hampshire	887
9	New Jersey	7,332	26	Iowa	2,902	43	Montana	786
10	Massachusetts	5,769	27	Oklahoma	2,892	44	Nevada	702
11	North Carolina	5,606	28	Colorado	2,772	45	South Dakota	689
12	Indiana	5,400	29	Oregon	2,527	46	North Dakota	657
13	Virginia	5,197	30	Arizona	2,450	47	District of Columbia	656
14	Georgia	5,117	31	Mississippi	2,429	48	Delaware	582
15	Missouri	4,867	32	Kansas	2,369	49	Vermont	493
16	Wisconsin	4,720	33	Arkansas	2,180	50	Wyoming	450
17	Tennessee	4,380	34	West Virginia	1,878	51	Alaska	406

LEADING STANDARD METROPOLITAN STATISTICAL AREAS: COUNTY COMPONENTS*

SOURCE: U.S. Bureau of the Census

Anaheim-Sta. Ana-Garden Grove, Calif.: Orange. **Atlanta, Ga.:** Butts, Cherokee, Clayton, Cobb, DeKalb, Douglas, Fayette, Forsyth, Fulton, Gwinnett, Henry, Newton, Paulding, Rockdale & Walton. **Baltimore, Md.:** Anne Arundel, Baltimore, Carroll, Harford, Howard & Baltimore city. †**Boston-Lowell-Brockton-Lawrence-Haverhill, Mass.-N.H.:** Essex, Middlesex, Norfolk, Plymouth & Suffolk, Mass.; Rockingham, N.H. **Buffalo, N.Y.:** Erie & Niagara. **Chicago, Ill.:** Cook, DuPage, Kane, Lake, McHenry & Will. **Cincinnati, Ohio-Ky.-Ind.:** Clermont, Hamilton & Warren, Ohio; Boone, Campbell & Kenton, Ky.; Dearborn, Ind. **Cleveland, Ohio:** Cuyahoga, Geauga, Lake & Medina. **Columbus, Ohio:** Delaware, Fairfield, Franklin, Madison & Pickaway. **Dallas-Ft. Worth, Tex.:** Collin, Dallas, Denton, Ellis, Hood, Johnson, Kaufman, Parker, Rockwall, Tarrant & Wise. **Dayton, Ohio:** Greene, Miami, Montgomery & Preble. **Denver-Boulder, Colo.:** Adams, Arapahoe, Boulder, Denver, Douglas, Gilpin & Jefferson. **Detroit, Mich.:** Lapeer, Livingston, Macomb, Oakland, St. Clair & Wayne. **Houston, Tex.:** Brazoria, Ft. Bend, Harris, Liberty, Montgomery & Waller. **Indianapolis, Ind.:** Boone, Hamilton, Hancock, Hendricks, Johnson, Marion, Morgan & Shelby. **Kansas City, Mo.-Kans.:** Cass, Clay, Jackson, Platte & Ray, Mo.; Johnson & Wyandotte, Kans. **Los Angeles-Long Beach, Calif.:** Los Angeles. **Louisville, Ky.-Ind.:** Bullitt, Jefferson & Oldham, Ky.; Clark & Floyd, Ind. **Memphis, Tenn.-Ark.-Miss.:** Shelby & Tipton, Tenn.; Crittenden, Ark.; De Soto, Miss. **Miami, Fla.:** Dade. **Milwaukee, Wis.:** Milwaukee, Ozaukee, Washington & Waukesha. **Minneapolis-St. Paul, Minn.-Wis.:** Anoka, Carver, Chisago, Dakota, Hennepin, Ramsey, Scott, Washington & Wright, Minn.; St. Croix, Wis. **Nassau-Suffolk, N.Y.:** Nassau & Suffolk. **Newark, N.J.:** Essex, Morris, Somerset & Union. **New Orleans, La.:** Jefferson, Orleans, St. Bernard & St. Tammany parishes. **New York, N.Y.-N.J.:** Bronx, Kings, New York, Putnam, Queens, Richmond, Rockland & Westchester, N.Y.; Bergen, N.J. **Philadelphia, Pa.-N.J.:** Bucks, Chester, Delaware, Montgomery & Philadelphia, Pa.; Burlington, Camden & Gloucester, N.J. **Phoenix, Ariz.:** Maricopa. **Pittsburgh, Pa.:** Allegheny, Beaver, Washington & Westmorland. **Portland, Oreg.-Wash.:** Clackamas, Multnomah & Washington, Oregon; Clark, Washington. †**Providence-Warwick-Pawtucket, Rhode Island:** Bristol, Kent, Providence & Washington. **Riverside-San Bernardino-Ontario, Calif.:** Riverside & San Bernardino. **Rochester, N.Y.:** Livingston, Monroe, Ontario, Orleans & Wayne. **Sacramento, Calif.:** Placer, Sacramento & Yolo. **St. Louis, Mo.-Ill.:** Franklin, Jefferson, St. Charles, St. Louis & St. Louis city, Mo.; Clinton, Madison, Monroe & St. Clair, Ill. **San Antonio, Tex.:** Bexar, Comal & Guadalupe. **San Diego, Calif.:** San Diego. **San Francisco-Oakland, Calif.:** Alameda, Contra Costa, Marin, San Francisco & San Mateo. **San Jose, Calif.:** Santa Clara. **Seattle-Everett, Wash.:** King & Snohomish. **Tampa-St. Petersburg, Fla.:** Hillsborough, Pasco & Pinellas. **Washington, D.C.-Md.-Va.:** Dist. of Columbia; Charles, Montgomery & Prince Georges, Md.; Arlington, Fairfax, Loudoun, Prince William, & cities of Alexandria, Fairfax, Falls Church, Manassas & Manassas Park, Va.

* Names are counties, unless otherwise specified. †New England County Metropolitan Area.

LARGEST U.S. METROPOLITAN AREAS   (Rank by 1977 Estimate)

SOURCE: U.S. Bureau of the Census (Series P-26)

Rank 1977	Standard Metropolitan Statistical Area	1970 Population	1977 Estimate
1	New York, N.Y.-N.J.	9,973,716	9,386,700
2	Los Angeles-Long Beach, Calif.	7,041,980	7,031,000
3	Chicago, Ill.	6,977,611	7,017,400
4	Philadelphia, Pa.-N.J.	4,824,110	4,793,900
5	Detroit, Mich.	4,435,051	4,370,200
6	Boston-Lowell-Brockton-Lawrence-Haverhill, Mass.-N.H.*	3,848,593	3,897,800
7	San Francisco-Oakland, Calif.	3,107,355	3,182,200
8	Washington, D.C.-Md.-Va.	2,910,111	3,020,100
9	Nassau-Suffolk, N.Y.	2,555,868	2,687,900
10	Dallas-Fort Worth, Tex.	2,378,353	2,673,300
11	Houston, Tex.	1,999,316	2,512,200
12	St. Louis, Mo.-Ill.	2,410,602	2,379,800
13	Pittsburgh, Pa.	2,401,362	2,294,500
14	Baltimore, Md.	2,071,016	2,146,900
15	Minneapolis-St. Paul, Minn.-Wis.	1,965,391	2,037,200
16	Newark, N.J.	2,057,468	1,969,200
17	Cleveland, Ohio	2,063,729	1,949,600
18	Atlanta, Ga.	1,595,517	1,831,500
19	Anaheim-Sta. Ana-Garden Grove, Calif.	1,421,233	1,800,800
20	San Diego, Calif.	1,357,854	1,683,000
21	Denver-Boulder, Colo.	1,239,477	1,464,300
22	Miami, Fla.	1,267,792	1,441,200
23	Seattle-Everett, Wash.	1,424,605	1,427,200
24	Milwaukee, Wis.	1,403,884	1,426,500
25	Tampa-St. Petersburg, Fla.	1,088,549	1,380,500
26	Cincinnati, Ohio-Ky.-Ind.	1,387,207	1,375,400
27	Buffalo, N.Y.	1,349,211	1,313,000
28	Riverside-San Bernardino-Ontario, Calif.	1,141,307	1,305,600
29	Kansas City, Mo.-Kans.	1,273,926	1,293,300
30	Phoenix, Ariz.	971,228	1,253,600
31	San Jose, Calif.	1,065,313	1,217,300
32	Indianapolis, Ind.	1,111,352	1,143,800
33	New Orleans, La.	1,046,470	1,133,100
34	Portland, Oreg.-Wash.	1,007,130	1,121,500
35	Columbus, Ohio	1,017,847	1,086,800
36	Hartford-New Britain-Bristol, Conn.*	1,035,195	1,052,000
37	San Antonio, Tex.	888,179	1,024,900
38	Rochester, N.Y.	961,516	970,200
39	Sacramento, Calif.	803,793	929,400
40	Memphis, Tenn.-Ark.-Miss.	834,103	886,500
41	Louisville, Ky.-Ind.	867,330	883,000
42	Fort Lauderdale-Hollywood, Fla.	620,100	864,400
43	Providence-Warwick-Pawtucket, R.I.*	855,495	852,000
44	Dayton, Ohio	852,531	833,100
45	Salt Lake City-Ogden, Utah	705,458	822,200
46	Bridgeport-Stamford-Norwalk-Danbury, Conn.*	792,814	807,000
47	Birmingham, Ala.	767,230	805,300
48	Norfolk-Virginia Beach-Portsmouth, Va.-N.C.	732,600	802,600
49	Albany-Schenectady-Troy, N.Y.	777,977	794,300
50	Toledo, Ohio-Mich.	762,658	777,400
51	Greensboro-Winston-Salem-High Point, N.C.	724,129	774,000
52	Nashville-Davidson, Tenn.	699,271	773,000
53	Oklahoma City, Okla.,	699,092	768,500
54	New Haven-West Haven-Waterbury-Meriden, Conn.*	744,948	758,900
55	Honolulu, Hawaii	630,528	723,400
56	Jacksonville, Fla.	621,827	694,200
57	Akron, Ohio	679,239	660,800
58	Syracuse, N.Y.	636,596	647,500
59	Gary-Hammond-E. Chicago, Ind.	633,367	644,300
60	Worcester-Fitchburg-Leominster, Mass.*	637,037	643,400
61	Northeast Pennsylvania, Pa.	621,882	628,700
62	Allentown-Bethlehem-Easton, Pa.-N.J.	594,382	624,100
63	Tulsa, Okla.	549,153	609,700
64	Richmond, Va.	547,542	603,300
65	Charlotte-Gastonia, N.C.	557,785	597,000
66	New Brunswick-Perth Amboy-Sayreville, N.J.	583,813	593,500
67	Orlando, Fla.	453,270	593,000
68	Springfield-Chicopee-Holyoke, Mass.*	583,031	589,400
69	Omaha, Nebr.-Iowa	542,646	580,900
70	Grand Rapids, Mich.	539,225	575,600
71	Jersey City, N.J.	607,839	564,100
72	Youngstown-Warren, Ohio	537,124	540,600
73	Greenville-Spartanburg, S.C.	473,454	526,400
74	Wilmington, Del.-N.J.-Md.	499,493	516,200
75	Flint, Mich.	508,664	514,400
76	Long Branch-Asbury Park, N.J.	461,849	491,600
77	Raleigh-Durham, N.C.	419,254	487,100
78	West Palm Beach-Boca Raton, Fla.	348,993	476,900
79	Austin, Tex.	323,158	474,300
80	Fresno, Calif.	413,329	471,900
81	New Bedford-Fall River, Mass.*	444,301	467,800
82	Oxnard-Simi Valley-Ventura, Calif.	378,497	467,800
83	Paterson-Clifton-Passaic, N.J.	460,782	461,600
84	Lansing-East Lansing, Mich.	424,271	455,100
85	Tucson, Ariz.	351,667	454,600
86	Knoxville, Tenn.	409,409	449,100
87	Baton Rouge, La.	375,628	435,200
88	El Paso, Tex.	359,291	434,700
89	Harrisburg, Pa.	410,505	428,900
90	Mobile, Ala.	376,690	425,100
91	Tacoma, Wash.	412,344	423,400
92	Johnson City-Kingsport-Bristol, Tenn.-Va.	373,591	408,200
93	Chattanooga, Tenn.-Ga.	370,857	403,200
94	Albuquerque, N. Mex.	333,266	401,900
95	Canton, Ohio	393,789	401,000
96	Wichita, Kans.	389,352	394,900
97	Charleston-N. Charleston, S.C.	336,125	385,400
98	Davenport-Rock I.-Moline, Iowa-Ill.	362,638	375,000
99	Columbia, S.C.	322,880	374,300
100	Fort Wayne, Ind.	361,984	370,400
101	Little Rock-N. Little Rock, Ark.	323,296	369,200
102	Newport News-Hampton, Va.	333,140	364,000
103	Beaumont-Port Arthur-Orange, Tex.	347,568	363,900
104	Bakersfield, Calif.	330,234	363,000
105	Peoria, Ill.	341,979	362,000
106	Las Vegas, Nev.	273,288	359,800
107	Shreveport, La.	333,826	356,500
108	York, Pa.	329,540	351,800
109	Lancaster, Pa.	320,079	347,900
110	Des Moines, Iowa	313,562	333,000
111	Utica-Rome, N.Y.	340,670	326,800
112	Trenton, N.J.	304,116	316,900
113	Madison, Wis.	290,272	313,000
114	Stockton, Calif.	291,073	311,400
115	Spokane, Wash.	287,487	310,200
116	Binghamton, N.Y.-Pa.	302,672	305,700

* New England County Metropolitan Area.

STANDARD CONSOLIDATED STATISTICAL AREAS (SCSA)   SOURCE: U.S. Bureau of the Census

Rank 1977	Standard Consolidated Statistical Area	1970 Population	1977 Estimate
1	New York—Newark—Jersey City, N.Y.-N.J.-Conn.	17,494,149	16,485,000
2	Los Angeles—Long Beach—Anaheim, Calif.	9,983,017	10,605,200
3	Chicago—Gary, Ill.-Ind.	7,610,978	7,661,700
4	Philadelphia—Wilmington—Trenton, Pa.-Del.-Md.-N.J.	5,627,719	5,627,000
5	San Francisco—Oakland—San Jose, Calif.	4,423,797	4,693,400
6	Detroit—Ann Arbor, Mich.	4,669,154	4,620,400
7	Boston—Lawrence—Lowell, Mass.-N.H.	3,848,593	3,525,000 (1976)
8	Cleveland—Akron-Lorain, Ohio	2,999,811	2,874,400
9	Houston—Galveston, Tex.	2,169,128	2,707,600
10	Miami-Fort Lauderdale, Fla.	1,887,892	2,305,600
11	Seattle—Tacoma, Wash.	1,836,949	1,850,600
12	Cincinnati—Hamilton, Ohio-Ky.-Ind.	1,613,414	1,625,900
13	Milwaukee—Racine, Wis.	1,574,722	1,603,300

VOTER PARTICIPATION: PRESIDENTIAL ELECTIONS
PERCENTAGE OF VOTING AGE POPULATION WHO VOTED

SOURCE: U.S. Bureau of the Census

	1976 election	1972 election	1968 election		1976 election	1972 election	1968 election
Sex:				**Residence:**			
Male	59.6	64.1	69.8	Metropolitan	59.2	64.3	68.0
Female	58.8	62.0	66.0	Nonmetropolitan	59.1	59.4	67.3
Race:				**School year completed:**			
White	60.9	64.5	69.1	8 or less	44.1	47.4	54.5
Black	48.7	52.1	57.6	9–11	47.2	52.0	61.3
Spanish origin*	31.8	37.4	N.A.	12	59.4	65.4	72.5
Age:				More than 12	73.5	78.8	81.2
18–20	38.0	48.3	33.3	**Employment:**			
21–24	45.6	50.7	51.1	Employed	62.0	66.0	71.1
25–34	55.4	59.7	62.5	Unemployed	43.7	49.9	52.1
35–44	63.3	66.3	70.8	Not in labor force	56.5	59.3	63.2
45–64	68.7	70.8	74.9				
65 and over	62.2	63.5	65.8				

* Persons of Spanish origin can be of any race.

IMMIGRATION TO THE UNITED STATES

SOURCE: U.S. Immigration and Naturalization Service

Years	Number	Years	Number	Years	Number	Years	Number
1820–1975	47,098,919	1871–1880	2,812,191	1941–1950	1,035,039	1970	373,326
1820	8,385	1881–1890	5,246,613	1951–1960	2,515,479	1971	370,478
1821–1830	143,439	1891–1900	3,687,564	1961–1965	1,450,312	1972	384,685
1831–1840	599,125	1901–1910	8,795,386	1966	323,040	1973	400,063
1841–1850	1,713,251	1911–1920	5,735,811	1967	361,972	1974	394,861
1851–1860	2,598,214	1921–1930	4,107,209	1968	454,448	1975	386,194
1861–1870	2,314,824	1931–1940	528,431	1969	358,579	1976	398,613
						1977	462,315
						1978	601,442

IMMIGRATION BY COUNTRIES: 1820–1978

SOURCE: U.S. Immigration and Naturalization Service

Countries	1978	Total (1820 to 1978)	Countries	1978	Total (1820 to 1978)
All countries	601,442	48,664,965	Romania	1,628	170,891
Europe	76,156	36,202,963	Spain	4,266	259,551
Albania	41	2,556	Sweden [2]	644	1,271,925
Austria [1]	504	4,315,642	Switzerland	860	349,103
Hungary [1]	626		USSR	4,677	3,373,314
Belgium	611	202,418	Yugoslavia [4]	2,227	113,549
Bulgaria [4]	135	67,827	Other Europe	407	55,605
Czechoslovakia	438	137,029			
Denmark	399	364,160	Asia	243,596	2,853,760
Estonia	6	1,128	China	2,278	515,550
Finland	313	33,441	India	19,145	163,698
France	2,741	750,424	Japan	4,500	406,438
Germany [1]	7,567	6,977,743	Turkey	1,022	385,555
Great Britain			Other Asia	216,651	1,382,519
England	14,982	3,178,558			
Scotland	955	820,063			
Wales	134	95,127	America	266,470	9,050,711
Not specified	354	804,822	Canada & Newfoundland	23,495	4,104,857
Greece	6,994	654,886	Mexico	92,681	2,123,727
Ireland	923	4,723,544	West Indies	87,717	1,686,801
Italy	7,032	5,294,418	Central America	20,481	312,863
Latvia	16	2,555	South America	42,080	713,024
Lithuania	30	3,852	Other America	16	109,439
Luxembourg	24	2,867			
Netherlands	1,182	359,641	Africa	10,336	132,059
Norway [2]	428	856,474	Australia & New Zealand	2,665	118,508
Poland [3]	4,495	514,496	Pacific Islands	137	24,571
Portugal	10,517	445,354	Not specified	2,082	282,393

[1] Data for Austria-Hungary were not reported until 1861; Austria and Hungary have been recorded separately since 1905. From 1938 to 1945 inclusive, Austria was included with Germany. [2] From 1820 to 1868, the figures for Norway and Sweden were combined. [3] Poland was recorded as a separate country from 1820 to 1898 and again since 1920. [4] Bulgaria, Serbia, and Montenegro were first reported in 1899. Bulgaria has been reported separately since 1920, while the Serb, Croat, and Slovene Kingdom has been recorded as Yugoslavia since 1922. Data collected from country of last residence.

WORLD POPULATION FACTS

SOURCE: *UN Demographic Yearbook 1978*, © United Nations

Regions	1950	Midyear Estimates (in Millions) 1970	1975	1978	Annual % Increase (1970-75)
WORLD	2,513	3,678	4,033	4,258	1.8
Africa	219	354	406	442	2.7
Americas	330	509	559	591	1.9
Asia*	1,380	2,091	2,319	2,461	2.1
Europe*	392	460	474	480	0.6
Oceania	13	19	21	22	1.8
USSR	180	244	254	262	0.8

*Excluding USSR

MOST POPULOUS URBAN AREAS

City	Population	Year	City	Population	Year
New York	16,485,000	1977 (E)	Peking	7,570,000	1970 (E)
Mexico City	13,993,866	1978 (E)	Seoul	7,500,000	1975
Tokyo	11,683,613	1976	São Paulo	7,198,608	1975 (E)
Shanghai	10,820,000	1970 (E)	Calcutta	7,031,382	1971
Los Angeles	10,605,200	1977 (E)	London	7,028,200	1976
Paris	9,863,000	1975	Bombay	5,970,575	1971
Buenos Aires	9,749,000	1978 (E)	Cairo	5,921,000	1975
Moscow	8,011,000	1979	Philadelphia	5,627,000	1977 (E)
Chicago	7,661,700	1977 (E)	Rio de Janeiro	5,157,000	1974 (E)

(E) Estimated data.

MOST POPULOUS CITIES

City	Population	Year	City	Population	Year
Shanghai	10,000,000	1976 (E)	São Paulo	5,186,752	1970
Mexico City	8,988,230	1978 (E)	Jakarta	5,000,000	1973 (E)
Tokyo	8,646,520	1975	Leningrad	4,588,000	1979
Cairo	8,500,000	1975 (E)	Tehran	4,400,000	1976
Moscow	8,011,000	1979	Tianjin	4,280,000	1970 (E)
Peking	7,570,000	1970 (E)	Rio de Janeiro	4,252,009	1970
Seoul	7,500,000	1977 (E)	Karachi	3,498,634	1972
New York	7,312,200	1977(E)	Delhi	3,287,883	1971
London	7,028,200	1976(E)	Calcutta	3,148,746	1971
Bombay	5,970,575	1971	Chicago	3,074,084	1976 (E)

(E) Estimated data.

MOST POPULOUS COUNTRIES

Country	Midyear 1978 Estimate (in Millions)	Annual % Increase 1975-78	Density per Sq. Mil	Area in Sq. Mi.
China	933.03	1.4	252.8	3,691,000
India	638.39	2.1	502.9	1,269,339
USSR	261.57	0.9	30.2	8,649,490
UNITED STATES	218.06	0.7	60.3	3,615,123
Indonesia	145.10	2.4	184.0	788,430
Brazil	115.40	2.8	35.1	3,286,470
Japan	114.90	1.0	788.4	145,730
Bangladesh	84.66	2.4	1,535.8	55,126
Nigeria	84.50	—	222.6	379,628
Pakistan	76.77	3.0	247.3	310,403
Mexico	66.94	3.6	87.9	761,600
Germany, West	61.31	− 0.3	640.6	95,704
Italy	56.70	0.5	487.5	116,303
United Kingdom	55.82	− 0.0	591.3	94,399
France	53.28	0.4	253.7	210,038
Vietnam	47.87	—	372.8	128,405
Philippines	46.35	3.3	400.6	115,707
Thailand	45.10	2.5	227.3	198,455
Turkey	43.21	2.3	143.6	300,946
Egypt	39.64	2.1	102.5	386,659
Spain	37.11	1.4	189.3	195,988
Korea, South	37.10	1.6	971.8	38,175
Iran	35.21	2.2	55.3	636,293
Poland	35.01	1.0	290.0	120,725
Burma	32.21	2.2	123.0	261,789
Ethiopia	29.71	2.6	63.0	471,776
Zaire	27.75	3.7	30.2	918,962
South Africa	27.70	2.8	58.6	472,359
Argentina	26.39	1.3	24.7	1,068,296
Colombia	25.65	2.7	58.3	439,735
Canada	23.50	1.1	6.1	3,851,809
Yugoslavia	21.91	0.9	221.8	98,766
Romania	21.86	0.9	238.4	91,699
Morocco	18.91	3.0	109.7	172,413

LARGEST COUNTRIES, BY GEOGRAPHICAL AREA

Rank	Country	Area in Sq. Mi.	Rank	Country	Area in Sq. Mi.
1	USSR	8,649,490	15	Libya	679,358
2	Canada	3,851,809	16	Iran	636,293
3	China (People's Rep.)	3,691,000	17	Mongolia	606,163
4	UNITED STATES	3,615,123	18	Peru	496,222
5	Brazil	3,286,470	19	Chad	495,752
6	Australia	2,967,909	20	Niger	489,189
7	India	1,269,339	21	Angola	481,351
8	Argentina	1,068,296	22	South Africa	472,359
9	Sudan	967,494	23	Ethiopia	471,776
10	Algeria	919,591	24	Mali	464,873
11	Zaire	918,962	25	Mauritania	452,702
12	Saudi Arabia	829,995	26	Colombia	439,735
13	Indonesia	788,430	27	Bolivia	424,163
14	Mexico	761,600			

NATION'S 50 LEADING COUNTIES* IN MEDIAN FAMILY INCOME: 1969†

SOURCE: U.S. Bureau of the Census, 1970 Census of Population: Characteristics of Population

Rank	County	Income	Rank	County	Income	Rank	County	Income
1.	Montgomery, Md.	$16,710	18.	Fairfield, Conn.	$13,086	35.	Suffolk, N.Y.	$12,084
2.	Fairfax, Va.	15,707	19.	Lake, Ill.	13,009	36.	Baltimore, Md.	12,081
3.	Nassau, N.Y.	14,632	20.	Waukesha, Wis.	12,795	37.	Arapahoe, Colo.	12,063
4.	Du Page, Ill.	14,458	21.	Norfolk, Mass.	12,749	38.	Hartford, Conn.	12,057
5.	Marin, Calif.	13,935	22.	Montgomery, Pa.	12,747	39.	Jefferson, Colo.	12,045
6.	Oakland, Mich.	13,826	23.	Ozaukee, Wis.	12,620	40.	Honolulu, Hawaii	12,035
7.	Westchester, N.Y.	13,784	24.	Union, N.J.	12,593	41.	Putnam, N.Y.	11,996
8.	Rockland, N.Y.	13,753	25.	Santa Clara, Calif.	12,456	42.	Middlesex, N.J.	11,982
9.	Arlington, Va.	13,743	26.	Prince Georges, Md.	12,450	43.	McHenry, Ill.	11,965
10.	Bergen, N.J.	13,597	27.	Monroe, N.Y.	12,423	44.	Lake, Ohio	11,964
11.	Anchorage, Alaska	13,593	28.	Contra Costa, Calif.	12,423	45.	Kane, Ill.	11,947
12.	Howard, Md.	13,472	29.	Geauga, Ohio	12,411	46.	Richmond, N.Y.	11,894
13.	Somerset, N.J.	13,433	30.	St. Louis, Mo.	12,392	47.	King, Wash.	11,886
14.	Morris, N.J.	13,421	31.	Washtenaw, Mich.	12,294	48.	Tolland, Conn.	11,874
15.	Johnson, Kans.	13,384	32.	Orange, Calif.	12,245	49.	Middlesex, Mass.	11,860
16.	San Mateo, Calif.	13,222	33.	De Kalb, Ga.	12,137	50.	Delaware, Pa.	11,822
17.	Macomb, Mich.	13,110	34.	Dakota, Minn.	12,120			

* With 50,000 or more population.   † Figures are for calendar year 1969, as gathered in 1970 census.

NATION'S 50 LARGEST CITIES* RANKED BY MEDIAN FAMILY INCOME: 1970 CENSUS

SOURCE: U.S. Department of Commerce, Bureau of Economic Analysis

Rank	City	SMSA*	City Only	Rank	City	SMSA*	City Only
1.	Honolulu, Hawaii	$12,035	$12,539	26.	Oakland, Calif.	$ 9,626	$ 9,626
2.	San Jose, Calif.	12,456	11,927	27.	Washington, D.C.	12,933	9,583
3.	Seattle, Wash.	11,676	11,037	28.	Nashville-Davidson, Tenn.	9,187	9,473
4.	Indianapolis, Ind.	10,754	10,754	29.	Philadelphia, Pa.	10,783	9,366
5.	St. Paul, Minn.	11,682	10,544	30.	Fort Worth, Texas	10,101	9,271
6.	Los Angeles, Calif.	10,972	10,535	31.	Boston, Mass.	11,449	9,133
7.	San Francisco, Calif.	11,802	10,503	32.	Cleveland, Ohio	11,407	9,107
8.	Toledo, Ohio	10,932	10,474	33.	Oklahoma City, Okla.	9,345	9,106
9.	Long Beach, Calif.	10,282	10,282	34.	Cincinnati, Ohio	10,257	8,894
10.	Milwaukee, Wis.	11,338	10,262	35.	Baltimore, Md.	10,577	8,815
11.	Chicago, Ill.	11,931	10,242	36.	Buffalo, N.Y.	11,430	8,804
12.	Omaha, Nebr.	10,204	10,208	37.	Pittsburgh, Pa.	9,737	8,800
13.	San Diego, Calif.	10,133	10,166	38.	Jacksonville, Fla.	8,671	8,671
14.	Detroit, Mich.	12,117	10,045	39.	Memphis, Tenn.	8,542	8,646
15.	Dallas, Tex.	10,405	10,019	40.	Louisville, Ky.	9,814	8,564
16.	Rochester, N.Y.	11,969	10,002	41.	Atlanta, Ga.	10,695	8,399
17.	Minneapolis, Minn.	9,960	9,960	42.	St. Louis, Mo.	10,504	8,182
18.	Phoenix, Ariz.	9,856	9,956	43.	El Paso, Tex.	7,792	7,963
19.	Kansas City, Mo.	10,588	9,910	44.	Norfolk, Va.	8,705	7,821
20.	Houston, Tex.	10,191	9,876	45.	Birmingham, Ala.	8,295	7,737
21.	Tulsa, Okla.	9,286	9,870	46.	Newark, N.J.	11,847	7,735
22.	Portland, Oreg.	10,463	9,799	47.	San Antonio, Tex.	7,981	7,734
23.	Columbus, Ohio	10,460	9,731	48.	Tampa, Fla.	7,883	7,678
24.	New York, N.Y.	10,870	9,682	49.	New Orleans, La.	8,670	7,445
25.	Denver, Colorado	10,777	9,654	50.	Miami, Fla.	9,245	7,304

* Standard Metropolitan Statistical Areas (city plus outlying areas); for definitions of largest areas, see page 220.

U.S. METROPOLITAN AREA PER CAPITA INCOME: 1978

SOURCE: U.S. Department of Commerce, Bureau of Economic Analysis

SMSA'S WITH HIGHEST INCOMES

Standard Metropolitan Statistical Area	Income
Anchorage, Alaska	$11,839
Reno, Nevada	11,161
Bridgeport-Stamford-Norwalk-Danbury, Connecticut	10,721
Midland, Texas	10,658
San Francisco-Oakland, California	10,492
Washington, DC-Maryland-Virginia	10,259
San Jose, California	9,771
Salinas-Seaside-Monterey, California,	9,666
Seattle-Everett, Washington	9,582
Detroit, Michigan	9,512
Chicago, Illinois	9,493
Newark, New Jersey	9,487
Nassau-Suffolk, New York	9,407
Los Angeles-Long Beach, California	9,399
Houston, Texas	9,398
Sarasota, Florida	9,310
Peoria, Illinois	9,309
Anaheim-Santa Ana-Garden Grove, California	9,298
West Palm Beach-Boca Raton, Florida	9,225
Cleveland, Ohio	9,204
Ann Arbor, Michigan	9,160
Portland, Oregon-Washington	9,140
Denver-Boulder, Colorado	9,080
New Brunswick-Perth Amboy-Sayreville, New Jersey	9,051
Las Vegas, Nevada	8,989

SMSA'S WITH LOWEST INCOMES

Standard Metropolitan Statistical Area	Income
Monroe, Louisiana	$ 6,313
Wilmington, North Carolina	6,313
Lawrence, Kansas	6,277
Tuscaloosa, Alabama	6,250
Johnson City-Kingsport-Bristol, Tennessee-Virginia	6,164
Pascagoula-Moss Point, Mississippi	6,154
Bryan-College Station, Texas	6,133
Clarksville-Hopkinsville, Tennessee-Kentucky	6,096
Albany, Georgia	6,063
Biloxi-Gulfport, Missssippi	6,013
Fort Smith, Arkansas-Oklahoma	6,013
Panama City, Florida	5,994
Pensacola, Florida	5,981
Bloomington, Indiana	5,961
St. Cloud, Minnesota	5,928
Anniston, Alabama	5,860
Alexandria, Louisiana	5,804
Fayetteville, North Carolina	5,784
Las Cruces, New Mexco	5,675
El Paso, Texas	5,639
Lawton, Oklahoma	5,596
Provo-Orem, Utah	5,331
Brownsvlle-Harlngen-San Benito, Texas	5,024
Laredo, Texas	4,529
McAllen-Pharr-Edinburg, Texas	4,323

URBAN INTERMEDIATE BUDGET FOR A 4-PERSON FAMILY IN SELECTED METROPOLITAN AREAS: 1979 (in dollars)

SOURCE: U.S. Bureau of Labor Statistics, Autunn 1979 Urban Family Budgets and Comparative Indexesfor Selected Urban Areas (USDL: 80-278)

Metropolitan Areas	All Items	Food	Metropolitan Areas	All Items	Food
Anchorage Alaska	$27,933	$6,215	St. Louis, Mo.-Ill.	$19,963	$5,307
Atlanta, Ga.	18,821	4,837	San Diego, Calif.	20,088	4,799
Baltimore, Md.	20,316	4,835	San Francisco-Oakland, Calif.	21,478	5,138
Boston, Mass.	24,381	5,338	Seattle-Everett, Wash.	20,719	5,026
Buffalo, N.Y.	21,806	5,157	Washington, D.C.-Md.-Va.	22,206	5,179
Chicago, Ill.-N.W. Ind.	20,564	5,114	Metropolitan Area Average	20,935	5,112
Cincinnati, Ohio-Ky.-Ind.	20,287	5,146			
Cleveland, Ohio	20,868	5,057	**Nonmetropolitan Areas**		
Dallas, Texas	18,301	4,750			
Denver, Colo.	20,468	4,864	Northeast	20,730	5,028
			North Central	18,876	4,717
Detroit, Mich.	20,821	5,005	South	17,454	4,622
Honolulu, Hawaii	25,799	6,339	West	19,348	4,732
Houston, Texas	19,025	4,939			
Kansas City, Mo.-Kans	19,618	4,917	Nonmetropolitan Area Average	18,651	4,739
Los Angeles-Long Beach, Calif.	19,871	4,903			
Milwaukee, Wis.	21,387	4,899	**URBAN U.S. AVERAGE**	**20,517**	**5,044**
Minneapolis-St. Paul, Minn.	21,426	5,094			
New York, N.Y.-N.E. N.J.	23,856	5,576			
Philadelphia, Pa.-N.J.	21,436	5,661			
Pittsburgh, Pa.	19,890	5,251			

WORLDWIDE COST OF LIVING—1979

SOURCE: United Nations, *Monthly Bulletin of Statistics*, May 1980

Country	All Items	Food	Country	All Items	Food
Argentina (Buenos Aires)	129,051.0	31,864.0	Japan	219.0	220.9
Austria	172.9	162.9	Jordan[2]	156.0	143.6
Bahamas (Nassau)	163.6	175.6	Korea, South	350.1	406.0
Bangladesh (Dacca)	354.8	340.5	Luxembourg	178.9	174.5
Barbados	330.8	363.1	Madagascar (Antananarivo)	205.3	220.4
Belgium	191.0	172.6	Malawi (Blantyre)	205.9	215.8
Brazil (São Paulo)	742.5	820.0	Malaysia (Sabah)	152.3	174.7
Canada	196.7	238.0	Morocco	156.7	155.8
Chile (Santiago)	310,499.0	368,167.0	Netherlands	190.5	118.8
Costa Rica (San Jose)	236.5	249.7	New Caledonia (Noumea)	200.5	204.1
Cyprus	117.6	112.8	New Zealand	277.2	282.3
Czechoslovakia	108.5	105.8	Norway	201.7	199.3
Denmark	277.6	148.0	Pakistan	273.1	279.0
El Salvador	108.7	108.8	Panama (Panama City)[2]	122.3	122.1
Fiji	227.5	235.2	Papua New Guinea	196.9	197.3
Finland	262.2	265.9	Paraguay (Asuncion)	279.9	324.9
France	220.8	230.1	Philippines	250.5	239.2
Gambia (Banjul-Kambo St. Mary)	250.4	275.8	Saint Lucia	303.6	341.2
Germany, West	155.8	147.2	Sierra Leone (Freetown)	256.9	280.3
Ghana (Accra)	276.4	283.7	Spain	358.6	341.7
Gibraltar	322.3	355.1	Sri Lanka (Colombo)	182.6	192.8
Greece	303.9	333.3	Sweden	212.4	223.2
Guadeloupe (Basse-Terre)	232.1	246.2	Switzerland	156.2	152.2
Guatemala[2]	149.9	140.3	Thailand (Bangkok, Metropolis)	207.5	228.2
Haiti (Port-au-Prince)	235.4	247.1	Trinidad and Tobago	289.1	300.1
Honduras (Tegucigalpa)	178.1	182.1	Tunisia (Tunis)[1]	113.5	116.2
Hong Kong[2]	139.0	136.0	United Kingdom	305.8	353.1
Hungary	142.4	145.8	UNITED STATES	187.2	199.0
Ireland	304.5	333.4	Venezuela (Caracas)	184.2	235.4
Israel	1,401.0	1,486.5	Yugoslavia	432.0	456.0
Italy	304.5	307.6	Zimbabwe	198.7	197.3
Ivory Coast (Abidjan)	272.3	304.0			

[1]1977 = 100; [2] 1975 = 100.

THE AMERICAN CONSUMER: PERSONAL EXPENDITURES (1978)

SOURCE: U.S. Department of Commerce, Bureau of Economic Analysis

	Personal Consumption Expenditures by Tye of Product (Millions of Dollars)		Personal Consumption Expenditures by Type of Product (Millions of Dollars)
Food (includes alcohol and tobacco)	$289,573	Recreation	$ 91,244
Clothing, accessories, and jewelry	107,642	Private education and research	20,770
Personal care	18,569	Religious and welfare activities	17,157
Housing	212,153	Foreign travel and other, net	5,177
Household operation	195,022	Total personal consumption expenditures	1,350,762
Medical care expenses	131,026	Durable commodities	200,299
Personal business	71,097	Nondurable commodities	530,643
Transporation	191,327	Services	619,820

CONSUMER PRICE INDEX* AND PURCHASING POWER OF THE CONSUMER DOLLAR (1967=100)   Source: Bureau of Labor Statistics

Year	All Items	Food & Beverages	Housing	Rent	Apparel & Upkeep	Trans-portation	Medical Care	Enter-tain-ment	Other Goods and Services	Purchasing power of the consumer dollar
1968	104.2	103.6	104.0	102.4	105.4	103.2	106.1	105.7	105.2	.960
1969	109.8	108.8	110.4	105.7	111.5	107.2	113.4	111.0	110.4	.911
1970	116.3	114.7	118.2	110.1	116.1	112.7	120.6	116.7	116.8	.860
1971	121.3	118.3	123.4	115.2	119.8	118.6	128.4	122.9	122.4	.824
1972	125.3	123.2	128.1	119.2	122.3	119.9	132.5	126.5	127.5	.799
1973	133.1	139.5	133.7	124.3	126.8	123.8	137.7	130.0	132.5	.752
1974	147.7	158.7	148.8	130.6	136.2	137.7	150.5	139.8	142.0	.678
1975	161.2	172.1	164.5	137.3	142.3	150.6	168.6	152.2	153.9	.621
1976	170.5	177.4	174.6	144.7	147.6	165.5	184.7	159.8	162.7	.587
1977	181.5	188.0	186.5	153.5	154.2	177.2	202.4	167.7	172.2	.551
1978	195.4	206.3	202.8	164.0	159.6	185.5	219.4	176.6	183.3	.512
1979	217.4	228.5	227.6	176.0	166.6	212.0	239.7	188.5	196.7	.461

* Consumer Price Index for All Urban Consumers (CPI-U)

AVERAGE U.S. RETAIL FOOD PRICES   Source: Bureau of Labor Statistics (in cents)

Year	Flour, wheat 10 lbs.	Rice lb.	White bread lb.	Round steak lb.	Rib roast lb.	Chuck roast lb.	Pork chops lb.	Bacon sliced lb.	Milk[1] qt.	Butter lb.	Cheese lb.	Pota-toes 15 lbs.	Sugar lb.	Eggs doz.	Coffee lb.
1913	33	8.7	5.6	22.3	19.8	16.0	21.0	27.0	8.9	38.3	22.1	25.5	5.5	34.5	29.8
1918	67	12.9	9.8	36.9	30.7	26.6	39.0	52.9	13.9	57.7	35.9	48.0	9.7	56.9	30.5
1919	72	15.1	10.0	38.9	32.5	27.0	42.3	55.4	15.5	67.8	42.6	57.0	11.3	62.8	43.3
1920	81	17.4	11.5	39.5	33.2	26.2	42.3	52.3	16.7	70.1	41.6	94.5	19.4	68.1	47.0
1924	49	10.1	8.9	34.8	31.3	21.6	31.0	38.4	13.4	52.2	36.2	42.0	9.0	51.0	42.6
1927	55	10.7	9.2	38.7	34.1	25.2	37.2	47.8	14.1	56.3	38.6	57.0	7.2	48.7	47.4
1929	51	9.8	8.8	46.0	39.1	31.4	37.5	43.9	14.4	55.5	39.5	48.0	6.4	52.7	47.9
1930	46	9.5	8.6	42.6	36.4	28.6	36.2	42.5	14.1	46.4	36.6	54.0	6.1	44.5	39.5
1932	32	6.6	7.0	29.7	25.6	18.5	21.5	24.2	10.7	27.8	24.4	25.5	5.0	30.2	29.4
1934	49	8.0	8.3	28.1	23.6	17.5	25.5	29.1	11.2	31.5	25.0	34.5	5.5	32.5	26.9
1937	47.9	8.4	8.6	39.1	32.8	25.7	36.7	41.3	12.5	40.7	29.4	41.9	5.6	36.2	25.5
1939	37.9	7.7	7.9	36.0	29.5	23.4	30.4	31.9	12.2	32.5	25.3	37.1	5.4	32.1	22.4
1941	45.2	8.7	8.1	39.1	31.1	25.5	34.3	34.3	13.6	41.1	30.0	35.2	5.7	39.7	23.6
1942	52.8	12.1	8.7	43.5	34.0	29.3	41.4	39.4	15.0	47.3	34.8	51.3	6.8	48.4	28.3
1944	64.7	12.8	8.8	41.4	33.4	28.8	37.3	41.1	15.6	50.0	36.0	69.8	6.7	54.5	30.1
1946	70.8	14.0	10.4	52.1	43.1	36.6	48.5	53.3	17.6	71.0	50.1	70.2	7.7	58.6	34.4
1948	98.0	20.8	13.9	90.5	73.7	64.4	77.2	76.9	21.8	86.7	65.6	83.8	9.4	72.3	51.4
1950	98.2	16.8	14.3	93.6	74.3	61.6	75.4	63.7	20.6	72.9	51.8	69.2	9.7	60.4	79.4
1954	107.2	19.6	17.2	90.7	70.3	51.4	86.3	81.7	23.0	72.4	57.6	78.9	10.5	58.5	110.8
1956	106.6	17.2	17.9	88.2	70.1	48.4	78.2	57.3	24.2	72.1	57.2	101.6	10.6	60.2	103.4
1958	110.4	18.4	19.3	104.2	81.6	63.3	91.8	79.3	25.3	74.2	58.0	93.9	11.3	60.4	90.7
1960	110.8	18.6	20.3	105.5	81.7	61.6	85.8	65.5	26.0	74.9	68.6	107.7	11.6	57.3	75.3
1962	114.0	19.1	21.2	107.8	84.1	62.3	89.8	70.3	26.1	75.2	72.4	94.8	11.7	54.0	70.8
1964	113.4	18.8	20.7	103.9	82.8	56.8	88.0	66.7	26.4	74.4	73.4	113.6	12.8	53.9	81.6
1965	116.2	19.0	20.9	108.4	89.7	59.5	97.3	81.3	26.3	75.4	75.4	140.6	11.8	52.7	83.3
1966	118.8	19.0	22.2	110.7	93.2	62.2	106.3	95.4	27.8	82.2	84.4	112.4	12.0	59.9	82.3
1967	119.2	18.6	22.2	110.3	94.0	60.7	100.4	83.7	28.7	83.0	87.2	112.1	12.1	49.1	76.9
1968	116.8	18.8	22.4	114.3	98.8	63.5	102.9	81.4	30.3	83.6	88.8	114.5	12.2	52.9	76.4
1969	116.2	18.8	23.0	126.7	109.3	70.4	112.2	87.8	31.5	84.6	94.0	122.4	12.4	62.1	76.5
1970	117.9	19.1	24.3	130.2	111.7	72.5	116.2	94.9	33.0	86.6	100.7	134.5	13.0	61.4	91.1
1971	119.9	19.6	25.0	136.1	118.0	75.0	108.1	80.0	33.9	87.6	105.5	129.2	13.6	52.9	93.4
1972	119.2	19.6	24.7	147.7	129.5	82.1	124.6	96.2	34.5	87.1	108.6	138.9	13.9	52.4	92.7
1973	151.2	26.0	27.6	174.6	152.2	102.8	155.9	132.5	37.6	91.6	120.8	205.4	15.1	78.1	104.0
1974	205.0	44.0	34.5	179.8	158.5	102.1	156.5	132.0	39.2	94.6	145.8	249.6	32.3	78.3	122.9
1975	198.8	41.1	36.0	188.5	179.6	102.8	185.6	175.6	39.3	102.5	153.6	201.6	37.2	77.0	133.4
1976	185.2	37.5	35.3	178.3	177.4	96.9	184.8	171.1	41.4	126.1	173.0	219.0	24.0	84.1	187.3
1977	169.2	35.3	35.5	176.1	182.1	92.0	181.2	156.2	42.0	133.1	172.0	224.6	21.6	82.3	347.2
1978[2]	169.0	40.2	35.8	189.5	200.2	103.3	193.2	173.2	42.8	139.6	92.3[3]	198.0	23.9	81.5	339.5

1) Milk — 1933 through 1973 = delivered milk; after 1973 milk purchased in grocery stores.
2) Data for 1978 are averages only for January through April.
3) American Process cheese.

THE CHANGING AMERICAN FOOD BASKET: 1914–1979   Source: U.S. Department of Agriculture

The table indicates the amount of food that could be purchased through the years with one hour of labor.

Item	Unit	1914	1919	1929	1939	1949	1959	1969	1977	1979
Bread, white	Lb.	3.5	4.7	6.4	7.9	9.8	11.1	13.9	15.9	15.8
Round steak	Lb.	0.9	1.2	1.2	1.7	1.6	2.0	2.5	3.2	N.A.
Pork chops	Lb.	1.0	1.1	1.5	2.1	1.9	2.6	2.8	3.1	N.A.
Sliced bacon	Lb.	0.8	0.9	1.3	2.0	2.1	3.3	3.6	3.6	N.A.
Butter	Lb.	0.6	0.7	1.0	1.9	1.9	2.9	3.8	3.6	N.A.
Cheese	Lb.	1.0	1.1	1.4	2.5	2.4	3.8	3.4	3.3	N.A.
Milk, fresh	Qt.	—	—	—	5.6	7.0	9.1	11.6	13.5	13.5
Eggs, fresh	Doz.	0.6	0.8	1.1	2.0	2.0	4.1	5.1	6.8	8.0
Oranges	Doz.	—	0.9	1.3	2.2	2.7	3.3	3.8	4.4	N.A.
Potatoes	Lb.	12.3	12.4	17.0	25.1	25.1	34.8	38.9	37.6	N.A.
Tomatoes* (canned)	—	—	2.9	4.4	7.3	9.1	14.1	16.2	15.0	N.A.
Margarine	Lb.	—	1.1	2.1	3.8	4.5	7.8	11.5	9.8	N.A.

* #2 can from 1914 to Sept. 1954; #303 can beginning Oct. 1954.

AMERICAN FAMILY CHARACTERISTICS: 1979

Source: U.S. Bureau of Census

Characteristic	Families	Percent	Characteristic	Families	Percent
All families	57,804,000	100.0	Farm	2,051,000	3.5
White	50,910,000	88.1	Headed by Women	8,458,000	14.6
Black and Other	6,894,000	11.9	Age of Family Head:		
Family Size:			Under 25 years	3,837,000	6.6
2 persons	22,485,000	38.9	25–34 years	13,478,000	23.3
3 persons	12,975,000	22.4	35–44 years	11,754,000	20.3
4 persons	12,037,000	20.8	45–54 years	10,883,000	18.8
5 persons	6,089,000	10.5	55–64 years	9,342,000	16.2
6 persons	2,524,000	4.4	65 years or older	8,510,000	14.7
7 persons or more	1,694,000	2.9	Marital Status of Household Heads:		
Own Children under 18 Years Old:			All Households	77,330,000	100.0
No children	27,433,000	47.5	Married	51,246,000	66.3
1 child	11,882,000	20.6	Separated	2,854,000	3.7
2 children	11,005,000	19.0	Widowed	10,372,000	13.4
3 children	4,913,000	8.5	Divorced	6,738,000	8.7
4 children or more	2,571,000	4.4	Single	8,974,000	11.6
Residence:					
Nonfarm	55,753,000	96.5			

SEX RATIO OF U.S. POPULATION

Source: U.S. Bureau of the Census (males per 100 females). Figures relate to July 1, and include Armed Forces overseas

Year	All ages	Under 15 years	15 to 24 years	25 to 44 years	45 to 64 years	65 or older	Year	All ages	Under 15 years	15 to 24 years	25 to 44 years	45 to 64 years	65 or older
1979	95.0	104.3	102.4	97.3	92.2	68.4	1968	96.2	103.7	102.2	96.9	92.4	73.8
1978	95.1	104.3	102.3	97.4	92.1	68.5	1966	96.7	103.7	102.1	96.9	93.2	75.7
1977	95.1	104.2	102.3	97.3	92.0	68.7	1964	97.1	103.6	101.8	97.0	94.1	77.9
1976	95.1	104.2	102.3	97.3	91.9	69.0	1962	97.5	103.4	101.5	97.0	94.9	80.2
1974	95.4	104.1	102.2	97.3	91.6	69.7	1960	97.8	103.4	101.4	96.9	95.7	82.6
1972	95.6	104.0	102.1	97.2	91.6	70.8	1956	98.4	103.7	100.6	97.2	97.0	85.8
1970	95.9	103.9	102.2	96.9	91.7	72.0	1950	99.3	103.8	100.0	97.2	100.1	89.5

MARITAL STATUS OF ADULTS (Persons 14 years old and over)

Source: U.S. Bureau of Census

Marital Status and Sex	1955*	1960	1970	1979	Marital Status and Sex	1955*	1960	1970	1979
Total (millions)	107	114	147	170	Male, total (cont.)				
Single (millions)	16	17	37	47	Widowed	4.6	4.1	3.0	2.4
Married (millions)	79	84	94	102	Divorced	1.9	2.1	2.2	4.3
Widowed (millions)	10	11	11	12	Female, total (millions)	56	59	77	89
Divorced (millions)	2	3	5	9	Percent distribution	100.0	100.0	100.0	100.0
Male, total (millions)	51	55	70	81	Single	12.0	11.8	22.1	24.2
Percent distribution	100.0	100.0	100.0	100.0	Married	71.9	71.3	62.0	58.0
Single	17.4	17.8	28.2	31.1	Husband separated	2.5	2.2	2.2	2.7
Married	76.1	76.0	66.6	62.2	Widowed	13.6	14.0	12.5	11.8
Wife separated	1.5	1.7	1.3	1.9	Divorced	2.4	2.9	3.5	6.0

* Excludes Alaska and Hawaii.

U.S. MARRIAGE AND DIVORCE RATES

Source: National Center for Health Statistics

Year	Marriages Number (thousands)	Divorces Number (thousands)	Marriage Rate (per thousand)	Divorce Rate (per thousand)	Year	Marriages Number (thousands)	Divorces Number (thousands)	Marriage Rate (per thousand)	Divorce Rate (per thousand)
1910	948	83	10.3	0.9	1963	1,654	428	8.8	2.3
1915	1,008	104	10.0	1.0	1964	1,725	450	9.0	2.4
1920	1,274	171	12.0	1.6	1965	1,800	479	9.3	2.5
1925	1,188	175	10.3	1.5	1966	1,857	499	9.5	2.5
1930	1,127	196	9.2	1.6	1967	1,927	523	9.7	2.6
1935	1,327	218	10.4	1.7	1968	2,069	584	10.4	2.9
1940	1,596	264	12.1	2.0	1969	2,145	639	10.6	3.2
1945	1,613	485	12.2	3.5	1970	2,159	708	10.6	3.5
1950	1,667	385	11.1	2.6	1971	2,190	773	10.6	3.7
1955	1,531	377	9.3	2.3	1972	2,282	845	11.0	4.1
1960	1,523	393	8.5	2.2	1973	2,284	915	10.9	4.4
1961	1,548	414	8.5	2.3	1974	2,230	977	10.5	4.6
1962	1,577	413	8.5	2.2	1975	2,153	1,036	10.1	4.9
					1976	2,155	1,083	10.0	5.0
					1977*	2,178	1,091	10.0	5.0

* Provisional figures.

ILLEGITIMATE BIRTHS IN AMERICA

Source: National Center for Health Statistics (Figures in thousands)

Categories	1940	1950	1960	1965	1970	1975	1976	1977	1978
Total Illegitimate Live Births	89.5	141.6	224.3	291.2	398.7	447.9	468.1	515.7	543.9
By age of mother:									
Under 15 years	2.1	3.2	4.6	6.1	9.5	11.0	10.3	10.1	9.4
15 to 19 years	40.5	56.0	87.1	123.1	190.4	222.5	225.0	239.7	239.7
20 to 24 years	27.2	43.1	68.0	90.7	126.7	134.0	145.4	168.6	186.5
25 to 29 years	10.5	20.9	32.1	36.8	40.6	50.2	55.4	62.4	70.0
30 to 34 years	5.2	10.8	18.9	19.6	19.1	19.8	21.0	23.7	26.5
35 to 39 years	3.0	6.0	10.6	11.4	9.4	8.1	8.6	8.8	9.4
40 and over	1.0	1.7	3.0	3.7	3.0	2.3	2.3	2.3	2.3
By color of mother:									
White	40.3	53.5	82.5	123.7	175.1	186.4	197.1	220.1	233.6
Nonwhite	49.2	88.1	141.8	167.5	215.1	261.6	271.0	295.5	310.2

DIVORCE LAWS 1980

SOURCE: Women's Bureau, U.S. Department of Labor and *The Book of the States* (1980-81) by the Council of State Governments

State or other Jurisdiction	Residence required before filing suit for divorce(c)	"No fault" divorce (a) Marriage breakdown (d)	"No fault" Separation	"No fault" Prior decree of limited divorce	"Traditional" Adultery	"Traditional" Mental and/or physical cruelty	"Traditional" Desertion	"Traditional" Alcoholism and/or drug addiction	"Traditional" Impotency	"Traditional" Non-support by husband	"Traditional" Insanity	"Traditional" Pregnancy at marriage	"Traditional" Bigamy	"Traditional" Unexplained absence	"Traditional" Felony conviction or imprisonment	"Traditional" Other	Period before remarry: Plaintiff	Period before remarry: Defendant
Alabama	6 mos.(g)	•	2 yrs.(h)	2 yrs.	•	—	1 yr.	•	•	•	5 yrs.	•	—	—	•	(i)	60 days(j)	60 days(j)
Alaska	90 days	•	—	—	•	•	1 yr.	•	•	•	18 mos.	—	—	—	•	—	—	—
Arizona	90 days	•	—	—	—	—	—	—	—	—	—	—	—	—	—	—	—	—
Arkansas	60 days(k)	—	3 yrs.	—	•	•	1 yr.	•	•	*(l)	3 yrs.	—	•	—	•	—	—	—
California	(m)	•	—	—	—	—	—	—	—	—	(n)	—	—	—	—	—	—	—
Colorado	90 days	•	—	—	—	—	—	—	—	—	—	—	—	—	—	—	—	—
Connecticut	1 yr.(o)	•	18 mos.	—	•	•	1 yr.	•	—	—	5 yrs.	—	—	7 yrs.	•	(p)	—	—
Delaware	6 mos.	*(q)	—	—	(q)	(q)	(q)	(q)	—	—	(q)	—	(q)	—	(q)	(q)	—	—
Florida	6 mos.	•	—	—	—	—	—	—	—	—	3 yrs.(r)	—	—	—	—	—	—	—
Georgia	6 mos.	•	—	—	•	•	1 yr.	•	•	—	2 yrs.	•	—	—	•	(p,s,t)	(u)	(u)
Hawaii	3 mos.	•	2 yrs.(h)	*(v)	•	•	—	•	•	—	—	—	—	—	—	—	—	—
Idaho	6 wks.	•	5 yrs.	—	•	•	•	•	•	•	3 yrs.	—	•	—	•	—	—	—
Illinois	90 days	—	—	—	•	•	1 yr.	2 yrs.	•	•	—	—	•	—	•	(w,x)	—	—
Indiana	6 mos.	•	—	—	—	—	—	—	—	—	2 yrs.	—	—	—	•	—	—	—
Iowa	1 yr.	•	—	—	•	•	—	•	—	•	—	—	—	—	•	—	1 yr.(j)	1 yr.(j)
Kansas	60 days	•	—	—	•	•	1 yr.	•	—	•	3 yrs.	—	—	—	•	—	30 days	30 days
Kentucky	180 days(y)	•	—	—	•	•	—	•	—	•	—	—	—	—	•	—	—	—
Louisiana	(z)	—	2 yrs.	*(aa)	•	—	—	—	—	—	—	—	—	—	•	—	—	—
Maine	6 mos.(o)	•	—	—	•	•	3 yrs.	•	•	•	—	—	—	—	•	—	—	—
Maryland	(ab)	—	(ac)	—	•	—	1 yr.	—	—	—	3 yrs.	—	—	—	•	(ad)	—	—
Massachusetts	(ae)	•	—	—	•	•	1 yr.	•	•	•	—	—	—	—	•	—	—	—
Michigan	180 days(o)	•	—	—	—	—	—	—	—	—	—	—	—	—	—	—	—	—
Minnesota	1 yr.(o)	•	—	—	—	—	—	—	—	—	—	—	—	—	—	—	6 mos.(j)	6 mos.(j)
Mississippi	1 yr.	•	—	—	•	•	1 yr.	•	•	•	3 yrs.	—	•	—	•	(s,af)	—	(ag)
Missouri	90 days	•	—	—	—	—	—	—	—	—	—	—	—	—	—	—	—	—
Montana	90 days	•	180 days	—	—	—	—	—	—	—	—	—	—	—	—	—	—	—
Nebraska	1 yr.	•	—	—	—	—	—	—	—	—	—	—	—	—	—	—	—	—
Nevada	6 wks.(o)	•	1 yr.(u)	—	—	—	—	—	—	—	2 yrs.	—	—	—	•	—	—	—
New Hampshire	1 yr.(o)	•	—	—	•	•	2 yrs.	•	•	•	—	—	—	2 yrs.	•	(ah,ai)	—	—
New Jersey	1 yr.	—	18 mos.	—	•	•	1 yr.	•	—	—	2 yrs.	—	—	—	•	(aj)	—	—
New Mexico	6 mos.	•	—	—	•	•	•	•	—	—	—	—	—	—	—	—	—	—
New York	1 yr.(o)	•	1 yr.(h)	—	•	•	1 yr.	—	(ak)	(al)	5 yrs.(ak)	—	—	—	•	—	—	—
North Carolina	6 mos.	•	1 yr.	—	•	—	—	—	•	*(l)	3 yrs.	•	—	—	•	(i)	—	—
North Dakota	1 yr.	•	—	1 yr.	•	•	1 yr.	•	•	*(l)	5 yrs.	—	•	—	•	(i)	(u)	(u)
Ohio	6 mos.	*(am)	2 yrs.	—	•	•	1 yr.	•	•	*(l)	4 yrs.	—	•	—	•	(p,an)	—	—
Oklahoma	6 mos.(ao)	•	—	—	•	•	1 yr.	•	•	*(l)	5 yrs.	•	—	—	•	(p,an)	6 mos.	6 mos.
Oregon	6 mos.	•	—	—	—	—	—	—	—	—	—	—	—	—	—	—	60 days	60 days
Pennsylvania	1 yr.	•	—	—	•	•	2 yrs.	•	•	—	3 yrs.	—	•	—	•	(j,s,ap)	—	(aq)
Rhode Island	2 yrs.	—	3 yrs.	—	•	•	5 yrs.(at)	•	•	•	—	—	—	—	•	(as,at)	6 mos.	6 mos.
South Carolina	3 mos.(au)	—	3 yrs.	—	•	•	1 yr.	•	—	—	—	—	—	7 yrs.	•	—	—	—
South Dakota	—	•	—	—	•	•	1 yr.	1 yr.	—	1 yr.	5 yrs.	—	•	—	•	—	—	—
Tennessee	6 mos.	•	—	2 yrs.(u)	•	•	1 yr.	•	•	1 yr.	—	—	—	—	•	(x,av)	—	—
Texas	6 mos.	—	3 yrs.	—	•	•	1 yr.	•	•	—	3 yrs.	—	—	—	•	—	30 days(j)	30 days(j)
Utah	3 mos.	—	3 yrs.(h)	—	•	•	1 yr.	•	•	*(j)	(aw)	—	•	—	•	—	—	—
Vermont	6 mos.(ax)	—	6 mos.	—	•	•	•	—	—	*(j)	5 yrs.	—	—	—	—	—	—	—

State or other Jurisdiction	"No fault" divorce (a)				"Traditional" Grounds for Absolute Divorce (b)												Period before parties may remarry after final decree (f)	
	Residence required before filing suit for divorce(c)	Marriage break-down (d)	Separa-tion	Prior decree of limited divorce	Adul-tery	Mental and/or physical cruelty	Deser-tion	Alco-holism and/or drug addiction	Impo-tency	Non-support by husband	In-sanity	Preg-nancy at mar-riage	Big-amy	Un-explained ab-sence	Felony convic-tion or imprison-ment	Other	Plaintiff	Defendant
Virginia	6 mos.	—	1 yr.	(ay)	•	•	1 yr.	—	—	—	—	—	—	—	•	—	—	—
Washington	—	•	—	—	—	—	—	—	—	—	—	—	—	—	—	—	—	—
West Virginia	1 yr.(o)	—	2 yrs.	—	•	•	1 yr.	•	—	—	3 yrs.	—	—	—	•	—	—	—
Wisconsin	6 mos.	—	1 yr.	1 yr.	•	•	1 yr.	1 yr.	—	•	1 yr.	—	—	—	•	—	6 mos.	6 mos.
Wyoming	60 days(o)	—	2 yrs.(az)	—	•	•	1 yr.	•	•	•	2 yrs.	•	—	—	•	(ba,bb)	—	—
District of Columbia	6 mos.	—	6 mos.(bc)	*(bd)	—	—	—	—	—	—	—	—	—	—	—	—	—	—
Puerto Rico	1 yr.(o)	*(bc)	2 yrs.	—	•	•	1 yr.	•	•	—	7 yrs.	—	—	10 yrs.	•	(bf)	—	(bg)

(a) "No fault" includes all proceedings where it is not necessary to prove one of the "traditional" grounds for divorce. In some states divorce can be obtained by the agreement of both parties; in others, unilaterally. (b) "Traditional" grounds enacted into English and American law during mid-1800s. (c) Local residence may also be required. (d) Expressed in statutes as irremediable or irretrievable breakdown of marriage relationship, irreconcilable differences, incompatibility, marriage insupportable because of discord, etc. (e) By another man; unknown to husband. (f) In contested divorce cases, many lawyers advise no remarriage until time for appeal has passed. (g) Two years for wife filing on grounds of nonsupport. (h) Under decree of separate maintenance and/or written separation agreement. (i) Crime against nature. (j) Except to each other. In Iowa, court can waive ban. (k) Three-month residency required before final judgment. (l) Grounds available to husband also. (m) No final decree until party is resident for 6 months. (n) Incurable. (o) In some cases, a lesser period of time may be allowed. (p) Fraud, force, or duress. (q) Grounds indicated, along with homosexuality, willful refusal to perform marriage obligations, and contracting venereal disease constitute basis for finding of marriage breakdown. (r) Mental incompetence. (s) Parties related by marriage or blood contrary to statute. (t) Mental incapacity at time of marriage. (u) In the discretion of the court. (v) After expiration of term of separation decree. (w) Loathsome disease. (x) Attempt on life of spouse by poison or other means showing malice. (y) No decree until parties have lived apart for 60 days. (z) Must be permanent residents (domiciliaries) of state and grounds must have occurred in state. (aa) Spouse who obtained separation may obtain absolute divorce 1 year after decree becomes final. Other party may obtain divorce 1 year and 60 days from date of separation decree. (ab) One year if cause occurred out of state; 2 years for insanity. (ac) Voluntary living apart for 1 year and no reasonable expectation of reconciliation, or living separate and apart without cohabitation or interruption for 3 years. (ad) Any cause which renders marriage null and void from the outset. (ae) One year if grounds occurred outside of Commonwealth (af) Insanity or idiocy at time of marriage not known to other party. (ag) When divorce is granted on grounds of adultery, court may prohibit remarriage. Disability may be removed after 1 year upon satisfactory evidence of reformation. (ah) Membership in religious sect not believing in marriage. (ai) Wife out of state 10 years without husband's consent. (aj) Deviant sexual contact without consent of spouse. (ak) Grounds for annulment. (al) Grounds for separation. (am) On petition of both spouses, accompanied by separation agreement executed and confirmed by both spouses in court appearance not less than 90 days after filing of petition. (an) Defendant obtained divorce from plaintiff in another state. (ao) Five years for insanity and spouse in out-of-state facility. (ap) Remarriage after 2 years upon false but well-founded rumor of death of spouse. (If first spouse reappears, he or she may seek divorce for bigamy within 6 months.) (aq) If divorce is granted for adultery, the guilty party cannot marry the accomplice in adultery during lifetime of former spouse. (ar) Shorter period in court's discretion. (as) Void or voidable marriage; in case party is deemed civilly dead from crime or other circumstances, party may be presumed dead. (at) Gross misbehavior or wickedness. (au) If both parties residents; 1 year if one is a nonresident. (av) Refusal by wife to move to state with husband. (aw) Adjudication of permanent and incurable insanity. (ax) Two years if grounds are insanity. (ay) Limited divorce granted on the grounds of cruelty, reasonable apprehension of bodily hurt, willful desertion, or abandonment may be merged into an absolute divorce after 1 year. (az) Two years' separation without material fault by plaintiff. (ba) Husband guilty of conduct constituting vagrancy. (bb) Conviction of felony before marriage. (bc) Voluntary separation, involuntary separation, 1 year. (bd) Granted for 6 months' voluntary separation, 1 year involuntary separation, adultery, or cruelty. (be) By mutual consent. (bf) Attempt by either parent to corrupt son or prostitute daughter, or proposal by husband to prostitute wife. (bg) If remarriage before 301 days, she must present certificate showing pregnancy or nonpregnancy if she has given birth. If pregnant, former spouse presumed to be father.

MEDIAN DURATION OF U.S. MARRIAGES PRIOR TO DIVORCE OR ANNULMENT (in years)

SOURCE: National Center for Health Statistics

State*	1950	1960	1970	1977
Reporting States Average	5.3	7.1	6.7	6.6
Alabama	(NA)	7.3	5.3	4.9
Alaska	5.0	6.2	5.4	5.0
California	(NA)	(NA)	(NA)	7.0
Connecticut	(NA)	(NA)	(NA)	8.3
Georgia	(NA)	6.3	5.4	5.3
Hawaii	(NA)	6.3	7.2	5.7
Idaho	4.2	4.8	4.6	5.0
Illinois	(NA)	(NA)	(NA)	6.2
Iowa	4.5	5.7	5.6	5.8
Kansas	(NA)	5.8	5.1	5.2
Kentucky	(NA)	(NA)	(NA)	5.6
Maryland	(NA)	9.0	8.8	8.4
Michigan	6.6	(NA)	7.0	7.0
Missouri	5.2	(NA)	5.4	5.5
Montana	(NA)	5.1	5.1	5.1
Nebraska	5.7	6.3	6.0	6.1
New York	(NA)	(NA)	(NA)	8.1
Ohio	(NA)	(NA)	6.3	6.0
Oregon	4.7	5.9	5.9	6.0
Pennsylvania	(NA)	9.2	8.1	7.7
Rhode Island	(NA)	(NA)	9.2	8.2
South Carolina	(NA)	(NA)	(NA)	6.8
South Dakota	4.8	6.3	5.9	5.8
Tennessee	4.6	6.3	5.6	5.3
Utah	(NA)	4.7	5.3	4.8
Vermont	(NA)	(NA)	(NA)	7.8
Virginia	8.2	8.3	7.7	7.8
Wisconsin	(NA)	8.2	7.9	7.0
Wyoming	4.2	5.4	4.6	4.6

(NA) Not Available. *Based on sample data.

MARRIAGE LAWS: 1980

SOURCE: Women's Bureau, U.S. Department of Labor and The Book of States, (1980-81), by the Council of State Governments

State	Age at Which Marriage Can be Contracted without Parental Consent		Age at Which Marriage Can be Contracted With Parental Consent		Blood Test and Other Medical Requirements — Period between Examination and Issuance of License (days)	Scope of Medical Examination	Waiting Period	
	Male	Female	Male	Female			Before Issuance of License	After Issuance of License
Alabama	18	18	17(a)	14(a)	30	(b)	—	—
Alaska	18	18	16(c)	16(c)	30	(b)	3 da.	—
Arizona	18	18	16(c)	16(c)	30	(b)	(d)	—
Arkansas	18	18	17(c)	16(c)	30	(b)	3 da.	—
California	18	18	18(a,c)	16(a,c)	30	(b,f,g,h)	—	—
Colorado	18	18	16(c)	16(c)	30	(b,g,i)	—	—
Connecticut	18	18	16(c)	16(c)	35	(b)	4 da.	—
Delaware	18	18	18(c)	16(c)	30	(b)	—	(k)
Florida	18	18	16(a,c)	16(a,c)	30	(b)	3 da.	—
Georgia	18(l)	18(l)	16(c,l)	16(c,l)	30	(b,f)	3 da.(m)	—
Hawaii	18	18	16	16(c)	30	(b)	—	—
Idaho	18	18	16(c)	16(c)	—	(g)	(o)	—
Illinois	18	18	16(c)	16(c)	15	(b,f)	3 da.	—
Indiana	18	18	17(c)	17(c)	30	(b,f)	3 da.	—
Iowa	18	18	16	16	20	(b)	3 da.	—
Kansas	18	18	18(c)	18(c)	30	(b)	3 da.	—
Kentucky	18	18	(a,q)	(a,q)	15	(b,f)	3 da.	—
Louisiana	18	18	18(c)	16(c)	10	(b)	—	72 hrs.
Maine	18	18	16(c)	16(c)	60	(b)	5 da.	—
Maryland	18	18	16(c)	16(c)	—	—	48 hrs.	—
Massachusetts	18	18	18(c)	18(c)	30	(b,g)	3 da.	—
Michigan	18	18	(r)	16	30	(b)	3 da.	—
Minnesota	18	18	18	16(s)	—	—	5 da.	—
Mississippi	21	21	17(c)	15(c)	30	(b)	3 da.	—
Missouri	18	18	15(c)	15(c)	15	(b)	3 da.	—
Montana	18	18	18(c)	18(c)	20	(b)	5 da.	3 da.
Nebraska	19	19	17	17	30	(b,g)	2 da.	—
Nevada	18	18	16(a,c)	16(a,c)	—	—	—	—
New Hampshire	18	18	14(s)	13(s)	30(t)	(b)	3 da.	—
New Jersey	18	18	16(c)	16(c)	30	(b)	72 hrs.	—
New Mexico	18	18	16(c)	16(c)	30	(b)	72 hrs.	—
New York	18	18	16	14(u)	30	(b,f)	—	24 da.(v)
North Carolina	18	18	16	16(c)	30	(b,g,w,x)	—	—
North Dakota	18	18	16	16	30	(b,y)	—	—
Ohio	18	18	18(c)	16(c)	30	(b)	5 da.	—
Oklahoma	18	18	16(c)	16(c)	30	(b)	(o)	—
Oregon	18	18	17	17	30	(b)	—	(z)
Pennsylvania	18	18	16(c)	16(c)	30	(b,aa)	3 da.	—
Rhode Island	18	18	18(c)	16(c)	40	(b,g,x)	—	—
South Carolina	18	18	16(c)	14(c)	—	—	24 hrs.	—
South Dakota	18	18	16(c)	16(c)	20	(b)	—	—
Tennessee	18	18	16(c)	16(c)	30	(b)	3 da.(ab)	—
Texas	18	18	14(c)	14(c)	21	(b)	—	—
Utah	18	18	16(a)	14(a)	30	(b)	—	—
Vermont	18	18	16(c)	16(c)	30	(b)	—	5 da.
Virginia	18	18	16(a,c)	16(a,c)	30	(b)	—	—
Washington	18	18	17(c)	17(c)	—	(b,x,ac)	3 da.	—
West Virginia	18	18	(q)	(q)	30	(b)	3 da.	—
Wisconsin	18	18	16	16	20	(b)	5 da.	—
Wyoming	19	19	17(c)	16(c)	30	(b)	—	—
District of Columbia	18	18	16(a)	16(a)	30	(b)	3 da.	—
Puerto Rico	21	21	18(c)	16(c)	10(ad)	(b,ac)	—	—

Note: Common law marriage is recognized in Alabama, Colorado, Georgia, Idaho, Iowa, Kansas, Montana, Ohio, Oklahoma, Pennsylvania, Rhode Island, South Carolina, Texas, and the District of Columbia. (a) Parental consent not required if previously married. (b) Venereal diseases. (c) Legal procedure for younger persons to obtain license. (d) Blood test must be on record at least 48 hours before issuance of license. (f) Sickle cell anemia. (g) Rubella immunity. (h) Tay-Sachs disease. (i) Rh factor (k) Residents, 24 hours; nonresidents, 96 hours. (l) Parental consent is not needed regardless of age in cases of pregnancy or when couple has a living child born out of wedlock. (m) Unless parties are 18 years of age or over, or woman is pregnant, or applicants are the parents of a living child born out of wedlock. (o) Three days if parties are under 18 years of age. (q) Non minimum age. (r) No provision in the law for parental consent for males. (s) Permission of judge also required. (t) Maximum period between blood test and date of intended marriage. (u) If under 16 years of age, consent of family court judge also required. (v) However, marriage may not be solemnized within 3 days of date on which specimen for blood test was taken. (w) Mental competence. (x) Tuberculosis. (y) Some marriages prohibited if a party is severely retarded. (z) License valid 3 days after application signed and valid for 30 days thereafter. (aa) Court order needed if party is weakminded, insane, or of unsound mind. (ab) May be waived if certain conditions are met. (ac) Affidavit of mental competence required. Also, no epilepsy in Puerto Rico. (ad) Maximum time from blood test to expiration of license.

SOCIAL SECURITY AND MEDICARE

SOURCE: U.S. Social Security Administration

The basic idea of social security is a simple one: during working years employees, their employers, and self-employed people pay social security contributions which are pooled in special trust funds. When earnings stop or are reduced because the worker retires, becomes disabled, or dies, monthly cash benefits are paid to replace part of the earnings the family has lost.

Part of the contributions made go into a separate hospital insurance trust fund so that when workers and their dependents reach 65 they will have help in paying their hospital bills. Medicare is available also to people under 65 who have been entitled to social security disability benefits for 2 consecutive years or more and to insured people of any age and their dependents who need a kidney transplant or dialysis treatment because of permanent kidney failure. Medical insurance, also available, helps pay doctors' bills and other medical expenses. This program is financed out of premiums partially paid for by those who are enrolled with the majority of the cost paid for by the Federal Government. Under present law, the Federal share can never be less than one-half the cost of the program. Starting July 1, 1980, enrollees pay $9.60 a month for this protection.

Nine out of 10 working people in the United States are now building protection for themselves and their families under social security.

FINANCING THE PROGRAMS

Federal retirement, survivors, and disability benefits and hospital insurance benefits are paid for by contributions based on earnings covered under social security.

If you are employed, you and your employer share the contributions. If you are self-employed, you pay contributions for retirement, survivors, and disability insurance at about 1½ times the rate for an employee. However, the hospital insurance contribution rate is the same for the employer, the employee, and the self-employed person.

As long as you have earnings that are covered by the law, you pay contributions regardless of your age and even if you are receiving social security benefits.

How Contributions Are Paid

If you are employed, your contribution is deducted from your wages each payday. Your employer sends it, with an equal amount as his own share of the contribution, to the Internal Revenue Service.

If you are self-employed and your net earnings are $400 or more in a year, you must report your earnings and pay your self-employment contribution each year when you file your individual income tax return. This is true even if you owe no income tax.

Your wages and self-employment income are entered on your individual record by the Social Security Administration. This record of your earnings will be used to determine your eligibility for benefits and the amount of cash benefits you will receive.

The maximum amount of earnings that can count for social security and on which you pay social security contributions is shown in the following table:

Year	Amount	Year	Amount
1937-50	$3,000	1974	13,200
1951-54	3,600	1975	14,100
1955-58	4,200	1976	15,300
1959-65	4,800	1977	16,500
1966-67	6,600	1978	17,700
1968-71	7,800	1979	22,900
1972	9,000	1980	25,900
1973	10,800	1981	29,700

Earnings over the maximums may have been reported to your social security record, but cannot be used to figure your benefit rate.

When you work for more than one employer in a year and pay social security contributions on wages over the social security maximum, you may claim a refund of the excess contributions on your income tax return for that year.

If you work for only one employer and he deducts too much in contributions, you should apply to the employer for a refund. A refund is made only when more than the required amount of contributions has been paid. Questions about contributions or refunds should be directed to the Internal Revenue Service. These tables show the schedule of contributions rates now in the law:

SOCIAL SECURITY TAX RATES (in percent)

Year	OASI[*1]	DI[*2]	HI[3]	Total
Employers & employees, each				
1977	4.375	0.575	0.90	5.85
1978	4.275	.775	1.00	6.05
1979-80	4.330	.750	1.05	6.13
1981	4.525	.825	1.30	6.65
1982-84	4.575	.825	1.30	6.70
1985	4.750	.950	1.35	7.05
1986-89	4.750	.950	1.45	7.15
1990 & later	5.100	1.100	1.45	7.65
Self-employed				
1977	6.1850	0.8150	0.90	7.90
1978	6.0100	1.0900	1.00	8.10
1979-80	6.0100	1.0400	1.05	8.10
1981	6.7625	1.2375	1.30	9.30
1982-84	6.8125	1.2375	1.30	9.35
1985	7.1250	1.4250	1.35	9.90
1986-89	7.1250	1.4250	1.45	10.00
1990 & later	7.6500	1.6500	1.45	10.75

*By allocation in law. [1]Old Age, Survivors Insurance. [2]Disability Insurance. [3]Hospital Insurance.

Social Security Cash Benefits

To get monthly cash payments for yourself and your family, or for your survivors to get payments in case of your death, you must first have credit for a certain amount of work under social security. This is measured in quarters of coverage. Credit may have been earned at any time after 1936.

In 1980, all employees and self-employed people earn one quarter of coverage for each $290 of their covered annual earnings. In 1979, they earned one quarter of coverage for each $260 of covered annual earnings; in 1978, one quarter of coverage for each $250. This quarter of coverage measure is increased each year to reflect increases in average wages. *No more than 4 quarters can be earned for any year, regardless of total earnings.*

For years before 1978, employees earned one quarter of coverage for a 3-month calendar quarter in which they were paid covered wages of $50 or more. Four quarters were counted for any year in which a person had $400 or more in self-employment income or in cash wages from farm work, or for any year a person had the maximum earnings that counted for social security.

You can be either fully or currently insured or both, depending on the total amount of credit you have for work under social security and the amount you have in the last 3 years.

If you stop working under social security before you have earned enough credit to be insured, no cash benefits will be payable to you. The earnings already credited to you will remain on your social security record; if you later return to work, regardless of your age, all your covered earnings will be considered.

Fully Insured

Just how much credit you must have to be fully insured depends upon the year you reach 62 or upon the date of your death or disabilty.

The amount of credit you will need is measured in quarters of coverage; but for convenience, the table on this page is given in years. The people in your social security office will be glad to give you further details if you have questions.

You are fully insured if you have credit for at least as many years as shown on the appropriate line of the following chart.

When you reach 62 or become disabled	You will be fully insured if you have credit for this much work
1975	6
1977	6½
1979	7
1981	7½
1983	8
1987	9
1991 or later	10

If you become disabled or die before reaching 62 you are fully insured if you have credit for ¼ year of work for each year after 1950 and up to the year of your disability or death. In counting the number of years after 1950, omit years before you were 22.

No one is fully insured with credit for less than 1½ years of work and no one needs more than 10 years of work to be fully insured.

Currently Insured

You will be currently insured if you have social security credit for at least 1½ years of work within the 3 years before you die. If you leave a widow or widower and young children, they are eligible for monthly benefits if you were currently insured.

AMOUNTS OF MONTHLY PAYMENTS

The amount of monthly social security benefits due you or your dependents or survivors is based on your average earnings under social security over a period of years.

The exact amount of your benefit cannot be figured until there is an application for benefits, and all of your earnings up to the time of the application are considered.

A worker who doesn't get any benefits before 65 and who delays his retirement past age 65 will get a special credit that can mean a larger benefit. The credit adds 1 percent for each year (½2 of 1 percent for each month) from age 65 to age 72 (3 percent for people reaching 65 after 1981).

The law provides a special minimum benefit at retirement for some people who worked under social security more than 20 years. This provision helps people who had low incomes, but above a specified amount, in their working years. The amount of the special minimum depends on the number of years of coverage. For a worker retiring at 65 with 30 or more years of coverage, the minimum would be $252.80.

DISABILITY PAYMENTS

If you become disabled before 65, you and certain members of your family may be eligible for benefits.

Do not wait too long after you are disabled to apply for benefits; if you wait more than a year, you may lose benefits. Payments may begin with the 6th full month of disability.

If you are found eligible for disability insurance benefits, you will remain eligible as long as you are disabled. When you reach 65, your benefit will be changed to retirement payments at the same rate.

Who Is Considered Disabled?

A person is considered disabled only if he has a severe physical or mental condition which—

*prevents him from working, and
is expected to last (or has lasted) for at least 12 months
or is expected to result in death.*

A person with a severe medical condition could be eligible even if he manages to do a little work.

How Much Work Credit Is Required for a Disabled Worker?

If you become disabled before you are 24, you need credit for 1½ years of work in the 3 years before you become disabled.

If you become disabled between 24 and 31, you need social security credits for half the time after you are 21 and before you become disabled.

To get disability benefits if you become disabled at 31 or later, you must be fully insured and have credit for 5 years of work out of the 10 years ending when you become disabled.

People who become disabled because of blindness can get benefits without having to meet the requirement of substantial recent work.

FAMILY PAYMENTS

Monthly payments can be made to certain dependents:
*When the worker gets retirement or disability benefits;
When the worker dies.*

These dependents are:

Unmarried children under 18, or between 18 and 22 if they are full-time students;

Unmarried children 18 or over who were severely disabled before they reached 22 and who continue to be disabled;

A wife, widow, or widower regardless of age, if caring for a child under 18 or disabled and the child gets payments based on the worker's record;

A wife 62 or widow 60 or older, even if there are no children entitled to payments;

A widow 50 or older (or widower 50 or older) who becomes disabled not later than 7 years after the death of the worker or not later than 7 years after the end of entitlement to benefits as a widow with a child;

A husband 62 or over or widower 60 or over;

Dependent parents 62 or over after a worker dies.

In addition to monthly benefits, a lump-sum payment of $255 may be made after the worker's death.

Payments may also be made to a divorced wife or husband at 62 or a surviving divorced wife at 60 (or a disabled surviving divorced wife 50 or older) if the marriage lasted at least 10 years.

Benefits also can be paid a dependent surviving divorced wife at any age if she is caring for her deceased former husband's child under 18 or disabled who is entitled to benefits.

For more information about this provision, get in touch with your social security office.

Generally, a marriage must have lasted at least 1 year before dependents of a retired or disabled worker can get monthly benefits; survivors can get benefits in most cases if the marriage lasted at least 9 months.

Examples of monthly social security retirement payments for workers who reach 62 before 1979

Average yearly earnings after 1950 covered by social security

Benefits can be paid to a:	$923 or less	$3,000	$4,000	$5,000	$6,000	$8,000	$10,000*
Retired worker at 65	133.90	276.80	325.60	377.60	426.70	530.40	587.70
Retired worker at 62	107.20	221.50	260.50	302.10	341.40	424.40	470.20
Wife or husband at 65	67.00	138.40	162.80	188.80	213.40	265.20	293.90
Wife or husband at 62	50.30	103.80	122.10	141.60	160.10	198.90	220.50
Wife under 65 and one child in her care	67.00	144.20	230.80	319.00	356.00	397.80	440.80
Maximum family payment	200.90	423.10	556.40	696.60	782.60	928.20	1028.40

*Maximum earnings covered by social security were lower in past years and must be included in figuring your average earnings. This average determines your payment amount. Because of this, the amount shown in the last column generally won't be payable until future years. The maximum retirement benefit generally payable to a worker who is 65 in 1980 is $572.00.

Amount of Your Family's Benefits

Cash benefits to your dependents, and to your survivors in case of your death, are figured from the amount of your retirement or disability benefit.

Permanently reduced benefits are received by:

Workers and their wives who choose to start receiving retirement benefits while they are between 62 and 65; Widows and widowers who choose to start receiving benefits between 60 and 65 and Disabled widows and disabled widowers 50 or older who receive benefits before they reach 65.

The amount of the reduction depends on the number of months they receive benefits before they reach 65. On the average, people who choose to get benefits early will collect about the same value in total benefits over the years, but in smaller installments to take account of the longer period during which they will be paid.

If a person is entitled to monthly benefits based on the social security records of two or more workers, he will receive no more than the largest of the benefits.

The lump-sum payment at a worker's death is $255.

Benefits Not Taxable

Social security benefits you receive are not subject to Federal income tax.

AN APPLICATION IS NECESSARY

Before payments can start, an application must be filed. When you are nearing 65 or if you become disabled, get in touch with your social security office.

It is important for you to inquire at your social security office 2 or 3 months before you reach 65, not only for the possibility of retirement benefits, but also for Medicare benefits, which are available whether or not you retire. If you wait until the month you reach 65 to apply for the medical insurance part of Medicare, you will lose at least one month of protection. It is always to your advantage to apply before you reach 65, even if you do not plan to retire. If you have high earnings which would increase the amount of your benefit in the year you are 65 or later, your benefit amount will be refigured. You will always be sure of receiving benefits at the highest possible rate.

If you plan to retire *before* you reach 65, it is important to apply for benefits no later than the last day of the month you want benefits to begin. Generally, benefits payable for months before age 65 can start no earlier than the month you apply.

When a person who has worked under the social security law dies, some member of his family should get in touch with the social security office.

If you cannot come to the social security office write or telephone. A representative can arrange to visit you.

Long delay in filing an application can cause loss of some benefits, since back payments for monthly cash benefits can be made for no more than 12 months.

An application for a lump-sum death payment must usually be made within 2 years of the worker's death.

HEALTH INSURANCE (MEDICARE)

Nearly all people 65 and over are eligible for health insurance protection under Medicare, including some people who do not have enough credit for work covered by social security to qualify for monthly cash benefits.

Medicare also covers people who have been getting disability checks for 2 years or more and insured people and their dependents who need a kidney transplant or dialysis treatment because of permanent kidney failure.

There are two parts to Medicare: hospital insurance and, for those who choose, medical insurance.

Eligibility for Hospital Insurance

If you are 65 or over and are entitled to social security or railroad retirement benefits or if you are disabled and have been getting disability for 2 consecutive years or more, you are automatically eligible for hospital insurance; if you are not entitled to either of these benefits, you should ask about hospital insurance and medical insurance at your social security office.

People 65 or older who are not automatically entitled to hospital insurance can buy this protection for a monthly premium of $77 for the 12-month period starting July 1, 1980, although you will also have to purchase medical insurance.

After you establish your eligibility, you receive a health insurance card, which shows that you have hospital insurance, medical insurance, or both.

YOUR HOSPITAL INSURANCE

Hospital insurance will help pay the cost of covered services for the following hospital and follow-up care:

Up to 90 days of hospital care in a participating hospital during a "benefit period."[1] For the first 60 days of care in 1980, your hospital insurance will pay all but the first $180 of expenses. For the 61 through the 90th day of care, your hospital insurance will pay all but $45 daily for covered services. (There is a lifetime limit of payment for 190 days of care in mental hospitals.)

You also have 60 reserve days which can be used after you have exhausted your 90 days of hospital care in a "benefit period." Reserve days are not replaced after you use them. Hospital insurance pays all but $90 a day of your covered expenses during the reserve days.

Hospital insurance in many cases also pays for up to 100 days of care in a participating skilled nursing facility after a hospital stay. Hospital insurance pays for all covered services for the first 20 days of care and all but $22.50 per day for up to 80 more days.

Up to 100 home health "visits" from a participating home health agency when prescribed by your physician may also be covered.

WHAT YOUR MEDICAL INSURANCE PAYS

Anyone who is 65 *or* older or entitled to hospital insurance is eligible for medical insurance. People who get monthly social security or railroad retirement benefits are automatically enrolled in medical insurance—unless they say they don't want it—at the same time they become entitled to hospital insurance. Other eligible people must apply for medical insurance at a social security office.

You will have protection at the earliest possible time if you enroll during the 3-month period just before the month you first become eligible for medical insurance. You may also enroll the month you become eligible and during the 3 following months, but your protection will not start until 1 to 3 months after that.

Anyone who declines enrollment in Medicare medical insurance during the initial enrollment period can enroll during any general enrollment period (January 1 through March 31 of each year). The premium will be 10 percent higher for each full year a person could have had medical insurance but didn't choose to.

Medical insurance is financed with monthly premiums paid by those who are enrolled and by the Federal Government. The basic medical insurance premium is currently $9.60 a month for the 12-month period starting July 1, 1980.

If you wish to drop your medical insurance, you may give notice to do so at any time. But, you can re-enroll only once and your premium will be higher.

YOUR MEDICAL INSURANCE

Generally, your medical insurance will pay 80 percent of the reasonable charges for the following services after the first $60 in a calendar year.

Physicians' and surgeons' services, no matter where you receive the services—in the doctor's office, in a clinic, in a hospital, or at home. (You do not have to meet the $60 deductible before your medical insurance will pay for X-ray or laboratory services of physicians when you are a bed patient in a hospital. The full reasonable charge will be paid, instead of 80 percent.) Home health services even if you have not been in a hospital—up to 100 visits during a calendar year. (Medical insurance pays the reasonable cost after you meet the $60 deductible.)

A number of other medical and health services, such as diagnostic tests, surgical dressings and splints, and rental or purchase of medical equipment.

Outpatient physical therapy services—whether or not you are homebound—furnished under supervision of a participating hospital, skilled nursing facility, home health agency, approved clinic, rehabilitation agency, or public health agency. All outpatient services of a participating hospital, including diagnostic tests or treatment.

Certain services by podiatrists (but not routine foot care or treatment of flat feet or partial dislocation). Limited services by chiropractors.

---

[1] A "benefit period" begins the first time you enter a hospital after your hospital insurance start. It ends after you have not been an inpatient for 60 days in a row in any hospital or in any facility that mainly provides skilled nursing or rehabilitation services.

For More Medicare Information

For more information on the health insurance programs, get in touch with your social security office and ask for a copy of the leaflet, "A brief explanation of Medicare."

MEDICAID

Both Medicare and Medicaid are part of the Social Security Act. They differ, however, in that the former is an insurance program intended to help those 65 (and some disabled people under 65), while Medicaid is designed for certain kinds of needy and low-income people: the aged (65 or older), the blind, the disabled, members of families with dependent children, and other cases involving children.

Medicaid programs, paid for by money from federal, state, and local taxes, were available in all states except Arizona as of April 1974. Under these programs, payment is made for at least the following services: inpatient hospital care; outpatient hospital services; other laboratory and X-ray services; skilled nursing home services; physicians' services; the screening, diagnosis, and treatment of children; and home health care services.

Medicaid can pay what Medicare does not pay for people who are eligible for both programs. For example, Medicaid can pay the $180 deductible amount for the first 60 days of hospital care under hospital insurance, and the $45 a day for the next 30 days of care. Medicaid also can pay the $60 deductible and the monthly premium for medical insurance.

OLD-AGE, SURVIVORS, AND DISABILITY INSURANCE PROGRAM

PROJECTED EXPENDITURES, INCOME, AND LEVEL OF THE COMBINED OASI AND DI TRUST FUNDS AFTER THE SOCIAL SECURITY AMENDMENTS OF 1977
(in billions)

Calendar Year	Expenditures	Income	Net increase in funds	Funds at beginning of year	Funds at beginnning of year as a percentage of outgo during year
1977	$ 87.6	$ 82.1	$ -5.5	$ 41.1	47%
1978	97.2	92.4	-4.8	35.6	37
1979	106.9	106.5	-0.4	30.8	29
1980	117.1	119.1	2.0	30.4	26
1981	127.4	137.1	9.6	32.4	25
1982	138.3	150.2	11.9	42.0	30
1983	149.2	161.3	12.1	53.9	36
1984	161.2	172.9	11.7	66.0	41
1985	174.0	194.2	20.1	77.7	45
1986	187.6	209.0	21.4	97.9	52
1987	202.0	223.7	21.7	119.3	59

SOCIAL SECURITY: 1985-2050 A.D.

SOURCE: Social Security Administration

Note: Social Security is not true insurance because reserves are not built up against all future liabilities. Due to its governmental status the administrators try only to insure that income for a given year is enough to pay all expenses and to add a certain percentage to the Social Security trust fund (they try to keep the fund equal to the sum of all payments the previous year).

In order to keep payments and the trust fund at the proper levels over a long period, the administrators compute probable benefit payments (outgo) and then determine what income will be necessary to make the payments. Because of fluctuations in employment, inflation, and population rates, both figures are very difficult to compute, but the table below shows the product of all the administrators' computations. In essence it shows the percentage of taxable payroll required to pay off Social Security obligations in any year. This may sound complicated, but it is not. In order to clarify it, let's look at one year; 1985: in that year it will take a total of 11.16 percent of the taxable payroll (roughly $1,116 for a worker earning $10,000) to keep the system solvent. (This means that for everyone receiving $4,000 in benefits, there will be 4 workers earning $10,000 and paying a tax of $1,000.) NOTE: each worker would not pay entire $1,000; it is divided equally between employee and employer. The table takes into account how many workers there will be, how much they'll be making, the effects of population change on the number of people eligible for benefits, etc.

OLD-AGE, SURVIVORS, AND DISABILITY INSURANCE AND MEDICARE PROGRAMS

PROJECTED EXPENDITURES, TAX INCOME, AND NET DIFFERENCES EXPRESSED AS A PERCENTAGE OF TAXABLE PAYROLL[1]

Year	Old-Age and Survivors Insurance Expend.	Income	Disability Insurance Expend.	Income	Medicare Hospital Insurance Expend.	Income	Total for OASDHI Expend.	Income	Medicare Supplementary Medical Ins. Expenditures[2]
1977	9.39	8.75	1.50	1.15	1.99	1.80	12.88	11.70	
1980	8.63	8.66	1.48	1.50	2.22	2.10	12.33	12.26	0.85
1985	8.79	9.50	1.66	1.90	2.98	2.70	13.43	14.10	0.96
1990	8.71	10.20	1.87	2.20	3.76	2.90	14.34	15.30	1.28
1995	8.68	10.20	2.07	2.20	4.52	2.90	15.27	15.30	1.64
2000	8.63	10.20	2.34	2.20	5.27	2.90	16.24	15.30	1.90
2025	13.49	10.20	2.91	2.20	7.44[3]	2.90	23.84	15.30	2.00
2050	13.35	10.20	2.82	2.20	7.61[3]	2.90	23.78	15.30	2.63
									2.52

[1]The effective taxable payroll is slightly different for OASDI and HI because of the tax treatment of self-employed persons; however, it does not materially affect the comparisons. In 1977, taxable payroll represented about 85 percent of total earnings in covered employment; in 1981 and later the corresponding percentage will be approximately 91 percent.

[2]Expenditures are approximately equal to total income from premiums and general revenue for the Medicare-SMI program. Although the Medicare-SMI program is not financed by payroll taxes, its cost is shown for comparison as a percentage of payroll which is taxable for HI purposes. Figures after 1977 are based upon unpublished estimates.

[3]Based upon unpublished estimates. For the purpose of this comparison, it was assumed that after the year 2000 medical care unit cost increases would be equal to average wage increases in covered employment.

DISADVANTAGED: A DEFINITION

The level of family income used to determine whether or not a person is poor has been raised an average of $460 by the U.S. Department of Labor to reflect increases in consumer prices over the past year.

The revised poverty-level guidelines for metropolitan area and farm families became effective April 1, 1979, based on the Office of Management and Budget (OMB) recommendations.

Income levels for families of one through six persons are:

Family Size	Income: Nonfarm*	Income: Farm*
1	$3,400	$2,910
2	4,500	3,840
3	5,600	4,770
4	6,700	5,700
5	7,800	6,630
6	8,900	7,560

* For Continental U.S.

Income limits for families of more than six persons may be determined by adding for the nonfarm and farm levels these amounts for each additional person: $1,100 and $930 for the Continental U.S.

They will have limited application to Federal, state and local employment and training programs under the Comprehensive Employment and Training Act (CETA). These levels will be modified by the Bureau of Labor Statistics family income data for use by CETA administrators.

The eligibility requirements for CETA titles II B, II D, VII, and most programs funded under title IV, include the definition of "economically disadvantaged" containing provisions incorporating the income poverty levels and the Lower Living Standard Income Levels.

The income guidelines or the Lower Living Standard Income Level (whichever is higher) is to be used in determining income eligibility for CETA.

The Labor Department's Employment and Training Administration (ETA) defines an economically disadvantaged person as one who is a member of a family that (1) receives cash welfare payments; or (2) has a family income that, in relation to family size and location, represents 70 percent of the lower living income level issued by the department's Bureau of Labor Statistics or poverty levels established by the Office of Management and Budget—whichever is higher.

POVERTY IN THE UNITED STATES:

SOURCE: Bureau of the Census (numbers in millions)

Year	Number below Poverty Level				Percent below Poverty Level			
	Total	White	Black and Other Races	Black Only	Total	White	Black and Other Races	Black Only
1978	24.5	16.3	8.2	7.6	11.4	8.7	22.8	30.6
1977	24.7	16.4	8.3	7.7	11.6	8.9	29.0	31.3
1976	25.0	16.7	8.3	7.6	11.8	9.1	29.4	31.1
1975	25.9	17.8	8.1	7.5	12.3	9.7	29.3	31.3
1974	23.4	15.7	7.6	7.2	11.2	8.6	28.3	30.3
1973	23.0	15.1	7.8	7.4	11.1	8.4	29.6	31.4
1972	24.5	16.2	8.3	7.7	11.9	9.0	31.9	33.3
1971	25.6	17.8	7.8	7.4	12.5	9.9	30.9	32.5
1970	25.4	17.5	7.9	7.5	12.6	9.9	32.0	33.5
1967	27.8	19.0	8.8	8.5	14.2	11.0	37.2	39.3
1965	33.2	22.5	10.7	NA	17.3	13.3	47.1	NA

FACTS ABOUT THE POOR

SOURCE: Community Services Administration

Based on 1979 population and 1978 income, there were 24,497,000 poor persons. Despite the fact that there are almost two poor white persons for every poor nonwhite person, the incidence of poverty among nonwhites was 28.2 percent as compared to 8.7 percent for whites. Children under 18 years of age made up 40.5 percent of the poor.

Between 1977 and 1978 the number of poor persons declined by 223,000. At the same time the number of poor persons aged 65 and over increased by 56,000.

For the 5,280,000 poor families the average income deficit in 1978 was $2,370. For the 5,435,000 poor unrelated individuals the deficit averaged $1,288.(*) In order to bring all the poor to the poverty income threshold it would require a direct payment amounting to $19,513,880,000.

(*) Average income deficit is the amount of income below the income poverty threshold level, which was as of May 7, 1979, for a non-farm family of four, $6,700; a farm family of four, $5,700.

POVERTY IN AMERICA BY STATES

There were 14,028,000 fewer poor persons in the United States in 1969 than in 1959, according to the office of Economic Opportunity (OEO). The national incidence of poverty dropped from 22.1 percent to 12.3 percent during this 10-year period.

Significant changes occurred in the numbers of poor within the individual states. Poor farmers moved to urban areas, often in other states; industry provided employment for increasing numbers of poor persons previously considered unemployable or, for one reason or another, undesirable; and more wives and youths worked to add to their family income. The total for the 1969 census differs from that shown above due to differences in survey methods and family definitions.

State	Thousands of Poor Persons 1959	1969*
Total	38,682	27,125
Alabama	1,374	857
Alaska	38	35
Arizona	314	264
Arkansas	843	523
California	2,199	2,153
Colorado	312	263
Connecticut	236	212
Delaware	73	58
District of Columbia	161	123
Florida	1,371	1,088
Georgia	1,505	924
Hawaii	102	69
Idaho	124	92
Illinois	1,446	1,112
Indiana	797	493
Iowa	583	319
Kansas	419	275
Kentucky	1,137	718
Louisiana	1,274	933
Maine	222	131
Maryland	523	387
Massachusetts	608	473
Michigan	1,216	819
Minnesota	646	398
Mississippi	1,173	767
Missouri	1,051	672
Montana	129	92
Nebraska	309	188
Nevada	35	43
New Hampshire	87	65
New Jersey	673	574
New Mexico	278	227
New York	2,319	1,986
North Carolina	1,796	996
North Dakota	169	93
Ohio	1,508	1,041
Oklahoma	680	465
Oregon	262	235
Pennsylvania	1,881	1,228
Rhode Island	135	100
South Carolina	1,049	595
South Dakota	202	120
Tennessee	1,374	836
Texas	2,970	2,047
Utah	135	118
Vermont	88	52
Virginia	1,164	691
Washington	397	336
West Virginia	637	380
Wisconsin	607	421
Wyoming	51	38

*Source: 1970 Census Fourth Count Summary Tapes

AID TO FAMILIES WITH DEPENDENT CHILDREN

SOURCE: U.S. Department of Health, Education and Welfare (Data for August 1979)

State	Families	NUMBER OF RECIPIENTS		PAYMENTS TO RECIPIENTS	Average per —		Percentage change from Aug. 1978	
		Total	Children	Total	Family	Recipient	Recipients	Amount
Total[1]	3,491,834	10,227,562	7,125,375	$953,047,711	$272.94	$ 93.18	−2.2	6.4
Ala.	61,089	177,320	128,339	6,805,134	111.40	38.38	2.0	3.2
Alaska[2]	5,933	14,386	9,960	1,944,972	327.82	135.20	18.9	25.5
Ariz.	17,214	48,583	36,089	2,902,048	168.59	59.73	.8	15.0
Ark.	29,514	86,027	63,298	4,439,469	150.42	51.61	−2.5	1.5
Calif.	456,809	1,326,137	898,678	177,927,400	389.50	134.17	−4.4	19.0
Colo.	26,793	74,162	51,876	5,958,015	222.37	80.34	−5.7	1.1
Conn.	46,184	135,680	95,057	15,900,694	344.29	117.19	− .8	4.8
Del.	11,236	31,547	22,146	2,411,070	214.58	76.43	1.9	3.7
D.C.	31,205	87,774	60,904	8,147,015	261.08	92.82	−5.0	8.4
Fla.	84,741	234,585	169,816	14,969,140	176.65	63.81	1.5	23.7
Ga.	80,750	212,775	155,888	10,019,617	124.08	47.09	− .6	16.2
Guam	1,260	4,538	3,378	257,660	204.49	56.78	−1.1	2.5
Hawaii	19,152	58,993	39,360	7,521,091	392.71	127.49	− .2	2.9
Idaho	7,446	20,230	13,923	1,996,280	268.10	98.68	4.3	4.6
Ill.	209,199	665,709	471,062	54,454,612	260.30	81.80	−4.5	−7.4
Ind.	51,032	147,662	105,848	9,665,776	189.41	65.46	−2.0	− .7
Iowa	34,322	95,140	64,160	10,596,080	308.73	111.37	2.5	10.6
Kans.	24,294	64,079	46,920	6,516,721	268.24	101.70	−7.0	9.7
Ky.	60,870	163,989	116,112	10,018,509	165.25	61.34	−1.4	.3
La.	65,519	206,741	152,923	9,220,421	140.73	44.60	1.3	11.3
Maine	20,672	59,850	39,999	4,641,459	224.53	77.55	.7	8.6
Md.	74,880	207,969	143,210	16,301,103	217.70	78.38	1.0	11.7
Mass.	123,593	351,600	229,984	39,159,550	316.84	111.38	−3.8	−3.0
Mich.	207,526	630,313	431,243	72,865,560	351.12	115.60	1.9	10.2
Minn.	47,685	129,057	87,589	15,464,004	324.29	119.82	.8	3.6
Miss.	55,877	173,587	127,313	4,900,247	87.70	28.23	4.7	36.0
Mo.	64,215	190,570	131,016	13,129,471	204.46	68.90	−6.3	*
Mont.	6,405	17,690	12,474	1,401,275	218.78	79.21	− .5	8.8
Nebr.	12,209	34,949	24,578	3,155,590	258.46	90.29	−2.6	−2.1
Nev.	3,786	10,456	7,386	778,335	205.58	74.44	8.9	17.7
N.H.	7,750	21,430	14,343	2,086,426	269.22	97.36	−2.5	15.7
N.J.	145,151	453,413	315,264	43,795,261	301,72	96.59	−1.1	2.2
N.M.	17,340	51,508	36,052	2,998,776	172.94	58.22	1.1	9.9
N.Y.	359,907	1,096,879	760,439	137,353,082	381.63	125.22	−3.9	1.1
N.C.	73,983	191,427	137,565	12,106,385	163.64	63.24	−1.5	5.2
N.D.	4,617	12,690	8,834	1,165,644	252.47	91.86	−5.8	.6
Ohio	165,514	472,266	324,597	45,740,761	276.36	96.85	−3.2	21.1
Okla.	29,139	87,108	63,951	7,396,828	253.85	84.92	− .3	15.7
Oreg.	35,793	94,551	60,939	11,188,908	312.60	118.34	−21.0	−12.5
Pa.[1]	213,452	628,776	433,825	59,501,947	278.76	94.63	−3.1	−1.7
P.R.	40,201	157,906	112,249	1,846,437	45.93	11.69	−9.5	−8.5
R.I.[2]	17,243	49,801	34,289	4,508,240	261.45	90.53	−3.1	−1.8
S.C.	52,662	144,792	104,153	6,015,410	114.23	41.55	2.2	26.6
S.D.	7,302	20,240	14,794	1,538,760	210.73	76.03	−3.7	1.5
Tenn.	57,066	153,759	110,862	6,477,000	113.50	42.12	−3.8	−2.0
Texas	94,995	294,113	216,211	10,127,975	106.62	34,43	1.3	−1.6
Utah	11,009	33,807	21,572	3,233,391	293.70	95.64	−8.6	−7.0
Vt.	6,803	20,237	13,185	2,248,251	330.48	111.10	6.5	11.0
V.I.	966	2,966	2,407	189,214	195.87	63.79	−10.7	43.9
Va.	58,146	160,679	113,007	11,998,309	206.35	74.67	−1.3	1.3
Wash.	49,033	136,392	87,916	16,765,895	341.93	122.92	−1.0	7.6
W. VA.	26,889	76,561	57,694	6,160,072	229.09	80.46	17.0	5.8
Wis.	72,938	197,800	136,174	24,469,815	335.49	123.71	1.6	6.6
Wyo.	2,525	6,343	4,524	626,606	248.16	98.79	5.5	21.5

*Increase or decrease of less than 0.05 percent.   [1]Estimated data.

DRUG LAW ENFORCEMENT SOURCE: Drug Enforcement Administration

Item	STATE AND LOCAL ARRESTS				DOMESTIC FEDERAL ARRESTS			
	1975	1976	1977	1978	1975	1976	1977	1978
Number of Arrests	508,189	500,540	569,293	596,940	7,404	9,240	9,369	7,943
Arrest Rate per 100,000	283.6	285.2	298.4	283.3				
Estimated % by Drug								
Narcotics (heroin, cocaine)	13.1%	9.9%	13.2%	13.2%	66.4%	56.8%	64.8%	55.3%
Cannabis	69.2%	72.4%	71.2%	70.9%	17.5%	29.5%	18.2%	21.3%
Dangerous Drug	17.7%	3.0%	15.6%	15.9%	15.6%	13.3%	16.5%	21.2%
Other	—	14.7%	—	—	0.5%	0.4%	.5%	2.2%
Estimated % by Race								
White	78.7%	77.0%	77.0%	76.5%	84.9%	82.5%	80.6%	80.1%
Nonwhite	21.3%	22.9%	22.9%	23.5%	15.1%	17.1%	19.4%	19.9%
Estimated % by Age								
Under 21	53.3%	52.4%	50.7%	50.4%	10.1%	9.3%	8.2%	5.6%
21-24	23.7%	76.1%	23.2%	23.0%	30.1%	29.8%	26.5%	16.7%
25-29	13.1%	14.0%	14.5%	14.3%	26.6%	27.3%	28.4%	27.6%
30-39	7.2%	7.2%	8.4%	6.3%	21.7%	22.6%	25.2%	34.1%
40 or Older	2.7%	2.5%	3.2%	6.0%	11.5%	10.9%	12.1%	16.0%
Estimated % by Sex								
Male	86.2%	86.4%	86.1%	86.3%	85.9%	85.6%	85.8%	87.2%
Female	13.8%	13.6%	13.9%	13.7%	14.1%	14.4%	14.2%	12.8%

DRUGS: USES AND ABUSES

Source: Smith Kline & French

Drugs	Pharmacologic Classification	Federal Controls	Medical Use	Potential for Physical Dependence	How Taken When Abused	Comments
Morphine (an opium derivative)	Central Nervous System Depressant	Narcotic: Schedule II Controlled Substances Act of 1970	To relieve pain	Yes	Orally or by injection	Morphine is the standard against which other narcotic analgesics are compared. Legally available on prescription only.
Heroin (a morphine derivative)	Depressant	Narcotic: Schedule I C. S. A. of 1970	To relieve pain	Yes	Sniffed or by injection	Not legally available in the United States. Used medically in some countries for relief of pain.
Codeine (an opium derivative)	Depressant	Narcotic C. S. A. of 1970	To relieve pain and coughing	Yes	Orally (usually as cough syrup)	Preparations containing specified minimal amounts of codeine are classified as "exempt" narcotics (Schedule V) and can be obtained without prescription in some states.
Paregoric (preparation containing opium)	Depressant	Narcotic: Schedule II C. S. A. of 1970	For sedation and to counteract diarrhea	Yes	Orally or by injection	Paregoric is often boiled to concentrate narcotic content prior to injection. Prescription only.
Meperidine (synthetic morphine-like drug)	Depressant	Narcotic: Schedule II C. S. A. of 1970	To relieve pain	Yes	Orally or by injection	Shorter acting than morphine. Frequent dosing required. Withdrawal symptoms appear quickly. Prescription only.
Methadone (synthetic morphine-like drug)	Depressant	Narcotic: Schedule II C. S. A. of 1970	To relieve pain	Yes	Orally or by injection	Longer acting than morphine. Withdrawal symptoms develop more slowly and are less intense and more prolonged. Prescription only.
Cocaine	Central Nervous System Stimulant	Schedule II C. S. A. of 1970	Local anesthetic	No	Sniffed or by injection	
Marijuana	Hallucinogen	Schedule I	No	No	Smoked or orally	Available legally only for research.
Barbiturates (e.g., amobarbital, pentobarbital, secobarbital)	Depressant	Schedule II and III C. S. A. of 1970	For sedation, sleep-producing, epilepsy, high blood pressure	Yes	Orally or by injection	Written prescription only. No refills for Schedule II barbiturates. For Schedule III barbiturates original prescription expires after 6 months. Only 5 refills permitted within this period. Dependence generally occurs only with the use of high doses for a protracted period of time.
Amphetamine drugs (e.g., amphetamine, dextroamphetamine, methamphetamine—also known as desoxyephedrine)	Stimulant	Schedule II C. S. A. of 1970	For antiappetite, narcolepsy, hyperkinetic behavior disorders	No	Orally or by injection	Written prescription only. No refills permitted.
LSD (also mescaline, peyote, psilocybin, DMT, STP, THC)	Hallucinogen	Schedule I C. S. A. of 1970	Medical research only	No	Orally or by injection	

U.S. INDEX OF CRIME Source: Federal Bureau of Investigation

TRENDS BY GEOGRAPHIC REGION (Percent change, 1979 over 1978)

	Total	Violent	Property	Murder	Forcible Rape	Robbery	Aggravated Assault	Burglary	Larceny-Theft	Motor Vehicle Theft
Northeastern States	+ 9	+11	+ 8	+11	+10	+14	+ 7	+ 5	+10	+ 8
North Central States	+ 7	+ 8	+ 7	+ 8	+13	+ 3	+10	+ 4	+ 8	+ 9
Southern States	+10	+12	+ 0	+10	+14	+17	+ 9	+10	+ 9	+16
Western States	+ 8	+11	+ 7	+ 8	+10	+10	+12	+ 2	+10	+ 9
TOTAL	+ 8	+11	+ 8	+ 9	+12	+12	+ 9	+ 6	+ 9	+10

TRENDS BY YEARS (Percent change 1968-1978, each year over previous year)

	Total	Violent	Property	Murder	Forcible Rape	Robbery	Aggravated Assault	Burglary	Larceny-Theft	Motor Vehicle Theft
1970/1969	+ 9	+12	+ 9	+ 8	+ 2	+17	+ 8	+11	+ 9	+ 6
1971/1970	+ 6	+11	+ 6	+11	+11	+11	+10	+ 9	+ 5	+ 2
1972/1971	− 4	+ 2	− 5	+ 5	+11	− 3	+ 7	− 1	− 6	− 6
1973/1972	+ 6	+ 5	+ 6	+ 5	+10	+ 2	+ 7	+ 8	+ 5	+ 5
1974/1973	+18	+11	+18	+ 5	+ 8	+15	+ 8	+18	+21	+ 5
1975/1974	+10	+ 5	+10	− 1	+ 1	+ 5	+ 6	+ 7	+14	+ 2
1976/1975	0	− 4	+ 1	− 8	+ 1	−10	+ 1	− 5	+ 5	− 4
1977/1976	− 3	+ 2	− 4	+ 2	+11	− 4	+ 6	− 1	− 6	+ 1
1978/1977	+ 2	+ 5	+ 2	+ 2	+ 7	+ 3	+ 7	+ 2	+ 1	+ 2

CRIME: U.S. CITIES (Offenses Known to the Police, 1978 and 1979)
Source: Federal Bureau of Investigation

Preliminary figures for cities over 100,000 population reporting more than 11,000 incidents.

City	Crime Index 1978	Crime Index 1979
Akron, Ohio	15,606	16,434
Albuquerque, N. Mex.	22,866	27,342
Anaheim, Calif.	15,417	17,009
Anchorage, Alaska	10,243	11,848
Atlanta, Ga.	53,870	58,785
Austin, Texas	24,719	27,237
Baltimore, Md.	69,463	73,744
Baton Rouge, La.	21,969	23,933
Berkeley, Calif.	11,838	12,765
Birmingham, Ala.	26,659	31,862
Boston, Mass.	65,366	70,231
Bridgeport, Conn.	12,467	12,358
Buffalo, N.Y.	27,313	26,975
Charlotte, N.C.	23,119	22,985
Chattanooga, Tenn.	12,109	13,362
Chicago, Ill.	190,815	186,728
Cincinnati, Ohio	30,296	33,121
Cleveland, Ohio	50,952	51,947
Colorado Springs, Colo.	13,259	14,871
Columbus, Ohio	44,839	50,605
Corpus Christi, Texas	17,326	17,544
Dallas, Texas	86,569	93,761
Dayton, Ohio	23,812	25,036
Denver, Colo.	50,993	51,990
Des Moines, Iowa	16,827	17,419
Detroit, Mich.	110,511	110,723
El Paso, Texas	23,609	26,439
Flint, Mich.	19,167	20,149
Fort Lauderdale, Fla.	16,726	19,309
Fort Wayne, Ind.	12,686	13,611
Fort Worth, Texas	36,008	42,690
Fresno, Calif.	22,997	23,265
Gary, Ind.	10,009	11,659
Grand Rapids, Mich.	12,544	14,620
Hartford, Conn.	18,594	20,643
Hollywood, Fla.	10,719	11,547
Honolulu, Hawaii	51,892	52,926
Houston, Texas	132,000	141,748
Huntsville, Ala.	10,770	11,936
Indianapolis, Ind.	34,837	35,105
Jackson, Miss.	12,366	14,351
Jacksonville, Fla.	36,274	39,349
Jersey City, N.J.	15,863	16,670
Kansas City, Kans.	15,460	16,199
Kansas City, Mo.	37,729	42,064
Knoxville, Tenn.	11,031	11,237
Las Vegas, Nev.	29,371	34,133
Lexington, Ky.	13,594	13,531
Little Rock, Ark.	16,071	15,470
Long Beach, Calif.	27,776	28,957
Los Angeles, Calif.	233,344	258,632
Louisville, Ky.	19,253	18,892
Lubbock, Texas	14,259	13,332
Madison, Wis.	12,294	13,663
Memphis, Tenn.	43,542	44,501
Miami, Fla.	34,860	37,180
Milwaukee, Wis.	33,822	38,370
Minneapolis, Minn.	30,542	32,406
Mobile, ALa.	15,210	16,580
Montgomery, Ala.	11,988	11,499
Nashville, Tenn.	26,444	28,612
Newark, N.J.	32,057	N.A.
New Haven, Conn.	17,524	17,602
New Orleans, La.	45,823	52,479
New York, N.Y.	570,354	621,110
Norfolk, Va.	19,472	19,907
Oakland, Calif.	38,854	41,269
Oklahoma City, Okal.	27,638	33,577
Omaha, Nebr.	21,459	24,352
Orlando, Fla.	12,992	14,022
Peoria, Ill.	10,929	13,471
Philadelphia, Pa.	72,949	82,586
Phoenix, Ariz.	71,575	75,147
Pittsburgh, Pa.	26,776	27,958
Portland, Ore.	35,614	36,077
Providence, R.I.	12,403	12,652
Richmond, Va.	16,943	18,826
Riverside, Calif.	13,394	13,675
Rochester, N.Y.	25,285	28,287
Rockford, Ill.	9,684	11,603
Sacramento, Calif.	29,188	31,652
St Louis, Mo.	54,485	57,213
St. Paul, Minn.	20,162	21,001
St. Petersburg, Fla.	16,272	18,021
Salt Lake City, Utah	16,103	17,452
San Antonio, Texas	52,526	54,981
San Bernardino, Calif.	13,668	14,285
San Diego, Calif.	66,838	72,093
San Francisco, Calif.	70,385	70,745
San Jose, Calif.	41,831	43,309
Santa Ana, Calif.	16,250	16,992
Savannah, Ga.	9,473	14,326
Seattle, Wash.	44,083	N.A.
Shreveport, La.	14,028	15,371
Spokane, Wash.	12,582	15,699
Springfield, Mass.	12,511	13,397
Springfield, Mo.	11,032	12,504
Stockston, Calif.	12,611	13,753
Syracuse, N.Y.	15,174	14,963
Tacoma, Wash.	13,464	N.A.
Tampa, Fla.	27,002	31,687
Toledo, Ohio	29,411	32,603
Tucson, Ariz.	29,111	30,799
Tulsa, Okla.	24,742	27,431
Virginia Beach, Va.	12,812	13,540
Washington, D.C.	50,950	56,430
Wichita, Kans.	19,894	20,391
Winston-Salem, N.C.	10,971	12,221
Worcester, Mass.	12,577	12,573

CAPITAL PUNISHMENT   SOURCE: National Coalition Against the Death Penalty

ABOLITION COUNTRIES

Argentina*	1921	India (Travencore)	1944
Australia		Northern Ireland	1966
Federal**	1945	Israel**	1954
New South Wales**	1955	Italy***	1944
Queensland**	1922	Liechtenstein	(1798)
Tasmania**	1968	Luxembourgb	(1821)
Austria	1968	Mexico†	1970
Belgiuma	1867	Monaco	1962
Bolivia	1962	Nepal	1950
Brazil***	1946	Netherlands	1886
Canada	1976	New Zealand	1961
Colombia	1910	Nicaragua*	(1892)
Costa Rica	1870	Norway***	1905
Denmark	1978	Panama	1915
Dominican Republic	1924	Portugal	1867
Ecuador	1897	San Marino	1848
Finland***	1949	Sweden***	1921
West Germany	1949	Switzerland	1942
Great Britain	1965	Uruguay	1907
Honduras	1957	Vatican City State	1969
Iceland	1940	Venezuela	1864

* Capital punishment abolished de jure as of year indicated; if abolished only de facto, date in parentheses indicates year of last execution. ** Death penalty retained for certain exceptional crimes other than murder, rape, burglary, robbery, arson, and kidnapping. *** Death penalty retained for use in wartime or under military law. a One murderer executed during World War I in 1918. b One multiple murderer executed in 1948. † Death penalty retained in 3 of 32 states.

Death Penalty States	Year of Last Execution	Death Penalty States	Year of Last Execution
Ala.	1965	Mo.	1965
Ariz.	1963	Mont.	1943
Ark.	1964	Neb.	1959
Calif.	1967	Nev.	1979
Conn.	1960	N.H.	1939
Colo.	1967	N.M.	1960
Del.	1946	N.C.	1961
D.C.	1957	Okla.	1966
Fla.	1979	Oregon	NA
Ga.	1964	Penn.	1962
Idaho	1957	S.C.	1962
Ind.	1961	S.D.	NA
Kan.	1965	Tenn.	1960
Ky.	1962	Texas	1964
La.	1961	Utah	1977
Mass.	NA	Va.	1962
Md.	1961	Wash.	1963
Miss.	1964	Wyo.	1965

UNITED STATES

In the United States, 14 states and the District of Columbia have no laws authorizing the use of the death penalty: Alaska, Hawaii, Iowa, Kansas, Maine, Michigan, Minnesota, New Jersey, New York, North Dakota, Ohio, West Virginia and Wisconsin.

Except for a few special cases, all states have abolished the mandatory death penalty for murder, rape, and other crimes, leaving the decision between death or life imprisonment to the discretion of the jury or the court. This is the result of the U.S. Supreme Court decision, known as the "Furman" decision, which ruled by a 5 to 4 vote in 1972 that the death penalty for murder and for rape, when imposed mandatorily by the jury, constitutes cruel and unusual punishment and is in violation of the U.S. Constitution's 8th and 14th amendments.

In 1976, the U.S. Supreme Court affirmed that the death penalty did not violate the Constitution's ban on "cruel and unusual" punishment. However, "mandatory" death sentences for crimes such as murder are held not valid. At the same time, the Court upheld state statutes passed in Georgia, Florida, and Texas, while striking down those of Louisiana and North Carolina. Since this 1976 "Gregg" ruling, 35 states have enacted capital punishment laws which have not been successfully challenged in the courts.

Capital punishment continued to cause debate in 1978.

On March 10, Maryland Acting Gov. Blair Lee III signed into law a bill reinstating the death penalty for 10 types of first-degree murder. In July, Ohio's capital punishment law was struck down by the U.S. Supreme Court on grounds that it failed to allow juries to consider mitigating circumstances before imposing a death sentence. California and Oregon voters upheld their respective states' death penalty laws on Nov. 7. Oregon voters reinstated the death penalty by a solid margin, and California voters increased the number of crimes for which death could be imposed. Governors in New York, New Jersey and Pennsylvania vetoed capital punishment bills, but Pennsylvania legislators overrode the veto. Idaho joined Oklahoma and Texas in approving injection of lethal chemicals as an alternative to more traditional methods of execution. As of Dec. 31, 1979, there were 567 persons on death row.

Prisoners on Death Row as of December 31, 1979

State	Total	Law	State	Total	Law
Ala.	43	post-Furman[1]	Mont.	3	post-Gregg
Ariz.	22	post-Furman	Nebr.	8	post-Furman
Ark.	12	post-Furman	N.H.	—	post-Gregg
Calif.	25	post-Gregg	Nev.	7	post-Gregg
Colo.	—	post-Furman	N.C.	8	post-Gregg
Conn.	—	post-Furman	Okla.	25	post-Gregg
Del.	1	post-Gregg	Oreg.	1	post-Gregg
Fla.	138	post-Furman	Pa.	4	post-Furman
Ga.	71	post-Furman	R.I.	—	post-Furman
Idaho	1	post-Gregg	S.C.	8	post-Gregg
Ill.	19	post-Gregg	Tenn.	11	post-Gregg
Ind.	3	post-Gregg	Tex.	117	post-Furman
Ky.	3	post-Gregg	Utah	7	post-Gregg
La.	2	post-Gregg	Vt.	—	pre-Furman
Md.	1	post-Gregg	Va.	8	post-Gregg
Mass.	—	post-Gregg	Wash.	5	post-Gregg
Miss.	11	post-Gregg	Wyo.	1	post-Gregg
Mo.	2	post-Gregg			

[1] Pre-Furman law for homicide by a person serving a life sentence only.

EXECUTIONS IN THE UNITED STATES   SOURCE: U.S. Dept. of Justice, Law Enforcement Assistance Administration

Year	Prisoners Executed			
	Total	White	Negro	Other
All years (1930-79)	3,862	1,754	2,066	42
Percent	100.0	45.4	53.5	1.1
1979	2	2	—	—
1978	—	—	—	—
1977	1	1	—	—
1967	2	1	1	—
1966	1	1	—	—
1965	7	6	1	—
1964	15	8	7	—
1963	21	13	8	—
1962	47	28	19	—
1961	42	20	22	—
1960	56	21	35	—
1959	49	16	33	—
1958	49	20	28	1
1957	65	34	31	—
1956	65	21	43	1
1955	76	44	32	—
1954	81	38	42	1
1953	62	30	31	1
1952	83	36	47	—

Year	Prisoners Executed			
	Total	White	Negro	Other
1951	105	57	47	1
1950	82	40	42	—
1949	119	50	67	2
1948	119	35	82	2
1947	153	42	111	—
1946	131	46	84	1
1945	117	41	75	1
1944	120	47	70	3
1943	131	54	74	3
1942	147	67	80	—
1941	123	59	63	1
1940	124	49	75	—
1939	160	80	77	3
1938	190	96	92	2
1937	147	69	74	4
1936	195	92	101	2
1935	199	119	77	3
1934	168	65	102	1
1933	160	77	81	2
1932	140	62	75	3
1930	155	90	65	—

CIVIL RIGHTS/RACE

CIVIL RIGHTS LEGISLATION

Source: Congressional Quarterly Inc.

Six major civil rights bills have been passed by Congress since 1957. Highlights of these bills are:

1957—The Civil Rights Act of 1957 (HR 6127–PL 85-315) was the first civil rights legislation passed by Congress since the Reconstruction period. It prohibited action to prevent persons from voting in federal elections, authorizing the Attorney General to bring suit when a person was deprived of his voting rights. It also created a Civil Rights Commission and set up a Civil Rights Division in the Department of Justice.

1960—The Civil Rights Act of 1960 (HR 8601–PL 86-449) strengthened provisions of the 1957 Act for court enforcement of voting rights and required that voting records be preserved. It also contained limited criminal penalty provisions relating to bombing and to obstruction of federal court orders.

1964—The Civil Rights Act of 1964 (HR 7152–PL 88-352) prohibited discrimination on the basis of race, sex, or national origin in public accommodations and in federally assisted programs. It also prohibited discrimination by employers and unions.

1965—The Voting Rights Act of 1965 (S 1564–PL 89-110) authorized the Attorney General to appoint federal examiners to register voters in certain areas.

1968—A civil rights bill (HR 2516–PL 90-284) prohibited discrimination in the sale or rental of about 80 percent of all housing. It also protected persons exercising specified rights, such as attending school.

1970—A bill (HR 4249–PL 91-285) amended and extended the Voting Rights Act of 1965. It extended its application to Northern cities or counties where literacy tests are required.

1975—The Voting Rights Act was extended for seven years.

COLOR AND RACE OF U.S. POPULATION: 1970

Source: Bureau of the Census

Regions and States	White	Black	Indian	Japanese	Chinese	Filipino	All other
United States, total	177,748,975	22,580,289	792,730	591,290	435,062	343,060	720,520
Northeast Region	44,310,504	4,344,153	49,466	38,978	115,777	31,424	150,401
Maine	985,276	2,800	2,195	348	206	453	770
New Hampshire	733,106	2,505	361	360	420	157	772
Vermont	442,553	761	229	134	173	53	427
Massachusetts	5,477,624	175,817	4,475	4,393	14,012	2,361	10,488
Rhode Island	914,757	25,338	1,390	629	1,093	1,761	1,757
Connecticut	2,835,458	181,177	2,222	1,621	2,209	2,177	6,845
New York	15,834,090	2,168,949	28,355	20,351	81,378	14,279	89,565
New Jersey	6,349,908	770,292	4,706	5,681	9,233	5,623	22,721
Pennsylvania	10,737,732	1,016,514	5,533	5,461	7,053	4,560	17,056
North Central Region	51,641,183	4,571,550	151,287	42,354	39,343	27,824	98,122
Ohio	9,646,997	970,477	6,654	5,555	5,305	3,490	13,539
Indiana	4,820,324	357,464	3,887	2,279	2,115	1,365	6,235
Illinois	9,600,381	1,425,674	11,413	17,299	14,474	12,654	32,081
Michigan	7,833,474	991,066	16,854	5,221	6,407	3,657	18,404
Wisconsin	4,258,959	128,224	18,924	2,648	2,700	1,209	5,067
Minnesota	3,736,038	34,868	23,128	2,603	2,422	1,456	4,456
Iowa	2,782,762	32,596	2,992	1,009	993	614	3,410
Missouri	4,177,495	480,172	5,405	2,382	2,815	2,010	6,222
North Dakota	599,485	2,494	14,369	239	165	204	805
South Dakota	630,333	1,627	32,365	221	163	83	715
Nebraska	1,432,867	39,911	6,624	1,314	551	324	1,902
Kansas	2,122,068	106,977	8,672	1,584	1,233	758	5,286
South Region	50,420,108	11,969,961	201,222	30,917	34,284	31,979	106,896
Delaware	466,459	78,276	656	359	559	392	1,403
Maryland	3,194,888	699,479	4,239	3,733	6,520	5,170	8,370
District of Columbia	209,272	537,712	956	651	2,582	1,662	3,675
Virginia	3,761,514	861,368	4,853	3,500	2,805	7,496	6,958
West Virginia	1,673,480	67,342	751	368	373	722	1,201
North Carolina	3,901,767	1,126,478	44,406	2,104	1,255	905	5,144
South Carolina	1,794,430	789,041	2,241	826	521	1,222	2,235
Georgia	3,391,242	1,187,149	2,347	1,836	1,584	1,253	4,164
Florida	5,719,343	1,041,651	6,677	4,090	3,133	5,092	9,457
Kentucky	2,981,766	230,793	1,531	1,095	558	612	2,351
Tennessee	3,293,930	621,261	2,276	1,160	1,610	846	2,604
Alabama	2,533,831	903,467	2,443	1,079	626	540	2,179
Mississippi	1,393,283	815,770	4,113	461	1,441	475	1,369
Arkansas	1,565,915	352,445	2,014	587	743	289	1,302
Louisiana	2,541,498	1,086,832	5,294	1,123	1,340	1,249	3,970
Oklahoma	2,280,362	171,892	98,468	1,408	999	612	5,488
Texas	9,717,128	1,399,005	17,957	6,537	7,635	3,442	45,026
West Region	31,377,180	1,694,625	390,755	479,041	245,658	251,833	365,101
Montana	663,043	1,995	27,130	574	289	236	1,142
Idaho	698,802	2,130	6,687	2,255	498	206	1,989
Wyoming	323,024	2,568	4,980	566	292	108	878
Colorado	2,112,352	66,411	8,836	7,831	1,489	1,068	9,272
New Mexico	915,815	19,555	72,788	940	563	386	5,953
Arizona	1,604,948	53,344	95,812	2,394	3,878	1,253	9,271
Utah	1,031,926	6,617	11,273	4,713	1,281	392	3,071
Nevada	448,177	27,762	7,933	1,087	955	817	2,007
Washington	3,251,055	71,308	33,386	20,335	9,201	11,462	12,422
Oregon	2,032,079	26,308	13,510	6,843	4,814	1,633	6,198
California	17,761,032	1,400,143	91,018	213,280	170,131	138,859	178,671
Alaska	236,767	8,911	16,276	916	228	1,498	35,786
Hawaii	298,160	7,573	1,126	217,307	52,039	93,915	98,441

AMERICANS OF SPANISH ANCESTRY   Source: Bureau of the Census

The March 1979 Current Population Survey furnished a statistical profile of Americans of Spanish origin. By census definition this group consists of those Americans of Mexican, Puerto Rican, Cuban, Central or South American, or other Spanish origin.

In March 1979 their estimated numbers were:

Mexican	7,326,000
Puerto Rican	1,748,000
Cuban	794,000
Central or South American	840,000
Other Spanish	1,371,000
Total	**12,079,000**

The latest available information, that of the 1970 Census, gave the following breakdown for those states having the largest Spanish origin population: California: 2,368,748; Texas: 1,840,862; New York: 1,352,302; Florida: 405,037; Illinois: 393,347; New Mexico: 308,340; New Jersey: 288,488; Arizona: 265,006; Colorado: 225,506; Michigan: 151,070.

The population of Spanish origin in March 1979 was a younger population than the overall population of the United States: Persons of Spanish origin had a lower median age, 22 years old, than the overall population, 29.8 years old. About 12.6 percent of all persons of Spanish origin were under 5 years of age, while the proportion of the total United States population under 5 years of age was 7.2 percent. Only about 4.5 percent of all persons of Spanish origin were 65 years old and over in March 1979 compared to 10.7 percent for the total population.

Since women in general marry at younger ages than men, there was a larger proportion of single Spanish origin men than of single Spanish origin women; about 35 percent of Spanish origin men 14 years old and over in 1978 were single, but only about 28 percent of Spanish origin women were single.

Younger persons of Spanish origin have achieved, in recent years, higher levels of educational attainment than their elders. For example, in 1979 about 54.3 percent of Spanish origin persons 25 to 34 years old had completed 4 years of high school or more, but only 32.5 percent of Spanish origin persons 45 to 64 years old had done so. In 1978 only 5.7 percent of all persons of Spanish origin 25 to 29 years old had completed less than 5 years of school, but about 25 percent of Spanish origin persons 45 to 64 years old had completed less than 5 years of school.

In March 1979 there were about 4.8 million employed persons of Spanish origin 16 years old and over in the United States, but only 7.6 percent of these persons were working in professional and technical fields. Among employed persons of Spanish origin, those of Mexican origin had the highest proportion, 4.8 percent, employed as farm laborers.

Family income in 1978 was lower for Spanish origin families than for all families in the population. Specifically, median income of families with a family head of Spanish origin was $12,600, as compared with $17,900 for all families. Also, the proportion of Spanish origin families with incomes of under $5,000 was 14.6 percent, but the proportion of all families with incomes under $5,000 was 8.2 percent.

In 1978 there was a marked difference between the individual incomes of men and women of Spanish origin. For example, about 34.7 percent of Spanish origin men with income earned less than $6,000, but about 69.5 percent of Spanish origin women with income had incomes of less than $6,000. At the higher income range, 3.8 percent of men of Spanish origin had incomes over $25,000, but only 0.3 percent of women of Spanish origin had incomes at this level.

There were about 263,000 families with head of Spanish origin in 1978 below the poverty level, or about one of every 10 families with head of Spanish origin. There was, however, a noticeable difference in the proportions of low-income families between the subcategories of Spanish origin. For example, although only 5 percent of families with head of Cuban origin were below the low-income level, about 16 percent of families with head of Puerto Rican origin were below the low-income level in 1978.

EMPLOYMENT IN URBAN POVERTY AREAS   Source: Bureau of Labor Statistics

	TOTAL		WHITE		BLACK AND OTHER	
U.S. Employment Status	1978	1979	1978	1979	1978	1979
Total United States						
Civilian labor force	100,420,000 ...	102,908,000	88,456,000 ...	90,602,000	11,964,000 ...	12,306,000
Unemployed	6,047,000 ...	5,963,000	4,620,000 ...	4,577,000	1,427,000 ...	1,386,000
Unemployment rate (percent)	6.0 ...	5.8	5.2 ...	5.1	11.9 ...	11.3
Poverty Areas						
Civilian labor force	16,285,000 ...	16,195,000	11,694,000 ...	11,695,000	4,591,000 ...	4,500,000
Unemployed	1,412,000 ...	1,318,000	732,000 ...	697,000	680,000 ...	621,000
Unemployment rate (percent)	8.7 ...	8.1	6.3 ...	6.0	14.8 ...	13.8

AMERICAN INDIANS   Source: Bureau of the Census

The Indian population in the United States was determined by the 1970 census to number 792,730, up from the 1960 figure of 523,591. Over fifty percent live in the five states of Arizona, California, New Mexico, North Carolina, and Oklahoma. One-fourth live in the South, one-fifth in the North Central states, and the remaining five percent in the Northeast.

The ten largest Indian tribes and their 1970 populations are:

Navajo	96,743
Cherokee	66,150
Sioux (Dakota)	47,825
Chippewa	41,946
Pueblo	30,971
Lumbee	27,520
Choctaw and Houma	23,562
Apache	22,993
Iroquois	21,473
Creek, Alabama and Coushatta	17,004

Almost one-half of America's Indians live in urban areas, 28 percent on 115 major reservations, and the rest on small reservations and in rural areas. The rural-to-urban migration of Indians has partly resulted in higher educational attainment, better jobs and housing, and higher income levels.

Poverty, however, remains a critical problem among the Indians. Almost forty percent of their population was found to be living below the poverty level in 1969. Their median family income was $5,832 versus the national average of $9,590. Hardest hit financially are the reservation Indians, who must cope with near-subsistence conditions.

Unemployment, nearly three times the national average, affects the reservation Indians most severely, too. This can be attributed in part to a reluctance to establish industrial plants and commercial businesses on the reservation.

Educational advances have taken place. One-third of Indians over 25 years of age have completed high school, while more than one-half of the total population had finished twelve years of school. Twenty-five percent of Indian males between 16 and 21 had dropped out of school. Reservation Indians again fared the worst. The Navajo Reservation Indians completed an average number of only 4.1 school years.

In the area of housing, over twenty-five percent of America's Indians live in overcrowded conditions of more than one person per room. Only seventy-two percent of Indian housing have complete plumbing, in contrast to the national average of ninety-two percent.

WOMEN'S RIGHTS: SOCIAL HISTORY OF AMERICAN WOMEN

1821 Emma Willard founds the Troy Female Seminary, the first endowed school for girls in America.

1848 Seneca Falls Convention held; Elizabeth Cady Stanton, Lucretia Mott and others draft the "Declaration of Sentiments," the first public protest against the inequality of the economic, political, and social positions of women in America.

1849 Elizabeth Blackwell completes her training at Geneva Medical College and becomes the first woman ever to receive an M.D. degree.

1868 New York women form the Working Women's Association to fight for better working conditions.

1868 Susan B. Anthony and Elizabeth Cady Stanton found *The Revolution,* a newspaper with the motto; "Men, their rights and nothing more; women, their rights and nothing less!"

1869 National Woman Suffrage Association founded; American Woman Suffrage Association founded; two organizations merge in 1890 to work for a voting rights amendment to the Constitution.

1873 State of Illinois passes the first women's equal employment legislation.

1890 Wyoming, the first territory to grant political equality to women, joins the Union.

1917 Miss Jeannette Rankin of Montana becomes the first woman to serve in Congress.

1920 Nineteenth Amendment to the Constitution adopted, giving women the right to vote.

1963 Congress passes the Equal Pay Act which stipulates that equal pay must be given for equal work.

1964 Under Title VII of the Civil Rights Act passed by Congress, discrimination based on sex by employers of 15 or more employees is prohibited.

1972 Ms. magazine, written and edited by women, begins publication.

1973 The Supreme Court issues two decisions rendering all state abortion laws unconstitutional.

1973 The Senate July 23 passes a bill to protect consumers against unfair billing practices and to prohibit lenders from discriminating on the basis of sex or marital status in all credit transactions.

1974 Little League Baseball allows girls to play.

1976 The military academies of the Army, Air Force and Navy admit women to their freshman classes.

1977 The National Women's Conference meets in Houston, Texas, in observance of International Women's Year.

1978 Congress passes the Pregnancy Disability Bill, making pregnancy an insurable disability.

1978 Congress passes a bill extending the time by three years three months for ratification of the Equal Rights Amendment.

THE EQUAL RIGHTS AMENDMENT (Pending)

SOURCE: National Organization for Women, 425 13th St. NW, Suite 1001, Washington, D.C. 20004

The Equal Rights Amendment, which would be Amendment XXVII to the U.S. Constitution, was proposed by Congress on March 22, 1972. A total of 38 states must ratify the ERA for its adoption. As of January 18, 1977, 35 states had done so. The text follows:

Section 1.   Equality of rights under the law shall not be denied or abridged by the United States or by any state on account of sex.

Section 2.   The Congress shall have the power to enforce, by appropriate legislation, the provisions of this article.

Section 3.   This amendment shall take effect two years after the date of ratification.

BLACK POPULATION OF LARGE U.S. CITIES

SOURCE: Bureau of the Census

Cities by Rank	Black Population 1960	1970	% of Total Population
New York City, N.Y.	1,087,931	1,668,115	21.2
Chicago, Ill.	812,637	1,102,620	32.7
Detroit, Mich.	482,223	660,428	43.7
Philadelphia, Pa.	529,240	653,791	33.6
Washington, D.C.	411,737	537,712	71.1
Los Angeles, Calif.	334,916	503,606	17.9
Baltimore, Md.	325,589	420,210	46.4
Houston, Texas	215,037	316,551	25.7
Cleveland, Ohio	250,818	287,841	38.3
New Orleans, La.	233,514	267,308	45.0
Atlanta, Ga.	186,464	255,051	51.3
St. Louis, Mo.	214,377	254,191	40.9
Memphis, Tenn.	184,320	242,513	38.9
Dallas, Texas	129,242	210,238	24.9
Newark, N.J.	138,035	207,458	54.2
Indianapolis, Ind.	98,049	134,320	18.0
Birmingham, Ala.	135,113	126,388	42.0
Cincinnati, Ohio	108,754	125,070	27.6
Oakland, Calif.	83,618	124,710	34.5
Jacksonville, Fla.	105,655	118,158	22.3
Kansas City, Mo.	83,146	112,005	22.1
Milwaukee, Wis.	62,458	105,088	14.7
Pittsburgh, Pa.	100,692	104,904	20.2
Richmond, Va.	91,972	104,766	42.0
Boston, Mass.	63,165	104,707	16.3
Columbus, Ohio	77,140	99,627	18.5
San Francisco, Calif.	74,383	96,078	13.4
Buffalo, N.Y.	70,904	94,329	20.4
Gary, Ind.	69,123	92,695	52.8
Nashville-Davidson, Tenn.	76,437	87,851	19.6
Norfolk, Va.	78,806	87,261	28.3
Louisville, Ky.	70,075	86,040	23.8
Ft. Worth, Texas	56,440	78,324	19.9
Miami, Fla.	65,213	76,156	22.7
Dayton, Ohio	57,288	74,284	30.5
Charlotte, N.C.	56,248	72,972	30.3
Mobile, Ala.	65,619	67,356	35.4
Shreveport, La.	56,607	62,152	34.1
Jackson, Miss.	51,556	61,063	39.7
Compton, Calif.	28,265	55,781	71.0
Tampa, Fla.	46,244	54,720	19.7
Jersey City, N.J.	36,692	54,595	21.0

BLACK-AMERICAN HISTORY

Year	Event

1619 The first Negroes to be brought to the American colonies arrived in Virginia as indentured servants.

1661 Virginia passed the first law making Negroes slaves.

1663 Slavery was legally recognized in Maryland.

1688 Quakers in Germantown, Pa., issued the first formal antislavery protest in the Western Hemisphere.

1770 Crispus Attucks, a runaway slave, was killed in the Boston Massacre.

1775 The Pennsylvania Abolition Society, the first antislavery society in America, was founded.

1776 The Declaration of Independence was signed, the final version omitting an attack on slavery by Thomas Jefferson contained in the draft version.

The Continental Congress approved a proposal by General George Washington to permit the enlistment of free Negroes in the Continental Army. About 5,000 Negroes served in the War of Independence.

1787 Congress barred the extension of slavery into the Northwest Territory.

1791 Eli Whitney invented the cotton gin, spurring the expansion of cotton plantations and the demand for slaves.

1800 Gabriel Prosser, a Virginia slave, led an unsuccessful insurrection and was hanged with 24 conspirators.

1807 British Parliament abolished the slave trade.
Congress barred the importation of new slaves into U.S. territory.

1816 The American Colonization Society was formed to resettle free American Negroes in Africa.

1820 Congress adopted the Missouri Compromise providing for the admission of Missouri into the Union as a slave state, and Maine's entry as a free state. All territory north of 36°30′ was declared free; all territory south of that line was left open to slavery.

1827 The first Negro newspaper, *Freedom's Journal*, began publication in New York City.
Slavery was abolished in New York State.

1830 The U.S. Census Bureau reported that 3,777 Negro heads of families owned slaves.

1831 Federal and state troops crushed a slave rebellion in Southampton County, Va., led by Nat Turner. The rebellion, in which more than 50 whites and more than 100 slaves were killed, ended in the capture and execution of Turner and led to the adoption of more rigid slave codes.

1847 Frederick Douglass, a former slave and a lecturer with the Massachusetts Anti-Slavery Society, began publishing *North Star*, an abolitionist newspaper.

1849 Harriet Tubman escaped from slavery in Maryland. She became one of the most venturesome conductors on the Underground Railroad, leading over 300 slaves to freedom.
Benjamin Roberts filed the first school integration suit on behalf of his daughter. The Massachusetts Supreme Court rejected the suit and established a "separate but equal" precedent.

1850 The Compromise of 1850 admitted California to the Union as a free state but strengthened the Fugitive Slave Law, giving greater inducement for the apprehension of runaway slaves.

1852 Harriet Beecher Stowe's novel *Uncle Tom's Cabin*, a vastly popular antislavery work, was published.

1853 *Clotelle: or the President's Daughter* by historian William Wells Brown was published—the first novel by an American Negro.

1854 James A. Healy was ordained a priest in Notre Dame cathedral, Paris. He later became America's first Negro Roman Catholic bishop.
The first Negro college, Lincoln University, was founded as Ashmun Institute in Oxford, Pa.

1855 The first Negro to win elective office in the United States, John Mercer Langston, was elected clerk of Brownhelm Township, Lorain Co., O.

1863 The Draft Riots took place in New York City. Blacks and abolitionists were attacked and killed.

1865 By the end of the Civil War, some 186,000 Negroes had served with the Union forces.
The Thirteenth Amendment, freeing all slaves, was passed by Congress.
The Freedman's Bureau was organized to aid and protect newly freed blacks in the South.
Dr. John S. Rock, a Boston physician and lawyer, was the first Negro admitted to the bar of the United States Supreme Court.
Southern states passed the "Black Codes" in an attempt to restrict the freedom of emancipated slaves.

1866 Charles L. Mitchell and Edward G. Walker were elected to the Massachusetts House of Representatives, becoming the first Negroes to serve in a U.S. legislature.

1867 Morehouse College, Atlanta, Ga., and Howard University, Washington, D.C., were founded.

1868 Oscar J. Dunn attained the highest elective office held by an American Negro up to that time, becoming lieutenant governor of Louisiana.

1869 Ebenezer Don Carlos Basset was appointed minister to Haiti, the first Negro diplomat to represent the United States.

1870 Hiram Revels was elected to fill the unexpired U.S. Senate term of Jefferson Davis of Mississippi, becoming the first Negro Senator. He served a year.
Joseph H. Rainey of South Carolina became the first Negro in the House of Representatives. He was subsequently reelected four times.

1875 Congress passed a civil rights act prohibiting discrimination in such public accommodations as hotels and theaters.

1877 Henry O. Flipper became the first Negro to graduate from West Point.

1881 Tennessee passed a "Jim Crow" law instituting segregated railroad travel that set a trend among other states in the South.
Booker T. Washington opened Tuskegee Institute in Alabama.

1883 The Supreme Court declared the 1875 Civil Rights Act unconstitutional.

1890 Mississippi instituted restrictions on voting, including a poll tax and literacy tests, which were designed to disenfranchise Negroes. During the decade, other Southern states followed. Louisiana added (1898) the exclusionary device of the "grandfather clause," which set educational and property qualifications for voting but exempted those whose ancestors had been eligible to vote as of Jan. 1, 1867.

1891 The Provident Hospital in Chicago—the first such interracial institution in America—was founded by Negro surgeon Daniel Hale Williams.

1895 Frederick Douglass, the Negro abolitionist whom Lincoln had called "the most meritorious man of the 19th century," died.

1896 The National Association of Colored Women was organized in Washington, D.C.; Mary Church Terrell served as its first president.

1898 Four Negro regiments in the regular army compiled an excellent combat record during the Spanish-American War. Dismounted elements of the black Ninth and Tenth Cavalry rescued the Rough Riders from near annihilation.

1905 Twenty-nine Negro intellectuals from 14 states, headed by Dr. W. E. B. DuBois, organized the Niagara Movement, which demanded the abolition of all racial distinctions. The meeting took place at Fort Erie, N.Y.

1909 Matthew Henson, a Negro member of Admiral Peary's expedition, placed the American flag at the North Pole.

1910 The National Association for the Advancement of Colored People (NAACP) was founded in New York. The "Great Migration" of more than 2 million Southern blacks began.

1911 The National Urban League was founded. It was originally made up of two groups: The Committee for Improving the Industrial Conditions of Negroes and The League for the Protection of Colored Women.

1915 The Association for the Study of Negro Life and History was established by the "father of Negro history," Dr. Carter G. Woodson.

1917 Ten thousand Negroes marched down Fifth Avenue in New York to protest the many lynchings in the South. The parade was led by W. E. B. DuBois. Race riots broke out in East St. Louis, Illinois.

1920 The pioneer black nationalist Marcus Garvey inaugurated the International Convention of the Universal Negro Improvement Association (UNIA) in Harlem. UNIA reached its greatest influence during the following two years.

1928 Oscar De Priest of Illinois was the first black Congressman from a northern state.

1935 Mary McLeod Bethune organized the National Council of Negro Women.

1936 Negro track star Jesse Owen won four gold medals in the Olympics at Berlin.

1937 William H. Hastie became the first Negro to serve as a U.S. Federal judge.

Joe Louis became heavyweight boxing champion of the world, defeating Jim Braddock for the title.

1939 Contralto Marian Anderson, denied the use of Constitution Hall in Washington by the Daughters of the American Revolution, sang on Easter Sunday before 75,000 people at the Lincoln Memorial.

1940 Benjamin O. Davis, Sr., was appointed the first black general in the U.S. armed forces.

Dr. Charles R. Drew did notable research into blood preservation and discovered blood plasma.

1941 A Negro threat to stage a massive protest march on Washington resulted in the issuance of Executive Order 8802 prohibiting racial discrimination in defense industries or the government (but not the armed forces).

1942 The Congress of Racial Equality (CORE), an action-oriented civil rights group, was founded by James Farmer in Chicago.

1947 Statistics amassed by Tuskegee Institute indicated that in the period 1882–1947 3,426 Negroes were lynched in the United States. Of these, 1,217 were lynched in the 1890–1900 decade.

1948 President Truman issued Executive Order 9981 calling for "equality of treatment and opportunity" in the armed forces.

1949 William L. Dawson became the first Negro to head a Congressional committee.

1951 Ralph J. Bunche, who won a Nobel Peace Prize in 1950, was appointed Under-Secretary of the United Nations, the highest ranking American employed by the international body.

Private First Class William Thompson was awarded the Congressional Medal of Honor for bravery in the Korean War, the first Negro to win it since the Spanish-American War.

1952 A Tuskegee Institute report indicated that for the first time in 71 years of compilation, no lynchings were reported in the United States.

1954 In "Brown v. Board of Education of Topeka" the U.S. Supreme Court held that segregation in public education denied equal protection of the laws.

1955 A bus boycott in Montgomery, Ala., was led by Dr. Martin Luther King, Jr., after Rosa Parks was arrested for refusing to give up her seat to a white man.

1957 Central High School in Little Rock, Ark., was integrated by nine Negro children, but not until President Eisenhower had called in troops to keep order.

1960 Four Negro North Carolina A & T College freshmen occupied places at a Woolworth lunch counter, launching a wave of nonviolent sit-ins.

1961 CORE began "Freedom Rides" that rolled through the South, protesting segregation.

1962 The Albany (Ga.) Movement—a citywide attempt, supported by the Southern Christian Leadership Conference, Student Nonviolent Coordinating Committee, NAACP, and CORE, to abolish discrimination in all public facilities—was formed.

James Meredith desegregated the University of Mississippi, after President Kennedy dispatched troops and riots killed two persons.

1963 NAACP leader Medgar Evers was murdered in the doorway of his home in Jackson, Miss.

Birmingham, Ala.: The plight of Negroes in the South and throughout the nation was dramatized here as fire hoses, police dogs, and rough handling by the police, followed by bomb blasts in the black ghetto, became the order of the day. September 15: A bomb blast at the Sixteenth Street Baptist Church killed four girls.

June 11: President Kennedy declared that the black struggle for civil rights is a "moral issue."

August 28: The March on Washington in which more than 200,000 Americans from all walks of life converged on the nation's capital constituted one of the largest single protests in American history. The marchers gathered on the steps of the Lincoln Memorial to dramatize discontent with the Negro's plight.

1964 Three young civil-rights workers—Michael Schwerner, Andrew Goodman, and James E. Chaney—were murdered in Mississippi.

Riots exploded in Harlem and elsewhere.

1965 Malcolm X., former Black Muslim and advocate of black nationalism, was assassinated in New York City.

Thurgood Marshall was named as the first Negro Solicitor General of the United States.

President Johnson signed the Voting Rights Act, under which federal examiners are authorized to register black voters who have been refused by state officials.

Riots erupted in the Watts section of Los Angeles; 35 people were killed, 883 others were injured, and 3,598 were arrested. Damage totaled more than $220 million.

1966 Robert Weaver was appointed head of the Department of Housing and Urban Development (HUD), the first Negro ever to serve at cabinet level.

Constance Baker Motley, former borough president of Manhattan, became the first Negro woman to become a federal judge in American history.

The U.S. Supreme Court outlawed all poll taxes.

The concept of "Black Power" was adopted by CORE.

1967 Solicitor General Thurgood Marshall became the first Negro Supreme Court Justice.

At a four-day Black Power conference—the largest of its kind in American history—more than 400 people representing 45 civil rights groups from 36 cities convened in Newark, N.J., expressing viewpoints that ranged from moderate to militant.

1968 April 4: While standing on the balcony of a Memphis motel, Dr. Martin Luther King, Jr., was shot and killed by a sniper.

The Kerner Commission reported that "our nation is moving toward two societies, one black, one white—separate and unequal."

1969 Educational institutions acceded to demands by black students for more black studies.

James Earl Ray pleaded guilty to the assassination of Martin Luther King; sentenced to 99 years in prison.

1970 The killing in December 1969 of a Black Panther leader, Fred Hampton, led to a federal investigation and the subsequent conclusion that the Chicago police had exercised undue force.

1971 Samuel L. Gravely, Jr., was made the first black admiral in the U.S. Navy.

Thirteen Black Panthers, including two who fled to Algeria during the trial, were acquitted in New York City on charges of conspiring to bomb department stores and police stations and to murder policemen.

The six-month trial in New Haven of Bobby G. Seale, chairman of the Black Panther party, and Mrs. Ericka Huggins, a New Haven Panther, for crimes arising from the death of Alex Rackley, ended in a mistrial as the jury was unable to reach a verdict. Rackley, a Panther, died in May 1969.

1972 Over 8,000 delegates and observers met in Gary, Indiana as the first National Black Political Convention voted to set up a permanent representative body to set the direction for black political and social actions.

Angela Davis, accused of conspiracy to kidnap and murder, was acquitted.

The busing of children, both black and white, from one neighborhood school district to another became an important political issue. The Nixon administration supported and signed into law a bill which prohibited busing solely to achieve racial integration.

1975 Black Muslims agreed to accept white members.

1976 U.S. Supreme Court outlawed discrimination in commercially operated nonsectarian private schools.

1977 The TV dramatization of Alex Haley's book *Roots* was seen by the largest audience ever. The story chronicled the black author's family history from mid-eighteenth century African beginnings.

1978 U.S. Supreme Court ruled that the University of California Medical School at Davis must admit Allan P. Bakke, a 38-year-old white engineer, as the school's minority-admissions plan was inflexible and racially biased. The justices ruled, however, that race could be considered as a university admission factor. Black leaders expressed concern regarding the decision.

PUBLIC HEALTH/MEDICINE

BIOLOGICAL AND MEDICAL SCIENCE REVIEW: 1979/80

Helen H. Swallow, C.N.M., Member, American Medical Writers Association, and W. J. Morse, Jr., M.D.

Progress against cancer: Hodgkin's disease, which attacks young adults, is a cancer of the lymph system. It begins with the painless enlargement of a lymph node, typically in the neck. If not diagnosed and treated, the process spreads to adjacent lymph glands. The glands become matted and the malignant cells spread to other glands and nearby structures. The spleen is invaded and eventually organs and tissues outside the lymphatic system are affected. Night sweats, loss of weight, anemia, fatigue, nausea, and increased susceptibility to infection develop as the disease spreads.

At Massachusetts General Hospital, researchers Alan C. Aisenberg, M.D., Ph.D., Rita M. Lingood, M.Sc., and Robert A. Lew, Ph.D., have reviewed the results of treatment (in Boston) for Hodgkin's disease over the last two decades. They report that 20 years ago only 1 in 3 patients with this ailment lived more than five years after the diagnosis. This year, 9 out of 10 who contracted the disease will be alive and well in 5 years. Furthermore, if relapse occurs, retreatment, or "salvage," usually results in "disease-free survival." Because retreatment is so successful, primary treatment can be conservative.

Hodgkin's disease is diagnosed by physical examination, blood tests, lymphangiogram (lymphatic system visualized on serial X-ray pictures after radio-opaque dye has been injected), exploratory surgery, and biopsy. After diagnosis, the disease can be "staged," i.e., assigned a symbol designating the extent of malignant growth. Stages I and II signify that the tumor is located on only one side of the diaphragm. Stages III and IV are more serious, involving tumor growth above and below the diaphragm. The spleen is removed when the diagnostic or exploratory operation is done. Now that this is common practice, survival without any trace of the disease is much more likely to occur.

The stage of the disease is taken into consideration in planning treatment. Almost always, combinations of anti-cancer drugs are given in cycles over a period of several months. The use of combinations like MOPP (nitrogen mustard, Oncovin, prednisone, and procarbazine) and ACDV (adriamycin, bleomycin, vinblastine, and imidazole) have had the greatest impact on improving the rate of cure in Hodgkin's disease. Formerly, one drug was used at a time. Radiation therapy still has a place in the treatment of this cancer, but today it will rarely be the only treatment.

Twenty years ago, many patients died from the treatment, the side effects of which are anemia, another cancer, and overwhelming infection. Today, recent advances in hematology (the study of blood) and immunology (the study of the body's defense systems) permit the oncologist to evaluate carefully the patient's response to these potent and potentially dangerous treatments.

The near victory over Hodgkin's disease is a rare example of a cure preceding knowledge of the cause of a disease. Current investigations by epidemiologists have found no meaningful association of the disease with its reported "clusters." Familial tendency to immune disorders and a variety of environmental, nutritional, genetic, and ethnic factors have been suggested as possible causes of or contributors to Hodgkin's disease, but all that is known for certain is that the (statistically) typical patient is from a small family of better-than-average socio-economic status and education.

Infectious diseases: Five different strains of herpesvirus cause cold sores, herpes genitalis, infectious mononucleosis, chicken pox, shingles, and cytomegalic inclusion disease. All herpesviruses are contagious, but unpredictably so. All have the ability to lie dormant in the nerve roots after the first or primary infection. Herpesviruses resemble each other when seen under the electron microscope, but immunologic tests have been successful in identifying them. Each has a shell of protein and a core of DNA (the genetic pattern necessary for the replication of any cell). Like all other viruses, the herpesviruses cannot live without a host cell. They are obligate parasites.

Herpes simplex I (HSVI) causes cold sores. Following infection, the virus sequesters itself in the root of the facial nerve for weeks, months, or years. Activated by emotional or physical stress, sunlight or fever, the virus moves out along the nerve to cause the familiar sore, usually on the lip or inside of the cheek, but sometimes on the eye. Cold sores begin as a prickling sensation under the skin, then become small, tender lumps. Blisters develop, open, and the characteristic painful ulcers are formed. Oral infection is called herpes labialis. Ocular infection, called herpes keratitis, can cause scarring, which is progressive with recurrence of infection, sometimes causing blindness. Herpes labialis usually leaves no scar.

Herpes simplex II (HSVII) causes herpes genitalis. The primary infection produces a small cluster of very painful lesions on the genitals that ulcerate and last for a week or more. The patient may develop flulike symptoms with fever, malaise, lack of appetite, and swollen glands. After the initial episode, HSVII lies dormant in the roots of certain spinal nerves. Recurrent infections are probable, but the sores are not as widespread, do not last as long, and are not accompanied by systemic illness. Herpes genitalis is very contagious and is spread by sexual contact. Each year, an estimated 300,000 women and men contract this venereal disease.

HSVII may produce life-threatening infection of the newborn when transmitted to babies at birth as they pass through an infected birth canal. If a pregnant woman has an active genital lesion or a vaginal or cervical culture indicative of HSVII during the last weeks of pregnancy, the baby will be delivered by cesarean section.

HSVII has an affinity for the transition zone of the cervix (the junction of the vaginal and cervical epithelium), where the virus may live quietly for years. Because women who have had HSVII infections have a greater statistical risk of developing cancer of the cervix, an association between the virus and cervical cancer is suspected.

Infectious mononucleosis is caused by the Epstein-Barr virus (EBV). This herpesvirus was discovered in 1964 by the British pathologist M. Anthony Epstein and graduate student Yvonne Barr. In young children, the disease is usually so mild that it passes unnoticed; it does, however, grant immunity for life. Adolescents call it the "kissing disease." For some, it is more serious than that. Fatigue, headache, swollen glands, enlarged spleen and liver, fever, and severe sore throat with large raw ulcers of the mouth and throat can make a young person ill for weeks.

Researchers have recovered EBV from several cancers: Burkitt's lymphoma (a malignant tumor of the jaw that grows to enormous size in only a few weeks, most common in teenaged African children); naso-pharyngeal cancer (the most frequently diagnosed cancer in China); and Hodgkin's disease (a cancer of the lymph system that occurs four times more often in young people who have had mononucleosis than in those who have not). Because EBV produces symptoms by causing the immune system to attack itself, Werner Henle, M.D., of Philadelphia, calls infectious mononucleosis a "self-limited leukemia."

Cytomegalovirus (CMV) causes cytomegalic inclusion disease. The infection is rarely diagnosed in healthy young people as it results in only a mild and brief episode of malaise and sore throat. Organ transplant patients, however, suffer a severe form of the infection. These patients cannot fight CMV because their normal immune abilities have been suppressed with medications administered to prevent rejection of the new organ. For them, and for other immunosuppressed people, CMV infection can be fatal. Infants born of women who were infected during the first three months of pregnancy may be born microcephalic, hydrocephalic, blind, deaf, or retarded.

Varicella zoster virus (VZV) causes chicken pox and shingles. In most cases, a child develops a fever and then an itchy rash on the trunk and face—usually 10 to 12 days after exposure. A week or so later, the scabs (or crust) that cover the lesions which accompany this disease, fall off, and the child is well. A few children do not recover so easily. Shortly after the onset of the initial fever, these children develop encephalitis (brain inflammation) or Reye's syndrome (acute encephalopathy with fatty degeneration of the internal organs), the frequent results being either permanent damage to the central nervous system, or death.

Immunosuppressed children (and adults) contract a severe form of chicken pox. Boston pediatrician John Saia notes that 7% of the children who are treated for cancer die of varicella virus infection because the drugs used to kill the cancer cells reduce the child's ability to fight infection.

Like all herpesviruses, VZV lies dormant in nerve roots after the symptoms of the initial infection have resolved. Shingles is the late expression of latent VZV. In old age, with stress or immunosuppression from disease or medication, VZV can cause a chain of vesicles to erupt along the line of a nerve to the skin, usually on the back. The vesicles are painful and last for many days.

For the first time, a vaccine against VZV has been developed. Tested first in Japan, it is now being used experimentally in the U.S. It seems to be effective in protecting healthy as well as leukemic, immunosuppressed children from chicken pox infection. The vaccine has not only prevented children from getting the disease, it has also produced measurable and apparently adequate levels of antibody to VZV, indicating immunity to chicken pox. The duration of immunity will not be known for years. There is concern that vaccinated children, prevented from developing the natural and enduring immuity conferred by a case of the chicken pox, will become susceptible again later in life, when the infection is far more serious.

Serial testing for continued immunity and repeated immunization may be necessary if large numbers of children are to be routinely immunized against chicken pox—as they are against measles, German measles, mumps, poliomyelitis, whooping cough, tetanus, and diphtheria.

Another herpes vaccine is being used experimentally to prevent—or minimize—the extent of cytomegalic inclusion disease in kidney-transplant patients. The results are promising, but the study is too small to evaluate statistically.

Both herpes vaccines are made of live, attenuated virus, i.e., viruses grown over generations in a laboratory that are weak enough not to cause infection but strong enough to provoke the immune system in the body to make antibodies to the disease-causing virus. Some oncologists (cancer specialists) feel that if the recently discovered association of herpesviruses with some cancers is real, the vaccines might, themselves, be carcinogenic. Others, Dr. Epstein among them, believe that the prevention of infectious mononucleosis would help prevent any cancers that might develop from the EBV virus.

It may be that another drug currently being used in controlled testing will minimize the effects of *all* herpes infections. *Acyclovir,* an anti-viral agent being applied topically to shingles vesicles, drastically reduces the pain associated with the disease and appears to inhibit the development of new blisters. Given intravenously to children who are at risk of developing a severe case of chicken pox, the new drug seems to provide them with protection from the danger.

Interferon: Manufactured in very small amounts by the body's lymphocytes (one type of white blood cell) in response to most viruses, interferon is a naturally occurring protein. It activates the immune system, prevents the invading virus from reproducing itself within the host cell, and changes the membrane of the invaded cell to interfere with the virus's ability to infect other cells. Since its discovery, in 1957, scientists have suspected that interferon could be used to treat viral infections—and cancers caused by viruses—if it could be produced synthetically in sufficient quantity. (Because it is present in the body in such minute amounts when there is no infection, it takes 65,000 pints of blood to collect 100mg of interferon.)

Kari Cantell, M.D., of the Finnish Red Cross, has developed a laboratory technique for inducing human white blood cells to produce interferon in small quantity. Charles Weissmann, M.D., Walter Gilbert, Ph.D., and others are using recombinant DNA technology to clone (asexually reproduce) bacteria capable of carrying a gene that will cause the production of interferon in fu-

ture bacterial generations. [Recombinant DNA technology, or "gene-splicing," describes the process of isolating that particular portion of deoxyribonucleic acid responsible for specific characteristics or abilities in one cell and implanting that specific DNA fragment in another cell. The implanted cell will then reproduce according to the new, recombined DNA pattern.] Weissmann, Gilbert, and their colleagues proved the biologic activity of the synthesized interferon by inhibiting the growth of a human virus in frog's eggs inoculated with interferon. This was the first human protein to be synthesized and proven biologically active.

Interferon has been hailed as a miracle drug by some, but researchers are more cautious. Practical uses of interferon now being carefully evaluated are those for the treatment of leukemic children, immunosuppressed because the anti-cancer drugs they must take suppress the infection-fighting responses of the body, and patients who have had organ transplants, since the drugs which help prevent rejection of transplanted organs also render these patients singularly susceptible to infection. (See Infectious diseases.)

Extensive animal studies suggest that interferon may inhibit the replication of malignant cells in the same way it inhibits reproduction of viruses, and this has led to carefully controlled clinical studies now under way in which cancer patients are being given interferon. As these studies are evaluated, and as new and more plentiful supplies of interferon become available, large, broad clinical trials will become a reality. Such trials will help researchers evaluate further the value of the drug as an anti-viral, anti-cancer agent.

Artificial blood: Called Fluosol, artificial blood was first given to a human patient in April 1979, in Japan, following fifteen years of animal testing there. In the past year, about one hundred patients in the U.S. and Japan have received it.

Fluosol is made from perfluorocarbons. These chemicals, originally developed to separate uranium isotopes for atomic bombs, are able to carry oxygen. Since transporting oxygen is the major function of the body's red blood cells, Fluosol holds great promise for patients who need red cells but cannot receive natural transfusions of fresh blood for a variety of reasons: they may be in remote areas where blood is not available, or reside in countries where there are no blood donor programs; also, transfusion of fresh blood is difficult on the battlefield and in disasters where demands for blood outstrip supplies; finally, there are those whose religion forbids natural transfusion.

Fluosol will not be helpful for patients who require white blood cells, antihemophilic factor, antibodies, or other blood constituents.

Artificial blood is being used currently only as a "humanitarian investigational new drug," but it is undergoing formal clinical study at a number of U.S. medical centers to satisfy F.D.A. requirements prior to approval for widespread use.

Tardive Dyskinesia: A recently recognized disorder resulting from the long-term use of neuroleptics (major tranquilizers), tardive dyskinesia develops slowly and increases in severity the longer the drugs are taken. Persons afflicted with the disorder experience repetitive, involuntary movements of the hands, feet, facial muscles, tongue, and jaw and may suffer blurring of vision, weakness, and fainting. Joseph DeVeaugh-Geiss, M.D., of Syracuse, estimates that 30 to 50% of patients taking neuroleptics will develop tardive dyskinesia. A cure for the syndrome has not been developed.

Some of the drugs implicated are Thorazine, Mellaril, Prolixin, Trilafon, Navane, Haldol, Loxitane, and Moban. These drugs have proved effective in the treatment of patients with severe mental disorders—patients who are suicidal, violent, or who suffer hallucinations or great anxiety. Unfortunately, the use of the drugs has not always been limited to serious disease: nursing homes, hospitals for the chronically ill, and correctional institutions (for children as well as adults) have used the drugs simply for sedation, sometimes against the will of the recipients, often on prescription by those who are not qualified psychiatrists. (Recently, the courts in Massachusetts upheld the right of mental patients to refuse *any* medication.)

Because any patient treated with a major tranquilizer has a significant chance of developing tardive dyskinesia, Shervert Frazier, M.D., president of the American College of Psychiatrists, has recommended that this risk be carefully considered when prescribing these drugs, pointing out that the potential benefit from their use must clearly outweigh the risks involved.

LONGEVITY IN THE UNITED STATES

SOURCE: 1979 data from Statistical Bureau, Metropolitan Life Insurance Company; earlier years from the National Center for Health Statistics

The expectation of life at birth for the resident population of the United States increased to an all-time high in 1979. Preliminary life tables indicate that the average length of life for the total population rose from 73.3 years in 1978 to 73.8 years in 1979—a gain of 3.1 years since 1969-71 and of 14.6 years since 1929-31, when the average was only about 59 years.

The expected lifetime rose to 70.0 years for the male newborn and to 77.7 years for the female. The favorable 1979 experience reflected a significant decline in infant mortality.

EXPECTATION OF LIFE IN THE U.S.: 1949-51 to 1979

Age	1949-51	1959-61	1969-71	1976	1977	1978†	1979*
0-1	68.1	69.9	70.7	72.8	73.2	73.3	73.8
1	69.2	70.7	71.2	72.9	73.2	73.3	73.8
15	55.9	57.3	57.7	59.3	59.6	59.7	60.2
25	46.6	47.9	48.4	50.0	50.3	50.4	50.8
35	37.3	38.5	39.1	40.6	40.9	41.0	41.5
45	28.5	29.5	30.1	31.5	31.8	31.9	32.3
55	20.6	21.4	22.0	23.2	23.5	23.6	23.9
65	13.8	14.4	15.0	16.0	16.3	16.3	16.7

†Provisional.   * Preliminary.

EXPECTATION OF LIFE—UNITED STATES: 1977

SOURCE: National Center for Health Statistics

AGE	Total (years)	White Male	White Female	All Other Male	All Other Female
Birth	73.2	70.0	77.7	64.6	73.1
1	73.2	70.0	77.6	65.2	73.6
2	72.3	69.1	76.6	64.3	72.7
3	71.3	68.1	75.7	63.4	71.7
4	70.4	67.2	74.7	62.4	70.8
5	69.4	66.2	73.7	61.5	69.8
6	68.4	65.2	72.8	60.5	68.9
7	67.5	64.3	71.8	59.6	67.9
8	66.5	63.3	70.8	58.6	66.9
9	65.5	62.3	69.8	57.6	65.9
10	64.5	61.3	68.8	56.6	65.0
11	63.5	60.4	67.9	55.7	64.0
12	62.6	59.4	66.9	54.7	63.0
13	61.6	58.4	65.9	53.7	62.0
14	60.6	57.4	64.9	52.8	61.0
15	59.6	56.5	63.9	51.8	60.0
16	58.7	55.5	62.9	50.8	59.1
17	57.7	54.6	62.0	49.9	58.1
18	56.8	53.7	61.0	49.0	57.1
19	55.9	52.8	60.1	48.1	56.2
20	54.9	51.9	59.1	47.2	55.2
21	54.0	51.0	58.1	46.3	54.3
22	53.1	50.1	57.2	45.4	53.3
23	52.1	49.1	56.2	44.5	52.4
24	51.2	48.2	55.2	43.6	51.4
25	50.3	47.3	54.3	42.8	50.5
26	49.3	46.4	53.3	41.9	49.5
27	48.4	45.5	52.3	41.1	48.6
28	47.5	44.6	51.4	40.2	47.7
29	46.5	43.6	50.4	39.4	46.7
30	45.6	42.7	49.4	38.6	45.8
31	44.7	41.8	48.5	37.7	44.9
32	43.7	40.8	47.5	36.9	43.9
33	42.8	39.9	46.5	36.0	43.0
34	41.8	39.0	45.6	35.2	42.1
35	40.9	38.0	44.6	34.3	41.2
36	40.0	37.1	43.6	33.5	40.3
37	39.0	36.2	42.7	32.6	39.3
38	38.1	35.3	41.7	31.8	38.4
39	37.2	34.3	40.8	31.0	37.5
40	36.3	33.4	39.8	30.2	36.7
41	35.4	32.5	38.9	29.4	35.8
42	34.5	31.6	38.0	28.6	34.9
43	33.6	30.7	37.0	27.9	34.1
44	32.7	29.8	36.1	27.1	33.2
45	31.8	29.0	35.2	26.3	32.4
46	30.9	28.1	34.3	25.6	31.5
47	30.0	27.2	33.4	24.8	30.7
48	29.2	26.4	32.5	24.1	29.9
49	28.3	25.5	31.6	23.4	29.1
50	27.5	24.7	30.7	22.7	28.3
51	26.7	23.9	29.8	22.0	27.5
52	25.9	23.1	29.0	21.3	26.7
53	25.0	22.3	28.1	20.7	26.0
54	24.2	21.5	27.2	20.0	25.2
55	23.5	20.8	26.4	19.4	24.5
56	22.7	20.0	25.5	18.8	23.7
57	21.9	19.3	24.7	18.2	23.0
58	21.2	18.5	23.9	17.6	22.3
59	20.4	17.8	23.1	17.0	21.6
60	19.7	17.1	22.3	16.5	21.0
61	19.0	16.4	21.5	15.9	20.3
62	18.3	15.8	20.7	15.4	19.7
63	17.6	15.2	19.9	15.0	19.1
64	16.9	14.5	19.2	14.5	18.4
65	16.3	13.9	18.4	14.0	17.8
66	15.6	13.3	17.7	13.5	17.1
67	15.0	12.7	16.9	13.0	16.4
68	14.3	12.2	16.2	12.4	15.8
69	13.7	11.6	15.5	11.9	15.1
70	13.1	11.1	14.8	11.4	14.5
71	12.5	10.5	14.1	11.0	14.0
72	11.9	10.0	13.4	10.6	13.6
73	11.4	9.6	12.7	10.3	13.2
74	10.9	9.1	12.1	10.0	12.8
75	10.4	8.6	11.5	9.7	12.5
76	9.9	8.2	10.9	9.5	12.2
77	9.4	7.8	10.4	9.2	11.9
78	9.0	7.5	9.8	9.0	11.7
79	8.6	7.1	9.3	8.9	11.5
80	8.2	6.8	8.8	8.7	11.3
81	7.8	6.5	8.4	8.6	11.1
82	7.4	6.2	7.9	8.4	10.9
83	7.1	5.9	7.5	8.2	10.7
84	6.7	5.6	7.1	7.9	10.2
85 & over	6.4	5.3	6.8	7.3	9.6

INFANT AND NEONATAL DEATH RATES IN THE UNITED STATES: 1977

SOURCE: National Center for Health Statistics (Deaths per 1,000 live births)

State	Infant Deaths[1]	Neonatal Deaths[2]	State	Infant Deaths[1]	Neonatal Deaths[2]	State	Infant Deaths[1]	Neonatal Deaths[2]	State	Infant Deaths[1]	Neonatal Deaths[2]
Ala.	16.9	11.1	Ill.	16.0	11.3	Mont.	13.7	8.9	R.I.	12.1	8.3
Alaska	15.1	8.5	Ind.	14.2	9.7	Nebr.	12.7	9.3	S.C.	17.6	12.2
Ariz.	13.5	8.7	Iowa	12.4	9.6	Nev.	13.9	8.9	S.D.	16.4	12.4
Ark.	15.4	9.8	Kans.	13.4	10.4	N.H.	10.2	7.9	Tenn.	15.4	10.8
Calif.	12.0	7.9	Ky.	14.4	9.9	N.J.	14.3	10.7	Texas	14.7	10.3
Colo.	12.0	7.4	La.	17.9	13.1	N.M.	13.8	9.6	Utah	10.1	6.8
Conn.	13.5	10.3	Maine	9.5	6.2	N.Y.	14.4	10.5	Vt.	10.0	6.8
Del.	13.6	9.4	Md.	14.3	10.7	N.C.	15.8	11.2	Va.	15.9	11.4
D.C.	27.4	20.5	Mass.	11.9	9.3	N.D.	13.7	10.5	Wash.	12.1	7.4
Fla.	15.5	10.6	Mich.	14.1	9.9	Ohio	13.9	10.1	W.Va.	14.6	10.3
Ga.	15.4	9.6	Minn.	11.1	7.9	Okla.	13.7	8.9	Wis.	11.3	7.5
Hawaii	11.5	7.7	Miss.	18.2	12.9	Oreg.	12.2	7.9	Wyo.	13.9	8.3
Idaho	11.3	6.7	Mo.	14.2	10.2	Pa.	14.0	10.6	U.S. avg.	14.1	9.9

[1] Under 1 yr.   [2] Under 28 days.

LEADING CAUSES OF DEATH IN THE UNITED STATES: 1977

Source: National Center for Health Statistics

Rank	Cause of Death	Number of Deaths	Death Rate per 100,000 Population	Rank	Cause of Death	Number of Deaths	Death Rate per 100,000 Population
	ALL CAUSES	1,899,597	878.1	5.	Influenza & Pneumonia	51,193	23.7
1.	Heart Diseases	718,850	332.3	6.	Diabetes Mellitus	32,989	15.2
2.	Cancer	386,686	178.7	7.	Cirrhosis of Liver	30,848	14.3
3.	Stroke	181,934	84.1	8.	Arteriosclerosis	28,754	13.3
4.	Accidents	103,202	47.7	9.	Suicide	28,681	13.3
	Motor Vehicular	49,510	22.9	10.	Diseases of Early Infancy	23,401	10.8
	All Other	53,692	24.8		All Other Causes	209,857	97.0

DEATH RATES FOR SPECIFIED CAUSES, BY COLOR AND SEX: UNITED STATES, 1977

Source: National Center for Health Statistics

(Rate per 100,000 population in specified group)

	Total			White			Nonwhite		
	Both sexes	Male	Female	Both sexes	Male	Female	Both sexes	Male	Female
All causes	878.1	994.1	768.2	882.2	998.2	783.3	813.0	967.1	672.5
Major cardiovascular diseases	444.5	478.8	412.0	460.6	495.5	427.4	340.0	368.3	314.1
Diseases of heart	332.3	376.7	290.2	346.0	392.4	301.8	243.5	273.3	216.4
Hypertension	2.6	2.6	2.7	2.4	2.4	2.5	4.0	4.2	3.8
Cerebrovascular diseases	84.1	73.5	94.1	85.1	73.2	96.5	77.3	75.2	79.2
Arteriosclerosis	13.3	11.1	15.4	14.2	11.7	16.7	7.2	6.9	7.4
Cancer	178.7	200.0	158.6	183.1	202.5	164.5	150.8	183.2	121.2
Accidents	47.7	68.4	28.1	47.1	66.7	28.4	51.6	79.1	26.6
Motor vehicle accidents	22.9	34.0	12.3	23.1	34.1	12.7	21.2	33.8	9.8
All other accidents	24.8	34.3	15.8	24.0	32.7	15.7	30.4	45.4	16.8
Influenza and pneumonia	23.7	26.2	21.2	23.9	25.9	22.0	22.1	28.6	16.2
Cirrhosis of liver	14.3	19.2	9.6	13.6	18.3	9.1	18.6	24.9	12.9
Diabetes mellitus	15.2	13.0	17.4	14.7	12.7	16.5	19.0	14.6	23.1
Suicide	13.3	20.1	6.8	14.2	21.4	7.3	7.3	11.4	3.5
Homicide	9.2	14.6	4.2	5.7	8.7	2.9	31.9	53.6	12.0
Bronchitis, emphysema, and asthma	10.3	15.3	5.6	11.2	16.5	6.1	5.0	7.4	2.8
Tuberculosis, all forms	1.4	1.9	0.8	1.1	1.5	0.7	3.3	5.0	1.7

DEATH RATES IN AMERICA 1977 (per 1,000)

Source: National Center for Health Statistics

Age Group	Total			White			Nonwhite		
	Both sexes	Male	Female	Both sexes	Male	Female	Both sexes	Male	Female
All ages[1]	8.8	9.9	7.7	8.9	10.0	7.8	8.1	9.7	6.7
Under 1	14.9	16.6	13.0	12.7	14.3	10.9	25.5	27.8	23.0
1–4	0.7	0.8	0.6	0.6	0.7	0.6	1.0	1.1	0.9
5–9	0.3	0.4	0.3	0.3	0.4	0.3	0.4	0.5	0.3
10–14	0.4	0.4	0.3	0.3	0.4	0.3	0.4	0.5	0.3
15–19	1.0	1.5	0.6	1.0	1.5	0.6	1.0	1.5	0.6
20–24	1.3	2.0	0.7	1.3	1.9	0.6	1.8	2.8	1.0
25–29	1.3	1.9	0.7	1.1	1.7	0.6	2.5	3.8	1.3
30–34	1.4	1.9	0.9	1.2	1.6	0.8	2.8	4.2	1.7
35–39	2.0	2.6	1.3	1.7	2.2	1.2	3.9	5.6	2.6
40–44	3.0	3.9	2.2	2.6	3.4	1.9	5.8	7.9	4.0
45–49	4.8	6.3	3.5	4.3	5.7	3.1	8.3	11.0	6.0
50–54	7.5	10.0	5.3	7.0	9.3	4.8	12.4	16.2	9.1
55–59	11.4	15.2	7.9	10.7	14.4	7.3	17.8	23.1	13.1
60–64	17.8	24.3	12.2	17.0	23.4	11.4	25.6	33.6	19.0
65–69	24.8	34.7	16.9	24.3	34.4	16.3	28.9	38.0	21.8
70–74	38.5	53.2	27.7	37.3	52.3	26.3	51.6	62.0	43.0
75–79	60.7	81.5	47.4	59.6	81.0	46.0	74.1	86.5	64.5
80–84	88.1	113.6	73.9	89.5	116.0	74.9	73.5	89.9	62.7
85 and over	147.3	173.0	135.4	152.9	180.4	140.4	96.0	112.9	86.7

[1] Figures for age not stated included in "All ages" but not distributed among age groups.

U.S. DEATHS FROM ACCIDENTS

Source: National Center for Health Statistics

Type of Accident	Deaths per 100,000 Population			Type of Accident	Deaths per 100,000 Population		
	1970	1973	1977		1970	1973	1977
All Accidents	56.4	55.2	47.7	Unspecified falls	5.6	5.5	4.4
Railway Accidents	0.4	0.4	0.3	Accidents caused			
Motor vehicle accidents	26.9	26.5	22.9	By fire and flames	3.3	3.1	2.9
Motor vehicle traffic	26.3	25.9	22.4	By firearms	1.2	1.2	0.9
Vehicle-pedestrian	4.4	4.3	3.6	Accidents mainly of industrial type			
Other road vehicle accidents	0.1	0.1	0.1	Cutting or piercing instrument	0.1	0.1	0.1
Water transport accidents	0.8	0.8	0.6	Explosive material	0.3	0.2	0.2
Air and space transport accidents	0.8	0.8	0.8	Hot substances, etc.	0.1	0.1	0.1
Accidental poisoning				Electric current	0.6	0.5	0.5
By solid and liquid substances	0.6	0.6	0.5	Other	1.9	1.8	1.5
By gases and vapors	0.8	0.8	0.7	Inhalation and ingestion of objects	1.4	1.4	1.4
Accidental falls	8.3	7.9	6.4	Accidental drowning	3.1	3.4	2.8
Fall from one level to another	2.4	2.0	1.8	Complications due to medical procedures	1.8	1.7	1.4
Fall on the same level	0.4	0.3	0.2	All other accidents	4.0	3.7	2.5

U.S. HOMICIDES AND SUICIDES

SOURCE: National Center for Health Statistics

	1960		1965		1970		1977	
Item	Male	Female	Male	Female	Male	Female	Male	Female
Homicide	**6,269**	**2,195**	**8,148**	**2,564**	**13,278**	**3,570**	**15,355**	**4,613**
Assault by:								
Firearms and explosives	3,460	1,167	4,807	1,351	9,209	2,004	10,520	2,354
Cutting and piercing instruments	1,442	394	1,847	445	2,229	551	2,747	795
Other means	1,069	631	1,216	768	1,512	1,010	1,821	1,462
Intervention of police	242	3	271	—	328	5	266	2
Execution	56	—	7	—	—	—	1	—
Suicide	**14,539**	**4,502**	**15,490**	**6,017**	**16,629**	**6,851**	**21,109**	**7,572**
Poisoning	2,631	1,699	3,179	2,816	3,299	3,285	3,340	3,147
Hanging and strangulation	2,576	79	2,453	744	2,422	831	2,982	848
Firearms and explosives	7,879	1,138	8,457	1,441	9,704	2,068	13,342	2,742
Other	1,453	875	1,401	1,016	1,204	667	1,445	835

— Represents zero.

ACCIDENTAL DEATH RATES: BY NATIONS

SOURCE: United Nations Demographic Yearbook, 1978 (Table 21), © United Nations

Nation	Latest Year Available	Accidental Deaths per 100,000 Population*
South Africa		
Nonwhite	1971	88.0
White	1971	70.9
Zimbabwe (European)	1977	75.0
France	1970	74.8
Austria	1976	69.8
Hungary	1977	63.3
Portugal	1975	63.3
Luxembourg	1976	62.6
Belgium	1976	60.5
Kuwait	1977	59.1
Czechoslovakia	1976	58.7
Venezuela	1977	57.9
Finland	1974	56.8
Iceland	1977	54.1
Ecuador	1975	53.1
Germany, East	1976	52.4
Germany, West	1976	51.5
New Zealand	1976	51.2
Italy	1972	48.9
Australia	1977	48.0
Sweden	1975	48.0
UNITED STATES	1976	46.9
Switzerland	1977	46.8
Norway	1977	46.0
Ireland	1975	45.2
Mexico	1975	45.1
Greece	1976	44.7
Yugoslavia	1975	43.9
Costa Rica	1977	42.9
Bulgaria	1976	40.4
Uruguay	1976	39.7
Spain	1975	38.6
Netherlands	1977	37.3
Denmark	1976	37.0
Israel	1977	33.4
Jordan	1976	31.4
England & Wales	1976	30.6
Canada	1976	30.0
Japan	1977	26.6
Chile	1976	24.8
Singpore	1977	21.8
Paraguay	1977	20.1
Malta	1977	19.8
Argentina	1977	19.5
Hong Kong	1977	19.5

* Based on population estimates for the designated year.

INTERNATIONAL SUICIDE RATES (per 100,000 population)

SOURCE: United Nations Demographic Yearbook, 1978 (Table 21), © United Nations

Nation	Year	Rate
Hungary	1977	40.3
Finland	1974	25.1
Denmark	1976	23.9
Switzerland	1977	23.8
Austria	1976	22.7
Germany, West	1976	21.7
Czechoslovakia	1976	20.8
Iceland	1977	20.4
Sweden	1975	19.4
Japan	1977	17.8
Belgium	1976	16.6
France	1970	15.4
Cuba	1971	15.0
Luxembourg	1976	14.6
Zimbabwe (European)	1977	14.6
South Africa		
White	1971	14.5
Nonwhite	1971	5.6
Bulgaria	1976	14.1
Yugoslavia	1975	13.4
Canada	1976	12.8
UNITED STATES	1976	12.5
Hong Kong	1977	12.3
Norway	1977	11.4
Australia	1977	11.1
Uruguay	1976	10.8
Singapore	1977	9.7
Netherlands	1977	9.2
New Zealand	1976	9.2
Trinidad & Tobago	1976	8.9
Portugal	1975	8.5
Argentina	1977	7.8
England & Wales	1976	7.8
Israel	1977	6.5
Mauritius	1977	6.4
Italy	1972	5.8
Chile	1976	5.7
Ireland	1975	4.7
Venezuela	1977	4.6
Costa Rica	1977	4.4
Spain	1975	3.9
Greece	1976	2.8
Parguay	1977	1.8
Mexico	1975	1.7
Kuwait	1977	0.4
Guyana	1976	0.3
Jordan	1976	0.2
Egypt	1975	0.1

VENEREAL DISEASE

SOURCE: American Social Health Association

Venereal disease, or more accurately, sexually transmissible disease, encompasses 20 conditions of which gonorrhea, nongonnococcal urethritis/cervicitis, genital herpes, syphilis, cytomegalovirus and group B streptococcal disease are the most dangerous. It is estimted that over ten million persons were affected with some form of VD this year. Complications from prolonged and untreated infection with some forms of VD can lead to serious medical conditions, some of which can be permanently debilitating and even fatal.

Most veneral diseases can be completely cured although at least two are viral and cannot. Genital herpes is spreading at an alarming rate, and is associated with cervical cancer in women and brain damage in newborn babies. With vaccines for any of the venereal diseases still some way off, major attention is given to educating the public. The American Social Health Association produces and distributes, films, literature and other material suited for home, classroom or clinic. Additionally, the VD National Hotline, an information and referral service in the continental U.S. is 800-227-8922 (Calif., 800-982-5883).

REFERENCE CHART: LEADING CANCER SITES, 1980 (ESTIMATED)

SOURCE: American Cancer Society. All figures rounded to nearest 1,000.

Site	Estimated New Cases 1980	Estimated Deaths 1980	Warning Signal; If you have one, see your doctor	Safeguards	Comment
BREAST	109,000	36,000	Lump or thickening in the breast or unusual discharge from nipple.	Regular checkup. Monthly breast self-examination.	The leading cause of cancer death in women.
COLON AND RECTUM	114,000	53,000	Change in bowel habits; bleeding.	Regular checkup, including digital, occult blood and proctoscopic exams, especially after age 40.	Because of accuracy of available tests, is potentially a highly curable disease.
LUNG	117,000	101,000	Persistent cough, or lingering respiratory ailment cigarettes.	80% of lung cancer would be prevented if no one smoked.	The leading cause of cancer death among men and rising mortality among women.
ORAL (INCLUDING PHARYNX)	26,000	9,000	Sore that does not heal. Difficulty in swallowing.	Regular checkup.	Many more lives should be saved because the mouth is easily accessible to visual examination by physicians and dentists.
SKIN	14,000[1]	6,000	Sore that does not heal, or change in wart or mole.	Regular checkup, avoidance of over-exposure to sun.	Skin cancer is readily detected by observation, and diagnosed by simple biopsy.
UTERUS	54,000[2]	11,000	Unusual bleeding or discharge.	Regular checkup, including pelvic examination with Pap test.	Uterine cancer mortality has declined 70% during the last 40 years with wider application of the Pap test. Postmenopausal women with abnormal bleeding should be checked.
KIDNEY AND BLADDER	52,000	18,000	Urinary difficulty bleeding, in which case consult doctor at once.	Regular checkup with urinalysis.	Protective measures for workers in high-risk industries are helping to eliminate one oof the important causes of these cancers.
LARYNX	11,000	4,000	Hoarseness—difficulty in swallowing.	Regular checkup, including larygoscopy.	Readily curable if caught early.
PROSTATE	66,000	22,000	Urinary difficulty	Regular checkup, including palpation.	Occurs mainly in men over 60, the disease can be detected by palpatation at regular checkup.
STOMACH	23,000	14,000	Indigestion	Regular checkup.	An 80% decline in mortality in 50 years, for reasons yet unknown
LEUKEMIA	22,000	16,000	Leukemia is cancer of blood-forming tissues and is characterized by the abnormal production of immature white blood cells. Acute lymphocytic leukemia strikes mainly children and is treated by drugs which have extended life from a few months to as much as ten years. Chronic leukemia strikes usually after age 25 and progresses less rapidly.		
LYMPHOMAS	39,000	21,000	These cancers arise in the lymph system and include Hodgkin's Disease and lymphosarcoma. Some patients with lymphatic cancers can lead normal lives for many years. Five-year survival rate for Hodgkin's Disease increased from 25% to 54% in 20 years.		

[1] Only melanoma. Estimate new cases of non-melanoma skin cancer over 400,000.

[2] If carcinoma in situ is included, cases total over 98,000.

PROGRESS AGAINST CANCER

Category	1937	1979
Saved (alive five years after treatment)	Fewer than one in five	One in three
Uterine cancer	Chief cause of cancer death in women	Death rate cut more than 70% since 1930 Could be reduced more
Lung cancer	Mounting: no prospect of control	Still mounting: but upward of 80% could be prevented
Research support	Less than $1,000,000	About $1,000,000
Cancer clinics and registries approved by American College of Surgeons	240 in United States and Canada	Over 800, plus expansion of teaching, research, treatment centers
State control measures	Seven states	All 50 states
Chemotherapy	Almost no research	Major research attack has produced more than 40 useful drugs

One in two patients could be saved today by early diagnosis and prompt treatment

CANCER DEATH RATES AROUND THE WORLD

SOURCE: American Cancer Society

Death Rates per 100,000 Population—1972-73

Male Cancer Death Rates		Male Cancer Death Rates		Female Cancer Death Rates		Female Cancer Death Rates	
Czechoslovakia*	213.2	New Zealand	174.5	Ireland	132.3	Iceland	115.4
Scotland	205.0	Northern Ireland	170.3	Hungary	129.0	Belgium	115.2
Belgium	200.4	Hong Kong	169.4	Scotland	128.7	Netherlands	113.8
Hungary	195.2	Italy*	169.2	Denmark	127.2	Sweden	112.3
France*	194.5	Denmark	165.5	Austria	123.4	Canada*	109.3
Netherlands	193.4	Ireland	165.1	England & Wales	123.2	UNITED STATES	106.1
Luxembourg*	193.4	Australia	163.2	Uruguay*	122.9	Luxembourg*	106.1
Uruguay*	192.9	Singapore	162.1	New Zealand	121.8	Costa Rica	106.0
England & Wales	189.7	Poland	160.4	Chile	121.4	Switzerland	103.5
Austria	189.4	UNITED STATES	159.4	Germany, West	121.3	Trinidad & Tobago*	102.9
Germany, West	182.4	Canada*	157.6	Israel	118.5	Australia	102.0
Finland*	182.0	Chile	147.0	Northern Ireland	118.1	Norway	101.8
Switzerland	175.2	Sweden	146.6	Czechoslovakia*	118.0	Poland	101.2

*1974 only.

ADJUSTED HOSPITAL EXPENSE PER INPATIENT DAY: COMMUNITY HOSPITALS, 1968-1978
SOURCE: American Hospital Association

Expenses per day related to inpatient care adjusted to exclude those expenses incurred for outpatient care.

Hospital Size	1968	1970	1972	1974	1975	1976	1977	1978
All Community Hospitals	$55.80	$73.73	$94.87	$113.55	$133.81	$151.79	$173.98	$194.34
6-24 Beds	41.98	59.68	75.76	83.44	100.43	117.46	132.19	152.34
25-49 Beds	41.10	54.15	68.68	82.73	98.97	113.42	132.33	151.68
50-99 Beds	45.24	58.85	72.98	86.58	101.96	117.95	134.53	149.68
100-199 Beds	51.11	65.87	84.31	101.06	119.14	135.04	154.64	172.50
200-299 Beds	56.22	74.32	92.43	111.35	129.93	148.37	169.76	186.94
300-399 Beds	59.24	77.96	99.34	116.80	137.82	155.99	177.72	200.70
400-499 Beds	60.67	79.68	100.23	122.11	140.68	160.35	183.55	208.78
500 or more Beds	66.27	87.37	115.34	136.73	161.97	179.80	206.40	228.53

HOSPITAL COSTS IN COMMUNITY HOSPITALS
SOURCE: American Hospital Association

Year	Adjusted Expenses per Inpatient Day	Average Length of Stay (Days)	Average Adjusted Expense per Patient Stay	Year	Adjusted Expenses per Inpatient Day	Average Length of Stay (Days)	Average Adjusted Expense per Patient Stay
1963	$35.11	7.7	$270.35	1972	$ 94.87	7.9	$ 749.47
1965	40.56	7.8	316.37	1973	102.44	7.8	799.03
1967	49.46	8.3	410.52	1974	113.55	7.8	885.69
1968	55.80	8.4	468.72	1975	133.81	7.7	1030.34
1969	64.26	8.3	533.36	1976	151.79	7.7	1168.78
1970	73.73	8.2	604.59	1977	173.98	7.6	1322.25
1971	83.43	8.0	667.44	1978	194.34	7.6	1474.41

ABORTION AND THE LAW

On January 22, 1973, the U.S. Supreme Court issued two landmark rulings in *Roe* v. *Wade* and *Doe* v. *Bolton* which declared the abortion laws of Texas and Georgia, respectively, unconstitutional. As a result of these decisions, state abortion laws are subject to the Court's three-fold guidelines (each of which determines the states' power to regulate abortion based on the trimester of pregnancy in question).

Since that time, state legislatures and the Congress have set up parental and spousal consent requirements or funding regulations pursuant to their legitimate interests "in the health of the mother and the potential life of the fetus."

In a 1976 decision, the Court ruled that the State cannot, in all cases, require parental consent to abortions for minors. The Court did decide, however, that statutory provisions requiring written consent of the aborting mother, and requiring recordkeeping and reporting which "are reasonably directed to the preservation of maternal health and that properly respect a patient's confidentiality and privacy," are constitutional.

In the 1977 decisions, *Maher* v. *Roe* and *Beal* v. *Doe*, the Court ruled that states have no Constitutional or statutorial obligation to provide Medicaid funding for elective nontherapeutic abortion. The Court maintained that "the State unquestionably has a 'strong and legitimate interest in encouraging normal childbirth...,' an interest honored over the centuries." Such "sensitive" issues, declared the Court, are properly decided by the legislature in a democratic society.

In June 1980, the Supreme Court, in *Harris* v. *McRae* and *Williams* v. *Zbarag*, extended its ruling by determining that neither Congress nor the States need provide funding for medically necessary abortions. Resolving a much contested element in the abortion controversy, the Court further declared that such funding restrictions are not violative of the First Amendment's Establishment Clause just because it "may coincide with the religious tenets of the Roman Catholic Church."

ABORTION DEBATE: 1980

Since 1973, opponents of abortion have sought to reverse the Court's decisions through legislation and litigation. Their major efforts have been directed in these areas:

Constitutional Amendments: "Right-to-life" and "states rights" amendments have been proposed. The former would accord personhood to the unborn child, while the latter would return abortion regulation to the states. As an alternative to amending the Constitution, abortion opponents are pursuing, at the state level, the route that would require Congress to convene a Constitutional Convention to adopt a "Human Life Amendment." As of August 1980, 19 state legislatures—of a required 34—have passed resolutions to attain this end.

Funding Restrictions: In 1976, Congress enacted the "Hyde Amendment" to the Labor-HEW Appropriations bill to cut off, in most cases, federal funds for abortion provided through the Medicaid program. Various versions, more or less restrictive than the 1976 bill, had been enacted by each successive Congress. A number of states had also continued to prohibit the use of public funds for abortion. Court challenges were brought against the Hyde Amendment and some of the state laws which restricted government funding of abortions. In two 1977 decisions, the U.S. Supreme Court held that funding of non-medically necessary abortions is not mandated by either the Constitution or the Medicaid provisions of the Social Security Act. These decisions plus the federal government's withdrawal of its state reimbursements led to two thirds of the states dropping abortion coverage from their Medicaid programs. As a result, in February-December 1978, there was a 99% decline in the number of Medicaid abortions reported by HEW. A total of 17 states and the District of Columbia were continuing Medicaid coverage for all or most abortions by May 1978. Subsequently, two federal judges, one each from Illinois and New York, declared the Hyde Amendment unconstitutional. The Illinois judge also ruled unconstitutional an Illinois statute prohibiting state funding of medically necessary abortions. Federal funding of abortion was then resumed pending action by the Supreme Court. In June 1980, the Court, extending the reasoning of the 1977 cases, decided that neither Congress nor the States was constitutionally compelled, nor were the States required by the Medicaid statute, to provide funding for medically necessary abortions. Its opinion also affirmed that "abortion is inherently different from other medical procedures because no other medical procedure involves the purposeful termination of a potential life." These latest decisions should, for the time being, put to an end most federal, and a substantial amount of state, abortion funding. They also place in doubt a 1979 New Jersey lower court decision declaring unconstitutional a New Jersey statute restricting state support of abortion.

Consent Requirements: Since the beginning of 1976, the Supreme Court has ruled various state consent requirements for abortion unconstitutional. A companion case to the 1976 Supreme Court decisions indicated that, while a parental veto was not constitutionally permissible, required parental consultation might be constitutional. Subsequently, some states have attempted to enact statutes consonant with the Court's suggestion. These laws are being or probably will be challenged. The courts are also considering the proposal of a mandatory 24-hour cooling-off period between the time consent is given for an abortion and the procedure itself.

"Informed Consent" Provisions: Laws mandating counseling procedures such as detailing fetal development and possible physical and psychological complications subsequent to abortion have been passed by several state legislatures and the Akron City Council. Such laws are being challenged in the courts.

AIR POLLUTION IN U.S. AIR QUALITY CONTROL AREAS: 1978

Source: Environmental Protection Agency

OZONE/OXIDANT

Note: The new ozone standard is 235 $\mu g/m^3$, daily maximum hour.

Number of Stations

Metropolitan Area	Total Valid	Exceeding 1-hour Average of 160$\mu g/m^3$	Range of Max. 1-Hr. Values ($\mu g/m^3$)*
New York	13	13	216–392
Los Angeles	22	19	176–686
Chicago	27	15	137–451
Philadelphia	16	14	216–392
Detroit	8	6	216–353
San Francisco	18	10	176–333
Boston	3	3	255–274
Washington, D.C.	14	11	216–372
Cleveland	11	8	137–412
St. Louis	16	13	157–412

*$\mu g/m^3$ = micrograms per cubic meter.

CARBON MONOXIDE

Note: The 8-hour standard is 10 milligrams per cubic meter of air ($\mu g/m^3$), arithmetic mean.

Number of Stations

Metropolitan Area	Total Valid	Exceeding 8-Hour Standard	Range of Max. 8-Hour Values ($\mu g/m^3$)*
New York	23	11	4.1–18.7
Los Angeles	24	12	6.2–22.6
Chicago	18	5	4.3–18.1
Philadelphia	20	7	4.1–16.1
Detroit	9	3	6.8–13.6
San Francisco	15	3	5.8–16.5
Boston	6	5	9.9–15.6
Washington, D.C.	14	10	15.8–24.4
Cleveland	3	1	6.5–13.1
St. Louis	13	7	5.0–16.0

*$\mu g/m^3$ = milligrams per cubic meter.

SULFUR DIOXIDE

Note: The primary annual standard is 80 $\mu g/m^3$, arithmetic mean.

Number of Stations

Metropolitan Area	Total Valid	Exceeding Annual Standard	Range of Annual Mean ($\mu g/m^3$)*
New York	25	0	15–56
Los Angeles	1	0	4–4
Chicago	20	0	11–79
Philadelphia	15	0	24–70
San Francisco	8	0	5–11
Detroit	7	0	20–44
Boston	3	0	21–51
Washington, D.C.	5	0	12–58
Cleveland	4	0	57–72
St. Louis	10	0	30–47

*$\mu g/m^3$ = micrograms per cubic meter.

TOTAL SUSPENDED PARTICULATES

Note: The primary annual standard is 75 $\mu g/m^3$, geometric mean.

Number of Stations

Metropolitan Area	Total Valid	Exceeding Annual Standard	Range of Annual Mean ($\mu g/m^3$)*
New York	91	6	26–95
Los Angeles	15	12	62–153
Chicago	91	27	38–138
Philadelphia	46	5	29–94
Detroit	40	13	39–151
San Francisco	14	1	40–114
Boston	16	1	37–82
Washington, D.C.	44	1	32–79
Cleveland	87	15	43–146
St. Louis	26	10	25–176

*$\mu g/m^3$ = micrograms per cubic meter.

WORLDWIDE TANKER* CASUALTIES, 1973 TO 1979

Source: Tanker Advisory Center, New York, N.Y.

Accidental Tanker Oil Spills

Year	Number	Amount (tons)
1973	36	84,458
1974	48	67,114
1975	45	188,042
1976	29	204,235
1977	49	213,080
1978	35	260,488
1979	65	723,533

*Includes tankers, ore/oil and bulk/oil ships of 6,000 deadweight tons and over.

Tanker Casualties by Flag of Registry, 1978

Country	Total	Percent of Total
U.S.	76	11.1
U.K.	87	12.7
Greek	96	14.0
Japanese	12	1.8
Liberian	187	27.3
Norwegian	18	2.6
Panamanian	33	4.8
USSR	8	1.2
Other nations	168	24.5
TotaL, 66 nations	685	100.00

MEDICAL CARE INDEXES

Source: U.S. Bureau of Labor Statistics

Year	All medical care items*	Physicians' services	Dental services	Optometric examination and eyeglasses	Hospital daily service charges	Prescriptions and drugs
1935	36.1	39.2	40.8	56.7	11.9	70.7
1945	42.1	46.0	49.6	63.9	16.2	74.8
1955	64.8	65.4	73.0	77.0	41.5	94.7
1960	79.1	77.0	82.1	85.1	56.3	104.5
1962	83.5	81.3	84.7	89.2	64.9	101.7
1963	85.6	83.1	87.1	89.7	69.0	100.8
1964	87.3	85.2	89.4	90.9	72.4	100.5
1965	89.5	88.3	92.2	92.8	76.6	100.2
1966	93.4	93.4	95.2	95.3	84.0	100.5
1967	100.0	100.0	100.0	100.0	100.0	100.0
1968	106.1	105.6	105.5	103.2	113.2	100.2
1969	113.4	112.9	112.9	107.6	127.9	101.3
1970	120.6	121.4	119.4	113.5	143.9	103.6
1971	128.4	129.8	127.0	120.3	160.8	105.4
1972	132.5	133.8	132.3	124.9	102.0†	105.6
1973	137.7	138.2	136.4	129.5	105.6†	105.9
1974	150.5	150.9	146.8	138.6	115.1†	109.6
1975	168.6	169.4	161.9	149.6	132.3†	118.8
1976	184.7	188.5	172.2	158.9	148.7†	126.0
1977	202.4	206.0	185.1	168.2	164.1†	134.1
1978	219.4	223.1	198.1	—	—	143.5
1979	239.7	243.6	214.8	—	—	153.8

*1967 = 100 † **Hospital Service Charges** (January 1972 = 100)

MILESTONES OF MEDICINE

Date	Milestone	Discoverer	Nationality
6th cent. B.C.	First recorded dietary and sanitary laws	Book of Leviticus	Hebrew
5th–4th cent. B.C.	Medicine moves from realm of superstition to that of observation; emergence of the idea of nature as healer	Hippocrates	Greek
4th cent. B.C.	Beginning of a systematic study of anatomy	Herophilus	Greek
2d cent. A.D.	Correlation of extant medical knowledge into a single great system that influenced medical thought until the 16th century	Clarissimus Galen	Greco-Roman
9th or 10th cent.	First-known description of smallpox and differentiation between that disease and measles; the approach was used until the 18th century	Rhazes or Rasis	Persian
16th cent.	Reaffirmation of nature as prime healer; also, beginning of chemotherapy	Paracelsus	Swiss
1543	Publication of **De humani corporis fabrica**, first anatomy textbook based entirely on observation, rather than on Galen's writings	Andreas Vesalius	Flemish
c. 1590	Invention of the microscope	Zacharias Janssen	Dutch
1628	Discovery of blood circulation	William Harvey	English
c. 1648	Founding of biochemistry	Jan Baptista van Helmont	Flemish
1661	Discovery that capillaries are vein-artery junctions, thus completing the explanation of blood circulation	Marcello Malpighi	Italian
1736	First successful appendectomy	Claudius Amyand	French
1757–66	Established physiology as a branch of science	Albrecht von Haller	Swiss
1796	First successful antitoxin vaccination (for smallpox)	Edward Jenner	English
1800	Founding of histology—the study of tissues	Marie F. X. Bichat	French
1816	Invention of the stethoscope	René Laënnec	French
1822	Description of the process of digestion	William Beaumont	American
1838–39	Establishment of cell theory founding of cytology	Matthias Schleiden, Theodor Schwann	German
1842	Use of ether as an anesthetic during surgery	Crawford W. Long	American
1844	Use of nitrous oxide as anesthetic during surgery	Horace Wells	American
1857	Development of the pasteurization process began	Louis Pasteur	French
1860	Experiments that finally destroyed the idea of spontaneous generation	Louis Pasteur	French
1865	Introduction of surgical antisepsis	Joseph Lister	English
1866	Invention of the clinical thermometer	Thomas C. Allbut	English
1870–1909	Founding of neuroanatomy	Camillo Golgi	Italian
c. 1872	Founding of bacteriology	Ferdinand Cohn	German
1877	Publication of postulates for determining the etiology of diseases	Robert Koch	German
1883–84	Discovery of the bacillus that causes diphtheria	Edwin Klebs, Friedrich Löffler	German
1890–95	Founding of serology and immunology	Paul Ehrlich, Emil von Behring	German
1894	Discovery of bubonic plague's causative bacillus	Alexandre Yersin	French
		S. Kitasato	Japanese
1892, 1895	Founding of virology	Dmitri Ivanovski	Russian
		(Independently, M. Beijerinck)	Dutch
1895	Publication of **Studies in Hysteria**; founding of psychoanalysis	Sigmund Freud	Austrian
1895	Discovery of X rays	Wilhelm Roentgen	German
1897	Development of method for making a differential blood count	Paul Ehrlich	German
1901	Establishment of etiology of yellow fever	Walter Reed and others	American
1906	Development of specific test for syphilis	August Wassermann and others	German
		(Independently, Lazlo Detre)	Hungarian
1906	Passage of U.S. Pure Food Law—the first legislation of its kind	Harvey W. Wiley	American
1912	Discovery of vitamins	Casimir Funk	American, b. Poland
1915	Discovery of pellagra cure	Joseph Goldberger	American, b. Austria-Hungary
1921	Isolation of insulin for use in diabetic therapy	Frederick Banting, Charles Best	Canadian
1926	Discovery of liver extract (vitamin B_1)	George Minot, William Murphy	American
1928	Invention of artificial respirator ("iron lung")	Philip Drinker, Louis Shaw	American
1928	Discovery of penicillin	Alexander Fleming	Scottish
c. 1932	First use of sulfa drugs in therapy	Gerhard Domagk	German
1940	Discovery of the Rh factor	Karl Landsteiner	American, b. Austria
1943	Discovery of streptomycin and its use in treating tuberculosis	Selman Waksman	American
1944	Introduction of corrective heart surgery to enable survival of "blue babies"	Alfred Blalock, Helen Taussig	American
1949	Cortisone introduced into medical therapy	Philip Hench and others	American
1953	Establishment of cryosurgery in which body temperature is lowered to slow circulation, allowing dry-heart surgery	Henry Swan	American
1954	Introduction of open-heart surgery	C. Walton Lillehei	American
1954	Development of hypodermic poliomyelitis vaccine	Jonas Salk	American
1955	Development of oral poliomyelitis vaccine	Albert Sabin	American
1963	First use of artificial heart for circulating blood during heart surgery	Michael De Bakey	American
1967	First surgical transplant of a human heart	Christiaan Barnard	South African
1969	Deciphering of structure of gamma globulin—one of the body's chief defenders against diseases	Gerald Edelman and others	American
1972	Research into the structure of antibodies	Gerald Edelman	American
		Rodney R. Porter	English
1978	First "test-tube" baby born	Patrick Steptoe, Robert Edwards	English
1979	First synthesis of a biologically active human protein, Interferon	Kari Cantell	Finnish
		Charles Weissmann	Swiss
		Walter Gilbert	American

MEDICAL GLOSSARY

Abscess: Collection of pus in a tissue cavity resulting from a localized infection associated with cellular disintegration.

Anemia: Decrease in the number of circulating red blood cells or in their hemoglobin (oxygen-carrying pigment) content. Can result from excessive bleeding or blood destruction (either inherited or disease caused) or from decreased blood formation (either nutritional deficiency or disease). In one form, sickle-cell anemia, it is inherited, occurring almost wholly among blacks. Pernicious anemia is caused by inability to absorb vitamin B_{12}.

Angina: Choking pain. Angina pectoris: chest pain resulting from insufficient blood circulation through the vessels supplying blood to the heart, precipitated by exertion or emotion and usually relieved by a vasodilator drug.

Arteriosclerosis: Generalized thickening, loss of elasticity, and hardening of the body's small and medium-size arteries.

Asthma: Disease characterized by repeated attacks of shortness of breath, with wheezing, cough, and choking feeling due to a spasmodic narrowing of the small bronchi (small air tubes opening into the lung respiratory alveoli or cavities).

Biopsy: Removal of a small piece of tissue from the living body for microscopic or chemical examination to assist in disease diagnosis.

Bronchitis: Inflammation of the bronchi (tubular passages leading to lung cavities). It may be acute or chronic and caused by infection or the action of physical or chemical agents.

Cancer (Neoplasm): A cellular tumor (swelling) resulting from uncontrolled tissue growth. Its natural evolution is to spread locally or to other body locations through the blood and lymph stream.

Cataract: Opacity of the normally transparent eye lens; this condition leads to impaired vision and stems from hereditary, nutritional, inflammatory, toxic, traumatic, or degenerative causes.

Catheterization: Introduction of a tubular instrument called a catheter into a body cavity for purposes of injecting fluids (as in intravenous therapy), of withdrawing fluids (as in bladder catheterization), or for observing body functions (as in cardiac catheterization).

Cerebrospinal Fluid Examination: Chemical, miscroscopic, and bacteriological examination of a sample of the usually clear and colorless liquid bathing the brain and spinal cord. The sample is usually removed by needle puncture of the lumbar spine.

Cirrhosis: Chronic liver ailment that results in a progressive destruction of liver cells and impairment of the organ's functions.

Computerized Axial Tomography (CAT Scan): The use of serial X-ray beams, recorders, and a computer to construct a visual, 3-dimensional description of any portion of the body for identification of abnormal structures or processes.

Conjunctivitis: Acute or chronic inflammation of the conjunctiva—the delicate transparent membrane lining the eyelids and covering the exposed surface of the eyeball. It results from the action of bacteria, allergens, and physical or chemical irritants.

Cyst: Any normal or abnormal sac in the body, especially one containing a liquid or semiliquid material.

Cystic Fibrosis: An inherited disease of the mucous-secreting glands that appears in infancy. Respiratory, excretory, and digestive functions are impaired by the copious production of thick secretions. There is no cure, but modern antibiotics and respiratory therapy enable children to live into adulthood.

Cystitis: Acute or chronic inflammation of the urinary bladder, caused by infection or irritation. The symptoms are frequent voiding accompanied by burning sensation and, sometimes, blood in the urine.

Diabetes (Mellitus): Hereditary or acquired disease of the insulin-secreting cells of the pancreas. Symptoms are thirst, weight loss, and frequent urination. Diabetes is diagnosed by use of urine and blood sugar tests. It is treated by regulating the sugar in the blood with diet, oral drugs, or, when necessary, with regular injections of insulin. Severe diabetes, if untreated, will result in kidney failure, blindness, and death.

Eczema: Inflammatory skin disease that produces a great variety of lesions, such as vesicles, thickening of skin, watery discharge, and scales and crusts, with itching and burning sensations. Eczema is caused by allergy, infections, and nutritional, physical, and sometimes unknown factors.

Edema: Excessive accumulation of water and salt in the tissue spaces, caused by kidney or heart disease (generalized edema) or by local circulatory impairment stemming from inflammation, trauma, or neoplasm (localized edema).

Electrocardiogram (ECG or EKG): Graphic tracing of the electric current that is produced by the rhythmic contraction of the heart muscle. Visually, a periodic wave pattern is produced. Changes in the wave pattern may appear in the course of various heart diseases; the tracing is obtained by applying electrodes on the skin of the chest and limbs.

Electroencephalogram (EEG): Graphic recording of the electric current created by the activity of the brain. The electrodes are placed on the scalp.

Embolism: Blocking of a blood vessel by a dislodged blood clot (after surgery), a fat globule (after a fracture), gas bubbles (after sudden decompression), clumps of bacteria (in certain infections), or by other matter.

Emphysema (Pulmonary): Lung disease characterized by over distention of the air sacs of the lungs (alveoli), their loss of elasticity, and destruction of the walls separating them. It results in a reduction of the respiratory surface, chronic shortness of breath, wheezing, and cough.

Epilepsy: Disease characterized by sudden and brief (in some forms momentary) convulsions, which are associated with impairment or loss of consciousness, psychic or sensory disturbances, and autonomic nervous system perturbations.

Gangrene: A form of necrosis (tissue death) due to an inadequate blood supply. Infection may also occur.

Gastritis: Acute or chronic inflammation of the lining of the stomach. It may be caused by the ingestion of alcohol, spices, medicines, chemicals, foods, as well as by infections or allergy.

Gastroscopy: Direct visualization of the stomach interior by means of an optical instrument called a gastroscope.

Gastrointestinal Series (G.I. Series): Serial X-ray examination of the stomach and intestines.

Glaucoma: Eye disease characterized by an increase in the internal pressure in the eye, caused by alteration of the intraocular fluid flow and resulting in visual impairment, and if untreated, blindness.

Goiter: Enlargement of the thyroid gland that shows as a swelling at the base of the neck. Goiter is often associated with iodine deficiency (endemic goiter), or with excessive secretion of thyroid hormones (exophthalmic goiter).

Gout: A disturbance of body chemistry, manifested by elevated uric acid blood levels and excessive deposits in tissues, particularly joints and cartilages. It is characterized by repeated attacks of acute and very painful inflammation of joints, especially those of the big toe but also of ankles, knees, wrists, and elbows.

Hematoma: Swelling produced by a collection of blood escaping from a ruptured blood vessel, resulting from trauma or injury. It is generally located under the skin and subcutaneous tissue, or under the bony structure of the skull.

Hemorrhage (Bleeding): Any copious blood loss from the circulation. If sufficiently severe or unchecked, it will lead to anemia, shock, and death.

Hemorrhoids (Piles): Abnormal dilatation of the veins of the rectum and anus, causing local swelling, pain, itching, bleeding, and induration.

Hepatitis: Liver inflammation, caused by infection or toxic substances. It is characterized by clay-colored stools, dark urine, fever, and jaundice (yellow coloration of the skin and white of the eye).

Hernia: Protrusion of a portion of an organ or tissue through an abnormal body opening. Inguinal hernia is one of the most common and consists of an intestinal loop protruding at the groin.

Hypertension: Disease characterized by elevated blood pressure, resulting from the functional or pathological narrowing of the peripheral small arteries. Except in limited instances, its cause is generally unknown.

Immunotherapy: a method of treating certain diseases by stimulating the body's natural immune response, resulting in partial or total immunization.

Intestinal Obstruction: Blocking of the normal flow of the intestinal contents, caused by twisting of a gut loop, benign tumor, cancer, or foreign body.

Kidney Failure (Renal Failure): Severe impairment of the excretory function of the kidney. The acute form occurs most frequently after crushing injuries, transfusion of mismatched blood, severe burns or shock, generalized infections, obstetric accidents, and certain chemical poisoning.

Laboratory Procedures: Laboratory tests performed to assist in disease diagnosis and treatment. Usually these tests are carried out on samples of blood, urine, or other body fluids. The most common are:

Blood Count: Determination of the number and percentage of red and white blood cells from a blood sample that is obtained by puncturing a vein or the skin. It consists of a red blood cell count (RBC), white blood cell count (WBC), and platelet count.

Blood Grouping: Classification of red blood cells by the demonstration of specific antigens in the blood. Always done prior to transfusion.

Blood Chemistry: Determination of the content of various blood chemicals; the most usual are: sugar, for diabetes; urea nitrogen (BUN), for kidney or liver disease; uric acid, for gout; and cholesterol, for vascular and liver disease.

Blood Culture: Investigation to detect the presence of pathogenic germs by special culturing in artificial media.

Urinalysis (Urine Analysis): Examination of urine constituents, both normal (urea, uric acid, total nitrogen, ammonia, chlorides, phosphate, and others) and abnormal (albumin, glucose, acetone, bile, blood, cells, and bacteria).

Meningitis: Inflammation of the enveloping membranes of the brain or spinal cord, caused by virus, bacteria, yeasts, fungi, or protozoa. It is frequently a serious complication of another infection.

Metabolism: The total of the physical and chemical processes occurring in the living organism by which its substance is produced, maintained, and exchanged with transformation of energy; this energy itself provides fuel for all body functions and heat production.

Metastasis: Transfer of a disease (usually cancer) or the causative agent of a disease (e.g. bacteria or cancer cells) from one organ or part of the body to another, through the blood or lymph vessels.

Multiple Sclerosis: A chronic and slowly progressive disease of unknown cause that is characterized by patches of fibrous tissue degeneration in brain and spinal cord, causing various nervous system symptoms. The disease's course is marked by occasional periods of worsening or improvement.

Muscular Dystrophy: An inherited disease that involves the progressive weakness and degeneration of voluntary skeletal muscle fibers without nerve involvement.

Myocarditis: Inflammation of the heart muscle that is associated with or caused by a number of infectious diseases, toxic chemicals, drugs, and traumatic agents.

Necrosis: Localized death of tissue, following interruption of the blood supply to the area.

Nephritis: Inflammatory, acute or chronic disease of the kidneys, which usually follows some form of infection or toxic chemical poisoning. It impairs renal function, causing headache, edema, elevated blood pressure, and appearance of albumin in urine.

Neuralgia: Brief attack of acute and severe shooting pain along the course of one or more peripheral nerves, usually without clear cause.

Neuritis: Inflammation or degeneration of one or more peripheral nerves, causing pain, tenderness, tingling sensations, numbness, paralysis, muscle weakness, and wasting and disappearance of reflexes in the area involved. The cause may be infectious, toxic, nutritional (vitamin B1 deficiency), or unknown.

Pancreatitis: Inflammation of the pancreas, either mild or acute and fulminating. The chronic form is characterized by recurrent attacks of diverse severity. Symptoms are sudden abdominal pain, tenderness and distention, vomiting and, in severe cases, shock and circulatory collapse.

Pap Smears (Papanicolau Smears): Method of staining smears of various body secretions—especially cervical but also respiratory, digestive, or genitourinary—to detect cancer by examining the normally shed cells in the smear. The procedure is named for its developer.

Parkinsonism (Paralysis Agitans): A usually chronic condition, marked by muscular rigidity, immobile face, excessive salivation, and tremor. These symptoms characterize Parkinson's disease; however, they are also observed in the course of treatment with certain psychotropic drugs or following encephalitis, or trauma.

Pericarditis: Acute or chronic inflammation of the pericardium (fibrous sac surrounding the heart), caused by infection, trauma, myocardial infarction, cancer, or complication from other diseases.

Peritonitis: Acute or chronic inflammation of the serous membrane lining abdominal walls and covering the contained viscera. Its symptoms are abdominal pain and tenderness, nausea, vomiting, moderate fever, and constipation. It is usually caused by infectious agents or foreign matter entering the abdominal cavity from the intestinal tract (perforation), female genital tract, blood stream, or the outside (wounds, surgery).

Phlebitis: Condition caused by inflammation of a vein wall, usually resulting in the formation of a blood clot inside its cavity. Phlebitis produces pain, swelling, and stiffness of the affected part, generally a limb.

Pleurisy: Acute or chronic inflammation of the pleura (serous membranes lining the thoracic cavity and covering the lungs). It often accompanies inflammatory lung diseases and may be caused by infection, cancer, or cardiac infarct.

Pneumonia: An acute inflammation of the lungs, usually caused by bacterial or viral infection. Chills, sharp chest pain, shortness of breath, cough, rusty sputum, fever, and headache are primary symptoms.

Pneumothorax: Accumulation of air or gas in the pleural cavity (between the chest wall and the lung), resulting in lung collapse. It may result from a penetrating chest wound or some disease, or may be deliberately induced for treatment of lung ailments (tuberculosis).

Polycythemia: an abnormal increase in the number of circulating red blood cells.

Polyp: A protruding excrescence or growth from a mucous membrane, usually of the nasal passages but also of the uterine cervix, alimentary tract, or vocal cords.

Psoriasis: Chronic, occasionally acute, recurrent skin disease of unknown cause, characterized by thickened red skin patches that are covered with whitish shiny scales (plaques). Psoriasis usually affects the scalp, elbows, knees, back, and buttocks.

Pulmonary Edema: An acute condition in which there is a waterlogging of the lung tissue, including its alveolar cavities. Respiration is impaired. If inadequately treated, it may lead to rapid death; it is often a complication of chronic heart disease.

Rheumatic Fever: Disease characterized by initial sore throat, chills, high fever, and painful inflammation of large joints. Frequently cardiac complications follow, leading to permanent organic heart disease.

Rickets: Generally a disease of infants and young children caused by vitamin D deficiency. There is defective bone calcification that causes skeletal deformities, such as bow legs, knock knees, and pigeon chest.

Sciatica: A severe pain along the sciatic nerve, which extends from the buttocks along the back of the thigh and leg to the ankle.

Spinal Curvature: A marked displacement of the normally straight vertical spine, which may be caused by disease or mechanical deviation of the bones or muscles of the spine, hips, or legs.

Septicemia: Presence of bacteria or bacterial toxins in the circulating blood caused by the breakdown of local defenses, permitting a circumscribed infection to spread.

Silicosis: Occupational disease, usually chronic, causing fibrosis of the lungs. It results from inhalation of the dust of stone, flint, or sand that contains silica (quartz). Called "grinders' disease," it is observed in workers who have breathed such dust for a period of years.

Slipped Disk: An acute or chronic condition, caused by the traumatic or degenerative displacement and protrusion of the softened central core of an intervertebral disk (cartilagenous disk between the spine bones), especially of the lower back. Symptoms are low back pain, which frequently extends to the thigh; muscle spasm; and tenderness.

Spastic Paralysis (Cerebral Palsy): A condition probably stemming from various causes present since birth. Associated with nonprogressive brain damage, cerebral palsy is characterized by spastic, jerky voluntary movements, or constant involuntary and irregular writhing.

Stroke (Cerebral Apoplexy): A sudden attack of paralysis, with disturbance of speech and thought. It is caused by the destruction of brain substance, as the result of brain hemorrhage, vascular damage, intravascular clotting, or local circulatory insufficiency.

Tardive Dyskinesia (TD): A condition in which there are repeated involuntary movements of the extremities, face, jaw, and tongue. TD afflicts many people who have taken antipsychotic medications for prolonged periods of time. It is disfiguring and usually not reversible.

Thermography: a diagnostic technique for locating the presence of underlying tumors by recording infrared radiations that emanate from the body surface: tumors radiate more heat than the surrounding tissues.

Thrombophlebitis: Condition caused by the inflammation of a vein complicated by the formation of an intravascular blood clot (thrombus). Circulation is obstructed in the affected area, usually the legs.

Thrombosis: Formation, development, or presence of a blood clot inside an artery or vein. This condition can be serious, if it affects the blood vessels of vital organs, such as the brain, heart, or lungs.

Tumor: A swelling or growth of new tissue; it develops independently of surrounding structures and serves no specific function of its own.

Uremia: Toxic clinical condition in which renal insufficiency allows the retention of urinary waste products in the circulating blood.

Varicose Veins: Abnormally distended and lengthened superficial veins caused by slowing and obstruction of the normal blood backflow. Varicose veins are most commonly observed in the legs, anus and rectum (hemorrhoids), and scrotum (varicocele).

MODERN DRUG ADVANCES

Acyclovir—Antiviral drug effective in preliminary studies for treatment of herpes infections.

Adrenocorticosteroids—More than 20 synthetic adrenal hormones and their chemical derivatives. They are used primarily in the treatment of "collagen diseases" (e.g., rheumatoid arthritis) and in the suppression of certain inflammatory diseases or immunological processes.

Allopurinol—An oral drug used in suppressing the symptoms of gout.

Ampicillin—A "broad-spectrum" semisynthetic penicillin effective in the treatment of many infections.

Antithyroid Agents—A group of unrelated compounds, ranging from propylthiouracil to radio-iodide; used for treating hyperthyroidism.

BCG (Bacille Calmette-Guérin)—a nonvirulent strain of tubercle bacillus used in vaccines for immunization against tuberculosis and experimentally in controlling some forms of cancer.

Chloramphenicol—An important broad-spectrum antibiotic that is used to treat typhoid fever, certain types of food poisoning, and other infections caused by microorganisms that are resistant to other antibiotics.

Chloroquin Compounds—Antimalarial and certain forms of extraintestinal amebiasis. They are also used in a few unrelated diseases, such as arthritis.

Chlorpromazine and Other Tranquilizers—Over 30 compounds with mild depressant action on the brain, used in certain mental illnesses and anxiety states, and for antinauseant and sedative effects.

Clofibrate—A drug capable of reducing elevated cholesterol and triglyceride concentrations in the blood.

Clomiphene Citrate—A drug that improves fertility, sometimes causing multiple births.

Diphenhydramine and 30 Other Antihistaminics—Employed mainly in treating certain allergic conditions and also for antiemetic and sedative effects.

Estrogen-Progestogen Contraceptives—Oral contraceptive agents.

Ganglionic Blocking Agents, Mostly Quaternary Ammonium Compounds—Used in the treatment of certain types of hypertension.

Griseofulvin—A drug taken orally that is effective against many fungal infections of the skin and fingernails and toenails.

Halogenated Hydrocarbon Anesthetics—Volatile liquids that are used for inhalation anesthesia.

Hydantoins—Used in the treatment of grand mal (epilepsy) and certain other convulsive states.

Hypnotic Barbiturates—Sedatives and sleeping pills.

Immune Globulins—A protein derived from human blood that, when injected into persons exposed to certain infectious diseases, confers temporary immunity.

Interferon—A protein, produced by the white blood cells, that activates immune systems, prevents an invading virus from reproducing itself within the host cell, and changes membranes of the invaded cell to interfere with the virus's ability to infect other cells. It was recently synthesized and is being used experimentally in the treatment of certain cancers and viruses.

Isoniazid—The most important drug in the treatment and prophylaxis of tuberculosis.

Isoproterenol—Used in the treatment of bronchial asthma, particularly to relieve the bronchial-tube spasm.

Lidocaine and Other Local Anesthetics—Injected locally to anesthetize tissues prior to minor surgical operations.

Lithium—A drug found effective in the treatment of manic-depressive psychoses.

Meperidine—A powerful pain-relieving drug.

Methantheline and Other Anticholinergics—Parasympatholytic agents used in cases of peptic ulcer and to decrease hypermotility (or spasm) of the gastrointestinal tract.

Methicillin—The first penicillin effective against staph (staphylococcus) infections that are resistant to ordinary penicillin.

Oral Antidiabetes Agents (e.g., isophane insulin and tolbutamide)—Insulin replacement for some types of diabetes.

Propranolol—A drug for heart-rhythm disorders.

Rauwolfia and Veratrum Alkaloids—Principles of plant origin used in treating hypertension or as a tranquilizer.

Streptomycin—An important antibiotic, and one of the primary drugs for treating tuberculosis.

Sulfonamides—Used in the treatment of infections of the respiratory and urinary tracts and in certain types of meningitis.

Surgical Skeletal Muscle Relaxants (About seven surgical, peripherally acting preparations)—These drugs are used to relax muscles during surgery.

Synthetic Anticoagulants—Used to prevent formation or extension of blood clots within arteries and veins.

Ten Basic Penicillins, Plus Salts and Esters—Antibacterial drugs that are used primarily to treat infections of the skin, respiratory tract, and of the genitourinary tract.

Tetracycline Derivatives, Plus Salts and Esters—Used in the treatment of a wide variety of infections caused by many different types of micro-organisms.

Thiazides, Organomercurial and Diuretics—To remove excess fluid from the body in certain types of heart and kidney diseases. Also used in the treatment of hypertension (high blood pressure).

Trihexyphenidyl, Amantadine Hydrochloride, L-Dopa, and Other Anti-Parkinsonism Agents—Used to relieve the muscle symptoms in patients with Parkinson's disease.

Vaccines—For the prevention or modification of infectious diseases, such as poliomyelitis, measles, and mumps.

PSYCHIATRIC TERMS

SOURCE: American Psychiatric Association

Alienation: The estrangement felt in cultural settings one views as foreign, unpredictable, or unacceptable.

Anal Character: In psychoanalysis a pattern of behavior in an adult that originates in the anal eroticism of infancy and is characterized by such traits as excessive orderliness, miserliness, and obstinacy.

Anorexia Nervosa: A disorder marked by severe and prolonged refusal to eat, resulting in significant weight loss, amenorrhea or impotence, disturbance of body image, and an intense fear of becoming obese. Most frequently encountered in girls and young women.

Anxiety: Apprehension, the source of which is largely unknown or unrecognized. It is different from fear, which is the emotional response to a consciously recognized and usually external danger.

Autistic Child: In child psychiatry, a child who responds chiefly to inner thoughts, who does not relate to his environment, and whose overall functioning is immature and often appears retarded.

Blocking: Difficulty in recollection, or interruption of a train of thought or speech, caused by unconscious emotional factors.

Catatonic State (catatonia): A state characterized by immobility with muscular rigidity or inflexibility and at times by excitability. Virtually always a symptom of schizophrenia.

Community Mental Health Center (CMHC): A mental health delivery system providing community-based services. Regulations require that the following services be provided: inpatient, outpatient, partial hospitalization, services for children and the elderly, half-way houses, alcohol and drug abuse programs, emergency services, follow-up care, assistance to the courts and other public agencies, and consultation and education.

Compensation: (1) A defense mechanism, operating unconsciously, by which the individual attempts to make up for (i.e., to compensate for) real or fancied deficiencies; (2) a conscious process in which the individual strives to make up for real or imagined defects in such areas as physique, performance, skills, or psychological attributes.

Complex: A group of associated ideas that have a common emotional tie. These are largely unconscious and significantly influence attitudes and associations. Examples are:

Inferiority complex: Feelings of inferiority stemming from real or imagined physical or social inadequacies that may cause anxiety or other adverse reactions. The individual may overcompensate by excessive ambition or by the development of special skills, often in the very field in which he was originally handicapped.

Oedipus complex: Attachment of the child for the parent of the opposite sex, accompanied by envious and aggressive feelings toward the parent of the same sex. These feelings are largely repressed (i.e., made unconscious) because of the fear of displeasure or punishment by the parent of the same sex. In its original use, the term applied only to the male child.

Compulsion: An insistent, repetitive, and unwanted urge to perform an act that is contrary to the person's ordinary conscious wishes or standards. Failure to perform the compulsive act results in overt anxiety.

Defense Mechanism: A specific process, operating unconsciously, that is employed to seek relief from emotional conflict and freedom from anxiety.

Depression: Psychiatrically, a morbid sadness, dejection, or melancholy; to be differentiated from grief, which is realistic and proportionate to what has been lost. A depression may be a symptom of any psychiatric disorder or may constitute its principal manifestation.

Ego: In psychoanalytic theory, one of the three major divisions of human personality, the others being the *id* and *superego*. The *ego*, commonly identified with consciousness of self, is the mental agent mediating among three contending forces: the external demands of social pressure or reality; the primitive instinctual demands arising from the *id* imbedded as it is in the deepest level of the unconscious; and the claims of the *superego*, born of parental and social prohibitions and functioning as an internal censor or "conscience."

Empathy: An objective awareness of the feelings, emotions, and behavior of another person. To be distinguished from sympathy, which is usually nonobjective and noncritical.

Epilepsy: A disorder characterized by periodic seizures, and sometimes accompanied by a loss of consciousness. May be caused by organic or emotional disturbances.

Major epilepsy (grand mal): Characterized by gross convulsive seizures, with loss of consciousness.

Minor epilepsy (petit mal): Minor nonconvulsive epileptic seizures; may be limited to only momentary lapses of consciousness.

Euphoria: An exaggerated feeling of physical and emotional well-being inconsonant with reality.

Extroversion: A state in which attention and energies are largely directed outward from the self, as opposed to interest primarily directed toward the self, as in introversion.

Free Association: In psychoanalytic therapy, spontaneous, uncensored verbalization by the patient of whatever comes to mind.

Fugue: A major state of personality dissociation characterized by amnesia and actual physical flight from the immediate environment.

Homosexuality: Sexual attraction or relationship between members of the same sex.

Latent homosexuality: A condition characterized by unconscious homosexual desires.

Overt homosexuality: Homosexuality that is consciously recognized or practiced.

Hypnosis: A state of increased receptivity to suggestion and direction, initially induced by the influence of another person. The degree may vary from mild suggestibility to a trance state so profound as to be used in surgical operations.

Hypochondriasis: Overconcern with the state of physical or emotional health, accompanied by various bodily complaints without demonstrable organic pathology.

Hysterical Personality: A personality type characterized by shifting emotional feelings, susceptibility to suggestion, impulsive behavior, attention seeking, and immaturity.

Id: *See* Ego.

Inhibition: Interference with or restriction of activities; the result of an unconscious defense against forbidden instinctual drives.

Insight: Self-understanding. A major goal of psychotherapy. The extent of the individual's understanding of the origin, nature, and mechanisms of his attitudes and behavior.

Mania: A suffix denoting a pathological preoccupation with some desire, idea, or activity; a morbid compulsion. Some frequently encountered manias are *dipsomania*, compulsion to drink alcoholic beverages; *egomania*, pathological preoccupation with self; *kleptomania*, compulsion to steal; *megalomania*, pathological preoccupation with delusions of power or wealth; *monomania*, pathological preoccupation with one subject; *necromania*, pathological preoccupation with the dead; *pyromania*, morbid compulsion to set fires.

Manic-Depressive Reaction (bi-polar disorder): A group of psychiatric disorders marked by conspicuous mood swings, ranging from normal to elation or to depression, or alternating. Officially regarded as a psychosis but may also exist in milder form.

Depressed phase: Characterized by depression of mood with retardation and inhibition of thinking and physical activity.

Manic phase: Characterized by heightened excitability, acceleration of thought, speech, and bodily motion, and by elation or grandiosity of mood, and irritability.

Masochism: Pleasure derived from undergoing physical or psychological pain inflicted by oneself or by others. It may be consciously sought or unconsciously arranged or invited. Present to some degree in all human relations and to greater degrees in all psychiatric disorders. It is the converse of sadism, in which pain is inflicted on another, and the two tend to coexist in the same individual.

Narcissism (narcism): Self-love, as opposed to object-love (love of another person). Some degree of narcissism is considered healthy and normal, but an excess interferes with relations with others.

Obsession: Persistent, unwanted idea or impulse that cannot be eliminated by logic or reasoning.

Overcompensation: A conscious or unconscious process in which a real or fancied physical or psychological deficit inspires exaggerated correction.

Paranoid State: Characterized by delusions of persecution. A paranoid state may be of short duration or chronic.

Phobia: An obsessive, unrealistic fear of an external object or situation. Some of the common phobias are *acrophobia,* fear of heights; *agoraphobia,* fear of open places; *claustrophobia,* fear of closed spaces; *mysophobia,* fear of dirt and germs; *xenophobia,* fear of strangers.

Projective Tests: Psychological tests used as a diagnostic tool. Among the most common projective tests is the Rorschach (inkblot) test.

Psychoanalysis: A theory of human development and behavior, a method of research, and a system of psychotherapy, originally described by Sigmund Freud (1856–1939). Through analysis of free associations and interpretation of dreams, emotions and behavior are traced to the influence of repressed instinctual drives in the unconscious. Psychoanalytic treatment seeks to eliminate or diminish the undesirable effects of unconscious conflicts by making the patient aware of their existence, origin, and inappropriate expression.

Psychoneurosis: One of the two major categories of emotional illness, the other being the psychoses. It is usually less severe than a psychosis, with minimal loss of contact with reality.

Psychosis: A major mental disorder of organic and/or emotional origin in which there is a departure from normal patterns of thinking, feeling, and acting. Commonly characterized by loss of contact with reality, distortion of perception, regressive behavior and attitudes, diminished control of elementary impulses and desires, and delusions and hallucinations. Chronic and generalized personality deterioration may occur. A majority of patients in public mental hospitals are psychotic.

Psychosomatic: Adjective to denote the constant and inseparable interdependence of the psyche (mind) and the soma (body). Most commonly used to refer to illnesses in which the manifestations are primarily physical with at least a partial emotional cause.

Psychotherapy: The term for any type of mental treatment that is based primarily upon verbal or nonverbal communication with the patient, in distinction to the use of drugs, surgery, or physical measures such as electric or insulin shock.

Regression: The partial or symbolic return to more infantile patterns of reacting.

Repression: A defense mechanism, operating unconsciously, that banishes unacceptable ideas, emotions, or impulses from consciousness or that keeps out of consciousness what has never been conscious.

Sadism: *See* **Masochism.**

Schizophrenia: A severe emotional disorder of psychotic depth characteristically marked by a retreat from reality with delusion formation, hallucinations, emotional disharmony, and regressive behavior. Formerly called dementia praecox. Its prognosis has improved in recent years.

Shock Treatment: A form of psychiatric treatment in which electric current, insulin, or carbon dioxide is administered to the patient and results in a convulsive reaction to alter favorably the course of mental illness.

Sublimation: A defense mechanism, operating unconsciously, by which instinctual but consciously unacceptable drives are diverted into personally and socially acceptable channels.

Superego: *See* **Ego.**

Unconscious: That part of the mind the content of which is only rarely subject to awareness. It is the repository for knowledge that has never been conscious or that may have been conscious briefly and was then repressed.

PATIENT CARE EPISODES IN MENTAL HEALTH FACILITIES

SOURCE: National Institute for Mental Health

Patient care episodes are defined as the number of residents in inpatient facilities at the beginning of the year (or the number of persons on the rolls of noninpatient facilities) plus the total additions to these facilities during the year. Total additions during the year include new admissions, readmissions, and returns from long-term leave. The index, patient care episodes, therefore, is not equal to a true annual prevalence rate nor the annual prevalence of treated mental disorder, since episodes of care are counted rather than cases. This index does present useful measures of the volume of services utilized by persons with mental disorders and as such are useful in describing the distribution of episodes by age, sex, modality and type of facility.

While trend data on day care episodes by type of facility are not available for more than a few years, such data are available for inpatient and outpatient episodes as illustrated below. The number of inpatient and outpatient care episodes in mental health facilities in 1977 — 6.6 million — was almost four times greater than the approximately 1.7 million episodes in 1955.

Number and percent distribution of inpatient and outpatient care episodes[1], in selected mental health facilities, by type of facility: United States, 1955, 1965, 1975 and 1977 (Provisional)

Year	Total All[1] Facilities	State & County Mental Hospitals	Private Mental[2] Hospitals	Gen. Hosp. Psychiatric Service (non-VA)	VA Psychiatric Inpatient Services	Federally Assisted Comm. Men. Health Cen.	Federally Assisted Comm. Men. Health Cen.	Other
			Inpatient Services of:				**Outpatient Psychiatric Services of:**	
				Number of Patient Care Episodes				
1977	6,639,278	574,226	184,189	571,725	217,507	268,966	1,741,729	3,080,936
1975	6,409,447	598,993	165,327	265,934	88,355	—	—	379,000
1965	2,636,525	804,926	125,428	542,642	176,800	130,088	622,906	1,693,848
1955	1,675,352	818,832	123,231	519,328	115,843	—	—	1,071,000
				Percent Distribution				
1977	100.0	8.6	2.8	8.6	3.3	4.1	26.2	46.4
1975	100.0	9.3	2.6	8.8	3.3	3.9	24.7	47.4
1965	100.0	30.5	4.8	19.7	4.4	—	—	40.6
1955	100.0	48.9	7.3	15.9	5.3	—	—	22.6

[1] In order to present trends on the same set of facilities over this interval, it has been necessary to exclude from this table the following: private psychiatric office practice; psychiatric service modes of all types in hospitals or outpatient clinics of Federal agencies other than the VA (e.g., Public Health Service, Indian Health Service, Department of Defense Bureau of Prisons, etc.); inpatient service modes of multiservice facilities not shown in this table; all partial care episodes, and outpatient episodes of VA hospitals. [2] Includes estimates of episodes of care in residential treatment centers for emotionally disturbed children.

Source (All years except 1977): The National Institute of Mental Health, Statistical Note 139—Provisional data on patient care—episodes in mental health facilities, August 1977.

Source (1977): Unpublished provisional data from the National Institute of Mental Health.

RECOMMENDED DAILY DIETARY ALLOWANCES FOR AMERICANS

The schedule is designed for the maintenance of good nutrition of normally active Americans in a temperate climate. The following abbreviations are used: Gm. for gram; Mg. for milligram; I.U. for International Unit.

Family Members	Weight (Pounds)	Height Feet Inches	Calories	Protein (Gms.)	Calcium (Gms.)	Iron (Mg.)	Vitamin A (I.U.)	Thiamine (Mg.)	Riboflavin (Mg.)	Niacin (Mg. Equiv.)	Ascorbic Acid (Mg.)	Vitamin D (I.U.)
MEN												
18–35 years ...	154	5–9	2,900	70	0.8	10	5,000	1.2	1.7	19	70	—
35–55 years ...	154	5–9	2,600	70	0.8	10	5,000	1.0	1.6	17	70	—
55–75 years ...	154	5–9	2,200	70	0.8	10	5,000	0.9	1.3	15	70	—
WOMEN												
18–35 years ...	128	5–4	2,100	58	0.8	15	5,000	0.8	1.3	14	70	—
35–55 years ...	128	5–4	1,900	58	0.8	15	5,000	0.8	1.2	13	70	—
55–75 years ...	128	5–4	1,600	58	0.8	10	5,000	0.8	1.2	13	70	—
CHILDREN												
1–3 years	29	2–10	1,300	32	0.8	8	2,000	0.5	0.8	9	40	400
3–6 years	40	3–6	1,600	40	0.8	10	2,500	0.6	1.0	11	50	400
6–9 years	53	4–1	2,100	52	0.8	12	3,500	0.8	1.3	14	60	400
BOYS												
9–12 years	72	4–7	2,400	60	1.1	15	4,500	1.0	1.4	16	70	400
12–15 years ...	98	5–1	3,000	75	1.4	15	5,000	1.2	1.8	20	80	400
15–18 years ...	134	5–8	3,400	85	1.4	15	5,000	1.4	2.0	22	80	400
GIRLS												
9–12 years	72	4–7	2,200	55	1.1	15	4,500	0.9	1.3	15	80	400
12–15 years ...	103	5–2	2,500	62	1.3	15	5,000	1.0	1.5	17	80	400
15–18 years ...	117	5–4	2,300	58	1.3	15	5,000	0.9	1.3	15	70	400

DESIRABLE WEIGHTS FOR ADULT MEN AND WOMEN

Height (in shoes, 1-in. heels) FT. IN.	MEN WEIGHT (LB.) IN INDOOR CLOTHING*			Height (in shoes, 2-in. heels) FT. IN.	WOMEN WEIGHT (LB.) IN INDOOR CLOTHING*		
	Small Frame	Medium Frame	Large Frame		Small Frame	Medium Frame	Large Frame
5 2	112–120	118–129	126–141	4 10	92–98	96–107	104–119
5 3	115–123	121–133	129–144	4 11	94–101	98–110	106–122
5 4	118–126	124–136	132–148	5 0	96–104	101–113	109–125
5 5	121–129	127–139	135–152	5 1	99–107	104–116	112–128
5 6	124–133	130–143	138–156	5 2	102–110	107–119	115–131
5 7	128–137	134–147	142–161	5 3	105–113	110–122	118–134
5 8	132–141	138–152	147–166	5 4	108–116	113–126	121–138
5 9	136–145	142–156	151–170	5 5	111–119	116–130	125–142
5 10	140–150	146–160	155–174	5 6	114–123	120–135	129–146
5 11	144–154	150–165	159–179	5 7	118–127	124–139	133–150
6 0	148–158	154–170	164–184	5 8	122–131	128–143	137–154
6 1	152–162	158–175	168–189	5 9	126–135	132–147	141–158
6 2	156–167	162–180	173–194	5 10	130–140	136–151	145–163
6 3	160–171	167–185	178–199	5 11	134–144	140–155	149–168
6 4	164–175	172–190	182–204	6 0	138–148	144–159	153–173

* For nude weight, deduct 5–7 lbs. (male) or 2–4 lbs. (female).

RECOMMENDED FOOD QUANTITIES IN TERMS OF SERVINGS

SOURCE: U.S. Department of Agriculture

Here follows a table of food groups and approximate amounts of foods as served per person per day, according to low-cost and moderate-cost plans. Servings allow for some plate waste. In addition to the food groups mentioned, some fats and oils (available in butter and margarine) and sugar (in its own form or in sweets and preserves) should be included in most diets.

NUMBER OF SERVINGS PER PERSON PER DAY

Food Group	Unit	Plan	Child 1–6 years[1]	Child 6–12 years[1]	Girl 12–20 years	Boy 12–20 years	Woman 20–55 years	Woman 55 years and over	Man 20–55 years	Man 55 years and over
Meat, poultry, fish or alternates	1 oz. cooked lean meat, 1 egg, ½ cup cooked dry beans, or 2 tbsp. peanut butter	Low Cost	3–3½	4–4½	4½–5	4½–6	5½–6	3½–4½	5½–6	4½–5½
		Moderate	3½–4½	5–7	7	7–8	7½	5½–6½	7½–8	7
Milk, cheese, ice cream, ice milk	1 8-oz. cup of milk as beverage or in cooking or cheese or ice cream	Low Cost	2¼	2¼–3	4	4	2	2	2	2
		Moderate	3	3	4	4	2	2	2	2
Vegetables and fruits	½ cup or equivalent vegetable or fruit as served	Low Cost	2–3½	4½–5½	5–6	5½–6½	4½–5½	3½–4½	5–6	4–5
		Moderate	2½–4	4½–6	5½–6½	6–7½	5–6	4–4½	5½–7	5–6
Cereal and bakery products	1 slice of bread or other bakery products with equal flour; 1 oz. ready-to-eat cereal; or ¾ cup cooked cereal or cereal product	Low Cost	5–7	8–9	8–9	14–16	7–8	5–7	12–14	8–9
		Moderate	4–6	8–9	7–8	13–15	7–8	4–5	11–13	7–8

[1] Smaller amount is for younger children.

EARTH: FACTS/FIGURES

EARTH: THIRD PLANET FROM THE SUN

The Earth, our planet, is located at an average distance of 93 million miles from the Sun, which it orbits in 365 days, 6 hours, 8 minutes, and 38 seconds. The Earth completes one rotation on its axis in 23 hours, 56 minutes, and 4 seconds, and its equator is inclined 23 degrees and 27 minutes to the plane of the ecliptic. The equatorial diameter of the Earth is 7,926 miles; its polar diameter is 7,900 miles. The Earth's average density is 5.52 grams/cm^3.

The circumference of the Earth around the equator has been estimated at 24,900 miles, while its circumference around the poles is thought to be about 24,820 miles. From these dimensions, it is obvious that the Earth is not a true sphere, but rather a *geoid*—a triaxial ellipsoid that is nearly spherical but flattened at the poles. Small bulges produce four "corners"—at Ireland, off Peru, south of Africa, and near New Guinea. Space-satellite measurements have further indicated two "dimples" in the Northern Hemisphere, giving the Earth a slightly pearlike appearance.

The Earth has an estimated mass of 5.883×10^{21} tons and an estimated volume of 2.6×10^{11} cubic miles. Its total surface area is approximately 197,272,000 square miles, of which the land area makes up only about 57,200,000 square miles. The average land elevation is 2,700 feet; the average ocean depth is 12,500 feet.

It is generally believed that the Earth and the other planets are 4.6 billion years old, although the oldest rocks found on the Earth are only 3.7 billion years old. Scientists have given names to the various geological time periods of Earth's history.

The largest segments of geologic time are called eras and are named according to the type of life that then existed. Eras are divided into periods, which are further divided into epochs. The period names usually refer to locations where rocks of the specific period were first studied (e.g., Devonian signifies Devonshire, England; Cretaceous, the chalk deposits that are found on both sides of the English Channel). Other names, such as Ordovician and Silurian, are actually the names of Celtic tribes that inhabited parts of Wales where rocks from this time interval were first studied.

Era	Period, Epoch	Age (Millions of Years Ago)	Evolution of Life
Cenozoic	Quaternary, Recent & Pleistocene	0 to 2.5	Man
	Tertiary, Pliocene	2.5 to 12	Higher Mammals
	Tertiary, Miocene	12 to 25	
	Tertiary, Oligocene	25 to 36	
	Tertiary, Eocene	36 to 58	
	Tertiary, Paleocene	58 to 63	
Mesozoic	Cretaceous	63 to 135	Modern Vegetation
	Jurassic	135 to 200	Birds
	Triassic	200 to 230	Mammals
Paleozoic	Permian	230 to 280	
	Carboniferous	280 to 345	Reptiles
	Devonian	345 to 405	Amphibians
	Silurian	405 to 425	Land Plants
	Ordovician	425 to 500	Agnathans, Fishes
	Cambrian	500 to 570	Invertebrate Animals
Pre-Cambrian	Late Pre-Cambrian	570 to 700	Higher Algae
	Upper Pre-Cambrian	700 to 1600	
	Middle Pre-Cambrian	1600 to 2700	Unicellular Organisms
	Lower Pre-Cambrian	2700 to 3500	Blue-green Algae
	Archaean	3500+	Bacteria

THE EARTH'S INTERIOR

The core at the Earth's center is the least-known part of the interior; our knowledge of it stems mostly from study of seismic (earthquake) waves and their propagation. However, it is known that the solid inner core of iron is surrounded by a liquid outer core of iron. The inner core, which has a radius of about 850 miles, is believed to have a very high pressure and high temperature (about 10,000° F) and a density of about 13.5 grams/cm^3 (13.5 times the density of water). The outer core has a thickness of about 1,200 miles. Surrounding the outer core is the mantle, which is 1,800 miles thick. The boundary between the mantle and the core is called the Gutenberg-Wiechert Discontinuity.

The mantle has an average density of 5 grams/cm^3 and consists of three layers: the plastic inner mantle that surrounds the liquid core, a transition region, and the outer solid mantle. The uppermost region of the Earth's interior is called the crust and is separated from the outer mantle by the Mohorovicic Discontinuity (or M-Discontinuity). The crust consists of continental crust and oceanic crust. The continental crust is composed of relatively light silicon rocks, such as granite, andesite, and various grades of metamorphic rocks known under the general name of *sial* (aluminum silicate, with silicon oxide comprising 60%) which has an average density of 2.7 grams/cm^3. The continental crust has an average thickness of 23 miles, reaching 40 to 45 miles under high mountain chains. The oceanic crust is composed of heavier basaltic rocks that contain greater proportions of metallic oxides, such as magnesium and iron, under the general name of *sima* (magnesium silicate, with silicon oxide comprising only 46%) which has an average density of 3.0 grams/cm^3. The oceanic crust has an average thickness of 4 miles. As well as being lighter and much thicker, the continental crust is considerably older than the ocean crust.

EARTH'S WATER-COVERED SURFACE

The oceans (hydrosphere) cover some 140 million square miles—70 percent of the Earth's total surface area—to an average depth of 12,500 feet. There are 340 million cubic miles of liquid water on the Earth's surface—making our planet a truly water-covered one. The greatest ocean depth is found in the Marianas Trench in the Western Pacific, being more than 37,500 feet deep.

Chemically, the ocean consists of water (96.5%) and numerous dissolved salts (3.5%), of which common salt (2.8%) is easily the most abundant. The principal elements in seawater are chlorine, sodium, magnesium, sulfur, oxygen, calcium, potassium, bromine, strontium, boron, and smaller amounts of carbon, fluorine, and iodine.

The features of the ocean floor, which result from deformations of the Earth's crust, are either elevations—ridges, rises, seamounts, and sills—or depressions—troughs, trenches, basins, and deeps. For example, the Atlantic Ocean is divided into two troughs by a north-south ridge, the Mid-Atlantic Ridge, which extends into both hemispheres. On either side of the ridge, depths exceeding 16,000 feet exist.

THE EARTH'S ATMOSPHERE

For its first 60 miles, the Earth's atmosphere has a nearly homogeneous composition consisting of the following gases:

Constituent	Percent by Volume
Nitrogen (N_2)	78.084
Oxygen (O_2)	20.946
Argon (Ar)	0.934
Carbon dioxide (CO_2)	0.033
Neon (Ne)	0.000018
Helium (He)	0.000005
Methane (CH_4) & Krypton (Kr)	0.000001

Water vapor (H_2O) varies within the lower atmosphere (the lowest 7 miles) from 0 to 4 percent, but it generally is present in concentrations of 0.1 to 1 percent. Water vapor is rarely found above the lower atmosphere.

Above 60 miles, the atmosphere is no longer homogeneous, but rather successive layers consisting of atomic oxygen (O), helium (He), and hydrogen (H).

Incoming solar radiation reaching our planet heats up the Earth's surface to about $-18°$ F. At this temperature, the Earth emits infrared radiation into space in all directions; however, the carbon dioxide and water vapor molecules in the Earth's lower atmosphere absorb and then reemit this infrared radiation. Part of the reemitted infrared radiation is directed downward and strikes the Earth's surface, increasing the surface temperature to a value of about 60° F, which is the Earth's actual mean temperature, averaged over the entire year. The absorption and reemission of infrared radiation by CO_2 and H_2O is known as the "Greenhouse Effect" or greenhouse temperature enhancement.

The Earth's neutral atmosphere can be divided into five distinct regions, depending on the region's temperature gradient, which is the variation of temperature with height within a particular atmospheric region. That is, a positive temperature gradient means that temperature increases with height; a negative temperature gradient means that temperature decreases with height; an undefined temperature gradient means that the density of molecules is too low to give a meaningful value to the temperature.

Atmospheric Region	Height	Temperature Gradient
Troposphere	0 to 7 miles	... Negative
Stratosphere	7 to 30 miles	... Positive
Mesosphere	30 to 50 miles	... Negative
Thermosphere ...	50 to 300 miles	... Positive
Exosphere	Above 300 miles	... Undefined

The troposphere contains about two-thirds of the total mass of the atmosphere. Within this layer, the temperature decreases with increasing height at a "lapse rate" of about 3.5° F per 1,000 feet. The decrease of temperature with height results from the atmosphere's being heated by solar radiation mainly from below. Whenever there is warmer below cooler air, vertical motions in the atmosphere result, since warm air is lighter than cool air. Such a condition causes vertical wind motions or convective currents within the troposphere. All of our weather, such as clouds and precipitation, occurs in the troposphere.

At the top of the troposphere, the temperature (about $-75°$ F) stops decreasing with height, and the stratosphere begins. Within the stratosphere, the temperature increases with height from heating that is caused by the absorption of solar ultraviolet radiation by the stratospheric ozone layer. Since ozone absorbs most of the incoming solar ultraviolet radiation, this lethal radiation does not reach the surface, where it would adversely affect life.

At the top of the stratosphere, the temperature reaches its maximum of about 35° F, and the mesosphere begins. Within the mesosphere, the temperature decreases approximately 1.5° F per 1,000 feet. The temperature minimum of the entire atmosphere, about $-130°$ F, is found at the top of the mesosphere.

Above this mesopause, the thermosphere begins. This is a region in which the temperature increases with height because of the absorption and subsequent heating of solar X rays and short wavelength ultraviolet radiation. The temperature of the higher layers of the thermosphere can reach about 2000° F. However, at the extremely low density prevailing in this region temperature is a somewhat meaningless concept. Above the thermosphere is the exosphere, which is the top of the Earth's neutral atmosphere.

In addition to the neutral atmosphere of Earth, there are several regions consisting of large amounts of positive atomic nuclei or ions and negative electrons. The absorption of solar X rays and ultraviolet radiation results in the ionization of the air, which, in turn, results in several ionized layers known as the ionosphere. Another region of charged particles—protons and electrons—comprises the Van Allen Radiation belts, which surround the Earth at distances from about 1250 to 3000 miles and 8000 to 12,000 miles. The protons and electrons are held within the radiation belts by the Earth's magnetic field. Most of the electrons and protons in the belt's outer portion come from the Sun in the form of the solar wind.

There is evidence to suggest that the Earth originally had an atmospheric composition similar to that of Jupiter: mostly hydrogen and helium, some methane and ammonia, and no oxygen. It is possible that life began in this atmosphere. However, at some point in the past, the entire original atmosphere was lost and the present one developed. It is believed that nitrogen came from the Earth's interior via volcanic outgassing, as did the carbon dioxide and water vapor in the present atmosphere. Most of the oxygen in our atmosphere was probably produced by plant photosynthesis. Atmospheric argon was produced by the decay of radioactive potassium in rocks and minerals in the Earth's interior.

ORIGIN OF LIFE ON EARTH

The Earth and the other planets are thought to be about 4.6 billion years old. The earliest known fossil records of living organisms on our planet are about 3 billion years old. It is estimated that life existed on our planet some 3.5 to 4 billion years ago, suggesting that up to 1 billion years elapsed before life evolved on Earth from the material then available. Fundamental to an understanding of the origin of life is knowledge of the chemical makeup of living cells.

Two types of molecules—proteins and nucleic acids—play basic functional roles in living cells. Proteins are large complex molecules consisting of a number of amino acids that are joined together to form a long chain. An amino acid is a carbon compound containing an acid group ($-COOH$) and a basic amino group ($-NH_2$). Some 21 different amino acids have been found in proteins. Enzymes are the biochemical catalysts that control many metabolic processes. Enzymes are proteins in which the amino-acid chain has been folded into a very specific shape.

Nucleic acids are formed in the cell nucleus, but some are produced in other cell parts. Like proteins, nucleic acids are complex molecules composed of chains of simpler units. The fundamental unit of nucleic acids is a complex molecule called a nucleotide, which consists of three separate parts: residues of a nitrogenous base, a sugar with five carbon atoms, and phosphoric acid.

In a given nucleic acid, all of the sugar residues are the same. They are either all ribose or all deoxyribose. When the sugar residues are all ribose, the nucleic acids are called ribonucleic acids (RNA) and, when they all are deoxyribose, the nucleic acids are called deoxyribonucleic acids (DNA). Both DNA and RNA are produced in the nuclei of nearly all living cells but, whereas RNA leaves the nucleus and enters the surrounding cytoplasm, essentially all the DNA remains within the nucleus.

Nucleic acids are the key materials for all terrestrial life forms, their presence being fundamental to life processes. DNA is the principal component of genes and chromosomes, passed from parents to offspring. The sequence of nucleotides in DNA comprises the genetic code, which determines the type and amount of protein synthesized in a particular living cell. Hence, it appears that the formation of nucleic acids is related to the origin of life. It has been suggested that viruses, which are larger than a single molecule but smaller than a cell nucleus, represent an intermediate stage between nonliving and living systems. However, the modern virus, which needs to inhabit a cell in order to live, is presumed to be a development of a more primitive precursor.

The probable inorganic elements and conditions on Earth during its first billion years, which together combined to form life, were first discussed by the Russian biochemist A. I. Oparin in his 1924 publication *The Origin of Life*. Oparin described the gradual step-by-step evolution of life from the simple inorganic elements of hydrogen, carbon, nitrogen, and oxygen. A somewhat similar view was expressed (1928) independently by the English biochemist J. B. S. Haldane. The first attempts to simulate early conditions on Earth and produce biological compounds in the laboratory were largely failures. Although oxygen is now the second most abundant gas in the Earth's atmosphere, accounting for some 21% by volume, it was probably not always so abundant.

If oxygen were as abundant in the past as it is today, then carbon would be present mainly as carbon dioxide. Oparin suggested that atmospheric carbon probably existed originally in the reduced form—methane (CH_4)—and not in oxidized form—carbon dioxide (CO_2). Similarly, nitrogen, now present in free state and accounting for some 78% by volume of the atmosphere, would have been in the reduced form of ammonia (NH_3). Like Oparin, but for entirely different reasons, Haldane also concluded that the Earth's primitive atmosphere probably contained little if any free oxygen but consisted mainly of carbon dioxide, ammonia, and water vapor.

In 1952, the American chemist H. C. Urey showed that the Earth's primitive atmosphere should have consisted of methane, ammonia, water vapor, and free hydrogen gas. Urey and S. Miller began a series of lab experiments attempting to synthesize the gases of his theoretical atmosphere into complex organic molecules. After exposing gases to ultraviolet radiation, to simulate the sun's radiation, Urey and Miller reported (1953) that they had successfully produced several amino acids, as well as other organic compounds of biological interest.

From similar laboratory experiments made by P. H. Abelson (1956) and by Pavlovskaya and A. G. Pasinsky (1957) in the USSR, it has been established that amino acids can be produced by passing an electrical discharge (simulating lightning discharges in the Earth's primitive atmosphere) through various gas mixtures other than those used by Urey and Miller. Provided the gaseous system has overall reducing characteristics, amino acids are always formed. Other experiments have shown that amino acids can even be formed in aqueous solutions.

As life evolved on Earth, it appears certain that later stages took place in a liquid water environment. This is evidenced by the presence of large amounts of water in all living organisms and the fact that the calcium/potassium ratio in seawater and blood is roughly similar. Furthermore the earliest organisms would have required the protection of the oceans from the damaging solar ultraviolet radiation. It seems likely that the primitive organisms in the oceans started to obtain hydrogen necessary for the synthesis of amino acids and other organic molecules by dissociating water using light energy. This is an important stage in the evoluton of life since free oxygen was released into the atmosphere. Once oxygen and then ozone built up in the atmosphere, the land was effectively shielded from solar ultraviolet. At this stage organisms appear to have emerged from the sea and colonized land.

Laboratory experiments have shown that amino acids and nucleic acids could have been synthesized in a reducing atmosphere of hydrogen, methane, ammonia, and water vapor. It is now believed that the Earth originally had such an atmosphere when life originated.

ANCIENT SUPERCONTINENTS

American scientists of the Environmental Science Services Administration reported in 1969 that they had established that Australia and Antarctica, which are now separated by about 2,000 miles of water, were once part of an ancient supercontinent.

The scientists, Walter Sproll and Dr. Robert S. Dietz, having processed oceanographic data obtained in 1967 by U.S. and Australian scientists during a global cruise of the Coast and Geodetic Survey Ship *Oceanographer*, relate that there was a fit between the two continents.

Sproll and Dietz are supporters of the continental-drift theory: that the continents constantly drift about 1–6 in. each year in the earth's mantle—the part of the earth's interior that rests between the molten central core and the crust. Among the scientists who espouse this theory, some believe that there was once a single supercontinent they call Pangaea; others, including Sproll and Dietz, contend that there were two supercontinents, which they refer to as Gondwana and Laurasia.

Supporters of the two-continent theory believe that Gondwana was composed of Australia, Antarctica, Africa, India, South America, Madagascar, and various submerged fragments, while Laurasia is thought to have consisted of North America and Eurasia.

It was generally believed of the two continents that southern Australia was once linked with another land mass, but opinions differed as to which one. Antarctica was the popular choice, but some thought it was Madagascar; others contended that it was the east coast of Africa, while still others believed it to have been the southwestern coast of South America.

Sproll and Dietz reported that their study shows that the south coast of Australia once joined Antarctica and identifies the exact position of fit: the SE end of Australia —including Tasmania—fitted into Antarctica's Ross Sea, while the SW end reached to just off Antarctica's Knox Coast; the concave Great Bight of Australia fitted against the convex outline of Wilkes Land.

"Recent geophysical findings on the ocean floor have demonstrated to the satisfaction of most earth scientists that the continents were once together," the ESSA scientists said. "About 200 to 250 million years ago, they commenced to separate and slowly drifted to their present scattered locations around the globe. One of the last units to be sundered—the Australia-Antarctica split—may have occurred as late as 40 million years ago.

The fit of continents is not the only evidence of continental drift. There is a very significant fit of rock formations and other geological structures in landmasses now separated by oceans. Studies of the past positions of the magnetic poles also indicate relative movement between continents. Again the scattered distribution of certain animals and plants in the distant past as well as that of ancient climatic zones can only be satisfactorily explained by continental drift: the discovery in Antarctica of a fossilized bone of an extinct amphibian points to a much milder Antarctic climate in the past.

Continental drift is now explained in terms of plate tectonics. The earth's outer shell is divided into at least 15 rigid rock segments, known as plates, that extend downward through the earth's crust and float on a semi-molten layer of the upper mantle. Seven of the plates are of major size and in most cases carry a continental landmass with surrounding ocean floor and island arcs. The plates are slowly moving relative to each other, driven by powerful forces within the earth's mantle. The movements of the plates have produced the present continent locations. At their boundaries plates are either slowly separating with new material added from the mantle, are converging with one plate being ground down and consumed under another, or are gliding past each other. Almost all earthquake, volcanic, and mountain-building activity closely follows these boundaries and is related to movements between them.

THE CONTINENTS

Name	Area (in square miles)	Percent of World's Land	Highest Point (in feet)	Lowest Point (in feet)
Asia	17,129,000	29.7	Mount Everest (29,028), Nepal-China	Dead Sea (1,296 below sea level), Israel-Jordan
Africa	11,707,000	20.0	Kibo (19,340), a peak of Mount Kilimanjaro, Tanzania	Lake Assal, Djibouti (510 below sea level)
North America	9,363,000	16.3	Mount McKinley (20,320), Alaska	Death Valley (282 below sea level), California
South America	6,886,000	12.0	Aconcagua (22,831), Argentina	Salinas Grandes (131 below sea level), Valdés Pen., Argentina
Europe	4,057,000	7.0	El'brus (18,510), USSR	Caspian Sea (92 below sea level), USSR
Australia	2,942,000	5.1	Mount Kosciusko (7,316), New South Wales	Lake Eyre (52 below sea level), South Australia
Antarctica	5,500,000	9.6	Vinson Massif (16,864)	Sea level

PREHISTORIC CREATURES

Allosaurus: This predator of 125 million years ago was the giant of its day: 34-feet long, more than eight feet high, and with a reach of about 15 feet above the ground. It had a massive skull that was nearly a yard long and a lower jaw hinged far back, enabling it to swallow food in unchewed lumps. Allosaurus remains have been found in Utah, Wyoming, and other Rocky Mountain states.

Anatosaurus (Trachodon): This 30-foot, duck-billed dinosaur lived in North America about 100 million years ago. It had a long narrow skull, a ducklike bill, and at the back of the jaws up to 2,000 grinding teeth, which were continuously replaced as they wore out. The anatosaurus could swim and wade, as evidenced by its webbed feet and deep oarlike tail.

Apatosaurus (Brontosaurus): This quadruped dinosaur probably grew to more than 70 feet in length and 30 tons in weight. Because of its size, the apatosaurus (as well as the brachiosaurus) had a huge pelvis and long, heavy shoulder blades. It had a short but deep body, a long neck, a massive tail, and a relatively tiny brain weighing about one pound. The apatosaurus was herbivorous and semiaquatic; as its nostrils were situated high on its head it could stand almost fully submerged. It lived about 125 million years ago in Colorado, Wyoming, Texas, and other Western states.

Archaeopteryx: Appearing about 150 million years ago, the archaeopteryx was the earliest known bird and was about the size of our crow. Although it had feathers, its bony tail, toothed jaws, and the claws on its forelimbs were reptilian. But its hindlimbs were birdlike, thus it could walk and run like a chicken. The archaeopteryx was probably warm-blooded, had weak flying muscles, and a gliding flight.

Baluchitherium: The largest land mammal ever to have lived. Found in Oligocene (circa 28–30 million years ago) deposits of Western and Central Asia, it was over 16 feet tall and weighed several tons; its head alone was over 4 feet long. Baluchitherium was related to the modern rhinoceros, but unlike the rhino it had no horns, long limbs, and a long neck, which would have suited it for swift running and browsing on leaves on the higher branches of trees.

Brachiosaurus: Ranging from 60 to 80 feet in length and weighing up to 80 tons, the brachiosaurus was one of the largest land animals that ever lived. The dinosaur's front legs were massive; consequently, its shoulders were high and sloped giraffe-fashion to the hips. Since its nostrils were located on a raised area of the head, the creature could breathe while standing in deep water. The brachiosaurus, which fed on vegetation, lived in Colorado, adjacent areas, and eastern Africa more than 125 million years ago.

Camptosaurus: Appearing in North America about 125 million years ago, the camptosaurus ranged between four and 15 feet in length. It had strong hind limbs; small, stout forelimbs; and a broad hand with full fingers. Its femur was curved, suggesting that this dinosaur sometimes walked on all fours. The camptosaurus was a nonpredatory planteater, with a flat, beak-like mouth.

Coelacanth: This subgroup of lobe-finned fishes ranged in weight from 125 to 150 pounds and were strong, armed with sharp teeth, and active. Early coelacanths were freshwater fish, but later forms were marine. They first appeared about 350 million years ago and were thought to have become extinct about 65 million years ago. However, in 1938 a fisherman caught a 4½-foot coelacanth off the coast of South Africa, and since then several other specimens have been caught.

Compsognathus: This dinosaur was no larger than a big fowl, and two-thirds of its body was neck and tail. Its toes were long and clawed, and its small jaws were lined with sharp teeth. This slender bipedal creature preyed on small reptiles, on the Baltic coast of what is now Germany, about 125 million years ago.

Eohippus (Hyracotherium): As its name implies, the "dawn (eo) horse (hippus)" was the earliest-known horse, appearing about 60 million years ago on the Great Plains of North America. The species varied from 10 to 20 inches high; all of these horses had four toes on each front foot and three on each hind foot. The eohippus was lightly built; its hindquarters were high and its simple teeth were suited for browsing on leaves. Some species of the eohippus migrated to Europe about 50 million years ago, becoming ancestors of the Old World horse. By the time that the Indians reached North America, the New World horse had become extinct.

Hesperornis: This flightless water bird ranged from Europe to North America about 100 million years ago. The hesperornis had an elongated body, about 6 feet long, with feet that enabled it to swim. It had a long bill, possibly toothed, and preyed on fish. Although its ancestors probably had wings, those of the hesperornis were useless evolutionary remnants.

Iguanodon: This genus of herbivorous dinosaurs varied in length from 15 to 30 feet and reached a height of 15 feet. All specimens had narrow bodies. They walked on hind feet, which had three large toes and one small one, and used their long heavy tails for balancing. Their small "forefeet" were five-fingered and had a thumb that was shaped into a bony spike. Iguanodon remains have been found in Europe and North Africa; the genus flourished between 100 and 140 million years ago.

Kronosaurus: Similar to the sperm whale of today, the kronosaurus paddled through Australian seas about 70 million years ago. Its neck was comparatively short, and its elongated skull measured 12 feet. The kronosaurus had large eyes and temporal openings, nostrils in front of the eyes, an almost solid palate, and long sharp teeth.

Lystrosaurus: A member of the dicynodont group of mammal-like reptiles, this animal is dated from the early Triassic Age (circa 220 million years ago) of both South Africa and Asia. It is believed that the dicynodonts may in general have preferred to live in marshy country, but Lystrosaurus is the only one which may have been aquatic to any extent. All dicynodonts were herbivorous and were the most common land animals of their time.

Megatherium: The largest of the extinct giant ground sloths, it flourished in both North and South America during the Pleistocene (circa 1.5 million to 10,000 years ago). This early mammal was slightly larger than the modern elephant and possessed extremely massive limbs. Its teeth grew continually throughout life and were adapted for a leaf-eating diet. It had a short, massive neck and tail, but a relatively long trunk. Its hands possessed powerful claws, which probably served to draw branches down towards its extensible tongue; the animal appears to have walked on the outside of its knuckles.

Pteranodon: This flying reptile lived between 85 and 100 million years ago, ranging from present-day Kansas to Europe and possibly around the world. Its body was small, bulking to about that of a small turkey. Its jaws formed a long toothless beak, and the back of the skull extended into a bony crest that was between about four and six feet long. The pteranodon's large wingspread, about 25 feet, and pelicanlike gular pouch gave it a most unreptilian appearance.

Stegosaurus: This "plated dinosaur" was a quadruped, about 20 feet long and weighing about 2 tons. It had short forelegs, two rows of bony plates down its back, and long pointed spikes on its tail. The brain of the stegosaurus, about the size of a walnut, weighed only about 2½ ounces. The bony plates, together with its tail spikes, may have been used for defense against predators; alternatively they may have functioned as heat exchangers. This herbivorous dinosaur roamed the American West about 125 million years ago.

Triceratops: This dinosaur was also herbivorous and also lived in the American West, about 100 million years ago. The head of the triceratops was about eight feet long and sheltered a two-pound brain. Its body, which was about 20 feet long, was bulky and shaped like a barrel. The dinosaur's four legs were of equal size. The name *triceratops* is derived from the creature's three horns: one on the nose and one over each eye.

Tyrannosaurus: The "tyrant" dinosaur was a flesh-eater and well equipped for predation with six-inch teeth that were housed in a four-foot-long skull. Existing for a short time, about 85 million years ago, this dinosaur was 40 feet long and 19 feet tall. It weighed up to eight tons. Its forelimbs were reduced to such a degree that it is believed that they were not utilitarian; therefore, the creature's predation was probably restricted to its use of its jaws and powerful clawed hind legs.

Uintatherium: The uintatheres were primitive rhinoceros-like ungulates of late Paleocene and Eocene times (circa 50 to 60 million years ago), and are distantly related to the elephants. Their long, low skulls were characterized by a number of large, horn-like bony swellings; they possessed large, saber-like upper canine teeth which were presumably very effective as defensive weapons.

FOSSIL MAN

Remains of what may be man's earliest ancestors were found on two continents in 1934 and in 1961. Fossil bones from sites in India and Africa indicate that these creatures (Ramapithecus and Kenyapithecus), in spite of having lived more than 14 million years ago, were more manlike than apelike.

However, the oldest bones to be placed with certainty in the category "Hominidae," or the family of Man, are about 4 million years old. Hominid remains have been found in several locations. Many archaeologists have given their finds a different name (e.g., Zinjanthropus, Paranthropus, Plesianthropus), but today we recognize that all of these individuals who lived between 2 million and 4 million B.C. have the same general characteristics and can be called by the general genus name, Australopithecus, or "southern ape."

The different genus and species names are given in the chart below to indicate that they probably represent different branches of the same group.

The brain of Australopithecus was about the same size as that of a modern large ape—half that of modern man. In spite of his apelike traits, Australopithecus walked erect.

Some of the specimens found by L. S. B. Leakey in 1960 have been given the classification name Homo, the genus to which modern man belongs. Homo habilis was only 3½ to 4½ feet tall but had a larger brain and more manlike features.

Homo erectus, sometimes called Pithecanthropus or "ape man" (e.g., Java Man, Peking Man), was probably the direct ancestor of modern man, Homo sapiens. He appeared at least 1½ million years ago and was structurally similar to us although he lacked a forehead and possessed a bony shelf over his eyes and a small chin. He made tools and knew how to use fire.

The next major evolutionary advance came approximately 100,000 years ago with the appearance of Neanderthal Man; he, too, was short in stature and had low brows, but his brain was equal in size to that of modern man, and he possessed a language. He was not a settler, but instead hunted widely.

At about 35,000 B.C., as the Neanderthals were disappearing, modern man, Homo sapiens (e.g., Cromagnon), appeared. He was taller and more delicate, and he fashioned intricate tools and clothing and drew paintings of his environment. However, it was not until 9,000 years ago that Homo sapiens became a domesticator of animals, a farmer, and a settler.

MAJOR FOSSIL MAN DISCOVERIES

Year	Scientific Name	Period and Estimated Date (B.C.)	Location	Remains	Discoverer
1848	Homo calpicus (Gibraltar Man)	Upper Pleistocene 50,000–120,000	Forbes Quarry, Gibraltar	skull	Lieutenant Flint
1856	Homo neanderthalensis (Neanderthal Man)	Upper Pleistocene 50,000	Neander Valley, nr. Dusseldorf, Germany	skull, bones	Johann C. Fuhlrott
1868	Homo sapiens (Cromagnon)	Upper Pleistocene 35,000	Cromagnon, France	4 skeletons, 1 fetus	Louis Lartet
1891	Pithecanthropus erectus (Java Man)	Lower Pleistocene 700,000	Trinil, Java	skull, femur	Eugene Dubois
1907	Homo heidelbergensis (Heidelberg Man)	Middle Pleistocene 450,000	Mauer, nr. Heidelberg, Germany	lower jaw	Otto Schoetensack
1909–13	Eoanthropus dawsoni* (Piltdown Man)	Holocene (Recent)	Piltdown, Sussex, England	composite skull	Charles Dawson
1924	Australopithecus africanus (Southern Ape)	Pleistocene c. 3,000,000	Taung, South Africa	skull	M. de Bruyn
1921–37	Sinanthropus pekinensis (Peking Man)	Middle Pleistocene 450,000	Choukoutien, nr. Peking, China	skulls, teeth, bones	Davidson Black
1929–34	Mt. Carmel Man	Upper Pleistocene 500,000	Tabūn and Skhūl, Israel	parts of 16 skeletons	Dorothy Garrod
1934	Ramapithecus	Upper Miocene 10,000,000	NW India	parts of jaws	G. E. Lewis
1935–55	Early Homo sapiens (Swanscombe Skull)	Middle Pleistocene 250,000	Swanscombe, Kent, England	parts of skull	A. T. Marston
1938	Paranthropus robustus	Lower Pleistocene c. 2,000,000	Kromdraai, Transvaal	skull part, bones	G. Terblanche
1947	Australopithecus prometheus (Southern Ape)	Lower Pleistocene c. 3,000,000	Makapansgat, Transvaal	skull fragments	J. Kitching
1953–60	Neanderthal Man	Upper Pleistocene 50,000	Shanidar, Iraq	skeletons	Ralph Solecki
1959	Zinjanthropus boisei (Nutcracker Man)	Lower Pleistocene c. 1,750,000	Olduvai, Tanzania	skull	Mary D. Leakey
1960	Homo habilis	Lower Pleistocene c. 1,750,000	Olduvai, Tanzania	skull fragments	Louis S. B. Leakey
1961	Kenyapithecus wickeri	Middle Miocene c. 14,000,000	Fort Ternan, Kenya	palate, teeth	Louis S. B. Leakey
1965	Homo erectus palaeo-hungaricus	Middle Pleistocene 450,000	Vertesszollos, Hungary	occipital bone	Laszlo Vertes
1967–72	Australopithecus boisei, Australopithecus africanus, Homo habilis	Upper Pliocene 4,000,000–1,500,000	Omo Valley, Ethiopa	various remains	Y. Coppens, F. C. Howell, and teams
1968–80	Australopithecus boisei, Homo habilis, Homo erectus	Pleistocene 2,200,000–1,300,000	Koobi Fora (formerly East Rudolf), Kenya	150 specimens	Richard Leakey and team
1971	Pithecanthropine? (Arago Man)	Middle Pleistocene 3,000,000	Arago, France	skull	H. de Lumley
1975–80	Australopithecus afarensis	Upper Pliocene c. 3,500,000	Laetoli, Tanzania	footprints, jaws, teeth, 8 adults, 3 children	Mary Leakey and team

* Exposed as a fraud in 1953 by radioactivity tests.

MAXIMUM LIFE-SPANS OF ANIMALS
The list below reflects the maximum life-span of various animals while in captivity.

Years	Animal	Years	Animal	Years	Animal	Years	Animal
190	Giant Tortoise	37	Chimpanzee	25	Tiger	17	Goat
138	Eastern Box Turtle	36	Toad	25	Zebra	16	Bullfrog
84	Elephant	33	Gorilla	23	Leopard	16	Cheetah
80	Freshwater Oyster	31	Gibbon	23	Domestic Cat	16	Kangaroo
68	Owl	31	Grizzly Bear	22	Domestic Dog	15	Pronghorn
55	Eagle	30	Dolphin	20	Cougar	15	Reindeer
51	Pelican	30	Lion	20	Cow	15	Timber Wolf
50	Domestic Horse	28	Giraffe	20	Moose	14	Chicken
46	Jackass	28	Sea Lion	20	Rattlesnake	14	Coyote
45	Baboon	25	Black Bear	20	Sheep	13	Rabbit
41	Polar Bear	25	Camel	19	Beaver	10	Pig

THE ANIMAL KINGDOM

This classification system of living animals is one of many types available. Subphyla are included only for phylum Chordata, subclasses only for class Mammalia, and orders only for Eutheria in class Mammalia.

SUBKINGDOM PROTOZOA—one-celled animals
- **Phylum Protozoa**—acellular animals (protozoans)
  - Class Mastigophora (Flagellata)—flagellates
  - Class Sarcodina (Rhizopoda)—sarcodines (Amoeba)
  - Class Sporozoa—spore-forming parasites
  - Class Ciliophora (Ciliata)—ciliates (Paramecium)
SUBKINGDOM MESOZOA—certain wormlike parasites
- **Phylum Mesozoa**—mesozoans
SUBKINGDOM PARAZOA—pore-perforated bodies
- **Phylum Porifera**—sponges
  - Class Calcarea—chalky sponges
  - Class Hexactinellida—glass sponges
  - Class Demospongiae—horny sponges
SUBKINGDOM METAZOA—multi-cellular animals
- **Phylum Coelenterata (Cnidaria)**—coelenterates
  - Class Hydrozoa—hydroids (Portuguese man-of-war)
  - Class Scyphozoa—jellyfish
  - Class Anthozoa—sea anemones and corals
- **Phylum Ctenophora**—ctenophores
  - Class Tentaculata—with tentacles
  - Class Nuda—without tentacles
- **Phylum Platyhelminthes**—flatworms
  - Class Turbellaria—free-living flatworms
  - Class Trematoda—flukes
  - Class Cestoda—tapeworms
  - Class Gnathostomulida—gnathostomulids
- **Phylum Nemertea**—nemertines (ribbon worms)
  - Class Anopla—unarmed proboscis
  - Class Enopla—armed proboscis
- **Phylum Acanthocephala**—thorny-headed worms
- **Phylum Aschelminthes**—aschelminths
  - Class Rotifera (Rotatoria)—rotifers
  - Class Gastrotricha—gastrotrichs
  - Class Kinorhyncha (Echinodera)—kinorhynchs
  - Class Nematoda—nematodes (roundworms)
  - Class Nematomorpha—horsehair worms
  - Class Priapulida—priapulids
- **Phylum Sipunculida**—sipunculids
- **Phylum Bryozoa (Ectoprocta)**—bryozoans
  - Class Phylactolaemata—fresh-water
  - Class Gymnolaemata—salt-water
- **Phylum Entoprocta**—entoprocts
- **Phylum Phoronida**—phoronids
- **Phylum Brachiopoda**—brachiopods
  - Class Inarticulata—without teeth
  - Class Articulata—with teeth
- **Phylum Mollusca**—mollusks
  - Class Amphineura—chitons
  - Class Monoplacophora—monoplacophs
  - Class Gastropoda—gastropods (snails, slugs)
  - Class Scaphopoda—tooth shells
  - Class Bivalvia (Lamellibranchia)—bivalve mollusks
  - Class Cephalopoda—cephalopods (squids, octopi)
- **Phylum Echiurida**—echiuroid marine worms
- **Phylum Annelida**—segmented worms
  - Class Polychaeta—sand-and bristleworms
  - Class Mysostomaria—mysostomarians
  - Class Oligochaeta—earthworms
  - Class Hirudinea—leeches
  - Class Archiannelida—no external segments
- **Phylum Onychophora**—velvet worms
- **Phylum Tardigrada**—tardigrades (water bears)

Phylum Pentastomida—tongue worms
Phylum Arthropoda—arthropods
- Class Merostomata—horseshoe & king crabs
- Class Arachnida—spiders, ticks, mites, scorpions
- Class Pycnogonida (Pantopoda)—sea spiders
- Class Crustacea—crustaceans
- Class Chilopoda—centipedes
- Class Diplopoda—millipedes
- Class Pauropoda—pauropods
- Class Symphyla—symphylids (garden centipede)
- Class Insecta—insects

Phylum Chaetognatha—arrowworms
Phylum Pogonophora—beard worms
Phylum Hemichordata—hemichordates
- Class Enteropneusta—acorn worms
- Class Pterobranchia—pterobranchs
- Class Planctosphaeroidea—planctosphaera

Phylum Echinodermata—echinoderms
- Class Echinoidea—sea urchins, sand dollars
- Class Holothuroidea—sea cucumbers
- Class Crinoidea—crinoids (sea lilies, feather stars)
- Class Asteroidea—starfish
- Class Ophiuroidea—brittle & basket stars

Phylum Chordata—chordates
- Subphylum Urochordata (Tunicata)—tunicates
  - Class Ascidiacea—sea squirts
  - Class Thaliacea—salps
  - Class Larvacea—larvaceans
- Subphylum Cephalochordata—lancelets
- Subphylum Vertebrata (Craniata)—vertebrates
  - Class Agnatha—jawless vertebrates
  - Class Chondrichthyes (Elasmobranchii)—cartilaginous fish (sharks, rays)
  - Class Osteichthyes—bony fish
  - Class Amphibia—amphibians
  - Class Reptilia—reptiles
  - Class Aves—birds
  - Class Mammalia—mammals
    - Subclass Prototheria—egg laying mammals (monotremes)
    - Subclass Theria—viviparous (live-bearing) mammals
      - Infraclass Metatheria—pouched mammals (marsupials)
      - Infraclass Eutheria—placental mammals
        - Order Insectivora—moles, shrews, hedgehogs
        - Order Dermoptera—flying lemurs (colugos)
        - Order Chiroptera—bats
        - Order Primates—lemurs, monkeys, apes, man
        - Order Edentata—sloths, anteaters, armadillos
        - Order Pholidota—pangolins
        - Order Lagomorpha—rabbits, hares, pikas
        - Order Rodentia—rodents
        - Order Cetacea—whales, dolphins, porpoises
        - Order Carnivora—carnivores (dogs, cats)
        - Order Pinnipedia—seals, sea lions, walruses
        - Order Tubulidentata—aardvark
        - Order Proboscidea—elephants
        - Order Hyracoidea—hyraxes (coneys)
        - Order Sirenia—sea cows (manatee, dugong)
        - Order Perissodactyla—odd-toe ungulates (horses, zebras, tapirs, rhinoceroses)
        - Order Artiodactyla—even-toed ungulates (cattle, deer, sheep, goats, pigs, camels)

ANIMAL GESTATION PERIODS AND LITTERS

SOURCE: Grace Davall, Assistant Curator, Mammals and Birds, New York Zoological Society

Animal	Gestation Period	Litter Size
AMERICAN BUFFALO (BISON)	270–285 days	1
BABOON	6 months	1–2
BLACK BEAR	7 months	1–4
CAMEL	12–13 months	1
CAT	63 days	1–6
CHIMPANZEE	226 days	1–2
CHINCHILLA	105–111 days	1–4
COW	280 days	1–2
DEER (WHITE-TAIL)	7 months	2
DOG	61 days	1–12
DOLPHIN	9 months	1
ELEPHANT	21 months	1
FOX	49–55 days	1–8
GERBIL	14 days	1–7
GIRAFFE	14–15 months	1
GORILLA	8½ months	1
HAMSTER	16–19 days	2–12
HORSE	11 months	1
KANGAROO	38–39 days	1–2
LION	108 days	1–4
MACAQUE	160–170 days	1–2
MINK	48–51 days	4–8
MOUSE	19–21 days	1–9
OPOSSUM	12–13 days	4–13
OTTER	9½–12½ months	1–4
PIG	112–115 days	4–6
RABBIT	1 month	1–13
RACCOON	63 days	1–6
SHEEP	150 days	1–3
SKUNK	52 days	4–7
SQUIRREL	44 days	2–5
TIGER	100–108 days	2–4
WOLF	60–63 days	1–13
YAK	just over 9 months	1
ZEBRA	11–12 months	1

ENDANGERED WILDLIFE   Source: Office of Endangered Species, U.S. Dept. of the Interior

Anyone wishing to know the status of any animal should contact the Office of Endangered Species, Dept. of the Interior, Washington, D.C. 20240. Below is a selection from official List of Endangered Fauna, including the 109 native to the United States.

BONY FISHES (Class *Osteichthyes/Phylum Chordata*)
Sturgeons & Paddlefishes (Order: *Acipenseriformes):* 1. Sturgeon, Shortnose.

Trout, Salmon & Relatives (Order: *Salmoniformes*): 1. Ala Balik; 2. Cisco, Longjaw; 3. Trout, Arizona (Apache); 4. Trout, Gila; 5. Trout, Greenback cutthroat; 6. Trout, Lahontan cutthroat; 7. Trout, Paiute cutthroat.

Carps, Minnows & Relatives (Order: *Cypriniformes*): 1. Ayumodoki; 2. Bonytail, Pahranagat; 3. Chub, Humpback; 4. Chub, Mohave; 5. Cicek; 6. Cui-ui; 7. Dace, Kendall Warm Springs; 8. Dace, Moapa; 9. Squawfish, Colorado River; 10. Tanago, Miyako; 11. Woundfin.

Sticklebacks (Order: *Solenichthyiformes):* 1. Stickleback, Unarmored threespine.

Silversides, Topminnows & Relatives (Order: *Atheriniformes*): 1. Gambusia, Big Bend; 2. Gambusia, Clear Creek; 3. Gambusia, Pecos; 4. Killifish, Pahrump; 5. Pupfish, Comanche Springs; 6. Pupfish, Devil's Hole; 7. Pupfish, Owens River; 8. Pupfish, Tecopa; 9. Pupfish, Warm Springs; 10. Topminnow, Gila.

Perches & Relatives (Order: *Perciformes*): 1. Darter, Fountain; 2. Darter, Maryland; 3. Darter, Okaloosa; 4. Darter, Watercress; 5. Pike, Blue.

AMPHIBIANS (Class *Amphibia/Phylum Chordata*)
Salamanders (Order: *Urodela*): 1. Salamander, Desert slender; 2. Salamander, Santa Cruz long-toed; 3. Salamander, Texas blind. **Frogs** (Order: *Anura*): 1. Frog, Stephen Island; 2. Frog, Israel painted; 3. Toad, Houston.

REPTILES (Class *Reptilia/Phylum Chordata*)
Turtles (Order: *Testudinata*): 1. Terrapin, River (Tuntong); 2. Tortoise, Galapagos; 3. Tortoise, Madgascar radiated; 4. Tortoise, Short-necked (swamp); 5. Turtle, Aquatic box; 6. Turtle, Atlantic Ridley; 7. Turtle, Hawksbill; 8. Turtle, Leatherback.

Crocodiles (Order: *Crocodilia*): 1. Alligator, American; 2. Crocodile, Cuban; 3. Crocodile, Morelet's.

Lizards & Snakes (Order: *Squamata*): 1. Lizard, Day gecko; 2. Lizard, Round Island day gecko; 3. Lizard, Anegada ground iguana; 4. Lizard, Barrington land iguana; 5. Lizard, Blunt-nosed leopard; 6. Snake, Jamaica boa; 7. Snake, Puerto Rican boa; 8. Snake, San Francisco garter.

BIRDS (Class *Aves/Phylum Chordata*)
Albatrosses, Petrels & Relatives (Order: *Procellariiformes*): 1. Albatross, Short-tailed; 2. Cahow (Bermuda petrel); 3. Petrel, Hawaiian dark-rumped.

Pelicans (Order: *Pelecaniformes*): 1. Pelican, Brown.
Ducks, Geese, Swans & Relatives (Order: *Anseriformes*): 1. Duck, Hawaiian (koloa); 2. Duck, Laysan; 3. Duck, Mexican; 4. Duck, White-winged wood; 5. Goose, Aleutian Canada; 6. Goose, Hawaiian (nene).

Eagles, Falcons, Vultures & Relatives (Order: *Falconiformes*): 1. Condor, Andean; 2. Condor, California; 3. Eagle, Monkey-eating; 4. Eagle, Southern bald; 5. Eagle, Spanish imperial; 6. Falcon, American peregrine; 7. Falcon, Arctic peregrine; 8. Goshawk, Christmas Island; 9. Hawk, Anjouan Island sparrow; 10. Hawk, Galapagos; 11. Hawk, Hawaiian (io); 12. Kite, Florida Everglade.

Pheasants, Grouse, Curassows & Relatives (Order: *Galliformes*): 1. Curassow, Red-billed; 2. Curassow, Trinidad white-headed; 3. Guan, Horned; 4. Megapode, Maleo; 5. Megapode, LaPerouse's; 6. Pheasant, Bar-tailed; 7. Pheasant, Blyth's tragopan; 8. Pheasant, Brown-eared; 9. Pheasant, Cabot's tragopan; 10. Pheasant, Chinese monal; 11. Pheasant, Edward's; 12. Pheasant, Imperial; 13. Pheasant, Mikado; 14. Pheasant, Palawan peacock; 15. Pheasant, Sclater's monal; 16. Pheasant, Swinhoe's; 17. Pheasant, Western tragopan; 18. Pheasant, White-eared; 19. Prairie Chicken, Attwater's greater; 20. Quail, Masked bobwhite.

Cranes, Rails, Bustards & Relatives (Order: *Gruiformes*): 1. Bustard, Great Indian; 2. Coot, Hawaiian; 3. Crane, Hooded; 4. Crane, Japanese; 5. Crane, Mississippi sandhill; 6. Crane, Siberian white; 7. Crane, Whooping; 8. Gallinule, Hawaiian; 9. Kagu (rail); 10. Rail, Auckland Island; 11. Rail, California clapper; 12. Rail, Light-footed clapper; 13. Rail, Yuma clapper; 14. Wanderer, Plains; 15. Takahe.

Plovers, Snipes, Gulls & Relatives (Order: *Charadriiformes):* 1. Curlew, Eskimo; 2. Gull, Audouin's; 3. Stilt, Hawaiian; 4. Tern, California least.

Pigeons, Doves, Sandgrouse & Relatives (Order: *Columbiformes*): 1. Dove, Cloven-feathered; 2. Dove, Grenada; 3. Dove, Palau ground; 4. Pigeon, Azores wood; 5. Pigeon, Chatham Island; 6. Pigeon, Puerto Rican plain.

Parrots (Order: *Psittaciformes):* 1. Parrot, Puerto Rican; 2. Parakeet, Splendid.

Owls (Order: *Strigiformes):* 1. Owl, Anjouan scops; 2. Owl, Palau; 3. Owl, New Zealand laughing.

Goatsuckers & Relatives (Order: *Caprimulgiformes*): 1. Whip-poor-will, Puerto Rican.

Woodpeckers, Puffbirds, Barbets & Relatives (Order: *Piciformes):* 1. Woodpecker, Imperial; 2. Woodpecker, Ivory-billed; 3. Woodpecker, Red-cockaded.

Perching Birds—Sparrows, Larks, Thrushes & Relatives (Order: *Passeriformes):* 1. Bulbul, Mauritius olivaceous; 2. Crow, Hawaiian (alala); 3. Cuckoo-Shrike, Mauritius; 4. Cuckoo-Shrike, Reunion; 5. Finch, Sao Miguel bullfinch; 6. Flycatcher, Chatham Island robin; 7. Flycatcher, Eyrean grass-wren; 8. Flycatcher, Grey-necked rock-fowl; 9. Flycatcher, Palau fantail; 10. Flycatcher, Seychelles black; 11. Flycatcher, Tahiti; 12. Flycatcher, Western bristlebird; 13. Flycatcher, White-necked rock-fowl; 14. Flycatcher (Tyrant), Euler's; 15. Flycatcher (Tyrant), Scarlet-breasted robin; 16. Flycatcher (Tyrant), Tinian monarch; 17. Grackle, Slender-billed; 18. Honeycreeper, Akiapolaau; 19. Honeycreeper, Crested (akohekohe); 20. Honeycreeper, Hawaii akepa (akepa); 21. Honeycreeper, Kauai akialoa; 22. Honeycreeper, Maui parrotbill; 23. Honeycreeper, Maui akepa (akepuie); 24. Honeycreeper, Molokai creeper (kakawahie); 25. Honeycreeper, Oahu creeper (alauwahio); 26. Honeycreeper, Ou; 27. Honeycreeper, Palila; 28. Honeycreepers, Laysan & Nihoa finches; 29. Honeycreepers, Kauai & Maui nukupuus; 30. Honey-eater, Helmeted; 31. Honey-eater, Kauai Oo (oo aa); 32. Scrub-bird, Noisy; 33. Sparrow, Cape Sable; 34. Sparrow, Dusky seaside; 35. Sparrow, Santa Barbara song; 36. Starling, Ponape Mountain; 37. Starling, Rothschild's (myna); 38. Thrasher, White-breasted; 39. Thrush, Large Kauai; 40. Thrush, Molokai (olomau); 41. Thrush, Seychelles magpie-robin; 42. Thrush, Small Kauai (puaiohi); 43. Thrush, Western whipbird; 44. Warbler, Nihoa millerbird; 45. Warbler, Bachman's; 46. Warbler, Kirtland's.

MAMMALS (Class *Mammalia/Phylum Chordata*)
Bats (Order: *Chiroptera*): 1. Bat, Indiana; 2. Bat, Hawaiian hoary.

Primates (Order: *Primates*): 1. Avahis; 2. Aye-aye; 3. Colobus, Red; 4. Colobus, Zanzibar red; 5. Gibbon, Kloss; 6. Gibbon, Pileated; 7. Gorilla; 8. Indris; 9. Langur, Douc; 10. Langur, Pagi Island; 11. Lemurs; 12. Lemurs, Gentle; 13. Lemurs, Sportive & Weasel; 14. Lemurs, Dwarf; 15. Lemurs, Mouse; 16. Lemurs, Forkmarked; 17. Macaque, Lion-tailed; 18. Mangabey, Tana River; 19. Marmoset, Goeldi's; 20. Monkey, Spider; 21. Monkey, Spider; 22. Orangutan; 23. Sifakas; 24. Tamarins, Golden-rumped; (Golden Marmosets); 25. Uakari.

Rodents (Order: *Rodentia*): 1. Rat, Morro Bay kangaroo; 2. Mouse, Salt marsh harvest; 3. Prairie dog, Utah; 4. Squirrel, Delmarva fox.

Whales, Dolphins & Porpoises (Order: *Cetacea*): 1. Whale, Blue; 2. Whale, Bowhead; 3. Whale, Finback; 4. Whale, Gray; 5. Whale, Humpback; 6. Whale, Right; 7. Whale, Sei; 8. Whale, Sperm.

Carnivores (Order: *Carnivora*): 1. Bear, Mexican grizzly; 2. Cat, Tiger; 3. Cheetah; 4. Cougar, Eastern; 5. Dog, Asiatic wild; 6. Ferret, Black-footed; 7. Fox, Northern kit; 8. Fox, San Joaquin kit; 9. Hyaena, Barbary; 10. Hyaena, Brown; 11. Jaguar; 12. Leopard; 13. Leopard, Formosan clouded; 14. Leopard, Snow; 15. Lion, Asiatic; 16. Lynx, Spanish; 17. Margay; 18. Marten, Formosan yellow-throated; 19. Ocelot; 20. Otter, Cameroon clawless; 21. Otter, Giant; 22. Otter, La Plata; 23. Panther, Florida; 24. Serval, Barbary; 25. Tiger; 26. Wolf, Eastern timber; 27. Wolf, Northern Rocky Mountain; 28. Wolf, Red; 29. Wolf, Maned.

Sirenians (Order: *Sirenia*): 1. Manatee, Florida.
Even-Toed Ungulates (Order: *Artiodactyla*): 1. Anoa; 2. Banteng; 3. Bison, Wood; 4. Deer, Columbian white-tailed; 5. Deer, Key; 6. Deer, Marsh; 7. Deer, McNeill's; 8. Deer, Swamp; 9. Gazelle, Cuviers; 10. Pronghorn, Sonoran; 11. Hartebeest, Swayne's; 12. Ibex, Pyrenean; 13. Impala, Black-faced.

LONG FOREIGN RIVERS

River	Empties into	Length (in miles)	River	Empties into	Length (in miles)
Amazon	Atlantic Ocean	3,915	Nile-Kagera	Mediterranean Sea	4,145
Amu-Dar'ya	Aral Sea	1,616	Ob'-Irtysh-Black Irtysh	Gulf of Ob' (Kara Sea)	3,362
Amur-Shilka-Onon	Tatar Strait	2,744	Oder	Baltic Sea	538
Angara	Yenisey River	1,135	Oka	Volga River	918
Araguaia	Tocantins River	1,367	Olenek	Laptev Sea	1,411
Athabasca	Lake Athabasca	765	Orange	Atlantic Ocean	1,350
Belaya	Kama River	889	Orinoco	Atlantic Ocean	1,600
Brahmaputra	Bay of Bengal	1,700	Ottawa	St. Lawrence River	790
Churchill	Hudson Bay	1,000	Paraguay	Paraná River	1,584
Congo (Zaire)	Atlantic Ocean	2,718	Paraná-La Plata	Atlantic Ocean	2,450
Cubango-Okovango	Okovango Swamps	994	Peace-Finlay	Slave River	1,195
Danube	Black Sea	1,775	Pechora	Pechora Sea	1,124
Darling	Murray River	1,160	Pilcomayo	Paraguay River	1,000
Dnieper	Black Sea	1,368	Po	Adriatic Sea	420
Dniester	Black Sea	876	Purus	Amazon River	1,995
Don	Sea of Azov	1,222	Rhine	North Sea	820
Dvina, Northern	White Sea	809	Rhone	Gulf of Lions	505
Ebro	Mediterranean Sea	565	Rio Grande	Gulf of Mexico	1,885
Elbe	North Sea	724	St. Lawrence	Gulf of St. Lawrence	1,900
Euphrates	Persian Gulf	1,700	Salween	Gulf of Martaban	1,770
Fraser	Strait of Georgia	850	São Francisco	Atlantic Ocean	1,811
Ganges	Bay of Bengal	1,550	Saskatchewan	Lake Winnipeg	1,205
Hwang Ho (Yellow)	Yellow Sea	2,877	Seine	English Channel	482
Indigirka	East Siberian Sea	1,228	Selenga	Lake Baykal	920
Indus	Arabian Sea	1,800	Si	South China Sea	1,650
Irrawaddy	Bay of Bengal	1,325	Sungari	Amur River	1,130
Japurá	Amazon River	1,500	Syr-Dar'ya—Naryn	Aral Sea	1,859
Kama	Volga River	1,262	Tagus (Tajo, Tejo)	Atlantic Ocean	565
Kasai	Congo River	1,338	Tigris	Euphrates River	1,181
Kolyma	East Siberian Sea	1,562	Tisza	Danube River	800
Lena	Laptev Sea	2,734	Tocantins	Pará River	1,677
Limpopo	Indian Ocean	995	Ural	Caspian Sea	1,509
Loire	Bay of Biscay	628	Uruguay	Río de La Plata	994
Mackenzie-Peace-Finlay	Beaufort Sea	2,635	Vistula	Gulf of Danzig	664
Madeira	Amazon River	2,013	Volga	Caspian Sea	2,194
Magdalena	Caribbean Sea	1,000	Volta	Atlantic Ocean	710
Mekong	South China Sea	2,610	Yangtze	East China Sea	3,434
Meuse	North Sea	590	Yellow (Hwang Ho)	Yellow Sea	2,877
Murray-Darling	Indian Ocean	2,310	Yenisey	Kara Sea	2,543
Negro	Amazon River	1,400	Yenisey-Angara	Kara Sea	3,100
Nelson-Saskatchewan	Hudson Bay	1,600	Yukon	Bering Sea	1,979
Niger	Gulf of Guinea	2,548	Zambezi	Indian Ocean	1,600

OCEANS AND SEAS

Ocean	Area (in square miles)	Percent of World's Water	Greatest Depth (in feet)	Sea	Area (in square miles)	Greatest Depth (in feet)
Pacific	64,186,000	46	Mariana Trench, off the Mariana Islands, 36,198	Caribbean	970,000	24,720
				Mediterranean Sea	969,000	16,896
				South China Sea	895,000	15,000
Atlantic	31,862,000	22.9	Puerto Rico Trench, (Milwaukee Deep), off Puerto Rico, 28,374	Bering Sea	875,000	15,800
				Gulf of Mexico	600,000	12,300
				Sea of Okhotsk	590,000	11,070
				East China Sea	482,000	9,500
				Sea of Japan	389,000	12,280
Indian	28,350,000	20.3	Java Trench, off Java, 25,344	Hudson Bay	317,500	846
				North Sea	222,000	2,200
Arctic	5,427,000	3.9	Eurasia Basin, north of Svalbard, 17,880	Black Sea	185,000	7,365
				Red Sea	169,000	7,200
				Baltic Sea	163,000	1,506

ELEMENTS IN SEAWATER

SOURCE: U.S. Office of Saline Water

Element	Milligrams per Kilogram*	Element	Milligrams per Kilogram*	Element	Milligrams per Kilogram*
Chlorine	18,980	Aluminum	0.5	Cesium	0.002
Sodium	10,561	Rubidium	0.2	Uranium	0.0015
Magnesium	1,272	Lithium	0.1	Molybdenum	0.0005
Sulfur	884	Phosphorus	0.001–0.10	Thorium	0.0005
Calcium	400	Barium	0.05	Cerium	0.0004
Potassium	380	Iodine	0.05	Silver	0.0003
Bromine	65	Arsenic	0.01–0.02	Vanadium	0.0003
Carbon	28	Iron	0.002–0.02	Lanthanum	0.0003
Strontium	13	Manganese	0.001–0.01	Yttrium	0.0003
Boron	4.6	Copper	0.001–0.01	Nickel	0.0001
Silicon	0.02–4.0	Zinc	0.005	Scandium	0.00004
Fluorine	1.4	Lead	0.004	Mercury	0.00003
Nitrogen (compound)	0.01–0.7	Selenium	0.004	Gold	0.000006

* Parts per million.

MAJOR GLACIERS OF THE WORLD

Based on statistics from "Fluctuation of Glaciers 1965-70," © IAHS/UNESCO, 1973, and other sources.

Name	Locality	*Area (sq. mi.)	*Length (mi.)
Aletsch	Swiss Alps	45	15
Amundsen	Antarctica	—	60
Baltoro	Asia (Karakoram)	290	35
Beardmore	Antarctica	130	100
Bering	Alaska	—	125
Bivachnyy	Asia (Pamir)	75	15
Chisana	Alaska	135	30
Columbia	Alaska	110	40
Denman	Antarctica	—	70
Fedchenko	Asia (Pamir)	350	45
Gangotri	Asia (Himalaya)	115	20
Garmo	Asia (Pamir)	60	15
Geographical Society	Asia (Pamir)	50	15
Grum-Grzhimaylo	Asia (Pamir)	60	25
Hispar	Asia (Karakoram)	240	35
Hofsjökull†	Iceland	260	—
Hubbard	Alaska-Yukon	—	75
Humboldt	Greenland	—	70
Inyl'chek, Yuzh.	Asia (Tien Shan)	110	40
Jostedalsbreen†	Norway	485	60
Kahiltna	Alaska	—	45
Lambert	Antarctica	—	270
Langjökull†	Iceland	265	40
Logan	Alaska-Yukon	—	70
Malaspina	Alaska-Yukon	1,350	75
Muir	Alaska	400	15
Muldrow	Alaska	735	45
Mýrdalsjökull†	Iceland	180	30
Nabesna	Alaska	775	50
Petermann	Greenland	—	90
Rennick	Antarctica	185	160
Rider	Greenland	125	—
Rimo	Asia (Karakoram)	200	30
Robert Scott	Antarctica	—	90
Shackleton	Antarctica	—	90
Shamrock	Alaska	40	15
Siachen	Asia (Karakoram)	450	50
Svartisen	Norway	200	20
Tasman	New Zealand	50	20
Temir-su	Asia (Tien Shan)	45	25
Totten	Antarctica	—	45
Triumvirate	Alaska	170	30
Vatnajökull†	Iceland	2,200	90
Zemu	Asia (Himalaya)	50	20
Zeravshan	Asia (Turkestan)	45	15

* Approximate, subject to continuous revision. † Icefield.

LARGE LAKES OF THE WORLD

Lake	Continent	Area (in sq. miles)	Length (in miles)	Max. Depth (in ft.)
Caspian Sea	Asia-Europe	143,243	746	3,264
Superior	N. America	31,700	383	1,301
Victoria	Africa	26,724	250	270
Aral Sea	Asia	25,676	266	256
Huron	N. America	23,010	247	748
Michigan	N. America	22,300	321	923
Tanganyika	Africa	12,650	420	4,700
Baykal	Asia	12,162	395	5,316
Great Bear	N. America	12,096	190	1,356
Nyasa (Malawi)	Africa	11,555	360	2,320
Great Slave	N. America	11,269	300	2,015
Chad	Africa	10,000–4,000*	175–125	25–15
Erie	N. America	9,910	241	209
Winnipeg	N. America	9,417	265	60
Ontario	N. America	7,340	193	775
Ladoga	Europe	7,104	124	738
Balkhash	Asia	7,027	376	87
Maracaibo	S. America	5,120	110	100
Bangweulu	Africa	4,500–1,900*	50	—
Tungting	Asia	4,500–1,500*	80	—
Onega	Europe	3,710	154	377
Eyre	Australia	3,500–0*	110	—
Titicaca	S. America	3,200	120	1,000
Nicaragua	N. America	3,100	100	230
Athabasca	N. America	3,064	200	400
Reindeer	N. America	2,568	143	—
Tonle Sap	Asia	2,500–1,000*	85	40–5
Turkana (Rudolf)	Africa	2,463	160	240
Issyk-Kul'	Asia	2,425	114	2,303
Urmia	Asia	2,300–1,500*	90	50
Torrens	Australia	2,230*	120	—
Vänern	Europe	2,156	85	328
Winnipegosis	N. America	2,075	125	38
Albert	Africa	2,075	100	160
Kariba	Africa	2,050	175	295
Nettilling	N. America	1,956	65	—
Chany	Asia	1,931–965*	56	39–23
Nipigon	N. America	1,872	70	540
Gairdner	Australia	1,825–0*	100	—
Mweru	Africa	1,800	75	60
Manitoba	N. America	1,794	140	12
Taymyr	Asia	1,737	125	85
Kyoga	Africa	1,700	75	25
Khanka	Asia	1,700	59	33
Lake of the Woods	N. America	1,679	70	70
Peipus	Europe	1,400	87	50
Koko Nor	Asia	1,625	70	125
Nasser-Nubia	Africa	1,550	350	—
Dubawnt	N. America	1,480	70	—
Van	Asia	1,470	80	—
Wollaston	N. America	1,035	70	—
Great Salt	N. America	940	75	27

* Max. and min. of fluctuating water area.

GREAT WORLD DESERTS

Desert	Location	Size
Arabian (Eastern)	North Africa-Red Sea coast	c. 70,000 sq. mi.
Atacama	Northern Chile	c. 140,000 sq. mi.; c. 600 mi. long
Colorado	Southern California	c. 2,500 sq. mi.
Dasht-i-Kavir	Iran	c. 450 mi. long; c. 175 mi. wide
Dasht-i-Lut	Iran	c. 300 mi. long; c. 175 mi. wide
Death Valley	California	c. 140 mi. long; c. 10 mi. wide
Gibson	Western Australia	c. 250,000 sq. mi.
Gobi	China and Mongolia	c. 500,000 sq. mi.; c. 1,000 mi. long
Great Salt Lake	Utah	c. 125 mi. long; c. 80 mi. wide
Great Sandy	Western Australia	c. 150,000 sq. mi.
Great Victoria	Western and South Australia	c. 250,000 sq. mi.
Kalahari	Southern Africa	c. 225,000 sq.mi.
Kara-Kum	Turkmen SSR, USSR	c. 115,000 sq. mi.; c. 650 mi. long
Kyzyl-Kum	Uzbek & Kazakh SSR, USSR	c. 100,000 sq. mi.
Mojave	Southern California	c. 15,000 sq.mi.
Namib	South-West African coast	c. 800 mi. long; c. 60 mi. wide
Nefud (An Nafud)	Northern Arabia	c. 180 mi. long; c. 140 mi. wide
Negev	Southern Israel	c. 5,000 sq. mi.
Nubian	Northern Sudan	c.150,000 sq. mi.
Rub al Khali	Southern Arabia	c. 235,000 sq.mi.
Sahara	Northern Africa	c. 3,500,000 sq. mi; c. 3,100 mi. long; c. 1,100 mi. wide
Sechura	Peruvian coast	c. 10,000 sq. mi.
Simpson	Central Australia	c. 45,000 sq.mi.
Syrian (El Hamad)	Northern Arabia, Iraq, Jordan & Syria	c. 450 mi. long; c. 350 mi. wide
Taklamakan	Sinkiang-Uigur Aut. Reg., China	c. 180,000 sq. mi.; c. 500 mi. long; c. 300 mi. wide
Thar (Great Indian)	India and Pakistan	c. 500 mi. long; c. 275 mi.wide
Vizcaíno	Baja California Sur, Mexico	c. 6,000 sq. mi.

HIGH MOUNTAIN PEAKS (See page 301 for U.S. peaks over 14,000 feet)

ASIA

Name	Location	Feet
Everest (Chomolungma)	Nepal-China (Tibet)	29,028
K2 (Godwin-Austen)	Pakistan-China	28,250
Kanchenjunga I	Nepal-India	28,208
Lhotse	Nepal-China (Tibet)	27,923
Makalu	Nepal-China (Tibet)	27,824
Kanchenjunga II	Nepal-India	27,803
Lhotse Shar	Nepal-China (Tibet)	27,504
Dhaulagiri I	Nepal	26,810
Manaslu I (Kutang)	Nepal	26,760
Cho Oyu I	Nepal-China (Tibet)	26,750
Nanga Parbat I	Pakistan	26,660
Annapurna I	Nepal	26,504
Gasherbrum I	Pakistan	26,470
Broad Peak	Pakistan	26,400
Gasherbrum II	Pakistan	26,362
Gosainthan (Shisha Pangma)	China (Tibet)	26,291
Gasherbrum IV	Pakistan	26,181
Gasherbrum III	Pakistan	26,090
Annapurna II	Nepal	26,041
Gyachung Kang	Nepal-China (Tibet)	25,990
Nanga Parbat II	Pakistan	25,953
Himalchuli	Nepal	25,895
Disteghil Sar	Pakistan	25,868
Nuptse	Nepal	25,850
Khinyang Chhish	Pakistan	25,760
Masherbrum	Pakistan	25,660
Nanda Devi	India	25,645
Cho Oyu II	Nepal-China (Tibet)	25,611
Chomo Lönzo	China (Tibet)	25,558
Rakaposhi	Pakistan	25,550
Batura Muztagh I	India (Kashmir)	25,540
Kanjut Sar	India (Kashmir)	25,460
Kamet	India-China (Tibet)	25,447
Namcha Barwa	China (Tibet)	25,445
Dhaulagiri II	Nepal	25,429
Saltoro Kangri	Pakistan	25,400
Batura Muztagh II	Pakistan	25,361
Gurla Mandhata	China (Tibet)	25,355
Ulugh Muztagh	China (Sinkiang-Tibet)	25,338
Trivor	Pakistan	25,330
Kungur	China (Sinkiang)	25,325
Jannu	Nepal	25,294
Dhaulagiri III	Nepal	25,271
Tirich Mir	Pakistan	25,230
Saser Kangri I	India (Kashmir)	25,170
Chogolisa	Pakistan	25,148
Dhaulagiri IV	Nepal	25,135
Kangchungtse (Makalu II)	Nepal-China (Tibet)	25,128
Dhaulagiri V	Nepal	24,992
Rathong	Nepal-India	24,912
Minya Konka	China	24,900
Annapurna III	Nepal	24,787
Kula Kangri	Bhutan-China (Tibet)	24,784
Changtse	China (Tibet)	24,780
Muztagh Ata	China (Sinkiang)	24,757
Annapurna IV	Nepal	24,688
Communism Peak	USSR	24,590
Noshaq	Pakistan-Afghanistan	24,581
Jongsong Peak	India-China (Tibet)	24,472
Malubiting	Pakistan	24,470
Pobeda Peak	USSR	24,406
Chomo Lhari	Bhutan-China (Tibet)	23,997
Muztagh	China (Sinkiang)	23,891
Amne Machin	China	23,490
Demavend	Iran	18,376
Ararat	Turkey	16,946
Djaja (Carstensz)	Indonesia (New Guinea)	16,503
Klyuchevskaya Sopka	USSR	15,584
Kinabalu	Malaysia (Sabah)	13,455
Kerintji	Indonesia (Sumatra)	12,484
Fuji	Japan	12,389
Semeru	Indonesia (Java)	12,060

AFRICA

Name	Location	Feet
Kilimanjaro (Kibo)	Tanzania	19,340
Kenya (Batian)	Kenya	17,058
Kilimanjaro (Mawenzi)	Tanzania	16,896
Margherita (Ruwenzori)	Uganda-Zaire	16,795
Ras Dashan	Ethiopia	15,157
Meru	Tanzania	14,979
Karisimbi	Rwanda-Zaire	14,787
Elgon (Wagagai)	Kenya-Uganda	14,178
Toubkal	Morocco	13,665
Cameroon (Fako Peak)	Cameroon	13,350
Teide	Canary Is.	12,198

AUSTRALIA and OCEANIA

Name	Location	Feet
Wilhelm	Papua New Guinea	14,793
Mauna Kea	US (Hawaii)	13,796
Mauna Loa	US (Hawaii)	13,680
Cook (Aorangi)	New Zealand	12,349
Kosciusko	Australia	7,316

ANTARCTICA

Name	Feet	Name	Feet
Vinson Massif	16,864	Markham	14,285
Tyree	16,289	Bell	14,117
Gardner	15,374	Mackellar	14,098
Kirkpatrick	14,856	Anderson	13,990
Elizabeth	14,698	Bentley	13,934

EUROPE (including Caucasus)

Name	Location	Feet
El'brus	USSR	18,510
Shkhara	USSR	17,064
Dykh-Tau	USSR	17,054
Koshtan-Tau	USSR	16,877
Dzhangi-Tau	USSR	16,565
Kazbek	USSR	16,558
Mont-Blanc	France	15,771
Dufourspitze (Mte. Rosa)	Switz.-Italy	15,203
Dom (Mischabel)	Switz.	14,911
Lyskamm	Switz.-Italy	14,852
Weisshorn	Switz.	14,780
Täschhorn	Switz.	14,733
Matterhorn	Switz.	14,692
Mont-Maudit	France-Italy	14,649
Dent-Blanche	Switz.	14,293
Nadelhorn	Switz.	14,196
Grand-Combin	Switz.	14,154
Lenzspitze	Switz.	14,098
Finsteraarhorn	Switz.	14,022
Rimpfischhorn	Switz.	13,776
Aletschhorn	Switz	13,763
Jungfrau	Switz.	13,642
Gran Paradiso	Italy	13,323
Piz Bernina	Switz.-Italy	13,284
Grossglockner	Austria	12,457
Mulhacén	Spain	11,411
Etna	Italy	11,053
Zugspitze	Germany-Austria	9,721
Olympus (Mytikas)	Greece	9,570
Glittertind	Norway	8,110
Ben Nevis	UK (Scotland)	4,406
Vesuvius	Italy	4,190

NORTH AMERICA

Name	Location	Feet
Logan	Canada	19,524
Citlaltépetl (Orizaba)	Mexico	18,855
St. Elias	Canada-US	18,008
Popocatépetl	Mexico	17,887
Iztaccíhuatl	Mexico	17,343
Lucania	Canada	17,147
King Peak	Canada	16,971
Steele	Canada	16,644
Wood	Canada	15,885
Vancouver	Canada-US	15,700
Fairweather	Canada-US	15,300
Toluca (Zinantécatl)	Mexico	15,015
Walsh	Canada	14,780
La Malinche	Mexico	14,635
Nevada de Colima	Mexico	14,205
Cofre de Perote	Mexico	14,050
Tajumulco	Guatemala	13,845
Robson	Canada	12,972
Chirripó Grande	Costa Rica	12,530
Parícutin	Mexico	10,400

SOUTH AMERICA

Name	Location	Feet
Aconcagua	Argentina	22,831
Ojos del Salado	Argentina	22,546
Bonete	Argentina-Chile	22,572
Tupungato	Argentina-Chile	22,310
Pissis	Argentina	22,245
Mercedario	Argentina	22,211
Huascarán	Peru	22,205
Llullaillaco	Argentina-Chile	22,057
Cumbre del Libertador Gen. San Martín	Argentina	22,047
Ancohuma	Bolivia	21,489
Sajama	Bolivia	21,391
Nacimiento	Argentina	21,302
Illampu	Bolivia	21,276
Illimani	Bolivia	21,184
Coropuna	Peru	21,079
Nevados de Huandoy	Peru	20,981
Toro	Argentina-Chile	20,932
Chimborazo	Ecuador	20,561
Cotopaxi	Ecuador	19,347
El Misti	Peru	19,199

DAMS, MAN-MADE LAKES, HYDROELECTRIC PLANTS

SOURCE: Water and Power Resources Service, Dept. of the Interior

HIGHEST DAMS

A = Arch; E = Earth or Rockfill; G = Gravity; M = Multi-Arch; UC = Under Construction

Name of Dam		Height Meters	Height Feet	Year Completed
1. Rogunsky, USSR	E	325	1,066	UC
2. Nurek, USSR	E	317	1,040	UC
3. Grand Dixence, Switzerland	G	285	935	1962
4. Inguri, USSR	A	272	892	UC
5. Chicoasen, Mexico	E	265	869	UC
6. Vaiont, Italy	A	262	858	1961
7. Mica, Canada	E	242	794	1974
8. Sayanskaya, USSR	A	242	794	UC
9. Chivor, Colombia	E	237	778	1975
10. Mauvoisin, Switzerland	A	237	777	1957
11. Oroville, U.S.A.	E	235	770	1968
12. Chirkey, USSR	A	233	764	1975
13. Bhakra, India	G	226	742	1963
14. El Cajon, Honduras	A	226	741	UC
15. Hoover, U.S.A.	A/G	221	726	1936
16. Contra, Switzerland	A	220	722	1965
17. Piva (Mratinje), Yugoslavia	A	220	722	1975
18. Dworshak, U.S.A.	G	219	717	1974
19. Glen Canyon, U.S.A.	A	216	710	1964
20. Daniel Johnson, Canada	M	214	703	1968
21. Toktogul, USSR	G	213	699	UC
22. Auburn, U.S.A.	A	209	685	UC
23. Luzzone, Switzerland	A	208	682	1963
24. Keban, Turkey	E/G	207	679	1974
25. Dez, Iran	A	203	666	1963
26. Almendra, Spain	A	202	662	1970
27. Koelbrein, Austria	A	200	656	1977

LARGEST DAMS

Based on total volume of dam structure.

Name of Dam	Volume (Thousands) Cubic Meters	Volume (Thousands) Cubic Yards	Year Completed
1. New Cornelia Tailings, U.S.A.	209,500	274,026	1973
2. Tarbela, Pakistan	121,000	158,268	1975
3. Fort Peck, U.S.A.	96,034	125,612	1940
4. Raul Leoni, Venezuela	78,000	102,014	UC
5. Ataturk, Turkey	73,700	96,400	UC
6. Oahe, U.S.A.	70,343	92,008	1963
7. Oosterschelde, Netherlands	70,000	91,560	UC
8. Yacyreta-Apipe, Argentina-Paraguay	70,000	91,560	UC
9. Mangla, Pakistan	65,651	85,872	1967
10. Gardiner, Canada	65,553	85,743	1968
11. Afsluitdijk, Netherlands	63,400	82,927	1932
12. Oroville, U.S.A.	59,639	78,008	1968
13. San Luis, U.S.A.	59,378	77,666	1967
14. Garrison, U.S.A.	50,846	66,506	1956
15. Cochiti, U.S.A.	49,417	64,631	1975
16. Tabka, Syria	46,000	60,168	1975
17. Kiev, USSR	44,000	57,552	1964
18. W.A.C. Bennett, Canada	43,733	57,203	1967
19. High Aswan (Sadd-el-Aali), Egypt	41,733	57,203	1970
20. Dantiwada Left Earthenbank, India	41,040	53,680	1965
21. Saratov, USSR	40,400	52,843	1967
22. Mission Tailings #2, U.S.A.	40,088	52,435	1973
23. Fort Randall, U.S.A.	38,383	50,205	1956
24. Kanev, USSR	37,860	49,520	1974
25. Kakhova, USSR	35,640	46,617	1955
26. Lauwerszee, Netherlands	35,575	46,532	1969
27. Beas, India	35,019	45,800	1975

GREATEST MAN-MADE LAKES

Name of Dam	Capacity Millions of Cubic Meters	Capacity Thousands of Acre-Feet	Year Completed
1. Owen Falls, Uganda	204,800	166,000	1954
2. Bratsk, USSR	169,270	137,220	1964
3. High Aswan (Sadd-el-Aali), Egypt	169,000	137,000	1970
4. Kariba, Zimbabwe-Zambia	160,368	130,000	1959
5. Akosombo, Ghana	148,000	120,000	1965
6. Daniel Johnson, Canada	141,852	115,000	1968
7. Raul Leoni, Venezuela	136,000	110,000	UC
8. Krasnoyarsk, USSR	73,300	59,425	1972
9. W.A.C. Bennett, Cananda	70,309	57,006	1967
10. Zeya, USSR	68,400	55,452	1975
11. Cabora Bassa, Mozambique	64,000	51,900	1974
12. LaGrande, Canada	62,260	50,475	UC
13. Ust-Ilimsk, USSR	59,300	48,100	UC
14. Volga-V.I.Lenin, USSR	58,000	47,020	1955
15. Bukhtarma, USSR	53,000	42,970	1960
16. Ataturk, Turkey	48,700	39,481	UC
17. Irkutsk, USSR	46,000	37,290	1956
18. Hoover, U.S.A.	36,703	29,755	1936
19. Vilyui, USSR	35,900	29,104	1967
20. Sobradinho, Brazil	34,200	27,700	UC
21. Tucurui, Brazil	34,000	27,564	UC
22. Volgograd-22nd Congress, USSR	33,500	27,160	1958
23. Glen Canyon, U.S.A.	33,305	27,000	1964
24. Keban, Turkey	31,000	25,110	1974
25. Garrison, U.S.A.	30,000	24,321	1956
26. Iroquois, Canada	29,960	24,288	1958
27. Oahe, U.S.A.	29,100	23,591	1963

LARGEST HYDROELECTRIC PLANTS

MW = Megawatts

Name of Dam	Rated Capacity MW Present	Rated Capacity MW Ultimate	Year of Initial Operation
1. Italpu, Brazil-Paraguay	—	12,870	UC
2. Grand Coulee, U.S.A.	6,263	6,494	1941/80
3. Guri, Venezuela	524	6,500	1967
4. Sayanskaya, USSR	—	6,400	UC
5. Krasnoyarsk, USSR	6,096	6,096	1968
6. LaGrande 2, Canada	—	5,328	UC
7. Churchill Falls, Canada	5,225	5,225	1971
8. Bratsk, USSR	4,100	4,600	1964
9. Sukhovo, USSR	—	4,500	UC
10. Ust-Ilimsk, USSR	720	4,320	1974
11. Cabora Bassa, Mozambique	2,000	4,000	1975
12. Tucurui, Brazil	—	3,960	UC
13. Rogunsky, USSR	—	3,600	UC
14. Paulo Afonso, Brazil	1,524	3,409	1955
15. Solteira, Brazil	3,200	3,200	1973
16. Inga I, Zaire	360	2,820	1974
17. John Day, U.S.A.	2,160	2,700	1968
18. Nurek, USSR	—	2,700	UC
19. Sao Simao, Brazil	—	2,680	UC
20. Volgograd-22nd Congress, USSR	2,560	2,560	1958
21. Chicoasen, Mexico	—	2,400	UC
22. Volga-V.I. Lenin, USSR	2,300	2,300	1955
23. Iron Gates I, Romania-Yugoslavia	2,300	2,300	1970
24. W.A.C.Bennett, Canada	1,816	2,270	1969
25. Foz Do Areia, Brazil	2,250	2,250	UC
26. High Aswan (Sadd-el-Aali), Egypt	2,100	2,100	1967
27. Bath County, U.S.A.	—	2,100	UC
28. Tarbela, Pakistan	700	2,100	1977
29. Itumbiara, Brazil	—	2,080	UC
30. Chief Joseph, U.S.A.	1,024	2,069	1956
31. Salto Santiago, Brazil	—	1,998	UC
32. Robert Moses-Niagara, U.S.A.	1,950	1,950	1961
33. Salto Grande, Argentina-Uruguay	—	1,890	UC
34. Dinorwic, U.K.	—	1,880	UC
35. Ludington, U.S.A.	1,872	1,872	1973
36. St. Lawrence Power Dam, U.S.A.-Canada	1,824	1,824	1958
37. The Dalles, U.S.A.	1,807	1,807	1957
38. Karakaya, Turkey	—	1,800	UC
39. Grand Maison, France	1,200	1,800	UC
40. Mica, Canada	—	1,740	UC
41. Itaparica, Brazil	—	1,700	UC
42. Kemano, Canada	813	1,670	1954
43. Blue Ridge, U.S.A.	—	1,600	UC
44. Beauharnois, Canada	1,021	1,574	1950
45. Kariba, Zimbabwe-Zambia	1,266	1,566	1959
46. San Carlos, Colombia	—	1,550	UC

VOLCANOES

Key to letters: (E) Last eruption, with year in parentheses; (R) Rumbling; (St) Steaming; (D) Dormant.

Name	Location	Height (in feet)
AFRICA		
Kibo (Kilimanjaro) (D)	Tanzania	19,340
Cameroon Mt. (E-1959)	Cameroon	13,350
El Teide (St)	Canary Is.	12,172
Nyiragongo (E-1977)	Zaire	11,385
Nyamulagira (E-1976)	Zaire	10,028
Fogo (E-1951)	Cape Verde Is.	9,281
Tristan da Cunha (E-1961)	South Atlantic	6,760
Teneguia (D)	Canary Is.	2,006
ANTARCTICA		
Deception Island (E-1970)		—
Erebus (E-1978)		12,450
Melbourne (St)		8,500
ASIA and AUSTRALASIA		
Klyuchevskaya (E-1962)	USSR	15,584
Kerintji (St)	Indonesia	12,484
Fuji (D)	Japan	12,389
Rindjani (E-1964)	Indonesia	12,224
Tolbachik (E-1941)	USSR	12,080
Semeru (E-1963)	Indonesia	12,060
Ichinskaya (St)	USSR	11,880
Kronotskaya (D)	USSR	11,575
Koryakskaya (E-1957)	USSR	11,339
Slamet (E-1953)	Indonesia	11,247
Raung (St)	Indonesia	10,932
Shiveluch (E-1964)	USSR	10,771
Dempo (St)	Indonesia	10,364
Welirang (D)	Indonesia	10,354
Agung (E-1964)	Indonesia	10,308
Sundoro (D)	Indonesia	10,285
Tjareme (E-1938)	Indonesia	10,098
Gede (E-1949)	Indonesia	9,705
Apo (D)	Philippines	9,369
Merapi (E-1969)	Indonesia	9,551
Bezymyannaya (E-1961)	USSR	9,514
Marapi (D)	Indonesia	9,485
Tambora (D)	Indonesia	9,353
Mayon (E-1978)	Philippines	7,940
Sinila (E-1979)	Indonesia	c. 7,000
Bulosan (E-1978)	Philippines	5,140
Usu (E-1978)	Japan	2,390
Taal (E-1977)	Philippines	990
MID-PACIFIC		
Mauna Kea (D)	Hawaii	13,796
Mauna Loa (E-1975)	Hawaii	13,680
Kilauea (E-1977)	Hawaii	4,077
EUROPE		
Etna (E-1979)	Sicily, Italy	11,053
Askja (E-1961)	Iceland	4,954
Hekla (E-1980)	Iceland	4,892
Vesuvius (St)	Italy	4,190
Stromboli (E-1971)	Lipari Is., Italy	3,038
Surtsey (E-1967)	Iceland	570
Eldfell (E-1973)	Iceland	327
NORTH AMERICA		
Popocatépetl (St)	Mexico	17,887
Colima (St)	Mexico	14,205
Wrangell (St)	Alaska	14,163
Torbert (E-1953)	Alaska	11,413
Spurr (E-1953)	Alaska	11,069
Lassen (D)	California	10,457
Paricutin (D)	Mexico	10,400
Redoubt (E-1966)	Alaska	10,197
Iliamna (St)	Alaska	10,016
St. Helens (E-1980)	Washington	9,677*
Shishaldin (St)	Aleutians	9,387
Pavlof (E-1950)	Alaska	8,261
Veniaminof (D)	Alaska	8,225
Griggs (St)	Alaska	7,600
Mageik (St)	Alaska	7,250
Douglas (St)	Alaska	7,064
Chiginagak (D)	Alaska	6,900
Katmai (E-1962)	Alaska	6,715
Kukak (St)	Alaska	6,700
Makushin (D)	Aleutians	6,680
Pogromni (E-1964)	Aleutians	6,568
Martin (E-1960)	Alaska	6,050
Trident (E-1963)	Alaska	6,010

* Height prior to 1980 eruption.

Name	Location	Height (in feet)
CENTRAL AMERICA and CARIBBEAN		
Tajumulco (R)	Guatemala	13,845
Tacaná (R)	Guatemala	13,428
Acatenango (R)	Guatemala	12,992
Fuego (E-1978)	Guatemala	12,582
Santa Maria (R)	Guatemala	12,362
Atitlan (R)	Guatemala	11,565
Irazú (E-1964)	Costa Rica	11,260
San Pedro (R)	Guatemala	9,921
Poãs (St)	Costa Rica	8,930
Pacaya (E-1970)	Guatemala	8,346
Izalco (E-1967)	El Salvador	6,184
Soufrière (E-1979)	St. Vincent	4,048
SOUTH AMERICA		
Guallatiri (E-1959)	Chile	19,882
Lascar (E-1951)	Chile	19,652
Cotopaxi (St)	Ecuador	19,347
Misti (D)	Peru	19,199
Cayambe (D)	Ecuador	18,996
Tupungatito (E-1959)	Chile	18,504
Sangay (E-1946)	Ecuador	17,159
Tungurahua (R)	Ecuador	16,512
Cotacachi (E-1955)	Ecuador	16,204
Pichincha (D)	Ecuador	15,696
Purace (E-1950)	Colombia	15,604
Lautaro (St)	Chile	11,090
Llaima (E-1955)	Chile	10,239
Villarrica (E-1964)	Chile	9,318
Osorno (R)	Chile	8,730
Shoshuenco (E-1960)	Chile	7,743

WORLD WATERFALLS

Location and Name		Height[1] (in feet)
AFRICA		
Aughrabies[3]	S. Africa	482
Baratieri	Ethiopia	460
Chirombo[2]	Zambia	880
Dianzundu (Duque de Braganca)	Angola	344
Finca	Ethiopia	508
Howick	S. Africa	358
Kalambo[2,3]	Tanz.-Zambia	726
Karkloof[2]	S. Africa	350
Livingstone[2]	Zaire	875
Lofoi	Zaire	1,115
Magwa	S. Africa	450
Maletsunyane	Lesotho	630
Murchison[2]	Uganda	400
Ruacana	Angola	406
Stanley[2]	Zaire	200
Tisisat[3]	Ethiopia	140
Tsitza	S. Africa	375
Tugela[2]	S. Africa	3,110
Verme	Ethiopia	229
Victoria[2,3]	Zimbabwe-Zambia	355
ASIA		
Diyaluma	Sri Lanka	600
Jog (Gersoppa)[2,3]	India	830
Kegon	Japan	330
Kirindi Ela	Sri Lanka	347
Kurundu Oya	Sri Lanka	620
Laksapana	Sri Lanka	377
Nachi	Japan	430
Ramboda	Sri Lanka	329
Ratna Ella	Sri Lanka	305
Sivasamudram (Kaveri)[2]	India	320
Yudaki	Japan	335
OCEANIA		
Akaka	Hawaii (US)	420
Barron	Australia	770
Bowen[2]	New Zealand	540
Helena	New Zealand	860
Leura[2]	Australia	308
Stirling	New Zealand	505
Sutherland[2]	New Zealand	1,904
Tully[2]	Australia	972
Wentworth[2]	Australia	518
Wollomombi[2]	Australia	1,580
EUROPE		
Aurstapet[2]	Norway	794
Gastein[2]	Austria	486
Gavarnie	France	1,385
Giessbach[2]	Switz.	1,312
Glomach	UK (Scotland)	370
Golling[2]	Austria	203
Iffigen	Switz.	394
Kile[2]	Norway	1,840
Krimml[2]	Austria	1,246
Låtefoss[2]	Norway	541
Mardalsfoss (E.)[2]	Norway	1,696
Mardalsfoss (W.)	Norway	1,535
Marmore[2]	Italy	525
Mongefossen[2]	Norway	2,539
Reichenbach[2]	Switz.	656
Rjoandefoss[2]	Norway	1,847
Rjukenfoss	Norway	983

[1] Height means total drop whether in one or more leaps. [2] Falls consisting of more than one leap.
[3] Falls that diminish greatly seasonally.

Location and Name		Height[1] (in feet)
Simme[2]	Switz.	459
Skjeggedalsfoss	Norway	525
Skykkjedalsfoss	Norway	820
Søtefoss	Norway	896
Stalheimsfoss	Norway	413
Staubbach	Switz.	984
Stäuber	Switz.	590
Stigfoss	Norway	590
Toce[2]	Italy	470
Trümmelbach[2]	Switz.	1,312
Tyssefoss[2]	Norway	1,749
Tyssestrengene[2]	Norway	2,795
Vermafoss	Norway	1,248
Vettisfoss[2]	Norway	1,214
Vøringfoss	Norway	597

NORTH AMERICA

Location and Name		Height[1] (in feet)
Basaseachic	Mexico	1,000
Bridalveil	US (Calif.)	620
Chequaga	US (N.Y.)	156
Churchill	Canada (Newf.)	245
Comet	US (Wash.)	320
Cumberland	US (Ky.)	68
Della	Canada (B.C.)	1,443
Fairy	US (Wash.)	700
Fall Creek	US (Tenn.)	256
Feather	US (Calif.)	640
Grand	Canada (N. Br.)	75
Grand	Canada (Ont.)	150
Granite	US (Wash.)	350
Illilouette	US (Calif.)	370
Juanacatlán, Salto de[3]	Mexico	70
Jumatán	Mexico	394
Manitou	US (Wis.)	165
Minnehaha[3]	US (Minn.)	52
Missouri (Great Falls)[2]	US (Mont.)	90
Montmorency	Canada (Que.)	274
Multnomah[2]	US (Oreg.)	620
Narada	US (Wash.)	168
Necaxa	Mexico	540
Nevada	US (Calif.)	594
Niagara[2]:		
American	US (N.Y.)	167
Canadian (Horseshoe)	U.S.-Canada	158
Palouse	US (Wash.)	198
Panther	Canada (Alta.)	600
Passaic (Great Falls)[3]	US (N.J.)	70
Potomac (Great Falls)[2]	US (Md.-Va.)	90
Ribbon[3]	US Calif.)	1,612
Saint Anthony	US (Minn.)	60
Seven	US (Colo.)	266
Shawinigan	Canada (Que.)	150
Shoshone[2][3]	US (Idaho)	210
Silver Strand	US (Calif.)	1,170
Sluiskin	US (Wash.)	300
Snoqualmie	US (Wash.)	270
Tahquamenon[2]	US (Mich.)	88
Takakkaw[2]	Canada (B.C.)	1,650
Taughannock	US (N.Y.)	215
Tower	US (Wyo.)	132
Twin[2][3]	US (Idaho)	125
Vernal	US (Calif.)	317
Virginia	Canada (N.W.T.)	315
Xico	Mexico	256

Location and Name		Height[1] (in feet)
Yellowstone[2]		
Upper	US (Wyo.)	109
Lower		308
Yosemite[2]	US (Calif.)	2,425
Upper		1,430

SOUTH AMERICA

Location and Name		Height[1] (in feet)
Angel[2]	Venezuela	3,212
Upper		2,648
Anta, Cascada da	Brazil	665
Candelas, Cataratas de	Colombia	984
Glass	Brazil	1,325
Grande	Arg.-Uruguay	75
Grande	Brazil	140
Great	Guyana	500
Iguazú (Iguaçu)[2]	Brazil	237
Itiquira	Brazil	395
Kaieteur[2]	Guyana	822
highest		741
King Edward VIII	Guyana	850
King George VI	Guyana	1,600
Kukenaam[2]	Venezuela	2,000
Marina[2]	Guyana	500
Papagaio	Brazil	350
Patos-Maribondo	Brazil	115
Paulo Afonso[2]	Brazil	275
Roraima[3]	Guyana	1,500
Sete Quedas (Guairá)	Brazil-Parag.	360
Tequendama	Colombia	482
Urubupungá	Brazil	33

[1] Height means total drop whether in one or more leaps. [2] Falls consisting of more than one leap. [3] Falls that diminish greatly seasonally.

OUTSTANDING WORLDWIDE WEATHER EXTREMES

SOURCE: National Oceanic & Atmospheric Administration

TEMPERATURE EXTREMES

Temperature extremes for any place on Earth are determined by a number of factors, including altitude, latitude, and physical characteristics. For an extreme to be recorded, an observation must be made at the precise time and place of occurrence; consequantity, more extreme temperatures undoubtedly have occurred.

THE HOTTEST

Area	Max. (°F.)	Place	Elevation (Ft.)	Date
Africa	136	Al'Aziziyah, Libya	380	Sept. 13, 1922
North America	134	Death Valley, California	−178	July 10, 1913
Asia	129	Tirat Tsvi, Israel	−722	June 21, 1942
Australia	128	Cloncurry, Queensland	622	Jan. 16, 1889
Europe	122	Seville, Spain	26	Aug. 4, 1881
South America	120	Rivadavia, Argentina	676	Dec. 11, 1905
Oceania	108	Tuguegarao, Philippines	72	Apr. 29, 1912
Antarctica	58	Esperanza, Palmer Peninsula	−26	Oct. 20, 1956

THE COLDEST

Area	Min. (°F.)	Place	Elevation (Ft.)	Date
Antarctica	−127	Vostok Station	11,220	Aug. 24, 1960
Asia	−90	Oymyakon, USSR	2,625	Feb. 6, 1933
Greenland	−87	Northice Station	7,690	Jan. 9, 1954
North America	−81	Snag, Yukon, Canada	1,925	Feb. 3, 1947
Europe	−67	Ust'-Shchugor, USSR	279	date unknown
South America	−27	Sarmiento, Argentina	879	June 1, 1907
Africa	−11	Ifrane, Morocco	5,364	Feb. 11, 1935
Australia	−8	Charlotte Pass, New South Wales	NA	July 22, 1947

RAINFALL EXTREMES

The total annual precipitation recorded at a place may vary greatly from year to year. The rainiest places show the greatest variations from year to year in actual amounts. The drier places show the greatest variation taken as a percentage of the mean value. At Cherrapunji, India, for example, the greatest amount of precipitation in a calendar year was 905.1 inches. The least was 282.6 inches, a difference of over 600 inches. At Arica, Chile, half of the total rainfall recorded from 1931 through 1960 fell in the single year of 1959. No rain at all fell in 19 of the 30 years. Because of such fluctuations, the average annual precipitation may be greatly influenced by the available years of record; the longer the record, the more reliable is the average.

THE WETTEST

Area	Average Annual Rainfall (Inches)	Place	Elevation (Ft.)	Years of Record
Oceania	460.0	Mt. Waialeale, Hawaii	5,075	33
Asia	450.0	Cherrapunji, India	4,309	75
Africa	404.6	Debundscha, Cameroon	30	33
South America	354.0	Quibdó, Colombia	240	11–17
North America	262.1	Henderson Lake, Br. Col.	12	15
Europe	182.8	Crkvice, Yugoslavia	3,337	23
Australia	179.0	Tully, Queensland	220	32

THE DRIEST

Area	Average Annual Rainfall (Inches)	Place	Elevation (Ft.)	Years of Record
South America	0.03	Arica, Chile	95	60
Africa	0.1	Wadi Halfa, Sudan	410	40
Antarctica	0.8	South Pole Station	9,186	11
North America	1.2	Bataques, Mexico	16	15
Asia	1.8	Aden, P.D.R. Yemen	22	51
Australia	4.05	Mulka, South Australia	NA	35
Europe	6.4	Astrakhan, USSR	45	26
Oceania	8.93	Puako, Hawaii	5	14

WORLD'S HIGHEST BUILDINGS

*Under construction. SOURCE: Council on Tall Buildings and Urban Habitat

Building	Location	Height (in feet)	Stories
Sears Tower	Chicago	1,454	110
World Trade Center (Twin Towers)	New York City	1,350	110
Empire State	New York City	1,250	102
Standard Oil (Indiana)	Chicago	1,136	80
John Hancock	Chicago	1,127	100
Texas Commerce Plaza*	Houston	1,049	75
Chrysler	New York City	1,046	77
American International	New York City	950	66
First Bank Tower	Toronto	935	72
40 Wall Tower	New York City	927	71
Citicorp Center	New York City	914	59
Water Tower Place	Chicago	859	74
United California Bank	Los Angeles	858	62
United California Bank	New York City	851	66
RCA Rockefeller Center	New York City	850	70
First National Bank	Chicago	844	60
Transamerica	San Francisco	843	48
U. S. Steel	Pittsburgh	841	64
One Chase Manhattan Plaza	New York City	813	60
Pan American	New York City	808	59
Woolworth	New York City	792	57
Palace of Science and Culture	Warsaw	790	42
John Hancock Tower	Boston	790	60
M.L.C. Centre	Sydney, Australia	786	70
Commerce Court West	Toronto	784	57
3 First National Plaza	Chicago	775	58
IDS Center	Minneapolis	772	57
One Penn Plaza	New York City	766	57
Maine Montparnasse	Paris	751	64
Prudential Center	Boston	750	52
Federal Reserve	Boston	750	32
Exxon	New York City	750	54
First International Plaza	Houston	748	55
1 Liberty Plaza (U.S. Steel)	New York City	743	54
Ikebukuro Office Tower	Tokyo	742	60
20 Exchange Place (Citibank)	New York City	741	55
Renaissance 1	Detroit	739	73
Security Pacific National Bank	Los Angeles	738	57
Bank of America	San Francisco	738	52
Toronto Dominion Bank Tower	Toronto	736	56
Shinjuku Center	Tokyo	733	54
One Astor Plaza	New York City	730	54
9 West 57th Street	New York City	725	50
Peachtree Center Plaza	Atlanta	723	71
Carlton Centre	Johannesburg	722	50
One Shell Plaza	Houston	714	52
First International	Dallas	710	56
Terminal Tower	Cleveland	708	52
Union Carbide	New York City	707	52
General Motors	New York City	705	50
Metropolitan Life	New York City	700	50
Atlantic Richfield Plaza A & B	Los Angeles	699	52
One Shell Square	New Orleans	697	51
500 Fifth Avenue	New York City	697	58
Shinjuku Mitsui	Tokyo	696	55
IBM	Chicago	695	52
Shinjuku Nomura	Tokyo	690	53
Neiman-Marcus*	Chicago	690	65
55 Water Street	New York City	687	53
Chemical Bank Trust	New York City	687	50
Three Allen Center	Houston	685	50
One Houston Center	Houston	681	46
Chanin	New York City	680	55
Gulf+Western	New York City	679	44
Marine Midland Bank	New York City	677	52
Southern Bell*	Atlanta	677	46
Metropolitan Tower	New York City	675	50
Lincoln Building	New York City	673	55
McGraw-Hill	New York City	670	51
1633 Broadway	New York City	670	48
Bank of Oklahoma Tower	Tulsa	667	50
Civic Center	Chicago	662	38
Overseas-Chinese Banking Corp.	Singapore	660	52
First City Tower*	Houston	660	49
Shinjuku Sumitomo	Tokyo	656	52
Parque Central Torre Oficinas	Caracas	656	56
1100 Milam	Houston	651	47
Michigan + Oak*	Chicago	650	60
Ukraine Hotel	Moscow	650	34
American Brands	New York City	648	47
Lake Point Towers	Chicago	645	70
A.T.&T.	New York City	645	70
1000 Lakeshore Plaza	Chicago	640	60
Irving Trust	New York City	640	53
345 Park Avenue	New York City	634	44
Yasuda Kasai	Tokyo	633	43

SELECTED WORLD STRUCTURES

SOURCE: Amer. Society of Civil Engineers

Structure	Location	Height in Feet
Polish National TV Service Tower	Plock, Poland	2,120
KTHI-TV	Fargo, N.D.	2,063
CN Communication Tower	Toronto	1,815
Ostankino TV tower	Near Moscow, USSR	1,762
Moscow TV tower	USSR	1,732
B.R.E.N. Tower	Nevada	1,527
Loran Mast	Snaefellsnes, Iceland	1,378
Danish Government Navigational Mast	Thule, Greenland	1,345
Peking Radio Antenna	China	1,312
Tower Zero	N.W. Cape, Western Australia	1,271
TV antenna	Emley Moor, England	1,265
TV antenna	Belmont, England	1,265
Zender Lopik TV Antenna	Near Lopik, Netherlands	1,253
American Electric Power smokestack	Cresap, W. Va.	1,206
Utah Copper Div. of Kennecott Copper Corp. Magna Smelter Chimney	Great Salt Lake, Utah	1,200
East Berlin Antenna	East Germany	1,185
Television Center	Moscow	1,179
TV tower	Vinnitsa, Ukraine, USSR	1,150
Loran Tower	Tomil, Yap Island	1,100
CHCHTV Antenna	Hamilton, Canada	1,093
TV tower	Tokyo	1,092
Leningrad antenna	USSR	1,065
TV Antenna	Kojál, Czechoslovakia	1,033
Weather tower	Obninsk, USSR	1,027
Lakihegg Antenna	Lakihegg, Hungary	1,006
ITA Antenna	Brynychain, Wales	1,000
Conemaugh Station Chimney (pair)	Johnstown, Pa.	1,000
TV antenna	Black Hill, Scotland	1,000
TV antenna	Durris, Scotland	1,000
TV antenna	Anglia-Mendlesham, England	1,000
ITA Antenna	Strabane, Northern Ireland	1,000
Factory chimney	Cracow, Poland	985
Eiffel Tower (with TV antenna, 1052)	Paris	984
TV Tower	Munich	951
Exxon Co. Oil Platform	Santa Barbara, Calif.	945
TV Tower	Hamburg, Germany	856
Ohio Edison Company Chimney	Stratton, Ohio	853
General Post Office Antennae (pair)	Rugby, England	820
TV antenna	Stuttgart, Germany	767
Radio tower	Transvaal, Rep. of So. Africa	760
BBC Antenna, Crystal Palace	London	710
TV antenna	West Berlin	696
National Cathedral Tower	Washington, D.C.	660
Gateway Arch	St. Louis	630
Tour du Maine	Paris	607
Space Needle	Seattle	606
Donauturm	Vienna	597
Radio Luxembourg Antenna	Junglinster	591
Post Office Tower	London	580
San Jacinto Column	Houston	570
Tower of the First Methodist Church	Chicago	568
Washington Monument	Washington, D.C.	555
American Smelting and Refining smokestack	Tacoma, Wash.	535
Ulm Cathedral	West Germany	530
Vertical Assembly Building	Cape Canaveral, Fla.	525
Cathedral of Learning	Pittsburgh	523
Blackpool Tower	England	519
Cologne Cathedral	West Germany	515
Mole Antonelliana	Turin, Italy	510
Kaknastornet Tower	Stockholm	502

EARTH'S EXTREMES

SOURCE: National Geographic Society

Wettest spot .... Mt. Waialeale, Hawaii; greatest annual average, 460 inches (12-month record, Cherrapunji, India: 1,042 inches between Aug. 1860 and July 1861)

Driest spot .... Atacama Desert, Chile; rainfall barely measurable

Coldest spot .... Vostok, Antarctica; −127°F. recorded in 1960

Hottest spot .... Al'Aziziyah, Libya; 136°F. recorded in 1922

Northernmost town ... Ny Alesund, Spitsbergen, Norway

Southernmost town ... Puerto Williams, Chile

Highest town .... Aucanquilcha, Chile; 17,500 feet

Lowest town .... Villages along the Dead Sea; 1,299 feet below sea level

Largest gorge .... Grand Canyon, Colorado River, Arizona; 277 miles long, 1–20 miles wide, 1 mile deep

Deepest gorge .... Hells Canyon, Snake River, Idaho; 7,900 feet deep

Strongest surface wind ... 231 mph; recorded in 1934 at Mount Washington, New Hampshire

Greatest tides .... Bay of Fundy, Nova Scotia; 53 feet

Biggest meteor crater .. New Quebec, Canada; 2 miles wide

PRINCIPAL WORLD ISLANDS

Island	Area (in sq. miles)	Island	Area (in sq. miles)	Island	Area (in sq. miles)
Greenland	840,000	New Caledonia (France)	6,530	Savaii (W. Samoa)	662
New Guinea	305,000	Hawaiian (U.S.)	6,450	Zanzibar (Tanzania)	641
Borneo	290,000	Nordaustlandet (Norway)	6,409	Oahu (Hawaii, U.S.)	608
Madagascar	226,400	Franz Josef Land (USSR)	6,216	Guadeloupe (France)	584
Baffin (Canada)	195,928	Kuriles (USSR)	6,025	Alands (Finland)	581
Sumatra (Indonesia)	164,000	Bahamas	5,382	Kauai (Hawaii, U.S.)	553
Japan	145,730	Samar (Philippines)	5,050	Shetlands (U.K.)	552
Philippines	115,707	New Hebrides (Vanuatu)	5,700	Rhodes (Greece)	542
New Zealand	103,736	Negros (Philippines)	4,906	Faeroes (Denmark)	540
Great Britain (U.K.)	88,764	Falklands (U.K.)	4,618	Marquesas (France)	492
Honshu (Japan)	88,000	Palawan (Philippines)	4,550	Carolines (Pacific Is.)	463
Victoria (Canada)	83,896	Panay (Philippines)	4,446	Okinawa (Japan)	454
Ellesmere (Canada)	75,767	Jamaica	4,232	Upolu (W. Samoa)	433
Celebes (Indonesia)	72,986	Aleutians (Alaska, U.S.)	4,201	Martinique (France)	425
South (N.Z.)	58,393	Hawaii (U.S.)	4,038	Tahiti (France)	402
Java (Indonesia)	48,842	Viti Levu (Fiji)	4,010	Pemba (Tanzania)	380
North (N.Z.)	44,187	Cape Breton (Canada)	3,981	Orkneys (U.K.)	372
Newfoundland (Canada)	42,031	Mindoro (Philippines)	3,759	Madeiras (Portugal)	307
Cuba	40,533	Kodiak (Alaska, U.S.)	3,670	Dominica	290
Luzon (Philippines)	40,420	Cyprus	3,572	Tonga	270
Iceland	39,768	Puerto Rico (U.S.)	3,435	Molokai (Hawaii, U.S.)	261
Mindanao (Philippines)	36,537	Corsica (France)	3,352	Bahrain	240
Moluccas (Indonesia)	32,307	New Ireland (PNG)	3,340	St. Lucia	238
Novaya Zemlya (USSR)	31,900	Crete (Greece)	3,218	Corfu (Greece)	229
Ireland	31,743	Galápagos (Ecuador)	3,075	Isle of Man (U.K.)	227
Sakhalin (USSR)	29,500	Anticosti (Canada)	3,066	Bornholm (Denmark)	227
Hispaniola (Haiti and Dominican Rep.)	29,399	Wrangel (USSR)	2,819	Singapore	226
Hokkaido (Japan)	28,983	Hebrides (U.K.)	2,812	Guam (U.S.)	212
Banks (Canada)	27,038	Canaries (Spain)	2,808	Isle Royale (Mich., U.S.)	196
Tasmania (Australia)	26,383	Leyte (Philippines)	2,786	Virgins (U.S.-U.K.)	192
Ceylon (Sri Lanka)	25,332	Kerguélen (France)	2,700	Marianas (excluding Guam) (Pacific Is.)	184
Svalbard (Norway)	23,957	Andamans (India)	2,448	Curaçao (Neth. Antilles)	182
Devon (Canada)	21,331	Guadalcanal (Solomon Islands)	2,180	Barbados	166
Bismarck Arch. (PNG)	18,976	Bali (Indonesia)	2,171	Isle of Wight (U.K.)	145
Marajó (Brazil)	17,991	Prince Edward (Canada)	2,170	Lanai (Hawaii, U.S.)	140
Tierra del Fuego (Chile and Argentina)	17,900	Balearics (Spain)	1,936	St. Vincent	131
Axel Heiberg (Canada)	16,671	Trinidad (Trinidad & Tobago)	1,864	Maltese	122
Melville (Canada)	16,274	Ryukyus (Japan)	1,767	Grenada	120
Southampton (Canada)	15,913	Madura (Indonesia)	1,752	Tobago (Trinidad & Tobago)	116
Solomons	15,600	Cape Verde	1,557	Antigua	108
New Siberian Is. (USSR)	14,672	South Georgia (U.K.)	1,450	Martha's Vineyard (Mass., U.S.)	93
Severnaya Zemlya (USSR)	14,285	Euboea (Greece)	1,411	Elba (Italy)	87
New Britain (PNG)	14,100	Long (N.Y., U.S.)	1,401	Seychelles	85
Taiwan (Formosa) (China)	13,836	Socotra (PDR Yemen)	1,400	Channel (U.K.)	74
Kyushu (Japan)	13,770	Samoa	1,209	Marshalls (Pacific Is.)	70
Hainan (China)	13,127	Gotland (Sweden)	1,153	Easter (Chile)	63
Prince of Wales (Canada)	12,872	Western Samoa	1,133	Staten (N.Y., U.S.)	58
Spitsbergen (Norway)	12,355	Manitoulin (Canada)	1,068	Tutuila (Amer. Samoa)	53
Vancouver (Canada)	12,079	Réunion (France)	969	St. Helena (U.K.)	47
Timor	11,527	Azores (Portugal)	902	Nantucket (Mass., U.S.)	46
Sicily (Italy)	9,926	Juventud (I. of Pines) (Cuba)	849	Hong Kong	30
Somerset (Canada)	9,570	Bioko (Fernando Po) (Equat. Guinea)	779	Manhattan (N.Y., U.S.)	22
Sardinia (Italy)	9,301	Tenerife (Spain)	745	Bermudas	21
Fiji	7,055	Maui (Hawaii, U.S.)	729	Iwo Jima (Japan)	7.8
Shikoku (Japan)	6,860	Mauritius	720	Nauru	7.7
		Skye (U.K.)	670	Governors (N.Y., U.S.)	180 acres

GEOGRAPHIC CENTERS OF THE UNITED STATES

SOURCE: U.S. Geological Survey

Because there is neither a generally accepted definition of a geographic center nor a completely satisfactory method for determining it, there may be as many geographic centers of a state or country as there are definitions of the term.

No marked or monumented point has been established by any government agency as the geographic center of either the 50 states, the conterminous United States, or the North American Continent. However, a monument was erected in Lebanon, Kansas, by a group of citizens who had hired engineers to determine the "geographic center" of the United States.

Sometimes confused with the geographic center of the United States is the reference point for all property lines and city, county, State, and international boundaries on the North American Continent that are tied to the National Triangulation networks of the United States, Canada, Mexico, and Central America. This point is Meades Ranch Triangulation station located at latitude 39°13'26.686", longitude 98°32'30.506", about 12 miles north of Lucas, Kansas. It is the base point or origin of geodetic positions and directions in the triangulation net of the United States because it is at the junction of the main east-west transcontinental triangulation arc stretching from the Atlantic to the Pacific Coasts and the main north-south arc, which follows approximately the 98th meridian from the Canadian border to the Rio Grande.

In determining the centers of the states, islands adjacent to their coastlines and large bodies of water on their boundaries were excluded.

The geographic centers and positions listed below should be considered as estimates. The center of the United States (without Alaska and Hawaii) is approximately Lebanon, Kansas.

Center	Latitude (N)	Longitude (W)
Conterminous United States (48 States) Near Lebanon, Smith County, Kansas	39°50'	98°35'
Continental United States (49 States) Near Castle Rock, Butte County, South Dakota	44°59'	103°38'
The United States (50 States) West of Castle Rock, Butte County, South Dakota	44°58'	103°46'
North American Continent 6 miles west of Balta, Pierce County, North Dakota	48°10'	100°10'

State	Geographic Center
Alabama	12 miles southwest of Clanton
Alaska	63°50'N., 152°00'W., 60 miles north-west of Mt. McKinley
Arizona	55 miles east-southeast of Prescott
Arkansas	12 miles northwest of Little Rock
California	35 miles east of Madera
Colorado	30 miles northwest of Pikes Peak
Connecticut	at East Berlin
Delaware	11 miles south of Dover
District of Columbia	near Fourth and L Streets NW
Florida	12 miles north-northwest of Brooksville
Georgia	18 miles southeast of Macon
Hawaii	20°15'N., 156°20'W., off Maui Island
Idaho	at Custer, southwest of Challis
Illinois	28 miles northeast of Springfield
Indiana	14 miles north-northwest of Indianapolis
Iowa	5 miles northeast of Ames
Kansas	15 miles northeast of Great Bend
Kentucky	3 miles north-northwest of Lebanon
Louisiana	3 miles southeast of Marksville
Maine	18 miles north of Dover-Foxcroft
Maryland	4½ miles northwest of Davidsonville
Massachusetts	north part of city of Worcester
Michigan	5 miles north-northwest of Cadillac
Minnesota	10 miles southwest of Brainerd
Mississippi	9 miles west-northwest of Carthage
Missouri	20 miles southwest of Jefferson City
Montana	12 miles west of Lewistown
Nebraska	10 miles northwest of Broken Bow
Nevada	26 miles southeast of Austin
New Hampshire	3 miles east of Ashland
New Jersey	5 miles southeast of Trenton
New Mexico	12 miles south-southwest of Willard
New York	12+ miles south of Oneida and 26+ miles southwest of Utica
North Carolina	10 miles northwest of Sanford
North Dakota	5 miles southwest of McClusky
Ohio	25 miles north-northeast of Columbus
Oklahoma	8 miles north of Oklahoma City
Oregon	25 miles south-southeast of Prineville
Pennsylvania	2½ miles southwest of Bellefonte
Rhode Island	1 mile south-southwest of Crompton
South Carolina	13 miles southeast of Columbia
South Dakota	8 miles northeast of Pierre
Tennessee	5 miles northeast of Murfreesboro
Texas	15 miles northeast of Brady
Utah	3 miles north of Manti
Vermont	3 miles east of Roxbury
Virginia	5 miles southwest of Buckingham
Washington	10 miles west-southwest of Wenatchee
West Virginia	4 miles east of Sutton
Wisconsin	9 miles southeast of Marshfield
Wyoming	58 miles east-northeast of Lander

EXTREME POINTS OF THE UNITED STATES

SOURCE: U.S. Geological Survey

The geographic center of an area may be defined as the center of gravity of the surface, or that point on which the surface of the area would balance if it were a cardboardlike plane of uniform thickness. Extreme points are measured from the various centers of the U.S. Because many factors, such as curvature of the earth, large bodies of water, and irregular surfaces, affect the determination of centers of gravity, the following positions should be considered as approximations only.

Location	Direction from Geographic Center	Coordinates Latitude (N)	Coordinates Longitude (W)	Distance from Geographic Center (in miles)
From geographic center of United States near Lebanon, Smith County, Kansas, 39°50', 98°35' to—				
Lake of the Woods, Minnesota	Northeast	49°23'	95°09'	680
Key West, Florida	Southeast	24°33'	81°48'	1,436
West Quoddy Head, Maine	East	44°49'	66°57'	1,640
Cape Alava, Washington	West	48°10'	124°44'	1,412
From geographic center of United States (including Alaska) near Castle Rock, Butte County, S.D., 44°59', 103°38' to—				
Point Barrow, Alaska	Northwest	71°23'	156°29'	2,504
Key West, Florida	Southeast	24°33'	81°48'	1,865
West Quoddy Head, Maine	East	44°49'	66°57'	1,779
Cape Wrangell, Attu Island, Alaska	Northwest	52°55'	172°27'(E)	3,623
From geographic center of United States (including Alaska and Hawaii) west of Castle Rock, S.D., 44°58', 103°46' to—				
Point Barrow, Alaska	Northwest	71°23'	156°29'	2,502
Ka Lae (South Cape), Hawaii Island, Hawaii	Southwest	18°56'	155°41'	3,456
West Quoddy Head, Maine	East	44°49'	66°57'	1,785
Cape Wrangell, Attu Island, Alaska	Northwest	52°55'	172°27'(E)	3,620

U.S. COASTLINE & SHORELINE Source: National Ocean Survey, National Oceanic and Atmospheric Administration

General coastline figures represent lengths of the seacoast outline. The coastlines of sounds and of bays are included to a point where they narrow to the width of 30 minutes of latitude, and the distance across at such point is included. Tidal shoreline figures include the outer coast, offshore islands, sounds, bays, and rivers to the head of tidewater or to a point where tidal waters narrow to a width of 100 feet.

	Coastline	Shoreline
UNITED STATES	12,383	88,633
(without Alaska and Hawaii)	4,993	53,677
Atlantic	2,069	28,673
Maine	228	3,478
New Hampshire	13	131
Massachusetts	192	1,519
Rhode Island	40	384
Connecticut	—	618
New York	127	1,850
New Jersey	130	1,792
Pennsylvania	—	89
Delaware	28	381
Maryland	31	3,190
Virginia	112	3,315
North Carolina	301	3,375
South Carolina	187	2,876
Georgia	100	2,344
Florida (Atlantic only)	580	3,331
Gulf of Mexico	1,631	17,141
Florida (Gulf only)	770	5,095
Alabama	53	607
Mississippi	44	359
Louisiana	397	7,721
Texas	367	3,359

	Coastline	Shoreline
Pacific	7,623	40,298
California	840	3,427
Oregon	296	1,410
Washington	157	3,026
Hawaii	750	1,052
Alaska (Pacific only)	5,580	31,383
Alaska (Arctic only)	1,060	2,521
EXTRATERRITORIAL		
Canal Zone	20	126
Atlantic		
Navassa	5	5
Puerto Rico	311	700
Virgin Islands	117	175
Pacific		
Baker Island	3	3
Guam Islands	78	110
Howland Island	4	4
Jarvis Island	5	5
Johnston Island	5	5
Midway Island	20	33
Palmyra Island	9	16
Samoa Islands	76	126
Wake Island	12	20

AVERAGE AND EXTREME U.S. ELEVATIONS Source: U.S. Geological Survey

State or Territory	Mean Elevation (feet)	HIGH Point	Mean Elevation (feet)	LOW Point	Mean Elevation (feet)
Alabama	500	Cheaha Mountain	2,407	Gulf of Mexico	(1)
Alaska	1,900	Mount McKinley	20,320	Pacific Ocean	(1)
American Samoa	1,300	Lata Mountain (Tau I.)	3,160	Pacific Ocean	(1)
Arizona	4,100	Humphreys Peak	12,633	Colorado River	70
Arkansas	650	Magazine Mountain	2,753	Ouachita River	55
California	2,900	Mount Whitney	14,494	Death Valley	—282
Canal Zone	280	Cerro Galera	1,205	Atlantic Ocean	(1)
Colorado	6,800	Mount Elbert	14,433	Arkansas River	3,350
Connecticut	500	Mount Frissell (So. Slope)	2,380	Long Island Sound	(1)
Delaware	60	On Ebright Road (New Castle County)	442	Atlantic Ocean	(1)
Florida	100	Sec. 30, T. 6N., R. 20W.	345	Atlantic Ocean	(1)
Georgia	600	Brasstown Bald	4,784	Atlantic Ocean	(1)
Guam	330	Mount Lamlam	1,329	Pacific Ocean	(1)
Hawaii	3,030	Mauna Kea	13,796	Pacific Ocean	(1)
Idaho	5,000	Borah Peak	12,662	Snake River	710
Illinois	600	Charles Mound	1,235	Mississippi River	279
Indiana	700	Franklin Township (Wayne County)	1,257	Ohio River	320
Iowa	1,100	Sec. 29, T. 100 N., R. 41 W.	1,670	Mississippi River	480
Kansas	2,000	Mount Sunflower	4,039	Verdigris River	680
Kentucky	750	Black Mountain	4,145	Mississippi River	257
Louisiana	100	Driskill Mountain	535	New Orleans	—5
Maine	600	Mount Katahdin	5,268	Atlantic Ocean	(1)
Maryland	350	Backbone Mountain	3,360	Atlantic Ocean	(1)
Massachusetts	500	Mount Greylock	3,491	Atlantic Ocean	(1)
Michigan	900	Mount Curwood	1,980	Lake Erie	572
Minnesota	1,200	Eagle Mountain	2,301	Lake Superior	602
Mississippi	300	Woodall Mountain	806	Gulf of Mexico	(1)
Missouri	800	Taum Sauk Mountain	1,772	St. Francis River	230
Montana	3,400	Granite Peak	12,799	Kootenai River	1,800
Nebraska	2,600	Johnson Township (Kimball County)	5,426	SE corner of state	840
Nevada	5,500	Boundary Peak	13,143	Colorado River	470
New Hampshire	1,000	Mount Washington	6,288	Atlantic Ocean	(1)
New Jersey	250	High Point	1,803	Atlantic Ocean	(1)
New Mexico	5,700	Wheeler Peak	13,161	Red Bluff Reservoir	2,817
New York	1,000	Mount Marcy	5,344	Atlantic Ocean	(1)
North Carolina	700	Mount Mitchell	6,684	Atlantic Ocean	(1)
North Dakota	1,900	White Butte	3,506	Red River	750
Ohio	850	Campbell Hill	1,550	Ohio River	433
Oklahoma	1,300	Black Mesa	4,973	Little River	287
Oregon	3,300	Mount Hood	11,235	Pacific Ocean	(1)
Pennsylvania	1,100	Mount Davis	3,213	Delaware River	(1)
Puerto Rico	1,800	Cerro de Punta	4,389	Atlantic Ocean	(1)
Rhode Island	200	Jerimoth Hill	812	Atlantic Ocean	(1)
South Carolina	350	Sassafras Mountain	3,560	Atlantic Ocean	(1)
South Dakota	2,200	Harney Peak	7,242	Big Stone Lake	962
Tennessee	900	Clingmans Dome	6,643	Mississippi River	182
Texas	1,700	Guadalupe Peak	8,751	Gulf of Mexico	(1)
Utah	6,100	Kings Peak	13,528	Beaverdam Creek	2,000
Vermont	1,000	Mount Mansfield	4,393	Lake Champlain	95
Virginia	950	Mount Rogers	5,729	Atlantic Ocean	(1)
Virgin Islands	750	Crown Mountain (St. Thomas)	1,556	Atlantic Ocean	(1)
Washington	1,700	Mount Rainier	14,410	Pacific Ocean	(1)
West Virginia	1,500	Spruce Knob	4,862	Potomac River	240
Wisconsin	1,050	Timms Hill	1,952	Lake Michigan	581
Wyoming	6,700	Gannett Peak	13,804	Belle Fourche River	3,100

(1) = Sea level.

PRINCIPAL U.S. RIVERS

SOURCE: U.S. Geological Survey

River	Empties Into:	Length (in miles)
Mississippi-Missouri-Red Rock	Gulf of Mexico	3,741
Missouri-Red Rock	Mississippi River	2,564
Mississippi	Gulf of Mexico	2,348
Missouri	Mississippi River	2,315
Yukon (U.S.-Canada)	Bering Sea	1,979
St. Lawrence (U.S.-Canada)	Atlantic Ocean	1,900
Rio Grande (U.S.-Mexico)	Gulf of Mexico	1,885
Arkansas	Mississippi River	1,450
Colorado (U.S.-Mexico)	Gulf of California	1,450
Brazos	Gulf of Mexico	1,309
Ohio-Allegheny	Mississippi River	1,306
Columbia (U.S.-Canada)	Pacific Ocean	1,243
Red (Okla.-Tex.-Ark.-La.)	Mississippi River	1,222
Mississippi, Upper	to mouth of Missouri River	1,171
Snake	Columbia River	1,000
Ohio	Mississippi River	981
Pecos	Rio Grande	926
Canadian	Arkansas River	906
Tennessee-N. Fk. Holston	Ohio River	900
Colorado (Texas)	Gulf of Mexico	894
Columbia, Upper (U.S.-Canada)	to mouth of Snake River	890
Kuskokwim	Bering Sea	800
Tanana	Yukon River	800
North Canadian	Canadian River	784
Kansas-Republican-Arikaree	Missouri River	743
Green (Wyo.-Colo.-Utah)	Colorado River	730
Milk (U.S.-Canada)	Missouri River	729
Trinity	Gulf of Mexico	715
James (N. Dak.-S. Dak.)	Missouri River	710
Cimarron	Arkansas River	698
Cumberland	Ohio River	687
White (Mo.-Ark.)	Mississippi River	685
North Platte	Platte River	680
Yellowstone	Missouri River	671
Tennessee	Ohio River	652
Mobile-Alabama-Coosa	Gulf of Mexico	639
Gila	Colorado River	630
Washita	Red River	626
Ouachita	Red River	605
Little Missouri	Missouri River	560
Smoky Hill	Kansas River	560
Porcupine (U.S.-Canada)	Yukon River	555
Koyukuk	Yukon River	554
Red River of the North (U.S.-Canada)	Lake Winnipeg	545
Tombigbee	Mobile River	525
Apalachicola-Chattahoochee	Gulf of Mexico	524
White (S. Dak.-Nebr.)	Missouri River	507
Osage-Marais des Cygnes	Missouri River	496
Pend Oreille-Clark Fork	Columbia River	490
Pearl	Gulf of Mexico	490
Powder	Yellowstone River	486
Kootenai (U.S.-Canada)	Columbia River	485
Wabash	Ohio River	475
Innoko	Yukon River	463
Susquehanna	Chesapeake Bay	458
Neosho	Arkansas River	450
South Platte	Platte River	442
Santee-Wateree-Catawba	Atlantic Ocean	438
Pee Dee-Yadkin	Atlantic Ocean	435
Niobrara	Missouri River	431
Wisconsin	Mississippi River	430

LARGE U.S. LAKES

SOURCE: U.S. Geological Survey and Statistics Canada

Natural U.S. lakes with areas of 100 sq. mi. or more are listed

Lake	State	Area (sq. mi.)
Superior	Canada, Minnesota, Wisconsin, and Michigan	31,700
Huron	Canada and Michigan	23,010
Michigan	Wisconsin, Illinois, Indiana, and Michigan	22,300
Erie	Canada, Michigan, Ohio, Pennsylvania, and New York	9,910
Ontario	Canada and New York	7,340
Great Salt[a]	Utah	1,685[b]
Lake of the Woods	Minnesota and Canada	1,679
Iliamna	Alaska	1,000
Okeechobee	Florida	700
Pontchartrain[a]	Louisiana	625
Becharof	Alaska	458
Red Lake (Upper and Lower)	Minnesota	451
Champlain	New York, Vermont, and Canada	435
St. Clair	Michigan and Canada	432
Salton Sea[a]	California	374[b]
Rainy	Minnesota and Canada	360
Teshekpuk	Alaska	315
Naknek	Alaska	242
Winnebago	Wisconsin	215
Mille Lacs	Minnesota	207
Flathead	Montana	197
Tahoe	California and Nevada	193
Leech	Minnesota	176
Pyramid[a]	Nevada	172[b]
Pend Oreille	Idaho	148
Ugashik (Upper and Lower)	Alaska	147
Upper Klamath	Oregon	142
Utah	Utah	140
Bear (including Mud Lake)	Idaho and Utah	136
Yellowstone	Wyoming	134
Moosehead	Maine	117
Tustumena	Alaska	117
Clark	Alaska	110
Winnibigoshish	Minnesota	109
Dall	Alaska	100

[a] Salty. [b] Variable.

HIGHEST U.S. MOUNTAIN PEAKS

SOURCE: U.S. Geological Survey

Peak	State	Elevation
Mt. McKinley	Alaska	20,320
Mt. St. Elias	Alaska	18,008
Mt. Foraker	Alaska	17,400
Mt. Blackburn	Alaska	16,523
Mt. Bona	Alaska	16,421
Mt. Sanford	Alaska	16,237
South Buttress	Alaska	15,885
Mt. Vancouver	Alaska	15,700
Mt. Churchill	Alaska	15,638
Mt. Fairweather	Alaska	15,300
Mt. Hubbard	Alaska	15,015
Mt. Bear	Alaska	14,831
East Buttress	Alaska	14,730
Mt. Hunter	Alaska	14,573
Mt. Alverstone	Alaska	14,565
Browne Tower	Alaska	14,530
Mt. Whitney	California	14,494
Mt. Elbert	Colorado	14,433
Mt. Massive	Colorado	14,421
Mt. Harvard	Colorado	14,420
Mt. Rainier	Washington	14,410
Mt. Williamson	California	14,375
Blanca Peak	Colorado	14,345
La Plata Peak	Colorado	14,336
Uncompahgre Peak	Colorado	14,309
Crestone Peak	Colorado	14,294
Mt. Lincoln	Colorado	14,286
Grays Peak	Colorado	14,270
Mt. Antero	Colorado	14,269
Torreys Peak	Colorado	14,267
Castle Peak	Colorado	14,265
Quandary Peak	Colorado	14,265
Mt. Evans	Colorado	14,264
Longs Peak	Colorado	14,255
Mt. Wilson	Colorado	14,246
White Mtn.	California	14,246
North Palisade	California	14,242
Shavano Peak	Colorado	14,229
Mt. Belford	Colorado	14,197
Mt. Princeton	Colorado	14,197
Crestone Needle	Colorado	14,197
Mt. Yale	Colorado	14,196
Mt. Bross	Colorado	14,172
Kit Carson Mtn.	Colorado	14,165
Mt. Wrangell	Alaska	14,163
Mt. Shasta	California	14,162
Mt. Sill	California	14,162
El Diente Peak	Colorado	14,159
Maroon Peak	Colorado	14,156
Tabeguache Mtn.	Colorado	14,155
Mt. Oxford	Colorado	14,153
Mt. Sneffels	Colorado	14,150
Mt. Democrat	Colorado	14,148
Capitol Peak	Colorado	14,130
Pikes Peak	Colorado	14,110
Snowmass Mtn.	Colorado	14,092
Windom Peak	Colorado	14,087
Mt. Russell	California	14,086
Mt. Eolus	Colorado	14,084
Mt. Columbia	Colorado	14,073
Mt. Augusta	Alaska	14,070
Missouri Mtn.	Colorado	14,067
Humboldt Peak	Colorado	14,064
Mt. Bierstadt	Colorado	14,060
Sunlight Peak	Colorado	14,059
Handies Peak	California	14,058
Split Mt.	Colorado	14,048
Culebra Peak	Colorado	14,047

U.S. TEMPERATURE EXTREMES

SOURCE: National Oceanic and Atmospheric Administration

HIGHEST TEMPERATURES

Greenland Ranch, Calif., with 134° on July 10, 1913, holds the record for the highest temperature ever officially recorded in the United States. This station is located in Death Valley, which is about 140 miles long, four to 16 miles wide, and runs north and south in southeastern California and southwestern Nevada. Death Valley is below sea level and flanked by towering mountain ranges with Mt. Whitney, rising to 14,495 feet, less than 100 miles to the west. It has the hottest summers in the Western Hemisphere and is the only known place in the United States where nighttime temperatures sometimes remain above 100°.

In the United States the station normally having the highest annual average is Key West, Fla., 78.2°; the highest summer average, Death Valley, Calif., 98.2°; and the highest winter average, Key West, Fla., 70.2°.

Amazing temperature rises of 40° to 50° in a few minutes occasionally may be brought about by Chinook winds. Some outstanding extreme temperature rises in short periods are:

12 hours: 83°, Granville, N. Dak., Feb. 21, 1918, from −33° to 50° from early morning to late afternoon.

15 minutes: 42°, Fort Assiniboine, Mont., Jan. 19, 1892, from −5° to 37°.

7 minutes: 34°, Kipp, Mont., Dec. 1, 1896; observer also reported that a total rise of 80° occurred in a few hours and that 30 inches of snow disappeared in one-half day.

2 minutes: 49°, Spearfish, S. Dak., Jan. 22, 1943, from −4° at 7:30 a.m., to 45° at 7:32 a.m.

HIGHEST TEMPERATURES IN CONTERMINOUS UNITED STATES BY MONTHS

Month	Temp. (°F.)	Year	Day	State	Place	Elevation Feet
Jan.	98	1936	17	Texas	Laredo	421
Feb.*	105	1963	3	Ariz.	Montezuma	735
Mar.*	108	1954	31	Texas	Rio Grande City	168
Apr.	118	1898	25	Calif.	Volcano Springs	−220
May*	124	1896	27	Calif.	Salton	−263
June*†	127	1896	15	Ariz.	Ft. Mohave	555
July	134	1913	10	Calif.	Greenland Ranch	−178
Aug.†	127	1933	12	Calif.	Greenland Ranch	−178
Sept.	126	1950	2	Calif.	Mecca	−175
Oct.*	116	1917	5	Ariz.	Sentinel	685
Nov.*	105	1906	12	Calif.	Craftonville	1,759
Dec.	100	1938	8	Calif.	La Mesa	539

* Two or more occurrences, most recent given. † Slightly higher temperatures in old records are not used owing to lack of information.

RECORD HIGHEST TEMPERATURES BY STATES

State	Temp. (°F.)	Date	Station	Elevation Feet
Ala.	112	Sept. 5, 1925	Centerville	345
Alaska	100	June 27, 1915	Fort Yukon	—
Ariz.	127	July 7, 1905*	Parker	345
Ark.	120	Aug. 10, 1936	Ozark	396
Calif.	134	July 10, 1913	Greenland Ranch	−178
Colo.	118	July 11, 1888	Bennett	—
Conn.	105	July 22, 1926	Waterbury	400
Del.	110	July 21, 1930	Millsboro	20
D.C.	106	July 20, 1930*	Washington	112
Fla.	109	June 29, 1931	Monticello	207
Ga.	112	July 24, 1952	Louisville	337
Hawaii	100	Apr. 27, 1931	Pahala	850
Idaho	118	July 28, 1934	Orofino	1,027
Ill.	117	July 14, 1954	E. St. Louis	410
Ind.	116	July 14, 1936	Collegeville	672
Iowa	118	July 20, 1934	Keokuk	614
Kans.	121	July 24, 1936*	Alton (near)	1,651
Ky.	114	July 28, 1930	Greensburg	581
La.	114	Aug. 10, 1936	Plain Dealing	268
Maine	105	July 10, 1911*	North Bridgton	450
Md.	109	July 10, 1936*	Cumberland & Frederick	623–325
Mass.	106	July 4, 1911*	Lawrence	51
Mich.	112	July 13, 1936	Mio	963
Minn.	114	July 6, 1936*	Moorhead	904
Miss.	115	July 29, 1930	Holly Springs	600
Mo.	118	July 14, 1954*	Warsaw & Union	687–560
Mont.	117	July 5, 1937	Medicine Lake	1,950
Nebr.	118	July 24, 1936*	Minden	2,169
Nev.	122	June 23, 1954*	Overton	1,240
N.H.	106	July 4, 1911	Nashua	125
N.J.	110	July 10, 1936	Runyon	18
N. Mex.	116	July 14, 1934*	Orogrande	4,171
N.Y.	108	July 22, 1926	Troy	35
N.C.	109	Sept. 7, 1954*	Weldon	81
N. Dak.	121	July 6, 1936	Steele	1,857
Ohio	113	July 21, 1934*	Gallipolis (near)	673
Okla.	120	July 26, 1943*	Tishomingo	670
Oreg.	119	Aug. 10, 1898*	Pendleton	1,074
Pa.	111	July 10, 1936*	Phoenixville	100
R.I.	102	July 30, 1949	Greenville	420
S.C.	111	June 28, 1954*	Camden	170
S. Dak.	120	July 5, 1936	Gannvalley	1,750
Tenn.	113	Aug. 9, 1930*	Perryville	377
Tex.	120	Aug. 12, 1936	Seymour	1,291
Utah	116	June 28, 1892	Saint George	2,880
Vt.	105	July 4, 1911	Vernon	310
Va.	110	July 15, 1954	Balcony Falls	725
Wash.	118	Aug. 5, 1961*	Ice Harbor Dam	475
W. Va.	112	July 10, 1936*	Martinsburg	435
Wis.	114	July 13, 1936	Wisconsin Dells	900
Wyo.	114	July 12, 1900	Basin	3,500

* Also on earlier dates at the same or other places.

LOWEST TEMPERATURES

In the United States, the lowest temperature on record, −79.8°, was recorded at Prospect Creek Camp, which is located in the Endicott Mountains of northern Alaska. The lowest temperature in the 48 states, −69.7°, occurred at Rogers Pass (Lewis and Clark County, Montana), which is mountainous and heavily forested terrain, about a half mile east of and 140 feet below the summit of the Continental Divide.

The lowest average annual temperature recorded in the United States is 9.3° at Barrow, Alaska, on the Arctic coast. Barrow also has the coolest summers (June, July, August) with an average of 36.4°. The lowest average winter (December, January, February) temperature is −15.7° at Barter Island on the Arctic coast of northeast Alaska. In Hawaii, average annual temperatures range from 44.0° at Mauna Loa Slope Observatory (elevation 11,146 feet) on the island of Hawaii to 76.6° at Honolulu on the island of Oahu.

In the 48 states, Mt. Washington, N.H. (elevation 6,262 feet) has the lowest mean annual temperature, 26.9° F, and the lowest mean summer (June, July, August) temperature, 46.8°. A few stations in the Northeast and upper Rockies have mean annuals in the high 30's, and at the same stations in the latter area summers may average in the high 40's. Winter (December, January, February) mean temperatures are lowest in northeastern North Dakota where the average is 5.9° at the Langdon Experiment Farm and northwestern Minnesota where the average is 6.1° at Hallock.

In continental areas of the Temperate Zone, 40° to 50° temperature falls in a few hours caused by advection (horizontal shifting) of cold air masses are not uncommon. Following these large drops, radiation sometimes may cause a further temperature fall resulting in remarkable changes. Some outstanding extreme temperature falls are:

24 hours: 100°, Browning, Mont., Jan. 23–24, 1916, from 44° to −56°.

12 hours: 84°, Fairfield, Mont., Dec. 24, 1924, from 63° at noon to −21° at midnight.

2 hours: 62°, Rapid City, S. Dak., Jan. 12, 1911, from 49° at 6 a.m., to −13° at 8 a.m.

27 minutes: 58°, Spearfish, S. Dak., Jan. 22, 1943, from 54° at 9 a.m., to −4° at 9:27 a.m.

15 minutes: 47°, Rapid City, S. Dak., Jan. 10, 1911, from 55° at 7 a.m. to 8° at 7:15 a.m.

LOWEST TEMPERATURES IN CONTERMINOUS UNITED STATES BY MONTHS

Month	Temp. (°F.)	Year	Day	State	Place	Elevation Feet
Jan.	−70	1954	20	Mont.	Rogers Pass	5,470
Feb.	−66	1933	9	Mont.	Riverside	6,700
Mar.	−50	1906	17	Wyo.	Snake River	6,862
Apr.	−36	1945	5	N. Mex.	Eagle Nest	8,250
May	−15	1964	7	Calif.	White Mtn. 2	12,470
June	2	1907	13	Calif.	Tamarack	8,000
July*	10	1911	21	Wyo.	Painter	6,800
Aug.*	5	1910	25	Mont.	Bowen	6,080
Sept.*	−9	1926	24	Mont.	Riverside	6,700
Oct.	−33	1917	29	Wyo.	Soda Butte	6,600
Nov.	−53	1959	16	Mont.	Lincoln 14 NE	5,130
Dec.*	−59	1924	19	Mont.	Riverside	6,700

* Two or more occurrences, most recent given.

RECORD LOWEST TEMPERATURES BY STATES

State	Temp. (°F.)	Date	Station	Elevation Feet
Ala.	−24	Jan. 31, 1966	Russellville	880
Alaska	−80	Jan. 23, 1971	Prospect Creek Camp	1,100
Ariz.	−40	Jan. 7, 1971	Hawley Lake	8,180
Ark.	−29	Feb. 13, 1905	Pond	1,250
Cal.	−45	Jan. 20, 1937	Boca	5,532
Colo.	−60	Feb. 1, 1951	Taylor Park	9,206
Conn.	−32	Feb. 16, 1943	Falls Village	585
Del.	−17	Jan. 17, 1893	Millsboro	20
D.C.	−15	Feb. 11, 1899	Washington	112
Fla.	− 2	Feb. 13, 1899	Tallahassee	193
Ga.	−17	Jan. 27, 1940	CCC Camp F−16	—
Hawaii	14	Jan. 2, 1961	Haleakala, Maui Island	9,750
Idaho	−60	Jan. 18, 1943	Island Park Dam	6,285
Ill.	−35	Jan. 22, 1930	Mount Carroll	817
Ind.	−35	Feb. 2, 1951	Greensburg	954
Iowa	−47	Jan. 12, 1912	Washta	1,157
Kans.	−40	Feb. 13, 1905	Lebanon	1,812
Ky.	−34	Jan. 28, 1963	Cynthiana	684
La.	−16	Feb. 13, 1899	Minden	194
Maine	−48	Jan. 19, 1925	Van Buren	510
Md.	−40	Jan. 13, 1912	Oakland	2,461
Mass.	−34	Jan. 18, 1957	Birch Hill Dam	840
Mich.	−51	Feb. 9, 1934	Vanderbilt	785
Minn.	−59	Feb. 16, 1903*	Pokegama Dam	1,280
Miss.	−19	Jan. 30, 1966	Corinth	420
Mo.	−40	Feb. 13, 1905	Warsaw	700
Mont.	−70	Jan. 20, 1954	Rogers Pass	5,470
Nebr.	−47	Feb. 12, 1899	Camp Clarke	3,700
Nev.	−50	Jan. 8, 1937	San Jacinto	5,200
N.H.	−46	Jan. 28, 1925	Pittsburg	1,575
N.J.	−34	Jan. 5, 1904	River Vale	70
N. Mex.	−50	Feb. 1, 1951	Gavilan	7,350
N.Y.	−52	Feb. 9, 1934	Stillwater Reservoir	1,670
N.C.	−29	Jan. 30, 1966	Mt. Mitchell	6,525
N. Dak.	−60	Feb. 15, 1936	Parshall	1,929
Ohio	−39	Feb. 10, 1899	Milligan	800
Okla.	−27	Jan. 18, 1930*	Watts	958
Oreg.	−54	Feb. 10, 1933*	Seneca	4,700
Pa.	−42	Jan. 5, 1904	Smethport	—
R.I.	−23	Jan. 11, 1942	Kingston	100
S.C.	−13	Jan. 26, 1940	Longcreek (near)	1,631
S. Dak.	−58	Feb. 17, 1936	McIntosh	2,277
Tenn.	−32	Dec. 30, 1917	Mountain City	2,471
Tex.	−23	Feb. 8, 1933*	Seminole	3,275
Utah	−50	Jan. 5, 1913*	Strawberry Tunnel east portal	7,650
Vt.	−50	Dec. 30, 1933	Bloomfield	915
Va.	−29	Feb. 10, 1899	Monterey	—
Wash.	−48	Dec. 30, 1968	Mazama	2,120
			Winthrop	1,765
W. Va.	−37	Dec. 30, 1917	Lewisburg	2,200
Wis.	−54	Jan. 24, 1922	Danbury	908
Wyo.	−63	Feb. 9, 1933	Moran	6,770

* Also on earlier dates at the same or other places.

WIND CHILL

Source: National Oceanic and Atmosphereic Administration

A very strong wind combined with a temperature slightly below freezing can have the same chilling effect as a temperature nearly 50°F lower in a calm atmosphere. Arctic explorers and military experts have developed what is called the "wind-chill factor," which shows the combined effects of wind and temperature as equivalent calm-air temperatures. In effect, the index describes the cooling power of the air on exposed flesh. The wind-chill table here shows this cooling power for various combinations of wind and temperature, and will help you gauge how much protection you really need.

Directions: 1) Find actual (calm) air temperature across top of table. 2) Determine wind speed and follow across to correct calm-air temperature. Number given is **equivalent temperature.**

For example, a 10° temperature with a 20 mph wind equals the equivalent of −24 degrees.

WIND CHILL

Equivalent Temperatures (°F)

Windspeed (Miles per hour)	35	30	25	20	15	10	5	0	−5	−10	−15	−20	−25	−30	−35	−40	−45
Calm	35	30	25	20	15	10	5	0	−5	−10	−15	−20	−25	−30	−35	−40	−45
5	33	27	21	16	12	7	1	−6	−11	−15	−20	−26	−31	−35	−41	−47	−54
10	21	16	9	2	−2	−9	−15	−22	−27	−31	−38	−45	−52	−58	−64	−70	−77
15	16	11	1	−6	−11	−18	−25	−33	−40	−45	−51	−60	−65	−70	−78	−85	−90
20	12	3	−4	−9	−17	−24	−32	−40	−46	−52	−60	−68	−76	−81	−88	−96	−103
25	7	0	−7	−15	−22	−29	−37	−45	−52	−58	−67	−75	−83	−89	−96	−104	−112
30	5	−2	−11	−18	−26	−33	−41	−49	−56	−63	−70	−78	−87	−94	−101	−109	−117
35	3	−4	−13	−20	−27	−35	−43	−52	−60	−67	−72	−83	−90	−98	−105	−113	−123
40	1	−4	−15	−22	−29	−36	−45	−54	−62	−69	−76	−87	−94	−101	−107	−116	−128
45	1	−6	−17	−24	−31	−38	−46	−54	−63	−70	−78	−87	−94	−101	−108	−118	−128
50	0	−7	−17	−24	−31	−38	−47	−56	−63	−70	−79	−88	−96	−103	−110	−120	−128

Zone labels within the table: VERY COLD — BITTER COLD — EXTREME COLD

U.S. CITY WEATHER I   Source: National Climatic Center

City	Record Temperature High (F°)	Record Temperature Low (F°)	Annual Average: Precip. (Water equiv.) (in.)	Annual Average: Snow and Sleet (in.)	Wind Speed (mph)	First Freeze Date 32 F° or less Average	First Freeze Date 32 F° or less Earliest on record	Last Freeze Date 32 F° or less Average	Last Freeze Date 32 F° or less Latest on record	Elevation of Station (feet)
Albany	104	—28	36.46	65.7	8.8	Oct. 13	Sept. 23	Apr. 27	May 20	292
Albuquerque	105	—17	8.33	10.7	9.0	Oct. 29	Oct. 11	Apr. 16	May 18	5,314
Atlanta	103	— 9	48.66	1.5	9.1	Nov. 12	Oct. 24	Mar. 24	Apr. 15	1,034
Baltimore	107	— 7	41.62	21.9	9.5	Oct. 26	Oct. 8	Apr. 15	May 11	155
Birmingham	107	—10	53.46	1.2	7.4	Nov. 10	Oct. 17	Mar. 17	Apr. 21	630
Bismarck	114	—45	16.15	38.4	10.6	Sept. 22	Sept. 6	May 11	May 30	1,660
Boise	111	—23	11.97	21.7	9.0	Oct. 12	Sept. 9	May 6	May 31	2,868
Boston	104	—18	41.55	41.9	12.6	Nov. 7	Oct. 5	Apr. 8	May 3	29
Buffalo	99	—21	35.19	88.6	12.3	Oct. 25	Sept. 23	Apr. 30	May 24	706
Burlington, Vt.	101	—30	32.54	78.4	8.8	Oct. 3	Sept. 13	May 10	May 24	340
Charleston, W. Va.	108	—24	43.66	28.8	6.5	Oct. 28	Sept. 29	Apr. 18	May 11	951
Charlotte	104	— 5	45.00	5.6	7.6	Nov. 4	Oct. 15	Apr. 2	Apr. 16	769
Cheyenne	100	—38	14.48	52.0	13.3	Sept. 27	Aug. 25	May 18	June 18	6,141
Chicago	105	—23	33.47	40.7	10.3	Oct. 26	Sept. 25	Apr. 20	May 14	623
Cincinnati	102	—19	40.40	23.2	9.1	Oct. 25	Sept. 28	Apr. 15	May 25	877
Cleveland	103	—19	34.15	51.5	10.8	Nov. 2	Sept. 29	Apr. 21	May 14	805
Columbia, S.C.	107	— 2	45.23	1.8	6.9	Nov. 3	Oct. 4	Mar. 30	Apr. 21	225
Columbus, Ohio	106	—20	36.98	27.7	8.7	Oct. 31	Oct. 7	Apr. 16	May 9	833
Concord, N.H.	102	—37	38.13	64.1	6.7	Sept. 24	Sept. 13	May 17	June 6	346
Dallas-Ft. Worth, Tex.	112	— 8	32.11	2.7	11.1	Nov. 21	Oct. 27	Mar. 16	Apr. 13	596
Denver	105	—30	14.60	60.1	9.0	Oct. 14	Sept. 16	May 2	May 28	5,332
Des Moines	110	—30	31.49	33.2	11.1	Oct. 10	Sept. 28	Apr. 20	May 11	963
Detroit	105	—24	31.49	31.7	10.2	Oct. 21	Sept. 23	Apr. 23	May 12	626
El Paso	109	— 8	8.47	4.4	9.6	Nov. 11	Oct. 31	Mar. 13	Apr. 11	3,916
Great Falls	107	—49	14.83	57.7	13.1	Sept. 26	Sept. 7	May 14	June 8	3,657
Hartford	102	—26	43.00	53.1	9.0	Oct. 15	Sept. 27	Apr. 22	May 10	179
Houston	108	5	47.07	0.4	7.6	Dec. 11	Oct. 25	Feb. 5	Mar. 27	108
Indianapolis	107	—25	39.98	21.3	9.7	Oct. 22	Sept. 27	Apr. 23	May 27	808
Jackson	107	— 5	50.96	0.8	7.7	Nov. 8	Oct. 9	Mar. 18	Apr. 25	331
Jacksonville	105	10	51.75	Trace	8.6	Dec. 16	Nov. 3	Feb. 6	Mar. 31	31
Juneau	90	—22	53.95	109.1	8.5	Oct. 21	Sept. 9	Apr. 22	June 8	24
Kansas City, Mo.	113	—22	36.66	19.7	10.2	Oct. 26	Sept. 30	Apr. 7	May 6	1,025
Little Rock	110	—13	48.17	5.3	8.2	Nov. 15	Oct. 23	Mar. 16	Apr. 13	265
Los Angeles	110	23	11.94	Trace	7.4	—	Dec. 9	—	Jan. 21	104
Louisville	107	—20	42.94	17.3	8.4	Oct. 25	Oct. 15	Apr. 10	Apr. 19	488
Memphis	106	—13	48.74	5.7	9.2	Nov. 5	Oct. 17	Mar. 20	Apr. 15	284
Miami	100	26	59.21	—	9.1	—	—	—	Feb. 6	12
Milwaukee	105	—25	30.18	45.2	11.8	Oct. 23	Sept. 20	Apr. 25	May 27	693
Minneapolis-St. Paul	108	—34	26.62	45.8	10.6	Oct. 13	Sept. 3	Apr. 29	May 24	838
Mobile	104	— 1	63.26	0.4	9.3	Dec. 12	Nov. 15	Feb. 17	Mar. 20	221
Nashville	107	—15	46.61	10.9	7.9	Oct. 31	Oct. 7	Apr. 3	Apr. 24	605
New Orleans	102	7	58.93	0.2	8.4	Dec. 3	Nov. 11	Feb. 15	Apr. 8	30
New York City	106	—15	43.56	29.1	9.4	Nov. 12	Oct. 19	Apr. 7	Apr. 24	87
Norfolk	105	2	45.22	7.2	10.6	Nov. 21	Nov. 7	Mar. 22	Apr. 14	30
Oklahoma City	113	—17	31.71	9.2	12.9	Nov. 7	Oct. 7	Apr. 1	May 3	1,304
Omaha	114	—32	28.48	32.5	10.9	Oct. 20	Sept. 24	Apr. 14	May 11	982
Philadelphia	106	—11	41.18	20.3	9.6	Nov. 17	Oct. 19	Mar. 30	Apr. 20	28
Phoenix	118	16	7.41	Trace	6.1	Dec. 11	Nov. 4	Jan. 27	Mar. 3	1,107
Pittsburgh	103	—20	36.21	45.5	9.4	Oct. 20	Oct. 10	Apr. 21	May 4	1,225
Portland, Me.	103	—39	42.15	74.3	8.8	Sept. 27	Sept. 17	May 12	May 31	63
Portland, Ore.	107	— 3	37.98	7.5	7.8	Dec. 1	Oct. 26	Feb. 25	May 4	39
Providence	104	—17	40.90	37.8	10.8	Oct. 26	Oct. 3	Apr. 14	Apr. 24	62
Reno	106	—19	7.65	26.8	6.4	Oct. 2	Aug. 30	May 14	June 25	4,400
Richmond	107	—12	43.77	14.3	7.6	Nov. 8	Oct. 5	Apr. 2	May 11	177
Sacramento	115	17	17.33	Trace	8.3	Dec. 11	Nov. 4	Jan. 24	Mar. 14	25
St. Louis	115	—23	36.70	17.8	9.5	Oct. 20	Sept. 28	Apr. 15	May 10	564
Salt Lake City	107	—30	15.63	58.1	8.7	Nov. 1	Sept. 25	Apr. 12	Apr. 30	4,227
San Francisco	106	20	18.88	Trace	10.5	—	Dec. 11	—	Jan. 21	18
Seattle	100	0	40.30	15.2	9.3	Dec. 1	Oct. 19	Feb. 23	Apr. 3	450
Spokane	108	—30	16.19	54.0	8.7	Oct. 12	Sept. 13	Apr. 20	May 16	2,365
Washington, D.C.	106	—15	40.00	16.8	9.2	Nov. 10	Oct. 2	Mar. 29	May 12	65
Wichita	114	—22	30.06	16.3	12.6	Nov. 1	Sept. 27	Apr. 5	Apr. 21	1,340
Wilmington, Del.	107	—15	43.63	20.1	9.1	Oct. 26	Sept. 27	Apr. 18	May 9	80

U.S. CITY WEATHER II

SOURCE: National Climatic Center (data based on normals for 1936-1975)

AVERAGE MONTHLY TEMPERATURES (in °F)

City	Jan.	Feb.	Mar.	April	May	June	July	Aug.	Sept.	Oct.	Nov.	Dec.	ANNUAL
Albany	23.0°	23.7°	33.5°	46.5°	58.4°	67.7°	72.5°	70.2°	62.7°	51.4°	39.7°	27.7°	48.1°
Albuquerque	34.5	39.5	46.3	54.8	63.8	73.3	77.1	75.1	68.4	56.8	43.9	35.1	55.7
Atlanta	43.5	45.6	52.6	61.3	69.6	76.4	78.5	77.8	73.1	62.9	52.0	44.7	61.5
Baltimore	33.2	35.0	42.6	53.6	63.1	72.1	76.8	75.3	68.5	57.3	46.0	36.4	55.0
Birmingham	45.6	47.1	55.0	62.9	70.7	77.8	79.9	79.6	75.2	64.6	53.4	46.3	63.2
Bismarck	8.1	12.2	25.3	42.9	54.6	64.1	70.6	68.5	57.9	45.7	28.6	15.4	41.1
Boise	29.9	35.5	42.3	49.6	57.8	65.4	74.5	72.5	62.7	52.3	40.6	32.1	51.3
Boston	28.9	29.1	36.9	46.9	57.7	67.0	72.6	70.7	64.0	54.2	43.5	32.6	50.3
Buffalo	25.1	24.5	32.3	43.3	54.6	64.7	70.3	68.9	62.6	51.8	40.0	29.5	47.3
Burlington, Vt.	18.0	18.4	29.3	42.6	55.2	64.8	69.7	67.3	59.6	48.8	36.6	23.3	44.5
Charleston, W. Va.	36.6	38.0	46.0	56.0	64.8	72.3	76.0	74.8	69.3	58.0	46.7	38.2	56.4
Charlotte	42.0	43.9	51.0	60.0	68.9	76.0	78.7	77.4	72.2	61.6	50.9	43.1	60.5
Cheyenne	26.1	27.7	32.4	41.4	51.0	61.0	67.7	66.4	57.3	46.4	35.2	28.6	45.1
Chicago	24.7	27.1	36.4	47.8	58.2	68.4	73.8	72.5	65.6	54.5	40.4	29.4	49.9
Cincinnati	30.8	33.6	41.7	53.5	63.3	71.9	75.5	74.2	67.3	56.3	43.6	34.4	53.9
Cleveland	27.5	27.8	35.9	47.0	58.3	67.9	72.2	70.6	64.6	53.8	41.6	31.3	49.9
Columbia, S.C.	46.6	48.1	55.1	63.5	71.9	78.5	80.8	79.9	75.1	64.5	54.4	47.2	63.8
Columbus, Ohio	29.4	30.8	40.0	51.1	61.9	70.9	74.8	72.9	66.6	55.0	42.3	32.4	52.3
Concord, N.H.	21.3	22.8	31.9	44.4	56.2	64.9	70.0	67.3	59.7	49.2	37.5	25.6	45.9
Dallas-Ft. Worth, Tex.	45.6	48.8	56.9	65.2	72.7	80.9	84.5	84.6	77.8	67.8	56.1	47.7	65.7
Denver	30.1	32.8	38.7	47.4	56.7	66.6	72.6	71.3	62.6	51.6	39.6	32.3	50.2
Des Moines	20.8	24.7	36.3	50.4	61.5	71.1	76.1	73.7	65.3	54.2	38.5	26.1	49.9
Detroit	25.3	25.8	34.5	46.7	58.1	68.2	73.0	71.1	64.2	53.1	40.1	29.5	49.2
El Paso	44.7	49.3	55.6	63.8	72.2	80.8	81.9	80.2	74.8	64.7	52.5	45.2	63.8
Great Falls	21.2	26.1	31.4	43.3	53.3	60.9	69.7	67.9	57.6	48.3	34.8	27.1	45.1
Hartford	27.1	27.7	36.9	47.9	59.0	67.9	73.1	70.9	63.7	53.3	42.1	30.4	50.0
Houston	53.2	54.6	62.0	67.9	74.3	79.8	82.4	81.3	77.5	70.2	59.6	55.5	68.2
Indianapolis	28.5	30.8	40.1	52.0	62.5	71.8	75.7	73.7	66.9	55.5	42.0	31.9	52.6
Jackson	48.4	50.9	57.3	65.3	72.6	79.6	81.8	81.5	76.9	66.5	55.7	49.5	65.5
Jacksonville	55.0	56.6	61.8	67.5	73.7	78.5	80.4	80.1	77.1	68.9	60.6	54.9	67.9
Juneau	22.2	27.3	31.2	38.4	46.4	52.8	55.5	54.1	49.0	41.5	32.0	26.9	39.8
Kansas City, Mo.	29.7	33.1	43.2	55.5	65.3	74.7	79.5	78.0	70.0	59.1	44.7	33.6	55.6
Little Rock	41.7	44.8	52.9	62.5	70.1	78.2	81.3	80.5	74.1	63.8	51.9	43.8	62.1
Los Angeles	54.6	55.9	56.9	59.3	62.1	64.9	68.3	69.5	68.5	65.2	60.4	56.4	61.8
Louisville	34.7	36.8	45.6	56.3	66.0	74.6	78.3	76.8	70.4	58.9	46.4	37.2	56.9
Memphis	41.3	44.1	52.2	62.1	70.5	78.2	81.2	80.0	74.1	63.5	51.6	43.6	61.9
Miami	67.5	68.0	71.3	74.9	78.0	80.9	82.2	82.7	81.6	77.8	72.3	68.5	75.5
Milwaukee	20.9	23.2	32.6	44.3	54.3	64.5	70.7	69.7	62.5	51.5	37.7	26.1	46.5
Minneapolis-St. Paul	13.2	16.7	29.6	45.7	57.9	67.8	73.1	70.7	61.5	50.0	33.0	19.5	44.9
Mobile	51.9	54.4	60.1	67.1	74.3	80.3	81.8	81.5	78.1	68.9	58.9	53.1	67.6
Nashville	39.1	41.0	49.5	59.5	68.2	76.3	79.4	78.3	72.2	61.1	48.9	41.1	59.6
New Orleans	54.3	56.5	61.7	68.9	75.4	80.8	82.2	82.0	78.8	70.7	60.7	55.6	69.0
New York City	32.3	32.7	40.6	51.1	61.9	70.9	76.1	74.6	68.0	58.0	46.7	35.7	54.1
Norfolk	41.6	42.3	48.8	57.4	66.7	74.7	78.6	77.5	72.4	62.2	52.1	43.6	59.8
Oklahoma City	37.2	40.8	49.8	60.2	68.2	77.0	81.4	81.1	73.7	62.7	49.4	39.9	60.1
Omaha	22.0	26.5	37.5	51.7	62.7	72.3	77.4	75.1	66.3	55.0	39.3	27.5	51.1
Philadelphia	33.1	33.8	41.6	52.2	63.0	71.8	76.6	74.7	68.4	57.5	46.2	36.2	54.6
Phoenix	51.6	55.4	60.5	67.7	76.0	85.2	90.8	89.0	83.6	71.7	59.8	52.4	70.3
Pittsburgh	30.7	31.3	39.9	51.1	62.0	70.6	74.6	72.8	66.6	55.2	43.2	33.6	52.7
Portland, Me.	22.4	23.4	32.3	42.8	53.2	62.4	68.2	66.6	59.6	49.6	38.6	26.9	45.5
Portland, Ore.	38.5	43.0	45.9	50.6	57.0	60.2	65.8	65.3	62.7	54.0	45.7	41.1	52.5
Providence	29.4	29.3	37.6	47.5	57.8	66.9	72.7	71.0	63.9	54.0	43.4	32.6	50.5
Reno	31.8	36.6	41.2	47.4	54.9	62.5	70.2	68.5	60.7	50.9	41.0	33.4	49.9
Richmond	38.0	39.4	46.9	56.9	66.1	74.0	77.6	76.1	69.9	58.9	48.7	39.7	57.7
Sacramento	44.9	49.8	53.1	58.1	64.5	70.8	75.4	74.3	71.6	63.4	52.9	45.7	60.4
St. Louis	31.7	34.8	44.3	56.1	65.9	75.1	79.3	77.5	70.1	59.0	45.3	35.3	56.2
Salt Lake City	28.0	33.2	40.7	49.0	58.3	68.1	77.2	75.4	65.1	53.1	40.5	31.4	51.7
San Francisco	48.0	50.9	52.9	54.6	57.3	60.3	61.5	62.0	62.9	60.0	54.3	49.3	56.2
Seattle	38.2	42.2	43.9	48.1	55.0	59.9	64.4	63.8	59.6	51.8	44.6	40.5	51.0
Spokane	26.8	31.7	39.4	47.6	55.8	62.5	70.2	68.7	59.5	48.7	37.0	30.4	48.2
Washington, D.C.	36.1	37.7	45.7	56.1	65.8	74.3	78.4	76.9	70.3	59.6	48.4	38.4	57.3
Wichita	31.6	35.2	44.7	56.3	65.4	75.3	80.3	79.3	70.9	59.6	45.2	35.0	56.5
Wilmington, Del.	32.6	33.1	41.9	52.2	62.7	71.4	76.0	74.1	67.9	56.8	45.7	35.2	54.2

THE NATIONAL WEATHER SERVICE

Although people are critical of the weather forecaster's failures, they seldom generously acknowledge his successes. Employing a vast network of radar stations, professional and amateur weather observers, orbiting satellites, and other sources of data on a regular basis, the National Weather Service, a major program element of the National Oceanic and Atmospheric Administration (in the Department of Commerce) has the impressive record of 87% accurate rain predictions for the same day and 80% for the next. The national average of success in forecasting shows that today's and tonight's temperatures are correct within about 3½ degrees and tomorrow's to within about 4½ degrees.

The National Weather Service employs about 5000 full-time people at 400 facilities within the 50 states and at 14 overseas stations. Its physical facilities are valued at approximately $75 million.

The National Meteorological Center receives the following observational reports daily: 20,000 synoptic and 29,000 hourly from surface observation; 3,000 synoptic from ships; 4,100 atmospheric soundings; 3,200 aircraft reports; and all available cloud and temperature data from weather satellites.

HURRICANE NAMES: 1981

Atlantic Ocean, Caribbean Sea, Gulf of Mexico

Arlene, Bret, Carla, Dennis, Emily, Floyd, Gert, Harvey, Irene, Jose, Katrina, Lenny, Maria, Nate, Ophelia, Philippe, Rita, Stan, Tammy, Vince, Wilma.

Eastern North Pacific

Adrian, Beatriz, Calvin, Dora, Eugene, Fernanda, Greg, Hilary, Irwin, Jova, Knut, Lidia, Max, Norma, Otis, Pilar, Ramon, Selma, Todd, Veronica, Wiley.

METEOROLOGICAL GLOSSARY

Anticyclone—An area of high pressure from which air spirals in all directions, usually accompanied by good weather. Anticyclones circulate in a clockwise direction in the northern hemisphere and in a counterclockwise direction in the southern (as seen from above).

Blizzard—A fall of fine, powdery snow accompanied by low temperatures and strong winds, often with low visibility and large accumulations.

Blizzard warning—Considerable amounts of snow will fall, with winds of at least 35 mph and temperatures not higher than 20°F.

Blowing snow—Snow lifted from the ground by the wind enough to restrict visibility.

Cold wave warning—A rapid and dramatic drop in temperature during the following 24 hrs requiring substantially increased protection for agricultural, industrial, commercial and social activities.

Convection—Motion of air produced by thermal or mechanical instability in the atmosphere.

Coriolis force—The force, apparently resulting from the earth's rotation, that causes high-pressure weather systems to circulate in a clockwise direction in the northern hemisphere and in a counterclockwise direction in the southern.

Cyclone—A rotary, usually columnar or funnel-shaped atmospheric system having its lowest pressure at the center of a circulating mass of air and water vapor. Cyclones circulate in a counterclockwise direction in the northern hemisphere and in a clockwise direction in the southern (as seen from above).

Drifting snow—Snow blown into significant drifts by strong winds either during or after a snowfall.

Eddy—(Within a fluid mass) a circulation pattern independent of the surrounding fluid.

Freezing drizzle—A light freezing rain.

Freezing rain—Another name for an ice storm.

Gale warning—Winds of 38–55 mph may be expected, with attendant strong wave action at sea.

Hail—Precipitation in the form of ice (hailstones) formed by the accumulation of sub-freezing water on a growing ice particle either by repeated circulation aloft or by long descent through layers of super-cooled water in clouds.

Hazardous driving (travelers') warning—Falling, blowing, or drifting snow, freezing rain or drizzle, sleet or strong winds will make driving dangerous.

Heavy snow warning—A fall of four inches or more in a 12-hr period or of six inches or more in a 24-hr period.

Hurricane—A well-defined weather system with winds of more than 74 mph and pronounced rotary circulation at the surface.

Hurricane warning—Winds of 74 mph or more may be expected within 24 hrs or high water or high waves may endanger life and property.

Hurricane watch—A hurricane that is nearby may affect the area; prepare for action if a hurricane warning is issued.

Ice storm—A winter storm in which falling rain rapidly freezes on all surfaces, causing hazardous driving conditions.

Inversion—A meteorological system in which temperature increases with an increase in altitude, the reverse of a normal system at lower altitudes.

Lightning—A discharge of electricity between clouds or between clouds and the earth resulting from an equalization between positively and negatively charged masses.

Livestock (stockmen's) warnings—Livestock will require protection from snow or ice accumulations, from a rapid drop in temperature, or from strong winds.

Neutercane—A storm, similar to and formerly identified as a cyclone or tropical storm, observed by weather satellites in areas of the oceans where hurricanes do not usually occur.

Ridge—An elongated high-pressure atmospheric system.

Seeding—The sprinkling of crystals, usually of silver iodide, into clouds and tropical storm formations in order to induce sudden freezing of super-cooled water vapor with a resultant release of latent heat of fusion, raising of cloud temperatures, and attendant reduction in maximum wind speeds. In some experiments, the intention of seeding is to increase the height and volume of storm clouds, thus dissipating the storm's energy over a wider area.

Severe blizzard warning—Considerable amounts of snow will fall, with winds of at least 45 mph and temperature not higher than 10°F.

Sleet storm—A winter storm in which falling rain freezes before striking the surface, usually bouncing on the ground.

Small-craft warning—Wind and water action may threaten the safety of small boats, which are best advised to remain in or return to port.

Snow flurries—Intermittent light snow for short periods with minimal accumulations.

Snow squalls—Brief, heavy snowfalls accompanied by gusty winds.

Storm warning—Winds of 55–74 mph may be expected, with attendant dangerous wave action at sea.

Thunder—A sound produced when lightning suddenly heats the surrounding air and causes it to expand with explosive force.

Thunderstorm—An atmospheric disturbance of varying severity, often accompanied by rain and characteristically by lightning. Thunderstorms are caused by unstable thermal convection currents of air that carry water vapor aloft creating a chimney-like effect. Exchanges of heated and cooled air and water increase and accelerate the effect, with attendant formation of ice and snow at upper altitudes and precipitation as water on the ground.

Tornado—A violently rotating column of air, moving counterclockwise at an estimated 300 mph, descending from a thunderstorm cloud system in a characteristically funnel-shaped form.

Tornado warning—A tornado has been sighted and all are advised to seek shelter.

Tornado watch—Tornadoes are expected to develop.

Tropical depression—A weather system with winds of not more than 39 mph and some circulation at the surface.

Tropical disturbance—Ill-defined weather phenomenon without strong wind and little or no circulation, sometimes better developed at higher altitudes.

Tropical storm—A well-defined weather system with winds of 39–73 mph and strong circulation at the surface.

Trough—An elongated low-pressure atmospheric system.

Waterspout—A tornado over water, in which water vapor is sucked skyward in a funnel-shaped vortex.

Wind-chill factor—The combined effect of temperature and wind velocity as compared with equivalent temperature in calm air.

NATIONAL OCEANIC AND ATMOSPHERIC ADMINISTRATION

The National Oceanic and Atmospheric Administration (NOAA) was formed on October 3, 1970, to explore, map and chart the ocean and its resources; to manage, use, and conserve those resources; and to describe, monitor, and predict conditions in all environments. It also is to issue warnings against impending destructive natural events while developing beneficial methods and assessing the consequences of environmental modification.

Among its principal functions and activities, NOAA reports the weather of the U.S. and provides weather forecasts to the general public, issues warning bulletins against destructive natural events, and provides services for such weather-sensitive activities as aviation, marine activities, and agriculture.

NOAA prepares and issues nautical and aeronautical charts and geodetic surveys. It conducts a broad range of research programs on the environment, including the use of satellites. The agency promotes wise and balanced management of the Nation's coastal zone, including the awarding of grants to states for their own development of their coastal zones. The agency also administers the Marine Mammal Protection Act of 1972.

The National Sea Grant program, which provides grants to institutions for marine research, education, and advisory services, is administered by the NOAA. It is also developing a system of data buoys for obtaining and disseminating marine environment data. Additionally, it tests and evaluates oceanographic instruments and maintains a national reference center for their specifications and characteristics.

DAYLIGHT SAVING TIME

In enacting the Uniform Time Act of 1966 (amended in 1972), the Congress made the observance of advanced (daylight) time automatic throughout the country for the six-month period extending from the last Sunday of April to the last Sunday of October.

That law, however, allows a state which falls in one time zone to exempt itself as a whole, and a state which falls in more than one time zone to exempt itself as a whole, or only that part in the most easterly zone, from the observance of advanced time. In 1977, in addition to the territories, only Arizona, Hawaii and the eastern time zone of Indiana did not observe daylight saving time from April 24 to October 30.

Faced with the energy crisis in 1974, the U.S. government required the use of daylight saving time throughout the year and, as amended later in 1974, it was temporarily observed from January 6 to October 27, 1974, and from February 23 to October 26, 1975.

Time-zone boundaries in the United States have been defined—and from time to time relocated—since 1918 by the Interstate Commerce Commission and by the Department of Transportation beginning in 1967. Prior to 1966, however, a number of communities in the vicinity of the defined boundaries chose not to recognize them. When the Uniform Time Act became effective in 1967 those communities were confronted with a problem. With its automatic advanced (daylight) feature, the 1966 act required a far greater degree of nationwide recognition of the boundaries defined by DOT. The result has been active urging by state, local, and municipal governments, as well as hundreds of requests from private citizens, for the relocation of time zones boundaries.

STANDARD TIME ZONES

Time zone boundaries for the United States are defined by the Secretary of Transportation under the Standard Time Act (1918) as amended by the Uniform Time Act (1966). In the map below, reading from east to west, when it is 5:00 P.M. Atlantic Time (a zone that runs along the Maine-New Brunswick border, and includes Puerto Rico and the Virgin Islands in the Caribbean), it is 4:00 P.M. Eastern Time; 3:00 P.M. Central Time; 2:00 P.M. Mountain Time; 1:00 P.M. Pacific Time; 12 noon Yukon Time; 11:00 A.M. Alaska-Hawaii Time; and 10:00 A.M. Bering Time (which includes Nome and Western Alaska). Thus, there is a seven-hour time difference between Nome, Alaska, and San Juan, Puerto Rico. Effective April 27, 1980, the Yukon Time Zone has been extended to include Juneau, Alaska, and parts of the surrounding area.

LATITUDE AND LONGITUDE OF U.S. CITIES

Source: National Ocean Survey

City and State	Lat. ° ′	Long. ° ′	City and State	Lat. ° ′	Long. ° ′	City and State	Lat. ° ′	Long. ° ′
Akron, Ohio	41 05	81 31	Durham, N.C.	36 00	78 54	Nashville, Tenn.	36 10	86 47
Albany, N.Y.	42 39	73 45	El Paso, Tex.	31 46	106 29	Newark, N.J.	40 44	74 10
Albuquerque, N.M.	35 05	106 39	Eugene, Ore.	44 03	123 05	New Haven, Conn.	41 18	72 55
Allentown, Pa.	40 36	75 28	Fairbanks, Alaska	64 48	147 51	New Orleans, La.	29 57	90 04
Amarillo, Tex.	35 12	101 50	Fargo, N.D.	46 53	96 47	New York, N.Y.	40 45	74 00
Anchorage, Alaska	61 12	149 48	Flagstaff, Ariz.	35 11	111 39	Niagara Falls, N.Y.	43 05	79 03
Ann Arbor, Mich.	42 17	83 45	Fort Wayne, Ind.	41 04	85 08	Nome, Alaska	64 30	165 25
Asheville, N.C.	35 35	82 33	Fort Worth, Tex.	32 45	97 20	Norfolk, Va.	36 51	76 17
Atlanta, Ga.	33 45	84 24	Gainesville, Fla.	29 39	82 19	Oakland, Calif.	37 48	122 16
Augusta, Ga.	33 28	81 58	Galveston, Tex.	29 18	94 48	Oklahoma City, Okla.	35 28	97 31
Austin, Tex.	30 16	97 45	Gary, Ind.	41 36	87 20	Omaha, Nebr.	41 16	95 56
Baltimore, Md.	39 17	76 37	Grand Rapids, Mich.	42 58	85 40	Peoria, Ill.	40 41	89 35
Bangor, Me.	44 48	68 46	Green Bay, Wisc.	44 30	88 00	Philadelphia, Pa.	39 57	75 09
Baton Rouge, La.	30 27	91 11	Greenville, S.C.	34 50	82 24	Phoenix, Ariz.	33 27	112 04
Biloxi, Miss.	30 23	88 53	Harrisburg, Pa.	40 15	76 52	Pittsburgh, Pa.	40 26	80 00
Birmingham, Ala.	33 31	86 49	Hartford, Conn.	41 46	72 40	Pocatello, Idaho	42 52	112 27
Bismarck, N.D.	46 48	100 47	Honolulu, Hawaii	21 20	158 00	Portland, Me.	43 39	70 15
Boise, Idaho	43 37	116 12	Houston, Tex.	29 45	95 22	Portland, Ore.	45 31	122 41
Boston, Mass.	42 21	71 03	Indianapolis, Ind.	39 46	86 10	Providence, R.I.	41 50	71 25
Brattleboro, Vt.	42 51	72 33	Iowa City, Iowa	41 39	91 31	Provo, Utah	40 14	111 39
Bridgeport, Conn.	41 11	73 11	Jacksonville, Fla.	30 19	81 39	Reno, Nev.	39 31	119 48
Buffalo, N.Y.	42 52	78 52	Joplin, Mo.	37 05	94 30	Richmond, Va.	37 32	77 26
Butte, Mont.	46 01	112 32	Juneau, Alaska	58 18	134 24	Rochester, N.Y.	43 09	77 36
Casper, Wyo.	42 51	106 19	Kalamazoo, Mich.	42 17	85 35	St. Louis, Mo.	38 38	90 12
Charleston, S.C.	32 47	79 56	Kansas City, Mo.	39 05	94 35	Salt Lake City, Utah	40 45	111 53
Charlotte, N.C.	35 14	80 51	Knoxville, Tenn.	35 58	83 55	San Francisco, Calif.	37 47	122 25
Chattanooga, Tenn.	35 03	85 19	Lancaster, Pa.	40 02	76 18	Santa Fe, N.M.	35 41	105 56
Cheyenne, Wyo.	41 08	104 49	Las Vegas, Nev.	36 10	115 09	Savannah, Ga.	32 04	81 05
Chicago, Ill.	41 52	87 38	Lincoln, Nebr.	40 49	96 42	Seattle, Wash.	47 37	122 20
Cincinnati, Ohio	39 06	84 31	Little Rock, Ark.	34 45	92 17	Shreveport, La.	32 30	93 44
Cleveland, Ohio	41 30	81 42	Los Angeles, Calif.	34 03	118 14	Sioux Falls, S.D.	43 32	96 43
Columbus, Ohio	39 58	83 00	Louisville, Ky.	38 14	85 45	Syracuse, N.Y.	43 03	76 09
Concord, N.H.	43 12	71 32	Macon, Ga.	32 50	83 37	Tallahassee, Fla.	30 26	84 16
Dallas, Tex.	32 47	96 48	Madison, Wisc.	43 04	89 23	Texarkana, Tex.	33 25	94 02
Dayton, Ohio	39 45	84 11	Memphis, Tenn.	35 09	90 03	Topeka, Kans.	39 03	95 40
Daytona Beach, Fla.	29 12	81 01	Miami, Fla.	25 47	80 12	Tulsa, Okla.	36 09	96 00
Denver, Colo.	39 45	104 59	Milwaukee, Wisc.	43 02	87 54	Tucson, Ariz.	32 13	110 58
Des Moines, Iowa	41 35	93 37	Minneapolis, Minn.	44 59	93 16	Utica, N.Y.	43 07	75 13
Detroit, Mich.	42 20	83 03	Mobile, Ala.	30 42	88 03	Washington, D.C.	38 54	77 01
Dubuque, Iowa	42 30	90 40	Montgomery, Ala.	32 23	86 19	Wichita, Kans.	37 41	97 20
Duluth, Minn.	46 47	92 06	Montpelier, Vt.	44 16	72 35	Wilmington, Del.	39 45	75 33

SUNRISE AND SUNSET: 1981

Source: U.S. Naval Observatory

Note: To determine Daylight Saving Time, add one hour to all times; e.g., sunrise at 20° latitude on January 2 is 7:36 D.S.T.

To determine sunrise or sunset for any location, follow these directions:

(1) From the table directly above, determine the latitude and longitude of the city closest to you;

(2) From the tables below, read the sunrise or sunset time for the desired date at the correct latitude (given in degrees at the top of the table);

(3) Determine your time zone:

(a) **Eastern Time Zone:** If longitude is less than 75°, subtract four minutes from the time on the table for each degree. If it is greater than 75°, add four minutes for each degree.

(b) **Central Time Zone:** If longitude is less than 90°, subtract four minutes from the time on the table for each degree. If it is greater, add four minutes for each degree.

(c) **Rocky Mountain Time:** If longitude is less than 105°, subtract four minutes from the time on the table for each degree. If it is greater, add four minutes for each degree.

(d) **Pacific Time:** If longitude is less than 120°, subtract four minutes from the time on the table for each degree. If it is greater, add four minutes for each degree.

SUNRISE (UPPER LIMB)

Date	+20° h m	+30° h m	+35° h m	+40° h m	+46° h m	+50° h m
Jan. −2	6 34	6 55	7 07	7 21	7 42	7 59
2	6 36	6 56	7 08	7 22	7 42	7 59
6	6 37	6 57	7 09	7 22	7 42	7 58
10	6 37	6 57	7 09	7 22	7 41	7 56
14	6 38	6 57	7 08	7 21	7 39	7 54
18	6 38	6 56	7 07	7 19	7 36	7 50
22	6 38	6 55	7 05	7 17	7 33	7 46
26	6 37	6 54	7 03	7 14	7 29	7 42
30	6 36	6 52	7 00	7 11	7 25	7 37
Feb. 3	6 35	6 49	6 57	7 07	7 20	7 31
7	6 33	6 47	6 54	7 03	7 15	7 25
11	6 31	6 43	6 40	6 58	7 09	7 18
15	6 29	6 40	6 46	6 53	7 03	7 11
19	6 27	6 36	6 42	6 48	6 57	7 03
23	6 24	6 32	6 37	6 42	6 50	6 56
27	6 21	6 28	6 32	6 37	6 43	6 48
Mar. 3	6 18	6 24	6 27	6 31	6 36	6 40
7	6 15	6 20	6 22	6 25	6 28	6 31
11	6 12	6 15	6 17	6 18	6 21	6 23
15	6 09	6 10	6 11	6 12	6 13	6 14
19	6 05	6 05	6 05	6 05	6 05	6 05
23	6 02	6 01	6 00	5 59	5 58	5 57
27	5 58	5 56	5 54	5 52	5 50	5 48
31	5 55	5 51	5 49	5 46	5 42	5 39
Apr. 4	5 51	5 46	5 43	5 40	5 35	5 31
8	5 48	5 41	5 38	5 33	5 27	5 22
12	5 45	5 37	5 32	5 27	5 20	5 14
16	5 41	5 32	5 27	5 21	5 12	5 05
20	5 38	5 28	5 22	5 15	5 05	4 57
24	5 35	5 24	5 17	5 10	4 59	4 50
28	5 33	5 20	5 13	5 04	4 52	4 42
May 2	5 30	5 16	5 08	4 59	4 46	4 35
6	5 28	5 13	5 04	4 54	4 40	4 28
10	5 26	5 10	5 01	4 50	4 34	4 22
14	5 24	5 07	4 57	4 46	4 29	4 16
18	5 23	5 05	4 54	4 42	4 25	4 10
22	5 22	5 03	4 52	4 39	4 21	4 05
26	5 21	5 01	4 50	4 36	4 17	4 01
30	5 20	5 00	4 48	4 34	4 14	3 57
June 3	5 20	4 59	4 47	4 32	4 12	3 55
7	5 20	4 58	4 46	4 31	4 10	3 52

SUNRISE (UPPER LIMB)

Latitude

Date	+20°	+30°	+35°	+40°	+46°	+50°
	h m	h m	h m	h m	h m	h m
11	5 20	4 58	4 45	4 31	4 09	3 51
15	5 20	4 58	4 45	4 30	4 08	3 50
19	5 21	4 59	4 46	4 31	4 09	3 50
23	5 22	5 00	4 47	4 32	4 09	3 51
27	5 23	5 01	4 48	4 33	4 11	3 53
July 1	5 24	5 02	4 49	4 35	4 13	3 55
5	5 25	5 04	4 51	4 37	4 15	3 58
9	5 27	5 06	4 53	4 39	4 18	4 01
13	5 28	5 08	4 56	4 42	4 22	4 05
17	5 30	5 10	4 58	4 45	4 26	4 09
21	5 31	5 12	5 01	4 48	4 30	4 14
25	5 33	5 15	5 04	4 52	4 34	4 19
29	5 34	5 17	5 07	4 55	4 38	4 25
Aug. 2	5 36	5 19	5 10	4 59	4 43	4 30
6	5 37	5 22	5 13	5 03	4 48	4 36
10	5 38	5 24	5 16	5 06	4 53	4 42
14	5 40	5 27	5 19	5 10	4 58	4 48
18	5 41	5 29	5 22	5 14	5 03	4 54
22	5 42	5 31	5 25	5 18	5 08	5 00
26	5 43	5 33	5 28	5 22	5 13	5 06
30	5 44	5 36	5 31	5 26	5 18	5 12
Sept. 3	5 45	5 38	5 34	5 29	5 23	5 18
7	5 46	5 40	5 37	5 33	5 28	5 24
11	5 46	5 42	5 40	5 37	5 33	5 30
15	5 47	5 44	5 43	5 41	5 38	5 35
19	5 48	5 47	5 46	5 44	5 43	5 41
23	5 49	5 49	5 48	5 48	5 48	5 47

Date	+20°	+30°	+35°	+40°	+46°	+50°
	h m	h m	h m	h m	h m	h m
27	5 50	5 51	5 51	5 52	5 53	5 54
Oct. 1	5 51	5 53	5 55	5 56	5 58	6 00
5	5 52	5 56	5 58	6 00	6 03	6 06
9	5 53	5 58	6 01	6 04	6 09	6 12
13	5 54	6 00	6 04	6 08	6 14	6 18
17	5 55	6 03	6 07	6 12	6 19	6 25
21	5 57	6 06	6 11	6 17	6 25	6 31
25	5 58	6 09	6 14	6 21	6 30	6 38
29	6 00	6 11	6 18	6 25	6 36	6 44
Nov. 2	6 02	6 15	6 22	6 30	6 42	6 51
6	6 04	6 18	6 26	6 35	6 47	6 58
10	6 06	6 21	6 29	6 39	6 53	7 04
14	6 08	6 24	6 33	6 44	6 59	7 11
18	6 11	6 27	6 37	6 48	7 04	7 17
22	6 13	6 31	6 41	6 53	7 10	7 24
26	6 15	6 34	6 45	6 57	7 15	7 30
30	6 18	6 37	6 49	7 01	7 20	7 35
Dec. 4	6 21	6 40	6 52	7 05	7 25	7 40
8	6 23	6 43	6 55	7 09	7 29	7 45
12	6 25	6 46	6 58	7 12	7 33	7 49
16	6 28	6 49	7 01	7 15	7 36	7 53
20	6 30	6 51	7 04	7 18	7 38	7 55
24	6 32	6 53	7 05	7 20	7 40	7 57
28	6 34	6 55	7 07	7 21	7 42	7 58
32	6 35	6 56	7 08	7 22	7 42	7 59
36	6 36	6 57	7 09	7 22	7 42	7 58

SUNSET (UPPER LIMB)

Latitude

Date	+20°	+30°	+35°	+40°	+46°	+50°
	h m	h m	h m	h m	h m	h m
Jan. −2	17 30	17 09	16 57	16 43	16 23	16 06
2	17 33	17 12	17 00	16 46	16 26	16 10
6	17 35	17 15	17 03	16 50	16 30	16 14
10	17 38	17 18	17 07	16 54	16 35	16 20
14	17 41	17 22	17 11	16 58	16 40	16 25
18	17 43	17 25	17 14	17 02	16 45	16 31
22	17 46	17 28	17 18	17 07	16 51	16 37
26	17 48	17 32	17 23	17 12	16 56	16 44
30	17 51	17 35	17 27	17 17	17 02	16 51
Feb. 3	17 53	17 39	17 31	17 21	17 08	16 58
7	17 55	17 42	17 35	17 26	17 14	17 04
11	17 57	17 45	17 39	17 31	17 20	17 11
15	17 59	17 49	17 43	17 36	17 26	17 18
19	18 01	17 52	17 46	17 40	17 32	17 25
23	18 03	17 55	17 50	17 45	17 38	17 32
27	18 04	17 58	17 54	17 49	17 43	17 39
Mar. 3	18 06	18 00	17 57	17 54	17 49	17 45
7	18 07	18 03	18 01	17 58	17 55	17 52
11	18 08	18 06	18 04	18 02	18 00	17 58
15	18 10	18 08	18 07	18 07	18 06	18 05
19	18 11	18 11	18 11	18 11	18 11	18 11
23	18 12	18 13	18 14	18 15	18 16	18 17
27	18 13	18 16	18 17	18 19	18 22	18 24
31	18 14	18 18	18 20	18 23	18 27	18 30
Apr. 4	18 15	18 20	18 24	18 27	18 32	18 36
8	18 16	18 23	18 27	18 31	18 38	18 43
12	18 17	18 25	18 30	18 35	18 43	18 49
16	18 18	18 28	18 33	18 39	18 48	18 55
20	18 20	18 30	18 36	18 43	18 53	19 01
24	18 21	18 33	18 40	18 47	18 59	19 08
28	18 22	18 35	18 43	18 51	19 04	19 14
May 2	18 24	18 38	18 46	18 55	19 09	19 20
6	18 25	18 40	18 49	18 59	19 14	19 26
10	18 27	18 43	18 53	19 03	19 19	19 32
14	18 28	18 46	18 56	19 07	19 24	19 38
18	18 30	18 48	18 59	19 11	19 29	19 43
22	18 32	18 51	19 02	19 15	19 33	19 49
26	18 33	18 53	19 05	19 18	19 37	19 54
30	18 35	18 55	19 07	19 21	19 41	19 58
June 3	18 36	18 57	19 10	19 24	19 45	20 02
7	18 38	18 59	19 12	19 26	19 48	20 06
11	18 39	19 01	19 14	19 29	19 50	20 09
15	18 40	19 02	19 15	19 30	19 52−	20 11
19	18 42	19 04	19 17	19 32	19 54	20 12
23	18 42	19 04	19 17	19 33	19 55	20 13
27	18 43	19 05	19 18	19 33	19 55	20 13
July 1	18 43	19 05	19 18	19 33	19 54	20 12

Date	+20°	+30°	+35°	+40°	+46°	+50°
	h m	h m	h m	h m	h m	h m
5	18 44	19 05	19 17	19 32	19 53	20 11
9	18 43	19 04	19 17	19 31	19 51	20 09
13	18 43	19 03	19 15	19 29	19 49	20 06
17	18 42	19 02	19 13	19 27	19 46	20 02
21	18 41	19 00	19 11	19 24	19 42	19 58
25	18 40	18 58	19 08	19 21	19 38	19 53
29	18 38	18 55	19 05	19 17	19 34	19 47
Aug. 2	18 37	18 53	19 02	19 13	19 28	19 41
6	18 34	18 49	18 58	19 08	19 23	19 35
10	18 32	18 46	18 54	19 03	19 17	19 28
14	18 29	18 42	18 50	18 58	19 11	19 20
18	18 27	18 38	18 45	18 53	19 04	19 13
22	18 24	18 34	18 40	18 47	18 57	19 05
26	18 20	18 30	18 35	18 41	18 50	18 57
30	18 17	18 25	18 30	18 35	18 42	18 49
Sept. 3	18 14	18 20	18 24	18 29	18 35	18 40
7	18 10	18 15	18 19	18 22	18 27	18 31
11	18 06	18 11	18 13	18 16	18 20	18 23
15	18 03	18 06	18 07	18 09	18 12	18 14
19	17 59	18 01	18 01	18 02	18 04	18 05
23	17 55	17 56	17 56	17 56	17 56	17 56
27	17 52	17 51	17 50	17 49	17 48	17 48
Oct. 1	17 48	17 46	17 44	17 43	17 40	17 39
5	17 45	17 41	17 39	17 36	17 33	17 30
9	17 41	17 36	17 33	17 30	17 25	17 22
13	17 38	17 32	17 28	17 24	17 18	17 13
17	17 35	17 27	17 23	17 18	17 11	17 05
21	17 32	17 23	17 18	17 12	17 04	16 57
25	17 30	17 19	17 13	17 07	16 57	16 50
29	17 27	17 16	17 09	17 02	16 51	16 42
Nov. 2	17 25	17 12	17 05	16 57	16 45	16 35
6	17 23	17 09	17 01	16 52	16 39	16 29
10	17 22	17 07	16 58	16 48	16 34	16 23
14	17 21	17 05	16 55	16 45	16 30	16 17
18	17 20	17 03	16 53	16 42	16 26	16 13
22	17 19	17 01	16 51	16 39	16 22	16 08
26	17 19	17 00	16 49	16 37	16 19	16 05
30	17 19	17 00	16 49	16 36	16 17	16 02
Dec. 4	17 20	17 00	16 48	16 35	16 16	16 00
8	17 21	17 00	16 48	16 35	16 15	15 58
12	17 22	17 01	16 49	16 35	16 15	15 58
16	17 24	17 02	16 50	16 36	16 15	15 59
20	17 25	17 04	16 52	16 37	16 17	16 00
24	17 27	17 06	16 54	16 40	16 22	16 02
28	17 30	17 09	16 56	16 42	16 22	16 05
32	17 32	17 11	16 59	16 45	16 25	16 09
36	17 35	17 14	17 02	16 49	16 29	16 13

CALENDARS: 1801-2000

Select the desired year from the table below. The number shown with each year tells you the calendar to use for that year.

Year	No.	Year	No.	Year	No.	Year	No.	Year	No.
1801	5	1841	6	1881	7	1921	7	1961	1
1802	6	1842	7	1882	1	1922	1	1962	2
1803	7	1843	1	1883	2	1923	2	1963	3
1804	8	1844	9	1884	10	1924	10	1964	11
1805	3	1845	4	1885	5	1925	5	1965	6
1806	4	1846	5	1886	6	1926	6	1966	7
1807	5	1847	6	1887	7	1927	7	1967	1
1808	13	1848	14	1888	8	1928	8	1968	9
1809	1	1849	2	1889	3	1929	3	1969	4
1810	2	1850	3	1890	4	1930	4	1970	5
1811	3	1851	4	1891	5	1931	5	1971	6
1812	11	1852	12	1892	13	1932	13	1972	14
1813	6	1853	7	1893	1	1933	1	1973	2
1814	7	1854	1	1894	2	1934	2	1974	3
1815	1	1855	2	1895	3	1935	3	1975	4
1816	9	1856	10	1896	11	1936	11	1976	12
1817	4	1857	5	1897	6	1937	6	1977	7
1818	5	1858	6	1898	7	1938	7	1978	1
1819	6	1859	7	1899	1	1939	1	1979	2
1820	14	1860	8	1900	2	1940	9	1980	10
1821	2	1861	3	1901	3	1941	4	1981	5
1822	3	1862	4	1902	4	1942	5	1982	6
1823	4	1863	5	1903	5	1943	6	1983	7
1824	12	1864	13	1904	13	1944	14	1984	8
1825	7	1865	1	1905	1	1945	2	1985	3
1826	1	1866	2	1906	2	1946	3	1986	4
1827	2	1867	3	1907	3	1947	4	1987	5
1828	10	1868	11	1908	11	1948	12	1988	13
1829	5	1869	6	1909	6	1949	7	1989	1
1830	6	1870	7	1910	7	1950	1	1990	2
1831	7	1871	1	1911	1	1951	2	1991	3
1832	8	1872	9	1912	9	1952	10	1992	11
1833	3	1873	4	1913	4	1953	5	1993	6
1834	4	1874	5	1914	5	1954	6	1994	7
1835	5	1875	6	1915	6	1955	7	1995	1
1836	13	1876	14	1916	14	1956	8	1996	9
1837	1	1877	2	1917	2	1957	3	1997	4
1838	2	1878	3	1918	3	1958	4	1998	5
1839	3	1879	4	1919	4	1959	5	1999	6
1840	11	1880	12	1920	12	1960	13	2000	14

1

JANUARY

S	M	T	W	T	F	S
1	2	3	4	5	6	7
8	9	10	11	12	13	14
15	16	17	18	19	20	21
22	23	24	25	26	27	28
29	30	31				

FEBRUARY

S	M	T	W	T	F	S
			1	2	3	4
5	6	7	8	9	10	11
12	13	14	15	16	17	18
19	20	21	22	23	24	25
26	27	28				

MARCH

S	M	T	W	T	F	S
			1	2	3	4
5	6	7	8	9	10	11
12	13	14	15	16	17	18
19	20	21	22	23	24	25
26	27	28	29	30	31	

APRIL

S	M	T	W	T	F	S
						1
2	3	4	5	6	7	8
9	10	11	12	13	14	15
16	17	18	19	20	21	22
23	24	25	26	27	28	29
30						

MAY

S	M	T	W	T	F	S
	1	2	3	4	5	6
7	8	9	10	11	12	13
14	15	16	17	18	19	20
21	22	23	24	25	26	27
28	29	30	31			

JUNE

S	M	T	W	T	F	S
				1	2	3
4	5	6	7	8	9	10
11	12	13	14	15	16	17
18	19	20	21	22	23	24
25	26	27	28	29	30	

JULY

S	M	T	W	T	F	S
						1
2	3	4	5	6	7	8
9	10	11	12	13	14	15
16	17	18	19	20	21	22
23	24	25	26	27	28	29
30	31					

AUGUST

S	M	T	W	T	F	S
		1	2	3	4	5
6	7	8	9	10	11	12
13	14	15	16	17	18	19
20	21	22	23	24	25	26
27	28	29	30	31		

SEPTEMBER

S	M	T	W	T	F	S
					1	2
3	4	5	6	7	8	9
10	11	12	13	14	15	16
17	18	19	20	21	22	23
24	25	26	27	28	29	30

OCTOBER

S	M	T	W	T	F	S
1	2	3	4	5	6	7
8	9	10	11	12	13	14
15	16	17	18	19	20	21
22	23	24	25	26	27	28
29	30	31				

NOVEMBER

S	M	T	W	T	F	S
			1	2	3	4
5	6	7	8	9	10	11
12	13	14	15	16	17	18
19	20	21	22	23	24	25
26	27	28	29	30		

DECEMBER

S	M	T	W	T	F	S
					1	2
3	4	5	6	7	8	9
10	11	12	13	14	15	16
17	18	19	20	21	22	23
24	25	26	27	28	29	30
31						

2

JANUARY

S	M	T	W	T	F	S
					1	2
7	8	9	10	11	12	13
14	15	16	17	18	19	20
21	22	23	24	25	26	27
28	29	30	31			

FEBRUARY

S	M	T	W	T	F	S
					1	2
4	5	6	7	8	9	10
11	12	13	14	15	16	17
18	19	20	21	22	23	24
25	26	27	28			

MARCH

S	M	T	W	T	F	S
					1	2
4	5	6	7	8	9	10
11	12	13	14	15	16	17
18	19	20	21	22	23	24
25	26	27	28	29	30	31

APRIL

S	M	T	W	T	F	S
1	2	3	4	5	6	7
8	9	10	11	12	13	14
15	16	17	18	19	20	21
22	23	24	25	26	27	28
29	30					

MAY

S	M	T	W	T	F	S
		1	2	3	4	5
6	7	8	9	10	11	12
13	14	15	16	17	18	19
20	21	22	23	24	25	26
27	28	29	30	31		

JUNE

S	M	T	W	T	F	S
					1	2
3	4	5	6	7	8	9
10	11	12	13	14	15	16
17	18	19	20	21	22	23
24	25	26	27	28	29	30

JULY

S	M	T	W	T	F	S
1	2	3	4	5	6	7
8	9	10	11	12	13	14
15	16	17	18	19	20	21
22	23	24	25	26	27	28
29	30	31				

AUGUST

S	M	T	W	T	F	S
				1	2	3
5	6	7	8	9	10	11
12	13	14	15	16	17	18
19	20	21	22	23	24	25
26	27	28	29	30	31	

SEPTEMBER

S	M	T	W	T	F	S
						1
2	3	4	5	6	7	8
9	10	11	12	13	14	15
16	17	18	19	20	21	22
23	24	25	26	27	28	29
30						

OCTOBER

S	M	T	W	T	F	S
		1	2	3	4	5
7	8	9	10	11	12	13
14	15	16	17	18	19	20
21	22	23	24	25	26	27
28	29	30	31			

NOVLMBER

S	M	T	W	T	F	S
					1	2
4	5	6	7	8	9	10
11	12	13	14	15	16	17
18	19	20	21	22	23	24
25	26	27	28	29	30	

DECEMBER

S	M	T	W	T	F	S
						1
2	3	4	5	6	7	8
9	10	11	12	13	14	15
16	17	18	19	20	21	22
23	24	25	26	27	28	29
30	31					

3

JANUARY

S	M	T	W	T	F	S
					1	2
6	7	8	9	10	11	12
13	14	15	16	17	18	19
20	21	22	23	24	25	26
27	28	29	30	31		

FEBRUARY

S	M	T	W	T	F	S
					1	2
3	4	5	6	7	8	9
10	11	12	13	14	15	16
17	18	19	20	21	22	23
24	25	26	27	28		

MARCH

S	M	T	W	T	F	S
					1	2
3	4	5	6	7	8	9
10	11	12	13	14	15	16
17	18	19	20	21	22	23
24	25	26	27	28	29	30
31						

APRIL

S	M	T	W	T	F	S
				1	2	3
7	8	9	10	11	12	13
14	15	16	17	18	19	20
21	22	23	24	25	26	27
28	29	30				

MAY

S	M	T	W	T	F	S
				1	2	3
5	6	7	8	9	10	11
12	13	14	15	16	17	18
19	20	21	22	23	24	25
26	27	28	29	30	31	

JUNE

S	M	T	W	T	F	S
						1
2	3	4	5	6	7	8
9	10	11	12	13	14	15
16	17	18	19	20	21	22
23	24	25	26	27	28	29
30						

JULY

S	M	T	W	T	F	S
				1	2	3
7	8	9	10	11	12	13
14	15	16	17	18	19	20
21	22	23	24	25	26	27
28	29	30	31			

AUGUST

S	M	T	W	T	F	S
				1	2	3
4	5	6	7	8	9	10
11	12	13	14	15	16	17
18	19	20	21	22	23	24
25	26	27	28	29	30	31

SEPTEMBER

S	M	T	W	T	F	S
1	2	3	4	5	6	7
8	9	10	11	12	13	14
15	16	17	18	19	20	21
22	23	24	25	26	27	28
29	30					

OCTOBER

S	M	T	W	T	F	S
		1	2	3	4	5
6	7	8	9	10	11	12
13	14	15	16	17	18	19
20	21	22	23	24	25	26
27	28	29	30	31		

NOVEMBER

S	M	T	W	T	F	S
					1	2
3	4	5	6	7	8	9
10	11	12	13	14	15	16
17	18	19	20	21	22	23
24	25	26	27	28	29	30

DECEMBER

S	M	T	W	T	F	S
1	2	3	4	5	6	7
8	9	10	11	12	13	14
15	16	17	18	19	20	21
22	23	24	25	26	27	28
29	30	31				

4

JANUARY

S	M	T	W	T	F	S
			1	2	3	4
5	6	7	8	9	10	11
12	13	14	15	16	17	18
19	20	21	22	23	24	25
26	27	28	29	30	31	

FEBRUARY

S	M	T	W	T	F	S
						1
2	3	4	5	6	7	8
9	10	11	12	13	14	15
16	17	18	19	20	21	22
23	24	25	26	27	28	

MARCH

S	M	T	W	T	F	S
						1
2	3	4	5	6	7	8
9	10	11	12	13	14	15
16	17	18	19	20	21	22
23	24	25	26	27	28	29
30	31					

APRIL

S	M	T	W	T	F	S
				1	2	3
6	7	8	9	10	11	12
13	14	15	16	17	18	19
20	21	22	23	24	25	26
27	28	29	30			

MAY

S	M	T	W	T	F	S
				1	2	3
4	5	6	7	8	9	10
11	12	13	14	15	16	17
18	19	20	21	22	23	24
25	26	27	28	29	30	31

JUNE

S	M	T	W	T	F	S
1	2	3	4	5	6	7
8	9	10	11	12	13	14
15	16	17	18	19	20	21
22	23	24	25	26	27	28
29	30					

JULY

S	M	T	W	T	F	S
		1	2	3	4	5
6	7	8	9	10	11	12
13	14	15	16	17	18	19
20	21	22	23	24	25	26
27	28	29	30	31		

AUGUST

S	M	T	W	T	F	S
					1	2
3	4	5	6	7	8	9
10	11	12	13	14	15	16
17	18	19	20	21	22	23
24	25	26	27	28	29	30
31						

SEPTEMBER

S	M	T	W	T	F	S
	1	2	3	4	5	6
7	8	9	10	11	12	13
14	15	16	17	18	19	20
21	22	23	24	25	26	27
28	29	30				

OCTOBER

S	M	T	W	T	F	S
			1	2	3	4
5	6	7	8	9	10	11
12	13	14	15	16	17	18
19	20	21	22	23	24	25
26	27	28	29	30	31	

NOVEMBER

S	M	T	W	T	F	S
						1
2	3	4	5	6	7	8
9	10	11	12	13	14	15
16	17	18	19	20	21	22
23	24	25	26	27	28	29
30						

DECEMBER

S	M	T	W	T	F	S
	1	2	3	4	5	6
7	8	9	10	11	12	13
14	15	16	17	18	19	20
21	22	23	24	25	26	27
28	29	30	31			

5

JANUARY

S	M	T	W	T	F	S
					1	2
4	5	6	7	8	9	10
11	12	13	14	15	16	17
18	19	20	21	22	23	24
25	26	27	28	29	30	31

FEBRUARY

S	M	T	W	T	F	S
1	2	3	4	5	6	7
8	9	10	11	12	13	14
15	16	17	18	19	20	21
22	23	24	25	26	27	28

MARCH

S	M	T	W	T	F	S
1	2	3	4	5	6	7
8	9	10	11	12	13	14
15	16	17	18	19	20	21
22	23	24	25	26	27	28
29	30	31				

APRIL

S	M	T	W	T	F	S
				1	2	3
5	6	7	8	9	10	11
12	13	14	15	16	17	18
19	20	21	22	23	24	25
26	27	28	29	30		

MAY

S	M	T	W	T	F	S
					1	2
3	4	5	6	7	8	9
10	11	12	13	14	15	16
17	18	19	20	21	22	23
24	25	26	27	28	29	30
31						

JUNE

S	M	T	W	T	F	S
	1	2	3	4	5	6
7	8	9	10	11	12	13
14	15	16	17	18	19	20
21	22	23	24	25	26	27
28	29	30				

JULY

S	M	T	W	T	F	S
				1	2	3
5	6	7	8	9	10	11
12	13	14	15	16	17	18
19	20	21	22	23	24	25
26	27	28	29	30	31	

AUGUST

S	M	T	W	T	F	S
						1
2	3	4	5	6	7	8
9	10	11	12	13	14	15
16	17	18	19	20	21	22
23	24	25	26	27	28	29
30	31					

SEPTEMBER

S	M	T	W	T	F	S
		1	2	3	4	5
6	7	8	9	10	11	12
13	14	15	16	17	18	19
20	21	22	23	24	25	26
27	28	29	30			

OCTOBER

S	M	T	W	T	F	S
				1	2	3
4	5	6	7	8	9	10
11	12	13	14	15	16	17
18	19	20	21	22	23	24
25	26	27	28	29	30	31

NOVEMBER

S	M	T	W	T	F	S
1	2	3	4	5	6	7
8	9	10	11	12	13	14
15	16	17	18	19	20	21
22	23	24	25	26	27	28
29	30					

DECEMBER

S	M	T	W	T	F	S
		1	2	3	4	5
6	7	8	9	10	11	12
13	14	15	16	17	18	19
20	21	22	23	24	25	26
27	28	29	30	31		

6

JANUARY

S	M	T	W	T	F	S
					1	2
3	4	5	6	7	8	9
10	11	12	13	14	15	16
17	18	19	20	21	22	23
24	25	26	27	28	29	30
31						

FEBRUARY

S	M	T	W	T	F	S
	1	2	3	4	5	6
7	8	9	10	11	12	13
14	15	16	17	18	19	20
21	22	23	24	25	26	27
28						

MARCH

S	M	T	W	T	F	S
	1	2	3	4	5	6
7	8	9	10	11	12	13
14	15	16	17	18	19	20
21	22	23	24	25	26	27
28	29	30	31			

APRIL

S	M	T	W	T	F	S
				1	2	3
4	5	6	7	8	9	10
11	12	13	14	15	16	17
18	19	20	21	22	23	24
25	26	27	28	29	30	

MAY

S	M	T	W	T	F	S
						1
2	3	4	5	6	7	8
9	10	11	12	13	14	15
16	17	18	19	20	21	22
23	24	25	26	27	28	29
30	31					

JUNE

S	M	T	W	T	F	S
		1	2	3	4	5
6	7	8	9	10	11	12
13	14	15	16	17	18	19
20	21	22	23	24	25	26
27	28	29	30			

JULY

S	M	T	W	T	F	S
				1	2	3
4	5	6	7	8	9	10
11	12	13	14	15	16	17
18	19	20	21	22	23	24
25	26	27	28	29	30	31

AUGUST

S	M	T	W	T	F	S
1	2	3	4	5	6	7
8	9	10	11	12	13	14
15	16	17	18	19	20	21
22	23	24	25	26	27	28
29	30	31				

SEPTEMBER

S	M	T	W	T	F	S
			1	2	3	4
5	6	7	8	9	10	11
12	13	14	15	16	17	18
19	20	21	22	23	24	25
26	27	28	29	30		

OCTOBER

S	M	T	W	T	F	S
					1	2
3	4	5	6	7	8	9
10	11	12	13	14	15	16
17	18	19	20	21	22	23
24	25	26	27	28	29	30
31						

NOVEMBER

S	M	T	W	T	F	S
	1	2	3	4	5	6
7	8	9	10	11	12	13
14	15	16	17	18	19	20
21	22	23	24	25	26	27
28	29	30				

DECEMBER

S	M	T	W	T	F	S
			1	2	3	4
5	6	7	8	9	10	11
12	13	14	15	16	17	18
19	20	21	22	23	24	25
26	27	28	29	30	31	

7

JANUARY
```
 S  M  T  W  T  F  S
                   1
 2  3  4  5  6  7  8
 9 10 11 12 13 14 15
16 17 18 19 20 21 22
23 24 25 26 27 28 29
30 31
```
FEBRUARY
```
 S  M  T  W  T  F  S
       1  2  3  4  5
 6  7  8  9 10 11 12
13 14 15 16 17 18 19
20 21 22 23 24 25 26
27 28
```
MARCH
```
 S  M  T  W  T  F  S
       1  2  3  4  5
 6  7  8  9 10 11 12
13 14 15 16 17 18 19
20 21 22 23 24 25 26
27 28 29 30 31
```
APRIL
```
 S  M  T  W  T  F  S
                1  2
 3  4  5  6  7  8  9
10 11 12 13 14 15 16
17 18 19 20 21 22 23
24 25 26 27 28 29 30
```
MAY
```
 S  M  T  W  T  F  S
 1  2  3  4  5  6  7
 8  9 10 11 12 13 14
15 16 17 18 19 20 21
22 23 24 25 26 27 28
29 30 31
```
JUNE
```
 S  M  T  W  T  F  S
          1  2  3  4
 5  6  7  8  9 10 11
12 13 14 15 16 17 18
19 20 21 22 23 24 25
26 27 28 29 30
```
JULY
```
 S  M  T  W  T  F  S
                1  2
 3  4  5  6  7  8  9
10 11 12 13 14 15 16
17 18 19 20 21 22 23
24 25 26 27 28 29 30
31
```
AUGUST
```
 S  M  T  W  T  F  S
    1  2  3  4  5  6
 7  8  9 10 11 12 13
14 15 16 17 18 19 20
21 22 23 24 25 26 27
28 29 30 31
```
SEPTEMBER
```
 S  M  T  W  T  F  S
             1  2  3
 4  5  6  7  8  9 10
11 12 13 14 15 16 17
18 19 20 21 22 23 24
25 26 27 28 29 30
```
OCTOBER
```
 S  M  T  W  T  F  S
                   1
 2  3  4  5  6  7  8
 9 10 11 12 13 14 15
16 17 18 19 20 21 22
23 24 25 26 27 28 29
30 31
```
NOVEMBER
```
 S  M  T  W  T  F  S
       1  2  3  4  5
 6  7  8  9 10 11 12
13 14 15 16 17 18 19
20 21 22 23 24 25 26
27 28 29 30
```
DECEMBER
```
 S  M  T  W  T  F  S
             1  2  3
 4  5  6  7  8  9 10
11 12 13 14 15 16 17
18 19 20 21 22 23 24
25 26 27 28 29 30 31
```

8

JANUARY
```
 S  M  T  W  T  F  S
 1  2  3  4  5  6  7
 8  9 10 11 12 13 14
15 16 17 18 19 20 21
22 23 24 25 26 27 28
29 30 31
```
FEBRUARY
```
 S  M  T  W  T  F  S
          1  2  3  4
 5  6  7  8  9 10 11
12 13 14 15 16 17 18
19 20 21 22 23 24 25
26 27 28 29
```
MARCH
```
 S  M  T  W  T  F  S
             1  2  3
 4  5  6  7  8  9 10
11 12 13 14 15 16 17
18 19 20 21 22 23 24
25 26 27 28 29 30 31
```
APRIL
```
 S  M  T  W  T  F  S
 1  2  3  4  5  6  7
 8  9 10 11 12 13 14
15 16 17 18 19 20 21
22 23 24 25 26 27 28
29 30
```
MAY
```
 S  M  T  W  T  F  S
       1  2  3  4  5
 6  7  8  9 10 11 12
13 14 15 16 17 18 19
20 21 22 23 24 25 26
27 28 29 30 31
```
JUNE
```
 S  M  T  W  T  F  S
                1  2
 3  4  5  6  7  8  9
10 11 12 13 14 15 16
17 18 19 20 21 22 23
24 25 26 27 28 29 30
```
JULY
```
 S  M  T  W  T  F  S
 1  2  3  4  5  6  7
 8  9 10 11 12 13 14
15 16 17 18 19 20 21
22 23 24 25 26 27 28
29 30 31
```
AUGUST
```
 S  M  T  W  T  F  S
          1  2  3  4
 5  6  7  8  9 10 11
12 13 14 15 16 17 18
19 20 21 22 23 24 25
26 27 28 29 30 31
```
SEPTEMBER
```
 S  M  T  W  T  F  S
                   1
 2  3  4  5  6  7  8
 9 10 11 12 13 14 15
16 17 18 19 20 21 22
23 24 25 26 27 28 29
30
```
OCTOBER
```
 S  M  T  W  T  F  S
    1  2  3  4  5  6
 7  8  9 10 11 12 13
14 15 16 17 18 19 20
21 22 23 24 25 26 27
28 29 30 31
```
NOVEMBER
```
 S  M  T  W  T  F  S
             1  2  3
 4  5  6  7  8  9 10
11 12 13 14 15 16 17
18 19 20 21 22 23 24
25 26 27 28 29 30
```
DECEMBER
```
 S  M  T  W  T  F  S
                   1
 2  3  4  5  6  7  8
 9 10 11 12 13 14 15
16 17 18 19 20 21 22
23 24 25 26 27 28 29
30 31
```

9

JANUARY
```
 S  M  T  W  T  F  S
    1  2  3  4  5  6
 7  8  9 10 11 12 13
14 15 16 17 18 19 20
21 22 23 24 25 26 27
28 29 30 31
```
FEBRUARY
```
 S  M  T  W  T  F  S
             1  2  3
 4  5  6  7  8  9 10
11 12 13 14 15 16 17
18 19 20 21 22 23 24
25 26 27 28 29
```
MARCH
```
 S  M  T  W  T  F  S
                1  2
 3  4  5  6  7  8  9
10 11 12 13 14 15 16
17 18 19 20 21 22 23
24 25 26 27 28 29 30
31
```
APRIL
```
 S  M  T  W  T  F  S
    1  2  3  4  5  6
 7  8  9 10 11 12 13
14 15 16 17 18 19 20
21 22 23 24 25 26 27
28 29 30
```
MAY
```
 S  M  T  W  T  F  S
          1  2  3  4
 5  6  7  8  9 10 11
12 13 14 15 16 17 18
19 20 21 22 23 24 25
26 27 28 29 30 31
```
JUNE
```
 S  M  T  W  T  F  S
                   1
 2  3  4  5  6  7  8
 9 10 11 12 13 14 15
16 17 18 19 20 21 22
23 24 25 26 27 28 29
30
```
JULY
```
 S  M  T  W  T  F  S
    1  2  3  4  5  6
 7  8  9 10 11 12 13
14 15 16 17 18 19 20
21 22 23 24 25 26 27
28 29 30 31
```
AUGUST
```
 S  M  T  W  T  F  S
             1  2  3
 4  5  6  7  8  9 10
11 12 13 14 15 16 17
18 19 20 21 22 23 24
25 26 27 28 29 30 31
```
SEPTEMBER
```
 S  M  T  W  T  F  S
 1  2  3  4  5  6  7
 8  9 10 11 12 13 14
15 16 17 18 19 20 21
22 23 24 25 26 27 28
29 30
```
OCTOBER
```
 S  M  T  W  T  F  S
       1  2  3  4  5
 6  7  8  9 10 11 12
13 14 15 16 17 18 19
20 21 22 23 24 25 26
27 28 29 30 31
```
NOVEMBER
```
 S  M  T  W  T  F  S
                1  2
 3  4  5  6  7  8  9
10 11 12 13 14 15 16
17 18 19 20 21 22 23
24 25 26 27 28 29 30
```
DECEMBER
```
 S  M  T  W  T  F  S
 1  2  3  4  5  6  7
 8  9 10 11 12 13 14
15 16 17 18 19 20 21
22 23 24 25 26 27 28
29 30 31
```

10

JANUARY
```
 S  M  T  W  T  F  S
       1  2  3  4  5
 6  7  8  9 10 11 12
13 14 15 16 17 18 19
20 21 22 23 24 25 26
27 28 29 30 31
```
FEBRUARY
```
 S  M  T  W  T  F  S
                1  2
 3  4  5  6  7  8  9
10 11 12 13 14 15 16
17 18 19 20 21 22 23
24 25 26 27 28 29
```
MARCH
```
 S  M  T  W  T  F  S
                   1
 2  3  4  5  6  7  8
 9 10 11 12 13 14 15
16 17 18 19 20 21 22
23 24 25 26 27 28 29
30 31
```
APRIL
```
 S  M  T  W  T  F  S
       1  2  3  4  5
 6  7  8  9 10 11 12
13 14 15 16 17 18 19
20 21 22 23 24 25 26
27 28 29 30
```
MAY
```
 S  M  T  W  T  F  S
             1  2  3
 4  5  6  7  8  9 10
11 12 13 14 15 16 17
18 19 20 21 22 23 24
25 26 27 28 29 30 31
```
JUNE
```
 S  M  T  W  T  F  S
 1  2  3  4  5  6  7
 8  9 10 11 12 13 14
15 16 17 18 19 20 21
22 23 24 25 26 27 28
29 30
```
JULY
```
 S  M  T  W  T  F  S
       1  2  3  4  5
 6  7  8  9 10 11 12
13 14 15 16 17 18 19
20 21 22 23 24 25 26
27 28 29 30 31
```
AUGUST
```
 S  M  T  W  T  F  S
                1  2
 3  4  5  6  7  8  9
10 11 12 13 14 15 16
17 18 19 20 21 22 23
24 25 26 27 28 29 30
31
```
SEPTEMBER
```
 S  M  T  W  T  F  S
    1  2  3  4  5  6
 7  8  9 10 11 12 13
14 15 16 17 18 19 20
21 22 23 24 25 26 27
28 29 30
```
OCTOBER
```
 S  M  T  W  T  F  S
          1  2  3  4
 5  6  7  8  9 10 11
12 13 14 15 16 17 18
19 20 21 22 23 24 25
26 27 28 29 30 31
```
NOVEMBER
```
 S  M  T  W  T  F  S
                   1
 2  3  4  5  6  7  8
 9 10 11 12 13 14 15
16 17 18 19 20 21 22
23 24 25 26 27 28 29
30
```
DECEMBER
```
 S  M  T  W  T  F  S
    1  2  3  4  5  6
 7  8  9 10 11 12 13
14 15 16 17 18 19 20
21 22 23 24 25 26 27
28 29 30 31
```

11

JANUARY
```
 S  M  T  W  T  F  S
          1  2  3  4
 5  6  7  8  9 10 11
12 13 14 15 16 17 18
19 20 21 22 23 24 25
26 27 28 29 30 31
```
FEBRUARY
```
 S  M  T  W  T  F  S
                   1
 2  3  4  5  6  7  8
 9 10 11 12 13 14 15
16 17 18 19 20 21 22
23 24 25 26 27 28 29
```
MARCH
```
 S  M  T  W  T  F  S
 1  2  3  4  5  6  7
 8  9 10 11 12 13 14
15 16 17 18 19 20 21
22 23 24 25 26 27 28
29 30 31
```
APRIL
```
 S  M  T  W  T  F  S
          1  2  3  4
 5  6  7  8  9 10 11
12 13 14 15 16 17 18
19 20 21 22 23 24 25
26 27 28 29 30
```
MAY
```
 S  M  T  W  T  F  S
                1  2
 3  4  5  6  7  8  9
10 11 12 13 14 15 16
17 18 19 20 21 22 23
24 25 26 27 28 29 30
31
```
JUNE
```
 S  M  T  W  T  F  S
    1  2  3  4  5  6
 7  8  9 10 11 12 13
14 15 16 17 18 19 20
21 22 23 24 25 26 27
28 29 30
```
JULY
```
 S  M  T  W  T  F  S
          1  2  3  4
 5  6  7  8  9 10 11
12 13 14 15 16 17 18
19 20 21 22 23 24 25
26 27 28 29 30 31
```
AUGUST
```
 S  M  T  W  T  F  S
                   1
 2  3  4  5  6  7  8
 9 10 11 12 13 14 15
16 17 18 19 20 21 22
23 24 25 26 27 28 29
30 31
```
SEPTEMBER
```
 S  M  T  W  T  F  S
       1  2  3  4  5
 6  7  8  9 10 11 12
13 14 15 16 17 18 19
20 21 22 23 24 25 26
27 28 29 30
```
OCTOBER
```
 S  M  T  W  T  F  S
             1  2  3
 4  5  6  7  8  9 10
11 12 13 14 15 16 17
18 19 20 21 22 23 24
25 26 27 28 29 30 31
```
NOVEMBER
```
 S  M  T  W  T  F  S
 1  2  3  4  5  6  7
 8  9 10 11 12 13 14
15 16 17 18 19 20 21
22 23 24 25 26 27 28
29 30
```
DECEMBER
```
 S  M  T  W  T  F  S
       1  2  3  4  5
 6  7  8  9 10 11 12
13 14 15 16 17 18 19
20 21 22 23 24 25 26
27 28 29 30 31
```

12

JANUARY
```
 S  M  T  W  T  F  S
             1  2  3
 4  5  6  7  8  9 10
11 12 13 14 15 16 17
18 19 20 21 22 23 24
25 26 27 28 29 30 31
```
FEBRUARY
```
 S  M  T  W  T  F  S
 1  2  3  4  5  6  7
 8  9 10 11 12 13 14
15 16 17 18 19 20 21
22 23 24 25 26 27 28
29
```
MARCH
```
 S  M  T  W  T  F  S
    1  2  3  4  5  6
 7  8  9 10 11 12 13
14 15 16 17 18 19 20
21 22 23 24 25 26 27
28 29 30 31
```
APRIL
```
 S  M  T  W  T  F  S
             1  2  3
 4  5  6  7  8  9 10
11 12 13 14 15 16 17
18 19 20 21 22 23 24
25 26 27 28 29 30
```
MAY
```
 S  M  T  W  T  F  S
                   1
 2  3  4  5  6  7  8
 9 10 11 12 13 14 15
16 17 18 19 20 21 22
23 24 25 26 27 28 29
30 31
```
JUNE
```
 S  M  T  W  T  F  S
       1  2  3  4  5
 6  7  8  9 10 11 12
13 14 15 16 17 18 19
20 21 22 23 24 25 26
27 28 29 30
```
JULY
```
 S  M  T  W  T  F  S
             1  2  3
 4  5  6  7  8  9 10
11 12 13 14 15 16 17
18 19 20 21 22 23 24
25 26 27 28 29 30 31
```
AUGUST
```
 S  M  T  W  T  F  S
 1  2  3  4  5  6  7
 8  9 10 11 12 13 14
15 16 17 18 19 20 21
22 23 24 25 26 27 28
29 30 31
```
SEPTEMBER
```
 S  M  T  W  T  F  S
          1  2  3  4
 5  6  7  8  9 10 11
12 13 14 15 16 17 18
19 20 21 22 23 24 25
26 27 28 29 30
```
OCTOBER
```
 S  M  T  W  T  F  S
                1  2
 3  4  5  6  7  8  9
10 11 12 13 14 15 16
17 18 19 20 21 22 23
24 25 26 27 28 29 30
31
```
NOVEMBER
```
 S  M  T  W  T  F  S
    1  2  3  4  5  6
 7  8  9 10 11 12 13
14 15 16 17 18 19 20
21 22 23 24 25 26 27
28 29 30
```
DECEMBER
```
 S  M  T  W  T  F  S
          1  2  3  4
 5  6  7  8  9 10 11
12 13 14 15 16 17 18
19 20 21 22 23 24 25
26 27 28 29 30 31
```

13

JANUARY
```
 S  M  T  W  T  F  S
                1  2
 3  4  5  6  7  8  9
10 11 12 13 14 15 16
17 18 19 20 21 22 23
24 25 26 27 28 29 30
31
```
FEBRUARY
```
 S  M  T  W  T  F  S
    1  2  3  4  5  6
 7  8  9 10 11 12 13
14 15 16 17 18 19 20
21 22 23 24 25 26 27
28 29
```
MARCH
```
 S  M  T  W  T  F  S
       1  2  3  4  5
 6  7  8  9 10 11 12
13 14 15 16 17 18 19
20 21 22 23 24 25 26
27 28 29 30 31
```
APRIL
```
 S  M  T  W  T  F  S
                1  2
 3  4  5  6  7  8  9
10 11 12 13 14 15 16
17 18 19 20 21 22 23
24 25 26 27 28 29 30
```
MAY
```
 S  M  T  W  T  F  S
 1  2  3  4  5  6  7
 8  9 10 11 12 13 14
15 16 17 18 19 20 21
22 23 24 25 26 27 28
29 30 31
```
JUNE
```
 S  M  T  W  T  F  S
          1  2  3  4
 5  6  7  8  9 10 11
12 13 14 15 16 17 18
19 20 21 22 23 24 25
26 27 28 29 30
```
JULY
```
 S  M  T  W  T  F  S
                1  2
 3  4  5  6  7  8  9
10 11 12 13 14 15 16
17 18 19 20 21 22 23
24 25 26 27 28 29 30
31
```
AUGUST
```
 S  M  T  W  T  F  S
    1  2  3  4  5  6
 7  8  9 10 11 12 13
14 15 16 17 18 19 20
21 22 23 24 25 26 27
28 29 30 31
```
SEPTEMBER
```
 S  M  T  W  T  F  S
             1  2  3
 4  5  6  7  8  9 10
11 12 13 14 15 16 17
18 19 20 21 22 23 24
25 26 27 28 29 30
```
OCTOBER
```
 S  M  T  W  T  F  S
                   1
 2  3  4  5  6  7  8
 9 10 11 12 13 14 15
16 17 18 19 20 21 22
23 24 25 26 27 28 29
30 31
```
NOVEMBER
```
 S  M  T  W  T  F  S
       1  2  3  4  5
 6  7  8  9 10 11 12
13 14 15 16 17 18 19
20 21 22 23 24 25 26
27 28 29 30
```
DECEMBER
```
 S  M  T  W  T  F  S
             1  2  3
 4  5  6  7  8  9 10
11 12 13 14 15 16 17
18 19 20 21 22 23 24
25 26 27 28 29 30 31
```

14

JANUARY
```
 S  M  T  W  T  F  S
                   1
 2  3  4  5  6  7  8
 9 10 11 12 13 14 15
16 17 18 19 20 21 22
23 24 25 26 27 28 29
30 31
```
FEBRUARY
```
 S  M  T  W  T  F  S
       1  2  3  4  5
 6  7  8  9 10 11 12
13 14 15 16 17 18 19
20 21 22 23 24 25 26
27 28 29
```
MARCH
```
 S  M  T  W  T  F  S
          1  2  3  4
 5  6  7  8  9 10 11
12 13 14 15 16 17 18
19 20 21 22 23 24 25
26 27 28 29 30 31
```
APRIL
```
 S  M  T  W  T  F  S
                   1
 2  3  4  5  6  7  8
 9 10 11 12 13 14 15
16 17 18 19 20 21 22
23 24 25 26 27 28 29
30
```
MAY
```
 S  M  T  W  T  F  S
    1  2  3  4  5  6
 7  8  9 10 11 12 13
14 15 16 17 18 19 20
21 22 23 24 25 26 27
28 29 30 31
```
JUNE
```
 S  M  T  W  T  F  S
             1  2  3
 4  5  6  7  8  9 10
11 12 13 14 15 16 17
18 19 20 21 22 23 24
25 26 27 28 29 30
```
JULY
```
 S  M  T  W  T  F  S
                   1
 2  3  4  5  6  7  8
 9 10 11 12 13 14 15
16 17 18 19 20 21 22
23 24 25 26 27 28 29
30 31
```
AUGUST
```
 S  M  T  W  T  F  S
       1  2  3  4  5
 6  7  8  9 10 11 12
13 14 15 16 17 18 19
20 21 22 23 24 25 26
27 28 29 30 31
```
SEPTEMBER
```
 S  M  T  W  T  F  S
                1  2
 3  4  5  6  7  8  9
10 11 12 13 14 15 16
17 18 19 20 21 22 23
24 25 26 27 28 29 30
```
OCTOBER
```
 S  M  T  W  T  F  S
 1  2  3  4  5  6  7
 8  9 10 11 12 13 14
15 16 17 18 19 20 21
22 23 24 25 26 27 28
29 30 31
```
NOVEMBER
```
 S  M  T  W  T  F  S
          1  2  3  4
 5  6  7  8  9 10 11
12 13 14 15 16 17 18
19 20 21 22 23 24 25
26 27 28 29 30
```
DECEMBER
```
 S  M  T  W  T  F  S
                1  2
 3  4  5  6  7  8  9
10 11 12 13 14 15 16
17 18 19 20 21 22 23
24 25 26 27 28 29 30
31
```

HOLIDAYS AND COMMEMORATED DAYS FOR 1981

Days in parentheses are not legal holidays. *—Holiday observed on following Monday; **—Holiday observed on preceding Friday. Note: applies to all states immediately following symbol

January

1 / New Year's Day (All states & Canada)
2 / Day after New Year's Day (KY)
8 / (Battle of New Orleans Day) (LA)
12 / Martin Luther King Day (MI)
15 / Martin Luther King Day (CT, FL, IL, MD, MA, NJ, SC, DC)
18 / Dr. Martin Luther King, Jr. Day (NY)
19 / Martin Luther King's Birthday (OH)
19 / Robert E. Lee's Birthday (AL, AR, FL, GA, MS, NC, SC)
    Confederate Heroes Day (TX);
    Lee-Jackson Day (VA)

February

2 / Abraham Lincoln's Birthday (DE, OR)
2 / (Groundhog Day)
9 / Abraham Lincoln's Birthday (AZ, OK)
12 / Abraham Lincoln's Birthday (AK, CA, CO, CT, FL, IL, IN, IA, KS, MD, MO, MT, NJ, NM, NY, PA, UT, VT, WA, WV)
14 / (St. Valentine's Day)
15 / Susan B. Anthony's Birthday (FL)
16 / George Washington's Birthday (All states except HI, KY, MI, MN, NE, OH, SD, UT, WI)
    Combined celebration of birthdays of George Washington & Abraham Lincoln (MN, WI); called Presidents' Day (HI, KY, MI, NE, OH, UT)

March

2 / Texas Independence Day (TX)
3 / Mardi Gras Day (AL)
3 / Town Meeting Day (VT)
17 / (St. Patrick's Day)
25 / Maryland Day (MD)
26 / Prince Jonah Kuhio Kalanianaole Day (HI)
30 / Seward's Day (AK)

April

2 / Pascua Florida Day (FL)
12 / Anniversary of signing of Halifax Resolves (*—NC)
13 / Thomas Jefferson's Birthday (AL)
17 / Good Friday (CT, DE, FL, HI, IN, LA, MD, NJ, ND, TN) (Canada); Good Friday Afternoon (KY, WI)
20 / Easter Monday (NC)
20 / Patriot's Day (ME, MA)
20 / Confederate Memorial Day (AL)
21 / San Jacinto Day (TX)
22 / Arbor Day (NE)
22 / Oklahoma Day (OK)
24 / (Arbor Day)
26 / Confederate Memorial Day (FL, *—GA)
27 / Confederate Memorial Day (MS)
27 / Fast Day (NH)

May

1 / (May Day)
4 / Rhode Island Independence Day (RI)
8 / Harry S Truman's Birthday (MO)
10 / Confederate Memorial Day (*—NC, SC)
10 / (Mother's Day)
17 / (Armed Forces Day)
19 / Primary Election Day (PA)
19 / Victoria Day (Canada)
20 / Anniversary of Mecklenburg Declaration of Independence (NC)
25 / Confederate Memorial Day (VA); Decoration Day (TN)
25 / Memorial Day (All states except AL, DE, MD, MS, NM, NH, SC, TN, VA, VT)
30 / Memorial Day (NH, NM); (**—DE, MD, VT)

June

1 / Jefferson Davis' Birthday (AL, MS)
3 / Jefferson Davis' Birthday (FL, GA, SC)
11 / King Kamehameha I Day (HI)
14 / (Flag Day)
19 / Emancipation Day (TX)
20 / West Virginia Day (WV)
21 / (Father's Day)

July

1 / Dominion Day (Canada)
4 / Independence Day (All states); (*—GA; **—AR, DE, ID, IL, IA, LA, MD, MN, NE, NV, ND, OR, SC, VT, VA, WY)
4 / (Indian Rights Day) (WI)
24 / Pioneer Day (UT)

August

2 / American Family Day (AZ)
3 / Colorado Day (CO)
10 / Victory Day (RI)
16 / Bennington Battle Day (*—VT)
21 / Admission Day (HI)
27 / Lyndon B. Johnson's Birthday (TX)
30 / Huey P. Long Day (LA)

September

7 / Labor Day (All states & Canada)
9 / Admission Day (CA)
12 / Defenders' Day (**—MD)
13 / (Grandparents' Day)
27 / (Indian Day) (OK)

October

8 / Yom Kippur (NC)
9 / (Leif Ericson Day)
12 / Columbus Day (All states except AK, AR, CO, HI, IA, KY, LA, MI, MS, NV, ND, OR, SC, SD, WA)
12 / Discoverers' Day (HI)
12 / Thanksgiving Day (Canada)
12 / Farmers' Day (FL)
12 / Pioneer's Day (SD)
18 / Alaska Day (AK)
24 / (United Nations Day)
31 / (Halloween)
31 / Nevada Day (**—NV)

November

1 / (All Saints' Day) (LA)
3 / Election Day (CO, KY, MT, NJ, NC, PA)
9 / Veterans Day (MI, OK)
11 / Veterans Day (All states except MI, OK); Armistice Day (RI, WI); Remembrance Day (Canada)
26 / Thanksgiving Day (All states)
27 / Thanksgiving Friday (IL, KY, NE, WA)

December

24 / Christmas Eve (AR, SC)
25 / Christmas Day (All states & Canada)
26 / Day after Christmas (KY, SC); Boxing Day (Canada)

NEW WORLD EXPLORERS
NORTH AMERICA

c. 1000 . . . Leif Ericsson (Norway) possibly sailed to Labrador and Newfoundland, from Greenland; others theorize that he reached Virginia, Nova Scotia, or New England

c. 1010 . . . Thorfinn Karlsefni (Iceland) sailed from Greenland to North America, probably Labrador or New England

1497–98 . . . John Cabot (England) sailed to North America, probably Cape Breton Island or Newfoundland

1513 . . . Juan Ponce de León (Spain) sailed to near St. Augustine, Florida, and south to Miami Bay

1519 . . . Alonso de Pineda (Spain) explored the Gulf of Mexico from Florida to the mouth of the Rio Grande

1524 . . . Giovanni da Verrazano (France) explored North American coast, probably from North Carolina to Maine, entering New York Bay

1528 . . . Pánfilo de Narváez (Spain) explored Florida from Tampa Bay as far as Tallahassee

1534–36 . . . Jacques Cartier (France) sailed to Strait of Belle Isle, Newfoundland, and discovered Prince Edward Island; he also discovered St. Lawrence River as far as Quebec and Montreal (1535–36)

1536 . . . Alvar Nuñez Cabeza de Vaca (Spain), shipwrecked on Texas coast, traveled as far as New Mexico, Arizona, and possibly California

1538–39 . . . Francisco de Ulloa (Spain) explored Gulf of California to its head, proving that present-day Baja California is a peninsula

1538–41 . . . Hernando de Soto (Spain) began (1539) exploring southern coast of United States, as far inland as Mississippi River, Arkansas, and Oklahoma

1539 . . . Marcos de Niza (Spain) explored southeastern Arizona and perhaps New Mexico

1540–42 . . . Francisco Vásquez de Coronado (Spain) explored New Mexico, Texas Panhandle, Oklahoma, and Kansas

1542 . . . Juan Rodríguez Cabrillo (Spain) discovered California mainland, landing at San Diego Bay

1565 . . . Pedro Menéndez de Avilés (Spain) founded St. Augustine, Florida, and explored Gulf Coast

1576–78 . . . Sir Martin Frobisher (England) explored Frobisher Bay, South Baffin Island, and Hudson Strait in northeastern Canada

1577–79 . . . Sir Francis Drake (England) sailed from Chile to Washington, stopping at San Francisco Bay

1585–87 . . . John Davis (England) discovered Cumberland Sound off Baffin Island in northeastern Canada

1598–1605 . . . Juan de Oñate (Spain) explored New Mexico (1598), Oklahoma, and the plains around Wichita, Kansas (1601), and went down the Colorado River to the Gulf of California (1605)

1602 . . . Bartholomew Gosnold (England) explored eastern coast from Maine to Narragansett Bay, naming Cape Cod

1603–9 . . . Samuel de Champlain (France) explored St. Lawrence River as far as Lachine (1603), New England south to Martha's Vineyard (1603–6); founded Quebec (1608); and discovered Lake Champlain (1609)

1607–9 . . . John Smith (England) helped to found (1607) Jamestown, Virginia, and explored adjacent areas

1609–10 . . . Henry Hudson (Netherlands) sailed up Chesapeake, Delaware, and New York Bays; under English flag, he sailed through Greenland, Labrador, Hudson Strait and Bay (1610)

1634 . . . Jean Nicolet (France) explored Lake Michigan, Green Bay, and Fox River, Wisconsin

1673 . . . Louis Jolliet, Father Jacques Marquette (France) navigated Mississippi, Arkansas, and Illinois Rivers to Chicago; first to establish the existence of a waterway from St. Lawrence River to the Gulf of Mexico

1678–79 . . . Frère Louis Hennepin (France) explored Great Plains and the upper Mississippi River region

1678–80 . . . Daniel Greysolon Duluth (Du Lhut) (France) claimed Lake Superior and upper Mississippi region for France; his treatment of the Indians gained their lasting friendship

1679–82 . . . Robert Cavalier de La Salle (France) crossed Great Lakes and navigated Mississippi River to its mouth

1691–92 . . . Henry Kelsey (England) explored the area around Reindeer Lake in western Canada

1692 . . . Arnout Viele (France) explored the area from the Great Lakes to the Ohio River

1701 . . . Antoine de la Mothe Cadillac (France) explored upper Michigan; founded Detroit

1710–18 . . . Jean Baptiste le Moyne, sieur de Bienville (France), founded Mobile (1710) and New Orleans (1718)

1731–43 . . . Pierre Gautier de Varennes, sieur de la Vérendrye (Canada), explored central Canada, Red River country, and the Missouri River (1731–34); discovered Lake Manitoba (1739) in central Canada; and traveled probably as far as the Black Hills in north central United States (1742–43)

1769–79 . . . Daniel Boone (United States) explored Kentucky territory (1769–71) and blazed the Wilderness Road (1775)

1770–72 . . . Samuel Hearne (England) opened areas of north central Canada, around Great Slave Lake and Coppermine River

1775–76 . . . Silvestre Vélez de Escalante (Spain) explored Arizona and Colorado; first white man known to travel in Utah

1792 . . . Robert Gray (United States) discovered Columbia River in northwestern United States

1789–93 . . . Sir Alexander Mackenzie (Canada) followed Mackenzie River in Canada to Arctic Ocean (1789); explored elsewhere in Canada, making first overland crossing of North America to the Pacific, north of Mexico (1793)

1797–1810 . . . David Thompson (Canada) explored Rocky Mountains and all of the Columbia River system

1803–6 . . . Meriwether Lewis, William Clark (United States) navigated Missouri River to Bismarck, North Dakota, traveled west through the mountains to the Clearwater, Snake, and Columbia Rivers as far as the Pacific Ocean

1805–7 . . . Zebulon Pike (United States) explored Minnesota (1805) and southwestern United States, sighted Pikes Peak (1806)

c. 1807 . . . John Colter (United States) crossed Teton Range in the Rocky Mountains, and discovered Yellowstone area

1819–27 . . . Sir John Franklin (England) explored northern Canada to the Arctic

1825 . . . James Bridger (United States) discovered Great Salt Lake in Utah

1825–27 . . . Jedediah Smith (United States) traveled from Great Salt Lake to Colorado River and San Diego, California; on return trip, he crossed Sierra Nevada and Great Salt Desert

1832–35 . . . Benjamin Bonneville (United States) helped open Rocky Mountain territory

1842–45 . . . John Frémont, Kit Carson (United States) explored Oregon, Nevada, and California

SOUTH AND CENTRAL AMERICA

1492–1502 . . . Christopher Columbus (Spain) discovered America: Bahamas, Cuba, and Hispaniola in the Caribbean (1492); Venezuela (1498); and Honduras (1502)

1499 . . . Alonso de Ojeda (Spain) explored northeastern coast of South America

1499–1509 . . . Vicente Pinzón (Spain) explored coast of Brazil and discovered mouth of the Amazon River in Brazil (1499–1500); skirted along Yucatán, Honduras, and Venezuela (1508–9)

1500 . . . Pedro Alvarez Cabral (Portugal) reached coast of Brazil, possibly before Pinzón

1501–2 . . . Amerigo Vespucci (Portugal) discovered Río de la Plata, explored about 6,000 miles of South American coast; he was the first to suggest that America was not part of Asia

1513 . . . Vasco Núñez de Balboa (Spain) discovered the Pacific Ocean by crossing Isthmus of Panama

1516 . . . Juan Díaz de Solís (Spain) sailed up Río de la Plata and explored Uruguay

1517 . . . Francisco Fernández de Córdoba (Spain) discovered Yucatán in Mexico

1519 . . . Gil González Dávila and Andrés Niño (Spain) explored Pacific coast of Central America from Panama to Nicaragua

1519–21 . . . Hernán Cortés (Spain) discovered Aztec capital Tenochtitlán (now Mexico City) and conquered Mexico

1520 . . . Ferdinand Magellan (Spain) explored Río de la Plata and Patagonia in Argentina, and discovered the strait at the tip of South America that bears his name

1524–33 . . . Francisco Pizarro (Spain) explored the San Juan River between Colombia and Ecuador; conqueror of Peru (1532–33)

1526–30 . . . Sebastian Cabot (Spain) explored Río de la Plata country along Paraguay, Plata, and Paraná Rivers

1530–35 . . . Nikolaus Federmann (Germany) explored northwestern Venezuela and interior of Colombia through the Andes

1533 . . . Sebastián de Belalcázar (Spain) explored and conquered Ecuador and southeastern Colombia

1535–37 . . . Diego de Almagro (Spain) explored from Peru south through the Andes as far as Coquimbo and the Atacama Desert in Chile

1535–37 . . . Pedro de Mendoza (Spain) explored Río de la Plata and founded Buenos Aires (1536)

1536 . . . Gonzalo Jiménez de Quesada (Spain) founded Bogotá, Colombia, and explored the Magdalena River, Colombia

1541 . . . Francisco de Orellana (Spain) floated down the Amazon's entire length

1549–52 . . . Pedro de Valdivia (Spain) explored Chile, founding Concepción and Valdivia (1552)

1595 . . . Sir Walter Raleigh (England) explored Orinoco River, penetrating 300 miles into Guiana's interior

1616 . . . Willem C. Schouten (Netherlands) rounded and named Cape Horn at the tip of South America, avoiding the Strait of Magellan

1799–1804 . . . Alexander von Humboldt (Germany) explored source of Orinoco and Amazon Rivers, establishing the connecting systems of the two

STARS/PLANETS/SPACE

ORIGIN AND EVOLUTION OF THE UNIVERSE

One of the major and perhaps most fundamental problems in astronomy is to develop a theory of the origin and evolution of the universe, based on actual observations of stars and galaxies and on known physical laws, in the attempt to determine how the universe changes with time. Cosmology deals with the physical structure of the universe, and with the origin of the universe and of its subsystems—that is, galaxies and systems of galaxies. Several different theories of the origin and evolution of the universe have been suggested.

The Einstein-Friedmann relativistic theories of cosmology, which were first formulated (1922) by Albert Friedmann, a Russian physicist, are based on Einstein's theory of general relativity. The relativistic theorists postulate a universe that is in constant motion and originated from one infinitesimal point and subsequently expanded. The expansion of the universe refers to the mutual recession of galaxies from each other, with a recessional velocity proportional to their distance from one another. The observational evidence for the recession of galaxies from one another was first discovered by the American astronomer Edwin Hubble in the late 1920s.

Most astronomers believe that the whole universe originated in a cataclysmic explosion. This is the basis of the "big-bang" theory. From the moment of the big bang the universe has expanded and as the galaxies formed they shared in this expansion. At the very beginning, the temperature in the universe was extremely high. As it decreased, particles of radiation (photons) and of matter were created. Within only a few minutes electrons and the nuclei of hydrogen, deuterium, and helium had been produced. Matter and radiation continued to cool and after many thousands of years the immense clouds of matter that had formed were able to condense into galaxies and stars.

According to the relativistic concept, the geometry of space determines the kind of expansion of the universe. If the curvature of space is positive, which means that space is finite, the relativistic equations predict that the expansion of the universe will come to a halt at some finite time. Thereafter, the universe will begin to contract with increasing velocity until it reaches its initial primordial state of very high density and very high temperature. This concept is sometimes referred to as a "closed" universe. If the curvature of space is negative, the expansion could be permanent; the universe could expand forever. In this "open" universe idea, even after the last star has stopped shining and the entire universe is in total darkness, the universe will still be expanding.

According to the "steady-state" or "continuous creation" theory of cosmology, galaxies recede from one another, but their spatial density remains constant. According to this theory, there is a continuous creation of new matter (hydrogen atoms) throughout space. The newly created matter subsequently condenses to form new stars and galaxies between the older galaxies, and a steady state or constant spatial density with time is maintained. In the steady-state concept, the universe had no beginning and has no end.

However, we can determine an upper limit for the age of the universe, since its rate of expansion has been continually slowing up. This is considered evidence of the primordial explosion postulated as first putting the universe in motion. Based on the present rate of the expansion, it appears that the age of the universe is between about 10 and 20 billion years.

The big-bang theory predicts that the radiation originally created in the big bang should by now have cooled to a very low temperature. It should in fact be observed as black-body radiation characteristic of a temperature of about 3 kelvin ($-270°C$), i.e., as very high frequency radio waves (microwaves) of very low intensity. In 1965, A. A. Penzias and R. W. Wilson of the Bell Telephone Laboratories in New Jersey, made an accidental discovery of major cosmological importance. They detected a background microwave emission of uniform intensity coming from all parts of the sky that corresponded to a temperature of about 3 kelvin. This is believed to be the relic radiation from the original big bang of the universe. Molecules found in interstellar space can be used as a cosmic thermometer: spectral measurements of CN absorption confirm the existence of the 3-kelvin universal background radiation.

Further evidence for the big bang comes from studies on the abundance of helium in the universe. Most of the helium in the universe is thought to have formed within minutes of the big bang. The amount predicted by theory is very close to what has been observed: helium forms about 25% (by mass) of the matter in the universe, hydrogen about 73%, with oxygen, carbon and other elements making up the balance.

According to the big-bang theory, the number of galaxies per volume of space should have been much greater in the past, before the universe began expanding, than it is today. The steady-state model holds that the number of galaxies per volume of space should be statistically the same everywhere at all times. Martin Ryle, the British Astronomer Roval, has presented very substantial radio astronomical evidence against the steady-state theory, based on counts of the numbers of radio galaxies that are very distant in space (looking farther out into space is really like looking back into time).

At present it appears that the balance of the observational evidence is against the steady-state concept and in favor of the big-bang theory.

STARS AND GALAXIES

Stars are the basic elements in the universe. More than 90 percent of the mass of our own galaxy—the Milky Way—is in the form of stars; the rest of the matter is interstellar hydrogen gas and dust that form stars. The mass of the Sun—the star of our solar system—is 2×10^{30} kg. The range of masses observed for most stars varies from 0.05 of the Sun's mass to 60 times the Sun's mass. The range of luminosity or absolute magnitude (brightness) varies from a tiny fraction of the Sun's luminosity for white dwarf stars to over a million times the Sun's luminosity for the most luminous stars. The range of stellar radii varies from 1/70,000 of the Sun's radius for neutron stars to over 1,000 times the Sun's radius for supergiants. The Sun's density is about 1.4 grams/cm^3 (a little heavier than water). White dwarfs may be over 1 million times as dense as the Sun and neutron stars even more dense; supergiants can be only one-millionth as dense as the Sun.

Multiple star systems consist of more than two stars linked by gravitational forces. Galactic or open clusters are loosely bound stellar systems with up to a few hundred stars. Globular or closed clusters are tightly bound spherical star clusters with maybe over a million stars. Galaxies are the largest stellar systems and are regarded as the basic mass elements of the universe. Galaxies, which occur in clusters, contain from a billion to a thousand billion stars each. It has been estimated that there are at least 10 billion galaxies in the universe. From observations, it appears that there are three distinct types. In spiral galaxies, spiral arms of gas and dust are distinctly visible. In elliptical galaxies, there are no visible spiral arms or gas, and the exterior shape is either elliptical or spherical. Irregular galaxies have no definite shape.

In 1944 Walter Baade reported that stars in the nucleus of spiral galaxies are different from the stars in the arms of the galaxy. Stars within the spiral arms are called Population I stars and are young and bluish in color. Population II stars are found in the galactic nucleus and galactic halo and are old and reddish in color.

Red giants are cool red stars that have undergone expansion; their luminosity may be well over 1,000 times the Sun's luminosity, and their radius several hundred times the Sun's radius. The red giant has already converted about 50 percent of its hydrogen into helium by thermonuclear processes. As this energy source becomes exhausted, expansion halts and contraction to a white dwarf may occur. White dwarfs have low luminosity, relatively high surface temperature and extremely high density. They are dying stars and are gradually cooling to become "black dwarfs" or nonluminous chunks of mass. The Sun will become a white dwarf in billions of years time.

The process by which a star dies depends on its mass. When its energy is exhausted, a star with a mass below 1.4 times the Sun's mass will become a white dwarf. One with a mass between 1.4 and about 3 times the Sun's mass will contract through the white-dwarf stage and become a tiny immensely dense neutron star. Supernovae are stars that suddenly increase their luminosity by more than 10 million times. The supernova luminosity increase reflects the fact that the star is exploding—literally blowing itself up. It is believed that the remnant of at least one supernova (the Crab Nebula) is a neutron star, which forms the pulsating radio source or "pulsar" observed in that region of the sky.

QUASARS

Quasars ("quasi-stellar radio sources") were first discovered in 1961 as starlike objects emitting extremely intense radio radiation. In 1963 optical astronomers identified these objects with faint sources of light. Since then hundreds of quasars have been found, all well beyond our galaxy. Over 99% are undetectable radio sources and are sometimes referred to as QSOs ("quasi-stellar objects"). It is still a most challenging problem to understand the physical process that leads to the tremendous radio emission in some quasars and the lack of it in others. The discovery that most quasars emit intense infrared radiation and X-rays must also now be explained.

In 1963, Maarten Schmidt, of the California Institute of Technology, discovered one of the main characteristics of quasars: a large red shift in the location of the emission lines in their spectra. It is generally accepted that these large red shifts are caused by the cosmological expansion of the universe. The red shift is used to determine the distance of receding extragalactic objects. The measured red shift of quasars would place them at a few billion light years—in fact, the most distant objects in the universe.

This interpretation also implies that to be detectable on Earth quasars must emit a thousand times more energy than entire galaxies, each containing about 100 billion stars. The radiative emission from quasars in the visible and in the short radio-wavelength region varies with time. The time scale and amplitude of these brightness variations place a limit on the geometrical size of the emitting object. Thus, the center of activity in a quasar is in the order of a few light months or less in diameter, compared to 100,000 light years for a galaxy. Detailed studies have been made of the complex emission lines and absorption lines that occur in the spectra of quasars. These studies indicate that the compact active region lies at the center of a group of dense, rapidly moving clouds of gas, which are enveloped in low density gas.

Despite the theories advanced, the actual origin of the tremendous energy output of quasars remains unknown. One theory is that the energy is generated in a compact cluster of stars by supernova explosions, numerous collisions between the closely packed stars, and by pulsars. In another theory the active center contains a supermassive black hole of a billion solar masses; the energy is released when gas and stars are drawn into the black hole.

Of late, there has been a growing awareness that quasars show similarities to Seyfert galaxies, which are a galaxy class characterized by the small size and high luminosity of their nuclei. Their outer parts, however, are inconspicuous. Since quasars appear photographically similar and have similar emission spectra to Seyfert galaxies, it appears that these two celestial phenomena may somehow be related.

PULSARS

In 1967 a new class of astronomical object was discovered by a Cambridge University group: a rapidly pulsating radio source, or "pulsar." The radio signals from this object, located in the constellation Vulpecula, were periodic in nature, consisting of brief radio pulses that were separated by about 1.3 seconds. Since then, more than 300 pulsars have been discovered.

The most interesting property of pulsars is the extreme regularity of their radio-emission period, which ranges from 0.033 to over 4 seconds. It was believed that this time period between radio pulses was remarkably constant, varying by not more than a few parts per million annually; however, recently it has been found that the periods of most pulsars are lengthening very slightly due to the transfer of internal rotational energy to the surroundings. Two of these pulsars have been identified with the remnants of exploding stars, the Crab Nebula and one in the constellation of Vela. These two pulsars have the shortest periods of any known—0.033 and 0.089 second, respectively—but their periods are increasing more rapidly than those of any other pulsars. A pulsar's radio pulses are of very short duration compared to the time periods between those pulses, which typically are some thousandths of a second.

Optical astronomers have gone to considerable lengths to determine if pulsars emit optical pulses as well as radio pulses. At the present time, only the Crab Nebula pulsar and the very faint Vela pulsar have been observed to emit periodic pulses of light. The former also emits X-rays, ultraviolet, and infrared radiation.

A pulsar is assumed to be a rapidly rotating neutron star, which is a very dense star with an intense magnetic field. The gravitational collapse of a massive dying star causes it to implode as a supernova and vast quantities of energy are given off. Any remaining core could be a pulsar, with a mass between 1.4 and about 3 times the Sun's mass but a diameter of only about 10 miles (the Sun's diameter is 865,000 miles). This kind of star rotates so rapidly that it can complete one rotation on its axis in less than a thousandth of a second.

STELLAR AND GALACTIC TERMS

Absolute Magnitude—Apparent magnitude that a star would have at a distance of 10 parsecs.

Albedo—Reflecting power of a nonluminous body.

Apparent Magnitude—A measure of the observed light flux received from a star or other object at Earth.

Astronomical Unit (AU)—The average distance between the Sun and the Earth. It is equal to 92,957,000 miles and is often used as a unit of measurement.

Bands (in spectra)—Emission or absorption lines, usually in the spectra of chemical compounds or radicals, coalesced into broad emission or absorption bands.

Binary Star—System of two stars revolving about a common center of gravity.

Black Body—A hypothetical perfect radiator that absorbs and reemits all radiation incident upon it.

Clouds of Magellan—Two neighboring galaxies visible to the naked eye from southern latitudes.

Cosmic Rays—Atomic nuclei (mostly protons) that are observed to strike the Earth's atmosphere with exceedingly high energies, probably from supernovae.

Cosmological Red Shift—Red shift of spectral lines in celestial objects arising from the expansion of the universe which, when interpreted with a cosmological model, indicates the distance of those objects.

Cosmology—The study of the organization and evolution of the universe.

Dark Nebula—A cloud of interstellar dust that obscures the light of more distant stars and appears as an opaque curtain.

Diffuse Nebula—A reflection or emission nebula produced by interstellar matter (not a planetary nebula).

Emission Nebula—A gaseous nebula that derives its visible light from the fluorescence of ultraviolet light from a star in or near the nebula.

Extragalactic—Beyond the galaxy.

Gamma Rays—Photons (of electromagnetic radiation) of energy higher than that of X rays—the most energetic form of electromagnetic radiation.

Gravitational Force—Force of attraction between two bodies, directly proportional to product of their masses, inversely proportional to square of distance between them.

"Heavy" Elements—In astronomy, usually those elements of greater atomic number than helium.

Hertzsprung-Russell Diagram—A basic classification of the properties of stars in which luminosity is related to effective surface temperature or star color.

Infrared Radiation—Electromagnetic radiation of wavelength longer than the longest visible (red) wavelengths but shorter than radio wavelengths.

Interstellar Dust—Microscopic solid grains, believed to be mostly dielectric compounds of hydrogen and other common elements, in interstellar space.

Interstellar Gas—Sparse gas in interstellar space.

Kelvin Temperature Scale—An absolute temperature scale, the zero point of which is $-273.15°$ C; temperature in kelvin = temperature in $°C - 273.15$.

Law of the Red Shifts—The relation between the radial velocity and distance of a remote galaxy: the radial velocity is proportional to the galaxy distance.

Light-year—The distance light travels in a vacuum in one year; 1 LY $= 9.46 \times 10^{12}$ km, or about 6×10^{12} mi.

Luminosity—The rate of radiation of electromagnetic energy into space by a star or other object.

Magnitude—A measure of the amount of light flux received from a star or other luminous object.

Nebula—Cloud of interstellar gas or dust.

Neutron Stars—A near-final stage in stellar evolution at which nuclear energy sources are exhausted, central densities are nuclear densities, and the stars are supported by degenerate neutron pressure. Rotating neutron stars are of current interest as pulsar models.

Nova—Suddenly exploding or erupting star gradually fading to original brightness.

Nuclear Transformation—Transformation of one atomic nucleus into another.

Occultation—An eclipse of a star or planet by the moon or some other celestial body, as seen from Earth.

Parsec—The distance of an object that would have a stellar parallax of one second of arc; 1 parsec $= 3.26$ light-years.

Planetary Nebula—A shell of gas ejected from, and enlarging about, a certain kind of extremely hot star.

Population I and II—Two classes of stars (and star systems) classified according to their spectral characteristics, chemical compositions, radial velocities, ages, and galaxy locations.

Proton-Proton Reaction—A chain of thermonuclear reactions by which hydrogen nuclei are built up into nuclei of helium, so producing huge amounts of energy.

Radio Waves—The lowest-energy electromagnetic radiation, lying beyond the infrared region of the spectrum. Narrow bands that can pass through the Earth's atmosphere are used in radio astronomy.

Recurrent Nova—A nova that has been known to erupt more than once.

Red Shift, Redshift—A shift to longer wavelengths of the light from remote galaxies; presumed to be produced by a Doppler shift.

Seyfert Galaxies—Galaxies having very bright nuclei and inconspicuous spiral arms. Their spectra show strong emission lines.

Solar Wind—Flow of high-energy particles (mainly protons and electrons) from the Sun.

Spectral Class (or Type)—A classification of a star according to the characteristics of its spectrum.

Spectrograph—An instrument for photographing a spectrum; usually attached to a telescope to photograph the spectrum of a star.

Spectroscope—An instrument for directly viewing the spectrum of a light source.

Spectrum—The array of colors or wavelengths obtained when light from a source is dispersed, as in passing it through a prism or grating.

Stellar Evolution—The changes that take place in the sizes, luminosities, structures, and the like of stars as they age.

Supergiants—Very bright stars that have undergone considerable expansion.

Ultraviolet Radiation—Electromagnetic radiation of wavelengths shorter than the shortest visible (violet) wavelengths and in the approximate range 10 to 300 nanometers.

X rays—Electromagnetic radiation lying between gamma rays and ultraviolet radiation in energy: totally absorbed by Earth's atmosphere.

THE TWENTY BRIGHTEST STARS*

The 20 brightest stars—stars with smallest apparent magnitude—contain one triple-star system and nine binary systems. The table gives the stars, their distance in parsecs, and the apparent and absolute magnitude of the stars and their components.

Star	Distance (Parsecs)	APPARENT VISUAL MAGNITUDES OF COMPONENTS			ABSOLUTE VISUAL MAGNITUDES OF COMPONENTS		
		1st	2d	3d	1st	2d	3d
Sirius	2.7	−1.47	+ 8.5	—	+1.4	+11.4	—
Canopus	34	−0.73	—	—	−3.3	—	—
Arcturus	11	−0.06	—	—	−0.3	—	—
α Centauri	1.3	−0.00	+ 1.4	+10.7	+4.4	+ 5.8	+15
Vega	8.0	+0.04	—	—	+0.6	—	—
Rigel	261	+0.08	+ 6.6	—	−7.0	− 0.4	—
Capella	14	+0.09	+ 0.5	—	+0.1	+ 0.4	—
Procyon	3.4	+0.34	+10.8	—	+2.6	+13.0	—
Betelgeuse	199	+0.41v	—	—	−5.5	—	—
Achernar	23	+0.47	—	—	−1.6	—	—
β Centauri	101	+0.59	+ 4	—	−4.4	− 0.8	—
Altair	4.9	+0.77	—	—	+1.9	—	—
α Crucis	86	+0.79	+ 1.9	—	−3.9	− 3.5	—
Aldebaran	20	+0.86	+13	—	−0.3	+12	—
Spica	80	+0.96	—	—	−3.5	—	—
Antares	132	+1.08	+ 5.1	—	−4.5	− 0.3	—
Pollux	11	+1.15	—	—	+0.2	—	—
Fomalhaut	7.0	+1.16	+ 6.5	—	+1.7	+ 7.3	—
β Crucis	175	+1.24v	—	—	−5.0	—	—
Deneb	460	+1.26	—	—	−7.0	—	—

* For information about the Sun, see page 321.   v = variable magnitude.

THE NEAREST STARS*

The following list gives the star, its distance in parsecs (a parsec is equal to 3.26 light-years), and the apparent and absolute magnitudes of the star and its components. The apparent magnitude is the brightness of the star as observed from Earth, while the absolute magnitude is the brightness that the star would have at a distance of 10 parsecs. The larger the magnitude, the fainter the star. A first-magnitude star appears roughly 2.5 times as bright as a second-magnitude star. A zero magnitude star is 2.5 times as bright as a first-magnitude star, and a —1 star is 2.5 times as bright as a zero-magnitude star.

Star	Distance (Parsecs)	APPARENT VISUAL MAGNITUDES OF COMPONENTS			ABSOLUTE VISUAL MAGNITUDES OF COMPONENTS		
		1st	2d	3d	1st	2d	3d
Proxima	1.31	10.7	—	—	15.1	—	—
α Centauri	1.31	0.00	+ 1.4	+10.7	+ 4.4	+ 5.8	+15
Barnard's Star	1.80	+ 9.54	—	—	+13.2	—	—
Wolf 359	2.33	+13.5	—	—	+16.7	—	—
Lalande 21185	2.48	+ 7.48	—	—	+10.5	—	—
Sirius	2.67	— 1.47	+ 8.5	—	+ 1.4	+11.4	—
Luyten 726–8	2.73	+12.5	+12.9	—	+15.4	+15.8	—
Ross 154	2.91	+10.6	—	—	+13.3	—	—
Ross 248	3.16	+12.24	—	—	+14.7	—	—
ε Eridani	3.28	+ 3.68	—	—	+ 6.1	—	—
Ross 128	3.31	+11.13	—	—	+13.5	—	—
Luyten 789–6	3.31	+12.28	—	—	+14.6	—	—
Procyon	3.37	+ 0.34	+10.7	—	+ 2.6	+13.0	—
61 Cygni	3.43	+ 5.19	+ 6.02	—	+ 7.5	+ 8.4	—
ε Indi	3.43	+ 4.71	—	—	+ 7.0	—	—
Σ 2398	3.53	+ 8.90	+ 9.69	—	+11.1	+11.9	—
BD+43°44	3.56	+ 8.07	+11.04	—	+10.3	+13.2	—
Lac 9352	3.59	+ 7.43	—	—	+ 9.6	—	—
τ Ceti	3.65	+ 3.49	—	—	+ 5.7	—	—
BD+5°1668	3.77	+10.9	—	—	+13.0	—	—
Lac 8760	3.83	+ 6.76	—	—	+ 8.8	—	—
Kapteyn's Star	3.90	+ 8.81	—	—	+10.8	—	—
Kruger 60	3.93	+ 9.85	+11.3	—	+11.9	+13.3	—
Ross 614	4.03	+11.13	+14.8	—	+13.1	+16.8	—
BD—12°4523	4.10	+10.13	—	—	+12.0	—	—
v. Maanen's Star	4.24	+12.36	—	—	+14.3	—	—

* For information about the Sun, see page 321.

THE CONSTELLATIONS

Constellations are configurations of stars supposedly resembling a particular object, person, or animal. Usually, the stars within a given constellation are named with a Greek letter plus the genitive of the constellation, with the brightest star getting the first Greek letter, alpha; the second brightest getting the second Greek letter, beta; and the like. The following table gives the constellation, its genitive, its English name or description, and the abbreviation for it that is usually found on star charts.

Constellation	Genitive	English name or description	Abbreviation
Andromeda	Andromedae	Chained Maiden	And
Antlia	Antliae	Air pump	Ant
Apus	Apodis	Bird of Paradise	Aps
Aquarius	Aquarii	Water bearer	Aqr
Aquila	Aquilae	Eagle	Aql
Ara	Arae	Altar	Ara
Aries	Arietis	Ram	Ari
Auriga	Aurigae	Charioteer	Aur
Boötes	Boötis	Herdsman	Boo
Caelum	Caeli	Chisel	Cae
Camelopardalis	Camelopardalis	Giraffe	Cam
Cancer	Cancri	Crab	Cnc
Canes Venatici	Canum Venaticorum	Hunting dogs	CVn
Canis Major	Canis Majoris	Great dog	CMa
Canis Minor	Canis Minoris	Little dog	CMi
Capricornus	Capricorni	Sea goat	Cap
*Carina	Carinae	Keel of Argonauts' ship	Car
Cassiopeia	Cassiopeiae	Queen of Ethiopia	Cas
Centaurus	Centauri	Centaur	Cen
Cepheus	Cephei	King of Ethiopia	Cep
Cetus	Ceti	Whale	Cet
Chamaeleon	Chamaeleontis	Chameleon	Cha
Circinus	Circini	Compasses	Cir
Columba	Columbae	Dove	Col
Coma Berenices	Comae Berenices	Berenice's hair	Com
Corona Australis	Coronae Australis	Southern crown	CrA
Corona Borealis	Coronae Borealis	Northern crown	CrB
Corvus	Corvi	Crow	Crv
Crater	Crateris	Cup	Crt
Crux	Crucis	Cross (southern)	Cru
Cygnus	Cygni	Swan	Cyg
Delphinus	Delphini	Dolphin	Del
Dorado	Doradûs	Swordfish	Dor
Draco	Draconis	Dragon	Dra
Equuleus	Equulei	Little horse	Equ
Eridanus	Eridani	River	Eri
Fornax	Fornacis	Furnace	For
Gemini	Geminorum	Twins	Gem
Grus	Gruis	Crane	Gru
Hercules	Herculis	Hercules	Her
Horologium	Horologii	Clock	Hor
Hydra	Hydrae	Sea serpent	Hya
Hydrus	Hydri	Water snake	Hyi
Indus	Indi	Indian	Ind
Lacerta	Lacertae	Lizard	Lac
Leo	Leonis	Lion	Leo
Leo Minor	Leonis Minoris	Little lion	LMi
Lepus	Leporis	Hare	Lep
Libra	Librae	Balance	Lib
Lupus	Lupi	Wolf	Lup
Lynx	Lyncis	Lynx	Lyn
Lyra	Lyrae	Lyre	Lyr
Mensa	Mensae	Table Mountain	Men
Microscopium	Microscopii	Microscope	Mic
Monoceros	Monocerotis	Unicorn	Mon
Musca	Muscae	Fly	Mus
Norma	Normae	Rule	Nor
Octans	Octantis	Octant	Oct
Ophiuchus	Ophiuchi	Serpent bearer	Oph
Orion	Orionis	Orion, the hunter	Ori
Pavo	Pavonis	Peacock	Pav
Pegasus	Pegasi	Pegasus, the winged horse	Peg
Perseus	Persei	Perseus, hero who saved Andromeda	Per
Phoenix	Phoenicis	Phoenix	Phe
Pictor	Pictoris	Easel	Pic

Constellation	Genitive	English name or description	Abbreviation
Pisces	Piscium	Fishes	Psc
Piscis Austrinus	Piscis Austrini	Southern fish	PsA
*Puppis	Puppis	Stern of the Argo-nauts' ship	Pup
*Pyxis	Pyxidis	Compass on the Argonauts' ship	Pyx
Reticulum	Reticuli	Net	Ret
Sagitta	Sagittae	Arrow	Sge
Sagittarius	Sagittarii	Archer	Sgr
Scorpius	Scorpii	Scorpion	Sco
Sculptor	Sculptoris	Sculptor's tools	Scl
Scutum	Scuti	Shield	Sct
Serpens	Serpentis	Serpent	Ser
Sextans	Sextantis	Sextant	Sex
Taurus	Tauri	Bull	Tau
Telescopium	Telescopii	Telescope	Tel
Triangulum	Trianguli	Triangle	Tri
Triangulum Australe	Trianguli Australis	Southern triangle	TrA
Tucana	Tucanae	Toucan	Tuc
Ursa Major	Ursae Majoris	Great bear	UMa
Ursa Minor	Ursae Minoris	Little bear	UMi
*Vela	Velorum	Sails of the Argonauts' ship	Vel
Virgo	Virginis	Virgin	Vir
Volans	Volantis	Flying fish	Vol
Vulpecula	Vulpeculae	Fox	Vul

* The four constellations Carina, Puppis, Pyxis, and Vela originally formed the single constellation Argo Navis.

SUPERNOVAE, "BLACK HOLES" AND THE GUM NEBULA

Astronomers have recently added two new objects to the growing list of strange and puzzling objects speculated about or found in the universe. A "black hole" is the hypothetical result of a runaway or uncontrolled gravitational collapse of a star or collection of stars. Eventually a collapsing object, such as a star, will reach a limiting size, called the Schwarzschild radius, which depends upon the mass of the object. For the Sun the Schwarzschild radius would be under two miles. If the contracting object continues to contract to less than its Schwarzschild radius it becomes a black hole. The gravitational forces exerted by this object are so strong that no matter or radiation can escape from it. The light emanating from this object is trapped and effectively removed from the "observable universe."

A supernova occurs when a star has evolved to such an unstable state that it blows itself up. The energy released in the holocaust is almost beyond comprehension. The material ejected with immense force from the exploding star forms a huge shell of gas which sweeps up interstellar gas as it expands. This is known as a supernova remnant. What remains of the star is possibly its dense central core. Astrophysicists have speculated that the core of a supernova can become either a neutron star or a black hole. The final mass of the remnant star determines whether gravitational collapse will stop at the stable neutron star stage, instead of running away and becoming a black hole. It is believed that if the star's mass is greater than about 3.0 times the Sun's mass a black hole should readily form. (Neutron stars should form for stars whose mass is above 1.4 times the Sun's mass.) A black hole almost certainly exists in the binary star Cygnus X-1 and maybe in other X-ray binaries. There is also possible evidence of massive black holes at the centers of certain galaxies, notably M87, that would tear apart and swallow stars in the immediate surroundings.

Nebulae are extended bright luminosities in the sky. Some nebulae are the glowing remnants of supernovae. Other nebulae are clouds of ionized hydrogen surrounding hot stars, which cause them to glow continuously. Such objects surrounding hot stars are called Stromgren spheres. The Gum Nebula (discovered by the Australian astronomer, Colin S. Gum, in 1952) combines certain characteristics of the other two types of nebulae. It is about 2,600 light-years across in its longest dimension and appears to be somewhat elliptical in shape. A group of astronomers from NASA and Kitt Peak National Observatory proposes that the Gum Nebula is a fossil Stromgren sphere produced by a supernova that exploded 11,000 years ago, giving off a tremendous blast of ultraviolet radiation, which ionized interstellar hydrogen clouds for hundreds of light years around. What is now glowing is not the material that was originally ejected from the supernova, but the interstellar hydrogen gas that was there before the supernova explosion. Unlike Stromgren spheres that are continuously being ionized by hot stars, the fossil Gum Nebula is gradually decaying, as the ionized hydrogen gas recombines in the absence of a new ionizing source.

INTERSTELLAR MOLECULES

Within the last 25 years astronomers have found that there is a continuous exchange of material between stars and the interstellar medium. Stars are continually being formed from diffuse interstellar material. This diffuse interstellar material somehow collects into interstellar clouds which may eventually contract under gravitational forces forming stars and, possibly, planetary systems. As stars evolve, material is ejected from them to again become part of the interstellar medium.

The first interstellar molecules ever found—CH, CH+, and CN (cyanogen)—were diatomic (consisting of only two atoms) and were found more than 40 years ago by optical astronomers.

In March 1951 radio astronomers detected interstellar atomic hydrogen (H) and in 1963 they discovered the hydroxyl radical (OH) in the interstellar medium. Up to this time no one had ever detected a polyatomic molecule (consisting of three or more atoms). The formation of molecules more complex than diatomic molecules in interstellar space was believed to be rare, since interstellar densities and temperatures are so low that molecule formation is very difficult.

This idea was upset in 1968 when radio astronomers detected interstellar ammonia (NH_3). In early 1969 radio astronomers detected interstellar water vapor (H_2O). In March 1969 interstellar formaldehyde (H_2CO)—the first polyatomic organic molecule—was discovered by radio astronomers. On March 13, 1970, a Naval Research Laboratory Aerobee rocket detected molecular hydrogen (H_2) in interstellar space.

Interstellar atomic hydrogen (H) has been observed by radio astronomers since 1951, but molecular hydrogen had previously eluded detection. In 1970 radio astronomers also found interstellar carbon monoxide (CO), hydrogen cyanide (HCN), cyanoacetylene (HC_3N), formic acid (HCOOH), and methanol or wood alcohol (CH_3OH). Another molecule, originally called "X-ogen" has since been identified as HCO^+. At present over 50 interstellar molecules have been detected, including deuterium (heavy hydrogen), hydrogen sulfide (H_2S), acetaldehyde (CH_3CHO), and silicon monoxide (SiO). Large numbers are found in massive dense interstellar clouds, such as the Great Nebula in Orion and Sagittarius B2.

Additional evidence for the existence of extraterrestrial organic molecules was given in December 1970, when it was announced that a meteorite that fell near Murchison, Victoria, Australia, on September 28, 1969, is believed to contain five of the 20 most common amino acids—glycine, alanine, glutamic acid, valine, and proline. This finding demonstrates that complex amino acids, the basic building blocks of proteins, can be and have been formed outside the Earth by natural chemical processes.

Hence, in recent years, astronomers have found that the interstellar medium is interspersed with molecules, a proportionately high fraction of which are organic compounds. As star and planet formation take place, these organic compounds may play an important role in the chemical evolution and origin of life.

OUR LOCAL GROUP OF GALAXIES

Our local group of galaxies contains over 30 members that cover a region about 3 million light-years in diameter. The largest members are both spiral galaxies—our Milky Way galaxy and the Andromeda galaxy (M-31). All together, there are three spirals, four irregulars, 11 ellipticals, and many dwarf irregulars and dwarf ellipticals. Some of our local galaxies are listed below, with apparent magnitude, distance in thousand parsecs (kiloparsecs), galactic diameter in kiloparsecs, and absolute magnitude.

Galaxy	Visual magnitude	Distance (kilopcs)	Diameter (kilopcs)	Absolute magnitude
The Milky Way	—	—	30	(—21)
Large Magellanic Cloud	0.9	48	10	—17.7
Small Magellanic Cloud	2.5	56	8	—16.5
Ursa Minor system	—	70	1	(—9)
Sculptor system	8.0	83	2.2	—11.8
Draco system	—	100	1.4	(—10)
Fornax system	8.3	190	6.6	—13.3
Leo II system	12.04	230	1.6	—10.0
Leo I system	12.0	280	1.5	—10.4
NGC 6822	8.9	460	2.7	—14.8
NGC 147	9.73	570	3	—14.5
NGC 185	9.43	570	2.3	—14.8
NGC 205	8.17	680	5	—16.5
NGC 221 (M32)	8.16	680	2.4	—16.5
IC 1613	9.61	680	5	—14.7
Andromeda galaxy	3.47	680	40	—21.2
NGC 598 (M33)	5.79	720	17	—18.9
Maffei 1	11.0	1000	—	—19.0

ASTRONOMICAL INSTRUMENTATION

The most important property of a telescope is its ability to gather light so that objects that are too remote or too faint to be seen with the naked eye are detectable. The light-gathering power of a telescope varies according to the total surface area of either the objective lens or the mirror in the telescope.

There are two main classes of telescopes that gather visible light: reflectors and refractors. In a reflector, a large curved mirror gathers the light; in a refractor, a large objective lens accomplishes this feat. The largest reflecting telescope now in operation has a 236″ mirror; the largest refracting telescope has a 40″ objective lens. The Schmidt camera is an optical system that utilizes both a mirror and a lens; it produces excellent star images over a large area of the sky and is in widespread use around the world.

In 1931, K. G. Jansky encountered interference in the form of radio radiation coming from an unknown source, which subsequent investigation showed was the Milky Way. In 1936, Grote Reber built the first antenna that was specifically designed to receive these cosmic radio waves. In 1942, radio radiation was first received from the Sun. After World War II, the technique of making radio astronomical observations was rapidly developed, especially in Australia, England, the Netherlands, and more recently in the United States. The 328-foot radio telescope at Bonn, West Germany is the world's largest fully steerable radio telescope.

In a radio telescope, the radiowave gathering is done by a parabolic metallic reflector, called a "dish," which focuses waves onto an antenna, or by a dipole antenna. Sensitivity is increased by using an array of such antennas.

Radio signals have been observed to come from the Sun, the Moon, certain planets, from the center of our galaxy, and from other galaxies. In addition, strong radio signals are given off by quasars while rapidly pulsating radio signals are received from pulsars. Radio signals can be used to determine both the surface and lower-atmosphere temperatures of the planets.

Other types of radio emission offer insight into the physical processes within the upper atmosphere of the planets and the Sun, as well as certain physical processes within galaxies. Signals at certain discrete radio wavelengths are caused by the presence of certain interstellar molecules. The amount and distribution of these molecules in space are determinable by using radio telescopes.

Radar astronomy systems consist of a powerful radio transmitter, capable of transmitting high-power radio signals out into space over long distances, and a sensitive antenna, with which the return radar echo is detectable. This returning radar echo can provide information about lunar and planetary surfaces, planetary atmospheres and rotation periods, and the precise values of the distances of different solar system objects. X-ray astronomy gains data from satellites and from rocket and balloon flights, X-rays being absorbed by the atmosphere. Since 1962 over 3,000 X-ray sources have been detected inside and outside our Galaxy and include supernova remnants, quasars, binary systems, and possible black holes.

Only a few bands of infrared wavelengths from space can penetrate the atmosphere. Special detectors of this radiation, on the ground and in rockets, have shown that huge quantities of infrared rays are emitted from dying stars and from stars being born.

MAJOR ASTRONOMICAL FACILITIES

This list includes the world's major astronomical observing facilities: reflecting and refracting optical telescopes, radio telescopes, and radar astronomy systems. UC = Under construction.

REFLECTING TELESCOPES AND SCHMIDT CAMERAS

Mirror Diameter (Inches)	Observatory	In Operation Since
236	Academy of Sciences of the USSR, near Zelenchukskaya, USSR	1976
200	Palomar Observatory, Mount Palomar, California	1948
176*	Smithsonian Astrophysical Observatory, Mount Hopkins, Arizona	1978
158	Kitt Peak National Observatory, Tucson, Arizona	1974
157	Cerro Tololo Observatory, La Serena, Chile	1976
153	Siding Spring Observatory, Siding Spring, NSW, Australia	1975
150	Mount Stromlo Observatory, Canberra, Australia	1972
142	European Southern Observatory, La Silla, Chile	1976
120	Lick Observatory, Mount Hamilton, California	1959
107	McDonald Observatory, Fort Davis, Texas	1968
104	Crimean Astrophysical Observatory, Simeis, Ukrainian SSR	1960
101	Las Campanas Observatory, La Serena, Chile	1977
100	Hale Observatory, Mount Wilson, California	1917
98	Royal Greenwich Observatory, Herstmonceux, Sussex, England	1967
90	Steward Observatory, University of Arizona, Tucson, Arizona	1969
88	Mauna Kea Observatory, University of Hawaii, Mauna Kea, Hawaii	1970
84	Kitt Peak National Observatory, Tucson, Arizona	1961
82	McDonald Observatory, Fort Davis, Texas	1938
80	Kitt Peak National Observatory Solar Telescope, Tucson, Arizona	1960
79	Astrophysical Observatory, Ondřejov, Czechoslovakia	1967
77	Observatoire de Haute-Provence, Saint Michel, France	1958
74	David Dunlap Observatory, Richmond Hill, Ontario, Canada	1935
74	Radcliffe Observatory, Pretoria, South Africa	1948
74	Mount Stromlo Observatory, Canberra, Australia	1955

* Light-gathering power of the six 72″ mirrors in the Multiple Mirror Telescope.

Mirror Diameter (Inches)	Observatory	In Operation Since
74	Helwan Observatory, Helwan, Egypt	1960
74	Okayama Astrophysical Observatory, Kamogata Machi, Japan	1960
73	Dominion Astrophysical Observatory, Victoria, British Columbia	1918
72	Astrophysical Observatory, University of Padua, Asiago, Italy	1973
72	(Schmidt) Palomar Observatory, Mount Palomar, California	1948
72	(Schmidt) Mount Stromlo Observatory, Canberra, Australia	1973
72	Lowell Observatory, Flagstaff, Arizona	1961
61	Agassiz Station, Harvard College Observatory, Cambridge, Massachusetts	1934
61	National Observatory, Bosque Alegre Station, Argentina	1942
61	U.S. Naval Observatory, Flagstaff, Arizona	1963
61	Lunar and Planetary Laboratory, Tucson, Arizona	1965
60	Hale Observatory, Mount Wilson, California	1908
60	Boyden Observatory, Bloemfontein, South Africa	1930
60	Steward Observatory, Tucson, Arizona	1964
60	Lunar and Planetary Laboratory, Tucson, Arizona	1967
60	Palomar Observatory, Mount Palomar, California	1972
60	University of Mexico, Baja, California	UC
60	Cerro Tololo Observatory, La Serena, Chile	1967
60	Smithsonian Astrophysical Observatory, Mount Hopkins, Arizona	1970

REFRACTING TELESCOPES

Lens Diameter (Inches)	Observatory	In Operation Since
40	Yerkes Observatory, Williams Bay, Wisconsin	1897
36	Lick Observatory, Mount Hamilton, California	1888
33	Observatory of Physical Astronomy, Meudon, France	1893
32	Astrophysical Observatory, Potsdam, Germany	1899
30	Nice Observatory, Nice, France	1880
30	Allegheny Observatory, Pittsburgh, Pennsylvania	1914
28	Royal Greenwich Observatory, Herstmonceux, England	1894
26.5	University Observatory, Vienna, Austria	1878
26.5	Union Observatory, Johannesburg, South Africa	1925
26	U.S. Naval Observatory, Washington, D.C.	1873
26	Leander-McCormick Observatory, Charlottesville, Virginia	1883
26	Royal Greenwich Observatory, Herstmonceux, England	1897
26	Observatory of Acad. of Sciences, Berlin-Babelsberg, Germany	1912
26	Astronomical Observatory, Belgrade, Yugoslavia	1929
26	Tokyo Astronomical Observatory, Mitaka, Tokyo, Japan	1930
26	Mount Stromlo Observatory, Canberra, Australia	1953
26	Astronomical Observatory of the USSR Academy of Sciences, Pulkova	1957
24	Lowell Observatory, Flagstaff, Arizona	1896
24	South African Astronomical Observatory, Cape of Good Hope	1901
24	Hamburg Observatory, Bergedorf, Hamburg, Germany	1908

RADIO TELESCOPES

Antenna Diameter (Feet)	Observatory	In Operation Since
1000	Arecibo Observatory, Arecibo, Puerto Rico	1963
1000 × 115	Observatory of Paris, Nançay, France	1964
600 × 400	University of Illinois, Danville, Illinois	1962
400	University of California, Hat Creek, California	1960
360 × 70	Ohio State-Ohio Wesleyan Radio Observatory, Delaware, Ohio	1962
350	Stanford Radio Astronomy Institute, Stanford, California	1959
328 × 131(2)	Lebedev Physics Institute, Serpukhov, USSR	1963
328	Max Planck Institute, Bonn, West Germany	1971
300	National Radio Astronomy Observatory, Green Bank, West Virginia	1962
250	Nuffield Radio Ast. Lab., Jodrell Bank, England	1957
210	Australian Nat. Radio Astron. Observatory (CSIRO), Parkes, New South Wales	1961
210	Jet Propulsion Laboratory, Goldstone, California	1968
150	Sagamore Hill Radio Observatory, Hamilton, Massachusetts	1963
150	Algonquin Radio Observatory, Lake Traverse, Ontario	1967
140	National Radio Astronomy Observatory, Green Bank, West Virginia	1964
130	California Institute of Technology, Owens Valley, California	1968
120	Haystack Lincoln Laboratory, Massachusetts Institute of Technology, Tyngsboro, Massachusetts	1963
120	Carnegie Institution, Derwood, Maryland	1964
120	University of Illinois, Danville, Illinois	1971
118	Heinrich Hertz Institute, Berlin-Adlershof, Germany	1958
90(2)	California Institute of Technology, Owens Valley, California	1958
85	University of Michigan, Dexter, Michigan	1959
85(2)	Jet Propulsion Laboratory, Goldstone, California	1960
85	Harvard Radio Astronomy Station, Fort Davis, Texas	1961
85	University of California, Hat Creek, California	1962
85(2)	National Radio Astronomy Observatory, Green Bank, West Virginia	1964
1 mile array	Westerbork Observatory, Westerbork, Netherlands	1970
3.1 mile array	Mullard Radio Astron. Observatory, Cambridge, England	1972
1 mile array	Molonglo Radio Observatory, Sydney University, Hoskinstown, New South Wales	1960

RADAR ASTRONOMY SYSTEMS

Antenna Diameter (Feet)	Observatory	Peak Power (Kilowatts)
1000	Arecibo Observatory, Arecibo, Puerto Rico	2,500
250	Nuffield Radio Ast. Lab., Jodrell Bank, Macclesfield, England	60
120	Haystack Lincoln Laboratory, Massachusetts Institute of Technology, Tyngsboro, Massachusetts	400
85	Jet Propulsion Laboratory, Goldstone, California	100
84	Millstone Lincoln Laboratory, Massachusetts Institute of Technology, Westford, Massachusetts	5,000
50 (8)	Crimean Astrophysical Observatory, Crimea, Ukrainian SSR	60

THE SUN, OUR NEAREST STAR

The Sun is of great importance because of its dominant influence on the Earth and the other planets and its role in the beginning and maintenance of life on our planet. But it is also important because the Sun is the only star near enough to be observed in any detail. Astronomers have inferred that physical processes on other stars are similar to those processes observed on the Sun.

This star is directly responsible for many phenomena on our planet, including the origin and survival of life, clouds, atmospheric motion and weather, and the thermal structure and composition of the Earth's atmosphere and the atmospheres of the other planets. Several billion years ago solar ultraviolet radiation supplied the energy needed to synthesize inorganic elements into the first organic molecules that formed the basis for life on Earth.

The average surface temperature of our planet, which must be within certain limits if life is to flourish and evolve, is determined by the amount of visible solar radiation the Earth's surface receives. Visible solar radiation causes water to evaporate from our oceans, and this atmospheric water vapor eventually condenses to form clouds and precipitation. Solar heating is responsible for the large-scale motions of the atmosphere and ocean, as well as small-scale phenomena, such as cumulus cloud formation. Solar X rays and ultraviolet radiation determine the temperature of the upper atmospheres of the planets, as well as the structure of planetary ionospheres.

Solar electrons and protons reaching the vicinity of the Earth, via solar wind or solar flares, are trapped by the Earth's magnetic field, forming the Van Allen radiation belts. Solar-emitted particles that collide with the atoms in our upper atmosphere cause auroral displays.

Solar particles are also responsible for radio and shortwave communication fadeouts, since clouds of these solar particles embedded in the Earth's upper atmosphere interfere with the radio reflection characteristics of the ionosphere. Sudden increases in the emission of solar X rays and energetic particles, during periods of high solar activity, may prove dangerous to astronauts orbiting above the protective blanket of atmosphere that shields life at the Earth's surface from the lethal solar radiation and particle flux.

It is believed that the formation of the Sun, the planets, and other stars began with the condensation of an interstellar gas cloud; this cloud consisted almost completely of pure hydrogen with a very small percentage of heavier elements that were produced during the explosion and ejections of exploding stars (supernovae). In fact, the interstellar medium is constantly being supplied with material rich in heavy elements that have been ejected from supernovae.

As a star contracts out of the interstellar cloud under gravitational forces, the temperature and pressure at the star's center (core) increase until the temperature reaches about 10 million degrees. At this temperature, four hydrogen nuclei in the star's core fuse together to form a single helium nucleus. However, four hydrogen nuclei weigh a little more than one helium nucleus. This small amount of mass has been converted to energy. Every second the Sun converts some 616 million tons of hydrogen into 612 million tons of helium. This thermonuclear reaction provides the tremendous amount of energy that the Sun radiates out in all directions into space in the form of electromagnetic radiation: X rays; ultraviolet, visible, and infrared rays; and radio waves. Every square meter of the Sun's surface emits 64 million watts into space.

Its high temperature causes the Sun to be a gaseous body or, more precisely, a plasma—the fourth state of matter that is attained when electrically neutral atoms break up into positively charged nuclei and negatively charged electrons. The diameter of the Sun is about 864,900 miles—more than 109 times that of the Earth. The Sun's mass is 2×10^{30} kg—or approximately 333,000 times the mass of the Earth. The mean density of the Sun is 1.4 grams/cm^3—only about one-quarter of the Earth's density—suggesting that the Sun primarily consists of very light elements. The period of the Sun's rotation on its axis depends on the solar latitude, being least (25 days) at the equator; its average rotation period is 27 days.

It is difficult to obtain any evidence that is based on direct observation about the core of the Sun. All of our knowledge of the solar core reflects theoretical considerations: it is a region of very high pressure and temperature, and thermonuclear reactions occur there. The solar energy is transported from the core by radiative processes, in which atoms absorb, reemit, and scatter the radiation. Close to the surface the energy is carried by large looping convection currents in the unstable region known as the convective zone. Shock waves from this zone carry energy into the solar atmosphere.

The solar surface (photosphere or "sphere of light") is what we see when looking up at the Sun. By using high-resolution telescopes, the convection currents' tops can actually be observed on the photosphere. The solar surface is not as smooth as had been thought; it is actually covered with a fine cellular structure (granulation), which is caused by the top of the convection cells breaking across the photosphere. Spectacular gaseous eruptions (prominences) from the surface can extend up to an altitude of 500,000 miles in great arching filaments.

Other photospheric features include sunspots and solar flares, which are discussed below. The convective motions are very important, because they appear to be the source of the mechanical energy that is responsible for heating and the observed temperature increase within the solar atmosphere. The immense temperature—2,000,000°C—of the outer layer of the atmosphere (the corona) has no dependence on the heat flowing from the photosphere.

The solar atmosphere consists of two regions: the chromosphere and the corona. The chromosphere is 6,000 to 9,000 miles thick, and its lower part is simply an extension of the photosphere at about 6,000° C, the density decreasing very considerably. The upper chromosphere has a temperature that approaches 100,000° C.

The corona, which surrounds the chromosphere, is the region that is observed during a total solar eclipse, when the Moon, which has the same angular size in the sky as the Sun, passes directly in front of it, blocking out the photospheric radiation and permitting the fainter light of the corona to be observed.

The solar atmosphere permeates through the interplanetary medium via a constant stream of solar protons and electrons ("solar wind"). The protons and electrons have enough energy by virtue of the high temperature of the solar atmosphere to escape from the Sun's gravitational field. The solar wind streams radially outward from the Sun, and is a regular feature of the Sun. Study of the X-ray emissions from the corona have revealed large low-density regions, known as coronal holes, usually extending as winding structures from the polar regions. They appear to be the source of the high-speed particles of the solar wind.

Complicated magnetic fields occur in the region extending from the convective zone to the corona and beyond. There is much evidence that magnetic fields are of considerable importance on the Sun. Their most spectacular manifestations are related to photospheric solar activity, particularly prominences, sunspots and solar flares. Sunspots are complicated hydromagnetic phenomena displaying very strong magnetic fields; they appear dark against the bright photosphere because their temperatures are several thousand degrees lower.

Associated with sunspots are solar flares, energetic phenomena that produce both electromagnetic radiation and solar particle emission. These flares occur because their material has gained enough energy—via solar magnetic fields—to be ejected from the Sun and shot into space. One of the remarkable features of both sunspots and solar flares is that they increase then decrease in number in an 11-year cycle of solar activity. Also associated with this cycle are increased emissions of solar X rays and centimeter radio waves.

In recent years, it has been shown from studies of the frictional atmospheric drag on orbiting satellites and from direct *in situ* measurements with instruments on board rockets and satellites that the temperature, composition, and density of the Earth's upper atmosphere is strongly responsive to changes in solar geometry and the level of solar activity. Some of these responses follow diurnal, 27-day (solar rotation period), and 11-year (sunspot cycle) variations.

THE PLANETS

It is thought that about 4.6 billion years ago, the Earth was formed from the same interstellar gas cloud that gave birth to the other planets of the solar system and the Sun. The gas cloud was mostly hydrogen, with heavier elements making up only a small fraction of its composition. As the gas cloud contracted under gravitational forces, the temperature and pressure of the central core increased tremendously until thermonuclear reactions—the conversion of hydrogen into helium with the accompanying release of huge amounts of light and heat energy—began, and a star, the Sun, formed. Dust grains in the now disk-shaped cloud constantly collided and coalesced into ever larger bodies, which in turn consolidated into planets surrounded by gaseous atmospheres.

During the following 4.6 billion years, the planets and their atmospheres have changed and evolved significantly. The following is a brief survey of the planets in our solar system, with the exception of the Earth, which is discussed in the section *Earth: Facts/Figures.*

MERCURY is the second smallest planet in the solar system and the closest to the Sun. This combination provides for a hot and gravitationally "weak" planet that cannot retain a gaseous atmosphere. Mercury rotates within a period of 58.65 days, or exactly two thirds of its period of revolution around the Sun: 88 days.

The U.S. Mariner 10 space probe has relayed to Earth invaluable information and photographs as it flew within 500 miles of Mercury. The surface resembles that of the Moon in being heavily cratered, little eroded, and with smooth areas similar but smaller than the lunar *maria.* The surface material has a low density. Thus the average density, measured accurately by Mariner 10, of 5.5 grams/cc implies a large core of heavy material, possibly iron. The planet could therefore be similar in composition to the Earth. An iron core would mean that Mercury has a magnetic field and in fact a very weak magnetic field was detected by the probe.

No gaseous atmosphere greater than 100-billionths that of the Earth was revealed. Traces of helium were detected but this gas would be rapidly boiled off. Measurements of surface temperature gave a daytime maximum of 350°C (660°F) and a night-time minimum of −170°C (−270°F). Mercury therefore has a greater surface temperature range than any other planet, although its maximum is less than that of Venus.

VENUS, "Earth's twin" in size and mass, is otherwise unlike it. Its surface is hot (about 890°F on dark and light side and from pole to pole), waterless, corrosive and lifeless, with a pressure averaging 90 terrestrial atmospheres (equivalent to an ocean depth of 1/2 mile) and gentle surface winds of 1 to 2 mph. It has no moon, no magnetic field, no aurorae and no radiation belts. Only about 2% of incident solar radiation reaches its surface, while 75% is reflected; the rest is absorbed in atmosphere and clouds. A "greenhouse effect" makes the surface abnormally hot. Atmospherically absorbed heat drives convective currents and strong winds aloft, creating wind speeds in excess of 400 mph in the middle of the cloud zone and about 200 mph atop the clouds.

Although no liquid or solid particles exist below about 21 miles, surface visibility is probably less than 1/2 mile (molecular light scattering) and a bright Venusian midday would compare to one heavily overcast on Earth. From 21 to about 31 miles there is smog and haze. The cloud layer lies at 31-41 miles and consists of tiny liquid droplets of sulfuric acid, tinged yellow with tiny grains of sulfur.

Sixteen space probes, beginning with Mariner 2 (1962) and culminating with Pioneer Venus 1 and 2 and Venera 11 and 12 (Dec. 1978) have vastly increased our knowledge. Some recently returned data have not yet been interpreted (as of May 1980). For example, the isotropic data for argon are presently contradictory, and reports of lightning and thunder need confirmation, as does the reported incandescent glow of the surface. The 890°F surface temperature is borderline for glowing, depending on the emissivity of the material.

Venera 9 and 10 returned surface photographs. Site 9 was rock-strewn, with 15-20° slopes. The rocks were sharp-edged, indicative of "young" topography. Site 10 was on a plain, with slab-like (layered?) pitted boulders and "rock outcrops." It is a comparatively "mature" topography, suggesting more corrosion and degradation. Gamma ray spectrometers and densitometers measured U, Th and K radioactivities, and densities compatible with basaltic rock.

Venus condensed too close to the Sun ever to have possessed much water. The ambient surface temperature of 890°F is too hot for water-bearing minerals such as micas and amphiboles to be stable. Probably there have never been oceans, or sedimentary rocks such as limestone. It is also doubtful that there has ever been life.

Water and life have greatly altered Earth's primitive atmosphere, locking up most of its CO_2 in the hydrosphere and carbonate rocks. Were this CO_2 released on Earth our atmosphere would be much like that of Venus in bulk, pressure and composition.

The atmosphere of Venus is about 97% CO_2, 3% N_2, with traces of H_2O, O_2, noble gases, CO, SO_2, and others. In its lesser gases it is inhomogeneous in its upper reaches where photochemical reactions occur, but is homogeneous below about 21 miles, where no liquid or solid particles condense. Both Earth and Venus lost their original hydrogen and helium in the "protoplanet" stage. Were all of the atmospheric water of Venus to condense onto a level, cool surface, its depth would be about 1.5 feet.

Like Earth, Venus has an ionosphere. Unlike Earth's it persists at night, and there is an ionopause—i.e., a sharp *upper* boundary where the ionosphere reacts with the solar wind, in the absence of a magnetosphere. The atmosphere of Venus is very dynamic in its upper reaches, driven by the solar energy absorbed. At both poles there is a huge zone of down-flowing air.

The cause of the anomalous 243-day *retrograde* rotation of Venus is unknown. The once suspected spin-orbit resonance control by Earth has been discounted. Venus' spin vector is apparently aligned with the angular momentum vector of the solar system. Since Pluto (in its highly inclined orbit) contributes to this alignment, ultimate determination of Pluto's mass may be possible.

High rock surface temperatures and out-flowing radioactive heat probably caused Venus to "outgas" (liberate gaseous materials from its interior into its atmosphere) early in its history. One might not expect to find current active volcanism, but two large suspected volcanic features have been reported. The hot "crustal" rocks should lack rigidity, eliminating strains that might cause severe "earthquakes."

Venus probably has a molten iron core. Slow rotation precludes the existence of a magnetic field. Earth-based radar mapping, enhanced by probe altimetry and imaging, has found a Tibet-sized plateau and Himalayan-height mountains, a huge valley and (apparently) large impact craters. With no erosional processes known, tectonic activity is suspected. Regional slopes are gentle (less than 5°). Total topographic relief is about 9 miles, comparable to Earth's, but not bi-modally distributed into continental interior plateaus and abysmal ocean basins, as is Earth's relief.

MARS, in direct contrast to Venus, with its hot, heavy, and opaque atmosphere, has one that is cold, thin, and transparent and readily permits observation of the planet's surface features. As observed from Earth, Mars's main surface features include white polar caps and bright and dark regions all of which show seasonal variations.

The bright areas, which constitute almost three-quarters of the total Martian surface area, give the planet its familiar ruddy color. The bright areas are believed to be siliceous, as was found from data sent back in 1971 from the Soviet probe Mars III. The dark areas cover roughly one third of the planet's surface.

Infrared observations have shown that the average temperature of the whole planet is −45° F, with a maximum equatorial noon temperature of 80° F. The daily temperature variation from noon to midnight at the equator is about 180° F, suggesting that the Martian atmosphere is very thin and thus does not retain heat. With an atmosphere much thinner than ours, the atmospheric surface pressure is only 7.7 mbar (Viking readings). Because the Martian atmosphere is so thin, it changes temperature rapidly, thus bringing about the large temperature contrasts that play a major role in driving the high Martian winds.

In 1971 three orbiting Mars probes were launched: two Russian (Mars II and III) and one American (Mariner 9). Mars III deposited a transmitter on the surface of the planet, but this failed almost immediately after arrival. Mariner 9 remained in orbit for almost a year and sent back photographs and scientific information that drastically altered man's ideas about the planet. Only half of the surface, mainly in the southern hemisphere, is substantially cratered. In the northern hemisphere, observed by Mariner 9, four immense volcanic mountains were found as well as a vast system of canyons, tributary gullies, and narrow channels. These features are far greater in scale than anything seen on earth. The largest volcanic mountain, Olympus Mons, the biggest known in the solar system, is more than 300 miles in diameter at the base and about 16 miles high. The sparsely cratered northern regions, strewn with wind-blown debris, are plains of lava that flooded the surface at different times after its earliest history. The heavily cratered southern terrain was also modified by volcanic activity.

Apparently, contrary to earlier ideas, there has been internal activity in the planet, maybe quite recently. This is also suggested by the series of huge canyons, 50 to 75 miles wide and 3 to 4 miles deep stretching along the equator to the east of the volcanic regions.

At the eastern extreme of the canyons lies a large area of chaotic terrain, first observed by Mariner 6 and 7. It is an irregular jumble of topographic forms, possibly the result of some kind of collapse related to that of the canyons. Channels, hundreds of miles long, extend from this terrain in a northwesterly direction. They also appear in other areas on the planet's surface. The channels may have been cut by large amounts of flowing water. The Viking spacecraft have since shown that in Mars' earliest history flowing water was significant in shaping its features. Since then, although surface dust and other debris have been extensively and continuously redistributed by high-speed winds, wind erosion of the surface has been negligible, leaving features sharply defined.

The bright circular region, Hellas, roughly 1000 miles across, is an example of basinlike depressions seen in several regions of the Martian surface. Mariner 7 showed it to be almost devoid of topographical features. It is exceptionally low—over a mile below the mean Martian elevation. Mariner 9 indicated that Hellas probably serves as a collection center for dust and may also be a source of dust.

The lower atmosphere can become filled with dust when the Martian winds become really strong. The dust storms are phenomena whose explanation may be similar to that of the initial stages of a hurricane. When Mariner 9 and the Soviet Mars probes reached Mars, the greatest dust storm in more than a century was raging. The mapping of the Martian surface was consequently delayed for almost three months.

The polar caps appear as a white cover over the north and south poles. This cover grows and recedes with seasonal regularity, alternating from one hemisphere to the other once every Martian year (687 Earth days). The Mariner 7 photographs showed snow-filled craters of the southern polar cap in sharp relief with snow-covered crater rims. The Viking orbiters have indicated that the residual (summer) northern and probably the southern caps are predominantly water ice not frozen carbon dioxide as hitherto suspected. The amount of water vapor in the atmosphere, although very small, was found to increase with latitude, reaching a peak at the edge of the polar caps. In addition infrared measurements showed that the surface temperature (about –70° C) is not cold enough for solid carbon dioxide to form.

The landings of Viking 1 and 2 on Mars on July 20 and September 3, 1976, respectively, have greatly increased our store of Martian information. The mission's purpose was to probe the planet's interior, surface properties, weather, atmosphere and biology. Photographs from the two Viking orbiters and the two landers have shown Mars as a planet that, like Earth, has been shaped by great forces, and have revealed Mars' characteristics to a greater degree than any other unmanned exploration of Mars has been able to accomplish.

Landing site locales were finalized only after the two spacecraft went into orbit around Mars. Viking 1 landed near a region heavily scoured by what are believed to have been ancient floods, while Viking 2 is on a vast flat plain pocked by fewer craters. The color pictures transmitted to earth showed a bright faintly pink sky and a salmon-pink surface. The dry pink dust covering most of the rock-strewn desert-like surface is composed of a mixture of iron-rich clay minerals and carbonate minerals, iron oxide probably giving Mars its red appearance.

The inorganic analysis of Martian soil showed the presence of silicon, iron, calcium, aluminum, titanium, and sulfur (in order of abundance). Analysis of the atmosphere found it to contain 95% carbon dioxide, 2.7% nitrogen, 1.6% argon, and traces of oxygen and water vapor. The presence of argon showed that there was probably a much denser atmosphere and hence a very different climate from today's. The discovery of nitrogen increases the possibility of some form of life having evolved.

Viking landers are the first spacecraft ever sent to another planet with equipment specifically designed to search for alien life forms. Information from biology experiments on Mars are inconclusive but could suggest "the possibility of biological activity in the samples being incubated." Life on Mars has of yet been neither confirmed nor ruled out, but if it does exist, it has made a different adaptation than life forms on Earth.

JUPITER has a dense, cloudy atmosphere of hydrogen and helium, with about 90% hydrogen and 2% CH_4 and NH_3 and traces of ethane and acetylene. It rotates rapidly (in approximately 9 hours 50 minutes), is flattened 1/15, has a low mean density, great mass, a large fraction of the solar system's angular momentum and 14 satellites. Its interior has a small rock-metal core, a liquid monatomic hydrogen "metallic" mantle 28,000 miles thick, and a liquid diatomic hydrogen mantle overlying that. Parallel clouds characterize its visible surface, divided into white-yellowish zones and reddish-brown belts. They probably consist of H_2O, ammonia, and NH_4SH crystals. Cloud-top temperatures average about −220°F.

Jupiter's central temperature theoretically is about 54,000°F and the planet radiates about two times as much energy as it receives, due possibly to continuing contraction.

The Great Red Spot — 24,000 × 9,000 miles — is an immense hurricane-like atmospheric disturbance, poorly understood. Other smaller, ephemeral spots are known. Since 1954 radio astronomers have detected radio signals, arising in strong magnetic fields and in Jupiter's magnetosphere. This magnetosphere is huge, complex and interacts with the solar wind, Jupiter's atmosphere, and the surface of Io (one of the planet's satellites). A "plasma torus" near Io's orbit surrounds Jupiter, containing ionized sulfur, with a temperature of 180,000°F. A "flux tube" connects Jupiter's magnetic poles and Io, and a powerful electric current flows (possibly as great as 5 million amperes). A system of rings lies in the equatorial plane.

The elongated satellite, Amalthea, is dark like an asteroid (166 × 88 miles). Io is fantastic! Seven currently active volcanoes were found spewing umbrella-shaped plumes up to 180 miles. Its surface is orange-red with no impact craters, but over 100 huge caldera-like depressions and lava flows—a "young" surface, renewed about every 10 million years.

Io and Europa are composed of rock; Ganymede and Callisto are composed of mixtures of "water-ice" and rock. Europa has few craters, Ganymede more, and craters are "shoulder-to-shoulder" on Callisto. Europa has a cracked, ice-encrusted surface. Ganymede, larger than Mercury, is also ice-encrusted, with a contorted, involuted and faulted pattern of lines and ridges. Icy Callisto has a huge bull's-eye formation (1,600 miles across), with concentric mountain ridges around a 200-mile central basin.

SATURN, the second largest planet in the solar system, has an internal and atmospheric structure similar to that of Jupiter. But it may have a greater amount of hydrogen and methane, as well as a smaller amount of ammonia in its atmosphere. The density of Saturn is so low—less than the density of water—that, if immersed in a large enough body of water, the planet would float.

First discovered by Galileo, the superb rings of Saturn have the appearance of a large, extremely thin, and flat circular sheet, lying centered on the planet in the equatorial plane. There are three prominent rings; the outer ring A is separated from the brightest ring, B, by a narrow gap called Cassini's Division. Interior to ring B is a faint, semitransparent one known as the "Crepe," or ring C. The rings are only about five miles thick and are probably composed of innumerable particles of ice.

The rings of Saturn are very large in extent. Ring A, which has an outer radius of 85,000 miles, is 10,000 miles wide. Cassini's Division is approximately 1,700 miles wide; ring B has a width of 16,500 miles. The Crepe ring is roughly 10,000 miles wide, reaching to within 9,000 miles of Saturn's cloud tops.

Despite reports of an additional ring (the D ring) inside the C ring and another broad one (the E ring) lying beyond the A ring, the U.S. Pioneer 11 probe, which flew past Saturn in Sept. 1979, found no evidence of them. Instead it discovered two very narrow rings, named the F and G rings, lying beyond the A ring.

Pioneer 11 also discovered at least one, and maybe as many as five new satellites; no evidence, however, was found of the moon Janus, reported in 1966. Saturn therefore has at least 10 satellites. The largest, Titan, is about the size of Mercury; it is the only satellite in the solar system observed to date that has an appreciable atmosphere, mainly of methane and possibly hydrogen, with a surface pressure which may be similar to that of Earth.

URANUS and **NEPTUNE** are the third- and fourth-largest planets, respectively, in the solar system. Because of their great distance from the Sun, little is known about either of them. Their mass can be calculated from the orbital period of their satellites. Their diameters have recently been recalculated by balloon measurement (Uranus: 32,200 miles) and by a stellar occultation (Neptune: 30,800).

Uranus was the first planet to be discovered with the aid of a telescope. It was discovered in 1781 by William Herschel. Neptune was telescopically discovered in 1846 by J. G. Galle; this discovery was based on orbital changes of Uranus brought about by the gravitational pull of Neptune. These gravitational perturbations were calculated by J. C. Adams and U. J. Leverrier.

Spectroscopic observations of their atmospheres have established the presence of molecular hydrogen and helium, as in the atmospheres of Jupiter and Saturn, and an increased proportion of methane.

Uranus has a system of five known moons, Neptune has two. Neptune's larger moon, Triton, Jupiter's Ganymede and Callisto, and Saturn's Titan comprise the four largest moons of the solar system.

Observations in 1977 and 1978 indicate that Uranus is surrounded by at least eight rings lying in its equatorial plane, similar to but much narrower than Saturn's rings.

PLUTO, the most distant and smallest planet in the solar system, was discovered in 1930 by C. W. Tombaugh. Although little is yet known about Pluto, it appears to be a small low-density body, too cold and small to retain an appreciable atmosphere and probably covered in a layer of methane ice.

Pluto has the most eccentric orbit in the solar system, bringing it at times closer to the Sun than Neptune. Because of its orbit, some theorists have suggested that Pluto may in fact be a runaway moon of Neptune.

In 1978 a moon was discovered in orbit around Pluto. The orbital distance and period of this moon has led to the first reasonably accurate measurement of Pluto's mass (0.2% of Earth's mass). Additional measurements now indicate a diameter of 1,500–2,000 miles.

THE SPECTRAL SEQUENCE

The spectral class or spectral type of a star is a classification that depends on the star's color or surface temperature. The spectral class and corresponding star color, approximate surface temperature, and principal features of the star's spectrum are:

Spectral Class	Color	Approximate Surface Temperature (K)	Principal Features of Spectrum
O ..	blue ...	>30,000 ..	Relatively few absorption lines in observable spectrum. Lines of ionized helium, nitrogen, silicon, and other atoms. Weak hydrogen lines.
B ...	blue-white	11,000–30,000	Lines of neutral helium, ionized silicon, oxygen, and magnesium. Hydrogen lines more pronounced.
A ...	white ...	7,500–11,000	Strong lines of hydrogen. Weak lines of ionized magnesium, silicon, iron, titanium, calcium, and others. Weak lines of some neutral metals.
F ...	white to yellowish	6,000–7,500	Hydrogen lines still conspicuous. Lines of ionized calcium, iron, and chromium, and of neutral iron and chromium. Lines of other neutral metals.
G ..	yellow ..	5,000–6,000	Very strong lines of ionized calcium. Many lines of ionized and neutral metals. Hydrogen lines weaker.
K ...	orange to red	3,500–5,000	Lines of neutral metals predominate. Hydrogen lines are quite weak. Bands of molecular titanium oxide.
M ..	red	<3,500 ..	Strong lines of neutral metals and strong bands of titanium oxide dominate.

IMPORTANT PLANETARY PROBES

Name of probe	Launching Local date	Rocket	Weight, lbs.	Period, min.	Inclination, degrees	Perigee, miles	Apogee, miles	Results of mission—Remarks
				SOVIET UNION				
Venera I	12 Feb. 1961	—	1,417	300 days	0.58	0.7183 A.U.	1.0190 A.U.	In solar orbit; Venus probe; radio contact lost at 4.6 million miles.
Mars I	1 Nov. 1962	—	1,965	519 days	2.683	0.9237 A.U.	1.604 A.U.	In solar orbit; Mars probe; radio contact lost at 66 million miles.
Zond I	2 Apr. 1964	—	1,700		solar orbit			In solar orbit; probe aimed at Venus; failed to send back information on its target.
Zond II	30 Nov. 1964	—			solar orbit			In orbit; probe aimed at Mars; failed to send back information on its target.
Venera II	12 Nov. 1965	—	2,123		solar orbit			In solar orbit; failed to send back data.
Venera III	16 Nov. 1965	—	2,116		duration of flight: 105 days			First space probe to impact on a planet; entry capsule sent back no data after landing.
Venera IV	12 June 1967	—	2,433		duration of flight: 128 days			Instrumented capsule deployed parachute 18.10.67.

Name	Date	Launch Vehicle	Weight	Period		Perihelion	Aphelion	Remarks
Venera V	5 Jan. 1969	—	2,500				—	Instrumented capsule deployed parachute 16.5.69.
Venera VI	10 Jan. 1969	—	2,500				—	Instrumented capsule deployed parachute 17.5.69.
Venera VII	16 Aug. 1970	—	2,500				—	Instrumented capsule transmitted data for 23 minutes 15.12.70.
Mars II	19 May 1971	—	—	duration of flight: 18 hrs.				Orbited Mars 27.11.72; sent back close-range photos.
Mars III	28 May 1971	—	—	duration of flight: 11 days				Instrumented capsule televised signals from surface.
Venera VIII	26 Mar. 1972	—	—				—	Ceased transmitting on entering atmosphere.
Mars IV	21 July 1973	—	10,250				—	Failed to go into Martian orbit.
Mars V	25 July 1973	—	10,250				—	Went into orbit March 1974.
Mars VI	5 Aug. 1973	—	10,250				—	Released descent module: ceased functioning.
Mars VII	9 Aug. 1973	—	10,250				—	Failed to go into orbit.
Venera IX	6 June 1975	—	—	duration of flight: 139 days				Descent modules landed on Venus at sites of different terrain, relaying data and clear photos of surface.
Venera X	14 June 1975	—	—	duration of flight: 134 days				
Venera XI	9 Sept. 1978	—	—	duration of flight: 108 days				Descent modules relayed detailed data and photographs.
Venera XII	14 Sept. 1978	—	—	duration of flight: 99 days				
UNITED STATES								
Pioneer 5	11 Mar. 1960	Thor-Able	95	312 days	3.55	0.8161 A.U.	0.995 A.U.	In solar orbit; launched toward Venus; studied interplanetary space.
Mariner 2	26 Aug. 1962	Atlas-Agena B	446	348 days	1.66	0.7046 A.U.	1.299 A.U.	In solar orbit; passed within 22,000 miles of Venus.
Mariner 3	5 Nov. 1964	Atlas-Agena D	575	448.7 days	0.524	0.6150 A.U.	0.8155 A.U.	In solar orbit; final speed too low.
Mariner 4	28 Nov. 1964	Atlas-Agena D	575	567.2 days	2.540	1.1089 A.U.	1.5730 A.U.	In solar orbit; highly successful; 22 photographs of Mars sent back in mid-July 1965.
Pioneer 6	16 Dec. 1965	TAID	139	311.3 days	0.1695	0.814 A.U.	0.985 A.U.	In solar orbit; studied Sun and interplanetary space.
Pioneer 7	17 Aug. 1966	TAID	139	402.9 days	0.097	1.010 A.U.	1.125 A.U.	In solar orbit; studied Sun and interplanetary space.
Mariner 5	14 June 1967	Atlas-Agena D	540	duration of flight: 127 days				In solar orbit; Venus probe; fly-by on 19.10.67.
Pioneer 8	13 Dec. 1967	TAID	145	—	—	1.0 A.U.	1.1 A.U.	In solar orbit; studied Sun and interplanetary space.
Mariner 6	24 Feb. 1969	Atlas-Agena D	—	duration of flight: 156 days				Passed within 2,000 miles of Mars on 31.7.69; relayed data and photos.
Mariner 7	27 Mar. 1969	Atlas-Agena D	—	duration of flight: 130 days				Passed within 2,000 miles of Mars on 5.8.69; sent photographs back to Earth.
Mariner 9	30 May 1971	Atlas Centaur	2,200	12 hrs.	65	800	11,000	Entered Mars orbit 14.11.71; sent photographs and instrument readings to Earth.
Pioneer 10	2 Mar. 1972	Atlas Centaur	570	—	—	—	—	Flew past Jupiter 4.12.73 relaying data and photos of planets and satellites.
Pioneer 11	6 Apr. 1973	Atlas Centaur	570	—	—	—	—	Investigated asteroid belt; passed Jupiter 3.12.74; passed Saturn 1.9.79.
Mariner 10	3 Nov. 1973	Atlas Centaur	—	—	—	—	—	Relayed data and photos of Venus, photos of Mercury.
Viking 1	20 Aug. 1975	Titan 3E/Centaur	7,550	entered Mars orbit 6/19/76; landed July 20, 1976				Orbiters studied atmosphere, photographed surface; landers studied surface geology and chemistry, testing soil for signs of life.
Viking 2	9 Sept. 1975	Titan 3E/Centaur	7,550	entered Mars orbit 8/7/76; landed Sept. 3, 1976				
Voyager 1	5 Sept. 1977	Titan 3 E/Centaur	1,820	—	flew by Jupiter March 1979; Saturn flyby Nov. 1980			Studied and photographed Jupiter's atmosphere and surfaces of main satellites in great detail.
Voyager 2	20 Aug. 1977	Titan 3 E/Centaur	1,820	—	flew by Jupiter July 1979; Saturn flyby Aug. 1981			
Pioneer Venus 1	20 May 1978	Atlas Centaur	—	—	—	—	—	Orbiters plus multiprobe atmospheric entry craft studied Venusian atmosphere and surface.
Pioneer Venus 2	8 Aug. 1978	Atlas Centaur	—	—	—	—	—	

THE MOON

The Moon is the closest celestial body to the Earth, at a mean distance of 238,857 miles. Because of its elliptical orbit, the Moon reaches a minimum distance—or perigee—of 221,463 miles and a maximum distance—apogee—of 252,710 miles. The Moon revolves around the Earth in 27 days/7 hours/43 minutes. The Moon's rotation about its axis is equal to its period of revolution, hence the Moon always shows the Earth the same face. However, since its revolution around the Earth is not uniform, speeding up at perigee and slowing down at apogee, and because its equator is inclined 6 degrees to the plane of its orbit, about 59 percent of the Moon's surface is visible at different times from the Earth. The Moon's mass is 1/81 of the Earth's mass, and its radius of 1,080 miles makes it about one-fourth of the Earth's radius. The mean density of the Moon is 3.34 grams/cm^3.

The Moon is visible, as are the Earth and the other planets, by virtue of its reflection of solar radiation. However, the Moon is a relatively poor reflector, with an albedo, or reflectivity, of only 7 percent. At full moon, the Earth is between the Sun and the Moon (although usually not in the same plane), and the whole lunar disk facing the Earth is completely illuminated. At new moon, the Moon is between the Sun and the Earth (usually not in the same plane), and the Sun's rays illuminate only the hemisphere facing it, leaving the side facing the Earth in complete darkness, making it invisible from Earth. After new moon, the waxing thin crescent turns into first quarter. Following full moon, the waning gibbous turns into last quarter, then into new moon again.

The origin of the Moon is still a major area of debate. Three different mechanisms have been suggested for its origin: independent formation in Earth orbit, formation via fission of the Earth, and capture by Earth's gravitational field after formation elsewhere.

In the independent-formation theory, the Moon is supposed to have been formed by accretion of small masses from the original interstellar gas cloud that gave birth to the Sun, the Earth, and other planets. The major difficulty with this hypothesis is the disparity in mean density between the Earth and the Moon. This density difference, which is generally believed to represent a difference in the composition—specifically in the proportion of metallic iron and silicates—makes it difficult to explain why objects accumulating in the same part of the gas cloud should have such different compositions.

In 1898, G. H. Darwin, the astronomer son of Sir Charles Darwin, concluded that the Earth and the Moon might have once formed one body that rotated at high speed (about five hours). This rapid rotation might have led to fission into one large and one or more smaller bodies, the latter eventually forming the Moon. However, mathematical objections to this theory have led modern astronomers to abandon it.

According to some hypotheses, the first large solid bodies to form in the solar system were approximately the size of the Moon. These bodies collided, forming the planets. The Moon is considered to be one of these bodies, which escaped destruction by accretion and was later gravitationally captured by the Earth.

The lunar surface is divided into bright highland areas (comprising about two thirds of the total surface) and dark lowland areas, called *maria*, because they were originally thought to be seas. Craters are the most conspicuous and most plentiful of all lunar surface features. The near side of the Moon has more *maria* than the far side, which is almost entirely covered by highland regions. The major mechanisms believed to be responsible for crater formation are meteoritic impact and lunar volcanism. Impact craters appear to be of two types. Primary craters stem from the actual impact of meteoritic material; secondary craters result in part from the rain of heavy debris ejected from the primary ones. Craters may also be formed by collapse triggered by seismic quakes, which result from the impact of a large meteorite. The frequency with which craters are found on the bright highland areas is more than 15 times that of their incidence on the dark lowland *maria*. It is known that the Moon, and also possibly Mars, Mercury, and Earth, suffered very intense bombardment by massive bodies (planetesimals) about 4 billion years ago. Shortly after this, volcanic lava flooded gigantic basins on the Moon's surface, covering many craters and creating the *maria*. Seismic waves indicate activity (moonquakes) still occurring in the Moon's core but its present thick rigid outer layers prevent any surface fracturing.

Lunar rilles, or deep canyons, some of them more than 100 miles long, were thought to be remnants of long-dried-out rivers on the Moon but are probably collapse features. One of them, the Hadley Rille, was studied at close range by the astronauts of Apollo 15 in 1971.

Mascons—dense lunar mass concentrations—were accidentally discovered in 1968 during analysis of small changes in the motion of Langley Research Center's Lunar Orbiter 5 during 80 consecutive orbits around the Moon. Five conspicuous mascons, ranging from 25 to 100 miles in extent and perhaps 25 miles below the lunar surface, were detected under all five large circular *maria* on the side of the Moon facing the Earth—Mare Imbrium, Mare Serenitatis, Mare Crisium, Mare Nectaris, and Mare Humorum. A sixth mascon is located in the central part of the lunar disk, between Sinus Aestuum and Sinus Medil. There is also some evidence that a large mascon exists under Mare Orientale. Mascons are absent from the bright lunar highlands and from the irregularly shaped *maria*. Both the presence of these features under every ringed *mare*, except Sinus Iridum, and their relative absence elsewhere, suggest a physical relationship.

In 1969, six more mascons were discovered—in Mare Smythii, Mare Humboldtianum, Mare Orientale, the ringed plain Grimaldi, and in two unnamed *maria*. As with the other mascons, the new mascons were discovered as lunar-orbiting spacecraft speeded up in passing over certain areas, which were revealed as places where the lunar gravitational attraction was stronger than average.

Due to the Moon's smaller mass, its gravitational attraction is only one sixth of the Earth's. Since the Moon is a weak gravitational body, it is believed that it could not retain any atmosphere it may have originally had for any length of time, since the atoms and molecules of the lunar atmosphere could easily drift off the planet. Observations first made with Apollo instruments have, however, revealed the presence of helium, neon, argon, and radon in very minute quantities.

The large day-to-night temperature variation observed on the Moon also suggests that it does not have an appreciable atmosphere. A planetary atmosphere acts as a heat insulator that keeps the planet's surface from experiencing wide temperature extremes from day to night. The day-to-night temperature variations on the Moon range from 300° F in the lunar equatorial region at noon to —220° F before sunrise—a daily change of over 500° F.

The samples of lunar material brought back by the Apollo astronauts consist of basaltic igneous rocks; breccias, which are composed of soil and rock fragments compacted into coherent rock; and lunar soil. The soil is a mixture of crystalline and glassy fragments with a variety of interesting shapes; it also contains fragments of iron meteorites. Most of the breccia rock fragments are similar to the larger igneous rocks and apparently were derived from them; the rocks in turn were probably once part of the underlying lunar bedrock.

The igneous rocks from the Moon contain the minerals pyroxene, plagioclase, ilmenite, olivine, and cristobalite. Three new minerals were found in these igneous rocks: pyroxmanganite, ferropseudobrookite, and a chromium-titanium compound. All of the lunar rocks were found to have unusually high concentrations of chromium, titanium, scandium, zirconium, hafnium, and yttrium, and very low concentrations of sodium. Many elements such as potassium, rubidium, cesium, chlorine, and thallium, which exist in great abundance in Earth rocks, were found to be very deficient in the lunar rocks.

Radioactive isotopic dating of the igneous rocks brought back by the astronauts shows that they were formed 3.3 to 3.7 billion years ago. In May 1970, G. Wasserburg reported that an Apollo 12 rock was found to be 4.6 billion years old, making it the oldest rock yet found on the Moon or Earth. For the soil and breccia such dating gives an age of 4.4 to 4.6 billion years. The existence of complex biological molecules in the lunar samples would be of tremendous significance, but some of the most sophisticated and sensitive analytical techniques ever devised failed to detect any. Lacking an atmosphere and an appreciable magnetic field, the moon is exposed to ultraviolet radiation as well as high-energy cosmic rays and the solar wind.

MODERN PLANETARY DATA

	Distance from Sun in Astronomical Units[1]	Period of Revolution Around Sun	Diameter[2]	Mass[3]	Density[6] (grams/cm³)
MERCURY	0.387	87.97 Days	0.38	0.055	5.5
VENUS	0.723	224.70 Days	0.95	0.815	5.25
EARTH	1.000	365.25 Days	1.00	1.00	5.517
MARS	1.524	1.88 Years	0.53	0.107	3.94
JUPITER	5.203	11.86 Years	11.20	317.9	1.330
SATURN	9.539	29.45 Years	9.36	95.2	0.706
URANUS	19.18	84.01 Years	4.06	14.6	1.21
NEPTUNE	30.06	164.79 Years	3.88	17.2	1.67
PLUTO	39.44	247.7 Years	0.23(?)	0.002	0.8(?)

	Period of Rotation (H = hours; M = minutes)	Amount of Incident Solar Radiation[4]	Albedo[5]	Observed Surface Temp.	Number of Satellites
MERCURY	58.65 Days	6.7	0.06	660°F (Dayside)	0
VENUS	243 Days (retrograde)	1.9	0.76	890°F	0
EARTH	$23^H 56^M 4^S$	1.0	0.36	70°F	1
MARS	$24^H 37^M 23^S$	0.43	0.16	— 45°F	2
JUPITER	$9^H 50^M$*	0.04	0.73	—220°F (Cloud-top)	14
SATURN	$10^H 14^M$**	0.01	0.76	—290°F (Cloud-top)	10
URANUS	$10^H 49^M$ (retrograde)	0.003	0.93	—350°F (Cloud-top)	5
NEPTUNE	$15^H 48^M$	0.001	0.84	—360°F (Cloud-top)	2
PLUTO	6.39 Days	0.0006	0.8(?)	—380°F	1

[1]The astronomical unit, defined as the mean distance from the Earth to the Sun, is approximately 93 million miles. [2]Diameter in terms of the Earth's diameter: 7,926 miles. [3]Mass in terms of the Earth's mass: 1.3×10^{25} pounds. [4]Amount of solar radiation falling on the planet in terms of the solar radiation the Earth receives: about 1.4 kilowatts falling on every square meter of the upper atmosphere per second. [5]The albedo is the percentage of the incoming solar radiation that is reflected back to space by the planet and its atmosphere. [6]Density of water is 1.0 gram/cm³. * For the latitudes greater than 12°, the rotation period is $9^H 55^M$. ** For temperate latitudes, the rotation period is $10^H 38^M$.

SATELLITES OF THE SOLAR SYSTEM

Planet		Satellites	Distance from the Planet (Miles)	Period of Revolution* (Days)	Radius (Miles)	Mass (Pounds)
Earth	1	Moon	238,850	27.32	1,080	162×10^{21}
‡Mars	1	Phobos	5,810	0.32	8.4 × 6.5 × 6	—
	2	Deimos	14,595	1.26	4.7 × 3.7 × 3.4	—
†Jupiter	1	Io	262,075	1.77	1,137	160×10^{21}
	2	Europa	416,980	3.55	900	104×10^{21}
	3	Ganymede	665,130	7.15	1,550	339×10^{21}
	4	Callisto	1,169,820	16.69	1,400	209×10^{21}
	5	Amalthea	112,470	0.50	60	—
	6	Hestia	7,131,940	250.57	30	—
	7	Hera	7,292,940	259.7	9	—
	8	Poseidon	14,594,300	739	6	—
	9	Hades	14,687,200	758	6	—
	10	Demeter	7,282,700	259	6	—
	11	Pan	14,036,000	692	6	—
	12	Adrastea	13,199,000	631	6	—
	13	Leda	6,906,700	240	—	—
Saturn	1	Mimas	115,320	0.94	150	0.09×10^{21}
	2	Enceladus	147,950	1.37	180	0.15×10^{21}
	3	Tethys	183,150	1.89	310	0.14×10^{21}
	4	Dione	234,580	2.74	310	2.20×10^{21}
	5	Rhea	327,590	4.52	400	5.06×10^{21}
	6	Titan	759,090	15.95	1,500	301×10^{21}
	7	Hyperion	921,340	21.28	150	0.68×10^{21}
	8	Iapetus	2,212,200	79.33	340	2.20×10^{21}
	9	Phoebe	8,047,700	550.34	60	—
	10	Janus	98,500	0.75	90	—
Uranus	1	Ariel	119,200	2.52	250	2.64×10^{21}
	2	Umbriel	166,020	4.14	190	1.10×10^{21}
	3	Titania	272,390	8.70	340	8.80×10^{21}
	4	Oberon	364,270	13.46	310	5.72×10^{21}
	5	Miranda	81,000	1.41	90	$.02 \times 10^{21}$
Neptune	1	Triton	220,700	5.88	1,150	308×10^{21}
	2	Nereid	3,456,000	360	90	0.07×10^{21}
Pluto	1	1978-P-1 (Charon)	12,000	6.39	c.400	—

* Around planets. ‡ Satellites are roughly ellipsoidal: principal radii are given.
† A 14th satellite of Jupiter was discovered in 1979 and a 15th in 1980.

THE ASTEROIDS OR MINOR PLANETS

Between the orbits of Mars and Jupiter are found several thousand small rocky bodies, density 2–2.5 grams/cm³, orbiting the Sun. Ceres was the first to be discovered in 1801, and is also the largest (620 miles in diameter). Some 2,000 asteroids—minor planets—have now been catalogued and their orbits determined. However, there may be as many as 50,000 asteroids in the asteroid belt, most of which probably have diameters of less than a mile.

Because of their large number and planetary positions, it was originally thought that asteroids were the remnants of an exploded planet; however, since the total mass of the asteroids is less than 1/1000 of the Earth's mass, it is unlikely. Evidence shows that most asteroids have a surface consisting of very primitive material (carbonaceous chondrites) so that they may be the solid primordial remnants of the original dust from which the Sun and Earth and other planets condensed.

Many asteroids are not confined to the zone between Mars and Jupiter but have highly eccentric orbits. Hermes and Icarus pass close to Earth's orbit, Hidalgo close to Saturn's. Chiron, discovered 1977 by C. Kowall, orbits between Saturn and Uranus and has been recognized as an asteroid rather than a comet.

COMETS

Comets are bodies that move around the Sun, most of them in highly elliptical orbits. As a comet approaches the Sun, a somewhat transparent envelope of gas and dust called the *coma* appears around the small compact icy nucleus. The nucleus and coma comprise the comet's head. If the comet comes within two astronomical units of the Sun, it may develop a luminous tail—a long straight gaseous one that always points away from the Sun and a shorter broad dust tail that also curves away from the Sun.

Spectroscopic analysis of the comet's head shows the existence of the following neutral molecules and atoms: H_2O, OH, C, O, CO, CH, CN, NH, NH_2, Fe, and Ni. The following ionized molecules are found in the comet's tail: CH^+, CO^+, CO_2^+, and N_2^+. In addition, large amounts of dust are found in both the head and tail.

The comet's head may be as large as 500,000 miles across, and some comet tails are more than 10 million miles long. Comets circle the Sun in one of three types of orbits: elliptical, parabolic, or hyperbolic. Comets with elliptical orbits are periodic comets: they will continually orbit the Sun, as do the planets. Parabolic or hyperbolic orbits are probably caused by strong planetary perturbation.

The exact origin of comets is unknown. There may be hundreds of millions of comet nuclei in a huge region (Oort cloud) centered on the Sun but way beyond the orbit of Pluto. Occasionally, one may become perturbed and enter into close orbit around the Sun. Comet nuclei, which are only a few miles in diameter, are believed to consist of rocky fragments and frozen gases. As it approaches the Sun, solar radiation and heat cause the frozen gases in the nucleus to vaporize, forming the coma and later, as it comes still closer to the Sun, the tail.

The coma and head shine as sunlight is scattered by the dust and is also reradiated by fluorescent gas molecules. The gas is ionized by the solar wind streaming out radially from the Sun, carrying the gas ions with it and forming the long gaseous tail.

An enormous cloud of hydrogen, 10 times as large as the Sun, was discovered around comet Bennett in April 1970 by the National Aeronautics and Space Administration's Orbiting Geophysical Observatory (OGO) 5 satellite during a special maneuver to view the comet with a hydrogen-sensing device. Comet Bennett had become visible over portions of the United States and Britain late in March. Its huge hydrogen gas envelope—not visible from Earth—is about 8 million miles across and is probably the largest entity ever observed orbiting the Sun.

The existence of large amounts of hydrogen around comets was first discovered in January 1970 by Orbiting Astronomical Observatory (OAO) 2 when it observed a cloud around the comet Tago-Sato-Kosaka. Hydrogen is the most abundant element in the universe, and the vast amounts of it measured by the OAO and OGO satellites clearly show it to be a major constituent of comets. So it now appears that the newly discovered hydrogen clouds are a fourth feature to be added to the classical three components of a comet: the center, or nucleus; the coma; and the tail, which streams out thousands, sometimes millions of miles, always in a direction away from the Sun.

SOME PERIODIC COMETS

Comet	Period (Years)	Perihelion Distance*	Average Distance from Sun*
Encke	3.3	0.339	2.21
Grigg-Skjellerup	5.12	0.855	2.89
Tempel-2	5.27	1.37	3.0
Giacobini-Zinner	6.3	0.94	3.4
Faye	7.42	1.644	3.8
Whipple	7.44	2.47	3.8
Comas Solá	8.94	1.87	4.3
Väisälä	11.28	1.745	4.79
Neujmin-1	17.9	1.54	6.8
Crommelin	27.9	0.744	9.2
Olbers	69.6	1.18	16.9
Pons-Brooks	70.9	0.775	17.2
Halley	76.0	0.587	17.9

* In astronomical units.

METEORS

Meteors are small, usually highly fragile particles that enter the Earth's atmosphere at great speeds. A meteor will burn up or vaporize from frictional heating as it enters the atmosphere. A burning meteor is popularly referred to as a "shooting star" or "falling star." A meteor is called a *meteoroid* before it enters the earth's atmosphere; meteors the size of dust particles are called *micrometeorites*. A *fireball* is a bright glowing meteor that is brilliant enough to cast shadows on the ground. A *bolide* is a fireball that explodes in the atmosphere.

In general, an observer at any one location may observe between five and 10 meteors an hour; however, worldwide, there are some 200,000 visible meteors a day that collectively represent a mass influx of about 10 tons. In addition micrometeorites may account for some 100 tons of extraterrestrial matter that falls to Earth each day.

Meteors usually become visible at about 70 miles above the Earth's surface. Larger bodies may not completely burn up in the Earth's atmosphere and survive the trip through the atmosphere to Earth. These survivors are called *meteorites*, and may weigh as much as 60 tons; they are fundamentally different from meteors both in their origin and in their composition, which is stony, or iron-nickel, or a mixture of these.

Meteor showers occur each year as the Earth runs into patches of particle swarms that are scattered about in the Earth's orbit. When the Earth runs into one of these swarms, meteors appear to burst out in all directions from a particular radiant point. The Leonid meteor showers of November 12, 1799, and November 13, 1833, produced some 300,000 meteors per hour. The Leonid shower on the morning of November 17, 1966, may have produced as many as 2,500 meteors per minute.

Analysis of orbits and periods indicates that meteor showers may be associated with the disintegration of comets. Meteorites are probably closely related to asteroids. Meteor showers, which are named after the constellations in which their radiant point appears to lie, usually are visible for several days before and after their date of maximum occurrence. Meteors associated with meteor showers are usually completely disintegrated within the Earth's upper atmosphere.

PRINCIPAL METEOR SHOWERS

Meteor Stream	Date of Maximum Occurrence	Maximum Hourly Rate	Associated Comet
Quadrantids	Jan. 3	110	
Lyrids	Apr. 22	12	1861 I
η Aquarids	May 5	21	Halley?
Arietids	June 8*	40	
ε Perseids	June 9*	30	
β Taurids	June 30*	20	Encke
δ Aquarids	July 28	35	
Perseids	Aug. 12	68	1862 III
Draconids	Oct. 10	—	1933 III, Giacobini-Zinner
Orionids	Oct. 21	30	Halley?
Taurids	Nov. 8	12	Encke
Andromedids	Nov. 10	—	Biela
Leonids	Nov. 17	10	1866 I
Geminids	Dec. 14	58	
Ursids	Dec. 22	5	Tuttle

* Daytime showers.

ASTRONOMICAL PHENOMENA: 1981 Source: U.S. Naval Observatory

The times in the following tables, dealing with the Moon, with eclipses, and with the seasons, are all given in Greenwich (England) Mean Time (GMT); the new day "begins" at 00 hours 00 minutes (midnight) at the Greenwich meridian and lasts 23 hours and 59 minutes, until one minute before the next day begins. In the United States, there are eight standard time zones, which differ from the Greenwich Mean Time by a fixed number of hours.

To convert any GMT value to that of a particular time zone, subtract from the GMT the number of hours in the table below. If the number of hours to be subtracted is greater than the GMT value, then add 24 hours to the GMT before subtracting. This will then give the time for the preceding day. If the difference is between 00 and 11 hours, the time is A.M.; if the difference is between 12 and 23 hours the time is P.M.

Local Time Zone	To Convert from GMT
Eastern Daylight	Subtract 4 hours
Eastern Standard/Central Daylight	Subtract 5 hours
Central Standard/Mountain Daylight	Subtract 6 hours
Mountain Standard/Pacific Daylight	Subtract 7 hours
Pacific Standard/Yukon Daylight	Subtract 8 hours
Yukon Standard/Alaska and Hawaii Daylight	Subtract 9 hours
Alaska and Hawaii Standard	Subtract 10 hours
Bering Standard	Subtract 11 hours

PHASES OF THE MOON: 1981 d = day; h = hour; m = minute (Universal Time or GMT)

	New Moon d	h	m		First Quarter d	h	m		Full Moon d	h	m		Last Quarter d	h	m
Jan.	6	07	24	Jan.	13	10	10	Jan.	20	07	39	Jan.	28	04	19
Feb.	4	22	14	Feb.	11	17	49	Feb.	18	22	58	Feb.	27	01	14
Mar.	6	10	31	Mar.	13	01	50	Mar.	20	15	22	Mar.	28	19	34
Apr.	4	20	19	Apr.	11	11	11	Apr.	19	07	59	Apr.	27	10	14
May	4	04	19	May	10	22	22	May	19	00	04	May	26	21	00
June	2	11	32	June	9	11	33	June	17	15	04	June	25	04	25
July	1	19	03	July	9	02	39	July	17	04	39	July	24	09	40
July	31	03	52	Aug.	7	19	26	Aug.	15	16	37	Aug.	22	14	16
Aug.	29	14	43	Sept.	6	13	26	Sept.	14	03	09	Sept.	20	19	47
Sept.	28	04	07	Oct.	6	07	45	Oct.	13	12	49	Oct.	20	03	40
Oct.	27	20	13	Nov.	5	01	09	Nov.	11	22	26	Nov.	18	14	54
Nov.	26	14	38	Dec.	4	16	22	Dec.	11	08	41	Dec.	18	05	47
Dec.	26	10	10												

PERIGEE (Moon closest to Earth)

	d	h		d	h		d	h
Jan.	15	04	June	1	14	Sept.	17	04
Feb.	8	23	June	29	19	Oct.	15	02
Mar.	8	12	July	27	09	Nov.	12	11
Apr.	5	19	Aug.	21	21	Dec.	11	00
May	4	05						

APOGEE (Moon farthest from Earth)

	d	h		d	h		d	h
Jan.	27	20	June	14	03	Oct.	3	01
Feb.	24	17	July	11	18	Oct.	30	16
Mar.	24	09	Aug.	8	12	Nov.	26	21
Apr.	20	16	Sept.	5	07	Dec.	23	23
May	17	18						

SEASONS 1981

Spring begins — Mar. 20: 17 h: 03 m
Summer begins — June 21: 11 h: 45 m
Autumn begins — Sept. 23: 03 h: 05 m
Winter begins — Dec. 21: 22 h: 51 m

SUN DISTANCES 1981

Perihelion (Earth closest to sun) — Jan. 2
Aphelion (Earth farthest from sun) — July 3

ECLIPSES: 1981 h = hour; m = minute

JANUARY 20 — PENUMBRAL ECLIPSE OF THE MOON

Visible in eastern Pacific Ocean, North America, South America, northwestern Africa, western Europe, the Atlantic Ocean, and the arctic regions.

Moon enters penumbra:	Jan. 20: 05 h: 35.9 m
Middle of the eclipse:	Jan. 20: 07 h: 49.9 m
Moon leaves penumbra:	Jan. 20: 10 h: 03.9 m

FEBRUARY 4-5—ANNULAR ECLIPSE OF THE SUN

Visible in Australia except western portion, New Zealand, Antarctica, and west of South America.

Eclipse begins:	Feb. 4: 19 h: 27.8 m
Central eclipse at local apparent noon:	Feb. 4: 21 h: 57.6 m
Eclipse ends:	Feb. 5: 00 h: 49.2 m

JULY 17—PARTIAL ECLIPSE OF THE MOON

Visible in eastern South Pacific Ocean, South America, North America except northwestern part, Africa except the northeastern part, southwestern Europe, Atlantic Ocean, and Antarctica.

Moon enters penumbra:	July 17: 02 h: 05.2 m
Middle of the eclipse:	July 17: 04 h: 46.8 m
Moon leaves penumbra:	July 17: 07 h: 28.4 m

JULY 31—TOTAL ECLIPSE OF THE SUN

Visible in Eastern Europe, Asia except extreme south, Hawaiian Islands, northwestern part of North America, and arctic regions.

Eclipse begins:	July 31: 01 h: 11.3 m
Central eclipse at local apparent noon:	July 31: 03 h: 35.6 m
Eclipse ends:	July 31: 06 h: 20.4 m

CONFIGURATIONS OF THE BRIGHT PLANETS: 1981

To locate the bright planets, their location in degrees north or south of the Moon is given. All times are GMT.

	d	h			d	h			d	h	
Jan.	4	09	Venus 3° S	June	3	13	Venus 4° N		1	06	Jupiter 4° S
	7	21	Mars 1.6° S		3	23	Mercury 3° N		1	15	Venus 5° S
	25	17	Saturn 2° S		10	09	Jupiter 3° S		24	05	Mars 0.04° S
	25	18	Jupiter 3° S		10	14	Saturn 2° S		30	02	Mercury 9° S
Feb.	3	17	Venus 1.6° S		30	06	Mars 4° N	Oct.	1	21	Venus 7° S
	5	20	Mars 0.6° S	July	3	13	Venus 1.3° N		22	17	Mars 1.4° S
	22	00	Jupiter 3° S		7	20	Jupiter 4° S		26	04	Saturn 3° S
	22	00	Saturn 2° S		7	23	Saturn 2° S	Nov.	1	03	Venus 6° S
Mar.	4	14	Mercury 2° N		29	00	Mars 3° N		20	04	Mars 2° S
	21	01	Jupiter 3° S	Aug.	2	13	Venus 2° S		22	16	Saturn 3° S
	21	04	Saturn 1.7° S		4	12	Jupiter 4° S		23	13	Jupiter 4° S
Apr.	17	01	Jupiter 3° S		4	12	Saturn 3° S		30	20	Venus 3° S
	17	06	Saturn 1.7° S		26	15	Mars 1.4° N	Dec.	18	13	Mars 3° S
May	14	03	Jupiter 3° S		30	23	Mercury 4° S		20	03	Saturn 3° S
	14	09	Saturn 1.8° S	Sept.	1	01	Saturn 3° S		21	06	Jupiter 4° S
									29	05	Venus 2° N

U.S. SPACE PROGRAM

SOURCE: National Aeronautics and Space Administration

SCIENTIFIC AND APPLICATIONS SATELLITES

Applications Technology Satellites—The Applications Technology Satellites (ATS) are designed to test in space promising techniques and equipment for use in future meteorological, navigation, and communications satellite systems. The satellites also carry scientific experiments such as instruments to measure radiation in space. The approximately 1,600-pound spacecraft was designed to include from 100 to 300 pounds of experimental equipment. A larger model, ATS-6, launched in 1974, weighs 3,000 pounds. Its transmitter was turned off in 1979. Orbits are at synchronous (approximately 22,235-mile) altitude.

Biosatellites—The biosatellites carried into space a wide variety of plants and animals ranging from microorganisms to primates. The experiments were aimed primarily at studying the biological effects of zero gravity—or weightlessness—weightlessness combined with a known source of radiation, and removal of living things from the influence of the Earth's rotation. They have contributed to knowledge in genetics, evolution, and physiology, and have provided new information about the effects of prolonged flight in space.

Discoverer—Discoverer is a U.S. military satellite program that, since its inception (February 28, 1959), has provided valuable data in such areas as radiation, meteoroids, and air density in space near Earth, as well as in aerospace medicine. A major contribution of the program was the development of the technology for midair recovery or sea recovery of packages sent from an orbiting satellite to Earth.

Early Bird—Early Bird (launched April 6, 1965) was the world's first operational commercial communications satellite. Its owner, the International Telecommunications Satellite Organization (INTELSAT), reimbursed NASA for costs involved in launching, tracking, and monitoring the satellite. Early Bird was guided by Earth stations into a nearby stationary position (relative to Earth's surface) over the Atlantic. From that point, it was able to furnish communications service (including telecasts) between Europe and North America.

Earth Resources Technology Satellites (LANDSAT)—LANDSAT is a technology development program designed to provide comprehensive observation of the Earth's surface. The first spacecraft, launched in 1972, carries television cameras and radiometric scanners which will collect global data on the earth's environment: the condition of the atmosphere and oceans, major ecological changes, and variations in weather systems. The 2,100-pound satellite circles the Earth four times a day and has a lifetime of more than a year to cover all four seasons and to account for seasonally-induced variations in the Earth's surface. The satellite's cameras view a 115-mile swath running north to south as the satellite orbits the Earth. This broad synoptic scanning shows more detail and contrast than the mosaic-like maps made from airplane surveys. A second spacecraft was launched in 1975 and a third in 1978. Only the third is still transmitting.

Echo—Echo 1 (orbited August 12, 1960) proved that it is possible to communicate between distant areas on Earth by reflecting radio microwaves from a manmade satellite. Echo 1 was fabricated of aluminum-vapor-coated polyester film 0.0005 inch thick (about half the thickness of cellophane wrapping on a cigarette package). It was 100 feet in diameter and weighed 123½ pounds. Radio signals were literally bounced off the satellite from one point on the Earth to another.

Echo 2 (launched January 25, 1964) was 135 feet in diameter—as tall as a 13-story building—and weighed 565 pounds. Made up of a laminate of aluminum foil and polymer plastic about 0.00075 inch thick, it was 20 times as rigid as Echo 1.

Explorers—Explorers comprise the largest group of satellites in the United States space program. Explorer 1 (launched February 1, 1958) was the nation's first satellite. It made one of the most significant contributions of the Space Age, confirming existence of the previously theorized Van Allen radiation belts—a zone of intense radiation surrounding the Earth.

Generally, Explorers are small satellites carrying a limited number of experiments. Their orbits vary to serve the particular purposes of the experiments. Their designs also differ.

Explorers have been put into orbit to measure the thin wisps of air in the upper atmosphere; determine air density by latitude and altitude; provide data on the composition of Earth's ionosphere, including the presence of electrons, which enable the ionosphere to bounce back certain radio waves, thus making possible long-range radio communications on Earth; study the composition, density, pressure, and other properties of the upper atmosphere; provide information on micrometeoroids (small particles of matter in space), and measure the small variations in Earth's gravity field and fix more precisely the locations of points on Earth.

High Energy Astronomy Observatory (HEAO)—The HEAO program studies some of the most intriguing mysteries of the universe — pulsars, black holes, neutron stars, quasars and supernovae. HEAO 1, launched Aug. 12, 1977, and HEAO 3, launched September 20, 1979, were designed to perform celestial surveys, mapping the sky for sources and background of X-rays. HEAO 2, launched Nov. 13, 1978, a celestial pointing mission, was to spend one year studying individual X-ray objects in detail by using an advanced X-ray telescope.

Interplanetary Explorers—Interplanetary Explorers are a special class of Explorers to provide data on radiation and magnetic fields between the Earth and Moon. The information has been of value to science and contributed to planning for the Apollo program that landed American explorers on the Moon.

Nimbus—Advanced equipment intended for use in future operational weather satellites is tested in Nimbus, a research and development project. Nimbus 1 (launched August 28, 1964) was equipped with advanced television cameras and with a high-resolution infrared observation system. The cameras provided daylight pictures; the infrared equipment, night pictures. Nimbus 1 ceased operation about a month after operation.

The thousands of day and night pictures taken by Nimbus 1 have contributed significantly not only to study and tracking of hurricanes and other weather phenomena but also to geology, geography, oceanography, and other earth sciences.

Nimbus 2 (launched May 15, 1966) contained equipment not only for providing day and night pictures of the Earth and its clouds but also for measuring the Earth's heat balance. Heat balance refers to how much of the Sun's radiation the Earth absorbs and how much it reflects back into the atmosphere. The Nimbus 2 experiment represents the first time such information was obtained on a global basis. Study of heat balance data may increase understanding of how storms are born, develop, and die.

Nimbus 3 (launched April 14, 1969), and Nimbus 4 (launched April, 1970), were both powered by a nuclear system, contained equipment to determine the variation of temperature with height within the atmosphere. Nimbus 5 (launched December 1972) carries instruments to measure temperature in clouds as an indicator of their height. Nimbus 6 was launched on June 12, 1975, and Nimbus 7, an advanced pollution-monitoring satellite, was lofted on October 24, 1978.

Orbiting Astronomical Observatory (OAO)—Man's study of the universe has been narrowly circumscribed because the atmosphere blocks or distorts much electromagnetic radiation (X-rays, infrared rays, ultraviolet rays) from space. These emissions can tell much about the structure, evolution, and composition of celestial bodies. OAO has made it possible to observe the universe in ultraviolet wavelengths for extended periods from a vantage point above the haze of the atmosphere that contains 99 percent of Earth's air.

Orbiting Geophysical Observatory (OGO)—Orbiting Geophysical Observatories are designed to broaden significantly knowledge about the Earth and space and how the Sun influences and affects both. The approximately 1,000-pound OGO furnishes many times the data provided by smaller satellites such as the Explorers.

The principal advantage of OGO is that it makes possible the observation of numerous phenomena simultaneously for prolonged periods of time. This permits study in depth of the relationships between the phenomena. For example, while some OGO experiments report on the erratic behavior of the Sun, others may describe concurrent fluctuations in Earth and interplanetary magnetic fields, space radiation, and properties of the Earth's atmosphere.

Orbiting Solar Observatory (OSO)—OSO is a series of satellites intended for intensive study of the Sun and solar phenomena from a point above the disruptive effects of the atmosphere. The observatory is designed to carry such instruments as X-ray and Lyman Alpha spectrometers, neutron flux sensors, and gamma-ray monitors. OSO scientific equipment is supplied to NASA by leading astronomers as it is to OAO.

Data from OSO have provided deeper insight into the functioning of the Sun, and suggest that techniques could be developed for forecasting the major solar flares that flood space with intensities of radiation lethal to man and detrimental to instruments.

Pegasus—Named for the winged horse of Greek mythology, Pegasus satellites are among the heaviest and largest of U.S. spacecraft. Deployed in space, the great wings of the Pegasus satellites span 96 feet while the center section, resembling the fuselage of an airplane, is 71 feet long. The wings are designed to report punctures by micrometeoroids, tiny particles of matter speeding through space. Data from Pegasus satellites not only have advanced man's understanding of space but are aiding him in design of large craft intended for prolonged missions in space.

Relay—Project Relay demonstrated the feasibility of intercontinental and transoceanic transmission of telephone, television, teleprint, and facsimile radio signals via a medium-altitude (several thousand to 12,000 miles) active-repeater (radio-equipped) satellite.

Syncom—NASA's Project Syncom (for *synchronous communication*) demonstrated the feasibility of employing synchronous-orbit active-repeater satellites for global communication. Syncom satellites have been used in many experiments and public demonstrations.

Telstar—Telstar—like Relay—was an experiment using active-repeater satellites in medium-altitude orbits. Because the two satellites differed in important structural and other features, they permitted comparison of different designs. This contributed to the acquisition of information needed to develop equipment for an operational communications satellite system.

TIROS—Originally a research and development project, TIROS has evolved into an operational weather observation system. TIROS stands for *Television* and *Infra-Red Observation Satellite*. The first TIROS satellite was launched on April 1, 1960. Since then, TIROS 1 and subsequent satellites have proved themselves the most effective storm detection system known. They have provided meteorologists with more than half a million usable cloud-cover pictures, enabling them to track, forecast, and analyze storms. Through TIROS observations, the U.S. Weather Service has issued thousands of storm bulletins to countries throughout the world.

Continued progress has been made in improving the observations made by TIROS and in making these observations available to weather services of other nations. TIROS satellites now provide almost global coverage as compared to the coverage of about 25 percent of the Earth's surface at the program's inception. They can provide high-quality pictures of Earth's cloud cover. Some are equipped with an automatic picture transmission (APT) system that permits receipt of TIROS cloud-cover photographs on the ground with relatively inexpensive ground equipment.

In addition to contributing significantly to the discovery and tracking of hurricanes and other weather phenomena, TIROS satellites are providing valuable data for meteorological research. Such research may lead to long-range weather forecasts and perhaps greater understanding of how hurricanes and other destructive storms breed and how their development can be curbed. TIROS pictures of the Earth are proving useful in geography and geology, in showing the magnitude of river and sea ice, and in furnishing information on snowcover and thus spring flooding. A new advanced TIROS-N satellite was launched on October 13, 1978.

TOS and NOAA—NASA's research and development work with meteorological satellites has led to the world's first operational weather satellite system, called TOS (for *TIROS Operational Satellite*). The TOS system is furnishing weathermen daily with pictures of the weather over nearly the whole Earth. TOS and an improved version called ITOS are financed, managed, and operated by the Weather Service, a part of the National Oceanic and Atmospheric Administration of the United States Department of Commerce.

Transit and the Navy Navigation Satellite System—Transit was a Department of Defense experimental navigation satellite program designed to lead to a worldwide operational navigation-satellite system for American military ships. The operational system, consisting of four satellites that are properly positioned relative to each other, is intended to provide accurate data for navigational fixes on an average of once every 1¾ hours. The system is designed to allow users to determine their precise position on Earth regardless of weather and time of day.

Vanguard—Project Vanguard was inaugurated as part of the American program for the International Geophysical Year. The first Vanguard satellite went into orbit on March 17, 1958. Among the valuable data acquired from this satellite was information regarding the relatively slight but significant distortion referred to as the "pear shape" of the Earth. Two other Vanguards were successfully launched in 1959 in this now completed program. The Vanguards provided valuable information on Earth and its space environment, including such phenomena as Earth's magnetic field, the Van Allen radiation belts, and micrometeoroids.

UNMANNED INTERPLANETARY MISSIONS

Lunar Orbiter—Lunar Orbiter 1 (launched August 10, 1966) was the first of a series of spacecraft designed to orbit the Moon and return closeup pictures and other information about Earth's only natural satellite. The photographs and other information returned to Earth by Lunar Orbiter spacecraft contributed to manned landings on the Moon and added significantly to knowledge. Analysis of Lunar Orbiter 5's motions around the Moon led to the surprise discovery of lunar mascons.

Mariner—Mariner 9 orbited Mars in 1971–72, sending back via television 7,000 photographs of the Martian surface. Mariner 10, launched in November 1973, flew by Venus and Mercury in February and March 1974, returning the first close-up pictures of those planets. After orbiting around the Sun, Mariner 10 again flew by Mercury on September 21, 1974, and for a third time on March 16, 1975.

Pioneer—Pioneer was the designation of NASA's first series of long-distance spacecraft. Of these, the most notable was Pioneer 5 (launched March 11, 1960), with which radio communication was maintained until June 26, 1960, when the craft was about 22.5 million miles from Earth—a record for the period.

NASA opened a new series of Pioneer experiments with the launch of Pioneer 6 (December 16, 1965). The series is designed to monitor on a continuing basis phenomena of interplanetary space such as radiation, magnetic fields, and the solar wind.

Some Pioneers are investigating space between Earth and Venus; others, between Earth and Mars. The knowledge gained is expected to advance scientific understanding and contribute to planning for manned interplanetary space flights.

Pioneer 10 (launched March 2, 1972) observed Jupiter close up in December, 1973 after passing beyond the orbit of Mars and through the Asteroid belt. Ultimately it should escape the solar system. Pioneer 11, launched March 6, 1973, followed a similar flight path, with a Jupiter encounter Dec. 4, 1974. Pioneer 11 flew past Saturn's rings in Sept. 1979.

Pioneer Venus 1 (launched May 20, 1978) and Pioneer Venus 2 (launched Aug. 8, 1978) began the most extensive study ever made of Venus upon arrival at the planet in December 1978. Swinging into orbit on Dec. 4, Pioneer Venus 1 was to sample upper atmospheric composition, make radar measurements of the surface elevations and roughness, and take daily ultraviolet and infrared pictures of the atmosphere for one Venusian year (225 Earth days) or more. On December 9, the four probes and transporter bus that comprised Pioneer Venus 2 plunged into the Venusian clouds at widely separated points for detailed measurements of the atmosphere from top to bottom.

Ranger—NASA's Project Ranger made possible the greatest single advance in lunar knowledge since Galileo first studied the Moon through a telescope more than three centuries ago. In the program, Ranger spacecraft telecast to Earth 17,255 closeups of the Moon. Features as small as 10 inches across on the lunar surface were made visible to man for the first time.

Ranger 7 through Ranger 9, the last of the Ranger series, began telecasting pictures when they were about 20 minutes away from the Moon and continued to telecast until crashing onto the surface. The Rangers with the television packages were about 5 feet in diameter at their hexagonal base and approximately 8¼ feet long. Cruising in space with appendages extended, Ranger spanned 15 feet across its winglike solar panels and measured 10¼ feet to the far edge of its dish-shaped antenna.

Surveyor—Surveyor was designed to decelerate from the lunar approach velocity of 6,000 mph (or 9,000 feet per second) to a touchdown speed of about 3½ mph.

The first Surveyors were designed as engineering test spacecraft intended primarily to test soft-landing techniques. Their legs were instrumented to return data on the Moon's surface hardness, and each carried a single scanning television camera which have transmitted over 90,000 photos of the lunar surface.

Viking—A decade of planning and work came to fruition with the landing of robot spacecraft on Mars to conduct detailed scientific investigation of the planet, including the search for life. After an 11-month journey, Viking 1 touched down on the boulder-strewn Martian plain called Chryse on July 20, 1976. On Sept. 3, its sister ship, Viking 2, landed at Utopia, about 1,600 km (1,000 mi.) nearer to Mars' polar cap.

Specially designed cameras on the craft took closeup pictures of the planet; miniature weather stations monitored the thin Martian air; other instruments noted magnetism, radiation; and Martian soil was analyzed in miniaturized biology laboratories aboard the spacecraft. The "life" experiments data both satisfied and puzzled scientists. The presence of compounds which were conceivably of biological origin was indicated by the data but the organic analysis data did not support that conclusion.

The end of the normal missions of the two spacecraft occurred in mid-November when solar conjunction produced a blackout of Viking-to-Earth communications. By mid-December, there was a return to post-conjunction operations, and the beginning of the "extended missions" which ended in 1978. The landers continued to operate during a "continued mission" phase through February 1979 and mission planners have advocated a plan to keep Viking Lander 1 operating on a reduced schedule through 1989.

Voyager—Two Voyager spacecraft, carrying instruments to conduct 11 science experiments, were launched on Aug. 20 and Sept. 5, 1977, toward Jupiter, Saturn and the outer reaches of the solar system. Voyager 1, launched on the later date, reached Jupiter on March 5, 1979, and almost immediately made two major discoveries — a ring around Jupiter and active volcanoes on Io, the planet's closest satellite. Boosted toward Saturn, Voyager 1 also examined three other satellites — Europa, Ganymede and Callisto; Voyager 2 made its closest approach to Jupiter on July 9, 1979, also surveyed Callisto, Ganymede, Europa and Amalthea. Both spacecraft continued to observe Jupiter as they headed for Saturn.

Voyager 1 was scheduled to begin studying Saturn in November 1980 and Voyager 2 in August 1981. On the inbound journey, Voyager 1 was to closely examine the big satellite, Titan, the only satellite known to have a dense atmosphere. Mission planners have left their options open for Voyager 2's course after Saturn and may go on to Uranus.

MANNED SPACE-FLIGHT PROGRAMS

Project Mercury—Project Mercury placed the first Americans into space. The pioneering project was organized (October 5, 1958) to orbit a manned spacecraft, investigate man's reaction to, and abilities in, space flight, and recover both man and spacecraft.

Project Mercury experiments demonstrated that the high-gravity forces of launch and of atmosphere entry as well as weightlessness in orbit for as much as 34 hours do not impair man's ability to control a spacecraft. It proved that man not only augments the reliability of spacecraft controls but also can conduct scientific observations and experiments that expand and clarify information from instruments.

Project Gemini—Project Gemini markedly extended the technology and experience gained through Project Mercury and vastly increased knowledge about space, Earth, and man. The last of the Gemini missions was Gemini 12 (completed November 15, 1966). In achieving all of its major objectives, the Gemini project demonstrated that man can maneuver his craft in space; leave his craft and do useful work in space if he is properly clothed and equipped; rendezvous (find and come near) and dock (link up) his craft with another vehicle in space; function effectively during prolonged space flight of a least two weeks and return to Earth in good physical condition; and control his spacecraft during its descent from orbit and land it within a selected area on Earth.

Project Apollo—Its goals: land American explorers on the Moon and bring them safely back to Earth (which was successfully accomplished by Apollo 11 in July 1969), and establish the technology to meet other national interests in space. The Apollo spacecraft is made up of three sections or modules:

1. COMMMAND MODULE—The command module is designed to accommodate three astronauts in a "shirtsleeve" environment; i.e., the astronauts are able to work, eat, and sleep in the module without pressure suits. The command module, like the crew compartment of an airliner, has windows, and contains controls and instruments (including a computer) of various kinds to enable the astronauts to pilot their craft. The command module weighs about 5 tons. It stands 11 feet tall and has a base diameter of about 13 feet.

2. SERVICE MODULE—The service module is equipped with rocket engines and fuel supplies to enable the astronauts to propel their craft into and out of lunar orbit and to change their course in space. The service module weighs 24 tons. It is 23 feet long and 13 feet in diameter.

3. LUNAR MODULE—The lunar module (LM) is the space ferry that takes two Apollo astronauts down to the Moon and carries them from the Moon's surface into lunar orbit and rendezvous with the Apollo command and service modules in lunar orbit. At launch from Earth, the LM weighs about 14½ tons. It is some 20 feet high and has a base diameter of 13 feet. After the two-man crew of the LM returns to the command module, the LM is jettisoned in lunar orbit.

Skylab—Skylab was America's first orbiting space laboratory, launched by NASA on May 14, 1973. Eleven days later, the first of three scheduled manned missions made a rendezvous with the space station, activating its extensive facilities to conduct solar astronomy experiments, to relay informaton on Earth's ecological systems and to study the effects of weightlessness on industrial processes. Most important, however, was the medical and life sciences information obtained from observation of the three-man crews as they lived in space for prolonged periods of time. The Skylab II (actually the first *manned* Skylab) mission lasted 28 days; its success prompted NASA to extend Skylab III's mission (launched July 28, 1973 to 59 days. A fourth (third manned) and final Skylab mission was launched on November 16, 1973, and the crew spent 84 days in space. Skylab descended from orbit and broke up over Australia on July 11, 1979.

Apollo Soyuz Test Project—The first international manned space flight was made by United States and U.S.S.R. spacecraft July 15-24, 1975. Its objective was to accomplish spacecraft rendezvous, docking, undocking, crew transfer, interaction of control centers, and interaction of spacecraft crews. The planned joint activities were carried out successfully and the many ceremonial activities were televised as were many of the other activities.

Space Shuttle—The key element in the United States' future Space Transportation System made its first appearance as the first Space Shuttle orbiter, the Enterprise, was rolled out at the NASA/Rockwell International facility at Palmdale, Calif., in September 1976. The spacecraft successfully completed a series of approach and landing flight tests in 1977. The second Space Shuttle orbiter, Columbia, was transported to the Kennedy Space Center, Florida, in March 1979 for the first orbital flight test in early 1981.

The agency named 15 pilot astronaut candidates and 20 mission specialist astronaut candidates to be crew members on flights of the Space Shuttle which will be operational in the 1980's.

MANNED SPACE FLIGHTS

Spacecraft	Launching Date	Astronauts	Revolutions	Flight Time	Flight Highlights
USSR Vostok I	Apr. 12, 1961	Yuri A. Gagarin	1	1 hr. 48 mins.	First manned flight.
U.S. Mercury-Redstone 3	May 5, 1961	Alan B. Shepard, Jr.	Suborbital	0 hrs. 15 mins.	First American in space.
U.S. Mercury-Redstone 4	July 21, 1961	Virgil I. Grissom	Suborbital	0 hrs. 16 mins.	Evaluated spacecraft functions.
USSR Vostok II	Aug. 6, 1961	Gherman S. Titov	16	25 hrs. 18 mins.	More than 24 hours in space.
U.S. Mercury-Atlas 6	Feb. 20, 1962	John H. Glenn	3	4 hrs. 55 mins.	First American in orbit.
U.S. Mercury-Atlas 7	May 24, 1962	M. Scott Carpenter	3	4 hrs. 56 mins.	Landed 250 miles from target.
USSR Vostok III	Aug. 11, 1962	Andrian G. Nikolayev	60	94 hrs. 22 mins.	First group flight (Vostok III and IV).
USSR Vostok IV	Aug. 12, 1962	Pavel R. Popovich	45	70 hrs. 57 mins.	Came within 3.1 miles of Vostok III on first orbit.
U.S. Mercury-Atlas 8	Oct. 3, 1962	Walter M. Schirra, Jr.	6	9 hrs. 13 mins.	Landed 5 miles from target.
U.S. Mercury-Atlas 9	May 15, 1963	L. Gordon Cooper, Jr.	22	34 hrs. 20 mins.	First long flight by an American.
USSR Vostok V	June 14, 1963	Valery F. Bykovsky	76	119 hrs. 6 mins.	Second group flight (Vostok V and VI).
USSR Vostok VI	June 16, 1963	Valentina V. Tereshkova	45	70 hrs. 50 mins.	Passed within 3 miles of Vostok V; first woman in space.
USSR Voskhod I	Oct. 12, 1964	Komarov; Feoktistov; Yegorov	15	24 hrs. 17 mins.	First 3-man craft.
USSR Voskhod II	Mar. 18, 1965	Leonov; Belyayev	16	26 hrs. 2 mins.	First man outside spacecraft in 10-minute "walk" (Leonov).
U.S. Gemini 3	Mar. 23, 1965	Virgil I. Grissom John W. Young	3	4 hrs. 53 mins.	First manned orbital maneuvers.
U.S. Gemini 4	June 3, 1965	James A. McDivitt Edward H. White, II	62	97 hrs. 48 mins.	21-minute "space walk" (White).
U.S. Gemini 5	Aug. 21, 1965	L. Gordon Cooper, Jr. Charles Conrad, Jr.	120	190 hrs. 56 mins.	First extended manned flight.
U.S. Gemini 7	Dec. 4, 1965	Frank Borman James A. Lovell, Jr.	206	330 hrs. 35 mins.	Longest space flight at the time.
U.S. Gemini 6-A	Dec. 15, 1965	Walter M. Schirra, Jr. Thomas P. Stafford	16	25 hrs. 52 mins.	World's first successful space rendezvous.
U.S. Gemini 8	Mar. 16, 1966	Neil A. Armstrong David R. Scott	6.5	10 hrs. 42 mins.	World's first docking (to Agena target); mission cut short.
U.S. Gemini 9-A	June 3, 1966	Thomas P. Stafford Eugene A. Cernan	44	72 hrs. 21 mins.	Rendezvous, extravehicular activity, precision landing.
U.S. Gemini 10	July 18, 1966	J. W. Young; M. Collins	43	70 hrs. 47 mins.	Rendezvous with 2 targets; Agena package retrieved.
U.S. Gemini 11	Sept. 12, 1966	C. Conrad, Jr.; R. F. Gordon, Jr.	44	71 hrs. 17 mins.	Rendezvous and docking.
U.S. Gemini 12	Nov. 11, 1966	J. A. Lovell, Jr., E. E. Aldrin, Jr.	59	94 hrs. 35 mins.	3 successful extravehicular trips.

MANNED SPACE FLIGHTS (Cont.)

Spacecraft	Launching Date	Astronauts	Revolutions	Flight Time	Flight Highlights
USSR Soyuz 1	Apr. 23, 1967	Vladimir M. Komarov	17	26 hrs. 40 mins.	Heaviest manned craft; crashed, killing Komarov.
U.S. Apollo 7	Oct. 11, 1968	W. M. Schirra, Jr.; D. F. Eisele; R. Walter Cunningham	163	260 hrs. 9 mins.	First manned flight of Apollo spacecraft.
USSR Soyuz 3	Oct. 26, 1968	Georgi T. Beregovoi	60	94 hrs. 51 mins.	Rendezous with unmanned Soyuz 2.
U.S. Apollo 8	Dec. 21, 1968	F. Borman; Wm. A. Anders; James A. Lovell, Jr.	Moon orbital (10 revolutions)	147 hrs.	First manned voyage around Moon.
USSR Soyuz 4	Jan. 14, 1969	Vladimir A. Shatalov	45	71 hrs. 14 mins.	Rendezvous with Soyuz 5.
USSR Soyuz 5	Jan. 15, 1969	Volynov; Khrunov; Yeliseyev	46	72 hrs. 46 mins.	Cosmonauts transfer to Soyuz 4.
U.S. Apollo 9	Mar. 3, 1969	J. A. McDivitt; D. R. Scott; Russell L. Schweickart	151	241 hrs. 1 min.	First docking with Lunar Module within Earth's atmosphere.
U.S. Apollo 10	May 18, 1969	Stafford; Cernan; Young	31 (Moon)	192 hrs. 3 mins.	Descent to within 9 miles of Moon.
U.S. Apollo 11	July 16, 1969	Neil A. Armstrong Edwin E. Aldrin, Jr. Michael Collins	Moon orbital for Command Module (31 revolutions)	195 hrs. 18 mins.	Armstrong and Aldrin, in Lunar Module, land in Sea of Tranquility. Collins remained in lunar orbit in Command Module. Remained on Moon for 21 hours, 36 minutes.
USSR Soyuz 6	Oct. 11, 1969	G. S. Shonin; V. N. Kubasov	79	118 hrs. 42 mins.	Welding of metals in space.
USSR Soyuz 7	Oct. 12, 1969	Filipchenko; Volkov; Gorbatko	79	118 hrs. 41 mins.	Tests for building an orbiting space laboratory.
USSR Soyuz 8	Oct. 13, 1969	V. A. Shatalov; A. S. Yeliseyev	79	118 hrs. 50 mins.	Test for building an orbiting space laboratory.
U.S. Apollo 12	Nov. 14, 1969	Charles Conrad, Jr.; A. L. Bean; R. F. Gordon, Jr.	Moon orbital for Command Module (45 revolutions)	244 hrs. 36 mins.	Conrad and Bean, in Lunar Module, land in Sea of Storms. Gordon remained in lunar orbit in Command Module.
U.S. Apollo 13	Apr. 11, 1970	J. A. Lovell, Jr.; F. W. Haise, Jr.; John L. Swigert, Jr.	Swung around Moon; returned to Earth	142 hrs. 52 mins.	Power failure en route to Moon led to the termination of the scheduled lunar landing of Lovell and Haise.
USSR Soyuz 9	June 1, 1970	Nikolayev; Sevastyanov	286	424 hrs. 59 mins.	Studied physical reactions to extended space travel.
U.S. Apollo 14	Jan. 31, 1971	Alan B. Shepard, Jr.; Stuart A. Roosa; Edgar D. Mitchell	Moon orbital for Command Module (34 revolutions)	216 hrs. 0.2 mins.	Shepard and Mitchell, in Lunar Module, land in Fra Mauro area. Roosa remained in lunar orbit in Command Module.
USSR Soyuz 10	Apr. 22, 1971	Shatalov; Yeliseyev; Rukavishnikov	32	47 hrs. 46 mins.	Aborted after linking up with unmanned satellite Salyut 1.
USSR Soyuz 11	June 6, 1971	Dobrovolsky; Volkov; Patsayev	360	570 hrs. 22 mins.	Docked with Salyut 1; dead on return.
U.S. Apollo 15	July 26, 1971	David R. Scott Alfred M. Worden James B. Irwin	Moon orbital for Command Module (64 revolutions)	295 hrs. 12 mins.	Scott and Irwin, in Lunar Module, landed in Hadley Rille and explored in Lunar Rover. Worden, from Command Module, performed experiments and first deep space walk.
U.S. Apollo 16	Apr. 16, 1972	Charles M. Duke, Jr. Thomas K. Mattingly John W. Young	Moon orbital for Command Module (74 revolutions)	265 hrs. 51 mins.	Young and Duke spent 71 hours, two minutes on the Moon's surface. They returned with 214 pounds of lunar rock and soil.

Mission	Date	Crew	Orbits/Revolutions	Duration	Remarks
U.S. Apollo 17	Dec. 7, 1972	Eugene A. Cernan Ronald E. Evans Harrison H. Schmitt	Moon orbital for Command Module (75 revolutions)	301 hrs. 51 mins.	Cernan and Schmitt spent a record 74 hours and 59 mins. on Moon and returned with 250 pounds of lunar material.
U.S. Skylab 2	May 25, 1973	Charles "Pete" Conrad, Jr. J. P. Kerwin; P. J. Weitz	393	672 hrs. 49 mins.	First manned flight to Skylab space station.
U.S. Skylab 2	July 28, 1973	Alan L. Bean, Owen K. Garriott, Jack R. Lousma	852	1427 hrs. 9 mins.	Second manned flight to space station demonstrating man's ability to function for long periods in space.
USSR Soyuz 12	Sept. 27, 1973	V. G. Lazarev; O. G. Makarov	29	47 hrs. 16 mins.	Testing of modifications in spacecraft.
USSR Soyuz 13	Dec. 18, 1973	P. I. Klimuk; V. V. Lebedev	119	188 hrs. 55 mins.	Cosmonauts grew nutritive protein samples.
U.S. Skylab 4	Nov. 16, 1973	G. P. Carr; Wm. R. Pogue; Edward G. Gibson	1,214	2017 hrs. 17 mins.	Weightless for 84 days, the astronauts each "grew" an inch.
USSR Soyuz 14	July 3, 1974	Popovich; Artyukhin	N.A.	377 hrs. 30 mins.	Occupied Salyut 3.
USSR Soyuz 15	Aug. 26, 1974	Sarafanov; Demin	N.A.	48 hrs. 12 mins.	Failed to achieve a link-up with Salyut 3.
USSR Soyuz 16	Dec. 2, 1974	Filipchenko; Rukavishnikov	96	142 hrs. 24 mins.	ASTP precursor flight to check out new Soyuz designs.
USSR Soyuz 17	Jan. 11, 1975	Grechko; Gubarev	N.A.	709 hrs. 20 mins.	Occupied Salyut 4 and set Soviet duration record.
USSR Soyuz 18	May 24, 1975	Klimuk; Sevastyanov	N.A.	1512 hrs. (est.)	Conducted experiments with Salyut 4.
USSR Soyuz 19 U.S. Apollo 18	July 15, 1975 July 15, 1975	Leonov; Kubasov Stafford; Slayton; Brand	96 Earth orbits 136 Earth orbits	143 hrs. 31 mins. 217 hrs. 30 mins.	ASTP joint flight, U.S. and USSR link up in space and hold a joint news conference.
USSR Soyuz 21	July 6, 1976	Volynov; Zholobov	N.A.	50 days	Conducted experiments with Salyut 5.
USSR Soyuz 22	Sept. 15, 1976	Bykovsky; Aksenov	N.A.	8 days	Photographed Earth's surface.
USSR Soyuz 23	Oct. 14, 1976	Zudov; Rozhdestvensky	N.A.	2 days	Failed to achieve link-up with Salyut 5.
USSR Soyuz 24	Feb. 7, 1977	Gorbatko; Glazkov	N.A.	425 hrs. 23 mins.	Conducted experiments with Salyut 5.
USSR Soyuz 25	Oct. 9, 1977	Kovalenak; Ryumin	N.A.	48 hrs. 46 mins.	Failed to dock with Salyut 6.
USSR Soyuz 26	Dec. 10, 1977	Romanenko; Grechko	1600 (approx.)	96 days, 10 hrs.	Docked with Salyut 6. Returned to Earth in Soyuz 27, March 16, 1978.
USSR Soyuz 27	Jan. 10, 1978	Dzhanibekov; Makarov	N.A.	6 days	Docked with Salyut 6. Returned to Earth in Soyuz 26, Jan. 16, 1978.
USSR Soyuz 28	March 2, 1978	Gubarev; Remek (Czech)	N.A.	7 days	Docked with Salyut 6. Returned to Earth, March 10, 1978.
USSR Soyuz 29	June 15, 1978	Kovalenak; Ivanchenkov	N.A.	139 days, 15 hrs.	Docked with Salyut 6. Returned to Earth in Soyuz 31, Nov. 2, 1978.
USSR Soyuz 30	June 27, 1978	Klimuk; Hermaszewski (Pole)	N.A.	8 days	Docked with Salyut 6. Returned to Earth, July 5, 1978.
USSR Soyuz 31	Aug. 26, 1978	Bykovsky; Jaehn (E. Ger.)	N.A.	8 days	Docked with Salyut 6. Returned to Earth in Soyuz 29, Sept. 3, 1978.
USSR Soyuz 32	Feb. 25, 1979	Lyakhov; Ryumin	N.A.	175 days	Docked with Salyut 6 space station; resupplied three times. Returned to Earth on Aug. 19, in Soyuz 34.
USSR Soyuz 33	Apr. 10, 1979	Rukavishnikov; Ivanov (Bulgarian)	N.A.	2 days	Aborted attempt to ferry two cosmonauts to the Salyut 6 space station. Returned to Earth, Apr. 12.
USSR Soyuz 35	Apr. 9, 1980	Ryumin; Popov	N.A.	185 days	Docked with Salyut 6 space station. In orbit for record endurance space flight. Returned to Earth, Oct. 11.
USSR Soyuz 36	May 25, 1980	Farkas (Hungarian); Kubasov	N.A.	7 days	Link-up with Salyut 6. Returned to Earth, June 3.
USSR Soyuz T2	June 5, 1980	Malyshev; Aksenov	N.A.	4 days	Link-up with Salyut 6. Returned to Earth, June 9.
USSR Soyuz 37	July 23, 1980	Gorbatko; Tuan (Vietnamese)	N.A.	8 days	Link-up with Salyut 6. Returned to Earth, July 31.

SCIENCE: PAST/PRESENT

ENGINEERING ACHIEVEMENTS

The following is a list of engineering projects that have received the American Society of Civil Engineers' Outstanding Civil Engineering Achievement Award.

St. Lawrence Seaway and Power Project. A swath for ocean-going vessels from the Atlantic to the Great Lakes, serving America's and Canada's energy and navigational needs.

John F. Kennedy International Airport, 1961—Designed to handle nearly all of the New York area's international air traffic, one-half of its domestic long-haul traffic, and one-quarter of its domestic short and medium air traffic.

Intercontinental Ballistic Missile Program, 1962—This program involved ICBM installations in 14 states.

Ohio River Basin Clean Streams Program, 1963—This complex of facilities for pollution control affected the economy of more than 1,500 municipalities in eight states adjacent to 1,000 miles of waterways in the Ohio River Basin.

The Glen Canyon Unit of the Colorado River Project, 1964—Rising 710 feet, the dam is only 16 feet less than Hoover Dam in height; its concrete volume is greater.

Chesapeake Bay Bridge-Tunnel, 1965 — This engineering achievement crosses over and under the open sea and links the Eastern Shore of Virginia with the mainland. Its 12.5 miles of low-level trestle, four man-made islands, two mile-long tunnels, a high and medium-level bridge and several miles of approach roads make up the project.

NASA Complex 39, 1966—This huge complex, the Apollo-Saturn assembly and launch facility at Cape Kennedy (Merritt Island), Florida, is dominated by the world's second largest building: the Vehicle Assembly Building.

St. Louis Gateway Arch, 1967—This 630-foot stainless steel arch commemorates the role of St. Louis as the historic "Gateway to the West."

San Mateo Hayward Bridge, 1968—Spans San Francisco Bay, is located 17 miles south of the city, accommodates 50,000 vehicles daily, and is 6.7 miles long.

Oroville Dam and Powerplant, 1969—This dam on California's Feather River is the highest (770 ft.) in the Western Hemisphere and the world's third largest.

Middletown, Ohio, Armco Steelworks, 1970—This steelmaking complex was cited for construction innovations, techniques, materials, and pollution control.

World Trade Center, 1971—When built, these twin towers were the world's two tallest buildings (110 stories, 1,350 feet high).

California State Water Project, 1972—The project to deliver 4.23 million acre-feet of water throughout California. Its major aqueduct extends 444 miles.

Ludington Pumped Storage Project, 1973—Water from Lake Michigan is pumped up to a reservoir from which it rushes through the turbines of the power plant, which has a generating capacity of over 1.8 million kw of electricity.

Land Reclamation Program of Fulton County, Ill., 1974 — Sludge is barged down the Illinois River to Fulton County, and pumped 11 miles underground until converted into liquid fertilizer.

The Keowee-Toxaway Project, 1975 — of the Duke Power Co., in the western part of North and South Carolina, a 700-million-dollar power generating complex that includes two hydroelectric projects and a major nuclear generating station, generating over 3.4 million kw of electricity.

Lower Snake River Project, 1976 — a 140-mile development in southeastern Washington — is designed to facilitate navigation and generate power through the construction of four dams and the Lewiston levee and parkway system.

Superior, Wis., Midwest Energy Terminal, 1977 — The nation's largest western coal transshipment terminal, this complex was designed to receive, store, and load Montana coal from rail cars onto Great Lakes carriers for Detroit Edison's fuel needs.

Trans-Alaska Pipeline, 1978 — An 800-mile system of highway, 48-inch steel pipeline from Prudhoe Bay to Valdez, eight pump stations along the route, and storage and tanker facilities at Valdez harbor.

Nation's Capital Metro Transit System, 1979—Some 30 miles of currently operational subway connecting suburban Maryland and Virginia with various sections of Washington, D.C., serving 300,000 weekday travellers.

Shell Oil's Cognac offshore drilling platform, 1980—Located off the coast of Louisiana, this is the tallest oil rig—1,265 ft. tall—and is capable of a daily peak oil production of 50,000 barrels and 150 mil. cu. ft. of gas.

PERIODIC TABLE OF ELEMENTS

The periodic table, first devised by the Russian chemist Dmitri I. Mendeleev (1834–1907) in 1869, is shown here in its present form. It is an orderly classification of the elements based on physical and chemical similarities. The atomic number of each element denotes the number of protons (positive charge) in the nucleus of its atoms as well as the number of electrons (negative charge) in its orbital shells when the atoms are neutral. In general, the higher the atomic number, the heavier the element. The table is arranged so that elements in the same vertical column possess similar properties (this similarity is related to the number of outer or valence electrons). Elements in the same horizontal row have the same number of electron shells. Numbers in brackets are atomic numbers of undiscovered elements.

	Group I A	II A	III B	IV B	V B	VI B	VII B		VIII		I B	II B	III A	IV A	V A	VI A	VII A	Inert Gases
1	H 1																	He 2
2	Li 3	Be 4											B 5	C 6	N 7	O 8	F 9	Ne 10
3	Na 11	Mg 12											Al 13	Si 14	P 15	S 16	Cl 17	Ar 18
4	K 19	Ca 20	Sc 21	Ti 22	V 23	Cr 24	Mn 25	Fe 26	Co 27	Ni 28	Cu 29	Zn 30	Ga 31	Ge 32	As 33	Se 34	Br 35	Kr 36
5	Rb 37	Sr 38	Y 39	Zr 40	Nb 41	Mo 42	Tc 43	Ru 44	Rh 45	Pd 46	Ag 47	Cd 48	In 49	Sn 50	Sb 51	Te 52	I 53	Xe 54
6	Cs 55	Ba 56	La 57	Hf 72	Ta 73	W 74	Re 75	Os 76	Ir 77	Pt 78	Au 79	Hg 80	Tl 81	Pb 82	Bi 83	Po 84	At 85	Rn 86
7	Fr 87	Ra 88	Ac 89	104	105	106	107	(108)	(109)	(110)	(111)	(112)	(113)	(114)	(115)	(116)	(117)	(118)

LANTHANIDE SERIES	Ce 58	Pr 59	Nd 60	Pm 61	Sm 62	Eu 63	Gd 64	Tb 65	Dy 66	Ho 67	Er 68	Tm 69	Yb 70	Lu 71
ACTINIDE SERIES	Th 90	Pa 91	U 92	Np 93	Pu 94	Am 95	Cm 96	Bk 97	Cf 98	Es 99	Fm 100	Md 101	No 102	Lr 103

ELEMENTS AND THEIR DISCOVERERS

Element and Symbol	Atomic Number	Atomic Weight	Discoverer and Date
Actinium (Ac)	89	(227)*	A. Debierne (1899)
Aluminum (Al)	13	27.0	F. Wöhler (1827)
Americium (Am)	95	(243)	G. Seaborg et al. (1944)
Antimony (Sb)	51	121.8	B. Valentine (1604)
Argon (Ar)	18	39.9	W. Ramsay and J. Rayleigh (1894)
Arsenic (As)	33	74.9	A. Magnus (1250) (?)
Astatine (At)	85	(210)	E. Segrè et al. (1940)
Barium (Ba)	56	137.3	H. Davy (1808)
Berkelium (Bk)	97	(247)	S. Thompson et al. (1949)
Beryllium (Be)	4	9.0	N. Vauquelin (1798)
Bismuth (Bi)	83	209.0	C. Geoffroy the Younger (1753)
Boron (B)	5	10.8	H. Davy et al. (1808)
Bromine (Br)	35	79.9	A. Balard (1826)
Cadmium (Cd)	48	112.4	F. Stromeyer (1817)
Calcium (Ca)	20	40.1	H. Davy (1808)
Californium (Cf)	98	(251)	S. Thompson et al. (1950)
Carbon (C)	6	12.0	Prehistoric
Cerium (Ce)	58	140.1	J. Berzelius and W. d'Hisinger (1803)
Cesium (Cs)	55	132.9	R. Bunsen and G. Kirchhoff (1860)
Chlorine (Cl)	17	35.5	K. Scheele (1774)
Chromium (Cr)	24	52.0	N. Vauquelin (1797)
Cobalt (Co)	27	58.9	G. Brandt (c.1735)
Copper (Cu)	29	63.5	Prehistoric
Curium (Cm)	96	(247)	G. Seaborg et al. (1944)
Dysprosium (Dy)	66	162.5	L. de Boisbaudran (1886)
Einsteinium (Es)	99	(254)	A. Ghiorso et al. (1952)
Erbium (Er)	68	167.3	C. Mosander (1843)
Europium (Eu)	63	152.0	E. Demarçay (1896)
Fermium (Fm)	100	(257)	A. Ghiorso et al. (1952)
Fluorine (F)	9	19.0	H. Moissan (1886)
Francium (Fr)	87	(223)	M. Perey (1939)
Gadolinium (Gd)	64	157.3	J. C. de Marignac (1880)
Gallium (Ga)	31	69.7	L. de Boisbaudran (1875)
Germanium (Ge)	32	72.6	C. Winkler (1886)
Gold (Au)	79	197.0	Prehistoric
Hafnium (Hf)	72	178.5	D. Coster and G. von Hevesy (1923)
Helium (He)	2	4.0	J. C. P. Janssen and N. Lockyer (1868)
Holmium (Ho)	67	164.9	J. Soret and M. Delafontaine (1878)
Hydrogen (H)	1	1.0	H. Cavendish (1766)
Indium (In)	49	114.8	F. Reich and T. Richter (1863)
Iodine (I)	53	126.9	B. Courtois (1811)
Iridium (Ir)	77	192.2	S. Tennant (1803)
Iron (Fe)	26	55.8	Prehistoric
Krypton (Kr)	36	83.8	W. Ramsay and M. Travers (1898)
Lanthanum (La)	57	138.9	C. Mosander (1839)
Lawrencium (Lr)	103	(257)	A. Ghiorso et al. (1961)
Lead (Pb)	82	207.2	Prehistoric
Lithium (Li)	3	6.9	A. Arfvedson (1817)
Lutetium (Lu)	71	175.0	G. Urbain (1907)
Magnesium (Mg)	12	24.3	Recognized by J. Black (1755)
Manganese (Mn)	25	54.9	Recognized by K. Scheele et al. (1774)
Mendelevium (Md)	101	(258)	A. Ghiorso et al. (1955)
Mercury (Hg)	80	200.6	Prehistoric
Molybdenum (Mo)	42	95.9	K. Scheele (1778)
Neodymium (Nd)	60	144.2	C. von Welsbach (1885)
Neon (Ne)	10	20.2	W. Ramsay and M. Travers (1898)
Neptunium (Np)	93	(237)	E. McMillan and P. Abelson (1940)
Nickel (Ni)	28	58.7	A. Cronstedt (1751)
Niobium (Columbium) (Nb)	41	92.9	C. Hatchett (1801)
Nitrogen (N)	7	14.0	D. Rutherford (1772)
Nobelium (No)	102	(255)	A. Ghiorso et al. (1958)
Osmium (Os)	76	190.2	S. Tennant (1803)
Oxygen (O)	8	16.0	J. Priestley (1774)
Palladium (Pd)	46	106.4	W. Wollaston (1803)
Phosphorus (P)	15	31.0	H. Brand (1669)
Platinum (Pt)	78	195.1	D. de Ulloa (1735)
Plutonium (Pu)	94	(244)	G. Seaborg et al. (1940)
Polonium (Po)	84	(209)	P. and M. Curie (1898)
Potassium (K)	19	39.1	H. Davy (1807)
Praseodymium (Pr)	59	140.9	C. von Welsbach (1885)
Promethium (Pm)	61	(145)	J. Marinsky et al. (1947)
Protactinium (Pa)	91	231.0	K. Fajans and A. H. Göhring (1913)
Radium (Ra)	88	226.1	P. and M. Curie (1898)
Radon (Rn)	86	(222)	E. Rutherford (thoron) (1899); E. Dorn (radon) (1900)
Rhenium (Re)	75	186.2	W. Noddack et al. (1925)
Rhodium (Rh)	45	102.9	W. Wollaston (1803)
Rubidium (Rb)	37	85.5	R. Bunsen and G. Kirchhoff (1861)
Ruthenium (Ru)	44	101.1	K. Claus (or Klaus) (1844)
Samarium (Sm)	62	150.4	L. de Boisbaudran (1879)
Scandium (Sc)	21	45.0	L. Nilson (1879)
Selenium (Se)	34	79.0	J. Berzelius (1817)
Silicon (Si)	14	28.1	J. Berzelius (1824)
Silver (Ag)	47	107.9	Prehistoric
Sodium (Na)	11	23.0	H. Davy (1807)
Strontium (Sr)	38	87.6	H. Davy (1808)
Sulfur (S)	16	32.1	Prehistoric
Tantalum (Ta)	73	180.9	A. Ekeberg (1802)
Technetium (Tc)	43	(97)	E. Segrè and C. Perrier (1937)
Tellurium (Te)	52	127.6	M. von Reichenstein (1782)
Terbium (Tb)	65	158.9	C. Mosander (1843)
Thallium (Tl)	81	204.4	W. Crookes (1861)
Thorium (Th)	90	232.0	J. Berzelius (1828)
Thulium (Tm)	69	168.9	P. Cleve (1879)
Tin (Sn)	50	118.7	Prehistoric
Titanium (Ti)	22	47.9	W. Gregor (1791)
Tungsten (Wolfram) (W)	74	183.9	J. and F. d'Elhuyar (1783)
Uranium (U)	92	238.0	E. M. Peligot (1841)
Vanadium (V)	23	51.0	A. del Rio (1801)
Xenon (Xe)	54	131.3	W. Ramsay and M. Travers (1898)
Ytterbium (Yb)	70	173.0	C. Marignac (1878)
Yttrium (Y)	39	88.9	J. Gadolin (1794)
Zinc (Zn)	30	65.4	Prehistoric
Zirconium (Zr)	40	91.2	M. Klaproth (1789)
Unnilquadium	104	(257)	A. Ghiorso et al. / G. Flerov et al.
Unnilpentium	105	(262)	A. Ghiorso et al. / G. Flerov et al.
Unnilhexium	106	(262)	A. Ghiorso et al. / G. Flerov et al.
Unnilseptium	107	(261)	G. Flerov et al. (1976)

* A number in parentheses under "Atomic Weight" is the mass number of the longest-lived isotope.

SELECTED NATIONAL ACADEMIES OF SCIENCE

Institution	Founded
National Academy of Sciences (Rome)	1603
The Royal Society (London)	1660
Academy of Sciences (Paris)	1666
The Royal Danish Academy of Sciences and Letters (Copenhagen)	1742
Royal Academy of Sciences, Letters, and Fine Arts of Belgium (Brussels)	1772
Royal Society of Edinburgh	1783
Royal Irish Academy (Dublin)	1786
Hungarian Academy of Sciences (Budapest)	1825
Austrian Academy of Science (Vienna)	1847
The Norwegian Academy of Science and Letters in Oslo	1857
National Academy of Sciences (Washington, D. C.)	1863
Yugoslav Academy of Sciences and Arts (Zagreb)	1867
Japan Academy (Tokyo)	1879
Royal Society of Canada (Ottawa)	1882
National Academy of Science (Mexico City)	1884
Brazilian Academy of Sciences (Rio de Janeiro)	1916
Academy of Athens	1926
Academia Sinica (Taipei)	1928
National Academy of Sciences of Buenos Aires	1937
Academy of the Socialist Republic of Rumania (Bucharest)	1948
Academy of Finland (Helsinki)	1947
Chinese Academy of Sciences (Peking)	1949
Czechoslovak Academy of Sciences (Prague)	1952
Polish Academy of Sciences (Warsaw)	1952
Australian Academy of Science (Canberra)	1954
Israel Academy of Sciences and Humanities (Jerusalem)	1961
Academy of Sciences of Cuba (Havana)	1962

LANDMARKS OF SCIENCE

Date	Landmark	Discoverer	Nationality
5th cent. B.C.	The atomic structure of matter postulated	Democritus	Greek
5th cent. B.C.	Postulation of causality in nature: the belief that every natural event has a natural cause	Leucippus	Greek
c. 300 B.C.	Compilation of **Elements**: the first formal statement of geometric principles	Euclid	Greek
3d cent. B.C.	Discovery of the laws of floating bodies, establishing the discipline of hydrostatics	Archimedes	Greek
c. 230 B.C.	First measurement of the Earth's circumference (accomplished without astronomical instruments)	Eratosthenes	Greek
3d cent. B.C.	Observations and calculations leading to the conclusions that the Earth is smaller than the Sun, rotates on an inclined axis, and revolves around the Sun; also, explanation of the seasons	Aristarchus of Samos	Greek
2d cent. B.C.	Measurement of size and distance of the Sun and the Moon	Hipparchus	Greek
2d cent. A.D.	Synthesis of current astronomical knowledge in the **Almagest**, which provided a system of celestial mechanics	Claudius Ptolemaeus (Ptolemy)	Greek
9th cent. A.D.	Establishment of the theory of numbers	Al-Khowarizmi	Arabian
1530	Publication of **De re metallica**, establishing the science of mineralogy	Georg Bauer (Agricola)	German
1543	Publication of **De revolutionibus orbium coelestium**; the solar system described as heliocentric	Mikolaj Kopernik (Copernicus)	Polish
1559	First cylindrical-projection map (commonly known as Mercator's projection), establishing mapmaking	Gerhard Kremer (Mercator)	Flemish
1589–92	Discovery of the laws of motion concerning falling bodies, the pendulum, and the inclined plane	Galileo Galilei	Italian
1600	Publication of **De magnete**: the basis for future work on magnetism and electricity	William Gilbert or Gylberde	English
1609/1619	Discovery of the three fundamental laws of planetary motion	Johannes Kepler	German
1614	Invention of logarithms as a powerful method of arithmetical calculation	John Napier	Scottish
1619	Formulation of analytic geometry	René Descartes	French
1620	Publication of **Novum Organum**, elucidating first formal theory of inductive logic	Francis Bacon	English
1643	Proof that air has weight; invention of the barometer	Evangelista Torricelli	Italian
1661	Formulation of the modern concept of the distinction between chemical elements and compounds	Robert Boyle	Anglo-Irish
1662	Discovery of law (Boyle's law) governing relation between pressure and volume of a gas	Robert Boyle	Anglo-Irish
c. 1670	Discovery of the calculus: the most powerful mathematical tool	Isaac Newton [Independently (1675–76) by Gottfried Leibniz, German]	English
1676	First measurement of the velocity of light	Olaus Römer	Danish
1687	Publication of **Philosophiae naturalis principia mathematica**, establishing the laws of gravitation and universal laws of motion	Isaac Newton	English
1690	Propounding of the wave theory of light	Christiaan Huygens	Dutch
1729	Distinction between electrical conductors and nonconductors (insulators)	Stephen Gray	English
1733	Distinction between two kinds of electricity (later called positive and negative); establishment of the fundamental law of electric charges	C. F. Du Fay	French
1735	Publication of **Systema naturae**: the foundation of taxonomy	Karl von Linné (Carolus Linnaeus)	Swedish
c. 1789	Discovery of true nature of combustion	Antoine Lavoisier	French
1795	Publication of **Theory of the Earth**, which paved the way to modern geological science	James Hutton	Scottish
1799	Discovery of the law of definite proportions of elements by weight in chemical compounds	Joseph Proust	French
1801	**Disquisitiones Arithmeticae** advances number theory	Karl F. Gauss	German
1802	Discovery of the dark lines in the solar spectrum	William Wollaston [Independently (1814) by Joseph von Fraunhofer, German]	English
1803	Proposal of an atomic theory of matter to explain the laws of chemical combination	John Dalton	English
1815	Establishment of stratigraphic geology for dating geological formations	William Smith	English
1820	Discovery of electromagnetism	Hans Christian Oersted	Danish
1825–26	Formulation of non-Euclidean geometry	Nikolai I. Lobachevski [Independently (1825–26) by Janos Bolyai, Hungarian]	Russian
1827	Statement of the law (Ohm's law) of electric conduction	Georg S. Ohm	German
1828	First synthesis of an organic compound from inorganic material	Friedrich Wöhler	German
1831	Discovery of electromagnetic induction	Michael Faraday [Independently (c. 1830) by Joseph Henry, American]	English
1840s	Formulation of the law of the conservation of energy (also known as the first law of thermodynamics)	Julius R. von Mayer / James P. Joule / Hermann L. F. von Helmholtz	German / English / German
1850	Formulation of the concept of entropy: the second law of thermodynamics	Rudolf J. E. Clausius	German
1850s	Establishment of the science of spectroscopy	Gustav R. Kirchhoff / Robert W. Bunsen	German / German

LANDMARKS OF SCIENCE (Continued)

Date	Landmark	Discoverer	Nationality
1852	Formulation of the concept of chemical valence	Edward Frankland	English
1854	Invention of Boolean algebra: the mathematization of logic	George Boole	English
1855	Founding of the science of oceanography	Matthew F. Maury	American
1859	Publication of **Origin of Species,** setting forth the idea of natural selection of living things	Charles Darwin [Independently (1858) by A. R. Wallace, English]	English
1861	Establishment of organic chemistry as the chemistry of carbon compounds	Friedrich A. Kekulé	German
1864	Formulation of the mathematical theory of electromagnetic radiation	James C. Maxwell	Scottish
1865	Formulation of the fundamental laws of genetics	Gregor J. Mendel	Austrian
1869	Formulation of the periodic law and periodic table of elements	Dmitri I. Mendeleev	Russian
1884	Formulation of the concepts of transfinite mathematics and the development of set theory, the basis of modern mathematical analysis	Georg Cantor	German
1884	Establishment of the concept of ionic dissociation in solution (ionization)	Svante A. Arrhenius	Swedish
1887	Propagation of electromagnetic waves (radio waves): demonstration that these waves travel at the velocity of light	Heinrich R. Hertz	German
1895	Discovery of X-rays	Wilhelm K. Roentgen	German
1896	Discovery of radioactivity in uranium	Antoine H. Becquerel	French
1897	Discovery of the electron	Joseph J. Thomson	English
1900	Postulation of quantum theory	Max Planck	German
1901	Enunciation of the idea of evolution by mutation	Hugo Marie De Vries	Dutch
	Established nature of radioactive disintegration	Ernest Rutherford	English, b. New Zealand
1905–15	Postulation of the special and general theories of relativity	Albert Einstein	American, b. Germany
1905–16	Completion of first cloud chamber for observing nuclear particles	Charles T. R. Wilson	Scottish
1911	Discovery of superconductivity	Heike Kammerlingh-Onnes	Dutch
1911	Formulation of the concept of the planetary atom	Niels H. D. Bohr	Danish
1913	Establishment of the concept of atomic number and that it is equal to the charge on the nucleus	Henry G. J. Moseley	English
1913	Completion of **Principia Mathematica,** a major contribution to symbolic logic	Bertrand A. W. Russell Alfred North Whitehead	English English
1916	First relativistic theory of ''black holes'' formed by high-density matter	Karl Schwarzschild	German
1924–26	Formulation of wave mechanics	Louis V. de Broglie Erwin Schroedinger	French German
1925	Formulation of matrix mechanics	Werner Heisenberg	German
1926	Publication of **Conditioned Reflexes**	Ivan Petrovich Pavlov	Russian
1931	Postulation of existence of the neutrino	Wolfgang Pauli	German
1932	Discovery of the neutron	James Chadwick	English
1932	Discovery of the positron	Carl D. Anderson	American
1934	Neutron bombardment of uranium leading to the production of transuranium elements	Enrico Fermi	American, b. Italy
1938	First nuclear fission of uranium	Lise Meitner Otto Hahn Fritz Strassmann	Austrian-Swedish German German
1942	Controlled nuclear fission of uranium	Enrico Fermi and others	American, b. Italy
1945	Explosion of first atomic bomb	J. Robert Oppenheimer and others	American
1947	Development of carbon-14 dating	Willard F. Libby	American
1948	Construction of the transistor	John Bardeen, Walter H. Brattain, & William Shockley	American
1951	First power-producing, nuclear-fission reactor	Atomic Energy Commission	American
1951	Explosion of first nuclear-fusion (hydrogen) bomb	Atomic Energy Commission	American
1953	Deciphering the double-helix structure of deoxyribonucleic acid (DNA) in the chromosome	Francis Crick, Maurice Wilkins, & James Watson	English American
1954	Construction of first maser	Charles H. Townes	American
1955	Production and detection of the antiproton	Emilio G. Segré Owen Chamberlain	American, b. Italy American
1958	Discovery of belts of high-energy radiation surrounding the Earth	James A. Van Allen	American
1960	First demonstration of laser action	Theodore H. Maiman	American
1967	Deciphering the structure of ribonuclease (RNA)	David Harker and others	American
1968	Synthesizing of ribonuclease molecule	R. Bruce Merrifield and others Ralph F. Hirschman and others	American American
1969	First men on the moon	Neil Armstrong Edwin Aldrin	American American
1971	Discovery of reverse transcriptase for synthesizing DNA from RNA	H. Temin	American
1974	Detection of psi particle	Sam Ting and others Burt Richter and others	American American
1976	Discovery of a charmed particle	Leon Lederman and others	American
	Completion of gene synthesis	Har Gobind Khorana	American, b. India
1978	Discovery that some animal genes are interrupted in structure with genetic material of unknown function	P. Chambon and others	French

THE BASIS OF MEASUREMENT

The International System of Units (Système International, SI) is the modernized version of the metric system, established by international agreement to provide a logical and interconnected framework for all measurements in science, industry, and commerce. The seven base units here given are the foundation for the entire system, and all other units are derived from them. (Use of metric weights and measures was legalized in the United States in 1866, and our customary units of weights and measures are defined in terms of the meter and kilogram.)

Length—*Meter*. The meter is defined as 1,650,763.73 wavelengths in vacuum of the orange-red line of the spectrum of krypton-86.

Time—*Second*. The second is defined as the duration of 9,192,631,770 cycles of the radiation associated with a specified transition of the cesium atom.

Mass—*Kilogram*. The standard for the kilogram is a cylinder of platinum-iridium alloy kept by the International Bureau of Weights and Measures at Paris. A duplicate at the National Bureau of Standards serves as the mass standard for the United States. The kilogram is the only base unit still defined by an artifact.

Temperature—*Kelvin*. The Kelvin scale has its base at absolute zero and has a fixed point at the triple point of water defined as 273.16 kelvins. This triple point, at which water forms an interface of solid, liquid, and vapor, is defined as 0. 01° C on the Celsius or centigrade scale, and 32.02° F on the Fahrenheit scale.

Electric Current—*Ampere*. The ampere is defined as the magnitude of the current that, when flowing through each of two long parallel wires separated by one meter in free space, results in a force between the two wires (due to their magnetic fields) of 2×10^{-7} newton for each meter of length. (A newton is the unit of force of such size that a body of one kilogram mass would experience an acceleration of one meter per second per second.)

Luminous Intensity—*Candela*. The candela is defined as the luminous intensity of 1/600,000 of a square meter of a radiating cavity at the temperature of solidifying platinum (2,042 K).

Amount of Substance—*Mole*. The mole is defined as the amount of a substance containing as many elementary units (specified as atoms, molecules, ions, electrons, photons, and so forth) as there are carbon atoms in 0.012 kilogram of carbon-12.

TABLES OF METRIC WEIGHTS AND MEASURES

LINEAR MEASURE

10 millimeters (mm)	= 1 centimeter (cm)	
10 centimeters	= 1 decimeter (dm)	= 100 millimeters
10 decimeters	= 1 meter (m.)	= 1,000 millimeters
10 meters	= 1 dekameter (dam)	
10 dekameters	= 1 hectometer (hm)	= 100 meters
10 hectometers	= 1 kilometer (km)	= 1,000 meters

AREA MEASURE

100 square millimeters	= 1 square centimeter	
10,000 square centimeters	= 1 square meter	= 1,000,000 square millimeters
100 square meters	= 1 are (a)	
100 ares	= 1 hectare (ha)	= 10,000
100 hectares	= 1 square kilometer	= 1,000,000 square meters

VOLUME MEASURE

one liter	= 0.001 cubic meter	
10 milliliters (ml)	= 1 centiliter (cl)	
10 centiliters	= 1 deciliter (dl)	= 100 milliliters
10 deciliters	= 1 liter (l)	= 1,000 milliliters

VOLUME MEASURE (Cont.)

10 liters	= 1 dekaliter (dal)	
10 dekaliters	= 1 hectoliter (hl)	= 100 liters
10 hectoliters	= 1 kiloliter (kl)	= 1,000 liters

WEIGHT

10 milligrams (mg)	= 1 centigram (cg)	
10 centigrams	= 1 decigram (dg)	= 100 milligrams
10 decigrams	= 1 gram (g)	= 1,000 milligrams
10 grams	= 1 dekagram (dag)	
10 dekagrams	= 1 hectogram (hg)	= 100 grams
10 hectograms	= 1 kilogram (kg)	= 1,000 grams
1,000 kilograms	= 1 metric ton (t)	

CUBIC MEASURE

1,000 cubic millimeters	= 1 cubic centimeter	
1,000 cubic centimeters	= 1 cubic decimeter	= 1,000,000 cubic millimeters
1,000 cubic decimeters	= 1 cubic meter	= 1 stere
		= 1,000,000 cubic centimeters
		= 1,000,000,000 cubic millimeters

TABLES OF EQUIVALENTS

The name of a unit enclosed in brackets [1 chain] indicates (1) that the unit is not in current use in the United States, or (2) that the unit is believed to be based on "custom and usage" rather than on formal definition. Equivalents involving decimals are, in most instances, rounded off to the third decimal place except where exact equivalents are so designated.

1 angstrom[1]	0.1 millimicron (exactly).
	0.000 1 micron (exactly).
	0.000 000 1 millimeter (exactly).
	0.000 000 004 inch.
1 cable's length	120 fathoms.
	720 feet.
	219.456 meters (exactly).
1 centimeter	0.393 7 inch.
1 chain (Gunter's or surveyor's)	66 feet.
	20.1168 meters (exactly).
[1 chain] (engineer's)	100 feet.
	30.48 meters (exactly).
1 decimeter	3.937 inches.
1 dekameter	32.808 feet.
1 fathom	6 feet.
	1.8288 meters (exactly).
1 foot	0.3048 meter (exactly).
1 furlong	10 chains (surveyor's).
	660 feet.
	220 yards.
	⅛ statute mile.
	201.168 meters (exactly).
[1 hand]	4 inches.
1 inch	2.54 centimeters (exactly).
1 kilometer	0.621 mile.
1 league (land)	3 statute miles.
	4.828 kilometers.
1 link (Gunter's or surveyor's)	7.92 inches (exactly).
	0.201 168 meter (exactly).
[1 link (engineer's)]	1 foot.
	0.3048 meter (exactly).
1 meter	39.37 inches.
	1.094 yards.
1 micron (μ [the Greek letter mu])	0.001 millimeter (exactly).
	0.000 039 37 inch.
1 mil	0.001 inch (exactly).
	0.025 4 millimeter (exactly).

1 mile (statute or land)	5,280 feet.
	1.609 kilometers.
1 mile (nautical, international)	1.852 kilometers (exactly).
	1.151 statute miles.
	0.999 U.S. nautical miles.
1 millimeter	0.039 37 inch.
1 millimicron (mμ [the English letter m in combination with the Greek letter mu])	0.001 micron (exactly).
	0.000 000 039 37 inch.
1 point (typography)	0.013 837 inch (exactly).
	1/72 inch (approximately).
	0.351 millimeter.
1 rod, pole, or perch	16½ feet.
	5½ yards.
	5.0292 meters (exactly).
1 yard	0.9144 meter (exactly).

AREAS OR SURFACES

1 acre	43,560 square feet.
	4,840 square yards.
	0.405 hectare.
1 are	119.599 square yards.
	0.025 acre.
1 hectare	2.471 acres.
[1 square (building)]	100 square feet.
1 square centimeter	0.155 square inch.
1 square decimeter	15.500 square inches.
1 square foot	929.030 square centimeters.
1 square inch	6.4516 square centimeters (exactly).
1 square kilometer	0.386 square mile.
	247.105 acres.
1 square meter	1.196 square yards.
	10.764 square feet.
1 square mile	258.999 hectares.
1 square millimeter	0.002 square inch.
1 square rod, sq. pole, or sq. perch	25.293 square meters.
1 square yard	0.836 square meter.

CAPACITIES OR VOLUMES

1 barrel, liquid	31 to 42 gallons.[2]
1 barrel, standard for fruits, vegetables, and other dry commodities except cranberries	7,056 cubic inches. 105 dry quarts. 3.281 bushels.
1 barrel, standard, cranberry	5,286 cubic inches. 86 45/64 dry quarts. 2.709 bushels, struck measure.
1 bushel (U.S.), struck measure	2,150.42 cubic inches. 35.239 liters.
[1 bushel, heaped (U.S.)]	2,747.715 cubic inches. 1.278 bushels, struck measure.[3]
[1 bushel (British Imperial) (struck measure)]	1.032 U.S. bushels. 2,219.36 cubic inches.
1 cord (firewood)	128 cubic feet.
1 cubic centimeter	0.061 cubic inch.
1 cubic decimeter	61.024 cubic inches.
1 cubic foot	7.481 gallons. 28.316 cubic decimeters.
1 cubic inch	0.554 fluid ounce. 4.433 fluid drams. 16.387 cubic centimeters.
1 cubic meter	1.308 cubic yards.
1 cubic yard	0.765 cubic meter.
1 cup, measuring	8 fluid ounces. ½ liquid pint.
1 dram, fluid or liquid (U.S.)	⅛ fluid ounce. 0.226 cubic inch. 3.697 milliliters. 1.041 British fluid drachms.
1 dekaliter	2.642 gallons. 1.135 pecks.
1 gallon (U.S.)	231 cubic inches. 3.785 liters. 0.833 British gallon. 128 U.S. fluid ounces.
[1 gallon (British Imperial)]	277.42 cubic inches. 1.201 U.S. gallons. 4.546 liters. 160 British fluid ounces.
1 gill	7.219 cubic inches. 4 fluid ounces. 0.118 liter.
1 hectoliter	26.418 gallons. 2.838 bushels.
1 liter	1.057 liquid quarts. 0.908 dry quart. 61.024 cubic inches.
1 milliliter	0.271 fluid dram. 16.231 minims. 0.061 cubic inch.
1 ounce, fluid or liquid (U.S.)	1.805 cubic inches. 29.574 milliliters. 1.041 British fluid ounces.
[1 ounce, fluid (British)]	0.961 U.S. fluid ounce. 1.734 cubic inches. 28.412 milliliters.
1 peck	8.810 liters.
1 pint, dry	33.600 cubic inches. 0.551 liter.
1 pint, liquid	28.875 cubic inches (exactly). 0.473 liter.
1 quart, dry (U.S.)	67.201 cubic inches. 1.101 liters. 0.969 British quart.
1 quart, liquid (U.S.)	57.75 cubic inches (exactly). 0.946 liter. 0.833 British quart.
[1 quart (British)]	69.354 cubic inches. 1.032 U.S. dry quarts. 1.201 U.S. liquid quarts.
1 tablespoon	3 teaspoons. 4 fluid drams. ½ fluid ounce.
1 teaspoon	⅓ tablespoon. 1⅓ fluid drams.

WEIGHTS OR MASSES

1 assay ton[4]	29.167 grams.
1 carat	200 milligrams. 3.086 grains.
1 dram, apothecaries	60 grains. 3.888 grams.
1 dram, avoirdupois	27 11/32 (= 27.344) grains. 1.772 grams.
1 grain	64.798 91 milligrams (exactly).
1 gram	15.432 grains. 0.035 ounce, avoirdupois.
1 hundredweight, gross or long[5]	112 pounds. 50.802 kilograms.
1 hundredweight, net or short	100 pounds. 45.359 kilograms.
1 kilogram	2.205 pounds.
1 microgram (μg [the Greek letter mu in combination with the letter g])	0.000 001 gram (exactly).
1 milligram	0.015 grain.
1 ounce, avoirdupois	437.5 grains (exactly). 0.911 troy or apothecaries ounce. 28.350 grams.
1 ounce, troy or apothecaries	480 grains. 1.097 avoirdupois ounces. 31.103 grams.
1 pennyweight	1.555 grams.
1 point	0.01 carat. 2 milligrams.
1 pound, avoirdupois	7 000 grains. 1.215 troy or apothecaries pounds. 453.592 37 grams (exactly).
1 pound, troy or apothecaries	5 760 grains. 0.823 avoirdupois pound. 373.242 grams.
1 ton, gross or long[5]	2,240 pounds. 1.12 net tons (exactly). 1.016 metric tons.
1 ton, metric	2,204.623 pounds. 0.984 gross ton. 1.102 net tons.
1 ton, net or short	2,000 pounds. 0.893 gross ton. 0.907 metric ton.

---

[1] The angstrom is basically defined as 10^{-10} meter. [2] There are a variety of "barrels," established by law or usage. For example, federal taxes on fermented liquors are based on a barrel of 31 gallons; many state laws fix the "barrel for liquids" at 31½ gallons; one state fixes a 36-gallon barrel for cistern measurement; federal law recognizes a 40-gallon barrel for "proof spirits"; by custom, 42 gallons comprise a barrel of crude oil or petroleum products for statistical purposes, and this equivalent is recognized "for liquids" by four states. [3] Frequently recognized as 1¼ bushels, struck measure. [4] The assay ton bears the same relation to the milligram that a ton of 2,000 pounds avoirdupois bears to the ounce troy; hence the weight in milligrams of precious metal obtained from one assay ton of ore gives directly the number of troy ounces to the net ton. [5] The gross or long ton and hundredweight are used commercially in the United States to only a limited extent, usually in restricted industrial fields. These units are the same as the British "ton" and "hundredweight."

ROMAN NUMERALS

These are letter symbols used to represent numbers. The seven basic letters and their number equivalents are: I = 1, V = 5, X = 10, L = 50, C = 100, D = 500, M = 1,000. All other numbers (there is no zero) are formed using combinations of these letters (reading left to right, highest to lowest) which, when added together, produce the desired total: MCLX = 1,160; LXXI = 71; XVIII = 18, etc.

In most cases a subtraction principle is used to show numbers containing 4's and 9's. Thus, instead of using four consecutive similar letters (IIII, XXXX or CCCC), only one letter is shown, followed by a larger value letter from which the smaller is to be subtracted. Examples of these cases are: IV = 4, IX = 9, XL = 40, XC = 90, CD = 400, CM = 900. 494 is written CDXCIV, 1979 becomes MCMLXXIX.

The addition of a bar line over the Roman numeral increases its value 1,000 times. V̄ represents 5,000, X̄IX is 19,000, L̄VI is 56,000. A large number such as 145,262 converts to C̄X̄L̄V̄C̄C̄LXII.

BINARY NUMBERS

This number system utilizes only two symbols, 1 and 0. The location of these symbols in the binary number indicates the presence (1) or absence (0) of a certain number of units which, when added together, produce a total numerical value. The number of units to be added is determined by the length of the binary number and the location(s) of the 1 symbol. The extreme right-hand place stands for one unit; each successive place to the left represents double (2 times) the quantity of the place to its right.

Number of Units	32	16	8	4	2	1	Add	Total Value
BINARY 1 =						1	1	1
NUMBERS 10 =					1	0	2+0	2
101 =				1	0	1	4+0+1	5
1010 =			1	0	1	0	8+0+2+0	10
11001 =		1	1	0	0	1	16+8+0+0+1	25
101110 =	1	0	1	1	1	0	32+0+8+4+2+0	46

UNIT CONVERSIONS

To Convert	Into	Multiply By
Acre	hectare	0.4047
Acres	square feet	43,560.0
Acres	square miles	1.562×10^{-3}
Ampere-hours	coulombs	3,600.0
Angstrom unit	inch	$3,937 \times 10^{-9}$
Angstrom unit	micron	1×10^{-4}
Astronomical unit	kilometers	1.495×10^{8}
Atmospheres	cms of mercury	76.0
Bolt (U.S. cloth)	meters	36.576
BTU	horsepower-hrs	3.931×10^{-4}
BTU	kilowatt-hrs	2.928×10^{-4}
BTU/hr	watts	0.2931
Bushels	cubic inches	2,150.4
Calories, gram (mean)	BTU (mean)	3.9685×10^{-3}
Centares	square meters	1.0
Centimeters	kilometers	1×10^{-5}
Centimeters	meters	1×10^{-2}
Centimeters	millimeters	10.0
Centimeters	feet	3.281×10^{-2}
Centimeters	inches	0.3937
Chain	inches	792.0
Circumference	radians	6.283
Coulombs	faradays	1.036×10^{-5}
Cubic centimeters	cubic inches	0.06102
Cubic centimeters	pints (U.S. liq.)	2.113×10^{-3}
Cubic feet	cubic meters	0.02832
Cubic feet/min	pounds water/min.	62.43
Cubic feet/sec	gallons/min.	448.831
Cubits	inches	18.0
Days	seconds	86,400.0
Degrees (angle)	radians	1.745×10^{-2}
Degrees/sec.	revolutions/min.	0.1667
Dynes	grams	1.020×10^{-3}
Dynes	joules/meter (newtons)	1×10^{-5}
Ell	inches	45.0
Em, pica	inch	0.167
Ergs	BTU	9.480×10^{-11}
Ergs	foot-pounds	7.3670×10^{-8}
Ergs	kilowatt-hours	2.778×10^{-14}
Faradays/sec.	amperes (absolute)	96,500
Fathoms	feet	6.0
Feet	centimeters	30.48
Feet	meters	0.3048
Feet	miles (nautical)	1.645×10^{-4}
Feet	miles (statute)	1.894×10^{-4}
Feet/min.	centimeters/sec.	0.5080
Feet/sec.	knots	0.5921
Feet/sec.	miles/hour	0.6818
Foot-pounds	BTU	1.286×10^{-3}
Foot-pounds	kilowatt-hours	3.766×10^{-7}
Furlongs	miles (U.S.)	0.125
Furlongs	feet	660.0
Gallons	liters	3.785
Gallons of water	pounds of water	8.3453
Gallons/min.	cubic feet/hour	8.0208
Grams	ounces (avoirdupois)	3.527×10^{-2}
Grams	ounces (troy)	3.215×10^{-2}
Grams	pounds	2.205×10^{-3}
Hand	centimeters	10.16
Hectares	acres	2.471
Hectares	square feet	1.076×10^{5}
Horsepower	BTU/min.	42.44
Horsepower	kilowatts	0.7457
Horsepower	watts	745.7
Hours	days	4.167×10^{-2}
Hours	weeks	5.952×10^{-3}
Inches	centimeters	2.540
Inches	miles	1.578×10^{-5}
International ampere	ampere (absolute)	0.9998
International volt	volts (absolute)	1.0003
Joules	BTU	9.480×10^{-4}
Joules	ergs	1×10^{7}
Kilograms	pounds	2.205
Kilometers	feet	3,281.0
Kilometers	meters	1,000.0
Kilometers	miles	0.6214
Kilometers/hr.	knots	0.5396
Kilowatts	horsepower	1.341
Kilowatt-hours	BTU	3,413.0
Knots	feet/hour	6,080.0
Knots	nautical miles/hr.	1.0
Knots	statute miles/hr.	1.151
League	miles (approximately)	3.0
Light year	miles	5.9×10^{12}
Links (surveyor's)	inches	7.92
Liters	cubic centimeters	1,000.0
Liters	cubic inches	61.02
Liters	gallons (U.S. liq.)	0.2642
Liters	milliliters	1,000.0
Liters	pints (U.S. liq.)	2.113
Meters	centimeters	100.0
Meters	feet	3.281
Meters	kilometers	1×10^{-3}
Meters	miles (nautical)	5.396×10^{-4}
Meters	miles (statute)	6.214×10^{-4}
Meters	millimeters	1,000.0
Microns	meters	1×10^{-6}
Miles (nautical)	feet	6,080.27
Miles (statute)	feet	5,280.0
Miles (nautical)	kilometers	1.853
Miles (statute)	kilometers	1.609
Miles (nautical)	miles (statute)	1.1516
Miles (statute)	miles (nautical)	0.8684
Miles/hour	feet/min.	88.0
Milligrams/liter	parts/million	1.0
Milliliters	liters	1×10^{-3}
Millimeters	inches	3.937×10^{-2}
Newtons	dynes	1×10^{5}
Ohms (international)	ohms (absolute)	1.0005
Ounces	grams	28.349527
Ounces	pounds	6.25×10^{-2}
Ounces (troy)	ounces (avoirdupois)	1.09714
Parsec	miles	19×10^{12}
Parsec	kilometers	3.084×10^{13}
Pints (liq.)	cubic centimeters	473.2
Pints (liq.)	cubic inches	28.87
Pints (liq.)	gallons	0.125
Pints (liq.)	quarts (liq.)	0.5
Pounds	kilograms	0.4536
Pounds	ounces	16.0
Pounds	ounces (troy)	14.5833
Pounds	pounds (troy)	1.21528
Pounds/sq. inch	grams/sq. cm.	70.31
Quarts (dry)	cubic inches	67.20
Quarts (liq.)	cubic inches	57.75
Quarts (liq.)	gallons	0.25
Quarts (liq.)	liters	0.9463
Quires	sheets	25.0
Radians	degrees	57.30
Radians	minutes	3,438.0
Reams	sheets	500.0
Revolutions	degrees	360.0
Revolutions/min.	degrees/sec.	6.0
Rods	meters	5.029
Rods	feet	16.5
Rods (surveyor's measure)	yards	5.5
Seconds	minutes	1.667×10^{-2}
Slug	pounds	32.17
Tons (long)	kilograms	1,016.0
Tons (short)	kilograms	907.1848
Tons (long)	pounds	2,240.0
Tons (short)	pounds	2,000.0
Tons (long)	tons (short)	1.120
Tons (short)	tons (long)	0.89287
Volt (absolute)	statvolts	3.336×10^{-3}
Watts	BTU/hour	3.4129
Watts	horsepower	1.341×10^{-3}
Watts (international)	watts (absolute)	1.0002
Yards	meters	0.9144
Yards	miles (nautical)	4.934×10^{-4}
Yards	miles (statute)	5.682×10^{-4}

MULTIPLES AND SUBMULTIPLES

Prefix	Symbol	Equivalent	Factor
atto-	a	quintillionth part	$\times 10^{-18}$
femto-	f	quadrillionth part	$\times 10^{-15}$
pico-	p	trillionth part	$\times 10^{-12}$
nano-	n	billionth part	$\times 10^{-9}$
micro-	μ	millionth part	$\times 10^{-6}$
milli-	m	thousandth part	$\times 10^{-3}$
centi-	c	hundredth part	$\times 10^{-2}$
deci-	d	tenth part	$\times 10^{-1}$
deca-	da	tenfold	$\times 10$
hecto-	h	hundredfold	$\times 10^{2}$
kilo-	k	thousandfold	$\times 10^{3}$
mega-	M	millionfold	$\times 10^{6}$
giga-	G	billionfold	$\times 10^{9}$
tera-	T	trillionfold	$\times 10^{12}$

TABLES OF UNITED STATES CUSTOMARY WEIGHTS AND MEASURES

LINEAR MEASURE

12 inches (in.) = 1 foot (ft.)
3 feet = 1 yard (yd.)
5½ yards = 1 rod (rd.), pole, or perch (16½ ft.)
40 rods = 1 furlong (fur.) = 220 yards = 660 feet
8 furlongs = 1 statute mile (mi.) = 1,760 yards = 5,280 feet

3 land miles = 1 league
5,280 feet = 1 statute or land mile
6,076.11549 feet = 1 international nautical mile

AREA MEASURE

Squares and cubes of units are sometimes abbreviated by using "superior" figures. For example, ft² means square foot, and ft³ means cubic foot.

144 square inches = 1 square foot
9 square feet = 1 square yard = 1,296 square inches
30¼ square yards = 1 square rod = 272¼ square feet
160 square rods = 1 acre = 4,840 square yards = 43,560 square feet
640 acres = 1 square mile
1 mile square = 1 section (of land)
6 miles square = 1 township = 36 sections = 36 square miles

CUBIC MEASURE

1,728 cubic inches = 1 cubic foot
27 cubic feet = 1 cubic yard

LIQUID MEASURE

When necessary to distinguish the liquid pint or quart from the dry pint or quart, the word "liquid" or the abbreviation "liq." should be used in combination with the name or abbreviation of the liquid unit.

4 gills (gi.) = 1 pint (pt.) (= 28.875 cubic inches)
2 pints = 1 quart (qt.) (= 57.75 cubic inches)
4 quarts = 1 gallon (gal.) (= 231 cubic inches) = 8 pints = 32 gills

APOTHECARIES FLUID MEASURE

60 minims (min.) = 1 fluid dram (fl. dr.) (= 0.2256 cubic inch)
8 fluid drams = 1 fluid ounce (fl. oz.) (= 1.8047 cubic inches)
16 fluid ounces = 1 pint (= 28.875 cubic inches) = 128 fluid drams
2 pints = 1 quart (= 57.75 cubic inches) = 32 fluid ounces = 256 fluid drams
4 quarts = 1 gallon (= 231 cubic inches) = 128 fluid ounces = 1,024 fluid drams

DRY MEASURE

When necessary to distinguish the dry pint or quart from the liquid pint or quart, the word "dry" should be used in combination with the name or abbreviation of the dry unit.

2 pints = 1 quart (= 67.2006 cubic inches)
8 quarts = 1 peck (pk.) (= 537.605 cubic inches) = 16 pints
4 pecks = 1 bushel (bu.) (= 2,150.42 cubic inches) = 32 quarts

AVOIRDUPOIS WEIGHT

When necessary to distinguish the avoirdupois dram from the apothecaries dram, or to distinguish the avoirdupois dram or ounce from the fluid dram or ounce, or to distinguish the avoirdupois ounce or pound from the troy or apothecaries ounce or pound, the word "avoirdupois" or the abbreviation "avdp." should be used in combination with the name or abbreviation of the avoirdupois unit.

(The "grain" is the same in avoirdupois, troy, and apothecaries weights.)

27 11/32 grains = 1 dram (dr.)
16 drams = 1 ounce (oz.) = 437½ grains
16 ounces = 1 pound (lb.) = 256 drams = 7,000 grains
100 pounds = 1 hundredweight (cwt.)*
20 hundredweights = 1 ton (tn.) = 2,000 pounds*

In "gross" or "long" measure, the following values are recognized:

112 pounds = 1 gross or long hundredweight*
20 gross or long hundredweights = 1 gross or long ton = 2,240 pounds*

TROY WEIGHT

24 grains = 1 pennyweight (dwt.)
20 pennyweights = 1 ounce troy (oz. t.) = 480 grains
12 ounces troy = 1 pound troy (lb. t.) = 240 pennyweights = 5,760 grains

APOTHECARIES WEIGHT

20 grains = 1 scruple (s. ap.)
3 scruples = 1 dram apothecaries (dr. ap.) = 60 grains
8 drams apothecaries = 1 ounce apothecaries (oz. ap.) = 24 scruples = 480 grains
12 ounces apothecaries = 1 pound apothecaries (lb. ap.) = 96 drams apothecaries = 288 scruples = 5,760 grains

GUNTER'S OR SURVEYOR'S CHAIN MEASURE

7.92 inches = 1 link (li.)
100 links = 1 chain (ch.) = 4 rods = 66 ft.
80 chains = 1 statute mile = 320 rods = 5,280 ft.

---

* When the terms "hundredweight" and "ton" are used unmodified, they are commonly understood to mean the 100-pound hundredweight and the 2,000-pound ton, respectively; these units may be designated "net" or "short" when necessary to distinguish them from the corresponding units in gross or long measure.

TEMPERATURE CONVERSIONS

The table offers temperature conversions that range from the freezing point of water (32° F., 0° C.) to its boiling point (212° F., 100° C.). For conversions below or beyond that range, apply these formulas: to convert Fahrenheit degrees into Celsius, subtract 32, multiply by 5, and divide by 9; to convert Celsius into Fahrenheit, multiply by 9, divide by 5, and add 32. A Fahrenheit degree is smaller than a Celsius degree, one Fahrenheit degree being 5/9 of a Celsius degree.

°F	°C	°F	°C	°F	°C	°F	°C	°F	°C
32	0	53	11.7	72	22.2	89.6	32	103	39.4
33.8	1	54	12.2	73	22.8	90	32.2	104	40
35.6	2	55	12.8	73.4	23	91	32.8	105	40.6
36.5	2.5	56	13.3	74	23.3	91.4	33	105.8	41
37.4	3	57	13.9	75	23.9	92	33.3	106	41.1
38	3.3	57.2	14	75.2	24	93	33.9	107	41.7
39	3.9	58	14.4	76	24.4	94	34.4	107.6	42
39.2	4	59	15	77	25	95	35	108	42.2
40	4.4	60	15.6	78	25.6	96	35.6	109	42.8
41	5	61	16.1	79	26.1	96.8	36	110	43.3
42	5.6	62	16.7	80	26.7	97	36.1	111	43.9
43	6.1	63	17.2	80.6	27	97.3	36.3	112	44.4
44	6.7	64	17.8	81	27.2	98	36.7	113	45
45	7.2	65	18.3	82	27.8	98.6	37	114	45.6
46	7.8	66	18.9	82.4	28	99	37.2	115	46.1
46.4	8	66.2	19	83	28.3	99.5	37.5	116	46.7
47	8.3	67	19.4	84	28.9	100	37.8	117	47.2
48	8.9	68	20	85	29.4	100.4	38	118	47.8
48.2	9	69	20.6	86	30	101	38.3	118.4	48
50	10	69.8	21	87	30.6	101.8	38.8	119	48.3
51	10.6	70	21.1	88	31.1	102	38.9	120	48.9
52	11.1	71	21.7	89	31.7	102.2	39	121	49.4
122	50	140	60	160	71.1	180	82.2	197	91.7
123	50.6	141	60.6	161	71.7	181	82.8	198	92.2
124	51.1	142	61.1	161.6	72	182	83.3	199	92.8
125	51.7	143	61.7	162	72.2	183	83.9	199.4	93
125.6	52	144	62.2	163	72.8	183.2	84	200	93.3
126	52.2	145	62.8	164	73.3	184	84.4	201	93.9
127	52.8	146	63.3	165	73.9	185	85	202	94.4
128	53.3	147	63.9	166	74.4	186	85.6	203	95
129	53.9	148	64.4	167	75	186.8	86	204	95.6
130	54.4	149	65	168	75.6	187	86.1	204.8	96
131	55	150	65.6	168.8	76	188	86.7	205	96.1
132	55.6	151	66.1	169	76.1	188.6	87	206	96.7
133	56.1	152	66.7	170	76.7	189	87.2	207	97.2
134	56.7	152.6	67	171	77.2	190	87.8	208	97.8
134.6	57	153	67.2	172	77.8	190.4	88	208.4	98
135	57.2	154	67.8	173	78.3	191	88.3	209	98.3
136	57.8	155	68.3	174	78.9	192	88.9	210	98.9
136.4	58	156	68.9	175	79.4	193	89.4	210.2	99
137	58.3	156.2	69	176	80	194	90	211	99.4
138	58.9	157	69.4	177	80.6	195	90.6	212	100
138.2	59	158	70	178	81.1	195.8	91		
139	59.4	159	70.6	179	81.7	196	91.1		

SCIENCE GLOSSARY

PHYSICS AND ATOMIC ENERGY

Absolute temperature—Temperature scale on which the zero point is absolute zero (−273.15° C).

Acceleration—Rate of change of velocity; increase or decrease in velocity per unit of time.

Alpha particle—Low-speed, low-penetration helium nucleus emitted during disintegration of radioactive elements.

Anode—The positive electrode in an electric cell or an electron tube.

Angstrom—A unit of length: 1/100,000,000 centimeter.

Atom—Smallest part of a chemical element that takes part in a chemical change.

Atomic number—Number of protons in an atomic nucleus.

Atomic weight—Ratio of the average mass per atom of an element to 1/12 of the mass of an atom of carbon 12.

Beta particle—High-speed, high-penetration electron emitted during radioactive disintegration.

British thermal unit (BTU)—The amount of heat required to raise the temperature of one pound of water through one Fahrenheit degree.

Calorie—The amount of heat required to raise the temperature of one gram of water through 1° C.

Cathode—The negative electrode in an electric cell or an electron tube.

Celsius scale—A temperature scale on which the range between the freezing point of water, 0°, and the boiling point, 100°, is divided into 100 equal degrees. Also called the *Centigrade* scale.

Centrifugal force—The apparent force experienced by a body moving in a curved path that acts outward from the center of the path.

Doppler effect—Apparent change in frequency of sound waves or light waves caused by relative motion of the source toward or away from an observer, and by motion of an observer toward or from a stationary source.

Electron—Negatively charged, stable elementary particle.

Fission—Specifically, the splitting of an atomic nucleus into two parts of approximately the same size, accompanied by the release of great amounts of energy.

Fusion, nuclear—Union of two light atomic nuclei to form a heavier, more complex one, accompanied by the release of great amounts of energy. Also called *thermonuclear fusion*.

Gamma rays—Shortwave, high-frequency electromagnetic radiation emitted during disintegration of radioactive elements.

Gravity—Attraction of the earth or a celestial body for other bodies at or near its surface.

Half life—The time required for half of a radioactive substance to decay.

Hertz—Unit of frequency equal to 1 cycle per second.

Infrared—Electromagnetic radiation with wavelengths longer than visible red.

Ion—Charged atom or group of atoms produced by loss or gain of electrons from the outer orbits.

Ionization—Any process resulting in the formation of ions from atoms or molecules.

Joule—Unit of energy equal to the work done when a force of one newton moves through one meter.

Kinetic energy—Energy due to motion.

Liquid—Fluid phase of matter in which the surface is free, the volume is definite, and the shape is determined by the container.

Magnetic field—Space permeated by magnetic lines of force.

Magnetic pole—One of the two points in a magnet or a celestial body where magnetism seems to concentrate.

Mass Number—Sum of the numbers of protons and neutrons in the nucleus of an atom.

Matter—Anything that has mass and occupies space.

Meson—Any of a group of elementary particles of small mass and very short life.

Neutron—Neutral particle found in the nuclei of atoms with a mass number greater than 1.

Newton—Unit of force equal to the force required to give a mass of 1 kilogram on acceleration of 1 meter per second per second.

Nuclear reactor—Device for starting and regulating nuclear fission for the purpose of producing heat.

Nucleon—Particle found in the structure of an atom's nucleus; a proton or neutron.

Nucleus—Central, positively charged part of an atom.

Ohm—Unit of electrical resistance.

Photoelectric effect—Emission of electrons by certain substances when struck by light or other radiation.

Photon—A quantum of radiation.

Physical change—An alteration that includes no change in the molecular composition of a substance.

Physics—The study of matter and energy and the interchange of energy among material things.

Positron—Positive electron.

Proton—Positively charged, stable particle found in the nuclei of all atoms.

Quantum mechanics—Modern mathematical form of the quantum theory.

Quantum theory—Theory that all energy is lost or gained in discrete amounts (quanta).

Quark—Type of particle with fractional electron charge, postulated to be components of other particles.

Radar—Electronic system for detecting distant objects by means of transmitted high-frequency radio waves and their reflection from the objects.

Radiation—Electromagnetic waves, or particles emitted from nuclei.

Radioactivity—Disintegration of the nuclei of the atoms of certain elements, during which electromagnetic waves and elementary particles are emitted.

Relative density—Ratio of density of a substance to the density of water. Formerly *specific gravity*.

Relativity—(1) Einstein's special theory: All motion is relative to observer, and velocity of light in space is constant regardless of motion of light source or observer. Mass may be changed into energy and vice versa according to the law $E = mc^2$ (2) Einstein's general theory: gravitation is a consequence of curved space.

Resistance—Opposition to passage of electric current offered by an electrical conductor.

Spectroscope—Optical instrument for the study of spectra.

Spectrum—Band of electromagnetic radiation in which the constituent parts are arranged according to their wavelengths or their frequencies.

Transformer—Device for changing the voltage of alternating current.

Transistor—Device made of semiconductor materials for the control of the flow of electric current.

Ultrasonic—Having a frequency above that audible to human beings: above about 20,000 hertz (cycles per second).

Ultraviolet—Electromagnetic radiation with wavelengths shorter than visible violet but longer than X-rays.

Velocity—Rate of motion in a given direction.

Watt hour—The energy of 1 watt acting for 1 hour.

Wavelength—Distance between two successive points of a wave in the same phase, such as crest to crest.

X-rays—Electromagnetic radiations of short wavelength and high penetration of matter.

MATHEMATICS

Additive inverse of a number—A number with its sign changed to minus if originally plus, or vice versa.

Algorism (Algorithm)—In modern mathematics, any systematic method or procedure for computation.

Analog computer—A calculating device in which magnitudes are determined by measurement along scales rather than by digital counting, e.g., slide rule.

Analytic geometry—The technique of dealing with geometry in terms of algebra.

Antilogarithm—The number corresponding to a given logarithm, e.g., 2 is the logarithm of 100, therefore, 100 is the antilogarithm of 2.

Axiom—In a system of mathematics or logic, a proposition or statement from which secondary propositions or statements are derived.

Binary arithmetic—A system of calculation in which the only numerals used are 0 and 1, and all real numbers are represented as powers of 2.

Bit—Condensation of *binary digit*. In computer and information theory, a single binary digit, either 0 or 1.

Boolean algebra—An algebra obeying special laws that make it suitable for such uses as the study of logic and planning switching circuits.

Calculus—Generally, any system of mathematical calculation, or any system of operations involving symbols, e.g., calculus of finite differences, calculus of probabilities, and the like. Specifically, a method of mathematical analysis (developed independently by Isaac Newton and Gottfried Leibniz) involving the rate of change of a variable function.

Cardinal number—Zero and the counting numbers 1, 2, 3, 4, . . ., as distinguished from the ordinal numbers.

Cartesian coordinates—Two or three lines intersecting at right angles and providing a reference system for locating points in two or three dimensional space; used in analytic geometry.

Compound interest—Interest paid periodically on the sum of a given principle and its accruing interest.

Decimal number system—The ordinary number system (sometimes called the Arabic system) that denotes real numbers according to the place values for multiples of 10 plus the digits 0 through 9.

Derivative—A measure of the rate at which one mathematical variable changes in response to changes in a related variable.

Digital computer—A calculating machine in which mathematical operations are performed by individually tallying every digit.

Duodecimal system—A system of numeration in which the base is 12. The numbers 10 and 11 of the decimal system are rendered in the duodecimal system by arbitrary symbols, two of which in use are *t* (called dek) and *e* (called el).

Function—In classical algebra, a variable y so related to another variable x, that for each value given to x there is a value that may be determined for y.

Hardware—The electronic equipment used in a computer system, in contrast to the software.

Infinity—A quantity that is greater than any assignable quantity.

Integral—Mathematical function used in calculus for finding the area under a curve.

Intersection—That portion of two or more sets common to all the sets considered.

Iterative procedure—A means of approximating the solution to an equation by repeating a given procedure several times to get successively closer answers, each based on the preceding approximation.

Logarithm—The exponent of the power to which a number is to be raised to produce a given number. Thus, using the base 10, the logarithm of 100 is 2, because the exponent of the power to which 10 must be raised in order to equal 100 is 2 ($10^2 = 100$).

Machine language—The characters and symbols and the rules for combining them that convey information and instruction to a computer for processing.

Matrix—Usually a rectangular array of numbers, including several columns and rows, that can be manipulated as though it were a single quantity.

Modular arithmetic—A form of arithmetic dealing with the remainders left over when all the numbers considered are divided by a single number, the modulus.

Multiplicative inverse of a number—The reciprocal of that number; for example, 1/5 is the reciprocal of 5.

Non-Euclidean geometry—Any of several geometries that substitute other postulates for Euclid's fifth postulate (in effect, through a point outside a given line, only one line may be drawn parallel to the given line).

Open sentence—An equation containing one or more unknown quantities.

Ordinal number—A number that indicates position or relation; thus, 2d, 3d, 8th.

Postulate—An unproved assumption accepted as basic to a mathematical system, and from which, in combination with other postulates, the propositions of the system are derived, or in terms of which the propositions are proved.

Problem language—The language used by a programmer to state the problem to be solved by a computer.

Program—A sequence of steps to be executed by a computer to solve a given problem.

Reciprocal—The number that results when 1 is divided by a given number. Thus, the reciprocal of 2 is ½; the reciprocal of 4 is ¼; and the reciprocal of a fraction is the fraction inverted, thus the reciprocal of ⅘ is ⅝.

Repeating decimal—A nonterminating decimal in which a pattern of numbers is established and is followed by a continuous repetition of the digit or pattern of digits, thus: .222222222222, .777777777777, .1515151515-15, .234523452345; a repeating decimal is also called a recurring decimal, periodic decimal, or circulating decimal.

Scalar—A quantity indicating magnitude but not direction, in contrast to a vector.

Set—A collection of objects, symbols, or ideas with some common property or attribute.

Slide rule—A computing device usually consisting of a frame and a horizontal slide, on both of which are printed scales graduated logarithmically. Also, usually, a transparent runner, or indicator, containing a hairline that is used to enable accurate reading of the results obtained by manipulation of the slide within the frame.

Software—Programs, procedures, and routines that support and augment a computer system.

Symbolic logic—Logic performed with the use of symbols subject to certain predetermined rules.

Topology—The study of those properties of geometric figures that remain unchanged despite radical distortions of considered figures.

Transformation—A rule for transforming one set of values into another; for example, $y = 2x$ transforms each x into a y twice as large.

Truth set—A set of solutions to an equation or group of equations.

Union—The total of all the members of all the sets of the union being considered.

Vector—A quantity having direction as well as magnitude. Thus, velocity is a vector because it is specified by its direction as well as its magnitude.

CHEMISTRY

Acid—A substance that in aqueous solution turns blue litmus red, furnishes hydronium ions, and contains hydrogen, which can be replaced by a metal.

Alkali—A water-soluble base that ionizes strongly to form hydroxide ions.

Anion—A negative ion.

Base—A substance that in aqueous solution turns red litmus blue, furnishes hydroxyl ions, and reacts with an acid to form a salt and water only.

Buffer—A solution containing either a weak acid and its salt or a weak base and its salt, thereby resisting changes in acidity or basicity.

Carbohydrate—A compound of carbon, hydrogen, and oxygen, usually having hydrogen and oxygen in the proportion of 2 to 1.

Catalyst—A substance that alters the rate at which a chemical reaction takes place, but which itself remains unchanged.

Cation—A positive ion.

Chemical change—Change in a substance involving a change in its identity due to an increase, decrease, or rearrangement of the atoms within its molecules; opposed to physical change, in which the substance keeps its identity.

346   SCIENCE: PAST/PRESENT

Colloid—Dispersion in a medium of particles that are very small aggregates of molecules. Also called *colloidal suspension*.

Combustion—Any chemical change that produces heat and, usually, light. Most commonly, the combination of the oxygen of the air with a substance: *burning*.

Compound—A homogeneous substance composed of two or more chemical elements, the proportions of which by weight are fixed and invariable.

Cracking—A method of changing the constituents of petroleum, using pressure, heat, and catalysts, in which the hydrocarbons of high molecular weight are broken down into those of lower molecular weight.

Crystal—A solid in which the component molecules, atoms, or ions are oriented in a definite and repeated geometric pattern.

Deliquescent substance—A substance that absorbs moisture from the air and dissolves in the water so absorbed.

Deuterium—An isotope of hydrogen of mass number 2.

Distillation—Vaporization of a liquid, followed by condensation of the vapor.

Electrolysis—Chemical decomposition of a substance by an electric current passed through the substance in dissolved or molten state.

Element—A substance which cannot be decomposed by ordinary types of chemical change, or made by chemical union.

Emulsion—Dispersion of minute droplets of one liquid (that does not dissolve) in another.

Ester—Organic compounds corresponding to inorganic salts, derived by replacing hydrogen of an acid by an organic group.

Fixation of nitrogen—The combination of atmospheric nitrogen with other elements to form chemical compounds.

Formula—The combination of chemical symbols showing the composition of a chemical element or compound.

Hard water—Water that contains chemicals in solution that react with soap to form a precipitate and which therefore only lathers with difficulty.

Hydrocarbon—A compound containing only carbon and hydrogen.

Hydrolysis—Chemical reaction of a substance with water.

Ion—An atom or group of atoms possessing an electrical charge.

Isomers—Molecules that have the same number and kinds of atoms but different molecular configurations.

Isotopes—Atoms of the same atomic number which differ in the number of protons in the nucleus.

Molecular weight—Relative weight of a molecule compared to the weight of an atom of carbon taken as exactly 12.00; the sum of the atomic weights of the atoms in a molecule.

Molecule—The smallest unit of a substance that can exist free, and retain all the chemical properties of that substance.

Osmosis—Diffusion of a solvent through a semipermeable membrane into a more concentrated solution.

Oxidation—A process in which an atom or group of atoms loses electrons; combination with oxygen.

pH—A symbol for the logarithm of the reciprocal of the hydrogen ion concentration of a solution; thus, an indication of the acidity or basicity of a solution. A neutral solution has a pH of 7; an acid solution has a pH lower than seven, an alkaline, higher.

Photosynthesis—A chemical change that utilizes light energy; e.g., the production in plants of starch from carbon dioxide and water in sunlight.

Polymorphism—The ability of a substance to exist in two or more crystalline forms.

Precipitate—An insoluble solid deposited from a solution.

Protein—Complex organic compounds of very high molecular weight that compose a large part of all living matter; protein molecules invariably contain the elements of carbon, hydrogen, oxygen, and nitrogen.

Radical—A group of atoms that functions as a unit in chemical change.

Reduction—A process in which an atom or group of atoms gains electrons: loss of oxygen or combination with hydrogen.

Salt—A compound made up of the positive ion of a base and the negative ion of an acid.

Solution—A homogeneous mixture of two or more substances of dissimilar molecular structure. In a solution there is a dissolving medium—*solvent*—and a dissolved substance—*solute*.

Standard conditions—0° C and 1 atmosphere (760 mm, or 29.92 in. of mercury) pressure.

Synthesis—The formation of a compound from its elements or from simpler compounds.

Tritium—An isotope of hydrogen of mass number 3.

Valence—A number that represents the combining power of an atom or radical referred to hydrogen as a standard.

MULTIPLICATION AND DIVISION TABLE

A number in the top line (14) multiplied by a number in the extreme left hand column (13) produces the number where the top line and side line meet (182).

A number in the table (208) divided by the number at the top of the same column (13) results in the number (16) in the extreme left hand column. A number in the table (208) divided by the number at the extreme left (16) results in the number (13) at the top of the column.

1	2	3	4	5	6	7	8	9	10	11	12	13
2	4	6	8	10	12	14	16	18	20	22	24	26
3	6	9	12	15	18	21	24	27	30	33	36	39
4	8	12	16	20	24	28	32	36	40	44	48	52
5	10	15	20	25	30	35	40	45	50	55	60	65
6	12	18	24	30	36	42	48	54	60	66	72	78
7	14	21	28	35	42	49	56	63	70	77	84	91
8	16	24	32	40	48	56	64	72	80	88	96	104
9	18	27	36	45	54	63	72	81	90	99	108	117
10	20	30	40	50	60	70	80	90	100	110	120	130
11	22	33	44	55	66	77	88	99	110	121	132	143
12	24	36	48	60	72	84	96	108	120	132	144	156
13	26	39	52	65	78	91	104	117	130	143	156	169
14	28	42	56	70	84	98	112	126	140	154	168	182
15	30	45	60	75	90	105	120	135	150	165	180	195
16	32	48	64	80	96	112	128	144	160	176	192	208
17	34	51	68	85	102	119	136	153	170	187	204	221
18	36	54	72	90	108	126	144	162	180	198	216	234
19	38	57	76	95	114	133	152	171	190	209	228	247
20	40	60	80	100	120	140	160	180	200	220	240	260
21	42	63	84	105	126	147	168	189	210	231	252	273
22	44	66	88	110	132	154	176	198	220	242	264	286
23	46	69	92	115	138	161	184	207	230	253	276	299
24	48	72	96	120	144	168	192	216	240	264	288	312
25	50	75	100	125	150	175	200	225	250	275	300	325

14	15	16	17	18	19	20	21	22	23	24	25
28	30	32	34	36	38	40	42	44	46	48	50
42	45	48	51	54	57	60	63	66	69	72	75
56	60	64	68	72	76	80	84	88	92	96	100
70	75	80	85	90	95	100	105	110	115	120	125
84	90	96	102	108	114	120	126	132	138	144	150
98	105	112	119	126	133	140	147	154	161	168	175
112	120	128	136	144	152	160	168	176	184	192	200
126	135	144	153	162	171	180	189	198	207	216	225
140	150	160	170	180	190	200	210	220	230	240	250
154	165	176	187	198	209	220	231	242	253	264	275
168	180	192	204	216	228	240	252	264	276	288	300
182	195	208	221	234	247	260	273	286	299	312	325
196	210	224	238	252	266	280	294	308	322	336	350
210	225	240	255	270	285	300	315	330	345	360	375
224	240	256	272	288	304	320	336	352	368	384	400
238	255	272	289	306	323	340	357	374	391	408	425
252	270	288	306	324	342	360	378	396	414	432	450
266	285	304	323	342	361	380	399	418	437	456	475
280	300	320	340	360	380	400	420	440	460	480	500
294	315	336	357	378	399	420	441	462	483	504	525
308	330	352	374	396	418	440	462	484	506	528	550
322	345	368	391	414	437	460	483	506	529	552	575
336	360	384	408	432	456	480	504	528	552	576	600
350	375	400	425	450	475	500	525	550	575	600	625

FOREIGN WEIGHTS AND MEASURES

Name of Unit	Country	U.S. Equivalent
Ardeb	Egypt	43.55 gals.
Arroba	Costa Rica	25.35 lbs.
Bak (opium)	Laos	57.9 grains
Barril	Mexico	16.72 gals.
Batman	Iran	6.546 lbs.
Beswa	Afghanistan	116.8 sq. yds.
Bhara	Malaysia	400.0 lbs.
Bocoy	Cuba	18.214 bu.
Botella	Honduras	1.216 pts.
Bu	Japan	.011930 in.
Caballería	El Salvador	111.11 acres
Cable (nautical)	United Kingdom	200.0 yds.
Cajuela	Costa Rica	3.74 gals.
Cân	South Vietnam	1.333 lbs.
Candy	Burma	18,000.0 lbs.
Caneca	Cuba	4.784 gals.
Cántaro (wine)	Spain	3.572 gals.
Cape inch	South Africa	1.033 ins.
Capicha	Iran	2.32 qts.
Carga	El Salvador	200.0 lbs.
Carga	Mexico	308.6 lbs.
Case (bananas)	Western Samoa	72.0 lbs.
Catty	Indonesia	1.3616 lbs.
Centner	Denmark	110.231 lbs.
Chang	Mongolia	3.50 yds.
Cheung	Hong Kong	4.063 yds.
Chi	South Korea	1.423 sq. ins.
Cho	Japan	119.30 yds.
Chum	Malaysia	1.475 ins.
Chupak	Malaysia	1.0 qt.
Cuadra	Ecuador	91.9 yds.
Cuadra	Peru	2.47 acres
Cuarta	Costa Rica	8.228 ins.
Cuartilla	Ecuador	50.7 lbs.
Cuartillo (oil)	Mexico	.890 pt.
Cubito	Somalia	22.0 ins.
Cuerdo	Puerto Rico	.971 acre
Dariba	Egypt	43.55 bu.
Dawulla	Ethiopia	220.46 lbs.
Dékare	Bulgaria	.247 acre
Dhira	Syria	29.5 ins.
Dira	Saudi Arabia	17.3 ins.
Djuim	Byelorussian SSR	1.0 in.
Dönüm	Cyprus	1,600.0 sq. yds.
Dönüm, metric	Israel	1,196.0 sq. yds.
Doppelzentner	West Germany	220.462 lbs.
Dra (textiles)	Jordan	26.8 ins.
Du	Mongolia	5.72 qts.
El	Surinam	2.26 ft.
Fan che	Mainland China	1.19599 sq. ft.
Fanega	Paraguay	63.4 gals.
Farsakh-song	Iran	3.88 mi.
Fatar	Muscat and Oman	Span from first finger to thumb
Fen	Mainland China	.1312 in.
Frasila	Tanzania	36.0 lbs.
Fuder	West Germany	220.0 gals.
Fun	Hong Kong	.14625 in.
Fuss	West Germany	12.36 ins.
Gallon	Haiti	.8326 gal.
Gang	South Vietnam	.4306 sq. ft.
Gantang	Sabah	1.0 gal.
Gaz	Iran	1.14 yds.
Gazi jerib	Afghanistan	29.0 ins.
Gian sheng	Mainland China	27.4961 bu.
Gong qing	Mainland China	2.471054 acres
Grain, colonial	Mauritius	.819 grain
Gun	Hong Kong	1.333 lbs.
Gurraf	Libya	2.03 qts.
Habba (gold)	Sudan	1.543 grains
Hand (height of horses)	United Kingdom	4.0 ins.
Heml	Egypt	550.3 lbs.
Hold (agriculture)	Hungary	1.422 acres
Izenbi	Morocco	2,153.0 sq. yds.
Jemba	Malaysia	144.0 sq. ft.
Jin	Mainland China	1.1023 lbs.
Jutro, katastarsko	Yugoslavia	1.422 acres
Kala	Morocco	19.69 ins.
Kantang	Cambodia	1.650 gals.
Kantar	Lebanon	565.3 lbs.
Kantar	Egypt	99.05 lbs.
Ken	Japan	1.988 yds.
Kettle	Sierra Leone	8.79 qts.
Kilates (troy)	Philippines	3.09 grains
Kin	Japan	1.32 lbs.
Koku	Japan	39.68 gals.
Kosh	Nepal	2.0 mi.
Kung chang	China (Taiwan)	10.9361 yds.
Kwien	Thailand	440.0 gals.
Kwintal	Poland	220.46 lbs.
Legua	Cuba	2.635 mi.
Legua	Uruguay	3.2 mi.
Leaguer	South Africa	127.0 gals.
Lei (Chinese mi.)	Hong Kong	706–745.0 yds.
Lelong	Malaysia	2,400.0 sq. ft.
Li	Mainland China	546.8 yds.
Li	South Korea	2.440 mi.
Libra	Spain	1.014 lbs.
Livre, colonial	Seychelles	1.079 lbs.
Load (cocoa)	Sierra Leone	60.0 lbs.
Ma (Chinese yd.)	Hong Kong	35.10 ins.
Manzana	Guatemala	1.74 acres
Marco	Mexico	1.015 oz.
Marco real	Spain	1.591 acres
Maund (Imperial)	Aden	82.28 lbs.
Mecate	Costa Rica	21.942 yds.
Medida	Honduras	2.527 qts.
Meripeninkulma	Finland	1.15 mi.
Mid (oil)	Jordan	15.8 qts.
Mil	Sweden	6.214 mi.
Mile (geographical)	Indonesia	4.60 mi.
Milla legal	Argentina	1.0 mi.
Misura	Libya	4.36 gals.
Mu	Mainland China	.16474 acre
Mud	Netherlands	2.471 acres
Mudu (rice)	Nigeria	2.5 lbs.
Nim-man	Iran	3.272 lbs.
Oke	Saudi Arabia	2.8 lbs.
Onza	Honduras	1.014 oz.
Ounce, Amsterdam	Indonesia	1.089 oz.
Peninkulma (mil)	Finland	6.21 mi.
Phân	South Vietnam	2.583 sq. ft.
Pié	Argentina	1.0 ft.
Pied anglais	Haiti	1.0 ft.
Pipa	Dominican Republic	15.75 bu.
Pond	Surinam	1.102 lbs.
Poud (grain)	USSR	36.11 lbs.
Pulgada	Philippines	1.0 in.
Quintal	Angola	220.5 lbs.
Quintal	El Salvador	100.0 lbs.
Raummeter	Austria	1.308 cu. yds.
Ri	Japan	2.440 mi.
Roupi (textiles)	Cyprus	3.00 ins.
Rute	West Germany	4.12 yds.
Sâa	Libya	26.13 gals.
Saco (coffee)	Colombia	137.8 lbs.
Saco (coffee)	Peru	152.1 lbs.
Seer	Nepal	2.057 lbs.
Shaku	Japan	.635 fl. oz.
Shō	Japan	1.587 qts.
Sildarmál (herring)	Iceland	4.12 bu.
Solar	Ecuador	.43 acre
Stone	United Kingdom	14.0 lbs.
Stoop (beer)	Netherlands	1.32 gals.
Sun	Japan	1.19303 ins.
Tael	Cambodia	1.323 avoir. oz.
Tanan	Thailand	.880 qt.
Tartous	Syria	1,099.0 sq. yds.
Tercia	El Salvador	1.0 ft.
Thail (opium)	Indonesia	1.241 avoir. oz.
Thôn	South Vietnam	2.870 sq. yds.
To	Japan	3.968 gals.
Tola (standard)	Pakistan	180.0 grains
Tomme	Denmark	1.030 ins.
Tondeland	Denmark	1.363 acres
Tonne	Schleswig-Holstein, W. Ger.	1.35 acres
Tonneau de mer	Belgium	100.0 cu. ft.
Topo (usual)	Peru	.86 acre
Tuuma	Finland	1.0 in.
Ud	Sudan	2.54 yds.
Uyên (rice)	South Vietnam	.880 qt.
Vara	Chile	32.91 ins.
Vara	Paraguay	2.84 ft.
Vara	Spain	2.74 ft.
Voet, Amsterdam	Netherlands	.928 ft.
War	Aden	1.0 yd.
Wari	Kenya	1.0 yd.
Wine gallon	Barbados	.83267 gal.
Wizna	Malta	8.750 lbs.
Yang	South Korea	1.32 oz.
Yarda	Colombia	35.43 ins.
Yen	South Vietnam	13.33 lbs.
Zentner	Austria	220.46 lbs.
Zoll	West Germany	1.03 ins.

SQUARES, CUBES, SQUARE ROOTS, AND CUBE ROOTS

No.	Squares	Cubes	Square roots	Cube roots
1	1	1	1.0000000	1.0000000
2	4	8	1.4142136	1.2599210
3	9	27	1.7320508	1.4422496
4	16	64	2.0000000	1.5874011
5	25	125	2.2360687	1.7099759
6	36	216	2.4494896	1.8171206
7	49	343	2.6457513	1.9129312
8	64	512	2.8284271	2.0000000
9	81	729	3.0000000	2.0800837
10	100	1000	3.1622777	2.1544347
11	121	1331	3.3166248	2.2239801
12	144	1728	3.4641016	2.2894286
13	169	2197	3.6055513	2.3513347
14	196	2744	3.7416574	2.4101422
15	225	3375	3.8729833	2.4662121
16	256	4096	4.0000000	2.5198421
17	289	4913	4.1231056	2.5712816
18	324	5832	4.2426407	2.6207414
19	361	6859	4.3588989	2.6684016
20	400	8000	4.4721360	2.7144177
21	441	9261	4.5825757	2.7589243
22	484	10648	4.6904158	2.8020393
23	529	12167	4.7958315	2.8438670
24	576	13824	4.8989795	2.8844991
25	625	15625	5.0000000	2.9240177
26	676	17576	5.0990195	2.9624960
27	729	19683	5.1961524	3.0000000
28	784	21952	5.2915026	3.0365889
29	841	24389	5.3851648	3.0723168
30	900	27000	5.4772256	3.1072325
31	961	29791	5.5677644	3.1413806
32	1024	32768	5.6568542	3.1748021
33	1089	35937	5.7445626	3.2075343
34	1156	39304	5.8309519	3.2396118
35	1225	42875	5.9160798	3.2710663
36	1296	46656	6.0000000	3.3019272
37	1369	50653	6.0827625	3.3322218
38	1444	54872	6.1644140	3.3619754
39	1521	59319	6.2449980	3.3912114
40	1600	64000	6.3245553	3.4199519
41	1681	68921	6.4031242	3.4482172
42	1764	74088	6.4807407	3.4760266
43	1849	79507	6.5574385	3.5033981
44	1936	85184	6.6332496	3.5303483
45	2025	91125	6.7082039	3.5568933
46	2116	97336	6.7823300	3.5830479
47	2209	103823	6.8556546	3.6088261
48	2304	110592	6.9282032	3.6342411
49	2401	117649	7.0000000	3.6593057
50	2500	125000	7.0710678	3.6840314
51	2601	132651	7.1414284	3.7084298
52	2704	140608	7.2111026	3.7325111
53	2809	148877	7.2801099	3.7562858
54	2916	157464	7.3484692	3.7797631
55	3025	166375	7.4161985	3.8029525
56	3136	175616	7.4833148	3.8258624
57	3249	185193	7.5498344	3.8485011
58	3364	195112	7.6157731	3.8708766
59	3481	205379	7.6811457	3.8929965
60	3600	216000	7.7459667	3.9148676
61	3721	226981	7.8102497	3.9364972
62	3844	238328	7.8740079	3.9578915
63	3969	250047	7.9372539	3.9790571
64	4096	262144	8.0000000	4.0000000
65	4225	274625	8.0622577	4.0207256
66	4356	287496	8.1240384	4.0412401
67	4489	300763	8.1853528	4.0615480
68	4624	314432	8.2462113	4.0816551
69	4761	328509	8.3066239	4.1015661
70	4900	343000	8.3666003	4.1212853
71	5041	357911	8.4261498	4.1408178
72	5184	373248	8.4852814	4.1601676
73	5329	389017	8.5440037	4.1793390
74	5476	405224	8.6023253	4.1983364
75	5625	421875	8.6602540	4.2171633
76	5776	438976	8.7177979	4.2358236
77	5929	456533	8.7749644	4.2543210
78	6084	474552	8.8317609	4.2726586
79	6241	493039	8.8881944	4.2908404
80	6400	512000	8.9442719	4.3088695
81	6561	531441	9.0000000	4.3267487
82	6724	551368	9.0553851	4.3444815
83	6889	571787	9.1104336	4.3620707
84	7056	592704	9.1651514	4.3795191
85	7225	614125	9.2195445	4.3968296
86	7396	636056	9.2736185	4.4140049
87	7569	658503	9.3273791	4.4310476
88	7744	681472	9.3808315	4.4479602
89	7921	704969	9.4339811	4.4647451
90	8100	729000	9.4868330	4.4814047
91	8281	753571	9.5393920	4.4979414
92	8464	778688	9.5916630	4.5143574
93	8649	804357	9.6436508	4.5306549
94	8836	830584	9.6953597	4.5468359
95	9025	857375	9.7467943	4.5629026
96	9216	884736	9.7979590	4.5788570
97	9409	912673	9.8488578	4.5947009
98	9604	941192	9.8994949	4.6104363
99	9801	970299	9.9498744	4.6260650
100	10000	1000000	10.0000000	4.6415888

DECIMAL EQUIVALENTS OF COMMON FRACTIONS

8ths	16ths	32ds	64ths	Equivalent
			1	.015625
		1	2	.031250
			3	.046875
	1	2	4	.062500
			5	.078125
		3	6	.093750
			7	.109375
1	2	4	8	.125000
			9	.140625
		5	10	.156250
			11	.171875
	3	6	12	.187500
			13	.203125
		7	14	.218750
			15	.234375
2	4	8	16	.250000
			17	.265625
		9	18	.281250
			19	.296875
	5	10	20	.312500
			21	.328125
		11	22	.343750

8ths	16ths	32ds	64ths	Equivalent
			23	.359375
3	6	12	24	.375000
			25	.390625
		13	26	.406250
			27	.421875
	7	14	28	.437500
			29	.453125
		15	30	.468750
			31	.484375
4	8	16	32	.500000
			33	.515625
		17	34	.531250
			35	.546875
	9	18	36	.562500
			37	.578125
		19	38	.593750
			39	.609375
5	10	20	40	.625000
			41	.640625
		21	42	.656250
			43	.671875
	11	22	44	.687500

8ths	16ths	32ds	64ths	Equivalent
			45	.703125
		23	46	.718750
			47	.734375
6	12	24	48	.750000
			49	.765625
		25	50	.781250
			51	.796875
	13	26	52	.812500
			53	.828125
		27	54	.843750
			55	.859375
7	14	28	56	.875000
			57	.890625
		29	58	.906250
			59	.921875
	15	30	60	.937500
			61	.953125
		31	62	.968750
			63	.984375
8	16	32	64	1.000000

INVENTORS AND INVENTIONS

Invention	Date	Inventor	Country
abacus	c. 500 B.C.	unknown	China (?)
achromatic lens	1758	John Dolland	England
adding machine	1642	Blaise Pascal	France
adding machine (commercial)	1885	William Burroughs	U.S.
addressing machine	1893	J. S. Duncan	U.S.
aerosol spray	1941	Lyle D. Goodhue	U.S.
air brake	1869	George Westinghouse	U.S.
air conditioning	1911	Willis H. Carrier	U.S.
air-cushion vehicle	1877	J. I. Thornycroft	England
airplane	1903	Orville and Wilbur Wright	U.S.
airplane (multi-motored)	1913	Igor Sikorsky	Russia
airship (nonrigid)	1852	Henri Giffard	France
airship (rigid)	1900	Ferdinand von Zeppelin	Germany
automatic pilot	1929	William Green	U.S.
automobile (electric)	1891	William Morrison	U.S.
automobile (internal combustion)	1887	Gottlieb Daimler / Karl Benz (independently)	Germany / Germany
Babbitt metal	1839	Isaac Babbitt	U.S.
Bakelite	1907	Leo H. Baekeland	U.S.
balloon	1783	J. M. and J. E. Montgolfier	France
barbed wire	1874	Joseph F. Glidden	U.S.
barometer	1643	Evangelista Torricelli	Italy
battery (electric)	1800	Alessandro Volta	Italy
benday process	1879	Benjamin Day	U.S.
Bessemer converter	1856	Henry Bessemer	England
Bessemer converter	1857	William Kelly (independently)	U.S.
betatron	1939	Donald W. Kerst	U.S.
bicycle	1816	Karl D. von Sauerbronn	Germany
bifocal lens	1780	Benjamin Franklin	U.S.
blast furnace	1828	J. B. Neilson	Scotland
bottlemaking machine	1903	Michael Owens	U.S.
Braille	1829	Louis Braille	France
breech-loading rifle	1810	John Hall	U.S.
bubble chamber	1952	Donald A. Glaser	U.S.
bulldozer	1923	unknown	U.S.
bullet (rifle)	1849	Claude E. Minié	France
Bunsen burner	1855	Robert W. Bunsen	Germany
calculating machine (digital)	1823	Charles Babbage	England
camera (photographic)	1822	Joseph N. Niepce	France
carburetor	1892	Gottlieb Daimler	Germany
cash register	1879	James Ritty	U.S.
cathode-ray tube	1878	William Crookes	England
cellophane	c. 1900	Jacques Brandenberger	Switzerland
celluloid	1855	Alexander Parkes	England
cement (portland)	1824	Joseph Aspdin	England
chronometer	1735	John Harrison	England
clock (pendulum)	1656	Christiaan Huygens	Holland
cloud chamber	1911	Charles T. R. Wilson	Scotland
color photography	1881	Frederic E. Ives	U.S.
combine (harvesting, threshing, cleaning)	1911	Benjamin Holt	U.S.
compressed-air rock drill	1871	Simon Ingersoll	U.S.
computer (differential analyzer)	1928	Vannevar Bush	U.S.
computer (electronic)	1946	J. Presper Eckert / John W. Mauchly	U.S.
condensed milk	1853	Gail Borden	U.S.
cotton gin	1793	Eli Whitney	U.S.
cylinder lock	1865	Linus Yale, Jr.	U.S.
cultivator	1820	Henry Burden	U.S.
daguerrotype	1837	Louis J. M. Daguerre	France
dictating machine	1885	Charles S. Taintor	U.S.
diesel engine	1892	Rudolf C. K. Diesel	Germany
disc brake	1902	Ferdinand W. Lanchester	England
dynamite	1866	Alfred B. Nobel	Sweden
electric flatiron	1882	Henry W. Seely	U.S.
electric generator	1832	Hippolyte Pixii	France
electric motor	1822	Michael Faraday	England
electric shaver	1928	Jacob Schick	U.S.
electric stove	1896	William S. Hadaway, Jr.	U.S.
electric vacuum cleaner	1907	James M. Spangler	U.S.
electromagnet	1824	William Sturgeon	England
electron microscope	1939	Vladimir K. Zworykin	U.S.
electroplating	1805	Luigi Brugnatelli	Italy
electrotype	1839	Moritz-Hermann Jacobi	Russia
elevator (passenger)	1852	Elisha G. Otis	U.S.
evaporated milk	1880	John B. Meyenberg	U.S.
firearm magazine	1854	Horace Smith and Daniel B. Wesson	U.S.
flanged railway rail	1831	Robert L. Stevens	U.S.
flying shuttle	1733	John Kay	England
frequency-modulation (FM) broadcasting	1933	Edwin H. Armstrong	U.S.
galvanometer	1819	Johann S. C. Schweigger	Germany
gas engine (four-cycle)	1876	Nikolaus August Otto	Germany
geiger counter	1913	Hans W. Geiger	England
glider	1853	George Cayley	England
gramophone (disc record)	1887	Emile Berliner	U.S.
gyrocompass	1911	Elmer A. Sperry	U.S.
halftone engraving process	1886	Frederic E. Ives	U.S.
helicopter (man-carrying)	1907	Paul Cornu	France
holography	1949	Denis Gabor	England
hydraulic press	1795	Joseph Brahmah	England
hydrometer	1768	Antoine Baumé	France
hydroplane	1911	Glenn H. Curtis	U.S.
internal combustion engine	1859	Jean J. E. Lenoir	France
internal combustion engine (high speed)	1880	Gottlieb Daimler	Germany
iron lung	1928	Philip Drinker and Louis A. Shaw	U.S.
jet engine	1937	Frank Whittle	England
kaleidoscope	1816	David Brewster	Scotland
knitting machine	c. 1589	William Lee	England
lamp (incandescent)	1879	Thomas A. Edison	U.S.
lamp (mercury vapor)	1901	Peter C. Hewitt	U.S.
lamp (neon)	1910	Georges Claude	France

Invention	Date	Inventor	Country
laser	1960	Theodore H. Naiman	U.S.
lathe (engine-driven)	1800	Henry Maudslay	England
Leyden jar	1746	John Bevis	England
		Pieter van Musschenbroek	Holland
life preserver	1805	John Edwards	England
lightning rod	1752	Benjamin Franklin	American colonies
linoleum	1860	Frederick Walton	England
linotype	1884	Ottmar Mergenthaler	U.S.
lithography	1798	Aloys Senefelder	Germany
long-playing (LP) record	1948	Peter C. Goldmark	U.S.
machine gun	1862	Richard J. Gatling	U.S.
match (friction)	1827	John Walker	England
match (safety)	1855	J. E. Lundstrom	Sweden
metronome	1816	Johann N. Mälzel	Austria
micrometer	1636	William Gascoigne	England
microphone	c. 1877	Thomas A. Edison	U.S.
microscope	1590	Zacharias Janssen	Holland
miner's lamp	1815	Humphry Davy	England
monotype	1887	Tolbert Lanston	U.S.
motion pictures	1872	Eadweard Muybridge and John D. Isaacs	U.S.
motorcycle	1885	Edward Butler	England
mowing machine	1810	Peter Gaillard	U.S.
multiplying machine	1671	Gottfried W. von Leibniz	Germany
nitroglycerine	c. 1846	Ascanio Sobrero	Italy
nylon	1935	Wallace H. Carothers	U.S.
oleomargarine	1868	Hippolyte Mége-Mouriez	France
parachute	1783	Louis S. Lenormand	France
parking meter	1935	Carlton C. Magee	U.S.
percussion cap	1816	Joshua Shaw	U.S.
phonograph (cylindrical record)	1877	Thomas A. Edison	U.S.
photocell	1895	Julius Elster and Hans Geitel	Germany
phototype-setting machine	1945	E. G. Klingberg Fritz Stadelmann H. R. Freund	U.S.
plow, iron	1784	James Small	England
plow (wooden)	c. 2500 B.C.	unknown	Egypt
polarizing glass (Polaroid)	1932	Edwin H. Land	U.S.
printing press (screw type)	c. 1450	Johann Gutenberg	Germany
printing with movable type	11th century	Pi-sheng	China
prism spectroscope	1859–60	Gustave Kirchhoff and Robert Bunsen	Germany
pump (air)	1650	Otto von Guericke	Germany
radar	1935	Robert A. Watson-Watt	England
radio-telegraph	1895	Guglielmo Marconi	Italy
radio-telephone	1902	Reginald A. Fessenden	U.S.
railway (electric)	1881	Werner von Siemens	Germany
railway signal (block)	1863	Ashbel Welch and Robert Stewart	U.S.
railway sleeping car	1859	George M. Pullman	U.S.
reaper	1826	Patrick Bell	Scotland
refrigerator	1858	Ferdinand Carré	France
revolver	1831	Samuel Colt	U.S.
rifle	1520	August Kotter	Germany
roller bearings	c. 1496	Leonardo da Vinci	Italy
rolling mill	c. 1496	Leonardo da Vinci	Italy
safety pin	1849	Walter Hunt	U.S.
sail	c. 3000 B.C.	unknown	Egypt
saw (circular)	1777	Samuel Miller	England
screw propeller	1804	John C. Stevens	U.S.
self-starter (automobile)	1911	Charles F. Kettering	U.S.

Invention	Date	Inventor	Country
sewing machine	1790	Thomas Saint	England
shrapnel shell	1784	Henry Shrapnel	England
silencer (firearm)	1908	Hiram P. Maxim	U.S.
slide rule	c. 1620	William Oughtred	England
spinning machine	1764	James Hargreaves	England
sprinkler (fire)	1723	Ambrose Godfrey	England
steamboat	1783	Marquis de Jouffroy d'Abbans	France
steam engine	1628	Edward Somerset	England
steam engine (condensing)	1765	James Watt	Scotland
steam hammer	1839	James Nasmyth	Scotland
stereoscope	1838	Charles Wheatstone	England
stereotyping	1725	William Ged	Scotland
stock ticker	1870	Thomas A. Edison	U.S.
storage battery	1803	Johann W. Ritter	Germany
street car	1834	Thomas Davenport	U.S.
submarine detector	1917	Max Mason	U.S.
switchboard	1877	Edgar T. Holmes	U.S.
tank, military	1914	Ernest D. Swinton	England
tape recorder (magnetic)	1899	Valdemar Poulsen	Denmark
telegraph (multiwire)	1809	Samuel T. von Soemmering	Germany
telegraph (single wire)	1835	Samuel F. B. Morse	U.S.
telegraph cable (submarine)	1866	Cyrus W. Field	U.S.
telephone	1876	Alexander G. Bell	U.S.
telescope	1608	Hans Lippershey	Holland
telescope (reflecting)	1661	James Gregory	Scotland
television	1926	James Logie Baird	Scotland
television iconoscope scanner	1938	Vladimir K. Zworykin	U.S.
thermometer (air and water)	c. 1592	Cornelius Drebbel	Holland
thermometer (mercury)	1714	Gabriel D. Fahrenheit	Germany
threshing machine	1732	Michael Menzies	Scotland
tire (pneumatic)	1843	Robert W. Thompson	England
toaster (automatic)	1918	Charles Strite	U.S.
tractor	1825	Robert Keeley	England
transformer (electric)	1885	William Stanley	U.S.
transistor	1948	J. Bardeen W. H. Brattain W. Shockley	U.S.
typecasting machine	1836	David Bruce	U.S.
typewriter	1714	Henry Mill	England
vacuum bottle	1873	James Dewar	England
vacuum tube (diode)	1904	John A. Flemming	England
vacuum tube (triode)	1906	Lee De Forest	U.S.
vulcanized rubber	1839	Charles Goodyear	U.S.
Wankel engine	1957	Felix Wankel	Germany
warship (steam)	c. 1860	John Ericsson	U.S.
washing machine	1858	Hamilton E. Smith	U.S.
weaving machine	1733	John Kay	England
wirephoto	1881	Shelford Bidwell	England
xerography	1948	Chester Carlson	U.S.
X-ray tube (hot-filament)	1913	William D. Coolidge	U.S.
zipper	1893	Whitcomb L. Judson	U.S.

UNITED STATES
POLYCONIC PROJECTION
SCALE OF MILES
0 100 200 300 400
SCALE OF KILOMETRES
0 100 200 300 400
Capitals of Countries
International Boundaries
State Capitals
State Boundaries
Copyright by C. S. HAMMOND & Co., N. Y.

TENNESSEE
MISSISSIPPI
GEORGIA
FLORIDA
GULF OF MEXICO
ALABAMA
MILES
KILOMETERS
State Capitals
County Seats
Longitude West of Greenwich
Copyright HAMMOND INCORPORATED, Maplewood, N.J.
CHICKAMAUGA AND CHATTANOOGA NAT'L MIL. PK.
KENNESAW MT. NAT'L BATTLEFIELD PK.
HORSESHOE BEND NAT'L MIL. PK.
WALTER F. GEORGE DAM
PICKWICK LANDING DAM
COLBERT
LAUDERDALE
LIMESTONE
MADISON
JACKSON
DE KALB
FRANKLIN
LAWRENCE
MORGAN
MARSHALL
MARION
WINSTON
CULLMAN
ETOWAH
CHEROKEE
WALKER
BLOUNT
ST. CLAIR
CALHOUN
FAYETTE
JEFFERSON
LAMAR
CLEBURNE
PICKENS
TUSCALOOSA
SHELBY
TALLADEGA
CLAY
RANDOLPH
GREENE
BIBB
COOSA
CHAMBERS
HALE
PERRY
CHILTON
TALLAPOOSA
LEE
SUMTER
AUTAUGA
ELMORE
MACON
RUSSELL
DALLAS
MONTGOMERY
BULLOCK
MARENGO
LOWNDES
BARBOUR
CHOCTAW
WILCOX
BUTLER
PIKE
CRENSHAW
DALE
HENRY
CLARKE
MONROE
COFFEE
WASHINGTON
CONECUH
COVINGTON
GENEVA
HOUSTON
ESCAMBIA
MOBILE
BALDWIN
Birmingham
Montgomery
Mobile
Huntsville
Tuscaloosa
Decatur
Gadsden
Florence
Sheffield
Muscle Shoals
Tuscumbia
Russellville
Hamilton
Jasper
Cullman
Guntersville
Ft. Payne
Albertville
Boaz
Attalla
Anniston
Jacksonville
Oxford
Heflin
Talladega
Sylacauga
Alexander City
Opelika
Auburn
Phenix City
Columbus
Selma
Prattville
Wetumpka
Tuskegee
Union Springs
Eufaula
Troy
Enterprise
Ozark
Dothan
Andalusia
Opp
Brewton
Atmore
Greenville
Camden
Monroeville
Evergreen
Andalusia
Bay Minette
Prichard
Chickasaw
Gulf Shores
Dauphin Island
Pensacola
Chattahoochee
Bainbridge
Atlanta
Rome
Cartersville
LaGrange
Columbus
Buena Vista
Cuthbert
Donaldsonville
Chattanooga
Cleveland
Dalton
Ellijay
Corinth
Booneville
Amory
Aberdeen
Columbus
Macon
Lauderdale
Pascagoula
Santa Rosa Island
Mobile Bay
Mississippi Sound
Ft. Walton Beach
Crestview
De Funiak Springs
Valparaiso
Lake Seminole
Lake Eufaula
Weiss Res.
Guntersville L.
Wheeler Lake
Logan Martin Lake
Lay Lake
Martin L.
Cheaha Mtn. 2,407
Tombigbee R.
Alabama R.
Black Warrior R.
Coosa R.
Tallapoosa R.
Chattahoochee River
Perdido R.
Escambia R.
Conecuh R.
Pea R.
Choctawhatchee R.
Sepulga R.
Cahaba R.
Sipsey R.
Tennessee R.
Pickwick Lake
Bankhead L.
L. M. Smith L.
Demopolis Lake
N
ALABAMA

THE FIFTY STATES

See pages 182 and 183 for selected 1980 Census population figures.

ALABAMA

Site of the first Confederate capital in the proverbial "Heart of Dixie," Alabama is a traditionally agricultural state in the Southern mold. A continuing concerted drive toward greater economic diversification in the state began in the 1930s, after costly boll weevil infestations and other problems demonstrated that the state was relying too heavily on cotton. Today, Birmingham has become the South's largest iron and steel producing center, while the Redstone Arsenal and George C. Marshall Space Flight Center in Huntsville have emerged as important research installations; in a single decade (1950-60), Huntsville's population more than quadrupled.

Hydroelectric power provided by the Tennessee Valley Authority has been a key factor in Alabama's growing industrialization. Tourist attractions include the Mound State Monument (Moundsville) and the George Washington Carver Museum at Tuskegee Institute, a school founded by Booker T. Washington, a former slave.

The state's diverse topography ranges from the Appalachian highlands in the northeast to the broad coastal plain comprising about two-thirds of the total area; in the plain's central region is the fertile "Black Belt." Swamps, bayous, and sandy beaches also mark the varied terrain. The state's abbreviated coastline is dominated by Mobile Bay; Dauphin Island lies at the bay's entrance. About 65 percent of the state is forested.

Mound Builders, who lived in the Alabama region in prehistoric times, were followed by a number of Indian tribes, including the Chickasaws, Cherokees, and Creeks. Spaniards Cabeza de Vaca and Hernando De Soto were among the region's early European explorers. The first permanent European settlement was made (1702) by Frenchmen at Fort Louis near present-day Mobile; it served as the capital of the Louisiana Territory until 1722. Other French settlements followed, but in 1763 France lost the region to the British.

After the American Revolution, England ceded to the United States all of the Alabama region except the southernmost British West Florida area that included Mobile; this region, together with East Florida, went to Spain.

In 1817, after a short period as part of the Territory of Mississippi, the region was organized as the Alabama Territory. Settlers spurred by the virtual ending of Indian troubles in the area helped the new territory's growth; statehood came in 1819. Slave-supported plantation farming, aided by the recent invention of the cotton gin, soon emerged as the main factor in the state's economy.

Alabama seceded from the Union and joined the Confederacy in 1861; Montgomery was briefly the Confederate capital. The state suffered a great deal from both the Civil War and the harsh, chaotic Reconstruction.

In the middle of the twentieth century, there were spectacular and sometimes bloody confrontations between supporters and opponents of racial segregation. Martin Luther King, Jr., led opponents of segregation in a boycott of Montgomery buses in 1955-56, in the 1963 demonstrations in Birmingham, and in a march from Selma to Montgomery in 1965. In 1978, a suspect in the 1963 bombing of a black church in Birmingham was convicted, and, in 1980, the state reopened its investigation of the murder of Viola Liuzzo during the Selma-to-Montgomery march. Democratic Governor George Wallace retired from politics in 1979 and was succeeded by Forrest James, a Democrat with no segregationist identity.

The U.S. Supreme Court in a nationally important 1980 decision ruled that the city of Mobile could select its officials through *at-large* elections.

Alabama ranked second only to Missouri in lives lost during the heat wave in summer 1980. The unofficial death toll as of July 20 stood at 121.

Full name: State of Alabama. **Origin of name:** From the Indian, Alba Amo meaning "I Clear the Thicket." **Inhabitant:** Alabamian. **Capital:** Montgomery. **State motto:** Andemus Jura Nostra Defendere (We Dare Defend Our Rights). **Flag:** Red cross of St. Andrew on white field. **Seal:** A circled map of Alabama with boundaries & rivers. **Flower:** Camellia. **Bird:** Yellowhammer. **Tree:** Southern pine. **Song:** "Alabama." **Nickname:** Yellowhammer State and The Heart of Dixie.

Governor: Forrest James, Jr. **Annual salary:** $50,000. **Term:** 4 years. **Current term expires:** Jan. 1983. **Voting requirements:** 18 yrs. old & U.S. citizen; resident of state 10 days. **U.S. Congressmen:** 7 **Entered Union:** 1819 (22nd state).

Location & boundaries: Southeastern state: bounded on the north by Tennessee; on the east by the Chattahoochee River & Georgia; on the south by Florida & the Gulf of Mexico; & on the west by Mississippi. **Total area:** 51,609 sq. mi. (ranks 29th). **Extreme length:** 330 mi. **Extreme breadth:** 200 mi. **Coastline:** 53 mi. **Chief rivers:** Mobile, Alabama, Tombigbee, Coosa. **Major lakes:** Wheeler, Guntersville, Wilson, Martin, Mitchell. **No. of counties:** 67.

Population (1979 est.): 3,769,000 (ranks 22nd). **Pop. increase (1970-79):** 9.4%. **Places over 25,000 pop.:** 15. **Places over 100,000:** 4. **Largest cities:** Birmingham, Mobile, Montgomery. **Pop. density:** 73.0 per sq. mi. (ranks 26th). **Pop. projection 1985:** 3,958,000. **Pop. distribution:** 61.8% metropolitan; 38.2% nonmetropolitan. **White:** 73.4%. **Black:** 26.4%. **Other:** 0.2%. **Marriage rate (1977):** 12.3 per 1,000 people. **Divorce rate:** 6.4 per 1,000 people.

State finances (1978). Revenue: $3,385,436,000. **Expenditures:** $3,251,165,000. **State taxes:** $424.58 per capita. **State personal income tax:** Yes. **Public debt (1978):** $267.22 per capita. **Federal aid (1979):** $356.04 per capita. **Personal income (1979 est.):** $6,976.

Sectors of the economy (% of labor force employed in 1970): Manufacturing (29%), Wholesale & retail trade (19%), Government (17%), Services (9%), Educational Services (7%), Construction (7%). **Leading products:** primary & fabricated metals, transportation equipment, machinery, food, textiles, apparel, paper, chemicals. **Minerals:** coal, cement, stone, petroleum. **Agricultural products:** broilers, cattle, eggs, corn, soybeans, peanuts. **Fishing:** shrimp, red snappers, blue crabs. **Avg. farm (1979 est.):** 236 acres. **Avg. value of farm per acre:** $515.

Highway expenditures per capita (1978): $104.47. **Persons per motor vehicle:** 1.32. **Minimum age for driver's license:** 16. **Gasoline tax:** 11¢ per gallon. **Diesel tax:** 12¢ per gallon. **Motor vehicle deaths:** 30.7 per 100,000 people.

Birthrate (1978): 16.2 per 1,000 people. **Infant mortality rate per 1,000 births (1977):** 16.9. **Physicians per 100,000 pop. (1977):** 117. **Dentists per 100,000 pop. (1977):** 32. **Acceptable hospital beds:** 6.8 per 1,000 people. **State expenditures per capita for health and hospitals (1978):** $70.10.

Education expenditures (1975-76): $369.88 per capita annually. **No. of pupils in public schools (1976 est.):** 741,000. **No. of institutions of higher learning (1976-77):** 56. **Public school expenditure per pupil in attendance (1975-76):** $1,195. **Avg. salary of public school teachers (1974-75 est.):** $9,503. **No. full-time teachers (1977 est.):** 39,790. **Educational attainment of adult population (1976):** 12.2 median yrs. of school completed; 6.8% with less than 5 years of education; 10.2% with 4 yrs. of college.

Telephones (1977): 62 per 100 people. **State Chamber of Commerce:** Alabama Chamber of Commerce, 468 South Perry Street, P.O. Box 76, Montgomery, Alabama 36101.

ALASKA

Alaska is a land of great extremes: first among the states in area, last in population. One of the na-

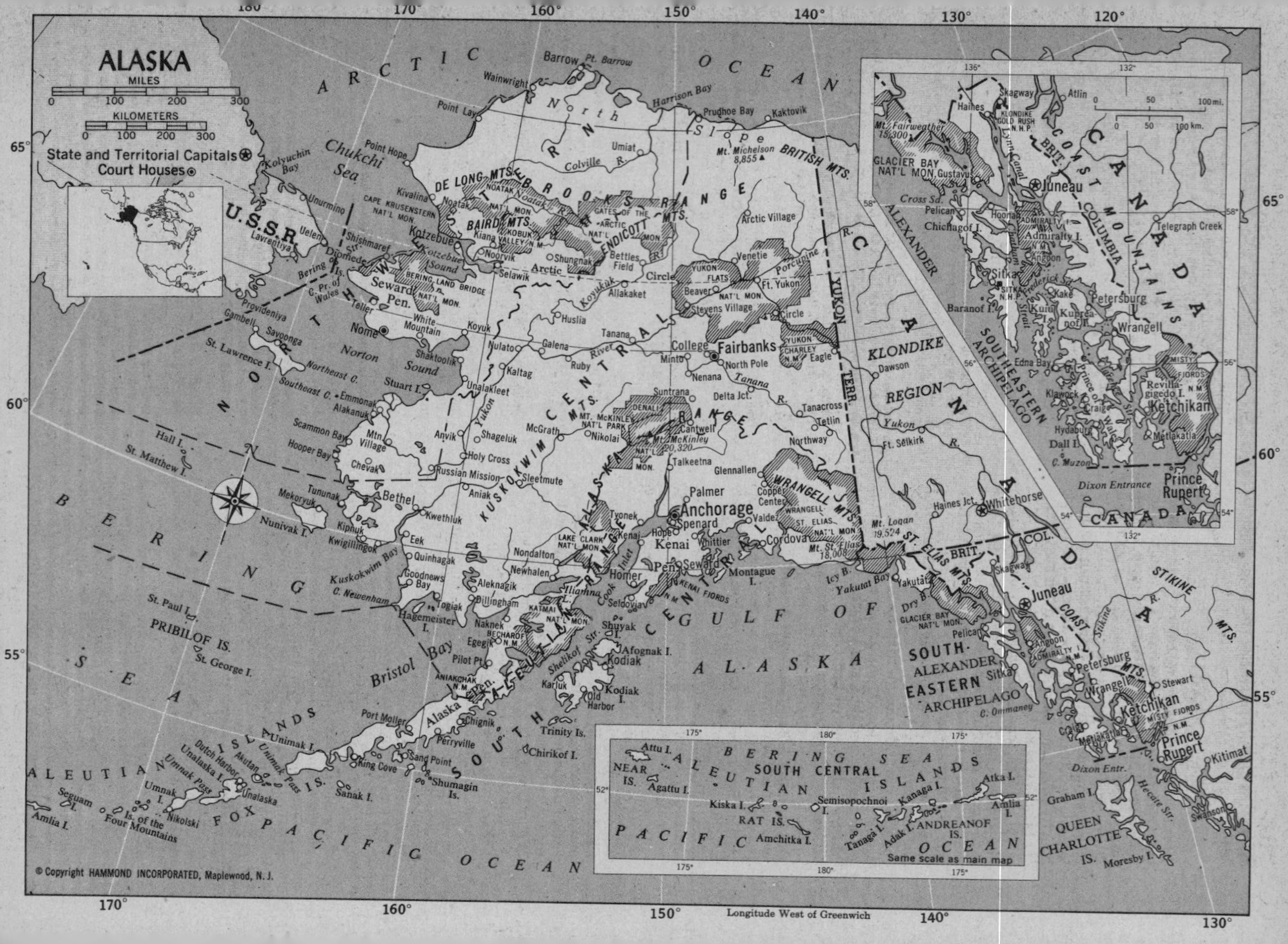
ALASKA
MILES
KILOMETERS
State and Territorial Capitals
Court Houses
Copyright HAMMOND INCORPORATED, Maplewood, N.J.
Longitude West of Greenwich
ARCTIC OCEAN
PACIFIC OCEAN
GULF OF ALASKA
BERING SEA
U.S.S.R.
CANADA
BRITISH COLUMBIA
YUKON TERR.
COAST MOUNTAINS
BROOKS RANGE
ALASKA RANGE
CENTRAL MTS.
DE LONG MTS.
BAIRD MTS.
ENDICOTT MTS.
WRANGELL MTS.
ST. ELIAS MTS.
KUSKOKWIM MTS.
BRITISH MTS.
STIKINE MTS.
NORTON SOUND
KOTZEBUE SOUND
Chukchi Sea
North Slope
SEWARD PEN.
ALEUTIAN RANGE
ALEUTIAN ISLANDS
NEAR IS.
RAT IS.
ANDREANOF IS.
FOX IS.
PRIBILOF IS.
SOUTHEASTERN ARCHIPELAGO
SOUTH-ALEXANDER EASTERN ARCHIPELAGO
ALEXANDER ARCHIPELAGO
KLONDIKE REGION
Barrow
Pt. Barrow
Wainwright
Point Lay
Point Hope
Prudhoe Bay
Kaktovik
Harrison Bay
Umiat
Colville R.
Mt. Michelson 8,855
Kivalina
Noatak
Kotzebue
Noorvik
Shungnak
Bettles Field
Venetie
Porcupine
Ft. Yukon
Circle
Beaver
Stevens Village
Allakaket
Koyukuk
Huslia
Tanana
Nulato
Galena
Ruby
Minto
North Pole
Nenana
College
Fairbanks
Eagle
Dawson
Ft. Selkirk
Yukon R.
Delta Jct.
Tanacross
Tetlin
Northway
Glennallen
Copper Center
Valdez
Cordova
Mt. Logan 19,524
Mt. St. Elias 18,008
Yakutat Bay
Yakutat
Icy B.
Dry B.
Haines Jct.
Whitehorse
Skagway
Juneau
Haines
Atlin
Telegraph Creek
Mt. Fairweather 15,300
Glacier Bay Nat'l Mon.
Gustavus
Pelican
Hoonah
Sitka
Chichagof I.
Baranof I.
Admiralty I.
Angoon
Kake
Kupreanof I.
Petersburg
Wrangell
Prince of Wales I.
Craig
Klawock
Hydaburg
Dall I.
C. Muzon
Ketchikan
Metlakatla
Prince Rupert
Kitimat
Stewart
Queen Charlotte Is.
Moresby I.
Graham I.
Hecate Str.
Dixon Entrance
Unurmino
Uelen
Lavrentiya
Providenya
Gambell
Savoonga
St. Lawrence I.
Northeast C.
Southeast C.
Emmonak
Alakanuk
Scammon Bay
Hooper Bay
Chevak
Mtn. Village
Shageluk
Holy Cross
Russian Mission
Sleetmute
Aniak
Bethel
Kwethluk
Eek
Quinhagak
Goodnews Bay
C. Newenham
Togiak
Hagemeister I.
Hall I.
St. Matthew I.
Nunivak I.
Mekoryuk
Tununak
Kipnuk
Kwigillingok
Kuskokwim Bay
Shishmaref
Teller
Nome
White Mountain
Koyuk
Shaktoolik
Unalakleet
Kaltag
Stuart I.
McGrath
Nikolai
Cantwell
Mt. McKinley 20,320
Denali Nat'l Mon.
Mt. McKinley Nat'l Park
Talkeetna
Palmer
Anchorage
Spenard
Tyonek
Kenai
Hope
Whittier
Seward
Homer
Kenai Pen.
Cook Inlet
Lake Clark Nat'l Mon.
Nondalton
Newhalen
Iliamna L.
Seldovia
Montague I.
Kenai Fjords
Nikiski
Katmai Nat'l Mon.
Aniakchak N.M.
Naknek
Egegik
Becharof N.M.
King Salmon
Dillingham
Aleknagik
Pilot Pt.
Port Moller
Sand Point
Perryville
Chignik
King Cove
Shumagin Is.
Sanak I.
Unimak I.
Unimak Pass
Dutch Harbor
Akutan
Unalaska
Umnak
Umnak Pass
Nikolski
Is. of the Four Mountains
Seguam I.
Amlia I.
Kodiak
Old Harbor
Karluk
Afognak I.
Shuyak I.
Trinity Is.
Chirikof I.
Shelikof Str.
St. Paul I.
St. George I.
Bristol Bay
Attu I.
Agattu I.
Kiska I.
Amchitka I.
Semisopochnoi I.
Kanaga I.
Tanaga I.
Adak I.
Atka I.
Amlia I.
Cross Sd.
Edna Bay
Misty Fjords N.M.
Revillagigedo I.
Stikine R.

tion's biggest bargains (Alaska's purchase price was less than 2¢ an acre), it is potentially one of the richest states—particularly in view of the spectacular oil strikes in Prudhoe Bay off the state's frigid Arctic (or North) Slope. Many believe that these strikes will fulfill the century-long promise of "The Last Frontier"; the find has already been called "one of the largest petroleum accumulations known to the world today." In 1969 about $900 million was bid for oil-land leases.

During the next decade, oil revenues so glutted state coffers that in April 1980 the state enacted a plan to share the wealth directly with Alaska's 400,000 residents. The state income tax was virtually abolished and each Alaskan was to receive annually at least $50 for every year he lived in the state since 1959. In early September 1980, the Alaska Supreme Court struck down the law which would have brought these plans to fruition. Later that month the State Legislature voted overwhelmingly to repeal the state personal income tax. The State Supreme Court has yet to rule on the share-the-wealth plan enacted earlier this year.

Alaska's awesome terrain has long challenged explorers and settlers. The state, which entered the Union in 1959, is cut into isolated areas by its craggy coast and high mountains, principally the Brooks Range in the north (an extension of the Rocky Mountains) and the Alaska Range in the south, which includes Mount McKinley, the highest peak in North America.

Sticking out into the sea in the northwest is the Seward Peninsula. Off the peninsula, in the Bering Strait, is U.S.-owned Little Diomede Island, separated from the USSR's Big Diomede by about two miles. Alaska is separated from the nearest state, Washington, by about 500 miles.

The Alaskan climate is widely variable. The southeast coast, protected by mountains from the north winds and influenced by the warm Japan Current, is generally temperate and rainy, while interior summers are short and very hot (with exceptionally long days), and the winters very cold.

Captain Vitus Bering, a Dane who explored for Russia, is thought to have been the first white man to visit Alaska (1741), after passing close to it on an earlier voyage. At this time there were about 75,000 Indians, Eskimos, and Aleuts in Alaska; some prehistoric campsites date back to the Ice Age.

Though several nations tried to get a foothold in the region, mainly for the trade in sea otter pelts it might support, Russia prevailed, establishing Alaska's first white settlement on Kodiak Island in 1784. By the 1850s, Russia, facing increased competition from Americans, British, and Canadians, plus a dwindling supply of fur-bearing animals, wanted to sell. In 1867, U.S. Secretary of State William H. Seward agreed to buy—for $7.2 million—thereby becoming a target of ridicule. Many Americans dubbed Alaska "Seward's Folly" or "Seward's Icebox," considering it a frozen wasteland that was relatively valueless.

But gold was discovered (1896) at Klondike in neighboring Yukon Territory, and in Alaska itself at Nome (1899) and at Fairbanks (1902). Settlement was spurred as prospectors poured in and the economy was strengthened—but the lasting gains were few.

During World War II, the region's importance as a military outpost was dramatized when the Japanese briefly occupied some of the Aleutians—the war's only North American enemy occupation. Today, Alaska contains the Distant Early Warning system (DEW line) and other defense installations, including military bases. Roughly half the state's personal income is from government sources, and 97 percent of the land is Federally owned.

With a long coastline punctuated by many bays and fjords, Alaska is a leading state in commercial fishing. Forest products account for a considerable share of the state's revenue, while the value of agricultural products remains for more potential than actual. Only a small fraction of the state's potential cropland of 2 to 3 million acres has so far been developed. Tourism is a major industry.

On Good Friday, March 27, 1964, an exceptionally powerful earthquake struck the south-central part of the state, killing 114 and causing property damage estimated at $750 million.

In 1971 Congres passed the Alaska Native Land Claims Settlement Act to extinguish the nearly 100-year old claims of Alaska's 55,000 Eskimos, Indians and Aleuts by providing 40 million acres of land and approximately $925 million in compensation. An enrollment of eligible natives began in 1972.

Construction on the $4.5 billion Trans-Alaska pipeline project, first proposed in 1969 and delayed by legal suits brought by environmentalists finally began in 1974. In June 1977 oil began to flow from Prudhoe Bay on the Arctic Ocean through the 799-mile, 48-inch hot-oil pipeline to the Gulf of Alaska port of Valdez. To get that oil to the American consumer, President Carter in January 1980 announced plans for a pipeline to extend from a Washington state port, where it was to receive oil from Alaska by sea, to Minnesota.

A proposed trans-Canadian pipeline to deliver natural gas from the Alaskan North Slope to the lower forty-eight states has been approved by the United States and Canada. In January 1980 the Alberta Gas Trunk Line Co., Ltd. announced plans to begin construction of a segment of the pipeline from Calgary to the U.S. border, while the Pacific Gas and Electric Co. was expected to extend the line to Oregon.

In 1979 the House of Representatives approved a land bill which set aside 126 million acres for 13 national parks, 21 wildlife refuges, 112 wild and scenic rivers and two national forest wildernesses. Of the 76 million acres designated for wildlife refuges, 67 million were classified as wilderness where neither commercial activity nor mechanized vehicles would be permitted. The approval of this bill was a blow to industry because it prevented much of the development of the economic potential in the area. Developers received another setback in February 1980, when the Interior Department imposed environmental restrictions on 40 million Federal acres to the end of the century.

Plans begun in 1974 to move the capital of Alaska from Juneau to Willow, a site chosen in 1977, have been delayed by the Alaska Legislature. State Senator Bill Ray and his supporters have blocked the move, citing the high cost to the Alaskans. The deadline for the proposal is October 1980.

Full name: State of Alaska. **Origin of name:** From Aleutian word meaning "Great Land." **Inhabitant:** Alaskan. **Capital:** Juneau. **State motto:** North to the Future. **Flag:** Blue field with seven gold stars, representing the Big Dipper; eighth star represents the North Star. **Seal:** Rising sun shines on lake, fishing boat, merchant ship, forests, mining & agricultural activities, symbols of Alaskan resources & occupations. **Flower:** Forget-me-not. **Bird:** Willow ptarmigan. **Tree:** Sitka spruce. **Song:** "Alaska's Flag." **Nickname:** The Great Land.

Governor: Jay S. Hammond. **Annual salary:** $70,068. **Term:** 4 years. **Current term expires:** Dec. 1982. **Voting requirements:** 18 yrs. old & U.S. citizen; resident of state 10 days. **U.S. Congressman:** 1. **Entered Union:** 1959 (49th state).

Location & boundaries: Pacific state: bounded on the north by the Arctic Ocean; on the east by Canada; on the south by the Pacific

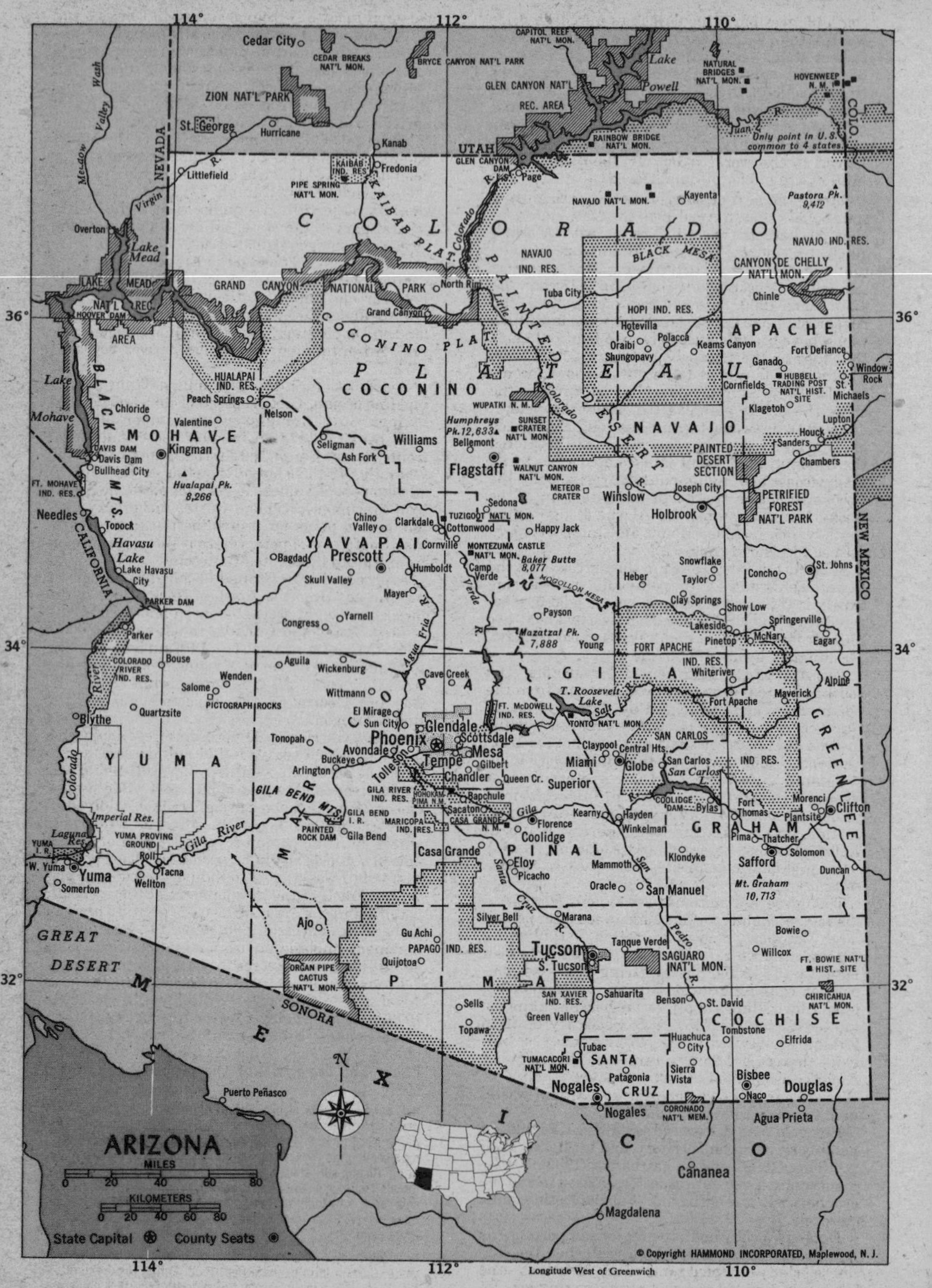
ARIZONA
MILES
0 20 40 60 80
KILOMETERS
0 20 40 60 80
State Capital ⊛   County Seats ●
© Copyright HAMMOND INCORPORATED, Maplewood, N.J.
Longitude West of Greenwich
114°   112°   110°

NEVADA
UTAH
COLORADO
NEW MEXICO
CALIFORNIA
SONORA
MEXICO

Cedar City
CEDAR BREAKS NAT'L MON.
ZION NAT'L PARK
BRYCE CANYON NAT'L PARK
CAPITOL REEF NAT'L MON.
GLEN CANYON NAT'L REC. AREA
Lake Powell
NATURAL BRIDGES NAT'L MON.
HOVENWEEP N. M.
St. George
Hurricane
Kanab
RAINBOW BRIDGE NAT'L MON.
Only point in U.S. common to 4 states.
Littlefield
KAIBAB IND. RES.
Fredonia
PIPE SPRING NAT'L MON.
GLEN CANYON DAM
Page
NAVAJO NAT'L MON.
Kayenta
Pastora Pk. 9,412
Overton
Lake Mead
NAVAJO IND. RES.
BLACK MESA
CANYON DE CHELLY NAT'L MON.
LAKE MEAD NAT'L REC. AREA
HOOVER DAM
GRAND CANYON NATIONAL PARK
North Rim
Tuba City
NAVAJO IND. RES.
Chinle
APACHE
Lake Mohave
Grand Canyon
HOPI IND. RES.
Hotevilla
Oraibi
Shungopavy
Polacca
Keams Canyon
Fort Defiance
Ganado
Chloride
HUALAPAI IND. RES.
Peach Springs
Nelson
WUPATKI N. M.
Cornfields
HUBBELL TRADING POST NAT'L HIST. SITE
St. Michaels
Window Rock
Valentine
Seligman
Williams
Humphreys Pk. 12,633
Bellemont
SUNSET CRATER NAT'L MON.
NAVAJO
Klagetoh
Lupton
DAVIS DAM
Davis Dam
Kingman
Ash Fork
Flagstaff
WALNUT CANYON NAT'L MON.
Houck
Sanders
Bullhead City
Hualapai Pk. 8,266
METEOR CRATER
Winslow
Joseph City
PAINTED DESERT SECTION
Chambers
FT. MOHAVE IND. RES.
BLACK MTS.
Sedona
Holbrook
PETRIFIED FOREST NAT'L PARK
Needles
Topock
Chino Valley
Clarkdale
TUZIGOOT NAT'L MON.
Happy Jack
Havasu Lake
Cottonwood
Cornville
MONTEZUMA CASTLE NAT'L MON.
Baker Butte 8,077
Snowflake
St. Johns
Lake Havasu City
YAVAPAI
Prescott
Bagdad
Humboldt
Camp Verde
Heber
Taylor
Concho
Skull Valley
Clay Springs
Show Low
PARKER DAM
Mayer
Payson
Lakeside
Springerville
Parker
Congress
Yarnell
MOGOLLON MESA
Mazatzal Pk. 7,888
Young
McNary
Eagar
COLORADO RIVER IND. RES.
Bouse
Aguila
Wickenburg
Cave Creek
GILA
FORT APACHE IND. RES.
Whiteriver
Alpine
Salome
Wenden
Wittmann
T. Roosevelt Lake
Fort Apache
Maverick
Quartzsite
PICTOGRAPH ROCKS
El Mirage
FT. McDOWELL IND. RES.
TONTO NAT'L MON.
Blythe
Sun City
Glendale
Scottsdale
SAN CARLOS
Central Hts.
GREENLEE
YUMA
Tonopah
Avondale
Phoenix
Tempe
Mesa
Claypool
Globe
San Carlos
San Carlos L.
Buckeye
Gilbert
Miami
IND. RES.
Arlington
Tolleson
Chandler
Queen Cr.
Superior
Morenci
GILA BEND MTS.
GILA RIVER IND. RES.
HOHOKAM PIMA N. M.
Bapchule
COOLIDGE DAM
Bylas
Plantsite
Clifton
Imperial Res.
PAINTED ROCK DAM
Sacaton
Gila
CASA GRANDE N. M.
Kearny
Hayden
Fort Thomas
Thatcher
Solomon
Laguna Res.
YUMA PROVING GROUND
Gila Bend I. R.
MARICOPA IND. RES.
Florence
Winkelman
Pima
GRAHAM
YUMA I. R.
Roll
Gila River
Gila Bend
Casa Grande
Coolidge
PINAL
Kearny
Kliondyke
Safford
Duncan
W. Yuma
Yuma
Tacna
Eloy
Picacho
Mammoth
Oracle
San Manuel
Mt. Graham 10,713
Somerton
Wellton
Ajo
Gu Achi
Silver Bell
Marana
Bowie
GREAT
PAPAGO IND. RES.
Quijotoa
Tucson
Tanque Verde
SAGUARO NAT'L MON.
Willcox
FT. BOWIE NAT'L HIST. SITE
DESERT
ORGAN PIPE CACTUS NAT'L MON.
S. Tucson
PIMA
CHIRICAHUA NAT'L MON.
Sells
SAN XAVIER IND. RES.
Sahuarita
Benson
St. David
Puerto Peñasco
Topawa
Green Valley
Huachuca City
Tombstone
Elfrida
COCHISE
TUMACACORI NAT'L MON.
Tubac
SANTA
Patagonia
Sierra Vista
Bisbee
Douglas
Nogales
CRUZ
Naco
Nogales
CORONADO NAT'L MEM.
Agua Prieta
Cananea
Magdalena

Ocean; & on the west by the Bering Sea & Arctic Ocean. **Total area:** 586,412 sq. mi. (ranks 1st). **Extreme length:** 2,200 mi. **Extreme breadth:** 1,200 mi. **Coastline:** 6,640 mi. **Chief rivers:** Yukon, Tanana, Kuskokwim. **Major lakes:** Iliamna, Becharof, Tustumena. **No. of boroughs:** 10.

Population (1979 est.): 406,000 (ranks 50th). **Pop. increase (1970-79):** 34.3%. **Places over 25,000 pop.:** 3. **Places over 100,000:** 1. **Largest cities:** Anchorage, Fairbanks. **Pop. density:** 0.7 per sq. mi. (ranks 50th). **Pop. projection 1985:** 455,000. **Pop. distribution:** 43.7% metropolitan; 56.3% nonmetropolitan. **White:** 78.8%. **Black:** 3%. **Other:** 17.2%. **Marriage rate (1977):** 12.5 per 1,000 people. **Divorce rate:** 8.8 per 1,000 people.

State finances (1978). Revenue: $1,317,902,000. **Expenditures:** $1,289,246,000. **State taxes:** $1,398.25 per capita. **State personal income tax:** No. **Public debt (1978):** $2,799.13 per capita. **Federal aid (1979):** $935.71 per capita. **Personal income (1979 est.):** $11,252.

Sectors of the economy (% of labor force employed in 1970): Government (37%), Wholesale & retail trade (19%), Educational Services (11%), Construction (9%), Services (8%), Manufacturing (7%). **Leading products:** seafood, timber, pulp, oil, gas, petrochemicals. **Minerals:** petroleum & natural gas, coal, sand & gravel. **Agricultural products:** dairy items, eggs, cattle, hay, vegetables, wool. **Fishing:** salmon, halibut, crab, shrimp, scallops. **Avg. farm (1979 est.):** 5,600 acres. **Avg. value of farm per acre:** Not available.

Highway expenditures per capita (1978): $421.59. **Persons per motor vehicle:** 1.51. **Minimum age for driver's license:** 16. **Gasoline tax:** 8¢ per gallon. **Diesel tax:** 8¢ per gallon. **Motor vehicle deaths:** 31.5 per 100,000 people.

Birthrate (1978): 21.6 per 1,000 people. **Infant mortality rate per 1,000 births (1977):** 15.1. **Physicians per 100,000 pop. (1977):** 127. **Dentists per 100,000 pop. (1977):** 55. **Acceptable hospital beds:** 4.1 per 1,000 people. **State expenditures per capita for health and hospitals (1978):** $98.68.

Education expenditures (1975-76): $973.64 per capita annually. **No. of pupils in public schools (1977 est.):** 90,000. **No. of institutions of higher learning (1976-77):** 9. **Public school expenditure per pupil in attendance (1975-76):** $3,710. **Avg. salary of public school teachers (1974-75 est.):** $16,906. **No. full-time teachers (1977 est.):** 4,510. **Educational attainment of adult population (1976):** 12.7 median yrs. of school completed; 2.8% with less than 5 years of education; 17.6% with 4 yrs. of college.

Telephones (1977): 55 per 100 people. **State Chamber of Commerce:** Alaska State Chamber of Commerce, 310 Second Street, Juneau, Alaska 99801.

ARIZONA

Arizona, the last mainland state to join the Union (1912), lies west of the Continental Divide and consists of three general areas: the desert in the southwest, the central highlands, and the Colorado Plateau in the northwest. Almost all of the state is within the Colorado drainage basin. Its principal tourist attraction, the awesome Grand Canyon, is one of the world's natural wonders: a multicolored fissure 217 miles long, four to eight miles wide at the brim, and about a mile deep.

The warm, dry, and reputedly health-restoring climate of the state's southern region—which includes Arizona's two largest cities, Phoenix and Tucson—has made it a popular winter resort area (as well as the site of many senior citizen retirement communities). Tourism is one of the leading industries in Arizona.

In addition to the Grand Canyon, state attractions include Hoover Dam, Lake Mead, 15 national monuments, various Indian villages and reservations (the state has the nation's largest Indian population: about 117,900), the Petrified Forest, and the Painted Desert. A new addition to the list is legendary London Bridge, which a private group has re-erected at Lake Havasu City.

Bolstered by defense contracts, manufacturing has lately become the state's leading industry, followed by mining and agriculture. Arizona produces a number of metals, including more than half of the country's supply of copper.

Mummies and ancient human relics—such as baskets and cloth—have been found in a strikingly well-preserved condition in Arizona. Several Indian cultures lived there from about 25,000 to 10,000 B.C., and the ancestors of the modern Navajos (or Navahos) and Apaches lived in northern Arizona. One of the oldest continuously inhabited settlements in the country, the community of Oraibi was built sometime in the 1100s by Hopi Indians, over 5,000 of whom presently live on a reservation in northeast Arizona. The first white men were 16th-century Spanish explorers. The United States obtained (1848) most of the land from Mexico following the Mexican War; the rest was included in the Gadsden Purchase (1853).

Arizona was organized as a territory in 1863, with the capital at Prescott (1865-67), then Tucson (1867-77), Prescott again (1877-89), and finally at Phoenix. Over many years, various bloody conflicts raged in Arizona—between the whites and the Apaches, whose leaders included the fabled fighters Cochise and Geronimo, between Confederate and Union troops during the Civil War, between labor and management during violent strikes in the mining communities, and between cattlemen and sheepmen in the range wars that continued until the turn of the century. Yet another subject of contention through the years has been the water rights along the Colorado River claimed not only by Arizona but by Nevada and California as well; distribution now follows a 1963 U.S. Supreme Court ruling.

Hopi and Navajo Indians of northeastern Arizona have been feuding for years over ownership of 1.8 million acres of desert plateau which acts as a buffer between the much smaller Hopi reservation and the Navajo nation which surrounds it. The U.S. Supreme Court ruled in the early 1960s that the two tribes should share the land equally, but Congress has failed to resolve the matter.

In 1979 Governor Babbitt declared a state emergency after it was discovered that a Tucson plant manufacturing tritium (used to make illuminated watch dials and signs) was leaking radioactivity. National Guardsmen seized the plant and confiscated more than 1,000 gallons of tritium.

Full name: State of Arizona. **Origin of name:** From the Indian, Alekzon, meaning "Small Spring." **Inhabitant:** Arizonan. **Capital:** Phoenix. **State motto:** Ditat Deus (God Enriches). **Flag:** A copper-colored star centered on radiating red & yellow stripes & a horizontal blue bar. **Seal:** Miner standing in mountains symbolizes state's mineral industry; irrigated fields & cow represent agriculture. **Flower:** Saguaro cactus. **Bird:** Cactus wren. **Tree:** Paloverde. **Song:** "Arizona." **Nickname:** Grand Canyon State.

Governor: Bruce E. Babbitt. **Annual salary:** $50,000. **Term:** 4 years. **Current term expires:** Jan. 1983. **Voting requirements:** 18 yrs. old & U.S. citizen; resident of state 50 days. **U.S. Congressmen:** 4. **Entered Union:** 1912 (48th state).

Location & boundaries: Southwestern state: bounded on the north by Utah; on the east by New Mexico; on the south by Mexico; & on the west by Baja California (Mexico), the Colorado River, California & Nevada. **Total area:** 113,909 sq. mi. (ranks 6th). **Extreme length:** 395 mi. **Extreme breadth:** 340 mi. **Chief rivers:** Colorado, Little Colorado, Gila. **Major lakes:** Mohave, Theodore Roosevelt, Lake Mead. No. of counties: 14.

Population (1979 est.): 2,450,000 (ranks 30th). **Pop. increase (1970-79):** 38.0%. **Places over 25,000 pop.:** 7. **Places over 100,000:** 3. **Largest cities:** Tucson, Phoenix, Mesa. **Pop. density:** 21.5 per sq. mi. (ranks 40th). **Pop. projection 1985:** 2,926,000. **Pop. distribution:** 74.7% metropolitan; 25.3% nonmetropolitan. **White:** 91.1%. **Black:** 3%. **Indian:** 5.4%. **Other:** 0.5%. **Marriage rate (1977):** 12.3 per 1,000 people. **Divorce rate:** 7.2 per 1,000 people.

ARKANSAS
MILES
KILOMETERS
State Capital   County Seats
Longitude West of Greenwich
© Copyright HAMMOND INCORPORATED, Maplewood, N.J.

State finances (1978). Revenue: $2,423,112,000. **Expenditures:** $2,067,347,000. **State Taxes:** $555.37 per capita. **State personal income tax:** Yes. **Public debt (1978):** $41.62 per capita. **Federal aid (1979):** $324.00 per capita. **Personal income (1979 est.):** $8,305.

Sectors of the economy (% of labor force employed in 1974): Wholesale & retail trade (21%), Government (19%), Services (15%), Manufacturing (14%), Educational Services (8%), Construction (7%). **Leading products:** electrical & other machinery; transportation equipment; food; primary metals; printing & publishing; stone, clay & glass products. **Minerals:** copper, sand & gravel, molybdenum, silver, cement. **Agricultural products:** cattle, dairy products, cotton lint, hay, lettuce. **Avg. farm (1979 est.):** 6,983 acres. **Avg. value of farm per acre:** $691.

Highway expenditures per capita (1978): $111.85. **Persons per motor vehicle:** 1.38. **Minimum age for driver's license:** 16. **Gasoline tax:** 8¢ per gallon. **Diesel tax:** 8¢ per gallon. **Motor vehicle deaths:** 43.6 per 100,000 people.

Birthrate (1978): 18.2 per 1,000 people. **Infant mortality rate per 1,000 births (1977):** 13.5. **Physicians per 100,000 pop. (1977):** 87. **Dentists per 100,000 pop. (1977):** 48. **Acceptable hospital beds:** 4.8 per 1,000 people. **State expenditures per capita for health and hospitals (1978):** $47.73.

Education expenditures (1975-76): $524.21 per capita annually. **No. of pupils in public schools (1977 est.):** 495,000. **No. of institutions of higher learning (1976-77):** 22. **Public school expenditure per pupil in attendance (1975-76):** $1,753. **Avg. salary of public school teachers (1974-75 est.):** $11,168. **No. full-time teachers (1977 est.):** 24,810. **Educational attainment of adult population (1976):** 12.6 median yrs. of school completed; 3.3% with less than 5 years of education; 15.7% with 4 yrs. of college.

Telephones (1977): 70 per 100 people. **State Chamber of Commerce:** Arizona State Chamber of Commerce, 3216 N. Third Street, Suite 103, Phoenix, Arizona 85012.

ARKANSAS

Gracing the Arkansas terrain are rugged hills, scenic valleys and streams, and impressive hardwood and pine forests. In the south and east are the generally flat West Gulf Coastal and Mississippi Alluvial Plains, while highlands make up the northwestern region. Magazine Mountain (2,853 feet) is the state's highest point. About three-fifths of the land is wooded, forming the basis for a sizable timber industry. Resources include two large national forests, the Ozark and Ouachita.

Arkansas ranks among the national leaders in cotton, rice, soybean and livestock production; it also contains one of the world's most famous spas (Hot Springs), as well as North America's first diamond mine, near Murfreesboro. No longer commercially operative, the mine is today a state park, popular among tourists; anyone finding a diamond there (up to five carats) is allowed to keep it. Excellent hunting and fishing also contribute to the state's increasingly significant tourism business as do such attractions as the Old Arsenal in Little Rock's MacArthur Park, which marks the birthplace of one of the most famous of Arkansans, General Douglas MacArthur.

The production of oil, the state's major mineral, is another important element in the economy. Arkansas is the nation's chief producer of bauxite ore, from which aluminum is extracted. A further vital asset is an abundant water supply, convertible to hydroelectric power. A modern navigational system on the Arkansas River connects the Gulf of Mexico and Little Rock, now a foreign trade zone, the 14th such zone established in the United States, and the only one on an inland waterway.

The so-called Bluff Dwellers of about A.D. 500 are considered to have been the first inhabitants of the Arkansas region, followed by the culturally superior Mound Builders and, later, by Quapaw, Osage, and Caddo Indians.

The first Europeans to visit (1541) the area were Spanish explorers led by Hernando De Soto. Frenchmen arrived more than a century later: Marquette and Jolliet exploring (1673) the land around the mouth of the Arkansas River, and La Salle claiming (1682) for France the Arkansas region and the rest of the Mississippi Valley. In 1686, Henri de Tonti, established Arkansas Post, the first permanent settlement. The United States obtained all of what is now Arkansas as part of the Louisiana Purchase (1803).

Much of the region's early history is shared with Louisiana, of which it was a part until 1812, when it was attached to the Territory of Missouri. Settlement was spurred by the cotton boom of 1818, and a year later Arkansas Territory, incorporating part of present-day Oklahoma, was created. The 1830s saw the emergence of the slavery-supported plantation system as the state's primary economic force. The virtual absence of Indian troubles encouraged immigration, and between 1830 and 1840 population tripled.

Statehood came (1836) at a time when the slavery issue was more and more seriously dividing the nation. In March 1861, the Arkansas convention voted to remain in the Union, but when President Lincoln asked for troops, the state refused and two months later decided to secede. Many relatively small battles were fought in the state, and from 1864-65 there existed two separate state governments: one at Little Rock controlled by the Union and a Confederate one at Washington, Arkansas. Recovery in the postwar period was slow in coming, and not helped by the violence-engendering struggle (1872-74) for the governorship between Republicans Elisha Baxter and Joseph Brooks, a struggle won by Baxter only after Presidential intervention.

On the cultural scene, the Arkansas Arts Center in Little Rock offers exhibits, plays, and classes in painting, sculpture, dance, photography, music and drama. The Arkansas Symphony Orchestra was established in 1966.

In addition to a fine public school system, there is the Arkansas School for the Deaf, established about 1866 as the Arkansas Deaf-Mute Institute, and the Arkansas School for the Blind. Arkansas Enterprises for the Blind opened in 1947 a rehabilitation center providing personal adjustment, pre-vocational and vocational training for the blind and visually impaired. It has served persons from the fifty states and over twenty-four foreign countries.

In 1966 the state made political history by electing a transplanted New Yorker, Winthrop Rockefeller (now deceased), governor on the Republican ticket, climaxing a six-year effort on his part to build a two-party system in this traditionally Democratic state. Rockefeller served two terms, but lost to a political unknown, Dale Bumpers, in a third term bid in 1970.

In November 1978, Pine Bluff was chosen for the location of a proposed nerve gas plant. According to the plan, production of nerve gas shells and bombs probably would not begin before 1982.

In May and June 1980 thousands of Cuban refugees were housed at Fort Chaffee near Barling. On two occasions rioting broke out and scores of Cubans escaped temporarily into the surrounding area.

Full name: State of Arkansas. **Origin of name:** From Algonquian name of the Quapaw Indians. **Inhabitant:** Arkansan. **Capital:** Little Rock. **State motto:** Regnat Populus (The People Rule). **Flag:** Star-studded blue & white diamond on a red field; diamond shape represents Arkansas, the only diamond-producing state. **Seal:** Shield design has steamboat, plow, beehive & sheaf of wheat, symbolizing industry & agriculture; angel of mercy & sword of justice guard American eagle; goddess of liberty stands above.

Counties indicated by numbers:
1 ALAMEDA
2 AMADOR
3 CALAVERAS
4 CONTRA COSTA
5 LAKE
6 MARIN
7 MERCED
8 NAPA
9 ORANGE
10 SACRAMENTO
11 SAN FRANCISCO
12 SAN JOAQUIN
13 SOLANO
14 STANISLAUS
15 SUTTER
16 YUBA

SAN FRANCISCO AND VICINITY
LOS ANGELES AND VICINITY

© Copyright HAMMOND INCORPORATED

CALIFORNIA
MILES
KILOMETERS
State Capitals   County Seats

Longitude West of Greenwich

PACIFIC OCEAN
OREGON
NEVADA
ARIZONA
MEXICO
BAJA CALIFORNIA

Flower: Apple blossom. **Bird:** Mockingbird. **Tree:** Pine. **Song:** "Arkansas." **Nickname:** Land of Opportunity.

Governor: William Clinton. **Annual salary:** $35,000. **Term:** 2 years. **Current term expires:** Jan. 1981. **Voting requirements:** 18 yrs. old & U.S. citizen; registered in county of residence 20 days. **U.S. Congressmen:** 4. **Entered Union:** 1836 (25th state).

Location & boundaries: South Central state: bounded on the north by Missouri; on the east by the Mississippi River & the states of Missouri, Tennessee & Mississippi; on the south by Louisiana; & on the west by Texas & Oklahoma. **Total area:** 53,104 sq. mi. (ranks 27th). **Extreme length:** 275 mi. **Extreme breadth:** 240 mi. **Chief rivers:** Mississippi, Arkansas, Ouachita, White. **Major lakes:** Bull Shoals, Ouachita, Beaver, Norfork. **No. of counties:** 75.

Population (1979 est.): 2,180,000 (ranks 33rd). **Pop. increase (1970-79):** 13.4%. **Places over 25,000 pop:** 8. Places over 100,000: 1. **Largest cities:** Little Rock, Fort Smith, N. Little Rock. **Pop. density:** 41.1 per sq. mi. (ranks 35th). **Pop. projection 1985:** 2,353,000. **Pop. distribution:** 38.4% metropolitan; 61.6% non-metropolitan. **White:** 81.4%. **Black:** 18.3%. **Other:** 0.2%. **Marriage rate (1977):** 11.2 per 1,000 people. **Divorce rate:** 9.0 per 1,000 people.

State finances (1978). Revenue: $1,839,706,000. **Expenditures:** $1,684,539,000. **State taxes:** $423.72 per capita. **State personal income tax:** Yes. **Public debt (1978):** $80.35 per capita. **Federal aid (1979):** $385.05 per capita. **Personal income (1979 est.):** $6,785.

Sectors of the economy (% of labor force employed in 1970): Manufacturing (26%), Wholesale and retail trade (19%), Government (15%), Services (8%), Educational Services (8%), Construction (7%). **Leading products:** food, lumber & wood, paper products, electrical machinery, chemicals, furniture & fixtures, apparel. **Minerals:** petroleum, natural gas, bauxite, stone, bromine, sand & gravel. **Agricultural products:** broilers, cattle, eggs, soybeans, rice, cotton lint. **Avg. farm (1979 est.):** 290 acres. **Avg. value of farm per acre:** $691.

Highway expenditures per capita (1978): $120.99. **Persons per motor vehicle:** 1.45. **Minimum age for driver's license:** 16. **Gasoline tax:** 9.5¢ per gallon. **Diesel tax:** 10.5¢ per gallon. **Motor vehicle deaths:** 26.2 per 100,000 people.

Birthrate (1978): 16.1 per 1,000 people. **Infant mortality rate per 1,000 births (1977):** 15.4. **Physicians per 100,000 pop. (1977):** 113. **Dentists per 100,000 pop. (1977):** 32. **Acceptable hospital beds:** 6.3 per 1,000 people. **State expenditures per capita for health and hospitals (1978):** $50.63.

Education expenditures (1975-76): $344.34 per capita annually. **No. of pupils in public schools (1977 est.):** 454,000. **No. of institutions of higher learning (1976-77):** 29. **Public school expenditure per pupil in attendance (1975-76):** $1,161. **Avg. salary of public school teachers (1974-75 est.):** $9,021. **No. full-time teachers (1977 est.):** 22,290. **Educational attainment of adult population (1976):** 12.2 median yrs. of school completed; 6.0% with less than 5 years of education; 9.1% with 4 yrs. of college.

Telephones (1977): 62 per 100 people. **State Chamber of Commerce:** Arkansas State Chamber of Commerce, 911 Wallace Building, Little Rock, Arkansas 72201.

CALIFORNIA

California, the most populous of the states, is the national leader in agriculture, commercial fishing, and motor vehicle ownership. It ranks first in manufacturing and third in land area and oil production.

The heart of the state is the fertile Central Valley, fenced in by two long north-south mountain ranges: the Sierra Nevada (on the east) and the Coast Range. Several small forested ranges of the Klamath Mountains cover the northwestern corner of the state, while below the Coast Range are the Los Angeles Ranges, and below these, the San Diego Ranges. More than 40 percent of the land is forested. Other important land areas are the Cascade Mountains extending northward from the Central Valley and the Basin and Range Region of the southeast and extreme northeast; within the southeastern part of this region are the Mojave and Colorado deserts.

Both the highest mountain peak in the conterminous United States, Mt. Whitney (14,494 feet) and the lowest point in the hemisphere (282 feet below sea level) can be seen from Dante's View, 5,475 feet high and about 3 miles east of that lowest point. Two island groups lie off the coast: the Santa Barbara (or Channel) Islands, consisting of eight major islands 20 to 60 miles from the southern mainland, and the six small rugged Farallon Islands, about 30 miles west of San Francisco. California's main harbors are San Francisco and San Diego Bays and the man-made Los Angeles harbor, San Pedro Bay. Great extremes mark the climate, with many areas enjoying generally mild and sunny weather, partially befouled in urban areas by palls of smog.

There were about 130,000 Indians living in the California region when Juan Rodriguez Cabrillo, a Portuguese in Spanish employ, discovered it in 1542. English interest in the area began with Sir Francis Drake, who claimed (1579) it for Queen Elizabeth I, but the first permanent European settlement was made by Spaniards, who established 21 missions northward along the coast from San Diego (1769) to Sonoma (1823). In 1812, Russian fur-traders from Alaska came down and established Fort Ross on the state's northern coast, but they did not prevail. In 1822, after Mexico won its independence from Spain, California became a Mexican province, and its social, economic, and political life was centered around large cattle ranches. The first organized group of American settlers came to the region by land in 1841; the United States offered to buy the province, but Mexico refused to sell. U.S. forces occupied the area early in the Mexican War, with Mexico formally ceding its claims in 1848.

Less than two weeks before the treaty was signed, an event of massive importance occurred at John A. Sutter's sawmill near Coloma: the discovery of gold, which set off the famous Gold Rush of '49. In the following seven years, the region produced $450 million worth of gold, while the population jumped from about 15,000 to almost 300,000. This influx virtually secured American possession of the territory. San Francisco, for example, grew from an outpost to a great city, in a turbulent, often lawless, atmosphere. Vigilante groups filled the "law-and-order" gap until more stable government was established, beginning with admission of California into the Union as a free state, under terms of the Compromise of 1850. Meanwhile, California's mountain-walled isolation was rapidly ending: the telegraph reached the area in 1861, and eight years later direct rail connection was made with the rest of the country.

The late 19th and early 20th centuries were marked by continued population growth, soaring land values, and economic-rooted social tensions between American-born Californians, Mexican-Americans and Oriental immigrants. Manufacturing, especially the canning and packing of food, increased greatly; and Hollywood became the world motion picture capital.

More recently, defense-contract industries, electronics and senior citizen retirement communities have played particularly large roles in the state's economy. Tourist attractions include Disneyland (in Anaheim), San Francisco's Golden Gate Bridge, 17 national forests, six national parks, and many scenic beaches.

With 20 million residents in 1970, California overtook New York as the most populous state, but population growth slowed in the following decade. California has recently experienced a net out-mi-

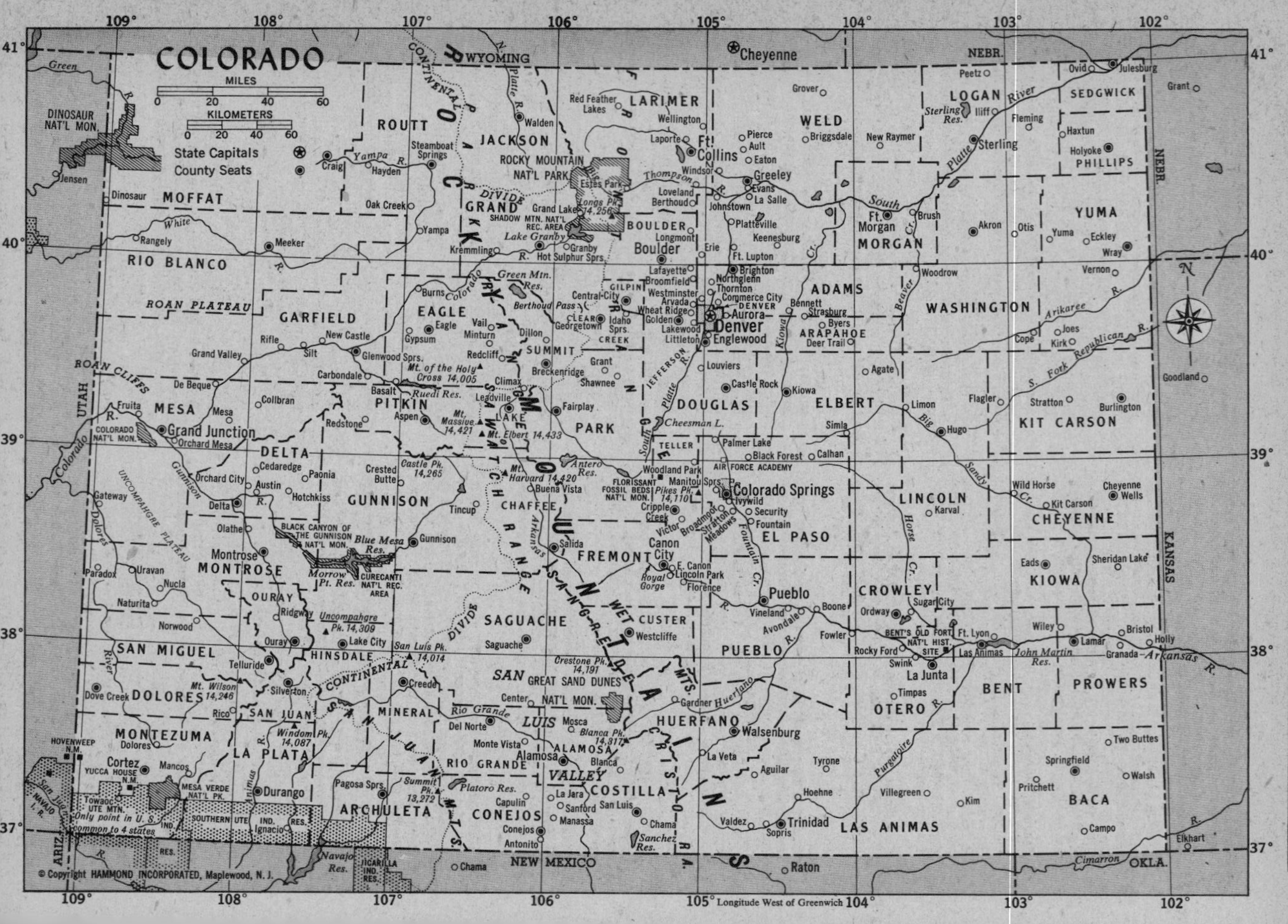

COLORADO
MILES
KILOMETERS
State Capitals
County Seats
NEBR.
KANSAS
WYOMING
UTAH
NEW MEXICO
OKLA.
ARIZ.
SEDGWICK
PHILLIPS
YUMA
WASHINGTON
KIT CARSON
CHEYENNE
KIOWA
PROWERS
BACA
LOGAN
WELD
MORGAN
ADAMS
ARAPAHOE
ELBERT
LINCOLN
CROWLEY
BENT
OTERO
LAS ANIMAS
LARIMER
BOULDER
DENVER
DOUGLAS
EL PASO
PUEBLO
HUERFANO
COSTILLA
JACKSON
GRAND
GILPIN
CLEAR CREEK
JEFFERSON
PARK
TELLER
FREMONT
CUSTER
SAGUACHE
ALAMOSA
CONEJOS
ARCHULETA
ROUTT
EAGLE
SUMMIT
LAKE
CHAFFEE
GUNNISON
HINSDALE
MINERAL
RIO GRANDE
GARFIELD
PITKIN
MESA
DELTA
MONTROSE
OURAY
SAN JUAN
LA PLATA
MOFFAT
RIO BLANCO
SAN MIGUEL
DOLORES
MONTEZUMA
ROCKY MOUNTAIN NAT'L PARK
CONTINENTAL DIVIDE
ROCKY
SAWATCH RANGE
SANGRE DE CRISTO MTS.
FRONT RANGE
SAN JUAN MTS.
SAN LUIS VALLEY
GREAT SAND DUNES NAT'L MON.
ROAN PLATEAU
ROAN CLIFFS
UNCOMPAHGRE PLATEAU
BLACK CANYON OF THE GUNNISON NAT'L MON.
MESA VERDE NAT'L PK.
DINOSAUR NAT'L MON.
COLORADO NAT'L MON.
HOVENWEEP N.M.
YUCCA HOUSE N.M.
JICARILLA IND. RES.
SOUTHERN UTE IND. RES.
UTE MTN. IND. RES.
NAVAJO I.R.
Cheyenne
Denver
Colorado Springs
Pueblo
Trinidad
Julesburg
Ovid
Sedgwick
Grant
Haxtun
Holyoke
Fleming
Sterling
Iliff
Peetz
Grover
Briggsdale
New Raymer
Ault
Pierce
Eaton
Greeley
Evans
La Salle
Johnstown
Platteville
Keenesburg
Brighton
Wellington
Laporte
Ft. Collins
Windsor
Loveland
Berthoud
Longmont
Lafayette
Broomfield
Westminster
Arvada
Wheat Ridge
Golden
Lakewood
Littleton
Englewood
Aurora
Commerce City
Northglenn
Thornton
Erie
Ft. Lupton
Walden
Steamboat Springs
Oak Creek
Yampa
Hayden
Craig
Meeker
Rangely
Dinosaur
Jensen
Fruita
Grand Junction
Mesa
Orchard Mesa
De Beque
Grand Valley
Rifle
Silt
New Castle
Glenwood Springs
Carbondale
Basalt
Aspen
Redstone
Gypsum
Eagle
Minturn
Redcliff
Vail
Leadville
Climax
Dillon
Breckenridge
Fairplay
Kremmling
Granby
Hot Sulphur Sprs.
Grand Lake
Estes Park
Central City
Idaho Springs
Georgetown
Shawnee
Grant
Buena Vista
Salida
Canon City
Florence
Cripple Creek
Victor
Woodland Park
Manitou Sprs.
Divide
Castle Rock
Kiowa
Simla
Calhan
Elizabeth
Bennett
Byers
Strasburg
Deer Trail
Agate
Limon
Hugo
Flagler
Stratton
Burlington
Cheyenne Wells
Kit Carson
Wild Horse
Eads
Sheridan Lake
Holly
Lamar
Granada
Las Animas
La Junta
Rocky Ford
Swink
Ordway
Sugar City
Fowler
Boone
Avondale
Vineland
Florence
Walsenburg
La Veta
Aguilar
Hoehne
Kim
Branson
Tyrone
Villegreen
Springfield
Pritchett
Walsh
Two Buttes
Campo
Wiley
Bristol
Salida
Poncha Springs
Saguache
Center
Monte Vista
Del Norte
Creede
Lake City
Gunnison
Crested Butte
Sapinero
Montrose
Olathe
Delta
Cedaredge
Paonia
Hotchkiss
Orchard City
Ouray
Ridgway
Telluride
Norwood
Nucla
Naturita
Paradox
Gateway
Silverton
Durango
Ignacio
Bayfield
Pagosa Springs
Chama
Antonito
Manassa
Sanford
San Luis
Blanca
Fort Garland
Mosca
Hooper
Center
Platoro Res.
Cortez
Mancos
Dolores
Rico
Dove Creek
Mt. Elbert 14,433
Mt. Massive 14,421
Mt. Harvard 14,420
La Plata Pk. 14,361
Blanca Pk. 14,317
Uncompahgre Pk. 14,309
Crestone Pk. 14,191
Mt. of the Holy Cross 14,005
Pikes Peak 14,110
Longs Peak 14,255
Castle Pk. 14,265
Grizzly Pk. 13,988
Windom Pk. 14,087
Mt. Wilson 14,246
Wheeler Peak
BLUE MESA RES.
CURECANTI NAT'L REC. AREA
MORROW PT. RES.
San Luis Pk. 14,014
Summit Pk. 13,272
FOSSIL BEDS NAT'L MON.
AIR FORCE ACADEMY
SHADOW MTN. NAT'L REC. AREA
Arkansas R.
South Platte River
Rio Grande
Gunnison River
Dolores River
Yampa R.
White R.
Green R.
Colorado R.
San Juan R.
Republican
Arikaree
Cimarron R.
Purgatoire
Sand Cr.
Horse Cr.
Big Sandy Cr.
Continental Divide
105° Longitude West of Greenwich
© Copyright HAMMOND INCORPORATED, Maplewood, N.J.
Only point in U.S. common to 4 states

gration to each of its less populated neighbors—Oregon, Nevada and Arizona.

The long struggle of Cesar Chavez' United Farm Workers to unionize farm workers drew increasingly intense competition from the Teamsters Union. Some growers who had signed contracts with Chavez' union in 1970 following a five-year strike and table grape boycott signed new contracts in 1973 with the Teamsters. In 1975 the United Farm Workers Union was overwhelmingly endorsed by farm workers as a legitimate union in California. Chavez continued in his fight for better wages by announcing a national boycott of iceberg lettuce on April 26, 1979, in support of his union's strike (which began January 19) against West Coast lettuce growers. Two confrontations between growers and workers resulted in one death and about a dozen injuries.

In the spring of 1978 a taxpayers' revolt against heavy government spending and high tax rates culminated in the adoption, by 65% of the vote, of Proposal 13, a state constitutional amendment mandating a 57% reduction in property taxes, and limiting the authority of state and local governments to raise taxes. No drastic reduction in government services followed—largely because the state was able to divide a huge surplus with local governments. In 1980, however, California voters rejected by a 3-2 margin another initiative (Proposition 9) which sought to reduce state income tax rates by half. Howard Jarvis, author of both propositions, has suggested he would continue his efforts in this matter by mounting an assault on state pension funds.

Full name: State of California. **Origin of name:** From an imaginary island in a 16th-century Spanish romance. **Inhabitant:** Californian. **Capital:** Sacramento. **State motto:** Eureka (I Have Found It). **Flag:** a bear & a red star on white field with red horizontal bar at the bottom. **Seal:** Grizzly bear stands near seated figure of Minerva; a miner, ships & peaks of Sierra Nevada in background; state motto. **Flower:** Golden poppy. **Bird:** California Valley quail. **Tree:** California redwood. **Song:** "I Love You, California." **Nickname:** Golden State.

Governor: Edmund G. Brown, Jr. **Annual salary:** $49,100. **Term:** 4 years. **Current term expires:** Jan. 1983. **Voting requirements:** 18 yrs. old & U.S. citizen; state resident 29 days. **U.S. Congressmen:** 43. **Entered Union:** 1850 (31st state).

Location & boundaries: Pacific state: bounded on the north by Oregon; on the east by Nevada & Arizona; on the southeast by the Colorado River; on the south by Mexico; & on the west by the Pacific Ocean. **Total area:** 158,693 sq. mi. (ranks 3rd). **Extreme length:** 1775 mi. **Extreme breadth:** 1360 mi. **Coastline:** 1,264 mi. **Chief rivers:** Sacramento, San Joaquin, Klamath. **Major lakes:** Salton Sea, Tahoe, Goose. **No. of counties:** 58.

Population (1979 est.): 22,694,000 (ranks 1st). **Pop. increase (1970-79):** 13.6%. **Places over 25,000 pop.:** 150. **Places over 100,000:** 21. **Largest cities:** Los Angeles, San Diego, San Francisco, San Jose. **Pop. density:** 143.0 per sq. mi. (ranks 14th). **Pop. projection 1985:** 23,767,000. **Pop. distribution:** 92.7% metropolitan; 7.3% nonmetropolitan. **White:** 89.1%. **Black:** 7%. **Other:** 3.9%. **Marriage rate (1977):** 6.9 per 1,000 people. **Divorce rate:** 6.0 per 1,000 people.

State finances (1978). Revenue: $29,486,935,000. **Expenditures:** $24,628,536,000. **State taxes:** $673.62 per capita. **State personal income tax:** Yes. **Public debt (1978):** $317.19 per capita. **Federal aid (1979):** $359.80 per capita. **Personal income (1979 est.):** $9,913.

Sectors of the economy (% of labor force employed in 1970): Manufacturing (22%), Wholesale and retail trade (21%), Government (18%), Services (9%), Educational Services (8%), Construction (5%). **Leading products:** transportation equipment, food, machinery, ordnance & accessories, fabricated metals, printing & publishing. **Minerals:** petroleum, natural gas, cement, sand & gravel. **Agricultural products:** cattle, dairy items, hay, tomatoes, cotton lint. **Fishing:** tuna, salmon, crabs. **Avg. farm (1979 est.):** 538 acres. **Avg. value of farm per acre:** $936.

Highway expenditures per capita (1978): $56.24. **Persons per motor vehicle:** 1.42. **Minimum age for driver's license:** 16. **Gasoline tax:** 7¢ per gallon. **Diesel tax:** 7¢ per gallon. **Motor vehicle deaths:** 23.8 per 100,000 people.

Birthrate (1978): 16.0 per 1,000 people. **Infant mortality rate per 1,000 births (1977):** 12.0. **Physicians per 100,000 pop. (1977):** 222. **Dentists per 100,000 pop. (1977):** 66. **Acceptable hospital beds:** 5.3 per 1,000 people. **State expenditures per capita for health and hospitals (1978):** $54.59.

Education expenditures (1975-76): $531.69 per capita annually. **No. of pupils in public schools (1977 est.):** 4,316,000. **No. of institutions of higher learning (1976-77):** 252. **Public school expenditure per pupil in attendance (1975-76):** $1,721. **Avg. salary of public school teachers (1974-75 est.):** $14,915. **No. full-time teachers (1977 est.):** 219,190. **Educational attainment of adult population (1976):** 12.7 median yrs. of school completed; 3.3% with less than 5 years of education; 16.8% with 4 yrs. of college.

Telephones (1977): 82 per 100 people. **State Chamber of Commerce:** California Chamber of Commerce, P.O. Box 1736, 455 Capitol Mall, Sacramento, California 95808.

COLORADO

Colorado, the Centennial State, is the state with the highest overall elevation; it has more than 1,000 peaks that soar at least 10,000 feet, including legendary Pikes Peak. In the east are the high plains, while the Rockies' peaks and ranges make up the central region; and in the west is the Colorado Plateau. The Continental Divide runs generally north and south through the west-central part of the state. As is typical of mountainous areas, there are great extremes of climate, yet a surprisingly diverse agriculture.

This state is part of the *real* Old West, not the West of romanticized Westerns. Ruthlessly competitive gold mining (starting in 1858) and silver mining (1875) and the decades-long wresting of crops from the arid land shaped Colorado and defined its character.

Many metals are mined in the mountains. Molybdenum, which hardens steel and is used in rocketry, is the state's most valuable: Colorado holds over half of the world's supply. Oil shale is the state's most important undeveloped resource.

Food and machinery are the state's two main industries. Only California has more irrigated acreage; however, two-thirds of Colorado's farm output consists of livestock and livestock products. It leads in the refining of beet sugar.

Cliff-dwelling Indians are believed to have built (c. A.D. 100) Colorado's first civilization in the Mesa Verde plateau, which lies in the southwest corner of the state; they carved irrigation ditches and built many-storied pueblos.

In the 1500s, Spanish explorers became the first Europeans to visit the region but, not finding gold, they did not stay. The United States got the eastern and central areas of Colorado as part of the Louisiana Purchase and the western part as a result of the Mexican War.

The gold rush of the late 1850s was followed by the Civil War. With fewer Federal troops in the area, the intense fighting between whites and the Arapaho and Cheyenne Indians posed the very real threat of general lawlessness.

The establishment (1861) of the Colorado Territory was a step toward unity and stability, and the advent of the railroads in the 1870s was another. Statehood came in 1876. This was the era in which the New York journalist Horace Greeley sponsored a Colorado farming colony and advised, "Go West, young man!"

The 1880s brought fiscal health and early growth as a state, but trouble and renewed bloodshed characterized the next decade.

CONNECTICUT
MASSACHUSETTS
RHODE ISLAND
NEW YORK
ATLANTIC OCEAN
LONG ISLAND SOUND
LONG ISLAND
TACONIC MTS
LITCHFIELD
TOLLAND
WINDHAM
HARTFORD
NEW HAVEN
MIDDLESEX
NEW LONDON
FAIRFIELD
Mt. Frissell 2,380
Twin Lakes
Canaan
E. Canaan
Salisbury
Lakeville
Falls Village
Norfolk
Colebrook
Millerton
Sharon
Amenia
Millbrook
Cornwall
W. Goshen
Goshen
Cornwall Bridge
Mohawk Mtn. 1,682
Torrington
Winchester Ctr.
Winsted
New Hartford
Harwinton
Litchfield
Bantam
Kent
L. Waramaug
New Preston
Bear Hill 1,281
Washington
Bethlehem
Roxbury
Bridgewater
Woodbury
Sherman
New Milford
Pawling
Watertown
Thomaston Res.
Thomaston
Terryville
Plymouth
Bristol
Plainville
Nepaug Res.
Burlington
Unionville
Collinsville
Canton
Canton Ctr.
Simsbury
Avon
Farmington
Granby
Tariffville
Hartford
W. Hartford
Elmwood
E. Hartford
Bloomfield
Windsor
S. Windsor
Wilson
Windsor Locks
Warehouse Point
Broad Brook
Suffield
Hazardville
Enfield
Thompsonville
Congamond Lakes
E. Hartland
Barkhamsted Res.
West Branch
E. Branch
Somersville
Longmeadow
Rockville
Ellington
Vernon
Talcottville
Manchester
Tolland
Willington
Stafford Springs
Staffordville
Storrs
Mansfield Ctr.
Coventry
Andover
Willimantic
Windham
Columbia
Hebron
Lebanon
Shenipsit L.
South Woodstock
Eastford
Pomfret
Abington
Hampton
Brooklyn
E. Brooklyn
Danielson
Dayville
E. Killingly
N. Grosvenor Dale
Thompson
Putnam
Quaddick Res.
Webster
Webster L.
Central Village
Moosup
Canterbury
Sterling
Plainfield
Baltic
Versailles
Yantic
Jewett City
Pachaug Pd.
Voluntown
Preston City
Norwich
Gardner L.
Montville
Uncasville
Chesterfield
Quaker Hill
N. Stonington
Newington
Wethersfield
Glastonbury
S. Glastonbury
Rocky Hill
New Britain
Berlin
Southington
Plantsville
Cromwell
Portland
Marlborough
E. Hampton
Colchester
Moodus
Middletown
Meriden
S. Meriden
Cheshire
Middlefield
Durham
Haddam
E. Haddam
Chester
Deep River
Essex
Ivoryton
Old Saybrook
Old Lyme
Waterbury
Waterville
Oakville
Union City
Naugatuck
Beacon Falls
Wallingford
N. Guilford
Gaillard L.
Montowese
Bethany
Hamden
Whitneyville
Ansonia
Derby
Seymour
Shelton
New Haven
W. Haven
E. Haven
Allingtown
Orange
Woodmont
Milford
Stratford
Stratford Pt.
Stony Creek
Guilford
Madison
Clinton
Niantic
Coast Guard Academy
Naval Submarine Base
New London
Groton
Poquonock Bridge
W. Mystic
Mystic
Stonington
Pawcatuck
Westerly
Morningside Pk.
Waterford
Watch Hill Pt.
Fishers I.
The Race
Plum I.
Orient Pt.
Greenport
Southold
Gardiners Bay
Gardiners I.
Montauk Pt.
Sag Harbor
Hammonasset Pt.
Sachem Head
Cornfield Pt.
Morgan Pt.
Danbury
Bethel
Newtown
Sandy Hook
Monroe
Redding
Ridgefield
Branchville
Easton
Easton Res.
Saugatuck Res.
Stepney
Trap Fall Res.
Trumbull
Fairfield
Bridgeport
Westport
Wilton
Mt. Kisco
New Croton Res.
Croton Falls Res.
Brewster
Kensico Res.
New Canaan
Norwalk
S. Norwalk
E. Norwalk
Norwalk Is.
Darien
Noroton Hts.
Stamford
Cos Cob
Riverside
White Plains
Greenwich
Wappinger Cr.
Fishkill Cr.
Housatonic River
Naugatuck River
Quinnipiac R.
Shepaug R.
Connecticut R.
Scantic R.
Farmington R.
Thames R.
Shetucket R.
Natchaug R.
Quinebaug R.
Willimantic R.
Candlewood Isle
Lake Candlewood
MILES
0 5 10 15 20
KILOMETERS
0 5 10 15 20
State Capital
Copyright HAMMOND INCORPORATED, Maplewood, N.J.
Longitude West of Greenwich
73° 30′ 73° 30′ 72°
42° 30′ 41°

Silver prices dropped badly after the repeal of the Sherman Silver Purchase Act (1893), and many great mines closed, leaving behind ghost towns with colorful names such as Cripple Creek and Eureka. Range warfare was rife, and bitter hassles took place over railway franchises. Long-simmering labor-management conflict came to a head in 1914 in a battle near Trinidad between striking coal miners and the militia in which innocent women and children were killed. Subsequent reforms included regular government inspection of mines.

The state's economy advanced sharply after both World Wars. In between were more years of struggle: the great Wall Street fiasco of 1929 was accompanied, in Colorado, by drought and high winds which created a disastrous dust bowl.

Today, Colorado is prosperous. Denver is an important business center, missile-plant site, and headquarters for Federal agencies. In addition, U.S. coins are minted there, while the National Bureau of Standards laboratory at Boulder has expanded greatly in recent years. Scientists at an observation station near Climax are studying the earth's atmosphere and conducting space research.

Because of the state's magnificent scenery, tourism has developed into a major industry. Tourist attractions include a dozen national forests, hunting and fishing, Balanced Rock in the Garden of the Gods, Buffalo Bill's Grave on Lookout Mountain, and cultural festivals at Aspen and Central City.

The U.S. Air Force Academy, founded in 1958, is located at Colorado Springs. In 1976 the academy admitted the first female cadets.

In 1979 the Interior Department proposed stricter air quality standards for the 50-mile-long Black Canyon of the Gunnison River in the western part of the state.

Full name: State of Colorado. **Origin of name:** From Spanish for "Colored Red." **Inhabitant:** Coloradan. **Capital:** Denver. **State motto:** Nil Sine Numine (Nothing Without Providence). **Flag:** A red letter C encloses gold ball & rests against blue, white & blue bars. **Seal:** A triangular figure, representing "all seeing" eye of God, bound rods, three mountains & pick & hammer. **Flower:** Rocky Mountain columbine. **Bird:** Lark bunting. **Tree:** Blue spruce. **Song:** "Where the Columbines Grow." **Nickname:** Centennial State.

Governor: Richard D. Lamm. **Annual salary:** $50,000. **Term:** 4 years. **Current term expires:** Jan. 1983. **Voting requirements:** 18 yrs. old & U.S. citizen; resident of state and precinct, 32 days. **U.S. Congressmen:** 7. **Entered Union:** 1876 (38th state).

Location & boundaries: Rocky Mountain state: bounded on the north by Wyoming & Nebraska; on the east by Nebraska & Kansas; on the south by Oklahoma & New Mexico; & on the west by Utah. **Total area:** 104,247 sq. mi. (ranks 8th). **Extreme length:** 387 mi. **Extreme breadth:** 276 mi. **Chief rivers:** Colorado, Arkansas, South Platte, Rio Grande. **Major lakes:** Blue Mesa, Dillon, John Martin, Granby. **No. of counties:** 63.

Population (1979 est.): 2,772,000 (ranks 28th). **Pop. increase (1970-79):** 25.5%. **Places over 25,000 pop.:** 18. **Places over 100,000:** 5. **Largest cities:** Denver, Colorado Springs, Lakewood, Aurora. **Pop. density:** 26.6 per sq. mi. (ranks 38th). **Pop. projection 1985:** 3,123,000. **Pop. distribution:** 80.6% metropolitan; 19.4% nonmetropolitan. **White:** 85.5%. **Spanish-surnamed:** 10.2%. **Black:** 3%. **Other:** 1.3%. **Marriage rate (1977):** 11.2 per 1,000 people. **Divorce rate:** 7.8 per 1,000 people.

State finances (1978). Revenue: $2,675,106,000. **Expenditures:** $2,279,059,000. **State taxes:** $453.97 per capita. **State personal income tax:** Yes. **Public debt (1978):** $116.27 per capita. **Federal aid (1979):** $330.19 per capita. **Personal income (1979 est.):** $8,945.

Sectors of the economy (% of labor force employed in 1970): Wholesale and retail trade (22%), Government (20%), Manufacturing (15%), Educational Services (10%), Services (8%), Construction (7%). **Leading products:** food; machinery; transportation equipment; electrical equipment; printing & publishing; stone, clay & glass items; fabricated metals; chemicals; lumber. **Minerals:** molybdenum, petroleum, coal, sand & gravel. **Agricultural products:** cattle, hay, dairy items, wheat, sugar beets, sheep. **Avg. farm (1979 est.):** 1,434 acres. **Avg. value of farm per acre:** $332.

Highway expenditures per capita (1978): $93.98. **Persons per motor vehicle:** 1.03. **Minimum age for driver's license:** 21. **Gasoline tax:** 7¢ per gallon. **Diesel tax:** 7¢ per gallon. **Motor vehicle deaths:** 26.0 per 100,000 people.

Birthrate (1978): 16.3 per 1,000 people. **Infant mortality rate per 1,000 births (1977):** 12.0. **Physicians per 100,000 pop. (1977):** 204. **Dentists per 100,000 pop. (1977):** 58. **Acceptable hospital beds:** 5.7 per 1,000 people. **State expenditures per capita for health and hospitals (1978):** $58.41.

Education expenditures (1975-76): $552.30 per capita annually. **No. of pupils in public schools (1977 est.):** 562,000. **No. of institutions of higher learning (1976-77):** 39. **Public school expenditure per pupil in attendance (1975-76):** $1,605. **Avg. salary of public school teachers (1974-75 est.):** $11,554. **No. full-time teachers (1977 est.):** 30,280. **Educational attainment of adult population (1976):** 12.8 median yrs. of school completed; 1.3% with less than 5 years of education; 19.4% with 4 yrs. of college.

Telephones (1977): 77 per 100 people. **State Chamber of Commerce:** Colorado Association of Commerce and Industry, 1390 Logan Street, Suite 308, Denver, Colorado 80203.

CONNECTICUT

Connecticut, one of the smallest states in area, is one of the most varied and most prosperous. Generally rectangular in shape, the state is divided by the Connecticut River and its fertile valley into two almost equal regions. Gently rolling hills rise from the southern coastal plain to an average elevation of about 1,000 feet at the northern boundary.

Highly industrialized cities contrast with the scenic, typically New England countryside, 60 percent of which is forested. The southern shore has a number of excellent harbors, and several small islands lie off the coast. The southern section, particularly Fairfield County, is home for many who work in New York City.

Among Connecticut's attractions are Yale University at New Haven, the American Dance Festival at Connecticut College in New London, and this hemisphere's first school for the deaf, at Hartford.

About 7,000 members of the Algonquian Indian family were living in Connecticut before the Europeans came; of these, the Pequot were most powerful. Uncas, chief of the Mohican branch of the Pequots, was immortalized by James Fenimore Cooper in *The Last of the Mohicans*. Relations between the Indians and early settlers were mostly friendly, except for the brief Pequot War (1637) and the more serious King Philip's War (1675-76).

Dutch navigator Adriaen Block was the first European of record to visit the state (1614), sailing up the Connecticut River. In 1633, colonists from Holland set up a trading post (near present-day Hartford), but the Dutch lost control of the area to the English; Puritans from the Massachusetts Bay Colony established the first permanent settlement at the site of modern Windsor that same year, and another at Wethersfield in 1634. English settlements at Hartford and Saybrook began in 1635, and representatives of the three "River Towns" of Windsor, Wethersfield, and Hartford united to form the Connecticut Colony and adopt (1639) the "Fundamental Orders" that gave citizens the right to elect government officials and omitted the religious test for citizenship; the document thus anticipated the U.S. Constitution and is considered the world's first written constitution.

Meanwhile, a wholly new colony came into being with the establishment of New Haven (1638) and other communities in the southern part of Connecticut; called the New Haven Colony, it was more rigidly Puritan than the older colony. In 1662, the Connecticut Colony procured an unusually democratic royal charter resembling the "Fundamental Orders" and providing for the incorporation (1665) of the New Haven Colony, which strongly opposed absorption but reluctantly acquiesced under threat of an alternative take-over by New York. Sir Edmund Andros, who had been named British governor of New England by James II, demanded surrender of the colony's charter; he arrived in Hartford in 1687 to seize the document, but the townspeople are said to have hidden it in the legendary Charter Oak tree.

Connecticut patriots, including Nathan Hale and Governor Jonathan Trumbull, took on a leading role in the Revolutionary War, and the colony served as the Continental Army's major supply area. After the war Connecticut gave up its claims to all western land except the so-called "Western Reserve." Statehood dates from 1788, but boundary disputes with New York, Massachusetts, and Rhode Island persisted until the present borders were established in 1799. Jefferson's Embargo Act of 1807 was highly unpopular in Connecticut, as it was elsewhere in New England. The state's contribution to the Union cause in the Civil War was exceptional; five times the quota of men volunteered.

Most early Connecticut colonists wrested their living from the land and made their own clothes and tools. Enterprising "Yankee peddlers" with horse and rig toured the nation, hawking well-turned wares. During and after the Civil War, better transportation and sharply increased immigration served to shift the economic focus from agriculture to industry. The state, sometimes called "The Arsenal of the Nation," became one of the most industrialized in the country. Its business pioneers included revolver inventor Samuel Colt, rubber magnate Charles Goodyear, and Eli Whitney, who innovated mass production of firearms and manufactured (1793) the cotton gin that proved a boon to the textile industry.

Often called the Insurance Capital of the World, Hartford is the headquarters city for nearly 40 firms in that field.

Connecticut is a leader in the production of such vital items as ball and roller bearings, electronic goods, chemicals and plastics, jet engines, helicopters, and nuclear submarines. United Technologies Corp., the state's largest employer with ten divisions and subsidiaries, and the Electric Boat Division of General Dynamics in Groton are important contributors to the nation's aerospace and submarine production. Electric Boat launched the world's first nuclear submarine in 1954. Shifting emphasis to commercial production has helped the state's numerous defense contractors withstand recent military cutbacks.

In the southwest section the industrial base is shifting from traditional skilled industry and manufacturing. A number of major companies have established headquarters facilities in the state, including Xerox, IBM, General Electric, Pepsico and Union Carbide. Connecticut ranks very high among the states in per capita income, and in the proportionate number of white-collar and professional workers in the work force.

Full name: State of Connecticut. **Origin of name:** From the Indian, Quinnehtukqut, meaning "Beside the Long Tidal River." **Inhabitant:** Nutmegger. **Capital:** Hartford. **State motto:** Qui Transtulit Sustinet (He Who Transplanted Still Sustains). **Flag:** State seal on blue field. **Seal:** Three grapevines symbolize transplanting of culture & traditions of Europe to the colony. **Flower:** Mountain laurel. **Bird:** Robin.

Tree: White oak. **Song:** "Yankee Doodle." **Nickname:** Constitution State.

Governor: Ella T. Grasso **Annual salary:** $42,000. **Term:** 4 years. **Current term expires:** Jan. 1983. **Voting requirements:** 18 yrs. old & U.S. citizen; resident of state. **U.S. Congressmen:** 6. **Entered Union:** 1788 (5th state).

Location & boundaries: New England state: bounded on the north by Massachusetts; on the east by Rhode Island; on the south by Long Island Sound; & on the west by New York. **Total area:** 5,009 sq. mi. (ranks 48th). **Extreme length:** 100 mi. **Extreme breadth:** 50 mi. **Coastline:** 253 mi. **Chief rivers:** Connecticut, Housatonic, Thames. **Major lake:** Candlewood. **No. of counties:** 8.

Population (1979 est.): 3,115,000 (ranks 24th). **Pop. increase (1970-79):** 2.7%. **Places over 25,000 pop.:** 35. **Places over 100,000:** 5. **Largest cities:** Hartford, Bridgeport, New Haven. **Pop. density:** 621.9 per sq. mi. (ranks 4th). **Pop. projection 1985:** 3,210,000. **Pop. distribution:** 88.2% metropolitan; 11.8% non-metropolitan. **White:** 93.5%. **Black:** 6%. **Other:** 0.5%. **Marriage rate (1977):** 7.4 per 1,000 people. **Divorce rate:** 3.9 per 1,000 people.

State finances (1978). Revenue: $2,908,740,000. **Expenditures:** $2,789,507,000. **State taxes:** $500.30 per capita. **State personal income tax:** No. **Public debt (1978):** $1,070.82 per capita. **Federal aid (1979):** $344.98 per capita. **Personal income (1979 est.):** $9,959.

Sectors of the economy (% of labor force employed in 1973): Manufacturing (34%), Wholesale & retail trade (22%), Services (14%), Government (14%), Educational Services (8%), Construction (5%). **Leading products:** transportation equipment, electrical and other machinery, primary and fabricated metals, chemicals, instruments. **Agricultural products:** dairy items, eggs, tobacco. forest and nursery truck crops. **Avg. farm (1979 est.):** 125 acres. **Avg. value of farm per acre:** $2,158.

Highway expenditures per capita (1978): $62.30. **Persons per motor vehicle:** 1.40. **Minimum age for driver's license:** 16. **Gasoline tax:** 11¢ per gallon. **Diesel tax:** 11¢ per gallon. **Motor vehicle deaths:** 14.5 per 100,000 people.

Birthrate (1978): 12.0 per 1,000 people. **Infant mortality rate per 1,000 births (1977):** 13.5. **Physicians per 100,000 pop. (1977):** 226. **Dentists per 100,000 pop. (1977):** 62. **Acceptable hospital beds:** 6.1 per 1,000 people. **State expenditures per capita for health and hospitals (1978):** $68.51.

Education expenditures (1975-76): $400.67 per capita annually. **No. of pupils in public schools (1977 est.):** 626,000. **No. of institutions of higher learning (1976-77):** 46. **Public school expenditure per pupil in attendance (1975-76):** $1,687. **Avg. salary of public school teachers (1974-75 est.):** $12,051. **No. full-time teachers (1977 est.):** 42,180. **Educational attainment of adult population (1976):** 12.6 median yrs. of school completed; 2.1% with less than 5 years of education; 18.3% with 4 yrs. of college.

Telephones (1977): 81 per 100 people. **State Chamber of Commerce:** Connecticut Business & Industry Association, Inc., 60 Washington Street, Suite 1202, Hartford, Connecticut 06106.

DELAWARE

Although only Rhode Island is smaller in size and few states are less populous, Delaware has a disproportionate worth because of its natural assets and strategic proximity to New York, Philadelphia, Baltimore, and Washington. This location and the state's convenient incorporation laws have made Delaware the home of about 70,000 chartered firms, including some of the country's largest.

The state is part of the Delmarva Peninsula separating Delaware and Chesapeake Bays, the peninsula being shared with Maryland and Virginia. Almost all of the state consists of a part of the Atlantic Coastal Plain extending from Florida to New Jersey; the exception is that part of the Piedmont Plateau crossing the state's northern tip and having a maximum width of about 10 miles. Rolling hills in the north slope to a nearly sea-level plain. The state has the nation's lowest mean elevation, and along the southern border is a 30,000-acre swamp. The climate is moderate though humid, with few prolonged periods of extreme temperature.

Before the Europeans arrived, the region was inhabited by the Lenni-Lenape (later called Delaware) Indians, of Algonquian linguistic stock. Although others from Europe may have preceded him, explorer Henry Hudson is credited with Delaware's discovery (1609). A year later, Captain Samuel Argall of Virginia named Delaware Bay for his colony's governor, Thomas West, Baron De La Warr. Several countries vied for control of the state; Swedes made the first permanent settlement (1638) at Fort Christina (now Wilmington); but New Sweden, as the colony as a whole was called, gave way (1655) to Dutch forces led by New Netherland Governor Peter Stuyvesant. The English seized the colony in 1664, administering it under the Duke of York until 1682. It was then annexed to Pennsylvania as The Three Lower Counties. In 1704 it became semiautonomous, and fought in the American Revolution as a separate state. It later became (1787) the first state to ratify the U.S. Constitution.

Meanwhile, the Wilmington area developed into the hub of the flour-milling business and, in 1802, Eleuthère Irénée du Pont established a gunpowder mill on nearby Brandywine Creek that was the foundation of the state's enormous chemical industry. British ships shelled Lewes during the War of 1812, but there was little damage. Great tensions were created in Delaware by the advent of the Civil War, for it was a border state, condoning slavery but remaining loyal to the Union. Antiadministration and neutralist views were common; true secessionists were rare throughout the conflict.

Aided by fertile soil and an abundant water supply, agriculture has long been an important part of Delaware's economy, although far superseded over the years by manufacturing, chiefly of chemicals, and food and food products. In the 1950s, there was a new surge of industrial expansion, while the population increased by about 40 percent. Among historical attractions are Fort Christina Monument, Hagley Museum, and Winterthur Museum, in and near Wilmington; central New Castle, a unique survival of a colonial capital, almost unchanged; Dover, with notable public and private buildings; and Lewes, site of the first attempted settlement. Recreation areas include Cape Henlopen, Delaware Seashore, and Trap Pond State Parks. Rehoboth Beach is a popular resort area.

Because the Delaware Bay contains a deep natural channel, a sheltered area, and a convenient route to major east coast oil refineries, the state has frequently been mentioned as a prime site for construction of a deepwater terminal. In 1971, under former Republican Gov. Russell W. Peterson, who later was named chairman of the President's Council on Environmental Quality, the state enacted a broad zoning law which flatly prohibited off-shore ports in state waters and refineries and other heavy industry in its coastal zone.

Supporters argue that the law spells out a policy of moderate growth and is needed to protect Delaware's environment and tourist industry. Environmentalists have introduced amendments to clarify the language of the 1971 acts which remain intact despite continuing opposition from petroleum companies and industrially related groups.

In November 1978, Dover Air Force Base was the scene of the return of the 913 bodies from Jonestown, Guyana, after the mass murder-suicides there. The base's mortuary staff, plus military pathologists and graves registration experts from the Washington area, undertook the difficult task of identifying and embalming the corpses. Base personnel took on a more pleasant mission in early 1980, as they hosted the six U.S. diplomats spirited out of Iran by Canadian embassy officials in Tehran. The diplomats spent two days in seclusion at Dover before returning to their homes.

Full name: State of Delaware. **Origin of name:** From Lord De La Warr, English governor of Virginia. **Inhabitant:** Delawarean. **Capital:** Dover. **State motto:** Liberty & Independence. **Flag:** State seal in a buff diamond on a blue field with date Delaware ratified Constitution. **Seal:** A sheaf of wheat, an ear of corn, an ox, a soldier & a farmer under the crest of a ship. **Flower:** Peach blossom. **Bird:** Blue Hen Chicken. **Tree:** American holly. **Song:** "Our Delaware." **Nicknames:** Blue Hen State; Diamond State; First State.

Governor: Pierre S. du Pont IV. **Annual salary:** $35,000. **Term:** 4 years. **Current term expires:** Jan. 1981. **Voting requirements:** 18 yrs. old & U.S. citizen; state resident, 1 year; county, 3 mos.; district, 30 days. **U.S. Congressmen:** 1. **Entered Union:** 1787 (1st state).

Location & boundaries: Middle Atlantic state: bounded on the north by Pennsylvania; on the east by New Jersey, Delaware Bay & the Atlantic Ocean; & on the south & west by Maryland. **Total area:** 2,057 sq. mi. (ranks 49th). **Extreme length:** 96 mi. **Extreme breadth:** 35 mi. **Coastline:** 28 mi. **Chief rivers:** Delaware, Nanticoke, Christina. **Major lakes:** None, but many small lakes and ponds. **No. of counties:** 3.

Population (1979 est.): 582,000 (ranks 47th). **Pop. increase (1970-79):** 6.2%. **Places over 25,000 pop.:** 2. **Places over 100,000:** None. **Largest cities:** Wilmington, Newark, Dover. **Pop. density:** 282.9 per sq. mi. (ranks 7th). **Pop. projection 1985:** 626,000. **Pop. distribution:** 68.5% metropolitan; 31.5% non-metropolitan. **White:** 85.1%. **Black:** 14.3%. **Other:** 0.6%. **Marriage rate (1977):** 6.9 per 1,000 people. **Divorce rate:** 5.2 per 1,000 people.

State finances (1978). Revenue: $800,842,000. **Expenditures:** $725,031,000. **State taxes:** $771.48 per capita. **State personal income tax:** Yes. **Public debt (1978):** $1,316.19 per capita. **Federal aid (1979):** $399.31 per capita. **Personal income (1979 est.):** $9,537.

Sectors of the economy (% of labor force employed in 1970): Manufacturing (30%), Wholesale and retail trade (19%), Government (15%), Services (8%), Educational Services (8%), Construction (8%). **Leading products:** chemicals & related items, food, apparel, primary & fabricated metals, textile mill items, automobiles, paper. **Agricultural products:** broilers, dairy items, corn, soybeans, potatoes. **Fishing:** clams, crabs. **Avg. farm (1979 est.):** 207 acres. **Avg. value of farm per acre:** $1,725.

Highway expenditures per capita (1978): $89.87. **Persons per motor vehicle:** 1.47. **Minimum age for driver's license:** 16. **Gasoline tax:** 9¢ per gallon. **Diesel tax:** 9¢ per gallon. **Motor vehicle deaths:** 21.6 per 100,000 people.

Birthrate (1978): 14.9 per 1,000 people. **Infant mortality rate per 1,000 births (1977):** 13.6. **Physicians per 100,000 pop. (1977):** 156. **Dentists per 100,000 pop. (1977):** 44. **Acceptable hospital beds:** 8.1 per 1,000 people. **State expenditures per capita for health and hospitals (1978):** $70.40.

Education expenditures (1975-76): $566.38 per capita annually. **No. of pupils in public schools (1977 est.):** 120,000. **No. of institutions of higher learning (1976-77):** 10. **Public school expenditure per pupil in attendance (1975-76):** $1,817. **Avg. salary of public school teachers (1974-75 est.):** $12,110. **No. full-time teachers (1977 est.):** 7,210. **Educational attainment of adult population (1976):** 12.5 median yrs. of school completed; 1.8% with less than 5 years of education; 15.5% with 4 yrs. of college.

Telephones (1977): 84 per 100 people. **State Chamber of Commerce:** Delaware State Chamber of Commerce, Inc., 1102 West Street, Wilmington, Delaware 19801.

FLORIDA

Florida, southernmost of the continental states, is a low-lying peninsula with a coastline second in

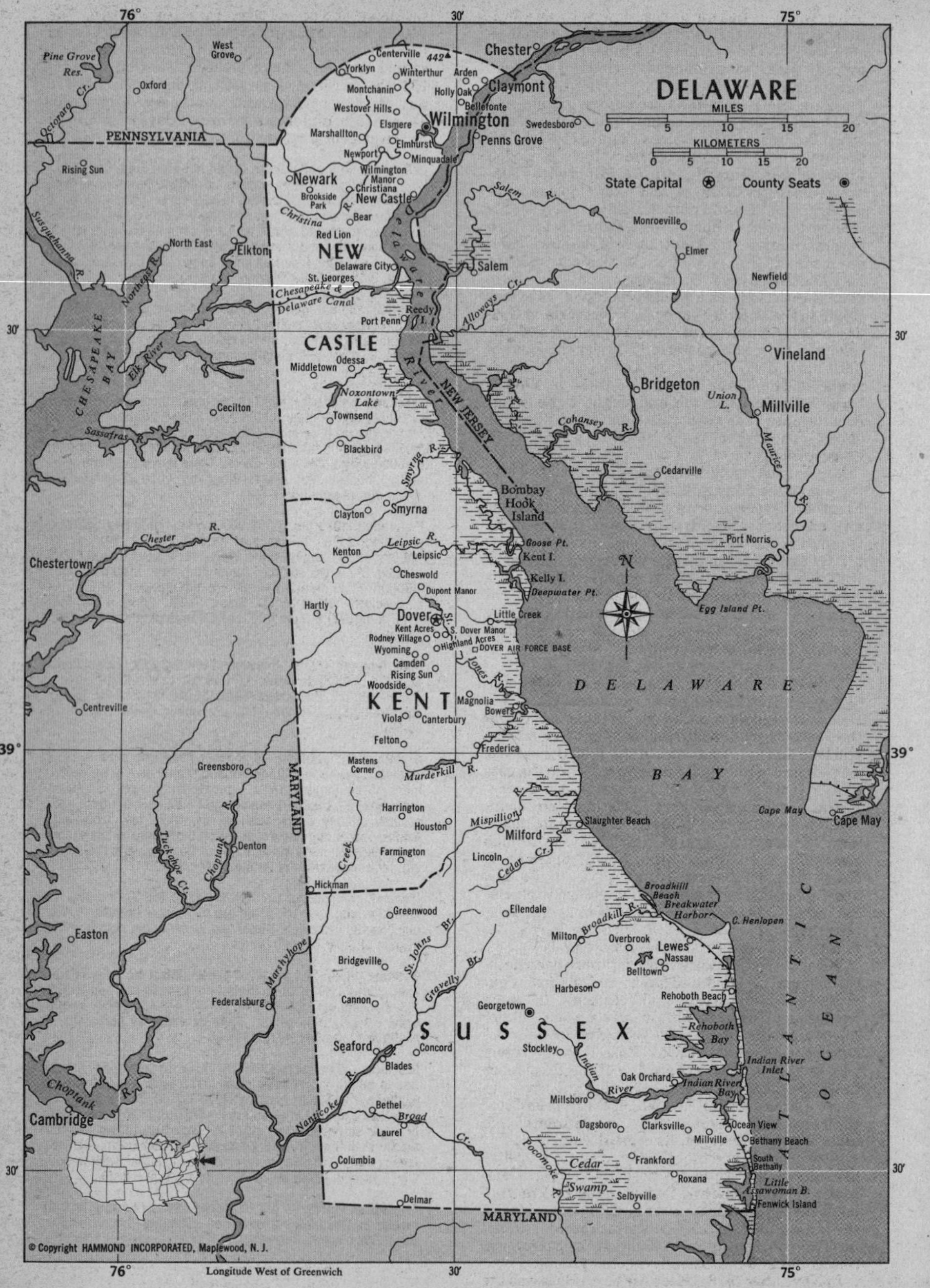
DELAWARE
MILES
0 5 10 15 20
KILOMETERS
0 5 10 15 20
State Capital County Seats
PENNSYLVANIA
Pine Grove Res.
West Grove
Oxford
Rising Sun
North East
Elkton
Chestertown
Centreville
Easton
Cambridge
Choptank R.
Tuckahoe Cr.
Denton
Greensboro
Greenwood
Bridgeville
Federalsburg
Seaford
Cannon
Bethel
Laurel
Columbia
Delmar
Concord
Blades
Broad Cr.
Nanticoke R.
Marshyhope Creek
Hickman
Farmington
Harrington
Houston
Mastens Corner
Felton
Viola
Canterbury
Magnolia
Woodside
Rising Sun
Camden
Wyoming
Hartly
Dover
Kent Acres
Rodney Village
Highland Acres
S. Dover Manor
DOVER AIR FORCE BASE
Dupont Manor
Cheswold
Kenton
Leipsic
Leipsic R.
Smyrna
Clayton
Smyrna R.
Blackbird
Townsend
Noxontown Lake
Middletown
Odessa
St. Georges
Delaware City
Chesapeake & Delaware Canal
Red Lion
Bear
New Castle
Christiana
Wilmington Manor
Brookside Park
Newark
Christina
Newport
Marshallton
Elsmere
Elmhurst
Minquadale
Wilmington
Bellefonte
Holly Oak
Westover Hills
Montchanin
Winterthur
Yorklyn
Centerville
442
Arden
Claymont
Chester
Swedesboro
Penns Grove
Salem
Salem R.
Alloways Cr.
Reedy I.
Port Penn
Monroeville
Elmer
Newfield
Vineland
Bridgeton
Millville
Union L.
Maurice R.
Cedarville
Cohansey R.
Port Norris
Bombay Hook Island
Goose Pt.
Kent I.
Kelly I.
Deepwater Pt.
Egg Island Pt.
Jones R.
Little Creek
DELAWARE
BAY
Bowers
Frederica
Murderkill R.
Milford
Mispillion R.
Lincoln
Cedar Cr.
Ellendale
Slaughter Beach
Broadkill Beach
Breakwater Harbor
C. Henlopen
Milton
Broadkill R.
Overbrook
Lewes
Nassau
Belltown
Harbeson
Rehoboth Beach
Rehoboth Bay
Indian River Inlet
Indian River Bay
Georgetown
Stockley
St. Johns Br.
Gravelly Br.
Oak Orchard
Indian River
Millsboro
Dagsboro
Clarksville
Millville
Ocean View
Bethany Beach
South Bethany
Frankford
Roxana
Selbyville
Little Assawoman B.
Fenwick Island
Pocomoke Cedar Swamp
MARYLAND
KENT
SUSSEX
NEW CASTLE
NEW JERSEY
Delaware River
Susquehanna R.
Octoraro Cr.
Chesapeake Bay
Elk River
Sassafras R.
Cecilton
Northeast R.
Chester R.
Choptank R.
ATLANTIC OCEAN
N
Copyright HAMMOND INCORPORATED, Maplewood, N.J.
Longitude West of Greenwich
76° 30′ 75°
39° 30′

length only to Alaska's, measuring 1,350 miles—580 on the Atlantic coast and 770 on the Gulf. The state has an average elevation of 100 feet. Curving southwestward for about 200 miles off the southern coast are the Florida Keys, including Elliott Key and Key Largo at the north and Key West at the south.

Indians are thought to have inhabited this region about 10,000 years ago. In 1513 Juan Ponce de León, a Spanish explorer said to be searching for the legendary Fountain of Youth, landed on the east coast and mistakenly thought his find was an island. He named it and claimed it for Spain. Except for an interlude of British rule (1763-1783), Spain kept a tenuous hold until 1819, when the United States bought the Spanish claim. Florida became a state in 1845, seceded from the Union in 1861, and was readmitted in 1868. Florida's early development was severely hampered by two bloody and costly wars with the Seminole Indians, who were not defeated until 1842. Many never surrendered, but fled instead to the Everglades wilderness, became the core of a new tribe, and, eventually, were settled on reservations. In May 1970, the Seminoles were awarded $12,347,500 for land taken from them by U.S. military forces. The Indians estimate there are now 1,500 Seminoles in Florida and 3,500 in Oklahoma.

Among the fastest-growing states in the nation, Florida has risen in population from 2.8 million in 1950 to over 8.8 million today. Land values and industry have grown proportionately, but rapid expansion has created such problems for the state as attempting to keep pace with the spiraling demand for new facilities.

Tourism is the state's leading industry, thanks to one of the mildest and most comfortable climates east of the Mississippi and an abundance of swimming, fishing, and other recreational resources. Resort centers along the "Gold Coast" include Miami Beach (a suburb of Miami), Palm Beach, Daytona Beach, and Fort Lauderdale. Formerly a winter industry, tourism is now significant all year round. Disney World, built on a 27,400-acre site near Orlando, is the state's newest attraction; eight times as large as California's Disneyland, it is the world's largest non-governmental construction project.

Everglades National Park, at Florida's southern tip, draws many visitors. The 5,000-square-mile preserve contains the country's largest remaining tropical wilderness and a multitude of plant and animal types. Other attractions include Cypress Gardens near Winter Haven, Monkey Jungle near Goulds (a Miami suburb), and the Ringling Museum of Art in Sarasota.

Commercial fishing is a major industry in the state, although much of the water is given over to sport fishermen. There are more kinds of fish in the waters in or off Florida than anywhere else in the country. The state is also important agriculturally; its leading crop—oranges—is worth over $400 million a year. Mining of phosphate is also significant.

An important connection point for North, Central, and South American air traffic, Florida has about 330 airports; Miami International is one of the busiest in the world in passenger traffic.

Natural dangers the state faces include crop damage by droughts and early frosts, and seasonal (July-October) hurricanes. Destructive hurricanes struck Florida in 1926, 1928, 1935, 1941, and 1964. Today, many Federal programs are being implemented to help arm the state against these tropical storms.

Cape Canaveral (called Cape Kennedy from 1963 to 1973) was the launching site of most U.S. space vehicles, including the first manned vehicle to land on the moon (1969), the first orbiting laboratory (Skylab 1973), and the first joint venture with the Soviet Union (1975).

All Florida courts were open in 1977 to news coverage by television and still picture cameras, thus making the state's judicial system the most open to media coverage in the nation.

John A. Spenkelink was put to death in the electric chair on May 25, 1979, at the Florida State Prison. He was the first person to be executed in the U.S. since 1977. His case attracted nationwide attention from those both for and against capital punishment, thereby paving the way for the reconsideration of death penalty sentences.

In 1980, Florida voters adopted a constitutional amendment to increase from $5,000 to $25,000 the homestead exemption from property taxes. The state compensated local governments for lost revenue out of a large surplus.

Tens of thousands of Cuban refugees journeyed in small boats from Mariel, Cuba, to Key West in May 1980. Many were then transferred to Eglin Air Force Base, near Fort Walton Beach in Florida's Panhandle region, before being sent to permanent settlement sites throughout the nation.

Full name: State of Florida. **Origin of name:** From Spanish, Pascua Florida, meaning "Feast of Flowers." **Inhabitant:** Floridian. **Capital:** Tallahassee. **State motto:** In God We Trust. **Flag:** State seal lies on white field crossed by diagonal red bars. **Seal:** Sun, steamboat & Indian girl strewing flowers. **Flower:** Orange blossom. **Bird:** Mockingbird. **Tree:** Sabal palm. **Song:** "Old Folks at Home." **Nickname:** Sunshine State.

Governor: Robert Graham. **Annual salary:** $56,000. **Term:** 4 years. **Current term expires:** Jan. 1983. **Voting requirements:** 18 yrs. old & U.S. citizen; resident of state and county. **U.S. Congressmen:** 15. **Entered Union:** 1845 (27th state).

Location & boundaries: South Atlantic state: bounded on the north by Alabama, the Chattahoochee River, Georgia & St. Mary's River; on the east by the Atlantic Ocean; on the south by the Straits of Florida; & on the west by the Gulf of Mexico, the Perdido River & Alabama. **Total area:** 58,560 sq. mi. (ranks 22nd). **Extreme length:** 447 mi. **Extreme breadth:** 361 mi. **Coastline:** 399 mi. on Atlantic; 798 mi. on Gulf Coast. **Chief rivers:** St. Johns, Apalachicola, Suwannee. **Major lakes:** Okeechobee, George, Kissimmee. **No. of counties:** 67.

Population (1979 est.): 8,860,000 (ranks 8th). **Pop. increase (1970-79):** 30.5%. **Places over 25,000 pop.:** 44. **Places over 100,000:** 8. **Largest cities:** Jacksonville, Miami, Tampa, St. Petersburg. **Pop. density:** 151.3 per sq. mi. (ranks 12th). **Pop. projection 1985:** 10,941,000. **Pop. distribution:** 85.9% metropolitan; 14.1% nonmetropolitan. **White:** 84.1%. **Black:** 15.5%. **Other:** 0.4%. **Marriage rate (1977):** 10.5 per 1,000 people. **Divorce rate:** 7.4 per 1,000 people.

State finances (1978). Revenue: $6,442,069,000. **Expenditures:** $5,712,824,000. **State taxes:** $438.01 per capita. **State personal income tax:** No. **Public debt (1978):** $272.75 per capita. **Federal aid (1979):** $270.08 per capita. **Personal income (1979 est.):** $8,532.

Sectors of the economy (% of labor force employed in 1970): Wholesale and retail trade (24%), Government (16%), Manufacturing (14%), Services (12%), Construction (9%), Educational Services (7%). **Leading products:** apparel products; transportation equipment; fabricated metal products; chemicals; paper items; food; printing & publishing; electrical machinery; limestone, clay & glass items; fabricated metals. **Minerals:** phosphate rock, stone, clay. **Agricultural products:** dairy items, cattle, citrus, tomatoes, sugarcane for sugar & seed, winter vegetables. **Fishing:** oysters and scallops, crabs, lobsters, shrimp. **Avg. farm (1979 est.):** 394 acres. **Avg. value of farm per acre:** $930.

Highway expenditures per capita (1978): $76.44. **Persons per motor vehicle:** 1.23. **Minimum age for driver's license:** 16. **Gasoline tax:** 8¢ per gallon. **Diesel tax:** 8¢ per gallon. **Motor vehicle deaths:** 26.3 per 100,000 people.

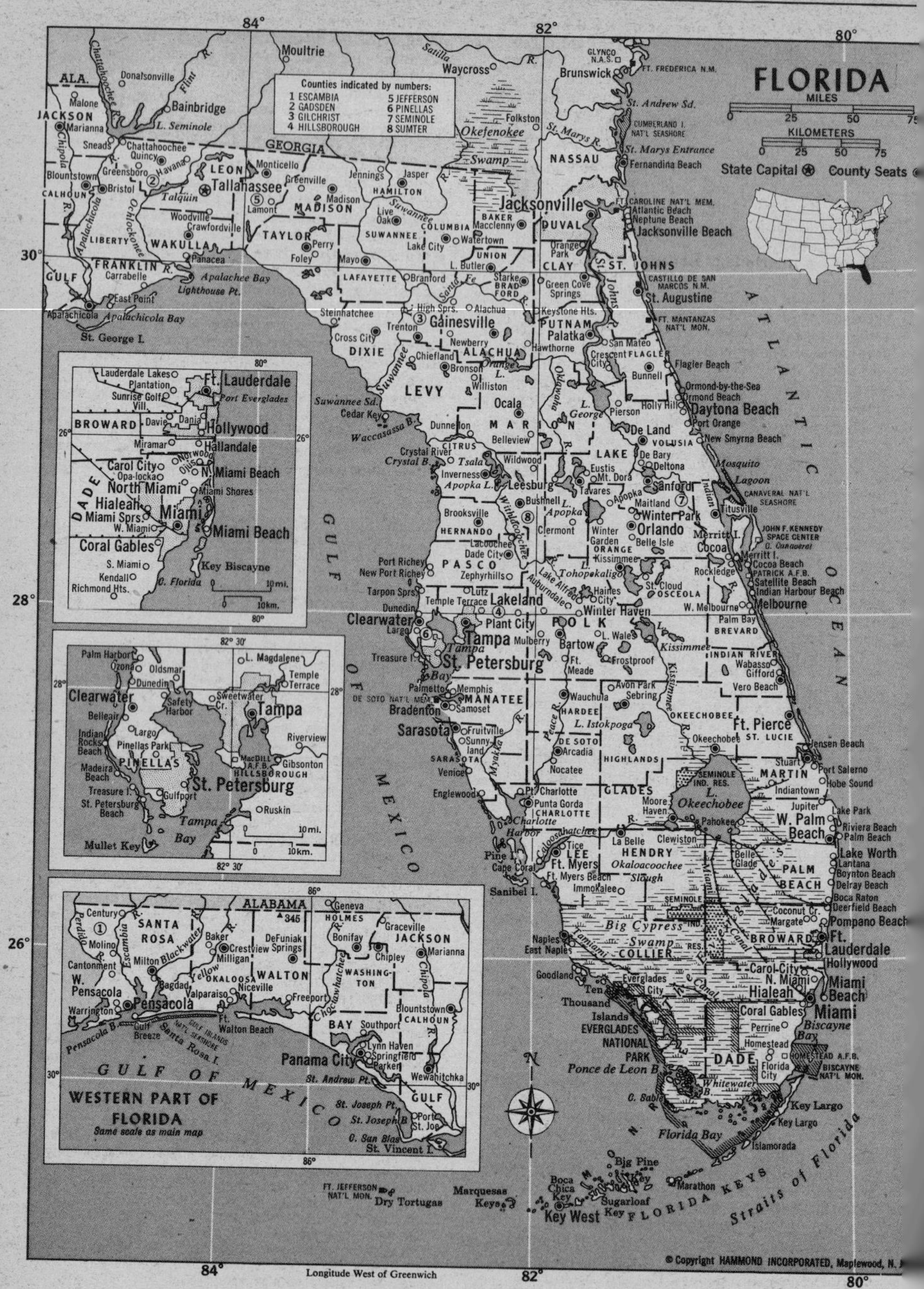
FLORIDA
MILES
KILOMETERS
State Capital   County Seats

Counties indicated by numbers:
1 ESCAMBIA   5 JEFFERSON
2 GADSDEN   6 PINELLAS
3 GILCHRIST   7 SEMINOLE
4 HILLSBOROUGH 8 SUMTER

ALA.
GEORGIA
Moultrie
Waycross
Brunswick
GLYNCO N.A.S.
FT. FREDERICA N.M.
Donalsonville
Bainbridge
Flint
Satilla R.
St. Andrew Sd.
CUMBERLAND I. NAT'L SEASHORE
St. Marys Entrance
Malone
Marianna
L. Seminole
Okefenokee
Swamp
St. Marys R.
NASSAU
Fernandina Beach
JACKSON
Sneads
Chattahoochee
Quincy
Havana
Greensboro
Bristol
Blountstown
Chipola
CALHOUN
Folkston
FT. CAROLINE NAT'L MEM.
Atlantic Beach
Neptune Beach
Jacksonville Beach
LEON
Tallahassee
Monticello
Greenville
Jennings
Jasper
HAMILTON
Jacksonville
BAKER
Macclenny
DUVAL
Talquin
Lamont
MADISON
Madison
Live Oak
COLUMBIA
Watertown
Orange Park
Woodville
Crawfordville
TAYLOR
Perry
Foley
SUWANNEE
Lake City
L. Butler
UNION
Starke
BRADFORD
CLAY
Green Cove Springs
ST. JOHNS
St. Augustine
CASTILLO DE SAN MARCOS N.M.
WAKULLA
Panacea
Mayo
Santa Fe
FT. MANTANZAS NAT'L MON.
LIBERTY
FRANKLIN
Carrabelle
LAFAYETTE
Branford
High Sprs.
Alachua
PUTNAM
Palatka
San Mateo
FLAGLER
Bunnell
Flagler Beach
GULF
Apalachicola
Apalachicola Bay
Lighthouse Pt.
Apalachee Bay
St. George I.
Steinhatchee
Cross City
Trenton
Gainesville
Newberry
Chiefland
Bronson
ALACHUA
Hawthorne
Crescent City
Ormond-by-the-Sea
Ormond Beach
DIXIE
LEVY
Williston
Ocala
MARION
L. George
Pierson
Holly Hill
Daytona Beach
Port Orange
Cedar Key
Suwannee Sd.
Waccasassa B.
Dunnellon
Belleview
De Land
VOLUSIA
New Smyrna Beach
Crystal River
Crystal B.
Tsala
CITRUS
Wildwood
LAKE
De Bary
Deltona
Mosquito Lagoon
Inverness
Apopka L.
Leesburg
Eustis
Mt. Dora
Tavares
Sanford
Apopka
Maitland
CANAVERAL NAT'L SEASHORE
Titusville
Brooksville
Bushnell
L. Apopka
Winter Park
Orlando
Indian R.
HERNANDO
Clermont
Winter Garden
Belle Isle
ORANGE
Merritt I.
Cocoa
JOHN F. KENNEDY SPACE CENTER
C. Canaveral
Lacoochee
Dade City
Kissimmee
Rockledge
Cocoa Beach
PATRICK A.F.B.
Satellite Beach
Indian Harbour Beach
Port Richey
New Port Richey
Zephyrhills
L. Tohopekaliga
St. Cloud
OSCEOLA
Melbourne
Tarpon Sprs.
Lutz
Temple Terrace
Haines City
Auburndale
Lake Alfred
W. Melbourne
Palm Bay
BREVARD
Dunedin
Clearwater
Largo
Plant City
Lakeland
Winter Haven
POLK
L. Wales
INDIAN RIVER
Wabasso
Gifford
Tampa
St. Petersburg
Treasure I.
Tampa Bay
Mulberry
Bartow
Frostproof
Kissimmee
Vero Beach
Palmetto
Memphis
MANATEE
Samoset
Ft. Meade
Avon Park
Sebring
OKEECHOBEE
Ft. Pierce
ST. LUCIE
DE SOTO NAT'L MEM.
Bradenton
Sarasota
Fruitville
Sunnyland
Wauchula
HARDEE
L. Istokpoga
HIGHLANDS
Jensen Beach
Stuart
Port Salerno
MARTIN
SARASOTA
Arcadia
Nocatee
DE SOTO
Okeechobee
L. Okeechobee
Hobe Sound
Venice
Englewood
Pt. Charlotte
Punta Gorda
CHARLOTTE
GLADES
Moore Haven
Indiantown
Jupiter
Lake Park
W. Palm Beach
Riviera Beach
Palm Beach
Charlotte Harbor
Pahokee
Cape Coral
Pine I.
Caloosahatchee
LEE
La Belle
Clewiston
SEMINOLE IND. RES.
Belle Glade
Lake Worth
Lantana
Boynton Beach
PALM BEACH
Ft. Myers
HENDRY
Okaloacoochee Slough
Delray Beach
Boca Raton
Sanibel I.
Ft. Myers Beach
Immokalee
Deerfield Beach
Pompano Beach
SEMINOLE
Big Cypress IND. RES.
Coconut Cr.
Margate
BROWARD
Ft. Lauderdale
Naples
East Naples
COLLIER
Swamp
Hollywood
Carol City
N. Miami
Miami Beach
Goodland
Everglades City
Hialeah
Coral Gables
Miami
Ten Thousand Islands
EVERGLADES NATIONAL PARK
Perrine
Biscayne Bay
DADE
Homestead
HOMESTEAD A.F.B.
Ponce de Leon B.
Florida City
BISCAYNE NAT'L MON.
C. Sable
Whitewater B.
Florida Bay
Key Largo
Key Largo
Islamorada
FT. JEFFERSON NAT'L MON.
Dry Tortugas
Marquesas Keys
Boca Chica Key
Big Pine Key
Sugarloaf Key
Marathon
FLORIDA KEYS
Key West
Straits of Florida
ATLANTIC OCEAN
GULF OF MEXICO
N

Longitude West of Greenwich
Copyright HAMMOND INCORPORATED, Maplewood, N.J.

Ft. Lauderdale
Lauderdale Lakes
Plantation
Sunrise Golf Vill.
Port Everglades
BROWARD
Davie
Dania
Hollywood
Miramar
Hallandale
Norwood
Carol City
Opa-locka
Ojus
N. Miami Beach
DADE
North Miami
Miami Shores
Hialeah
Miami Sprs.
Miami
W. Miami
Miami Beach
Coral Gables
S. Miami
Kendall
Key Biscayne
Richmond Hts.
C. Florida

Palm Harbor
Ozona
Oldsmar
L. Magdalene
Dunedin
Temple Terrace
Sweetwater Cr.
Clearwater
Safety Harbor
Tampa
Belleair
Riverview
Indian Rocks Beach
Largo
Pinellas Park
PINELLAS
MacDill A.F.B.
Gibsonton
HILLSBOROUGH
Madeira Beach
Treasure I.
St. Petersburg
St. Petersburg Beach
Gulfport
Ruskin
Tampa Bay
Mullet Key

WESTERN PART OF FLORIDA
Same scale as main map
ALABAMA
Century
Molino
SANTA ROSA
Geneva
Graceville
HOLMES
Baker
DeFuniak Springs
Bonifay
JACKSON
Marianna
Cantonment
Milton
Crestview
Milligan
Chipley
W. Pensacola
Bagdad
OKALOOSA
WALTON
WASHINGTON
Warrington
Pensacola
Valparaiso
Niceville
Freeport
Blountstown
CALHOUN
Pensacola B.
Gulf Breeze
Santa Rosa I.
Ft. Walton Beach
BAY
Southport
GULF ISLANDS NAT'L SEASHORE
Lynn Haven
Springfield
Parker
Wewahitchka
Panama City
GULF
St. Andrew Pt.
St. Joseph Pt.
St. Joseph B.
Port St. Joe
C. San Blas
St. Vincent I.
GULF OF MEXICO

Birthrate (1978): 13.1 per 1,000 people. **Infant mortality rate per 1,000 births (1977):** 15.5. **Physicians per 100,000 pop. (1977):** 183. **Dentists per 100,000 pop. (1977):** 47. **Acceptable hospital beds:** 6.5 per 1,000 people. **State expenditures per capita for health and hospitals (1978):** $54.73.

Education expenditures (1975-76): $375.65 per capita annually. **No. of pupils in public schools (1977 est.):** 1,515,000. **No. of institutions of higher learning (1976-77):** 73. **Public school expenditure per pupil in attendance (1975-76):** $1,576. **Avg. salary of public school teachers (1974-75 est.):** $10,780. **No. full-time teachers (1977 est.):** 78,920. **Educational attainment of adult population (1976):** 12.4 median yrs. of school completed; 3.7% with less than 5 years of education; 13.7% with 4 yrs. of college.

Telephones (1977): 80 per 100 people. **State Chamber of Commerce:** Florida State Chamber of Commerce, P.O. Box 5497, 311 S. Calhoun Street, Tallahassee, Florida 32301.

GEORGIA

The largest state east of the Mississippi, and the last of the 13 Colonies to be founded, Georgia consists of three main land regions: in the north is a small section of the Appalachian Mountains; the Piedmont Plateau constitutes the middle; and in the south, coastal flatlands make up about three-fifths of the state's total area. Landmarks include the Okefenokee Swamp, one of the country's largest.

Mound Builders were the first known inhabitants of the Georgia region, followed in modern times by Creek and Cherokee Indians. Spanish explorer De Soto is thought to have been the first European to visit (1540) the area, but British claims soon conflicted with those of Spain; in 1733, English philanthropist James Oglethorpe led a group of his countrymen in launching the first permanent settlement at Savannah as an asylum for debtors. England ended the Spanish threat in 1742, as forces under Oglethorpe defeated their rivals in the battle of Bloody Marsh.

The sale of rum and the introduction of Negro slaves into the region were at first outlawed, but by about 1750 new legislation ended these restrictions. Many foreigners were among the early immigrants, soon followed by settlers mainly from Virginia and the Carolinas.

After the American Revolution, Georgia became a stronghold of slavery and cotton culture—fostered by the invention of the cotton gin, in 1793, by Eli Whitney, who was living near Savannah. Georgia seceded in 1861, and suffered great damage in the Civil War. The war ended slavery, but black Georgians suffered many disabilities until the civil rights movement of the 1950s and 1960s.

Changes in social patterns are evident. Public accommodations throughout the state are generally desegregated, in accordance with law, as are most school systems, although residential housing patterns in many areas limit the amount of actual school integration. In 1980 violence occurred between blacks and whites in rural Wrightsville.

As in many other parts of the country, Georgians expressed concern over busing pupils to achieve racial balance in schools. In February, 1972, classroom boycotts to protest busing cut into school attendance at Augusta. There were efforts to promote a statewide boycott, but they failed.

Georgia, the first state (1943) to grant 18-year-olds the right to vote, in 1973 lowered from 21 to 18 the legal age for adults.

Georgia is today involved in the same agriculture-to-industry transformation which the South as a whole is undergoing. Its extensive resources include a wealth of largely untapped hydroelectric power and some of the most valuable marble and gravel deposits in the country. Favorable climate, natural resources and an abundant labor supply have caused many industries to establish plants in the state. Industrialization has brought efforts at unionization, and resistance to these efforts. In 1980, the mayor and police chief of Milledgevile settled out of court with a union which had sued them for alleged illegal surveillance of union organizers. Georgia is the nation's largest supplier of peanuts and poultry, and also ranks high in textiles, egg production, lumber, cotton, peaches, and tobacco production, while Atlanta has become one of the South's most important transportation and distributing centers.

Tourism is another significant revenue source, and is aided by such attractions as the Chattahoochee and Oconee National Forests, FDR's "Little White House" at Warm Springs, and Andersonville Prison Park and National Cemetery on the site of the infamous Confederate prison. A major attraction is the enormous Confederate Memorial carving, the world's largest single piece of sculpture, cut into the sheer north face of historic Stone Mountain, near Atlanta; the work, centerpiece of a 3,200-acre park, depicts General Robert E. Lee, Confederate President Jefferson Davis, and General Stonewall Jackson.

Former Gov. Jimmy Carter, often hailed as one of the South's "new breed" of young progressive chief executives, was inaugurated as President of the United States in 1977, the first Southern president since the Civil War.

Full name: State of Georgia. **Origin of name:** In honor of King George II of England. **Inhabitant:** Georgian. **Capital:** Atlanta. **State motto:** Wisdom, Justice & Moderation. **Flag:** State seal on a vertical blue bar; Confederate flag to the right. **Seal:** Arch representing state constitution; three columns with Georgia's motto; date 1776 is year Georgia signed Declaration of Independence. **Flower:** Cherokee rose. **Bird:** Brown thrasher. **Tree:** Live oak. **Song:** "Georgia." **Nickname:** Peach State and The Empire State of the South.

Governor: George D. Busbee. **Annual salary:** $61,050. **Term:** 4 years. **Current term expires:** Jan. 1983. **Voting requirements:** 18 yrs. old & U.S. citizen. **U.S. Congressmen:** 10. **Entered Union:** 1788 (4th state).

Location & boundaries: South Atlantic state: bounded on the north by Tennessee & North Carolina; on the east by South Carolina, the Atlantic Ocean & the Savannah, Tugaloo & Chattooga Rivers; on the south by St. Mary's River & Florida; & on the west by Florida, Alabama & the Chattahoochee River. **Total area:** 58,876 sq. mi. (ranks 21st). **Extreme length:** 315 mi. **Extreme breadth:** 250 mi. **Coastline:** 100 mi. **Chief Rivers:** Altamaha, Chattahoochee, Savannah. **Major lakes:** Lanier, Allatoona, Seminole. **No. of counties:** 159.

Population (1979 est.): 5,117,000 (ranks 14th). **Pop. increase (1970-79):** 11.5%. **Places over 25,000 pop.:** 12. **Places over 100,000:** 3. **Largest cities:** Atlanta, Columbus, Macon, Savannah. **Pop. density:** 86.9 per sq. mi. (ranks 22nd). **Pop. projection 1985:** 5,721,000. **Pop. distribution:** 56.8% metropolitan; 43.2% non-metropolitan. **White:** 73.8%. **Black:** 25.9%. **Other:** 0.3%. **Marriage rate (1977):** 13.3 per 1,000 people. **Divorce rate:** 6.1 per 1,000 people.

State finances (1978). Revenue: $4,137,333,000. **Expenditures:** $3,892,982,000. **State taxes:** $429.53 per capita. **State personal income tax:** Yes. **Public debt (1978):** $264.70 per capita. **Federal aid (1979):** $425.29 per capita. **Personal income (1979 est.):** $7,515.

Sectors of the economy (% of labor force employed in 1970): Manufacturing (27%), Wholesale and retail trade (20%), Government (16%), Services (9%), Educational Services (7%), Construction (7%). **Leading products:** textile mill items, apparel, food, transportation equipment, lumber, pulp & paper products, chemicals. **Minerals:** clays, stone, cement, sand & gravel. **Agricultural products:** broilers, eggs, cattle, peanuts, tobacco, corn. **Fishing:** shrimp. **Avg. farm (1979 est.):** 291 acres. **Avg. value of farm per acre:** $609.

GEORGIA
Counties indicated by numbers:
1 BALDWIN
2 BARROW
3 CATOOSA
4 CHEROKEE
5 CLAYTON
6 DADE
7 DE KALB
8 DOUGLAS
9 FAYETTE
10 GLASCOCK
11 MONTGOMERY
12 OCONEE
13 ROCKDALE
14 SCHLEY
15 TALIAFERRO
16 TOWNS
17 WALTON
18 WHITFIELD
MILES
KILOMETERS
State Capitals.
County Seats
Copyright HAMMOND INCORPORATED, Maplewood, N.J.
Longitude West of Greenwich
GULF OF MEXICO
ATLANTIC OCEAN
FLORIDA
ALABAMA
TENN.
NORTH CAROLINA
SOUTH CAROLINA
SAVANNAH RIVER ATOMIC ENERGY RESERVATION

Highway expenditures per capita (1978): $100.70. **Persons per motor vehicle:** 1.35. **Minimum age for driver's license:** 16. **Gasoline tax:** 7.5¢ per gallon.* **Diesel tax:** 7.5¢ per gallon.* **Motor vehicle deaths:** 28.9 per 100,000 people. *Plus 3% of retail sales price.

Birthrate (1978): 16.6 per 1,000 people. **Infant mortality rate per 1,000 births (1977):** 15.4. **Physicians per 100,000 pop. (1977):** 141. **Dentists per 100,000 pop. (1977):** 39. **Acceptable hospital beds:** 6.2 per 1,000 people. **State expenditures per capita for health and hospitals (1978):** $65.27.

Education expenditures (1975-76): $354.73 per capita annually. **No. of pupils in public schools (1977 est.):** 1,079,000. **No. of institutions of higher learning (1976-77):** 67. **Public school expenditure per pupil in attendance (1975-76):** $1,323. **Avg. salary of public school teachers (1974-75 est.):** $10,641. **No. full-time teachers (1977 est.):** 48,200. **Educational attainment of adult population (1976):** 12.3 median yrs. of school completed; 8.0% with less than 5 years of education; 12.3% with 4 yrs. of college.

Telephones (1977): 73 per 100 people. **State Chamber of Commerce:** Georgia Chamber of Commerce, 1200 Commerce Building, Atlanta, Georgia 30303.

HAWAII

Hawaii, 50th state to join (1959) the Union, is a chain of 132 islands near the center of the North Pacific Ocean, about 2,400 miles from San Francisco. The islands were formed by volcanoes erupting from the ocean floor; there are some still-active volcanoes at the easterly end of the island chain, which extends 1,523 miles, and may be divided into three groups: the sand and coral islands of the northwest, rock islets in the center, and the eight major islands at the southeast end.

The eight major islands make up all except three square miles of the entire area: Hawaii, Oahu, Maui, Kahoolawe, Lanai, Molokai, Kauai, and Niihau. Hawaii is the largest of these islands (4,038 sq. mi.), while Oahu has the highest population (over 80 percent of the state's total). On Oahu are Honolulu and Pearl Harbor. Of these eight islands, only Kahoolawe is uninhabited; it is used as a target island for bombing and artillery training. The coastline of the islands is approximately 750 miles long. Cooling trade winds make for a pleasantly mild climate all year round. Rainfall varies from hundreds of inches in the mountains to less than 10 inches in the lowlands.

A melting pot of nationalities and racial groups, Hawaii was first settled by seagoing Polynesians, most likely from the Marquesas Islands, during the eighth century. The early Hawaiians, who practiced a religion that included human sacrifice and idolatry, developed a feudal form of government. Europe learned of the islands after British explorer Captain James Cook came upon them (1778); he named them the "Sandwich Islands" in honor of the Earl of Sandwich.

Local chieftain King Kamehameha I took control (1795) of the main islands—except Kauai and Niihau—after thirteen years of warfare with other aspirants. The other two islands accepted his rule in 1810.

Missionaries were active on the islands in the 1800s. In 1840, the Kingdom of Hawaii adopted its first constitution. The growth of the vital sugar and pineapple industries increased U.S. business and political involvement, leading to the establishment (1900) of Hawaii as a United States Territory following annexation (1898). The present population includes significant numbers of Polynesians, Chinese, Filipinos, and Japanese, as well as Caucasians.

The "date which will live in infamy"—Dec. 7, 1941—saw the Japanese attack on Pearl Harbor, which drew the nation into World War II.

Hawaii has since consolidated its importance as a strategic U.S. military outpost: Army, Navy, and Air Force units of the Pacific are under a single command located there. The salaries of military personnel and civilians employed at this command constitute one of Hawaii's principal sources of income. Tourism is the major revenue source. Sugar and pineapple are still exported but are diminishing in the face of foreign competition.

The building boom which critics say created a "concrete jungle" in Waikiki to provide for the tourists is now shifting toward housing for local residents, giving rise to cries of "urban sprawl." There is considerable focus on environmental quality control, with frequent calls for preserving the land. In addition, there is growing concern over the traditional land development pattern. Most of the undeveloped land has been in the hands of a few owners who in the past leased but would not sell to private individuals, who then built homes on their leaseholds. With pressure on landowners to sell rather than lease, and with escalating land values, the future of the real estate market is uncertain.

In addition to such pleasures as swimming, boating and surfing, the islands have much to offer the scientist, historian and general sightseer, including the Bishop Museum in Honolulu—an important center for Polynesian studies; Iolani Palace in Honolulu, the only royal palace in the United States; the world's most active volcano, Kilauea, on Hawaii Island; the extinct Haleakala Crater on Maui Island; and the Waimea Canyon on Kauai Island, often called the "Grand Canyon of the Pacific." The cliff Nuuanu Pali (1,188 feet high) offers a fine view of Oahu's northeast coast.

In 1979, blue-collar state employees went on a six-week strike, causing accumulation of trash and school closings, and there was a three-day work stoppage by most of the state's police officers.

Full name: State of Hawaii. **Origin of name:** Perhaps from native name of the Polynesians' original home. **Inhabitant:** Hawaiian. **Capital:** Honolulu. **State motto:** Ua Mau Ke Ea O Ka Aina I Ka Pono (The Life of the Land Is Perpetuated in Righteousness). **Flag:** Eight alternating white, red & blue bars, representing main islands of state; Union Jack in upper left. **Seal:** Coat of arms of Hawaiian monarchy with King Kamehameha I on right & goddess of liberty on left. **Flower:** Hibiscus. **Bird:** Hawaiian goose. **Tree:** Candlenut (kukui). **Song:** "Hawaii Ponoi." **Nickname:** Aloha State.

Governor: George R. Ariyoshi. **Annual salary:** $50,000. **Term:** 4 years. **Current term expires:** Dec. 1982. **Voting requirements:** 18 yrs. old & U.S. citizen. **U.S. Congressmen:** 2. **Entered Union:** 1959 (50th state).

Location & boundaries: Pacific state composed of a chain of 132 islands, located about 2,397 miles SW of San Francisco; major islands from east to west are Hawaii, Maui, Kahoolawe, Lanai, Molokai, Oahu, Kauai & Niihau. **Total area:** 6,450 sq. mi. (ranks 47th). **Coastline:** 750 mi. **No. of counties:** 5 (inc. Kalawao County—a leprosy settlement).

Population (1979 est.): 915,000 (ranks 40th). **Pop. increase (1970-79):** 18.8%. **Places over 25,000 pop.:** 4. **Places over 100,000:** 1. **Largest cities:** Honolulu, Kailua. **Pop. density:** 141.9 per sq. mi. (ranks 15th). **Pop. projection 1985:** 1,017,000. **Pop. distribution:** 80.5% metropolitan; 19.5% nonmetropolitan. **White:** 37.4%. **Black:** 1%. **Other:** 61.6%. **Marriage rate (1977):** 11.5 per 1,000 people. **Divorce rate:** 5.1 per 1,000 people.

State finances (1978). Revenue: $1,555,968,000. **Expenditures:** $1,495,221,000. **State taxes:** $841.33 per capita. **State personal income tax:** Yes. **Public debt (1978):** $1,888.71 per capita. **Federal aid (1979):** $445.57 per capita. **Personal income (1979 est.):** $9,353.

Sectors of the economy (% of labor force employed in 1975): Wholesale and retail trade (24%), Government (23%), Services (21%), Construction (8%), Manufacturing (7%). **Leading products:** food, printing & publishing, stone, clay, glass items, fabricated metals, lumber & wood. **Agricultural products:** dairy items, cattle,

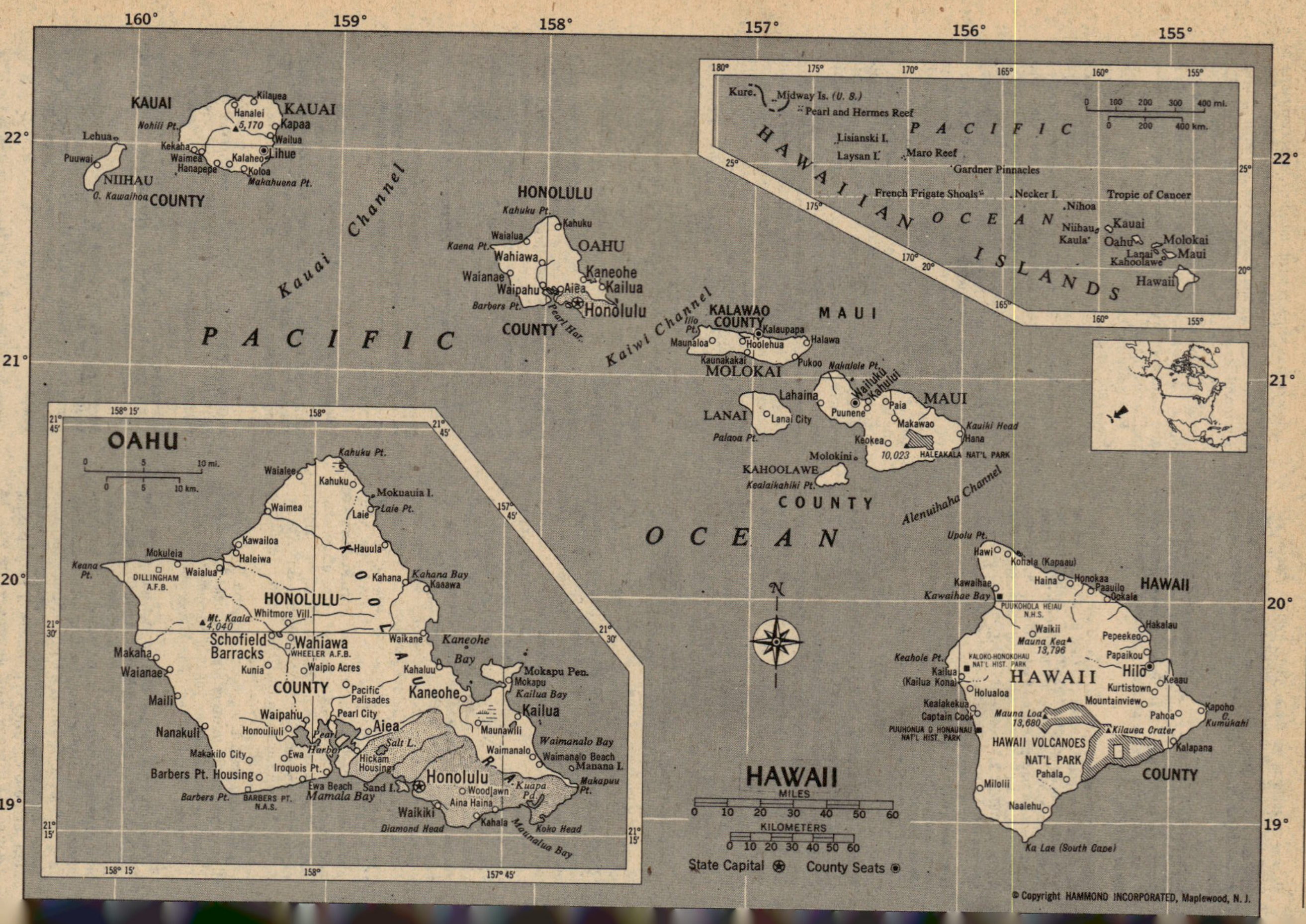
KAUAI
Kilauea
Hanalei
5,170
Kapaa
Wailua
Lihue
Koloa
Kalaheo
Hanapepe
Kekaha
Waimea
Nohili Pt.
Lehua
Puuwai
NIIHAU
O. Kawaihoa
KAUAI COUNTY
Makahuena Pt.
Kauai Channel
PACIFIC
HONOLULU
Kahuku Pt.
Kahuku
Waialua
Kaena Pt.
Wahiawa
OAHU
Kaneohe
Waianae
Waipahu
Aiea
Kailua
Barbers Pt.
Pearl Har.
Honolulu
HONOLULU COUNTY
Kaiwi Channel
Ilio Pt.
KALAWAO COUNTY
Kalaupapa
MAUI
Maunaloa
Hoolehua
Halawa
Kaunakakai
Pukoo
MOLOKAI
Nahalele Pt.
Lahaina
Wailuku
Kahului
Paia
MAUI
LANAI
Lanai City
Puunene
Makawao
Kauiki Head
Hana
Palaoa Pt.
Keokea
Molokini
10,023 HALEAKALA NAT'L PARK
KAHOOLAWE
Kealaikahiki Pt.
COUNTY
Alenuihaha Channel
OCEAN
N
HAWAII
MILES
0 10 20 30 40 50 60
KILOMETERS
0 10 20 30 40 50 60
State Capital
County Seats
Kure
Midway Is. (U. S.)
Pearl and Hermes Reef
Lisianski I.
Laysan I.
Maro Reef
Gardner Pinnacles
French Frigate Shoals
Necker I.
Nihoa
Niihau
Kaula
Kauai
Oahu
Molokai
Lanai
Maui
Kahoolawe
Hawaii
Tropic of Cancer
PACIFIC
HAWAIIAN OCEAN ISLANDS
Upolu Pt.
Hawi
Kohala (Kapaau)
Haina
Honokaa
Paauilo
Ookala
Kawaihae
Kawaihae Bay
PUUKOHOLA HEIAU N.H.S.
Waikii
Mauna Kea 13,796
Hakalau
Pepeekeo
Papaikou
HAWAII
Hilo
Keaau
HAWAII
Keahole Pt.
Kailua
(Kailua Kona)
KALOKO-HONOKOHAU NAT'L. HIST. PARK
Kealakekua
Captain Cook
Holualoa
Mauna Loa 13,680
Kurtistown
Mountainview
Pahoa
Kapoho
C. Kumukahi
PUUHONUA O HONAUNAU NAT'L. HIST. PARK
Kilauea Crater
Kalapana
HAWAII VOLCANOES NAT'L PARK
Pahala
Milolii
COUNTY
Naalehu
Ka Lae (South Cape)
OAHU
10 mi.
10 km.
5
5
Waialee
Kahuku Pt.
Kahuku
Mokuauia I.
Waimea
Laie
Laie Pt.
Keana Pt.
Mokuleia
Kawailoa
Haleiwa
Hauula
DILLINGHAM A.F.B.
Waialua
Kahana
Kahana Bay
Kaaawa
HONOLULU
Whitmore Vill.
Mt. Kaala 4,040
Schofield Barracks
Wahiawa
WHEELER A.F.B.
Waikane
Kaneohe Bay
Makaha
Kunia
Waipio Acres
COUNTY
Kahaluu
Kaneohe
Waianae
Pacific Palisades
Mokapu Pen.
Mokapu
Kailua Bay
Maili
Waipahu
Pearl City
Aiea
Kailua
Honouliuli
Maunawili
Nanakuli
Salt L.
Makakilo City
Pearl Harbor
Ewa
Hickam Housing
Waimanalo
Waimanalo Bay
Waimanalo Beach
Manana I.
Barbers Pt. Housing
Iroquois Pt.
Kuapa Pd.
Makapuu Pt.
Barbers Pt.
BARBERS PT. N.A.S.
Ewa Beach
Sand I.
Honolulu
Woodlawn
Mamala Bay
Aina Haina
Waikiki
Kahala
Koko Head
Diamond Head
Maunalua Bay
Copyright HAMMOND INCORPORATED, Maplewood, N. J.

hogs, sugarcane, pineapples, vegetables. **Fishing:** Aku, Ahi, Akule, tuna, big-eyed scad, marlin. **Avg. farm (1979 est.):** 619 acres. **Avg. value of farm per acre:** Not available.

Highway expenditures per capita (1978): $78.68. **Persons per motor vehicle:** 1.67. **Minimum age for driver's license:** 15. **Gasoline tax:** 11.5¢ per gallon in Hawaii Cty., 12¢ in Honolulu Cty., 12.5¢ in Kauai Cty., 13.5¢ in Maui Cty. **Diesel tax:** 11.5¢ per gallon in Hawaii Cty., 15¢ in Honolulu Cty., 12.5¢ in Kauai Cty., 13.5¢ in Maui Cty. **Motor vehicle deaths:** 21.6 per 100,000 people.

Birthrate (1978): 18.6 per 1,000 people. **Infant mortality rate per 1,000 births (1977):** 11.5. **Physicians per 100,000 pop. (1977):** 196. **Dentists per 100,000 pop. (1977):** 69. **Acceptable hospital beds:** 4.4 per 1,000 people. **State expenditures per capita for health and hospitals (1978):** $119.92.

Education expenditures (1975-76): $481.80 per capita annually. **No. of pupils in public schools (1977 est.):** 172,000. **No. of institutions of higher learning (1976-77):** 11. **Public school expenditure per pupil in attendance (1975-76):** $1,817. **Avg. salary of public school teachers (1974-75 est.):** $13,665. **No. of full-time teachers (1977 est.):** 8,930. **Educational attainment of adult population (1976):** 12.7 median yrs. of school completed; 5.5% with less than 5 years of education; 16.8% with 4 yrs. of college.

Telephones (1977): 70 per 100 people. **State Chamber of Commerce:** Chamber of Commerce of Hawaii, Dillingham Building, 735 Bishop Street, Honolulu, Hawaii 96813.

IDAHO

Idaho is a rugged, mountainous state that does not yield its resources easily. It has the nation's deepest canyon (Hells Canyon, on the Oregon border), as well as 50 mountain peaks more than 10,000 feet high. There are three main regions: the southern, dominated by the Snake River plains and desolate volcanic terrain; the central, a primitive area of craggy mountains and canyons, dominated by the Salmon River Mountains; and the northern region, featuring the Cabinet Mountains and the Selkirk Mountains lying on the Canadian border. Forests of fir, pine, spruce, and other varieties cover about 40 percent of the state. Many peaceful, relatively unspoiled lakes set off the rough beauty of these areas and of the snow-capped mountains.

Indians are thought to have been living in the area 10,000 years ago. The region was acquired by the United States in the Louisiana Purchase (1803) and explored two years later by Lewis and Clark, who crossed the Bitterroot Range and camped near the present site of Lewiston (founded 1861). Throughout the 1860s, Idaho experienced a gold rush that drew scores of prospectors but left a legacy of ghost towns. Mining, however, is still important; Idaho ranks first nationally in the production of silver, garnets, and cobalt.

In the 1870s, the growing white occupation of Indian lands—particularly for cattle ranging—led to a series of battles between U.S. forces and the Nez Percé, Bannock, and Sheepeater tribes. Idaho gained statehood in 1890.

During the 1890s, disputes between miners and mineowners often resulted in violence and bloodshed. In 1892, in the Coeur d'Alene area, unionized miners used dynamite and guns to fight nonunion men and mineowners. There was violence again in 1899. Governor Frank Steunenberg declared martial law then and called in Federal troops to restore order. Six years later, Steunenberg, no longer in office, was murdered by a member of the Western Federation of Miners; the confessed killer, defended by Clarence Darrow in a famous trial, was sentenced to life imprisonment.

Despite recent ravages by forest fires (including a 78,000-acre blaze in 1967) and troublesome mountain pine beetle infestations, agriculture is still the state's leading industry; crops include potatoes, wheat, apples, corn, barley, and hops. In 1979, the state's small poultry industry was devastated by the discovery of PCBs in chicken feed.

Irrigation, which has been crucially important, was begun on a large scale under the Federal government's Carey Act (1894) and Reclamation Act (1902). By 1950, Idaho had more than 5,000 diversion dams, 360 reservoirs (with 5 million acre-feet of water capacity), and more than 15,000 miles of irrigation canals and ditches. In 1968, the Idaho Power Company completed Hells Canyon Dam in the Snake River Valley, which also includes Oxbow and Brownlee dams. In recent years thousands of acres of new land have been brought into cultivation on high desert plateaus in the Boise area, largely possible through increased water pumping efficiency. With the completion of the Snake River navigation project in 1975, Idaho now has water access to the Pacific Ocean.

Manufacturing has been steadily increasing, particularly the dehydrating and freezing of potatoes of which Idaho produces about one-fourth of the nation's yield. Nearly 75 percent of this crop is now processed before it goes to the consumer.

Tourism, now the third-ranked industry, is also on the rise, with an estimated 6 million yearly visitors.

Soda Springs, Champagne Springs, Steamboat Spring, and Hooper Spring boast ice-cold, as well as hellishly hot, water discharges. Lava Hot Springs, the site of a state park, has yielded mineral-rich waters since Indian times.

Other attractions of Idaho include the Craters of the Moon National Monument; Sun Valley that offers skating, swimming, skiing and other attractions; and the Sawtooth Mountains in central Idaho, where a new national recreation area was created in 1972. In 1978 Federal legislation established the large new Gospel-Hump Wilderness Area in north-central Idaho.

In June 1976 the Teton dam burst in the eastern part of the state, causing an estimated one billion dollars damage. Loss of human life was relatively light, but thousands of acres of farmland were destroyed and much of the Idaho cattle industry was temporarily wiped out by floodwaters. Reports indicate the collapse was in part due to poor design.

The eruption of Mount St. Helens in the neighboring state of Washington dumped volcanic ash on northern Idaho in May 1980.

Full name: State of Idaho. **Origin of name:** Probably from the Indian word meaning "Gem of the Mountains." **Inhabitant:** Idahoan. **Capital:** Boise. **State motto:** Esto Perpetua (It Is Forever). **Flag:** State seal centered on blue field. **Seal:** Woman holding scales & a spear; miner; trees & river; elk's head; horns of plenty & sheaves of grain. **Flower:** Syringa. **Bird:** Mountain bluebird. **Tree:** Western pine. **Song:** "Here We Have Idaho." **Nickname:** Gem State.

Governor: John V. Evans. **Annual salary:** $40,000. **Term:** 4 years. **Current term expires:** Jan. 1983. **Voting requirements:** 18 yrs. old & U.S. citizen; registered 5 days with county clerk or 10 days with registrar. **U.S. Congressmen:** 2. **Entered Union:** 1890 (43rd state).

Location & boundaries: Rocky Mountain state: bounded on the north by Canada; on the east by Montana & Wyoming; on the south by Utah & Nevada; & on the west by Oregon, the Snake River & Washington. **Total area:** 83,557 sq. mi. (ranks 13th). **Extreme length:** 483 mi. **Extreme breadth:** 310 mi. **Chief rivers:** Snake, Salmon, Clearwater. **Major lakes:** Pend Oreille, Coeur d'Alene, Priest. **No. of counties:** 44.

Population (1979 est.): 905,000 (ranks 41st). **Pop. increase (1970-79):** 26.9%. **Places over 25,000 pop.:** 4. **Places over 100,000:** 1. **Largest cities:** Boise, Pocatello, Idaho Falls. **Pop. density:** 10.3 per sq. mi. (ranks 43rd). **Pop. projection 1985:** 979,000. **Pop. distribution:** 16.9% metropolitan; 83.1% nonmetropolitan. **White:** 98.1%. **Black:** 0.3%. **Other:** 1.6%. **Marriage rate (1977):** 15.7 per 1,000 people. **Divorce rate:** 7.0 per 1,000 people.

IDAHO
MILES
KILOMETERS
State Capitals ⊛ County Seats ⊛
BRITISH COLUMBIA
WATERTON-GLACIER
WATERTON LAKES NAT'L PARK
ALBERTA
INT'L PEACE PK.
GLACIER
BLACKFEET
INDIAN
RESERVATION
NATIONAL
PARK
Metaline Falls
BOUNDARY
Lake Koocanusa
Priest L.
Bonners Ferry
KALISPEL IND. RES.
Pend Oreille
Sandpoint
BONNER
Priest River
Clark Fork
Libby
Kalispell
Hungry Horse Res.
Flathead L.
FLATHEAD
INDIAN
RESERVATION
Spirit Lake
Lake Pend Oreille
Rathdrum
Spokane R.
Hayden
KOOTENAI
Post Falls
Coeur d'Alene
Spokane
Smelterville
Osburn
Coeur d'Alene L.
Kellogg
Mullan
Wallace
Avery
SHOSHONE
St. Maries
BENEWAH
St. Joe
E. Sister Pk. 6,866
Great Falls
Teton R.
Missouri R.
Smith R.
N
Canyon Ferry Res.
Helena ⊛
Missoula
Blackfoot R.
Clark Fork
Bitterroot R.
MONTANA
BITTERROOT
Potlatch
Colfax
LATAH
Troy
Moscow
Pullman
Genesee
Clearwater
Elk River
Fork
CLEARWATER
Lolo Pass 5,187
Lochsa R.
NEZ PERCE NAT'L HIST PARK
Lewiston
Lapwai
Orofino
Headquarters
Pierce
Weippe
CLEARWATER
Nezperce
Kamiah
Craigmont
Kooskia
Cottonwood
Selway
NEZ PERCE
LEWIS
Snake R.
River
Grangeville
White Bird
High Mtn. Sheep Res.
IDAHO
Elk City
MOUNTAINS
Butte
BEAVERHEAD MTS.
Continental Divide
CONTINENTAL DIVIDE
Big Hole R.
Lost Trail Pass 6,990
Dillon
Bozeman
Yellowstone R.
Enterprise
Riggins
He-Devil Mtn. 9,387
Salmon River
Waugh Mtn. 8,882
Salmon
Baker
Cobalt
LEMHI
LEMHI RANGE
Madison R.
Jefferson R.
Hebgen L.
YELLOWSTONE
OXBOW DAM
BROWNLEE DAM
ADAMS
New Meadows
McCall
Council
Cambridge
Cascade Res.
Cascade
Warm Lake
South Fork
Middle Fork
SALMON RIVER MTS.
VALLEY
Mormon Mtn. 9,545
Twin Pks. 10,328
Leadore
Challis
Salmon
Clayton
LOST RIVER
Island Park Res.
MONTANA
CENTENNIAL MTS.
CLARK
Dubois
Shoshone L.
FREMONT
Ashton
St. Anthony
Jackson L.
WASHINGTON
Weiser
Payette
Cape Horn Mtn. 9,600
Castle Pk. 11,820
CUSTER
SAWTOOTH NAT'L REC. AREA
Borah Pk. 12,662
Big Lost R.
Mackay
Moore
Arco
NAT'L REACTOR TESTING STA. U.S.A.E.C. RES.
Mud L.
JEFFERSON
MADISON
Rexburg
Rigby
Iona
Ammon
TETON
Driggs
GRAND TETON NAT'L PARK
Vale
New Plymouth
Fruitland
PAYETTE
GEM
Payette
Emmett
Garden City
Caldwell
Boise
Meridian
NAMPA
ADA
Murphy
MOUNTAIN HOME A.F.B.
ELMORE
Mountain Home
Garden Valley
BOISE
Idaho City
Atlanta
Anderson Ranch Res.
Arrowrock Res.
CAMAS
Fairfield
Wood R.
Ketchum
Sun Valley
Hailey
Bellevue
Carey
BLAINE
CRATERS OF THE MOON NAT'L MON.
7,659
Atomic City
BUTTE
Springfield
Aberdeen
BINGHAM
Shelley
Idaho Falls
BONNEVILLE
Palisades Res.
Grays L.
Blackfoot
FORT HALL IND. RES.
Chubbuck
Blackfoot River Res.
CARIBOU
Snake River
Homedale
Owyhee L.
OREGON
CANYON
Snake River
Bruneau R.
Owyhee R.
Riddle
Three Creek
WESTERN SHOSHONE IND. RES.
SNAKE
OWYHEE
C. J. Strike Res.
Hammett
Glenns Ferry
Bliss
Bruneau
GOODING
Gooding
Wendell
Bliss
Shoshone
Richfield
LINCOLN
Big Wood R.
JEROME
Jerome
Buhl
Filer
Kimberly
Twin Falls
TWIN FALLS
Shoshone Falls
Salmon Cr. Res.
Oakley
Albion
CASSIA
Cache Pk. 10,340
Almo
MINIDOKA
Rupert
Paul
Heyburn
Burley
Walcott Res.
American Falls Res.
American Falls
McCammon
POWER
Pocatello
Inkom
Lava Hot Spgs.
Soda Sprs.
BANNOCK
Grace
Downey
Malad City
ONEIDA
FRANKLIN
Preston
Franklin
Montpelier
Paris
BEAR LAKE
Bear L.
WYOMING
Jackson
Jackson L.
UTAH
NEVADA
© Copyright HAMMOND INCORPORATED, Maplewood, N.J.
Longitude West 114° of Greenwich
116°
114°
112°
48°
46°
44°
42°

State finances (1978). Revenue: $887,700,000. **Expenditures:** $837,069,000. **State taxes:** $479.31 per capita. **State personal income tax:** Yes. **Public debt (1978):** $147.83 per capita. **Federal aid (1979):** $348.51 per capita. **Personal income (1979 est.):** $7,446.

Sectors of the economy (% of labor force employed in 1970): Wholesale and retail trade (23%), Government (17%), Manufacturing (15%), Educational Services (9%), Services (8%), Construction (7%). **Leading products:** food; lumber & chemicals; electronics; printing & publishing; stone, clay & pumice. **Minerals:** silver, phosphate rock, lead, zinc. **Agricultural products:** potatoes, cattle, sheep, dairy items, wheat, hay, sugar beets. **Avg. farm (1979 est.):** 661 acres. **Avg. value of farm per acre:** $485.

Highway expenditures per capita (1978): $162.96. **Persons per motor vehicle:** 1.65. **Minimum age for driver's license:** 16. **Gasoline tax:** 9.5¢ per gallon. **Diesel tax:** 9.5¢ per gallon. **Motor vehicle deaths:** 37.2 per 100,000 people.

Birthrate (1978): 22.0 per 1,000 people. **Infant mortality rate per 1,000 births (1977):** 11.3. **Physicians per 100,000 pop. (1977):** 109. **Dentists per 100,000 pop. (1977):** 49. **Acceptable hospital beds:** 4.3 per 1,000 people. **State expenditures per capita for health and hospitals (1978):** $47.36.

Education expenditures (1975-76): $412.04 per capita annually. **No. of pupils in public schools (1977 est.):** 197,000. **No. of institutions of higher learning (1976-77):** 9. **Public school expenditure per pupil in attendance (1975-76):** $1,368. **Avg. salary of public school teachers (1974-75 est.):** $9,573. **No. full-time teachers (1977 est.):** 9,510. **Educational attainment of adult population (1976):** 12.6 median yrs. of school completed; 1.5% with less than 5 years of education; 13.5% with 4 yrs. of college.

Telephones (1977): 71 per 100 people. **State Chamber of Commerce:** Idaho Association of Commerce & Industry, 805 Idaho St., Rm. 414, P.O. Box 389, Boise, Idaho 83701.

ILLINOIS

Illinois, the nation's fifth most populous state, consists almost entirely of gently rolling plains that slope gradually from north to south, although there is a range of relatively small hills, known as the Shawnee Hills (or the "Illinois Ozarks"), in the southern part of the state. In the north is Chicago, with 28.8 miles of shoreline along Lake Michigan; it is the state's largest city by far, and the country's second largest after New York. More than 60 percent of the state's population lives in or around Chicago.

Fertile soil, excellent drainage, and a long growing season have made Illinois one of the nation's major agricultural states, despite a climate that also includes spring and summer tornadoes and wide temperature extremes. The state is usually first or second (to Iowa) in corn production, first in soybeans, and a leading producer of hogs.

Manufacturing and mining are other important revenue sources for the state, which ranks high in oil and coal production and has the nation's largest soft coal reserves. Since 1842, Illinois has been the country's leading producer of fluorspar, or fluorite, which is used in making steel.

Transportation has been a key factor in the state's growth, thanks to its strategic position between the two seaboards and its proximity to important waterways, including Lake Michigan (and the Saint Lawrence Seaway) and the Mississippi River. Canals and an extensive highway system have also helped. Chicago has been the nation's railroad hub for many years, and today is a leading air travel center.

Prehistoric Indians called Mound Builders lived in the Illinois region and left a legacy of more than 10,000 burial and temple mounds. Later inhabitants included a union of Indian tribes known as the "Illinois Confederacy." The Frenchmen Marquette and Jolliet were the first Europeans of record (1673) to visit the region and, two years later, Marquette founded a mission at the Indian town of Kaskaskia, near the present site of Utica. The first permanent European settlement, founded (1699) by French priests of the Seminary of Foreign Missions, was at Cahokia. The territory was ceded by France to Britain in 1763. In 1779, during the Revolutionary War, the Commonwealth of Virginia set up the "County of Illinois." The area passed to the Northwest Territory in 1787. The first county, St. Clair, was established in 1790. Illinois became a territory in 1809 and entered the Union as a state in 1818.

Early landmarks in the state's history included the growing migration of eastern settlers following the opening (1825) of the Erie Canal; the Black Hawk War (1832), which virtually ended Indian troubles in the area; and the "Lincoln" years (1831-60), during which Abraham Lincoln rose from New Salem laborer to Springfield lawyer and president-elect. Lincoln's seven 1858 debates on the slavery issue with prominent Democrat Stephen A. Douglas, which were held in seven different Illinois towns, did not win him the Senate seat both men were seeking, but instead won him the national attention that led to his becoming the nation's Civil War President.

Illinois made great economic advances after the Civil War, despite such setbacks as the Chicago fire (October 1871) and a number of serious labor disputes, particularly the Haymarket Square Riot (1886) and the Pullman strike (1894).

Industry boomed during World War II, which also served to put the state into the vanguard of the Atomic Age: in 1942, at the University of Chicago, Enrico Fermi and other scientists set off the world's first controlled atomic reaction.

The state's current problems are many but not unique. There have been racial tensions in the major cities, and critical unemployment in some southern cities. In recent years, Chicago has been plagued by civil unrest and corruption, and there have been violence, security problems and a number of escapes from Illinois prisons.

The state's tourist attractions include Old Town, the Art Institute, and the Museum of Science and Industry in Chicago; the reconstructed state park in New Salem, where Lincoln lived (1831-37); the Lincoln home and tomb in Springfield; the Dickson Indian Mounds near Havana; and Shawnee National Forest. Chain O'Lakes, a group of lakes in the northeastern part of the state, is a popular summer resort area.

In 1980, Illinois was shocked by the conviction of its Attorney General, William J. Scott, on charges of evading Federal income taxes.

Full name: State of Illinois. **Origin of name:** From Indian name meaning "The Men." **Inhabitant:** Illinoisan. **Capital:** Springfield. **State motto:** State Sovereignty—National Union. **Flag:** Adaptation of state seal centered on white field. **Seal:** An American eagle holds shield with stars & stripes, representing 13 original states; olive branch stands for peace; prairies & rising sun represent plains of Illinois. **Flower:** Native violet. **Bird:** Cardinal. **Tree:** Oak. **Song:** "Illinois." **Nickname:** Prairie State.

Governor: James R. Thompson. **Annual salary:** $58,000. **Term:** 4 years. **Current term expires:** Jan. 1983. **Voting requirements:** 18 yrs. old & U.S. citizen; resident of state, county, and district 30 days. **U.S. Congressmen:** 24. **Entered Union:** 1818 (21st state).

Location & boundaries: Midwestern state: bounded on the north by Wisconsin; on the east by Lake Michigan, Indiana & the Wabash River; on the southeast by Kentucky; on the southwest by Missouri; & on the west by the Mississippi River, Missouri & Iowa. **Total area:** 56,400 sq. mi. (ranks 24th). **Extreme length:** 381 mi. **Extreme breadth:** 211 mi. **Shoreline:** 63 mi. **Chief rivers:** Mississippi, Illinois, Kaskaskia. **Major lakes:** Michigan, Chain O'Lakes. **No. of counties:** 102.

ILLINOIS
MILES
0 10 20 30 40 50 60
KILOMETERS
0 10 20 30 40 50 60
State Capital
County Seats
Longitude West of Greenwich
© Copyright HAMMOND INCORPORATED, Maplewood, N.

Population (1979 est.): 11,229,000 (ranks 5th). **Pop. increase (1970-79):** 1.1%. **Places over 25,000 pop.:** 65. **Places over 100,000:** 3. **Largest cities:** Chicago, Rockford, Peoria. **Pop. density:** 199.1 per sq. mi. (ranks 10th). **Pop. projection 1985:** 11,454,000. **Pop. distribution:** 81.3% metropolitan; 18.7% nonmetropolitan. **White:** 86.4%. **Black:** 12.8%. **Other:** 0.8%. **Marriage rate (1977):** 9.6 per 1,000 people. **Divorce rate:** 4.4 per 1,000 people.

State finances (1978). Revenue: $10,317,928,000. **Expenditures:** $9,952,914,000. **State taxes:** $513.60 per capita. **State personal income tax:** Yes. **Public debt (1978):** $457.52 per capita. **Federal aid (1979):** $336.76 per capita. **Personal Income (1979 est.):** $9,823.

Sectors of the economy (% of labor force employed in 1970): Manufacturing (30%), Wholesale and retail trade (20%), Government (13%), Services (7%), Educational Services (7%), Construction (5%). **Leading products:** machinery, food, electrical machinery, primary & fabricated metals, chemicals, printing & publishing. **Minerals:** coal; petroleum; stone, sand & gravel. **Agricultural products:** hogs, cattle, dairy items, corn, soybeans, wheat. **Avg. farm (1979 est.):** 268 acres. **Avg. value of farm per acre:** $1,786.

Highway expenditures per capita (1978): $78.06. **Persons per motor vehicle:** 1.53. **Minimum age for driver's license:** 16. **Gasoline tax:** 7.5¢ per gallon. **Diesel tax:** 7.5¢ per gallon. **Motor vehicle deaths:** 19.0 per 100,000 people.

Birthrate (1978): 15.5 per 1,000 people. **Infant mortality rate per 1,000 births (1977):** 16.0. **Physicians per 100,000 pop. (1977):** 171. **Dentists per 100,000 pop. (1977):** 52. **Acceptable hospital beds:** 6.8 per 1,000 people. **State expenditures per capita for health and hospitals (1978):** $48.77.

Education expenditures (1975-76): $464.94 per capita annually. **No. of pupils in public schools (1977 est.):** 2,205,000. **No. of institutions of higher learning (1976-77):** 149. **Public school expenditure per pupil in attendance (1975-76):** $1,848. **Avg. salary of public school teachers (1974-75 est.):** $13,469. **No. full-time teachers (1977 est.):** 129,230. **Educational attainment of adult population (1976):** 12.5 median yrs. of school completed; 2.6% with less than 5 years of education; 13.7% with 4 yrs. of college.

Telephones (1977): 84 per 100 people. **State Chamber of Commerce:** Illinois State Chamber of Commerce, 20 North Wacker Drive, Chicago, Illinois 60606.

INDIANA

Although it is the smallest state in the continental United States west of the Alleghenies, Indiana ranks among the national leaders in population, agriculture, and manufacturing. Huge steel mills and oil refineries make the state's 45-mile Lake Michigan waterfront one of the world's great industrial centers, while the fertile plains of the central region produce an abundance of food (especially grain crops) for market and livestock. Mining, especially of coal and oil, is also significant; and the state's vast southern quarries produce two-thirds of the nation's building limestone. The automotive industry maintains a large number of plants in the state.

There are three main land regions: the Great Lakes Plain in the north, the central Till Plains (the largest single area), and, in the south, the Interior Low Plateau, characterized by hills, ridges, knolls, caves, and waterfalls. (The two plains regions are subdivisions of the Central Lowlands.) The generally mild, humid climate is marked by occasional temperature extremes.

The first inhabitants of the Indiana region were the prehistoric Mound Builders, followed by a number of Indian tribes, chiefly the Miamis. Many of the Indians came into the area from the east after losing their land to the white settlers. The first European of record to visit the region was Robert Cavelier, Sieur de La Salle, who made two explorations (1679, 1681) and paved the way for

French fur-trading posts (in the 1720s) and the first European permanent settlement at Vincennes (fortified 1732). The English sharply challenged French control, however, and by the 1763 Treaty of Paris they gained dominance in the area; in 1774 the British government attached the territory to the province of Quebec.

During the American Revolution, George Rogers Clark and a small army financed by Virginia Governor Patrick Henry captured (1778) Vincennes from the British, lost it, and then in the following year recaptured it. Virginia relinquished (1784) its claim to the Northwest Territory, of which Indiana was the south central part; three years later, the Northwest Ordinance provided for the territory's government, the permanent exclusion of slavery, and basic individual rights. Indiana Territory was created as an entity separate from Ohio in 1800 and initially included the present states of Indiana, Illinois, and Wisconsin, as well as parts of Michigan and Minnesota. After Michigan and Illinois became separate territories (1805, 1809), Indiana had almost the same boundaries as it has today. (The present boundaries were finally established when statehood was attained, in 1816.)

Indian troubles in the area were serious and persistent during the whole early period of white settlement. Anthony Wayne's victory at Fallen Timbers in Ohio (1794) brought peace but it was short-lived. Governor William Henry Harrison, who played a primary role in Indiana's early development, purchased (1809) for the Federal Government nearly 3 million acres of Indian lands in southern Indiana; this outraged the Shawnee chief Tecumseh, who led several tribes on the warpath. Troops led by Harrison won (1811) the Battle of Tippecanoe (near present-day Lafayette) and, during the War of 1812, defeated combined Indian and British forces in the Battle of the Thames, at Moraviantown, Ontario. Thus was British influence in the region ended, and the Indian threat virtually broken.

Indiana's famous "Hoosier" personality was forged in the first half of the 19th century, and its hallmarks were rustic simplicity, self-sufficient isolation, and an almost reflexive conservatism. Attempts were made, most notably at New Harmony (1814), to reorganize society fundamentally along idealistic lines; although the experiments failed, they were the basis for the eventual development in the state of enlightened social and legal institutions and practices. The Hoosier spirit has been immortalized by such authors as Edward Eggleston, James Whitcomb Riley, Booth Tarkington, and George Ade, as well as songwriter Paul Dresser ("On the Banks of the Wabash") and artist John T. McCutcheon, whose cartoon "Injun Summer" has become a classic of its kind. And although his themes were more universal, novelist Theodore Dreiser *(Sister Carrie, An American Tragedy)* was also a Hoosier, and the brother of Paul Dresser.

Internal strife, led by the proslavery Knights of the Golden Circle, marked the Civil War period in Indiana, which, however, largely supported the Union cause. Except for occasional raids, the state saw little action.

Indiana's first public port opened in 1970 on Lake Michigan near Portage after a prolonged battle between proponents of industrial expansion and environmentalists over destruction of the unique dunelands between Gary and Michigan City. A compromise produced the Dunes National Lakeshore.

While the port permits worldwide waterborne trade via the St. Lawrence Seaway, much greater

INDIANA
MILES
0 10 20 30 40 50
KILOMETERS
0 10 20 30 40 50
State Capital
County Seats
Longitude West of Greenwich
© Copyright HAMMOND INCORPORATED, Maplewood, N.J.

tonnage moves on the Ohio River, where there is a port at Mount Vernon; another port is planned near Jeffersonville.

Railroads and trucks remain the most important transport in Indiana, where Indianapolis is favored by being the crossroads of five interstate highways. Virtually all livestock now moves by truck, and there have been forecasts that Indianapolis will become the largest collecting point in the nation for meat animals.

Hoosiers also brag of the Army Finance Center at Ft. Benjamin Harrison, largest U.S. military building aside from the Pentagon.

Claremont is the site of Raceway Park, home of drag racing.

In 1980, the Ford Motor Co. was prosecuted at Winamac, Indiana, for negligent homicide, the state claiming that faulty car design was responsible for the deaths of three teenagers. The company was acquitted, in a case with important implications for all manufacturers.

Later that year, the United States Supreme Court ruled that the boundary between Indiana and Kentucky was the high-water mark of the Ohio River as it was in 1792—not, as Kentucky claimed, the contemporary high-water mark. The ruling made it impossible for Kentucky to sue to stop construction of a nuclear power plant at Marble Hill, Indiana, but Kentucky gained jurisdiction over some land on the Indiana side of the river.

Full name: State of Indiana. **Origin of name:** Denoted that state was domain of Indians. **Inhabitant:** Hoosier. **Capital:** Indianapolis. **State motto:** The Crossroads of America. **Flag:** Gold torch & 19 gold stars on blue field. **Seal:** Pioneer scene represents westward expansion. **Flower:** Peony. **Bird:** Cardinal. **Tree:** Tulip poplar. **Song:** "On the Banks of the Wabash Far Away." **Nickname:** Hoosier State.

Governor: Otis R. Bowen, M.D. **Annual salary:** $48,000. **Term:** 4 years. **Current term expires:** Jan. 1981. **Voting requirements:** 18 yrs. old & U.S. citizen; resident of state 30 days; township 60 days; precinct 30 days. **U.S. Congressmen:** 11. **Entered Union:** 1816 (19th state).

Location & boundaries: Midwestern state: bounded on the north by Lake Michigan & Michigan; on the east by Ohio; on the southeast & south by the Ohio River & Kentucky; & on the west by the Wabash River & Illinois. **Total area:** 36,291 sq. mi. (ranks 38th). **Extreme length:** 280 mi. **Extreme breadth:** 160 mi. **Shoreline:** 45 mi. **Chief rivers:** Wabash, Ohio, White. **Major lakes (other than border-forming):** Monroe Reservoir, Mississinewa Reservoir, Wawasee. **No. of counties:** 92.

Population (1979 est.): 5,400,000 (ranks 12th). **Pop. increase (1970-79):** 3.9%. **Places over 25,000 pop.:** 23. **Places over 100,000:** 6. **Largest cities:** Indianapolis, Fort Wayne, Gary, Evansville. **Pop. density:** 148.8 per sq. mi. (ranks 13th). **Pop. projection 1985:** 5,481,000. **Pop. distribution:** 67.8% metropolitan; 32.2% nonmetropolitan. **White:** 92.8%. **Black:** 6.9%. **Other:** 0.3%. **Marriage rate (1977):** 10.6 per 1,000 people. **Divorce rate:** 6.3 per 1,000 people.

State finances (1978). Revenue: $4,223,579,000. **Expenditures:** $3,729,223,000. **State taxes:** $456.77 per capita. **State personal income tax:** Yes. **Public debt (1978):** $110.66 per capita. **Federal aid (1979):** $257.56 per capita. **Personal income (1979 est.):** $8,686.

Sectors of the economy (% of labor force employed in 1970): Manufacturing (36%), Wholesale and retail trade (19%), Government (13%), Educational Services (8%), Services (6%), Construction (5%). **Leading products:** electrical & other machinery, transportation equipment, food, chemicals, primary & fabricated metals. **Minerals:** coal, cement, stone, petroleum. **Agricultural products:** hogs, cattle, dairy items, corn, soybeans, wheat. **Avg. farm (1979 est.):** 190 acres. **Avg. value of farm per acre:** $1,498.

Highway expenditures per capita (1978): $83.61. **Persons per motor vehicle:** 1.40. **Minimum age for driver's license:** 16. **Gasoline tax:** 8.5¢ per gallon. **Diesel tax:** 8.5¢ per gallon. **Motor vehicle deaths:** 24.3 per 100,000 people.

Birthrate (1978): 15.5 per 1,000 people. **Infant mortality rate per 1,000 births (1977):** 14.2. **Physicians per 100,000 pop. (1977):** 120. **Dentists per 100,000 pop. (1977):** 39. **Acceptable hospital beds:** 6.5 per 1,000 people. **State expenditures per capita for health and hospitals (1978):** $47.01.

Education expenditures (1975-76): $413.36 per capita annually. **No. of pupils in public schools (1977 est.):** 1,146,000. **No. of institutions of higher learning (1976-77):** 64. **Public school expenditure per pupil in attendance (1976-77):** $1,446. **Avg. salary of public school teachers (1974-75 est.):** $11,358. **No. full-time teachers (1977 est.):** 57,830. **Educational attainment of adult population (1976):** 12.4 median yrs. of school completed; 1.9% with less than 5 years of education; 11.0% with 4 yrs. of college.

Telephones (1977): 73 per 100 people. **State Chamber of Commerce:** Indiana State Chamber of Commerce, Inc.; 201-212 Board of Trade Building, Indianapolis, Indiana 46204.

IOWA

With about two-thirds of its land mass between 800 and 1,400 feet above sea level, Iowa is a gently rolling plain quilted almost entirely by farms. The border-forming Mississippi and Missouri Rivers provide an abundant water supply and transportation routes.

The soil of Iowa is considered the finest in America and accounts for the fact that Iowa produces a tenth of the nation's food supply. It alternately shares the lead with Illinois in corn production, is second in soybeans and is a major producer of oats. The state's high crop yield supports the country's largest livestock industry; Iowa is the leading hog state and ranks high in cattle.

Because of the soil's economic importance, floods and the quest of greater productivity have made Iowans conservation conscious. In fact, in 1960 it was recognized that only a quarter of the state's water supply was being effectively harnessed.

As impressive as Iowa's agriculture is, manufacturing income is greater. The chief industrial centers are Des Moines; Cedar Rapids, site of its first nuclear power plant (1974); Dubuque and Waterloo. Except for gypsum—Iowa is the nation's third-largest producer—mining is not significant.

The state's climate is of the continental, long-summer type, marked by great extremes; there is generally less precipitation in the western regions than in the eastern.

A civilization of Mound Builders—sedentary farmers who lived in permanent villages—predated the Indians in Iowa; the Effigy Mounds National Monument contains numerous examples of their building in bird, animal, and serpentine forms. The first Europeans to visit the region were Jacques Marquette and Louis Jolliet (1673); almost a century later (1788), the Indians allowed Julien Dubuque, a French-Canadian, to mine lead in the area of the city named for him. The United States obtained control of the state under the Louisiana Purchase (1803). Formation of Iowa Territory dates from 1838.

There was much fighting between white settlers and Indians of the area. A rich strip of land 50 miles wide along the Mississippi was won from the Sauk and Fox in 1832, after Black Hawk and his braves were defeated in battle. Other areas were taken from the Indians in 1836 and 1837. The Sioux ceded their claims in 1851, although an outlaw band of their numbers six years later killed 33 settlers in the Spirit Lake Massacre.

When Iowa became (1846) a state, its capital was at Iowa City; the more centrally located Des Moines became the capital in 1857. It was at this time, too, that the state's present boundaries were drawn up.

IOWA
MILES
KILOMETERS
State Capital
County Seats
MINNESOTA
WISCONSIN
ILLINOIS
NEBRASKA
MISSOURI
S. DAKOTA
MISSISSIPPI RIVER
MISSOURI RIVER
LYON
OSCEOLA
DICKINSON
EMMET
KOSSUTH
WINNEBAGO
WORTH
MITCHELL
HOWARD
WINNESHIEK
ALLAMAKEE
SIOUX
O'BRIEN
CLAY
PALO ALTO
HANCOCK
CERRO GORDO
FLOYD
CHICKASAW
FAYETTE
CLAYTON
PLYMOUTH
CHEROKEE
BUENA VISTA
POCAHONTAS
HUMBOLDT
WRIGHT
FRANKLIN
BUTLER
BREMER
BLACK HAWK
BUCHANAN
DELAWARE
DUBUQUE
WOODBURY
IDA
SAC
CALHOUN
WEBSTER
HAMILTON
HARDIN
GRUNDY
MONONA
CRAWFORD
CARROLL
GREENE
BOONE
STORY
MARSHALL
TAMA
BENTON
LINN
JONES
JACKSON
HARRISON
SHELBY
AUDUBON
GUTHRIE
DALLAS
POLK
JASPER
POWESHIEK
IOWA
JOHNSON
CEDAR
CLINTON
SCOTT
POTTAWATTAMIE
CASS
ADAIR
MADISON
WARREN
MARION
MAHASKA
KEOKUK
WASHINGTON
MUSCATINE
MILLS
MONTGOMERY
ADAMS
UNION
CLARKE
LUCAS
MONROE
WAPELLO
JEFFERSON
HENRY
LOUISA
DES MOINES
FREMONT
PAGE
TAYLOR
RINGGOLD
DECATUR
WAYNE
APPANOOSE
DAVIS
VAN BUREN
LEE
Sioux Falls
Sioux City
Council Bluffs
Omaha
Des Moines
Cedar Rapids
Davenport
Dubuque
Waterloo
Ft. Dodge
Mason City
Rock Island
Moline
Galesburg
Burlington
Keokuk
Ottumwa
Fairfield
Mt. Pleasant
Washington
Muscatine
Iowa City
Marshalltown
Grinnell
Newton
Boone
Ames
Nevada
Perry
Atlantic
Clarinda
Shenandoah
Red Oak
Creston
Osceola
Chariton
Albia
Centerville
Bloomfield
Corydon
Leon
Mount Ayr
Bedford
Glenwood
Hamburg
Sidney
Nebraska City
Plattsmouth
Fremont
Clinton
Maquoketa
Anamosa
Marion
Vinton
Independence
West Union
Decorah
Waukon
Cresco
Osage
Charles City
New Hampton
Waverly
Forest City
Algona
Estherville
Spencer
Le Mars
Cherokee
Storm Lake
Sac City
Carroll
Denison
Harlan
Audubon
Guthrie Ctr.
Adel
Winterset
Indianola
Knoxville
Oskaloosa
Sigourney
Wellman
Tipton
Manchester
Elkader
Guttenberg
McGregor
Lansing
New Albin
Caledonia
Austin
Albert Lea
Fairmont
Worthington
Tecumseh
Maryville
Princeton
NORTH

From the beginning, the character of Iowa has been a paradoxical amalgam of free-thinking liberalism and close-to-the-vest conservatism. Education has long had a high priority in the state, resulting in the nation's lowest illiteracy rate. Iowa has 3 state-supported universities, over 30 private colleges and approximately 10 private junior colleges. In 1965 a system of 15 area community colleges and vocational-technical schools was established.

The 1976-77 legislative session brought about a revision in the property tax law, limiting increases in taxable value of residential and agricultural buildings for a period of two years and changing the method of taxing farm land from 50 percent on value and 50 percent on productivity to a tax on productivity alone. Land use policy planning committees were set up, and the building code commission was directed to establish energy efficiency standards for new buildings.

Full name: State of Iowa. **Origin of name:** From name of Sioux tribe—the Ioways or Aiouez—meaning "Sleepy Ones." **Inhabitant:** Iowan. **Capital:** Des Moines. **State motto:** Our Liberties We Prize & Our Rights We Will Maintain. **Flag:** Vertical blue, white & red bars; flying eagle carrying state motto. **Seal:** Prairie scene represents Iowa's pioneer days; an eagle flies over scene carrying streamer with state motto. **Flower:** Wild rose. **Bird:** Eastern goldfinch. **Tree:** Oak. **Song:** "The Song of Iowa." **Nickname:** Hawkeye State.

Governor: Robert D. Ray. **Annual salary:** $60,000. **Term:** 4 years. **Current term expires:** Jan. 1983. **Voting requirements:** 18 yrs. old & U.S. citizen; resident of state; registration 10 days before election. **U.S. Congressmen:** 6. **Entered Union:** 1846 (29th state).

Location & boundaries: Midwestern state: bounded on the north by Minnesota; on the east by the Mississippi River, Wisconsin & Illinois; on the south by the Des Moines River & Missouri; & on the west by the Missouri River, Nebraska, the Big Sioux River & South Dakota. **Total area:** 56,290 sq. mi. (ranks 25th). **Extreme length:** 324 mi. **Extreme breadth:** 210 mi. **Chief rivers:** Des Moines, Mississippi, Missouri, Big Sioux. **Major lakes:** Clear, Spirit, Storm Red Rock. **No. of counties:** 99.

Population (1979 est.): 2,902,000 (ranks 26th). **Pop. increase (1970-79):** 2.7%. **Places over 25,000 pop.:** 15. **Places over 100,000:** 3. **Largest cities:** Des Moines, Cedar Rapids, Davenport. **Pop. density:** 51.6 per sq. mi. (ranks 29th). **Pop. projection 1985:** 2,957,000. **Pop. distribution:** 37.4% metropolitan; 62.6% nonmetropolitan. **White:** 98.5%. **Black:** 1.2%. **Other:** 0.3%. **Marriage rate (1977):** 9.2 per 1,000 people. **Divorce rate:** 3.8 per 1,000 people.

State finances (1978). Revenue: $2,774,463,000. **Expenditures:** $2,742,151,000. **State taxes:** $484.18 per capita. **State personal income tax:** Yes. **Public debt (1978):** $78.46 per capita. **Federal aid (1979):** $302.24 per capita. **Personal income (1979 est.):** $8,589.

Sectors of the economy (% of labor force employed in 1970): Wholesale and retail trade (22%), Manufacturing (20%), Government (14%), Educational Services (9%), Services (7%), Construction (5%). **Leading products:** food; electrical & other machinery; chemicals; printing & publishing; primary & fabricated metals; stone, clay & glass items. **Minerals:** cement; stone, sand & gravel; gypsum. **Agricultural products:** cattle, hogs, dairy items, corn, soybeans, hay. **Avg. farm (1979 est.):** 281 acres. **Avg. value of farm per acre:** $1,458.

Highway expenditures per capita (1978): $143.32. **Persons per motor vehicle:** 1.20. **Minimum age for driver's license:** 16. **Gasoline tax:** 10¢ per gallon. **Diesel tax:** 11.5¢ per gallon. **Motor vehicle deaths:** 22.1 per 100,000 people.

Birthrate (1978): 15.3 per 1,000 people. **Infant mortality rate per 1,000 births (1977):** 12.4. **Physicians per 100,000 pop. (1977):** 117. **Dentists per 100,000 pop. (1977):** 44. **Acceptable hospital beds:** 7.4 per 1,000 people. **State expenditures per capita for health and hospitals (1978):** $59.88.

Education expenditures (1975-76): $476.95 per capita annually. **No. of pupils in public schools (1977 est.):** 596,000. **No. of institutions of higher learning (1976-77):** 61. **Public school expenditure per pupil in attendance (1975-76):** $1,653. **Avg. salary of public school teachers (1974-75 est.):** $10,598. **No. full-time teachers (1977 est.):** 36,790. **Educational attainment of adult population (1976):** 12.5 median yrs. of school completed; 1.0% with less than 5 years of education; 12.8% with 4 yrs. of college.

Telephones (1977): 74 per 100 people. **State Chamber of Commerce:** Iowa Manufacturers Association, 706 Employers Mutual Building, 717 Mulberry Street, Des Moines, Iowa 50309.

KANSAS

The popular notion that Kansas consists wholly of flat prairie land is false; the land, in fact, rises from an elevation of about 700 feet in the southeast to more than 4,000 feet in the northwest, where the foothills of the Rockies begin. Three main land regions make up the state: the Great Plains, covering the western two-thirds; the Dissected Till Plains, covering a small area in the northeast corner; and the Southeastern Plains, often subdivided by geographers into the Osage Plains in the east and the Flint Hills in the west. Thousands of rolling hills between 100 and 400 feet high dot the state's terrain, which also features many valleys and picturesque chalk and sandstone formations. The relatively small natural water area is augmented by more than a hundred artificial lakes.

The eastern half of Kansas contains the overwhelmingly larger part of the population: the three largest cities—Wichita, Kansas City, and Topeka—are all in this section. Kansas City, on the eastern border, adjoins Kansas City, Missouri, but the two are separate municipalities.

A number of Indian tribes—including the Kansa, Wichita, Pawnee, and Comanche—were living in the Kansas region before the coming (1541) of the first European, Spanish explorer Francisco Vásquez de Coronado; he and his men were seeking the gold of a land called Quivira and, finding none, departed without establishing settlements. La Salle's far-reaching land claims (1682) on behalf of France included the Kansas region but, although French fur traders dealt with area Indians in the years immediately following, the Indians retained actual possession of the land. France yielded its claim to West Louisiana (including Kansas) to Spain in 1763, and Spain retroceded it to France (1800), which three years later sold it in the Louisiana Purchase to the United States.

Lewis and Clark, Zebulon M. Pike, and Major Stephen H. Long made (1803-19) the first serious explorations of the area, but their reports were incomplete and such as to discourage immediate American settlement. Erroneously considered a part of the "Great American Desert," the Kansas region was primarily used (1825-42) as a resettlement area for uprooted Indian tribes.

With the establishment of the Santa Fe Trail (1821), which cut across the region diagonally from northeast to southwest, and the Oregon Trail (c. 1830), which traversed part of the northeastern region, the first permanent non-Indian settlements (Fort Leavenworth-1827, Fort Scott-1842, and Fort Riley-1853) were founded as outposts to protect travelers against Indian raids.

The passage of the Kansas-Nebraska Act (1854), repealing the slavery-prohibiting Missouri Compromise of 1821 in favor of "squatter sovereignty," thrust Kansas into a bloody tug-of-war between proslavery and antislavery forces who rushed into the territory and fought savagely for political control. This was the era of "Bleeding Kansas," which saw the free-state "Jayhawkers" (including famed abolitionist John Brown) pitted against the advocates of slavery; the Jayhawkers ultimately won

KANSAS
MILES
KILOMETERS
⊛ State Capital ◉ County Seats
Counties indictaed by numbers:
1 GEARY
2 JEFFERSON
3 LEAVENWORTH
4 SHAWNEE
5 WYANDOTTE
NEBRASKA
COLORADO
OKLAHOMA
MISSOURI
TEXAS
CHEYENNE
RAWLINS
DECATUR
NORTON
PHILLIPS
SMITH
JEWELL
REPUBLIC
WASHINGTON
MARSHALL
NEMAHA
BROWN
DONIPHAN
ATCHISON
JACKSON
POTTAWATOMIE
RILEY
CLAY
CLOUD
MITCHELL
LINCOLN
OSBORNE
ROOKS
GRAHAM
SHERIDAN
THOMAS
SHERMAN
WALLACE
LOGAN
GOVE
TREGO
ELLIS
RUSSELL
RUSH
BARTON
ELLSWORTH
RICE
SALINE
DICKINSON
OTTAWA
MARION
MORRIS
WABAUNSEE
SHAWNEE
DOUGLAS
JOHNSON
MIAMI
FRANKLIN
OSAGE
LYON
CHASE
BUTLER
GREENWOOD
ELK
CHAUTAUQUA
COWLEY
SUMNER
HARPER
KINGMAN
RENO
HARVEY
SEDGWICK
MC PHERSON
PRATT
KIOWA
EDWARDS
PAWNEE
STAFFORD
HODGEMAN
NESS
LANE
SCOTT
FINNEY
GRAY
FORD
CLARK
MEADE
SEWARD
STEVENS
GRANT
HASKELL
KEARNY
HAMILTON
STANTON
MORTON
GREELEY
WICHITA
BARBER
COMANCHE
COFFEY
ANDERSON
LINN
BOURBON
ALLEN
NEOSHO
WILSON
MONTGOMERY
LABETTE
CHEROKEE
CRAWFORD
WOODSON
GEARY
FLINT HILLS
SMOKY HILLS
OSAGE IND. RES.
Maryville
St. Joseph
Kansas City
Topeka
Lawrence
Leavenworth
Atchison
Manhattan
Junction City
Abilene
Salina
Concordia
Belleville
Washington
Marysville
Seneca
Hiawatha
Sabetha
Holton
Centralia
Frankfort
Hanover
Beatrice
Falls City
Fairbury
Red Cloud
Superior
Mankato
Smith Ctr.
Lebanon
Phillipsburg
Norton
Oberlin
Atwood
St. Francis
Bird City
Goodland
Colby
Hoxie
Hill City
Stockton
Osborne
Beloit
Cawker City
Downs
Natoma
Lucas
Russell
Victoria
Hays
La Crosse
Ness City
Dighton
Scott City
Leoti
Tribune
Syracuse
Johnson
Ulysses
Lakin
Elkhart
Richfield
Hugoton
Liberal
Meade
Plains
Satanta
Sublette
Garden City
Cimarron
Dodge City
Montezuma
Fowler
Ashland
Minneola
Bucklin
Coldwater
Protection
Medicine Lodge
Kiowa
Anthony
Harper
Attica
Kingman
Cunningham
Pratt
St. John
Stafford
Larned
Great Bend
Hoisington
Claflin
Ellinwood
Sterling
Lyons
Hutchinson
Nickerson
Buhler
Newton
Halstead
Hesston
McPherson
Lindsborg
Marquette
Gypsum
Kanopolis
Ellsworth
Holyrood
Wilson
Lincoln
Minneapolis
Delphos
Glasco
Clyde
Clay Ctr.
Wakefield
Miltonvale
Bennington
Solomon
Chapman
Enterprise
Herington
Council Grove
Strong City
Cottonwood Falls
Eskridge
Alma
Wamego
Wabaunsee
St. Marys
Rossville
Onaga
Westmoreland
Ogden
Ft. Riley
Waterville
Greenleaf
Clifton
Scandia
Jewell
Emporia
Madison
Eureka
Howard
Moline
Sedan
Cedar Vale
Arkansas City
Winfield
Oxford
Wellington
Belle Plaine
Mulvane
Derby
Augusta
El Dorado
Towanda
Potwin
Andover
Wichita
Clearwater
Cheney
Colwich
Conway Sprs.
Argonia
Caldwell
Ponca City
Enid
Burden
Douglass
Eudora
Baldwin City
Wellsville
Ottawa
Garnett
Burlingame
Lyndon
Osage City
Olpe
Burlington
Le Roy
Yates Ctr.
Iola
Humboldt
Moran
Chanute
Erie
St. Paul
Neosho Falls
Toronto
Fredonia
Neodesha
Cherryvale
Independence
Coffeyville
Caney
Columbus
Baxter Sprs.
Galena
Weir
Pittsburg
Girard
Arcadia
Arma
Frontenac
Ft. Scott
Pleasanton
Mound City
La Cygne
Paola
Louisburg
Spring Hill
Gardner
Olathe
Overland Pk.
Prairie Village
Bonner Sprs.
Lansing
Tonganoxie
Perry
Oskaloosa
Valley Falls
Nortonville
Effingham
Troy
Elwood
Wathena
Highland
Horton
Forbes A.F.B.
McConnell A.F.B.
Bartlesville
Pawhuska
Tulsa
Claremore
Oologah Res.
Lake O' The Cherokees
Marais des Cygnes
Arkansas River
Smoky Hill River
Solomon River
Saline River
Republican River
Big Blue
Little Blue
Platte
North Fork Solomon
South Fork Solomon
Walnut River
Neosho River
Cottonwood River
Verdigris River
Fall River
Cimarron R.
North Canadian
Salt Fork
Medicine Lodge R.
Pawnee R.
Cheyenne Bottoms
Cedar Bluff Res.
Kirwin Res.
Webster Res.
Waconda Res.
Glen Elder Res.
Wilson Res.
Kanopolis Res.
Milford Res.
Tuttle Creek Res.
Pomona Res.
Marion Res.
John Redmond Res.
Toronto Res.
Fall River Res.
Elk City Res.
Perry Res.
Pretty Prairie
Cheney Res.
Harlan Co. Res.
Norton Res.
Swanson L.
Red Willow
Great Salt Plains Res.
Keystone Res.
HOMESTEAD NAT'L MON.
FT. LARNED NAT'L HIST. SITE
POTAWATOMI IND. RES.
KICKAPOO I.R.
SAC & FOX/IOWA IND. RES.
Mt. Sunflower 4,039
Russell Sprs.
Sharon Sprs.
Quinter
Gove
Oakley
Palco
Plainville
WaKeeney
Lake McKinney
McCook

out and, in 1861 Kansas entered the Union as a free state.

Often called the Nation's Breadbasket, Kansas is the leading wheat producer and flour miller as well as one of the most important mining states. Today, Kansas is moving toward economic diversification, and manufacturing has now surpassed agriculture as the primary revenue source. The massive wheat and cattle raising operations have spawned an impressive manufacturing segment producing farm and heavy equipment. Hesston Corporation is now a world leader in farm machinery and exemplifies Kansas' growth in this area.

The production of transportation equipment is the major industrial activity. Wichita produces more than half the nation's aircraft, while Topeka is a center for the manufacture and repair of railroad cars, and is also a major tire production center. Kansas' strategic location in the center of America makes it attractive to industries with nationwide distribution.

Occasional periods of drought or flood have prompted a massive program of flood control, water conservation and utilization. More than 30 federal reservoirs have been constructed or authorized along with dozens of watershed districts.

The reservoirs and lesser impoundments assure cities and industries of a stable water supply and provide facilities for camping, fishing, swimming, boating and water skiing. There are state park facilities at many of the reservoirs and an outstanding system of roadside parks.

Among the top tourist attractions is the Dwight D. Eisenhower Center at Abilene, featuring the boyhood home, Museum, Presidential Library, and Chapel where the former President and World War II commander is buried. Reconstruction of Early Day Front Street at Dodge City and Old Ft. Larned are other tourist attractions.

As a result of the food shortage of recent years, thousands of acres of Kansas farmland were pressed back into production. Bumper crops of wheat and corn were harvested in 1976 and 1977, both here and abroad, with the result that U.S. stockpiles were at their highest level in many years and prices dropped sharply in the face of a lessening demand for American grains abroad. Kansas farmers were among the leaders of the American Agriculture movement, which withheld grain and influenced the price support increases of 1978.

In the fall of 1979, a controversial Federal court order requiring the Wichita public schools to reassign thousands of pupils in order to improve racial balance was implemented with no serious incidents. However, a violent racial confrontation between blacks and the Wichita police, unrelated to the school reassignment order, took place in April 1980.

Full name: State of Kansas. **Origin of name:** From name of Sioux tribe, meaning "People of the South Wind." **Inhabitant:** Kansan. **Capital:** Topeka. **State motto:** Ad Astra per Aspera (To the Stars through Difficulties). **Flag:** Blue field with wreath & yellow sunflower over state seal. **Seal:** Rising sun represents east; buffalo, log cabin, riverboat, wagon & plowing farmer suggest early history of region. **Flower:** Sunflower. **Bird:** Western meadowlark. **Tree:** Cottonwood. **Song:** "Home on the Range." **Nickname:** Sunflower State.

Governor: John Carlin. **Annual salary:** $45,000. **Term:** 4 years. **Current term expires:** Jan. 1983. **Voting requirements:** 18 yrs. old & U.S. citizen; resident of state and voting area; registration 20 days before election. **U.S. Congressmen:** 5. **Entered Union:** 1861 (34th state).

Location & boundaries: Midwestern state: bounded on the north by Nebraska; on the east by the Missouri River & Missouri; on the south by Oklahoma; & on the west by Colorado. **Total area:** 8,264 sq. mi. (ranks 14th). **Extreme length:** 411 mi. **Extreme breadth:** 208 mi. **Chief rivers:** Arkansas, Missouri, Kansas. **Major lakes:** Tuttle Creek, Cedar Bluff, Cheney, Perry. **No. of counties:** 105.

Population (1979 est.): 2,369,000 (ranks 32nd). **Pop. increase (1970-79):** 5.3%. **Places over 25,000 pop.:** 10. **Places over 100,000:** 3. **Largest cities:** Wichita, Kansas City, Topeka. **Pop. density:** 28.8 per sq. mi. (ranks 37th). **Pop. projection 1985:** 2,380,000. **Pop. distribution:** 46.2% metropolitan; 53.8% nonmetropolitan. **White:** 94.4%. **Black:** 4.8%. **Other:** 0.8%. **Marriage rate (1977):** 10.1 per 1,000 people. **Divorce rate:** 5.4 per 1,000 people.

State finances (1978). Revenue: $1,902,986,000. **Expenditures:** $1,746,638,000. **State taxes:** $447.67 per capita. **State personal income tax:** Yes. **Public debt (1978):** $179.67 per capita. **Federal aid (1979):** $304.22 per capita. **Personal income (1979 est.):** $9,055.

Sectors of the economy (% of labor force employed in 1975): Wholesale and retail trade (18.7%), Government (16.9%), Manufacturing (15.8%), Services (13.1%). **Leading products:** aerospace equipment, food, chemicals, crude oil & natural gas items, machinery, printing & publishing. **Minerals:** petroleum, helium, natural gas & gas liquids. **Agricultural products:** cattle, hogs, dairy items, wheat, sorghum grain, hay. **Avg. farm (1979 est.):** 669 acres. **Avg. value of farm per acre:** $437.

Highway expenditures per capita (1978): $100.17. **Persons per motor vehicle:** 1.20. **Minimum age for driver's license:** 16. **Gasoline tax:** 8¢ per gallon. **Diesel tax:** 10¢ per gallon. **Motor vehicle deaths:** 24.4 per 100,000 people.

Birthrate (1978): 15.7 per 1,000 people. **Infant mortality rate per 1,000 births (1977):** 13.4. **Physicians per 100,000 pop. (1977):** 145. **Dentists per 100,000 pop. (1977):** 44. **Acceptable hospital beds:** 7.8 per 1,000 people. **State expenditures per capita for health and hospitals (1978):** $50.25.

Education expenditures (1975-76): $432.04 per capita annually. **No. of pupils in public schools (1977 est.):** 430,000. **No. of institutions of higher learning (1976-77):** 52. **Public school expenditure per pupil in attendance (1975-76):** $1,538. **Avg. salary of public school teachers (1974-75 est.):** $9,770. **No. full-time teachers (1977 est.):** 27,230. **Educational attainment of adult population (1976):** 12.6 median yrs. of school completed; 1.0% with less than 5 years of education; 14.6% with 4 yrs. of college.

Telephones (1977): 77 per 100 people. **State Chamber of Commerce:** Kansas Assn. of Commerce and Industry, 500 First National Tower, One Townsite Plaza, Topeka, Kansas 66603.

KENTUCKY

Kentucky, renowned for the quality of its tobacco, whiskey, and racehorses, was the first state west of the Alleghenies to be settled by pioneers. A state of sometimes bizarre contrasts, Kentucky has the nation's gold reserves (at Fort Knox) and many fine farms and estates, yet much of its land has been devastated by reckless lumbering and strip-mining practices, and in some eastern areas chronic unemployment prevails. Two Kentuckians, Abraham Lincoln and Jefferson Davis, were the opposing presidents in the Civil War.

Roughly triangular in shape, the state consists of the Appalachian Plateau (known locally as the Cumberland Plateau and constituting the largest single area—more than a fourth of the total), the northcentral Bluegrass Region, the Pennyroyal Region (or Southwestern Mississippian Embayment), the Western Coal Field, and the East Gulf Coastal Plain (or Jackson Purchase Region), which makes up the state's western tip. A double hairpin turn in the Mississippi River separates a small bit of extreme southwestern Kentucky from the rest of the state. Most of the state's surface is a much-furrowed plain sloping gently to the west. The state's northern boundary, the Ohio River, has been shifting gradually north- and westward for centuries. Kentucky thus had stood to gain territory with the border's expansion, but the Supreme Court ruled in January 1980 that the boundary remains fixed at its original position regardless of the movement of the Ohio River.

About half the land is farmed, and agriculture (especially tobacco) is still important, although it has been surpassed in recent years by manufacturing. Commercial fishing is limited, while mining continues as a major activity; Kentucky ranks as the country's leading coal producer. Spurred by the building of new roads, tourism is also a significant revenue source; attractions include Mammoth Cave National Park, Abraham Lincoln Birthplace National Historical Site, Daniel Boone National Forest, Natural Bridge, and the annual Kentucky Derby.

Indians are thought to have lived in the forests of what is now western Kentucky as long as 15,000 years ago. Although other Europeans visited the region during the latter part of the 17th century, the first serious exploration of record was conducted (1750) by Dr. Thomas Walker, who passed through, and named, Cumberland Gap. About this time, a number of Indian tribes—including the Cherokee, Iroquois, and Shawnee—who were using the region as hunting grounds strongly resisted the advance of the white man. Daniel Boone explored eastern Kentucky (1767) and later spent two years in the Bluegrass Region. In 1773 he led a group of settlers into Kentucky, but Indians forced him out. James Harrod established (1774) the first permanent non-Indian settlement at Harrodsburg; in the following year Daniel Boone, acting as an agent for the Transylvania Company, returned to hack out the Wilderness Road and establish Boonesboro.

Indian raids were a continuing menace until General Anthony Wayne's victory in the Battle of Fallen Timbers in Ohio (1794) virtually ended them. Kentucky was originally a county of Virginia known as Fincastle before gaining statehood in 1792. The 1795 Pinckney's Treaty with Spain and the 1803 Louisiana Purchase made travel on the Mississippi more secure and aided development.

Kentucky's growth has been marked by conflict and violence. Kentuckians fought hard against the Alien and Sedition Acts (1798), vigorously supported the War of 1812 and the Mexican War (1846-48), and, although neutral in the Civil War, supplied each side with thousands of troops. The slavery issue, a particularly contentious one for a slaveholding state containing many abolitionists, was officially resolved in 1865 with the adoption of the 13th Constitutional Amendment. Lesser conflicts included the Hatfield-McCoy wrangle (1882-96), troubles surrounding the assassination of Democratic gubernatorial candidate William Goebel (1900), the so-called Black Patch War (1904-09) between tobacco farmers and buyers, and frequent strife between mine owners and the United Mine Workers.

In response to the energy crisis forced in the early 1970s by the oil shortage and rising prices, coal mines were reopened, resulting in a drop in the state's unemployment. After two methane gas explosions which claimed 26 lives in 1976, a mine safety bill was passed.

Full name: Commonwealth of Kentucky. **Origin of name:** From Wyandot name, Ken-tah-teh, meaning "Land of Tomorrow." **Inhabitant:** Kentuckian. **Capital:** Frankfort. **State motto:** United We Stand, Divided We Fall. **Flag:** State seal on a blue field. **Seal:** Two men greeting each other; state motto. **Flower:** Goldenrod. **Bird:** Cardinal. **Tree:** Kentucky coffee tree. **Song:** "My Old Kentucky Home." **Nickname:** Bluegrass State.

Governor: John Y. Brown, Jr. **Annual salary:** $45,000. **Term:** 4 years. **Current term expires:** Jan. 1984. **Voting requirements:** 18 yrs. old & U.S. citizen; resident of state 6 months; county 30 days; precinct 30 days. **U.S. Congressmen:** 7. **Entered Union:** 1792 (15th state).

Location & boundaries: Southeastern state: bounded on the north by the Ohio River, Illinois, Indiana & Ohio; on the east by the Big Sandy & Tug Fork Rivers, West Virginia & Virginia; on the south by Tennessee; & on the west by the Mississippi River & Missouri. **Total area:** 40,395 sq. mi. (ranks 37th). **Extreme length:** 350 mi. **Extreme breadth:** 175 mi. **Chief rivers:** Ohio, Kentucky, Tennessee. **Major lakes:** Kentucky, Barkley & Cumberland Reservoirs. **No. of counties:** 120.

Population (1979 est.): 3,527,000 (ranks 23rd). **Pop. increase (1970-79):** 9.5%. **Places over 25,000 pop.:** 8. **Places over 100,000:** 2. **Largest cities:** Louisville, Lexington, Owensboro, Covington. **Pop. density:** 87.3 per sq. mi. (ranks 21st). **Pop. projection 1985:** 3,751,000. **Pop. distribution:** 45.1% metropolitan; 54.9% nonmetropolitan. **White:** 92.6%. **Black:** 7.2%. **Other:** 0.2%. **Marriage rate (1977):** 9.8 per 1,000 people. **Divorce rate:** 4.5 per 1,000 people.

State finances (1978). Revenue: $3,354,533,000. **Expenditures:** $3,241,028,000. **State taxes:** $526.63 per capita. **State personal income tax:** Yes. **Public debt (1978):** $748.27 per capita. **Federal aid (1979):** $380.18 per capita. **Personal income (1979 est.):** $7,342.

Sectors of the economy (% of labor force employed in 1970): Manufacturing (26%), Wholesale and retail trade (19%), Government (16%), Educational Services (8%), Services (7%), Construction (7%). **Leading products:** food, chemicals, tobacco items, machinery, primary & fabricated metals, transportation equipment. **Minerals:** coal, petroleum, stone, natural gas. **Agricultural products:** cattle, hogs, tobacco, dairy items, corn, hay. **Avg. farm (1979 est.):** 150 acres. **Avg. value of farm per acre:** $792.

Highway expenditures per capita (1978): $148.39. **Persons per motor vehicle:** 1.33. **Minimum age for driver's license:** 16. **Gasoline tax:** 9¢ per gallon. **Diesel tax:** 9¢ per gallon. **Motor vehicle deaths:** 25.1 per 100,000 people.

Birthrate (1978): 16.4 per 1,000 people. **Infant mortality rate per 1,000 births (1977):** 14.4. **Physicians per 100,000 pop. (1977):** 128. **Dentists per 100,000 pop. (1977):** 40. **Acceptable hospital beds:** 5.4 per 1,000 people. **State expenditures per capita for health and hospitals (1978):** $44.38.

Education expenditures (1975-76): $369.85 per capita annually. **No. of pupils in public schools (1977 est.):** 684,000. **No. of institutions of higher learning (1976-77):** 38. **Public school expenditure per pupil in attendance (1975-76):** $1,122. **Avg. salary of public school teachers (1974-75 est.):** $9,240. **No. full-time teachers (1977 est.):** 35,290. **Educational attainment of adult population (1976):** 12.1 median yrs. of school completed; 5.7% with less than 5 years of education; 10.0% with 4 yrs. of college.

Telephones (1977): 61 per 100 people. **State Chamber of Commerce:** Kentucky Chamber of Commerce, Versailles Rd., P.O. Box 817, Frankfort, Kentucky 40602.

LOUISIANA

With its French and Spanish background, Louisiana is rich in history and among the nation's leaders in oil and natural gas, salt, sulphur, commercial fishing, fur trapping and rice, sugar cane and sweet potato production. The Michoud plant at New Orleans was a vital rocket-assembly installation during NASA's earth orbit and Apollo moon shots, contributing to the emergence of manufacturing as a major industry in the state.

New Orleans lies 100 miles up the Mississippi River from the Gulf of Mexico. It has been the nation's second-busiest seaport since 1840 but is perhaps better known as the site of the annual Mardi Gras. The world's longest bridge, the 24-mile Lake Pontchartrain Causeway, connects New Orleans to Mandeville. A sizeable timber industry is fed by extensive forest lands.

In the north are low rolling hills, and in the east

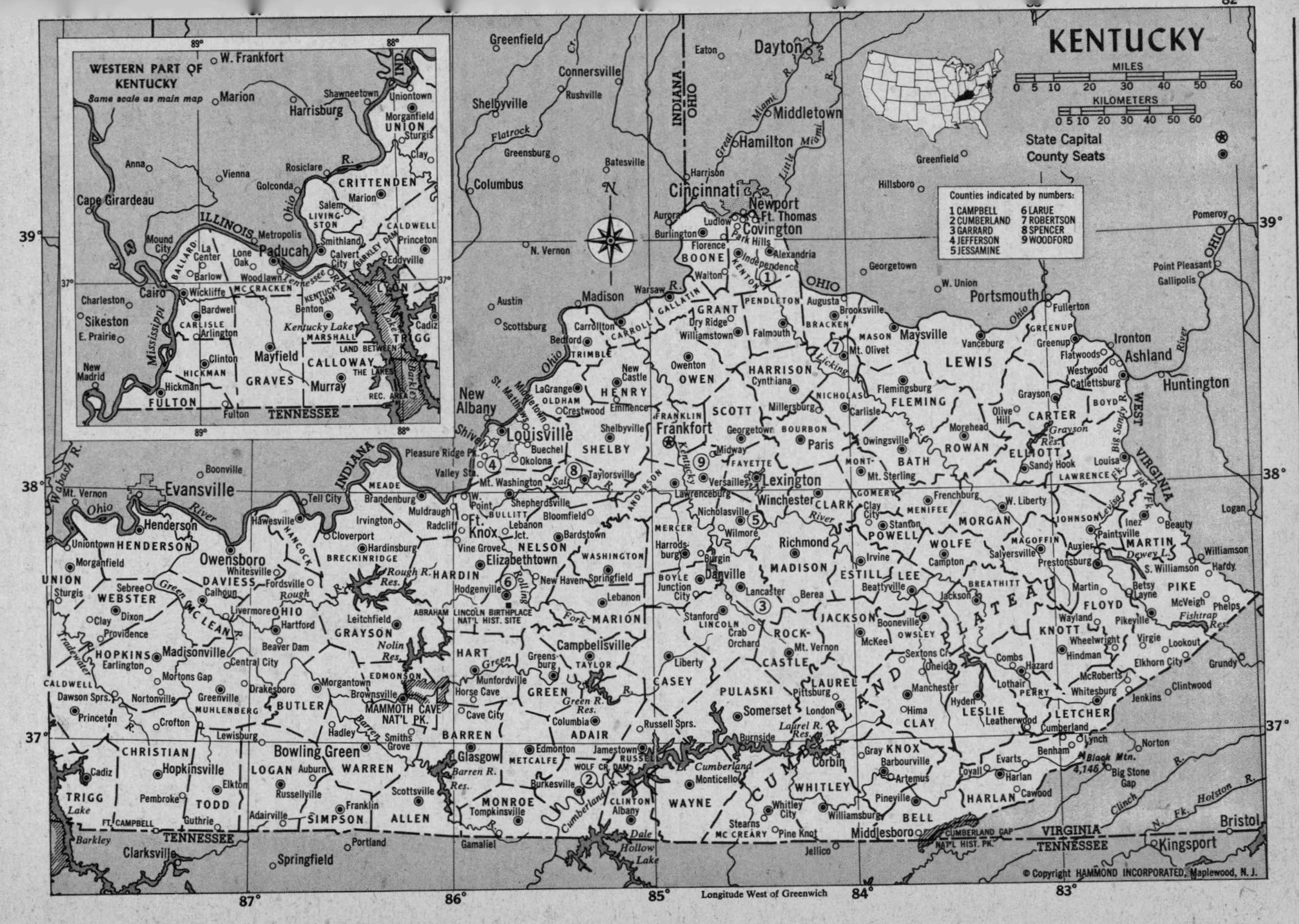

KENTUCKY
MILES
KILOMETERS
State Capital
County Seats
Counties indicated by numbers:
1 CAMPBELL
2 CUMBERLAND
3 GARRARD
4 JEFFERSON
5 JESSAMINE
6 LARUE
7 ROBERTSON
8 SPENCER
9 WOODFORD
WESTERN PART OF KENTUCKY
Same scale as main map
© Copyright HAMMOND INCORPORATED, Maplewood, N.J.
Longitude West of Greenwich

many bluffs dot the river plain. Coastal marshes and sluggish streams (bayous) are features of the southern terrain. The Mississippi Delta, a fertile sedimentary deposit, comprises a third of the state's total area.

Indians are thought to have lived in the northern part of the Louisiana region over 3,000 years ago. Spanish explorer Cabeza de Vaca may have visited the area about 1530, and Hernando De Soto did so (1540-42). Approximately 12,000 Indians were then living in the region.

In 1682 Robert Cavelier, Sieur de La Salle, reached the mouth of the Mississippi and claimed all the land drained by it and its tributaries for King Louis XIV of France.

Permanent French settlement of the Louisiana region began (1699) with its founding as a royal colony and the establishment of a community near present-day Biloxi, Mississippi. In 1717 the area was granted to a company headed by John Law, who initially centered his development in the region that is now Arkansas, but then moved south. New Orleans was founded in 1718 and four years later became the capital. Law's venture spurred immigration, but eventually failed.

French control of the region gave way (1762) to Spanish; France regained possession in 1800. Three years later, Napoleon Bonaparte, seeking funds to support his European military activities, sold the land to the United States, as part of the vast Louisiana Purchase. In 1804 the territory was divided at the state's present northern border: the northern portion, now made up of other states, was at first called the District of Louisiana, then the Territory of Louisiana, and later Missouri Territory; the southern portion, originally the Territory of Orleans, became the present state of Louisiana. The period between 1760 and 1790 was marked by an influx of French-speaking Acadians, or Cajuns, from what is now Nova Scotia, who settled mainly in the southern region.

In the early 19th century, the natives of Louisiana were a heterogeneous mixture of French, Spanish, Isleños from the Canary Islands, and Germans. Although the Louisianians generally did not welcome the coming of the Americans, they did unite behind Andrew Jackson to defeat (1815) the British in the Battle of New Orleans at the end of the War of 1812. The state, which entered the Union in 1812, was enlarged by the settlement of the West Florida Controversy, which had stemmed from conflicting Spanish and American land claims involving portions of Florida, Alabama, Mississippi, and Louisiana; the Transcontinental Treaty of 1819 gave control of the disputed regions to the United States.

Early statehood was marked by the advent of the Mississippi steamboat trade and its attendant prosperity, and by the rise of plantation agriculture. The Civil War and the Reconstruction period brought considerable hardship and chaos. White rule was ultimately reestablished and farm tenancy and sharecropping replaced the plantation system. The discovery of oil (1901) and natural gas (1916) greatly aided the state's economic recovery.

The 1927 Mississippi flood, which forced 300,000 people from their homes, remains the worst on record. But the 1973 high water flooded nearly four million acres of Louisiana for months before the crisis ebbed away into the Gulf. Enormous damage was averted by the levee system.

Huey P. Long, elected governor in 1927 and assassinated in 1935, remains the state's most renowned political figure. His term as governor launched a political dynasty that continued even after he was killed. As governor and later (1930) as U.S. senator, Long was an advocate of a "Share the Wealth" program that challenged powerful Louisiana oil interests. He was responsible for much material progress but also was blamed for considerable political corruption.

Louisiana today is becoming increasingly industrialized, often to the detriment of its tradition-ripe picturesqueness. One reason for the spurt is that the state grants 10-year tax exemptions to new industries. Tourism also has grown, and today accounts for over $1 billion annually. Those seeking to preserve the traces of the past were heartened by the Federal government's refusal (July 1969) to grant funds for part of a highway system that would have "seriously impaired the historic quality of New Orleans' famed French Quarter." An alternate route was not acceptable because of its disruptive effects on the city, excessive costs, and construction hazards to the city's river levee. The ruling was believed to be the first denial of Federal funds for a highway on the basis of preserving a historic area.

The Louisiana Offshore Oil Port (Loop) is being constructed 18 miles off Grand Isle. Tankers too large to dock at any existing U.S. ports will unload their cargo at the superport, and the oil will be sent to the mainland by pipeline. The port is scheduled to be operational by 1980.

On March 10, 1980, David C. Treen was inaugurated as Louisiana's first Republican governor in 103 years. He had been elected by a slim margin in a run-off on Dec. 8, 1979, having promised to end the state's notorious political corruption.

Full name: State of Louisiana. **Origin of name:** In honor of King Louis XIV of France. **Inhabitant:** Louisianian. **Capital:** Baton Rouge. **State motto:** Union, Justice & Confidence. **Flag:** State seal & motto on a blue field. **Seal:** Mother pelican feeding brood. **Flower:** Magnolia. **Bird:** Brown pelican. **Tree:** Bald cypress. **Song:** "Give Me Louisiana." **Nickname:** Pelican State.

Governor: David C. Treen. **Annual salary:** $52,400. **Term:** 4 years. **Current term expires:** Mar. 1984. **Voting requirements:** 18 yrs. old & U.S. citizen; resident of state 1 yr.; county, 6 mos.; district, 3 mos.; valid I.D. **U.S. Congressmen:** 8. **Entered Union:** 1812 (18th state).

Location & boundaries: Gulf state: bounded on the north by Arkansas; on the east by the Mississippi & Pearl Rivers & Mississippi; on the southeast & south by the Gulf of Mexico; & on the west by Texas & the Sabine River. **Total area:** 48,523 sq. mi. (ranks 31st). **Extreme length:** 237 mi. **Extreme breadth:** 236.5 mi. **Coastline:** 397 mi. **Chief rivers:** Mississippi, Atchafalaya, Red, Ouachita. **Major lakes:** Pontchartrain, Grand, White. **No. of parishes (counties):** 64.

Population (1979 est.): 4,018,000 (ranks 20th). **Pop. increase (1970-79):** 10.2%. **Places over 25,000 pop.:** 11. **Places over 100,000:** 3. **Largest cities:** New Orleans, Baton Rouge, Shreveport. **Pop. density:** 82.8 per sq. mi. (ranks 24th). **Pop. projection 1985:** 4,096,000. **Pop. distribution:** 63.2% metropolitan; 36.8% non-metropolitan. **White:** 69.7%. **Black:** 29.9%. **Other:** 0.4%. **Marriage rate (1977):** 9.8 per 1,000 people. **Divorce rate:** Not Available.

State finances (1978). Revenue: $4,115,184,000. **Expenditures:** $3,918,087,000. **State taxes:** $499.30 per capita. **State personal income tax:** Yes. **Public debt (1978):** $514.84 per capita. **Federal aid (1979):** $375.63 per capita. **Personal income (1979 est.):** $7,477.

Sectors of the economy (% of labor force employed in 1970): Wholesale & retail trade (21%), Government (17%), Manufacturing (16%), Services (10%), Educational Services (9%), Construction (8%). **Leading products:** chemicals, food, petroleum and paper items, transportation equipment, lumber, primary metals. **Minerals:** petroleum, natural gas, sulfur. **Agricultural products:** cattle, dairy items, rice, sugar cane, soybeans. **Fishing:** shrimp, menhaden, oysters. **Avg. farm (1979 est.):** 294 acres. **Avg. value of farm per acre:** $763.

LOUISIANA
MILES
KILOMETERS
State Capital
Parish Seats
Parishes indicated by numbers:
1 JEFFERSON
2 ORLEANS
3 ST. CHARLES
4 ST. JAMES
5 ST. JOHN THE BAPTIST
6 WEST BATON ROUGE
ARKANSAS
TEXAS
MISSISSIPPI
ALABAMA
GULF OF MEXICO
Longitude West of Greenwich
© Copyright HAMMOND INCORPORATED, Maplewood, N. J.

Highway expenditures per capita (1978): $126.34. **Persons per motor vehicle:** 1.50. **Minimum age for driver's license:** 15. **Gasoline tax:** 8¢ per gallon. **Diesel tax:** 8¢ per gallon. **Motor vehicle deaths:** 27.2 per 100,000 people.

Birthrate (1978): 18.1 per 1,000 people. **Infant mortality rate per 1,000 births (1977):** 17.9. **Physicians per 100,000 pop. (1977):** 143. **Dentists per 100,000 pop. (1977):** 38. **Acceptable hospital beds:** 6.4 per 1,000 people. **State expenditures per capita for health and hospitals (1978):** $83.93.

Education expenditures (1975-76): $385.08 per capita annually. **No. of pupils in public schools (1977 est.):** 827,000. **No. of institutions of higher learning (1976-77):** 31. **Public school expenditure per pupil in attendance (1975-76):** $1,391. **Avg. salary of public school teachers (1974-75 est.):** $9,800. **No. full-time teachers (1977 est.):** 46,620. **Educational attainment of adult population (1976):** 12.3 median yrs. of school completed; 8.7% with less than 5 years of education; 11.5% with 4 yrs. of college.

Telephones (1977): 66 per 100 people. **State Chamber of Commerce:** Louisiana Association of Business & Industry, P.O. Box 3988, Baton Rouge, Louisiana 70821.

MAINE

Four-fifths of Maine is covered by forests that feed an enormous wood-processing industry. There are three general land areas: the White Mountains region in the northwest, the New England Uplands extending through the heart of the state, and the coastal lowlands of the southeast. Many bays and harbors dot the craggy, convoluted coastline. Southwest of Portland, the rockbound coast is supplanted by sandy beaches. Sailors coasting downwind from Boston gave the shore its nickname, "Down East." Fishermen are attracted by the state's 2,500 lakes and ponds and 5,000 rivers and streams. Waterpower availability is correspondingly excellent. Ten mountains rise more than 4,000 feet; undersea peaks form 400 offshore islands.

The climate is marked by generally severe winters, and summer evenings occasionally so cool that people heat their homes. Yet this very ruggedness of terrain and climate has proved an asset in drawing tourists. Skiing, camping, and other outdoor activities are especially popular, and many city-worn visitors seek out the unspoiled Allagash wilderness, the 92-mile-long Allagash Wilderness Waterway, and Mount Katahdin (5,268 ft.), which is the first place in the nation to catch the rays of the rising sun. Other attractions include Bar Harbor on Mount Desert Island, most of which is part of Acadia National Park.

Maine may have been sighted by Norse explorer Leif Ericsson as early as A.D. 1000, and English-employed Italian sea captain John Cabot is considered to have been the first European to reach the area, in 1498. Thousands of Abnaki and Etchemin Indians were living there at the time. They peaceably coexisted with the earliest settlers but occasionally joined together to fight off raiding Iroquois. The legendary city of Norumbega, thought to have contained vast riches, drew adventurers up the Penobscot River, upon which the city was said to have been located.

Maine lands were granted (1622) by the Council for New England (successor to the Plymouth Company) to two wealthy Englishmen, Sir Ferdinando Gorges and Captain John Mason. Gorgeana (now York) became (1641) the first chartered English city in the New World. After Gorges' death (1647), Maine was largely neglected. Its settlers came under the jurisdiction of Massachusetts, which later bought (1677) the proprietary rights of Gorges' heirs for about $6,000. French efforts to control the region ended with the Treaty of Paris (1763), termi-

nating the French and Indian Wars that had begun in 1689.

Revolt against England was in the air in the 1760s because of taxes and restrictions. In 1774, Maine men followed Boston's example of a year earlier and burned a supply of British tea (York Tea Party). The first naval encounter of the American Revolution took place (June 1775) off Machias, as patriots captured the British ship *Margaretta*. The eastern part of the state passed under British control during the War of 1812.

Maine stayed a part of Massachusetts until 1820, when it was admitted to the Union as a free state under the terms of the Missouri Compromise, thus balancing Missouri's admission as a slave state. A long-simmering boundary dispute with New Brunswick was settled by the Webster-Ashburton Treaty (1842), which ended the bloodless Aroostook War.

Maine was the first state to outlaw (1851) alcohol, which remained illegal until 1934. From 1909 to 1955, to keep the state's hydroelectric power within its borders and thus attract new industries, the sale of such power outside the state was prohibited. The state's textile business has declined since the 1920s, while the food-processing industry has grown significantly. Lobsters, canned sardines, potatoes, and blueberries are among the state's most famous products, as well as shoes, beet sugar and wood pulp and paper. Mining is limited, despite large deposits of granite, limestone, and slate. The communications satellite station near Andover (completed 1962) is part of a worldwide satellite communications system.

The New York Mercantile Exchange, the only market for the round, white Maine potatoes, suspended trading in 1979, on contracts for delivery in March, April, and May. While the NYME said it acted to prevent a collapse of the market which could have resulted from the shortage of high-quality Maine potatoes, Maine farmers, who lost millions of dollars because of the halt, contended that the supply problems were caused by manipulation of the market by a few big traders. In March 1980 Maine farmers blockaded Canadian border crossings to protest the flooding of U.S. markets by Canadian potato imports.

In March 1980 members of the Penobscot Indian tribe approved an $81 million settlement proposal for their claims to half of Maine's territory.

In a referendum in March 1980, Maine voters strengthened a five-year-old ban on slot machines operated for profit to eliminate even those gambling devices operated for charity.

Full name: State of Maine. **Origin of name:** From name of ancient province in France. **Inhabitant:** Mainer. **Capital:** Augusta. **State motto:** Dirigo (I Guide). **Flag:** State seal on a blue field. **Seal:** Farmer & seaman represent two chief occupations; pine tree symbolizes forests; moose, wildlife; northern star stands for northern location. **Flower:** White pine cone & tassel. **Bird:** Chickadee. **Tree:** White pine. **Stone:** Tourmaline. **Song:** "State of Maine Song." **Nickname:** Pine Tree State.

Governor: Joseph E. Brennan. **Annual salary:** $35,000. **Term:** 4 years. **Current term expires:** Jan. 1983. **Voting requirements:** 18 yrs. old & U.S. citizen; resident of state and municipality of registration. **U.S. Congressmen:** 2. **Entered Union:** 1820 (23rd state).

Location & boundaries: New England state; bounded on the north & east by Canada; on the south by New Hampshire & the Atlantic Ocean; & on the west by New Hampshire & Canada. **Total area:** 33,215 sq. mi. (ranks 39th). **Extreme length:** 332 mi. **Extreme breadth:** 207 mi. **Coastline:** 228 mi. **Chief rivers:** Androscoggin, Kennebec, Penobscot, St. Croix. **Major lakes:** Moosehead, Chesuncook, Sebago, Rangeley. **No. of counties:** 16.

Population (1979 est.): 1,097,000 (ranks 38th). **Pop. increase (1970-79):** 10.4%. **Places over 25,000 pop.:** 3. **Places over**

MAINE
MILES
KILOMETERS
State and Provincial Capitals
County Seats
© Copyright HAMMOND INCORPORATED, Maplewood, N.J.
Longitude West of Greenwich
ATLANTIC OCEAN
CANADA
QUÉBEC
NEW BRUNSWICK
NEW HAMPSHIRE
AROOSTOOK
PENOBSCOT
SOMERSET
FRANKLIN
OXFORD
KENNEBEC
WALDO
HANCOCK
WASHINGTON
LINCOLN
KNOX
ANDROSCOGGIN
CUMBERLAND
YORK
SAGADAHOC
ST. LAWRENCE RIVER
LAURENTIDES PROV. PK.
Baie-St-Paul
Montmagny
Île d'Orléans
Québec
Etchemin R.
Chaudière R.
Tring Jonction
Lac-Mégantic
L. Mégantic
L. St-François
QUÉBEC
L. de l'Est
St. Francis
Allagash R.
Saint John R.
St. Francis
Soldier Pond
Allagash
Eagle Lake
▲1,981
Fish River L.
Square L.
Edmundston
Madawaska
Ft. Kent
Frenchville
St. Agatha
Long L.
Keegan
Van Buren
Stockholm
Grand Falls
LORING A.F.B.
Limestone
Caribou
Washburn
Ft. Fairfield
Ashland
Mapleton
Presque Isle
Squa Pan L.
Mars Hill
Bridgewater
Aroostook R.
Chemquasabamticook L.
Eagle L.
Chamberlain L.
Allagash L.
Caucomgomoc L.
Grand Lake Seboeis
Monticello
Houlton
Woodstock
Saint John R.
Chesuncook L.
Seboomook L.
Mt. Katahdin ▲5,268
East Branch
Patten
Mattawamkeag L.
Sherman Mills
Island Falls
Oakfield
Moosehead Lake
Jackman
Rockwood
Pemadumcook L.
Millinocket L.
Millinocket
E. Millinocket
Danforth
Chiputneticook Lakes
Grand L.
Magaguadavic L.
Oromocto L.
Big Squaw Mtn. 3,196
Greenville
Seboeis L.
Mattawamkeag
Baskahegan L.
St. Croix R.
Brownville Jct.
Monson
Brownville
Milo
Schoodic L.
Penobscot R.
Lincoln
West Grand L.
Princeton
Grand Falls L.
St. Stephen
Flagstaff L.
West Forks
Guilford
Sebec L.
Howland
Nicatous L.
Big L.
Woodland
Calais
ST. CROIX NAT'L MON.
Eustis
Caratunk
Wyman L.
Dover-Foxcroft
Meddybemps L.
Pembroke
PASSAMAQUODDY IND. RES.
Eastport
Stratton
Bigelow Mtn. 4,150
Bingham
Dexter
PENOBSCOT IND. RES.
Milford
Machias R.
Lubec
Aziscohos L.
Oquossoc
Rangeley
Kingfield
Saddleback Mtn. 4,116
Solon
Corinna
Pushaw L.
Old Town
Orono
Narraguagus R.
W. Quoddy Hd.
Grand Manan Chan.
Richardson Lakes
Phillips
N. Anson
Hartland
Newport
Bangor
Brewer
Machias
E. Machias
Grand Manan I.
Mooselookmeguntic L.
Madison
Pittsfield
Hampden
Cherryfield
Umbagog L.
Farmington
Wilton
Skowhegan
Burnham
Winterport
Bucksport
Orland
Graham L.
Milbridge
Jonesport
Machias B.
Great Wass I.
Andover
Mexico
Norridgewock
Ellsworth
Hancock
Gouldsboro
Rumford
Dixfield
Chisholm
Waterville
Fairfield
Blue Hill
Petit Manan Pt.
Peru
Winslow
Searsport
Bar Harbor
Bethel
Livermore Falls
China
Palermo
Belfast
Castine
Blue Hill Falls
W. Paris
Livermore
Augusta
Lincolnville
Deer I.
S.W. Harbor
Mt. Desert I.
ACADIA NAT'L PK.
Norway
S. Paris
Winthrop
Hallowell
Camden
Penobscot Bay
Oxford
Gardiner
Randolph
Rockport
Warren
Rockland
Stonington
Swans I.
Auburn
Richmond
Waldoboro
Thomaston
Vinalhaven
Isle au Haut
ACADIA NAT'L PK.
Poland
Lewiston
Lisbon Falls
Wiscasset
Damariscotta
Tenants Harbor
Matinicus I.
Bridgton
Topsham
Bath
Bristol
Muscongus B.
Fryeburg
Naples
Gray
Brunswick
Freeport
Boothbay Harbor
Monhegan I.
Sebago L.
Cornish
Yarmouth
Phippsburg
Kezar Falls
Cumberland Ctr.
Falmouth Foreside
Casco Bay
Cape Small
Gorham
Limerick
Westbrook
Portland
S. Portland
C. Elizabeth
York
Saco
Old Orchard Beach
Springvale
Alfred
Biddeford
Salmon Falls R.
Sanford
Kennebunk
Kennebunkport
Rochester
Berwick
Wells
Ogunquit
S. Berwick
York
Kittery
Portsmouth
Isles of Shoals
Kennebec R.
Androscoggin R.

100,000: None. **Largest cities:** Portland, Lewiston, Bangor. **Pop. density:** 33.0 per sq. mi. (ranks 36th). **Pop. projection 1985:** 1,196,000. **Pop. distribution:** 23.0% metropolitan; 77.0% nonmetropolitan. **White:** 99.3%. **Black:** 0.3%. **Other:** 0.4%. **Marriage rate (1977):** 10.6 per 1,000 people. **Divorce rate:** 5.2 per 1,000 people.

State finances (1978). Revenue: $1,161,242,000. **Expenditures:** $1,118,225,000. **State taxes:** $483.41 per capita. **State personal income tax:** Yes. **Public debt (1978):** $639.76 per capita. **Federal aid (1979):** $458.61 per capita. **Personal income (1979 est.):** $7,057.

Sectors of the economy (% of labor force employed in 1970): Manufacturing (32%), Wholesale and retail trade (20%), Government (15%), Educational Services (8.2%) Services (7%), Construction (6%). **Leading products:** paper items, leather items, food, textile items, lumber & wood, transportation equipment, printing & publishing. **Minerals:** sand & gravel, cement, stone, peat. **Agricultural products:** broilers, dairy items, potatoes, hay, apples. **Fishing:** lobster, ocean perch, clams. **Avg. farm (1979 est.):** 216 acres. **Avg. value of farm per acre:** $485.

Highway expenditures per capita (1978): $102.94. **Persons per motor vehicle:** 1.51. **Minimum age for driver's license:** 15. **Gasoline tax:** 9¢ per gallon. **Diesel tax:** 9¢ per gallon. **Motor vehicle deaths:** 21.8 per 100,000 people.

Birthrate (1978): 14.5 per 1,000 people. **Infant mortality rate per 1,000 births (1977):** 9.5. **Physicians per 100,000 pop. (1977):** 143. **Dentists per 100,000 pop. (1977):** 42. **Acceptable hospital beds:** 6.7 per 1,000 people. **State expenditures per capita for health and hospitals (1978):** $47.28.

Education expenditures (1975-76): $378.56 per capita annually. **No. of pupils in public schools (1977 est.):** 245,000. **No. of institutions of higher learning (1976-77):** 25. **Public school expenditure per pupil in attendance (1975-76):** $1,406. **Avg. salary of public school teachers (1974-75 est.):** $13,202. **No. full-time teachers (1977 est.):** 14,390. **Educational attainment of adult population (1976):** 12.5 median yrs. of school completed; 1.2% with less than 5 years of education; 13.6% with 4 yrs. of college.

Telephones (1977): 68 per 100 people. **State Chamber of Commerce:** Maine State Chamber of Commerce, One Canal Plaza, Box 65, Portland, Maine 04112.

MARYLAND

Maryland has been called "America in Miniature" because, although small in area, it is uncommonly diverse and rich in history. Hills, valleys, rolling plains, swamps, and plateaus are all found there, and contrasting life-styles abound: from tobacco farmers in the southern part of the state to the missile makers of the highly industrialized Baltimore area, where more than half of the state's population lives. It was from Maryland that Washington, D.C. received (1791) part of its land (the rest was ceded by Virginia); when the capital was threatened by Confederate forces, Maryland became the scene of much fighting, including one of the bloodiest Civil War battles of all: Antietam (1862). Earlier, during the War of 1812, Marylander Francis Scott Key, watching the British bombardment of Baltimore's Fort McHenry, was inspired to write "The Star-Spangled Banner."

Maryland's coastline along the Atlantic Ocean is short, but Chesapeake Bay, which divides the state into an Eastern and Western Shore, provides many fine harbors, and a number of important islands dot the bay. A section of the Atlantic Coastal Plain, sometimes called "Tidewater Maryland," makes up all of the low-lying Eastern Shore. Fishing is a significant industry, and wild fowl abound.

Indians, mainly of the Algonquian family, were living in what is now Maryland before John Cabot, probably the region's first European explorer, sailed along the eastern coast in 1498. Virginian William Claiborne established the first settlement, a fur-trading post, on Kent Island.

The Maryland region was named for Henrietta Maria, queen consort of Charles I, who granted it (1632) to George Calvert, first Baron Baltimore. But Calvert died the same year, and his son Cecilius, second Baron Baltimore, was given the grant. He soon began developing the colony as both an income source and a religious haven for persecuted fellow Catholics. The Act of Toleration (1649) was passed in behalf of the Catholics, but when the Puritans gained control of the area they repealed this instrument (1654). A short civil war followed (1655), from which the Puritans emerged victors. In 1657 a compromise briefly restored the proprietorship to Lord Baltimore.

The English government eventually (1691) made Maryland a royal province. Commercial development proceeded rapidly in the next century, particularly in the Baltimore area. Indian troubles were infrequent and comparatively mild. Boundary quarrels with Pennsylvania were settled by the drawing of the Mason-Dixon Line (1767). Marylanders staged (1774) a Boston-style "tea party" in Annapolis, protesting British rule, and fought so well in the American Revolution that George Washington nicknamed Maryland "The Old Line State," in honor of its dependable "troops of the line." The state, which entered the Union in 1788, prospered early, thanks largely to the famous Baltimore clipper ships and the opening (1830) of the Baltimore and Ohio Railroad, first in the hemisphere to carry both passengers and freight.

During the Civil War, Maryland was a sharply divided slave state that remained loyal to the Union under great pressure; the state's inherited racial problems are compounded by such factors as inadequate urban housing and public apathy.

Maryland becomes increasingly less a part of the Old South and seems to grow smaller every year. Expressways now link all areas of the state; two of them serve the rapidly developing Baltimore-Washington corridor, while Interstate 70 reaches into Western Maryland and the dual-lane U.S. 50 and U.S. 13 funnel traffic through the Eastern Shore. The Francis Scott Key Bridge opened in 1977. It is Baltimore's second harbor crossing and teams with the Harbor Tunnel. A second span of the Chesapeake Bay Bridge opened in 1973.

Maryland's tourist attractions include a wide variety of parks and forests stretching from Appalachia to the Atlantic Ocean. Annapolis is the site of the U.S. Naval Academy, with the nation's oldest statehouse in use and more original colonial buildings than any other U.S. city. Columbia, the planned city built by James Rouse halfway between Baltimore and Washington, celebrated its 10th anniversary in 1977.

In 1975 Maryland's Governor Mandel and five associates were indicted by a Federal grand jury on charges of mail fraud and "racketeering" activity. The trial ended abruptly in 1976 with two separate cases of tampering. A second trial held in 1977 resulted in conviction, and Mandel was sentenced to four years in prison. The sentence was voided when the 4th U.S. Circuit Court of Appeals set aside his conviction on technical grounds on January 11, 1979, but, following a review, it was reinstated on July 20. In a separate charge filed in January 1980, the state alleged that Governor and Mrs. Mandel, upon leaving the governor's mansion in 1977, had illegally removed such state property as furniture and liquor.

Full name: State of Maryland. **Origin of name:** From Queen Henrietta Maria of England, wife of Charles I. **Inhabitant:** Marylander. **Capital:** Annapolis. **State motto:** "Fatti maschi, parole femine" ("Manly deeds, womanly words"). **Flag:** Geometric black

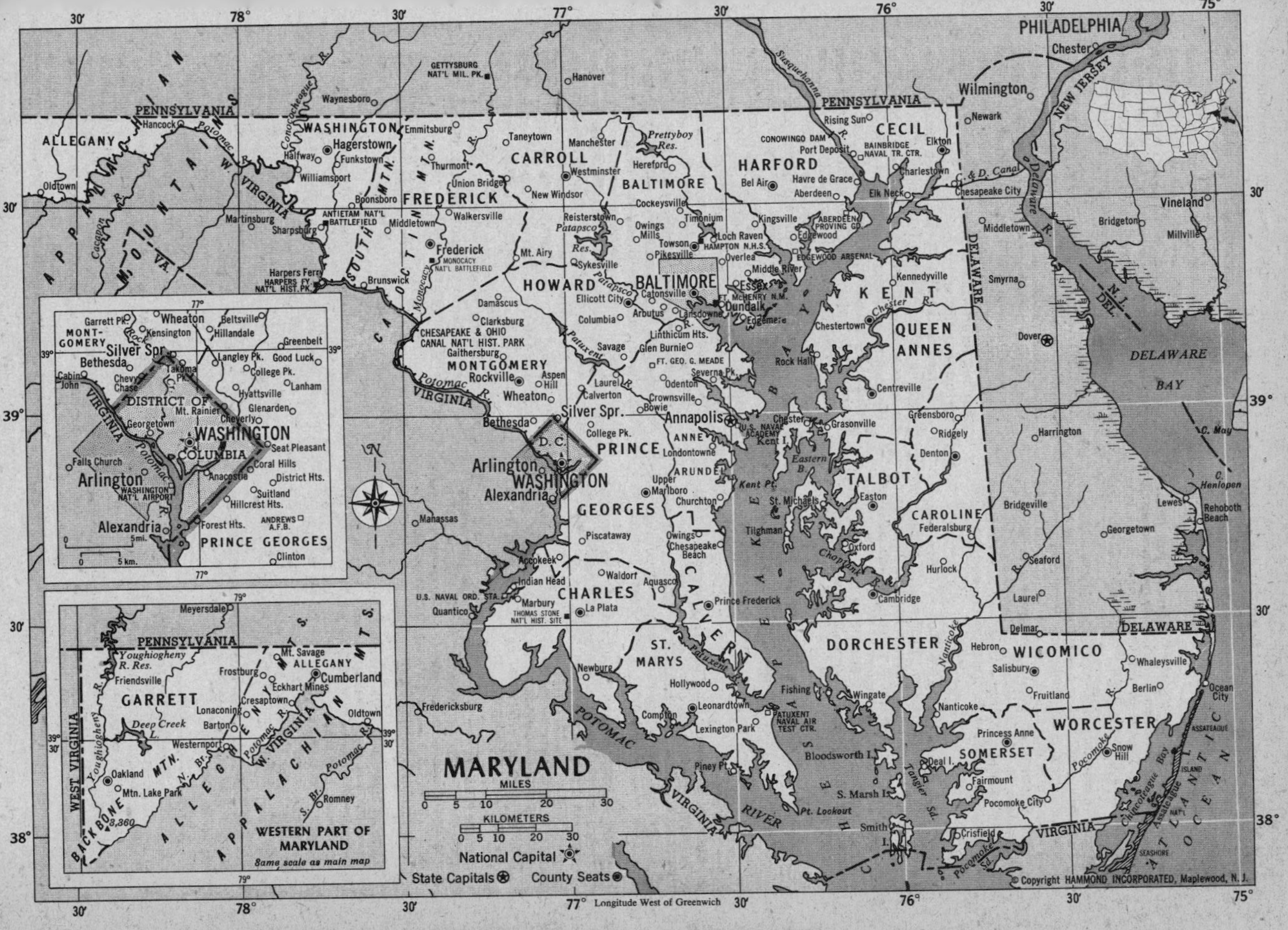
MARYLAND
MILES
KILOMETERS
National Capital
State Capitals
County Seats
WESTERN PART OF MARYLAND
Same scale as main map
© Copyright HAMMOND INCORPORATED, Maplewood, N.J.
Longitude West of Greenwich

& gold pattern in opposite quarters; red & white crosses in the others. **Seal:** Shield with coats of arms of Calvert & Crossland families; farmer represents Maryland; fisherman, Lord Baltimore's Avalon colony in Newfoundland. **Flower:** Black-eyed Susan. **Bird:** Baltimore oriole. **Tree:** White oak. **Song:** "Maryland, My Maryland." **Nickname:** Old Line State.

Governor: Harry R. Hughes. **Annual salary:** $60,000. **Term:** 4 years. **Current term expires:** Jan. 1983. **Voting requirements:** 18 yrs. old & U.S. citizen; resident of state and county 30 days. **U.S. Congressmen:** 8. **Entered Union:** 1788 (7th state).

Location & boundaries: Middle Atlantic seaboard state: bounded on the north by Pennsylvania; on the east by Delaware & the Atlantic Ocean; on the south by the Potomac River, Virginia & West Virginia; & on the west by West Virginia. **Total area:** 10,577 sq. mi. (ranks 42nd). **Extreme length:** 198.6 mi. **Extreme breadth:** 125.5 mi. **Coastline:** 31 mi. (coastline including Chesapeake Bay, 3,190 mi.). **Chief rivers:** Potomac, Susquehanna, Patuxent. **Major lakes:** Deep Creek Lake (man-made). **No. of counties:** 23, plus 1 independent city.

Population (1979 est.): 4,148,000 (ranks 18th). **Pop. increase (1970-79):** 5.7%. **Places over 25,000 pop.:** 7. **Places over 100,000:** 1. **Largest cities:** Baltimore, Rockville, Hagerstown, Bowie. **Pop. density:** 392.2 per sq. mi. (ranks 5th). **Pop. projection 1985:** 4,637,000. **Pop. distribution:** 84.8% metropolitan; 15.2% nonmetropolitan. **White:** 81.5%. **Black:** 17.9%. **Other:** 0.7%. **Marriage rate (1977):** 10.9 per 1,000 people. **Divorce rate:** 4.0 per 1,000 people.

State finances (1978). Revenue: $4,538,033,000. **Expenditures:** $4,128,035,000. **State taxes:** $580.55 per capita. **State personal income tax:** Yes. **Public debt (1978):** $915.67 per capita. **Federal aid (1979):** $385.75 per capita. **Personal income (1979 est.):** $9,150.

Sectors of the economy (% of labor force employed in 1970): Manufacturing (20%), Government (26%), Wholesale and retail trade (19%), Educational Services (8%), Services (7%), Construction (7%). **Leading products:** food and kindred products, primary metals, electrical equipment and supplies, transportation equipment, chemical and allied products, apparel, printing. **Agricultural products:** dairy items, broilers, cattle, corn, hay, tobacco. **Fishing:** oysters, crabs, clams. **Avg. farm (1979 est.):** 175 acres. **Avg. value of farm per acre:** $1,799.

Highway expenditures per capita (1978): $96.65 **Persons per motor vehicle:** 1.49. **Minimum age for driver's license:** 16. **Gasoline tax:** 9¢ per gallon. **Diesel tax:** 9¢ per gallon. **Motor vehicle deaths:** 17.1 per 100,000 people.

Birthrate (1978): 13.3 per 1,000 people. **Infant mortality rate per 1,000 births (1977):** 14.3. **Physicians per 100,000 pop. (1977):** 268. **Dentists per 100,000 pop. (1977):** 57. **Acceptable hospital beds:** 6.0 per 1,000 people. **State expenditures per capita for health and hospitals (1978):** $83.04.

Education expenditures (1975-76): $516.83 per capita annually. **No. of pupils in public schools (1977 est.):** 848,000. **No. of institutions of higher learning (1976-77):** 52. **Public school expenditure per pupil in attendance (1975-76):** $2,054. **Avg. salary of public school teachers (1974-75 est.):** $13,282. **No. full-time teachers (1977 est.):** 48,400. **Educational attainment of adult population (1976):** 12.6 median yrs. of school completed; 2.1% with less than 5 years of education; 18.6% with 4 yrs. of college.

Telephones (1977): 78 per 100 people. **State Chamber of Commerce:** Maryland Chamber of Commerce, 60 West Street, Annapolis, Maryland 21401.

MASSACHUSETTS

Today a key New England state, Massachusetts was also one of the most important of the 13 Colonies. It was at Plymouth in 1620 that the Pilgrims landed. And the Boston Massacre (1770) and Tea Party (1773) were major, irreversible steps on the road to the American War of Independence, which began at Lexington and Concord in 1775. Statehood dates from 1788.

The topography of the state is unusually varied. The eastern third is a low coastal plain that includes the Cape Cod peninsula and the islands due south: the Elizabeth Islands, Martha's Vineyard, and Nantucket. The New England Uplands, part of a high plateau stretching from Maine to New Jersey, extend westward for roughly 50 miles. Due west of this area is the Connecticut Valley, which extends from Massachusetts to southern Connecticut; the Connecticut River flows through it, providing fine soil for farming. Farther west lies the Berkshire Valley, surrounded by the Berkshire Hills and, near the northwestern border, the Taconic Mountains.

Besides its historic sites, the state's attractions include the Museum of Fine Arts and Symphony Hall in Boston, the summer Tanglewood music festival in the Berkshires, and literary landmarks, such as the homes of Emerson, Hawthorne and Thoreau in Concord. Cape Cod is a leading Eastern summer resort area, with long, sandy beaches and picturesque towns.

Norsemen including Leif Ericsson may have visited the region about A.D. 1000, but this remains more conjecture than fact. In 1602 English explorer Bartholomew Gosnold landed on Cuttyhunk Island in the Elizabeth chain and gave Cape Cod its name, and Captain John Smith explored the coast in 1614. Oddly enough, the arrival of the Pilgrims at Plymouth six years later, after a brief stop at what is now Provincetown, was purely accidental; the *Mayflower's* destination was a point south of the Hudson River, but a severe storm diverted the ship north. Because this area was beyond the bounds of the sponsoring company in London, a provisional instrument of government called the "Mayflower Compact" was drawn up. Designed to serve until more permanent institutions could be established, this covenant of the Massachusetts Bay Colony, as the settlement was called, formed the foundation of American democracy. But it was not originally a very democratic democracy, because while the Puritans insisted on religious freedom for themselves, they denied it to others, and some they banished from the colony. Roger Williams and the Reverend Thomas Hooker were exiled in 1636, and settled in Rhode Island and Connecticut respectively. Puritan oppression climaxed with the Salem witch trials at the end of the seventeenth century; about 20 persons accused of witchcraft were put to death.

Indian troubles began with an engagement with the Pequot Indians in 1637. In 1675-76, settlers and Wampanoag Indians, led by Metacom, who was known as King Philip, battled in "King Philip's War," which the colonists won at great expense. At various times from 1689 to 1763, the colonists fought against the French and their Indian allies, and ultimately prevailed. Soon after, they began resisting the royal tax laws, setting the stage for general revolt. In 1775 General George Washington arrived in Cambridge to assume command of the Continental Army. A year later, he routed the redcoats from Boston in the war's first major American victory. Then the scene of battle shifted to New York, New Jersey, and Pennsylvania.

The American Revolution was followed in Massachusetts by hard times. There came a business depression, and friction between the legislature and farmers, many of whom suffered foreclosures for debts and taxes; an insurrection (1786-87) led by former army captain Daniel Shays became known as Shays' Rebellion. But prosperity gradually returned, only to fade away again as Jefferson's 1807 Embargo Act, intended to keep the country from involvement in European wars, seriously hurt the state's sea-oriented economy. As it happened, the precaution was a failure: war came

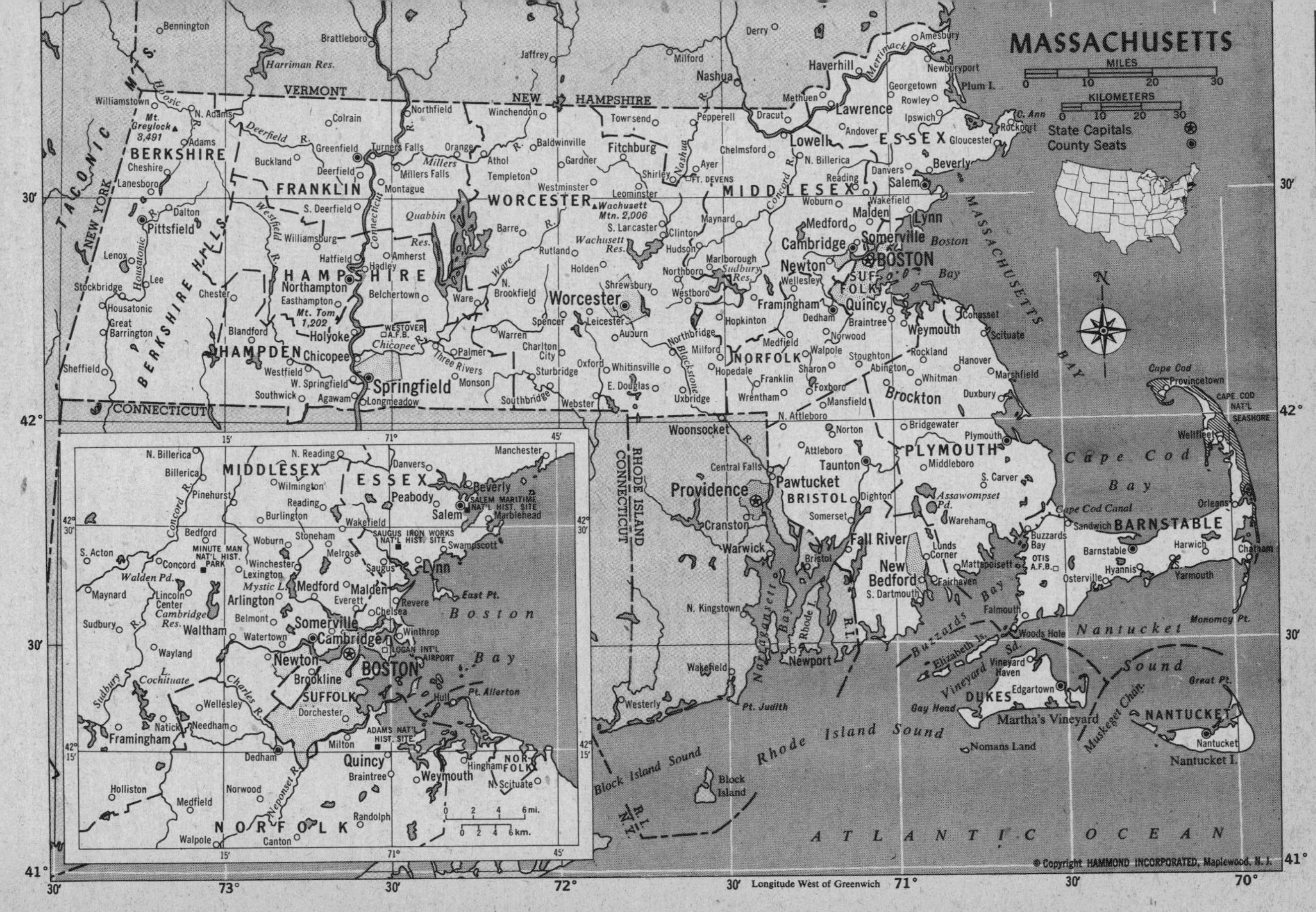

MASSACHUSETTS
MILES
KILOMETERS
State Capitals
County Seats
Copyright HAMMOND INCORPORATED, Maplewood, N.J.
Longitude West of Greenwich
ATLANTIC OCEAN
MASSACHUSETTS BAY
Cape Cod Bay
CAPE COD NAT'L SEASHORE
Cape Cod
Cape Cod Canal
Provincetown
Wellfleet
Orleans
Chatham
Harwich
Yarmouth
Monomoy Pt.
BARNSTABLE
Sandwich
Barnstable
Hyannis
Osterville
Woods Hole
Falmouth
Mattapoisett
Fairhaven
Buzzards Bay
OTIS A.F.B.
Lunds Corner
Nantucket Sound
NANTUCKET
Nantucket
Nantucket I.
Muskeget Chan.
Great Pt.
DUKES
Edgartown
Vineyard Haven
Gay Head
Martha's Vineyard
Nomans Land
Sd.
Elizabeth Is.
Buzzards Bay
Assawompset Pd.
S. Carver
VERMONT
NEW HAMPSHIRE
NEW YORK
CONNECTICUT
RHODE ISLAND
Bennington
Brattleboro
Harriman Res.
Williamstown
N. Adams
Mt. Greylock 3,491
Adams
Cheshire
Lanesboro
Dalton
Pittsfield
Lenox
Lee
Stockbridge
Housatonic
Great Barrington
Sheffield
BERKSHIRE
TACONIC
Hoosic R.
BERKSHIRE HILLS
Housatonic R.
Chester
Blandford
Colrain
Northfield
Jaffrey
Winchendon
Towsend
Deerfield R.
Greenfield
Turners Falls
Buckland
Deerfield
Millers Falls
Montague
Orange
Athol
Templeton
Baldwinville
Fitchburg
Westminster
Gardner
FRANKLIN
S. Deerfield
Williamsburg
Hatfield
Hadley
Amherst
Northampton
Easthampton
Mt. Tom 1,202
Holyoke
Chicopee
WESTOVER A.F.B.
HAMPSHIRE
HAMPDEN
Westfield
W. Springfield
Agawam
Southwick
Longmeadow
Springfield
Belchertown
Quabbin Res.
Barre
Ware
Rutland
Holden
N. Brookfield
Warren
Palmer
Three Rivers
Monson
Spencer
Leicester
Charlton City
Sturbridge
Southbridge
Webster
Oxford
Auburn
WORCESTER
Worcester
Wachusett Mtn. 2,006
Wachusett Res.
Leominster
S. Lancaster
Clinton
Hudson
Marlborough
Northboro
Westboro
Shrewsbury
Hopkinton
Framingham
Milford
Hopedale
Whitinsville
Northbridge
E. Douglas
Uxbridge
Blackstone R.
Milford
Bellingham
Franklin
Wrentham
Foxboro
Mansfield
N. Attleboro
Attleboro
Norton
Medfield
Walpole
Sharon
Stoughton
Norwood
NORFOLK
Dedham
Wellesley
Newton
Needham
Quincy
Braintree
Weymouth
Rockland
Abington
Whitman
Brockton
Bridgewater
Duxbury
Marshfield
Hanover
Scituate
Cohasset
Milford
Nashua
Derry
Merrimack R.
Haverhill
Methuen
Lawrence
Andover
Lowell
Dracut
Pepperell
N. Billerica
Chelmsford
Ayer
Shirley
Ft. Devens
Maynard
Concord R.
Reading
Danvers
Woburn
Wakefield
MIDDLESEX
Medford
Malden
Cambridge
Somerville
Newton
BOSTON
SUFFOLK
Boston Bay
Amesbury
Newburyport
Plum I.
Georgetown
Rowley
Ipswich
C. Ann
Rockport
Gloucester
ESSEX
Beverly
Salem
Lynn
Sudbury Res.
Connecticut R.
Westfield R.
Ware R.
Woonsocket
Central Falls
Pawtucket
Providence
Cranston
Warwick
BRISTOL
Dighton
Somerset
Bristol
Fall River
New Bedford
S. Dartmouth
Taunton
Middleboro
PLYMOUTH
Plymouth
Narragansett Bay
N. Kingstown
Wakefield
Westerly
Newport
Pt. Judith
Rhode I.
R.I.
R.I. N.Y.
Block Island
Block Island Sound
Rhode Island Sound
INSET (BOSTON area):
MIDDLESEX
ESSEX
NORFOLK
SUFFOLK
Boston Bay
N. Billerica
Billerica
Pinehurst
Wilmington
N. Reading
Reading
Burlington
Wakefield
Stoneham
Melrose
Danvers
Peabody
Salem
SALEM MARITIME NAT'L HIST. SITE
Marblehead
Beverly
Manchester
SAUGUS IRON WORKS NAT'L HIST. SITE
Swampscott
Saugus
Lynn
East Pt.
Bedford
Concord
MINUTE MAN NAT'L HIST. PARK
Walden Pd.
Lincoln Center
Lexington
Winchester
Woburn
Arlington
Mystic L.
Medford
Malden
Everett
Revere
Chelsea
Winthrop
LOGAN INT'L AIRPORT
Belmont
Watertown
Waltham
Cambridge Res.
Somerville
Cambridge
BOSTON
Newton
Brookline
Dorchester
Hull
Pt. Allerton
ADAMS NAT'L HIST. SITE
Milton
Quincy
Braintree
Weymouth
Hingham
N. Scituate
NORFOLK
S. Acton
Maynard
Sudbury
Wayland
L. Cochituate
Framingham
Natick
Needham
Wellesley
Holliston
Medfield
Norwood
Dedham
Walpole
Canton
Randolph
Charles R.
Sudbury R.
Neponset R.
45'
30'
15'
42° 30'
42° 15'
0 2 4 6 mi.
0 2 4 6 km.
15'
71°
45'
73°
72°
71°
70°
30'
42°
41°

anyway in 1812, and Massachusetts turned to manufacturing for its principal livelihood.

Over the years, steady influxes of immigrants provided a plentiful source of labor, and workers were often exploited. Labor unions fought hard for recognition, and there were strikes, occasionally marked by violence as in the 1912 textile strike at Lawrence. Governor Calvin Coolidge gained national prominence when he broke a policemen's strike in Boston in 1919.

Today Massachusetts still ranks among the national leaders in manufacturing, as well as commercial fishing. The electronics industry, tourism, and its many private colleges and universities are important to the state's economy.

In February 1980 a controversial new state law took effect requiring daily spoken prayers in public schools.

Full name: Commonwealth of Massachusetts. **Origin of name:** From Algonquian name, Massa-dchu-es-at, meaning "Great-Hill-Small-Place." **Inhabitant:** Bay Stater. **Capital:** Boston. **State motto:** Ense Petit Placidam Sub Libertate Quietem (By the Sword We Seek Peace, but Peace Only under Liberty). **Flag:** State seal on white field is on one side; other side has green pine tree on blue field. **Seal:** Coat of arms of Commonwealth of Massachusetts; Indian points arrow downward, symbolizing peace; star over his right shoulder represents Massachusetts as a state. **Flower:** Mayflower. **Bird:** Chickadee. **Tree:** American elm. **Song:** "Hail Massachusetts." **Nickname:** Bay State.

Governor: Edward J. King. **Annual salary:** $60,000. **Term:** 4 years. **Current term expires:** Jan. 1983. **Voting requirements:** 18 yrs. old & U.S. citizen; resident of state. **U.S. Congressmen:** 12. **Entered Union:** 1788 (6th state).

Location & boundaries: New England state: bounded on the north by Vermont & New Hampshire; on the east by the Atlantic Ocean; on the south by the Atlantic Ocean, Rhode Island & Connecticut; on the west by New York. **Total area:** 8,257 sq. mi. (ranks 45th). **Extreme length:** 190 mi. **Extreme breadth:** 110 mi. **Coastline:** 192 mi. **Chief rivers:** Connecticut, Merrimack, Charles, Housatonic. **Major lakes:** Assawompset Pond; Quabbin, Wachusett Reservoirs. **No. of counties:** 14.

Population (1979 est.): 5,769,000 (ranks 10th). **Pop. increase (1970-79):** 1.4%. **Places over 25,000 pop.:** 59. **Places over 100,000:** 4. **Largest cities:** Boston, Worcester, Springfield, Cambridge. **Pop. density:** 698.7 per sq. mi. (ranks 3rd). **Pop. projection 1985:** 6,209,000. **Pop. distribution:** 86.1% metropolitan; 13.9% nonmetropolitan. **White:** 96.3%. **Black:** 3.1%. **Other:** 0.6%. **Marriage rate (1977):** 6.9 per 1,000 people. **Divorce rate:** 2.9 per 1,000 people.

State finances (1978). Revenue: $6,259,387,000. **Expenditures:** $5,894,639,000. **State taxes:** $571.67 per capita. **State personal income tax:** Yes. **Public debt (1978):** $876.26 per capita. **Federal aid (1979):** $472.44 per capita. **Personal income (1979 est.):** $8,844.

Sectors of the economy (% of labor force employed in 1970): Manufacturing (29%), Wholesale and retail trade (20%), Government (15%), Educational Services (9%), Services (6%), Construction (5%). **Leading products:** electrical machinery, apparel, leather items, fabricated metals, printing, food. **Agricultural products:** dairy items, poultry, greenhouse & nursery items, vegetables, tobacco. **Fishing:** haddock, flounder, scallops. **Avg. farm (1979 est.):** 135 acres. **Avg. value of farm per acre:** $1,366.

Highway expenditures per capita (1978): $67.84. **Persons per motor vehicle:** 1.54. **Minimum age for driver's license:** 17. **Gasoline tax:** 8.5¢ per gallon. **Diesel tax:** 8.5¢ per gallon. **Motor vehicle deaths:** 15.0 per 100,000 people.

Birthrate (1978): 11.9 per 1,000 people. **Infant mortality rate per 1,000 births (1977):** 11.9. **Physicians per 100,000 pop. (1977):** 241. **Dentists per 100,000 pop. (1977):** 67. **Acceptable hospital beds:** 8.2 per 1,000 people. **State expenditures per capita for health and hospitals (1978):** $77.07.

Education expenditures (1975-76): $434.26 per capita annually. **No. of pupils in public schools (1977 est.):** 1,152,000. **No. of institutions of higher learning (1976-77):** 119. **Public school expenditure per pupil in attendance (1975-76):** $2,059. **Avg. salary of public school teachers (1974-75 est.):** $12,468. **No. full-time teachers:** Not available. **Educational attainment of adult population (1976):** 12.6 median yrs. of school completed; 2.4% with less than 5 years of education; 16.8% with 4 yrs. of college.

Telephones (1977): 74 per 100 people. **State Chamber of Commerce:** Massachusetts Commonwealth Chamber of Commerce, c/o New Bedford Area Chamber of Commerce; P.O. Box G-827, New Bedford, Massachusetts 02742.

MICHIGAN

Michigan, the world's largest producer of automobiles and among the most populous of the states, extends across two peninsulas and consists of two land regions: the Great Lakes Plain that makes up all of the mitten-shaped Lower Peninsula (where 90 percent of the people live) and the eastern portion of the irregularly shaped Upper Peninsula and the Superior Upland that comprise the rest. The state is touched by four of the five Great Lakes (all but Ontario) and has a longer shoreline than any other inland state.

Dividing the peninsulas and linking Lakes Michigan and Huron are the Straits of Mackinac, crossed by one of the world's longest suspension bridges. Largest among the state's approximately 500 islands is the 209-square-mile Isle Royale (a national park) in Lake Superior. Many mountains, forests, rivers, and waterfalls make the state a sportsman's paradise. The somewhat moist climate is marked by well-defined seasons.

Several Indian tribes were living in the Michigan region when the first European, Étienne Brulé of France, arrived (1618). Other Frenchmen, including Marquette, Jolliet, and La Salle, followed, and the first permanent settlement was established (1668) at Sault Sainte Marie. By 1700 there were French missions, fur-trading posts, and forts on both peninsulas; Fort Pontchartrain (founded 1701) was to become the city of Detroit. But the French were more interested in the lucrative pelt trade than in extensive development of the territory; while Mackinac Island became a busy trading center, most of the rest of the region remained sparsely settled and vulnerable to attack by the British, who gained possession in 1763. The Indians in the area, who had lived in peace with the French, detested the British and tried to drive them out, but eventually they joined with them to fight the Americans in the American Revolution and in the War of 1812.

Michigan, initially part of the Northwest Territory and then of Indiana Territory, was made a separate territory in 1805, with Detroit as its capital (succeeded by Lansing in 1847). Statehood was delayed by a boundary dispute with Ohio and Southern opposition to forming another free state. Compromises broke the impasse, as Michigan's admission (1837) was offset by that of slave state Arkansas, while Ohio was given the disputed land in return for awarding to Michigan the Upper Peninsula, which had been a part of the Territory of Wisconsin.

Michigan's development as a state was rapid, and a number of important roads, rail lines, and canals were soon built—including the vital Soo Ship Canal at Sault Sainte Marie (completed 1855), which allows ships to travel between Lakes Huron and Superior; these new routes spurred the state's mining industry. In the political sphere, the Republican party was founded in 1854 at Jackson, and abolitionist sentiment was strong throughout the state which contributed 100,000 troops to the Union cause during the Civil War.

Today Michigan is both a center of tourism and

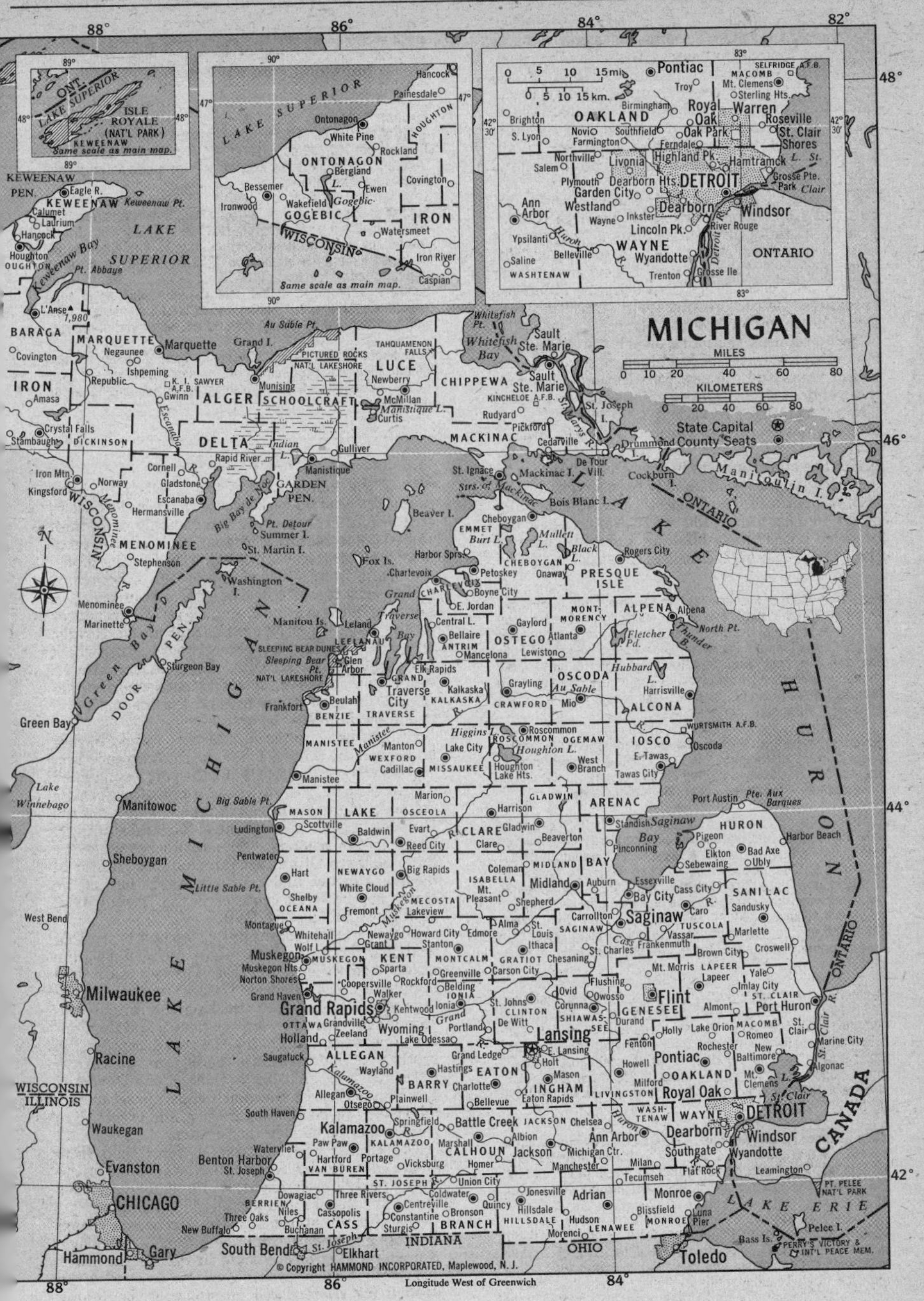
MICHIGAN
MILES
KILOMETERS
State Capital
County Seats
ONT. LAKE SUPERIOR
ISLE ROYALE (NAT'L PARK)
KEWEENAW
Same scale as main map.
LAKE SUPERIOR
ONTONAGON
GOGEBIC
IRON
WISCONSIN
Same scale as main map.
Ontonagon
White Pine
Rockland
Bergland
Ewen
Covington
Bessemer
Wakefield
Ironwood
Watersmeet
Iron River
Caspian
Hancock
Painesdale
Houghton
OAKLAND
WAYNE
WASHTENAW
ONTARIO
SELFRIDGE A.F.B.
MACOMB
Mt. Clemens
Sterling Hts.
Pontiac
Troy
Birmingham
Royal Oak
Warren
Roseville
St. Clair Shores
Brighton
S. Lyon
Novi
Southfield
Oak Park
Ferndale
Highland Pk.
Hamtramck
L. St. Clair
Northville
Livonia
Salem
Plymouth
Dearborn Hts.
DETROIT
Grosse Pte. Park
Ann Arbor
Garden City
Westland
Dearborn
Windsor
Wayne
Inkster
Lincoln Pk.
River Rouge
Ypsilanti
Belleville
Wyandotte
Grosse Ile
Saline
Trenton
KEWEENAW PEN.
Eagle R.
Calumet
Laurium
Hancock
Houghton
Keweenaw Pt.
Keweenaw Bay
Pt. Abbaye
LAKE SUPERIOR
L'Anse
7,980
BARAGA
Covington
MARQUETTE
Negaunee
Ishpeming
Republic
Marquette
Grand I.
Au Sable Pt.
PICTURED ROCKS NAT'L LAKESHORE
TAHQUAMENON FALLS
Whitefish Pt.
Whitefish Bay
Sault Ste. Marie
MICHIGAN
IRON
Amasa
K. I. SAWYER A.F.B.
Gwinn
Munising
ALGER
SCHOOLCRAFT
LUCE
Newberry
McMillan
Curtis
CHIPPEWA
Sault Ste. Marie
KINCHELOE A.F.B.
Crystal Falls
Stambaugh
DICKINSON
DELTA
Indian L.
Manistique L.
Manistique
Rapid River
Gulliver
Rudyard
Pickford
St. Joseph I.
Cedarville
De Tour Vill.
State Capital
County Seats
Drummond I.
Cockburn I.
Manitoulin I.
Iron Mtn.
Norway
Kingsford
Cornell
Gladstone
Escanaba
Hermansville
WISCONSIN
Menominee
GARDEN PEN.
St. Ignace
Mackinac I.
Strs. of Mackinac
Bois Blanc I.
ONTARIO
MENOMINEE
Stephenson
Big Bay de Noc
Pt. Detour
Summer I.
St. Martin I.
Beaver I.
Cheboygan
EMMET
Burt L.
Mullett L.
Black L.
Rogers City
LAKE
HURON
Menominee
Marinette
Washington I.
Fox Is.
Harbor Sprs.
Charlevoix
Petoskey
CHEBOYGAN
Onaway
PRESQUE ISLE
Green Bay
DOOR PEN.
Manitou Is.
Leland
Charlevoix
Boyne City
E. Jordan
Gaylord
MONT- MORENCY
Atlanta
ALPENA
Alpena
North Pt.
Thunder B.
Sturgeon Bay
Washington I.
SLEEPING BEAR DUNES
LEELANAU
Central L.
Bellaire
Mancelona
Lewiston
Fletcher Pd.
Beulah
Sleeping Bear Pt.
NAT'L LAKESHORE
Glen Arbor
GRAND TRAVERSE
Traverse City
Elk Rapids
ANTRIM
OSTEGO
OSCODA
Hubbard L.
Harrisville
Frankfort
BENZIE
TRAVERSE
Kalkaska
KALKASKA
Grayling
CRAWFORD
Au Sable
Mio
ALCONA
WURTSMITH A.F.B.
Lake Winnebago
Manistee
MANISTEE
Manton
WEXFORD
Cadillac
Higgins L.
Lake City
MISSAUKEE
Roscommon
ROSCOMMON
Houghton Lake Hts.
Houghton L.
OGEMAW
West Branch
IOSCO
Oscoda
E. Tawas
Tawas City
Manistee
Big Sable Pt.
MASON
Scottville
LAKE
OSCEOLA
Marion
Harrison
GLADWIN
ARENAC
Port Austin
Pte. Aux Barques
Manitowoc
Ludington
Baldwin
Evart
CLARE
Gladwin
Standish
Saginaw Bay
HURON
Pigeon
Harbor Beach
Pentwater
Reed City
Clare
Beaverton
Pinconning
Elkton
Bad Axe
Sebewaing
Ubly
Sheboygan
Hart
NEWAYGO
Big Rapids
Coleman
MIDLAND
BAY
Essexville
Auburn
Bay City
Cass City
SANILAC
West Bend
Shelby
OCEANA
White Cloud
Fremont
MECOSTA
Lakeview
ISABELLA
Mt. Pleasant
Shepherd
Midland
Carrollton
Caro
Sandusky
Little Sable Pt.
Montague
Whitehall
Wolf L.
Newaygo
Grant
Howard City
Stanton
Edmore
Alma
St. Louis
Ithaca
SAGINAW
Saginaw
Cass R.
Frankenmuth
Vassar
TUSCOLA
Marlette
Croswell
Muskegon
Muskegon Hts.
Norton Shores
MUSKEGON
Sparta
KENT
MONTCALM
Greenville
Carson City
GRATIOT
Chesaning
St. Charles
Brown City
Yale
Coopersville
Rockford
Belding
Ovid
Flushing
Mt. Morris
LAPEER
Imlay City
ST. CLAIR
Grand Haven
Walker
IONIA
Ionia
St. Johns
Corunna
Owosso
Lapeer
Almont
Port Huron
Grand Rapids
OTTAWA
Grandville
Kentwood
Grand R.
CLINTON
De Witt
SHIAWAS- SEE
Durand
GENESEE
Flint
Holly
Lake Orion
MACOMB
Romeo
St. Clair
Marine City
Holland
Zeeland
Wyoming
Portland
Lansing
E. Lansing
Fenton
Howell
Rochester
New Baltimore
Algonac
Saugatuck
ALLEGAN
Wayland
Grand Ledge
Holt
Mason
Milford
Pontiac
Mt. Clemens
L. St. Clair
Allegan
Hastings
EATON
INGHAM
LIVINGSTON
OAKLAND
Royal Oak
South Haven
Otsego
BARRY
Charlotte
Eaton Rapids
Bellevue
WASH- TENAW
WAYNE
DETROIT
Kalamazoo
Plainwell
Springfield
Battle Creek
JACKSON
Chelsea
Ann Arbor
Dearborn
Windsor
Watervliet
Paw Paw
KALAMAZOO
Marshall
Albion
Jackson
Michigan Ctr.
Southgate
Wyandotte
Benton Harbor
St. Joseph
Hartford
Portage
Vicksburg
Homer
Manchester
Milan
CANADA
VAN BUREN
CALHOUN
Tecumseh
Flat Rock
Leamington
CHICAGO
Dowagiac
Three Rivers
ST. JOSEPH
Coldwater
Jonesville
Adrian
Monroe
PT. PELEE NAT'L PARK
Waukegan
BERRIEN
Centreville
Union City
Quincy
Hillsdale
Hudson
Blissfield
Luna Pier
LAKE ERIE
Evanston
Three Oaks
Niles
Cassopolis
Constantine
Bronson
HILLSDALE
LENAWEE
MONROE
Bass Is.
Pelee I.
New Buffalo
Buchanan
CASS
Sturgis
BRANCH
Morenci
Hammond
Gary
South Bend
Elkhart
INDIANA
OHIO
Toledo
PERRY'S VICTORY & INT'L PEACE MEM.
Milwaukee
Racine
WISCONSIN
ILLINOIS
St. Joseph R.
© Copyright HAMMOND INCORPORATED, Maplewood, N.J.
Longitude West of Greenwich

industry. Greenfield Village in Detroit's suburban Dearborn, to which Ford moved some of early America's famous landmarks, including the courthouse where Abraham Lincoln practiced, attracts over a million sightseers annually. The spectacular, colorful turning of the Upper Peninsula's forests in fall attract thousands there, and the state has many annual events aimed at attracting others. Summer resorts abound along both the inland and Great Lakes.

The United Automobile, Aerospace and Agricultural Implement Workers of America (UAW), now the nation's third-largest union with over 1.4 million members, got its start in the famed "Sit-Down Strikes" of the 1930s with workers refusing to leave auto plants until their fledgling union was recognized as bargaining agent. UAW international headquarters are in Detroit.

Social reforms, including open housing, have occurred in a number of Michigan communities in recent years and the new constitution created an independent Civil Rights Commission with police powers. A state referendum in 1976 banned the use of throwaway containers for beer and soft drinks.

The recession in 1980 was particularly damaging to the state's auto industry, whose grip on the American market had already been shaken by foreign competitors. The bad news was only partially offset in February 1980 when Volkswagen announced plans to establish an assembly plant in the Detroit suburb of Sterling Heights.

Full name: State of Michigan. **Origin of name:** From Michigama, meaning "Great Water." **Inhabitant:** Michiganian. **Capital:** Lansing. **State motto:** Si Quaeris Peninsulam Amoenam, Circumspice (If You Seek a Pleasant Peninsula, Look Around You). **Flag:** State seal on a blue field. **Seal:** Sun rising over water & man in field appear on shield supported by an elk & a moose. **Flower:** Apple blossom. **Bird:** Robin. **Tree:** White pine. **Song:** "Michigan, My Michigan." **Nickname:** Wolverine State.

Governor: William G. Milliken. **Annual salary:** $65,000. **Term:** 4 years. **Current term expires:** Jan. 1983. **Voting requirements:** 18 yrs.-old & U.S. citizen; registered resident of state 30 days. **U.S. Congressmen:** 19. **Entered Union:** 1837 (26th state).

Location & boundaries: Midwestern state: bounded on the north by Lake Superior, the Straits of Mackinac & Lake Huron; on the east by Lakes Huron & St. Clair, Canada & Lake Erie; on the south by Ohio & Indiana; & on the west by Wisconsin & Lake Michigan. **Total area:** 58,218 sq. mi. (ranks 23rd). **Extreme length:** Upper peninsula 334 mi.; lower peninsula 286 mi. **Extreme breadth:** Upper peninsula 215 mi.; lower peninsula 200 mi. **Shoreline:** 2,232 mi. **Chief rivers:** Grand, Kalamazoo, Escanaba, Saginaw. **Major lakes (other than border-forming):** Houghton, Torch, Charlevoix, Burt. **No. of counties:** 83.

Population (1979 est.): 9,207,000 (ranks 7th). **Pop. increase (1970-79):** 3.7%. **Places over 25,000 pop.:** 45. **Places over 100,000:** 6. **Largest cities:** Detroit, Grand Rapids, Warren, Lansing. **Pop. density:** 158.1 per sq. mi. (ranks 11th). **Pop. projection 1985:** 9,546,000. **Pop. distribution:** 81.3% metropolitan; 18.7% nonmetropolitan. **White:** 88.2%. **Black:** 11.2%. **Other:** 0.6%. **Marriage rate (1977):** 9.4 per 1,000 people. **Divorce rate:** 4.7 per 1,000 people.

State finances (1978). Revenue: $10,505,213,000. **Expenditures:** $9,490,177,000. **State taxes:** $592.55 per capita. **State personal income tax:** Yes. **Public debt (1978):** $234.06 per capita. **Federal aid (1979):** $387.25 per capita. **Personal income (1979 est.):** $9,269.

Sectors of the economy (% of labor force employed in 1970): Manufacturing (36%), Wholesale and retail trade (19%), Government (14%), Educational Services (8%), Services (6%), Construction (5%). **Leading products:** primary & fabricated metals, food, electrical machinery, paper. **Minerals:** iron ore, cement, sand & gravel, copper. **Agricultural products:** cattle, poultry, dairy items, corn, hay, wheat. **Fishing:** whitefish, chubs, lake herring. **Avg. farm (1979 est.):** 168 acres. **Avg. value of farm per acre:** $955.

Highway expenditures per capita (1978): $77.46. **Persons per motor vehicle:** 1.42. **Minimum age for driver's license:** 16. **Gasoline tax:** 11¢ per gallon. **Diesel tax:** 11¢ per gallon, reduced to 9¢ effective May 1, 1981. **Motor vehicle deaths:** 22.2 per 100,000 people.

Birthrate (1978): 15.2 per 1,000 people. **Infant mortality rate per 1,000 births (1977):** 14.1. **Physicians per 100,000 pop. (1977):** 142. **Dentists per 100,000 pop. (1977):** 49. **Acceptable hospital beds:** 5.7 per 1,000 people. **State expenditures per capita for health and hospitals (1978):** $66.49.

Education expenditures (1975-76): $526.25 per capita annually. **No. of pupils in public schools (1977 est.):** 2,006,000. **No. of institutions of higher learning (1976-77):** 94. **Public school expenditure per pupil in attendance (1975-76):** $1,902. **Avg. salary of public school teachers (1974-75 est.):** $14,224. **No. full-time teachers (1977 est.):** 99,360. **Educational attainment of adult population (1976):** 12.5 median yrs. of school completed; 1.8% with less than 5 years of education; 12.6% with 4 yrs. of college.

Telephones (1977): 74 per 100 people. **State Chamber of Commerce:** Michigan State Chamber of Commerce, Business and Trade Center, Suite 400, 200 North Washington Square, Lansing, Michigan 48933.

MINNESOTA

Site of the headwaters of the Mississippi, Minnesota is one of the most scenic states in the nation, rich in natural resources and boasting more than 15,000 lakes. Manufacturing, mainly of farm products, has in recent years become the leading industry, while improved techniques and new copper, nickel, and taconite finds signal a resurgence in mining. Tourism is today a major revenue producer for the state, which also ranks high agriculturally, with livestock and corn recently surpassing wheat in importance. Politically, Minnesota has gained a reputation for voter independence, experimentation in local government, and the institution of Scandinavian-type cooperatives.

Duluth has the nation's largest inland harbor and, since the completion of the St. Lawrence Seaway and Power Project (1959), the port has handled an increasingly significant amount of foreign trade. In Minneapolis are the central offices of the University of Minnesota, one of the largest universities in the country, while in Rochester is the famous Mayo Clinic, an international center of medical practice and research. About half of the state's population is centered in the "Twin Cities" of Minneapolis and St. Paul.

Minnesota's topography is marked by rolling prairies, fertile valleys, high bluffs, deep pine woods, and wilderness areas. The two main land regions are the Superior Upland (or, locally, the "arrowhead country"), consisting of a roughly triangular northeastern land segment, and the Central Lowlands, comprising the rest except, in the south, a small projection of the Wisconsin Driftless Area and two small projections of the Dissected Till Plains. The state's continental climate has a relatively low mean temperature, and is subject to wide and often sudden fluctuation.

The timber industry, which flourished from about 1870 to the early 1900s, was vital to the state's early development, while incidentally fostering the well-known legend of Paul Bunyan.

The first inhabitants of the Minnesota region are thought to date from about 20,000 years ago. Norsemen may have visited in the 14th century, but the first Europeans of record to do so were the French fur traders and missionaries, beginning with Radisson and Groseilliers (1659-61) and including La Salle, Marquette and Jolliet, and Daniel Greysolon—Sieur Du Lhut, or Duluth—who claimed (1679) the region for King Louis XIV.

MINNESOTA
MILES
0 20 40 60 80
KILOMETERS
0 20 40 60 80
State Capital
County Seats
CANADA
Woodridge
Angle Inlet
Whitemouth Lake
Lake of the Woods
Sprague
Emerson
MANITOBA
Roseau R.
Warroad
KITTSON
Hallock
Greenbush
Williams
ROSEAU
Baudette
Rainy
ONTARIO
Ft. Frances
Karlstad
Two Rivers
Stephen
Thief L.
LAKE OF THE WOODS
International Falls
Littlefork
Kabetogama L.
Rainy Lake
QUETICO PROV. PK.
Saganaga
90°
ONTARIO
Eagle Mtn. 2,301
MISQUAH HILLS
GRAND PORTAGE NAT'L. MON.
Grand Portage
48°
Hovland
COOK
Grand Marais
LAKE SUPERIOR
Tofte
NORTHEASTERN MINNESOTA
Same scale as main map
90°
Argyle
Middle R.
Warren
MARSHALL
Grygla
BELTRAMI
KOOCHICHING
Big Falls
Nett L.
VOYAGEURS NAT'L PARK
Crane Lake
Lac La Croix
Basswood
Thief River Falls
POLK
PENNINGTON
Upper Red L.
Ponemah
Big Fork
Little Fork
Pelican
Orr
Vermilion L.
Burntside L.
Ely
Vermilion R.
Alice L.
48°
East Grand Forks
Grand Forks
NORTH DAKOTA
Red Lake Falls
RED LAKE
Lower Red L.
Redlake
Cook
Tower
VERMILION R.A.
Birch L.
Sawbill Landing
COOK
Oklee
CLEARWATER
Redlake
Blackduck
Bigfork
ITASCA
Mountain Iron
Chisholm
Virginia
Aurora
Biwabik
Gilbert
Hoyt Lakes
LAKE
Taconite Harbor
Tofte
Crookston
Erskine
McIntosh
Clearbrook
Bagley
Bowstring L.
Nashwauk
Hibbing
Keewatin
Eveleth
ST.
Silver Bay
Maple L.
Fertile
Fosston
Bemidji
Winnibigoshish L.
Cass L.
Deer River
Bovey
Coleraine
Goodland
Cotton
LOUIS
LAKE SUPERIOR
Hillsboro
Halstad
Ada
NORMAN
MAHNOMEN
Rice
Mahnomen
Twin Valley
Mississippi R.
Cass Lake
L. Itasca
Walker
Leech L.
Remer
Grand Rapids
MESABI
Independence
Two Harbors
Fargo
Dilworth
Hawley
CLAY
BECKER
Lake Park
HUBBARD
CASS
Floodwood
St. Louis R.
Proctor
Duluth
Moorhead
Barnesville
Detroit Lakes
Frazee
Menagha
Park Rapids
Pine River
Whitefish L.
CROW
McGregor
CARLTON
Cloquet
Carlton
Superior
Washburn
L. Lida
Pelican Rapids
Perham
New York Mills
WADENA
Nisswa
Crosby
WING R.A.
Aitkin
Moose Lake
Ashland
Wahpeton
Breckenridge
Dead L.
Otter Tail L.
Wadena
Gull L.
AITKIN
PINE
WILKIN
OTTER TAIL
Henning
TODD
Baxter
Brainerd
Sandstone
Fergus Falls
Battle Lake
Parkers Prairie
Eagle Bend
CUYUNA
Mille Lacs Lake
Isle
Hinckley
St. Croix R.
GRANT
Elbow Lake
Browerville
MORRISON
Onamia
N.D. S.D.
Traverse
Wheaton
Alexandria
Long Prairie
Little Falls
Pierz
MILLE LACS
Mora
KANABEC
WISC.
TRAVERSE
STEVENS
Morris
DOUGLAS
Osakis
Mississippi R.
BENTON
Foley
Milaca
Pine City
Browns Valley
Graceville
Glenwood
Sauk Centre
Melrose
Albany
Sauk Rapids
Princeton
Cambridge
Rush City
Center City
CHISAGO
BIG STONE
Starbuck
L. Minnewaska
STEARNS
St. Joseph
St. Cloud
SHERBURNE
North Branch
Lindstrom
Ortonville
SWIFT
Benson
Belgrade
Cold Spring
Monticello
Elk River
Forest L.
ANOKA
WASHINGTON
Milbank
Marsh L.
Appleton
Kerkhoven
Green L.
Paynesville
New London
Annandale
Maple Lake
Buffalo
Anoka
Champlin
Stillwater
Bayport
Lac qui Parle
Willmar
KANDIYOHI
Litchfield
WRIGHT
Corcoran
HENNEPIN
RAMSEY
Madison
Dawson
Montevideo
Clara City
MEEKER
Cokato
Winsted
Hutchinson
Minneapolis
Orono
St. Paul
S. St. Paul
CHIPPEWA
Olivia
Bird Island
MC LEOD
Waconia
Bloomington
Burnsville
SOUTH DAKOTA
LAC QUI PARLE
Canby
Clarkfield
Granite Falls
Renville
Hector
Glencoe
Chaska
CARVER
Jordan
Shakopee
DAKOTA
Hastings
YELLOW MEDICINE
Minnesota R.
Fairfax
Gaylord
Arlington
Belle Plaine
SCOTT
Farmington
Red Wing
Durand
Mondovi
Hendricks
Ivanhoe
Minneota
Marshall
REDWOOD
Redwood Falls
Morgan
Winthrop
SIBLEY
Le Sueur
New Prague
GOODHUE
Cannon Falls
Lake City
Pepin
Wabasha
Arcadia
LINCOLN
Tyler
LYON
Tracy
Springfield
Sleepy Eye
NICOLLET
New Ulm
LE SUEUR
Le Center
Montgomery
RICE
Northfield
Kenyon
Zumbrota
WABASHA
Brookings
Lake Benton
PIPESTONE
Shetek
Lamberton
BROWN
Swan L.
N. Mankato
St. Peter
Waterville
Faribault
Pine Island
Galesville
PIPESTONE NAT'L. MON.
Flandreau
MURRAY
COTTONWOOD
Westbrook
Madelia
Lake Crystal
Mankato
Waseca
Mantorville
Rochester
Plainview
Winona
44°
Dell Rapids
Pipestone
Slayton
Edgerton
Fulda
Mountain Lake
St. James
BLUE EARTH
Owatonna
Dodge Ctr.
Kasson
St. Charles
Chatfield
WINONA
La Crescent
ROCK
STONE
Windom
WATONWAN
Mapleton
WASECA
STEELE
DODGE
OLMSTED
La Crosse
Sioux Falls
Luverne
NOBLES
Worthington
Lakefield
MARTIN
Truman
FARIBAULT
Wells
FREEBORN
Austin
MOWER
Preston
FILLMORE
Houston
Caledonia
WISCONSIN
Lennox
Rock Rapids
Sibley
Adrian
JACKSON
Jackson
Fairmont
Blue Earth
Elmore
Albert Lea
Le Roy
Spring Valley
Harmony
Spring Grove
IOWA
Estherville
Northwood
Cresco
Decorah
Longitude West of Greenwich
Copyright HAMMOND INCORPORATED, Maplewood, N.J.

Principal Indian tribes in the region at the time were the Sioux in the west and south and the Ojibwa in the heavily wooded northern section; the two groups, often at war with one another, were generally friendly to the French, who built up a vast pelt-marketing empire but ultimately lost it (1763) to the British.

Serious American development began after the War of 1812, with the powerful American Fur Company leading the way. Eastern Minnesota at this time was still part of the Northwest Territory, while the western region had been acquired (1803) as part of the Louisiana Purchase. A short-lived Spanish claim to the region (dating from 1762) was never effectively enforced. The year 1819 saw the building of Fort St. Anthony (later called Fort Snelling), and in 1832 Henry R. Schoolcraft discovered the source of the Mississippi at Lake Itasca. Six years later, Pierre Parrant settled on the site of present-day St. Paul.

In 1849 the Minnesota region—which in whole or part had been successively a portion of the French, English, and Spanish empires, the Northwest Territory, and seven U.S. territories—was made a territory in its own right. A comprehensive Indian treaty (1851) and statehood (1858) both spurred settlement, which was not deterred by a brief, ill-fated Sioux uprising in 1862.

In the 1890s, the mining of the high-grade iron ore of the Mesabi Ranges became a major industry. As the rich Mesabi mines dwindled after World War II, iron companies began to mine a low-grade ore called taconite, which abounds in Minnesota, and to extract high-grade iron pellets from it. Extraction leaves useless tailings, which contain asbestos and other dangerous substances.

Tailings caused a near-crisis in the city of Silver Bay. In 1975, the Reserve Mining Company, one of Silver Bay's largest employers, was ordered by a Federal court to stop dumping tailings into Lake Superior. At first, the company claimed that it would have to go out of business, thus ruining Silver Bay's economy. Eventually, a compromise allowed the company a "reasonable time" to change. In 1980, the company opened a land dump, linked to its plant by a slurry system, and ended dumping in the lake.

Violence broke out in mid-May 1979 on the Chippewa Indian Reservation at Red Lake because of discontent with the leadership of tribal chairman Roger Jourdain. Two youths were killed and seven buildings and 45 vehicles were destroyed by fire. Five Indians were convicted of conspiracy and assault charges in the incident.

In the summer and autumn of 1979, a long strike by grain handlers at the port cities of Duluth, Minnesota, and Superior, Wisconsin, cost farmers in Minnesota and the Dakotas almost a billion dollars.

Full name: State of Minnesota. **Origin of name:** From the Sioux meaning "Sky-Tinted Water." **Inhabitant:** Minnesotan. **Capital:** St. Paul. **State motto:** L'Etoile du Nord (The Star of the North). **Flag:** State seal & 19 gold stars on blue field. **Seal:** Indian riding into sunset, farmer plowing field, waterfall, forest. **Flower:** Pink & white lady's-slipper. **Bird:** Common loon. **Tree:** Norway (Red) pine. **Song:** "Hail! Minnesota." **Nickname:** North Star State.

Governor: Albert H. Quie. **Annual salary:** $62,000. **Term:** 4 yrs. **Current term expires:** Jan. 1983. **Voting requirements:** 18 yrs. old & U.S. citizen; registered state resident 20 days. **U.S. Congressmen:** 8. **Entered Union:** 1858 (32nd state).

Location & boundaries: Northern Midwestern state: bounded on the north by Canada; on the east by Lake Superior, Wisconsin & the Mississippi River; on the south by Iowa; & on the west by South Dakota, North Dakota & Red River of the North. **Total area:** 84,068 sq. mi. (ranks 12th). **Extreme length:** 406 mi. **Extreme breadth:** 358 mi. **Coastline:** 180 mi. **Chief rivers:** Mississippi, Red River of the North, Minnesota. **Major lakes:** Superior, Red, Lake of the Woods. **No. of counties:** 87.

Population (1979 est.): 4,060,000 (ranks 19th). **Pop. increase (1970-79):** 6.7%. **Places over 25,000 pop.:** 21. **Places over 100,000:** 2. **Largest cities:** Minneapolis, St. Paul, Duluth, Rochester. **Pop. density:** 48.3 per sq. mi. (ranks 33rd). **Pop. projection 1985:** 4,179,000. **Pop. distribution:** 63.9% metropolitan; 36.1% nonmetropolitan. **White:** 98.2%. **Black:** 0.9%. **Other:** 0.9%. **Marriage rate (1977):** 7.9 per 1,000 people. **Divorce rate:** 3.5 per 1,000 people.

State finances (1978). Revenue: $4,799,408,000. **Expenditures:** $4,473,952,000. **State taxes:** $688.46 per capita. **State personal income tax:** Yes. **Public debt (1978):** $441.69 per capita. **Federal aid (1979):** $372.41 per capita. **Personal income (1979 est.):** $8,760.

Sectors of the economy (% of labor force employed in 1970): Wholesale and retail trade (22%), Manufacturing (21%), Government (15%), Educational Services (9%), Services (7%), Construction (6%). **Leading products:** food; electrical & other machinery; printing & publishing; paper items; chemicals; stone, clay & glass items. **Minerals:** iron ore, taconite, sand & gravel, cement, stone. **Agricultural products:** cattle, hogs, dairy items, corn, soybeans. **Fishing:** yellow pike, lake herring, tullibee. **Avg. farm (1979 est.):** 291 acres. **Avg. value of farm per acre:** $854.

Highway expenditures per capita (1978): $103.12. **Persons per motor vehicle:** 1.47. **Minimum age for driver's license:** 16. **Gasoline tax:** 11¢ per gallon. **Diesel tax:** 11¢ per gallon. **Motor vehicle deaths:** 24.0 per 100,000 people.

Birthrate (1978): 15.4 per 1,000 people. **Infant mortality rate per 1,000 births (1977):** 11.1. **Physicians per 100,000 pop. (1977):** 178. **Dentists per 100,000 pop. (1977):** 60. **Acceptable hospital beds:** 7.8 per 1,000 people. **State expenditures per capita for health and hospitals (1978):** $60.01.

Education expenditures (1975-76): $549.00 per capita annually. **No. of pupils in public schools (1977 est.):** 850,000. **No. of institutions of higher learning (1976-77):** 65. **Public school expenditure per pupil in attendance (1975-76):** $1,911. **Avg. salary of public school teachers (1974-75 est.):** $12,852. **No. full-time teachers (1977 est.):** 50,950. **Educational attainment of adult population (1976):** 12.5 median yrs. of school completed; 1.1% with less than 5 years of education; 13.2% with 4 yrs. of college.

Telephones (1977): 74 per 100 people. **State Chamber of Commerce:** Minnesota Association of Commerce and Industry, 200 Hanover Bldg., 480 Cedar Street, St. Paul, Minnesota 55101.

MISSISSIPPI

Without renouncing the history that has been both its pride and its handicap, this Deep South state has begun to rework its economic and social structures after a period of transition that began during the Great Depression.

In 1936, wealthy lumberman Hugh White became governor and instituted a "Balance Agriculture with Industry" (BAWI) program which allowed cities to issue bonds and build plants for private industry. By 1965, industrial employment had inched ahead of agricultural employment.

Tourists from outside the state enrich Mississippi's economy by over $500 million yearly as they flock to the beaches of the Gulf Coast winter resort area and other attractions.

The petroleum industry has become a major factor since the discovery of oil in the Tinsley field in 1939. Mississippi is a leading producer of oil and natural gas in the U.S.

The state is made up of two main land regions: the flat and fertile Delta area along the Mississippi River in northwest Mississippi and the rolling hills which cover most other areas, though broken by occasional river valleys. The Bay of St. Louis and Biloxi or Back Bay break the coastline and a chain of small islands lie offshore.

MISSISSIPPI
MILES
KILOMETERS
State Capitals
County Seats
Copyright HAMMOND INCORPORATED, Maplewood, N.J.
89° Longitude West of Greenwich

Mississippi was inhabited by the Choctaw, Chickasaw, Natchez and Yazoo Indians before De Soto explored it for Spain in 1540. French explorers La Salle, Iberville and Bienville came later.

The French ceded Mississippi to the British under the Treaty of Paris in 1763 but the Spanish claimed it along with West Florida in 1781. Spanish influence virtually ended in 1798 when Mississippi flew the United States flag as a territory of the new republic.

The early settlement of the state was handicapped by conflicting land claims, Indian troubles and the Yazoo Land Fraud in which Georgia, claiming the region, sold lots to speculators. Georgia finally ceded its claim to the Federal Government in 1802 and the Louisiana Purchase in 1803 insured free access to the Mississippi River. Mississippi became a state in 1817.

By the time the Civil War began, Mississippi was among the wealthiest states in the nation. Property assessments totaled $509 million in 1860. By 1880 property assessments had fallen to $110 million. Not until 1920 did assessments reach the pre-Civil War level.

Most black people were effectively disfranchised until the passage of the Federal Voting Rights Act of 1965.

Attacks on segregation brought turbulence. Two persons were killed in rioting at the University of Mississippi; NAACP leader Medgar Evers was shot to death in ambush at his Jackson home in 1963; and three civil rights workers were killed in 1964 near Philadelphia, Miss. However, the state joined the FBI in a massive crackdown on the Ku Klux Klan group behind much of the trouble, and tensions then eased.

Massive public school desegregation came later and Mississippi experienced less trouble than Northern and Eastern states under similar orders. Mississippi experienced some campus unrest as the 1960s closed and two persons were shot to death in a riot at Jackson State College in 1970.

In recent years blacks have made important gains, with an improvement in job opportunities and an increase in numbers elected to public office. The 1979 elections increased the number of blacks in the legislature from four to seventeen.

Mississippi's recent bid for trade with Middle Eastern and South American countries has paid off in massive sales of such products as farm machinery, food products, soybeans an cotton.

The Tennessee-Tombigbee Waterway project, one of a number of such measures cancelled by President Carter as an economy move, was reinstated after Congressional pressure was brought to bear. The project, estimated to cost $1.8 billion, is expected to be a shot in the arm for Mississippi's economy.

Full name: State of Mississippi. **Origin of name:** From the Indian, Maesi, meaning "Large," & Sipu, meaning "River." **Inhabitant:** Mississippian. **Capital:** Jackson. **State motto:** Virtute et Armis (By Valor & Arms). **Flag:** Horizontal red, white & blue bars with Confederate battle flag in upper left. **Seal:** American eagle holds olive branch, representing peace, & three arrows, symbolizing war. **Flower:** Magnolia. **Bird:** Mockingbird. **Tree:** Magnolia. **Song:** "Go, Mississippi." **Nickname:** Magnolia State.

Governor: William F. Winter. **Annual salary:** $53,000. **Term:** 4 years. **Current term expires:** Jan. 1984. **Voting requirements:** 18 yrs. old & U.S. citizen; resident and registered 30 days. **U.S. Congressmen:** 5. **Entered Union:** 1817 (20th state).

Location & boundaries: Southeastern state bounded on the north by Tennessee; on the east by Alabama; on the south by the Gulf of Mexico & Louisiana; & on the west by the Mississippi River, Louisiana & Arkansas. **Total area:** 47,716 sq. mi. (ranks 32nd). **Extreme length:** 352 mi. **Extreme breadth:** 188 mi. **Coastline:** 44 mi. **Chief rivers:** Mississippi, Yazoo, Pearl, Big Black. **Major lakes:** Grenada, Barnett, Sardis, Enid, Okatibbee Reservoirs. **No. of counties:** 82.

Population (1979 est.): 2,429,000 (ranks 31st). **Pop. increase (1970-79):** 9.6%. **Places over 25,000 pop.:** 8. **Places over 100,000:** 1. **Largest cities:** Jackson, Biloxi, Meridian. **Pop. density:** 50.9 per sq. mi. (ranks 31st). **Pop. projection 1985:** 2,521,000. **Pop. distribution:** 26.6% metropolitan; 73.4% nonmetropolitan. **White:** 62.8%. **Black:** 36.8%. **Other:** 0.4%. **Marriage rate (1977):** 11.1 per 1,000 people. **Divorce rate:** 5.3 per 1,000 people.

State finances (1978). Revenue: $2,342,334,000. **Expenditures:** $2,059,724,000. **State taxes:** $455.14 per capita. **State personal income tax:** Yes. **Public debt (1978):** $539.47 per capita. **Federal aid (1979):** $426.31 per capita. **Personal income (1979 est.):** $6,167.

Sectors of the economy (% of labor force employed in 1970): Manufacturing (26%), Wholesale and retail trade (18%), Government (18%), Educational Services (9%), Construction (8%), Services (7%). **Leading products:** food, lumber & wood, apparel, chemicals, transportation equipment. **Minerals:** petroleum, natural gas, sand & gravel. **Agricultural products:** cattle, broilers, eggs, cotton lint, soybeans, cottonseed. **Fishing:** menhaden, shrimp, oysters. **Avg. farm (1979 est.):** 274 acres. **Avg. value of farm per acre:** $520.

Highway expenditures per capita (1978): $103.31. **Persons per motor vehicle:** 1.47. **Minimum age for driver's license:** 15. **Gasoline tax:** 9¢ per gallon. **Diesel tax:** 10¢ per gallon. **Motor vehicle deaths:** 32.6 per 100,000 people.

Birthrate (1978): 18.4 per 1,000 people. **Infant mortality rate per 1,000 births (1977):** 18.2. **Physicians per 100,000 pop. (1977):** 105. **Dentists per 100,000 pop. (1977):** 30. **Acceptable hospital beds:** 7.1 per 1,000 people. **State expenditures per capita for health and hospitals (1978):** $54.69.

Education expenditures (1975-76): $363.00 per capita annually. **No. of pupils in public schools (1977 est.):** 503,000. **No. of institutions of higher learning (1976-77):** 45. **Public school expenditure per pupil in attendance (1975-76):** $1,072. **Avg. salary of public school teachers (1974-75 est.):** $8,338. **No. full-time teachers (1977 est.):** 27,510. **Educational attainment of adult population (1976):** 12.1 median yrs. of school completed; 7.9% with less than 5 years of education; 11.5% with 4 yrs. of college.

Telephones (1977): 58 per 100 people. **State Chamber of Commerce:** Mississippi Economic Council, 656 N. State Street, P.O. Box 1849, Jackson, Mississippi 39205.

MISSOURI

Traditional "Gateway to the West," centrally located Missouri owes much of its industrial and agricultural importance to the nation's two largest rivers—the Mississippi and Missouri—which form part of the state's borders while facilitating transportation and enriching its soil. Lead mining, in which the state ranks first nationally, has been important in the region for 200 years, being conducted chiefly in the Viburnum and Bixby areas. Most of the state's manufacturing activity is concentrated in and around St. Louis and Kansas City.

The state is made up of four principal land regions: the Dissected Till Plains, lying north of the Missouri; the Osage Plains in the west; the West Gulf Coastal Plain (known locally as the Mississippi Alluvial Plain), covering the southeastern corner; and the Ozark Plateau, making up most of the southern section and constituting the largest single region. The Dissected Till and Osage Plains are considered subdivisions of the Central Lowlands. Ten major artificial lakes formed by dams in the Ozark region have helped make that area a popular vacationland, contributing greatly to the state's $1 billion annual tourism business. Although two-thirds of the state was once covered by forests, today only half that amount remains, including Mark Twain and Clark National Forests.

MISSOURI
MILES
KILOMETERS
State Capitals
County Seats
Copyright HAMMOND INCORPORATED, Maplewood, N.J.

The Mound Builders, the earliest known inhabitants of the Missouri region, predated the Osage and Missouri Indians, who were living there when the first European explorers—Frenchmen Marquette and Jolliet—visited (1673). France's claim to the entire Mississippi Valley, including what is now Missouri, was based on La Salle's travels in 1682. In the following years, French fur trading posts were established along the river, and the working of the lead mines was begun. Established about 1735, Ste. Genevieve was the first permanent white settlement.

Having met defeat in the French and Indian Wars, France secretly yielded (1762) to Spain all its territory west of the Mississippi; even so, Frenchmen Laclede and Chouteau founded St. Louis two years later. Napoleon regained (1800) possession of the region for France, then sold it three years later as part of the Louisiana Purchase. A year later, in 1804, President Thomas Jefferson sent Meriwether Lewis and William Clark westward up the Missouri River on the famous expedition that tied the United States together as a continental nation. The area was briefly a district of the Territory of Indiana, but was made a separate territory in 1805, comprising at that time all U.S. land west of the Mississippi and north of 33° north latitude and therefore including the future state of Missouri.

The question of admitting Missouri to the Union became bound up, in Congress, with the volatile slavery issue. Bitter controversy was arduously resolved by the Missouri Compromise (1820), which provided for the admission of Missouri (1821) as a slave state and Maine as a free one, while banning slavery in the rest of the Louisiana Purchase north of 36°30′N. Missouri was at this time the nation's western frontier, and fur trading was still its foremost economic pursuit. The state's six northwestern counties were added by the Platte Purchase (1837). An unusual boundary dispute between Missouri and Illinois was settled early in 1970, giving Illinois the site of Old Kaskaskia, the state's original capital, now an island as a result of shifts by the Mississippi River. Illinois received Kaskaskia and Beaver islands, and Missouri, Cottonwoods and Roth islands.

The years preceding the Civil War were marked by growing prosperity in an increasingly tense political climate. The town of Independence became the starting point of the much-traveled Santa Fe and Oregon Trails, while St. Louis prospered as a thriving inland port. St. Joseph was the eastern starting point of the briefly active (1860-61) Pony Express. But bitter Missouri-Kansas border wars over the slavery issue had begun, and although Missouri voted (February 1861) not to secede from the Union, Missourians were sharply divided in their allegiances, supplying both sides with troops.

Missouri today seeks to attract new industry by stressing its central location, good transportation facilities, availability of labor, and relatively low taxes. Tourism has emerged in recent years as one of Missouri's leading businesses.

The unrelenting heat wave in summer 1980 most tragically affected Missouri in terms of human lives lost. The unofficial death toll as of July 20 had reached 275. Governor Teasdale declared a state of emergency and the National Guard was on alert to assist the elderly and other victims of 100°-plus temperatures.

Full name: State of Missouri. **Origin of name:** From name of Sioux tribe. **Inhabitant:** Missourian. **Capital:** Jefferson City. **State motto:** Salus Populi Suprema Lex Esto (Let the Welfare of the People Be the Supreme Law). **Flag:** State seal centered on horizontal red, white & blue bars. **Seal:** Two grizzly bears hold shields of United States & Missouri; 24 stars represent Missouri's entrance into Union.

Flower: Hawthorn. **Bird:** Bluebird. **Tree:** Flowering dogwood. **Song:** "Missouri Waltz." **Nickname:** Show-Me State.

Governor: Joseph P. Teasdale. **Annual salary:** $37,500. **Term:** 4 years. **Current term expires:** Jan. 1981. **Voting requirements:** 18 yrs. old & U.S. citizen; registered in state. **U.S. Congressmen:** 10. **Entered Union:** 1821 (24th state).

Location & boundaries: Southern Midwestern state: bounded on the north by Iowa; on the east by Illinois, Kentucky, Tennessee & the Mississippi River; on the south by Arkansas; & on the west by Oklahoma, Kansas, Nebraska & the Missouri River. **Total area:** 69,686 sq. mi. (ranks 19th). **Extreme length:** 284 mi. **Extreme breadth:** 308 mi. **Chief rivers:** Missouri, Mississippi, Osage. **Major lakes:** Lake of the Ozarks; Stockton, Taneycomo, Clearwater, and Wappapello lakes; Table Rock & Pomme de Terre Reservoirs. **No. of counties:** 114 & the city of St. Louis.

Population (1979 est.): 4,867,000 (ranks 15th). **Pop. increase (1970-79):** 4.1%. **Places over 25,000 pop.:** 16. **Places over 100,000:** 3. **Largest cities:** St. Louis, Kansas City, Springfield, Independence. **Pop. density:** 69.8 per sq. mi. (ranks 27th). **Pop. projection 1985:** 4,985,000. **Pop. distribution:** 63.5% metropolitan; 36.5% nonmetropolitan. **White:** 89.3%. **Black:** 10.3%. **Other:** 0.4%. **Marriage rate (1977):** 10.9 per 1,000 people. **Divorce rate:** 5.3 per 1,000 people.

State finances (1978). Revenue: $3,401,585,000. **Expenditures:** $3,009,139,000. **State taxes:** $367.16 per capita. **State personal income tax:** Yes. **Public debt (1978):** $114.09 per capita. **Federal aid (1979):** $310.07 per capita. **Personal income (1979 est.):** $8,132.

Sectors of the economy (% of labor force employed in 1970): Manufacturing (24%), Wholesale and retail trade (22%), Government (15%), Educational Services (8%), Services (7%), Construction (6%). **Leading products:** transportation equipment, food, chemicals, printing & publishing, machinery, fabricated metals. **Minerals:** stone, cement, lead, iron ore. **Agricultural products:** cattle, hogs, dairy items, corn, soybeans, hay. **Avg. farm (1979 est.):** 274 acres. **Avg. value of farm per acre:** $520.

Highway expenditures per capita (1978): $85.50. **Persons per motor vehicle:** 1.50. **Mininum age for driver's license:** 16. **Gasoline tax:** 7¢ per gallon. **Diesel tax:** 7¢ per gallon. **Motor vehicle deaths:** 24.5 per 100,000 people.

Birthrate (1978): 15.0 per 1,000 people. **Infant mortality rate per 1,000 births (1977):** 14.2. **Physicians per 100,000 pop. (1977):** 152. **Dentists per 100,000 pop. (1977):** 47. **Acceptable hospital beds:** 7.4 per 1,000 people. **State expenditures per capita for health and hospitals (1978):** $54.48.

Education expenditures (1975-76): $368.55 per capita annually. **No. of pupils in public schools (1977 est.):** 936,000. **No. of institutions of higher learning (1976-77):** 83. **Public school expenditure per pupil in attendance (1975-76):** $1,389. **Avg. salary of public school teachers (1974-75 est.):** $10,257. **No. full-time teachers (1977 est.):** 53,210. **Educational attainment of adult population (1976):** 12.4 median yrs. of school completed; 2.5% with less than 5 years of education; 11.8% with 4 yrs. of college.

Telephones (1977): 73 per 100 people. **State Chamber of Commerce:** Missouri Chamber of Commerce, P.O. Box 149, Jefferson City, Missouri 65101.

MONTANA

As its Spanish name suggests, Montana is a mountainous region: the Rocky Mountains cover the western two-fifths of the state and the high, gently rolling Great Plains make up the rest. The state is large, ranking fourth nationally in area, but it is sparsely populated. The Rockies' Bitterroot Range, marking the Montana-Idaho boundary, is one of the most rugged and remote areas in the country. Many of the state's mountains are thick with forests below the timber line; fir, pine, and spruce abound. The state produces about three million Christmas trees a year.

Montana's climate is generally cool to cold, and dry. Tourists—mainly hunters, fishermen, and dude ranch patrons—have been coming to the state in growing numbers, attracted by plentiful fish and game and the varied scenery. As an industry, tourism has become increasingly vital in recent years. Attractions include Glacier National Park, 11 national forests, the Lewis and Clark Cavern (one of the country's largest), and a number of annual rodeos and Indian ceremonials. Yellowstone National Park, most of which is in Wyoming, has three entrances in Montana.

Arapaho, Blackfoot, Cheyenne, Crow, Atsina, Bannock, Kalispel, Kutenai, and Shoshoni Indians were living in the region before the arrival of the first Europeans, who were probably fur trappers of the Hudson Bay Company or the Northwest Company. In 1805, Lewis and Clark explored the area on their journeys to and from the Pacific Coast. The American Fur Company, in 1829 and 1846, built two of Montana's earliest non-Indian settlements: Forts Union and Benton.

The major Indian wars (1867-77) included the famous 1876 Battle of Little Bighorn, popularly known as "Custer's Last Stand," in which Cheyennes and Sioux killed General Custer and more than 200 of his men. But the Indians' moment of glory was something of a brief one, for in 1877, when Chief Joseph and his Nez Percé warriors surrendered to Federal troops near the Canadian border, Indian resistance in Montana virtually ended. Today, the state has some 30,000 Indians, almost all of whom live on seven reservations.

The United States obtained most of Montana as part of the Louisiana Purchase (1803). The remaining northwestern section passed into U.S. hands following the 1846 treaty with England. Montana was originally part of the Territory of Idaho, created in 1863; Montana Territory came into being in 1864. Statehood came in 1889.

Much of Montana's early history was bound up with mining, which is still a leading industry: oil, coal, copper, and sand and gravel are important products. The capital of Helena was originally a mining camp called Last Chance Gulch. The Anaconda Company branched out from Butte ("the richest hill on earth") to become a giant conglomerate of its day, with interests in railroading, journalism, banking, and other fields.

Another of Montana's major occupations, ranching, came into its own in 1866 when a cattleman by the name of Nelson Story drove his herd of a thousand longhorn from Texas to Montana, setting an example that many others soon followed. The coming of the railroad in 1883 was another impetus. But the severe winter of 1886-87 spelled disaster; thousands of cattle perished in subzero blizzards. Although the industry eventually recovered, for a long time profit margins were narrow. Ranching is economically important: the state has over three times as many cattle (including calves) and about as many sheep as it has people.

Montana today is attempting to attract new industry while preserving clean air and water. The aims have touched off a clash between environmentalists and the energy companies which are developing reserves of strippable coal.

In May 1980, volcanic ash from the eruption of Mount St. Helens in Washington fell thickly in six counties in western Montana. Streets became impassable, and schools and businesses were closed.

Full name: State of Montana. **Origin of name:** From Spanish word meaning "Mountainous." **Inhabitant:** Montanan. **Capital:** Helena. **State motto:** Oro y Plata (Gold & Silver). **Flag:** State seal on blue field. **Seal:** A plow, pick & shovel rest on soil, symbolizing Montana's agricultural & mineral industries; Great Falls of Missouri River & mountain scenery. **Flower:** Bitterroot. **Bird:** Western meadowlark. **Tree:** Ponderosa pine. **Song:** "Montana." **Nicknames:** Treasure State; the Big Sky Country; Land of the Shining Mountains.

Governor: Thomas L. Judge. **Annual salary:** $37,500. **Term:** 4 years. **Current term expires:** Jan. 1981. **Voting requirements:** 18 yrs. old & U.S. citizen; registered resident of state & county 30 days. **U.S. Congressmen:** 2. **Entered Union:** 1889 (41st state).

Location & boundaries: Rocky Mountain state: bounded on the north by Canada; on the east by North Dakota & South Dakota; on the south by Wyoming & Idaho; & on the west by Idaho. **Total area:** 147,138 sq. mi. (ranks 4th). **Extreme length:** 570 mi. **Extreme breadth:** 315 mi. **Chief rivers:** Missouri, Yellowstone, Kootenai. **Major lakes:** Flathead; Fort Peck & Canyon Ferry Reservoirs. **No. of counties:** 56.

Population (1979 est.): 786,000 (ranks 43rd). **Pop. increase (1970-79):** 13.2%. **Places over 25,000 pop.:** 4. **Places over 100,000:** None. **Largest cities:** Billings, Great Falls, Missoula. **Pop. density:** 5.3 per sq. mi. (ranks 48th). **Pop. projection 1985:** 843,000. **Pop. distribution:** 24.4% metropolitan; 75.6% nonmetropolitan. **White:** 95.5%. **Black:** 0.3%. **Other:** 4.2%. **Marriage rate (1977):** 9.9 per 1,000 people. **Divorce rate:** 6.2 per 1,000 people.

State finances (1978). Revenue: $922,568,000. **Expenditures:** $868,334,000. **State taxes:** $430.90 per capita. **State personal income tax:** Yes. **Public debt (1978):** $173.52 per capita. **Federal aid (1979):** $517.05 per capita. **Personal income (1979 est.):** $7,412.

Sectors of the economy (% of labor force employed in 1970): Wholesale and retail trade (22%), Government (21%), Manufacturing (10%), Educational Services (10%), Services (7%), Construction (6%). **Leading products:** lumber & wood; primary metals; food; petroleum & coal items; printing & publishing; stone, clay & glass items; chemicals. **Minerals:** copper, petroleum, lead & zinc, sand & gravel, phosphate rock, silver, gold. **Agricultural products:** cattle, dairy items, sheep, wheat, hay, barley, flax seed, sugar beets. **Avg. farm (1979 est.):** 2,857 acres. **Avg. value of farm per acre:** $186.

Highway expenditures per capita (1978): $187.85. **Persons per motor vehicle:** .87. **Minimum age for driver's license:** 15. **Gasoline tax:** 9¢ per gallon. **Diesel tax:** 11¢ per gallon. **Motor vehicle deaths:** 34.5 per 100,000 people.

Birthrate (1978): 17.4 per 1,000 people. **Infant mortality rate per 1,000 births (1977):** 13.7. **Physicians per 100,000 pop. (1977):** 128. **Dentists per 100,000 pop. (1977):** 54. **Acceptable hospital beds:** 6.7 per 1,000 people. **State expenditures per capita for health and hospitals (1978):** $64.84.

Education expenditures (1975-76): $540.40 per capita annually. **No. of pupils in public schools (1977 est.):** 168,000. **No. of institutions of higher learning (1976-77):** 12. **Public school expenditure per pupil in attendance (1975-76):** $1,745. **Avg. salary of public school teachers (1974-75 est.):** $10,160. **No. full-time teachers (1977 est.):** 10,110. **Educational attainment of adult population (1976):** 12.6 median yrs. of school completed; 1.2% with less than 5 years of education; 14.2% with 4 yrs. of college.

Telephones (1977): 71 per 100 people. **State Chamber of Commerce:** Montana Chamber of Commerce, 110 Neill Avenue, P.O. Box 1730, Helena, Montana 59601.

NEBRASKA

Nebraska is rich with grass (with more forage varieties than any other state) and grain; agriculture is its mainstay. The grassy Sand Hills make up the state's central region, and rolling farmland, found in the east, rises gradually from 840 feet above sea level to 5,300 feet in the western High Plains region. A portion of the South Dakota Badlands takes up about 1,000 square miles of the northwest corner of the state. The climate of Nebraska is one of extremes: severe winters and sweltering summers.

Nebraska annually harvests large crops of corn, sorghum, oats, wheat, rye, soybeans, alfalfa and dry edible beans. Omaha, with its surrounding area, forms the nation's largest meat-packing center, and it is the second-largest cattle market of both the United States and the world.

MONTANA
MILES
KILOMETERS
State Capital ⊛   County Seats ⊙
© Copyright HAMMOND INCORPORATED, Maplewood, N. J.
CANADA
BRITISH COLUMBIA
ALBERTA
SASKATCHEWAN
NORTH DAKOTA
S. DAK.
WYOMING
IDAHO
WYO.
LINCOLN
FLATHEAD
LAKE
SANDERS
MINERAL
MISSOULA
RAVALLI
GRANITE
POWELL
LEWIS AND CLARK
DEER LODGE
SILVER BOW
BEAVERHEAD
MADISON
GALLATIN
JEFFERSON
BROADWATER
PARK
GLACIER
TOOLE
LIBERTY
HILL
BLAINE
PHILLIPS
VALLEY
DANIELS
SHERIDAN
ROOSEVELT
TETON
PONDERA
CHOUTEAU
CASCADE
MEAGHER
JUDITH BASIN
FERGUS
PETROLEUM
GARFIELD
PINEY BUTTES
McCONE
RICHLAND
DAWSON
PRAIRIE
WIBAUX
ROSEBUD
MUSSEL SHELL
GOLDEN VALLEY
WHEATLAND
SWEET GRASS
STILL WATER
CARBON
YELLOWSTONE
TREASURE
BIG HORN
CUSTER
FALLON
POWDER RIVER
CARTER
Cranbrook
Fernie
Pincher Creek
Lethbridge
Shaunavon
Assiniboia
Radville
Plentywood
Scobey
Medicine L.
Froid
Culbertson
Rexford
Eureka
Fortine
Troy
Libby
Whitefish
Columbia Falls
Kalispell
Lakeside
Somers
Polson
Ronan
Charlo
St. Ignatius
Plains
Thompson Falls
St. Regis
Superior
Alberton
Missoula
Seeley L.
Lincoln
Helena
Drummond
Philipsburg
Deer Lodge
Anaconda
Butte
Whitehall
Boulder
Centerville
Townsend
Three Forks
Belgrade
Bozeman
Manhattan
Livingston
Big Timber
Victor
Hamilton
Darby
Stevensville
Florence
Corvalis
Dillon
Sheridan
Twin Bridges
Virginia City
Ennis
Lima
Dubois
W. Yellowstone
Gardiner
Salmon
Sunburst
Kevin
Shelby
Cut Bank
Browning
Valier
Dupuyer
Conrad
Choteau
Dutton
Fairfield
Augusta
Chester
Rudyard
Big Sandy
Havre
Chinook
Harlem
Gildford
Ft. Benton
Black Eagle
Geraldine
Cascade
Belt
Great Falls
Sand Coulee
Denton
Stanford
Wolf Creek
Winifred
Roy
Lewistown
Winnett
Jordan
Circle
Richey
Lambert
Sidney
Glendive
Savage
Beach
Terry
Wibaux
Plevna
Baker
Ekalaka
Hammond
Alzada
Broadus
Sheridan
Buffalo
Gillette
Worland
Cody
Greybull
Powell
Glasgow
Nashua
Frazer
Wolf Point
Poplar
Hinsdale
Saco
Malta
Dodson
Hays
Ft. Peck
Opheim
Judith Gap
White Sulphur Sprs.
Harlowton
Melville
Ryegate
Roundup
Melstone
Musselshell
Hysham
Forsyth
Miles City
Hardin
Crow Agency
Lame Deer
Lodge Grass
Billings
Laurel
Fromberg
Bridger
Red Lodge
Columbus
Park City
Absarokee
Joliet
Nye
Livingston
Big Timber
Bozeman
Ballantine
Pompeys Pillar
Meagher
Judith
Crazy Pk. 11,214
Koch Pk. 11,293
Electric Pk. 11,155
Granite Pk. 12,799
Cloud Pk. 13,165
Hebgen
Earthquake L.
Hap Hawkins Lake
WATERTON LAKES NAT'L PK.
GLACIER INT'L PEACE PARK
GLACIER NATIONAL PARK
BLACKFEET IND. RES.
FLATHEAD IND. RES.
ROCKY BOY'S IND. RES.
FT. BELKNAP IND. RES.
FORT PECK IND. RES.
CROW IND. RES.
NORTHERN CHEYENNE IND. RES.
TONGUE R. IND. RES.
CYPRESS HILLS PROV. PARKS
MALMSTROM A.F.B.
BIG HOLE NAT'L BATTLEFIELD
BIGHORN CANYON NAT'L REC. AREA
CUSTER BATTLEFIELD NAT'L MON.
DEVILS TOWER NAT'L MON.
YELLOWSTONE NATIONAL PARK
GRAND TETON NAT'L PK.
FT. UNION TRADING POST NAT'L HIST. SITE
CONTINENTAL DIVIDE
BITTERROOT RANGE
BIG BELT MTS.
LITTLE BELT MTS.
BULL MTS.
BEAVERHEAD MTS.
CENTENNIAL MTS.
BIGHORN MTS.
RANGE
Lake Koocanusa
Kootenai R.
Clark Fork
Flathead Lake
Flathead R.
Lookout Pass
Lolo Pass
Marias Pass
Milk R.
Marias R.
Teton R.
Missouri R.
Judith R.
Musselshell R.
Dry R.
Little Dry
Yellowstone R.
Tongue R.
Bighorn R.
Little Bighorn
Powder R.
Little Missouri R.
Belle Fourche R.
Fort Peck Lake
Fresno Res.
Tiber Res.
Hungry Horse Res.
Canyon Ferry L.
Bighorn Lake
Tongue R. Res.
Frenchman R.
Pakowki L.
Poplar R.
Buffalo Bill Res.
Shoshone R.
Selway R.
Bitterroot R.
Big Hole
Beaverhead R.
Jefferson R.
Madison R.
Gallatin R.
Yellowstone L.
Salmon R.
MEDICINE ROCKS
Ft. Peck Dam

The state's numerous rivers and lakes are vitally important to its agricultural and allied processing industries. Many conservation practices, such as dam construction, systematic tree-planting, and irrigation, are widely employed to keep the land productive. Larger farms, more modern equipment, and improved farming techniques have resulted in vastly increased production even with a smaller farm population.

Judging by stone tool and weapon remnants that have been unearthed, the first inhabitants of Nebraska arrived between 10,000 and 25,000 years ago. In the early 1700s, Spanish and French explorers found, among others, the Omaha and Oto Indians living peacefully along the region's rivers. The buffalo-hunting Pawnee, however, battled other tribes—especially the Sioux—but were generally friendly to whites. The Sioux, Arapaho, and Cheyenne Indians constituted the white settlers' principal resistance, waging a losing battle to keep their hunting grounds.

The United States gained possession of the area with the Louisiana Purchase (1803). Pioneers going west along the Oregon Trail, which followed the Platte Valley, stimulated trading and settlement; many early Nebraskans earned a living supplying food, lodging, and fresh mounts. Statehood came in 1867.

Early times were very hard for settlers. There was bitter, protracted conflict between them and the cattlemen, who wanted the land for their herds. (This struggle was not fully resolved until the 1904 Kinkaid Act gave over the last of the state's open range land to the homesteaders.) And there were harsh blows from nature: blizzards, locust infestations, and droughts.

World War I brought prosperity, but hard times returned: depression and drought hit the state simultaneously. Overextended farmers faced foreclosure. Violence was averted by the enactment of a series of farm mortgage moratorium acts; New Deal legislation also helped. In 1937, the Nebraska legislature was reorganized into a "one house" (unicameral) system, under which state senators are elected on a nonpartisan basis.

Border disputes with Iowa have plagued Nebraska ever since the Missouri River was made the dividing line (1867). Through the years, the river's shifting has transferred parcels of land from one state to the other.

Full name: State of Nebraska. **Origin of name:** From Omaha Indian name for the Platte River. **Inhabitant:** Nebraskan. **Capital:** Lincoln. **State motto:** Equality Before the Law. **Flag:** State seal on blue field. **Seal:** Blacksmith represents mechanical arts; settler's cabin, growing corn & shocks of grain stand for agriculture; steamboat & train symbolize transportation. **Flower:** Goldenrod. **Bird:** Western meadowlark. **Tree:** Cottonwood. **Song:** "Beautiful Nebraska." **Nickname:** Cornhusker State.

Governor: Charles Thone. **Annual salary:** $40,000. **Term:** 4 years. **Current term expires:** Jan. 1983. **Voting requirements:** 18 yrs. old & U.S. citizen; state resident and registered voter. **U.S. Congressmen:** 3. **Entered Union:** 1867 (37th state).

Location & boundaries: Midwestern state: bounded on the north by South Dakota; on the east by Iowa, the Missouri River & Missouri; on the south by Kansas; on the southwest by Colorado; & on the west by Wyoming. **Total area:** 77,227 sq. mi. (ranks 15th). **Extreme length:** 415 mi. **Extreme breadth:** 205 mi. **Chief rivers:** Missouri, North Platte, South Platte. **Major lakes:** Lewis & Clark, McConaughy. **No. of counties:** 93.

Population (1979 est.): 1,574,000 (ranks 35th). **Pop. increase (1970-79):** 6.0%. **Places over 25,000 pop.:** 3. **Places over 100,000:** 2. **Largest cities:** Omaha, Lincoln, Grand Island. **Pop. density:** 20.4 per sq. mi. (ranks 41st). **Pop. projection 1985:** 1,665,000. **Pop. distribution:** 44.6% metropolitan; 55.4% nonmetropolitan. **White:** 96.6%. **Black:** 2.7%. **Other:** 0.7%. **Marriage rate (1977):** 8.3 per 1,000 people. **Divorce rate:** 3.9 per 1,000 people.

State finances (1978). Revenue: $1,231,625,000. **Expenditures:** $1,144,827,000. **State taxes:** $434.64 per capita. **State personal income tax:** Yes. **Public debt (1978):** $35.79 per capita. **Federal aid (1979):** $300.70 per capita. **Personal income (1979 est.):** $8,341.

Sectors of the economy (% of labor force employed in 1970): Wholesale and retail trade (22%), Government (16%), Manufacturing (14%), Educational Services (9%), Services (7%), Construction (6%). **Leading products:** food, electrical & other machinery, chemicals, fabricated metal items, printing & publishing, primary metals, transportation equipment. **Agricultural products:** cattle, hogs, dairy items, corn, hay, wheat, sorghums. **Avg. farm (1979 est.):** 759 acres. **Avg. value of farm per acre:** $470.

Highway expenditures per capita (1978): $131.70. **Persons per motor vehicle:** 1.27. **Minimum age for driver's license:** 16. **Gasoline tax:** 11.5¢ per gallon*. **Diesel tax:** 11.5¢ per gallon*. **Motor vehicle deaths:** 22.3 per 100,000 people. * Plus 5% of cost of fuel.

Birthrate (1978): 16.0 per 1,000 people. **Infant mortality rate per 1,000 births (1977):** 12.7. **Physicians per 100,000 pop. (1977):** 139. **Dentists per 100,000 pop. (1977):** 56. **Acceptable hospital beds:** 7.4 per 1,000 people. **State expenditures per capita for health and hospitals (1978):** $61.94.

Education expenditures (1975-76): $435.53 per capita annually. **No. of pupils in public schools (1977 est.):** 307,000. **No. of institutions of higher learning (1976-77):** 29. **Public school expenditure per pupil in attendance (1975-76):** $1,477. **Avg. salary of public school teachers (1974-75 est.):** $9,715. **No. full-time teachers (1977 est.):** 20,040. **Educational attainment of adult population (1976):** 12.5 median yrs. of school completed; 1.0% with less than 5 years of education; 12.8% with 4 yrs. of college.

Telephones (1977): 77 per 100 people. **State Chamber of Commerce:** Nebraska Association of Commerce & Industry, P.O. Box 81556, 424 Terminal Bldg., Lincoln, Nebraska 68501.

NEVADA

Except for its northeast and southeast corners, Nevada lies entirely within the Great Basin, a broad plateau averaging 5,500 feet in elevation and broken by mountain ranges. The Sierra Nevadas on the California border interrupt moisture-carrying clouds from the Pacific, making Nevada the driest state in the country; its average annual rainfall is only 3.73 inches. Much of the state is uninhabited, sagebrush-covered desert dotted by alkali sinks in which rivers have dried up. Only three states have fewer inhabitants than Nevada, which in 1970 had but 4.5 persons per square mile.

Nevada's minimal agriculture depends largely on irrigation. Most crops go for livestock feed. Leading income sources have been, first, tourism, then mining—followed by a modest mineral and metals processing industry. In the Reno area, warehousing, aided by a free port law, is growing substantially. Thanks mainly to legalized gambling and lenient divorce laws, tourism today accounts for billions of dollars in revenue. The Las Vegas and Reno metropolitan areas, where nearly four of every five Nevadans live, are the principal tourist attractions. Others include Lake Tahoe on the California-Nevada border and Death Valley National Monument.

Indians are thought to have inhabited the Nevada region between 10,000 and 20,000 years ago. In more recent times, the Shoshoni, Washoe, Northern Paiute, and other tribes lived there.

In 1775 a Spanish missionary named Francisco Garcés passed through what is now Nevada on his way to the West Coast. In the early 1800s, trappers searched the area for new fur sources. John C. Frémont and Kit Carson explored (1843-45) the Great Basin and Sierra Nevada.

NEBRASKA
MILES
KILOMETERS
MINN.
SOUTH DAKOTA
IOWA
WYOMING
COLORADO
KANSAS
MO.
Spencer
Storm Lake
Cherokee
Sioux City
Dakota City
Vermillion
Sioux Falls
Mitchell
Andes
L. Andes
FT. RANDALL DAM
Tyndall
Yankton
Lewis and Clark Lake
GAVINS PT. DAM
Center
Bloomfield
Hartington
Laurel
Randolph
Osmond
Creighton
Plainview
Wausa
Niobrara
Verdigre
Springview
Valentine
Ainsworth
Bassett
Stuart
Atkinson
O'Neill
Ewing
Butte
Winner
Martin
Hay Sprs.
Rushville
Gordon
Hemingford
Alliance
Chadron
Crawford
Harrison
Mitchell
Morrill
Scottsbluff
Gering
Minatare
Bayard
Bridgeport
Harrisburg
Kimball
Potter
Sidney
Dalton
Lodgepole
Chappell
Big Sprs.
Oshkosh
Lewellen
Ogallala
Paxton
Grant
Benkelman
Wauneta
Imperial
Trenton
Culbertson
McCook
Cambridge
Oxford
Beaver City
Alma
Franklin
Red Cloud
Nelson
Superior
Hebron
Deshler
Fairbury
Edgar
Sutton
Geneva
Clay Ctr.
Minden
Holdrege
Bertrand
Elwood
Gosper
Arapahoe
Oberlin
Phillipsburg
Smith Ctr.
Beloit
Concordia
Marysville
Manhattan
Topeka
Holton
Falls City
Humboldt
Pawnee City
Tecumseh
Auburn
Peru
Nebraska City
Shenandoah
Plattsmouth
Bellevue
Omaha
Council Bluffs
OFFUTT A.F.B.
Papillion
Millard
Ralston
Boys Town
Lincoln
Crete
Wilber
Friend
Milford
Seward
York
Aurora
Central City
St. Paul
Grand Island
Wood River
Shelton
Gibbon
Kearney
Ravenna
Loup City
Sherman
Ord
Burwell
Taylor
Sargent
Broken Bow
Ansley
Callaway
Arnold
Stapleton
North Platte
Sutherland
Paxton
Brady
Gothenburg
Cozad
Lexington
Curtis
Stockville
Hayes Ctr.
Wallace
Wray
Akron
Sterling
Ft. Morgan
WYOMING
BADLANDS NAT'L MON.
WIND CAVE NAT'L PK.
JEWEL CAVE N.M.
Hot Sprs.
Edgemont
Cheyenne River
PINE RIDGE INDIAN RES.
ROSEBUD IND. RES.
White River
Cheyenne
Niobrara
Snake R.
Merritt Res.
Loup River
Dismal R.
Middle Loup R.
North Loup R.
Calamus R.
Platte River
North Platte River
South Platte River
Republican River
Frenchman Cr.
Beaver Cr.
Blue River
Little Blue River
Big Blue R.
Missouri River
Nemaha R.
Platte R.
Elkhorn R.
Logan Cr.
Keya Paha R.
SIOUX
DAWES
BOX BUTTE
SHERIDAN
CHERRY
BROWN
ROCK
HOLT
KEYA PAHA
BOYD
KNOX
CEDAR
DIXON
DAKOTA
THURSTON
CUMING
BURT
WASHINGTON
DOUGLAS
SARPY
CASS
OTOE
NEMAHA
RICHARDSON
PAWNEE
JOHNSON
GAGE
JEFFERSON
THAYER
FILLMORE
SALINE
LANCASTER
SAUNDERS
DODGE
COLFAX
PLATTE
STANTON
MADISON
PIERCE
WAYNE
ANTELOPE
WHEELER
GARFIELD
LOUP
BLAINE
THOMAS
HOOKER
GRANT
ARTHUR
McPHERSON
LOGAN
CUSTER
VALLEY
GREELEY
BOONE
NANCE
MERRICK
HOWARD
SHERMAN
BUFFALO
HALL
HAMILTON
YORK
SEWARD
BUTLER
POLK
CLAY
ADAMS
KEARNEY
PHELPS
GOSPER
DAWSON
LINCOLN
KEITH
PERKINS
CHASE
HAYES
FRONTIER
HARLAN
FURNAS
RED WILLOW
HITCHCOCK
DUNDY
DEUEL
GARDEN
MORRILL
CHEYENNE
KIMBALL
BANNER
SCOTTS BLUFF
PINE RIDGE
SAND HILLS
BADLANDS
SOUTH DAKOTA
104° 102° 100° 98° 96°
42° 40°

The United States obtained (1848) the region, following the Mexican War, and the first permanent settlement (1851) was a Mormon trading post called Mormon Station (now Genoa). Amid the conflicting pressures of the Civil War, Nevada was made a state (1864), although the territory did not meet the population requirement.

In 1859 the discovery of the Comstock (silver and gold) Lode, near what became Virginia City, brought an influx of both settlers and adventurers. During the next 20 years, the lode yielded more than $300 million of mineral wealth which helped the Union to win the Civil War and was the basis of many American fortunes. Today copper is the major ore mined with plants at McGill (Kennecott) and Yerington (Anaconda).

The Federal Government owns 87% of the land in Nevada. The first Federal irrigation project anywhere was the Newlands Irrigation Project, completed in 1907, which helped west central Nevada's agriculture. Another Federal irrigation project—the Southern Nevada Project—was completed in 1971. In the early 1950s, the Federal Government began to test nuclear devices on Federal land in the Nevada desert.

As the 1970s drew to a close, Nevadans became increasingly annoyed by the limitation which Federal ownership of so much land was putting on agriculture, commercial, and residential growth. Moreover, in 1979, reports that nuclear testing may have caused a high rate of cancer in areas near the test site led to a storm of protest. In July 1979, the Nevada legislature declared the state to be owner of 49,000,000 acres of Federal land—apparently in order to facilitate judicial review of Federal policies. Three months later, officials of Nevada and of other Western states met at Reno to discuss common problems.

In 1980, a Federal study advised construction in Nevada of covered mobile launching sites for MX missiles. Many Nevadans complained that the plan would encourage saturation bombing of Nevada in the event of war.

Full name: State of Nevada. **Origin of name:** From Spanish for "Snow-Clad." **Inhabitant:** Nevadan. **Capital:** Carson City. **State motto:** All for Our Country. **Flag:** Blue field with gold & green insignia in upper left; words "Battle Born" recall that Nevada gained statehood during Civil War. **Seal:** Plow & sheaf of wheat represent Nevada's agricultural resources; quartz mill, mine tunnel & carload of ore symbolize mineral wealth of state; 36 stars. **Flower:** Sagebrush. **Animal:** Nelson (Desert) bighorn sheep. **Bird:** Mountain bluebird. **Tree:** Single-leaf piñon. **Song:** "Home Means Nevada." **Nickname:** Silver State.

Governor: Robert F. List. **Annual salary:** $50,000. **Term:** 4 years. **Current term expires:** Jan. 1983. **Voting requirements:** 18 yrs. old & U.S. citizen; state resident 30 days. **U.S. Congressmen:** 1. **Entered Union:** 1864 (36th state).

Location & boundaries: Rocky Mountain state: bounded on the north by Oregon & Idaho; on the east by Utah & Arizona; & on the south & west by California. **Total area:** 110,540 sq. mi. (ranks 7th). **Extreme length:** 483 mi. **Extreme breadth:** 320 mi. **Chief rivers:** Humboldt, Colorado, Truckee. **Major lakes:** Pyramid, Walker, Tahoe, Mead. **No. of counties:** 17.

Population (1979 est.): 702,000 (ranks 44th). **Pop. increase (1970-79):** 43.6%. **Places over 25,000 pop.:** 5. **Places over 100,000:** 1. **Largest cities:** Las Vegas, Reno, North Las Vegas. **Pop. density:** 6.4 per sq. mi. (ranks 47th). **Pop. projection 1985:** 734,000. **Pop. distribution:** 81.3% metropolitan; 18.7% nonmetropolitan. **White:** 91.7%. **Black:** 5.7%. **Other:** 2.6%. **Marriage rate (1977):** 170.6 per 1,000 people. **Divorce rate:** 16.2 per 1,000 people.

State finances (1978). Revenue: $911,469,000. **Expenditures:** $774,145,000. **State taxes:** $591.82 per capita. **State personal income tax:** No. **Public debt (1978):** $373.28 per capita. **Federal aid (1979):** $375.64 per capita. **Personal income (1979 est.):** $10,204.

Sectors of the economy (% of labor force employed in 1970): Services (22%), Wholesale and retail trade (19%), Government (18%), Construction (8%), Educational Services (6%), Manufacturing (5%). **Leading products:** stone, clay & glass items; chemicals; printing & publishing; food items; lumber; electrical machinery; fabricated metals. **Minerals:** copper, gold, sand & gravel, diatomite. **Agricultural products:** sheep, cattle, hay, alfalfa seed, wheat, dairy items. **Avg. farm (1979 est.):** 4,495 acres. **Avg. value of farm per acre:** $104.

Highway expenditures per capita (1978): $165.19. **Persons per motor vehicle:** 1.11. **Minimum age for driver's license:** 16. **Gasoline tax:** 6¢ per gallon. **Diesel tax:** 6¢ per gallon. **Motor vehicle deaths:** 46.4 per 100,000 people.

Birthrate (1978): 16.5 per 1,000 people. **Infant mortality rate per 1,000 births (1977):** 13.9. **Physicians per 100,000 pop. (1977):** 136. **Dentists per 100,000 pop. (1977):** 49. **Acceptable hospital beds:** 5.0 per 1,000 people. **State expenditures per capita for health and hospitals (1978):** $52.51.

Education expenditures (1975-76): $459.82 per capita annually. **No. of pupils in public schools (1977 est.):** 140,000. **No. of institutions of higher learning (1976-77):** 6. **Public school expenditure per pupil in attendance (1975-76):** $1,617. **Avg. salary of public school teachers (1974-75 est.):** $12,854. **No. full-time teachers (1977 est.):** 6,050. **Educational attainment of adult population (1976):** 12.6 median yrs. of school completed; 1.2% with less than 5 years of education; 13.1% with 4 yrs. of college.

Telephones (1977): 98 per 100 people. **State Chamber of Commerce:** Nevada Chamber of Commerce Association, P.O. Box 2806, Reno, Nevada 89505.

NEW HAMPSHIRE

New Hampshire is a relatively small but well wooded and scenic state of mountains, lakes, and rapid rivers that provide a good water supply and large hydroelectric-power potential. There are three main land areas: the coastal lowlands covering the southeast corner; the New England Uplands, covering most of the southwest, west central, and south central area; and the White Mountains region in the north, which includes Mount Washington, the Northeast's highest peak (6,288 feet). Near the coast are the rough-hewn Isles of Shoals, three of which belong to New Hampshire. The state's largest harbor is at Portsmouth, near the mouth of the Piscataqua. The climate features cool summers with low humidity and winters marked by heavy snowfall. The ocean tempers the weather along the 17.8 mile Atlantic coastline, shortest of any state bordering an ocean.

About 5,000 Indians were living in the New Hampshire region before the Europeans came. The various tribes coexisted peacefully but often banded together to fight the Iroquois. The first explorers in the area are thought to have been Captain Martin Pring (1603), Samuel de Champlain (1605), and Captain John Smith (1614). Permanent settlement began in 1623, when David Thomson established Little Harbour, now in the town of Rye. Captain John Mason, who had a hand in the founding (1630) of Portsmouth, gave New Hampshire its name. Though the state was once part of Massachusetts, it became a separate royal colony in 1679; the two states had the same governor from 1699 to 1741. New Hampshire established an independent government (1776), one designed to be only temporary but which in fact operated until 1784, when the present constitution was adopted. New Hampshire was the ninth state to ratify the U.S. Constitution (1788), and the one that made that document legal.

Complicated boundary disputes with all its neighbors have marked New Hampshire's history. Royal orders eventually defined the Massachusetts (1741) and New York (1764) boundaries, while the

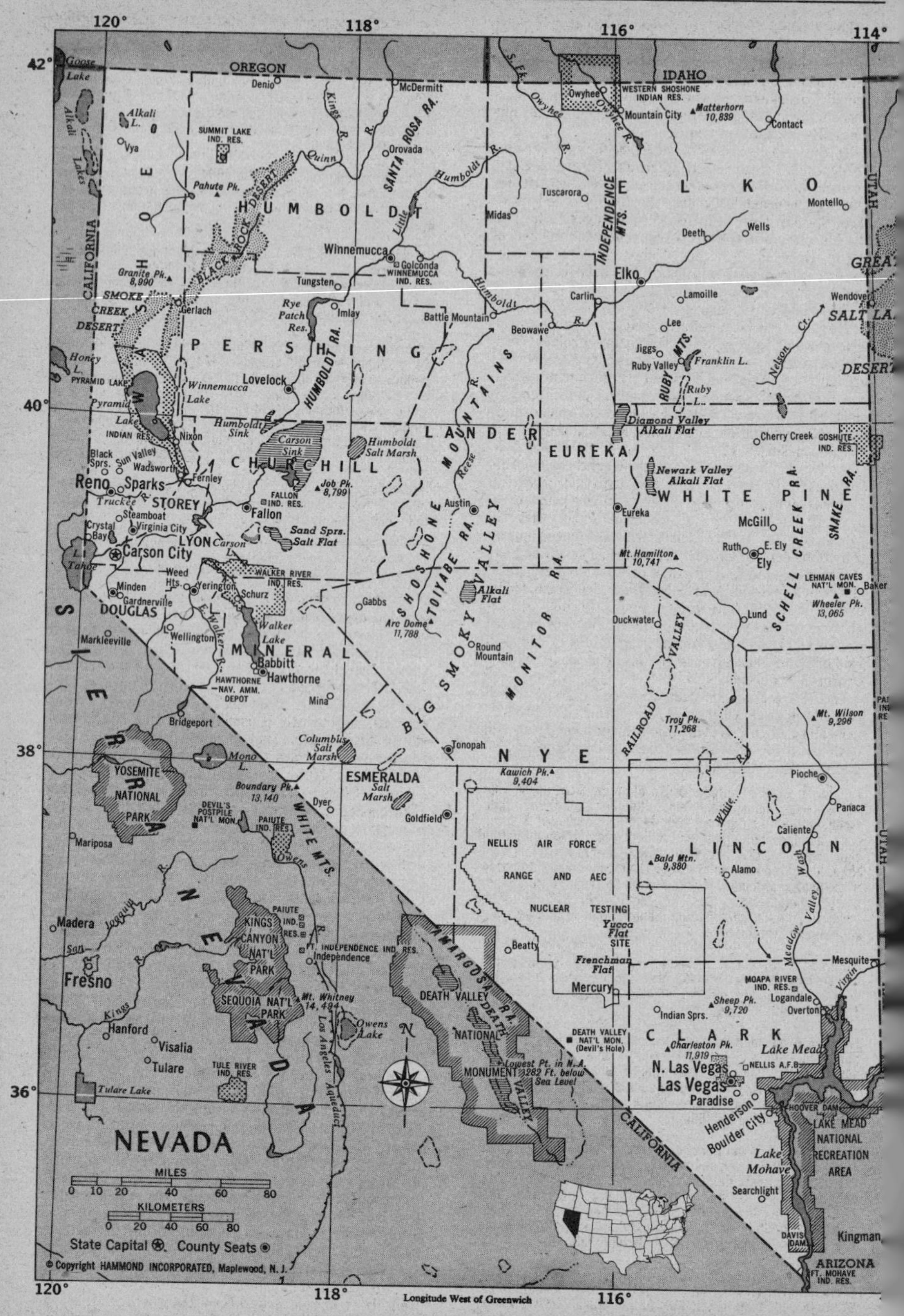
NEVADA
120° 118° 116° 114°
42° 40° 38° 36°
OREGON
IDAHO
CALIFORNIA
UTAH
ARIZONA
Goose Lake
Alkali Lakes
Alkali L.
Vya
Denio
McDermitt
Kings R.
Quinn
Orovada
SANTA ROSA RA.
Little Humboldt R.
Humboldt R.
Tuscarora
WESTERN SHOSHONE INDIAN RES.
Mountain City
Matterhorn 10,839
Contact
Owyhee
S. Fk. Owyhee R.
Owyhee R.
Montello
SUMMIT LAKE IND. RES.
Pahute Pk.
HUMBOLDT
BLACK ROCK DESERT
Midas
Deeth
Wells
ELKO
Granite Pk. 8,990
Winnemucca
Golconda
WINNEMUCCA IND. RES.
Tungsten
INDEPENDENCE MTS.
Elko
Carlin
Lamoille
Lee
Wendover
GREAT
SALT LAKE
SMOKE CREEK DESERT
Gerlach
Rye Patch Res.
Imlay
Battle Mountain
Beowawe
Humboldt R.
Jiggs
Ruby Valley
RUBY MTS.
Franklin L.
Ruby L.
Nelson Cr.
DESERT
Honey L.
PYRAMID LAKE
PERSHING
Lovelock
Humboldt Sink
LANDER
Reese R.
Diamond Valley Alkali Flat
Cherry Creek
GOSHUTE IND. RES.
Pyramid Lake
INDIAN RES.
Nixon
Black Sprs.
Sun Valley
Wadsworth
Winnemucca Lake
CHURCHILL
Humboldt Salt Marsh
Carson Sink
EUREKA
Newark Valley Alkali Flat
Eureka
WHITE PINE
McGill
SNAKE RA.
SCHELL CREEK RA.
Reno
Sparks
STOREY
Truckee
Fernley
FALLON IND. RES.
Job Pk. 8,799
Austin
SHOSHONE MOUNTAINS
TOIYABE RA.
Ruth
E. Ely
Ely
Steamboat
Virginia City
Fallon
Sand Sprs. Salt Flat
Mt. Hamilton 10,741
Crystal Bay
L. Tahoe
Carson City
LYON
Carson L.
BIG SMOKY VALLEY
Alkali Flat
Duckwater
Lund
LEHMAN CAVES NAT'L MON.
Baker
Wheeler Pk. 13,065
Weed Hts.
WALKER RIVER IND. RES.
Gabbs
MONITOR RA.
Minden
Yerington
Schurz
Arc Dome 11,788
Round Mountain
RAILROAD VALLEY
Gardnerville
DOUGLAS
Walker R.
Walker Lake
MINERAL
Wellington
Babbitt
Hawthorne
Markleeville
HAWTHORNE NAV. AMM. DEPOT
Mina
Troy Pk. 11,268
Mt. Wilson 9,296
Bridgeport
Columbus Salt Marsh
Tonopah
NYE
SIERRA
Mono L.
Boundary Pk. 13,140
Dyer
ESMERALDA
Salt Marsh
Kawich Pk. 9,404
Pioche
YOSEMITE NATIONAL PARK
DEVIL'S POSTPILE NAT'L MON.
PAIUTE IND. RES.
Goldfield
Panaca
Mariposa
WHITE MTS.
Owens R.
NELLIS AIR FORCE
RANGE AND AEC
NUCLEAR TESTING
SITE
LINCOLN
Bald Mtn. 9,380
Alamo
Caliente
NEVADA
PAIUTE IND. RES.
FT. INDEPENDENCE IND. RES.
Independence
Yucca Flat
Beatty
AMARGOSA RA.
DEATH VALLEY
Mesquite
Madera
KINGS CANYON NAT'L PARK
Fresno
San Joaquin R.
Kings R.
SEQUOIA NAT'L PARK
Mt. Whitney 14,494
Owens Lake
Los Angeles Aqueduct
Frenchman Flat
Mercury
MOAPA RIVER IND. RES.
Indian Sprs.
Sheep Pk. 9,720
Logandale
Overton
DEATH VALLEY NATIONAL MONUMENT
Lowest Pt. in N.A. 282 Ft. below Sea Level
DEATH VALLEY NAT'L MON. (Devil's Hole)
Charleston Pk. 11,919
CLARK
Lake Mead
N. Las Vegas
NELLIS A.F.B.
Hanford
Visalia
Tulare
TULE RIVER IND. RES.
Tulare Lake
Las Vegas
Paradise
Lake Mohave
Henderson
Boulder City
HOOVER DAM
LAKE MEAD NATIONAL RECREATION AREA
Searchlight
DAVIS DAM
Kingman
FT. MOHAVE IND. RES.
N
MILES
0 10 20 40 60 80
KILOMETERS
0 20 40 60 80
State Capital ✪ County Seats ⊙
© Copyright HAMMOND INCORPORATED, Maplewood, N.J.
120° 118° 116°
Longitude West of Greenwich

state's northern border was set by the Webster-Ashburton Treaty (1842), which established the international line between the United States and Canada. But not until a 1934 U.S. Supreme Court ruling was the Vermont boundary decided. A border dispute with Maine over 2,400 acres of coastal waters that began in 1974 was resolved in 1976, when the U.S. Supreme Court awarded the bulk of the disputed territory to Maine.

The state is one of the most industrialized in the nation, based on the percentage of its population working in manufacturing. The electronic, chemical, and machinery industries are major employers.

New Hampshire, with its beneficial tax climate, is experiencing an influx of new industrial development, especially in the southern sections along the Massachusetts border. In the absence of a general sales or income tax, state government is financed through the state-operated liquor monopoly, pari-mutuel betting on racing, state taxes on business profits and rooms and meals. Education is funded by the local property tax.

Tourism, meanwhile, has mushroomed into an annual $500-million business. One fifth of the land is in public parklands, including 724,000 acres of the White Mountain National Forest, which extends into Maine. Hiking, boating, and camping are popular, and the state has more than 60 ski lifts. Attractions include Strawbery Banke, a preservation project that has restored about 30 buildings and homes of the original settlement at Portsmouth, N.H., the Kancamagus Highway between Lincoln and Conway, Daniel Webster's birthplace near Franklin, the Mount Washington Cog Railway, the first (1869) in North America, and the famous "Old Man of the Mountain" granite head profile at Franconia, the state's official emblem.

New Hampshire today functions as an exceptionally democratic entity, with the state's 222 towns (nicknamed "little republics") using the traditional town meeting to provide a forum for all voters. The state, which for decades had a sometimes disputed reputation as a political bellwether, has been relieved of its position as the first to hold a presidential primary by Puerto Rico, which in 1980 held its first such election.

Nuclear power remains controversial in New Hampshire. In 1976 construction began on a nuclear power plant in the environmentally sensitive seacoast area at Seabrook. Anti-nuclear power forces from all over New England focused on the issue, and in May 1977, a mass occupation of the construction site resulted in the arrest of 1,414 demonstrators by authorities. In October 1979 and again in May 1980, protestors renewed attempts to occupy the site, but their repeated assaults were repelled by state troopers and National Guardsmen armed with nightsticks and high-pressure water hoses. Some injuries were reported.

Full name: State of New Hampshire. **Origin of name:** From the English county of Hampshire. **Inhabitant:** New Hampshirite. **Capital:** Concord. **State motto:** Live Free or Die. **Flag:** State seal on a blue field. **Seal:** A reproduction of Revolutionary War frigate "Raleigh" is surrounded by nine stars in a laurel wreath to symbolize victory. **Flower:** Purple lilac. **Bird:** Purple finch. **Tree:** White birch. **Songs:** "Old New Hampshire" & "New Hampshire, My New Hampshire." **Nickname:** Granite State.

Governor: Hugh J. Gallen. **Annual salary:** $44,520. **Term:** 2 years. **Current term expires:** Jan. 1981. **Voting requirements:** 18 yrs. old & U.S. citizen; registered voter and state resident. **U.S. Congressmen:** 2. **Entered Union:** 1788 (9th state).

Location & boundaries: New England state: bounded on the north by Canada; on the east by Maine & the Atlantic Ocean; on the south by Massachusetts; & on the west by Vermont, Canada & the Connecticut River. **Total area:** 9,304 sq. mi. (ranks 44th). **Extreme length:** 180 mi. **Extreme breadth:** 93 mi. **Coastline:** 17.8 mi. **Chief rivers:** Connecticut, Merrimack, Androscoggin. **Major lake:** Winnipesaukee. **No. of counties:** 10.

Population (1979 est.): 887,000 (ranks 42nd). **Pop. increase (1970-79):** 20.2%. **Places over 25,000 pop.:** 3. **Places over 100,000:** None. **Largest cities:** Manchester, Nashua, Concord. **Pop. density:** 95.3 per sq. mi. (ranks 19th). **Pop. projection 1985:** 935,000. **Pop. distribution:** 36.6% metropolitan; 63.4% nonmetropolitan. **White:** 99.4%. **Black:** 0.3%. **Other:** 0.3%. **Marriage rate (1977):** 10.4 per 1,000 people. **Divorce rate:** 5.2 per 1,000 people.

State finances (1978). Revenue: $742,887,000. **Expenditures:** $708,329,000. **State taxes:** $275.99 per capita. **State personal income tax:** No, except on interest & dividends. **Public debt (1978):** $482.30 per capita. **Federal aid (1979):** $328.75 per capita. **Personal income (1979 est.):** $8,231.

Sectors of the economy (% of labor force employed in 1970): Manufacturing (36%), Wholesale and retail trade (19%), Government (14%), Educational Services (8%), Construction (7%), Services (6%). **Leading products:** leather items, electrical & other machinery, textile mill items, paper items, food items, printing & publishing. **Agricultural products:** dairy items, eggs, cattle, hay, apples, potatoes. **Avg. farm (1979 est.):** 193 acres. **Avg. value of farm per acre:** $802.

Highway expenditures per capita (1978): $122.49. **Persons per motor vehicle:** 1.30. **Minimum age for driver's license:** 16. **Gasoline tax:** 11¢ per gallon. **Diesel tax:** 11¢ per gallon. **Motor vehicle deaths:** 19.6 per 100,000 people.

Birthrate (1978): 14.3 per 1,000 people. **Infant mortality rate per 1,000 births (1977):** 10.2. **Physicians per 100,000 pop. (1977):** 161. **Dentists per 100,000 pop. (1977):** 52. **Acceptable hospital beds:** 5.9 per 1,000 people. **State expenditures per capita for health and hospitals (1978):** $63.95.

Education expenditures (1975-76): $389.87 per capita annually. **No. of pupils in public schools (1977 est.):** 173,000. **No. of institutions of higher learning (1976-77):** 24. **Public school expenditure per pupil in attendance (1975-76):** $1,493. **Avg. salary of public school teachers (1974-75 est.):** $10,016. **No. full-time teachers (1977 est.):** 11,180. **Educational attainment of adult population (1976):** 12.6 median yrs. of school completed; 1.1% with less than 5 years of education; 15.3% with 4 yrs. of college.

Telephones (1977): 75 per 100 people. **State Chamber of Commerce:** Business and Industry Association of New Hampshire, 23 School Street, Concord, New Hampshire 03301.

NEW JERSEY

New Jersey's importance is disproportionate to its modest size. Strategically located, amid many rich markets, the state has extraordinary transportation facilities and a correspondingly large volume of interstate traffic: railway trackage, highways, tunnels, and bridges abound. The nation's most densely populated state, it is a manufacturing giant with limited but valuable farming and fishing industries.

Many sandy beaches, coupled with a generally mild climate marked by ocean breezes, have made New Jersey popular with vacationers, and tourism is today a major industry. Attractions include such resort areas as Atlantic City and Wildwood, as well as the Thomas A. Edison National Historic Site in West Orange, the Walt Whitman House in Camden, the Garden State Arts Center in Telegraph Hill Park, and several ski areas.

Before the coming of the Europeans, the region was inhabited by Lenni-Lenape (later called Delaware) Indians of the Algonquian group. The area's early colonial history is bound up with that of New York (then New Netherland), of which it was a part. With the passing of power from Dutch to English hands (1664), New Jersey began to emerge as a more distinct entity. Proprietorship of lands

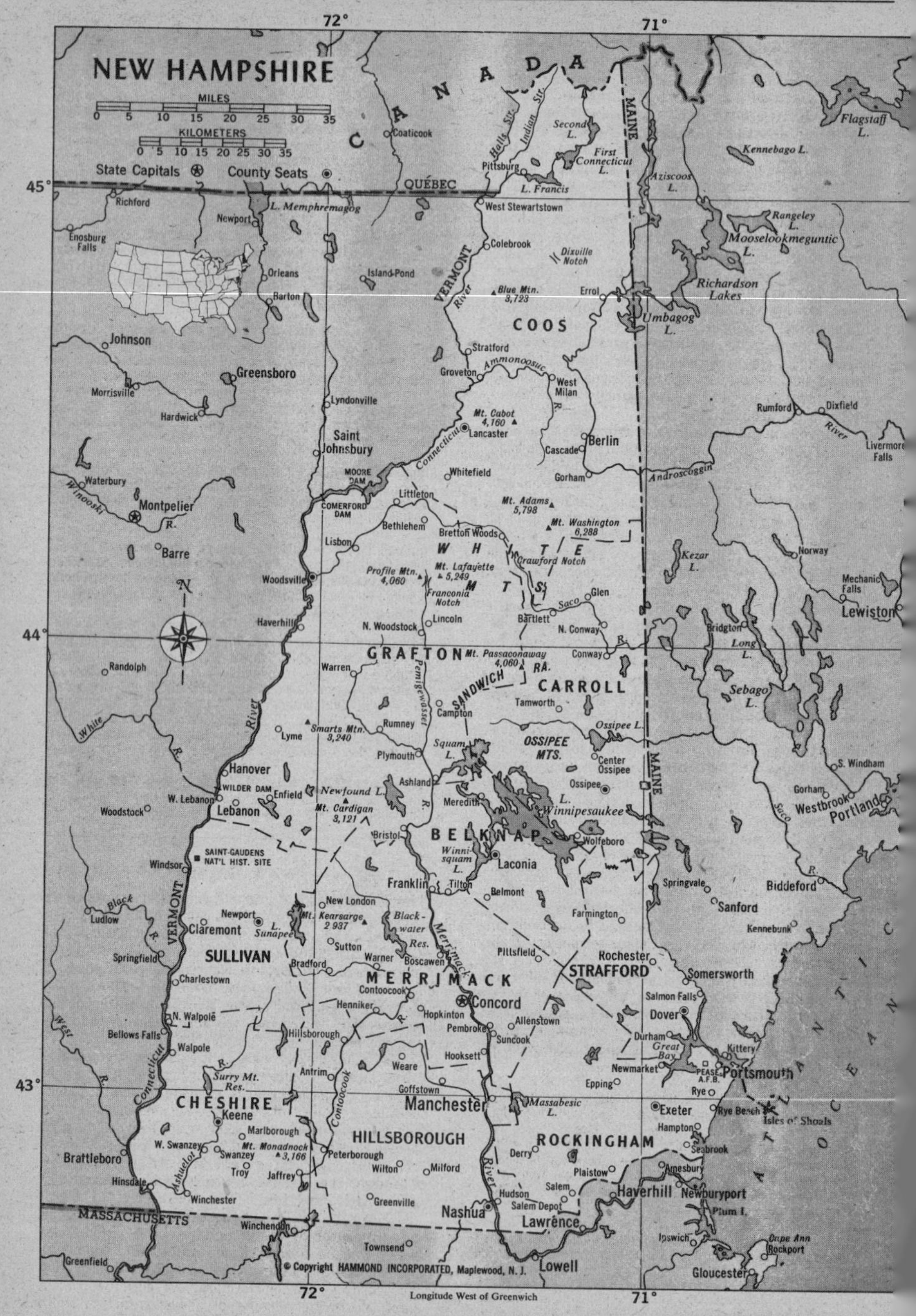

NEW HAMPSHIRE
MILES
0 5 10 15 20 25 30 35
KILOMETERS
0 5 10 15 20 25 30 35
State Capitals ⊛ County Seats ◉
45°
44°
43°
72°
71°
CANADA
QUÉBEC
VERMONT
MAINE
MASSACHUSETTS
ATLANTIC OCEAN
Longitude West of Greenwich
COOS
GRAFTON
CARROLL
BELKNAP
SULLIVAN
MERRIMACK
STRAFFORD
CHESHIRE
HILLSBOROUGH
ROCKINGHAM
WHITE MTS.
OSSIPEE MTS.
SANDWICH RA.
Coaticook
Richford
Newport
Enosburg Falls
Orleans
Barton
Island Pond
L. Memphremagog
Johnson
Greensboro
Morrisville
Hardwick
Lyndonville
Saint Johnsbury
Waterbury
Winooski R.
Montpelier
Barre
MOORE DAM
COMERFORD DAM
Woodsville
Haverhill
Randolph
Woodstock
Ludlow
Springfield
Charlestown
N. Walpole
Bellows Falls
Walpole
Brattleboro
Hinsdale
Winchester
Greenfield
Winchendon
Townsend
Pittsburg
Second L.
First Connecticut L.
L. Francis
West Stewartstown
Colebrook
Dixville Notch
Errol
Blue Mtn. 3,723
Stratford
Groveton
West Milan
Mt. Cabot 4,160
Lancaster
Cascade
Berlin
Gorham
Whitefield
Littleton
Bethlehem
Bretton Woods
Mt. Adams 5,798
Mt. Washington 6,288
Crawford Notch
Lisbon
Profile Mtn. 4,060
Mt. Lafayette 5,249
Franconia Notch
Glen
Saco
Bartlett
N. Conway
N. Woodstock
Lincoln
Conway
Warren
Mt. Passaconaway 4,060
Tamworth
Rumney
Campton
Smarts Mtn. 3,240
Lyme
Plymouth
Squam L.
Center Ossipee
Ossipee L.
Ossipee
Hanover
Ashland
Meredith
WILDER DAM
W. Lebanon
Enfield
Newfound L.
Mt. Cardigan 3,121
Winnipesaukee
Lebanon
Bristol
Wolfeboro
SAINT-GAUDENS NAT'L HIST. SITE
Winnisquam L.
Laconia
Windsor
Franklin
Tilton
Belmont
New London
Mt. Kearsarge 2,937
Black-water Res.
Newport
L. Sunapee
Claremont
Farmington
Sutton
Warner
Boscawen
Pittsfield
Rochester
Somersworth
Bradford
Contoocook
Henniker
Hopkinton
Concord
Pembroke
Allenstown
Suncook
Durham
Salmon Falls
Dover
Great Bay
Hillsborough
Weare
Hooksett
Newmarket
Kittery
PEASE A.F.B.
Portsmouth
Antrim
Surry Mt. Res.
Goffstown
Epping
Rye
Keene
Manchester
Massabesic L.
Exeter
Rye Beach
Marlborough
Hampton
W. Swanzey
Mt. Monadnock 3,166
Peterborough
Derry
Seabrook
Swanzey
Troy
Jaffrey
Wilton
Milford
Plaistow
Amesbury
Greenville
Hudson
Salem
Haverhill
Newburyport
Nashua
Salem Depot
Lawrence
Plum I.
Ipswich
Greenfield
Townsend
Lowell
Gloucester
Cape Ann Rockport
Isles of Shoals
Connecticut River
Ammonoosuc
Androscoggin River
Saco R.
Merrimack R.
Pemigewasset R.
Contoocook R.
Ashuelot R.
West R.
Black R.
White R.
Connecticut R.
Kezar L.
Umbago g L.
Richardson Lakes
Mooselookmeguntic L.
Rangeley L.
Kennebago L.
Flagstaff L.
Aziscoos L.
Norway
Rumford
Dixfield
Livermore Falls
Lewiston
Mechanic Falls
Bridgton
Long L.
Sebago L.
S. Windham
Gorham
Westbrook
Portland
Springvale
Sanford
Biddeford
Kennebunk
Salmon Falls
Winnisquam
© Copyright HAMMOND INCORPORATED, Maplewood, N.J.

between the Hudson and Delaware Rivers was granted by James II to Lord John Berkeley and Sir George Carteret, who then offered territory to settlers in return for sworn allegiance to the king and payment of quitrent (fixed rent). Berkeley eventually sold (1676) his land share to a group of Quakers, who then agreed with Carteret to divide the region into East and West Jersey, the line running southeastward from the Delaware River near the Water Gap to the Atlantic Ocean near Little Egg Harbor. Carteret owned East Jersey—about three-eighths of the total area—until his death (1680), while West Jersey became the nation's first Quaker settlement. Control of both Jerseys eventually reverted to England which governed it jointly with New York from 1702 to 1738, when Lewis Morris was made governor of New Jersey alone.

The region remained turbulent for many years. A decade of virtual lawlessness began in 1745, ended only by the advent of the French and Indian War of the mid-1750s, which served to unify New Jerseyans against a common enemy. Because of its location between New York City and Philadelphia, New Jersey was the scene of many important battles of the American Revolution. In 1783 Princeton served briefly as the nation's capital. Statehood dates from 1787.

After the Revolution, many scientific breakthroughs took place in the state, and the country's first model factory town was founded in 1791 at the site of the present Paterson, under the auspices of Alexander Hamilton's Society for the Establishment of Useful Manufactures. (A few years later, Hamilton was killed in Weehawken in a notorious duel with Aaron Burr.)

The state was sharply divided by the Civil War. Most New Jerseyans accepted the ending of slavery, but many businessmen were against the war because of the profitable Southern market. When peace came, the state's population and economy continued their rapid growth, interrupted by the Panic of 1873. Powerful special-interest groups grasped undue political control, bringing a counterwave of reform under Governor Woodrow Wilson, who was elected in 1910. But after Wilson left in 1913 to become president, much of the impetus toward reform in the state withered away.

The institution (1966) of a general sales tax has helped lighten the state's severe financial problems, as has the March 1970 hike in that tax, from three to five percent. One side effect of these measures has been to detract somewhat from the state's traditionally favorable tax climate which, together with streamlined corporation laws, has been a vital weapon in the continuing battle with other states for new industry. New Jersey enacted an income tax in 1976 as a replacement for portions of local property tax burdens, and in December 1977 the tax was made permanent.

Large-scale urban-renewal projects that would eliminate blight while creating jobs are seen as a means of alleviating a major part of the problem. A vast $300-million Hackensack Meadowlands project built on land from ten different north Jersey towns opened in 1976, with the National Football League Giants and the Cosmos professional soccer team as the major long-term tenants and including a racetrack. In 1977 the New York Nets announced plans to move to a permanent home to be constructed in the complex. Port Jersey, a 707-acre, $160-million industrial center with a 17-berth terminal for containerships has been planned for the New Jersey side of Upper New York Bay, adjoining the U.S. Military Ocean Terminal in Bayonne.

In mid-1977 the courts lifted the ban on drilling East Coast offshore oil leases, and exploration commenced by the end of the year. After six months there had been no announcement of any profitable strikes in the Baltimore Canyon off the New Jersey Coast. Since that time, however, both Texaco Inc. and the U.S. Geological Survey have announced offshore gas finds.

In 1976 New Jersey passed a constitutional amendment authorizing the establishment of gambling casinos in Atlantic City as a means of rejuvenating the ailing resort and rebuilding the tourist industry in general. The first casino opened in May 1978 and has proved successful. Since then additional casinos have opened and others are being constructed.

Full name: State of New Jersey. **Origin of name:** From Channel Island of Jersey. **Inhabitant:** New Jerseyite. **Capital:** Trenton. **State motto:** Liberty & Prosperity. **Flag:** State seal on yellow field. **Seal:** Three plows & goddess Ceres holding a cornucopia represent agriculture; a horse's head lies above sovereign's helmet. **Flower:** Purple violet. **Bird:** Eastern goldfinch. **Tree:** Red oak. **Song:** (unofficial) "New Jersey Loyalty Song." **Nickname:** Garden State.

Governor: Brendan T. Byrne. **Annual salary:** $65,000. **Term:** 4 years. **Current term expires:** Jan. 1982. **Voting requirements:** 18 yrs. old & U.S. citizen; resident of state & county 30 days. **U.S. Congressmen:** 15. **Entered Union:** 1787 (3rd state).

Location & boundaries: Middle Atlantic state: bounded on the north by New York; on the east by New York, the Hudson River & the Atlantic Ocean; on the south by Delaware Bay; on the southwest by Delaware & the Delaware River; & on the west by Pennsylvania & the Delaware River. **Total area:** 7,836 sq. mi. (ranks 46th). **Extreme length:** 166 mi. **Extreme breadth:** 57 mi. **Coastline:** 130 mi. **Chief rivers:** Raritan, Delaware, Hudson, Passaic. **Major lakes:** Hopatcong, Budd, Culvers. **No. of counties:** 21.

Population (1979 est.): 7,332,000 (ranks 9th). **Pop. increase (1970-79):** 2.2%. **Places over 25,000 pop.:** 64. **Places over 100,000:** 4. **Largest cities:** Newark, Jersey City, Paterson, Elizabeth. **Pop. density:** 935.7 per sq. mi. (ranks 1st). **Pop. projection 1985:** 7,741,000. **Pop. distribution:** 92.1% metropolitan; 7.9% nonmetropolitan. **White:** 88.6%. **Black:** 10.7%. **Other:** 0.7%. **Marriage rate (1977):** 6.8 per 1,000 people. **Divorce rate:** 2.8 per 1,000 people.

State finances (1978). Revenue: $7,437,860,000. **Expenditures:** $6,936,901,000. **State taxes:** $469.48 per capita. **State personal income tax:** Yes. **Public debt (1978):** $646.02 per capita. **Federal aid (1979):** $370.35 per capita. **Personal income (1979 est.):** $9,702.

Sectors of the economy (% of labor force employed in 1970): Manufacturing (32%), Wholesale and retail trade (19%), Government (14%), Services (7%), Educational Services (7%), Construction (5%). **Leading products:** chemicals, machinery, food items, primary & fabricated metals, transportation equipment, apparel. **Agricultural products:** dairy items, cattle, tomatoes, potatoes, corn, hay, asparagus. **Fishing:** clams, flounder, oysters. **Avg. farm (1979 est.):** 130 acres. **Avg. value of farm per acre:** $2,222.

Highway expenditures per capita (1978): $43.13. **Persons per motor vehicle:** 1.54. **Minimum age for driver's license:** 17. **Gasoline tax:** 8¢ per gallon. **Diesel tax:** 8¢ per gallon. **Motor vehicle deaths:** 15.3 per 100,000 people.

Birthrate (1978): 12.8 per 1,000 people. **Infant mortality rate per 1,000 births (1977):** 14.3. **Physicians per 100,000 pop. (1977):** 173. **Dentists per 100,000 pop. (1977):** 60. **Acceptable hospital beds:** 6.2 per 1,000 people. **State expenditures per capita for health and hospitals (1978):** $57.66.

Education expenditures (1975-76): $440.96 per capita annually. **No. of pupils in public schools (1977 est.):** 1,406,000. **No. of institutions of higher learning (1976-77):** 65. **Public school expenditure per pupil in attendance (1975-76):** $2,122. **Avg. salary of public school teachers:** Not available. **No. full-time teachers (1977 est.):** 91,320. **Educational attainment of adult population (1976):** 12.4 median yrs. of school completed; 2.7% with less than 5 years of education; 14.9% with 4 yrs. of college.

NEW JERSEY
MILES
KILOMETERS
State Capitals
County Seats
Longitude West of Greenwich
© Copyright HAMMOND INCORPORATED, Maplewood, N.J.
ATLANTIC OCEAN
Delaware Bay
DELAWARE
MARYLAND
PENNSYLVANIA
NEW YORK
KITTATINNY MT.
PINE BARRENS
BERGEN
PASSAIC
SUSSEX
WARREN
MORRIS
ESSEX
HUDSON
UNION
HUNTERDON
SOMERSET
MIDDLESEX
MERCER
MONMOUTH
OCEAN
BURLINGTON
CAMDEN
GLOUCESTER
SALEM
ATLANTIC
CUMBERLAND
CAPE MAY
Newark
Jersey City
Paterson
Trenton
PHILADELPHIA
Wilmington
Camden
Atlantic City
New Brunswick
Elizabeth
Long Island
Brooklyn
NEW YORK
Staten I.
Sandy Hook
Asbury Park
Long Branch
Toms River
Lakewood
Point Pleasant
Barnegat
Barnegat Light
Long Beach
Ship Bottom
Beach Haven
Little Egg Inlet
Ocean City
Sea Isle City
Avalon
Stone Harbor
Wildwood
Cape May
Cape May Court House
Vineland
Bridgeton
Millville
Salem
Woodstown
Glassboro
Clayton
Elmer
Hammonton
Mays Landing
Egg Harbor City
Buena
Northfield
Pleasantville
Linwood
Somers Point
Brigantine
Ventnor City
Margate City
Great Egg Harbor Inlet
Woodbine
Port Norris
Cedarville
Greenwich
Dover
Smyrna
Greensboro
Middletown
Elkton
Newark
Oxford
Chester
West Chester
Phoenixville
Norristown
Hatboro
Doylestown
Levittown
Bristol
Morrisville
Trenton
W. Trenton
Hightstown
Allentown
Bordentown
Florence
Burlington
Willingboro
Riverside
Palmyra
Pennsauken
Collingswood
Cherry Hill
Haddonfield
Audubon
Gloucester City
Woodbury
Somerdale
Lindenwold
Berlin
Pine Hill
Williamstown
Batsto
Mullica R.
Great Egg Harbor R.
Maurice R.
Cohansey R.
Delaware R.
Schuylkill River
Brandywine Cr.
C. & D. Canal
Sassafras R.
Chester
Elk R.
Tuckahoe R.
Choptank Cr.
Ben Davis Pt.
Deep Water Pt.
Egg Island Pt.
Hereford Inlet
Villas
Seabrook
Vineland
Union L.
Dorothy
Absecon
Tuckerton
New Gretna
Little Egg Harbor
Great Bay
Mullica R.
Forked River
Manahawkin
Beachwood
Seaside Park
Seaside Hts.
Lavallette
Island Hts.
Island Beach
Barnegat Bay
Manasquan
Neptune
Bradley Beach
Belmar
Sea Girt
Spring L. Hts.
Brick
Candlewood
New Egg
Freehold
Eatontown
W. Long Branch
Red Bank
Rumson
Little Silver
FORT MONMOUTH
Keansburg
Atlantic Highlands
Middletown
Strathmore
Keyport
Spotswood
Sayreville
South River
Old Bridge
Cranbury
Princeton
Pennington
Hopewell
Lambertville
Flemington
Frenchtown
Manville
Raritan
Somerville
Bound Brook
Middlesex
Metuchen
Edison
Perth Amboy
Woodbridge
Rahway
Linden
Westfield
Plainfield
Scotch Plains
Summit
Bernardsville
High Bridge
Round Valley Res.
Spruce Run Res.
Alpha
Phillipsburg
Easton
Washington
Belvidere
Hackettstown
Morris Plains
Morristown
Parsippany
Denville
Dover
Wharton
Budd L.
Boonton
Livingston
Madison
MORRISTOWN NAT'L HIST. PARK
PICATINNY ARSENAL
Montclair
E. Orange
Irvington
Newark
Jersey City
Bloomfield
Passaic
Clifton
Hackensack
Cliffside Park
Paterson
Dumont
Oradell Res.
Ridgewood
Hawthorne
Wyckoff
Oakland
Butler
Ringwood
Wanaque Res.
Greenwood L.
Suffern
Ramsey
Warwick
Haverstraw
Ossining
Peekskill
Chester
Port Jervis
Matamoras
Delaware River
Montague
High Pt. 1,803
DELAWARE WATER GAP NAT'L REC. AREA
Layton
Sussex
Branchville
Hamburg
Franklin
Newton
Sparta
L. Mohawk
L. Hopatcong
Hopatcong
Blairstown
Stroudsburg
Delaware Water Gap
Bangor
Pequest R.
Musconetcong R.
Paulins Kill
Wallkill R.
Ramapo R.
Hackensack River
Hudson River
Passaic R.
Millstone R.
Manasquan R.
Toms R.
Rancocas Cr.
Crosswicks Cr.
Neshaminy Cr.
Oldmans Cr.
Raccoon Cr.
FORT DIX
McGUIRE A.F.B.
LAKEHURST NAVAL AIR STA.
Lakehurst
Wrightstown
New Egypt
Mt. Holly
Medford
Medford Lakes
Moorestown
Mercerville
Smyrna
N
75° 30' 75° 30' 74°
41° 30' 40° 30' 39°
76° 30' 75° 30' 74°
Inset:
BERGEN
PASSAIC
ESSEX
HUDSON
UNION
MIDDLESEX
MONMOUTH
N.Y.
NEW YORK
Wanaque
Ramsey
Oakland
Wyckoff
Upper Saddle Riv.
Park Ridge
Waldwick
Westwood
L. Tappan
Pompton Lakes
Ridgewood
Oradell Res.
New Milford
Dumont
Tenafly
Bergenfield
Englewood
Ft. Lee
Cliffside Park
Teaneck
Hackensack
Lodi
Garfield
Paramus
Fair Lawn
Paterson
Clifton
Passaic
Little Falls
Totowa
Elmwood Park
Cedar Grove
Verona
Nutley
Belleville
Lyndhurst
N. Bergen
Union City
Hoboken
Jersey City
Newark
NEWARK AIRPORT
Montclair
Bloomfield
W. Orange
Orange
E. Orange
Maplewood
Millburn
Irvington
Kearny
EDISON NAT'L HIST. SITE
Union
Roselle
Elizabeth
Linden
Rahway
Carteret
Woodbridge
Perth Amboy
S. Amboy
Staten Island
Brooklyn
Long Island
Bayonne
STATUE OF LIBERTY N.M.
Upper Bay
Lower Bay
Newark Bay
The Narrows
FT. WADSWORTH
FT. HANCOCK
Sandy Hook
Raritan Bay
Arthur Kill
Kill Van Kull
Hackensack R.
Passaic R.
Hudson R.
Manhattan
Union Beach
Keyport
Keansburg
Matawan
Hazlet
Atlantic Highlands
Highlands
N.J.
Wynona
N. Haledon
Haledon
Wayne
Glen Rock
Rock Ridge
8 mi.
4 km.

Telephones (1977): 84 per 100 people. **State Chamber of Commerce:** New Jersey State Chamber of Commerce, 5 Commerce Street, Newark, New Jersey 07102.

NEW MEXICO

New Mexico is a land of great contrast. It is rich in history yet in the forefront of the Atomic Era—the world's first A-bomb, produced at Los Alamos, was exploded (1945) at Trinity Site near Alamogordo. Three major cultures intermingle—Spanish, Indian, and Anglo-American—and within each is a variety of types and subcultures.

Indians are thought to have lived in this region between 20,000 and 25,000 years ago. In 1975, a total of 100,280 Indians—mainly Navajo, Apache, and Pueblo—were to be found in New Mexico, living much as their ancestors had, despite a few modern trappings. Within the state is the country's largest Indian reservation (more than 16 million acres), which is inhabited by Navajos. At Gallup each August is held the colorful Inter-tribal Indian Ceremonial.

Sharp contrasts also mark the face of the land, a complex blending of deserts, rugged blue-rimmed mesas, and forested mountain regions, with an average mean elevation of 5,700 feet. The generally thin, dry air cools rapidly at night, making for wide daily temperature variations. Because of the great ranges in altitude and rainfall, the state supports six distinct life zones and a correspondingly large variety of plants and animals.

Water is generally scarce in New Mexico, and irrigation difficult. Much of the land, however, is devoted to grazing, sustaining a sizable ranching industry. Cotton lint is the main crop in the irrigated areas. In the dry-farming regions (about two thirds of the state's farmland), hay and wheat are among the significant outputs. Dry-farmers are gradually shifting to irrigation, as more dams and wells are built. In the river valleys, especially along the Rio Grande, fruits and vegetables are grown.

Francisco Vásquez de Coronado, in search of the fabled "Seven Cities of Cibola," explored (1540-42) the region that became New Mexico, but found no treasure. In 1598 the first Spanish colony was established at the Pueblo of San Juan de Los Caballeros. Santa Fe was founded in 1610 and made provincial capital. Roman Catholic missionaries set up schools in the region. Subjected to harsh treatment and forbidden to worship their gods, the Pueblo Indians revolted in 1680; Spain regained control in 1692. Mexico governed from 1821 until the United States took possession via the 1848 Mexican treaty and the 1853 Gadsden Purchase. Vital to early-day commerce, the Santa Fe Trail between New Mexico and Missouri was opened in 1821; today, east of Santa Fe, the Trail is still in use as U.S. 85.

The surrender (1886) of Geronimo terminated the Apache Wars and marked the virtual end of area Indian troubles. During the 1880s, the mining and ranching industries boomed. New Mexico entered the Union in 1912.

New Mexico is one of the largest energy-producing states in the nation. The state is the leading producer of potash and uranium. It has almost half of the nation's uranium reserves and large deposits of low-sulphur coal and natural gas. Historically, it has been a massive exporter of energy, sending out of the state more than half the electricity it has produced, about three-quarters of the gas generated and almost all of the petroleum pumped in the state.

Since 1945, the state has been a leader in the field of energy research and development. It helps the nation solve its energy needs through research conducted by Los Alamos Scientific Laboratory and Sandia Laboratories in the nuclear, solar and geothermal fields. Northwest New Mexico is presently undergoing a massive coal gasification project that will provide additional energy for the Western United States.

The increased demand for domestic energy and the pattern of growth it shares with other states of the sunbelt have brought problems as well as prosperity. School systems are overcrowded and there is a housing shortage in some places. Urban sprawl is spreading around Grants, Albuquerque and Santa Fe, intensifying the contrast between the relatively low economic level of the rural areas and the prosperity of some cities and mining communities. As a result, political power, which has been in the hands of agricultural interests (ranching is still the state's chief industry), is shifting to represent newcomers from out of state and the growing Mexican-American population.

Tourist attractions in New Mexico include the Carlsbad Caverns National Park, Inscription Rock at El Morro National Monument, and the ruins of Fort Union, which in its day was one of the largest U.S. military outposts on the southwest frontier. At Lincoln are mementos of Billy the Kid, the outlaw who was involved (1878) in the Lincoln County cattle war. And near Aztec are Indian ruins, including a 500-room, E-shaped pueblo dating from A.D. 800-1200.

In February 1980 a prison revolt at the New Mexico state penitentiary left more than 30 inmates dead and about 90 prisoners and guards injured. During the 36-hour siege, convicts turned on one another, torturing and killing suspected informers. The worst U.S. prison riot since that at Attica, New York, nine years before, it focused national attention on the explosive atmosphere in many of the nation's prisons.

Full name: State of New Mexico. **Origin of name:** From the Aztec, Mexitli, meaning "War God." **Inhabitant:** New Mexican. **Capital:** Santa Fe. **State motto:** Crescit Eundo (It Grows As It Goes). **Flag:** Stylized red sun, symbol of Zia pueblo of Indians, on a yellow field. **Seal:** Two eagles represent annexation of New Mexico by the United States; scroll under eagles bears state's motto. **Flower:** Yucca. **Bird:** Roadrunner. **Tree:** Piñon or nut pine. **Gem:** Turquoise. **Vegetable:** Chile and Pinto Beans. **Song:** "O, Fair New Mexico." **Nickname:** Land of Enchantment.

Governor: Bruce King. **Annual salary:** $48,000. **Term:** 4 years. **Current term expires:** Dec. 1982. **Voting requirements:** 18 yrs. old & U.S. citizen; registered state resident 42 days (30 days for Pres. election). **U.S. Congressmen:** 2. **Entered Union:** 1912 (47th state).

Location & boundaries: Southwestern state: bounded on the north by Colorado; on the east by Oklahoma & Texas; on the south by Texas & Mexico; & on the west by Arizona. **Total area:** 121,666 sq. mi. (ranks 5th). **Extreme length:** 391 mi. **Extreme breadth:** 352 mi. **Chief rivers:** Rio Grande, San Juan, Pecos, Canadian. **Major lakes:** Navajo, Conchas, Cochiti, Elephant Butte Reservoir. **No. of counties:** 32.

Population (1979 est.): 1,241,000 (ranks 37th). **Pop. increase (1970-79):** 22.1%. **Places over 25,000 pop.:** 7. **Places over 100,000:** 1. **Largest cities:** Albuquerque, Santa Fe, Las Cruces. **Pop. density:** 10.2 per sq. mi. (ranks 44th). **Pop. projection 1985:** 1,361,000. **Pop. distribution:** 33.6% metropolitan; 66.4% non-metropolitan. **White:** 90.1%. **Indian:** 7.2%. **Black:** 1.9%. **Other:** 0.8%. **Marriage rate (1977):** 10.5 per 1,000 people. **Divorce rate:** 7.7 per 1,000 people.

State finances (1978). Revenue: $1,638,729,000. **Expenditures:** $1,329,250,000. **State taxes:** $627.95 per capita. **State personal income tax:** Yes. **Public debt (1978):** $284.47 per capita. **Federal aid (1979):** $431.43 per capita. **Personal income (1979 est.):** $7,294.

NEW MEXICO
UTAH
COLORADO
OKLA.
TEXAS
ARIZONA
MEXICO
CHIHUAHUA
SONORA
San Juan
Rio Arriba
Taos
Colfax
Union
Navajo
McKinley
Sandoval
Santa Fe
Mora
Harding
Valencia
Bernalillo
Torrance
Guadalupe
Quay
Curry
Catron
Socorro
De Baca
Roosevelt
Lincoln
Chaves
Grant
Sierra
Dona Ana
Luna
Otero
Eddy
Lea
Hidalgo
San Miguel
Monticello
Mt. Wilson 14,246
Silverton
Crestone Pk. 14,294
Great Sand Dunes Nat'l Mon.
La Junta
Center
Del Norte
Monte Vista
Alamosa
Blanca Pk. 14,317
Walsenburg
Huerfano R.
Purgatoire R.
Hovenweep Nat'l Mon.
Yucca House N.M.
Cortez
Mesa Verde Nat'l Park
Durango
Pagosa Sprs.
Trinidad
Only point in U.S. common to 4 states.
Aztec Ruins N.M.
Dulce
Chama
Raton
Dry Cimarron R.
Farmington
Aztec
Blanco
Navajo Res.
Jicarilla
Tierra Amarilla
Questa
Cimarron
Maxwell
Clayton
Shiprock
Bloomfield
Wheeler Pk. 13,161
Eagle Nest L.
Carrizo Cr.
Toadlena
Canjilon
Arroyo Hondo
Taos
Springer
Capulin Mtn. Nat'l Mon.
Chuska Mts.
Indian
El Rito
Pueblo
Ranches of Taos
Canyon De Chelly Nat'l Mon.
Chaco Canyon Nat'l Mon.
Velarde
Dixon
Penasco
Wagon Mound
Reservation
La Jara
San Juan Pueblo
Espanola
Truchas
Mora
Ft. Union N.M.
Roy
Mosquero
Cuba
Los Alamos
Chimayo
Continental
Crownpoint
Bandelier Nat'l Mon.
Pueblo I.R.
Tesuque
Watrous
Gamerco
Puerco
Ft. Wingate Army Depot
Jemez Pueblo
Santa Fe
Glorieta
Las Vegas
Manuelito
Gallup
Thoreau
San Mateo
Pueblo Ind. Res.
San Felipe
Pecos
Pecos Nat'l Mon.
Conchas Res.
Conchas Dam
Logan
Bluewater
Milan
Mt. Taylor 11,389
Corrales
Santo Domingo Pueblo
Rowe
Ute Res.
Zuni R.
Grants
Paguate
Bernalillo
Santa Fe
San Miguel
Zuni
San Rafael
El Morro N.M.
Acomita
Albuquerque
Anton Chico
Santa Rosa
Tucumcari
Zuni Ind. Res.
Lava Beds
Acoma
Pueblo Ind. Res.
Kirtland A.F.B.
Isleta
Tijeras
Moriarty
Guadalupe
Quemado
Los Lunas
Estancia
Laguna del Perro
Encino
Alamogordo Res.
Melrose
Clovis
Belen
Mountainair
Vaughn
Cannon A.F.B.
Texico
Jarales
Manzano Mts.
Ft. Sumner
Magdalena
Lemitar
Gran Quivira Nat'l Mon.
Corona
De Baca
Portales
Salt L.
Socorro
Fifteenmile
Elida
San Antonio
Llano
Reserve
San Francisco R.
Lava Beds
Carrizozo
Roswell
Whitewater Baldy 10,892
White
Capitan
Sierra Blanca Pk. 12,003
Lincoln
Estacado
Elephant Butte Res.
Sands
Ruidoso
Tatum
Gila Cliff Dwellings Nat'l Mon.
Truth or Consequences
Missile
Mescalero
Mescalero Apache Ind. Res.
Dexter
Hagerman
Lovington
Buckhorn
Caballo Res.
Range
Tularosa
Alamogordo
Artesia
Silver City
Hanover
Santa Rita
Rincon
White Sands Nat'l Mon.
Holloman A.F.B.
L. McMillan
Oil Center
Central
Bayard
Hurley
Hatch
L. Avalon
Hobbs
Lordsburg
Mesilla
University Park
Carlsbad
Eunice
Deming
La Mesa
Loving
Jal
Animas
Columbus
Anthony
Carlsbad Caverns Nat'l Pk.
La Union
El Paso
Texas
Guadalupe Mts. Nat'l Park
Red Bluff L.
Kermit
Continental
Ft. Bliss
Chamizal Nat'l Mem.
Ciudad Juarez
Fabens
Salt Lakes
Pecos
Grandes
L. Guzman
L. Sta. Maria
Rio Grande
Toyah Lake
Copyright Hammond Incorporated, Maplewood, N.J.
Sangre de Cristo Mts.
San Juan Mts.
Jornada del Muerto
Black Ra.
San Andres Mts.
Sacramento Mts.
Guadalupe Mts.
Divide
Rio Grande
Pecos R.
Canadian R.
Delaware Cr.
Penasco
Hondo
Salt Cr.
Arroyo
Blanco Cr.
MILES
0 20 40 60 80 100
KILOMETERS
0 20 40 60 80 100
State Capital
County Seats
Longitude West of Greenwich
38°
36°
34°
32°
108°
106°
104°

Sectors of the economy (% of labor force employed in 1970): Government (27%), Wholesale and retail trade (21%), Educational Services (12%), Services (11%), Construction (7%), Manufacturing (7%). **Leading products:** food items, petroleum & coal items, electronics, apparel. **Minerals:** coal, lead, zinc, gold, petroleum, silver, natural gas, potassium salts, copper, uranium, molybdenum. **Agricultural products:** cattle, sheep, dairy items, cotton lint, hay, sorghum, grain, poultry. **Avg. farm (1979 est.):** 4,170 acres. **Avg. value of farm per acre:** $100.

Highway expenditures per capita (1978): $135.44. **Persons per motor vehicle:** 1.18. **Minimum age for driver's license:** 15. **Gasoline tax:** 8¢ per gallon. **Diesel tax:** 8¢ per gallon. **Motor vehicle deaths:** 54.5 per 100,000 people.

Birthrate (1978): 19.7 per 1,000 people. **Infant mortality rate per 1,000 births (1977):** 13.8. **Physicians per 100,000 pop. (1977):** 147. **Dentists per 100,000 pop. (1977):** 41. **Acceptable hospital beds:** 5.5 per 1,000 people. **State expenditures per capita for health and hospitals (1978):** $69.47.

Education expenditures (1975-76): $495.82 per capita annually. **No. of pupils in public schools (1977 est.):** 281,000. **No. of institutions of higher learning (1976-77):** 17. **Public school expenditure per pupil in attendance (1975-76):** $1,509. **Avg. salary of public school teachers (1974-75 est.):** $10,200. **No. full-time teachers (1977 est.):** 13,600. **Educational attainment of adult population (1976):** 12.5 median yrs. of school completed; 5.7% with less than 5 years of education; 15.3% with 4 yrs. of college.

Telephones (1977): 63 per 100 people. **State Chamber of Commerce:** Association of Commerce and Industry of New Mexico, 117 Quincy, N.E., Albuquerque, New Mexico 87108.

NEW YORK

New York is a state of superlatives, ideally located and richly endowed. In many respects, it is a nerve center of the nation, a major marketplace, and a national leader in manufacturing, finance, fashion, art, and communications. Second to California in population, New York is the region that George Washington foresaw as a "seat of empire"—hence its nickname, the Empire State. New York City, the nation's largest city, was the first U.S. capital (1789-90), and Washington was first inaugurated (1789) there.

Roughly triangular in shape, the state has a highly diversified terrain, with many lakes, wooded hills, and fertile valleys. Most of the area south of the Mohawk Valley falls within the province of the Appalachian Plateau, which covers more than half the state and slopes upward from northwest to southeast. New York's land features include the scenic Adirondack Mountains in the north and the Catskill range in the south, as well as imposing Niagara Falls. New York is the only state to border both the Atlantic Ocean and the Great Lakes.

Florentine explorer Giovanni da Verrazano is thought to have discovered New York by entering New York Bay in 1524. In 1609 Henry Hudson, an Englishman in the employ of the Dutch, sailed up the river bearing his name and the same year Samuel de Champlain discovered what is now Lake Champlain. The Dutch West India Company began (1624) settlement of the region, then called New Netherland, at Fort Orange (now Albany). Soon after, Governor Peter Minuit is said to have bought Manhattan Island from the Indians for trinkets worth about $24.

Indian troubles, misgovernment, and other woes hindered the colony's development. As a countermeasure, the Dutch began (1629) the "patroon" (landholder's) system that tended to concentrate economic and governmental power in the hands of a few. Squabbling broke out among the patroons, other settlers, and the home company, and Minuit was recalled (1631) for granting the patroons undue privileges. He then entered the service of Sweden; its colony (New Sweden), along the Delaware River south of Dutch interests, was viewed by the Dutch as a territorial threat. Minuit's successors—Wouter Van Twiller and Willem Kieft—were failures, but Peter Stuyvesant for a time did better. In 1655 he captured New Sweden for the Dutch and reorganized New Amsterdam (now New York City). Stuyvesant was a strict Calvinist whose tactics often provoked resentment.

Meanwhile, English penetration of Long Island and the southeastern part of what is now the mainland state was steadily progressing. In the north and west of the state, Canadian French allied themselves with the Huron Indians, but met with hostility from the Iroquois. Comprised of five tribes confederated about 1570, the Iroquois greatly influenced the struggle for control of the region between France and England that ensued after the Dutch surrender (1664) of the land to the British. New Netherland thus became the colonies New York and New Jersey, granted by King Charles II to his brother, the Duke of York (later James II). The Dutch recaptured New York in 1673, but had to yield it again a year later.

The period was marked by the development of English governmental institutions, amid a welter of conflicts and confrontations. A popular legislative assembly was formed in 1683, after years of struggle by townspeople wanting a meaningful voice in their government; but two years later the assembly was dissolved by James II. In 1686 the king sought to combine New York, New Jersey, and the New England colonies under the vice-regal authority of governor general Edmund Andros, but Andros was very unpopular, and when the king was dethroned in England in 1688, Andros was forced out of power by irate citizens. New York City merchant Jacob Leisler, hoping to foster more democratic government, then seized control, but was soon replaced by a royal governor and executed.

New York played a major role in the French and Indian Wars (1689-1763) in which France was helped by Algonquian Indians, while the Iroquois aided the English. The region also saw much action in the American Revolution and the War of 1812. (Statehood dates from 1788.) With the opening of the Erie Canal (1825), which linked the Hudson and the Great Lakes, the state entered an era of great prosperity, reinforced a few years later by the massive industrial demands of the Civil War. The state contributed more men (nearly 500,000), supplies, and money to the Union cause than any other.

The postwar period was marked by continued industrialization, large-scale immigration, and a corrupt political climate that often led to ineffective reform pressures: it was the notorious era of Boss Tweed and Tammany Hall. The most successful reform efforts were those made between World Wars I and II.

Recent important state developments include a $1 billion state office building complex called the Empire State Plaza in Albany; the Artpark near Niagara Falls, an area devoted to the visual and performing arts, with summer artists-in-residence; and the expansion of the higher education system. The State University of New York is the largest higher education system in the country, with 21 campuses throughout the state and an enrollment of over 225,000.

In 1978, residents of the Love Canal area in Niagara Falls learned they were living on top of a chemical time-bomb. Leakage from toxic wastes dumped 30 years before by the Hooker Chemical Corp., forced 239 families to evacuate the area. In

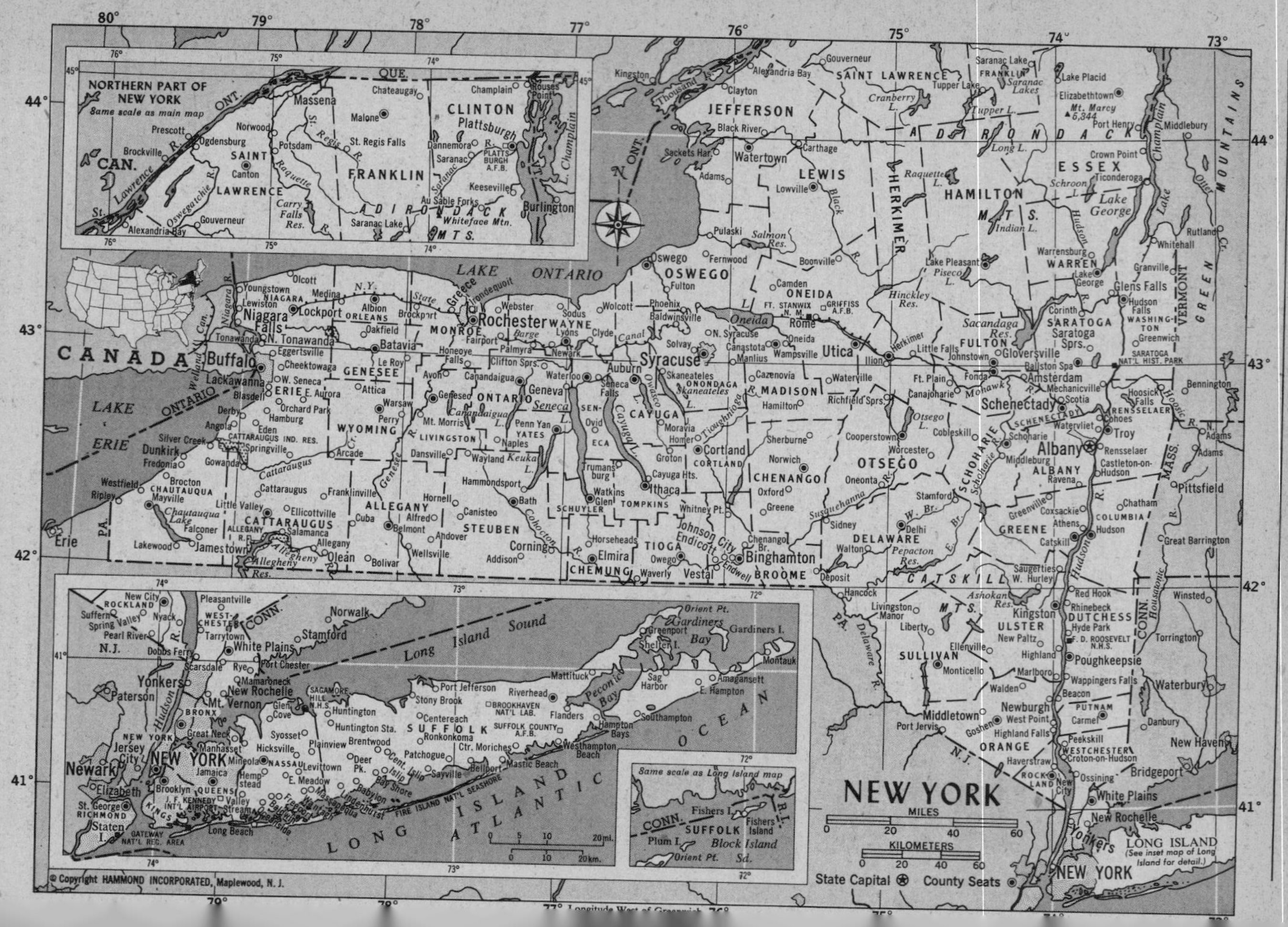
NEW YORK
MILES
KILOMETERS
State Capital   County Seats
LONG ISLAND
(See inset map of Long Island for detail.)
NORTHERN PART OF NEW YORK
Same scale as main map
Same scale as Long Island map
© Copyright HAMMOND INCORPORATED, Maplewood, N.J.
Longitude West of Greenwich

May 1980, the Environmental Protection Agency revealed that 30 percent of Love Canal residents suffered from chromosome damage linked to higher incidences of miscarriages, birth defects and cancer. Federal authorities have now allowed for the temporary relocation of the 710 remaining families at government expense.

Full name: State of New York. **Origin of name:** In honor of the Duke of York. **Inhabitant:** New Yorker. **Capital:** Albany. **State motto:** Excelsior (Ever Upward). **Flag:** State coat of arms on blue field. **Seal:** Coat of arms surrounded with legend "The Great Seal of State of New York." Coat of arms has figures representing Liberty & Justice, a typical New York river scene & an eagle perched on globe. **Flower:** Rose. **Bird:** Bluebird. **Tree:** Sugar maple. **Gem:** Garnet. **Song:** "I Love New York." **Nickname:** Empire State.

Governor: Hugh L. Carey. **Annual salary:** $85,000. **Term:** 4 years. **Current term expires:** Jan. 1983. **Voting requirements:** 18 yrs. old & U.S. citizen; resident of state and county for 30 days; registered. **U.S. Congressmen:** 39. **Entered Union:** 1788 (11th state).

Location & boundaries: Middle Atlantic state; bounded on the north by the St. Lawrence River & Canada; on the east by Vermont, Massachusetts & Connecticut; on the south by the Atlantic Ocean, New Jersey, the Delaware River & Pennsylvania; & on the west by Pennsylvania, Lake Erie, Niagara River, Lake Ontario & Canada. **Total area:** 49,576 sq. mi. (ranks 30th). **Extreme length (exclusive of Long Island):** 20 mi. **Extreme breadth:** 310 mi. **Coastline:** 127 mi. on Atlantic; 371 mi. on Lakes Ontario & Erie. **Chief rivers:** St. Lawrence, Hudson, Mohawk. **Major lakes:** Finger Lakes, Champlain, Erie, Ontario. **No. of counties:** 62.

Population (1979 est.): 17,648,000 (ranks 2nd). **Pop. increase (1970-79):** −3.3%. **Places over 25,000 pop.:** 36. **Places over 100,000:** 6. **Largest cities:** New York, Buffalo, Rochester, Syracuse, Cheektowaga. **Pop. density:** 356.0 per sq. mi. (ranks 6th). **Pop. projection 1985:** 17,927,000. **Pop. distribution:** 88.4% metropolitan; 11.6% nonmetropolitan. **White:** 86.8%. **Black:** 11.9%. **Other:** 1.3%. **Marriage rate (1977):** 7.3 per 1,000 people. **Divorce rate:** 3.1 per 1,000 people.

State finances (1978). Revenue: $23,425,988,000. **Expenditures:** $21,395,740,000. **State taxes:** $616.08 per capita. **State personal income tax:** Yes. **Public debt (1978):** $1,261.84 per capita. **Federal aid (1979):** $502.62 per capita. **Personal income (1979 est.):** $9,098.

Sectors of the economy (% of labor force employed in 1970): Manufacturing (24%), Wholesale and retail trade (20%), Government (17%), Services (8%), Educational Services (8%), Construction (5%). **Leading products:** printing & publishing, apparel, machinery, instruments, transportation equipment, food items. **Minerals:** cement, stone, sand & gravel, salt. **Agricultural products:** dairy items, poultry, fruit, vegetables. **Fishing:** clams, scallops, flounder. **Avg. farm (1979 est.):** 222 acres. **Avg. value of farm per acre:** $642.

Highway expenditures per capita (1978): $45.89. **Persons per motor vehicle:** 2.11. **Minimum age for driver's license:** 17. **Gasoline Tax:** 8¢ per gallon. **Diesel tax:** 10¢ per gallon. **Motor vehicle deaths:** 13.8 per 100,000 people.

Birthrate (1978): 13.2 per 1,000 people. **Infant mortality rate per 1,000 births (1977):** 14.4. **Physicians per 100,000 pop. (1977):** 243. **Dentists per 100,000 pop. (1977):** 76. **Acceptable hospital beds:** 7.9 per 1,000 people. **State expenditures per capita for health and hospitals (1978):** $94.14.

Education expenditures (1975-76): $516.47 per capita annually. **No. of pupils in public schools (1977 est.):** 3,330,000. **No. of institutions of higher learning (1976-77):** 287. **Public school expenditures per pupil in attendance (1975-76):** $2,580. **Avg. salary of public school teachers (1974-75 est.):** $15,000. **No. full-time teachers (1977 est.):** 211,540. **Educational attainment of adult population (1976):** 12.5 median yrs. of school completed; 3.0% with less than 5 years of education; 16.0% with 4 yrs. of college.

Telephones (1977): 74 per 100 people. **State Chamber of Commerce:** Empire State Chamber of Commerce, Inc., 150 State Street, Albany, New York 12207.

NORTH CAROLINA

One of the 13 Colonies and the Southeast's foremost industrial state, North Carolina presents an unusual amalgam of tradition and progress. It is a leader in both small-farm agriculture and business-applied research, and the nation's major producer of tobacco and tobacco products. The state also ranks high as a producer of textiles, bricks, wood products, and seafood. The first sustained airplane flight, by Orville and Wilbur Wright, took place (1903) near Kitty Hawk. Today, the state boasts of its famous "Research Triangle" at the University of North Carolina, Duke University, and North Carolina State University; the schools use their pooled resources to assist industry.

The state is topographically similar to South Carolina, sharing the same three principal land regions: (from east to west) the Atlantic Coastal Plain, the Piedmont Plateau, and the Blue Ridge Mountains. Mount Mitchell is the highest peak east of the Mississippi. Beyond the state's coastline are the islands, reefs, sheltered sounds, dunes, and capes of the Outer Banks, including Capes Fear and Hatteras—the latter so treacherous to ships that it is often called the graveyard of the Atlantic. About 60 percent of the state is forested.

The headwaters of the scenic New River in North Carolina were saved from inundation by power company dams in legislation enacted in Congress in 1976 and backed by every major environmental group in the country. The river is considered one of the oldest in the Western Hemisphere.

Much of North Carolina's early history is shared with South Carolina, of which it was a part until 1712. Highlights of this period include Sir Walter Raleigh's unsuccessful attempts (1585, 1587) to establish a colony on Roanoke Island. Although it lasted only about a year, Raleigh's initial settlement was the first English colony in the New World; when all members of his second settlement (1587-?) disappeared, it came to be called the "Lost Colony"; among the missing was Virginia Dare, first child of English parentage born in America.

Among the region's problems were Culpeper's Rebellion (1677), involving colonists angered by the English Navigation Acts; and the Cary Rebellion (1708), brought about by Quakers and other dissenters who refused to support the established Anglican church. In 1705, French Huguenots from Virginia established North Carolina's first permanent settlement at Bath.

Growth in the Carolinas was slow. Swamps and dense forests made land communication difficult, and there were serious Indian troubles, especially during the Tuscarora War (1711-13). Pirates, too, were a hindrance, often menacing the colony's seabound trade; the slaying (1718) of the infamous "Blackbeard" (Edward Teach) in a battle near Ocracoke Island eased the problem. From 1712 to 1729, the proprietors appointed separate governors to administer North and South Carolina. A bitter North Carolina-Virginia boundary dispute was settled in 1728. Dissatisfied with the proprietary system, England eventually made (1729) the region a royal colony, a move that marked a period of progress in which farming and industry expanded as the population rose.

North Carolina contributed troops and materials to help England in its various colonial wars, while a persistent east-west sectionalism began to develop; this rift was caused by sharp differences in geography, politics, economics, and religion. Indian troubles were virtually ended in 1761 by a treaty with the Cherokees, but their final removal from the area did not begin until 1835. In 1768 irate back-country farmers, protesting taxes they considered excessive, organized the short-lived Regulator Movement for reform. The insurgents were

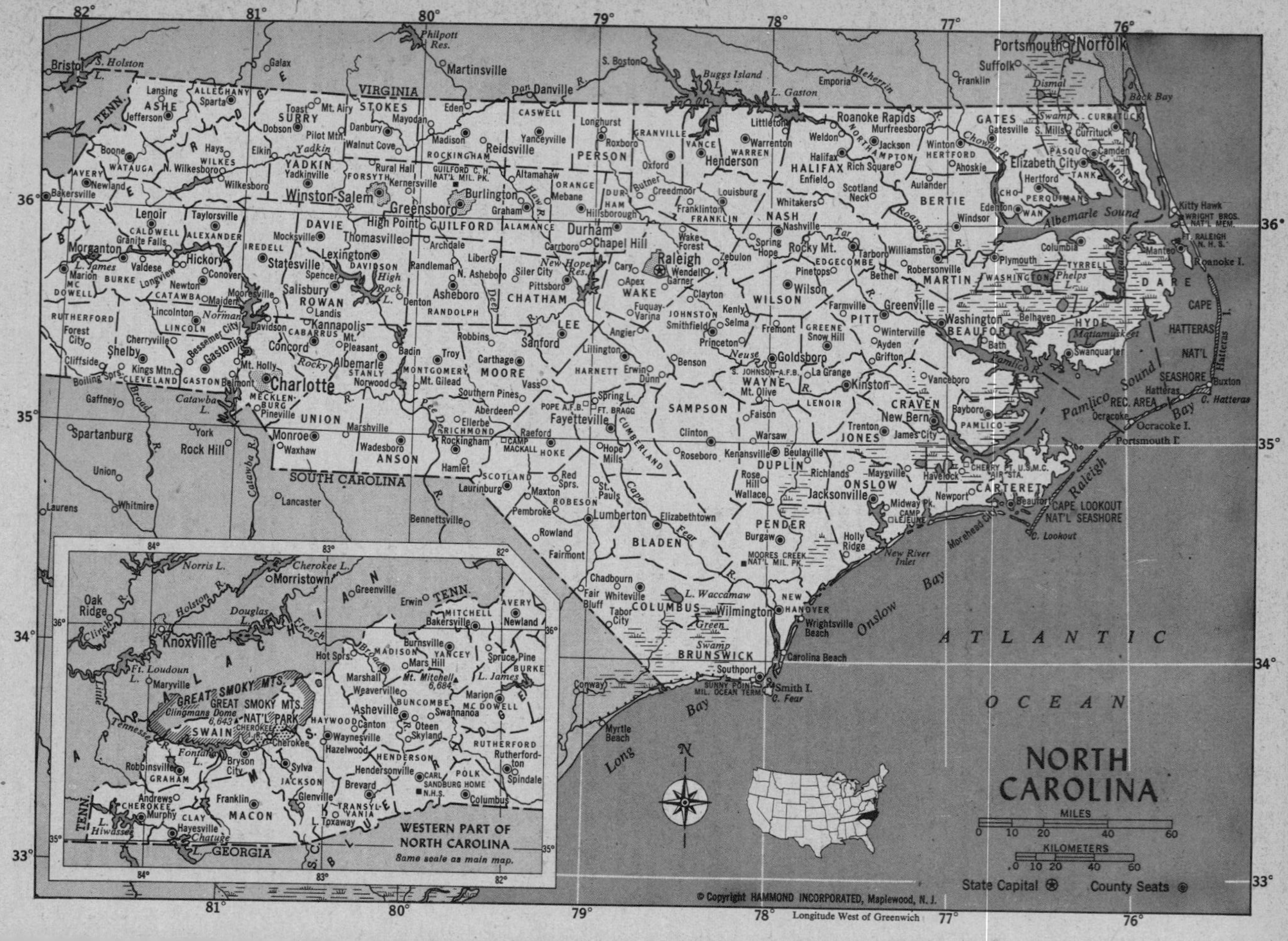
NORTH CAROLINA
MILES
KILOMETERS
State Capital ⊛   County Seats ⊙
© Copyright HAMMOND INCORPORATED, Maplewood, N.J.
Longitude West of Greenwich
ATLANTIC OCEAN
WESTERN PART OF NORTH CAROLINA
Same scale as main map.
VIRGINIA
TENN.
GEORGIA
SOUTH CAROLINA
Raleigh
Charlotte
Greensboro
Winston-Salem
Durham
High Point
Fayetteville
Wilmington
Asheville
Knoxville
Morristown
Great Smoky Mts. Nat'l Park
Great Smoky Mts.
Clingmans Dome 6,643
Mt. Mitchell 6,684

eventually suppressed (1771) at Alamance by the provincial militia.

During the American Revolution, there was relatively little fighting on the state's soil, but many North Carolinians saw action elsewhere. In 1779 North Carolina annexed an area of present-day Tennessee settled by the Watauga Association, which lay immediately beyond North Carolina's present border. North Carolina administered the region until 1784, when it ceded its claim to the United States. The "Watauga" settlers then established the independent state of Franklin. Failing to gain official recognition, the new state's territory was again absorbed in 1789 by North Carolina, which later that same year ceded it once more to the Federal government; North Carolina's statehood dates from that year.

From 1815 to 1835, North Carolina languished in backwardness and apathy, and came to be called the "Rip Van Winkle State"; this period was followed until 1860 by one of progress, which saw a resurgence of political democracy and a lessening of unproductive sectionalism.

Despite the presence of considerable pro-Union and antislavery sentiment, North Carolina joined the Confederacy after the Civil War began. During the conflict, the port of Wilmington became a haven for Confederate blockade-runners. In the postwar period, Reconstruction was followed by the return of white supremacy and a suffrage amendment (1900) that again disenfranchised the Negro.

Among modern North Carolina's most pressing preoccupations is the continued strengthening and diversification of its economy, to curb reliance upon any single factor, such as tobacco. Another task is the peaceable achievement of racial integration. A majority of the rural and small-city school districts in the state are headed toward complete desegregation, but in the larger cities, such as Charlotte, Raleigh, Winston-Salem, and Durham, breaking down the dual systems has been difficult because there are more all-black schools and more rigid residential patterns.

The U.S. Supreme Court, in an historic ruling in the spring of 1971, upheld U.S. District Judge James B. McMillan's ruling that busing was a legitimate tool to use in ending racial segregation. The decision was applied to several school districts and by the fall, few racially identifiable schools remained in the state.

A conflict between extremist groups in Greensboro resulted in the deaths of five persons in November 1979. The slayings occurred at an anti-Ku Klux Klan rally sponsored by the Workers' Viewpoint Organization (WVO), a left-wing group also known as the Communist Workers party, U.S.A. As the protest rally began in a black area of Greensboro, Klansmen and American Nazi party members appeared and taunted the demonstrators. When the WVO group retaliated the Klan and Nazi members opened fire with pistols, rifles and shotguns. The gunfire was returned by the demonstrators. Police arrested 15 Klansmen and American Nazis for killing five of the anti-Klan group; 14 were indicted for murder or felonious rioting in December.

Full name: State of North Carolina. **Origin of name:** In honor of Charles I of England. **Inhabitant:** North Carolinian. **Capital:** Raleigh. **State motto:** Esse Quam Videri (To Be Rather Than to Seem). **Flag:** Gold scrolls & NC (separated by white star) on blue bar; a red & white horizontal bar to right. **Seal:** Liberty holds scroll inscribed "Constitution"; seated figure of plenty; date "May 20, 1775." **Flower:** Dogwood. **Bird:** Cardinal. **Tree:** Pine. **Song:** "The Old North State." **Nickname:** Tar Heel State.

Governor: James B. Hunt, Jr. **Annual salary:** $60,085. **Term:** 4 years. **Current term expires:** Jan. 1981. **Voting requirements:** 18 yrs. old & U.S. citizen; resident of state, 1 yr.; district, 30 days. **U.S. Congressmen:** 11. **Entered Union:** 1789 (12th state).

Location & boundaries: South Atlantic state; bounded on the north by Virginia; on the east by the Atlantic Ocean; on the south by South Carolina & Georgia; & on the west by Tennessee. **Total area:** 52,586 sq. mi. (ranks 28th). **Extreme length:** 503 mi. **Extreme breadth:** 187 mi. **Coastline:** 301 mi. **Chief rivers:** Yadkin, Cape Fear, Neuse, Roanoke. **Major lakes:** Fontana, Mattamuskeet, Norman. **No. of counties:** 100.

Population (1979 est.): 5,606,000 (ranks 11th). **Pop. increase (1970-79):** 10.3%. **Places over 25,000 pop.:** 18. **Places over 100,000:** 5. **Largest cities:** Charlotte, Greensboro, Winston-Salem, Raleigh. **Pop. density:** 106.6 per sq. mi. (ranks 17th). **Pop. projection 1985:** 6,185,000. **Pop. distribution:** 45.2% metropolitan; 54.8% nonmetropolitan. **White:** 76.6%. **Black:** 22.4%. **Other:** 1%. **Marriage rate (1977):** 7.9 per 1,000 people. **Divorce rate:** 4.5 per 1,000 people.

State finances (1978). Revenue: $4,854,529,000. **Expenditures:** $4,672,085,000. **State taxes:** $467.71 per capita. **State personal income tax:** Yes. **Public debt (1978):** $139.51 per capita. **Federal aid (1979):** $318.53 per capita. **Personal income (1979 est.):** $7,359.

Sectors of the economy (% of labor force employed in 1970): Manufacturing (36%), Wholesale and retail trade (18%), Government (13%), Services (8%), Educational Services (7%), Construction (7%). **Leading products:** textile items, tobacco items, furniture & fixtures, food items, electrical machinery, chemicals, apparel. **Agricultural products:** broilers, dairy items, tobacco, corn, soybeans. **Fishing:** shrimp, menhaden, crabs. **Avg. farm (1979 est.):** 125 acres. **Avg. value of farm per acre:** $819.

Highway expenditures per capita (1978): $100.27. **Persons per motor vehicle:** 1.25. **Minimum age for driver's license:** 16. **Gasoline tax:** 9¢ per gallon. **Diesel tax:** 9¢ per gallon. **Motor vehicle deaths:** 23.9 per 100,000 people.

Birthrate (1978): 14.8 per 1,000 people. **Infant mortality rate per 1,000 births (1977):** 15.8. **Physicians per 100,000 pop. (1977):** 143. **Dentists per 100,000 pop. (1977):** 36. **Acceptable hospital beds:** 6.2 per 1,000 people. **State expenditures per capita for health and hospitals (1978):** $72.66.

Education expenditures (1975-76): $410.23 per capita annually. **No. of pupils in public schools (1977 est.):** 1,174,000. **No. of institutions of higher learning (1976-77):** 116. **Public school expenditure per pupil in attendance (1975-76):** $1,394. **Avg. salary of public school teachers (1974-75 est.):** $11,275. **No. full-time teachers (1977 est.):** 54,280. **Educational attainment of adult population (1976):** 12.2 median yrs. of school completed; 6.4% with less than 5 years of education; 11.8% with 4 yrs. of college.

Telephones (1977): 67 per 100 people. **State Chamber of Commerce:** North Carolina Citizens Association, P.O. Box 2508, Insurance Building, Raleigh, North Carolina 27602.

NORTH DAKOTA

North Dakota is the most rural of the states, with more than 90 percent of the land in farms. Agriculture and mining are two of its economic mainstays. Only Kansas produces more wheat, and the state's coal and oil reserves are among the nation's largest. Manufacturing is limited but growing, with food processing leading the way. Tourism is aided by excellent hunting and fishing and such attractions as the Theodore Roosevelt National Park in the Badlands and numerous historic sites including Fort Abercrombie (established 1857), the first U.S. military post in the region. A number of rodeos and fairs take place in the state in the summer and early fall.

Three main regions make up the state: the Red River Valley, comprising a ten-to-forty-mile-wide strip along the eastern border; the Young Drift Plains, just west of this strip; and, covering the state's southwestern half, the Great Plains (also known locally as the Missouri Plateau). The state's continental climate is marked by wide temperature variation, light-to-moderate precipitation, and considerable windiness.

North Dakota's prestatehood history is shared with that of South Dakota. The first Europeans to explore the area were the Sieur de la Vérendrye and sons who visited in 1738, four years before their travels in South Dakota. First settlement attempts were made (1812) at Pembina by Scottish and Irish families. After statehood (1889) separated it from its sister state, North Dakota experienced a spurt in population, growing from about 191,000 in 1890 to more than 577,000 in only 20 years.

The Nonpartisan League was founded in 1915 by farmers who advocated state involvement in the storage and processing of grain to break the power of out-of-state interests, increased funds for rural schools, and tax incentives to improve farms. The legislature which took office in 1919 was controlled by persons elected with the League's support; they enacted the League's educational and tax programs, and established a state-owned bank, a state-owned flour mill, and a state-owned grain elevator.

Work was begun in 1968 on the first stage of an irrigation system to carry water through nearly 2,000 miles of canals to irrigate a million acres of North Dakota soil. The entire project is expected to cost over $500 million. The Lonetree Reservoir and Dam project has come under fire from the Federal Government, the State of Minnesota, and the Canadian government, so work has been halted on the partially completed construction.

The $9 million Omega all-weather navigation system permitting any ship or aircraft with a proper receiver to determine its exact position was completed near Lamoure in 1973. Unique in North America, it is one of eight in the world.

In 1975, legislature was 34th in the nation to ratify the ERA constitutional amendment. Legislature also passed an education reciprocity plan whereby resident students of North Dakota and Minnesota may attend school in either state without paying "out of state" tuition.

The recent energy crisis resulted in the exploitation, chiefly by strip mining, of the coal reserves in the western part of the state, over the objections of environmentalists.

North Dakota's farmers suffered heavy losses in 1979 because of a strike by grain handlers in the ports of Duluth, Minnesota, and Superior, Wisconsin, and because of the discovery of PCBs in chicken feed and hog feed.

Full name: State of North Dakota. **Origin of name:** From the Sioux meaning "Alliance with Friends." **Inhabitant:** North Dakotan. **Capital:** Bismarck. **State motto:** Liberty & Union, Now & Forever, One & Inseparable. **Flag:** Eagle with American shield on breast, holding sheaf of arrows in left claw & olive branch in right & carrying in beak a banner inscribed "E Pluribus Unum"; above eagle is sunburst enclosing 13 stars, beneath is scroll inscribed "North Dakota"—all on blue field with yellow fringe. **Seal:** Elm tree & setting sun; plow, sheaves of wheat & anvil symbolize agriculture; bow & arrows & Indian hunting a buffalo represent North Dakota's history. **Flower:** Wild prairie rose. **Bird:** Western meadowlark. **Tree:** American elm. **Song:** "North Dakota Hymn." **Nickname:** Flickertail State and The Sioux State.

Governor: Arthur A. Link. **Annual salary:** $47,000. **Term:** 4 years. **Current term expires:** Jan. 1981. **Voting requirements:** 18 yrs. old & U.S. citizen; resident of precinct 30 days. **U.S. Congressmen:** 1. **Entered Union:** 1889 (39th state).

Location & boundaries: Northern Midwestern state: bounded on the north by Canada; on the east by Minnesota at the Red River of the North; on the south by South Dakota; & on the west by Montana. **Total area:** 70,664 sq. mi. (ranks 17th). **Extreme length:** 360 mi. **Extreme breadth:** 210 mi. **Chief rivers:** Red River of the North,

Missouri, Sheyenne. **Major lakes:** Devils, Sakakawea Reservoir. **No. of counties:** 53.

Population (1979 est.): 657,000 (ranks 46th). **Pop. increase (1970-79):** 6.3%. **Places over 25,000 pop.:** 4. **Places over 100,000:** None. **Largest cities:** Fargo, Grand Forks, Bismarck, Minot. **Pop. density:** 9.3 per sq. mi. (ranks 45th). **Pop. projection 1985:** 675,000. **Pop. distribution:** 22.7% metropolitan; 77.3% nonmetropolitan. **White:** 97%. **Black:** 0.4%. **Other:** 2.6%. **Marriage rate (1977):** 8.7 per 1,000 people. **Divorce rate:** 3.0 per 1,000 people.

State finances (1978). Revenue: $771,064,000. **Expenditures:** $699,144,000. **State taxes:** $474.83 per capita. **State personal income tax:** Yes. **Public debt (1978):** $124.89 per capita. **Federal aid (1979):** $445.20 per capita. **Personal income (1979 est.):** $7,774.

Sectors of the economy (% of labor force employed in 1970): Wholesale and retail trade (23%), Government (19%), Educational Services (11%), Services (7%), Construction (6%), Manufacturing (5%). **Leading products:** food items, printing & publishing, machinery. **Minerals:** petroleum, sand & gravel, natural gas, lignite coal. **Agricultural products:** cattle, dairy items, poultry, potatoes, sugar beets, wheat, barley, hay. **Avg. farm (1979 est.):** 1,017 acres. **Avg. value of farm per acre:** $306.

Highway expenditures per capita (1978): $166.54. **Persons per motor vehicle:** 1.07. **Minimum age for driver's license:** 16. **Gasoline tax:** 8¢ per gallon. **Diesel tax:** 8¢ per gallon. **Motor vehicle deaths:** 27.9 per 100,000 people.

Birthrate (1978): 17.3 per 1,000 people. **Infant mortality rate per 1,000 births (1977):** 13.7. **Physicians per 100,000 pop. (1977):** 120. **Dentists per 100,000 pop. (1977):** 46. **Acceptable hospital beds:** 9.2 per 1,000 people. **State expenditures per capita for health and hospitals (1978):** $52.02.

Education expenditures (1975-76): $474.78 per capita annually. **No. of pupils in public schools (1977 est.):** 127,000. **No. of institutions of higher learning (1976-77):** 15. **Public school expenditure per pupil in attendance (1975-76):** $1,408. **Avg. salary of public school teachers (1974-75 est.):** $9,176. **No. full-time teachers (1977 est.):** 8,120. **Educational attainment of adult population (1976):** 12.5 median yrs. of school completed; 1.7% with less than 5 years of education; 12.2% with 4 yrs. of college.

Telephones (1977): 73 per 100 people. **State Chamber of Commerce:** Greater North Dakota Association—State Chamber of Commerce, P.O. Box 2467, 107 Roberts Street, Fargo, North Dakota 58108.

OHIO

A leading industrial state and the first to be carved out of the Northwest Territory, Ohio enjoys a variety of important natural resources and a strategic location near many rich markets. Predominantly a producer of iron and steel and their products, the state also ranks high in mining and agriculture (especially livestock). It is among the most populous of states, and only Virginia has produced more U.S. Presidents than Ohio, which claims eight.

Four land regions make up the state: the Appalachian Plateau, making up almost all of the eastern half; the fertile Till Plains, constituting the bulk of the western half; a five-to-50-mile-wide strip of the Great Lakes Plain bordering Lake Erie; and, in the south, an extension of Kentucky's Bluegrass Region forming a small wedge between the plateau and the lowlands. The climate is generally temperate but marked somewhat by extremes and sudden changes. Many dams and reservoirs have been built as a bulwark against disasters such as the floods of 1913 that killed about 500 persons and caused some $150 million in property loss.

Early Amerindian peoples are thought to have lived in the Ohio region between 5,000 and 7,000 years ago, followed by the Adena and Hopewell Mound Builders (c. 800 B.C.—A.D. 1300).

Algonquian and Iroquois Indians were living in the region when the first Europeans arrived.

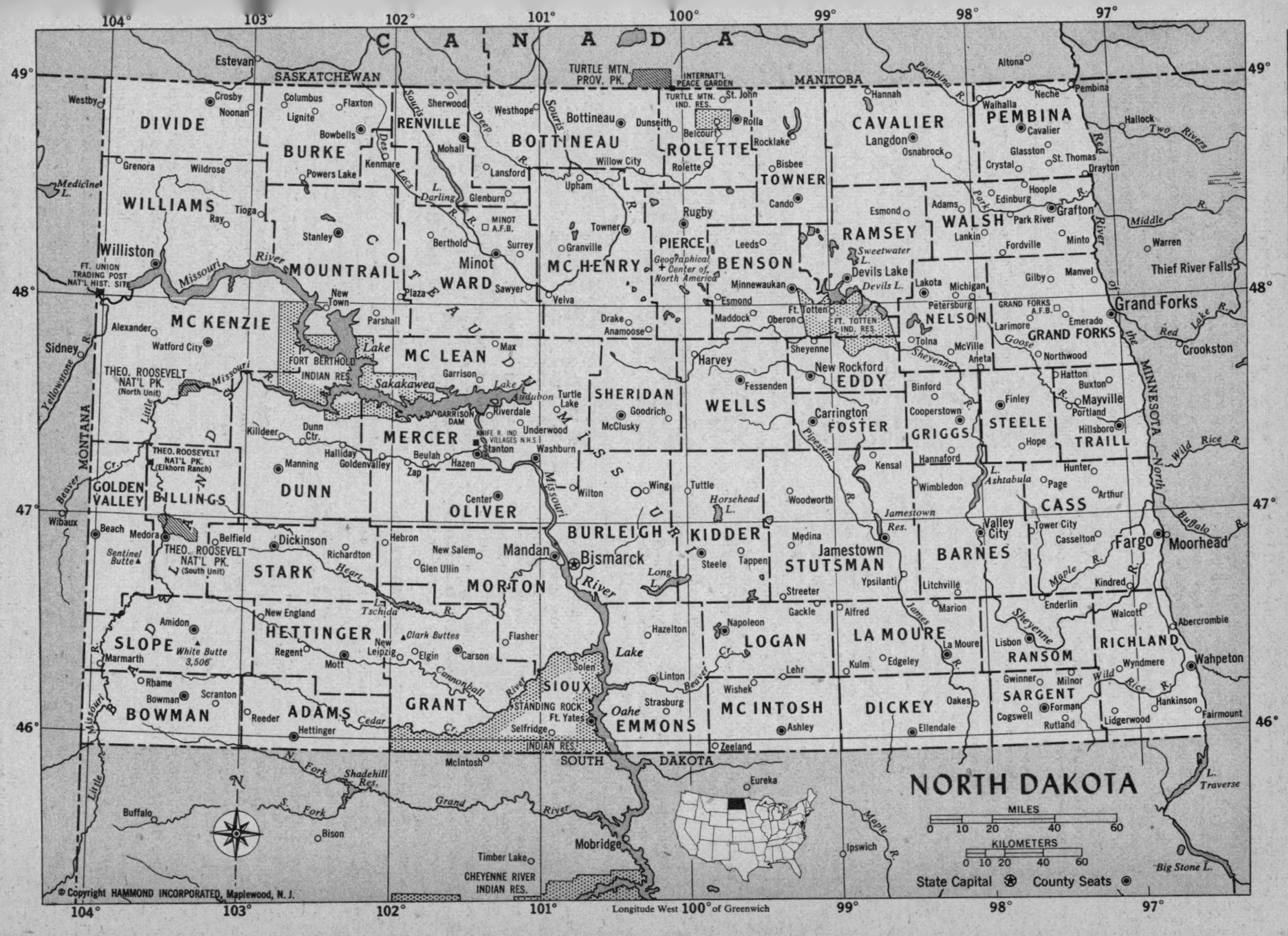
NORTH DAKOTA
State Capital
County Seats
MILES
KILOMETERS
Longitude West 100° of Greenwich
© Copyright HAMMOND INCORPORATED, Maplewood, N.J.

CANADA
SASKATCHEWAN
MANITOBA
MINNESOTA
SOUTH DAKOTA
MONTANA

DIVIDE
BURKE
WILLIAMS
MCKENZIE
MOUNTRAIL
WARD
RENVILLE
BOTTINEAU
MCHENRY
PIERCE
ROLETTE
TOWNER
CAVALIER
PEMBINA
WALSH
RAMSEY
BENSON
NELSON
GRAND FORKS
STEELE
TRAILL
CASS
BARNES
GRIGGS
FOSTER
EDDY
WELLS
SHERIDAN
MCLEAN
MERCER
OLIVER
DUNN
BILLINGS
GOLDEN VALLEY
SLOPE
BOWMAN
ADAMS
HETTINGER
STARK
MORTON
GRANT
SIOUX
EMMONS
MCINTOSH
LOGAN
LA MOURE
DICKEY
SARGENT
RANSOM
RICHLAND
STUTSMAN
KIDDER
BURLEIGH

Estevan
Westby
Crosby
Noonan
Columbus
Lignite
Flaxton
Bowbells
Sherwood
Westhope
Bottineau
Dunseith
Belcourt
St. John
Rolla
Rocklake
Rolette
Bisbee
Langdon
Osnabrock
Altona
Hannah
Walhalla
Neche
Pembina
Cavalier
Hallock
Two Rivers
Glasston
Crystal
St. Thomas
Drayton
Hoople
Edinburg
Park River
Grafton
Minto
Warren
Thief River Falls
Gilby
Manvel
Fordville
Lankin
Adams
Esmond
Grenora
Wildrose
Williston
Tioga
Ray
Stanley
Berthold
Powers Lake
Kenmare
Mohall
Lansford
Glenburn
Minot A.F.B.
Towner
Surrey
Granville
Willow City
Upham
Rugby
Cando
Sweetwater L.
Devils Lake
Devils L.
Lakota
Michigan
Minnewaukan
Maddock
Oberon
Esmond
Sheyenne
Tolna
McVille
Aneta
Petersburg
Larimore
Emerado
Grand Forks A.F.B.
Grand Forks
Crookston
Northwood
Hatton
Buxton
Mayville
Portland
Hillsboro
Hope
Finley
Cooperstown
Binford
Hannaford
Kensal
Carrington
New Rockford
Fessenden
Harvey
Drake
Anamoose
Velva
Sawyer
Plaza
New Town
Parshall
Garrison
Max
Riverdale
Audubon
Turtle Lake
Goodrich
McClusky
Underwood
Washburn
Stanton
Hazen
Zap
Beulah
Goldenvalley
Halliday
Dunn Ctr.
Killdeer
Manning
Alexander
Watford City
Sidney
Minot
Ashtabula L.
Wimbledon
Page
Hunter
Arthur
Valley City
Tower City
Casselton
Fargo
Moorhead
Jamestown Res.
Jamestown
Medina
Steele
Tappen
Woodworth
Tuttle
Wing
Horsehead L.
Center
Wilton
Bismarck
Mandan
Glen Ullin
Hebron
New Salem
Richardton
Dickinson
Belfield
Beach
Medora
Sentinel Butte
Amidon
White Butte 3,506'
Marmarth
Rhame
Bowman
Scranton
Reeder
Hettinger
Buffalo
Bison
Mobridge
Timber Lake
McIntosh
Eureka
Zeeland
Ellendale
Ashley
Oakes
Wishek
Ipswich
Strasburg
Selfridge
Ft. Yates
Standing Rock
Solen
Linton
Napoleon
Hazelton
Lehr
Kulm
Edgeley
La Moure
Gackle
Alfred
Streeter
Ypsilanti
Litchville
Marion
Lisbon
Enderlin
Gwinner
Milnor
Cogswell
Forman
Rutland
Lidgerwood
Wyndmere
Wahpeton
Hankinson
Fairmount
Walcott
Abercrombie
Kindred
Flasher
Carson
Elgin
New Leipzig
Mott
Regent
New England
Clark Buttes
Steele
Medina
Stutsman

Medicine L.
Missouri River
Little Missouri
Yellowstone R.
Beaver Cr.
Cr.
Heart R.
La Tschida L.
Cannonball River
Grand River
N. Fork
S. Fork
Shadehill Res.
Cedar Cr.
Oahe
Lake
Lake Sakakawea
Garrison Dam
Souris R.
Deep R.
Des Lacs R.
Darling L.
Pipestem
Sheyenne R.
Goose R.
Red River of the North
Red R.
Park R.
Pembina R.
Middle R.
Wild Rice R.
North R.
Maple R.
Big Stone L.
Traverse L.
Devils L.

FT. UNION TRADING POST NAT'L HIST. SITE
THEO. ROOSEVELT NAT'L PK. (North Unit)
THEO. ROOSEVELT NAT'L PK. (Elkhorn Ranch)
THEO. ROOSEVELT NAT'L PK. (South Unit)
FORT BERTHOLD INDIAN RES.
KNIFE R. IND. VILLAGES N.H.S.
TURTLE MTN. PROV. PK.
INTERNAT'L PEACE GARDEN
TURTLE MTN. IND. RES.
FT. TOTTEN IND. RES.
Ft. Totten
Geographical Center of North America
STANDING ROCK INDIAN RES.
CHEYENNE RIVER INDIAN RES.

49° 48° 47° 46°
104° 103° 102° 101° 100° 99° 98° 97°

Robert Cavelier, Sieur de La Salle, passed through about 1670, providing a basis for French claims to the region that were sharply contested by the British, who claimed all the territory extending westward from their colonies. Victory in the French and Indian Wars (1689-1763) gave England the upper hand until the American Revolution. Massachusetts, Connecticut, and Virginia land claims in the area were resolved by the Northwest Ordinance (1787). A band of New Englanders led by General Rufus Putnam established (1788) the first permanent white settlement at Marietta. Early settlers were beset by serious Indian troubles that were largely ended after troops under General Anthony Wayne won (1794) the Battle of Fallen Timbers, near present-day Toledo. The Division Act of 1800 created the Indiana Territory out of the western part of the region, then still called the Northwest Territory. In 1803, Ohio entered the Union. A border dispute with the Territory of Michigan gave rise (1835) to the "Toledo War" but, before any actual fighting broke out, Congress awarded the area—about 520 square miles along Lake Erie—to Ohio. At present another land controversy between the two states—over a 200-square-mile area beneath Lake Erie that is rich in oil and natural gas—remains to be resolved. The state's southern boundary, the Ohio River, has been receding gradually north- and westward for centuries. Fortunately for Ohio, the U.S. Supreme Court ruled in January 1980 that the boundary is to remain fixed at its original position regardless of the river's shifting course.

Ohio was in the forefront of events leading to the Civil War. The abolition movement began at St. Clairsville, and many Ohioans helped slaves escape to Canada via the Underground Railroad. Although there was relatively little actual fighting on its soil, Ohio contributed heavily to the Union cause. In the postwar period the state rapidly emerged as an industrial power while retaining its agricultural status. In the years just prior to the turn of the century, big business became inordinately involved in Ohio politics, causing discontent among the less well-off. Labor troubles developed that culminated in Jacob S. Coxey's march on Washington, D.C. (1894) and a voting shift toward reform candidates. More recent troubles of this nature include major strikes during the mid-1930s, 1949, and 1959.

Tourism, aided by a surge in new highway construction, has developed into a valuable revenue-producer, now bringing in over $3 billion a year. Attractions include numerous state park and recreation areas, prehistoric Indian mounds, and historic sites such as Commodore Perry's Victory and International Peace Memorial at Put-in-Bay on Lake Erie, which commemorates his vital victory there during the War of 1812. Annual events include the All-American Soap Box Derby, held in Akron each summer.

In 1979 Honda Motor Company Ltd. of Japan opened a motorcycle assembly plant (its first in the U.S.) northwest of Columbus. At nearby Marysville, Honda plans to construct an auto assembly complex to employ about 2,000 persons. It is scheduled to open in 1982 or 1983.

Full name: State of Ohio. **Origin of name:** From Iroquois name meaning "Great." **Inhabitant:** Ohioan. **Capital:** Columbus. **State motto:** With God, All Things Are Possible. **Flag:** Pennant-shaped flag; white-bordered red circle & white stars on a blue triangle, with red & white bars. **Seal:** Sheaf of wheat; bundle of arrows; sun rising behind mountains, indicating Ohio was first state west of Allegheny Mountains. **Flower:** Scarlet carnation. **Bird:** Cardinal. **Tree:** Buckeye. **Song:** "Beautiful Ohio." **Nickname:** Buckeye State.

Governor: James A. Rhodes. **Annual salary:** $50,000. **Term:** 4 years. **Current term expires:** Jan. 1983. **Voting requirements:** 18 yrs. & U.S. citizen; resident of county and precinct 30 days. **U.S. Congressmen:** 23. **Entered Union:** 1803 (17th state).

Location & boundaries: Midwestern state; bounded on the north by Michigan & Lake Erie; on the east by Pennsylvania & West Virginia; on the south by West Virginia, Kentucky & the Ohio River & on the west by Indiana. **Total area:** 41,222 sq. mi. (ranks 35th). **Extreme length:** 230 mi. **Extreme breadth:** 210 mi. **Shoreline:** 312 mi. **Chief rivers:** Ohio, Miami, Muskingum. **Major lakes:** Erie, Grand. **No. of counties:** 88.

Population (1979 est.): 10,731,000 (ranks 6th). **Pop. increase (1970-79):** 0.7%. **Places over 25,000 pop.:** 46. **Places over 100,000:** 7. **Largest cities:** Cleveland, Columbus, Cincinnati, Toledo. **Pop. density:** 260.3 per sq. mi. (ranks 8th). **Pop. projection 1985:** 10,861,000. **Pop. distribution:** 79.8% metropolitan; 20.2% nonmetropolitan. **White:** 90.6%. **Black:** 9.1%. **Other:** 0.3%. **Marriage rate (1977):** 9.1 per 1,000 people. **Divorce rate:** 5.4 per 1,000 people.

State finances (1978). Revenue: $10,095,426,000. **Expenditures:** $8,876,800,000. **State taxes:** $384.67 per capita. **State personal income tax:** Yes. **Public debt (1978):** $320.02 per capita. **Federal aid (1979):** $286.10 per capita. **Personal income (1979 est.):** $8,775.

Sectors of the economy (% of labor force employed in 1970): Manufacturing (36%), Wholesale and retail trade (19%), Government (13%), Educational Services (7%), Services (6%), Construction (5%). **Leading products:** transportation equipment, primary & fabricated metals, machinery, rubber & plastic items. **Minerals:** bituminous coal, limestone, sand & gravel, salt, oil. **Agricultural products:** milk, hogs, cattle & calves, corn, soybeans. **Fishing:** yellow perch, catfish, white bass, yellow pike. **Avg. farm (1979 est.):** 168 acres. **Avg. value of farm per acre:** $1,516.

Highway expenditures per capita (1978): $73.44. **Persons per motor vehicle:** 1.32. **Minimum age for driver's license:** 16. **Gasoline tax:** 7¢ per gallon. **Diesel tax:** 7¢ per gallon. **Motor vehicle deaths:** 19.1 per 100,000 people.

Birthrate (1978): 15.0 per 1,000 people. **Infant mortality rate per 1,000 births (1977):** 13.9. **Physicians per 100,000 pop. (1977):** 150. **Dentists per 100,000 pop. (1977):** 46. **Acceptable hospital beds:** 6.3 per 1,000 people. **State expenditures per capita for health and hospitals (1978):** $64.09.

Education expenditures (1975-76): $415.77 per capita annually. **No. of pupils in public schools (1977 est.):** 2,217,000. **No. of institutions of higher learning (1976-77):** 131. **Public school expenditure per pupil in attendance (1975-76):** $1,481. **Avg. salary of public school teachers (1974-75 est.):** $9,176. **No. full-time teachers (1977 est.):** 118,810. **Educational attainment of adult population (1976):** 12.4 median yrs. of school completed; 1.7% with less than 5 years of education; 11.5% with 4 yrs. of college.

Telephones (1977): 70 per 100 people. **State Chamber of Commerce:** Ohio Chamber of Commerce, Huntington Bank Building, 17 South High Street, 8th Floor, Columbus, Ohio 43215.

OKLAHOMA

Oil-rich Oklahoma, the nation's Indian Territory in the early 19th century, has the largest Indian population of any state (1970). Generally considered an agricultural state, even though the value of its manufacturing and mining output exceeds cash farm revenue, the state earns more from livestock and livestock products (especially cattle) than it does from crops. Manufacturing, although becoming more diverse, is still based largely on the processing of the state's farm and mineral products. Most industry is located in and around Oklahoma City and Tulsa, which also rank among the world's foremost gas and oil centers.

Topographically, the state is largely a rolling plain sloping from northwest to southeast, with a mean altitude of 1,300 feet. About three-fourths of the state, especially the central area, consists of the Osage Plains section of the Central Lowlands.

OHIO
MILES
0 10 20 30 40 50
KILOMETERS
0 10 20 30 40 50
State Capital
County Seats
DETROIT
Ann Arbor
Dearborn
Ypsilanti
Windsor
CANADA
L. St. Clair
Chatham
RONDEAU PROV. PK.
Pt. Aux Pins
Amherstburg
Leamington
ONTARIO
L A K E   E R I E
Conneaut
Ashtabula
Edgewood
Geneva
Jefferson
Pymatuning
Res.
Pelee Pt.
POINT PELEE NAT'L PARK
Pelee I.
PERRYS VICTORY AND INTERNAT'L PEACE MEM.
Kelleys I.
Fairport Harbor
Mentor-on-the-Lake
CLEVELAND
Lakewood
Painesville
Mentor
ASHTABULA
Andover
Orwell
GEAUGA
Chardon
Kinsman
Monroe
Raisin R.
MICHIGAN
Toledo
Sylvania
Ottawa Hills
Oregon
L U C A S
OTTAWA
Bass Islands
Sheffield Lake
Avon Lake
Euclid
Cleveland Hts.
Shaker Hts.
Burton
Mosquito Cr. Res.
Cortland
Shenango R. Res.
Montpelier
Tiffin R.
FULTON
Wauseon
Delta
Maumee
Port Clinton
Vermilion
Avon
Rocky River
CUYAHOGA
Parma
Solon
Aurora
Windham
TRUMBULL
WILLIAMS
Archbold
Bryan
Perrysburg
Oak Harbor
Lorain
Amherst
N. Ridgeville
Berea
Brunswick
Warren
Niles
Girard
Hubbard
Joseph R.
DEFIANCE
Napoleon
HENRY
Bowling Green
Gibsonburg
Fremont
Sandusky
Huron
ERIE
Oberlin
Elyria
LORAIN
Medina
SUMMIT
Cuyahoga Falls
Stow
Ravenna
PORTAGE
Kent
Newton Falls
Austintown
Youngstown
Campbell
Boardman
Struthers
Hicksville
Defiance
Maumee R.
Baltimore
N. Fostoria
Clyde
Bellevue
Norwalk
Wellington
New London
Wadsworth
MEDINA
Akron
Tallmadge
Mogadore
Berlin Res.
Canfield
MAHONING
Paulding
Ottawa
PUTNAM
Blanchard R.
WOOD
SANDUSKY
SENECA
Tiffin
Willard
HURON
Rittman
WAYNE
Orrville
Mansfield
Barberton
N. Canton
STARK
Alliance
Sebring
Salem
Columbiana
PAULDING
Findlay
HANCOCK
Carey
CRAWFORD
Shelby
ASHLAND
Ashland
RICHLAND
Wooster
Massillon
Canton
Louisville
Minerva
Lisbon
E. Palestine
VAN WERT
Van Wert
Columbus Grove
Bluffton
WYANDOT
Bucyrus
Crestline
Galion
Loudonville
Millersburg
Dover
Brewster
Malvern
COLUMBIANA
E. Liverpool
Delphos
ALLEN
Lima
Ada
Upper Sandusky
Ontario R.
Lakeville
HOLMES
New Philadelphia
Atwood Res.
CARROLL
Carrollton
Wellsville
MERCER
Celina
AUGLAIZE
Ft. Shawnee
Kenton
HARDIN
MARION
Marion
Mt. Gilead
MORROW
Mohican R.
KNOX
Mt. Vernon
COSHOCTON
Coshocton
TUSCARAWAS
Uhrichsville
Newcomerstown
Dennison
Leesville Res.
JEFFERSON
Wintersville
Steubenville
St. Marys
Wapakoneta
Scioto R.
Olentangy R.
L. St. Marys
Coldwater
Minster
SHELBY
Sidney
LOGAN
Bellefontaine
Richwood
UNION
Delaware
DELAWARE
Utica
Johnstown
Tuscarawas R.
HARRISON
Cadiz
Mingo Jct.
Clendening Res.
Tiltonsville
Versailles
Indian L.
Campbell Hill 1,550
Marysville
Hoover Res.
LICKING
Newark
Dillon Res.
Salt Fk. L.
Piedmont Res.
Martins Ferry
Bradford
Greenville
Covington
Piqua
CHAMPAIGN
Urbana
Plain City
Westerville
Worthington
Granville
Heath
GUERNSEY
St. Clairsville
Bridgeport
Wheeling
DARKE
MIAMI
Troy
New Carlisle
Mad R.
Upper Arlington
Buckeye Lake
Cambridge
Byesville
Barnesville
BELMONT
Shadyside
Bellaire
Tipp City
Springfield
Grandview Hts.
FRANKLIN
Columbus
Whitehall
Bexley
Zanesville
Powhatan Point
Vandalia
CLARK
London
Grove City
Baltimore
MUSKINGUM
Woodsfield
Brookville
Fairborn
MADISON
Groveport
FAIRFIELD
Crooksville
Caldwell
NOBLE
MONROE
Eaton
MONTGOMERY
Dayton
Yellow Sprs.
Oakwood
GREENE
Xenia
Lancaster
New Lexington
PERRY
New Straitsville
MORGAN
McConnelsville
WASHINGTON
PREBLE
Kettering
Centerville
FAYETTE
Washington C.H.
PICKAWAY
Circleville
Logan
Hocking R.
N
Germantown
Miamisburg
Franklin
Sabina
Paint Cr.
Marietta
Oxford
Trenton
Middletown
WARREN
Lebanon
CLINTON CO. A.F.B.
Wilmington
MOUND CITY GROUP NAT'L MON.
Kingston
HOCKING
Nelsonville
The Plains
Athens
Belpre
Parkersburg
BUTLER
Hamilton
Fairfield
Mason
CLINTON
Greenfield
Scioto R.
Chillicothe
VINTON
McArthur
ATHENS
Ohio River
Cheviot
Reading
HAMILTON
Blanchester
ROSS
Bainbridge
Wellston
MEIGS
Pomeroy
Cincinnati
Batavia
Hillsboro
Lynchburg
Rocky Fork L.
Waverly
PIKE
Jackson
Middleport
Covington
CLERMONT
Williamsburg
HIGHLAND
Piketon
Gallipolis
WEST VIRGINIA
New Richmond
Mt. Orab
Bethel
Peebles
BROWN
Georgetown
ADAMS
W. Union
SCIOTO
Lucasville
Oak Hill
JACKSON
GALLIA
Raccoon Cr.
Ohio
Ripley
Manchester
W. Portsmouth
New Boston
Wheelersburg
Portsmouth
KENTUCKY
River
LAWRENCE
Ironton
Coal Grove
South Point
Chesapeake
Huntington
Longitude West of Greenwich
Copyright HAMMOND INCORPORATED, Maplewood, N.J.

84°30'
Harrison
Gt. Miami R.
Greenhills
Mt. Healthy
Lincoln Hts.
N. College Hill
Wyoming
HAMILTON
St. Bernard
Cheviot
Norwood
Cleves
Bridgetown
Covedale
Cincinnati
WILLIAM H. TAFT N.H.S.
Sharonville
Blue Ash
Reading
Deer Park
Silverton
Little Miami R.
Covington
Newport
Ft. Thomas
KENTUCKY
Silver Grove
Erlanger
Loveland
CLERMONT
Milford
Owensville
Newtown
Forestville
Withamsville
Amelia
Batavia
East Fork
Ohio R.
0 4 8 mi.
0 4 8 km.
84°30'

LAKE ERIE
81°30'
CLEVELAND
Lakewood
Bay Village
Rocky River
Fairview Pk.
Brooklyn
CLEVELAND-HOPKINS AIRPORT
Olmsted
Berea
Parma Hts.
Strongsville
Middleburg Hts.
N. Royalton
Brecksville
Eastlake
Willowick
Wickliffe
Willoughby
LAKE
E. Cleveland
Euclid
S. Euclid
Cleveland Hts.
Shaker Hts.
Garfield Hts.
Maple Hts.
Bedford
Parma
Independence
CUYAHOGA
Broadview Hts.
Macedonia
SUMMIT
Boston Hts.
Univ. Hts.
Lyndhurst
Mayfield Hts.
Warrensville Hts.
Chagrin Falls
Solon
Twinsburg
Chagrin R.
W. Br. Rocky R.
E. Br. Rocky R.
Cuyahoga R.
0 4 8 mi.
0 4 8 km.
81°30'
41°30'
41°

The Great Plains region, making up the northwestern panhandle, slopes from 4,973 feet at Black Mesa in the west (the state's highest point) to about 287 feet in the extreme Southeast. Vast wheat fields and broad grazing lands characterize much of the terrain, punctuated by such features as the Wichita, Arbuckle, Ouachita, and Ozark mountains in the southwest, southcenter, southeast and northeast, respectively. A segment of the West Gulf Coastal Plains covers the extreme southeastern corner of the state. A quarter of the land is forested, but only pine and hardwood in the southeast are commercially significant.

Various bands of buffalo-hunting Indians roamed the Oklahoma region before the coming of the first European, Spanish explorer Coronado, who crossed (1541) what is today the Oklahoma panhandle. All the area except it came under U.S. sovereignty via the Louisiana Purchase (1803), and a year later that part of the purchase north of present-day Louisiana was made the District of Louisiana, governed as part of Indiana Territory. The district became in turn the Territory of Louisiana (1805) and the Missouri Territory (1812).

In 1819, Arkansas Territory, including the present state of Oklahoma, was formed from a part of Missouri Territory. A few years later, the U.S. Government designated part of the region Indian Territory and used it for the forcible resettlement of the Five Civilized Tribes (Cherokee, Choctaw, Chickasaw, Creek, and Seminole), who had been living in relatively close contact with white men of the southeastern states for more than 100 years. Some of these Indians pursued farming in the traditional Southern mold, even maintaining slaves. When the Civil War erupted, the Indians were caught up in it, fighting on both sides and suffering invasions from both Confederate and Union forces.

After the war, the five tribes were punished collectively for those Indians who had supported the Confederacy; the western part of the Indian Territory was taken from them, and much of it was assigned to other tribes in the country that the government wanted resettled. White encroachments, led by Kansas-bound Texas cattlemen, soon followed despite laws and Indian treaties; a number of cattle trails, including the famed Chisholm Trail, were forged across the state. The first railroad across the region (built 1870-72) brought still more white settlers. The influx was legalized when a large strip of land was opened for settlement on April 22, 1889. Some of the settlers who entered before the proper time were called "sooners," giving rise to Oklahoma's nickname, the Sooner State.

The western section of present-day Oklahoma was made Oklahoma Territory in 1890, and for a time Oklahoma and Indian (the "twin") Territories existed side by side. The Indians wanted separate admission to the Union, as the state of Sequoyah, but in 1907 the territories were merged and admitted as a single state.

Oklahoma's advances in the economic sphere include expanding aerospace facilities in Tulsa, several tire manufacturing plants, one of the world's largest paper mills at Valliant in the southeastern section, and Western Electric, General Motors and Honeywell plants, the FAA center and Wilson & Co., all in Oklahoma City. The Arkansas River navigation project, the largest single domestic project ever undertaken by the Army Corps of Engineers, has made Tulsa a port city via a new channel and system of locks dredged from Tulsa across Arkansas to the Mississippi River. In agriculture, conservation methods have been inaugurated since the Dust Bowl days of the 1930s and, in some areas, irrigation is used to offset frequent droughts. Wheat is the principal crop.

Tourism in recent years has boomed with an increased advertising program, with much of the emphasis put on the state parks, lodges and recreation areas located on the system of large man-made lakes. Other tourist attractions include the Will Rogers Memorial (at Claremore, near his birthplace at Oologah), the Philbrook Art Center (Tulsa), Indian City U.S.A. (near Anadarko) with authentic copies of Indian villages of the early 1800s, Tsa-La-Gi Cherokee Indian village (Tahlequah) where "The Trail of Tears" pageant depicting the Cherokee removal to Oklahoma is performed during the summer, and the National Cowboy Hall of Fame and Western Heritage Center (Oklahoma City).

In January 1980 racial violence shook the small farming and lumbering city of Idabell in the southeast corner of the state, leaving two dead.

Full name: State of Oklahoma. **Origin of name:** From Choctaw meaning "Red People." **Inhabitant:** Oklahoman. **Capital:** Oklahoma City. **State motto:** Labor Omnia Vincit (Labor Conquers All Things). **Flag:** Symbols of war & peace on a blue field. **Seal:** Indian & white man shaking hands before justice, representing cooperation of all people of state; large star has symbols of the Five Civilized Tribes from the southeastern states, forced by the government to resettle in this region. **Flower:** Mistletoe. **Bird:** Scissor-tailed flycatcher. **Tree:** Redbud. **Song:** "Oklahoma!" **Nickname:** Sooner State.

Governor: George Nigh. **Annual salary:** $48,000. **Term:** 4 years. **Current term expires:** Jan. 1983. **Voting requirements:** 18 yrs. old & U.S. citizen; resident of state; registered with County Election Board. **U.S. Congressmen:** 6. **Entered Union:** 1907 (46th state).

Location & boundaries: South Central state: bounded on the north by Colorado & Kansas; on the east by Missouri & Arkansas; on the south by Texas & the Red River; & on the west by Texas & New Mexico. **Total area:** 69,919 sq. mi. (ranks 18th). **Extreme length:** 464 mi. **Extreme breadth:** 230 mi. **Chief rivers:** Red, Arkansas, Cimarron, Canadian. **Major lakes:** Texoma, Eufaula, Oologah Reservoir. **No. of counties:** 77.

Population (1979 est.): 2,892,000 (ranks 27th). **Pop. increase (1970-79):** 13.0%. **Places over 25,000 pop.:** 13. **Places over 100,000:** 2. **Largest cities:** Oklahoma City, Tulsa, Lawton, Norman. **Pop. density:** 41.4 per sq. mi. (ranks 34th). **Pop. projection 1985:** 3,016,000. **Pop. distribution:** 55.6% metropolitan; 44.4% nonmetropolitan. **White:** 88.9%. **Black:** 7%. **Other:** 4.1%. **Marriage rate (1977):** 14.7 per 1,000 people. **Divorce rate:** 7.8 per 1,000 people.

State finances (1978). Revenue: $2,625,829,000. **Expenditures:** $2,315,432,000. **State taxes:** $456.76 per capita. **State personal income tax:** Yes. **Public debt (1978):** $383.48 per capita. **Federal aid (1979):** $327.01 per capita. **Personal income (1979 est.):** $8,226.

Sectors of the economy (% of labor force employed in 1974): Government (20%), Manufacturing (14.4%), Wholesale & retail trade (14.8%), Services (12.7%), Educational Services (9%), Construction (4.2%). **Leading products:** food items; machinery; petroleum and coal items; stone, clay & glass items; transportation equipment; fabricated metals; apparel. **Minerals:** petroleum and coal, natural gas & natural gas liquids, cement. **Agricultural products:** cattle, dairy items, hogs, wheat, hay, sorghum grain. **Avg. farm (1979 est.):** 479 acres. **Avg. value of farm per acre:** $442.

Highway expenditures per capita (1978): $93.66. **Persons per motor vehicle:** 1.14. **Minimum age for driver's license:** 16. **Gasoline tax:** 6.5¢ per gallon. **Diesel tax:** 6.5¢ per gallon. **Motor vehicle deaths:** 31.3 per 100,000 people.

Birthrate (1978): 16.1 per 1,000 people. **Infant mortality rate per 1,000 births (1977):** 13.7. **Physicians per 100,000 pop. (1977):** 123. **Dentists per 100,000 pop. (1977):** 39. **Acceptable hospital beds:** 6.1 per 1,000 people. **State expenditures per capita for health and hospitals (1978):** $45.38.

Education expenditures (1975-76): $381.21 per capita annually. **No. of pupils in public schools (1977 est.):** 589,000. **No. of

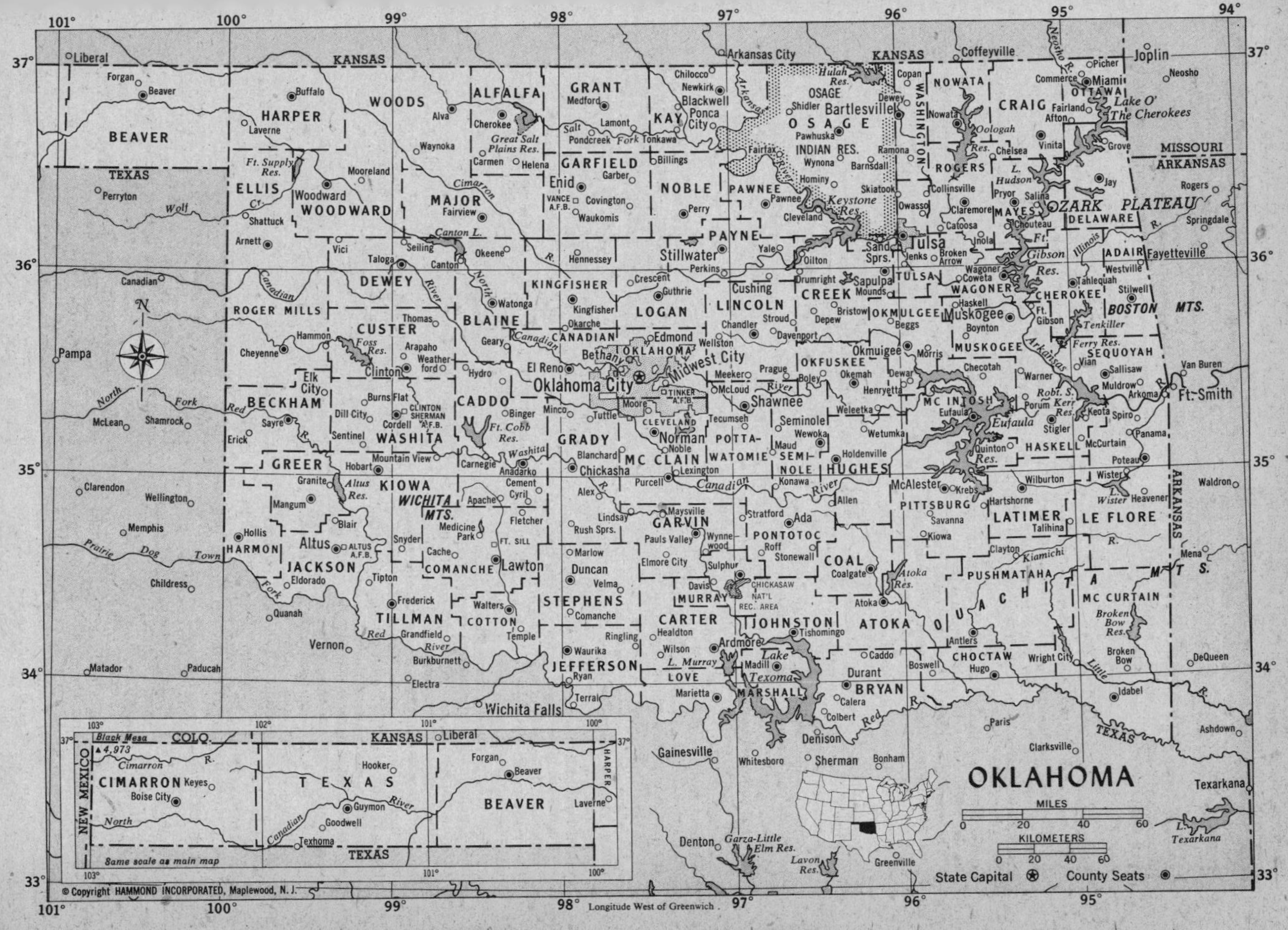
OKLAHOMA
MILES
KILOMETERS
State Capital
County Seats
Longitude West of Greenwich
Copyright HAMMOND INCORPORATED, Maplewood, N. J.
U.S. STATES/CITIES/TERRITORIES
427

KANSAS
MISSOURI
ARKANSAS
TEXAS
NEW MEXICO
COLO.

BEAVER
HARPER
WOODS
ALFALFA
GRANT
KAY
OSAGE
WASHINGTON
NOWATA
CRAIG
OTTAWA
ELLIS
WOODWARD
MAJOR
GARFIELD
NOBLE
PAWNEE
ROGERS
MAYES
DELAWARE
ADAIR
DEWEY
KINGFISHER
PAYNE
CREEK
TULSA
WAGONER
CHEROKEE
ROGER MILLS
CUSTER
BLAINE
CANADIAN
LOGAN
LINCOLN
OKMULGEE
MUSKOGEE
SEQUOYAH
BECKHAM
CADDO
OKLAHOMA
CLEVELAND
OKFUSKEE
McINTOSH
HASKELL
WASHITA
GRADY
McCLAIN
POTTA-
WATOMIE
SEMI-
NOLE
HUGHES
PITTSBURG
LATIMER
LE FLORE
GREER
KIOWA
GARVIN
PONTOTOC
COAL
PUSHMATAHA
HARMON
JACKSON
COMANCHE
STEPHENS
MURRAY
ATOKA
McCURTAIN
TILLMAN
COTTON
CARTER
JOHNSTON
JEFFERSON
LOVE
MARSHALL
BRYAN
CHOCTAW
OZARK PLATEAU
BOSTON MTS.
OUACHITA MTS.
WICHITA MTS.
INDIAN RES.

Liberal
Forgan
Beaver
Buffalo
Laverne
Perryton
Shattuck
Arnett
Woodward
Mooreland
Waynoka
Alva
Cherokee
Carmen
Helena
Medford
Chilocco
Newkirk
Blackwell
Ponca City
Tonkawa
Lamont
Pondcreek
Billings
Enid
Garber
Covington
Waukomis
Fairview
Vici
Seiling
Canton
Okeene
Hennessey
Watonga
Kingfisher
Okarche
Crescent
Guthrie
Perkins
Stillwater
Yale
Cleveland
Pawnee
Perry
Arkansas City
Copan
Dewey
Bartlesville
Shidler
Pawhuska
Ramona
Barnsdall
Hominy
Skiatook
Wynona
Fairfax
Nowata
Collinsville
Owasso
Catoosa
Claremore
Chelsea
Vinita
Jay
Grove
Pryor
Salina
Chouteau
Hudson
Springdale
Rogers
Fayetteville
Westville
Tahlequah
Stilwell
Coffeyville
Picher
Commerce
Miami
Ottawa
Fairland
Afton
Joplin
Neosho
Oilton
Drumright
Cushing
Chandler
Stroud
Depew
Bristow
Sapulpa
Mounds
Sand Sprs.
Jenks
Broken Arrow
Coweta
Wagoner
Tulsa
Haskell
Boynton
Muskogee
Checotah
Warner
Vian
Sallisaw
Muldrow
Arkoma
Ft. Smith
Van Buren
Keota
Spiro
Panama
Poteau
Stigler
Quinton
McCurtain
Wister
Heavener
Talihina
Clayton
Kiamichi
Mena
Waldron
Pampa
McLean
Shamrock
Clarendon
Wellington
Memphis
Hollis
Childress
Matador
Paducah
Quanah
Vernon
Electra
Burkburnett
Wichita Falls
Cheyenne
Hammon
Foss Res.
Elk City
Sayre
Erick
Dill City
Burns Flat
Cordell
Clinton
Weatherford
Arapaho
Thomas
Geary
Hydro
El Reno
Bethany
Oklahoma City
Moore
Edmond
Wellston
Midwest City
Tinker A.F.B.
Meeker
McLoud
Shawnee
Prague
Okemah
Boley
Henryetta
Dewar
Morris
Okmulgee
Weleetka
Wewoka
Maud
Seminole
Tecumseh
Norman
Noble
Purcell
Lexington
Konawa
Allen
Holdenville
Eufaula
McAlester
Krebs
Hartshorne
Savanna
Kiowa
Wilburton
Granite
Mangum
Altus
Blair
Snyder
Medicine Park
Apache
Cache
Cyril
Cement
Fletcher
Ft. Sill
Tipton
Eldorado
Frederick
Grandfield
Temple
Walters
Comanche
Waurika
Ryan
Terral
Marietta
Madill
Lake Texoma
Tishomingo
Atoka
Coalgate
Atoka Res.
Caddo
Durant
Calera
Colbert
Denison
Sherman
Bonham
Paris
Clarksville
Ashdown
DeQueen
Broken Bow
Wright City
Hugo
Boswell
Idabel
Texarkana
Anadarko
Carnegie
Mountain View
Hobart
Lawton
Marlow
Duncan
Velma
Comanche
Rush Sprs.
Lindsay
Alex
Maysville
Pauls Valley
Wynnewood
Elmore City
Sulphur
Stratford
Ada
Roff
Stonewall
Davis
Chickasha
Blanchard
Chickasaw Nat'l Rec. Area
Ardmore
L. Murray
Healdton
Wilson
Ringling
Gainesville
Whitesboro
Denton
Greenville

Great Salt Plains Res.
Ft. Supply Res.
Canton L.
Keystone Res.
Ft. Cobb Res.
Altus Res.
Robt. S. Kerr Res.
Ferry Res.
Lake O' The Cherokees
Tenkiller
Broken Bow Res.
Hulah Res.
Oologah Res.
Garza-Little Elm Res.
Lavon Res.
L. Texarkana

Canadian River
North Canadian River
Cimarron River
Arkansas River
Red River
Washita River
North Fork
Wolf Cr.
Dog Town Cr.
Prairie Dog Town Fork
Illinois R.
Little R.
Neosho R.

N

Black Mesa ▲ 4,973
CIMARRON
Keyes
Boise City
Cimarron
North Canadian
Texhoma
Goodwell
Guymon
Hooker
Forgan
Beaver
Laverne
Liberal
HARPER
BEAVER
NEW MEXICO
COLO.
KANSAS
TEXAS
Same scale as main map

institutions of higher learning (1976-77): 44. **Public school expenditure per pupil in attendance (1975-76):** $1,278. **Avg. salary of public school teachers (1974-75 est.):** $9,208. **No. full-time teachers (1977 est.):** 31,050. **Educational attainment of adult population (1976):** 12.4 median yrs. of school completed; 2.8% with less than 5 years of education; 11.7% with 4 yrs. of college.

Telephones (1977): 75 per 100 people. **State Chamber of Commerce:** Oklahoma State Chamber of Commerce, 4020 N. Lincoln Blvd., Oklahoma City, Oklahoma 73105.

OREGON

With more than 30 million acres of trees (nearly half the state's total area), Oregon is the nation's leading lumber state. Its awesome scenery includes mountains, plains, lush valleys, and immense forests. The 400-mile Pacific coast is marked by the thickly forested Coast Range and the Klamath Mountains that parallel it.

There are four other general land areas: the Cascade Mountains, the Willamette Valley between the coastal elevations and the Cascades, the Columbia Plateau, and the Basin and Range Region.

The Cascade Range is a climatic dividing line: there is mild, moist weather in the west, and in the east dry weather that is warmer in summer and colder in winter than the west's.

Except for the section in the southeast known as the Basin and Range Region, the entire area east of the Cascades is called the Columbia Plateau; this plateau, comprising two-thirds of the state, was formed thousands of years ago when lava gushed forth from the Earth's crust, which has since been covered by rolling plains, and, along the desolate southern edge, the Harney Desert. It was across these plains that settlers from the East came, along the Oregon Trail.

Portland, 100 miles inland, is reached from the Pacific via the Columbia River, and is one of the West Coast's major ports; the Portland area contains about half of Oregon's total population.

Oregon produces about a fifth of the nation's lumber and a majority of our plywood. Centered in the Willamette Valley, wood processing is the state's leading manufacturing industry.

There is some mining in the state, principally of nickel, gemstones, and construction materials. Agriculture, shipping, fishing (mainly for Chinook and silver salmon), metal and food processing, and tourism are also economically significant. Attractions include Hells Canyon, Mount Hood, and Crater Lake, a brilliantly blue, clear body of water that is the principal feature of the national park bearing its name; the nation's deepest lake (1,932 feet), it is six miles wide and was formed 6,600 years ago when the peak of Mount Mazama, in which the lake is set, collapsed after violent volcanic activity. Another tourist attraction is Kah-Nee-Ta Vacation Resort in the Warm Springs Indian Reservation, which was developed by 2,000 Northwest tribesmen; it offers hot mineral baths, swimming, fishing, and riding.

Chinook, Tillamook, Clackama, and Multnomah Indians were among the Oregon Country's earliest known inhabitants. Spanish seamen, sailing from Mexico to the Philippines, are thought to have been the first Europeans to sight the Oregon coast, in the 1500s and 1600s. Captain Cook, seeking the Northwest Passage to the Atlantic, charted some of the coastline in 1778. The Columbia River was discovered in 1792, and the Lewis and Clark expedition passed through the region in 1805.

The nineteenth century was marked by the conflict of British and American claims to the area that were eventually resolved by treaty in 1846.

Two years later, Oregon became a territory, which until 1853 also included present-day Washington. Statehood came in 1859. In 1860 the discovery of gold in what is now Idaho turned Portland into a vital trade center for the Pacific Northwest. Transcontinental rail service came to Oregon in 1883.

In the early part of the 20th century, a series of reform measures were enacted in what came to be known as the Oregon System; this system, designed to make government more responsive to those governed, featured a referendum amendment, a direct primary, and a recall provision. Oregon women were given the vote in 1912.

The state also has developed a broad program for improving the environment and has given its Dertment of Environmental Quality the power to enforce the regulations. In addition, Oregon has adopted a Scenic Waterways plan for state ownership of land along many rivers in the state as well as a law for public ownership of the ocean beaches. Oregon was a pioneer in outlawing throwaway beverage containers and fluorocarbon aerosol cans. One of the first states to abolish criminal penalties for the possession of small amounts of marijuana, Oregon in 1979 legalized the sale of marijuana for legitimate medical purposes.

The great eruption of Mount St. Helens volcano in neighboring Washington on May 18, 1980, had little effect on Oregon, but the lesser eruption of May 24 sprayed dust and ash over parts of northern Oregon, damaging crops and making roads impassable.

Full name: State of Oregon. **Origin of name:** Probably from Spanish, Orejon, meaning "Big-eared men." **Inhabitant:** Oregonian. **Capital:** Salem. **State motto:** The Union. **Flag:** State seal & lettering in yellow on a blue field. **Seal:** Departing British man-of-war & arriving American merchant ship symbolize end of British influence & rise of American power; sheaf of grain, pickax & plow represent mining & agriculture. **Flower:** Oregon grape. **Bird:** Western meadowlark. **Fish:** Chinook salmon; **Rock:** Thunderegg. **Tree:** Douglas fir. **Song:** "Oregon, My Oregon." **Nickname:** Beaver State.

Governor: Victor G. Atiyeh. **Annual salary:** $53,394. **Term:** 4 years. **Current term expires:** Jan. 1983. **Voting requirements:** 18 yrs. old & U.S. citizen; must be registered and resident 20 days before election. **U.S. Congressmen:** 4. **Entered Union:** 1859 (33rd state).

Location & boundaries: Pacific state: bounded on the north by the Columbia River & Washington; on the east by Idaho & the Snake River; on the south by Nevada & California; & on the west by the Pacific Ocean. **Total area:** 96,981 sq. mi. (ranks 10th). **Extreme length:** 295 mi. **Extreme breadth:** 395 mi. **Coastline:** 360 mi. **Chief rivers:** Columbia, Snake, Willamette. **Major lakes:** Upper Klamath, Malheur, Crater. **No. of counties:** 36.

Population (1979 est.): 2,527,000 (ranks 29th). **Pop. increase (1970-79):** 20.8%. **Places over 25,000 pop.:** 7. **Places over 100,000:** 1. **Largest cities:** Portland, Eugene, Salem. **Pop. density:** 26.1 per sq. mi. (ranks 39th). **Pop projection 1985:** 2,610,000. **Pop. distribution:** 59.9% metropolitan; 40.1% nonmetropolitan. **White:** 97.2%. **Black:** 1.2%. **Other:** 1.6%. **Marriage rate (1977):** 8.8 per 1,000 people. **Divorce rate:** 6.9 per 1,000 people.

State finances (1978). Revenue: $3,052,187,000. **Expenditures:** $2,593,369,000. **State Taxes:** $474.17 per capita. **State personal income tax:** Yes. **Public debt (1978):** $1,271.97 per capita. **Federal aid (1979):** $347.09 per capita. **Personal income (1979 est.):** $8,842.

Sectors of the economy (% of labor force employed in 1970): Wholesale and retail trade (22%), Manufacturing (21%), Government (17%), Educational Services (10%), Services (7%), Construction (6%). **Leading products:** lumber & wood items, food items, paper items, machinery, fabricated metals, printing & publishing. **Agricultural products:** wheat, livestock, barley, oats, hops, legumes, potatoes, berries, fruits, nuts, truck crops, dairy and poultry products, sugar beets, corn, green beans and peppermint. **Fishing:** salmon, tuna, bottom fish (sole, rockfish, halibut, cod, etc.) and shellfish. **Avg. farm (1979 est.):** 622 acres. **Avg. value of farm per acre:** $330.

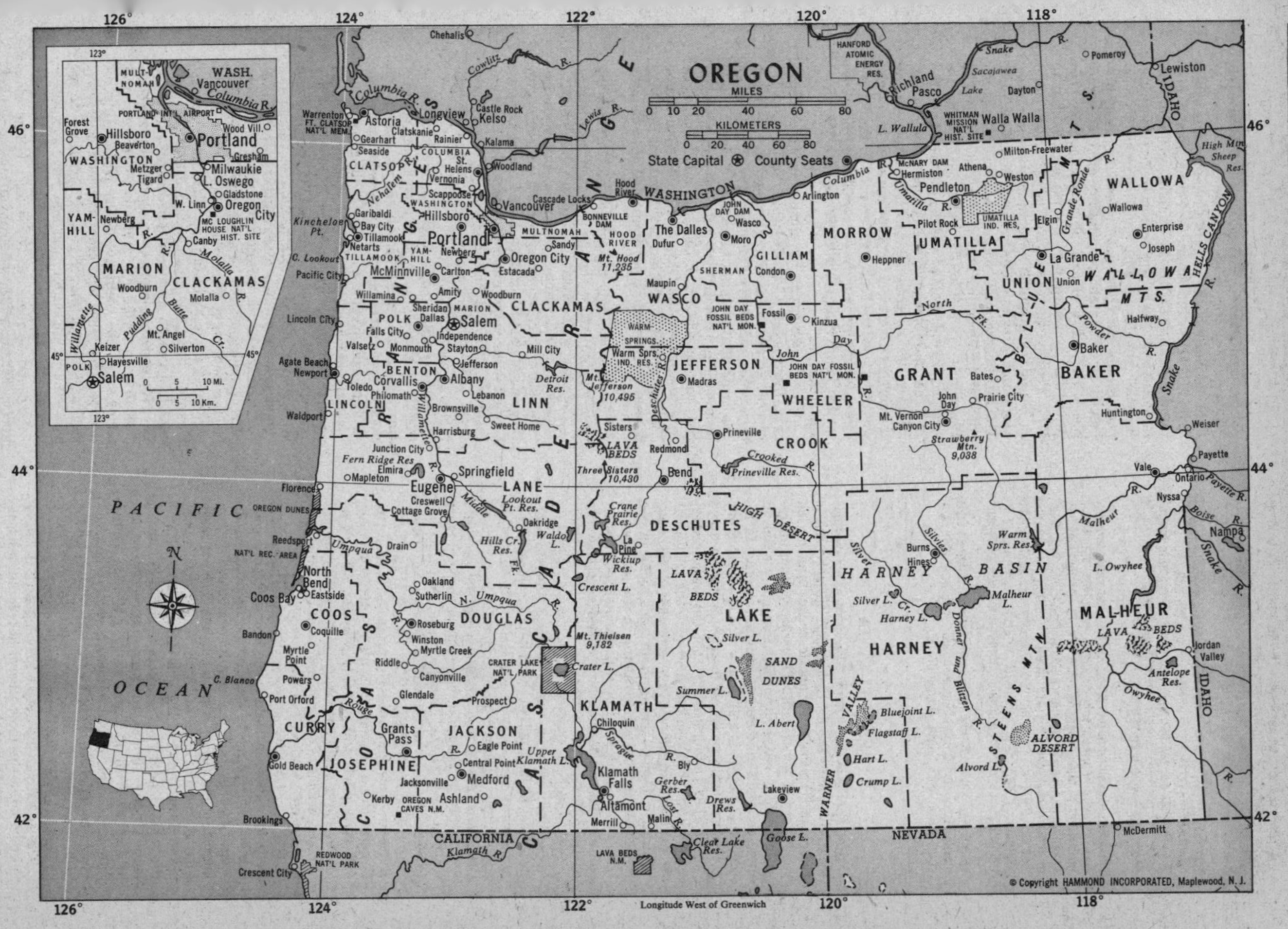
OREGON
MILES
KILOMETERS
State Capital
County Seats
WASH.
WASHINGTON
IDAHO
NEVADA
CALIFORNIA
PACIFIC OCEAN
MULTNOMAH
MARION
CLACKAMAS
YAMHILL
POLK
CLATSOP
TILLAMOOK
LINCOLN
BENTON
LINN
LANE
POLK
WASHINGTON
WALLOWA
UNION
UMATILLA
MORROW
GILLIAM
WASCO
SHERMAN
JEFFERSON
WHEELER
GRANT
BAKER
CROOK
DESCHUTES
LAKE
KLAMATH
JACKSON
JOSEPHINE
CURRY
COOS
DOUGLAS
HARNEY
MALHEUR
CASCADE RANGE
HELLS CANYON
WALLOWA MTS.
BLUE MTS.
STEENS MTN.
WARNER VALLEY
HARNEY BASIN
HIGH DESERT
SAND DUNES
LAVA BEDS
Chehalis
Pomeroy
Lewiston
Dayton
Walla Walla
Milton-Freewater
Weston
Athena
Hermiston
Pendleton
Pilot Rock
Arlington
Heppner
Condon
Moro
Wasco
The Dalles
Dufur
Maupin
Madras
Kinzua
Fossil
Elgin
Wallowa
Enterprise
Joseph
La Grande
Union
Halfway
Baker
Bates
Prairie City
John Day
Canyon City
Mt. Vernon
Huntington
Weiser
Payette
Ontario
Nyssa
Nampa
Vale
McDermitt
Jordan Valley
Burns
Hines
Prineville
Redmond
Bend
Sisters
Three Sisters 10,430
Mt. Jefferson 10,495
Mt. Hood 11,235
Mt. Thielsen 9,182
Strawberry Mtn. 9,038
Lakeview
Klamath Falls
Altamont
Merrill
Malin
Chiloquin
Medford
Ashland
Jacksonville
Central Point
Eagle Point
Grants Pass
Kerby
Gold Beach
Brookings
Crescent City
Port Orford
Powers
Myrtle Point
Bandon
Coquille
Coos Bay
Eastside
North Bend
Reedsport
Florence
Oakland
Sutherlin
Roseburg
Winston
Myrtle Creek
Riddle
Canyonville
Glendale
Prospect
Drain
Cottage Grove
Creswell
Oakridge
Eugene
Springfield
Mapleton
Elmira
Junction City
Harrisburg
Brownsville
Sweet Home
Lebanon
Albany
Jefferson
Mill City
Stayton
Philomath
Corvallis
Waldport
Newport
Agate Beach
Toledo
Valsetz
Monmouth
Falls City
Independence
Salem
Dallas
Sheridan
Willamina
Amity
Carlton
McMinnville
Newberg
Oregon City
Estacada
Sandy
Woodburn
Hillsboro
Portland
Vancouver
Cascade Locks
Hood River
Scappoose
St. Helens
Vernonia
Woodland
Kalama
Rainier
Clatskanie
Castle Rock
Kelso
Longview
Astoria
Warrenton
Gearhart
Seaside
Garibaldi
Bay City
Netarts
Tillamook
Pacific City
Lincoln City
Richland
Pasco
Columbia R.
Willamette R.
Deschutes R.
Snake R.
Sacajawea Lake
L. Wallula
Grande Ronde R.
Powder R.
Malheur R.
Owyhee R.
Boise R.
Silvies R.
Donner und Blitzen R.
Klamath R.
Sprague R.
Rogue R.
Umpqua R.
N. Umpqua R.
Middle Fk.
Lewis R.
Cowlitz R.
Crater L.
Upper Klamath L.
L. Abert
Summer L.
Silver L.
Goose L.
Clear Lake Res.
Gerber Res.
Drews Res.
Silver L.
Malheur L.
Harney L.
Bluejoint L.
Flagstaff L.
Hart L.
Crump L.
Alvord L.
Antelope Res.
L. Owyhee
Warm Sprs. Res.
Crescent L.
Wickiup Res.
Crane Prairie Res.
Prineville Res.
Detroit Res.
Fern Ridge Res.
Lookout Pt. Res.
Hills Cr. Res.
Warm Sprs. Ind. Res.
Umatilla Ind. Res.
HANFORD ATOMIC ENERGY RES.
WHITMAN MISSION NAT'L HIST. SITE
McNARY DAM
JOHN DAY DAM
BONNEVILLE DAM
JOHN DAY FOSSIL BEDS NAT'L MON.
JOHN DAY FOSSIL BEDS NAT'L MON.
CRATER LAKE NAT'L PARK
OREGON CAVES N.M.
LAVA BEDS N.M.
REDWOOD NAT'L PARK
FT. CLATSOP NAT'L MEM.
OREGON DUNES NAT'L REC. AREA
High Mtn. Sheep Res.
Kinchelo Pt.
C. Lookout
C. Blanco
La Pine
Waldo L.
ALVORD DESERT
LAVA BEDS
Copyright HAMMOND INCORPORATED, Maplewood, N.J.
Longitude West of Greenwich
46°
44°
42°
118°
120°
122°
124°
126°

WASH.
Vancouver
Columbia R.
MULT-NOMAH
PORTLAND INT'L AIRPORT
Wood Vill.
Gresham
Portland
Milwaukie
L. Oswego
Gladstone
Oregon City
MC LOUGHLIN HOUSE NAT'L HIST. SITE
Canby
Hillsboro
Beaverton
Metzger
Tigard
W. Linn
WASHINGTON
YAM-HILL
Newberg
Forest Grove
MARION
CLACKAMAS
Woodburn
Mt. Angel
Silverton
Molalla
Molalla R.
Butte Cr.
Pudding R.
Willamette R.
Keizer
Hayesville
Salem
POLK
123°
45°
10 Mi.
10 Km.

Highway expenditures per capita (1978): $115.41. **Persons per motor vehicle:** 1.27. **Minimum age for driver's license:** 16. **Gasoline tax:** 7¢ per gallon. **Diesel tax:** 7¢ per gallon. **Motor vehicle deaths:** 28.9 per 100,000 people.

Birthrate (1978): 15.9 per 1,000 people. **Infant mortality rate per 1,000 births (1977):** 12.2. **Physicians per 100,000 pop. (1977):** 174. **Dentists per 100,000 pop. (1977):** 68. **Acceptable hospital beds:** 5.0 per 1,000 people. **State expenditures per capita for health and hospitals (1978):** $61.17.

Education expenditures (1975-76): $548.98 per capita annually. **No. of pupils in public schools (1977 est.):** 468,000. **No. of institutions of higher learning (1976-77):** 43. **Public school expenditure per pupil in attendance (1975-76):** $1,995. **Avg. salary of public school teachers (1974-75 est.):** $10,958. **No. full-time teachers (1977 est.):** 25,150. **Educational attainment of adult population (1976):** 12.7 median yrs. of school completed; 1.1% with less than 5 years of education; 15.4% with 4 yrs. of college.

Telephones (1977): 73 per 100 people. **State Chamber of Commerce:** Associated Oregon Industries, Inc., P.O. Box 12519, 1149 Court Street, N.E., Salem, Oregon 97309.

PENNSYLVANIA

Called the "Keystone State" because of its central location among the 13 Colonies, Pennsylvania is today an important economic center and a rich repository of Americana. The state, which enjoys an abundant water supply, is the nation's fourth most populous, and manufacturing, mining, farming, and tourism are all important to its economy.

Pennsylvania produces nearly all the country's hard coal and a fourth of its steel. Oil is also important, although not so much so as in the 1890s; the first oil well in the world was drilled (1859) near Titusville. Dairy farming flourishes today in the northeast, as does cattle raising in the southwest; throughout the fertile, well-farmed southeast countryside can be seen the highly decorated barns of the Pennsylvania Dutch.

Pittsburgh was the home (1920) of the first radio broadcasting station, and the first electric computer was built (1945) in Philadelphia; these cities, along with Erie, provide the state with three fine ports. Philadelphia is the dominantly large city of the eastern region (as Pittsburgh is of the western).

Roughly rectangular, the state is crossed from west to east by the Erie Lowland, Appalachian Plateau (by far the largest single region), Great Appalachian Valley, Blue Ridge, Piedmont Plateau, New England Uplands, and Atlantic Coastal Plain. Among the many attractions are 495 state park and recreation areas, as well as Valley Forge and Gettysburg Battlefield national shrines, scenes of decisive events in the American Revolution and the Civil War.

The state's early history is shared in large part with neighboring Delaware, which it once contained. Swedes made the first permanent settlement (1643) in the Pennsylvania region at Tinicum Island in the Schuylkill River, but Swedish rule soon gave way (1655) to Dutch. The English supplanted the Dutch in 1664, as King Charles II put the region under the control of his brother James, Duke of York. In 1681, the king granted the region to Quaker William Penn, naming it after Penn's father, an admiral in the Royal Navy to whom the king was indebted. Penn's era, which except for a brief interruption (1692-94) lasted until his death in 1718, was an enlightened and fruitful one.

The so-called Charter of Privileges (1701) gave Pennsylvania the most liberal of colonial governments, and there shortly followed a cultural flowering as well. Benjamin Franklin of Philadelphia published *The Pennsylvania Gazette* (1729-1766) and the *Poor Richard's Almanack* (1732-1757), in addition to pursuing his interest in politics and science. The nation's first magazine, *The American Magazine, or A Monthly View of the Political State of the British Colonies,* was established (1741) in Philadelphia. Penn's notably fair-minded dealings with the Indians, including his famous treaty, kept the region free of the usual frontier bloodshed. But Penn's successors—especially his son Thomas, who took over in 1746—lacked his vision and conciliatory gifts, and troubles with the French and Indians lasted from 1754 until the suppression of Pontiac's Rebellion in 1763. Pennsylvania was involved at various times in boundary disputes with four other colonies: Maryland, Virginia, Connecticut, and New York. The bitterest wrangle was the one with Connecticut over the Wyoming Valley, which gave rise to the Pennamite Wars (1769-71 and 1784). The northwestern "Erie triangle" was bought first from the Indians, and later from the Federal Government, following a 1789 agreement with New York setting the northern border at the 42nd parallel; the parcel was purchased to secure an Erie port for the colony. The establishment of the Mason-Dixon line (1767) settled Pennsylvania's differences with Maryland and Virginia.

After the American Revolution, in which Pennsylvania played a central role, settlement increased in the western region and in the upper Susquehanna Valley. The country's first paved road, the Philadelphia-Lancaster Turnpike, was completed in 1794. In 1811, a Robert Fulton steamboat was launched at Pittsburgh and became the first to traverse the Ohio and Mississippi rivers. The Schuylkill Canal, one of the nations first long canals (completed 1825), connected Philadelphia and Reading.

The state strongly supported the Union in the Civil War; only New York contributed more troops.

The most widespread flood in the state's history struck in 1972, when Hurricane Agnes, diminished to a tropical storm, remained stationary over the central part of the state for 24 hours. Officials termed it the worst natural disaster in the state's history. In 1975 the Susquehanna again overflowed in the wake of Hurricane Eloise, with damage estimated at over $200 million.

On March 28, 1979, a reactor cooling system at the Three Mile Island nuclear power plant south of Harrisburg malfunctioned in the nation's worst nuclear accident in history. The possibility of a core meltdown or an explosion of the hydrogen gas bubble that had formed in the overheated reactor posed a real threat to nearby residents. Although neither catastrophe occurred, some 144,000 people were evacuated at a cost of $18 million. A 12-member commission appointed by President Carter to investigate the accident issued its report in October 1979: It blamed the plant operator Metropolitan Edison for, among other things, failing to train its personnel adequately to cope with malfunctions. However, the study also concluded that the accident had caused no significant health problems. The Nuclear Regulatory Commission fined Metropolitan Edison $155,000, and only a tie vote on the panel saved the utility company from losing its license. The NRC also cited Babcock & Wilcox, designer of the damaged reactor, for failure to report safety information that may have avoided or lessened the malfunction.

A second accident at Three Mile Island took place in February 1980 when about 1,000 gallons of radioactive water leaked into an auxiliary building. Small amounts of radioactivity were released into the atmosphere and 11 workers were evacuated

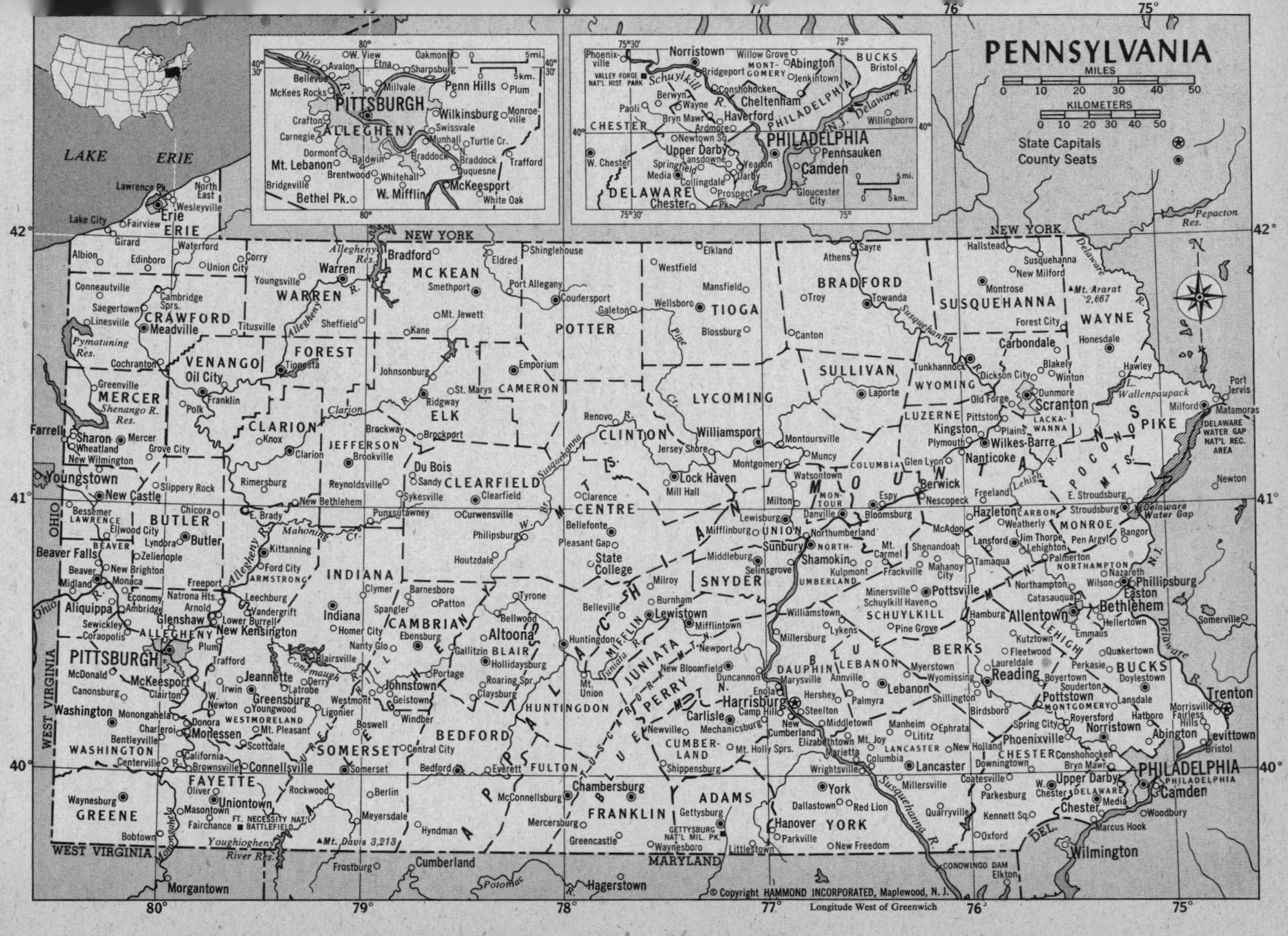

PENNSYLVANIA
MILES
KILOMETERS
State Capitals
County Seats
U.S. STATES/CITIES/TERRITORIES
431
© Copyright HAMMOND INCORPORATED, Maplewood, N.J.
Longitude West of Greenwich
LAKE ERIE
NEW YORK
OHIO
WEST VIRGINIA
MARYLAND
DEL.
N.J.
PITTSBURGH
ALLEGHENY
W. View
Etna
Oakmont
Sharpsburg
Penn Hills
Plum
Bellevue
Avalon
Millvale
Monroeville
McKees Rocks
Wilkinsburg
Crafton
Carnegie
Swissvale
Munhall
Turtle Cr.
Dormont
Braddock
Trafford
Mt. Lebanon
Baldwin
Braddock
Duquesne
Brentwood
Whitehall
Bridgeville
McKeesport
Bethel Pk.
W. Mifflin
White Oak
Ohio R.
PHILADELPHIA
DELAWARE
CHESTER
MONTGOMERY
BUCKS
Phoenixville
Norristown
Willow Grove
Abington
Bristol
VALLEY FORGE NAT'L. HIST. PARK
Bridgeport
Jenkintown
Schuylkill R.
Conshohocken
Berwyn
Wayne
Cheltenham
Paoli
Bryn Mawr
Haverford
Philadelphia
Willingboro
Ardmore
Newtown Sq.
Upper Darby
Pennsauken
W. Chester
Springfield
Lansdowne
Yeadon
Camden
Media
Darby
Collingdale
DELAWARE
Chester
Prospect Pk.
Gloucester City
Delaware R.
Lawrence Pk.
North East
Wesleyville
Lake City
Fairview
Erie
ERIE
Girard
Waterford
Corry
Albion
Edinboro
Union City
Warren
Bradford
Shinglehouse
Elkland
Sayre
Hallstead
Conneautville
Cambridge Sprs.
Youngsville
Eldred
Westfield
Athens
Susquehanna
New Milford
Saegertown
Titusville
WARREN
MCKEAN
Smethport
Port Allegany
Coudersport
Mansfield
BRADFORD
Troy
Towanda
Montrose
Mt. Ararat 2,667
Linesville
CRAWFORD
Meadville
Sheffield
Kane
Mt. Jewett
POTTER
Galeton
Wellsboro
TIOGA
Canton
SUSQUEHANNA
Forest City
WAYNE
Carbondale
Honesdale
Pymatuning Res.
Allegheny Res.
Cochranton
VENANGO
Oil City
FOREST
Tionesta
Johnsonburg
Emporium
SULLIVAN
Tunkhannock
WYOMING
Dickson City
Winton
Hawley
Greenville
Franklin
CAMERON
St. Marys
LYCOMING
Laporte
Old Forge
Dunmore
Scranton
Shenango R. Res.
Polk
Clarion
Ridgway
ELK
Renovo
Williamsport
LUZERNE
Pittston
Plains
LACKA-WANNA
Wallenpaupack
Milford
Port Jervis
Farrell
Sharon
Mercer
Grove City
Knox
Brockway
Brockport
CLINTON
Jersey Shore
Montoursville
Kingston
Plymouth
Wilkes-Barre
Nanticoke
Matamoras
Wheatland
New Wilmington
CLARION
Clarion
JEFFERSON
Brookville
Du Bois
Sandy
CLEARFIELD
Muncy
Montgomery
COLUMBIA
Glen Lyon
DELAWARE WATER GAP NAT'L REC. AREA
Youngstown
New Castle
Chicora
Rimersburg
Reynoldsville
Sykesville
Clearfield
Clarence
Mill Hall
Lock Haven
Watsontown
Milton
MONTOUR
Berwick
Espy
Nescopeck
Newton
Bessemer
BUTLER
E. Brady
Punxsutawney
Curwensville
CENTRE
Bellefonte
Lewisburg
Danville
Bloomsburg
Freeland
E. Stroudsburg
LAWRENCE
Ellwood City
Butler
Philipsburg
Pleasant Gap
UNION
Northumberland
McAdoo
Hazleton
CARBON
Stroudsburg
Delaware Water Gap
BEAVER
Lyndora
Zelienople
Kittanning
Houtzdale
State College
Mifflinburg
Sunbury
NORTH-
Mt. Carmel
Shenandoah
Weatherly
Jim Thorpe
MONROE
Bangor
Beaver Falls
Ford City
Middleburg
Shamokin
Lansford
Lehighton
Pen Argyl
Beaver
New Brighton
INDIANA
Clymer
Barnesboro
Tyrone
SNYDER
Selinsgrove
Kulpmont
Frackville
Mahanoy City
Tamaqua
Palmerton
NORTHAMPTON
Midland
Monaca
Freeport
ARMSTRONG
Patton
Milroy
Belleville
Burnham
Williamstown
CUMBERLAND
Minersville
Schuylkill Haven
Pottsville
Hamburg
Allentown
Nazareth
Northampton
Wilson
Phillipsburg
Aliquippa
Economy
Ambridge
Natrona Hts.
Arnold
Leechburg
Spangler
Bellwood
MIFFLIN
Lewistown
Mifflintown
Lykens
Pine Grove
Easton
Bethlehem
Hellertown
Sewickley
Coraopolis
Glenshaw
Lower Burrell
New Kensington
Indiana
Homer City
Nanty Glo
CAMBRIAN
Ebensburg
Altoona
Gallitzin
BLAIR
Huntingdon
JUNIATA
Millersburg
Hershey
SCHUYLKILL
Myerstown
Annville
BERKS
LEHIGH
Emmaus
Somerville
ALLEGHENY
PITTSBURGH
Plum
Trafford
Blairsville
Holidaysburg
Roaring Spr.
Mt. Union
New Bloomfield
PERRY
Duncannon
Marysville
DAUPHIN
Palmyra
Lebanon
Wyomissing
Reading
Kutztown
Fleetwood
Perkasie
Quakertown
BUCKS
McDonald
McKeesport
Jeannette
Derry
Latrobe
Westmont
Geistown
Portage
Johnstown
Claysburg
HUNTINGDON
Enola
Harrisburg
Camp Hill
Steelton
Shillington
Laureldale
Boyertown
Souderton
Doylestown
Canonsburg
Clairton
Irwin
Greensburg
Youngwood
Ligonier
Windber
BEDFORD
Carlisle
Newville
Mechanicsburg
New Cumberland
Middletown
Manheim
Lititz
Birdsboro
Spring City
Montgomery
Lansdale
Trenton
Washington
Monongahela
Newton
WESTMORELAND
Mt. Pleasant
Boswell
Central City
Mt. Holly Sprs.
Elizabethtown
Mt. Joy
New Holland
Ephrata
Phoenixville
Norristown
Hatboro
Morrisville
Fairless Hills
Charleroi
Donora
Monessen
Scottdale
SOMERSET
Somerset
Bedford
Everett
FULTON
CUMBER-LAND
Marietta
Columbia
LANCASTER
Downingtown
CHESTER
Conshohocken
Bryn Mawr
Abington
Levittown
Bristol
WASHINGTON
Centerville
California
Brownsville
Connellsville
Shippensburg
Wrightsville
Lancaster
Millersville
Coatesville
W. Chester
Upper Darby
DELAWARE
PHILADELPHIA
Waynesburg
FAYETTE
Oliver
Uniontown
Rockwood
Berlin
McConnellsburg
Chambersburg
ADAMS
York
Parkesburg
Media
Camden
GREENE
Masontown
Meyersdale
Hyndman
Mercersburg
FRANKLIN
Gettysburg
Dallastown
Red Lion
Quarryville
Kennett Sq.
Chester
Woodbury
Bobtown
FT. NECESSITY NAT'L BATTLEFIELD
Fairchance
Mt. Davis 3,213
GETTYSBURG NAT'L MIL. PK.
Hanover
YORK
Oxford
Marcus Hook
Youghiogheny River Res.
Frostburg
Greencastle
Waynesboro
Littlestown
Parkville
New Freedom
Conowingo Dam
Elkton
Wilmington
Morgantown
Cumberland
Hagerstown
Potomac R.
Pepacton Res.

during the 90-minute crisis, but no health injury was reported.

It is expected to take four years and about $400 million to repair the nuclear facility.

Full name: Commonwealth of Pennsylvania. **Origin of name:** In honor of William Penn, father of the founder. **Inhabitant:** Pennsylvanian. **Capital:** Harrisburg. **State motto:** Virtue, Liberty & Independence. **Flag:** State seal & motto supported by two horses on gold-bordered blue field. **Seal:** Eagle, ship, plow & sheaves of wheat stand for strength, commerce & agricultural abundance; stalk of corn & olive branch represent peace & plenty. **Flower:** Mountain laurel. **Bird:** Ruffed grouse. **Tree:** Hemlock. **Song:** None. **Nickname:** Keystone State.

Governor: Richard L. Thornburgh. **Annual salary:** $66,000. **Term:** 4 years. **Current term expires:** Jan. 1983. **Voting requirements:** 18 yrs. old & U.S. citizen; resident of state (or district) for 60 days. **U.S. Congressmen:** 25. **Entered Union:** 1787 (2nd state).

Location & boundries: Middle Atlantic state: bounded on the north by New York; on the east by the Delaware River, New York & New Jersey; on the southeast by Delaware & the Delaware River; on the south by Maryland & West Virginia; on the west by West Virginia & Ohio; & on the northwest by Lake Erie. **Total area:** 45,333 sq. mi. (ranks 33rd). **Extreme length:** 307 mi. **Extreme breadth:** 169 mi. **Shoreline:** 51 mi. **Chief rivers:** Delaware, Allegheny, Susquehanna. **Major lakes:** Erie, Wallenpaupack; Pymatuning & Bear Creek Reservoirs. **No. of counties:** 67.

Population (1979 est.): 11,731,000 (ranks 4th). **Pop. increase (1970-79):** −0.6%. **Places over 25,000 pop.:** 23. **Places over 100,000:** 4. **Largest cities:** Philadelphia, Pittsburgh, Erie, Allentown. **Pop. density:** 258.8 per sq. mi. (ranks 9th). **Pop. projection 1985:** 12,032,000. **Pop. distribution:** 80.4% metropolitan; 19.6% nonmetropolitan. **White:** 91.1%. **Black:** 8.6%. **Other:** 0.3%. **Marriage rate (1977):** 7.8 per 1,000 people. **Divorce rate:** 3.2 per 1,000 people.

State finances (1978). Revenue: $12,106,282,000. **Expenditures:** $11,723,405,000. **State taxes:** $533.24 per capita. **State personal income tax:** No. **Public debt (1978):** $555.02 per capita. **Federal aid (1979):** $349.20 per capita. **Personal income (1979 est.):** $8,559.

Sectors of the economy (% of labor force employed in 1970): Manufacturing (34%), Wholesale and retail trade (19%), Government (13%), Educational Services (7%), Services (6%), Construction (5%). **Leading products:** primary and fabricated metals, food items, machinery, chemicals, apparel. **Minerals:** coal, cement, stone, sand & gravel. **Agricultural Products:** dairy items, cattle, hogs, hay, corn, oats, wheat. **Avg. farm (1979 est.):** 151 acres. **Avg. value of farm per acre:** $1,245.

Highway expenditures per capita (1978): $73.15. **Persons per motor vehicle:** 1.70. **Minimum age for driver's license:** 17. **Gasoline tax:** 11¢ per gallon. **Diesel tax:** 11¢ per gallon. **Motor vehicle deaths:** 17.8 per 100,000 people.

Birthrate (1978): 12.9 per 1,000 people. **Infant mortality rate per 1,000 births (1977):** 14.0. **Physicians per 100,000 pop. (1977):** 172. **Dentists per 100,000 pop. (1977):** 53. **Acceptable hospital beds:** 7.6 per 1,000 people. **State expenditures per capita for health and hospitals (1978):** $72.42.

Education expenditures (1975-76): $407.55 per capita annually. **No. of pupils in public schools (1977 est.):** 2,162,000. **No. of institutions of higher learning (1976-77):** 179. **Public school expenditure per pupil in attendance (1975-76):** $1,914. **Avg. salary of public school teachers (1974-75 est.):** $12,200. **No. full-time teachers (1977 est.):** 135,270. **Educational attainment of adult population (1976):** 12.4 median yrs. of school completed; 2.3% with less than 5 years of education; 11.9% with 4 yrs. of college.

Telephones (1977): 79 per 100 people. **State Chamber of Commerce:** Pennsylvania Chamber of Commerce, 222 North Third Street, Harrisburg, Pennsylvania 17101.

RHODE ISLAND

Rhode Island, the nation's smallest state, is not an island, although many small islands are contained within it, including one in Narragansett Bay, Aquidneck Island.

The Bay, which extends inland 28 miles from the Atlantic Ocean, is the predominant feature of the state's eastern section, which comprises about two-thirds of the total area and includes Providence, Pawtucket, and most of Rhode Island's other major cities. The remaining northeastern third of the state is rough, hilly terrain rising east to northwest from 200 to 800 feet above sea level—this section being a part of the New England Uplands, which extend from Maine to Connecticut. Offshore, ten miles south of the mainland, is Block Island, an important navigation landmark. Sixty-seven percent of the state's area is forested, but mostly with "restocked" trees not yet suitable for lumber. Damaging hurricanes occasionally plague the coast.

Once dominated economically by the textile industry, Rhode Island has added many new industries, in a continuing drive toward greater diversification. Small commercial fishing fleets operate out of several ports.

Explorer Giovanni da Verrazano is thought to have been the first European to visit (1524) the region. Adriaen Block explored there in 1614. In 1636, Roger Williams, looking for a place where "persons distressed for conscience" could go, left Puritan-controlled Massachusetts and founded Providence, the state's first settlement. Two years later Williams organized the country's first Baptist congregation.

Despite harsh, costly combat with the Indians in King Philip's War (1675-76), the region prospered, thanks in large measure to the "triangular trade"—vessels carried rum from Newport to Africa, slaves from there to the West Indies, and molasses from there to Newport, where it was made into rum. Later, Rhode Island renounced slavery, prohibiting (1774) the importation of slaves; it also strongly backed the Union in the Civil War. The economic gap that the passing of the triangular trade left was soon filled by the rapid growth of manufacturing, spurred by Samuel Slater's pioneering in mechanized textile production and by a heavy influx of European immigrants who provided an ample labor pool.

From its beginnings, Rhode Island has been famous for its insistence on political and religious freedom, attracting oppressed and refuge-seeking settlers, and the state's rebellious, iconoclastic character streak soon became evident. In 1769, Newport rebels scuttled the British revenue ship *Liberty* and, three years later, in protest to British trade and navigation laws, a group of Providence men burned the English ship *Gaspee* to the water's edge in Narragansett Bay where it had run aground. Rhode Island was the last of the original 13 states to ratify (1790) the Constitution.

Rhode Island also balked at Jefferson's Embargo Act of 1807, and in the War of 1812 it refused to allow its militia to serve outside its borders. Thomas Wilson Dorr and other Rhode Islanders made an abortive revolution in 1842 ("Dorr's Rebellion"), which nonetheless effected a small measure of legislative reform.

In the late 1800s Newport became a fashionable summer home for the very rich, and many palatial mansions were built, some of which are now open for tourists to visit. Today Newport is the country's yachting capital, host to the America's Cup, Newport-Bermuda, and transatlantic races. In 1976, Newport was the first port of welcome for the spectacular fleet of Tall Ships, which sailed from throughout the world to commemorate the bicen-

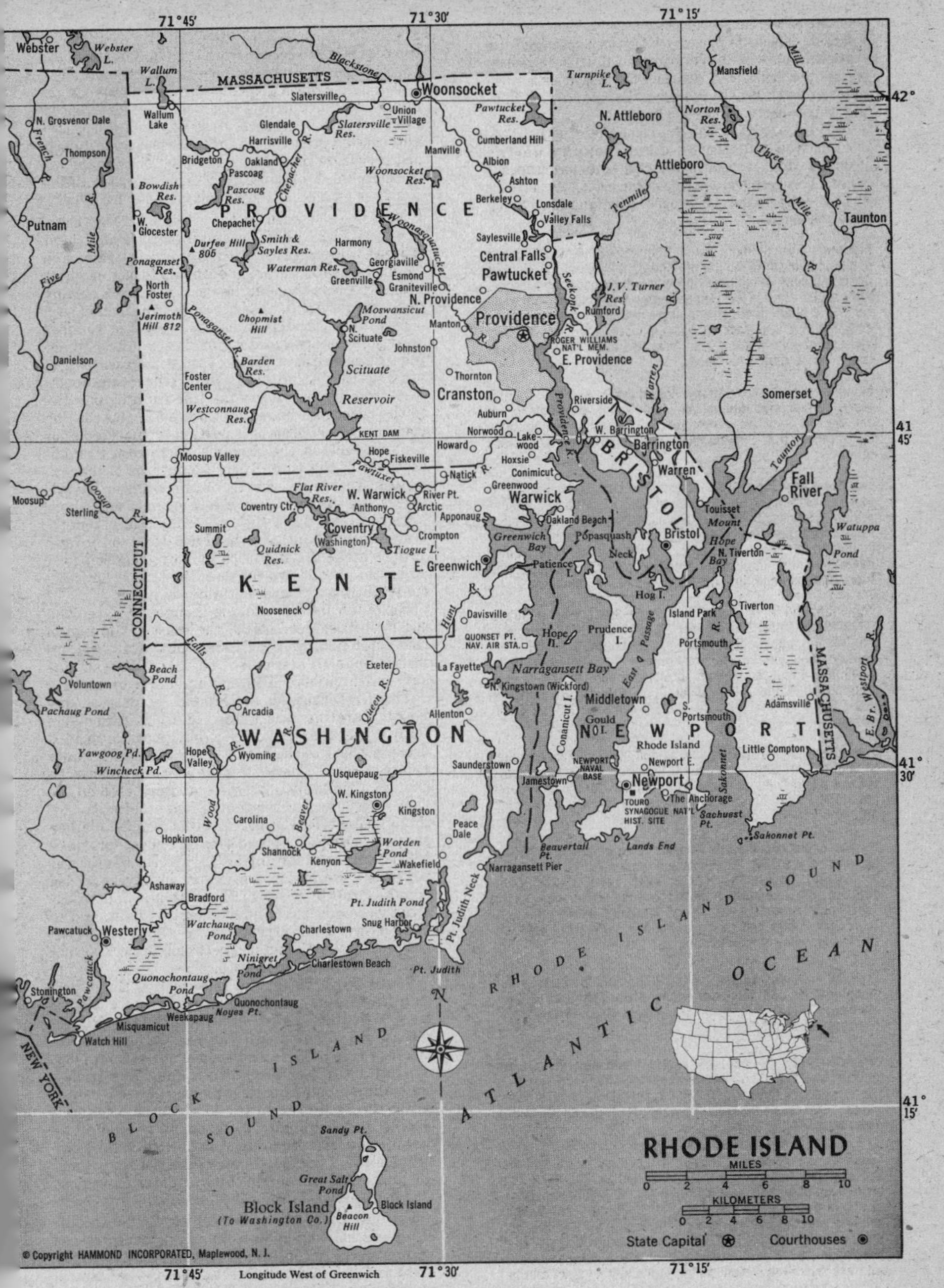
RHODE ISLAND
MILES
KILOMETERS
Longitude West of Greenwich
State Capital
Courthouses
MASSACHUSETTS
CONNECTICUT
NEW YORK
PROVIDENCE
KENT
WASHINGTON
NEWPORT
BRISTOL
Narragansett Bay
RHODE ISLAND SOUND
BLOCK ISLAND SOUND
ATLANTIC OCEAN
Block Island
(To Washington Co.)
© Copyright HAMMOND INCORPORATED, Maplewood, N.J.
Webster
Webster L.
Wallum L.
Wallum Lake
Slatersville
Woonsocket
Pawtucket Res.
Turnpike L.
Mansfield
N. Grosvenor Dale
Glendale
Slatersville Res.
Union Village
N. Attleboro
Norton Res.
Thompson
Harrisville
Manville
Cumberland Hill
Attleboro
Bridgeton
Oakland
Woonsocket Res.
Albion
Pascoag
Ashton
Bowdish Res.
Pascoag Res.
Chepachet
Berkeley
Lonsdale
Valley Falls
Taunton
Putnam
W. Glocester
Durfee Hill 805
Smith & Sayles Res.
Harmony
Saylesville
Central Falls
Ponaganset Res.
Waterman Res.
Georgiaville
Esmond
Pawtucket
North Foster
Greenville
Graniteville
N. Providence
J.V. Turner Res.
Five Mile R.
Jerimoth Hill 812
Chopmist Hill
Moswansicut Pond
Manton
Rumford
Danielson
N. Scituate
Johnston
Providence
ROGER WILLIAMS NAT'L MEM.
E. Providence
Somerset
Ponaganset R.
Barden Res.
Scituate
Thornton
Cranston
Riverside
Foster Center
Reservoir
Auburn
Warren R.
W. Barrington
Westconnaug Res.
KENT DAM
Norwood
Lakewood
Barrington
Moosup Valley
Hope
Fiskeville
Howard
Hoxsie
Warren
Fall River
Pawtuxet R.
Natick
Conimicut
Flat River Res.
W. Warwick
River Pt.
Greenwood
Warwick
Watuppa Pond
Moosup
Coventry Ctr.
Anthony
Arctic
Oakland Beach
Touisset Mount
Sterling
Summit
Apponaug
Popasquash Neck
Bristol
Hope
Quidnick Res.
Coventry (Washington)
Crompton
Greenwich Bay
Hope Bay
N. Tiverton
Tiogue L.
Patience I.
E. Greenwich
Hog I.
KENT
Nooseneck
Hunt R.
Davisville
Prudence I.
Island Park
Tiverton
Beach Pond
QUONSET PT. NAV. AIR STA.
Hope I.
Portsmouth
Voluntown
Falls R.
Exeter
La Fayette
Narragansett Bay
Pachaug Pond
Arcadia
Queen R.
Allenton
Middletown
Adamsville
Yawgoog Pd.
WASHINGTON
Gould I.
S. Portsmouth
Winicheck Pd.
Hope Valley
Wyoming
Saunderstown
Rhode Island
Little Compton
Hopkinton
Wood R.
Usquepaug
Jamestown
NEWPORT NAVAL BASE
Newport E.
Carolina
Beaver R.
W. Kingston
Kingston
Peace Dale
Newport
Shannock
Kenyon
Worden Pond
Wakefield
TOURO SYNAGOGUE NAT'L HIST. SITE
The Anchorage
Sachuest Pt.
Ashaway
Bradford
Narragansett Pier
Beavertail Pt.
Lands End
Sakonnet Pt.
Watchaug Pond
Charlestown
Snug Harbor
Pt. Judith Neck
Pawcatuck
Westerly
Ninigret Pond
Charlestown Beach
Pt. Judith
Quonochontaug Pond
Stonington
Quonochontaug
Weekapaug
Noyes Pt.
Misquamicut
Watch Hill
Sandy Pt.
Great Salt Pond
Beacon Hill
Block Island
Pawcatuck R.
Moosup R.
Blackstone R.
Chepachet R.
Woonasquatucket R.
Seekonk R.
Providence R.
Tenmile R.
Three Mile R.
Mill R.
Taunton R.
Sakonnet R.
East Passage
Conanicut I.
Westport R.
E. Br. Westport R.
71°45'
71°30'
71°15'
42°
41°45'
41°30'
41°
41°15'

tennial of the United States. The flotilla assembled was one of the largest ever.

Rhode Island is presently trying to broaden its economic base by expanding its tourist industry. Music festivals and dramas highlight the summer's entertainment possibilities, along with fishing tournaments and regattas.

In February 1979, the Supreme Court of the state overturned the state's death penalty on the grounds that it was cruel and unusual punishment. The court ruled that the 1973 law did not allow a judge to consider mitigating circumstances.

Full name: State of Rhode Island & Providence Plantations. **Origin of name:** In honor of the Isle of Rhodes: name chosen by General Court of Colony. **Inhabitant:** Rhode Islander. **Capital:** Providence. **State motto:** Hope. **Flag:** Golden anchor & 12 gold stars on white field. **Seal:** State motto printed above anchor, symbolizing hope; date 1636 was year Roger Williams founded Providence. **Flower:** Violet. **Bird:** Rhode Island red. **Tree:** Red maple. **Song:** "Rhode Island." **Nickname:** Little Rhody.

Governor: John Joseph Garrahy. **Annual salary:** $42,500. **Term:** 2 years. **Current term expires:** Jan. 1981. **Voting requirements:** 18 yrs. old & U.S. citizen; resident of city or town 30 days; positive identification. **U.S. Congressmen:** 2. **Entered Union:** 1790 (13th state).

Location & boundaries: New England state: bounded on the north & east by Massachusetts; on the west by Connecticut; & on the south by New York where Block Island Sound meets Long Island Sound in the Atlantic Ocean. **Total area:** 1,214 sq. mi. (ranks 50th). **Extreme length:** 48 mi. **Extreme breadth:** 37 mi. **Coastline:** 40 mi. **Chief rivers:** Sakonnet, Blackstone, Woonasquatuket, Pawtuxet. **Major lakes:** Worden Pond, Scituate Reservoir. **No. of counties:** 5.

Population (1979 est.): 929,000 (ranks 39th). **Pop. increase (1970-79):** −2.1%. **Places over 25,000 pop.:** 11. **Places over 100,000:** 1. **Largest cities:** Providence, Warwick, Cranston. **Pop. density:** 765.2 per sq. mi. (ranks 2nd). **Pop. projection 1985:** 1,003,000. **Pop. distribution:** 92.2% metropolitan; 7.8% non-metropolitan. **White:** 96.6%. **Black:** 2.7%. **Other:** 0.7%. **Marriage rate (1977):** 7.6 per 1,000 people. **Divorce rate:** 3.7 per 1,000 people.

State finances (1978). Revenue: $1,086,921,000. **Expenditures:** $1,066,996,000 **State taxes:** $490.12 per capita. **State personal income tax:** Yes. **Public debt (1978):** $921.38 per capita. **Federal aid (1979):** $443.70 per capita. **Personal income (1979 est.):** $8,266.

Sectors of the economy (% of labor force employed in 1970): Manufacturing (35%), Wholesale and retail trade (19%), Government (16%), Educational Services (8%), Services (6%), Construction (5%). **Leading products:** jewelry & silverware, textile items, primary metals, machinery, fabricated metals, electrical equipment, rubber and plastic items. **Avg. farm (1979 est.):** 94 acres. **Avg. value of farm per acre:** $2,133.

Highway expenditures per capita (1978): $40.95. **Persons per motor vehicle:** 1.38. **Minimum age for driver's license:** 16. **Gasoline tax:** 10¢ per gallon. **Diesel tax:** 10¢ per gallon. **Motor vehicle deaths:** 11.6 per 100,000 people.

Birthrate (1978): 12.4 per 1,000 people. **Infant mortality rate per 1,000 births (1977):** 12.1. **Physicians per 100,000 pop. (1977):** 197. **Dentists per 100,000 pop. (1977):** 49. **Acceptable hospital beds:** 7.3 per 1,000 people. **State expenditures per capita for health and hospitals (1978):** $116.45.

Education expenditures (1975-76): $433.78 per capita annually. **No. of pupils in public schools (1977 est.):** 170,000. **No. of institutions of higher learning (1976-77):** 12. **Public school expenditure per pupil in attendance (1975-76):** $1,722. **Average salary of public school teachers (1974-75 est.):** $12,885. **No. full-time teachers (1977 est.):** 10,960. **Educational attainment of adult population (1976):** 12.4 median yrs. of school completed; 3.4% with less than 5 years of education; 14.9% with 4 yrs. of college.

Telephones (1977): 73 per 100 people. **State Chamber of Commerce:** Rhode Island Chamber of Commerce Federation, 206 Smith Street, Providence, Rhode Island 02908.

SOUTH CAROLINA

South Carolina, where the Civil War began, was the first state to secede from the Union. One of the 13 Colonies, it is particularly rich in historic sites, which help draw a growing number of tourists annually. Vivid contrasts often confront the visitor: inlet-dotted swampland gives way to hill country, and estates graced by handsome Georgian homes are set off by poor areas in which shacks are not uncommon. A major U.S. Marine Corps training center is located at Parris Island, near Beaufort.

Vast projects such as the Atomic Energy Commission's $1.2-billion Savannah River Plant (near Aiken) underscore South Carolina's transition from a basically agrarian economy to one in which industry plays the leading part. Livestock raising and commercial fishing are also significant.

Two main land regions make up the roughly triangular-shaped state: the "low country," making up two-thirds of the total area and consisting of a part of the Atlantic Coastal Plain rising northwest from the ocean to a fall line running parallel to the coast and bisecting Columbia; and the "up country," consisting of a portion of the Piedmont Plateau and, in the extreme northwest, a small segment of the Blue Ridge Mountains of the Appalachian range. South of the Santee River's mouth are the Sea Islands, a long chain of offshore isles reaching down the rest of the state's length. Water is abundant, and the sharp drops in the land surface make the state rich in hydroelectric-power potential. About two-thirds of the land is forested, contributing to a sizable timber industry.

Giovanni da Verrazano is thought to have been the first to explore (1524) the coast of the region that later became North and South Carolina; an initial Spanish settlement (1526) at Winyah Bay suffered a malaria outbreak and did not endure.

The first English settlement in present-day South Carolina was made (1670) at Albemarle Point on the Ashley River, but poor conditions drove settlers to the site of Charleston (originally Charles Town). There grew the core of a prosperous though ultimately unstable economy based on the slave-supported cultivation of rice and indigo. Although North and South Carolina were officially a single province, they had separate governors until 1691; from that year until 1712, a sole governor was based at Charleston while his deputy governed North Carolina. After 1712, North and South Carolina were governed independently again, and in 1729 they officially became separate royal provinces; the boundary between them was not defined, however, until 1815.

South Carolina, in the years before the American Revolution, progressed economically despite wars with the Spanish and French, and with pirates and Indians; there was a revolt against proprietary rule in 1719, and a slave uprising in 1739. An influx of Germans, Swiss, and Scots-Irish—from abroad and from neighboring states—helped settle the uplands and the lower middle country. Social and economic differences between the small-scale farmers of the up country and the plantation lords of the low country gave rise to regional disputes, culminating in the Regulator Movement for up country reforms. Statehood dates from 1788.

The early part of the 19th century in South Carolina was marked by a decline in agriculture and an increasingly contentious dialogue between the state and the Federal government on the issue of states' rights. South Carolina's Nullification Act (1832) declared a new, higher U.S. tariff act null and void; the immediate issue was resolved (1833) by compromise, but the larger question of the divi-

SOUTH CAROLINA
MILES
KILOMETERS
State Capital
County Seats
ATLANTIC OCEAN
NORTH CAROLINA
GEORGIA
Long Bay
Copyright HAMMOND INCORPORATED, Maplewood, N.J.
Longitude West of Greenwich

OCONEE
PICKENS
ANDERSON
GREENVILLE
SPARTANBURG
CHEROKEE
YORK
UNION
LAURENS
NEWBERRY
LANCASTER
CHESTER
FAIRFIELD
RICHLAND
KERSHAW
LEE
CHESTERFIELD
MARLBORO
DILLON
MARION
HORRY
FLORENCE
DARLINGTON
WILLIAMSBURG
GEORGETOWN
SUMTER
CLARENDON
CALHOUN
LEXINGTON
SALUDA
GREENWOOD
ABBEVILLE
McCORMICK
EDGEFIELD
AIKEN
ORANGEBURG
BERKELEY
CHARLESTON
DORCHESTER
COLLETON
BAMBERG
BARNWELL
ALLENDALE
HAMPTON
BEAUFORT
JASPER

Columbia
Charleston
Greenville
Spartanburg
Anderson
Florence
Myrtle Beach
Conway
Georgetown
Sumter
Camden
Orangeburg
Walterboro
Beaufort
Aiken
Greenwood
Abbeville
Newberry
Union
Laurens
Clinton
Chester
Lancaster
Rock Hill
York
Fort Mill
Gaffney
Easley
Pickens
Seneca
Walhalla
Westminster
Clemson
Pendleton
Honea Path
Due West
Calhoun Falls
McCormick
Edgefield
Johnston
Batesburg
Leesville
Swansea
Lexington
West Columbia
Cayce
Forest Acres
Eastover
St. Matthews
Cameron
Bowman
Branchville
St. George
Summerville
Moncks Corner
Ridgeville
Harleyville
Holly Hill
Eutawville
Santee
Summerton
Manning
Kingstree
Andrews
Hemingway
Johnsonville
Lake City
Timmonsville
Darlington
Hartsville
Cheraw
Bennettsville
McColl
Clio
Dillon
Latta
Mullins
Marion
Nichols
Loris
Aynor
North Myrtle Beach
Myrtle Beach A.F.B.
Murrells Inlet
Pawleys Island
North I.
Isle of Palms
Sullivans Island
Mt. Pleasant
Folly Beach
Kiawah I.
Edisto Island
Hilton Head I.
Port Royal
Hardeeville
Ridgeland
Estill
Varnville
Hampton
Brunson
Allendale
Fairfax
Barnwell
Blackville
Williston
New Ellenton
Jackson
Bath
Clearwater
N. Augusta
Denmark
Bamberg
Springfield
North

ATLANTIC OCEAN
Cape Romain
Bulls Bay
Winyah Bay
St. Helena Sound
Port Royal Sound
Tybee Roads

Pee Dee River
Little Pee Dee River
Lynches River
Black River
Santee River
Wateree River
Congaree R.
Broad River
Saluda R.
Savannah River
Edisto R.
Combahee R.
Cooper R.
Ashley R.

L. Marion
L. Moultrie
L. Murray
Clark Hill Res.
Hartwell Res.
Lake Keowee
Lake Hartwell

BLUE RIDGE
Sassafras Mtn. 3,560
KINGS MTN. NAT'L MIL. PK.
COWPENS NAT'L BATTLEFIELD
NINETY SIX N.H.S.
CONGAREE SWAMP NAT'L MON.
SHAW A.F.B.
FT. JACKSON
SAVANNAH RIVER ATOMIC ENERGY RESERVATION
SANTEE DAM
HARTWELL DAM
CLARK HILL DAM
SUMTER NAT'L MON.

Charlotte
Gastonia
Fayetteville
Lumberton
Whiteville
Elizabethtown
Rockingham
Laurinburg
Wadesboro
Monroe
Savannah
Augusta
Athens
Thomson
Statesboro
Sylvania
Millen
Waynesboro
Louisville
Sandersville
Milledgeville
Madison
Commerce
Cornelia
Toccoa
Clayton

sion of power between nation and state remained. A leading national figure of the period was South Carolina's Senator John C. Calhoun, who defended not only the values and rights of his own state, but of the South as a whole. After South Carolina led the way to secession (1860), Confederate artillery fire on Federal troops at Fort Sumter in Charleston Harbor started (April 12, 1861) the Civil War.

During the conflict, there was much fighting along the state's coast, and a Union blockade of Charleston Harbor crippled the economy. In 1865, troops led by General William T. Sherman marched across the state, destroying many plantations and burning Columbia. Reconstruction brought a measure of material recovery, but there was also much waste and political corruption. White supremacy and Negro disenfranchisement soon returned.

The South Carolina legislature in 1977 reinstated the death penalty along the lines of a Georgia measure that has been declared constitutional by the U.S. Supreme Court. It also passed a constitutional amendment that will do much to equalize property taxes in South Carolina.

In 1979 the nation's only commercial nuclear waste disposal facility in operation was at Barnwell, S.C. To prevent the state from becoming a national nuclear dumping ground, Gov. Richard Riley in October ordered a severe reduction in the amount of out-of-state nuclear waste to be processed at Barnwell.

Full name: State of South Carolina. **Origin of name:** In honor of Charles I of England. **Inhabitant:** South Carolinian. **Captial:** Columbia. **State mottoes:** Animis Opibusque Parati (Prepared in Mind & Resources); Dum Spiro, Spero (While I Breathe, I Hope). **Flag:** White palmetto & crescent on blue field. **Seal:** Palmetto tree, symbolizing successful defense (1776) of fort on Sullivan's Island against British; figure of hope carrying laurel branch across sword-covered beach. **Flower:** Carolina (Yellow) jessamine. **Bird:** Carolina wren. **Tree:** Palmetto. **Song:** "Carolina." **Nickname:** Palmetto State.

Governor: Richard W. Riley. **Annual salary:** $60,000. **Term:** 4 years. **Current term expires:** Jan. 1983. **Voting requirements:** 18 yrs. old & U.S. citizen; resident of state; registration 30 days before election. **U.S. Congressmen:** 6. **Entered Union:** 1788 (8th state).

Location & boundaries: South Atlantic state: bounded on the north & northeast by North Carolina; on the east by the Atlantic Ocean; & on the south & west by Georgia & the Savannah River. **Total area:** 31,055 sq. mi. (ranks 40th). **Extreme length:** 273 mi. **Extreme breadth:** 210 mi. **Coastline:** 281 mi. **Chief rivers:** Pee Dee, Santee, Edisto, Savannah. **Major lakes:** Marion, Moultrie, Murray. **No. of counties:** 46.

Population (1979 est.): 2,932,000 (ranks 25th). **Pop. increase (1970-79):** 13.2%. **Places over 25,000 pop.:** 10. **Places over 100,000:** 1. **Largest cities:** Columbia, Charleston, Greenville, North Charleston. **Pop. density:** 94.4 per sq. mi. (ranks 20th). **Pop. projection 1985:** 3,261,000. **Pop. distribution:** 48.3% metropolitan; 51.7% nonmetropolitan. **White:** 69.3%. **Black:** 30.4%. **Other:** 0.3%. **Marriage rate (1977):** 17.8 per 1,000 people. **Divorce rate:** 3.7 per 1,000 people.

State finances (1978). Revenue: $2,768,427,000. **Expenditures:** $2,584,661,000. **State taxes:** $467.60 per capita. **State personal income tax:** Yes. **Public debt (1978):** $604.15 per capita. **Federal aid (1979):** $335.57 per capita. **Personal income (1979 est.):** $7,027.

Sectors of the economy (% of labor force employed in 1970): Manufacturing (36%), Wholesale and retail trade (17%), Government (15%), Services (9%), Educational Services (7%), Construction (7%). **Leading products:** textile items, chemicals, paper items, food items, machinery, lumber & wood items. **Agricultural products:** dairy items, cattle, tobacco, soybeans, cotton, peaches, corn. **Fishing:** shrimp, oysters, crabs. **Avg. farm (1979 est.):** 186 acres. **Avg. value of farm per acre:** $635.

Highway expenditures per capita (1978): $71.70. **Persons per motor vehicle:** 1.48. **Minimum age for driver's license:** 16. **Gasoline tax:** 10¢ per gallon. **Diesel tax:** 10¢ per gallon. **Motor vehicle deaths:** 30.3 per 100,000 people.

Birthrate (1978): 17.1 per 1,000 people. **Infant mortality rate per 1,000 births (1977):** 17.6. **Physicians per 100,000 pop. (1977):** 129. **Dentists per 100,000 pop. (1977):** 37. **Acceptable hospital beds:** 6.0 per 1,000 people. **State expenditures per capita for health and hospitals (1978):** $85.32.

Education expenditures (1975-76): $398.40 per capita annually. **No. of pupils in public schools (1977 est.):** 612,000. **No. of institutions of higher learning (1976-77):** 56. **Public school expenditure per pupil in attendance (1975-76):** $1,278. **Avg. salary of public school teachers (1974-75 est.):** $9,770. **No. full-time teachers (1977 est.):** 32,570. **Educational attainment of adult population (1976):** 12.2 median yrs. of school completed; 6.9% with less than 5 years of education; 10.4% with 4 yrs. of college.

Telephones (1977): 65 per 100 people. **State Chamber of Commerce:** South Carolina Chamber of Commerce, 1002 Calhoun St., Columbia, South Carolina 29201.

SOUTH DAKOTA

South Dakota contains (near Castle Rock) the geographical center of the United States, as well as the largest gold mine in the world, Homestake, at the town of Lead. Rich in Old West lore, with such place names as Belle Fourche, Deadwood, and Wounded Knee, the state is home for nearly 30,000 Indians (mostly Sioux), living on 8,400 square miles of reservations. Within the state's borders is one of the country's most famous landmarks and tourist attractions, Mount Rushmore, in the Black Hills; carved into its granite face, at an altitude of more than a mile, are 60-foot-high busts of Presidents Washington, Jefferson, Lincoln, and Theodore Roosevelt. Badlands National Park contains fantastic pinnacles and canyons in a desert setting.

The state, which has less than five percent forested land, is cut by the Missouri into broadly contrasting, irregularly shaped halves. In the west are the Badlands, the spectacular Black Hills, and the rolling grasslands of the Great Plains, while in the east are the rich farmlands that continue to make agriculture South Dakota's main industry. There is a heavy emphasis on livestock, including large numbers of cattle, hogs and sheep. Manufacturing consists mainly of meat processing.

Early inhabitants were the Mound Builders, dating from about 1200. Living there after 1600 were the Arikara Indians, an advanced agricultural people, eventually forced out by the more warlike Sioux, or Dakota, Indians. South Dakota and southwestern North Dakota were part of the vast territory claimed (1682) for France by Robert Cavelier, Sieur de La Salle, but Frenchmen did not actually visit the region until 1742-43, when the brothers François and Louis Joseph Vérendyre made explorations and planted a lead plate at the site of what is now Pierre. The area was ceded to Spain in 1762, and toward the end of the century it became part of the St. Louis fur-trading empire. Napolean Bonaparte reclaimed (1800) the territory for France, but three years later sold it to the United States, as part of the Louisiana Purchase.

The Lewis and Clark Expedition explored the region which is now the Dakotas in 1804 and 1806. Fort Pierre, the first non-Indian settlement (1817), became a major fur-trading center, and in 1831 the first steamboat on the upper Missouri began operations.

Dakota Territory—comprising both Dakotas and parts of Montana and Wyoming—was created in 1861. In 1868, the Sioux—their way of life disrupted by the decline of the buffalo herds—made a treaty with the U.S., accepting a food subsidy and a reservation which included the Black Hills. But the

SOUTH DAKOTA
MILES
0 10 20 40 60 80
KILOMETERS
0 10 20 40 60 80
State Capital
County Seats
Longitude West 100° of Greenwich
© Copyright HAMMOND INCORPORATED, Maplewood, N.J.
MONTANA
NORTH DAKOTA
WYOMING
NEBRASKA
MINNESOTA
IOWA
HARDING
PERKINS
BUTTE
MEADE
CORSON
DEWEY
ZIEBACH
WALWORTH
POTTER
FAULK
EDMUNDS
MC PHERSON
CAMPBELL
BROWN
MARSHALL
ROBERTS
DAY
CODINGTON
GRANT
DEUEL
HAMLIN
CLARK
SPINK
SULLY
HYDE
HAND
BEADLE
KINGSBURY
LAKE
MOODY
MINNEHAHA
BROOKINGS
STANLEY
HUGHES
HAAKON
JONES
SANBORN
MINER
LAKE
BRULE
JERAULD
AURORA
HANSON
MC COOK
HUTCHINSON
TURNER
LINCOLN
BUFFALO
LYMAN
TRIPP
BRULE
CHARLES
MIX
DOUGLAS
GREGORY
YANKTON
CLAY
UNION
PENNINGTON
JACKSON
WASHABAUGH
(UNORGANIZED)
MELLETTE
BENNETT
SHANNON
(UNORGANIZED)
TODD
(UNORGANIZED)
CUSTER
FALL RIVER
LAWRENCE
BLACK HILLS
Bowman
Mott
Linton
Edgeley
LaMoure
Rice R.
Wahpeton
Hankinson
Wheaton
Lake Traverse
Browns Valley
Big Stone L.
Ortonville
Madison
Milbank
Watertown
Clear L.
Gary
White
Estelline
Hayti
Bryant
Arlington
Volga
Elkton
Brookings
Oldham
Preston
Iroquois
DeSmet
Carthage
Madison
Flandreau
Pipestone
NAT'L MON.
PIPESTONE
Colman
Dell Rapids
Garretson
Colton
Luverne
Harrisburg
Canton
Centerville
Rock Valley
Beresford
Irene
Viborg
Menno
Hurley
Parker
Freeman
Marion
Sioux Falls
Lennox
Scotland
Tyndall
Avon
Yankton
Wakonda
Vermillion
Elk Point
N. Sioux City
Sioux City
S. Sioux City
Ponca
Randolph
Hartington
Bloomfield
Plainview
O'Neill
Bassett
Valentine
Niobrara
Springfield
Bon Homme
Pickstown
Ft. Randall Dam
Gavins Pt. Dam
Lewis & Clark L.
Bonesteel
Burke
Dallas
Colome
Gregory
Wagner
Avon
L. Andes
Delmont
Olivet
Tripp
Armour
Geddes
Platte
Corsica
Parkston
Bridgewater
Emery
Ethan
Canistota
Hartford
Salem
Alexandria
White L.
Stickney
Kimball
Plankinton
Letcher
Woonsocket
Howard
Artesian
Canova
Mitchell
Davison
Chamberlain
Oacoma
Kennebec
Presho
Murdo
Vivian
Wood
White River
Winner
Okreek
Mission
St. Francis
Parmelee
Martin
Allen
Kyle
Pine Ridge
Wanblee
Kadoka
Belvidere
Philip
Bad
Midland
Milesville
Cherry Creek
Wall
New Underwood
Ellsworth A.F.B.
Rapid City
Hill City
Keystone
Mt. Rushmore Nat'l Mem.
Custer
Wind Cave Nat'l Park
Jewel Cave Nat'l Mon.
Newcastle
Edgemont
Igloo
Hot Springs
Angostura Res.
Chadron
Badlands Nat'l Park
Deadwood
Lead
Central City
Sturgis
Ft. Meade
Spearfish
Belle Fourche
Newell
Belle Fourche Res.
Buffalo
Bison
Timber Lake
Isabel
Dupree
Eagle Butte
La Plant
Trail City
Mobridge
Selby
Bowdle
Hoven
Gettysburg
Faulkton
Redfield
Doland
Conde
Clark
Willow L.
Onida
Highmore
Miller
Wessington
Wolsey
Huron
Wessington Springs
Gannvalley
Pierre
Ft. Pierre
Blunt
Oahe Dam
Lake Oahe
Maurine
Faith
Lemmon
Hettinger
McIntosh
McLaughlin
Herreid
Mound City
Eureka
Leola
Frederick
Hecla
Columbia
Hosmer
Ipswich
Groton
Aberdeen
Bristol
Webster
Waubay
Waubay L.
Wilmot
Sisseton
Veblen
Britton
Claremont
Langford
Rosholt
Crow Creek Ind. Res.
Lower Brule Ind. Res.
Big Bend Dam
Lake Sharpe
Lake Francis Case
Standing Rock Ind. Res.
Ft. Yates
Cheyenne River Ind. Res.
Rosebud Ind. Res.
Pine Ridge Ind. Res.
Harney Pk. 7,242
+ Geographical Center of the United States
Missouri River
James River
Cheyenne River
White River
Grand River
Moreau River
Belle Fourche River
Bad River
Niobrara River
Keya Paha R.
Elkhorn R.
Big Sioux R.
Vermillion River
Wolf Cr.
Snake R.
Cedar Cr.
Cannonball R.
Thunder Butte
Shadehill Res.
Little Missouri R.
N. Fork
S. Fork
Fork
46° 45° 44° 43°
104° 103° 102° 101° 100° 99° 98° 97°

discovery of gold in the Black Hills caused non-Indian prospectors to pour in. Open war broke out between the Sioux and the prospectors. The Sioux agreed in 1876 to abandon the Black Hills, after the government threatened to cut off their food supply. Rough mining towns grew up, and population soared from about 98,000 (1880) to nearly 350,000 (1890). North and South Dakota were admitted to the Union on November 2, 1889.

The Pine Ridge Indian Reservation was the focus of recurring violence in the early 1970s. Wounded Knee, the site of a massacre of Indians in 1890, was the scene of a 71-day takeover by members of the militant American Indian Movement (AIM) in 1973. There were also numerous incidents on the reservation, including the shooting deaths of two FBI agents in 1975, for each of which a member of AIM was sentenced to life imprisonment in 1977. On June 13, 1979, the U.S. Court of Claims ruled that the removal of the Sioux from the Black Hills in 1876 had violated the tribe's constitutional rights as well as its treaty rights. The Federal Government was ordered to pay the Sioux $17,500,000 for the loss of the Black Hills—and to pay it with interest because of the constitutional violation. The total was estimated to be about $100,000,000—the largest award ever made to a U.S. Indian tribe. The government appealed to the Supreme Court.

Full name: State of South Dakota. **Origin of name:** From the Sioux meaning "Alliance with Friends." **Inhabitant:** South Dakotan. **Capital:** Pierre. **State motto:** Under God the People Rule. **Flag:** State seal surrounded by gold circle, stylized sun & lettering in yellow on a blue field. **Seal:** Smelter chimney, represents mining; plowman stands for farming; riverboat symbolizes transportation. **Flower:** Pasqueflower. **Bird:** Ringnecked pheasant. **Tree:** Black Hills spruce. **Song:** "Hail, South Dakota." **Nickname:** Coyote State; Sunshine State.

Governor: William J. Janklow. **Annual salary:** $45,000. **Term:** 4 yrs. **Current term expires:** Jan. 1983. **Voting requirements:** 18 yrs. old & U.S. citizen; registered to vote; no durational residency requirements. **U.S. Congressmen:** 2. **Entered Union:** 1889 (40th state).

Location & boundaries: Northern Midwestern state: bounded on the north by North Dakota; on the east by Minnesota, Iowa & Big Sioux & Red Rivers; on the south by Nebraska & the Missouri River; & on the west by Wyoming & Montana. **Total area:** 77,047 sq. mi. (ranks 16th). **Extreme length:** 380 mi. **Extreme breadth:** 245 mi. **Chief rivers:** Missouri, James, Cheyenne. **Major lakes:** Lewis & Clark, Big Stone. **No. of counties:** 67.

Population (1979 est.): 689,000 (ranks 45th). **Pop. increase (1970-79):** 3.4%. **Places over 25,000 pop.:** 2. **Places over 100,000:** None. **Largest cities:** Sioux Falls, Aberdeen, Rapid City. **Pop. density:** 8.9 per sq. mi. (ranks 46th). **Pop. projection 1985:** 707,000. **Pop. distribution:** 27.9% metropolitan; 72.1% non-metropolitan. **White:** 94.7%. **Black:** 0.3%. **Other:** 5%. **Marriage rate (1977):** 14.9 per 1,000 people. **Divorce rate:** 3.5 per 1,000 people.

State finances (1978). Revenue: $597,683,000. **Expenditures:** $581,674,000. **State Taxes:** $324.06 per capita. **State personal income tax:** No. **Public debt (1978):** $560.15 per capita. **Federal aid (1979):** $451.96 per capita. **Personal income (1979 est.):** $7,334.

Sectors of the economy (% of labor force employed in 1970): Wholesale and retail trade (22%), Government (19%), Educational Services (10%), Services (7%), Construction (5%), Manufacturing (4%). **Leading products:** food items; printing & publishing; machinery; stone, clay & glass items; lumber; fabricated metals. **Agricultural products:** cattle, hogs, dairy items, wheat, corn, hay. **Avg. farm (1979 est.):** 1,095 acres. **Avg. value of farm per acre:** $257.

Highway expenditures per capita (1978): $142.04. **Persons per motor vehicle:** 1.15. **Minimum age for driver's license:** 16. **Gasoline tax:** 12¢ per gallon. **Diesel tax:** 12¢ per gallon. **Motor vehicle deaths:** 27.7 per 100,000 people.

Birthrate (1978): 17.7 per 1,000 people. **Infant mortality rate per 1,000 births (1977):** 16.4. **Physicians per 100,000 pop. (1977):** 103. **Dentists per 100,000 pop. (1977):** 43. **Acceptable hospital beds:** 8.7 per 1,000 people. **State expenditures per capita for health and hospitals (1978):** $71.86.

Education expenditures (1975-76): $451.94 per capita annually. **No. of pupils in public schools (1977 est.):** 146,000. **No. of institutions of higher learning (1976-77):** 17. **Public school expenditure per pupil in attendance (1975-76):** $1,445. **Avg. salary of public school teachers (1974-75):** $8,860. **No. full-time teachers (1977 est):** 8,830. **Educational attainment of adult population (1976):** 12.5 median yrs. of school completed; 1.1% with less than 5 years of education; 11.4% with 4 yrs. of college.

Telephones (1977): 68 per 100 people. **State Chamber of Commerce:** Greater South Dakota Chamber of Commerce, P.O. Box 190, Pierre, South Dakota 57501.

TENNESSEE

Traces of Tennessee's traditionally hardy frontier spirit remain today in its museums and restored buildings, as well as in the character and life-style of many Tennesseans themselves. The first state to be created out of national territory, Tennessee came to be called the Volunteer State because of its readiness to furnish troops in the War of 1812 and the Mexican War. Its history and culture have been deeply influenced by its three main land regions—East, Middle, and West Tennessee.

In East Tennessee, with the heaviest population outside of the major urban areas in the state, are the Great Smoky Mountains and the eastern slope of the Cumberland Mountains, both in the Appalachian range. Middle Tennessee consists of the fertile Nashville Basin and an elevated plain (the Highland Rim) and the western slope of the Cumberlands, which divide the two sections of the state, the features being part of the Interior Low Plateaus. Middle Tennesseans of this gently rolling bluegrass region tend to identify with the Old South. West Tennessee lies between the western bend of the Tennessee River and the Mississippi River and includes a portion of the East Gulf Coastal Plain and a thin strip of the Mississippi Alluvial Plain. Here farming predominates. About half of the state is forested.

Tennessee, once a basically rural region, has become a largely industrial state. Chemicals, textiles, and food and metal products are among the major manufactures. Massive hydroelectric installations, developed (beginning 1933) by the Tennessee Valley Authority (TVA), provide power for Tennessee and six other states. Mining, lumbering, cotton, tobacco, and livestock are also vital elements of the state's economy.

Indians similar to the Mound Builders are thought to have been the early inhabitants of the Tennessee region. The Chickasaw, Cherokee, and Shawnee were among the tribes living there when the first Europeans, led by De Soto, arrived in 1540. De Soto was soon followed by countryman Juan Pardo, but the Spaniards were seeking gold and did not settle. A long period of French-British contention over the land was foreshadowed by the arrival in the same year (1673) of Marquette and Jolliet, and Englishmen James Needham and Gabriel Arthur. In 1682, La Salle and his party paused in their exploration of the Mississippi Valley and built Fort Prudhomme at the mouth of the Hatchie River.

Spurred by reports of scouts such as Daniel Boone, a steady stream of settlers from Virginia and the Carolinas soon began to enter the region. French influence waned, and by 1763 the British were in control, despite strong resistance from the

TENNESSEE
MILES
KILOMETERS
State Capital   County Seats
Longitude West of Greenwich
Copyright HAMMOND INCORPORATED, Maplewood, N.J.

Cherokees. Between 1772 and 1790 several abortive attempts were made by settlers to establish self-government and achieve statehood.

In 1790 Congress organized the region into the "Territory of the United States South of the River Ohio," commonly called the Southwest Territory. Tennessee entered the Union in 1796.

Tennessee began life as a state with what Jefferson called the nation's "least imperfect and most republican" constitution. By 1800, immigration had swelled the population to 100,000, and the coming of steam and rail transportation did much to develop the state's economy. When the Cherokees and the Chickasaws were forced to move west in the late 1830s, another, smaller wave of immigration ensued. Politically, the new state's dominant figure was Andrew Jackson, who served as a U.S. representative and senator from Tennessee before becoming (1829) president.

Although a slaveholding state, Tennessee was at first pro-Union in the years before the Civil War, but after Fort Sumter a referendum was held and two-thirds of the people backed secession (1861). Tennessee was the last Confederate state to secede, and the first to be readmitted.

The Reconstruction Era triggered a strong reaction that included the founding (1866) of the Ku Klux Klan in Pulaski and the adoption (1870) of a new constitution limiting Negro suffrage via a poll tax. On the farms, a tenancy system replaced the plantations, and the state's crippled economy turned toward increased industrialization for new life. In 1878, the worst yellow-fever epidemic in U.S. history hit Memphis, killing thousands.

Among the state's attractions is Great Smoky Mountains National Park, which it shares with North Carolina. Parts of five states can be seen from Lookout Mountain on the Tennessee River near Chattanooga. The Historic State Capital and a reproduction of the Parthenon are in Nashville, the home of the famed "Grand Ole Opry." The new Opry House and Opryland, U.S.A., a 300-acre theme park are popular tourist attractions. Libertyland, a theme park at Memphis, was opened during the nation's bicentennial.

In 1973, six years after the repeal of the ban on the teaching of the theory of evolution, a new version was enacted. It requires that equal emphasis be given to Genesis in the classroom as well as other theories of man's origin. The original law resulted in the 1925 trial of biology teacher John Scopes in the little town of Dayton, Tenn. The trial pitted Clarence Darrow for the defense against special prosecutor William Jennings Bryan.

The Clinch River nuclear energy project was opposed by President Carter as unnecessary, too expensive and, as a producer of plutonium as a by-product, a substance likely to cause proliferation of atomic weapons technology. Nevertheless, after much controversy, a House committee approved going ahead with the reactor early in 1979.

Lamar Alexander replaced Governor Ray Blanton on January 17, 1979 (three days before the appointed inauguration day), to stop further convicted criminals from being granted executive clemency. Blanton's clemency grants were in question because of their possible link to a Federal probe of his administration's alleged clemency-for-sale scandal. On April 10, the Tennessee Court of Criminal Appeals upheld 52 grants of clemency allowed by Blanton the day before he left office. Six persons (Blanton not among them) were indicted in connection with the pardon sales.

Nuclear Fuel Services, Inc. of Erwin, Tenn., a manufacturer of atomic fuel, was shut down from September 1979 to January 1980 amid reports that 20 lbs. of uranium was missing from the plant. Since investigators detected no evidence of theft, the Nuclear Regulatory Commission allowed the company to reopen but ordered stricter security measures.

Full name: State of Tennessee. **Origin of name:** From Tennese, name of leading Cherokee town. **Inhabitant:** Tennessean. **Capital:** Nashville. **State motto:** Agriculture & Commerce. **Flag:** Three white stars in a white-bordered blue circle on a red field; narrow white & blue stripe at right. **Seal:** Plow, sheaf of wheat & cotton plant represent agriculture; riverboat symbolizes commerce; Roman numerals indicate Tennessee was 16th state to be admitted to Union. **Flower:** Iris. **Bird:** Mockingbird. **Tree:** Tulip poplar. **Song:** "The Tennessee Waltz," "When It's Iris Time in Tennessee," "Tennessee, My Homeland Tennessee," "My Tennessee," & "Oh! Tennessee." **Nickname:** Volunteer State.

Governor: A. Lamar Alexander. **Annual salary:** $68,226. **Term:** 4 years. **Current term expires:** Jan. 1983. **Voting requirements:** 18 yrs. old & U.S. citizen; resident of state for 20 days. **U.S. Congressmen:** 8. **Entered Union:** 1796 (16th state).

Location & boundaries: Southeastern state: bounded on the north by Kentucky & Virginia; on the east by North Carolina; on the south by Georgia, Alabama & Mississippi; & on the west by Arkansas, Missouri & the Mississippi River. **Total area:** 42,244 sq. mi. (ranks 34th). **Extreme length:** 432 mi. **Extreme breadth:** 110 mi. **Chief rivers:** Mississippi, Tennessee, Cumberland. **Major lakes:** Watts, Chickamauga, Douglas, Cherokee. **No. of counties:** 95.

Population (1979 est.): 4,380,000 (ranks 17th). **Pop. increase (1970-79):** 11.6%. **Places over 25,000 pop.:** 11. **Places over 100,000:** 4. **Largest cities:** Memphis, Nashville, Knoxville, Chattanooga. **Pop. density:** 103.7 per sq. mi. (ranks 18th). **Pop. projection 1985:** 4,592,000. **Pop. distribution:** 63.0% metropolitan; 37.0% nonmetropolitan. **White:** 83.7%. **Black:** 16.1%. **Other:** 0.2%. **Marriage rate (1977):** 12.9 per 1,000 people. **Divorce rate:** 6.4 per 1,000 people.

State finances (1978). Revenue: $3,275,928,000. **Expenditures:** $3,091,556,000. **State taxes:** $391.08 per capita. **State personal income tax:** No, except on interest and dividends. **Public debt (1978):** $317.45 per capita. **Federal aid (1979):** $329.30 per capita. **Personal income (1979 est.):** $7,299.

Sectors of the economy (% of labor force employed in 1973): Wholesale and retail trade (16.9%), Government (15.8%), Services (13.9%), Manufacturing (13.8%), Educational Services (7%), Construction (6.1%). **Leading products:** chemicals, food items, electrical equipment, apparel, textile items, primary metals. **Minerals:** stone, coal, zinc, cement, copper. **Agricultural products:** cattle, soybeans, dairy items, cotton, tobacco. **Avg. farm (1979 est.):** 146 acres. **Avg. value of farm per acre:** $669.

Highway expenditures per capita (1978): $99.41. **Persons per motor vehicle:** 1.45. **Minimum age for driver's license:** 16. **Gasoline tax:** 7¢ per gallon. **Diesel tax:** 8¢ per gallon. **Motor vehicle deaths:** 28.4 per 100,000 people.

Birthrate (1978): 15.4 per 1,000 people. **Infant mortality rate per 1,000 births (1977):** 15.4. **Physicians per 100,000 pop. (1977):** 148. **Dentists per 100,000 pop. (1977):** 46. **Acceptable hospital beds:** 7.3 per 1,000 people. **State expenditures per capita for health and hospitals (1978):** $49.10.

Education expenditures (1975-76): $352.65 per capita annually. **No. of pupils in public schools (1977 est.):** 830,000. **No. of institutions of higher learning (1976-77):** 67. **Public school expenditure per pupil in attendance (1975-76):** $1,214. **Avg. salary of public school teachers (1974-75 est.):** $9,878. **No. full-time teachers (1976 est.):** 42,130. **Educational attainment of adult population (1977):** 12.2 median yrs. of school completed; 6.4% with less than 5 years of education; 10.5% with 4 yrs. of college.

Telephones (1977): 67 per 100 people. **State Chamber of Commerce:** State Chamber Division of the Tennessee Taxpayers Assoc., 1070 Capitol Hill Bldg., Nashville, Tennessee 37219.

TEXAS

Second largest of the states and among the most populous, Texas is a fiercely independent land of awesome expanses and great natural resources. It leads the nation in the production of oil, natural gas, cattle, and cotton, and ranks high in fishing and electric power. Texas is also a major agricultural state, as well as a growing industrial region. It contains the facilities of 19 of the top 20 U.S. chemical companies, and is the home of the Manned Spacecraft Center (Houston) and other space age projects. And while keeping pace technologically, it can also claim a richly varied heritage, having flown the flags of six nations: Spain, France, Mexico, the Republic of Texas, the Confederate States of America, and the United States.

The state consists of four main land regions: the West Gulf Coastal Plain, the largest single area, making up more than two-fifths of the total area and consisting of a 150- to 350-mile-wide strip of land in the east and southeast extending from the Gulf of Mexico to the Balcones Escarpment; the Central Lowland, known locally as the Osage Plains and extending southward to a line running roughly from Fort Worth, through Abilene, to Big Springs and including the southern fringe of the Texas panhandle; the Great Plains, reaching mostly westward (but also north and southward) from the Central Lowland into New Mexico and including the bulk of the panhandle; and the Basin and Range (or Trans-Pecos) Region, making up the westernmost part of the state below New Mexico and including high, rugged, partly arid plains crossed by spurs of the Rocky Mountains; in this region are the Guadalupe Mountains and the state's highest point, Guadalupe Peak (8,751 feet).

Texas has more farmed area than any other state, and about half the land consists of forest, woodland, or brush land. The state's widely varied climate ranges from the warm, damp, subtropical Gulf Coast and lower Rio Grande Valley to the continental weather of the northern panhandle. Hot, dry weather is typical of the far south as are frequent droughts. Narrow sand bars, enclosing shallow lagoons, lie along the coast and afford some protection against ocean storms and tidal waves. The U.S.-Mexican border, where it follows the Rio Grande has been a continuing problem for the state, because the riverbed shifts occasionally, cutting off land from one or the other country. These shifts have given rise to nearly a century of minor but annoying border disputes. In August 1970, however, Presidents Nixon and Diaz met in Mexico and announced agreement on current disputes and ways to prevent future ones. New, major reservoirs, built in cooperation with Mexico, will prevent any substantial change in the Rio Grande.

Indians inhabited what is now Texas about 20,000 years before the coming of the Europeans. Spaniards (including Cabeza de Vaca and Francisco Vásquez Coronado) visited the region in the 16th and 17th centuries, settling (1682) at Ysleta (near present-day El Paso). Spain increased its settlement efforts after French explorer Robert Cavelier, Sieur de La Salle, established (1685) a short-lived colony near Matagorda Bay. The first Spanish mission, San Francisco de los Tejas, was founded in 1690 and others soon followed, but generally Spain's efforts to exploit the region's wealth and convert the Indians were not very successful. After the Louisiana Purchase (1803) gave the United States a common border with Texas, Americans began challenging Spanish rule there.

Moses Austin secured (1821) a grant from local authorities permitting him, as an *empresario*, to bring in American settlers; when he died that same year, his son, Stephen F. Austin, established the first permanent Anglo-American settlement at San Felipe de Austin. Often called the "Father of Texas," Austin brought approximately 8,000 colonists to the region. Other *empresarios* brought hundreds more, and during the next 15 years the total approached 30,000. Preoccupied with its birth as an independent republic (1824), Mexico was not effective in curbing what it saw as a growing encroachment on its territory, despite an 1830 law restricting immigration, and the establishment of customs stations and a military force in Texas.

The Anglo-Americans were moved to action when Antonio López de Santa Anna set up (1835) a Mexican dictatorship in Texas; the Texans then proclaimed (1836) a provisional government at Washington-on-the-Brazos and turned command of the revolutionary army over to Sam Houston. Santa Anna and his men quickly gained the upper hand in the struggle, recapturing San Antonio, which had initially fallen to the Texans; the Mexican victory came despite the famous heroic defense of the Alamo by greatly outnumbered Texans (including Davy Crockett and Jim Bowie). After more than 300 Texas prisoners were shot at Goliad, Houston rallied his still relatively small army and, with a surprise attack, won (April 21, 1836) the Battle of San Jacinto, ending the war and bringing to birth the Independent Republic of Texas.

Under its famed Lone Star flag, Texas remained independent for nearly a decade, with Houston serving as president. The country was beset by many grave problems, including Indian and Mexican raids and a money shortage. The issue of annexation by the United States, which most Texans favored, arose early. Slavery, condoned in Texas, made the issue highly controversial: the Southern states favored annexation, while the Northern ones opposed it. Annexation, which came in 1845, precipitated the Mexican War (1846-48).

Settlers, drawn by inexpensive land, came to Texas in great numbers in the pre-Civil War period. Partly because of its slave-holding status but more importantly because of states' rights views, the state sided with the Confederacy, seceding in 1861. Texas saw little action during the war, but contributed 50,000 troops and much matériel to the Southern cause. The state suffered much during the excesses of Reconstruction.

The development of modern Texas was spurred by the growth of the cattle industry, the coming of the railroad, and the discovery, among others before it, of the spectacular Spindletop oil field (1901) near Beaumont. Texas today, while enjoying great growth, faces serious challenges, such as ways to irrigate with surface water its dry western areas where shrinking underground supplies now help to grow vast crops.

The planned Seadock superport, a project similar to the Loop superport being constructed off Louisiana, remained a possibility through the establishment in July 1977 of a state authority which could fund the project. In October 1979, the U.S. Department of Transportation gave tentative approval, subject to a study of the authority's financial soundness and its ability to compensate victims of oil spills.

In 1979, inland Texas was damaged by a system of tornados, and the coast by a tropical storm and resulting floods, and by oil spills from a Liberian freighter and from a damaged oil well in Mexican waters.

Texas suffered numerous adverse effects from the summer 1980 heat wave which swept much of the nation. While the mercury climbed beyond 100° in most cities for more than a week, 100 heat-related deaths were reported (unofficially, as of July 20), forest fires destroyed thousands of acres,

TEXAS
MILES
State Capital ⊛   County Seats ⊙
KEY TO NUMBERS ON MAP
County — County Seat
1 DELTA — Cooper
2 FRANKLIN — Mt. Vernon
3 CAMP — Pittsburg
4 MORRIS — Daingerfield
5 ROCKWALL — Rockwall
6 RAINS — Emory
7 GREGG — Longview
8 SOMERVELL — Glen Rose
9 SAN JACINTO — Coldspring
WESTERN PART OF TEXAS
Same scale as main map
HOUSTON
GULF OF MEXICO
NEW MEXICO
OKLAHOMA
ARKANSAS
MEXICO
Longitude West of Greenwich
© Copyright HAMMOND INCORPORATED, Maplewood, N.J.

crops wilted in the fields, and milk production was reported down by as much as 20 percent.

Full name: State of Texas. **Origin of name:** From the Indian meaning "Friends" or "Allies." **Inhabitant:** Texan. **Capital:** Austin. **State motto:** Friendship. **Flag:** Single star on vertical blue bar with a red & a white bar to the right. **Seal:** Single star with branch of oak, representing strength, on left; olive branch, symbolizing peace, to the right. **Flower:** Bluebonnet. **Bird:** Mockingbird. **Tree:** Pecan. **Song:** "Texas, Our Texas." **Nickname:** Lone Star State.

Governor: William P. Clements, Jr. **Annual salary:** $71,400. **Term:** 4 years. **Current term expires:** Jan. 1983. Voting requirements: 18 yrs. old & U.S. citizen; registered resident of state 30 days. **U.S. Congressmen:** 24. **Entered Union:** 1845 (28th state).

Location & boundaries: Southwestern state: bounded on the north by Oklahoma & the Red River; on the northeast by Arkansas; on the east by Louisiana & the Sabine River; on the south by the Gulf of Mexico, the Rio Grande River & Mexico, & on the west by New Mexico. **Total area:** 267,338 sq. mi. (ranks 2nd). **Extreme length:** 801 mi. **Extreme breadth:** 773 mi. **Coastline:** 367 mi. **Chief rivers:** Rio Grande, Red, Pecos, Brazos, Colorado. **Major lakes:** Texoma, Toledo Bend, Amistad, Falcon. **No. of counties:** 254.

Population (1979 est.): 13,380,000 (ranks 3rd). **Pop. increase (1970-79):** 19.5%. **Places over 25,000 pop.:** 46. **Places over 100,000:** 9. **Largest cities:** Houston, Dallas, San Antonio, El Paso. **Pop. density:** 50.1 per sq. mi. (ranks 32nd). **Pop. projection 1985:** 14,277,000. **Pop. distribution:** 79.4% metropolitan; 20.6% nonmetropolitan. **White:** 86.6%. **Black:** 12.7%. **Other:** 0.7%. **Marriage rate (1977):** 12.6 per 1,000 people. **Divorce rate:** 6.4 per 1,000 people.

State finances (1978). Revenue: $9,925,190,000. **Expenditures:** $8,553,508,000. **State taxes:** $414.17 per capita. **State personal income tax:** No. **Public debt (1978):** $163.11 per capita. **Federal aid (1979):** $268.18 per capita. **Personal income (1979 est.):** $8,649.

Sectors of the economy (% of labor force employed in 1970): Wholesale and retail trade (22%), Manufacturing (19%), Government (16%), Services (9%), Educational Services (8%), Construction (8%). **Leading products:** chemicals, petroleum & coal items, food items, transportation equipment, machinery, primary & fabricated metals. **Minerals:** petroleum, natural gas & natural gas liquids, cement. **Agricultural products:** cattle, sheep, swine, dairy items, mohair, sorghum grain, cotton lint, rice, wheat, oats, barley, pecans. **Fishing:** shrimp, oysters, menhaden. **Avg. farm (1979 est.):** 872 acres. **Avg. value of farm per acre:** $354.

Highway expenditures per capita (1978): $71.86. **Persons per motor vehicle:** 1.25. **Minimum age for driver's license:** 16. **Gasoline tax:** 5¢ per gallon. **Diesel tax:** 6.5¢ per gallon. **Motor vehicle deaths:** 30.3 per 100,000 people.

Birthrate (1978): 18.2 per 1,000 people. **Infant mortality rate per 1,000 births (1977):** 14.7. **Physicians per 100,000 pop. (1977):** 152. **Dentists per 100,000 pop. (1977):** 41. **Acceptable hospital beds:** 6.1 per 1,000 people. **State expenditures per capita for health and hospitals (1978):** $52.54.

Education expenditures (1975-76): $427.48 per capita annually. **No. of pupils in public schools (1977 est.):** 2,781,000. **No. of institutions of higher learning (1976-77):** 146. **Public school expenditure per pupil in attendance (1975-76):** $1,487. **Avg. salary of public school teachers (1974-75 est.):** $10,136. **No. full-time teachers (1977 est.):** 49,180. **Educational attainment of adult population (1976):** 12.4 median yrs. of school completed; 6.0% with less than 5 years of education; 13.7% with 4 yrs. of college.

Telephones (1977): 74 per 100 people. **State Chamber of Commerce:** Texas State Chamber of Commerce, 7701 N. Lamar, Suite 302, Austin, Texas 78752.

UTAH

Utah is a rough-hewn, scenically spectacular state consisting of two relatively arid regions (eastern and western), divided by the rain-catching Wasatch Range of the Rocky Mountains. In the west is the Great Basin, which includes the Great Salt Lake (about 75 miles long and 30 miles wide) and the 4,000-square-mile Great Salt Lake Desert. East of the Wasatch Range are the Uinta Mountains (with 11 peaks that rise more than 13,000 feet) and the awesome, many-hued Colorado Plateau. Most of the towns and cities, situated at the base of the mountains, enjoy a pleasant climate with few temperature extremes.

A number of factors—mainly scarcity of water—have limited the state's agricultural growth. Nearly three-quarters of the annual farm revenue comes from livestock and livestock products.

The struggle for better irrigation in Utah began with the early Mormon settlers and still goes on. In 1967 the $325-million Central Utah Project was begun; if completed, it will consist of a vast complex of dams, canals, and aqueducts.

Stimulated by the demands of World War II, manufacturing has become increasingly vital. Leading manufactures include food products; fabricated steel; stone, clay and glass products; missiles; chemicals; and in recent years, electronics equipment. In rural communities, the fabric and apparel industries are active.

In the last ten years, distribution services have become an important part of the Utah economy. Since the state legislature eliminated all taxes on inventories, the state has become an important shipping and receiving point for the entire Western market.

Tourism is important, attracting visitors to the Great Salt Lake; Arches, Bryce Canyon, Canyonlands, Capitol Reef and Zion National Parks; Natural Bridges National Monument, Glen Canyon National Recreation Area, and Golden Spike National Historic Site.

Disfavored by the agrarian Mormons, mining got off to a slow start, but in 1863 huge deposits of copper, silver, and lead were unearthed in Bingham Canyon, which contains the largest open-pit copper mine in the country. The industry came into its own with the coming of the railroad in 1869. Since 1948, significant quantities of oil, natural gas and uranium have been found. In 1980 an important gas field was opened in the Overthrust Belt near the Wyoming border east of Ogden. Recent discoveries of large oil-shale and tar-sands deposits have raised hopes of further energy development, but uncertainties in the economy and a lagging technology have slowed the exploitation of these resources.

Archaeological findings (1968) in the Great Basin at Hogup Cave, 75 miles northwest of Salt Lake City, show that there was continuous Indian habitation in the area from 6400 B.C. to A.D. 1600. An even older human habitation, Danger Cave near Wendover, was excavated a decade ago and dates to 9000 B.C. Some doubt exists as to whether or not Spanish explorers visited the region in 1540 when they explored the Grand Canyon, but it has been established that in 1776 two Spanish Franciscan friars—Silvestre Velez de Escalante and Francisco Atanasio Domínguez—did explore the area. They recommended colonization, but Spain was apparently not interested. Between 1811 and 1840 British and American fur trappers hunted their prey there.

Permanent occupation of the territory was begun in 1847 by the persecuted Mormons—members of the Church of Jesus Christ of Latter-day Saints—who had emigrated from New York via Missouri, Ohio, and Illinois to Utah in search of "a [secluded] gathering place for Zion." From the time of its founding (1847) Salt Lake City has been the world headquarters of the L.D.S. church.

The Utah region at that time belonged to Mexico, but after the Mexican War (1846-48), it became the property of the United States. At least 70 percent of the state's area is still federally owned and

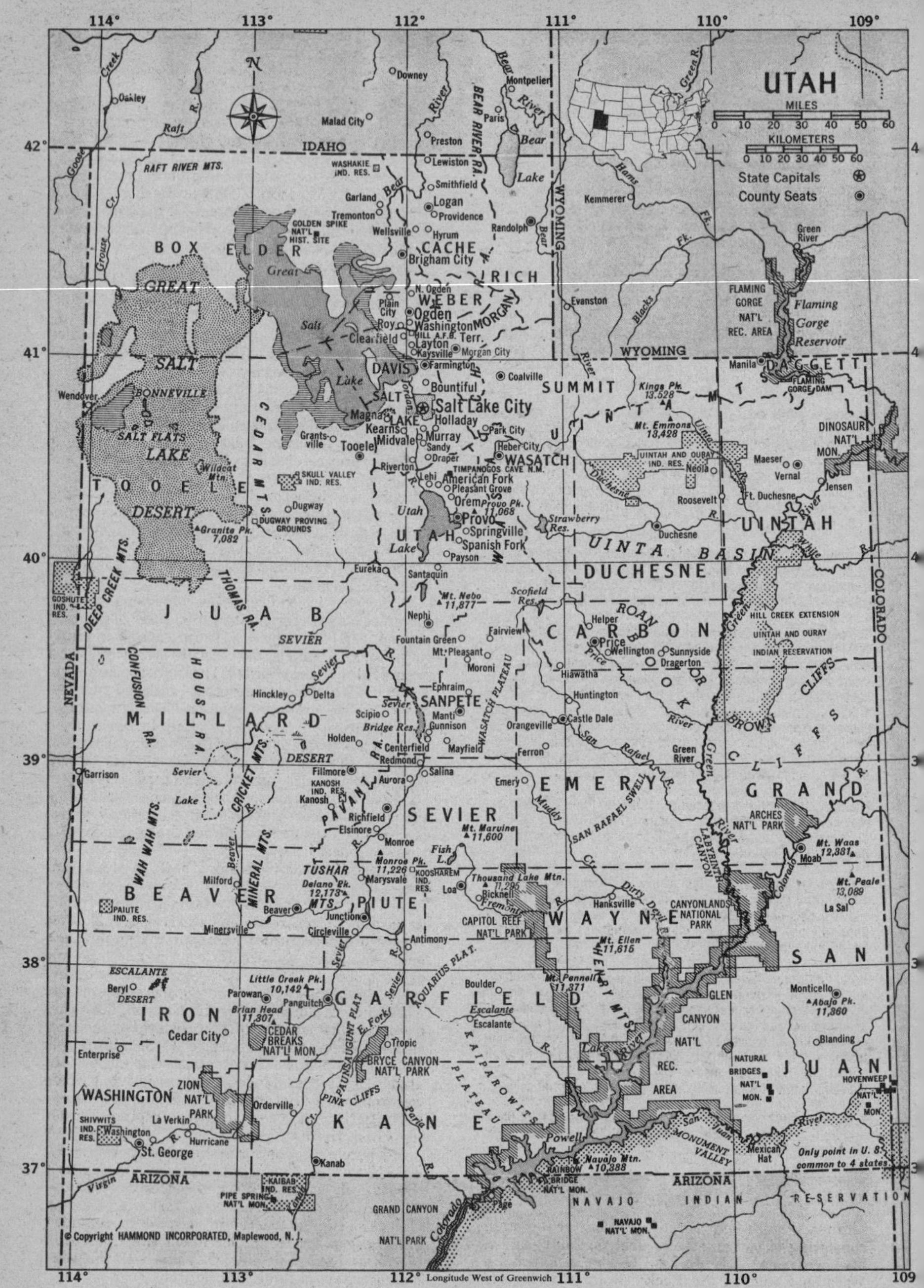
UTAH
MILES
KILOMETERS
State Capitals
County Seats
0 10 20 30 40 50 60

114° 113° 112° 111° 110° 109°

Oakley
Raft
Goose Cr.
Grouse Cr.
Malad City
Downey
Montpelier
Paris
Bear River
Bear
Lake
Preston
Lewiston
Smithfield
Logan
Providence
Randolph
Kemmerer
Green River
IDAHO
42°
RAFT RIVER MTS.
WASHAKIE IND. RES.
Garland
Tremonton
Wellsville
Hyrum
CACHE
Brigham City
RICH
Evanston
WYOMING
FLAMING GORGE NAT'L REC. AREA
Flaming Gorge Reservoir
BOX ELDER
GOLDEN SPIKE NAT'L HIST. SITE
Great
GREAT
Salt
SALT
Lake
N. Ogden
Plain City
Ogden
Washington Terr.
Roy
Clearfield
HILL A.F.B.
Layton
Kaysville
Farmington
WEBER
MORGAN
Morgan City
Coalville
SUMMIT
Kings Pk. 13,528
Mt. Emmons 13,428
Manila
DAGGETT
FLAMING GORGE DAM
41°
LAKE
DAVIS
Bountiful
Salt Lake City
Holladay
Park City
Heber City
UINTA MTS
UINTAH AND OURAY IND. RES.
Maeser
Vernal
Neola
DINOSAUR NAT'L MON.
Jensen
BONNEVILLE
SALT FLATS
Wendover
Magna
Kearns
Midvale
Murray
Sandy
Draper
WASATCH
Roosevelt
Ft. Duchesne
LAKE
TOOELE
Grantsville
Tooele
Riverton
Lehi
American Fork
Pleasant Grove
Orem
Provo Pk. 11,068
TIMPANOGOS CAVE N.M.
Strawberry Res.
Duchesne
UINTAH
Wildcat Mtn.
SKULL VALLEY IND. RES.
Dugway
DESERT
Granite Pk. 7,082
DUGWAY PROVING GROUNDS
Provo
Springville
Spanish Fork
Payson
UTAH
Utah Lake
UINTA BASIN
40°
CEDAR MTS.
THOMAS RA.
Eureka
Santaquin
Mt. Nebo 11,877
Scofield Res.
DUCHESNE
GOSHUTE IND. RES.
DEEP CREEK MTS.
JUAB
SEVIER
Nephi
Fountain Green
ROAN
Helper
Price
Wellington
Sunnyside
Dragerton
HILL CREEK EXTENSION
UINTAH AND OURAY INDIAN RESERVATION
NEVADA
CONFUSION RA.
HOUSE RA.
Fairview
CARBON
Hiawatha
CLIFFS
BROWN
Hinckley
Delta
Ephraim
Mt. Pleasant
Moroni
SANPETE
Huntington
Scipio
Manti
Gunnison
Orangeville
Castle Dale
Ferron
Green River
MILLARD
Centerfield
Mayfield
WASATCH PLATEAU
San Rafael
Holden
Redmond
DESERT
39°
Garrison
Sevier Lake
Fillmore
Aurora
Salina
Emery
EMERY
GRAND
ARCHES NAT'L PARK
Mt. Waas 12,331
CRICKET MTS.
KANOSH IND. RES.
Kanosh
Richfield
Elsinore
SEVIER
Mt. Marvine 11,600
SAN RAFAEL SWELL
Muddy
LABYRINTH CANYON
Moab
Mt. Peale 13,089
WAH WAH MTS.
PAVANT RA.
Monroe
Fish L.
Monroe Pk. 11,226
KOOSHAREM IND. RES.
Loa
Thousand Lake Mtn. 11,290
Bicknell
Fremont
Hanksville
Dirty Devil
CANYONLANDS NATIONAL PARK
La Sal
MINERAL MTS.
TUSHAR MTS
Delano Pk. 12,173
Marysvale
Milford
Beaver
BEAVER
PIUTE
Junction
CAPITOL REEF NAT'L PARK
WAYNE
Mt. Ellen 11,615
SAN
Minersville
Circleville
Antimony
38°
ESCALANTE DESERT
Beryl
Parowan
Little Creek Pk. 10,142
Brian Head 11,307
Panguitch
GARFIELD
AQUARIUS PLAT.
Boulder
Escalante
Mt. Pennell 11,371
HENRY MTS.
GLEN CANYON NAT'L REC. AREA
Monticello
Abajo Pk. 11,360
IRON
Cedar City
CEDAR BREAKS NAT'L MON.
Tropic
BRYCE CANYON NAT'L PARK
KAIPAROWITS PLATEAU
Blanding
NATURAL BRIDGES NAT'L MON.
JUAN
Enterprise
PINK CLIFFS
HOVENWEEP NAT'L MON.
WASHINGTON
ZION NAT'L PARK
Orderville
PAUNSAUGUNT PLAT.
KANE
Lake Powell
MONUMENT VALLEY
Mexican Hat
Only point in U.S. common to 4 states
SHIVWITS IND. RES.
Washington
La Verkin
Hurricane
St. George
Kanab
RAINBOW BRIDGE NAT'L MON.
Navajo Mtn. 10,388
San Juan River
37°
Virgin
ARIZONA
KAIBAB IND. RES.
PIPE SPRING NAT'L MON.
NAVAJO
INDIAN
RESERVATION
ARIZONA
© Copyright HAMMOND INCORPORATED, Maplewood, N.J.
GRAND CANYON NAT'L PARK
Colorado R.
NAVAJO NAT'L MON.
Longitude West of Greenwich
114° 113° 112° 111° 110° 109°

administered, and about ten percent of the people work for Federal agencies.

Two Indian wars were fought: the Walker War (1853-54) and the Black Hawk War (1865-68), involving a number of tribes but principally the Utes, who were eventually placed on a reservation in the Uinta basin.

As early as 1849 Utah asked to be admitted to the Union, but Congress refused—mainly because the Mormon practice of polygamy was frowned upon.

The dismissal of the Mormon leader, Brigham Young, as territorial governor led to the "Utah" or "Mormon" War (1857-58). Federal troops were dispatched to the area, but there was more bad feeling than actual fighting. When the Civil War broke out in 1861, the troops were recalled and peace reigned, although there remained a residue of bitterness between the Mormon stronghold and the "outside" world which time has gradually erased. Utah finally entered the Union in 1896.

Some residents of St. George have filed claims against the Energy Department charging that nuclear blasts which occurred some 25 years ago at the Nevada Testing Site caused cancer deaths among members of their families who lived in the area.

Full name: State of Utah. **Origin of name:** From the Indian tribe of Utes. **Inhabitant:** Utahn. **Capital:** Salt Lake City. **State motto:** Industry. **Flag:** State seal in a gold circle on blue field. **Seal:** Beehive on shield represents industry; sego lilies surrounding beehive symbolize time when Mormon pioneers ate lily bulbs to avoid starvation. **Flower:** Sego lily. **Bird:** Seagull. **Tree:** Blue spruce. **Song:** "Utah, We Love Thee." **Nickname:** Beehive State.

Governor: Scott M. Matheson. **Annual salary:** $40,000. **Term:** 4 years. **Current term expires:** Dec. 1980. **Voting requirements:** 18 yrs. old & U.S. citizen; state resident 30 days. **U.S. Congressmen:** 2. **Entered Union:** 1896 (45th state).

Location & boundaries: Rocky Mountain state: bounded on the north by Idaho; on the northeast by Wyoming; on the east by Colorado; on the south by Arizona; & on the west by Nevada. **Total area:** 84,916 sq. mi. (ranks 11th). **Extreme length:** 345 mi. **Extreme breadth:** 275 mi. **Chief rivers:** Colorado, Green, Sevier. **Major lakes:** Great Salt Lake, Utah, Sevier, Bear Lake. **No. of counties:** 29.

Population (1979 est.): 1,367,000 (ranks 36th). **Pop. increase (1970-79):** 29.1%. **Places over 25,000 pop.:** 7. **Places over 100,000:** 1. **Largest cities:** Salt Lake City, Ogden, Provo. **Pop. density:** 16.1 per sq. mi. (ranks 42nd). **Pop. projection 1985:** 1,449,000. **Pop. distribution:** 78.7% metropolitan; 21.3% nonmetropolitan. **White:** 97.4%. **Black:** 0.6%. **Other:** 2%. **Marriage rate (1977):** 12.0 per 1,000 people. **Divorce rate:** 5.5 per 1,000 people.

State finances (1978). Revenue: $1,432,247,000. **Expenditures:** $1,299,885,000. **State taxes:** $463.63 per capita. **State personal income tax:** Yes. **Public debt (1978):** $222.32 per capita. **Federal aid (1979):** $316.75 per capita. **Personal income (1979 est.):** $7,185.

Sectors of the economy (% of labor force employed in 1970): Government (25%), Wholesale and retail trade (22%), Manufacturing (15%), Educational Services (12%), Services (7%), Construction (6%). **Leading products:** food items; stone, clay, & glass items; machinery; printing & publishing; fabricated metals; petroleum & coal items. **Minerals:** copper, petroleum, coal, molybdenum. **Agricultural products:** cattle, dairy items, turkeys, hay, wheat, barley. **Avg. farm (1979 est.):** 1,049 acres. **Avg. value of farm per acre:** $265.

Highway expenditures per capita (1978): $90.73. **Persons per motor vehicle:** 1.36. **Minimum age for driver's license:** 16. **Gasoline tax:** 9¢ per gallon. **Diesel tax:** 9¢ per gallon. **Motor vehicle deaths:** 28.3 per 100,000 people.

Birthrate (1978): 29.5 per 1,000 people. **Infant mortality rate per 1,000 births (1977):** 10.1. **Physicians per 100,000 pop. (1977):** 166. **Dentists per 100,000 pop. (1977):** 63. **Acceptable hospital beds:** 3.9 per 1,000 people. **State expenditures per capita for health and hospitals (1978):** $59.50.

Education expenditures (1975-76): $570.03 per capita annually. **No. of pupils in public schools (1977 est.):** 310,000. **No. of institutions of higher learning (1976-77):** 14. **Public school expenditure per pupil in attendance (1975-76):** $1,471. **Avg. salary of public school teachers (1974-75 est.):** $10,150. **No. full-time teachers (1977 est.):** 13,110. **Educational attainment of adult population (1976):** 12.8 median yrs. of school completed; 1.0% with less than 5 years of education; 17.5% with 4 yrs. of college.

Telephones (1977): 73 per 100 people. **State Chamber of Commerce:** None.

VERMONT

Vermont, the only New England state lacking an ocean coastline, is noted for the independence of thought and action that stem, in part, from this relative insularity; there is much truth to the saying, "Vermonters will do nothing that you tell them to; most anything that you ask them to."

Four main land areas make up the state: the extensively forested Green Mountains, forming a north-south backbone through the center (and inspiring the state's French-rooted name); the White Mountains in the northeast, Lake Champlain and the Champlain Valley in the northwest, and the Taconic Hills in the southwest. Many lakes, ponds, streams, and rivers—including the eastern-border-forming Connecticut River—provide an abundant water supply. Forests cover about 60 percent of the area.

Called a "state in a very natural state" by poet Robert Frost (who lived the latter part of his life near Ripton), Vermont is famous for the rustic charm of its towns and villages, winding roads, covered bridges, and largely unspoiled scenery. In the early 1900s, manufacturing began to replace agriculture in importance through small-scale industralization: only a quarter of the state's land is now devoted to agriculture. Maple sugar and syrup and the finest marble in the United States are among Vermont's better-known products, while about nine-tenths of the nation's asbestos comes from the Hyde Park region. Machine tools, computer components and armaments are the state's leading industrial products.

Four-season tourism has grown enormously in recent years (Vermont's skiing industry alone accounts for over $50 million annual revenue), and attractions include the Green Mountain National Forest, Shelburne and Bennington museums, and many state parks.

French explorer Samuel de Champlain was most likely the first European to visit the region, discovering (1609) the lake now bearing his name. The British established (1724) the first permanent settlement at Fort Dummer (near present-day Brattleboro), and the English assumed control at the end of the French and Indian War (1763). Beginning in the mid-1700s New Hampshire and New York made conflicting claims on the region, and violence erupted when Ethan Allen and his "Green Mountain Boys" resisted New York officers who sought to take possession of the territory.

These differences were soon overshadowed by the American Revolution, in which the Vermonters played an important part, including the capture of Fort Ticonderoga and Crown Point. In 1777, Vermont proclaimed its independence, drawing up the first state constitution that outlawed slavery and established universal manhood suffrage without property qualifications. Land disputes continued, but were finally ended (1791) when Vermont paid New York a $30,000 claims settle-

QUEBEC
CANADA
QUEBEC
45°
30'
73°
30'
72°
30'
Rouses Point
Alburg
Missisquoi Bay
Highgate Ctr.
Swanton
Richford
N. Troy
Jay Pk. 3,861
Troy
Newport
Derby Line
Norton
Canaan
Beecher Falls
Gore Mtn. 3,330
Derby
Isle La Motte
Missisquoi R.
Enosburg Falls
ORLEANS
Seymour L.
Island Pond
Colebrook
GRAND ISLE
N. Hero
St. Albans
Bakersfield
Eden
Irasburg
Orleans
Willoughby L.
Bloomfield
Plattsburgh
FRANKLIN
Barton
W. Burke
ESSEX
Grand Isle
Fairfax
Lamoille River
Johnson
Burke Mtn. 3,267
Guildhall
Groveton
S. Hero
Milton
Cambridge
Jeffersonville
Hyde Park
Caspian L.
Greensboro
Lyndon
Lyndonville
Keeseville
Colchester
Essex
Smugglers Notch
Morrisville
LAMOILLE
Hardwick
CALEDONIA
Lunenburg
Lancaster
Winooski
Mt. Mansfield 4,393
Stowe
30°
Au Sable Forks
Burlington
Essex Jct.
S. Burlington
Richmond
Waterbury Res.
Danville
Concord
St. Johnsbury
Gilman
Shelburne
CHITTENDEN
Waterbury
Cabot
MOORE DAM
Moore Res.
Hinesburg
Winooski
WASHINGTON
Marshfield
E. Barnet
Littleton
Camels Hump 4,083
E. Montpelier
Plainfield
Barnet
COMERFORD DAM
River
Vergennes
Montpelier
Barre
Groton
S. Ryegate
Ammonoosuc
Waitsfield
Northfield
S. Barre
Mad R.
Gran

Mt. Ellen 4,135
Graniteville
Websterville
Wells River
Woodsville
WHITE
Bristol
Williamstown
Newbury
Addison
Roxbury
Lincoln
Port Henry
Bread Loaf Mtn. 3,823
ORANGE
Bradford
MOUNTAINS
44°
Middlebury
ADDISON
Granville
Chelsea
E. Middlebury
Randolph
Post Mills
Ticonderoga
L. Dunmore
Squam L.
Forest Dale
Bethel
Thetford
Plymouth
Orwell
Brandon
White R.
Royalton
Sharon
Newfound L.
Lake George
Hubbardton
Pittsford
Chittenden Res.
Norwich
Hanover
Lake Winnipesaukee
L. Bomoseen
Proctor
Pico Pk. 3,967
Wilder
WILDER DAM
Hartford
Poultney
Rutland
Woodstock
White River Jct.
Lebanon
Laconia
Fair Haven
Castleton
Killington Pk. 4,241
W. Rutland
Bridgewater
Hartland
Poultney
RUTLAND
Black R.
WINDSOR
SAINT-GAUDENS NAT'L HIST. SITE
30°
L. St. Catherine
Wallingford
Windsor
Lake George
Wells
Okemo Mtn. 3,372
Mt. Ascutney 3,144
Claremont
L. Sunapee
Franklin
Glens Falls
Pawlet
Danby
Ludlow
Proctorsville
Newport
Hudson Falls
Dorset
N. Springfield
Springfield
Chester
Manchester Ctr.
Bromley Mtn. 3,260
Manchester Depot
Londonderry
Schuylerville
Mt. Equinox 3,816
Manchester
Saxtons River
Bellows Falls
N. Westminster
Concord
Arlington
Stratton Mtn. 3,859
Jamaica
Westminster
NEW HAMPSHIRE
43°
Somerset Res.
WINDHAM
Newfane
Putney
Keene
VERMONT
Mechanicville
N. Bennington
W. Dover
Deerfield
Wilmington
Brattleboro
MILES
Hoosick Falls
Bennington
Harriman Res.
Hinsdale
KILOMETERS
Troy
BENNINGTON
Pownal
Readsboro
Whitingham
Vernon
State Capitals
County Seats
N. Adams
MASSACHUSETTS
Northfield
Longitude West of Greenwich
Copyright HAMMOND INCORPORATED, Maplewood, N.J.
NEW YORK
Connecticut River
Lake Champlain
Otter Creek
GREEN MOUNTAINS

ment and was admitted to the Union, the first state to be added to the original 13.

The Embargo Act of 1807 and the War of 1812 were unpopular with Vermonters, who relied heavily on trade with Canada. But involvement in the war was unavoidable. Invasion by the British from Canada was averted when Americans, led by Captain Thomas Macdonough, gained a vital naval victory on Lake Champlain in 1814. Two years later, disastrous frosts ruined the state's crops, and thousands of farmers went west; immigration, which had been significant, fell sharply and never regained its former level.

Abolition was popular in the state, which strongly supported Abraham Lincoln in the 1860 presidential election. Vermont's casualties in the Civil War, as a proportion of the male population, were among the heaviest of any Northern state.

Historically a Republican state, Vermont has increasingly become a state in which the two parties are in close balance. The first Democratic governor was elected in 1962 and served until 1968. A second Democrat was elected for two terms beginning in 1972. The Republicans recaptured the governor's chair in 1976 and 1978, although in 1976 they lost control of the House of Representatives for the first time since the early 19th century. The House seat was regained by the GOP with the 1978 elections. The first Democratic U.S. Senator in the state's history was elected in 1974.

Full name: State of Vermont. **Origin of name:** From the French words meaning "Green Mountain." **Inhabitant:** Vermonter. **Capital:** Montpelier. **State motto:** Freedom & Unity. **Flag:** State seal on a blue field. **Seal:** Pine tree with 14 branches represents 13 original states & Vermont; cow & sheaves of wheat stand for dairying & agriculture; wavy lines at top & bottom symbolize sky & sea. **Flower:** Red clover. **Bird:** Hermit thrush. **Tree:** Sugar maple. **Song:** "Hail, Vermont." **Nickname:** Green Mountain State.

Governor: Richard A. Snelling. **Annual salary:** $44,800. **Term:** 2 years. **Current term expires:** Jan. 1981. **Voting requirements:** 18 yrs. old & U.S. citizen; registered state resident. **U.S. Congressmen:** 1. **Entered Union:** 1791 (14th state).

Location & boundaries: New England state: bounded on the north by Canada; on the east by New Hampshire & the Connecticut River; on the south by Massachusetts; & on the west by New York & Lake Champlain. **Total area:** 9,609 sq. mi. (ranks 43rd). **Extreme length:** 159 mi. **Extreme breadth:** 86 mi. **Chief rivers:** Connecticut, Winooski, Lamoille. **Major lake:** Champlain. **No. of counties:** 14.

Population (1979 est.): 493,000 (ranks 48th). **Pop. increase (1970-79):** 10.9%. **Places over 25,000 pop.:** 1. **Places over 100,000:** None. **Largest cities:** Burlington, Rutland. **Pop. density:** 51.3 per sq. mi. (ranks 30th). **Pop. projection 1985:** 517,000. **Pop. distribution:** 100% nonmetropolitan; 0.0% metropolitan. **White:** 99.6%. **Black:** 0.2%. **Other:** 0.2%. **Marriage rate (1977):** 10.0 per 1,000 people. **Divorce rate:** 4.4 per 1,000 people.

State finances (1978). Revenue: $603,546,000. **Expenditures:** $570,955,000. **State taxes:** $480.17 per capita. **State personal income tax:** Yes. **Public debt (1978):** $947.54 per capita. **Federal aid (1979):** $489.45 per capita. **Personal income (1979 est.):** $7,280

Sectors of the economy (% of labor force employed in 1970): Manufacturing (24%), Wholesale and retail trade (18%), Government (15%), Educational Services (11%), Services (8%), Construction (8%). **Leading products:** machinery, food items, computer components, printing, stone items, lumber, wood & paper items, rubber & plastic items. **Agricultural products:** dairy items, cattle, apples, hay, maple items. **Avg. farm (1979 est.):** 295 acres. **Avg. value of farm per acre:** $657.

Highway expenditures per capita (1978): $118.30. **Persons per motor vehicle:** 1.31. **Minimum age for driver's license:** 18. **Gasoline tax:** 9¢ per gallon. **Diesel tax:** none. **Motor vehicle deaths:** 25.9 per 100,000 people.

Birthrate (1978): 14.6 per 1,000 people. **Infant mortality rate per 1,000 births (1977):** 10.1. **Physicians per 100,000 pop. (1977):**

200. **Dentists per 100,000 pop. (1977):** 55. **Acceptable hospital beds:** 6.4 per 1,000 people. **State expenditures per capita for health and hospitals (1978):** $78.21.

Education expenditures (1975-76): $497.47 per capita annually. **No. of pupils in public schools (1977 est.):** 103,000. **No. of institutions of higher learning (1976-77):** 23. **Public school expenditure per pupil in attendance (1975-76):** $1,504. **Avg. salary of public school teachers (1974-75 est.):** $9,206. **No. full-time teachers (1977 est.):** 7,170. **Educational attainment of adult population (1976):** 12.5 median yrs. of school completed; 1.0% with less than 5 years of education; 15.6% with 4 yrs. of college.

Telephones (1977): 68 per 100 people. **State Chamber of Commerce:** Vermont State Chamber of Commerce, P.O. Box 37, Montpelier, Vermont 05602.

VIRGINIA

Virginia, home of the first English settlement in North America (Jamestown, 1607), is a state particularly rich in American history. A Virginian, Richard Henry Lee, introduced (June 7, 1776) the motion for separation of the 13 Colonies from England; Virginian Thomas Jefferson was the main author of the Declaration of Independence; and Virginian George Washington led the way to victory in the American Revolution. Eight U.S. Presidents were Virginians, including four of the first five: Washington (1st), Jefferson (3rd), James Madison (4th), and James Monroe (5th); the latter three, in office 24 consecutive years, made up the so-called "Virginia Dynasty." Famed Chief Justice John Marshall was also a Virginian.

The state, which is named for Elizabeth I ("The Virgin Queen"), has acquired several nicknames including "The Mother of States," because all or part of eight other states were formed from western territory it once claimed: West Virginia, Kentucky, Illinois, Indiana, Michigan, Minnesota, Ohio, and Wisconsin. In the American Revolution, General Charles Cornwallis's surrender (1781) to Washington at Yorktown virtually ended hostilities. During the Civil War, Virginia was the central battleground. Among the major battles fought within it were First and Second Bull Run (Manassas), Fredericksburg, Chancellorsville, the Wilderness, and Richmond; Confederate General Robert E. Lee, another Virginian, surrendered at Appomattox (April 9, 1865).

Roughly triangular in shape, the state has four principal land regions (west to east): the Appalachian Plateau, the Great Appalachian Valley (known also locally as the Valley of Virginia, a series of ridges and valleys including the historic Shenandoah Valley), the Piedmont Plateau (the largest single area), and the Atlantic Coastal Plain, also called the Tidewater Region. Prominent local features of the Appalachian range include the Allegheny Mountains along the western border and the Blue Ridge range rising between the Valley and Piedmont sections. Across Chesapeake Bay, making up the lower part of the Delmarva Peninsula, is the state's Eastern Shore. About two-thirds of the land is forested.

Significant agriculture includes fruit, hay, corn, peanuts, and tobacco, the largest crop and a crucial factor in the state's development. Leading manufactures include chemical and tobacco products. Fishing and, to a lesser degree, mining (especially of coal) are considerable, as is tourism. Attractions include the reconstructed colonial town of Williamsburg, Washington's birthplace (Wakefield) and residence (Mount Vernon), Jefferson's Monticello, Virginia Beach, Shenandoah National Park, Arlington National Cemetery, and various Civil War battlegrounds.

WESTERN PART OF VIRGINIA
Same scale as main map
VIRGINIA
MILES
KILOMETERS
National Capital
State Capitals
County Seats
Independent Cities *Bristol
ALLEGHENY MOUNTAINS
BLUE RIDGE MOUNTAINS
SHENANDOAH MTS.
ATLANTIC OCEAN
CHESAPEAKE BAY
DELAWARE
MARYLAND
PA.
MD.
W. VA.
TENN.
N.C.
KENTUCKY
NORTH CAROLINA
LOUDOUN
FAIRFAX
WASHINGTON
© Copyright HAMMOND INCORPORATED, Maplewood, N.J.

Indians of three major language groups (Algonquian, Siouan, and Iroquoian) were living in the region when the first British arrived, about 25 years after an unsuccessful settlement by Spanish Jesuits. English settlement proceeded despite great hardship, mainly through the efforts of such men as Captain John Smith and Thomas West, Baron De La Warr, Virginia's first governor. The House of Burgesses, first legislative body in the New World, convened (1619) at Jamestown, and five years later Virginia became England's first royal colony. The importation of Negroes, first as indentured servants and later as slaves, was begun. The production and exportation of tobacco, which was first cultivated (1612) by John Rolfe, spurred the colony's growth, and the plantation became the earliest social unit. Rolfe's marriage (1614) to Pocahontas helped induce a brief period of peace with the Indians, but there were massacres in 1622 and 1644, and not until Lord Dunmore's War (1774) did Indian troubles decrease.

At the time of Sir William Berkeley's governorship (1641-52, 1660-77), the colony was thriving, with freeholders and merchants controlling the government. Hard times came (1660) with the Restoration's Navigation Acts, which stipulated the exclusive use of English ships and ports for the tobacco trade, causing initial transport bottlenecks, price drops, and widespread discontent. This unrest was aggravated by Berkeley's increasingly unpopular practices (including a slacking of vigilance against the Indians), and an abortive revolt (Bacon's Rebellion, 1676) was mounted; when Berkeley harshly overreacted, England recalled him.

Inflamed by such orators as Patrick Henry ("Give me liberty or give me death!"), Virginians in the 18th century traveled a path of inevitable revolt and, after Washington's final military victory had decided the issue, they provided the first Federal leadership. In 1788 Virginia ratified the Constitution and relinquished all its western land claims except Kentucky and West Virginia (Kentucky became an independent state in 1792, as did West Virginia in 1863; two counties were added to the latter state in 1866). Virginia seceded from the Union in 1861 and was readmitted in 1870.

A new constitution was drafted (1902) that imposed a poll tax, virtually disenfranchising Blacks, but state and Federal court decisions in the 1960s held the poll tax unconstitutional as a requisite for voting, and a new state constitution approved by voters in 1970 eliminated the tax.

Virginia undertook "massive resistance" to public school desegregation after the Supreme Court's 1954 desegregation ruling, and a few schools were temporarily closed to avoid integration. During the 1960s and 1970s racial tensions have sharply declined. Tension was renewed, however, when federal courts issued orders for massive busing of pupils, climaxed by the decision of a U.S. District Judge ordering the consolidation of the school systems of Richmond and two adjacent, mostly white counties. That order later was overturned.

In January 1980 state health officials authorized Eastern Virginia Medical School at Norfolk to open a "test tube baby" clinic, the first such facility in the U.S.

Full name: Commonwealth of Virginia. **Origin of name:** In honor of Queen Elizabeth of England, the "Virgin Queen." **Inhabitant:** Virginian. **Capital:** Richmond. **State motto:** Sic Semper Tyrannis (Thus Always to Tyrants). **Flag:** State seal on blue field. **Seal:** State motto; standing figure representing virtue, dressed as woman warrior, standing triumphant over figure of tyranny. **Flower:** American Dogwood. **Bird:** Cardinal. **Tree:** American Dogwood. **Song:** "Carry Me Back to Old Virginia." **Nickname:** Old Dominion State.

Governor: John N. Dalton. **Annual salary:** $60,000. **Term:** 4 years. **Current term expires:** Jan. 1982. **Voting requirements:** 18 yrs. old & U.S. citizen; registered in precinct of residence. **U.S. Congressmen:** 10. **Entered Union:** 1788 (10th state).

Location & boundaries: South Atlantic state: bounded on the north by Maryland; on the west by West Virginia & Kentucky; on the south by Tennessee & North Carolina; & on the east by the Atlantic Ocean. **Total area:** 40,817 sq. mi. (ranks 36th). **Extreme length:** 440 mi. **Extreme breadth:** 200 mi. **Coastline:** 342 mi.; 112 mi. along the Atlantic Ocean & 230 mi. along Chesapeake Bay. **Chief rivers:** James, Potomac, Rappahannock. **Major lakes:** Smith Mountain, John H. Kerr Reservoir. **No. of counties:** 95.

Population (1979 est.): 5,197,000 (ranks 13th). **Pop. increase (1970-79):** 11.7%. **Places over 25,000 pop.:** 15. **Places over 100,000:** 9. **Largest cities:** Norfolk, Richmond, Virginia Beach. **Pop. density:** 127.3 per sq. mi. (ranks 16th). **Pop. projection 1985:** 5,730,000. **Pop. distribution:** 65.6% metropolitan; 34.4% nonmetropolitan. **White:** 80.9%. **Black:** 18.5%. **Other:** 0.6%. **Marriage rate (1977 est.):** 11.3 per 1,000 people. **Divorce rate:** 4.2 per 1,000 people.

State finances (1978). Revenue: $4,706,668,000. **Expenditures:** $4,321,663,000. **State taxes:** $453.72 per capita. **State personal income tax:** Yes. **Public debt (1978):** $243.93 per capita. **Federal aid (1979):** $330.11 per capita. **Personal income (1979 est.):** $8,605.

Sectors of the economy (% of labor force employed in 1970): Government (24%), Manufacturing (22%), Wholesale and retail trade (18%), Services (8%), Educational Services (8%), Construction (7%). **Leading products:** chemicals, textile items, apparel, food items, transportation equipment, furniture & fixtures, electrical equipment & supplies. **Minerals:** coal, stone, sand & gravel, lime. **Fishing:** crabs, oysters, menhaden. **Agricultural products:** livestock & livestock items, dairy items, poultry & poultry items, tobacco, corn, hay. **Avg. farm (1979 est.):** 164 acres. **Avg. value of farm per acre:** $864.

Highway expenditures per capita (1978): $134.61. **Persons per motor vehicle:** 1.48. **Minimum age for driver's license:** 16. **Gasoline tax:** 9¢ per gallon. **Diesel tax:** 9¢ per gallon. **Motor vehicle deaths:** 20.6 per 100,000 people.

Birthrate (1978): 14.2 per 1,000 people. **Infant mortality rate per 1,000 births (1977):** 15.9. **Physicians per 100,000 pop. (1977):** 167. **Dentists per 100,000 pop. (1977):** 48. **Acceptable hospital beds:** 6.3 per 1,000 people. **State expenditures per capita for health and hospitals (1978):** $82.13.

Education expenditures (1975-76): $417.42 per capita annually. **No. of pupils in public schools (1977 est.):** 1,085,000. **No. of institutions of higher learning (1976-77):** 72. **Public school expenditure per pupil in attendance (1975-76):** $1,488. **Avg. salary of public school teachers (1974-75 est.):** $11,279. **No. full-time teachers (1977 est.):** 63,560. **Educational attainment of adult population (1976):** 12.4 median yrs. of school completed; 4.6% with less than 5 years of education; 16.4% with 4 yrs. of college.

Telephones (1977): 68 per 100 people. **State Chamber of Commerce:** Virginia State Chamber of Commerce, 611 East Franklin Street, Richmond, Virginia 23219.

WASHINGTON

Washington, traditional gateway to Alaska and the Far East, is a leader in the vital areas of aircraft production, nuclear research, lumbering, and actual and potential waterpower production. It is also a land of rugged beauty that particularly appeals to lovers of the great outdoors.

The Cascade Mountains, running north and south, divide the state in two, the eastern part comprising about three-fifths of the total area. The Olympic Mountains make up the northwest corner of the state, while the Puget Sound Lowland lies between the Olympic Mountains on the west and the Cascades on the east. In the southwest corner is the Coast Range, which extends south into Oregon. East of the Cascades are the Rocky Mountains in the north and the Columbia Plateau in the south. Most of the state's larger cities, including Seattle

WASHINGTON
MILES
KILOMETERS
State and Provincial Capitals
CANADA
BRITISH COLUMBIA
VANCOUVER ISLAND
Str. of Juan de Fuca
PACIFIC OCEAN
IDAHO
OREGON
WHATCOM
Bellingham
Mt. Baker 10,778
OKANOGAN
FERRY
STEVENS
PEND OREILLE
SKAGIT
Mt. Vernon
SNOHOMISH
Everett
CHELAN
DOUGLAS
OKANOGAN
LINCOLN
SPOKANE
Spokane
KING
SEATTLE
CLALLAM
Port Angeles
JEFFERSON
OLYMPIC NATIONAL PARK
Mt. Olympus 7,965
MASON
Shelton
KITSAP
Bremerton
GRAYS HARBOR
Aberdeen
Hoquiam
THURSTON
Olympia
KITTITAS
Ellensburg
GRANT
ADAMS
WHITMAN
Pullman
GARFIELD
COLUMBIA
WALLA WALLA
Walla Walla
BENTON
Richland
Pasco
Kennewick
FRANKLIN
PIERCE
Tacoma
MT. RAINIER NAT'L PK.
Mt. Rainier 14,410
YAKIMA
Yakima
LEWIS
Centralia
Chehalis
PACIFIC
COWLITZ
Kelso
Longview
SKAMANIA
Mt. St. Helens
KLICKITAT
Goldendale
CLARK
Vancouver
Portland
Mt. Hood 11,235
Mt. Adams 12,307
Columbia River
Snake River
GRAND COULEE DAM
Franklin D. Roosevelt L.
BONNEVILLE DAM
The Dalles
CASCADE RANGE
WENATCHEE MTS.
COAST RANGES
Columbia River
Spokane
Coeur d'Alene
Lewiston
ASOTIN
KING
SEATTLE
Bremerton
Tacoma
KITSAP
PIERCE
Bellevue
Renton
Auburn
Kent
Maple Valley
Snoqualmie
10 mi.
10 km.

and Tacoma, are in the western region along Puget Sound, an unusual 200-mile-long arm of the Pacific Ocean; it varies in width up to 40 miles and harbors more than 300 islands. This area has a milder climate than any other in the country that is as far north. Generally, the weather is drier in the east than in the west, which receives moist Pacific winds and considerable rainfall. Principal irrigated regions are in the Columbia Basin and the valleys of the Walla Walla, Snake, and Yakima rivers. The Lower Granite Dam and Lock System extends navigation on the Columbia and Snake rivers as far inland as Lewiston, Idaho.

Washington is a leading producer of apples, wheat, and hops. Livestock and livestock products make up a third of the total farm revenue, while commercial fishing is significant. Mineral production, including coal and stone, accounted for $216 million in 1977. Aircraft, lumber and food industries dominate the manufacturing sector of the economy.

Today, the state is trying to diversify and stabilize its industry, with less dependency on federal defense contracts. One area of concentration is the brisk tourist trade, which has gained greatly in recent years as more facilities are built to augment the exceptional hunting, fishing, and skiing available. Mount Rainier and Olympic National Parks, and the Grand Coulee Dam National Recreation Area, are among the major attractions. Seattle Center, consisting of structures from the 1962 Century 21 Exposition, includes a monorail and 606-foot "Space Needle." Whitman Mission National Historic Site denotes the place Marcus Whitman founded an Indian mission in 1836; it is also the site of the 1847 Indian massacre in which Whitman and others were killed.

A part of the Oregon country claimed by both Britain and the United States in the 1830s, Washington became U.S. territory by a compromise treaty with Britain in 1846. It became a state in 1889.

The period after World War I was one of discontent and strife in the labor field. There were many disputes, especially between businessmen and the Industrial Workers of the World (IWW); violence erupted at Centralia. During World War II, the state's sizable Japanese-American population suffered discrimination and disruption; over 15,000 people were displaced eastward.

In 1979, Gov. Dixy Lee Ray closed a nuclear waste dump near Hanford, accusing users of carelessness in shipments. The dump was reopened after Gov. Ray made an agreement with the governors of the other two states with similar dumps—Richard Riley of South Carolina and Robert List of Nevada—to require dump users to certify that each shipment met all Federal and state standards.

In November 1979, Washington voters approved a proposal forbidding the state budget to increase faster than personal income.

In March 1980, Mount St. Helens, a volcano which had been dormant since 1857, began to rumble and to spew out smoke and ash. Tremors and thunderstorms followed, and Gov. Ray ordered the area five miles around the mountain evacuated. An eruption on May 18 blew 1,300 feet off the mountain, spewed volcanic ash throughout western Washington and into Idaho and Montana, sent streams of mud through low-lying areas, and overturned 2,500 acres of timber. The ash disabled vehicles and closed hundreds of miles of highways. A stream of mud moved slowly down the Toutle River, and Spirit Lake filled up with mud and ash and was cut in half by a dam of debris. Steam and ash continued out of the mountain; the ground

rumbled; an eruption on May 24 blew 200 feet off the mountain, spreading more ash and mud. On the night of June 12-13, a third major eruption sent pebbles of pumice the size of marbles into the air; pebble fallout forced the evacuation of the entire town of Cougar.

On July 22, after almost six weeks of silence, and following a series of increasingly frequent earthquakes, Mount St. Helens spewed forth ash three times within a two-hour period. This trio of eruptions resulted in the lava dome being completely blown apart and a new, glowing inner crater being revealed.

Full name: State of Washington. **Origin of name:** In honor of George Washington. **Inhabitant:** Washingtonian. **Capital:** Olympia. **State motto:** Alki (By & By). **Flag:** State seal on green field. **Seal:** Portrait of George Washington & date 1889, the year state was admitted to Union. **Flower:** Western rhododendron. **Bird:** Willow goldfinch. **Tree:** Western hemlock. **Song:** "Washington, My Home." **Nickname:** Evergreen State.

Governor: Dixy Lee Ray. **Annual salary:** $63,000. **Term:** 4 years. **Current term expires:** Dec. 1980. **Voting requirements:** 18 yrs. old & U.S. citizen; registered and state resident 30 days. **U.S. Congressmen:** 7. **Entered Union:** 1889 (42nd state).

Location & boundaries: Pacific state: bounded on the north by Canada; on the east by Idaho; on the south by Oregon & the Columbia River; & on the west by the Pacific Ocean. **Total area:** 68,192 sq. mi. (ranks 20th). **Extreme length:** 358 mi. **Extreme breadth:** 240 mi. **Coastline:** 157 mi. **Chief rivers:** Columbia, Snake, Yakima. **Major lakes:** Chelan, Franklin D. Roosevelt. **No. of counties:** 39.

Population (1979 est.): 3,926,000 (ranks 21st). **Pop. increase (1970-79):** 15%. **Places over 25,000 pop.:** 14. **Places over 100,000:** 3. **Largest cities:** Seattle, Spokane, Tacoma. **Pop. density:** 57.6 per sq. mi. (ranks 28th). **Pop. projection 1985:** 3,792,000. **Pop. distribution:** 71.1% metropolitan; 28.9% non-metropolitan. **White:** 95.4%. **Black:** 2.1%. **Other:** 2.5%. **Marriage rate (1977):** 11.3 per 1,000 people. **Divorce rate:** 7.3 per 1,000 people.

State finances (1978). Revenue: $4,965,154,000. **Expenditures:** $4,250,017,000. **State taxes:** $648.66 per capita. **State personal income tax:** No. **Public debt (1978):** $382.90 per capita. **Federal aid (1979):** $351.83 per capita. **Personal income (1979 est.):** $9,435.

Sectors of the economy (% of labor force employed in 1970): Manufacturing (22%), Wholesale and retail trade (22%), Government (19%), Educational Services (9%), Services (7%), Construction (6%). **Leading products:** transportation equipment, machinery, food items, lumber & wood, paper items, chemicals, primary metals, printing & publishing. **Agricultural products:** dairy items, cattle, poultry, wheat, apples, hay. **Fishing:** salmon, oysters, crabs. **Avg. farm (1979 est.):** 488 acres. **Avg. value of farm per acre:** $586.

Highway expenditures per capita (1978): $104.13. **Persons per motor vehicle:** 1.26. **Minimum age for driver's license:** 16. **Gasoline tax:** 12¢ per gallon. **Diesel tax:** 12¢ per gallon. **Motor vehicle deaths:** 26.1 per 100,000 people.

Birthrate (1978): 15.5 per 1,000 people. **Infant mortality rate per 1,000 births (1977):** 12.1. **Physicians per 100,000 pop. (1977):** 183. **Dentists per 100,000 pop. (1977):** 68. **Acceptable hospital beds:** 4.4 per 1,000 people. **State expenditures per capita for health and hospitals (1978):** $50.65.

Education expenditures (1975-76): $515.16 per capita annually. **No. of pupils in public schools (1977 est.):** 769,000. **No. of institutions of higher learning (1976-77):** 48. **Public school expenditure per pupil in attendance (1975-76):** $1,684. **Avg. salary of public school teachers (1974-75 est.):** $12,538. **No. full-time teachers (1977 est.):** 36,000. **Educational attainment of adult population (1976):** 12.7 median yrs. of school completed; 1.0% with less than 5 years of education; 16.1% with 4 yrs. of college.

Telephones (1977): 76 per 100 people. **State Chamber of Commerce:** Association of Washington Business, P.O. Box 658, Olympia, Washington 98507.

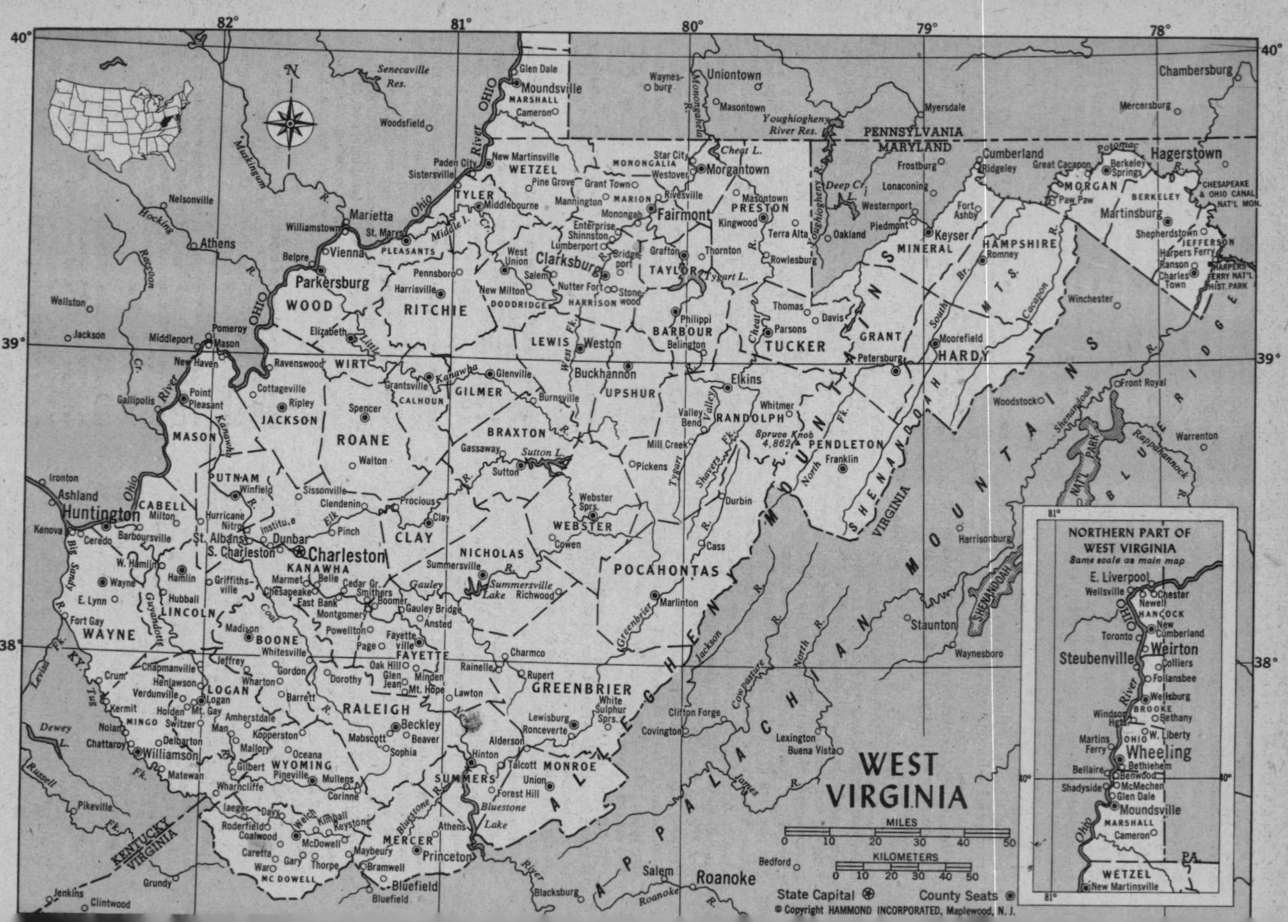

WEST VIRGINIA
State Capital
County Seats
Copyright HAMMOND INCORPORATED, Maplewood, N. J.
MILES
KILOMETERS
PENNSYLVANIA
MARYLAND
VIRGINIA
KENTUCKY
APPALACHIAN MOUNTAINS
SHENANDOAH MOUNTAINS
BLUE RIDGE
SHENANDOAH NAT'L PARK
CHESAPEAKE & OHIO CANAL NAT'L MON.
HARPERS FERRY NAT'L HIST. PARK
Chambersburg
Mercersburg
Hagerstown
Cumberland
Frostburg
Lonaconing
Westernport
Piedmont
Ridgeley
Great Cacapon
Paw Paw
Berkeley Springs
Martinsburg
Shepherdstown
Harpers Ferry
Charles Town
Ranson
JEFFERSON
BERKELEY
MORGAN
Potomac R.
Myersdale
Uniontown
Masontown
Youghiogheny River Res.
Monongahela R.
Deep Cr. L.
Oakland
Cheat L.
Morgantown
Star City
Westover
MONONGALIA
Grant Town
Riversville
Masontown
Fort Ashby
Keyser
MINERAL
Romney
HAMPSHIRE
Winchester
Woodstock
Front Royal
Warrenton
Rappahannock R.
Shenandoah R.
Staunton
Waynesboro
Harrisonburg
Moorefield
HARDY
Petersburg
GRANT
Franklin
PENDLETON
Thomas
Davis
Parsons
TUCKER
Terra Alta
Rowlesburg
Kingwood
Thornton
PRESTON
Mannington
MARION
Monongah
Fairmont
Enterprise
Shinnston
Lumberport
Bridgeport
Grafton
TAYLOR
Tygart L.
Whitmer
Spruce Knob 4,862
RANDOLPH
Valley Bend
Elkins
Mill Creek
Pickens
Durbin
Cass
North Fk.
SHENANDOAH MTS.
South Br.
Cacapon
Glen Dale
Moundsville
MARSHALL
Cameron
Woodsfield
New Martinsville
Paden City
Sistersville
WETZEL
Pine Grove
TYLER
Middlebourne
Marietta
Williamstown
St. Marys
Middle I.
Belpre
Vienna
PLEASANTS
West Union
Clarksburg
Salem
New Milton
DODDRIDGE
Nutter Fort
Stonewood
HARRISON
Philippi
Belington
BARBOUR
Cheat R.
West Fk.
LEWIS
Weston
Buckhannon
UPSHUR
Senecaville Res.
Muskingum R.
Hocking R.
Nelsonville
Athens
Jackson
Wellston
Raccoon Cr.
Pomeroy
Middleport
Mason
New Haven
Gallipolis
Ironton
Ashland
Kenova
Ceredo
Huntington
Barboursville
Milton
CABELL
Parkersburg
WOOD
Pennsboro
Harrisville
RITCHIE
Elizabeth
Little Kanawha R.
WIRT
Ravenswood
Cottageville
Ripley
JACKSON
Spencer
ROANE
Walton
Grantsville
CALHOUN
Glenville
GILMER
Burnsville
Gassaway
Sutton L.
Sutton
BRAXTON
Point Pleasant
MASON
PUTNAM
Winfield
Sissonville
Clendenin
Elk R.
Nitro
Institute
St. Albans
Dunbar
S. Charleston
Charleston
KANAWHA
Marmet
Belle
Chesapeake
East Bank
Cedar Gr.
Smithers
Montgomery
Boomer
Gauley Bridge
Ansted
Powelltton
Page
Fayetteville
FAYETTE
Oak Hill
Glen Jean
Minden
Mt. Hope
Lawton
Rainelle
Charmco
Procious
Clay
CLAY
Webster Sprs.
Cowen
WEBSTER
NICHOLAS
Summersville
Summersville Lake
Richwood
Gauley R.
POCAHONTAS
Marlinton
Greenbrier R.
W. Hamlin
Hamlin
Griffithsville
LINCOLN
Hurricane
Coal R.
Madison
Whitesville
BOONE
Hubball
E. Lynn
Fort Gay
WAYNE
Wayne
Guyandotte R.
Big Sandy R.
Chapmanville
Henlawson
Verdunville
Mt. Gay
Holden
Switzer
Man
Amherstdale
LOGAN
Logan
Barrett
Gordon
Dorothy
Wharton
Jeffrey
RALEIGH
Beckley
Mabscott
Beaver
Sophia
Oceana
Mullens
Corinne
Pineville
WYOMING
Gilbert
Mallory
Kopperston
Kermit
MINGO
Switzer
Delbarton
Williamson
Nolan
Chattaroy
Matewan
Wharncliffe
Iaeger
Davy
Welch
Kimball
Keystone
Roderfield
Coalwood
Caretta
War
Gary
Thorpe
MC DOWELL
McDowell
Maybeury
Bramwell
MERCER
Princeton
Bluefield
Bluewell
Athens
Hinton
SUMMERS
Forest Hill
Union
Talcott
MONROE
Alderson
Ronceverte
Lewisburg
White Sulphur Sprs.
GREENBRIER
Rupert
Clifton Forge
Covington
Lexington
Buena Vista
Bedford
Salem
Roanoke
Blacksburg
Roanoke R.
Bluestone Lake
Bluestone R.
James R.
Jackson R.
North R.
Cow Pasture R.
Kanawha R.
Kentucky
Virginia
Levisa Fk.
Tug Fk.
Russell Fk.
Dewey L.
Grundy
Pikeville
Jenkins
Clintwood
KY.
Crum
Cool R.
Shavers Fk.
Tygart R.
Jackson R.

NORTHERN PART OF
WEST VIRGINIA
Same scale as main map
E. Liverpool
Wellsville
Chester
Newell
New Cumberland
HANCOCK
Toronto
Weirton
Steubenville
Colliers
Follansbee
Wellsburg
BROOKE
Bethany
Windsor Hgts.
W. Liberty
Martins Ferry
Wheeling
Bethlehem
Benwood
McMechen
Glen Dale
Bellaire
Shadyside
Moundsville
MARSHALL
Cameron
New Martinsville
WETZEL
Ohio River
PA.

WEST VIRGINIA

West Virginia, second leading coal producer in the U.S., has rugged, ravine-slashed terrain and highly irregular boundaries. There are two main land regions: the Appalachian Plateau constitutes more than 80 percent of its area, and the Great Appalachian Valley consists of a wide strip along the eastern border and includes an expanse of the Allegheny Mountains and a small section of the Blue Ridge. Most of the state's coal, oil, gas, and salt deposits are in the plateau region. Moderately cold winters, warm summers, and adequate rainfall are features of the climate, but the craggy land is not conducive to large-scale farming.

Manufacturing and commerce buttress the state's mineral-oriented economy. The state's numerous glass factories include the Fostoria works at Moundsville and the Fenton plant at Williamstown. The Ohio and Kanawha Valleys are vital chemical centers. Fine scenery, mineral springs, and 40 state parks make for a sizable tourism business. Attractions include the Harpers Ferry National Historical Park, the Monongahela National Forest, and Wheeling's Oglebay Park.

West Virginia's early history is largely shared with Virginia, of which it was a part until Virginia joined the Confederacy in 1861; the western counties then adopted their own government and sided with the Union; statehood dates from 1863. Two counties were added to the state in 1866.

Indians known as Mound Builders were the region's earliest inhabitants, but they were gone long before the advent of the Europeans in the 1670s. Several Indian tribes continued, however, to use the area as hunting grounds. Welsh, Scots-Irish, and Germans may have lived in the region before him, but credit is often given to Morgan Morgan for having established (1731) the first known permanent settlement on Mill Creek in the eastern panhandle. In 1742 coal was discovered on the Coal River, an event that was a major determinant of West Virginia's destiny. The Indians' hold on the region virtually ended in 1774 but fighting erupted three years later and continued until 1794.

When the state broke away from Virginia, many West Virginians, including General Thomas J. (Stonewall) Jackson, remained loyal to the mother state. A famous long-running (1882-96) feud between the Hatfields of West Virginia and the McCoys of Kentucky resulted in many killings and involved the governors of those states in an acrimonious rift.

Industrial expansion marked the late 19th and early 20th centuries, despite serious labor disputes, especially in the coal mining industry. Not until the 1930s were the mines unionized and working conditions appreciably improved.

A public employee strike for union recognition in 1968 resulted in mass dismissals of state highway workers. The coal mines were shut down 45 days in late 1971 as the United Mine Workers negotiated a new contract. Wildcat strikes have erupted in the mines over such issues as safety and health benefits. Some 25,000 coal miners stayed off the job for three weeks in early 1974 in a protest over gas rationing measures at the height of the fuel crisis.

Recently the coal industry has come under attack by labor activists charging that priority is given to production and profits over the health of miners, and by environmentalists who charge the state's land is being destroyed for the benefit of out-of-state interests.

In 1975 there was a major resurgence in the state's coal industry. In 1976 progress was slowed by a wildcat strike which began in Logan, spreading to eight other states before it ended. With the announcement of President Carter's energy program in 1977, increased importance was placed on West Virginia's industry, but again production was hampered by a series of wildcat strikes. In the longest coal strike in U.S. history, the United Mine Workers shut down the mines from December 1977 to March 1978. And 5,200 wildcat strikers stayed off the job for 11 days in February and March 1980.

A $1.4 billion energy facility is slated to be constructed near Morgantown by 1984. It will be the first plant of commercial size to produce liquid fuel directly from coal.

Full name: State of West Virginia. **Origin of name:** In honor of the "Virgin Queen," Elizabeth I of England. **Inhabitant:** West Virginian. **Capital:** Charleston. **State motto:** Montani Semper Liberi (Mountaineers Are Always Free). **Flag:** State seal on blue-bordered white field. **Seal:** Rock (with date June 20, 1863, when state entered Union) stands between farmer & miner, symbolizing state's industries. **Flower:** Big rhododendron. **Bird:** Cardinal. **Tree:** Sugar maple. **Songs:** "The West Virginia Hills," "This Is My West Virginia," & "West Virginia, My Home Sweet Home." **Nickname:** Mountain State.

Governor: John D. Rockefeller IV. **Annual salary:** $50,000. **Term:** 4 years. **Current term expires:** Jan. 1981. **Voting requirements:** 18 yrs. old & U.S. citizen; resident of state, 60 days, registered, 30 days. **U.S. Congressmen:** 4. **Entered Union:** 1863 (35th state).

Location & boundaries: Southeastern state: bounded on the north by the Ohio River, Pennsylvania, Maryland & the Potomac River; on the east by Maryland & Virginia; on the south by Virginia; & on the west by Kentucky, Ohio & the Ohio River. **Total area:** 24,181 sq. mi. (ranks 41st). **Extreme length:** 265 mi. **Extreme breadth:** 237 mi. **Chief rivers:** Ohio, Potomac, Kanawa. **Major lake:** East Lynn Reservoir. **No. of counties:** 55.

Population (1979 est.): 1,878,000 (ranks 34th). **Pop. increase (1970-79):** 7.7%. **Places over 25,000 pop.:** 7. **Places over 100,000:** None. **Largest cities:** Huntington, Charleston, Wheeling. **Pop. density:** 77.2 per sq. mi. (ranks 25th). **Pop. projection 1985:** 1,907,000. **Pop. distribution:** 36.1% metropolitan; 63.9% nonmetropolitan. **White:** 95.6%. **Black:** 4.2%. **Other:** 0.2%. **Marriage rate (1977):** 9.4 per 1,000 people. **Divorce rate:** 5.2 per 1,000 people.

State finances (1978). Revenue: $2,080,435,000. **Expenditures:** $2,054,400,000. **State taxes:** $527.29 per capita. **State personal income tax:** Yes. **Public debt (1978):** $382.90 per capita. **Federal aid (1979):** $410.06 per capita. **Personal income (1979 est.):** $7,470.

Sectors of the economy (% of labor force employed in 1970): Manufacturing (23%), Wholesale and retail trade (19%), Government (17%), Educational Services (8%), Services (7%), Construction (7%). **Leading products:** chemicals; stone, clay & glass items; primary & fabricated metals; food items; machinery; printing & publishing. **Minerals:** coal, natural gas & natural gas liquids, stone. **Agricultural products:** cattle, dairy items, hay, apples, corn. **Avg. farm (1979 est.):** 214 acres. **Avg. value of farm per acre:** $472.

Highway expenditures per capita (1978): $198.49. **Persons per motor vehicle:** 1.55. **Minimum age for driver's license:** 18. **Gasoline tax:** 10.5¢ per gallon. **Diesel tax:** 10.5¢ per gallon. **Motor vehicle deaths:** 25.1 per 100,000 people.

Birthrate (1978): 15.7 per 1,000 people. **Infant mortality rate per 1,000 births (1977):** 14.6. **Physicians per 100,000 pop. (1977):** 134. **Dentists per 100,000 pop. (1977):** 34. **Acceptable hospital beds:** 8.4 per 1,000 people. **State expenditures per capita for health and hospitals (1978):** $55.58.

Education expenditures (1975-76): $377.18 per capita annually. **No. of pupils in public schools (1977 est.):** 399,000. **No. of institutions of higher learning (1976-77):** 28. **Public school expenditure per pupil in attendance (1975-76):** $1,382. **Avg. salary of public school teachers (1974-75 est.):** $9,124. **No. full-time teachers (1977 est.):** 20,670. **Educational attainment of adult population (1976):** 12.1 median yrs. of school completed; 5.0% with less than 5 years of education; 9.2% with 4 yrs. of college.

WISCONSIN
MILES
KILOMETERS
State Capitals   County Seats
Longitude West of Greenwich
© Copyright HAMMOND INCORPORATED, Maplewood, N.J.

Telephones (1977): 55 per 100 people. **State Chamber of Commerce:** West Virginia Chamber of Commerce, P.O. Box 2789, 1101 Kanawha Valley Bldg., Charleston, West Virginia 25330.

WISCONSIN

Although Wisconsin is best known as the leading U.S. dairy state, manufacturing today represents its major economic activity; top products include nonelectrical machinery and the many pulp and paper items that the state's forests make possible. Wisconsin is also the country's largest supplier of beer, with brewers concentrated most heavily in the Milwaukee area. Politically, the state has gained a reputation for progress and reform.

The land itself, rich and diverse, consists of two principal regions: the Superior Upland in the north and the Central Lowlands, covering the lower two-thirds of the state and consisting of the Wisconsin Driftless Area in the west and the Great Lakes Plain in the east. Rolling hills, ridges, and fertile valleys and plains, punctuated by many clear lakes, have made Wisconsin famous for its scenic beauty, and, despite past exploitation, forests still cover almost half the state. By far the largest part of the population lives in the southeastern region. The state's climate is marked by sharply defined seasons that are tempered somewhat by Lakes Superior and Michigan.

Frenchman Jean Nicolet was the first European to explore the Wisconsin region, landing (1634) at Green Bay in search of a fur-trading fortune and the legendary "Northwest Passage" to the Orient. At the time, Ottawa, Huron, and other Indians from the east were forcing indigenous Indians (including the Winnebago) westward, and only the Menominees were settled there. The arrival of Nicolet and other Frenchmen soon after established France's claim to the region that was valid until 1763, when the British gained possession.

After the American Revolution, England ceded (1783) the region to the United States, but the British retained actual control until after the War of 1812. A part of the Northwest Territory until 1800, the Wisconsin region became, successively, a part of the territories of Indiana (1800-09), Illinois (1809-18), and Michigan (1818-36). When it was made a separate territory in 1836, Wisconsin included its present area in addition to parts of Iowa, Minnesota, and sections of North and South Dakota east of the Missouri and White Earth Rivers. In 1838, the territory west of the Mississippi was organized as the Territory of Iowa, Wisconsin retaining its present area and a northward extension to Lake of the Woods in what is now Minnesota. A decade later, Wisconsin entered the Union.

Wisconsin's Indian troubles reached a climax in the Black Hawk War (1832), which virtually ended the Indian threat in the area and caused a settlement boom. There followed a substantial influx of immigrants—especially Germans, Irish, English, and Welsh. Liberal leaders, like Carl Schurz, settled in Wisconsin and added to the intellectual development of the state. In 1871, Wisconsin was hit by the great Peshtigo forest fire, the worst natural disaster in its history, which killed more than 1,000 persons and destroyed more than $5 million worth of property. An extensive reforestation program is part of Wisconsin's current far-reaching conservation efforts.

Wisconsin is the home of the three major league sports teams. The Green Bay Packers have won the NFL championship eleven times and the Milwaukee Bucks became the NBA champions in 1971. Major league baseball returned to the state in 1970 when the Seattle club of the American League became the Milwaukee Brewers.

In 1976 Wisconsin became the first of the 1976 primary states to hold an open presidential primary election. The Democratic National Committee decided in 1978 to bar open primaries in this state as well as in Michigan and Montana.

Full name: State of Wisconsin. **Origin of name:** From an Indian name. **Inhabitant:** Wisconsinite. **Capital:** Madison. **State motto:** Forward. **Flag:** State seal on a blue field. **Seal:** A sailor & a miner hold shield with symbols representing Wisconsin's industries; badger is state's nickname; horn of plenty; pyramid of lead. **Flower:** Wood violet. **Bird:** Robin. **Tree:** Sugar maple. **Rock:** Granite. **Mineral:** Galena. **Domestic Animal:** Dairy Cow. **Song:** "On, Wisconsin!" **Nickname:** Badger State.

Governor: Lee Sherman Dreyfus. **Annual salary:** $65,801. **Term:** 4 years. **Current term expires:** Jan. 1983. **Voting requirements:** 18 yrs. old & U.S. citizen; resident of voting district 10 days. **U.S. Congressmen:** 9. **Entered Union:** 1848 (30th state).

Location & boundaries: Midwestern state: bounded on the north by Lake Superior & the state of Michigan; on the east by Lake Michigan; on the south by Illinois; & on the west by Iowa, Minnesota, the Mississippi River & the St. Croix River. **Total area:** 56,154 sq. mi. (ranks 26th). **Extreme length:** 315 mi. **Extreme breadth:** 289 mi. **Shoreline:** 785 mi. **Chief rivers:** Mississippi, Wisconsin, St. Croix, Black, Fox. **Major lakes:** Winnebago, Poygan, Mendota, Pentenwell, Castle Rock. **No. of counties:** 72.

Population (1979 est.): 4,720,000 (ranks 16th). **Pop. increase (1970-79):** 6.8%. **Places over 25,000 pop.:** 23. **Places over 100,000:** 2. **Largest cities:** Milwaukee, Madison, Racine, Green Bay. **Pop. density:** 84.0 per sq. mi. (ranks 23rd). **Pop. projection 1985:** 4,972,000. **Pop. distribution:** 63.0% metropolitan; 37.0% nonmetropolitan. **White:** 96.4%. **Black:** 2.9%. **Other:** 0.7%. **Marriage rate (1977):** 8.0 per 1,000 people. **Divorce rate:** 3.1 per 1,000 people.

State finances (1978). Revenue: $5,524,752,000. **Expenditures:** $4,755,651,000. **State taxes:** $660.23 per capita. **State personal income tax:** Yes. **Public debt (1978):** $425.46 per capita. **Federal aid (1979):** $365.13 per capita. **Personal income (1979 est.):** $8,419.

Sectors of the economy (% of labor force employed in 1970): Manufacturing (31%), Wholesale and retail trade (20%), Government (14%), Educational Services (8%), Services (6%), Construction (5%). **Leading products:** machinery, food items, transportation equipment, paper items, primary & fabricated metals. **Agricultural products:** dairy items, cattle, hogs, hay, corn, oats. **Fishing:** whitefish, lake herring, chubs, carp, buffalo. **Avg. farm (1979 est.):** 197 acres. **Avg. value of farm per acre:** $807.

Highway expenditures per capita (1978): $82.15. **Persons per motor vehicle:** 1.63. **Minimum age for driver's license:** 16. **Gasoline tax:** 9¢ per gallon. **Diesel tax:** 9¢ per gallon. **Motor vehicle deaths:** 20.9 per 100,000 people.

Birthrate (1978): 14.7 per 1,000 people. **Infant mortality rate per 1,000 births (1977):** 11.3. **Physicians per 100,000 pop. (1977):** 144. **Dentists per 100,000 pop. (1977):** 55. **Acceptable hospital beds:** 6.4 per 1,000 people. **State expenditures per capita for health and hospitals (1978):** $58.77.

Education expenditures (1975-76): $525.51 per capita annually. **No. of pupils in public schools (1977 est.):** 932,000. **No. of institutions of higher learning (1976-77):** 58. **Public school expenditure per pupil in attendance (1975-76):** $1,792. **Avg. salary of public school teachers (1974-75 est.):** $13,046. **No. full-time teachers (1977 est.):** 57,970. **Educational attainment of adult population (1976):** 12.1 median yrs. of school completed; 1.4% with less than 5 years of education; 12.7% with 4 yrs. of college.

Telephones (1977): 70 per 100 people. **State Chamber of Commerce:** Wisconsin Association of Manufacturers & Commerce, 111 E. Wisconsin Ave., Room 1600, Milwaukee, Wisconsin 53202.

WYOMING

Wyoming, an awesome, sparsely settled state of alternating plains and mountains, is crossed by the Continental Divide—the junction of the Great

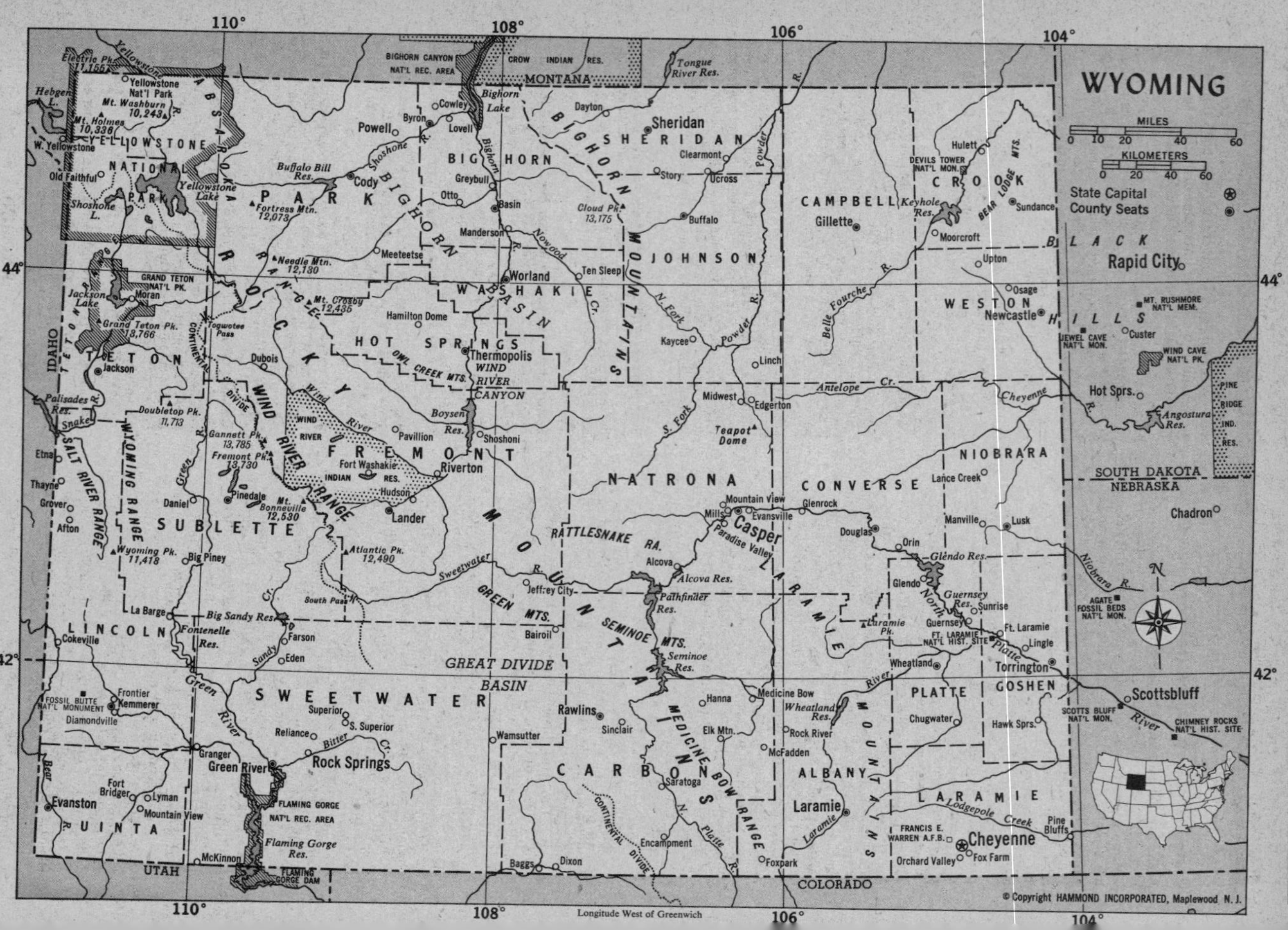

WYOMING
MILES
KILOMETERS
State Capital
County Seats
Copyright HAMMOND INCORPORATED, Maplewood N.J.
MONTANA
SOUTH DAKOTA
NEBRASKA
COLORADO
UTAH
IDAHO
Longitude West of Greenwich
BLACK HILLS
BEAR LODGE MTS.
CROOK
CAMPBELL
Gillette
WESTON
Newcastle
Osage
Upton
Sundance
Hulett
Moorcroft
DEVILS TOWER NAT'L MON.
Keyhole Res.
Rapid City
MT. RUSHMORE NAT'L MEM.
Custer
JEWEL CAVE NAT'L MON.
WIND CAVE NAT'L PK.
Hot Sprs.
Angostura Res.
CHEYENNE RIVER IND. RES.
PINE RIDGE IND. RES.
Chadron
NIOBRARA
Lance Creek
Lusk
Manville
CONVERSE
Douglas
Glenrock
Orin
Glendo
Glendo Res.
North Platte River
Guernsey
Guernsey Res.
Sunrise
FT. LARAMIE NAT'L HIST. SITE
Ft. Laramie
Lingle
Torrington
PLATTE
GOSHEN
Wheatland
Wheatland Res.
Chugwater
Hawk Sprs.
LARAMIE
Lodgepole Creek
Horse Creek
Pine Bluffs
FRANCIS E. WARREN A.F.B.
Cheyenne
Orchard Valley
Fox Farm
SCOTTS BLUFF NAT'L MON.
Scottsbluff
AGATE FOSSIL BEDS NAT'L MON.
Niobrara R.
CHIMNEY ROCKS NAT'L HIST. SITE
SHERIDAN
BIGHORN
Sheridan
Dayton
Clearmont
Ucross
Story
JOHNSON
Buffalo
Kaycee
BIGHORN MOUNTAINS
Cloud Pk. 13,175
Ten Sleep
CROW INDIAN RES.
Tongue River Res.
Powder R.
N. Fork
Antelope Cr.
Belle Fourche R.
Linch
Edgerton
Midwest
Teapot Dome
NATRONA
Mountain View
Casper
Mills
Evansville
Paradise Valley
Alcova
Alcova Res.
Pathfinder Res.
Seminoe Res.
RATTLESNAKE RA.
SEMINOE MTS.
Hanna
Elk Mtn.
Medicine Bow
Rock River
McFadden
ALBANY
Laramie
Foxpark
MEDICINE BOW RANGE
CARBON
Saratoga
Sinclair
Rawlins
Encampment
CONTINENTAL DIVIDE
Dixon
Baggs
Wamsutter
GREAT DIVIDE BASIN
GREEN MTS.
Bairoil
Jeffrey City
LARAMIE MOUNTAINS
Laramie River
Laramie Pk.
Platte R.
N. Platte R.
BIG HORN
Basin
Worland
Manderson
Greybull
Otto
Lovell
Cowley
Byron
Powell
Cody
PARK
Shoshone R.
Bighorn Lake
Bighorn R.
Nowood R.
Buffalo Bill Res.
Fortress Mtn. 12,073
Needle Mtn. 12,130
Mt. Crosby 12,435
ABSAROKA RANGE
BIGHORN CANYON NAT'L REC. AREA
WASHAKIE
HOT SPRINGS
Thermopolis
WIND RIVER CANYON
OWL CREEK MTS.
Hamilton Dome
Meeteetse
Shoshoni
Boysen Res.
FREMONT
Riverton
Hudson
Lander
Pavillion
Fort Washakie
WIND RIVER INDIAN RES.
Atlantic Pk. 12,490
ROCKY MOUNTAINS
WIND RIVER RANGE
Wind River
Dubois
Gannett Pk. 13,785
Fremont Pk. 13,730
Pinedale
Mt. Bonneville 12,530
Doubletop Pk. 11,720
CONTINENTAL DIVIDE
Togwotee Pass
Jackson
GRAND TETON NAT'L PK.
Grand Teton 13,766
Moran
Jackson Lake
Jenny Lake
TETON RANGE
YELLOWSTONE NATIONAL PARK
Yellowstone L.
Shoshone L.
Old Faithful
W. Yellowstone
Mt. Washburn 10,243
Mt. Holmes 10,336
Electric Pk. 11,155
Hebgen L.
Palisades Res.
Snake R.
SALT RIVER RANGE
Etna
Thayne
Grover
Afton
WYOMING RANGE
Wyoming Pk. 11,418
Daniel
Big Piney
La Barge
SUBLETTE
Fontenelle Res.
Green River
Big Sandy Res.
Farson
Eden
South Pass
SWEETWATER
Sweetwater R.
Superior
S. Superior
Reliance
Rock Springs
Granger
Bitter Cr.
FLAMING GORGE NAT'L REC. AREA
Flaming Gorge Res.
FLAMING GORGE DAM
McKinnon
LINCOLN
Cokeville
Kemmerer
Frontier
Diamondville
FOSSIL BUTTE NAT'L MONUMENT
UINTA
Fort Bridger
Lyman
Mountain View
Evanston
Bear R.
104° 106° 108° 110°
42° 44°

Plains and the Rocky Mountains, which slash across the state's rectangle from the northwest corner to the center of the southern boundary.

The plains-mountains dividing line is less marked in the central and northern "intermontane" areas. The horizons are distant, and the land generally high—its average altitude of 6,700 feet is second only to Colorado's. The spectacular Devil's Tower—the country's first national monument—is a volcanic plug in the northeastern plains that stands 865 feet above its 415-foot base and can be seen for many miles.

The face of the land provides a clue to its economy. Short, tough grass covers much of the terrain, 80 percent of which is used for cattle and sheep grazing (Wyoming is second only to Texas in wool production). Recent consolidations have increased the size but decreased the number of farms and ranches within the state. About 20 percent of the farms produce commercial crops; the others are devoted to livestock production.

The growth of agriculture, however, is limited by the state's water supply. Although Wyoming has sufficient precipitation and underground springs to foster crop growth, as late as 1966 only ten percent of these resources were being utilized effectively. The perennial problem is distribution: in some places, where the soil is suitable for farming, the streamflow and precipitation are too light, while many large rivers like the Yellowstone and Tongue run through steep, rocky canyons.

More important to the state than agriculture is mining. In 1975, the assessed valuation on minerals was 48 percent of the entire state valuation. With the rise in oil prices, Wyoming has become one of the most intensively explored states in the Union. The Overthrust Belt near the Utah border shows great promise. Oil and oil products are among Wyoming's leading industries. Other minerals include bentonite, trona, coal, uranium, and iron ore. Wyoming is the second largest uranium producing state. Devastated by the conversion of railroad locomotives to diesel power, coal is making a comeback following formulation of emission standards which make Wyoming's low sulphur coal very much in demand. The state's coal reserves are estimated at 36 billion tons, of which two thirds is recoverable through strip mining and underground mining methods.

John Colter, a fur-trapper and a member of the Lewis and Clark expedition (1804-06), is the first European known to have entered the state; in 1807 he explored the Yellowstone area and brought back news of its geysers and hot springs.

By 1850, pioneers were "going west" via three famous trails, all of which passed through Wyoming: the California, Mormon (to Utah), and Oregon (to the Pacific Northwest). Meanwhile the Plains Indians, their homeland challenged, grew increasingly hostile, raiding wagon trains and defying accompanying troops. These troubles climaxed in 1865-66, then tapered off.

The Union Pacific Railroad was built (1867-68) across southern Wyoming, following the coal deposits and bringing in laborers to work the mines. The scant farmland caused many homesteaders to bypass Wyoming, leaving it open for cattlemen, who enjoyed bonanza days from 1865 to 1887.

Rustlers, declining market prices, and the severe winter of 1886-87 in which one-sixth of the herds starved all helped to curtail the cattle industry's dominance. About this time, sheep raising began to increase, leading to conflict between sheepmen and cattlemen over grazing rights.

Today tourism is increasingly vital to Wyoming's economy: over nine million persons—including many sportsmen—visit the state annually. Yellowstone and Grand Teton National Parks are prime attractions. Wyoming has been decisively thrust into the missile age by Warren AFB (Cheyenne), one of the largest in the nation's ICBM complex.

Full name: State of Wyoming. **Origin of name:** Named after Wyoming Valley, Pennsylvania; Indian word means "Alternating Mountains & Valleys." **Inhabitant:** Wyomingite. **Capital:** Cheyenne. **State motto:** Equal Rights. **Flag:** State seal & buffalo on a red-&-white-bordered blue field. **Seal:** Woman & motto, "Equal Rights," symbolize equal treatment women have had in state; two men represent Wyoming's livestock & mining industries; dates Wyoming became territory & state. **Flower:** Indian paintbrush. **Bird:** Meadowlark. **Tree:** Cottonwood. **Song:** "Wyoming." **Nickname:** Equality State.

Governor: Ed Herschler. **Annual salary:** $55,000. **Term:** 4 years. **Current term expires:** Jan. 1983. **Voting requirements:** 18 yrs. old & U.S. citizen; resident of state & registered to vote before or at primary for general election. **U.S. Congressmen:** 1. **Entered Union:** 1890 (44th state).

Location & boundaries: Rocky Mountain state: bounded on the north by Montana; on the east by South Dakota & Nebraska; on the south by Colorado & Utah; & on the west by Utah, Idaho & Montana. **Total area:** 97,914 sq. mi. (ranks 9th). **Extreme length:** 365 mi. **Extreme breadth:** 265 mi. **Chief rivers:** North Platte, Bighorn, Green, Snake. **Major lakes:** Yellowstone, Jackson, Flaming Gorge Reservoir. **No. of counties:** 23.

Population (1979 est.): 450,000 (ranks 49th). **Pop. increase (1970-79):** 35.3%. **Places over 25,000 pop.:** 2. **Places over 100,000:** None. **Largest cities:** Cheyenne, Casper, Laramie. **Pop. density:** 4.6 per sq. mi. (ranks 49th). **Pop. projection 1985:** 442,000. **Pop. distribution:** 0.0% metropolitan; 100.0% non-metropolitan. **White:** 97.2%. **Black:** 0.8%. **Other:** 2%. **Marriage rate (1977):** 14.3 per 1,000 people. **Divorce rate:** 7.6 per 1,000 people.

State finances (1978). Revenue: $670,888,000. **Expenditures:** $507,006,000. **State taxes:** $682.75 per capita. **State personal income tax:** No. **Public debt (1978):** $237.11 per capita. **Federal aid (1979):** $363.33 per capita. **Personal income (1979 est.):** $9,657.

Sectors of the economy (% of labor force employed in 1970): Government (22%), Wholesale and retail trade (20%), Educational Services (11%), Services (9%), Construction (7%), Manufacturing (6%). **Leading products:** petroleum & coal items; food items; stone, clay & glass items; lumber & wood; printing & publishing. **Minerals:** petroleum, natural gas, sodium salts, iron ore, uranium. **Agricultural products:** cattle, sheep, wool, hay, sugarbeets, wheat. **Avg. farm (1979 est.):** 4,875 acres. **Avg. value of farm per acre:** $119.

Highway expenditures per capita (1978): $247.56. **Persons per motor vehicle:** 1.03. **Minimum age for driver's license:** 16. **Gasoline tax:** 8¢ per gallon. **Diesel tax:** None. **Motor vehicle deaths:** 56.8 per 100,000 people.

Birthrate (1978): 20.4 per 1,000 people. **Infant mortality rate per 1,000 births (1977):** 13.9. **Physicians per 100,000 pop. (1977):** 113. **Dentists per 100,000 pop. (1977):** 50. **Acceptable hospital beds:** 6.4 per 1,000 people. **State expenditures per capita for health and hospitals (1978):** $55.88.

Education expenditures (1975-76): $624.03 per capita annually. **No. of pupils in public schools (1977 est.):** 89,000. **No. of institutions of higher learning (1976-77):** 8. **Public school expenditure per pupil in attendance (1975-76):** $2,142. **Avg. salary of public school teachers (1974-75 est.):** $10,350. **No. full-time teachers (1977 est.):** 5,080. **Educational attainment of adult population (1976):** 12.6 median yrs. of school completed; 1.2% with less than 5 years of education; 14.5% with 4 yrs. of college.

Telephones (1977): 77 per 100 people. **State Chamber of Commerce:** None.

REPRESENTATIVE AMERICAN CITIES

See pages 182 and 183 for Selected 1980 Census population figures.

ALBUQUERQUE

Location: North-central New Mexico, on upper Rio Grande **County:** Bernalillo **City Area:** 95.22 sq. miles (246.62 sq. kilometers) **Altitude:** 4,958 feet (1506.6 meters)
Mayor: David Rusk **Chief Administrative Officer:** Jim Jaramillo
City Population: 243,751 (1970 census), 284,617 (1976 est.)
Metro Area Population: 333,266 (1970 census), 401,900 (1977 est.)
Daily Newspapers: 2 **No. of Radio Stations:** 21 (1980) **No. of TV Stations:** 5 (1980)
City Chamber of Commerce: Greater Albuquerque Chamber of Commerce, 401 2nd Street, NW, Albuquerque, New Mexico 87102

Albuquerque, seat of Bernalillo County, is the largest city in New Mexico; a fast-growing center of trade, clean industry, and Federal agencies; and a health resort. On a per capita basis, more solar-heated homes stand here than in any other large U.S. city.

The old town of Albuquerque was founded in 1706 and named for the Duke of Alburquerque. After the Mexican War (1846-48), New Mexico was organized as a U.S. territory. Albuquerque was occupied by Confederate forces briefly in 1862. The new Albuquerque was mapped out in 1880 in connection with railroad construction.

After World War II, the city grew rapidly, primarily because of Sandia Laboratory (a nuclear weapons laboratory and the city's largest employer) and Kirtland Air Force Base, a nuclear effects research laboratory and satellite tracking station. Lovelace Foundation for medical research is also located here. Albuquerque now has railroad shops, lumber mills, and food-processing plants. Manufactures include brick and tile, wood products, Indian jewelry, clothing, and business machines. Several national electronic firms have announced plans to open facilities recently. New office buildings and hotels are being constructed and a major redevelopment of the downtown area is underway.

Of historic interest is the Old Town Plaza, laid out by Spanish settlers in 1706. Some of the buildings are two centuries old and have recently been restored. The Church of San Felipe de Neri (1706), once used as a fortress against the Indians, is in the Old Town. Other attractions are the University of New Mexico, founded in 1889, with pueblo-style buildings; the Ernie Pyle Memorial Branch Library, former home of the war correspondent; the annual state fair; and the magnificent vistas from the Sandia Peak Aerial Tramway.

ATLANTA

Location: Northwest Georgia, at foot of Blue Ridge Mountains, about 75 miles from northern border **County:** mostly in Fulton, part in DeKalb **City Area:** 136 sq. miles (352 sq. kilometers) **Altitude:** 1,050 feet (319.1 meters)
Mayor: Maynard H. Jackson
City Population: 495,039 (1970 census), 425,666 (1976 est.)
Metro Area Population: 1,595,517 (1970 census), 1,831,500 (1977 est.)
Daily Newspapers: 3 **No. of Radio Stations:** 23 (1980) **No. of TV Stations:** 8 (1980)
City Chamber of Commerce: Atlanta Chamber of Commerce, 1300 North Omni International, Atlanta, Georgia 30303

Atlanta, seat of Fulton County and capital and largest city of Georgia, is the leading commercial, industrial, and distribution center of the southeastern United States. It is also a port of entry and cultural center.

The first settler, Hardy Ivy, built a cabin on former Creek Indian land in 1833. The town, founded as Terminus in 1837, was later called Marthasville and in 1845 assumed the name Atlanta. It is said that the name was given it by railroad builder J. E. Thomson for its location at the end of the Western and Atlantic Railroad. It was incorporated as a city in 1847.

An important Confederate communications center during the Civil War, Atlanta fell to General W. T. Sherman on September 2, 1864, and on November 15 was put to the torch and almost completely destroyed. After the war, a new city was constructed and industrialization proceeded rapidly. In 1868 Atlanta became the state capital.

Today there are more than 1,500 manufacturing plants in the area. Products include automobiles, airplanes, chemicals, furniture, steel, paper, fertilizers, soft drinks, and processed foods. Atlanta is a major garment manufacturing center and is the home of the Apparel Mart, opened in 1979 as a showcase for southeastern clothing buyers. It is also a financial center and home of a Federal Reserve district bank. The National Center for Disease Control of the U.S. Public Health Service has its national headquarters here.

In 1973 Andrew J. Young was elected from the racially mixed metro area Fourth District, the first black Georgia Congressman since Reconstruction days, and in 1977 was appointed as U.S. Ambassador to the UN. Maynard H. Jackson, the first black mayor in modern times, was elected to a second term in 1977.

A billion-dollar building boom has included major privately financed projects plus several public facilities: a stadium and coliseum are in operation; the $70-million Georgia World Congress convention complex opened in September 1976. The Atlanta Memorial Arts Center, in memory of the 100 members of the Atlanta Art Association killed in a plane crash, opened in 1968. The Metropolitan Atlanta Rapid Transit Authority's $2.1-billion Federally financed subway system started services July 1, 1979.

In recent years Atlanta has developed its international trade, with a dozen foreign banks, 11 consulates and 10 foreign trade bureaus opening, earning the nickname "Paris of the South." Atlanta's new William B. Hartsfield International Airport is the global air hub of the southeast.

Of historic interest are the capitol and state library; the state archives building; the Cyclorama of the Battle of Atlanta; Oakland Cemetery of Civil War dead; Fort McPherson; and Wren's Nest, the home of Joel Chandler Harris, noted fabulist.

BALTIMORE

Location: In Maryland, 40 miles northeast of Washington, D.C., on the Patapsco River **County:** Baltimore is an independent city **City Area:** 79 sq. miles (205 sq. kilometers) **Altitude:** 20 feet (6.1 meters)
Mayor: William Donald Schaefer
City Population: 905,787 (1970 census), 804,900 (1977 est.)
Metro Area Population: 2,071,016 (1970 census), 2,146,900 (1977 est.)
Daily Newspapers: 3 **No. of Radio Stations:** 24 (1980) **No. of TV Stations:** 5 (1980)
City Chamber of Commerce: Greater Baltimore Committee, Inc., Suite 900, Two Hopkins Plaza, Charles Center, Baltimore, Maryland 21201

Baltimore, largest city in Maryland, is an industrial and commercial center and major seaport. Named for Lord Baltimore, first proprietor of Maryland, it was settled in the early 1600s and officially founded in 1729.

The shipbuilding industry grew highly profitable during the Revolution and War of 1812. The famous Baltimore clippers were built in the early 1800s. During the First and Second World Wars, the city was a major shipbuilder and supply port.

Baltimore was the site of the Continental Congress after the British occupation of Philadelphia (1777-78). The city's location, near the eastern terminus of the National Road that eventually ran from Cumberland to St. Louis, helped it develop into a major center of commerce. The opening in 1825 of the Erie Canal, in New York State, diverting trade, led to the chartering of the Baltimore & Ohio Railroad to bolster Baltimore's position.

During the Civil War, Maryland remained in the Union, but many Baltimore residents were pro-Southern and in 1861 some of them attacked Union troops. The city suffered a disastrous fire in 1904 but emerged as a better-planned metropolis.

Of historic interest are the Maryland Historical Society; the Baltimore Cathedral, the 175-year-old U.S. Frigate *Constellation*; Edgar Allan Poe's grave in Westminster Churchyard, and Ft. McHenry.

Today Baltimore handles the fourth largest volume of foreign trade of any American port. It has attracted diverse industries, including sugar and food processing. Petroleum and chemicals, aircraft, guided missiles, and steel and gypsum products are important industries. Bethlehem Steel Company's Sparrows Point complex, the largest tidewater steel plant in the world, is located here.

Baltimore, which suffers from the deterioration and shrinking population common to all Eastern cities, has attacked these problems vigorously. Through careful planning, long-term renewal efforts have begun to reverse the trend without adding to the city's debt load. A 8.5 mile subway is under construction and a major program of urban redevelopment has reshaped the downtown area. Charles Center, begun twenty years ago, is virtually complete, as is the Civic Center. In the Inner Harbor area, an Academy of Science has been completed, the Convention Center opened in August 1979, the Harborplace Shopping Pavilions opened in July 1980, and the National Aquarium will open in 1981.

To ease traffic jams plaguing the city's harbor tunnel, a $100-million federal grant was approved in 1980 for construction of a second connection, to be named Fort McHenry Tunnel.

BIRMINGHAM

Location: North-central Alabama, in the Jones Valley at the foot of Red Mt. **County:** Jefferson **City Area:** 89.7 sq. miles (232.4 sq. kilometers) **Altitude:** 600 feet (182.3 meters)
Mayor: Richard Arrington
City Population: 305,893 (1970 census), 280,544 (1976 est.)
Metro Area Population: 767,230 (1970 census), 805,300 (1977 est.)
Daily Newspapers: 2 **No. of Radio Stations:** 16 (1980) **No. of TV Stations:** 4 (1980)
City Chamber of Commerce: Birmingham Area Chamber of Commerce, P.O. Box 10127, Birmingham, Alabama 35202

Birmingham, seat of Jefferson County, is Alabama's principal industrial city and the South's leading iron-and-steel center.

Named after Birmingham, England, the city was founded and incorporated in 1871. A decade earlier the iron ore, coal, and limestone deposits in the region were used by Confederate forces to produce cannonballs and rifles. As railroads expanded and the steel industry developed, Birmingham prospered. A financial panic briefly interrupted its growth in 1900.

Since World War II, the city's economy has undergone diversification. Birmingham, "the Pittsburgh of the South," is now a leader in transportation equipment, construction materials, chemicals, and food processing.

Birmingham experienced a building boom during the 1960s; a $37.5-million civic center includes a coliseum, music hall, theater, and exhibit hall. Development of the University of Alabama in Birmingham is entering its final phase of completion on a 236-acre site adjacent to downtown. The $100-million complex of 40 buildings is expected to outstrip U.S. Steel as the area's biggest employer. By 1990, an estimated 50,000 people will be either an employee, a student, or both.

Of interest is the Arlington Historical Shrine, one of Alabama's few remaining antebellum homes. Overlooking the city on nearby Red Mountain is a giant statue of Vulcan, the largest iron figure ever cast. The Birmingham Museum of Art has recently been enlarged. The city is also the home of the Southern Research Institute, which has a technical staff of 360.

BOSTON

Location: In Massachusetts, on Massachusetts Bay, between Neponset River and the mouths of the Charles and Mystic rivers **County:** Suffolk **City Area:** 49.9 sq. miles (129.2 sq. kilometers) **Altitude:** 27 feet (8.2 meters)
Mayor: Kevin H. White

City Population: 641,071 (1970 census), 618,250 (1976 est.)
Metro Area Population: 3,848,593 (1970 census), 3,897,800 (1977 est.)
Daily Newspapers: 2 **No. of Radio Stations:** 28 (1980) **No. of TV Stations:** 7 (1980)
City Chamber of Commerce: Greater Boston Chamber of Commerce, 125 High Street, Boston, Massachusetts 02110

Boston, seat of Suffolk County and capital of Massachusetts, is New England's largest city. It was settled in 1630 by Puritan colonists. It became the center of American Puritanism and a fount of culture and intellect. The Boston Public Latin School, founded in 1635, and Harvard College, founded the following year in nearby Cambridge, were the first American schools.

An important commercial center because of its busy harbor, Boston became a leader in opposing British rule. Among pre-Revolutionary War actions were the Boston Massacre (1770) and the Boston Tea Party (1773). The Battle of Bunker Hill, one of the first of the Revolution, was fought close by in June 1775.

After the war, Boston prospered steadily and became a city in 1822. Prominent families such as the Cabots, Lowells, and Lodges ("the Boston Brahmins") made fortunes in shipping, textiles, and shoes. Because of the cultivated tastes of wealthy Bostonians, the city became known as "the Athens of America." Despite the conservative and wealthy atmosphere, however, it was a center of abolitionism before the Civil War.

A 19th-century flood of immigrants, largely Irish at first, converted Boston into a thriving industrial metropolis. Although it declined during the first half of the 20th century, primarily because industries moved to the South, Boston remained a cultural center and is still the financial and trading center of New England, a leading port, and an important market for fish, seafood, and wool. The electronics industry has helped revive Boston's economy.

Boston is also noted for its hospitals and its universities, among them Northeastern, Boston University and Boston College, as well as Harvard and MIT across the Charles River in Cambridge. In October 1979 the new John F. Kennedy Library was dedicated.

History-steeped Boston has many points of interest from colonial and Revolutionary War times, including the Old North Church, Old South Meeting House, Old State House, Paul Revere House, King's Chapel, Boston Common and Faneuil Hall.

Downtown has undergone major redevelopment in recent years, with the building of commercial and residential high-rises, the Government Center and the renovation of Faneuil Hall Marketplace, including Quincy, South and North Markets, the Downtown Crossing Pedestrian shopping mall, and Boston Waterfront Park.

Boston celebrated its 350th birthday in September 1980, climaxing months of festivities that had begun in May with a parade of tall ships in Boston harbor.

BUFFALO

Location: Western New York, at mouth of Niagara River on Lake Erie **County:** Erie **City Area:** 42.6 sq. miles (110.3 sq. kilometers) **Altitude:** 585 feet (177.8 meters)
Mayor: James D. Griffin
City Population: 462,768 (1970 census), 400,234 (1976 est.)
Metro Area Population: 1,349,211 (1970 census), 1,313,000 (1977 est.)
Daily Newspapers: 2 **No. of Radio Stations:** 19 (1980) **No. of TV Stations:** 5 (1980)
City Chamber of Commerce: Buffalo Area Chamber of Commerce, 107 Delaware Ave., Buffalo, New York 14202

Buffalo, seat of Erie County and second largest city in New York State, was named after a local creek, which in turn derived its name from that of an Indian who once lived in the area.

A village was laid out on the site of the present city by Joseph Ellicott for the Holland Land Company in 1803. Almost completely destroyed by fire during the War of 1812, Buffalo grew slowly until the opening of the Erie Canal in 1825 after which it mushroomed. Buffalo was chartered as a city in 1832, became an important transportation center, a major Great Lakes port, and since the opening of the St. Lawrence Seaway, a world port.

The city has had a long association with the Presidency. Millard Fillmore, Buffalo resident, was elected Vice-President in 1848 and two years later became President after the death of Zachary Taylor. Grover Cleveland, mayor of Buffalo in 1881, was elected President in 1884 and 1892. During the 1901 Pan-American Exposition, President McKinley was assassinated in Buffalo.

Industry in the Buffalo area has flourished, largely because of hydroelectric power from Niagara Falls augmented by the Niagara Power Project, one of the largest hydroelectric power projects in the world. Buffalo is the largest grain-milling center in the world. Bethlehem Steel and General Motors are the two largest industrial employers in the area, while the State University at Buffalo is the single largest employer.

Downtown Buffalo has undergone a tremendous facelift in the past ten years. In Oct. 1978, the Buffalo Convention Center was completed, strengthening the Niagara Frontier as a prime locale for conventions. The rapid transit rail system is underway and will be completed by 1984.

Of interest in the area are nearby Niagara Falls; the Buffalo Museum of Science, Historical Museum, and Zoological Gardens; the Albright-Knox Art Gallery; Roswell Park and Children's Hospitals; the Eye Bank; and Niagara Square.

Buffalo's professional sports teams include the Bills (NFL), Sabres (NHL), Bisons (Eastern-League baseball), Stallions (indoor soccer) and Bisons (women's softball).

CHARLESTON

Location: In southeastern part of South Carolina, along coast, on peninsula between Ashley and Cooper Rivers **County:** Charleston **City Area:** 20.6 sq. miles (53.5 sq. kilometers) **Altitude:** sea level **Mayor:** Joseph P. Riley, Jr.
City Population: 66,945 (1970 census), 60,772 (1976 est.) **Metro Area Population:** 336,125 (1970 census), 385,400 (1977 est.)
Daily Newspapers: 2 **No. of Radio Stations:** 10 (1980) **No. of TV Stations:** 3 (1980)
City Chamber of Commerce: Charleston Trident Chamber of Commerce, P.O. Box 975, Charleston, South Carolina 29401

Charleston is a major Atlantic seaport and, as one of America's oldest cities, a leading tourist center. It was originally called Charles Towne in honor of Charles II by the English settlers who first landed in 1670 at Albemarle Point, about 7 miles from modern Charleston. Ten years later they moved to Oyster Point, where the city had been laid out according to the Grande Modell sent from England by the Lords Proprietor. It was incorporated in 1783 as Charleston and became the economic and social center of the region.

By the time of the Revolution, Charleston was the most important city south of Philadelphia. It was a wealthy cultural center to which French Huguenots and other non-English immigrants gave a cosmopolitan touch.

Charleston's role in the Civil War began when the South Carolina ordinance of secession was passed there in December 1860. The city's harbor was also the site of the first hostile act of the war: the firing on Fort Sumter on April 12, 1861. Although under continuous siege from 1863 to 1865, Charleston did not fall to Union forces until February 1865.

Despite the ravages of two wars, disastrous fires, a violent earthquake in 1886, and periodic hurricanes, Charleston has retained many historic buildings and colonial mansions. Of interest are: Fort Sumter, a national monument since 1948; Patriot's Point, a naval museum; the Dock Street Theater, opened in 1735; the original Catfish Row, made famous in Gershwin's *Porgy and Bess*; the Charleston Museum, founded in 1773; the Huguenot Church built in 1680 and rebuilt in 1844, and numerous ante-bellum homes in the peninsula city. Nearby are notable plantation homes and three world famous gardens: Cypress, Magnolia and Middleton. Charles Towne Landing (a park, pavilion, and natural zoo), was established at the time of the city's tricentennial anniversary in 1970.

The city's growing economy is linked to port and transportation expansion and commerce; diversified business, industrial, and education centers; and military installations and facilities maintained by the Army, Navy, Air Force, and the Coast Guard. New construction projects, such as the proposed Charleston Convention Center and a $13-million hotel, will bring in more tourists and more tax revenue, revitalizing the downtown area. However, controversy over the location of the convention center site, on land surrounded by areas under restoration, has held up construction.

Spoleto Festival USA, "the world's most comprehensive art festival," has become an annual event, featuring music, drama, ballet, films, opera, dance and visual arts.

CHICAGO

Location: Northeastern corner of Illinois on shore of Lake Michigan **County:** Cook **City Area:** 228.1 sq. miles (590.8 sq. kilometers) **Altitude:** 578.5 feet (175.8 meters)
Mayor: Jane Byrne
City Population: 3,369,357 (1970 census), 3,074,084 (1976 est.)
Metro Area Population: 6,977,611 (1970 census), 7,017,400 (1977 est.)
Daily Newspapers: 2 **No. of Radio Stations:** 26 (1980) **No. of TV Stations:** 9 (1980)
City Chamber of Commerce: Chicago Association of Commerce and Industry, 130 S. Michigan Ave., Chicago, Illinois 60603

Chicago, seat of Cook County, Illinois, is the largest city between the Eastern seaboard and the Pacific Coast, the most important Great Lakes port, and the world's largest railroad terminal. Its O'Hare International Airport is considered the world's busiest.

Father Marquette and Louis Jolliet visited the site of Chicago in 1673, but more than a century elapsed before a trading post was established, by Jean Baptiste Point du Sable. He was succeeded in 1804 by the first permanant non-Indian settler, John Kinzie, who is usually regarded as the "father of Chicago."

The Erie Canal, which was opened in 1825, stimulated growth and helped convert Chicago into a prosperous commercial town. Incorporated as a city in 1837, it developed into a major rail hub and the nation's mid-continent shipping center soon after the arrival of the railroads in the 1840s. By the time of the Civil War, meatpacking had become a leading industry.

In 1871 the city was almost completely destroyed by a great fire. It was quickly rebuilt, and its booming industry attracted immigrants from all over the world. In the 1890s Chicago replaced Philadelphia as the nation's second largest city, a position it held until 1980. Labor problems led to violent eruptions, such as the Haymarket Riot of 1886 and Pullman strikes in 1894.

Chicago is a leading producer of steel, telephone equipment, appliances, electrical machinery, plastic products, and diesel engines. It boasts a Federal Reserve district bank, the Midwest Stock Exchange, the Chicago Mercantile Exchange, and the Chicago Board of Trade—the world's largest commodity futures market.

The skyscraper was Chicago's contribution to American architecture. The first skyscraper, designed by William Le Baron Jenney, was built here in 1883, and of the world's ten tallest buildings, four are in Chicago. Two of the nation's greatest architects, Louis H. Sullivan and Frank Lloyd Wright, worked in Chicago.

Landmarks of interest in the Chicago area include the Sears Tower, the world's tallest skyscraper; the Chicago Mercantile Exchange, a major international commodity and monetary market; the Merchandise Mart, the largest commercial building in the world; the Art Institute; the Museum of Science and Industry; the Shedd Aquarium; the Adler Planetarium; the Oriental Institute Museum of the University of Chicago; the Lincoln Park and Brookfield Zoos; and the Water Tower, one of the few structures to survive the 1871 fire. In 1974 the Chagall mosaic was unveiled at the First National Bank Plaza; it consists of a colorful wall of glass and stone from all over the world.

Chicago's first female mayor was elected by a landslide margin of 82% on April 3, 1979, after previously defeating incumbent Michael A. Bilandic in the Democratic primary of Feb. 27. Bilandic's defeat was an upset for the old-line Daley political machine.

Chicago's school system was closed down for two weeks by a teachers' strike which began on Jan. 28, 1980. The dispute between the teachers' union and the school board over layoffs and delinquent paychecks was settled by Feb. 11.

CINCINNATI

Location: Southwestern Ohio, on Ohio River **County:** Hamilton
City Area: 78 sq. miles (202 sq. kilometers) **Altitude:** 550 feet (167.1 meters)
Mayor: J. Kenneth Blackwell **City Manager:** Sylvester Murray
City Population: 453,514 (1970 census), 410,441 (1976 est.)
Metro Area Population: 1,387,207 (1970 census), 1,375,400 (1977 est.)
Daily Newspapers: 2 **No. of Radio Stations:** 19 (1980) **No. of TV Stations:** 5 (1980)
City Chamber of Commerce: Greater Cincinnati Chamber of Commerce, 120 West Fifth Street, Cincinnati, Ohio 45202

Cincinnati, seat of Ohio's Hamilton County, is an industrial, commercial, and cultural center. The first settlers arrived in 1788 and named it Losantiville. In 1790 General Arthur St. Clair, first governor of the Northwest Territory, renamed it Cincinnati for the Society of the Cincinnati, which was formed by Continental Army officers at the end of the American Revolution. Cincinnati was the first seat of the legislature of the Northwest Territory; it was incorporated in 1802 and chartered as a city in 1819.

Completion of the Miami Canal (1827) and the Ohio and Erie Canal in the 1830s increased the growth of Cincinnati and its importance as a shipping center. The city was also a major station on the Underground Railroad.

Cincinnati suffered disastrous floods in 1884 and 1937. The Cincinnati riot (March 28-31, 1884) was the result of a crime wave and corrupt politics. Later the notorious political boss G. B. Cox took control, but a reform movement in the 1920s led to the establishment (1924) of the city-manager type of government.

Located on the Ohio River, Cincinnati is a major manufacturing center and a leading producer of machine tools, soap products, and playing cards. Cosmetics, radar equipment, automobiles, jet engines, and metal goods also are important to the economy. In 1976 the Environmental Protection Agency Laboratory opened here.

Recent additions to the refurbished downtown area are the new Cincinnati Plaza Hotel and the First National Bank Center. The architecturally renowned Union Terminal has been given a new lease on life as an urban shopping mall.

Riverfront Stadium, built in 1970, houses the Cincinnati Bengals Football Team and the Cincinnati Reds Baseball Team.

In December 1979, 11 rock fans were trampled to death at the Riverfront Coliseum in a frenzied scramble for limited unreserved seats at a concert by the British rock group "The Who."

CLEVELAND

Location: Northeastern Ohio, on Lake Erie at mouth of the Cuyahoga River **County:** Cuyahoga **City Area:** 76 sq. miles (196.8 sq. kilometers) **Altitude:** 680 feet (206.6 meters)
Mayor: George V. Voinovich
City Population: 750,879 (1970 census), 625,643 (1976 est.)
Metro Area Population: 2,063,729 (1970 census), 1,949,600 (1977 est.)
Daily Newspapers: 2 **No. of Radio Stations:** 9 (1980) **No. of TV Stations:** 5 (1980)
City Chamber of Commerce: Greater Cleveland Growth Association, 690 Union Commerce Building, Cleveland, Ohio 44115

Cleveland, seat of Cuyahoga County and largest city in Ohio, is a port of entry on Lake Erie. It was laid out in 1796 by General Moses Cleaveland, an ancestor of President Grover Cleveland. Three years later a permanent settlement was established by Lorenzo Carter, and in 1836 Cleveland was chartered as a city.

After the completion of the Ohio and Erie Canal in the 1830s and the arrival of the railroad in 1851, Cleveland became a significant link between the interior of Ohio and eastern markets. Coal from Pennsylvania and iron ore shipped from Minnesota by way of the Great Lakes made the city an important iron and steel producer. It also developed into the main refining area for Pennsylvania oil, and in 1870 John D. Rockefeller began his oil dynasty in Cleveland. Immigrants from all over the world settled in the city to work in the industries. Many of their descendants still live in pleasant suburbs.

Besides iron and steel production, mainstays of the economy today are the manufacture of electrical equipment, machine tools, automobile parts, and chemicals.

Cleveland has experienced a decline common to many large cities, its own accelerated by riots in the 1960s. However, cooperative efforts have produced an almost new downtown skyline, with new commercial and federal and local government buildings. The old flats area along the river has been restored, providing evening entertainment in the many restaurants and pubs.

The Cuyahoga River, Lake Erie, and the air itself have had a notorious reputation for pollution, but extensive efforts to clean up the environment have met with some success.

Of special interest is the Emerald Necklace—a system of parks, trails, and bridle paths looping the city—along with the downtown Convention Center and Municipal Stadium. The East Side's University Circle area is a cultural center housing the Art Museum, Museum of Natural History, Western Reserve Historical Society Museum and Severance Hall, home of the world-reknowned Cleveland Orchestra.

In December 1978, the city failed to pay $14 million worth of promissory notes that had fallen due and thus became the first major U.S. city to default since the Great Depression. To generate additional revenue, voters approved a 50% increase in city income taxes in February 1979. The increase, plus a 20% lay-off of municipal employees, enabled the city to retire $3.5 million of debt by September 1979. Renegotiation of the notes is expected to save Cleveland from bankruptcy. The city suffered a 15-week school closing from mid-October 1979 to January 8, 1980 because of a teachers' strike.

COLUMBUS

Location: Central Ohio, on Scioto River **County:** Franklin **City Area:** 180.9 sq. miles (468.5 sq. kilometers) **Altitude:** 780 feet (237.0 meters)
Mayor: Tom Moody
City Population: 540,025 (1970 census), 533,075 (1976 est.)
Metro Area Population: 1,017,847 (1970 census), 1,086,800 (1977 est.)
Daily Newspapers: 2 **No. of Radio Stations:** 7 (1980) **No. of TV Stations:** 4 (1980)
City Chamber of Commerce: Columbus Area Chamber of Commerce, 50 West Broad Street, P.O. Box 1527, Columbus, Ohio 43216

Columbus, capital of Ohio and seat of Franklin County, is the state's largest city in area. It was laid out to be the capital in 1812, a position it assumed four years later, and chartered as a city in 1834. A feeder canal (1831) to the Ohio and Erie Canal, along with the National Road (1833), spurred development. By the middle of the 19th century the railroad had arrived, making Columbus a commercial and transportation center.

During the Civil War Columbus was an assembly point for recruits and the site of a Union arsenal. A cemetery at Camp Chase, a Civil War prison, contains the graves of 2,260 Confederate soldiers. By the end of the century the city was a leader in the manufacture of buggies, producing about 20,000 a year. In 1913 the Scioto River flooded, causing the death of more than 100 people.

Today about 20 percent of the working population is employed by the federal, state, or municipal government. Industry is also a large employer; among the city's products are coal-mining machinery, concrete mixers, auto parts, paints, shoes, glassware, and refrigerators. Columbus is the headquarters of the Battelle Memorial Institute, an organization engaged in scientific, technological, and economic research.

Several downtown construction projects have generated excitement and confidence about Columbus as a place to work, to shop, and to live. Completion of the Ohio Center (convention center) and the Capitol South recreation center insure continued growth of the downtown area.

The Columbus *Dispatch* announced plans to offer subscribers with home computers the opportunity to receive the newspaper electronically on their home screens. Effective July 1980, the service is the first to be offered by a daily newspaper in the U.S.

DALLAS

Location: Northeastern Texas on Trinity River, about 75 miles south of Oklahoma border **County:** Dallas **City Area:** 350 sq. miles (906.5 sq. kilometers) **Altitude:** 481 feet (146.2 meters)
Mayor: Robert Folsom **City Manager:** George Schrader
City Population: 844,303 (1970 census) 848,829 (1976 est.)
Metro Area Population: 2,378,353 (1970 census) 2,673,300 (1977 est.)
Daily Newspapers: 3 **No. of Radio Stations:** 43 (1980) **No. of TV Stations:** 6 (1980)
City Chamber of Commerce: Dallas Chamber of Commerce, 1507 Pacific Avenue; Dallas, Texas 75201

Dallas, seat of Dallas County and second largest city in Texas, is the financial and commercial center of the Southwest.

John Neely Bryan settled here in 1841 and later founded Dallas, probably naming it after George M. Dallas, then Vice President under James K. Polk.

In 1858 followers of the French social philosopher Charles Fourier abandoned their nearby socialist community, La Réunion, and moved to Dallas. Two years later a fire destroyed most of the town, but residents quickly rebuilt it. During the Civil War the Confederate Army had quartermaster, commissary, and administrative headquarters here.

Oil was discovered in eastern Texas in the 1930s, increasing the growth of Dallas, which was the site of the Texas Centennial Exposition in 1936. During and after World War II, population boomed following introduction of first the aircraft and then the electronics industries. Today the city's economy is highly diversified, with a strong manufacturing base and many corporate headquarters of the electronics, oil, gas, finance and insurance industries.

President Kennedy was assassinated in Dallas in 1963.

Dallas is the home of the annual Texas state fair, the Cotton Bowl football stadium, the NFL Dallas Cowboys, and shares with Fort Worth the American Baseball League's Texas Rangers. Dallas hosts annually final matches of the $100,000 World Championship of Tennis, the Byron Nelson Golf Classic, the U.S. Karate National Championships, and the Avon Futures Tennis Finals.

Another advantage which Dallas has created for itself is its role as a tourist/convention center. Its role as a merchandise distribution center helped make it a major buyers' market. Dallas/Fort Worth Airport is one of the world's largest airports.

Dallas is also the cultural center of Texas. Each year the city is host to the Metropolitan Opera and has its own Civic Opera and Symphony as well. There are other community enterprises in the cultural field including the Summer Musicals, the Civic Ballet, the Civic Chorus, the Dallas Theatre Center, and the Bob Hope Theatre.

DENVER

Location: North-central Colorado, on South Platte River **County:** Denver; city and county are coextensive **City Area:** 117 sq. miles (303 sq. kilometers) **Altitude:** 5,280 feet (1604.5 meters)
Mayor: William H. McNichols, Jr.
City Population: 514,678 (1970 census) 476,200 (1977 est.)
Metro Area Population: 1,239,477 (1970 census) 1,464,300 (1977 est.)
Daily Newspapers: 2 **No. of Radio Stations:** 17 (1980) **No. of TV Stations:** 6 (1980)
City Chamber of Commerce: Denver Chamber of Commerce, 1301 Welton, Denver, Colorado 80204

Denver, capital and largest city of Colorado, is a major commercial and financial center. It was settled in 1858 after the discovery of placer gold at the junction of the South Platte River and Cherry Creek, and named for James W. Denver, governor of the Kansas Territory, which then included eastern Colorado.

Denver was incorporated in 1861 and became the capital of the Colorado Territory six years later. During the 1870s and 1880s rich lodes of silver, gold, and copper were found in the Rockies, bringing fortune seekers to the area. The city boasted plush opera houses with singers imported from the East, makeshift boarding houses, and noisy saloons, such as the famous Silver Dollar.

By the end of the 19th century, Denver was beginning to develop into a large processing, shipping, and distributing point for an extensive agricultural area, making mining and metalworking less important. A federal mint has been in operation for more than a century. Today the aerospace industry makes a significant contribution to Denver's economy, and food processing is also a major occupation. In addition, the city is the regional center for many federal agencies. The Atomic Energy Commission's Rocky Flats plant is nearby, and the federal Solar Energy Research Institute opened in 1978. In nearby Golden, Colo. Denver is fast becoming a national energy capital, rivalling Houston in importance. The city is the center for the development of the West's energy resources—oil, gas, coal, shale oil, uranium, synthetic fuels and solar energy. As a result, new office construction is booming in Denver.

Military establishments in the area include Lowry Air Force Base; the Air Force Accounting and Finance Center; the army's Rocky Mountain Arsenal, where the army stores nerve-gas weapons; and Fitzsimmons General Hospital. The Air Force Academy is in Colorado Springs, less than 100 miles south of Denver.

In March of 1979, the Environmental Protection Agency began searching within the Denver city limits for radioactive dump sites, used by local radium refineries over 50 to 60 years ago. EPA officials confirmed 15 sites of excessive radiation emission.

Denver, which maintains the largest system of public parks and recreational facilities in the world, is a tourist mecca. Of interest are the Colorado State Historical Museum, the tomb of Buffalo Bill, the Cody Museum, and the $6.1-million Denver Art Museum, a block-square, fortresslike structure set against a distant backdrop of Rocky Mountains, and the Denver Botanic Gardens.

DETROIT

Location: Southeastern Michigan, on Detroit River, between Lakes St. Clair and Erie, 18 miles north of Lake Erie **County:** Wayne **City Area:** 139.6 sq. miles (361.6 sq. kilometers) **Altitude:** 581 feet (176.6 meters)
Mayor: Coleman A. Young
City Population: 1,514,063 (1970 census), 1,314,206 (1976 est.)
Metro Area Population: 4,435,051 (1970 census), 4,370,200 (1977 est.)
Daily Newspapers: 2 **No. of Radio Stations:** 7 (1980) **No. of TV Stations:** 9 (1980)
City Chamber of Commerce: Greater Detroit Chamber of Commerce, 150 Michigan Ave., Detroit, Michigan 48226

Detroit, seat of Wayne County, is the largest city in Michigan and one of the largest in the United States. Antoine de la Mothe Cadillac established a French fort (Pontchartrain) and settlement on the site in 1701.

The settlement took the name Detroit from the French word for "strait," because it was on the water link between Lake Erie and Lake St. Clair. Detroit was ceded to the British in 1763, turned over to the United States in 1796, destroyed by fire in 1805, rebuilt, and occupied by the British for a year during the War of 1812. It became an important commercial center after the opening of the Erie Canal in 1825.

From 1837, when Michigan became a state, until 1847, Detroit was the capital. It was connected by rail to Chicago in 1852 and to New York two years later. The city was a key terminus of the Underground Railroad.

Detroit assumed great importance after the middle of the 19th century because of its shipping, shipbuilding, and manufacturing.

Today, Greater Detroit serves as international headquarters for General Motors, American Motors, Ford and Chrysler. But with the auto industry in a severe slump, the unemployment rate in the "Motor City" soared to nearly twice the national average during the recession of 1980. The Detroit-Pontiac-Flint corridor produces some 25 percent of all the cars and trucks built in the United States. Detroit is linked to Windsor, Ont., by a bridge over and a tunnel under the Detroit River.

The city also is international headquarters for the United Automobile, Aerospace and Agricultural Implement Workers of America (UAW), which has been embroiled in many labor disputes.

Detroit has had two major racial riots. One in 1943 and the other in 1967.

Renaissance Center, a $350-million complex along Detroit's downtown riverfront, the new Joe Louis Arena, and the Senator Philip A. Hart Plaza are three of the new construction projects completed or underway. The Horace E. Dodge & Son Memorial Fountain, designed by Isamu Noguchi, has become the center of community activity and the permanent home of Detroit's famous international ethnic festivals. The city was host to the 1980 Republican convention.

The Detroit Symphony Orchestra, Detroit Institute of Arts, and the Detroit Zoo are rated among the nation's best. Henry Ford Museum and Greenfield Village, which contains Thomas A. Edison's original laboratories and many early American landmarks, attract more than 1.6 million visitors annually to suburban Dearborn. Belle Isle, a 1,000-acre park in the Detroit River, is a major recreation center, with gardens, a conservatory, children's zoo and aquarium among attractions.

FORT WORTH

Location: Northern Texas, at the junction of the Clear and West forks of the Trinity River about 30 miles west of Dallas **Counties:** Tarrant, Hood, Wise, Parker and Johnson **City Area:** 244 sq. miles (632 sq. kilometers) **Altitude:** 670 feet (203.6 meters)
Mayor: Woodie Woods **City Manager:** Robert Herchert
City Population: 393,455 (1970 census), 367,909 (1976 est.)
Metro Area Population: 2,378,353 (1970 census), 2,673,300 (1977 est.)
Daily Newspapers: 3 **No. of Radio Stations:** 22 (1980) **No. of TV Stations:** 6 (1980)
City Chamber of Commerce: Fort Worth Area Chamber of Commerce, 700 Throckmorton, Fort Worth, Texas 76102

Fort Worth, often considered in conjunction with nearby Dallas, is the seat of Tarrant County and a prime cog in the massive North Texas industrial complex, serving as a transportation center, oil-pipeline hub and a major grain and livestock market. It is one of the nation's largest producers of aircraft, an outgrowth of World War II, when aircraft assembly first flourished there.

Settlement of the area began in 1843. Four years later Camp Worth (later Fort Worth) was established by Major Ripley A. Arnold as a frontier outpost to protect settlers against Comanche Indian raids; it was named in honor of Major General William J. Worth, then commander of U.S. troops in Texas, and proved of great use to the Army during the Mexican War.

After the Army departed (1853), the town suffered a brief decline, but soon began to boom. Cowboys driving Longhorn cattle up the Chisholm Trail to the railheads of Kansas would bed their herds outside of Fort Worth and go into town for supplies and relaxation. This brought a heavy influx of merchants and contributed much to the city's growth, which was further spurred by the coming of the railroad in 1876, three years after the city's incorporation. Meat-packing and the milling and shipping of grain were the mainstays of the fledgling town's economy. With the 20th century, came widespread industrialization and a continuing trend toward greater diversification. Besides those mentioned, other of the city's chief industries include brewing, electronics, food processing, and the manufacture of automobiles, containers, furniture, leather goods and machinery.

Despite the bustle of its industry, Fort Worth today retains a distinctive, easy-going Western flavor. It is known all over the world as "Cowtown" or "Where the West Begins," and is committed to retaining its Western heritage. Fort Worth has become increasingly involved in the arts, rivaling Dallas as the state's cultural leader. Its attractions include Casa Mañana, a theater-in-the-round that presents Broadway productions; a renowned museum complex including the Fort Worth Art Museum, the Kimbell Art Museum, the Amon Carter Museum of Western Art, and the Fort Worth Museum of Science and History; the Fort Worth Opera and Symphony; and Trinity Park. In addition, the area boasts the Fort Worth Water Garden Park, the Will Rogers Memorial Complex, and the Tarrant County Convention Center. Fort Worth is host to the Van Cliburn Piano Competition and the Colonial Invitational Golf Tournament and is the home of Six Flags Over Texas. Popular annual events include the Southwestern Exposition, Fat Stock Show and Rodeo.

HONOLULU

Location: In Hawaii, in Pacific Ocean, 2,397 miles southwest of San Francisco **County:** Honolulu **City Area:** 608 sq. miles 574.7 sq. kilometers) **Altitude:** 21 feet (6.4 meters)
Mayor: Frank F. Fasi **Managing Director:** Edward Y. Hirata
City Population: 324,871 (1970 census), 723,400 (1977 est.)
Metro Area Population: 630,528 (1970 census), 723,400 (1977 est.)
Daily Newspapers: 2 **No. of Radio Stations:** 25 (1980) **No. of TV Stations:** 5 (1980)
City Chamber of Commerce: The Chamber of Commerce of Hawaii, Dillingham Building, 735 Bishop Street, Honolulu, Hawaii 96813

Honolulu, capital and principal city of Hawaii, is on the island of Oahu at the crossroads of the Pacific. (The name "Honolulu" is Hawaiian for "sheltered harbor.") Although Honolulu city and county are usually thought of as consisting of Oahu only, Honolulu is technically the largest city in the nation, with boundaries extending officially 1,381 miles northwest to Kure Island. (Oklahoma City, with 621 square miles of contiguous territory, thus ranks second in extent but first in landmass.)

Honolulu became the seat of the Kamehameha dynasty, which had succeeded in unifying the Hawaiian Islands in 1810, and in 1845 it was named the permanent capital of the Kingdom of Hawaii. During the 19th century, American and European whalers and sandalwood traders came to Honolulu, and it was occupied successively by Russian, British, and French forces. It developed into an important commercial city after U.S. annexation of Hawaii in 1898.

In the early 20th century, the U.S. Navy established its famous base at Pearl Harbor, now the headquarters of the U.S. Pacific Fleet. Honolulu was bombed during Japan's surprise attack on Pearl Harbor on Dec. 7, 1941, and during World War II became a major staging area for U.S. forces in the Pacific.

The postwar years saw a tourist boom coupled with a diversification of industry. The military, with all branches represented in Hawaii, continued as a mainstay of the economy, but tourism surpassed it as the leading industry. In 1979 alone, 3.9 million visitors came to the islands. However, high air fares and the economic recession on the mainland caused the number of tourists to decline in 1980.

Numerous new high-rise office buildings have changed the skyline and helped revitalize downtown Honolulu. Harbor facilities have been expanded and the Honolulu International Airport has been enlarged.

Structures of interest in the city are Iolani Palace, former home of Hawaii's monarchs and the only royal palace in the U.S.; the state capitol; the Bishop Museum (of Polynesian Ethnology and Natural History); Washington Place, former private home of Queen Lilioukalani; and the Neal Blaisdell Center, a 22-acre complex of public buildings.

HOUSTON

Location: Southeastern Texas, on Houston Ship Channel, 50 miles from Gulf of Mexico **Counties:** Brazoria, Harris, Fort Bend, Liberty, Montgomery and Waller. **City Area:** 556.3 sq. miles (1440.8 sq. kilometers) **Altitude:** 49 feet (15 meters)
Mayor: Jim McConn
City Population: 1,253,479 (1970 census), 1,737,000 (1979 est.)
Metro Area Population: 1,999,316 (1970 census), 2,884,000 (1979 est.)
Daily Newspapers: 2 **No. of Radio Stations:** 31 (1980) **No. of TV Stations:** 6 (1980)
City Chamber of Commerce: Houston Chamber of Commerce, 1100 Milam, 25th Floor, Houston, Texas 77002

Houston, seat of Harris County, is the leading industrial metropolis not only of Texas but also of the surrounding region. It is the largest city in the Southwest and South, the fifth largest in the nation (1979), and the country's third-largest seaport.

Founded in 1836 by J. K. and A. C. Allen, the city was named for General Sam Houston, hero of the Battle of San Jacinto (1836), by which Texas gained independence from Mexico. The city served as capital of the Republic of Texas from 1837 until 1840.

The discovery of oil in Southeast Texas at Spindletop in 1901 and the opening of the man-made Houston Ship Channel in 1914 stimulated the rapid development of the Houston area.

Strategically situated in an area rich in oil, gas, sulfur, salt, lime, timber, industrial soil, seawater and freshwater, the Houston metropolitan area ranks first in the nation in petroleum refining, petrochemical manufacturing, manufacturing and distribution of petroleum equipment and pipeline transmission of oil and gas.

Houston, which became the U.S. center of manned spacecraft activities in the early 1960s, has experienced increasing economic diversification over the past two decades. The city emerged as a corporate center in the 1960s, and since 1970 over 200 major companies have moved their headquarters, subsidiaries or divisions to Houston, capitalizing on the growing nucleus of energy, space and medical technology available in the area.

The Texas Medical Center is a $694-million complex of 24 institutions and organizations on 235 acres in central Houston. More than 80 research firms maintain research-facilities in Houston. The number of life, earth, and physical scientists in metropolitan Houston has risen to 11,100, up 92 percent since 1970, while technical engineers have increased 63 percent in the same period, to stand at 29,400.

In addition, the city is growing in prominence in international business. More than 40 foreign banks maintain representative offices in Houston, and 51 nations maintain consular offices there. Houston Intercontinental Airport provides direct service to Europe, the Middle East, South and Central America, the Caribbean, Mexico and Canada.

Bordering the City of Houston on the southeast is the Lyndon B. Johnson Space Center, a $202-million complex for astronaut training, equipment testing, and flight control for the Skylab and Space Shuttle programs.

Houston's Nina Vance Alley Theatre is nationally known, performing repertory works as well as new plays. Elegant Jones Hall for the Performing Arts features the Houston Symphony Society, the Houston Ballet, and the Houston Grand Opera; all tour nationally. The Astrodome, a huge, enclosed and air-conditioned arena, has convertible seating arrangements which allow the presentation of widely varied sports events. The Summit, another sports and entertainment arena, is located in Houston's Greenway Plaza.

Houston is home of the Houston Astros of the National Baseball League, the Houston Oilers of the American Conference of the National Football League, the Houston Rockets of the National Basketball Association, and the Houston Hurricanes of the North American Soccer League.

Prominent tourist attractions in the area include the Harris County Domed Stadium and Astrohall; Astroworld, a 65-acre family amusement park; the Museum of Fine Arts and several other museums; Johnson Space Center; and San Jacinto Battleground, plus the battleship *Texas*, a veteran of two World Wars.

INDIANAPOLIS

Location: In central Indiana, on White River **County:** Marion **City Area:** 379.4 sq. miles (982.6 sq. kilometers) **Altitude:** 710 feet (215.8 meters)
Mayor: William H. Hudnut, III
City Population: 729,768 (1970 census), 708,867 (1976 est.)
Metro Area Population: 1,111,352 (1970 census), 1,143,800 (1977 est.)
Daily Newspapers: 2 **No. of Commercial Radio Stations (AM):** 8 (1980) **No. of TV Stations:** 5 (1980)
City Chamber of Commerce: Indianapolis Chamber of Commerce, 320 North Meridian Street, Indianapolis, Indiana 46204

Indianapolis, seat of Marion County and capital of Indiana, is the largest city in the state. Its name combines "Indiana" with "polis," the Greek term for "city." It was settled in 1820.

Indianapolis grew slowly until the arrival of the first railroad in 1847. Toward the end of the 19th century the discovery of nearby natural gas, plus the beginning of the automobile industry, helped the city's expansion. On Jan.

1, 1970, the City of Indianapolis merged with surrounding Marion County in the nation's first major city-county consolidation to occur without a popular referendum since modern New York City was formed in 1898. Some autonomy was retained by local units, including eleven school corporations.

Leading products are processed foods, electronics equipment, heavy machinery, and pharmaceuticals. Indianapolis is also an insurance center, with offices of more than 70 firms.

Indianapolis might be called the educational hub of Indiana. It includes the Indiana University Medical School and Center, Butler University, Indiana Central University, Indiana University/Purdue University at Indianapolis (IUPUI), and Marian College.

Urban renewal has made enormous changes in the city's skyline in the last ten years. Indianapolis has kept its famous Soldiers' and Sailors' Monument on Monument Circle, but the city is now dominated by such structures as the Indiana National Bank Tower, Indiana Bell Telephone Building, the Market Square Arena, a new Hyatt Hotel, the new Federal Building, and the Indiana Convention and Exposition Center.

Three of Indianapolis' newest points of interest are: the Museum of Art, the Indiana State Museum, and the Children's Museum, the largest of its kind in the nation. Indianapolis is national headquarters for the American Legion and the home of the Army Finance Center at Fort Harrison. Tourist attractions include the homes of President Benjamin Harrison, James Whitcomb Riley and Booth Tarkington. Eagle Creek Park is the country's largest municipal park.

The city has professional baseball and basketball teams and is the home of the Indianapolis 500 motor speedway track. Indianapolis is also the home of the Amateur Athletic Union and the U.S. Automobile Club.

KANSAS CITY

Location: Western Missouri, on Kansas-Missouri border, on Kansas and Missouri rivers **Counties:** Jackson, Clay, Platte **City Area:** 316 sq. miles (818 sq. kilometers) **Altitude:** 750 feet (227.9 meters)
Mayor: Richard L. Berkley **City Manager:** Robert A. Kipp
City Population: 507,330 (1970 census), 458,251 (1976 est.) **Metro Area Population:** 1,273,926 (1970 census), 1,293,300 (1977 est.)
Daily Newspapers: 2 **No. of Commercial Radio Stations (AM):** 14 (1979) **No. of TV Stations:** 5 (1980)
City Chamber of Commerce: Chamber of Commerce of Greater Kansas City, 600 Ten Main Center, 920 Main Street, Kansas City, Missouri 64105

Kansas City, Missouri's second largest metropolis, is an important industrial, commercial, and banking center. It is separated from Kansas City, Kansas, by the state line, but both are served by the same railroad terminals and transit and telephone systems.

The area was explored by the French early in the 18th century and toward the end of the century by Daniel Morgan Boone (son of the famous frontiersman), who was probably the first American to set foot in the vicinity. François Chouteau established a trading post in 1826, and a settlement later developed known as Westport Landing. The city was incorporated in 1850 as the Town of Kansas, it became the City of Kansas in 1853, and under a new charter (1889) was named Kansas City. Its name reflects its location on the Kansas (Kaw) River, which in turn honors an Indian tribe.

Kansas City grew into an important trade and transportation hub for pioneers migrating westward over the Oregon and Santa Fe Trails; it was an early center of the nation's cattle business. In 1865 the railroad arrived, and four years later Hannibal Bridge, the first structure to span the Missouri River, was opened.

Today Kansas City is a major market for winter wheat and cattle. Its stockyards are among the nation's busiest. It leads the nation in the manufacture of vending machines, is the country's second largest assembly center for cars and trucks, and is an important warehousing center.

On March 27, 1980, a six-day strike by 900 Kansas City firefighters ended. Following the settlement, Gov. Joseph Teasdale of Missouri agreed to pardon 71 strikers who had been jailed for violating a county court's no-strike order.

LOS ANGELES

Location: Southwestern California, between Santa Monica and San Pedro bays, near the Pacific coast **County:** Los Angeles **City Area:** 464 sq. miles (1201.8 sq. kilometers) **Altitude:** 275 feet (83.6 meters)
Mayor: Thomas Bradley
City Population: 2,811,801 (1970 census), 2,743,994 (1976 est.)
Metro Area Population: 7,041,980 (1970 census), 7,031,000 (1977 est.)
Daily Newspapers: 2 **No. of Commercial Radio Stations (AM):** 35 (1979) **No. of TV Stations:** 11 (1980)
City Chamber of Commerce: Los Angeles Chamber of Commerce, 400 South Bixel Street, Los Angeles, California 90017

Los Angeles, seat of California's Los Angeles County, displaced Chicago as the nation's second most populous city according to advance 1980 Census reports.

Gaspar de Portolá led an expedition to the site in 1769, and in 1781 El Pueblo de Nuestra Señora la Reina de los Angeles de Porciuncula (The Town of Our Lady the Queen of the Angels of Porciuncula) was founded. The name was later shortened to Los Angeles.

In 1846 during the Mexican War, U.S. military forces took the town. Four years later, Los Angeles was incorporated as a city; that same year California entered the Union. It was soon linked with the Eastern seaboard as railroads arrived: the Southern Pacific in 1876 and the Santa Fe nine years later. Discovery of oil in the 1890s stimulated commercial growth, and the opening of the Panama Canal in 1914 brought further expansion. The motion-picture industry grew up in the early 20th century and more recent years have seen the establishment of television studios.

The Los Angeles area is rich in agricultural resources and well known for its citrus fruit. It ranks third nationally in manufacturing, finance, and trade, and leads the U.S. in production of aircraft and aircraft parts. In addition, Greater Los Angeles is the nation's sportswear center and the world's second largest garment manufacturer. Other important industries are food processing and the production of machinery, chemicals, and electronics equipment. As a port Los Angeles handles the largest cargo tonnage of deep-sea vessels on the Pacific Coast and is a major fishing complex. In 1979, it was reported that 16 industrial corporations with sales exceeding $1 billion were headquartered in the Los Angeles area.

Los Angeles County has the heaviest per-capita concentration of automobiles in the world, and the city is famous for its vast system of freeways radiating from the center of town to outlying areas. Dozens of independent municipalities are incorporated in the county, some completely surrounded by the city. Shore areas include Santa Monica, Manhattan Beach, Hermosa Beach, Redondo Beach, and Long Beach. The industrial section includes Lynwood, Downey, Norwalk, and Torrance.

Los Angeles is the home of a $33.5 million Music Center, the Los Angeles County Museum of Art and the recently constructed Los Angeles Convention Center.

Of interest to the thousands of tourists who flock to the Los Angeles area are Disneyland, at nearby Anaheim, considered the biggest attraction in the West; Mount Wilson Observatory; Mission San Gabriel Arcángel, dedicated in 1771; Santa Catalina Island; the Hollywood Bowl; Griffith Park with its zoo, golf course, and observatory; and Laguna Beach.

Los Angeles will host the 1984 Summer Olympics. The decision by the city to ratify a contract with the International Olympic Committee came after 15 months of conflict between the two over who would bear financial responsibility. Under a compromise incorporated into the agreement, Los Angeles would have no financial liability. The burden would be shared by the U.S. Olympic Committee and a private group.

The city is celebrating a yearlong bicentennial observance which will culminate on September 4, 1981, the 200th anniversary of its founding. Art shows, ballet and plays will be presented under the slogan "L.A.'s the Place."

LOUISVILLE

Location: Northwest Kentucky, at the falls of the Ohio River **County:** Jefferson **City Area:** 65.2 sq. miles (168.9 sq. kilometers) **Altitude:** 477 feet (144.9 meters)
Mayor: William B. Stansbury

City Population: 361,706 (1970 census) 330,011 (1976 est.) **Metro Area Population:** 867,330 (1970 census), 883,000 (1977 est.)
Daily Newspapers: 2 **No. of Commercial Radio Stations (AM):** 10 (1980) **No. of TV Stations:** 6 (1980)
City Chamber of Commerce: Louisville Area Chamber of Commerce, 300 West Liberty, Louisville, Kentucky 40202

Louisville, seat of Jefferson County, is the largest city in Kentucky and a major Southern industrial center. The city lies over a mammoth glacial deposit called an "aquifer," which is drawn upon for water.

Laid out in 1773 by General George Rogers Clark and settled six years later, it was named Louisville in 1780 by the Virginia legislature in honor of King Louis XVI of France. Two years later at Louisville, General Clark built Fort Nelson, which served as headquarters for his expeditions to the Northwest. It was then widely known as the "Settlement at the Falls."

Louisville was incorporated as a city in 1828 and grew into an important river port after the opening of the Louisville and Portland Canal in 1830. Arrival of the railroad in 1851 enhanced its position as a transportation center. During the Civil War it was a major Union base, despite the divided loyalties of its citizens.

Today the city has the world's largest electrical appliance and neoprene plants. Other important industries are the manufacture of bourbon whiskey, aluminum products, bathroom fixtures, tobacco processing, auto and truck manufacturing, and meat packing. The American Printing House for the Blind, the world's largest publisher of Braille books and magazines and talking books, is located in Louisville. More than $300-million in private and public funds have been committed to the redevelopment of the downtown area. A $135-million Galleria office, shopping and apartment complex will open in 1982, as will the $70-million Riverfront development.

Of historic interest are the grave of George Rogers Clark, in Cave Hill Cemetery, and the site of Fort Nelson. The state's tourist attractions include Churchill Downs, scene of the annual Kentucky Derby; the State Fair Grounds; the Louisville Zoological Garden featuring a children's zoo, and the Filson Club, which houses a Kentucky history museum.

MEMPHIS

Location: Southwestern corner of Tennessee, on Mississippi River **County:** Shelby **City Area:** 290 sq. miles (651.1 sq. kilometers) **Altitude:** 275 feet (83.6 meters)
Mayor: Wyeth Chandler **Chief Administrative Officer:** Henry Evans
City Population: 657,007 (1970 census), 667,880 (1976 est.)
Metro Area Population: 834,103 (1970 census), 886,500 (1977 est.)
Daily Newspapers: 2 **No. of Radio Stations:** 24 (1980) **No. of TV Stations:** 4 (1980)
City Chamber of Commerce: Memphis Area Chamber of Commerce, 555 Beale Street, P.O. Box 224, Memphis, Tennessee 38101

Memphis, seat of Shelby County, is the largest city in Tennessee and a port of entry. It is the commercial center for much of Tennessee, Arkansas, and Mississippi, as well as parts of Missouri and Alabama. It was named after the ancient Egyptian city.

According to tradition, De Soto crossed the Mississippi River in 1540 at the site of this Tennessee city. In 1682 La Salle built Fort Prudhomme overlooking the river, and for almost a century the area was involved in the imperial rivalries of Great Britain, France, and Spain. The United States built Fort Adams in 1797, and in 1819 Memphis was laid out. Thirty years later it was incorporated as a city, having become an important port noted for its gambling casinos and glittering wealth.

The fall of Memphis to Union forces on June 6, 1862, ended the city's early prosperity. After the Civil War, yellow-fever epidemics caused about 25,000 people to flee.

Today Memphis is a major hardwood-lumber center and manufacturer of furniture and flooring. It is also a leading cotton and livestock market and home of the Memphis Cotton Exchange. The city's products include rubber goods, cottonseed oil, textiles, farm machinery, drugs, and livestock feeds. It is headquarters for Plough, Inc., Holiday Inns of America, Inc. and Cook Industries, grain exporters, and the site of Sharp Electronics Corporation, a Japanese microwave and television production plant.

The Tennessee Chute Project has provided Memphis with a dam connecting the mainland to Presidents Island in the Mississippi and has given the city a stillwater harbor with two barge terminals. A 963-acre industrial park is now on the island; across the harbor is the 6,800-acre Frank C. Pidgeon Industrial Park.

Of interest in Memphis is Confederate Park, which contains ramparts used in defense against Union gunboats in 1862, and Beale Street, which was immortalized by jazz composer W.C. Handy. It is the site of Graceland, the mansion and gravesite of Elvis Presley, and two memorials to Rev. Martin Luther King, Jr., who was assassinated in the city in 1968. Memphis is the only four-time winner of the Ernest T. Trigg (Cleanest City in the Nation) Award.

MIAMI

Location: Southeastern Florida, on Biscayne Bay **County:** Dade **City Area:** 34 sq. miles (88.1 sq. kilometers) **Altitude:** 25 feet (7.6 meters)
Mayor: Maurice A. Ferre **City Manager:** Joseph R. Grassie
City Population: 334,859 (1970 census), 352,424 (1976 est.)
Metro Area Population: 1,267,792 (1970 census), 1,441,200 (1977 est.)
Daily Newspapers: 4 **No. of Commercial Radio Stations (AM):** 13 (1980) **No. of TV Stations:** 8 (1980)
City Chamber of Commerce: Greater Miami Chamber of Commerce, 391 N.E. 15 St., Miami, Florida 33132

Miami, seat of Florida's Dade County, is an international banking and trade center, and the focal point of a world-famous resort area. The city was founded in 1870 at the site of Fort Dallas, which the United States had built in the 1830s during the war against the Seminoles. "Miami" is an Indian word meaning "big water."

In 1896 the financier Henry M. Flagler extended the Florida East Coast Railroad to Miami, built the Royal Palm Hotel, and dredged the city's harbor. The city was incorporated the same year. By 1910 it was booming.

During the 1920s the Miami region was the scene of wild land speculation in which many fortunes were lost. However, the city continued to grow, despite disastrous hurricanes in 1926 and 1935.

Miami has the largest population of Cuban refugees in the United States—in excess of 500,000. The 1980 boat exodus of thousands of new Cuban refugees strained the resources of Miami's existing first- and second-generation Cuban community. An additional influx of sea-borne refugees from Haiti also taxed public services in the South Florida metropolis.

A major rail, air and shipping point, Miami is considered the principal gateway to Latin America; the Dodge Island passenger terminal is home base for the many cruise ships serving South America and the Caribbean. The Greater Miami Foreign-Trade Zone is the largest of its kind in the U.S.

Although tourism is the leading industry in the area, the city is the nation's third largest garment manufacturing center. Concrete, metal, meat products, and commercial fishing also make substantial contributions to Miami's economy. Miami's booming trade with Latin America and the Caribbean has been spurred by the siting of 13 major overseas banks in the city. The U.S. Environmental Science Services Administration's Oceanographic and Meteorological Laboratories have made Miami a world leader in undersea studies. Construction of the $900-million, 20.5-mile elevated rail system, linking downtown Miami with its suburbs, began in June, 1979.

Greater Miami, which consists of over two dozen independent municipalities, is renowned for its luxurious resort hotels and fine beaches. Recently, many of the visitors have come from Latin America and Europe. Tourist attractions include Bicentennial-New World Center Park, the Museum of Science, the Miami Seaquarium, and Vizcaya, formerly the estate of James Deering and now the Dade County Art Museum. Everglades National Park, a preserve for tropical birds and flora, is nearby. The area has year-round horse racing at Hialeah, Gulfstream and Calder racetracks. Miami is home to the annual Orange Bowl Festival and January 1 football classic, and to the National Football League's Miami Dolphins.

Fourteen people were killed in May 1980 riots within the black community of Liberty City following the acquittal of four policemen accused of killing a black businessman. Further rioting occurred in July.

MILWAUKEE

Location: Southeastern Wisconsin, on Lake Michigan **County:** Milwaukee **City Area:** 96.5 sq. miles (249.9 sq. kilometers) **Altitude:** 581 feet (176.6 meters)
Mayor: Henry W. Maier
City Population: 717,372 (1970 census) 661,082 (1976 est.) **Metro Area Population:** 1,403,884 (1970 census) 1,426,500 (1977 est.)
Daily Newspapers: 2 **No. of Radio Stations:** 26 (1980) **No. of TV Stations:** 6 (1980)
City Chamber of Commerce: Metropolitan Milwaukee Association of Commerce, 756 North Milwaukee Street, Milwaukee, Wisconsin 53202

Milwaukee, seat of Milwaukee County and largest city in Wisconsin, is a leading Great Lakes port and major industrial metropolis.

French missionaries and the French explorer La Salle visited the site in the late 17th century. French Canadian fur traders came to barter with the Indians, and in 1795 the North West Company established a trading post. The first permanent settler, Solomon Juneau, an agent of the American Fur Company, arrived in 1818. His settlement and several neighboring villages merged after 1835 to form Milwaukee, which was incorporated as a city in 1846. Its name is derived from an Indian term interpreted to mean either "gathering place by the waters" or "beautiful land."

The city's excellent harbor, accessible raw materials, and growing population made it a shipping and industrial center, and German immigrants, arriving after 1848, stimulated its political, economic, and social development.

Milwaukee produces more beer than any other city and is the home of three of the four largest breweries. However, machinery manufacturing is the area's largest industry. Milwaukee is also a leading grain market and a major meat packer.

Of interest in the city are the Greek Orthodox Annunciation Church, designed by Frank Lloyd Wright; the War Memorial Center, on the lakeshore, designed by Eero Saarinen and housing the Milwaukee Art Center; the Milwaukee County Zoo, one of the most modern in the nation; the Mitchell Park Botanical Conservatory, three domed buildings for display of plants under arid, moist and temperate conditions; and the world-famous breweries, which offer tours to the public. A $12-million Performing Arts Center with a large park and fountains is the home of the Milwaukee Symphony Orchestra and the Repertory Theatre. MECCA, the Milwaukee Exposition and Convention Center and Arena, one of Milwaukee's newest buildings, has won national attention because of its artistic design and colors.

Milwaukee has gained recognition from national organizations for cleanliness and beautification for many years and is one of the safest areas in the nation.

MINNEAPOLIS

Location: East-central Minnesota, on both sides of Mississippi River at Falls of St. Anthony **County:** Hennepin **City Area:** 58.8 sq. miles (152.2 sq. kilometers) **Altitude:** 815 feet (247.7 meters)
Mayor: Donald Fraser **Chief Administrative Officer:** David C. Niklaus
City Population: 434,400 (1970 census) 371,896 (1976 est.) **Metro Area Population:** 1,965,391 (1970 census), 2,037,200 (1977 est.)
Daily Newspapers: 2 **No. of Commercial Radio Stations (AM):** 7 (1980) **No. of TV Stations:** 5 (1980)
City Chamber of Commerce: Greater Minneapolis Chamber of Commerce, 15 South Fifth Street, Minneapolis, Minnesota 55402

Minneapolis, seat of Hennepin County, is the largest city in Minnesota and an important industrial and railroad center. It is contiguous to St. Paul, its twin city and the state capital.

Father Louis Hennepin visited the site in 1680 and gave the Falls of Saint Anthony their name. In 1819 the U.S. government established Fort Snelling, and two years later a sawmill was built at the falls. The village of St. Anthony was soon settled on the east bank of the Mississippi River, while Minneapolis grew up (c. 1847) on the west bank. Minneapolis, from the local Indian "minnea," or water, combined with "polis," Greek for city, was incorporated as a town in 1856 and as a city the following year. In 1872 St. Anthony was annexed.

During the 1890s the lumber business thrived as logs were floated downstream to the sawmills of Minneapolis from the great forests of the north. Minneapolis was also known as the "Flour City of the World" until a change in freight rates after World War I shifted the center of the flour-milling industry to Buffalo.

Today the city is the home of the Minneapolis Grain Exchange, the world's largest cash grain market, and headquarters for a Federal Reserve district bank. A leading industry is the manufacture of linseed oil, paint, and industrial finishes. Other important products are precision instruments and farm machinery; printing and publishing are also important.

Minneapolis and St. Paul constitute the financial and industrial center of a large area rich in natural resources, power, and transportation facilities. The two cities are connected by a massive freeway system that runs through the suburban areas, plus a $300-million Minneapolis Gateway Center in the Loop. A $65-million domed stadium is under construction in the downtown area. Minneapolis has 25 industrial parks and a 12-acre river terminal to handle shipping and storage of grain, fertilizer, petroleum products, sand gravel, salt and coal.

The major landmarks in Minneapolis are the 57-story IDS skyscraper and Nicollet Mall. Within the city are 153 parks with 22 lakes; Minnehaha Park with its Stevens House, dating from 1849; the Tyrone Guthrie Theater; the $5.5-million Walker Art Center; and the Minnesota Orchestra's new concert hall.

NEWARK

Location: Northeastern New Jersey, on Passaic River and Newark Bay **County:** Essex **City Area:** 24 sq. miles (62.2 sq. kilometers) **Altitude:** 55 feet (16.7 meters)
Mayor: Kenneth A. Gibson
City Population: 381,930 (1970 census), 331,495 (1976 est.)
Metro Area Population: 2,057,468 (1970 census), 1,969,200 (1977 est.)
Daily Newspapers: 1 **No. of Radio Stations:** 2 (1980) **No. of TV Stations:** 2 (1980)
City Chamber of Commerce: Greater Newark Chamber of Commerce, 50 Park Place, Newark, New Jersey 07102

Newark, seat of Essex County and largest city in New Jersey, is an important industrial and commercial center.

It was settled in 1666 by Puritans from Connecticut led by Robert Treat and is said to have been named after the town of Newark, England, although some contend its name was New Ark and had a religious connotation.

During the Revolutionary War, the city was the scene of several skirmishes; General George Washington passed through in 1776 leading his troops south to the Delaware River.

Newark's industrial growth began in the early 19th century. The arrival of railroads and canals in the 1830s stimulated the expansion of shoemaking and tanning and the development of the jewelry, insurance, and shipbuilding industries. After 1880 swarms of immigrants arrived, living in hastily built tenements. In 1915 Port Newark opened; during World War I Newark was the nation's leading shipbuilding city.

Today Newark is the country's third leading insurance center. A significant factor in its economic life is the Port of New York Authority, which operates Port Newark and Newark International Airport. Among the city's products are leather goods, jewelry, malt liquors, plastics, electrical equipment, auto parts, and chemicals.

Of interest in the city are Trinity Cathedral, the Sacred Heart Cathedral (begun in 1898), the First Presbyterian Church (1791); and the old County courthouse (1906), designed by Cass Gilbert.

Newark began to deteriorate economically and politically in the 1930s, a process which continued for 30 years or more. The city suffered the same ills which plagued many of the country's major cities—an exodus of population and business from the central city, with the concommitant drop in revenues, and a high unemployment rate among the remaining population, which is now over 75 percent Black and Hispanic. Newark is fighting hard to lure business back to the downtown area and to improve the lot of its underprivileged citizens. Local efforts aided by the receipt of large federal health-care funds have dramatically reduced the death rate over a ten-year period since the mid 60s.

The Prudential and Mutual Benefit life insurance companies have since built new headquarters here, Blue Cross-Blue Shield of New Jersey is also headquartered here, and Public Service Electric and Gas Company, a major utility, has replaced its downtown headquarters with a new $60-million, 27-story corporate complex on an adjacent site. Since then millions of dollars have been spent to rebuild the city. The New Jersey Institute of Technology expanded its facilities. In 1974 New Jersey College of Medicine and Dentistry, Essex County College, Seton Hall and Rutgers University began construction of university facilities. In 1976 construction was completed at Seton Hall Law School, the School of Dentistry, Rutgers University and Essex County College.

In 1979, the Federal Communications Commission ordered 7 New York City and 3 Philadelphia TV stations to establish offices and studios in New Jersey if they wished to have their licenses renewed. New Jersey and Delaware are the only states in the nation without their own VHF television stations.

NEW ORLEANS

Location: Southeastern Louisiana, on Mississippi River, near Lake Pontchartrain, about 100 miles from Gulf of Mexico **Parish:** Orleans **City Area:** 366 sq. miles (947.9 sq. kilometers) **Altitude:** 5 feet (1.5 meters)
Mayor: Ernest N. Morial **Chief Administrative Officer:** Reynaud Rochon
City Population: 593,471 (1970 census), 561,200 (1977 est.)
Metro Area Population: 1,046,470 (1970 census), 1,133,100 (1977 est.)
Daily Newspapers: 2 **No. of Radio Stations:** 26 (1980) **No. of TV Stations:** 5 (1980)
City Chamber of Commerce: Chamber of Commerce of New Orleans and the River Region, P.O. Box 30240, New Orleans, Louisiana 70190

New Orleans, coextensive with Louisiana's Orleans Parish (county), is one of the largest cities in the South, the nation's second largest port, and the third largest port in the world. It was founded in 1718 by the Sieur de Bienville and named for Philippe II, duke of Orleans. Four years later it became the capital of the French colony of Louisiana. In 1762 the city passed to Spain, but remained culturally French.

New Orleans was returned to France in 1800 and in 1803 came under U.S. jurisdiction with the Louisiana Purchase. It developed into a flourishing cotton and slave-trade center, and was an important stopover on the southern routes to the West. After Andrew Jackson's victory over the British at New Orleans (January 8, 1815), the city's prosperity reached great heights, and New Orleans became famous for gaiety and elegance. (Today its colorful Mardi Gras, which is held every February, is one of the country's best-known festivals.)

In 1862 the city fell to Admiral David G. Farragut and did not fully recover from occupation by Union troops under General Benjamin Butler and the subsequent Reconstruction era until the end of World War I. Discovery of oil and the renewed commercial importance of sugar and cotton helped the city regain prosperity.

Today New Orleans is the banking and business center of the New South. It has the world's largest sugar refinery and is surrounded, offshore and on, by some of the most productive sources of oil in the nation. Other important industries are aerospace and shipbuilding.

The city's Vieux Carré, the French quarter, which comprised the original settlement, is a popular tourist attraction. Among the points of interest are Royal Street (Rue Royale) and the French Market on Decatur Street. Dixieland jazz was born on Bourbon Street.

The Lake Pontchartrain Causeway, completed in 1956, is the world's longest overwater highway bridge (126,055 feet). A second causeway was opened to traffic in 1969.

Other landmarks include the Hibernia Tower, 33-story International Trade Mart, and the 52-story One Shell Square. The $178-million air-conditioned Superdome, the largest in the world, was dedicated August 3, 1975. The downtown area is being developed with five large-scale multi-use projects, provided for by some $1 billion in investments by private and public sectors. These projects are the Poydras Plaza, the International Rivercenter, the Pan-American Life Insurance Company. Headquarters, the Canal Place, and the Piazza D'Italia.

NEW YORK CITY

Location: Southeastern New York, at mouth of Hudson River **Counties:** New York, Bronx, Kings, Queens, and Richmond **City Area:** 320 sq. miles (828.8 sq. kilometers) **Altitude:** 55 feet (16.7 meters)
Mayor: Edward I. Koch
City Population: 7,895,563 (1970 census), 7,312,200 (1977 est.)
Metro Area Population: 9,973,716 (1970 census), 9,386,700 (1977 est.)
Daily Newspapers: 7 **No. of Commercial Radio Stations (AM):** 16 (1980) **No. of TV Stations:** 9 (1980)
City Chamber of Commerce: New York Chamber of Commerce and Industry, 65 Liberty Street, New York, New York 10005

New York, the nation's largest city and richest port, is a national leader in business, finance, manufacturing, communications, service industries, fashion, and the arts. It is also one of the world's largest cities, one of the world's leading ports, and headquarters of the United Nations.

As the financial headquarters of the world, New York is the home of some of the world's largest corporations and the New York and American Stock Exchanges.

As a cultural capital and influential arbiter of taste, the city has its renowned theater district and the cultural complex of Lincoln Center for the Performing Arts. It also has innumerable museums, art galleries, and related attractions, as well as scientific collections, libraries, and educational institutions.

Giovanni da Verrazano, a Florentine, was probably the first European to visit (1524) the site of New York. Henry Hudson's explorations (1609) up the river named after him led to the first permanent European settlements. In 1625 the colony of New Netherland was established, with its capital, New Amsterdam, located at the southern tip of Manhattan Island. The following year Peter Minuit of the Dutch West India Company bought the entire island from the Indians for the equivalent of about $24 in trinkets and beads. In 1664 the English seized the city for the Duke of York, for whom it was renamed. Later the Dutch regained control for a brief period (1673-74).

New York was active in the colonial opposition to British rule, and during the first year of the Revolution several battles were fought in the area. In 1776 the British captured the city and controlled it for the rest of the war.

New York, the first capital (1789-90) of the United States under the Constitution, was the site of George Washington's first inauguration. Until 1797 the city was also the capital of New York State.

The opening of the Erie Canal (1825) accelerated the growth of the city, already the nation's largest, and established its dominance over Boston and Philadelphia. The New York and Harlem Railroad was completed in 1832. By 1840 New York was the country's leading port.

During the 19th century, the city expanded northward from the tip of Manhattan, until by 1874 it covered the entire island. That same year saw annexation of parts of Westchester County that later formed the Bronx. New York assumed its present boundaries in 1898, after annexing Brooklyn, Queens County and Staten Island.

New York's best known attractions include Central Park, the Bronx Zoo and Botanical Gardens, the Aquarium at Coney Island, Hayden Planetarium, the Fifth Avenue shops, the Broadway theatrical district, the United Nations Headquarters, Radio City Music Hall, the Statue of Liberty and the Staten Island ferry, Rockefeller and Lincoln Centers, Madison Square Garden, Yankee and Shea Stadiums, Greenwich Village, Chinatown and the Financial District, the Metropolitan Museum of Art, St. Patrick's Cathedral and the World Trade Center.

1979 saw a further easing of New York City's fiscal problems. A group of out-of-state and foreign banks agreed to join city banks in acting as "backup" lenders for up to $600 million in short-term notes. This was the first time this had happened since the crisis began in 1975.

New York's mass transit system, the nation's largest, ground to a halt on April 1, 1980, when 33,000 subway and bus workers went out on strike. The Long Island Railroad, the nation's largest commuter line, was also shut down by strikers for a short period. New Yorkers and commuters managed to reach their jobs by walking, driving, bicycling and even rollerskating to work for the eleven days of the strike's duration.

New York City was host to the 1980 Democratic Convention on August 11-14, which saw the renomination of Jimmy Carter and Walter Mondale to the presidency and vice-presidency.

OKLAHOMA CITY

Location: Central Oklahoma, on North Canadian River **Counties:** Oklahoma, Canadian, Cleveland and McClain **City Area:** 621 miles (1,608 sq. kilometers) **Altitude:** 1,207 feet (366.8 meters)
Mayor: Patience Latting **City Manager:** James J. Cook
City Population: 368,164 (1970 census), 369,438 (1976 est.)
Metro Area Population: 699,092 (1970 census), 768,500 (1977 est.)
Daily Newspapers: 3 **No. of Radio Stations:** 23 (1980) **No. of TV Stations:** 5 (1980)
City Chamber of Commerce: Oklahoma City Chamber of Commerce, One Santa Fe Plaza, Oklahoma City, Oklahoma 73102

Oklahoma City, seat of Oklahoma County and state capital, is the largest municipality in Oklahoma. It is also the state's financial, commercial, and industrial center.

The city's origin is one of the most colorful in American history. When the first land run into Indian Territory took place on April 22, 1889, a small Santa Fe Railroad water and coaling station blossomed into a city of 10,000 people between noon and sundown. The name of the city and territory means "red people" and had been proposed by a Choctaw chief in 1866 to designate the area set off for Indians. Oklahoma City was incorporated in 1890 and became the state capital in 1910.

Oil was struck in 1928, and it soon became apparent that rich oil and gas lands lay beneath the city itself. An extensive system of oil wells in the metropolitan area, reaching almost to the governor's mansion, is a large factor in the city's economy.

Oklahoma City is a rapidly growing regional, national and international marketing center. The U.S. Customs Bureau opened an office in 1967 to expedite exports and imports. Industry includes meat packing, including the headquarters of Wilson & Co., electronics components and the production of transportation equipment and oil field supplies. General Motors opened a huge auto assembly plant in 1979. The city also is noted as a convention site.

Oklahoma City has grown into an aeronautical complex with such Federal Aviation Administration facilities as the Aeronautical Center and Civil Aeromedical Institute. Nearby is Tinker Air Force Base with equipment and inventory of over $2 billion.

Of interest are the National Cowboy Hall of Fame and Western Heritage Center, with western art and a recreation of a western scene; the State Historical Society Building and Museum; the zoo; Kirkpatrick Center, with its science, air and space museum; and the State Capitol. The Oklahoma National Stockyards, the nation's largest cattle feeder market, has been designated as a national historical landmark.

OMAHA

Location: East-central Nebraska, on Missouri River **County:** Douglas **City Area:** 87.8 sq. miles (226.5 sq. kilometers) **Altitude:** 985 feet (299.3 meters)
Mayor: Al Veys
City Population: 358,452 (1970 census), 371,012 (1976 est.)
Metro Area Population: 542,646 (1970 census) 580,900 (1977 est.)
Daily Newspapers: 1 **No. of Radio Stations (AM):** 9 (1980) **No. of TV Stations:** 4 (1980)
City Chamber of Commerce: Greater Omaha Chamber of Commerce, Suite 2100, 1620 Dodge, Omaha, Nebraska 68102

Omaha, seat of Douglas County, is the largest city in Nebraska. It is an important cattle market and the nation's largest meat packing center. It took its name from the Omaha Indians living nearby, who were known as "those who go upstream or against the current."

Omaha's history is associated with the opening of the West beginning with Lewis and Clark's conference with the Indians in 1804. A trading post was set up by Jean Pierre Cabanne in 1825, and the first settlement came in 1846-47, when the Mormons spent the winter there on their way to Utah. The city was officially founded in 1854 after Indians ceded the present Douglas County to the United States. Three years later Omaha was incorporated as a city and was capital of the Nebraska Territory from 1855 to 1867.

As a supply point for westward migration, Omaha grew quickly. The Union Pacific Railroad arrived in 1865, augmenting river traffic and making Omaha, on the west bank of the Missouri, a major transportation and shipping center.

Despite floods, droughts, and a plague of grasshoppers later in the 19th century, the city continued to expand. Today it is an important market for livestock and farm produce and has large meat-packing and food-processing plants, grain elevators, and stockyards. It also has oil refineries, a large lead smelter, and factories manufacturing farm implements and appliances.

The headquarters of the Strategic Air Command are located here as are the regional headquarters of the Farm Credit Administration and the Reconstruction Finance Corporation. Boys Town, the youth community founded by Father Edward J. Flanagan in 1917, is 11 miles west of the city.

Of interest are Fort Omaha, built in 1868, and the Mormon Cemetery with the Winter Quarters Monument. Riverview Park contains a monument to Friedrich von Schiller and Levi Carter Park has a lake and picnic grounds. The Joslyn Art Museum contains paintings by many of the world's greatest artists.

PHILADELPHIA

Location: Southeastern Pennsylvania, at the junction of the Delaware and Schuylkill rivers, 88 miles from Atlantic Ocean **County:** Philadelphia **City Area:** 129 sq. miles (334.1 sq. kilometers) **Altitude:** 100 feet (30.4 meters)
Mayor: William J. Green **Managing Director:** W. Wilson Goode
City Population: 1,949,996 (1970 census), 1,784,500 (1977 est.)
Metro Area Population: 4,824,110 (1970 census), 4,793,900 (1977 est.)
Daily Newspapers: 5 **No. of Commercial Radio Stations (AM):** 9 (1979) **No. of TV Stations:** 6 (1980)
City Chamber of Commerce: The Greater Philadelphia Chamber of Commerce, Suburban Station Building, 1617 John F. Kennedy Blvd., Philadelphia, Pennsylvania 19103

Philadelphia, coextensive with Philadelphia County, is the largest city in Pennsylvania and the fourth largest in the nation. The site was originally settled by Swedes early in the 17th century. In 1682 William Penn founded a Quaker settlement, naming it Philadelphia from the Greek phrase for "brotherly love."

The city was the largest and wealthiest in the 13 Colonies and served, except during a brief British occupation, as the capital from 1777 to 1788—the period of the adoption of the Articles of Confederation (1778) and the drafting of the United States Constitution (1787). From 1790 to 1800 it was the capital of the United States.

Philadelphia was the site of both Banks of the United States—the first from 1791 to 1811, and the second from 1816 to 1836. It was also an important center of the abolition movement and a major station on the Underground Railroad.

Philadelphia was host to the 1876 Centennial Exposition, commemorating the 100th anniversary of American independence, and the 1926 Sesquicentennial Exposition.

Today its diversified economy includes such industries as printing and publishing, shipbuilding, and the manufacture of machinery, chemicals, clothing, carpets, instruments, cigars and textiles. It is the largest petroleum refining center on the East Coast and the second largest in the nation. It has the largest freshwater port in the world, with 50 miles of waterfront, and is also a major financial center.

A major renovation of the waterfront, referred to as Penn's Landing, is in progress, and a University City Science Center is being developed. Ground was broken in April 1972 for a $300-million complex called Market Street East, which has transformed Philadelphia's main shopping street from City Hall to Independence Mall into a mall and transportation center. In November 1975 the Chestnut Street Transitway opened to transform the 10 blocks between 8th and 18th streets into a buses-only transitway and a modern shrub-lined pedestrian promenade and shopping mall.

Former Representative William J. Green was elected mayor in 1979 to succeed Frank L. Rizzo. Earlier, voters had rejected by a 3-1 margin a city charter amendment to permit Rizzo to run for a third term.

There are numerous historic monuments in the city. Independence Hall, where the Declaration of Independence was signed, is in Independence National Park. Nearby is Congress Hall, seat of Congress from 1790 to 1800; Carpenters' Hall, meeting place for the First Continental Congress; the First and Second U.S. Banks; the Jacob Graff House; old City Hall; and the Merchants' Exchange. Other points of interest are Elfreth's Alley, one of the nation's oldest streets; Christ Church; the Society Hill area; and the Betsy Ross House. Fairmount Park, one of the largest in the world, contains many historic monuments and a famous zoo. Among the city's many outstanding museums are the world-famous Museum of Art, the Franklin Institute Science Museum and the University Museum.

PHOENIX

Location: South-central Arizona on Salt River **County:** Maricopa **City Area:** 325 sq. miles (842 sq. kilometers) **Altitude:** 1,117 feet (340.4 meters)
Mayor: Margaret Hance **City Manager:** Marvin Andrews
City Population: 589,016 (1970 census), 680,000 (1976 est.)
Metro Area Population: 971,228 (1970 census), 1,253,600 (1977 est.)
Daily Newspapers: 2 **No. of Commercial Radio Stations (AM):** 19 (1980) **No. of TV Stations:** 7 (1980)
City Chamber of Commerce: Phoenix Metropolitan Chamber of Commerce, 34 W. Monroe Street, Phoenix, Arizona 85003

Phoenix, seat of Maricopa County and state capital, is the largest city in Arizona and one of the fastest growing in the nation. Because Phoenix grew up on a site that showed traces of an ancient Hohokam Indian settlement, it was named after the mythological bird that rose from its own ashes.

The area was probably visited by the Spanish explorers Cabeza de Vaca in 1536, Marcos de Niza in 1539, and Coronado in 1540. John Y. T. Smith established a hay camp on the Salt River in 1866, and the following year Phoenix was officially founded. It was incorporated as a city in 1881 and replaced Prescott as the territorial capital in 1889, two years after the first railroad arrived. In 1912 Arizona was admitted to the Union, and Phoenix became the state capital.

The completion in 1911 of Roosevelt Dam, part of the first successful large-scale irrigation project in the country, made it possible to grow citrus fruits, dates and other crops in the desert climate. The city has also prospered from rich mineral deposits in the region. Since 1945 electronics, computer, aircraft, furniture, steel, aluminum and chemical manufacturing have become important.

In 1972 the Phoenix Civic Plaza, a $19-million commercial and cultural complex, and the 40-story Valley National Bank Building, Arizona's tallest, were completed.

Abundant sunshine has made Phoenix a health resort and winter vacationland. Of interest in the area are the city's museums; nearby South Mountain Park; and Taliesin West, home of the late Frank Lloyd Wright and now an architectural school directed by Mrs. Wright. An annual rodeo simulates the atmosphere of the Old West each spring.

Phoenix has a mushrooming population—people are moving into this city at a rate of more than 400 a day. Newcomers are discovering that the reasons they moved away—air pollution, traffic congestion, inflation, overburdened utilities and suburban sprawl—are problems that already exist in Phoenix. Major long-range plans for the city are in the beginning stages, with redevelopment and "in-filling" of areas within the inner city being the new direction taken.

As Phoenix has mushroomed in population and development, so it has in athletic stature. Professional sports teams such as the National Basketball Association Phoenix Suns have found a home in the Valley of the Sun and are popular drawing cards.

PITTSBURGH

Location: Southwestern Pennsylvania, at junction where the Allegheny and Monongahela rivers form the Ohio River **County:** Allegheny **City Area:** 55.5 sq. miles (143.8 sq. kilometers) **Altitude:** 745 feet (226.4 meters)
Mayor: Richard Caliguiri
City Population: 520,089 (1970 census), 449,092 (1976 est.)
Metro Area Population: 2,401,362 (1970 census), 2,294,500 (1977 est.)
Daily Newspapers: 2 **No. of Commercial Radio Stations (AM):** 11 (1979) **No. of TV Stations:** 6 (1980)
City Chamber of Commerce: The Greater Pittsburgh Chamber of Commerce, 411 Seventh Avenue, Pittsburgh, Pennsylvania 15219

Pittsburgh, seat of Allegheny County, is the second largest city in Pennsylvania, an important inland port, and one of the world's great steel centers.

It was founded on the site of Shannopin, an Indian settlement that was a fur-trading post in the late 17th century. In the 18th century the French built Fort Duquesne on the site, and after it fell to the British it was renamed Fort Pitt in honor of William Pitt. The fort withstood attack in 1763 during Pontiac's Rebellion, and in the ensuing years a village grew up around it.

When the Northwest Territory opened up, the village became an important trading and shipping center. Anthony Wayne negotiated (1795) with Indian tribes in the area, allowing Pittsburgh to develop in peace. It was incorporated as a city in 1816. Completion of the Pennsylvania Canal in 1837 and rail lines in 1851 further stimulated industrial and commercial development. One of the world's first cable suspension bridges was constructed here in 1847.

In 1936 Pittsburgh suffered the most disastrous flood of its history when the Allegheny and the Monongahela rivers rose 46 feet, inundating much of the business and industrial district, paralyzing the city, and taking 45 lives. Damages amounted to $25 million.

The city is headquarters for some of the country's biggest corporations. Among them are U.S. Steel, Gulf Oil, Rockwell International, Heinz foods, Westinghouse, Alcoa, Consolidation Coal, PPG Industries, and Koppers Co. The reactors for the Nautilus and Skate, the first nuclear submarines, were built here.

Pittsburgh's revolutionary urban-renewal program began when public-spirited citizens formed the Allegheny Conference on Community Development in 1943. Demolition work began in 1950 for the famous Gateway Center and $22-million Civic Auditorium with a retractable dome. The program has been eminently successful in rebuilding the Golden Triangle—the triangular-shaped business district bounded by the Allegheny, Monongahela, and Ohio rivers. It has also been so successful in controlling smoke emitted by the steelmaking and other industrial complexes that Pittsburgh is no longer "Smoky City," a nickname it bore for more than a century. Other redevelopment highlights are the Market Square Redevelopment Project, a downtown block filled with night spots and restaurants, and a $25-million Convention Center and Exhibition Hall. However, a proposal by PPG Industries to build a $150-million office complex on five acres now occupied by small businesses met strong opposition from area merchants. They received $2 million in an out-of-court settlement from PPG in 1980.

Pittsburgh has a fine park system. City landmarks include the Carnegie-Mellon University, established by Andrew Carnegie in 1895; the University of Pittsburgh and its Cathedral of Learning, noted for its medical and law schools; the Buhl Planetarium and Institute of Popular Science; and Highland Park, site of the Pittsburgh Zoo and a memorial to Stephen Foster, who was born there. Heinz Hall for the Performing Arts opened in September 1971. It is home for the Pittsburgh Symphony,

Pittsburgh Opera, Civic Light Opera, Pittsburgh Ballet and Pittsburgh Youth Symphony.

The bold skyline of Pittsburgh is clearly visible from the top of Mount Washington reached from the south bank of the Monongahela by the "incline," one of two in the city, which acts as a near-verticle tramway up the steep slope.

PORTLAND

Location: Northwestern Oregon, near the junction of the Willamette and Columbia rivers **Counties:** Multnomah and Washington **City Area:** 107 sq. miles (277 sq. kilometers) **Altitude:** 77 feet (23.4 meters)
Mayor: Francis Ivancie
City Population: 382,352 (1970 census), 379,826 (1976 est.)
Metro Area Population: 1,007,131 (1970 census) 1,121,500 (1977 est.)
Daily Newspapers: 2 **No. of Radio Stations:** 21 (1980) **No. of TV Stations:** 5 (1980)
City Chamber of Commerce: Portland Chamber of Commerce, 824 S.W. 5th Avenue, Portland, Oregon 97204

Portland, seat of Multnomah County and largest city in Oregon, is a trading, transportation, and manufacturing center, an important deepwater port with shipyards and the world's third-largest floating dry dock.

When it was founded in 1845, a coin was flipped to decide whether it should be named after Boston, Massachusetts or Portland, Maine. Incorporated in 1851, it expanded with the establishment of the salmon industry after the Civil War, the arrival of the railroad (1883), the Alaska gold rush (1897-1900), and the Lewis and Clark Centennial Exposition (1905). A disastrous fire in 1873 destroyed part of the city, but it was rapidly rebuilt. The city made history in 1889 with the first long-distance transmission of electricity; power from a plant on the Willamette Falls at Oregon City was sent over wires to light the streets of Portland. During World War II, Portland emerged as a major shipbuilding port.

Today the city is a major export point for wheat, wool, bauxite and lumber, and the leading manufacturer of specialized lumbering equipment. Also important to the city's economy are the numerous chemical industries. Portland has become a major electronics manufacturing center. It is the home of Tektronics, a major producer of display and signal equipment.

Portland instituted a popularly elected regional government that embraces parts of three counties. The reorganization is the first of its kind in the nation, and calls for a two-tiered government of municipal, county and other local jurisdictions and a regional government.

A $16-million transit mall was completed in the central business district in late 1977. The mall provides partial separation of buses, pedestrians and cars for improved transportation flow and lower pollutant levels in the downtown area. A new transit project is the $161-million light rail route which will extend 15 miles from downtown Portland to a suburb.

The 1980 eruption of Mount St. Helens in neighboring Washington state coated the city with volcanic ash for several days.

Of interest in Portland are the annual rose festival, the Pacific International Livestock Exposition, the Portland Zoo, the Portland Art Museum, and the fine views of various mountains, occasionally including distant Mount Rainier and Mount Jefferson. Mount Tabor, an extinct volcanic crater, is located in Portland.

PROVIDENCE

Location: Northeastern Rhode Island, at the head of the Narragansett Bay, on Providence River **County:** Providence **City Area:** 20 sq. miles (51.8 sq. kilometers) **Altitude:** 80 feet (24.3 meters)
Mayor: Vincent A. Cianci, Jr.
City Population: 179,116 (1970 census), 164,989 (1976 est.)
Metro Area Population: 855,495 (1970 census), 852,000 (1977 est.)
Daily Newspapers: 2 **No. of Radio Stations:** 16 (1980) **No. of TV Stations:** 3 (1980)
City Chamber of Commerce: Greater Providence Chamber of Commerce, 10 Dorrance Street, Providence, Rhode Island 02903

Providence, seat of Providence County and state capital, is the largest city in Rhode Island and a port of entry. It was founded by Roger Williams in 1636 after he was exiled from Massachusetts. The Narragansett Indians granted him title to the site, which he named in gratitude for "God's merciful providence." Early settlers formed (1638) a "Proprietors Company" cooperative.

The settlement developed slowly during the 17th century and suffered much destruction during King Philip's War (1675-76) when Indians raided it and burned more than a third of its homes. Later, however, Providence developed into an important commercial center, and many families amassed fortunes as ships engaged in the West Indian trade.

Providence served the patriotic cause during the Revolutionary War and signed the Rhode Island Independence Act two months before the signing of the Declaration of Independence. After the War of 1812, Providence became a jewelry and textile manufacturing center. In 1832 the city charter became effective.

In 1842 Thomas Wilson Dorr, a Providence man, led a rebellion that collapsed; however, it was influential in the formation of a more democratic state constitution. In 1900 Providence became Rhode Island's sole capital, having been joint capital with other communities since colonial days.

Today Providence is still noted as a jewelry manufacturing center. Silverware, textiles, machinery, metal products, and rubber goods are also important products.

Among the city's historic structures are the old market building (1773), the Stephen Hopkins House (c. 1755), the John Brown House (1786), and the First Baptist Meetinghouse (1775). Roger Williams Park contains a museum of natural history and a natural amphitheater where concerts are given.

Westminster Mall and downtown Providence are under reconstruction.

Providence is the home of Brown University, Providence College, Rhode Island College, and Rhode Island School of Design, one of the country's leading art schools.

ROCHESTER

Location: Western New York State, at the mouth of the Genesee River on Lake Ontario, 65 miles east of Buffalo **County:** Monroe **City Area:** 36 sq. miles (93.2 sq. kilometers) **Altitude:** 510 feet (154.9 meters)
Mayor: Thomas P. Ryan, Jr. **City Manager:** L. Joe Miller
City Population: 295,011 (1970 census), 262,766 (1976 est.)
Metro Area Population: 961,516 (1970 census), 970,200 (1977 est.)
Daily Newspapers: 2 **No. of Commercial Radio Stations (AM):** 16 (1979) **No. of TV Stations:** 5 (1980)
City Chamber of Commerce: Rochester Area Chamber of Commerce, Ind., 55 St. Paul Street, Rochester, New York 14604

Rochester, seat of Monroe County, is situated on the falls of the Genesee River, the New York State Barge Canal and Lake Ontario. Known as the home of Eastman Kodak, Bausch & Lomb, R. T. French, and Xerox, the city enjoys an unusually diverse economy; major industries include machinery, optical goods, foundry products, nurseries, food packing and processing, leather goods, printing and publishing. It also has great natural beauty, its many parks and gardens earning for it the nickname, "The Flower City."

The Rochester region was originally the home of the Seneca Indians. In 1789 Ebenezer Allen built a mill at the falls of the Genesee, on land he had been granted on condition he serve the Senecas' needs. But the mill failed, and Allen's land was sold to Colonel Nathaniel Rochester and two friends. In 1811 Colonel Rochester laid out the village and a year later the first white settlement was made; its original name, Rochesterville, was shortened in 1812. The village was incorporated in 1817, the city in 1834.

Blessed with abundant waterpower, and the rich yields of the Genesee Valley, a significant milling industry developed and played a large part in Rochester's early growth. The industry's success was assured by the opening of the Erie Canal to the city in 1823.

Before the Civil War, the city was in the forefront of the anti-slavery movement and a station on the Underground Railroad; it was in Rochester that black abolitionist Frederick Douglass published a newspaper, *The North Star*. The period 1850-1900 saw the decline of milling as the city's chief economic pursuit, and the rise of the nursery trade and a number of technical industries to take its place. In 1916 the city was extended northward, in a strip along the banks of the Genesee, to Lake Ontario.

Among the city's attractions are the Eastman Kodak Company, whose plants are open to tours; the George Eastman House of Photography; the Rochester Museum of Arts and Sciences; the Strassenburgh Planetarium; Eastman Theatre, home of the Rochester Philharmonic and the Susan B. Anthony House, commemorating the women's rights pioneer and former Rochester resident.

SACRAMENTO

Location: North-central California, at the confluence of the Sacramento and American rivers, 90 miles northeast of San Francisco **County:** Sacramento **City Area:** 93.8 sq. miles (242.9 sq. kilometers) **Altitude:** 17 feet (5.2 meters)
Mayor: Phillip Isenberg **City Manager:** Walter Slipe
City Population: 257,105 (1970 census), 262,305 (1976 est.)
Metro Area Population: 803,793 (1970 census), 929,400 (1977 est.)
Daily Newspapers: 2 **No. of Radio Stations:** 16 (1980) **No. of TV Stations:** 6 (1980)
City Chamber of Commerce: Sacramento Metropolitan Chamber of Commerce, P.O. Box 1017, Sacramento, California 95805

Sacramento, capital of California and seat of Sacramento County, is a rare amalgam of industrial strength and natural beauty, and the focal point of the profusely fertile Sacramento Valley. Fruits, vegetables, cattle and dairy products abound, supporting a large food packing and processing industry. Other important resources include oil, natural gas, timber, lead, pottery clay and a plentiful supply of waterpower for generating electricity. In 1963 the city opened deep-water port facilities, with direct access to the Pacific Ocean. The city is also an important missile development and electronics center.

The history of Sacramento is rich in drama and color, dating from its founding in 1839 by John Augustus Sutter, a German-born Swiss citizen who received permission from the Mexican governor to establish a colony for fellow Swiss immigrants. Originally called New Helvetia, it received its present name (from the river which ran beside it) in 1848, when it was laid out as a town.

The following year brought the new community immediate and widespread renown, when gold was discovered (by James W. Marshall) on Sutter's property, triggering the legend-engendering Gold Rush of 1849. Fortune followed fame in swift abundance, as Sacramento became the supply center for prospectors, in an often ruthless seller's market. (Ironically, the Gold Rush brought only impoverishment to Sutter himself, as hordes of prospectors pillaged his property and put him heavily in debt.)

Sacramento was incorporated as a town in 1850 and selected as the state capital four years later. City incorporation came in 1863.

From 1849 to 1862, Sacramento was plagued by a series of disasters, including a serious fire and three devastating floods; yet always the town came back to flourish anew. (Over the years, the development of flood control techniques has greatly aided the city's growth.) A hub of river transport since its inception, Sacramento also became (in 1856) the terminus of California's first railroad and (in 1860) the western terminus of the Pony Express. In 1863 the Central Pacific Railroad began laying track east from Sacramento to meet the westward-reaching Union Pacific, and six years later the link was made, giving the country its first transcontinental rail route.

In 1978, a comprehensive plan was issued to guide public and private efforts in developing and revitalizing the center city. A $30-million redevelopment project is under way in an effort by retailers to move back into the downtown area.

Among Sacramento's many attractions are old Fort Sutter, built by Sutter and now maintained as a museum; the 1860 State Capitol; the old Governor's Mansion; the Crocker Art Gallery; Old Sacramento, a recreation of the original city, including restaurants, theaters, shops and such museums as the Pony Express Museum and the Railroad Museum.

ST. LOUIS

Location: East-central Missouri, near junction of Mississippi and Missouri rivers **County:** St. Louis is an independent city **City Area:** 61 sq. miles (158 sq. kilometers) **Altitude:** 455 feet (138.3 meters)
Mayor: James F. Conway
City Population: 622,236 (1970 census), 514,100 (1977 est.)
Metro Area Population: 2,410,602 (1970 census), 2,379,800 (1977 est.)
Daily Newspapers: 2 **No. of Commercial Radio Stations (AM):** 13 (1980) **No. of TV Stations:** 6 (1980)
City Chamber of Commerce: St. Louis Regional Commerce and Growth Association, 10 Broadway, St. Louis, Missouri 63102

St. Louis, the largest city in Missouri and the Mississippi River Valley, is surrounded by, but independent of, St. Louis County.

In 1763 the French fur trader Pierre Laclede chose the site for a trading post and a year later dispatched René Auguste Chouteau to build it. It was named St. Louis after Louis IX, the patron saint of France.

The settlement, which became part of the United States in 1803 with the Louisiana Purchase, was an important point of embarkation for expeditions to the West, such as that of Lewis and Clark in 1804. Incorporated in 1808, it did not expand rapidly until after the War of 1812, when immigrants coming by flatboat began to settle the West. Great Americans associated with the city include Charles Lindbergh, Thomas Hart Benton and Joseph Pulitzer.

Today manufacturing is the most important aspect of the economy. The St. Louis industrial area is the only one in the nation producing six basic metals: iron, lead, zinc, copper, aluminum, and magnesium. The city is also a major center for chemical industries and research. St. Louis is second only to Detroit in automobile assembly; it has one of the pioneer aerospace manufacturers; and it claims the world's largest brewery, Anheuser-Busch, Inc.

In 1966 St. Louis completed its 50,000-seat Busch Memorial Stadium. The following year the Jefferson National Expansion Memorial, a project of the National Park Service, was dedicated. The city erected the 630-foot stainless steel Gateway Arch, tallest monument in the country, as part of the memorial. The Arch attracts between 4- and 6-million visitors a year.

St. Louis, like many other cities, is seeking to rejuvenate its downtown area. In the Laclede's Landing section on the riverfront, old warehouses are being restored, and new restaurants and nightspots have revived night life in the area. A new $25-million Convention Center and new hotels are bringing more visitors to the city.

Points of interest in St. Louis include the Old Courthouse, scene of the Dred Scott case; Forest Park; the Missouri Botanical Garden; the Municipal Opera; the McDonnell Planetarium; and the Powell Symphony Hall.

ST. PAUL

Location: Eastern Minnesota, adjacent to Minneapolis at the junction of the Minnesota River with the Mississippi **County:** Ramsey **City Area:** 52.2 sq. miles (135.2 sq. kilometers) **Altitude:** 780 feet (237.0 meters)
Mayor: George Latimer
City Population: 309,866 (1970 census), 272,465 (1976 est.)
Metro Area Population: 1,965,391 (1970 census), 2,037,200 (1977 est.)
Daily Newspapers: 2 **No. of Commercial Radio Stations (AM):** 7 (1980) **No. of TV Stations:** 3 (1980)
City Chamber of Commerce: St. Paul Area Chamber of Commerce, Suite 300, Osborn Bldg., St. Paul, Minnesota 55102

St. Paul, capital of Minnesota and seat of Ramsey County, is contiguous with Minneapolis, with which it forms the Twin Cities metropolitan area, home for about half the state's population. A port of entry and a major transportation and industrial center, the city is situated on bluffs overlooking the Mississippi, close to the head of navigation. Its diverse economy includes meat packing, printing, publishing, steel fabrication, and the manufacture of automobiles, machinery, petroleum products, aerospace equipment, computers, food products, abrasives and cosmetics.

Permanent white settlement in the area began in 1819 with the establishment of an army post on the Minnesota River, on the site of Mendota, now a St. Paul suburb. The following year, the post was moved across the river, where Josiah Snelling built Fort St. Anthony, later named Fort Snelling. Thanks to its strategic location and a large supply of game, fur-trading flourished at Mendota, as did the trading of food and dry goods. After treaties with the Indians paved the way for settlement, many traders, lumbermen and others came from the East to make the area home.

In 1838 a community was begun on the site of present-day St. Paul, which was originally named Pig's Eye, after one of the settlers, a French-Canadian trader named Pierre "Pig's Eye" Parrant. But it soon came to be called St. Paul, in honor of the church built there in 1841 by Father Lucian Galtier. St. Paul was made the capital of Minnesota Territory in 1849, and was incorporated five years later. It was made the state capital in 1858, when Minnesota was admitted to the Union. With the advent of the railroad and the ready availability of immigrant labor (especially German and Irish), St. Paul's early prosperity was assured. The city limits were extended to the Minneapolis line in 1884.

Among the city's attractions are the Capitol Building (completed in 1904), which has the world's largest supported marble dome; the Cathedral of St. Paul; the St. Paul Arts and Science Center; the St. Paul Civic Opera, which specializes in light opera and operettas; Indian Mounds Park; and, on the outskirts of the city, Fort Snelling State Park. A major annual event is the St. Paul Winter Carnival, for which an ice palace is sculptured and a pageant enacted.

SALT LAKE CITY

Location: North-central Utah, southeast of the Great Salt Lake, at the foot of the Wasatch range **County:** Salt Lake **City Area:** 56 sq. miles (145 sq. kilometers) **Altitude:** 4,260 feet (1294.5 meters)
Mayor: Ted Wilson
City Population: 175,885 (1970 census), 168,667 (1976 est.)
Metro Area Population: 705,458 (1970 census), 822,200 (1977 est.)
Daily Newspapers: 2 **No. of Radio Stations:** 23 (1980) **No. of TV Stations:** 6 (1980)
City Chamber of Commerce: Salt Lake Area Chamber of Commerce, 19 East 2nd. South, Salt Lake City, Utah 84111

Salt Lake City, seat of Salt Lake County, is Utah's capital, its largest city, and headquarters of the 4 million members of the Mormon faith—the Church of Jesus Christ of Latter-day Saints. It was founded in 1847 by the Mormon leader Brigham Young. Mormon settlers soon transformed the arid region into irrigated farmland.

After 1849 Salt Lake City (called Great Salt Lake City until 1868) was a supply point for California-bound pioneers. A link to the transcontinental railroad in 1870 brought non-Mormons to the city and contributed to its growth. When Utah entered the Union in 1896, Salt Lake City became its capital.

Today the metropolis is an important distribution point for a rich agricultural and mining area, as well as an important air and rail hub. Its industries include printing and publishing, oil refining, copper refining, and the smelting of copper and iron. Electronics manufacturing is increasingly becoming an important industry. Major employers are Hill Air Force Base, 30 miles to the north, local defense industries, and the Kennecott Copper Corp.

The city lies at the foot of the beautiful Wasatch Mountains. The magnificent Utah State Capitol with its copper dome houses noted works of art and many interesting exhibits. The Salt Palace, a $17-million civic auditorium complex, was completed in 1969, since enlarged.

Centrally located Temple Square contains the most important buildings of the Mormon Church—the Mormon Temple, a mammoth granite structure designed under Brigham Young's direction and built between 1853 and 1893; and the Tabernacle, housing one of the world's largest organs.

Now completed is the tallest building in Salt Lake City, a 28-story office building for the Mormon church. A multimillion dollar arts project is the latest phase of the city's building boom. The Bicentennial Arts Center includes a concert hall for the Utah Symphony and a performing arts center. Under construction is Crossroads Plaza, a downtown shopping mall-hotel complex.

SAN ANTONIO

Location: South-central Texas, on the San Antonio River about 190 miles west of Houston **County:** Bexar **City Area:** 267 sq. miles (692 sq. kilometers) **Altitude:** 701 feet (231.3 meters)
Mayor: Lila Cockrell **City Manager:** Tom Huebner
City Population: 708,582 (1970 census), 783,765 (1976 est.)
Metro Area Population: 888,179 (1970 census), 1,024,900 (1977 est.)
Daily Newspapers: 3 **No. of Radio Stations:** 21 (1980) **No. of TV Stations:** 5 (1980)
City Chamber of Commerce: Greater San Antonio Chamber of Commerce, 602 East Commerce Street, P.O. Box 1628, San Antonio, Texas 78296

San Antonio, port of entry and seat of Bexar County, has developed into the banking and commerce hub of south central Texas, while retaining its history-rich Spanish-Mexican character, redolent of the days when Indian, Spanish, Mexican, Texan and United States forces all sought dominion there. Only 154 miles from the U.S.-Mexico border at Laredo, it is a bilingual city whose old missions and historic landmarks offer charming contrast to its modern factories, refineries and military installations.

Although the federal government is San Antonio's largest employer, farming, stock-raising, food processing and diversified manufacture are also important to its economy. The city's mild climate and natural beauty have made it a popular winter resort.

The site of San Antonio had been known to the Spanish, and to the Coahuiltecan Indians, long before 1718, when a military expedition led by Martín de Alarcón, Spanish governor of Coahuila and Texas, founded a town and fort there, the Villa (and Presidio) de Béjar. At the same time, missionaries founded the Mission San Antonio de Valero nearby; in 1724 the mission was moved from its original site to where the Alamo stands today.

In 1731 Spanish colonists from the Canary Islands founded San Fernando de Béjar, just west of Alarcón's settlement. By 1791 the three settlements—Villa de Béjar, Mission San Antonio de Valero and San Fernando de Béjar—came to be known as one, San Antonio de Béjar (later, simply, San Antonio).

The settlement grew in prominence and was the principal objective of the Mexican and Texas Revolutions (1821, 1836). In the latter conflict, on March 6, 1836, the famous battle of the Alamo took place, in which all of the nearly 200 defenders (including Davy Crockett) were killed by Mexican forces numbering over 2,400. However, the following month, spurred by the battlecry "Remember the Alamo!," the Texans gained ultimate victory at San Jacinto, and the Texas republic was born; a year later, San Antonio was incorporated.

During the later part of the 19th century, the town became a major cattle center, where herds were assembled and started on overland drives up the Chisholm Trail to the Kansas railheads. San Antonio's prosperity was aided by the advent of the railroad and, later, by the increased military presence there.

Among the city's attractions are the Alamo; La Villita, a reconstructed old Spanish settlement; the historic Governor's Palace and San Fernando Cathedral, both restored; the Arneson River Theater; and the Tower of the Americas, built during HemisFair '68. San Antonio is the home of five major universities and has one of the largest medical centers in the country at the University of Texas (San Antonio campus).

SAN DIEGO

Location: Southern California, on east side of San Diego Bay **County:** San Diego **City Area:** 319.5 sq. miles (810.7 sq. kilometers) **Altitude:** sea level
Mayor: Pete Wilson **City Manager:** Ray Blair
City Population: 697,027 (1970 census), 789,059 (1976 est.)
Metro Area Population: 1,357,854 (1970 census), 1,683,000 (1977 est.)
Daily Newspapers: 2 **No. of Commercial Radio Stations (AM):** 11 (1979) **No. of TV Stations:** 4 (1980)
City Chamber of Commerce: San Diego Chamber of Commerce, 110 W. "C" Street, Suite 3600, San Diego, California 92101

San Diego, seat of San Diego County, is a port of entry and the oldest permanent European settlement in California. The city has risen rapidly in size, from fifteenth largest in the country in 1970, and now ranks as the ninth largest in the United States.

Since Juan Rodriguez Cabrillo sailed into its bay in 1542, the area has been under four flags—that of Spain, Mexico, California, and the United States. In 1769 San Diego de Alcalá Mission was established by Junípero Serra, a Franciscan missionary. A settlement grew up and was incorporated (1850) as a city after California became part of the Union.

San Diego's excellent natural harbor has made it an important commercial center and the site of several large U.S. Navy installations. It is the distribution and processing hub for the surrounding farm and dairy region and has a wide variety of manufactures. It is the home of the Atlas missile, an aircraft producer, and it is an important oceanographic and health sciences center. San Diego has a large electronics industry. Recently 30 new companies have relocated to San Diego because of the availability of land and workers. Its magnificent climate and proximity to Mexico have made tourism a significant part of the economy.

San Diego's Balboa Park contains an art gallery, museums, gardens, a zoo, and some buildings from the Panama-California International Exposition (1915-16) and the California Pacific International Exposition (1935-36). In the Old Town area is a state park containing adobes from the Spanish and Mexican era. The Mission Bay park includes boat landings, water ski, fishing and swimming areas, hotels and Sea World, a huge marine animal amusement park.

A 16-mile trolley line, linking downtown San Diego with the Mexican border at Tijuana, will open in July 1981. The new light rail system is expected to carry 30,000 passengers daily and will operate with 14 modern trolley cars built in West Germany.

SAN FRANCISCO

Location: West-central California, on a peninsula between Pacific Ocean and San Francisco Bay **County:** San Francisco **City Area:** 46.3 sq. miles (119.9 sq. kilometers) **Altitude:** 65 feet (19.6 meters)
Mayor: Dianne Feinstein **Chief Administrative Officer:** Roger Boas
City Population: 715,674 (1970 census), 654,400 (1977 est.)
Metro Area Population: 3,107,355 (1970 census), 3,182,200 (1977 est.)
Daily Newspapers: 2 **No. of Commercial Radio Stations (AM):** 16 (1979) **No. of TV Stations:** 10 (1980)
City Chamber of Commerce: San Francisco Chamber of Commerce, 465 California Street, San Francisco, California 94104

San Francisco, coextensive with California's San Francisco County, is the financial center of the West and, together with the San Francisco Bay area, the largest port on the Pacific Coast.

In 1579 Sir Francis Drake stopped in the vicinity on his voyage around the world. In 1776 a mission, later known as Mission Dolores, and fort were founded at a site chosen by Juan Bautista de Anza. In 1846, during the Mexican War, a U.S. naval force under John Montgomery took Yerba Buena, the settlement that had grown up. The following year the community assumed the name of its bay, which, according to tradition, had been named after St. Francis of Assisi by Spanish voyagers in 1595.

In 1848 the California gold rush began and a flood of fortune seekers, adventurers, and settlers brought a period of lawlessness, during which San Francisco's waterfront section became notorious as the Barbary Coast, and vigilantes were organized to restore order. Newcomers from all over the world, including China, gave the city a cosmopolitan air. It was incorporated in 1850 and linked with the East by railroads in 1869.

On April 18, 1906, a disastrous earthquake and fire almost completely destroyed the city; an estimated 700 persons perished.

The opening of the Panama Canal, which stimulated trade, was celebrated by the Panama-Pacific Exposition of 1915. By 1939, the year of the Golden Gate International Exposition, San Francisco had become the leading industrial and commercial center of the Pacific Coast. During the Second World War, the city was the major mainland supply point and port of embarkation for the struggle in the Pacific.

San Francisco is the home of the Pacific Coast Stock Exchange and a Federal Reserve district bank. More than 65 industrial parks lie within a 50-mile radius of the city. Major industries include food processing, ship-building, petroleum refining, and the manufacture of metal products and chemicals. The city is also a noted cultural center.

Situated among steep hills, San Francisco is a colorful city of lovely vistas, graceful bridges, ornate mansions, imposing public buildings, and unusual districts. The Golden Gate Bridge (1937) links the city with Marin County to the north. San Francisco's scenic hills now hold apartment complexes and shopping centers, but despite the changes the city maintains its warm personality.

Rejuvenation of the inner city has come from the creation of block and merchant associations and the arrival of new department stores in the downtown area.

San Francisco is famous for its fine restaurants; its cable car system, preserved as a historic landmark; Chinatown—the country's largest—with its Oriental architecture, tearooms, and temples; Telegraph Hill, where in earlier times a signal tower sent word to the city of the arrival of ships and is now crowned with the Coit Memorial Tower; and Nob Hill, once the home of millionaires, is the site of the Cable Car Barn. Also of interest are Fisherman's Wharf, with its fishing fleet and seafood restaurants; the nearby National Maritime Museum and its historic ships; Ghirardelli Square and the Cannery, converted factories housing shops and restaurants; the Cow Hollow district, scene of art, book and specialty shops in an area of Victorian houses; and Golden Gate Park, with its planetarium, museum of natural history, aquarium, and flower gardens. The Cow Palace is the home of political conventions, sports events, and livestock exhibitions. In 1980 San Francisco celebrated the opening of the Louise M. Davies Symphony Hall, a fitting home for the great San Francisco Symphony.

SAN JOSE

Location: Western California, about 40 miles southeast of San Francisco in the Santa Clara Valley **County:** Santa Clara **City Area:** 136.2 sq. miles (352.8 sq. kilometers) **Altitude:** 90 feet (27.3 meters)
Mayor: Janet Gray Hayes **City Manager:** Francis Fox
City Population: 461,212 (1970 census), 573,806 (1976 est.)
Metro Area Population: 1,065,313 (1970 census), 1,217,300 (1977 est.)
Daily Newspapers: 2 **No. of Commercial Radio Stations (AM):** 13 (1979) **No. of TV Stations:** 3 (1980)
City Chamber of Commerce: San Jose Chamber of Commerce, One Paseo De San Antonio, San Jose, California 95113

San Jose, seat of Santa Clara County, is virtually contiguous with the city of Santa Clara, the two communities together forming the focal point of the fertile Santa Clara Valley, the world's largest dried fruit packing and canning region. In addition to its agricultural importance, San Jose has developed into a significant center for electronics research and diversified manufacturing. The "Silicon Valley" area is the nation's leading producer of semi-conductors.

San Jose (originally the Pueblo de San José de Guadalupe) was founded in 1777 by José Joaquin Moraga, as a Spanish military supply base, and soon also became an ecclesiastical center. After the territory came under U.S. control, San Jose was made (in 1849) California's first capital, although statehood was not officially achieved until 1850, the year San Jose also became the state's first incorporated city. It remained the capital until 1851, when the seat of state government shifted to Vallejo.

In its early years, San Jose served as a supply base for gold prospectors and as a bustling fruit trade depot. The coming of the railroad (in 1864), connecting the community to San Francisco, consolidated its importance as a distribution point for the increasingly bountiful produce of the Santa Clara Valley. This in turn gave rise to the growth of industries to equip the region's farms and service the needs of a growing populace.

Between 1940 and 1960, San Jose's population increased three-fold; from 1960 to 1970, it more than doubled, making San Jose-Santa Clara one of the nation's largest urban areas. This rapid growth was seen as a plus by developers, politicians and retailers. However, the growth has led to the decay of the downtown area, air pollution and traffic congestion. A rethinking of San Jose's growth future has come with Mayor Hayes' reelection. Initial efforts at "in-filling" and redevelopment of areas within the city, instead of continued urban sprawl, appears to be successful.

Places of interest in San Jose include the Municipal Rose Garden; Mission San José de Guadalupe, dating from 1779; the home of poet Edwin Markham; Winchester Mystery House; Rosicrucian Park; and, nearby the Lick Observatory (atop Mount Hamilton) and Alum Rock Park, a popular 687-acre spa well known for its mineral springs and scenic allure.

SEATTLE

Location: West-central Washington, on Puget Sound and west shore of Lake Washington **County:** King **City Area:** 92 sq. miles (238 sq. kilometers) **Altitude:** 10 feet (3.0 meters)
Mayor: Charles Royer
City Population: 530,831 (1970 census), 490,586 (1976 est.)
Metro Area Population: 1,424,605 (1970 census), 1,427,200 (1977 est.)
Daily Newspapers: 2 **No. of Commercial Radio Stations (AM):** 19 (1980) **No. of TV Stations:** 4 (1980)
City Chamber of Commerce: Seattle Chamber of Commerce, 215 Columbia Street, Seattle, Washington 98104

Seattle, seat of King County, is Washington's largest city and the largest in the Pacific Northwest. It is a manufacturing, trade, and transportation center, and a major port of entry. The city is situated on seven hills and is flanked by the majestically beautiful Cascade and Olympic Mountains. Within its limits are four lakes, 48 parks and more than 22 miniparks.

Seattle began as a small lumber settlement in 1851. It was platted two years later and named for a chief of the Duwamish and Suquamish Indians. Incorporated in 1869, it remained a small lumber town until the arrival of the railroad in 1884. Subsequent strikes, anti-Chinese riots, and a great fire in 1889 did not prevent the city from growing rapidly. With the 1897-98 Alaska gold rush, Seattle became a boom town and was the nation's chief link with Alaska. Further growth came with the Alaska-Yukon-Pacific Exposition (1909), the opening of the Panama Canal (1914), and the completion (1917) of a canal and locks making the city both a saltwater and freshwater port. In 1919 the Industrial Workers of the World (IWW) led a general strike in Seattle, long a center of the radical labor movement. A series of various municipal scandals led to the election in 1926 of a reform candidate, Bertha K. Landis, the first woman mayor of a large American city.

World War II made the city a center of aircraft manufacturing and shipbuilding. The Boeing Company is the largest employer in the area. Although the region underwent a severe recession in the early 1970s due to a slackening of the aerospace industry, the area's economy and the aircraft industry are booming again. The construction of the trans-Alaska crude oil pipeline did much to bolster Seattle's economy. Other important industries today are electronics, food processing, lumber, chemical products, metal goods and machinery production.

The Seattle downtown area has taken on a new look. Since 1970 almost half of the downtown has been rebuilt. Seattle has become an important cultural center on the West Coast. It boasts a first-rate Opera House, the Seattle Symphony Orchestra, several active theater companies, and a fine arts museum. Of interest in the city is the Seattle Center, site of the Century 21 Exposition. It is connected to the downtown area by a monorail line and contains the opera house, arena, coliseum, and International Fountain, the world-famous 606-foot Space Needle, and the Pacific Science Center. Also of interest are Pike Place Market, Underground Seattle and the old Pioneer Square district.

Seattle is the home of the Mariner Baseball Team, the Seahawks Football Team, the Sounders Soccer Team, and the Smashers Volleyball Team.

TAMPA

Location: On the west coast of Florida at the mouth of the Hillsboro River on Tampa Bay. **County:** Hillsborough **City Area:** 84.5 sq. miles (218.9 sq. kilometers) **Altitude:** 15 feet (4.6 meters)
Mayor: Bob Martinez
City Population: 277,714 (1970 census), 271,365 (1976 est.)
Metro Area Population: 1,088,549 (1970 census), 1,380,500 (1977 est.)
Daily Newspapers: 2 **No. of Radio Stations:** 13 (1980) **No. of TV Stations:** 4 (1980)
City Chamber of Commerce: Greater Tampa Chamber of Commerce, P.O. Box 420, Tampa, Florida 33601

Tampa, a port of entry and the closest port to the Panama Canal, is located on Tampa Bay, an inlet of the Gulf of Mexico. Once known almost exclusively as a vacation spot and a source of fine cigars, Tampa, which is the seat of Hillsborough County, today has also emerged as one of Florida's most industrialized cities and the trade center of the state's west coast. Its economy ranges from food processing and phosphate shipping to the manufacture of a wide variety of goods, including fertilizer, paint, cement, cigars, fabricated steel, and electronic equipment. Nearby is MacDill Air Force Base, headquarters for the U.S. Readiness Command. Tampa International Airport, which is served by 16 airlines, has been called "the best airport in the world" in the press. The downtown area is undergoing major redevelpment activity.

At least two Spanish explorers, and probably more, visited the site of Tampa in the 16th century: Panfilo de Narváez (1528) and Hernando de Soto (1539). Seminole Indians successfully resisted white men's efforts to settle in the area until 1823, when a contingent of U.S. troops established Fort Brooke there. By 1831 the settlement that had grown up around the fort had come to be known by its former Indian name of Tampa; it was incorporated in 1849. During the Civil War, Tampa was bombarded by gunboats.

Development of Tampa began in earnest in 1885 with the coming of Henry B. Plant's narrow-gauge South Florida Railroad—and his port improvements and tourism promotions. The economy got another boost when the manufacture of cigars was begun (in 1886) at Ybor City, which soon became a part of Tampa proper. Tourism was spurred in 1891 by the completion of the lavish, Moorish-style Tampa Bay Hotel, which today houses the University of Tampa. In 1898, during the Spanish-American War, Tampa served as the embarkation point for Colonel "Teddy" Roosevelt and his "Rough Riders." In the mid-1920s the man-made Davis Islands in Tampa Bay were completed, providing choice sites for hotels, residences and various resort facilities.

Among Tampa's attractions are Ybor city, the city's Latin quarter, famous for its Spanish restaurants and shops, and the Busch Gardens, Florida's second-largest attraction. Tampa Museum, opened in July, 1979, is the city's first major public effort at a permanent art museum. Under construction is the Center for Science and Industry, expected to be completed in 1980. It has already won the Owen Corning Energy Conservation Award for its energy conservation design and for its use of solar panels. The Gasparilla Festival, a one-day event in honor of the alleged pirate José Gaspar, is celebrated in February with a mock invasion of the city.

WASHINGTON, D.C.

Location: Between Virginia and Maryland, on Potomac River **City Area:** 68.2 sq. miles (176.7 sq. kilometers) **Altitude:** 72 feet (21.9 meters)
Mayor: Marion S. Barry, Jr. **City Administrator:** Elijah B. Rogers
City Population: 756,668 (1970 census), 685,000 (1977 est.)
Metro Area Population: 2,910,111 (1970 census), 3,020,100 (1977 est.)
Daily Newspapers: 2 **No. of Commercial Radio Stations (AM):** 18 (1980) **No. of TV Stations:** 6 (1980)

City Chamber of Commerce: District of Columbia Chamber of Commerce, 1319 F Street, N.W., Suite 904, Washington, D.C. 20004

Washington, D.C., is not only the capital of the United States but an important business and financial center, with over 1,800 professional and trade associations headquartered there. Since 1895, when Georgetown became part of Washington, it has been coextensive with the District of Columbia. Washington's large government work force insures a more recession-proof climate than in other major markets.

The District was established by Congress in 1790-91, and George Washington selected the exact site for the "Federal City," which was designed by Pierre L'Enfant and laid out by Andrew Ellicott. Maryland and Virginia ceded land for the District, and the capital moved there from Philadelphia in 1800. Thomas Jefferson was the first President to be inaugurated in Washington.

During the War of 1812, the city fell to the British, who burned the Capitol, White House, and other public buildings. During the Civil War, the city was threatened by Confederate forces.

1878 marked the end of home rule for the district, with city officials thereafter being appointed by the President. Since 1961, however, when residents were given the right to vote in Presidential elections, Washingtonians have sought to increase local self-government and national political representation. Residents were allowed to elect their own school board in 1968, and full home rule followed in 1975. Under the Nixon Administration, the District of Columbia was granted non-voting representation in Congress, with Walter E. Fauntroy sworn in on April 19, 1971, as Washington's first Representative in nearly 100 years. And in an historic move, Congress voted in 1978 to approve a constitutional amendment giving the District full elected representation in both the House and the Senate. The amendment gives Washington two Senators—expanding the Senate from 100 to 102—and either one or two Representatives, based on the District's 1980 census. The amendment must now be ratified by at least 38 state legislatures by the summer of 1985 for it to become law. So far, nine states have ratified and twelve have rejected the amendment (Sept. 1980).

Washington, with its broad tree-shaded thoroughfares and open vistas, has many imposing buildings. The Capitol and White House are the most historic. Other leading tourist attractions are the Washington Monument and Lincoln and Jefferson Memorials. The many additional points of interest in or near the city include the Library of Congress; the National Archives, which houses the Declaration of Independence, the Constitution, and the Bill of Rights; the Supreme Court Building; Constitution Hall; the Smithsonian Institution; the National Gallery of Art; the numerous embassies; the Pentagon; the U.S. Naval Observatory; and Mount Vernon. The fashionable Georgetown area was designated a national monument in 1967.

The Arlington Memorial Bridge across the Potomac River connects Washington with Arlington National Cemetery. Among the city's beautiful parks are West Potomac Park, which includes the Tidal Basin with the famous Japanese cherry trees; East Potomac Park; Rock Creek Park and the adjoining National Zoological Park; and Anacostia Park.

Washington's Metro, the computerized subway system which opened in 1976, is having mixed results. While linking the downtown area with the airport, Capitol Hill and Washington's suburbs, the Metro must accommodate the multitude of passengers with a shortage of cars due to malfunctions.

Public and private redevelopment has given downtown Washington a new face. Currently under way is the joint $500-million public-private Pennsylvania Avenue Development Plan for combined residential-commercial use, and the $60-million expansion of the Sheraton Park Hotel in northwest Washington. In 1980, construction began on a $99-million convention center north of the Mall that officials hope will one day attract the city's first national political convention.

U.S. OUTLYING AREAS

The areas under United States sovereignty or otherwise associated with some type of American jurisdiction extend through the Caribbean and almost across the Pacific. From east to west, the Virgin Islands of the United States, in the Caribbean, lie 160° from the Palau Islands in the American-administered Trust Territory of the Pacific Islands, nearly halfway around the world. The distance between Point Barrow in northern Alaska, 71.5° north of the equator, and American Samoa in the southwest Pacific, 14° south of the equator, is nearly half of that from pole to pole.

American Samoa—*Status:* Unorganized unincorporated territory. *Population:* 31,500 (1977 est.). *Area:* 83 sq. mi. *Seat of government:* Pago Pago (2,451).

American Samoa consists of six small Pacific islands in that part of the Samoan islands lying east of 171°W., plus Swains Island, 250 miles north of Tutuila. It is roughly 2,200 miles southwest of Hawaii and 1,600 miles northeast of the northern tip of New Zealand.

In 1977 American Samoa held its first popular election for governor. The victor, Peter Tali Coleman, a native of the islands, was inaugurated on January 3, 1978. There is a legislature, the *Fono*, with limited authority, the House of Representatives being elected by universal suffrage, the Senate by the native chiefs. Samoan society is rigidly stratified, and the chiefs, of whom there are some 600 of varying ranks, have firm, paternalistic control over their followers.

The six islands in the Samoan group came under American hegemony in 1899, when Great Britain and Germany renounced their claims in favor of the United States, and Swains was added in 1925. American Samoa's native inhabitants are U.S. nationals; they are not American citizens but may migrate freely to the United States. In October 1978, President Carter signed into law an act of Congress giving the islands a nonvoting delegate to the U.S. House of Representatives.

Guam—*Status:* Organized unincorporated territory. *Population:* 115,000 (1977 est.). *Area:* 212 sq. mi. *Capital* Agana (2,110).

This island in the western Pacific is the most southerly of the Marianas, 1,300 miles east of the Philippines and 1,475 miles south of Japan, at 13°27'N. and 144°47'E. Of volcanic origin, it is mountainous in the south, a plateau in the north. The climate is tropical, with moderately heavy rainfall. The indigenes—the Chamorros—make up about half the population. Most of the rest are military or other government transients. English is the official language. About 95 percent of the native Guamanians are Roman Catholics.

U.S. military installations and tourism are the most significant factors in the economy. Guam is the only American territory without excise duties (except for tobacco, liquid fuel, and liquor).

Guam's administration is under the U.S. Department of the Interior. Its people are U.S. citizens (however, they do not vote in national elections but do have a nonvoting delegate in the House of Representatives). The governor and lieutenant governor are elected by the people. There is an elected unicameral legislature. On August 4, 1979, Guam residents rejected a proposed constitution drafted in December 1977 which allowed the island more self-government. Most islanders felt that it did not provide residents with the same rights as other Americans.

Howland, Baker, and Jarvis Islands—*Status:* Unincorporated possession. *Population:* Uninhabited. *Area:* 2.77 sq. mi.

These three small islands are situated in the South Pacific: Howland at 48°N.,176°38'W., Baker at 0°15'N.,176°27'W. and Jarvis at 0°23'S.,160°02'W. Howland and Baker are coral atolls about 35 miles apart and some 2,000 miles southwest of Honolulu. Jarvis lies some 1,500 miles south of Honolulu. They had rich guano deposits that were worked by American interests in the 1850s; however, when that industry faded, the islands had no value until the trans-Pacific aviation era began in the 1930s. In 1934 the United States reasserted its claim to them, based on the fact that they had been mentioned in the Guano Act of 1856.

Johnston Atoll—*Status:* Unincorporated possession. *Population:* 1,007 (1970 census). *Area:* .91 sq. mi.

This Pacific atoll lies 715 miles southwest of Honolulu, at 16°45'N. and 169°30'W. It consists of a reef around four islets. Johnston was annexed in 1858 by both the United States and the Kingdom of Hawaii. A quantity of guano was removed during the next 50 years, and for a long time the area was also a bird reservation. It was taken over by the U.S. Navy in 1934.

In 1958 and 1962 it was the site of high-altitude nuclear tests. In 1971 the Defense Department started to move 13,000 tons of nerve and mustard gas stored on Okinawa to igloo-shaped structures on Johnston.

Kingman Reef—*Status:* Unincorporated possession. *Population:* Uninhabited. *Area:* .01 sq. mi.

This bare reef in the Pacific lies 35 miles northwest of Palmyra Island and 1,000 miles south of Honolulu at 6°24'S. 162°22'W. It was annexed by the United States in 1922 and placed under the U.S. Navy in 1934.

Midway Islands—*Status:* Unincorporated possession. *Population:* 2,000 (1977 est.). *Area:* 1.9 sq. mi.

Midway is near the western end of the Hawaiian chain, 1,200 miles northwest of Honolulu, at 28°12'-17'N. and 177°19'-26'W. It consists of an atoll with two islets.

Made a possession in 1867 and placed under the U.S. Navy in 1903, Midway was the scene of one of the great air/sea battles of World War II. Today it is a naval installation; its chief executive is a naval officer. Midway is noted as a nesting site for seabirds.

Navassa Island—*Status:* Unincorporated possession. *Population:* Uninhabited. *Area:* 2 sq. mi.

Navassa lies in the Caribbean between Jamaica and Haiti, 30 miles west of the latter. It was certified in 1865 as appertaining to the United States under the Guano Act of 1856. A presidential proclamation of 1916 declared it to be under the sole jurisdiction of the United States and reserved it for lighthouse purposes. It is administered by the Coast Guard.

Palmyra Island—*Status:* Unincorporated possession. *Population:* Uninhabited. *Area:* 3.85 sq. mi.

An atoll of more than 50 islets, Palmyra is located in the Pacific 1,000 miles south of Honolulu, at 5°52'N. and 162°06'W. It is covered with dense foliage, coconut trees, and pisonis grandis, a 100-foot-tall balsalike tree.

Claimed by the Kingdom of Hawaii in 1862, the atoll was annexed by the United States with Hawaii in 1898. Excluded from Hawaii's boundaries when the latter became a state in 1959, it was placed under the administration of the U.S. Secretary of the Interior in 1961. In 1979 the U.S. government proposed purchasing the privately-owned island for use as a nuclear waste storage site.

Puerto Rico—*Status:* Commonwealth (Estado Libre Asociado). *Population:* 3,214,000 (1977 est.). *Area:* 3,435 sq. mi. *Capital:* San Juan (452,749).

Puerto Rico, 885 miles southeast of the southern coast of Florida, is the easternmost island of the Greater Antilles in the Caribbean. It is separated from the Dominican Republic to the west by the 61 miles of Mona Passage. To the east, St. Thomas of the U.S. Virgin Islands is 34 miles away. Among the offshore islands are Vieques and Culebra to the east, Mona to the west.

The island is crossed by mountain ranges and ringed by a coastal plain that is 15 miles wide at its broadest. The climate is mildly tropical. Rainfall is moderate in the coastal areas, but heavier in the interior mountains.

Many of the people are of mixed African-Spanish descent. (The original Arawak Indians were destroyed in the 16th century.) English and Spanish are the official languages, but Spanish is commonly spoken. Roman Catholicism predominates.

Before World War II, the Puerto Rican economy was based on sugar and such related products as rum. Needlework, mostly piecework produced by women at home, was the second most important activity, and tobacco growing the third. Unemployment was high, poverty widespread; however, after the war a determined drive was begun to foster industrialization on the island.

Under then Governor Rexford Guy Tugwell and the Puerto Rican legislative leader Luis Muñoz Marin, the framework for economic expansion was established. In 1948, "Operation Bootstrap" commenced, giving tax exemptions to new or expanded industry. By 1971 the program had attracted $2 billion in industrial investments and 2,000 plants. The successor program will continue or expand incentives and hopes to attract $4 billion more through 1980.

Today, income from manufacturing is more than three times that from agriculture, although sugar, coffee, tobacco, and rum are still produced and exported. Among the industries attracted by the tax abatement and lower wage scales in Puerto Rico are textiles and apparel, leather and shoes, electronic components, pharmaceuticals, tuna canning, and—increasingly—such heavy industries as metal products and petrochemicals.

In addition, tourist facilities and tourism have greatly expanded. Despite the general economic advance, unemployment continues to be much higher than in the United States. The per capita income, while far below that of the United States, exceeds that of any Latin American country.

Puerto Ricans are U.S. citizens and, if they migrate to this country, vote subject only to local electoral requirements. Puerto Rico does not send members to Congress (although it has a Resident Commissioner in the House of Representatives who may introduce legislation but does not have a vote) and Puerto Rico is not liable to federal taxation.

Beginning in 1948 (as the first elected governor), Luis Muñoz Marin—leader of the Popular Democratic party and the force behind "Operation Bootstrap"—served four terms, retiring in 1964. During this period the main minority faction was the Statehood Republican party, which advocated U.S. statehood for Puerto Rico as opposed to the commonwealth status championed by the Popular Democrats. In a plebiscite held in 1967, the vote was 60.5 percent for continuation of commonwealth status, and 38.9 percent for statehood.

In the 1968 gubernatorial election, however, Luis A. Ferré, long a prominent Statehood Republican, who ran as the candidate of the New Progressive party (which he had helped form during the plebiscite campaign), won with more than 44 percent of the vote. Although Ferré's platform advocated statehood for Puerto Rico, he had made it clear that such a step would depend on a plebiscite "separate from the general elections." In 1972 Ferré was defeated by Rafael Hernández-Colón of the Popular Democratic party, but in 1976 the New Progressives returned to power under Carlos Romero Barcelo.

Although advocates of Puerto Rican independence have had little impact at the polls, there has long been such a movement on the island. Perhaps its leading figure was the Harvard-educated Pedro Albizu Campos, who died in 1965, aged 73. A leader of the Nationalist party in Puerto Rico, in 1950 he staged an abortive armed revolt, which included an attempt by some of his followers to assassinate President Truman.

Columbus claimed the island for Spain in 1493 on his second voyage to the New World. Spanish colonization began under Ponce de León in 1508. Occupied by American troops during the Spanish-American War, the island was ceded to the United States by Spain in 1898. Congress provided for its civil government by the Foraker Act of 1900 and granted Puerto Ricans U.S. citizenship in 1917 by an "Organic Act," known as the Jones Act. In 1947 Puerto Rico obtained the right to elect its governor. Commonwealth status in free association with the United States was achieved in 1952. Operating under a constitution much like that of the United States, Puerto Rico has an elected legislature consisting of a Senate and a House of Representatives. In 1977, the Puerto Rican legislature provided for the selection of delegates to the Democratic and Republican conventions by presidential primary. More than 600,000 voters participated in the 1980 election of delegates to the two parties' national conventions.

Migration from Puerto Rico to the mainland has varied with the economic conditions here and on the island. It was very heavy during much of the 1950s, and the 1970 census counted more than 1.8 million persons of Puerto Rican birth in the United States. Substantial numbers of Puerto Ricans have also returned to the island from the United States.

In September 1978, the United Nations Decolonization Committee passed a Cuban-sponsored resolution calling for self-determination for Puerto Rico, recommending that it be included on the UN's list of nongoverning territories as a U.S. colony. In response, committees in both houses of Congress approved resolution in 1979 reaffirming American support of self-determination for the island's people; Gov. Romero-Barceló has pledged to call a referendum on the island's status after the 1980 gubernatorial elections.

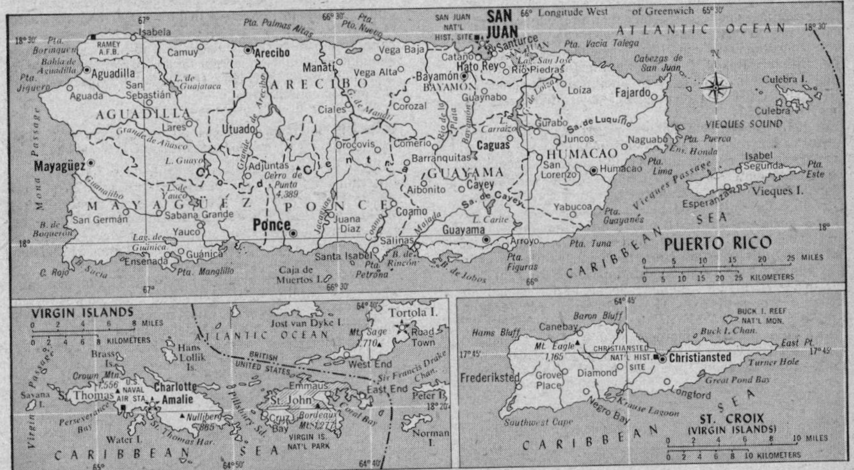

Trust Territory of the Pacific Islands—*Status:* UN Trust Territory. *Population:* 140,000 (1979 est.), Northern Mariana Is. 15,700 (1976 est.). *Area:* 8,511 sq. mi. including lagoons (707 sq. mi. of land). *Administrative Center:* Saipan, Northern Mariana Islands.

These islands and atolls, generally known as Micronesia, are scattered over an area of more than three million sq. mi. There are more than 3,000 of them, about 100 inhabited. They stretch 2,300 miles from some 500 miles east of the Philippines almost as far east as the international date line, from about 1° to 22°N. and from 130° to 172°E. The islands fall into three major groups—the Carolines (including the Palau Islands), the Marshalls, and the Marianas (excluding Guam). A number of the islands were the scene of bitter fighting during World War II—Peleliu in the Carolines, Saipan in the Marianas, Kwajalein in the Marshalls. Bikini and Enewetak in the Marshalls have been used as nuclear-test sites.

Subsistence agriculture (coconuts, cassava, copra, bananas, yams) and fishing are the main economic activities; copra and fish are the chief exports. Tourism is being developed.

The area is under the jurisdiction of the U.S. Secretary of the Interior; administrative authority is vested in a high commissioner who is appointed by the president. Following the establishment of the new island governments beginning in 1976 (see below), the duties of the high commissioner were limited to carrying out UN Trust Territory policy.

Beginning in 1565 the islands gradually came under tenuous Spanish control. Strong German penetration into the Marshall Islands in the late nineteenth century resulted in the sale of the whole area to Germany by Spain in 1899. Following Germany's defeat in the First World War, they were placed under Japanese mandate. In 1947, following the end of World War II, they entered the UN Trusteeship system under American administration as a "strategic" trust: one in which military bases are permissible.

For many years after assuming its trusteeship, the United States neglected the area, permitting the Japanese-built road system and sanitary facilities to deteriorate. In 1966, the World Health Organization reported that health conditions were bad; the United States has pledged improvements in this field.

In 1969, Secretary of the Interior Hickel visited the islands and promised immediate steps would be taken to increase the territory's self-government and assure that equal wages would be paid to Micronesians and Americans for doing comparable work. At the same time, it was reported that a political status commission, appointed by the Trust Territory-wide Congress of Micronesia in 1967, had recommended that the territory be made a self-governing nation in free association with the United States or, failing that, seek complete independence. An offer by the United States of "Commonwealth status" like that of Puerto Rico was rejected by the Congress of Micronesia in 1970. The Trust Territory's Congress of Micronesia was dissolved in 1978.

In 1975 the **Northern Mariana Islands** voted in favor of future commonwealth status and in 1976 the U.S. Congress approved a plan making the islands a commonwealth associated with the United States. Following a March 1977 referendum approving a new constitution—providing for an elected bicameral legislature and an elected governor—Carlos S. Camacho became the islands' first democratically elected chief executive, and the first native islander to administer the Northern Marianas in over 400 years of foreign domination. The bicameral Legislature consists of a 9-member Senate and a 14-member House of Representatives. The administrative center is on Saipan.

In a July 12, 1979, referendum, four of the six island districts of the Trust Territory—Ponape, Yap, Kosrae and Truk—voted to accept "free association" with the U.S. as the **Federated States of Micronesia (FSM)**. Such status entails continued American financial support for 15 years, with Washington to retain responsibility for defense; otherwise the islands will become fully self-governing when the United States terminates its UN Trusteeship in 1981. Tosiwo Nakayama was elected president in 1979. The federal Congress consists of a Senate and a House of Representatives. The capital is Kolonia on Ponape.

The **Marshall Islands** electorate rejected membership in the FSM in the July 1979 referendum. Under May 1979 constitution, legislation is the function of the *Nitijela* which meets at the government center on Majuro atoll. The president is Amata Kabua. Bikini and Kwajalein, scene of postwar nuclear tests, are located in the Marshalls.

The Palau group, now the **Republic of Belau**, also rejected inclusion in the FSM. Under the republican constitution of 1979, the government consists of a president and a legislature *(the Olbiil era Kelulau)* with 28 elected representatives and 16 non-voting chiefs. The seat of government is on Koror.

Virgin Islands—*Status:* Organized unincorporated territory. *Population:* 110,000 (1977 est.). *Area:* 133 sq. mi. *Capital:* Charlotte Amalie (12,220), on St. Thomas.

The Virgin Islands of the United States form the western end of the Lesser Antilles between the Caribbean and the Atlantic, about 34 miles east of Puerto Rico. They comprise nearly 100 islands and cays, but only three islands are significant—St. Thomas (27 sq. mi.), St. Croix (82 sq. mi.), and St. John (19 sq. mi.). The United States bought the Virgin Islands from Denmark for $25 million in 1917.

St. Thomas is mountainous, with many harbors, of which Charlotte Amalie is one of the finest in the Caribbean. The climate is subtropical, moderated by the trade winds. Rainfall is variable and sometimes so light as to cause drought. Seventy percent of the population is black, many of whom are immigrants from other Antillean islands. Of the rest, considerably more than half are from the United States. English is the official language.

Since the phasing out of the peasant-based sugarcane agriculture, there has been little farming on the islands. Tourism is the major industry, and the area has the greatest number of cruise-ship calls in the world. Oil refining and bauxite processing are important; labor-intensive light industry has been introduced. More than half the island of St. John is occupied by the Virgin Islands National Park.

The U.S. Department of the Interior has jurisdiction over the islands. The governor has been elected since 1970. Juan Luis became governor in January 1978 on the death of Cyril E. King. Virgin Islanders are U.S. citizens, but cannot vote in national elections and have no Congressional representation, except for a non-voting delegate in the House since April 1972. In March 1979 voters rejected a proposed constitution.

Wake Island—*Status:* Possession. *Population:* 150 (1974 est.). *Area:* 2.5 sq. mi. *Administrative Center:* Wake Islet.

Wake lies in the Pacific some 2,000 miles west of Honolulu and 1,500 miles northeast of Guam, at 19°17'N. and 166°35'E. It is an atoll comprising three islets—Wake, Wilkes, and Peale. They are formed of coral built up on the rim of an underwater volcano; the land averages only 12 feet above sea level. Waves driven by 200-knot winds from Typhoon Sarah swept over the three islets in 1967.

The island has an aviation base with a 9,800-foot runway. Responsibility for its civil administration was vested in the U.S. Secretary of the Interior in 1962, but since 1974 has been under the Air Force Department.

Wake Island was annexed in 1899. It was attacked by the Japanese on December 7, 1941, and later that month fell after an heroic defense by the small Marine garrison.

U.S. TERRITORIAL ACQUISITIONS, POSSESSIONS, AND LEASEHOLDS

Year	Acquisition

— **Gross Area (888,685 sq. mi.)** Original territory of the first 13 states and their claims, including part of drainage basin of Red River of the North, south of the 49th parallel, sometimes considered part of Louisiana Purchase; completely acquired by independence treaty (1783; ratified, 1784) with Great Britain.

1803 **Gross Area (827,192 sq. mi.)** Louisiana Purchase acquired from France for about $15 million (60 million francs); total payment, including interest: $23,213,567.73.

1819 **Gross Area (72,003 sq. mi.)** Florida and adjacent areas purchased from Spain for amount not exceeding $5 million; treaty ratified 1821.

1845 **Gross Area (390,144 sq. mi.)** Independent Republic of Texas annexed and admitted as a state.

1846 **Gross Area (285,580 sq. mi.)** Oregon Territory acquired by treaty with Great Britain, terminating joint occupation.

1848 **Gross Area (529,017 sq. mi.)** Mexican Cession acquired out of the Mexican War; the United States paid $15 million.

1853 **Gross Area (29,640 sq. mi.)** Gadsden Purchase negotiated with Mexico for $10 million; treaty ratified 1854.

1858 **Gross Area (.91 sq. mi.)** By terms of the Guano Island Act (1856), stipulating that the United States could take possession of any uninhabited guano island, Johnston and Sand Islands in the Pacific were claimed; they constitute a possession.

1862 **Gross Area (3.85 sq. mi.)** Palmyra Island, 1,000 miles south of Honolulu, annexed by Hawaii but not included in the state; it constitutes a possession.

1863 **Gross Area (1 sq. mi.)** Under the Guano Island Act (1856), the Swan Islands in the Caribbean were claimed by the United States. The U.S. recognized Honduran sovereignty over the islands on September 1, 1972.

1865 **Gross Area (2 sq. mi.)** Under the Guano Island Act (1856), Navassa in the Caribbean was claimed; it constitutes a possession.

1867 **Gross Area (586,412 sq. mi.)** Alaska purchased from Russia for $7.2 million.
Gross Area (1.9 sq. mi) Midway Islands, 1,200 miles NW of Honolulu, annexed; they are a possession.

1898 **Gross Area (6,450 sq. mi.)** Independent Republic of Hawaii annexed.
Gross Area (212 sq. mi.) Guam, in the Western Pacific area, conquered from Spain and formally annexed by peace treaty (ratified, 1899); it constitutes an organized unincorporated territory.
Gross Area (115,707 sq. mi.) Philippines conquered from Spain; peace treaty (ratified, 1899) stipulated payment of $20 million for the islands; the Philippines became independent on July 4, 1946.
Gross Area (3,435 sq. mi.) Puerto Rico conquered from Spain and formally annexed by peace treaty (ratified, 1899); granted commonwealth status by Act of Congress on July 25, 1952.

1899 **Gross Area (2.5 sq. mi.)** Wake Island in Central Pacific claimed; it constitutes a possession.

1899 **Gross Area (83 sq. mi.)** American Samoa acquired by partition treaty (ratified, 1900) with Great Britain and Germany; it constitutes an unorganized, unincorporated territory.

1903 **Gross Area (647 sq mi.)** Canal Zone leased from Panama (treaty ratified, 1904); United States paid $10 million supplemented by annual amounts of $250,000 (1913-33); $430,000 (1934-55); $1.93 million (1956-1971); $2.095 million (1972); and $2.33 million (1974 to date). Under the terms of the 1977 treaty, the Canal Zone reverted to Panama on October 1, 1979.
Gross Area (30 sq. mi.) Guantanamo leased from Cuba for coaling and naval station.

1914 **Gross Area (4.6 sq. mi.)** Corn Islands leased for 99 years from Nicaragua for payment of $3 million; treaty (ratified, 1916) included perpetual right to construct and maintain a ship canal through Lake Nicaragua. The canal rights and the lease of the islands were terminated on April 25, 1971.

1916 **Gross Area (133 sq. mi.)** Virgin Islands purchased from Denmark for $25 million by treaty (ratified in 1917); they constitute an organized unincorporated territory.

1919 **Gross Area (each less than 0.5 sq. mi.)** By terms of the Guano Island Act (1856), Quita Sueño Bank, Roncador Cay, and Serrana Bank in the Caribbean were claimed; 1928 treaty provided Colombia with fishing rights in adjacent waters. On September 8, 1972, the United States renounced all claims.

1922 **Gross Area (.01 sq. mi.)** Kingman Reef in the South Pacific annexed by Act of Congress; it constitutes a possession.

1925 **Gross Area (1.33 sq. mi.)** Swains Island in the Pacific annexed by Resolution of Congress and incorporated in American Samoa.

1934 **Gross Area (2.77 sq. mi. combined)** U.S. control of Howland, Baker, and Jarvis islands in the South Pacific was reasserted under terms of the Guano Island Act (1856); they are possessions.

1939 **Gross Area (27 sq. mi.)** Canton and Enderbury Islands, 1,660 miles SW of Honolulu, controlled jointly by Britain and the United States. They are to be ceded to Kiribati, when the 1979 draft treaty comes into force.

1947 **Gross Land Area (707 sq. mi)** Trust Territory of the Pacific Islands, about 3,000 Micronesian islands and atolls including the Caroline, Marshall, and Mariana groups (except Guam) placed under U.S. jurisdiction by UN Trusteeship System.

1952 **Gross Area (848 sq. mi.)** Ryukyu Islands, including Okinawa, under U.S. jurisdiction by peace treaty with Japan; other islands included in treaty but returned to Japan by an agreement, June 26, 1968, are: Volcano Islands, including Iwo Jima (11 sq. mi.), Bonin Islands (40 sq. mi.), Marcus Island (1 sq. mi.), Rosario Island (less than 0.5 sq. mi.), and Parece Vela. All of the remaining territory was formally returned to Japan on May 15, 1972.

1968 **Gross Area (193 acres)** Mexico ceded to the United States the northern half of Cordova Island in the Rio Grande in return for the Chamizal (630 acres) on December 13, 1968, readjusting the border near El Paso, Texas.

ADMISSION DATES OF STATES TO THE UNION

State	Date	State	Date	State	Date
Delaware	Dec. 7, 1787	Louisiana	April 30, 1812	West Virginia	June 20, 1863
Pennsylvania	Dec. 12, 1787	Indiana	Dec. 11, 1816	Nevada	Oct. 31, 1864
New Jersey	Dec. 18, 1787	Mississippi	Dec. 10, 1817	Nebraska	March 1, 1867
Georgia	Jan. 2, 1788	Illinois	Dec. 3, 1818	Colorado	Aug. 1, 1876
Connecticut	Jan. 9, 1788	Alabama	Dec. 14, 1819	North Dakota	Nov. 2, 1889
Massachusetts	Feb. 6, 1788	Maine	March 15, 1820	South Dakota	Nov. 2, 1889
Maryland	April 28, 1788	Missouri	Aug. 10, 1821	Montana	Nov. 8, 1889
South Carolina	May 23, 1788	Arkansas	June 15, 1836	Washington	Nov. 11, 1889
New Hampshire	June 21, 1788	Michigan	Jan. 26, 1837	Idaho	July 3, 1890
Virginia	June 26, 1788	Florida	March 3, 1845	Wyoming	July 10, 1890
New York	July 26, 1788	Texas	Dec. 29, 1845	Utah	Jan. 4, 1896
North Carolina	Nov. 21, 1789	Iowa	Dec. 28, 1846	Oklahoma	Nov. 16, 1907
Rhode Island	May 29, 1790	Wisconsin	May 29, 1848	New Mexico	Jan. 6, 1912
Vermont	March 4, 1791	California	Sept. 9, 1850	Arizona	Feb. 14, 1912
Kentucky	June 1, 1792	Minnesota	May 11, 1858	Alaska	Jan. 3, 1959
Tennessee	June 1, 1796	Oregon	Feb. 14, 1859	Hawaii	Aug. 21, 1959
Ohio	March 1, 1803	Kansas	Jan. 29, 1861		

CANADA

Area: 3,851,809 sq. mi. **Population:** 23,809,800 (Jan. 1, 1980 est.)

Official Name: Canada **Capital:** Ottawa **Nationality:** Canadian **Language:** English and French are both official languages. About 13% of the population is bilingual; 67% speaks English only, 18% French only, and 2% other languages, such as Italian, German and Ukrainian **Religion:** Roman Catholic 46%, United Church 18% and Anglican 12%. The rest is made up of Presbyterian, Lutheran, Baptist, Jewish, etc. **Flag:** A single red maple leaf with eleven points, centered on a white square; flanked by vertical red bars one half the width of the square. **Anthem:** O Canada; God Save the Queen (royal anthem) **Currency:** Canadian Dollar (1.17 per U.S. $1 as of March, 1980)

Location: North America, occupying all of the continent north of the United States except for Alaska and the French islands of St. Pierre and Miquelon, in the Gulf of St. Lawrence. The second largest country in the world, Canada is bordered on the north by the Arctic Ocean; on the east by Baffin Bay, Davis Strait and the Atlantic Ocean; on the south by the United States; and on the west by the Pacific Ocean and Alaska **Features:** The Shield, a rugged area of pre-Cambrian rock, covers most of eastern and central Canada, or roughly half the entire country. To the north is the Arctic Archipelago and to the west of the Shield is a vast prairie region stretching to the Canadian Rockies. Westernmost Canada, which comprises most of British Columbia, is laced with towering mountain ranges **Chief Rivers:** Mackenzie, Yukon, St. Lawrence, Nelson, Columbia, Churchill

Head of State: Queen Elizabeth II, represented by a governor-general, Edward R. Schreyer, born 1936, assumed office 1978 **Head of Government:** Prime Minister Pierre Elliott Trudeau, born 1921, elected Feb. 18, 1980 **Effective Date of Present Constitution:** The British North America Act of 1867 provides Canada with a form of written constitution; however, as in Britain, many of the country's legal and parliamentary practices are based on unwritten conventions **Legislative Body:** Parliament (bicameral), consisting of a Senate and a House of Commons. The Senate is composed of a maximum of 104 members, appointed until age 75 by the governor-general on the advice of the prime minister. The House of Commons has 282 members, elected for 5 years **Local Government:** 10 provinces, governed by a premier and an elected legislature. There are also 2 large northern territories, Yukon and the Northwest Territories. Yukon is governed by a federal government commissioner and a council of 7 elected members. The Northwest Territories are governed by a commissioner and a council of 9, of whom 5 are appointed and 4 elected

Ethnic Composition (1971): 44.6% of the population is of British Isles descent; 28.7% of French origin; German 6.1%; Italian, 3.4%; Ukrainian 2.7%; Netherlands 2.0% and others 12.5% **Population Distribution:** 75.5% urban **Density:** 6.5 inhabitants per square mile Density: 6.5 inhabitants per square mile

Largest Cities (M.A. = Metropolitan Area 1978) 1976: Toronto, 633,318 (M.A. 2,856,500); Montreal, 1,080,546 (M.A. 2,823,000); Vancouver, 410,188 (M.A. 1,173,300); Ottawa, 304,462 (M.A. 726,400); Winnipeg, 560,874 (M.A. 589,100); Edmonton, 461,361 (M.A. 581,400); Quebec, 177,082 (M.A. 554,500); Hamilton, 312,003 (M.A. 536,300); Calgary, 469,917 (M.A. 504,900); Kitchener, 131,870 (M.A. 280,100); London, 240,392 (M.A. 274,100); Halifax, 117,882 (M.A. 271,200); Windsor, 196,526 (M.A. 246,300); Victoria, 62,551 (M.A. 222,500); Sudbury, 97,604 (M.A. 155,000); Regina, 149,593 (M.A. 160,000)

Per Capita Income: $8,049 (1978) **Gross National Product (GNP):** $260.5 billion (1979) **Economic Statistics:** Manufacturing accounts for 21% of Gross National Product (chief industries: motor vehicles manufacturers, pulp and paper mills, meat slaughtering and processors, petroleum refining, iron and steel mills, motor vehicles parts and accessories manufacturers, dairy products industry, sawmills and planing mills, miscellaneous machinery and equipment manufacturers, and smelting and refining); about 29% is derived from public administration and services; 24% from trade and finance; 9% from primary industries (agriculture, forestry, fishing, trapping, and mining) **Minerals and Mining:** Crude petroleum, copper, nickel, iron ore, zinc, natural gas, natural gas by-products, sand and gravel, and coal, are exploited in large quantities. Value of mineral production: $26.1 billion (1979) **Labor Force:** 10,354,000 employed (April 1980) with 20% employed in manufacturing, 36% in services and public administration, 7% in primary industries and 23% in trade and finance **Average industrial earnings (Feb. 1980):** $306.56 per week. The average monthly wage for agricultural workers is $663.00 with board **Foreign Trade:** Exports, chiefly motor vehicles and parts, crude petroleum, fabricated metals, other machinery and equipment, other fabricated inedible materials, metal ores and concentrates, wheat, totaled $64.0 billion in 1979. Imports, chiefly machinery and equipment, motor vehicles and parts, crude petroleum, food, fabricated metals and other fabricated inedible materials, totaled $62.5 billion **Principal Trade Partners:** United States, Britain, Japan, West Germany, Venezuela, Italy, France, Australia, Netherlands, Saudi Arabia

Vital Statistics: Birthrate, 15.3 per 1,000 of population; death rate, 7.2 **Life Expectancy:** males 70.19, females 77.48 **Health Statistics:** 7.9 hospital beds per 1,000 inhabitants **Infant Mortality:** 12 per 1,000 births **Education Statistics:** 15,344 primary and secondary schools, with combined enrollment of 5,279,481 **Enrollment in Higher Education:** 616,795 **GDP Expended on all forms of Education:** 7.8%

Transportation: Surfaced roads total 712 938 km; earth roads 171 336; total roads 884 273 **Passenger Cars:** 9,744,994 **Railway Mileage (in km):** 67 890 of first main track; total 94 085 **Principal Ports:** Vancouver, Sept Iles, Port Cartier, Montreal, Halifax, Quebec City, Saint John, Hamilton, Baie Comeau, Sarnia **Major Airlines:** Air Canada, the government line, and Canadian Pacific Airlines, a private carrier, operate domestic and international services

Communications: There are both government and privately owned radio and TV stations **No. of Radio Stations:** 449 AM; 416 FM; 8 short wave: 98.4% of homes have radios (excludes car radios) **No. of TV Stations:** 1,045: 97.8% of homes have TV's; 76.7% have color TV's **No. of Telephones:** 15,172,000: 97.2% of homes have telephones **No. of Newspapers:** 120 dailies; daily circulation 5,193,852

Weights and Measures: Old British standards with gradual implementation of the metric system **Travel Requirements:** for entry into Canada, proper identification and valid passport

---

Barely six months after he assumed office, Prime Minister Joe Clark and his Progressive Conservative government were voted out of office. His short-lived government underlines the internal tensions and increased instability facing the Canadian federation as it enters the 1980s.

Clark had campaigned against Prime Minister Pierre Trudeau's Liberal rule by calling for tax cuts and a lowering of mortgage and interest rates to help boost the economy. He hoped these measures would cure the nation's economic ills, as unemployment reached 7.5 percent in April 1979, and inflation continued unchecked at 9.1% annually. But economic realities—and an $11.2 billion federal budget deficit—forced Clark to submit an austerity budget to Parliament. He called for a federal hiring freeze, and proposed raising taxes by $3.5 billion in fiscal 1980.

In addition, Clark acted to change the policies of Petro-Canada—the government-owned petroleum corporation—which fixed prices for domestic oil far below prevailing world market levels. Clark scorned that policy as both unfair to the energy-rich provinces and bad for Canada's energy self-sufficiency, and proposed increasing federal taxes on gasoline sales nearly 18 percent to 35 cents on the gallon. He also moved to raise prices on domestic oil by $4 a barrel from the current $13.75 cost.

Clark's fiscal policies and attempts to decontrol oil prices resulted in the resounding defeat of his government's proposed budget by parliament December 13, 1979, in a vote of no confidence. With a minority of 136 seats in the 282-member house of commons, the PC had stayed in office with the support of five MPs from Quebec's Social Credit party. But the *Créditistes* abstained in the vote, allowing the Liberals and the socialist New Democratic party to defeat the budget. Clark called for the dissolution of parliament, and set February 18, 1980 as the date for new elections.

CANADA
CONIC PROJECTION
SCALE OF MILES
0 100 200 300 400 500
SCALE OF KILOMETRES
0 100 200 300 400 500
Capitals of Countries
Provincial & Territorial Capitals
Canals
Copyright by C. S. Hammond & Co., N. Y.
GREENLAND
BAFFIN BAY
DAVIS STRAIT
ATLANTIC OCEAN
BAFFIN ISLAND
FRANKLIN
DISTRICT OF FRANKLIN
FOXE BASIN
NORTHWEST TERRITORIES
DISTRICT OF KEEWATIN
DISTRICT OF MACKENZIE
HUDSON BAY
James Bay
LABRADOR
NEWFOUNDLAND
QUEBEC
ONTARIO
MANITOBA
SASKATCHEWAN
ALBERTA
BRITISH COLUMBIA
ROCKY MOUNTAINS
COAST MTS.
YUKON
ALASKA
UNITED STATES
BEAUFORT SEA
PARRY CHANNEL
Victoria I.
District of
Banks Island
Devon I.
Cornwallis I.
Bathurst
Melville I.
Somerset I.
Prince of Wales I.
Boothia Pen.
King William L.
Gjoa Haven
Melville Pen.
Prince Charles I.
Southampton I.
Coral Har.
Cumberland Sd.
Frobisher Bay
Resolution I.
C. Chidley
Nettilling L.
Amadjuak L.
Cape Dorset
Foxe Pen.
Foxe Chan.
Igloolik
Repulse Bay
Baker Lake
Chesterfield Inlet
Eskimo Point
Churchill
Tavani
Padlei
Coats I.
Mansel I.
Cape Smith
Nottingham I.
Saglouc
Maricourt
Bellin
Povungnituk
Ottawa Is.
Inoucdjouac
L. Minto
Clearwater
Richmond Gulf
Belcher Is.
Poste-de-la-Baleine
Ft-George
East-Main
Ft-Rupert
Fort Albany
Akimiski
Moosonee
Albany
Mistassini
L. Pletipi
Mingan
Sept-Iles
Anticosti I.
Gulf of St. Lawrence
St. Lawrence
Cap-Chat
Rimouski
Gaspé
Port-aux-Basques
C. Race
St. Johns
Carbonear
Bonavista
Grand Falls
Gander
White Bay
C. Bauld
Battle Harbour
Cartwright
Goose Bay
Hopedale
Nain
Nutak
George River
Ungava Bay
L. Chimo
Fort McKenzie
Schefferville
Amery
Nelson
York Factory
Lynn Lake
Reindeer L.
Brochet
Nueltin L.
Dubawnt L.
Chesterfield
Wollaston L.
Cree L.
Chipewyan
Uranium City
L. Athabasca
Ft. Smith
Ft. Resolution
Great Slave Lake
Ft. Reliance
Garr. L.
Ft. Providence
Yellowknife
Rae
Ft. Liard
Trout L.
Lac la Martre
Ft. Simpson
Wrigley
Fort Norman
Norman Wells
Great Bear Lake
Port Radium
Coppermine
Paulatuk
Coronation Gulf
Holman I.
Amundsen Gulf
Tuktoyaktuk
Inuvik
Arctic Red River
Aklavik
Mackenzie Bay
Peel
Porcupine
Fort Yukon
Circle
Fairbanks
Tanana
Dawson
Mayo
Fort Selkirk
Whitehorse
Pelly
Teslin L.
Watson Lake
Skagway
Juneau
Sitka
Mt. St. Elias 18,008
Mt. Logan 19,524
Fairweather 15,300
Prince of Wales I.
Ketchikan
Prince Rupert
Hecate Str.
Queen Charlotte Is.
Queen Charlotte Sd.
Smithers
Terrace
Kitimat
Burns Lake
Vanderhoof
Prince George
Quesnel
Dawson Cr.
Grande Prairie
Peace River
Fort Vermilion
Hay River
Athabasca
Fort McMurray
Peace River
St. Paul
Meadow Lake
Lloydminster
Vermilion
Edson
Edmonton
Wetaskiwin
Leduc
Camrose
Jasper
Mt. Waddington 13,260
Courtenay
Vancouver I.
Nanaimo
Victoria
Str. of Juan de Fuca
New Westminster
Vancouver
Kamloops
Revelstoke
Kelowna
Vernon
Trail
Cranbrook
Nelson
Banff
Lake Louise
Red Deer
Calgary
Drumheller
Biggar
North Battleford
Prince Albert
The Pas
Melfort
Humboldt
Saskatoon
Winnipegosis
Swift Current
Medicine Hat
Lethbridge
Cardston
Shaunavon
Moose Jaw
Regina
Brandon
Weyburn
Estevan
Souris
Morden
Dauphin
Yorkton
Melville
Kamsack
Winnipeg
St. Boniface
Steep Rock
Kenora
Lake of the Woods
Rainy River
Fort Frances
Red L.
Sioux Lookout
L. Nipigon
Geraldton
Armstrong
Hearst
Kapuskasing
Cochrane
Timmins
Kirkland Lake
Rouyn
Val d'Or
Amos
La Tuque
Shawinigan
Trois-Rivières
Rivière-du-Loup
Edmundston
Campbellton
Chicoutimi
Jonquière
Gouin Res.
Québec
Montréal
Sherbrooke
Fredericton
Moncton
Saint John
Truro
Halifax
Dartmouth
Bridgewater
Yarmouth
Sable I.
NEW BRUNSWICK
NOVA SCOTIA
PRINCE EDWARD I.
Charlottetown
Sydney
Glace Bay
Cape Breton I.
Cabot Str.
MAINE
N. H.
VT.
MASS.
CONN.
R. I.
N. Y.
PA.
New York
Boston
Portland
Augusta
Montpelier
Albany
Buffalo
Niagara Falls
Cleveland
Windsor
Detroit
London
Sarnia
Toronto
Hamilton
Owen Sound
Manitoulin I.
Sault Ste. Marie
Sudbury
North Bay
Blind River
White River
Chapleau
Sturgeon Falls
Hull
Ottawa
Cornwall
Kingston
Peterborough
Parry Sound
Pembroke
Georgian Bay
Lake Simcoe
Sault Ste. Marie
Lake Superior
Lake Michigan
Lake Huron
Lake Erie
Milwaukee
Duluth
Minneapolis
St. Paul
Fargo
Bismarck
Pierre
Niobrara
Missouri
Seattle
Spokane
Portland
Columbia
Thunder Bay
Nipigon
Port Arthur
WASH.
IDA.
MONT.
N. DAK.
S. DAK.
NEBR.
IOWA
MINN.
WIS.
MICH.
UNITED STATES
Longitude West of 90° Greenwich
MICH.
Port Huron
Detroit
Windsor
Sandwich
Walkerville
St. Clair
Chatham
Wallaceburg
Leamington
Pt. Pelee
Lake Erie
Long Pt.
Welland Canal
Welland
Lake Huron
Goderich
Listowel
Walkerton
Orangeville
Fergus
Kitchener
Stratford
Woodstock
London
St. Thomas
Sarnia
Simcoe
Brantford
Galt
Guelph
Hamilton
St. Catharines
Niagara Falls
Niagara Falls N.Y.
Buffalo N.Y.
Brampton
Toronto
Oshawa
Newmarket
Cobourg
Erie
Miles 0 20 40
Miles 0 10 20
Sorel
Joliette
Drummondville
St. Jérôme
Lachine
Laval
Verdun
Montréal
St-Jean
Valleyfield
St-Hyacinthe
Sherbrooke
Granby
Magog

At thirty-nine, the youngest prime minister in Canada's history, Clark from the start was beset by low public recognition and an image as a weak leader. His proposed tax increases and the specter of rising oil prices—derisively called "the 18 percent solution" by the press—plus reversal of his early campaign pledge to transfer Canada's embassy in Israel from Tel Aviv to Jerusalem after threatened retaliation by oil-rich Arab states—led to his defeat in the February 18 general elections. The Liberals won an absolute majority of 144 seats in the House of Commons, with the New Democrats, led by Edward Broadbent, increasing its total to 32 seats. The PC fell from 136 to 103 seats in the house, holding its own only in its traditional Western strongholds. The *Créditistes*, tainted by their support to Clark's government, were totally wiped out from parliament.

With the rising fortunes of the Liberal party came the political resurrection of its leader, Pierre Elliott Trudeau. Trudeau had resigned as party chief November 21, but accepted a December 18 draft to head the Liberal ticket. His campaign theme was a familiar one: Unity. Trudeau pledged he would be a 'caretaker' prime minister, and not serve out his full five-year term. He declared his goal was to lay the constitutional basis for a strong, united Canadian confederation that he and his party had always envisioned—a "just society" for all Canadians. His campaign broadened traditional Liberal support in Quebec to include the economically hard-pressed Maritime provinces, and the crucial Ontario vote to ensure his return to office.

But Trudeau faces an uphill battle in seeking to bind the nation together. Clark's concessions to the oil and mineral-rich Western provinces was a genuine recognition that the provinces have been economically and politically dominated by the "Eastern" establishment. Clark had promised greater powers to the provinces, and despite his belief in a strong central government, Trudeau cannot ignore the clamor of the ten disparate local governments for more control over their own affairs.

Trudeau's biggest immediate problem remains Quebec. Since November 1976, when the separatist *Parti Québécois* won a legislative majority in the provincial assembly, Premier René Lévesque has pursued a policy calculated to make Quebec an independent state. In 1979, Lévesque called for accepting a "sovereign" Quebec within an economic association with Canada, moderating demands for total independence in order to gain acceptance of greater autonomy for the province by the rest of the nation. When Quebec's National Assembly called a referendum on association for 1980, Trudeau came out in support of Quebec Liberal leader Claude Ryan's proposals for more provincial autonomy within the federal system. He attacked the referendum as a ploy by Lévesque and the PQ to gain a yes vote by presenting independence as autonomy. On May 20, 1980, fully 58 percent of those Quebecers who turned out voted *non* to sovereignty-association, with only 42 percent casting *oui* ballots. These results had been preceeded by a Liberal resurgence in local by-elections, in recent opinion polls showing separatist sentiment waning, and by the December 13, 1979 ruling of Canada's Supreme Court striking down Quebec's Bill 101—making French the official and primary language of that province—as unconstitutional.

Following his impressive victory in Quebec, Trudeau called for a new constitutional conference to spell out the scope of proposed increased territorial powers and self-government for Quebec and the other provinces. The British North American Act of 1867 makes the Canadian charter an act of British Parliament. Despite revisions such as the Citizenship Act of 1977, ending Canadians' status as "British subjects," any change must be approved in London, after unanimous approval by Ottawa and the provinces. Trudeau has long sought patriation—i.e., to bring the constitution solely under Canadian jurisdiction—and remove the amendment procedure from British control.

Trudeau has proposed three main areas of constitutional change he feels are necessary for confederation to work: establishment of a federal parliament with real national powers, authorizing provincial assemblies to exert equally valid territorial powers, and codification of a bill of rights, including preservation of language rights for the French-speaking minority. Provincial leaders met in Ottawa in July 1980 to consider these latest proposals, with Trudeau setting a September deadline for completing negotiations.

HISTORY: Although the Vikings are believed to have visited Canada about A.D. 1000, the first recorded landing was made by John Cabot in 1497. Cabot, an Italian-born explorer in the service of Henry VII of England, landed near Newfoundland and claimed the area for the English king. In 1534, Jacques Cartier planted a cross on the Gaspé Peninsula and claimed the region for France. The intense rivalry that followed as each country tried to extend its claims was to dominate the history of Canada for more than two centuries

1689-1763: French and Indian Wars, a series of colonial wars in North America that reflect Anglo-French rivalry in Europe, culminate in the loss of French control of Canada and the establishment of British rule

1774: Quebec Act is passed, reversing favored treatment accorded British in Quebec and providing for preservation of French culture; the act is to prove instrumental in maintaining loyalty of Canada to Britain following outbreak of the American Revolution

1791: Constitutional Act divides Lower Canada, now southern Quebec, from Upper Canada, now southern Ontario, and establishes limited self-government

1837-41: Rebellions in the two Canadas and growing movement for responsible government cause British government to reunite the two Canadas

1867: British North America Act establishes Dominion of Canada, a confederation of Nova Scotia, New Brunswick, and Lower and Upper Canada, the latter two becoming the provinces of Quebec and Ontario, respectively. (The other components of present-day Canada are added in subsequent years, the last, Newfoundland, not until 1949.)

1914-18: Canada fights on Allied side in World War I; issue of conscription arouses strong opposition from French Canadians, deepening split between the French- and English-speaking

1931: Statute of Westminster establishes equality of Canadian Parliament with that of Britain

1939-45: Canada plays vital role in World War II and emerges as one of the major nations of the world

1957: Conservatives, led by John Diefenbaker, take office after 22 years of Liberal party rule

1963: Liberals, led by Lester Pearson, return to power

1967: French President Charles de Gaulle, on a visit to Canada, calls for a "free Quebec" during speech in Montreal; his speech prompts a sharp rebuke from the Canadian government, causing the French leader to cut short his Canadian visit

1968: Pearson retires and is succeeded by Pierre Elliott Trudeau, a French Canadian lawyer and former justice minister; new elections are held in which decisive Liberal victory gives Canada its first majority government in six years

1969: Canada opens negotiations with Communist China for the establishment of diplomatic relations between the two countries; Commons passes government-sponsored language bill requiring bilingual federal facilities wherever 10 percent of the people of any district speak French

1970: Government invokes wartime powers after separatist terrorists kidnap British diplomat and Quebec labor minister, who is subsequently slain

1971: Trudeau and Kosygin sign a protocol agreement in Moscow calling for regular, high-level consultations; Communist China and Canada exchange ambassadors

1974: Trudeau reelected with parliamentary majority

1975: Wage and price controls are imposed for three years

1976: The death penalty is abolished throughout Canada. Parti Québécois takes the Quebec provincial elections

1977: Bill establishing French as primary language in government and education introduced into Quebec's National Assembly. Berger Commission calls for 10-year halt to construction of natural gas pipeline in Northwest until native land claims settled. Citizenship Act becomes law

ALBERTA
MILES
0 20 40 60 80 100
KILOMETERS
0 20 40 60 80 100
Provincial Capital
ALBERTA
NORTHERN PART

BR. COLUMBIA
SASKATCHEWAN
MONTANA
WASH.
IDAHO
Longitude West of Greenwich
© C.S. HAMMOND & Co., Maplewood, N.J.

120° 118° 116° 114° 112° 110°
56° 54° 52° 50°

Dawson Creek
Gordondale
Hines Creek
Manning
North Star
Fairview
Whitelaw
Bluesky
Berwyn
Grimshaw
Nampa
Peace River
Hythe
Beaverlodge
Wembley
Spirit River
Rycroft
Woking
Sexsmith
Wanham
Grande-Prairie
Eaglesham
Girouxville
Falher
Donnelly
McLennan
High Prairie
Grouard Mission
Enilda
Faust
Kinuso
Canyon Creek
Lesser Slave L.
Slave Lake
Valleyview
House Mt. 3,950
Wallace Mt. 4,130
Swan Hills
Fox Creek
Ft. Assiniboine
Atikameg
Utikuma Lake
Trout Mt. 2,709
Peerless Lake
Wabasca
N. Wabasca L.
Calling Lake
Smith
Flatbush
Fawcett
Colinton
Boyle
Athabasca
Dapp
Rochester
Legend L.
Bitumount
Ft. McKay
Ft. McMurray
Waterways
THICKWOOD HILLS
Conklin
Winefred L.
Methy Lake
Peter Pond Lake
Imperial Mills
Lac La Biche
Egg L.
Craigend
Grandin
Primrose Lake
Cold L.
Cold L.
Grand Centre
Bonnyville
Ft. Kent
Therien
Mallaig
Glendon
Vilna
St. Paul
Elk Point
Grande Cache
WILLMORE WILDERNESS PROV. PARK
Barrhead
Westlock
Thorhild
Smoky L.
Waskatenau
Whitecourt
Blue Ridge
Pickardville
Mayerthorpe
Sangudo
Morinville
Legal
Redwater
Andrew
Willingdon
Two Hills
Myrnam
Derwent
Edson
Marlboro
Bickerdike
Wildwood
Evansburg
Entwistle
St-Albert
Ft. Saskatchewan
Lamont
Mundare
Clandonald
Marwayne
Stony Plain
Sherwood Pk.
ELK I. N.P.
Vegreville
Innisfree
Kitscoty
Hinton
Mercoal
Luscar
Foothills
Mountain Park
Violet Grove
Drayton Valley
Breton
Calmar
Leduc
Devon
EDMONTON
Tofield
Ryley
Holden
Mannville
Vermilion
Lloydminster
Jasper
JASPER NATIONAL PARK
Mt. Robson 12,972
MT. ROBSON PROV. PK.
WELLS GRAY PROV. PARK
HAMBER PROV. PK.
Mt. Columbia 12,294
Nordegg (Brazeau)
Saunders
Rocky Mtn. House
Sylvan Lake
Eckville
Bentley
Caroline
Winfield
Rimbey
Gull L.
Ponoka
Wetaskiwin
Pigeon L.
Thorsby
Millet
New Norway
Daysland
Killam
Sedgewick
Camrose
Viking
Irma
Edgerton
Chauvin
Hardisty
Hughenden
Wainwright
Mirror
Alix
Lacombe
Red Deer
Delburne
Donalda
Forestburg
Alliance
Provost
Stettler
Castor
Coronation
Consort
Penhold
Innisfail
Big Valley
Veteran
Compeer
Bowden
Trochu
Endiang
Sundre
Olds
Westward Ho
Didsbury
Three Hills
Morrin
Hanna
Youngstown
Cereal
Oyen
Carstairs
Acme
Midlandvale
Drumheller
Rosedale
Crossfield
Newcastle
E. Coulee
Airdrie
Cochrane
Rockyford
Standard
Acadia Valley
BANFF NAT'L. PK.
Lake Louise
YOHO NAT'L. PK.
Field
Mt. Eisenhower 8,950
Banff
Canmore
Exshaw
KOOTENAY NAT'L. PK.
MT. ASSINIBOINE PROV. PK. 11,870
Calgary
Strathmore
Gleichen
Bassano
Duchess
Brooks
Cessford
Empress
Black Diamond
Turner Valley
Okotoks
Milo
Tilley
Hilda
High River
Longview
Vulcan
Lomond
Ralston
Schuler
Nanton
Champion
Vauxhall
Redcliff
Medicine Hat
Stavely
Carmangay
Barons
Claresholm
Picture Butte
Bow Island
Irvine
Granum
Taber
Grassy Lake
Burdett
Coleman
Hillcrest
Bellevue
Blairmore
Pincher Cr
Welling
Coaldale
Lethbridge
Stirling
Raymond
Foremost
Etzikom
Manyberries
Hill Spring
Magrath
Warner
Pakowki L.
Ft. Macleod
WATERTON LAKES NAT'L. PARK
Cardston
Milk River
Aden
WATERTON-GLACIER INT'L PEACE PK.
Waterton Pk.
GLACIER NAT'L PK.
Coutts
MONTANA

N.W. TERRITORIES
WOOD BUFFALO NATIONAL PARK
CARIBOU MTS.
Habay
Meander River
Assumption
Ft. Vermilion
Keg River
BIRCH MTS.
Bitumount
Lake Athabasca
Lake Claire
Ft. Chipewyan
SASK.
BR. COL.
60° 58°
120° 118° 116° 114° 112° 110°
50 100 mi.
50 100 km.

1978: Soviet nuclear-powered satellite crashes in northern Canada; radiation threat minimal. Trudeau introduces new federal constitution to supercede 1867 Dominion Act. Government halts all development in northern Yukon, considers measures to protect caribou migration. Four western provinces join Ontario in opposing any future economic association with an independent Quebec

1979: Progressive Conservatives come to power under Joe Clark, ending 11-year term of Prime Minister Trudeau. Task Force on Canadian Unity report calls for recognition of Quebec's right to self-determination and secession, proposes granting province powers to "protect and develop its distinctive character" within the Canadian federation. U.S. and Canada sign pact on disputed Atlantic and Pacific fishing grounds; but "fish war" continues with seizure of U.S. tuna boats and American ban on Canadian tuna imports as treaty is stalled in U.S. Senate. Supreme Court Dec. 13 voids Quebec's French-language Bill 101 as unconstitutional. U.S. and Canada agree to pollution controls along border to prevent "acid rain." Clark government is defeated Dec. 13 in no-confidence vote on austerity budget. Yukon territorial council becomes legislative assembly and appoints a cabinet, in step towards provincial status

1980: Ottawa announces Jan. 29 that Canadian diplomats aided six Americans to escape Tehran after takeover of U.S. Embassy. Joe Clark's Progressive Conservatives are defeated in Feb. 18 general elections; Liberals win majority in parliament, as Pierre Trudeau gains new term as prime minister. Federal report issued March 6 rejects provincial status for Northwest Territories for the immediate future. Quebec Liberals call for revision of constitution to give provinces more self-rule. Voters reject Quebec sovereignty in May 20 referendum. Trudeau and Alberta's Premier Peter Lougheed break off talks July 25 on federal energy policy and price increases for province's oil and natural gas

ALBERTA

Area: 255,219 square miles **Population:** 1,838,037 (1976 Census); 2,012,500 (June 1, 1979 est.) ranks fourth; population density 7.9 per sq. mi.; urban, 75.0%; rural 25.0%

Capital: Edmonton **Major Cities, (1976 Census metropolitan area populations):** Edmonton, 554,228; Calgary, 469,917

Ethnic Composition: British Isles, 47%; German, 14%; Ukrainian, 8%; Scandinavian, 6%; French, 6%; Netherlands, 4%; and Native Indian, 3%; other, 12% **Religion:** United Church, 28%; Roman Catholic, 24%; Anglican, 10%; Lutheran, 8%; Presbyterian, 4%; other, 26% **Vital Statistics (per 1,000 population, 1979):** birth rate, 17.3; death rate, 6.0; marriage rate, 8.8; divorce rate (1978), 3.1; infant mortality (per 1,000 live births, 1977), 11.1

Location and Geography: Except for the northeast corner and the mountainous fringe on its western border, Alberta is underlain with arable soil, and irrigation has made the semi-arid far south and east productive for agricultural purposes. Most of the province is now very fertile agricultural land

Government: Alberta became a province in 1905 and is represented in the federal government by 21 members in the House of Commons and 6 Senators. The provincial government is unicameral with a Legislative Assembly of 79 members. In March 1979, 74 Progressive Conservatives, four members of the Social Credit party and one New Democrat were elected to the legislature **Premier:** Honourable Peter Lougheed **Salary and Allowance:** $51,511

Education (1978-79): In Alberta, there are 1,405 primary and secondary schools; 19,307 schoolrooms; 23,867 teachers; and 418,715 grades 1-12 students enrolled. Total full-time winter session students enrolled at 3 universities, 30,847, and 10,091 full-time students enrolled at 6 Alberta public colleges

Net value of production in goods-producing industries (1979 est.): $20,962,000,000. Mining represented 56.9% of this total, construction 20.4%, agriculture 6.2% and manufacturing 14.5%. Value of oil and natural gas production is increasing annually and has made the province Canada's leading producer of mineral products with a value of $12,885 million in 1979. In 1979 Alberta produced 88% of the crude petroleum, 91% of the natural gas and 27% of the coal in the nation **Leading manufacturing industries (1979):** slaughtering and meat processors, petroleum refining, metal fabricating industries, chemical & chemical products industries, primary metals industries **Average industrial earnings (Dec. 1979):** $312.33 per week **Cash receipts from farming operations (1979):** $2,835,669,000; 41.2% derived from cattle and calves, 16.0% from wheat, 12.3% from rapeseed, 8.8% from barley, and 4.8% from dairy products **Families with incomes over $15,000 (1977):** 65.7% **Per capita personal income (1978):** $8,407

Provincial Finances: Gross budgetary revenue (est., fiscal year 1980-81): $7.16 billion (excl. funds allocated to the Alberta Heritage Savings Trust Fund). Gross budgetary expenditures (est., fiscal year 1980-81): $5.31 billion

Daily newspapers: 9 **Telephones in service (December 1979):** 1,542,958 **Radio stations:** 127 **Homes with radios (1978):** 98% **Homes with TV's (1978):** 96%

Hospital beds (March 1978-79): 14,575 (7.5 beds per 1,000 population, 1978-79) **Residents per physician (Dec. 1979):** 690

Motor vehicles (1979-80): 1,783,158 **Residents per motor vehicle:** 1.1 **Motor vehicle deaths (1979):** 692

The first European to explore Alberta was Pierre Boucher, Sieur de Boucherville, in 1751. Boucher was an agent of the English Hudson's Bay Company, but it was not until over forty years later, in 1795, that the Company and its rival, the French Northwest Company, established the first European settlements in the province. Both of the companies set up their trading posts near Edmonton, although trapping activities were concentrated further north.

In 1869 the government of the region was transferred from the Hudson's Bay Company to the newly formed Dominion of Canada, but widespread settlement was delayed until the Canadian Pacific Railroad reached the province in the mid-1880's. After the railroad made eastern markets accessible, settlers—mostly ranchers and farmers—began trickling into the region. They found that although it is far north in latitude, most of the land in Alberta is fertile.

With the development and introduction of early-ripening Marquis wheat in the early part of the 20th century, settlers poured into the west, coming in almost equal numbers from the U.S., the U.K., eastern Canada, and northern Europe. Alberta's population rose from 73,000 in 1901 to 374,000 in 1911. Since then its population has risen steadily, although less spectacularly.

Following World War II, the agricultural nature of the province began to change with the discovery of new oil fields near Leduc in 1947. During 1978 the search for new supplies of conventional petroleum and natural gas reached one of the highest levels of the 1970s.

Alberta's long term supplies of petroleum are assured by the vast reserves of oil recoverable from Alberta's oil sands. The largest oil sands deposit is found in northeastern Alberta and two plants, Suncor and Syncrude, are currently producing from these deposits. Three additional oil sands mining plants have been proposed and are in various stages of planning.

Abundant deposits of natural gas are found in Alberta and the province produces approximately 95% of Canada's pentanes plus propane and butanes, the bulk of which are transported to other Canadian provinces or exported to the United States. Alberta also has reserves of more than 100 billion tons of high quality coking coal.

Increasing revenues from the sale of petroleum and natural gas enabled the Alberta government to establish the Alberta Heritage Savings Trust Fund in 1976. The Fund was created to invest a portion of the province's non-renewable resource revenue to provide economic and social benefits to Albertans now and in the future. As of December 31, 1979, the assets of the Fund totalled $5.9 billion.

BRITISH COLUMBIA

Area: 366,255 square miles **Population:** 2,466,608 (1976 Census); 2,611,700 (Jan. 1, 1980 estimate); ranks third in both area & population; population density (1980): 7.1 per sq. mi.; urban, 75.7%; rural 24.3% **Capital:** Victoria **Major Cities (1976 Census Metropolitan Areas):** Vancouver, 1,173,300; Victoria, 222,500

Ethnic Composition: British Isles, 58%; German, 9%; Scandinavian, 5%; French, 4%; Netherlands, 3%; Ukrainian, 3%; Italian, 2%; and Native Indians, 2% **Religion:** United Church, 25%; Roman Catholic, 19%; Anglican, 18%; Lutheran, 6%; Presbyterian, 5%; Baptist, 3%; no religion, 13% **Vital Statistics (per 1,000 popula-

BRITISH COLUMBIA
MILES
KILOMETERS
Provincial and State Capitals
Longitude West of Greenwich

BRITISH COLUMBIA NORTHERN PART
YUKON TERR.
N.W.T.
PACIFIC OCEAN
COAST MTS.
CASSIAR MTS.
CONTINENTAL DIVIDE
GLACIER BAY NAT'L MON.
Juneau
Sitka
Atlin L.
Tulsequah
Cassiar
Lower Post
Liard
Old Ft. Nelson
MUNCHO LAKE PROV. PK.
Ft. Nelson
STIKINE R.
MT. EDZIZA PROV. PK. & REC. AREA

VANCOUVER ISLAND
Vancouver
Qualicum Beach
Parksville
Port Alberni
Alberni
Nanaimo
Alberni Inlet
Ladysmith
Cassidy
Gibson's Ldg.
W. Vancouver
N. Vancouver
Port Moody
Coquitlam
GOLDEN EARS PROV. PK.
Mission City
Burnaby
Haney
Hatzic
Agassiz
Richmond
New Westminster
Langley
Surrey
Delta
White Rock
Chilliwack
Chemainus
Youbou
Cowichan L. Lake
ISLAND
Port Renfrew
Centre Saanich
Sidney
Saanich
Duncan
Orcas I.
San Juan I.
Sooke
Victoria
Esquimalt
Bellingham
Anacortes
WASH.
Str. of Juan de Fuca

COAST MTS.
SKEENA MTS.
OMINECA MTS.
ROCKY MTS.
HAZELTON MTS.
CONTINENTAL DIVIDE
CARIBOO MTS.
MONASHEE MTS.
SELKIRK MTS.
COAST MOUNTAINS
PACIFIC OCEAN
ALASKA
ALBERTA
WASHINGTON
IDAHO
MONTANA
Kupreanof I.
Petersburg
Mitkof I.
Wrangell
Etolin I.
Caremboo I.
Prince of Wales
Ketchikan
Revilla gigedo
Iskut R.
Premier
Stewart
Alice Arm
Portland Canal
Dall I.
C. Knox
Dundas I.
Dixon Entrance
Prince Rupert
Port Simpson
Port Edward
Skeena R.
Masset
Porcher I.
Pitt I.
Port Essington
Terrace
Usk
Graham I.
Port Clements
McCauley I.
Queen Charlotte
Skidegate
Banks I.
QUEEN CHARLOTTE ISLANDS
Moresby I.
HECATE STRAIT
Gill I.
Princess Royal I.
Aristazabal I.
Kunghit I.
O. St. James
QUEEN CHARLOTTE SOUND
Kitimat
NANIKA DAM
Kemano
Butedale
Ocean Falls
Bella Coola
Hagensborg
King I.
Hunter I.
Campbell I.
Calvert I.
Rivers Inlet
Aiyansh
Kincolith
Kitwanga
Hazelton
New Hazelton
Smithers
Telkwa
Babine L.
Quick
Houston
Decker Lake
Burns Lake
François Lake
François L.
Fort Fraser
Fraser Lake
Vanderhoof
Stuart L.
Fort St. James
Willow River
Aleza Lake
Giscome
South Ft. George
Prince George
McBride
KENNEY DAM
Tetachuck L.
TWEEDSMUIR PROV. PARK
Takla L.
Thutade L.
Manson Cr.
Finlay Forks
Ware
Ft. Grahame
Sikanni R.
Chief R.
Sikanni River
Finlay R.
Peace R.
Parsnip R.
Wonowon
Hudson Hope
Fort St. John
Taylor
Dawson Cr.
East Pine
Chetwynd
Rolla
Pouce-Coupé
Tupper
Sinclair Mills
WILLMORE WILDERNESS PROV. PK.
Quesnel
BOWRON LAKE PROV. PK.
Narcosli Creek
Likely
Quesnel L.
Wells
MT. ROBSON PROV. PK.
Valemount
JASPER NAT'L PARK
HAMBER PROV. PK.
WELLS GRAY PROV. PK.
Blue River
Williams Lake
150 Mile House
Fraser R.
Chilcotin R.
Chilko L.
Mt. Waddington 13,260
Alkali Lake
100 Mile House
Clearwater
Bridge Lake
Little Fort
70 Mile House
Clinton
Louis Cr.
Cache Cr.
Thompson R.
Chase
MT. REVELSTOKE NAT'L PK.
Revelstoke
GLACIER NAT'L PK.
YOHO NAT'L PK.
Golden
KOOTENAY NAT'L PK.
BANFF NATIONAL PARK
Banff
Edgewater
MT. ASSINIBOINE PROV. PARK
Invermere
Salmon Arm
Enderby
Arrow Lakes
Nakusp
Gold Bridge
Bralorne
Lillooet R.
Lillooet
Ashcroft
N. Kamloops
Kamloops
Armstrong
Vernon
Okanagan L.
KOKANEE GLACIER PROV. PK.
Kaslo
Kootenay Lake
Canal Flats
Claresholm
Lytton
Merritt
Kelowna
Peachland
Summerland
Penticton
Nelson
Castlegar
Kinnaird
Marysville
Kimberly
Fernie
Cranbrook
Sparwood
Fort Macleod
Taber
Lethbridge
Hedley
Princeton
Copper Mtn.
Oliver
Greenwood
Grand Forks
Warfield
Fruitvale
Creston
Grasmere
WATERTON LAKES NAT'L PK.
WATERTON-GLACIER INTERNAT'L PEACE PK.
Osoyoos
Rossland
Trail
Colville
Sandpoint
Kootenai R.
Kootenay R.
Koocanusa L.
GLACIER NATIONAL PARK
Whitefish
Kalispell
Cut Bank
N. Vancouver
GARIBALDI PROV. PK.
Squamish
Britannia Beach
Pt. Coquitlam
Harrison L.
Hope
MANNING PROV. PK.
Ladner
White Rock
Mission City
Chilliwack
NORTH CASCADES NAT'L PARK
SKAGIT ROSS L. N.R.A.
CHELAN NAT'L REC. AREA
WASHINGTON
Okanogan
Columbia R.
VANCOUVER ISLAND
Campbell River
Courtenay
Comox
Cumberland
STRATHCONA PROV. PARK
Powell River
Refuge Cove
Simoom Sound
Kelsey Bay
Tahsis
Nootka L.
Nootka Sd.
Port Hardy
Port Alice
Alert Bay
Sointula
Quatsino
Quatsino Sd.
O. Scott
O. Cook
C. Cook
Tofino
Ucluelet
Barkley Sd.
PACIFIC RIM NAT'L PARK
Flores I.
Bamfield
Port Albern.
Nanaimo
Ladysmith
Duncan
Vancouver
New Westminster
Esquimalt
Victoria
Bellingham
Anacortes
C. Flattery
Str. of Juan de Fuca
© C. S. HAMMOND & Co., Maplewood, N. J.

tion, 1979): birth rate, 15.0; death rate, 7.4; marriage rate, 8.3 divorce rate, 3.6; infant mortality (per 1,000 live births), 12.4

Location and Geography: Parallel ranges of mountains and fertile valleys cover all but the northeast corner of the province. There is also a deeply indented Pacific shoreline. Because it is warmed by the Japanese Current, the climate of the coastal region is moderate

Government: British Columbia became a province in 1871 and is represented in the federal government by 29 members in the House of Commons and 6 Senators. The provincial government is unicameral with a Legislative Assembly of 57 members. In May 1979, 31 members of the Social Credit party and 26 members of the New Democratic party were elected to the legislature **Premier:** Honourable William R. Bennett **Salary and allowance:** $59,500

Education: Of the population fifteen years of age and over, 18% have less than Grade 9 education, 63% have a secondary school education and 19% have a post-secondary degree or certification (1976 Census). **Total expenditures on education (1978):** $1,514,050,579 **Schools:** 1,606 primary and secondary schools (Sept. 1979) with a combined enrollment of 511,671 **Colleges:** Three degree-granting universities, 14 vocational schools and community colleges and seven provincial institutes with a combined enrollment of 120,941 (1979-80)

Value added in goods-producing industries (1977): $9,894,289,000; manufacturing represents 46.5% and construction 24.7%. Slightly more than half of the manufacturing total comes from wood industries and paper and allied industries. Mining, which accounted for 20% of the province's industry in the 1940's, now accounts for only 11.7% **Leading manufacturing industries (1977):** Pulp and paper mills, sawmills and planing mills, and veneer and plywood mills **Average industrial earnings (1979):** $327.14 per week Value of fishery products (1978): $518 million **Cash receipts from farming operations (1979):** $635.9 million, of which 23% is derived from dairy products, and 18% from poultry and eggs **Families with incomes of $16,000 and over (1976):** 62% **Per capita personal income (1979):** $9,615 **Unemployment (1979):** 7.7%

Provincial Finances: Gross general revenue (fiscal year 1979-80): $5,520 million; gross general expenditure, $5,270 million

Daily Newspapers: 21 Combined circulation (1978): 571,227 **Telephones (1979):** 1,752,639 **Homes with radios (1979):** 98% **Homes with TV's (1979):** 97%

Hospital beds (1980): 17,893 (6.9 beds per 1,000 population) **Physicians (1979):** 5,244 (2.0 per 1,000 population)

Motor vehicles (1979): 1,553,100 **Residents per motor vehicle (1979):** 1.7 **Motor vehicle deaths (1979):** 738

The first European to visit what is now the province of British Columbia was a Spaniard, Juan Perez, who came while on a voyage in search of the Northwest Passage. Two years later Capt. James Cook explored and established the general outline of the northwest coast. Cook stopped only briefly on the coast of Vancouver Island, but while there he obtained several sea-otter pelts from the Indians. When he arrived in Macao, on the south China coast, and traded the pelts, the potential profits of the sea-otter became clear. Soon after Cook published an account of his voyage, a legion of trading ships descended on the coast, setting the stage for a decades-long controversy between Spain and England over which was the rightful claimant to the area.

With the coming of trappers and traders after the 1790's, English control was established, and the merged Northwest and Hudson Bay Companies controlled the region until the middle of the nineteenth century. In 1849 and 1858 Vancouver Island and mainland British Columbia, respectively, were made English colonies. In 1866 the two were united and agreed to become part of the Dominion of Canada in 1871 on condition that a transcontinental railroad be built.

The completion of the railroad in 1885 spurred the development of agriculture, forestry and mining. The economy received a second boost in 1914 when the Panama Canal opened, giving Vancouver direct sea-borne access to European markets.

During the twentieth century the province has continued to grow. The demands of World War II sparked spectacular growth in the forest industries, hydroelectric power, and manufacturing. These additional jobs contributed to a trebling of the population since 1941.

In December 1975, the New Democratic party was unseated by the Social Credit party headed by William Bennett. The "Socreds" pledged to repeal the Mineral Royalties Act of the previous administration, legislation which had been strongly opposed by the mining industry. But the May 1979 elections saw the Social Credit majority reduced to 31 seats in the assembly, with the NDP winning the remaining 26 seats.

MANITOBA

Area: 251,000 square miles **Population:** 1,021,506 (1976 Census); 1,026,200 (Jan. 1, 1980 estimate): ranks fifth; population density 4.8; urban, 69.9%; rural, 30.1% **Capital:** Winnipeg **Largest Cities (1976 Census):** Winnipeg, 578,217; Brandon, 34,901

Ethnic Composition: British Isles, 42%; German, 12%; Ukrainian, 12%; French, 9%; Native Indian, 4%; Polish, 4% and Scandinavian, 4% **Religion:** United Church, 26%; Roman Catholic, 25%; Anglican, 12%; Lutheran, 7%; Mennonite, 6%; Ukrainian Catholic, 6% **Vital Statistics (per 1,000 population):** birth rate, 15.9; death rate, 8.0; marriage rate, 8.0; divorce rate, 2.12; infant mortality (per 1,000 live births), 13.7

Location and Geography: Located between Ontario and Saskatchewan, Manitoba is a vast plain which rises gradually to the west and south. On the southern prairie the fertility of the land varies greatly, from the black gumbo of the Red River valley to sandy soil in the southwest and stonier soil between Lakes Winnipeg and Manitoba

Government: Manitoba became a province in 1870 **No. of representatives in Parliament:** 14 members in the House of Commons and 6 Senators **Type of legislature:** Unicameral with a Lieutenant-Governor, Executive Council and a Legislative Assembly of 57 members **Current government:** In October 1977, 33 Progressive Conservatives, 23 New Democrats and one Liberal were elected to the legislature **Premier:** Honourable Sterling Lyon **Salary and allowance:** $38,799

Education (April 1980): 24.4% of the population 15 years of age and over had Grade 8 or less; 51.5% attended high school; 7.2% had some post-secondary education; 9.1% had a post-secondary certificate or diploma; 8.0% had a university degree **Total education expenditures (1978-79):** $720,341,000 **Schools:** 809 primary and secondary schools (1978-79) with a combined enrollment of 232,470 **Colleges:** Seven degree-granting universities and eight post-secondary non-university institutions with a combined enrollment of 20,049

Value added in goods-producing industries (1977): $2,801,235,000; manufacturing represented 42.9% of this total, construction 23.5%, agriculture 19.3%, and electric power 7.9% **Value of manufacturing shipment (1977):** $2,840,894,000 **Leading manufacturing industries:** slaughtering and meat processing, agricultural implements, dairy products, feed, publishing and printing, miscellaneous food processing, aircraft manufacturing, women's clothing factories **Average industrial earnings (Feb. 1980):** $272.83 per week **Cash receipts from farming operations (1979):** $1,299,354,000 with 23.5% from cattle and calves, 21.5% derived from wheat, 9.2% from hogs, 7.8% from barley, 9.2% from rapeseed, 4.8% from diary products and 5.8% from flaxseed **Per capita personal income (1978):** $7,456 **Unemployment (1979):** 5.4%

Provincial Finances: Estimated gross general revenue, fiscal year 1978-79, $1,744.7 million; estimated gross general expenditure, $1,863.3 million

Daily newspapers: 9 Total circulation: 268,397 **Number of telephones per 100 population (1978):** 63.8 **Homes with radios:** 98.2% **Homes with TV's:** 96.4%

Hospital beds (1979): 7,869 (7.6 beds per 1,000 population) **Physicians (1977):** 1,811 (population per physician, 572)

Motor Vehicles (1978): 628,427 **Residents per motor vehicle:** 1.6 **Motor vehicle deaths (1978):** 203

Despite the fact that it is known as a "prairie province," only a small southern portion of Manitoba's 251,000 square miles is actually treeless grassland. The remainder ranges from forest land,

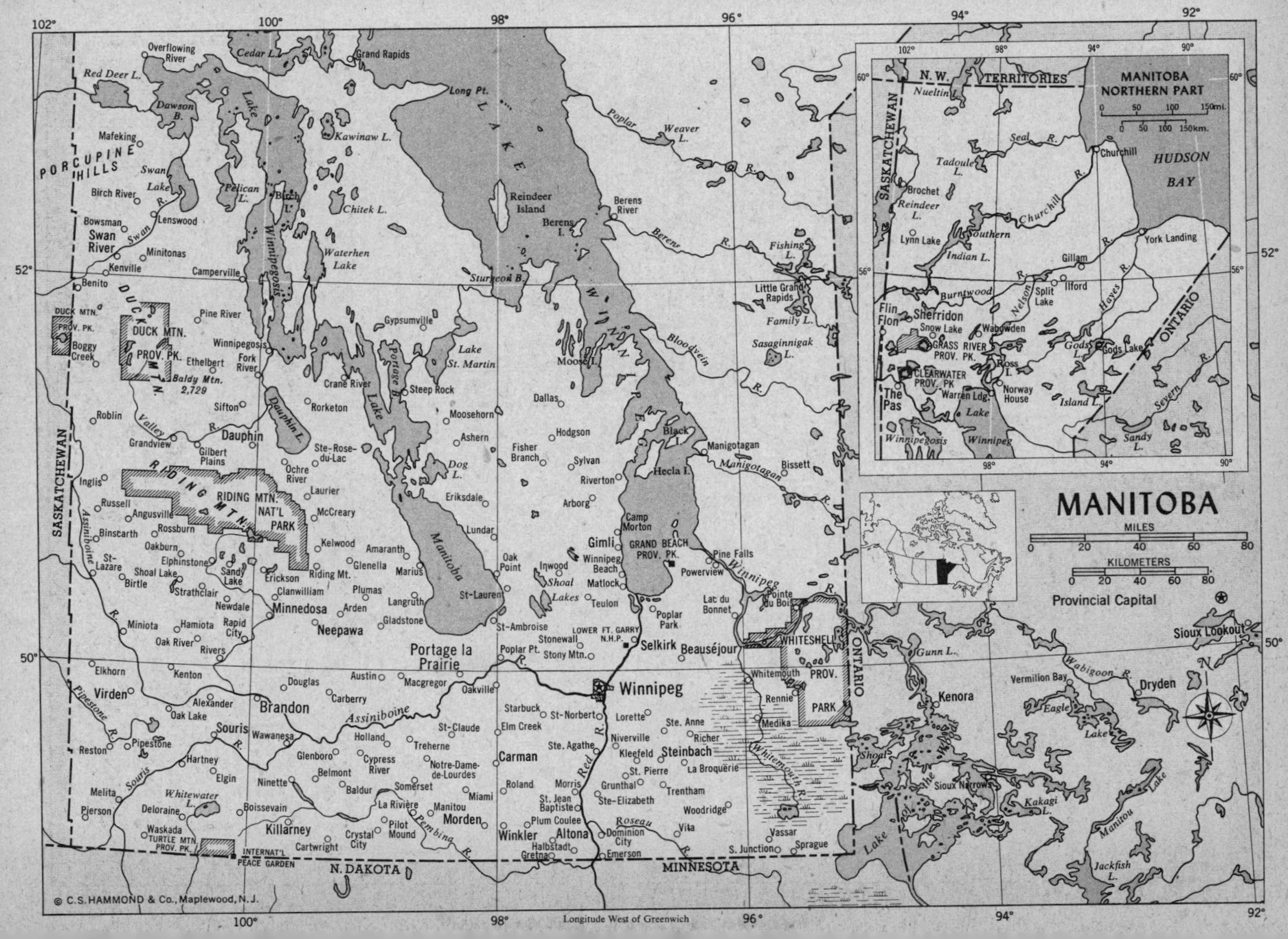

MANITOBA
MILES
KILOMETERS
Provincial Capital

MANITOBA
NORTHERN PART
N. W. TERRITORIES
SASKATCHEWAN
ONTARIO
HUDSON BAY
Nueltin L.
Tadoule L.
Brochet
Reindeer L.
Lynn Lake
Indian L.
Seal R.
Churchill
Southern
Churchill
York Landing
Gillam
Ilford
Split Lake
Burntwood
Nelson
Flin Flon
Sherridon
Snow Lake
Wabowden
GRASS RIVER PROV. PK.
Ross I.
Gods L.
Gods Lake
CLEARWATER PROV. PK.
The Pas
Warren Ldg.
Norway House
Island L.
Hayes
Severn
Sandy L.
Winnipegosis
Winnipeg Lake

Overflowing River
Red Deer L.
Cedar L.
Grand Rapids
Long Pt.
Poplar
Weaver L.
Mafeking
PORCUPINE HILLS
Swan Lake
Birch River
Pelican L.
Birch I.
Kawinaw L.
Chitek L.
Reindeer Island
Berens River
Berens I.
Bowsman
Lenswood
Swan River
Minitonas
Kenville
Benito
Camperville
Winnipegosis
Waterhen Lake
Sturgeon B.
Berens R.
Fishing L.
Little Grand Rapids
Family L.
Sasaginnigak L.
DUCK MTN. PROV. PK.
Boggy Creek
DUCK MTN. PROV. PK.
Pine River
Gypsumville
Bloodvein
Ethelbert
Fork River
Baldy Mtn. 2,729
Lake St. Martin
Moose I.
Winnipegosis
Crane River
Portage B.
Steep Rock
Dallas
Sifton
Rorketon
Moosehorn
Hodgson
Black
Manigotagan
Bissett
Roblin
Valley
Dauphin L.
Ashern
Fisher Branch
Sylvan
Hecla I.
Manigotagan
Dauphin
Ste-Rose-du-Lac
Dog L.
Riverton
Grandview
Gilbert Plains
Ochre River
Laurier
Eriksdale
Arborg
Camp Morton
Inglis
RIDING MTN. NAT'L PARK
McCreary
Lundar
Gimli
GRAND BEACH PROV. PK.
Pine Falls
Russell
Angusville
Rossburn
Kelwood
Amaranth
Oak Point
Winnipeg Beach
Powerview
Winnipeg R.
Binscarth
Oakburn
Elphinstone
Riding Mt.
Glenella
Marius
Inwood
Shoal Lakes
Matlock
Lac du Bonnet
Pointe du Bois
St-Lazare
Shoal Lake
Sandy Lake
Erickson
Clanwilliam
Plumas
Langruth
St-Laurent
Teulon
Poplar Park
Birtle
Strathclair
Newdale
Minnedosa
Arden
Gladstone
St-Ambroise
LOWER FT. GARRY N.H.P.
Miniota
Hamiota
Rapid City
Neepawa
Stonewall
Poplar Pt.
Stony Mtn.
Selkirk
Beauséjour
WHITESHELL PROV. PARK
Whitemouth
Rennie
Medika
ONTARIO
Gunn L.
Sioux Lookout
Oak River
Rivers
Portage la Prairie
Elkhorn
Kenton
Douglas
Austin
Macgregor
Oakville
Winnipeg
Whitemouth R.
Kenora
Vermilion Bay
Wabigoon R.
Dryden
Virden
Alexander
Oak Lake
Brandon
Carberry
Assiniboine
Starbuck
St-Norbert
Lorette
Ste. Anne
Richer
Eagle Lake
Souris
Wawanesa
St-Claude
Elm Creek
Niverville
Kleefeld
Steinbach
Whitemouth
Shoal
Sioux Narrows
Reston
Pipestone
Holland
Treherne
Ste. Agathe
Carman
St. Pierre
La Broquerie
Kakagi L.
Hartney
Glenboro
Cypress River
Notre-Dame-de-Lourdes
Roland
Morris
Grunthal
Trentham
Manitou L.
Elgin
Ninette
Belmont
Somerset
Baldur
Miami
St. Jean Baptiste
Ste-Elizabeth
Woodridge
Melita
Whitewater L.
Boissevain
La Rivière
Manitou
Morden
Plum Coulee
Roseau R.
Vita
Vassar
Jackfish L.
Pierson
Deloraine
Killarney
Crystal City
Pilot Mound
Pembina R.
Winkler
Altona
Dominion City
S. Junction
Sprague
Waskada
TURTLE MTN. PROV. PK.
Cartwright
INTERNAT'L PEACE GARDEN
Halbstadt
Gretna
Emerson
N. DAKOTA
MINNESOTA
Souris R.
Assiniboine
Red R.
Lake of the Woods
Manitou Lake
© C.S. HAMMOND & Co., Maplewood, N.J.
Longitude West of Greenwich

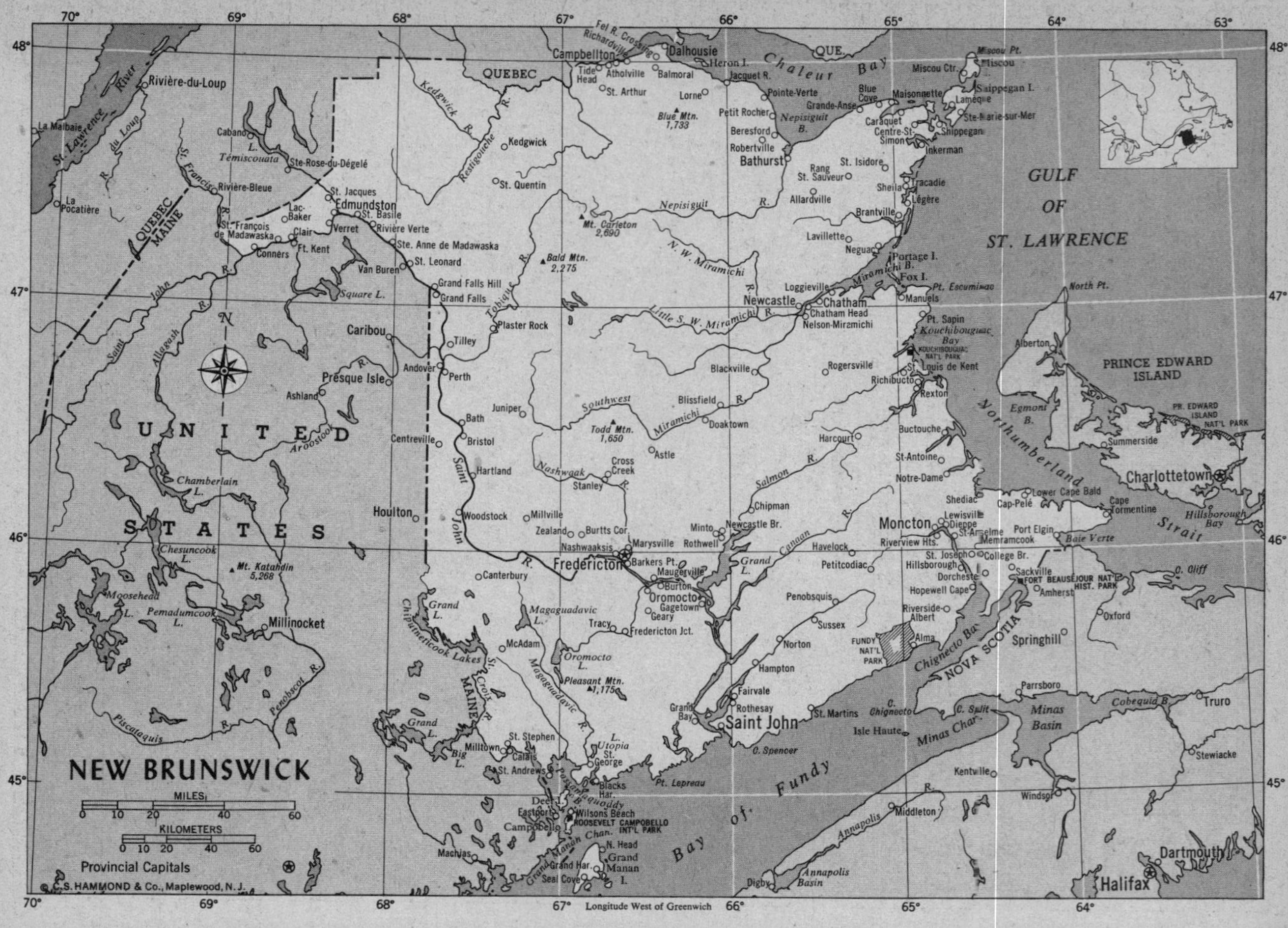
NEW BRUNSWICK
Provincial Capitals
MILES
KILOMETERS
C.S. HAMMOND & Co., Maplewood, N.J.
QUEBEC
QUE.
GULF OF ST. LAWRENCE
PRINCE EDWARD ISLAND
NOVA SCOTIA
MAINE
UNITED STATES
Bay of Fundy
Chaleur Bay
Northumberland Strait
Charlottetown
Summerside
Alberton
Egmont B.
North Pt.
Pt. Escuminac
Shediac
Dieppe
Moncton
Riverview Hts.
Lewisville
St. Joseph
Dorchester
Hillsborough
Hopewell Cape
Riverside
Albert
Alma
FUNDY NAT'L PARK
Sackville
FORT BEAUSÉJOUR NAT'L HIST. PARK
Amherst
Springhill
Parrsboro
Minas Basin
Chignecto Bay
C. Chignecto
Isle Haute
Windsor
Kentville
Middleton
Annapolis
Annapolis Basin
Digby
Truro
Stewiacke
Dartmouth
Halifax
Cobequid B.
C. Split
Saint John
Rothesay
Fairvale
Hampton
Norton
Sussex
Penobsquis
Havelock
Petitcodiac
Chipman
Minto
Newcastle Br.
Grand L.
Maugerville
Oromocto
Burton
Gagetown
Geary
Fredericton Jct.
Fredericton
Marysville
Nashwaaksis
Barkers Pt.
Burtts Cor.
Zealand
Millville
Stanley
Cross Creek
Astle
Juniper
Bristol
Hartland
Woodstock
Canterbury
McAdam
St. Stephen
Milltown
Calais
St. Andrews
Machias
ROOSEVELT CAMPOBELLO INT'L PARK
Campobello
Eastport
Grand Manan
N. Head
Seal Cove
Deer I.
Pt. Lepreau
St. George
Blacks Har.
Lepreau
St. Martins
C. Spencer
Passamaquoddy Bay
Grand L.
Chiputneticook Lakes
St. Croix R.
Houlton
Centreville
Andover
Perth
Tilley
Grand Falls
Grand Falls Hill
Plaster Rock
Bath
Bristol
Millinocket
Mt. Katahdin 5,268
Ashland
Presque Isle
Caribou
Van Buren
Ft. Kent
Conners
Clair
St. Jacques
Edmundston
Rivière Verte
Ste. Anne de Madawaska
St. Leonard
St. Basile
Lac-Baker
St. François de Madawaska
Ste-Rose-du-Dégelé
Temiscouata L.
Cabano
Rivière-Bleue
St. Francois
La Pocatière
La Malbaie
Rivière-du-Loup
St. Lawrence River
QUEBEC MAINE
Chamberlain L.
Chesuncook L.
Moosehead L.
Pemadumcook L.
Piscataquis R.
Penobscot R.
Aroostook R.
Allagash R.
Square L.
Kedgwick
St. Quentin
Kedgwick R.
Restigouche R.
Campbellton
Dalhousie
Fel R. Crossing
Richardville
Tide Head
Atholville
St. Arthur
Balmoral
Lorne
Blue Mtn. 1,783
Mt. Carleton 2,690
Bald Mtn. 2,275
Nepisiguit R.
N.W. Miramichi R.
Little S.W. Miramichi R.
S.W. Miramichi R.
Southwest Miramichi R.
Tobique R.
Nashwaak R.
Salmon R.
Canaan R.
Kennebecasis R.
Magaguadavic R.
Oromocto R.
Todd Mtn. 1,650
Pleasant Mtn. 1,175
Miscou Pt.
Miscou
Shippegan I.
Lamèque
Miscou Ctr.
Maisonnette
Shippegan
Inkerman
Tracadie
Légère
Sheila
Caraquet
Centre-St-Simon
Grande-Anse
Pointe-Verte
Beresford
Robertville
Petit Rocher
Bathurst
Nepisiguit B.
Rang St. Sauveur
St. Isidore
Allardville
St. Sauveur
Brantville
Neguac
Lavillette
Loggieville
Newcastle
Nelson-Miramichi
Chatham
Chatham Head
Fox I.
Portage I.
Pt. Sapin
Kouchibouguac
KOUCHIBOUGUAC NAT'L PARK
St. Louis de Kent
Rexton
Richibucto
Buctouche
Notre-Dame
St-Antoine
Manuels
Rogersville
Harcourt
Blackville
Blissfield
Doaktown
Rothwell
Gagetown
Oromocto L.
Magaguadavic L.
Victoria L.
Utopia L.
Saint John R.
C. Tormentine
Cape Tormentine
Port Elgin
Baie Verte
Memramcook
College Br.
Selme
St-Paul
Lower Cape
Cape Bald
Pr. Edward Island Nat'l Park
C. Cliff
Oxford
Longitude West of Greenwich

to lakes, subarctic tundra, and—most surprisingly of all for a "prairie" province—nearly 400 miles of salt-water coast on Hudson Bay. Its name and reputation derives from the fact that only the prairie area south of the infertile Pre-Cambrian shield is suitable for large-scale settlement.

Manitoba is bounded on the south by the U.S., on the west by Saskatchewan, on the north by the Keewatin District, and on the east by Ontario, but it was through its Hudson Bay sea coast that early European explorers, trappers, and settlers first came to the province. The first European to enter the territory was probably Sir Thomas Button in 1612. Nearly 60 years later, in 1670, the Hudson's Bay Company began building forts in the area, principally at the mouths of the Nelson and Churchill rivers. Throughout the 18th century the area was affected by the feud between the English Hudson's Bay Company and the French Northwest Company. The feud between the two fur-trading companies continued until 1821 when the rivals amalgamated.

Until the advent of the steamship and railroad in the mid-19th century, white men came to the provinces mostly as trappers and traders. An exception was the historic Red River Settlement (now Winnipeg), which was established in 1812, but it was not until the late 1860's that steam navigation from the north and railroads from the south and east made the area accessible to large numbers of settlers.

In 1870 the province of Manitoba was organized. It was linked by rail to the U.S. in 1878 and with eastern Canada in 1881, and the population, which was a mere 25,000 in 1871, grew to 250,000 in 1901 and 700,000 in 1931.

Like their prairie neighbors in both Canada and the U.S., Manitobans suffered during the 1920s and '30s, but since the hard years of the Great Depression, the growth of mineral, forest, and manufacturing industries, and the return of markets for its agricultural products have helped the province become one of Canada's richest. While it was once solely dependent on agriculture, its economy is now substantially diversified. Manufacturing accounts for over 40 percent of the province's net produced value; agriculture less than 20 percent.

In 1969 the New Democratic party won control after eleven years of Conservative rule. The NDP introduced public automobile insurance, medicare, and other wide-ranging social programs. In 1974, the province agreed to fund 25 percent of a pilot project which would give a guaranteed minimum income to 2,500 residents, the federal government paying the balance.

An upset victory in the October 1977 elections returned the Progressive Conservatives to office after eight years.

NEW BRUNSWICK

Area: 27,633 square miles **Population:** 677,250 (1976 Census); 705,700 (Apr. 1, 1980 estimate); ranks eighth; population density 24.5 per square mile; urban, 52%; rural, 48% **Capital:** Fredericton **Major cities (1976 census agglomeration) populations:** Fredericton, 45,885; Moncton, 77,571; Saint John, 112,974

Ethnic Composition: British Isles, 58%; French, 37% **Religion:** Roman Catholic, 52%; Baptist, 14%; United Church, 13%; Anglican, 11% **Vital Statistics (per 1,000 population 1978):** birth rate, 15.5; death rate, 7.5; marriage rate, 7.6; divorce rate, 1.66; infant mortality (per 1,000 live births), 11.8

Location and Geography: Nearly rectangular in shape, New Brunswick has an extensive sea coast: on the Bay of Chaleur on the north, the Gulf of St. Lawrence and Northumberland Strait on the east, and the Bay of Fundy on the south. Much of the soil is rocky and unfit for agriculture, but generous rainfall produces prolific forest growth. The Bay of Fundy, which separates New Brunswick and Nova Scotia, has the world's highest tides, and there are proposals to harness these to produce electric power

Government: New Brunswick became a province in 1867 and is represented in the federal government by 10 members in the House of Commons and 10 Senators. The provincial government is unicameral with a Legislative Assembly of 58 members. In October 1978, 30 Progressive Conservatives and 27 Liberals, plus the speaker were elected to the legislature **Premier:** Honourable Richard Hatfield **Salary and allowance:** $46,023

Education (1972): In the Atlantic Provinces (New Brunswick, Newfoundland, Nova Scotia, and Prince Edward Island) 95% of the population had over Grade IV education; 28.8%, secondary school; and 4.5%, university **Total expenditures on education (school year ended June 30, 1979):** $233,383,000 **Schools:** 465 primary and secondary schools (1979-80) with a combined enrollment of 155,819 (Sept. 30, 1979) **Colleges:** Four degree-granting universities with a total enrollment of 10,770. There are 8 campuses known as New Brunswick Community Colleges which comprise what used to be trade schools and institutes of technology with a full-time enrollment of 4,195 (Sept. 30, 1979)

Value added in goods-producing industries (1978 est.): $1,688,400. Manufacturing represented 47% of this total, construction 28%, electric power 8%, mining 5%, forestry 4%, agriculture 4% **Leading manufacturing industries (1977):** pulp and paper mills, sawmills and planing mills, and fishery products **Average industrial earnings (Mar. 1980):** $277.48 per week **Cash receipts from farming operations (1979):** $137,952,000 **Families with incomes over $10,000 (1978 est.):** 66.5% **Per capita personal income (1979):** $6,506 **Unemployment (1979):** 11.1%

Provincial Finances: Estimated gross general revenue, fiscal year 1979-80, $1,392.5 million; estimated gross general expenditure, $1,330.8 million

Daily newspapers (1979): 6 **Circulation:** 150,536 **Telephones per 100 population (1979):** 54 **Homes with radios:** 98.0% **Homes with TV's:** 98.0%

Hospital beds (excluding provincial hospitals, 1979): 4,270 (6.1 per 1,000 population) **Physicians (1979):** 720 (population per physician, 973)

Motor vehicles (1978): 340,777 **Residents per motor vehicle:** 2.0 **Motor vehicle deaths (1978):** 226

There was little settlement of New Brunswick during the French period, and for 20 years following the beginning of British rule (1763), the sea coasts and river valleys were largely left to the fur traders. Then "Tories"—"Loyalists" as they are called in New Brunswick—escaping from the rebelling American Colonies southward, settled the area in 1783. At that time the County of Sunbury was split from Nova Scotia and made a separate province named New Brunswick, after the family name of the reigning monarch, George III.

Other immigrations brought Scottish farmers and laborers and immigrants from Great Britain after the Napoleonic wars of the next century. By 1842 the population had swelled to 74,000.

The 600 mile long New Brunswick coast and the softwood forests of the interior encouraged the development of lumbering, shipbuilding, and fisheries and, helped by preferential tariffs and trade agreements with England, the colony was initially prosperous. Its resources were a mixed blessing, however, for they hindered the development of a well balanced economy and political system.

By 1866 declining economic fortunes forced the colony into a not wholly welcome union with the nascent Dominion of Canada. A major railroad link with Montreal was established as a result of a pre-unification agreement, but its promise of economic salvation was dimmed as the coming of the steamship, and the depletion of its forest reserves brought economic ruin to many provincial industries.

Since World War II some success has occurred in developing a more balanced economy. Although still heavily oriented towards extractive industries and their exportation, the province has attempted to develop manufacturing industries for processing the raw materials.

The service sector accounts for 70 percent of provincial employment; nearly one-quarter of the labor force works in the public sector, including military establishments at Oromocto and Chatham.

NEWFOUNDLAND

Area: 156,185 square miles **Population:** 557,725 (1976 Census); 577,400 (Jan. 1, 1980 estimate); ranks ninth; population density 3.9; urban 58.9%; rural 41.1% **Capital:** St. John's **Major cities (1976 metropolitan area populations):** St. John's, 143,390; Corner Brook, 25,198

Ethnic Composition: British Isles, 94%; French, 3% **Religion:** Roman Catholic, 37%; Anglican, 28%; United Church, 19% **Vital Statistics (per 1,000 population):** birth rate, 18.4; death rate, 5.5; marriage rate, 6.8; divorce rate, 0.81; infant mortality (per 1,000 live births), 12.2

Location and Geography: Newfoundland includes the island of Newfoundland (43,359 square miles) and the coast of Labrador (112,828 square miles) on the mainland. They are separated by the Strait of Belle Isle which is nine and a half miles wide at its narrowest point. The island's surface is low, rolling, and rocky. Its highest point is Lewis Hill (2,672 feet) in the Northern peninsula. The west coast and river valleys are thickly forested

Government: Newfoundland became a province in 1949 and is represented in the federal government by 7 members in the House of Commons and 6 Senators. The provincial government is unicameral with a House of Assembly of 52 members. In June 1979, 33 Progressive Conservatives and 19 Liberals were elected to the house **Premier:** Honourable Brian Peckford **Salary and allowance:** $43,690

Education (April 1980): 34.8% of the population 15 years of age and over had Grade 8 or less; 43.9% attended high school; 6.8% had some post-secondary education; 10.0% had a post-secondary certificate or diploma; 4.5% had a university degree **Total expenditures on education (1978-79):** $371,238,000 **Schools:** 692 primary and secondary schools (1978-79) with a combined enrollment of 153,576 **Colleges:** One degree-granting university and six non-university post-secondary institutions with enrollment of 8,121

Value added in goods-producing industries (1977): $1,402,998,000; Construction represented 22.0% of this total; mining 31.1%, manufacturing 25.0%, electric power 11.8% and fisheries 6.1%. (The development of the huge iron ore deposits in Labrador has boosted Newfoundland to 6th position in the nation's production of minerals. In 1979 production was valued at $1,100,152,000. Iron ore contributed 86.3% of the total and represented 50.3% of the total Canadian production.) **Value of manufacturing shipments (1977):** $697,466,000 **Leading manufacturing industry:** fishery products **Average industrial earnings (Feb. 1980):** $283.73 per week **Families with incomes over $12,000 (1977):** 57.8% **Per capita personal income (1978):** $5,313 **Unemployment (1979):** 15.4%

Provincial Finances: Estimated gross general revenue, fiscal year 1978-79: $1,179.1 million; estimated gross general expenditure, $1,242.1 million

Daily newspapers (1977): 3 **Circulation:** 50,302 **Telephones per 100 population (1978):** 40.6 **Homes with radios:** 97.1% **Homes with TV's:** 98.6%

Hospital beds (1979): 3,624 (6.3 per 1,000 population) **Physicians (1977):** 803 (population per physician, 704)

Motor Vehicles (1978): 188,357 **Residents per motor vehicle:** 3.0 **Motor vehicle deaths:** 73

Newfoundland, which consists of the island of Newfoundland itself and the coast of Labrador, is a land of great natural resources. Huge forests of spruce and pine cover much of the area; the inland wilderness has an abundance of wildlife; great mineral wealth lies hidden beneath the surface; hydroelectric power is abundant; and the Grand Banks, in which it is located, is a fishing ground of legendary richness.

Despite these resources, the history of Newfoundland is largely one of great promise only partially fulfilled. It was discovered by John Cabot in 1497, and Sir Humphrey Gilbert made a formal claim for Britain in 1583, but the island remained a distant outpost visited only by fishing boats until the end of the 18th century. By then a court system and land-based commerce had been established, but by 1850 the population had only increased to 30,000.

Fishing and forestry gave the island limited prosperity through the 1860s and '70s, and fueled by this the small province chose not to join the Canadian nation when it was granted dominion status in 1867. The question of union was taken up again in the 1890s, but by then the province's precarious economic condition made it impossible. It remained independent until February 16, 1934 when, after surveying the province's debts, Britain reestablished direct rule, which was then maintained until Newfoundland was united with Canada in 1949.

Many economists today believe that Newfoundland's continuing economic problems can be solved only by developing resource industries and increasing the volume of local processing and refining, as opposed to the continuing export of raw natural resources. In 1979, it was reported that a large oil deposit had been discovered off the coast.

Provincial elections on June 18, 1979 saw the Progressive Conservatives increase their majority in the 52-member assembly to 33, with the Liberals winning the remaining 19 seats.

NOVA SCOTIA

Area: 20,396.55 square miles **Population:** 828,571 (1976 Census); 851,000 (Jan. 1, 1980 estimate); ranks seventh; population density 41.7 **Capital:** Halifax **Major city populations (1976 metropolitan populations):** Halifax, 235,440; Dartmouth, 65,341

Ethnic Composition: British Isles, 77%; French, 10%; German, 5% **Religion:** Roman Catholic, 36%; United Church, 21%; Anglican, 17%; Baptist, 13%; Presbyterian, 5% **Vital Statistics (per 1,000 population, 1978):** birth rate, 14.9; death rate, 8.2; marriage rate, 7.8; divorce rate, 2.3; infant mortality (per 1,000 live births), 11.9

Location and Geography: The province is a 359.6-mile long peninsula. The Atlantic coast is generally rocky; the slopes facing the Bay of Fundy and Gulf of St. Lawrence, sheltered from the Atlantic storms by a series of low ridges that run through the center of the province, consist of fertile plains and river valleys. Cape Breton Island, the northeast portion of the province, is mostly rugged upland and is divided almost in two by the saltwater Bras d'Or Lake, in reality a land-enclosed extension of the sea

Government: Nova Scotia became a province in 1867 and is represented in the federal government by 11 members in the House of Commons and 10 Senators. The provincial government is unicameral with a House of Assembly of 52 members. In October 1978, 31 Progressive Conservatives, 17 Liberals and four New Democrats were elected to the house **Premier:** Honourable John M. Buchanan, Q.C.

Education (1976 census): In Nova Scotia 25.3% of the population 15 years of age and over have completed a Grade 8 education; 44.9% have attended high school; 23.9% have taken post-secondary education; and 5.9% have university degrees **Total expenditures on education (1978-79):** $380 million **Schools:** 615 primary and secondary schools with a combined enrollment of 198,715 **Colleges:** 10 degree-granting universities and colleges with a full-time enrollment of 17,932 in 1978-79

Value added in goods-producing industries (1977): $1,722,700,000; manufacturing represents 45.1% of this total; construction, 27.9%; fisheries, 7.7%; and mining, 7.0%. The province vies with British Columbia each year as the nation's leading producer of fish products. These in 1978 had a total value of $441,305,000 **Leading manufacturing industries (1979):** Petroleum and coal products, food and beverage, paper and allied industries, and transportation equipment industries **Average industrial earnings (1979):** $245.23 per week **Cash Receipts from farming operations (1979):** $175,262,000, with 27.8% derived from dairy products, 23.2% from livestock, 16.1% from crops, 19.5% from poultry and eggs **Families with incomes over $10,000 (1978):** 76% **Per capita personal income (1979 est.):** $7,183 **Unemployment (1979):** 10.2%

Provincial Finances: Revenue plus recoveries, forecast fiscal year 1979-80, $1,555,364,700; estimated 1980-81, $1,714,383,700. Expenditure, forecast 1979-80, $1,523,906,400; estimated 1980-81, $1,730,618,300

NEWFOUNDLAND
LABRADOR (PART OF NEWFOUNDLAND)
Provincial Capital
MILES
0 10 20 40 60 80 100
KILOMETERS
0 10 20 40 60 80 100
ST. PIERRE & MIQUELON (France)
© C.S. HAMMOND & Co., Maplewood, N.J.
Longitude West of Greenwich
LABRADOR
QUEBEC
Lake Melville
MEALY MTS.
Rigolet
Indian Har.
Hamilton Inlet
George I.
West Bay
North R.
Sand Hill R.
3,700
Sandwich B.
Cartwright
Separation Point
Table Bay
Huntingdon I.
Labrador Sea
I. of Ponds
HIGH MTS.
2,080
Eagle R.
Paradise R.
Hawke I.
Stony I.
Gilbert R.
Square Islands
Alexis R.
1,920
Port Hope Simpson
St. Lewis R.
Fox Har.
Battle Har.
Mary's Har.
Henley Har.
Belle Isle
Red Bay
R. St. Paul
R. St. Augustin
W. St-Modeste
L'Anse-au-Loup
Forteau
Blanc-Sablon
Strait of Belle Isle
Pistolet B.
Griquet
St. Anthony
Cook's Har.
St-Augustin
R. Petit Mécatina
Flower's Cove
Hare Bay
Mutton Bay
Harrington Harbour
Gulf of St. Lawrence
Ten Mile L.
Bartlett's Har.
St. John I.
Roddickton
Englee
Groais I.
Grey Is.
Bell I.
Ingornachoix B.
Port Saunders
Canada B.
Daniel's Har.
Harbour Deep
White Bay
St. Barbe Is.
Fleur-de-Lys
C. St. John
Cow Head
GROS MORNE NAT'L PK.
Jackson's Arm
Seal Cove
Baie-Verte
La Scie
LONG RANGE MTS.
Bonne B.
Gros Morne 2,644
Nippers Har.
Notre Dame Bay
Twillingate
Fogo
Joe Batt's Arm
Fogo I.
Trout River
Trout River Pond
Norris
Hampden
King's Pt.
New World I.
Sir Chas. Hamilton Sd.
Bay of Islands
SIR R. A. SQUIRES MEM. PK.
Springdale
Robert's Arm
Carmanville
Lumsden
Lark Har.
Deer Lake
Cook's Cove
Humber R.
Sandy L.
Main Topsail 1,822
Howley
Botwood
Lewisporte
Norris Arm
Wesleyville
Greenspond
Corner Brook
Grand Lake
Badger
Windsor
Gander R.
Gander
Hare Bay
Bonavista Bay
Port au Port B.
SERPENTINE PROV. PK.
Buchans
Red Indian L.
Bishop's Falls
Grand Falls
Gander L.
Bonavista
Lourdes
Port au Port Pen.
Stephenville
Stephenville Crossing
Exploits R.
NEWFOUNDLAND
TERRA NOVA NAT'L PARK
Catalina
C. St. George
St. George's Bay
St. George's
Meelpaeg L.
Great Burnt L.
Mt. Sylvester 1,250
Terra Nova R.
Port Blandford
Trinity
Random I.
Trinity Bay
Grates Pt.
Robinsons
Victoria L.
Clarenville
Bay de Verde
LONG RANGE MTS.
Round Pond
Sunnyside
Conception Bay
Pouch Cove
C. Anguille
Port-aux-Basques
St. Alban's
Milltown
Gisburn L.
Victoria
Carbonear
Bell I.
Torbay
C. Ray
Rose-Blanche
Terrenceville
Harbour Grace
Wabana
St. John's
Channel
Burgeo
La Poile B.
Ramea
François
Hermitage B.
Belleoram
Harbour Breton
Fortune B.
Garnish
Marystown
Creston
Burin
Placentia Bay
Bay Roberts
Holyrood
Avalon Pen.
Bay Bulls
Mt. Carmel
Cape Broyle
Cabot Strait
Miquelon
Grand Bank
Fortune
St-Pierre
Lamaline
Burin Pen.
St. Lawrence
Placentia
Branch
St. Mary's
St. Mary's B.
St. Vincent's
C. Pine
Ferryland
Renews
Trepassey
C. Race
ATLANTIC OCEAN
Ungava Bay
Akpatok I.
Killinek I.
Button Is.
C. Chidley
N. Aulatsivik I.
Ft. Chimo
George R.
R. de la Baleine
TORNGAT MTS.
QUEBEC
LABRADOR
Cirque Mtn. 5,160
Saglek B.
Hebron
Nutak
S. Aulatsivik I.
Nain
Tunungayualok I.
Davis Inlet
Hopedale
Schefferville
Makkovik
C. Harrison
Canairiktok R.
Menihek Lakes
Smallwood Res.
Rigolet
Hamilton Inlet
Labrador City
Churchill Falls
North West River
L. Melville
Cartwright
Lac Joseph
Churchill R.
Goose Bay
Ashuanipi L.
Atikonak L.
Eagle R.
Port Hope Simpson
SAGUENAY PROVINCIAL PARK
Havre-St-Pierre
QUEBEC
St-Augustin
Str. of Belle Isle
Ste. Anthony
Sept-Îles (Seven Islands)
Anticosti I.
G. of St. Lawrence
Harrington Har.
Port Saunders
NEWFOUNDLAND
Labrador Sea

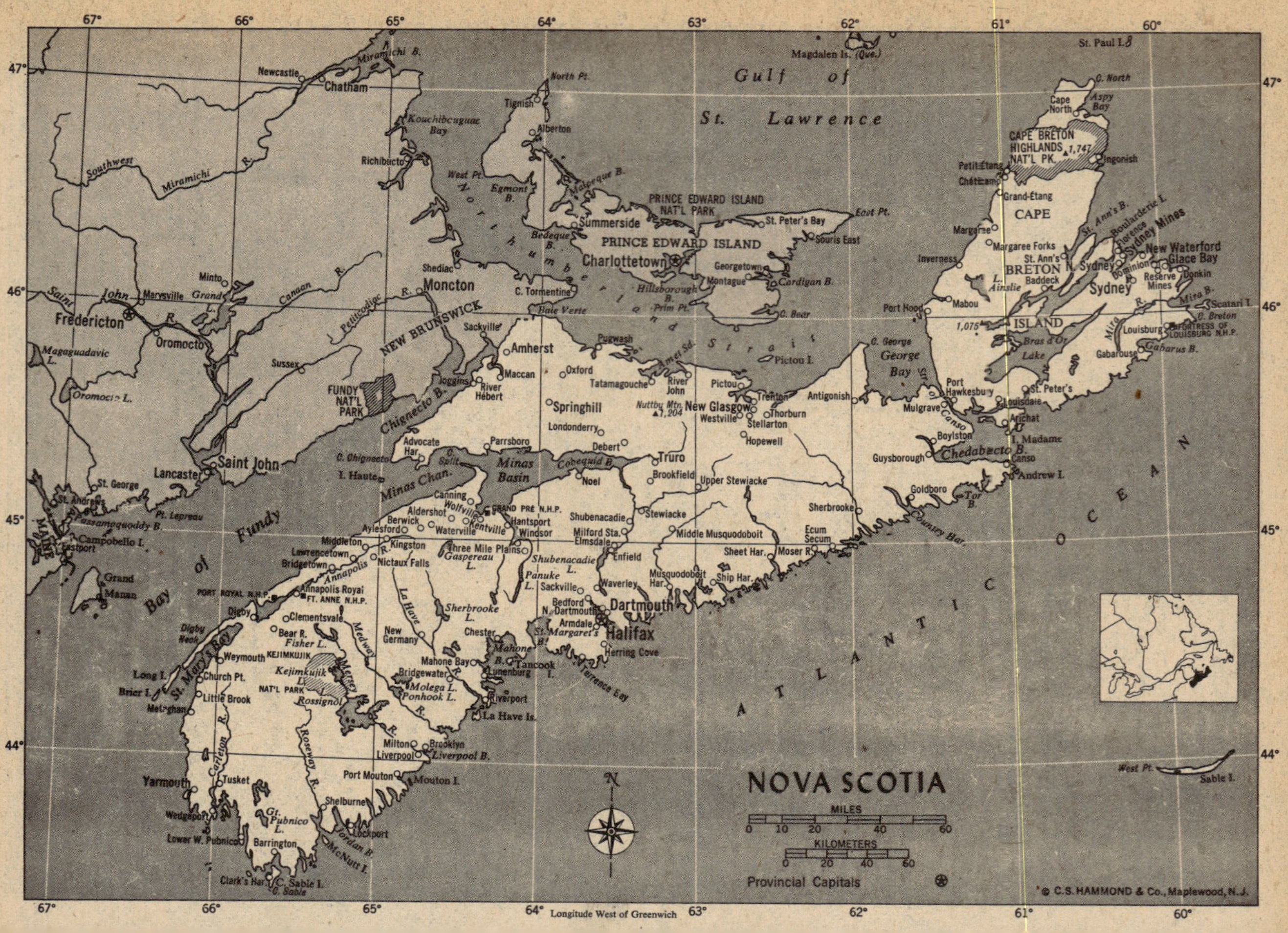
NOVA SCOTIA
MILES
KILOMETERS
Provincial Capitals
Longitude West of Greenwich
© C.S. HAMMOND & Co., Maplewood, N.J.
Gulf of St. Lawrence
Magdalen Is. (Que.)
St. Paul I.
C. North
Cape North
Aspy Bay
Ingonish
CAPE BRETON HIGHLANDS NAT'L PK. 1,747
Petit-Etang
Chéticamp
Grand-Etang
CAPE
Margaree
Margaree Forks
St. Ann's B.
Boularderie I.
Florence
Sydney Mines
New Waterford
Glace Bay
Inverness
St. Ann's
L. Ainslie
BRETON
N. Sydney
Baddeck
Dominion
Reserve Mines
Donkin
Sydney
Mira B.
Scatari I.
C. Breton
ISLAND
1,075
Bras d'Or Lake
Mabou
Port Hood
Louisburg
FORTRESS OF LOUISBURG N.H.P.
Mira R.
Gabarous
Gabarus B.
G. George Bay
Port Hawkesbury
Louisdale
Arichat
I. Madame
St. Peter's
Chedabucto B.
Canso
Andrew I.
Goldboro
Tor B.
Newcastle
Chatham
Miramichi B.
Southwest Miramichi
Kouchibouguac Bay
Richibucto
Tignish
Alberton
North Pt.
West Pt.
Egmont B.
Malpeque B.
Northumberland
PRINCE EDWARD ISLAND NAT'L PARK
Summerside
St. Peter's Bay
East Pt.
Souris East
PRINCE EDWARD ISLAND
Charlottetown
Bedeque B.
Georgetown
Montague
Cardigan B.
Hillsborough B.
Prim Pt.
C. Bear
Strait
Minto
Marysville
Grand
Canaan R.
Shediac
Moncton
C. Tormentine
Baie Verte
Saint John R.
Fredericton
Oromocto
Magaguadavic L.
Oromocto L.
Petitcodiac R.
NEW BRUNSWICK
Sackville
Amherst
Maccan
Pugwash
Oxford
Tatamagouche
River John
Pictou I.
Pictou
Trenton
Antigonish
Mulgrave
Boylston
Guysborough
Canso
Sussex
FUNDY NAT'L PARK
Joggins
River Hébert
Chignecto B.
Springhill
Londonderry
Nuttby Mtn. 1,204
New Glasgow
Thorburn
Westville
Stellarton
Hopewell
Advocate Har.
Parrsboro
Debert
Truro
Hantsport
Wolfville
Brookfield
Upper Stewiacke
Sherbrooke
St. George
Lancaster
Saint John
St. Andrews
Pt. Lepreau
Passamaquoddy B.
Campobello I.
Eastport
Grand Manan
MAINE
Bay of Fundy
O. Chignecto
Split
I. Haute
Minas Chan.
Minas Basin
Cobequid B.
Noel
Canning
Aldershot
Berwick
Aylesford
Waterville
Kentville
GRAND PRE N.H.P.
Windsor
Three Mile Plains
Gaspereau L.
Shubenacadie
Milford Sta.
Elmsdale
Shubenacadie L.
Panuke L.
Stewiacke
Middle Musquodoboit
Enfield
Waverley
Musquodoboit Har.
Ecum Secum
Sheet Har.
Moser R.
Ship Har.
Sunary Bar
Middleton
Lawrencetown
Bridgetown
R. Kingston
Nictaux Falls
PORT ROYAL N.H.P.
Annapolis
Annapolis Royal
FT. ANNE N.H.P.
Digby
Digby Neck
Clementsvale
Bear R.
Fisher L.
Weymouth
KEJIMKUJIK
La Have
Sherbrooke L.
New Germany
Chester
Bedford
N. Dartmouth
Armdale
St. Margaret's B.
Dartmouth
Halifax
Herring Cove
Terrence Bay
Long I.
Brier I.
Church Pt.
Little Brook
Meteghan
St. Mary's Bay
Carleton
Medway R.
Kejimkujik L.
NAT'L PARK
Molega L.
Ponhook L.
Rossignol L.
Mahone B.
Mahone Bay
Bridgewater
Lunenburg
Tancook I.
Riverport
La Have Is.
Milton
Brooklyn
Liverpool
Liverpool B.
Yarmouth
Tusket
Wedgeport
Lower W. Pubnico
Gt. Pubnico L.
Barrington
Mersey R.
Shelburne
Jordan B.
McNutt I.
Lockport
Port Mouton
Mouton I.
Roseway R.
Clark's Har.
C. Sable I.
C. Sable
West Pt.
Sable I.
ATLANTIC OCEAN
N

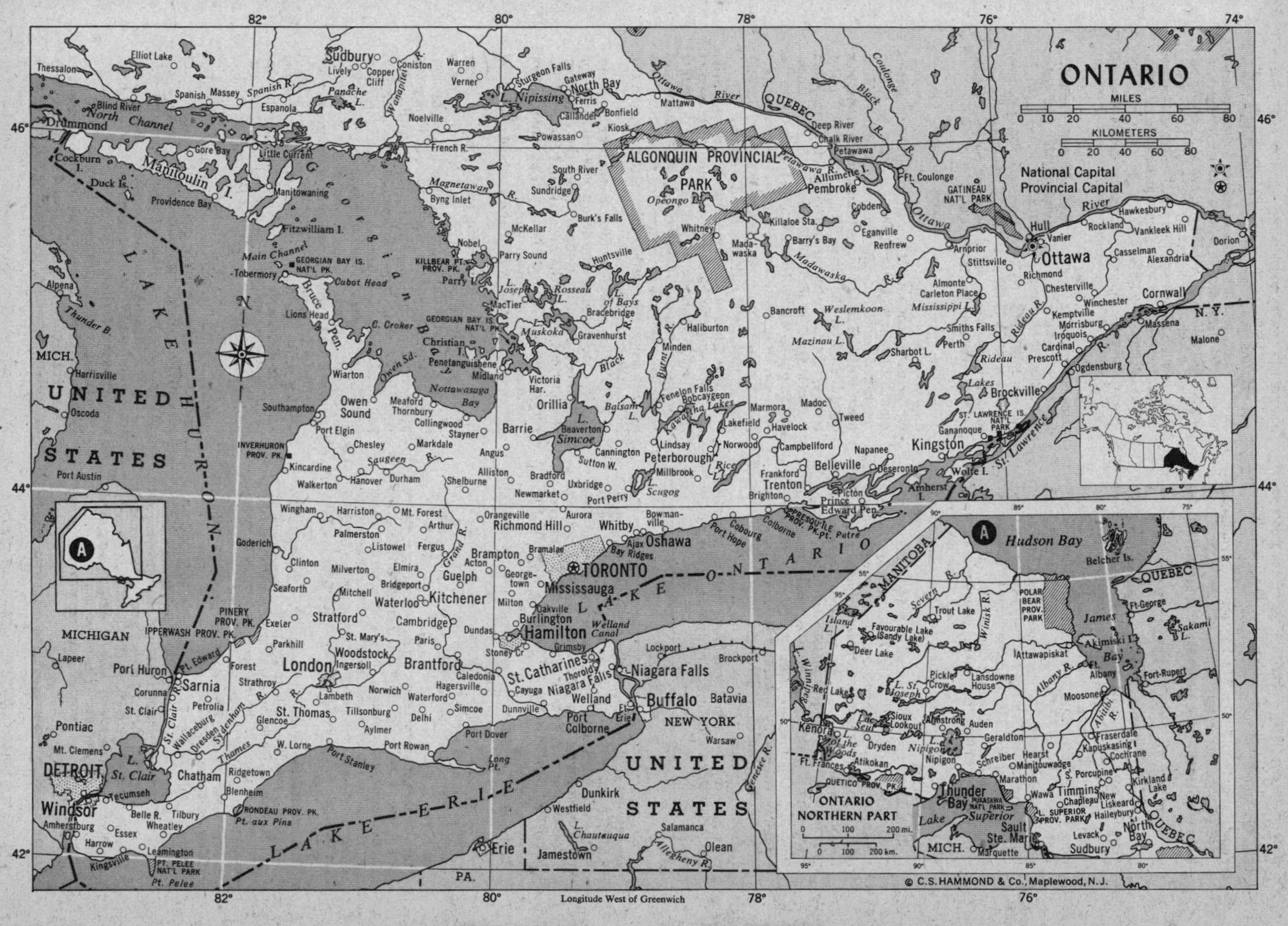

ONTARIO
MILES
KILOMETERS
National Capital
Provincial Capital
Thessalon
Elliot Lake
Sudbury
Coniston
Warren
Lively
Copper Cliff
Panache L.
Verner
Sturgeon Falls
Gateway
North Bay
Spanish
Massey
Spanish R.
Espanola
Wanapitei L.
Noelville
L. Nipissing
Ferris
Bonfield
Callander
Mattawa
Ottawa
River
QUEBEC
Black
Coulonge
Blind River
North Channel
Drummond
Gore Bay
Little Current
French R.
Kiosk
Powassan
Deep River
Chalk River
Petawawa
Petawawa R.
Cockburn I.
Duck Is.
Manitoulin I.
Providence Bay
Manitowaning
Magnetawan
South River
Sundridge
ALGONQUIN PROVINCIAL PARK
Opeongo L.
Allumette I.
Ft. Coulonge
GATINEAU NAT'L PARK
Pembroke
Cobden
Eganville
Renfrew
River
Hull
Vanier
Ottawa
Hawkesbury
Rockland
Vankleek Hill
Dorion
Fitzwilliam I.
Byng Inlet
Burk's Falls
Killaloe Sta.
Barry's Bay
Whitney
Madawaska
Madawaska
Arnprior
Stittsville
Almonte
Carleton Place
Mississippi L.
Richmond
Ottawa
Casselman
Alexandria
MICH.
Alpena
Thunder B.
LAKE HURON
Main Channel
GEORGIAN BAY IS. NAT'L PK.
KILLBEAR PT. PROV. PK.
Tobermory
Cabot Head
Bruce Pen.
Lions Head
McKellar
Nobel
Parry Sound
Parry I.
MacTier
L. Joseph
Rosseau L.
L. of Bays
Bracebridge
Huntsville
Bancroft
Weslemkoon L.
Mississippi L.
Smiths Falls
Perth
Sharbot L.
Rideau
Rideau R.
Kemptville
Morrisburg
Iroquois
Cardinal
Prescott
Winchester
Chesterville
Cornwall
N.Y.
Massena
Malone
Ogdensburg
Harrisville
Oscoda
C. Croker
GEORGIAN BAY IS. NAT'L PK.
Christian I.
Penetanguishene
Muskoka
Gravenhurst
Black
Minden
Haliburton
Mazinau L.
Lakes
Brockville
Gananoque
ST. LAWRENCE IS. NAT. PARK
St. Lawrence
Port Austin
UNITED STATES
Wiarton
Owen Sd.
Midland
Victoria Har.
Nottawasaga Bay
Orillia
Balsam L.
Burnt R.
Fenelon Falls
Bobcaygeon
Kawartha Lakes
Marmora
Madoc
Tweed
Wolfe I.
Amherst I.
Kingston
Deseronto
Napanee
Southampton
Owen Sound
Meaford
Thornbury
Collingwood
Stayner
Barrie
Simcoe
Beaverton L.
Lindsay
Lakefield
Havelock
Campbellford
Belleville
Picton
Prince Edward Pen.
INVERHURON PROV. PK.
Port Elgin
Chesley
Markdale
Angus
Saugeen R.
Kincardine
Hanover
Durham
Alliston
Shelburne
Newmarket
Bradford
Uxbridge
Port Perry
Sutton W.
Cannington
Scugog L.
Millbrook
Peterborough
Rice L.
Norwood
Frankford
Trenton
Brighton
Presqu'ile
Amherst
MICHIGAN
A
Wingham
Harriston
Mt. Forest
Arthur
Goderich
Palmerston
Listowel
Fergus
Clinton
Milverton
Elmira
Bridgeport
Seaforth
Mitchell
Waterloo
Kitchener
Stratford
Cambridge
St. Mary's
Parkhill
Dundas
Paris
Woodstock
Ingersoll
Orangeville
Richmond Hill
Aurora
Brampton
Bramalea
Bay Ridges
Acton
Georgetown
Guelph
Milton
Oakville
Mississauga
TORONTO
Whitby
Ajax
Oshawa
Bowmanville
Cobourg
Port Hope
Colborne
PRESQU'ILE PROV. PK.-Pt. Putre
LAKE ONTARIO
Welland Canal
Burlington
Hamilton
Grimsby
Stoney Cr.
St. Catharines
Thorold
Niagara Falls
Lockport
Brockport
PINERY PROV. PK.
Exeter
IPPERWASH PROV. PK.
Pt. Edward
Forest
London
Strathroy
Brantford
Caledonia
Hagersville
Norwich
Waterford
Delhi
Simcoe
Cayuga
Niagara Falls
Welland
Port Colborne
Buffalo
NEW YORK
Batavia
Warsaw
Lapeer
Port Huron
Corunna
Sarnia
Petrolia
St. Clair
St. Clair
Wallaceburg
Dresden
Sydenham
Thames
St. Thomas
W. Lorne
Lambeth
Tillsonburg
Aylmer
Port Rowan
Port Dover
Dunnville
Port Stanley
Long Pt.
LAKE ERIE
Dunkirk
Westfield
L. Chautauqua
Salamanca
Olean
Genesee R.
Allegheny R.
UNITED STATES
Pontiac
Mt. Clemens
DETROIT
L. St. Clair
Tecumseh
Windsor
Amherstburg
Harrow
Belle R.
Tilbury
Essex
Wheatley
Kingsville
Leamington
PT. PELEE NAT'L PARK
Pt. Pelee
Glencoe
Blenheim
Ridgetown
RONDEAU PROV. PK.
Pt. aux Pins
Chatham
Erie
Jamestown
PA.
Longitude West of Greenwich
CANADA
493
Hudson Bay
Belcher Is.
QUEBEC
Ft-George
Sakami L.
Akimiski I.
James Bay
Fort-Rupert
Albany
Moosonee
Attawapiskat
Winisk R.
POLAR BEAR PROV. PARK
MANITOBA
Severn
Trout Lake
Favourable Lake (Sandy Lake)
Deer Lake
Island L.
L. Winnipeg
Red Lake
Lac Seul
L. St. Joseph
Crow
Sioux Lookout
Lansdowne House
Pickle
Armstrong
Auden
Geraldton
Fraserdale
Kapuskasing
Cochrane
Kenora
Lake of the Woods
Dryden
Atikokan
QUETICO PROV. PK.
Ft. Frances
Nipigon
Nipigon L.
Schreiber
Hearst
Manitouwadge
S. Porcupine
Marathon
Wawa
Timmins
New Liskeard
Haileybury
Chapleau
L. SUPERIOR PROV. PARK
PUKASKWA NAT'L PARK
Thunder Bay
ONTARIO NORTHERN PART
Lake Superior
Sault Ste. Marie
MICH.
Marquette
Levack
Sudbury
North Bay
QUEBEC
Abitibi R.
Albany R.
© C.S. HAMMOND & Co., Maplewood, N.J.

Daily newspapers (1978): 6 **Circulation:** 183,417 **Telephones per 100 population (1979):** 56.0 **Homes with radios:** 98.8% **Homes with TV's:** 98.0%

Hospital beds (1979): 6,164 (7.5 per 1,000 population) **Physicians:** 1,446 (population per physician approx. 586)

Motor vehicles (1979): 493,371 **Motor vehicle deaths (1979):** 189

John Cabot is regarded, on the basis of his 1497 visit to Cape Breton Island, as the "discoverer" of Nova Scotia, despite the belief that Norsemen and European fishermen probably visited the island long before Columbus arrived in the New World. Britain's claim to Nova Scotia began with Cabot's visit, but its sovereignty was contested by France until Halifax was firmly established as a naval and military base in 1749, and the Acadians were expelled in 1755. Following the American Revolution, nearly 30,000 "Loyalists" emigrated to Nova Scotia, becoming its first citizens. The province was a founding member of the Canadian confederation.

Population growth, increased trade, and wealth marked the first half of the 19th century. In 1846 the colony had one-third as much shipping tonnage as France, but today Nova Scotia shares many of the problems of its neighboring provinces. Its economy is largely dependent on low-technology industries such as fishing and mining, and though the federal government is attempting to diversify the economy, unemployment and economic disparity between the Maritime Provinces and the rest of Canada remains.

A growing vacationland, Nova Scotia has two national parks and nine designated historic parks.

ONTARIO

Area: 412,582 square miles **Population:** 8,264,465 (1976 Census); 8,543,300 (Jan. 1, 1980 estimate); ranks first; population density, 23.3; urban, 81.2% rural, 18.8% **Capital:** Toronto **Major cities (1978 metropolitan area population estimates):** Toronto, 2,856,500; Ottawa, 726,400; Hamilton, 536,300; St. Catharines-Niagara Falls, 306,000; London, 274,100; Kitchener, 280,100; Sudbury, 155,000; Thunder Bay, 120,700; Oshawa, 139,300

Ethnic Composition: British Isles, 59%; French, 10%; German, 6%; Italian, 6% **Religion:** Roman Catholic, 33%; United Church, 22%; Anglican, 16%; Presbyterian, 7%; Baptist, 4%; Lutheran, 3% **Vital Statistics (per 1,000 population):** birth rate, 14.3; death rate, 7.2; marriage rate, 8.0; divorce rate, 2.43; infant mortality (per 1,000 live births), 11.3

Location and Geography: Located in the center of Canada, Ontario is a geographic and cultural transition between eastern Quebec and the midwestern prairie provinces. It has a freshwater shoreline of 1,700 miles on the Great Lakes and St. Lawrence River and 750 miles of salt-water shorelines on Hudson and James Bays. The northern part is within the Canadian Shield, but nearly 17.5 million acres are arable

Government: Ontario became a province in 1867 and is represented in the federal government by 95 members in the House of Commons and 24 Senators. The provincial government is unicameral with a Legislative Assembly of 125 members. In June 1977, 58 Progressive Conservatives, 34 Liberals, and 33 New Democrats were elected to the legislature **Premier:** Honourable William G. Davis **Salary and allowance:** $55,892

Education (April 1980): 21.7% of the population 15 years of age and over had Grade 8 or less; 52.3% attended high school; 8.5% had some post-secondary education; 9.1% had a post-secondary certificate or diploma; 8.5% had a university degree **Total expenditures on education (1978-79):** $6,654,418,000 **Schools:** 5,200 primary and secondary schools (1978-79), with a combined enrollment of 1,974,702 **Colleges:** 22 degree-granting universities and 30 non-university post-secondary institutions with enrollment of 220,231

Value added in goods-producing industries (1977): $34,537,717,000, 38.2% of Canada's total; manufacturing contributed 70.3%; construction, 15.7%; mining, 4.1%; and agriculture, 4.6%. The province is the second largest producer of mineral products with a total value of $3,271 million in 1979 **Value of manufacturing shipments (1977):** $55,590,930,000, 51.1% of the national total **Leading manufacturing industries:** motor vehicles and their parts and accessories, iron and steel mills, slaughtering and meat processing, miscellaneous machinery and equipment, pulp and paper mills and petroleum refining **Average industrial earnings (Feb. 1980):** $301.80 per week **Cash receipts from farming operations (1979):** $3,941,730,000, with 27.3% derived from cattle and calves, dairy products 17.2%, hogs 11.4%, tobacco 6.9%, poultry 6.2% and vegetables 4.9% **Families with incomes over $12,000 (1978):** 79.2% **Per capita personal income (1978):** $8,735 **Unemployment (1979):** 6.5%

Provincial finances: Estimated gross general revenue, fiscal year 1978-79 was $14.0 billion; estimated gross general expenditure, $15.0 billion

Daily newspapers: 48 English and 1 French **Combined circulation:** 2,247,821 **Telephones per 100 population (1978):** 68.5 **Homes with radios:** 98.5% **Homes with TV's:** 98.0%

Hospital beds (1979): 60,597 (7.1 beds per 1,000 population) **Physicians (1977):** 15,602 (population per physician, 538)

Motor vehicles (1978): 4,496,105 **Residents per motor vehicle:** 1.9 **Motor vehicle deaths (1978):** 1,439

Ontario was the site of the first European settlement in the interior of North America. In 1639 a combined Jesuit mission, French fort, and Norman town, called Sainte-Marie Among the Hurons, was established on the River Wye, nearly 800 miles from Quebec. The colony lasted for ten years, when it was burned by its founders in the face of attacking Iroquois, who with the Huron Indians were the settlers' chief rivals in the fur trade. Archaeologists and historians have recently restored the outpost on its site 90 miles north of Toronto.

At the time of the founding of Sainte-Marie, Huronia was the most densely populated area of what is now Canada. It was the home of 30,000 Hurons, who controlled the best trade routes and acted as middlemen, trading for furs with more distant tribes and with white settlements on the St. Lawrence River.

In 1774, eleven years after cession to England, the Quebec Act made the area a western extension of Quebec. Loyalist refugees from the American Revolution settled the area around the St. Lawrence, and in 1791 a division was effected, Upper Canada being the future Ontario.

During the War of 1812 the Loyalists defended their lands against the U.S., the town of York suffering invasion and burning by U.S. forces. After the war, emigration by U.S. and British citizens seeking land brought rapid population expansion. The fur trade was slowly replaced with lumbering and wheat production, and by the mid-19th century the economy began to boom as development of railroads and canal systems started a major transportation network. The establishment of the Dominion of Canada in 1867 and of the capital of Ottawa added to the importance of the province.

Today Ontario is the largest province in terms of wealth and population. Its industrial production accounts for nearly 40 percent of the national income and it is the major industrial center of Canada, producing 97 percent of the motor vehicle parts, and over 90 percent of all office and store machinery, motor vehicles and household radios and televisions manufactured domestically. Yet the province's farming, lumber and fishing are still vitally important to the Canadian economy. And its famous lake regions have made Ontario a favorite summer and winter vacationland for Canadians and Americans alike.

For all its wealth, Ontario still suffers from some unemployment. Resentment over the extent of American control of Canadian business is growing, as are accusations of the exertion of undue U.S. influence on the affairs of the Canadian nation. With proposals for independence in Quebec, Ontario's position as the center of commerce and industry for Canada has been enhanced by the exodus of businesses from its eastern neighbor.

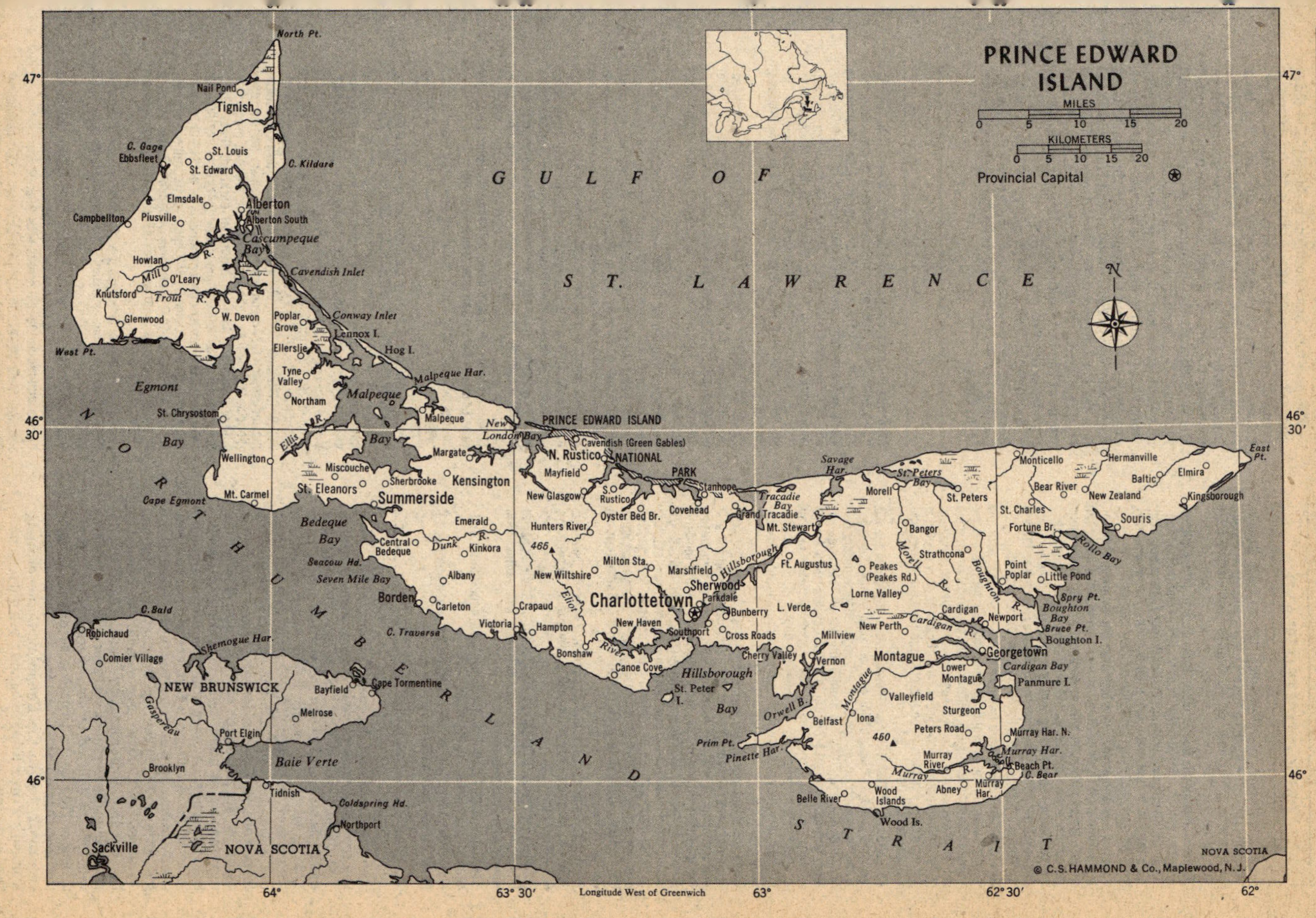
PRINCE EDWARD ISLAND
MILES
KILOMETERS
Provincial Capital
GULF OF ST. LAWRENCE
NORTHUMBERLAND STRAIT
CANADA
495
Longitude West of Greenwich
© C.S. HAMMOND & Co., Maplewood, N. J.
NOVA SCOTIA
North Pt.
Nail Pond
Tignish
C. Gage
Ebbsfleet
St. Louis
St. Edward
C. Kildare
Elmsdale
Campbellton
Piusville
Alberton
Alberton South
Cascumpeque Bay
Howlan
Mill R.
O'Leary
Knutsford
Trout R.
Glenwood
W. Devon
Cavendish Inlet
West Pt.
Poplar Grove
Conway Inlet
Lennox I.
Hog I.
Ellerslie
Tyne Valley
Northam
Egmont Bay
St. Chrysostom
Ellis R.
Malpeque
Malpeque Har.
Malpeque Bay
New London Bay
PRINCE EDWARD ISLAND NATIONAL PARK
Cavendish (Green Gables)
Wellington
Mt. Carmel
Cape Egmont
Miscouche
Sherbrooke
Kensington
Margate
St. Eleanors
Summerside
Bedeque Bay
Central Bedeque
Seacow Hd.
Seven Mile Bay
Dunk R.
Kinkora
Emerald
Albany
Borden
Carleton
C. Bald
Robichaud
Comier Village
NEW BRUNSWICK
Gasperau R.
Shemogue Har.
C. Traverse
Bayfield
Cape Tormentine
Melrose
Port Elgin
Brooklyn
Baie Verte
Tidnish
Coldspring Hd.
Northport
Sackville
NOVA SCOTIA
N. Rustico
Mayfield
New Glasgow
S. Rustico
Oyster Bed Br.
Stanhope
Covehead
Hunters River
New Wiltshire
Milton Sta.
465
Eliot R.
Crapaud
Victoria
Hampton
Bonshaw
Canoe Cove
New Haven
Southport
Charlottetown
Parkdale
Sherwood
Marshfield
Hillsborough
Ft. Augustus
Tracadie Bay
Grand Tracadie
Tracadie
Mt. Stewart
Savage Har.
Morell
St. Peters Bay
St. Peters
Bangor
Strathcona
Morell R.
Peakes (Peakes Rd.)
Lorne Valley
L. Verde
Bunberry
Cross Roads
Cherry Valley
Millview
Vernon
New Perth
Montague R.
Lower Montague
Montague
Valleyfield
Belfast
Iona
Orwell B.
Prim Pt.
Pinette Har.
St. Peter I.
Hillsborough Bay
Bangor
Point Poplar
Little Pond
Spry Pt.
Boughton Bay
Bruce Pt.
Boughton I.
Boughton R.
Cardigan
Cardigan R.
Newport
Georgetown
Cardigan Bay
Panmure I.
Sturgeon
Peters Road
450
Murray Har. N.
Murray River
Murray
Beach Pt.
C. Bear
Murray Har.
Abney
Belle River
Wood Islands
Wood Is.
Monticello
Bear River
St. Charles
Fortune Br.
Rollo Bay
Hermanville
Baltic
New Zealand
Elmira
Kingsborough
Souris
East Pt.

PRINCE EDWARD ISLAND

Area: 2,184 square miles **Population:** 118,229 (1976 Census); 123,900 (Jan. 1, 1980 estimate); ranks tenth; population density, 54.1; urban, 37.1%; rural, 62.9% **Capital:** Charlottetown (1976 population), 17,063

Ethnic Composition: British Isles, 83%; French 14% **Religion:** Roman Catholic, 46%; United Church, 25%; Presbyterian, 12%; Anglican, 6%; Baptist, 6% **Vital Statistics (per 1,000 population):** birth rate, 16.3; death rate, 8.1; marriage rate, 7.7; divorce rate, 1.11; infant mortality (per 1,000 live births), 7.6

Location and Geography: Separated from the mainland by Northumberland Strait, nine to 25 miles wide, the island is about 120 miles in length and has an average width of 20 miles. The irregular coastline has many large bays and deep inlets and all inland waters are tidal except for one river and one lake. The rich soil is of a distinctive red color; more than half of the area is farmed. There is no mining and forestland is limited to small farm woodlots

Government: Prince Edward Island became a province in 1873 and is represented in the federal government by four members in the House of Commons and four Senators. The provincial government is unicameral with a Legislative Assembly of 32 members. In April 1979, 21 Progressive Conservatives and 11 Liberals were elected to the legislature **Premier:** Honourable Angus MacLean **Salary and allowance:** $44,000

Education (April 1980): 26.7% of the population 15 years of age and over had grade 8 or less; 51.1% attended high school; 7.8% had some post-secondary education; 8.9% had a post-secondary certificate or diploma; 5.6% had a university degree **Total expenditures on education (1978-79):** $80,430,000 **Schools (1978-79):** 73 primary and secondary schools with a combined enrollment of 27,225. In the same year full-time enrollment in one degree-granting university and two post-secondary non-university institutions was 2,179

Value added in goods-producing industries (1977): $167,212,000. Agriculture represented 27.8% of the total; construction, 31.9%; manufacturing, 26.9%; and fisheries, 9.1% **Leading manufacturing industries:** fish products, dairy products, fruit and vegetable processing **Average industrial earnings (Feb. 1980):** $222.82 per week **Cash receipts from farming operations (1979):** $110,606,000, with 27.1% derived from potatoes, 18.8% from cattle and calves, 15.2% from hogs, and 15.2% from dairy products **Per capita personal income (1978):** $5,574 **Unemployment (1979):** 11.3%

Provincial Finances: Estimated gross general revenue, fiscal year 1978-79, $268.4 million; estimated gross general expenditure, $268.6 million

Daily Newspapers: 3 **Combined circulation:** 31,922 **Number of telephones:** 48.6 per 100 population **Homes with radios:** 99% **Homes with TV's:** 98%

Hospital beds (1979): 975 (8.0 beds per 1,000 population) **Physicians:** 141 (population per physician, 865)

Motor Vehicles (1978): 65,501 **Residents per motor vehicle:** 1.9 **Motor vehicle deaths (1978):** 30

The great explorer Jacques Cartier, in 1534, was the first European to visit Prince Edward Island. The French called it Ile St. Jean and used the island as a fishery. When the British took over in 1758 most of the nearly 5,000 Acadians living there were deported. The British divided their newly won territory into lots which were granted to persons in Britain, largely Scots, who had a claim on the patronage of the Crown. Few of the new owners fulfilled their obligation to develop their holdings, however, and a century of struggle followed between tenant farmers and nonresident proprietors. It was resolved only after Confederation in 1873 when the Dominion government advanced $800,000 to the provincial government to buy out the landlords and resell the land to tenants. The development of Prince Edward Island was further delayed by its separation from Nova Scotia in 1769 by the British government. Despite the fact that an 1864 meeting in Charlottetown eventually led to the Canadian Confederation, ironically Prince Edward Island itself did not enter the Dominion until 1873.

The province has abundant good soil, and today agriculture remains a principal industry. However, farmers have become overly dependent on potatoes, a crop that generates 25% of total farm income. Silver fox farming originated on the island. From 1910 to 1940 the island was world-famous for the breed, which is now virtually extinct there. Although its isolation from the mainland has mad the island increasingly attractive to tourists, it must import its energy needs and thus pays more for electricity and other power sources than any other province. A replica of the house from *Anne of Green Gables*, found in the National Park, is a favorite of travelers. Fort Amherst National Historic Park, at Rocky Point, contains earthworks of the fort built by the British after its capture from the French in 1758.

By the mid-1980s, the Ministry of Veterans Affairs is to be relocated to Charlottetown, thus becoming the first federal ministry to be transferred from Ottawa.

QUEBEC

Area: 594,860 square miles **Population:** 6,234,445 (1976 Census); 6,288,300 (Jan. 1, 1980 estimate); ranks second; population density, 11.9; urban, 79.1%; rural, 20.9% **Capital:** Québec **Major cities (1978 metropolitan estimates):** Montréal, 2,823,000; Québec, 554,500; Chicoutimi-Jonquière, 129,700 (1976 metropolitan area population): Laval, 246,243; Longueuil, 122,429; Montréal-Nord, 97,250; Sherbrooke, 76,804; Verdun, 68,013; La Salle, 76,713; Ste-Foy, 71,237; Hull, 61,039; St-Laurent, 64,404; Trois Rivières, 52,518; St-Léonard, 78,452

Ethnic Composition: French, 79%; British Isles, 11% **Religion:** Roman Catholic, 87%; United Church, 3%; Anglican, 3% **Vital Statistics (per 1,000 population):** birth rate, 15.1; death rate, 6.9; marriage rate, 7.3; divorce rate, 2.31; infant mortality (per 1,000 live births), 11.9

Location and Geography: The province's northern four-fifths lies in the Canadian Shield, a lake-dotted, partly wooded, rolling plateau. The St. Lawrence Lowlands have climate and soil well suited for general farming. The Appalachian region, south of the St. Lawrence River and including the Gaspé peninsula, is a succession of plateaus and plains, much of it arable and the remainder wooded

Government: Québec became a province in 1867 and is represented in the federal government by 75 members in the House of Commons and 24 Senators. The provincial government is unicameral with a National Assembly of 110 members. In November 1976, party standings were: *Parti Québécois* 71, Liberals 26, Union Nationale 11, Social Credit one, Independent one **Prime Minister:** Honourable René Lévesque **Salary and allowance:** $78,668

Education (April 1980): 29.5% of the population 15 years of age and over had Grade 8 or less; 48.2% attended high school; 5.3% had some post-secondary education; 10.1% had a post-secondary certificate or diploma; 6.8% had a university degree **Expenditures on Education (1978-79):** $5,492,596,000 **Schools (1978-79):** 3,021 primary and secondary, with a combined enrollment of 1,297,690 **Colleges:** Seven degree-granting universities and 74 post-secondary non-university institutions with a total enrollment of 220,049

Value added in goods-producing industries (1977): $19,742,501,000; manufacturing represented 62.4% of this total and construction, 21.7% **Value of manufactured shipments (1977):** $27,951,262,000, 25.7% of the national total **Leading manufacturing industries (1977):** pulp and paper, petroleum refining, dairy products, smelting and refining, slaughtering and meat processing, women's clothing **Average industrial earnings (Feb. 1980):** $304.96 per week **Mineral production (1979):** $2,247,850,000 **Cash Receipts from farming operations (1979):** $1,916,951,000; dairy products contributed 32.6%; hogs, 22.1%; cattle and calves, 12.3%; and poultry, 10.0% **Families with incomes over $12,000:** 74.0% **Per capita personal income (1978):** $7,628 **Unemployment (1979):** 9.6%

Provincial Finances: Estimated gross general revenue (fiscal year 1978-79), $14.0 billion; estimated gross general expenditure, $14.8 billion

Daily newspapers: 10 French language, three English **Combined Circulation:** 1,173,154 **Telephones per 100 population (1978):** 61.5 **Homes with radios:** 98.6% **Homes with TV's:** 98.5%

Hospital beds (1979): 53,401 (8.5 beds per 1,000 population) **Physicians (1977):** 11,545 (population per physician, 544)

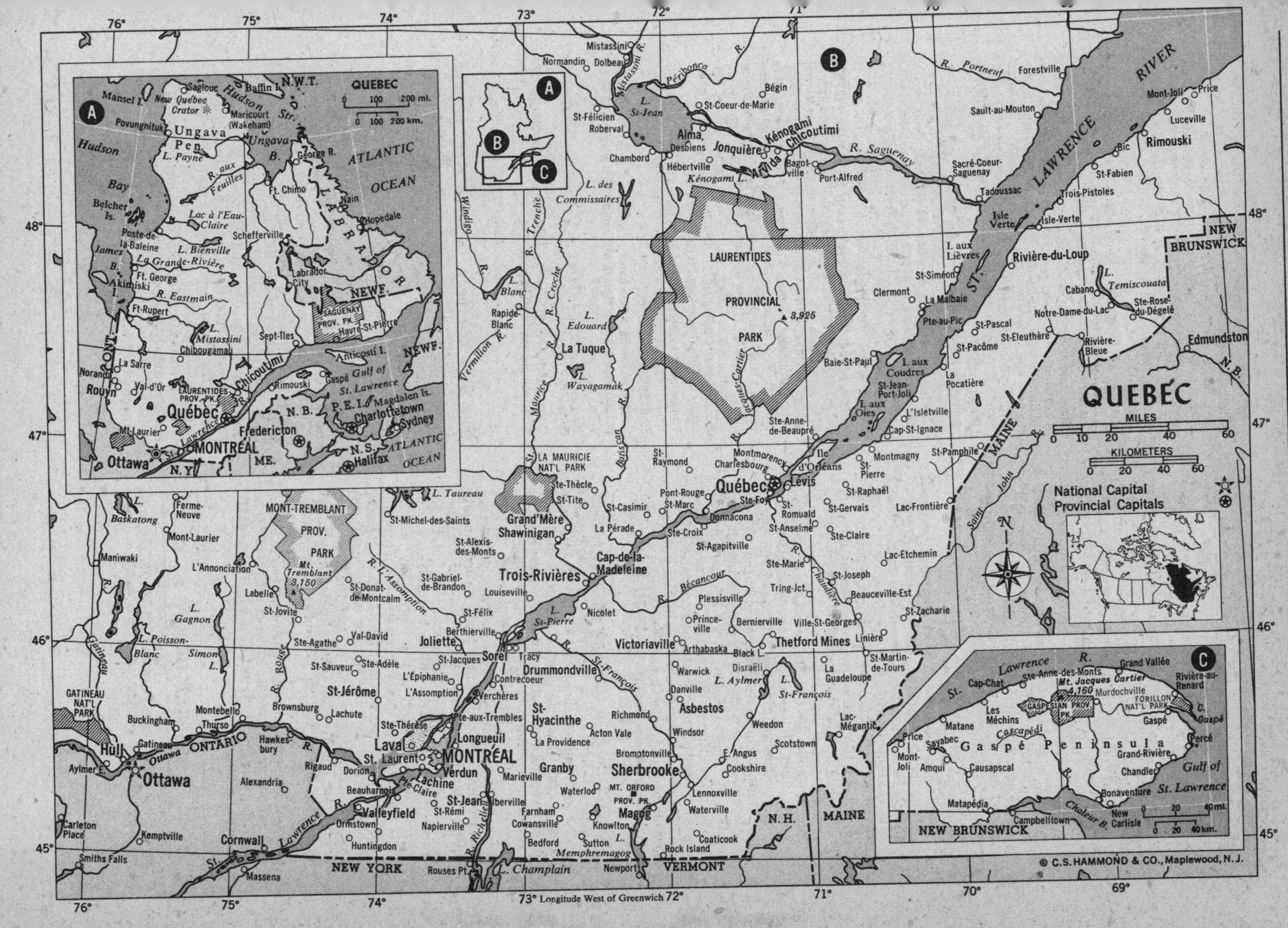
QUEBEC
MILES
KILOMETERS
National Capital
Provincial Capitals
ST. LAWRENCE RIVER
LAWRENCE RIVER
Mistassini R.
Normandin
Dolbeau
Péribonca R.
Bégin
St-Coeur-de-Marie
St-Félicien
Roberval
L. St-Jean
Alma
Desbiens
Jonquière
Kénogami
Chicoutimi
R. Saguenay
Chambord
Hébertville
Kénogami L.
Bagotville
Port-Alfred
Sacré-Coeur-Saguenay
Tadoussac
R. Portneuf
Forestville
Sault-au-Mouton
Mont-Joli
Price
Luceville
Bic
Rimouski
St-Fabien
Trois-Pistoles
Isle Verte
Isle-Verte
Rivière-du-Loup
St-Siméon
Clermont
La Malbaie
Pte-au-Pic
Cabano
Temiscouata
Ste-Rose-du-Dégelé
Notre-Dame-du-Lac
Rivière-Bleue
Edmundston
N.B.
NEW BRUNSWICK
St-Pascal
St-Pacôme
St-Eleuthère
L. des Commissaires
LAURENTIDES
PROVINCIAL
PARK
3,925
Jacques-Cartier R.
Baie-St-Paul
I. aux Coudres
St-Jean-Port-Joli
La Pocatière
I. aux Oies
L'Isletville
Cap-St-Ignace
Ste-Anne-de-Beaupré
Montmorency
Charlesbourg
Ile d'Orléans
Montmagny
St-Pierre
St-Pamphile
Québec
Lévis
Ste-Foy
St-Romuald
St-Raphaël
St-Gervais
Ste-Claire
Lac-Frontière
Lac-Etchemin
Donnacona
St-Anselme
Ste-Marie
St-Joseph
Beauceville-Est
St-Zacharie
Chaudière
L. Blanc
L. Croche
Trenche R.
Windigo
L. Edouard
Rapide-Blanc
Vermillon R.
L. Wayagamak
La Tuque
Batiscan R.
St-Maurice R.
LA MAURICIE NAT'L PARK
St-Raymond
Ste-Thècle
St-Tite
Pont-Rouge
St-Marc
St-Casimir
La Pérade
Ste-Croix
St-Agapitville
Bécancour R.
Plessisville
Princeville
Bernierville
Ville-St-Georges
Linière
St-Martin-de-Tours
Thetford Mines
Arthabaska
Black L.
Disraëli
La Guadeloupe
Lac-Mégantic
L. Aylmer
St-François
L. St-François
Warwick
Danville
Asbestos
Windsor
Richmond
Acton Vale
Weedon
E. Angus
Scotstown
Cookshire
Lennoxville
Waterville
Coaticook
Rock Island
Grand'Mère
Shawinigan
Cap-de-la-Madeleine
Trois-Rivières
Louiseville
Nicolet
L. St-Pierre
Victoriaville
Drummondville
St-François R.
St-Hyacinthe
La Providence
Bromptonville
Sherbrooke
MT. ORFORD PROV. PK.
Magog
Knowlton
Sutton
Memphremagog
Newport
N.H.
MAINE
VERMONT
Ferme-Neuve
Baskatong L.
Mont-Laurier
Maniwaki
MONT-TREMBLANT PROV. PARK
Mt. Tremblant 3,150
L'Annonciation
Labelle
St-Jovite
St-Donat-de-Montcalm
L. Gagnon
L. Poisson-Blanc
L. Simon
Rouge R.
Ste-Agathe
Val-David
Ste-Adèle
St-Sauveur
St-Jérôme
L. Taureau
St-Michel-des-Saints
St-Alexis-des-Monts
St-Gabriel-de-Brandon
St-Félix
R. L'Assomption
Berthierville
St-Pierre L.
Joliette
St-Jacques
Sorel
Tracy
Contrecoeur
L'Epiphanie
L'Assomption
Verchères
St-Thérèse
Pte-aux-Trembles
Laval
Longueuil
MONTRÉAL
St-Laurent
Verdun
Lachine
Pte-Claire
Marieville
Granby
Waterloo
Iberville
St-Jean
St-Rémi
Farnham
Cowansville
Bedford
Napierville
Ormstown
Huntingdon
GATINEAU NAT'L PARK
Hull
Gatineau
Aylmer E.
Ottawa
ONTARIO
Montebello
Thurso
Buckingham
Brownsburg
Lachute
Hawkesbury
Rigaud
Dorion
Beauharnois
Valleyfield
Alexandria
Cornwall
Carleton Place
Kemptville
Smiths Falls
Massena
NEW YORK
Rouses Pt.
L. Champlain
St. Lawrence
Richelieu R.
Ottawa R.
Gatineau R.
Saint John R.
MAINE
QUEBEC
100
200 ml.
100
200 km.
N.W.T.
Baffin I.
Mansel I.
Saglouc
Hudson Str.
New Québec Crater
Maricourt (Wakeham)
Povungnituk
Ungava Pen.
Ungava B.
Hudson Bay
L. Payne
R. aux Feuilles
George R.
ATLANTIC OCEAN
Belcher Is.
Ft. Chimo
Nain
Hopedale
LABRADOR
Lac à l'Eau-Claire
Schefferville
Labrador City
NEWF.
Poste-de-la-Baleine
L. Bienville
James B.
La Grande-Rivière
Ft. George
Akimiski I.
R. Eastmain
Ft-Rupert
L. Mistassini
Chibougamau
SAGUENAY PROV. PK.
Sept-Iles
Havre-St-Pierre
Anticosti I.
NEWF.
Noranda
Rouyn
La Sarre
Val-d'Or
LAURENTIDES PROV. PK.
Chicoutimi
Rimouski
Gaspé
Gulf of St. Lawrence
Magdalen Is.
P.E.I.
Charlottetown
Mt-Laurier
Québec
MONTRÉAL
Fredericton
N.B.
Sydney
N.S.
Halifax
ATLANTIC OCEAN
Ottawa
N.Y.
ME.
C
Lawrence R.
St. Lawrence R.
Cap-Chat
Ste-Anne-des-Monts
Mt. Jacques Cartier 4,160
Murdochville
Grand Vallée
Rivière-au-Renard
FORILLON NAT'L PARK
C. Gaspé
Gaspé
Les Méchins
Matane
Cascapédi
Gaspé Peninsula
Grand-Rivière
Percé
Price
Sayabec
Mont-Joli
Amqui
Causapscal
Chandler
Bonaventure
Chaleur B.
Gulf of St. Lawrence
St. Lawrence
Matapédia
Campbellton
New Carlisle
NEW BRUNSWICK
20
40 ml.
20
40 km.
© C.S. HAMMOND & CO., Maplewood, N.J.
Longitude West of Greenwich
CANADA

Motor vehicles (1978): 3,042,726 **Residents per motor vehicle:** 2.1 **Motor vehicle deaths (1978):** 1,505

It was at Quebec that Cartier landed in 1534, proclaiming French sovereignty. In 1608 Champlain established a settlement at the site of Quebec City, and by 1750 65,000 French-Canadian descendants of the original settlers inhabited the land around the St. Lawrence River. When New France, subject of the crown of France, was ceded to Britain in 1763, and the colony officially became the "province of Quebec," it was a land where French law, religion and custom were firmly entrenched. The confusion created by the co-existence of French-Canadian and British rule was somewhat resolved in 1774 by an act guaranteeing maintenance of French civil law and customs, freedom of worship and education, but the problem remains a source of great controversy to this day.

The French nationalist sentiment has become increasingly strident since the late 1950s. French-speaking Canadians have insisted on greater control of their province's industry and commerce, with demands that Quebec become a separate nation. In 1974, the legislature gave voice to the separatists' demands and established French as the province's official language.

The November 1976 elections in Quebec gave the majority of legislative seats to the separatist *Parti Québécois*. Provincial Prime Minister René Lévesque announced his government's intention to seek independence from the federal government and create a sovereign Quebec. A white paper declaring an end to bilingualism in this "French society" was issued and promptly attacked by Ottawa. Canada's Prime Minister Trudeau called for a referendum on the question of Quebec's secession, with the resignation of Lévesque if the results did not indicate support for his proposal.

In 1977, the *Parti Québécois* exhibited moderation in its drive for independence, reversing it's previous stand on abolition of English language schools and easing language demands on large, English-using corporations. But Lévesque and the PQ remain adamant on demanding greater autonomy and self-rule for the French province. In 1978 French was established as the primary language of government, education and legal record, despite charges by the federal government and the other provinces that this would "sabotage" national unity. However, a 1979 ruling of the federal Supreme Court struck down this legislation. In 1979, the Lévesque government proposed a referendum on a "sovereign-association" plan that would give Quebec greater self-government while maintaining economic ties to the rest of the Canadian federation. The May 20, 1980 referendum resulted in a defeat for separatism. 58% of Quebec's voters, including 54% of the French-speaking electorate, rejected the proposal. Lévesque remained in office, and called for a new Canadian constitution that would guarantee Quebec's right to self-determination.

SASKATCHEWAN

Area: 251,633 square miles **Population:** 921,325 (1976 Census); 967,400 (June 1, 1980 estimate); ranks sixth; population density, 3.84; urban, 55.5%; rural, 44.5% **Capital:** Regina **Major cities (1978 population):** Regina, 160,000; Saskatoon, 139,200

Ethnic Composition: British Isles, 42%; German, 19%; Ukrainian, 9%; Scandinavian, 6%; French, 6%; and Native Indian, 4% **Religion:** United Church, 30%; Roman Catholic, 28%; Lutheran, 10%; Anglican, 9%; Ukrainian Catholic, 4%; Mennonite, 3% **Vital Statistics (per 1,000 population 1977):** birth rate, 17.7; death rate, 8.1; marriage rate, 7.7; divorce rate, 1.6; infant mortality (per 1,000 live births), 15.0

Location and Geography: Situated between Manitoba and Alberta, the southern portion of the province consists of a rolling plain. The northern third begins the Canadian shield

Government: Saskatchewan became a province in 1905 and is represented in the federal government by 14 members in the House of Commons and six Senators. The provincial government is unicameral with a Legislative Assembly of 61 members. In October 1978, 44 New Democrats and 17 Conservatives were elected to the legislature **Premier:** Honourable Allan E. Blakeney **Salary and allowance:** $53,580

Education (1976): In Saskatchewan, 94% of the population had completed Grade IV; 49.4%, secondary schools and 6.2%, university **Total expenditures on education (1979-80):** $706,508,000 **Schools and students:** 1,064 primary and secondary schools with a combined enrollment of 220,979 **Colleges:** Two degree-granting universities and 15 community colleges, and technical and vocational institutes, with an enrollment of 237,882

Value added in goods-producing industries (1979): $5,397,000,000; agriculture represented 37% of this total, mining 27%, construction 19%, and manufacturing 13% **Value of Mineral Shipments (1979):** $1,802,000,000 **Leading manufacturing industries:** slaughtering and meat processing, petroleum refining, dairy products, metal fabricating and potash mining **Average industrial earnings (1979):** $285.17 per week **Cash receipts from farming operations (1979):** $2,905,193,000; with 43% derived from wheat, 17% from cattle and calves, and 5% from barley **Families with incomes over $10,000 (1977):** 67% **Per capita personal income (1979):** $8,235 **Unemployment (1979):** 4.2%

Provincial Finances: Estimated gross general revenue, fiscal year 1980-81, $2,019 million; estimated gross general expenditure, $2,018 million

Daily newspapers: 4 **Combined circulation:** 136,067 **Telephones per 100 population:** 62 **Homes with radios:** 99% **Homes with TV's:** 97%

Hospital beds (1979): 7,876 (8.2 per 1,000 population) **Physicians (1979):** 947 (1,012 population per physician)

Motor Vehicles (1978): 722,643 **Residents per motor vehicle:** 1.3 **Motor vehicle deaths (1978):** 257

The first European to reach what is now Saskatchewan and to see the vast buffalo herds that roamed the central plains was Henry Kelsey, an agent of the Hudson's Bay Company. In 1690 he was sent into the Northwest to explore the vast territory and ensure the Company's fur supply by pacifying the Indians. For two centuries fur trading continued, and settlement only began in 1870 with the building of the railroad and the practice of homesteading.

Today the province has Canada's largest area of occupied agricultural land. Yet, after the disasters of the dust bowl of the 1930s, diversification has been a priority and now 65 percent of the province's gross product is from industry, only 35 percent from farming. Petroleum, mining and manufacturing are the major industries; farms are large and highly mechanized.

The 1978 elections affirmed support for the NDP and Premier Blakeney's policy of taking over one-half of the potash mining industry, much of which is owned by United States interests.

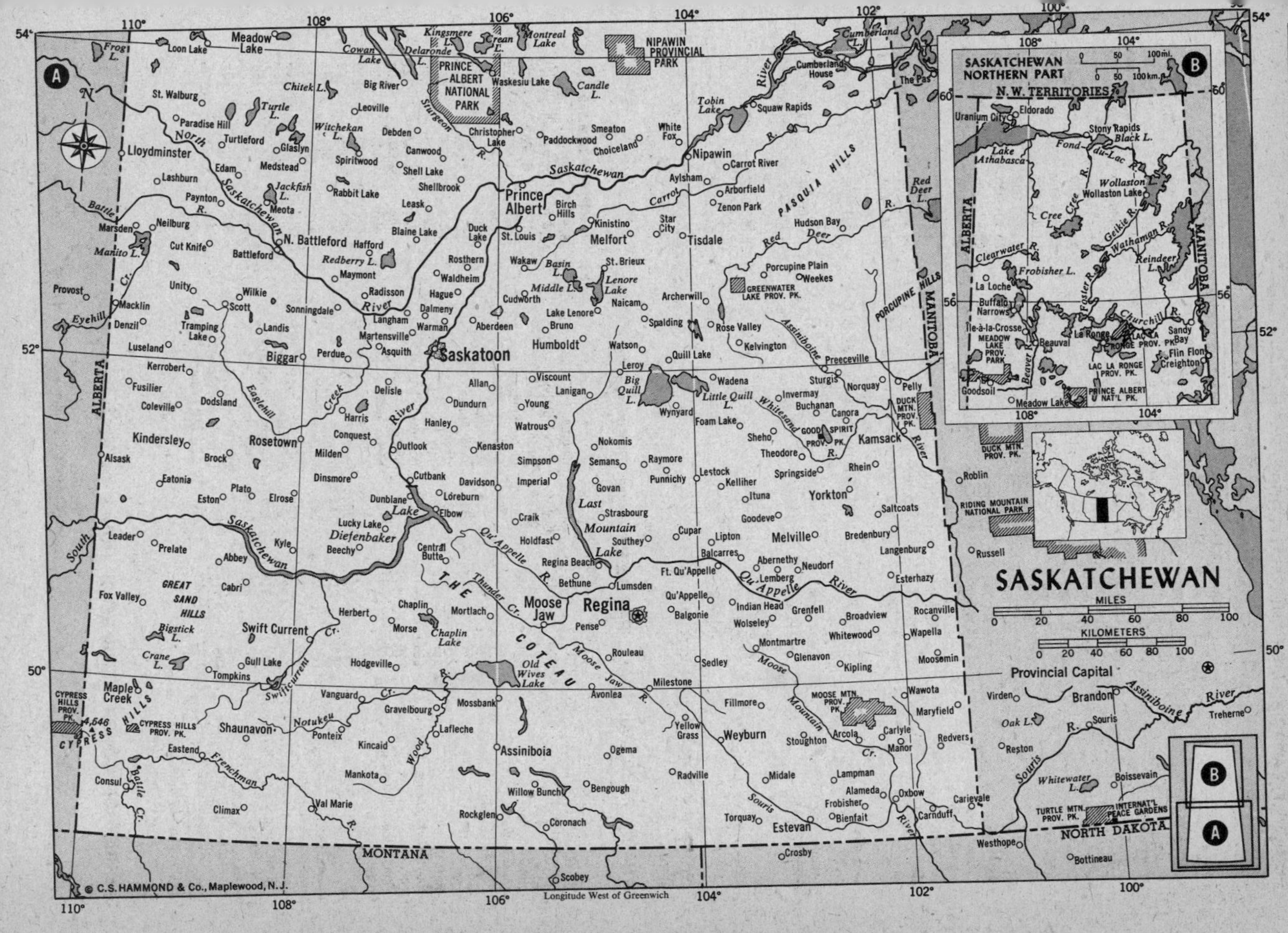
SASKATCHEWAN
MILES
KILOMETERS
Provincial Capital
Longitude West of Greenwich
© C.S. HAMMOND & Co., Maplewood, N.J.
CANADA
ALBERTA
MONTANA
NORTH DAKOTA
MANITOBA
NIPAWIN PROVINCIAL PARK
PRINCE ALBERT NATIONAL PARK
SASKATCHEWAN NORTHERN PART
N.W. TERRITORIES
Uranium City
Eldorado
Lake Athabasca
Stony Rapids
Black L.
Fond du Lac
Wollaston
Wollaston Lake
Cree L.
Clearwater
Frobisher L.
La Loche
Buffalo Narrows
Île-à-la-Crosse
MEADOW LAKE PROV. PARK
Beauval
La Ronge
LAC LA RONGE PROV. PK.
Sandy Bay
Flin Flon
Creighton
Churchill R.
Reindeer L.
Foster R.
Geikie R.
Wathaman R.
Goodsoil
Meadow Lake
PRINCE ALBERT NAT'L PK.
RIDING MOUNTAIN NATIONAL PARK
DUCK MTN. PROV. PK.
Roblin
Russell
Frog L.
Loon Lake
Meadow Lake
St. Walburg
Paradise Hill
Chitek L.
Turtle L.
Turtleford
Leoville
Big River
Kingsmere L.
Delaronde L.
Crean L.
Montreal Lake
Waskesiu Lake
Candle L.
Cumberland L.
Cumberland House
The Pas
Lloydminster
Lashburn
Edam
Medstead
Glaslyn
Spiritwood
Debden
Canwood
Shell Lake
Shellbrook
Christopher Lake
Sturgeon R.
Paddockwood
Smeaton
Choiceland
White Fox
Nipawin
Carrot River
Tobin Lake
Squaw Rapids
North Saskatchewan R.
Saskatchewan
Jackfish L.
Meota
Rabbit Lake
Leask
Birch Hills
Prince Albert
Kinistino
Melfort
Star City
Tisdale
Aylsham
Arborfield
Zenon Park
Carrot R.
Red Deer R.
PASQUIA HILLS
Hudson Bay
Porcupine Plain
Weekes
PORCUPINE HILLS
Marsden
Neilburg
Cut Knife
Battleford
N. Battleford
Hafford
Redberry L.
Blaine Lake
Duck Lake
St. Louis
Rosthern
Waldheim
Maymont
Wakaw
Basin L.
Lenore Lake
St. Brieux
Middle L.
Lake Lenore
Naicam
Spalding
Rose Valley
Archerwill
Kelvington
GREENWATER LAKE PROV. PK.
Assiniboine
Preeceville
Sturgis
Norquay
Pelly
DUCK MTN. PROV. PK.
Manito L.
Provost
Macklin
Denzil
Eyehill
Luseland
Tramping Lake
Landis
Unity
Scott
Wilkie
Sonningdale
Langham
Warman
Martensville
Hague
Aberdeen
Dalmeny
Cudworth
Saskatoon
Humboldt
Bruno
Watson
Leroy
Quill Lake
Wadena
Big Quill L.
Little Quill L.
Invermay
Buchanan
Canora
Whitesand R.
GOOD SPIRIT PROV. PK.
Sheho
Theodore
Rhein
Kamsack
Kerrobert
Fusilier
Coleville
Dodsland
Biggar
Perdue
Asquith
Delisle
Harris
Conquest
Milden
Dinsmore
Allan
Dundurn
Hanley
Kenaston
Outlook
Cutbank
Davidson
Viscount
Lanigan
Young
Watrous
Simpson
Nokomis
Semans
Raymore
Punnichy
Govan
Lestock
Kelliher
Springside
Ituna
Goodeve
Yorkton
Melville
Saltcoats
Bredenbury
Langenburg
Esterhazy
Kindersley
Alsask
Brock
Rosetown
Eatonia
Plato
Eston
Elrose
Loreburn
Dunblane
Lucky Lake
Diefenbaker
Lake Diefenbaker
Beechy
Elbow
Central Butte
Craik
Holdfast
Last Mountain Lake
Strasbourg
Southey
Cupar
Lipton
Balcarres
Abernethy
Lemberg
Neudorf
Leader
Prelate
Kyle
Abbey
Cabri
South Saskatchewan River
Eaglehill Creek
GREAT SAND HILLS
Bigstick L.
Crane L.
Fox Valley
Maple Creek
CYPRESS HILLS PROV. PK.
4,546
CYPRESS HILLS
Swift Current
Shaunavon
Eastend
Consul
Climax
Frenchman R.
Battle Cr.
Gull Lake
Tompkins
Herbert
Morse
Chaplin
Chaplin Lake
Mortlach
Hodgeville
Vanguard
Notukeu Cr.
Ponteix
Kincaid
Gravelbourg
Lafleche
Mossbank
Assiniboia
Mankota
Willow Bunch
Bengough
Coronach
Rockglen
Val Marie
THE COTEAU
Thunder Cr.
Qu'Appelle R.
Moose Jaw
Regina
Pense
Bethune
Lumsden
Regina Beach
Ft. Qu'Appelle
Qu'Appelle
Balgonie
Rouleau
Sedley
Milestone
Avonlea
Old Wives Lake
Moose Jaw R.
Indian Head
Wolseley
Grenfell
Broadview
Whitewood
Montmartre
Glenavon
Kipling
Wapella
Moosomin
Rocanville
Fillmore
Weyburn
Yellow Grass
Stoughton
Moose Mountain
MOOSE MTN. PROV. PK.
Arcola
Carlyle
Manor
Wawota
Maryfield
Redvers
Midale
Lampman
Frobisher
Bienfait
Alameda
Oxbow
Carnduff
Carievale
Estevan
Souris R.
Ogema
Radville
Torquay
Crosby
Scobey
Provincial Capital
Virden
Brandon
Assiniboine River
Treherne
Oak L.
Souris
Reston
Whitewater L.
Boissevain
Westhope
Bottineau
TURTLE MTN. PROV. PK.
INTERNAT'L PEACE GARDENS

PRINCIPAL CANADIAN AGRICULTURAL CROPS   Source: Statistics Canada

	Area in Acres		Yield per Acre		Total Production	
	1978	1979	1978	1979*	1978	1979°
			Bushels		Bushels	
Winter wheat	735,000	770,000	40.5	43.4	29,737,000	33,406,000
Spring wheat	21,757,100	22,377,500	29.5	24.7	642,422,000	552,544,000
Durum wheat	3,650,000	2,800,000	28.7	23.6	104,800,000	66,100,000
All wheat	26,142,100	25,947,500	29.7	25.1	776,959,000	652,050,000
Oats for grain	4,518,000	3,806,500	52.0	50.7	234,757,000	193,093,000
Barley for grain	10,533,400	9,199,700	45.3	42.2	477,084,000	388,573,000
Fall rye	736,000	769,000	30.6	25.5	22,528,000	19,632,000
Spring rye	52,000	46,000	25.1	22.3	1,305,000	1,025,000
All rye	788,000	815,000	30.2	25.3	23,833,000	20,657,000
Mixed grains	1,497,000	1,468,900	53.6	55.8	80,301,000	01,911,000
Flaxseed	1,300,000	2,290,000	17.3	14.4	22,500,000	32,900,000
Rapeseed	6,980,000	8,500,000	22.1	18.5	154,200,000	157,000,000
Corn for grain	1,933,000	2,200,000	82.1	88.8	158,753,000	195,398,000
Buckwheat	149,000	164,000	22.5	10.3	3,346,000	1,695,000
Peas, dry	97,000	108,000	30.2	26.4	2,930,000	2,850,000
Soybeans	705,000	700,000	26.9	35.3	18,944,000	24,680,000
			Cwt			
Beans, dry	148,000	94,000	11.4	16.1	1,687,000	1,517,000
			Pounds			
Mustard seed	242,000	155,000	942	758	228,000,000	117,500,000
Sunflower seed	226,000	405,000	1,173	1,202	265,000,000	487,000,000
			Tons			
Tame hay	13,847,000	13,620,000	2.14	2.14	29,665,000	29,168,000
Fodder corn	1,226,500	1,202,200	12.70	13.46	15,582,000	16,178,000
Sugar beets	61,002	58,754	17.10	16.17	1,043,400	950,300

* As indicated on or about November 15, 1979.

CANADA: PRINCIPAL TRADE PARTNERS   Source: Statistics Canada

Country	EXPORTS $000,000			Country	IMPORTS $000,000		
	1979*	1978	1977		1979*	1978	1977
United States	43,439	36,455	30,404	United States	45,420	35,246	29,815
Japan	4,077	3,052	2,513	Japan	2,157	2,268	1,793
United Kingdom	2,589	1,985	1,929	United Kingdom	1,929	1,600	1,279
Germany, West	1,368	782	768	Germany, West	1,556	1,244	967
Netherlands	1,082	563	513	Venezuela	1,505	1,283	1,360
USSR	763	567	358	Saudi Arabia	1,242	749	712
Italy	729	481	498	France	778	684	522
Venezuela	671	686	568	Italy	636	525	400
Belgium/Luxembourg	668	475	511	Taiwan	522	397	321
France	620	460	360	Australia	466	350	353
People's Repub. China	596	503	369	Korea, South	463	363	323
Australia	557	412	409	Hong Kong	427	332	280
Brazil	422	417	282	Sweden	383	325	260
Korea, South	364	216	144	Iran	351	594	537
Argentina	284	96	107	Switzerland	323	285	221
Norway	279	144	223	Brazil	313	248	214
Poland	262	224	156	Netherlands	252	227	191
Cuba	257	218	189	Belgium/Luxembourg	241	202	160
Saudi Arabia	252	235	109	South Africa	240	149	150
Mexico	236	229	220	Mexico	208	185	195
Other Countries	4,495	3,719	3,053	Other Countries	3,041	2,682	2,279
All Countries	64,010	51,919	43,683	All Countries	62,453	49,938	42,332

* Preliminary, by order of rank.

SALARIES OF SENIOR MEMBERS OF HOUSE OF COMMONS

Position	Sessional Allowance	Expense Allowance	Salary	Motor Vehicle	Total
Prime Minister	$30,600	$13,500	$37,800	$2,000	$83,900
Cabinet Ministers and Leaders of Opposition in the House of Commons	30,600	13,500	22,600	2,000	68,700
Members of Parliament	30,600	13,500°	—	—	44,100°

* Certain members for larger northern constituencies have larger expense allowances.

YUKON TERRITORY
MILES
0 25 50 75 100 125
KILOMETERS
0 25 50 75 100 125
Territorial and State Capitals
BEAUFORT SEA
Demarcation Pt.
Herschel I.
Herschel
Kugmallit Bay
Mackenzie Bay
Richards I.
Tuktoyaktuk
Eskimo (Husky) Lakes
Reindeer Sta.
Sitidgi L.
Kingaluk R.
Inuvik
Aklavik
Liverpool Bay
BRITISH MTS.
Firth R.
Old Crow R.
Porcupine
Old Crow
RICHARDSON MOUNTAINS
Eagle R.
River
McDougall Pass
Ft. McPherson
Travaillant Lake
Arctic Red River
N. W. TERRS.
Arctic R.
Red
River
Mackenzie
Arctic Circle
Ft. Good Hope
L. Belot
L. des Bois
FRANKLIN
Smith Arm
Great Bear Lake
Mt. Burgess 5,580
Peel
R.
Bonnet Plume R.
Snake R.
ROCKY
MACKENZIE
Norman Wells
Canol
Ft. Franklin
65°
OGILVIE
Ogilvie
Hart R.
Chapman Lake
MOUNTAINS
SELWYN
Mountain R.
Ft. Norman
ALASKA
Eagle
Yukon
Forty Mile
Mt. Campbell 7,750
Beaver R.
MOUNTAINS
Keele R.
Redstone R.
Wrigley
Glacier Creek (Sixtymile)
Bear Cr.
Dawson
Klondike
Wernecke Elsa
Clear Creek
Keno Hill
R.
River
Keele Pk. 9,750
MTS.
Sulphur
Granville
Barlow
McQuesten
Mayo
Hess R.
Macmillan Pass
Christie Pass
Stewart River
Stewart
River
KLONDIKE
TINTINA
Coffee Creek
River
Pelly Crossing
Macmillan
R.
Mt. Selous 7,140
MOUNTAINS
Donjek R.
Ft. Selkirk
Pelly
Minto
McCabe Crossing
River
VALLEY
South Nahanni R.
Snag
Beaver Creek
Nisling R.
Yukon Crossing
Carmacks
Faro
Ross River
Mt. Sir James MacBrien 9,000
NAHANNI
NAT'L PARK
Koidern
White R.
Aishihik
Aishihik L.
Big Salmon
Yukon
Big Salmon R.
Hyland R.
Coal R.
N. W. TERRS.
Burwash Landing
Kluane
Kluane Lake
Destruction Bay
KLUANE
Kluane
Canyon
Takhini
Lower Laberge
L. Laberge
Upper Laberge
Teslin
Frances Lake
Frances Lake
Mt. Lucania 17,147
ST. ELIAS
NAT'L PARK
Champagne
Haines Jct.
MacRae
Whitehorse
Johnsons Crossing
Liard R.
Mt. Logan 19,524
MOUNTAINS
Robinson
Kusawa L.
Tagish
Teslin
Watson Lake
60°
Mt. St. Elias 18,008
Klukshu
Carcross
Lake
Teslin Lake
Swift River
Upper Liard
Lower Post
Smith River
0°
Yakutat Bay
Yakutat
Alsek R.
BRITISH COLUMBIA
Atlin
Atlin Lake
CASSIAR
Liard River
River
GULF
OF
ALASKA
Chilkat Pass
Chilkoot Pass
Skagway
Haines
ALASKA
N
Cassia r
McDame
Kechika R.
MUNCHO LAKE PROV. PK.
MTS.
GLACIER BAY
Glacier Bay
NAT'L MON.
Juneau
Tulsequah
Dease Lake
STONE MTN. PROV. PK.
© C.S. HAMMOND & Co., Maplewood, N.J.
140°
135°
Longitude West of Greenwich
130°
125°
70°
140°
135°
130°
125°

NORTHWEST TERRITORIES
MILES
KILOMETERS
State and Territorial Capitals
ARCTIC OCEAN
QUEEN ELIZABETH ISLANDS
SVERDRUP IS.
Borden I.
Isachsen Ellef Ringnes I.
Amund Ringnes I.
North Magnetic Pole
Prince Patrick I.
Mackenzie King I.
Meuld Bay
Lands End
Hazen Str.
PARRY ISLANDS
Melville I.
Bathurst I.
Cornwallis I.
Resolute Bay
Devon I.
Lancaster Sd.
Barrow Str.
C. Pr. Alfred
M'Clure Str.
Viscount Melville Sound
Stefansson
Banks I.
Sachs Har.
Hadley Bay
Prince of Wales I.
Somerset I.
Pr. Regent Inlet
Brodeur Pen.
Borden Pen.
Arctic Bay
Pond Inlet
Bylot I. 6,200
DISTRICT OF FRANKLIN
Baffin Island
Baffin Bay
UNITED STATES RA.
C. Columbia
Alert
Hazen L.
Kennedy Chan.
Ellesmere Island
Eureka
Axel Heiberg
9,500
Smith Sd.
Nares Basin
Kane Basin
Grise Fiord
C. Parry
Thule
C. Atholl
C. York
Melville Bay
Hayes Pen.
Jones Sd.
Philpots I.
GREENLAND
(KALÅTDLIT-NUNÅT)
(Denmark)
Disko I.
Disko Bay
Davis Strait
C. Adair
Clyde
C. Henry Kater
Home Bay
AUYUITTUQ NAT'L PARK
8,500
Cumberland Sd.
Pângnirtung
Cumberland Pen.
C. Mercy
Broughton I.
Padloping I.
C. Dyer
Netilling L.
Lemieux Is.
Amadjuak L.
Frobisher Bay
Hall Pen.
Loks Land
Frobisher B.
Lake Harbour
Resolution I.
Port Burwell
Akpatok I.
Beaufort Sea
DISTRICT OF MACKENZIE
Victoria Island
Holman I.
Amundsen Gulf
Cape Parry
C. Bathurst
C. Lambton
Letty Har.
Paulatuk
Stanton
Wollaston Pen. 1,700
Read Island
Bluenose L.
Cambridge Bay
Coronation Gulf
Coppermine
Victoria Str.
Queen Maud Gulf
King William I.
Gjoa Haven
Spence Bay
Boothia Pen.
Gulf of Boothia
Boothia
Igloolik
Melville Pen.
Pelly Bay
Chantrey Inlet
Foxe Basin
C. Wilson
Foxe Pen.
Prince Charles I.
C. Dorset
Coats I.
Mansel I.
Repulse Bay
Roes Welcome Sd.
Southampton I.
Coral Har.
Nottingham
Sea-horse
Hudson Strait
Saglouc
New Québec Crater
QUEBEC
Ungava Peninsula
Ungava Bay
Ft. Chimo
L. Minto
UNITED STATES
BROOKS RA.
Barrow
Pt. Barrow
Yukon
Fairbanks
ALASKA
Old Crow
Aklavik
6,500
Mackenzie
Herschel Bay
Tuktoyaktuk
Inuvik
Ft. McPherson
7,750
Dawson
Mayo
Elsa
Beaver Cr.
Yukon
Pelly
YUKON TERR.
Keele Pk. 9,750
Cristie Pass
Carmacks
Haines Jct.
Mt. Logan 19,524
Carcross
Skagway
Whitehorse
Teslin
Haines
Ross R.
MACKENZIE MTS.
9,062 Mt. Sir James MacBrien
NAHANNI NAT'L PARK
Watson L.
Ft. Simpson
Wrigley
Norman Wells
Ft. Norman
Ft. Franklin
Great Bear Lake
Port Radium
Mackenzie River
Good Hope
Fort
Arctic Circle
Back R.
Contwoyto L.
Garry L.
Bathurst Inlet
Thelon
DISTRICT OF KEEWATIN
Dubawnt L.
Baker L.
Chesterfield Inlet
C. Low
Rankin Inlet
Whale Cove
Yathkyed L.
Tavani
Eskimo Pt.
Padlei
Ennadai
Wholdaia L.
Kasba L.
Nueltin L.
Wager B.
Hudson Bay
Lac la Martre
Rae
Discovery
Yellowknife
Great Slave Lake
Ft. Reliance
Snowdrift
Nonacho L.
Ft. Resolution
Ft. Providence
Hay River
Pine Pt.
Ft. Smith
WOOD BUFFALO NAT'L PK.
Meander R.
Uranium City
ALBERTA
SASKATCHEWAN
MANITOBA
Ft. Liard
Ft. Nelson
MUNCHO L. PROV. PK.
Liard
BRITISH COLUMBIA
ROCKY MTS.
COAST MTS.
GLACIER BAY N'M.
Juneau
Petersburg
ALASKA
All islands in Hudson and James Bays
lie within the District of Keewatin

CANADIAN IMPORTS BY LEADING COMMODITIES ($000)

SOURCE: Statistics Canada

	1979*	1978	1977
1. Motor vehicle parts excluding engines	6,846,724	6,330,520	5,624,037
2. Crude petroleum	4,507,214	3,471,138	3,215,267
3. Passenger automobiles and chassis	4,378,071	3,816,594	3,366,915
4. Trucks, truck tractors and chassis	1,777,274	1,215,620	1,005,618
5. Motor vehicle engines	1,120,060	807,619	545,414
6. Electronic computers	1,102,088	852,664	562,074
7. Precious metals, incl. alloys	1,097,810	244,466	58,946
8. Other telecommunication and rel. equipment	970,485	779,632	652,782
9. Organic chemicals	895,082	681,954	493,635
10. Coal	865,021	632,441	617,663
11. Other end products, inedible	854,840	613,857	465,378
12. Miscellaneous equipment and tools	768,692	679,084	577,268
13. Aircraft complete with engines	679,426	263,395	89,246
14. Wheel tractors, new	655,319	441,696	425,049
15. Plate, sheet and strip, steel	648,149	379,840	270,613
16. Other chemical products	616,395	512,536	381,185
17. Other special transactions, trade	567,508	389,615	421,221
18. Plastics materials, not shaped	560,717	483,741	376,016
19. Other metals in ores, conc., scrap	503,838	208,897	229,573
20. Other photographic goods	479,226	440,063	340,437

* Ranked by value.

CANADIAN EXPORTS BY LEADING COMMODITIES ($000)

SOURCE: Statistics Canada

	1979*	1978	1977
1. Passenger automobiles and chassis	4,260,489	5,007,464	4,474,162
2. Lumber, softwood	3,820,586	3,158,220	2,338,643
3. Motor vehicle parts excl. engines	3,660,677	3,417,021	2,673,705
4. Newsprint paper	3,221,678	2,886,235	2,381,500
5. Wood pulp	3,084,253	2,180,905	2,157,594
6. Natural gas	2,889,054	2,190,294	2,028,053
7. Trucks, truck tractors and chassis	2,715,255	2,703,264	2,136,758
8. Crude petroleum	2,404,582	1,572,662	1,750,637
9. Wheat	2,180,282	1,912,830	1,881,546
10. Petroleum and coal products	1,883,655	776,580	649,100
11. Iron ores and concentrates	1,354,086	782,793	1,063,922
12. Fertilizers and fertilizer materials	987,310	734,933	658,969
13. Precious metals incl. alloys	954,771	567,511	416,488
14. Aluminum incl. alloys	917,521	1,140,562	769,580
15. Other inorganic chemicals	839,651	653,611	352,506
16. Coal and other crude bitum products	835,277	751,872	650,240
17. Motor vehicle engines and parts	817,638	1,061,954	944,934
18. Electricity	729,234	478,875	376,965
19. Organic chemicals	704,665	401,529	301,399
20. Other telecommunication and rel. equipment	655,349	460,407	347,416

* Ranked by value.

CANADA: POPULATION, 1851–1979 SOURCE: Statistics Canada

	1851	1871	1891	1931	1951	1971	1979[3]
Newfoundland	—	—	—	—	361,416	522,104	574,000
Prince Edward Island	62,678[1]	94,021	109,078	88,038	98,429	111,641	122,800
Nova Scotia	276,854	387,800	450,396	512,846	642,584	788,960	846,900
New Brunswick	193,800	285,594	321,263	408,219	515,697	634,557	701,000
Quebec	890,261	1,191,516	1,488,535	2,874,662	4,055,681	6,027,764	6,298,800
Ontario	952,004	1,620,851	2,114,321	3,431,683	4,597,542	7,703,106	8,499,800
Manitoba	—	25,228	152,560	700,139	776,541	988,247	1,030,500
Saskatchewan	—	—	—[2]	921,785	831,728	926,242	957,100
Alberta	—	—	—[2]	731,605	939,501	1,627,874	2,008,900
British Columbia	55,000	36,247	98,173	694,263	1,165,210	2,184,621	2,566,900
Yukon	—	—	—	4,230	9,096	18,388	21,600
Northwest Territory	5,700	48,000	98,967	9,316	16,004	34,807	43,200
Total Canada	2,436,297	3,689,257	4,833,239	10,376,786	14,009,429	21,568,311	23,671,500

[1] 1848 figure. [2] Included with the Northwest Territories. [3] Postcensal estimate.

LARGEST CANADIAN CITIES SOURCE: Statistics Canada

	1851	1901	1951	1961	1971	1976
Calgary, Alberta	—	4,091	129,060	249,641	403,343*	469,917
Edmonton, Alberta	—	—	159,631	281,027	438,152	461,361
Halifax, Nova Scotia	20,749	40,832	85,589	92,511	122,035	117,882
Hamilton, Ontario	14,112	52,634	208,321	273,991	309,173	312,003
London, Ontario	—	37,981	95,343	169,569	223,222	240,392
Montreal, Quebec	57,715	267,730	1,021,520	1,191,062	1,214,352	1,080,546
Ottawa, Ontario	—	59,928	202,045	268,206	302,341	304,462
Quebec, Quebec	42,052	68,840	164,016	171,979	187,833*	177,082
Regina, Saskatchewan	—	—	71,319	112,141	139,479*	149,593
Saint John, N.B.	22,745	40,711	50,779	55,153	89,039	85,956
St. John's Newfoundland	—	—	52,873	63,633	88,414*	86,576
Toronto, Ontario	30,775	208,040	675,754	672,407	712,786	633,318
Vancouver, British Columbia	—	26,133	344,833	384,522	426,298*	410,188
Windsor, Ontario	—	12,153	120,049	114,367	203,300	196,526
Winnipeg, Manitoba	—	42,340	235,710	265,429	504,150*	560,874

* Revised, based on 1976 areas.

WORLD NATIONS

AFGHANISTAN

Area: 250,775 sq. mi. **Population:** 15,540,000 (1979 census)
Official Name: Democratic Republic of Afghanistan **Capital:** Kabul **Nationality:** Afghan **Languages:** Pushtu, spoken by the Pathans, and Dari, a Persian dialect spoken by the Tajiks, are official languages **Religion:** About 99% of the population are Moslems, most of whom belong to the Sunni sect. Islam is the state religion **Flag:** Three equal horizontal stripes of black, red and green with the national coat of arms set near the hoist at the intersection of the black and red stripes **Anthem:** N.A. **Currency:** Afghani (44.2 per U.S. $1)

Location: Central Asia. Landlocked Afghanistan is bordered by the USSR on the north, China on the extreme northeast, Pakistan on the east and south, and Iran on the west **Features:** The towering Hindu Kush range and its parallel extensions run through the center of the country from northeast to southwest. Mountains and desert country are interspersed by small, fertile valleys irrigated by snow-fed mountain streams **Chief Rivers:** Helmand, Farah Rud, Hari Rud, Khulm, Amu Darya

Head of State and Government: Prime Minister Babrak Karmal, born 1930, named head of state, prime minister, Chairman of the Revolutionary Council and General Secretary of the People's Democratic party, following the Soviet-backed coup of December 1979 **Effective Date of Present Constitution:** April 14, 1980 (provisional constitution) **Legislative Body:** Revolutionary Council of 57 members. A Grand National Assembly (Supreme Council) is to be elected under the terms of the provisional constitution of 1980 **Local Government:** 28 provinces, each headed by a governor

Ethnic Composition: The Pathans (Pushtus) make up about half the total population; the rest is made up largely of Tajiks, Uzbeks, Hazara, and Turkmen **Population Distribution:** 15% urban **Density:** 62 inhabitants per sq. mi.

Largest Cities: (1976 estimates) Kabul 603,969, Kandahar 160,684, Herat 115,165; (1973 est.) Baghlan 110,874, Tagab 106,777, Charikar 100,443

Per Capita Income: $193 (1979 est.) **Gross National Product (GNP):** $2.9 billion (1979) **Economic Statistics:** about 53% of GNP comes from agriculture (wheat, corn, fruit, nuts, barley, rice, cotton, sugar beets and cane) and animal husbandry (sheep, cattle, goats); 16% from trade and services; 11% from industry and handicrafts (textiles, cement, flour, sugar, fruit processing, hand-woven carpets); 20% from other activities **Minerals and Mining:** Fields of natural gas in northern Afghanistan are being developed with Soviet assistance. There are large coal deposits; known deposits of iron ore, chromite and beryl are unexploited; lapis lazuli of world-renowned quality is produced. Hydroelectricity is an important source of energy **Labor Force:** 4,600,000 (1970), with 67% in agriculture, and 8% in industry **Foreign Trade:** Exports, chiefly fruit, karakul skins, natural gas, wool and carpets, totaled $313 million in 1977. Imports, mainly textiles, used clothing, petroleum products, tea, tires, thread, sugar and medicine, totaled $491 million **Principal Trade Partners:** USSR, Japan, West Germany, India, Pakistan, Czechoslovakia

Vital Statistics: Birthrate, 43.2 per 1,000 of pop. (1974); death rate, 21 **Life Expectancy:** 40.3 years **Health Statistics:** 5,879 inhabitants per hospital bed (1976); 28,313 per physician (1974) **Illiteracy:** 90% **Infant Mortality:** 185 per 1,000 births **Primary and Secondary School Enrollment:** 943,326 (1976) **Enrollment in Higher Education:** 12,256 (1975) **GNP Expended on Education:** 1.3% (1974)

Transportation: Paved roads total 1,900 mi. (1975) **Motor Vehicles:** 64,500 (1971) **Passenger Cars:** 38,400 **Railway Mileage:** None **Ports:** None **Major Airlines:** Ariana Afghan Airlines operates international flights **Communications:** Government owned **Radio Transmitters:** 6 **Receivers:** 115,000 (1976) **Television Stations:** 1 **Telephones:** 28,000 (1976) **Newspapers:** 17 dailies, 27 per 1,000 inhabitants (1975)

Weights and Measures: Metric system and local units are used **Travel Requirements:** The U.S. Government advises against travel to Afghanistan (1980)

Divided by tribal loyalties and the country's mountainous terrain, many in Afghanistan live now as their forefathers did: as herdsmen, nomads, and farmers. The cities, especially the capital, Kabul, show tentative signs of modernity, but the gap between the way urban and rural Afghans live and think has long been a major problem in attempts to consolidate the national mosaic.

Afghanistan's modern history has seen tribal rebellions, bloody royal successions and military coups, but no foreign interference ever had resulted in virtually total conquest until the Soviet Union invaded in late December 1979, and quickly became an occupying force—beset, however, by guerrilla resistance in the countryside.

King Mohammed Zahir Shah, who succeeded his assassinated father in 1933 at the age of 19, was a near-prisoner of relatives for years. He did not assume full governmental powers until 1963. Zahir attempted to introduce reforms and presented his people with the first democratic constitution in 1964. Lasting political changes did not take place, however, and a two-year drought in 1971-72 brought an already poor economy to a crisis condition, sealing the fate of the monarchy.

In July 1973 a group of young military officers deposed the king and proclaimed a republic. The leader of the coup, Lt. Gen. Mohammad Daud Khan, a cousin of the king and a former prime minister (1953-1963), became both president and prime minister of the new republic. The constitution of 1964 was put aside and rule by decree instituted. In April 1978 President Daud, members of his family and some 100 police officers and other officials were among an undetermined number who were killed as leftist military elements overthrew the government in two days of fierce fighting in Kabul. The rebels set up a Revolutionary Council to run the country by decree and installed a civilian, Nur Mohammad Taraki, general secretary of the Marxist Khalq Party, as president and prime minister of what became "the Democratic Republic of Afghanistan." On Dec. 5, Taraki signed a 20-year Afghan-USSR friendship treaty in Moscow.

Protesting the Taraki government's atheistic policies, village tribesmen began sporadic attacks on government forces in 1978. Without forming a united front, fervent but poorly armed Moslem bands gained control of an estimated 22 of the country's 28 provinces in 1979. In Herat, Moslems and defecting troops rioted in March and killed hundreds of loyal troops; a government response with helicopter gunships caused an estimated 20,000 deaths in the city. In April, in Kerala in Kunar province, Afghan soldiers and police and Soviet advisors massacred more than 1,000 men and boys.

The Revolutionary Council named Hafizulla Amin as prime minister in March 1979; six months later, in a shootout that took 60 lives at Kabul's People's House, Taraki was apparently slain and Amin became president. But in a Dec. 27 coup backed by Soviet troops, Babrak Karmal, back from exile in Eastern Europe, was installed as head of state, and Amin was executed for "crimes against the people." A 3½-hour battle preceded the takeover of Radio Kabul by the Soviets.

By the start of 1980 the Soviet troops had fanned out to control towns, passes, and key roads throughout the country. Even so, "holy warriors"— organized into some 60 guerrilla groups—retained control of the barren countryside, and they took over the roads and passes at night. Urban unrest ran high. In February, Kabul merchants shuttered their shops; the demonstrations that followed were quelled with from 400 to 1,500 deaths. In April, Kabul schoolgirls made protest marches; eventually, helicopters strafed the university campus, killing from 60 to 200 students. Months after the occupation began, 80,000 Soviet troops were bogged down with security duties.

HISTORY: Afghanistan has suffered invasions from east and west— by Persians, Greeks, Mongols, and Turks. Among the foreign conquerors was Alexander the Great, in the 4th century B.C. After him came the independent kingdom of Bactria, which lasted until the middle of the 2nd century B.C. Buddhism spread from the east but was superseded by Islam in the 7th century A.D., after which several Moslem kingdoms were set up

11th cent.: Mahmud of Ghazni, an Afghan Moslem, forms kingdom stretching from Caspian Sea to the Ganges River

13th cent.: Genghis Khan and his hordes overrun the country

18th cent.: Persians under Nadir Shah conquer Afghanistan; after Nadir's death in 1747, Ahmad Shah unifies the country for the first time and sets up the Durrani dynasty

1838-42: Attempts by Emir Dost Mohammed to exploit Anglo-Russian rivalry in central Asia and to seize control of British possessions in India lead to first Afghan War, which ends with British withdrawal from Afghanistan

1878-80: Dost Mohammed's son, Shere Àli, turns to Russia for aid, setting off second Afghan War with Britain; Shere Ali is ousted and replaced by Anglophile Abd ur-Rahman

1907: Anglo-Russian agreement guarantees independence of Afghanistan under British influence

1926-29: Afghanistan becomes kingdom, with Amanullah as first king; he attempts to modernize the country but ultra-conservative elements force him to abdicate

1930-33: His successor, Mohammed Nadir Shah, continues reforms until killed; Mohammed Zahir Shah becomes king

1964-65: A new, liberal constitution goes into effect and parliamentary elections are held for the first time

1973: King Mohammed Zahir Shah is overthrown by brother-in-law, General Mohammad Daud Khan; Daud proclaims Afghanistan a republic, declares himself president and prime minister

1974: Daud and Brezhnev sign a joint statement of interest in a collective Asian security system and establishment of a commission to expand Soviet-Afghan cooperation

1975: Daud nationalizes all banks and land reform laws are announced. Increased foreign aid is received

1978: Daud killed as leftist military coup succeeds; Nur Mohammad Taraki becomes president and prime minister. Rural Moslem conservatives begin guerrilla warfare

1979: U.S. Ambassador Adolph Dubs, kidnapped by rebels, is killed in a rescue attempt by government security officers. Hafizullah Amin becomes prime minister in March and advances to president in a coup on Sept. 16, when Taraki reportedly is killed. In a Dec. 27 coup, Babrak Karmal becomes head of state, and Amin is executed. Soviet troops, airlifted into Kabul, win a battle for Radio Kabul, which announces the coup

1980: Soviet troops occupy the country, but the rebels fight on in widespread guerrilla resistance. Kabul merchants shutter their shops, and many die in street protests

---

ALBANIA

Area: 11,100 sq. mi. **Population:** 2,608,000 (1978 est.)

Official Name: People's Socialist Republic of Albania **Capital:** Tirana **Nationality:** Albanian **Languages:** Albanians are divided into two main language groups: Gheg, north of the river Shkumbi, and Tosk in the south. The official language is based on Tosk. Greek is spoken by the Greek minority in the south **Religion:** 50% Moslem, 20% Orthodox, 10% Roman Catholic. In 1967, however, all religious institutions were closed by the government **Flag:** A red field, with a double-headed black eagle and a gold-edged, five-pointed star above it **Anthem:** Anthem of the Flag **Currency:** Lek (7 per U.S. $1)

Location: Southeast Europe, on the west coast of the Balkan peninsula. Albania is bordered on the north and east by Yugoslavia, on the south by Greece, and on the west by the Adriatic Sea **Features:** About 20% of the country consists of a flat-to-rolling coastal plain. Most of the country, however, consists of hills and mountains, frequently covered with scrub forest **Chief Rivers:** Drin, Mat, Shkumbi, Semun, Vijosë

Political Leader: First Secretary of the Albanian (Communist) Party of Labor: Enver Hoxha, born 1908; in power since 1945 as First Secretary of the Central Committee **Head of State:** Chairman of the Presidium of the People's Assembly: Haxhi Lleshi, born 1913,

reelected by People's Assembly 1978 **Head of Government:** Chairman of the Council of Ministers (premier): Mehmet Shehu, born 1913, reappointed by the People's Assembly in 1978 **Effective Date of Present Constitution:** 1976 **Legislative Body:** People's Assembly (unicameral), consisting of 250 members, elected for 4 years. The People's Assembly is nominally the supreme organ of government, but in practice meets only a few days each year. Real power is vested in the Politburo and Central Committee of the Communist party **Local Government:** 27 districts and one independent city, more than 200 localities, and 2,500 villages, with locally elected people's councils in each of these subdivisions

Ethnic Composition: The population is homogeneous, with a small Greek minority **Population Distribution:** 34% urban (1971) **Density:** 235 inhabitants per sq. mi.

Largest Cities: (1975 estimates) Tirana 170,000, Durrës 80,000, Vlorë 57,000, Korcë 53,000, Shkodër 49,000

Per Capita Income: $720 (1979 est.) **Gross National Product (GNP):** $1.9 billion (1979 est.) **Economic Statistics:** GNP components are not available. In 1968, however, industrial production accounted for 61.5% of total production in the country; the principal industries are oil refining, chemicals, fertilizers, construction materials, textiles, pig iron, processed minerals, and agricultural products. Agricultural production is chiefly devoted to corn, sugar beets, wheat, cotton, tobacco, and livestock **Minerals and Mining:** Chrome ore, oil, coal, copper, iron, and nickel are exploited and are among Albania's chief exports. Hydroelectric and thermoelectric plants provide the country with full electrification **Labor Force:** In 1972, 343,228 workers were employed in the socialist sector of the economy, with about 30% in industry and 60% in agriculture **Foreign Trade:** Exports, chiefly chrome ores, crude petroleum, bitumen, olives, fruit and tobacco, amounted to $91 million in 1970. Imports, chiefly machinery and equipment, rolled steel and wheat, totaled about $159 million **Principal Trade Partners:** Yugoslavia, Greece, Italy

Vital Statistics: Birthrate, 33.3 per 1,000 of pop.; death rate, 8.1 (1971) **Life Expectancy:** 69 years **Health Statistics:** 164 inhabitants per hospital bed; 159 per physician (1972) **Infant Mortality:** 86.8 per 1,000 births (1965) **Illiteracy:** 25% **Education Statistics:** 1,429 schools with a combined enrollment of 750,000 pupils (1975) **Enrollment in Higher Education:** 28,668 (1971) **GNP Expended on Education:** N.A.

Transportation: There were 4,200 mi. of paved roads in 1969 **Motor Vehicles:** 10,100 (1967) **Passenger Cars:** 2,600 (1967) **Railway Mileage:** 188 **Ports:** Durrës, Vlorë **Major Airlines:** Albtransport operates international flights **Communications:** Government owned **Radio Transmitters:** 19 **Receivers:** 180,000 (1976) **Television Transmitters:** 1 **Receivers:** 4,500 (1976) **Telephones:** 10,150 (1963) **Newspapers:** 2 dailies, 46 copies per 1,000 inhabitants (1975)

Weights and Measures: Metric system **Travel Requirements:** (1971) Passport, visa obtainable in Paris or Rome

---

Albania's present, like its past, is influenced by its forbidding hills and poor soil. In a land unattractive to migrants, the Albanians have preserved their ancient culture. But the land cannot feed the people; Albania is a food-importing nation. Fearful of strangers, Albania must depend on strangers for its survival.

Since 1946, Albania has been dominated by the Albanian Party of Labor—a party fanatically devoted to Marxist-Leninist ideology. The Party's leaders have rejected calls for de-Stalinization and for détente with the West and have maintained a rigid police state. The government has fallen out, successively, with Yugoslavia, the Soviet Union and China, as these states have moved away from ideological rigidity.

At the beginning of the 20th century, Albania was part of the Ottoman Empire. Serbia took from that Empire much territory inhabited by ethnic Albanians before an alarmed Austria, in 1912, helped the rest of the country to win independence. After World War I, Albania was caught up in the rivalry between Yugoslavia and Italy; the latter annexed Albania in 1939.

Nominally independent under Communist rule in 1946, Albania was virtually a Yugoslav satellite. The two countries joined in aiding Communist guerrillas in Greece. But Albania broke with

Yugoslavia in 1947 and ended the Greek adventure, after Yugoslavia broke with the Soviet Union. Territorial claims against Yugoslavia and loyalty to Joseph Stalin led Albania to remain in the Soviet camp, and the Soviet Union took over the task of supplying most of Albania's food.

In 1961, however, Albania's relations with the Soviet Union soured because of Soviet policies of de-Stalinization. Albania turned to Communist China for friendship and food. For practical reasons Albania resumed relations with Yugoslavia in 1970 and with Greece in 1971. Later, China's course became increasingly pragmatic, and Albania criticized the lack of devotion to the Communist cause. After Mao's death in 1976, Albania became hostile to his successors, and in 1978 China ended its assistance to Albania. In February 1979, Albania condemned China for its temporary armed invasion of Vietnam.

HISTORY: Around 300 B.C., the Illyrian kingdom covered much of what is now Albania. Greek colonies were established along the coast, but the hinterland remained independent. In the 6th century A.D., while nominally under Byzantine rule, Albania was invaded by the Slavs and in the 9th century was annexed to Bulgaria. The Turks conquered the country in the 15th century

1912-20: Albania proclaims its independence with the support of Austria-Hungary. During World War I, Albania is occupied by Allied troops but reasserts its independence

1925-28: Ahmed Zogu, chief of the Mat district, seizes power with Yugoslav support. He rules as president until 1928, when he establishes a monarchy and becomes King Zog I

1939: Italy occupies Albania and unites it with Italian crown

1946: Albania becomes a people's republic under the leadership of Enver Hoxha, head of the Communist resistance group during the Italian occupation

1955-60: Backed by the USSR, Albania joins the Warsaw Pact and the United Nations. Relations with the Soviet Union soon cool, however, as Moscow attempts to improve relations with Yugoslavia, behind whose frontiers live more than 750,000 ethnic Albanians; estrangement is sharpened by Albania's support for Peking in Sino-Soviet ideological split

1961: USSR breaks diplomatic relations with Albania

1968: Albania withdraws from Warsaw Pact

1970: Albania signs trade pact with Yugoslavia

1971: Greece and Albania resume full diplomatic relations

1973: Purge of eight officials for anti-party activity

1976: A new constitution is approved by People's Assembly

1978: Chinese aid ended. New agreement with Greece increases trade and opens air route

---

ALGERIA

Area: 919,591 sq. mi. **Population:** 19,130,000 (1979 est.)

Official Name: Democratic and Popular Republic of Algeria **Capital:** Algiers **Nationality:** Algerian **Languages:** Arabic is the official and principal language. French is also widely spoken and serves as a quasi-official language. Berber dialects are spoken by one-fourth the population **Religion:** 99% Moslem; Islam was declared the state religion in 1976 **Flag:** A red star in a red crescent in center of background of green (left hand of flag) and white (right hand) **Anthem:** We Pledge **Currency:** Algerian dinar (3.8 per U.S. $1)

Location: North Africa. Algeria is bordered on the north by the Mediterranean Sea, on the east by Tunisia and Libya, on the south by Niger and Mali, and on the west by Mauritania, Western Sahara, and Morocco **Features:** Two mountain chains, the Tell Atlas and the Saharan Atlas. The mountains of the Tell Atlas rise from a narrow coastal plain along the Mediterranean and are separated from the Saharan Atlas by a corridor of semiarid plateaus dotted with salt marshes and shallow salt lakes. To the south lies the Sahara itself, broken only by a few oases **Chief River:** Chéliff

Head of State and of Government: President: Chadli Bendjedid, born 1929, elected 1979. He is assisted by Premier Mohamed Ben Ahmed Abdelghani, appointed 1979 **Effective Date of Present Constitution:** 1976 **Legislative Body:** A new National Popular Assembly of 261 members was elected in February 1977 for 5-year terms **Local Government:** 31 departments, each administered by a governor who is responsible to the Minister of the Interior

Ethnic Composition: The population is of Arabo-Berber stock **Population Distribution:** 52% urban **Density:** 20.8 inhabitants per sq. mi.

Largest Cities: (1978 census) Algiers 1,365,400, Oran 491,900, Constantine 335,100, Annaba 255,900, Blida 160,900

Per Capita Income: $1,648 (1979) **Gross National Product (GNP):** $27 billion (1979) **Economic Statistics:** In 1976, 7% of the GNP came from agriculture (wheat, vineyard, orchards), livestock raising (sheep, cattle, donkeys, mules, horses, pigs, goats) and fishing; 35% from trade and services; and 44% from mining and industry (food processing and beverages, textiles, leather, chemicals, building materials, steel, and engineering) **Minerals and Mining:** Vast deposits of oil and gas, iron ore, phosphates, and coal; small amounts of lead, zinc and copper **Labor Force:** 2.6 million (1975 est.), of which 60% is engaged in agriculture, 12% in industry, and the rest in services **Foreign Trade:** Exports, chiefly petroleum, natural gas, fruit and wine, totaled $4.9 billion in 1976. Imports, mainly textiles, cereals, chemicals, motor vehicles, iron and steel products, sugar, machinery, and electrical apparatus, totaled $5.5 billion (1976) **Principal Trade Partners:** France, West Germany, Italy, United States, USSR, Japan, Spain, Canada

Vital Statistics: Birthrate, 47.8 per 1,000 of pop. (1975); death rate, 15.4 **Life Expectancy:** 53.3 years (1975) **Health Statistics:** 356 inhabitants per hospital bed, 8,192 per physician (1976) **Infant Mortality:** 70 per 1,000 births **Illiteracy:** 70% **Primary and Secondary School Enrollment:** 3,400,531 (1976) **Enrollment in Higher Education:** 59,100 (1977) **GNP Expended on Education:** 9% (1977) **Transportation:** Paved roads total 22,125 mi. (1977) **Motor Vehicles:** 440,800 (1975) **Passenger Cars:** 286,100 **Railway Mileage:** 2,423 **Ports:** Algiers, Oran, Annaba, Bejaia, Arzew **Major Airlines:** Air Algérie operates international and domestic flights **Communications:** Government owned **Radio Transmitters:** 27 **Receivers:** 3,220,000 (1974) **Television Transmitters:** 75 **Receivers:** 525,000 (1976) **Telephones:** 273,000 (1976) **Newspapers:** 4 dailies, 17 copies per 1,000 inhabitants (1975)

Weights and Measures: Metric system **Travel Requirements:** Passport, tourist visa, $3.75, valid for 3 months, 4 photos

---

Algeria won independence from France in a long struggle organized by a disciplined party—the National Liberation Front (NLF). Independence brought one-party rule, economic dislocation, and a period of military control. The NLF is a party of Islam, socialism, and concern for the aspirations of the Third World in general and of the Arab states in particular. It is strident in its support of those it considers oppressed, and has made Algeria a haven for many kinds of self-proclaimed revolutionaries—including airplane hijackers. Israel is a favorite target of Algerian rhetoric, although not of Algerian military action. Ironically, Algeria's only actual military adventure is that against Morocco—in support of the Polisario movement for Western Saharan independence.

Despite its ideology, Algeria must trade with the capitalist West. Its economy was ruined by the departure of its European inhabitants after independence, and recovery is incomplete. Fortunately, Algeria has oil and gas which the West needs.

France agreed to independence in 1962, after a plebiscite showed a majority to favor "independence in cooperation with France." Benyoussef Ben Khedda, who had headed the NLF's exile government, became Premier. But his power was broken by Ahmed Ben Bella, a firebrand NLF official who had spent most of the struggle in a French jail. Ben Bella established a one-party system that tended toward personal dictatorship. He was deposed in 1965 by Colonel Houari Boumédienne, who established military rule within the NLF framework.

Boumédienne created most of the salient features of the new Algeria. Finding that cooperation with France was working to France's advantage, he ended it in 1971. Then, he increased trade with the United States, although he had broken diplomatic relations with the U.S. in 1967 because of U.S. support for Israel. Discontent of NLF leaders with military rule led to the adoption of a new constitution in 1976 and to ratification by the voters of the NLF's choice of Boumédienne as President. The constitution did not bring democracy, but it broadened the limits within which divergent views were tolerated.

The system of semi-democratic one-party rule was tried and found workable in 1978, when Boumédienne died after weeks in a coma. As the constitution provided, Rabah Bitat, the President of the National Popular Assembly, became interim President. In 1979, the Congress of the NLF nominated Colonel Chadli Bendjedid, the Minister of Defense, for a six-year term as President, and he was approved by the voters. In 1980 the government, acknowledging the country's poor use of its resources and chronic shortages of goods, announced plans to limit costly foreign imports and to start conserving oil reserves for future domestic needs.

HISTORY: In prehistoric times, Algeria was inhabited by a mixture of peoples from whom the Berbers of today are probably descended. About 1200 B.C. the Phoenicians made settlements in the area, and it eventually fell under the control of Carthage. After the destruction of Carthage in 146 B.C., the Romans gradually gained control of the entire North African coast. With the weakening of the Roman Empire, Algeria fell prey to Vandals from Europe and eventually to the Arabs

7th cent.: Algeria, along with the rest of North Africa, falls to Moslem conquerors from Arabia. Islam takes root

11th cent.: Saharan nomads sweep into the country and destroy farms and pastures, forcing the coastal Berbers into seafaring and piracy. The Berbers spread through North Africa and, in the Moorish Conquest, move to the Iberian peninsula to occupy much of Spain

16th cent.: Spain gains a foothold in Algeria and Algerians turn to Turkish corsairs for help in 1518. Turkish rule is established

1830: France sends an expedition to pacify turbulent tribes along the coast and in the interior. French naval forces seize Algiers, depose the bey, and establish French rule

1942: Allies invade North Africa during World War II

1954-61: Discontent with French rule erupts in a widespread rebellion. Rebel leaders form a "provisional government of Algeria" in Cairo, but the fighting continues until the opening of peace talks with the French

1962-63: Algeria becomes an independent republic. Benyoussef Ben Khedda, premier of the provisional government in exile, takes control but is ousted by Vice-Premier Ahmed Ben Bella who later becomes President under one-party constitution

1965: A military revolt led by Colonel Houari Boumédienne overthrows Ben Bella. A revolutionary council assumes power; Ben Bella placed in "comfortable" confinement

1967-68: Algeria declares war on Israel, but no Algerian troops take part in Middle East fighting. Boumédienne fosters closer economic and military ties with USSR

1969: Algeria accuses U.S. State Department and CIA of involvement in a conspiracy to overthrow the government

1971: French oil companies in Algeria partly nationalized; France ends "special relations" with Algeria

1973: The United States arranges to import 1 billion cubic feet of Algerian liquefied natural gas daily for 25 years

1974: Algeria resumes diplomatic relations with U.S. after severance in 1967

1976: Algerian troops clash with Moroccan and Mauritanian forces in Western Sahara. New constitution approved and elections held. Boumédienne elected President

1978: Boumédienne dies

1979: Chadli Bendjedid elected President. Confinement of Ben Bella lifted

---

ANDORRA

Area: 188 sq. mi. **Population:** 31,000 (1979 est.)

Official Name: Principality of Andorra **Capital:** Andorra la Vella **Nationality:** Andorran **Languages:** Catalan is the official language. French and Spanish are also spoken **Religion:** Roman Catholic **Flag:** Vertical blue, yellow, and red stripes, with the national coat of arms in the center **Anthem:** The Great Charlemagne **Currency:** French franc (4.2 per U.S. $1) and Spanish peseta (70.8 per U.S. $1)

Location: Eastern Pyrenees, between France and Spain **Features:** Drained by the Valira River, Andorra consists of narrow valleys and gorges, bounded by high peaks **Chief Rivers:** Valira

Head of State: Andorra is a co-principality under the joint sovereignty of the president of France and the Spanish bishop of Urgel, each of whom is represented by a viguier, or agent **Head of Government:** Syndic-General Estanislau Sangrá Font, elected 1978

Legislative Body: Parliament (unicameral General Council) **Effective Date of Present Constitution:** 1866 Plan of Reform **Local Government:** 7 parishes, each with an elected council

Ethnic Composition: Native Andorrans, who constitute one-third of the population, are of Catalan stock. The rest of the population is primarily Spanish and French **Population Distribution:** 81% urban **Density:** 165 inhabitants per sq. mi. **Largest Towns:** (1977 est.) Andorra la Vella 19,764, Sant Juliá 3,510, Encamp 2,268

Per Capita Income: N.A. **Gross National Product (GNP):** N.A. **Economic Statistics:** Tourism is the chief source of income. Cereals, potatoes, livestock raising and tobacco are dominant, while tobacco processing is the chief industry. Timber production and building are also important activities. There is considerable smuggling of merchandise shipped between France and Spain **Minerals and Mining:** Small amounts of iron ore and lead are mined **Labor Force:** 9,500, with about 80% in local industries and 20% in agriculture **Foreign Trade:** Principal exports are timber, cattle and derivatives, and furniture; the chief imports are fuel, perfumes, clothing, radio and television sets. Imports in 1979 totaled $840 million **Principal Trade Partners:** France, Spain, West Germany, Japan

Vital Statistics: Birthrate, 16.5 per 1,000 of pop. (1976); death rate, 5.0 **Life Expectancy:** 70 years **Health Statistics:** N.A. **Infant Mortality:** .16 per 1,000 births **Illiteracy:** negligible **Primary and Secondary School Enrollment:** 5,555 (1975) **Enrollment in Higher Education:** N.A. **GNP Expended on Education:** The French government pays part of the costs of the French-language schools. Schools in the southern areas, near Spain, are supported by the Spanish government

Transportation: Surfaced roads total 77 mi. **Motor Vehicles:** 9,346 (1970) **Passenger Cars:** 8,200 (1969) **Railway Mileage:** None **Ports:** None **Major Airlines:** No air service **Communications:** Privately owned **Radio Stations:** 4 **Licenses:** 6,600 (1976) **Television Stations:** None **Receivers:** 3,000 (1976) **Telephones:** 4,000 (1977) **Newspapers:** One daily established in 1974; French and Spanish periodicals are imported and sold locally

Weights and Measures: Metric system **Travel Requirements:** See France

---

Modern tourism, bringing about a million visitors a year, has altered the formerly leisurely pace of life in Andorra. And the pace is destined to quicken even more with easier access to the tiny state in the fastness of the Pyrenees, for France is building a modern highway to Andorra from Toulouse, by way of Foix, on the Ariège River.

Motoring tourists—and automobile traffic in general—are especially important to Andorra, which obtains more than a third of its revenue from gasoline taxes and automobile fines. Tourism as an industry supplements Andorran wool-combing, spinning, tobacco processing, and the manufacture of sandals. Smuggling of goods from France into Spain is also a substantial industry.

What draws tourists is the attraction of towering passes; peaks topped with snow as late as June; a countryside dotted with sheep, goats, and mules; and bargains. Despite the state's need of revenue, there are no sales taxes or customs duties.

HISTORY: According to tradition, Charlemagne granted the people of Andorra a charter because of their help in battling the Moors. In 843 Charles the Bald made the Spanish count of Urgel overlord of Andorra. In 1278 the bishop of Urgel was made joint suzerain after contending that Andorra was part of the endowment of his cathedral. The rights of the count eventually passed by inheritance to Henry IV of France and eventually to the presidents of France

1793: French revolutionary government renounces its claims to Andorra

1806: Napoleon restores co-principality at Andorrans' request

1933: Suffrage is granted to all men over the age of 25

1941: Suffrage is restricted to heads of families

1970: Limited women's suffrage granted

1971: New bishop of Urgel installed as the 80th co-prince

1977: Personal income tax voted by the General Council

ANGOLA

Area: 481,351 sq. mi. **Population:** 7,000,000 (1978 est.)

Official Name: People's Republic of Angola **Capital:** Luanda **Na-**

tionality: Angolan **Languages:** Portuguese is the official language. A number of African languages, chiefly of Bantu origin, are commonly spoken **Religion:** Animist 84%, Roman Catholic 12%, Protestant 4% **Flag:** Two equal horizontal stripes of red over black, with yellow five-pointed star, machete, and half a cogwheel in the center **Anthem:** N.A. **Currency:** Kwanza (49.3 per U.S. $1)

Location: West-central Africa. Bounded by the Atlantic Ocean on the west, Namibia on the south, and Zaire and Zambia on the north and east. The exclave of Cabinda lies on the Atlantic coast north of the Congo River mouth **Features:** A narrow coastal strip rises sharply toward an interior plateau, which ranges from 3,000 to 5,000 feet in elevation. A highland area of 6,000 to 7,000 feet lies in the west-central region. Cabinda consists of a low-lying rain forest **Chief Rivers:** Cubango, Cuanza, Cunene, Cuango, Cassai, Cuando, Congo, Cuito

Head of State and of Government: President: José Eduardo dos Santos, born 1942, elected 1979 **Effective Date of Present Constitution:** 1975 **Legislative Body:** The MPLA-Labor party's Central Committee and Political Bureau governs **Local Government:** 17 provinces, under appointed commissars

Ethnic Composition: Predominantly indigenous Bantus, with the Ovimbundu constituting 38%, Kimbundu 23%, Bakongo 13%. Only 30,000 Portuguese remained at independence **Population Distribution:** N.A. **Density:** 14.5 inhabitants per sq. mi.

Largest Cities: (1972 est.) Luanda 540,000; (1970 census) Huambo 61,885; Lobito 59,528; Benguela 40,996; Lubango 31,674; Malanje 31,599; Cabinda 21,124

Per Capita Income: $442 (1979 est.) **Gross National Product (GNP):** $3.4 billion (1979) **Economic Statistics:** The economy remains heavily dependent upon agriculture (subsistence and cash crops such as coffee, sisal, cotton, wheat, sugar, and tobacco, with fish and timber of importance). Industry (cement, oil refining, paper, agricultural processing, and metal products) has declined since independence **Minerals and Mining:** Iron ore and diamonds are exploited, and petroleum is being produced in the Cabinda exclave **Labor Force:** Total currently unknown, with an estimated 80% in agriculture, and 10% in industry **Foreign Trade:** Exports, chiefly petroleum, coffee, iron ore, diamonds, cotton, and fish meal, totaled $840 million in 1977. Imports, mainly machinery, textiles, transportation and construction equipment, iron and steel products, rice, and electrical products, totaled $680 million **Principal Trade Partners:** Portugal, USSR, West Germany, United States, Britain, Spain, Japan, France

Vital Statistics: Birthrate, 47.2 per 1,000 of pop. (1975); death rate, 27 (1974) **Life Expectancy:** 38.5 years **Health Statistics:** 322 inhabitants per hospital bed; 15,404 per physician (1972) **Infant Mortality:** 24.1 per 1,000 births **Illiteracy:** 85% **Education Statistics:** N.A. **Higher Education:** N.A. **GNP Expended on Education:** N.A.

Transportation: Surfaced roads total 8,371 mi. (1974) **Motor Vehicles:** 183,031 (1973) **Passenger Cars:** 127,271 **Railway Mileage:** 1,895 **Ports:** Lobito, Luanda, Moçamades, Cabinda **Major Airlines:** Domestic flights are by TAAG (Angolan Airlines) **Communications:** Government owned **Radio Transmitters:** 19 (1972) **Receivers:** 116,000 (1976) **Television:** None **Telephones:** 31,000 (1976) **Newspapers:** 1 daily, 2 copies per 1,000 inhabitants (1975)

Weights and Measures: Metric system **Travel Requirements:** No U.S. representation in Angola. Contact Angola UN Mission in New York for travel information

---

Fifteen years of rebellion against colonial rule culminated in the granting of Angolan independence by Portugal on November 11, 1975. However, independence did not bring peace to Angola, the largest and most important territory of the former Portuguese overseas empire. Three factions contended for power in this resource-rich country: the Marxist-oriented Popular Movement for the Liberation of Angola (MPLA), the pro-Western National Front for the Liberation of Angola (FNLA), and the pro-Western National Union for the Total Independence of Angola (UNITA). The MPLA, backed by the Soviet Union and Cuba, held the Angolan capital, Luanda, while the pro-Western forces occupied most of the country north and south of the capital.

Initially, following independence, the pro-Western FNLA and UNITA forces scored military successes against the Marxist MPLA in the central area around Luanda. Both sides employed foreign troops in their fight for full control of the nation. Particularly important was the contribution to the MPLA of trained manpower by Cuba and of arms by the USSR. South African armed forces crossed into Angola from Namibia (South-West Africa) to aid the FNLA and UNITA.

In late November of 1975 the military tide turned in favor of the MPLA as a result of the massive Soviet and Cuban assistance. The situation grew increasingly grim for the pro-Western factions on December 19 when the U.S. Senate voted to cut off covert financial aid to the combatants. By mid-February 1976 the MPLA forces had smashed the two pro-Western factions and had overrun most of Angola. South African troops withdrew into Namibia in late March. But elements of both the defeated FNLA and UNITA continue to wage guerrilla warfare today.

The violent conditions of this period resulted in the flight of most of the Portuguese population. The departure of the educationally and technically advanced segment of Angolan society resulted in a drastic decline in the economic life of the country.

The leader of the MPLA, Agostinho Neto, a poet and doctor, became president of independent Angola in November 1975. Faced with massive economic problems, he sought better relations with Western governments, but because of the continued presence of Cuban troops in the country, the United States refused to establish diplomatic relations

Neto died in a Moscow hospital in Sept. 10, 1979, after an operation for cancer. The central committee of the MPLA-Labor party (as the MPLA was renamed in 1977) unanimously elected José Eduardo dos Santos, then Minister of Planning, to succeed Neto. In his inauguration address, dos Santos affirmed support for his predecessor's objectives and programs.

HISTORY: Prior to the coming of the Portuguese in 1483, present-day Angola was part of the African Kingdom of the Kongo. During the 16th century Portugal established trading posts along the coast and exploited Angola as a prime source of the lucrative slave trade. The Dutch captured and held the Angolan port cities for seven years until the Portuguese recaptured them in 1648

1884-85: At Berlin Conference the Portuguese receive "right of occupation" to Angola while losing all claim to central African territory

1910-20: Portugal begins serious colonizing effort in Angola

1926: Portuguese Republic overthrown. Subsequent authoritarian regime of Salazar tightens Portuguese rule over colony

1961: Rebellion against Portugal breaks out, beginning 15-year violent struggle for independence

1962: UN General Assembly votes condemnation of Portuguese administration of colonies

1975: Portugal grants Angolan independence. Rival factions battle for supremacy

1976: Marxist MPLA group wins control of Angola. Angola admitted to the UN

1978: In April 5,000 Cuban troops lead government offensive against pro-Western guerrillas. In May South African forces enter Angola from South-West Africa in "limited military operation" against guerrillas of SWAPO (South-West African People's Organization) South Africa's action is unanimously condemned by UN Security Council

1979: President Neto dies Sept. 10 and is succeeded by his Minister of Planning, José Eduardo dos Santos, a Soviet-educated petroleum engineer

1980: South African forces raid Namibian guerrilla camps in Angola

---

ARGENTINA

Area: 1,068,296 sq. mi. **Population:** 26,729,000 (1979 est.)
Official Name: Argentine Republic **Capital:** Buenos Aires **Nationality:** Argentine **Languages:** Spanish is the official and principal language. Italian, French, and German are also frequently spoken **Religion:** About 95% of the population belongs to the Roman Catholic Church, which is officially recognized in the Constitution. There are small minorities of Protestants and Jews **Flag:** Horizontal stripes of blue, white, and blue, with the sun on the white stripe **Anthem:** Argentine National Anthem, beginning "Hear, mortals, the sacred cry of Liberty" **Currency:** New Argentine peso (1,786 per U.S. $1)

Location: Southern South America. Argentina is bordered on the north by Bolivia and Paraguay, on the northeast by Brazil and Uruguay, on the east and south by the Atlantic Ocean, and on the west by Chile **Features:** The heartland of Argentina is the rich, temperate plains area known as the Pampas, which fans out from the east-central sector of the country. The north consists of sub-tropical lowlands, while the west is dominated by the Andean Mountains and the south by the Patagonian steppe and the rainy Tierra del Fuego **Chief Rivers:** Paraná, Negro, Salado, Colorado, Chubut

Head of State and Government: President: Lt. Gen. Jorge Rafael Videla, born 1925, took office following the coup of March 1976, confirmed for three-year term in May 1978 by the 3-man junta. The junta, which reserves final executive power, will serve a 3-year term, and is advised by a military Legislative Advisory Commission **Effective Date of Present Constitution:** Although the constitution of 1853 is still in effect, its provisions have been made subject to the Statutes of the Revolution, issued after a military coup in 1966 **Legislative Body:** The National Congress was dissolved in 1976 **Local Government:** 22 provinces, 1 national territory, and 1 federal district, each administered by an appointed governor

Ethnic Composition: 97% of the population is of European origin; persons of Arab descent, Indians and mestizos constitute about 3% **Population Distribution:** 81.1% urban (1975) **Density:** 25 inhabitants per sq. mi.

Largest Cities (M.A. = Metropolitan Area): Buenos Aires (1974 est.) 2,976,000 (M.A. 8,925,000); others (1970 census) Córdoba 781,565 (M.A. 790,508), Rosario 750,455 (M.A. 806,942), Lanús 449,824, Lomas de Zamora 410,806, La Plata 391,247 (M.A. 478,666)

Per Capita Income: $2,180 (1979) **Gross National Product (GNP):** $52 billion (1979) **Economic Statistics:** In 1975, 48% of the GNP came from trade and services; 36% from industry (iron and steel, automobiles, machinery, chemicals, cement); 11% from agriculture (meat, hides, grain, fruits); and 8% from mining and construction **Minerals and Mining:** Oil and natural gas supply domestic needs; copper, low-grade iron ore and small amounts of coal, lead, zinc, silver, bismuth, vanadium, beryllium, tantalite, and tungsten are mined **Labor Force:** 9,928,234 in 1975, of which 29% is employed in manufacturing and 15% in agriculture; approximately 2.5 million are organized in unions **Foreign Trade:** Exports, chiefly grains, meat, wool, hides, linseed oil and other agricultural products totaled $7.8 billion in 1979. Imports, mainly machinery and equipment, iron and steel products, chemicals, textiles and fuels, totaled $6.4 billion **Principal Trade Partners:** United States, Brazil, West Germany, Netherlands, Italy, Britain, Japan, USSR

Vital Statistics: Birthrate, 21.8 per 1,000 of pop. (1975); death rate, 8.8 **Life Expectancy:** 68 years **Health Statistics:** 176 inhabitants per hospital bed; 479 per physician (1972) **Infant Mortality:** 59 per 1,000 births (1970) **Illiteracy:** 7% **Primary and Secondary School Enrollment:** 4,945,515 (1977) **Enrollment in Higher Education:** 619,950 **GNP Expended on Education:** 1.6% (1976)

Transportation: Paved roads total 23,000 mi. (1975) **Motor Vehicles:** 3,500,000 (1976) **Passenger Cars:** 2,160,000 (1974) **Railway Mileage:** 25,794 **Ports:** Buenos Aires, Bahía Blanca, La Plata, Rosario **Major Airlines:** Aerolíneas Argentinas is the major international and domestic carrier **Communications:** Partly government owned **Radio Transmitters:** 163 (1974) **Receivers:** 26,000,000 (1973) **Television Transmitters:** 82 **Receivers:** 4,500,000 (1974) **Telephones:** 2,400,000 (1976) **Newspapers:** 167 dailies, 179 copies per 1,000 inhabitants (1974)

Weights and Measures: Metric system **Travel Requirements:** Passport and visa required. Check embassy or consulate for specific requirements. No fee

---

Extending 2,300 miles from north to south and with an Atlantic coastline 1,600 miles long, Argentina is the second-largest country on the South American continent, after Brazil. Its topography and climate are as varied as those of the United States, the terrain ranging from the subtropical lowlands of the north to the towering Andean Mountains in the west and the bleak Patagonian steppe and rainy Tierra del Fuego in the south. More than 60 percent of the country's area is suitable for agriculture, of which about 8 percent is under cultivation and the remainder is pastureland upon which a massive livestock population thrives (there are currently more than two animals for every Argentine man, woman and child). The heartland of Argentina is the rich, temperate plains area known as the Pampas, which fans out for almost 500 miles from Buenos Aires in the east-central sector; here is found some of the richest topsoil in the world.

Politically, the dominant factor of life in Argentina has been turmoil. In the early months of 1976, Argentina was a country on the edge of anarchy, racked by daily kidnappings and bombings. Its treasury, down to its last foreign reserves, was about to default on its overseas debt. Then, on March 24, in a bloodless coup led by the Commander in Chief of the army, Jorge Rafael Videla, the military deposed Isabel Perón, the first woman chief of state in the Americas, from the presidency, her inept government falling along with her.

Mrs. Perón had come into power on the death of her husband, Juan Perón, in July 1974. He had returned to Argentina in June 1973, after 18 years of exile, which had been preceded by an 11-year rule as Argentina's president. He was reelected to the presidency in September of that year, with his wife as vice-president.

After the ouster of Mrs. Perón, Videla was sworn in as president on March 29, 1976. The final executive power was entrusted to a military junta that set two goals: crushing terrorism and reviving the economy. Despite the opposition of President Videla and other moderates who have demanded an end to uncontrolled kidnappings and arrests by security forces of the Army, more than 5,000 Peronist and Marxist guerrillas and guerrilla suspects are believed to have been killed since 1976. In 1979, Amnesty International estimated the number of missing at 15,000. A UN subcommission on prevention of discrimination named Argentina among seven countries guilty of "a pattern of gross violation of human rights." On Sept. 29, 1979, Gen. Luciano Menéndez, commander of the III Corps in Córdoba and a hardline rightist, called for an army uprising against what he termed the softness of the government in dealing with subversion. He gained little support and was subsequently arrested and relieved of his command.

Meanwhile, despite assurances from Videla that the war against terrorism was over, attacks on the lives and property of government officials and leaders of banking and industry continued.

A new "Professional Associations Law," aimed at curbing the political thrust of the trade unions, which were the backbone of Peronist power, took effect Nov. 16, 1979.

On Dec. 19, 1979, the ruling junta issued a document, "Political Bases for the Process of National Reorganization," setting guidelines for a return to more democratic government, as Videla had promised in 1978. The plan calls for a republican form of government and substantial autonomy for the provinces. The armed forces would retain power for making decisions on the conduct of national strategy, national security and defense of the constitution." Totalitarian ideologies (evidently referring to communist and Peronist) would be excluded. Interior Minister Albano Harguindeguy had indicated earlier that a sharing of power with civilians would begin at the municipal level and move upward to state and federal governments.

On the economic front the government's program scored some successes, notably in boosting agricultural production, expanding hydroelectric power facilities, and lifting foreign reserves to $7 billion—up from virtually nothing at the end of the Perón regime. Still, inflation persisted with prices rising at an annual rate of 170 percent in 1979.

In March 1980 the government contracted with a Swiss firm to manufacture a heavy water plant which will give Argentina full control over the nuclear fuel cycle that generates a growing share of its electric power. The plant is to be assembled near Arroyito and completed in 1984.

HISTORY: The treeless plains of the Pampas were inhabited by fierce nomadic Indian tribes of unknown origin for centuries before 1516, when a band of eight conquistadors led by Juan Díaz de Solís landed on the shores of Río de la Plata. Magellan and Sebastian Cabot soon followed on other voyages of exploration and in 1580 Juan de Garay reached what is now Buenos Aires by way of Paraguay. By the 18th century Buenos Aires had become the capital of a vast Spanish viceroyalty that included Argentina

1810: Argentine revolutionists depose Spanish viceroy and form their own government

1817-19: General José de San Martín crosses the Andes with 5,000 men, defeats Spanish crown forces at Battle of Maipú (1818), and goes on to liberate Chile and Peru. New Argentine constitution sets off civil war between "federalists" and "unitarians," with the latter favoring a central government dominated by Buenos Aires

1829: Juan Manuel de Rosas, the federalist leader, establishes one-man rule

1845-52: Rosas interferes in neighboring countries; aided by Brazil, Uruguay, France and Britain, Justo José de Urquiza overthrows Rosas, who flees to England

1880-81: Long struggle between Buenos Aires and federalist forces ends, with the city becoming a federal district; settlers end Indians' resistance by virtually wiping them out

1916-30: Period of vast immigration and prosperity begins; Hipólito Irigoyen, leader of the Radicals, a bourgeois reform party, is elected president and enacts wide social-reform legislation. He is succeeded in 1922 by another Radical, but returns to power in 1928. Two years later he is overthrown by the military

1943-45: The latest in a string of military coups places Colonel Juan Domingo Perón in a relatively unimportant post as labor secretary. Perón, effecting sweeping social and economic reforms, wins popularity among masses; he is thrown in jail by frightened military men. Released after nine days, Perón asks for election

1946: Perón wins election. A widower, he takes as his second wife Eva Duarte, a radio star, who helps Perón establish trade unions along militant, Fascist lines

1952-55: Eva Perón dies (1952); Perón, unsettled, faces charges of immorality and corruption. After thwarting several coups, he is overthrown and makes his way to Spain

1973: Following a long succession of civilian and military presidents, Perón returns from exile on June 20 and, running on a coalition ticket, is elected president in September

1974: Perón dies and is succeeded by his wife, Isabel Perón

1976: Coup topples Mrs. Perón's government. Argentina is governed by a junta led by Gen. Jorge Rafael Videla

1979: Jacobo Timerman, outspoken former publisher of La Opinión, is released Sept. 25 after spending 29 months under house arrest. He is deprived of Argentine citizenship and is placed on a plane to join his family in Israel

1980: Argentina signs 5-year agreement to supply the USSR with feed grain

---

AUSTRALIA

Area: 2,967,909 sq. mi. **Population:** 14,418,000 (1979 est.)

Official Name: Commonwealth of Australia **Capital:** Canberra **Nationality:** Australian **Languages:** English **Religion:** 36% Anglican, 31% Roman Catholic, 10% Methodist, 9% Presbyterian, 2% Baptist, 12% others **Flag:** A blue field, with the Union Jack in the upper left corner, a large, 7-pointed white star directly beneath, and five smaller white stars in the right half **Anthem:** God Save the Queen **National Song:** Advance Australia Fair **Currency:** Australian dollar (0.90 per U.S. $1)

Location: An island continent between the Indian and Pacific oceans, lying southeast of Asia. It is bounded on the north by the Torres Strait and the Timor Sea, on the east by the Coral and Tasman seas, and on the south and west by the Indian Ocean. The continent and the island of Tasmania, off the eastern part of the south coast, make up the Commonwealth of Australia **Features:** The continent is roughly a low, irregular plateau, with a flat, arid center. The southeastern quarter of the continent is a huge fertile plain covering some 500,000 sq. mi. Relatively low mountains lie close to the east coast **Chief Rivers:** Murray, Darling, Murrumbidgee, Burdekin, Fitzroy, Ord

Head of State: Queen Elizabeth II, represented by a governor-general, Sir Zelman Cowen, born 1919, appointed 1977 **Head of Government:** Prime Minister John Malcolm Fraser, born 1930, reelected 1977 **Effective Date of Present Constitution:** 1900, revised 1977 **Legislative Body:** Federal Parliament (bicameral), consisting of a Senate and House of Representatives. There are 64 Senators, elected for 6-year terms. The House consists of 124 members, elected every 3 years **Local Government:** 6 states, each

headed by a governor appointed by the sovereign and with an elected legislature, premier, and a cabinet. There is also one internal territory, one capital territory, and six external territories

Ethnic Composition: The population is mainly of British origin; Aborigines (excluding mixed-bloods) number 40,000 **Population Distribution:** 86% urban **Density:** 4.6 inhabitants per sq. mi.

Largest Cities (Metropolitan Area): (1976 census) Sydney 3,021,300, Melbourne 2,603,000, Brisbane 957,000, Adelaide 900,000, Perth 805,000, Canberra 215,400, Hobart 162,000

Per Capita Income: $7,646 (1979) **Gross National Product (GNP):** $110 billion (1979 est.) **Economic Statistics:** About 30% of GNP comes from industry (steel, automobiles, ships, textiles, chemicals, petroleum refining, electrical equipment). Agriculture and mining, however, are the mainstays of the economy. Australia is the world's foremost wool-growing country, producing almost one-third of the world's wool, and is a leading producer of meats and dairy products. Mining, which accounts for 3% of GNP, plays an important role in the country's export trade **Minerals and Mining:** Coal, iron ore, bauxite, copper, lead, zinc, uranium, nickel, crude oil, and other minerals are mined. A major diamond field is to be exploited. Australian wells provide 50% of the nation's crude oil requirements. About 90% of indigenous oil production is from offshore wells in the Bass Strait, discovered in 1964 and estimated to have reserves of 1,500 million barrels. There have been several natural gas finds; reserves are estimated at 20 trillion cu. ft. of gas **Labor Force:** 6.2 million (1978), of which 22% is employed in manufacturing, 6% in agriculture, and 51% in services **Foreign Trade:** Exports, chiefly wool, wheat, meat, dairy products, and iron ore, totaled $14.2 billion in 1978. Imports, mainly machinery and transportation equipment, manufactured goods, chemicals, mineral fuels, crude materials, food and beverages, totaled $14 billion **Principal Trade Partners:** Japan, United States, Britain, West Germany, New Zealand, Canada, Singapore, France

Vital Statistics: Birthrate, 16.1 per 1,000 of pop. (1977); death rate, 7.7 **Life Expectancy:** 71 years **Health Statistics:** 80 inhabitants per hospital bed; 600 per physician (1975) **Infant Mortality:** 14 per 1,000 births **Illiteracy:** Negligible **Primary and secondary school enrollment:** 2,725,463 (1976) **Enrollment in Higher Education:** 274,738 (1975) **GNP Expended on Education:** 6.3% (1975)

Transportation: Paved roads total 261,170 mi. (1973) **Motor Vehicles:** 6,880,000 (1977) **Passenger Cars:** 5,550,000 **Railway Mileage:** 25,166 **Ports:** Sydney, Melbourne, Newcastle, Port Kembla, Fremantle, Port Hedland, Port Adelaide, Dampier, Brisbane **Major Airlines:** Qantas Airways is the major international carrier; domestic flights are operated by Trans-Australia Airlines and the privately-owned Ansett Airlines of Australia **Communications:** Both government and privately owned **Radio Transmitters:** 219 **Receivers:** 10,500,000 (1976) **Television Transmitters:** 198 **Licenses:** 4,785,000 (1976) **Telephones:** 5,502,000 (1976) **Newspapers:** 70 dailies, 394 copies per 1,000 inhabitants (1975)

Weights and Measures: British standards are being replaced by the metric system **Travel Requirements:** Passport; visa valid for 48 months or life of passport; no fee

---

Political and economic pressures of the postwar era, enhanced by the communications revolution of the times, have propelled Australia out of easygoing isolation into an increasing involvement in world and regional affairs.

Australia is one of the foremost donors of foreign aid compared with the national income. Much of this aid goes to Papua New Guinea, which became independent on September 16, 1975. The emergence of new independent island states in the South Pacific has thrust demands for leadership on Australia as the most advanced and affluent power in its geopolitical sphere.

Ties between Australians and the "mother country," Britain, loosened significantly in World War II when it became clear that the hard-pressed British forces were unable to defend Australia against the Japanese onslaught. Americans filled the breach, and from that time on the Australians have looked toward the United States as the guarantor of national security. The new relationship was cemented after the war in the ANZUS (Australia, New Zealand, United States) Treaty of Mutual Security.

Japan has emerged as Australia's foremost customer overseas, taking more than one-fourth of the country's total exports. Japan's late Prime Minister Masayoshi Ohira, in a 1979 visit, expressed hopes for making further deals for long-term supply of raw materials and discussed formation of a Pacific Basin Community.

Assistance to the country's 40,000 full-blood aborigines and 150,000 part-aborigines has been stepped up, but advancement programs have foundered because of administrative problems. Aborigines have been demanding a greater say in their own affairs. In November 1978, the government agreed to grant Northern Territory aborigines a 4.25 percent royalty (estimated $11 million per year) on uranium oxide extracted from a ranger site.

The application of postwar technology to the exploitation of vast mineral resources revolutionized the Australian economy. By the 1970s, Australia had become the leading supplier of lead and zinc, the chief iron ore exporter and furnished 90 percent of the world's rutile and zircon.

At the outset of the 1980s, the country was literally riding a minerals boom as the world sought energy sources other than costly oil. Ranked second (behind the U.S.) in coal exports, Australia was expected to advance to No. 1 in a few years. Uranium, shale, and natural gas exports also were to rise sharply. Reynolds Metals Co., with a consortium of five other companies, signed a 1980 agreement for a billion-dollar bauxite mining and alumina refining project southeast of Perth. Conzinc Riotinto of Australia Ltd. announced in 1980 that its two-year-old Western Australia find had turned out to be one of the world's largest diamond fields, with "pipes" larger than any in South Africa. About 60% of the stones are of gem quality.

Development of underground wealth required massive importation of capital, principally from Japan, Britain and the United States. A major consequence has been a nationalist backlash against the extent of foreign ownership of business, particularly in the mining industry. Foreign takeover bids for major Australian companies are subject to government approval. To protect local firms from exploitation by foreign mineral buyers, the government announced in October 1978 that it would supervise all mineral exportation negotiations.

HISTORY: Long before it was first sighted by European explorers in the 17th century, Australia was inhabited by primitive native groups with various languages and customs. In 1770, Captain James Cook explored the east coast of the continent and claimed it for Britain. Within 50 years, the whole of Australia became a British dependency, serving as a penal colony and dumping ground for British criminals and undesirables

1851-59: Gold strikes in Victoria and New South Wales in 1851 attract thousands of new settlers; within two decades the rising population is settled in six self-governing colonies

1901: Constitution providing for federation of colonies is approved by British Parliament; Commonwealth of Australia comes into being

1914-18: Australia fights on Allied side during World War I

1939-45: Australia fights alongside Allies in World War II

1946-48: Immigrants, numbering 2 million by 1965, begin to pour into Australia

1952-54: Australia signs Pacific defense pact (ANZUS) with New Zealand and United States and joins SEATO

1972: The first Labor Party government in 23 years is elected, recognizes the People's Republic of China

1975: The Labor Party government is dismissed. Liberal-Country Party coalition government is elected by a large majority vote. Papua New Guinea is granted independence

1977: Liberal-Country Party government decisively reelected

1978: In November worsening economy prompts division of Ministry of Employment and Industsrial Relations into two separate cabinet departments

1979: In January Cyclone Peter causes extensive damage in north Queensland. In February, Prime Minister Fraser streamlines cabinet, delegating more authority to ministers

1980: A diamond field found in Western Australia may be one of the world's largest. A vast bauxite mining and alumina refining venture will be started near Perth.

AUSTRIA

Area: 32,375 sq. mi. **Population:** 7,506,000 (1979 est.)

Official Name: Republic of Austria **Capital:** Vienna **Nationality:** Austrian **Languages:** German is the official and principal language. Slovenian, Croatian, and Hungarian are spoken by small minorities **Religion:** 90% Roman Catholic **Flag:** Red, white, and red horizontal stripes, with the national emblem centered on the white stripe **Anthem:** Land of Mountains, Land on the River **Currency:** Schilling (12.9 per U.S. $1)

Location: Central Europe. Landlocked Austria is bordered by West Germany and Czechoslovakia on the north, Hungary on the east, Yugoslavia and Italy on the south, and Switzerland and Liechtenstein on the west **Features:** The country is 70% mountainous, with the Alps and their outliers dominating the west and south. The east and Vienna are located in the Danube basin **Chief Rivers:** Danube, Inn, Mur, Drau, Enns

Head of State: President Rudolf Kirchschlaeger, born 1915, reelected 1980 **Head of Government:** Chancellor Bruno Kreisky, born 1911, took office April 1970, reappointed May 1979 **Effective Date of Present Constitution:** 1920, reinstated 1945 **Legislative Body:** Federal Assembly (bicameral parliament), consisting of the Federal Council (upper house), or *Bundesrat*, with 58 members, and the National Council (lower house), or *Nationalrat*, with 183 members. Members of the Upper House are appointed by provincial diets for 4 to 6-year terms; members of the Lower House are elected for 4 years **Local Government:** 9 provinces, each administered by an elected governor and provincial legislature

Ethnic Composition: Austrians are generally of South Germanic stock, with Slavic admixtures. The only sizeable minority group consists of some 70,000 Slovenes in Carinthia **Population Distribution:** 52% urban **Density:** 232 inhabitants per sq. mi.

Largest Cities: (1976 est.) Vienna 1,592,800, Graz 250,893, Linz 208,000, Salzburg 139,000, Innsbruck 120,355

Per Capita Income: $6,308 (1979) **Gross National Product (GNP):** $47 billion (1979 est.) **Economic Statistics:** About 61% of GNP comes from industry (machinery, iron and steel, food and beverages, electronics, chemicals, textiles, ceramics, stone and glass, and metal goods); 5% from agriculture and forestry **Minerals and Mining:** Iron ore, petroleum, magnesite, lignite, and natural gas **Labor Force:** 2,700,000 (1978), of which 60% is employed in commerce and industry, 14% in agriculture, and 26% in services **Foreign Trade:** Exports, mainly machinery, iron and steel, textiles, chemicals, wood and paper, totaled $15 billion in 1979. Imports, chiefly machinery, transportation equipment, textiles, mineral fuels and chemicals, totaled $20 billion **Principal Trade Partners:** West Germany, Switzerland, Italy, Britain, United States, Sweden, Netherlands, France, USSR, Poland, Yugoslavia

Vital Statistics: Birthrate, 11.3 per 1,000 of pop. (1977); death rate, 12.2 **Life Expectancy:** 73 years **Health Statistics:** 88 inhabitants per hospital bed; 444 per physician (1976) **Infant Mortality:** 16.9 per 1,000 births (1977) **Illiteracy:** Negligible **Primary and Secondary School Enrollment:** 1,263,298 (1976) **Enrollment in Higher Education:** 104,525 (1975) **GNP Expended on Education:** 5.7% (1976)

Transportation: Surfaced roads total 20,357 mi. **Motor Vehicles:** 2,337,400 (1977) **Passenger Cars:** 1,865,300 **Railway Mileage:** 4,081 **Ports:** None **Major Airlines:** Austrian Airlines operates international and domestic flights **Communications:** Government owned **Radio Transmitters:** 399 **Licenses:** 2,185,000 (1976) **Television Transmitters:** 461 **Licenses:** 1,772,000 (1976) **Telephones:** 2,281,000 (1976) **Newspapers:** 30 dailies, 320 copies per 1,000 inhabitants (1975)

Weights and Measures: Metric system **Travel Requirements:** Passport, no visa for 3 months

Once the core of the Hapsburg Empire that covered much of Central and Southern Europe, Austria has been reduced by wars to a relatively small state and, by its geographical position, to a land that is officially neutral between East and West. But its actual sympathies and economic ties lie with the West.

Because Austria was forced by Hitler's 1938 *Anschluss* to become part of the Nazi war machine, the victors of World War II granted it a special state treaty in 1955, which specified the country's official neutrality.

But most of Austria's trade is with Western Europe. After the European Economic Community (EC) was organized in 1958, Austria sought association with it, despite the objections of the Soviet Union, which argued that association was incompatible with neutrality. Austria joined the European Free Trade Association in 1960, and, over token Soviet opposition, negotiated a special agreement with the EC in 1973.

Internal politics have been influenced by an almost equal division of voting strength between the People's party—which professes Christian values and respect for property— and the Socialist party. From 1945 to 1966, the People's party had a plurality, but not a majority, in the *Nationalrat* and governed in coalition with the Socialists. The two parties made this arrangement because neither trusted the small Freedom party, which held the rest of the seats, and because memories of the chaos of the 1930s caused a desire for stability. This "grand coalition" ended in 1966, when a special election gave the People's party a one-seat majority; the Socialists were offered a coalition, but imposed conditions which the winners thought unreasonable. In 1970 the Socialists won a plurality, but not a majority, and formed a minority government with Bruno Kreisky as chancellor after attempts to reorganize the grand coalition broke down. This government remained in office after winning majorities in the elections of 1971, 1975 and 1979. There is little real difference between the parties, and the economy has remained basically capitalist, but with much state intervention.

Aside from the basic industries, an important source of income in Austria is tourism, as visitors are attracted to Alpine ski slopes and lakes and to city attractions such as the summer festival in Mozart's native city, Salzburg, and the spring festival week in Vienna.

HISTORY: Austria was settled by various tribes in prehistoric times and was subject to numerous invasions long before the Roman conquest around 15 B.C. About A.D. 800 it became a province of Charlemagne's empire and was joined to the Holy Roman Empire two centuries later. German-speaking rulers sponsored migrations, and the German language became predominant. By the end of the 13th century most of Austria was firmly under the rule of the Hapsburgs, who were to build a huge empire in central and southern Europe. By 1815, Austria had also become the leading power in the German Confederation, only to lose that position half a century later

1848: Nationalistic minorities in the Austrian Empire revolt against the monarchy but are subdued by Austrian forces

1866: Austro-Prussian War ends in Austrian defeat and terminates Austrian influence in German Confederation

1867: Hungary gains equal rights with Austria under a dual monarchy

1914-18: On June 28, 1914, a Serbian nationalist assassinates Archduke Francis Ferdinand, triggering World War I; Austria is allied with Germany and other Central Powers and shares in their defeat; Hapsburg monarchy collapses and Austria is proclaimed a republic

1932-34: Engelbert Dollfuss becomes chancellor and opposes *Anschluss* (union) with Germany; the outlawed Nazi party carries out his assassination (1934)

1938: Hitler annexes Austria to Germany

1945: United States, USSR, Britain, and France divide Austria into occupation zones following World War II. People's party wins elections; forms coalition with Socialist party

1955: Occupation forces leave and Austria proclaims permanent neutrality

1966: The conservative People's Party gains absolute majority in parliamentary election, ending 20-year rule of Socialist-conservative coalition

1969: Parliament, by overwhelming majority, ratifies treaty to prevent spread of nuclear weapons. Austria and Italy agree to give major autonomy to the 230,000 German-speaking inhabitants of the Italian province of Alto Adige. Socialists win, but without majority; their leader, Bruno Kreisky, becomes chancellor of minority government

1975: Socialist government wins second majority

1976: 12th Winter Olympics are held in Innsbruck

BAHAMAS

Area: 5,382 sq. mi. **Population:** 225,000 (1978 est.)

Official Name: Commonwealth of the Bahamas **Capital:** Nassau **Nationality:** Bahamian **Language:** English **Religion:** There are Baptist, Methodist, Anglican, and Roman Catholic congregations **Flag:** Three horizontal stripes, the upper and lower aquamarine, the middle gold, with a black equilateral triangle on the hoist **Anthem:** March on, Bahamaland **Currency:** Bahamian dollar (1.00 per U.S. $1)

Location: An archipelago located in the northern portion of the West Indies in the Atlantic **Features:** The Bahamas include 700 islands and 2,000 rocks and cays, but less than 30 of the islands are inhabited. The islands are generally low and flat, with many splendid beaches. The climate is pleasantly warm throughout the year

Head of State: Queen Elizabeth II, represented by acting governor-general Gerald C. Cash **Head of Government:** Prime Minister Lynden O. Pindling, reelected 1977 **Effective Date of Present Constitution:** July 1973 **Legislative Body:** A General Assembly consists of a Senate with 16 members and a House of Assembly with 38 elected members **Local Government:** 18 districts, administered by appointed commissioners

Ethnic Composition: 85% Negro; the rest are of British, Canadian, and U.S. descent **Population Distribution:** 57.9% urban **Density:** 42 inhabitants per sq. mi.

Largest Cities: (1970 census) Nassau 105,352, Freeport 15,546

Per Capita Income: $4,000 (1979) **Gross National Product (GNP):** $900 million (1979 est.) **Economic Statistics:** Tourism is the main source of income. About 7% of the work force is engaged in agriculture, and about 54% in industry. **Minerals and Mining:** Salt is extracted from brine by solar radiation; cement and petroleum products are produced **Labor Force:** 69,791 (1970), with 20% in industry, 7% in agriculture, and the rest in trade and services **Foreign Trade:** Exports, mainly cement, petroleum products, alcoholic beverages, pulpwood, pharmaceuticals, crawfish, and salt extracted from brine by solar radiation totaled about $2.4 billion in 1977. Imports of food, drink, tobacco, crude oil, manufactured articles, and animals totaled $2.1 billion **Principal Trade Partners:** United States, Saudi Arabia, Nigeria, Angola, Libya, Britain

Vital Statistics: Birthrate, 18.1 per 1,000; death rate, 3.9 per 1,000 **Life Expectancy:** 68.8 years **Infant Mortality:** 29.2 per 1,000 (1975) **Illiteracy:** 7% **Health Statistics:** 140 inhabitants per hospital bed; 2,100 per physician (1976) **Primary and Secondary School Enrollment:** 31,928 (1976) **Enrollment in Higher Education:** 2,160 (1975) **GNP Expended on Education:** 5.4% (1973)

Transportation: Surfaced roads total about 1,000 mi. **Motor Vehicles:** 41,800 (1976) **Passenger Cars:** 36,500 **Railway Mileage:** None **Ports:** Nassau, Freeport **Major Airlines:** Nassau is served by numerous international carriers, and Bahamasair services the Family Islands **Communications:** Government owned **Radio Transmitters:** 6 **Receivers:** 96,000 (1976) **Television Transmitters:** 1 **Telephones:** 58,000 (1976) **Newspapers:** 2 dailies, 152 copies per 1,000 inhabitants (1975)

Weights and Measures: British and metric systems **Travel Requirements:** Passport and visa not required of tourist with onward/return ticket and citizenship identification

After three centuries as a British colony, the Bahamas became an independent nation on July 10, 1973. The new country at the same time became an independent member of the British Commonwealth—the 33rd British possession to gain its freedom since World War II. Bahamian Prime Minister Lynden O. Pindling and his ruling Progressive Liberal Party had received a mandate for independence in elections held in September 1972. The party was formed in 1953 by blacks discontented with the policies of the white-dominated government.

In opposition to Pindling's ruling party is the Free National Movement, made up of whites and black PLP dissidents.

Because of the warm climate and beautiful beaches, tourism is the major industry. The islands host over 1,700,000 visitors a year.

A real estate boom drove land prices up so high that in 1979 the government restricted land sales for foreigners. Some $250 million in construction was expected in a three-year span ending in 1982.

Citrus fruit, bananas, and vegetables are grown, but most food must still be imported. Pulpwood, cement, rum, and salt are exported. Nassau, the capital, is a major center for banking and insur-

* For flags of ANGOLA, CAPE VERDE, COMOROS, DJIBOUTI and DOMINICA see page 517

* For flags of GRENADA, GUINEA-BISSAU and KIRIBATI see page 517

* For flags of MOZAMBIQUE and PAPUA NEW GUINEA see page 517

* For flags of ST. LUCIA, ST. VINCENT, SÃO TOMÉ E PRÍNCIPE, SEYCHELLES, SOLOMON IS., SURINAME, TUVALU and VANUATU see next page.

YEMEN (PEOPLES REP.)
YEMEN ARAB REP.
YUGOSLAVIA
ZAIRE
INDEPENDENT NATIONS 1974-1980
ZAMBIA
GRENADA (1974)
GUINEA-BISSAU (1974)
MOZAMBIQUE (1975)
CAPE VERDE (1975)
COMOROS (1975)
SÃO TOMÉ E PRÍNCIPE (1975)
PAPUA NEW GUINEA (1975)
ANGOLA (1975)
SURINAME (1975)
SEYCHELLES (1976)
DJIBOUTI (1977)
SOLOMON ISLANDS (1978)
TUVALU (1978)
DOMINICA (1978)
ST. LUCIA (1979)
KIRIBATI (1979)
ST. VINCENT & GRENS. (1979)
ZIMBABWE (1980)
VANUATU (1980)
TIME ZONES OF THE WORLD
NOTE: Standard time zones in the U.S.S.R. are always advanced one hour.
6PM 7PM 8PM 9PM 10PM 11PM MID-NIGHT 1AM 2AM 3AM 4AM 5AM 6AM 7AM 8AM 9AM 10AM 11AM NOON 1PM 2PM 3PM 4PM 5PM 6
MERIDIAN
INTERNATIONAL DATE LINE
MONDAY
SUNDAY
GREENWICH
STANDARD
TIME
ZONES
Areas using half hour deviations.
Areas not using zone system.
90° E 120° E 150° E 180° 150° W 120° W 90° W 60° W 30° W 0° 30° E 60° E 90° E
60° N 40° N 20° N 0° 20° S 40° S

THE WORLD
MERCATOR PROJECTION
Capitals of Countries
Copyright by C.S. HAMMOND & Co., N.Y.
Longitude East of Greenwich
Longitude West of Greenwich
International Date Line
Arctic Circle
Tropic of Cancer
Equator
Tropic of Capricorn
ARCTIC OCEAN
NORTH ATLANTIC OCEAN
SOUTH ATLANTIC OCEAN
NORTH PACIFIC OCEAN
SOUTH PACIFIC OCEAN
INDIAN OCEAN
NORTH AMERICA
SOUTH AMERICA
AFRICA
ASIA
AUSTRALIA
GREENLAND
(KALÅTLLIT-NUNÅT)
(Den.)
UNION OF SOVIET SOCIALIST REPUBLICS
CANADA
UNITED STATES
MEXICO
CENTRAL AMERICA
BRAZIL
ARGENTINA
CHILE
PERU
BOLIVIA
COLOMBIA
VENEZUELA
UNITED KINGDOM
IRELAND
FRANCE
SPAIN
PORTUGAL
GERMANY
POLAND
SWEDEN
NORWAY
FINLAND
ITALY
TURKEY
SAUDI ARABIA
IRAN
IRAQ
EGYPT
LIBYA
ALGERIA
MOROCCO
NIGERIA
NIGER
CHAD
SUDAN
ETHIOPIA
SOMALIA
ZAIRE
ANGOLA
ZAMBIA
TANZANIA
KENYA
NAMIBIA
SOUTH AFRICA
MOZAMBIQUE
MADAGASCAR
INDIA
CHINA
MONGOLIA
MANCHURIA
JAPAN
KOREA
PHILIPPINES
INDONESIA
MALAYSIA
THAILAND
BURMA
VIETNAM
NEW ZEALAND
SVALBARD (Nor.)
FRANZ JOSEF LAND (U.S.S.R.)
NOVAYA ZEMLYA
SEVERNAYA ZEMLYA
ICELAND
BARENTS SEA
KARA SEA
NORWEGIAN SEA
GREENLAND SEA
BAFFIN BAY
HUDSON BAY
BEAUFORT SEA
BERING SEA
SEA OF OKHOTSK
GULF OF ALASKA
CORAL SEA
TASMAN SEA
CARIBBEAN SEA
MEDITERRANEAN SEA
BLACK SEA
ARABIAN SEA
BAY OF BENGAL
SOUTH CHINA SEA
YELLOW SEA
SEA OF JAPAN
Moscow
Leningrad
Stockholm
Oslo
Helsinki
London
Paris
Madrid
Lisbon
Rome
Warsaw
Ottawa
Washington
New York
Chicago
Los Angeles
San Francisco
Seattle
Denver
Houston
Mexico City
Havana
Caracas
Bogotá
Lima
Santiago
Buenos Aires
Montevideo
Rio de Janeiro
São Paulo
Brasília
Cairo
Tripoli
Dakar
Cape Town
Nairobi
Delhi
Calcutta
Bombay
Madras
Peking
Shanghai
Tokyo
Manila
Jakarta
Singapore
Sydney
Melbourne
Canberra
Auckland
Wellington
Hawaiian Is. (U.S.)
Honolulu
Anchorage
Fairbanks

EUROPE
LAMBERT AZIMUTHAL EQUAL-AREA PROJECTION
SCALE OF MILES
0 100 200 300 400 500 600
SCALE OF KILOMETRES
0 100 200 300 400 500 600
Capitals of Countries
International Boundaries
Internal Boundaries
Copyright by C. S. HAMMOND & CO., N.Y.

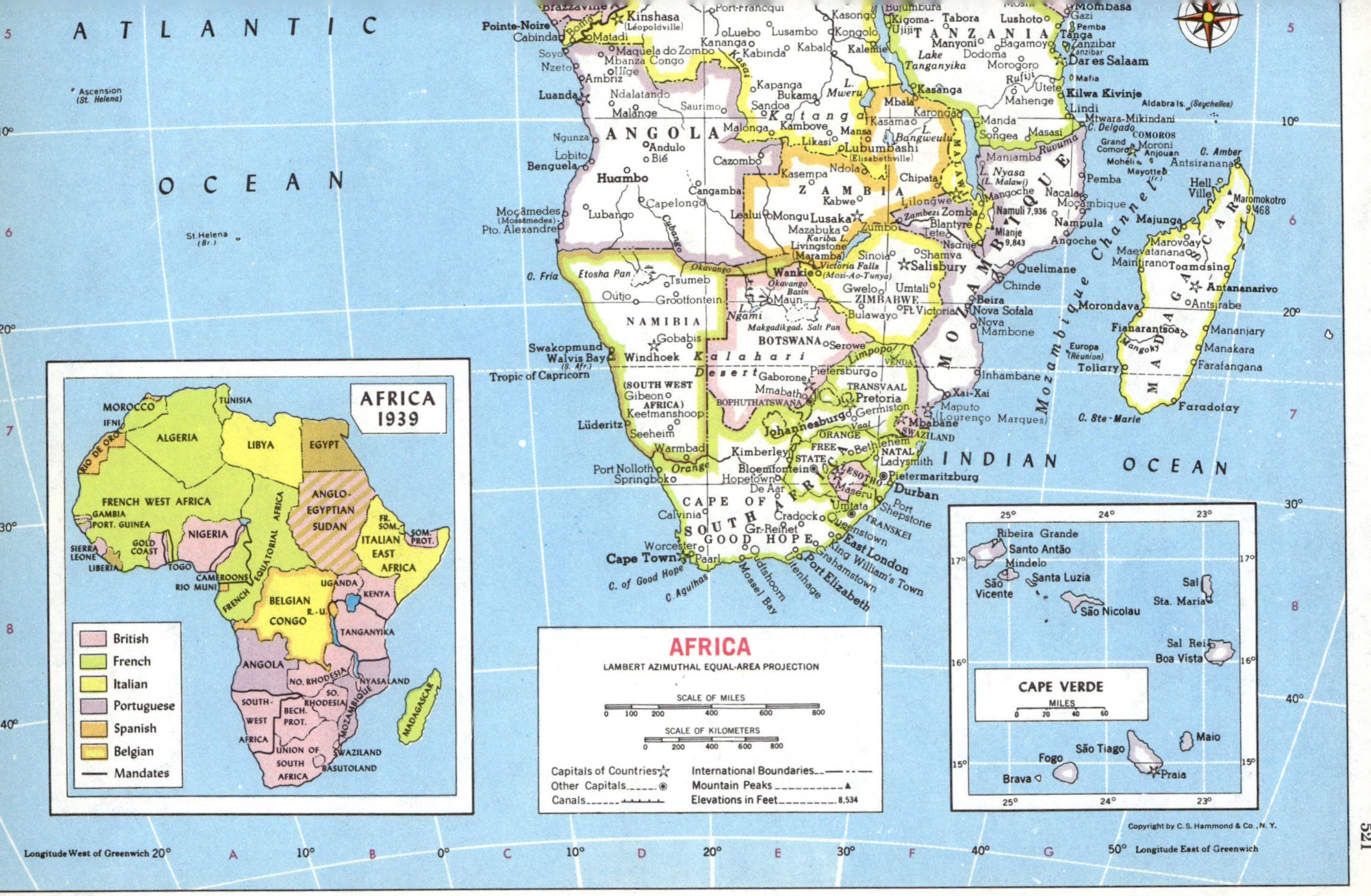

AFRICA
LAMBERT AZIMUTHAL EQUAL-AREA PROJECTION
SCALE OF MILES
0 100 200 400 600 800
SCALE OF KILOMETERS
0 200 400 600 800
Capitals of Countries
Other Capitals
Canals
International Boundaries
Mountain Peaks
Elevations in Feet 8,534

AFRICA 1939
British
French
Italian
Portuguese
Spanish
Belgian
Mandates
MOROCCO
IFNI
RIO DE ORO
ALGERIA
TUNISIA
LIBYA
EGYPT
ANGLO-EGYPTIAN SUDAN
FR. SOM.
SOM. PROT.
ITALIAN EAST AFRICA
FRENCH WEST AFRICA
GAMBIA
PORT. GUINEA
SIERRA LEONE
LIBERIA
GOLD COAST
TOGO
NIGERIA
CAMEROONS
RIO MUNI
FRENCH EQUATORIAL AFRICA
BELGIAN CONGO
R. U.
UGANDA
KENYA
TANGANYIKA
ANGOLA
NO. RHODESIA
SO. RHODESIA
BECH. PROT.
NYASALAND
MOZAMBIQUE
SOUTH WEST AFRICA
SWAZILAND
UNION OF SOUTH AFRICA
BASUTOLAND
MADAGASCAR

CAPE VERDE
MILES
0 20 40 60
Ribeira Grande
Santo Antão
Mindelo
São Vicente
Santa Luzia
São Nicolau
Sal
Sta. Maria
Sal Rei
Boa Vista
Fogo
São Tiago
Maio
Brava
Praia

ATLANTIC OCEAN
INDIAN OCEAN
Ascension (St. Helena)
St. Helena (Br.)
Brazzaville
Pointe-Noire
Cabinda
Matadi
Soyo
Nzeto
Kinshasa (Léopoldville)
Maquela do Zombo
Mbanza Congo
Ollfe
Ambriz
Luanda
Ndalatando
Malange
Saurimo
Port-Francqui
Luebo
Lusambo
Kananga
Kasongo
Bujumbura
Kongolo
Kigoma
Ujiji
Tabora
Lushoto
Kabalo
Kabinda
Kalemie
Manyoni
Dodoma
Morogoro
Bagamoyo
Gazi
Pemba
Tanga
Zanzibar
Dar es Salaam
TANZANIA
Lake Tanganyika
L. Mweru
Kapanga
Bukama
Sandoa
Katanga
Kasama
Karonga
Mbala
L. Bangweulu
Manda
Mahenge
Rufiji
Utete
Mafia
Kasanga
Kilwa Kivinje
Lindi
Mtwara-Mikindani
Aldabra Is. (Seychelles)
Songea
Masasi
C. Delgado
COMOROS
Grand Comoro
Moroni
Anjouan
Mohéli
Mayotte (Fr.)
C. Amber
Antsiranana
Hell Ville
ANGOLA
Ngunza
Lobito
Benguela
Huambo
Andulo
Bié
Malonga
Likasi
Lubumbashi (Elisabethville)
Mansa
Cazombo
Cangamba
Lubango
Capelongo
Moçâmedes (Mossâmedes)
Pto. Alexandre
ZAMBIA
Kabwe
Ndola
Kasempa
Chipata
Lilongwe
Lealui
Mongu
Lusaka
Mazabuka
Kariba L.
Livingstone (Maramba)
Zumbo
Zambezi
Zomba
Teteo
Blantyre
Nsanje
Mlanje 9,843
Namuli 7,936
Maniamba
L. Nyasa (L. Malawi)
Mangoche
Nacala
Mozambique
Pemba
Nampula
Angoche
MALAWI
MOZAMBIQUE
Maromokotro 9,468
Majunga
Marovoay
Maevatanana
Maintirano
Toamasina
Antananarivo
Antsirabe
Morondava
Mananjary
Manakara
Fianarantsoa
Mangoky
Toliary
Europa (Réunion)
Faradofay
C. Ste-Marie
MADAGASCAR
Mozambique Channel
C. Fria
Etosha Pan
Tsumeb
Outjo
Grootfontein
Okavango
Cubango
Wankie (Mosi-Ao-Tunya)
Victoria Falls
Sinoia
Salisbury
Shamva
Quelimane
Chinde
Beira
Nova Sofala
Nova Mambone
Gwelo
Umtali
Ft. Victoria
Bulawayo
ZIMBABWE
L. Ngami
Maun
L. Dow
Makgadikgadi Salt Pan
Okavango Basin
NAMIBIA
Swakopmund
Walvis Bay (S. Afr.)
Windhoek
Gobabis
Kalahari Desert
BOTSWANA
Serowe
Gaborone
Mmabath
Limpopo
VENDA
Pietersburg
Inhambane
Xai-Xai
Maputo
Lourenço Marques
TRANSVAAL
BOPHUTHATSWANA
Pretoria
Germiston
Johannesburg
Vaal
Tropic of Capricorn
(SOUTH WEST AFRICA)
Gibeon
Keetmanshoop
Lüderitz
Seeheim
Warmbad
Port Nolloth
Springbok
Kimberley
Orange
Hopetown
De Aar
Bloemfontein
ORANGE FREE STATE
Bethlehem
LESOTHO
Maseru
NATAL
Ladysmith
Pietermaritzburg
Durban
SWAZILAND
Mbabane
Umtata
TRANSKEI
Port Shepstone
King William's Town
East London
Grahamstown
Queenstown
Cradock
Gr. Reinet
Port Elizabeth
Uitenhage
Oudtshoorn
Calvinia
Worcester
CAPE OF GOOD HOPE
SOUTH AFRICA
Cape Town
Paarl
C. of Good Hope
C. Agulhas
Mossel Bay
Copyright by C.S. Hammond & Co., N.Y.
Longitude West of Greenwich 20°
Longitude East of Greenwich

ATLANTIC OCEAN
ARCTIC OCEAN
PACIFIC OCEAN
BERING SEA
SEA OF OKHOTSK
BARENTS SEA
KARA SEA
LAPTEV SEA
WHITE SEA
BALTIC SEA
NORTH SEA
BLACK SEA
CASPIAN SEA
ADRIATIC SEA
MEDITERRANEAN SEA
RED SEA
YELLOW SEA
E. CHINA SEA
SEA OF JAPAN
Greenland
Iceland
Jan Mayen (Nor.)
Faeroe Is. (Den.)
Shetland Is.
Hebrides
North Pole
Spitsbergen
Svalbard (Spitsbergen) (Nor.)
Bear I. (Nor.)
Hope I.
Edge I.
Alexandra Ld.
Wilczek Land
Franz Josef Ld.
Komsomolets I.
Severnaya Zemlya
October Revolution I.
Bol'shevik I.
Novaya Zemlya
New Siberian Is.
Bol'shoy Lyakhov I.
Wrangel I.
Nunivak I.
St. Lawrence I.
Aleutian Is.
Kamchatka Pen.
Sakhalin
Kuril Is.
Hokkaido
Honshu
Shikoku
Kyushu
UNITED STATES ALASKA
Bering Str.
C. Dezhnev
Chukchi Pen.
G. of Anadyr'
Kolyma Range
Omolon
Taymyr Pen.
Yamal
North Cape
Arctic Circle
RUSSIAN SOVIET FEDERATED SOCIALIST REPUBLIC
UNION OF SOVIET SOCIALIST REPUBLICS
S I B E R I A
KAZAKH S.S.R.
UZBEK S.S.R.
TURKMEN S.S.R.
KIRGIZ S.S.R.
TADZHIK S.S.R.
MONGOLIA
INNER MONGOLIA
XINJIANG
TIBET
CHINA
TURKEY
SYRIA
IRAQ
IRAN (PERSIA)
AFGHANISTAN
SAUDI
KUWAIT
CYPRUS
LEBANON
JORDAN
ISRAEL
Caucasus
Urals
Tian Shan
Altun Shan
Kunlun Shan
Pa Hingan Ling
Sikhote-Alin
Stanovoy Ra.
Hindu Kush
Pamir
London
Paris
Dublin
Belfast
Glasgow
Edinburgh
Milan
Rome
Berlin
Vienna
Budapest
Belgrade
Bucharest
Sofia
Tirana
Athens
Istanbul
Ankara
Warsaw
Prague
Brussels
Amsterdam
Hamburg
Copenhagen
Oslo
Stockholm
Helsinki
Tallinn
Riga
Kaunas
MOSCOW
Leningrad
Kiev
Voronezh
Volgograd (Stalingrad)
Astrakhan
Sverdlovsk
Chelyabinsk
Magnitogorsk
Perm
Nizhniy Tagil
Zlatoust
Troitsk
Kustanay
Aktyubinsk
Novokazalinsk
Kzyl-Orda
Karaganda
Tselinograd
Semipalatinsk
Ayaguz
Zaysan
Panfilov
L. Balkhash
Aral Sea
L. Tengiz
Gur'yev
Chelkar
Tashkent
Frunze
Namangan
Andizhan
Khiva
Bukhara
Samarkand
Ashkhabad
Mary
Tehran (5,600 m)
Meshed
Gorgan
Qazvin
Isfahan
Abadan
Shiraz
Kerman
Kabul
Herat
Meymaneh
Qandahar
Islamabad
Srinagar
Amritsar
Gilgit
Baghdad
Mosul
Kirkuk
Basra
Karbala
Beirut
Damascus
Alexandria
Cairo
Tel Aviv-Jaffa
Nicosia
Salonika
Trabzon
Erzurum
Diyarbakir
Adana
Samsun
Sinop
Izmir
Taymyr
Surgut
Tyumen
Tobol'sk
Tara
Barabinsk
Omsk
Novosibirsk
Tomsk
Anzhero-Sudzhensk
Kemerovo
Krasnoyarsk
Nizhneudinsk
Prokop'yevsk
Novokuznetsk
Barnaul
Gorno-Altaysk
Minusinsk
Zima
Tulun
Cheremkhovo
Irkutsk
Ulan-Ude
Kyakhta
Ulaanbaatar
Sühbaatar
Kyzyl
Chita
Nerchinsk
Sretensk
Severobaykal'sk
L. Baykal
Bodaybo
Kirensk
Olekminsk
Aldan
Neryungri
Yakutsk
Vilyuysk
Vilyuy
Lena
Verkhoyansk
Ust'-Maya
Aldan
Nel'kan
Chumikan
Ayan
Nikolayevsk
Komsomol'sk
Khabarovsk
Skovorodino
Blagoveshchensk
Svobodnyy
Zeya
Oktuch'ye
Amur
Vladivostok
Nakhodka
Sovetskaya Gavan'
Nizhnevartovsk
Khanty-Mansiysk
Salekhard
Novyy Urengoy
Berezovo
Igarka
Dudinka
Noril'sk
Turukhansk
Golchikha
Khatanga
Ust'-Olenek
Ust'-Olenek
Dzhelinde
Bulun
Yana
Srednekolymsk
Chersky
Cherskiy
Provideniya
Anadyr'
Petropavlovsk-Kamchatskiy
Okhotsk
Magadan
Bilibino
Tara
Yenisey
Ob
Irtysh
Ural
Syr-Dar'ya
Amu-Dar'ya
Tarim He
Taklimakan Shamo
Qaidam Pendi
Tsaidam
Ürümqi
Yining
Kashi
Aksu
Korla
Hami
Turpan
Hotan
Yutian
Qiemo
Lop Nur
Golmud
Xining
Lanzhou
Yumen
Jiuquan
Zhangye
Wuwei
Yinchuan
Baotou
Hohhot
Zhangjiakou
PEKING (Beijing)
Tianjin
Baoding
Taiyuan
Xi'an
Zhengzhou
Xinxiang
Kaifeng
Luoyang
Wuhan
Yichang
Chengdu
Chongqing
Kunming
Guiyang
Changsha
Nanchang
Hangzhou
NANJING
SHANGHAI
Hefei
Jinan
Qingdao
Yantai
Xuzhou
Ji'nan
Dalian
Lüda
Shenyang
Changchun
Jilin
Harbin
Qiqihar
Chengde
Chaoyang
Jinzhou
Dandong
Tonghua
Yanji
Songhua
Huang He
Yangtze
GOBI
Bayan Dobo Sumu
Bayan Dobo Sumu
Erenhot
Sühbaatar
Kerulen
Karakorum
Hovd
Uliastay
Ulaangom
Seoul
Pusan
Inch'ŏn
KOREA
TOKYO
Yokohama
Nagoya
Kyoto
Kobe
Osaka
Shizuoka
Kitakyushu
Nagasaki
Kumamoto
Kagoshima
Kanazawa
Niigata
Akita
Aomori
Hakodate
Sapporo
Sendai
Wakayama
Toyohashi
Okayama
Hiroshima
Tropic of Cancer
Okinawa Is. (Jap.)
Amami Is. (Jap.)
Daito (Jap.)
Parece Vela (Jap.)
Sakishima
Naha
Nile
Rhine
Elbe
Oder
Vistula
Danube
Loire
Bern
Volga
Don
Dnieper
Pechora
N. Dvina
W. Dvina
Mezen'
L. Onega
L. Ladoga
G. of Bothnia
Muonio
Kaunas
Berezniki
English Chan.
50° 60° 70° 80° 80° 70° 60° 50°
40° 30° 20°
20° 30° 40°

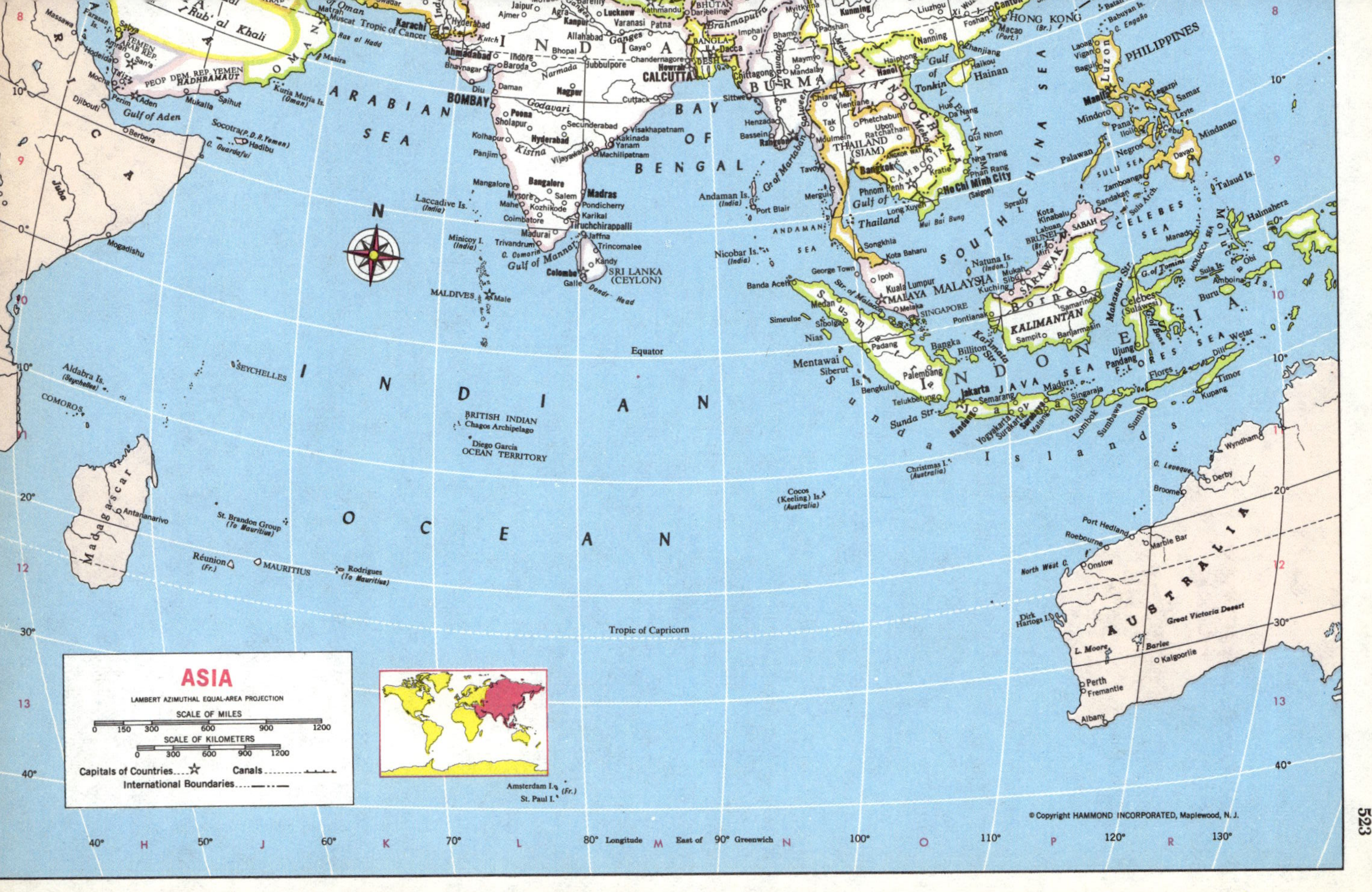
ASIA
LAMBERT AZIMUTHAL EQUAL-AREA PROJECTION
SCALE OF MILES
0 150 300 600 900 1200
SCALE OF KILOMETERS
0 300 600 900 1200
Capitals of Countries
Canals
International Boundaries
© Copyright HAMMOND INCORPORATED, Maplewood, N.J.

PHILIPPINES
Manila
Luzon
Mindoro
Samar
Leyte
Negros
Mindanao
Davao
Zamboanga
Talaud Is.
Halmahera
CELEBES SEA
MOLUCCA SEA
SULU SEA
Celebes (Sulawesi)
Buru
Amboina
Wetar
FLORES SEA
Dili
Timor
Kupang
Flores
Sumbawa
Lombok
Bali
JAVA SEA
Madura
Surabaya
Semarang
Yogyakarta
Surakarta
Jakarta
JAVA
BORNEO
KALIMANTAN
Banjarmasin
Samarinda
Pontianak
SARAWAK
Kuching
SABAH
Kota Kinabalu
Sandakan
BRUNEI (Br.)
Labuan
Macassar Str.
Makassar (Ujung Pandang)
G. of Tomini
Sula Is.
Obi

INDONESIA
SUMATRA
MALAYSIA
MALAYA
SINGAPORE
Kuala Lumpur
Melaka
Str. of Malacca
Medan
Banda Aceh
Padang
Palembang
Bengkulu
Bangka
Billiton
Karimata
Siberut
Mentawai Is.
Nias
Simeulue
Sibolga
Telukbetung
Sunda Str.
Natuna Is. (Indon.)
Spratly

SOUTH CHINA SEA
HONG KONG
Macao (Port.)
Canton
Foshan
Zhanjiang
Haikou
Hainan
Nanning
Kunming
Liuzhou
Xi...
Paoshan

BURMA
Myitkyina
Bhamo
Maymyo
Mandalay
Sittwe
Henzada
Bassein
Rangoon
Moulmein
Tak
Tavoy
Mergui
Chiang Mai
Phetchabun
Ubon Ratchathani
THAILAND (SIAM)
Bangkok
Gulf of Thailand
CAMBODIA
Phnom Penh
Kratie
INDO-CHINA
Ho Chi Minh City (Saigon)
Phan Rang
Nha Trang
Qui Nhon
Da Nang
Hue
Vientiane
Hanoi
Haiphong
Gulf of Tonkin
Mekong
Long Xuyen
Mui Bai Bung

BHUTAN
Darjeeling
Kathmandu
Brahmaputra
BANGLA DESH
Dacca
Chittagong
Ganges
CALCUTTA
Cuttack

INDIA
Jaipur
Agra
Bareilly
Lucknow
Kanpur
Varanasi
Patna
Allahabad
Ajmer
Bhopal
Indore
Gaya
Jubbulpore
Chandernagore
Howrah
Nagpur
Godavari
Hyderabad
Secunderabad
Visakhapatnam
Kakinada
Yanam
Machilipatnam
Vijayawada
BOMBAY
Poona
Sholapur
Kolhapur
Panjim
Daman
Diu
Bhavnagar
Baroda
Ahmadabad
Narmada
Kistna
Mangalore
Mysore
Salem
MADRAS
Coimbatore
Kozhikode
Mahe
Pondicherry
Karikal
Tiruchchirappalli
Madurai
C. Comorin
Trivandrum
Bangalore
Hyderabad
Kutch

Karachi
Tropic of Cancer
Hyderabad

OMAN
Matrah
Muscat
Ras al Hadd
Masira
Sur
Kuria Muria Is. (Oman)
Rub' al Khali
YEMEN ARAB REP.
San'a
Mocha
PEOP. DEM. REP. YEMEN
HADHRAMAUT
Mukalla
Saihut
Perim
Aden
Gulf of Aden
Socotra (P.D.R. Yemen)
Hadibu
C. Guardafui

ARABIAN SEA
AFRICA
Massawa
Djibouti
Berbera
Mogadishu
Juba
C. Guardafui

BAY OF BENGAL
Gr. of Martaban
Andaman Is. (India)
Port Blair
Nicobar Is. (India)
ANDAMAN SEA
Laccadive Is. (India)
Minicoy I. (India)
MALDIVES
Male
Gulf of Mannar
SRI LANKA (CEYLON)
Colombo
Galle
Dondra Head
Kandy
Trincomalee
Jaffna

Equator

INDIAN OCEAN
SEYCHELLES
Aldabra Is. (Seychelles)
COMOROS
Madagascar
Antananarivo
St. Brandon Group (To Mauritius)
Réunion (Fr.)
MAURITIUS
Rodrigues (To Mauritius)
BRITISH INDIAN OCEAN TERRITORY
Chagos Archipelago
Diego Garcia
Christmas I. (Australia)
Cocos (Keeling) Is. (Australia)
Amsterdam I. (Fr.)
St. Paul I.

OCEAN
Tropic of Capricorn

AUSTRALIA
Wyndham
C. Leveque
Derby
Broome
Port Hedland
Roebourne
North West C.
Onslow
Marble Bar
Dirk Hartog I.
L. Moore
Bartee
Kalgoorlie
Perth
Fremantle
Albany
Great Victoria Desert

40° 50° 60° 70° 80° Longitude East of 90° Greenwich 100° 110° 120° 130°
H J K L M N O P R
8 9 10 11 12 13

THE NEAR and MIDDLE EAST
CONIC PROJECTION
SCALE OF MILES
0 100 200 300 400
KILOMETERS
0 100 200 300 400
Capitals of Countries
Other Capitals
International Boundaries
Other Boundaries
BLACK SEA
CASPIAN SEA
MEDITERRANEAN SEA
AEGEAN SEA
ARABIAN SEA
RED SEA
PERSIAN GULF
GULF OF OMAN
G. of Aden
MEDITERRANEAN SEA
Istanbul
Edirne
Salonika
Athens
Canea
Crete
Candia
Rhodes
CYPRUS
Nicosia
TURKEY
Ankara
Izmir
Bursa
Eskisehir
Balikesir
Denizli
Antalya
Konya
Adana
Mersin
Kayseri
Sivas
Samsun
Trabzon
Zonguldak
Sinop
Adapazari
Corum
Afyon
Malatya
Maras
Urfa
Diyarbakir
Erzurum
Kars
Tbilisi
Batumi
Poti
Kutaisi
Kirovabad
Baku
Erivan
Tabriz
Ardebil
Khoi
Nukha
Derbent
Krasnovodsk
Kizyl-Arvat
Ashkhabad
Mary
Bayram-Ali
Termez
Tashauz
Urgench
Khiva
Bukhara
Leninabad
Dushanbe
Samarkand
Chardzhou
Tashkent
Andizhan
Kokand
Kyzyl-Kum Desert
Kara-Kum Desert
S. S. R.
CHINA
SINKIANG
Chitral
Kabul
Charikar
Peshawar
Rawalpindi
Islamabad
Srinagar
Khyber Pass
Feyzabad
Khanabad
Mazar-e-Sharif
Meymaneh
Andkhui
AFGHANISTAN
Herat
Ghazni
Sabzawar (Shindand)
Farah
Qandahar
Kalat-i-Ghilzai
Sangar
Rudbar
Zabul
Chagal
Hamun-i-Helmand
Namakzar
Hamun-i-Jaz Murian
PAKISTAN
Dera Ismail Khan
Sialkot
Amritsar
Lahore
Multan
Bahawalpur
Dera Ghazi Khan
Quetta
Kalat
Kharan Kalat
Shikarpur
Larkana
Sukkur
Nawabshah
Bela
Hyderabad
Karachi
INDIA
Bikaner
Jodhpur
Udaipur
Ahmadabad
Porbandar
Bhavnagar
Surat
Daman
Diu
Great Indian Desert
Rann of Kutch
G. of Kutch
Turbat
Tump
Gwadar
Chahbar
Makran
Jask
Bandar Abbas
Iranshahr
Bam
Zahedan
Kerman
Sirjan (Saidabad)
Lar
Bushehr
Kazerun
Shiraz
Isfahan
Yazd
Gavkhaneh
Dasht-i-Lut
Tabas (Tabas-Masina)
IRAN
Tehran
Qum
Dasht-i-Kavir
Darya-yi-Namak
Kashan
Arak
Hamadan
Kermanshah
Kashmar
Nishapur
Sabzawar
Meshed
Gorgan
Atrek
Babol
Bandar-i-Torkaman
Enzeli Resht
Zenjan
Qazvin
Demavend 18,376
Elburz
Hit
Kut
Baghdad
Karbala
Hilla
An Najaf
An Nasiriya
Basra
Abadan
Khorramshahr
Kuwait
Al Kuwait
Neutral Zone
KUWAIT
Mesopotamia
Syrian Desert
IRAQ
Mosul
Erbil
Kirkuk
Tigris
Euphrates
Aleppo
El Haseke
SYRIA
Latakia
Tripoli
Homs
Palmyra
Hama
LEBANON
Beirut
Damascus
Sea of Galilee
ISRAEL
Haifa
Tel Aviv-Jaffa
Jerusalem
Gaza
Dead Sea
Amman
JORDAN
Wadi Sirhan
Jauf
Sakaka
Taima
Hail
Jebel Shammar
Nefud
Buraida
W. er Rumna
Khaibar
Umme Lajj
Medina
Mahd Dhahab
Shaqra
Riyadh
Hauta
Laila
SAUDI ARABIA
Rub' al Khali
Dhahran
Hofuf
BAHRAIN
Manama
QATAR
Doha
Abu Dhabi
UN. ARAB EMIRATES
Ras al Khaimah
Buraimi
Sohar
Matrah
Muscat
Akhdar
Nizwa
Sur
Ras al Hadd
Masira
OMAN
Dhofar
Salala
Murbat
Qamr Bay
Sauqira Bay
Kuria Muria Is.
Bahr as Safi
Najran
Sa'da
YEMEN
Sa'ada
Dhamar
Ta'izz
Hodeida
Mocha
PEOPLES DEM. REP. OF YEMEN
ARAB REP.
Shibam
Seiyun
Hadhramaut
Shihr
Mukalla
Haura
W. Hadhramaut
Madinat ash Sha'b
Lahej
Aden
Perim I.
Kamaran I. (P.D.R. Yemen)
Farasan Is.
Massawa
Dahlak Arch.
Socotra (P.D.R. Yemen)
DJIBOUTI
ETHIOPIA
Asmara
Agordat
Aduwa
Gondar
L. Tana
Ras Dashan 15,157
Aduwa
Gedaref
Kassala
EGYPT
Alexandria
Cairo
Port Said
Suez Canal
Tanta
Giza
El Faiyum
El Minya
Asyut
Sohag
Qena
El Karnak
Kharga Oasis
Dakhla Oasis
Aswan
Aswan High Dam
Arabian Desert
Libyan Desert
Qattara Depression
Siwa Oasis
Sidi Barrani
Nile
L. Nasser
Lake
Sinai Pen.
Gulf of Suez
Gulf of Aqaba
Elath 'Aqaba
Midian
Wejh
Yenbo
Rabigh
Jidda
Mecca
Taif
Qunfidha
Abha
SUDAN
Khartoum
Khartoum North
Omdurman
Wad Medani
Atbara
Merowe
Abu Hamed
Dongola
Suakin
Port Sudan
3rd Cataract
4th Cataract
5th Cataract
6th Cataract
Nubian Desert
Jebel Oda 7,412
Blue Nile
White Nile
Kosti
El Obeid
En Nahud
Gedaref
Wad Medani
Wadi el Milk
Barka
Atbara
Aswan
Jebel Shammar
N
ARABIA
Tropic of Cancer
Copyright by C. S. HAMMOND & Co., N. Y.

SOUTH AMERICA
LAMBERT AZIMUTHAL EQUAL-AREA PROJECTION
SCALE OF MILES
0 100 200 400 600
SCALE OF KILOMETERS
0 200 400 600
Capitals of Countries
International Boundaries
Copyright by C.S. Hammond & Co., N.Y.
Longitude West of Greenwich

ARCTIC OCEAN
ATLANTIC OCEAN
PACIFIC
ASIA
U.S.S.R.
UNITED KINGDOM
ICELAND
GREENLAND
(KALÂTDLIT-NUNÂT)
(Den.)
GREENLAND SEA
Denmark Str.
KING CHRISTIAN IX LAND
KING FREDERIK VI COAST
KING CHRISTIAN X LAND
KING FREDERIK VIII LAND
KNUD RASMUSSEN LAND
Arctic Circle
North Pole
BEAUFORT SEA
BAFFIN BAY
Baffin Island
Davis Strait
Hudson Strait
LABRADOR SEA
LABRADOR
NEWFOUNDLAND
Ellesmere I.
QUEEN ELIZABETH ISLANDS
Victoria I.
Banks I.
Amundsen Gulf
Great Bear Lake
Great Slave Lake
Mackenzie
NORTHWEST TERRITORIES
HUDSON BAY
James Bay
C A N A D A
YUKON TERR.
BRITISH COLUMBIA
ALBERTA
SASKATCHEWAN
MANITOBA
ONTARIO
QUEBEC
Vancouver I.
QUEEN CHARLOTTE IS.
ALEXANDER ARCH.
UNITED STATES
ALASKA
Mt. McKinley
20,320
Brooks Range
SEWARD PEN.
Kodiak I.
ALASKA PEN.
BERING SEA
Bering Strait
St. Lawrence I.
Nunivak I.
St. Matthew I.
Bristol Bay
Wrangel I.
Anadyr
ROCKY MOUNTAINS
Coast Mountains
Cascade Range
WASH.
OREG.
IDAHO
MONT.
WYO.
N. DAK.
S. DAK.
NEBR.
MINN.
IOWA
WIS.
MICH.
L. Superior
L. Michigan
L. Huron
L. Erie
L. Ontario
N.Y.
PA.
N.J.
New York
Philadelphia
Baltimore
Boston
MAINE
N.H.
VT.
MASS.
Winnipeg
L. Winnipeg
Regina
Calgary
Edmonton
Saskatoon
Montreal
Ottawa
Toronto
Quebec
Chicago
Detroit
Duluth
Minneapolis
St. Paul
Missouri
Mississippi
Fairbanks
Anchorage
Seward
Whitehorse
Dawson
Faeroe Is.
(Den.)
Jan Mayen
(Nor.)
C. Farewell
C. Chidley
St. Pierre & Miquelon (Fr.)
Sable I.
Prince Edward I.
Cape Breton I.
Gulf of St. Lawrence
Belcher Is.
Southampton I.
Devon I.
Somerset I.
Prince of Wales I.
Melville I.
Gulf of Boothia
BOOTHIA PEN.
MELVILLE PEN.
Foxe Basin
Foxe Chan.
Cumberland Sd.
Lancaster Sd.
Bylot I.
Disko
Peace R.
Athabasca
L. Athabasca
Churchill
Nelson
Yukon

NORTH AMERICA
LAMBERT AZIMUTHAL EQUAL-AREA PROJECTION
SCALE OF MILES
0 100 200 400 600 800
SCALE OF KILOMETERS
0 200 400 600 800
Capitals of Countries
International Boundaries
Other Boundaries
Canals
Copyright by C.S. HAMMOND & Co., N.Y.
UNITED STATES
Los Angeles
SANTA BARBARA IS.
San Diego
San Bernardino
L. Mead
Havasu L.
ARIZ.
Phoenix
Tucson
Yuma
Douglas
N. MEX.
Santa Fe
Albuquerque
Roswell
Gila
Colorado
Rio Grande
El Paso
Ciudad Juárez
Wichita
Oklahoma City
OKLA.
Tulsa
Muskogee
Amarillo
Wichita Falls
Ft. Worth
Dallas
Abilene
San Angelo
TEXAS
Austin
Waco
San Antonio
Houston
Beaumont
Galveston
Corpus Christi
Brownsville
Laredo
Del Rio
Pecos
ARK.
Little Rock
Ft. Smith
Shreveport
LA.
Monroe
Vicksburg
Jackson
Baton Rouge
New Orleans
MISS.
Meridian
Montgomery
ALA.
Birmingham
TENN.
Nashville
Memphis
Chattanooga
Knoxville
GA.
Atlanta
Augusta
Macon
Columbus
Savannah
Columbia
S.C.
Charleston
N.C.
Raleigh
Charlotte
Wilmington
Springfield
Louisville
Nashville
Trinidad
Canadian
Red
Arkansas
FLA.
Jacksonville
St. Augustine
Tallahassee
Pensacola
Mobile
Orlando
Tampa
St. Petersburg
W. Palm Beach
Miami
C. Canaveral
Key West
Florida Keys
Straits of Florida
Bermuda (Br.)
Tropic of Cancer
MEXICO
Gulf of California
LOWER CALIFORNIA
Guadalupe I. (Mex.)
Cedros I.
C. San Lucas
Hermosillo
Chihuahua
Sierra Madre Occidental
Conchos
Torreón
Saltillo
Monterrey
Culiacán
Durango
Mazatlán
Aguascalientes
León
Santiago
Guadalajara
C. Corrientes
Manzanillo
San Luis Potosí
Querétaro
Morelia
Toluca
Mexico City
Puebla
Orizaba
Jalapa
Veracruz
Tampico
Llave
Bay of Campeche
Acapulco de Juárez
Oaxaca
Villahermosa
YUCATÁN PENINSULA
Valladolid
Mérida
Cozumel
Yucatán Chan.
REVILLAGIGEDO IS. (Mex.)
Tropic of Cancer
Gulf of Mexico
Mississippi Delta
GUATEMALA
Guatemala
BELIZE
Belmopan
Belize
G. of Honduras
Ceiba
HONDURAS
Tegucigalpa
EL SALVADOR
San Salvador
NICARAGUA
León
Managua
L. Nicaragua
COSTA RICA
San José
Limón
PANAMA
Panamá
G. of Panamá
Panama Canal
Colón
C. Gracias a Dios
BAHAMA
Bahama
Gt. Abaco
Nassau
Eleuthera
Cat I.
Andros I.
Gt. Exuma
Long I.
Acklins I.
Gt. Inagua
Mayaguana
TURKS AND CAICOS IS. (Br.)
CUBA
Havana
Pinar del Río
Matanzas
Sta. Clara
Cienfuegos
Camagüey
Holguín
Santiago de Cuba
Juventud
Isle of Pines
Grand Cayman I. (Br.)
JAMAICA
Kingston
HAITI
Port-au-Prince
DOMINICAN REP.
Santo Domingo
Hispaniola
Guantánamo
Windward Pass.
Mona Pass.
PUERTO RICO (U.S.)
San Juan
Virgin Is. (U.S. & Br.)
St. Christopher
Guadeloupe (Fr.)
Anguilla (Br.)
Barbuda (Br.)
Antigua (Br.)
DOMINICA
Martinique (Fr.)
ST. LUCIA
ST. VINCENT
GRENADA
BARBADOS
TOBAGO
TRINIDAD
WEST INDIES
GREATER ANTILLES
LESSER ANTILLES
NETH. ANTILLES
CARIBBEAN SEA
SOUTH AMERICA
VENEZUELA
Caracas
Maracaibo
Valencia
Barquisimeto
Cumaná
Orinoco
Ciudad Bolívar
COLOMBIA
Bogotá
Cúcuta
Medellín
Cali
Neiva
Buenaventura
Popayán
Tumaco
Barranquilla
Cartagena
Magdalena
Meta
ECUADOR
Quito
Ibarra
Guayaquil
Riobamba
Cuenca
Putumayo
PERU
Marañón
Iquitos
Piura
Chiclayo
Cajamarca
Trujillo
Ucayali
Amazon
Juruá
BRAZIL
Rio Negro
Madre de Dios
PACIFIC OCEAN
ATLANTIC OCEAN
Clipperton (Fr.)
Cocos I. (C.R.)
Malpelo I. (Col.)
GALÁPAGOS IS. (Ecuador)
Fernandina
Isabela
S. Salvador
S. Cristóbal
Sta. Cruz
Equator
Longitude West of Greenwich

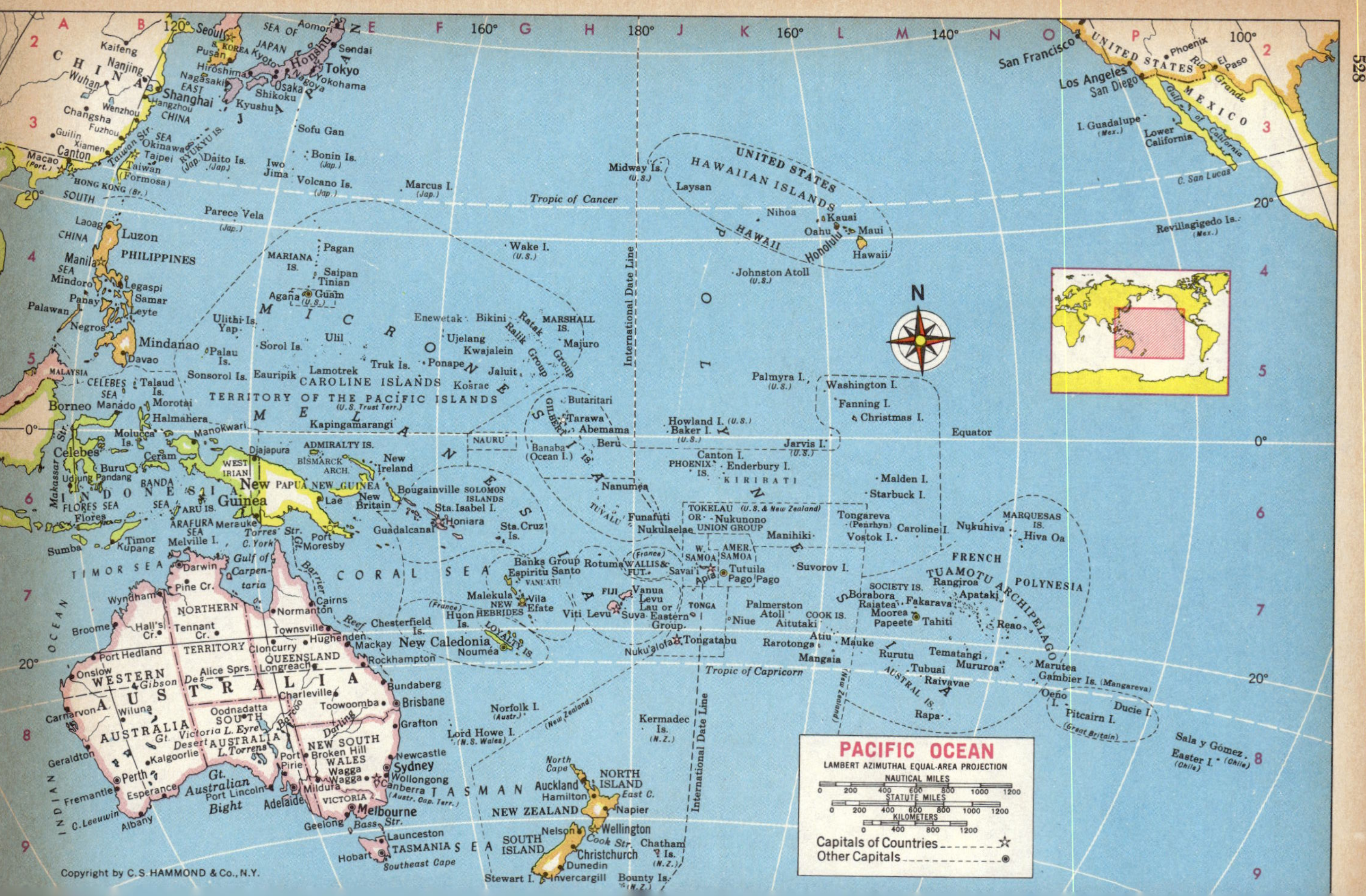
PACIFIC OCEAN
LAMBERT AZIMUTHAL EQUAL-AREA PROJECTION
NAUTICAL MILES
STATUTE MILES
KILOMETERS
Capitals of Countries
Other Capitals
Copyright by C. S. HAMMOND & Co., N.Y.
UNITED STATES
Los Angeles
San Diego
San Francisco
MEXICO
Lower California
Gulf of California
C. San Lucas
El Paso
Phoenix
Rio Grande
I. Guadalupe (Mex.)
Revillagigedo Is. (Mex.)
Sala y Gomez (Chile)
Easter I. (Chile)
Ducie I. (Great Britain)
Pitcairn I.
Gambier Is. (Mangareva)
Mangareva
Oeno I.
Rapa
Raivavae
Tubuai
Rurutu
AUSTRAL IS.
Tematangi
Mururoa
Maria
Marutea
Reao
Rangiroa
Apataki
Rajatea
Fakarava
Anaa
Bora Bora
Moorea
Tahiti
Papeete
SOCIETY IS.
TUAMOTU ARCHIPELAGO
FRENCH POLYNESIA
MARQUESAS
Nukuhiva
Hiva Oa
Tongareva
(Penrhyn)
Caroline I.
Vostok I.
Suvorov I.
Starbuck I.
Malden I.
Christmas I.
Fanning I.
Washington I.
Palmyra I. (U.S.)
Jarvis I. (U.S.)
Howland I. (U.S.)
Baker I. (U.S.)
Enderbury I.
Canton I.
PHOENIX IS.
KIRIBATI
TOKELAU (U.S.A New Zealand)
Nukulaelae
Manihiki
UNION GROUP
COOK IS.
Rarotonga
Mangaia
Mauke
Atiu
Mitiaro
Aitutaki
Palmerston Atoll
Niue (New Zealand)
Tropic of Capricorn
International Date Line
Equator
Tropic of Cancer
HAWAIIAN ISLANDS
UNITED STATES
HAWAII
Nihoa
Kauai
Oahu
Maui
Hawaii
Honolulu
Laysan
Midway Is. (U.S.)
Johnston Atoll (U.S.)
POLYNESIA
W. AMER.
SAMOA
Tutuila
Pago Pago
W. SAMOA
Savaii
Apia
Upolu
TONGA
Nukualofa
Tongatabu
FIJI
Viti Levu
Vanua Levu
Suva
Lau or Eastern Group
Rotuma (France)
WALLIS & FUT.
Funafuti
TUVALU
Nukufetau
Nanumea
Abemama
Beru
Tarawa
Butaritari
GILBERT IS.
Banaba (Ocean I.)
NAURU
Kosrae
Ponape
Kwajalein
Jaluit
Majuro
Ralik Group
Ratak Group
MARSHALL IS.
Bikini
Enewetak
Ujelang
Wake I. (U.S.)
Marcus I. (Jap.)
CAROLINE ISLANDS
TERRITORY OF THE PACIFIC ISLANDS
(U.S. Trust Terr.)
MICRONESIA
Truk Is.
Uli
Uhi
Lamotrek
Eauripik
Kapingamarangi
Sonsorol
Sorol Is.
Morotai
Halmahera
Palau
Ulithi Is.
Yap
Pagan
Saipan
Tinian
Agana
Guam (U.S.)
MARIANA IS.
Bonin Is. (Jap.)
Volcano Is. (Jap.)
Iwo Jima (Jap.)
Sofu Gan
Parece Vela (Jap.)
Daito Is. (Jap.)
JAPAN
Tokyo
Osaka
Nagoya
Yokohama
Kyoto
Kobe
Hiroshima
Nagasaki
Fukuoka
Kyushu
Shikoku
Honshu
Sendai
Aomori
SEA OF JAPAN
Okinawa
RYUKYUS
EAST CHINA SEA
Seoul
Pusan
KOREA
CHINA
Shanghai
Hangzhou
Wenzhou
Fuzhou
Xiamen
Canton
Macao (Port.)
HONG KONG (Br.)
Taipei
Taiwan (Formosa)
Nanjing
Kaifeng
Wuhan
Changsha
Guilin
PHILIPPINES
Luzon
Manila
Legaspi
Samar
Leyte
Mindoro
Panay
Negros
Palawan
Mindanao
Davao
Manado
Talaud
Morotai
CELEBES SEA
SOUTH CHINA SEA
SULU SEA
MALAYSIA
Borneo
Celebes
Ceram
Buru
Ujung Pandang
Makassar
FLORES SEA
BANDA SEA
Flores
Sumba
Timor
Kupang
INDONESIA
WEST IRIAN
Manokwari
Merauke
ARU IS.
Fakfak
ARAFURA SEA
TIMOR SEA
Djajapura
NEW GUINEA
PAPUA NEW GUINEA
Port Moresby
Lae
BISMARCK ARCH.
ADMIRALTY IS.
Manus
New Ireland
New Britain
Bougainville
SOLOMON ISLANDS
Guadalcanal
Honiara
Sta. Isabel I.
Sta. Cruz Is.
CORAL SEA
Banks Group
Espiritu Santo
Luganville
NEW HEBRIDES
Efate
Vila
Malekula
VANUATU
LOYALTY IS.
New Caledonia (France)
Noumea
Chesterfield Is.
NORTH
Barrier Reef
Great Barrier Reef
AUSTRALIA
QUEENSLAND
Cairns
Townsville
Mackay
Rockhampton
Bundaberg
Brisbane
Toowoomba
Charleville
Longreach
Cloncurry
Normanton
Cooktown
NORTHERN TERRITORY
Darwin
Pine Cr.
Katherine
Tennant Cr.
Alice Springs
Wyndham
Halls Cr.
WESTERN AUSTRALIA
Broome
Port Hedland
Onslow
Carnarvon
Geraldton
Perth
Fremantle
Kalgoorlie
Esperance
Albany
C. Leeuwin
Wiluna
Gt. Sandy Desert
Gt. Victoria Desert
Gibson Desert
Nullarbor Plain
Gt. Australian Bight
SOUTH AUSTRALIA
Oodnadatta
L. Eyre
Port Augusta
Port Pirie
Port Lincoln
L. Torrens
Adelaide
NEW SOUTH WALES
Broken Hill
Dubbo
Newcastle
Sydney
Wollongong
Wagga Wagga
VICTORIA
Melbourne
Geelong
Bendigo
Ballarat
Mildura
Canberra (Aust. Cap. Terr.)
Bass Str.
TASMANIA
Hobart
Launceston
Southeast Cape
NEW ZEALAND
NORTH ISLAND
SOUTH ISLAND
Auckland
Hamilton
Wellington
Napier
Nelson
Christchurch
Dunedin
Invercargill
Stewart I.
Cook Str.
Chatham Is. (N.Z.)
Bounty Is. (N.Z.)
North Cape
TASMAN SEA
Norfolk I. (Austr.)
Lord Howe I. (N.S. Wales)
Kermadec Is. (N.Z.)
INDIAN OCEAN
N
20°
0°
20°
40°
100°
120°
140°
160°
180°
160°

ance and for corporate operations. There is one bank for every 600 Bahamians. The Bahamas is also an oil transshipment point to the United States and has large refineries.

A fleet of nine government patrol boats enforces laws prohibiting foreigners from commercial fishing in Bahamian waters. One patrol boat, the *Flamingo*, was sunk by Cuban jets, with the loss of four seamen, on May 10, 1980, while towing two impounded Cuban fishing vessels.

HISTORY: On Oct. 12, 1492, Christopher Columbus made his first landfall in the Western Hemisphere at San Salvador (now known as Watling Island) in the Bahamas. At the time the islands were inhabited by the Arawak Indians
1647: First permanent European settlement in the Bahamas
1860: Royal Victoria Hotel first attracts winter tourists
1964: Bahamas granted complete internal self-government
1973: Britain grants independence July 10
1975: A five-year treaty is signed with the European Community
1979: Land sales to foreigners are restricted
1980: Cuban jets sink a Bahamian patrol boat; four seamen killed

BAHRAIN

Area: 255 sq. mi. **Population:** 345,000 (1978 est.)
Official Name: State of Bahrain **Capital:** Manama **Nationality:** Bahraini **Languages:** Predominantly Arabic; English used widely **Religion:** Moslem, the Sunni sect predominating in urban centers and the Shi'a sect in rural areas **Flag:** Red, with vertical serrated white band on the hoist **Anthem:** "National Anthem" **Currency:** Bahraini dinar (0.38 per U.S. $1)
Location: Southwest Asia. Eleven islands in the Persian Gulf. The main island, Bahrain, and those nearby lie 15 miles east of the coast of Saudi Arabia and about the same distance west of the coast of Qatar
Head of State: Emir Isa ibn Salman al Khalifa, born 1933 **Head of Government:** Prime Minister: Sheikh Khalifa ibn Salman al Khalifa, assisted by a cabinet **Effective Date of Present Constitution:** 1973 **Legislative Body:** Rule is by the emir's decree **Local Government:** 6 municipalities—4 urban, each administered by a partly elected municipal council; and 2 rural
Ethnic Composition: 80% Arab, with about 12% Indians, Pakistanis, and Iranians and about 3,000 Europeans **Population Distribution:** 78.1% urban **Density:** 1,353 inhabitants per sq. mi.
Largest Cities: (1977 est.) Manama 100,000; (1972 est.) Muharraq 50,000
Per Capita Income: $4,744 (1979) **Gross National Product (GNP):** $1.7 billion (1979 est.) **Economic Statistics:** Petroleum refining and the production of crude oil are the most important economic resources. About 50% of the oil refined is piped from Saudi Arabia. There is in addition an aluminum smelter, a major dry dock and smaller industrial plants. The islands produce dates, rice, and vegetables; fishing is important regionally **Minerals and Mining:** Considerable deposits of natural gas exist, in addition to oil deposits **Labor Force:** 110,000 (1977 est.), with 5% in agriculture and 90% in industry (chiefly petroleum and aluminum refining) **Foreign Trade:** Exports, chiefly crude oil, totaled $1.9 billion in 1978. Imports, including machinery, foods, chemicals, industrial equipment, and vehicles, totaled $1.8 billion **Principal Trade Partners:** Britain, Saudi Arabia, United States, Japan, Kuwait, UAE
Vital Statistics: Birthrate, 46 per 1,000 of pop. (1974); death rate, 9 **Infant Mortality:** 23 per 1,000 births (1974) **Health Statistics:** 270 inhabitants per hospital bed; 218 per physician (1977) **Illiteracy:** 48% **Primary and Secondary School Enrollment:** 45,640 (1976) **Enrollment in Higher Education:** 703 (1975) **GNP Expended on Education:** 4.6% (1975)
Transportation: Roads total about 58 mi. **Motor Vehicles:** 48,700 (1977) **Passenger Cars:** 35,500 **Ports:** Sitra, Mina Salman **Major Airlines:** Gulf Air and several international companies service the country **Radio Transmitters:** 5 **Receivers:** 150,000 (1976) **Television Transmitters:** 1 **Receivers:** 31,000 (1976) **Telephones:** 31,000 (1976) **Newspapers:** 1 daily, 11 weeklies, 29 copies per 1,000 inhabitants
Weights and Measures: Metric system, plus local measures **Travel Requirements:** Passport and visa required, $14 fee

Bahrain consists of a number of desert islands in the west central Persian Gulf, chief among these

being Bahrain, Muharraq, Sitra, Umm Na'san, and the Hawar group. Bahrainis, who are Moslem Arabs, constitute about 80 percent of the population. There are also Arabs from elsewhere, Iranians, Indians, and Europeans.

The oil industry and transit trade are the mainstays of the economy. There is a large refinery on Sitra, and trade passes through Manama and Mina Salman, a duty-free transit center. "Offshore" service banking is a source of revenue.

Internally, the ruler, or emir, wields almost absolute power. In 1970 a Council of State was established, responsible to the ruler and serving at his pleasure. In 1971 Bahrain declared independence, ending its special relationship with Britain. Iran informally became Bahrain's protector, but in 1979 Bahrain expelled the special envoy of Iran's new revolutionary government.

HISTORY: Bahrain may have been "Dilmun," a trade center mentioned in Sumerian records, but little is known of its history before it was occupied by Portugal (1501-1602). The present dynasty was founded in 1783 by an adventurer from Arabia
1820: British protectorate status begins
1971: Bahrain declares independence on August 15, and is admitted to the UN and the Arab League
1973: New constitution is in effect
1975: National Assembly is dissolved by Emir Khalifa

BANGLADESH

Area: 55,126 sq. mi. **Population:** 85,645,000 (1979 est.)
Official Name: People's Republic of Bangladesh **Capital:** Dacca **Nationality:** Bangladeshi **Languages:** Bengali is official; English is also widely used **Religion:** About 85% Moslem and 14% Hindu, with some Buddhists and Christians **Flag:** Rectangular, in bottle green, with a red circle, slightly left of center, on the green body **Anthem:** Amar Sonar Bangla (My Golden Bengal) by Rabindranath Tagore **Currency:** Taka (15.37 per U.S. $1)
Location: Bangladesh is bordered on the north, east, and west by India, on the southeast by Burma, and on the south by the Bay of Bengal **Features:** a subtropical alluvial plain, with many river valleys and deltas. Average annual temperature 49°F-80°F. Jute fields, rice paddies, tea plantations, tropical jungles, and swamps are prominent features of its landscape **Chief Rivers:** Ganges and Brahmaputra
Head of State: President: Maj. Gen. Ziaur Rahman, born 1936, assumed office in April 1977, elected June 1978 for a 5-year term **Head of Government:** Shah Azizur Rahman, born 1925, appointed 1979 **Effective Date of Present Constitution:** Nov. 1972 **Legislative Body:** Unicameral 330-member Parliament; 30 seats are reserved for women **Local Government:** 19 districts grouped into 4 divisions
Ethnic Composition: The population is overwhelmingly Bengali, with a few tribal peoples in the hills near the Burma border **Population Distribution:** 8.8% urban (1974) **Density:** 1,554 inhabitants per sq. mi.
Largest Cities: (1974 census), Dacca 1,310,976, Khulna 436,000, Chittagong 416,733
Per Capita Income: $109 (1979) **Gross National Product (GNP):** $9.6 billion (1979) **Economic Statistics:** In 1976 about 60% of GNP was from agriculture (jute, rice, tea, sugarcane, chillies, wheat, and tobacco); 10% from industry and 22% from trade and services **Minerals and Mining:** There are large reserves of natural gas and some deep-lying coal **Labor Force:** 28,000,000 (1978), with 78% engaged in agriculture; some 8% are employed in industry **Foreign Trade:** Exports are chiefly raw jute and jute products, hides and skins and tea, and totaled about $497 million in 1978. Imports, chiefly fuels, machinery, clothing, foodstuffs, and chemicals, totaled $1.3 billion **Principal Trade Partners:** United States, Britain, Canada, India, Japan, USSR, Italy, UAE, Mozambique, Pakistan
Vital Statistics: Birthrate, 49.5 per 1,000 of pop. (1975); death rate, 28.1 **Life Expectancy:** 47 years **Health Statistics:** 4,868 inhabitants per hospital bed; 14,178 per physician (1976) **Infant Mortality:** 140 per 1,000 births **Illiteracy:** 75% **Primary and Secondary School Enrollment:** 11,800,209 (1976) **Enrollment in Higher Education:** 121,155 **GNP Expended on Education:** 1.4% (1975)
Transportation: Paved roads total 2,511 miles **Motor Vehicles:** 56,500 (1972) **Passenger Cars:** 31,700 **Railway Mileage:** 1,806 **Ports:** Chittagong, Chalna **Major Airlines:** Biman (Air Bangladesh) operates both international and domestic services **Communica-

tions: Government owned **Radio Transmitters:** 16 **Receivers:** 350,000 (1973) **Television Stations:** 1 **Telephones:** 80,000 (1975) **Newspapers:** 30 dailies (1975)

Weights and Measures: Metric system and British standards

Travel Requirements: Passport and visa required

In December 1970 the Awami League, a Bengali nationalist party concentrated in East Pakistan and led by the enormously popular Sheik Mujibur Rahman, won a majority of the seats in the Pakistan National Assembly. This unexpectedly strong showing in the first national elections held in Pakistan since independence emphasized the fissure between the Bengalis in East Pakistan and their rulers in Islamabad.

The old state of Bengal, now Bangladesh, has been a perennial disaster zone. It has virtually no industry, and the market for jute—its main export crop—has declined steadily with the introduction of synthetic fibers. Its population density is among the highest in the world, and most of its people live at the subsistence level. Bengalis long resented the relative prosperity of West Pakistan, contending it was the result of exploitative economic policies.

Demands for Bengali autonomy came to a head in the campaign of the Awami League. Sheik Mujib's six-point program called for a loose federation amounting to internal self-government for the Bengalis.

On March 1, 1971, Pakistan's President Yahya Khan announced that the convening of the National Assembly would be postponed. Leaders of the Awami League claimed they were being cheated of the fruits of the election, which had made them the majority party of Pakistan.

Widespread rioting and strikes in the Bengali province ensued, and on March 25, President Yahya Khan ordered the national army into the province to crush the separatist movement by force and arrest Sheik Mujib as a traitor. The next day, before his arrest, Sheik Mujib in a radio broadcast declared the independence of Bangladesh. The East Bengal Regiment of the army promptly defected to form the Bangladesh armed forces. For a few days the national army was pinned down. On April 10 a constituent assembly of the Awami League candidates elected to the National Assembly convened and confirmed the declaration of Bengali independence, naming Sheik Mujib president of the republic. But a military campaign of great ferocity, resulting in a death toll in the hundreds of thousands, quickly subdued the Bangladesh forces and cowed the population. In addition, several million Bengalis fled to neighboring India, and an occupation army remained.

Reports of clashes between Indian and Pakistani forces began to be heard. On December 3, Pakistani planes attacked western Indian military airfields, and Indian troops launched an attack in Bangladesh. Three days later India recognized the Bangladesh provisional government. After a whirlwind Indian campaign, the Pakistani forces in Bangladesh surrendered on December 16.

Sheik Mujib, freed from jail in Pakistan, returned to Bangladesh early in 1972, and on January 12 was named prime minister. The Sheik rapidly lost his charismatic hold as Bangladesh suffered from a disintegrating economy, corruption and famine.

Following the assassination of Sheik Mujib during a military coup in August 1975, Bangladesh experienced the turmoil of two new leaders within a period of two and a half months. Khandakar Mushtaque Ahmed was sworn in as president, but was forced to resign in November. Mohammad Sayem, chief justice of the Supreme Court, succeeded to the presidency. On assuming office, Sayem dissolved parliament.

Public opinion in Bangladesh, and especially in the armed forces, on which the Sayem regime largely depended for support, was divided in the first part of 1976 among four main forces: the supporters of Gen. Ziaur Rahman, the army chief of staff; the supporters of the late Sheik Mujib and the Awami League; the Islamic right; and the left-wing National Socialist party. Unrest was widespread inside the army.

Taking advantage of these divisive conditions, General Rahman assumed full power as chief martial law administrator on November 30, 1976, and arrested at least 11 prominent political leaders, including former Pres. Khandakar Mushtaque Ahmed. National elections that had been promised for early 1977 were postponed. On April 21, 1977, General Rahman was sworn in as president following the resignation of Sayem. On October 2, 1977, at Dacca Airport, dissident junior officers attempted unsuccessfully to overthrow the government. Some reports put the death toll as high as 230.

In a field of 10 candidates, General Rahman won a five-year presidential term on June 3, 1978, by garnering about 75 percent of the votes cast. In February 1979, his Bangladesh Nationalist party swept 207 of the 300 contested parliament seats in national elections. The Awami League was left far behind, winning only 40 seats. Martial law was lifted and parliament restored with Shah Azizur Rahman as prime minister.

The country turned into the 1980s with its food production rising and food imports down by 50%. "Exporting" of workers helped the economy as 100,000 Bangladesh men sent money home from jobs in Persian Gulf states.

In 1980 jail guards in Rajshahi killed three prisoners and wounded 37 with gunfire during a demonstration. This led to a general strike by 10 opposition parties in Dacca, where police killed two persons and injured more than 50.

HISTORY: In the 12th century, Moslem invaders brought Islam to Bengal, part of which is now Bangladesh. Moslem power and culture in the Indian subcontinent reached their zenith under the Mogul empire (1526-1857). Despite cultural interchange with the Hindus, the Moslem community continued to maintain its distinct identity under British rule

1970: In November a massive cyclone kills 200,000

1971: The Awami League, a Bengali nationalist party, leads a movement and civil war for Bengali independence

1972: Awami leader Sheik Mujibur Rahman is named prime minister. New constitution is effected

1973: First parliamentary elections held; Awami League controls the National Assembly

1975: Sheik Mujib is assassinated in a military coup and Khandakar Mushtaque Ahmed is named president. He is forced to resign during a power struggle within the army, and Mohammad Sayem assumes the presidency. Sayem dissolves parliament

1977: A martial law court in Dacca convicts and sentences former president Khandakar Mushtaque Ahmed to 5 years in prison on charges of corruption and abuse of official power. Gen. Ziaur Rahman is sworn in as president. Coup attempt by dissident officers fails; government, charging involvement, bans Democratic League, National Socialist party and Soviet Bangladesh Communist party

1978: Gen. Ziaur Rahman is elected to presidency for five-year term

1979: President Rahman's Bangladesh Nationalist party wins parliamentary elections. Martial law lifted

---

BARBADOS

Area: 166 sq. mi. **Population:** 265,000 (1978 est.)

Official Name: Barbados **Capital:** Bridgetown **Nationality:** Barbadian **Languages:** English is the official and universal language **Religion:** About 70% of the population belongs to the Anglican Church. The rest are mainly Methodists, Moravians, and Roman Catholics **Flag:** Vertical bands of blue, gold, and blue, with a black trident centered on the gold band **Anthem:** National Anthem of Barbados, beginning "In plenty and in time of need" **Currency:** Barbadian dollar (2.01 per U.S. $1)

Location: West Indies. The most easterly of the Caribbean islands, Barbados lies immediately east of the Windward Islands and about 270 miles northeast of the mainland of South America **Features:** The island, which is of coral origin, is relatively flat, rising gently from the west coast in a series of terraces to a ridge in the center **Chief Rivers:** None

Head of State: Queen Elizabeth II, represented by a governor-general, Sir Deighton Harcourt Lisle Ward **Head of Government:** Prime Minister John Michael Geoffrey ("Tom") Adams, born 1932, elected 1976 **Effective Date of Present Constitution:** 1966 **Legislative Body:** Parliament (bicameral), consisting of a House of Assembly and a Senate. The House of Assembly is composed of 24 members, elected for 5 years. The Senate consists of 21 members, 12 of whom are appointed by the governor-general on the advice of the prime minister, 2 on the advice of the leader of the opposition, and 7 appointed by the governor-general to represent various social and economic groups **Local Government:** 11 parishes and the city of Bridgetown

Ethnic Composition: About 80% of the population is of African descent; 4% is white, mainly of British origin **Population Distribution:** 37% urban **Density:** 1,596 inhabitants per sq. mi.

Largest City: (1970 census) Bridgetown 8,868 (Metropolitan Area 97,565)

Per Capita Income: $2,150 (1979) **Gross National Product (GNP):** $588 million (1979) **Economic Statistics:** In 1973 about 42% of GNP was derived from trade and services; 16% from agriculture (sugarcane), fishing and animal husbandry; 11% from industry (sugar, rum, molasses, electronic parts) **Minerals and Mining:** Limestone and coral are quarried for domestic needs; there are small quantities of natural gas **Labor Force:** 97,000 (1973), of which 16% is employed in agriculture and 28% in industry **Foreign Trade:** Exports, chiefly sugar, rum, molasses and clothing, totaled $95 million in 1977. Imports, mainly food, machinery, transportation equipment, chemicals and petroleum products, totaled $274 million **Principal Trade Partners:** Britain, United States, Canada, West Indies, Japan

Vital Statistics: Birthrate, 18.6 per 1,000 of pop. (1976); death rate, 9.2 **Life Expectancy:** 70 years **Health Statistics:** 119 inhabitants per hospital bed; 1,250 per physician (1976) **Infant Mortality:** 28.3 per 1,000 births **Illiteracy:** 2% **Primary and Secondary School Enrollment:** 62,666 (1976) **Enrollment in Higher Education:** 1,417 (1973) **GNP Expended on Education:** 7.5% (1976)

Transportation: Paved roads total 840 mi. **Motor Vehicles:** 28,700 (1976) **Passenger Cars:** 24,700 **Railway Mileage:** None **Ports:** Bridgetown **Major Airlines:** Barbados is served by numerous international airlines **Communications:** Both government and privately owned **Radio Transmitters:** 3 **Receivers:** 130,000 (1976) **Television Transmitters:** 1 **Receivers:** 48,000 (1976) **Telephones:** 44,000 (1976) **Newspapers:** 1 daily, 98 copies per 1,000 inhabitants (1975)

Weights and Measures: Metric system **Travel Requirements:** Passport or proof of citizenship

Four centuries ago, the Portuguese sailors who sighted the 21-mile-long strip of coral first noticed its trees, their long branches drooping to the ground, and gave their name, Barbados—the bearded fig tree—to the island. The name is the only sign that Barbados has not always been British, perhaps even more British than Britain.

Nevertheless, since it won independence in 1966, the West Indian country has moved to expand its regional and hemispheric ties. It was admitted to the United Nations immediately after gaining independence and has also joined the Organization of American States and the Inter-American Development Bank.

In recent years the Barbadian economy, once totally dependent on the sugar crop, has been diversified by the development of tourism and light manufacturing industries.

After a year of unsuccessful negotiations for a new agreement, the United States announced in 1978 that it would close its naval facility in Barbados. Operated for 22 years, the facility dealt with underwater research and communications.

The oil tanker *Atlantic Empress*, carrying 2 million barrels of crude oil, sank 150 miles off Barbados in 1979 after a collision with another tanker.

HISTORY: Although both Arawak and Carib Indians had at one time inhabited Barbados, the island was uninhabited when the first white settlers arrived from England in 1627. In less than a decade slaves were brought from Africa to work the sugar plantations, which continue to serve as the mainstay of the island's economy. Slavery was abolished in 1834, but the island's political life continued to be dominated by a small white upper class until well into the 20th century

1954: Sir Grantley Adams, a Negro Barbadian and founder of the Barbados Labour Party, becomes the first prime minister of the island

1966: Barbados achieves full independence

1968-69: Barbados joins Caribbean Free Trade Area and Inter-American Development Bank

1973: Prime ministers of Barbados, Trinidad and Tobago, Guyana, and Jamaica establish CARICOM, a Caribbean common market and community

1975: A five-year treaty is signed with the EC

1976: J.M.G. Adams is elected prime minister

BELGIUM

Area: 11,781 sq. mi. **Population:** 9,841,000 (1978 est.)

Official Name: Kingdom of Belgium **Capital:** Brussels **Nationality:** Belgian **Languages:** French, Flemish (Dutch), and German are the official and principal spoken languages. Flemish is spoken by the Flemings (Dutch) in the north and west, and French by the Walloons in the south and east; Brussels is bilingual **Religion:** The population is predominantly Roman Catholic, but there are several Protestant denominations and a Jewish community **Flag:** Vertical stripes of black, yellow, and red **Anthem:** La Brabançonne ("Song of Brabant") **Currency:** Belgian franc (29.1 per U.S. $1)

Location: Northwest Europe. Belgium is bordered by the Netherlands and the North Sea on the north, by Germany and Luxembourg on the east, and by France on the southwest and west **Features:** Although generally flat, Belgium has increasingly hilly and forested terrain toward the Ardennes region in the southeast **Chief Rivers:** Scheldt, Meuse

Head of State: King Baudouin I, born 1930, ascended the throne 1951 **Head of Government:** Premier Wilfried Martens, born 1936, appointed 1979 **Effective Date of Present Constitution:** 1831, amended December 1970 **Legislative Body:** Parliament (bicameral), consisting of a Senate and Chamber of Representatives. The Senate, consisting of 182 members elected for 4 years, is partly elected directly and in part chosen by provincial councils and fellow senators. The Chamber, with 212 members, is elected by direct universal suffrage for 4 years **Local Government:** 9 provinces and 589 (1976) communes, with considerable autonomy in local matters. Four regions have been established: Flanders and Wallonia, each with a large degree of autonomy, and Brussels and a German-speaking region with lesser powers

Ethnic Composition: Flemings 58%, French (Walloons) 41%, Germans 1% **Population Distribution:** 94.6% urban **Density:** 835 inhabitants per sq. mi.

Largest Cities: (1971 est.) Brussels 1,071,194, Antwerp 226,570, Ghent 149,265, Liège 147,277, Bruges 117,220

Per Capita Income: $7,971 (1979) **Gross National Product (GNP):** $78.6 billion (1979) **Economic Statistics:** 30% of the GNP comes from industry (steel, metal manufacturing, nonferrous metal, textile, diamond cutting, chemical, glass); 25% from commerce; 24% from services; 7% from construction; 8% from transport and communications; 4% from agriculture (livestock, sugar beets, hay, potatoes, grain) **Minerals and Mining:** Coal is the only mineral resource of major importance. Iron, lead, zinc, copper, manganese, and phosphates are mined in small quantities **Labor Force:** 4 million (1978), with 47% in services, 30% in industry, 8% in construction, 3% in agriculture and 12% in civil service **Foreign Trade:** Exports, chiefly chemicals, textiles, diamonds, iron and steel products, machinery, automotive vehicles, glass, and nonferrous metals, totaled $44.8 billion in 1978. Imports, mainly grains, ores, petroleum, chemicals, textiles, diamonds, metals and products, machinery, electrical equipment and automotive vehicles, totaled $48.3 billion **Principal Trade Partners:** West Germany, Netherlands, France, Italy, United States, Britain, Switzerland

Vital Statistics: Birthrate, 12.4 per 1,000 of pop. (1977); death rate, 11.4 **Life Expectancy:** 71 years **Health Statistics:** 111 inhabitants per hospital bed; 493 per physician (1976) **Infant Mortality:** 14 per 1,000 births **Illiteracy:** 3% **Primary and Secondary School Enrollment:** 1,773,614 (1976) **Enrollment in Higher Education:** 159,660 (1975) **GNP Expended on Education:** 6.2% (1976)

Transportation: Paved roads total 32,800 mi. **Motor Vehicles:** 3,168,400 (1977) **Passenger Cars:** 2,871,300 **Railway Mileage:** 2,620 **Ports:** Antwerp, Zeebrugge, Ghent, Ostend **Major Airlines:** Sabena airline operates both domestic and international services

Communications: Government controlled **Radio Transmitters:** 48 **Licenses:** 4,044,000 (1976) **Television Transmitters:** 28 **Licenses:** 2,646,000 (1976) **Telephones:** 2,949,000 (1976) **Newspapers:** 30 dailies, 239 copies per 1,000 inhabitants (1975)

Weights and Measures: Metric system **Travel Requirements:** Passport, no visa for 3 months

---

The geography of Belgium has brought it misfortune and fortune: the misfortune of having a largely low-lying countryside that served as a route for foreign armies, and the fortune of a location in Western Europe that helps to make the country a key trading and manufacturing center.

In its military misadventures, Belgium was the scene of Caesar's conquest of the Gallic tribes; the site of Napoleon's ultimate defeat, at Waterloo; and the stage for invasion by German armies in both world wars. But conflict also brought Belgium independence; the Belgians revolted against Dutch domination in 1830.

The northern part of the country, in which Belgian basic industry is largely situated, is inhabited by Dutch-speaking Flemings. Most of the rest of Belgium is Walloon country, where French is spoken. Currently the Flemings are dominant, with a majority in both the Senate and Chamber. The bilingual nature of the land has led to much friction.

In 1970, in order to reduce linguistic tensions, the unitary constitution of 1831 was revised to recognize "three cultural communities: French, Dutch, and German." Four linguistic regions—the Flemish and Walloon areas, a small German area along the border of West Germany, and bilingual Brussels—were created. Each has a council with limited authority over education, culture, and the economy. But proposals to increase their authority have been the most divisive issue of the 1970s. In 1980 the coalition government backed down on its proposal to grant Brussels self-governing status because of objections by the Walloons. However, wider powers were granted to the Flemish and Walloon areas in August.

Dependent on trade, Belgium has been a leader in the movement for European integration. It merged its customs with those of Luxembourg in 1921. The Netherlands joined this union to form *Benelux* by an agreement which took full effect in 1950. The Benelux countries joined the European Economic Community in 1958, and their earlier experience has helped to guide the Community. European integration helped to make Belgium prosperous in the 1960s; the Walloon region gained new industries.

In addition to industry, Belgium has gained as the headquarters of major international organizations—NATO, which had run out of its welcome in France, and the European Community, which is headquartered in Brussels.

HISTORY: Belgium, named after ancient Celtic settlers, the Belgae, was conquered by Julius Caesar about 50 B.C. and later formed part of Charlemagne's empire. Ruled by Burgundy in the 15th century, it passed to the Hapsburgs of Austria and then of Spain. In the 16th century, the Low Countries (including modern Belgium, Luxembourg, and the Netherlands) revolted against Spanish rule. But while the northern and predominantly Protestant Netherlands provinces won their independence, Belgium remained under Spanish rule until the 18th century
1713: Belgium is ceded to Austria by the Treaty of Utrecht, which ends the War of the Spanish Succession
1792-97: French armies invade Belgium; country is ceded to France by Treaty of Campo Formio
1815: Belgium is united with the Netherlands by Treaty of Paris
1830-39: Belgians revolt against affiliation with Protestant Netherlands, a provisional government declares Belgium independent; Dutch invade Belgium but are forced by Britain and France to recognize the country's independence. Belgian Parliament chooses Prince Leopold of Saxe-Coburg-Gotha as ruler of the new kingdom

1885-1908: Leopold II becomes absolute monarch of Congo Free State. Belgium reluctantly annexed the area in 1908
1914-18: Germans invade and occupy neutral Belgium
1940-44: Germany again invades Belgium; King Leopold III surrenders unconditionally. Belgian cabinet sets up government-in-exile in London and declares surrender illegal; Belgian underground continues to fight German invaders
1950-51: Belgian electorate votes for return of king, but uprisings against Leopold by Socialists and Liberals force him to abdicate in favor of his son, Baudouin
1960: Belgium grants Congo independence
1968: Cultural-language conflict between Flemish and French-speaking population (Walloons) leads to fall of center-right coalition government; new coalition of Christian Socialists and Socialists is formed
1969: Cultural conflict continues to simmer as Senate studies constitutional reform proposals for regional autonomy
1970: Belgium amends constitution giving autonomous cultural and economic powers to each of the two communities, Flemings and Walloons
1973: Heretofore provisional double presidency (one Fleming, one Walloon) is made permanent part of Socialist party structure
1974: Iran's withdrawal from joint oil refining project adds to Belgium's economic woes and topples Leburton government. Leo Tindemans forms three-party coalition government
1975: Severe inflation and 6 percent unemployment force wage-price measures
1977: Tindemans' coalition government wins April election after cabinet crisis brought on by withdrawal of leftist Walloons
1978: Linguistic tensions trouble coalition. Crisis is resolved in June, but Tindemans resigns in October. Paul Vanden Boeynants becomes caretaker premier, and elections produce no major changes. Belgian Army enters Zaire to rescue victims of violence
1979: Wilfried Martens becomes premier in five-party coalition
1980: Greater authority is given to Flemish and Walloon regions, but not to Brussels

---

BENIN

Area: 43,483 sq. mi. **Population:** 3,377,000 (1978 est.)

Official Name: People's Republic of Benin **Capital:** Porto Novo **Nationality:** Beninese or Beninois **Languages:** French is the official language; the most common African dialects are Fon, Mina, Yoruba, and Dendi **Religion:** Animists 65%, Moslems 15%, Roman Catholics 14%, Protestants 6% **Flag:** A green flag with a red five-pointed star in the upper left **Anthem:** The New Dawn **Currency:** CFA Franc (210.2 per U.S. $1)

Location: West Africa. Benin is bordered on the north by Upper Volta and Niger, on the east by Nigeria, on the south by the Bight of Benin, and on the west by Togo **Features:** A 75-mile coastline of sandy beaches and lagoons is unbroken by natural harbors; north of it is a flat area that is the main oil palm region; further inland, a swampy depression is succeeded by hills, plateaus; and the Atakora Mountains, which stretch into Togo **Chief Rivers:** Ouémé, Mono, Couffo

Head of State and of Government: President and Prime Minister: Col. Mathieu Kérékou, assumed power in 1972; he also is defense minister **Effective Date of Present Constitution:** August 1977 **Legislative Body:** A 336-member National Revolutionary Assembly was elected in Nov. 1979 **Local Government:** 6 departments

Ethnic Composition: Of some 42 distinctive African groups the main ones are the Fon, Yoruba, Adja, Bariba, Peul, and Somba. There are also about 5,500 Europeans **Population Distribution:** 13.7% urban (1975) **Density:** 78 inhabitants per sq. mi.

Largest Cities: (1975 est.) Cotonou 178,000, Porto Novo 104,000; (1973 est.) Natatingou 49,000, Abomey 38,000

Per Capita Income: $133 (1978) **Gross National Product (GNP):** $500 million (1978 est.) **Economic Statistics:** In 1978, 33% of GDP came from agriculture (coffee, cotton, peanuts, cassava, fish, yams, corn, oil palm products); 16% from industry (palm oil products, textiles, kenaf, beverages, furniture, ceramics and cement) and mining **Minerals and Mining:** Some low-grade iron ore and limestone deposits are located in the north **Labor Force:** 1.5 million, 48% in agriculture and some 50,000 salaried workers **Foreign Trade:** Exports, chiefly palm kernel oil, cotton, and cocoa beans, totaled $115 million in 1978. Imports, chiefly food products, textiles, machinery, vehicles, and iron and steel products, totaled $289 million **Principal Trade Partners:** France, United States, West Germany, Netherlands, Nigeria, Japan, Britain

Vital Statistics: Birthrate, 49.9 per 1,000 of pop. (1975); death rate, 23 **Life Expectancy:** 41 years **Health Statistics:** 727 inhabitants per hospital bed; 35,555 per physician (1976) **Infant Mortality:** 109.6

per 1,000 births **Illiteracy:** 80% **Primary and Secondary School Enrollment:** 348,723 (1977) **Enrollment in Higher Education:** 2,118 (1975) **GNP Expended on Education:** 7.4% (1976)

Transportation: Paved roads total 446 mi. **Motor Vehicles:** 26,500 (1976) **Passenger Cars:** 17,000 **Railway Mileage:** 360 **Ports:** Cotonou **Major Airlines:** Air Afrique provides intercontinental and regional services **Communications:** State controlled **Radio Transmitters:** 4 (1972) **Receivers:** 150,000 (1976) **Television Stations:** None **Receivers:** 100 (1972) **Telephones:** 8,000 (1974) **Newspapers:** 1 daily, 0.3 copies per 1,000 inhabitants (1975)

Weights and Measures: Metric system **Travel Requirements:** Passport and visa required. Transit visa $3.00 for 24 hours; 1-3 days, $3.00, 2 photos

---

In addition to being one of the smallest, poorest, and most densely populated countries in West Africa, Benin has the unenviable distinction of having had more changes of government than any other newly independent African nation.

Counting the government that was in office when the former French territory won independence in 1960 under the name Dahomey, there were 11 governments between 1960 and 1972. Six of these were installed by military coups. In many cases, governments resigned or were ousted simply because they could not meet a payroll.

In 1970 the government sought to bring a measure of stability to the country by creating a civilian presidential commission which consisted of three former leaders who had served as president or premier in the past. Starting with Hubert Maga, as first president, the chairmanship of the commission was to rotate every two years.

According to schedule Mr. Maga stepped down in May 1972 and was replaced by Justin Ahomadegbe. Five months later, however, the transfer of power by military coup was again the case. On October 26 junior and middle-grade army officers seized power, replacing Ahomadegbe's regime with an 11-man military government headed by then Maj. Mathieu Kérékou.

The Kérékou government represented a clear break from earlier regimes. Persons long in positions of power were swept aside and replaced by a younger generation. A guiding principle of "Marxist-Leninist Scientific Socialism" was proclaimed by President Kérékou and some changes in the political and economic system began to appear. Reports of corruption, incompetence in government and attempted coups followed by wholesale arrests continue to come from Benin, however.

In elections held Nov. 20, 1979, for a National Revolutionary Assembly, more than 80 percent of the electorate voted. The count was overwhelmingly in favor of the single list of candidates of the People's Revolutionary party of Benin (PRPB).

Much of Benin's political instability has been caused by the country's weak economy and dependence on French aid. Producing only a small quantity of palm products, cotton and cocoa beans for export, Benin has been unable to earn enough revenue to meet development requirements.

Benin's imports climbed to an annual level of $289 million in 1978 while exports lagged at $115 million. Membership in the French franc pool is the only thing that makes such a deficit possible.

HISTORY: In the 17th century, the powerful Kingdom of Abomey gained dominance over neighboring kingdoms; it maintained its pre-eminent position until the late 19th century, when it was occupied by the French. Abomey armies, which included an elite corps of women soldiers, warred constantly with Yorubas in the east and raided Ashanti territory to the west. Until well into the 19th century, much of the fighting was stimulated by the slave trade, since prisoners were readily sold to European slavers
1851: French make treaty with King Gezo of Cotonou, where they establish trading post
1892-1904: French crush Abomey rebellion, push inland, and make country part of French West Africa

1958-59: Territory of Dahomey becomes autonomous state within French community; constitution is adopted and, in National Assembly elections Hubert Maga becomes premier
1960: Dahomey becomes fully independent, with Maga as president
1963: Maga government is forced to resign in coup led by Col. (later General) Christophe Soglo, army chief of staff, who forms provisional government
1964: In national elections, Sourou Migan Apithy is chosen as president, Justin Ahomadegbe as vice-president
1965: Dissension among government leaders prompts second coup by General Soglo; provisional civilian government is formed and elections are announced, but Soglo again intervenes, proclaims himself president and premier of military regime, bans political activity
1967: Soglo government is overthrown by military junta
1968: Military regime returns government to civilian administration headed by Emile-Derlin Zinsou
1972: Dahomey's first peaceful transition of power is aborted by the country's fifth coup since independence. Maj. Mathieu Kérékou assumes power
1975: Rebellion led by Minister of Labor quashed. Dahomey is renamed the People's Republic of Benin by President Kérékou
1977: In January, foreign airborne assault fails to overthrow Kérékou, who claims invasion was French inspired
1979: In November first general elections for a National Revolutionary Assembly are held in accordance with the new constitution which had been announced in 1977

BHUTAN

Area: 18,147 sq. mi. **Population:** 1,240,000 (1978 est.)

Official Name: Kingdom of Bhutan **Capital:** Thimphu **Nationality:** Bhutanese **Languages:** Dzongka, a Tibetan dialect, is the official and principal language; Nepali and tribal dialects are also spoken **Religion:** About 75% are Mahayana Buddhists and many live in Buddhist monasteries; the Nepalese of southern Bhutan (25%) are predominantly Hindu **Flag:** Divided diagonally with saffron to the left and red to the right, with a white dragon outlined in black in the center **Anthem:** National Anthem, beginning "In the sandal-wood ornamented Kingdom of Dragonland" **Currencies:** Ngultrum (8.1 per U.S. $1) and Indian rupee (8.1 per U.S. $1)

Location: Eastern Himalayas of Central Asia. Bhutan is bordered by China (Tibet) on the north and northwest, and by India on the east, west and south **Features:** The undemarcated northern boundary with Tibet stretches along 300 miles of snow-capped peaks that are almost inaccessible. The inner Himalayan region in central Bhutan contains densely populated, fertile valleys; the Duar Plain of southern Bhutan contains dense forests **Chief Rivers:** Manas, Sankosh, Tongsa, Torsa, Raidak

Head of State and of Government: King Jigme Singye Wangchuk, born 1955, ascended the throne 1972. The king governs with the aid of a 4-man council of ministers **Effective Date of Present Constitution:** No formal written constitution **Legislative Body:** Tsongdu (unicameral national assembly), consisting of 150 members, 40 appointed by the king, 10 by the organizations of lamas, and the rest nominated by villages for 3-year terms. Parliamentary government is still rudimentary **Local Government:** 4 regions under appointed governors

Ethnic Composition: Bhutanese, or Bhotias, who are ethnically related to the Tibetans, make up 60% of the population. Nepalese constitute about 25% and the rest consist of various tribal groups, including the Lepcha, an indigenous people, and the Santal, descendants of migrants from India **Population Distribution:** The population is chiefly rural **Density:** 68 inhabitants per sq. mi.

Largest Cities: (1970 est.) Thimphu 50,000, Paro Dzong 35,000, Taga Dzong 18,000, Punakha 12,000, Bumthang 10,000

Per Capita Income: $80 (1979) **Gross National Product (GNP):** $135 million (1979) **Economic Statistics:** The economy is still at a primitive level and many transactions are on a barter basis. The country is self-sufficient in food; the main crops are rice, wheat, and barley, and together with butter from yaks provide a sufficient diet. Large forests provide the potential for lumber and paper-processing plants, and several turbulent rivers furnish a potential source of hydroelectric power. Bhutan's first 5-year development plan was begun in 1961 with the aid of India, the fourth plan covers the years 1976-1981 **Minerals and Mining:** Copper, dolomite, graphite, and coal deposits have been discovered **Labor Force:** Virtually the entire working population is engaged in agriculture and pastoral activities **Foreign Trade:** Almost all external trade is with India, chiefly exports ($1 million) of rice, dolomite and handicrafts, and imports ($1.4 million) of textiles and light equipment

Vital Statistics: Birthrate, 43.6 per 1,000 of pop. (1975); death rate,

20.5 **Life Expectancy:** 43.6 years **Health Statistics:** N.A. **Infant Mortality:** N.A. **Illiteracy:** 95% **Primary and Secondary School Enrollment:** 20,357 (1976) **Enrollment in Higher Education:** Bhutanese students are studying in India, New Zealand, Australia and the U.S. **GNP Expended on Education:** N.A.

Transportation: Paved roads total 250 mi. **Motor Vehicles:** N.A. **Passenger Cars:** N.A. **Railway Mileage:** None **Ports:** None **Major Airlines:** An Indian airline operates flights from Hashimara, West Bengal, to Paro Dzong **Communications:** Teleprinter and postal services link Bhutan with India and the rest of the world **Radio Transmitters:** 1 A.M. station **Receivers:** 6,000 **Television:** None **Telephones:** 1,000 **Newspapers:** A weekly government newspaper is published in 3 languages

Weights and Measures: Traditional and metric standards are used **Travel Requirements:** Tourists are admitted only in groups by prearrangement with the Ministry of Tourism, Thimphu. Passport, visa, smallpox and cholera immunizations are required. India requires special passes to enter Bhutan.

Well into the 20th century, the Buddhist kingdom of Bhutan was still living in the 19th, content to be isolated politically from the rest of the world. In 1959 the Chinese takeover of Tibet, Bhutan's northern neighbor, jolted the country into closing its trade routes to Tibet and into building a road to the south.

It took six days then, on the back of a mule, to travel from Bhutan to India. The same trip now, by bus, takes five hours. With the help of foreign, mainly Indian, aid and advisers, similar advances have been made in other sectors in the agrarian kingdom. Where only 2,600 of Bhutan's people had gone even to primary school a decade ago, now 20,000 are studying in schools of all levels. About 500 have studied abroad at universities and returned to Bhutan.

Bhutan's king from 1952 to 1972 was Jigme Dorji Wangchuk, whose name means "fearless thunderbolt master of the cosmic powers." Despite his awesome appellation, the king was surprisingly informal and genuinely loved by his people. To give his rule a popular base, he persuaded the National Assembly to pass a bill (dropped by his successor) empowering it by a two-thirds vote to replace the king with the next in the royal line of succession if the monarch loses the assembly's confidence. After his death, he was succeeded by his son, Jigme Singye Wangchuk.

Bhutan is largely independent and insists that it is not an Indian protectorate, though by a treaty of 1949 it "agrees to be guided by the government of India in regard to external relations." Until 1978, Bhutan was under an agreement to sell its goods only to India. Bhutan has no plans to open its mountain border with China; it has diplomatic missions only at the United Nations, in India and in Bangladesh.

Bhutan's people are thinly spread over a beautiful, mountainous country. Most Bhutanese live as farmers on their own land, bartering for what they need. Since 1974, Bhutanese planners have permitted group tours of rich travelers—a maximum of 200 at a time—who stay in excellent new facilities. In 1979 some 1,500 tourists put $700,000 into Bhutan's economy.

HISTORY: Bhutan's early history is obscure. In the 16th century it was conquered by Tibet and nominally came under a dual spiritual and temporal rule. In the 19th century the southern part of the country was occupied by the British and annexed to India, and Britain began paying Bhutan an annual subsidy. In 1907 Sir Ugyen Wangchuk, a former local governor, established a hereditary monarchy, and in a 1910 treaty Bhutan agreed to British direction of its external affairs
1949: India signs treaty with Bhutan assuming Britain's role in subsidizing kingdom and directing its foreign relations; India returns areas annexed by Britain in 1865
1959: Communist China publishes maps showing parts of Bhutan as Chinese territory; Communist spokesmen claim Bhutan be-

longs to greater Tibet. Indian government warns that any attack on Bhutan will be regarded as an act of aggression against India
1971: Bhutan is admitted to the United Nations
1973: Bhutan signs agreement with UN under which Bhutan will receive $2.5 million in aid to carry out projects under third five-year plan
1974: King Jigme Singye Wangchuk formally crowned

BOLIVIA

Area: 424,163 sq. mi. **Population:** 5,425,000 (1979 est.)

Official Name: Republic of Bolivia **Capital:** La Paz is the administrative capital, Sucre the legal and judicial capital **Nationality:** Bolivian **Languages:** Spanish, the official language, is spoken by about 55% of the population (but only 36% as a mother tongue). The rest speak a variety of Indian dialects, chiefly Quechua and Aymara **Religion:** The population is about 95% Roman Catholic **Flag:** Red, yellow, and green horizontal stripes, with the national coat of arms on the yellow stripe **Anthem:** National Anthem, beginning "Bolivians, provident destiny" **Currency:** Bolivian peso (24.5 per U.S. $1)

Location: South America. Landlocked Bolivia is bordered on the north and east by Brazil, on the south by Paraguay and Argentina, and on the west by Chile and Peru **Features:** The country is divided into three distinct regions: the Altiplano, a bleak plateau lying between two ranges of the Andes Mountains and one of the world's highest inhabited regions; an intermediate region (yungas) containing the eastern mountain slopes and valleys, and the Amazon-Chaco lowlands (llanos) **Chief Rivers:** Beni, Guaporé-Iténez, Mamoré-Río Grande, Pilcomayo, Paraguay

Head of State and of Government: President: Gen. Luis García Meza, assumed office in July 1980 coup **Effective Date of Present Constitution:** 1967; many provisions suspended after 1969 coup **Legislative Body:** Bicameral National Congress (disbanded July 1980) with 27 Senators and 117 Deputies **Local Government:** 9 departments, each headed by an appointed prefect

Ethnic Composition: 65% Amerindian (mainly Quechua and Aymará), 10% of European origin, 25% of mixed origin (Cholo) **Population Distribution:** 38.6% urban (1975) **Density:** 12.8 inhabitants per sq. mi.

Largest Cities: (1975 est.) La Paz 660,700, Cochabamba 184,340, Santa Cruz 149,230, Oruro 110,490, Sucre 106,590

Per Capita Income: $543 (1979) **Gross National Product (GNP):** $3.4 billion (1979) **Economic Statistics:** In 1973 about 21% of GNP came from agriculture (sugar, corn, potatoes, wheat, and rice); 12% from manufacturing (food processing, textiles, leather goods, cement, and glass ceramics); 15% from mining; 28% from trade and services; 4% from construction; 9% from transportation **Minerals and Mining:** Mining is the most important element of the nation's economy and accounts for the major share of the country's exports. Tin still dominates these exports, which also include lead, zinc, silver, copper, tungsten, bismuth, antimony, gold, petroleum, natural gas, and sulphur **Labor Force:** 2.8 million (1977); 70% in agriculture, 10% in services and utilities, 7% in manufacturing, 3% in mining, 10% other **Foreign Trade:** Exports, chiefly tin, natural gas, petroleum, tungsten, silver, antimony, copper, lead, zinc, sugar, cotton and coffee, totaled $670 million in 1978. Imports, mainly machinery, vehicles, iron and steel, and food staples, totaled $764 million **Principal Trade Partners:** United States, Argentina, West Germany, Britain, Brazil, Japan, Switzerland, Netherlands

Vital Statistics: Birthrate, 48 per 1,000 of pop. (1976); death rate, 18 **Life Expectancy:** 47 years **Health Statistics:** 526 inhabitants per hospital bed; 2,583 per physician (1975) **Infant Mortality:** 77.3 per 1,000 births **Illiteracy:** 37% **Primary and Secondary School Enrollment:** 1,050,931 (1976) **Enrollment in Higher Education:** 51,585 (1976) **GNP Expended on Education:** 3.2% (1976)

Transportation: Paved roads total 714 mi. **Motor Vehicles:** 59,700 (1977) **Passenger Cars:** 34,300 **Railway Mileage:** 2,400 **Ports:** None **Major Airlines:** Lloyd Aéreo Boliviano (LAB) operates domestic and international services **Communications:** Government controlled **Radio Transmitters:** 106 (1976) **Receivers:** 476,000 (1975) **Television Transmitters:** 2 **Receivers:** 100,000 (1976) **Telephones:** 49,000 (1974) **Newspapers:** 14 dailies, 35 copies per 1,000 inhabitants (1975)

Weights and Measures: Metric system; old Spanish units are still used **Travel Requirements:** Passport and tourist visa, 90-day extendable, no fee

---

Often called the "Tibet of South America," landlocked Bolivia is made up of three distinct topographical regions: a mineral-rich high plateau region, an extensively farmed middle region of semitropical rain forests and somewhat drier valleys, and the sparsely populated Amazon-Chaco lowlands.

Bolivia is among the poorest countries in Latin America, with its Andean Indian peasants and its miners widely separated from the urban minorities of European origin.

Signs of economic and social advance, however, include skyscraper office buildings, modern jet airliner service between La Paz and the tropical lowlands, and the large growth in primary school enrollment.

Bolivia's economy is based on natural gas and petroleum, which make the country self-sufficient in energy, and nonferrous minerals, including tin, of which Bolivia is one of the world's leading producers. The prevailing economic philosophy is nationalist capitalism.

From 1943, when the pro-miner National Revolutionary Movement (MNR) led a revolt against poor working conditions and suppression of strikes, power shifted back and forth between the MNR and rightist military juntas. In August 1971 the regime of Gen. Juan José Torres was overthrown by Col. Hugo Banzer Suárez with support of both the MNR and the rightist Bolivian Socialist Falange. By foiling a series of attempts to unseat him and by establishing (in 1974) an all-military government, Banzer attained a relatively long period of political stability. In 1978, in response to a popular cry for more democratic government, he announced a presidential election to be held in July. Gen. Juan Pereda Asbún, backed by Banzer, received more than half of the popular votes, but Bolivia's electoral court declared the election void on the grounds of fraud. Two days later, Pereda launched a bloodless coup from Santa Cruz, and Banzer went into self-imposed exile in Argentina.

In turn, the Pereda regime was toppled on November 24 without bloodshed, and the army's Gen. David Padilla Arancibia became the interim president. His government promised a presidential election by "universal democratic vote" in July 1979. Because no candidate received a majority of votes, it was left to the National Congress to choose a president. Walter Guevara Arze emerged as the first civilian president in 10 years. However, when he was toppled by a coup in November, Lidia Gueiler Tejada, president of the Chamber of Deputies, was selected to serve as interim president until a new election scheduled for June 29, 1980. A former president, Hernán Siles Zuazo, won a plurality in the 1980 election, but not a majority, of votes. Before the National Congress could meet on August 3 to choose a president, a three-man military junta seized power on July 17 to prevent the choice of the left-wing Siles Zuazo. Gen. Luis García Meza, representing the army in the junta, was proclaimed president by the group.

HISTORY: The Bolivian Altiplano was a center of Indian life long before the days of the Incas, who conquered the region in the 13th century. The Spanish conquest began in the 1530s, and the Indians were soon virtually enslaved to work the rich silver mines of Upper Peru, as Bolivia was then called. Following the occupation of Spain by Napoleon in 1809, Upper Peru became one of the first Spanish colonies to revolt against Spain

1824-26: Revolutionary army under Antonio José de Sucre, chief lieutenant of Simón Bolívar, defeats Spanish forces at Ayacucho. Bolivian independence is proclaimed in 1825

1879-84: Bolivia and Peru fight Chile in War of the Pacific. Chile is victorious and Bolivia is forced to cede province of Atacama, nation's only coastal territory

1903: After bitter conflict, Bolivia cedes large rubber-tree area on Acre River to Brazil

1932-35: Discovery of oil at the foot of the Bolivian Andes precipitates Chaco War with Paraguay, which lays claim to region. More than 100,000 lives are lost on both sides; a defeated Bolivia loses three-quarters of disputed Chaco Boreal area to Paraguay

1943: Economic unrest culminates in widespread strikes by miners; pro-miner Movement of the National Revolution (MNR) stages revolt and takes power

1951-56: Victor Paz Estenssoro, the MNR candidate, wins presidential elections but is prevented from taking office by military junta; he is finally swept into power by a party-led uprising

1964-66: Second administration headed by Paz is overthrown and a military junta installed. Air Force General René Barrientos Ortuño is elected president in 1966

1967: Cuban guerrilla leader Ernesto "Che" Guevara, who had been waging a "liberation" movement in Bolivia, is executed

1969: Barrientos is killed in helicopter crash and is succeeded by Vice-President Luis Adolfo Siles Salinas; Siles is ousted, however, in coup led by General Alfredo Ovando Candia

1970: Ovando regime is overthrown in leftist coup led by General Juan José Torres

1971: Torres is overthrown in rebel uprising; Col. Hugo Banzer Suárez is appointed president

1974: Banzer's government orders price rises to cope with a food shortage; labor strikes and a peasant revolt result

1976: Negotiations are entered into with Chile and Peru concerning their granting Bolivia an outlet to the Pacific Ocean. Juan José Torres is slain in Argentina, resulting in massive strikes and unrest. State takes over all iron ore and manganese deposits

1977: Civilian-military coup attempt fails

1978: Gen. Juan Pereda Asbún seizes presidency in coup following elections but is toppled four months later by Gen. David Padilla Arancibia

1979: When no presidential candidate gains a majority in July elections, congress chooses Walter Guevara Arze to be interim executive. Guevara is unseated by a coup in November and replaced by Lidia Gueiler Tejada pending new elections in 1980. Playing host to the General Assembly of the Organization of American States in La Paz, Oct. 22-31, Bolivia requests and, by a 25 to 0 vote, wins that body's support of "a sovereign and useful access to the Pacific Ocean"

1980: June election results in plurality, but not majority, for Hernán Siles Zuazo. Before congress can pick a new president, a military junta seizes power and names Gen. García Meza as head of state

---

BOTSWANA

Area: 224,764 sq. mi. **Population:** 791,000 (1979 est.)

Official Name: Botswana **Capital:** Gaborone **Nationality:** Botswana **Languages:** English is the official language; Setswana is the main African language. Various dialects of the Khoisan "click" language are spoken by the Bushmen; Afrikaans is also used **Religion:** About 15% Christian; the rest practice tribal religions **Flag:** A blue field divided by a black horizontal band edged in white **Anthem:** Our Land **Currency:** Pula (0.79 per U.S. $1)

Location: Southern Africa. Landlocked Botswana is bordered by Namibia on the north and west, by Zambia and Zimbabwe on the east, and by South Africa on the southeast and south **Features:** Most of the country is a tableland, with a mean altitude of 3,300 feet. The Kalahari Desert covers much of the southwest; in the northwest the waters of the Okavango River form a great inland delta, known as the Okavango Swamps, which extend over 6,500 sq. mi. **Chief Rivers:** Okavango, Molopo, Shashi, Limpopo

Head of State and of Government: President: Dr. Quett K.J. Masire, elected by the National Assembly in July 1980 **Effective Date of Present Constitution:** September 30, 1966 **Legislative Body:** Parliament (unicameral), consisting of a 36-member National Assembly. Of the total membership, 32 are directly elected and 4 chosen by the elected members. The constitution also provides for a House of Chiefs, which plays an advisory role in government affairs **Local Government:** 10 districts and 3 independent towns, governed by local councils

Ethnic Composition: The majority in Botswana are Bantu, grouped into 8 main tribes; in addition, there are some 30,000 Bushmen, 5,000 Europeans, and smaller groups of Asians, Hottentots, and those of mixed origin **Population Distribution:** 12.3% urban **Density:** 3.5 inhabitants per sq. mi.

Largest Cities: (1974 est.) Francistown 22,000, Gaborone 21,000, Selebi-Pikwe 20,572 (1975)

Per Capita Income: $337 (1978) **Gross National Product (GNP):** $250 million (1978) **Economic Statistics:** In 1973, 36% of GNP came from animal husbandry (cattle, goats, sheep) and agriculture (corn, sorghum); 17.3% from trade and services; and 16% from industry (meat processing) and mining **Minerals and Mining:** Manganese, copper and copper/nickel, coal, and diamonds are mined **Labor Force:** About 385,000, with most in agriculture **Foreign Trade:** Exports, chiefly livestock, hides and skins, copper, nickel, diamonds, canned meats, beans and sorghum, totaled $184 million in 1978. Imports, chiefly cereals, petroleum products, textiles, sugar, and motor vehicles, totaled $294 million **Principal Trade Partners:** South Africa, Britain, Zambia, United States

Vital Statistics: Birthrate, 45.6 per 1,000 of pop. (1975); estimated death rate, 23 **Life Expectancy:** 45 years **Health Statistics:** 328 inhabitants per hospital bed; 10,476 per physician (1976) **Infant Mortality:** 24.1 **Illiteracy:** 67% **Primary and Secondary School Enrollment:** 141,863 (1976) **Enrollment in Higher Education:** 469 (1975) **GNP Expended on Education:** 9.2% (1975)

Transportation: Paved roads total 360 mi. **Motor Vehicles:** 14,200 (1977) **Passenger Cars:** 3,400 **Railway Mileage:** 436 **Ports:** None **Major Airlines:** Air Botswana operates domestic flights and maintains services to South Africa and Zambia **Communications:** Government owned **Radio Transmitters:** 4 (1974) **Receivers:** 6,000 (1976) **Television:** None **Telephones:** 8,000 (1975) **Newspapers:** 1 daily, 20 per 1,000 inhabitants (1975)

Weights and Measures: Metric system **Travel Requirements:** Passport, no visa

---

Since gaining independence in 1966, the former British protectorate of Bechuanaland has seen its previously bleak economic prospects brightened by the discovery of substantial mineral wealth—diamonds, copper, and nickel.

The mineral wealth found in the country's arid northeastern area includes a diamond "pipe" (the core of an ancient volcano) at Orapa, which is one of the largest ever discovered anywhere. Development of the diamonds and other minerals by American and South African companies involves an investment of some $130 million.

With mineral development and new industry, this impoverished African country hopes to gain economic independence that will significantly add to its political independence.

Nearly surrounded by white-ruled areas, Botswana previously had seemed destined to be no more than a cattle ranch for South Africa. As head of a newly independent black African state, Botswana's late president, Sir Seretse Khama, had asserted opposition to South Africa's racist policies, but acknowledged his country's economic dependence on its southern neighbor. Still, Botswana is devoted to strengthening its commercial and psychological ties with Zambia and other independent states of black Africa, while refusing to have diplomatic relations with Pretoria.

Relations between Botswana and white-ruled Zimbabwe Rhodesia became strained as a result of incidents arising out of the guerrilla war between Zimbabwe Rhodesian black nationalists and Zimbabwe Rhodesian security forces. The Botswana deeply resented the infiltration of Zimbabwe Rhodesian security forces into their country. In a series of clashes with police in 1978, residents registered their protest over the arrest of Ompatile Tswaipe, a member of the Botswana Defense Force, who was charged with the murder of a British student and two South African game wardens. Tswaipe, whom many Botswana believed was quite properly defending his country from foreign infiltration when the incident occurred, was later acquitted.

Sir Seretse, an Oxford-educated lawyer, caused a controversy in his homeland as well as in South Africa by his marriage to an Englishwoman in 1948. However, his popularity gained him victory in the preindependence elections of 1965. He maintained a policy of non-racial democracy for Botswana. Sir Seretse was reelected overwhelmingly for a third term as president Oct. 20, 1979. He died on July 13, 1980, and was succeeded by Dr. Quett K.J. Masire, Vice President and Finance Minister under Sir Seretse.

HISTORY: Little is known of the origins of Botswana's peoples. The early inhabitants, the Bushmen, who now are dying out, have no recorded history. The ancestors of most of the present-day population, the Botswana, probably arrived centuries ago in Bantu migra-

tions from Central or East Africa. In the 19th century, the great chief Khama III loosely united the Botswana against incursions of the neighboring Matabele people and Boer trekkers from the Transvaal. Under British protection, the southern area was made part of the South African Cape Colony, while the northern part, known as Bechuanaland, remained under direct British administration until it became independent Botswana

1909: Constitution of Union (now Republic) of South Africa is drafted, with a provision that Bechuanaland and other British protectorates in southern Africa, Basutoland (now Lesotho) and Swaziland, will some day be included in the union

1920-61: Advisory councils, one representing Africans, the other, Europeans, are established by British Central Authority. Central Authority establishes a Joint Advisory Council with African and European membership, which resolves to form legislative council to assist in governing the territory. A constitution for this purpose is promulgated

1965: New constitution is made effective and general elections are held for new National Assembly; seat of government is moved from Mafeking in South Africa to Gaborone

1966: Bechuanaland becomes independent member of the British Commonwealth and adopts name of Botswana

1973: Botswana severs diplomatic relations with Israel as a result of Middle East war

1975: A five-year treaty is signed with EC

1977: UN Security Council adopts a resolution demanding the cessation of all hostile acts against Botswana by Rhodesia

1979: Sir Seretse Khama is reelected president for a third term as the candidate of the Botswana Democratic party; with 60 percent of the electorate voting, he receives 100,398 votes to only 17,480 for his nearest rival, Dr. Kenneth Koma, chairman of the pro-Marxist Botswana National Front

1980: Sir Seretse dies and is succeeded by Dr. Quett K.J. Masire

---

BRAZIL

Area: 3,286,470 sq. mi. **Population:** 118,645,000 (1979 est.)

Official Name: Federative Republic of Brazil **Capital:** Brasília **Nationality:** Brazilian **Languages:** Portuguese is the official and principal language. In central and southern Brazil, Italian, German, and Japanese immigrants still use their native languages **Religion:** About 93% of the population is Roman Catholic. There are about 8 million Protestants and 150,000 Jews **Flag:** Green, with a yellow diamond enclosing a blue globe containing 23 white stars and a white band inscribed with the words "Ordem e Progresso" (Order and Progress) **Anthem:** Brazilian National Hymn, beginning "From peaceful Ypiranga's banks" **Currency:** Cruzeiro (50.6 per U.S. $1)

Location: South America. The fifth-largest nation in the world, Brazil is bordered by every country in South America except Chile and Ecuador. It is bounded by French Guiana, Suriname, Guyana, Venezuela, and Colombia on the north, by Peru, Bolivia, and Paraguay on the west, and by Uruguay and Argentina on the south **Features:** The country is divided into four distinct major regions: the northern tropical basin of the Amazon, which flows more than 1,500 miles within the country, bordered on the north by the Guiana Highlands; the semiarid scrub land of the northeast; the agricultural and mineral heartland of the south-central plains, plateaus and highlands; and the narrow coastal belt, fringed by interior mountain ranges, extending from Natal to Porto Alegre **Chief Rivers:** Amazon, São Francisco, Paraná, Uruguay, Paraguay

Head of State and of Government: President João Baptista de Oliveira Figueiredo, born 1921, inaugurated on Mar. 15, 1979, following selection by Electoral College in 1978 for six-year term **Effective Date of Present Constitution:** January 24, 1967, extensively revised in 1969 **Legislative Body:** National Congress (bicameral), composed of the Chamber of Deputies and the Senate **Local Government:** 22 states, each with an indirectly elected governor and legislature, 4 federal territories, and 1 federal district

Ethnic Composition: The primary elements are 60% European, 12% African and a complex mixture (28%) of both **Population Distribution:** 61.2% urban **Density:** 36.1 inhabitants per sq. mi.

Largest Cities: (1975 est.—Metropolitan Areas) São Paulo 7,198,608, Rio de Janeiro 4,857,716, Belo Horizonte 1,557,464, Recife 1,249,821, Salvador 1,237,393, Fortaleza 1,109,839

Per Capita Income: $1,371 (1979) **Gross National Product (GNP):** $214.9 billion (1979) **Economic Statistics:** 38% of GNP comes from industry (food processing, chemicals, textiles, metallurgical products, vehicles and accessories, electrical and communications equipment), mining and construction; 32% from services; 8% from agriculture (rice, corn, coffee, sugarcane, soybeans, livestock, manioc, cotton); 16% from trade, and 6% from transportation and communications **Minerals and Mining:** Large deposits of iron, manganese, and bauxite; nickel, lead, tin, asbestos, chrome ore, gold, tungsten, and copper are also mined but supplies must be augmented by imports. Coal and petroleum production are also supplemented by imports **Labor Force:** Approximately 38,000,000 (1978); of which 38% is employed in agriculture, 24% in industry **Foreign Trade:** Exports, chiefly coffee, soybeans, cotton, iron ore, cane sugar, pine wood, corn, and cocoa beans, totaled $15.1 billion in 1979. Imports, mainly wheat, crude petroleum, machinery, chemicals, metals and heavy equipment, totaled $17.2 billion **Principal Trade Partners:** United States, West Germany, Argentina, Italy, The Netherlands, United Kingdom, France, Japan, Saudi Arabia, Canada, Poland

Vital Statistics: Birthrate, 37.1 per 1,000 of pop. (1975); death rate, 8.8 **Life Expectancy:** 61 years **Health Statistics:** 526 inhabitants per hospital bed; 2,117 per physician (1975) **Infant Mortality:** about 88 per 1,000 births **Illiteracy:** 17% **Primary and Secondary School Enrollment:** 20,968,339 (1974) **Enrollment in Higher Education:** 1,316,640 (1976) **GNP Expended on Education:** 2.3% (1976)

Transportation: Paved roads total 47,000 mi. **Motor Vehicles:** 7,313,500 (1976) **Passenger Cars:** 5,916,300 **Railway Mileage:** 20,447 **Ports:** Santos, Rio de Janeiro, Vitória, Salvador, Rio Grande, Recife, Paranagua, Macapá **Major Airlines:** VARIG and Cruzeiro do Sul operate domestic and international services **Communications:** Government controlled **Radio Transmitters:** 999 **Receivers:** 16,980,000 (1975) **Television Transmitters:** 66 (1973) **Receivers:** 10,680,000 (1975) **Telephones:** 4,036,000 (1976) **Newspapers:** 280 dailies, 39 per 1,000 inhabitants (1973)

Weights and Measures: Metric system **Travel Requirements:** Passport and visa required. Tourists need onward/return ticket or financial guarantee; $2.00 fee

---

Long considered the country of the future, Brazil has begun to grow visibly through industrialization within its vast geographical outline. Since 1930 the activist governments of the country, the largest in Latin America and the fifth largest in the world in area, have—despite wide ideological differences—followed roughly similar policies of industrial development and national integration of the huge hinterland and the urban coast. As a result, Brazil is the industrial leader of South America, with by far the largest gross national product.

For all its economic progress, Brazil has had more than its share of political upheaval. It has been by turns a Portuguese colony, an independent empire, a republic, a dictatorship, and, up to 1964, a representative democracy. Since the ousting of a civilian president, João Goulart, in that year, Brazil has had a succession of five army generals as presidents.

Leaving the economy largely under civilian management, the first three military administrations reformed the tax structure, began the reorganization of the state's inefficient bureaucracy, shifted some resources to the country's backward regions, attracted large amounts of U.S. and other foreign investment capital, and whipped up the pace of industrial expansion. The result is often described as Brazil's "economic miracle."

Brazil's economy fared less well under the fourth military administration, in which Ernesto Geisel, a career artillery general, served a five-year term that ended in 1979. The nation's industrial and farm exports were still growing, but these advantages were offset by increased imports, strikes, and the rapidly rising cost of living.

Gen. João Baptista Figueiredo, who had been the chief of intelligence, was sworn in as president on March 15, 1979. He had been elected five months earlier in Brazil's first contested presidential election since the coup that ousted Goulart. The print media—but not television and radio—received full freedom during the campaign.

Figueiredo inherited the economic problems of his predecessor. Almost immediately he had to send troops to restore calm and bring about a settlement of a strike by 180,000 metalworkers in São Paulo. A wave of other strikes ensued. At the root of this labor discontent was the cost of living which rose 77 percent through 1979. The São Paulo metalworkers struck again in October 1979 and April 1980, demanding large wage increases. Brazil's trade deficit also grew at a very rapid rate.

Brazil depends heavily on foreign oil and, to deal with soaring petroleum prices, in mid-1979 the government instituted an energy-saving program. Curbs were placed on imports. A six-year plan was launched for development of vehicles built or modified to run on alcohol made from the country's bountiful sugarcane crop. In November, Brazil got a loan of $1.2 billion from international banks for its alcohol fuel program. In the area of nuclear energy, Brazil is buying eight power plants and a uranium reprocessing facility from West Germany.

On Dec. 7, 1979, Figueiredo announced sweeping changes in economic policy. There would be no more export subsidies, and a tax was instituted to limit exports of essential foods, a shortage of which contributed to inflation at home. Restrictions on foreign borrowing were eased. The cruzeiro was devalued by 30 percent, bringing total devaluation in 1979 to 93 percent.

In his inauguration speech, Figueiredo had announced his "unswerving purpose" of restoring democracy to Brazil in the future. In August 1979, he signed a law granting amnesty to political prisoners and exiles except those held for "acts of terrorism." In November he put into effect legislation dissolving the two political parties that had been decreed by the government in 1965. The formation of opposition parties would be allowed as long as they were democratic and in accord with the constitution.

HISTORY: In 1500 Pedro Alvares Cabral landed on the Brazilian coast and claimed the land for Portugal. The first Portuguese governor-general of Brazil was appointed in 1549. In 1727 coffee was introduced in Brazil. In 1808 King John VI, fleeing the Napoleonic invasion of Portugal, arrived in Rio de Janeiro, and in 1815 all Portuguese dominions were designated the United Kingdom of Portugal, Brazil, and the Algarves. The king returned to Portugal in 1821, leaving behind Dom Pedro, his son, as regent

1822: Dom Pedro, later Pedro I, declares Brazil independent of Portugal and assumes title of emperor

1840: Dom Pedro II begins his 40-year rule as emperor

1888: Slavery is abolished and 700,000 slaves are emancipated

1889: The monarchy is toppled by a bloodless revolution and Brazil becomes a republic

1930: Getúlio Vargas comes to power through a revolution and establishes dictatorial rule

1942: Brazil enters WW II and declares war against Axis powers

1945-54: Military coup topples the Vargas dictatorship and restores democracy. In 1951 Vargas again becomes president. Faced with army opposition and threatened with impeachment, he commits suicide in 1954

1956-61: Presidency of Juscelino Kubitschek; capital moved from Rio de Janeiro to Brasília

1964: The elected government of João Goulart is ousted in a military coup led by General Humberto de Alencar Castelo Branco

1974: General Ernesto Geisel "elected" as the fourth successive president from the military

1975: Geisel rejects any return to democratic system of 1954-64

1979: General João Baptista de Oliveira Figueiredo sworn in as president after winning a two-party contest in late 1978

1980: Hundreds of criminal and political suspects are murdered by vigilante "death squads" around *favelas* (slums) of São Paulo and Rio de Janeiro, marking a new wave of violence. Pope John Paul II visits Brazil

---

BULGARIA

Area: 42,823 sq. mi. **Population:** 8,814,000 (1978 est.)
Official Name: People's Republic of Bulgaria **Capital:** Sofia **Nationality:** Bulgarian **Languages:** Bulgarian is the official and principal language; Turkish, Greek, and Armenian are spoken by minority groups **Religion:** Bulgarian Orthodox 85%, Moslem 13%; other denominations are Roman Catholicism, Protestantism, and Judaism. The government is officially atheist **Flag:** Horizontal stripes of white, green, and red, with the state emblem, a lion framed by wheatstalks, located on the white stripe near the hoist **Anthem:** Mila Rodino (Dear Fatherland) national anthem (1964) **Currency:** Lev (0.85 per U.S. $1)

Location: Southeast Europe, on the eastern part of the Balkan peninsula. Bulgaria is bordered on the north by Romania, on the east by the Black Sea, on the south by Turkey and Greece, and on the west by Yugoslavia **Features:** The country is divided into several roughly parallel east/west zones: the Danubian tableland in the north; the Stara Planina (Balkan) Mountains through the central part; and the Thracian Plain and Rhodope Mountains in the south and southwest **Chief Rivers:** Danube, Maritsa, Iskur, Tundzha

Political Leader and Head of State: Todor Zhivkov, born 1911; First Secretary of the Central Committee of the Communist party since 1954, reelected 1976. In 1971 he was elected chairman of the State Council **Head of Government:** Stanko Todorov, born 1920, Chairman of the Council of Ministers (premier). The Chairman of the National Assembly is Vladimir Bonev **Effective Date of Present Constitution:** May 1971 **Legislative Body:** Parliament (unicameral National Assembly), consisting of 400 members elected for 5 years. Although the National Assembly is nominally the supreme organ of state power, real power is, in fact, wielded by the Politburo and Secretariat of the Communist party **Local Government:** 27 provinces and one city commune, each governed by an elective people's council

Ethnic Composition: 85% of the population consists of ethnic Bulgarians; the only sizable minority is the Turks, who make up about 9%. Macedonians, Armenians, Gypsies, and Greeks constitute smaller ethnic groups **Population Distribution:** 59.4% urban **Density:** 206 inhabitants per sq. mi.

Largest Cities: (1975 census) Sofia 965,355, Plovdiv 305,091, Varna 269,980, Ruse 171,264, Burgas 148,236

Per Capita Income: $3,034 (1979) **Gross National Product (GNP):** $27 billion (1979) **Economic Statistics:** About 43% of GNP comes from industry (food processing, engineering and metallurgy, textiles, chemicals, rubber); 20% from agriculture (wheat, corn, barley, sugar beets); 7% from commerce; and the rest from other activities **Minerals and Mining:** Lead, iron ore, zinc, and copper are produced in substantial quantities. Large coal reserves exist but the coal is of low caloric value **Labor Force:** 4.3 million (1975), of which 57% is employed in industry and construction, and 38% in agriculture (1974) **Foreign Trade:** Exports, mainly foodstuffs, machines and equipment and dairy products, fuels, raw materials and minerals, rose oil, totaled $7.1 billion in 1978. Imports, chiefly machines and equipment, fuels, minerals, raw materials, metals, animal and vegetable products, totaled $6.6 billion **Principal Trade Partners:** USSR, East Germany, Czechoslovakia, West Germany, Poland, Romania, France

Vital Statistics: Birthrate 16.1 per 1,000 of pop. (1977); death rate 10.7 **Life Expectancy:** 71 years **Health Statistics:** 115 inhabitants per hospital bed; 453 per physician (1976) **Infant Mortality:** 23.7 per 1,000 births (1977) **Illiteracy:** 5% **Primary and Secondary School Enrollment:** 1,317,659 (1976) **Enrollment in Higher Education:** 128,593 (1975) **GNP Expended on Education:** 5.4% (1976)

Transportation: Surfaced roads total 7,884 mi. **Motor Vehicles:** 39,000 (1967) **Passenger Cars:** 11,400 (1967) **Railway Mileage:** 3,780 **Ports:** Burgas, Varna **Major Airlines:** Bulgarian Civil Aviation-Balkan operates domestic and international services **Communications:** Government controlled **Radio Transmitters:** 32 **Licenses:** 2,750,000 (1976) **Television Transmitters:** 154 **Licenses:** 1,546,000 (1976) **Telephones:** 853,000 (1976) **Newspapers:** 13 dailies, 232 per 1,000 inhabitants (1975)

Weights and Measures: Metric system **Travel Requirements:** Passport and visa required; transit visa, up to 30 hours, $9.00; tourist visa, 30 hours-2 months, $14.00

Long one of the more backward countries of Eastern Europe, Bulgaria has sought to modernize itself under Communist rule along several directions. The country has expanded its industry, often in close coordination with the Soviet Union. Bulgaria and Romania are the only East European countries in which Soviet troops were not stationed.

Bulgaria produces early fruits and vegetables for the rest of the Soviet bloc. The country's Black Sea coast has been developed as a summer resort area.

At the 10th congress of the Bulgarian Communist Party, held in April 1971 and attended by Soviet leader Leonid Brezhnev, a new constitution and a new party program were adopted. The congress reaffirmed the dominance of Todor Zhivkov, the country's veteran Communist Party boss, while the new party program hailed the "indissoluble Bulgar-Soviet friendship."

This show of solidarity was at least partially cosmetic, a public closing of ranks amid undercurrents of domestic unrest, principally among workers seeking higher pay and better living conditions. In June 1973, the government responded to repeated pressures from the trade unions by authorizing a 23 percent raise in minimum wages.

HISTORY: Bulgaria, part of ancient Thrace and Moesia, was settled by Slavic tribes in the 6th century. In the 7th century the Slavs were conquered by Turkic-speaking Bulgars, who in time fully merged with the Slavs and whose domain continued to expand until the early part of the 11th century, when the Bulgarian state was annexed by the Byzantine Empire. Bulgaria again became a major Balkan power in the 12th and 13th centuries. In the 14th century, however, it was overrun by the Ottoman Turks and remained under their rule for 5 centuries

1876: Bulgarians revolt against Turkish rule but rebellion is crushed by brutal Turkish reprisals

1878: A large Bulgaria is created under Treaty of San Stefano ending Russo-Turkish Wars. However, treaty is revised by Congress of Berlin, making northern Bulgaria a principality under Turkish suzerainty and leaving southern Bulgaria, known as Eastern Rumelia, under direct Turkish rule

1885-1908: Alexander of Battenberg, first prince of Bulgaria, annexes Eastern Rumelia. His successor, Prince Ferdinand of Saxe-Coburg-Gotha, profiting from revolution of Young Turks in 1908, proclaims Bulgaria's independence

1912-13: Bulgaria, allied with Serbia, Greece, and Montenegro, enters first Balkan War against Turkey, which is expelled from all of Europe except the Constantinople area. Bulgarian claims to Macedonia result in second Balkan War, with Bulgaria fighting the armies of Serbia, Romania, Greece, and Turkey; Bulgaria is defeated and loses territory to all its enemies

1915-1918: Bulgaria enters World War I on side of Germany and Austria-Hungary, is defeated and loses territory

1941-44: Bulgaria joins Axis powers in World War II, declaring war on Britain and United States but not on USSR; in 1944 USSR declares war on Bulgaria and occupies country; Communists seize power with Soviet help

1946-48: Monarchy is abolished and a people's republic established. Industry is nationalized and resistance to collectivization of agriculture is broken

1955: Bulgaria joins Warsaw Pact

1969: Zhivkov regime launches campaign against Western influences in arts and culture and warns against anti-Soviet "revisionist" nationalism

1971: New constitution and new Bulgarian Communist Party program adopted

1976: Bulgaria meets with other Balkan nations for first conference on Balkan cooperation since WW II

1978: Bulgaria extradites suspected West German terrorists. Diplomatic problems arise over steel dumping and assassinations of Bulgarian exiles

---

BURMA

Area: 261,789 sq. mi. **Population:** 32,913,000 (1979 est.)

Official Name: Socialist Republic of the Union of Burma **Capital:** Rangoon **Nationality:** Burmese **Languages:** Burmese, the official language, is spoken by 80%; the rest speak a variety, including Tamil, Hindi, Chinese, Shan, Karen, Kachin, Chin and Kayah; English is used in business **Religion:** 85% of the people are Buddhists; minority religions are Hinduism, Islam, Christianity, and animism **Flag:** A red field with a blue rectangle in the upper left corner containing a cog wheel and ear of paddy surrounded by 14 white stars **Anthem:** Our Free Homeland **Currency:** Kyat (6.6 per U.S. $1)

Location: Southeast Asia. Burma is bordered on the north and northeast by China, on the east by Laos and Thailand, on the south by the Andaman Sea and the Bay of Bengal, and on the west by Bangladesh and India **Features:** The country is rimmed on the north, east, and west by mountain ranges forming a giant horseshoe. Enclosed within this mountain barrier is a central basin containing most of the country's agricultural land and population. The Salween River, cutting deep gorges through the Shan Plateau and Karenni hills in the east separates the narrow Tenasserim coast from the central basin. A similar narrow coastal strip lies in the west between the Bay of Bengal and the Arakan Yoma mountain range **Chief Rivers:** Irrawaddy, Salween, Sittang, Mekong

Head of State and of Government: President: General U Ne Win, born 1911, chairman of the Council of State, elected president in 1974, reelected 1978 for four years. He is assisted by a Cabinet headed by Prime Minister U Maung Maung Kha, elected 1977 **Effective Date of Present Constitution:** January 1974 **Legislative Body:** Parliament (unicameral People's Assembly) with 464 members elected for 4-year terms **Local Government:** 7 states and 7 divisions. Since March 1974, Peoples Councils have been elected at various local levels

Ethnic Composition: Burmans, ethnically related to the Tibetans, make up about 72% of the population; the Karens (7%), the Shans (6%), the Kachins (2%), and the Chins (2%) are the next largest ethnic groups. Chinese (3%) and Hindus and Pakistanis (6%) constitute the other major ethnic groups **Population Distribution:** 19% urban **Density:** 126 inhabitants per sq. mi.

Largest Cities: (1973 est.) Rangoon 2,055,000; Mandalay 417,000; Moulmein 202,000

Per Capita Income: $165 (1979) **Gross National Product (GNP):** $5.6 billion (1979) **Economic Statistics:** In 1973, 37% of GNP came from agriculture, fishing, and forestry; 11% from industry and mining; and 43% from trade and services **Minerals and Mining:** Burma is rich in minerals, but production is low; petroleum, copper and tin are exploited; small quantities of tungsten, lead, zinc, nickel, cobalt, and precious stones are produced **Labor Force:** 12.2 million, of which 67% is employed in agriculture, and 9% in industry **Foreign Trade:** Exports, chiefly rice, teak and various ores, totaled $243 million in 1978. Imports, mainly textiles, machinery, transport equipment, and foodstuffs, totaled $309 million **Principal Trade Partners:** Singapore, Japan, Indonesia, West Germany, China, Hong Kong, France, Britain

Vital Statistics: Birthrate 39.5 per 1,000 pop. (1975); death rate 15.8 **Life Expectancy:** 53 years **Health Statistics:** 1,125 inhabitants per hospital bed; 5,408 per physician (1976) **Infant Mortality:** 60 per 1,000 births **Illiteracy:** 30% **Education Statistics:** 18,670 primary and secondary schools with a total enrollment of 4,370,987 (1976) **Enrollment in Higher Education:** 56,083 (1975) **GNP Expended on Education:** 1.7% (1976)

Transportation: Surfaced roads total 13,000 mi. **Motor Vehicles:** 79,900 (1977) **Passenger Cars:** 38,600 **Railway Mileage:** 2,040 **Ports:** Rangoon, Sittwe, Bassein, Moulmein, Tavoy, Mergui **Major Airlines:** Burma Airways operates both domestic and international services **Communications:** Government owned **Radio Transmitters:** 5 **Licenses:** 665,000 (1976) **Television:** None **Telephones:** 32,000 (1976) **Newspapers:** 7 dailies, 10 copies per 1,000 inhabitants (1975)

Weights and Measures: British weights and measures as well as local units are used **Travel Requirements:** Passport; visa; transit visa, 24 hours, $1.65, 2 photos; tourist visa, one week, $4.85, 3 photos

A neglected adjunct of imperial India until 1937, Burma started its modern nationhood doubly colonialized: by the British and by the Indians, who ran the lower levels of government and, with the Chinese, dominated commerce.

The Japanese occupation of Burma during World War II turned the lush, rich land into a battlefield on which Burmese nationalists first fought the British and then the Japanese, whom they found to be worse oppressors.

The inability of the government to mollify the rebellious hill peoples, the demise of the coalition which had ruled since 1948, and the prevalence of corruption led to the unopposed military take-over of General Ne Win in 1958. He gave Burma two years of comparatively able government and then returned authority to civilians. While U Nu's faction won a convincing victory, the country's troubles proved too powerful for his new government.

In 1962 Ne Win again took over, jailing many politicians and banning all parties but the army's. The 15-man Revolutionary Council began broad nationalization, driving out Indians and generally sealing off Burma. The replacement of Indians and Chinese with Burmese proved politically popular but economically disastrous.

Under a new constitution adopted in 1974, Ne Win was elected president, and in 1978 he was reelected for another four-year term. The 1978 national elections gave the appearance of unity, since all candidates were members of Burma's single party, the Socialist Program party. Burma was beset, however, by internal disunity, underscored by the exodus of Moslems and in stepped-up guerrilla strife.

In the Arakan division in western Burma, about 200,000 Moslems fled into Bangladesh in the first half of 1978, voicing fear of the Burmese army. And on Burma's eastern border, Communists were increasingly active. For the first time in years of guerrilla activity, they were joined by minorities who have been traditionally anti-Communist. The nation's economy suffered as the sporadic fighting limited mining and lumbering.

HISTORY: A Mongoloid race from Tibet, the Burmese moved southward before the 9th century and settled along the Irrawaddy. In the 11th century, King Anawratha established supremacy over the Irrawaddy delta and introduced Hinayana Buddhism. His kingdom fell to Kublai Khan in 1287, after which it passed to the Shans, who ruled until 1546 as tributaries of China. Following the rise of new Burmese dynasties, Burma was once again unified, only to be annexed piecemeal by Britain in the 19th century

1937: Burma obtains dominionlike status

1942-45: Japan invades Burma during World War II and expels the British from most of the country. U.S., British, and Chinese forces mount a counterattack and expel the Japanese

1948: The Union of Burma is set up as an independent republic. U Nu becomes the first premier

1962: General Ne Win takes over from U Nu

1970: Government troops clash with rebels in northern Burma

1971: Large Karen minority plans new drive against government; Chinese-backed Burmese Communists launch widespread attacks on troop positions in northeast Burma

1974: New constitution adopted by referendum. Ne Win installed as president

1975: Army claims defeat of insurgents. Students riot

1976: Karen rebels and Communist Shan insurgents renew fighting with government forces. Military plot to overthrow Ne Win aborted

1978: Ne Win reelected for second four-year term. About 200,000 Moslems flee into Bangladesh, telling of beatings, rapes and executions

1979: Burma leaves the nonaligned nations movement, saying it was disillusioned by Cuban handling of a summit meeting

---

BURUNDI

Area: 10,747 sq. mi. **Population:** 4,256,000 (1978 est.)

Official Name: Republic of Burundi **Capital:** Bujumbura **Nationality:** Burundi **Languages:** Kirundi (Rundi), a Bantu tongue, and French are the official languages; Swahili is the trade language **Religion:** 60% are Christians, chiefly Roman Catholic; 2% Moslems and the rest are animists **Flag:** A white saltire (diagonal cross) with green and red quarters, and a white circle in the center bearing 3 red six-pointed stars outlined in green **Anthem:** Dear Burundi, O Sweet Land **Currency:** Burundi franc (90 per U.S. $1)

Location: East-central Africa. Burundi is bordered by Rwanda on the north, Tanzania on the east and south, Lake Tanganyika on the southwest, and Zaire on the northwest **Features:** Most of the country consists of grassy uplands and high plateaus. The Ruzizi River Valley and Lake Tanganyika, both along the western boundary with the Congo, constitute part of the Great Rift Valley **Chief Rivers:** Kagera, Ruvubu, Malagarazi, Ruzizi

Head of State and Government: President: Col. Jean-Baptiste Bagaza, born 1946, seized power in 1976 and appointed president **Effective Date of Present Constitution:** 1974, suspended 1976 **Legislative Body:** None. Rule is by the Supreme Revolutionary Council **Local Government:** 8 provinces, each headed by a military governor

Ethnic Composition: 85% are Bahutu (Hutu), farmers of Bantu origin; 14% are Tutsi (Watusi, Batutsi), a tall warrior people of Hamitic origin; and 1% Twa (Batwa), aboriginal pygmies **Population Distribution:** 5% urban **Density:** 396 inhabitants per sq. mi.

Largest Cities: (1976 est.) Bujumbura 160,000, Gitega 25,000; (1970 est.) Ngozi 5,000

Per Capita Income: $122 (1978) **Gross National Product (GNP):** $490 million (1978) **Economic Statistics:** In 1977, 58% of GNP was derived from agriculture (coffee, cotton, tea, bananas, sweet potatoes, cassava, millet and sorghum); and 12% from industry (chiefly food processing and textiles) **Minerals and Mining:** Bastnaesite, used for the manufacture of color TV tubes, and small amounts of cassiterite, tungsten, and gold are mined. Important nickel deposits are to be exploited **Labor Force:** 800,000 (1978), with 95% in agriculture **Foreign Trade:** Exports, chiefly coffee, cotton, tea, hides, and minerals, totaled $66 million in 1978. Imports, mainly textiles and leather, vehicles, machinery, food products, petroleum, consumer goods, totaled $97 million **Principal Trade Partners:** United States, Belgium, Luxembourg, West Germany, France, Kenya, Tanzania, Britain, Italy

Vital Statistics: Estimated birth rate, 46.8 per 1,000 of pop. (1975); death rate, 20.4 **Life Expectancy:** 41 years **Health Statistics:** 857 inhabitants per hospital bed; 45,432 per physician (1975) **Infant Mortality:** 150 per 1,000 births **Illiteracy:** 90% **Primary and Secondary School Enrollment:** 274,931 (1976) **Enrollment in Higher Education:** 1,002 (1975) **GNP Expended on Education:** 2.2% (1976)

Transportation: Of some 3,700 miles of road only about 75 miles are paved **Motor Vehicles:** 7,300 (1976) **Passenger Cars:** 5,100 **Railway Mileage:** None **Ports:** None **Major Airlines:** Air Burundi provides service to neighboring countries **Communications:** Government owned **Radio Transmitters:** 6 **Receivers:** 105,000 (1976) **Television:** None **Telephones:** 4,000 (1976) **Newspapers:** 2 dailies, 0.3 per 1,000 inhabitants (1974)

Weights and Measures: Metric system **Travel Requirements:** Passport, visa, $11 fee, 3 pictures

---

One of Africa's least-known and poorest countries, Burundi was until independence in 1962 the southern half of the former Belgian trust territory of Ruanda-Urundi. The landlocked country—Bujumbura, the capital, is nearly 1,000 miles by lake-rail routes from the nearest seaport, Dar es Salaam, in Tanzania—remains a geophysical, ethnic and economic twin of neighboring Rwanda.

Like Rwanda, Burundi is small, densely populated, heavily eroded, and the home of diverse peoples—the tall Tutsi (better known as Watusi), the traditional ruling minority; the medium-height Hutu, the majority peasant folk; and the dwindling pygmy Twa. However, in contrast to Rwanda where the majority Hutu rule, in Burundi the minority Tutsi caste has control and is reluctant to better the lives of the Hutu masses. As a result, foreign assistance to Burundi is less than half that provided to Rwanda, since donors assume their aid would end up serving the Tutsi elite.

The overthrow of the monarchy and proclamation of a republic in 1966 by a young Tutsi prime minister, Capt. Michel Micombero, opened the way to relative stability and concentration on needed economic development. While there have been gains in fiscal stability, Burundi continues to depend primarily on a small and fluctuating production of coffee.

Discontent among the Hutu has been an obstacle to more rapid development. In 1970 an alleged Hutu plot to massacre the Tutsi and seize power led to executions. In 1972-73 hostilities between the ruling Tutsis and the more numerous Hutus escalated, as Hutu tribesmen entered the country from Tanzania and Rwanda, precipitating fighting in which more than 100,000 were killed.

In November 1976 Burundi's armed forces deposed the president without violence, and the Uprona, the only political party, was dissolved. A Belgian-trained political scientist, Col. Jean-Baptiste Bagaza, is now in control.

HISTORY: Burundi's earliest inhabitants, the pygmy Twa, were supplanted by the Hutu, a Bantu people, who, in turn, were subjugated in the 15th or 16th century by the Tutsi, a tall, warrior people, coming probably from Ethiopia. Although Burundi was visited briefly by European explorers, it was not until the late 19th century that serious efforts at colonization were attempted
1899: Burundi, along with neighboring Rwanda, is made part of German East Africa
1916: Belgian forces from the Congo defeat Germans, occupy Burundi and Rwanda
1923-61: Burundi and Rwanda become Belgian mandated territory known as Ruanda-Urundi which in 1946 is made United Nations trusteeship. Louis Rwagasore, son of the Tutsi Mwami (king), becomes premier; he is assassinated
1962: Kingdom of Burundi attains full independence under Mwami Mwambutsa IV
1965: Premier Pierre Ngendandumwe assassinated; Dr. Pie Masumbuko becomes acting premier
1966: Premier Michel Micombero deposes King Ntare V, declares himself President of Republic
1972-73: Tutsi-Hutu war results in more than 100,000 deaths
1978: In Oct., outbreak of cholera draws foreign medical teams
1979: Approximately 85 missionaries, mostly Catholic, are expelled in June on grounds of preaching against the government

---

CAMBODIA

Area: 69,898 sq. mi. **Population:** 5,200,000 (1980 est. CIA)

Official Name: People's Republic of Kampuchea (pro-Vietnamese, in Phnom Penh); Democratic Kampuchea (functions in countryside) **Capital:** Phnom Penh **Nationality:** Cambodian or Kampuchean **Languages:** Cambodian, or Khmer, is the official and predominant language **Religion:** The vast majority practice Theravada Buddhism **Flag (People's Republic):** Red, with a stylized yellow five-towered temple in the middle **Flag (Democratic Kampuchea):** Red, with a stylized yellow three-towered temple in the middle **Currency:** Riel

Location: Southeast Asia. Cambodia is bounded by Thailand and Laos on the north, by Vietnam on the southeast, by the Gulf of Thailand on the southwest, and by Thailand on the west **Features:** The country largely consists of a saucer-shaped alluvial plain drained by the Mekong River and shut off by mountains **Chief Rivers:** Mekong, Stung Sen

Head of State (People's Republic): President Heng Samrin, born 1934, is head of the People's Revolutionary Council **Head of State (Democratic Kampuchea):** Khieu Samphan is Chairman of the State Presidium **Effective Date of Present Constitution:** None **Local Government:** 19 provinces

Ethnic Composition: Cambodians, or Khmer, make up about 87% of the population; Chinese 5%, and Chams (Moslems descended from the people of the ancient kingdom of Champa) make up the rest **Density:** 74 inhabitants per sq. mi.

Largest Cities: Phnom Penh 600,000 (1970 est.); reported to be c. 300,000 in 1980; (1972 est.) Battambang 80,000, Kompong Cham 50,000, Pursat 20,000

Per Capita Income: $114 (1979) **Gross National Product (GNP):** $660 million (1979) **Economic Statistics:** In normal times overwhelmingly agricultural (rice, rubber, beans, corn), with a little industry (textiles, cement, rubber products) **Minerals and Mining:** Phosphates, gemstones and gold were produced, and there are known quantities of unexploited iron ore, manganese, and phosphates **Foreign Trade:** Rubber and dried fish are known exports, and oil and machinery are imported **Principal Trade Partners:** Vietnam, Laos, Soviet Bloc

Transportation: Roads totaled 3,225 mi. in 1970 **Railway Mileage:** 400 (1970) **Port:** Kompong Som **Communications:** Government owned

Weights and Measures: Metric system **Travel Requirements:** No U.S. relations exist, and tourists are not accepted at present

---

During 22 years of existence as an independent nation, caught in the middle of the East-West political and military struggle in Southeast Asia, Cambodia managed to walk the tightrope of neutrality. Its success was credited to the diplomatic skill of Prince Norodom Sihanouk, who started as a youthful king under the French, abdicated to fill a more active political role as premier, and then became the country's first chief of state.

Sihanouk managed to maintain Cambodia's neutrality even as the Vietnam War intruded increasingly on—and over—the eastern border. Then, in March 1970, while he was out of the country, his government was overthrown in a coup led by Lt. Gen. Lon Nol.

Within a month, Cambodia's small and ill-equipped army was fighting the Vietnamese Communists and Prince Sihanouk was forming a government in exile based in Peking. The war went badly for the Cambodians, who appealed to the world for help against the enemy's sudden consolidation of its enclaves in the east. Late in April there was a response: South Vietnamese and

American troops drove across the border to smash the sanctuaries. Many Vietnamese Communists moved west and assumed control of large sections of the country, including the temples at Angkor. Phnom Penh itself was often isolated from the only seaport.

In mid-1973, the United States was hoping to nudge Cambodia's exiled Prince Sihanouk and Khmer insurgent leaders into serious peace talks with members of General Lon Nol's regime. The diplomatic pressure was being brought to bear against a backdrop of urgency caused by the steady advance of Communist troops toward Phnom Penh and the imminent end of U.S. bombing raids in the country. It was at this time that the Pentagon admitted having secretly bombed Communist forces in Cambodia as early as 1969 and supplying false statistics to the U.S. Senate.

The war, with U.S. help, continued through 1974 and into 1975, with Khmer Rouge forces moving ever closer to the capital city of Phnom Penh. The end came swiftly in April 1975, with the departure of President Lon Nol and the evacuation of U.S. civilians and embassy personnel. According to Cambodian estimates, nearly 800,000 people had been killed in the war and 200,000 wounded.

In the first months after the war, refugees who escaped to Thailand reported that hundreds of thousands of people had been forcibly moved from the cities to rural areas. Almost the entire population of Phnom Penh—a city swollen by 2 million refugees—was evacuated and put to work in the rice fields. Refugees spoke of long forced marches, starvation and wholesale killings by the Khmer Rouge.

In January 1976 a new constitution went into effect and the state took a new name: Democratic Kampuchea. Elections were held on March 20 and a People's Representative Assembly of 250 was selected. Prince Sihanouk, who had returned to Phnom Penh in late 1975, announced his resignation as Head of State on April 5 and Khieu Samphan became President of the State Presidium. In September 1977, Pol Pot ended his country's virtual isolation by making a trip to Peking, where he was identified as the Secretary of the Central Committee of the Cambodian Communist Party, Prime Minister and the prime force in making sweeping changes.

Under Pol Pot—he had been Saloth Sar, a schoolteacher, according to Prince Sihanouk—the country's economy and manpower were reshaped drastically. All lands and means of production belonged to the state. Private plots, permitted even in China and the USSR, were forbidden. Wages were paid as food rations, but they were meager, and no money was circulated. The foremost economic activity was the rebuilding of irrigation canals and dikes that had been destroyed in the civil war.

The outside world was ignored, except for China, which sent technical advisers and delivered supplies through Kompong Som, Cambodia's only port. Reports carried to neighboring countries said that the harsh treatment had produced a high death toll—possibly somewhere between 500,000 and 2 million. U.S. President Carter accused Cambodia of being the world's worst violator of human rights.

Enemies for centuries, Cambodia and Vietnam fought frequent border clashes in 1977 and 1978. In December 1978, Vietnamese troops moved steadily across Cambodia with, Hanoi said, the aid of Cambodian insurgents. On Jan. 9, 1979, Phnom Penh fell, and Pol Pot's government was replaced with the Hanoi-backed People's Revolutionary Council of Cambodia. A Cambodian, Heng Samrin took over as president, and he declared that "during the last three years, they [the Khmer Rouge under Pol Pot] killed millions." Entire villages and communes had been slaughtered, he said. On Feb. 18,

he signed a treaty of peace and friendship with Vietnam.

Despite the change in governments, the fighting continued. Khmer Rouge loyalists fled into the jungles or mixed with the population, and Pol Pot reportedly was with them. The Khmer Rouge recaptured the port of Kompong Som in January for their first major victory. Soon they were cutting roads and thus denying supplies to Vietnam troops, but they pursued a policy of avoiding big-scale confrontations. Estimates were that Vietnam had 100,000 soldiers in Cambodia, and they were joined by 1,000 Laotians, whose homeland was being used as a staging ground for incursions. Prince Sihanouk, in Geneva, estimated that the Pol Pot forces had 40,000 to 50,000 men and said they were getting aid through Thailand. In July the pro-Vietnam government of Heng Samrin reported that total victory had been achieved over the Pol Pot forces, but the fighting continued on into 1980.

Fearing that 2.25 million Cambodians may starve because crops had not been planted or were destroyed in the fighting, UNICEF and the International Red Cross took charge of receiving food from 51 nations. Massive tie-ups in port and in warehouses occurred in early 1980. The U.S. Ambassador to Thailand, Morton I. Abramowitz, said in April that "the occupiers of Cambodia and their allies have so far not permitted this effort to go forward in the manner and on the scale necessary." Estimates were that, from 1975 through 1979, possibly as many as 4 million Cambodians died.

HISTORY: Modern Cambodia is what remains of the great Khmer Empire, which by the 1200s stretched across Southeast Asia from the South China Sea westward into Burma. By the 1800s the Khmer holdings had been steadily reduced to the present size of Cambodia by the invasions of the Vietnamese and Siamese

1863: French protectorate is established over Cambodia

1887: Cambodia is incorporated in the Union of Indo-China

1945: Japanese invade Cambodia, driving out the Vichy French

1946: French return and grant Cambodia autonomy within the French Union

1953-54: Cambodia achieves full independence; leaves French Union

1970: Prince Sihanouk is ousted in pro-Western coup; U.S. and South Vietnamese troops enter Cambodia in drive against North Vietnamese forces; Cambodians and South Vietnamese continue fighting after withdrawal of U.S. ground troops. Cambodia is declared a republic

1971: United States expands bombing strikes and troop-ferrying missions; South Vietnamese driven from Cambodia

1973: Pentagon admits it conducted 14 months (1969/70) of secret bombings in Cambodia. Bombing halted Aug. 15

1974: Government troops and insurgents continue military operations. Long Boret forms 15-member wartime cabinet to replace the coalition government, which resigned June 13. The U.S. airlifts supplies

1975: U.S. triples its airlift to overcome effect of insurgents' blockade of roads into Phnom Penh and of Mekong River. April 1: Lon Nol leaves country. Government resistance begins to crumble. April 12: U.S. closes Phnom Penh embassy and evacuates staff. April 16: Government surrenders and insurgents enter Phnom Penh. War ends. May 14: U.S. air, sea and ground forces battle Cambodians after seizure of the American merchant ship *Mayaguez* in the Gulf of Siam. The ship and crew of 39 were freed. American casualties in the rescue operations were 15 killed, 3 missing and 50 wounded

1976: New constitution adopted in December goes into effect. Elections held on March 20. April 5: Prince Sihanouk resigns as Head of State

1977: Pol Pot identified as nation's leader

1978: Border clashes with Vietnam and Thailand intensify

1979: Phnom Penh falls, Pol Pot's government ("Democratic Kampuchea") retreats to the countryside, and the Vietnam-backed People's Revolutionary Council takes over, with Heng Samrin as presidentof the "People's Republic of Kampuchea"

1980: UNICEF and the Red Cross direct a famine-relief effort, but distribution of food apparently is slowed by government inertia. In the "Democratic Kampuchea" government, Khieu Samphan replaces Pol Pot as head of state

CAMEROON

Area: 183,568 sq. mi. **Population:** 8,058,000 (1978 est.)

Official Name: United Republic of Cameroon **Capital:** Yaoundé **Nationality:** Cameroonian **Languages:** French (spoken by 75%) and English (25%) are both official languages; 24 African languages are spoken **Religion:** 33% Christian (mainly in the south); 15% Moslem (mainly in the north); the rest are animists **Flag:** Vertical green, red, and yellow stripes, with a yellow star in the center of the red stripe **Anthem:** O, Cameroon, Cradle of Our Ancestors **Currency:** CFA Franc (210.2 per U.S. $1)

Location: West-central Africa. Cameroon is bordered by Lake Chad on the north, by Chad and the Central African Republic on the east, by the Congo, Gabon, and Equatorial Guinea on the south, by the Gulf of Guinea on the west, and by Nigeria on the west and northwest **Features:** Of the country's four distinct regions, the south consists of a low coastal plain with equatorial rain forests, the center forms a transitional plateau, the west is an area of mountainous forests, and the north is low rolling savanna **Chief Rivers:** Sanaga, Nyong

Head of State and of Government: President Ahmadou Ahidjo, born 1924, reelected to fifth 5-year term in April 1980, assisted by a cabinet headed by the premier, Paul Biya **Effective Date of Present Constitution:** May 1972 **Legislative Body:** National Assembly (unicameral), consisting of 120 members elected by universal suffrage for 5 years **Local Goverment:** 7 provinces with appointed governors

Ethnic Composition: Estimates of the number of tribal groups run as high as 200. The main divisions are the Bantus and semi-Bantus, which include the Beti and Bamiléké; the Sudanese, mainly Kirdis; and the Arab Foulbé. Pygmies inhabit the equatorial forest **Population Distribution:** 25% urban **Density:** 44 inhabitants per sq. mi.

Largest Cities: (1975 estimates) Douala 435,000, Yaoundé 274,000, N'Kongsamba 67,000

Per Capita Income: $439 (1979) **Gross National Product (GNP):** $3.6 billion (1979) **Economic Statistics:** 33% of GNP came from agriculture (coffee, cocoa, bananas, cotton, peanuts, livestock, rubber, palm oil) and 24% from industry (aluminum, paper, chemicals) **Minerals and Mining:** Large deposits of bauxite ore, iron ore, and limestone; traces of mica and phosphates; small deposits of tin and gold. Petroleum and natural gas exploitation has begun **Labor Force:** Over 3 million; 75% in agriculture **Foreign Trade:** Exports, chiefly coffee, cocoa beans, aluminum, wood, cotton, and rubber, totaled $888 million in 1978. Imports, mainly vehicles and transportation equipment, industrial machinery and other capital goods, consumer goods, food, beverages, and tobacco, totaled $1 billion **Principal Trade Partners:** EC countries (mainly France), United States, Japan, Chad, adjacent African nations

Vital Statistics: Birthrate, 40.4 per 1,000 of pop. (1975); death rate, 22 **Life Expectancy:** 41 years **Health Statistics:** 390 inhabitants per hospital bed; 15,820 per physician (1976) **Infant Mortality:** 137 per 1,000 births **Illiteracy:** 82% **Primary and Secondary School Enrollment:** 1,375,548 (1977) **Enrollment in Higher Education:** 7,191 (1975) **GNP Expended on Education:** 4.6% (1976)

Transportation: Paved roads total about 1,338 miles **Motor Vehicles:** 110,700 (1976) **Passenger cars:** 59,500 **Railway Mileage:** 727 **Ports:** Douala, Tiko, Victoria, Kribi **Major Airlines:** Air Cameroun and Cameroons Air Transport operate internal services; Air Afrique operates international services **Communications:** Government owned **Radio Transmitters:** 4 **Receivers:** 603,000 (1974) **Television:** None **Telephones:** 22,000 (1973) **Newspapers:** 2 dailies, 4 copies per 1,000 inhabitants (1975)

Weights and Measures: Metric system **Travel Requirements:** Passport, visa required beyond 1 month stay, valid up to 3 months, $5 fee, 2 pictures

Cameroon has been one of the main racial crossroads of Africa as a result of Bantu migrations from the east and links to the Sahara caravan trade to the north. Extending nearly 800 miles in length from the Gulf of Guinea to Lake Chad, the country is a cross section of Africa from desert north through central plateau and grasslands to southern rain forest.

Formerly a German colony, Cameroon was divided between France and Britain after World War I, with the French getting about four-fifths of the area. The country was reunited as a federal republic in 1961, after a UN plebiscite had resulted in the addition of the northern part of former British Cameroons to Nigeria.

The two areas, West Cameroon (formerly British) and the larger East Cameroon (formerly French) were governed as constituent states, each with its own legislature. The new constitution which went into effect in May 1972 calls for a unitary state with a strong executive authority and an elected national assembly.

Cameroon is the only African country in which both French and English are official languages. The Federal University of Cameroon, established in Yaoundé in 1962, is the first in Africa to teach courses in French and English, as well as one of the first to establish a medical school.

Cameroon has been one of Africa's "quiet" countries, in which the single-party government of President Ahmadou Ahidjo has maintained a measure of political and economic stability.

Before Cameroon became an independent republic in 1960, the former French eastern area was torn by a terrorist revolt. Protracted rebel activities in the central part of the country were suppressed in 1970. Despite the diversity of its peoples, cultures, and religions, however, Cameroon has escaped the coups and civil wars that have plagued neighboring countries.

Cameroon's great diversity of tropical produce—timber, cocoa, coffee, rubber, palm oil, cotton, and a wide range of food crops—has been the basis for an economic growth that has been averaging nine percent a year. Although France remains the country's chief partner in trade and investment, British, American, West German, and Japanese interests have been attracted by the favorable economic and investment climate. Petroleum production began in 1978.

Education and health services also are increasing and Cameroonians take pride in the fact that 70 percent of the country's children attend school, a high rate for developing Africa.

HISTORY: The country was given its name by 15th century Portuguese explorers. Impressed with the number of shrimp in one of the rivers, they called it Rio dos Camarões (River of Shrimp) and extended the name to the entire region. After being made a German colony in the late 19th century, the country was occupied during World War I by the French and British, who divided it under League of Nations mandates

1946: French and British mandates are converted into United Nations Trusteeships

1959: UN General Assembly votes end of French trusteeship

1960: On Jan. 1, French Cameroon becomes independent Cameroon Republic; draft constitution is approved by referendum; National Assembly names Premier Ahmadou Ahidjo president

1961: In UN-supervised plebiscites, southern part of British Cameroons votes for reunification with Cameroon Republic, northern part for union with Nigeria; federation of East and West Cameroon is established

1966: After unification of major political parties in East and West Cameroon, all opposition parties are dissolved or join in single new party, the Cameroon National Union

1970: President Ahidjo is reelected for third successive term

1971: Political trials and executions end 10-year guerrilla insurrection

1972: Cameroon Labor Minister Ekangaki is elected Secy.-Gen. of the Organization of African Unity

1975: Paul Biya is named as Cameroon's first premier

1979: Deposits of good quality light crude oil and natural gas are discovered 50 to 75 miles offshore

1980: President Ahidjo is reelected to his fifth five-year term

CANADA
(See separate Canada section)

CAPE VERDE

Area: 1,557 sq. mi. **Population:** 314,000 (1978 est.)

Official Name: Republic of Cape Verde **Capital:** Praia **Nationality:** Cape Verdean **Languages:** Officially Portuguese, with most speaking a dialect, Crioulo **Religion:** 65% Roman Catholic, and 30% animist **Flag:** Two horizontal stripes, yellow over green, with a red vertical stripe at the hoist, the latter having an emblem of a black star over a yellow seashell, framed by two cornstalks **Anthem:** This Is Our Beloved Country **Currency:** Cape Verdean escudo (38.3 per U.S. $1)

Location: In the Atlantic Ocean, 390 miles west of Dakar, Senegal, off the coast of Africa, centering on 16°N. and 24°W. Ten islands and 5 islets comprise the nation **Features:** Summer climate is extremely hot and there is a lack of potable water. Three of the main islands are flat; the other seven are mountainous, volcanic in origin **Chief Rivers:** No large rivers

Head of State: President Aristides Pereira, named 1975 **Head of Government:** Premier Pedro Pires, appointed 1975 **Effective Date of Constitution:** Not yet formulated **Legislative Body:** National Assembly (unicameral), with 56 members. The only political party permitted to operate in the Republic is the PAIGC **Local Government:** 24 Electoral Districts

Ethnic Composition: 70% are Creoles (mulattoes) of mixed African and Portuguese descent, 28% are Africans, and 2% Europeans **Population Distribution:** 19.7% urban **Density:** 202 inhabitants per sq. mi.

Largest Cities: (1970 census) Mindelo 28,797, Praia 21,494, Espargos 3,978

Per Capita Income: $180 (1978) **Gross National Product (GNP):** $57 million (1978 est.) **Economic Statistics:** The main economic function of the country is ship and aircraft refueling. The soil is poor and dry, and although some food (corn, beans, coffee, sugar) is grown, much must be imported. Fishing is important **Minerals and Mining:** Salt, pozzolana (used in making cements) **Labor Force:** 84,869 in 1970, with 67% in agriculture, and 5% in industry **Foreign Trade:** Exports, chiefly fish products, bananas, salt, coffee, pozzolana, totaled $2.3 million in 1978. Imports, chiefly corn, wheat, cement, petroleum products, totaled $25.4 million **Principal Trade Partners:** Portugal, EC, Angola, United States

Vital Statistics: Birthrate, 27.6 per 1,000 of pop. (1975); death rate, 9.4 **Life Expectancy:** 45 years **Health Statistics:** 516 per hospital bed; 7,750 per physician (1977) **Infant Mortality:** 104.9 per 1,000 births (1975) **Illiteracy:** 86% **Primary and Secondary School Enrollment:** 71,790 (1972) **Enrollment in Higher Education:** N.A. **GNP Expended on Education:** 1.5% (1972)

Transportation: Paved roads total 380 mi. **Motor Vehicles:** 4,000 (1977) **Passenger Cars:** 3,100 **Railway Mileage:** None **Ports:** Mindelo, Praia **Major Airlines:** T.A.P. provides international service, and Cape Verde Air Transport domestic service **Communications:** Government owned **Radio Transmitters:** 4 **Receivers:** 36,000 (1976) **Television:** None **Telephones:** 2,000 (1976) **Newspapers:** Three, several times a week

Weights and Measures: Metric system **Travel Requirements:** Passport, visa

---

Cape Verde became independent on July 5, 1975, ending 515 years of Portuguese rule. In 1460 the Portuguese navigators Diego Gomes and Antonio da Noli discovered Maio and São Tiago Islands, and in 1462 the first settlers landed on São Tiago.

Cape Verde, one of five territories relinquished by Portugal (the others being Guinea-Bissau, Mozambique, São Tomé and Príncipe, and Angola), has strong ties with Guinea-Bissau. Aristedes Pereira and Pedro Pires, heroes of the guerrilla war waged against Portugal in Guinea-Bissau, were named president and premier, respectively in 1975.

The islands have been afflicted with disastrous drought and famine in recent years. Since the mid-1900s, an estimated 300,000 Cape Verdeans have emigrated because of the difficulty in earning a living. Workers' remittances sent home from abroad are estimated at $8 million annually.

HISTORY: The islands were discovered in 1460 by Portuguese navigators in the service of Prince Henry the Navigator. Settlement began two years later. The archipelago was a center for the slave trade with the West African coast

1975: On June 30, the Party for the Independence of Guinea-Bissau and Cape Verde (PAIGC) is the only political group to run candidates for the 56-member Assembly at the first general election. The Assembly is to write a constitution and decide whether Cape Verde should form a nation with Guinea-Bissau. Officials of the U.S. Agency for International Development sign a $5-million assistance agreement with Cape Verde's new government. Admitted to the UN

1976: Cape Verde and USSR sign pact granting reciprocal use of each other's ports

1979: Unrest in ruling party leads three cabinet ministers to resign

---

CENTRAL AFRICAN REPUBLIC

Area: 236,293 sq. mi. **Population:** 2,370,000 (1978 est.)

Official Name: Central African Republic **Capital:** Bangui **Nationality:** Central African **Languages:** French is the official language; Sangho is the national language **Religion:** 40% Protestant, 28% Roman Catholic, 24% animist, 8% Moslem **Flag:** Horizontal bars of blue, white, green, and yellow, bisected by a vertical red bar. A yellow star appears on the blue band at the upper left **Anthem:** La Renaissance **Currency:** CFA Franc (210.2 per U.S. $1)

Location: At almost the exact center of the African continent. The landlocked country is bordered by Chad on the north, Sudan on the east, Zaire and Congo on the south, and Cameroon on the west **Features:** The country is a huge, well-watered plateau drained by 2 major river systems **Chief Rivers:** Ouham, Ubangi, Kotto, Lobaye, Sangha

Head of State and of Government: President David Dacko, born 1930, assumed office following the coup of September 1979. He is assisted by a premier, Bernard Christian Ayandho **Effective Date of Present Constitution:** None, at present **Legislative Body:** None, at present **Local Government:** 14 prefectures

Ethnic Composition: Of some 80 different ethnic groups, the main ones (66%) are the Banda in the east-central area; the Baya and the Mandjia in the west and in the west-central area; 7% are M'baka **Population Distribution:** 20% urban **Density:** 10 inhabitants per sq. mi.

Largest Cities: (1974 est.) Bangui 301,000, Bouar 48,000, Bangassou 46,000, Bambari 35,000

Per Capita Income: $194 (1978 est.) **Gross National Product:** $370 million (1978 est.) **Economic Statistics:** Agriculture (cotton, coffee, rice, tobacco, rubber, peanuts, palm oil) and livestock (cattle, sheep, goats, pigs, poultry) make up 34% of the GNP; diamond and uranium mining, and small-scale manufacturing (textiles, beer, shoes, bicycles and motor bikes, plastics) 16%; and trade and services 29% **Minerals and Mining:** Diamonds, uranium and gold are exploited. Deposits of iron ore, zinc, copper, and tin exist **Labor Force:** 80% of the population is engaged in farming **Foreign Trade:** Exports, chiefly diamonds, wood, cotton, and coffee, totaled $79 million in 1978. Imports, mainly machinery and equipment, textiles, and petroleum products, totaled $71 million **Principal Trade Partners:** France, other EC countries, United States, Japan, Cameroon, Congo

Vital Statistics: Birthrate, 43.4 per 1,000 of pop. (1975); death rate, 22.5 **Life Expectancy:** 40 years **Health Statistics:** 522 inhabitants per hospital bed; 20,833 per physician (1975) **Infant Mortality:** 190 per 1,000 births **Illiteracy:** 93% **Primary and Secondary School Enrollment:** 245,307 (1975) **Enrollment in Higher Education:** 555 **GNP Expended on Education:** 3.9% (1973)

Transportation: Paved roads total 116 mi. **Motor Vehicles:** 13,000 (1974) **Passenger Cars:** 9,100 **Railway Mileage:** None **Ports:** None **Major Airlines:** Air Banguie and Air Centrafrique operate domestic services; Air Afrique, Aeroflot, and UTA operate international services **Communications:** Government owned **Radio Transmitters:** 6 (1972) **Receivers:** 75,000 (1976) **Television Transmitters:** 1 **Telephones:** 5,000 (1973) **Newspapers:** One, several times a week

Weights and Measures: Metric system **Travel Requirements:** Passport, visa

---

Isolation in the heart of Africa constitutes the main problem of the Central African Republic *(the Central African Empire* from 1976 until 1979), a problem that is compounded by a paucity of resources and a small population.

Most of the former French colony of Ubangi-Shari is a plateau of 2,000-foot elevation, a condition that makes for a relatively temperate climate during the dry season. Stretches of grassy savanna and woodland, in which there is an abundance of wildlife, give the land a magnificent beauty.

With modern techniques, cotton production has increased more than three times to 60,000 metric tons a year and provides a major export. Diamond production and small quantities of coffee and peanuts have also added to exports and income.

While the diamonds may be shipped by air, the

other products must be transported at considerable cost by road or river to the nearest ports. Aid from France, the World Bank, and other sources has helped improve roads and create small industry, but clearly a rail link is needed for further crop expansion and development of timber resources.

The recent exploitation of uranium at Bakouma, 540 miles east of Bangui, has brightened economic prospects and, with new exploration indicating deposits of iron ore, manganese, and copper, has heightened the need for a railroad.

On becoming fully independent Aug. 13, 1960, the Central African Republic adopted a parliamentary form of government. David Dacko became president. His cousin, Col. Jean-Bédel Bokassa, a former French army sergeant, led a military coup in 1966 which dissolved the national assembly and established Bokassa as head of the ruling revolutionary council. Ten years later, he proclaimed himself emperor and was crowned in a $22-million ceremony in December 1977. He ruled by imperial decree and sometimes with brutal discipline.

One government decree, that students wear state uniforms, prompted protest demonstrations in the capital in January 1979, resulting in 12 deaths. Amnesty International reported the killing of more than 100 schoolchildren following their arrest for further rioting in April. A later report by judges from five African nations stated that Emperor Bokassa was present at the prison during the massacre of the 8 to 16-year-old children.

Emperor Bokassa was overthrown with French assistance on Sept. 20, 1979, in a bloodless coup led by David Dacko who resumed the presidency he had held from 1960 to 1965. Bokassa sought asylum in France, claiming citizenship, but was refused entry. He then settled in Ivory Coast.

HISTORY: For centuries, what is now the Central African Republic was a crossroads for numerous migrations by various groups, mainly of Bantu origin. In the 19th century, French expeditions penetrated the country, which was named Ubangi-Shari after its two main rivers. Early in the 20th century, the country was joined with Chad and became one of the territories of French Equatorial Africa

1946: French constitutional reform confers French citizenship on people of Ubangi-Shari

1958: In a referendum, Ubangi-Shari votes to become an autonomous republic within the French Community. The Central African Republic is proclaimed, with Barthélémy Boganda as president

1959: Boganda, founder of the republic and its mass political party, Social Evolution Movement of Black Africa, is killed in plane crash and succeeded by his cousin, David Dacko

1960-65: Republic becomes a fully independent nation under President Dacko, who dissolves all political parties. He is reelected in an election in which he is the only candidate

1966: Colonel Jean-Bedel Bokassa, chief of staff of the armed forces, overthrows Dacko government, ousts Communist Chinese mission, and establishes rule by revolutionary council

1969: Central African Republic suspends relations with Congo (later Zaire) after latter's accusation that Bokassa regime had murdered a number of Congolese

1970: C.A.R. resumes relations with Zaire and Chad

1972: Congress of the sole political party appoints Bokassa president for life

1974: Bokassa promotes himself to Marshal of the Republic. French consulate ordered closed; French journals prohibited

1975: Bokassa names Elizabeth Domitien as Africa's first woman premier

1976: Bokassa escapes assassination attempt in February. He dismisses Domitien and declares his country a parliamentary monarchy with himself as emperor

1979: Following disclosure that Bokassa was responsible for mass killings of schoolchildren, David Dacko leads a coup that unseats the emperor and forces him into exile

CHAD

Area: 495,752 sq. mi. **Population:** 4,309,000 (1978 est.)
Official Name: Republic of Chad **Capital:** N'Djamena **Nationality:** Chadian **Languages:** French is the official language. An Arabic dialect is spoken in northern and central Chad; in the south the main tribal languages are Sara, Massa, and Moudang **Religion:** More than 50% of the population is Moslem, 40% animist, and 5% Christian **Flag:** Vertical stripes of blue, yellow, and red **Anthem:** La Tchadienne, beginning "Chadians, Stand up and Set to Work!" **Currency:** CFA Franc (210.2 per U.S. $1)

Location: North-Central Africa. Landlocked Chad is bordered by Libya on the north, Sudan on the east, the Central African Republic on the south, and by Niger, Nigeria, and Cameroon on the west **Features:** The country is shaped like a shallow basin, rimmed by mountain ranges on the north and east. The northern part of the country is desert, the central part a savanna, and the south tropical, with wooded savanna. Lake Chad on the western border is believed to be the remnant of an inland sea **Chief Rivers:** Shari, Logone

Head of State and of Government: President Goukouni Oueddei, born 1944, assumed power in 1979 **Effective Date of Present Constitution:** 1962; suspended 1975 **Legislative Body:** None **Local Government:** 14 prefectures, under appointed governors

Ethnic Composition: The population is about evenly divided between the northern and eastern people, of predominantly Sudanic origin, and the Nilotic southerners. There are some 5,000 Europeans, mainly French **Population Distribution:** 13.9% urban **Density:** 9 inhabitants per sq. mi.

Largest Cities: (1972 est.) N'Djamena 179,000, Sarh 43,700, Moundou 39,600, Abécher 28,100

Per Capita Income: $86 (1978 est.) **Gross National Product (GNP):** $370 million (1978 est.) **Economic Statistics:** In 1973 about 50% of GNP came from agriculture (cotton, sorghum, rice, sugar, peanuts, gum arabic, livestock) and fishing, 8% from industry and mining, and 23% from trade and services **Minerals and Mining:** Natron, a low-grade salt, is the only exploited mineral. Traces of shale oil, uranium, kaolin, and tungsten have been found in the north. Petroleum has been discovered **Labor Force:** 1.3 million (1970), with about 88% in agriculture **Foreign Trade:** Exports, chiefly cotton and cattle, totaled $102 million in 1978. Imports, mainly mineral products (including petroleum products), foodstuffs and beverages, electrical machinery and parts, textiles, and transportation equipment, totaled $192 million **Principal Trade Partners:** Nigeria, France, Japan, Britain

Vital Statistics: Birthrate, 44 per 1,000 of pop.; death rate, 24 **Life Expectancy:** 43 years **Health Statistics:** 1,140 inhabitants per hospital bed; 44,382 per physician (1974) **Infant Mortality:** 160 per 1,000 births **Illiteracy:** 95% **Primary and Secondary School Enrollment:** 230,462 (1976) **Enrollment in Higher Education:** 547 (1975) **GNP Expended on Education:** 2.4% (1976)

Transportation: Paved roads total 150 mi. **Motor Vehicles:** 12,100 (1973) **Passenger Cars:** 5,800 **Railway Mileage:** None **Ports:** None **Major Airlines:** Air Chad is the domestic carrier; Air Afrique, Air Cameroun, UTA, and Sudan Airways operate services to Chad **Communications:** Government owned **Radio Transmitters:** 6 **Receivers:** 76,000 (1976) **Television Transmitters:** 1 **Telephones:** 5,000 (1975) **Newspapers:** 4 dailies, 0.4 copies per 1,000 inhabitants (1975)

Weights and Measures: Metric system **Travel Requirements:** (1971) Passport, visa, $6.25; 3 photos, round-trip ticket

The remote outpost of former French Equatorial Africa, landlocked Chad suffers from isolation, internal strife, and a loss of arable land.

With its productive area more than 1,000 miles from any seaport, Chad is difficult to reach except by air. There is no railroad and a good part of the network of dirt roads and tracks is impassable during the rainy season.

Since 1968 Arab guerrillas in the northern and eastern part of the country have waged a rebellion against the Bantu-dominated government. Some 3,500 French troops were sent to help the Chadian government quell the revolt, an action that has raised controversy both in France and in Africa. French forces actively fighting the rebels were withdrawn in 1971.

The chief cause of the nomadic northerners' enmity toward the Chadian government was the fact that it had been dominated by southerners—Negroid river peoples whom the Arabs traditionally scorned as slaves. In addition, the northerners, mainly the Toubous, resented the government's tax on their cattle.

The regime of François Tombalbaye, which had been in power since 1962, was toppled by a military coup in 1975. General Félix Malloum, the new

Bantu ruler, became the object of a coup attempt hemself in February 1979 when the Moslem premier, Hissene Habré, tried to oust him. Hundreds were killed in streetfighting in the capital. At a conference arranged by Nigeria in Kano, agreement was reached on a cease-fire. A provisional government was set up and Nigerian troops were sent to N'Djamena to maintain order as armies of the contending factions were being withdrawn. Malloum's forces withdrew, but guerrilla forces remained and looted the city.

As fighting continued, Malloum fled in March to Nigeria. For months control passed from one provisional government to another. On Nov. 10 a transitional government of national unity was formed with Goukouni Oueddei as president and Habré as defense minister. The power struggle between these rival Moslem leaders was quieted for only a few months, however. On March 22, 1980, guerrilla forces loyal to the president and the minister fought each other in the streets of N'Djamena, using tanks, artillery and rockets. the number of persons killed, both military and civilian, ran into the hundreds. About 400 Europeans, Americans and others were evacuated by French aircraft. Small French and Congolese peacekeeping forces stood aside. The French withdrew in May.

In addition to the ravages of political strife the economy of Chad was damaged by six years of severe drought from 1967. Thousands of persons died, cattle perished and valuable grazing land became sandy desert.

The main export crop, cotton, has declined recently. Because of the high cost of transportation, Chad's exports of cotton require a high subsidy by France, which also provides about half of Chad's national budget. Chad developed little during colonialism and seems to rely more on France, economically, since independence.

HISTORY: Chad is believed to have been a center of ancient cultures before the southward encroachment of the Sahara. The varied ethnic make-up of present-day Chadians is evidence also of a succession of migrations and invasions in past centuries by Bantu southerners, Sudanese Moslems, and Nilotic peoples. Throughout the ages, Chad was the domain of conquerors and warrior slave traders, some of whom held sway until the late 19th century. Among the last of these was Rabah Amoney, a Sudanese ex-slave turned slave merchant and chieftain, whose conquest of the Bornu Kingdom was to lead to French intervention

1897-1900: Traditional rulers, threatened by Rabah's army, seek protection of French, whose forces march across the Sahara from Algeria, defeat Sudanese, and impose own rule

1910: Chad is made one of the four territories of French Equatorial Africa, along with Gabon, the present Congo (Brazzaville), and Ubangi-Shari (now the Central African Empire)

1940: Chad becomes first territory to rally to Free French

1959-60: Chad becomes autonomous member of French Community. On Aug. 11, 1960, complete independence and the Republic of Chad are proclaimed

1962: All opposition parties are banned under new constitution and single-party rule is set up by Chadian Progressive party, led by President François Tombalbaye

1963: State of emergency is declared after abortive coup d'état and arrest of Moslem leaders; constitutional amendments are adopted and new elections are held in an effort to heal the rift between Moslem north and Bantu south

1969: Moslem guerrillas step up attacks on government installations as Arab-Bantu split widens; President Tombalbaye calls in French troops to help quell growing revolt

1973: UN reports Chad is most severly affected of the sub-Saharan countries suffering from drought

1975: President Tombalbaye assassinated (April 13). Military junta headed by Gen. Félix Malloum takes control

1977: Attempted coup against Malloum fails

1979-1980: Malloum is ousted in coup and rival factions battle for control of country; one provisional government follows another in rapid succession; hundreds of persons are killed in streetfighting in the capital in March 1980

CHILE

Area: 292,256 sq. mi. **Population:** 10,917,000 (1979 est.)

Official Name: Republic of Chile **Capital:** Santiago **Nationality:** Chilean **Languages:** The official and virtually universal language is Spanish **Religion:** 90% Roman Catholic **Flag:** A white horizontal stripe over a longer red stripe, with a blue square in the upper left corner containing a 5-pointed white star **Anthem:** National Anthem; refrain "Sweet Country, receive the pledge" **Currency:** Chilean peso (39 per U.S. $1)

Location: Southwest coast of South America. Chile is bordered on the north by Peru, on the east by Argentina and Bolivia, on the south by Drake Passage, and on the west by the Pacific Ocean **Features:** The country stretches some 2,650 miles along the Pacific coast and is at no point wider than 250 miles. The north is desert, the central region agricultural, and the south is forest land. The towering Andes dominate most of the eastern frontier **Chief Rivers:** Loa, Maule, Bio-Bio, Valdivia

Head of State and of Government: President: Maj. Gen. Augusto Pinochet Ugarte, born 1915, assumed power September 1973 as head of a 4-man military junta **Effective Date of Present Constitution:** 1980 **Legislative Body:** Congress (dissolved) **Local Government:** 12 regions, subdivided into 40 provinces, and the metropolitan region of Santiago

Ethnic Composition: About 68% of the population is of Spanish-Indian descent, 30% of European (mainly Spanish) descent, and less than 1% Indian **Population Distribution:** 79% urban **Density:** 37 inhabitants per sq. mi.

Largest Cities: (1976 est.) Santiago 3,361,000, Viña del Mar 250,670, Valparaíso 248,440, Talcahuano 197,287, Concepción 172,510, Antofagasta 159,980, Temuco 150,560

Per Capita Income: $1,848 (1979 est.) **Gross National Product (GNP):** $17.8 billion (1979 est.) **Economic Statistics:** In 1979, 50% of GNP was derived from trade and services; 21% from industry (paper and paper products, iron and steel, petrochemicals, chemicals, and metal products); 11% from mining; and 9% from agriculture (wheat, wine grapes, potatoes, sugar beets, tobacco, fruit), forestry and fishing **Minerals and Mining:** Chile is one of the world's leading copper producers; iron ore is second in importance; natural nitrates, iodine, molybdenum and coal are also exploited **Labor Force:** 3,500,000 (1978), with 28% in agriculture **Foreign Trade:** Exports, mainly copper and copper manufactures, iron ore, pulp and paper, fishmeal, wine, seafood, wool, and fruit, totaled $3.8 billion in 1979. Imports, mainly machinery and equipment, agricultural products, and transport equipment, totaled $4.2 billion **Principal Trade Partners:** United States, Latin American Free Trade Association, EC, Japan

Vital Statistics: Birthrate, 23.9 per 1,000 of pop. (1976); death rate, 7.8 **Life Expectancy:** 67 years **Health Statistics:** 277 inhabitants per hospital bed; 2,177 per physician (1976) **Infant Mortality:** 39.7 per 1,000 births (1978) **Illiteracy:** 8% **Primary and Secondary School Enrollment:** 2,729,375 (1977) **Enrollment in Higher Education:** 149,647 (1975) **GNP Expended on Education:** 3.7% (1975)

Transportation: Paved roads total 5,744 mi. (1978) **Motor Vehicles:** 479,100 (1977) **Passenger Cars:** 297,100 **Railway Mileage:** 5,511 **Ports:** Valparaíso, Arica, Antofagasta, Coquimbo, Iquique, Talcahuano **Major Airlines:** LAN-Chile, the government-owned airline, operates domestic and international services **Communications:** Government controlled **Radio Transmitters:** 229 (1971) **Receivers:** 3,100,000 (1974) **Television Transmitters:** 27 **Receivers:** 1,000,000 (1975) **Telephones:** 451,000 (1976) **Newspapers:** 47 dailies (1975); 94 copies per 1,000 inhabitants (1972)

Weights and Measures: Metric system **Travel Requirements:** Passport, no visa up to 3 months

---

Chile has long had an outstanding potential—immense natural resources and a relatively sophisticated population—but efforts to match living standards to promise have fallen short. Inflation, once chronic and at runaway rates—it rose 340 percent in 1975, for instance—has been brought down to a manageable 30-40 percent a year, but at the expense of large-scale unemployment and other social problems.

Nature is largely responsible for the economic and social status of Chile, a land dominated by the geological immaturity of the Andes, a mountain range that runs the entire length of the long and narrow country. Relatively "new" and earthquake-prone, the Andes yield the copper and other metals that account for more than half of Chile's foreign-exchange earnings.

Politically, Chile has also been a victim of abrupt

change and contrasts. The pride of South American democracies from 1932 until the 1970s, the country since 1973 has seen its military employ coercion at the expense of human rights to remove all vestiges of the Marxist experiment of Salvador Allende Gossens. Allende in 1970 became the first Marxist to be elected president in South America, but on September 11, 1973, one week after the third anniversary of Allende's election, a military junta staged the first successful coup against a civilian government in Chile since 1927. President Allende was reported to have committed suicide. A year later it was learned that the United States had funneled more than $8 million through the CIA to anti-Allende groups.

The current military regime, headed by Chile's president, Gen. Augusto Pinochet Ugarte, is facing world criticism for political repression, torture and news censorship. The regime continues to hold political prisoners, but, under pressure from the U.S. and other democratic nations, the number has been reduced. The junta's aim has been to entrench political power by dictatorial rule, and Pinochet has succeeded in establishing an "authoritarian democracy."

After the UN General Assembly reported that Chile was violating human rights, President Pinochet ordered a national referendum on Jan. 4, 1978, that upheld his government. "In the face of the international aggression against the government of the homeland," the referendum read in part, "I [the voter] support President Pinochet in his defense of the dignity of Chile." The "yes" vote was announced as 75 percent. Despite this ringing support, the government eased up by restoring some autonomy to civil judges and by limiting the president's punitive powers. Also, an amnesty program was set in motion, leading to pardons or voluntary exile for some prisoners.

In July 1978, the junta removed one of its members, Air Force Gen. Gustavo Leigh, who had advocated a swifter return to civilian rule. His replacement, Gen. Fernando Matthei, supports the retention of Pinochet as president through 1985.

On Feb. 14, 1979, the U.S. District Court in Washington, D.C., found three Cuban exiles guilty in the murder of Orlando Letelier, who had been Allende's ambassador to the United States. Letelier, Chile's most prominent political exile, was killed when a bomb blew up his car in Washington in 1976. An American, Michael V. Townley, said he made and planted the bomb on orders of DINA, the old Chilean secret police force. On May 14, Chile's chief justice refused to extradite three Chilean army officers to the United States for trial.

Chile has been receiving considerable foreign investment, notably in mining and banking, but also in diversified industries. Several U.S. companies—Anaconda, Exxon, Dow Chemical—were among the principal investors in 1979. Development of the wood-products industry is helping to alleviate dependence on a one-product (copper) industry.

HISTORY: Prior to the Spanish conquest of Chile in the 16th century, the northern portion of the country was under the rule of the Inca Empire and the south was mainly controlled by the Araucanian Indians, who were to prove fiercely hostile to the Spanish colonists until almost the end of the 19th century. During most of its colonial history, Chile was a captaincy general dependent on the viceroyalty of Peru

1817-18: Argentine revolutionist José de San Martín brings an army over the Andes from Argentina to Chile and, in 1818, defeats Spanish army at Battle of Maipú. Bernardo O'Higgins, who had been chosen supreme director, formally proclaims Chile's independence (Feb. 12)

1879-83: Chile defeats Peru and Bolivia in the War of the Pacific, acquiring the mineral-bearing northern desert region

1891-1925: Internal struggle between executive and legislative branches culminates in overthrow of President José Balmaceda (1891); congressional dictatorship lasts until 1925

1932-38: President Arturo Alessandri, elected for second term, institutes a kind of state capitalism in efforts to wipe out aftermath of 1929 depression; however, he turns to repressive measures and alienates working class

1946-48: Economic dislocations lead to riots and strikes encouraged by aggressive Communist activity

1964-68: Eduardo Frei Montalva is elected president and his Christian Democratic Party wins control of Chamber of Deputies after defeating coalition of Marxist parties. Frei launches reform program

1969: National discontent becomes manifest in congressional elections, when Frei's party retains majority in lower house but loses more than a third of its former seats; right-wing National party scores heavy gains

1970: Salvador Allende Gossens becomes the first Marxist to be elected president of a Latin American country

1971: Government nationalizes all U.S. copper investments

1972: Chile furthers relations with Communist countries

1973: Allende coalition gains 14 Chamber and 3 Senate seats. On September 11, Allende government is overthrown by a military junta. Allende dies in coup. State of siege declared

1974: Military junta returns to private ownership 150 companies nationalized by left-wing Allende government. CIA bankrolling of anti-Allende groups is revealed

1975: Government accelerates expulsion of political prisoners and grants safe conduct to Chilean refugees in foreign embassies, allowing them to leave the country

1978: Referendum shows wide support for Pinochet; opposition charges fraud. Government declares amnesty for political prisoners and exiles and lifts state of siege. Border disputes with neighbors continue; Bolivia breaks diplomatic relations, alleging Chile has hindered negotiations to grant it a corridor to Pacific

1979: Minister of Labor issues decrees allowing employer lockouts and limited collective bargaining; unions are prevented from collecting dues from workers through company payrolls

1980: President Pinochet breaks diplomatic relations with the Philippines (Mar. 24) after Filipino president Ferdinand E. Marcos declines to meet Pinochet on his planned trip to Asia. Voters approve new Constitution and 8½-year term for Pinochet

---

CHINA (PEOPLE'S REPUBLIC)

Area: 3,691,000 sq. mi. **Population:** 953,578,000 (1979 est.)

Official Name: People's Republic of China **Capital:** Peking (Beijing) **Nationality:** Chinese **Languages:** Chinese, spoken with many regional phonetical differences but written with a uniform script, is the principal language. Mandarin, based on the Peking dialect, forms the basis of the new national language being promoted by the government; Shanghai, Cantonese, Fukienese, and Hakka dialects are spoken in the south. Among the national minorities, the Tibetans have their own highly distinctive language and script, while the Uigurs of Xinjiang (Sinkiang) speak a Turkic language **Religion:** Freedom of religion is guaranteed under the constitution. The 3 long-established religions are Confucianism, Buddhism, and Taoism; the average Chinese has practiced a mixture of all 3 faiths. About 5% of the people are Moslems, and there is a very small minority of Christians **Flag:** A red field with a gold star and an arc of 4 smaller stars to the right in the upper left corner **Anthem:** Anthem beginning, "March on, brave people of our nation," set to the music of The March of the Volunteers **Currency:** Yuan (renminbi) (1.51 per U.S. $1)

Location: East Asia. China, the third-largest country in the world after the USSR and Canada, is bounded on the north by Mongolia and the USSR; on the east by the USSR, North Korea, the Yellow Sea, and the East China Sea; on the south by the South China Sea, Vietnam, Laos, Burma, India, Bhutan, and Nepal; and on the west by Afghanistan, Pakistan, and the USSR **Features:** Two-thirds of the country is mountainous or semidesert. The eastern part consists of fertile plains and deltas **Chief Rivers:** Chang Jiang (Yangtze), Huang (Yellow), Amur, Xi (Si)

Head of State: Executive responsibility is vested in a State Council, headed by the premier. Control is exercised by the Standing Committee of the Central Committee's Politburo, within the National People's Congress **Head of Government:** Premier Zhao Ziyang, born 1919, elected by the National People's Congress, Sept. 1980 **Head of Party:** Hua Guofeng, born c. 1920, Chairman of the Politburo of the Communist party **Effective Date of Present State Constitution:** March 15, 1978 **Legislative Body:** National People's Congress (unicameral), consisting of 3,497 members elected for 5-year terms. The provinces elect 1 deputy for every 800,000 inhabitants; municipalities directly under central authority elect 1 deputy for every 100,000 inhabitants. Ethnic minorities are represented by 381 deputies, the armed forces by 505 deputies, and overseas

CHINA
CONIC PROJECTION
MILES
KILOMETERS
Capitals of Countries
Provincial Capitals
International Boundaries
Provincial Boundaries
© Copyright HAMMOND INCORPORATED, Maplewood, N. J.
PACIFIC OCEAN
SEA OF OKHOTSK
SEA OF JAPAN
YELLOW SEA
EAST CHINA SEA
SOUTH CHINA SEA
PHILIPPINE SEA
MONGOLIA
INNER MONGOLIA
MONGGOL ZIZHIQU
NEI MONGOL
XINJIANG UYGUR
XINJIANG UYGUR ZIZHIQU
QINGHAI
XIZANG ZIZHIQU
TIBET
GANSU
NINGXIA HUIZU ZIZHIQU
SHANXI
SHAANXI
HEBEI
SHANDONG
HENAN
HUBEI
ANHUI
JIANGSU
SICHUAN
GUIZHOU
HUNAN
JIANGXI
ZHEJIANG
FUJIAN
YUNNAN
GUANGXI ZHUANGZU ZIZHIQU
GUANGDONG
LIAONING
JILIN
HEILONGJIANG
NORTH KOREA
SOUTH KOREA
JAPAN
U. S. S. R.
INDIA
NEPAL
BHUTAN
BURMA
LAOS
THAILAND
VIETNAM
PHILIPPINES
TAIWAN (Formosa)
HAINAN
PEKING (Beijing)
SHANGHAI
TIANJIN
Taiyuan
Xi'an
Chengdu
Chongqing
Kunming
Canton (Guangzhou)
HONG KONG (Br.)
Macao (Port.)
Victoria
Shenyang
Harbin
Changchun
Jilin
TOKYO
Yokohama
Osaka
Nagoya
Kyoto
Kobe
Seoul
Pyongyang
Tropic of Cancer
110° Longitude East of Greenwich 120°
WORLD NATIONS
547

Chinese by 35 deputies **Local Government:** 21 provinces, 5 autonomous regions, and 3 municipalities directly under central authority. Revolutionary committees and people's congresses are the principal local organs of power

Ethnic Composition: 94% Han Chinese; 6% Chuang, Uigur, Hui, Yi, Tibetan, Miao, Manchu, Mongol, Korean, and numerous lesser minorities **Population Distribution:** 20% urban **Density:** 258 inhabitants per sq. mi.

Largest Cities: (1976 est.) Shanghai 10,000,000; (1970 est.) Peking (Beijing) 7,570,000, Tianjin 4,280,000, Shenyang 2,800,000, Wuhan 2,560,000, Canton 2,500,000, Chongqing 2,400,000, Nanjing 1,750,000, Harbin 1,670,000, Luda 1,650,000

Per Capita Income: $370 (1979) **Gross National Product (GNP):** $375 billion (1979) **Economic Statistics:** Agriculture is still the foundation of the economy. GNP components are not available but official figures disclosed in 1971 indicate that industrial capacity is still comparatively small. The State Statistical Bureau had estimated $409 billion for the gross value of industrial, transport and agricultural production in 1979. Grain output for 1979 was 332 million metric tons; chemical fertilizer, 11 million metric tons; cotton cloth, 12 billion meters; petroleum output, more than 106 million metric tons **Minerals and Mining:** Coal, petroleum, iron ore, tin, molybdenum, tungsten, mercury, manganese, antimony **Labor Force:** The working age population is about 476 million, with 75% in agriculture **Foreign Trade:** Exports are estimated at about $14 billion for 1979, with imports of about $16.1 billion. Exports are chiefly agricultural and food products, minerals, and textiles. Imports are mainly wheat, chemical fertilizers, iron and steel, transport equipment, machinery, advanced technology equipment, insecticides, cotton and rubber **Principal Trade Partners:** Japan, Hong Kong, West Germany, Romania, Singapore, Britain, United States, Malaysia, Canada, France, Australia

Vital Statistics: Birthrate, 26.9 per 1,000 pop. (1975); death rate, 10.3 **Life Expectancy:** 62 years **Illiteracy:** 45%. **Recent Statistics on Health and Infant Mortality:** N.A. **Primary and Secondary School Enrollment:** 200,000,000 (1977) **Enrollment in Higher Education:** 600,000 **GNP Expended on Education:** N.A.

Transportation: Surfaced roads total 300,000 mi. **Motor Vehicles:** N.A. **Passenger Cars:** N.A. **Railway Mileage:** 32,000 **Ports:** Shanghai, Tianjin, Luda, Canton **Major Airlines:** The Civil Aviation Administration of China operates domestic flights and international flights abroad **Communications:** Government owned **Radio Transmitters:** 250 **Receivers:** 45,000,000 (1978) **Television Transmitters:** 120 **Receivers:** 1,250,000 (1978) **Telephones:** 5,000,000 (1978) **Newspapers:** N.A.

Weights and Measures: Metric System and local standards **Travel Requirements:** Passport, visa; contact Chinese Embassy, Washington, D.C.

Developments of the early 1970s made the world dramatically aware that domestic conditions in the world's most populous country had stabilized; that China had come out of the disorders of the Cultural Revolution and that a new posture had been taken to break out of the diplomatic isolation of the 1950s and 60s.

The resulting circumstances have brought about a pronounced change for the better in a country the economy of which had been dislocated by factional strife and nationalistic excesses during the Cultural Revolution in 1966-69.

The Peking regime initiated a fresh approach in foreign affairs in April 1971 by inviting an American table-tennis team, with accompanying journalists, to tour China. This gesture was a surprise even in the context of the new moderation that had become increasingly evident during the year before.

Relations had been established with Canada, Italy, and a number of smaller countries; more Chinese delegations had been sent abroad; more foreign trade agreements had been signed; and Chinese diplomatic missions in foreign countries, which operated without ambassadors during the Cultural Revolution, had been restaffed.

After April 1972 there came a small but steady flow of Americans and other Western nationals. These visitors made possible illuminating new appraisals of internal conditions, and Peking climaxed their visits in July by arranging to receive President Nixon.

Impressed by Washington's new policy of military pullback in Asia, the Chinese moved to ease relations with the United States. Simultaneously Peking acted to strengthen the home front by slowing the pace of the Cultural Revolution and stabilizing conditions under a reshuffled, pragmatic leadership built with the assent of Communist party Chairman Mao Zedong, around Premier Zhou Enlai.

Thus a situation was created of far-ranging significance for today and the future. Peking's move has shaken loose accustomed world-power alignments and brought about a "big three" constellation susceptible to shifting and jockeying of unpredictable ramifications.

The new Peking policy also led to formal diplomatic relations with Japan in 1972 and culminated in the signing of a 10-year treaty of peace and friendship in 1978.

Trade with the United States began in 1972 following the lifting of the American trade embargo, and by 1979 had reached more than $2.3 billion, and is expected to be about $3.5 billion in 1980. In May 1979, China concluded an agreement on establishing formal commercial relations with the United States, which provided for the lowering of United States tariff restrictions on Chinese imports and the granting of a most-favored nation trade status (approved February 1, 1980).

Following the death of Premier Zhou Enlai on January 8, 1976, the succession of crises intensified. A mounting debate between moderates and radicals culminated in April in the most serious riots since the Cultural Revolution of 1966-69. The Politburo, acting quickly to defuse the potentially explosive situation, dismissed the "moderate" Deng Xiaoping from all his posts, and elevated Hua Guofeng to the premiership.

With the death of Mao Zedong the main task facing Hua Guofeng, Mao's successor, was to resolve the conflict between radical and moderate factions in the party. Late in 1976, he moved decisively against the radicals, known as the "Gang of Four," led by Mao's widow, Jiang Jing. After their arrest in October, the Peking regime seemed to embark on a moderate course. In July 1977, in an apparent effort to liberalize Maoist doctrine along pragmatic lines, Deng Xiaoping was brought back into the government as first deputy premier. Together with Chairman Hua and the honorary head of state, Ye Jianying, he is part of China's ruling triumvirate.

Slowly through the succeeding months, Deng's power grew with the implementation of the slogan "four modernizations"—rapid development of agriculture, industry, defense, and science and technology. Organizational changes were planned in the agricultural sector which included more state aid to poorer areas, state planning becoming more centralized, and the return of private plots to the farmers. In the industrial sphere, workers were granted a 60 percent wage increase as part of an effort to spur the economy and to achieve "comprehensive modernization" by the year 2000. Change was evident in the science technology and education areas, with the emergence of new journals, new institutes and academies, new exchanges with foreign scientists and the reduction of time spent by scientists in political activity. Also, university admission by entrance examination was reinstated.

China's chief defense goal is to achieve parity with the United States and the Soviet Union. To do this, the Peking regime has called for the introduction of foreign technology and the purchase of foreign weapons as part of the modernization effort for China's military, considered by Westerners as 20 years behind the Russians.

Relations with the United States improved in 1978 with the announcement of the formal establishment of official diplomatic relations between the two countries, effective on March 1, 1979. At the same time, the announcement included the abrogation of the mutual defense treaty between the United States and the offshore Republic of China and the termination of formal diplomatic relations with Taiwan.

On February 17, 1979, China invaded Vietnam which after four weeks resulted in no territorial gains, heavy casualties on both sides, and a drain on China's economy.

China's "four modernization" program in 1980 became less ambitious than as first envisioned by Deng Xiaoping, and was modified to make it more economically viable. China's leading economists and some high officials opposing Deng have stated that China must realize that modernization is dependent on the weather for agricultural production, on the international economy for the cost of imported and exported capital goods, and on the size of the off-shore oil deposits necessary for payment of imports. Therefore, policy has changed from the importation of complete facilities and consumer goods to that of importing foreign technology and manufacturing processes compatible with China's financial situation. China thus cancelled large contracts with the West, including a $2.5 billion one with Japan. At the same time, China changed her policy of self-sufficiency to that of borrowing or obtaining credit from abroad, with US$10 billion in loans from Japan and $17 billion credit from France and Britain. Following China's admission to the International Monetary Fund and the World Bank in 1980, her borrowing power will increase and her credit rating will continue to remain good.

In 1980, along with the ousting of four members of the party's Politburo who rose to power during the Cultural Revolution and were proteges of Mao Zedong, a general reassessment of Mao's merits and mistakes was made and his standing has been slowly declining. Another indication of "de-Mao-ification," the late Liu Shaoqi, former chief of state before his dismissal in 1968 by Mao, was memorialized and posthumously rehabilitated.

In late summer of 1980, the third annual session of the 5th National People's Congress (NPC), convened to review national problems, to approve recommendations made by the State Council, to vote on a resolution for an amendment to the constitution outlawing criticisms on big character posters, to raise the minimum marriage age to 22 for men and 20 for women, and to approve greater management autonomy for industrial enterprises. The NPC formally elected Zhao Ziyang to replace Hua Guofeng as premier, accepted the resignations of several vice premiers including Deng Xiaoping, and elected three new vice premiers. Hua and Deng remain as chairman and vice-chairman respectively of the party's Politburo. Deng, who is considered the main moving force of China's current developmental advancement, succeeded since his rehabilitation in 1977 in placing his proteges throughout many sectors of the government and party, and thereby promote effective measures in his modernization program.

HISTORY: The home of the oldest continuing civilization on earth, China has a recorded history dating back more than 2,000 years before the birth of Christ. By the advent of the Christian era, the Chinese had lived under a succession of dynasties that succeeded in unifying the country and protecting it from the outside world by building the Great Wall. In the end, however, the wall was to prove useless against invaders

1644: Manchu (Ching) dynasty is established, completing the gradual conquest of China by the Manchu peoples of the north

1839-42: Britain provokes Opium War and defeats Chinese; China opens ports and grants extraterritorial rights to British traders, cedes Hong Kong to Britain

1894-95: China and Japan war for control over their co-protectorate of Korea; a defeated China is forced to cede Formosa (Taiwan), Liaotung peninsula, and Pescadores to Japan

1898-1900: Resentment against foreign influence erupts in Boxer Rebellion; revolt is quelled after intervention by European, U.S., and Japanese forces. U.S. Open Door policy, calling for equal treatment for all nations in Chinese ports and respect for China's territorial integrity, wins lip service from European powers

1911-12: Manchu dynasty is overthrown in revolution led by Sun Yat-sen; a republic is established with Sun as president

1917-30: Civil war breaks out between supporters of Sun's Kuomintang Party in the south and the national government and its warlords in the north; Kuomintang army, led by Chiang Kai-shek, sweeps north and defeats warlords. A new civil war breaks out, however, after Chiang breaks alliance formed by Sun with Chinese Communists

1931-39: Japan, taking advantage of turmoil in China, invades Manchuria and sets up puppet government. In 1934, some 100,000 Communist troops led by Mao Zedong, Lin Biao, and Zhou Enlai, begin 6,000-mile march to the north to avoid encirclement by Kuomintang army. More than three-quarters of the troops are lost during the 12-month "Long-March." Kuomintang and Communists later agree to truce to repel Japanese, but agreement collapses and sporadic fighting resumes

1945-49: U.S. attempts to mediate civil war fail; Communists launch offensive and drive Chiang's forces from mainland to Taiwan; People's Republic of China is proclaimed Oct. 1, 1949

1950: China overruns Tibet; Chinese Communist forces intervene on side of North Korea in Korean War

1960-64: Growing rift between USSR and "hard-line" Chinese Communist leaders breaks into open. China explodes its first nuclear bomb

1966-67: Mao Zedong launches "Cultural Revolution" in attempt to reverse trend toward "revisionist" Communism. New policy is marked by widespread purge of leading officials and wave of terrorism by Mao's youthful followers, known as Red Guards. China explodes its first hydrogen bomb

1969: Chinese and Soviet troops exchange fire along borders

1971: People's Republic of China replaces Nationalist China (Taiwan) in the UN. Lin Biao, Mao's designated successor, dies following an abortive coup

1972: Nixon visits China, meets Zhou Enlai and Mao Zedong

1975: China adopts a revised constitution of 30 articles endorsing the doctrines that emerged from the "Great Proletarian Cultural Revolution" of the late 1960s. Ford and Kissinger visit China

1976: Mao Zedong, Zhou Enlai and Zhu De die. Hua Guofeng confirmed premier and chairman of Communist party. Tangshan earthquake kills an estimated 700,000

1977: Deng Xiaoping returns to Politburo

1978: Chairman Hua reappointed, travels to North Korea, Eastern Europe, and Iran. Deng Xiaoping signs friendship treat in Tokyo

1979: Deng Xiaoping visits the United States and signs scientific and cultural exchange agreement. China invades Vietnam in February. China and the U.S. establish formal diplomatic relations on March 1. Hua Guofeng visits France, West Germany, United Kingdom, and Italy

1980: China admitted to International Monetary Fund and World Bank. Hua Guofeng travels to Yugoslavia for Tito's funeral and to Japan for Ohira's funeral, meeting President Carter in Tokyo. U.S. reopens consulates in Shanghai and Canton. National People's Congress convenes and elects Zhao Ziyang as premier to replace Hua Guofeng. Deng Xiaoping and several premiers resign from State Council and are replaced

---

NATIONALIST CHINA (TAIWAN)

Area: 13,971 sq. mi. **Population:** 17,342,083 (1979 est.)

Official Name: Republic of China **Capital:** Taipei **Nationality:** Chinese **Languages:** Mandarin Chinese is the official language; native Taiwanese speak a variant of the Amoy dialect, although the Hakka dialect is used in northwestern Taiwan; Japanese and English are also widely used by the inhabitants **Religion:** The predominant religion (93%) is a blend of Buddhism, Confucianism and Taoism. 4.5% are Christians **Flag:** A red field with a blue rectangle in the upper left corner containing a 12-pointed white sun **Anthem:** National Anthem of the Republic of China, beginning "Our aim shall be to found a free land" **Currency:** New Taiwan yuan (dollar) (36 per U.S. $1)

Location: The seat of the Republic of China is the island of Taiwan, 90 miles off the southeast coast of the Chinese mainland. In addition to the island proper, Taiwan comprises 14 islands in the Taiwan group and 63 in the Penghu group, known as the Pescadores. The islands of Quemoy and Matsu, just off Fukien province on the China mainland, are also under the control of the Republic of China. Taiwan, also known as Formosa, is bordered on the north by the East China Sea, on the east by the Pacific Ocean, on the south and southwest by the South China Sea, and on the west by the Taiwan

(Formosa) Strait **Features:** About two-thirds of the island of Taiwan is composed of rugged foothills and mountain chains. The mountains, towering along the eastern coast, run from northeast to southwest. A flat coastal plain, running from north to south, occupies the western third and supports most of the population **Chief Rivers:** Cho-shui, Tan-shui, Hsia-tan-shui

Head of State: President Chiang Ching-kuo, born 1910, elected 1978 **Head of Government:** Premier Sun Yün-hsüan, appointed 1978 **Effective Date of Present Constitution:** 1947 **Legislative Body:** The National Assembly (unicameral); its members (elected 1947) are serving indefinitely. Of the original 3,045 there are now about 1,300. The 5 branches of government are the Legislative, Executive, Control, Examination, and Judicial yuans. The Legislative Yuan is the highest body and now has 410 members; both it and the National Assembly have some parliamentary function, and are dominated by the Nationalist Party (the Kuomintang) under its chairman, the premier **Local Government:** The Provincial Government is under a governor appointed by the national government. There is an elective Provincial Assembly with limited powers

Ethnic Composition: With the exception of about 250,000 aborigines of Indonesian origin, the Taiwanese are descendants of Chinese who migrated from the provinces of Fukien and Kwangtung of mainland China during the past 3 centuries; post-World War II refugees from the mainland constitute about 14% of the population **Population Distribution:** 77% urban (1975) **Density:** 1,241 inhabitants per sq. mi.

Largest Cities: (1977 est.) Taipei 2,165,519; (1979 est.) Kaohsiung 1,002,000, Taichung 549,000, Tainan 525,000, Keelung 343,000

Per Capita Income: $1,535 (1979) **Gross National Product (GNP):** $27.7 billion (1979 est.) **Economic Statistics:** 30% of GNP comes from industry (textiles, electronics, plastics, furniture, other goods), and 12% from agriculture (rice, sweet potatoes, bananas, sugarcane, pineapple, peanuts, and soybeans are the major crops) **Minerals and Mining:** Taiwan is deficient in minerals with the exception of coal. There are reserves of volcanic sulphur and deposits of natural gas and petroleum **Labor Force:** 6.1 million (1978), 39% employed in manufacturing, mining and construction, 35% in commerce and services, 26% in agriculture **Foreign Trade:** Exports, chiefly textiles, chemicals, metals and machinery, plywood, sugar, bananas, and canned mushrooms, totaled $12.7 billion in 1978. Imports, chiefly machinery, chemicals, transportation equipment, soybeans, raw cotton, timber, crude oil, and wheat, totaled $11 billion **Principal Trade Partners:** United States, Japan, Hong Kong, West Germany, Australia, Britain, Singapore, Canada, Thailand, Saudi Arabia, South Korea, Kuwait

Vital Statistics: Birthrate, 26 per 1,000 of pop (1976); death rate, 5 **Life Expectancy:** 70 years **Health Statistics:** 580 inhabitants per hospital bed; 1,377 per physician **Infant Mortality:** 14 per 1,000 births **Illiteracy:** 10% **Education Statistics:** 3,269 primary and secondary schools, with combined enrollment of 3,932,000 (1975) **Enrollment in Higher Education:** 282,300 **GNP Expended on Education:** 4.8%

Transportation: Surfaced roads total 5,496 mi. (1974) **Motor Vehicles:** 2,600,000 (1976) **Passenger Cars:** 122,517 (1974) **Railway Mileage:** 2,795 (1978) **Ports:** Kaohsiung, Keelung, Hualien, Taichung, Suao **Major Airlines:** China Airlines operates domestic and international services **Communications:** Both government and privately owned **Radio Stations:** 111 **Receivers:** 3,000,000 **Television Stations:** 3 **Receivers:** 747,444 **Telephones:** 598,504 **Newspapers:** 31 dailies, 80 copies per 1,000 inhabitants

Weights and Measures: Metric system and local units are used **Travel Requirements:** Passport, visa

---

The government of the Republic of China, defeated on mainland China by the Communists in 1949, established itself on Taiwan, with the goal of regaining power over all of China. That goal, with time, has become more and more remote. In the meantime, with the help of massive American aid, the government has built Taiwan into a prosperous, industrializing island state.

In 1971 a steady stream of countries switched diplomatic recognition from Taiwan to Communist China. With the shift in U.S. policy on China and American support for the seating of Peking in the United Nations, the Nationalist diplomatic position underwent further erosion. Nationalist China was eventually expelled from the UN and replaced by the Communist-led People's Republic of China.

Because of its insistence that it was not only the government of Taiwan, 90 miles off the China mainland, but also the only legal government of all China, the Nationalist regime would not sanction elections that would change the central leadership. But it has held local elections.

The government has been dominated by the Kuomintang, or Nationalist party, and the party in turn was dominated by President Chiang Kai-shek until his death in April 1975. Criticism of government policies and officials is permitted in the press, though the president and his relatives are an exception. Editors practice a form of self-censorship.

Nationalist officials, who like to refer to Taiwan as "Free China," readily concede that the province is still under martial law and freedom is in some respects limited. But they point out that freedom and democracy have to be understood in an Asian context, and declare that, whatever Taiwan's shortcomings, it is infinitely more free and democratic than the People's Republic.

Taiwan, which was devastated when China regained control from Japan after World War II, is flourishing, if overpopulated. The 17.3 million people, the vast majority of whom are native-born Taiwanese, enjoy one of the highest standards of living in Asia. But critics, especially those who advocate an independent Taiwan, say that the current huge military expenditures impede more rapid economic growth. The island developed its economy partly because it has enjoyed U.S. military protection and received U.S. military aid.

In a November 1977 election for local offices, independent candidates scored their largest, if still limited, victory since 1949. Moreover, the unusual fairness of the election was seen as reflecting a decision by the government to allow native Taiwanese a greater share in the political process than did Chiang Kai-shek.

When President Yen Chia-kan (C.K. Yen) retired in March 1978 the National Assembly named Premier Chiang Ching-kuo to succeed him, in an election in which he was the only candidate. The former Economics Minister, Sun Yün-hsüan, was named premier in May.

Formal diplomatic relations between Taiwan and the United States were terminated on March 1, 1979, while cultural, commercial and quasi-official relations continue. The Taiwan-U.S. trade in 1979 amounted to $9.03 billion as compared to $7.3 billion in 1978. Taiwan's total worldwide trade in 1979 was $30.87 billion, a 30% increase over 1978, and included trade with several communist countries. With the abrogation of the mutual defense treaty with the United States on December 31, 1979, Taiwan has made progress toward self sufficiency both industrially and militarily.

HISTORY: Chinese emigration to Taiwan began in the 7th century. In the 16th century the Portuguese arrived, naming the island Formosa, meaning "beautiful." The Dutch assumed control in 1641 but were driven out in 1662 by Ming dynasty forces fleeing the Manchu takeover in mainland China. In 1683 Taiwan, too, fell to the Manchus. At the end of the Sino-Japanese War of 1894-95 it was ceded to Japan, which held it until the conclusion of World War II, when it was restored to China

1949: The Nationalist government of Chiang Kai-shek and remnants of his army flee to Taiwan, as the Communist forces of Mao Zedong gain control of the Chinese mainland

1950: President Truman orders U.S. Seventh Fleet to patrol the Taiwan Strait, thwarting a planned invasion of Taiwan by Communist China

1955: Following shelling of Nationalist-held offshore islands, the United States pledges to defend Taiwan and the Pescadores

1965: Because of Taiwan's impressive economic growth, U.S. aid is terminated except for surplus-food shipments

1966: Chiang Kai-shek is reelected president for fourth term

1969: Chiang Ching-kuo, elder son of Chiang Kai-shek, is named deputy premier

1971: Nationalist China replaced in UN by Mainland China

1972: Chiang Kai-shek is reelected president for fifth term; Chiang Ching-kuo is named premier

1973: U.S. announces gradual withdrawal of its forces on Taiwan as relations with Communist China improve

1974: U.S. pledges to continue to "safeguard the security of Taiwan"

1975: Generalissimo Chiang Kai-shek, 87, dies of a heart attack in Taipei, April 5, and Yen Chia-kan (C.K. Yen) succeeds him

1978: Yen Chia-kan retires; Chiang Ching-kuo succeeds him in presidency. Taiwan terminates treaty with Japan following the signing of a treaty of friendship between Japan and the People's Republic of China

1979: American and Taiwan embassies are closed on March 1, quasi-official offices are established in each country

1980: Taiwan loses membership in both the International Monetary Fund and the World Bank

COLOMBIA

Area: 439,735 sq. mi. **Population:** 26,360,000 (1979 est.)

Official Name: Republic of Colombia **Capital:** Bogotá **Nationality:** Colombian **Languages:** Spanish is the official language and is spoken by all but a few Indian tribes **Religion:** Roman Catholicism is the state religion and that of 95% of the population **Flag:** The top half of the flag is yellow; the bottom half consists of a blue stripe and red stripe of equal widths **Anthem:** National Anthem, beginning "O unwithering glory, immortal joy" **Currency:** Colombian peso (46 per U.S. $1)

Location: Northwest South America. Colombia is bordered on the north by the Caribbean Sea, on the east by Venezuela and Brazil, on the south by Peru and Ecuador, and on the west by the Pacific Ocean and Panama **Features:** Colombia is divided by the Andes Mountains into flat coastal areas, a highland or plateau area, and an eastern plains area **Chief Rivers:** Magdalena, Cauca, Amazon

Head of State and of Government: President Julio César Turbay Ayala, born 1916, elected June 1978 **Effective Date of Present Constitution:** August 1886 **Legislative Body:** Congress (bicameral), consisting of a Senate and a Chamber of Representatives. The Senate has 112 members; the Chamber has 199 members **Local Government:** 22 departments, the Special District of Bogotá, 3 intendencies, and 5 commissaries, under appointed governors and administrators

Ethnic Composition: 58% Mixed European and Indian descent, 20% European stock, 14% European and African descent, 4% African stock, and 1% Indian **Population Distribution:** 64% urban **Density:** 60 inhabitants per sq. mi.

Largest Cities: (1973 census) Bogotá 2,855,065, Medellín 1,070,924, Cali 898,253, Barranquilla 661,009, Cartagena 292,512, Bucaramanga 291,661, Manizales 199,904

Per Capita Income: $808 (1979) **Gross National Product (GNP):** $22.8 billion (1979) **Economic Statistics:** 23% of GNP comes from agriculture (coffee, rice, cotton, potatoes, bananas, sugar); 17% from trade; 20% from industry (food, beverages, tobacco, textiles, chemicals, metal products and machinery) **Minerals and Mining:** Petroleum, gold, salt, limestone, sand and gravel, platinum and emeralds are exploited **Labor Force:** Wage earners totaled 7,841,742 (1975), with 41% in agriculture, 23% in industry, and 14% in services **Foreign Trade:** Exports, chiefly coffee, crude petroleum, agricultural products, textiles, cattle, and emeralds, totaled $2.9 billion in 1978. Imports, chiefly machinery and electronic equipment, chemicals, transport vehicles, metals and metal products, totaled $3.4 billion **Principal Trade Partners:** United States, West Germany, Japan, Netherlands, Italy, Britain, Sweden, the Andean Group

Vital Statistics: Birthrate, 30 per 1,000 of pop. (1976); death rate, 8.8 **Life Expectancy:** 61 years **Health Statistics:** 530 inhabitants per hospital bed; 1,818 per physician (1975) **Infant Mortality:** 62.8 per 1,000 births **Illiteracy:** 19% **Primary and Secondary School Enrollment:** 5,776,638 (1977) **Enrollment in Higher Education:** 186,635 (1975) **GNP Expended on Education:** 1.9% (1976)

Transportation: Paved roads total 5,092 mi. **Motor Vehicles:** 558,100 (1977) **Passenger Cars:** 453,600 **Railway Mileage:** 2,134 **Ports:** Buenaventura, Sta. Marta, Barranquilla, Cartagena, Tumaco **Major Airlines:** Avianca and Aerocondor operate domestic and international services **Communications:** Government and privately owned **Radio Transmitters:** 340 **Receivers:** 2,850,000 (1976) **Television Transmitters:** 3 **Receivers:** 1,700,000 (1976) **Telephones:** 1,769,000 (1976) **Newspapers:** 36 dailies, 69 copies per 1,000 inhabitants (1974)

Weights and Measures: Metric system **Travel Requirements:** Passport, tourist card valid for visits up to 90 days, 2 photos

---

Colombia, in effect, is a federation of city-states that are reflections of the isolation imposed by the Andes. Traditionally, the economy has been based on coffee on the rocks: Small farmers strive to raise quality coffee beans on the steep and rocky slopes of the Andes. Their crop accounts for the largest part of the nation's legal exports. In recent years, however, the illicit growing and exporting of marijuana and cocaine has risen fast as a major economic activity, estimated at from $1 billion to $2 billion a year even in the face of a government crackdown.

Colombia's social problems are staggering; its population is growing by 2.1 percent a year, despite efforts to expand family-planning programs, and its cities are swelling because of migration from rural areas. (Bogotá's population has doubled in the past 10 years.)

With illiteracy widespread, Colombia has a high unemployment rate and the income distribution of her population is highly skewed in favor of the upper fifth of the population. Access to health services and the quality of health care are even more unequally distributed.

Colombia's people are as varied as its geography. The top hundred or so families are basically European, and American-educated. The bulk of the people are of part-Indian stock, and some are descendants of African slaves. About 18 percent of the population is black or mulatto. There are small groups of nomads who wander the deserts of the northern fringe of the land as well as primitive Amazon Indians in the forests of the south. Indians make up 1 percent of the population.

Politically, Colombia is the largest working democracy in Latin America. Its 26 million people are still awed by *La Violencia*, the bloody period of anarchy from 1948 to 1958, which cost about 200,000 lives. Its cause is still debated. *La Violencia* gave the Spanish language a new word, *bogotazo*, referring to the sudden eruption of violence in the capital on April 9, 1948, an uprising not clearly linked to a specific cause.

In any event, the civil war led first to the military dictatorship (1953-57) of General Gustavo Rojas Pinilla, then to a return to democracy on the basis of cooperation between the two traditional parties, the Liberals and the Conservatives, who began to rotate the presidency. Colombia permits its notably ineffectual Communist party to operate openly and legally.

With the advent to power of President Misael Pastrana Borrero in August 1970, following an election bitterly contested by General Rojas, Colombia began to achieve substantial progress for the people as a whole. In 1973, however, there were renewed indications that the violence that had marked so much of her history was not yet dead. After a number of bloody guerrilla actions, the government adopted several emergency security measures, including the establishment of special groups within the armed forces to pursue guerrilla bands operating in rural areas.

The 1974 elections offered the first open polls after 16 years of alternate rule by Liberals and Conservatives. Alfonso López Michelsen, the Liberal party candidate, won a constitutional mandate for a four-year term in coalition with the Conservatives. His term was marred somewhat by strikes of workers and students and by attacks and kidnappings by left-wing guerrillas.

The Liberals were again big winners in the 1978 congressional elections, and their candidate, Julio César Turbay Ayala, won the presidency in a close race. He became involved very soon in the twin problems of increased terrorism and rising drug traffic. On January 1, 1979, guerrillas of the M-19 group seized 5,300 weapons from the main Bogotá military arsenal. M-19, the Movement of April 19, got its name from the date in 1970 on which General Rojas was defeated for the presidency. Its original members were radical followers of Rojas. M-19 advocates establishing a socialist state through force of arms. In the wake of the arsenal raid, soldiers arrested several hundred left-wing guerrillas and imprisoned them.

M-19 struck again on February 27, 1980, as a group of masked young men and women shot their way into the Dominican Republic's embassy in Bogotá where a diplomatic reception was being held. They demanded $50 million ransom and release of 311 political prisoners as part of the price for freeing more than 50 hostages, among whom were the Spanish-born U.S. ambassador, Diego C. Asencio, and top-level diplomats of 15 other countries. During two months of negotiations, many of the hostages, including all of the women, were released gradually. The Uruguayan ambassador escaped on March 17, breaking a leg in jumping from a second-story window. For its part, the Colombian government speeded up the trials of political prisoners and acquitted many. On April 27 the siege ended peacefully when the 16 guerrillas settled for an alleged ransom of $2.5 million from unknown sources and safe escort to Cuba. They were flown to Havana with 12 of their hostages who were released on arrival.

M-19 claimed success in bringing the world's attention to their allegations of torture and infringement of human rights by the Colombian military. The government won accolades for its painstaking negotiations and for avoiding the use of force to free the hostages. President Turbay invited the Inter-American Human Rights Commission to investigate M-19's charges of torture and to monitor the trials of guerrillas held in jails.

Inflation rose to about 30 percent in 1979. Exports of coffee increased more than 50 percent, but revenue from this source remained flat as world prices dropped.

The government, meanwhile, was trying to stop another kind of export—illicit drugs. Soldiers swarmed over the Guajira Peninsula, a major point for shipping marijuana to the United States, in late 1978 and in 1979, and the government reported the seizure and burning of more than 100,000 tons of marijuana.

HISTORY: Colombia was inhabited perhaps as early as 5000 B.C. by Indian tribes of whom little is known. Prominent among pre-Colombian cultures was that of the highland Chibchas, a sedentary agricultural people located in the eastern chain of the Andes, in the center of the country. European colonization began about five years after Spanish explorers came to Colombia in 1499. With the founding of Bogotá in 1538, Colombia became the nucleus of New Granada, a vast territory that included parts of Panama, Venezuela, and Ecuador. The struggle for Colombian independence was, as elsewhere in Latin America, precipitated by Napoleon's invasion of Spain in the early 19th century

1810: Revolutionary leaders stage uprising in Bogotá

1819: By defeating Spanish royalist forces, Simón Bolívar secures independence of the new republic of Greater Colombia, which includes the former territory of New Granada

1830: Greater Colombia breaks up and New Granada (now Colombia and Panama) becomes a separate state

1863: New Granada becomes a federal republic, the United States of Colombia

1899: Civil war breaks out between liberal and conservative elements and results in more than 100,000 deaths and virtual economic ruin for the country

1903: Panama proclaims its independence from Colombia and achieves it with U.S. support

1948-53: Assassination of left-wing liberal leader Jorge Gaitán in 1948 sets off a major revolt, ultimately costing 200,000 lives and leading to the declaration of a state of siege. President Laureano Gómez, an archconservative, takes power in 1950 but is ousted in a coup d'état led by the chief of the armed forces, General Gustavo Rojas Pinilla

1957: Rojas, in turn, is ousted by a military junta, which promises and provides presidential and congressional elections within the year. An amendment to the constitution is approved by plebiscite, providing for 12 years of parity (equal representation) between Liberal and Conservative parties in the 3 branches of government

1969: Colombia joins Andean common market

1970: Departmental and municipal elections result in overwhelming defeat for Rojas and victory for Conservative party

1973: Agrarian reform bill is passed to reduce amount of land held by any person and to expropriate poorly farmed estates

1974: Alfonso López Michelsen elected in landslide Liberal victory

1975: President López declares a state of siege because of unrest

1977: Protests against high prices and continued martial law rule erupt in violence; 13 die, 4,000 arrested

1978: Following Liberal party election victory, Julio César Turbay Ayala wins presidency

1979: M-19 guerrilla group captures arms from arsenal; hundreds of persons are taken as political prisoners

1980: Diplomats of 16 countries are held hostage for two months by M-19 guerrillas who seize Dominican Republic embassy Feb. 27. Liberal party victorious in March 9 by-elections

---

COMOROS

Area: 719 sq. mi. **Population:** 290,000 (1978 est.)

Official Name: Federal and Islamic Republic of the Comoros **Capital:** Moroni **Nationality:** Comoran **Languages:** Arabic, French, Swahili **Religion:** Moslem, some Christians **Flag:** A green field with a white crescent in the center, set at an angle and encompassing four five-pointed stars in a line **Anthem:** N.A. **Currency:** CFA Franc (210.2 per U.S. $1)

Location: The Comoros (12°S., 44E.) lie in the Mozambique Channel of the Indian Ocean 300 miles northwest of Madagascar. There are three main islands: Anjouan, Mohéli and Grand Comoro, and a number of minor ones. The Republic claims nearby Mayotte as part of its territory **Features:** The islands are of volcanic origin and Karthala (elevation 8,399 ft.) on Grand Comoro is still active. The climate is tropical with a hot rainy season from November to April, becoming more temperate the rest of the year **Chief Rivers:** There are no large rivers

Head of State: President Ahmed Abdallah, born 1919, elected October 1978, following the coup of May 1978 **Head of Government:** Prime Minister Salim Ben Ali, appointed 1978 **Effective Date of Constitution:** 1978 **Legislative Body:** Federal Assembly (unicameral) of 39 members **Local Government:** The 3 islands are organized into 7 regions

Ethnic Composition: The people are largely descendants of Moslem settlers with strains from Africa and Madagascar; there is a small European colony **Population Distribution:** N.A. **Density:** 403 inhabitants per sq. mi.

Largest City: (1974 est.) Moroni 12,000

Per Capita Income: $153 (1976 est.) **Gross Domestic Product (GDP):** $51 million (1976) **Economic Statistics:** A wide variety of crops flourish in the rich volcanic soil: rice, cassava, ambrevade (a pea-family plant), sweet potatoes, citrus fruits, and some European vegetables. The chief commercial crops are vanilla, perfume plants, and copra. Fishing and stock raising are important. In 1976, 40% of GDP came from agriculture, 34% from industry **Minerals and Mining:** There are practically no mineral resources **Labor Force:** 184,000 (1976) with 87% in agriculture **Foreign Trade:** Exports chiefly vanilla, ilang-ilang essence for perfumes, copra, cloves and sisal totaled $9 million in 1978. Imports, primarily rice, vegetables, mineral products, textiles, metals and automobiles, totaled $21 million **Principal Trade Partners:** France, Madagascar, Kenya, Italy, West Germany, Tanzania, United States

Vital Statistics: Birthrate, 46.6 per 1,000 of pop. (1975); death rate, 21.7 **Life Expectancy:** 49 years **Health Statistics:** 458 inhabitants per hospital bed; 13,810 per physician (1972) **Infant Mortality:** 51.7 per 1,000 births **Illiteracy:** 85% **Primary and Secondary School Enrollment:** 26,391 (1973) **Enrollment in Higher Education:** N.A. **GDP Expended on Education:** 8.7% (1971)

Transportation: Paved roads total 183 mi. **Motor Vehicles:** N.A. **Passenger Cars:** N.A. **Railway Mileage:** None **Ports:** Mutsamudu, Moroni, Fomboni, Bambao **Major Airlines:** Air Comores provides domestic service **Communications:** Government controlled **Radio Transmitters:** 3 (1973) **Receivers:** 36,000 (1976) **Television:** None **Telephones:** 2,000 (1976) **Newspapers:** None; imported from Madagascar

Weights and Measures: Metric system **Travel Requirements:** N.A.

After 133 years as, successively, a French colony attached to Madagascar and a French Overseas Territory, three of the four Comoro Islands unilaterally declared independence on July 6, 1975. Still French territory but claimed by the Republic of the Comoros is the fourth island, Mayotte.

Ahmed Abdallah was elected president of the new nation. These actions followed a vote in favor of independence in a referendum of December 1974.

In 1975, Ahmed Abdallah was overthrown in a bloodless coup led by Ali Soilih who was selected as president on January 2, 1976. The new nation has been vexed with the problem of the status of the largely Christian island of Mayotte. In 1976, the inhabitants of Mayotte voted to remain within the French Republic and not to join with the other largely Moslem Comoro Islands in independence. An April 12 referendum showed a preference for departmental status within France.

President Ali Soilih was overthrown on May 13, 1978, in a coup led by a French-born mercenary, Bob Denard, and Said Atthoumani, Interior Minister in the former Ahmed Abdallah government of 1975. The new government, headed by Ahmed Abdallah and Mohammed Ahmed, announced the release of political detainees and the restoration of rights and religious freedom. Mohammed Ahmed resigned in October 1978, leaving Ahmed Abdallah in sole command.

HISTORY: The original settlers of the Comoros came from mainland Africa. The first detailed knowledge of the area is undoubtedly due to Arab sailors, although the Phoenicians probably visited the islands much earlier. Two Arab invasions swept over the Comoros, the last coming from the Persian Gulf in the 15th century. In the 16th century the islands were visited by Portuguese, Dutch, French and Malagasy navigators

1843: French seize Mayotte

1886: Anjouan, Grand Comoro and Mohéli come under French protection

1912: The islands join administratively with Madagascar

1946: The Comoros become partially autonomous and receive the status of an Overseas Territory

1961: The islands receive complete internal autonomy

1975: Independence is declared. Comoros is admitted to UN. Government of Ahmed Abdallah overthrown by Ali Soilih

1976: Mayotte votes to remain French

1978: Ali Soilih overthrown in coup. Political-Military Directory under Ahmed Abdallah emerges; voters approve new constitution in Oct. 1 referendum. Ahmed Abdallah elected president

1979: UN General Assembly reaffirms Comoran sovereignty over Mayotte

---

CONGO

Area: 132,046 sq. mi. **Population:** 1,459,000 (1978 est.)

Official Name: People's Republic of the Congo **Capital:** Brazzaville **Nationality:** Congolese **Languages:** French is the official language; Lingala and Kikongo are the principal spoken languages **Religion:** 49% animist, 49% Christian (mainly Roman Catholic), and 1% Moslem **Flag:** A red field; in the upper left corner is a yellow 5-pointed star above crossed yellow hammer and hoe, surrounded by green palm branches **Anthem:** The Internationale **Currency:** CFA Franc (210.2 per U.S. $1)

Location: West-central Africa. The Congo is bordered on the north by Cameroon and the Central African Republic, on the east and south by Zaire, on the southwest by the Angolan exclave of Cabinda and the Atlantic Ocean, and on the west by Gabon and Cameroon **Features:** The country consists of a coastal plain, savanna, highlands, and a plateau. Roughly half the land area is covered by dense equatorial forest, and a quarter of the country covered by marshes **Chief Rivers:** Congo, Ubangi, Sangha, Kouilou-Niari

Head of State and Government: President: Col. Denis Sassou-Nguesso, born 1941, elected July 1979. He is assisted by a Prime Minister, Col. Louis-Sylvain Goma, born 1941, appointed 1979 by the central committee of the Congolese Workers' party (PCT) **Effective Date of Present Constitution:** 1979 **Legislative Body:** Power is in the hands of the sole political party, the Congolese Workers party (PCT). A National People's Assembly was elected in 1979 **Local Government:** 9 regions and a capital district, under appointed commissioners

Ethnic Composition: The 15 groups and 75 tribes are predominantly Bantu; major ones include the Bakongo, Bateke, M'Boshi, and Sangha. Pygmies number about 5,000. There are about 8,500 Europeans, mostly French **Population Distribution:** 40% urban (1976) **Density:** 11 inhabitants per sq. mi.

Largest Cities: (1974 census) Brazzaville 298,967, Pointe-Noire 141,700

Per Capita Income: $500 (1978 est.) **Gross National Product (GNP):** $710 million (1978 est.) **Economic Statistics:** In 1978 about 19% of GNP was from agriculture (peanuts, palm kernels, coffee, cocoa, bananas, sugarcane, rice, corn, manioc, and sweet potatoes), forestry, and fishing; 10% from industry (forest products, sugar refining, palm and peanut oil, brewing, flour milling) **Minerals and Mining:** Crude petroleum is the major exploited mineral resource. There are high-grade iron-ore reserves, and some zinc, gold, copper, lead, and natural gas are produced. Potash production ended in 1977 **Labor Force:** 600,000, with 80% engaged in subsistence agriculture **Foreign Trade:** Exports, chiefly petroleum, wood, sugar, tobacco, and industrial diamonds, totaled $294 million in 1978. Imports, mainly machinery, electrical equipment, vehicles, textiles, clothing, foods, and chemicals, totaled $238 million **Principal Trade Partners:** France, West Germany, United States, Italy

Vital Statistics: Birthrate, 45.1 per 1,000 of pop. (1975); death rate, 20.8 **Life Expectancy:** 43.5 years **Health Statistics:** 201 inhabitants per hospital bed (1976); 6,338 per physician (1975) **Infant Mortality:** 180 per 1,000 births **Illiteracy:** 80% **Primary and Secondary School Enrollment:** 421,211 (1975) **Enrollment in Higher Education:** 3,249 **GNP Expended on Education:** 8.2% (1975)

Transportation: Surfaced roads total 345 miles **Motor Vehicles:** 33,000 (1976) **Passenger Cars:** 20,000 **Railway Mileage:** 500 **Ports:** Pointe-Noire **Major Airlines:** Air Congo and Lina Congo operate internal services; Air Afrique, Aeroflot, Air France, KLM, Sabena, and UTA operate international services **Communications:** Government owned **Radio Transmitters:** 10 (1973) **Receivers:** 83,000 (1976) **Television Transmitters:** 1 **Receivers:** 3,300 (1976) **Telephones:** 11,000 (1976) **Newspapers:** 3 dailies, 1 copy per 1,000 inhabitants (1974)

Weights and Measures: Metric system **Travel Requirements:** Passport; visa. Contact Congo UN Mission in New York City

---

Since gaining independence from France in 1960, Congo has swung sharply from right to left politically while moving forward very slowly economically.

Despite much leftist rhetoric, Congo's Marxist-Leninist "orientation" remains confusing—perhaps more expedient than orthodox. China and the Soviet Union appear to wield considerable influence over the government and speculation about which of them is in the ascendancy is a popular pastime in Brazzaville.

But it is capitalistic France that continues to be Congo's chief trading partner and source of economic and financial aid. Private French companies control most of the country's commerce and small industry.

President Marien Ngouabi, who came to power in 1968 and set up the ruling Congolese Workers' party (PCT), was assassinated March 18, 1977. Gen. Joachim Yhombi-Opango, who succeeded him, was ousted early in 1979 and replaced by Col. Denis Sassou-Nguesso in a leftist reaction against alleged bourgeois tendencies of the former regime.

In response to an October 1979 Paris report, the new president acknowledged that more than a thousand Congolese children, most said to be under 15 years of age, had been sent to Cuba for up to 15 years of training. He denied, however, the assertion that this action had been taken without parents' consent.

HISTORY: When the Portuguese explorer Diego Cão arrived off the mouth of the Congo River in 1482, he found two long-established Bantu empires. To the north lay the Kingdom of Loango and its vassal states, and to the south, the great Mani-Congo stretching into Angola. Four centuries later, Count Pierre Savorgnan de Brazza (for whom Brazzaville is named) established French control over the area north of the river. In 1885, the Congress of Berlin recognized French claims to the region, later renamed Middle Congo

1910: Middle Congo becomes part of French Equatorial Africa, which also includes Gabon, Ubangi-Shari (now the Central African Republic), and Chad

1958: The Congo becomes an autonomous member of French Community

1960: Full independence is proclaimed Aug. 15, and Fulbert Youlou becomes first president of the republic

1963: Youlou is overthrown in a revolt and succeeded by Alphonse

Massamba-Débat who founds (in 1964) a Marxist-Leninist party. Chinese mission takes over direction of the economy

1965: Following arrests of American diplomats, United States closes Brazzaville embassy

1968: Capt. Marien Ngouabi, popular northern army officer, leads coup that ousts Massamba-Débat

1970: Ngouabi proclaims a people's republic, the first in Africa

1972: Production in offshore oil fields begins

1977: Ngouabi assassinated March 18. Emile Cardinal Biayenda murdered; Massamba-Débat executed for his role in assassination plot. Col. Joachim Yhombi-Opango, named president April 13 by military junta, abolishes national assembly. U.S. reopens its embassy

1978: Attempted coup to overthrow President Yhombi-Opango fails

1979: Col. Denis Sassou-Nguesso named president by PCT in February, following ouster of Yhombi-Opango who is accused of treason. Official PCT list of National People's Assembly candidates approved in July elections; new constitution also approved

COSTA RICA

Area: 19,652 sq. mi. **Population:** 2,193,000 (1979 est.)

Official Name: Republic of Costa Rica **Capital:** San José **Nationality:** Costa Rican **Languages:** Spanish is the official and predominant language; a Jamaican dialect of English is spoken by many of the country's Negroes, descendants of Jamaican workers who emigrated to Costa Rica in the 19th century **Religion:** Overwhelmingly Roman Catholic **Flag:** A blue stripe at top and bottom, separated by two white stripes from a broad center red stripe bearing the national coat of arms on the lefthand side **Anthem:** National Anthem, beginning "Noble country, thy beautiful banner" **Currency:** Colón (8.57 per U.S. $1)

Location: Central America. Costa Rica is bordered on the north by Nicaragua, on the east by the Caribbean Sea, on the southeast by Panama, and on the west by the Pacific Ocean **Features:** About two-thirds of the country is covered by forests. There is a fairly wide coastal plain on the eastern side and a narrower plain on the Pacific coast. A volcanic mountain system composed of 3 ranges crosses the country lengthwise **Chief Rivers:** Rio Grande, San Carlos

Head of State and of Government: President: Rodrigo Carazo Odio, born 1926, elected 1978 **Effective Date of Present Constitution:** November 1949 **Legislative Body:** Legislative Assembly (unicameral), consisting of 57 members elected by popular vote for 4 years **Local Government:** 7 provinces, each with a governor appointed by the president

Ethnic Composition: The population is predominantly of European (mainly Spanish) descent, with a large mestizo (mixed European and Indian) minority. Negroes of Jamaican origin number about 2% of the population **Population Distribution:** 41% urban **Density:** 112 inhabitants per sq. mi.

Largest Cities: (1973 census) San José 215,441, Alajuela 33,122, Limón 29,621, Puntarenas 26,331, Heredia 22,700, Cartago 21,753

Per Capita Income: $1,431 (1979) **Gross National Product (GNP):** $3.4 billion (1979) **Economic Statistics:** In 1979 about 22% of GNP came from agriculture (coffee, bananas, cocoa, sugarcane, rice, beans, and livestock), forestry, and fishing; 20% from industry (food and beverages, textiles, fertilizers, shoes, furniture) **Minerals and Mining:** Gold and manganese are mined **Labor Force:** 740,000 (1979); 34% in agriculture, 36% in industry and commerce, 25% in services and government **Foreign Trade:** Exports, chiefly coffee, bananas, meat, sugar, cocoa, and fertilizers, totaled $858 million in 1978. Imports, mainly manufactures, machinery and transport equipment, chemicals, foodstuffs, and petroleum, totaled $1.2 billion **Principal Trade Partners:** United States, West Germany, Nicaragua, El Salvador, Guatemala, Japan

Vital Statistics: Birthrate, 29.7 per 1,000 of pop. (1976); death rate, 4.6 **Life Expectancy:** 68 years **Health Statistics:** 261 inhabitants per hospital bed; 1,524 per physician (1975) **Infant Mortality:** 33.6 per 1,000 births **Illiteracy:** 10% **Primary and Secondary School Enrollment:** 481,994 (1976) **Enrollment in Higher Education:** 38,629 (1977) **GNP Expended on Education:** 5.2% (1974)

Transportation: Paved roads total 1,200 mi. **Motor Vehicles:** 107,300 (1976) **Passenger Cars:** 64,900 **Railway Mileage:** 661 **Ports:** Limón, Puntarenas, Golfito **Major Airlines:** LACSA (Costa Rican Airlines) operates domestic and international flights **Communications:** Government controlled **Radio Transmitters:** 65 **Receivers:** 254,774 (1979) **Television Transmitters:** 12 **Receivers:** 155,000 (1976) **Telephones:** 145,000 (1979) **Newspapers:** 6 dailies, 88 copies per 1,000 inhabitants (1975)

Weights and Measures: Metric system and old Spanish weights and measures are used **Travel Requirements:** Passport and visa not required if tourist card obtained prior to departure (valid 30 days, $2.00 fee)

Born in the bloodshed of civil war in 1948, the stable and progressive political institutions of Costa Rica have since provided relative peace and democracy despite severe pressures.

The country's republican form of government, in which presidential power is held in check by a strong Assembly, has been able to renew itself every four years through peaceful and honest elections held under the exclusive authority of a jealously independent electoral board.

The sophistication of Costa Rica's politics goes hand in hand with economic and social levels much higher than the rest of Central America has been able to achieve. For example, per capita income is considerably higher than in most of the rest of Central America. Although there are extremes of wealth and poverty here as elsewhere, distribution is generally more equitable.

Even with its orderly process of government, Costa Rica has experienced political problems. In 1966 the country retained the reformist National Liberation party in control of the Assembly while electing as president the candidate of a conservative anti-Liberation coalition, José Joaquín Tréjos Fernández. Legislative and executive branches were at constant loggerheads in a period of financial difficulty requiring decisive action. The voters remedied this in 1970 when they elected the Liberation candidate for president, José Figuéres Ferrer, and his party kept control in the Assembly. In 1974, the National Liberation party retained the presidency with the election of its candidate, Daniel Oduber Quirós.

In the 1978 elections, political power passed peacefully to a new president, Rodrigo Carazo Odio, an economist and businessman, and his Unity party, a coalition of four parties. For years, the biggest issue in the nation's political life had been the presence in Costa Rica of Robert Vesco, a fugitive from U.S. charges of embezzling $224 million from a mutual fund he controlled. Carazo had vowed, as his first order of business, to expel Vesco "for the nation's health." When Vesco left on a business trip to the Bahamas, Carazo acted on his pledge by ordering all ports of entry to bar Vesco's return.

The first electricity from the vast Arenal Project in Guanacaste province was generated in 1979. Construction on the project in the next five years will double the country's electrical capacity and will increase irrigation considerably.

During the civil war in Nicaragua in 1978-79, thousands of Sandinista rebels crossed the border into Costa Rica and used that country as a training and staging area for their offensive against the Somoza regime. Having no army, Costa Rica was virtually powerless. When two of its border guards were killed by Nicaraguan troops in November 1978, Costa Rica severed relations with its neighbor.

HISTORY: Prior to Costa Rica's discovery in 1502 by the Spanish, the country was inhabited by the Guaymi Indians. During the Spanish colonial period, Costa Rica was largely ignored by the mother country because of the paucity of minerals, and administered as part of the captaincy general of Guatemala

1821: Costa Rica obtains independence from Spain, and along with the rest of Central America is annexed to Mexico

1823: Costa Rica and the other Central American countries secede from Mexico and establish the Central American Federation

1838: Costa Rica becomes an independent republic

1856-57: William Walker, an American adventurer, attempts to conquer Costa Rica but is defeated by Central American alliance

1917-19: Revolution breaks out; dictatorship is set up by Frederico Granados

1948-49: President Teodoro Picado annuls elections won by presidential candidate Otilio Ulate. José Figuéres leads civilian uprising, installs own junta, then turns presidency over to Ulate

1962: Costa Rica joins Central American Common Market

1963: The volcano Irazú erupts, destroying productive land

1968: The volcano Arenal erupts, bringing new devastation

1970: José Figuéres wins presidential election

1974: Daniel Oduber Quirós is elected president
1976: Trade relations restored with Cuba
1978: Rodrigo Carazo Odio is elected president
1979: Sandinista rebels from Nicaragua use Costa Rica as a base for a successful assault on Somoza regime
1980: Strike by banana workers, which threatened Costa Rica's second most important export crop, is ended after 26 days

CUBA

Area: 42,827 sq. mi. **Population:** 9,728,000 (1978 est.)

Official Name: Republic of Cuba **Capital:** Havana **Nationality:** Cuban **Languages:** Spanish is the official and universal language **Religion:** Predominantly Roman Catholic before Castro **Flag:** Three horizontal blue stripes separated by two white stripes, with an equilateral red triangle at the left containing a 5-pointed white star **Anthem:** Hymn of Bayamo **Currency:** Cuban peso (0.72 per U.S. $1)

Location: Northern rim of the Caribbean Sea. The largest and most westerly island of the West Indies, Cuba lies at the entrance of the Gulf of Mexico and some 90 miles south of Florida **Features:** About three-fifths of the country consists of flat to gently rolling terrain with many wide and fertile valleys and plains. The rest is mountainous or hilly **Chief Rivers:** Cauto, Sagua la Grande, Zaza, Caonao, San Pedro, Toa

Political Leader, Head of State and of Government: President Fidel Castro Ruz, born 1926, First Secretary of the Central Committee of the Cuban Communist party, and president of the councils of state and of ministers, seized power in 1959 **Effective Date of Present Constitution:** December 1976 **Legislative Body:** National Assembly of People's Power (unicameral), with 481 deputies elected for 5-year terms. Power lies in the Communist party Politburo **Local Government:** 14 provinces, including Havana city and the special municipality of Isla de la Juventud (Isle of Pines), with locally elected assemblies

Ethnic Composition: 51% mulatto (mixed European and black), 37% European ancestry, 11% black, 1% Chinese **Population Distribution:** 60.5% urban (1971) **Density:** 227 inhabitants per sq. mi.

Largest Cities: (1976 est.) Havana 1,949,000, Santiago de Cuba 322,000, Camagüey 228,000, Guantánamo 158,000, Holguín 153,000, Santa Clara 150,000

Per Capita Income: $1,297 (1979) **Gross National Product (GNP):** $12.7 billion (1979) **Economic Statistics:** 10% of GNP is derived from agriculture (sugar, tobacco, cattle, coffee); 41% from industry (mainly sugar refining, cigarettes and cigars, rum, and textiles); and 33% from trade and finance (1974) **Minerals and Mining:** Cuba has the world's largest deposit of nickel; reserves of iron ore, manganese, cobalt, copper, chromite, salt, petroleum, gold, silver **Labor Force:** 2,700,000 (1976), with 39% in transportation and services, 33% in agriculture, and 26% in industry and construction **Foreign Trade:** Exports, chiefly sugar, nickel, tobacco, shrimp, lobster, and beef, were $3.6 billion (1978). Imports, mainly petroleum, equipment and machinery, and food, totaled $4.2 billion **Principal Trade Partners:** Soviet bloc, Japan, Spain, Canada, Britain

Vital Statistics: Birthrate, 19.8 per 1,000 of pop. (1976); death rate, 5.6 **Life Expectancy:** 72 years **Health Statistics:** 235 inhabitants per hospital bed; 1,121 per physician (1976) **Infant Mortality:** 23 per 1,000 births (1976) **Illiteracy:** 3.1% **Primary and Secondary School Enrollment:** 2,463,545 (1976) **Enrollment in Higher Education:** 82,688 (1975) **GNP Expended on Education:** 9.9% (1974)

Transportation: Paved roads total 5,470 mi. **Motor Vehicles:** 120,000 (1976) **Passenger Cars:** 80,000 **Railway Mileage:** 9,100 **Ports:** Havana, Matanzas, Nuevitas, Cienfuegos, Santiago de Cuba **Major Airlines:** Cubana de Aviación, the government-owned airline, operates domestic and international flights **Communications:** Government controlled **Radio Transmitters:** 115 (1975) **Receivers:** 2,100,000 (1976) **Television Transmitters:** 19 **Receivers:** 650,000 (1976) **Telephones:** 289,000 (1974) **Newspapers:** 15 dailies (1975), 107 per 1,000 inhabitants

Weights and Measures: Metric system **Travel Requirements:** Passport, visa; tourist visa, $6.00 fee, apply to Czechoslovak Embassy, Washington, D.C. 20009

Cuba, largest of the West Indies and the only Communist-controlled country in the Western Hemisphere, lies only 90 miles south of Key West, Florida. Cuba's capital, Havana, is less than an hour's flight southwest from Miami. The country's largest city and principal port, Havana, was originally important as a well-situated way station between Spain and her colonies in the Western Hemisphere. Eventually, settlers moved inland, devoting themselves mainly to growing sugarcane and tobacco.

Despite the physical proximity of Cuba to the U.S. and the potential trade and other ties, the relationship between the two countries has never developed quite as one might expect. Cuba was the last Latin American nation to gain independence from Spain. The United States actually opposed the first attempt to free Cuba begun by Simón Bolívar. A native-based liberation movement starting in 1868 sputtered out after 10 years of fighting. It was not until 1895 that a revolution led by José Martí successfully challenged Spain. The revolutionaries also won strong sentiments of support in the U.S. After the mysterious sinking of the *Maine*, the U.S. declared war on Spain.

When a freely elected Cuban government took office in 1902, it found it had little to sell except land. Many foreign investors, chiefly Americans, stepped forward and purchased enormous areas and began to rebuild the sugar industry. For years after, Cuba was locked into a one-crop agricultural economy with American ownership of the land, mines and other resources. Income was, and still is, almost totally dependent on the world price of sugar. American interests were protected by the Platt Amendment that allowed U.S. to intervene in Cuban affairs, which it did in 1906-1909 and again in 1912.

Fulgencio Batista, a former army sergeant, dominated the political scene either directly or indirectly from 1934 to 1944 and from 1952 to 1959. Cuba's basic problems went unresolved during the Batista era and various groups sought his downfall.

President Batista's regime became repressive and increasingly unpopular, and on July 26, 1953, an armed opposition group led by a young lawyer, Fidel Castro, attacked the Moncada army barracks at Santiago de Cuba. The attack failed and many of those not killed were imprisoned, including Castro. He was released by President Batista under an amnesty in May 1955 and went into exile in Mexico, where he formed his "26th of July Movement." While a number of other groups in Cuba also actively opposed Batista, it was Castro's forces, eventually numbering several thousands, who finally succeeded in forcing Batista to flee the country, on January 1, 1959.

The Castro regime's early promises of agrarian reform to benefit the peasants resulted in state ownership of most of the land and in the organization of state farms. Cuba's business and industrial sectors were nationalized and placed under the direction of the state, which has also effectively abolished all opposition political activity.

A major element of Cuba's foreign policy under Castro has been the "exporting" of revolutionary techniques. To this end, Cuba has supported guerrilla movements in various countries in the Western Hemisphere and elsewhere—notably Africa—by providing weapons, financing, propaganda and, in some cases, advisory personnel.

A nod toward normalizing U.S.-Cuban relations was made in 1975 by U.S. Secretary of State Henry Kissinger. But the nod became a "no" when Cuba dispatched troops to help Russian-backed forces in Angola's civil war. After Jimmy Carter became president, he first tested the water with some qualified public overtures toward Cuba, and then on March 9, 1977, announced an end to travel restrictions in Cuba. The two countries soon negotiated fishing and maritime rights agreements.

Still, the United States kept a wary eye on Soviet military gifts to Cuba—MiG-23 jet planes in 1978, a non-nuclear submarine in 1979. In August 1979 the Carter Administration affirmed reports that the Soviet Union had a combat brigade of 2,500 to 3,000 men stationed in Cuba. Both Havana and Moscow insisted that Soviet military personnel were there only for training and advisory purposes.

Cuba's economic plight has steadily worsened, so much so that in a December 1979 speech Castro admitted that his country is "sailing on a sea of difficulties." The plunge in world sugar prices from a peak of 60¢ a pound in 1960 to 10¢ in 1979 had had a devastating effect on Cuban life; a severe blight had destroyed most of the 1979 tobacco crop; a lack of foreign exchange had resulted in the virtual disappearance of Western goods from store shelves; food shortages were growing and rationing was strictly enforced; prices were extremely high in the black market. To keep the economy going at all, Cuba had to depend on a subsidy of $8 million a day from the Soviets.

Out of such conditions, as well as widespread dissatisfaction with political suppression under the Communist regime, erupted a determined effort by thousands of Cubans in 1980 to get out of the country. On April 1 six persons crashed a bus through the gates of the Peruvian embassy in Havana to gain asylum. Within a week more than 10,000 men, women and children had crowded into the embassy compound. Castro promised safe passage to the refugees, either to return to their homes or to emigrate to other countries that would take them in. Some 700 of them departed by plane to Costa Rica within 11 days, and some were flown on to Peru and other destinations. On April 21 a flotilla of small boats sent from Florida by Cuban-American sympathizers began to pick up refugees at the port of Mariel and take them to Key West. The numbers of Cubans reaching the U.S. to join about 800,000 others who had fled there since 1959 swelled to tens of thousands. The Cuban government reluctantly cooperated in the exodus, calling the refugees "antisocials and bums." There were indications that Castro was emptying his jails of ordinary criminals and shipping them out as refugees.

HISTORY: Following the discovery of Cuba by Columbus in 1492, the island remained under Spanish rule until almost the end of the 19th century. A revolt against Spain broke out in 1895 and evoked strong sympathy in the United States. After the brief Spanish-American War of 1898, Cuba became an independent republic, though under U.S. protection. With the abrogation of the Platt Amendment in 1934, the U.S. gave up the right to intervene in Cuban affairs, but retained its right to the naval base at Guantánamo

1934-59: Fulgencio Batista y Zaldívar, an army sergeant, overthrows regime and becomes dominant figure in Cuban politics. After ruling through puppet presidents, Batista proclaims new constitution in 1940 and is elected president for four-year term. In 1952 he returns to power through an army coup but his regime is increasingly threatened by rebel uprisings led by Fidel Castro, who finally forces Batista to flee

1960: Castro begins to transform Cuba into socialist state modeled on Soviet pattern and installs Communists in leading government posts. Most U.S.-owned property is nationalized without compensation; United States rescinds Cuban sugar quota

1961: United States severs diplomatic relations with Havana. Castro turns increasingly to Soviet Union for aid and protection, receiving supplies of arms and oil. Cuban exiles in United States, trained and equipped by Central Intelligence Agency, land invasion force at Bay of Pigs in abortive attempt to overthrow Castro

1962: Organization of American States excludes Cuba from membership. Installation of Soviet missiles in Cuba leads to U.S. demand for their removal and to imposition of naval blockade of island to bar further Soviet shipments. Strong U.S. reaction results in Soviet backdown and missiles are withdrawn

1970: Castro concedes that sugar harvest fell far below 10-million-ton goal

1971: Cuba signs economic pact with the Soviet Union

1972: Premier Castro makes his third official visit to Moscow at the end of a two-month world tour of socialist countries

1975: OAS passes resolution to lift the 11 years of formal diplomatic and economic isolation of Cuba

1976: A new constitution is approved by referendum

1978: U.S.-Cuba thaw is stalled, principally on issues of U.S.

economic blockade against Cuba, $1.8 billion in claims against Cuba by American companies and individuals, and continued Cuban presence in Africa (estimated at 26,000 men, mostly military, in Angola, Ethiopia and 14 other nations). U.S. accuses Cuba of having role in rebel invasion of Zaire from Angolan bases. Castro denies charge

1979: At Jan. 1 celebration of 20th anniversary of his seizure of power, Castro denounces the United States. During visit to Mexico he notes that that country was the only one in Latin America that kept up diplomatic relations with Cuba throughout past 20 years. As host to the sixth summit conference of Third World nations, in September, he defends use of Cuban troops to fight for "just causes" in Africa. Addressing UN General Assembly, he calls for U.S. and "other imperialists" to contribute $300 billion to developing nations over next 10 years

1980: Thousands of Cubans flee from economic hardships and political repression, seeking a better life in U.S. and other countries

---

CYPRUS

Area: 3,572 sq. mi. (including the 99 sq. mi. British-leased Sovereign Base Area) **Population:** 621,000 (1979 est.)

Official Name: Republic of Cyprus **Capital:** Nicosia **Nationality:** Cypriot **Languages:** Greek and Turkish are the official languages. English is widely understood **Religion:** 78% Greek Orthodox, 18% Moslem, 4% Maronite, Armenian and Apostolic Christians **Flag:** An outline map of Cyprus in gold above crossed green olive branches on a white field **Anthem:** None established **Currency:** Cypriot pound (0.36 per U.S. $1)

Location: Middle East. The third largest island in the Mediterranean, Cyprus lies 44 miles south of Turkey, 60 miles west of Syria, and 260 miles east of Rhodes, the nearest part of Greece **Features:** The Troodos Mountains in the southwest and the Kyrenia range along the northern coast dominate the island. The central plain, or Mesaoria, lies between the two mountain ranges **Chief River:** Pedieos (Pedias)

Head of State and of Government: President: Spyros Achilles Kyprianou, born 1932, succeeded August 1977, reelected for full 5-year term 1978 **Effective Date of Present Constitution:** 1960 **Legislative Body:** House of Representatives (unicameral), consisting of 35 Greek Cypriot members, elected for 5 years. Turkish Cypriots declared their independence and established in February 1975 the Turkish Federated State of Cyprus, with a president (Rauf R. Denktash elected in 1976), premier (Mustafa Cagatay, appointed 1978), and a 40-member unicameral Constituent Assembly; a referendum in 1976 approved a constitution **Local Government:** 6 districts

Ethnic Composition: About 78% of the population is of Greek descent, 18% of Turkish origin, and the rest composed of Armenians, Maronites, and other minorities **Population Distribution:** 42.2% urban (1974) **Density:** 174 inhabitants per sq. mi.

Largest Cities: (1973 census) Nicosia 116,125; (1972 estimates) Limassol 61,400, Famagusta 44,200, Larnaca 21,800, Paphos 12,100, Kyrenia 5,200

Per Capita Income: $2,387 (1979) **Gross National Product (GNP):** $1.5 billion (1979) **Economic Statistics:** About 18% of GNP was derived from agriculture and 26% from manufacturing and mining **Minerals and Mining:** Copper is the most important mineral, but the mines are becoming depleted; asbestos is becoming increasingly important. Other minerals are iron pyrites, chromite, umber, and yellow ocher **Labor Force:** 202,700 (1977, Greek area only), with 26% in industry, 23% in agriculture, forestry and fishing, 15% employed overseas or in military, 5% in government **Foreign Trade**—*Republic of Cyprus area (Greek):* Exports, chiefly fruits and vegetables, wine, cement and clothing, totaled $327 million in 1978. Imports, mainly machinery, manufactures, fuel and food, totaled $684 million *Turkish area:* Exports, chiefly fruits and vegetables and pyrites, totaled $16 million in 1976. Imports, chiefly food, fuels and machinery, totaled $66 million **Principal Trade Partners**—*Republic of Cyprus area (Greek):* Britain, Saudi Arabia, West Germany, France, Japan, Greece, Iraq, U.S., Lebanon, Kuwait *Turkish area:* Turkey, Britain, West Germany, France, Italy, Netherlands

Vital Statistics: Birthrate, 19.6 per 1,000 of pop. (1976); death rate, 9.8 **Life Expectancy:** 73 years **Health Statistics:** 177 inhabitants per hospital bed; 1,092 per physician (Greek area-1977) **Infant Mortality:** 27.2 per 1,000 births **Illiteracy:** 11% **Primary and Secondary School Enrollment:** (Greek area) 104,524 (1977) **Enrollment in Higher Education:** 782 (1976) **GNP Expended on Education:** 4.1% (1976)

Transportation: Paved roads total 2,800 mi. **Motor Vehicles:**

93,100 (1977) **Passenger Cars:** 74,500 **Railway Mileage:** None **Ports:** Famagusta, Limassol, Larnaca, Karavostassi **Major Airlines:** Cyprus Airways (government owned) operates domestic and international flights; there is also a Turkish-Cypriot airline **Communications:** State controlled **Radio Transmitters:** 16 **Licenses:** 200,000 (1976) **Television Transmitters:** 7 **Licenses:** 57,000 (1976) **Telephones:** 77,000 (1976) **Newspapers:** 12 dailies (1975), 107 copies per 1,000 inhabitants (1970)

Weights and Measures: Both British standards and the metric system are used along with local units **Travel Requirements:** Passport, no visa

---

The picturesque island of Aphrodite, Cyprus has been an independent but strife-torn nation since 1960. Previously, its strategic location had attracted many foreign conquerors, including the Egyptians, Phoenicians, Assyrians, Persians, Romans, Greeks, Turks and British. Today Cyprus is divided into two separate states and its future as a single nation is in doubt.

The island is the homeland of two antagonistic peoples—some half-million ethnic Greeks and slightly more than 120,000 ethnic Turks. The Greek Cypriots have traditionally favored *enosis* (union) with Greece, while the Turkish Cypriots want partition or cantonization of the country. In any case, virtually all Cypriots regard themselves as Greeks or Turks, Christians or Moslems first and as Cypriots second.

More than half the total area of Cyprus is cultivated, a noteworthy accomplishment in the largely arid Middle East. Mineral resources maintain a modest industrial complex. Light manufacturing is growing in the Greek area.

The constitution, in effect after independence in 1960, required that the president be a Greek Cypriot and the vice-president a Turkish Cypriot. Archbishop Makarios III, head of the Greek Orthodox Church on Cyprus became president. The Greek and Turkish communities lived under a form of de facto segregation.

Civil war between the two communities erupted in 1963, and terroristic campaigns became a part of Cypriot life. In 1964, the United Nations sent a peace-keeping force to minimize clashes. Turkish Cypriot leaders withdrew from active participation in the government of Cyprus. In 1967 war between Greece and Turkey over Cyprus was narrowly averted, mainly through the mediation of the United States. Turkey had threatened to invade the island but Greece finally agreed to remove nearly all of the 8,000 troops it had there.

The Cypriot national guard which was dominated by officers from Greece continued to press for union with Greece. In 1971 the EOKA B, a guerrilla movement favoring ties to Greece and led by Gen. George Grivas, stepped up its terrorist activities, which tended to undermine the government of President Makarios, who began his third five-year term in February 1973. (His second term had been extended.)

On July 15, 1974, Greek officers of the Cypriot national guard led a coup which overthrew President Makarios and replaced him with an EOKA B terrorist, Nikos Sampson. Turkey responded by invading Cyprus on July 20, and quickly conquered the northern two-fifths of the island. Most of the Greek Cypriots in the conquered territory fled south, and most of the Turkish Cypriots elsewhere moved north. Sampson's government collapsed.

Amid fears of a wider conflict, the UN ordered a cease-fire. Fighting continued sporadically but order was restored with Glafkos Clerides, president of the Cyprus House of Representatives, as interim president. By the time international pressure effected a real cease-fire on August 16, 200,000 Greek Cypriots were refugees. Makarios returned to power in December 1974.

In February 1975 a Turkish-Cypriot Federated State of Cyprus was created in the occupied area without the approval of Makarios, and in June a Turkish Cypriot referendum established a constitution for the state. Talks to establish a unified form of government continue, but accord at times seems distant. In April 1978 the Cypriot government rejected Turkish proposals for a settlement of the dispute between the island's Greeks and Turks, charging they were aimed at permanently dividing the island into two states. But there was still hope that unity could be restored. In January 1980, President Kyprianou offered the Turkish Cypriots certain economic benefits, including jobs and old-age pensions, as a first step toward rapprochement between the Turkish and Greek communities.

HISTORY: Cyprus, which derives its name from "kypros," the Greek word for copper, was settled first by the Greeks c. 1500 B.C. and passed to the Romans in 58 B.C. Later a part of the Byzantine Empire, the island slumbered until 1191, when Richard I of England conquered Cyprus and it became a base for the Crusaders. In the 16th century, the island was conquered by Turkey. Administration was transferred to Britain in 1878 and in 1928 the island became a Crown Colony

1946: Greece demands union (*enosis*) with Cyprus

1956: Archbishop Makarios, spiritual and political leader of the Greek Cypriots, is deported by British

1959: Greek-Turkish conferences in Zurich and London reach agreement on independence for Cyprus. Archbishop Makarios returns and is elected president

1960: Independence is officially proclaimed

1963: Violence between Greeks and Turks erupts in Nicosia

1964: Turks withdraw from active participation in government. Threat of war between Greece and Turkey over Cyprus brings United Nations peace-keeping force to island

1968: Makarios announces restoration of freedom of movement for Turkish Cypriots, ending blockade of Turkish sectors

1973: Struggle for *enosis* erupts into widespread violence

1974: Cypriot National Guard ousts President Makarios. Turkish forces invade Cyprus and gain control of 40 percent of the island. Two-way migration makes occupied territory predominantly Turkish, rest of island predominantly Greek. Makarios returns and resumes the presidency

1975: Turkish Cypriots proclaim their own state in northern Cyprus

1976: Turkish Cypriots elect Rauf Denktash to serve as president of the Turkish Cypriot Zone

1977: Turkish and Greek Cypriot leaders begin talks. Makarios dies. Spyros Kyprianou succeeds him

1978: Cypriot-Egyptian diplomatic relations severed after Cypriot troops in Larnaca kill 15 Egyptian commandos who were storming a Cyprus Airways jet in which two Palestinians held hostages. Deadlock in talks between Cypriot leaders continues

1980: Kyprianou offers economic benefits to Turkish Cypriots

CZECHOSLOVAKIA

Area: 49,373 sq. mi. **Population:** 15,247,000 (1979 est.)

Official Name: Czechoslovak Socialist Republic **Capital:** Prague **Nationality:** Czechoslovak **Languages:** Czech and Slovak are the official and principal languages; Hungarian and German are minority languages **Religion:** About 77% of the population is Roman Catholic; 8% are members of the Czechoslovak Church; and 8% are Protestants. All churches are under close government control **Flag:** A blue triangle on the hoist with its apex toward the center; the rest of the flag consists of a white band on top and a red band on the bottom **Anthem:** Where Is My Home? **Currency:** Koruna (10.4 per U.S. $1)

Location: Central Europe. Landlocked Czechoslovakia is bordered on the north by Poland, on the east by the USSR, on the south by Hungary and Austria, on the west by West Germany, and on the northwest by East Germany **Features:** Bohemia, Moravia, and Slovakia are the country's principal regions. Bohemia, in the west, is a plateau surrounded by mountains; Moravia, in the central region, is somewhat hillier; and Slovakia, in the east, is partly mountainous and partly lowland **Chief Rivers:** Labe, Vltava, Danube, Morava, Váh, Nitra, Hron, Ohre, Hornád

Political Leader and Head of State: President Gustáv Husák, born 1913, reelected 1980; general secretary of the Central Committee of the Communist Party **Head of Government:** Premier Lubomir Strougal, born 1935, appointed January 1, 1970 **Effective Date of Present Constitution:** 1960; the constitution was amended in 1969 to provide for Czech and Slovak local autonomy within a federal state, and again in 1971 and 1975 **Legislative Body:** Federal Assembly (bicameral), consisting of 2 equal chambers, the Chamber of the People and the Chamber of the Nations. The Chamber of the People has 200 members. The Chamber of the Nations consists of 75 representatives from the Czech Republic and 75 from the Slovak Republic. Both houses are elected for 5 years. The Federal Assembly is subordinate to the Central Committee of the Presidium of the Communist Party **Local Government:** The two republics have separate premiers and national councils, subordinate to the Federal Assembly. They are divided into 10 regions and 2 independent cities

Ethnic Composition: Czechs make up about 65% of the population and Slovaks 30%; Hungarians, Germans, Poles, Ukrainians, and Gypsies make up the rest **Population Distribution:** 66.7% urban (1974) **Density:** 309 inhabitants per sq. mi.

Largest Cities: (1976 est.) Prague 1,173,031, Brno 361,561, Bratislava 345,515, Ostrava 302,111, Kosice 179,143, Plzen 157,306

Per Capita Income: $5,039 (1979) **Gross National Product (GNP):** $76.6 billion (1979) **Economic Statistics:** About 45% of GNP comes from industry (iron and steel, glass, leather products, brewing, and textiles); 12% from agriculture (grains, sugar beets, hops, fruits and vegetables); 8% from construction; 9% from transport and communications; 9% from trade; 5% from housing; 11% from government and other services **Minerals and Mining:** Coal, antimony, magnesite, lignite and uranium **Labor Force:** 8.3 million (1976), with about 37% in industry and construction, and 18% in agriculture **Foreign Trade:** Exports, chiefly machinery, motor vehicles, iron and steel, and chemicals, totaled $11.7 billion in 1978. Imports, mainly machinery, industrial raw materials, food, fuel, and manufactured goods, totaled $12.5 billion **Principal Trade Partners:** USSR, East Germany, Poland, Hungary, Romania, West Germany, Britain, Bulgaria, Switzerland, China, Austria, Yugoslavia

Vital Statistics: Birthrate, 18.7 per 1,000 of pop. (1977); death rate, 11.5 **Life Expectancy:** 71 years **Health Statistics:** 99 inhabitants per hospital bed; 404 per physician (1976) **Infant Mortality:** 19.6 per 1,000 births (1977) **Illiteracy:** Negligible **Primary and Secondary School Enrollment:** 2,210,915 (1976) **Enrollment in Higher Education:** 155,059 (1975) **GNP Expended on Education:** 4.5% (1976)

Transportation: Paved roads total 37,350 mi. **Motor Vehicles:** 2,117,500 (1977) **Passenger Cars:** 1,827,700 **Railway Mileage:** 8,228 **Ports:** None **Major Airlines:** Czechoslovak Airlines operates domestic and international services **Communications:** State owned **Radio Transmitters:** 123 **Licenses:** 3,928,000 (1976) **Television Transmitters:** 788 **Licenses:** 3,793,000 (1976) **Telephones:** 2,743,000 (1976) **Newspapers:** 29 dailies, 300 copies per 1,000 inhabitants (1975)

Weights and Measures: Metric system **Travel Requirements:** Passport, visa, 2 pictures, $8 fee

---

The problem of Czechoslovakia today is trying to mold a socialist state of Marxist-Leninist traditions as determined by its Russian guardians while satisfying a native desire for the freedom and openness of a Western democracy.

The Communist party seized power in 1948, and established one of the world's least free societies. In the 1960s, with a new constitution, a cautious liberalizing movement emerged. A flowering of Czechoslovak artistry in films, the theater and other arts began. When the economy stagnated, Slovak Communists found a chance to replace hard-liner Antonin Novotny with Alexander Dubcek as first secretary of the Communist Party in January 1968.

Under Dubcek the trend toward freedom accelerated. Press censorship was reduced and grievances were aired, thus adding to the pressure for reforms while at the same time arousing the fears of Soviet leaders. The radical experiment to establish "socialism with a human face" ended abruptly on August 20, 1968. Armored units of the Warsaw Pact countries, led by Soviet tanks, entered Czechoslovakia at night to ensure the restoration of a more orthodox brand of Communism.

The dramatic incursion was characterized by its initiators as necessary to thwart a "threatened counterrevolution" by "imperialist forces." It was seen by Western observers—and most Czechs—as a final desperate move by Leonid I. Brezhnev, the Soviet Communist party chief, to curtail Dubcek's essay in socialist democracy.

Dubcek was forced in succeeding days to sign a protocol in Moscow accepting the military "assistance." He was formally replaced in April 1969 by Gustav Husák, who has since moved resolutely to restore the former system of state control in Czechoslovakia.

The aftermath of Dubcek's "Prague Spring" has been characterized by a reversal of his reforms; a broad purge of liberal economists, writers, educators and artists; and a "cleansing" of party ranks as well as the removal of the former leader himself from public life.

Dubcek's error had been to move too quickly, too prominently, and certainly too radically to shed the restrictions and repressions of the earlier Stalinist period of postwar Communist rule.

The new Czech party chief, Husák, has spent the intervening years walking a line between hardliners in the party, who want to carry the anti-Dubcek purges beyond the stages of ousters and restrictions to arrests and trials, and the many Czechs—revisionists, in party terminology—who watch now with sullen hostility to the withering of a brief, bright flowering of intellectual freedom.

As politically adroit as Dubcek was unsophisticated, Husák removed 400,000 members from the Czech Communist party—one-fifth of the national membership—but only a few have been tried for "anti-State" activities. Many leading educators, commentators, economists, and other leaders who supported Dubcek left the country.

In recent years a slight easing can be detected. Husák has given a second chance to lesser participants in the reform movement and hard-liners were unable to dominate the Communist party congress in April 1975. But the government has harassed dissidents who spread the ideas of the 1968 "Prague Spring"; in 1980 the well-known playwright Pavel Kohout was deprived of citizenship and not allowed to return to Prague from Vienna. Dissident attacks on Husák's "normalization" manage to circulate and are leaked to the West where they hinder Czech officials seeking better trade contacts with the non-Communist world.

HISTORY: In the 6th and 7th centuries, Slavic migrants absorbed Celtic, Germanic, and other cultures. The Czechs, in Bohemia and Moravia, and the Slovaks, in Slovakia, were united in the Great Moravian Empire in the ninth century, a period that also saw the introduction of Christianity. After the empire's collapse in the 10th century, the Slovaks were incorporated into the Kingdom of Hungary and the Czechs established the Kingdom of Bohemia. The 14th century, with its Hussite Revolution, marked the beginning of religious wars in the Czech lands that were to continue through the Reformation and Counter-Reformation. During the decline of the Kingdom of Bohemia, the Czechs came under foreign dynasties, ending up, along with the Slovaks, in the Austro-Hungarian Empire

1918: Following the defeat of Austria-Hungary in World War I, Czechoslovakia, incorporating the Czech lands and Slovakia, is proclaimed an independent republic with nationalist leader Thomas Masaryk its first president

1935: Masaryk dies. Eduard Beneš elected president

1938: Britain, France, Germany, and Italy, without having invited Czechoslovakia to the negotiating table, sign the Munich Pact, a capitulation to German demands for the Sudetenland, the border region of Bohemia inhabited by a large German minority. President Eduard Beneš resigns and goes into exile

1939-46: German troops occupy Czechoslovakia during World War II. The country is liberated by Soviet and U.S. forces. Beneš returns and resumes presidency

1948: Communists seize power; Beneš resigns; Foreign Minister Jan Masaryk, son of Thomas Masaryk, plunges to death from a window. Though officially termed a suicide, he is believed to have been murdered by the Communists

1955: Czechoslovakia joins the Warsaw Pact, the Soviet-bloc military organization

1968: Alexander Dubcek, a progressive, becomes first secretary of the Czechoslovak Communist party, replacing Antonin Novotny. The Soviet Union, alarmed by liberalization measures in Czechoslovakia, invades the country

1969: Gustav Husák replaces Dubcek as leader of the Czechoslovak Communist party and rescinds liberalization; Dubcek is ousted from ruling Presidium in purge of party progressives

1970: Dubcek is expelled from the Communist party and removed from his post as ambassador to Turkey

1973: First direct consular agreement between Communist Czechoslovakia and the United States is signed

1974: U.S. and Czechoslovakia reach preliminary agreement on settlement of postwar financial counterclaims

1975: Husák is elected president by Federal Assembly

1977: Czech dissidents publish manifesto (Charter 77) protesting the suppression of human rights; detention of signers follows

1978: Subdued public protests and destruction of statue mark 10th anniversary of invasion

1979: Charter 77 group falters, elects new leaders

DENMARK

Area: 16,629 sq. mi. **Population:** 5,118,000 (1979 est.)

Official Name: Kingdom of Denmark **Capital:** Copenhagen **Nationality:** Danish **Languages:** Danish is the official and universal language **Religion:** About 96% of the people belong to the established Lutheran Church **Flag:** A white cross on a red field **Anthem:** There is a Lovely Land **Currency:** Danish krone (5.6 per U.S. $1)

Location: Northwest Europe. Denmark is bordered on the north by the Skagerrak; on the east by the Kattegat, Öresund, and the Baltic Sea; on the south by West Germany; and on the west by the North Sea **Features:** Low-lying elevation, with flat or rolling landscape **Chief Rivers:** Stora, Skjern, Varde, Gudena

Head of State: Queen Margrethe II, born 1940, ascended the throne 1972 **Head of Government:** Premier Anker Joergensen, born 1922, appointed 1972 and 1975, reappointed 1979 **Effective Date of Present Constitution:** 1953 **Legislative Body:** Parliament (unicameral *Folketing*), with 179 members, including 2 each from Greenland and the Faeroe Islands, elected on the basis of proportional representation for 4 years **Local Government:** 14 counties and two urban communes, with elected chief administrative officers and councils

Ethnic Composition: Except for foreign "guest workers" the population is almost entirely Scandinavian **Population Distribution:** 80% urban **Density:** 308 inhabitants per sq. mi.

Largest Cities (M.A. = Metropolitan Area) (1976 est.): Copenhagen 699,300 (M.A. 1,327,940), Aarhus 246,111, Odense 167,911, Aalborg 154,605

Per Capita Income: $8,466 (1979) **Gross National Product (GNP):** $43.3 billion (1979) **Economic Statistics:** About 35% of GNP (1978) comes from manufacturing (food processing, machinery, chemicals), crafts, building and construction; 8% from agriculture (dairy and poultry farming, cattle raising, hog breeding, grain and root crops), forestry and fisheries **Minerals and Mining:** Oil and gas produced from North Sea wells **Labor Force:** 2,625,223 (1979); 25% in manufacturing, 15% in trade, 9% in agriculture, 8% in construction **Foreign Trade:** Exports, chiefly machinery and equipment, textiles and agricultural commodities, totaled $11.8 billion in 1978. Imports, mainly machinery and fittings, fuels, chemicals, iron and steel, totaled $14.8 billion **Principal Trade Partners:** Sweden, West Germany, Britain, United States, Norway, Netherlands

Vital Statistics: Birthrate, 12.2 per 1,000 of pop. (1977); death rate, 9.9 **Life Expectancy:** 73 years **Health Statistics:** 103 inhabitants per hospital bed; 624 per physician (1972) **Infant Mortality:** 8.9 per 1,000 (1977) **Illiteracy:** Negligible **Primary and Secondary School Enrollment:** 854,442 (1976) **Enrollment in Higher Education:** 110,271 (1975) **GNP Expended on Education:** 8.3% (1975)

Transportation: Roads total 40,000 mi. **Motor Vehicles:** 1,655,200 (1977) **Passenger Cars:** 1,381,300 **Railway Mileage:** 1,609 **Ports:** Copenhagen, Aalborg, Aarhus, Esbjerg **Major Airlines:** Scandinavian Airlines System (SAS) operates domestic and international services. Danair operates domestic routes **Communications:** Government owned **Radio Transmitters:** 19 **Licenses:** 1,851,000 (1976) **Television Transmitters:** 34 **Licenses:** 1,637,000 (1976) **Telephones:** 2,734,000 (1977) **Newspapers:** 49 dailies, 341 copies per 1,000 inhabitants (1974)

Weights and Measures: Metric system **Travel Requirements:** Passport, no visa for 3 months

Denmark, located strategically at the mouth of the Baltic Sea, consists of the Jutland Peninsula (projecting north from West Germany) and about 500 islands, of which 100 are inhabited. It is one of the smallest countries in the world if only its low-lying islands and the Jutland Peninsula are considered. However, the kingdom also embraces the Faeroe Islands and the island of Greenland, both of which now enjoy great autonomy.

Occupied during World War II by the Nazis, Denmark did not return in the postwar era to the policy of neutrality that it had followed through World War I. Instead it became a charter member of the North Atlantic Treaty Organization in 1949 and joined with the West Germans in forming a joint Baltic command within the alliance in 1961. But the Danes, like the Norwegians, have limited their NATO membership by declaring that neither foreign troops nor nuclear weapons may be stationed on their territory in peacetime.

Small-scale production of oil from wells on the Danish share of the North Sea continental shelf began in 1972, and surface mining of iron ore began in Greenland on a limited scale in 1973. But so far Denmark's natural resources remain largely limited to its rich farmland, and the nation relies heavily upon imports.

Through membership in the British-led European Free Trade Association (EFTA), Denmark and its neighbors—Norway, Sweden and Finland—created what amounted to a Nordic common market in 1960. Most of this was retained when Denmark, along with Britain and Ireland, opted out of EFTA to join the European Communities (European Community, European Coal and Steel Community and European Atomic Energy Community) on January 1, 1973.

The political process is firmly democratic. But no election since 1945 has given any party a majority in the Folketing. The Social Democratic party is the largest and usually leads the governing coalition, but decision-making is slow and marked by compromise. Efforts to reduce unemployment and to promote needed exports also require the help of unions and businesses, which are reluctant to help unstable coalitions and which resent the country's high taxes. A two-year austerity program, involving strict wage controls, took effect in 1977 after strikes thwarted it for eight months.

HISTORY: During the Viking age the Danes figured importantly in the Norse raids on Western Europe. Denmark became at once an Atlantic and a Baltic power and warred with the English, with German princes, and with Norwegian and Swedish kings. Denmark's period of expansion lasted until about 1600 and was followed by a losing struggle against Swedish and German rivals

1643-60: Wars with Sweden determine eastern borders

1815: Denmark, having sided with France in the Napoleonic Wars, is among the losers and is forced by Sweden to cede Norway

1864: War with Prussia and Austria ends with the loss of Schleswig-Holstein, a third of Denmark's territory, to Prussia

1914-18: Denmark remains neutral in World War I

1920: Denmark's present southern border is established as northern Schleswig is recovered in a plebiscite

1940-45: Nazi troops invade Denmark and occupy country until its liberation by British forces in May 1945

1949: Denmark joins in forming NATO

1960: Denmark joins European Free Trade Association

1968: Social Democrats, Denmark's largest party, are ousted in general elections after 15 years in office

1972: King Frederik IX dies; is succeeded on the throne by Queen Margrethe II, Denmark's first reigning queen in six centuries

1973: Denmark joins the EC

1978: Social Democratic Prime Minister Anker Joergensen forms minority coalition with Liberals and others

1979: Greenland is granted autonomy. Liberals quit government, forcing elections in which Social Democrats increase plurality in parliament; Joergensen forms new coalition

DJIBOUTI

Area: 8,880 sq. mi. **Population:** 250,000 (1978 est.)

Official Name: Republic of Djibouti **Capital:** Djibouti **Nationality:** Djibouti **Languages:** French is the official language; Somali (Issa) and Afar are spoken by their communities; Arabic **Religion:** 94%

Moslem, 6% Christian **Flag:** Horizontal stripes of light blue over green, with a red star on a white triangle at the hoist **Anthem:** N.A. **Currency:** Djibouti franc (178 per U.S. $1)

Location: Northeastern Africa, around the Gulf of Tadjoura at the western end of the Gulf of Aden, near the southern entrance to the Red Sea. Bordered on the north, west and southwest by Ethiopia, and on the southeast by Somalia **Features:** An arid rocky coastal plain (with salt and freshwater pans) fringed by foothills of the Ethiopian ranges, and an interior plateau in the north and west **Chief Rivers:** None

Head of State: President Hassan Gouled Aptidon, born 1916, assumed office June 1977 **Head of Government:** Premier Barkat Gourad Hamadou, appointed October 1978 **Effective Date of Present Constitution:** Not yet drafted **Legislative Body:** Parliament (unicameral Assembly), with 65 members (33 Issas, 30 Afars, 2 Arabs) elected for 5 years **Local Government:** 5 districts

Ethnic Composition: Somalis (chiefly Issas), Afars (including seasonal nomads), French, Arabs, Italians, Greeks, Sudanese and Indians **Population Distribution:** c. 65% urban **Density:** 28 inhabitants per sq. mi.

Largest City: (1977 est.) Djibouti 130,000

Per Capita Income: $1,727 (1978 est.) **Gross National Product (GNP):** $190 million (1978 est.) **Economic Statistics:** Derivation from GNP not available. Nomadic herding (goats, cattle, sheep, camels, donkeys) is the chief occupation in the hinterland. In the capital, shipbuilding, repair and servicing, construction, and the production of liquid gas and foodstuffs (bottling) are the chief activities **Minerals and Mining:** No production other than salt panning **Labor Force:** N.A. **Foreign Trade:** Exports (transit from Ethiopia), chiefly hides and skins, sugar, and Ethiopian coffee, totaled $5 million in 1976. Imports, chiefly machinery, fuels, steel products, chemicals, foods, and grain, totaled $72 million **Principal Trade Partners:** France, Ethiopia, Japan

Vital Statistics: Birthrate, 42 per 1,000 of pop. (1970); death rate, 7.6 **Life Expectancy:** N.A. **Health Statistics:** 107 inhabitants per hospital bed; 1,964 per physician (1976) **Infant Mortality:** N.A. **Illiteracy:** 95% **Primary and Secondary School Enrollment:** 11,758 (1975) **Enrollment in Higher Education:** N.A. **GNP Expended on Education:** 4.9% (1971)

Transportation: Surfaced roads total 137 mi. **Motor Vehicles:** 15,100 (1977) **Passenger Cars:** 11,800 **Railway Mileage:** 60 **Port:** Djibouti **Major Airlines:** Air France and five other lines provide international service; Air Djibouti, which also flies to Ethiopia, Yemen, Southern Yemen and Somalia, provides domestic service **Communications:** Government controlled **Radio Transmitters:** 4 (1974) **Receivers:** 15,000 (1976) **Television Transmitters:** 1 **Receivers:** 3,500 (1976) **Telephones:** 4,000 **Newspapers:** 1 several times a week, 34 copies per 1,000 inhabitants (1975)

Weights and Measures: Metric system **Travel Requirements:** Passport, visa; contact French embassy or Consulate for requirements

On June 27, 1977, the last remnant of France's once-vast empire on the African continent achieved independence as the Republic of Djibouti.

During its first 83 years of existence, the dependency was known as French Somaliland, but in 1967 this small coastal area was renamed the French Territory of Afars and Issas, in recognition of the two major ethnic groups comprising the population. The Republic of Djibouti takes its name from its capital city, a Red Sea port with a majority of the nation's population.

Economic prospects for the Republic of Djibouti are not auspicious, as the barren tract, smaller in area than New Hampshire, lacks resources. The sole economic reason for the existence of the Republic is the commercial activity at the port of Djibouti, which is the terminus of the 486-mile railway from Addis Ababa, Ethiopia. The line carries half of Ethiopia's exports along its single track, and Djibouti is the transshipment point to the outer world for this trade. Out beyond the urban environment of the capital, the meager population subsists through nomadic herding.

The indigenous population is divided between the Afars, or Danakils, and the Issas, a branch of the Somali ethnic family. Though the two groups had disagreed in the past about the timing of independence, a majority of voters approved an independence proposal on May 8, 1977. France, by agreement, continues to maintain a military force in Djibouti.

In March 1978, Ethiopian forces, aided by 1,000 Soviet advisors, and 11,000 Cuban troops, ended the eight-month Ogaden war by driving the Somalis from the region. But Ethiopia said there would be no cease-fire until Somalia formally renounced its territorial claims on the Ogaden, as well as on Djibouti and northern Kenya. Meanwhile, thousands of refugees have flooded Djibouti, thus placing greater strains on the fledgling nation. Further complicating matters in 1979 was the fighting between North and South Yemen. Showing its concern, Djibouti welcomed U.S. warships to its port in March.

HISTORY: French interest in the area began in the 1840s, culminating in the signing of friendship treaties with the local sultans. The purchase of the anchorage at Obock signaled the beginning of French occupation. The opening of the Suez Canal in 1869 and growing Anglo-French competition for territorial spoils in Africa caused France to expand its toehold to include all of the shores of the Gulf of Tadjoura

1884-85: The protectorate of French Somaliland is established
1896: The administrative capital is moved from Obock to Djibouti
1897-1917: The Franco-Ethiopian railway is built from Djibouti to Addis Ababa
1958: French Somaliland becomes an Overseas Territory of the French community
1967: In a referendum on independence, 60 percent of the voters choose to continue the ties with France. The area is renamed the French Territory of Afars and Issas
1977: Following a majority vote for independence, the independent Republic of Djibouti is proclaimed. Premier Ahmed Dini resigns after renewal of tensions between Afars and Issas
1978: Abdallay Mohamed Kamil appointed premier in February. In October, he is followed in office by Barkat Gourad Hamadou

---

DOMINICA

Area: 291 sq. mi. **Population:** 81,000 (1976 est.)

Official Name: Commonwealth of Dominica **Capital:** Roseau **Nationality:** Dominican **Languages:** English is the official language and is everywhere understood, but a patois, based on French and containing many African elements, is widely spoken **Religion:** Mainly Roman Catholic; some Anglicans and Methodists **Flag:** A dark green field quartered by three equal vertical and horizontal stripes of yellow, white and black. In the center a large red disk bears a parrot surrounded by a circle of ten five-pointed stars **Anthem:** Isle of Beauty, Isle of Splendour **Currency:** Dominican dollar (2.7 per U.S. $1)

Location: The island, located in the Windward Islands of the West Indies, lies between the French islands of Guadeloupe to the north and Martinique to the south. It is 20 miles long and 16 miles wide with a thickly forested mountainous terrain

Head of State: President Aurelius Marie, born 1903, appointed 1980 **Head of Government:** Prime Minister Mary Eugenia Charles, born 1919, appointed July 1980 **Effective Date of Present Constitution:** November 3, 1978 **Legislative Body:** House of Assembly (unicameral) with 21 elected representatives and 9 appointed senators **Local Government:** 2 town councils and 25 village councils

Ethnic Composition: Nearly all of the population is of African or mixed African-European origin. There is a small Carib Indian community **Density:** 278 inhabitants per sq. mi.

Largest Cities: (1976 est.) Roseau 16,800, Portsmouth 3,500

Per Capita Income: $410 (1977) **Gross National Product (GNP):** $32 million (1977). **Economic Statistics:** The economy is primarily agricultural, with bananas dominant. Citrus fruit and coconut production are also important. Industry and tourism are to be developed **Minerals and Mining:** None **Labor Force:** 25,150 (1976), primarily employed in agriculture **Foreign Trade:** Exports, chiefly bananas, grapefruit, lime juice, essential oils and coconuts, totaled $10 million in 1976. Imports, chiefly foods, machinery and consumer goods, totaled $18 million **Principal Trade Partners:** Britain, United States, Canada, Caribbean nations

Vital Statistics: Birthrate, 21.8 per 1,000 of pop. (1977); death rate, 6.7 **Life Expectancy:** N.A. **Health Statistics:** 234 inhabitants per hospital bed (1973); 5,385 per physician (1973) **Infant Mortality:** 24.1 per 1,000 births (1977) **Illiteracy:** 20% **Primary and Secondary School Enrollment:** 24,106 (1976) **Enrollment in Higher Education:** N.A. **GNP Expended on Education:** N.A.

Transportation: Surfaced (paved) roads total 300 mi. **Motor Vehicles:** 4,000 (1975) **Passenger Cars:** N.A. **Railway Mileage:** None **Port:** Roseau **Major Airlines:** LIAT, Air Martinique and Air Guadeloupe provide service to neighboring islands **Communications:** Government and privately owned **Radio Transmitters:** 2 **Receivers:** N.A. **Television Transmitters:** 1 **Receivers:** N.A. **Telephones:** 4,000 (1976) **Newspapers:** 2 weeklies

Weights and Measures: British and metric systems **Travel Requirements:** N.A.

The northernmost of the Windward Islands, Dominica has a pleasant climate and a great natural beauty that make it a haven for the sightseer, but its sparse, rocky soil makes life difficult for its predominantly black population, one of the poorest in the Caribbean.

One of the country's most urgent priorities since gaining independence in 1978 is the balanced development of the island's economy. Unemployment is chronic, over 20 percent, and agriculture is the mainstay of most islanders, with one crop—bananas—representing almost 80 percent of exports. Yet barely one third of the arable land is cultivated, mainly because of the mountainous and heavily wooded terrain. Foreign aid has become increasingly important, with Britain being Dominica's chief benefactor since independence.

Since achieving nationhood, Dominica has tottered on the brink of civil turmoil, with islanders divided betweeen two political factions; the social-democratic Dominica Labor party (DLP), which had pressed for independence by termination of the association with the United Kingdom, and the more conservative Dominica Freedom party (DFP), which had opposed independence except by referendum.

On May 29, 1979, amid charges of governmental corruption, anti-democratic moves and secret ties to South Africa, police fired on a demonstration of 15,000 in Roseau called to protest legislation curtailing press freedoms and banning the right to strike; two bystanders were killed. This sparked an island-wide general strike by all labor unions, and businessmen and political opponents joined in demanding that the DLP's Patrick R. John quit as prime minister. He resigned in June and was suceeded by James Oliver Seraphine, formerly Minister of Agriculture. On Aug. 29, Hurricane David killed 42 persons, made 65,000 homeless, virtually flattened Roseau, and destroyed the banana and grapefruit crops. Massive U.S. aid was received quickly. The Dominica Freedom party won a landslide victory in the July 1980 elections. The DFP's leader, Mary Eugenia Charles, became the first woman prime minister of a Caribbean nation on July 21. Miss Charles, an ardent anti-communist, favors a free enterprise course for the island nation.

HISTORY: The warlike Carib Indians are thought to have migrated north from South America to the West Indies in the 1300s, capturing the islands from the more peaceful Arawaks. Columbus first sighted the island on a Sunday in 1493 (by tradition) and named it Dominica after the Latin for that day of the week. Permanent European occupation did not occur until the mid-eighteenth century, when the French established settlements along the coast. Since that time the island has changed hands three times: captured by the British in 1759, retaken by the French in 1778, and restored to Britain by the Treaty of Paris in 1783. With the abolition of the slave trade in 1834, restricted local government developed under British colonial administration

1871: Dominica and other British islands to the north are formed into a federation of the Leeward Islands

1940: Dominica transferred to jurisdiction of Windward Islands group, under same government as Grenada, St. Vincent and St. Lucia

1958: Dominica joins Federation of the West Indies; remains member until its dissolution in 1962

1960: Windward Islands Group dissolved; direct rule by Britain reestablished

1967: Dominica becomes self-governing member of the West Indies Associated States within British Commonwealth

1970: DLP led by Premier Edward O. LeBlanc wins first general election under Associated status

1974: Legislature approves emergency powers to combat "Dread" Black Power terrorist movement; Dominica joins Caribbean Community and Common Market (CARICOM)

1975: DLP under Patrick R. John, who succeeds LeBlanc, retains power in March 24 elections against opposition DFP

1978: Dominica becomes fully independent November 3, the second Associated State (following Grenada in 1974) to achieve nationhood

1979: Antigovernment demonstrations in Roseau May 29 fired on by police, sparking general strike that forces Prime Minister John to resign a month later. James Oliver Seraphine takes over as prime minister. Hurricane David makes 65,000 homeless

1980: DFP wins landslide election victory. Its leader, Mary Eugenia Charles, becomes prime minister

---

DOMINICAN REPUBLIC

Area: 18,816 sq. mi. **Population:** 5,275,000 (1979 est.)

Official Name: Dominican Republic **Capital:** Santo Domingo **Nationality:** Dominican **Languages:** Spanish is the official and universal language **Religion:** About 95% of the people are Roman Catholic, the state religion **Flag:** Four rectangular sections divided by a white cross bearing the national coat of arms in the center; the upper left and lower right sections are dark blue and the other two sections are red **Anthem:** National Anthem, beginning "Brave men of Quisqueya" **Currency:** Dominican peso (1 per U.S. $1)

Location: West Indies, occupying the eastern two-thirds of the Island of Hispaniola. The Dominican Republic is bounded on the north by the Atlantic Ocean; on the east by the Mona Passage, which separates the country from Puerto Rico; on the south by the Caribbean Sea; and on the west by Haiti **Features:** The country is crossed by four east-west mountain ranges, the principal one being the Cordillera Central, which runs across the middle of the country. In the upper central part of the country lies the Cibao valley, often known as the nation's "food basket" **Chief Rivers:** Yaque del Norte, Jaina, Ozama, Yaque del Sur

Head of State and of Government: President Antonio Guzmán Fernández, born 1911, elected May 1978 to a 4-year term **Effective Date of Present Constitution:** November 28, 1966 **Legislative Body:** National Congress (bicameral), consisting of a 27-member Senate and a 91-member Chamber of Deputies, with members of both houses elected every 4 years by popular vote **Local Government:** 26 provinces and 1 national district, each headed by a governor appointed by the president

Ethnic Composition: 73% mulatto, 16% of European (chiefly Spanish) origin, 11% Negro **Population Distribution:** 46.8% urban (1976) **Density:** 280 inhabitants per sq. mi.

Largest Cities: (1970 census—Metropolitan Areas) Santo Domingo 802,619, Santiago 173,975, San Cristóbal 69,875, La Vega 64,370

Per Capita Income: $953 (1979) **Gross National Product (GNP):** $5.4 billion (1979) **Economic Statistics:** In 1977 about 21% of GNP came from agriculture (sugar, coffee, cocoa, rice, cotton, tobacco, bananas); 35% from trade and services; 19% from manufacturing (sugar refining, processing of other food products, beverages, tobacco, chemicals) **Minerals and Mining:** Bauxite, nickel, gold, silver and some iron ore are exploited **Labor Force:** 1.4 million (1977), with 55% in agriculture **Foreign Trade:** Exports, chiefly sugar, coffee, chocolate, tobacco, bauxite, gold, silver and nickel, totaled $676 million in 1978. Imports, mainly wheat, petroleum, automobiles, tractors, and pharmaceutical products, totaled $859 million **Principal Trade Partners:** United States, Netherlands, West Germany, Venezuela, Japan, Morocco, Spain, Switzerland

Vital Statistics: Birthrate, 45.8 per 1,000 of pop. (1975); death rate, 11 **Life Expectancy:** 61 years **Health Statistics:** 351 inhabitants per hospital bed; 1,866 per physician (1973) **Infant Mortality:** 43.5 per 1,000 births (1975) **Illiteracy:** 33% **Primary and Secondary School Enrollment:** 984,039 (1973) **Enrollment in Higher Education:** 41,352 (1974) **GNP Expended on Education:** 2.6% (1973)

Transportation: Paved roads total 3,500 mi. **Motor Vehicles:** 116,700 (1976) **Passenger Cars:** 77,300 **Railway Mileage:** 1,000 **Ports:** Santo Domingo, Haina, Barahona, Puerto Plata, La Romana, San Pedro de Macoris **Major Airlines:** Dominicana, the national airline, provides internal and limited international services **Communications:** Partly government controlled **Radio Transmitters:** 146 **Receivers:** 200,000 (1976) **Television Transmitters:** 7 **Receivers:** 160,000 (1976) **Telephones:** 160,000 (1979) **Newspapers:** 10 dailies, 42 copies per 1,000 inhabitants (1975)

Weights and Measures: Metric system **Travel Requirements:** Passport, visa, tourist card valid for 60 days, $6.00 fee

With the possible exception of Cuba, the Dominican Republic has been the most disrupted Latin American country of this century. Its proximity—physically, historically, and economically—to the United States has produced two armed interventions ordered by Washington since 1916. In the years between 1930 and 1961, the country, which occupies the eastern two-thirds of the island of Hispaniola, lived under the oppression of Generalissimo Rafael Leonidas Trujillo Molina.

Since 1966 the Dominican Republic has enjoyed a measure of stability, thanks to improved economic planning and agrarian reform. With massive assistance from the United States and from international lending agencies, the country continues to be one of the most dynamic and stable nations in Latin America.

In May 1978, after 12 years in office, President Joaquín Balaguer was defeated in his bid for a fourth straight four-year term by Antonio Guzmán of the opposition Dominican Revolutionary party (a centrist movement despite its misleadingly radical name). The election was marked by an armed intervention by Dominican troops who seized the electoral commission headquarters in Santo Domingo and stopped the ballot-count after a tally of a fourth of the votes showed Guzmán ahead by about a 3-to-2 margin. Several Latin American leaders spoke out against the action, as did President Carter, who threatened to cut off U.S. aid that includes a $38 million-a-year sugar-import program. At that point, Balaguer met with his generals, who may have acted without his consent, and (after some 30 hours) the counting resumed.

In his first state-of-the-nation speech, made in 1979, President Guzmán announced that agricultural development would be stressed in an effort to overcome a stagnant economy. And in its first venture into the Eurodollar market, the Dominican Republic signed a $185-million loan agreement with a group of international banks.

Memories of romantic earlier days were revived with the announcement that the Spanish galleon *Concepcíon*, which sank in 1641, had been found in the waters off the Dominican Republic by Burt Webber, Jr., of Annville, Pa., a treasure hunter, in November 1978. The government is to get half the artifacts recovered, and it plans to build a museum to house them.

HISTORY: The eastern part of the island of Hispaniola was known in pre-Columbian times as Quisqueya and was first settled by Carib and Arawak Indians. The island was discovered by Columbus in 1492 and soon became the springboard for Spanish conquest of the Caribbean. The western third of Hispaniola (Haiti) was ceded to France in 1697, and in 1795 France acquired the eastern part, known as Santo Domingo. The French were expelled from the eastern region in 1809 and in 1814 it reverted to Spain

1821: Dominicans proclaim their independence and attempt to unite with the Republic of Gran Colombia, founded by Bolívar

1822: Dominicans are conquered by Haiti and the whole island of Hispaniola falls under oppressive Haitian rule

1844: Dominicans revolt against Haiti and regain independence; a republic is established under Pedro Santana

1861-69: Widespread revolts and continued attacks from Haiti lead Santana to place country under Spanish rule, but popular opposition forces Spain to withdraw (1865). Opposition leader Buenaventura Báez, who succeeds Santana, negotiates treaty calling for annexation of country to the United States; U.S. Senate, however, refuses to ratify it

1905-24: United States takes over administration of Dominican customs to forestall intervention by foreign powers seeking to collect their debts; following mounting disorders, the republic is brought under U.S. military rule from 1916 until 1924

1930-61: Republic is ruled by dictator Rafael Leonidas Trujillo Molina, who is assassinated in 1961

1962-63: Juan Bosch, a leader of the democratic left, is elected president in republic's first free elections since 1924; after only seven months in office Bosch is overthrown by the military

1965: Civilian triumvirate installed by leaders of the 1963 coup is overthrown, precipitating civil war between left-wing forces seeking to restore Bosch and right-wing and military elements; U.S. troops intervene against pro-Bosch forces but fail to halt civil war, which ends after mediation by the OAS

1966: Joaquín Balaguer defeats Bosch for the presidency

1970: Balaguer is reelected president in a disputed election

1974-75: Balaguer is reelected to third consecutive term. Anti-government violence and political uncertainty plague the country

1976: King Juan Carlos and Queen Sofia of Spain visit, the first ruling Spanish monarchs ever to set foot in Latin America

1978: Antonio Guzmán is elected president

1979: Two hurricanes devastate republic, leaving 1,300 dead, 500 missing, 100,000 homeless. Over 100 followers of Balaguer are arrested Sept. 25 and charged with plotting to overthrow the government. Rosario Dominica gold mines nationalized

1980: Dominican embassy in Bogotá, Colombia, seized and held with hostage diplomats for two months

ECUADOR

Area: 109,483 sq. mi. **Population:** 8,078,000 (1979 est.)

Official Name: Republic of Ecuador **Capital:** Quito **Nationality:** Ecuadorean **Languages:** Spanish, the official language, is spoken by about 93% of the population, and Quechua by 7% **Religion:** Overwhelmingly Roman Catholic **Flag:** Half the width of the flag is yellow and the remaining half consists of blue and red bands; in the center is the national coat of arms **Anthem:** Hail, O Fatherland **Currency:** Sucre (25 per U.S. $1)

Location: South America. Crossed by the Equator, from which the country gets its name, Ecuador is bordered on the north by Colombia, on the east and south by Peru, and on the west by the Pacific Ocean. The Galápagos Islands, some 600 miles west of the mainland, are part of the national territory **Features:** About a fourth of the country consists of a coastal plain, and another fourth of the Sierra, or highlands, lying between two chains of the Andes Mountains. The Oriente, or eastern jungle, covers the remaining half of the country **Chief Rivers:** Guayas, Esmeraldas

Head of State and of Government: President Jaime Roldós Aguilera, born 1940, inaugurated August 10, 1979, for seven-year term **Effective Date of Present Constitution:** August 10, 1979 **Legislative Body:** Congress (unicameral) with 12 national and 57 provincial deputies **Local Government:** 20 provinces, each headed by an appointed governor

Ethnic Composition: 40% Indian, 40% mestizo, 10% of European (chiefly Spanish) origin, 5% African, 5% Oriental and other **Population Distribution:** 42.4% urban (1977) **Density:** 74 inhabitants per sq. mi.

Largest Cities: (1974 census) Guayaquil 814,064, Quito 597,133, Cuenca 104,667, Ambato 77,052, Machala 68,379

Per Capita Income: $1,103 (1979) **Gross National Product (GNP):** $7.7 billion (1979) **Economic Statistics:** In 1976 about 22% of GNP was derived from agriculture (bananas, coffee, cocoa, rice, sugar, cotton, grains, fruits and vegetables), forestry, and fishing; 16% from manufacturing (textiles, food processing, petroleum refining, cement) and mining; and 22% from trade and services **Minerals and Mining:** Petroleum is the primary mineral product. There are large deposits of calcium carbonate and copper; small quantities of gold are mined **Labor Force:** 2,400,000 (1978), of which 55% is employed in agriculture **Foreign Trade:** Exports, chiefly bananas, petroleum, coffee, cocoa, sugar and fish products, totaled $1.6 billion in 1978. Imports, mainly machinery, transportation equipment, chemicals, and paper products, totaled $1.3 billion **Principal Trade Partners:** United States, West Germany, Japan, Britain, Italy, Colombia

Vital Statistics: Birthrate, 41.8 per 1,000 of pop. (1975); death rate, 9.5 **Life Expectancy:** 57 years **Health Statistics:** 495 inhabitants per hospital bed; 2,017 per physician (1973) **Infant Mortality:** 65.8 per 1,000 births **Illiteracy:** 43% **Primary and Secondary School Enrollment:** 1,709,717 (1976) **Enrollment in Higher Education:** 170,173 **GNP Expended on Education:** 3.3% (1971)

Transportation: Paved roads total 2,050 mi. **Motor Vehicles:** 128,500 (1975) **Passenger Cars:** 51,300 **Railway Mileage:** 726 **Ports:** Guayaquil, Puerto Bolívar, Manta, Bahía de Caráquez, Salinas, Esmeraldas **Major Airlines:** AREA and Ecuatoriana de Aviación operate internal and international flights **Communications:** Government and privately owned **Radio Transmitters:** 232 (1972) **Receivers:** 1,700,000 (1970) **Television Transmitters:** 19 **Receivers:** 300,000 (1976) **Telephones:** 202,000 (1976) **Newspapers:** 29 dailies, 49 copies per 1,000 inhabitants (1975)

Weights and Measures: Metric system; Spanish measures are also used **Travel Requirements:** Passport, migratory control card, valid for 90 days, tourist visa valid for 180 days, no fee

Despite incredibly rich mineral and agricultural resources, Ecuador remains one of the least developed countries in South America—the result of sharp racial, geographic, and political differences.

Two fifths of Ecuador's population is Indian—people held in low esteem by those of mixed blood, African heritage, and the small ruling élite of European background. Although many of the Indians retain their languages and customs, they have been stripped of the rest of their culture by four centuries of European domination.

Aside from the Indians in the Andean highlands and the Amazonian tribes in the east, most of the rest of Ecuador's people live along the western littoral that borders the Pacific Ocean. Mainly of mixed African/Indian/European background, the coastal people have a tropical culture that differs markedly from the highlanders.

In a further division, Ecuador is dominated by the mutual dislike of two "city-states"—Quito, the capital, and Guayaquil, the industrial port.

Some 9,300 feet above sea level in the Andes, long considered the most beautiful city in South America and certainly the cleanest, Quito is a conservative, gracious administrative center. Its residents look with distaste on the boisterous, tropical people of Guayaquil, who, for their part, resent their tax payments to the capital. Despite their industry and commercial aggressiveness, they say, the appalling slums of their city reflect the indifference of Quito.

Since petroleum exports started in 1972, there has been a spurt in overall economic development. The oil, which is pumped out of the Amazon jungles by Texaco and by the government oil company, CEPE, is Ecuador's No. 1 export. The banana trade, in which a long-term contract is held with the Del Monte company, is another large source of export revenue. The country is now accustomed to trade and balance-of-payments surpluses, and its inflation rate—reaching 15% in 1979—is below the South American average.

In 1978 and 1979 the country held its first free national elections since the military seized power in 1972. First, in a referendum on Jan. 15, 1978, the voters chose a new constitution over a revision of the 1945 constitution. Then, on July 16, Jaime Roldós Aguilera, a law professor and a member of the Concentration of Popular Forces (CFP), led the first-round balloting for president. The military, wary because Roldós is a protégé of populist leader Assad Bucaram, delayed the final election for six months, but Roldós won handily in a two-party contest on April 29, 1979, and was inaugurated without incident on August 10. Soon afterward, however, a struggle developed between Roldós and his former chief, Bucaram, the leader of the CPF in congress. The president's program of social reform and economic development was stymied in congress, and he in turn vetoed bills that had been passed on Bucaram's initiative.

HISTORY: Ecuador was ruled by the Incas until their empire fell to the Spanish conquistadors in 1533. Spanish rule, which lasted until the early 19th century, was marked by ruthless exploitation of the native Indians and bloody rivalry among the Spaniards

1822: Ecuador is freed from Spanish rule after Spanish forces are defeated at Battle of Pichincha; country becomes part of Greater Colombia, a confederation consisting of the present territories of Ecuador, Colombia, Panama, and Venezuela, constituted under the leadership of Simón Bolívar

1830-45: Federation is dissolved in 1830; Republic of Ecuador is proclaimed, with Juan José Flores as first president; his conservative dictatorial rule arouses liberal opposition

1861-75: Gabriel García Morena rules as virtual dictator; he consolidates country after years of domestic strife and carries out major economic and social reforms, but his strong conservatism results in bitter strife that culminates in his assassination

1895-1912: Liberals dominate Ecuador's politics; separation of church and state is clearly defined, and basic personal freedoms are established

1913-44: Liberals continue to dominate political scene, but rival factions, supported by military juntas, bring about rapid changes in government

1948-52: Galo Plazo Lasso becomes president; his regime is marked by unprecedented political freedom

1961: President José María Velasco Ibarra is forced into exile; Vice-President Julio Arosemena Monroy succeeds as president

1963: Arosemena is ousted in military coup; a four-man military junta, headed by R. Adm. Ramon Castro Jijon, takes over. Junta dissolves Congress, decrees martial law, suspends the constitution, and bans Communist party

1968-69: In the first election held in seven years, Velasco Ibarra is elected president for fifth time as Ecuador experiences widespread economic and social unrest. Within eight months after taking office, president loses support of Liberal party

1970: President Velasco assumes dictatorial powers

1971: U.S. imposes financial sanctions on Ecuador following seizure of U.S. tuna boats

1972: Brig. Gen. Guillermo Rodriguez Lara replaces Velasco Ibarra in bloodless military coup. Lara declares a "nationalist, military, and revolutionary government"

1974: President Lara suspends elections and other political activities for five years

1975: Seizure of American fishing boats continues. Gen. Raúl González Alvear leads unsuccessful revolt against Lara

1976: President Lara is overthrown in a bloodless coup led by armed forces commanders, who form a military junta

1977: Ecuadorean government buys the local assets of Gulf Oil Corp. of the U.S., giving the government a 62.5 percent share in Ecuador's petroleum operations

1978: Elections held to choose new president; Jaime Roldós Aguilera is leader in first round

1979: In a run-off that had been delayed by the military for six months, Roldós wins and is inaugurated on Aug. 10

EGYPT

Area: 386,659 sq. mi. **Population:** 40,983,000 (1979 est.)

Official Name: Arab Republic of Egypt **Capital:** Cairo **Nationality:** Egyptian **Languages:** Arabic is the official and national language **Religion:** About 90% of the population is Sunni Moslem and Islam is the state religion; about 7% belongs to the Coptic Church (perhaps as high as 18%) **Flag:** Red, white, and black horizontal stripes with a golden hawk and Arabic inscription on the white stripe **Anthem:** National Anthem, beginning "The Time Has Come to Reach for Our Arms" **Currency:** Egyptian pound (0.70 per U.S. $1)

Location: Northeast Africa. Egypt is bordered on the north by the Mediterranean Sea; on the east by Israel and the Red Sea; on the south by the Sudan; and on the west by Libya **Features:** About 95% of the country is desert, with only the Nile Valley and delta, and a few oases, under cultivation **Chief River:** Nile

Head of State and of Government: President Anwar el-Sadat, born 1918, reelected for 6 years in 1976. He assumed the post of premier in May 1980 **Effective Date of Present Constitution:** 1971 **Legislative Body:** People's Assembly (unicameral), consisting of 392 members **Local Government:** 26 governorates headed by governors appointed by the president

Ethnic Composition: The homogeneous population is mainly Hamitic **Population Distribution:** 44% urban **Density:** 106 inhabitants per sq. mi.; inhabitable areas 3,000

Largest Cities: (1975 est.) Cairo 5,921,000; Alexandria 2,320,000, Giza 893,100, Suez 381,000

Per Capita Income: $492 (1979) **Gross National Product (GNP):** $20 billion (1979) **Economic Statistics:** 30% of GNP comes from agriculture (cotton, wheat, corn, rice); 22% from industry (food processing, textiles, petroleum and petroleum products, iron and steel manufactures, chemicals) and mining; 25% from services; 19% from trade and finance **Minerals and Mining:** Petroleum is the chief mineral resource; others are phosphate, iron ore, salt, manganese, and limestone **Labor Force:** 13,000,000, of which 50% is in agriculture, and 13% in industry **Foreign Trade:** Exports, chiefly cotton and cotton goods, rice, crude oil, and oil products, totaled $1.7 billion in 1978. Imports, mainly wheat, petroleum, industrial machinery, vehicle parts, and edible oils, totaled $6.7 billion **Principal Trade Partners:** USSR, EC countries, United States, East Germany, Japan, Czechoslovakia, Greece

Vital Statistics: Birthrate, 37.7 per 1,000 of pop. (1977); death rate, 11.8 **Life Expectancy:** 54 years **Health Statistics:** 479 inhabitants per hospital bed (1976); 1,516 per physician (1973) **Infant Mortality:** 101.3 per 1,000 births **Illiteracy:** 56% **Primary and Secondary School Enrollment:** 6,228,827 (1975) **Enrollment in Higher Education:** 455,097 **GNP Expended on Education:** 5.4% (1976)

Transportation: Paved roads total 7,640 mi. **Motor Vehicles:**

347,200 (1977) **Passenger Cars:** 283,200 **Railway Mileage:** 4,200 **Ports:** Alexandria, Port Said, Suez, Mersa Matruh, Safaga **Major Airlines:** Egypt Air operates internal and international services **Communications:** Government owned **Radio Transmitters:** 43 (1973) **Receivers:** 5,250,000 (1976) **Television Transmitters:** 28 (1977) **Receivers:** 1,300,000 (1977) **Telephones:** 503,000 (1974) **Newspapers:** 14 dailies, 21 copies per 1,000 inhabitants (1974)

Weights and Measures: Metric system is official but various local units are also used **Travel Requirements:** Passport, visa good for stay up to 3 months, $2.80 contribution to Abu Simbel fund

---

For Egypt, recent years have brought one pressing challenge after another: adjustments to the death of President Gamal Abdel Nasser, fateful decisions on war or peace with Israel, conspiracies against President Anwar el-Sadat, friendship with the United States at the expense of Soviet-Egyptian amity, and relentless economic problems.

Added to these challenges are the realities of Egypt's difficulties as the most populous country in the Arab world and the second most populous on the African continent, with 99 percent of its people compressed into 3.5 percent of its area.

President Sadat, who had been a leading figure in the 1952 revolution led by Nasser against King Farouk, quickly emerged as an unexpectedly strong president in the "collective leadership" that succeeded Nasser. He won support by curbing arbitrary police procedures and surveillance, calling for a society based on "the sovereignty of law," and outlining a program for accelerated economic development.

Egypt's economic problems are extensive and resistant to ready solutions. There are few natural resources, limited cultivable land and investment funds; in addition, bureaucracies are swollen with unproductive workers. Unemployment and inflation are rising, and illiteracy is 56%. The increasing number of university-trained graduates have little prospect for professional advancement.

To present a more progressive image while dealing with these economic difficulties, Sadat has implemented limited political reforms, including an upgrading of the People's Assembly. In late 1976, he announced that he would allow the formation of independent political parties, which had been banned since 1953, when the Arab Socialist Union was made the only legal political organization. Three parties were subsequently formed, but in 1978, new restrictions on them were enacted.

The peace treaty with Israel, signed in 1979, calls for Israel's phased withdrawal from Sinai within three years. By the end of 1979, Israel had returned most of the Sinai territory, including oil fields and Mt. Sinai itself, to Egypt. The treaty binds Egypt to sell oil to Israel, and other trade with Israel, plus increased U.S. aid, and reduced military needs have helped Egypt economically. But other Arab nations have tried to isolate Egypt and have suspended her from the Arab League and other Arab organizations. Yet Sadat got overwhelming domestic support for the treaty.

The treaty was the result of 14 months of difficult negotiations, which began in 1977, when President Sadat visited Israel and Israeli Prime Minister Menachem Begin returned the visit. After this dramatic opening, Palestinian raids on Israel, Israeli strikes at Palestinians in southern Lebanon, and arguments about the future of Palestinian territory slowed the negotiations. United States officials, including President Jimmy Carter, helped at crucial times to prevent a rupture.

On Feb. 26, 1980, Egypt exchanged ambassadors with Israel as another step toward normalization of relations. But the countries were deadlocked on the issue of granting Palestinian autonomy in the Gaza Strip and on the West Bank of the Jordan. Sadat has protested Israel's policy of establishing settlements on the West Bank, calling them "ill-conceived and illegal."

HISTORY: The history of Egypt dates back about 5,000 years. The country was united into a single kingdom about 3200 B.C. and was ruled by a succession of dynasties down to the time of Alexander the Great, who conquered Egypt in 332 B.C. Less than three centuries later, the country was under Roman rule. In 616, Egypt was conquered by the Persians before being invaded by the Arabs, who introduced Islam

1517: Egypt becomes part of the Ottoman Empire

1798: Napoleon conquers Egypt

1801-5: British and Turkish troops drive out the French; Mohammed Ali, an Albanian soldier, is appointed Egyptian pasha

1869: The Suez Canal is completed

1914: Egypt becomes a British protectorate

1936: Britain agrees to withdraw eventually from all of Egypt, except the Suez Canal Zone

1940-42: British forces use Egypt as a base to fight Italy and Germany in World War II

1948-49: Egypt plays major role in war between Arab states and the newly established state of Israel, but suffers humiliating defeats; war ends with an armistice

1952: King Farouk is deposed in army coup

1953-54: A republic is proclaimed, with Gen. Mohammed Naguib as president; Naguib is forced out of office and replaced by Col. Gamal Abdel Nasser

1956: Nasser nationalizes Suez Canal. Israel, barred from the canal, invades the Gaza Strip and the Sinai peninsula; England and France attack Egypt. Forces of all three invading countries are forced to withdraw under pressure from the United States, the USSR and the United Nations

1958: Egypt and Syria form the United Arab Republic (U.A.R.)

1961: Syrian army revolts and proclaims Syria's withdrawal from U.A.R.

1962: Egypt sends troops to Yemen to aid a republican revolution

1967: In the Six-Day War with Israel, Egypt loses the entire Sinai peninsula and the Gaza Strip, which are occupied by Israeli armies; Egypt withdraws its troops from Yemen

1968: Widespread student riots break out in protest against Nasser regime, which is accused of police-state rule. Egyptian and Israeli troops engage in repeated artillery duels along Suez Canal

1970: Egypt agrees to U.S.-sponsored truce with Israel as step toward peace talks; talks are stalled after Israel charges truce is being violated by the installation of Soviet-built missiles in the Suez Canal zone. Nasser dies of heart attack and is succeeded by Vice-President Anwar el-Sadat

1971: Sadat allows cease-fire with Israel to lapse but defers warfare. Conspiracy against Sadat erupts; six cabinet members, Vice-President Aly Sabry, and dozens of others are arrested. New constitution approved by national referendum

1972: Dr. Aziz Sidky replaces Dr. Mahmoud Fawzi as premier. President Sadat orders the departure of all Soviet military advisors (about 10,000)

1973: Sadat forces Sidky to resign, assumes premiership; Egypt launches attack across the Suez Canal, beginning fourth Arab-Israeli War. The Arabs attack on Yom Kippur, the holiest day of the year for Jews. It takes several days for the Israelis to mobilize, but they soon outmaneuver the Arab armies. Iraq, Tunisia, Morocco, and other Arab countries send troops to aid Egypt and Syria. Egypt and Israel negotiate ceasefire

1974: President Sadat changes the date of Egypt's national holiday from July 23 to October 6 to commemorate the onset of the Yom Kippur War; Sadat relinquishes the office of premier and appoints Abdul Aziz Hegazy in his place

1975: Premier Hegazy resigns and is replaced by Mamdouh Salem. The Suez Canal, closed since 1967, reopens. With the assistance of U.S. Secretary of State Kissinger, Egypt and Israel agree on removal of troops in the Sinai Peninsula. American Congress approves of U.S. civilian presence in Sinai to supervise electronic early warning stations

1976: Egyptian parliament approves of President Sadat's proposal to end 15-year Treaty of Friendship and Cooperation with the USSR. Saudi Arabia, Kuwait, Qatar and the United Arab Emirates establish the Gulf Authority for Egyptian Development with a capital of $2 billion. Sadat is elected to a second six-year term

1977: Egyptian and Libyan forces clash along desert border. President Sadat launches peace initiative; he and Israeli Premier Begin trade historic visits

1978: Peace talks bog down as Israeli troops enter southern Lebanon following Palestinian terror raid in Israel. Diplomatic relations with Cyprus severed after Cypriot troops kill 15 Egyptian commandos who were storming jet at Larnaca Airport in which Palestinian terrorists held 16 hostages. Egypt to get 50 F-5E fighter-bombers from the U.S. National referendum gives Sadat mandate to carry out proposals for curtailing political dissent, "to protect the home front and social peace"

1979: Egypt and Israel sign peace treaty, calling for phased Israeli withdrawal from Sinai within three years. Arab states suspend Egypt from several Arab organizations. Referendum in Egypt approves treaty. Sadat dissolves parliament; his National Democratic party wins overwhelming victory in June election

1980: Two thirds of Sinai territory is returned to Egypt as Israel completes 2nd phase of withdrawal; countries exchange ambassadors; negotiations continue on Palestinian issue. Sadat assumes premiership. Deposed Shah of Iran dies in Egyptian military hospital

EL SALVADOR

Area: 8,260 sq. mi. **Population:** 4,353,000 (1978 est.)

Official Name: Republic of El Salvador **Capital:** San Salvador **Nationality:** Salvadorean **Languages:** Spanish is the official and predominant language; a small number of Indians still speak Nahuatl **Religion:** Overwhelmingly Roman Catholic **Flag:** Blue, white, and blue horizontal stripes, with the national coat of arms centered on the white stripe **Anthem:** National Anthem, beginning "We proudly hail thee, motherland" **Currency:** Salvadorean colón (2.5 per U.S. $1)

Location: Central America. El Salvador is bordered on the north, northeast, and east by Honduras, on the south and southwest by the Pacific Ocean, and on the west and northwest by Guatemala **Features:** Mountain ranges running east to west divide the country into a narrow Pacific coastal belt on the south; a subtropical central region of valleys and plateaus, where most of the population lives; and a mountainous northern region **Chief Rivers:** Lempa, Grande de San Miguel

Head of State and of Government: Rule is by a five-man junta since the coup of Oct. 15, 1979 **Effective Date of Present Constitution:** 1962 **Legislative Body:** National Assembly (unicameral), consisting of 54 members elected by popular vote every 2 years **Local Government:** 14 departments, each headed by an appointed governor

Ethnic Composition: 89% mestizo (of mixed European—mainly Spanish—and Indian descent); the rest consists of small minorities of European and of Indian ancestry **Population Distribution:** 41.9% urban (1975) **Density:** 527 inhabitants per sq. mi.

Largest Cities: (1973 est.) San Salvador 368,000; (1971 census) Santa Ana 96,306, San Miguel 59,304

Per Capita Income: $751 (1979) **Gross National Product (GNP):** $3.3 billion (1979) **Economic Statistics:** In 1973 about 27% of GNP was from agriculture (coffee, cotton, sugar, rice, livestock); and 19% from industry (food processing, textiles, shoes, chemicals) **Minerals and Mining:** Substantial deposits of quartz, diatomaceous earth, kaolin, gypsum, limestone, and pumice **Labor Force:** 1,500,000 with 57% in agriculture and 14% in industry **Foreign Trade:** Exports, chiefly coffee, cotton, shrimp, sugar, cottonseed cakes, and cotton fabric, totaled $855 million in 1978. Imports, mainly transport equipment, chemical products, fuels and lubricants, raw materials, industrial machinery, and consumer goods, totaled $946 million **Principal Trade Partners:** United States, Latin America, Japan

Vital Statistics: Birthrate, 41.7 per 1,000 of pop. (1977); death rate, 7.8 **Life Expectancy:** 64 years **Health Statistics:** 597 inhabitants per hospital bed; 3,745 per physician (1976) **Infant Mortality:** 59.5 per 1,000 births (1977) **Illiteracy:** 60% **Primary and Secondary School Enrollment:** 887,872 (1977) **Enrollment in Higher Education:** 28,281 **GNP Expended on Education:** 3.3% (1975)

Transportation: Paved roads total 930 mi. **Motor Vehicles:** 61,000 (1974) **Passenger Cars:** 41,000 **Railway Mileage:** 432 **Ports:** La Unión (Cutuco), Acajutla, La Libertad **Major Airlines:** TACA operates internal and international flights **Communications:** Partly government controlled **Radio Transmitters:** 65 **Receivers:** 1,400,000 (1976) **Television Transmitters:** 3 **Receivers:** 136,000 (1976) **Telephones:** 70,000 **Newspapers:** 12 dailies, 51 copies per 1,000 inhabitants (1974)

Weights and Measures: Metric system is official but various local units are also used **Travel Requirements:** Proof of citizenship for issuance of tourist card on arrival, valid 90 days

As the most densely populated country on the entire American mainland, El Salvador has long aroused suspicions of expansionism among its neighbors, particularly Honduras, which has had up to 600,000 immigrant Salvadoreans among its populace. The constant pressure of too many people for El Salvador's diminutive land area has led to frequent border clashes with Honduras and, in July 1969, to a four-day war. In late 1976, an agreement was signed between the two countries providing for mediation by a third country in this recurrent, and often violent, dispute.

Much of the populace of this agriculturally-based economy is poverty-stricken, living on small plots of land owned by a few controlling families. Social reform is seen by the oligarchy as a communist concept to give political power to peasants.

Violence erupted immediately after the disputed 1977 election won by Gen. Carlos Humberto Romero. Three leftist guerrilla groups emerged, and a wave of bombings, kidnappings and murders by both leftists and extreme rightists ensued. On May 9, 1979, at least 24 persons died when police opened fire on demonstrators on the steps of the Metropolitan Cathedral in San Salvador.

With the situation worsening, two colonels deposed Romero on Oct. 15 and exiled him with his top aides, including all active generals. With three civilians they formed a Revolutionary Junta, promising moderate government and free elections by 1982. They called on both rightists and leftists to "end violence and respect the will of the majority."

However, violence actually increased in 1980. During the first three months at least 700 persons were killed, more than in all of 1979. Archbishop Oscar Arnulfo Romero, a highly respected figure and outspoken champion of peace, human rights and aid for the oppressed was assassinated March 24. During his funeral, bomb blasts set off a panic in which about 30 persons were killed. On May 2 a coup attempt by aides of former President Romero (not related to the archbishop) was crushed by the military-civilian junta.

HISTORY: El Salvador was the home of the Pipil Indians before the arrival of Pedro de Alvarado, who conquered the country for Spain in the 1520s. Until its independence in the 19th century, El Salvador was administered as part of the captaincy general of Guatemala

1821: El Salvador and the other Central American countries gain independence from Spain and are annexed to Mexico

1824-39: Central American countries withdraw from Mexico and establish the Central American Federation; the union is dissolved in 1839

1841-56: El Salvador's independence is decreed in January 1841; a republic is formally proclaimed in 1856

1931-44: Gen. Maximiliano Hernández Martínez seizes power

1945-61: Nation is wracked by political instability as governments rise and fall in numerous coups d'état; in 1961 a civilian-military directorate is formed

1962-67: A new constitution is promulgated and Lt. Col. Adalberto Rivera is elected president; during his term nation's currency is stabilized, an income tax is introduced, and pro-labor laws are passed. In 1967 Col. Fidel Sánchez Hernández is elected president

1968: Government's National Conciliation party suffers setback as reform-minded Christian Democrats score gains in legislative and municipal elections

1969: El Salvador wages brief war with Honduras, the underlying cause of which is immigration of Salvadoreans into Honduras. OAS mediation helps end fighting

1970: El Salvador and Honduras agree to set up demilitarized zone along border

1973: Peace talks break down and border disputes resume

1977: Violent unrest grips the country after Gen. Carlos Humberto Romero wins the presidency amid charges of fraud

1978: Scores die as widespread unrest continues

1979: Two colonels oust Romero, deport him with his aides, and form a governing junta along with three civilians

1980: Hundreds killed as violence increases. Junta begins expropriation of arable land in large estates for distribution to peasants

EQUATORIAL GUINEA

Area: 10,831 sq. mi. **Population:** 346,000 (1978 est.)

Official Name: Republic of Equatorial Guinea **Capital:** Malabo **Nationality:** Equatorial Guinean **Languages:** Spanish is the official language. On the mainland Fang is spoken, while the principal local language on Bioko island is Bubi **Religion:** About 80% of the population is Roman Catholic, the rest chiefly animists, with a small number of Moslems **Flag:** Green, white, and red horizontal stripes, with a blue triangle joining them at the staff side; in the center is the national coat of arms **Anthem:** National Anthem, beginning "Let's walk through the jungle of our immense happiness" **Currency:** ekuele (66.1 per U.S. $1)

Location: West Africa. Equatorial Guinea consists of 2 areas: the mainland—Río Muni (Mbini), bordered by Cameroon on the north, Gabon on the east and south, and the Atlantic Ocean on the west; and Bioko (Fernando Po), consisting of the main island of that name, Pagalu, and other small islands **Features:** There are 2 large volcanic formations on the main island, separated by a valley which crosses the island from east to west at its narrowest point. Río Muni consists of a coastal plain, and a series of valleys separated by low hills and spurs of the Crystal Mountains **Chief Rivers:** Benito, Muni, Campo

Head of State and of Government: President: Lt. Col. Teodoro Obiang Nguema Mbasogo. He is head of the Supreme Military Council **Effective Date of Present Constitution:** July 1973 **Legislative Body:** Power is in the hands of the Supreme Military Council **Local Government:** 2 provinces

Ethnic Composition: On Bioko the aboriginal Bubis are the major ethnic group; others include the descendants of liberated slaves. In Río Muni the main tribes are the Fang, Kombe, and Bujeba **Population Distribution:** 15% urban **Density:** 40 inhabitants per sq. mi.

Largest Cities: (1973 est.) Malabo 60,000, Bata 30,000

Per Capita Income: $312 (1978) **Gross National Product (GNP):** $100 million (1978) **Economic Statistics:** Production is predominantly agricultural, although forestry and fishing are also important. High-grade cocoa, coffee, bananas, and palm oil are the main crops. There is little industry **Minerals and Mining:** Geological surveys have raised hopes for the eventual discovery of petroleum; uranium deposits have been found and there are indications of iron ore **Labor Force:** More than 95% of the working population is engaged in agriculture **Foreign Trade:** Exports, chiefly cocoa, wood, and coffee, totaled $36 million in 1976. Imports, principally foodstuffs, building materials, petroleum products, textiles, motor vehicles, and pharmaceutical products, totaled $12 million **Principal Trade Partners:** Spain, United States, Britain, West Germany, France

Vital Statistics: Birthrate, 36.8 per 1,000 of pop. (1975); death rate 19.7 **Life Expectancy:** 43.5 years **Health Statistics:** 171 inhabitants per hospital bed (1967); 62,000 per physician (1975) **Infant Mortality:** 53.2 per 1,000 births **Illiteracy:** 80% **Primary and Secondary School Enrollment:** 40,500 (1975) **Enrollment in Higher Education:** N.A. **GNP Expended on Education:** N.A.

Transportation: Surfaced roads total 94 mi. **Motor Vehicles:** about 1,000 **Passenger Cars:** N.A. **Railway Mileage:** None **Ports:** Malabo, Bata **Major Airlines:** Iberia Airlines provides an international service **Communications:** State controlled **Radio Transmitters:** 2 **Receivers:** 80,000 (1976) **Television:** None **Telephones:** 2,000 **Newspapers:** 1 daily, 3 copies per 1,000 inhabitants

Weights and Measures: Metric system **Travel Requirements:** Passport, visa

---

One of the smallest of Africa's nations, Equatorial Guinea gained independence from Spain in 1968. For 11 years the country experienced repressive rule by President Masie Nguema Biyogo Negue Ndong, along with economic deterioration.

While severing all ties with Spain and taking a sharply anti-Western stance, President Masie welcomed new links with the Soviet Union, Communist China and North Korea.

Equatorial Guinea consists chiefly of the island of Bioko (Fernando Po), site of the capital, Malabo, and, 100 miles to the southeast, the larger area of Río Muni, a square of land between Cameroon and Gabon.

The island people of Bioko, until recently more prosperous, include the native Bubis; Fernandinos, descendants of freed African slaves; Nigerians, who have been contract laborers on cocoa plantations; and a number of Europeans. The poorer, majority mainland people, the Fangs, looked to independence and the leadership of President Masie, a Fang, to improve their lot, a hope as yet unmaterialized.

Europeans, mainly Spanish and Portuguese, who ran the high-quality cocoa plantations, coffee and lumber production, and other businesses, numbered 7,000 in 1968. But with increasing physical terrorism by government and a youth movement, the Juventud, only a few hundred Europeans remain in the country. Thousands of citizens were reportedly killed by the Masie regime, and more thousands fled to other countries.

President Masie was overthrown in a bloodless coup on August 3, 1979, and executed Sept. 29 following a public trial which the International Commission of Jurists deemed to be fair. Masie was replaced by a Supreme Military Council led by his nephew, Lt. Col. Teodoro Nguema Mbasogo. Relations were reestablished with Spain which began to send economic aid to its former colony.

HISTORY: Equatorial Guinea's island province of Fernando Po was discovered in the late 15th century by the Portuguese explorer Fernão do Po. It was ceded to Spain, along with mainland trading rights, in 1778. In the early 19th century, the island port of Santa Isabel was leased for a time to the British, who made it a naval base and refuge for freed slaves. Not until the 20th century did Spain actively begin administering and developing the colony, known as Spanish Guinea

1958-60: Spain makes colony a Spanish province, grants inhabitants Spanish citizenship and representation in *Cortés*

1963-64: Colony is renamed Equatorial Guinea; limited self-government is instituted

1968: After numerous appeals to United Nations and long negotiations, Equatorial Guinea becomes an independent republic

1969: Rivalry between the continental and island portions results in serious riots. President Masie assumes dictatorial powers, purges opposition leaders

1979: President Masie is deposed in coup

1980: Soviet personnel evacuate deep-sea fishing depot as Nguema Mbasogo declines to renew 15-year-old pact

---

ETHIOPIA

Area: 471,776 sq. mi. **Population:** 30,421,000 (1979 est.)

Official Name: Ethiopia **Capital:** Addis Ababa **Nationality:** Ethiopian **Languages:** Amharic is the official and predominant language; English is frequently used. Arabic is spoken by about one-third of the population; other spoken languages are Gallinya, Tigrinya, Ge'ez, and Italian **Religion:** About 40% of the population belongs to the established Ethiopian Orthodox (Coptic Christian) Church; 40% is Moslem and the rest animist **Flag:** Green, yellow, and red horizontal stripes **Anthem:** National Anthem, beginning "Let Ethiopia be joyous!" **Currency:** Birr (2.07 per U.S. $1)

Location: Eastern Africa. Ethiopia is bordered on the north by the Sudan and the Red Sea, on the east by Djibouti and Somalia, on the south by Kenya, and on the west by the Sudan **Features:** The center of the country consists of a high, partly mountainous plateau cut by numerous rivers and split diagonally by the Rift Valley. The terrain gradually slopes to lowlands in the west and to a plains region in the southeast **Chief Rivers:** Shibeli, Abbai (Blue Nile), Ganale Dorya, Awash, Omo

Head of State and of Government: Lt. Col. Mengistu Haile-Mariam, born 1942, named chairman of the Provisional Military Administrative Council (*Dergue*) in 1977 **Effective Date of Present Constitution:** 1955 (suspended) **Legislative Body:** The bicameral National Assembly was dissolved in 1974. All decisions are made by the *Dergue* **Local Government:** 14 provinces

Ethnic Composition: The Amharas and the Tigreans are of Semitic origin and make up 37% of the population; the Gallas, a Hamitic people, account for 40%. There are also numerous mixed, Negroid, and other groups, including the Falashas, or so-called "Black Jews," Sidamas, Somalis, and Yemenite Arabs, as well as some 30,000 Europeans, chiefly Italians **Population Distribution:** 12.4% urban (1975) **Density:** 64 inhabitants per sq. mi.

Largest Cities: (1977 est.) Addis Ababa 1,133,200, Asmara 364,020; (1972 est.) Dire Dawa 63,700, Dessye 49,750, Harar 48,440

Per Capita Income: $117 (1979) **Gross National Product (GNP):** $3 billion (1979) **Economic Statistics:** About 52% of GNP comes from agriculture (coffee, cotton, corn, sugar, wheat, sorghum, oilseeds, pulses) and livestock raising; 5% from industry (textiles, food processing, building materials, printing, leather, chemicals) **Minerals and Mining:** Limited output of gold, platinum, salt, iron, and manganese ore. Deposits of potash, copper, nickel, and asbestos have been discovered **Labor Force:** 11,300,000 (1971), with some 86% engaged in subsistence agriculture **Foreign Trade:** Exports, chiefly coffee, hides and skins, oilseeds, and pulses, totaled $305 million in 1978. Imports, mainly machinery and transport equipment, textiles, yarns and fabrics, foodstuffs, building materials, and petroleum products, totaled $518 million **Principal Trade Partners:** United States, Yugoslavia, Korea, West Germany, Saudi Arabia, Italy, Japan, Britain, Djibouti

Vital Statistics: Birthrate, 49.4 per 1,000 of pop. (1975); death rate, 25.8 **Life Expectancy:** 38 years **Health Statistics:** 3,277 inhabitants per hospital bed; 93,966 per physician (1976) **Infant Mortality:** 84.2 per 1,000 births **Illiteracy:** 95% **Primary and Secondary School Enrollment:** 1,150,194 (1974) **Enrollment in Higher Education:** 6,474 **GNP Expended on Education:** 2.3% (1975)

Transportation: Paved roads total about 2,000 mi. **Motor Vehicles:** 65,600 (1976) **Passenger Cars:** 52,500 **Railway Mileage:** 680 **Ports:** Massawa, Assab; a substantial portion of Ethiopia's trade moves through Djibouti **Major Airlines:** Ethiopian Airlines, the government line, operates domestic and international services **Communications:** State controlled **Radio Transmitters:** 8 (1975) **Receivers:** 210,000 (1976) **Television Transmitters:** 8 (1975) **Receivers:** 21,000 (1976) **Telephones:** 73,000 (1976) **Newspapers:** 8 dailies, 2.5 copies per 1,000 inhabitants (1975)

Weights and Measures: Metric system is official but traditional units are also used **Travel Requirements:** Passport, visa; check with Ethiopian embassy or consulates for requirements

---

The 44-year reign of Emperor Haile Selassie ended September 12, 1974, when a group of army officers completed a process which months before had begun to strip the emperor of most of his powers. This Provisional Military Administrative Council (PMAC) or *Dergue* removed him and installed his son, Asfa Wossen, 57, as a figurehead king. And in March 1975 a proclamation ended the monarchy, annulling the Crown Prince's appointment.

Since he became emperor in 1930, the Lion of Judah had promoted economic innovation and political reform, but progress was slow. Strong resistance came from farmers, aristocratic landowners and the Coptic Church, which owns about a third of all land in a country where agriculture is a livelihood for 86 percent of the population.

Civilian rioting and strikes protesting soaring prices, unemployment, and the government's mismanagement of relief efforts dealing with the country's drought and famine undermined Selassie's power. What finally led to his downfall was the cover-up of the 1973 famine, which caused the deaths of over 100,000 peasants.

In February 1974 an army mutiny forced Selassie's cabinet to resign. Selassie sought to maintain control of the country by naming a new premier, Endalkachew Makonnen, installing a new cabinet, and raising army wages. Meanwhile, Ethiopia remained under military control.

In March, Selassie agreed to call a constitutional convention that could lead to a replacement of his absolute monarchy by a more democratic form of government. Finally, in September, came the coup which ousted him. He died in 1975.

A turning point for the ruling PMAC came in November 1974 when its members voted to execute 60 Ethiopians, including their chairman, Lt. Gen. Aman Michael Andom. These executions solidified the powers of Maj. Mengistu Haile-Mariam, the First Deputy Chairman, and Lt. Col. Atnafu Abate, the Second Deputy Chairman, while the chairman of the Military Council, Brig. Gen. Teferi Bante, remained a figurehead. In February 1977 Bante and six other members of the *Dergue* were killed in a shootout.

With Lt. Col. Mengistu now in control of one of the most brutal and arbitrary regimes in power today, Ethiopia's secretive council has turned into a one-man dictatorship. Among the problems Mengistu faces are the implementation of the land reform program ending 2,000 years of feudalism, domestic dissidence (especially that of the Ethiopian People's Revolutionary party) and the consolidation of the "Socialist revolution."

Under his rule the government is taking a harder and more violent path in dealing with its enemies, both in and outside the country. Among the regime's enemies in arms are three different forces of Eritrean guerrillas fighting for the past 17 years for independence of the northernmost province, containing Ethiopia's entire 540-mile Red Sea coastline; a right-wing army of exiles loyal to the era of Haile Selassie that has made gains in the provinces of Gojjam and Gondar; Somali irredentists along the Somali frontier; and guerrillas who control one-third of Tigre province.

In March 1978 Ethiopian forces, aided by some 16,000 Cuban troops and 1,500 Soviet military advisors, captured the last major towns in the Ogaden region after an eight-month campaign. An estimated one million Somalis had fled to Somalia by early 1980, but at least 20,000 guerrillas continued the fight and claimed to control 70 percent of the countryside. Ethiopia launched two full-scale offensives, again with Cuban and Soviet help, against Eritrean rebels in 1978 and 1979. The Ethiopian forces reportedly abandoned the second campaign in December 1979 after being forced to evacuate Nakfa, the only major town in Eritrea held by the rebels, who also controlled the countryside. In March 1980 the rebels accused Ethiopia of moving thousands of Ethiopians into Eritrea and attempting to drive out Eritrean civilians from their own country.

The Ethiopian Orthodox Christian church, a dominant force under Haile Selassie, is struggling against government attempts to control or crush it. In March 1979, Mengistu launched a full-scale crackdown on the country's 12 million Christians, forcing some to register with the government and others to renounce their faith. Some reportedly were executed for refusing to cooperate.

HISTORY: Long isolated from outside influences, Ethiopia developed a culture still suggestive of biblical times. Among its proudest traditions is that of the descent of Ethiopian emperors from King Solomon and the Queen of Sheba, who according to legend was the Ethiopian Queen Makeda of Aksum. Christianity was introduced by Coptic missionaries in the 4th century A.D. Over the centuries, repeated incursions by Arabs and constant feuding by feudal lords disrupted the empire, and it was not until the reign of Menelik II (1889-1913) that it was consolidated. In 1896, Menelik defeated an invading Italian army, but the invaders later took over Eritrea

1916: Menelik's grandson, Lij Yasu, suspected of Moslem leanings, is deposed; Menelik's daughter, Judith, is installed as empress, with her cousin, Ras Tafari Makonnen, as regent and heir

1930-31: Following death of the empress in 1930, Ras Tafari becomes emperor, taking the name Haile Selassie, meaning "Power of the Trinity"; he proclaims the first constitution

1935-36: Italians occupy Ethiopia; emperor flees the country and appeals vainly to the League of Nations for protection

1941: Following Italian defeat in World War II East African campaign, Haile Selassie, with Ethiopian and British forces, returns in triumph to Addis Ababa

1942: Emperor begins modernization and reforms

1952: United Nations approves federation of Eritrea, former Italian colony, with Ethiopia

1955: Revised constitution provides for popularly elected Chamber of Deputies and first elections are held

1960: Military coup involving crown prince is crushed

1974: Army mutiny and general strikes cause Selassie to appoint new cabinet and premier and promise reforms; Haile Selassie's rule ended. Lt. Gen. Aman Michael Andom is appointed premier and chairman of the military government (Sept.). Andom shot to death. Brig. Gen. Teferi Bante emerges as figurehead controlled by Maj. Mengistu Haile-Mariam and Lt. Col. Atnafu Abate

1975: Fighting erupts between Eritrean rebels and government troops in Asmara, provincial capital of Eritrea. Selassie dies

1977: Bante is killed. Mengistu becomes chief of state and commander in chief of armed forces

1978: Eight-month Ogaden War ends as Cuban and Soviet-aided Ethiopian forces drive Somalis from region. Ethiopia launches major offensive against Eritrean rebels, again with Cuban and Soviet help. A million-and-a-half Ethiopians are reportedly starving in nation's worst famine since 1973. In November Ethiopia and the Soviet Union sign a 20-year friendship pact

569
WORLD NATIONS

1979: Ethiopia abandons second full-scale offensive in Eritrea
1980: Government moves Ethiopians into Eritrea to displace Eritrean civilians; rebels hold Nakfa and countryside

---

FIJI

Area: 7,055 sq. mi. **Population:** 612,000 (1978 est.)

Official Name: Fiji **Capital:** Suva **Languages:** English is the official language; Fijian, Hindi **Religion:** Almost all indigenous Fijians are Christians, mainly Methodist. The Indian population is mostly Hindu **Flag:** A light blue field with the Union Jack in the upper left and the shield of the Fiji coat of arms in the fly **Anthem:** God Bless Fiji **Currency:** Fijian dollar (0.81 per U.S. $1)

Location: Southwest Pacific. Fiji consists of about 320 islands, grouped around the Koro Sea, about 1,100 miles north of New Zealand. The largest of the islands, Viti Levu (18°S., 178°E.), constitutes more than half the land area and is the seat of the capital. The island of Rotuma, about 240 miles north of Vanua Levu, is part of the Fijian group **Features:** The larger islands are of volcanic origin, mountainous, and surrounded by coral reefs. The windward sides of the islands are covered with dense tropical forests; the leeward sides contain grassy plains **Chief Rivers:** Rewa, Dreketi, Sigatoka, Navua, Mba

Head of State: Queen Elizabeth II, represented by a governor-general, Ratu Sir George Cakobau, appointed 1972 **Head of Government:** Prime Minister: Ratu Sir Kamisese Mara, born 1920, appointed Chief Minister in 1967, assumed the office of prime minister in 1970, and reappointed in 1977 **Effective Date of Present Constitution:** October 1970 **Legislative Body:** Parliament (bicameral), consisting of the Senate and the House of Representatives. The Senate has 22 members, half of whom are appointed for 6 years and the other half for 3 years. The House of Representatives has 52 members elected on a communal basis for 5 years **Local Government:** 4 administrative divisions, each headed by a government-appointed commissioner; 8 urban areas have elected councils

Ethnic Composition: 51% of the population is descended from Indian laborers who came to Fiji in the late 19th century; the indigenous Fijians, who number 44%, are Melanesians, but with a considerable admixture of Polynesian blood. 2% are Europeans and part Europeans, 2% Rotumans and other Pacific islanders, and 1% Chinese **Population Distribution:** 37% urban **Density:** 87 inhabitants per sq. mi.

Largest Cities: (1976 census) Suva 66,622, Lautoka 22,672, Nadi 6,938, Ba 5,917, Nausori 5,262, Labasa 4,328

Per Capita Income: $1,313 (1978) **Gross National Product (GNP):** $790 million (1978) **Economic Statistics:** In 1973 about 27% of GNP was from agriculture (sugar, coconuts, rice, bananas, ginger); 16% from industry (sugar milling, coconut oil) and mining; and 41% from trade and services **Minerals and Mining:** Gold is mined and exported, and there has been some mining of copper and bauxite; iron ore and phosphate are known to exist in some of the islands but it is not yet known whether they are commercially valuable. Manganese ore is also mined **Labor Force:** 149,000 (1970), with about 52% in agriculture, 11% in manufacturing, 22% in construction and engineering, and 13% in services **Foreign Trade:** Exports, chiefly sugar, coconut oil, unrefined gold, molasses, and lumber, totaled $187 million in 1977. Imports, mainly machinery, fuels, clothing, cotton fabrics, and food, totaled $279 million **Principal Trade Partners:** Australia, Japan, Britain, New Zealand, United States, Canada, Malaysia, Singapore

Vital Statistics: Birthrate, 28.6 per 1,000 of pop. (1976); death rate, 4.4 **Life Expectancy:** 70 years **Health Statistics:** 320 inhabitants per hospital bed; 1,763 per physician (1976) **Infant Mortality:** 9.1 per 1,000 births (1977) **Illiteracy:** 15% **Primary and Secondary School Enrollment:** 167,260 (1976) **Enrollment in Higher Education:** 1,810 (1975) **GNP Expended on Education:** 5.1% (1976)

Transportation: All-weather roads total 2,000 mi. **Motor Vehicles:** 30,300 (1977) **Passenger Cars:** 19,300 **Railway Mileage:** 400 miles of narrow-gauge track **Ports:** Suva, Lautoka, Levuka **Major Airlines:** Fiji and Polynesian Airlines operate domestic or regional services **Communications:** State owned **Radio Transmitters:** 11 **Receivers:** 300,000 (1976) **Television:** None **Telephones:** 31,000 (1976) **Newspapers:** 1 daily, 35 copies per 1,000 inhabitants (1975)

Weights and Measures: British standards are used **Travel Requirements:** Passport and onward/return ticket required. Visa issued on arrival for 4 months stay

---

In 1874, when Fiji was the haunt of cannibals, its chiefs ceded the islands to Queen Victoria. Ninety-six years to the day later, on October 10, 1970, Britain granted Fiji independence. With independence, domestic problems have risen to the surface, such as differences between mainly urban-dwelling Indians, who make up more than half of the population, and the indigenous Melanesians, who number about a sixth less than the Indians, but who own over 80 percent of the land.

Political equanimity is kept by an arrangement in which each group elects an equal number of members of government, the balance of power being held by representatives of the minority of voters who are neither Indian nor Melanesian.

Since 1975, political harmony has been threatened because of the formation of splinter groups from both major parties. This imbalance was exemplified in the 1976 elections in which Prime Minister Sir Kamisese Mara resigned after his ruling Alliance party suffered defeat in the general election. The defeat meant political turmoil for Fijians, with no party able to gain an overall majority in the House of Representatives. As a result of this impasse, the governor-general reappointed Mara prime minister. A measure of stability was regained in September 1977 when the Alliance party, led by Mara, won by a landslide in the general elections. The victory was seen as vindicating Mara's determination to preserve Fiji's multiracial society.

Today, Fiji is more than a tourist haven. In education, Fiji draws islanders to its University of the South Pacific, its medical school, and even its Protestant theological school. It is a leading voice of the South Pacific in the United Nations. In commerce, Fiji is a transshipment point for trade to the Pacific islands. Exports include sugar, coconut products, and gold.

HISTORY: Vanua Levu, Taveuni and some smaller islands in the northeast of the Fiji archipelago were discovered by the Dutch navigator Tasman in 1643. Other islands in the group were discovered in the following century by Captain James Cook and other British explorers, but it was not until 1804 that the first European settlement was established, at Levuka. Missionaries soon followed and succeeded in abolishing cannibalism and in converting Cakobau, the most influential of the native chiefs, to Christianity

1874: Britain annexes the islands at the request of the tribal chiefs
1879: Importation begins of indentured Indian laborers for work on the sugar plantations
1900: Plan by European settlers for federation with New Zealand is rejected
1904: Europeans win elective representation in a 10-man Legislative Council, whose one Indian member and two Fijian members are nominated by governor
1929: Indians win right to elective representation in council
1963: Legislative Council is reconstituted, giving Fijians elective representation
1965: New constitution is introduced, providing for greater self-government
1970: Fiji wins independence and joins the UN
1972: First general elections since independence are held
1975: Treaty is signed with EC
1976: Prime Minister Sir Kamisese Mara resigns, but is reappointed by the governor-general
1977: Alliance party wins by landslide in general elections
1978: Fiji contributes 500-man contingent to the United Nations Interim Force in Lebanon (UNIFIL) peacekeeping force
1979: Two Fijian soldiers of the UNIFIL peacekeeping force are killed Feb. 3 in clashes with Palestinian guerrillas. Cyclone Meli devastates part of Fiji archipelago (March 27); 52 are killed, thousands left homeless. Fiji provides 1,300-man contingent for peacekeeping force in Zimbabwe-Rhodesia

---

FINLAND

Area: 130,128 sq. mi. **Population:** 4,764,000 (1979 est.)

Official Name: Republic of Finland **Capital:** Helsinki **Nationality:** Finnish **Languages:** Finnish, the dominant tongue, and Swedish, spoken by 6.5% of the population, are both official languages. Lappish is spoken by a small minority **Religion:** More than 92% of the population belongs to the established Evangelical Lutheran Church; less than 8% belongs to the Orthodox Church of Finland and the so-called free churches **Flag:** An extended blue cross on a white field with the national coat of arms centered on the cross **Anthem:** Our Land **Currency:** Markka (3.67 per U.S. $1)

Location: Northern Europe. Finland is bordered by Norway on the north, by the USSR on the east, by the Gulf of Finland and the Baltic Sea on the south, and by the Gulf of Bothnia and Sweden on the west. A third of Finland's total length lies north of the Arctic Circle **Features:** Finland is a land of 60,000 lakes, nearly all of them in the southern half of the country. About 70% of the land area is covered with forests; swamps, many of them wooded, cover about 30%. The generally low-lying coastal belt rises slightly to a forested plateau. The far north is marked by low, mountainous terrain **Chief Rivers:** Kemijoki, Oulujoki, Muoniojoki-Torniojoki

Head of State: President Urho Kaleva Kekkonen, born 1900, in office since 1956, reelected (to fifth term) in 1978 **Head of Government:** Premier Mauno Koivisto, appointed May 1979 **Effective Date of Present Constitution:** 1919 **Legislative Body:** Parliament (unicameral Edhuskunta), consisting of 200 members elected by direct universal suffrage for 4-year terms **Local Government:** 12 provinces, (including autonomous Ahvenanmaa—the Aland Islands), each headed by a governor. Urban and rural communes have elected councils

Ethnic Composition: Finnish-speaking Finns make up 93.2% of the population and Swedish-speaking Finns 6.6%. Lapps number about 3,000 and "Kazan Turks" 1,000 **Population Distribution:** 59% urban **Density:** 37 inhabitants per sq. mi.

Largest Cities: (1976 est.) Helsinki 493,324, Tampere 166,179, Turku 164,520, Espoo 123,954, Vantaa 122,301

Per Capita Income: $5,815 (1979) **Gross National Product (GNP):** $27.7 billion (1979) **Economic Statistics:** 31% of GNP comes from industry (metals, engineering, foodstuffs, paper and paper products, furniture, textiles, chemicals); 9% from agriculture (oats, barley, wheat, rye), fishing and forestry; 14% from commerce and finance **Minerals and Mining:** Copper, nickel, iron, zinc, vanadium, silver and lead are mined in substantial quantities **Labor Force:** 2.2 million (1977), with 14% in agriculture and forestry, 34% in industry and construction, and 38% in trade and services **Foreign Trade:** Exports, chiefly paper products, machinery, transport equipment, chemicals, textiles, dairy products totaled $8.6 billion in 1978. Imports, mainly raw materials for industry, fuels and lubricants, machinery, automobiles, aircraft, foodstuffs, and textiles, totaled $7.9 billion **Principal Trade Partners:** Britain, Sweden, USSR, West Germany, United States

Vital Statistics: Birthrate, 13.9 per 1,000 of pop. (1977); death rate, 9.4 **Life Expectancy:** 72 years **Health Statistics:** 66 inhabitants per hospital bed; 703 per physician (1975) **Infant Mortality:** 12 per 1,000 births (1977) **Illiteracy:** Negligible **Primary and Secondary School Enrollment:** 869,894 (1976) **Enrollment in Higher Education:** 77,206 (1975) **GNP Expended on Education:** 7.1% (1976)

Transportation: Paved roads total 19,261 mi. (1976) **Motor Vehicles:** 1,220,400 (1977) **Passenger Cars:** 1,075,400 **Railway Mileage:** 3,705 **Ports:** Helsinki, Turku, Naantali, Hamina, Hanko, Kemi, Oulu, Pori, Kotka, Sköldvik **Major Airlines:** Finnair operates domestic and international flights **Communications:** Government owned **Radio Transmitters:** 101 **Licenses:** 2,199,575 (1976) **Television Transmitters:** 83 **Licenses:** 1,779,469 (1976) **Telephones:** 1,936,000 (1976) **Newspapers:** 57 dailies, 537 copies per 1,000 inhabitants (1976)

Weights and Measures: Metric system **Travel Requirements:** Passport; no visa for 3 months

---

With a self-assurance that has grown over the last decade, neutral Finland, which borders the Soviet Union, has been playing a role in international affairs unthinkable a decade ago.

It has served a two-year term (1969-70) on the UN Security Council, where small powers, in taking their turn in the chair, find themselves presiding at times over big-power disputes. Ministers of 35 nations, including the United States and Canada, met in Helsinki in June 1973 to lay groundwork for a European détente. The Conference on Security and Cooperation in Europe (CSCE), held in August 1975 in Helsinki, dealt with the inviolability of frontiers, economic cooperation, and freer movement of people and ideas. The conference was regarded by Finland as an assurance of its independence from the Soviet Union.

To the Finns, these actions are among a series of initiatives that would have been out of the question at the beginning of the 1960s, a period of uneasy relations with the neighboring Soviets.

At the time, a major Finnish political organiza-

tion, the Social Democratic party, was being kept out of government to avoid repercussions in Moscow. But the Social Democrats returned to cabinet posts in 1966 and were part of the coalition government that achieved the signing of the Free Trade Agreement with the European Community (EC). President Kekkonen's third six-year term was lengthened by parliamentary decision after the major parties failed to find a candidate who could run Finland's sensitive foreign policy—especially Finland's relations to the Soviet Union—as well as Kekkonen, at the helm since 1956.

The Free Trade Agreement with the EC came after 13 months of hesitation and often bitter political debate in which Finland's relations with the Soviet Union played a significant part.

In January 1978, in the first presidential election in a decade, President Kekkonen was reelected to his fifth consecutive term. In May 1979, Kekkonen appointed Mauno Koivisto premier of a new centrist coalition government, which was formed without the leftist Liberal party.

HISTORY: The earliest known inhabitants of Finland were the Lapps. By the 8th century A.D., however, they had been pushed northward by the Finns, coming from the south and southeast. In the 12th century Finland was Christianized by the Swedes and in the 16th century became a grand duchy under the Swedish crown. Russia acquired the province of Vyborg in 1721 and was ceded the rest of the duchy in 1809. Although Finland enjoyed considerable autonomy under Russian rule, Finnish nationalism developed into a powerful movement

1899-1906: Tsar Nicholas II begins strong Russification program, evoking stiff Finnish resistance. Russian governor-general is assassinated and a general strike breaks out. Finns win concessions, set up a unicameral diet and introduce universal suffrage

1917-20: Following the Bolshevik seizure of power in the Russian Revolution, Finnish diet proclaims Finland's independence. Civil war breaks out between Russian sympathizers (Reds) and Finnish nationalists (Whites), led by Marshal Carl Gustav Mannerheim and aided by German troops. Whites are victorious and after a brief regency under Mannerheim a republic is set up. The Soviet Union recognizes Finland

1939-40: Soviet Union, which has been given a free hand in Finland under Moscow's nonagression pact with Nazi Germany, demands demilitarization of Finnish fortifications on Karelian Isthmus north of Leningrad, use of a naval base in Finland, and the cession of islands in Gulf of Finland. Finns refuse to bow to demands and Soviet troops attack. Despite strong resistance by Finnish troops, led by Mannerheim, Finland is defeated and is forced to cede one-tenth of its territory to USSR

1941-45: Finland is caught up in war between the Soviet Union and Nazi Germany, the Finns fighting what they regard as the Continuation War against the Russians and not as allies of Germany. Full-scale Soviet offensive results in Finnish defeat in 1944. Armistice terms oblige Finns to expel German troops; resulting warfare leads to further devastation of Finland

1947: Under peace treaty signed in Paris, Finland cedes more territory to USSR and agrees to pay heavy indemnity

1955-61: Finland joins Nordic Council, and becomes associate member of European Free Trade Association; continues policy of neutrality and cooperation with Soviet Union

1973: Finland signs Free Trade Agreement with the EC. President Kekkonen's term extended by four years

1975: Finland hosts concluding session of the Conference on Security and Cooperation in Europe (CSCE)

1976: Finland hit by first police strike in postwar Europe

1977: Kalevi Sorsa succeeds Martti Miettunen as premier

1978: President Kekkonen reelected to fifth straight term

1979: Mauno Koivisto succeeds Sorsa as premier

FRANCE

Area: 210,038 sq. mi. **Population:** 53,478,000 (1979 est.)

Official Name: French Republic **Capital:** Paris **Nationality:** French **Languages:** French is the official and predominant language. Other languages spoken include Breton (akin to Welsh) in Brittany; a German dialect in Alsace and Lorraine; Flemish in northeastern France; Spanish, Catalan, and Basque in the southwest; and Italian in the southeast and on the island of Corsica **Religion:** Chiefly Roman Catholic, 4% Moslem (mostly immigrants from North Africa), 2% Protestant, 1% Jewish **Flag:** A tricolor of blue, white, and red vertical stripes **Anthem:** La Marseillaise **Currency:** Franc (4.2 per U.S. $1)

Location: Western Europe. France is bounded on the north by the English Channel and the Strait of Dover; on the northeast by the North Sea, Belgium and Luxembourg; on the east by Germany, Switzerland, and Italy; on the southeast by the Mediterranean Sea; on the south by Andorra and Spain; and on the west by the Atlantic Ocean **Features:** About two thirds of the country consists of flat or gently rolling terrain, and the remaining third is mountainous. A broad plain covers most of northern and western France, from the Belgian border in the northeast to Bayonne in the southwest. The lowland plains area is bounded on the south by the Pyrenees; on the southeast by the mountainous Massif Central; and on the east by the Alps, Jura, and Vosges mountains **Chief Rivers:** Seine, Loire, Garonne, Rhône, Rhine

Head of State: President Valéry Giscard d'Estaing, born 1926, elected 1974 for 7 years **Head of Government:** Premier Raymond Barre, born 1924, reappointed 1978 **Effective Date of Present Constitution:** 1958 **Legislative Body:** Parliament (bicameral), with a National Assembly and the Senate. The National Assembly, elected by direct universal suffrage for 5 years, is composed of 491 deputies. The Senate is composed of 295 members, elected indirectly for 9 years by an electoral college made up of National Assembly members, the General Departmental Councils, and the delegates of the Municipal Councils. The National Assembly can be dissolved by the president with the advice of the premier **Local Government:** Metropolitan France is divided into 96 departments, each headed by a prefect appointed by the central government and each under the authority of an elected General Council. The departments are divided into cantons and communes, with each commune electing its own municipal council and designated mayor

Ethnic Composition: The French are a mixture of the 3 basic European stocks: Nordic, Alpine, and Mediterranean. The largest foreign-born groups are North Africans, Italians, Portuguese, Spaniards, Czechoslovaks, Poles, and Yugoslavs **Population Distribution:** 71% urban **Density:** 255 inhabitants per sq. mi.

Largest Cities: (1975 census) Paris 2,291,554 (Metropolitan Area 9,878,524), Marseille 901,421, Lyon 454,265, Toulouse 371,143, Nice 331,002, Nantes 252,537, Strasbourg 251,520, Bordeaux 220,830, Saint-Étienne 218,289, LeHavre 216,917, Rennes 194,094, Toulon 180,508, Reims 177,320, Lille 171,010, Grenoble 165,431, Brest 163,940

Per Capita Income: $8,619 (1979) **Gross National Product (GNP):** $461 billion (1979) **Economic Statistics:** About 38% of GNP comes from industry (metalworking, machinery, chemicals, transport equipment, food and beverages, textiles, clothing) and construction; 57% from trade and services; 5% from agriculture and fishing (wheat, barley, potatoes, beet sugar, apples, wine, fish, beef cattle, and pigs) **Minerals and Mining:** The country is an important producer of iron ore, potash, bauxite, coal, natural gas, sulphur, and building raw materials. It also has deposits of zinc, lead, pyrites, phosphates, and uranium **Labor Force:** 20.5 million, with 47% in trade and services, 38% in manufacturing and construction, 10% in agriculture, fishing, and forestry **Foreign Trade:** Exports, chiefly machinery, chemicals, textiles, automobiles, steel, grain, and aircraft, totaled $79.2 billion in 1978. Imports, mainly machinery, foodstuffs, petroleum, chemicals, steel, nonferrous metals, and transportation equipment, totaled $78.7 billion **Principal Trade Partners:** West Germany, Belgium, Luxembourg, Italy, United States, Switzerland, Britain, Netherlands, Algeria, Japan, Saudi Arabia

Vital Statistics: Birthrate, 14.0 per 1,000 of pop. (1977); death rate, 10.1 **Life Expectancy:** 72 years **Health Statistics:** 97 inhabitants per hospital bed, 678 per physician (1976) **Infant Mortality:** 11.4 per 1,000 births **Illiteracy:** Negligible **Primary and Secondary School Enrollment:** 9,511,719 (1976) **Enrollment in Higher Education:** 1,038,576 (1975) **GNP Expended on Education:** 5.8% (1976)

Transportation: Surfaced roads total 520,000 mi. **Motor Vehicles:** 19,340,000 (1977) **Passenger Cars:** 16,700,000 **Railway Mileage:** 26,380 **Ports:** Marseille, Le Havre, Dunkirk, Nantes, St-Nazaire, Rouen, Bordeaux, Brest, Nice **Major Airlines:** Air France and UTA operate international flights; Air-Inter operates domestic flights **Communications:** Government owned **Radio Transmitters:** 290 **Licenses:** 26,000,000 (1976) **Television Transmitters:** 3,001 (1974) **Licenses:** 14,197,000 (1975) **Telephones:** 15,554,000 (1976) **Newspapers:** 98 dailies, 214 copies per 1,000 inhabitants (1975)

Weights and Measures: Metric system **Travel Requirements:** Passport; no visa for 3 months

---

For a country with a reputation for being ungovernable, France has moved and is continuing to move through a difficult period of transition, politically, economically, and socially, with an uncharacteristic amount of smoothness.

That there is some unrest and dissatisfaction is attested to by strikes, demonstrations, manifestations of violence, and angry meetings. But these fits of temper surge up and die down quickly, and the appearance of crisis they create is quickly dissipated.

Despite some dire predictions, France has moved out of the Gaullist era into more prosaic leadership with the institutions that General de Gaulle had bequeathed intact. A people that history books describe as undisciplined and individualistic appear to accept strong executive power as a fact of political life, particularly when it concentrates as it now does on domestic problems and eschews to a large extent the kind of global diplomacy practiced by de Gaulle.

The main goal of de Gaulle's successor, Georges Pompidou, was to eliminate France's industrial backwardness and move her into the forefront of advanced technical nations. The rich, varied soil of France that produces the food and wines that have contributed to the French art of living have also produced a powerful, conservative rural society that over the centuries has dominated the country.

The shift to an urban, industrialized society is one of the great central facts of contemporary France. As people move from farm to city and enter into radically different ways of life and work, tensions are created. They are aggravated by the failure of the cities to accommodate ever increasing populations with adequate housing and transport. More and more, once sleepy provincial centers are starting to take on the bustle, noise, and discomfort of Paris.

More than just the rural population is in transition. Shopkeepers and artisans who flourished in a slow-moving, small-scale economy are finding themselves squeezed out of the market by the demand for more efficient and cheaper ways of making and distributing goods and services. Workers in small inefficient plants or in traditional industries that are dying out are finding themselves having to adjust to new lines of work in new places. Students and educational authorities are trying to make their schools relevant to a new kind of society that places a premium on technical proficiency and accords declining prestige to the contemplative man of letters.

All these are long-range problems that are more or less painful to resolve and create tensions that sometimes may cause explosions. In May 1968, students and workers exploded together, bringing the government of General de Gaulle and the whole regime into peril. Although de Gaulle weathered the storm, it was the beginning of the end for him; the following year he was defeated in a referendum and was forced into lonely and somewhat bitter retirement. When he died in November 1970, there was a great national and international outpouring of sentiment for him.

The events of May 1968 left a decided impact. The franc was no longer sacrosanct and monetary policies henceforth were more closely coordinated with those of France's European partners. The upheaval has led to a style of government that places great importance on discussion and participation in decisions. At the same time, the memory of the 1968 disorders made most Frenchmen very law-and-order conscious. How to protect civil liberties while putting down the disorders that continue to crop up has become a major subject of debate.

Another great theme of debate is how to loosen the power of one of the most highly centralized countries in the world without destroying national unity. The move is on to satisfy municipal and regional desires for more of a say over personal futures, but the habit of deciding everything in Paris is deep-rooted and hard to change.

Abroad, France, no longer a colonial power, has paid the greatest attention to the movement toward western European unity. Under Pompidou, European unity, long blocked by his predecessor's refusal to accept Britain as a European partner, began again to show movement. The successful negotiation with Britain for entry into the Common Market was due largely to Pompidou.

In April 1974 Pompidou died at the age of 62. On May 19, Finance Minister Valéry Giscard d'Estaing was elected president by a narrow margin. In his years in office, Giscard d'Estaing has displayed an informal style and a willingness to attack France's problems. He received a resounding vote of confidence in the legislative elections of March 1978 when candidates of his center-right coalition won a formidable 291-200 majority in the new National Assembly. It was a surprising and humiliating defeat for the alliance of Socialists and Communists, which the public opinion polls had projected as winning. Giscard, magnanimous in victory and seeking to substitute a political consensus for the left-right polarization so characteristic of French politics, vowed to bring the leftists "on the sidelines" into active participation in the government. Following the elections, Giscard reappointed Premier Raymond Barre, who has been given much of the credit for keeping the annual inflation rate under 10 percent, substantially reducing unemployment and cutting the international payments deficit.

In foreign affairs, President Giscard has pursued independent policies often conflicting with those of the United States. Although he supported NATO defense and condemned the Soviet invasion of Afghanistan in late 1979, Giscard defied U.S. wishes and met with Soviet leader Leonid Brezhnev at Warsaw, Poland, in May 1980. They discussed international tensions caused by the Soviet aggression. Earlier the same month, the French government had incurred U.S. displeasure by permitting the French Olympic Committee to approve France's participation in the 1980 Moscow games despite President Carter's call for a boycott.

HISTORY: The land of France was inhabited in ancient times by the Gauls, who, by 51 B.C., had been subdued by the Romans. The Latin language predominated by the 5th century A.D., when Roman power collapsed, and the Franks from Germany made the land part of a large domain. Charlemagne ruled from 768 to 814 and extended the domain, but it was divided in 838—"Francia," with its Latin-based language, going to Charles the Bald. The kings lost power to local nobles in the 10th century, but recovered it slowly in later centuries

1337: The Hundred Years War breaks out, actually a series of short wars and truces between France and England, whose kings lay claim to the French throne

1429-53: Joan of Arc successfully leads French armies in lifting the siege of Orléans but is burned at the stake in 1431 after falling into English hands; English are finally driven out

1643-1715: Louis XIV gains military and political primacy for France in continental Europe, creates a great overseas empire, and establishes an absolute monarchy with a highly centralized government; his reign marks the golden age of French culture

1789-94: The French Revolution sweeps away Old Regime. A National Convention is formed, the monarchy abolished, Louis XVI executed, and a republic proclaimed. The Reign of Terror sets in, leading to arrest and execution of a huge number of royalists and members of minority political blocs. France's neighbors form an alliance to suppress the Revolution

1799-1804: Napoleon Bonaparte becomes first consul under the Consulate, a tripartite executive body; he restores domestic stability and defeats Austrian-British coalition

1804-14: Napoleon proclaims himself emperor, leads French armies in a series of unequaled victories against the other powers of Europe. His attempt to conquer Russia, however, results in a decisive defeat for France and the formation of an armed European coalition which forces his abdication

1815: Napoleon escapes from exile on Elba, rallies a French army, and is decisively defeated at Waterloo

1848: Revolution overthrows Bourbon monarchy, restored after Napoleon; the Second Republic is formed

1852: Louis Napoleon, Bonaparte's nephew, engineers coup d'état and overthrows republic; as Napoleon III, he establishes the Second Empire

1870-71: France defeated in Franco-Prussian War; Second Empire collapses and the Third Republic is formed

1914-18: France plays a major role in World War I against the Austro-German coalition. Nation shares in Allied victory but its economy is devastated by the war

1939: France joins Britain in declaring war on Germany following Nazi invasion of Poland

1940: France suffers ignominious defeat by Germany. Marshal Henri Pétain forms government at Vichy and sues for peace; Germans occupy half of France. Gen. Charles de Gaulle escapes to London, forms a wartime government and the Free French army

1944: Paris is liberated by Allied armies. De Gaulle's provisional exile government is officially recognized by the Allies

1945-46: De Gaulle is unanimously elected provisional president of the Fourth Republic but resigns after leftists withdraw support

1958-61: De Gaulle is recalled to power as the Fourth Republic is threatened with collapse because of the Algerian conflict. He engineers a new constitution vesting strong powers in the executive and establishing the Fifth Republic; despite considerable opposition, he negotiates Algerian independence

1966: De Gaulle withdraws French forces from NATO

1968: Student-worker uprisings paralyze France and threaten to topple Gaullist regime, but de Gaulle weathers the storm; his Gaullist party wins smashing victory in parliamentary election

1969: President de Gaulle resigns after the defeat of a referendum for constitutional reform; Gaullist candidate Georges Pompidou is elected president; he devalues the franc

1970: President Pompidou initiates broad reforms designed to benefit blue-collar workers

1974: Pompidou dies; Giscard d'Estaing is elected president. Laws on voting age of 18 and legalized abortion are passed

1975: Giscard d'Estaing visits Algeria; first such trip by French head of state since Algerian independence

1976: Political parties of the left win a majority in nationwide local elections in March. Premier Jacques Chirac resigns, reconstitutes Gaullist party into the Assembly for the Republic. Raymond Barre, nonpartisan technocrat, becomes premier

1977: Socialists and Communists gain in municipal elections, Chirac elected mayor of Paris. Territory of Afars and Issas (Djibouti), last French colony in Africa, gains independence

1978: Center-right candidates win large majority in legislative elections, repulsing strong leftist challenge. France reportedly explodes neutron bomb at South Pacific test base

1980: President Giscard meets with Soviet leader Brezhnev, explores Middle East tensions caused by Soviet invasion of Afghanistan; France participates in Moscow Olympic Games

---

GABON

Area: 103,346 sq. mi. **Population:** 538,000 (1978 est.)

Official Name: Gabonese Republic **Capital:** Libreville **Nationality:** Gabonese **Languages:** French is the official language; Fang is spoken in the north and a variety of Bantu tongues in the rest of the country **Religion:** About 46% of the population is Christian, mainly Roman Catholic; there are about 3,000 Moslems and the rest are animists **Flag:** Green, yellow, and blue horizontal stripes **Anthem:** Harmony **Currency:** CFA Franc (210.2 per U.S. $1)

Location: West-central Africa. Gabon is bordered on the north by Equatorial Guinea and by Cameroon, on the east and south by the Congo, and on the west by the Atlantic Ocean **Features:** About 85% of the entire country is covered by dense equatorial rain forest. The coastal plain is deeply indented in the north, while inland there are plateaus and mountains through which rivers have carved deep valleys and channels **Chief Rivers:** Ogooué, Ngounié, Abanga

Head of State and of Government: President: El Hadj Omar (Albert-Bernard) Bongo, born 1935; succeeded 1967; reelected 1979. He is assisted by the appointed prime minister, Léon Mébiame **Effective Date of Present Constitution:** 1961 **Legislative Body:** National Assembly (unicameral), consisting of 93 members **Local Government:** 9 regions divided into 36 prefectures, and 8 urban communes, with appointed officials

Ethnic Composition: Almost all Gabonese are of Bantu origin. The Fang are the largest of the country's tribes, followed by the Eshira, Bapounou, Bateke, and Okandé **Population Distribution:** 32% urban **Density:** 5.2 inhabitants per sq. mi.

Largest Cities: (1973 est.) Libreville 57,000, Port-Gentil 35,000, Franceville 5,000

Per Capita Income: $4,833 (1979) **Gross National Product (GNP):** $2.7 billion (1979) **Economic Statistics:** In 1973 about 18% of GNP was from agriculture (cocoa, coffee, palm oil, rice, cassava, bananas, yams, corn, and peanuts) and forestry; 14% from manufacturing and construction; (largely timber and mineral processing); 30% from mining; 22% from trade and services **Minerals and Mining:** Very rich deposits of manganese and iron ore; uranium and gold are also produced; there are known deposits of lead, zinc, phosphate, and diamonds. Rich offshore oil and natural gas deposits are being developed **Labor Force:** About 280,000, of which 58% are engaged in agriculture **Foreign Trade:** Exports, wood, petroleum, uranium, manganese and coffee, totaled $1.1 billion in 1978. Imports, chiefly machinery, foods, transportation equipment, metal products, tobacco, refined petroleum products, and industrial chemicals, totaled $633 million **Principal Trade Partners:** France, United States, West Germany, Netherlands, Britain, Japan, Argentina, Brazil

Vital Statistics: Birthrate, 32.2 per 1,000 of pop. (1975); death rate, 22.2 **Life Expectancy:** 39 years **Health Statistics:** 132 inhabitants per hospital bed; 5,208 per physician (1975) **Infant Mortality:** 83 per 1,000 births **Illiteracy:** 70% **Primary and Secondary School Enrollment:** 153,858 (1976) **Enrollment in Higher Education:** 1,014 (1975) **GNP Expended on Education:** 4.5% (1976)

Transportation: Paved roads total 400 mi. **Motor Vehicles:** 17,400 (1974) **Passenger Cars:** 10,100 **Railway Mileage:** 184 miles; the 400-mile Transgabon line is under construction **Ports:** Libreville, Port-Gentil **Major Airlines:** Air Service and Air Affaires are domestic carriers; Air Gabon provides international services **Communications:** Government owned **Radio Transmitters:** 10 **Receivers:** 93,000 (1976) **Television Transmitters:** 8 **Receivers:** 8,500 (1976) **Telephones:** 11,000 (1976) **Newspapers:** 1 daily, 1 copy per 1,000 inhabitants (1975)

Weights and Measures: Metric system **Travel Requirements:** Passport, visa, $10 fee

---

As the smallest territory of French Equatorial Africa, jungle-matted Gabon was noted chiefly as a source of tropical hardwoods and as the unhealthy land where for 53 years the famous medical missionary, the late Dr. Albert Schweitzer, operated a hospital at Lambaréné.

Most of Gabon is still a humid tangle of trees and creepers, but the increasing number of roads slicing through the jungle attest to the dramatic change that has made the country potentially one of the richest in Africa.

Not long after gaining independence from France in 1960, Gabon was found to possess some of the world's largest deposits of manganese, iron ore, and uranium.

Development of these resources is proceeding impressively, and the airline passenger approaching Libreville, the capital and chief port, may see evidence of new wealth also in the offshore oil rigs glinting above the gray Atlantic.

While tropical woods, particularly those from which the best plywood is made, are still a major export, the rising production of minerals has given Gabon a continuing trade surplus and the highest per capita annual income in black Africa.

Meanwhile, on the economic scene, because of the attractions of newfound mineral wealth, French participation in Gabon's development has grown even greater than it was in the colonial period. In February 1974 the two nations agreed that a detachment of French troops, would remain in Gabon, which was to stay within the French zone.

Frenchmen run the new enterprises, the schools, banks, shops, and most businesses, and six French advisors serve in the President's office. President Bongo is actively seeking trade ties and investment from the United States, Britain, and West Germany in an effort to reduce French domination.

By 1976, relations with France had grown increasingly cool, with verbal attacks by President Bongo against "savage capitalism" and "exploitation" of Gabon's natural resources, becoming more frequent. However, Gabon still participates in the annual French-African summit, and severing of ties between the two nations does not appear to be imminent.

HISTORY: In the 15th century, Portuguese voyagers became the first Europeans to explore the coastal area of Gabon. However, because of dense jungles and impenetrable highlands the country remained relatively undisturbed by Europeans until the mid-19th century, when the French began making treaties with coastal chieftains and penetrating the interior. In 1890 Gabon formally became part of the French Congo and in 1910 was made a separate colony as part of French Equatorial Africa

1913: Dr. Albert Schweitzer, Alsatian-born physician, theologian, and musicologist, establishes medical mission at Lambaréné

1958-59: Republic of Gabon is established as autonomous member of the French Community; Léon M'Ba, leader of Gabonese Democratic party, becomes premier of provisional government

1960: Republic proclaims full independence

1961-63: Two main parties agree on joint list of candidates for election, in which M'Ba becomes president; factional disputes disrupt coalition and new elections are called

1964: When election decrees bar opposition candidates, Gabonese Army overthrows M'Ba government, but it is promptly restored by French military intervention; in subsequent elections in which opposition participates, M'Ba forces win 31 seats, compared with 16 for the opposition

1967: President M'Ba dies and is succeeded by Vice-President Albert-Bernard Bongo

1968: President Bongo declares Gabon a one-party state and forms new Gabonese Democratic party open to all citizens

1971: A new $500-million four-year plan is begun to further develop timber and mineral resources that include large deposits of manganese, iron ore, and uranium

1973: Bongo is elected to a seven-year term as president

1975: Léon Mébiame is named premier. Treaty is signed with EC. Gabon is admitted to full membership in OPEC

1976: Gabon becomes world's largest exporter of manganese

1978-79: Nation's financial status improves considerably as a result of government's stabilization program

---

THE GAMBIA

Area: 4,127 sq. mi. **Population:** 585,000 (1979 est.)

Official Name: Republic of The Gambia **Capital:** Banjul **Nationality:** Gambian **Languages:** English is the official language; Malinke and Wolof are the main spoken languages **Religion:** Approximately 85% of the population is Moslem; about 14% Christian; and the rest animist **Flag:** Red, blue, and green horizontal stripes, with the center blue stripe edged in white **Anthem:** For the Gambia, Our Homeland **Currency:** Dalasi (1.72 per U.S. $1)

Location: West Africa. The Gambia is a narrow strip 7-20 miles wide on either side of the Gambia River, extending eastward 200 miles from the Atlantic, and surrounded by Senegal on the land sides **Features:** Coastal mangrove swamps and salt water flats graduate to sand hills and inland plateaus **Chief River:** Gambia

Head of State and of Government: President: Alhaji Sir Dawda Kairaba Jawara, born 1924; prime minister since 1962, he became president in April 1970, and was reelected in 1977 **Effective Date of Present Constitution:** 1970 **Legislative Body:** House of Representatives (unicameral); 35 members elected by universal suffrage for a 5-year term, and 8 special members **Local Government:** Banjul, and 6 administrative divisions

Ethnic Composition: The principal groups are the Mandingo (38%), Fula (16%), Wolof (14%), Jola (9%), and Serahuli (8%) **Population Distribution:** 16% urban **Density:** 142 inhabitants per sq. mi.

Largest Cities: (1977 est.) Banjul 43,890; (1973 census) Sarrekunda 16,637

Per Capita Income: $196 (1978) **Gross National Product (GNP):** $110 million (1978) **Economic Statistics:** 58% of GNP is from agriculture (chiefly peanuts), 26% from trade and services **Minerals and Mining:** No known resources of value apart from laterite and stone **Labor Force:** 165,000, about 85% being engaged in agriculture **Foreign Trade:** Exports, mainly peanuts, fish and palm kernels, totaled $46 million (1978). Imports, chiefly food, textiles and clothing, oil, machine and transport equipment, totaled $117 million **Principal Trade Partners:** Britain, Netherlands, France, United States, Japan, West African countries

Vital Statistics: Birthrate, 43.3 per 1,000 of pop. (1975); death rate, 24.1 **Life Expectancy:** 33 years **Health Statistics:** 771 inhabitants per hospital bed; 13,500 per physician (1976) **Infant Mortality:** 82.6 per 1,000 births **Illiteracy:** 90% **Primary and Secondary School Enrollment:** 32,969 (1976) **Enrollment in Higher Education:** 947 (1971) **GNP Expended on Education:** 4.4% (1976)

Transportation: Paved roads total 180 mi. **Motor Vehicles:** 6,092 (1973) **Passenger Cars:** 3,000 **Railway Mileage:** None **Ports:** Banjul **Major Airlines:** Gambia Airways, Air Senegal, British United

Airways, and Nigeria Airways operate international and regional flights **Communications:** Partly government owned **Radio Stations:** 4 **Receivers:** 61,000 (1976) **Television:** None **Telephones:** 3,000 (1976) **Newspapers:** 1 newspaper published 3 times a week

Weights and Measures: British Imperial system is used; transfer to metric system started in 1976 **Travel Requirements:** Passport, transit visa $1.25, other visas $5.00

The Gambia, Africa's smallest country, has been gaining increasing self-reliance through the unlikely combination of peanut production, Scandinavian tourists, and careful fiscal management. Recently, attention has been focused on The Gambia because of the 1976 bestseller by Alex Haley, *Roots*, which chronicles the story of Haley's ancestors from tribal life in The Gambia to slavery in America.

Formerly Britain's oldest African colony, The Gambia became independent in 1965 and proclaimed itself a republic in 1970. It added "The" to its official name to avoid confusion with Zambia, another African country.

Except for a short Atlantic coast, the country is enclosed within Senegal. A sandy strip of land, it stretches some 200 miles in length along either side of the Gambia River and varies in width from seven to 30 miles.

The broad mouth of the Gambia River is one of West Africa's finest harbors and the site of the capital, Banjul. Mandingoes, a handsome, friendly people, form the main element of the population.

Peanuts, planted on most of the available land, account for 95 percent of exports, but, in recent years, tourism has become a welcome and fast-growing addition to the economy, luring 25,000 Scandinavians a year.

Old hotels have been enlarged and new ones built to meet growing demand. With tourist organizations in other countries now showing interest in The Gambia, prospects are bright for a continuance of the boom and creation of more jobs and revenue. With Soviet, Chinese and British aid, The Gambia is beginning fishery development and irrigation projects.

HISTORY: Along with neighboring Senegal, The Gambia was inhabited in past ages by peoples associated with the great empires of Ghana, Mali, and Songhay. Reached by Portuguese navigators in the 15th century, in 1588 the territory became, through purchase, the first British colony in Africa. After prolonged struggle, the British and French fixed the borders of Senegal and Gambia; in 1888 the latter became a crown colony

1965: The Gambia becomes a fully independent member of the British Commonwealth; a referendum to make the country a republic fails to receive necessary two-thirds majority

1966: Elections give Prime Minister Sir Dawda Jawara's People's Progressive party an increased majority

1967-69: Britain loans The Gambia over $10 million

1970: The Gambia becomes a republic

1975: Treaty is signed with EC

1979: Pres. Jawara announces formation of a special court to handle charges of corruption. An agricultural development fund is set up to boost farm production

---

EAST GERMANY

Area: 41,768 sq. mi. **Population:** 16,745,000 (1979 est.)

Official Name: German Democratic Republic **Capital:** East Berlin **Nationality:** German **Languages:** German is the official and universal language **Religion:** 53% Protestant, 8% Roman Catholic, 39% no affiliation. Although the constitution provides for religious freedom, all churches are closely regulated by the state **Flag:** Black, red, and gold horizontal stripes, with the national emblem in the center **Anthem:** Arisen from the Ruins **Currency:** GDR mark (1.77 per U.S. $1)

Location: North-central Europe. East Germany is bordered on the north by the Baltic Sea, on the east by Poland, on the southeast by Czechoslovakia, and on the southwest and west by the Federal Republic of Germany **Features:** In the north are the lakes and low

hills typical of the Baltic Sea country; the center is partly mountainous and in addition consists of a sandy arid section and a fertile plain. The heavily forested southern region consists of the Mittelgebirge, and the extension of the North German lowlands **Chief Rivers:** Elbe, Oder, Saale, Havel, Spree, Neisse

Political Leader and Head of State: Erich Honecker, born 1912, secretary general of the Central Committee of the Socialist Unity Party and chairman of the State Council **Head of Government:** Willi Stoph, born 1914, appointed October 1976 chairman of the Council of Ministers (premier) **Effective Date of Present Constitution:** 1968, amended 1974 **Legislative Body:** Volkskammer (unicameral) consisting of 500 members, elected by universal suffrage for 5-year terms; final decisions are made by the party's Politburo **Local Government:** 15 administrative districts named after their respective chief towns. All urban and rural divisions have locally elected bodies

Ethnic Composition: The population is ethnically homogeneous. The only minority is a Slavic group called the Sorbs which makes up about 0.2% of the population **Population Distribution:** 75.5% urban **Density:** 401 inhabitants per sq. mi.

Largest Cities: (1976 estimates) East Berlin 1,101,123, Leipzig 565,392, Dresden 509,253, Karl-Marx-Stadt (Chemnitz) 305,874, Magdeburg 278,023, Halle 235,546, Rostock 215,044, Erfurt 204,468, Zwickau 122,209, Potsdam 120,333

Per Capita Income: $5335 (1979) **Gross National Product (GNP):** $89 billion (1979) **Economic Statistics:** About 54% of GNP comes from industry, and 20% from agriculture. The chief industries are iron and steel, chemicals, fertilizers, machinery, transport equipment, synthetic rubber and fibers, drugs, plastics, and vehicles. The chief crops are barley, oats, potatoes, rye, sugar beets, and wheat **Minerals and Mining:** The arbitrary division of Germany left the East with few natural resources. Its only major resources are lignite, potash and uranium **Labor Force:** 8,600,000 (1975), with 39% in industry, 21% in services, 10% in commerce, 9% in agriculture **Foreign Trade:** Exports, chiefly machinery, railway rolling stock, chemicals, fertilizers and pesticides, fuel oil, construction materials, ships, motor vehicles, clothing and textiles, were estimated at $15.2 billion in 1979. Imports, mainly mineral ores, coal, rolled steel, fertilizer, tires, crude oil, wood, cotton and wool, paper pulp, foodstuffs, forage and feeds, and raw skins, were estimated at $17.6 billion **Principal Trade Partners:** USSR, Czechoslovakia, Poland, Hungary, France, Britain, West Germany, Bulgaria, Netherlands, Sweden

Vital Statistics: Birthrate, 13.3 per 1,000 of pop. (1977); death rate, 13.4 **Life Expectancy:** 72 years **Health Statistics:** 93 inhabitants per hospital bed; 523 per physician (1976) **Infant Mortality:** 13.1 per 1,000 births (1977) **Illiteracy:** Negligible **Primary and Secondary School Enrollment:** 3,014,086 (1976) **Enrollment in Higher Education:** 386,000 (1975) **GNP Expended on Education:** 5.6% (1974)

Transportation: Surfaced roads total 8,032 mi., with 1,000 mi. of superhighways **Motor Vehicles:** 2,806,700 (1977) **Passenger Cars:** 2,236,700 **Railway Mileage:** 8,856 (1974) **Ports:** Rostock, Wismar, Stralsund, Sassnitz **Major Airlines:** Interflug operates domestic and international services **Communications:** State controlled **Radio Transmitters:** 66 **Licenses:** 6,167,000 (1976) **Television Transmitters:** 461 **Licenses:** 5,180,000 (1976) **Telephones:** 2,751,000 (1976) **Newspapers:** 40 dailies, 472 copies per 1,000 inhabitants (1975)

Weights and Measures: Metric system **Travel Requirements:** Passport; visa obtainable at border or at East German embassy; visa entitlement certificate

---

The German Democratic Republic is mainly the work of one man, Walter Ulbricht, a ruthless and fanatical leader. Without his dedication and his seemingly tireless efforts from 1945 to 1971, his ruling Communist party and state apparatus, East Germany would undoubtedly have remained in a kind of Central European limbo.

Throughout the 1960s his prestige and power increased dramatically. In this period East Germany grew to be the 10th largest industrial power in the world and the country with the best living standard in the Communist world. Working to his advantage was the desire for security and comfort of the East Germans and their willingness to persevere under adverse conditions.

A major threat to Ulbricht's rule was posed by the reform program of the new Czechoslovak Communist leadership in 1968. The reform aims proclaimed in Prague by Alexander Dubcek were viewed in East Berlin as an elemental danger to the more or less orthodox, militant Marxism/Leninism practiced by the Ulbricht team. The East German leader recommended suppression; his advice was followed by the Soviet leaders who ordered the August 21, 1968, invasion of Czechoslovakia. Ulbricht was at his zenith in the wake of this move, and it seemed, for a while, that he was setting the tone of Russian foreign policy in Central Europe until his dismissal in 1971 as First Party Secretary for bypassing the Central Committee, overemphasizing large-scale development projects and obstructing Soviet aims for an accommodation with West Germany.

Ulbricht's successor, Erich Honecker, negotiated agreements of recognition with West Germany in 1974. Apparently in return for Honecker's support of Soviet policy, visiting Soviet leader Leonid Brezhnev announced in October 1979, during the German Democratic Republic's 30th anniversary celebrations, that the USSR would withdraw 20,000 of its troops from East Germany. The token troop withdrawal began in December, but its completion within a year still left an estimated 360,000 Soviet troops in East Germany.

HISTORY: The Germans made their first major appearance in recorded history when they came into contact with the Romans in the 1st century B.C. By the 5th century A.D. various Germanic tribes had overrun the Roman Empire. After the division of Charlemagne's possessions in 843, the kingdom of the Eastern Franks emerged as the nucleus of Germany, but for most of Germany's history political unification was to prove beyond reach. In 1517 Martin Luther precipitated the Protestant Reformation and Germany was torn by religious strife until the end of the Thirty Years' War (1618-48). In the 18th century Prussia began to emerge as an important power and in the next century successfully challenged Austria for domination of Germany

1815: Congress of Vienna perpetuates the political divisions of Germany and provides for a German Confederation

1862: Bismarck becomes chancellor of Prussia; his goal is to create a unified Germany dominated by Prussia and excluding Austria

1866: Prussia is victorious in the Austro-Prussian War

1870-71: Prussia defeats France in the Franco-Prussian War, enabling Bismarck to achieve his goal of a unified Germany under Prussia; in 1871 William I of Prussia is proclaimed German Emperor

1914-19: Germany is ranged against Allied Powers in World War I and suffers crushing defeat; German Empire collapses and newly formed Weimar Republic is forced to accept harsh terms of Versailles Treaty

1933-36: Hitler is appointed chancellor in 1933 and assumes dictatorial powers; Germany is transformed into a brutal police state; anti-Semitism becomes official policy, culminating eventually in the extermination of six million European Jews; intensive rearmament begins

1938: Hitler annexes Austria and later takes over the Sudetenland from Czechoslovakia

1939-45: Hitler seizes the rest of Czechoslovakia in March 1939; six months later Nazi forces invade Poland, triggering World War II; Nazi forces overrun Western Europe and in 1941 invade the Soviet Union; by 1945, however, Germany is totally defeated, its cities in ruins, and its territory under U.S., Soviet, British, and French occupation; Hitler commits suicide

1945-48: East Germany and part of Berlin come under Soviet occupation and are brought under the control of the Communist-dominated Socialist Unity party. A separate East German state is established under Soviet auspices as a result of the failure of the USSR and the Western occupying powers to agree on a uniform policy for all of Germany

1948-49: Soviet opposition to the plans of the three other Allies for Germany's future results in breakdown of joint Four Power rule; Russians attempt to blockade Berlin, whereupon Western Allies mount gigantic airlift to bring food to West Berliners; in October 1949, following the creation of the Federal Republic of Germany, Russians set up the German Democratic Republic

1953: Anti-Communist revolt in East Germany is crushed by Soviet forces

1955: Soviet Union signs treaty declaring East Germany a sovereign state

1961: Wall is erected around non-Soviet sectors of Berlin to prevent flight of East Germans to the west via West Berlin

1968: East German leader Walter Ulbricht meets with other East European leaders and calls for concerted action to halt liberalization in Czechoslovakia; within months, East German troops join in Soviet-led invasion of Czechoslovakia

1961: Wall is erected around non-Soviet sectors of Berlin to prevent flight of East Germans to the west via West Berlin

1968: East German leader Walter Ulbricht meets with other East European leaders and calls for concerted action to halt liberalization in Czechoslovakia; within months, East German troops join in Soviet-led invasion of Czechoslovakia

1971: Ulbricht resigns as head of Socialist Unity party, is succeeded by Erich Honecker of the party's Central Committee

1972: Traffic Treaty is signed with West Germany, providing for access to West Berlin

1973: East and West Germany ratify a treaty calling for closer relations. Later in the year, both join the UN. Ulbricht dies

1974: U.S. establishes diplomatic relations with East Germany in September. The two Germanys exchange representatives

1978: Agreement reached with West Germany on construction of new highway to West Berlin and other transit matters. Diplomatic problems arise over status of East Berlin

1979: Soviets begin token withdrawal of 20,000 troops

WEST GERMANY

Area: 95,704 sq. mi. **Population:** 61,439,000 (1979 est.)

Official Name: Federal Republic of Germany **Capital:** Bonn **Nationality:** German **Languages:** German is the official and universal language **Religion:** 49% Protestant, 45% Roman Catholic **Flag:** Black, red, and gold horizontal stripes **Anthem:** The official national anthem consists of the third verse of the old Deutschlandlied, beginning "Unity and Justice and Freedom" **Currency:** Deutsche Mark (1.80 per U.S. $1)

Location: North-central Europe. West Germany is bordered by Denmark and the North Sea on the north, by East Germany and Czechoslovakia on the east, by Austria and Switzerland on the south, and by France, Luxembourg, Belgium, and the Netherlands on the west **Features:** The country is generally flat in the north and hilly in the central and western areas, rising to more than 4,000 feet in the Black Forest and to more than twice that height in the Bavarian Alps **Chief Rivers:** Rhine, Danube, Ems, Weser, Elbe, Main, Mosel, Neckar, Isar

Head of State: President Karl Carstens, born 1914, elected 1979 for 5 years **Head of Government:** Chancellor Helmut Schmidt, born 1918, appointed 1974, elected 1976 **Effective Date of Present Constitution:** May 23, 1949 **Legislative Body:** Parliament (bicameral), consisting of the *Bundestag* and *Bundesrat*. The *Bundestag* has 496 elected members and 22 nonvoting members representing West Berlin, chosen for a term of 4 years. The *Bundesrat* has 41 members appointed by the state governments and 4 consultative members appointed by the West Berlin Senate **Local Government:** 10 states (*Länder*), each with its own legislative and ministerial government. West Berlin, though not legally a component state of West Germany, is closely integrated into the government's political and administrative system

Ethnic Composition: With the exception of a small Danish population in Schleswig-Holstein, the population is German **Population Distribution:** 86% urban **Density:** 642 inhabitants per sq. mi.

Largest Cities: (1976 est.) Berlin (West) 1,984,837, Hamburg 1,717,383, Munich 1,314,865, Cologne 1,013,771, Essen 677,568, Düsseldorf 664,336, Frankfurt-am-Main 636,157, Dortmund 630,609, Stuttgart 600,421

Per Capita Income: $9,501 (1979) **Gross National Product (GNP):** $583 billion (1979) **Economic Statistics:** About 54.6% of GNP is derived from manufacturing (food industry, chemicals, iron and steel, electrical engineering, machinery); 18.5% is from trade, transportation and communications; 13.5% is from agriculture (rye, wheat, oats, barley, potatoes), forestry and fishing **Minerals and Mining:** Coal is the most important mineral resource. There are also substantial deposits of iron ore (mostly low grade), lead and zinc, potash, salt, fluorspar, barites, pyrites, graphites, and basalt. Some natural gas is produced **Labor Force:** 26 million, with 37% in services, 36% in industry, and 6% in agriculture **Foreign Trade:** Exports, chiefly mechanical engineering products, motor vehicles, chemicals, electrical engineering products, and iron and steel, totaled $172 billion in 1979. Imports, mainly foodstuffs, crude oil, nonferrous metals and semifinished products, chemical products, iron and steel, textiles, totaled $160 billion **Principal Trade Partners:** United States, Canada, France, Netherlands, Great Britain, Belgium, Italy, Japan, Switzerland, Austria, Sweden

Vital Statistics: Birthrate, 9.5 per 1,000 of pop. (1977); death rate, 11.5 **Life Expectancy:** 71 years **Health Statistics:** 84 inhabitants per hospital bed, 503 per physician (1976) **Infant Mortality:** 15.5 per 1,000 births **Illiteracy:** Negligible **Primary and Secondary School**

Enrollment: 10,262 047 (1976) **Enrollment in Higher Education:** 836,002 (1975) **GNP Expended on Education:** 5.2% (1975)

Transportation: Surfaced roads total 104,487 mi., with 4,200 mi. of superhighways **Motor Vehicles:** 21,410,100 (1977) **Passenger Cars:** 20,020,200 **Railway Mileage:** 19,876 **Ports:** Hamburg, Wilhelmshaven, Bremen, Kiel, Emden, Lübeck **Major Airlines:** Lufthansa operates domestic and international services **Communications:** Partly government controlled **Radio Transmitters:** 346 **Licenses:** 20,909,000 (1975) **Television Transmitters:** 1,153 **Licenses:** 19,226,000 (1975) **Telephones:** 22,800,000 (1977) **Newspapers:** 320 dailies, 289 copies per 1,000 inhabitants (1974)

Weights and Measures: Metric system **Travel Requirements:** Passport, no visa for 90 days

---

The Federal Republic of Germany was created in 1949 in the British, French, and U.S. occupation zones of Germany, as a vehicle for solving the German problem. Located in the center of Europe and in the center of big-power politics, Germany was divided for centuries; in eight decades as a unified nation, it twice frightened the world. At first resentful of their division into two after 1949, the Germans gradually became accustomed to it.

The Christian Democratic Union/Christian Social Union (CDU/CSU) has been the largest party in every West German *Bundestag*, but has had a majority in only one. Konrad Adenauer, CDU/CSU Chancellor from 1949 to 1963, aligned West Germany with NATO, and presided over an "economic miracle" in which the country recovered from the ravages of war and absorbed millions of ethnic German immigrants from East Germany and Eastern Europe. The free-enterprise policies of Adenauer's Minister of Economics, Ludwig Erhard, were credited with the country's surprising growth, but West Germany was aided by having inherited most of prewar Germany's iron ore, coal, and hydropower, and—after 1958—by membership in the European Community.

The Social Democratic party of Germany (SPD) has been the second-largest in every *Bundestag*; the Free Democratic party (FDP) has held the balance of power between the CDU/CSU and the SPD since 1961. The FDP went into coalition with the CDU/CSU in 1961, forced the aging Adenauer to retire in favor of Ludwig Erhard in 1963, and brought down Erhard by withdrawing from the coalition in 1966. Kurt Kiesinger then became leader of the CDU/CSU, formed a "grand coalition" with the SPD, and served as chancellor until 1969.

Originally a socialist party, the SPD has become a party of moderate reform within capitalism. Willy Brandt, former Mayor of West Berlin, was its leader in 1969, when it took power in coalition with the FDP. He concentrated on foreign policy, and shocked many Germans by abandoning talk of reunification and by recognizing the East German regime. He also improved relations with other Communist countries and worked to strengthen and expand the EC. Forced to resign because of an espionage scandal in 1974, he was succeeded by Helmut Schmidt, also a Social Democrat. Two successive SPD chancellors have done little to modify their predecesors' free-enterprise policies, and West Germany has remained an economic giant. Growth is slower than in the heady years of the economic miracle, but inflation and unemployment are lower than elsewhere. Prosperity has not eliminated discontent. Terrorist activity has been severe, especially in 1977. In 1978, a controversial new law increased the authority of the police.

Under Chancellor Schmidt, West Germany has continued to support both NATO and U.S. policy toward Europe. In 1980, Schmidt condemned the Soviet invasion of Afghanistan, and West Germany was the only major European nation to join the U.S.-sponsored boycott of the 1980 Olympic Games held in Moscow.

HISTORY: The history of West Germany is bound up with that of Germany as a whole until the years immediately following World War II (*See* East Germany *for pre-WW II chronology*)

1948-49: Western Allies mount massive airlift to Berlin, thwarting Soviet attempt to blockade city; West German constituent assembly adopts provisional constitution for the Federal Republic of Germany; Konrad Adenauer is elected chancellor; East Germany, under Soviet occupation, is set up as a Communist state named the German Democratic Republic

1961: East German government erects Berlin Wall in effort to halt flight of East Germans to the west via West Berlin

1963: Adenauer retires and is succeeded by Ludwig Erhard

1966: Kurt Kiesinger becomes chancellor

1968: Country is rocked by student demonstrations following attempted slaying of left-wing student leader in West Berlin

1969: Willy Brandt becomes chancellor

1970: A nonaggression treaty, recognizing present European borders, is signed with Soviet Union

1972: Nonaggression pact with Soviet Union and Poland ratified. U.S., USSR, Britain, and France sign Final Quadripartite Protocol in Berlin, putting into effect earlier agreements on civilian travel in and around Berlin

1974: Chancellor Willy Brandt resigns over a spy scandal involving a member of his staff. Helmut Schmidt succeeds him. Legal age of majority is lowered from 21 to 18. Two German states recognize each other

1975: Economy is slowed by inflation and high unemployment

1976: Treaty with Poland to allow ethnic Germans to emigrate is ratified. Ruling coalition of Social Democrats and Free Democrats wins close victory in nationwide parliamentary elections

1978: Controversial anti-terrorist laws enacted

1979: Karl Carstens is elected president by the Federal Convention (the *Bundestag* plus members of the *Länder* parliaments)

1980: Signs agreement with East Germany to improve road, rail, and canal links between the two countries

---

GHANA

Area: 92,099 sq. mi. **Population:** 10,969,000 (1978 est.)

Official Name: Republic of Ghana **Capital:** Accra **Nationality:** Ghanaian **Languages:** English is the official and commercial language; of some 50 tribal languages and dialects spoken, the chief ones are Twi, Fanti, Ga, Ewe, Hausa, Dagbani, and Akan **Religion:** About 43% Christian, 12% Moslem, and the rest animist **Flag:** Red, gold, and green horizontal stripes, with a 5-pointed black star centered on the gold stripe **Anthem:** National Anthem, beginning "Lift high the flag of Ghana" **Currency:** Cedi (2.75 per U.S. $1)

Location: West Africa. Ghana is bordered on the north by Upper Volta, on the east by Togo, on the south by the Gulf of Guinea, and on the west by the Ivory Coast **Features:** Half of Ghana is less than 500 feet above sea level. The coastline is largely a low sandy shore, backed by plains and intersected by rivers. Northward is a belt of tropical rain forest, broken by densely forested hills and rivers. The far north is a region covered by savanna and grassland plains **Chief Rivers:** Volta, Pra, Tano

Head of State and of Government: President Hilla Limann, born 1934, elected 1979 **Effective Date of Present Constitution:** 1979 **Legislative Body:** National Parliament with 140 members **Local Government:** 9 regions divided into districts; each region is administered by a regional commissioner

Ethnic Composition: Ghanaians are chiefly of black Sudanese stock, the principal groups being the Akan, living mostly along the coast, and the Ashanti, in the forest areas immediately to the north; the Guans, living on the plains of the Volta River; the Gaand Ewe-speaking peoples of the south and southeast; and the Moshi-Dagomba-speaking tribes of the north **Population Distribution:** 31% urban **Density:** 119 inhabitants per sq. mi.

Largest Cities (M.A. = Metropolitan Area): (1970 census) Accra 564,194 (M.A. 738,498); Kumasi 260,286 (M.A. 345,117); Sekondi-Takoradi 91,874 (M.A. 160,868); Tema 60,767

Per Capita Income: $384 (1979) **Gross National Product (GNP):** $5.5 billion (1979) **Economic Statistics:** In 1975 about 45% of GNP was from agriculture (cocoa, of which Ghana is the world's leading producer, livestock, fish); 15% from manufacturing and mining; and 40% from trade and services. Industry consists of aluminum smelting and the processing of cocoa, kola nuts, coffee, coconuts, oil palms, and rubber **Minerals and Mining:** Gold is the most important mineral exploited, followed by diamonds. There are large reserves of manganese and bauxite; other minerals include low-grade deposits of iron ore, and deposits of beryl, ilmenite, nickel, graphite, and chromite **Labor Force:** 3.4 million, of which 57% is employed in agriculture, forestry, and fishing, 15.5% in industry and mining, and 27.5% in trade and services **Foreign Trade:** Exports, chiefly cocoa, cocoa butter, manganese, gold, diamonds, timber and aluminum, totaled $979 million in 1978. Imports, mainly machinery and transport equipment, cereals, alumina, petroleum, and textiles, totaled $843 million **Principal Trade Partners:** Britain, United States, Netherlands, West Germany, Switzerland

Vital Statistics: Birthrate, 47 per 1,000 of pop. (1976); death rate, 22 **Life Expectancy:** 52 years **Health Statistics:** 648 inhabitants per hospital bed; 10,310 per physician (1976) **Infant Mortality:** 59 per 1,000 births **Illiteracy:** 70% **Primary and Secondary School Enrollment:** 1,790,270 (1976) **Enrollment in Higher Education:** 9,079 (1975) **GNP Expended on Education:** 4.2% (1976)

Transportation: Paved roads total 3,500 mi. **Motor Vehicles:** 121,700 (1977) **Passenger Cars:** 72,400 **Railway Mileage:** 600 **Ports:** Tema, Takoradi **Major Airlines:** Ghana Airways operates internal and international services **Communications:** Government controlled **Radio Transmitters:** 10 **Receivers:** 10,080,000 (1976) **Television Transmitters:** 4 **Receivers:** 35,000 (1976) **Telephones:** 62,000 (1976) **Newspapers:** 4 dailies, 51 copies per 1,000 inhabitants (1975)

Weights and Measures: British standards are being replaced by the metric system **Travel Requirements:** Passport, visa, valid up to 14 days, $2.25 fee, 3 photos

---

The first of Britain's African possessions to gain freedom in the postwar decolonization era, Ghana has gone from a democratic parliamentary system, through dictatorship, rule by a military junta, a return to democracy, back to military rule for a short period, and, at present, democratic rule.

During this time, the country also experienced overly ambitious industrialization and near bankruptcy as a result of the extravagances of Kwame Nkrumah, its first leader. Nkrumah was deposed in 1966, and died in exile in 1972.

Ghana, however, possesses a potentially strong economy; major resources range through cocoa, timber, manganese, gold, and electric power. Her people are capable and progressive.

As the Gold Coast, the country had moved steadily toward self-government prior to independence in 1957 and with its new name of Ghana—that of an ancient African empire—was otherwise well prepared for complete sovereignty.

Ghana has many educators, lawyers, doctors, economists, and a well-trained civil service. Development programs are concentrating on diversification of agriculture, an increase of arable land, and the improvement of rural communities. The prime objective is to reduce Ghana's dependency on cocoa exports by increasing exports and self-sufficiency in other products.

Ghana is still the world's leading supplier of cocoa, but with lagging production and increases by other countries, her share of the market has declined.

In April 1978 the Ghana government banned three political organizations (and arrested 17 leading civilian politicians) after a nationwide referendum showed a majority of voters favor single-party rule. In 1977 those outlawed had spearheaded an "intellectual's revolt" that posed the gravest crisis to the government since its seizure of power in 1972. Students, doctors, lawyers, engineers and other professionals had joined in accusing the nation's military rulers of repression, corruption and fiscal mismanagement, and had demanded they resign.

Gen. Ignatius Kutu Acheampong, head of state since 1972, resigned on July 5, 1978, and was succeeded by Lt. Gen. Fred W.K. Akuffo. His first act was to release the civilians who had been arrested earlier in 1978. Strikes by civil servants and energy industry workers prompted the government to declare a state of emergency, which lasted from November to the end of 1978. While lifting the state of emergency on January 1, 1979, officials also legalized political activity for the first time in seven years.

On June 4 the government of General Akuffo was overthrown in a coup staged by junior army officers, and an Armed Forces Revolutionary Council, headed by Flight Lieut. Jerry Rawlings, took control. Former heads-of-state Akwasi Afrifa, Ignatius Acheampong and Fred Akuffo were executed shortly thereafter, in spite of an appeal for mercy from UN Secretary-General Waldheim. Nigeria halted oil deliveries to Ghana to register its displeasure.

Hilla Limann, leader of the People's National party, was victorious in a runoff following the July 1979 elections and took office as president of the Third Republic of Ghana on Sept. 24.

HISTORY: Ghana was dominated by independent black kingdoms in precolonial times. Following the arrival of the Portuguese in the 15th century, the coastal region soon became known as the Gold Coast because of the rich trade in gold. The gold trade later gave way to the slave trade, which was eventually abolished by the British in the 19th century. In 1874, Britain established the colony of the Gold Coast and in 1901 annexed the neighboring Ashanti kingdom. In the same year a region to the north, known as the Northern Territories, became a British protectorate

1922: Part of neighboring Togoland, a former German colony, is mandated to Britain by League of Nations and administered as part of the Gold Coast

1942-48: Africans are admitted into the government of the Gold Coast, but native agitation for independence mounts under the leadership of United Gold Coast Convention party; party leaders Joseph B. Danquah and Kwame Nkrumah are imprisoned

1949: Nkrumah, following his release, breaks with Danquah and forms his own party, the Convention People's party, and leads campaign of civil disobedience against the British

1951-52: Britain grants new constitution and elections are held; Nkrumah becomes prime minister

1957: The state of Ghana, comprising the Gold Coast and British Togoland, obtains independence, becoming the first black African colony to do so. Joins the UN

1960: Ghana becomes a republic within the British Commonwealth; Nkrumah becomes both chief of state and head of government, and is given the power to rule without parliament whenever he deems it necessary

1962-64: Nkrumah establishes one-party rule; several attempts on his life lead to arrests of numerous leaders in his own Convention People's party and of opposition leader Joseph Danquah, who dies in prison

1966: Nkrumah is deposed by a military coup; a National Liberation Council, headed by Lt. Gen. Joseph A. Ankrah, is set up to rule the country

1969: Ankrah resigns after admitting he received money for political purposes and is succeeded by Gen. Akwasi Afrifa. Civilian government is restored under new constitution

1970: Three-man presidential commission headed by Afrifa is dissolved; former Chief Justice Edward Akufo-Addo is elected president by electoral college

1972: Col. Ignatius Kutu Acheampong leads military coup against the Busia Government and assumes power as head of state; offices of president and prime minister abolished and constitution withdrawn. Kwame Nkrumah dies and his body is returned from Guinea for burial in Ghana

1975: Treaty is signed with EC

1978: Acheampong is replaced as head of state by Lt. Gen. Fred W.K. Akuffo

1979: Akuffo is overthrown on June 4, and is replaced by an Armed Forces Revolutionary Council, headed by Flight Lieut. Jerry Rawlings. Hilla Limann is elected president and takes office Sept. 24

1980: Pope John Paul II, visiting Ghana, calls on people to increase production on their farms

---

GREECE

Area: 50,944 sq. mi. **Population:** 9,360,000 (1978 est.)

Official Name: Hellenic Republic **Capital:** Athens **Nationality:** Greek **Languages:** Modern Greek; Turkish and Albanian are minority languages **Religion:** 97% of the population belongs to the Greek Orthodox Church; 2% are Moslems **Flag:** Nine equal horizontal stripes of blue and white with a white cross on a blue field in the upper left corner **Anthem:** Hymn of Liberty **Currency:** Drachma (42.5 per U.S. $1)

Location: Southeast Europe, occupying the southern part of the Balkan peninsula and more than 3,000 offshore islands. The Greek mainland is bordered on the north by Bulgaria, Yugoslavia, and Albania; on the east by Turkey and the Aegean Sea; on the south by the Mediterranean Sea; and on the west by the Ionian Sea **Features:** The country is predominantly mountainous, with much of the land dry and rocky **Chief Rivers:** Aliakmon, Peneus, Vardar, Achelous, Nestos, Alpheus, Struma

Head of State: President Constantine Karamanlis, born 1907, elected May 1980 **Head of Government:** Premier George Rallis, born 1918, appointed May 1980 **Effective Date of Present Constitution:** June 1975 **Legislative Body:** Parliament (unicameral), consisting of 300 deputies **Local Government:** 51 prefectures, each headed by an appointed prefect and the autonomous Mt. Athos district

Ethnic Composition: About 96% of the population is Greek. Minorities include Turks (1%), Slavs, Vlachs, Albanians and Bulgarians **Population Distribution:** 64.8% urban **Density:** 184 inhabitants per sq. mi.

Largest Cities (M.A. = Metropolitan Area): (1971 census) Athens 867,023 (M.A. 2,566,775), Salonika 345,799 (M.A. 482,361), Piraeus 187,362, Patras 111,607 (M.A. 112,228)

Per Capita Income: $2,882 (1979) **Gross National Product (GNP):** $27.2 billion (1979) **Economic Statistics:** Agriculture accounted for about 17% of the GNP in 1975 (the principal crops are wheat, tobacco, currants, grapes, olives, citrus fruits, and cotton); the industrial sector contributed about 31% (major industries include textiles; aluminum, nickel and chemical refineries; food processing; mining); services accounted for 50% **Minerals and Mining:** Lignite, bauxite, iron ore, chromite, barite and magnesite are exploited **Labor Force:** 3,400,000 (1978), with 38% in agriculture, 30% in services, and 19% in industry **Foreign Trade:** Exports, mainly tobacco, currants, cotton, unprocessed aluminum, iron, nickel, and citrus fruits, totaled $3 billion (1978). Imports, chiefly machinery, iron and steel, crude oil, meat, passenger cars and trucks, totaled $7.4 billion **Principal Trade Partners:** West Germany, Italy, United States, France, Japan, Saudi Arabia, Britain, Libya, Netherlands

Vital Statistics: Birthrate, 15.4 per 1,000 of pop. (1977); death rate, 8.2 **Life Expectancy:** 71 years **Health Statistics:** 156 inhabitants per hospital bed; 475 per physician (1976) **Infant Mortality:** 20 per 1,000 births (1977) **Illiteracy:** 10% **Primary and Secondary School Enrollment:** 1,615,286 (1975) **Enrollment in Higher Education:** 111,435 (1975) **GNP Expended on Education:** 1.8% (1974)

Transportation: Paved roads total 10,000 mi. **Motor Vehicles:** 894,900 (1977) **Passenger Cars:** 618,800 **Railway Mileage:** 1,580 mi. **Ports:** Piraeus, Salonika, Iraklion, Patras, Eleusis, Volos **Major Airlines:** Olympic Airways operates domestic and international services **Communications:** Government controlled **Radio Transmitters:** 61 **Receivers:** 2,750,000 (1976) **Television Transmitters:** 54 **Receivers:** 1,165,000 (1976) **Telephones:** 2,180,000 (1975) **Newspapers:** 106 dailies, 107 copies per 1,000 inhabitants (1975)

Weights and Measures: Metric system **Travel Requirements:** Passport, no visa for 2 months

---

The Hellenes (Greeks) inhabit a mountainous peninsula and its neighboring rocky islands. Agriculture is difficult—and so is administration. Trade and navigation—fostered by excellent harbors—have been vital for thousands of years. Individualism and loyalty to locality are strong.

The ancient Greeks had no national unity, but they were leaders in art, literature, and philosophy; and some of their city-states were the world's first democracies.

Conquered by Macedonia, then by Rome, then by the Ottoman Empire, Greece achieved independence and unity in struggles against the last in the 19th and 20th centuries. Disputes with Turkey concerning land and—more recently—territorial waters are still troublesome. Political stability within Greece has been rare.

Greece was occupied by Germany in World War II and needed considerable assistance from the United States to quell a Communist guerrilla movement in the war's aftermath. Greece entered NATO, despite the misgivings of many Greeks about U.S. influence, and Turkish membership, in the alliance. Later, the troubles in Cyprus aggravated ill-feelings toward Turkey.

Governed by short-lived coalition governments from 1946 until 1952, Greece achieved stability under Premier Alexander Papagos in 1952. He died

in 1955, and Constantine Karamanlis succeeded him, serving until 1963, when he went into exile after a squabble with King Paul. George Papandreou formed a stable government in 1964, but anti-NATO elements in his past worried many. King Constantine II fired him in 1965, and political unrest followed until the army seized power in 1967.

Col. George Papadopoulous emerged as strong man and premier. He abolished the monarchy and made himself president in 1973, only to be deposed by military colleagues. Gen. Demetrios Ioannides ran the government from behind the scenes until 1974, when he sponsored the ill-fated coup against President Makarios of Cyprus. His fellow-officers deposed him and invited Constantine Karamanlis to resume the premiership.

Karamanlis held an election, which his own New Democracy party won handily. He loosened Greece's connection with NATO and objected to the decision of the United States to end the arms embargo against Turkey. Despite his party's reduced mandate after special elections in 1977, Karamanlis took bold initiatives in foreign affairs. He negotiated a trade treaty with Albania in 1978 that opened the outside world for the strict Albanian Communist regime. In 1979 his government signed an even more important treaty making Greece a full member of the European Community effective in 1981. An associate member for years, Greece will be the first full member outside the heavily industrial region of Western Europe.

After serving six years as premier, Karamanlis was elected president of Greece by the parliament to succeed Konstantinos Tsatsos on May 5, 1980. The new president pledged to stay out of party politics and to represent the entire nation. The former foreign minister, George John Rallis, was elected premier by caucus of the New Democracy party.

HISTORY: Ancient Greece, a small land fragmented into frequently warring city-states, attained its golden age in the Athens of the 5th century B.C. In the following century it fell to the forces of Philip of Macedon, whose son, Alexander the Great, spread Hellenistic civilization widely. In the 2nd century B.C., Greece became a territory of the Roman Empire and eventually was incorporated into the Byzantine Empire. Turkish conquests, completed in the 15th century, made Greece part of the Ottoman Empire

1821-30: Greeks wage war of independence against Turks, who gain help of Egypt; following intervention by Britain, France, and Russia, Greece wins autonomy and finally independence

1832-63: European powers choose Prince Otto of Bavaria to be king of a fully independent Greece; he is deposed in 1862. The following year a Danish prince is chosen as monarch, becoming King George I of the Hellenes

1912-22: Greece takes part in the Balkan Wars of 1912-13 and increases its territory. Outbreak of World War I leads to split between pro-Allied government and neutralist King Constantine I; king abdicates in 1917; Greece joins Allied side and gains additional territory in the postwar settlements; Greece invades Asia Minor and is defeated by Turks

1923: Hostility to dynasty forces George II to leave Greece

1924-35: Greece is proclaimed a republic; after more than a decade of political strife, a plebiscite restores the monarchy

1936-41: John Metaxas becomes premier and institutes a dictatorship that lasts through Italy's World War II invasion of Greece, begun in 1940, and continues up to his death in 1941

1941-50: Germany invades in 1941 and Greece is occupied by Axis forces. With the expulsion of the last of the German troops in 1944, rivalry between Greek Communist and royalist guerrillas erupts into civil war. Under the Truman Doctrine, announced in 1947, the United States sends advisers to the Greek Army and provides $300 million in economic and military aid; Communist forces are finally defeated in 1950

1967: Military junta seizes power. King Constantine II and the royal family flee to Rome after an abortive countercoup; Col. George Papadopoulos becomes premier

1973: Papadopoulos decrees end to monarchy, appoints himself head of new "Hellenic Republic." He is toppled by a bloodless coup. Gen. Phaedon Gizikis becomes president with Dimitrios Ioannides as military dictator; elections are postponed indefinitely

1974: Ioannides sponsors coup in Cyprus. Turkish army invades Cyprus. Military junta leaders turn government over to civilians, ending seven years of military rule. Former Premier Constantine Karamanlis returns from self-imposed exile in Paris and is sworn in as premier by President Gizikis. Britain, Turkey, and Greece, meeting in Geneva, impose new cease-fire on Cyprus. Soon after, when Geneva peace talks break down, Turkish forces resume their advance on Cyprus. Greece withdraws its armed forces from NATO. First free elections in more than a decade result in decisive victory for Premier Karamanlis. In national referendum voters reject monarchy in favor of republican form of government

1975: Parliament adopts a new constitution and elects Konstantinos Tsatsos as president. Trial of the principal organizers of the 1967 coup results in their death sentences being commuted by cabinet to life imprisonment

1977: Karamanlis's New Democracy party loses 41 seats in parliamentary election, Panhellenic Socialist Movement gains 77 seats

1978: Greek leaders deplore U.S. ending its arms embargo against Turkey. New law makes terrorism a capital offense

1979: Agreement reached on Greece's full membership in European Community, effective 1981

1980: Karamanlis becomes president; George John Rallis is selected as premier

---

GRENADA

Area: 133 sq. mi. **Population:** 97,000 (1978 est.)

Official Name: Grenada **Capital:** St. George's **Nationality:** Grenadine **Languages:** English, with a rarely used Franco-African patois **Religion:** Roman Catholicism, Protestantism **Flag:** A diagonally divided field, yellow at top and bottom and green at sides, with red border on all sides, bearing along top and bottom three yellow stars each; in center a yellow star on a red disk; in hoist a green triangle with a nutmeg with yellow shell and brown fruit **Anthem:** Hail Grenada **Currency:** East Caribbean dollar (2.70 per U.S. $1)

Location: The southernmost of the Windward Islands in the West Indies. Includes the southern Grenadines, the largest of which is Carriacou **Features:** Volcanic in origin, the islands are chiefly mountainous **Chief Rivers:** There are no large rivers

Head of State: Queen Elizabeth II, represented by a governor-general, Sir Paul Scoon **Head of Government:** Prime Minister Maurice Bishop, born 1944, seized power in 1979 **Effective Date of Present Constitution:** 1967, suspended 1979 **Legislative Body:** Rule is by a 14-member People's Revolutionary Government (PRG) **Local Government:** 7 parishes

Ethnic Composition: Largely of mixed descent, with strains of white settlers, Africans brought in as slaves, and Carib Indians **Population Distribution:** N.A. **Density:** 729 inhabitants per sq. mi.

Largest Cities: (1970 census) St. George's 6,313, Gouyave 2,498, Grenville 1,723, Victoria 1,673·

Per Capita Income: $520 (1978 est.) **Gross Domestic Product (GDP):** $56 million (1978 est.) **Economic Statistics:** The economy is agricultural, with sugar, coconuts, nutmeg, cocoa, and bananas the chief exports. Yams, rice, breadfruit, and corn are grown for food. Tourism is increasingly important **Minerals and Mining:** Offshore exploration for gas and oil in progress **Labor Force:** 30,196, of which 40% are employed in agriculture, forestry and fishing **Foreign Trade:** Exports, chiefly cocoa, nutmeg and bananas, totaled $17 million (1978 est.). Imports totaled $36 million **Principal Trade Partners:** Britain, United States, Canada, Caribbean countries, Netherlands

Vital Statistics: Birthrate, 27.4 per 1,000 of pop. (1975); death rate, 5.9 **Life Expectancy:** 63 years **Health Statistics:** 144 inhabitants per hospital bed; 4,000 per physician (1974) **Infant Mortality:** 23.5 per 1,000 births **Illiteracy:** 24% **Education Statistics:** 71 primary and secondary schools with a combined enrollment of 34,863 (1971) **Enrollment in Higher Education:** c. 100 (1974) **GNP Expended on Education:** 9.4% (1975)

Transportation: Surfaced roads total 560 mi. **Motor Vehicles:** 3,900 (1971) **Passenger Cars:** 3,800 **Railway Mileage:** None **Ports:** St. George's, Grenville, Hillsborough **Major Airlines:** LIAT **Communications:** Government owned **Radio Transmitters:** 5 **Receivers:** 22,000 (1976) **Television:** None **Telephones:** 5,000 (1976) **Newspapers:** N.A.

Weights and Measures: British and metric systems **Travel Requirements:** Passport or proof of citizenship

---

Formerly a dependency of the United Kingdom and later a member of the British-controlled Federation of the West Indies, Grenada became an internally self-governing state on March 3, 1967. The United Kingdom retained responsibility for defense and external affairs. On February 7, 1974, Grenada became independent within the British Commonwealth of Nations, with a parliamentary system of government based on Great Britain's.

Grenada, known as the "Isle of Spice," is famous for its nutmeg, cocoa and cinnamon. Tourism is another mainstay of the island's economy.

Politically, Grenada has been the scene of widespread unrest since independence. The controversy centered on Prime Minister Eric Gairy's rule, considered by many Grenadians to be dictatorial. Rioting broke out in 1973 and 1974, and a secret police squad retaliated by employing strong-arm tactics. Subsequently, tourism declined and many Grenadians fled. In late 1976 Gairy was narrowly reelected with rural support.

In a coup marked by the killing of two policemen, Maurice Bishop, a London-educated lawyer, and the socialistic New Jewel Movement seized the government on March 13, 1979, while Gairy was in New York. The coup was accomplished by seizing the radio station and police barracks, along with government officials in their homes. Bishop became prime minister, and a 14-member People's Revolutionary Government took office. The constitution was suspended, but Grenada remained within the British Commonwealth. Bishop invited Cuban instructors to train his new People's Revolutionary Army and made a deal for Cuban workers to build a jet airport near St. George's. He shut down *Torchlight*, the island's only independent newspaper, after it criticized his government.

HISTORY: The original inhabitants of the islands were Arawak Indians who were expelled by the warlike Caribs shortly before the visit of Columbus in 1498. An abortive English settlement in 1609 was followed by French settlement and control from 1650 to 1762. Britain controlled the islands for over 200 years, except for five years of French rule (1779-83) during the American Revolution

1833: Slavery is abolished

1967: Grenada assumes Associated State status

1974: Independence is attained. Grenada is admitted to UN

1975: Treaty is signed with EC

1979: The New Jewel (for Joint Endeavor for Welfare, Education and Liberation) Movement seizes the government, and Maurice Bishop becomes prime minister. Grenada joins the "nonaligned" nations in a summit meeting in Cuba

1980: Bombing assassination attempt against the life of Bishop fails

---

GUATEMALA

Area: 42,042 sq. mi. **Population:** 7,046,000 (1979 est.)

Official Name: Republic of Guatemala **Capital:** Guatemala **Nationality:** Guatemalan **Languages:** Spanish is the official and predominant language; 20 varieties of the Maya-Quiché Indian dialects are spoken in the countryside **Religion:** Overwhelmingly Roman Catholic **Flag:** Blue, white, and blue vertical bands, with the national coat of arms in the center **Anthem:** National Anthem, beginning "Blessed Guatemala" **Currency:** Quetzal (1 per U.S. $1)

Location: Central America. Guatemala is bordered on the north by Mexico, on the east by Belize and the Caribbean, on the southeast by Honduras and El Salvador, on the southwest by the Pacific Ocean, and on the west by Mexico **Features:** The central highland region constitutes about one-fifth of the country's land surface. The Pacific plain is a narrow belt between mountains and ocean, while the Caribbean lowlands consist of fertile river valleys. The northern part of the country is dominated by the lowland forest of Petén **Chief Rivers:** Motagua, Usumacinta, Polochic, Samalá

Head of State and of Government: President: Gen. Fernando Romeo Lucas García, born 1924, elected 1978 **Effective Date of Present Constitution:** September 15, 1965 **Legislative Body:** National Congress (unicameral), consisting of 61 deputies elected by universal suffrage for 4 years **Local Government:** 22 departments, administered by governors appointed by the president and a central district, the capital city

Ethnic Composition: Pure-blooded descendants of the Maya Indians make up almost 50% of the population; the rest is largely of mixed Spanish and Indian descent **Population Distribution:** 36% urban **Density:** 168 inhabitants per sq. mi.

Largest Cities: (1973 census) Guatemala 700,538, Tiquisate 67,555, Quezaltenango 65,526, Escuintla 64,851

Per Capita Income: $1,115 (1979) **Gross National Product (GNP):** $6.7 billion (1979 est.) **Economic Statistics:** In 1973 about 28% of GNP came from agriculture (coffee, cotton, sugar cane, bananas, corn, beans, rice, wheat); 16% is derived from industry (foodstuffs, tobacco, textiles, furniture, paper and paper products, leather goods, chemical products, machinery and metal products); and 44% from trade and services **Minerals and Mining:** Zinc, silver, lead, nickel, and limestone are exploited **Labor Force:** 1,895,168 (1975), of which 58% is employed in agriculture, 24% in trade and services and 18% in industry **Foreign Trade:** Exports, chiefly coffee, bananas, cotton, sugar and meat, totaled $1.2 billion in 1978. Imports, mainly industrial machinery, textiles, chemicals and pharmaceutical products, and construction materials, totaled $1.3 billion **Principal Trade Partners:** United States, Central American countries, West Germany, Japan, Venezuela

Vital Statistics: Birthrate, 42.6 per 1,000 of pop. (1976); death rate, 9.3 (1976) **Life Expectancy:** 52 years **Health Statistics:** 457 inhabitants per hospital bed; 4,338 per physician (1973) **Infant Mortality:** 77 per 1,000 births (1976) **Illiteracy:** 70% **Primary and Secondary School Enrollment:** 749,450 (1975) **Enrollment in Higher Education:** 25,978 (1976) **GNP Expended on Education:** 1.7% (1976)

Transportation: Paved roads total 1,700 mi. **Motor Vehicles:** 132,800 (1976) **Passenger Cars:** 82,700 **Railway Mileage:** 605 **Ports:** Pto. Barrios, Sto. Tomás de Castilla, San José, Champerico **Major Airlines:** AVIATECA operates domestic and international services **Communications:** Partly government controlled **Radio Transmitters:** 95 **Receivers:** 265,000 (1976) **Television Transmitters:** 12 **Receivers:** 120,000 **Telephones:** 53,000 (1974) **Newspapers:** 11 dailies, 39 copies per 1,000 inhabitants (1972)

Weights and Measures: Metric system and local units **Travel Requirements:** Proof of citizenship; tourist card good for stay up to 6 months but usable only within 6 months of issue; $1 fee

---

Assassinations and kidnappings by extremists of both the left and right continue to plague Guatemala, the largest and potentially the wealthiest of the Central American republics.

In effect, there are two Guatemalas—one Spanish and one Indian. The Indians, concentrated in the picturesque central highlands, speak little Spanish and cling to peasant ways that originated with their Mayan ancestors well before the Spanish conquest. Constituting almost half the population, they account for the low economic and social standards of the country as a whole.

The educational deficit alone is staggering. Illiteracy still hovers at over 50 percent, and about half the children of school age get little or no schooling despite some progress in school construction. The problem is complicated by the necessity of teaching in the Indian languages before transferring to Spanish. Those who hold economic power in Guatemala have been reluctant to provide funds for education and other improvements.

Guatemala's wealth has traditionally been land-based. Coffee and cotton, the major products, are picked by the Indian population at low wages. In recent years, wider industrial opportunities have been provided by the Central American Common Market. Tires, clothing, foodstuffs, and pharmaceuticals have helped to diversify the economy although many of the industries are little more than assembly operations employing few workers. Oil reserves were discovered in 1976.

Since the election to the presidency in 1978 of Gen. Romeo Lucas Garcia, Guatemala has been virtually in a state of civil war. On one side is a coalition of guerrillas, Social Democratic politicians, unions, professors, students and Indian peasants. On the other side is the army, whose frequent brutal attacks on suspected rebel leaders have been abetted by right-wing "death squads." Assassinations, kidnappings, and other violent acts have been commonplace.

HISTORY: The Mayas, one of the most advanced of the Indian tribes, flourished in Guatemala for centuries before the arrival of the Spanish conquistadors. In the 12th century, however, Mayan civilization began to decline and its downfall was completed by the Spanish conquest in the 16th century. Under Spanish rule Guatemala was the seat of a captaincy general

1821: Guatemala is granted independence from Spain and with the other Central American countries is annexed to Mexico

1823-1825: Central American nations secede from Mexico and establish United Provinces of Central America

1839-1944: Guatemala becomes an independent republic and for more than a century is governed by the military

1951-57: Col. Jacobo Arbenz Guzmán, a leftist-leaning president, institutes social and agrarian reforms and expropriates holdings of foreign plantation owners, including United Fruit Co. Communist influence in Arbenz regime leads to strained relations with United States. With U.S. support, Col. Carlos Castillo Armas overthrows Arbenz in 1954 and returns expropriated land; Castillo Armas is assassinated in 1957

1958-63: Country is thrown into political turmoil and ruled by military juntas. State of siege is declared in 1963 to deal with growing terrorism and sabotage by extremists of right and left

1965-68: A new constitution takes effect in 1965; free elections are held the following year and Julio César Méndez Montenegro, candidate of moderately leftist Revolutionary party, becomes president. He suspends constitutional guarantees in January 1968 following terrorist slayings of two U.S. military officials. In August, U.S. Ambassador John Mein is killed

1970: Carlos Arana Osorio, leading a right-wing coalition, wins presidential election. Terrorists kidnap several foreign diplomats, kill West German Ambassador. State of siege imposed

1974: Alleged vote fraud installs Gen. Kjell Laugerud Garcia as president; violence ensues

1975: Britain agrees to resume talks with Guatemala on future of Belize (British Honduras). Guatemala has claimed sovereignty over the British dependency for more than 100 years

1976: Severe damage and 22,500 deaths are caused by a series of earthquakes

1978: Gen. Romeo Lucas García, government-backed moderate conservative, is elected president in runoff vote in Congress

1979: Two popular democratic leaders, as well as the Army Chief of Staff, and dozens of political, labor and student leaders and professors are assassinated

1980: Indian peasants seize Spanish embassy in Guatemala City to protest government strong-arm measures; police storm building and 39 persons die in ensuing fire; Spain breaks off relations

---

GUINEA

Area: 94,925 sq. mi. **Population:** 4,890,000 (1979 est.)

Official Name: People's Revolutionary Republic of Guinea **Capital:** Conakry **Nationality:** Guinean **Languages:** French is the official language; the languages of 8 ethnic groups are recognized as national languages. The two main languages are Peul (Fulani) and Mandé **Religion:** About 75% Moslem, 24% animist, less than 1% Christian **Flag:** Red, yellow, and green vertical stripes **Anthem:** Liberty **Currency:** Syli (19.1 per U.S. $1)

Location: West Africa. Guinea is bordered by Senegal and Mali on the north, the Ivory Coast on the east, Liberia and Sierra Leone on the south, the Atlantic Ocean on the west, and Guinea-Bissau on the northwest **Features:** The country consists of a low-lying coastal area, a pastoral plateau, a forest region along the Liberian border, and a dry area in the north **Chief Rivers:** Niger, Bafing, Konkouré, Koliba, Milo

Head of State: President Ahmed Sékou Touré born 1922; in power since 1958, reelected 1975 for 7 years; he is secretary-general of the country's only party **Head of Government:** Premier: Dr. Lansana Béavogui took office April 1972 **Effective Date of Present Constitution:** November 12, 1958 **Legislative Body:** National Assembly (unicameral), consisting of 150 members elected for 5 years. All members belong to the Democratic party of Guinea **Local Government:** 29 administrative regions, headed by appointed governors

Ethnic Composition: Of about 18 tribes in the country the most important are the Peuls (Fulani), Malinké (Mandingo), and Soussou **Population Distribution:** 9% urban **Density:** 52 inhabitants per sq. mi.

Largest City: (1973 est.) Conakry 198,000

Per Capita Income: $178 (1978) **Gross National Product (GNP):** $850 million (1978) **Economic Statistics:** About 40% of GNP is from agriculture (coffee, palm products, corn, millet, pineapples, bananas, rice, cassava), forestry, and fishing; 20% from mining, 14% from manufacturing (textiles, truck assembly, sawmilling, canning, paints, soap, cigarettes, plastics, furniture) **Minerals and Mining:** Bauxite and iron ore deposits are among the richest in the world; other minerals are diamonds and gold **Labor Force:** About 85% of the working population is engaged in plantation and subsistence agriculture. About 136,000 are wage earners (1976), mostly in public service **Foreign Trade:** Exports, chiefly alumina, pineapples, coffee, palm kernels, bananas, and iron ore, totaled $342 million in 1976. Imports, cotton textiles, rice, vehicles, cement, machinery, petroleum products, and sugar, totaled $279 million **Principal Trade Partners:** United States, France, West Germany, Spain, Italy, Romania, Canada, USSR, Britain

Vital Statistics: Birthrate, 47 per 1,000 of pop. (1975); death rate, 23 **Life Expectancy:** 41 years **Health Statistics:** 588 inhabitants per hospital bed; 15,100 per physician (1976) **Infant Mortality:** 172 per 1,000 births **Illiteracy:** 90% **Education Statistics:** 2,287 primary and secondary schools, with combined enrollment of 241,033 (1971) **Enrollment in Higher Education:** 2,874 (1972) **GNP Expended on Education:** 5.9% (1972)

Transportation: Paved roads total 2,969 mi. **Motor Vehicles:** 21,000 (1972) **Passenger Cars:** 10,200 **Railway Mileage:** 410 **Ports:** Conakry, Kassa, Benty, Kamsar **Major Airlines:** Air Guinée is the local carrier; 7 other lines provide international service **Communications:** State owned **Radio Transmitters:** 5 **Receivers:** 120,000 (1976) **Television:** None **Telephones:** 10,000 (1974) **Newspapers:** 1 daily, 1 copy per 1,000 inhabitants (1975)

Weights and Measures: Metric system **Travel Requirements:** Passport, visa, valid 3 months, $5 fee, 3 pictures

---

Committed by its militant leader, Ahmed Sékou Touré, in 1958 to "poverty in freedom rather than riches in slavery," Guinea has followed a tortuous course that has assured poverty but little freedom.

In 1958 Guinea was the only French colony to vote non to General de Gaulle's proposed community of semiautonomous nations still closely linked to France. Although, for France's former colonies, the community was to be a step toward eventual sovereignty, accompanied by aid and trade, Guinea opted for independence.

Hostility between France and Guinea persisted for the next two decades and ended officially only with a state visit by French President Valéry Giscard d'Estaing in December 1978.

Until recently, Guinea's huge mineral resources and great hydroelectric potential had been neglected. In addition to iron ore, gold, and diamonds, Guinea possesses bauxite deposits estimated to be a third of the world's total. An international consortium of aluminum companies, in which the Guinean government holds 49 percent interest, is now operating a big bauxite mining complex at Boké in northern Guinea. Production at more than nine million tons a year is expected to earn Guinea $500 million over a 20-year period.

In late 1970, Touré's long rule was shaken by the landing at Conakry of a small, seaborne guerrilla force, which Touré charged was an invasion by Portuguese mercenaries and Guinean renegades, backed by Portugal and launched from neighboring Portuguese Guinea. Denied by Portugal, the charge was supported by a UN commission.

HISTORY: Guinea possesses a rich ethnic and cultural heritage derived from the empires of Ghana, Mali, and Songhai, which ranged from the western Sudan to the West African coast between the 10th and 15th centuries. In the 15th century, the Portuguese, followed by the Dutch, English, and French, opened the country to European contacts and trade. Following the establishment of a protectorate by France in 1849, French penetration inland met with strong resistance from Fulani and Malinké chieftains. Resistance was finally crushed with the defeat in 1898 of the popular hero and chieftain Samory Touré, from whom President Sékou Touré is said to be descended

1958: Guinea, the only French West African territory to vote against membership in the French Community, becomes an independent republic; Sékou Touré, an acknowledged Marxist although rejecting Marxism as inapplicable to Africa, becomes president and his Democratic party of Guinea becomes the only political party; France abruptly withdraws all aid

1959–61: Guinea turns to the Soviet bloc and Communist China for assistance, and promotes African unity by forming short-lived union with Ghana and Mali

1965: Guinea suspends relations with France after charging that France encouraged a plot to overthrow Touré government

1966: Touré grants asylum to deposed Ghanaian President Nkrumah and names him honorary co-president of Guinea; new Ghanaian government breaks relations with Guinea

1970: Dispute with Portugal develops over charges of rebel infiltration from Guinea to Portuguese Guinea. Post of prime minister is created and the government is reorganized. Dr. Louis Lansana Béavogui becomes prime minister

1975: Relations restored with France. Touré elected for third term

1976: Discovery of a series of assassination plots on the life of President Touré announced by his administration. Government and military officials are implicated and arrested

1978: Guinea and Senegal restore diplomatic relations; French President Giscard d'Estaing visits

1979: In move to improve human-rights situation, several hundred political prisoners are freed. Touré visits United States

1980: Touré escapes assassination attempt May 14, but one person is killed and 30 are injured by exploding grenade

---

GUINEA-BISSAU

Area: 13,948 sq. mi. **Population:** 777,214 (1979 census)

Official Name: Republic of Guinea-Bissau **Capital:** Bissau **Nationality:** Guinean **Languages:** Portuguese and Crioulo, a creole lingua franca **Religion:** 66% animist, 30% Moslem, 4% Christian **Flag:** A black star on a red vertical stripe at the hoist and equal horizontal stripes in the fly of gold over light green **Anthem:** Long Live the Glorious Country **Currency:** Guinea-Bissau escudo (33.6 per U.S. $1)

Location: On the west coast of Africa, bounded by the Atlantic Ocean on the west, Senegal on the north, and Guinea on the east and south **Features:** A low-lying coastal plain with savanna, swamps, and rain forest. Large sections are frequently covered by tidal waters. There are 18 main offshore islands, including the Bijagós Archipelago **Chief Rivers:** Cacheu, Mansoa, Geba, Grande de Buba, Corubal

Head of State: President Luiz de Almeida Cabral, head of the State Council **Head of Goverment:** Premier (Chief Commissioner) Maj. João Bernardo Vieira, appointed 1978 **Effective Date of Constitution:** 1973 **Legislative Body:** National Assembly, 150 members of the PAIGC party elected for periods up to three years. It is the supreme organ of government, meets at least once a year and elects the president. The 15-member State Council serves for 3-year terms **Local Government:** 12 administrative regions, with elected regional councils

Ethnic Composition: Except for small groups of Portuguese and mulattos the people are mostly indigenous (Balanta, Fulani, Mandyako, Malinké, and Pepel) **Population Distribution:** N.A. **Density:** 56 inhabitants per sq. mi.

Largest Cities: (1970 census) Bissau 71,169, Bafata 7,717

Per Capita Income: $280 (1978) **Gross Domestic Product (GDP):** $174 million (1978) **Economic Statistics:** Agriculture probably accounts for well over 50% of the GDP. About 70% of the agricultural production is consumed locally **Minerals and Mining:** No commercial mining exists. There are potentially large deposits of bauxite **Labor Force:** 410,000; 94% are employed in agriculture **Foreign Trade:** Exports, chiefly peanuts, coconuts, frozen shrimp and fish, wood, totaled $11 million in 1978. Imports, chiefly textiles, vehicles, rice, consumer goods, fuel totaled approximately $50 million **Principal Trade Partners:** Portugal, Angola, Spain, West Germany, Sweden, Britain, U.S., Cape Verde

Vital Statistics: Birthrate, 40.1 per 1,000 of pop. (1975); death rate 25.1 **Life Expectancy:** 34 years **Health Statistics:** 481 inhabitants per hospital bed; 7,571 per physician (1976) **Infant Mortality:** 47.1 per 1,000 births **Illiteracy:** 95% **Primary and Secondary School Enrollment:** 86,756 (1976) **Enrollment in Higher Education:** N.A. **GNP Expended on Education:** 1.2% (1972)

Transportation: Paved roads total 265 mi. **Motor Vehicles:** 5,124 **Passenger Cars:** 3,268 **Railway Mileage:** None **Ports:** Bissau, Bolama **Major Airlines:** TAP **Communications:** Government owned **Radio Transmitters:** 2 **Licenses:** 11,000 (1976) **Television:** None **Telephones:** 3,000 (1973) **Newspapers:** 1 daily, 11 copies per 1,000 inhabitants (1975)

Weights and Measures: Metric system **Travel Requirements:** Passport, visa

---

Poor, diseased and subject to forced labor, Africans of Portuguese Guinea developed a national liberation movement in the early 1960s. By 1970 rebels claimed control of two-thirds of the country. The movement was led by the African Party for the Independence of Guinea and Cape Verde (PAIGC), whose basic tenet of doctrine was the "unity" of Guinea-Bissau and Cape Verde Islands, and was headed by Amilcar and Luis Cabral. The PAIGC proclaimed independence in 1973, but Portugal rejected the claim. However, the 1974 coup in Portugal ultimately resulted in an agreement granting independence for Guinea-Bissau on September 24 of that year, making Guinea-Bissau the first Portuguese African territory to achieve independence. Luis de Almeida Cabral became president, Amilcar Cabral having been killed in 1973.

Guinea-Bissau is currently struggling with all the problems that face developing nations, especially in the areas of education, health care, road development and electrification.

HISTORY: The Portuguese, sailing for Prince Henry the Navigator, reached the area in 1446. Slave trading was important in the 17th and 18th centuries
1879: Portuguese Guinea is separated from the administrative control of the Cape Verde Islands
1962: Revolt against Portuguese rule begins
1974: Portuguese Guinea attains independence as Guinea-Bissau
1978: Premier Francisco Mendes dies in auto crash
1979: President Antonio Ramalho Eanes of Portugal visits Guinea-Bissau; agreements reached on judicial and consular affairs

GUYANA

Area: 83,000 sq. mi. **Population:** 820,000 (1978 est.)
Official Name: Cooperative Republic of Guyana **Capital:** Georgetown **Nationality:** Guyanese **Languages:** English is the official language; other spoken languages include various East Indian dialects, Chinese, Portuguese, and a patois used by those of African origin **Religion:** About 57% Christian (chiefly Anglican), 33% Hindu, 9% Moslem **Flag:** A green field with a black-edged red triangular pennant superimposed on a white-edged yellow triangular pennant **Anthem:** Dear land of Guayana **Currency:** Guyana dollar (2.55 per U.S. $1)
Location: Northeast coast of South America. Guyana is bordered on the north by the Atlantic Ocean, on the east by Suriname, on the south and southwest by Brazil, and on the northwest by Venezuela **Features:** The country is divided into a low-lying coastal region, a heavily forested interior, and a region of mountains and savannas in the south and west **Chief Rivers:** Essequibo, Courantyne, Berbice, Mazaruni, Cuyuni, Demerara
Head of State: President Raymond Arthur Chung, born 1918, elected the republic's first president in 1970, and reelected in 1976 for 6 years **Head of Government:** Prime Minister Linden Forbes Sampson Burnham, born 1923, reappointed 1973 to 3rd term **Effective Date of Present Constitution:** 1966; a new one is in preparation **Legislative Body:** National Assembly (unicameral), consisting of 53 members elected by proportional representation for 5 years. The life of the present Assembly was extended 15 months beyond its normal July 10, 1978, closing, so that it might act as a Constituent Assembly to draft a new constitution. On Oct. 22, 1979, the Assembly's term was extended for another year **Local Government:** 10 regions, with regional ministers
Ethnic Composition: About 51% of the population is of East Indian descent; 31% African and African mixed; 6% indigenous Amerindians, and small groups of Portuguese and Chinese **Population Distribution:** 40% urban **Density:** 9.9 inhabitants per sq. mi.
Largest Cities (M.A. = Metropolitan Area): (1971 estimates) Georgetown 100,855 (M.A. 195,250); Linden 23,956; New Amsterdam 17,782; Corriverton 10,502; Rosehall 5,018
Per Capita Income: $660 (1979) **Gross National Product (GNP):** $577 million (1979) **Economic Statistics:** In 1973 about 20% of GNP came from agriculture (sugar, rice, corn, coconuts, coffee); 12% from manufacturing (cigarettes, matches, margarine, edible oils, beverages, sugar milling, aluminum smelting, wood and pulp); 18% from mining; and 22% from trade and services **Minerals and Mining:** Bauxite is the principal mineral. Diamonds and gold are also mined **Labor Force:** 242,000 (1975), with 31% in industry and mining and 29% in agriculture **Foreign Trade:** Exports, chiefly bauxite and aluminum, sugar, rice, timber, shrimp, gold, and diamonds, totaled $296 million in 1978. Imports, mainly foodstuffs, manufactured goods, machinery, petroleum products, beverages, and tobacco, totaled $279 million **Principal Trade Partners:** Britain, United States, Commonwealth Caribbean countries, Canada, Japan

Vital Statistics: Birthrate 26.6 per 1,000 of pop. (1976); death rate, 7.1 **Life Expectancy:** 67 years **Health Statistics:** 199 inhabitants per hospital bed; 3,249 per physician (1975) **Infant Mortality:** 40 per 1,000 births **Illiteracy:** 13% **Primary and Secondary School Enrollment:** 213,679 (1976) **Enrollment in Higher Education:** 2,307 (1973) **GNP Expended on Education:** 7.0% (1976)

Transportation: Paved roads total 480 mi. **Motor Vehicles:** 41,400 (1977) **Passenger Cars:** 28,400 **Railway Mileage:** 68 **Port:** Georgetown **Major Airlines:** Guyana Airways Corp. operates domestic passenger and international cargo flights **Communications:** Government and privately owned **Radio Transmitters:** 8 **Receivers:** 275,000 (1976) **Television:** None **Telephones:** 23,000 (1976) **Newspapers:** 3 dailies, 155 copies per 1,000 inhabitants (1974)

Weights and Measures: British standards **Travel Requirements:** Passport; no visa for 30 days; onward ticket

---

Aptly termed the "land of the waters" by the indigenous Amerindians, Guyana, along most of its coastline, is below sea level. The land along the Atlantic, where most people of the South American country live, is made habitable by the 300-year-old seawalls and drainage system built by the Dutch.

Until the early 19th century, under the British, various colonization plans failed before the lucrative sugar industry was introduced. The British imported African slaves, indentured Portuguese and East Indians, and Chinese. These waves of immigration have determined Guyana's racial composition and the experience of slavery and indentured servitude has molded the country's political and social life.

Guyana has unresolved boundary disputes with two of its neighbors, Venezuela and Suriname. Venezuela claims the area west of the Essequibo River, more than half the size of Guyana as now constituted, while the dispute with Suriname relates to which interior river—the Courantyne or the New River—is the Guyana/Suriname border.

Independent from Britain since 1966, Guyana insists on traveling the autonomous line of a "cooperative republic." As Prime Minister Forbes Burnham puts it, his government will "pursue relentlessly the policy of owning and controlling our natural resources." Burnham has established the only Marxist government in South America.

The most far-reaching initiatives taken by the government in furtherance of its socialist aims have been in the assertion of local control of the country's national economy. On January 1, 1975, the government nationalized the local mining operations of Reynolds Metal Co., completely bringing the country's bauxite mining industry under state control. By June 1976, when the British-owned Booker-McConnell Sugar Co. was nationalized, 80 percent of the nation's goods and services was in government hands.

In 1979, Guyana joined three Caribbean states—Jamaica, Grenada, and Saint Lucia—in a declaration accusing the U.S. of warmongering in beefing up airpower at Key West, Fla., in response to reports of increased Soviet military presence in Cuba.

On the homefront, Burnham, leader of the ruling People's National Congress, on October 22 postponed scheduled parliamentary elections for a year. This drew protests from two opposition parties—the Working People's Alliance, which, during a bauxite strike in 1979, declared itself a political party, and the People's Progressive party.

A mass-murder suicide on an appalling scale at Jonestown, a community set up in the jungle by the San Francisco-based People's Temple, turned world attention to Guyana in November 1978. The bizarre tragedy began with the murders of U.S. Representative Leo J. Ryan of California, who had flown to Guyana to investigate reports that cult members were being held against their will, and four members of his party. The five were killed at the Port Kaituma airport on November 18, just after visiting Jonestown and getting word that 20 Temple members wanted to defect. After news of the murders was radioed to Jonestown, the Rev. Jim Jones, self-proclaimed messiah, led the whole community in a previously rehearsed suicide plan. It was carried out mainly by mixing a flavored drink with cyanide, but there was also some gunfire. The U.S. military removed 913 bodies of Temple members by air to Dover (Del.) Air Force Base. Guyana officials declared that none of their citizens were involved.

HISTORY: Little is known of the history of Guyana before the arrival of Europeans. When European explorers came to Guyana in the late 1500s and early 1600s, they found Arawak, Carib, and Warrau Indians living in the area. In the late 17th century the country was settled by the Dutch and in the following century alternated between Dutch and British rule. By 1815, British rule was firmly established

1831: Three colonies of Berbice, Essequibo, and Demerara are united into the colony of British Guiana

1837: Slaves are emancipated

1928: British Guiana gains limited representative government

1953-57: A new constitution is adopted providing for a bicameral legislature and ministerial responsibility. Elections are held, People's Progressive party (PPP), led by Cheddi Jagan and generally supported by East Indians, captures 18 of the 24 elective seats. Six months after the election, the British suspend the constitution, charging Communist subversion of the British Guiana government; interim regime takes over

1961: Colony is granted full internal self-government, a new constitution is introduced; the PPP wins 20 of the 35 seats in the Legislative Assembly, Jagan is named prime minister

1962-64: Rivalry between PPP and People's National Congress (PNC), supported by the Negroes, leads to violence

1964: Two parties, PNC and the United Force, form a coalition government, with PNC leader Forbes Burnham as prime minister. Communal rioting re-erupts, a state of emergency is declared, and British troops are brought in to restore order

1966: Guyana becomes an independent state within the British Commonwealth and joins the UN

1968: Burnham's PNC wins general election

1970: Guyana is proclaimed a republic

1973: Guyana joins with Barbados, Jamaica, and Trinidad-Tobago to establish the Caribbean Community and Common Market (CARICOM)

1976: People's Progressive party (PPP), led by Dr. Cheddi Jagan, ends its three-year boycott of the National Assembly

1978: More than 900 die in murder-suicide tragedy of the People's Temple cult in Jonestown

1979: Burnham postpones scheduled parliamentary elections for a year

---

HAITI

Area: 10,683 sq. mi. **Population:** 4,919,000 (1979 est.)

Official Name: Republic of Haiti **Capital:** Port-au-Prince **Nationality:** Haitian **Languages:** French is the official language but is spoken by only about 10% of the population; Creole, a mixture of 17th century French, African dialects, and English, Spanish, and Indian words, is spoken by 90% **Religion:** Most of the population professes Roman Catholicism, the state religion; voodoo is widely practiced, especially in the rural areas **Flag:** Black and red vertical halves **Anthem:** Song of Dessalines **Currency:** Gourde (5 per U.S. $1)

Location: West Indies, occupying the western third of the island of Hispaniola in the Caribbean Sea. Haiti's only land border is with the Dominican Republic, on the east **Features:** About two thirds of the country is mountainous terrain unsuitable for cultivation **Chief Rivers:** Artibonite, Guayamouc

Head of State and of Government: President Jean-Claude Duvalier, born 1951; elected president in February 1971, he assumed the title "President for Life" on the death of his father, François Duvalier, in April 1971 **Effective Date of Present Constitution:** June 1964, amended in 1971 **Legislative Body:** Legislative Chamber (unicameral), consisting of 58 deputies, elected for 6 years but with little power **Local Government:** 5 departments, each headed by an appointed prefect

Ethnic Composition: Over 90% of the population is of African descent, nearly 10% is mulatto **Population Distribution:** 23.7% urban **Density:** 460 inhabitants per sq. mi.

Largest Cities: (1977 est.) Port-au-Prince 493,932, (1971 census) Cap-Haïtien 46,217, Pétionville 35,257, Gonaives 29,261

Per Capita Income: $269 (1979) **Gross National Product (GNP):** $1.4 billion (1979) **Economic Statistics:** 44.7% of GNP comes from agriculture (coffee, sugar, sisal, cotton); 37% from services, of which 21.8% is derived from tourism; 14.4% from manufacturing (processing of coffee, sugarcane, sisal, and edible oils; textiles, soap, cement); 3.9% from mining **Minerals and Mining:** Bauxite and copper are mined; deposits of gold, silver, antimony, tin, sulphur, coal, nickel, and gypsum are undeveloped **Labor Force:** 3,004,544 (1975), with 80% self-employed in agriculture **Foreign Trade:** Exports, mainly coffee, sugar, bauxite, essential oils, baseballs and softballs, sisal, shellfish, and fruits, totaled $148 million in 1978. Imports, mainly wheat, fish, fats and oils, paper, cotton fabrics, vehicles, petroleum, machinery, electrical equipment, and raw materials, totaled $209 million **Principal Trade Partners:** United States, EC countries, Japan, Curaçao

Vital Statistics: Birthrate, 35.8 per 1,000 of pop. (1975); death rate, 16.3 **Life Expectancy:** 50 years **Health Statistics:** 1,037 inhabitants per hospital bed (1976); 8,505 per physician (1973) **Infant Mortality:** 200 per 1,000 births **Illiteracy:** 85% **Primary and Secondary School Enrollment:** 566,499 (1976) **Enrollment in Higher Education:** 3,309 **GNP Expended on Education:** 0.9% (1976)

Transportation: Paved roads total 400 mi. **Motor Vehicles:** 21,100 (1976) **Passenger Cars:** 18,700 **Railway Mileage:** 50 **Ports:** Port-au-Prince, Miragoâne, Les Cayes **Major Airlines:** Cohata, the state-owned airline, operates internal services **Communications:** Partly government controlled **Radio Transmitters:** 72 **Receivers:** 95,000 (1976) **Television Transmitters:** 1 **Receivers:** 14,000 (1976) **Telephones:** 18,000 (1976) **Newspapers:** 7 dailies, 20 copies per 1,000 inhabitants (1975)

Weights and Measures: Metric system **Travel Requirements:** Proof of citizenship; tourist card valid for 30 days; no fee

---

Fourteen years of implacable dictatorship, with little economic or social progress for compensation, ended for Haiti in 1971 with the death of Dr. François Duvalier at the age of 64. Under the harsh rule of his police state, the country had become an anachronism in the Western Hemisphere after having been in the vanguard to win freedom from foreign rule.

Haiti's politics and economy are primitive. The country is nominally a republic with a president, but Dr. Duvalier—"Papa Doc"—was all-powerful. For most of Haiti's independent life, the country was dominated by a cultured and literate, generally mulatto, minority.

Illiteracy persists at nearly 85 percent, and most people lead subsistence lives on little plots of land amid luxuriant and colorful vegetation set against stark, eroded mountains. Roman Catholicism is the dominant religion, but it is mixed with voodoo, a religion of fetish and incantation rooted in the Haitians' African past. Manifestations of Duvalier rule include a force called the *Tontons Macoute*, or Bogeymen, a bulwark of the regime feared for its arbitrary dealings with ordinary people.

All in all, Papa Doc left a staggering legacy to his successor as "President for Life," his son Jean-Claude. When "Baby Doc" assumed power in April 1971, at the age of 19, there were few who assumed he could last long. But so far he has been successful in walking a political tightrope between the "old dinosaurs" of his father's era, who seek to hold the status quo, and the younger technocrats and businessmen who, while not desiring a dramatic change in the form of government, do seek a modernization of Haitian life. The young Duvalier has also had to contend with the political power wielded by his mother, Simone Duvalier. Early in 1980 he defied her wishes in several instances of appointments to his cabinet.

He has acted to ease repression somewhat, in an apparent attempt to gain favor with the Carter Administration, which has been critical of Haiti's bleak human rights record. The government said that it released the last political prisoners in 1977, and it invited the Red Cross and the Inter-American Commission on Human Rights to inspect its jails. On the other hand, there are reliable reports that conditions are improved solely for such visits and that inhumane conditions prevail again soon afterward.

The country has few resources with which to solve its staggering economic and social problems and has been characterized as an "environmental disaster." The destruction of the forests for charcoal has triggered massive soil erosion, reducing the amount of arable land. Exports remain largely confined to primary products such as sugar, coffee, essential oils, sisal, and some minerals. Over 150 U.S. companies now have plants in Haiti, and Haitian-controlled companies assemble imported U.S. components. Another major resource is tourism.

HISTORY: Haiti was largely ignored by Spain following the discovery of the island of Hispaniola by Columbus in 1492. While most Spanish colonists settled on the eastern part of the island, Haiti became a base for English and French pirates and was eventually ceded to France in the late 17th century. French colonists began to settle in the area, developing a plantation economy based on sugar and worked by black slaves. Following the outbreak of the French Revolution, the slaves rebelled and murdered most of their former masters

1793: A French army sent to crush the rebellion is defeated by guerrilla bands led by Toussaint L'Ouverture, a former slave

1801-03: Toussaint occupies the entire island of Hispaniola, abolishes slavery, and introduces a constitution: his rule ends when he is captured by a French force sent by Napoleon

1804-11: Jean Jacques Dessalines, another black general, continues the struggle against the French and defeats their army; he assumes title of emperor but is soon assassinated; nation becomes split into a northern kingdom ruled by Henri Christophe, a black, and a southern republic governed by a mulatto, Alexandre Pétion

1820-44: Haiti is reunited by Jean Pierre Boyer, who also brings Santo Domingo, in the eastern part of the island, under Haitian control; Boyer overthrown; nation regains independence

1849-59: Haiti is ruled by a former president and self-declared emperor, Faustin Élie Soulouque, a black; he is dethroned in a revolution led by a mulatto, Nicholas Fabre Geffrard

1905-34: United States takes Haiti's customs into receivership in 1905; in 1915, United States takes full control of country; occupation, which lasts for 19 years, results in many material improvements but arouses hostility throughout Latin America

1957-64: François Duvalier, a black middle-class physician, is elected president; with the help of a secret police force known as *Tontons Macoute*, he establishes dictatorship; in 1964 Duvalier has himself declared president for life

1968: Haitian exiles attempt to invade the country but fail

1969: The Organization of American States charges Duvalier government with terrorism

1970: Haitian Coast Guard vessels shell presidential palace in abortive coup

1971: François Duvalier dies after 14-year rule; his son, Jean-Claude, succeeds him

1977: Severe drought brings hundreds of thousands to brink of starvation and causes major shortages of electricity

1979-80: Thousands of Haitians, fleeing from economic and political conditions in their homeland, reach Florida in small boats to seek asylum. A new law, April 1980, provides for jail terms of up to three years for criticizing Duvalier in the press

---

HONDURAS

Area: 43,277 sq. mi. **Population:** 3,563,000 (1979 est.)

Official Name: Republic of Honduras **Capital:** Tegucigalpa **Nationality:** Honduran **Languages:** Spanish is the official and predominant language; English is spoken along the north coast and on the Bay Islands **Religion:** Overwhelmingly Roman Catholic **Flag:** Two blue horizontal stripes separated by a white stripe bearing a cluster of five blue stars **Anthem:** National Anthem, beginning "Thy flag is a heavenly light" **Currency:** Lempira (2 per U.S. $1)

Location: Central America. Honduras is bordered on the north by the Caribbean Sea; on the southeast by Nicaragua; on the southwest by El Salvador and the Pacific Ocean; and on the west by Guatemala **Features:** Except for the Caribbean and Pacific coastal plains, the country is generally mountainous **Chief Rivers:** Guayape, Patuca, Aguán, Ulúa

Head of State and of Government: President: Gen. Policarpo Paz García, born 1932, reported to have been designated as "provisional president" by the Constitutional Assembly (July 20, 1980) **Effective Date of Present Constitution:** A new constitution is being prepared **Legislative Body:** A 71-member Constitutional Assembly is fashioning a new constitution and election laws **Local Government:** 18 departments, each with a governor appointed by the president

Ethnic Composition: About 90% of the population is mestizo (of mixed European and Indian origin); Indians, Negroes, and Caucasians constitute small minorities **Population Distribution:** 31% urban **Density:** 82 inhabitants per sq. mi.

Largest Cities: (1976 est.) Tegucigalpa 316,500, San Pedro Sula 213,600, Choluteca 51,700, La Ceiba 49,900

Per Capita Income: $596 (1979) **Gross National Product (GNP):** $1.4 billion (1979) **Economic Statistics:** About 35% of GNP comes from agriculture (bananas, coffee, lumber, corn, meat, cotton, forestry and fishing; about 15% from industry (light consumer goods; processing of sugar, fruit juices, vegetable oils; meat packing); and 14% from trade **Minerals and Mining:** Gold, silver, lead, zinc, cadmium, mercury, and lime are extracted; other minerals are antimony, iron, copper, tin, coal, limestone, marble, and pitchblende. Petroleum exploration is under way **Labor Force:** 938,159 (1975), with some 62% in agriculture, 24% in trade and services, 12% in manufacturing and mining **Foreign Trade:** Exports, chiefly bananas, coffee, lumber, silver, meat, shellfish, cotton and tobacco, totaled $616 million in 1978. Imports, mainly transportation equipment, machinery, chemicals, fertilizer, petroleum products, and consumer durables, totaled $704 million **Principal Trade Partners:** United States, West Germany, Japan, Britain, Venezuela, Nicaragua, Guatemala

Vital Statistics: Birthrate, 47 per 1,000 of pop. (1976); death rate, 12 **Life Expectancy:** 56 years **Health Statistics:** 598 inhabitants per hospital bed; 2,992 per physician (1975) **Infant Mortality:** 31 per 1,000 births (1976) **Illiteracy:** 43% **Primary and Secondary School Enrollment:** 546,096 (1976) **Enrollment in Higher Education:** 15,499 **GNP Expended on Education:** 3.2% (1974)

Transportation: Paved roads total 900 mi. **Motor Vehicles:** 50,700 (1976) **Passenger Cars:** 20,500 **Railway Mileage:** 350 **Ports:** Puerto Cortés, Tela, La Ceiba, Amapala, Trujillo **Major Airlines:** SAHSA and TAN operate domestic and international services **Communications:** Partly government controlled **Radio Transmitters:** 151 **Receivers:** 161,000 (1976) **Television Transmitters:** 5 **Receivers:** 48,000 (1976) **Telephones:** 19,000 (1976) **Newspapers:** 8 dailies (1975), 44 copies per 1,000 inhabitants

Weights and Measures: Metric system, but local units are also used **Travel Requirements:** Passport, visa, no fee

---

The weak link in the Central American Common Market, Honduras is the archetype of a Central American banana republic, with a slow economic growth rate and 62 percent of the population involved in agriculture. It is a small country, constantly struggling to keep up with its neighbors and always falling further behind; its politics are frequently subject to military intervention; its economy did bow for many years to the wishes of United Brands and Standard Fruit—the leading businesses—and, of course, the leading export is bananas. However, in 1975 the government canceled the special privileges and concessions of these foreign companies after United Brands was involved in a bribery scandal attempting to bring about a reduction in the banana export tax. By 1980 relations between the government and the big producers seemed to have returned to normal.

Economically, Honduras seems to have little hope of catching up to its neighbors. Its few resources have been squandered by administrative incompetence and inexperience. Hopes for new growth are in part pinned on development of timbering in a 3-million-acre forest in northern Honduras.

In foreign affairs, Honduras' principal problem has been its border dispute with El Salvador. At least 600,000 Salvadoreans have left their crowded country for Honduras' limited opportunities. There were reports in 1980 that Cuba was using Honduras as a staging area for guerrillas to overthrow the government in San Salvador.

In January 1978 President Juan Melgar announced he would convene a Constitutional Assembly to "reform" the constitution. In August he was overthrown by a three-member military junta, headed by Gen. Policarpo Paz García, which promised free elections by 1980. On April 20, 1980, the Liberal party surprisingly defeated the National party, backed by the military, in close elections for the Constitutional Assembly that was to return Honduras to civilian rule.

HISTORY: Honduras was a center of Mayan civilization centuries before the arrival of Columbus in 1502. Following attempts by rival Spanish factions in Central America to gain control of it, Honduras was made part of the captaincy general of Guatemala
1821: Honduras declares independence from Spain and, along with the other Central American countries, is annexed to Mexico
1825: Honduras seceder from Mexico and becomes part of the Central American Federation
1838: Honduras becomes an independent republic in 1838
1933-49: Tiburcio Carias Andino rules as dictator
1957-63: Ramón Villeda Morales is elected first Liberal president in 25 years; he is overthrown by a military coup led by Oswaldo López Arellano, who takes over government
1965: Honduras returns to democratic rule when a constituent assembly elects López president and adopts a new constitution
1969: Honduras invaded by El Salvador. The two nations wage a short war
1970: Honduras and El Salvador agree to set up demilitarized zone along disputed border
1971: Honduras holds first direct election of a president since 1932; National party candidate Ramón Ernesto Cruz wins. U.S. recognizes Honduran sovereignty over long-disputed Swan Islands
1972: Bloodless coup puts Gen. López Arellano back in power
1974: Hurricane Fifi strikes, killing about 9,000
1975: Pres. López Arellano overthrown in bloodless coup after reports that he accepted $1.25 million bribe from United Brands. Juan Alberto Melgar Castro, Commander in Chief of armed forces, becomes president
1978: Melgar overthrown by three-member military junta
1980: Liberal party gains majority in Constitutional Assembly to write new constitution and set time for presidential election. Assembly designates junta head, Gen. Paz García, as provisional president

HUNGARY

Area: 35,919 sq. mi. **Population:** 10,710,000 (1979 est.)
Official Name: Hungarian People's Republic **Capital:** Budapest **Nationality:** Hungarian **Languages:** Hungarian (Magyar) is the official and universal language **Religion:** 68% Roman Catholic, 20% Calvinist, 5% Lutheran, 7% other (Unitarian, Jewish, etc.) **Flag:** Red, white, and green horizontal stripes **Anthem:** God bless the Hungarians **Currency:** Forint (20.3 per U.S. $1)

Location: East-central Europe. Landlocked Hungary is bordered on the north by Czechoslovakia, on the northeast by the USSR, on the east by Romania, on the south by Yugoslavia, and on the west by Austria **Features:** Most of the country is a flat plain, with the exception of low mountain ranges in the north-central and northeastern portions and to the north and south of Lake Balaton in the west **Chief Rivers:** Danube, Tisza, Drava, Rába

Political Leader: First Secretary of the Hungarian Socialist Workers' (Communist) party: János Kádár, born 1912, reappointed 1970 **Head of State:** The Presidential Council is collectively the head of state, usually represented by its president, Pál Losonczi, born 1919, reappointed 1975 **Head of Government:** Premier György Lázár, appointed 1975 **Effective Date of Present Constitution:** 1949, amended 1972 **Legislative Body:** National Assembly (unicameral) consisting of 352 members elected for 5 years **Local Government:** 19 counties (each divided into districts with locally elected councils); 4 autonomous cities and the capital, all with county status

Ethnic Composition: Hungarians (Magyars) make up 97% of the population; minority groups include Germans, Slovaks, Gypsies, Serbs, Croats, and Romanians **Population Distribution:** 50.6% urban **Density:** 298 inhabitants per sq. mi.

Largest Cities: (1976 est.) Budapest 2,076,331, Miskolc 201,647, Debrecen 189,511, Szeged 171,851, Pécs 164,213, Gyor 120,394

Per Capita Income: $3,336 (1979) **Gross National Product (GNP):** $36 billion (1979) **Economic Statistics:** About 38.5% of GNP is derived from industry (mining, chemical refining, metallurgy, food processing); 18.6% from agriculture (corn, wheat, sugar beets, vegetables, wine grapes); 12% from trade; 11% from services **Minerals and Mining:** Coal, bauxite, iron ore, and lignite are mined **Labor Force:** 5,230,000 (1977), of which 34% is employed in industry and construction, and 20% in agriculture **Foreign Trade:** Exports, chiefly transport equipment, medicine, machinery and shoes, totaled $8.8 billion in 1978. Imports, mainly crude oil, raw cotton, passenger cars, trucks, and rolled steel, totaled $10 billion **Principal Trade Partners:** USSR, E. Germany, Czechoslovakia, Poland, Italy, W. Germany, Austria

Vital Statistics: Birthrate, 16.7 per 1,000 of pop. (1977); death rate, 12.4 **Life Expectancy:** 70 years **Health Statistics:** 114 inhabitants per hospital bed; 439 per physician (1976) **Infant Mortality:** 26.2 per 1,000 births **Illiteracy:** 2% **Primary and Secondary School Enrollment:** 1,438,785 (1976) **Enrollment in Higher Education:** 107,555 (1975) **GNP Expended on Education:** 4.6% (1976)

Transportation: Surfaced roads total 21,561 mi. **Motor Vehicles:** 973,600 (1977) **Passenger Cars:** 744,700 **Railway Mileage:** 5,293 **Ports:** None **Major Airlines:** Malev, the state-owned airline, operates domestic and international services **Communications:** Government owned **Radio Transmitters:** 37 **Licenses:** 2,538,000 (1975) **Television Transmitters:** 22 **Licenses:** 2,495,000 (1976) **Telephones:** 1,076,000 (1976) **Newspapers:** 27 dailies, 233 copies per 1,000 inhabitants (1975)

Weights and Measures: Metric system **Travel Requirements:** Passport, visa valid for 30 days, fee $6, 2 photos

---

"Socialism with gaiety" is the way a top Hungarian has described his country's political formula to an American audience. The slogan is not far from the Czechoslovakian idea of "Socialism with a human face"—a concept that brought the violent downfall of Alexander Dubcek and his reformist government in 1968. However, the implementation of the formula in Hungary is so cautious, moderate, and delicate that no analogy with Czechoslovakia is appropriate.

In the midst of ideological regimentation, the breakdown of which brought Warsaw Pact troops into Prague, there is gaiety in Hungary. Political cabarets in Budapest pull few punches in criticizing bureaucratic ineptness and stuffiness. A television forum in which listeners quiz political leaders on their performance and promises brings sharp questions out into public discussion. Music, dancing, and plentiful good food add esthetic grace notes to the sense of gradual political progress.

The country is no longer traumatized by the uprising that Russian tanks crushed in 1956 and that caused some 200,000 Hungarians to flee to the West. The regime of János Kádár, imposed to fight the liberal ideas of the 1956 revolt, has proved far more progressive than was first thought possible. A surprising degree of dissent is allowed, though there are definite if generally unexpressed limits. Hungary remains, after all, a Communist state, basically faithful to the party line.

Thus, when it was necessary for someone to attack Romania for flirting with Communist China, a Hungarian editor was detailed to fire the first critical salvo. Similarly, the economic liberalization has been only partially mirrored in an effort to develop local political autonomy in small towns and not reflected at all in the repressive policies toward the Catholic Church.

What has emerged in Hungary, however, is a consumer-oriented economy that is the envy of all its neighbors. Hungarians have refined their New Economic Model since its introduction in 1968 to boost exports and imports.

The economy, however, is not without its problems. The high degree of centralization in Budapest sometimes results in mismanagement and inefficiencies, and in return for supplying oil needs in excess of rigid, outdated quotas, the Soviet Union requires agricultural surpluses that might otherwise earn valuable hard currency in the West. In April 1978, the regime adopted a two-year program of phasing out most price controls, subsidies for consumer goods, and heavy producer taxes. At the 12th Communist Party Congress in March 1979, Kádár called for greater productivity to increase workers' incomes (which had risen only 9 percent since 1975) and to combat the high inflation rate of more than 15 percent in 1979.

HISTORY: The Magyars migrated from beyond the Urals about the end of the 9th century A.D., conquered most of present-day Hungary, and established a dynasty that lasted more than four centuries. Pre-Magyar inhabitants had included Celts, Germans, Huns, Slavs, and Avars. In the last years of the 10th century, the Magyars embraced Christianity and made alliances with the Holy Roman Empire. Following a disastrous defeat by the Turks in 1526, a faction of Hungarian nobles elected Ferdinand I of Austria as king of Hungary, laying the foundations of Hapsburg rule

1686: Budapest is liberated from the Turks, who cede most of Hungary proper and Transylvania to Austria

1713: Hungarian Diet accepts Pragmatic Sanction aimed at guaranteeing the integrity of the Hapsburg possessions, thereby binding Hungary to Austria

1848-49: Hungarian revolt against Austrian rule is suppressed by Austrian and Russian armies

1867: Austro-Hungarian monarchy is established, giving Hungary nearly equal status with Austria

1918-19: Monarchy collapses in the aftermath of World War I defeat. A Hungarian republic is proclaimed but is soon supplanted by a Communist regime headed by Bela Kun; Romanian troops invade Hungary and help to suppress leftist government

1920: Under Treaty of Trianon, Hungary is deprived of three-fourths of its territory and over one-third of its population; country becomes a kingdom without a king, under the regency of Admiral Nicholas Horthy

1938-40: Aided by Italy and Germany, Hungary recovers lands lost to Czechoslovakia and Romania. In 1940 Hungary joins Axis powers and enters World War II

1944: Soviet troops occupy Hungary; a provisional government is set up and declares war against Germany

1947: Communists win 22 percent of vote in general elections

1948-49: Hungarian Communists seize power with Soviet support; in 1949 Hungary is proclaimed a People's Republic

1955: Hungary joins the UN

1956: Popular anti-Communist uprising breaks out in Budapest and spreads to rest of the country; a new coalition government under Imre Nagy declares Hungary neutral and withdraws country from Warsaw Pact; János Kádár sets up counter-government and calls for Soviet support; Soviet troops and tanks suppress revolution, causing nearly 200,000 Hungarians to flee the country

1958: Imre Nagy and some of his ministers are executed. János Kádár resigns as premier and is succeeded by Ferenc Münnich

1961: Kádár resumes premiership

1965: Gyula Kallai becomes premier; Kádár remains First Secretary of ruling Hungarian Socialist Workers' party

1967: Hungary signs a new 20-year friendship and mutual assistance pact with Soviet Union, replacing one signed in 1948. Jeno Fock succeeds Gyula Kallai as premier

1968: Hungarian troops march with Soviet troops when Soviets invade Czechoslovakia

1971: Government holds first general elections in which voters could choose between nonofficial and official candidates. Newcomers unseat eight incumbents in parliament

1975: György Lázár becomes premier

1978: Crown of St. Stephen, 1,000-year-old traditional symbol of Hungary's nationhood, is returned by U.S. after having been held in protective custody since the end of World War II. Government announces measures to phase out most subsidies for consumer goods and end heavy producer taxes

1979: 12 Communist Party Congress reduces Politburo to 13 members, including young associates of Kádár

---

ICELAND

Area: 39,768 sq. mi. **Population:** 224,000 (1978 est.)

Official Name: Republic of Iceland **Capital:** Reykjavík **Nationality:** Icelandic **Languages:** Icelandic is the official and universal language **Religion:** 95% of the population belongs to the state church, the Evangelical Lutheran Church **Flag:** A red cross edged in white on a field of blue **Anthem:** Our Country's God **Currency:** Króna (452 per U.S. $1)

Location: North Atlantic. A large island extending about 300 miles from east to west and about 190 miles from north to south, Iceland is the westernmost state of Europe, lying 600 miles west of Norway. The Arctic Circle runs through the small island of Grímsey off Iceland's northern coast **Features:** Almost three fourths of the country's land area, which is of recent volcanic origin, consists of glaciers, lakes, a mountainous lava desert, and other wasteland, with the remainder used for cultivation or grazing. Most of the inhabited areas are on the coast, particularly, in the southwest **Chief Rivers:** Thjórsá, Jökulsa, Ölfusá-Hvítá, Skjálfandafljót

Head of State: President: Mrs. Vigdís Finnbogadóttir, born 1930,

elected June 1980 **Head of Government:** Premier Gunnar Thoroddsen, born 1910, appointed February 1980 **Effective Date of Present Constitution:** 1874, amended 1903 and 1944 **Legislative Body:** Parliament *(Althing)*, composed of 60 members elected for 4 years. After elections it becomes bicameral, dividing itself into 2 chambers with equal powers, one of 20 members and the other of 40 members. The 2 houses often meet together **Local Government:** 16 counties, each with a council, and 14 urban municipalities

Ethnic Composition: The population is homogeneous **Population Distribution:** 87.1% urban **Density:** 5.6 inhabitants per sq. mi.

Largest Cities: (1976 est.) Reykjavík 84,493; (1973 est.) Kópavogur 11,639, Akureyri 11,484, Hafnarfjördhur 10,926

Per Capita Income: $6,400 (1979) **Gross National Product (GNP):** $1.5 billion (1979) **Economic Statistics:** About 14% of GNP comes from fishing and fish processing; 18% from industry other than fish processing (manufacture of electric motors, fertilizer, chemicals, cement, clothing, furniture, books); 7% from agriculture (sheep raising, dairy products, hay, potatoes); 32% from services; 15% from construction **Minerals and Mining:** Diatomite, peat, lignite, perlite; hydroelectric power **Labor Force:** 100,000 (1977), of which 42% is employed in fishing, fish processing, and other industries; 11% in agriculture; 46% in trade and services **Foreign Trade:** Exports, chiefly fish and fish products (about 75% of the total), aluminum ingots, and agricultural products, totaled $649 million in 1978. Imports, mainly machinery, textiles, petroleum products, metals and metal products, ships, and food grains, totaled $680 million **Principal Trade Partners:** United States, West Germany, Britain, USSR, Norway, Denmark, Portugal, Sweden

Vital Statistics: Birthrate, 18 per 1,000 of pop. (1977); death rate, 6.5 **Life Expectancy:** 75 years **Health Statistics:** 64 inhabitants per hospital bed; 550 per physician (1974) **Infant Mortality:** 9.5 per 1,000 births **Illiteracy:** Negligible **Primary and Secondary School Enrollment:** 52,271 (1975) **Enrollment in Higher Education:** 2,970 (1975) **GNP Expended on Education:** 4.2% (1975)

Transportation: Paved roads total 120 miles; there are over 6,000 miles of gravel road **Motor Vehicles:** 78,000 (1977) **Passenger Cars:** 70,100 **Railway Mileage:** None **Ports:** Reykjavík, Akureyri **Major Airlines:** Icelandair operates domestic and international services **Communications:** Government owned **Radio Transmitters:** 29 **Licenses:** 64,000 (1976) **Television Transmitters:** 80 **Licenses:** 53,000 (1976) **Telephones:** 91,000 (1976) **Newspapers:** 5 dailies, 431 copies per 1,000 inhabitants (1975)

Weights and Measures: Metric system **Travel Requirements:** Passport, no visa for 3 months

---

Out in the North Atlantic, closer to Greenland than to Western Europe, lies the rugged, largely desolate island of volcanic origin called Iceland, with 222,000-plus fiercely individualistic inhabitants who have a tradition of preserving their heritage. Their language, for example, has remained virtually unchanged since the 12th century.

Although Iceland has no armed forces, it joined in the cold-war days of 1949 in forming the North Atlantic Treaty Organization. As its contribution, it granted NATO the right to maintain a base, manned by Americans, at Keflavík, 30 miles outside of Reykjavík, the capital. A leftist coalition formed in 1971 announced plans to phase out the installation, but in 1974 a coalition of the former governing and opposition parties agreed to allow the base to remain.

The government extended the fishing limits in 1972 from 12 miles offshore to 50, and in 1975 from 50 to 200 miles. With fish and fish products accounting for 14 percent of the country's gross national product and 75 percent of its total exports, the moves were a logical progression of a conservation drive begun in 1958 when Iceland extended its fishing limits from four miles to 12.

Foreign reaction to these extensions has been far more serious than in 1958. In 1973 and 1975-76, Britain, which gets 45 percent of its fish from the waters off Iceland, sent heavily armed frigates into the disputed waters, touching off a "cod war" between the two countries, with shots being fired, boats rammed and nets cut.

In 1976 the two countries reached a diplomatic settlement and British ships were removed. In conjunction with this agreement, important tariff concessions by the European Community (EC) for fish products became effective for Iceland. The EC's adoption of a common 200-mile fishing limit imposed new problems, as it excludes Icelandic vessels from rich waters to which they had previously had access.

Parliamentary elections were called December 1979 after the Social Democrats withdrew from the coalition government. A political crisis ensued when no party won a sizable plurality in the new parliament. After the major parties failed to form a new government, Gunnar Thoroddsen deserted his own conservative Independence party and formed a new coalition government with the People's Alliance and Progressive party in February 1980.

Vigdís Finnbogadóttir, manager of the Reykjavík Theater Company, became the world's first popularly elected female head of state by winning the June 1980 presidential election.

HISTORY: The first permanent settler of Iceland was Ingolfur Arnason of Norway, who arrived with his family around 870. Others of Norwegian origin followed, some bringing with them Irish and Scottish wives and slaves. In 930 a commonwealth was established and a general assembly, the *Althing*, instituted. Christianity was introduced in the year 1000. Iceland came under the Norwegian crown in the 13th century, but in 1380 both Iceland and Norway passed under the Danish crown. The former was destined to remain linked to Denmark until the 20th century

1918: Iceland is declared a sovereign state in union with Denmark
1940-41: British troops occupy Iceland following Germany's World War II occupation of Denmark; U.S. forces take over Iceland's defense in 1941
1944: Icelanders vote to terminate union with Denmark; Iceland is proclaimed a republic
1949: Iceland joins in forming NATO
1958-61: Fishing limits are extended from four miles to 12; so-called "cod war" begins, with Britain challenging the Icelandic pronouncement by sending in trawlers backed by warships; in 1961 Britain finally agrees to the 12-mile limit
1970: Iceland becomes member of European Free Trade Association. Premier Bjarni Benediktsson perishes in fire; Justice Minister Johann Hafstein is designated his successor
1971: Government defeated in elections. Hafstein resigns. New left-wing coalition government announces it will close the American-manned NATO base at Keflavík
1972-73: Fishing limits are extended from 12 miles to 50, touching off new "cod war" with Britain; West Germany joins Britain in protesting extension
1973: Iceland signs agreement with Britain giving limited fishing rights within the new zone
1974: Iceland signs agreement with U.S. allowing U.S. to maintain NATO base at Keflavík
1975: Fishing limits extended from 50 to 200 miles
1976: British and Icelandic foreign ministers sign an interim pact to end the "cod war" between the two countries and restore diplomatic relations which had been severed. British frigates, sent into fishing zone in November '75 to protect British trawlers from harassment by Icelandic patrol boats, withdraw. Dr. Kristján Eldjárn is unopposed for third four-year term as president
1978: Strike by government workers temporarily isolates nation by cutting international flights, mail and telephone links
1980: New center-left coalition govenment is formed under Premier Gunnar Thoroddsen. Vigdís Finnbogadótir is elected president

---

INDIA

Area: 1,269,339 sq. mi. **Population:** 650,982,000 (1979 est.)

Official Name: Republic of India **Capital:** New Delhi **Nationality:** Indian **Languages:** Hindi is the official language; English is an associate language. In addition to Hindi; the constitution recognizes 14 national languages, although as many as 1,652 languages and dialects are spoken in the country. Hindi, however, is spoken by 38% of the population. Telugu 9%, Bengali 8%, Marathi 8%, Tamil 7%, Urdu 6%, Gujarati 5%, Kanarese 4%, Punjabi 3%, Oriya 3%, Malayalam 3% **Religion:** 84% Hindu, 10% Moslem, 3% Christian, 2% Sikh, 1% Buddhist, Jain and others **Flag:** Saffron, white, and green horizontal stripes, with the 24-spoke Wheel of Asoka (chakra) in blue on the white stripe **Anthem:** Morning Song of India **Currency:** Rupee (8 per U.S. $1)

Location: Southern Asia, occupying most of the Indian sub-continent. India is bordered on the north by Afghanistan, China, Nepal, and Bhutan; on the east by Bangladesh, Burma, and the Bay of Bengal; on the south by the Indian Ocean's Gulf of Mannar and Palk Strait, which separate India from Sri Lanka; on the west by the Arabian Sea; and on the northwest by Pakistan **Features:** The country consists of three major topographical areas: the Himalaya mountains extending along the whole of the northern border; the Indo-Gangetic Plain, a fertile and heavily populated region; and the southern peninsula, including the Deccan Plateau, which is of moderate elevation and less densely populated **Chief Rivers:** Ganges, Brahmaputra, Godavari, Kistna (Krishna), Narbada, Mahanadi

Head of State: President Neelam Sanjiva Reddy, born 1913, elected July 1977 **Head of Government:** Prime Minister: Mrs. Indira Gandhi, born 1917, appointed Jan. 1980. She held the same office from 1966 to 1977 **Effective Date of Present Constitution:** 1950 **Legislative Body:** Parliament (bicameral), consisting of the *Lok Sabha* (House of the People) and the *Rajya Sabha* (Council of States). The *Lok Sabha* has 542 members, elected by universal suffrage for 6 years. The *Rajya Sabha* has 244 members, 13 of whom are appointed by the president and the rest elected for 6 year terms by the state and territorial legislatures **Local Government:** 22 states and 9 union territories, each with an appointed governor and with its own elected legislature

Ethnic Composition: Two major strains predominate: the Indo-Aryan (72%) in the north and the Dravidian (25%) in the south. There is also an aboriginal population in the central part, and some Mongoloid peoples in the north **Population Distribution:** 21% urban **Density:** 513 inhabitants per sq. mi.

Largest Cities: (1971 census) Bombay 5,970,575, Delhi 3,287,883, Calcutta 3,148,746 (with suburbs 7,031,382), Madras 2,469,449, Hyderabad 1,607,396, Ahmadabad 1,585,544, Bangalore 1,540,741, Kanpur 1,154,388

Per Capita Income: $154 (1979) **Gross National Product (GNP):** $121 billion (1979) **Economic Statistics:** About 43% of GNP comes from agriculture (rice, wheat, tea, jute, pulses, cotton, sugar, peanuts); 23% from mining and manufacturing (iron and steel, textiles, chemicals, cement, industrial machinery and equipment); 16% from commerce, transportation, and communications **Minerals and Mining:** Coal and iron are the country's main mineral assets; mica, manganese, and bauxite are also abundant. Iron ore reserves are estimated at about one fourth of the world's total; oil supplies less than half of the nation's refinery requirements **Labor Force:** 240 million (1976), of which 72% is engaged in agriculture, 11% in industry, and 17% in trade and services **Foreign Trade:** Exports, chiefly cotton and jute textiles, tea, sugar, coffee, metallic ores, and iron and steel manufactures, totaled $6.4 billion in 1977. Imports, mainly petroleum, food grains, nonelectrical machinery and fertilizer, totaled $6.5 billion **Principal Trade Partners:** United States, Japan, Britain, USSR, Iran, West Germany

Vital Statistics: Birthrate, 35.2 per 1,000 of pop. (1975); death rate, 15.9 **Life Expectancy:** 51 years **Health Statistics:** 1,465 inhabitants per hospital bed; 3,961 per physician (1973) **Infant Mortality:** 130 per 1,000 births (1974) **Illiteracy:** 66% **Primary and Secondary School Enrollment:** 93,310,864 (1976) **Enrollment in Higher Education:** 3,198,550 **GNP Expended on Education:** 2.7% (1975)

Transportation: Surfaced roads totaled about 370,000 mi. **Motor Vehicles:** 1,495,800 (1977) **Passenger Cars:** 805,400 **Railway Mileage:** 38,614 **Ports:** Calcutta, Bombay, Madras, Mormugao, Cochin, Kandla, Visakhapatnam, Paradeep, Mangalore, Tuticorin **Major Airlines:** Indian Airlines Corporation is the domestic carrier and Air India the international line **Communications:** Government controlled **Radio Transmitters:** 153 **Licenses:** 14,848,000 (1976) **Television Transmitters:** 18 **Licenses:** 280,000 (1976) **Telephones:** 2,096,000 (1976) **Newspapers:** 835 dailies, 16 copies per 1,000 inhabitants (1975)

Weights and Measures: Metric system and local units are used **Travel Requirements:** Passport, no visa required for stay up to 30 days

---

Successive invasions and a long period of subjugation under alien rule have made India what it is today—a land of diverse, often conflicting cultures, religions, and people that is held in unity by a complicated yet resilient political system. The British, who were the masters of the subcontinent for a century and a half, brought its disparate regions under one administration. To overcome the myriad languages and dialects, they made English the communication medium of the elite, the tiny minority that still dominates the government, industry, education, and art.

Indian leaders, as fruit of their long fight for freedom, inherited a truncated land after the carving out of Pakistan as a homeland for Moslems; they have been struggling with the overwhelming problems of the subcontinent ever since.

The country's successive five-year plans, while laying the foundation for a prosperous industrial nation at some future date, have not so far produced any substantial improvement in the average Indian's quality of life. All the benefits of the large development expenses over the last 25 years have been neutralized by a runaway population increase—now almost two percent a year—that has pushed more and more people below the poverty line. Unemployment has risen sharply. Pressure is increasing on living space, schools, and hospitals. Despite recent record food crops and a rise in industrial output, the population increase, on which only a marginal dent has been made by a costly birth-control program, has resulted in deteriorating living conditions for most Indians.

The social structure, ever in conflict, throws up many obstacles to progress. The Hindus, who make up 84 percent of the population, are divided into countless subcastes. The downtrodden untouchables, who constitute one seventh of the population, have begun asserting their rights. Clashes with upper-caste Hindus have become frequent and often violent.

The Moslem minority, 10 percent of the population, has remained suspect in the eyes of the majority ever since the creation of Pakistan. They live in constant insecurity and threat from militant Hindus. Bloody riots between Hindus and Moslems erupt periodically. The smaller minorities, the Sikhs, Buddhists, Jains, Parsis, and Christians, live in relative security, but the chances of their assimilation into the Hindu-dominated national life are remote.

In 1975 India went through the most important political crisis in its years as a republic when in April the government declared a state of emergency, arrested political leaders opposed to Prime Minister Indira Gandhi, began press censorship and suspended protection of fundamental rights. This repressive action was precipitated by Gandhi's conviction on charges of corrupt practices in the 1971 general election.

In July 1975 Mrs. Gandhi's power was restored when new laws approved by parliament permitted her to rule by proclamation, barred the courts from reviewing her actions and changed the election law retroactively to remove any criminal offenses. In December Gandhi's Congress party delayed general elections, due in March 1976, for at least a year and extended the state of emergency for six months.

In January 1977 Mrs. Gandhi announced the elections that had been postponed would be held in March; press censorship was subsequently lifted. In what was hailed as a victory for Indian democracy, Morarji R. Desai, 81, and his Janata party defeated Mrs. Gandhi and her 30-year-old son, Sanjay, in the election. It was the first defeat suffered by the ruling Congress party in the 30 years of India's independence. The new government immediately revoked the emergency rule legislation and released the political prisoners who had been jailed without charges. And since Desai himself was one of the thousands of political prisoners detained during Mrs. Gandhi's 19-month "emergency rule" period, it came as no surprise when the new government launched a series of civil and criminal investigations into her alleged abuses of power.

What was surprising, though, was a swift—even though relatively short-lived—upturn in Mrs. Gandhi's fortunes. In February 1978, a month after leaving the Congress party to form a splinter group, she reemerged as a major force in Indian politics when her Congress-I (for Indira) party entered a series of state elections and won decisively in two important states and did better than expected in a third. Her comeback surge possibly contributed to the split, two months later, in the ruling Janata party, resulting in the creation of a separate West Bengal Janata party. Moreover, Mrs. Gandhi was elected to parliament in November 1978, defeating 27 candidates in a by-election in Chickmagalur in the state of Karnataka.

However, Mrs. Gandhi found herself fighting for political survival a month later when the *Lok Sabha*, the lower house of parliament, expelled her on charges of contempt of the house and breach of privilege for her actions while as prime minister. In addition, the government set up special courts that would keep her tied up in litigation. In February 1979 her son, Sanjay, was convicted of the theft and burning of a film (during the "emergency rule" period) that ridiculed his mother's conduct in office. Sentenced to prison, he was freed on bail pending appeal.

Desai meanwhile grappled with an increase in crime, caste violence, chronic power shortages, labor unrest, and soaring inflation. Food grain production was a bright spot, rising almost high enough to meet all of the country's needs. In March 1979, Desai and Soviet Premier Kosygin, meeting in New Delhi, signed trade and scientific and technological agreements. India will exchange rice for Soviet oil of equal value, and the Soviet Union will join in oil exploration in India. The Soviets will build one new steel mill in India and expand two others. In general, however, Desai's government turned India away from large-scale industrialism and toward a "cottage industry" system.

On July 15, 1979, Prime Minister Desai resigned following growing defections from and splits within his Janata party. President Reddy appointed Chaudhury Charan Singh to serve as prime minister on July 28, but Singh resigned on August 20 when Mrs. Gandhi withdrew support from the Singh coalition. Singh did, however, lead a caretaker government until elections in January 1980.

Campaigning on the slogans "Law and Order" and "Banish Poverty," Mrs. Gandhi upset predictions and won office by an overwhelming majority—351 seats out of 542 in the lower house. No other party even got the required number of seats (54) to win recognition as the official opposition. Her son Sanjay also won a parliamentary seat; subsequently, the Supreme Court acquitted him in the film case. That had been the only conviction resulting from the old charges against mother and son. Sanjay was killed in an airplane crash in June.

HISTORY: The Indus Valley was the site of a flourishing civilization from the 3rd millennium to about 1500 B.C., when the region was conquered by the Aryans who, over the next 2,000 years, developed a Brahmanic civilization and introduced a caste system. In 327-325 B.C., Alexander the Great invaded northwest India, only to be driven out, and in the following century most of the subcontinent was united under Asoka the Great, who established Buddhism as the state religion. After his death, however, Buddhism declined in India as Hinduism experienced a resurgence

4th cent.: Hindu kingdoms are established

8th cent.: Islam is introduced into Sind by Arab invaders

1498-1510: European contact with India, begun with the arrival of Portuguese explorer Vasco da Gama, is followed by Portuguese conquest of Goa and spurs rivalry among European powers for trade with subcontinent

1526-1707: India is ruled by Mogul dynasty; a large Moslem population grows up and a new culture evolves, developing a characteristic Indo-Islamic style in art and architecture, as evidenced by the Taj Mahal

1746-63: India is turned into a battleground for the forces of France and Britain as each tries to carve out colonial domains; with the 1763 Treaty of Paris, British supremacy is assured

1857-58: Sepoy Rebellion by native soldiers in the employ of British East India Company is brutally suppressed; company is dissolved and India is placed under the direct rule of the British Crown

1919: Mohandas K. Gandhi, later known as the Mahatma or "great-souled," organizes the first of many passive resistance campaigns against British rule; he is imprisoned

1942-45: Indian National Congress, largely Hindu-supported, splits with Moslem League, which favors creation of Pakistan as a separate Moslem state, over support for Britain during World War II; Congress is outlawed, while League, which supports Britain, gains strength

1947: Subcontinent is partitioned into the independent nations of India and Pakistan; Jawaharlal Nehru becomes India's first prime minister; bloody riots break out between Hindus and Moslems and millions flee in crisscross migration to new states; India and Pakistan fight over Kashmir

1948: Gandhi is assassinated by Hindu fanatic who blames him for partition; Kashmir fighting ends with UN cease-fire

1950: India becomes republic within Commonwealth of Nations

1954: India signs nonaggression pact with Communist China

1956: Constitutional amendment redrawing state boundaries along linguistic lines put into effect

1962: Chinese Communist troops occupy Ladakh region of Kashmir

1964: Nehru dies and is succeeded by Lal Bahadur Shastri

1965-66: India and Pakistan fight three-week war in 1965 over Kashmir; hostilities end in a truce, followed by accord signed in 1966 at Tashkent, in the Soviet Union. Indian Prime Minister Lal Bahadur Shastri dies at Tashkent and is succeeded by Mrs. Indira Gandhi, daughter of the former prime minister, Jawaharlal Nehru

1969: Death of President Zakir Husain touches off power struggle in governing Congress party as Mrs. Gandhi and old guard party bosses clash over choice of successor; party splits following election of V.V. Giri, the candidate backed by Mrs. Gandhi, as president; bulk of party members remain with her New Congress party but she loses majority strength in parliament, forcing her to rely on Communists and independents for crucial votes

1970: Supreme Court rules bank nationalization law unconstitutional; prime minister counters court's action by issuing new ordinance nationalizing the banks. Mrs. Gandhi dissolves lower house of parliament and orders new elections

1971: Mrs. Gandhi's party is landslide victor in the elections held in March, winning two-thirds of the parliamentary seats. Civil war breaks out in Pakistan. Millions of East Pakistani refugees flee to India. India supports East Pakistan in fight against West Pakistan, and latter is soon defeated. East Pakistan becomes Bangladesh

1972: At Simla Conference India and Pakistan agree to observe "lines of control" in Kashmir

1973: At Delhi Conference India and Pakistan agree to repatriation of 93,000 Pakistani POWs held since their 1971 war. Soviet Union lends India two million tons of wheat and rice

1974: World Health Organization estimates 30,000 have died in northern India in worst smallpox epidemic of the century. Sikkim becomes an associated state of India. Worst famine since 1943 in West Bengal, Assam, and Bihar

1975: India is first non-Arab country to give full diplomatic status to Palestine Liberation Organization. Prime Minister Gandhi is convicted on charges of illegal activities in connection with her election. Gandhi suspends civil liberties and orders arrest of hundreds of political opponents. Gandhi's powers are restored by parliament and the Supreme Court

1976: Suspension of civil liberties continues throughout the year. India and Pakistan formally establish diplomatic ties

1977: Morarji R. Desai elected prime minister. President Fakhruddin Ali Ahmed dies; he is succeeded by Neelam Sanjiva Reddy. Government launches probes into alleged abuses of power by Mrs. Gandhi during her "emergency rule" period. India acts to improve relations with neighbors and U.S. while stressing friendship with Soviet Union, along with policy of "genuine nonalignment" less subject to Soviet influence than was the case in Mrs. Gandhi's administration

1978: High-level talks between India and Pakistan begin; disputed state of Kashmir tops agenda. Mrs. Gandhi's newly formed Congress-I party wins two important state elections and does better than expected in a third. Elected to parliament, she is expelled; special courts are set up to try her for actions taken when prime minister

1979: The Soviet Union and India sign agreements covering trade and technological and scientific cooperation for 10 to 15 years. Indian rice will be traded for Soviet oil. Simultaneously, the government curtails some large-scale industry and encourages "cottage industry" such as production of matches, candy, and cookies. Desai resigns and is succeeded by Chaudhury Charan Singh on July 28. Singh resigns on Aug. 20

1980: Indira Gandhi's Congress-I party wins by a landslide—351 out of 542 seats—in the *Lok Sabha* in January, and she is swept back into power as prime minister for a second time. In the state of Assam, students lead a move to expel illegal immigrants (Bangladeshis). The campaign, extended through northeast In-

dia and directed against "outsiders" (Bengalis), shuts colleges and reduces oil production. In May, the Congress-I party wins easily in eight out of nine states holding elections

INDONESIA

Area: 788,430 sq. mi. **Population:** 145,100,000 (1978 est.)

Official Name: Republic of Indonesia **Capital:** Jakarta **Nationality:** Indonesian **Languages:** Bahasa Indonesia, a form of Malay developed as a product of Indonesia's nationalist movement, is the official language; English is the second language and is compulsory in secondary schools **Religion:** 90% Moslem, 5% Christian, 3% Hindu (Bali has retained its Buddhist/Hindu heritage) **Flag:** A red horizontal stripe above a white stripe **Anthem:** Great Indonesia **Currency:** Rupiah (628 per U.S. $1)

Location: Southeast Asia, in the Malay archipelago. Indonesia consists of six large and 13,662 lesser islands, which form an arc between Asia and Australia. The principal group of islands is the Greater Sunda Islands, which include Java, Bali, Sumatra, Borneo (Kalimantan), and Celebes (Sulawesi). The country shares land borders with Malaysia, Brunei, and Papua New Guinea **Features:** The large islands have a central mountain range rising from fairly extensive lowlands and coastal plains. Many islands throughout the archipelago are dotted with volcanoes, both active and dormant **Chief Rivers:** Kapuas, Digul, Barito, Mahakam, Kajan, Hari, Mamberamo, Idenburg

Head of State and of Government: President: Gen. Suharto (Soeharto), born 1921, reelected 1978 **Effective Date of Present Constitution:** 1945 **Legislative Body:** Peoples' Consultative Assembly, consisting of 920 members, within it a 460-member (360 elected and 100 nominated by the president) House of Representatives (Parliament) **Local Government:** 23 provinces, each with an appointed governor and an elected legislature, 2 autonomous regions, 1 capital region, and the special territory of East Timor

Ethnic Composition: Malayans and Papuans constitute the main ethnic groups, each with numerous subdivisions. Chinese make up the largest nonindigenous group **Population Distribution:** 18.2% urban **Density:** 184 inhabitants per sq. mi.

Largest Cities: (1973 est.) Jakarta 5,000,000, Surabaya 2,000,000, Bandung 2,000,000, Medan 1,000,000, Yogyakarta 500,000; (1971 census) Semarang 646,590, Palembang 582,961

Per Capita Income: $344 (1979) **Gross National Product (GNP):** $56.6 billion (1979) **Economic Statistics:** About 36% of GNP comes from agriculture (rubber, copra, tea, coffee, tobacco, sugar, palm oil, rice), 16% from manufacturing (chiefly processing of agricultural and mineral products and light manufactures), 12% from mining **Minerals and Mining:** The country is one of the world's leading producers of tin and rubber and is the leading oil producer in the Far East. Other minerals are bauxite, nickel, copper, natural gas, and coal **Labor Force:** 55,000,000, of which some 64% is in agriculture and 7% in industry **Foreign Trade:** Exports, chiefly petroleum and petroleum products (60%), tin ore, copper, nickel, copra, coffee, and tobacco, totaled $11.6 billion in 1977. Imports, mainly textiles, machinery, transportation equipment, rice, fertilizer, and chemicals, totaled $6.7 billion **Principal Trade Partners:** Japan, United States, West Germany, Netherlands, Singapore, Britain, Trinidad & Tobago

Vital Statistics: Birthrate, 42.9 per 1,000 of pop. (1975); death rate, 16.9 **Life Expectancy:** 48 years **Health Statistics:** 1,625 inhabitants per hospital bed; 16,390 per physician (1975) **Infant Mortality:** 126 per 1,000 births **Illiteracy:** 40% **Primary and Secondary School Enrollment:** 22,613,072 (1976) **Enrollment in Higher Education:** 278,200 (1975) **GNP Expended on Education:** 1.4% (1976)

Transportation: Paved roads total c. 16,500 mi. **Motor Vehicles:** 806,400 (1977) **Passenger Cars:** 479,300 **Railway Mileage:** 4,800 **Ports:** Jakarta, Surabaya, Semarang, Palembang, Belawan, Dumai, Balikpapan, Samarinda **Major Airlines:** Garuda Airways and Merapti Nusantara operate domestic and international services **Communications:** Government controlled **Radio Transmitters:** 588 **Licenses:** 5,100,000 (1976) **Television Transmitters:** 29 **Licenses:** 325,000 (1976) **Telephones:** 314,000 (1976) **Newspapers:** 172 dailies (1975), 10 copies per 1,000 inhabitants

Weights and Measures: Metric system and traditional units are used **Travel Requirements:** Passport, tourist visa (to 30 days, $2.80 fee), 2 photos

Indonesia, with 13,662 tropical islands (992 of them inhabited), strung like a necklace along the equator, is one of the world's most beautiful nations. It is green and fertile, but until recently political upheavals guaranteed its backward, impoverished status among nations.

Ruled by Dutch colonialists for about 300 years, Indonesia declared its independence on August 17, 1945, following Japanese occupation during World War II. Four years of fighting and negotiation followed and its sovereignty was recognized in 1949.

The colonial economic and administrative machinery decayed under President Sukarno, who concentrated on building a national identity and pride among a conglomeration of races and religions scattered throughout the islands. He also sought to cast Indonesia in the role of leader of the "third world" while slowly moving closer to Communist China for support.

It was the gradual growth of the ideology of Communism that eventually led to Sukarno's downfall and plunged Indonesia not only into political and economic chaos but also into one of the worst bloodbaths in history.

On the night of September 30, 1965, the Communists and other leftists attempted a coup that was put down by anti-Communist military units under General Suharto. In an ensuing purge of Communists, more than 300,000 Indonesians were slaughtered. Political prisoners were held for years, but the government, pressured by Amnesty International and others, released 10,000 in 1977, 10,000 more in 1978, and still more thousands in 1979.

President Sukarno was gradually eased out of power and General Suharto became president, running the country under the tight rein of the military. The Communist party was banned.

President Suharto found Indonesia in financial ruin and deeply in debt to other nations for money Sukarno had borrowed to spend on military equipment and prestige projects such as public buildings and monuments. Under the new regime capital was lured into the country with tempting interest rates and guarantees.

Indonesia faces enormous problems, and tremendous overcrowding of the island of Java, where an estimated 80 million people live, tops the list. Efforts to move people to underpopulated outer island regions have largely failed. Despite development of roads, electrification, hospitals and schools, much of the outer island area still remains a wilderness.

However, a vast natural treasure of oil, minerals and forests is beginning to be harvested, to the benefit of both Indonesia and the foreign investors who have poured in the money and technical skills to exploit it. Currently, Indonesia is East Asia's main oil exporter and the world's eighth-largest exporter. Its oil and gas revenues topped $10 billion in 1979—up 50 percent in a year—and oil prices were raised again in 1980. Caltex Pacific Indonesia, a joint venture of Texaco and Standard Oil Co. of California, produces about half of Indonesia's oil.

In March 1978 President Suharto was unanimously reelected to a third five-year term by Indonesia's Congress. Adam Malik, chairman of the Congress, was elected vice-president. A new cabinet was also installed; its makeup—including 10 generals, double the number in the last cabinet— underscored the fact that the president's power base remains the military. The losers were the two elements most vocal in criticizing the government in the often tense months since Indonesia's last parliamentary election in May 1977. These were the activist university and high school students, who demanded that Suharto step down, and the Moslem Unitary Development party, which opposes Suharto's insistence on giving formal recognition in this predominantly Moslem nation to widespread mystical practices that take place mainly in Java and Bali.

HISTORY: The complex racial mixture found in Indonesia today is the result of two waves of invasions from Asia and the Pacific. Early in the Christian era the country came under the influence of Indian civilization and of Hinduism and Buddhism. In the 16th century, however, both of these were replaced by Islam as the dominant religion. In the 17th century, the Dutch emerged as the dominant power in Indonesia, maintaining their rule almost uninterruptedly until World War II, when the islands were occupied by Japan

1945-49: Nationalist leaders Sukarno and Mohammad Hatta proclaim Indonesia an independent republic following Japanese defeat in World War II. Attempts to reestablish Dutch rule evoke nationalist resistance; agreement is finally reached for creation of the United States of Indonesia, linked to Netherlands

1950-54: United States of Indonesia is dissolved; Republic of Indonesia is proclaimed, with Sukarno as president. Netherlands-Indonesian Union is dissolved

1959-60: Sukarno combines premiership with office of president and adopts authoritarian system of "guided democracy"; following disagreement with Hatta, who resigns as vice-president, Sukarno dissolves parliament and bans political parties

1962: Dutch withdraw from West Irian, on island of New Guinea, under agreement with United Nations, on condition that territory's people be permitted to decide their own political future

1965-66: Indonesia withdraws from UN; Sukarno adopts policy of collaboration with Communist China, which the Indonesian Communist party (PKI) supports in Sino-Soviet split. An attempted Communist coup is suppressed by army and is followed by anti-Communist riots in which more than 300,000 Indonesians are killed; General Suharto emerges as new strong man

1967-68: Sukarno is stripped of power and Suharto named acting president. Abandonment of pro-Peking stance is followed by riots directed against Indonesia's economically important Chinese minority; Suharto is formally elected president by People's Consultative Congress

1969: Government quells uprising by Papuan natives in West Irian; despite widespread native opposition, Indonesia annexes territory with the approval of tribal leaders

1971: July parliamentary elections are first to be held since 1955. The government party wins a majority of House seats

1973: Suharto reelected to second five-year term

1974: Japanese Premier Tanaka visits Jakarta. Students demonstrate against alleged policy of economic exploitation of the region

1975-76: Portuguese Timor is incorporated into Indonesia, becoming its 27th province

1977: Ruling Golkar party wins elections. Government releases 10,000 political prisoners

1978: Weeks of student protests precede presidential election; hundreds arrested, some campuses occupied; Suharto is reelected to third five-year term by Indonesian Congress. Government says it freed another 10,000 political prisoners. The rupiah is devalued 34% against the U.S. dollar to make rubber, coffee, copper, and other nonoil products more competitive in world markets

1979: A volcanic eruption on Mount Sinila, in central Java, kills 175 persons and injures 1,000. Food and medicine are rushed to the province of East Timor, where more than 100,000 persons suffer from famine and disease

---

IRAN

Area: 636,293 sq. mi. **Population:** 35,509,000 (1978 est.)

Official Name: Islamic Republic of Iran **Capital:** Tehran **Nationality:** Iranian **Languages:** Persian, or Farsi, an Aryan language of the Indo-European group and written Arabic characters, is the official and dominant language. Kurdish, various forms of Turkic, and Arabic are among the other languages spoken **Religion:** About 98% of the population is Moslem, with 90% belonging to the Shi'a sect of Islam and the rest to the Sunni sect. Minority religious groups include Jews, Baha'is, Zoroastrians, and Christian Armenians and Assyrians **Flag:** Green, white, and red horizontal stripes, with a golden lion brandishing a sword, and a rising sun behind him, centered on the white stripe **Anthem:** N.A. **Currency:** Iranian rial (70.5 per U.S. $1)

Location: Southwest Asia. Iran is bordered on the north by the USSR and the Caspian Sea, on the east by Afghanistan and Pakistan, on the south by the Persian Gulf, and on the west by Iraq and Turkey **Features:** The country is largely a semiarid plateau, with high mountain ranges and much barren desert. The Caspian coastal region is semitropical and fertile; the area around the Persian Gulf is extremely hot and dry **Chief Rivers:** Karun, Safid, Karkheh, Zayandeh, Dez

Religious Leader: Ayatollah Ruhollah Khomeini, born 1900?, is the *faghi* (religious leader) for life, according to the new constitution. The executive, legislative and judicial branches of the government are under the authority of the *faghi*. **Head of State:** President

Abolhassan Bani-Sadr, born 1933, elected Jan. 25, 1980, sworn in July 23, 1980 **Head of Government:** Prime Minister Mohammed Ali Rajai, born 1934, appointed Aug. 1980 **Effective Date of Present Constitution:** December 3, 1979 (approved by electorate in special referendum) **Legislative Body:** *Majlis* or Parliament (unicameral), consisting of 270 members popularly elected for a four-year term **Local Government:** 23 provinces

Ethnic Composition: Iranians (Persians) make up about 60% of the population. In addition, there are approximately 5 million Azerbaijanis, over 4 million Kurds, 2 million Arabs, 1 million Turkomans, 1 million Baluchis, 500,000 Qashqais, and smaller numbers of Lurs and Bakhtiaris **Population Distribution:** 46.8% urban **Density:** 56 inhabitants per sq. mi.

Largest Cities: (1976 est.) Tehran 4,400,000, Isfahan 800,000, Meshed 600,000, Tabriz 550,000, Shiraz 380,000, Ahwaz 350,000, Abadan 340,000, Kermanshah 250,000

Per Capita Income: $2,162 (1979) **Gross National Product (GNP):** $56.1 billion (1979) **Economic Statistics:** About 25% of GNP comes from agriculture (wheat, cotton, barley, rice, fresh and dried fruits and vegetables, pulses, oilseeds, sugar beets), forestry, and fishing; 27% from oil; 17% from industry (textiles, food processing, building materials, rubber tires and mining); 5% from construction; and 21% from trade and services **Minerals and Mining:** Oil (Iran has 10% of the world's known oil resources), iron ore, chromite, natural gas, copper, lead, zinc, coal, gypsum, gold, manganese, and salt **Labor Force:** 10,000,000 (1976) of which 37% is engaged in agriculture and 30% in industry **Foreign Trade:** Exports, mainly oil, carpets, cotton, and fruits, totaled $21.7 billion in 1978. Imports, chiefly machinery, iron and steel, chemicals and drugs, totaled $17.7 billion **Principal Trade Partners:** (1978) West Germany, United States, Britain, USSR, Japan, France, Italy, India, Eastern European countries

Vital Statistics: Birthrate, 41.7 per 1,000 of pop (1976); death rate, 13 **Life Expectancy:** 54 years **Health Statistics:** 650 inhabitants per hospital bed; 2,696 per physician (1975) **Infant Mortality:** 100 per 1,000 births (1977) **Illiteracy:** 63% **Primary and Secondary School Enrollment:** 7,125,466 (1976) **Enrollment in Higher Education:** 154,215 **GNP Expended on Education:** 5.4% (1976)

Transportation: Paved roads total 11,620 mi. (1976) **Motor Vehicles:** 1,136,700 (1977) **Passenger Cars:** 932,700 **Railway Mileage:** 3,700 **Ports:** Khorramshahr, Bandar Khomeini (Bandar Shahpur), Bushire, Bandar Abbas, Kharg, Abadan, Enzeli (Pahlavi) **Major Airlines:** Iran National Airlines operates internal and international services **Communications:** Government controlled **Radio Transmitters:** 64 **Receivers:** 6,500,000 (1976) **Television Transmitters:** 157 **Receivers:** 1,720,000 (1976) **Telephones:** 1,000,000 (1977) **Newspapers:** 20 dailies, 15 copies per 1,000 inhabitants (1974)

Weights and Measures: Metric system **Travel Requirements:** The U.S. government has banned all travel to Iran by American citizens, except for newsmen

---

Iran's revolution of 1979, a popular uprising of civilians, overthrew Shah Mohammed Reza Pahlavi and opened the way for creation of the Islamic Republic of Iran. Shock waves surged through the world with the exit of the Shah, long regarded as an ally of the U.S., a stalwart defender of the spread of communism in the Middle East, and a key figure in assuring the flow of petroleum so vital to the Western world. Terrorism intensified the turmoil later, on Nov. 4, 1979, when young militants seized the U.S. embassy compound in Tehran and vowed to hold the American diplomatic personnel as hostages until the Shah was returned to Iran for trial. A 79-year-old religious leader, Ruhollah Khomeini, successor to the Shah in power, gave his blessing to the capture. Meantime, as negotiations wore on into the following year, Iran's oil production dropped to an estimated 10% to 15% of that under the Shah. Unemployment climbed to 33%, and inflation was running at an annual rate of 50%.

Iran is a country about two and one-half times larger than Texas. Prone to earthquakes, the country has arable portions that are divided from one another by mountain ranges and deserts. Its most important ethnic group are the Farsi (Persians, whence the traditional name of the country—Persia), but over a third of the population are of other ethnic groups, most of them Indo-European, as are the Farsi. Its oil industry, founded in 1908, is the oldest in the Middle East and the backbone of the national economy. The wells, although they are beginning to run out, still have enormous potential.

Seat of ancient empires, Iran was conquered by Moslem Arabs in the 7th century A.D. Over centuries, most Iranians became Moslems, but kept their Indo-European languages. In the 15th century, Iran adhered to the Shi'a movement, turning away from Arab leadership.

Shah Reza Pahlavi, an army colonel, who seized power in a military coup in 1921, was favorable to the army and to the promotion of Western ways. Britain and the USSR ousted him in 1941 because he looked to Nazi Germany as a counterweight to British and Soviet influence.

His son and successor, Mohammed Reza Pahlavi, ruled mostly as a figurehead until 1953, when, with the help of the army and Western governments, he ousted Prime Minister Mohammed Mossadegh. The Shah was identified with foreign influence, and he became more and more dictatorial. The Shah launched a "revolution from the throne" in 1961, and carried out plans to modernize the country, improve public health, and raise the status of women and poor people. But he did not consult the people. Moreover, he offended the mullahs by disregarding their interpretations of the Koran and by seizing mosque property. SAVAK, his secret police, dealt harshly with those he considered to be enemies of progress. Wealth increasingly concentrated in the cities, and city ways became strange and offensive to country people.

When Britain withdrew its soldiers from the Persian Gulf region in 1970, the Shah began to give military assistance to neighboring countries. U.S. strategists considered his army crucial to the stability of the region. The army supported him, and the United States gave him aid.

The mosques became the centers of opposition to the Shah—even the opposition of Moslems who favored loose construction of the Koran and of socialists and others with little or no attachment to Islam. In 1978, riots broke out in the name of Khomeini, an exiled mullah who bore the holy title *Ayatollah.*

In 1979, the Shah left Iran, after appointing Shahpur Bakhtiar, a Mossadegh partisan, prime minister. Khomeini, still in exile, mocked the government and appointed a Council of the Islamic Revolution. He returned to Iran and designated Mehdi Bazargan, another Mossadegh partisan, prime minister. There were violent demonstrations on behalf of Bazargan. The armed forces at first supported Bakhtiar, but the defection of a few air force cadets and the strength of the revolution led the chiefs of staff to call for neutrality. Bakhtiar's government collapsed.

Khomeini, Bazargan, and the Council of the Islamic Revolution became power centers—not always in cooperation with each other. Mullahs and *ad hoc* militia units took most of the local authority. But the new order ran into multiple troubles. The Kurds, who had joined in overthrowing the Shah, pursued guerrilla tactics against the Islamic regime and claimed to have shot down a jet fighter; other ethnic groups, the Azerbaijanis and the Baluchis, also objected to governmental and religious control. Educated women launched demonstrations against Khomeini's suggestion that they wear *chador*, favored by the more rigid Moslems as the only suitable modest dress. Firing squads were active, executing more than 700 persons—political and military figures under the Shah as well as those accused of breaking Islamic ethical rules.

Sixteen days after the embassy seizure, the mili-

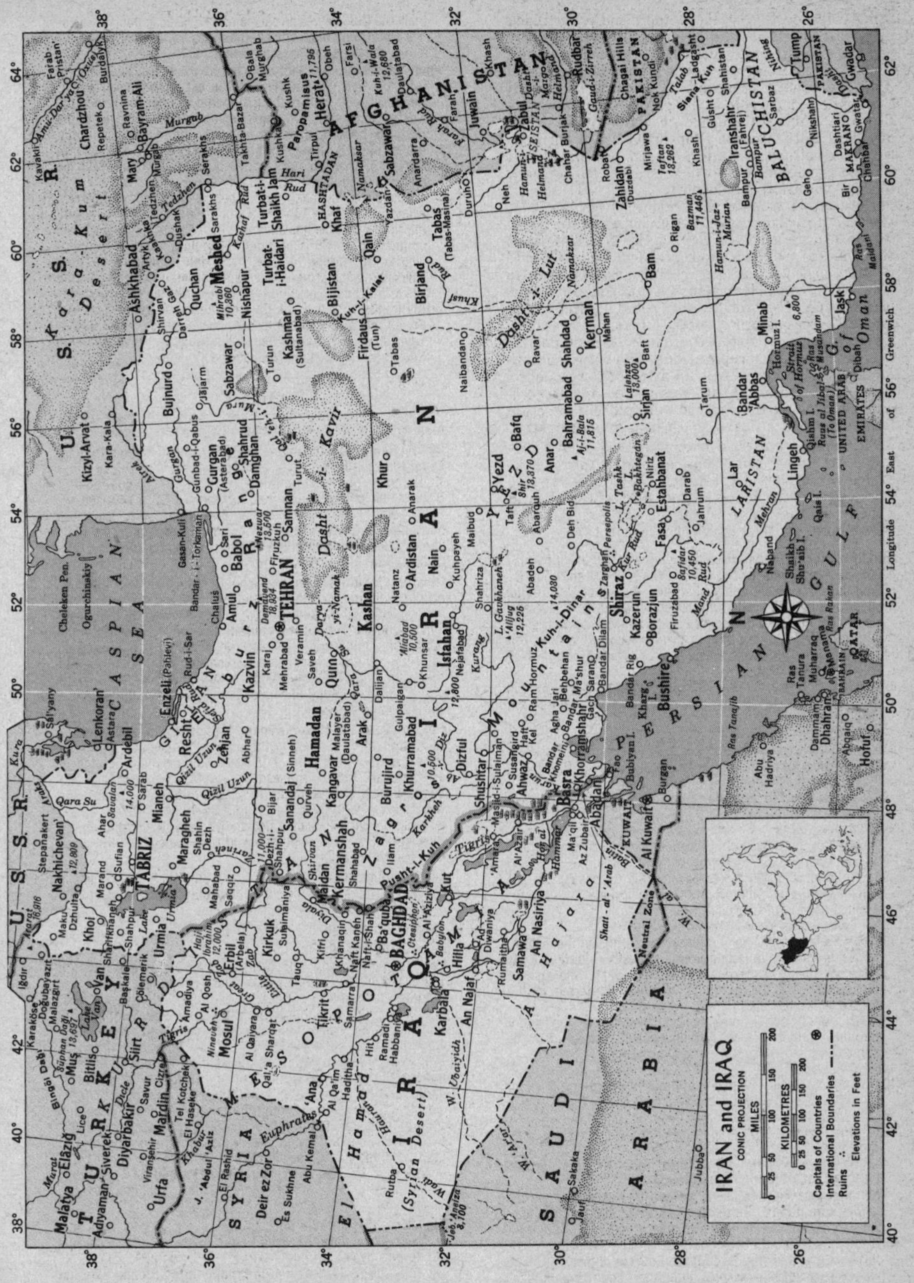
IRAN and IRAQ
CONIC PROJECTION
MILES
0 25 50 100 150 200
KILOMETRES
0 25 50 100 150 200
Capitals of Countries
International Boundaries
Ruins
Elevations in Feet

tants released five white women and eight black men—although all had been denounced initially as "spies." Still held were 50 in the embassy and three in the Foreign Ministry. When Bazargan and his government resigned in protest, Khomeini strengthened the role of the clergy by making the Revolutionary Council the government. In January 1980, following the adoption of the new constitution, Abolhassan Bani-Sadr, an economist, was elected president, a post nevertheless subservient to the Ayatollah's authority.

Retaliatory steps by the U.S., in November 1979, were a cutoff of oil imports from Iran and the freezing of Iranian assets in U.S. banks. A month later, the International Court of Justice, or "World Court," in a preliminary ruling, ordered Iran to free the hostages. Iran retorted that the court lacks jurisdiction. The World Court acted again on May 24, 1980, restating its order to free the hostages, warning Iran not to put them on trial, and declaring Iran liable for reparations. The court admonished the U.S. for its Apr. 24 attempt to rescue the hostages—a mission that was halted, before combat, when three helicopters were put out of action by mechanical failures on an Iranian salt desert.

Skirmishes between Iran and Iraq over a disputed boundary alignment escalated into a full-scale war in late September 1980. Iraqi troops drove deep into Iran's Khuzistan province and heavily damaged the oil refinery at Abadan. Iranian planes struck at Iraqi targets in turn.

HISTORY: An agricultural civilization existed in Iran as far back as 4000 B.C. The Aryans arrived about 2000 B.C. and split into two main groups, the Medes and the Persians. About 550 B.C., Cyrus the Great founded the Persian Empire, which later fell to successive invaders. The Arabs conquered the country and introduced Islam in the 7th century A.D.; they were in turn replaced by the Turks and Mongols. Internal order was restored by the Safavid dynasty, which ruled from 1499 to 1736

1736-47: Nadir Shah establishes Afshar dynasty; he invades India in 1738 and brings back great riches; a despotic ruler, he is assassinated in 1747

1794: Aga Mohammad Khan established Kajar dynasty

19th cent.: Iran loses vast territories to Afghanistan and Russia

1901: Discovery of oil intensifies the rivalry between Britain and Russia over Iran

1907: Anglo-Russian agreement divides Iran into spheres of influence

1921-25: Reza Khan, an army officer, stages coup d'état, overthrows Kajar dynasty, and establishes military dictatorship; he is elected shah and founds Pahlavi dynasty

1941: British and Soviet forces occupy Iran to counter German threat; Reza Shah abdicates and is succeeded by his son, Mohammad Reza Pahlavi

1946: Soviet troops are withdrawn from Iran

1951-53: Premier Mohammad Mossadegh, a militant nationalist, forces parliament to nationalize oil industry, which virtually collapses after Britain imposes a blockade. Shah, who opposes Mossadegh, flees the country but returns a few days later after Mossadegh is ousted

1961-62: Shah launches "revolution from the throne," calling for the end of serfdom, for land distribution, and electoral reform; he personally distributes crown land to peasants

1963: Women gain vote

1971: U.S. and Britain underwrite a $1-billion defense program for Iran as prelude to British withdrawal from the Persian Gulf

1972: Earthquake leaves over 5,000 dead

1974: Seven persons sentenced to death for plotting to assassinate the Shah

1975: Shah dissolves two-party system. U.S. and Iran sign $15 billion economic pact for non-oil trade

1978: Ultraconservative Moslems, leftist extremists and others join in widespread riots. Theater fire kills about 380 in port city of Abadan; government blames extremists

1979: Shah appoints Shahpur Bakhtiar, former Mossadegh partisan, prime minister, and leaves country. Exiled Ayatollah Ruhollah Khomeini condemns government and returns to Iran, designating Mehdi Bazargan as prime minister. Mass uprising sweeps out Bakhtiar government. Ethnic minorities revolt against government for local autonomy. Bazargan government holds referendum which results in 98% majority for "Islamic republic." Young militants seize the U.S. embassy compound, vowing to hold the hostages until the Shah is returned to Iran for trial. The U.S. freezes an estimated $12 billion in Iranian assets. The World Court orders that the hostages be freed. New constitution is approved in a special referendum

1980: Abolhassan Bani-Sadr is elected president, a position subservient to a *faghi* (religious leader); the leading theologian of Iran, Khomeini; later, part of the 270-member *Majlis* (parliament) is elected. In March, a UN inquiry commission, unable to see the hostages because Khomeini supports the militants' position, leaves Tehran in failure. The Shah leaves Panama to live in Cairo. On Apr. 5, Khomeini rules that the hostages will remain with the militants rather than be turned over to the government; the U.S. breaks diplomatic relations and puts an embargo on American exports to Iran. On Apr. 24, the U.S starts a nighttime military mission to free the hostages, but the effort is aborted, without combat, when three of eight helicopters suffer mechanical failures. In starting to leave Iran, eight Americans die as a helicopter and a plane collide on the ground. Ironically, Tehran has its own hostage crisis as 19 are held prisoner six days in May (by Iranian Arabs) in the Iranian embassy in London; an elite British military regiment rescues the hostages. Shah dies in Egypt on July 27. Iraqi armed forces invade Iran in all-out war in September. Abadan refinery damaged

---

IRAQ

Area: 172,476 sq. mi. **Population:** 12,767,000 (1979 est.)

Official Name: Republic of Iraq **Capital:** Baghdad **Nationality:** Iraqi **Languages:** Arabic is the official and dominant language; Kurdish is spoken in the northeast **Religion:** About 90% of the population is Moslem, almost evenly divided between the Shi'a sect and the Sunni sect; about 8% is Christian **Flag:** Red, white, and black horizontal stripes, with three five-pointed green stars on the white stripe **Anthem:** Anthem of the Republic, no words **Currency:** Iraqi dinar (.29 per U.S. $1)

Location: Southwest Asia. Iraq is bordered on the north by Turkey, on the east by Iran, on the southeast by Kuwait and the Persian Gulf, on the southwest by Saudi Arabia, and on the west by Jordan and Syria **Features:** The country consists of a mountain region in the northeast, a rugged and sparsely wooded area with some good pastures; the vast Syrian Desert, contiguous with the Arabian desert; and a fertile lowland region between the mountains and the desert, watered by the Euphrates and Tigris rivers **Chief Rivers:** Tigris, Euphrates

Head of State and of Government: President: Gen. Saddam Hussein, born 1935, elevated to Presidency on retirement of Ahmad Hassan al-Bakr on July 16, 1979. He is chairman of the Revolutionary Command Council and leads the Arab Socialist (Ba'ath) party **Effective Date of Present Constitution:** A provisional constitution was issued in 1970; a National Charter was drafted in 1971 as a basis for a permanent constitution **Legislative Body:** National Assembly (unicameral) of 250 members **Local Government:** 18 provinces, each headed by a governor

Ethnic Composition: Arabs constitute about 71% of the population; Kurds constitute an estimated 18% **Population Distribution:** 66% urban **Density:** 74 inhabitants per sq. mi.

Largest Cities: (1970 estimates) Baghdad 1,028,083, Mosul 333,177, Basra 286,955

Per Capita Income: $2,729 (1979) **Gross National Product (GNP):** $32 billion (1979) **Economic Statistics:** In 1976, 8% of GNP was from agriculture (dates, wheat, barley, rice, cotton, wool, hides, and skins); 16% from industry, excluding the petroleum industry (foodstuffs, water and power services, bricks and cement, beverages, cigarettes and textiles); 26% from trade and services; and 50% from oil industry **Minerals and Mining:** Petroleum, sulphur, phosphate, natural gas, and salt are exploited **Labor Force:** 3,200,000, of which 53% is employed in agriculture, 17% in industry, 11% in services **Foreign Trade:** Exports, chiefly petroleum (96% of total), agricultural products, livestock, and cement, totaled $11.2 billion in 1978. Imports, mainly industrial machinery, iron and steel, automobiles, tea, sugar, clothing, and pharmaceutical products, totaled $5.8 billion **Principal Trade Partners:** EC countries, USSR, Japan, UAE, China, United States, Lebanon, Kuwait, Yugoslavia

Vital Statistics: Birthrate, 48.1 per 1,000 of pop. (1975); death rate, 14.6 **Life Expectancy:** 62 years **Health Statistics:** 491 inhabitants per hospital bed; 2,555 per physician (1976) **Infant Mortality:** 27.5 per 1,000 births **Illiteracy:** 49% **Primary and Secondary School Enrollment:** 2,552,347 (1976) **Enrollment in Higher Education:** 86,111 (1975) **GNP Expended on Education:** 4.3% (1976)

Transportation: Paved roads total 4,000 mi. **Motor Vehicles:** 224,900 (1977) **Passenger Cars:** 150,400 **Railway Mileage:** 1,462 **Ports:** Basra, Umm Qasr, Fao, Az Zubair **Major Airlines:** Iraqi Airways operates domestic and international services **Communica-

tions: Government controlled **Radio Transmitters:** 12 **Receivers:** 1,252,000 (1975) **Television Transmitters:** 7 **Receivers:** 425,000 (1976) **Telephones:** 320,000 (1976) **Newspapers:** 7 dailies (1975), 22 copies per 1,000 inhabitants (1974)

Weights and Measures: Metric system and native units are used
Travel Requirements: Passport, visa, valid 3 months, 1 photo

Iraq, known to archaeologists as Mesopotamia—the site of the ancient Sumerian, Babylonian, and other civilizations, was among the first Arab countries to free itself from Western European domination, joining the League of Nations in 1932, at the termination of British-mandate rule.

In 1958, after the monarchy was overthrown in a bloody military coup, Iraq became a republic. Ten years later, in the fourth coup in a decade, Maj. Gen. Ahmed Hassan al-Bakr came to power as the head of a military junta. Thirteen days later, he deposed his two partners in the junta and proclaimed himself president. But his ill health resulted in the rise to prominence of Saddam Hussein, Deputy Chairman of the Revolutionary Command Council. On July 16, 1979, Bakr resigned and Saddam Hussein became president.

It is generally accepted that the country is ruled today by the inner core of the Ba'ath party, an ultranationalistic, left-wing, Pan-Arab group, a rival faction of which controls Syria. The Iraqi inner core consists of young intellectual zealots, who rarely appear in public, leaving such functions to the president. The ruling Ba'ath party controls the 22-member Revolutionary Command Council, which is the nation's highest authority.

Although the Iraqi authorities have tended to isolate themselves even from the rest of the Arab world, there have been some recent indications that they are beginning to make an effort to enhance their reputation abroad.

The mainstay of Iraq's economy is oil. The revenue it receives through its petroleum exports pays for the bulk of the national expenditure. The oil revenues have been handled sensibly by Iraqi officials and not squandered on prestige projects as in other oil-producing Middle Eastern lands. There has been a gradual improvement in general living standards.

In 1978, Iraq clashed with the Palestine Liberation Organization. A series of terrorist attacks and counterattacks took place, directed at Iraqi and PLO offices and officials in various European and Middle Eastern cities. Relations with the Soviet Union grew strained.

The militant Kurdish minority in the north has long been a problem to Iraqi officials. The Kurds, a nomadic non-Arab people, have traditionally been hostile to rule from Baghdad, and in recent years they engaged the Iraqi army in sporadic guerrilla warfare. Early in 1974, Iraq announced its plan for the autonomy of the Kurdish minority; the Kurds, however, rejected the government's terms for self-rule, and Kurdish leaders declared all-out war in April.

Closely related to the issue of the Kurds, who have ethnic ties to the Persians, is Iraq's conflict with Iran over navigation rights in the Shatt al Arab, the estuary formed by the confluence of the Tigris and Euphrates that forms part of a mutual border. In 1975 Iran and Iraq signed a reconciliation agreement, with Iraq abandoning its claim to the estuary and with Iran ending its support of the Kurdish rebellion, which shortly collapsed.

After the Iranian revolution of 1979 the two countries resumed their boundary dispute, resulting in border patrol clashes in early 1980. In April Iraq expelled about 7,000 Iranians and cancelled the 1975 agreement on September 27, Iraqi armed forces then invaded deep into Iran's oil-rich Khuzistan province and heavily damaged the major oil refinery at Abadan. Iranian air force planes attacked numerous targets in Iraq, including the nuclear power plant under construction near Baghdad.

HISTORY: About 3000 B.C. the Sumerians, already long established in the region, founded city-states in southern Mesopotamia. Among the civilizations that flourished there later were the Akkadian, Babylonian, and Assyrian. After about 500 B.C., Persia, and later Macedonia, dominated the area. In the 7th century A.D., Mesopotamia was overrun by the Arabs, who established their capital at Baghdad. Mongol invasions followed in the 12th and 15th centuries, and in the 16th century the region fell to the Ottoman Turks, under whose rule it remained until World War I

1920: Iraq is made a British mandate under the League of Nations

1932: An independent Iraq is admitted to the League

1941: A pro-Axis government, briefly in power, collapses under British military attack

1948-49: Iraq and the other Arab League member-states send their forces into Palestine during Arab/Israeli War. The war ends with an armistice

1958: Army coup led by Brig. Gen. Abdul Karim Kassem overthrows monarchy and proclaims a republic; King Faisal and Crown Prince Abdul Illah, the king's uncle, are slain

1961: Civil war flares as Kurdish tribesmen rebel

1963: A Ba'athist military coup, headed by Col. Abdul Salem Aref, ousts regime of Kassem, who is executed

1964: Cease-fire is arranged between army and Kurdish rebels, but fighting soon resumes

1966: Abdul Salem Aref is killed in helicopter crash; he is succeeded by his brother Abdul Rahman Aref

1967: Following Arab defeat in Six-Day War with Israel, Aref forms a new government under Lt. Gen. Tahir Yahya

1968: Bloodless coup overthrows Aref and Yahya; Revolutionary Command Council takes control under Gen. Ahmed Hassan al-Bakr

1969: Iraq executes about 40 Iraqis, many of them Jews, convicted of spying for Israel, the United States, and Iran

1970: Periodic war with Kurds is ended by granting of a degree of autonomy. Dispute with Iran over Persian Gulf area grows

1971: Iraq, in support of Palestinian militants, closes its border with Jordan. U.S. Embassy properties in Iraq are seized

1973: Coup attempt led by Col. Nazem Kazzar, Iraqi security chief, fails; Kazzar and 35 followers are executed

1974: Kurds declare war on Iraq

1975: Agreement with Iran, which had supported Kurds. Iraqi troops complete the takeover of former Kurdish strongholds

1977: President Bakr's power base is widened as Revolutionary Command Council is increased from 5 to 22 members

1978: Amid signs of growing strain in Iraq's relations with the Soviet bloc, the government reportedly executes 14 Communists. Iraq feuds with Palestine Liberation Organization

1979: Iraq helps to settle dispute between North Yemen and South Yemen, and hosts conference of Arab ministers protesting Israel-Egypt peace treaty. Bakr resigns on July 16, turning the presidency over to Saddam Hussein

1980: Iraqi border patrols clash with Iranian forces; Iraqi students battle Iranian students in Baghdad; government expels Iran's diplomats and about 7,000 Iranian nationals

---

IRELAND

Area: 27,136 sq. mi. **Population:** 3,365,000 (1979 est.)

Official Name: Ireland **Capital:** Dublin **Nationality:** Irish **Languages:** Irish (Gaelic) and English are the official languages; English, however, is the language in common use **Religion:** About 94% of the population is Roman Catholic, about 5% Protestant Episcopal **Flag:** Green, white, and orange vertical stripes **Anthem:** The Soldier's Song **Currency:** Irish Pound (.48 per U.S. $1)

Location: The republic of Ireland is situated on the second largest of the British Isles, occupying all of the island of Ireland with the exception of Northern Ireland (part of the United Kingdom) with which the republic has its only land border. It is bounded on the east by the Irish Sea, on the southeast by St. George's Channel, and on the west by the Atlantic Ocean **Features:** The country is shaped like a basin, with high coasts sloping inland to low-lying plains **Chief Rivers:** Shannon, Liffey, Suir, Boyne, Blackwater, Erne, Barrow

Head of State: President: Dr. Patrick John Hillery, born 1923, inaugurated 1976 **Head of Government:** Prime Minister Charles J. Haughey, born 1925, appointed December 1979 **Effective Date of Present Constitution:** December 29, 1937 **Legislative Body:** Parliament (bicameral *Oireachtas*) consisting of the Senate *(Seaned)* and the House of Representatives *(Dáil)*. The Senate is composed of 60 members, of whom 11 are nominated by the prime minister, 6 elected by the National University of Ireland and the University of

Dublin, and 43 from 5 panels of candidates established on a vocational basis. The *Dáil* has 148 elected members. The maximum term of office is 5 years in both houses **Local Government:** 26 administrative counties and 4 county boroughs, each with popularly elected councils

Ethnic Composition: The population is mainly Irish, with an Anglo-Irish minority **Population Distribution:** 52.2% urban **Density:** 124 inhabitants per sq. mi.

Largest Cities: (1971 census) Dublin 567,866, Cork 128,645, Limerick 57,161, Dún Laoghaire 53,171, Waterford 31,968

Per Capita Income: $3,425 (1979) **Gross National Product (GNP):** $11.5 billion (1979) **Economic Statistics:** In 1977 about 17% of GNP came from agriculture (cattle, dairy products, barley, wheat, oats, potatoes, sugar beets); 33% from industry (food processing, metal and engineering products, beverages, tobacco, textiles, chemicals, clothing, and footwear) **Minerals and Mining:** Rich deposits of lead, zinc, copper, iron ore, natural gas, and silver. Offshore oil resources are being investigated **Labor Force:** 1,133,000 (1978), of which 26% is employed in agriculture and fishing, 19% in industry **Foreign Trade:** Exports, chiefly meat, livestock, textiles, machinery and transportation equipment, dairy products, and metal ores, totaled $6 billion in 1978. Imports, mainly machinery and transportation equipment, chemicals, grains and other foodstuffs, textiles, metals and metal products, and petroleum, totaled $7.5 billion **Principal Trade Partners:** Britain, United States, West Germany, France, Netherlands, Japan

Vital Statistics: Birthrate, 21.4 per 1,000 of pop. (1977); death rate, 10.5 **Life Expectancy:** 72 years **Health Statistics:** 94 inhabitants per hospital bed; 831 per physician (1976) **Infant Mortality:** 15.7 per 1,000 births **Illiteracy:** Negligible **Primary and Secondary School Enrollment:** 547,824 (1977) **Enrollment in Higher Education:** 34,615 (1976) **GNP Expended on Education:** 6.2% (1976)

Transportation: Surfaced roads total 54,290 mi. **Motor Vehicles:** 645,900 (1977) **Passenger Cars:** 577,600 **Railway Mileage:** 1,334 **Ports:** Dublin, Cork, Limerick, Waterford, Rosslare, New Ross **Major Airlines:** Aer Lingus–Irish International Airlines operates domestic and international services **Communications:** Government controlled **Radio Transmitters:** 18 **Licenses:** 949,000 (1976) **Television Transmitters:** 28 **Receivers:** 655,000 (1976) **Telephones:** 480,000 (1976) **Newspapers:** 7 dailies, 222 copies per 1,000 inhabitants (1975)

Weights and Measures: British standards and the metric system are used **Travel Requirements:** Passport, no visa for 90 days

---

After 30 years of something of an economic miracle in which Ireland turned from an agrarian to an industrial society, a little of the power has gone out of Ireland's boom. A period of relatively slow growth, high inflation and unemployment, and problems with its balance of payments has confronted the government with warnings of trouble. Even so, Ireland has come a long way.

Over a half a century ago, when the 26 counties constituting the republic became an independent state, the economy was unbalanced and in indifferent shape. More than 90 percent of exports were agricultural and went to one market—Britain. Beyond a few established businesses—breweries, distilleries, and bakeries—there was no industry. As a result, the drain upon the nation's young through emigration—first to the United States, and later to Britain—was excessive.

Ireland has been greatly aided by foreigners—both as tourists and as developers. Canadians were given mining rights and their exploration and development have shown that Ireland has rich deposits of zinc, lead, copper, and silver. Additionally, Germans helped harness the Shannon River and gave Ireland its first big hydroelectric generators. Beet sugar production was begun, and for many years Ireland has been self-sufficient in sugar supplies. And promising reserves of oil and gas have recently been discovered off the Irish coast in the Irish Sea. In 1977 foreign investment in Ireland amounted to $1 billion.

Ireland, although committed to upholding the rights of private property and private enterprise, has governmental industries. The national transport company, the airline, the sugar company, the tourist board, the peat board, the radio and television service, and the electricity supply board are all owned by the state and administered by semi-governmental bodies. In January 1973, Ireland's economic prospects were brightened somewhat by its entry into the European Common Market.

Economic progress, however, has not erased the age-old "Irish Question," which again came to the fore with the 1969 outbreak of violence between Catholics and Protestants in Northern Ireland. Sporadic street violence has continued since that time. A series of bombings and bank and post-office raids, coupled with the 1976 assassination of British ambassador Christopher Ewart-Biggs by I.R.A. members, unleashed a chain of events which disrupted the government. An Emergency Powers Bill and a Criminal Law Bill, giving police broad powers in dealing with extremist groups was passed; President Cearbhall O'Dálaigh resigned over the laws and was succeeded as president by Patrick J. Hillery.

Prime Minister Jack Lynch resigned the post after two years in office on Dec. 5, 1979, after his Fianna Fáil party lost some local elections. The party chose Charles Haughey to replace him. In May 1980, Haughey met with British Prime Minister Margaret Thatcher and declared that Ireland could be unified only by agreement with the Protestant majority in Northern Ireland.

In September 1979, John Paul II became the first Roman Catholic pope to visit Ireland and received an exuberant Irish welcome. The pope's pleas to eschew violence were rejected by the I.R.A., however.

HISTORY: Celtic tribes from Gaul or Iberian Galicia conquered Ireland about the 4th century B.C. and established a Gaelic civilization. By the 3rd century A.D., five Gaelic kingdoms had been established and gradually became Christianized. Until the 8th century arrival of the Vikings, Ireland remained free from foreign invasion, escaping even the Roman conquest that befell neighboring Britain. In the end, however, beginning with the 12th-century Anglo-Norman conquest, that neighbor was to prove the most troublesome invader of all

1542: Henry VIII of England assumes the title of King of Ireland

1649: Oliver Cromwell confiscates nine-tenths of Irish land and distributes it among English Protestant settlers

1801: United Kingdom of Great Britain and Ireland is formed

1846-54: About one million Irish die of starvation as a result of famine, brought on by recurring potato blight; more than 1.5 million Irish emigrate, mostly to the United States

1916-20: Easter Rebellion against British rule breaks out in 1916 under leadership of Sinn Fein, a nationalist movement; rebellion is crushed and its leaders executed

1921-22: Irish Free State is set up as a British dominion; six northern counties of Ulster remain in United Kingdom. Sinn Fein splits into conservative and republican groups, the latter headed by Eamon de Valera and opposed to division of Ireland; civil war breaks out but conservative elements prevail

1931: Equality with Britain is affirmed by Statute of Westminster

1932: De Valera becomes prime minister

1937: New Constitution makes British monarch ceremonial head of Ireland for external purposes only

1939-45: Ireland remains neutral during World War II, but many Irish volunteer for service with British forces

1949: Ireland declares itself a republic, withdraws from British Commonwealth, and maintains jurisdictional claims over Northern Ireland

1951-59: De Valera becomes prime minister, following victory by Fianna Fáil in parliamentary elections; De Valera resigns his post as prime minister to take over presidency

1966: De Valera is reelected president for seven-year term; Jack Lynch becomes prime minister

1969: Lynch's Fianna Fáil party wins overall majority in parliament in general elections; government sends troops to northern border as Catholics battle Protestants in Ulster

1973: Erskine Childers succeeds De Valera as president. Liam Cosgrave is elected prime minister

1974: Cearbhall O'Dálaigh becomes fifth president on death of Childers

1975: Severe drought conditions imperil crops

1976: British ambassador to Ireland, Christopher Ewart-Biggs, is killed in Dublin by a land mine explosion. O'Dálaigh resigns presidency; Dr. Patrick J. Hillery becomes president

1977: Jack Lynch's Fianna Fáil Party wins election, making him new prime minister
1979: Prime Minister Lynch resigns and Charles Haughey becomes prime minister. Pope John Paul II visits Ireland

ISRAEL

Area: 7,847 sq. mi. **Population:** 3,800,000 (1979 est.)

Official Name: State of Israel **Capital:** Jerusalem; Tel Aviv is the diplomatic capital **Nationality:** Israeli **Languages:** Hebrew is the official and dominant language; Arabic is spoken by about 15% of the population; English is the most commonly used foreign language **Religion:** Judaism is the predominant religion; the Arab minority is largely Moslem and the Christian Arabs chiefly Greek Catholic and Greek Orthodox **Flag:** A white field with a blue six-pointed Star of David bordered above and below by blue horizontal stripes **Anthem:** The Hope **Currency:** Shekel (4.3 per U.S. $1)

Location: Middle East, at the eastern end of the Mediterranean. Israel is bordered on the north by Lebanon, on the east by Syria and Jordan, on the south by Egypt, and on the west by the Mediterranean Sea **Features:** The Negev Desert in the south constitutes about 50% of the country. The rest of the country consists of a narrow coastal plain in the center and a hilly region to the north **Chief Rivers:** Jordan, Kishon

Head of State: President Yitzhak Navon, born in 1921, elected by parliament in 1978 for a 5-year term **Head of Government:** Prime Minister Menachem Begin, born 1913, assumed office June 1977 **Effective Date of Present Constitution:** There is no written constitution; the structure of government is defined by fundamental laws **Legislative Body:** Parliament (unicameral *Knesset*) consisting of 120 members elected by universal suffrage for 4 years **Local Government:** 6 administrative districts, headed by appointed commissioners

Ethnic Composition: Jews constitute about 85% of the population, with the rest mainly Arabs **Population Distribution:** 82% urban **Density:** 484 inhabitants per sq. mi.

Largest Cities: (1975 est.) Tel Aviv 357,600, Jerusalem 344,200, Haifa 225,000, Ramat Gan 120,200, Bat Yam 114,000

Per Capita Income: $4,478 (1979) **Gross National Product (GNP):** $16.9 billion (1979) **Economic Statistics:** 7% of GNP comes from agriculture (citrus fruits, eggs, vegetables); 29% from manufacturing (food processing, metals and machinery, textiles, chemicals, and petroleum products), mining, and quarrying; 20% from commerce and finance; 19% from services **Minerals and Mining:** Potash, phosphate, bromine, phosphate rock, copper, iron, ceramic clays and glass sand, and gypsum are exploited **Labor Force:** 1,200,000 (1977), of which 25.3% is employed in industry, 32.8% in services, 12.2% in commerce, 6.5% in agriculture **Foreign Trade:** Exports, chiefly polished diamonds, citrus fruits, textiles, clothes, food products, chemicals, fertilizers, and mining products, totaled $4.2 billion in 1978. Imports, chiefly rough diamonds, machinery, transport equipment, nonmetallic mineral manufactures, food and live animals, raw materials, and chemicals, totaled $7.1 billion **Principal Trade Partners:** United States, Britain, West Germany, Netherlands, Belgium, France, Switzerland, Hong Kong, Japan, Italy

Vital Statistics: Birthrate, 26.1 per 1,000 of pop. (1977); death rate, 6.8 **Life Expectancy:** 72 years **Health Statistics:** 178 inhabitants per hospital bed; 351 per physician (1976) **Infant Mortality:** 20.1 per 1,000 births **Illiteracy:** 10% **Primary and Secondary School Enrollment:** 705,488 (1975) **Enrollment in Higher Education:** 75,338 (1974) **GNP Expended on Education:** 6.8% (1975)

Transportation: Paved roads total 3,350 mi. **Motor Vehicles:** 420,300 (1977) **Passenger Cars:** 312,700 **Railway Mileage:** 476 **Ports:** Haifa, Ashdod, Eilat **Major Airlines:** El Al Israel Airlines, the government airline, handles foreign travel, while Arkia, its subsidiary, handles domestic travel **Communications:** State controlled **Radio Transmitters:** 39 **Receivers:** 655,000 (1976) **Television Transmitters:** 28 **Receivers:** 475,000 (1976) **Telephones:** 888,000 (1976) **Newspapers:** 23 dailies, 208 copies per 1,000 inhabitants (1975)

Weights and Measures: Metric system **Travel Requirements:** Passport, no visa for 3 months

---

The proclamation of Israel as a nation in 1947 again established after an absence of many centuries a Hebrew state in a land regarded by Jews as their homeland. The ancient kingdoms of Israel and Judah had been conquered repeatedly through several centuries, and the Jews had scattered through many lands. Following the Moslem conquest of the 7th century A.D., Arab culture had become predominant. The 19th-century Zionist movement for restoration of the Jewish homeland promoted Jewish migration to the land—then the Ottoman province of Palestine. Palestine was occupied during World War I by Britain, which governed it as a mandate of the League of Nations from 1919 to 1946, and of the United Nations from 1946 to 1948. Jewish immigration continued, especially after the Nazi persecutions; by 1947, the Jews were in the majority in many areas of Palestine.

The UN moved to divide Palestine into an Arab and a Jewish state, over the objections of the Palestine Arabs, who rejected the UN proposal to organize a state. Israel declared its independence on May 14, 1948, and was attacked by five Arab nations. An uneasy cease-fire in 1949 gave Israel almost 50 percent more territory than originally granted; Jordan (then Transjordan) annexed the rest.

Arab-Israeli hostilities continued to seethe under the surface until they erupted in war on October 29, 1956, when Israel staged a "preemptive attack" on Egypt's Sinai during the Suez Canal crisis. A UN cease-fire ended the fighting on November 6, 1956, and Israel withdrew its forces under pressure.

During the Six Day War of 1967, Israel made large-scale territorial gains in the Gaza Strip, Sinai Peninsula, Old Jerusalem, the Golan Heights, and Jordan's West Bank. The memory of these gains set the stage for the war of 1973-74, when Egyptian, Syrian, and Iraqi forces attacked on October 6. The Arab forces first made large gains, but these were considerably reduced by the time a truce ended the fighting on November 7.

Despite the truce, sporadic fighting continued between Israel and Syrian troops, until U.S. Secretary of State Henry Kissinger arranged a cease-fire on May 31, 1974.

Border agreements with Syria and Egypt which included UN buffer zones were a stabilizing factor in those areas, but in November 1974 there was increased Israeli concern for the future of the West Bank of the Jordan River when the UN General Assembly voted that Palestinians should be entitled to return to their land and property, and granted the Palestine Liberation Organization (PLO) permanent observer status.

In September 1975 Kissinger completed negotiations for a second Egyptian-Israeli disengagement agreement setting out details of the new military position in the Sinai Peninsula and the extent of Israeli withdrawal to the eastern entrances of the Giddi and Mitla passes and from the Abu Rudays and Ras Sudar oil fields, which had been supplying 55 percent of Israel's oil needs. By February 1976 the final phase of the troop disengagement agreement was implemented.

Meanwhile, many Israelis had settled in the occupied territory, claiming that all of the historic homeland was as their land.

In 1977, the Labor Alignment, which had been the largest bloc in every previous legislature, suffered scandal and internal discord. The Likud party won the ensuing election and with two religious groups formed a coalition government more favorable to private enterprise and to Jewish religious tradition. Menachem Begin became prime minister.

Despite Begin's reputation as a hard-liner, President Anwar el-Sadat of Egypt visited Israel in 1977 as an initiative to peace. Begin returned the visit, and negotiations for peace opened. Despite disagreement over Jewish settlements Israel had established in the occupied territory, Begin and Sadat, with the help of U.S. President Jimmy Carter's diplomacy, signed a peace treaty in March 1979. Israel agreed to withdraw from occupied Sinai within three years, and from the oil fields there within a year, and agreed to take steps toward Palestinian self-government. The treaty also obligated Egypt to sell oil to Israel. By early 1980, Israel had withdrawn from two thirds of the Sinai, and the two countries opened their borders to each other and exchanged ambassadors.

The deadline of May 26, 1980, for resolving the Palestinian autonomy issue for the West Bank and Gaza was missed, and talks were suspended. Israel continued to establish settlements on the West Bank despite Egypt's protests and Arab terrorism. In May, after six Jews were killed by terrorists in Hebron, the Israeli government deported three Palestinian leaders in the West Bank to Lebanon. The UN Security Council called on Israel to undo the deportation. The United States abstained from the vote, but in March it had aroused a furore in Israel by voting for an Arab resolution condemning the Israeli resettlement policy. The U.S. vote was later disavowed by President Carter.

Begin's handling of the Palestinian issue also had repercussions in the Israeli cabinet. Ezer Weizman resigned as defense minister in late May. Previously, in October 1979, Moshe Dayan had quit as foreign minister over the same issue.

Poor in soil and minerals, beset by inflation, high taxes, and an enormous military budget, Israel nevertheless attracts many Jewish immigrants by promising a them a new life. Tourists are also attracted by sites of historic importance and places sacred to Islam and Christianity, as well as to Judaism.

HISTORY: In biblical times Israel (then Canaan and later Palestine) was the home of scattered Hebrew tribes. By about 1000 B.C. a Hebrew kingdom was firmly established at Jerusalem, under King David. After the reign of Solomon, the kingdom split into two states, Israel and Judah, which were respectively destroyed by Assyria and Babylonia. Palestine later fell to the Greeks and finally to the Romans. In the 7th century, the region was conquered by the Moslems. Later, it was an Ottoman province. During World War I, it came under British control. Modern Israel marks the culmination of the Zionist movement for the reconstitution of a Jewish state

1947: United Nations adopts Palestine partition plan to divide Palestine into two states, one Jewish and one Arab

1948: Israel is proclaimed a nation and British withdraw from Palestine. Armies of surrounding Arab states attack Israel

1949: Fighting ends with Israel in possession of almost 50 percent more territory than originally granted. Armistice agreements, but no peace treaties, are signed with Arab countries

1956: Israeli forces invade Egypt and occupy Sinai Peninsula and Gaza Strip

1957: Under American and Soviet pressure, Israel completes withdrawal to old borders. United States guarantees Israeli passage into Red Sea through previously blockaded Strait of Tiran

1964: Palestine Liberation Organization is formed

1967: Egyptians reimpose blockade. Israel attacks in Sinai and then into Jordan and Syria. At end of Six-Day War, Israelis occupy all of Sinai Peninsula, Gaza, and east bank of Suez Canal, the Gaza Strip, all of west bank of Jordan, and Golan Heights of Syria

1969: Prime Minister Levi Eshkol dies and is succeeded by Mrs. Golda Meir of the Israel Labor party. Arab guerrilla activity continues; Labor Alignment is returned to power

1972: Terrorist activity by PLO guerrillas and sympathizers increases, extending to a random massacre at Lod Airport and the kidnapping and death of Israeli athletes at the Olympic games in Munich. Israel carries out retaliatory raids on guerrilla settlements in Lebanon

1973: David Ben-Gurion, first prime minister and principal founder of the state of Israel, dies

1973-74: Fourth Arab-Israeli war breaks out when Egyptian, Syrian, and Iraqi forces launch surprise attack on October 6, 1973, Yom Kippur, the holiest day of the year for Jews. In January, Israel and Egypt agree on disengagement of forces. Fighting with Syria continues through May 1974

1975: Sporadic raids and bombing incidents, are carried out chiefly by the PLO, followed by Israeli reprisals on PLO camps in Syria; tension makes settlement of Arab-Israeli differences difficult

1976: Israeli airborne commandos rescue 103 hostages held at Uganda's Entebbe Airport by pro-Palestinian hijackers of an Air France airliner

1977: Israeli troops cross into Southern Lebanon and fight with Palestinians in the first direct clash between the two sides in more than two years. Likud party is victorious in general elections; Menachem Begin becomes prime minister. Begin confers with President Carter in Washington. Austerity moves, defense spending cuts, and Israeli pound devaluation are announced. President Sadat's Mideast "peace initiative" spurs round of talks

1978: PLO terror attack, worst in Israel's history, leaves 37 dead and 82 wounded; Israeli forces retaliate by invading southern Lebanon and occupy area for three months

1979: Peace treaty with Egypt signed. Treaty requires Israel to withdraw from Egypt within three years, from remaining oil fields within one year; and requires Egypt to sell oil to Israel

1980: Israeli forces complete withdrawal from Sinai oil fields; government opens borders to Egypt and exchanges ambassadors. Israeli-Egyptian talks on Palestinian autonomy are suspended after May 26th deadline under peace treaty is missed. A Knesset bill reaffirms *all* of Jerusalem as the Israeli capital

---

ITALY

Area: 116,303 sq. mi. **Population:** 56,954,000 (1979 est.)

Official Name: Italian Republic **Capital:** Rome **Nationality:** Italian **Languages:** Italian is the official and predominant language; German, French, Friulian, Slovene, Ladin, Albanian, and Greek are spoken by minorities **Religion:** Roman Catholicism is the religion of about 99% of the population **Flag:** Green, white, and red vertical stripes **Anthem:** Hymn of Mameli **Currency:** Italian lira (847 per U.S. $1)

Location: Southern Europe. Italy has common land frontiers in the west with France, and in the north with Switzerland, Austria, and Yugoslavia. Its boot-shaped peninsular coastline is bordered by three branches of the Mediterranean: the Tyrrhenian Sea on the west, the Ionian Sea on the south, and the Adriatic Sea on the east. Major offshore islands are Sicily and Sardinia **Features:** The country is rugged and mountainous, except for the Po Valley area in the north, the heel of "the boot" in the south, and small coastal areas **Chief Rivers:** Po, Tiber, Arno, Adige

Head of State: President Alessandro Pertini, born 1896, elected in 1978 by Electoral Assembly (Parliament plus 58 regional representatives) **Head of Government:** Premier Francesco Cossiga, born 1928, appointed 1979 **Effective date of Present Constitution:** January 1, 1948 **Legislative Body:** Parliament (bicameral), consisting of the Senate and the Chamber of Deputies. The Senate is composed of 322 members elected for 5 years. The Chamber of Deputies has 630 members elected for 5 years **Local Government:** 94 provinces, each headed by a prefect appointed by the central government. These are grouped into 20 regions, with limited governing powers

Ethnic Composition: The population is virtually homogeneous, with small minority groups of Germans, Friulians, Slovenes, Albanians, Ladins and French **Population Distribution:** 48% urban **Density:** 490 inhabitants per sq. mi.

Largest Cities: (1975 est.) Rome 2,868,248, Milan 1,731,281, Naples 1,223,785, Turin 1,202,215, Genoa 805,855, Palermo 662,567, Bologna 491,330, Florence 465,823

Per Capita Income: $4,189 (1979) **Gross National Product (GNP):** $238 billion (1979) **Economic Statistics:** 43% of GNP comes from industry (automobiles, oil refining, textiles, machinery, chemicals, food processing); 7% from agriculture (wheat, rice, grapes, olives, fruit and vegetables) **Minerals and Mining:** Italy is a leading producer of mercury, but is poor in most other minerals. Iron ore, petroleum, natural gas, lignite, pyrites, and sulphur are produced in small quantities **Labor Force:** 21.6 million, with some 38% in industry and 16% in agriculture **Foreign Trade:** Exports, chiefly industrial machinery, office machines, motor vehicles, textiles, and footwear, totaled $56 billion in 1978. Imports, mainly crude oil, minerals, machinery iron and steel, totaled $56 billion **Principal Trade Partners:** EC and EFTA countries, Latin America, United States, Libya, Saudi Arabia, Iraq, USSR

Vital Statistics: Birthrate, 13.2 per 1,000 of pop. (1977); death rate, 9.6 **Life Expectancy:** 70 years **Health Statistics:** 95 inhabitants per hospital bed; 502 per physician (1973) **Infant Mortality:** 17.6 per 1,000 births **Illiteracy:** 5% **Primary and Secondary School Enrollment:** 9,799,953 (1976) **Enrollment in Higher Education:** 976,712 **GNP Expended on Education:** 5.0% (1975)

Transportation: Surfaced roads total 179,241 mi., including 3,600 mi. of superhighways **Motor Vehicles:** 17,607,300 (1977) **Passenger Cars:** 16,371,200 **Railway Mileage:** 12,624 **Ports:** Genoa, Augusta, Venice, Naples, Trieste, Taranto, La Spezia **Major Airlines:** Alitalia, a government airline, conducts international flights while Itavia and ATI are domestic **Communications:** Partly government controlled **Radio Transmitters:** 1,964 **Licenses:** 13,024,000

(1976) **Television Transmitters:** 1,199 **Licenses:** 12,377,000 (1976) **Telephones:** 15,246,000 (1976) **Newspapers:** 78 dailies, 113 copies per 1,000 inhabitants (1974)

Weights and Measures: Metric system **Travel Requirements:** Passport, no visa for 3 months

---

Italy—one of the younger of Europe's nation-states, home of one of its oldest civilizations—is a society undergoing profound political, economic, and cultural transformations.

Unified politically only a century ago, Italians still seek a common sense of nationhood that will bridge their vast regional differences and rivalries. The Brenner Pass, in the Alps, and Cape Correnti, on the southern tip of Sicily, lie 750 miles apart, but the distance between them is far greater in terms of the environment, culture, traditions, and temperaments of their peoples.

The northerner is the heir to the Renaissance and *risorgimento:* vigorous, forward-looking, in the mainstream of European life, living in a temperate climate on land endowed with the lion's share of Italy's slender resources.

The southerner, on the other hand, has been less favored both by nature and by history. His land is poor, his climate marked by extremes, his political and cultural tradition still rooted in the aftermath of a feudalism that long resisted the liberating winds of the Renaissance, the French Revolution, and 19th-century liberalism.

The task of molding and governing a postwar republican Italy that will reconcile these vastly divergent interests and enlist equally the loyalties of the Milan industrialist, Roman aristocrat or shopkeeper, and Calabrian peasant has fallen on shifting coalitions of the democratic parties of the center and moderate left.

As of 1980, the Christian Democratic party has been the largest in every parliament—and has supplied every premier—since 1946. But it has never had a majority, and has had to negotiate agreements for coalition or support with other parties. Some coalitions included parties suspected of lacking dedication to democracy. The Christian Democrats lost much support in the 1970s because of corruption of their leadership.

The Communist party of Italy (PCI) became the second-largest in parliament by professing dedication to democracy and to national independence and by governing a number of cities with scrupulous honesty. But participation in the Cabinet eluded it because the Christian Democrats and others feared both the PCI's motives and the difficulties that a government with Communist ministers would face with the United States.

In 1978, for the first time, a coalition including the Communists was formed—to support a Cabinet consisting entirely of Christian Democrats. The Communists withdrew in 1979 after being rebuffed in their demand for seats in the cabinet. In 1979 Giulio Andreotti resigned as premier and was succeeded by Francesco Cossiga, who formed a new coalition government in April 1980.

Italy has been troubled by acts of political terrorism, the most spectacular being the kidnap and murder of former Premier Aldo Moro in 1978, and the bombing of the Bologna railroad station in August 1980, which killed 81 people.

HISTORY: About 500 B.C. Rome began its rise to power, supplanting the earlier Etruscan civilization. The Roman Empire fell in the 5th century A.D. and thereafter the Italian peninsula was largely politically fragmented until modern times. After the great cultural and intellectual flowering of the Renaissance, which reached its height in the late 15th century, much of Italy, divided into kingdoms, principalities, duchies, city-republics, and the Papal States, fell increasingly under foreign sway

1815: Following collapse of Napoleonic Empire, former states of Italian peninsula are reconstituted—some under Austrian rule

1848-49: Movement for the unification of Italy, known as the *risorgimento*, leads to revolts, but these are suppressed after initial successes

1859: Kingdom of Sardinia, aided by France, defeats Austrians at Solferino

1860-70: The Italian unification movement, whose most notable figures were Giuseppe Garibaldi, Giuseppe Mazzini, and Camillo di Cavour, moves ahead as various Italian states vote for union with Sardinia; following conquest of Kingdom of Two Sicilies by Garibaldi, that kingdom also votes for union with Sardinia, and in 1861 the Kingdom of Italy is proclaimed under Victor Emmanuel II. With the seizure of the papal possessions, Italian unification is completed by 1870

1915-18: Italy engages in World War I on side of Allies after initially declaring neutrality; country suffers heavy losses

1922: Benito Mussolini comes to power in wake of severe depression and establishes a fascist dictatorship

1935-36: Italy conquers Ethiopia

1940-43: Italy enters World War II as ally of Nazi Germany; Italian defeats in Greece and North Africa, and the Allied invasion of Sicily, help topple Mussolini's regime. New government is set up and an armistice signed with the Allies

1945: Mussolini is executed by Italian partisans

1946: Italy becomes a republic after voters decide by plebiscite to abolish the monarchy

1947: Peace treaty is ratified; Italy loses Fiume, Zara, Pula, and Istria to Yugoslavia and the Dodecanese Islands to Greece; its African colonies are placed under UN supervision

1949: Italy becomes a founding member of NATO

1966: Floods in northern and central Italy destroy or damage many art treasures, especially in Florence

1974: Premier Aldo Moro forms Christian-Democratic/Republican minority government

1975: Voting age is lowered to 18. The 1954 partition of Trieste territory becomes official

1976: Death toll from earthquake in Friuli reaches 1,200. Aldo Moro's government falls and new elections held. Italian Communist party makes major gains but Christian Democrats retain slight edge. Giulio Andreotti is sworn in as premier

1977: Italy and Yugoslavia ratify agreement ending World War II border dispute over area south of Trieste, with Italy ceding territory to Yugoslavia. Public protest and extremist violence erupts over Italy's economic crisis

1978: Government resigns as wave of violence continues; Communists withdraw tacit support and demand cabinet seats in emergency coalition. President Giovanni Leone reappoints Premier Andreotti to form new government, nation's 40th since World War II. Red Brigades kidnap former Permier Aldo Moro on same day Andreotti presents new government to parliament; Communists given direct role (short of cabinet-level) for first time since 1947. Red Brigades demand release of 13 leftist prisoners for Moro's life; government refuses to negotiate, as huge manhunt is mounted; government decree enhances power of police; Moro found dead; public reaction against Red Brigades noted. Abortion is legalized. President Leone resigns in face of corruption charges and is replaced by Alessandro Pertini. Trial of Red Brigades members ends (29 are sentenced up to 15 years in prison; 16 are acquitted)

1979: Communists withdraw from coalition after their demand for cabinet seats is rebuffed. Andreotti resigns; parliament is dissolved; Communists lose seats in elections for new parliament; Francesco Cossiga becomes premier

1980: Premier Cossiga forms new coalition of Social Democrats, Socialists, and Republicans stronger than his previous government. 81 people are killed in the bombing of the Bologna railroad station by right-wing terrorists

---

IVORY COAST

Area: 127,520 sq. mi. **Population:** 7,920,000 (1979 est.)

Official Name: Republic of the Ivory Coast **Capital:** Abidjan **Nationality:** Ivorian **Languages:** French is the official and commercial language, but the most common African language is Dioula **Religion:** 66% animist, 22% Moslem, 12% Roman Catholic **Flag:** Orange, white, and green vertical stripes **Anthem:** L'Abidjanaise, beginning "Greetings, O land of hope" **Currency:** CFA Franc (210.2 per U.S. $1)

Location: West Africa. Ivory Coast is bordered on the north by Mali and Upper Volta, on the east by Ghana, on the south by the Gulf of Guinea, and on the west by Liberia and Guinea **Features:** From the coast, a rain forest extends over about 40% of the country. The remainder is wooded and grassy savanna, with a mountainous area in the northwest **Chief Rivers:** Bandama, Sassandra, Komoé, Nzi, Cavally

Head of State and of Government: President Félix Houphouët-Boigny, born 1905, reelected November 1975 for fourth 5-year term **Effective Date of Present Constitution:** 1960, amended 1975 **Legislative Body:** National Assembly (unicameral), consisting of 120 members elected for 5 years. All members belong to the Democratic Party of the Ivory Coast, the nation's only party **Local Government:** 24 administrative departments, each headed by an elected council, and 2 autonomous municipalities

Ethnic Composition: About 60 groups, the largest being the Mande (26%), Akan (25%), Krou (18%), Sénoufo (13%), Lagoon people (7%) **Population Distribution:** 32.4% urban **Density:** 62 inhabitants per sq. mi.

Largest Cities: (1977 est.—Metropolitan Area) Abidjan 950,000; (1974 est.) Bouaké 140,000

Per Capita Income: $885 (1979) **Gross National Product (GNP):** $6.6 billion (1979) **Economic Statistics:** In 1976 about 31% of GNP came from agriculture (coffee, palm oil, cocoa, cotton, bananas, pineapples, rice, coconuts, sugar, rubber, yams, cassava, corn, millet, sorghum, livestock, tropical woods), 15% from industry (tuna-packing, sawmilling, agricultural processing, textiles, clothing, auto, truck and bus assembly, oil refining) **Minerals and Mining:** Small quantities of diamonds and manganese have been produced and exploitation of petroleum, iron ore, oil, nickel and gold is under way **Labor Force:** 2,600,000 (1970), with 78% in agriculture and 14% in industry and trade. Only 356,000 are wage earners **Foreign Trade:** Exports, chiefly coffee, wood, cocoa, palm oil, cotton, bananas, and pineapples, totaled $2.5 billion in 1978. Imports, mainly machinery, transport equipment, electrical equipment, and petroleum products, total $2.1 billion **Principal Trade Partners:** France, Netherlands, West Germany, Italy, Japan, United States

Vital Statistics: Birthrate, 45.6 per 1,000 of pop. (1975); death rate, 20.6 **Life Expectancy:** 43 years **Health Statistics:** 589 inhabitants per hospital bed; 15,234 per physician (1975) **Infant Mortality:** 138 per 1,000 births **Illiteracy:** 75% **Primary and Secondary School Enrollment:** 792,189 (1975) **Enrollment in Higher Education:** 8,701 (1976) **GNP Expended on Education:** 7.4% (1975)

Transportation: Surfaced roads total 1,500 mi. **Motor Vehicles:** 128,400 (1976) **Passenger Cars:** 84,900 **Railway Mileage:** 398 **Ports:** Abidjan, Sassandra, San Pedro **Major Airlines:** State-owned Air Ivoire is the domestic carrier; Air Afrique, a multinational airline, provides the main regional service **Communications:** Government owned **Radio Transmitters:** 17 **Receivers:** 600,000 (1976) **Television Transmitters:** 10 **Receivers:** 257,000 (1976) **Telephones:** 70,000 (1976) **Newspapers:** 3 dailies, 7 copies per 1,000 inhabitants (1975)

Weights and Measures: Metric system **Travel Requirements:** Passport; visa; onward ticket

---

The Ivory Coast, the richest and most economically self-sufficient state in former French West Africa (now Senegal, Guinea, Mali, Upper Volta, Mauritania, Benin, Niger, and Ivory Coast), is located on the south side of the African bulge and is slightly larger than New Mexico. The southern boundary is a 340-mile coastline on the Gulf of Guinea, characterized by heavy surf and a lack of natural harbors. Early European voyagers were discouraged by this coastline and the dense tropical forest, as well as by the scant gold to be found there. As a result, they established their forts farther to the east on the Gold Coast, now Ghana.

Shortly after the former French colony became independent in 1960, officials of the International Monetary Fund advised Ivorian leaders to coordinate fiscal and development planning, encourage competitive private enterprise, and create a favorable investment climate—advice Ivorians followed with huge success.

Ivorian President Félix Houphouët-Boigny, who continues to head the government, set up incentives for foreign investors. Himself an experienced administrator in French government service, he brought in top French economic planners to minutely map development.

Helped by high earnings from coffee and cocoa, the Ivory Coast concentrated initially on diversifying agriculture. Systematically, large new plantations of rubber, palm oil, pineapples, sugarcane, rice, and cotton were established. Proven pe-

troleum reserves have been found that could make Ivory Coast self-sufficient for fuel.

Since 1960 the Ivorian gross national product has grown by more than 11 percent a year, and the per capita income is among the highest in black Africa. Projects are under way to spread the prosperity of Abidjan, the capital, to other parts of the country. The new port of San Pedro, designed to open up the little-developed southwestern area, has been completed and iron-ore deposits in the northwest are being readied for development.

Although the French still maintain a strong economic position, they have had to share it with increasing numbers of German, Dutch, British, American, Italian, and Israeli enterprises.

Despite the impressive progress, along with increases of public housing, education, and health facilities, there remains an urgent need for raising rural living standards and creating employment.

HISTORY: Although evidence of a neolithic culture has been found in the Ivory Coast, little is known of the country's past before the first contacts by Portuguese and French in the 16th century. The Baoulés and the Agnis, both related to the Ashantis of Ghana, did not arrive until the 18th century, and most of the other tribal groups have their main centers in neighboring countries. The French began to establish control over the area in the 19th century and succeeded in colonizing it after much local resistance

1893: Ivory Coast is organized as a French protectorate

1898: Anti-French resistance collapses with the defeat of Almamy Samory, the Malinké warrior chief

1946-57: Félix Houphouët-Boigny founds African Democratic Rally, the first all-African political party; he is elected to the French National Assembly and wins far-reaching freedoms for France's African territories

1947: Upper Volta is detached from the Ivory Coast

1958: Ivory Coast becomes an autonomous republic within the French Community

1959: Houphouët-Boigny becomes premier

1960: Ivory Coast achieves full independence; Houphouët-Boigny is elected president

1963: More than 80 persons, including government ministers and Guinean nationals, are convicted of plotting to stage a coup and assassinate the president

1967: Ivory Coast and Guinea exchange prisoners in effort to smooth relations

1970: President Houphouët-Boigny, unopposed, is elected to his third term as president

1974: Proposals for dialogue between black African nations and South Africa lead to talks between South African Premier John Vorster and President Houphouët-Boigny

1975: President Houphouët-Boigny reelected without opposition for another five-year term. Constitution is amended so that in event of his death or incapacity the automatic successor would be the president of the National Assembly

1979: Asylum is granted to Bokassa I, deposed ruler of Central African Empire

1980: Oil begins to flow from offshore drilling site

JAMAICA

Area: 4,244 sq. mi. **Population:** 2,133,000 (1978 est.)

Official Name: Jamaica **Capital:** Kingston **Nationality:** Jamaican **Languages:** English is the official and dominant language; a Jamaican Creole, a mixture of archaic English and African, is also used **Religion:** 75% Protestant, 5% Roman Catholic, 20% other religions or no affiliation **Flag:** A gold diagonal cross, or saltire, divides the flag into four triangles; the top and bottom triangles are green and the remaining two are black **Anthem:** National Anthem, beginning "Eternal Father bless our land" **Currency:** Jamaican dollar (1.78 per U.S. $1)

Location: West Indies. The island of Jamaica lies in the Caribbean Sea, about 90 miles south of Cuba and 100 miles west of Haiti **Features:** Mountains cover about 80% of the island; lowlands stretch across the western end and a narrow plain covers the south **Chief Rivers:** Black, Minho, Cobre

Head of State: Queen Elizabeth II, represented by a governor-general, Florizel Glasspole, appointed June 1973 **Head of Government:** Prime Minister Michael N. Manley, born 1924?, appointed 1972 and again in 1976 **Effective Date of Present Constitution:** 1962 **Legislative Body:** Parliament (bicameral), consisting of the Senate and the House of Representatives. The Senate is composed of 21 members, 13 of whom are appointed by the governor-general on the advice of the prime minister and the rest on the advice of the leader of the opposition. The 60-member House of Representatives is elected; terms in both houses cannot exceed 5 years **Local Government:** 14 parishes, 12 of which are administered by elected councils. Kingston and St. Andrew are jointly governed by a corporation

Ethnic Composition: About 95% of the population is of African and mixed descent; other racial and nationality groups are Chinese, East Indian, Syrian, and European **Population Distribution:** 41% urban **Density:** 503 inhabitants per sq. mi.

Largest Cities: (1975 est.) Kingston 600,000 (metro area), Montego Bay 50,000, Spanish Town 50,000, May Pen 26,074 (1970)

Per Capita Income: $1,404 (1979) **Gross National Product (GNP):** $3.4 billion (1979) **Economic Statistics:** About 15% of GNP comes from manufacturing (sugar processing, rum, beer, clothing, furniture); 14% from wholesale and retail trade; 11% from agriculture (sugar, bananas, cocoa, coffee, citrus fruits, copra), forestry and fishing; 11% from construction; and 10% from mining and refining **Minerals and Mining:** Jamaica is one of the world's largest producers of bauxite; other minerals of commercial significance are gypsum, silica, marble, and limestone **Labor Force:** 859,500 (1975), with 31% in agriculture, forestry, fishing and mining; 26% in public administration and commerce; 19% in manufacturing and construction; 4% in transport and communication; and 20% in other services **Foreign Trade:** Exports, chiefly bauxite, alumina, sugar, rum, molasses, and bananas, totaled $807 million in 1978. Imports, mainly fuel, foodstuffs, manufactured goods, machinery and transportation equipment, totaled $800 million **Principal Trade Partners:** United States, Britain, Canada, Venezuela, Caribbean countries

Vital Statistics: Birthrate, 30 per 1,000 of pop. (1976); death rate, 7 **Life Expectancy:** 69 years **Health Statistics:** 257 inhabitants per hospital bed; 3,509 per physician (1974) **Infant Mortality:** 20 per 1,000 births (1976) **Illiteracy:** 18% **Primary and Secondary School Enrollment:** 593,366 **Enrollment in Higher Education:** 9,039 **GNP Expended on Education:** 6.9% (1976)

Transportation: Paved roads total about 4,700 mi. **Motor Vehicles:** 151,591 (1974) **Passenger Cars:** 109,628 **Railway Mileage:** 205 **Ports:** Kingston, Portland Bight **Major Airlines:** Air Jamaica operates international service; Trans-Jamaican Air Service provides domestic flights **Communications:** Government owned **Radio Transmitters:** 21 **Receivers:** 555,000 (1976) **Television Transmitters:** 13 **Receivers:** 111,000 (1976) **Telephones:** 109,000 (1976) **Newspapers:** 3 dailies, 91 copies per 1,000 inhabitants (1976)

Weights and Measures: Metric and British standards are used **Travel Requirements:** Proof of U.S. citizenship; return ticket

---

Like other Caribbean countries, Jamaica is trying to deal with an economy and a society in difficult transition. From slave days, Jamaica's mountains and lush fields, under British ownership, produced sugar, coffee, bananas, and spices. While these are still the economic mainstays, the island is striving now for more balance.

Industry and tourism are the watchwords, and investment in both in the last decade has been considerable. The sugar industry remains the island's single biggest employer, but, agriculture overall has fallen behind industry in its contribution to the gross national product.

Disaffection with agriculture—particularly with the sugar industry, an activity associated with slave exploitation—has caused an influx into Kingston in search of industrial and service jobs. Industry and tourism have not kept pace with the demand, and the result has been a jobless rate currently of about 30 percent and heavy emigration to the U.S. and Britain.

Prime Minister Michael Manley won a huge mandate for his program of democratic socialism in 1976. The government has purchased eight of the island's 12 sugar estates, and it operates a cement company and a banana company. But the economy has experienced a long decline. Sugar and cement production fell in 1979, and the banana operation reportedly lost money. Late that year, foreign banks, which had lent Jamaica $450 million, declined to lend more. Jamaica turned to the International Monetary Fund, but in January 1980, Manley broke off talks when the IMF wanted him

to lay off 11,000 government workers as a loan precondition. In May, he reported that a $50 million loan from Libya and $58 million worth of help from six other sources would stave off "a predicted collapse of the country's economy."

In February 1980, Manley called for elections to be held later in the year. More than a score of persons were killed in pre-election political violence.

HISTORY: Jamaica was inhabited by Arawak Indians when Columbus discovered the island in 1494. It was settled by the Spaniards early in the 16th century and remained under Spanish rule until 1655, when it was captured by the English. By the 18th century most of the Arawaks had died off, but a huge population of black slaves grew up around the island's sugar plantations. With the abolition of slavery in 1833, the plantation economy suffered a severe blow, resulting in long-lasting poverty and social unrest

1865-66: Uprising by blacks leads to imposition of martial law; British parliament establishes a crown colony government

1944: Britain grants the island a new constitution based on adult suffrage and a wide measure of self-government

1953: Island is granted full internal autonomy

1958-62: Jamaica joins West Indies Federation in 1958 along with nine other British possessions in the Caribbean; three years later, however, the island withdraws; in August 1962, Jamaica wins full independence, with Sir Alexander Bustamente, the island's labor leader, as prime minister

1967: Hugh Shearer becomes prime minister following sudden death of Sir Donald Sangster, leader of Jamaica Labor party

1968: Jamaica joins Caribbean Free Trade Association

1972: Jamaica Labor party is defeated in general election by People's National party; Michael Manley becomes prime minister

1974: The Suppression of Crime Act passed unanimously by the legislature. Its purpose is to reduce the rash of murders and other violent crimes on Jamaica. It provides for secret trials, no bail, and, for convicted offenders, indeterminate prison sentences

1975: Jamaica signs treaty with EC and reaches agreements with foreign companies mining bauxite on the island whereby the government would purchase controlling shares of stock

1976: Martial law is declared in Kingston because of violence among warring extremist factions of Prime Minister Manley's People's National party (PNP) and the opposition Jamaica Labor party (JLP). PNP wins overwhelming victory

1977: U.S. announces $63.3-million aid package to help Jamaica with its economic problems

1978: Government launches five-year economic program based on land reform

1979: Tourism drops after seven die in gasoline-price riots. A June storm kills 40 and damages crops

1980: The debt-plagued government breaks off loan talks with the International Monetary Fund, and commercial banks refuse to lend more, causing a foreign-exchange shortage that slows industry. A nursing home fire in Kingston kills at least 144 elderly women. In February, Manley calls for elections later in the year

---

JAPAN

Area: 145,730 sq. mi. **Population:** 115,870,000 (1979 est.)

Official Name: Japan **Capital:** Tokyo **Nationality:** Japanese **Languages:** Japanese is the official and universal language **Religion:** Buddhism and Shintoism are the chief religions; virtually all Japanese practice one or the other and most subscribe to both **Flag:** A red sun on a white field **Anthem:** The Reign of Our Emperor **Currency:** Yen (239 per U.S. $1)

Location: Japan is an archipelago forming a 2,360-mile-long arc off the east coast of Asia, between the Sea of Japan and the Pacific Ocean proper. It consists of four main islands: Hokkaido, Honshu, Shikoku, and Kyushu, and more than 3,000 smaller islands **Features:** 72% of the country is covered by hills and mountains, many of them active or dormant volcanoes. Because of the country's unstable geological position beside the Pacific deeps, numerous earthquakes are felt throughout the islands **Chief Rivers:** Tone, Shinano, Ishikari, Kitakami

Head of State: Emperor Hirohito, born 1901, ascended the throne 1926 **Head of Government:** Prime Minister Zenko Suzuki, born 1911, elected July 1980 **Effective Date of Present Constitution:** May 3, 1947 **Legislative Body:** Parliament, or Diet (bicameral), consisting of the House of Representatives and the House of Councillors. The House of Representatives has 511 members elected for 4 years. The House of Councillors has 252 members elected for 6 years

Local Government: 43 prefectures, each with an elected governor and local assembly, 2 urban prefectures, 1 metropolitan prefecture, and 1 territory

Ethnic Composition: The Japanese are a Mongoloid people, closely related to the other groups of east Asia, although there is evidence of admixture with Malayan and Caucasoid strains. Over 700,000 Koreans constitute the only important minority group; about 15,000 Ainu in Hokkaido, physically similar to Caucasians, are rapidly being assimilated **Population Distribution:** 76% urban **Density:** 795 inhabitants per sq. mi.

Largest Cities: (1975 census) Tokyo 8,646,520, Osaka 2,778,987, Yokohama 2,621,771, Nagoya 2,079,740, Kyoto 1,461,059, Kobe 1,360,605, Sapporo 1,240,613, Kitakyushu 1,058,058, Kawasaki 1,014,951

Per Capita Income: $7,245 (1979) **Gross National Product (GNP):** $839 billion (1979) **Economic Statistics:** 36.8% of GNP comes from industry (transportation equipment, electrical machinery, iron and steel, ships, chemicals), 8.1% from agriculture (rice, vegetables, fruit, wheat, barley, fish, and potatoes), 23.1% from trade, 11.1% from services **Minerals and Mining:** Coal is plentiful, but only about 25% can be used for industrial purposes. There are small amounts of zinc, limestone, lead, and sulphur **Labor Force:** 54,500,000 (1977) with 36% employed in industry, 12% in agriculture, and 52% in trade and services **Foreign Trade:** Exports, chiefly iron and steel, textiles, electronic equipment, motor vehicles, ships, totaled $98 billion in 1978. Imports, chiefly mineral fuels, metal ores and scrap, machinery and equipment, and foodstuffs, totaled $80 billion **Principal Trade Partners:** United States, Australia, Canada, Iran, South Korea, West Germany, Kuwait, Britain, Saudi Arabia, Indonesia, China

Vital Statistics: Birthrate, 15.5 per 1,000 of pop. (1977); death rate, 6.1 **Life Expectancy:** 74 years **Health Statistics:** 95 inhabitants per hospital bed; 845 per physician (1976) **Infant Mortality:** 8.9 per 1,000 births **Illiteracy:** Negligible **Primary and Secondary School Enrollment:** 20,069,305 pupils (1977) **Enrollment in Higher Education:** 2,354,841 **GNP Expended on Education:** 5.5% (1975)

Transportation: Paved roads total 243,212 mi. **Motor Vehicles:** 31,379,000 (1977) **Passenger Cars:** 19,826,000 **Railway Mileage:** 31,000 mi. **Ports:** Yokohama, Kobe, Tokyo, Nagoya, Osaka, Chiba, Kawasaki, Hakodate **Major Airlines:** Japan Air Lines, partly government owned and partly privately financed, operates international and domestic flights **Communications:** Government and privately owned **Radio Transmitters:** 944 **Receivers:** 59,650,000 (1976) **Television Transmitters:** 6,117 **Receivers:** 26,545,000 (1975) **Telephones:** 50,600,000 **Newspapers:** 180 dailies, 526 copies per 1,000 inhabitants (1974)

Weights and Measures: Metric system **Travel Requirements:** Passport, visa, valid 60 days

---

Japan, having soared from crushing defeat in World War II to a position among the world's leading industrial nations, is today building for itself an international role commensurate with its economic power, while attempting at the same time to resolve the great social problems caused by swift industrialization.

Crowded into a small island territory off the Asian mainland and isolated from the world by their own choice for centuries prior to 1854, the Japanese created a distinctive society and culture. There has been a large measure of modernization and Westernization, but traditional customs, social practices, and business procedures still are deep-rooted.

Close government/business ties and encouragement for export industries enabled Japan to build a huge international trade throughout the 1970s, while curbs on imports and foreign investments continued to afford protection for domestic industry. Eventually, the trade gap between Japan and the U.S. widened so greatly that relations between the two countries became acrimonious. As protectionist sentiment rose in the U.S., the Japanese voluntarily cut down on their shipments of TV sets and automobiles, removed some restraints on importing foreign goods, and sent buying missions to the U.S. On June 30, 1980, the U.S. lifted a three-year quota agreement on imports of color TV sets from Japan—in part because seven Japanese manufacturers had set up plants in the U.S.

By the start of the 1980s, the Japanese clearly had moved beyond the roles of traders and merchants engaged in export and had also become worldwide investors, producing Japanese goods overseas. In 1980, for example, Honda and Nissan announced plans to build cars in the U.S.; a deal was made with Rolls-Royce to build jet engines in Britain and Japan; and Japanese heavy industry companies joined with Australia's state of Victoria in plans to build a coal liquefaction plant. The country's Ministry of International Trade and Industry (MITI) provides a cohesive business-government approach—sometimes called "Japan Inc."—that has proved effective in economic expansion. The approach includes official subsidy and direction, such as "administrative guidances" in concentrating computer research efforts.

With only one brief interruption, Japan has been ruled by conservatives during the postwar years under the "no-war" 1946 constitution, which was imposed by American occupation authorities. The constitution provided the framework for democratic development and made the emperor, who had served as the nationalistic symbol for prewar militarism, a largely ceremonial chief of state.

Support for the ruling Liberal Democratic party (LDP), which derived much of its strength in rural areas, has gradually declined as a result of the migration, within two decades, of more than one-third of Japan's population from the countryside to the cities. The 1976 Lockheed scandal, involving LDP members accused of accepting bribes from the U.S.-based Lockheed Aircraft Corporation in exchange for lucrative sales contracts, also damaged the party's standing. The 1979 McDonnell Douglas and Grumman scandal, also arising from aircraft sales, again turned the spotlight on the activities of the trading companies and Japanese politicians. The LDP entered the 1980 elections fearing that it would win with such small margins that it would have to share power in a coalition. Instead, it won handily—thanks, in part, to a sympathy vote when Prime Minister Masayoshi Ohira died during the campaign—but questions remained as to whether long-squabbling factions could achieve unity. In July a little-known LDP politician, Zenko Suzuki, was chosen as prime minister.

Pollution of air and water have reached near-crisis proportions. Despite depletion of the rural population, farmland remains fragmented and an outdated subsidy system has caused huge overproduction of rice. A critical housing shortage persists, transport systems are overburdened, the educational structure is in need of broad reform, and social welfare systems are on a modest scale.

In recent years American troops and bases in Japan have been substantially reduced and, though still sheltered under the American nuclear umbrella, Japan has assumed responsibility for its own defense against any conventional attack. The security treaty with the United States, which provoked a major crisis in 1960, was quietly allowed to remain in effect, but the pace and extent of rearmament is once again a vital political issue. Japan has been spending less than 1% of its gross national product on defense. Worries have been increased by the USSR's rising sea strength and troop deployments on the Asian mainland and on nearby islands, and by Japan's almost total dependence on imported energy, principally Mideast oil.

Although in 1972 Japan restored diplomatic ties with China, its giant neighbor and source of much of its cultural tradition, the peace treaty was not ratified until October 1978, because special care had to be exercised to avoid offending another giant neighbor and traditional enemy, the Soviet Union.

HISTORY: Legend attributes the founding of the Japanese empire to Jimmu, a lineal descendant of the sun goddess and ancestor of the present imperial dynasty, in 660 B.C. Reliable records of Japanese history, however, date back only to about 400 A.D. From the 6th to 8th century, Japan came under the strong cultural influence of China and Buddhism was introduced. The development of a feudal system weakened the already diminished power of the emperors, who were to remain in obscurity for 700 years

1192: Yoritomo, leader of the feudal family of Minamato, takes the title of shogun (military governor) and sets up dictatorship

1542: First European contact is established with the arrival of Portuguese sailors

1637: Tokugawa shogunate bans all intercourse with the outside world, with the exception of Dutch traders in Nagasaki

1854: Commodore Matthew C. Perry, a U.S. naval officer, forces the opening of Japanese trade with the West

1867-68: Shogunate collapses and power is restored to Emperor Mutsuhito; Meiji Restoration, so called after emperor's reign name, is followed by formation of a pro-Western government which proceeds to modernize Japan

1894-95: Japan defeats China in Sino-Japanese War and annexes Formosa, the Pescadores, and Liaotung peninsula

1904-05: Russian power is smashed by Japanese in Russo-Japanese War

1910: Japan annexes Korea

1931: Japan seizes Manchuria from China and sets up puppet state of Manchukuo

1937: Japan invades China's northern provinces; Chinese resistance leads to full-scale though undeclared war

1940: Japan signs military alliance with Germany and Italy

1941-45: Surprise Japanese attack on Pearl Harbor in December 1941 triggers U.S. entry into World War II; successive Japanese victories give Japan control over vast territories stretching from India to the Aleutians; in late 1942, however, tide begins to turn and Japan loses ground to Allies; with the dropping of U.S. atomic bombs on Hiroshima and Nagasaki, Japan is forced to surrender and is occupied by U.S. forces

1946-47: The occupation, under direction of General Douglas MacArthur, initiates series of reforms aimed at democratization and demilitarization of Japan; a new constitution is adopted and emperor publicly disclaims his divinity

1954: Japan and United States sign military assistance pact

1960: Antigovernment riots and protests against military pacts force cancellation of visit by U.S. President Eisenhower

1964: Eisaku Sato becomes prime minister

1969: Japan steps up demand for the return of Okinawa, occupied by U.S. forces since World War II

1970: Japan renews security pact with United States

1971: Agreement is reached on reversion of Okinawa from U.S. to Japanese rule; Emperor Hirohito becomes first reigning monarch to leave Japan, visiting seven countries in Europe

1972: Okinawa is returned to Japan; Japan opens diplomatic relations with China. Eisaku Sato resigns as prime minister and is succeeded by Kakuei Tanaka

1974: Tanaka resigns as a result of accusations that he used his political office to amass a personal fortune. Takeo Miki becomes prime minister

1975: Emperor Hirohito makes first visit to U.S. by a reigning Japanese monarch

1976: Revelations emerge concerning $12.6 million in alleged payoffs by Lockheed Aircraft Corp. (U.S.) to secure Japanese aircraft contracts. Tanaka is arrested. Miki resigns after his party (LDP) suffers setback in elections. LDP leader, Takeo Fukuda, is elected prime minister by House of Representatives

1977: Prime Minister Fukuda shuffles cabinet in effort to better deal with Japan's mounting trade surplus and strained economic relations with industrial nations; he calls it the "gravest situation" since World War II

1978: New Tokyo International Airport opens under heavy guard as protesters try to disrupt flights (the facility has long been opposed by displaced farmers and leftist radicals, who delayed its opening five years). Earthquake near Tokyo is worst in 14 years; 21 persons are killed, 350 injured. On October 23, four decades after Japan invaded China, the two countries exchange ratifications of a peace treaty. Masayoshi Ohira defeats Fukuda in a party election and as a result becomes Japan's prime minister on Dec. 7

1979: Ohira visits U.S. President Carter and they jointly pledge to seek "over the next several years a more harmonious pattern of international trade and payments." The LDP wins a September election but lacks a majority until independents lend support; Ohira then narrowly defeats Fukuda in a parliamentary contest for prime minister

1980: Honda Motor Co. announces that it will build a U.S. plant (at Marysville, Ohio), and Nissan Motor Co. (Datsun cars and trucks) also says it will establish a U.S. plant. Japan and the U.S. sign an agreement for joint research on high-risk, high-technology problems. A no-confidence vote topples the Ohira government in May. Ohira dies on June 12—10 days before the next

parlimentary elections, in which he is a candidate—but the LDP wins by strong majorities and Zenko Suzuki becomes prime minister

---

JORDAN

Area: 37,737 sq. mi. **Population:** 2,984,000 (1978 est.)

Official Name: Hashemite Kingdom of Jordan **Capital:** Amman **Nationality:** Jordanian **Languages:** Arabic is the official and universal language **Religion:** 95% Sunni Moslem, 5% Christian **Flag:** Horizontal black, white, and green stripes, with a seven-pointed white star on a red triangle at the staff **Anthem:** The Royal Salute **Currency:** Jordanian dinar (.30 per U.S. $1)

Location: Southwest Asia. Jordan is bordered by Syria on the north, Iraq on the northeast, Saudi Arabia on the east and south, and Israel on the west **Features:** About four fifths of the country consists of desert. The Jordan River valley divides the land into the small, rocky West Bank (controlled by Israel) and the large East Bank, the latter forming a dry plateau that slopes to flat terrain in the northeast **Chief Rivers:** Jordan, Yarmuk

Head of State: King Hussein Ibn Talal, born 1935, ascended the throne 1953. He has veto power over the National Assembly **Head of Government:** Prime Minister Mudar Badran, born 1934, reappointed August 1980 **Effective Date of Present Constitution:** 1952, amended 1974 and 1976 **Legislative Body:** National Assembly (bicameral) consists of a 60-seat House of Representatives (dissolved by the King in 1976) and a Senate of 30 members, appointed by the King. A National Consultative Council, with advisory functions, was established in 1978 **Local Government:** 8 governorates, each headed by an appointed governor; 3 are in the Israeli-occupied West Bank

Ethnic Composition: Virtually 100% Arab **Population Distribution:** 44% urban **Density:** 79 inhabitants per sq. mi.

Largest Cities: (1976 est.) Amman 671,560, Zarqa 251,430, Irbid 130,880

Per Capita Income: $988 (1979) **Gross National Product (GNP):** $2.2 billion (1979) **Economic Statistics:** About 10% of GNP comes from agriculture (wheat, citrus fruits, olives, grapes, melons, vegetables, barley), 25% from industry (phosphate mining, cement, beverages, tobacco, soap, oil refining, tanning, vegetable oils), and 65% from trade and services **Minerals and Mining:** Exploited minerals include phosphates, potash, copper, and marble; manganese, iron, sulphur and oil deposits also exist **Labor Force:** 638,000, with 20% in agriculture, 20% in industry, and 60% in trade and services **Foreign Trade:** Exports, chiefly fruits and vegetables, phosphates, cement, and marble, totaled $310 million in 1978. Imports, mainly foodstuffs, machinery, vehicles, petroleum, and textiles, totaled $1.5 billion **Principal Trade Partners:** EC countries, United States, Lebanon, Iraq, Kuwait, Saudi Arabia, Japan, Syria, Romania

Vital Statistics: Birthrate, 41.0 per 1,000 of pop. (1977); death rate, 14.7 **Life Expectancy:** 52 years **Health Statistics:** 937 inhabitants per hospital bed; 2,438 per physician (1974) **Infant Mortality:** 21.6 per 1,000 births **Illiteracy:** 38% **Primary and Secondary School Enrollment:** 588,101 (1976) **Enrollment in Higher Education:** 9,302 **GNP Expended on Education:** 3.5% (1976)

Transportation: Paved roads total 3,440 mi. **Motor Vehicles:** 78,000 (1977) **Passenger Cars:** 57,000 **Railway Mileage:** 500 **Port:** Aqaba **Major Airlines:** Royal Jordanian Airlines (ALIA) operates international services **Communications:** Government owned **Radio Transmitters:** 7 **Receivers:** 531,000 (1976) **Television Transmitters:** 3 **Receivers:** 125,000 (1976) **Telephones:** 44,000 (1976) **Newspapers:** 4 dailies, 18 copies per 1,000 inhabitants (1975)

Weights and Measures: Metric system **Travel Requirements:** Passport, visa valid for 4 years for multiple entry, no fee

---

The Hashemite Kingdom of Jordan is a largely uninhabited desert, about the size of Indiana. In 1921, after centuries of Turkish rule, the area now comprising Jordan and Israel was awarded to the United Kingdom by the League of Nations as the Mandates for Palestine and Transjordan. In 1922, Britain divided the administration of the Mandate and established Abdullah, grandfather of the present King Hussein, as ruler of a semi-autonomous Amirate of Transjordan in the area east of the Jordan River. The western portion (Palestine) remained under the administration of a British High Commissioner.

Britain granted the eastern territory full independence in 1946, with Abdullah as king. When Arab Palestinians and Jews fought each other and the British for the control of Palestine, Britain asked the UN to help settle the conflict. The UN suggested that Palestine be divided into two states, one Jewish and one Arab.

In the fighting which broke out upon the proclamation of Israeli statehood in 1948, the Transjordan Arab Legion occupied most of the West Bank territories allotted to the Arab Palestinians in the United Nations partition plan, including East Jerusalem, and the Jews established the state of Israel, in large measure on the land given to them in the UN plan. Transjordan became the Hashemite Kingdom of Jordan in 1949.

The present ruler, Hussein Ibn Talal, became king in 1953. In 1967, during the Six-Day War, Israel occupied the West Bank territories.

The problems of the Middle East—particularly, resolution of Arab-Israeli issues—dominate Jordan's foreign policy. The current Mideast peace negotiations, with respect to Jordan, revolve around the ultimate disposition of the Israeli-occupied West Bank and Arab Jerusalem and the issue of the roles for Jordan and the Palestinian Liberation Organization (PLO) in the negotiations. Within Jordan, there is friction between the Palestinian refugees and the Bedouins—the principal ethnic group of unoccupied Jordan.

Following the decision of the Rabat summit conference of Arab heads of state in October 1974 to recognize the PLO's right to represent all Palestinians, King Hussein gave the PLO and its leader, Yassir Arafat, the responsibility for the West Bank. The king dissolved parliament and reorganized his cabinet, reducing its Palestinian membership. He summoned a new parliament in 1976 for a brief session.

Hussein's foreign policy—long pro-Western—has become increasingly favorable to Arab aspirations—largely because of increasing foreign aid from Arab oil states to his resource-poor kingdom. In 1980, Hussein refused again to commit Jordan to joining the peace negotiations under the Israeli-Egyptian 1979 peace treaty, which had promised Palestinian autonomy in the West Bank. Nevertheless, the United States agreed to sell Jordan 100 M-20 tanks to bolster its defenses.

HISTORY: The present territory of Jordan was the biblical home of the Moabites, the Ammonites, the Edomites, and some Hebrew tribes. It was conquered in 64 B.C. by Rome, in the 7th century A.D. by Moslem Arabs (from whom it derived its now-prevailing language and religion), in the 16th century by the Ottoman Empire, and in 1916 by Britain

1916: Sykes-Picot Agreement between France and Britain divides Ottoman holdings, with Transjordan (the present East Bank) in British sphere of influence

1921: British recognize Abdullah as ruler of Transjordan and Hashemite dynasty is founded

1928: Britain recognizes Transjordan as independent but retains suzerainty in the form of military and financial control

1946: Kingdom of Transjordan is proclaimed

1948: British mandate ends, fighting breaks out with new state of Israel

1949: Transjordan and Israel sign armistice, with Transjordan in control of West Bank and part of Jerusalem. Transjordan adopts name of Hashemite Kingdom of Jordan

1950: Arab Palestine (West Bank) is formally annexed by Jordan

1951: King Abdullah is assassinated in Jerusalem. His son, Talal, becomes king

1952: Talal is declared insane and ousted; his son, Hussein, becomes king

1967: King Hussein and President Nasser of Egypt sign mutual defense pact. Jordan is drawn into Six-Day War with Israel, which occupies all of Jerusalem and all of West Bank

1968-69: Israel attacks Arab guerrilla bases on East Bank

1970: Guerrillas hijack four Western airliners to Jordan and hold crews and passengers hostage; all are later released. Civil war breaks out between guerrillas and Jordanian forces

1971: Jordanian army's July offensive virtually eliminates all guerrilla bases. Syria severs relations with Jordan. Prime Minister Wasfi Al Tal is assassinated in Cairo

1973: Jordan joins in war against Israel

1974: Arab leaders at a summit conference recognize the Palestine Liberation Organization as the sole representative of the Palestinian people; King Hussein concurs

1975: Syria and Jordan establish a joint military command

1976: Syria and Jordan co-ordinate their foreign diplomatic representation in countries where either one maintains a mission. King Hussein reconvenes parliament, with representatives of the West Bank in attendance, after having dissolved it in 1974 to decrease Palestinian participation in Jordanian politics. Prime Minister Zaid al-Rifai resigns and King Hussein asks Mudar Badran, chief of the cabinet, to form a new government

1977: Queen Alia is killed in helicopter crash

1978: King Hussein marries Elizabeth Halaby, 26-year-old American and proclaims her Jordan's new queen

1980: Hussein visits Washington, D.C., for talks with President Carter; refuses to join Israeli-Egyptian peace negotiations

---

KENYA

Area: 224,960 sq. mi. **Population:** 15,322,000 (1979 est.)

Official Name: Republic of Kenya **Capital:** Nairobi **Nationality:** Kenyan **Languages:** Swahili and English are used officially; of more than 30 languages, Kikuyu and Luo are the most used **Religion:** 56% are Christian, 36% animist, 7% Moslem, 1% Hindu **Flag:** Horizontal stripes of black, red, and green, with the center red stripe bordered in white; a shield with black and white markings, and crossed spears behind, appears in the center of the flag **Anthem:** National Anthem, beginning "O, God of all Creation" **Currency:** Kenya shilling (7.4 per U.S. $1)

Location: East Africa. Kenya is bordered on the north by Sudan and Ethiopia, on the east by Somalia and the Indian Ocean, on the south by Tanzania, and on the west by Uganda **Features:** The Great Rift Valley in the center and west is girded by rugged plateaus and mountains. To the east are dry bush land and a marshy coastal plain. In the north the land turns to scrub and desert. Kenya has numerous lakes, including a portion of Lake Victoria **Chief Rivers:** Tana, Athi-Galana, Suam-Turkwel, Keiro

Head of State and of Government: President Daniel arap Moi, born 1924, took office in 1978, elected 1979 **Effective Date of Present Constitution:** 1963, revised 1969 **Legislative Body:** National Assembly (unicameral), consisting of 158 members elected for up to 5 years and 12 members nominated by the president **Local Government:** 7 provinces and the Nairobi area

Ethnic Composition: 30-40 groups fall into four main linguistic divisions: the Bantu, who constitute the majority, Nilo-Hamitics, Nilotics, and Hamitics. The largest tribes are the Kikuyu, Luhya, Luo, Kamba, Kisii and Meru. There are some 200,000 non-Africans, including Arabs, Europeans, and Hindu and Moslem Indians **Population Distribution:** 10% urban **Density:** 68 inhabitants per sq. mi.

Largest Cities: (1977 est.) Nairobi 776,000, Mombasa 371,000, (1976 est.) Nakuru 66,000, Kisumu 46,000

Per Capita Income: $291 (1979) **Gross National Product (GNP):** $4.5 billion (1979) **Economic Statistics:** About 20% of GNP comes from manufacturing (chiefly agricultural processing, oil refining, and small-scale consumer goods), mining and quarrying; 18% from trade, transportation and communications; 27% from services and about 31% from agriculture (coffee, tea, pyrethrum, sisal, livestock, meat and dairy products, wool, hides, corn, wheat, millet, and cassava), forestry, and fishing **Minerals and Mining:** Small quantities of soda ash, fluorspar, limestone, salt, copper, gold, and silver are produced **Labor Force:** 5,400,000 (1971), 86% in agriculture and 13% in industry **Foreign Trade:** Exports, chiefly coffee, tea, sisal, pyrethrum extract and flowers, meat and meat preparations, totaled $958 million in 1978. Imports, mainly machinery, transport equipment, manufactured goods, lubricants, and chemicals, totaled $1.8 billion **Principal Trade Partners:** EC countries, United States, Japan, Saudi Arabia, Iran, Zambia, India, Sweden, Uganda, China

Vital Statistics: Birthrate, 48 per 1,000 of pop.; (1976) death rate, 14 **Life Expectancy:** 51 years **Health Statistics:** 759 inhabitants per hospital bed; 16,292 per physician (1973) **Infant Mortality:** 51.4 per 1,000 births **Illiteracy:** 70% **Primary and Secondary School Enrollment:** 3,183,673 (1976) **Enrollment in Higher Education:** 11,351 (1974) **GNP Expended on Education:** 5.7% (1974)

Transportation: Paved roads total 2,700 mi. **Motor Vehicles:** 198,000 (1977) **Passenger Cars:** 114,100 **Railway Mileage:** 1,500 **Port:** Mombasa **Major Airlines:** Kenya Airways operates domestic and international services **Communications:** Government controlled **Radio Transmitters:** 18 **Receivers:** 514,000 (1976) **Television Transmitters:** 5 **Receivers:** 50,000 (1976) **Telephones:** 144,000 **Newspapers:** 3 dailies, 10 copies per 1,000 inhabitants (1975)

Weights and Measures: Metric system, with some English measures still used **Travel Requirements:** Passport, visa, valid 6 months. $3.15 fee

---

Kenya is one of Africa's best-known countries; the land of the safari, gameparks, and the lure of the green hills Ernest Hemingway made famous. Tourism has grown spectacularly, with annual earnings rivaling those from coffee export.

The Asian population is being rapidly reduced under a phased program of canceling government permits for Asians to carry on businesses. The influence of the European community is also declining.

Kenya has made considerable progress in industry and in agriculture, particularly in the success of African farmers settled on the former large British holdings in the old "White Highlands." But these gains have been offset by high population growth, unemployment, and drought. A slump in world demand for coffee and tea produced a severe trade deficit in 1978, continuing into 1979, and prompting the government to restrict imports. Kenya is energy-poor, but is developing hydroelectric power on the Tana River.

In leading the former British colony to independence in 1963, President Jomo Kenyatta stressed the need for unity with the slogan of *Harambee!* (Swahili for "Let us all pull together"). Kenyatta, affectionately known as *Mzee* ("the Old One"), was able to hold Kenya together, but not without strain. The Kenyatta government's strength was tested in 1975 when a wave of political unrest was touched off by the murder of Josiah Kariuki, a popular member of parliament and critic of Kenyatta. An investigation committee implicated police officials and top aides of Kenyatta, and the Assembly voted to accept the committee's report on the murder.

Although all Assembly members belong to Kenya's only party, the Kenya African National Union (KANU), dissident members formed an opposition group, which resulted in a KANU leadership decree that any Assembly member not following the party position would be expelled.

In August 1978, Kenyatta died peacefully in his sleep. Daniel arap Moi, 54, became president.

HISTORY: Kenya's coast was a familiar area to mariners of past eras, including Phoenicians, Egyptians, and Greeks. Arab coastal colonies were established as early as the 8th century and in the 15th century Portuguese joined in the thriving spice and slave trade. Britain gained a foothold in the 19th century and in 1895 established a protectorate over the area, then known as British East Africa. With the influx of British and South African settlers, Kenya continued to be dominated by the white population

1944: Africans win token political representation with the appointment of the first black member of the Legislative Council

1952-59: Mau Mau rebellion, led by secret terrorist organization comprising mainly Kikuyu tribesmen, results in brutal slayings of whites and Africans serving whites, and equally brutal retaliation by white community; Africans are granted larger, but still minority, representation in Legislative Council

1960-61: Britain agrees to new elections for Legislative Council, in which Africans win majority

1961-62: Jomo Kenyatta, imprisoned as alleged Mau Mau leader, is released; he enters Legislative Council as leader of the Kenya African National Union (KANU), backed largely by the Kikuyu and Luo tribes, and forces cooperation with the governing Kenya African Democratic Union (KADU), which is chiefly supported by the smaller tribal units

1963: Kenyatta leads KANU to overwhelming election victory; Kenya gains independence, with Kenyatta as prime minister

1964: Kenya becomes a republic within the British Commonwealth, under the presidency of Kenyatta; KADU voluntarily dissolves itself and Kenya becomes a one-party state

1966: Vice-President Oginga Odinga, an early Kenyatta follower and Luo tribal leader, resigns, charging KANU government with

being "capitalistic"; he forms new opposition party, the Kenya People's Union

1969: Economics Minister Tom Mboya, a Luo, is slain by a Kikuyu; slaying sparks antigovernment demonstrations and arrest of Oginga Odinga. KPU party is dissolved

1971: Opposition leader Oginga Odinga is released from detention

1974: Kenyatta orders all unauthorized noncitizen traders to leave. Swahili declared official language. Severe drought affects 70 percent of country

1975: Josiah Kariuki, one of Kenya's most popular politicians, who championed Kenya's poor, is murdered, allegedly by political enemies

1977: Tanzania closes 500-mile border with Kenya indefinitely. This action follows Kenya's withdrawal from participation in East African Airways, which forced the airline to close. Government bans all game hunting in an effort to save wildlife from extinction. Kenya claims Somali troops cross border. The two nations set up border commission to prevent recurrence

1978: Kenyatta dies. Daniel arap Moi becomes president

1979: Kenya launches 5-year development plan to eliminate poverty, disease and illiteracy, and to reduce unemployment. Moi retains office in November elections

1980: President Moi visits United States in February and gets increased economic aid. United States acquires military bases in Kenya for Middle East defense

---

KIRIBATI

Area: 264 sq. mi. **Population:** 58,000 (1978 est.)

Official Name: Republic of Kiribati **Capital:** Bairiki, on Tarawa **Nationality:** Kiribati **Languages:** I-Kiribati (Gilbertese) and English **Religion:** Evenly divided between Protestant and Roman Catholic **Flag:** Bottom half consists of six wavy, horizontal white stripes over navy blue; top half is red with a flying yellow frigate bird over a yellow sun, displaying nine straight and eight wavy yellow rays **Anthem:** Stand Up Kiribati **Currency:** Australian dollar (0.90 per U.S. $1)

Location: The island nation extends widely over the western Pacific, from 5°N to 11°S and 169°E to 150°W, and is scattered over two million sq. mi. of ocean. It includes 33 islands and atolls in the Gilbert, Phoenix and Line groups, plus Banaba (Ocean Island). All but Banaba have coral-ringed lagoons circling the tops of submerged mountains

Head of State and of Government: President Ieremia Tabai, born 1950, assumed office, July 12, 1979. The governor general is Reginald James Wallace **Effective Date of Present Constitution:** July 12, 1979 **Legislative Body:** a unicameral House of Assembly *(Maneaba ni Maungatabu)* of 35 elected members, one nominated representative of Banaba and the attorney general **Local Government:** 23 election districts

Ethnic Composition: Predominantly Micronesian with some Polynesians, mixed Micronesian-Polynesian, and Europeans **Population Distribution:** 30 % urban **Density:** 220 inhabitants per sq. mi.

Largest City: Bairiki 1,300

Per Capita Income: $730 (1974) **Gross National Product (GNP):** $40 million (1974) **Economic Statistics:** The economy is based largely on the export of copra. The brine shrimp industry on Christmas Island grows shrimps and shrimp eggs for fish farms throughout the world. There is a soft drink factory, a biscuit factory and a boatbuilding concern **Minerals and Mining:** Phosphate mining on Banaba (Ocean Island) is due to end in 1980 **Labor Force:** N.A. **Foreign Trade:** Exports, chiefly phosphate rock and copra, totaled $15.7 million in 1977. Imports totaled $10.3 million **Principal Trade Partners:** Britain, Australia

Vital Statistics: Birthrate, 22.3 per 1,000 of pop. (1971); death rate, 6.5 **Life Expectancy:** 58 years **Health Statistics:** 201 inhabitants per hospital bed (1977); 2,692 per physician (1975) **Infant Mortality:** 48.9 per 1,000 births (1971) **Illiteracy:** under 50% **Primary and Secondary School Enrollment:** 14,511 (1977) **Enrollment in Higher Education:** N.A. **GNP Expended on Education:** N.A.

Transportation: Motorable roads total 300 mi. **Motor Vehicles:** N.A. **Passenger Cars:** N.A. **Railway Mileage:** None **Ports:** Tarawa, Canton Island **Major Airlines:** Air Tunguru provides domestic service. Air Nauru and Air Pacific provide international service **Communications:** Government owned **Radio Transmitters:** 1 **Receivers:** 8,200 (1975) **Television Transmitters:** None **Telephones:** 250 **Newspapers:** 4 non-dailies, 89 copies per 1,000 inhabitants (1974)

Weights and Measures: British and metric **Travel Requirements:** not available

---

In November 1943, U.S. Marines landed on Tarawa, the central island in the far-flung Gilbert chain, and fought one of the bloodiest battles of the Second World War, defeating an entrenched Japanese garrison of 5,000. Although time seemed to have forgotten these peaceful islands since, the realities of the modern world have caught up to this newly independent nation—one of the world's poorest—of 33 coral atolls stretched across two million square miles of the South Pacific, at the crossroads of the equator and the international date line.

Independence came to the former Gilbert Islands on July 12, 1979, after 87 years of British rule. One of the most pressing problems facing Kiribati (pronounced "Kíribass") is economic; 99 percent of its $18-million annual income derives from phosphate mining, located only on Banaba (Ocean Island). But the joint Australian-New Zealand authority that controls mining there states the phosphate will run out by the end of 1980. Diversification is thus the main priority facing the new government on Tarawa. Agriculture is limited by poor soil, although the export of copra—derived from the native coconut palms—has been a source of revenue. There are plans to develop local industries—mainly fruit canning and handicrafts—as well as to exploit the potentially rich fishing grounds within Kiribati's 200-mile offshore boundaries. British pledges of $35 million in continued aid over the next four years, coupled with the approximately $60 million in royalties due from the British Phosphate Commission, also hold promise for future economic development.

Although fourteen of the islands in the Phoenix and Line groups have long been claimed by both Britain and the United States—including Kanton (Canton), Enderbury and Christmas Islands—the U.S. has agreed to relinquish Canton and Enderbury in 1980, and will cede the rest to Kiribati by treaty in the near future.

But the birth pangs of the new nation have caused other political problems the new government must face. The former residents of Banaba (Ocean Island), who were relocated following World War II after mining had despoiled their island, have fought for 10 years to reassert their claims to their traditional homes, and continue to oppose being part of an independent Kiribati. Kiribati, while assuring the islanders of their continued rights on Banaba, has refused so far to agree to Banaban demands for separation.

HISTORY: The main wave of Micronesian settlement of the area is thought to have originated from Samoa around the thirteenth century. Although Spanish navigators are credited with sighting some of the islands in 1537 and 1606, true European discovery of the area came only much later, with the first white settlement dating from the 1830s. Missionaries visited the islands in 1857, and by the 1860s a flourishing trade in coconut oil and copra had been established. Between 1850 and 1875 the islands were raided by "blackbirders" for slave labor in South America, Fiji, Tahiti, Hawaii and Austrlia. To stamp out this activity, the British established the High Commmision for the Western Pacific over the area in 1877

1888-89: Britain annexes Christmas, Fanning and Washington Islands

1892: Britain establishes protectorate over Gilberts and neighboring Ellice Islands

1915: Protectorate reorganized as Gilbert and Ellice Islands Colony, extended to include Ocean Island (Banaba) and the Northern Line Islands by 1919

1937: Phoenix Islands incorporated into Gilbert and Ellice Islands Colony

1939: Britain and U.S. sign treaty providing for joint control of Kanton (Canton) and Enderbury

1941-45: Japanese seize Tarawa and Ocean Island (Banaba) from British at outset of World War II. U.S. forces land on Tarawa November 1943, defeating Japanese occupation force. Australian forces liberate Ocean Island (Banaba) in 1945

1945-47: Banabans, dispersed during conflict, are resettled on Rabi, in Fiji Islands

1972: Gilbert and Ellice Islands, removed from jurisdiction of Western Pacific Commission, are placed under a British governor

1975: Ellice Islands separate from Gilberts, becoming Tuvalu (independent in 1978)

1978: London conference, Nov. 21-Dec. 7, sets constitutional framework for independence; Banaba representatives bolt meeting after Gilbertese officials reject demands for separation

1979: Gilberts become independent nation of Kiribati, July 12

NORTH KOREA

Area: 46,540 sq. mi. **Population:** 17,072,000 (1978 est.)
Official Name: Democratic People's Republic of Korea **Capital:** Pyongyang **Nationality:** Korean **Languages:** Korean is the official and universal language **Religion:** The traditional religions are Buddhism, Confucianism, Shamanism, and Ch'ondokyo, which combines elements of Buddhism and Christianity; the practice of religion has been discouraged by the government **Flag:** A broad center red stripe bordered on top and bottom by a thin white stripe and a broader blue stripe: left of center is a white disc containing a five-pointed red star **Anthem:** National Anthem, beginning "Morning sun, shine over the rivers and mountains" **Currency:** Won (1.79 per U.S. $1)

Location: North Korea occupies the northern portion of a peninsula in northeast Asia projecting southeast from Manchuria. It is bordered on the north by China, on the extreme northeast by the USSR, on the east by the Sea of Japan, on the south by South Korea, and on the west by the Yellow Sea and Korea Bay **Features:** A land of mountains, North Korea contains thousands of peaks, leaving less than one fifth of the total area as cultivable **Chief Rivers:** Tumen, Yalu, Ch'ongch'on, Taedong, Yesong

Head of State and Political Leader: President: Marshal Kim Il Sung, born 1912, reelected 1977. The premier is Li Jong Ok **Effective Date of Present Constitution:** 1972 **Legislative Body:** Supreme People's Assembly (unicameral), consisting of 579 members elected by universal suffrage for 4 years. It actually does little more than ratify decisions taken by the Central People's Committee of the Korean Workers' (Communist) party **Local Government:** 9 provinces

Ethnic Composition: North Koreans, like the South Koreans, are believed to be of Tungusic stock, ethnically related to the Mongols with some Chinese mixture. There are no ethnic minorities **Population Distribution:** 38.1% urban **Density:** 367 inhabitants per sq. mi.

Largest Cities: (1972 est.) Pyongyang 1,500,000, Hamhung 484,000, Chongjin 306,000, Sinuiju 300,000, Wonsan 275,000

Per Capita Income: $759 (1979) **Gross National Product (GNP):** $14.1 billion (1979) **Economic Statistics:** About 70% of GNP comes from industry and mining (coal, iron ore, steel, machinery, textiles); 15% from agriculture (rice, corn, barley, wheat, cotton) and the rest from other activities **Minerals and Mining:** Large deposits of coal, iron ore, lead, zinc, molybdenum, gold, graphite, and tungsten **Labor Force:** 7,500,000, with 55% in industry and services, and 45% in agriculture **Foreign Trade:** Exports, mainly ferrous and nonferrous metals, minerals, chemicals, fuel and oil, machinery and equipment, totaled $967 million in 1978. Imports, chiefly machinery and equipment, fuels, chemicals, and textiles, totaled $902 million **Principal Trade Partners:** USSR, China and other Communist countries, Japan, West Germany, France

Vital Statistics: Birthrate, 35.7 per 1,000 of pop. (1975); death rate, 9.4 **Life Expectancy:** 61 years **Health Statistics:** 333 inhabitants per hospital bed; 909 per physician **Infant Mortality:** N.A. **Illiteracy:** 10% **Primary School Enrollment:** 2,561,674 (1976) **Enrollment in Higher Education:** 214,000 (1973) **GNP Expended on Education:** N.A.

Transportation: Total road mileage is c. 12,600 **Motor Vehicles:** 60,000 (1971) **Railway Mileage:** 2,950 **Ports:** Chongjin, Hamhung, Nampo, Wonsan, Unggi **Major Airlines:** Civil Aviation Administration operates both international and domestic flights **Communications:** State controlled **Radio Transmitters:** 19 **Receivers:** 800,000 (1971) **Television Transmitters:** 1 **Receivers:** 50,000 (1973) **Telephones:** N.A. **Newspapers:** 11 dailies

Weights and Measures: Metric system **Travel Requirements:** N.A.

To the West, North Korea is one of the most isolated and least-known Communist countries. Personal contacts even between North and South Koreans are almost nonexistent since North and South are still in a technical state of war; the demilitarized zone across the peninsula, set up by the armistice in 1953, is probably the world's most tightly closed border.

The division of Korea along the 38th parallel at the end of World War II left the North with almost all the country's mineral resources and a major share of the industries developed by the Japanese in the former colony. The three-year Korean War devastated much of the industry, but planning, regimentation, and utilization of a trained labor force brought great strides in production by the early 1960s.

The highly authoritarian, military-dominated government of Marshal Kim Il Sung has sought to steer an independent course between the Soviet Union and China, while remaining antagonistic toward United States "imperialism" and what it calls the "puppet" South Korean regime.

Premier Kim, previously a guerrilla against the Japanese, arrived in Pyongyang with Soviet troops in October 1945 as a leader in the émigré forces trained by the Russians to take over in Korea. He established his dominance as premier when the Democratic People's Republic of Korea was set up in September 1948.

North Korea's military forces were strengthened rapidly as Soviet troops were withdrawn, and in June 1950 a North Korean military attack came close to seizing the entire peninsula before United Nations forces, led by American troops, gained the initiative.

The end of the war was followed by collectivization of agriculture; industry in the North had already been nationalized. Economic progress has been notable, educational facilities have been expanded, and extreme poverty has been sharply reduced.

However, life in the North is highly regimented. Consumer goods are scarce, the vast housing projects are drab, travel is tightly controlled and freedom of expression is restricted.

In a June 1973 dispatch, Kim was quoted as saying: "We hold that the North and the South should not enter the United Nations separately but as one state under a confederation." Since that time, he has reiterated his wish for a unified Korea under Communist rule.

Tension between the two countries increased after the finding in November 1974 of tunnels under the demilitarized zone emerging into South Korea. The victories of the Communists in South Vietnam and Cambodia and a visit to China by Kim, allegedly to seek Chinese support for military pressure on South Korea, had a negative effect on relations between the two Koreas. A new era was in prospect after the 1977 announcement by the U.S. that it planned the gradual withdrawal of all American ground forces from the demilitarized zone over the next five years.

When South Korea proposed, on Jan. 19, 1979, that fresh talks be held in an effort to prevent war and to unify the two countries, North Korea answered, only six days later, that a "new start" would be a good idea. Delegations began talks almost immediately—one day in February and another in March—but quickly got bogged down with procedures. UN Secretary-General Kurt Waldheim visited both Koreas in 1979, but no new peace initiatives developed. In 1980, however, talks were started with a view to a conference between the two Korean leaders. At the same time South Korea asserted that North Korea was attempting to send in armed espionage agents, apparently in hopes of exploiting the South's civil unrest.

HISTORY: Korean history goes back into a legendary past, with one of the earliest legends centering around Kitze, or Kija, a scholar credited with the introduction of Chinese culture into the Korean peninsula in the 12th century B.C. Chinese influence remained strong until well after the emergence of separate Korean kingdoms in the early centuries of the Christian era, and it was with Chinese help that one of these, the kingdom of Silla, conquered its rivals in the 7th century A.D. and unified the peninsula. In the 10th century Silla fell to the Koryo dynasty of Kaesong, under whose rule Confucianism gradually replaced Buddhism as the dominant religion

1231-60: Mongols occupy Korea

1392: Yi Sung-ke, a Korean general, seizes Korean throne

1592: Yi dynasty, aided by China, repels invasion by Japanese

1637: Korea is made a vassal of Manchu China, beginning a period of isolation from the rest of the world and giving Korea the name of "hermit kingdom"

1876-82: Korean ports are opened to Japanese, U.S. and European trade after Japan compels Korea to agree to commercial treaty

1894-1905: Japanese victories in Sino-Japanese and Russo-Japanese wars end in complete control of Korea by Japan

1910: Japan formally annexes Korea

1919: Nationalist leader Syngman Rhee sets up Korean government-in-exile in Shanghai

1945: Soviet and U.S. forces occupy Korea after Japan's defeat in World War II; they establish the 38th parallel as the dividing line between their occupation zones, with the Russians in the north and the Americans in the south

1948: Division of the peninsula is formalized with the establishment of the two separate regimes of North Korea and South Korea; Democratic People's Republic of North Korea is set up in 1948 under Premier Kim Il Sung, a Moscow-trained military man; Soviet forces evacuate North Korea

1950-53: North Korea invades South Korea in 1950; in response to UN request, the U.S. and 15 other member nations send troops to aid South Korea; after initial retreats, UN forces stage counteroffensive and drive North Koreans deep into North Korea; in October 1950 Chinese Communists join North Koreans in successful counterattack; fighting continues until a cease-fire is reached in 1953, leaving Korea divided as before

1954-61: Kim Il Sung pushes ambitious program of industrialization; North Korea is economically integrated with Soviet Union and Communist China; military aid treaties are signed with both

1968: North Korea seizes U.S. intelligence ship *Pueblo*, charging vessel violated North Korean territorial waters; crew is released after 11 months when U.S. signs a statement, which it labels false, admitting the *Pueblo's* intrusion

1970: Kim government proposes a federated Korea, conditional upon U.S. withdrawal from the south

1975: North Korea becomes first Communist country to not meet payment of Western debts

1976: North Korean soldiers kill two U.S. Army officers at Panmunjom

1977: Travel restrictions for U.S. citizens to North Korea are lifted

1978: Working-level talks between North and South Korea break down. Communist Chinese Premier Hua visits, describes North Korea as "sole legitimate sovereign Korean state" and calls for complete withdrawal of U.S. forces from Korea. North Korea denounces "slow" pace of U.S. troop pullout, calls for direct talks with U.S. on reunification of Korea

1979: In response to a South Koean suggestion, North Korea enters into unification talks. Foreigners get a rare glimpse of Pyongyang in April and May as 900 table-tennis players from 70 countries participate in a world tournament. Press dispatches emphasize the physical splendor of Pyongyang which, virtually leveled during the Korean War, has been rebuilt with broad avenues and vistas extending toward many monuments

1980: South Korea reports killing three North Korean frogmen who, it says, crossed a river near the DMZ. At sea, in March and in June, South Korea sinks two vessels it contends were North Korean spy boats

SOUTH KOREA

Area: 38,175 sq. mi. **Population:** 37,605,000 (1979 est.)

Official Name: Republic of Korea **Capital:** Seoul **Nationality:** Korean **Languages:** Korean is the official and universal language **Religion:** The traditional religions are Buddhism, Confucianism, Shamanism, and Ch'ondokyo, which combines elements of Buddhism and Christianity. However, accurate figures of the numbers of their adherents are not available. There are at least 4 million Christians, chiefly Protestant **Flag:** A divided circle of red (top) and blue (bottom) centered on a white field. A black bar design appears in each corner of the flag **Anthem:** National Anthem, beginning "Until the Eastern Sea is drained" **Currency:** Won (590 per U.S. $1)

Location: South Korea occupies the southern portion of a peninsula in northeast Asia projecting southeast from Manchuria. It is bounded on the north by North Korea, on the east by the Sea of Japan, on the south by the Korea Strait, and on the west by the Yellow Sea **Features:** The country is largely mountainous, with the limited arable land in the lowlands and river valleys of the south and southwest **Chief Rivers:** Somjin, Kum, Naktong, Han, Pukhan

Head of State and of Government: President Chun Doo Hwan, born 1931, elected by the National Conference for Unification Aug. 1980. He is assisted by a Prime Minister, Nam Duck Woo **Effective Date of**

Present Constitution: 1972. A new constitution is being prepared **Legislative Body:** National Assembly (unicameral), consisting of 231 members partly elected for 6 years **Local Government:** 9 provinces administered by appointed governors, and 2 specially administered cities

Ethnic Composition: The Korean population is one of the most homogeneous in the world. The primary stock is believed to be Tungusic, related to the Mongols with some Chinese mixture **Population Distribution:** 60% urban **Density:** 985 inhabitants per sq. mi.

Largest Cities: (1977 est.) Seoul 7,500,000; (1975 census) Pusan 2,454,051; Taegu 1,311,078, Inchon 799,982, Kwangju 607,058

Per Capita Income: $1,056 (1979) **Gross National Product (GNP):** $41 billion (1979) **Economic Statistics:** 30% of GNP comes from manufacturing (textiles, chemicals, food processing, clay, glass and stone products, transportation equipment) and mining; 21% from agriculture (rice, barley, soybeans, potatoes, wheat, millet, livestock raising), forestry and fishing **Minerals and Mining:** South Korea has less than 30% of the peninsula's estimated reserves of gold, silver, tungsten, molybdenum, and graphite, and about 10% of its coal and iron ore. It nevertheless produces anthracite coal, tungsten, iron ore, lead, amorphous graphite, fluorite, kaolite, and talc **Labor Force:** 13.9 million (1978), with 38% in agriculture and forestry; 23% in manufacturing and mining **Foreign Trade:** Exports, chiefly clothing and textiles, plywood, ships, iron and steel products, wigs, marine products, raw silk, and electronic products, totaled $15 billion in 1979. Imports, mainly fuel, nonelectric machinery, transportation equipment, food grains, electric machinery, textiles yarns and fabrics, totaled $20.3 billion **Principal Trade Partners:** United States, Japan, Saudi Arabia, Kuwait, West Germany

Vital Statistics: Birthrate, 28.8 per 1,000 of pop. (1975); death rate 8.9 **Life Expectancy:** 68 years **Health Statistics:** 1,310 inhabitants per hospital bed; 2,128 per physician (1976) **Infant Mortality:** 38 per 1,000 births **Illiteracy:** 6.8% **Primary and Secondary School Enrollment:** 9,060,787 (1977) **Enrollment in Higher Education:** 325,460 (1976) **GNP Expended on Education:** 4.1% (1974)

Transportation: Paved roads total 8,400 mi. **Motor Vehicles:** 270,500 (1977) **Passenger Cars:** 125,600 **Railway Mileage:** 3,594 **Ports:** Pusan, Inchon, Pohang, Masan, Mokpo, Gunsan, Mukho **Major Airlines:** Korean Airlines operates domestic and international services **Communications:** Government and privately owned **Radio Transmitters:** 94 **Receivers:** 12,300,000 (1978) **Television Transmitters:** 59 **Receivers:** 5.135.496 (1978) **Telephones:** 2,000,000 **Newspapers:** 36 dailies, 173 copies per 1,000 inhabitants (1975)

Weights and Measures: Metric system and old Korean units are used **Travel Requirements:** Passport, tourist visa valid for initial period of 2 months, no fee; 1 photo; affidavit of support

---

The Korean peninsula has often been described as a dagger pointed from the Asian heartland toward Japan, and its strategic position made it several times a battleground for more powerful neighbors. Long a "hermit kingdom" with a strong indigenous culture, Korea was annexed by the Japanese in 1910. Until the end of World War II it was ruled by a repressive colonial regime and exploited for its mineral resources, living space, and markets.

Considerable dislocation occurred when the primarily agricultural and densely populated South was separated from the industrial North in 1945 and put under United States occupation. After unsuccessful attempts to arrange nationwide elections under United Nations supervision, voting was held in 1948 in the South only and the government of the Republic of Korea was established under the presidency of Syngman Rhee.

The Korean War caused more than 800,000 military and civilian casualties in South Korea and approximately $3 billion worth of property damage. For a decade thereafter the huge U.S. aid effort, coupled with international assistance, was directed toward providing food and shelter, repairing war damage, and laying the groundwork for eventual economic development. During the 1970s, the South Korean economy flourished, and the nation became an important industrial power. In 1980, however, the auto industry was in distress, wage rates had doubled in three years, and some Japanese companies had pulled out of South Korea because production of goods for export had proved unprofitable.

President Rhee won reelection in 1952 and 1956, but as he grew more despotic and ruthless, police repression and official corruption aroused wide protests. Finally, rigging of elections in 1960 set off student demonstrations that overthrew Dr. Rhee. The subsequent government of Dr. John M. Chang proved ineffective and a military coup in May 1961 brought to power a junta led by Park Chung Hee, then a major general. General Park retired from the army, won the presidency in a national election in 1963, and was reelected in 1967 and 1972. In 1978 his presidency was extended for six years; no other name was on the ballot as the electoral college, the National Conference for Unification, elected him, 2,577 to 0. At the time of voting, all opposition leaders were under house arrest in Seoul.

Threatened by North Korean military power, Park maintained close ties with the U.S. to ensure military assistance, but relations became frayed, especially after the banning of all political dissent from 1975 on. In 1979, in the wake of nationwide student demonstrations, Park and his chief bodyguard were slain by Kim Jae Kyu, chief of the Korean Central Intelligence Agency. Simultaneously, five of Kim's associates killed five other presidential bodyguards. Said Kim: "I will be judged as one who tried to restore democracy, and as a hero." Kim and four accomplices were hanged on May 24, 1980.

The title of president passed to Park's prime minister, Choi Kyu Hah, who was constitutionally elected by the National Conference for Unification. Power, however, went to the military, which in late May 1980 announced the Special Committee for National Security Measures, headed by Lt. Gen. Chun Doo Hwan and made up principally of generals, plus some civilian cabinet members. Demonstrations in May 1980 were capped by the 10-day student rule of Kwangju. The protest was ended by a predawn strike by paratroopers, backed with tanks, that cost 200 to 300 lives. In August Chun Doo Hwan was elected president by the National Conference for Unification.

HISTORY: The history of South Korea is bound up with that of Korea as a whole up until 1948 when the government of the Republic of Korea was established under the presidency of Syngman Rhee

1950-53: Korean War, brought on by North Korea's invasion of South Korea, rages for three years as U.S. troops and forces of 15 other nations, responding to a request for help by the United Nations, try to repel the invaders; the conflict, broadened in 1951 with the entry of Communist China on the side of North Korea, ends with the establishment of a cease-fire and the continued division of the peninsula at the 38th parallel

1960: Rhee is elected for fourth term as president but is accused of rigging the elections; after widespread rioting he is forced from office and goes into exile

1961: South Korean armed forces overthrow government; Gen. Park Chung Hee takes power

1963-67: Park is elected president in 1963 and is reelected in 1967 amid charges by his opponents that elections were rigged

1969: South Korean voters approve a constitutional amendment that allows president to seek a third consecutive term

1970: United States agrees to bolster South Korean army after announcing U.S. troop cuts in South Korea

1972: Following secret talks, governments of North and South Korea announce agreement in principle on unification. Park institutes constitutional changes that increase his power

1973: Opposition leader Kim Dae-Jung is kidnapped in Japan, resulting in widespread demonstrations. Brought back to Korea, he is placed under house arrest and later released

1975: Assassination attempt on President Park fails but wife is victim. North Korea rejects a South Korean proposal to renew talks on unification

1978: Economy continues on uptrend. Strained relations between South Korea and U.S. worsen over planned pullout of American ground forces (as withdrawal begins); U.S. bugging of South Korean executive mansion is alleged, and influence-buying scandal comes to light, in which South Korean businessman Tongsun Park and former ambassador Kim Dong Jo allegedly paid U.S. Congressmen for continued American economic and military aid; Kim Dong Jo resigns post as national security adviser. Park, unopposed, is reelected for another six-year presidential term

On Dec. 27, Park's inauguration day, Kim Dae-jung is released from jail again after serving 31 months for criticizing the government

1979: Park asks North Korea for talks "any time, any place" to reunify the countries; delegations meet but bog down on procedural questions. U.S. President Carter visits Seoul in June, prompting government's release of many political dissidents. Student demonstrations sweep the cities in October. President Park and his chief bodyguard are killed on October 26 by Kim Jae Kyu, director of the Korean Central Intelligence Agency. Five of Kim's associates kill five other presidential bodyguards. Premier Choi Kyu Hah is elected president in December

1980: Student protests against martial law start in Seoul in May and spread to other cities. Rebel students seize Kwangju and hold it for 10 days, until paratroopers win back the city in a 3:30 A.M. assault on May 27. The death toll is 200 to 300. A paratroop officer, Lt. Gen. Chun Doo Hwan, head of the Defense Security Command, virtually takes charge of the government through the Special Committee for National Security Measures, made up mostly of generals. In June, the Martial Law Command announced that Kim Jong Pil, a former prime minister, and nine other politicians accused of gaining wealth through "abuse of power" have agreed to turn over their fortunes to the government. Chun Doo Hwan is elected president in August

KUWAIT

Area: 7,780 sq. mi. **Population:** 1,272,000 (1979 est.)

Official Name: State of Kuwait **Capital:** Kuwait **Nationality:** Kuwaiti **Languages:** Arabic is the official and universal language; English is widely spoken **Religion:** About 99% Moslem, chiefly of the Sunni sect; and 1% of other or no affiliation **Flag:** Green, white, and red horizontal stripes with a black trapezoid at the staff **Anthem:** National Anthem (no words) **Currency:** Kuwaiti dinar (.27 per U.S. $1)

Location: Northeast corner of the Arabian Peninsula. Kuwait is bordered on the north and west by Iraq, on the east by the Persian Gulf, and on the south by Saudi Arabia **Features:** The country is mainly flat desert, with a few oases **Chief Rivers:** There are no rivers

Head of State and of Government: Emir: Sheikh Jabir al-Ahmad al-Jabir as-Sabah, born 1928, acceded 1977. The emir is assisted by a council of ministers headed by a prime minister, Sheikh Saad al-Abdullah al-Salim as-Sabah, appointed 1978 **Effective Date of Present Constitution:** 1962, partly suspended in August 1976; a revision is planned **Legislative Body:** National Assembly (unicameral), dissolved in August 1976, with rule by royal decree **Local Government:** 3 governorates

Ethnic Composition: The population is about 85% Arab but only 48% are native-born. Non-Kuwaitis include Palestinians, Iraqis, Iranians, Egyptians, Indians, Syrians, Lebanese, and others **Population Distribution:** 99% urban **Density:** 163 inhabitants per sq. mi.

Largest Cities: (1975 census) Hawalli 130,302, Salimiya 113,874, Kuwait 108,211

Per Capita Income: $18,100 (1979 est.) **Gross National Product (GNP):** $16 billion (1979) **Economic Statistics:** The economy is based almost entirely on oil, which accounts for about 70% of GNP. About 15% comes from trade and services; the remainder from nonoil industries (chemical fertilizers, building materials, fishing) **Minerals and Mining:** Kuwait possesses nearly one fifth of the world's oil reserves. Oil concessions are held by the Kuwait Petroleum Establishment and British, American, and Japanese firms. Large amounts of natural gas are produced from the oil fields **Labor Force:** 300,000, with 70% held by non-Kuwaitis. 40% of the labor force is employed by the government, 34% are in industry (less than 5% in the heavily automated oil industry), and 1% in agriculture **Foreign Trade:** Exports, 96% crude oil and petroleum products, totaled $10.4 billion in 1978. Imports, chiefly foodstuffs, building materials, automobiles, industrial equipment and electrical products, totaled $4.6 billion **Principal Trade Partners:** Japan, United States, Britain, West Germany, Italy, Korea, Netherlands, Saudi Arabia

Vital Statistics: Birthrate, 43.3 per 1,000 of pop. (1976); death rate, 4.4 **Life Expectancy:** 69 years **Health Statistics:** 240 inhabitants per hospital bed; 883 per physician (1976) **Infant Mortality:** 34.3 per 1,000 births **Illiteracy:** 20% **Primary and Secondary School Enrollment:** 215,451 (1976) **Enrollment in Higher Education:** 9,934 **GNP Expended on Education:** 2.8% (1976)

Transportation: Paved roads total 1,400 mi. **Motor Vehicles:** 380,900 (1977) **Passenger Cars:** 285,800 **Railway Mileage:** None **Ports:** Mina al-Ahmadi, Shuwaikh, Shuaibah, Mina Abdullah **Major Airlines:** Kuwait Airways, government owned, operates international flights **Communications:** Government owned **Radio Transmitters:** 8 **Receivers:** 502,000 (1976) **Television Transmitters:** 7

Receivers: 375,000 (1978) **Telephones:** 153,000 **Newspapers:** 8 dailies, 86 copies per 1,000 inhabitants (1976)

Weights and Measures: Metric system **Travel Requirements:** Passport, transit visa, valid 2 days, $1.00; entry visa, valid 1 month, 1 entry, $4.00, 2 photos

---

Tiny, torrid Kuwait, an opulent strip of desert at the northwestern end of the Persian Gulf, enjoys one of the world's highest standards of living. In 1979 it ranked third among all nations in per capita gross national product with $18,100 GNP per person.

Since 1967 Kuwait has helped to subsidize the national economies of Egypt and of Jordan, both of which were defeated in the war with Israel. It must import all of its food but exports enough oil to pay for the people's basic needs.

As a capitalistic welfare state, where poverty is virtually unknown, it provides lavish public services that include: free universal medical service, free education through the university level (including free food and clothing for students), free telephone service, subsidized housing for which only token rentals are paid, and subsidies for those wishing to start business enterprises.

Kuwait has a higher proportion of the latest American cars than any country outside the United States, and the cars are driven over wide, well-surfaced roads. It has more than twice as many air-conditioning units as people, and there is said to be a millionaire for every 230 citizens.

As late as the 1940s, before large-scale oil exports began, Kuwait was little more than a feudal wilderness. It was a primitive, forbidding land, where the temperature would often reach 125 degrees in the shade.

Abd Allah al-Salim as-Sabah, who was emir when the oil boom began, developed the growth program. Following his death in 1965, his policies were continued by his successor, Sheikh Sabah al-Salim as-Sabah. On December 31, 1977, Sheikh Sabah died and his cousin, Sheikh Jabir al-Ahmad al-Jabir as-Sabah, became emir.

The Kuwaitis themselves are a minority of the population of their own country, and they make up only 30 percent of the work force. Of those Kuwaitis who are employed, 70 percent are on the government payroll. Non-Kuwaitis (mainly Palestinians, Saudis, Egyptians, Iraqis, Pakistanis, Indians, and Americans), share in the welfare services, but are not permitted to own property or to vote.

Kuwaiti society generally consists of five layers, with the members of the ruling family at the top, followed by the old Kuwaiti merchant families. Then come the former Bedouins now living in luxurious urban surroundings, the Arabs from other countries who have been granted Kuwaiti citizenship, and, last, the foreigners.

Many foreigners feel unappreciated by the Kuwaitis, and members of a large Palestinian underground have tried to force the government to take a stronger position than it has against Israel. The activities of this underground were cited by the government in explaining its decision to dissolve the National Assembly and restrict the press in 1976.

A British protectorate from 1897 to 1961, Kuwait received informal military protection from the Shah of Iran after 1970. After the Shah fell in 1979, Britain's Queen Elizabeth and Foreign Secretary David Owen visited Kuwait to indicate continuing commitment.

Despite the connection with Britain, Kuwait is very much involved in the Arab bloc. It sent soldiers to fight in the Yom Kippur War against Israel in 1973. The Kuwaiti government joined other Arab states in breaking relations with Cairo after Egypt made peace with Israel in 1979. Kuwait has raised its oil prices along with other Arab oil-producing nations, and in 1980 it cut back crude oil production to maintain high prices.

HISTORY: Kuwait was settled by Arab tribes in the early 18th century. The present dynasty was established in 1756 by Sheikh Sabah Abdul Rahim. Nominally an Ottoman province, Kuwait asked for British protection in 1897, when the ruling sheikh feared that the Turks wanted to make their authority effective

1899: In return for British protection, Kuwait undertakes not to cede or lease any of its territory without Britain's approval

1914-22: Britain declares Kuwait independent of Turkey and under British protection. British troops help repel invasion by Saudi Arabia; Saudis and Kuwait set up neutral zone in which they share sovereignty

1934: Kuwait's ruler grants a concession to Kuwait Oil Company, a joint American-British enterprise, to drill for oil

1961: Britain recognizes Kuwait as an independent state and pledges protection against foreign aggression; Iraq claims Kuwait as a province; British troops prevent Iraqi invasion

1967: During Arab-Israeli war, Kuwait declares support for the Arab cause and contributes large subsidies to Egypt and Jordan

1969: Government shows increasing alarm over growing Soviet inroads in Persian Gulf area; proposal for the formation of a federation of nine neighboring sheikhdoms raises fear that many will succumb to revolutionary movements

1973: Kuwait's forces fight along Suez Canal during Yom Kippur War. Along with other oil-producing nations, Kuwait announces huge increase in oil prices

1975: Government announces it intends to acquire 100 percent ownership of domestic oil operations

1977: An arms buildup begun in 1976 continues with the purchase of sophisticated Soviet weaponry

1980: Kuwait reduces oil output to 1.5 million bbls. daily

LAOS

Area: 91,428 sq. mi. **Population:** 3,546,000 (1978 est.)

Official Name: Lao People's Democratic Republic **Capital:** Vientiane **Nationality:** Laotian **Languages:** Lao, a tonal language of the Thai group, is the official and dominant language; French serves as the second language **Religion:** Theravada Buddhism is the official and predominant religion (90%); the country's mountain tribes are principally animist **Flag:** Two narrow red bands either side of a wide blue band, with a white disc in the middle **Anthem:** N.A. **Currency:** Kip (16 per U.S. $1)

Location: Southeast Asia. Landlocked Laos is bordered on the north by China, on the east by Vietnam, on the south by Cambodia, on the west by Thailand, and on the northwest by Burma **Features:** Northern Laos is laced with jungle-covered mountains and plateaus cut by narrow valleys. Lower Laos is marked by arid limestone terraces, sparsely forested and descending westward to the Mekong River Valley **Chief Rivers:** Mekong, Nam Hou

Head of State: President Souphanouvong, named in 1975 **Head of Government:** Premier: Kaysone Phoumvihan, born 1920, appointed 1975; he is also secretary general of the party **Effective Date of Present Constitution:** none, at present **Legislative Body:** An appointed 45-member People's Supreme Assembly. The government is actually controlled by the Central Committee of the Lao People's Revolutionary (Communist) Party under its secretary general **Local Government:** 13 provinces

Ethnic Composition: More than half of the people are ethnic Lao, descendants of the Thai, a people who migrated from southwestern China in the 13th century. Mountain tribes of Sino-Tibetan and Thai strains are found in the north; many of these tribes, as well as others of Malay background, inhabit central and south Laos **Population Distribution:** 15% urban **Density:** 39 inhabitants per sq. mi.

Largest Cities: (1970 est.) Vientiane 150,000, Savannakhet 39,000, Pakse 37,200, Luang Prabang 25,000, Khammouane 13,000

Per Capita Income: $86 (1979) **Gross National Product (GNP):** $310 million (1979) **Economic Statistics:** Components of GNP are not available. The economy of the country, the least developed of the nations of the Indochinese peninsula, is 85% agricultural. Major crops are rice, corn, coffee, cotton, tea, and tobacco. Industry is limited to light consumer goods, with some cottage and family-type production. Lumber, cigarettes, alcohol, and cement are produced in small plants **Minerals and Mining:** Tin is the major mineral resource; surveys indicate deposits of iron ore, gold, copper, and manganese **Labor Force:** About 90% of the population is engaged in agriculture **Foreign Trade:** Exports, chiefly wood, tin, coffee, and resins, totaled $15 million in 1979. Imports, mainly foods, petroleum products, and transportation equipment, totaled $80 million **Principal Trade Partners:** Thailand, Japan, Malaysia, Singapore, Vietnam

Vital Statistics: Birthrate, 44.6 per 1,000 of pop. (1975); death rate, 22.8 **Life Expectancy:** 35 years **Health Statistics:** 401 inhabitants per hospital bed (1975); 21,667 per physician (1976) **Infant Mortality:** N.A. **Illiteracy:** 88% **Primary and Secondary School Enrollment:** 346,649 (1976) **Enrollment in Higher Education:** 828 (1974) **GNP Expended on Education:** N.A.

Transportation: Improved roads total about 2,175 mi. **Motor Vehicles:** 16,600 (1974) **Passenger Cars:** 14,100 **Railway Mileage:** None **Ports:** None **Major Airlines:** Air Lao operates domestic and international flights **Communications:** Government owned **Radio Transmitters:** 9 **Licenses:** 200,000 (1976) **Television:** None **Telephones:** 5,000 (1973) **Newspapers:** 8 dailies (1975)

Weights and Measures: Metric system **Travel Requirements:** Passport, visa; check Laotian embassy for requirements

The old Kingdom of Laos, which formed part of French Indochina, was little known to the outside world until the Vietnam War made its strategic location significant. The largest segment of French Indochina, it was also the most remote and the least developed. French rule did little to turn the local and ethnic groups into a united Laotian nation.

Most of the people live in the western quarter of the nation, where they practice subsistence agriculture. Widely scattered hill tribes inhabit the rest of the country, which is mountainous and jungle-covered. Laos lacks modern industrial facilities and technological resources. The country has few significant exports.

The development of Laos has been impeded both by warfare and by the country's physical features. The absence of a network of roads makes communication between the Mekong Valley towns and the rest of the country difficult. The North Vietnamese supply trails into South Vietnam ran through Laos, and these had been the target of intense bombing by U.S. planes. The land war itself spilled over from Vietnam into Laos in 1971, when the South Vietnamese launched a drive into eastern Laos with the stated intention of cutting off the Ho Chi Minh Trail.

The fighting was not confined to the southeast. A civil war was waged, with varying intensity, elsewhere in the country, with the United States supporting the Laotian government forces and the North Vietnamese helping the pro-Communist Pathet Lao.

On February 21, 1973, the war in Laos officially ended, as the Pathet Lao and the government signed a cease-fire agreement. By the end of July, a political settlement was reached, whereby the two Laotian parties agreed on the sharing of ministries, the creation of two deputy premierships, and the formation of a political consultative council. On the military side, the parties agreed to the neutralization of the two capitals, Vientiane and Luang Prabang, and the division of the country into two zones.

In April 1974, a third coalition government of neutralists, rightists and pro-Communist Pathet Lao was established and in May and June Thai and U.S. forces withdrew, ending their 10 years of military involvement.

By December of 1975, as an indirect result of the South Vietnamese collapse, a relatively low-key Pathet Lao takeover of Laos was completed with the abolition of both the 600-year-old monarchy and the coalition government and the establishment of a People's Democratic Republic. Prince Souphanouvong, titular leader of the Pathet Lao, was named president and Kaysone Phoumvihan, head of the Marxist-Leninist Laos People's party, was appointed premier.

The tide of refugees flowing out of Vietnamese-dominated Laos has drained the country of most of its professional and commercial elite. The refugees are estimated variously at 130,000 to 250,000, imposing a heavy burden on neighboring Thailand and other Southeast Asian countries. But Laotian refugees had official Thai status as refugees, and living conditions were good when Rosalyn Carter paid a 1979 visit to a camp in northeast Thailand. Moreover, Thailand announced that it would accept more Laotian refugees rather than force them back across the border. Other Laotians, possibly 40,000, many of whom had been civilian officials and military officers in the previous government, are being detained in "political re-education" centers.

HISTORY: The Lao began moving south from China in the 13th century, gradually settling in the territory of the Khmer Empire. After centuries of warfare among the small feudal states of the region, the ruler of Luang Prabang state united most of what is now Laos and Northeast Thailand in the Kingdom of Lan Xang (Kingdom of the Million Elephants). The kingdom split into 2 states in 1707; after constant quarreling they were overrun by neighboring armies. By the early 1800s the Thai had won ascendancy and retained this hold until the French moved in and established a protectorate in 1893

1945-46: Japanese invade Lao region of French Indochina. French return and reestablish control

1949: Laos becomes independent state within French Union

1950: Pathet Lao, a Communist nationalist movement, is founded by Prince Souphanouvong

1953: Government battles Pathet Lao and Viet Minh, Vietnamese Communist forces

1954: Under terms of Geneva Conference agreement ending Indochina war, Laos becomes fully independent and Pathet Lao is permitted to occupy country's two northern provinces

1960: Neutralist-Pathet Lao coalition breaks down. Tug-of-war between Moscow-backed neutralists, American-backed rightists, and Pathet Lao erupts. Rightist Gen. Phoumi Nosavan drives neutralists from Vientiane; Premier Souvanna Phouma, the neutralist leader, flees to Cambodia

1962: U.S. troops move into northeast Thailand to discourage Pathet Lao drive on Vientiane. Three factions reach accord on coalition, and second Geneva Conference agrees on Laotian neutrality. Prince Souvanna Phouma returns as premier

1963: Pathet Lao abandons its role in the government as neutralist and leftist forces renew fighting

1965: Right-wing faction seizes government, banishing Gen. Phoumi Nosavan and reinstating Souvanna Phouma as premier. Neutralist-led government agrees to U.S. flights over Laos and to bombing of Ho Chi Minh Trail

1967: The premier, Prince Souvanna Phouma, states that Laos has been invaded by more than 40,000 North Vietnamese troops

1969: U.S. planes bomb Ho Chi Minh Trail and other North Vietnamese infiltration routes through Laos

1971: South Vietnamese troops supported by U.S. planes and artillery invade Laos in a drive against North Vietnamese supply lines; invasion ends after the retreat of South Vietnamese

1973: War in Laos ends as government, Pathet Lao sign cease-fire in February and agree on political settlement in July

1974: King Savang Vatthana dissolves Vientiane government and installs new coalition cabinet under Prince Souvanna Phouma, who remains premier

1975: National Assembly is dissolved by Pathet Lao. Prince Souphanouvong becomes president

1977: Rebels mount attacks against government throughout Laos. Vietnam and Laos sign a 25-year agreement for military and economic cooperation

1978: Laos faces flood and drought-caused food shortages and likelihood of famine in many areas. Rebel attacks continue; government is helped by Vietnamese troops. U.S. promises Laos $5 million worth of rice to help ease food shortages, the first U.S. aid to an Indochinese country since the Communist victories in 1975

1979: The 1977 Vietnam-Laos pact is alluded to indirectly in the 1979 Vietnam-Cambodia pact, which says that the three countries "must unite with one another in political, military, diplomatic, and other affairs." Soon Laos contributes 1,000 soldiers to the Vietnamese operations in Cambodia. Laos becomes involved in China's brief invasion of Vietnam in that Chinese troops, by Laotian accounts, invade Laotian territory on three occasions while maneuvering against the Vietnamese

LEBANON

Area: 4,015 sq. mi. **Population:** 3,012,000 (1978 est.)
Official Name: Republic of Lebanon **Capital:** Beirut **Nationality:** Lebanese **Languages:** Arabic is the official and dominant language; French and English are also widely used **Religion:** 62% Moslem (Sunni and Shi'ite) and 37% Christian (Maronite, Greek Orthodox, Armenian, Greek and Roman Catholic). There are also about 90,000 Druzes and 7,000 Jews **Flag:** A broad white horizontal stripe between narrower red stripes; in the center is a green cedar tree with a brown trunk **Anthem:** National Anthem, beginning "All of us" **Currency:** Lebanese pound (3.4 per U.S. $1)

Location: Southwest Asia. Lebanon is bordered on the north and east by Syria, on the south by Israel, and on the west by the Mediterranean Sea **Features:** The country consists of a narrow costal plain behind which are the high Lebanese Mountains. Farther east are the fertile Beqaa Valley and finally the Anti-Lebanon Mountains extending to the Syrian frontier **Chief Rivers:** Litani, Hasbani

Head of State: President Elias Sarkis, born 1924, assumed office in September 1976. By convention, the president is a Maronite **Head of Government:** Premier Takieddin Solh, born 1909, appointed July 1980. By convention, the premier is a Sunni Moslem **Effective Date of Present Constitution:** 1926, amended 1976 **Legislative Body:** Parliament (unicameral National Assembly), consisting of 99 members elected for 4 years. By convention, the speaker is a Shi'ite Moslem **Local Government:** 5 provinces

Ethnic Composition: 93% Arab, 6% Armenian, and 1% others **Population Distribution:** 60% urban **Density:** 750 inhabitants per sq. mi.

Largest Cities: (1972 est.) Beirut 1,000,000, Tripoli 200,000

Per Capita Income: $975 (1979) **Gross National Product (GNP):** $1.4 billion (1979) **Economic Statistics:** In 1973 about 55% of GNP came from trade and services; 9% from agriculture (citrus fruits, vegetables, tobacco, livestock production); 21% from industry (food processing, textiles, cement, oil refining) **Minerals and Mining:** Small amounts of bitumen, iron ore, lime, and salt **Labor Force:** 1,000,000, with about 49% in agriculture, and 11% in industry **Foreign Trade:** Exports, chiefly fruits, vegetables, and textiles, totaled $626 million in 1978. Imports, mainly aircraft, motor vehicles, cigarettes, household appliances, wheat and corn, totaled $1.4 billion **Principal Trade Partners:** Saudi Arabia, Kuwait, Jordan, United States, West Germany, France, Britain

Vital Statistics: Birthrate 39.8 per 1,000 of pop. (1975); death rate, 9.9 **Life Expectancy:** 63 years **Health Statistics:** 260 inhabitants per hospital bed; 1,330 per physician (1973) **Infant Mortality:** 82 per 1,000 births **Illiteracy:** 14% **Primary and Secondary School Enrollment:** 672,434 (1972) **Enrollment of Higher Education:** 44,296 (1971) **GNP Expended on Education:** 3.0% (1973)

Transportation: Paved roads total 3,775 mi. **Motor Vehicles:** 243,600 (1974) **Passenger Cars:** 220,200 **Railway Mileage:** 250 **Ports:** Beirut, Tripoli, Sidon **Major Airlines:** Middle East Airlines operates international services **Communications:** Government and privately owned **Radio Transmitters:** 6 **Receivers:** 1,600,000 (1976) **Television Transmitters:** 8 **Receivers:** 425,000 (1976) **Telephones:** 222,000 (1975) **Newspapers:** 33 dailies (1975), 92 copies per 1,000 inhabitants

Weights and Measures: Metric system **Travel Requirements:** Passport, 6-month visa valid for 2 entries, $5 fee

Lebanon is situated on the eastern shore of the Mediterranean and has an area slightly smaller than that of Connecticut. Bounded on the north and east by Syria and on the south by Israel, its chief topographic features are a narrow coastal plain behind which are the Lebanese Mountains, then the fertile Beqaa Valley, and finally the Anti-Lebanon Mountains extending to the Syrian border. An estimated 64 percent of the land is desert, waste, or urban; 27 percent farmland; and nine percent forest. The Litani River, flowing into the sea north of Tyre, is the main river.

Traditionally a part of Greater Syria, which in turn was a sector of the Ottoman Empire, Lebanon became a separate entity after World War I to satisfy its Christian inhabitants. It was administered by France from 1920 to 1941, when it was declared independent by the Free French. With few natural resources besides a good location, Lebanon became a center of commerce and banking. For a time, general prosperity and a desire to keep peace discouraged challenges to the privileged position of the Christians. Uneasy political stability prevailed. So did laissez-faire capitalism and personal freedom; the government governed as little as possible to avoid offending anybody.

In the 1970s, however, Palestinian guerrillas established bases in Lebanon and began raids on Israel, prompting Israeli retaliation. Bitter disputes resulted between the Moslems, who tended to sympathize with the Palestinian cause, and the Christians, who had less sympathy for it. Open war broke out in the spring of 1975, with armed Christian bands on one side, Palestinians and Lebanese Moslem and Druse bands on the other. Israel armed the Christians, but their opponents came close to winning, and Syria sent in army units to protect the Christians and deny Israel a pretext for intervening. Later, under the nominal command of the Arab League, the Syrians actually became a disturbing element, clashing with the Christians, whom they were supposed to protect.

The worst fighting ended in 1976, but Lebanon remained functionally divided along communal lines and unable to repair the damage of the war or to return to its former commercial and banking activities. Most of the soldiers in its army had joined warring bands, but the government retained its ability to collect taxes—and paid soldiers for fighting each other. The legislature elected Elias Sarkis, a Christian respected by Moslems, as president, and he appointed a Moslem, Selim al-Hoss, premier; their conciliatory efforts were of little avail.

Israel occupied much of southern Lebanon in 1978, in order to create a buffer zone there. The United Nations sent soldiers from many countries to police the area, and Israel withdrew, but turned some of the area over to Lebanese Christian warriors, instead of the UN. Meanwhile, Christian factions in northern Lebanon clashed with each other. Warriors of all factions sometimes attacked UN soldiers. Low-level fighting continued with Christians pitted against Syrian soldiers, Moslems, Druzes, and other Christians. Palestinian raids into Israel and Israeli raids on Palestinian bases took place. There were heavy losses on both sides; between 1975 and 1980, an estimated 42,000 people were killed and property destruction amounted to more than $6 million.

HISTORY: In ancient times, Hittite and Aramaean kingdoms occupied the area that is now Lebanon. The Lebanese coast later became the base for the sea-trading Phoenicians, but their cities soon fell prey to the Assyrians, Persians, and Greeks. Along with neighboring Syria, Lebanon was then brought under Roman rule and afterwards became part of the Byzantine Empire. Maronite Christians established themselves in the area, and even after the spread of Islam by the Arabs, who invaded Lebanon in the 7th century, the country long remained largely Christian

1516-17: Lebanon and Syria are absorbed into the Ottoman Empire, but Lebanon retains considerable autonomy

1841-64: Massacres of Maronite Christians by Druzes cause European governments to force Ottoman sultans to agree to a pro-Christian government for the area and to the establishment of autonomous province of Mount Lebanon

1918: Anglo-French force occupies Lebanon following collapse of Ottoman Empire in World War I

1920: Lebanon, along with Syria, becomes a French mandate

1941-45: Lebanon, under Free French occupation, is declared independent in 1941; however, French retain actual control of country until 1945

1958: Opposition to pro-Western policies of President Camille Chamoun erupts in rebellion; at Chamoun's request, U.S. troops are ordered to Lebanon by President Eisenhower; troops are withdrawn after formation of new Lebanese government

1968: Israeli commandos raid Beirut airport, destroying 13 civil aircraft; Israel claims raid was in retaliation for an earlier attack on Israeli airliner in Athens, carried out by two Arab terrorists from Beirut; Lebanon disclaims responsibility for commandos operating against Israel from Lebanese territory

1970: Suleiman Franjieh is elected president by legislature; Saeb Salaam succeeds Rashid Karami as premier

1972: Israel raids guerrilla bases in Lebanon in retaliation for the killing of Israeli athletes at the Munich Olympics

1973: Israeli commando raid on Beirut in which three guerrilla leaders are slain forces resignation of Premier Saeb Salaam and sparks two weeks of fighting in Beirut between guerrillas and Lebanese army; new Premier Takieddin Solh negotiates uneasy truce, but guerrilla activity and Israeli reprisals continue before and after Arab-Israeli war in October

1974: Border clashes between Israeli forces and Palestinian guerrillas based in Lebanon continue

1975-76: Some 60,000 die in 19-month civil war between Christians and Moslems; army disintegrates; economy nears collapse. Syria invades; Arab summit arranges cease-fire and establishes Arab League peacekeeping forces—consisting mostly of Syrians who are already there. Elias Sarkis becomes president; he appoints Selim al-Hoss premier

1977: Moslem leader Kamal Jumblat is assassinated

1978: Israelis, avenging a PLO terror raid, invade southern Lebanon, attacking PLO bases there; about 200,000 Lebanese and 65,000 Palestinian refugees flee to the north; most return as Israelis pull out three months later. UN peacekeeping forces form buffer zone between Israelis and PLO guerrillas. Conflict develops in southern border zone between central government, attempting to reassert its authority, and Israeli-backed Christian militia units. Israeli planes raid Palestinian camps in retaliation for terrorist attack on airline bus in London

1979: Continued fighting on all fronts. Saad Haddad, Christian militia officer, proclaims independent "Free Lebanese State" in Christian region along Israeli border. Premier al-Hoss forms new Moslem-Christian coalition government

1980: Israeli forces occupy Lebanon's southern border region for five days, in retaliation for Palestinian terrorist raid. Takieddin Solh succeeds al-Hoss as premier

---

LESOTHO

Area: 11,720 sq. mi. **Population:** 1,279,000 (1978 est.)

Official Name: Kingdom of Lesotho **Capital:** Maseru **Nationality:** Basotho **Languages:** Sesotho, the language of the Sotho people, and English are the official languages **Religion:** About 70% Christian, chiefly Roman Catholic, the rest being mostly animist **Flag:** Green and red vertical stripes to the left of a blue field bearing a white conical Sotho hat **Anthem:** National Anthem, beginning "Lesotho, the country of our fathers" **Currency:** South African rand (.80 per U.S. $1)

Location: An enclave within the east-central part of the Republic of South Africa, Lesotho is bordered on the west and north by the Orange Free State Province, on the east by the Province of Natal, and on the south by Cape Province and Transkei **Features:** About a fourth of the western sector is lowland terrain; the rest of the country is mountainous **Chief Rivers:** Orange, Caledon

Head of State: King Moshoeshoe II, born 1938; formerly Paramount Chief, he became king in 1966 **Head of Government:** Prime Minister, Dr. Leabua Jonathan, born 1914, appointed 1965; he seized power in 1970, acts also as defense and internal security minister, and rules by decree **Effective Date of Present Constitution:** 1966, suspended 1970 **Legislative Body:** Parliament (bicameral), suspended 1970. An interim National Assembly with limited powers was formed in 1973, the members being nominated by the government **Local Government:** 9 districts, with appointed administrators

Ethnic Composition: The population is almost entirely Bantu, with 85% Sotho and 15% Nguni. There are less than 1% South Africans, Asians and mixed **Population Distribution:** 1% urban **Density:** 109 inhabitants per sq. mi.

Largest City: (1972 est.) Maseru 29,049

Per Capita Income: $251 (1978) **Gross National Product (GNP):** $323 million (1978) **Economic Statistics:** In 1976 about 40% of GNP came from agriculture (corn, sorghum, wheat, beans, peas, livestock), 10% from industry (printing, carpet weaving, brewing, candlemaking, tire retreading) and mining **Minerals and Mining:** Few known mineral deposits except for diamonds **Labor Force:** 87% of population engaged in subsistence agriculture. 150,000 to 200,000 work six months to many years as wage earners in South Africa **Foreign Trade:** Exports, mainly diamonds, wool, mohair, and livestock, totaled $34.8 million in 1978. Imports, chiefly foodstuffs, textiles; clothing, transportation equipment, and chemicals, totaled $262 million **Principal Trade Partners:** South Africa, Britain, United States

Vital Statistics: Birthrate, 39 per 1,000 of pop. (1975); death rate, 19.7 **Life Expectancy:** 46 years **Health Statistics:** 552 inhabitants per hospital bed; 20,570 per physician (1976) **Infant Mortality:** 114.4 per 1,000 births **Illiteracy:** 60% **Primary and Secondary School Enrollment:** 239,943 (1976) **Enrollment in Higher Education:** 577 (1974) **GNP Expended on Education:** 3.7% (1973)

Transportation: Improved roads total 625 mi. **Motor Vehicles:** 7,800 (1975) **Passenger Cars:** 4,600 **Railway Mileage:** One mile of track links Maseru with South Africa **Ports:** None **Major Airlines:** Government-owned Lesotho Airways operates domestic services

Communications: Government owned **Radio Transmitters:** 3 Licenses: 23,000 (1976) **Television:** None **Telephones:** 4,000 (1974) **Newspapers:** Several weeklies

Weights and Measures: Metric and British standards **Travel Requirements:** Passport, visa valid for 20 days

An enclave in the southeastern area of South Africa, Lesotho, the former British protectorate of Basutoland, is an island of black African nationalism in a sea of apartheid. The small mountainous kingdom is the remnant of a larger realm, the refuge to which the Basotho were driven by tribal wars and Boer incursions.

In 1818, Moshesh I, a tribal chief from the north, succeeded in uniting the Basotho people. He ruled from about 1820 to 1870 and consolidated various tribes that had been scattered earlier by Zulu and Matabele warriors. During his reign, a series of wars with the Orange Free State (1856-68) resulted in the loss of a large area to the Free State, now known as the "Conquered Territory." Moshesh appealed to the British for help, and in 1868 the country was annexed by Britain.

For a considerable time thereafter the energies of the British administrators were absorbed largely in the task of settling intertribal disputes and in maintaining the position of the Paramount Chief as a symbol of national unity. From 1884 to 1959 legislative and executive authority was vested in a British High Commissioner. In 1910, the Basutoland Council, which had come into existence on an informal basis in 1903, was formally established as a consultative body.

Badly eroded and subject to droughts, the country produces mohair, wool, and hides from livestock. There are only about 1,000 square miles of cultivable land and many food supplies must be imported.

Although there has been an increase of revenue under a revised customs union with South Africa, much of Lesotho's income is derived from the wages of Basotho men who work as contract laborers in South African gold and coal mines.

There has been some development of light industry, tourism, and an increase of diamond mining, but Lesotho has little prospect of ending its economic dependence on South Africa. To a large extent, Lesotho is little more than one of the bantustans, or separate African homelands, that have been created in South Africa itself.

With the attainment of political independence in 1966, the traditional ruler, King Moshoeshoe II, tried to reassert royal authority, but after being forced into exile by the prime minister, Chief Leabua Jonathan, agreed to accept a titular, symbolic position.

Although professing to abhor apartheid, Chief Jonathan has advocated what he calls a realistic "bread-and-butter good-neighbor policy." But despite extreme poverty, Lesotho has achieved considerable progress in education—it has one of the highest literacy rates in Africa—and many Basotho, who are well educated and highly politicized, resent South Africa's racist regime.

When in early 1970, Jonathan appeared to have lost the country's first national elections, he declared the results invalid, jailed his leading opponents, and seized control. Although threatened with withdrawal of British aid, the plump, disarmingly jolly Jonathan has since ruled by decree.

Chief Jonathan has welcomed back the king from exile, talked of political reconciliation, and successfully suppressed several outbreaks of rebellion, including one in 1974 in which 20 rebels were killed in a plot allegedly hatched by the opposition Congress party.

HISTORY: Decimated by Zulu and Matabele raids in the early 19th century, the Basotho were later fused into a new nation in the mountains of Basutoland (Lesotho) by Moshesh (Moshoeshoe) I. The king soon had to contend with Boers in the neighboring Orange Free State and sought the protection of the British Cape Colony. Annexation by the colony in 1868, however, led to more fighting, and in 1884 Basutoland again was made a British protectorate. In 1909 a British act of Parliament, establishing the Union of South Africa, stipulated that Basutoland, as well as Bechuanaland (Botswana) and Swaziland, would not be transferred to their more powerful neighbor without prior consent of the inhabitants

1910: A consultative Basutoland Council, made up of Basotho chiefs and leaders, is established by the British

1959-60: A constitution is promulgated and a more representative legislative body, the Basutoland National Council, is set up

1961: South Africa's apartheid policies cause Britain to reaffirm that Basutoland and other protectorates will not be handed over to South African rule

1966: Basutoland gains independence as Lesotho

1967: Held under house arrest after attempting to assert absolute authority, King Moshoeshoe II accedes to Prime Minister Leabua Jonathan's demands that he reign as constitutional monarch

1970: Prime Minister Jonathan seizes control, suspends constitution, declares a state of emergency (ended in 1973); imprisons his opponent, Ntsu Mokhehle, following disputed election

1975: Miners recruited from Lesotho strike gold mine in South Africa to protest a Lesotho law requiring miners to remit 60 percent of their pay and deposit it in Lesotho banks

1979: Bombings attributed to outlawed Congress party cause great damage and loss of life; Jonathan converts paramilitary police unit into regular army to suppress violence

---

LIBERIA

Area: 43,000 sq. mi. **Population:** 1,742,000 (1978 est.)

Official Name: Republic of Liberia **Capital:** Monrovia **Nationality:** Liberian **Languages:** English, the official and commerical language, is spoken by about 20% of the population; some 28 African dialects are also spoken **Religion:** 75% animist, 10% Christian, 15% Moslem **Flag:** Eleven red and white horizontal stripes, with a five-pointed white star on a blue field in the upper left corner **Anthem:** National Anthem, beginning "All hail, Liberia, hail!" **Currency:** U.S. (Liberian) dollar

Location: West Africa. Liberia is bordered on the northeast by Guinea, on the east by the Ivory Coast, on the south and west by the Atlantic Ocean, and on the north by Sierra Leone **Features:** The country is flat, with the exception of some hills in the region of Monrovia, the Bomi Hills, and the Guinea Highlands. About 40% of the country is covered by tropical woodlands **Chief Rivers:** Mano, Lofa, St. Paul, St. John, Cestos

Head of State and of Government: Master Sgt. Samuel Kanyon Doe, born 1951?, took power following the coup of April 12, 1980. He is Chairman of the People's Redemption Council, the highest body of the new government **Effective Date of Present Constitution:** 1847 **Legislative Body (prior to coup of April 1980):** Congress (bicameral), consisting of a Senate and a House of Representatives. The Senate has 18 members elected for 6 years. The House of Representatives has 70 members elected for 4 years **Local Government:** 9 counties, headed by appointed superintendents

Ethnic Composition: More than 97% of the population is made up of indigenous Africans belonging to about 16 tribal groups. About 2.5% of the population are Americo-Liberian descendants of 19th century emancipated black American slaves **Population Distribution:** 28% urban **Density:** 41 inhabitants per sq. mi.

Largest Cities: (1976 est.) Monrovia 204,000, Harbel 60,000, Buchanan 25,000, Yekepa 16,000, Harper 14,000

Per Capita Income: $670 (1979) **Gross National Product (GNP):** $937 million (1979) **Economic Statistics:** About 33% of GNP comes from mining; 17% from agriculture (rubber, casava, rice, bananas, plantains), forestry, and fishing; and 11% from wholesale and retail trade **Minerals and Mining:** Liberia is the world's 10th largest producer of high-grade iron ore. Diamonds are of importance, and there are unexploited reserves of manganese, gold, columbite, tantalite, and bauxite **Labor Force:** 600,000, with 72% in agriculture, and only 25% in the monetary economy, chiefly on rubber plantations, in government, construction, and mining **Foreign Trade:** Exports, chiefly iron ore, rubber, and diamonds, totaled $486 million in 1978. Imports, mainly manufactured goods, machinery, transportation equipment, fuel, and food, totaled $481 million **Principal Trade Partners:** United States, West Germany, Japan, Britain, Italy

Vital Statistics: Birthrate, 49.8 per 1,000 of pop. (1971); death rate, 20.9 **Life Expectancy:** 46 years **Health Statistics:** 652 inhabitants per hospital bed; 11,761 per physician (1973) **Infant Mortality:** 159.2

per 1,000 births **Illiteracy:** 76% **Primary and Secondary School Enrollment:** 191,972 (1975) **Enrollment in Higher Education:** 2,404 (1975) **GNP Expended on Education:** 2.4% (1975)

Transportation: Paved roads total 325 mi. **Motor Vehicles:** 22,100 (1974) **Passenger Cars:** 12,100 **Railway Mileage:** 304 **Ports:** Monrovia, Buchanan, Greenville, Harper **Major Airlines:** Air Liberia operates internal services **Communications:** Partly government owned **Radio Transmitters:** 15 **Receivers:** 265,000 (1976) **Television Transmitters:** 4 **Receivers:** 18,800 (1974) **Telephones:** 7,500 (1974) **Newspapers:** 3 dailies, 8 copies per 1,000 inhabitants

Weights and Measures: U.S. standards are used **Travel Requirements:** Passport, visa valid for 90 days, $2 fee, 3 pictures

---

A green, rainy land settled in the 1820s by freed slaves from the United States, Liberia is Africa's oldest independent republic. As more and more blacks were being liberated early in the 19th century, some Americans became uneasy about their numbers. In 1816 the American Colonization Society was chartered by Congress to promote a "back-to-Africa" movement. The society purchased land from African chiefs in a region that had been largely depopulated by the slave trade, and the first group of an eventual 15,000 settlers established their colony at the present site of Monrovia.

Although it was a neglected stepchild, Liberia modeled its constitution, institutions and flag after those of the United States. It established itself as a sovereign nation in 1847, a status which the United States did not recognize until 1862, long after European powers had done so.

Lacking money and technology, as well as outside interest, the early Liberians were unable to progress beyond a simple rural economy. Contemporary Liberians often say, "We missed out on the benefits of colonialism." However, in the 1920s the Firestone Tire and Rubber Company started to develop a rubber industry which today employs about half of Liberia's wage earners. During World War II, American money and manpower poured in to give the country the big Robertsfield Airport, a new seaport at Monrovia, and the first network of modern roads. There followed the iron-ore boom of the 1950s with huge investments by foreign mining companies.

The making of Liberia into a modern country, with a viable economy and position of leadership in African affairs, has been almost entirely the work of the late William V.S. Tubman, Liberia's president from 1944 until his death in 1971.

A forceful and sometimes autocratic leader, Mr. Tubman spurred economic development through industry and iron-ore mining at a time when Liberia seemed to be lagging behind newer African nations.

Tubman was succeeded as president in 1971 by Vice-President William R. Tolbert, Jr., son of a former South Carolina slave who had prospered as a farmer in Liberia. Tolbert launched a program of widespread reform, but dissatisfaction increased with his autocratic rule and with continued control of the government and economy by the 2½% minority of descendants of American slaves. In April 1979, when police and soldiers opened fire on student-led demonstrators protesting an increase in the price of rice, 74 persons were killed and hundreds injured. Tolbert adopted unpopular repressive measures and had many opposition leaders jailed.

On April 12, 1980, Tolbert was killed in a coup by army enlisted men, and 27 of his aides were summarily executed in a blood bath. The leader of the coup, Master Sgt. Samuel K. Doe, 28, took over as head of state.

HISTORY: Before being colonized early in the 19th century by freed black slaves from the United States, Liberia was known as the Grain Coast for its production of grains of melegueta pepper. The indigenous peoples, among them Kru, Gola, Mandingo, and Vai, are believed to derive from ancient black nations of sub-Saharan regions farther north. During the several centuries of the slave trade, the country was steadily drained of population

1816: American Colonization Society is founded to send freed slaves to Western Africa

1822: First group of settlers arrives from United States and establishes colony on Providence Island, at present site of Monrovia, purchased by American Colonization Society

1824: Name "Liberia" is adopted and chief settlement is named Monrovia in honor of U.S. President James Monroe

1847: Joseph Jenkins Roberts, governor of the Liberian Commonwealth, a Virginia-born freeman of part-black ancestry, proclaims independent Republic of Liberia and becomes first president

1850-1920: Territory is lost to neighboring British, French colonies; economy and finances deteriorate, but government rejects proposal for international receivership

1923-26: Firestone Tire and Rubber Company assists government financially and begins development of rubber

1943: True Whig party candidate William V.S. Tubman becomes president; begins programs of social unification to speed assimilation of indigenous population into the rest of the community, and policy of "open door" for foreign investment

1955: Opposition Reformation and Independent True Whig parties are charged with plot to overthrow government by force and are banned; True Whig party becomes dominant

1967: President Tubman is reelected to sixth successive term

1971: Tubman dies and is succeeded by Vice-President Tolbert

1975: Tolbert is elected for an eight-year term as president

1979: Police and army fire on demonstrators against food-price increases in April, killing 74. Tolbert closes University of Liberia and suspends right of habeas corpus

1980: Tolbert is killed in coup April 12 by enlisted men of army; Master Sgt. Samuel K. Doe becomes head of state

---

LIBYA

On September 10, 1980, Colonel Qaddafi of Libya and President Assad of Syria issued a proclamation stating that Libya and Syria had become a single state.

Area: 679,358 sq. mi. **Population:** 2,748,000 (1978 est.)

Official Name: Socialist People's Libyan Arab Jamahiriya **Capital:** Tripoli **Nationality:** Libyan **Languages:** Arabic is the official and dominant language; English and Italian are also used **Religion:** 97% Sunni Moslem **Flag:** A plain green field Anthem: Almighty God **Currency:** Libyan dinar (.30 per U.S. $1)

Location: North Africa. Libya is bordered on the north by the Mediterranean Sea, on the east by Egypt, on the southeast by the Sudan, on the south by Chad and Niger, on the west by Algeria, and on the northwest by Tunisia **Features:** About 90% of the terrain consists of barren, rock-strewn plains and deserts, with three elevated regions in the northwest, northeast and extreme south **Chief Rivers:** There are no permanent rivers

Head of State: Colonel Muammar Qaddafi, born 1943; seized power in 1969; elected Revolutionary Leader (Head of State) in 1977. He also is defense minister **Head of Government:** Abdul Ati Obeidi is Secretary General of the General Secretariat of the General People's Congress, appointed 1979. Jadallah Azzuz al Talhi is secretary of the General People's Committee, appointed 1979 **Effective Date of Present Constitution:** The political structure is guided by the principles announced at the General People's Congress in March 1977 **Legislative Body:** General People's Congress (unicameral), closely controlled by the central government **Local Government:** 10 governorates, each under an appointed governor

Ethnic Composition: The population is chiefly a racial mixture of Arabs and Berbers **Population Distribution:** 30% urban **Density:** 4 inhabitants per sq. mi.

Largest Cities: (1973 census) Tripoli 281,497, Benghazi 131,970, Zawia 52,327, Misurata 45,146, Sabratha 30,817, Tarhuna 23,338

Per Capita Income: $6,897 (1979) **Gross National Product (GNP):** $20.2 billion (1979) **Economic Statistics:** In 1975 about 52% of GNP came from oil, 3% from agriculture (wheat, barley, tomatoes, dates, citrus fruits, olives, livestock); and 13% from manufacturing (food processing, textiles, soaps, detergents, paper bags and wrapping paper) **Minerals and Mining:** Libya is one of the world's largest oil producers. Other minerals are gypsum, natural gas, marble, iron ore, and potassium **Labor Force:** 900,000 (1977) of which 350,000 are resident foreigners **Foreign Trade:** Exports, consisting almost exclusively of crude oil, totaled $9.5 billion in 1978. Imports, mainly oil drilling equipment and machinery, iron and steel pipes, tubes, and fittings, manufactured goods, and food products, totaled $6.1 billion **Principal Trade Partners:** West Germany, Britain, Italy, United States, France, Japan

Vital Statistics: Birthrate, 45 per 1,000 of pop. (1975); death rate, 14.7 **Life Expectancy:** 53 years **Health Statistics:** 200 inhabitants per hospital bed; 938 per physician (1976) **Infant Mortality:** N.A. **Illiteracy:** 64% **Primary and Secondary School Enrollment:** 790,569 (1976) **Enrollment in Higher Education:** 11,997 **GNP Expended on Education:** 5.2% (1975)

Transportation: Paved roads total 4,800 mi. **Motor Vehicles:** 394,400 (1975) **Passenger Cars:** 263,100 **Railway Mileage:** none **Ports:** Tripoli, Benghazi, El Brega, Ras Lanuf, Zueitina, Syrte, El Hariga, Derna, Tobruk **Major Airlines:** Libyan Arab Airways operates domestic and international services **Communications:** Government-owned **Radio Transmitters:** 12 **Licenses:** 110,000 (1976) **Television Transmitters:** 2 **Licenses:** 10,000 (1975) **Telephones:** 45,000 (1975) **Newspapers:** 2 dailies, 17 copies per 1,000 inhabitants (1975)

Weights and Measures: Metric system and local units are used **Travel Requirements:** Passport (with Arabic translation), visa valid for 3 months; $7 fee, 2 pictures

---

Consisting mostly of arid desert, the land that is now Libya was a bone of contention among empires for thousands of years. Its most influential conquerors were the Moslem Arabs of the seventh century A.D.; they gave Libya the language and the religion that now prevail. Its most recent conqueror was Italy. After losing World War II, Italy was forced to grant independence to Libya in 1951. Idris, a Moslem chieftain, became king. But, with no natural resources except a location that was strategic in the Cold War, Libya was heavily dependent on the United States, which gave considerable assistance in return for the use of Wheelus Air Force Base.

With the discovery of oil in 1959, Libya, with less than 3 million people, became potentially a power in its own right. King Idris used the oil revenue to build schools, hospitals, highways, and low-cost housing.

But Libya did not achieve its real international potential until after the overthrow of King Idris by the army in 1969. A Revolutionary Command Council of military officers, headed by Col. Muammar Qaddafi, took control of the nation. Desert-born, with little understanding of the non-Moslem world, Qaddafi made Libya a bastion of strict Moslem traditionalism. He outlawed liquor, imposed a strict dress code for women, and made amputation the standard penalty for theft. A bitter enemy of big powers, he closed Wheelus Air Force Base, published manifestos condemning both the U.S. and USSR, and helped Malta to force the closing of British bases. A strident foe of Israel, he joined other Arab militant leaders in denouncing Egypt for making a separate peace with Israel in 1979. Qaddafi tried to intervene surreptitiously in Uganda to keep President Idi Amin Dada in power; after Amin's overthrow, he gave him asylum in Libya. In November, Uganda released the last of 56 Libyan soldiers captured during its civil war. On December 2, a mob in Tripoli attacked and damaged the U.S. embassy, but the American staff escaped without injury. The United States closed the embassy in May 1980.

Qaddafi moved in 1980 to silence his opponents and warned Libyan exiles to return or "be liquidated." After four anti-Qaddafi exiles were killed in London and Rome, the United States, in May, expelled four Libyan diplomats charged with threatening Libyan students in America. Libya immediately expelled 25 Americans it charged were spies and detained two others.

HISTORY: In ancient times, Libya was successively ruled by Carthage, Rome, and the Vandals. The Arabs conquered the country in the 7th century A.D. In the Middle Ages, Egypt and Tunisia vied for control of the country, and in the early 16th century Spain and the Knights of Malta replaced the African rivals in dominating Libya. The Ottoman Empire seized control in 1551, although Libya's local pashas continued to enjoy autonomy
1830: Turks reassert control over Libya

1911-33: Italy occupies Libya following Turco-Italian War (1911-12) and engages in long series of wars of pacification against the Sanusi, a Moslem religious brotherhood
1943-49: Libya is conquered by Allied forces in World War II; Tripolitania and Cyrenaica are placed under British administration and the Fezzan under French administration
1951: Kingdom of Libya gains formal independence, with Idris I, leader of the Sanusi brotherhood, as the country's first king
1954: United States is granted military air base in Libya
1959-61: Oil is discovered in Tripolitania and Cyrenaica in 1959
1967: Libya charges United States with helping Israel in Six-Day Middle Eastern War, calls on United States to liquidate Wheelus Air Force Base
1969: Monarchy is overthrown by a military junta composed of young nationalist army officers. Colonel Qaddafi, their leader, becomes prime minister in 1970
1970: Junta takes over Wheelus Air Force Base, buys Mirage jets from France, and renegotiates contracts with Western oil companies to gain greater share of oil revenues
1973: Qaddafi introduces the "cultural revolution," an attempt to govern Libya according to the tenets of Islam. Establishes "people's committees" to carry out the revolution
1974: Qaddafi relinquishes political and administrative functions; announces he will concentrate on ideology and organization. Premier Abdul Salam Jalloud assumes Qaddafi's former duties
1975: Creation of 618-member General National Congress is decreed to implement theories of Colonel Qaddafi
1976: Relations with Egypt deteriorate when Libyan soldiers are arrested in Cairo in connection with a plot to kidnap Maj. Omar Meheishi, a dissident member of the Revolutionary Command Council who fled Libya in 1975 after an attempted coup against Colonel Qaddafi. In retaliation Egyptians are expelled from Libya
1977: Libyan and Egyptian troops and aircraft battle along border
1979: Libya secretly sends soldiers to Uganda to defend government of President Idi Amin Dada against Tanzanian attack; grants asylum to Amin. Tripoli mob damages U.S. embassy
1980: Qaddafi orders Libyan exiles to return to Libya; four of his political opponents are murdered in Europe; U.S. expels four Libyan diplomats who allegedly threatened Libyan students, withdraws diplomatic staff and closes embassy in Tripoli. In Washington it is revealed that Billy Carter acted as an agent for Libya and received a loan from the Libyan government. Qaddafi and Syrian President Assad sign merger agreement proclaiming Libya and Syria a single state

---

LIECHTENSTEIN

Area: 61 sq. mi. **Population:** 25,000 (1978 est.)

Official Name: Principality of Liechtenstein **Capital:** Vaduz **Nationality:** Liechtensteiner **Languages:** German is the official language; Alemannic, a dialect, is spoken by most **Religion:** Roman Catholicism is the official religion and claims about 92% of the population **Flag:** Blue and red horizontal stripes, with a golden crown near the staff end of the blue stripe **Anthem:** National Anthem, beginning "Above on the German Rhine" **Currency:** Swiss franc (1.66 per U.S. $1)

Location: Western Europe. Liechtenstein, situated in the Rhine River Valley, is bordered by Austria on the east and by Switzerland on the south and west **Features:** One third of the area is level land bordering the right bank of the Rhine, and an upland and mountainous area occupies the remainder **Chief Rivers:** Rhine, Samina

Head of State: Prince Franz Josef II, born 1906, ascended the throne 1938 **Head of Government:** Prime Minister: Hans Brunhart, chairman of the 5-man Collegial Board, appointed April 1978 **Effective Date of Present Constitution:** 1921 **Legislative Body:** Parliament (unicameral *Landtag*), consisting of 15 members, elected for 4 years by male suffrage **Local Government:** 11 communes, with limited powers of self-government

Ethnic Composition: The population is of Germanic descent; one third is alien, mostly Swiss, Italian, Austrian and German **Population Distribution:** Predominantly rural **Density:** 410 inhabitants per sq. mi.

Largest Towns: (1974 est.) Vaduz 7,500; (1970 census) Schaan 3,890, Balzers 2,704, Triesen 2,637, Mauren 2,055

Per Capita Income: $11,330 (1979) **Gross National Product (GNP):** $340 million (1979) **Economic Statistics:** Some 40% of the land is used for raising crops (corn and other cereals, potatoes, garden produce, fruits), but the main source of income from land use is raising beef and dairy cattle. Industry is mainly devoted to the small-scale production of precision manufactures (calculating machines, optical lenses, high vacuum pumps), false teeth and textiles. Between 20,000 and 30,000 foreign firms maintain nominal headquarters in Vaduz, because of liberal tax incentives. Tourism and the sale of stamps are also important sources of income **Minerals and Mining:** Except for some quarrying, there is no mining **Labor Force:** 11,368 (5,078 foreign workers) with 54% in industry, trade and construction, 42% in services and 4% in agriculture, forestry and hunting **Foreign Trade:** Exports are chiefly special machinery and tools, artificial teeth, textiles, chemicals, and food. Liechtenstein has a customs union with Switzerland and there are no records of foreign trade totals **Principal Trade Partners:** EFTA and Common Market countries

Vital Statistics: Birthrate, 12.5 per 1,000 of pop. (1977); death rate, 6.1 **Life Expectancy:** 65 years **Health Statistics:** Hospital facilities exist in nearby Switzerland; 1,633 inhabitants per physician (1971) **Infant Mortality:** 6.5 per 1,000 births **Illiteracy:** Negligible **Primary and Secondary School Enrollment:** 4,445 pupils (1972) **Enrollment in Higher Education:** 243 **GNP Expended on Education:** N.A.

Transportation: Good paved roads serve the principality **Motor Vehicles:** 11,000 (1976) **Passenger Cars:** 10,000 **Railway Mileage:** 11.5 **Ports:** None **Major Airlines:** None **Communications:** Served by Switzerland **Radio Stations:** None **Licenses:** 5,000 (1976) **Television Stations:** None **Licenses:** 4,500 (1976) **Telephones:** 16,000 (1976) **Newspapers:** 1 daily, 286 copies per 1,000 inhabitants

Weights and Measures: Metric system **Travel Requirements:** Passport, no visa for 3 months

---

Since 1923 the tiny principality of Liechtenstein, wedged between Austria and Switzerland, has had a customs union with Switzerland, and that country also provides Liechtenstein's currency, administers its postal, telegraph, and telephone services, and handles Liechtenstein's international affairs. In World War II, Liechtenstein, like Switzerland, was a neutral.

Though bucolic, with lush green valleys and houses with red-tile roofs, the state has mainly an industrial economy. Only four percent of the population is engaged in agricultural pursuits.

Liechtenstein has become industrialized in the last quarter of a century; it contains Europe's biggest producer of false teeth and dental supplies, and is noted for such precision products as thin optic coatings and electronic microscopy. The industrialization has brought an influx of Swiss, Austrian, and German workers.

The principality is a tax haven for corporations and holding companies. Additional sources of income are tourism and the sale of postage stamps. Though Liechtenstein has neither a broadcasting station nor an airport, it is the repository of art valued at somewhere near $150 million, the holdings of Liechtenstein's monarch, Prince Franz Josef II.

In 1978, Liechtenstein joined the Council of Europe, although other nations represented in the Council objected to the principality's voting laws; alone in Europe, Liechtenstein does not allow women to vote for members of its national legislature. Women may vote in local elections in Vaduz.

HISTORY: The principality of Liechtenstein was created in 1719 as a fief of the Holy Roman Empire by uniting the barony of Schellenberg and the county of Vaduz, both of which had been purchased from the counts of Hohenem by the Austrian family of Liechtenstein. During the Napoleonic Wars, the principality was invaded by the French. In 1815, after Napoleon's downfall, Liechtenstein joined the newly formed Germanic Confederation

1866: Germanic Confederation is dissolved after Prussia's victory over Austria in the Seven Weeks' War, thus ending Liechtenstein's ties to other German states

1868: Liechtenstein, which had furnished Austria with 80 soldiers during the war with Prussia, disbands its military force and adopts policy of permanent neutrality

1919-24: Switzerland assumes control of Liechtenstein's external affairs and forms customs union with principality

1938: Prince Franz I is succeeded by his great-nephew, who, as Franz Josef II, becomes the first ruler to make Liechtenstein his permanent home

1945-65: Having avoided involvement in World War II, Liechtenstein enjoys rapid economic growth, developing into a center of tourism, trade, and small-scale manufacturing

1970: Traditional minority Patriotic Union wins one-vote majority in *Landtag*, ending 42-year leadership of coalition government by Progressive Citizens party

1973: Electorate again denies women the franchise

1974: Progressive Citizens party regains majority in parliament

1978: Hans Brunhart of Fatherland Union party is appointed prime minister; government is virtually paralyzed for two months as outgoing prime minister balks at relinquishing post of foreign minister, in addition to prime ministership; president rules former prime minister and his successor may share foreign ministership

---

LUXEMBOURG

Area: 999 sq. mi. **Population:** 358,000 (1978 est.)

Official Name: Grand Duchy of Luxembourg **Capital:** Luxembourg **Nationality:** Luxembourgian **Languages:** French is the official language. German is used in local newspapers. Letzeburgisch is the everyday language **Religion:** 97% Roman Catholic; 3% Protestant and Jewish **Flag:** A tricolor of red, white, and blue horizontal stripes **Anthem:** Our Homeland **Currency:** Luxembourg franc (29 per U.S. $1)

Location: Western Europe. Landlocked Luxembourg is bordered on the north and west by Belgium, on the east by the Federal Republic of Germany, and on the south by France **Features:** The northern part of the country contains the rugged uplands of the Ardennes plateau, while the south consists of undulating terrain with broad valleys **Chief Rivers:** Alzette, Sûre, Moselle, Our

Head of State: Grand Duke Jean, born 1921, ascended the throne 1964 **Head of Government:** Premier Pierre Werner, appointed 1979 **Effective Date of Present Constitution:** 1868 **Legislative Body:** Parliament (bicameral), consisting of a Chamber of Deputies of 59 members, elected for 5 years, and a Council of State appointed by the Grand Duke **Local Government:** 12 cantons grouped into 3 districts

Ethnic Composition: Luxembourgers are ethnically a mixture of French and German. Throughout the 20th century, a considerable number of immigrants from Italy and other Mediterranean countries have settled in Luxembourg **Population Distribution:** 68% urban **Density:** 358 inhabitants per sq. mi.

Largest Cities: (1974 est.) Luxembourg 78,403; (1970 census) Esch/Alzette 27,574, Differdange 17,964, Dudelange 14,615

Per Capita Income: $7,689 (1979) **Gross National Product (GNP):** $2.8 billion (1979) **Economic Statistics:** About 41% of GNP comes from industry (steel, chemicals, auto parts, rubber, synthetic fibers), 3% from agriculture (livestock, dairy products, wine) **Minerals and Mining:** Vast deposits of iron ore are mined; slate is also quarried in commercial quantities **Labor Force:** 146,500 (50% aliens) of which 48% is in services, 46% in industry, 6% in agriculture (grapes, livestock) **Foreign Trade:** Exports, chiefly steel, chemical products, plastic fibers, rubber and textiles, totaled $2.4 billion in 1978. Imports, mainly coal and iron ore, machinery, transportation equipment, and food, totaled $2.8 billion **Principal Trade Partners:** EC countries

Vital Statistics: Birthrate, 11.4 per 1,000 of pop. (1977); death rate, 11.5 **Life Expectancy:** 73 years **Health Statistics:** 85 inhabitants per hospital bed; 900 per physician (1976) **Infant Mortality:** 10.6 per 1,000 births (1977) **Illiteracy:** 2% **Primary and Secondary School Enrollment:** 53,423 (1976) **Enrollment in Higher Education:** 446 **GNP Expended on Education:** 5.2% (1973)

Transportation: Surfaced roads total 3,085 mi. **Motor Vehicles:** 152,200 (1977) **Passenger Cars:** 141,400 **Railway Mileage:** 168 **Ports:** None **Major Airlines:** LUXAIR operates regular services to Western Europe; Icelandair maintains a regular service to the United States **Communications:** Privately owned **Radio Transmitters:** 7 **Licenses:** 205,000 (1976) **Television Transmitters:** 4 **Licenses:** 105,000 (1976) **Telephones:** 158,000 (1976) **Newspapers:** 7 dailies, 560 copies per 1,000 inhabitants (1975)

Weights and Measures: Metric system **Travel Requirements:** Passport, no visa for less than 3 months

---

The Grand Duchy of Luxembourg, covering an area of 999 square miles, and with a population of over 350,000, is the equal of Sweden in the production of iron and steel. Centered at Esch-sur-Alzette, Luxembourg's iron and steel industry uses iron ore mined in the area for about half of its needs and imports the remainder, as well as coal. The duchy's steel mills, among the largest and oldest in Europe, were hard hit by the worldwide reduced demand for steel in 1979-80. But Luxembourg has many other manufacturing industries, of which the principal ones are chemicals and automotive parts. American capital was the source of much of this diversification, with investments coming also from Luxembourg's Common Market partners.

Agriculture is of the small-scale, mixed-farming type, and livestock breeding is important. Among Luxembourg's exports are dairy products, pigs, and roses, and its vineyards in the Moselle Valley produce fine white wines. Trilingual Luxembourgers, speaking their own patois plus French and German, call the southern part of the grand duchy *Bon Pays* or *Gutland*—in English, the "Good Land"—because of its agricultural qualities.

Most industry is concentrated in the extreme south, and, all-in-all, Luxembourg offers the tourist picturesque scenery, good food and drink, an excellent road system, and, for the hiker, extensive paths between old villages.

On the darker side is the fact that the duchy has twice been overrun in this century by German troops, with liberation coming both times with the arrival of American forces. At Hamm, outside Luxembourg City, more than 5,000 American soldiers, including General George S. Patton, Jr., lie buried.

Since the war Luxembourg has officially abandoned neutrality. In 1949 it became a charter member of the North Atlantic Treaty Organization and has since been one of the leading promoters of closer European cooperation. It was a pioneer in the kind of economic cooperation now exemplified by the European Community, having formed, in 1921, a customs union with Belgium; the union became *Benelux* when the Netherlands joined in 1948.

HISTORY: The county of Luxembourg, including the present Belgian province of Luxembourg, emerged in the 10th century and rose to prominence in 1308, when its ruler was elected Holy Roman Emperor. Raised to a duchy in 1354, Luxembourg passed to the Hapsburgs in 1482. During the next three centuries, the duchy's history was bound up with the southern Netherlands, which passed from Spanish to Austrian rule in 1714. France occupied the duchy during the French Revolutionary Wars and formally annexed it in 1797

1815: Congress of Vienna makes Luxembourg a grand duchy, in personal union with the Kingdom of the Netherlands

1839: Belgium, having won its independence from the Netherlands, annexes the present Belgian province of Luxembourg; it constituted the major part of the grand duchy

1867: Luxembourg is declared an independent, neutral state in personal union with the Netherlands by the Treaty of London

1890: William III of the Netherlands dies and is succeeded on the Dutch throne by his daughter Wilhelmina; however, Luxembourg passes to Duke Adolf of Nassau, who becomes grand duke

1914-18: Luxembourg, its neutrality violated by Germany, is occupied by German forces during World War I

1940: German forces invade grand duchy in World War II; ducal family and cabinet flee to London

1944: Luxembourg is liberated by Allied forces

1949: Grand duchy formally abandons its perpetual neutrality and joins North Atlantic Treaty Organization

1964: Grand Duchess Charlotte abdicates in favor of son Jean

1968-69: Christian Socialist/Socialist coalition government of Premier Pierre Werner falls in October 1968 after government refuses to agree to demands by Socialist trade union leaders for higher wages and greater welfare benefits; following new elections, Werner forms a new government of Christian Socialists and Socialists and is reappointed premier in 1969

1972: Voting age is lowered from 21 to 18

1974: Premier Werner's government falls, ending 55 years of unbroken control by Christian Socialists. Democrat Gaston Thorn becomes premier, leading a coalition of socialists and liberals

1979: Christian Democrats regain control of parliament following new elections; Pierre Werner replaces Thorn as premier and forms Christian Democrat-Liberal coalition

MADAGASCAR

Area: 226,657 sq. mi. **Population:** 8,289,000 (1978 est.)
Official Name: Democratic Republic of Madagascar **Capital:** Antananarivo **Nationality:** Malagasy **Languages:** Malagasy and French are the official languages; Hova and other dialects are also widely spoken **Religion:** About 55% animist, 40% Christian, and 5% Moslem **Flag:** A white vertical band at the staff and 2 horizontal bands, the upper red, the lower green **Anthem:** O, Our Beloved Fatherland **Currency:** Malagasy franc (210.2 per U.S. $1)

Location: Indian Ocean. The 4th-largest island in the world—after Greenland, New Guinea, and Borneo—Madagascar is situated some 250 miles off the east coast of Africa, from which it is separated by the Mozambique Channel **Features:** The terrain consists of a central belt of eroded highlands extending from the northeast to the southwest, sloping steeply eastward to a narrow, swampy coast and passing gradually to more extensive lowlands in the west. An inland plateau rises to 9,450 feet **Chief Rivers:** Mangoro, Ikopa, Onilahy, Tsiribihina, Mangoky, Sofia

Head of State and of Government: President: Cmdr. Didier Ratsiraka, born 1936, assumed power in a coup in June 1975 as head of Supreme Revolutionary Council, and elected president in December 1975; he is aided by a cabinet headed by the premier, Desire Rakotoarijaona, appointed August 1977 **Effective Date of Present Constitution:** 1975 **Legislative Body:** National Popular Assembly (unicameral) consisting of 137 members, elected for five years **Local Government:** 6 provinces

Ethnic Composition: The population is of Malayan-Indonesian origin, with an admixture of Arab and African strains; of 18 major groups, the most numerous are the Merina (Hova), Betsileo, Betsimisaraka, Sakalava and Tsimihety. There are about 10,000 French, 17,000 Indians, 9,000 Chinese, and 34,000 immigrants from the Comoros **Population Distribution:** 14% urban **Density:** 37 inhabitants per sq. mi.

Largest Cities: (1971 est.) Antananarivo 400,000, Antsirabe 70,000, Toamasina (Tamatave) 59,000, Fianarantsoa 59,000, Majunga 55,000, Antsiranana (Diégo-Suarez) 45,000, Toliary (Tuléar) 39,000

Per Capita Income: $300 (1979) **Gross National Product (GNP):** $2.5 billion (1979) **Economic Statistics:** In 1978 about 40% of the GNP came from agriculture (rice, coffee, tobacco, cloves, cocoa, vanilla, livestock), 17% from industry (including oil refining) and mining **Minerals and Mining:** Graphite, mica, gold, and industrial beryl are mined, but are not extensive **Labor Force:** 3.4 million, of which 90% is in agriculture **Foreign Trade:** Exports, chiefly coffee, vanilla, sugar, rice, cloves, and raffia, totaled $379 million in 1978. Imports, mainly transportation machinery, crude oil, textiles, chemicals, pharmaceuticals, machinery, and electrical appliances, totaled $344 million **Principal Trade Partners:** France, United States, West Germany, Japan, Italy, United Arab Emirates, Spain

Vital Statistics: Birthrate, 46.0 per 1,000 of pop. (1966); death rate 25.0 **Life Expectancy:** 46 years **Health Statistics:** 417 inhabitants per hospital bed; 10,337 per physician (1976) **Infant Mortality:** 53.2 per 1,000 births (1972) **Illiteracy:** 55% **Primary and Secondary School Enrollment:** 1,264,849 (1975) **Enrollment in Higher Education:** 8,385 (1975) **GNP Expended on Education:** 3.1% (1975)

Transportation: Paved roads total 2,800 mi. **Motor Vehicles:** 109,700 (1977) **Passenger Cars:** 57,400 **Railway Mileage:** 549 **Ports:** Toamasina (Tamatave), Majunga, Nossi-Be, Antsiranana (Diégo-Suarez), Toliary (Tuléar) **Major Airlines:** Air Madagascar operates domestic and international services **Communications:** Government controlled **Radio Transmitters:** 16 **Receivers:** 609,000 (1975) **Television Transmitters:** 4 **Receivers:** 8,000 (1976) **Telephones:** 32,000 (1976) **Newspapers:** 9 dailies, 9 copies per 1,000 inhabitants (1974)

Weights and Measures: Metric system **Travel Requirements:** Passport, visa valid for stay up to 1 month, $6.76 fee, 4 photos

Madagascar, known as the Malagasy Republic until 1976, is "the land at the end of the earth," a blend of Shangri-la and Lost World. Although near Africa—250 miles off the continent's southeast coast—Madagascar and its people, the Malagasy, appear to be more a part of southeast Asia. The island was settled, according to Malagasy folklore, more than 2,000 years ago by people who drifted or sailed across the Indian Ocean from the Malay-Indonesia area. Their descendants speak a language considered to be of Malayan-Polynesian origin and, while some show admixtures of African and Arab settlers, most have an Indochinese physique.

While unknown to much of the world, Madagascar was prized as a naval base in the contest of the British and French imperialisms. Triumph by the French brought an overthrow of the Malagasy monarchy, but not submission.

Despite their placid appearance, the Malagasy rose in a bloody and unsuccessful revolt against French rule in 1947. When, in 1960, the island became a fully sovereign republic under President Philibert Tsiranana, the Malagasy regarded the event as a return to self-rule rather than a granting of independence by a colonial power.

With self-rule, Madagascar has faced problems of resolving internal conflicts, mainly between the traditionally dominant Merina, or plateau people, and the *côtiers*, or coastal peoples. President Tsiranana was a *côtier* and former professor who sought to promote both national unity and the development of a sluggish agricultural economy.

Tsiranana favored continued close ties with France and, despite Madagascar's membership in the Organization of African Unity and his own condemnation of apartheid, he welcomed investment and economic aid from South Africa. That policy changed in 1972.

The economy is overwhelmingly agricultural, largely of a subsistence type. Rice is the main crop. New development efforts have been concentrated in mining, with occasional investments made in light manufacturing.

A major change in Madagascar's political life came in 1972 when President Tsiranana was removed from office. Student riots had begun to plague his administration, and a formal referendum was held which transferred power to a new military government headed by Premier Gabriel Ramanantsoa, a moderate leftist.

In February 1975, Ramanantsoa turned over full power to Col. Richard Ratsimandrava after 12 days of political crisis. After six days, Ratsimandrava was assassinated by paramilitary policemen.

The National Military Guidance Committee governed the country until June 15 when it invested Cmdr. Didier Ratsiraka as head of state and dissolved itself. In a referendum, Ratsiraka's presidency and a new constitution were approved by 95 percent of the voters. The nation was to be known henceforth as the Democratic Republic of Madagascar. The military, in control since 1972, has sought to nationalize important segments of the economy.

HISTORY: Despite Madagascar's proximity to Africa, Malagasy tradition and language support the belief that the first waves of migration came from the Sunda Islands (present-day Indonesia), starting a century or two before the Christian era. About A.D. 900, Arab settlers and Africans, brought by slave traders, were added to the population. Beginning in the 16th century, Portuguese, French, and English contested with rival Malagasy kingdoms for dominance of the island, which finally became a French protectorate in the 19th century

1885-1905: France invades Madagascar and establishes a limited protectorate. French consolidate control, but local resistance continues for many years

1942-43: British occupy Vichy-ruled Madagascar to prevent seizure by Japanese; Free French take over

1947: Armed revolt by Malagasy nationalists breaks out in opposition to "French Union" self-rule, lasts nearly a year before French suppress it; death toll is put as high as 80,000

1958: After reforms in 1956 paving way for independence, Madagascar votes "yes" in referendum creating Malagasy Republic within the French Community

1959: Philibert Tsiranana, a former teacher and founder of the Social Democratic party, is elected first president of the republic

1960: Madagascar is proclaimed a sovereign, independent nation

1965: President Tsiranana is reelected by smashing majority

1972: Executive powers are transferred to Gen. Ramanantsoa as premier of a military government

1975: Ramanantsoa turns over power to Col. Richard Ratsimandrava, who is assassinated after six days. A military committee invests Cmdr. Didier Ratsiraka as head of state. Nation renamed Democratic Republic of Madagascar

1978: Madagascar lays claim to four Indian Ocean islands administered by French Réunion

1979: Contract made with China to build a 1,200-kw. hydroelectric plant 60 miles from Antananarivo

MALAWI

Area: 45,747 sq. mi. **Population:** 5,817,000 (1978 est.)

Official Name: Republic of Malawi **Capital:** Lilongwe **Nationality:** Malawian **Languages:** English is the official language and Chichewa is the national language. Among the other various Bantu languages are Nyanja, Tumbuka, Yao, Tonga, and Ngoni **Religion:** About 35% of the people are Christians, 12% Moslems, and the rest animists **Flag:** 3 horizontal stripes of black, red, and green with a red rising sun on the black stripe **Anthem:** National Anthem, beginning "O God, bless our land of Malawi" **Currency:** Malawian kwacha (.80 per U.S. $1)

Location: East Africa. Landlocked Malawi is bordered on the north and northeast by Tanzania, on the southeast and southwest by Mozambique, and on the northwest by Zambia **Features:** The Great Rift Valley traverses the country from north to south, its deep trough containing the 360-mile-long Lake Nyasa (Malawi). West of the valley, the land rises to form high plateaus between 3,000 and 4,000 feet above sea level, while in the north the Nyika uplands rise to 8,500 feet. South of Lake Nyasa are the Shire Highlands, which rise to steep mountains ranging up to 10,000 feet **Chief Rivers:** Shire, Bua, Rukuru

Head of State and of Government: President: Dr. Hastings Kamuzu Banda, born 1906, elected by National Assembly in 1966, made president for life by constitutional amendment in November 1970; he also holds 5 cabinet posts **Effective Date of Present Constitution:** July 1966 **Legislative Body:** National Assembly (unicameral); 87 members for 5-year terms **Local Government:** 3 regions, divided into 24 districts. Each region has an appointed regional minister

Ethnic Composition: The people are almost all descended from Bantu tribes that arrived between the 16th and 19th centuries. They include the Chewa and the Nyanja, descendants of the Maravi, who emigrated from present-day Zaire; the Yao; the Tumbuka; the Lonwe; and the Sena **Population Distribution:** 10% urban **Density:** 127 inhabitants per sq. mi.

Largest Cities: (1976 est.) Blantyre-Limbe 219,000, Lilongwe 75,000, Zomba 16,000

Per Capita Income: $159 (1978) **Gross National Product (GNP):** $910 million (1978) **Economic Statistics:** In 1973 over 50% of the GNP was derived from agriculture (tea, tung nuts and oil, sugarcane, tobacco), 13% from industry, and 19% from trade and services **Minerals and Mining:** Production is limited to quarrying constructional stone and limestone; however there are unexploited deposits of bauxite and coal **Labor Force:** 1,500,000, with 85% in subsistence agriculture **Foreign Trade:** Exports, chiefly tobacco, tea, sugar, peanuts, corn, and cotton, totaled $189 million in 1978. Imports, mainly textiles, motor vehicles, petroleum products, medical and pharmaceutical goods, and food products, totaled $328 million **Principal Trade Partners:** Britain, South Africa, Netherlands, United States, Japan, West Germany

Vital Statistics: Birthrate, 50.5 per 1,000 of pop. (1974); death rate, 26 **Life Expectancy:** 42 years **Health Statistics:** 576 inhabitants per hospital bed; 48,462 per physician (1977) **Infant Mortality:** 142.1 per 1,000 births **Illiteracy:** 85% **Primary and Secondary School Enrollment:** 680,089 (1976) **Enrollment in Higher Education:** 1,148 (1975) **GNP Expended on Education:** 2.0% (1975)

Transportation: Improved roads total 1,071 mi. **Motor Vehicles:** 20,800 (1976) **Passenger Cars:** 10,200 **Railway Mileage:** 420 (1970) **Ports:** None **Major Airlines:** Air Malawi, Ltd., the national airline, operates domestic and international services **Communications:** Government controlled **Radio Transmitters:** 15 **Receivers:** 130,000 (1976) **Television:** None **Telephones:** 21,000 (1976) **Newspapers:** 1 daily, 1.8 copies per 1,000 inhabitants (1975)

Weights and Measures: Metric and British standards **Travel Requirements:** Passport, no visa required for stay up to 1 year

Malawi is among Africa's most picturesque yet poorest countries. It is distinguished also in being one of the few independent black African countries to establish official relations with South Africa and in having a despotic president, Dr. H. Kamuzu Banda, who banned the miniskirt, set rules on the length of men's shorts, and, in 1978, banned foreign journalists from the country indefinitely for what he considered unfair, false reporting of recent elections.

Soaring mountains and the long inland sea of Lake Nyasa have won the country the title of "Switzerland of Africa." But the resemblance ends with the scenery. Malawi's economy has been gaining with increased production of tea and tobacco and industrial investment from South Africa and Rhodesia, but with a dense population and per capita income of $159 a year, the country is still far from economic takeoff.

Dr. Banda, an associate and admirer of Ghana's erstwhile ruler, Kwame Nkrumah, has been president of Malawi since the former British protectorate became independent in 1964. In 1970 he had himself made president for life.

While maintaining that he is as much opposed to South Africa's racial policies as any black African leader, Dr. Banda has cited Malawi's need and landlocked position in southern Africa as necessitating close economic ties with her white-ruled neighbors. "I would do business with the Devil himself to help Malawian development," he has said. Nevertheless, Malawi joined 14 other African nations in 1973 in calling for diplomatic and economic sanctions against nations which cooperate with South Africa.

Tourism has become an important business for Malawi. Many hotels, however, have recently reported a drop in bookings as a result of Dr. Banda's rulings about dress, which were aimed at tourists.

Pressures for "Africanization" of property and jobs have been aimed at European landowners and Asian traders. As many as 200,000 Asians have had their businesses "Africanized."

The building of a new capital at Lilongwe, a pet project of Dr. Banda's, was aided by South African loans. Most of the $60-million cost of the new capital is being underwritten by South Africa.

In addition to increasing industry, plans are progressing for bauxite mining and construction of a large aluminum plant. Dr. Banda has said that Malawi either will become economically viable in the next 5 to 10 years or will cease to exist as a truly independent state.

HISTORY: Little is known about the history of Malawi, formerly Nyasaland, prior to the arrival of the Scottish missionary and explorer David Livingstone in 1859. His revulsion at the Arab slave trade moved him to promote establishment of Scottish missions and business groups to develop legitimate commerce as a substitute for the trade in human beings. Britain, in fighting the slave trade and also seeking to prevent encroachment by the Portuguese and Germans, gradually gained control of Nyasaland and set up a protectorate in 1891

1953: Nyasaland, despite strong Nyasa opposition, is joined to new Central African Federation, including also Northern and Southern Rhodesia

1959: Dr. Hastings Kamuzu Banda, leader of Nyasaland African Congress, and more than 1,000 of his followers, are imprisoned, charged with plotting massacre of white officials; after they were absolved they set up Malawi Congress party

1960-61: Britain grants Nyasaland constitution assuring African majority in Legislative Council; Malawi party wins overwhelming victory in council election

1963: Nyasaland secedes from Central African Federation, which is dissolved; Banda becomes prime minister under new constitution

1964-65: Nyasaland becomes independent Malawi

1966: Malawi becomes a republic within British Commonwealth, with Banda as president

1969: Malawi, at meeting of East and Central African States, refuses to join in manifesto criticizing white-dominated governments of Rhodesia and South Africa

1970: Prime Minister John Vorster of South Africa makes official visit to Malawi, the first such visit by a South African leader to a black African state

1971: President Banda visits South Africa, continuing close relations between Malawi and South Africa

1973: President Banda takes over control of press and radio

1975: Official transfer to new capital at Lilongwe takes place on January 1. Jehovah's Witnesses movement protests alleged persecution of 30,000 members by government

1977: President Banda dismisses his entire cabinet

MALAYSIA

Area: 128,308 sq. mi. **Population:** 12,960,000 (1978 est.)

Official Name: Malaysia **Capital:** Kuala Lumpur **Nationality:** Malay-

sian **Languages:** Malay (Bahasa Malaysia) is the official language; English, Tamil, and a variety of native, Chinese, and Indian dialects are also spoken **Religion:** Chiefly Moslem, and Islam is the state religion; in Sabah and Sarawak there are many animists. Most of the Chinese follow Buddhism, Confucianism, and Taoism. Of the Indian community, about 70% are Hindu, 20% Moslem, 5% Christian, and 2% Sikh **Flag:** Fourteen red and white stripes with blue field in upper left corner containing crescent and star in yellow **Anthem:** Our Country **Currency:** ringgit (2.23 per U.S. $1)

Location: Southeast Asia. Malaysia consists of West Malaysia (Malaya), and East Malaysia (Sabah and Sarawak). West Malaysia, on the Malay Peninsula, is bordered on the east by the South China Sea, on the south by the Strait of Johore, on the west by the Strait of Malacca and the Andaman Sea, and on the north by Thailand. Sarawak and Sabah, on the northwestern coast of the island of Borneo, are bordered by Brunei, and by the Indonesian province of Kalimantan on the southeast; on the west, north, and east are the South China, Sulu, and Celebes seas **Features:** Some 80% of the total land area of the country is forested. The Malay Peninsula consists of a spinal mountain range running roughly north and south and flanked by coastal plains. In Sabah and Sarawak, coastal plains rise to mountainous interiors **Chief Rivers:** Perak and Pahang in Malaya; Rajang in Sarawak, Kinabatangan in Sabah

Head of State: Paramount Ruler: Tuanka Haji Ahmad Shah Al-Mustain Billah Ibni Al-Marhum Sultan Abu Bakar Ri'ayatuddin Al-Mu'adzam Shah, shah of Pahang, elected April 1979 by the Conference of Rulers for a 5-year term **Head of Government:** Prime Minister Datuk Hussein bin Onn, born 1922, appointed 1976 **Effective Date of Present Constitution:** 1957 **Legislative Body:** Parliament (bicameral), consisting of a Senate (Dewan Negara) and a House of Representatives (Dewan Rakyat). The Senate is composed of 58 members, 32 appointed by the Paramount Ruler and 26 elected by state assemblies, for 6-year terms. The House of Representatives consists of 154 members, 114 from West Malaysia, 24 from Sarawak, and 16 from Sabah, all elected for a 5-year term **Local Government:** 13 states, headed by titular rulers and governors. Effective power is in the hands of the chief ministers, selected from the state assemblies

Ethnic Composition: Malayans constitute about 45% of the population, Chinese 36%, non-Malay indigenous peoples 8%, and Indians and Pakistanis 9.1% **Population Distribution:** 29% urban **Density:** 101 inhabitants per sq. mi.

Largest Cities: (1970 census) Kuala Lumpur 451,810, Pinang (Penang, George Town) 269,247, Ipoh 247,969

Per Capita Income: $1,207 (1979) **Gross National Product (GNP):** $16.4 billion (1979) **Economic Statistics:** In 1978, 30% of GNP was derived from agriculture (rubber, timber, rice, palm oil, coconut oil, fruits, sago, tea, and pepper); 16% from manufacturing (oil and sugar refining, steel plants, fertilizers, and many smaller import-substitute industries); and 6% from mining (tin, oil, iron) **Minerals and Mining:** Tin, oil and iron ore are the chief minerals. Petroleum from offshore wells is of growing importance in Sarawak and Sabah **Labor Force:** About 4,800,000 (1978 est.), with approximately 50% engaged in agriculture and fishing, and 14% in industry **Foreign Trade:** Exports, chiefly rubber, oil, tin, petroleum, and forest products, totaled $7.7 billion in 1978. Imports, mainly foodstuffs, industrial machinery, transportation equipment, metals, electrical equipment, and petroleum products, totaled $6.3 billion **Principal Trade Partners:** Britain, Singapore, Japan, United States, Australia, China, West Germany

Vital Statistics: Birthrate, 30.9 per 1,000 of pop. (1977); death rate, 6.1 **Life Expectancy:** 68 years **Health Statistics:** 347 inhabitants per hospital bed; 8,319 per physician (1974) **Infant Mortality:** 30.7 per 1,000 births **Illiteracy:** 39% **Primary and Secondary School Enrollment:** 2,462,682 (1977) **Enrollment in Higher Education:** 39,658 **GNP Expended on Education:** 5.1% (1971)

Transportation: Paved roads total 10,480 mi. **Motor Vehicles:** 658,200 (1977) **Passenger Cars:** 491,200 **Railway Mileage:** 1,416 **Ports:** Pinang, Port Dickson, Klang, Malacca, Kuching, Miri, Sandakan, Tawau, Kota Kinabalu **Major Airlines:** Malaysian Airline System operates international and domestic flights **Communications:** Government owned **Radio Transmitters:** 92 **Receivers:** 1,450,000 (1976) **Television Transmitters:** 38 **Receivers:** 555,000 (1976) **Telephones:** 320,000 (1976) **Newspapers:** 31 dailies, 87 copies per 1,000 inhabitants (1975)

Weights and Measures: British standards are used; metric conversion scheduled for 1976-1982 **Travel Requirements:** Passport, no visa for 3 months

For more than a century Malaya, with its rich deposits of tin and its ideal climate for growing rubber trees, has been prosperous and sought after.

With the addition in 1963 of Sarawak and Sabah, the former British colonies on the island of Borneo, the new Federation of Malaysia now contains one of the largest undeveloped areas in Asia.

The long center spine of Malaya and vast sections of Sarawak and Sabah are covered solidly with towering rain forests and low mountain ranges. Only the coastal areas and the occasional valleys are open and settled. Malaya, economically balanced and commercially progressive, continues to clear new tracts of jungle land for planting for rubber and coconut palm oil. But the efforts to enlarge the slender bands of modern development in Sarawak and Sabah have barely crept along since British colonial rule over these remote territories ended.

Although Malaysia enjoys a healthy balance of trade and its people have the highest per capita income in Southeast Asia after Singapore's, the economy suffers from overspecialization. Two commodities, rubber and tin, account for about half of the export trade. Both are vulnerable to price swings in world markets. In addition, synthetic rubber has been gaining favor while readily exploitable tin reserves are dwindling. On the plus side the new oil fields in Sabah are now producing; they now account for almost half of Malaysia's exports. The Malaysian Industrial Development Authority has used the "hard sell" since the early 1970s, and the country has attracted 600 multinational companies, most of them with plants in 60 widely dispersed industrial estates. Penang has become an electronics center, and Johore has received many companies that left Singapore.

Malaysia, which was actively anti-Communist, has since 1970 modified her foreign policy in favor of peaceful coexistence. In 1974, Prime Minister Abdul Razak visited Peking and established full diplomatic relations with Communist China.

The level of living in Malaysia's cities and small towns is the highest in Southeast Asia and there are no pressures on the land from the population. Malaya has been notably successful in completing a series of five-year development plans. Similar, though less ambitious, plans have been prepared for East Malaysia. The British, whose business firms reaped impressive profits from Malaya, left behind in that region an excellent civil service, comparatively good medical facilities, and a soundly administered school system that has been markedly successful in the cities and towns where most of the ethnic Chinese and Indians are concentrated.

But amid the prosperity of Malaysia there runs a continuing struggle between the Moslem Malays, who consider themselves the indigenous owners of Malaya, and the ethnic Chinese. The Chinese own 90 percent of the federation's commercial outlets, occupy the majority of the positions in medical, legal, and engineering circles, and possess an energy and drive that the graceful, deliberate, and highly religious Malays do not admire. Since Malaya first became independent in 1957 there has been a subsurface fear among the Malays that the ethnic Chinese may take control by winning a majority in the elected parliament.

The Malays, who now dominate the government, are also in conflict with the native groups in Sarawak and Sabah, with whom they are neither religiously nor culturally allied.

The bloody race riots of 1969 led to a 21-month suspension of parliament and rule by decree. Though parliament reconvened in February 1971, full democracy did not return. A constitutional amendment to outlaw discussion of sensitive issues likely to inflame race hatred was adopted. The 48-member National Unity Council became the sole body permitted to question the government's racial and linguistic policies.

A heavy tide of refugees from Vietnam, known as the "boat people" because of their arrival from across the South China Sea, caused political turbulence in Malaysia in 1978 and 1979. They were mostly Chinese and therefore were viewed by the Malays as a threat to the country's delicate political and social balance. The government had about 70,000 refugees in makeshift camps at the peak in 1979, and it tried to persuade other nations—especially those that had been involved in the war in Indochina—to accept them. At the start of 1980, Malaysia still had 34,000 Indochinese refugees; the United States was accepting them at that time at the rate of 3,000 a month.

HISTORY: By the beginning of the 13th century the coasts of Malaya, Sarawak, and Sabah, which now are joined in the Federation of Malaysia, were dotted with small trading ports where the natives, most of them of ethnic Malay stock, fished and produced spices. The lure of this spice trade brought the Portuguese, Dutch, and British merchant adventurers. As their trade grew, they found it profitable to take control of the ports to protect their enterprises from the natives and from the other European merchants. In 1511 the Portuguese occupied Malacca, on the west coast of Malaya, and in 1592 the British East India Company appeared at Penang

1867: British establish the Straits Settlements—Penang, Malacca, Singapore—as a crown colony

1888: British declare North Borneo (Sabah), Sarawak, and Brunei British protectorates

1941: Japanese invade Malaya in World War II, eventually driving the British and Dutch from the East Indies

1946: After Japanese surrender, British form Union of Malaya by uniting Penang and Malacca with the nine Malay states; Singapore, Sabah, and Sarawak become crown colonies

1948: Union of Malaya is succeeded by Federation of Malaya; Communist insurrection by ethnic Chinese breaks out, and government declares state of emergency

1957: Malaya becomes independent and member of British Commonwealth

1960: Emergency is ended with defeat of Communist guerrillas

1962-63: Britain and Malaya agree on formation of new Federation of Malaysia that is to include Malaya, Sarawak, Sabah, the tiny Sultanate of Brunei, and Singapore. Brunei decides at last minute to remain outside federation; Malaysia is officially created and joins Commonwealth

1965: After months of dispute over status of ethnic Chinese and Malays, stimulated by Malay fear of Chinese dominance, Singapore secedes from federation

1966: After three years of sporadic guerrilla war and threats of invasion from Indonesia, which had opposed the creation of the federation, Malaysia and Indonesia agree to peace

1969: Tension and rioting between Chinese and Malays in capital leads to suspension of the constitution and formation of a state-of-emergency ruling council

1970: Prime Minister Abdul Rahman, the founder and leader of Malaysia, resigns and is succeeded by Abdul Razak

1971: State of emergency, in effect for 21 months, is ended on February 19 and parliamentary government restored

1974: Prime Minister Razak's National Front Coalition wins an overwhelming election victory

1975: Prosperity of early 1970s ends and government faces an ailing economy, student unrest and guerrilla war by the Communists

1976: Razak dies on January 14, Deputy Prime Minister Datuk Hussein bin Onn takes office. Government tightens security measures in drive on Communist insurgents. Ethnic Chinese professionals flee to avoid racial discrimination

1978: Hoping to gain by the relative political and economic stability, Prime Minister Hussein bin Onn calls parliamentary elections a year earlier than required and wins large majority. Number of refugee "Boat People" who crossed the South China Sea from Vietnam rises to a total of about 53,000 "illegal immigrants" by year-end. After a freighter bearing 2,500 is denied permission to land in November, 197 of those aboard set out in a small boat but drown when it upsets in rough water

1979: On Jan. 5, Prime Minister Hussein announces that the government will accept no more refugees. On March 3, a Vietnamese boat is turned back by naval gunfire; eventually it capsizes and 104 persons drown. Meanwhile, Malaysia gets 100,000 more refugees—Moslems from the southern Philippines who flee to the state of Sabah (formerly northeast Borneo). The elected figurehead king, Sultan Yahya Petra, died; Sultan Ahmad Shah, Shah of Pahang, is elected for a five-year term

---

MALDIVES

Area: 115 sq. mi. **Population:** 141,000 (1978 est.)
Official Name: Republic of Maldives **Capital:** Male **Nationality:**

Maldivian **Languages:** Divehi, a dialect of Sinhalese, is the official and universal language; Arabic is also spoken **Religion:** Virtually all Maldivians are Sunni Moslems and Islam is the state religion **Flag:** A green rectangle with a white crescent superimposed on a red field **Anthem:** National Anthem **Currency:** Maldivian rupee (7.6 per U.S. $1)

Location: Indian Ocean. The Maldive Islands are a 500-mile-long archipelago of some 2,000 coral islands, 400 miles southwest of Sri Lanka. Male, the capital, is located at 4° 10′ N., 73°30′W. **Features:** The Maldives rest on a submarine ridge, believed to be of volcanic origin. They are grouped into 19 atolls, or rings of coral islands, each ring encircling a lagoon. Most of the islands are covered with coconut palms **Chief Rivers:** None

Head of State and of Government: President: Maumoon Abdul Gayoom, named president by legislature in 1978 **Effective Date of Present Constitution:** 1964, amended 1968, 1970, 1972, 1975 **Legislative Body:** Majlis (unicameral), 54 members, of whom 8 are appointed by the president and 46 are popularly elected for a 5-year term **Local Government:** Each of the 19 atolls has an elected committee with a head man *(Verin)* appointed by the government

Ethnic Composition: The people are of mixed Indian, Sinhalese, and Arabic descent **Population Distribution:** 12% urban **Density:** 1,226 inhabitants per sq. mi. (215 islands are inhabited)

Largest City: (1977 est.) Male 25,000

Per Capita Income: $85 (1978 est.) **Gross National Product (GNP):** $10 million (1978) **Economic Statistics:** The economy has a narrow base, being almost totally dependent on fisheries for its export earnings. Fishing is the basic industry, the catch consisting mainly of bonito and tuna. Cooked and smoked, they are known as Maldive fish and are used as a condiment. The second-largest commercial industry is copra and coconut oil production. A cottage industry based on coir yarn weaving provides work for many of the women in the islands. Tourism is growing **Minerals and Mining:** There are no mineral resources **Labor Force:** 50% of the population is engaged in fishing **Foreign Trade:** Exports, chiefly fish, coconuts, copra, coir, cowrie shell, tortoise shell, and local handicraft products, totaled $3.5 million in 1977. Imports, mainly rice, flour, kerosene, oil, sugar, textiles, and drugs, totaled $9.1 million **Principal Trade Partners:** Sri Lanka, India, Pakistan, Burma, Japan, Britain, Czechoslovakia, the Netherlands

Vital Statistics: Birthrate, 40.5 per 1,000 of pop. (1977); death rate, 11.8 **Health Statistics:** 3,500 inhabitants per hospital bed; 15,555 per physician (1977) **Infant Mortality:** 118.8 per 1,000 births **Illiteracy:** 42% **Primary and Secondary School Enrollment:** 3,549 (1977) **GNP Expended on Education:** 3% (1970)

Transportation: N.A. **Motor Vehicles:** 97 (1969) **Passenger Cars:** 20 (1969) **Railway Mileage:** None **Port:** Male **Major Airlines:** Air Maldives, established in 1974, connects Male with India and Sri Lanka **Communications:** Government controlled **Radio Transmitters:** 5 **Licenses:** 3,500 (1976) **Television Transmitters:** 1 **Telephones:** 227 (1969) **Newspapers:** 1 daily (1975), 182 copies per 1,000 inhabitants

Weights and Measures: Local units are used **Travel Requirements:** Passport, no visa required

---

The 2,000 islands that comprise the Maldives in the Indian Ocean consist of atolls, none of which are more than 20 feet in elevation. The islands are mostly protected by reefs, which have been the scene of numerous shipwrecks. The total land area is a third that of New York City. The 141,000 Maldivians inhabit only 215 of the islands.

Coconut palms cover the larger islands, on which breadfruit, figs, millet, and edible nuts are grown. Widespread in the hot and humid Maldive climate, malaria has been fought by the World Health Organization.

The Maldivian people live at a more or less subsistence level, and their basic economy is of the one-crop type—what is known as "Maldive fish." This is bonito, caught in local waters, cut up, boiled, smoked, and dried until it resembles hardwood. It is considered a delicacy in Sri Lanka and India, where it is whittled into fragments, cooked with onions and spices, and served as a condiment.

The staple foods of the Maldives are fish and rice. The rice has to be imported along with a host of other necessities, such as salt, sugar, kerosene, oil, and textiles.

There is no income tax, and the bulk of internal revenue is derived from customs duties, the rental of uninhabited islands, the licensing of boats and vehicles, and sale of postage stamps. Tourism is booming, reaching a total of 30,000 visitors annually, most of them West Germans traveling in tour groups that promise sun-and-swim vacations at soft, white beaches.

According to native legend, it was a Sinhalese prince who was the first sultan, having stayed on to rule after becoming becalmed in the Maldives with his royal bride. The country, with one brief exception in 1953, was a sultanate for eight centuries before adopting a republican form of government in 1968.

The role of the Maldives in international affairs has thus far been a limited one, but in 1974 the Maldives and India issued a joint communiqué expressing "full support for the concept of the Indian Ocean as a zone of peace, free from great power rivalries, tensions and military escalations." To stay clear of big-power involvement, the Maldives declined, in 1977, a Soviet offer to move into the Gan Island air base—the site of an 8,700-foot runway—that the British had abandoned two years earlier. But in 1980 a new Maldivian regime signed a cultural agreement with the Soviets. The Western world feared that the real Soviet objective was the air base, which is 450 miles north of Diego Garcia, the only U.S. base in the Indian Ocean. Peaceful international ventures include Indian and Japanese aid to the fishing industry through canneries and boat-building in the Maldives.

HISTORY: Sighted and described by Ibn Batuta in the 14th century, the Maldive Islands were occupied by the Portuguese from 1518 until the 17th century, when they came under the protection of the Dutch, then in control of Ceylon. The Maldives retained a similar status under the British, who expelled the Dutch from Ceylon during the occupation of the Netherlands by French Revolutionary forces

1887: British protection of the Maldives is formally recorded in an exchange of letters between the sultan and the governor of Ceylon

1948: After Ceylon achieves full independence, new agreement provides that British will control Maldivian foreign affairs but not interfere internally

1953: Sultanate is abolished and Maldives become a republic; efforts at reform by the new president arouse opposition from conservative elements; National Assembly votes to restore the sultanate

1957: An agreement allowing Britain to reactivate an air base on Gan Island stirs wide opposition

1960: Government makes "free gift" to Britain of Gan Island until 1986 in return for British help in quelling a rebellion in the three southernmost atolls

1965: Maldives achieve full independence

1968: Republican form of government is adopted; Ibrahim Nasir is elected president

1975: Premier Ahmed Zaki deposed for attempted coup and exiled in March. British withdraw from base on Gan

1977: USSR proposal to use the old air base is declined

1978: President Nasir go es into exile under unclear circumstances. He is succeeded by Maumoon Abdul Gayoom

1979: About 20 officials of the Nasir government are tried and sentenced. The usual punishment is banishment to a remote island for three or four years

1980: The USSR and the Maldives sign a cultural agreement

MALI

Area: 464,873 sq. mi. **Population:** 6,290,000 (1978 est.)

Official Name: Republic of Mali **Capital:** Bamako **Nationality:** Malian **Languages:** French is the official language and is the language of instruction in the nation's schools. The chief native languages are Bambara, Malinké, and Dyula **Religion:** About 90% Moslem, 9% animist, 1% Christian **Flag:** 3 vertical stripes of green, yellow, and red **Anthem:** National Anthem, beginning "At thy call, O Mali" **Currency:** Mali franc (416 per U.S. $1)

Location: West Africa. Landlocked Mali is bordered on the north by Algeria, on the east by Niger, on the south by Upper Volta, Ivory Coast, and Guinea, and on the west by Senegal and Mauritania **Features:** The country is mainly flat and dry, varying from the desolate Sahara in the north to pasture and croplands in the center and savanna scrub land in the south. The flatness of the landscape is broken in places by striking sandstone mountains and plateaus **Chief Rivers:** Niger, Senegal

Head of State and of Government: President: Gen. Moussa Traoré, born 1936; seized power in 1968, reelected June 1979 **Effective Date of Present Constitution:** Approved by referendum June 2, 1974, effective June 1979 **Legislative Body:** National Assembly (unicameral) of 82 members, elected for 4-year terms **Local Government:** 6 regions, each headed by an appointed governor

Ethnic Composition: Of some 23 ethnic groups, about 50% are Mandé, 17% Peul (Fulani), 12% Voltaic, 6% Songhai, and 5% Tuareg and Moor **Population Distribution:** 17% urban **Density:** 14 inhabitants per sq. mi.

Largest Cities: (1976 est.) Bamako 404,022, (1972 est.) Mopti 32,400, Kayes 28,500, Ségou 28,100, Sikasso 21,800, Gao 15,400

Per Capita Income: $87 (1978) **Gross National Product (GNP):** $540 million (1978) **Economic Statistics:** In 1977 about 45% of GNP was from agriculture (millet, sorghum, rice, cotton), livestock-raising, and fishing; 19% was derived from industry (textiles, cement, fruit processing) **Minerals and Mining:** Unexploited deposits of bauxite, uranium, oil, copper, manganese, phosphates, and iron. Salt and a small amount of gold are mined **Labor Force:** 2,800,000 with about 90% engaged in agriculture and livestock-raising **Foreign Trade:** Exports, mainly cotton, livestock, peanuts, and fish, totaled $133 million in 1978. Imports, chiefly vehicles and parts, cotton cloth, iron and steel, and petroleum products, totaled $312 million **Principal Trade Partners:** France, West Germany, Ivory Coast, Senegal, Britain, China, USSR, United States

Vital Statistics: Birthrate, 44.8 per 1,000 of pop. (1975); death rate, 24.9 **Life Expectancy:** 38 years **Health Statistics:** 1,426 inhabitants per hospital bed; 58,400 per physician (1976) **Infant Mortality:** 187 per 1,000 births **Illiteracy:** 95% **Primary and Secondary School Enrollment:** 307,858 (1975) **Enrollment in Higher Education:** 2,936 **GNP Expended on Education:** 4.7% (1975)

Transportation: Paved roads total 1,050 mi. **Motor Vehicles:** 24,200 (1976) **Passenger Cars:** 15,000 **Railway Mileage:** 401 **Ports:** None **Major Airlines:** Air Mali operates both domestic and international services **Communications:** Government owned **Radio Transmitters:** 14 **Receivers:** 82,000 (1976) **Television:** None **Telephones:** 5,000 (1971) **Newspapers:** 1 daily, 0.5 copies per 1,000 inhabitants (1972)

Weights and Measures: Metric system **Travel Requirements:** Passport, visa valid 1 week, $8 fee, 2 photos

---

Once the center of a succession of mighty African empires, present-day Mali lives in the shadow of past glories. The old empires gained power and wealth from conquest and the caravan trade in slaves, gold, and salt. But with the decay of this trade and the imposition of French colonial rule, the country reverted to a meager agricultural and pastoral economy.

Now independent, modern Mali, while hoping for the discovery of oil or other minerals, struggles to improve a limited production of cotton, livestock, and food crops.

Mali's most famous city—the fabled Timbuktu— is a symbol of lost prosperity and also of the efforts to regain some of that prosperity. This golden city of the 14th-century Songhai empire, built at the edge of the Sahara on the northern bend of the Niger River, is today a dusty town of 9,000 inhabitants. Malian officials have discovered that the old lure of Timbuktu has lost none of its appeal for tourists.

The majority of Malians, on the other hand, are more concerned with regaining a healthy economy and restoration of traditional freedom of enterprise.

Under former President Modibo Keita, Mali was set "irreversibly" on a path of socialism mainly of the Maoist variety. Large numbers of Communist Chinese were brought in to manage the economy, state enterprises were created and a program of farm collectivization started.

Keita acquired all power and even began wearing Mao tunics in place of the traditional boubou. The people were increasingly terrorized by the president's private militia, which also became a threat to the regular army.

The "irreversible" Keita socialism was reversed in 1968 with a bloodless coup by a group of young army officers. Although aware of growing opposition, the former president took no measures to prevent the military revolt and seemed to accept his ouster fatalistically.

Under the new government, the Military Committee of National Liberation, headed by Lt. Moussa Traoré, farm collectivization was abolished and a start made, with French help, on converting state enterprises into mixed-economy enterprises. While ties were retained with China and Russia the government adopted incentives for private foreign investment.

The ending of farm collectives has brought a marked increase in crop production, and in Bamako and other cities, private business and availability of goods have increased substantially. An American company is exploring for oil and a West German company for uranium. Financial aid has come also from France, the United States, and West Germany, as well as from the Soviet Union and East European countries.

Ten years of military government ended in June 1979 with elections under the new constitution. President Traoré, the only presidential candidate, retained the office for another five years. All 82 elected members of the National Assembly belonged to the only political party, the Democratic Union of the Malian People.

HISTORY: Modern Mali was a major part of past Sudanic empires— Ghana, Malinké (Mali), and Songhai—that flourished from the 8th through the 16th century. Ancient Mali reached its zenith about 1325 with the conquest of Gao and Timbuktu, the fabulous Saharan center of trade and learning. Following destruction of the Songhai empire by Moroccan invaders, the country came under the shifting rule of local chieftains. Two of these, Al-Haji Umar, a Tukulor, and Samory Touré, the Mandingo warrior hero and slave trader, waged fierce resistance against the incursions of French forces during the 19th century. With the defeat of Samory in 1898, French control was effectively extended over the country, which became known as French Sudan

1946: Sudanese Territorial Assembly is established with limited internal authority

1957: Territorial Assembly is given increased powers

1958: Sudan votes in constitutional referendum to become autonomous republic within the French Community

1959: Sudan and Senegal form union as the Federation of Mali

1960: Federation collapses as result of political and economic differences; Sudan proclaims itself the independent Republic of Mali with Modibo Keita as president

1963: Relations with Senegal are resumed

1964: Under single-party socialist rule, President Keita and his Sudanese Union are reelected

1968: Army officers overthrow Keita government in bloodless coup; set up military junta with Lt. Moussa Traoré as president

1969-74: Severe drought and famine take heavy toll in human life and livestock; refugees flock to the cities

1974: Referendum approves the new constitution calling for elections of president and National Assembly by universal suffrage

1975: Fighting occurs along frontier with Upper Volta

1978: Malian defense minister, foreign minister and two others are accused of treason. They are convicted in 1979

1979: Traoré, the only candidate, is reelected to presidency in June; civilians outnumber military in new government

---

MALTA

Area: 122 sq. mi. **Population:** 354,000 (1979 est.)

Official Name: Republic of Malta **Capital:** Valletta **Nationality:** Maltese **Languages:** Maltese, a Semitic dialect, and English are the official languages. Maltese is the principal spoken language but Italian is also widely spoken **Religion:** Roman Catholicism is the official religion and about 98% of the population is Catholic **Flag:** Two vertical stripes of white and red with a George Cross edged in red in the upper left corner **Anthem:** To This Sweet Land **Currency:** Maltese pound (0.34 per U.S. $1)

Location: Mediterranean Sea, about 58 miles south of Sicily and 180 miles from the coast of North Africa. Malta is comprised of 2 main islands, Malta and Gozo, and several smaller ones **Features:**

The country consists of a series of low hills, with terraced fields on the slopes **Chief Rivers:** The country has no rivers

Head of State: President: Dr. Anton Buttigieg, elected December 1976 **Head of Government:** Prime Minister Dominic Mintoff, born 1916, appointed June 1971; he is also foreign affairs and interior minister **Effective Date of Present Constitution:** 1964, revised 1974 **Legislative Body:** House of Representatives (unicameral), consisting of 65 members elected for 5-year terms **Local Government:** There is no formally organized local government

Ethnic Composition: Chiefly of Carthaginian and Phoenician stock, later mixed with Arabs, Italians, and British **Population Distribution:** 94% urban **Density:** 2,902 inhabitants per sq. mi.

Largest Cities: (1973 est) Sliema 21,768, Valletta 15,525, Rabat (Victoria) 5,505

Per Capita Income: $2,331 (1979) **Gross National Product (GNP):** $831 million (1979) **Economic Statistics:** Tourism, ship repair and light manufacturing are the bases of the economy **Minerals and Mining:** There are no mineral resources except for salt and stone **Labor Force:** 119,554 (1977) of which 26% is employed in industry, 6% in agriculture and fishing, and most of the rest in trade and services **Foreign Trade:** Exports, chiefly textiles, potatoes, flowers and seed, totaled $345 million in 1978. Imports, mainly machinery, chemicals, meat, mineral fuels and lubricants, and motor vehicles, totaled $668 million **Principal Trade Partners:** Britain, EC countries, Libya

Vital Statistics: Birthrate, 17.9 per 1,000 of pop. (1977); death rate, 8.6 **Life Expectancy:** 70 years **Health Statistics:** 96 inhabitants per hospital bed; 864 per physician (1971) **Infant Mortality:** 13.5 per 1,000 births **Illiteracy:** 17% **Primary and Secondary School Enrollment:** 61,148 (1976) **Enrollment in Higher Education:** 2,158 **GNP Expended on Education:** 4% (1976)

Transportation: Surfaced roads total 760 mi. **Motor Vehicles:** 73,200 (1977) **Passenger Cars:** 60,700 **Railway Mileage:** None **Ports:** Valletta **Major Airlines:** Air Malta operates flights to Europe and Africa **Communications:** Both government and privately owned **Radio Transmitters:** 2 **Licenses:** 63,000 (1976) **Television Transmitters:** 1 **Licenses:** 63,000 (1976) **Telephones:** 55,000 (1976) **Newspapers:** 6 dailies (1975)

Weights and Measures: Metric and English standards are used **Travel Requirements:** Passport, visa for stay exceeding 3 months

Over the centuries, the islands of Malta have been occupied by powers that sought control of the Mediterranean. And while under such occupations, the strategically placed islands have suffered much from attackers: in 1565, held by the Knights Hospitalers, a Turkish siege was defied; in World War II, Malta, as the "unsinkable aircraft carrier," withstood merciless Axis aerial bombardment, earning Britain's George Cross for heroism.

Independent from Britain since 1964, a republic since 1974, Malta has asserted some control over its own destiny. In 1971, Dominic Mintoff returned to power as Labor party prime minister following the defeat of the coalition of Giorgio Borg Olivier, the pro-Catholic prime minister. Mintoff took a neutral position between the Soviet and Western blocs. He forced Britain to renegotiate its lease on Maltese military facilities providing for increased rent to be paid to Malta and fixed an expiration date of April 1, 1979. Britain withdrew on schedule, and Malta was free of foreign soldiers for the first time in centuries.

Mintoff promoted light industry, notably textiles and plastics, and cultivated relations with the Arab states. Libya especially has been a good customer for the new industries—and a good provider of foreign aid. But loss of the revenue from the bases is expected to cause problems.

HISTORY: The strategic importance of Malta was recognized as far back as the time of the Phoenicians, whose occupation of the island was followed by invasions by the Greeks, Carthaginians, Romans, Byzantines, and Arabs. Malta was seized by the Normans in 1091. In 1530 it was given by Holy Roman Emperor Charles V to the Knights Hospitalers, who became known as the Knights of Malta and who in 1565 successfully withstood a siege by the Turks. The Knights continued to hold the island until 1798, when it was surrendered to Napoleon
1800: The French are ousted from the island by Britain, with the aid of a revolt by the Maltese

1814: Treaty of Paris confirms British possession
1921: Malta is granted limited self-government
1939-45: Malta sustains heavy bombing by Germans and Italians during World War II; entire population is awarded the George Cross in 1942
1964: Malta becomes independent
1969: Last British warships leave Malta
1972: Malta signs new financial and defense agreements with Britain and NATO, replacing the 1964 agreements
1974: Malta becomes a republic. Sir Anthony Mamo sworn in as first president
1976: Dr. Anton Buttigieg is elected president
1977: China promises continued economic and technical aid
1979: British lease of military bases ends; last British soldiers leave island

MAURITANIA

Area: 397,954 sq. mi. **Population:** 1,544,000 (1978 est.)

Official Name: Islamic Republic of Mauritania **Capital:** Nouakchott **Nationality:** Mauritanian **Languages:** Arabic, known in Mauritania as Hassaniyah, is the language most spoken, and with French is the official one; Wolof and Tukolor are also spoken in the South **Religion:** The population is almost entirely Moslem, and Islam is the state religion **Flag:** A gold star and crescent centered on a green field **Anthem:** National Anthem (no words) **Currency:** Ouguiya (45.9 per U.S.$1)

Location: West Africa. Mauritania is bordered on the north by Morocco, Algeria and the contested Western Sahara area, on the east and southeast by Mali, on the southwest by Senegal, and on the west by the Atlantic Ocean **Features:** The country on the whole is fairly flat. The Sahara zone in the north consists of shifting dunes and gravel plains, while the south is more fertile and suitable for cultivation **Chief River:** Senegal

Head of State and of Government: President and Prime Minister: Lt. Col. Mohamed Khouna Ould Haidalla, born 1939, appointed prime minister May 1979, assumed presidency on deposing President Louly on Jan. 4, 1980 **Effective Date of Present Constitution:** 1961, suspended 1978 **Legislative Body:** Mauritania is now governed by a Military Committee of National Salvation **Local Government:** 12 regions and one district (Nouakchott)

Ethnic Composition: Divided into three groups: 40% Arab-Berber-Negroid, 30% Arab-Berber (Moors), 30% Negroid **Population Distribution:** 23% urban, **Density:** 3.9 inhabitants per sq. mi.

Largest Cities: (1976 est.) Nouakchott 134,986; (1972 est.) Nouadhibou 24,000, Zouérate 16,000, Kaédi 15,700, Rosso 11,400, Boghé 10,600, F'Derick 10,000

Per Capita Income: $213 (1978) **Gross National Product (GNP):** $330 million (1978) **Economic Statistics:** In 1977 about 22% of the GNP was derived from agriculture (livestock, millet, corn, rice, sweet potatoes, peanuts, beans, gum arabic); 21% from industry, mining, and fish processing **Minerals and Mining:** Mauritania is second only to Liberia in West African iron-ore production. There are large deposits of gypsum **Labor Force:** 420,00 (1975), of which 90% is in agriculture **Foreign Trade:** Exports, chiefly iron ore, livestock, fish, dates, and gum arabic, totaled $133 million in 1978. Imports, mainly machinery, vehicles, electrical equipment, petroleum products, cement, tires, and tea, totaled $309 million **Principal Trade Partners:** France, Italy, Britain, West Germany, Senegal, Japan, Spain, United States

Vital Statistics: Birthrate, 44.8 per 1,000 of pop. (1975); death rate, 24.9 **Life Expectancy:** 39 years **Health Statistics:** 2,328 inhabitants per hospital bed; 15,172 per physician (1975) **Infant Mortality:** 187 per 1,000 births **Illiteracy:** 88% **Primary and Secondary School Enrollment:** 83,029 (1977) **Enrollment in Higher Education:** c. 1,000 study abroad **GNP Expended on Education:** 4.3% (1972)

Transportation: Paved roads total 370 mi. **Motor Vehicles:** 11,800 (1974) **Passenger Cars:** 4,400 (1972) **Railway Mileage:** 450 **Ports:** Nouadhibou, Nouakchott **Major Airlines:** Air-Mauritanie operates domestic and regional services; Air Afrique is the major international carrier **Communications:** Government controlled **Radio Transmitters:** 4 **Receivers:** 95,000 (1976) **Television Transmitters:** 1 **Telephones:** 1,300 est. (1969) **Newspapers:** 1 daily, 0.2 per 1,000 inhabitants (1972)

Weights and Measures: Metric system **Travel Requirements:** Passport, visa valid for 3 months, $10 fee, 3 photos

Mauritania is a borderland between Moorish/Arab North Africa and black West Africa. Although cast in the mold of a modern state and with membership in the Organization of African Unity, the former West African territory continues to be divided by racial distinctions dating from the medieval migrations of light-skinned Arabs and Berbers, who forced the darker-skinned natives into the southern region and enslaved many of them. French rule, established by 1920, favored the blacks, who were more inclined than the Arabs to take advantage of European education.

President Moktar Ould Daddah, the country's leader from 1960 to 1978, steered an enlightened and adroit course racially and politically. While promoting more education for the Moorish/Arab majority, President Moktar sought to gain foreign aid from both Western and Eastern sources. In July 1978 the president was overthrown in a bloodless coup led by military officers. Col. Mustapha Ould Salek was named president. In June 1979 Salek resigned and was succeeded by Col. Ahmed Louly.

Although France continues to provide most of the country's aid and development funds, Communist China recently has played a major role in such projects as rice-growing, irrigation, and cement manufacture and in drilling numerous wells to tap ground water.

Mauritania's main source of wealth has been rich deposits of iron ore and copper, which have been developed since independence by French interests. These have provided substantial earnings that have made it possible for the government to embark on the improvement of social services and of agriculture, on which more than 80 percent of Mauritanians depend. Copper production ceased in 1978.

Meanwhile, in addition to French and Chinese aid, Mauritanian development is being aided by countries such as the United States, Yugoslavia, and Spain.

Mauritanian gains in territory from the southern part of former Spanish Sahara were offset by the disruption to the nation's economy caused by raids of the *Polisario Front*, a Saharan liberation guerrilla group based in Algeria. But, after the seizure of power by the army in 1978, the *Polisario* proclaimed a unilateral cease-fire. The military government informally decided to respect the truce, and fighting fell to a sporadic level. On August 5, 1979, Mauritania signed a peace agreement with the *Polisario* under which it renounced all claim to its portion of the contested Western Sahara area. Morocco promptly occupied the region. Mauritania then resumed diplomatic relations with Algeria, ending a three-year break.

HISTORY: Mauritania's original inhabitants, a Sudanic black people, were enslaved or driven southward by the 11th-century Berber invasion that destroyed the empire of Ghana to the east. The Berbers in turn were conquered in the 16th century by Arab invaders, the Beni Hassan. Trade with Europeans, opened by the Portuguese in the 15th century, attracted the Dutch, English, and French. Throughout the 19th century, the French gradually extended control over the country, and established a protectorate in 1903. Mauritania was made a French colony in 1920

1946-56: Internal self-rule gradually increases along with Mauritanian representation in French parliament and Assembly of the French Union

1958: In referendum, Mauritania votes to become autonomous republic within new French Community

1960: Mauritania wins full independence, with Moktar Ould Daddah continuing as prime minister

1961: With adoption of presidential system, Daddah, the only candidate, is elected president; new People's party becomes the sole political organization

1963-66: Completion of iron-ore mining project by French-led consortium and development of extensive copper deposits give strong boost to nation's economy

1973-74: Drought causes widespread famine

1975: Agreement is signed among Spain, Morocco and Mauritania providing for withdrawal of the Spanish presence from Western Sahara. Daddah is reelected president

1976: Morocco and Mauritania partition Western Sahara, giving Mauritania the southern third. The proclamation of an independent republic by the *Polisario Front*, the Saharan liberation movement, is ignored. *Polisario* guerrillas raid Nouakchott

1977: *Polisario* units raid iron-mining center at Zouérate

1978: Group of Western and Arab banks lends Mauritania $360 million for exploitation of iron ore mines. French military planes help government forces stop *Polisario* rebels advancing on Zouérate. President Moktar Ould Daddah is overthrown in a bloodless coup by military officers, led by Col. Mustapha Ould Salek who becomes Chairman of Military Committee for National Recovery and president. *Polisario* proclaims cease-fire

1979: Premier Ahmed Oul Boucif and 10 other Mauritanian delegates to the Economic Community of West African States die in air crash. He is succeeded by Lt. Col. Mohamed Khouna Ould Haidalla. President Salek resigns. Lt. Col. Mohamed Mahmoud Ould Ahmed Louly is chosen by the MCNR to replace him

1980: President Louly resigns; Prime Minister Haidalla becomes president

---

MAURITIUS

Area: 790 sq. mi. **Population:** 940,000 (1979 est.)

Official Name: Mauritius **Capital:** Port Louis **Nationality:** Mauritian **Languages:** English is the official language, but a Creole patois, basically French, is spoken by 52% of the people; Chinese, Hindi, Urdu, and French are also spoken **Religion:** About 51% Hindu, 33% Christian (chiefly Roman Catholic), and 16% Moslem **Flag:** Four horizontal stripes of red, blue, yellow, and green **Anthem:** Motherland **Currency:** Mauritian rupee (7.6 per U.S. $1)

Location: Indian Ocean. Mauritius (20°S.,57°30'E.) lies about 500 miles east of Madagascar. Dependencies include Rodrigues and distant smaller islands **Features:** The island is volcanic in origin and almost entirely surrounded by coral reefs. The land rises to a central plateau, surrounded by mountains believed to be the rim of an ancient volcano **Chief Rivers:** Grand (S.E. and N.W.), Rempart, Poste

Head of State: Queen Elizabeth II, represented by a governor-general, Sir Dayendranath Burrenchobay **Head of Government:** Prime Minister: Sir Seewoosagur Ramgoolam, born 1900; reappointed 1976 **Effective Date of Present Constitution:** 1968 **Legislative Body:** Parliament (unicameral Legislative Assembly), 70 members with 5-year terms, 62 of whom are elected **Local Government:** 9 administrative districts, with local councils

Ethnic Composition: Indo-Mauritians (67%), Creoles (29%), Sino-Mauritians, and Franco-Mauritians **Population Distribution:** 44% urban **Density:** 1,190 inhabitants per sq. mi.

Largest Cities: (1975 est.) Port Louis 138,161, Beau Bassin/Rose Hill 81,353, Curepipe 53,068, Quatre Bornes 52,134

Per Capita Income: $817 (1978 est.) **Gross National Product (GNP):** $730 million (1978 est.) **Economic Statistics:** 29% of the GNP comes from agriculture (sugar [90%], tea, ginger, tobacco, vegetables, bananas, peanuts), 23% from industry (sugar processing, rum, beer) and construction, and 16% from services **Minerals and Mining:** There are no known mineral deposits **Labor Force:** 260,000 in 1975, with 28% in agriculture and 12% in industry, and 34% in services **Foreign Trade:** Exports, sugar and sugar products, tea, clothing, and molasses, totaled $300 million in 1978. Imports, chiefly foodstuffs, manufactured goods, machinery and transportation equipment, fuel, chemicals and fertilizers, totaled $494 million **Principal Trade Partners:** Britain, France, South Africa, Japan, Bahrain, United States, China, Belgium

Vital Statistics: Birthrate, 41.4 per 1,000 of pop. (1977); death rate, 7.0 **Life Expectancy:** 67 years **Health Statistics:** 271 inhabitants per hospital bed; 2,900 per physician (1976) **Infant Mortality:** 58 per 1,000 births **Illiteracy:** 20% **Primary and Secondary School Enrollment:** 208,272 (1976) **Enrollment in Higher Education:** 1,096 (1975) **GNP Expended on Education:** 4.5% (1976)

Transportation: Paved roads total 1,020 mi. **Motor Vehicles:** 37,300 (1977) **Passenger Cars:** 24,300 **Railway Mileage:** None **Ports:** Port Louis **Major Airlines:** Air Mauritius and several foreign airlines link Mauritius with Europe, Africa, and Asia **Communications:** Government controlled **Radio Transmitters:** 3 **Licenses:** 200,000 (1976) **Television Transmitters:** 4 **Licenses:** 41,000 (1976) **Telephones:** 27,000 (1976) **Newspapers:** 12 dailies, 91 copies per 1,000 inhabitants (1975)

Weights and Measures: Metric system **Travel Requirements:** Passport, visa, no charge except postage

---

Encircled by coral reefs and the blue-green Indian Ocean, Mauritius looks like the perfect model of a placid tropical island. The former British crown colony, lying nearly 1,500 miles east of southern Africa—its closest proximity to any continent—is renowned as the source of rare postage stamps and as the last refuge of the extinct dodo bird.

The remote volcanic island is also a microcosm of the present-day problems of less-developed countries: overpopulation, racial conflict, and dependence on a single crop, sugar. With no solutions in sight, it seems only a matter of time before the combined pressures of these problems bring an eruption. Indeed, a ban on 12 unions was imposed by the government in 1971 and only lifted in 1974, following lengthy negotiations between dockworkers and government officials.

Within the island's 790 square miles, there are, in addition to a large Indian-Hindu majority, major groups of Africans, Europeans (mainly French), and Creoles (an Afro-French mixture), and a small element of Chinese. Despite efforts of a coalition government headed by Prime Minister Sir Seewoosagur Ramgoolam to promote harmony, racial rivalries are intense. Violent racial rioting and also labor unrest preceded and accompanied Mauritius' independence in 1968.

Since elimination of malaria recently, the island's population is growing by 1.5 percent a year and birth control is opposed equally by Hindu, Catholic, and Moslem groups.

Some 90 percent of cultivated land is planted with sugarcane, but production is often drastically reduced by cyclones. In addition to depressed sugar prices, Mauritius has been faced with the loss of a preferential market through Britain's entry into the European Common Market.

At the same time, the Mauritian government has found itself in a dilemma in being opposed to white minority rule in South Africa even though South Africa is one of Mauritius' main trading partners. South Africa itself has shown interest in aiding Mauritius in return for a less anti-Pretoria stand and, in view of the island's problems, Mauritian officials appear inclined to accept.

It has been a rule of thumb on Mauritius that one ton of sugar exports was needed for each inhabitant. But sugar production is unlikely to exceed 700,000 tons a year, although population is now climbing toward the one million mark.

HISTORY: Originally uninhabited, Mauritius was first settled and named by the Dutch in the 17th century. The island was abandoned early in the 18th century, after which it was claimed by the French, who renamed it Ile-de-France and laid the foundations of a slave-owning plantation economy based on sugar. In 1814, the island was ceded to Britain and reverted to its original name. Slavery was abolished in 1834, and the planters began importing indentured Indians. Although they soon came to form a majority, the Indians long remained politically powerless because of a restricted franchise based on property qualifications

1948: Franchise is broadened by new constitution; in new elections, Indians win majority in legislative council, overthrowing dominance of Franco-Mauritians but causing other minority groups to fear Indian domination

1961: Constitutional conference in London paves way toward full self-government, but talks are marred by disputes between Hindu-dominated majority Labour party and minority parties

1967: Mauritius becomes self-governing; Labour party leader Seewoosagur Ramgoolam is appointed prime minister; island is wracked by racial and labor unrest

1968: Mauritius wins independence amid Creole-Moslem rioting

1970: Government begins drafting plans for crop diversification, light industry, and tourism

1971: Government declares state of emergency because of strikes

1975: Cyclone Gervaise leaves 90,000 homeless and destroys 30 percent of sugar harvest

1979: General strike in support of sugar workers paralyzes economy. Inflation rate is more than 30 percent

1980: Organization of African Unity condemns U.S. base on Diego Garcia, calls for island's return to Mauritius

MEXICO

Area: 761,600 sq. mi. **Population:** 69,381,000 (1979 est.)
Official Name: United Mexican States **Capital:** Mexico City **Nationality:** Mexican **Languages:** Spanish is the official and predominant language; 7% speak only Indian dialects **Religion:** 97% Roman Catholic; there are some 600,000 Protestants and 100,000 Jews **Flag:** Green, white, and red vertical stripes with the national emblem in the center **Anthem:** National Anthem, beginning "Mexicans, to the call of war" **Currency:** Mexican peso (22.8 per U.S. $1)

Location: North America. Mexico is bordered on the north by the United States, on the east by the Gulf of Mexico, on the south by Belize and Guatemala, and on the west by the Pacific Ocean **Features:** The country consists of a large central plateau, flanked by the eastern and western coastal ranges of the Sierra Madre. From a low desert plain in the north, the plateau rises to 8,000 feet near Mexico City **Chief Rivers:** Rio Bravo (Rio Grande), Lerma, Santiago, Usumacinta, Grijalva, Balsas, Pánuco

Head of State and of Government: President José López Portillo y Pacheco, born 1920, elected 1976 for 6-year term **Effective Date of Present Constitution:** 1917 **Legislative Body:** Congress (bicameral), consisting of the Senate and the Chamber of Deputies. The Senate is composed of 64 members elected for 6-year terms. The Chamber of Deputies has 400 members elected for 3 years **Local Government:** 31 states, 1 federal district. Each state has its own governor and popularly elected legislature

Ethnic Composition: About 60% of the population are mestizos of mixed Indian and Spanish descent. 30% are pure Indian, while 9% are of Spanish or other European ancestry **Population Distribution:** 64% urban **Density:** 91 inhabitants per sq. mi.

Largest Cities: (1975 est.) Mexico City 8,591,750, Guadalajara 1,560,805, Monterey 1,049,957, Ciudad Juárez 520,539, León 496,598, Puebla 482,155, Tijuana 386,852, Acapulco 352,673

Per Capita Income: $1,388 (1979) **Gross National Product (GNP):** $117.4 billion (1979) **Economic Statistics:** In 1977 about 12% of GNP came from agriculture (farming, livestock), forestry, and fishing, 37% from industry (cars, machinery, construction, petrochemicals, steel, cement) and mining (including oil) **Minerals and Mining:** Mexico is the world's largest producer of silver and a major producer of oil, gas, gold, sulfur, lead, and zinc. Coal, tin, antimony, mercury, copper, and iron are also mined **Labor Force:** 16.6 million (1975), 41% in agriculture, 34% in industry and mining, and 25% in services **Foreign Trade:** Exports, chiefly petroleum, cotton, sugar, fruits, vegetables, coffee, sulfur, and shrimp, totaled $6.5 billion in 1978. Imports, mainly industrial machinery, motor vehicles and parts, chemicals, communications and transportation equipment, and electric power equipment, totaled $8 billion **Principal Trade Partners:** United States, West Germany, Britain, Japan, France, Spain, Canada

Vital Statistics: Birthrate, 34.6 per 1,000 of pop. (1976); death rate, 6.8 **Life Expectancy:** 65 years **Health Statistics:** 530 inhabitants per hospital bed; 1,385 per physician (1972) **Infant Mortality:** 54.7 per 1,000 births (1976) **Illiteracy:** 16% **Primary and Secondary School Enrollment:** 15,389,642 (1976) **Enrollment in Higher Education:** 539,372 (1976) **GNP Expended on Education:** 4.3% (1976)

Transportation: Paved roads total 42,727 mi. **Motor Vehicles:** 3,759,600 (1977) **Passenger Cars:** 2,682,000 **Railway Mileage:** 20,000 **Ports:** Veracruz, Tampico, Coatzacoalcos, Guaymas, Salina Cruz, Mazatián, Manzanillo **Major Airlines:** Aeroméxico, the government-owned line and Mexicana, a privately owned line, operate both international and domestic flights **Communications:** Partly government controlled **Radio Transmitters:** 668 **Receivers:** 17,514,000 (1974) **Television Transmitters:** 150 **Receivers:** 4,885,000 **Telephones:** 3,309,000 (1976) **Newspapers:** 256 dailies (1975), 116 copies per 1,000 inhabitants (1975)

Weights and Measures: Metric system **Travel Requirements:** Tourist card, valid for stay up to 6 months; no charge

Mexico experienced the world's first social and political revolution of the 20th century, but to this day it still suffers seriously from economic underdevelopment. The bloody struggle that began in 1910 and cost over a million lives gave Mexico stable institutions and a strong constitution, yet most of the revolution's high-sounding principles have yet to be implemented. Glittering long-term hopes for economic advancement were raised, however, with major oil discoveries in the 1970s.

Today this third-largest of Latin American republics, and the most populous Spanish-speaking country in the world, enjoys a large measure of political solidity, under a system of government that falls somewhere between dictatorship and democracy. But the benefits of an economic "miracle" have reached only a small part of Mexico's 69 million inhabitants, and the country's large peasant

MEXICO
CONIC PROJECTION
SCALE OF MILES
0 100 200 300
SCALE OF KILOMETERS
0 100 200 300
National Capitals ..... ⊛
State Capitals ..... ◉
© Copyright HAMMOND INCORPORATED, Maplewood, N.J.
States Indicated by Numbers:
1 Tlaxcala
2 Morelos
3 Distrito Federal
4 México
5 Hidalgo
6 Querétaro
7 Guanajuato
8 Aguascalientes
9 Nayarit
10 Colima
Longitude West 102° of Greenwich
UNITED STATES
PACIFIC OCEAN
GULF OF MEXICO
Gulf of Tehuantepec
Gulf of Honduras
Bay of Campeche
Campeche Bank
Tropic of Cancer
BAJA CALIFORNIA NORTE
BAJA CALIFORNIA SUR
SONORA
CHIHUAHUA
COAHUILA
NUEVO LEON
TAMAULIPAS
SINALOA
DURANGO
ZACATECAS
SAN LUIS POTOSI
NAYARIT
JALISCO
MICHOACAN
GUERRERO
OAXACA
VERACRUZ
TABASCO
CHIAPAS
CAMPECHE
YUCATAN
QUINTANA ROO
GUATEMALA
BELIZE
HONDURAS
Sierra Madre Occidental
Sierra Madre Oriental
Rio Grande
Rio Bravo
REVILLAGIGEDO IS. (Colima)
Tijuana
Mexicali
Ensenada
San Vicente
Rosario
Yuma
Nogales
Tucson
Las Cruces
El Paso
Ciudad Juárez
San Angelo
Roswell
Lubbock
Abilene
Globe
Bisbee
Douglas
Heroica Nogales
Agua Prieta
Cananea
Pitiquito
Pto. Peñasco
Magdalena
Cumpas
Nacozari
Hermosillo
Moctezuma
Buenaventura
Madera
Chihuahua
Manuel Benavides
Ojinaga
Ciudad Acuña
Del Rio
Piedras Negras
Eagle Pass
Zaragoza
Allende
Sabinas
Muzquiz
Monclova
Nuevo Laredo
Laredo
Corpus Christi
Guaymas
Empalme
Sta. Rosalía
Mulegé
Ciudad Obregón
Navojoa
Alamos
Huatabampo
Topolobampo
Los Mochis
El Fuerte
Guadalupe
Guasave
Navolato
Culiacán
El Dorado
San Ignacio
Mazatlán
Rosario
Durango
Sombrerete
Fresnillo
Ciudad García
Zacatecas
Charcas
Matehuala
Ciudad Victoria
Santander Jiménez
Aldama
Jaumave
C. Mante
Ciudad Madero
Tampico
Pánuco
Reinosa
Matamoros
Brownsville
Gómez Palacio
Lerdo
Torreón
Parras
Saltillo
Monterrey
Cadereyta
Montemorelos
Linares
Hidalgo
Monclova
Concepción del Oro
Cedral
San Pedro
Guanaceví
Santa Bárbara
Parral
San Francisco del Oro
Ciudad Camargo
Jiménez
Ocampo
Villa Frontera
Saucillo
Aquiles Serdán
Cusihuiriáchic
Nonoava
Casas Grandes
Guzmán
Cumpas
Sahuaripa
Ures
Villa de Seris
I. Tiburón
I. Ángel de la Guarda
Cabo S. Lázaro
I. Sta. Margarita
Cabo S. Lucas
San José del Cabo
San Antonio
La Paz
I. Cerralvo
El Dorado
Tres Marías Is.
I. S. Benedicto
I. Socorro
Cabo Corrientes
B. de Banderas
Mascota
Tepic
Ixtlán
Aguascalientes
Pinos
San Luis Potosí
Río Verde
Cárdenas
Cerritos
Djocaliente
Colotlán
Tuxpan
Sánchez Román
Lagos
León
Guanajuato
Querétaro
Salamanca
Irapuato
Silao
La Piedad
Ocotlán
Ameca
Guadalajara
Zamora
Morelia
Ciudad Guzmán
Colima
Manzanillo
Tecomán
Coalcomán
Uruapan
Zitácuaro
Toluca
MEXICO CITY
Pachuca
Tulancingo
Teziutlán
Tlaxcala
Puebla
Cuernavaca
Taxco
Iguala
Teloloapan
Chilpancingo
Acapulco
Ometepec
Pta. Maldonado
Puerto Angel
Tlaxiaco
Oaxaca
Tixtla
Huajuapan
Tehuacán
Orizaba
Jalapa
Veracruz Llave
Alvarado
San Andrés Tuxtla
Coatzacoalcos (Pto. México)
Minatitlán
Villahermosa
Frontera
Carmen
Lag. de Campeche
Campeche
Champotón
Sabancuy
Mérida
Progreso
Hunucmá
Tizimín
Valladolid
Ticul
Tekax
Hopelchén
Felipe Carillo Puerto
Chetumal
Xcalak
Belize City
Belmopán
Stann Creek
Cobán
Zacapa
Quezaltenango
Huehuetenango
Guatemala
Sta. Rosa
Comitán
Ciudad de las Casas (S. Cristóbal)
Tuxtla Gutiérrez
Juchitán
Salina Cruz
Tonalá
Huixtla
Tapachula
Romero
Matías
Tierra Blanca
Tuxtepec
San Gabriel
Papantla de Olarte
Mineral del Monte
Tantoyuca
Huejutla
Jalpan
Cayo Arenas
Cayo Arcas
I. Pérez
Cabo Catoche
Cozumel
HIDALGO
Coyotepec
Zumpango
Teotihuacán
Azcapotzalco
Texcoco
Coyoacán
Xochimilco
Amecameca
Cuautla
Cuernavaca
Xochitepec
Jojutla
Jonacatepec
Izúcar de Matamoros
MEXICO CITY
D.F.
S. Martín
Texmelucan
Apizaco
Tlaxcala
Cholula
Puebla
Atlixco
Tepeaca
Tecamachalco
San Gabriel
Chignahuapan
Apan
San Salvador el Seco
Cuyoaco
Libres
Huamantla
Acatzingo
Serdán
Chapulco
Izúcar
Teziutlán
Misantla
Altotonga
Jalapa
Jico
Coatepec
R. J. García
Río Pescados
Huatusco de Chicuellar
Orizaba
Ciudad Mendoza
Zongolica
Córdoba
Soledad de Doblado
Río Blanco
Veracruz Llave
Villa Ursulo Galván
Villa Vicente Guerrero
Calpulalpam
Nauhcampatépetl 14,045
Iztaccíhuatl 17,343
Popocatépetl 17,887
Citlaltépetl 18,855
MILES
0 10 20 30
GULF OF MEXICO

population is only marginally better off now than in 1910. The unemployed and underemployed exceed 50 percent of the work force.

In politics, as in other fields, the contrasts between theory and practice in Mexico are vast. Under the republican form of government, contending parties are permitted, and six of them participated in the 1979 elections. In reality, however, Mexican politics is dominated by one amorphous party—the Revolutionary Institutional party (PRI)—which has provided every president since its creation in 1929.

During his six-year term, the president is an immensely powerful figure, but it is the party that reflects a wide spectrum of national opinion and eventually dictates the limits within which he can move. All significant support for and opposition to a president's policies come from within the ruling party. However, because the constitution forbids immediate reelection for members of the Senate and Chamber of Deputies, many talented politicians are attracted to the bureaucracy instead. Congress traditionally has been regarded as little more than a rubber stamp that ratifies executive decisions.

Although the PRI is technically structured around the three pillars of the peasant, worker, and popular movements, business interests have gained increasing control over the party and government in the past 20 years, giving weight to the saying that "in Mexico business is government and government is business." The economic boom that gave political strength to the business sector also spawned a host of conservative politicians.

The Roman Catholic Church has carried little political weight in Mexico, unlike most Latin American countries, since the revolution, although most people are nominally Catholic and there was a trememdous outburst of enthusiasm when Pope John Paul II visited the country in 1979. The constitution defends religious freedom, and in practice there is considerable tolerance of different creeds.

Mexico's economy, which had been growing at a remarkable average of 6.5 percent annually for the past 20 years, reversed that trend beginning in 1973 with an accelerating inflation rate. In an effort to stimulate exports, investments, and job creation, the government devalued the peso in 1976 for the first time in 22 years. The extremely high unemployment rate also increased the number of Mexicans crossing the border to the U.S. illegally to search for work.

Despite a fundamental agrarian reform following the revolution, which gave most peasants their own small plots of land and established a system of farm cooperatives, the shortage of irrigation, credit, and marketing facilities has kept most peasants living at subsistence level.

Mexico's considerable social and economic problems are made more acute by the country's population growth rate, at present about 3.3 percent per year. Improved health facilities have brought down the death rate dramatically since World War II, but successive governments have strongly opposed an official family planning program.

In foreign policy, Mexico has long followed a policy of nonintervention, which led it to maintain diplomatic relations with Cuba when all other members of the Organization of American States broke their ties in 1964.

Because of proximity and close economic ties, the United States has considerable influence in Mexican politics. This reality sometimes leads Mexico to take strongly nationalist stands, although differences between the countries are usually settled amicably.

Mexico has been in the oil business since the beginning of the century when foreign companies began to produce "black gold" there. By 1918 Mexico was second only to the United States in output. After the government nationalized the petroleum industry in 1938, production declined, then recovered slowly. In 1972, before new discoveries of oil in the Reforma area of Chiapas and Tabasco, Mexico's known petroleum reserves were put at 2.5 billion barrels. Since then, with new findings of oil and natural gas in the Gulf and Pacific coastal regions and offshore in the Gulf of Campeche, proven reserves have grown by leaps and bounds. In March 1980 they were put at 50 billion barrels. Morover, potential reserves were estimated at over 200 billion barrels, more than those of Saudi Arabia.

By reason of its oil wealth and large labor pool, Mexico was being acclaimed by economists at the outset of the 1980s as one of a handful of less-developed countries likely to gain rapidly in economic power and worldwide political influence.

HISTORY: Before the Spanish conquest of Mexico in 1519, Indian civilizations had flourished there for centuries, with that of the Mayas dating as far back as about 1500 B.C. With the conquest of the Aztecs by Hernán Cortéz, Indian culture was modified and the Indians themselves reduced to peonage on the land and in the mines. Corruption in the Spanish administration helped fan growing discontent among the Creoles, Mexican-born descendants of the Spaniards, leaving the country ripe for the revolutionary ideals spread by the French Revolution

1810: Miguel Hidalgo y Costilla, a Creole priest, begins the fight for independence; revolutionary armies spring up under various leaders

1821: Mexico is granted independence; anarchy, corruption, and political rivalry are rife

1836-45: Texas, under domination of U.S. settlers, secedes from Mexico and declares its independence; it is ultimately annexed by the United States

1846-48: Annexation brings on Mexican War with the United States; Mexico is defeated, signs Treaty of Guadalupe Hidalgo ceding vast block of territory to the United States

1857-61: Benito Juárez, reform-minded minister of justice and later president, introduces liberal constitution transferring power from Creoles to mestizos and secularizing church lands; conservative opposition leads to War of the Reform (1858-61), which ends in victory for liberals

1864-67: France establishes puppet empire under Austrian-born Emperor Maximilian; Juárez leads popular resistance; empire collapses

1876-1909: Porfirio Díaz leads successful revolt and establishes ruthless dictatorship; he reforms Mexico's finances, but despite nation's growing prosperity vast numbers of people are reduced to virtual slavery when their communal lands are apportioned to large estate owners; almost three-quarters of Mexico's mineral resources become by purchase the property of foreign interests

1910-17: Francisco I. Madero organizes rebellion and forces Díaz to resign; Mexico is thrown into ferment of revolt culminating in rise of leaders such as Venustiano Carranza, Francisco (Pancho) Villa, and Emiliano Zapata. Villa breaks with Carranza, who has U.S. support, and Villa's irregulars raid New Mexico (1916); U.S. Gen. John J. Pershing leads punitive expedition into Mexico in pursuit of Villa. Carranza frames liberal constitution of 1917 nationalizing mineral resources and restoring communal lands to Indians

1934-40: President Lázaro Cárdenas undertakes extensive land reform and expropriates foreign-owned companies

1968: Army and police clash with students protesting alleged government repression and violation of constitutional rights

1970: Luis Echeverría Alvarez is elected president

1973: Echeverría tours the world hoping to make strong trade agreements with the European Community, China and the Soviet Union. Mexican terrorists kidnap diplomatically and politically prominent people and ransom them for the release of political prisoners and for money to support their cause

1974: Mexico signs agreement for commercial co-operation with European Community, the first Latin American nation to do so

1976: José López Portillo is elected president

1977: President López Portillo visits U.S., stressing Mexico's independent stance, yet seeking cooperation. U.S. and Mexico sign first formal trade agreement since 1942

1978: Carter Administration couples promise of "no massive deportations" of Mexicans working illegally in the U.S. with offers of U.S. support for job-producing loans. Government legalizes Communist party for first time in 40 years. Government continues campaign of spraying marijuana fields with toxic chemical known as "paraquat." President López Portillo, visiting Japan, makes arrangements to sell oil there and concludes agreements by which Japanese banks will finance oil-related projects

1979: Pope John Paul II draws enthusiastic throngs when he comes to Mexico to open third meeting of Latin American Episcopal Conference in Puebla and visit major cities. U.S. President Carter receives cool official reception in February; promises that Mexico will no longer be treated as a "junior partner." Government announces a National Plan for Industrial Development (NPID) to utilize resources to spur productivity and overcome bottlenecks in transportation of goods. On June 3, a flaming gusher erupts at offshore Ixtoc I well, creating oil slick in Gulf of Mexico which fouls fishing grounds and beaches as far north as Texas. In July 1 congressional elections, PRI wins 296 of 300 seats in Chamber of Deputies; 100 new seats are apportioned among minority parties. Agreement is reached to sell natural gas to U.S. at price above U.S. domstic price. Crude-oil output reaches 1.9 billion barrels a day of which U.S. buys about 70%

1980: Expiration of 3-year-old treaty Jan. 1 marks end of U.S. shrimp fishing in Mexican waters. Government introduces a 10% value added tax (VAT) to replace 4% sales tax and increase revenues. U.S. government absolves Mexican growers of "dumping" excess tomatoes on American markets. Valve in newly completed pipeline is opened, allowing natural gas to flow into U.S. at an initial rate of 300 million cu. ft. per day. In March, PEMEX, the government-owned oil company, sets 1980 production goal of 2.25 to 2.5 million barrels of oil a day with exports of 1.17 million barrels a day. Agreement is reached to sell 300,000 barrels a day to Japan. Pres. López Portillo visits France, West Germany, Sweden and Canada negotiate oil deals in exchange for joint investment in Mexican enterprises and exchange of scientific and technical knowledge. Ixtoc I well is at last fully capped after a 3-billion-barrel oil spill, the worst in history

---

MONACO

Area: 0.708 sq. mi. (453 acres) **Population:** 25,000 (1978 est.)

Official Name: Principality of Monaco **Capital:** Monaco **Nationality:** Monacan or Monégasque **Languages:** French is the official language; the principal spoken languages are French, Monégasque, English and Italian **Religion:** 95% Roman Catholic, the official religion **Flag:** Red over white horizontal stripes **Anthem:** Monacan Hymn, beginning "Principality of Monaco, my fatherland" **Currency:** French franc (4.2 per U.S. $1)

Location: A coastal enclave within the Alpes-Maritimes department of southeastern France, bordering the Mediterranean Sea **Features:** The principality consists of 3 main areas: La Condamine, the business district around the port; Monte Carlo, the site of the famous casino, which is at a higher elevation; and Monaco, the capital, known also as the Rock because of its situation on a high promontory extending into the sea **Chief Rivers:** There are no rivers

Head of State: Prince Rainier III, born 1923, succeeded to the throne in 1949 **Head of Government:** Minister of State André Saint-Mleux (by law a French citizen), appointed 1972. He is assisted by a 3-man Council of Government **Effective Date of Present Constitution:** 1911, revised December 1962 **Legislative Body:** National Council (unicameral), consisting of 18 members elected for 5 years **Local Government:** 1 commune (with 4 quarters), under a mayor and a 15-member elected council

Ethnic Composition: The native Monacans are a minority (19%); 58% are French, and 17% Italian **Population Distribution:** 100% urban

Largest Cities: (1968 census) La Condamine 11,438, Monte Carlo 9,948; (1972 est.) Monaco 1,685

Per Capita Income: N.A. **Gross National Product (GNP):** N.A. **Economic Statistics:** About 55% of the income is derived from tourism, 30% from local industry, and 4% from the casino. The substantial part of the tourist revenue is derived from the government controlled Société Anonyme des Bains de Mer, which operates the gambling casino at Monte Carlo as well as hotels and motion picture theaters. Many foreign companies have established their headquarters in Monaco because of the low taxation **Minerals and Mining:** There are no minerals **Labor Force:** Most of the working population is employed by SBM; and some are employed by the small handicraft industry and by service establishments **Foreign Trade:** Statistical information is not available **Principal Trade Partners:** France

Vital Statistics: Birthrate 7.5 per 1,000 of pop. (1977); death rate, 10.6 **Life Expectancy:** 75 years **Health Statistics:** 75 inhabitants per hospital bed; 500 per physician (1976) **Infant Mortality:** 9.3 per 1,000 births (1970) **Illiteracy:** Negligible **Primary and Secondary**

School Enrollment: 4,227 (1973) **Enrollment in Higher Education:** N.A. **GNP Expended on Education:** N.A.

Transportation: Surfaced roads total about 30 mi. **Motor Vehicles:** N.A. **Passenger Cars:** N.A. **Railway Mileage:** 0.6 **Port:** La Condamine **Major Airlines:** None **Communications:** Both government and privately owned **Radio Transmitters:** 6 **Receivers:** 7,500 (1976) **Television Transmitters:** 3 **Receivers:** 16,000 (1976) **Telephones:** 24,000 (1976) **Newspapers:** French and other newspapers are on sale; the Journal de Monaco, an official weekly, is the only local newspaper

Weights and Measures: Metric system **Travel Requirements:** Passport, no visa for 3 months

---

Monaco has been a principality of three towns covering an area about half the size of New York's Central Park, but Monaco is growing and expanding into the sea. A land-filling program added more than 20 percent to Monaco's area, to a total of 453 acres, or about 0.7 square miles.

Still, the microscopic principality is a state, the second smallest independent state in the world, after the Vatican City. Crammed into its small size are Riviera weather, scenery to match, the gambling paradise of Monte Carlo's casino, a reigning Prince Rainier with a movie-queen wife (Grace Kelly), the world-famous Oceanographic Museum (under the direction of France's Jacques Cousteau), and the daily changing of the Caribinier Guard at Palace Square.

Of course, as a long-time vacation resort, Monaco is filled with noted hotels. To keep pace with modernization of the principality, existing hotels are being modernized and new ones built, all with government help.

Monaco has a customs union and interchangeable currency with France, whose consent, by a treaty of 1918, is required for accession to the throne of the principality. The birth of Princess Grace's son in 1958 assured a male ruler to follow Prince Rainier.

Without this royal line, Monaco would come under French protection, making the Monégasques, now free of income taxes, subject to French levies. Tax freedom for Monaco-based companies was curtailed by a 1963 fiscal convention with France, under which concerns in Monaco doing more than 25 percent of their business elsewhere must pay taxes. The convention also applies French income taxes to French citizens who moved to Monaco after mid-October 1957.

HISTORY: Monaco was occupied by the Phoenicians from the 10th to the 5th century B.C. and then by the Greeks. During the early Christian era it was dominated by Rome until occupied by the barbarians and Saracens. In 1191, the Genoese took possession of Monaco; the Grimaldi family took control in 1297. The male line died out in 1731, but the French Goyon-Matignon family, which succeeded by marriage, assumed the name Grimaldi, still used by the ruling prince

1793: Monaco is annexed to France

1815: Monaco is placed under the protection of the Kingdom of Sardinia

1861: Monaco becomes a French protectorate

1918: Principality signs treaty with France, stipulating that succession to the throne of Monaco must be approved by the French government

1949: Prince Rainier III succeeds his father, Prince Louis II, as ruler

1956: Prince Rainier marries American movie star, Grace Kelly

1963: "Tax war" with France ends in signing of new fiscal convention under which Monégasques and others remain free of direct taxation, but French citizens who had taken up residence in Monaco after October 13, 1957, have to pay income taxes, and companies doing more than a quarter of their business outside Monaco are made subject to a levy

1967: Prince Rainier wrests control of Société des Bains de Mer (SBM) from Greek shipping magnate Aristotle Onassis, principal stockholder and director of the company, which through its control of the Monte Carlo casino and the principality's hotels, was accused of impeding Monaco's tourist development

1978: Princess Caroline, daughter of Prince Rainier and Princess Grace, marries Philippe Junot, French investment banker. They separate in 1980

MONGOLIA

Area: 606,163 sq. mi. **Population:** 1,576,000 (1978 est.)

Official Name: Mongolian People's Republic **Capital:** Ulaanbaatar **Nationality:** Mongol **Languages:** Khalkha Mongolian, one of the large dialect groups of the Mongolian branch of the Altaic language family, is the official and dominant spoken language (90%). About 7% of the population speak Turkic languages **Religion:** Lamaistic Buddhism is the predominant religion (95%), but religious activity is discouraged by the Communist regime; Moslem 4% **Flag:** Vertical stripes of red, blue, and red with a yellow star and traditional symbols on the left **Anthem:** Our Free Revolutionary Land **Currency:** Tughrik (2.85 per U.S. $1)

Location: North Central Asia. Landlocked Mongolia is bordered on the north by the USSR, and on the east, south, and west by China **Features:** The country is essentially a huge steppe plateau with an average elevation of 4,000 feet. It is fringed by forested mountains in the north, while the south includes much of the Gobi Desert **Chief Rivers:** Selenge, Kerulen, Orhon, Dzavhan

Political Leader, Head of State and of Government: Yumjaagiyn Tsedenbal, born 1916; first secretary of the Mongolian People's Revolutionary (Communist) party since 1958; chairman of the presidium of the Hural since June 1974. He is assisted by Jambyn Batmonh, chairman of the Council of Ministers **Effective Date of Present Constitution:** July 1960 **Legislative Body:** People's Great Hural (unicameral), 354 members elected for a 4-year term by universal suffrage; actual power lies with the Politburo of the Party's Central Committee **Local Government:** 18 provinces and 2 independent cities

Ethnic Composition: Khalkha Mongols make up about 76% of the population, Oirat Mongols and Buryat Mongols 13%, and Kazakhs, a Turkic-speaking people about 2%. Russians, Chinese, Khotan Turks, and Tuvinians form smaller minorities **Population Distribution:** 48% urban **Density:** 2.6 inhabitants per sq. mi.

Largest Cities: (1977 est.) Ulaanbaatar 345,000, Darhan 32,900; (1969 census) Choybalsan 20,500, Nalayn 14,100

Per Capita Income: $800 (1979) **Gross National Product (GNP):** $1.3 billion (1979) **Economic Statistics:** In 1976, 25% of GNP was derived from industry, related to the processing of livestock products, 21% was from animal husbandry (sheep, goats, camels, cattle, and horses) and some field crops. Coal, copper, and molybdenum are the chief mining industries **Minerals and Mining:** Coal, copper, fluorspar and molybdenum **Labor Force:** Most work in state farms and collectives. Agriculture employs 55%, industry 11%, and services 10% **Foreign Trade:** Exports are chiefly cattle, coal, copper, molybdenum, wool, raw hides, and butter and meat products. Imports are mainly consumer goods, machinery, equipment, and industrial raw materials **Principal Trade Partners:** USSR (80%), Czechoslovakia, East Germany, Hungary, Poland, Romania

Vital Statistics: Birthrate, 37.1 per 1,000 of pop. (1976); death rate, 9.9 **Life Expectancy:** 64 years **Health Statistics:** 94 inhabitants per hospital bed; 493 per physician (1977) **Infant Mortality:** N.A. **Illiteracy:** 20% **Primary and Secondary School Enrollment:** 341,500 (1976) **Enrollment in Higher Education:** 9,861 (1975) **GNP Expended on Education:** N.A.

Transportation: Surfaced roads total 992 mi. **Motor Vehicles:** 24,000 **Passenger Cars:** N.A. **Railway Mileage:** 940 **Ports:** None **Major Airlines:** Air Mongol flies internally and to the Soviet Union **Communications:** Government owned **Radio Transmitters:** 90 **Receivers:** 124,000 (1976) **Television Stations:** 1 **Receivers:** 33,800 (1976) **Telephones:** 38,000 (1976) **Newspapers:** 1 daily, 78 copies per 1,000 inhabitants (1975)

Weights and Measures: Metric system **Travel Requirements:** Passport, visa (obtainable in London, Paris, or Moscow)

One of the most thinly populated countries in the world, Mongolia is three times as large as France, but most of its territory is desert and semiarid rangeland. Mongolia's importance in international politics is less a matter of its size than of its position: wedged directly between Communist China and the Soviet Union, and long a cause for friction between them.

All of Mongolia was considered part of China for centuries. A Mongol movement to gain independence at the turn of the century, supported by the tsarist Russian government, resulted in "autonomy" for Outer Mongolia. However, in 1919, after the tsarist government itself was overthrown by the 1917 revolution, the Chinese sent troops into Mongolia and canceled its autonomy. The Chinese troops were expelled in the early 1920s by White Russian forces, which in turn were defeated by the Soviet Red Army. Outer Mongolia was then established as the second socialist state in the world and the first Soviet satellite.

Lavish Soviet aid has enabled Mongolia to make impressive economic advances. The economy still relies heavily on its livestock base—the country's most important resource—but collective farms for stockbreeding have been established and there are a few nomadic herdsmen left. Industrial production has increased sharply.

The help given by the Soviet Union has not gone unnoticed in China. In a 1973 speech before the UN General Assembly, Chinese Deputy Foreign Minister Chiao Kuan-hua challenged the Soviet Union to remove its troops from Mongolia. China's problem is that there are more Mongols in China—in Inner Mongolia—than there are in the Mongolian Republic, and fears that Mongol nationalism might result in efforts to detach further segments of Chinese territory are apparently real. Possibly to guard against a Mongol nationalist movement in China, Peking in 1970 assigned large segments of Inner Mongolia to neighboring provinces, since rescinded.

In 1968 and 1969 there were small flare-ups along the 2,500-mile Chinese/Mongolian border, and the Mongols charged that the Chinese had sought to subvert their government and install a pro-Peking regime.

A nation of pivotal importance, Mongolia seems to have no alternative but to try to maneuver between Moscow and Peking while striving to maintain its independence.

HISTORY: The Mongols, loosely organized nomadic tribes living in Mongolia, China, and Siberia, were united in the 13th century under the leadership of Genghis Khan, who established a far-flung Eurasian empire. After his death, the empire was divided and eventually disintegrated, and a cleavage developed between the southern, or inner, Mongols, ruled by the Chinese and the northern, or outer, Mongols. In 1691 the northern Mongols accepted Chinese authority and remained under their rule until the 20th century

1911: Mongol princes proclaim Outer Mongolia an independent monarchy following the overthrow of China's Manchu dynasty; the throne is given to Bogdo Gegen, the Living Buddha of Urga

1915: Outer Mongolia signs treaty with republican China and tsarist Russia accepting autonomous status under Chinese authority; Russia gains control over Mongolia's foreign affairs

1919-21: Attempts by China to reassert sovereignty over Outer Mongolia following the Russian Revolution are defeated; Russian forces expel Chinese, and Outer Mongolia again proclaims its independence

1924: Mongolian People's Republic is proclaimed following the death of the Living Buddha; Communist rule is inaugurated with Soviet help

1950: Communist China and USSR sign treaty guaranteeing Mongolia's independence

1962: Mongolia and Communist China sign treaty fixing their 2,500-mile border. Premier Tsedenbal backs Soviet policy on peaceful coexistence, challenged by Peking

1963: Mongolia establishes diplomatic relations with Britain in the first such pact with a Western power. Mongolia asks Communist China to withdraw laborers sent by Peking to work on Mongolian construction projects

1964: Pro-Peking sympathizers are purged from Mongolian Communist party

1966-67: Relations between Mongolia and Communist China become strained. Soviet troops are stationed on Mongolia border

1969: Soviet and Communist Chinese troops clash at the Ussuri River, and tension rises on the Chinese-Mongolian frontier. Yumjaagiyn Tsedenbal reelected premier

1970: Soviet-Mongolian five-year economic plan drafted. Border troubles with Communist China continue

1976: Tsendenbal reelected first secretary for the fifth time

1978: The government introduces restrictions to stop the flow of rural people to the cities

1979: During a round of talks in Moscow, China asks, unsuccessfully, that the USSR withdraw three divisions from the Mongolian border

MOROCCO

Area: 172,413 sq. mi. **Population:** 19,470,000 (1979 est.)

Official Name: Kingdom of Morocco **Capital:** Rabat **Nationality:** Moroccan **Languages:** Arabic, the official language, is spoken by about 65%; Berber dialects are spoken by about 35%. French is also widely used **Religion:** The majority of Moroccans are Sunni Moslems and Islam is the state religion; there are small minorities of Christians and Jews **Flag:** A red field with a green 5-pointed star in the center **Anthem:** National Anthem (no words) **Currency:** Moroccan dirham (3.8 per U.S. $1)

Location: Northwest Africa. Morocco is bordered on the north by the Mediterranean Sea, on the east by Algeria, on the south, with the contested Western Sahara area interposed, by Mauritania, and on the west by the Atlantic Ocean **Features:** The center is occupied by the dry, rocky Atlas Mountains, which slope downward to narrow fertile coastal plains along the Mediterranean and the Atlantic. The south is occupied by the Sahara **Chief Rivers:** Oum-er-Rbia, Dra, Moulouya, Sous, Sebou

Head of State: King Hassan II, born 1929, ascended the throne 1961. Under the 1972 constitution, the king has limited authority to circumvent parliament by proclaiming a state of emergency or putting major issues to a referendum, which cannot be appealed **Head of Government:** Prime Minister Maati Bouabid, appointed March 1979 **Effective Date of Present Constitution:** March 1972 **Legislative Body:** Parliament (unicameral Chamber of Representatives), with 264 members elected for 4 years **Local Government:** 31 provinces and 2 urban prefectures, each headed by an appointed governor

Ethnic Composition: The majority of Moroccans are of Arab descent; about 35% are of Berber origin **Population Distribution:** 38% urban **Density:** 113 inhabitants per sq. mi.

Largest Cities: (1973 est.—Metropolitan Areas) Casablanca 1,753,400, Rabat 596,600, Marrakech 436,300, Fez 426,000, Meknès 403,000, Oujda 394,400, Kénitra 341,600, Tetuan 308,700, Safi 214,600, Tangier 208,000, Agadir 189,000

Per Capita Income: $563 (1979) **Gross National Product (GNP):** $11.4 billion (1979) **Economic Statistics:** 22% of the GNP is derived from agriculture (wheat, barley, fruits, corn, sugar, livestock), forestry and fishing; 21% from commerce; 16% from transportation and services; 12% from industry (food processing and canning, sugar refining, milling, tobacco production); and 4% from mining **Minerals and Mining:** Leading minerals are phosphates (45% of all minerals produced by the state), iron ore, coal, manganese, fluorite, cobalt, lead, zinc, copper **Labor Force:** 4.1 million in 1977, with 51% in agriculture, 20% in industry, and 29% in services **Foreign Trade:** Exports, chiefly vegetables, citrus fruit, phosphates, wine, and canned fish, totaled $1.3 billion in 1978. Imports, mainly wheat, sugar, fuel, industrial machinery and equipment, cotton and synthetic textile yarn, iron and steel products, are estimated at $3 billion **Principal Trade Partners:** EC countries, Poland, United States, USSR, Spain

Vital Statistics: Birthrate, 46.2 per 1,000 of pop. (1975); death rate, 15.7 **Life Expectancy:** 54 years **Health Statistics:** 739 inhabitants per hospital bed; 11,143 per physician (1976) **Infant Mortality:** 117 per 1,000 births **Illiteracy:** 79% **Primary and Secondary School Enrollment:** 2,196,800 (1976) **Enrollment in Higher Education:** 45,322 (1975) **GNP Expended on Education:** 6% (1976)

Transportation: Paved roads total 10,727 mi. **Motor Vehicles:** 493,100 (1976) **Passenger Cars:** 347,400 **Railway Mileage:** 1,156 **Ports:** Casablanca, Safi, Kénitra, Mohammedia, Agadir, Essaouira **Major Airlines:** Royal Air Maroc operates both domestically and internationally **Communications:** Government controlled **Radio Transmitters:** 33 **Receivers:** 1,500,000 (1976) **Television Transmitters:** 27 **Receivers:** 522,000 (1976) **Telephones:** 204,000 (1976) **Newspapers:** 9 dailies; 21 copies per 1,000 inhabitants (1975)

Weights and Measures: Metric system **Travel Requirements:** Passport, no visa for 3 months

---

Geographically, Morocco is the westernmost Arab country, the only one with a border on the Atlantic coast of North Africa. It stands almost as close to the United States as to the eastern end of the Arab world, and at one point—the Strait of Gibraltar—it is literally within sight of Europe.

Politically, too, Morocco shows Western tendencies. Although nominally a member of the Arab League, it remains outside the main thrust of Arab politics, commerce, and culture. In recent years, it has made great efforts to cultivate the friendship of the United States and Western Europe, with which it seems to have closer interests than with the militant Arab countries to its east.

Since independence from France in 1956, Morocco has been a monarchy with a liberal-sounding constitution, but King Hassan II has been as absolute as any ruler in the world.

Dissolving the National Assembly in 1965, the king instituted a "state of exception" that gave him virtually unlimited power. In 1970, by national referendum, a new constitution provided a modified form of parliamentary government; the 1972 constitution further limited the king's powers to challenge legislative decisions. He retains the power to declare a state of emergency.

The nation's chief problems are its rapidly expanding population—the growth rate is three percent a year—and the inability of its economy to keep pace. Since independence, investment has been mostly in agriculture, dams, and irrigation projects.

Although there has been some economic progress, considerably more is still needed. It is estimated that 40 percent of the youth between 20 and 30 are unemployed. Unemployment has forced workers to emigrate to western Europe to find jobs. The money they have returned to their families in Morocco has provided a valuable addition to the Moroccan balance of payments. Tourism has increased greatly in recent years.

A Marxist party exists in the country, but most Moroccan intellectuals, like their Algerian neighbors, have their own ideas about socialism and are not particularly attracted by either the Soviet or Chinese brand. The main support for the king—who is also the country's religious leader—comes from the rural areas.

By Arab-world standards, Morocco has a large middle class, imbued with both Arab and French culture, whose high standard of living coexists with the feudal rural society. In addition, it has the largest remaining French community—numbering some 100,000—in North Africa. The coexistence of the Arab and French cultures, however, adds to the frustration of many young intellectuals, who are increasingly demanding the Arabization of their country.

In March 1973 King Hassan reacted to steadily mounting pressures for an economic shake-up by decreeing the nationalization of farmlands in foreign hands and the elimination of foreign ownership of businesses.

In 1974 opposition to Spain's plans to grant self-rule to the Spanish Sahara, which Morocco claimed, united all Moroccan political elements behind the monarchy for the first time since the early 1960s. By November 1975 Spain agreed to partition Spanish Sahara. Despite Algeria's opposition to the partition, the northern two-thirds, including rich phosphate deposits at Bu Craa, went to Morocco and the southern third to Mauritania, and in December Moroccan officials proclaimed the annexation of Western Sahara as Moroccan troops marched into its capital.

When Mauritania and Morocco divided Western Sahara and the Saharan assembly ratified its annexation in 1976, they did not recognize the proclamation of the *Polisario Front*, the Saharan liberation movement, of the Saharan Arab Democratic Republic (SADR). Algeria's recognition of the SADR caused Morocco to sever diplomatic relations. After the Mauritanian army deposed President Moktar Ould Daddah in 1978, the *Polisario* made a tacit cease-fire with the new Mauritanian government and concentrated its energies on Morocco. In 1979 Mauritania gave up its claim to the southern portion of Western Sahara, which Morocco promptly occupied. The conflict has placed a burden on the Moroccan economy.

In 1979, Ahmed Osman resigned as premier, and

King Hassan appointed Maati Bouabid, a former labor leader, to succeed him.

HISTORY: In ancient times, Morocco was part of the empire of Carthage. Under the Romans it was formed into the province of Mauritania and later experienced successive invasions until conquered by the Arabs c. A.D. 683. Morocco became an independent kingdom in 788, but by the 10th century had broken up into several tribal states. The country was ultimately united under the Almoravids, a Berber Moslem dynasty that established a kingdom stretching from Senegal to Spain

15th cent.: Portugal and Spain capture all Moroccan ports

17th cent.: Morocco recaptures many European strongholds

1906: Algeciras Conference grants France special privileges in Morocco

1912: Morocco becomes a protectorate; under a French-Spanish agreement the country is divided administratively into French Morocco, Spanish Morocco, and a Southern Protectorate of Morocco, administered as part of the Spanish Sahara, and the international zone of Tangier

1953: Faced with growing movement for independence, French depose Sultan Sidi Mohammed ben Youssef and exile him to Madagascar

1955: French permit sultan to return

1956-57: Morocco gains independence in 1956; Tangier is restored. In 1957 Sidi Mohammed ben Youssef becomes King Mohammed V

1961-62: King Mohammed dies and is succeeded by his son, Hassan II. In 1962 a draft constitution presented by Hassan is approved by referendum

1965: Hassan declares state of emergency and assumes executive and legislative power

1970: New constitution is adopted ending king's absolutist rule

1971: Hassan survives attempted coup by rebellious army officers and cadets; king charges Libya with inciting the rebellion

1972: Hassan survives second attempted coup within 13 months. Defense Minister Oufkir, who had exercised wide civil and military powers after the 1971 attempt, found dead after leading counterattack on rebels. He is charged by Hassan with organizing the attempted takeover

1974: Massive deposit of oil shale discovered in Middle Atlas Mountains. King Hassan presses Spain to return Spanish Sahara territory to Morocco

1975: Some 200,000 unarmed Moroccans who moved over the border in the "Green March" into Spanish Sahara "to regain the Sahara peacefully," are called back by Hassan

1976: Morocco and Mauritania divide the disputed Western Sahara. Relations are severed with Algeria because of Algeria's support of *Polisario* guerrillas

1977: Moroccan troops are sent to Zaire to help repel invaders of Shaba province

1978: Moroccan government sends troops to Shaba Province in Zaire following invasion there by Katangan rebels. Railway workers and civil servants strike for higher pay

1979: Maati Bouabid succeeds Ahmed Osman as premier. Morocco occupies southern third of Western Sahara, after Mauritania renounces claim to area

MOZAMBIQUE

Area: 303,769 sq. mi. **Population:** 9,935,000 (1978 est.)

Official Name: People's Republic of Mozambique **Capital:** Maputo **Nationality:** Mozambican **Languages:** Bantu languages; Portuguese is the official language **Religion:** 66% animist, 22% Christian, 11% Moslem **Flag:** Four diagonal wedges of green, red, black and yellow separated by narrow white wedges, the national emblem of a white cogwheel with red star, white book, black silhouettes of hoe and rifle is at the upper left **Anthem:** N.A. **Currency:** Metical (35 per U.S. $1)

Location: On the east coast of Africa, bounded by the Mozambique Channel on the east, Swaziland on the south, South Africa on the south and west, Zimbabwe on the west, Zambia and Malawi on the northwest, and Tanzania on the north **Features:** Lowlands along the 1,700-mile-long coast rise to an 8,000-ft. plateau, with mountains to the north. The northern coastal plain is hot and humid, but is cooler to the south and inland **Chief Rivers:** Ruvuma, Lurio, Zambezi, Save, Limpopo

Head of State and of Government: President Samora Moisés Machel, born 1934, installed June 1975. He is head of the Frelimo party **Effective Date of Present Constitution:** 1975 **Legislative Body:** People's Assembly of 210 members **Local Government:** 10 provinces

Ethnic Composition: The people are mostly of Bantu stock, with a minority (perhaps 10,000) Europeans (mostly Portuguese) **Population Distribution:** 8% urban **Density:** 33 inhabitants per sq. mi.

Largest Cities: (1970 census) Maputo 101,754 (Metro Area—383,775), Beira 46,293, Nampula 23,072, Quelimane 10,522, Xai-Xai 5,234

Per Capita Income: $200 (1979) **Gross National Product (GNP):** $2.4 billion (1979) **Economic Statistics:** In 1975 the service sector (including transportation and tourism) accounted for 30% of the GNP; agriculture, 40%; and industry 20% **Minerals and Mining:** Copper, coal, beryl, columbite, fluorite, bauxite and tantalite **Labor Force:** 600,000 wage earners, with 80% of the population in subsistence agriculture **Foreign Trade:** Exports, chiefly cashew nuts, cotton and cotton products, sugar, copra, sisal fiber, tea and vegetable oils, amounted to $284 million in 1978. Imports, chiefly machinery, transportation equipment, metals and metal products, petroleum and wheat, reached $597 million **Principal Trade Partners:** South Africa, France, Britain, Portugal, Iran, United States, Japan

Vital Statistics: Birthrate, 43 per 1,000 of pop. (1975); death rate, 20 **Life Expectancy:** 43.5 years **Health Statistics:** 772 inhabitants per hospital bed; 16,392 per physician (1972) **Infant Mortality:** 92.5 per 1,000 births **Illiteracy:** 88% Primary and **Secondary School Enrollment:** 632,647 (1972) **Enrollment in Higher Education:** 906 (1976) **GNP Expended on Education:** 1.1% (1972)

Transportation: Paved roads total 2,686 mi. **Motor Vehicles:** 110,800 (1972) **Passenger Cars:** 89,300 **Railway Mileage:** 1,964 miles **Ports:** Maputo, Beira, Nacala, Pemba, Quelimane **Major Airlines:** DETA provides domestic and international service **Communications:** Government controlled **Radio Transmitters:** 49 **Licenses:** 225,000 (1976) **Television Transmitters:** None **Telephones:** 52,000 (1976) **Newspapers:** 5 dailies, 9 copies per 1,000 inhabitants (1975)

Weights and Measures: Metric system **Travel Requirements:** Apply to Permanent Mission of the People's Republic of Mozambique, New York 10017

Portuguese rule left an inheritance of poverty and disease for much of Mozambique's population. Forced labor was widespread, political rights and education limited. Ten years of pre-independence guerrilla war, the flight of skilled whites and the imposition of doctrinaire socialism have also taken their toll.

Nationalist forces aiming at independence began guerrilla warfare in 1964, starting in the north. The chief rebel movement was the Front for the Liberation of Mozambique (FRELIMO) which had been working for independence since 1962.

Clashes between the Portuguese army and insurgents increased in early 1974. In September after the military overthrew the home government in Portugal, FRELIMO and the Portuguese High Commissioner signed an agreement under which Mozambique would be ruled by a joint transitional government until full independence.

On June 25, 1975, Mozambique achieved full independence after 500 years of colonial rule, becoming the 45th African state to do so. Samora Moisés Machel, the first president, pledged to transform the country into the "first truly Marxist state in Africa." FRELIMO became the country's sole political party in the new state and the nucleus for the new People's Republic of Mozambique government. Since then the government has been establishing its authority and Marxist-oriented philosophy at all levels of society and planning a post-colonial economy. Among the goals of the FRELIMO program is the eradication of tribalism, regionalism, and racism.

At first Mozambique's future looked relatively bright in comparison to Portugal's other African territories, but most of the 220,000 whites fled, leaving the country almost without skilled and professional workers. All land was nationalized and food production declined by 75 percent in some areas while production of major cash crops was off by half. Many factories have been abandoned and the government now offers incentives for Portuguese managers to stay on. The major income remaining is foreign exchange earned by Mozambique miners in South Africa.

In March 1976 Machel closed the border with Rhodesia (now Zimbabwe), imposed sanctions and proclaimed a state of war. As Mozambique increased its efforts to train Rhodesian guerrillas and help them infiltrate the white-ruled nation, it was itself having greater economic and political problems. The border closing shut off Mozambique's major source of food and cost the country $165 million a year.

HISTORY: Bantu peoples entered Mozambique after 1000 A.D. from Central Africa. Arab traders touched on the coast prior to the coming of the Portuguese under Vasco da Gama in 1498. The Portuguese developed trading posts and a thriving slave trade during the following centuries. Mozambique's colonial boundaries were fixed by the end of the 19th century

1951: Portugal establishes Mozambique as an Overseas Province

1964: Independence forces begin guerrilla warfare

1974: FRELIMO (Mozambique Liberation Front) and Portugal agree to joint rule prior to independence

1975: Mozambique achieves independence

1976: Mozambique closes border with Rhodesia and declares a state of war. Intermittent border clashes occur

1977: Border clashes continue. Black refugees from Rhodesia fill camps in Mozambique

1978: Virtually all foreign and local banks are nationalized

1979: Government closing of 15 Catholic missions strains relations with the Church. National Resistance Movement, based in Zimbabwe-Rhodesia, commits acts of sabotage aimed at overthrow of Machel. Mozambique rejects Soviet request for naval base

1980: Though still committed to Marxism, Machel seeks economic aid from capitalist West; announces plan to encourage private enterprise and promises incentives for former white businessmen who return to Mozambique. Main camp of resistance movement captured. New currency, the metical, replaces the escudo

---

NAMIBIA

(See Territories and Dependencies section)

NAURU

Area: 7.7 sq. mi. **Population:** 7,100 (1978 est.)

Official Name: Republic of Nauru **Capital:** Yaren (district) **Nationality:** Nauruan **Languages:** Nauruan and English **Religion:** Christian, mainly Protestant **Flag:** A blue field halved by a horizontal gold bar, with a white star at the lower left **Anthem:** N.A. **Currency:** Australian dollar (0.90 per U.S. $1)

Location: Central Pacific, 0°30'S.,166°55'E. The island of Nauru lies just south of the equator, about 1,300 miles northeast of Australia **Features:** The island is completely surrounded by a coral reef. A narrow, fertile coastal strip lying between a sandy beach and coral cliffs is the most populated part of the island. The interior consists of a barren plateau containing extensive phosphate deposits, Nauru's major economic resource **Chief Rivers:** There are no rivers

Head of State and of Government: President Hammer De Roburt, born 1922, took office in 1978 **Effective Date of Present Constitution:** 1968 **Legislative Body:** Parliament (unicameral Legislative Assembly), consisting of 18 members elected by universal suffrage for 3 years **Local Government:** The island is divided into 14 districts, grouped into 8 electoral units

Ethnic Composition: The Nauruans are believed to be a mixture of Polynesian, Micronesian, and Melanesian, with Polynesian predominating. Other Pacific Islanders number about 1,800, Chinese 1,100, and Europeans 500 **Population Distribution:** Virtually the entire population is concentrated in settlements along the coast **Density:** 922 inhabitants per sq. mi.

Per Capita Income: $17,000 (1975) **Gross National Product (GNP):** $120 million (1975) **Economic Statistics:** Nauru's economy is built around the phosphate industry, which produces a revenue of more than $100 million annually and enables the islanders to enjoy one of the highest per capita incomes in the world. Although some food products are grown on the island, the inhabitants are largely dependent on imports of food supplies and all manufactured goods **Labor Force:** Nauruans, as a rule, do not engage in manual labor, and the phosphate industry is largely dependent on outside labor, employing 1,389 Chinese, Gilbertese, Australians, and Nauruans in 1975. About 60% of Nauruans are employed in the civil service **Foreign**

Trade: Exports, consisting entirely of phosphates, totaled $123 million in 1975. Imports, chiefly hardware, food, vehicles, machinery, timber, furniture, medicines, and fuels, amounted to $15 million **Principal Trade Partners:** Australia, New Zealand, Britain, Hong Kong, Japan, South Korea, China (Taiwan), Mexico

Vital Statistics: Birthrate, 19.8 per 1,000 of pop. (1976); death rate, 8.3 **Life Expectancy:** 53 years **Health Statistics:** 34 inhabitants per hospital bed; 700 per physician (1971) **Infant Mortality:** 19 per 1,000 births **Illiteracy:** Negligible **Primary and Secondary School Enrollment:** 1,973 (1975) **Enrollment in Higher Education:** 92 studying abroad (1975) **GNP Expended on Education:** 2.8% (1970)

Transportation: A road 18-22 feet wide circles the island; another, 16 feet wide, runs to the Buada district **Motor Vehicles:** There are more than 1,000 vehicles of all kinds on the island **Railway Mileage:** A three-and-one-quarter-mile stretch of railway links the phospate workings with the coast **Ports:** None. Nauru's shores go nearly straight down into deep waters, requiring the construction of special moorings for ships **Major Airlines:** Air Nauru operates flights to Pacific and Asian cities **Communications:** Government owned **Radio Transmitters:** 1 **Receivers:** 3,600 (1976) **Television:** None **Telephones:** 700 **Newspapers:** 1 fortnightly

Weights and Measures: British standards are used **Travel Requirements:** Applications for permission to enter Nauru must be made in writing to the Secretary of Justice in Nauru or to the Nauruan representative in Melbourne, Australia

---

The barren central plateau of Nauru, the tiny Pacific island, which is the smallest independent republic in the world, consists of large phosphate deposits, the result of centuries of bird droppings, that provide Nauru with a good source of income: the phosphate, much prized as fertilizer, is the island's main natural resource and only export.

This unique export helps to give the people of Nauru one of the highest per capita incomes in the world, as well as shops filled with luxury goods, free medical care, good housing, good schools, no taxes, and jobs for all.

Only 12 miles in circumference and three-and-a-half-miles wide, Nauru was named Pleasant Island by the captain of a British whaling ship who discovered it in 1798. Early contacts with Europeans brought guns and disease, and a consequent ravaging of the population. The people of Nauru now are more concerned with depletion of the phosphate deposits. Estimated to total 45 million tons, the deposits are expected to be exhausted in the 1990s or sooner.

Intense debate over the nation's course once the phosphate has been depleted has led to a rare period of political instability. In April 1978 President Dowiyogo, reelected the preceding November, resigned; his plan to raise a $22-million development loan overseas had been opposed by parliament. He was succeeded by Lagumot Harris, who himself resigned a month later after a money bill of his met a similar fate. Harris was succeeded by Hammer de Roburt, the man who led Nauru to independence in 1968.

HISTORY: Nauru, discovered by a British whaling team in 1798, was long known as Pleasant Island. In 1888 it was annexed by Germany and henceforth known by its native name. Phosphate was discovered on the island in the late 1890s and exploitation begun in 1901. With the outbreak of World War I, Australian forces occupied the island. After the war, Nauru was administered by Australia under a League of Nations mandate, which also named Britain and New Zealand as cotrustees

1942-45: Nauru is occupied by Japanese forces; 1,200 islanders are deported to Truk as forced labor

1947: Island is placed under United Nations Trusteeship, with Australia acting as administrator on behalf of the Australian, New Zealand, and British governments

1964: In anticipation of the exhaustion of Nauru's phosphate deposits, expected in about 30 years, Australia proposes that inhabitants be resettled on Curtis Island, off the Queensland coast; islanders reject proposal, choosing to remain on Nauru

1968: Nauru becomes independent republic; islanders reject proposals that Australia handle their defense and external affairs. Hammer De Roburt is elected president

1970: Nauru assumes management of its phosphate industry

1976: Bernard Dowiyogo is elected president
1977-78: Debate over nation's "post-phosphate" future leads to period of instability. President Dowiyogo resigns; Lagumot Harris succeeds him. Harris resigns; Hammer de Roburt succeeds Harris

NEPAL

Area: 54,663 sq. mi. **Population:** 13,713,000 (1979 est.)
Official Name: Kingdom of Nepal **Capital:** Kathmandu **Nationality:** Nepalese **Languages:** Nepali, the official language, is the first language of roughly 50% of the population and is spoken by another 30%; Tibeto-Burman languages (chiefly Newari), Indo-Aryan dialects, and English are also spoken **Religion:** Hinduism, the official religion, is the dominant faith (90%); Mahayana Buddhism is the dominant religion in the sparsely inhabited north, and both faiths are followed by many people of the central region **Flag:** Two red right-angled triangles bordered in blue at the hoist; the upper with a white moon crescent, the lower with a white sun **Anthem:** National Anthem, beginning "May glory crown our illustrious sovereign"
Currency: Nepalese rupee (12 per U.S. $1)

Location: Central Asia. Landlocked Nepal is bordered on the north by China (Tibet), and on the east, south and west by India **Features:** The country is mountainous, with dense swampy jungles. Across the south lies the 20-mile-wide Terai, a region of plain and swamp. Most of the country, a band across the center, is broken by sharp mountain ranges and traversed by high, fertile valleys. Along the northern border lies the high Himalaya, with 8 of the world's 12 highest peaks, including Mount Everest, whose 29,028-ft. elevation is the highest in the world **Chief Rivers:** Kali, Karnali, Gandak, Kosi

Head of State: King Birendra Bir Bikram Shah Dev, born 1946, acceded to the throne January 1972 **Head of Government:** Prime Minister: Surya Bahadur Thapa, born 1928, appointed June 1979 **Effective Date of Present Constitution:** December 1962, amended December 1975 **Legislative Body:** Parliament (unicameral National *Panchayat*), with 135 representatives from zonal assemblies and class groups, and 23 nominees of the king. A third of the members are elected for 6 years; the others serve for 2 or 4 years. The king has absolute veto power over parliamentary bills **Local Government:** 14 zones, each headed by an appointed commissioner, and 75 districts, each with a district assembly and 11-member executive committee known as the district *panchayat*. The latter, in turn, form a zonal assembly

Ethnic Composition: The Nepalese are descendants of 3 major migrations from India and Tibet. In addition to the Brahmans and Chetris whose ancestors came from India, the numerous tribes, called castes, include the Gurungs and Magars in the west; Tamangs and Newars in the center; Bhotias in the north; Rais, Limbus, and Sherpas in the east; and Tharus in the south **Population Distribution:** 5% urban **Density:** 251 inhabitants per sq. mi.

Largest Cities: (1971 census) Kathmandu 150,402, Lalitpur 59,049, Biratnagar 45,100, Bhaktapur 40,112

Per Capita Income: $111 (1979) **Gross National Product (GNP):** $1.6 billion (1979) **Economic Statistics:** In 1973 about 65% of GNP was from agriculture (paddy rice, maize, wheat, millet, jute) and forestry; 12% from mining and manufacturing (jute, textiles, yarns, cigarettes, vegetable oil crushing); and 17.3% from trade and services **Minerals and Mining:** Coal is mined. There are unexploited deposits of iron ore, copper, mica, lead, zinc, cobalt, nickel, and talc **Labor Force:** 4,852,524 (1971), 94% of which is in agriculture and 2% in industry **Foreign Trade:** Exports, chiefly rice, jute and jute products, ghee, oilseeds, timber, and herbs, totaled $98 million in 1977. Imports, mainly textiles, foodstuffs, petroleum products, machinery and equipment, vehicles and parts, totaled $169 million **Principal Trade Partner:** India

Vital Statistics: Birthrate, 42.9 per 1,000 of pop. (1975); death rate, 20.3 **Life Expectancy:** 40 years **Health Statistics:** 6,630 inhabitants per hospital bed; 36,450 per physician (1974) **Infant Mortality:** 152 per 1,000 births **Illiteracy:** 80% **Primary and Secondary School Enrollment:** 1,031,797 (1977) **Enrollment in Higher Education:** 23,504 **GNP Expended on Education:** 1.5% (1975)

Transportation: All-weather roads total 1,906 (1973) **Motor Vehicles:** 12,646 (1970) **Passenger Cars:** 7,281 **Railway Mileage:** 40 **Ports:** None **Major Airlines:** Royal Nepal Airlines operates domestic and international services **Communications:** Government owned **Radio Transmitters:** 5 **Receivers:** 150,000 (1976) **Television:** None **Telephones:** 9,162 (1974) **Newspapers:** 29 dailies (1975), 3 copies per 1,000 inhabitants (1974)

Weights and Measures: Metric system and local standards used
Travel Requirements: Passport, visa valid for 30-day stay, $5 fee, 1 photo

Beguiled by the slightly touristic, but not untrue, face that Nepal presents to the outside world, mountaineers, tourists, and hippies have flocked there and found what they sought: a peaceful Himalayan kingdom, backward but pleasant, a land of green valleys and towering mountains (including the world's highest, 29,028-ft. Mt. Everest, shared with Tibet), all presided over by the world's only Hindu king, thought by his people to be an incarnation of the god Vishnu.

The other side of Nepal's character is harsher, but no less true. Nepal is a primitive, divided, stratified society caught between two powerful and jealous neighbors, China and India, and unsettled by the pressures of modernization. With its history marked by bitter political feuding, Nepal is in a difficult position to shape the modernity its leaders want.

In recent years Nepal has halted Indian interference in its internal affairs and has established close relations with China.

Rising taxes, high prices, and shortages have contributed to recent unrest. In 1979, what began as student demands for academic changes turned into a broad call for parliamentary democracy joined by peasants, laborers, and the middle class. About 20 persons died in riots in several towns. In national elections in May 1980, voters settled the issue by casting 54% of their ballots for a streamlined version of the present system of indirect representation, called *panchayat*, in which King Birenda retains virtually absolute power. The defeated plan—parliamentary democracy—would have allowed political parties to compete for the first time since 1960.

HISTORY: Nepal, the world's only Hindu kingdom, has a long historical continuity, although little is known about the country before the 15th century. The modern kingdom of Nepal was established in the 18th century by the ruler of Gurkha, a small principality west of Kathmandu. His descendants introduced Hinduism as the state religion and established most of the present boundaries
1790-93: Gurkhas invade Tibet. A large Chinese army counterattacks and forces the Gurkhas to come to terms. Seeking assistance against the Chinese, the Gurkhas sign treaty with the British in India
1814-16: Series of frontier incidents leads to war between the British and Nepal. Nepal surrenders much of its territory and permits a British residency to be set up at Kathmandu
1846: Jung Bahadur Rana seizes the government and reduces the king to a figurehead
1951: An end is made to more than a century of rule by a succession of hereditary prime ministers from a noble family, the Ranas, during which the royal family played little part in governing. King Tribhuvana assumes power with Indian help, promises elections to a constituent assembly to formulate new constitution
1955: King Tribhuvana dies and is succeeded by Crown Prince Mahendra. Nepal joins UN
1959: King Mahendra declares Nepal a constitutional monarchy. In the country's first election, the Nepali Congress party wins an absolute majority
1960: King Mahendra dismisses the cabinet, dissolves parliament, bans political parties, and assumes powers of government; many political leaders are arrested
1962: New constitution is promulgated, introducing *panchayat* system of government from the village to the national level
1963: King Mahendra forms a state council with the right to advise the monarch
1972: King Mahendra dies and is succeeded by his son, Crown Prince Birendra Bir Bikram Shah Dev
1974: Nepal and China sign trade pact
1975: King Birendra, who received part of his education at Harvard, is formally crowned. Prime Minister Nagendra Prasad Rijal is replaced by Dr. Tulsi Giri. Heavily armed Khampa refugees from Tibet are driven from the Himalayan passes by Nepalese troops
1977: Prime Minister Tulsi Giri resigns; Kirti Nidhi Bista, who has held the post three times in eight years, succeeds him
1978: King Birendra slightly eases his stern control of Nepalese life
1979: Students, joined by other dissidents, stage violent demonstrations to demand that the monarchy be liberalized. B.P. Koirala, former prime minister who leads efforts for constitutional reform, is charged with sedition and incitement to armed rebellion. Prime Minister Bista resigns; Surya Bahadur Thapa is appointed in his place

1980: Voters reject a parliamentary democracy and instead approve a modified version of partyless government, leaving King Birenda and his advisors almost unlimited power

---

THE NETHERLANDS

Area: 15,892 sq. mi. **Population:** 14,083,000 (1979 est.)

Official Name: Kingdom of the Netherlands **Capital:** Amsterdam, but the seat of government is at The Hague **Nationality:** Netherlands or Dutch **Languages:** Hollands, or Dutch, is the official and predominant language; Frisian is spoken in the northern province of Friesland **Religion:** About 40.4% Roman Catholic, 32.9% Protestant, and 23.6% no religion **Flag:** Red, white, and blue horizontal stripes **Anthem:** Wilhelmus van Nassouwen (William of Nassau) **Currency:** Guilder (florin) (1.99 per U.S. $1)

Location: Northwest Europe. The Netherlands is bounded on the west and north by the North Sea, on the east by West Germany, and on the south by Belgium **Features:** The country is low and flat except for some hills in the southeast. About one-third of the land area is below sea level, and more than one-fifth reclaimed from the sea and protected by dikes **Chief Rivers:** Maas, IJssel, Waal, Lek

Head of State: Queen Beatrix, born 1938, invested April 30, 1980 **Head of Government:** Premier Andries A.M. van Agt, born 1931, appointed 1977 **Effective Date of Present Constitution:** 1814; frequently revised **Legislative Body:** The States General (bicameral), consisting of the First Chamber, or upper house, and the Second Chamber, or lower house. The First Chamber consists of 75 members chosen by the 11 provincial legislatures for 6 years. The Second Chamber has 150 members elected directly for 4 years **Local Government:** 11 provinces, with elected provincial executive councils and appointed commissioners, and the IJsselmeer polders

Ethnic Composition: 99% Dutch, 1% Indonesian and other **Population Distribution:** 77% urban **Density:** 886 inhabitants per sq. mi.

Largest Cities: (1976 est.) Amsterdam 751,156, Rotterdam 614,767, The Hague 479,369, Utrecht 250,887, Eindhoven 192,562, Haarlem 164,672, Groningen 163,357, Tilburg 151,513

Per Capita Income: $7,057 (1979) **Gross National Product (GNP):** $99 billion (1979) **Economic Statistics:** About 42.3% of GNP comes from industry (capital and consumer goods, food processing, chemicals, textiles), mining, construction, and utilities; 17.8% from commerce, banking, and finance; 6.5% from agriculture; and the rest from other activities **Minerals and Mining:** Large reserves of natural gas are exploited along with some salt, and crude oil **Labor Force:** 4,800,000 (1977), of which 35% is employed in industry, 7% in agriculture, 58% in services **Foreign Trade:** Exports, mainly meats, flower bulbs, petroleum products, natural gas, chemicals, textiles, machinery, and electrical equipment, totaled $50 billion in 1978. Imports, chiefly grains, petroleum, chemicals, textiles, iron and steel products, machinery and electrical equipment, and motor vehicles, totaled $53 billion **Principal Trade Partners:** EC countries, United States, Saudi Arabia

Vital Statistics: Birthrate, 12.5 per 1,000 of pop. (1977); death rate, 7.9 **Life Expectancy:** 72 years **Health Statistics:** 99 inhabitants per hospital bed; 601 per physician (1976) **Infant Mortality:** 9.5 per 1,000 births **Illiteracy:** Negligible **Primary and Secondary School Enrollment:** 2,779,065 (1976) **Enrollment in Higher Education:** 288,026 (1975) **GNP Expended on Education:** 8.7% (1975)

Transportation: Surfaced roads total 53,470 mi. **Motor Vehicles:** 4,206,000 (1977) **Passenger Cars:** 3,851,000 **Railway Mileage:** 1,760 **Ports:** Rotterdam, Amsterdam, IJmuiden, Terneuzen, Vlissingen, Delfzijl **Major Airlines:** K.L.M. (Royal Dutch Airlines) operates domestic and international flights **Communications:** Government owned **Radio Transmitters:** 30 **Licenses:** 3,997,000 (1976) **Television Transmitters:** 21 **Licenses:** 3,774,000 (1976) **Telephones:** 5,412,000 (1976) **Newspapers:** 93 dailies, 311 copies per 1,000 inhabitants (1973)

Weights and Measures: Metric System **Travel Requirements:** Passport, no visa up to 90 days

---

The Netherlands is just that, as much of the country lies below sea level. To a large extent it is manmade and is still being made. In 1932 a barrier dam closed the North Sea mouth of the Zuyder Zee, creating a vast freshwater lake, the IJsselmeer, out of which the hard-working Dutch have been carving habitable tracts, which by 1980 will have increased the Netherlands' arable land by a tenth. Spurred by a destructive storm in 1953, the country began to erect dams to create lakes and keep the sea out of southern estuaries.

This age-old battle against the depredations of the sea and the Rhine, Maas, and Scheldt rivers mirrors the centuries-old struggle of the Dutch against encroachment by man, from the conquest by Julius Caesar's legions in 55 B.C. to German occupation in World War II.

Aside from enlarging the country and bringing it freedom, the unity of purpose in the Netherlands' struggles has produced a people able to get along harmoniously and tolerant of other cultures, as shown in the integration of more than 300,000 nonwhite colonials from the former far-flung overseas empire. However the recent seizures of hostages by South Moluccan terrorists has led to a deterioration in relations between the Moluccans and the Dutch. The South Moluccans had emigrated to the Netherlands in the late 1940s when their islands became part of Indonesia.

Binding the loyalty of its citizens to the state is the four-centuries-old House of Orange, now headed by Queen Beatrix, who succeeded her mother, Juliana, when she abdicated on her 71st birthday, April 30, 1980. Though political parties are organized on religious and ideological principles, recent cabinets have been coalitions. A constitutional democracy, the Netherlands reflects rule by Burgundian kings five centuries ago, Dutch republicanism, and modern liberalism.

Ultimate power lies with parliament, which presides over jammed cities that blend charming old architecture with the new, and a countryside filled with canals, broad rivers, and tidy farms, few of which are larger than 50 acres. In fact, though the Netherlands is popularly believed to be an agricultural land, national income depends more on commerce and industry than on farming.

HISTORY: At the time of the conquest of the Lowland areas by Julius Caesar in 55 B.C., the region was settled by Celtic and Germanic tribes. The dominant tribes were the Saxons and Frisians. In the 3rd century A.D. the West Franks (Salic Franks) invaded the Low Countries and gradually conquered the region. Following the breakup of Charlemagne's empire in the 9th century, the Lowlands were parceled up into numerous duchies and counties. In the 16th century, the area passed to Charles V of the House of Hapsburg and then to his son, Philip II of Spain.

1568-81: Dutch wage war of independence against Spain under leadership of William the Silent, Prince of Orange, who unites the seven northern provinces; Spanish garrisons are expelled and United Provinces declare their independence

17th cent.: Treaty of Westphalia (1648), ending the Thirty Years War, recognizes independence of United Provinces. Meanwhile, Dutch build vast overseas empire and by 1700 the Netherlands is the world's leading maritime and commercial power

18th cent.: Dutch power begins to decline after 1715. In 1794, French revolutionary forces invade Netherlands; the following year French set up the Batavian Republic

1815: Congress of Vienna establishes Kingdom of Netherlands composed of Belgium and Holland

1830: Belgium revolts and gains independence

1914-39: Netherlands pursues policy of neutrality

1940-45: During World War II German forces overrun the Netherlands and subject country to ruthless occupation

1948: Queen Wilhelmina abdicates and is succeeded by her daughter, Juliana

1949: Netherlands grants Indonesia independence after four years of bitter strife

1954: The colonies of Surinam and Netherlands Antilles are incorporated into the Kingdom of the Netherlands

1957: Netherlands joins Common Market (EC)

1962-63: Netherlands turns western New Guinea (West Irian) over to the United Nations, which places it under Indonesian jurisdiction pending a referendum

1975: Independence is granted to Surinam (now Suriname) after 300 years of Dutch rule

1976: South Moluccan terrorists, who in support of the independence of South Molucca from Indonesia had in December 1975 hijacked a train and laid siege to the Indonesian consulate, are convicted and sentenced

1977: Prime Minister den Uyl's Labor party captures a plurality in parliament in May elections. South Moluccan terrorists hold 100 children hostage in a school and 50 others hostage in a train in an effort to force the Dutch government to help them in their independence struggle. The siege is ended by a Dutch military team staging a raid in which six terrorists and two hostages are killed. After collapse of his coalition, den Uyl presides over caretaker government until appointment in December of Christian Democrat Andries van Agt as prime minister; van Agt heads center-right coalition of Christian Democrats and Liberals

1978: In Assen, South Moluccan terrorists seize hostages for fourth time since 1975, in attempt to force granting of various demands; the three captors kill one of the 72 hostages, though one is killed in crossfire; terrorists arrested

1979: Parliament rejects U.S. proposal to deploy medium-range nuclear missiles in Europe

1980: Queen Juliana, 71, abdicates throne in favor of her daughter, Beatrix, 42

NEW ZEALAND

Area: 103,736 sq. mi. **Population:** 3,096,000 (1979 est.)

Official Name: New Zealand **Capital:** Wellington **Nationality:** New Zealand **Languages:** English is the official and predominant language; Maori, a Malayo-Polynesian language, is also spoken, but for the Maoris English is the first language **Religion:** 34% Anglican, 22% Presbyterian, 15% Roman Catholic, 7% Methodist, 22% other denominations or non-affiliated **Flag:** A blue field, with the British Union Jack in the upper left and the four stars of the Southern Cross in red edged in white on the right **Anthem:** God Save the Queen; **National Song:** God Defend New Zealand **Currency:** New Zealand dollar (1.0 per U.S. $1)

Location: South Pacific, about 1,200 miles southeast of Australia. New Zealand consists of two principal islands, North Island and South Island, separated by Cook Strait; Stewart Island lies off the southern tip of South Island; the Chatham Islands are about 400 miles east of South Island **Features:** North Island contains 72% of the country's population. The northern part of the island has rolling hills and low mountains; the southern half rises from fertile coastal plains to volcanic mountain peaks in the center. South Island is narrow and contains 28% of the population. The Southern Alps extend the entire length of the island and include New Zealand's highest peak, Mount Cook, with an elevation of 12,349 feet. Stewart Island is covered with rugged, forested peaks that rise more than 3,000 feet **Chief Rivers:** Waikato, Clutha, Taieri, Clarence, Oreti, Rangitikei, Wanganui, Waitaki, Mataura

Head of State: Queen Elizabeth II, represented by a governor-general, Sir Keith Jacka Holyoake, appointed March 1977 **Head of Government:** Prime Minister Robert D. Muldoon, born 1922, re-elected November 1978 **Effective Date of Present Constitution:** No written constitution **Legislative Body:** Parliament (unicameral House of Representatives), with 92 members elected by universal suffrage for 3 years **Local Government:** In 1976 there were 362 local authority areas

Ethnic Composition: About 92% of the population is of European descent; Maoris number 8% **Population Distribution:** 77.4% urban **Density:** 30 inhabitants per sq. mi.

Largest Cities (Urban Areas): (1976 census) Auckland 742,786, Wellington 327,414, Christchurch 295,296, Dunedin 113,222, Lower Hutt Valley 97,194, Hamilton 94,777, Palmerston North 63,873

Per Capita Income: $5,587 (1979) **Gross National Product (GNP):** $17.4 billion (1979) **Economic Statistics:** In 1972, agriculture, forestry and fishing accounted for 14.2% of the GNP, industry and mining 34.8%, and services 51.2%. The chief industries are food processing (meat and dairy products), transport equipment, textiles, cement, oil refining, and fertilizers. Wool, meat, and dairy products form the bulk of agricultural output **Minerals and Mining:** Iron sands, natural gas, coal, gold, and industrial minerals such as aggregate, limestone, pumice, serpentine, clays, and bentonite **Labor Force:** 1,255,000 (1976) of which 36% is engaged in industry, 12% in agriculture, 52% in services **Foreign Trade:** Exports, chiefly meat, dairy products, and wool, amounted to $3.6 billion in 1978. Imports, mainly machinery and related equipment, fuel, and industrial raw materials, totaled $3.1 billion **Principal Trade Partners:** Britain, Australia, United States, Japan, Canada, West Germany

Vital Statistics: Birthrate, 17.8 per 1,000 of pop. (1976); death rate, 8.2 **Life Expectancy:** 72 years **Health Statistics:** 97 inhabitants per hospital bed; 772 per physician (1977) **Infant Mortality:** 13.9 per 1,000 births (1976) **Illiteracy:** Negligible **Primary and Secondary School Enrollment:** 755,303 (1976) **Enrollment in Higher Education:** 74,929 **GNP Expended on Education:** 5.5% (1976)

Transportation: Paved roads total 29,000 mi. **Motor Vehicles:** 1,427,100 (1976) **Passenger Cars:** 1,205,400 **Railway Mileage:** 2,987 **Ports:** Auckland, Wellington, Lyttelton, Whangarei, Tauranga, Dunedin, Napier, Nelson **Major Airlines:** Air New Zealand operates domestic and international services **Communications:** Both government and privately owned **Radio Transmitters:** 64 **Receivers:** 2,715,000 (1976) **Television Transmitters:** 144 **Receivers:** 813,000 (1976) **Telephones:** 1,610,000 (1976) **Newspapers:** 39 dailies, 376 copies per 1,000 inhabitants (1975)

Weights and Measures: Metric system **Travel Requirements:** Passport, no visa for 30 days, onward ticket

---

Blessed with an equable climate that lets grass grow green the year around, New Zealand is renowned for butter, race horses, and lush scenery. The New Zealand dairy industry is said to be the most efficient anywhere, and the export of dairy products is the largest in the world despite the country's small size and population.

The reorganization of overseas markets for pastoral products resulting from the formation of the European Community (Common Market), particularly the prospective phasing out of special trading advantages in Britain for New Zealand butter and cheese, accelerated the postwar trend toward economic diversification. Many dairy farmers have turned successfully to raising meat animals, especially sheep, with government encouragement. In recent years New Zealand has been developing rich new outlets for its farm products in Asia and the Middle East. In 1979, Iran became the country's second-largest customer for lamb (after England), and Iraq also signed a big lamb contract.

Geothermal wells, hydropower, natural gas, and coal abound. New Zealand has no oil, but its Maui natural gas field, discovered in 1969, will be used to make gasoline in the first commercial application of a process developed by Mobil Oil Co. A plant to be built near New Plymouth will use gas provided by Maui Development Ltd., which is a partnership made up of the New Zealand government, Todd Petroleum Mining, Shell Oil (N.Z.), and British Petroleum. The diverse economy includes steel and aluminum production and varied forest products.

With the appearance of new independent states in the South Pacific, New Zealand began providing needed guidance and assistance to the fledgling nations. The first conference of the island heads of government, attended also by high-ranking representatives of Australia and New Zealand, was held in Wellington in August 1971 at the joint request of all the new states—Fiji, Western Samoa, Tonga, Nauru, and the Cook Islands, a self-governing dependency of New Zealand.

The island peoples are attracted to New Zealand by a variety of factors, including the high quality of education available to islanders and the easy interracial relationships. (Eight percent of the New Zealand population are Maoris, a branch of the Polynesian race; Auckland is said to be the biggest Polynesian city in the world, with more than 70,000 Maoris, Cook Islanders, Samoans, Tongans and others in the population.)

Like their Australian neighbors, the New Zealanders are overwhelmingly of British stock. Many of the hardworking pioneer white settlers came from Scotland, some to escape religious conflicts.

With a small population heavily endowed with skills, New Zealand enjoys one of the highest standards of living in the world. Government welfare programs provide "womb-to-tomb" security.

The New Zealanders have shared with the Australians a growing consciousness since World War II of belonging to the Pacific and Asian region. New Zealand has joined with Australia and Britain in a five-power pact for the defense of Singapore and Malaysia, and is a partner in the ANZUS (Australia, New Zealand, United States) Treaty of Mutual Security, the keystone of national defense.

The year 1975 saw the replacement of Wallace Rowling's Labour government by Robert Muldoon and the National party after a period of economic uncertainty and acrimonious political debate. Prime Minister Muldoon launched a campaign against abortion and came into conflict with the nation's intellectuals and the media. His party won reelection in November 1978, but its 22-seat majority in the legislature dwindled to seven.

HISTORY: The first European to discover New Zealand was the Dutch explorer Abel Tasman, who sighted the islands in 1642 but was prevented from landing by hostile Maori natives. The British explorer Captain James Cook visited the islands in 1769, and by the end of the century British whaling settlements were established along the coast. It was not until the 19th century, however, that large-scale British immigration began

1840: By the Treaty of Waitangi, Maoris surrender sovereignty to Britain in exchange for guarantees that they would be allowed to remain in possession of their lands; British New Zealand Company begins first organized attempt to colonize islands with British settlers

1845-48: Maoris, angered by Britain's failure to honor land guarantees, rebel against British rule until uprisings are suppressed by military force

1860-70: Maori Wars against Britain are resumed; Maoris are again defeated by superior British force after 10 years of fighting; immigrant population continues to rise, spurred by discovery of gold in 1861

1907: New Zealand wins dominion status

1914-18: New Zealand fights on Allied side in World War I

1939-45: New Zealand fights on Allied side again in World War II

1945: New Zealand becomes a founding member of the UN

1951: United States, New Zealand, and Australia sign ANZUS treaty binding three nations in mutual defense alliance

1960: National party defeats ruling Labour party in general election; Keith J. Holyoake becomes prime minister

1972: Norman E. Kirk becomes prime minister when Labour party wins

1973: New Zealand and Australia unsuccessfully attempt to block French nuclear testing in the Pacific

1974: Wallace Rowling succeeds after Kirk's death

1975: The EC, in renegotiating Britain's membership terms, agrees that duty-free butter imports from New Zealand after 1977 will remain at the current level until 1980. Rowling is defeated by Robert Muldoon of National party

1978: Muldoon reelected with reduced majority

1979: A sightseeing flight over the South Pole costs 257 lives when an Air New Zealand DC-10 hits a mountain

1980: To reduce the country's dependence on imported oil, the government makes a deal with Mobil Oil Co. to build a $500-million plant near New Plymouth to convert natural gas first into methanol and then into gasoline

---

NICARAGUA

Area: 50,193 sq. mi. **Population:** 2,481,000 (1979 est.)

Official Name: Republic of Nicaragua **Capital:** Managua **Nationality:** Nicaraguan **Languages:** Spanish is the official and universal language; some English is spoken on the east coast **Religion:** 95% Roman Catholic **Flag:** Horizontal stripes of blue, white, blue with the national coat of arms in the center Anthem: Hail Nicaragua **Currency:** Córdoba (10.0 per U.S. $1)

Location: Central America. Nicaragua, the largest of the Central American republics, is bounded on the north by Honduras, on the east by the Caribbean Sea, on the south by Costa Rica, and on the west by the Pacific Ocean **Features:** The western part of the country consists of a coastal plain, gradually rising toward rugged mountains. Beyond these mountains lies the interior, a sparsely populated wilderness of timbered plains and rolling hills cut by rivers. The eastern coastal plain extends about 50 miles inland and is partly swampland **Chief Rivers:** Grande de Matagalpa, Escondido, Coco, San Juan

Head of State and of Government: The country is governed by a 5-member junta: Sergio Ramírez Mercado, Moisés Hassan Morales, Daniel Ortega Saavedra, Arturo José Cruz and Rafael Cordoba Rivas **Effective Date of Present Constitution:** April 1974, abrogated 1979 **Legislative Body:** A 47-member Council of State acts as a legislative body **Local Government:** 16 departments

Ethnic Composition: 70% of the population is mestizo (of mixed European and Indian ancestry), 17% of European ancestry, 9% Negro, and 4% Indian **Population Distribution:** 50% urban **Density:** 49 inhabitants per sq. mi.

Largest Cities: (1976 est.) Managua 437,666, León 73,757, Granada 50,094, Masaya 40,907, Chinandega 38,646

Per Capita Income: $732 (1979) **Gross National Product (GNP):** $1.8 billion (1979) **Economic Statistics:** In 1973 about 40% of GNP came from trade and services, 26% from agriculture (cotton, coffee, cattle), forestry and fishing; 10% from industry (chemicals, insecticides, food processing, textiles), and mining **Minerals and Mining:** Copper, gold, silver, tungsten, gypsum, and precious stones **Labor Force:** 641,497 (1975), of which 48% is in agriculture, 30% in trade and services, and 14% in manufacturing and construction **Foreign Trade:** Exports, mainly cotton, cottonseed, coffee, meat, gold, sesame, and wood, totaled $646 million in 1978. Imports, mainly machinery, transportation equipment, manufacturing products, chemical products, and raw materials for industry, totaled $547 million **Principal Trade Partners:** Central American Common Market countries, United States, Venezuela, Japan, West Germany

Vital Statistics: Birthrate, 48.3 per 1,000 of pop. (1975); death rate, 13.9 **Life Expectancy:** 54 years **Health Statistics:** 474 inhabitants per hospital bed; 1,592 per physician (1976) **Infant Mortality:** 37 per 1,000 births **Illiteracy:** 48% **Primary and Secondary School Enrollment:** 741,477 (1975) **Enrollment in Higher Education:** 17,184 **GNP Expended on Education:** 2.5% (1974)

Transportation: Paved roads total 975 mi. **Motor Vehicles:** 52,000 (1973) **Passenger Cars:** 32,000 **Railway Mileage:** 235 **Ports:** Corinto, San Juan del Sur **Major Airlines:** Lineas Aéreas de Nicaragua (LANICA) operates domestic and international flights **Communications:** Partly government controlled **Radio Transmitters:** 7 **Receivers:** 126,000 (1974) **Television Transmitters:** 2 **Receivers:** 90,000 (1976) **Telephones:** 55,000 (1976) **Newspapers:** 7 dailies, 26 copies per 1,000 inhabitants (1975)

Weights and Measures: Metric system **Travel Requirements:** Passport, visa, valid for 30 days, one photo, no fee

---

A civil war that cost an estimated 15,000 lives brought an end in 1979 to the Somoza family's political and economic rule of Nicaragua after more than four decades. President Gen. Anastasio ("Tacho") Somoza Debayle, who had made a Managua bunker his home and command post for almost two years, fled by helicopter and airplane to the United States on July 17. In August he went into exile in Paraguay. The Sandinist National Liberation Front (FSLN), winner over the National Guard that the Somozas had headed since 1933, named a five-member junta as the provisional government during the war. At war's end, the junta appointed a 15-member cabinet made up of all shades of political opinion.

On the victory day, July 19, cheering Managua crowds toppled the statue of Tacho Somoza's father, Gen. Anastasio Somoza García, founder of the family dynasty. The elder Somoza had taken command of the National Guard in 1933, just after the U.S. Marines ended intermittent intervention that had begun in 1912. It was allegedly Somoza's guardsmen who, in 1934, assassinated Gen. Augusto César Sandino, the revolutionary hero from whom the Sandinists took their name. The elder Somoza seized the presidency on Jan. 1, 1937, and held virtually complete control of Nicaragua—the largest country in Central America—until his assassination in 1956. A son, Luis, president of the senate, was named president immediately; Luis' brother, Anastasio, a West Point graduate, became president in a 1967 election in which charges of fraud and intimidation arose.

The assassination of Pedro Joaquín Chamorro, publisher of *La Prensa* and a longtime critic of Somoza, in downtown Managua in January 1978 was widely attributed to the Somoza regime. Massive unrest and violence followed, culminating in the seizure of the National Palace by the FSLN seven months later. That action won release of 58 political prisoners and safe conduct out of the country. But the National Guard largely succeeded in putting the lid back on the violence until the Sandinists launched a successful revolution from the Costa Rican border on May 29, 1979.

In the closing weeks of warfare, central American neighbor nations, and through them the United States, conducted complex negotiations on the makeup of the new government, which ranges from avowed leftists to conservative businessmen. The U.S. quickly recognized the new regime, led by a 5-member junta, and made emergency food shipments.

A large segment of the population is impoverished, and the war's displacement of 600,000 persons aggravated this. Rampant unemployment, food shortages and war-ruined industries have led to illegal seizures of private farms and factories, and strikes have abounded. The government has jailed some extreme leftists, but is reluctant to deal harshly with the workers and peasants who aided in the overthrow of Somoza. It hopes that increased income from its exports, mainly of cotton and coffee, will soon moderate the nation's economic difficulties. One of its problems has been to replace the management of confiscated transportation, communication, agricultural, banking and industrial enterprises that were controlled by the Somoza family whose holdings have been estimated at $500 million. Nicaragua has joined the non-aligned nations and has been seeking good relations with both Communist and Western blocs.

HISTORY: Various Indian tribes inhabited Nicaragua before the arrival of the Spanish conquistador Gil González de Ávila in 1552. During the Spanish colonial period, Nicaragua was administered as part of the captaincy general of Guatemala

1821: Nicaragua wins independence from Spain and along with the other countries of Central America becomes annexed to Mexico

1825-38: Nicaragua secedes from Mexico and joins Central American Federation. In 1838 the federation is dissolved, and Nicaragua becomes an independent republic

1856-57: U.S. soldier of fortune William Walker seizes presidency but is ousted by alliance of Central American states

1912-33: Prolonged political turmoil between Liberals and Conservatives leads Provisional President Adolfo Díaz to ask for intervention of U.S. Marines to maintain order. In 1916 the Bryan-Chamorro Treaty is ratified, giving United States an option on route for a canal, but Liberals continue guerrilla warfare in protest against American intervention. U.S. Marines, withdrawn in 1925, again occupy country from 1926 to 1933

1934: Gen. Augusto César Sandino, who had defied efforts of U.S. Marines to catch him and who later had won concessions from the government, is assassinated, apparently by members of Gen. Anastasio Somoza's National Guard

1936-57: General Somoza seizes power; until his death by an assassin's bullet in 1956 he rules country as virtual private estate. His son, Luis, finishes his father's term and is reelected

1967: Anastasio Somoza Debayle, brother of Luis and head of armed forces, is elected president

1972: On December 23, earthquakes destroy much of Managua, killing an estimated 10,000; injuring about 15,000 and leaving half the city's population homeless

1974: Somoza is reelected for second presidential term, after resigning in 1972 because of election provisions but retaining full power in the interim as commander of the armed forces

1975: Somoza reimposes martial law following the kidnapping of prominent officials by Sandinist Liberation Front in 1974

1977: Leftist guerrillas make series of attacks on National Guard barracks

1978: Widespread civil unrest follows assassination of publisher Pedro Joaquín Chamorro, longtime Somoza foe. National Palace seized by leftist guerrillas, who hold members of congress hostage until they win release of 58 political prisoners and safe conduct out of country. Guerrillas gain broad support in efforts to oust Somoza, who vows to serve out term. Even the National Federation of the Chambers of Commerce joins a general strike in August, and the guerrillas capture several towns. However, in heavy fighting, the National Guard recaptures the places

1979: On May 29, Sandinist rebels launch a five-pronged attack from Costa Rican border. They quickly take León and other towns, and control the *barrios* of Managua. World television audiences see a National Guardsman execute U.S. TV reporter Bill Stewart at a roadblock. President Somoza flees the country on July 17. A five-member junta appoints a 15-member cabinet dominated by moderates

1980: Delegation of Nicaraguan leaders signs accords with Soviet Union to increase trade and obtain technical aid. U.S Congress authorizes $75 million in economic aid to Nicaragua May 19 after long delay. Cuba's President Fidel Castro heads guest list at first anniversary celebration of the July revolution

NIGER

Area: 489,189 sq. mi. **Population:** 4,994,000 (1978 est.)

Official Name: Republic of Niger **Capital:** Niamey **Nationality:** Nigerien **Languages:** French is the official language; the principal African languages are Fulani, Tamashek, Djerma, Songhai, and Hausa, used primarily in trade **Religion:** The population is predominantly Moslem **Flag:** Horizontal stripes of orange, white, and green with an orange disc in the center **Anthem:** La Nigérienne **Currency:** CFA Franc (210.2 per U.S. $1)

Location: West-central Africa. Landlocked Niger is bordered on the north by Algeria and Libya, on the east by Chad, on the south by Nigeria and Benin, on the southwest by Upper Volta, and on the west by Mali **Features:** Four fifths of the country (north) is arid desert, and the remainder (south) is mostly savanna **Chief River:** Niger

Head of State and of Government: President of the Supreme Military Council: Lt. Col. Seyni Kountché, born 1931, assumed power in 1974 **Effective Date of Present Constitution:** 1960, suspended 1974 **Legislative Body:** All powers are in the hands of the Council **Local Government:** 7 departments under appointed prefects, divided into 32 districts

Ethnic Composition: Hausa make up almost 50% of the population and Djerma-Songhai 23%, the rest are nomadic and seminomadic Peuls, or Fulani (15%), Tuaregs (12%), Toubous, and others **Population Distribution:** 8% urban **Density:** 10 inhabitants per sq. mi.

Largest Cities: (1975 est.) Niamey 130,299; (1972 est.) Zinder 39,000, Maradi 37,000, Tahoua 31,000

Per Capita Income: $127 (1978) **Gross National Product (GNP):** $640 million (1978) **Economic Statistics:** In 1973 over 50% of GNP was derived from agriculture (peanuts, cotton, tobacco, millet, sorghum, beans, rice, livestock), 27% from trade and services and 12% from manufacturing (textiles, peanut oil, oxygen-acetylene) and mining **Minerals and Mining:** Niger's uranium deposits, the fifth largest in the world, are mined in the Arlit and Akouta regions. Two more are to open by 1985. Tin and phosphates are also mined, and coal deposits are to be exploited **Labor Force:** 1,900,000 (1970), with about 90% in agriculture and stockraising **Foreign Trade:** Exports, mainly peanuts, uranium and livestock, totaled $308 million in 1978. Imports, chiefly fuels, machinery, motor vehicles and parts, food and clothing, totaled $318 million **Principal Trade Partners:** France, Nigeria, West Germany, Ivory Coast, Japan, United States

Vital Statistics: Birthrate, 52.2 per 1,000 of pop. (1975); death rate, 25.5 **Life Expectancy:** 39 years **Health Statistics:** 1,200 inhabitants per hospital bed; 47,300 per physician (1974) **Infant Mortality:** 162 per 1,000 births **Illiteracy:** 94% **Primary and Secondary School Enrollment:** 177,613 (1976) **Enrollment in Higher Education:** 541 (1975) **GNP Expended on Education:** 3.2% (1976)

Transportation: Paved roads total 1,080 mi. **Motor Vehicles:** 21,700 (1976) **Passenger Cars:** 9,900 **Railway Mileage:** None **Ports:** None **Major Airlines:** Air-Niger, a government-owned company, operates domestic and international flights **Communications:** Government owned **Radio Transmitters:** 13 **Receivers:** 150,000 (1971) **Television Transmitters:** 1 **Receivers:** N. A. **Telephones:** 8,000 (1976) **Newspapers:** 2 dailies, 0.5 copy per 1,000 inhabitants (1974)

Weights and Measures: Metric system **Travel Requirements:** Passport, visa valid for 7 days, no fee; for stay up to 3 months, $6.25 fee; 2 photos, onward ticket or guarantee from a bank

Niger has been called "a land where the harvest is won with the soul's scythe." For most of this neglected hinterland of former French West Africa is rocky desert, broken by bleak mountains. The productive southern area, watered in part by the Niger River, is semiarid and subject to droughts and floods.

While rich uranium deposits are being developed in the northern desert area and there is hope for discovery of oil and exploitation of other minerals, Niger still must depend on cattle and on limited export and food crops, chiefly peanuts, cotton, and grains. A hostile climate and need for irrigation are obstacles to increased production.

Lack of transportation is Niger's most serious problem. The landlocked country has no railroad and the rapids-strewn Niger River, a potentially low-cost route to the seacoast, has yet to be made navigable. The nearest seaport, Cotonou, in Benin, is 600 miles from Niamey, Niger's capital, and it is often noted that it takes more than two gallons of gasoline to import a single gallon.

Internal roads and links to neighboring countries, however, are gradually being built with French, American, World Bank, and United Nations aid. Canada, through new ties with French-speaking African countries, has recently become a major aid source for Niger.

A $60-million uranium project at Arlit, which began production in 1971, is a joint Nigerien/French/German/Italian undertaking. A second uranium project, organized in 1974 under a company started by the Nigerien government, the French Atomic Energy Commission, and a Japanese company, will develop uranium deposits in the Akouta district. Meanwhile, several American companies are prospecting for oil.

Like the other nations of the West African Sahel, Niger suffered greatly during the drought and famine of 1968-74. In 1973 cattle were dying; in 1974 people were dying. An estimated two million were starving in the Tuareg tribe alone. By October 1974, the drought was ended though massive international relief efforts, largely from the U.S. and the UN, were required to prevent starvation and malnutrition. Appeals for emergency food supplies continue as the problems of marginally productive land and overgrazing remain.

Hamani Diori, Niger's president from the time the country gained independence from France in 1960 until 1974, sought to promote national development and to unify Niger's traditionally hostile nomadic and settled farming peoples. He emphasized government stability; gradual improvement of agriculture, health, and education; and economic aid from numerous sources.

However, in 1974 when Diori was unable to stop his people's starvation in the famine resulting from the drought in the Sahel, he was overthrown by Lt. Col. Seyni Kountché who formed a 12-member military government with himself as president. Kountché dissolved the National Assembly, suspended the constitution and banned all political groups.

HISTORY: The region around Niger was probably known to Egyptians before the beginning of recorded history. Through the next 1,000 years it was a battleground for Arabs; Berbers; Toubous; the Ghana, Mali, Songhai, and Bornu empires; the Hausa states; and the Djermas, Fulanis, and Tuaregs. The first European explorers arrived in the late 18th century and were soon followed by French forces pushing forward still another empire

1901-22: French build chain of forts, crush Tuareg resistance, and establish colony of Niger

1946: French set up local advisory assembly, grant people of Niger French citizenship

1958: Niger becomes an autonomous republic within the French Community

1960: Complete independence is declared and Niger joins the UN

1964-65: Terrorist attacks and attempts to assassinate President Hamani Diori are quelled by government forces

1968-74: Drought and famine strike the Sahel

1974: Army Chief of Staff Lt. Col. Seyni Kountché ousts Diori, and declares himself head of state. Drought ends

1979: Rich uranium deposits discovered near Agadez in the Sahara

---

NIGERIA

Area: 379,628 sq. mi. **Population:** 84,500,000 (1978 est.)

Official Name: Federal Republic of Nigeria **Capital:** Lagos **Nationality:** Nigerian **Languages:** English is the official and business language. Among the 250 African languages and dialects, the most widely spoken are Hausa, Yoruba, Ibo, and Edo. Sizable minorities speak Fulani, Kanuri, Ijaw, Ibibio, and Tiv **Religion:** Northern Nigeria is largely Moslem, while the south and west have been strongly influenced by Christianity. About 47% of the population are Moslem, 34% Christian and 19% animist **Flag:** Vertical stripes of green, white, green **Anthem:** National Anthem, beginning "Nigeria, we hail thee" **Currency:** Naira (.56 per U.S. $1)

Location: West Africa. Nigeria is bounded on the northwest and north by Niger, on the northeast by Lake Chad, on the east by Cameroon, on the south by the Gulf of Guinea, and on the west by Benin **Features:** The coastal area consists of a belt of mangrove swamps intersected by delta branches of the Niger and innumerable smaller rivers and creeks. Inland, a belt of tropical rain forest extends up to 100 miles over gradually rising country. The country then rises to a plateau, which reaches an elevation of over 6,000 feet in the east. In the north, the savanna approaches the southern part of the Sahara **Chief Rivers:** Niger, Benue, Sokoto, Yobe, Gana, Kaduna, Cross, Gongola, Ogun

Head of State and of Government: President Alhaji Shehu Shagari, born 1925, elected Aug. 1979, took office Oct. 1 **Effective Date of Present Constitution:** 1979 **Legislative Body:** National Assembly (bicameral) consisting of a Senate and a House of Representatives. The Senate is composed of 95 members with each of the 19 states sending 5 members. The House of Representatives has 449 members. Both branches are directly elected and their maximum terms are 4 years **Local Government:** 19 states

Ethnic Composition: Of the country's 250 tribal groups, the dominant ones are the Yoruba (15%) in the west, the Ibo (16%) in the east, and the Hausa (19%) and Fulani (10%) in the north. Other large groups are the Edo (900,000) in the west, the Ibibio (about 1 million) and the Ijaw (900,000) in the east, and the Kanuri (2.9 million), Nupe (500,000), and Tiv (1.5 million) in the north **Population Distribution:** 23% urban **Density:** 223 inhabitants per sq. mi.

Largest Cities: (1975 est.) Lagos 1,060,848, Ibadan 847,000, Ogbomosho 432,000, Kano 399,000, Oshogbo 282,000, Ilorin 282,000, Abeokuta 253,000, Port Harcourt 242,000

Per Capita Income: $515 (1979) **Gross Domestic Product (GDP):** $38 billion (1979) **Economic Statistics:** More than 33% of GDP comes from oil and mining, an estimated 23% from agriculture (cocoa, peanuts, African oil palm products, rubber and cotton), and 7% from manufacturing (mainly food processing, oil refining, cotton textiles and cement) **Minerals and Mining:** Nigeria is the world's sixth-largest oil producer; other minerals are tin, coal, and limestone. Large natural gas deposits are being developed **Labor Force:** 30 million of which 64% are in agriculture, forestry and fishing, and 10% in industry **Foreign Trade:** Exports, crude petroleum (94%), cocoa, peanuts, palm nuts, rubber, tin and raw cotton, totaled $10 billion in 1978. Imports, chiefly machinery, transport equipment, industrial raw materials, manufactured goods, chemicals and food, amounted to $12 billion **Principal Trade Partners:** Britain, United States, West Germany, Japan, Netherlands, France

Vital Statistics: Birthrate, 49.3 per 1,000 of pop (1975); death rate, 22.7 **Life Expectancy:** 50 years **Health Statistics:** 1,378 inhabitants per hospital bed; 19,000 per physician (1976) **Infant Mortality:** 150 per 1,000 births **Illiteracy:** 65% **Primary and Secondary School Enrollment:** 5,458,160 (1973) **Enrollment in Higher Education:** 32,971 (1975) **GDP Expended on Education:** 2.6% (1975)

Transportation: Paved roads total 11,000 mi. **Motor Vehicles:** 255,000 (1975) **Passenger Cars:** 150,000 **Railway Mileage:** 2,680 **Ports:** Lagos, Port Harcourt, Bonny, Burutu **Major Airlines:** Nigeria Airways operates international and domestic services **Communications:** Government controlled **Radio Transmitters:** 46 **Licenses:** 5,100,000 (1976) **Television Transmitters:** 10 **Licenses:** 121,000 (1976) **Telephones:** 121,000 (1976) **Newspapers:** 12 dailies, 9 copies per 1,000 inhabitants (1974)

Weights and Measures: Metric system **Travel Requirements:** Passport, visa valid 3 months from date of issue, $2.30 fee

---

Nigeria, a country of extraordinary potential—oil, agricultural diversity, talented political leaders, a population that embraces fully a fifth of the black people in Africa—is also a country with extraordinary problems of instability. One of the underlying reasons for that instability is the nation's great ethnic diversity.

Nigeria's major tribal divisions consist of the seminomadic Hausa-Fulani of the north, the urbanized Yorubas in the west, and in the east, the industrious Ibos. Under British rule, the three regions, together with Lagos, the administrative center, were amalgamated into one vast colonial possession.

As Britain prepared Nigeria for self-government after World War II, it was recognized that the country could achieve its great economic potential only if it remained intact. Nigerian leaders and British authorities were confident, however, that old animosities could be submerged. In 1960 Britain granted full independence and in 1963 Nigeria became a republic.

The largely Moslem north dominated the new government. Distrust soon fanned tribal rivalries into open conflict after incidents of corruption, nepotism, and rigged elections. Ibos grew increasingly resentful as they saw excessive shares of the oil revenues from their region go to northern projects.

Early in 1966, a coup led by young Ibo army officers was accompanied by the murder of many Northern and Western officials, including Prime Minister Sir Abubakar Tafawa Balewa. Gen. Johnson Aguiyi-Ironsi, an Ibo who promised a government free of corruption and tribalism, was installed as president.

However, in a countercoup led by northern officers in July 1966, Ironsi was murdered. He was replaced by Lt. Col. (later Maj. Gen.) Yakubu Gowon, who, as a Christian and member of a minor tribe, was regarded as a neutralist in the tribal conflicts.

Late in 1966 thousands of Ibos working in the north were massacred. Thousands more fled back to their homeland and Gowon's efforts for new political cooperation were frustrated by Ibo fear and distrust. Ibo leader Lt. Col. Odumegwu Ojukwu unsuccessfully sought autonomy for the Eastern Region, then, in May 1967, proclaimed a Republic of Biafra.

In the ensuing conflict Biafran forces were at first victorious, but with growing federal strength, the rebel state was gradually reduced to a small area. As the war dragged on, starvation ravaged the East—a densely populated, food-deficient region. Despite relief efforts by many groups, Biafran resistance collapsed in January 1970, and Ojukwu fled to the Ivory Coast. The struggle took an estimated one million lives. In the years since there has been a gradual reintegration of Ibos into the national economy.

The Biafra trouble was scarcely over when prolonged drought desiccated the Sahel region in northern Nigeria. Cattle died by the thousands, farm lands suffered and fishing industry on Lake Chad collapsed as the lake shrank in size. The area is recovering, but many problems remain.

In October 1974 General Gowon announced that a previously scheduled return to civilian government (1976) had been canceled because of dispute over the 1973 census and the violent sectional political ambitions that were emerging. This announcement led to student demonstrations. Labor unrest increased over pay demands.

On July 29, 1975, Gowon was deposed in a bloodless coup; Brig. Gen. Murtala Rufai Mohammed was named head of state. In February 1976 Brig. Gen. Mohammed was assassinated by a group of "young revolutionaries" who later failed to gain control of the government. The nation's ruling Supreme Military Council named Lt. Gen. Olusegun Obasanjo as head of state.

A total of 37 persons were executed for their alleged involvement in the abortive coup and assassination. Nigeria's request that Great Britain extradite former Head of State Gowon, so that he could defend himself against accusations of involvement in the attempted coup, was denied.

Political activity, banned since 1966, was restored in September 1978. Four parties sprang up to compete for the right to form the long-promised civilian government. In August 1979 Alhaji Shehu Shagari was declared the winner of the election balloting for president, held under Nigeria's new constitution. The military surrendered control to a civilian government on Oct. 1.

Oil, first discovered in 1958, has made Nigeria the wealthiest black African nation. Oil exports account for more than 90 percent of the nation's foreign-exchange earnings and provide most of its government revenues. The country supplies about six percent of the oil consumed in the U.S. and is its second-largest source. Within OPEC Nigeria has joined those advocating the steepest hikes in oil export prices.

Backed by its oil revenues, Nigeria has increasingly pushed its image as a leading power in Africa. The country is still plagued, however, by deep-rooted corruption in public office, widespread poverty, backward living conditions, and acute shortages of trained manpower. Earnings from oil exports could support more imports but port facilities at Lagos cannot handle the increased amount of goods.

Nigeria has pushed for closer trading ties with its West African neighbors. The government is also seeking greater "Nigerianization" of foreign-owned-and-run enterprises to give Nigerians a greater share of the wealth. Although militant on anti-colonial issues involving the white-ruled nations of Africa, Nigeria maintains a moderate foreign policy.

HISTORY: Nigeria's earliest known culture, Nok, flourished around 700-200 B.C. During the 12th century, Nigeria's next great culture grew up around Ife, a sacred Yoruba city. In medieval times, northern Nigeria had contact with the large kingdoms of the western Sudan and by the end of the 14th century A.D. Islam was firmly established in the north. Between the 15th and 17th centuries, the Portuguese and British engaged in commerce and slave trading on the coast

1861-1914: British annex Lagos (1861); gradually establish administrative control over Nigeria

1947-54: Successive steps are taken to allow participation in the government by Africans in preparation for self-government

1960: Nigeria becomes an independent federal state within the British Commonwealth

1963: Nigeria becomes a federal republic within the Commonwealth

1966: Government is ousted by a military coup and a military government is established under Gen. Johnson Aguiyi-Ironsi (an Ibo from the Eastern Region); Ironsi is murdered when another military coup is staged by anti-Ibo elements in the army; a federal military government is set up under Lt. Col. (later Maj. Gen.) Yakubu Gowon. Thousands of Ibos are massacred and more than a million are driven from the north

1967: Military government announces the creation of 12 ethnically based states to replace the previous four regions. The Eastern Region, under the leadership of Lt. Col. Odumegwu Ojukwu, secedes from the Federation of Nigeria and proclaims itself the independent Republic of Biafra. Federal troops invade Biafra, marking the start of civil war

1968-69: Mass starvation threatens millions in Biafra as a result of the federal government's blockade of the region

1970: Surrender of Biafran forces brings end to 30-month civil war; federal government chief, Gen. Yakubu Gowon, pledges protection and political rights to former Biafrans

1972: Many small foreign-owned businesses are "Nigerianized"

1975: General Gowon is deposed in a bloodless coup. Brig. Gen. Murtala Rufai Mohammed is named head of state

1976: Mohammed assassinated in unsuccessful coup. Lt. Gen. Olusegun Obasanjo is named head of state. Nigeria discards British Parliament as a model for its upcoming 1979 civilian government and looks instead to presidential system of the U.S.

1978: Oil production down; yearly inflation rate is put at 25-40 percent. Nigeria warns Soviets and Cubans "not to overstay their welcome" in Africa. Twelve-year-old ban on political activity lifted

1979: Alhaji Shehu Shagari is elected president under new constitution. Daily oil output reaches 2.5 million barrels

1980: New government eases restraints on wage increases and imports. Directors of state oil company caught in $8-billion swindle

NORWAY

Area: 125,053 sq. mi. **Population:** 4,080,000 (1979 est.)

Official Name: Kingdom of Norway **Capital:** Oslo **Nationality:** Norwegian **Languages:** Norwegian is the official and predominant language; Lappish and Finnish are spoken in the north **Religion:** The state church, the Evangelical Lutheran Church, includes 94% of the population **Flag:** An extended white bordered blue cross on a red field **Anthem:** Yes, We Love This Land of Ours **Currency:** Norwegian krone (4.9 per U.S. $1)

Location: Northern Europe, occupying the smaller, western part of the Scandinavian peninsula. Norway has common land frontiers in the east with Sweden, Finland, and the Soviet Union. It is bounded on the north by the Arctic Ocean, on the west by the Norwegian Sea, and on the south by the Skagerrak, an arm of the North Sea **Features:** The country has a 2,125-mile coastline, deeply indented by numerous fjords. From the coast, the land rises to high plateaus and mountain ranges, the highest of which, Glittertind, reaches 8,110 feet. The highlands are cut by fertile valleys and rapid rivers and are dotted with lakes. Forests cover roughly one-fourth of the country, which also has numerous glaciers. Jostedalsbreen, in the southwest, is the largest ice field in Europe **Chief Rivers:** Glomma, Lagen

Head of State: King Olav V, born 1903, acceded to the throne in 1957 **Head of Government:** Premier Odvar Nordli, born 1928, reappointed 1977 **Effective Date of Present Constitution:** 1814 **Legislative Body:** *Storting* (bicameral parliament) consisting of 155 members elected by universal suffrage for a 4-year term. When assembled, parliament divides itself by election into 2 chambers, one of 39 members, the other of 116. Bills are introduced in the larger chamber and, when passed, are sent to the smaller one. If the chambers disagree, a joint session is held in which the fate of the bill is decided by a two-thirds majority **Local Government:** 19 counties and the city county of Oslo, each with a council and a governor

Ethnic Composition: Norwegians are mainly of Nordic origin; there has been some mixture with the Finns and Lapps, especially in the north, where some 20,000 Lapps still live **Population Distribution:** 57% urban **Density:** 33 inhabitants per sq. mi.

Largest Cities: (1976 est.) Oslo 462,732, Bergen 213,434, Trondheim 134,910, Stavanger 86,639, Kristiansand 59,488

Per Capita Income: $8,762 (1979) **Gross National Product (GNP):** $36 billion (1979) **Economic Statistics:** 6% of GNP comes from agriculture (dairy farming, beef, pork, eggs and poultry), including animal husbandry, forestry, fishing and whaling; 20% from industry (transport equipment, shipbuilding, metal products, food manufactures, chemicals and chemical products, printing and publishing, paper and paper products, electrical and other machinery, nonmetallic mineral products); 19% from trade and finance **Minerals and Mining:** Offshore oil and natural gas, limestone, pyrites, ilmenite, iron ore, coal, molybdenite, copper, zinc, lead **Labor Force:** 1,800,000, of which 29% is employed in services, 25% in industry, and 11% in agriculture **Foreign Trade:** Exports, chiefly petroleum, ships, nonferrous metals, paper and paperboard, paper pulp, iron and steel, totaled $10 billion in 1978. Imports, mainly industrial machinery, petroleum and petroleum products, iron and steel, and textiles, amounted to $11.4 billion **Principal Trade Partners:** Britain, West Germany, Sweden, Denmark, United States, Japan, Netherlands, Liberia, France

Vital Statistics: Birthrate, 12.5 per 1,000 of pop. (1977); death rate, 9.7 **Life Expectancy:** 75 years **Health Statistics:** 68 inhabitants per hospital bed; 567 per physician (1976) **Infant Mortality:** 10.5 per 1,000 births **Illiteracy:** Negligible **Primary and Secondary School Enrollment:** 726,011 (1976) **Enrollment in Higher Education:** 66,628 **GNP Expended on Education:** 7.7% (1976)

Transportation: Paved roads total 22,976 mi. **Motor Vehicles:** 1,268,500 (1977) **Passenger Cars:** 1,106,600 **Railway Mileage:** 2,635 **Ports:** Oslo, Narvik, Bergen, Stavanger, Tonsberg, Porsgrunn, Trondheim, Tromso **Major Airlines:** Scandinavian Airlines System (SAS), a consortium owned by the governments of Norway, Denmark, and Sweden, operates domestic and international services **Communications:** Government owned **Radio Transmitters:** 347 **Radio Licenses:** 1,288,000 (1976) **Television Transmitters:** 665 **Licenses:** 1,087,000 (1976) **Telephones:** 1,476,000 (1976) **Newspapers:** 80 dailies, 412 copies per 1,000 inhabitants (1975)

Weights and Measures: Metric system **Travel Requirements:** Passport, no visa for 3 months

---

Lying atop Western Europe with nearly half its 1,100-mile length north of the Arctic Circle, Norway—a rugged land of mountains, forests, glaciers, and a coastline deeply cut by fjords—is the most sparsely populated country on the Continent. It has, however, one of the highest living standards in Europe and, like the other Nordic lands, a far-reaching social welfare system.

Norway helped to form NATO in 1949, following its experience during World War II as a country invaded and occupied by the Germans. In doing so, it departed from the strict neutrality that it had observed since 1814, when it was forced during brief hostilities to enter with Sweden into a dual monarchy. Like Denmark, Norway, which, with Denmark, Sweden, and Finland, is a member of the Nordic Council, limits its membership in NATO by stipulating that neither foreign troops nor nuclear weapons may be stationed on its soil. The only Western European country that shares a frontier with the Soviet Union, Norway has a small garrison guarding that border, which is 122 miles long, in the far northeast.

The Norwegians were charter members of the British-led European Free Trade Association, organized in 1960, and for a time sought entry to the European Economic Community (formerly the Common Market). But in a national referendum held September 24-25, 1972, the Norwegian electorate decisively rejected such entry. However, the government negotiated a free trade agreement with the EC to gain advantages for Norway's major exports, particularly fish, aluminum, paper, and steel.

Rich in hydroelectric power, Norway has developed into an industrial nation that produces more than a fifth of its gross national product through manufacturing. All but about nine percent of Norwegian enterprises are privately owned. Small and medium-size plants predominate, with about 70 percent employing fewer than 10 persons.

Along with its promise of considerable riches, the 1968 discovery of huge oil and gas deposits on the continental shelf of the North Sea has brought Norway some major economic problems as well. After borrowing heavily to finance development, the government has found reserves to be smaller than first thought, and production costs higher. In April 1977 a spectacular oil well blowout cost $111 million in lost revenues and has delayed development of the Statfjord fields, where the nation expects to get most of its future oil. In March 1980, a tragic accident claimed the lives of 123 workers when a floating platform at Norway's Ekofisk offshore oil field capsized during a storm. Output of oil and natural gas amounted to only about two thirds of the projected 25 million tons in 1977, while the nation's balance of payments showed a record $5.3 billion deficit. As a result, the government devalued the krone by eight percent, froze prices and tightened credit. Further austerity measures are likely.

HISTORY: The history of Norway before the age of the Vikings is indistinct from that of the rest of Scandinavia. Norse Vikings emerge as an identifiable group in the 8th century, when the Anglo-Saxon Chronicle records their arrival in Britain. Norway itself, split into kingdoms and earldoms, was united in the 11th century and reached its peak in the 13th century, holding sway over Iceland and Greenland. Briefly united with Sweden in 1319, Norway formally joined with Denmark and Sweden in the Union of Kalmar in 1397, which lasted until the end of the Napoleonic Wars, although Sweden seceded in the 16th century

1814: Denmark, having sided with France in the Napoleonic Wars, is among the losers and is forced to cede Norway to Sweden. The Norwegians react by adopting a constitution of their own and choose a Danish prince to be king of Norway, but a Swedish army forces Norway to agree to a dual monarchy with Sweden

1905: Union with Sweden is dissolved and Norway becomes independent. Prince Charles of Denmark is elected king of Norway and ascends throne as Haakon VII

1914-18: Norway remains neutral during World War I, but its merchant fleet suffers heavy losses

1940-45: Nazi Germany attacks Norway and quickly occupies most of country despite strong Norwegian resistance. King Haakon and his cabinet leave the country and set up a government in exile in London. In occupied Norway, meanwhile, a puppet government is established under Norwegian Nazi leader Vidkun Quisling; despite his attempts to promote collaboration with Germans, the Norwegians continue to defy invaders. Norway is liberated in May 1945

1945: Norway becomes founding member of the UN. Trygve Lie elected first UN Secretary-General

1957: King Haakon dies and is succeeded by son, Olav V

1965: Labor party, which has been dominant for 30 years, is swept out of office in general elections; Per Borten, leader of Center party, forms non-socialist coalition government, which remains in power till 1971

1968: Huge oil and gas deposits are discovered in Norwegian sector of North Sea

1972: Voting in a national referendum, the Norwegian electorate rejects entry to the European Community (Common Market), toppling Labor government of Premier Bratteli, in power since 1971 and a strong advocate of EC entry; Lars Korvald of the Christian People's party forms a minority coalition government

1973: In general elections the Labor party obtains 35.29 percent of popular vote as the largest single group and returns to power with a minority government headed by Premier Trygve Bratteli

1974: Norway and the Soviet Union open negotiations to define the disputed boundary of the potentially oil-rich continental shelf of the Barents Sea

1975: The *Storting* (parliament) passes a tax law providing for a large surtax on North Sea oil production by oil companies, which will bring the government $1 billion a year

1976: Odvar Nordli becomes premier

1977: Oil well blowout in the Ekofisk Field is capped after a spill lasting eight days; the cost to Norway is put at $111 million

1978: Further austerity measures proposed as Norway's foreign debt nears $19 billion. Work proceeds on nation's third major oil find, the Statfjord field (discovered in 1974)

1980: Floating platform at Ekofisk oil field collapses, killing 123 workers, most of whom are Norwegians

---

OMAN

Area: 120,000 sq. mi. **Population:** 839,000 (1978 est.)

Official Name: Sultanate of Oman **Capital:** Muscat **Nationality:** Omani **Languages:** Arabic is the official and predominant language; Hindi, Baluchi, English, Farsi, and Urdu are spoken by the minorities **Religion:** 50% are Ibadi Moslems and about 25% Sunni Moslems. Islam is the official religion **Flag:** Horizontal white, red, and green bands, with a vertical red band at the hoist, a white symbol of crossed swords in the upper left **Anthem:** National Anthem, beginning "God save our sultan" **Currency:** Omani rial (0.35 per U.S. $1)

Location: Southeast Arabia. Bounded on the north and northwest by the Gulf of Oman and the United Arab Emirates, on the east and south by the Arabian Sea, and on the west by Southern Yemen and Saudi Arabia **Features:** The coastline extends for about 1,000 miles, with fertile coastal plain (the Batina), a range of barren hills, and a plateau and desert area with an average height of 1,000 feet. Also included are the detached tip of the Musandam Peninsula, and offshore the Kuria Muria and Masira islands **Chief Rivers:** There are no permanent rivers

Head of State and of Government: Sultan Qabus ibn Said al Bu Said, born 1939, seized power in July 1970. The sultan is an absolute monarch and also premier **Constitution and Legislative Body:** None **Local Government:** 37 regions, one province and the capital area, ruled by appointed governors

Ethnic Composition: The population is almost evenly divided between those of South and North Arabian stock. Minorities (60,000) of Iranians, Pakistanis, Indians, and East Africans **Population Distribution:** 10% urban **Density:** 7 inhabitants per sq. mi.

Largest Cities: (1974 estimate) Matrah 20,000, Salala 10,000, Nizwa 10,000, Muscat 7,000

Per Capita Income: $5,434 (1979) **Gross National Product (GNP):** $3 billion (1979) **Economic Statistics:** About 74% from industry (oil providing 70% of the total GNP, fishing, date-drying) and 2% of GNP is derived from agriculture (dates, bananas, onions, limes, tobacco, oranges, coconuts, melons, grapes, wheat, livestock) **Minerals and Mining:** Oil is the country's chief mineral resource, and there are deposits of asbestos, marble, chrome and copper **Labor Force:** 250,000 of which 36% are non-Omani **Foreign Trade:** Exports, oil (95%), dates, fish, and limes, totaled $1.6 billion in 1978. Imports, chiefly foods, machinery, manufactured goods, materials, and clothing, totaled $1.2 billion **Principal Trade Partners:** India, Pakistan, Australia, UAE, Britain, Japan, United States, West Germany

Vital Statistics: Birthrate, 50 per 1,000 of pop. (1974); death rate, 19 **Life Expectancy:** 47 years **Health Statistics:** 658 inhabitants per hospital bed; 1,975 per physician (1976) **Infant Mortality:** 145 per 1,000 births **Illiteracy:** 75% **Primary and Secondary School Enrollment:** 65,000 (1976) **GNP Expended on Education:** 7.4% (1975)

Transportation: Paved roads total 800 mi. **Motor Vehicles:** 8,168 **Railway Mileage:** None **Ports:** Muscat (Port Qabus), Matrah, Mina al Fahal, Rasyut **Major Airlines:** Gulf Air provides international service **Communications:** Government controlled **Radio Transmitters:** 4 **Receivers:** 1,000 **Television Transmitters:** 2 **Receivers:** 55,000 **Telephones:** 9,000 (1976) **Newspapers:** 1 daily

Weights and Measures: Metric system **Travel Requirements:** Passport; business visa, $9.00 fee, valid 7 days, 2 photos, letter from applicant's company and from sponsor in Oman

---

In 1970, Sultan Qabus ibn Said al Bu Said changed the name of Muscat and Oman to simply Oman, but he has not been able to change the fact that Oman is, in a sense, several countries. He belongs to the dynasty of the ancient port city of Muscat, the dynasty which survived the long-standing rivalry among port cities and foreign conquerors for control of the coast. And whoever has controlled the coast has also tried to control the nomads of the desert interior—part of which is traditionally known as Oman. Despite Sultan Qabus's attempt to give a single name to his dominion, Oman is more a dynastic conglomeration than a nation-state. It has no definite boundaries; control of the interior is weak; and the port cities have little loyalty to the dynasty, and less to an entity called "Oman."

For more than a century, the dynasty has relied on British assistance, and many of the high-ranking officers in the army are on loan from the British army. During most of the 1970s, Sultan Qabus could also borrow entire army units from Shah Mohammed Reza Pahlavi of Iran. The shah's overthrow in 1979 increased Oman's strategic importance in the Middle East to the West. On June 4, 1980, Oman agreed to allow the United States to use some ports and air bases in return for U.S. military and economic aid, estimated at $100 million in 1980-81.

Sultan Qabus, who had been educated in Britain, came to power in 1970 by overthrowing his father, Said ibn Taimur, who had been sultan since 1932. The older man had tried to keep his domain together by fear and by preventing change; he had forbidden nomads to enter the cities and city people to enter the interior, outlawed the cultivation of new land, and required his personal approval to build a new house or to repair an old one. Long an exporter of dates and camels, Muscat and Oman began to export oil in 1967. Although not a member of the Organization of Petroleum Exporting Countries (OPEC), Oman has followed its lead in raising oil prices. At the end of 1979, Oman increased the price for a barrel of crude oil by $4.00 to $28.20, about the average OPEC price.

An open revolt against the government which began in Dhofar in 1969 was put down by Sultan Qabus with the assistance of Iraq, Jordan, Iran, and Britain by 1975. However, in 1979 he risked isolation from the Arab world by endorsing the peace treaty between Egypt and Israel. While wishing to become the constitutional monarch of a democratic country, the sultan has indicated that Oman is not yet ready for democracy.

HISTORY: Muscat and Oman was converted to Islam in the 7th century, during the lifetime of Mohammed. In 1508, the Portuguese conquered the the coastal region. In the 17th century, they were driven out by the Turks, who were themselves expelled in 1741 by Ahmed Ibn Said of Yemen, founder of the present ruling family. In the early 19th century, Muscat and Oman was the most powerful state in Arabia, controlling Zanzibar, much of the Persian coast, and part of present-day West Pakistan, but during this period Muscat lost control of Oman—the interior region

1856-61: Rival heirs dispute succession to throne on death of Said ibn Sultan in 1856; dispute is settled through British mediation under an arrangement in 1861 calling for separation of Zanzibar from Muscat

1913-20: Tribes in interior of Oman rebel against sultan of Muscat, who controls only the cities of Muscat and Matrah, and elect Imam spiritual head of country; Imam is murdered in 1920, and sultan signs treaty with his successor calling for internal tribal autonomy and mutual nonaggression

1951: Traditional association with Britain is confirmed by new treaty of friendship, commerce, and navigation

1954-57: Imam dies in 1954; his successor breaks 1920 treaty and is driven from his capital; Muscat regains control of Oman

1958: Port of Gwadar and its hinterland in Baluchistan is sold to Pakistan

1965-66: UN General Assembly adopts resolution in 1965 calling for elimination of British presence in Muscat and Oman

1969: Leftist rebels in Dhofar province engage in guerrilla warfare in effort to overthrow sultan

1970: Sultan Said ibn Taimur is overthrown by son, Qabus ibn Said, who promises to establish modern government, end country's isolation, and use oil revenues for the good of the people

1971: Oman joins the UN

1975: Victory over rebels in Dhofar province is declared by sultan

1977: Britain closes its military base on the Omani island of Masira

1980: Oman and United States sign agreement to permit U.S. access to country's ports and airfields in exchange for American military and economic aid

PAKISTAN

Area: 342,750 sq. mi. **Population:** 76,770,000 (1978 est.)

Official Name: Islamic Republic of Pakistan **Capital:** Islamabad **Nationality:** Pakistani **Languages:** Urdu (spoken by only 7%) is the official language, but English is also widely used in government and commerce; Punjabi (64%), Sindhi (12%), Pushtu, Brahui, and Baluchi are regional languages **Religion:** Islam is the state religion and is practiced by 97% of the population; the rest are Hindus, Christians, Buddhists, or of no religious affiliation **Flag:** Green with a white vertical stripe at the hoist and a white crescent and a 5-pointed star in the center **Anthem:** National Anthem, beginning "Blessed be the sacred land" **Currency:** Pakistani rupee (9.9 per U.S. $1)

Location: South Asia. It extends c. 1,000 miles from the sea north to the mountain wall of the Hindu Kush and the towering peaks of the Karakoram. It adjoins Iran and Afghanistan on the west and northwest, China on the northeast, India on the east, and the Arabian Sea on the south **Features:** A barren plain stretches along the foothills of the mountains; in the center is the fertile Indus plain **Chief Rivers:** Indus, Sutlej, Chenab, Ravi

Head of State and of Government: President: Gen. Mohammad Zia-ul-Haq, born 1924, assumed office in 1978. He is also Chief Martial Law Administrator, an office he has occupied since the coup of July 1977 **Effective Date of Present Constitution:** 1973, amended 1976, temporarily suspended 1977 **Legislative Body:** Parliament (bicameral), with a National Assembly and a Senate, dissolved 1977; rule is by President Zia and a council of military chiefs **Local Government:** 4 provinces, presently governed by the provincial chief justices, and a federal capital territory plus tribal areas

Ethnic Composition: The population of Pakistan is made up chiefly of Punjabi, Sindhi, Pathan, and Baluchi. Several small tribes live in the mountainous areas **Population Distribution:** 26% urban **Density:** 224 inhabitants per sq. mi.

Largest Cities: (1972 census) Karachi 3,498,634, Lahore 2,165,372, Lyallpur 822,263, Hyderabad 628,310, Rawalpindi 615,392, Multan 542,195, Gujranwala 360,419; (1974 est.) Islamabad 250,000

Per Capita Income: $214 (1979) **Gross National Product (GNP):** $18 billion (1979) **Economic Statistics:** In 1977 about 33% of GNP came from agriculture (wheat, cotton, rice); 16% from manufacturing (textiles, food processing, chemicals, cement, paper, metal manufacturing) and mining; 15% from trade; and 6% from construction **Minerals and Mining:** There are large reserves of natural gas, copper, and some crude oil **Labor Force:** 22 million, with 60% in agriculture **Foreign Trade:** Exports, chiefly cotton, cotton products, leather goods, rugs, fish and rice, amounted to $1.3 billion in 1977. Imports, mainly machinery, transportation equipment, iron and steel, animal and vegetable oils and fats, petroleum and products, chemicals, tea and food grains, amounted to $2.7 billion **Principal Trade Partners:** United States, Japan, Saudi Arabia, Britain, Hong Kong, Sri Lanka, West Germany, Australia

Vital Statistics: Birthrate, 40.5 per 1,000 of pop. (1976); death rate, 12 **Life Expectancy:** 51 years **Health Statistics:** 1,871 inhabitants per hospital bed; 4,049 per physician (1973) **Infant Mortality:** 115 per 1,000 births (1970) **Illiteracy:** 79% **Primary and Secondary School Enrollment:** 7,325,303 (1975) **Enrollment in Higher Education:** 114,913 (1974) **GNP Expended on Education:** 2.1% (1976)

Transportation: Surfaced roads total 16,000 mi. **Motor Vehicles:** 287,800 (1975) **Passenger Cars:** 196,100 **Railway Mileage:** 5,475 **Ports:** Karachi, Port Qasim **Major Airlines:** Pakistan International Airlines, operates domestic and international services **Communications:** Partly government owned **Radio Transmitters:** 27 **Licenses:** 1,200,000 (1976) **Television Transmitters:** 16 **Receivers:** 350,000 (1976) **Telephones:** 240,000 (1975) **Newspapers:** 102 dailies (1975), 18 copies per 1,000 inhabitants

Weights and Measures: Metric system **Travel Requirements:** Passport, visa not required for stay up to 30 days

Throughout its relatively short history, Pakistan has been shot through with powerfully divisive forces. When the Indian subcontinent was granted independence from Britain in 1947, it was decided that a national homeland for Moslems should be created as a nation separate from predominantly Hindu India. For centuries there had been periodic bloodbaths resulting from communal rioting between Hindus and Moslems, and an independent Pakistan was seen as the solution.

Unfortunately, Indian Moslems were concentrated in two widely separated parts. The first consisted of all or part of four provinces now known as Pakistan, which borders Afghanistan, Iran, India, and China. The second and more populous part was carved from the old state of Bengal and is now Bangladesh, bordering India and Burma.

The gulf between the two wings of Pakistan was reflected in and intensified by the 1970 election, the first since independence. Of the 313 seats that were to be filled in the new National Assembly, 167 were won by the Awami League—a Bengali nationalist party, all the strength of which was in Bangladesh. The runner-up was the Pakistan People's party with 88 seats, all for West Pakistan. There was no major national party to bridge the two wings, and virtually the only cement holding them together was a common religion.

On March 1, 1971, at the urging of the Pakistan People's party, Gen. Yahya Khan announced that the convening of the National Assembly would be postponed pending further discussions of major constitutional issues. Leaders of the Awami League claimed they were being cheated.

Widespread rioting in Bangladesh ensued, and strikes crippled the cities. Bengali extremists murdered substantial numbers of non-Bengalis.

On March 25, President Yahya Khan ordered the national army into Bangladesh to crush the separatist movement. The East Bengal Regiment of the army promptly defected to join Bangladesh armed forces, and key bridges, railroads, and communications were blown up or damaged.

An occupation army remained in Bangladesh and had to contend with hostility from the province, sniping and sabotage from Bangladesh guerrillas, and a vast economic drain on the nation as a whole. Millions of refugees fled and hundreds of civilians were killed in the conflict.

In the ensuing months tension between India and Pakistan increased, and on December 4 Indian troops entered the Bengali province. On December 16 the Pakistani armed forces there surrendered to the Indian and Bangladesh command.

This defeat, and the secession of Bangladesh, for which the Pakistani public had been unprepared, led to the resignation of President Yahya Khan and the succession of Zulfikar Ali Bhutto, leader of the People's party, as the first civilian president. Bhutto negotiated the release of 90,000 prisoners and, as a spellbinding orator, set out to restore national pride. He put in train a series of reforms in education, politics, and social life and announced that the state would assume control, but not ownership, of ten basic industries.

In July 1977, following four months of political violence in which at least 350 people were killed, the Pakistani army seized power in a bloodless coup. The Army Chief of Staff, Gen. Mohammad Zia-ul-Haq, then became chief martial law administrator. The initial violence was touched off by alleged election fraud by the ruling People's party.

In March 1978, Bhutto, the most popular civilian politician in Pakistan's history, was convicted of a 1974 political murder and sentenced to hang. Denying his guilt, he appealed to the nation's Supreme Court but lost, 4-3. Hundreds of leaders of his Pakistan party were jailed in what Bhutto supporters said was a campaign to eliminate a political opponent; Zia, however, called the actions a continuing "process of accountability." Despite pleas for clemency from Pope John Paul II, U.S. President Carter, Soviet Union's Leonid Brezhnev, and China's Hua Guofeng, Bhutto was hanged secretly on April 4, 1979. Later in the year, Zia postponed the scheduled national elections and placed Bhutto's widow, the head of the People's party, and her daughter, Benazir, a Harvard graduate, under house arrest. Detention was not lifted until the following April.

In 1979, the U.S. cut off economic aid after accusing Pakistan of secret efforts to build nuclear weapons by importing various pieces and materials from Europe and the U.S. After the USSR invasion of Afghanistan put 80,000 Soviet troops at Pakistan's border, the U.S., in early 1980, offered Zia $400 million in military and economic aid over two years. But he rejected that sum as "peanuts"—and later he portrayed the offer as "devoid of credibility and durability." Eventually, Pakistan said it would accept $200 million—the economic proportion—if no strings were attached.

HISTORY: In the 8th century Moslems from Arabia introduced Islam to the lower reaches of what is now West Pakistan. Two centuries later, Moslem warriors swept from the northwest down through the Khyber Pass and conquered the upper reaches of West Pakistan, converting millions of the inhabitants to Islam. In the 13th century, Moslem invaders brought Islam to Bengal, part of which is now Bangladesh. Moslem power and culture on the Indian subcontinent reached their zenith under the Mogul empire (1526-1857). Despite cultural interchange with the Hindus, the Moslem cummunity continued to maintain its distinct identity under British rule, which lasted until the middle of the 20th century

1906-40: The Moslem League is founded as a separate political organization. Led by Mohammad Ali Jinnah, it demands the establishment of a Moslem state in India

1947: Pakistan is set up as a separate British dominion, with Jinnah as governor-general and Liaqat Ali Khan as prime minister. Establishment of the new state is followed by widespread communal strife between Moslems and Hindus, costing more than a million lives and uprooting millions of Hindus and Moslems

1948-49: Pakistan and India are involved in an undeclared war over the state of Jammu and Kashmir (a state whose predominantly Moslem population is ruled by a Hindu prince who signs Kashmir over to India). A cease-fire is arranged, and the state partitioned by a temporary demarcation line

1951-56: Liaqat Ali Khan is assassinated (1951), ushering in a period of political instability and tension between East and West Pakistan. A new constitution is adopted, and Pakistan becomes a republic within the British Commonwealth with Gen. Iskander Mirza as president

1958-62: Following continued turmoil in both parts of the country, Mirza abrogates the constitution, dismisses the cabinet, and hands over power to the army under Gen. Ayub Khan. Ayub takes over the presidency, dismisses the prime minister, and rules by decree. The new president proclaims new constitution

1965: Ayub Khan is elected president. Pakistan and India fight a brief war over the Rann of Kutch and Kashmir

1969: Ayub resigns in the face of widespread political unrest. Martial law is proclaimed under Gen. Agha Mohammad Yahya Khan, who takes over as president

1970: Yahya Khan proclaims Pakistan an Islamic federal state

1971: Civil war breaks out between Bengali and federal forces and Bengalis are defeated; in December brief war between India and Pakistan results in defeat of Pakistan and the secession of the Bengali province, now Bangladesh. Yahya Khan resigns and Zulfikar Ali Bhutto becomes president

1972: Pakistan and India sign Simla agreement to stabilize relations

1973: New constitution is adopted. Fazal Elahi Chaudhry is elected president by the National Assembly. Former President Bhutto becomes prime minister with no loss of power

1974: Civil rights restored. Earthquake kills more than 5,000. Pakistan recognizes Bangladesh

1975: Assassination of Provincial Minister Sherpao leads to opposition Awami party being declared illegal. U.S. lifts 10-year ban on sale of arms to Pakistan

1976: India and Pakistan agree to resume diplomatic relations

1977: Pakistani army under Gen. Mohammad Zia-ul-Haq seizes power in a bloodless coup, ending the Bhutto regime. Elections,

promised for October, are canceled; political activity is banned; martial-law rule is extended indefinitely; General Zia calls measures needed because of nation's "political turmoil"

1978: Bhutto is convicted of a 1974 murder and sentenced to die; denying charge, he appeals to Supreme Court; worldwide reaction includes appeals for clemency from the U.S. and several of Pakistan's Moslem neighbors. General Zia assumes the office of president following the resignation of Chaudhry

1979: On April 4, Bhutto, still declaring his innocence, is hanged. Days of rioting follow; 30,000 march in protest in Larkana, his hometown. The U.S. cuts off economic aid, contending that Pakistan is secretly trying to build nuclear weapons with equipment and materials purchased—often through dummy organizations—in Europe and the U.S. Zia declares Islamic law to be the country's law; two bank robbers are sentenced to have their right hands and left feet amputated. On October 16, Zia indefinitely postpones national elections scheduled for November 17. He dissolves all political parties, detains opposition leaders without charge or trial, expands the jurisdiction of military courts, and shuts three newspapers. On November 21, a mob, inflamed by erroneous radio reports from Iran, attacks and sets fire to the U.S. embassy in Islamabad, killing an American marine and a soldier; the Pakistani army, sluggish in responding, rescues the rest of the embassy personnel after six hours

1980: The Soviet invasion of Afghanistan sends more than 500,000 Afghans rushing to government refugee camps in Pakistan. Offered $400 million over two years by the U.S. to improve military defenses against the Soviet threat, Zia scoffs at it as "peanuts"

PANAMA

Area: 29,762 sq. mi. **Population:** 1,900,000 (1979 est.)

Official Name: Republic of Panama **Capital:** Panama **Nationality:** Panamanian **Languages:** Spanish is the official and predominant language; English is widely used in the capital and Colón; and small minorities of Italians, French, Greeks, East Indians, and indigenous Cuna Indians retain their national languages **Religion:** 93% Roman Catholic, 6% Protestant **Flag:** Divided into 4 rectangles: the lower left is blue; the upper right red; the upper left white with a blue star in the center; the lower right white with a red star in the middle **Anthem:** Istmeño Hymn **Currency:** Balboa (1 per U.S. $1)

Location: Latin America, occupying the southern end of the Isthmus of Panama, which forms the land connection between the North and South American continents. Panama is bounded on the north by the Caribbean Sea, on the east by Colombia, on the south by the Gulf of Panama and the Pacific Ocean, and on the west by Costa Rica **Features:** The country is largely mountainous and hilly, with 2 mountain ranges forming the backbone of the isthmus. Lowlands lie along both coastlines; the Atlantic side and eastern Panama are covered almost entirely by tropical rain forests. The Panama Canal bisects the country **Chief Rivers:** Tuira, Bayano, Santa María, Chepo, Indio

Head of State and of Government: President Aristides Royo, born 1940, elected 1978 for 6 years. The former Head of Government, Gen. Omar Torrijos, Commander of the National Guard, retains important decision-making powers **Effective Date of Present Constitution:** October 11, 1972 **Legislative Body:** A National Assembly of Community Representatives, with 505 members elected for 6 years, a National Legislative Council performs legislative functions when the Assembly is not in session **Local Government:** 9 provinces, each headed by an appointed governor, and one intendency (territory)

Ethnic Composition: The population is 70% mestizo, 14% Antilleans (immigrants from the West Indies and their descendants), 10% white and 6% Indian **Population Distribution:** 53.7% urban **Density:** 64 inhabitants per sq. mi.

Largest Cities: (1978 est.) Panama 438,000, San Miguelito 139,000, Colón 85,600, David 70,700

Per Capita Income: $1,436 (1979) **Gross National Product (GNP):** $2.7 billion (1979) **Economic Statistics:** In 1973 about 18% came from agriculture (rice, sugar, and bananas); 18% from trade; and 16% from industry (food processing, textiles, clothing, shoes, cement, pharmaceuticals, oil refining, sugar refining) **Minerals and Mining:** There are many minerals that remain unexploited because of poor quality; however, major copper and molybdenum deposits are to be exploited **Labor Force:** 543,000 (1978), of which 45% was engaged in services and commerce, 29% in agriculture, 10% in manufacturing, and 4% in canal activities **Foreign Trade:** Exports, chiefly bananas, shrimp, sugar and petroleum derivatives, totaled $292 million in 1978. Imports, mainly machinery, vehicles and parts, petroleum and food totaled $889 million **Principal Trade Partners:** United States, Saudi Arabia, Ecuador, Venezuela

Vital Statistics: Birthrate, 29.5 per 1,000 of pop. (1977); death rate, 7.1 (1975) **Life Expectancy:** 59 years **Health Statistics:** 284 inhabitants per hospital bed; 1,335 per physician (1977) **Infant Mortality:** 28.5 per 1,000 births **Illiteracy:** 18% **Primary and Secondary School Enrollment:** 502,932 (1977) **Enrollment in Higher Education:** 32,063 (1976) **GNP Expended on Education:** 4.9% (1976)

Transportation: Paved roads total 1,700 mi. **Motor Vehicles:** 103,900 (1975) **Passenger Cars:** 83,800 **Railway Mileage:** 225 **Ports:** Colón, Cristobal, Balboa, Bocas del Toro, Puerto Armuelles **Major Airlines:** Air Panama and Compañía Panameña de Aviación operate international and domestic services **Communications:** Partly government controlled **Radio Transmitters:** 120 **Receivers:** 270,000 (1976) **Television Transmitters:** 13 **Receivers:** 186,000 (1976) **Telephones:** 155,000 (1976) **Newspapers:** 6 dailies, 79 copies per 1,000 inhabitants (1975)

Weights and Measures: British standards and the metric system are used **Travel Requirements:** Passport, visa or 30-day tourist card obtainable from airline, $2 fee

Panama, the narrow serpentine isthmus connecting North and South America, is a largely mountainous country, bisected by a 51-mile-long Panama Canal. Since Nov. 1, 1979, Panama has been building up its financial and commercial status through possession of the land, dry docks, ports, and railroads of the former Canal Zone. (The waterway itself is scheduled to be controlled until Dec. 31, 1999, by the U.S.-operated Canal Commission, in which Panama is a junior partner.) As the home of 85 international banks, and well situated for the distribution or transshipment of goods, Panama is rapidly becoming the business center of Central America—and it has hopes of becoming the Hong Kong of the West.

Within the country, access roads are sparse, a handicap that the government, with outside help, has been trying to remedy. The eastern half of the country, down to the Colombian border, consists largely of impenetrable jungle inhabited by a few primitive Indian tribes.

The Panama Canal dominates life in the central populated areas, and it has played an overriding role in Panamanian politics, at the same time emerging as a symbol of North American domination.

On June 16, 1978, in Panama City, President Carter and Panamanian head of state Brig. Gen. Omar Torrijos Herrera took part in ceremonies formally concluding the two new Panama Canal treaties, thus bringing to fruition 13 years of often difficult negotiations. Basically, one treaty covers control of the canal while the other establishes its future neutrality. Under the accords, Panama will obtain full control of the canal in the year 2000, the U.S. will pay Panama $10 million annually in toll revenues (plus added amounts dependent on traffic), and the U.S. has the right to intervene unilaterally in Panama if the canal's operation is ever threatened after the year 2000.

In the final phase of the canal talks, both leaders absorbed considerable criticism from countrymen who felt too much was being given to the other nation. Carter narrowly averted a serious political setback in April 1978 when the U.S. Senate ratified, with but one vote to spare, the second of the two treaties. In order to gain ratification, the Administration accepted reservations favorable to the U.S. but politically embarrassing for Torrijos, who nonetheless accepted them.

A new oil transshipment port was opened on the Pacific Coast in 1979. It will transfer Alaskan oil from supertankers to smaller craft that can go through the canal. In addition, a new $20-million convention hall was announced for Panama City.

HISTORY: Little is known about the Indians inhabiting Panama before the arrival of the Spanish explorer Rodrigo de Bastidas in 1502. The region soon fell under the control of Balboa, who in 1513 made his famous crossing of the isthmus and discovered the Pacific. Under Spanish occupation the isthmus became the route by which Inca treasures were shipped to Spain. But Panama was to lose most of its importance in the carrying trade with the collapse of the Spanish Empire

1821: Panama breaks away from Spain and becomes part of Colombia

1848-49: California gold rush enhances importance of Panama as westward-bound U.S. settlers use isthmus as bridge between Atlantic and Pacific; crossings stimulate interest in a canal

1881-89: French company headed by Ferdinand de Lesseps begins work on a canal in 1881; disease among workers and financial problems drive company into bankruptcy within the decade

1903: Panamanians revolt when Colombian senate refuses to ratify Hay-Herrán Treaty granting United States right to build a canal across Panamanian isthmus; United States prevents Colombia from quelling rebellion and Panamanians declare their independence; new republic grants United States exclusive control of a canal zone in perpetuity and permits United States to intervene to protect Panamanian independence

1914: Panama Canal is opened

1939: Canal treaty is amended, eliminating U.S. right to intervene in Panamanian affairs

1959: Mobs of Panamanian youths invade Canal Zone in protest against U.S. sovereignty and demand revision of canal treaty

1964: Riots break out in Canal Zone as Panamanians protest U.S. failure to abide by agreement calling for simultaneous display of Panamanian and American flags

1967: United States and Panama negotiate new treaties under which United States would give up sovereignty over canal to U.S.-Panamanian authority and provide military defense for canal, and under which construction of a new canal might be undertaken; treaties, however, remain unratified

1968: National Assembly impeaches President Marco Aurelio Robles for having violated constitution by backing government candidate in presidential election; Assembly's decision is voided by Supreme Court. Following a dispute over the outcome of the election, opposition candidate Arnulfo Arias is declared president but is overthrown on October 1, 11 days after taking office, in coup led by National Guard; National Assembly is dissolved and constitutional guarantees suspended; Col. José M. Pinilla is sworn in as provisional president

1969: Brig. Gen. Omar Torrijos Herrera, one of the principal leaders of the 1968 coup, emerges as nation's strong man after banishing other leaders

1972: Torrijos acquires full civil and military powers

1975: Government moves toward nationalization of banana industry. U.S. and Panama sign a preliminary agreement to end U.S. jurisdiction over the Panama Canal and Zone

1977: President Carter and General Torrijos sign two new Panama Canal treaties in Washington, providing for transfer of canal to Panama by the year 2000 and establishing its future neutrality. Panamanians approve treaties in referendum

1978: U.S. Senate barely ratifies second of two treaties; last-minute reservations favorable to U.S. prove a political embarrassment to Torrijos but he finally accepts them; Carter visits Panama for formal conclusion of pacts. Aristides Royo, a lawyer and former education minister who helped negotiate the canal treaties, is elected president by the National Assembly. Torrijos continues as commander of National Guard

1979: Canal Zone is transferred to Panama on Oct. 1

1980: Panama turns down Iran's request for extradition of deposed Shah who had gained asylum there Dec. 15, 1979. Shah departs for Cairo Mar. 23

PAPUA NEW GUINEA

Area: 183,540 sq. mi. **Population:** 3,079,000 (1979 est.)

Official Name: Papua New Guinea **Capital:** Port Moresby **Nationality:** Papua New Guinean **Languages:** Melanesian Pidgin and Hiri (Police) Motu serve as linguas franca, but are not universal; English is the official language; about 750 localized Papuan languages are spoken **Religion:** About 1,400,000 (52%) profess Christianity, with half a million Roman Catholics and the rest Protestants; the rest practice animistic forms of worship **Flag:** Divided diagonally from upper left to lower right; the upper section is red with a gold bird of paradise, and the lower section is black with the five principal stars of the Southern Cross in white **Anthem:** O Arise All You Sons **Currency:** Kina (.67 per U.S. $1)

Location: Southwest Pacific. About 100 miles northeast of Australia, it occupies the eastern half of the island of New Guinea and is bordered on the west by Indonesia. 15% of the area is on islands to the north and east: the Bismarck Archipelago, the northwestern Solomons, and the smaller Trobriand, Woodlark, D'Entrecasteaux and Louisiade groups **Features:** A high mountain ridge bisecting the New Guinea portion rises to about 15,000 feet, graduating north and

National Anthem, beginning "We are free, let us always be so"
Currency: Sol (279 per U.S. $1)

Location: West coast of South America. Peru is bordered on the north by Ecuador and Colombia, on the east by Brazil and Bolivia, on the south by Chile, and on the west by the Pacific Ocean **Features:** The country is divided into a narrow coastal desert; the high sierra, the zone of the great Andean cordilleras; and the eastern lowlands (montaña), with uncharted hills, forests, and tropical jungles **Chief Rivers:** Amazon, Ucayali-Apurímac, Marañón-Huallaga

Head of State and of Government: President Fernando Belaúnde Terry, born 1912, elected May 1980, took office July 28, 1980. He is assisted by a cabinet headed by Prime Minister Manuel Ulloa **Effective Date of Present Constitution:** July 28, 1980 **Legislative Body:** Congress (bicameral), consisting of a Senate of 60 members elected on a regional basis for 5 years plus the former presidents of constitutional governments as life senators, and a Chamber of Deputies of 180 members elected for 5 years **Local Government:** 23 departments and the constitutional province of Callao

Ethnic Composition: 46% Indian, 38% mestizo, 15% white **Population Distribution:** 63% urban **Density:** 35 inhabitants per sq. mi.

Largest Cities: (1972 census) (M.A. = Metropolitan Area) Lima 2,981,292 (M.A. 4,000,000), Arequipa 304,653, Callao 296,220, Chimbote 159,045, Chiclayo 148,932

Per Capita Income: $1,074 (1979) **Gross National Product (GNP):** $18.4 billion (1979) **Economic Statistics:** 24% of the GNP is derived from manufacturing (textiles, foodstuffs, iron and steel, ships, metal products and chemicals, automobile assembly) and 12% from agriculture (cotton, sugar, rice, coffee), fisheries, and forestry **Minerals and Mining:** Copper, silver, lead, zinc, iron, petroleum, natural gas, bismuth, molybdenum, gold, and tungsten **Labor Force:** 5.3 million (1978), with 42% engaged in agriculture, 20% in services, and 13% in industry **Foreign Trade:** Exports, mainly copper, fishmeal, silver, iron, petroleum, sugar, cotton, and coffee, totaled $3.4 billion in 1979. Imports, chiefly capital goods, industrial raw materials, and intermediate goods, totaled $2 billion **Principal Trade Partners:** United States, Japan, West Germany, Britain, Ecuador, Argentina, Chile, Netherlands

Vital Statistics: Birthrate, 41 per 1,000 of pop. (1975); death rate, 11.9 **Life Expectancy:** 58 years **Health Statistics:** 463 inhabitants per hospital bed; 1,556 per physician (1975) **Infant Mortality:** 58.2 per 1,000 births (1972) **Illiteracy:** 39% **Primary and Secondary School Enrollment:** 3,988,753 (1977) **Enrollment in Higher Education:** 233,420 (1977) **GNP Expended on Education:** 3.6% (1976)

Transportation: Paved roads total 3,350 mi. **Motor Vehicles:** 466,600 (1977) **Passenger Cars:** 300,400 **Railway Mileage:** 1,550 **Ports:** Callao, Talara, Chimbote, Matarani, Ilo, Paita, Pisco **Major Airlines:** Compañía de Aviación Faucett and Aeroperú fly internationally and domestically **Communications:** Government controlled **Radio Transmitters:** 279 **Receivers:** 2,068,000 (1976) **Television Transmitters:** 52 **Receivers:** 600,000 (1976) **Telephones:** 389,000 (1976) **Newspapers:** 35 dailies (1975), 118 copies per 1,000 inhabitants (1974)

Weights and Measures: Metric system **Travel Requirements:** Passport, 90-day tourist card obtainable at port of entry, $10 fee

---

Peru's economy and social structure were long controlled by a few rich families and foreign mining interests. The aristocrats, however, have always been reluctant to see to the business of government themselves, and consequently the army and, occasionally, popular governments have filled the gap. Racial strains between the three major groups— Indian, mestizo, and white—have further complicated politics.

Inflation and crippling political infighting led, on October 3, 1968, to a coup by a military junta, which named Gen. Juan Velasco Alvarado as president. Despite broad social and economic reforms— including land reform and redistributions, a half share in business profits for the workers in Peruvian companies, and nationalization of large industries and public utilities—no protest was heard when Velasco was deposed by Gen. Francisco Morales Bermúdez in August 1975. By that time a faltering economy with rampant unemployment and a rise in the cost of living had offset any benefits gained from the socioeconomic changes. Morales at once consolidated his position by reaffirming the social and economic policies of the 1968 revolution.

Morales' government suffered from internal unrest, however, when it imposed an unpopular austerity program in its efforts to cope with an immense foreign debt. Its rule was marked by repression of extremist political publications and expulsions of leftist military officers and labor leaders. Nevertheless, a Constituent Assembly elected in 1978 drew up a new constitution in the following year. Fernando Belaúnde Terry, Peru's last civilian president, was reelected to that office in the May 1980 elections and was inaugurated on July 28.

HISTORY: At the time of the Spanish Conquest, Peru was the heartland of the great Inca Empire extending from northern Ecuador to central Chile. In 1532 the empire, which had recently undergone a civil war, fell to Spaniards led by Francisco Pizarro. In the colonial era the Indians of Peru were reduced to a serfdom from which the majority still have not fully emerged. In 1824 Spain's colonial rule came to an end with the defeat of Spanish forces by the revolutionary armies led by José de San Martín and Simón Bolívar

1862-79: Futile attempts by Spain to regain its former colonies lead to an intermittent war of small naval engagements; in a peace treaty signed in 1879 Spain finally recognizes the independence of Peru

1879-84: Peru and Bolivia fight unsuccessful War of the Pacific with Chile; Peru is forced to cede the nitrate province of Tarapacá to Chile and to allow Chilean occupation of the provinces of Tacna and Arica

1924: Victor Raúl Haya de la Torre founds APRA (Alianza Popular Revolucionaria Americana), dedicated to radical economic and social reforms to improve the lot of the lower classes, especially the Indians, and nationalization of foreign enterprises

1929: A controversy over Tacna and Arica dating back to the War of the Pacific is resolved through U.S. mediation; Arica is awarded to Chile and Tacna is returned to Peru

1945-48: APRA, though barred from putting up candidates, helps elect José Luis Bustamante to the presidency; he is deposed by a military junta led by General Manuel Odría

1956: Ex-President Manuel Prado is elected president with APRA support and legalizes the party

1962: Haya de la Torre wins slim plurality in disputed presidential elections; attempts to form a coalition government fail and army seizes power

1963-68: Military junta permits new elections and Fernando Belaúnde Terry, a moderate, becomes president; his government confronts rising opposition from legislature and a deteriorating economy; in 1968 Belaúnde is overthrown by a military junta headed by Gen. Juan Velasco Alvarado, which nationalizes U.S.-owned oil property

1969: Junta seizes American tuna boats

1970: An earthquake hits northern Peru, killing 50,000

1971: Government takes over U.S. copper concession

1972: Government seizes U.S. potash and phosphate concessions

1974: Major newspapers are expropriated and transferred to community guilds by the military regime

1975: Government action against striking civil employees results in widespread rioting in Lima, where hundreds are arrested as army quells demonstrations. Velasco overthrown by Morales

1976: Government declares a state of emergency after students and workers riot to protest a new set of austerity measures and call for a return to elected civilian government. Entire cabinet resigns after Prime Minister Fernandez Maldonado quits following an army crisis. Morales replaces resigning leftists with moderates. Huge foreign debt is accumulated

1977: Trans-Andean oil pipeline begins operation. Peru, in grave cash squeeze, is told by international banking community to enact austerity measures as condition for further credit

1978: Peru's foreign debt is put at $5.5 billion; annual inflation rate reaches 80 percent; unemployment and recession deepen. Government launches austerity program; its announcement of steep price hikes on consumer staples triggers two-day nationwide general strike and sets off wave of violence in which 31 persons are killed. Government, blaming "leftist agitators" for violence, declares brief period of martial law. APRA wins largest bloc of Constituent Assembly seats in Peru's first nationwide election since 1963; the Assembly has the task of rewriting the constitution and leading the nation to civilian government by 1980

1979: New constitution is signed by APRA founder Haya de la Torre in July, shortly before he dies; it gains limited approval by Morales. Inflation rate is reduced to 40%, but a comparable drop in real wages leads to a general strike, which soon collapses

1980: Military government decrees new laws Jan. 1 to create jobs, give workers better wages and stimulate trade. Country suffers worst drought in 70 years. Peru buys two squadrons of fighter bombers from USSR. Fernando Belaunde Terry is elected president

---

PHILIPPINES

Area: 115,707 sq. mi. **Population:** 47,719,000 (1979 est.)

Official Name: Republic of the Philippines **Capital:** Manila **Nationality:** Filipino **Languages:** Pilipino (the national language based on Tagalog), English and Spanish are the official languages; almost 90 Philippine languages and dialects are spoken **Religion:** 74% Roman Catholic, 9% Protestant, 7% Moslem, and the rest of other or no affiliation **Flag:** Top half blue, bottom, red, with a white triangle at the hoist containing a gold star in each corner and a golden sun in the center **Anthem:** National Anthem *(Pambansang Awit)*, beginning "Land of the morning, child of the sun returning" **Currency:** Philippine peso (piso) (7.52 per U.S. $1)

Location: Southeast Asia. The Philippines is an archipelago of 7,107 islands stretching about 1,100 miles along the southeastern rim of Asia, with the northern islands about 330 miles from China and the southwestern tip about 30 miles from Malaysia **Features:** 11 islands account for 94% of the total land area and population. Most of the larger islands are mountainous, and are also characterized by extensive coastal plains, wide valleys, volcanoes, mineral and hot springs **Chief Rivers:** Cagayan, Agno, Pampanga, Agusan, Cotabato

Head of State and of Government: President and Prime Minister Ferdinand E. Marcos, born 1917, elected 1965, reelected 1969 assuming full powers under martial law in 1972. In 1978, he became prime minister **Effective Date of Present Constitution:** 1973 (not yet fully implemented), amended 1976 **Legislative Body:** Interim National Assembly of 187 members, subject to override by president **Local Government:** 73 provinces, each headed by a governor appointed by the president, and 61 chartered cities

Ethnic Composition: The dominant racial stock of the Philippines is Malay, with an admixture of Indonesian and Chinese strains. Chinese, Americans, and Spaniards constitute the largest alien minorities **Population Distribution:** 32% urban **Density:** 412 inhabitants per sq. mi.

Largest Cities: (1975 est.) Manila 1,438,252 (Metropolitan Area 4,500,000), Davao 515,520, Cebu 418,517, Iloilo 247,956, Bacolod 196,492

Per Capita Income: $528 (1979) **Gross National Product (GNP):** $25 billion (1979) **Economic Statistics:** 39% of the GNP is derived from services, 29% from agriculture (including rice cultivation, sugar, copra, abaca, logs, coconuts); 24% from industry (mining, textiles, and other durable items manufacture) **Minerals and Mining:** There are deposits of iron ore, copper, gold, manganese, chromite, nickel, zinc, coal, and molybdenum. Oil production is beginning **Labor Force:** 15,400,000 (1976), with 60% in agriculture, forestry, and fishing; about 12% are in industry **Foreign Trade:** Exports, mainly copra, logs and lumber, sugar, coconut oil, copper concentrates, abaca, and canned pineapple, totaled $3.5 billion in 1978. Imports, chiefly nonelectrical machinery, transportation equipment, mineral fuel and lubricants, base metals, cereals, electric machinery, and textiles, totaled $4.7 billion **Principal Trade Partners:** United States, Japan, EEC, Australia, Indonesia, Saudi Arabia

Vital Statistics: Birthrate, 43.8 per 1,000 of pop. (1975); death rate, 10.5 **Life Expectancy:** 58 years **Health Statistics:** 639 inhabitants per hospital bed (1973); 3,154 per physician (1975) **Infant Mortality:** 58.9 per 1,000 births (1974) **Illiteracy:** 17% **Primary and Secondary School Enrollment:** 10,210,725 (1976) **Enrollment in Higher Education:** 764,725 **GNP Expended on Education:** 1.4% (1976)

Transportation: Paved roads total 11,500 mi. **Motor Vehicles:** 667,200 (1976) **Passenger Cars:** 386,200 **Railway Mileage:** 1,268 **Ports:** Cebu, Manila, Zamboanga, Iloilo, Davao, Batangas **Major Airlines:** Philippine Air Lines, privately owned, operates domestic and international flights **Communications:** Partly government controlled **Radio Transmitters:** 333 **Receivers:** 1,875,000 (1976) **Television Transmitters:** 24 **Receivers:** 800,000 (1976) **Telephones:** 542,000 (1976) **Newspapers:** 15 dailies, 18 copies per 1,000 inhabitants (1975)

Weights and Measures: Metric system **Travel Requirements:** Passport, no visa for 21 days, onward ticket

---

The Philippines, an island nation of plentiful resources, has been unable thus far to realize its rich potential for development. Independence, gained in 1946, has failed to produce effective democratic government. A high rate of population growth has eaten up much of the slow increase in gross national product, while the gap between the ruling rich and the restless poor remains wide.

Among the bright spots have been the dramatic advance in food production and the modest growth of industry, particularly electronics companies, which swarmed to Manila in 1978 and 1979. Aided by new agricultural technology, the Philippines progressed from being a major rice importer to self-sufficiency in the staple. The birth rate is one of the highest in the world, and the country needs 500,000 new jobs a year, more than it has been able to provide.

Three hundred years of Spanish rule made the Filipinos, a people of basic Malayan stock, the only Roman Catholic nation in Asia, and left a deep Latin imprint. The subsequent 48-year administration of the extensive archipelago by the United States helped impose a Western educational and political structure, but surging nationalism has recently led the people to try to cast off their long dependence on the United States.

Philippine elections have never been free of violence and corruption, and Ferdinand E. Marcos' decisive victory in the November 1969 race was accompanied by widespread charges of fraud, vote-buying, and intimidation, as well as by huge spending. Marcos, assaulted by a mob in January 1970 as he was leaving the national Congress building, blamed Communism for the climate of violence, while acknowledging that the discontent could be resolved only by creating more jobs, removing social inequities, reforming the machinery of government and developing a constructive nationalism.

In September 1972, Marcos tightened his grip on the reins of power by imposing martial law. In January 1973, he proclaimed the ratification of a new constitution changing the Philippines from a presidential to a parliamentary form of government. Yet he also extended martial law.

Miffed by U.S. criticism of reported human rights violations, Marcos called a national election for April 1978 (the first in six years) to choose members of an interim parliament that is to legislate until martial law is lifted and a regular parliament is formed. (Before permitting the vote, Marcos guaranteed himself a seat in the new assembly, along with the offices of president and prime minister.)

Marcos' strategy, however, backfired badly, as his brief cautious relaxation of restrictions on political activity just prior to the election led to an outburst of antigovernment sentiment, punctuated by public demonstrations against his authoritarian rule. (His main rival, former Senator Benigno Aquino, had to campaign from prison, where he faced a death sentence on a questionable murder conviction.) Though the election results—widely considered fraudulent—showed Aquino to have done poorly, the episode is thought to have gained him considerable new support. At one rally, 30,000 persons cheered as youthful protestors burned Marcos in effigy. An attempted march on Manila, protesting the disputed election, led to the arrest of 600 workers, students and nuns.

In 1979, Marcos ran into a slumping economy, a phenomenal jump in the cost of imported oil, and an open statement by Jaime Cardinal Sin, the Roman Catholic archbishop of Manila, that Filipinos he has talked with "have lost all hope of a peaceful solution to our present ills and are seriously thinking of something violent." The cardinal, who with other bishops spoke out against alleged military abuses, urged Marcos to "prepare the machinery" for elections. In the southern Philippines, the Moslem insurrection dragged on; in central Luzon and the central islands, the Communist New People's Army, with possibly 3,000 members, harassed government troops in rural areas.

HISTORY: For centuries after the birth of Christ the Philippine archipelago was an area of trade and settlement for Southeast Asian people of Malay stock. The area came into the sphere of European influence when it was discovered in 1521 by Magellan. By 1571 the Spanish had assumed control over the Philippines (named for Philip II of Spain) and for next 300 years ruled the islands as a colony
1898: Control of Philippines is ceded to the United States following Spanish-American War
1899: Guerrilla war breaks out against the Americans, ending with complete pacification of islands by 1905
1934: United States passes Philippine independence law providing for a 10-year period for final transfer of sovereignty
1941: Japanese attack Philippines without warning
1945: All of Philippines are freed of Japanese troops
1946: On July 4 the Republic of the Philippines is proclaimed. Independence is followed by widespread unrest and violence by Communist-led Huk guerrillas
1947: Under a 99-year treaty (amended, 1959), Philippines grants U.S. use of 23 strategically vital military bases
1954: Huk rebellion is largely put down
1970: Leftist students stage antigovernment demonstrations; Manila is crippled by general strike
1971: Urban disturbances and guerrilla violence continue. President Marcos accuses Communists of inciting rebellion
1972: Marcos imposes martial law
1973: New constitution goes into effect. Marcos assumes indefinite rule; extends martial law; receives endorsement by electorate, voting in national referendum. Conflict triggered by Moslem insurgency grows
1976: Manila absorbs the national capital area of Quezon City
1977: Voters reject a plan calling for a provisional government in the southwestern portion of the Philippines. Talks are deadlocked over the demands of the Moro National Liberation Front for control of the proposed autonomous region
1978: With an eye on U.S. and world opinion, Marcos briefly lifts ban (imposed in 1972) on political activity, prior to election of "interim" national assembly. Election results, allegedly fraudulent, show big win for Marcos' New Society Movement. Propaganda value is mitigated by antigovernment demonstrations and mass arrests. Two Moslem countries, Malaysia and Indonesia, fail in attempts to settle conflict between Marcos' government and the Mindanao-Sulu Moslems
1979: The total of Moslems fleeing the southern Philippines for Sabah, a nearby Malaysian state, passes the 100,000 mark. A treaty gives the U.S. "unhampered use" of Clark Air Force Base and the Subic Bay naval facility, over which the Filipino flag is raised for the first time; the U.S. agrees to give $500 million in military and economic aid over five years
1980: Moslem rebel activity continues. Typical, on the island of Mindanao in March, are grenade attacks that kill 20 and injure 200 in movie theaters and other public places in the towns of Ozamiaz and Iligan

---

POLAND

Area: 120,725 sq. mi. **Population:** 35,409,000 (1980 est.)
Official Name: Polish People's Republic **Capital:** Warsaw **Nationality:** Polish **Languages:** Polish is the official and universal language **Religion:** About 95% of the population is Roman Catholic; the rest are Eastern Orthodox, Protestant, Jewish, and of other or no affiliation **Flag:** Horizontal bands of white over red **Anthem:** National Anthem, beginning "Poland still is ours forever" **Currency:** Zloty (33 per U.S. $1)

Location: Eastern Europe. Poland is bounded on the north by the Baltic Sea, on the east by the Soviet Union, on the south by Czechoslovakia, and on the west by East Germany **Features:** The country consists mainly of lowlands, except the mountains on its southern border **Chief Rivers:** Vistula, Oder, Bug, Warta, Narew, San

Political Leader: First Secretary of the Central Committee of the United Workers' Party: Stanislaw Kania, born 1927, elected Sept. 6, 1980 **Head of State:** Chairman of the Council of State: Henryk Jablonski, born 1909, reelected 1976 **Head of Government:** Chairman of the Council of Ministers (Premier): Józef Pińkowski, born 1929 ?, appointed Aug. 24, 1980 **Effective Date of Present Constitution:** July 1952, amended 1976 **Legislative Body:** Parliament (unicameral Sejm), with 460 members elected for 4 years. The Sejm is virtually a rubber stamp for the endorsement of party programs **Local Government:** 49 provinces and 3 city provinces, each with a local people's council and a presidium

Ethnic Composition: The population is virtually homogeneous (98% Polish), with Ukrainians and Byelorussians constituting tiny minorities **Population Distribution:** 56% urban **Density:** 293 inhabitants per sq. mi.

Largest Cities: (1976 est.) Warsaw 1,448,900, Lodz 804,300, Cracow 693,800, Wroclaw 579,600, Poznan 521,600, Gdańsk 426,800, Szczecin 372,900

Per Capita Income: $3,384 (1979) **Gross National Product (GNP):** $119 billion (1979) **Economic Statistics:** 65.9% of the GNP is derived from industry (mining, steel, ships, machine manufacture, chemicals, power production, and foodstuffs); 9.1% is derived from commerce, and 8.9% from agriculture (wheat, rye, potatoes, oats, barley, sugar beets) **Minerals and Mining:** There are large deposits of coal, lignite, sulphur, copper ore, salt, vanadium, titanium, natural gas and zinc **Labor Force:** 18,800,000 (1977), with 32% in agriculture and forestry, 25% in industry **Foreign Trade:** Exports, chiefly copper, sulphur, coal, ships, textiles, steel, cement, chemicals, and foodstuffs, totaled $13.5 billion (1978). Imports, mainly oil, iron ore, fertilizers, wheat, and leather footwear, totaled $15.3 billion **Principal Trade Partners:** USSR, East Germany, Czechoslovakia, West Germany, Britain, United States, Iran, Italy, France, Romania, Austria

Vital Statistics: Birthrate, 19 per 1,000 of pop. (1977); death rate, 9.0 **Life Expectancy:** 71 years **Health Statistics:** 129 inhabitants per hospital bed; 615 per physician (1976) **Infant Mortality:** 24 per 1,000 births (1977) **Illiteracy:** negligible **Primary and Secondary School Enrollment:** 5,627,132 (1976) **Enrollment in Higher Education:** 575,499 (1975) **GNP Expended on Education:** 6% (1976)

Transportation: Paved roads total 40,000 mi. **Motor Vehicles:** 2,116,300 (1977) **Passenger Cars:** 1,547,300 **Railway Mileage:** 16,683 **Ports:** Gdansk, Gdynia, Szczecin **Major Airlines:** Polish Airlines LOT operates both domestically and internationally **Communications:** Government controlled **Radio Transmitters:** 51 **Licenses:** 8,230,000 (1976) **Television Transmitters:** 69 **Licenses:** 6,822,000 (1976) **Telephones:** 2,753,000 (1976) **Newspapers:** 44 dailies, 248 copies per 1,000 inhabitants (1975)

Weights and Measures: Metric system **Travel Requirements:** Passport, visa (2 photos, $10 fee) for 90 days

---

Four times in Poland's postwar history workers' revolts have set the nation on new economic and political courses. The first was in 1956, when factory employees in Poznan took to the streets to demand food. A political convulsion followed, bringing Wladyslaw Gomulka to power as first secretary of the Polish United Workers (Communist) party and ending much of the repression of the Stalinist period. Fourteen years later, in December 1970, port workers in Gdańsk marched in protest and set in motion the riots that led to Gomulka's downfall. His replacement, Edward Gierek, charted new policies in an effort to repair the errors of Gomulka's autocratic rule and improve the living conditions of the average Polish citizen. The June 1976 riots over food-price increases were a warning to Gierek's regime of what had happened twice before. The fourth great upheaval occurred in July and August 1980, when thousands of workers went on strike in Gdańsk and other Baltic cities. The strike caused a major shakeup in the government.

Gierek with his premier, Piotr Jaroszewicz, a trained economist, recharted Poland's five-year economic plan for 1971-75, emphasizing consumer industries and raising wages significantly. Following the 1976 riots, a system of compulsory deliveries for farmers was replaced by long-term contract deliveries, and planning has been even more consumer-oriented. Gierek also opened the state-controlled press to a limited measure of meaningful debate. Poland has expanded business and political relations with the West, especially West Germany, Britain, and the U.S.

Gierek sought to resume normal relations with the Roman Catholic Church. In 1979, the Polish-born Pope John Paul II visited Poland—according to the government as sovereign of the Vatican City-State on the occasion of the 35th anniversary of the Communist regime. But the Pope ostensibly paid tribute to the 900th anniversary of the murder of Saint Stanislaw, whose festival the government had refused to allow him to attend, and praised the saint as an opponent of oppressive government. The large crowds attending the Pope strengthened the church's hand against the government.

The national crises of 1980 began in July 1980, when scattered work stoppages in Gdańsk, Ursus, and a few other cities protested large price increases for certain meats. By mid-August over 150,000 workers in the Baltic area were on strike demanding not only improvement in economic conditions but also greater liberalization of political rights. On August 24 Gierek announced that Józef Pińkowski had replaced Edward Babiuch as premier. Three other members of the Central Committee of the party were dismissed in the shakeup. At the month's end, strikes had spread to mining and manufacturing centers throughout the country, and the government agreed to the formation of independent trade unions. On September 6, Gierek resigned as party chief for health reasons, and was replaced by Stanislaw Kania, a party chief concerned with security matters.

HISTORY: The recorded history of Poland dates from the 10th century, when Slavic tribes in the region united and their conversion to Christianity began. The medieval era was one of incessant wars, culminating in the defeat of the Teutonic Knights by Poland and Lithuania, united under the Jagiello dynasty. After the last Jagiello king died in 1572, Polish power began a gradual decline as a result of internal weaknesses and external conflicts. Beginning in 1772, and despite the national uprising of 1794 led by Thaddeus Kosciusko, successive partitions eliminated Poland as a sovereign state, a condition that persisted until the close of World War I

1918-21: Independent Polish republic is proclaimed; Versailles Treaty gives Poland access to Baltic Sea through Polish Corridor, free city of Danzig is set up; attempts by Allies to award Poland's eastern provinces to Russia lead to war between the 2 countries in 1920; Poles, aided by French, defeat Russians and win most of territorial claims in 1921 Treaty of Riga

1926-35: General Joseph Pilsudski, former chief of state, governs as virtual dictator after overthrowing democratic government; at his death in 1935, he is succeeded by Edward Smigly-Rydz

1939-45: Germany and Soviet Union, allied in nonaggression pact, invade Poland in September 1939, and the country is once again partitioned; all Poland comes under Nazi rule after Germany attacks USSR in 1941; about six million Poles, half of them Jews, are exterminated by Nazis, and 2.5 million more are deported to Germany as slave labor; Soviet troops reenter Poland in 1944; in August, Poles stage Warsaw uprising, which is crushed by Germans while Soviet forces remain inactive outside city; Germans are expelled in 1945

1947: Soviet-dominated government claims huge majority in the officially controlled elections of 1947; Communist regime proceeds to Sovietize country

1956: Workers and students in Poznan stage mass demonstration against Communist rule and Soviet control; Wladyslaw Gomulka becomes leader of the Polish United Workers' (Communist) party; Stefan Cardinal Wyszynski, under arrest since 1953, is released

1968: Poland joins Soviet Union and other Warsaw Pact members in invasion of Czechoslovakia. At home a campaign against "Zionists" and "revisionists" is waged

1970: Agreement is reached with West Germany on diplomatic relations, including acceptance of Oder-Neisse line as border between Germany and Poland. Economic unrest leads to ouster of Gomulka, who is succeeded by Edward Gierek

1973: Rapprochement with the Vatican

1974: Land reform law reorganizes small farms into larger units in exchange for increased social benefits

1975: Administrative reform changes the three-level system of local government into a two-level system, increasing Gierek's power. Gierek is named first secretary for a second five-year term

1976: Workers stage violent demonstrations and strikes to protest proposed drastic increases in food prices

1978: World's first Polish astronaut accompanies Russian on eight-day mission in Soviet spacecraft during which they rendezvous with two Russian astronauts aboard Salyut 6 space lab

1979: Polish-born Pope John Paul II draws huge crowds during visit to Poland

1980: Edward Babiuch replaces Piotr Jaroszewicz as premier. At 8th Communist Party Congress, Gierek admits economy is in bad shape, says economic recovery in 1980s will be slow. Workers in Gdańsk and other cities protest meat price hikes with work stoppages. Strike spreads until 350,000 workers are on strike. Józef Pińkowski supplants Babiuch as premier; other party leaders dismissed in major change. Government gives into the strikers' demand for independent trade unions. Gierek resigns; he is succeeded by Stanislaw Kania as party leader

PORTUGAL

Area: 35,549 sq. mi. **Population:** 9,866,000 (1979 est.)

Official Name: Portuguese Republic **Capital:** Lisbon **Nationality:** Portuguese **Languages:** Portuguese is the official and universal language **Religion:** 97% Roman Catholic **Flag:** Green and red vertical stripes, the red covering two-thirds of the flag; at the dividing line is the national coat of arms encircled in gold **Anthem:** The Portuguese **Currency:** Escudo (49.1 per U.S. $1)

Location: Western Europe, occupying the western portion of the Iberian peninsula. Portugal is bounded on the north and east by Spain and on the south and west by the Atlantic Ocean **Features:** The Tagus River divides the country into 2 distinct regions, the north being mountainous and the south consisting of rolling plains **Chief Rivers:** Tagus, Douro, Guadiana, Sado, Mondego

Head of State: President: Gen. António dos Santos Ramalho Eanes, born 1935, elected 1976 **Head of Government:** Premier Francisco Sá Carneiro, born 1934, appointed Dec. 29, 1979 **Effective Date of Present Constitution:** April 1976 **Legislative Body:** Parliament (unicameral Assembly), with 246 members elected for 4 years. An all-military Revolutionary Council reviews Assembly laws as to their constitutionality **Local Government:** 22 districts (including locally autonomous Madeira and the Azores), each with an appointed governor and district assembly

Ethnic Composition: The people are a homogeneous mixture of ethnic strains, including Celtic, Arab, Berber, Roman, Germanic, and Iberian **Population Distribution:** 37% urban **Density:** 278 inhabitants per sq. mi.

Largest Cities: (1975 est.) Lisbon 829,900, Oporto 335,700; (1973 est.) Amadora 65,870, Coimbra 55,985, Barreiro 53,690

Per Capita Income: $1,754 (1979) **Gross National Product (GNP):** $17.3 billion (1979) **Economic Statistics:** 43% of the GNP is derived from mining, manufacturing, and construction (electronics, textiles, wines, cork, food processing, ship-building, and ship repair) 18% from agriculture (grains, fruits, vegetables, wines); 14% from commerce and finance; and 25% from services **Minerals and Mining:** Wolfram, cassiterite, beryl, copper pyrites, and iron ore **Labor Force:** 4.1 million (1978), with 34% in services, 33% in agriculture, and 33% in industry **Foreign Trade:** Exports, chiefly cork, sardines, wines, textiles, minerals, machinery, and diamonds, totaled $2.4 billion in 1978. Imports, mainly machinery and industrial equipment, petroleum products, optical instruments, cotton, steel, wheat, and corn, amounted to $4.7 billion **Principal Trade Partners:** West Germany, United States, Britain, France, Italy, Spain, Sweden, Iraq

Vital Statistics: Birthrate, 19.2 per 1,000 of pop. (1976); death rate, 10.5 **Life Expectancy:** 69 years **Health Statistics:** 187 inhabitants per hospital bed; 817 per physician (1975) **Infant Mortality:** 39 per 1,000 births (1975) **Illiteracy:** 29% **Primary and Secondary School Enrollment:** 1,676,378 (1975) **Enrollment in Higher Education:** 79,702 **GNP Expended on Education:** 3.7% (1975)

Transportation: Paved roads total 24,800 mi. **Motor Vehicles:** 1,322,000 (1976) **Passenger Cars:** 1,034,000 **Railway Mileage:** 2,214 **Ports:** Lisbon, Leixões, Setúbal, Funchal, Douro **Major Airlines:** Transportes Aéreos Portugueses (TAP) flies internationally **Communications:** Government owned **Radio Transmitters:** 180 **Licenses:** 1,525,000 (1976) **Television Transmitters:** 42 **Licenses:** 723,000 (1976) **Telephones:** 1,119,000 (1976) **Newspapers:** 30 dailies, 70 copies per 1,000 inhabitants (1975)

Weights and Measures: Metric system **Travel Requirements:** Passport, no visa for 60 days

Portugal is the poorest country in Western Europe. Most of its people still make their living from the soil, but there is a bitter division between the hilly north, with its small independent farmers, and the more level south, where landless peasants lived for centuries in fear of the owners of huge estates. Portugal's experiment in democratic socialism, which began in 1976, has been complicated by misunderstanding between the individualistic northerners and the southern peasants, who tend to favor collectivism.

Another complicating factor is Portugal's relative lack of experience with democracy. António de Oliveira Salazar, who was premier from 1932 to 1968, governed as a harsh dictator, and his successor, Marcello Caetano, made few meaningful changes.

Salazar and Caetano hoped that Portugal would become a developed capitalist state, and favored the tiny class of entrepreneurial families. But these families drew most of their surplus capital from Portugal's African territories, which revolted against Portuguese rule in the 1960s. Linked to the entrepreneurial class and caught up in romantic nationalism, Salazar and Caetano drained Portugal of manpower and resources to suppress the revolts in Africa.

Caetano was overthrown in 1974 by the Armed Forces Movement (MFA), a coalition of soldiers who were tired of the struggle in Africa and sympathetic to socialism. The MFA government granted independence to the African territories— destroying the entrepreneurial class and all chance of development along completely capitalistic lines.

A National Assembly was elected in April 1975. "Rightist" parties had been outlawed, but the Social Democratic Center became the voices of those favoring a role for private enterprise. The Socialist party won a plurality in the Assembly, but the MFA remained in control of the government.

Despite continued unrest, a new constitution was adopted in 1976; it is distinctly socialist, and is democratic in all its essentials, although it reserves some power for the military-dominated Revolutionary Council. Gen. António dos Santos Ramalho Eanes was elected president; the National Assembly became an effective legislature; most restrictions on freedom of expression ended; and peace returned to the country.

The weak economy and continued arguments over the return to private ownership of farms illegally seized in 1974 have troubled the fledgling democracy. Mário Soares was premier in a minority socialist government from July 1976 to December 1977. In January 1978, he formed a majority coalition with the Social Democratic Center—actually the most non-socialist of the major parties. President Eanes dismissed him in July after the coalition broke down, and appointed a government of technocrats who were not members of the Assembly. Soares complained that a government drawn from outside the Assembly was unconstitutional, and the Assembly rejected the technocratic government. But Soares did not object at first when a second government of technocrats, with Carlos Alberto Mota Pinto as premier, took office in October with the Assembly's approval. However, in June 1979, Soares and the socialists joined the Communists in forcing Mota Pinto to submit to his government's resignation. Maria de Lurdes Ruivo da Silva Matos Pintassilgo was appointed to head a caretaker government.

In the elections of Dec. 2, 1979, the moderate Democratic Alliance won 45 percent of the popular vote, while the Socialist party got only 27 percent. The alliance gained a three-seat majority in the National Assembly and formed a new government with Francisco Sá Carneiro as premier. the cabinet which took office in early 1980 was without military representation for the first time since the 1974 coup. The new government's proposals for economic reform were blocked by the Revolutionary Council, pending new elections.

HISTORY: Lusitania, the western part of the Iberian peninsula, was conquered by Julius Caesar and Augustus. The Visigoths gained control over most of the region in the 5th century A.D. and maintained their rule until the coming of the Moors three centuries later. Portugal was established as an independent state by 1185 and was consolidated after the final expulsion of the Moors in 1249. Its independence, however, remained threatened by Castile until 1385, when the Castilians were defeated in battle

15th cent.: Prince Henry the Navigator captures Ceuta, on northwest African coast, in 1415; under his aegis, Portuguese navigators undertake series of voyages that result in rediscovery of Madeira Islands and penetration of Africa; Vasco da Gama becomes first European to sail to India (1497-99)

1500-20: Pedro Cabral reaches coast of Brazil in 1500 and claims land for Portugal

1580-1640: Philip II of Spain seizes Portuguese throne, beginning Portugal's 60-year period of "Spanish Captivity"; Portuguese revolt against Spanish rule and regain independence under John of Braganza, who becomes king

1807: Napoleon's forces march on Portugal

1822: Brazil declares its independence

1910: Manuel II is deposed by revolution; Portugal is declared a republic

1932: António de Oliveira Salazar, former finance minister, becomes premier after a long period of civil unrest and political instability; he institutes dictatorial rule

1961: India annexes Portuguese enclave of Goa; Portuguese crush insurrection in Angola, in southwest Africa

1968: Marcello Caetano becomes premier

1974: Liberal reforms initiated following bloodless coup which toppled Caetano and installed António de Spínola as president. He is succeeded later the same year by Francisco da Costa Gomes. Violent clashes occur between revolutionary and rightist forces

1975: In April, the first free elections in almost half a century give an Assembly majority to moderates and centrists. Azevedo replaces Gonçalves as premier

1976: New constitution is enacted. António dos Santos Ramalho Eanes is elected president and appoints Mário Soares premier

1977-78: International Monetary Fund issues stringent conditions as price to Portugal for $750-million loan; ensuing austerity measures lead to collapse of government. Soares forms new government of Socialists and conservatives, which also collapses; President Eanes dismisses him. Carlos Alberto Mota Pinto becomes premier in government of technocrats

1979: Mota Pinto submits government's resignation; Senhorita Pintassilgo is appointed caretaker premier. Democratic Alliance wins plurality in parliamentary elections

1980: New cabinet is headed by Premier Francisco Sá Carneiro

QATAR

Area: 4,247 sq. mi. **Population:** 250,000 (1979 est.)

Official Name: State of Qatar **Capital:** Doha **Nationality:** Qatari **Language:** Arabic is the official and dominant language; English and Farsi are spoken by some **Religion:** 98% of Qataris are Sunni Moslems of the Wahabi sect. **Flag:** Maroon with white serrated border near the hoist **Anthem:** National Anthem (no words) **Currency:** Qatari riyal (3.65 per U.S. $1)

Location: Southwest Asia. Qatar forms a 100-mile long peninsula stretching north into the Persian Gulf. It borders Saudi Arabia and the United Arab Emirates on the south **Features:** A low, hot, dry plain, consisting of nearly flat limestone with loose sand and gravel on top **Rivers:** None

Head of State and of Government: Emir: Khalifa ibn Hamad al-Thani, born 1937, assumed power in 1972. He is advised by an appointed Council of Ministers which he heads as prime minister **Effective Date of Present Constitution:** 1970; not fully implemented **Legislative Body:** A 30-member advisory council **Local Government:** 6 municipal councils

Ethnic Composition: Arabs (38%), Pakistanis (29%), Iranians (15%), others (18%). The population is almost 80% non-native **Population Distribution:** 71% urban **Density:** 59 inhabitants per sq. mi.

Largest Cities: Doha 150,000, (1976 est.); Umm Said 5,500 (1972 est.)

Per Capita Income: $38,743 (1979) **Gross National Product (GNP):** $6.5 billion (1979) **Economic Statistics:** Qatar's national income derives almost wholly from oil recovery; revenues totaled $3.5 billion in 1978 **Minerals and Mining:** Oil is the chief resource; natural gas deposits are being developed; limestone and clay are also mined **Labor Force:** 80,000 (82% non-Qatari) with about 70% in industry, service and commerce, 20% in government and 10% in agriculture **Foreign Trade:** Exports totaled $2.5 billion in 1978, 99% from oil. Imports, chiefly consumer goods and industrial equipment, totaled $1.2 billion **Principal Trade Partners:** EC countries, United States, Japan, India

Vital Statistics: Birthrate, 50 per 1,000 of pop. (1974); death rate, 19 **Life Expectancy:** 47 years **Health Statistics:** 96 inhabitants per hospital bed; 938 per physician (1974) **Infant Mortality:** 42 per 1,000 births (1972) **Illiteracy:** 75% **Primary and Secondary School Enrollment:** 35,613 (1976) **Enrollment in Higher Education:** 910 **GNP Expended on Education:** 2.0% (1975)

Transportation: Paved roads total 275 mi. **Motor Vehicles:** N.A. **Railway Mileage:** None **Ports:** Doha, Umm Said **Major Airlines:** Gulf Air serves Doha **Communications:** Government owned **Radio Transmitters:** 6 **Receivers:** 40,000 (1976) **Television Transmitters:** 3 **Receivers:** 30,000 (1976) **Telephones:** 29,400 (1978) **Newspapers:** 2 dailies

Weights and Measures: Metric system **Travel Requirements:** Passport, visa, valid 6 months, 2 photos

Oil production, begun shortly after World War II and now valued at roughly $3.5 billion a year, is the country's economic base. With oil proceeds, roads have been built, a sea-distilled water supply established, an educational program instituted, and free medical services introduced. Steps toward diversification have included the exploitation of the Gulf's fishery potential, the production of cement from local raw materials, encouragement of investment in domestic projects, investigation of the mechanics of natural gas recovery, transportation, marketing and usage, and the introduction of domestic refining. Qatar has developed a steel and petrochemical industry.

After Britain declared it would withdraw its military forces from the Persian Gulf area by the end of 1971, Qatar declared its independence on September 1, 1971. The ruler of Qatar, Emir Ahmad ibn Ali ben Abdullah al-Thani, was deposed in a bloodless coup by his cousin, Emir Khalifa ibn Hamad al-Thani, on February 22, 1972.

Qatar is a member of the Organization of Petroleum Exporting Countries (OPEC), and the government has gone along with the organization's anti-Israeli policies. Qatar severed diplomatic relations with Egypt in 1979 in concert with other Arab countries after the Egyptian-Israeli peace treaty was signed. It has increased oil prices periodically to the OPEC base price of $32 per barrel of crude oil as of June 1980.

HISTORY: For a long time Qatar was under Persian rule, and paid a bounty to the governor of Bushire for the right to fish for pearls. In the 19th century it became independent of Persia under Thani, the founder of the al-Thani dynasty
1871-1913: Qatar is occupied by Ottoman Turks
1916: Qatar comes under British protection
1971: Qatar declares its independence
1973: Qatar announces embargo on oil to U.S.
1977: Government completes nationalization of all oil operations
1979: Qatar cuts diplomatic ties with Egypt after Egyptian-Israeli peace treaty

---

ROMANIA

Area: 91,699 sq. mi. **Population:** 21,855,000 (1978 est.)
Official Name: Socialist Republic of Romania **Capital:** Bucharest
Nationality: Romanian **Languages:** Romanian is the official and dominant language. Hungarian, German, Ukrainian, and Yiddish are minority languages **Religion:** About 80% of the population nominally belongs to the Romanian Orthodox Church, and about 9% to the Roman Catholic Church. The rest are mainly Protestant, Jewish, and Moslem **Flag:** Blue, yellow, and red vertical stripes with the national coat of arms in the center **Anthem:** The Tricolored Song **Currency:** Leu (4.47 per U.S. $1)
Location: Southeastern Europe. Romania is bounded on the northeast by the Soviet Union, on the east by the Black Sea, on the south by Bulgaria, on the southwest by Yugoslavia, and on the west by Hungary **Features:** The Carpathian Mountains and Transylvanian Alps form a semi-circle through the center of the country, separating the plains in the east and south from the Transylvanian plateau in the northwest **Chief Rivers:** Danube, Prut, Siret, Olt, Ialomita, Jiu, Mures
Political Leader and Head of State: President Nicolae Ceausescu, born 1918, elected 1974, reelected 1975; since 1965, Secretary-General of the Central Committee of the Romanian Communist Party, and since 1967 president of the State Council, the primary legislative body **Head of Government:** Prime Minister Ilie Verdet, born 1924, appointed 1979 **Effective Date of Present Constitution:** August 1965 **Legislative Body:** Grand National Assembly (unicameral), consisting of 349 members elected for 5 years; it actually performs little legislative work **Local Government:** 39 counties with people's councils elected for 5 years, and Bucharest municipality
Ethnic Composition: 88% of the population is of Romanian stock, tracing its ancestry back to the Latin settlers of the Roman Empire. Hungarians (8%) are the leading ethnic minority, with smaller numbers of Germans, Ukrainians, Serbo-Croats, Jews, and Turks

Population Distribution: 48% urban **Density:** 238 inhabitants per sq. mi.
Largest Cities: (1977 est.—Metropolitan Areas) Bucharest 1,934,025, Constanta 290,226, Iasi 284,308, Timisoara 282,691, Cluj 262,421, Brasov 262,041
Per Capita Income: $3,586 (1979) **Gross National Product (GNP):** $79 billion (1979) **Economic Statistics:** In 1975 industry and construction accounted for 70% of the national income, while agriculture accounted for 16% **Minerals and Mining:** Large deposits of petroleum, natural gas, copper, lead, zinc, bauxite, manganese, bismuth, mercury, silver, iron ore, and coal **Labor Force:** 12 million (1977) with 40% in agriculture and 25% in industry **Foreign Trade:** Exports, mainly oilfield equipment, farm and other machinery, furniture and textiles totaled $8 billion in 1978. Imports, chiefly machinery and equipment, iron ores, coke, fuel, and electric motors, totaled $9 billion **Principal Trade Partners:** West Germany, USSR, Czechoslovakia, Italy, Britain, France, East Germany, Poland, China, United States, Iran, Switzerland, Libya
Vital Statistics: Birthrate, 19.6 per 1,000 of pop. (1977); death rate, 9.6 **Life Expectancy:** 70 years **Health Statistics:** 108 inhabitants per hospital bed; 750 per physician (1976) **Infant Mortality:** 31.2 per 1,000 births (1977) **Illiteracy:** negligible **Primary and Secondary School Enrollment:** 4,110,930 (1975) **Enrollment in Higher Education:** 381,321 (1976) **GNP Expended on Education:** N.A.
Transportation: Paved roads total 17,680 mi. **Motor Vehicles:** 45,100 (1970) **Railway Mileage:** 6,910 **Ports:** Constanta, Galati, Braila **Major Airlines:** Tarom flies internationally and domestically **Communications:** Government owned **Radio Transmitters:** 62 **Licenses:** 3,104,000 (1976) **Television Transmitters:** 194 **Licenses:** 2,963,000 (1976) **Telephones:** 1,076,000 (1974) **Newspapers:** 20 dailies, 129 copies per 1,000 inhabitants (1974)

Weights and Measures: Metric system **Travel Requirements:** Passport, visa, valid 60 days

---

For centuries a rural, backward country, Romania has the largest oil fields (now declining) of any country in Eastern Europe. Building on oil wealth, the Romanians have invested in modern chemical, steel, machinery, and related industries. Close economic ties have been fostered with Western Europe as well as with the Soviet bloc.

Although it remains a member of the Warsaw Pact military alliance and of the Communist Council for Mutual Economic Assistance, Romania has successfully asserted its right to conduct its own foreign affairs. Alone among the Eastern European conutries, Romania was outspoken in criticizing the Russian invasion of Afghanistan in late 1979.

Not wanting to be merely a supplier of raw materials and agricultural products to the more developed Communist countries, Romania has persistently refused to subordinate its desire for rapid economic development to Soviet plans for complete integration of Eastern European and Soviet economies. The nation's industrial production was expected to increase by 8.5% in 1980—the largest gain among Eastern European countries. But Romania's trade deficit with the West totaled about $1 billion in 1979, mainly because of a decline in exports and a rise in the cost of imports.

The heart of Romanian tactics aimed at resisting Moscow's pressure is a balancing act. Its essence is the matching of moves that irritate Moscow with moves that are pleasing. For instance, President Nicolae Ceausescu was the first East European leader to establish (1967) diplomatic relations with West Germany and the first leader of a Communist country in a quarter century to be visited by a U.S. president (Nixon in 1969).

More recently, this balancing act has become noticeable in Ceausescu's handling of political dissidents. In 1978 the government freed a group of political dissidents as part of an amnesty program in celebration of Romania's 100th anniversary of independence from Turkey. However, Ceausescu continues to keep a tight rein on the dissidents.

Ceausescu in 1974 strengthened his position as undisputed leader by naming himself president, installing a colorless loyalist, Manea Manescu, as premier, and abolishing the nine-member presidium, the top ruling body of the Communist party. He replaced the presidium with a twenty-three-member Executive Committee which is packed with loyalists. In 1979 President Ceaucescu appointed Ilie Verdet as premier on the retirement of Manescu.

HISTORY: Ancient Dacia, comprising most of present-day Romania, was part of the Roman Empire until the 3rd century A.D. After the Romans legions withdrew, the region was overrun by Goths, Huns, Avars, Slavs, and Mongols. The withdrawal of the Mongols in the 13th century was followed by the establishment of the principalities of Walachia and Moldavia, which soon fell under Turkish rule. Both were to remain in the Ottoman Empire until well into the 19th century

1828-29: Walachia and Moldavia are occupied by Russia in Russo-Turkish War; although technically remaining part of the Ottoman Empire, they actually become Russian protectorates

1859-66: Alexander John Cuza is elected prince of Walachia and Moldavia, which are officially united as Romania in 1861; 5 years later, Cuza is deposed and is succeeded by Carol I of the house of Hohenzollern-Sigmaringen

1878: Congress of Berlin grants Romania full independence

1916-19: Romania fights on Allied side in World War I; overrun by Austro-German forces, it is forced to accept a harsh peace treaty, which is later annulled by the Allied victory; Romania seizes Bessarabia from Russia, Bukovina from Austria, and Transylvania from Hungary

1938: King Carol II establishes Fascist dictatorship

1940-45: Under German pressure, Romania returns territories taken from Russia and Hungary; King Carol is overthrown by Marshal Ion Antonescu, aided by Iron Guard, a militaristic Fascist group; in 1941, Romania enters World War II on Axis side; following the invasion of Soviet troops in 1944, Antonescu is overthrown and Romania switches to Allied side; a Communist-led government is set up in 1945

1964: Showing increasing independence of the Soviet Union, Romanian Communist party asserts the right of each Communist party to form its own political program without interference

1968: Romania supports liberalization program in Czechoslovakia and refuses to join in invasion of Czechoslovakia by Soviet and other Warsaw Pact forces

1971: After declining to do so a year earlier, Romania joins the Soviet bloc's new international investment bank

1974: Communist Party Central Committee approves constitutional change establishing the office of President, which is assumed by Ceausescu. Manea Manescu becomes premier

1975: U.S. Congress passes resolution granting Romania most-favored-nation trade status

1977: Earthquake kills at least 1,500. Ceausescu asks for eight more years of austerity and sacrifice to raise Romania to ranks of developed nations

1979: Government established regional councils to supervise agriculture. Ilie Verdet becomes premier

RWANDA

Area: 10,169 sq. mi. **Population:** 4,819,000 (1978 est.)

Official Name: Republic of Rwanda **Capital:** Kigali **Nationality:** Rwandan **Languages:** Kinyarwanda (the national language) and French are the official languages; Kiswahili is spoken in the commercial centers **Religion:** More than 55% of the population is Christian, chiefly Roman Catholic; the rest are animist and Moslem **Flag:** Vertical stripes of red, yellow, and green with a black "R" in the center **Anthem:** Our Rwanda **Currency:** Rwanda franc (92.8 per U.S. $1)

Location: Central Africa. Landlocked Rwanda is bordered on the north by Uganda, on the east by Tanzania, on the south by Burundi, and on the west by Zaire **Features:** Known as the "Land of a Thousand Hills," the country consists largely of grassy uplands and hills, which roll down southeastward from the chain of volcanoes in the northwest **Chief Rivers:** Kagera, Nyabarongo, Akanyaru

Head of State and Government: President: Maj. Gen. Juvénal Habyarimana seized power in a bloodless coup July 1973 **Effective Date of Present Constitution:** Dec. 17, 1978 **Legislative Body:** National Development Council (unicameral) of 50 members **Local Government:** 10 prefectures, administered by appointed prefects

Ethnic Composition: 89% Hutu, a Bantu farming people; 10% Tutsi, a pastoral people of Hamitic origin; 1% Twa pygmies **Population Distribution:** 5% urban **Density:** 474 inhabitants per sq. mi.

Largest Cities: (1975 est.) Kigali 60,000, Butare 20,000

Per Capita Income: $174 (1978) **Gross National Product (GNP):**

$760 million (1978) **Economic Statistics:** 60% of the GNP is derived from agriculture (bananas, coffee, pyrethrum, tea, cotton, manioc, corn, spices, sweet potatoes); 18% from mining (cassiterite, columbo-tantalite, wolfram, amblygonite, beryl), 16% from commerce, and 6% from construction and manufacturing **Minerals and Mining:** Cassiterite is the most abundant mineral, although columbo-tantalite, wolfram, amblygonite, and beryl are also mined. There are unexploited deposits of bismuth, phosphates, monazite, magnatite, and natural gas **Labor Force:** 1,940,000 (1970), with 95% engaged in small handicrafts or agriculture, and less than 5% in industry. Wage earners numbered 70,000 in 1973 **Foreign Trade:** Exports, mainly Arabica coffee, cassiterite, tea, and wolfram, totaled $103 million in 1978. Imports, chiefly textiles, iron, petroleum, and vehicles, totaled $102 million **Principal Trade Partners:** Belgium, France, United States, Britain, Japan, Kenya, Iran, West Germany

Vital Statistics: Birthrate, 50 per 1,000 of pop. (1975); death rate, 23.6 **Life Expectancy:** 44 years **Health Statistics:** 510 inhabitants per hospital bed; 42,900 per physician (1976) **Infant Mortality:** 132.9 per 1,000 births **Illiteracy:** 75% **Primary and Secondary School Enrollment:** 446,720 (1976) **Enrollment in Higher Education:** 1,108 (1975) **GNP Expended on Education:** 2.6% (1976)

Transportation: Paved roads total 200 mi. **Motor Vehicles:** 11,300 (1975) **Passenger Cars:** 6,500 **Railway Mileage:** None **Ports:** None **Major Airlines:** Transport Airline of Rwanda operates international and domestic flights **Communications:** Government controlled **Radio Transmitters:** 4 **Receivers:** 70,000 (1976) **Television:** None **Telephones:** 3,000 (1975) **Newspapers:** 1 daily, .04 copies per 1,000 inhabitants (1975)

Weights and Measures: Metric system **Travel Requirements:** Passport, visa for stay up to 3 months, $10 fee, 4 photos

Rwanda, formerly part of the Belgian UN trust territory of Ruanda-Urundi, is Africa's most densely populated country. Nearly four and a half million people live in an area slightly smaller than the state of Maryland. Small and landlocked, it lies atop the mountainous western slope of the Great Rift Valley known as "the Roof of Africa." Through centuries of migratory settlement and population increase, the clearing of land for food production, together with overgrazing of cattle, has made Rwanda one of tropical Africa's most eroded areas. Its people contend with drought as well as poor soil in raising their crops of beans, bananas, sorghum, cassava, corn, and potatoes.

Despite erosion, Rwanda possesses scenic grandeur and great touristic potential, especially around Lake Kivu, considered by many the most beautiful of African lakes. However, the serene-looking highlands have known dark tragedy. In 1959-60, the Hutu people, the short stocky peasants who made up 85 percent of the population, rose up in bloody revolt against the Tutsi (or Watusi), the tall aristocratic people who kept the Hutu in feudal bondage for centuries. Thousands of Tutsi were killed or fled into neighboring countries. Neither willing nor able to stem the tide of Hutu unrest, the Belgian administration gave support to the Hutu on the eve of independence. In 1961 the Tutsi king, Mwami Kigeri V, was deposed and a republic declared, causing more than 160,000 Tutsi to flee to Burundi. Many returned later but in 1963-64 an armed invasion by Tutsi refugees set off another massacre of the tall people and put an apparent end to their minority caste domination.

Since independence, the government has concentrated on food production and the building of internal roads and road links into neighboring coastal countries. More than a fourth of national expenditures are for education and there has been some progress in light industry, but the major problems—population pressures, malnutrition, and poverty—remain largely unsolved.

In July 1973 Rwanda's manifold problems were compounded further as the government of President Grégoire Kayibanda was overthrown in a bloodless military coup, after months of tribal unrest between the governing Hutu majority and the Tutsi minority. The leader of the coup, Maj. Gen.

Juvénal Habyarimana emerged as the apparent leader of the country.

HISTORY: Rwanda, along with neighboring Burundi, originally was inhabited by the pygmy Twa people, and later occupied by Bantu Hutus from the Congo basin. By the 15th century, the Tutsi, or Watusi, a tall, cattle-keeping people believed to have originated in Ethiopia, had arrived in both countries and imposed a feudal overlordship on the more numerous Hutus. European explorers reached the area in the 19th century, and in 1885 the region was taken over by Germany. It was made a Belgian League of Nations mandate after World War I and remained under Belgian control after World War II. With the growth of African nationalism, Hutu leaders in Rwanda began seeking independence and emancipation from Tutsi domination

1955-58: Tutsi extremists, viewing Belgian political reforms as threat, repress Hutu movement and murder several Hutu leaders

1959: Bloody Hutu revolt overthrows Tutsi monarchy; Tutsis suffer heavy casualties and 120,000 of them flee to Burundi and other neighboring countries

1960: Leaders of Hutu Emancipation Movement (PARMEHUTU) establish provisional government

1961: Belgium recognizes PARMEHUTU regime, but United Nations, hoping to preserve ethnic-economic union of Rwanda and Burundi, rules it unlawful and orders elections; PARMEHUTU scores overwhelming victory

1962: UN resolution ends Belgian trusteeship and grants Rwanda full independence

1963: Abortive Tutsi invasion from Burundi results in massacre of 12,000 Tutsi in Rwanda and renewed Tutsi exodus

1970: Rwanda signs friendship pact with Belgium; work is begun on road link to Kampala, Uganda

1973: President Grégoire Kayibanda overthrown in bloodless military coup; Maj. Gen. Juvénal Habyarimana takes over

1974: Death sentences of ex-President Kayibanda and seven other government officials commuted to life imprisonment

1976: Ugandan oil blockade brings economic hardship

1978: Habyarimana is elected to a 5-year term as president

1979: Rwanda plays host to 6th Franco-African summit conference

---

SAINT LUCIA

Area: 238 sq. mi. **Population:** 112,000 (1978 est.)

Official Name: Saint Lucia **Capital:** Castries **Nationality:** Saint Lucian **Languages:** English is the official language; a French patois containing many African elements is widely spoken **Religion:** Chiefly Roman Catholic (90%), with several Protestant churches represented **Flag:** A blue field containing a white-bordered black triangle covered at the bottom by a yellow triangle **Anthem:** N.A. **Currency:** East Caribbean dollar ($2.70 per U.S. $1)

Location: St. Lucia, the second largest of the Windward Islands, lies south of Martinique and northeast of St. Vincent in the Eastern Caribbean **Features:** The island is of volcanic origin and mountainous, with magnificent scenery; there is a good harbor at Castries. The climate is tropical and humid, with heavy rainfall in the summer

Head of State: Queen Elizabeth II through Acting Governor-General Boswell Williams **Head of Government:** Prime Minister Allan Louisy, born 1916, appointed July 2, 1979 **Effective Date of Present Constitution:** Feb. 22, 1979 **Legislative Body:** Parliament (bicameral) consisting of a House of Assembly with 17 elected members and a Senate of 11 members, of whom 6 are appointed on the advice of the prime minister, 3 by the Opposition, and two by the Governor-General. The Parliament has a five-year term unless dissolved before that time **Local Government:** 16 parishes

Ethnic Composition: Chiefly African or of mixed origin **Population Distribution:** N.A. **Density:** 471 inhabitants per sq. mi.

Largest Cities: (1970 est.) Castries 40,451, Micoud 10,145, Vieux Fort 8,108, Soufrière 7,250

Per Capita Income: $590 (1977) **Gross Domestic Product (GDP):** $65 million (1977) **Economic Statistics:** The economy is primarily agricultural, with tourism and industry gaining in importance. The chief crops are bananas, coconuts, cocoa, citrus fruits, sugar, spices; there is a limited amount of timber production and commercial fishing. Industrial development is increasing rapidly. An oil refining and transshipment facility and an industrial free port zone are under construction **Labor Force:** 26,339 (1970), with 40% engaged in agriculture, 33% in industry, and 21% in services **Foreign Trade:** Exports, including bananas and a growing amount of manufactured goods, totaled $12.7 million in 1978, and imports, including manufactured goods, machinery, food, fuel and clothing, totaled $37.2 million **Prinicipal Trade Partners:** Britain, Commonwealth and CARICOM countries, United States

Vital Statistics: Birthrate, 35.0 per 1,000 of pop. (1975); death rate, 7.3 **Life Expectancy:** 57 years **Health Statistics:** 202 inhabitants per hospital bed; 4,231 per physician (1975) **Infant Mortality:** 19.2 per 1,000 births (1977) **Illiteracy:** 20% **Primary and Secondary School Enrollment:** 25,386 (1976) **Enrollment in Higher Education:** N.A. **GDP Expended on Education:** N.A.

Transportation: Paved roads total 280 mi. **Motor Vehicles:** 5,500 (1975) **Passenger Cars:** 3,700 **Railway Mileage:** None **Port:** Castries **Major Airlines:** St. Lucia Airways and major international airlines **Communications:** Government and privately owned **Radio Transmitters:** 3 **Receivers:** 82,000 (1975) **Television Transmitters:** 1 **Receivers:** 1,700 (1974) **Telephones:** 7,000 (1976) **Newspapers:** 3: 1 twice weekly, 1 weekly, 1 fortnightly; 78 copies per 1,000 inhabitants

Weights and Measures: Metric and British systems are used **Travel Requirements:** Passport and/or return ticket

---

A former British possession in the Windward Islands, Saint Lucia is an island nation characterized by its African heritage, French accent, British political system and all the social and economic burdens attendant on many newly independent mini-states. Independence was attained on February 22, 1979.

Traditionally tied to agriculture for its livelihood, the island had embarked on the path of new industrial and commercial development. The largest single project is a combined oil transshipment terminal and free trade zone being developed by American oil interests. The manufacturing sector has been expanded, accounting for nearly half of the island's exports. The island's even climate and great beauty has made tourism a major industry, especially since the construction of a modern jetport outside Castries in 1975. In addition, traditional cash crops such as bananas, cocoa and coconuts have been bolstered under a development plan supported by the World Bank and the International Monetary Fund.

Yet, although St. Lucia's future appears bright in comparison with some of its neighbors, it shares many of their problems. Dependence on imports of finished goods was responsible for a balance of payment deficit of $24 million in 1978. And unemployment remains endemic, at a staggering 30 percent annually. These economic woes, plus continued political strife over the progress towards independence, has sometimes marred the tranquility of this tropical paradise.

A landslide victory for the opposition Labor party in the July 2, 1979, general elections turned Prime Minister Compton and his United Workers party out of power after 15 years. A moderate, Compton had sought close cooperation with the Caribbean Economic Community (CARICOM) and closer ties with oil-rich Venezuela, as well as opting for termination of the islands's colonial status by mutual agreement with Britain. The new prime minister is Allan Louisy, a retired judge.

HISTORY: Little is known of the island's early history, but successive waves of Amerindian migration are thought to have populated the island in the 1300s. By the time of the first European landing, in the 16th century, the island was inhabited by the war-like Caribs. Initially a Spanish possession, the first attempts at settlement were made by the English, in 1605 and 1638-40; both succumbed to the Caribs. Subsequent French settlement proved more successful. Britain and France fought for control of the island over the next 150 years, with the last British occupation—in June, 1803—finally accepted by France in the Treaty of Paris in 1814. A plantation economy flourished, based on slavery; by 1834, when slavery was abolished in all British possessions, the island's African population numbered over 13,000.

1838: St. Lucia, administered as a separate colony, is merged with the government of the Windward Islands

1958: St. Lucia joins Federation of the West Indies; remains member until its dissolution is 1962

1959: St. Lucia separated from Windward group, becomes dependency under direct British administration

1962-65: Discussions ensue between St. Lucia and other smaller British territories on federation with Barbados, without success

1967: St. Lucia becomes self-governing member of the West Indies Associated States May 3
1974: Elections return United Workers party government to power; Prime Minister John G.N. Compton promises full independence
1977: July 24-27 constitutional conference in London agrees on framework for independence
1979: Independence attained Feb. 22; Labor party boycotts ceremony, as striking teachers and civil servants threaten the new nation's stability. Labor party scores upset victory over Compton's UWP, winning 12 of 18 Assembly seats in first post-independence election. Allan Louisy becomes prime minister. Saint Lucia joins three other Caribbean states—Jamaica, Grenada, and Guyana—in charging the United State with warmongering when President Carter establishes a Caribbean Contingency Joint Task Force in Key West, Fla.

SAINT VINCENT AND THE GRENADINES

Area: 150 sq. mi. **Population:** 104,000 (1978 est.)
Official Name: Saint Vincent and the Grenadines **Capital:** Kingstown **Nationality:** Saint Vincentian **Languages:** English, with some French patois spoken **Religion:** Methodist, Anglican and Roman Catholic **Flag:** Five unequal vertical stripes of blue, white, yellow, white and green with a breadfruit leaf, scroll, sprig of cotton and coat of arms centered on the yellow stripe **Anthem:** National Anthem, beginning "St. Vincent! Land So Beautiful" **Currency:** East Caribbean dollar (2.70 per U.S. $1)

Location: Eastern Caribbean. The islands are situated south of St. Lucia and north of Carriacou Island, a part of Grenada **Features:** The island of St. Vincent, 18 miles long and 11 miles wide, is volcanic in origin with a mountain ridge running its length and rising in the north to Soufrière volcano. The climate is tropical with heavy summer rains. The Grenadines portion consists of the islands of Bequia, Canouan, Mayreau, Mustique, Prince, Palm, Petite St. Vincent and Union, among others

Head of State: Queen Elizabeth II, represented by a governor-general, Sir Sydney Douglas Gun-Munro **Head of Government:** Prime Minister Robert Milton Cato, born 1915, appointed Dec. 1979 **Effective Date of Present Constitution:** Oct. 27, 1979 **Legislative Body:** House of Assembly (unicameral) with 13 elected representatives and 6 senators (4 appointed on the advice of the prime minister and 2 on the advice of the opposition leader). The normal term is 5 years **Local Government:** 5 parishes plus the Grenadines

Ethnic Composition: Mainly of African or mixed origin **Population Distribution:** N.A. **Density:** 693 inhabitants per sq. mi.

Largest City: (1978 est.) Kingstown 25,000

Per Capita Income: $300 (1976) **Gross National Product (GNP):** $33.5 million (1976) **Economic Statistics:** About 20% of GNP is from agriculture (bananas, arrowroot, coconuts, nutmeg, mace, sugar, vegetables). St. Vincent is the world's largest producer of arrowroot. 9% of GNP is from industry (agricultural and food processing, furniture, clothing, sugar refining, flour). Tourism is important **Minerals and Mining:** None **Labor Force:** 50,000 (1972) **Foreign Trade:** Exports, chiefly bananas, arrowroot, copra and mace, totaled $9.9 million in 1977. Imports, mainly fuel, fertilizer, transportation equipment and textiles, totaled $30.3 million **Principal Trade Partners:** Britain, Trinidad and Tobago, Barbados, Canada, United States

Vital Statistics: Birthrate, 31 per 1,000 of pop. (1977); death rate, 10.0 (1973) **Life Expectancy:** N.A. **Health Statistics:** 170 inhabitants per hospital bed (1972) **Infant Mortality:** 55 per 1,000 births (1977) **Illiteracy:** 5% **Primary and Secondary School Enrollment:** 26,938 (1975) **Enrollment in Higher Education:** N.A. **GNP Expended on Education:** N.A.

Transportation: Surfaced roads total 280 mi. **Motor Vehicles:** 4,300 (1976) **Passenger Cars:** 3,500 **Railway Mileage:** None **Port:** Kingstown **Major Airlines:** LIAT and Caribbean Airways provide service **Communications:** Privately owned **Radio Transmitters:** 2 **Receivers:** N.A. **Television Transmitters:** None **Telephones:** 5,000 (1977) **Newspapers:** 1 weekly

Weights and Measures: British system **Travel Requirements:** N.A.

On October 27, 1979, Saint Vincent and its dependent islands, the Grenadines, gained independence after 10 years as a British Associated State. But along with its newly independent neighbors in the Caribbean, St. Vincent faces acute growing pains from social and economic problems as it enters the 1980s.

Dependent on tourism and agriculture for their livelihood, the residents of this tiny nation in the Lesser Antilles average an annual per capita income of $300. Unemployment is estimated at 20 percent of the labor force, and the annual growth rate in the population is 2%, which threatens to put an even greater strain on the country's resources.

Despite these inherent problems, the island prospered in the 1970s, with gross domestic product growing 14 percent between 1976 and 1978. Its favorable climate encouraged good harvests and a booming tourist industry, matched by a modest growth in the manufacturing sector aided by government investment. But the eruption of the long-dormant volcano, Soufrière, on April 13, 1979, proved a heavy blow to the island's fragile economy. Although no one was injured—unlike the last major eruption in 1902, in which 2,000 died—the volcano spewed clouds of ash and smoke over the northern half of St. Vincent, forcing evacuation of 20,000 local residents and gravely damaging the important banana crop. Prospects for immediate relief include $23 million in post-independence aid promised from Great Britain, and $20 million in credits available from the Caribbean Development Bank.

General elections held December 5 of 1979 saw Milton Cato and his moderately socialist Saint Vincent Labour party returned to power. The SVLP won 11 of the 13 seats in the House of Assembly, with the others going to the centrist New Democrats; the conservative People's Political party — which had split with the SVLP after supporting it in the 1974 elections—failed to gain one seat. But balloting was followed by violence from rebels on Union and Palm Islands, who had threatened to secede if the elections did not go their way. Prime Minister Cato declared a state of emergency Dec. 7, and sent the island's police—it has no army—to quell the rebellion. After brief fighting in which one insurgent was killed, the revolt collapsed with the arrest of 19 rebels, including their Rastafarian leader, Rasta Bomba.

HISTORY: The earliest known inhabitants of the island were the Arawak Indians, soon supplanted by the warlike Caribs, who migrated from South America to people most of the Lesser Antilles from 1300 to 1600. Christopher Columbus was the first European to see the island, landing there on January 22, 1498 (Saint Vincent Day). Claimed by the British since 1627, a dispute ensued with France for control of the island, ending only with its formal ceding to Britain in the Treaty of Versailles in 1783. After an abortive uprising by the Caribs in 1795-96, most of the native population was deported to the island of Rattan in the Bay of Honduras, with the island thereafter peopled mainly by African slaves and their descendants
1833: St. Vincent is included in the Government of the Windward Islands, remaining a part of that colony until its dissolution in 1960, when it becomes a separately administered territory
1902: Volcano of Soufrière erupts, killing over 2,000 people
1958: St. Vincent participates in Federation of West Indies until its dissolution in 1962
1962-65: St. Vincent joins in discussions on federation of the Windward Island territories—including Grenada and St. Lucia—with Barbados; talks prove fruitless
1969: St. Vincent becomes an internally self-governing Associated State, with Britain retaining defense and foreign relations responsibility
1974: Milton Cato and St. Vincent Labour party swept into power in Dec. 9 elections, with support of Ebenezer Joshua's People's Progressive party; Cato becomes chief minister
1978: Constitutional talks are held in London Sept. 18-21, with parties agreeing on framework for independence
1979: Soufrière erupts April 13; 20,000 inhabitants are evacuated, crops destroyed and tourism disrupted. St. Vincent and the Grenadines gain their independence from Britain Oct. 27. Dec. 5 general elections to the House of Assembly result in victory for Milton Cato and the SVLP, which wins 11 of 13 seats; but secessionist violence erupts Dec. 7 on Palm and Union Islands; rebellion is quelled Dec. 8
1980: St. Vincent continues ongoing discussions with St. Lucia and Barbados on forming a common coast guard. Prime Minister Cato lifts Dec. 7, 1979, state of emergency May 16

SAN MARINO

Area: 23.4 sq. mi. **Population:** 21,000 (1978 est.)

Official Name: Most Serene Republic of San Marino **Capital:** San Marino **Nationality:** Sanmarinese **Language:** Italian is the official and universal language **Religion:** Roman Catholicism **Flag:** Horizontal bands of white and blue with the national coat of arms in the center **Anthem:** National Anthem, beginning "Honor to you, O ancient Republic" **Currency:** Italian lira (847 per U.S. $1)

Location: Landlocked San Marino is situated in the Apennines, southwest of Rimini, Italy **Features:** The town of San Marino is situated on the slopes of Mount Titano, and much of the republic is coextensive with the mountain, which has three pinnacles **Chief Rivers:** San Marino, Fumicello

Head of State and of Government: 2 Captains Regent, elected by the Council for six-month terms, assisted by a Congress of State (cabinet) **Effective Date of Present Constitution:** October 1600 **Legislative Body:** Great and General Council (unicameral), with 60 members elected every 5 years **Local Government:** 9 parishes (*castelli*), headed by Captains of the Castle and elected committees

Ethnic Composition: The Sanmarinese are of Italian origin. A small number of aliens reside in the republic. **Population Distribution:** 92% urban **Density:** 897 inhabitants per sq. mi.

Largest Town: (1976 est.) San Marino 4,563

Per Capita Income: N.A. **Gross National Product (GNP):** N.A. **Economic Statistics:** The principal occupations are farming, manufacturing, and animal husbandry. Main agricultural products are wheat, cheese and wine, while chief industrial goods are textiles, cement, paper, leather, and furs. Tourism (3 million a year) and the sale of postage stamps are major sources of income **Minerals and Mining:** Building stones are quarried for export **Labor Force:** 4,300 mostly employed in the agricultural sector. The rest work for manufacturing and service industries **Foreign Trade:** Exports consist of wine, woolens, furniture, ceramics, and postage stamps. Manufactured goods of all kinds make up the main imports. Because of a customs union with Italy, exports and imports are not subject to customs duties, and no record is kept of foreign payment transactions **Principal Trade Partner:** Italy

Vital Statistics: Birthrate, 14.8 per 1,000 of pop. (1977); death rate, 6.9 **Life Expectancy:** 72 years **Health Statistics:** Public health institutions include a hospital, a dispensary, and a laboratory of hygiene; 750 inhabitants per physician **Infant Mortality:** 14.8 per 1,000 births **Illiteracy:** Negligible **Primary and Secondary School Enrollment:** 2,884 (1976) **Enrollment in Higher Education:** N.A. **GNP Expended on Education:** N.A.

Transportation: Streets and roads total more than 60 miles **Motor Vehicles:** 9,584 **Passenger Cars:** 4,724 **Railway Mileage:** 20 miles of electric funicular railway **Ports:** None **Radio Transmitters:** There are no local radio or television transmitters; broadcasts are received from Italy **Radio Licenses:** 6,000 (1976) **Television Licenses:** 4,000 (1976) **Telephones:** 6,000 (1976) **Newspapers:** No dailies, but an edition of *Il Resto Del Carlino* of Bologna gives special attention to San Marino news; there are 3 fortnightlies

Weights and Measures: Metric system **Travel Requirements:** Passport, no visa

The Apennine slopes shelter a tiny country with a legendary beginning and an existence almost as fabled. Its founder is said to be Marinus, a Christian stonecutter from Dalmatia seeking refuge from persecution in the fourth century. The republic, named San Marino after the canonized Saint Marinus, is the world's smallest and oldest, having remained independent for some 1,600 years. It lived on after the collapse of the Roman Empire and survived such upheavals as an interdiction by the pope in the Middle Ages, occupation by troops of Giulio Cardinal Alberoni in 1739-40, the conquests of Napoleon, and the unification of Italy in the late 19th century.

San Marino's knack for survival carried it through the Mussolini era and World War II. In 1943 it rid itself of the Fascistlike regime of the Mussolini period, and from 1945 to the autumn of 1957 was ruled by a coalition of Communists and left-wing Socialists. After the defection of six members of the ruling group, an anti-Communist coalition gained control and went on to win subsequent elections. In 1973 that coalition resigned over economic policy disputes. The Christian Democrats formed a new coalition cabinet with Socialists and a splinter party. A coalition of Christian Democrats and Socialists governed from 1976 to 1977; in 1978, a coalition of Communists and Socialists formed a government. No major changes in government policy were made.

San Marino, situated on three-peaked Mount Titano, derives approximately 80 percent of its gross national product from tourism and the sale of postage stamps to collectors. The tourists, numbering about 3 million annually, are afforded a magnificent view of Rimini and the Adriatic Sea from three old fortresses and may visit stately buildings, churches, and museums.

HISTORY: According to tradition, San Marino was founded in the 4th century A.D. by Marinus, a Christian stonecutter from Dalmatia who was later canonized. Reputedly the world's oldest republic, it is the last of the Italian peninsula's once-numerous city-states

1631: Pope Urban VIII recognizes the independent status of San Marino

1739-40: San Marino is occupied by a military force under a papal legate, Giulio Cardinal Alberoni, who attempts to establish sovereignty over republic; occupation is terminated by Pope Clement II

1862: San Marino and Italy form a customs union

1939-44: San Marino, although officially neutral in World War II, is occupied by the German army and is the scene of heavy fighting during Allied advance into northern Italy

1945: Communist and left-wing Socialist coalition wins majority of seats in elections for the Grand Council

1957: Defection of six Council members leads to fall of coalition; anti-Communist councillors form new government

1973: Coalition government resigns; new cabinet is formed with Socialists and Christian Democrats; women are given expanded legal rights

1974: General elections are held and coalition of Christian Democrats and Socialists remains in power. New cabinet is formed. Three women win seats in the Council

1975: Socialists withdraw from the two-party coalition, leaving the Christian Democrats without an absolute parliamentary majority

1976: New coalition of Socialists and Christian Democrats is formed

1977: Socialist-Christian Democrat coalition collapses; Communists fail to form new government

1978: Communists form new government after Christian Democrats, winners of a plurality in May elections, fail to do so

SAO TOME and PRINCIPE

Area: 372 sq. mi. **Population:** 83,000 (1978 est.)

Official Name: Democratic Republic of São Tomé and Principe **Capital:** São Tomé **Nationality:** São Tomean **Languages:** Portuguese is the main language, and a local creole is also spoken **Religion:** Roman Catholicism is the predominant religion **Flag:** Three equal horizontal stripes of green, yellow and green with a red triangle at the hoist and two black stars on the yellow stripe **Anthem:** Total Independence **Currency:** Dobra (34.5 per U.S. $1)

Location: These two islands are in the Gulf of Guinea, about 125 miles off the west coast of Africa **Features:** Hilly, wooded interiors and flat coastal plains **Chief Rivers:** Grande, Abade

Head of State and of Government: President Manuel Pinto da Costa, elected 1975 **Effective Date of Constitution:** 1975 **Legislative Body:** Popular Assembly (unicameral), with members elected for 4 years. Control is in the hands of the MLSTP party, headed by the president **Local Government:** 2 island provinces

Ethnic Composition: The native population is mostly African, with some Portuguese admixture **Population Distribution:** N.A. **Density:** 223 inhabitants per sq. mi.

Largest Cities: (1970 census) São Tomé 7,681; Santo António 1,618

Per Capita Income: $260 (1977) **Gross Domestic Product (GDP):** $19.7 million (1977) **Economic Statistics:** Most of the population is engaged in the growing of plantation agricultural products and fishing **Minerals and Mining:** None **Labor Force:** 40,000, with 62% in agriculture (coffee, cocoa, coconuts, bananas), 7% in industry (beverages, copra, palm oil and fish processing) and commerce **Foreign Trade:** Exports, mostly palm products, coffee, cocoa and fruit, totaled $23 million (1977). Imports totaled $13 million **Principal Trade Partners:** Portugal, Netherlands

Vital Statistics: Birthrate, 45 per 1,000 of pop. (1972); death rate, 11.2 **Life Expectancy:** N.A. **Health Statistics:** 160 inhabitants per hospital bed; 6,666 per physician (1976) **Infant Mortality:** 64.3 per

1,000 births (1973) **Illiteracy: 90% Primary and Secondary School Enrollment:** 17,329 (1976) **Enrollment in Higher Education:** N.A. **GDP Expended on Education:** 2.2% (1972)

Transportation: All roads total 179 mi. **Motor Vehicles:** 2,000 (1973) **Passenger Cars:** 1,600 **Railway Mileage:** None **Ports:** São Tomé (on São Tomé) and Santo António (on Príncipe) **Major Airlines:** Air Gabon and TAG have mainland links **Communications:** Government owned **Radio Transmitters:** 4 **Licenses:** 20,000 (1976) **Television:** None **Telephones:** 900 **Newspapers:** 2 weeklies (1972)

Weights and Measures: Metric system **Travel Requirements:** Passport, visa

---

One of Africa's smallest countries, São Tomé and Príncipe is part of an extinct volcanic mountain range.

The islands' economy is based on cocoa, with copra and coffee also important. A steep drop in the world price of cocoa has greatly affected the new country's financial outlook. The crops are grown on company-owned plantations worked by labor imported from Mozambique and Angola. This temporary labor force outnumbers the permanent population, which largely refuses to work on the plantations, where conditions have been much criticized. Most of the 1,000 white settlers, who ran the plantations, and the Cape Verdeans, who served as foremen, left the islands after independence was declared. Malnutrition is a major health problem.

São Tomé and Príncipe, which lie 150 miles west of Gabon in the Gulf of Guinea, became independent on July 12, 1975, after 500 years of Portuguese rule, the fourth and smallest of Portugal's African territories to emerge from colonial status. Manuel Pinto da Costa was proclaimed first president by the political bureau of the Gabon-based Movement for the Liberation of São Tomé and Príncipe.

HISTORY: São Tomé and Príncipe were discovered in 1471 by the Portuguese, who began to settle convicts and exiled Jews on the islands and to establish sugar plantations using slaves from the African mainland

1951: The islands are designated a Portuguese Overseas Province

1975: São Tomé and Príncipe becomes independent

1979: Miguel Trovoada, whose post as prime minister had been abolished in April is reported to have staged an unsuccessful coup in September and taken refuge in UN mission

---

SAUDI ARABIA

Area: 829,995 sq. mi. **Population:** 7,866,000 (1978 est.)

Official Name: Kingdom of Saudi Arabia **Capital:** Riyadh (Jidda serves as the administrative center, and Taif is the summer capital) **Nationality:** Saudi Arabian **Languages:** Arabic is the official and universal language **Religion:** The overwhelming majority of the population is Sunni Moslem, and Islam is the state religion **Flag:** Green, with a white sword below the Arabic inscription "There is no god but God, and Mohammed is His Prophet" **Anthem:** Royal Anthem of Saudi Arabia, a short instrumental selection **Currency:** Saudi riyal (3.32 per U.S. $1)

Location: Arabian peninsula in Southwest Asia, Saudi Arabia is bounded on the north by Jordan, Iraq, and Kuwait; on the east by the Persian Gulf, Qatar, the United Arab Emirates, and Oman; on the south by Yemen and Southern Yemen, and on the west by the Red Sea **Features:** Nine-tenths of the country is covered by a barren plateau, including the Rub al-Khali and Al-Nafud desert regions. In the west, the Hejaz mountains border the narrow coastal plain along the Red Sea; to the east of the central plateau is the low-lying coastal region along the Persian Gulf **Chief Rivers:** There are no permanent rivers

Head of State and of Government: King Khalid ibn Abdul-Aziz Al Saud, born 1913, succeeded to the throne in March 1975. He named himself premier and his brother, Crown Prince Fahd ibn Abdel Aziz Al Saud, first deputy premier **Effective Date of Present Constitution:** None. Authority is based on Islamic law (Shari'a) and on Bedouin tradition **Legislative Body:** None. The appointed Council of Ministers performs some legislative functions **Local Government:** 18 provinces, 6 major and 12 minor, each with an appointed governor

Ethnic Composition: The population is largely homogeneous, descended from indigenous Arab tribes, with some admixture of Africans, Turks, Iranians, Indians, and Indonesians. At present about 30% are expatriates **Population Distribution:** 28% urban **Density:** 9.5 inhabitants per sq. mi.

Largest Cities: (1974 census) Riyadh 666,840, Jidda 561,104, Mecca 366,801, Taif 204,857, Medina 198,186, Dammam 127,844

Per Capita Income: $10,958 (1979) **Gross National Product (GNP):** $71 billion (1979) **Economic Statistics:** 62% of GNP is derived from industry, (oil refining, electrical goods, fertilizers, cement, iron and steel) and mining (80% in oil); 15% from trade and services; and 4% from agriculture (dates, grain, vegetables, livestock) **Minerals and Mining:** Saudi Arabia is the world's second-largest producer of oil. Other abundant minerals are natural gas, gypsum, copper, salt, manganese, silver, gold, sulphur, and lead **Labor Force:** About 2.7 million (one-half foreign), with 44% in commerce, services and government, 28% in agriculture, 21% in construction, 4% in industry and 3% in oil **Foreign Trade:** Exports, 99% petroleum and petroleum products, totaled $45 billion in 1978. Imports, principally motor vehicles, cereals, and power generating machinery, totaled $18 billion **Principal Trade Partners:** United States, West Germany, Japan, Italy, Netherlands, Britain, France

Vital Statistics: Birthrate, 49.5 per 1,000 of pop. (1975); death rate, 20.2 **Life Expectancy:** 45 years **Health Statistics:** 840 inhabitants per hospital bed; 2,200 per physician (1976) **Infant Mortality:** over 110 per 1,000 births (1976) **Illiteracy:** 70% **Primary and Secondary School Enrollment:** 908,905 (1975) **Enrollment in Higher Education:** 26,437 (1975) **GNP Expended on Education:** 10% (1977)

Transportation: Paved roads total 10,000 mi. **Motor Vehicles:** 112,000 (1974) **Passenger Cars:** 59,400 **Railway Mileage:** 357 **Ports:** Jidda, Dammam, Yenbo, Ras Tanura, Jubail **Major Airlines:** Saudia (Saudi Arabian Airlines), government owned, operates both domestic and international flights **Communications:** Government controlled **Radio Transmitters:** 20 **Receivers:** 260,000 (1976) **Television Transmitters:** 11 **Receivers:** 130,000 (1976) **Telephones:** 200,000 **Newspapers:** 11 dailies, 11 copies per 1,000 inhabitants (1974)

Weights and Measures: Metric system **Travel Requirements:** Passport, transit visa valid 72 hours, no charge, onward ticket. No tourist visas issued

---

The world's 587 million adherents of Islam regard Saudi Arabia with a special reverence because it contains Mecca, the holiest of holy sites. The birthplace of the Prophet Mohammed, Mecca is the direction to which these Moslems turn as they bow in prayer five times each day. It is the destination of some half million people a year from all parts of the world who follow the Koranic exhortation of making the pilgrimage, or *Haj*, during one's lifetime. Closed to non-Moslems, the city contains the Great Mosque, or *Haram*, and the *Kaaba*, with its sacred Black Stone.

The ruler of Saudi Arabia is considered the custodian of the holy sites and the chief defender of Islam. In addition, the present ruler, King Khalid, is the secular head of one of the world's leading oil-exporting countries and, consequently, one of its richest men, although his realm consists mostly of vast expanses of trackless desert. The combination of these functions has long given the Saudi king a strong voice in the Arab world.

Saudi Arabia has been also a country in which the deep Arab tradition of hospitality conflicts with an equally strong xenophobic tendency. It is a country where distrust of Western "imperialism" and American support for Zionism is often overshadowed by dependence on American technology and a fear of Communism.

The assassination of King Faisal by a nephew in 1975 caused reverberations throughout the Middle East. Faisal's brother, Crown Prince Khalid, succeeded him as king and named himself premier and Crown Prince Fahd first deputy premier. The new leaders are less concerned with fierce anti-Communism and are slightly more moderate on the Arab-Israel dispute.

Saudi Arabia has used its tremendous financial power to exert diplomatic pressure and has assumed a major role as a mediator in Middle Eastern affairs. Saudi Arabia has exercised a moderating influence on other Arab nations in raising oil prices in recent years.

The Saudi position in regard to the United States is ambivalent. On the one hand, the government maintains close ties with Washington as the leader of the non-Communist world and admires American know-how; but Saudi Arabia does not hesitate to pressure the United States to stop supporting Israel. In practice, the chief link between Saudi Arabia and the United States is their oil relationship. Saudi Arabia has the largest known oil reserves in the world (180 billion barrels), and the United States has been the world's leading consumer, by far, of Saudi Arabian oil, now being produced at the rate of about 9.5 million barrels a day. Soon after oil was discovered in the Saudi deserts in the 1930s, King Ibn Saud, Khalid's father, granted primary exploitation rights to the Standard Oil Company of California. The concession was subsequently transferred to the Arabian American Oil Company, known as Aramco, a conglomerate of several oil companies. Still 40 percent owned by four American oil companies, Aramco is the world's largest oil-producing company.

Aside from Islam, Aramco is perhaps the dominant force in Saudi Arabia. The Saudis have made some attempts to diversify the economy by encouraging agricultural and industrial development, but even the new projects involve Aramco because the company is often the final contractor. It has become almost an administrative arm of the Saudi government; it builds and runs schools and housing, constructs and maintains roads, and manages other important projects.

Before his assassination, King Faisal drafted a far-reaching and comprehensive plan calling for $142 billion in investment and affecting all areas of development. Cities are being transformed with modern buildings; new highway systems are complete, even with rush-hour traffic jams; and two major new industrial centers are being built at Jubail in the midst of Saudi Arabia's Gulf Coast oil fields and at Yanbu, the Red Sea port for Medina. A $15-20 billion gas-gathering system—a project larger than the trans-Alaska pipeline—is being built by an Arabian-American company. Other projects are giant desalination plants and a new airport the size of Manhattan Island to serve Jidda.

Although much of Saudi Arabia's oil revenue goes either to these projects or to the armed forces, some of it is now being spent for social welfare. Free medical service has been made available to all citizens, and elementary, secondary, and higher education is also free, although not compulsory. By contrast, the religious tenets of Islam, which form the common law of the land, are enforced with fundamentalist zeal.

On November 20, 1979, the Grand Mosque in Mecca, which is Islam's holiest shrine, was seized by a band of some 500 Islamic militants, whose leader claimed to be the *Mahdi*, or messiah of the Shiite Moslems. Saudi soldiers retook the mosque by December 4, but some 300 militants and 60 soldiers were killed. Another 63 raiders were executed in early 1980. The Saudi government unofficially declared that the seizure had been led by religious fanatics but was supported by certain international leftist forces.

The Saudi government protested the showing in the United States of a controversial television film, based on the actual 1977 execution of a Saudi princess for adultery, which was broadcast by about 100 Public Broadcasting stations on May 12, 1980. The *Death of a Princess* documentary drama had been broadcast earlier in Britain, and to show its displeasure, the Saudi government had forced the British ambassador to leave the country temporarily. The U.S. State Department conveyed the Saudis' concern over the showing of the film to the Public Broadcasting Service, but made clear that the Federal government could not exercise censorship to prevent the film from being shown.

HISTORY: Arabia has been inhabited for thousands of years by nomadic Semitic tribes. Followers of Mohammed, who was born in Mecca in the 6th century A.D., conquered most of the area between Persia on the east and Spain on the west, but Arabia itself declined in importance. As a political unit, Saudi Arabia is of relatively recent origin, dating from the 18th century, when the Saud family, adherents of the puritanical Wahabi movement, gained control over most of the Arabian peninsula

19th cent.: Wahabi movement is crushed (1811) by Egyptian expedition led by Mohammed Ali; movement revives temporarily, only to be defeated by Rashid dynasty, which gains control of central Arabia and expels Saud family

1902-32: Ibn Saud, the exiled Wahabi leader, conquers the Nejd, Hasa, and Hejaz regions and forms the kingdom of Saudi Arabia

1936: Oil is discovered near the Persian Gulf

1953: Ibn Saud dies and is succeeded by his eldest son, Saud

1962: Saud dispatches aid to royalist troops in Yemen after pro-Nasser revolutionaries depose Imam. Relations with Egypt are severed

1964: Saud is deposed and succeeded by Crown Prince Faisal, who introduces sweeping government reorganization and abolishes slavery. Relations with Egypt are restored

1967-68: Saudi Arabian troops are sent to Jordan during six-day Arab-Israeli war but take no part in fighting. King Faisal halts aid to Yemeni royalists in return for withdrawal of Egyptian troops; however, aid is temporarily resumed to counteract support for republicans by Soviet Union, Syria, and Southern Yemen

1969: Hundreds are arrested as government acts to head off attempt at coup d'état

1970: Resumption of ties to Yemen is marked by financial aid from Saudi Arabia

1973: The Yom Kippur War prompts King Faisal to cut exports of oil to the U.S. by 10 percent in order to compel the U.S. to demand a cease-fire and Israeli withdrawal from Arab territory

1975: King Faisal is assassinated by his nephew, Prince Faisal ibn Musad Abdel Aziz, 31; the king's brother, Crown Prince Khalid ibn Abdul-Aziz al Saud, 62 succeeds him

1976: Saudis hold down OPEC price increases to 5 percent

1978: Saudi Arabia buys 60 F-15 jet fighter-planes from U.S.

1979: Moslem militants seize and hold Grand Mosque in Mecca for two weeks before Saudi soldiers retake the holy shrine

1980: Saudi Arabian jetliner burns at Riyadh airport killing 301

SENEGAL

Area: 76,124 sq. mi. **Population:** 5,381,000 (1978 est.)

Official Name: Republic of Senegal **Capital:** Dakar **Nationality:** Senegalese **Languages:** French is the official language; among the spoken African languages, Wolof is used by nearly 50%, and Peul (Fulani), Mende, Diola and Mandingo are other main languages **Religion:** More than 80% of the population are Moslems; about 5% are Christians, and the rest animists **Flag:** Vertical stripes of green, yellow, and red with a green star in the center **Anthem:** National Anthem, beginning "Pluck your koras, strike the balafons" **Currency:** CFA Franc (210.2 per U.S. $1)

Location: West Africa. Senegal is bounded on the north by Mauritania, on the east by Mali, on the south by Guinea and Guinea-Bissau, and on the west by the Atlantic Ocean. The nation of The Gambia is an enclave within Senegal **Features:** The country is a transitional zone between the Sahara and the equatorial jungle with semidesert in the north, and open savanna in the center and south **Chief Rivers:** Senegal, Saloum, Gambia, Casamance

Head of State: President Léopold Sédar Senghor, born 1906, re-elected 1978 **Head of Government:** Premier Abdou Diouf, born 1935, reappointed 1978 **Effective Date of Present Constitution:** March 3, 1963, amended 1976 **Legislative Body:** National Assembly (unicameral), consisting of 100 members elected for 5 years **Local Government:** 8 regions, each headed by an appointed governor

Ethnic Composition: The largest ethnic group, the Wolof, makes up about 36% of the population. Other important groups are the Peul (Fulani), with 17.5%; the Serere, with 16.5%; the Tukulor, with 9%; Diola, with 9%; and the Mandingo, with 6.5%. A small non-African population, largely French, is concentrated in Dakar **Population Distribution:** 35% urban **Density:** 71 inhabitants per sq. mi.

Largest Cities: (1976 census) Dakar 798,792, Thiès 117,353, Kaolack 106,899, St-Louis 88,404, Ziguinchor 72,726, Rufisque 66,995, Diourbel 50,618, Mbour 37,663, Louga 35,063

Per Capita Income: $359 (1979) **Gross National Product (GNP):** $2 billion (1978) **Economic Statistics:** In 1978 about 38% of GNP was derived from trade and finance; 30% from agriculture and fishing (peanuts, accounting for about half of total production; fish; millet; sorghum; rice; cassava; potatoes; livestock); 20% from manufacturing (peanut oil mills, cement, food processing, textiles, leather, shoes, chemicals, and phosphate mining) **Minerals and Mining:** Calcium and aluminum phosphates, limestone, titanium, salt, and ilmenite are being worked **Labor Force:** Of 1,732,000, 80% are engaged in agriculture **Foreign Trade:** Exports, chiefly peanuts, phosphates, and canned fish, totaled $391 million in 1978. Imports, mainly food, textiles, machinery, chemical and petroleum products, totaled $716 million **Principal Trade Partners:** France, United States, Britain, Netherlands

Vital Statistics: Birthrate, 47.6 per 1,000 of pop. (1975); death rate, 23.9 **Life Expectancy:** 44 years **Health Statistics:** 853 inhabitants per hospital bed; 17,066 per physician (1976) **Infant Mortality:** 62.7 per 1,000 births (1972) **Illiteracy:** 90% **Primary and Secondary School Enrollment:** 373,534 (1975) **Enrollment in Higher Education:** 8,213 (1975) **GNP Expended on Education:** 3.0% (1976)

Transportation: Paved roads total 1,840 mi. **Motor Vehicles:** 69,800 (1974) **Passenger Cars:** 44,800 **Railway Mileage:** 642 **Ports:** Dakar, Kaolack, Ziguinchor, Saint-Louis **Major Airlines:** Air Senegal **Communications:** Government controlled **Radio Transmitters:** 14 **Receivers:** 290,000 (1976) **Television Transmitters:** 2 **Receivers:** 35,000 (1974) **Telephones:** 39,000 (1976) **Newspapers:** 2 dailies (1975), 7 copies per 1,000 inhabitants (1974)

Weights and Measures: Metric system **Travel Requirements:** Passport, visa, valid 3 months, 2 photos, $4.75 fee

---

Ever since it gained independence, discouraging economic reverses have beset Senegal, the former administrative and commercial center of the defunct French West African empire. In colonial times, the French federation, with a population of 20 million, was the market for industry and business based on the great port of Dakar, the Senegalese capital.

With the grant of independence also to other French African possessions, the federation was divided into nine separate and sovereign states. Although still closely tied to France economically, all were eager for their own commercial and industrial development as well as new trade outlets through other countries.

Forced to rely on its own meager resources and limited aid from France and other sources, Senegal has experienced increasing economic difficulty. Peanuts, introduced by the French more than a century ago, are the main cash crop. In the past, they have accounted for nearly 80 percent of exports and provided the main income for more than 90 percent of Senegalese. But with the end of French subsidies, lower prices and droughts, production has fallen sharply and, despite urgent government appeals, growing numbers of farmers have stopped planting peanuts.

American and other foreign assistance is gradually increasing production of rice, millet, sorghum, sugar, and livestock, but the effort is offset by the rapid fall in export earnings, rising debt, and tightened budgets.

Compounding these problems have been the continuing severe drought and famine plaguing not just Senegal but other countries of the sub-Sahara. An estimated 100,000 people died in 1973 and millions more were starving in the sub-Sahara region. Relief efforts were hampered by poor transportation and communications facilities.

President Léopold Senghor, Senegal's leader before and since independence, has shown considerable skill in maintaining stability despite his many problems. A longtime Francophile and also a poet of note, Senghor has appeared confident that economic problems would be solved by France. In March 1974 Senegal and France signed 44 agreements constituting a total renegotiation of the accords reached upon Senegal's independence in 1960. Terms of the accords included partial withdrawal of French troops and the transfer of a military base at Dakar to Senegal. Relations with Arab countries, however, have become closer. Senegal

broke off diplomatic relations with Israel in October 1973, and in 1976 sponsored a UN Commission on Human Rights resolution accusing Israel of war crimes in the occupied Arab territories. Relations with Israel grew more hostile in 1979 as Jerusalem refused to permit Senegalese troops to cross its borders with the rest of the UN Interim Force in Lebanon after Israeli authorities had arrested a Senegalese officer on charges of aiding Arab guerrillas.

In the 1970s the aging Senghor brought younger men and union leaders into his government. His choice as new premier was Abdou Diouf, an industrious and capable administrator. A 1976 constitutional amendment providing for the succession of the head of state makes Diouf the successor-designate to Senghor.

HISTORY: Senegal was largely dominated by the Moslem Tukuler tribe until 1893, when the Tukuler dynasty was overthrown by the French. European settlement, however, had begun as early as the 15th century, when the Portuguese settled along the Senegalese coastline. The French established a foothold in the area in the 17th century and by the 19th century Senegal was the center of French West Africa. In 1946, along with other parts of French West Africa, Senegal became part of the French Union

1958: Senegal becomes an autonomous republic within the newly formed French Community. Léopold-Sédar Senghor elected president

1959-60: Senegal is joined with the Sudanese Republic in the short-lived Mali Federation, which is dissolved after strong political differences develop between the two states

1962-63: Premier Mamadou Dia is ousted after bitter conflict with National Assembly; Senghor takes control of government and new constitution is adopted incorporating the office of premier with the presidency; new elections are held and Senghor, the only presidential candidate, is reelected

1964: All opposition parties are banned, except for small African Reunion party

1968: Senghor is reelected for five-year term and an unopposed list of 80 candidates of his party, the Senegalese Progressive Union, is elected to National Assembly. Widespread strikes by students and workers break out in protest against government austerity measures

1969: Senghor declares state of emergency to deal with unrest

1970: Senegal denies use of its roads as supply route for Portuguese Guinea rebels. Constitution revised; post of premier is reinstated and Abdou Diouf is chosen to fill it

1973: Severe drought affects crop production

1974: New political party, Senegalese Democratic party, formed

1976: At a conference of the Organization of African Unity and the Arab League in Dakar, President Senghor calls for a union of the two groups and for the establishment of an Arab-African arbitration and conciliation court

1978: Senghor is reelected in first multiparty election in 12 years. Senegal secures $26-million loan from International Monetary Fund to offset economic effects of drought

1979: Work begins on $550-million three-nation Senegal River irrigation and hydroelectric project

1980: Senghor pays ceremonial visit to the United States

SEYCHELLES

Area: 171 sq. mi. **Population:** 63,000 (1979 est.)

Official Name: Republic of Seychelles **Capital:** Victoria **Nationality:** Seychellois **Languages:** Creole is spoken by 94% of the population; English and French are official **Religion:** 91% Roman Catholic, 8% Anglican **Flag:** A field of red over green separated by a wavy white band **Anthem:** National Anthem, beginning "Seychellois staunch and true" **Currency:** Seychellois rupee (6.34 per U.S. $1)

Location: Indian Ocean. The republic lies about 1,000 miles east of Kenya, just south of the Equator **Features:** An archipelago of about 90 islands, it is divided almost equally between a Granitic Group and a Coralline Group. Mahé (4°45′S.,55°30′E.), the mountainous main island, comprises just over half of the total area, and contains most of the population **Chief Rivers:** None

Head of State and of Government: President France Albert René, born 1934, assumed office in coup in June 1977, elected 1979 **Effective Date of Present Constitution:** March 26, 1979 **Legislative Body:** National Assembly (unicameral) consists of 25 members. The Seychelles People's Progressive Front is the only party **Local Government:** 8 districts, one including all outlying island groups

Ethnic Composition: Most are descendants of 18th century French settlers and their African slaves, with a later mixture of other Europeans and Asians; there is a small minority of Indians and Chinese **Population Distribution:** 26% urban **Density:** 368 inhabitants per sq. mi.

Largest City: (1971 census) Victoria 13,736

Per Capita Income: $1,470 (1977) **Gross Domestic Product (GDP):** $89 million (1977) **Economic Statistics:** Percentages of GDP not available. Plantation agriculture (coconuts, vanilla, cinnamon, patchouli, fibers) and fishing at a subsistence level engage most of the population. Tourism is the chief income-making industry, and there is processing of coconuts and vanilla **Minerals and Mining:** None **Labor Force:** 19,827 in 1971; 55% of the wage earners are engaged in tourism and agricultural processing, and 27% in plantation agriculture **Foreign Trade:** Exports, chiefly copra, coconut oil, cinnamon bark, dried fish, vanilla oil, and patchouli, totaled $3 million (1978). Imports, mainly foods, manufactured goods, textiles, machinery, and petroleum products, totaled $55 million **Principal Trade Partners:** Pakistan, Britain, Kenya, Mauritius, South Africa

Vital Statistics: Birthrate, 25.9 per 1,000 of pop. (1977); death rate, 7.7 **Life Expectancy:** 65 years **Health Statistics:** 200 inhabitants per hospital bed; 2,857 per physician (1975) **Infant Mortality:** 43.2 per 1,000 births (1977) **Illiteracy:** 20% **Primary and Secondary School Enrollment:** 12,986 (1976) **Enrollment in Higher Education:** 142 (1976) **GDP Expended on Education:** 6.2% (1972)

Transportation: Surfaced roads (entirely on Mahé and Praslin islands) total 90 mi. **Motor Vehicles:** 3,900 (1977) **Passenger Cars:** 3,000 **Railway Mileage:** None **Port:** Victoria **Major Airlines:** Air Mahé operates domestic flights **Communications:** Partly government owned **Radio Transmitters:** 2 **Receivers:** 17,000 (1976) **Television:** None **Telephones:** 4,600 **Newspapers:** 2 dailies, 60 copies per 1,000 inhabitants (1975)

Weights and Measures: British system is used **Travel Requirements:** Passport, no visa, onward ticket

---

This 90-island archipelago is a beautiful tropical paradise largely isolated from the rest of the world. The climate is equable and healthful, although quite humid, since the islands are small and subject to marine influences. Temperatures on the main island of Mahé vary from 75° to 85°F, and high winds are rarely encountered, as this "lotus land" lies outside the cyclone belt. The fortunate natural environment once caused an early visitor to declare seriously that the Seychelles archipelago was the home of the original Garden of Eden.

Although the new republic is promoting agriculture, its principal hopes lie in tourism. The opening of the islands' first commercial airport in 1971 has increased the number of tourists attracted by the beautiful beaches, impressive scenery and fine climate. The government has made considerable effort to assure that the expansion of tourism neither disrupts the islands' cultural life nor spoils the natural beauty. Hotels and condominiums are well spaced so not to "wall off" the beaches. Whale-watching is promoted as a tourist attraction.

Under the stimulus of development and tourism, the Seychelles has virtually obtained full employment for its work force. But even paradise must pay a price, and in the Seychelles, like elsewhere, progress has brought inflation.

Under the nation's first president, James Mancham, the Seychelles remained neutral in foreign affairs, with a pro-Western outlook. The only intrusion of big-power presence is the hosting of an American satellite tracking station on Mahé.

In 1977 Mancham was overthrown by leftist rebels thought to have been supplied with Chinese and Soviet weapons from Tanzania. Mancham's ouster was attributed to his playboy lifestyle, his frequent absences from the country, and his proposal to postpone the 1979 elections. Former Prime Minister France Albert René subsequently became president and vowed some form of socialism for the country, as well as an emphasis on housing, agriculture, fishing and tourism.

HISTORY: Although the islands appeared on Portuguese charts as early as 1505 and may have been visited by Arabs much earlier, the Seychelles remained unclaimed and uninhabited until 1742. In that year the French governor of Mauritius, Mahé de Labourdonnais, sent an expedition to the islands. However, the full settlement of the archipelago did not take place until 1794. As a result of French defeat in the Napoleonic Wars, the Seychelles passed to the British in 1814 and became a dependency of Mauritius

1903: The Seychelles become a separate crown colony

1970: Limited internal self-government is granted

1976: Independence is proclaimed on June 29

1977: President Mancham overthrown in leftist coup. Former Prime Minister France Albert René assumes presidency

1979: René reelected to 5-year term under new one-party constitution. Some 100 persons arrested amid rumors of coup plot arising from dissatisfaction with René's socialist policies

---

SIERRA LEONE

Area: 27,925 sq. mi. **Population:** 3,470,000 (1978 est.)

Official Name: Republic of Sierra Leone **Capital:** Freetown **Nationality:** Sierra Leonean **Languages:** English is the official language. Mende and Temne are widely spoken, but the most commonly spoken language is Krio, a form of pidgin English **Religion:** 70% are animists, 25% Moslems, and 5% Christians **Flag:** Horizontal stripes of green, white, and blue **Anthem:** National Anthem, beginning "High we exalt thee, realm of the free" **Currency:** Leone (1.04 per U.S. $1)

Location: West Africa. Sierra Leone is bounded on the north and east by Guinea, on the southeast by Liberia, and on the west by the Atlantic Ocean **Features:** The country consists of a coastal plain of mangrove swamps that gradually gives way to wooded hills and upland plateaus in the interior, with mountains near the eastern border **Chief Rivers:** Rokel, Sewa, Moa, Jong, Little and Great Scarcies, Sherbro

Head of State and of Government: President Siaka P. Stevens, born 1905, elected April 1971, reelected 1976 for 5 years, sworn in for 7-year term in 1978 under new constitution **Effective Date of Present Constitution:** 1978 **Legislative Body:** Parliament (unicameral House of Representatives), with 104 members; 85 are elected by universal suffrage, 12 indirectly elected paramount chiefs, and 7 appointed by the president, all for 5 years. The All-People's Congress is the sole officially recognized party **Local Government:** 3 provinces governed by a minister with cabinet rank, and the Western (Freetown) area, under a council

Ethnic Composition: 18 tribal groups, with the Mende and Temne each making up about 30% of the population; others include the Limba, Loko, Kono, Sherbro, Vai, Gallina, Susu, Kissi, Mandingo, and Peul (Fulani). Less than 2% are Creoles, descendants of freed slaves, mostly from the Americas **Population Distribution:** 18% urban **Density:** 124 inhabitants per sq. mi.

Largest Cities: (1974 est.) Freetown 214,443, Bo 45,000, Kenema 30,000

Per Capita Income: $222 (1978) **Gross National Product (GNP):** $710 million (1978) **Economic Statistics:** 31% of the GNP is derived from agriculture (palm kernels, cocoa, coffee, rice, piassava, ginger, cola nuts); 26% from trade and services; 19% from extractive industries (diamonds, rutile, bauxite); and 6% from manufacturing (soap, flour, mineral water, furniture) **Minerals and Mining:** Chiefly diamonds, iron ore, bauxite and the world's largest deposits of rutile **Labor Force:** 1.5 million, with 80% engaged in agriculture **Foreign Trade:** Exports, diamonds, palm kernels, bauxite, rutile, coffee, and cocoa, totaled $186 million in 1978. Imports, chiefly manufactured goods, fuel, machinery and transportation equipment, and food, totaled $280 million **Principal Trade Partners:** Britain, Japan, United States, EC countries, China, Nigeria

Vital Statistics: Birthrate, 44.7 per 1,000 of pop. (1975); death rate, 20.7 **Life Expectancy:** 44 years **Health Statistics:** 927 inhabitants per hospital bed; 17,114 per physician (1972) **Infant Mortality:** 136.3 per 1,000 births **Illiteracy:** 90% **Primary and Secondary School Enrollment:** 256,388 (1975) **Enrollment in Higher Education:** 1,642 **GNP Expended on Education:** 3.1% (1976)

Transportation: Paved roads total 700 mi. **Motor Vehicles:** 25,200 (1976) **Passenger Cars:** 18,900 **Railway Mileage:** 52 **Ports:** Freetown, Bonthe, Pepel **Major Airlines:** Sierra Leone Airways, government owned, operates domestic flights **Communications:** Government owned **Radio Transmitters:** 3 **Receivers:** 62,000 (1975) **Television Transmitters:** 2 **Receivers:** 8,500 **Telephones:** 15,000 (1976) **Newspapers:** 1 daily, 10 copies per 1,000 inhabitants (1975)

Weights and Measures: Metric system **Travel Requirements:** Passport, visa valid for 1 month, $6.50 fee, 3 photos

One of the oldest and most progressive of Britain's former West African colonies, Sierra Leone got off to a favorable start on independence in 1961 with stable government and promising economic development. But since then the small nation, which depends mainly on the production of diamonds, coffee and cocoa, has experienced increasingly violent political upheaval.

In addition to the tendency of some officials to seek personal fortunes at public expense, Sierra Leone has been plagued by coups, states of emergency and, in March 1971, an attempted assassination of the country's present leader, President Siaka Stevens. In the process, economic improvements—particularly in agriculture—have been repeatedly disrupted and new development programs delayed.

Serious trouble began with elections in 1967. Then opposition leader, Stevens appeared to have won by a narrow margin over the bumptious Sir Albert Margai, whose government had been marked by corruption. But almost as soon as Stevens had been sworn in as prime minister, a group of army officers ousted him in a coup. The junta said it had acted to prevent a civil war between the Mende, the largest tribal group, and the rival Temne, a main source of Stevens' strength.

Rule by the military group proved unpopular, and in 1968 it was ousted by a counter-coup led by noncommissioned officers and police. This group promptly restored Stevens to the premiership and the country settled down to legally elected government. Two years later, however, opposition to Stevens' party resumed, with clashes that led to the declaration of a state of emergency.

Then in March 1971 Brig. Gen. John Bangura, the army commander, led an attempted coup and assassination plot. The coup fizzled when other army officers arrested Bangura and proclaimed their loyalty to the Stevens government. Another state of emergency was declared and, under a new mutual defense pact by Stevens and Guinean President Sékou Touré, 200 Guinean troops were flown into Freetown to bolster local troops. Bangura and three followers were executed.

On April 19, 1971, Stevens proclaimed Sierra Leone a republic and two days later he was sworn in as president. His power was reconfirmed by elections in 1973 and 1976. In 1978 Stevens pushed through legislation introducing a new constitution which extended the presidential term of office to seven years, abolished the office of prime minister and made the All-People's Congress the only legal party.

On the economic scene, Sierra Leone has taken strides toward the development of the production of bauxite, which amounted to 700,000 tons in 1974. Another resource, rutile, a mineral used in paint manufacture, is being developed under a U.S. investment agreement. Sierra Leone's deposits are among the world's largest.

HISTORY: Sierra Leone was originally divided into numerous kingdoms or chiefdoms. The Portuguese explorer Pedro da Cintra visited the coastal area in 1460 and named the mountainous peninsula at the mouth of the Rokel River Serra Lyoa (Lion Mountain), later corrupted to Sierra Leone. Until the 18th century, the region was an important source of slaves. In 1787, a group of abolitionists founded Freetown to resettle freed slaves from Britain, and in 1808 the settlement became a crown colony. In 1896, the interior was made a British protectorate

1924: New constitution is introduced permitting nomination of protectorate chiefs to legislative council but fails to satisfy nationalist aspirations

1943: Africans are admitted to the executive council

1951: New constitution is introduced, providing a framework for decolonization

1957-58: Elected House of Representatives replaces legislative council; Dr. Milton Margai, whose Sierra Leone People's party wins a majority of seats, becomes prime minister

1961: Sierra Leone becomes an independent Commonwealth state

1964: Prime Minister Milton Margai dies; his brother, Finance Minister Albert Margai, is asked by governor-general to form new government

1967: Siaka Stevens, leader of the opposition All People's Congress, is appointed prime minister after hotly contested election but is ousted by army chief; group of young army officers stage bloodless coup and a National Reformation Council composed of army and police officers is set up under chairmanship of Col. Andrew Juxon-Smith; House of Representatives is dissolved and constitution is suspended

1968: Military coup is staged by noncommissioned officers and police; House of Representatives is reconvened and asks Stevens to resume premiership

1969: Sierra Leone People's party loses strength in House of Representatives following by-elections; party leaders charge that losses were due to government intimidation of voters

1971: An attempted coup led by Brig. Gen. John Bangura, the army commander, is crushed; Prime Minister Stevens calls in troops from Guinea to help suppress dissident elements. Sierra Leone is declared a republic

1973: A plot to overthrow the government is uncovered. Sierra Leone increases its military capacity. The All People's Congress wins election, taking 84 of 97 parliamentary seats

1976: President Stevens is elected for second five-year term

1977: Students demand that Stevens resign, but APC wins elections decisively amid charges of vote fraud

1978: New constitution increases presidential term to seven years and makes APC sole recognized party

1979: Rising prices and shortage of rice cause discontent

1980: Public outcry against U.S. firm's proposal to dump chemical wastes in Sierra Leone leads Stevens to reject it. Organization of African Unity meets in Freetown. Stevens elected OAU president

---

SINGAPORE

Area: 233 sq. mi. **Population:** 2,363,000 (1979 est.)

Official Name: Republic of Singapore **Capital:** Singapore **Nationality:** Singaporean **Languages:** Malay, the national language, and English, Chinese, and Tamil are all official languages **Religion:** The majority of the ethnic Chinese are Buddhists, Taoists, or Confucianists; the Malays and Pakistanis are Moslems; and the Indians mainly Hindus. The Europeans and Eurasians are almost all Christians **Flag:** Horizontal stripes of red and white with a white crescent and 5 white stars in the upper left-hand corner **Anthem:** Forward Singapore **Currency:** Singapore dollar (2.14 per U.S. $1)

Location: Southeast Asia. The island of Singapore lies south of the Malay peninsula, separated by the Strait of Johore. A three-quarter-mile-long causeway connects the island with Malaysia; 54 small islets lie offshore **Features:** Except for a central plateau, most of the island is low lying and originally consisted of swamp and jungle. The city of Singapore occupies land that for the most part was reclaimed from the sea **Chief Rivers:** Sungei Seletar, Singapore

Head of State: President: Dr. Benjamin Henry Sheares, born 1908, in office since 1971 **Head of Government:** Prime Minister Lee Kuan Yew, born 1923, appointed 1965, reelected 1976 **Effective Date of Present Constitution:** 1959 (pre-independence) **Legislative Body:** Parliament (unicameral), consisting of 69 members elected by adult suffrage for 5 years

Ethnic Composition: About 76% of the population is ethnically Chinese, 15% Malays, and 7% Indians and Pakistanis. The rest are largely Europeans and Eurasians **Population Distribution:** 100% urban **Density:** 10,142 inhabitants per sq. mi.

Largest City: (1977 est.) Singapore 2,308,200

Per Capita Income: $3,863 (1979) **Gross National Product (GNP):** $9.1 billion (1979) **Economic Statistics:** In 1973 about 56% of GNP came from trade and services (including banks, financial institutions, transportation and communications); 21% from quarrying and manufacturing; and 3% from agriculture and fishing **Minerals and Mining:** None **Labor Force:** 919,000, with 27% in industry and 24% in commerce **Foreign Trade:** Exports, mainly crude rubber, petroleum products, electrical machinery, electronics, textiles, timber and coffee, totaled $10 billion in 1978. Imports, chiefly rubber, petroleum products, machinery, vehicles, and woven fabrics other than cotton, totaled $13 billion **Principal Trade Partners:** Malaysia, United States, Japan, Saudi Arabia, Britain, China, Hong Kong, Australia, West Germany

Vital Statistics: Birthrate, 16.6 per 1,000 of pop. (1977); death rate, 5.3 **Life Expectancy:** 69 years **Health Statistics:** 265 inhabitants per hospital bed; 1,341 per physician (1976) **Infant Mortality:** 12.4 per 1,000 births **Illiteracy:** 25% **Primary and Secondary School Enrollment:** 506,008 (1976) **Enrollment in Higher Education:** 22,607 (1975) **GNP Expended on Education:** 2.7% (1976)

Transportation: Paved roads total 1,286 mi. **Motor Vehicles:** 197,000 (1977) **Passenger Cars:** 142,100 **Railway Mileage:** 24 **Port:** Singapore **Major Airlines:** Singapore Airlines operates international flights **Communications:** Government controlled **Radio Transmitters:** 16 **Licenses:** 356,000 (1976) **Television Transmitters:** 2 **Licenses:** 294,000 **Telephones:** 329,000 (1976) **Newspapers:** 10 dailies, 201 copies per 1,000 inhabitants (1974)

Weights and Measures: Metric system; British, Chinese, and local standards are used **Travel Requirements:** Passport, no visa

---

Since 1819, when Singapore was created out of a mangrove swamp by Sir Stamford Raffles, the visionary agent of the British East India Company, it has served as East Asia's major transshipping point, as the wholesaler for other countries' products, as the bastion of the British Empire, and, more recently, as the area's leading processor of other countries' raw materials.

Blessed with one of the few natural harbors in the region, Singapore grew to become the largest port in Southeast Asia and the fourth largest in the world. Through this port have flowed rubber and tin from Malaysia and Indonesia to the markets of Europe and the United States.

The expanding rubber and tin industries early this century spurred immigration, mainly from southern China. In fact, up to 1957, Singapore's population consisted predominantly of noncitizen aliens. Today, Singapore is the only nation in the world with a population made up primarily of overseas Chinese, although immigration has now been slowed to a minimum. Malays, Indians, and Pakistanis are the other dominant ethnic groups.

Economically, Singapore has continued to thrive and maintains the highest per capita income in Southeast Asia, as well as virtually full employment. The Jurong area, a sprawling section of the island devoted to industrial development, today pulses with the processing of many types of raw materials and the manufacturing of finished goods. In 1977 it was announced that a consortium of Japanese companies plans to build an $800-million petrochemical complex which will be half owned by the Singapore government, on one of Singapore's offshore islands. At the outset of the 1980s, Singapore appeared to be veering away from labor-intensive industry, with large and inexpensive work forces, and toward capital-intensive industry. The ministry of trade and industry said that, for the decade, it expected an 8 percent real growth rate and diversification into computers, medical equipment, optical equipment, and machine tools.

Business travel and tourism have increased sharply, raising the number of Singapore's visitors from less than one million in 1973 to more than two million in 1978. In the latter year Singapore Airlines placed the largest single order ever made for commericial aircraft—$900 million to the Boeing Company for 10 long-range 747 jumbo jets and four medium-range 727 trijets.

Since 1959, when Singapore was granted internal self-government, the People's Action party, headed by Lee Kuan Yew, has controlled the island's affairs. In recent years the government has been accused of authoritarianism and repression. In 1974 drastic penalties were decreed for armed robbers, gun runners, and traffickers in illegal immigrants.

The Internal Security Act provides for detention without trial for those accused of pro-Communist activities. In 1977 a new campaign was begun to repress dissent—a series of arrests of prominent critics of government policies, who subsequently were pressured into signing confessions and appearing on television to recant.

In 1975 Foreign Minister S. Rajaratnam responded to Peking's more moderate attitude by leading Singapore's first goodwill mission to China where he met with the late Premier Zhou Enlai. In 1976 Prime Minister Lee was one of the last foreign officials to be allowed to meet with Chairman Mao Zedong. With a population that is overwhelmingly of Chinese ancestry, many of whom retain warm feelings for their ancestral land, Singapore cannot afford to antagonize Peking, but neither does it want to be a Chinese satellite.

HISTORY: For centuries the island of Singapore was little more than a mangrove swamp occupied by Malay fishermen who owed allegiance to the Sultan of Johore. In 1819, Sir Stamford Raffles of the British East India Company, who saw in Singapore potential for a great trading port, founded a trading post on the island
1824: Sultan of Johore cedes Singapore to the British East India Company
1826: Singapore becomes part of the British Straits Settlements
1942: Supposedly impregnable fortress of Singapore is captured by the Japanese in World War II
1946: Singapore becomes a separate British crown colony
1959: Singapore becomes a self-governing colony
1963: Federation of Malaysia is formed and Singapore joins Malaya, Sarawak, and Sabah in new nation
1965: Singapore withdraws from Malaysia federation
1971: Singapore, Malaysia, Britain, Australia, and New Zealand sign accord on joint defense arrangements for Singapore and Malaysia
1972-73: Australia announces that it will withdraw all but about 150 support troops by July 1973
1976: Prime Minister Lee's ruling People's Action party, in its fifth straight election victory, wins all 69 seats in parliament
1978: Amnesty International alleges serious human rights violations in Singapore, including detention without trial of at least 70 political dissenters
1979: As one of five countries making up the Association of Southeast Asian Nations (ASEAN), Singapore joins in a decision June 30 to accept no more Vietnamese refugees

---

SOLOMON ISLANDS

Area: 11,500 sq. mi. **Population:** 215,000 (1978 est.)

Official Name: Solomon Islands **Capital:** Honiara **Nationality:** Solomon Islander **Language:** English is the official language; Melanesian Pidgin is the universal lingua franca. A variety of Melanesian tongues are spoken throughout most of the islands. On Vella Lavella, Savo and the Russell Islands the dominant languages are of the Papuan family. Polynesian languages, closely related to Maori, are spoken on the outlying islands of Ontong Java, Rennell and Tikopia **Religion:** 33% Anglican, 17% Roman Catholic, 17% South Sea Evangelical Church. The remainder of the inhabitants are members of the United Church and the Christian Fellowship Church, except for 5%, who are animists **Flag:** A blue triangle with five white stars in the upper left and a plain green triangle in the lower right separated by a diagonal yellow stripe **Anthem:** God Save Our Solomons **Currency:** Solomon Islands dollar (.87 per U.S. $1)

Location: Southwest Pacific Ocean. About 1000 miles northeast of Australia, the islands form a scattered archipelago stretching 900 miles in a southeasterly direction from Papua New Guinea. The six major islands are Choiseul, New Georgia, Santa Isabel, Guadalcanal, Malaita and San Cristobal **Features:** The large islands have a mountainous spine which on one side drops steeply to sea level and on the other drops through a series of foothills to the coast. The highest peaks are found on Guadalcanal, which possesses the only extensive coastal plains in the Solomons. The weather varies from warm to hot and is humid, with annual rainfall exceeding 100 inches **Chief Rivers:** There is an abundance of short rivers on the larger islands

Head of State: Queen Elizabeth II, represented by a governor-general, Baddeley Devesi, born 1941, sworn in July 1978 **Head of Government:** Prime Minister Peter Kenilorea, born 1943, sworn in July 1978 **Effective Date of Present Constitution:** July 1978 **Legislative Body:** National Parliament (unicameral) consisting of 38 members elected for 4 years **Local Government:** At present 4 districts; provinces are to be established

Ethnic Composition: Melanesians 93%, Polynesians 4%, Gilbertese 1%, European stock 1% **Population Distribution:** 9% urban **Density:** 19 inhabitants per sq. mi.

Largest City: (1976 census) Honiara 14,942

Per Capita Income: $330 (1976) **Gross Domestic Product (GDP):** $64 million (1976) **Economic Statistics:** Copra and rice are the only important cash crops. Fisheries contribute to the economy, and the timber industry is being developed **Minerals and Mining:** Copper, bauxite and nickel deposits are being developed **Labor Force:**

14,184 (1974) **Foreign Trade:** Exports, chiefly fish, timber, and copra, amounted to $23.8 million in 1976. Imports, mainly machinery, transport equipment, food and fuels totaled $26.8 million **Principal Trade Partners:** Japan, Australia, Britain, American Samoa, EEC, Malaysia, Singapore

Vital Statistics: Birthrate, 41 per 1,000 of pop. (1970); death rate, 11 **Life Expectancy:** 51 years **Health Statistics:** 120 inhabitants per hospital bed; 5,135 per physician (1975) **Infant Mortality:** 68 per 1,000 births **Illiteracy:** 40% **Primary and Secondary School Enrollment:** 29,243 (1976) **Enrollment in Higher Education:** 160 (1976) **GDP Expended on Education:** 3.7% (1972)

Transportation: All weather roads total 283 miles **Motor Vehicles:** 1,796 (1972) **Passenger Cars:** 727 **Railway Mileage:** None **Ports:** Honiara, Gizo, Yandina **Major Airlines:** Solomon Islands Airways operates domestic and international flights **Communications:** Government owned **Radio Transmitters:** 3 **Radio Receivers:** 11,000 (1976) **Television Transmitters:** None **Television Receivers:** None **Telephones:** 1,726 **Newspapers:** 2 weeklies

Weights and Measures: Imperial weights and measures are still in use, but the metric system has been adopted as the future standard **Travel Requirements:** Passport, no visa

---

For a short period during World II the Solomon Islands were a focus of world attention as Japan and the United States engaged in land, air and sea battles for the control of the South Pacific. Guadalcanal, New Georgia, "the Slot," and Iron Bottom Sound—scenes of major clashes in 1942 and 1943—are all within the confines of the newly independent Solomon Islands.

Following hostilities, the islands returned to the peaceful obscurity of being a remote British protectorate unbothered by the tides of history. However, the worldwide retreat of colonialism during the 1960s resulted in a growing interest in eventual independence for the Solomons on the part of both the British and the islanders. Finally, on July 7, 1978, the Duke of Gloucester, representing Queen Elizabeth II, handed over power to the government of the new nation.

The most pressing problem facing the Solomon Islands is the maintenance of unity among the diverse and geographically separated peoples of the island chain. The commercially developed western islands have demanded more autonomy, and the non-Melanesian minority fears the neglect of its needs by the central government.

One of the main objectives of the government is to diversify the economy. In the past, production has been limited to copra planting, timber cutting and fishing. It is hoped that plans for the introduction of beef cattle and the growing of rice and oil palm will be implemented. Another source of future economic growth would be the successful exploitation of the islands' copper, bauxite and nickel ores.

HISTORY: Ancestors of the present Melanesian inhabitants entered the area from the Malay Archipelago some time between 1000 and 500 B.C. Polynesians came to the islands much later, from Uvea in the Wallis group, northeast of Fiji. The Spaniards reached Santa Isabel in the Solomons in 1568. During the 19th century missionaries and coconut traders made contact with the Solomon Islanders, and many of the inhabitants were recruited, sometimes forcibly, for labor in Fiji, Australia and New Caledonia
1893-98: Britain establishes a protectorate over the Solomons
1899: Germany transfers Santa Isabel, Choiseul, the Shortlands and Ontong Java to Britain
1942-43: Japanese invade the Solomons. American counteroffensive recaptures Guadalcanal; fighting continues on the islands until Allied forces move on to Bougainville
1946-52: Opposition to British rule is carried on by "Marching Rule" movement, a nativist cargo-cult
1960: Legislative Council established
1976: The protectorate is abolished, and the Solomons become a self-governing dependency
1977: Constitutional conference is held in London to plan for independence
1978: Full independence is achieved on July 7
1979: Government opens talks with Papua New Guinea on boundary dispute in North Solomons island group

SOMALIA

Area: 246,200 **Population:** 3,443,000 (1978 est.)
Official Name: Somali Democratic Republic **Capital:** Mogadishu **Nationality:** Somali **Languages:** Somali is the official language; Arabic, English, and Italian are still used extensively **Religion:** 99% are Sunni Moslems and Islam is the state religion **Flag:** Blue field with a 5-pointed white star in the center **Anthem:** Long Live Somalia **Currency:** Somali shilling (Somalo) (6.30 per U.S. $1)

Location: East Africa. Somalia is bounded on the north by the Gulf of Aden and Djibouti, on the southeast by the Indian Ocean, and on the west by Kenya and Ethiopia **Features:** Much of the country is arid or semiarid. The northern region is mountainous; the southern part is mostly desert, but with a large fertile area crossed by two large rivers flowing from Ethiopia **Chief Rivers:** Juba, Shebelli

Head of State and of Government: President: Maj. Gen. Mohamed Siad Barré, born 1919, secretary general of the Somali Socialist Revolutionary Party (SRSP), assumed power in 1969 **Effective Date of Present Constitution:** Sept. 23, 1979 **Legislative Body:** People's Assembly (unicameral) of 171 members, elected for 5 years. The SRSP is the only legal party **Local Government:** 15 regions divided into 78 districts

Ethnic Composition: The Hamitic population is mainly Somali. Other sizable ethnic groups include some 35,000 Arabs, 1,000 Indians and Pakistanis, and about 2,000 Italians **Population Distribution:** 9% urban **Density:** 14 inhabitants per sq. mi.

Largest City: (1973 est.) Mogadishu 400,000

Per Capita Income: $70 (1978) **Gross National Product (GNP):** $260 million (1978) **Economic Statistics:** Industry accounts for only about 8% of the GNP with the rest from livestock (cattle, camels, sheep, goats), the mainstay of the Somali economy; banana growing; wild animal hides such as Somali leopard skins; spices, fishing, and some minerals **Minerals and Mining:** Commercial production is confined to salt, charcoal, limestone, and meerschaum; uranium, iron ore and certain rare earths are currently being explored **Labor Force:** 1,100,000 (1970). Livestock production employs about 60% of the total; and agriculture 20% **Foreign Trade:** Exports, chiefly livestock, bananas, hides, meat and tuna, totaled $90 million in 1978. Imports, mainly manufactured goods, fuel, cereals, food preparations, transportation equipment, and chemicals, totaled $346 million **Principal Trade Partners:** Italy, Britain, United States, Saudi Arabia, USSR, Kuwait, Guatemala, Yugoslavia

Vital Statistics: Birthrate, 47.2 per 1,000 of pop. (1975); death rate, 21.7 **Life Expectancy:** 41 years **Health Statistics:** 569 inhabitants per hospital bed; 15,544 per physician (1972) **Infant Mortality:** 177 per 1,000 births **Illiteracy:** 80% **Primary and Secondary School Enrollment:** 241,419 (1976) **Enrollment in Higher Education:** 2,100 (1976) **GNP Expended on Education:** 4.8% (1976)

Transportation: Paved roads total 1,181 mi. **Motor Vehicles:** 16,000 (1972) **Passenger Cars:** 8,000 **Railway Mileage:** None **Ports:** Mogadishu, Berbera, Merka, Kismayu **Major Airlines:** Somali Airlines operates domestically and internationally **Communications:** Government owned **Radio Transmitters:** 5 **Receivers:** 69,000 (1976) **Television:** None **Telephones:** 6,000 (1971) **Newspapers:** 1 daily, 1 copy per 1,000 inhabitants (1973)

Weights and Measures: Metric system **Travel Requirements:** Passport, visa valid 3 months, $14 fee, 4 photos, onward ticket

---

Major power changes in the strategically located Horn of Africa have spotlighted Somalia, an arid East African country at the juncture of the Indian Ocean and the Gulf of Aden, as a link important to both the Middle East and Africa. A union of the former Italian and British Somalilands, Somalia became independent in 1960, but efforts at transforming its seminomadic society into a modern state have made scarcely any headway.

Somalis, a lean, handsome, fiercely proud people, have an oral history going back 2,000 years. Because of disputes among scholars, the Somali language had no written form until, in 1972, President Siad announced a system would be developed using the Roman alphabet.

Western and Communist aid has added some modern facilities—an American-built seaport and a Russian-built slaughterhouse—but the Somali economy remains largely a low-yield herding/farming system.

The current regime of Major General Mohamed Siad Barré, who overthrew the government of Premier Mohammed Ibrahim Egal in 1969, until recently had been marked by close ties with the Soviet Union and vociferous anti-Westernism. In exchange for military aid, Somalia provided the Soviets with a missile storage base. Angered by the Soviet buildup in Ethiopia, Somalia's arch-foe, Siad Barré, expelled the Soviets from Somalia in mid-1977, and the Somali army invaded Ogaden, an area of Ethiopia claimed by Somalia, to help the Somali rebels operating in the region. But the Ethiopian forces, aided by some 11,000 Cuban troops and 1,000 Soviet military advisors, drove the Somali troops from Ogaden by early 1978. Ethiopia has stated that there can be no lasting peace in the area until Somalia renounces its territorial claims on Ogaden, Djibouti and northern Kenya, and pays for damages caused in the war. Meanwhile, two "western Somali" liberation groups continue to fight on, guerrilla-style.

As a result of the eight-month Ogaden War, Somalia was burdened by the influx of about 1,300,000 refugees who fled from the region. The government has been hard pressed to feed 673,555 persons living in 25 refugee camps as of May 1980. Food has been supplied by Iraq, Saudi Arabia, Western European countries, and the United States, which shipped 80,000 tons of the total 110,000 tons provided to the refugees in the first half of 1980.

HISTORY: Although arid and desolate in many areas, Somalia was known as the Land of Punt (God's Land) in ancient Egyptian writings. It was reputedly the source of the biblical frankincense and myrrh, and was probably also the breeding ground of the locusts that invaded Egypt in the time of Joseph. Over the centuries the Somalis, a blend of Asian and African peoples, formed a confederation of closely knit clans in which Arab trading enclaves and sultanates evolved. Later, the nation was divided into British and Italian possessions, and, with union of these in 1960, it began a new era as the Somali Republic

19th cent.: British and Italians, through treaties with sultans and mutual agreements, divide country, with British occupying northwestern portion, Italians, the east and south

1901-20: Mohammed bin Abdallah Hasan, the "Mad Mullah," wages holy war against British

1936: Italian Somaliland is merged with Eritrea and Ethiopia as "Italian East Africa," following Ethiopian defeat in Italo-Ethiopian War of 1935-36

1940-41: Italians occupy British Somaliland during World War II; they are ousted by British, who take over Italian Somaliland

1947-50: Italy renounces colonial rights and is given 10-year UN trusteeship to prepare former possession for independence

1960: British and Italian Somaliland are united as Somali Republic

1961-64: Droughts and floods deplete crops, livestock; food shipments by United States and other countries avert famine

1969: President Abdirashid Ali Shermarke is slain by an assassin; army, with police backing, seizes power

1975: 120,000 Somali nomads are airlifted by Soviet planes from drought-stricken areas of north to southern regions

1977: Kenya and Somalia pledge maintenance of peace along border, following Kenya's charge of a Somali invasion

1978: Eight-month Ogaden war ends in March as Cuban and Soviet-aided Ethiopian forces drive Somalis from region. Somalia reports that army officers "influenced by foreign powers" attempted coup which failed; thwarted rebels are said to have killed 20 people and injured 34. Ethiopian jets bomb Somali towns and villages while Somali guerrillas recapture major military base in southern part of Ogaden region

1979: Somalia criticizes U.S. for failure to deliver $15 million in weapons as promised. New constitution adopted

1980: People's Assembly, meeting for first time in ten years, reconfirms Siad Barré as president for new six-year term. Somalia gets food from U.S. and other countries for Ogaden refugees. U.S. and Somalia sign agreement granting U.S. use of Berbera naval and air base, in exchange for arms aid

SOUTH AFRICA

Area: 472,359 sq. mi. (inc. Bophuthatswana, Transkei and Venda)
Population: 27,700,000 (1978 est.) (inc. Bophuthatswana, Transkei and Venda)

Official Name: Republic of South Africa **Capitals:** Cape Town (legislative), Pretoria (administrative), and Bloemfontein (judicial) **Nationality:** South African **Languages:** English and Afrikaans are the official languages. Of the white population, 63% speak Afrikaans and 37% speak English. In the *Bantustans*, the individual African languages are official. Indians, who constitute the bulk of the Asian minority, speak Tamil, Hindi, Gujarati, and Telugu **Religion:** Most of the population is Christian, chiefly Protestant. About 50% of the Africans in the *Bantustans* are animists. Most of the Asians are Hindus and Moslems **Flag:** Horizontal stripes of orange, white, and blue with small replicas of the Union Jack, the Boer flag of the Orange Free State, and old Transvaal Vierkleur banner in the center **Anthem:** Die Stem (The Voice of South Africa) **Currency:** Rand (0.78 per U.S. $1)

Location: Southern tip of the African continent, between the South Atlantic Ocean on the west and the Indian Ocean on the east. South Africa is landbound on the north and northeast by Namibia, Botswana, Zimbabwe, Swaziland, and Mozambique. Independent Lesotho lies entirely within the borders of South Africa. Walvis Bay, on the Namibian coast, is an exclave of the Cape Province **Features:** On the west, south, and east is a narrow coastal belt of lowlands extending into an extensive interior plateau **Chief Rivers:** Orange, Limpopo

Head of State: President Marais Viljoen, born 1915, elected 1979 **Head of Government:** Prime Minister Pieter W. Botha, born 1916, appointed 1978 **Effective Date of Present Constitution:** May 1961, a new constitution is being considered **Legislative Body:** Parliament (bicameral), consisting of the Senate and the House of Assembly. The Senate is composed of 51 members, of whom 42 are elected by provincial electoral colleges and 9 by the state president. The House of Assembly consists of 165 members directly elected by voters. Only white candidates and voters take part in parliamentary elections **Local Government:** 4 provinces, each with an appointed administrator and an elected provincial council. Ten self-governing *Bantustans* have been created since 1963, three of which, Transkei, Bophuthatswana and Venda have been granted independence

Ethnic Composition: Africans (Bantus) constitute 69.9% of the population, whites (largely of Dutch and British descent) 17.8%, coloreds (mixed white and African) 9.4%, and Asians 2.9% **Population Distribution:** 48% urban **Density:** 59 inhabitants per sq. mi.

Largest Cities: (1970 census) (M.A. = Metropolitan Area) Johannesburg 654,232 (M.A. 1,417,818), Cape Town 697,514 (M.A. 833,731), Durban 736,852 (M.A. 975,494), Soweto 602,043, Pretoria 545,450 (M.A. 573,283), Port Elizabeth 392,231 (M.A. 413,961), Germiston 221,972 (M.A. 293,257)

Per Capita Income: $1,507 (1979) **Gross National Product (GNP):** $41.9 billion (1979) **Economic Statistics:** About 32% of GNP is derived from trade and services; 28% from manufacturing (textiles, iron and steel, chemicals, fertilizer, automobile assembly, metalworking, electrical and nonelectrical machinery and equipment, mining machinery); 12% from mining (gold, platinum, coal, diamonds, antimony, iron ore, copper, uranium, manganese, chrome, asbestos); 8% from agriculture (sugar, tobacco, wool, corn, fruit, dairy products, wheat, fish) **Minerals and Mining:** Extensive mineral deposits, including gold, platinum, coal, diamonds, vanadium, antimony, iron ore, copper, uranium, manganese, chrome, asbestos **Labor Force:** 9,532,000 (1976), with 22.8% in industry, 23.4% in services, and 9.6% in agriculture **Foreign Trade:** Exports, chiefly diamonds, wool, fruit, copper, iron and steel, and gold, amounted to $8.5 billion in 1978 (excluding gold bullion). Imports, mainly industrial machinery and equipment, transportation equipment, and precision instruments, totaled $7.2 billion (excluding petroleum and munitions) **Principal Trade Partners:** Britain, West Germany, Japan, United States

Vital Statistics: Birthrate, 42.9 per 1,000 of pop. (1975); death rate, 15.5 **Life Expectancy:** 52 years **Health Statistics:** 152 inhabitants per hospital bed; 2,016 per physician (1973) **Infant Mortality:** 59 per 1,000 births (1974) **Illiteracy:** Negligible (white); 50% (others) **Primary and Secondary School Enrollment:** 4,653,452 (1972) **Enrollment in Higher Education:** 98,577 **GNP Expended on Education:** N.A.

Transportation: Paved roads total 20,000 mi. **Motor Vehicles:** 2,984,700 (1977) **Passenger Cars:** 2,163,500 **Railway Mileage:** 13,950 **Ports:** Durban, East London, Port Elizabeth, Cape Town, Richards Bay, Saldanha Bay **Major Airlines:** South African Airways, the government-owned airline, operates international and domestic flights **Communications:** Government controlled **Radio Transmitters:** 177 **Radio Receivers:** 2,500,000 (1976) **Television Transmitters:** 34 **Licenses:** 719,000 (1977) **Telephones:** 2,300,000 **Newspapers:** 24 dailies, 70 copies per 1,000 inhabitants (1975)

Weights and Measures: Metric system **Travel Requirements:** Passport, visa valid for 1 year

BOPHUTHATSWANA

Area: 15,570 sq. mi. **Population:** 1,200,000 **Density:** 77 inhabitants per sq. mi. **Official Name:** Republic of Bophuthatswana **Capital:** Mmabatho **Flag:** An orange diagonal stripe across a blue field with a white disk bearing a black leopard head in the upper hoist **Head of State and of Government:** President and Prime Minister: Chief Lucas Mangope, born 1923, elected December 1977 **Legislative Body:** Legislative Assembly (unicameral), with 99 members of which 48 are elected, 48 appointed by the 12 regional authorities, and 3 appointed by the president **Largest Cities:** (1970 census) Garankuwa 45,631, Mabopane 22,559

TRANSKEI

Area: 16,910 sq. mi. **Population:** 2,000,000 **Density:** 118 inhabitants per sq. mi. **Official Name:** Republic of Transkei **Capital:** Umtata **Flag:** Ochre, white, and green horizontal stripes **Head of State and of Government:** President: Dr. Kaiser Daliwonga Matanzima, born 1915, took office October 1976 as prime minister, December 1978 as president **Legislative Body:** National Assembly (unicameral), with 150 members, composed of 75 elected, 70 nominated chiefs, and 5 paramount chiefs, all serving 5-year terms **Largest Cities:** (1974 est.) Umtata 28,100, Butterworth (Gcuma) 24,000

VENDA

Area: 2,510 sq. mi. **Population:** 449,000 **Density:** 179 inhabitants per sq. mi. **Official Name:** Republic of Venda **Capital:** Thohoyandou **Flag:** Three equal horizontal stripes of green, yellow and brown with a vertical blue stripe at the hoist. A brown "V" is centered on the yellow stripe **Head of State and of Government:** Chief Patrick R. Mphephu **Legislative Body:** N.A. **Largest Centers:** Thohoyandou, Sibasa, Makwarela

---

South Africa is a land of great physical beauty and harsh social contrasts. Its rugged coastlines, steep escarpments, sweeping plateaus, and magnificent mountains afford unparalleled vistas. The setting of Cape Town, the country's oldest city, is among the most beautiful in the world. The modern skyscrapers of Johannesburg tower above the rolling countryside of the plateau highveld. The 19th century buildings that dominate the center of the administrative capital, Pretoria, form reminders of the period of conflict between Boer and Briton and the emergence of the Union of South Africa, predecessor of the present Republic.

Contrasted against the wealthy suburbs, modern highways, beach resorts and golf courses lie the bleak, much poorer African townships that house the urban labor reservoirs, the crowded workers' quarters near the mines, the traditional but often deteriorated African villages in the Bantu homelands. Rich South Africa is white South Africa; poorer South Africa tends to be the domain of the black, colored, and to a lesser extent the Asian communities. All *nationwide* statistics relating to the Republic should be considered in this context.

Although racial segregation as a way of life had characterized South Africa for many decades, a turning point came in 1948 when D. F. Malan's National party defeated the United party led by J. C. Smuts. Apartheid now became official state policy, and even the slightest trend toward racial integration was reversed. Public facilities became rigorously segregated, the major universities were restricted to whites, and numerous other steps were taken to eliminate racial contact in daily life. More significantly, however, the Nationalist government also embarked on a program of racial-territorial separation for the country as a whole, with the ultimate aim of the creation of a set of autonomous African states within South Africa's borders. Initially these areas were called *Bantustans*, and the first such territory to be awarded a degree of self-government was the Transkei in

1963. Transkei was declared to be an independent "homeland" in 1976. Two more such black homelands have since been granted independence, Bophuthatswana in 1977 and Venda in 1979. The homeland plan involves land exchanges, population movements, and numerous hardships for many of the people affected. Other nations have withheld recognition of the independence of these homelands which receive most of their income from South Africa.

South Africa's policies of separate development have been the target of increasingly sharp criticism throughout the world, and especially in black Africa. Demands have been voiced for boycotts on trade, business, and sports contests with the Republic. In South Africa itself, leaders of the African Homelands also have begun to put pressure on the government for greater sovereignty than the *Bantustan* plan had first envisaged, and for better conditions for Africans still residing and working in "white" South Africa. The response has been comparatively slight. Some concessions have been made in areas of job opportunity for blacks, equalization of salaries, acceptance of some interracial sports events and in ending discrimination in the use of restrooms and elevators. However, the legacy of apartheid and the straightjacket of separate development continue to dominate life in the Republic.

In 1979 a major political scandal rocked Pretoria, forcing John Vorster to resign the ceremonial post of president. An official investigation alleged that Vorster, while prime minister, had approved, and later tried to cover up, a propaganda program under which some $90 million in secret funds were funneled to friendly politicians and other leaders in Europe and the U.S. Pieter W. Botha, who became prime minister in 1978, was absolved of complicity and attempted to set his government on a reform course of relaxation in apartheid rules and more skilled jobs for blacks. Marais Viljoen, former president of the senate, became the republic's president in June 1979.

HISTORY: When European settlers first arrived, there were several distinct native groups occupying different parts of the territory, including the Bushmen, nomadic hunters of the western desert upland country, and the Hottentots, a pastoral people who occupied the southern and eastern coastal areas. At the same time, Bantu people were moving toward the Cape of Good Hope, having already occupied territories in the north and east

1488: Portuguese led by Bartholomew Diaz arrive at Cape

1652: First Dutch settlers establish Cape Colony

1814: Britain gains formal possession of the Cape Colony as a result of the Napoleonic Wars. Dutch begin eastward movement

1835-36: In a migration known as the Great Trek, the Boers (descendants of the Dutch settlers) leave Cape Colony for the north in protest against British rule

1899-1902: Boer War breaks out with Britain. By the Treaty of Vereeniging, the Boers acknowledge British sovereignty over Transvaal and the Orange Free State

1910: Union of South Africa is constituted under the terms of the South Africa Act passed by the British Parliament

1926-47: Ruling whites initiate separatist policies

1948: Afrikaner National Party, led by D. F. Malan, defeats J. C. Smuts' governing United Party and apartheid is introduced as official state policy

1959: Promotion of Bantu Self-Government Act is passed, providing for eight self-governing African states

1960: Seventy-two blacks are killed in protest demonstration against forced carrying of identity passes in Sharpeville

1961: South Africa becomes a republic and formally withdraws from British Commonwealth

1963: The first partially self-governing *Bantustan* (Bantu "homeland"), the Transkei, is established

1966: Prime Minister Hendrik Verwoerd is assassinated and is succeeded by Balthazar J. Vorster

1969: UN Security Council condemns South Africa for its refusal to permit the UN to take control of South-West Africa following the termination of a League of Nations mandate

1971: World Court rules that South Africa's administration of South-West Africa is illegal

1976: South African troops intervene unsuccessfully in Angolan civil war. Forced use of Afrikaans language in black schools precipitates rioting in Soweto, leaving 380 dead. Transkei homeland granted independence in October

1977: Black political activist Stephen Biko dies under suspicious circumstances while in police custody. UN Security Council unanimously orders worldwide mandatory embargo on arms supplies to South Africa because of its racial policies. Government scores overwhelming victory in general elections. Bophuthatswana granted independence

1978: Transkei breaks diplomatic relations with South Africa. South African forces enter Angola in "limited military operation" against guerrillas of SWAPO (South-West African People's Organization); action is condemned by UN Security Council. Prime Minister Vorster resigns and is named president. Pieter W. Botha is appointed prime minister

1979: Vorster resigns amid scandal, is succeeded by Marais Viljoen. Botha, exonerated, shuffles cabinet, removes hard-line minister of justice, proposes new approach to race relations. His program to provide more skilled jobs for blacks prompts wildcat strike by mine workers. Botha expels U.S. embassy personnel, asserting ambassador's airplane was used for reconnaissance missions over South Africa. Venda is granted independence. White-dominated Namibian National Assembly is organized and given legislative powers

1980: Clashes between South African troops and SWAPO guerrillas intensify. Angola reports large-scale occupation of its territory by South African force. Soaring international gold prices aid economy. Blacks and coloreds step up protests as Botha becomes more hesitant on reform policies; terrorists attack police stations and vehicles; thousands of colored (mixed-race) students in cities demonstrate against comparatively lower spending for their schools. Nine southern African nations agree on economic development plan to decrease their dependence on South Africa

---

SPAIN

Area: 195,988 sq. mi. **Population:** 36,775,000 (1978 est.)

Official Name: Spanish State **Capital:** Madrid **Nationality:** Spanish **Languages:** Spanish is the official and predominant language; Catalan, Galician, Valencian, and Basque are regional languages officially recognized for legal purposes since 1976 **Religion:** The population is overwhelmingly Roman Catholic **Flag:** Three unequal horizontal stripes of red, yellow and red with the greater arms of Spain near the hoist **Anthem:** Royal March **Currency:** Peseta (70 per U.S. $1)

Location: Southwest Europe, occupying most of the Iberian peninsula. Spain is bounded on the north by the Bay of Biscay, on the northeast by France and Andorra, on the east and south by the Mediterranean Sea, and on the west by Portugal and the Atlantic Ocean **Features:** Most of the country consists of a high plateau divided by mountains and broad depressions. The landmass rises sharply from the sea, leaving a narrow coastal plain except in the Andalusian lowlands in the south **Chief Rivers:** Ebro, Guadalquivir, Duero, Tajo, Guadiana, Miño

Head of State: King Juan Carlos I (de Borbón), born 1938, proclaimed king in 1975 **Head of Government:** Premier Adolfo Suárez González, born 1932, reappointed March 1979 **Effective Date of Present Constitution:** December 29, 1978 **Legislative Body:** *Cortes* (bicameral), with an elected 350-member Chamber of Deputies, and a Senate with 208 members, all for 4 years **Local Government:** 50 provinces, each headed by an appointed governor and a provincial council, and the 2 African presidios of Ceuta and Melilla. Catalonia and the Basque country have received regional autonomy

Ethnic Composition: The Castilians of central Spain, the Basques in the north, the Catalans in the northeast, the Galicians in the northwest, the Valencians in the east, and the Andalusians in the south represent separate cultural groups **Population Distribution:** 49% urban **Density:** 188 inhabitants per sq. mi.

Largest Cities: (1975 est.) Madrid 3,520,320, Barcelona 1,809,722, Valencia 713,026, Seville 588,784, Saragossa 542,317, Bilbao 457,655, Málaga 402,978

Per Capita Income: $2,830 (1979) **Gross National Product (GNP):** $105 billion (1979) **Economic Statistics:** About 53% of GNP is derived from trade and services; 37% from mining, manufacturing, construction, energy; and 10% from agriculture (cereals, fruits, vegetables, olive oil). Tourism is of great importance **Minerals and Mining:** Coal, iron, mercury, pyrites, zinc, copper and potash are produced **Labor Force:** 13,300,000 (1978), with 40% in services, 36% in industry and construction, and 20% in agriculture **Foreign Trade:** Exports, mainly footwear, textiles and clothing, steel products, transportation equipment, machinery, chemicals, and furniture, totaled $13 billion in 1978. Imports, chiefly feed grains, machinery, transportation and electrical equipment, fuels, metals,

chemicals, and tobacco, totaled $18.7 billion **Principal Trade Partners:** United States, West Germany, France, Britain, Saudi Arabia, Iran, Netherlands, Italy

Vital Statistics: Birthrate, 18 per 1,000 of pop. (1977); death rate, 7.7 **Life Expectancy:** 72 years **Health Statistics:** 190 inhabitants per hospital bed; 647 per physician (1975) **Infant Mortality:** 10.7 per 1,000 births (1976) **Illiteracy:** 3% **Primary and Secondary School Enrollment:** 6,812,755 (1976) **Enrollment in Higher Education:** 540,238 (1975) **GNP Expended on Education:** 1.7% (1974)

Transportation: Surfaced roads total 86,665 mi. **Motor Vehicles:** 7,102,600 (1977) **Passenger Cars:** 5,944,900 **Railway Mileage:** 10,824 **Ports:** Barcelona, Bilbao, Valencia, Cartagena, Sta. Cruz de Tenerife, Gijón, Huelva, Algeciras, Cádiz, Vigo **Major Airlines:** Iberia operates domestic and international flights, Aviaco operates domestic flights **Communications:** Government controlled **Radio Transmitters:** 430 **Receivers:** 9,300,000 (1976) **Television Transmitters:** 791 **Receivers:** 6,640,000 (1976) **Telephones:** 9,530,000 **Newspapers:** 115 dailies, 48 copies per 1,000 inhabitants (1975)

Weights and Measures: Metric system is official **Travel Requirements:** Passport, no visa for 6 months

---

Since the death of the dictatorial head of state, Francisco Franco, on November 20, 1975, Spain has moved steadily toward democracy. Two days after the passing of *El Caudillo*, the 500-year-old monarchy was restored with the proclamation of Juan Carlos de Borbón as king of Spain. King Juan Carlos I is the grandson of Alfonso XIII, who lost his throne in 1931.

In 1977, in the first free election in 41 years, Premier Adolfo Suárez González and his Democratic Center Union, a center-right grouping, captured 34 percent of the popular vote, with the Socialists coming in a close second with 28 percent. Suárez, a former Franco supporter, has held the premiership since his appointment by the King in 1976. The pardoning of more than half of the country's 1,600 political prisoners, the granting of the right of assembly, a loosening of press controls and legalization of the Communist party have all occurred since the new monarch promised "profound improvements" at his swearing-in ceremony on November 22, 1975. A new bicameral parliament was instituted in place of the appointed parliament left by Franco.

However, the problem of the "nations within the Spanish nation" still remains; Basque and Catalan separatism and Galician and Valencian regionalism present difficulties. Some concessions have been made to the aspirations to cultural freedom of the non-Castilian peoples, but many more will be required before the ethnic sensibilities of these ethnic groups will be satisfied.

In its economic life, Spain has progressed far from the devastation left by the 1936-1939 civil war. A good part of the prosperity results from the popularity of Spain as a tourist haven for other Europeans and for North Americans. The beauty of the Iberian seaside, plus its easy accessibility from Western Europe and relative inexpensiveness, have turned sleepy fishing villages into thriving vacation resorts.

Burgeoning industry, flourishing foreign trade and an ever-increasing middle class are all signs pointing to the fact that Spain has become a prosperous, 20th-century nation. Though there are still wide areas of poverty, the better life is noticeable in the cities—such as Madrid, Barcelona and Seville—and the wealthier provinces—such as Castile and Catalonia. However, the rising curve of economic growth has not been without its dips, and in 1978 a definite downturn began.

A new constitution was adopted in December 1978. It limited the king to an essentially ceremonial role, contained firm guarantees of human rights, and protected the electoral system which favored the rural areas. It also provided for the establishment of autonomous regions. The Basque country and Catalonia became autonomous provinces on January 11, 1980. When the government slowed the full implementation of limited self-rule until 1983, however, the Basque Nationalist party refused to participate in the proceedings of the National Assembly.

HISTORY: About 1000 B.C. the Iberian peninsula was invaded by Celtic tribes from the north, and two centuries later Phoenicians and Greeks began to establish colonies along the Spanish coast. The Carthaginians conquered most of the peninsula in the 3rd century B.C., but were forced out by the Romans, during whose rule political unity was established and Christianity introduced. Early in the 5th century, Spain was overrun by the Germanic Vandals and Visigoths. After forcing the Vandals to emigrate to Africa, the Visigoths were themselves conquered by the Moors

711-18: Roderick, the last of the Visigothic kings, is defeated in battle by the Moors, who gain control over virtually the entire peninsula. Asturias, the only remnant of Visigothic Spain, becomes the focus of the Christian reconquest

1492: King Ferdinand of Aragon and his wife, Queen Isabella of Castile, complete the reconquest of Spain by capturing Granada, the last remaining Moorish stronghold. The Catholic rulers order the expulsion of the Jews. Columbus wins the monarchs' support for his voyages and discovers America, where a vast Spanish empire is soon to be established

1588: Defeat of the Spanish Armada by England hastens the demise of Spanish power

1808-14: Napoleon's armies invade Spain and his brother Joseph is placed on the Spanish throne. The French are finally driven out by Spanish resistance fighters and British troops led by Wellington. Wars of independence break out in Spanish America, leading to the disruption of the empire

1898: Spanish-American War destroys remaining empire

1931-36: Alfonso XIII is deposed and a republic established. Economic and political unrest culminate in an army revolt against the republic, under the leadership of General Francisco Franco. The revolt precipitates the Spanish Civil War

1936-39: The war rages for two and a half years, with the Loyalists (Republicans), aided by the Soviet Union and foreign volunteers, gradually defeated by Franco's forces, aided by Nazi Germany and Fascist Italy. The Loyalist government flees to France, and Franco sets up a dictatorship, with the Fascist Falange as the only legal party

1942-47: Franco reestablishes the *Cortes* but on Fascist lines without genuine popular representation. The Law of Succession is promulgated, declaring Spain a kingdom and setting up a regency council, with Franco as head of state

1966-68: A new constitution curbing the political power of the National Movement and its political organ, the Falange, is approved by referendum. The position of president of government (premier) is created. However, dissatisfaction with the regime makes itself felt in strikes and university unrest, which lead to severe police repression

1969: Franco designates Prince Juan Carlos de Borbón y Borbón to be chief of state and king upon Franco's death or incapacitation

1970-71: Military court sentences six Basque separatists to death; Franco commutes sentences following world outcry

1973: Spain establishes full diplomatic relations with East Germany and Communist China; Premier Carrero Blanco is assassinated; Carlos Arias Navarro becomes premier

1975: Right of U.S. military to use Spanish bases is renewed. Franco dies. Prince Juan Carlos becomes head of state as King Juan Carlos I

1976: Spain withdraws from Western Sahara, last remnant of this once-vast colonial empire. Carlos Arias Navarro resigns premiership. He is replaced by Adolfo Suárez González

1977: Communist party is legalized and declared eligible for participation in national elections. Premier Suárez' Democratic Center Union emerges victorious in first free elections in 41 years. Government devalues peseta by 22 percent as economy continues slump. Catalonians and Basques granted provisional self-rule

1978: Basques legally celebrate their national day for first time since civil war. Communist party, holding its ninth congress (first since 1932), drops "Leninist" label despite strong Soviet advice against doing so. Suárez government suffers setback as Senate by-elections show victory for opposition Socialists and big surge by Communists. Government grants provisional autonomy to Balearic Islands and two other regions. Annual running-of-the-bulls festival in Pamplona is cancelled by violence sparked by police reaction to clash of Basques and Navarrese nationalists; disorders spread to San Sebastián and elsewhere (leaving two dead). New constitution limits king's role and contains detailed bill of rights

1979: Democratic Center Union wins plurality in new elections; Suárez is reappointed premier

1980: Basque country and Catalonia become autonomous regions

SRI LANKA

Area: 25,332 sq. mi. **Population:** 14,184,000 (1978 est.)

Official Name: Democratic Socialist Republic of Sri Lanka **Capital:** Colombo **Nationality:** Sri Lankan **Languages:** Sinhala is the official language; both Sinhala and Tamil are national languages. English is used widely **Religion:** 64% Hinayana Buddhist, 20% Hindu, 9% Christian (mainly Roman Catholic), 6% Moslem, 1% other **Flag:** Narrow green and orange vertical stripes on the left side, with a yellow lion carrying a sword in one upraised paw against a red background occupying the rest of the flag. The entire flag is bordered in yellow, with a vertical yellow band separating the orange and green stripes from the red background of the rest of the flag **Anthem:** Hail, Hail, Motherland **Currency:** Sri Lanka rupee (16.0 per U.S. $1)

Location: Island in the Indian Ocean, off the southeastern tip of India. Sri Lanka is bounded on the north by the Palk Strait, on the east by the Bay of Bengal, on the south by the Indian Ocean, and on the west by the Gulf of Mannar **Features:** A low-lying plain makes up the northern half of the island and continues around the southern coast. The south-central part is mountainous **Chief Rivers:** Mahaweli, Ganga, Kelani, Walawe, Kalu, Gal

Head of State and of Government: President Junius Richard Jayewardene, born 1906, sworn in 1978 for a 6-year term. He is assisted by a prime minister, Ranasinghe Premadasa, born 1924, appointed 1978 **Effective Date of Present Constitution:** September 7, 1978 **Legislative Body:** Parliament (unicameral), with 196 members for 6-year terms **Local Government:** 22 districts, each headed by a governor

Ethnic Composition: 72% Sinhalese and 20% Tamil. (11% of the Tamil population are "Sri Lanka Tamils," citizens whose ancestors have lived in Sri Lanka for many generations and who have full voting rights. The 9% "Indian Tamils" came from south India in the 19th century) **Population Distribution:** 22.4% urban **Density:** 560 inhabitants per sq. mi.

Largest Cities: (1974 est.) Colombo 592,000, Dehiwala-Mount Lavinia 162,000, Jaffna 114,000, Moratuwa 100,000; (1971 census) Kandy 93,602, Kotte 93,042, Galle 72,720

Per Capita Income: $284 (1979) **Gross National Product (GNP):** $4.1 billion (1979) **Economic Statistics:** In 1973 about 34% of GNP was from agriculture (tea, rice, rubber, pineapples, coconuts), forestry, and fishing; 33% from trade and services; and 13% from industry (foodstuffs, tobacco products, chemicals, garments, leather and footwear, cement, paper and paperboard, tires and tubes, metal products) and mining **Minerals and Mining:** Graphite mining is the principal mineral industry; there are also gemstones, mineral sands and limestone **Labor Force:** 5.2 million (1977), with 45% in agriculture, and 13% in industry **Foreign Trade:** Exports, chiefly tea, rubber, gems, graphite, and coconut products, totaled $846 million in 1978. Imports, mainly rice and other food products, textiles, machinery and transport equipment and petroleum, totaled $983 million **Principal Trade Partners:** Britain, China, United States, Japan, India, West Germany, Pakistan, Saudi Arabia

Vital Statistics: Birthrate, 26.5 per 1,000 of pop. (1976); death rate, 9 **Life Expectancy:** 68 years **Health Statistics:** 334 inhabitants per hospital bed; 4,007 per physician (1976) **Infant Mortality:** 43 per 1,000 births **Illiteracy:** 18% **Primary and Secondary School Enrollment:** 2,462,141 (1977) **Enrollment in Higher Education:** 14,568 (1974) **GNP Expended on Education:** 3.1% (1976)

Transportation: Paved roads total 15,000 miles **Motor Vehicles:** 143,000 (1976) **Passenger Cars:** 93,800 **Railway Mileage:** 1,016 **Ports:** Colombo, Trincomalee, Galle **Major Airlines:** Air Lanka operates domestic and international services **Communications:** Government controlled **Radio Transmitters:** 24 **Receivers:** 800,000 (1976) **Television Transmitters:** 1 **Telephones:** 72,000 (1975) **Newspapers:** 18 dailies (1975), 42 copies per 1,000 inhabitants (1971)

Weights and Measures: The metric system is being introduced **Travel Requirements:** Passport, no visa for 30 days, onward ticket

Isolated from global and regional rivalries at independence in 1948, Sri Lanka, formerly known as Ceylon, was without an enemy and appeared to be assured of peace and prosperity. But parliamentary democracy has been a forum for radical communal nationalism that has divided the Sinhalese

Buddhist majority and the large Tamil minority and often brought the country near civil war. A positive action was the program to settle the "Indian Tamils" question through the naturalization of some and the repatriation to India of others. However, the Tamils have continued to press for a separate state.

In April 1971 ultraleftist students plunged the country into a full-scale guerrilla war before they faded into the jungled countryside. The movement was believed to have been born in 1964 when youth wings of the various Communist party factions split from adult leaders, accusing them of being both corrupt and irrelevant to the needs of Sri Lanka's peasantry.

The revolutionary movement had an obvious attraction to the many students who were the sons of peasants and who had taken advantage of free college education only to find no jobs available upon graduation. The 1971 uprising led to the declaration of a state of emergency that did not end until February 1977.

Mrs. Sirimavo Bandaranaike, the prime minister from 1960-65 and again from 1970-77, was defeated in the general elections of 1977 by Junius Jayewardene's United National party. Nepotism, abuses of power, and corruption, in addition to the poor economic situation, were the major issues in the campaign. In 1976 there had been severe student and labor unrest.

Under the Jayewardene government, Sri Lanka made a dramatically swift turn away from socialism and toward capitalism. The tea plantations, for instance, had been allowed to run down after being seized by the government in the early 1970s; under Jayewardene, private managers were put in charge of money-losing state corporations, particularly in efforts to boost the major exports—tea, rubber, and coconut. Foreign investment increased sharply, aided by tax holidays and other incentives, as well as what Sri Lankans said was worker productivity second only to Singapore in Asian industry. The government set out to increase electricity generation and farm irrigation by drafting plans for five major dams and reservoirs to be built within six years. To bring hope to the rural poor, Prime Minister Ranasinghe Premadasa, who is also Minister of Housing, built the first of what he said would be 25,000 model villages.

HISTORY: The earliest inhabitants of Sri Lanka (formerly Ceylon) have left few traces. The Sinhalese, who form the bulk of the present population, came to the island from northern India in the 6th century B.C. They founded their capital at Anuradhapura, which became a major religious center following the conversion of Sri Lanka to Buddhism in the 3rd century B.C. Invasions from south India, notably by the Tamils, forced the Sinhalese into the southwest of the island. In the 12th century A.D., Arab traders appeared in Ceylon. The island's coastal areas were occupied by the Portuguese in the 16th century. By the middle of the 17th century, their possessions had been taken over by the Dutch

1795: The Dutch possessions are taken over by Britain

1802: The Crown Colony of Ceylon is established

1815: All of the island of Ceylon is brought under British rule

1948: Sri Lanka becomes independent, with dominion status in the British Commonwealth

1956-59: S.W.R.D. Bandaranaike becomes prime minister, heading a leftist coalition. His term is marked by bloody riots between Sinhalese and Tamils, and ends with his assassination

1960-65: New elections bring another leftist coalition to power, with Mrs. Sirimavo Bandaranaike, wife of the slain leader, as the world's first woman prime minister. Her government adopts a neutralist policy and nationalizes a number of Western oil companies. A dispute with the United States and Britain results

1965-66: Elections result in the victory of the pro-Western United National party, led by Dudley Senanayake. His government agrees to compensation for the expropriated oil companies, and the United States agrees to resume economic aid to Sri Lanka, cut off at the time the companies were nationalized

1968: Sri Lanka becomes first of the developing nations to achieve the goal of a 5 percent rise in per capita income

1970: Mrs. Bandaranaike returns to power

1971: Revolutionary students, seeking to replace the government with one more militantly socialist, lead an uprising that results in the death of thousands of rebels and civilians

1972: Ceylon becomes a republic within the Commonwealth and is renamed Sri Lanka under a new constitution; William Gopallawa is appointed the republic's first president by Mrs. Bandaranaike; National Assembly approves land reform plan

1977: Sirimavo Bandaranaike's Freedom party is defeated in general elections; Junius Richard Jayewardene becomes prime minister following his United National party's victory. Sri Lanka amends constitution to give nation French-style presidential governing system which dilutes power of elected assembly, reduces prime minister and cabinet to figureheads and concentrates power in hands of popularly elected, all-powerful president, to be chosen every six years (after initial term by Prime Minister Jayewardene). Opposition attempts to stir antigovernment feeling over the changes prove futile

1978: At ceremony combining presidential inauguration with celebration of Sri Lanka's 30th year of independence, Prime Minister Jayewardene is sworn in as first president under new system. Tamil is granted the status of a national language. New constitution becomes effective

1979: Foreign investment, encouraged by President Jayewardene's politics, rises to an annual rate of $40 million, 13 times greater than in the last year of the previous government. The Liberation Tigers, young Tamil extremists, stage a wave of killings, with more conservative Tamils as the main victims

SUDAN

Area: 967,494 sq. mi. **Population:** 17,376,000 (1978 est.)

Official Name: Democratic Republic of the Sudan **Capital:** Khartoum **Nationality:** Sudanese **Languages:** Arabic, the official language is the native tongue of about 51% of the population; the Negroes of southern Sudan speak about 32 different languages, with English the chief commercial language **Religion:** The religion of the 12 northern provinces is Islam, whose adherents include about 70% of the population; most of the southern tribes are animist (25%). There are also some small Christian communities (5%) **Flag:** Horizontal stripes of red, white, and black, with a green triangle at the hoist **Anthem:** Soldiers of God **Currency:** Sudanese pound (.50 per U.S. $1)

Location: Northeast Africa. Sudan, the largest country in Africa is bounded on the north by Egypt, on the east by the Red Sea and Ethiopia, on the south by Kenya, Uganda, and Zaire, and on the west by the Central African Republic, Chad, and Libya **Features:** An immense plateau sprawls over 3 distinct natural regions, ranging from the Libyan and Sahara deserts and plateaus in the north to grassy plains in the center to a great swamp and tropical savanna in the south **Chief Rivers:** Nile (the Blue Nile and White Nile join at Khartoum)

Head of State and of Government: President: Gen. Jaafar Muhammad al-Nimeiry, born 1929, seized power in 1969, became the first elected president in 1971 and was reelected in 1977. He is also prime minister (since 1977) **Effective Date of Present Constitution:** 1973 **Legislative Body:** People's Assembly (unicameral), with 304 members (274 popularly elected) belonging to the Sudanese Socialist Union party **Local Government:** 18 provinces, headed by appointed commissioners and councils; the 6 provinces of the Southern Region have a joint semiautonomous government

Ethnic Composition: The population of the 12 northern provinces is comprised mainly of Moslem Arabs and Nubians, who together constitute more than two thirds of the population; in the south are Nilotic, Sudanic and black tribes **Population Distribution:** 20% urban **Density:** 18 inhabitants per sq. mi.

Largest Cities: (1975 est.) Khartoum 321,666, Omdurman 305,308, Khartoum North 161,278, Port Sudan 123,000

Per Capita Income: $318 (1979) **Gross National Product (GNP):** $5.8 billion (1979) **Economic Statistics:** In 1973, 39% of GNP was from agriculture (long-staple cotton, peanuts, sugarcane, gum arabic, livestock), 27% from trade and services, and 11% from industry (food, and vegetable oil processing) **Minerals and Mining:** Small-scale production of iron ore, chromite, manganese ore, slate, gold, and gypsum; deposits of asbestos, slate and tin exist **Labor Force:** 8.2 million (1978), with 85% in agriculture **Foreign Trade:** Exports, mainly cotton, gum arabic, sesame, peanuts, oil cake and meal, and sheep and goats, totaled $674 million in 1978. Imports, chiefly cotton textiles, motor vehicles and parts, electrical and nonelectrical machinery, base metals and manufactures, chemicals and petroleum products, totaled $1.4 billion **Principal Trade Partners:** Britain, India, Japan, France, Iraq, China, West Germany, Italy, United States, Egypt, Saudi Arabia

Vital Statistics: Birthrate, 47.8 per 1,000 of pop. (1975); death rate,

17.5 Life Expectancy: 50 years **Health Statistics:** 932 inhabitants per hospital bed; 9,488 per physician **Infant Mortality:** 93.6 per 1,000 births **Illiteracy:** 85% **Primary and Secondary School Enrollment:** 1,544,553 (1976) **Enrollment in Higher Education:** 21,342 (1975) **GNP Expended on Education:** 5.5% (1974)

Transportation: Paved roads total 350 mi. (1976) **Motor Vehicles:** 50,400 (1972) **Passenger Cars:** 29,200 **Railway Mileage:** 2,895 **Ports:** Port Sudan, Suakin **Major Airlines:** Sudan Airways, government owned, operates domestically and internationally **Communications:** Government owned **Radio Transmitters:** 7 **Licenses:** 1,300,000 (1973) **Television Transmitters:** 2 **Receivers:** 100,000 (1975) **Telephones:** 60,000 (1976) **Newspapers:** 4 dailies, 8 copies per 1,000 inhabitants (1975)

Weights and Measures: Metric system is the legal standard, but British and Egyptian standards are also used **Travel Requirements:** Passport, visa valid 3 months, $13.13 fee, 3 photos

---

The Sudan is Africa's largest country, almost one-third the size of the continental United States, but only a small part of its area, ranging from barren desert to tropical rain forest, is productive. Forty percent of the potentially arable land in the Arab world lies within its boundaries, but only 10 percent of this is under cultivation. Long-staple cotton, the chief export, is grown mainly in the irrigated triangle of land known as the Gezira Plain. This fertile area, just below the confluence of the White and Blue Niles at Khartoum, the capital, and other irrigated areas are a major source also of food and fodder crops.

Crops are raised also in the central rainlands, but production is uncertain because of droughts. Waters of the White Nile backing up into northern Sudan behind Egypt's Aswan Dam will eventually fill the need for additional irrigation.

Of all the African nations only Benin has had a greater number of coups and countercoups. Only Nigeria and Zaire have fought civil wars as cruel as the 17-year conflict, during which 500,000 died, between the Sudan's majority-status Arabs in the north and the minority Christian and pagan blacks in the south. Maj. Gen. Jaafar al-Nimeiry, who himself had seized power in a coup in May 1969, negotiated an end to the war in 1972 by granting regional autonomy to the south.

Nimeiry has survived numerous assassination attempts and two coups that were uncovered before they were begun. Three that were attempted did not succeed, including the revolt led by dissident army elements in July 1976. In this most recent attempt the rebels were defeated by loyal soldiers after having managed to travel 1,000 miles across the desert undetected. Accusing Libya of being behind the uprising, the Sudanese government severed diplomatic relations with the Libyans.

In foreign affairs, the Sudan is a member of the UN, the Arab League, and the Organization of African Unity. The nation participated on the Arab side in the Yom Kippur War. Relations with the U.S. had been troubled by the Arab-Israeli War, by the commutation in 1974 of the sentences of eight Black September terrorists found guilty of the murders of three diplomats 15 months earlier, and by their subsequent release to the Palestinians. But more recently, Nimeiry, following Egypt's lead, brought the Sudan closer to the West.

In 1979, the Sudan was one of only three Arab states to endorse Egypt's peace treaty with Israel.

HISTORY: Nubia, the northern half of Sudan, was colonized by Egypt centuries before the Christian era. In the 6th century A.D., the Nubians embraced Coptic Christianity, but in the 15th century were converted to Islam by conquering Arabs. Although the Arabs extended their conquests to the south, it was not until 1821 that all of Sudan was unified by Egypt

1881-85: Sudanese, led by the Mahdi, a Moslem religious fanatic, revolt against Egyptian rule and win control over most of Sudan

1898-99: Anglo-Egyptian army defeats Mahdi's followers; Sudan is proclaimed an Anglo-Egyptian condominium under a governor-general; however, Britain dominates the administration of the Sudan

1924: Egyptian troops mutiny in the Sudan; the British governor-general is murdered; the British expel the Egyptians from the Sudan and assume its rule

1936: Status of Sudan is affirmed by Anglo-Egyptian treaty

1948: In Sudan's first elections, Independence Front, favoring an independent republic, wins large majority over National Front, which favors union with Egypt

1953: Britain and Egypt conclude an agreement providing for Sudanese self-government

1956: Sudan is proclaimed an independent republic

1958: Gen. Ibrahim Abboud seizes power in military coup, dissolves parliament, nullifies constitution, and promises reforms

1964-65: Abboud resigns following popular rioting against his regime and a civilian government is set up; elections are held for a constituent assembly to draft new constitution; Mohammed Ahmed Mahgoub becomes prime minister of a coalition government; black Sudanese rebels in southern provinces launch widespread attacks against government forces

1968: Constituent assembly is dissolved and new elections are held; new assembly elects a supreme council, with Ismail al-Azhari as president

1969: A military coup led by Col. (now Maj. Gen.) Jaafar al-Nimeiry overthrows supreme council, annuls provisional constitution, and establishes revolutionary council

1971: Nimeiry is briefly toppled by Communist-backed rebel officers but regains power in countercoup and is elected president

1973: Sudan adopts a new constitution. Oil discovered in Red Sea

1976: Diplomatic relations with Libya are severed following Libyan support of an abortive coup against Nimeiry

1977: U.S. agrees to sell 12 F-5 jet fighters to Sudan

1978: Government and opposition announce reconciliation, formally ending nine years of intermittent conflict

---

SURINAME

Area: 60,239 sq. mi. **Population:** 374,000 (1978 est.)

Official Name: Republic of Suriname **Capital:** Paramaribo **Nationality:** Surinamese **Languages:** Dutch is the official language; English is also widely used. The majority speak a Creole lingua franca called Sranang Tongo, or Taki Taki **Religion:** 26% Hindu, 26% Moslem, 24% Protestant, and 23% Roman Catholic **Flag:** A wide horizontal red band with a centered golden yellow star, separated by narrow white stripes from green stripes top and bottom **Anthem:** Elevating Our Glorious Land **Currency:** Suriname guilder (florin) (1.785 per U.S. $1)

Location: Northeast coast of South America. It is bordered on the north by the Atlantic Ocean, on the east by French Guiana, on the south by Brazil, and on the west by Guyana **Features:** The three chief zones are the coastal belt (partly protected by dikes), the central zones of forests and savannas, and the southern hill zone, comprising 75% of the area, and rising to over 4,000 feet **Chief Rivers:** Suriname, Saramacca, Coppename, Nickerie, Tapanahoni, Marowijne (Maroni), Corantijn (Courantyne)

Head of State and of Government: Henk R. Chin A Sen, installed as prime minister by a National Military Council following coup of Feb. 25, 1980. He was named president following a second coup by the same group on Aug. 14, 1980 **Effective Date of Present Constitution:** November 1975 **Legislative Body:** Parliament (unicameral), called the *Staten*, with 39 members elected for 4 years **Local Government:** 9 districts, under appointed commissioners

Ethnic Composition: 37% Hindustanis (descendants of Indian laborers), 31% Creoles (of African descent), 17% Javanese, 11% Bush Negroes (descendants of escaped African slaves), 3% Amerindians (of Carib and Arawak stock), and minorities of 7,000 Chinese and 7,000 Europeans (chiefly Dutch) and Lebanese. More than 100,000 Surinamese Hindustani are currently living in the Netherlands **Population Distribution:** N.A. **Density:** 6.2 inhabitants per sq. mi.

Largest Cities: (1974 est.) Paramaribo 150,000; (1964 census) Nieuw-Nickerie 7,400, Meerzorg 5,000, Marienburg 3,500, Moengo 2,100

Per Capita Income: $1,721 (1979) **Gross National Product (GNP):** $685 million (1979) **Economic Statistics:** About 36% of the GNP is derived from the bauxite industry. Most of the balance comes from agriculture (rice, coffee, sugar, citrus fruits, coconuts, corn, cocoa, tobacco), fishing and shrimping, and lumbering. Industry, other than the processing of alumina and aluminum from bauxite, is confined to sawmilling, rice and sugar milling, and the production of rum and cement **Minerals and Mining:** Suriname is a major source of bauxite, producing more than 10% of the world supply; gold is also mined commercially **Labor Force:** 118,000; in 1974, 29% of the workers were engaged in agriculture and 15% in industry **Foreign Trade:** Exports, more than 90% of which was bauxite ore, alumina and aluminum, the rest being citrus fruits, bananas, shrimp, rice, and plywood, totaled $348 million in 1977. Imports, mainly machinery, manufactured goods, textiles, vehicles, petroleum products, iron and steel, and foods, totaled $388 million **Principal Trade Partners:** United States, Netherlands, Britain, Norway, Venezuela, Japan, Trinidad and Tobago

Vital Statistics: Birthrate, 40.9 per 1,000 of pop.; death rate, 7.2 **Life Expectancy:** 66 years **Health Statistics:** 184 inhabitants per hospital bed; 2,030 per physician (1975) **Infant Mortality:** 30.4 per 1,000 births **Illiteracy:** 20% **Primary and Secondary School Enrollment:** 120,224 (1976) **Enrollment in Higher Education:** 2,138 **GNP Expended on Education:** 4.7%

Transportation: Paved roads total about 300 mi. **Motor Vehicles:** 39,000 (1976) **Passenger Cars:** 28,800 **Railway Mileage:** 100 **Ports:** Paramaribo, Nieuw-Nickerie, Albina **Major Airlines:** Suriname Airways handles domestic and international flights **Communications:** Government and privately owned **Radio Transmitters:** 7 **Receivers:** 112,000 (1976) **Television Transmitters:** 3 **Receivers:** 38,000 (1976) **Telephones:** 21,000 **Newspapers:** 7 dailies (1975), 52 copies per 1,000 inhabitants (1974)

Weights and Measures: Metric system **Travel Requirements:** Passport, no visa, onward ticket

---

On attaining independence in 1975, Suriname immediately faced a major problem stemming from its multiracial composition—37 percent Hindustani, 31 percent Creole of African descent, 17 percent Javanese, 11 percent Bush Negro. Owing to Hindustani fears of the Creole-dominated government, over 100,000 Surinamers emigrated to the Netherlands prior to independence, thus stripping the emerging nation of between a quarter and a third of its human resources. The emigrants were predominantly well-educated middle and upper-class entrepreneurs, managers and technicians. The Surinamese government has appealed for the émigrés to return home to help in the development of the resource-rich former colony. To assist in this development the Netherlands has promised to grant Suriname $1.5 billion in aid over the next decade. It has been suggested that the Dutch generosity is based on a desire to improve economic conditions in Suriname enough so that the Surinamese refugees will return to their tropical homeland and leave poor-paying jobs and welfare rolls in Amsterdam. Another problem is the migration from the countryside to the city, with the result that Suriname may have to import food rather than export it.

Suriname is rich in minerals, forests and potential water power. The country's bauxite deposits are believed to be among the richest in the world. The mining, processing, and exporting of this resource (and since 1965 of alumina and aluminum) constitute the backbone of the economy. Sites of the two major bauxite deposits—Moengo and Paranam—are accessible to navigable rivers emptying into the Atlantic. Food processing and lumbering account for other important industries. Alcoa Aluminum, at a cost of $150 million, has built a dam for the production of hydroelectric energy on the Suriname River.

A government headed by Premier Henck Arron took power in the 1973 elections, when the National Party Coalition, composed mostly of Creoles, unseated the United Reformed Party, led by Jaggernath Lachmon and composed mainly of Hindustanis and Javanese. The Arron government was toppled in February 1980 by a sergeants' coup that appeared to be outside party lines; the army had just been denied the right to form a labor union to seek higher pay and better working conditions. Henk Chin A Sen was chosen to head a civilian government supervised by the newly formed National Military Council. In August 1980 the military installed Chin in the presidency as well.

HISTORY: Christopher Columbus sighted the coast of the area in 1498; but the first successful settlement was not established until 1651 by the British. The colony prospered on a plantation economy based on slave labor imported from Africa. Notable among the emigrants from other New World colonies were Jews from Brazil, who in 1665 erected the first synagogue in the Western Hemisphere. The Netherlands acquired Suriname from Britain in exchange for Dutch rights in Nieuw Amsterdam (Manhattan Island, New York). In the 18th and early 19th centuries the colony, as a result of wars and treaties, was shuffled among England, France and the Netherlands

1815: Netherlands finally regains Suriname at Vienna Congress

1863: Slavery is abolished. Importation of Hindustani, Javanese and Chinese contract laborers follows

1954: Suriname is granted internal autonomy

1973: Creole-dominated National Party Coalition (NPK) wins elections. NPK leader Henck Arron becomes premier

1975: Suriname gains independence

1978: National Party Coalition reelected by landslide in nation's first elections since independence

1980: The army is denied the right to form a labor union. On February 25, a sergeants' coup, staged at the cost of six lives and the burning of a police station, ousts the Arron government. Henk Chin A Sen becomes head of a military-supervised civilian government. In May, 300 mercenaries—Dutch, Belgians, Venezuelans and South Moluccans—cross the border from French Guiana into Suriname but all are captured. Their leader, Frits Ormskerk, a former soldier in the Surinamese army, is executed by a firing squad. In August Chin is made president by the military

---

SWAZILAND

Area: 6,705 sq. mi. **Population:** 544,000 (1978 est.)

Official Name: Kingdom of Swaziland **Capital:** Mbabane **Nationality:** Swazi **Languages:** The official languages are English and si-Swati; Zulu is used by a minority **Religion:** About 43% are animists, with about 500 Moslems; the rest of the population is Christian **Flag:** Horizontal stripes of blue, yellow, red, yellow, and blue with a traditional Swazi shield, spears and staff in black and white in the center **Anthem:** National Anthem, beginning "O God, Bestower of the blessings of the Swazi" **Currency:** Lilangeni (0.78 per U.S. $1)

Location: Southern Africa. Swaziland is almost entirely surrounded by South Africa, except for a 70-mile-long border with Mozambique on the east **Features:** The country consists of three well-defined regions known locally as the high, middle, and low velds, all roughly of equal breadth. The humid *highveld* in the west is mountainous; a plateau lies in the center, and to the east is a subtropical low plain **Chief Rivers:** Komati, Umbuluzi, Great Usutu, Mkonda

Head of State: King Sobhuza II, born 1899; Ngwenyama (the Lion), head of the Swazi nation since 1921, made head of state in 1968 **Head of Government:** Prime Minister: Prince Mabandla Fred Dlamini, appointed Nov. 1979 **Effective Date of Present Constitution:** October 13, 1978 **Legislative Body:** Parliament, or *Liblandla*, (bicameral) consists of a 20-member Senate, and a 50-member House of Assembly; 10 of each are appointed by the king, the rest are chosen by an electoral college. There are no political parties, and the function of parliament is restricted to advising the king and debating proposals **Local Government:** 4 districts

Ethnic Composition: The African population is predominantly Swazi, with a Zulu minority; both belong to the Bantu group. About 3% are non-Africans **Population Distribution:** 15% urban **Density:** 81 inhabitants per sq. mi.

Largest Cities: (1976 est.) Manzini 26,000, Mbabane 22,000

Per Capita Income: $634 (1978) **Gross National Product (GNP):** $340 million (1978) **Economic Statistics:** The main activity is subsistence agriculture (maize, the subsistence crop, and such commercial crops as sugar, timber, citrus fruits, cotton, rice, and pineapples), which accounts for about 29% of GNP. Mining and manufacturing (machinery, beverages, chemicals, apparel, metal products, processed agricultural products) contribute about 37% of GNP **Minerals and Mining:** Deposits of iron ore, asbestos, and coal are exploited; kaolin, barites, gold, and pyrophyllite are exploited on a smaller scale **Labor Force:** 120,000 (1978), with 60,000 engaged in subsistence agriculture and 18,114 employed in South African mines **Foreign Trade:** Exports, chiefly iron ore, sugar, wood pulp and other forest products, and asbestos, totaled $207 million in 1978. Imports, mainly manufactured goods, machinery and transport equipment, fuel, food and beverages, and tobacco, totaled $270 million **Principal Trade Partners:** South Africa, Britain, Japan

Vital Statistics: Birthrate, 49 per 1,000 of pop. (1975); death rate, 21.8 **Life Expectancy:** 44 years **Health Statistics:** 294 inhabitants per hospital bed; 10,000 per physician (1976) **Infant Mortality:** N.A. **Illiteracy:** 75% **Primary and Secondary School Enrollment:** 111,071 (1976) **Enrollment in Higher Education:** 1,150 (1976) **GNP Expended on Education:** 5% (1975)

Transportation: Paved roads total 241 mi. **Motor Vehicles:** 15,000 (1976) **Passenger Cars:** 7,900 **Railway Mileage:** 192 **Ports:** None **Major Airlines:** Royal Swazi National Airways operates international flights **Communications:** Government and private **Radio Transmitters:** 7 **Receivers:** 60,000 (1976) **Television Transmitters:** 1 **Telephones:** 9,000 **Newspapers:** 1 daily, 111 copies per 1,000 inhabitants (1974)

Weights and Measures: Metric system **Travel Requirements:** Passport, no visa

---

The smallest of three former British protectorates in southern Africa to attain independence, Swaziland is the home of a gentle Bantu people. For the Swazis, British protection was not merely a colonialist device. It saved them from Zulu and Boer invasions and was also the shield against absorption into South Africa's apartheid system when the black African nation of Swaziland became independent in 1968.

Along with the other former protectorates, Botswana and Lesotho, Swaziland is geographically and economically linked to South Africa, but all three nations have asserted a determination to preserve political independence. Although all are members of the South African Customs and Monetary Area, in 1974 Swaziland issued its own currency, and political and economic tensions with South Africa have increased.

Despite its small size and landlocked situation between South Africa's *highveld* and the Mozambique border, Swaziland possesses exceptional potential for economic independence. In addition to major resources of iron ore, asbestos, and coal, the country produces sugar, rice, tobacco, cotton, citrus fruits, and other crops. It also has a wood-pulp industry based on a rapidly growing forest of pine and eucalyptus. Japan has become a major customer for iron ore, and rice production has been increased with the help of Nationalist China.

Most of the country's industries are still owned by British and South African interests, but, particularly in farmland, there is a program in operation under which Swazis are buying back foreign-owned property.

One of the major revenue producers for the government is the gambling casino of the Royal Swazi Hotel, near Mbabane, the capital. Since gambling is illegal in South Africa, a large part of the clientele is made up of white South Africans. But those around the gaming tables also include whites from Europe and black Africans.

In 1973 King Sobhuza discarded Swaziland's five-year-old constitution and, in 1977, replaced the nation's parliamentary system with an assembly of tribal leaders. The electoral process was restored in October 1978, under a new constitution, as Swazis voted for members of an electoral college, which in turn, was to name 40 members of the 50-man National Assembly and 10 of the nation's 20 senators. The remaining legislators were to be appointed by King Sobhuza.

HISTORY: The Swazis settled in present-day Swaziland in 1820 after being expelled by the Zulus from the land north of the Pongola River. Continued harassment by the Zulus led them to seek aid from the British, who succeeded in establishing friendly relations between the two tribes. The country's independence was guaranteed by the British and Transvaal governments in 1881 and 1884, and was followed by the establishment in 1890 of a provisional government representative of the Swazi and the two guarantors

1902-7: The Transvaal's rights in Swaziland pass to Britain following the Boer War; after a period of administration by the British governor of the Transvaal, Swaziland becomes a high commission territory ruled by a British commissioner

1921: Sobhuza II becomes Ngwenyama, head of the Swazi nation, after 20-year regency of his mother

1949: Opposition to South Africa's apartheid policy causes Britain to reject request that Swaziland, along with Basutoland (now Lesotho) and Bechuanaland (now Botswana), be transferred to South African control

1967: Swaziland wins self-government under a new constitution with Sobhuza as king

1968: Swaziland becomes independent state and a UN member

1969: Swaziland, disappointed by aid offered by Britain, moves to expand trade with African neighbors to boost national revenue; joins in customs union with South Africa

1973: Sobhuza repeals constitution; assumes supreme power

1976: Colonel Maphevu Dlamini becomes prime minister

1977: King Sobhuza abolishes the parliamentary system and replaces it with an assembly based on tribal leadership

1978: Voters create electoral college under new constitution. New railroad to South African coast completed

1979: Prime Minister Dlamini dies and is replaced by Prince Mabandla Fred Dlamini

---

SWEDEN

Area: 173,665 sq. mi. **Population:** 8,294,000 (1979 est.)

Official Name: Kingdom of Sweden **Capital:** Stockholm **Nationality:** Swedish **Languages:** Swedish, the official language, is spoken by the vast majority; in the north there are Lapp and Finnish-speaking minorities **Religion:** About 94% of the population is Lutheran, the state religion **Flag:** An extended yellow cross on a field of blue **Anthem:** Thou Ancient, Thou Freeborn **Currency:** Swedish Krona (4.2 per U.S. $1)

Location: Northern Europe, occupying the eastern part of the Scandinavian Peninsula. It is bordered on the northeast by Finland, on the east and south by the Gulf of Bothnia and the Baltic Sea, on the southwest by the Öresund, Kattegat, and Skagerrak, and on the west by Norway **Features:** The land is gently rolling in the south and mountainous in the north. About half the country is wooded, and lakes cover some 9% of the area **Chief Rivers:** Göta-Klar, Lule, Ume, Angerman, Dal

Head of State: King Carl XVI Gustaf, born 1946, succeeded 1973 **Head of Government:** Prime Minister Thorbjörn Fälldin, born 1926, assumed office Oct. 12, 1979 **Effective Date of Present Constitution:** January 1975 **Legislative Body:** Parliament (unicameral). The *Riksdag* consists of 349 members elected for 3-year terms **Local Government:** 24 counties, with appointed governors and elected councils

Ethnic Composition: The population is largely homogeneous, with a Lapp minority of 17,000. There are 425,000 immigrants, mainly from other Nordic countries, Greece, Yugoslavia, and Turkey **Population Distribution:** 83% urban **Density:** 48 inhabitants per sq. mi.

Largest Cities: (M.A. = Metropolitan Area) (1977 est.) Stockholm 658,743 (M.A. 1,374,897), Göteborg 440,211 (M.A. 693,562), Malmö 238,567 (M.A. 453,914), Uppsala 141,234, Norrköping 120,669, Västeras 118,131

Per Capita Income: $10,071 (1979) **Gross National Product (GNP):** $84 billion (1979) **Economic Statistics:** About 59% of the GNP is derived from trade and services; 36% from manufacturing, construction and mining and 5% from agriculture (chiefly oats, wheat, rye, barley, potatoes, and dairy produce) **Minerals and Mining:** High grade iron ore is the primary mineral but there are also smaller deposits of gold, silver, lead, copper, zinc, pyrites, tungsten, manganese, granite, quartz, and marble **Labor Force:** 4.2 million (1978), with 37% in mining, manufacturing and construction; 31% in public service; 22% in trade and transportation; 6% in agriculture **Foreign Trade:** Exports, chiefly lumber, pulp and paper, ships, iron ore, machinery, and base metals totaled $21.7 billion in 1978. Imports, mainly machinery, chemicals and fuel products, and base metals, totaled $20.4 billion **Principal Trade Partners:** EC countries, United States, Canada, Norway, Finland, USSR, Saudi Arabia

Vital Statistics: Birthrate, 11.6 per 1,000 of pop. (1977); death rate, 10.7 **Life Expectancy:** 74 years **Health Statistics:** 66 inhabitants per hospital bed; 580 per physician (1975) **Infant Mortality:** 8.0 per 1,000 births (1977) **Illiteracy:** Negligible **Primary and Secondary School Enrollment:** 1,229,611 (1976) **Enrollment in Higher Education:** 162,640, (1975) **GNP Expended on Education:** 7.7% (1976)

Transportation: Surfaced roads total 17,514 mi. (1973) **Motor Vehicles:** 3,045,400 (1976) **Passenger Cars:** 2,881,000 **Railway Mileage:** 7,538 **Ports:** Göteborg, Stockholm, Malmö, Helsingborg, Trelleborg, Gävle, Luleå, Sundsvall, Norrköping **Major Airlines:** Scandinavian Airlines System (SAS), owned jointly by Sweden, Norway and Denmark, operates internationally; AB Linjeflyg, the Swedish affiliate of SAS, operates domestically **Communications:** Government controlled **Radio Transmitters:** 282 **Licenses:** 3,203,000 (1976) **Television Transmitters:** 358 **Licenses:** 2,988,000 (1976) **Telephones:** 5,673,000 (1976) **Newspapers:** 135 dailies, 572 copies per 1,000 inhabitants (1975)

Weights and Measures: Metric system **Travel Requirements:** Passport, no visa for 3 months

Once upon a time Sweden was world-renowned for its idyllic stability; for life without hunger, war, or other material distress; for an overall reasonableness in settling its affairs. Intruding on the Swedish idyll in the last few years, however, have been such extraordinary developments as strikes by workers in defiance of union leaders now considered part of the Establishment, a new militance among organized salaried employees in the face of heavy taxes and an increasingly steep cost of living. However, Swedish unemployment is still among the world's lowest, and Swedish per capita gross national product is among the highest.

Although Sweden is often described abroad as a socialist state, it is not so in the Marxist sense. According to Swedish authorities, theirs is a pragmatic socialism dedicated to assuring material security for all and establishing state-owned enterprises only in areas that private enterprise cannot or will not enter. Roughly 90 percent of Swedish industry is privately owned. A little more than 5 percent is in public hands, and the remaining enterprises are cooperatives.

The high cost of social welfare, for which roughly one third of the budget is earmarked, is met from the high taxes and from contributions to compulsory insurance plans. Among the principal features of the social welfare state are a national health insurance, a pension system, free prenatal care and child delivery, annual allowances to the mother until a child reaches 16, free tuition at Swedish universities, home-furnishing loans for newlyweds, and rent rebates for large families.

Under a national policy of full employment, the state operates a job service, moves unemployed persons to areas where work is available and offers retraining to those who lose jobs through automation or disability. Despite recent labor troubles, Sweden's union-management relations, compared with those of most other highly industrialized countries, have on the whole been placid since the 1930s. In general, labor's demands have been tempered by the need to compete in world markets; exports account for roughly one fourth of the GNP.

Figuring largely in Sweden's economic and social achievements is its policy of neutrality, under which it has managed to avoid war for close to 160 years. But Sweden's neutrality, the Swedes insist, is an avoidance of alliances, not a neutrality of opinion. This policy, they say, is not abridged by strong stands taken on conflicts far from their shores, notably denunciations by government ministers of U.S. involvement in Vietnam and the military takeover in Chile.

The welfare programs were developed by the Social Democratic party, which dominated Swedish politics from 1936 until 1976. A majority of voters, reacting to high taxes and an unimaginative bureaucracy, then voted into power a coalition of three nonsocialist parties, with Thorbjörn Fälldin as prime minister. The coalition broke down in 1978 and was replaced by a minority Liberal government under Ola Ullsten. In the 1979 parliamentary elections, the Social Democrats failed by only one seat of regaining power as the three nonsocialist parties won 175 seats in the *Riksdag*. Fälldin again became prime minister.

In a nonbinding referendum on the nation's nuclear energy held March 23, 1980, Swedes chose not to abandon nuclear power as an energy source. A plurality of voters elected to continue operation of the country's six nuclear plants, but to limit their number to 12 in all and to phase out nuclear energy after 25 years.

Sweden's first nationwide strike in 70 years involved nearly one million workers for ten days in May, before the unions agreed to a 6.8 percent wage increase.

HISTORY: The earliest known reference to the Swedes is by the Roman historian Tacitus, who wrote in A.D. 98 that the Suiones (of the Lake Mälaren area) had a mighty fleet and a host of warriors, and were ruled by an absolute king. By the 6th century they had conquered their southern neighbors, the Götar, and merged with them. During the Viking period (9th—12th centuries), Swedes extended their influence across Russia to the Black Sea and joined with Danes and Norwegians in raids and voyages to Western Europe and the British Isles

829: Christianity is introduced by a Frankish monk, St. Anskar

1150-60: Erik IX stamps out paganism among the Swedes and undertakes a crusade against the Finnish heathens, adding Finland to the Kingdom of Sweden

1319: Sweden and Norway are united under Norway's Magnus VII

1397: Denmark, Sweden, and Norway are united under Denmark's Queen Margrethe to combat the superiority of the German mercantile organization, the Hanse

1523-60: Gustav Eriksson, elected king as Gustavus I, establishes Vasa dynasty, ends the union with Denmark and Norway, cuts ties to the Roman Catholic Church, and establishes a Lutheran state church

1611-32: Gustavus II establishes Sweden as a great European power, expanding the kingdom in wars with Russia and Poland and in the Thirty Years War against the Hapsburgs

1648: Peace of Westphalia gives Sweden German territory and makes Swedish kings princes of the Holy Roman Empire

1700-21: Charles XII launches a brilliant defensive campaign against Russia, Poland, and Denmark in the Northern War, but a series of victories is followed by a disastrous invasion of Russia, capped by the capitulation of the Swedish Army at Poltava (1709). After further defeats, Sweden declines as a major European power, having been forced to give up most of its continental conquests and possessions

1805-09: Sweden joins the Allies against Napoleon, loses its German Territories to France and Finland to Russia. Gustavus IV is overthrown; constitutional monarchy is established

1813-14: Entering its last major war, Sweden again joins the Allies against Napoleon, with Swedish forces led by the former French Marshal Jean Bernadotte, the chosen successor to the Swedish throne. He compels Denmark to cede Norway to Sweden

1818: Bernadotte ascends throne as Charles XIV; he steers Sweden toward a policy of neutrality

1905: Union with Norway is terminated peacefully

1917: Parliamentary form of government is established

1920: Sweden's first Social Democratic government is formed

1959: Sweden joins European Free Trade Association

1973: Carl XVI Gustaf succeeds to the throne upon the death of his grandfather, Gustaf VI Adolf

1975: A new constitution comes into effect which restricts the function of the king to a ceremonial role and approves the unicameral parliament in effect since 1971

1976: King Carl XVI Gustaf marries Sylvia Sommerlath. Swedish parliament adopts a law giving employees of certain companies the right to place two worker-delegates on the board of directors. Nonsocialist bloc (Center, Liberal and Moderate Unity parties) wins election; Thorbjörn Fälldin becomes prime minister

1977: Swedish cradle-to-grave "welfare state" palls as economy continues slumping badly, with many once-profitable exports reaching uncompetitive price levels due to high labor costs and sated world markets. Three of nation's largest shipbuilders are nationalized and merged. Three devaluations of krona improve its monetary position; investments, GNP decline

1978: Economy reaches crisis stage as prices and unemployment continue rising; recession is considered nation's worst in 40 years. *Riksdag* abrogates Salic Law, thus allowing female succession to the throne; second parliamentary vote needed to make this part of constitution. Liberal and Moderate Unity parties reject plans of Fälldin's Center party to stop building nuclear power plants. Fälldin resigns. Ola Ullsten becomes prime minister in minority Liberal government

1979: Nonsocialist bloc wins parliamentary elections by one seat over Social Democrats; Fälldin again becomes prime minister

---

SWITZERLAND

Area: 15,943 sq. mi. **Population:** 6,298,000 (1978 est.)

Official Name: Swiss Confederation **Capital:** Bern **Nationality:** Swiss **Languages:** German (65%), French (18%), Italian (12%), and Romansch, a Romance language spoken in eastern Switzerland (1%) are official languages. Many Swiss speak more than one language **Religion:** About 48% Protestant, 49% Roman Catholic, 0.3% Jewish **Flag:** A square red field with a white cross in the center **Anthem:** Swiss Psalm **Currency:** Swiss franc (1.66 per U.S. $1)

Location: Central Europe. Switzerland is bounded on the north by Germany, on the east by Austria and Liechtenstein, on the south by Italy, and on the west by France **Features:** About 60% of the country is covered by the great Alpine mountain chain running through the south. The Jura Mountains in the west make up about 10% of the land. The rest is a plateau between the two mountain ranges **Chief Rivers:** Rhine, Rhône, Aare, Inn

Head of State and of Government: Executive authority is vested in the Federal Council, composed of 7 councilors elected for 4 years by the Federal Assembly; each year a president and vice-president are elected. The council, whose members head the 7 federal departments, is the directing power in the nation. President (for 1980): Georges-André Chevallaz **Effective Date of Present Constitution:** 1848, amended 1874 **Legislative Body:** Federal Assembly (bicameral), consisting of the Council of State, with 46 members and either 3 or 4 year terms, and the National Council, with 200 members elected directly for 4 years **Local Government:** 26 cantons, with elected unicameral legislatures, divided into communes

Ethnic Composition: Traditionally 4 ethnic groups: German, French, Italian, and Romansch, with 932,743 resident foreigners (1978) **Population Distribution:** 58% urban **Density:** 395 inhabitants per sq. mi.

Largest Cities: (1975 est.) Zürich 396,300, Basel 195,700, Geneva 159,200, Bern 152,800, Lausanne 135,200

Per Capita Income: $9,439 (1979) **Gross National Product (GNP):** $60 billion (1979) **Economic Statistics:** 47% of GNP is derived from industry (machinery, chemicals, watches); 46% from commerce and services; and 7% from agriculture (dairy products, grains, fruit and vegetables, and wine-growing) **Minerals and Mining:** None; rich in forests and waterpower **Labor Force:** 2,800,000 (1978). About 23% are foreigners. Of the total, some 49% are in trade and services, 43% in industry, and 8% in agriculture and forestry **Foreign Trade:** Exports, chiefly machinery, watches, chemicals, and textiles, totaled $24 billion in 1978. Imports, mainly chemicals, crude oil, clothing, machines, and motor vehicles, totaled $24 billion **Principal Trade Partners:** West Germany, France, United States, Italy, Britain, Austria

Vital Statistics: Birthrate, 11.5 per 1,000 of pop. (1977); death rate, 8.8 **Life Expectancy:** 75 years **Health Statistics:** 87 inhabitants per hospital bed; 524 per physician (1976) **Infant Mortality:** 10.7 per 1,000 births (1977) **Illiteracy:** Negligible **Primary and Secondary School Enrollment:** 946,048 (1977) **Enrollment in Higher Education:** 64,720 (1975) **GNP Expended on Education:** 5.2% (1976)

Transportation: Surfaced roads total 37,000 mi. **Motor Vehicles:** 2,086,800 (1977) **Passenger Cars:** 1,932,800 **Railway Mileage:** 3,166 (1972) **Ports:** None **Major Airlines:** Swissair operates domestic and international flights **Communications:** Government controlled **Radio Transmitters:** 211 **Licenses:** 2,108,000 (1976) **Television Transmitters:** 583 **Licenses:** 1,809,000 (1976) **Telephones:** 4,016,000 (1976) **Newspapers:** 95 dailies, 402 copies per 1,000 inhabitants (1975)

Weights and Measures: Metric system **Travel Requirements:** Passport, no visa for 3 months

---

If pacifists want proof of their contentions, they can point to Switzerland, the country that has not sent its troops into foreign wars since 1815. Switzerland has low unemployment amid growing joblessness in much of the rest of the world, and it ranks among the world's wealthiest countries. But, like other countries, it has been plagued by growing inflation rates during the past few years, and federal budgets recently ceased to be balanced.

The Swiss guard their neutrality with a modern army. Switzerland's neutrality was guaranteed by the Congress of Vienna in 1815; dedication to neutrality has even kept Switzerland out of the United Nations. However, Switzerland is a member of several special agencies of the UN and has a permanent observer at the UN.

A member of the Council of Europe, Switzerland in 1972 was one of five members of the European Free Trade Association that signed a free-trade agreement with the EEC.

In part, the Swiss have been able to remain neutral because of the rugged Alps, which cover half the country and are uninviting as a battleground. At the same time, the country, which lacks actual mineral resources, has in its terrain and geographical location features that act as natural resources, and which are in fact the bases of the country's prosperity.

Snow-clad Alpine peaks from whose rushing

streams hydroelectric power has been widely developed also constitute a winter vacation mecca, and the central European location of their country has enabled the hardworking Swiss to make it a center for trade, shipping, freight-forwarding, banking, and insurance. And more than a third of Swiss exports consists of machinery, precision instruments, and watches.

The Swiss spirit of tolerance is more recent than the policy of neutrality; religious disputes produced a civil war as late as 1847—a revolt of Catholic rural cantons against the increasing influence of the Protestant cities over the federal government. But division along ethnic lines of French-, German-, and Italian-speaking peoples has been avoided by giving the cantons much power and keeping the federal government tightly reined. Taxes, for example, cannot be increased without a constitutional amendment, which requires a national referendum.

Hard-fought issues are usually absent, because Switzerland has been governed for decades by a coalition of major parties. One of the hardest-fought issues was resolved when the male electorate voted in 1971 to enfranchise Swiss women in federal elections, ending Swiss political backwardness and reversing a decision of 12 years before. The national trend of reaching decisions by consensus has produced a well-ordered country where even strikes are almost unknown, and there are no drastic extremes of wealth and poverty.

In 1979, after long discussion, the French-speaking communes of the Canton of Bern were organized into a new canton—Jura. Nuclear power, on which Switzerland become heavily dependent, became an issue in 1979; a referendum in February rejected a constitutional amendment to restrict it, but, after the Three Mile Island accident in the United States, the Swiss voted to forbid the construction of any new plant without the approval of the Federal Assembly.

HISTORY: The Helvetii, a Celtic tribe, were the first known inhabitants of Switzerland. The land was conquered by the Romans in 58 B.C. and remained a Roman province for approximately 300 years. In the 5th century, it was overrun by the Alemanni and the Burgundii, and then passed to the Franks. After being split between Swabia and Transjurane Burgundy in the 9th century, it was united under the Holy Roman Empire in 1033

1291: Forest cantons of Schwyz, Uri, and Unterwalden form defensive league in face of growing encroachments by House of Hapsburg

1315: League defeats Austrian armies at Morgarten Pass

1386-88: Joined by five other cantons, the league decisively defeats Austrians, insuring existence of the confederation

1499: Swiss gain virtual independence from Holy Roman Emperor Maximilian I

1519: Ulrich Zwingli, vicar of Zurich Cathedral, attacks practices of Roman Catholic Church; his lectures on New Testament mark beginning of Protestant Reformation in Switzerland

1541: John Calvin introduces Protestantism into Geneva and establishes a theocratic state

1648: Switzerland's formal independence is recognized in the Peace of Westphalia, which ended the Thirty Years War

1798-1803: French Revolution results in creation of Helvetic Republic, which is governed as a French appendage

1815: Perpetual Swiss neutrality is guaranteed by Congress of Vienna

1914-18: Swiss remain neutral in World War I

1939-45: Swiss maintain neutrality during World War II

1959: Women's suffrage, in federal elections, although advocated by federal council and federal assembly, is rejected in referendum

1971: Constitutional amendment gives Swiss women the vote in federal elections and the right to hold federal office

1974: A plebiscite in the French-speaking Jura region of the largely German-speaking canton of Bern results in a narrow majority favoring a separate Jura canton

1978: Acting to stem rise of Swiss franc and protect its export industry and tourism business, government decides to ban further foreign capital investment

1979: Canton of Jura established

SYRIA

On September 10, 1980, President Assad of Syria and Colonel Qadaffi of Libya issued a proclamation stating that Syria and Libya had become a single state.

Area: 71,722 sq. mi. **Population:** 8,088,000 (1978 est.)

Official Name: Syrian Arab Republic **Capital:** Damascus **Nationality:** Syrian **Languages:** Arabic is the official and predominant language; French and English are also used, and Armenian and Kurdish are spoken by minorities **Religion:** 74% Sunni Moslem, 16% other Moslem, and 10% Christian **Flag:** Three equal horizontal stripes of red, white and black with five-pointed green stars symmetrically aligned on the white stripe **Anthem:** National Anthem, beginning "Defenders of the homeland, salute" **Currency:** Syrian pound (3.95 per U.S. $1)

Location: Southwest Asia. Syria is bounded on the north by Turkey, on the east by Iraq, on the south by Jordan and Israel, and on the west by Lebanon and the Mediterranean Sea **Features:** The country consists of a narrow coastal plain, east of which is a highland region that is continued to the south by the Lebanon and Anti-Lebanon Mountains. Fertile plains form the central region, with the Syrian Desert to the southeast. North of the desert region lies the fertile Euphrates River Valley **Chief Rivers:** Euphrates, Orontes

Head of State and of Government: President: Lt. Gen. Hafez al-Assad, born 1928, reelected in 1978 for 7 years. He is assisted by Prime Minister Abdel Rauf al-Kasm, appointed Jan. 1980 **Effective Date of Present Constitution:** 1973 **Legislative Body:** People's Council (unicameral), consisting of 195 elected members **Local Government:** 13 provinces, each headed by an appointed governor and a partly elected council, and the municipality of Damascus

Ethnic Composition: 90% are Arabs; minorities include Circassians, Armenians, Turks, and Kurds **Population Distribution:** 48% urban **Density:** 113 inhabitants per sq. mi.

Largest Cities: (1977 est.) Damascus 1,097,205, Aleppo 842,606, Homs 292,280, Latakia 191,329, Hama 173,459

Per Capita Income: $983 (1979) **Gross National Product (GNP):** $8.3 billion (1979) **Economic Statistics:** 36% of the GNP is derived from services; 26% from industry (petroleum refining, textiles, cement, glass, apparel, soap, food processing); 19% from commerce; and 18% from agriculture (wheat, barley, cotton) **Minerals and Mining:** Oil, natural gas, phosphates, asphalt, gypsum and rock salt **Labor Force:** 1.8 million; 32% engaged in agriculture and 26% in industry **Foreign Trade:** Exports, chiefly petroleum (70% of total) and raw cotton, totaled $1 billion in 1978. Imports, mainly textiles, machinery, petroleum products, vehicles, and foodstuffs, totaled $2.4 billion **Principal Trade Partners:** EC countries, USSR, Arab countries, United States, Romania

Vital Statistics: Birthrate, 45.4 per 1,000 of pop. (1975); death rate, 14.8 **Life Expectancy:** 57 years **Health Statistics:** 956 inhabitants per hospital bed; 2,529 per physician (1977) **Infant Mortality:** 15.3 per 1,000 births (1976) **Illiteracy:** 47% **Primary and Secondary School Enrollment:** 1,828,339 (1976) **Enrollment in Higher Education:** 73,660 **GNP Expended on Education:** 5.8% (1975)

Transportation: Paved roads total 7,484 mi. **Motor Vehicles:** 118,700 (1976) **Passenger Cars:** 62,800 **Railway Mileage:** 958 **Ports:** Latakia, Baniyas, Tartus **Major Airlines:** Syrian Arab Airlines, government owned, operates domestically and internationally **Communications:** Government owned **Radio Transmitters:** 13 **Receivers:** 2,500,000 (1972) **Television Transmitters:** 7 **Receivers:** 230,000 (1976) **Telephones:** 193,000 **Newspapers:** 6 dailies (1975), 9 copies per 1,000 inhabitants

Weights and Measures: Metric system and local units are used **Travel Requirements:** Check with Syrian embassy, Washington, D.C.

Once the center of one of the most ancient civilizations on earth, Syria today seeks a leadership role in the Arab world. As an ardent champion of the Palestinian Liberation Organization, Syria has trained and armed guerrillas at bases within the country.

Syria merged with Egypt in 1958, but seceded in 1961. In the 1970s, it established a joint command and diplomatic coordination with Jordan. In 1979, President Hafez al-Assad of Syria and President Ahmed Hassan al-Bakr of Iraq formed a joint political command. They also agreed to merge their two Ba'ath socialist countries, but took no immediate steps to implement the agreement. Relations between Syria and Iraq have been marred by squab-

bles about ideological points and national goals. Each expelled the other's diplomats in August 1980.

President Assad is a military man who took power in a coup in 1970 and has brought stability to Syria.

Before World War I, Syria was part of the Ottoman Empire and loosely included all of what is now Lebanon, Israel, and Jordan, as well as Syria itself. Even today some people speak wistfully of a "Greater Syria." Between the two world wars, the country was under French mandate; it became independent in 1946.

The Syrian people are considered among the most sophisticated in the Arab world, largely because for centuries the country has been a passageway between the Mediterranean world and the Far East.

In recent years Syria has aligned itself closely with the Soviet Union. Its armed forces are equipped by Moscow, and there are believed to be upward of 1,000 Soviet military and civilian advisors in the country. However, Syrian intervention in Lebanon has placed a strain on Soviet relations because Russia has been a supporter of the Palestinians in Lebanon and the use of Soviet weapons by Syria against them has embarrassed Moscow. President Assad tried to patch up the differences in his spring 1977 trip to Moscow.

In spite of the Soviet presence, the left-wing military rulers have outlawed the Syrian Communist party. President Assad's Ba'ath (Socialist) party is predominant. The press and radio are directly controlled by the state.

Israeli soldiers have occupied part of southwestern Syria since 1967. A demilitarized zone, patrolled by a multinational force under United Nations command, has been established between the Israeli and Syrian forces. The Israeli-occupied area is of strategic importance, and many Israelis want their government to annex it. Syria has little to gain from negotiations with Israel and opposes Egypt's negotiations.

Most recently Syria has been concerned with the civil war in Lebanon, having historically regarded Lebanon as part of "Greater Syria" and not wanting a radical state on its western frontier. In the final phase of the 19-month conflict, Syrian troops and tanks intervened against Palestinian-led forces when it appeared they might win, install a radical state and incite war with Israel. In 1978, Syrian-dominated peacekeeping forces began battling Lebanese troops and right-wing militia in and around Beirut. Syrian and Israeli airplanes clashed in Lebanese air space during 1979.

Recent clashes between the minority Moslem Alawite sect and the extremist Moslem Brotherhood of the majority Sunnis have threatened the Alawite-dominated government. In 1979, 60 Syrian army cadets, mostly Alawites, were killed in an attack by the brotherhood's militants on an academy in Aleppo, and other such attacks occurred. In March 1980, following antigovernment riots in Aleppo and Hama, a general strike by merchants and professional people demanded democratic freedoms, release of political prisoners, and free elections for a new parliament. The government promised to consider the strikers' demands.

HISTORY: Ancient Syria was the home of Amorites, Aramaeans, Phoenicians, and Hebrews. After a succession of invaders that included Assyrians, Babylonians, Egyptians, Hittites, and Persians, the country was unified under Alexander the Great in 331 B.C. It later fell under Roman rule, becoming part of the Byzantine Empire when the Roman Empire was divided between East and West. In the 7th century, the country was conquered by the Arabs and became the center of a vast Islamic domain

11th cent: Seljuk Turks invade Syria from Asia Minor

12th cent: Crusaders gain control over Syrian coastal areas (1189-92) and fight the Moslems led by Saladin

1516-1918: Syria is conquered by the Ottoman Empire, remains largely stagnant during four centuries of Turkish rule

1920: Syria is made a French mandate
1941-46: Free French and British forces occupy Syria during World War II; French proclaim an independent Syrian republic but complete independence is not achieved until 1944. All foreign troops are withdrawn in 1946
1958-61: Egypt and Syria form United Arab Republic under presidency of Egypt's President Nasser; attempts to integrate the two economies, nationalization of Syrian industry, and domination of Syrian army posts by Egyptian officers cause widespread discontent, culminating in military coup and restoration of Syrian independence
1963-66: Series of military coups results in succession of governments, although left-wing Ba'ath party continues to dominate political scene. In 1966, a new coup leads to installation of Nureddin al-Attassi as president
1967: Syria shares in Arab defeat in Six-Day War with Israel, whose forces occupy Golan Heights in southwestern Syria
1968-71: Struggle between factions of Ba'ath party led by President Attassi and those of Gen. Hafez al-Assad ends with Assad's seizing power in 1970 and being elected president in 1971
1971: Syria breaks off relations with Jordan after border clash
1973: Syria settles her differences with Jordan, joins other Arab nations in a full-scale war against Israel and adopts a new constitution
1975: King Hussein of Jordan and President Assad announce that their countries will establish a Permanent Joint High Commission to coordinate political, economic, and cultural policies
1976: Syria sends troops into Lebanon during the civil war there
1977: Syria rejects Egyptian proposals for preliminary meeting to prepare for Geneva Middle-East peace talks involving Israel; it takes part in so-called "refusal summit" with Iraq, Algeria, Libya, Southern Yemen and the PLO; events constitute virtual rupture between Syria and Egypt
1978: Syrians and Lebanese Christians battle in Beirut area in heaviest fighting there since Lebanese civil war. Assad, first Syrian president to serve full seven-year term since nation gained independence in 1946, runs unopposed and is reelected in "yes-or-no" referendum; overwhelming "yes" vote seen as indicating broad support for his opposition to peace initiatives of Egyptian President Sadat. Mohammad Ali al-Halabi appointed prime minister. Cost of Syria's 30,000-man presence in Lebanon is put at $3 million a day; death toll includes estimated 600-700 Syrian troops
1979: Syrian and Israeli warplanes clash in Lebanese air space. President Assad and President Ahmed Hassan al-Bakr of Iraq establish joint political command and discuss eventual merger. Militant Moslem Brotherhood attacks Alawite minority in Aleppo
1980: President Assad purges 14 members of Ba'ath Socialist party from cabinet, including Premier Halabi; forms new 37-member cabinet with Abdel Rauf al-Kasm as premier. Syria and Iraq expel each other's diplomats. Assad and Libyan leader Qaddafi sign merger agreement proclaiming Syria and Libya a single state

TANZANIA

Area: 363,708 sq. mi. **Population:** 17,048,000 (1979 est.)
Official Name: United Republic of Tanzania **Capital:** Dar es Salaam (future capital by 1990—Dodoma) **Nationality:** Tanzanian **Languages:** English and Swahili, the national language, are official languages. Some 120 dialects, mostly Bantu, are also spoken **Religion:** 35% Moslem, 35% Christian, and the rest animist **Flag:** A green triangle in the upper left and a blue one in the lower right, separated by a diagonal black band edged in yellow **Anthem:** National Anthem, set to new words of hymn "God Bless Africa" **Currency:** Tanzanian shilling (8.24 per U.S. $1)

Location: East Africa, comprising the former republics of Tanganyika and Zanzibar. Mainland Tanzania (Tanganyika) is bounded on the north by Lake Victoria, Kenya and Uganda, on the east by the Indian Ocean, on the south by Mozambique, Malawi, and Zambia, and on the west by Rwanda, Burundi, and Zaire. The island of Zanzibar lies some 20 miles to the east of Tanganyika's coastline, in the Indian Ocean **Features:** Tanganyika consists of a low-lying eastern coastal area, a high plateau in the west-central region, and scattered mountainous zones. Zanzibar is a low-lying island of coral limestone **Chief Rivers:** Pangani, Wami, Rufiji, Malagarasi, Ruvuma

Head of State and of Government: President Julius Kambarage Nyerere, born 1922, reelected 1975, head of the Revolutionary Party. He is assisted by the first vice-president (chairman of the Zanzibar Revolutionary Council), Sheikh Mwinyi Aboud Jumbe, born 1920, and by a prime minister, Edward M. Sokoine, born 1938, appointed February 1977 **Effective Date of Present Constitution:** April 1977 **Legislative Body:** National Assembly (unicameral), with

233 members, of whom 106 were elected for 5 years by universal suffrage and the rest appointed **Local Government:** 25 regions, including 20 on the mainland and 5 in Zanzibar, each administered by an appointed regional commissioner

Ethnic Composition: About 99% of the population are Africans who belong to some 130 different tribes, mostly Bantu. Only the Sukuma numbers over a million members. European, Arab, and Indo-Pakistani minorities total about 150,000 **Population Distribution:** 7% urban **Density:** 47 inhabitants per sq. mi.

Largest Cities: (1975 est.) Dar es Salaam 517,000, Zanzibar 80,000; (1967 census) Tanga 61,058, Dodoma 35,000, Mwanza 34,861, Arusha 32,452

Per Capita Income: $182 (1979) **Gross National Product (GNP):** $3.2 billion (1979) **Economic Statistics:** In 1977, 51% of GNP was from agriculture (sisal, cotton, coffee, oilseeds, nuts, tea, tobacco, sugar, livestock; Zanzibar is the world's largest producer of cloves); 12% from trade and services; and 9% from manufacturing and mining **Minerals and Mining:** Diamonds and gold are the most important minerals being exploited, in addition to salt, mica sheets, gem stones and tin concentrates. Coal and iron deposits are to be exploited **Labor Force:** 5,600,000 (1970), with 90% engaged in subsistence agriculture, and 15% in industry. The monetary-sector employment in 1977: 457,000 workers **Foreign Trade:** Exports, chiefly cotton, coffee, diamonds, sisal, petroleum products, cloves, and cashew nuts, totaled $574 million in 1977. Imports, mainly machinery and transportation equipment, manufactured goods, fuel, and textiles, totaled $784 million **Principal Trade Partners:** Britain, China, United States, West Germany, Zambia, India

Vital Statistics: Birthrate, 47 per 1,000 of pop. (1967); death rate, 22 **Life Expectancy:** 48 years **Health Statistics:** 619 inhabitants per hospital bed; 18,480 per physician (1975) **Infant Mortality:** 152 per 1,000 births **Illiteracy:** 55% **Primary and Secondary School Enrollment:** 2,024,179 (1976) **Enrollment in Higher Education:** 3,064 **GNP Expended on Education:** 4.4% (1976)

Transportation: Paved roads total 2,228 mi. **Motor Vehicles:** 90,000 (1977) **Passenger Cars:** 43,600 **Railway Mileage:** 2,788 **Ports:** Dar es Salaam, Tanga, Mtwara, Lindi **Major Airlines:** Air Tanzania flies domestically and internationally **Communications:** Government owned **Radio Transmitters:** 10 **Receivers:** 300,000 (1976) **Television Transmitters:** 1 **Receivers:** 4,000 (1970) **Telephones:** 75,000 (1976) **Newspapers:** 3 dailies, 5 copies per 1,000 inhabitants (1974)

Weights and Measures: Metric system **Travel Requirements:** Passport, visa, $3.15 fee, 1 photo, onward ticket

---

Tanzania, a union of Tanganyika and Zanzibar, is the site of some of the oldest and newest forms of human society. Its link to man's past was established in 1959 at Olduvai Gorge in the northern part of what was then Tanganyika. There Dr. Louis S. B. Leakey, the British-born anthropologist, unearthed one of the oldest human fossils ever found, the skull of *Homo zinjanthropus*. Its age was estimated to be more than 1.5 million years.

Now, over a decade after independence from Britain, Tanzania is the testing ground for a form of African Socialism—*ujamaa*—as conceived by President Julius K. Nyerere. *Ujamaa*, which means familyhood in Swahili, refers to kibbutz-like rural developments whose members join in communal farming and general improvement on a basis of "love, sharing, and work." On a broader scale, it means a joint effort by which all Tanzanians may gain an equal share of the nation's resources. In 1973 the ruling party, the Tanganyika African National Union (TANU), decided that all peasants had to join *ujamaa* villages, making the movement no longer voluntary.

The Nyerere government has progressively nationalized private business, banks, and privately owned buildings and homes. The economy depends largely on agriculture—coffee, tea, cotton, sisal and other crops—and between rising population and the vagaries of African weather, there has been little gain on a per-capita share basis.

The government, while striving for self-reliance, has not scorned foreign aid. U.S. funds are providing new highways, but the main new project is the Tanzam Railway, which was built with money, equipment, and labor provided by Communist China, and was handed over to Tanzania and Zambia by China in July 1976 after six years of construction. Although Tanzania had seemed to favor the Chinese, Soviet President Podgorny's 1977 visit to Tanzania was warmly received because of the Zimbabwe nationalist cause, which was actively supported by both countries.

In November 1978 Tanzanian forces invaded neighboring Uganda after Idi Amin had occupied more than 700 square miles of Tanzanian soil. Within five months Tanzanians and Ugandan rebels captured Kampala and drove the Ugandan dictator into exile. The war cost Tanzania more than $500 million, crippling its internal economy. Some Tanzanian troops remained in Uganda into 1980.

HISTORY: Archaeological discoveries indicate that man inhabited Tanzania more than one million years ago. However, little is known about the early history of the area. Zanzibar, colonized by the Arabs in the 8th century, controlled the East African coastal region until the early 16th century, when both the island and the coast came under Portuguese rule. Arab rule was reestablished in the 17th century by the sultans of Muscat, under whom a large trade in ivory and slaves was established

1861: Zanzibar, under British pressure, is separated from control of Sultan of Muscat and becomes an independent sultanate

1885: Germany establishes a protectorate over the mainland region, which becomes known as German East Africa

1920: As a result of Germany's defeat in World War I, German East Africa is mandated to Britain; territory's name is changed to Tanganyika and German settlers are expelled

1946: Tanganyika becomes a trust territory

1961: Tanganyika wins independence; Julius K. Nyerere, head of Tanganyika African National Union (TANU) party, becomes prime minister

1962: Tanganyika becomes independent republic within Commonwealth; Nyerere is named as republic's first president

1963: Zanzibar achieves independence within the Commonwealth

1964: Afro-Shirazi party, representing the African majority in Zanzibar, overthrows Arab minority government and forces sultan to flee; Zanzibar becomes a republic, with Sheik Abeid Amani Karume as president. Tanganyika and Zanzibar agree to form United Republic of Tanzania, with Nyerere as president and Karume as first vice-president

1965-69: Tanzania becomes one-party state, with TANU constituting the one party in Tanganyika and the Afro-Shirazi party in Zanzibar, and both sharing power on national level. In 1967 government announces plans for socialist development and embarks on widespread nationalization in industry and agriculture; in 1969 it accepts offer of loan by Communist China to finance railroad linking Dar es Salaam with Zambian capital of Lusaka

1971: Refusal of Tanzania to recognize Uganda government of General Idi Amin leads to bitter dispute and border clashes

1972: Sheik Abeid Amani Karume, Chairman of the Revolutionary Council which governed Zanzibar, assassinated. General Amin charges Tanzania with invading Uganda and threatens retaliation

1975: Kenya reopens Tanzanian border saying that outbreak of cholera was under control. Tanzania agrees to meet with Kenya and Zambia to settle road and border disputes. Nyerere is elected to a fourth term as president

1976: Tanzania is a training ground for Zimbabwe (Rhodesia) guerrillas. Tanzam Railway is completed

1977: Tanzania closes its border with Kenya after Kenya withdraws from jointly-operated East African Airways in order to form separate Kenya Airlines. The Tanganyika African National Union and the Afro-Shirazi party of Zanzibar merge into one party called the Revolutionary party, headed by President Nyerere

1978: Government takes steps to combat cholera epidemic, which it reports has killed more than 400 persons. War with Uganda erupts as Idi Amin's troops occupy 710 square miles of northwestern Tanzania before being driven back

1979: Idi Amin is ousted. Nyerere denounces continuing white domination of Zimbabwe

1980: Voters of Zanzibar elect 40-member House of Representatives in first elections under a separate constitution approved by the Revolutionary party in December 1979

THAILAND

Area: 198,455 sq. mi. **Population:** 46,142,000 (1979 est.)
Official Name: Kingdom of Thailand **Capital:** Bangkok **Nationality:** Thai **Languages:** Thai is the official language and is spoken by most of the population; minority languages are Chinese, Malay, Khmer, and Lao **Religion:** Hinayana Buddhism is the religion of 95.5% of the population; Islam (4%), Confucianism and Christianity are minority religions **Flag:** Horizontal stripes of red, white, blue (double width), white, red **Anthem:** National Anthem, beginning "Thailand is the place for all Thais" **Currency:** Baht (20.4 per U.S. $1)

Location: Southeast Asia. Thailand is bounded on the north and east by Laos, on the east by Cambodia, on the south by Malaysia, and on the west and north by Burma. It extends down the Malay Peninsula between the Andaman Sea and the Gulf of Thailand **Features:** The core of the country is the central plain, with flat alluvial lands watered by a network of canals and irrigation projects. The north consists of parallel north-south mountain ranges and narrow, fertile valleys, while the region east of the central plain, the Khorat Plateau, is relatively barren. North-south mountain ranges also dominate peninsular Thailand **Chief Rivers:** Chao Phraya, Mekong, Nan, Ping, Mun, Pa Sak, Mae Klong

Head of State: King Bhumibol Adulyadej (Phumiphol Aduldet), born 1927, succeeded 1946 **Head of Government:** Prime Minister: Gen. Prem Tinsulanond, born 1920, appointed March 1980 **Effective Date of Present Constitution:** December 1978 **Legislative Body:** Parliament (bicameral), consisting of 225-member Senate, appointed on the recommendation of the prime minister, and a popularly elected 301-member House of Representatives **Local Government:** 72 provinces, under appointed governors

Ethnic Composition: 75% Thai, 14% Chinese, 11% minorities (Malays, northern hill tribes, Khmer, Lao) **Population Distribution:** 25% urban **Density:** 223 inhabitants per sq. mi.

Largest Cities: (1975 est.) Bangkok 4,178,000; (1970 census) Thonburi 628,015, Chiengmai 83,729, Nakhon Ratchasima 66,071

Per Capita Income: $528 (1979) **Gross National Product (GNP):** $24.7 billion (1979) **Economic Statistics:** 33% of 1974 GNP was derived from industry (mining and quarrying, manufacturing, construction, transportation and communications); 28% from agriculture; 25% from commerce and finance (wholesale and retail trade, banking, insurance, real estate, ownership of dwellings); 10% from services **Minerals and Mining:** Major offshore natural gas fields are being exploited. Sizable tin, tungsten and lignite deposits. Other minerals are manganese, molybdenum, antimony and gem stones **Labor Force:** 16,243,000 (1975); 67% agriculture and forestry, 10% industry **Foreign Trade:** Exports, chiefly tapioca, rubber, rice, maize, tin, sugar, brought in $5 billion in 1979. Imports, mainly machinery, spare parts, fuel, iron, steel, automobiles, electrical equipment, totaled $6.9 billion **Principal Trade Partners:** United States, Japan, Malaysia, Hong Kong, Singapore, West Germany, Britain, Netherlands, Saudi Arabia

Vital Statistics: Birthrate, 35 per 1,000 of pop. (1976); death rate, 10 **Life Expectancy:** 61 years **Health Statistics:** 808 inhabitants per hospital bed (1974); 8,374 per physician (1975) **Infant Mortality:** 25 per 1,000 births (1976) **Illiteracy:** 18% **Primary and Secondary School Enrollment:** 8,069,829 (1976) **Enrollment in Higher Education:** 130,965 (1975) **GNP Expended on Education:** 4.1% (1976)

Transportation: Paved roads total 12,150 mi. (1975) **Motor Vehicles:** 532,800 (1975) **Passenger Cars:** 266,100 **Railway Mileage:** 2,378 **Ports:** Bangkok, Sattahip **Major Airlines:** Thai Airways, domestic and international (gov't owned) **Communications:** Government controlled **Radio Transmitters:** 217 **Receivers:** 5,500,000 (1976) **Television Transmitters:** 48 **Receivers:** 761,000 (1976) **Telephones:** 334,000 (1976) **Newspapers:** 56 dailies, 24 copies per 1,000 inhabitants (1975)

Weights and Measures: Metric system and local units are used **Travel Requirements:** Passport, no visa for 15 days

---

One of the largest countries in Southeast Asia, Thailand is favored with superb rice land, vast stands of teak, and a guaranteed rainfall that insures agricultural abundance. Thailand is the only Southeast Asian nation that has never been colonized: the word *thai* itself means free, and the Thai people are proud of this heritage.

For generations they have successfully resisted pressure not only of China to the north but also of Cambodia to the east. The Thais, the vast majority of whom are Buddhists, have lived for centuries under the cohesive influence of their line of kings.

A constitutional monarchy replaced the absolute rule of the kings in 1932, but parliamentary democracy was placed in abeyance in 1958, when a military junta seized control of the government in a bloodless coup. Since that time, a series of coups has occurred—the most recent being a bloodless coup in October 1977 led by Defense Minister Sangad Chaloryu, a former admiral who said he was deposing Premier Thanin Kraivchien's civilian government because it was taking too long to restore democracy.

Thailand's military commander, Gen. Kriangsak Chamanan, was named to replace Thanin as premier. Kriangsak stayed in power as a result of the elections of April 1979. None of the 36 political groupings won a majority in the 301-seat lower house; he appointed all 225 senators as called for by the constitution, and then the members of the two houses, meeting jointly, reelected him premier. But his government fell on February 19, 1980, after permitting, withdrawing, and reimposing big price rises in electricity and petroleum, and drawing criticism for rising crime and labor unrest. Gen. Prem Tinsulanond, on record as a liberal who has spoken out against monopolies and unfair distribution of wealth, became premier on March 3.

Thailand continues to be beset by insurgent activities in the south, north and northeastern provinces, involving groups as diverse as the Thai Communists, the Thai-Muslim separatists and a group of Meo mountain tribesmen. Thai troops have been kept active; in one action they smashed concentrations of guerrillas by capturing 30 jungle camps in four provinces in April 1979.

With an economy that is based on agriculture and is rising 7 percent annually even when inflation is taken into account, Thailand is prospering. The tapioca root, exported to Europe as an animal feed, became the nation's top agricultural money-earner in 1978, surpassing rice. Rubber and tin remain important, but light industry is adding further economic strength. The discovery of gas in the Gulf of Siam, to be piped ashore by Union Oil Co., will ease the shock of higher fuel prices.

An influx of Indochinese refugees into Thailand's "rice bowl" threatens to overwhelm the country's economy. Once Cambodia had been a buffer against Vietnam, but the Vietnamese takeover of that nation put Cambodia on the front lines in 1970. An initial wave of 80,000 Cambodians crossed the border into Thailand to escape hunger and death; the Thais at first responded by forcibly returning 45,000 of them. But then Thailand gave international officials assurance that it would let refugees stay in camps "for a short and specified period" while third countries arranged resettlement. By mid-1980, Thailand had at least 300,000 Cambodians—a figure exclusive of 130,000 refugees from the 1975 Communist takeover of Indochina.

HISTORY: In the 11th century the Thai people, living in Yunnan Province of what is now China, began moving southward under pressure from the expanding Chinese. They settled in the valleys of the Chao Phraya and Mekong Rivers and formed political states, many of which were under the rule of King Rama Kamhaeng. In the 15th century they were united with other Thais around Chiang Mai, in the northeast, and with the northern Malays in the south. By the 18th century trade had been established with Europe and Thailand began to consolidate as a nation

1833: Trade agreement is signed with the United States

1917: Siam (as Thailand was then called) declares war on Germany and sends expeditionary force to Europe

1932: Coup d'état by army officers establishes constitutional government to replace absolute monarchy

1941: Japanese troops enter Thailand, which is forced to sign alliance

1946: King Ananda Mahidol is found shot to death and is succeeded on throne by his younger brother, Bhumibol Adulyadej

1947: Coup by military officers forces change in government

1957-58: In another bloodless coup, government is replaced by a short-lived military junta. This is followed by another shift of power when Field Marshal Sarit Thanarat seizes control

1962: U.S. military unit is sent to northeast Thailand as Lao Communists threaten to sweep to Mekong River

1963: Sarit dies and is replaced by Marshal Thanom Kittikachorn

1970: United States discloses it has been paying $50 million annually for support of Thai combat division in South Vietnam

1971: On November 17, Thanom's government takes absolute power in bloodless coup

1973: U.S. congressional order ends U.S. bombing flights from Thai bases. Antigovernment protests organized by students result in violence. Thanom's government resigns and university rector Sanya Thammasak is named premier

1974: Exiled former premier Thanom Kittikachorn returns and is expelled. Agreement reached for U.S. to withdraw two of its six remaining air bases by the end of 1974. Air America, funded by CIA, ceases operations in Thailand

1975: Kukrit Pramoj becomes premier. Government accepts U.S. apology for unauthorized use of territory by airlifting 1,100 U.S. Marines to Thailand in military operations to free ship *Mayaguez* and her crew from Cambodian gunboats

1976: Seni Pramoj becomes premier. All operations are ended at U.S. installations and military personnel are withdrawn

1977: Thai and Cambodian troops fight along the border. Thai military leadership takes power under Gen. Kriangsak Chamanan; 23-member Revolutionary Council is established; new government proclaims interim constitution promising elections by 1979; parliament is dissolved; King appoints 360-member national legislature, made up mostly of active or retired members of the military

1978: Amnesty International, estimating there are possibly up to 1,000 political prisoners in Thailand, calls for their release. Thailand and Cambodia agree to try to end bloody border fighting and to exchange ambassadors

1979: Premier Kriangsak visits President Carter, who declares that the U.S. "is deeply committed to the integrity of Thailand's borders." A tide of 80,000 Cambodian refugees flees into Thailand, whose military eventually forces 45,000 back across the border. By midyear, Thailand relents and lets Cambodians enter UN transit camps, pending resettlement elsewhere

1980: Kriangsak, facing a no-confidence vote over economic policies, quits as premier; Gen. Prem Tinsulanond, formerly defense minister and army chief, succeeds him. Vietnamese troops attack Cambodian refugees in two camps inside Thailand for two days in June to show displeasure over shipping of some armed Cambodian refugees back to their own country. This incursion prompts 100,000 more Cambodians to flee to Thailand, raising the total to an estimated 300,000 since January 1979

TOGO

Area: 21,853 sq. mi. **Population:** 2,472,000 (1979 est.)

Official Name: Togolese Republic **Capital:** Lomé **Nationality:** Togolese **Languages:** French is the official language; the dominant indigenous languages are Ewe, Twi, and Hausa. In all, more than 44 different languages are spoken **Religion:** 75% animist, 20% Christian (mostly Roman Catholics), 5% Moslem **Flag:** Five alternating horizontal stripes of green (3) and yellow (2), with a white star on a red square in the upper left **Anthem:** National Anthem, beginning "Hail to thee, land of our forefathers" **Currency:** CFA Franc (210.2 per U.S. $1)

Location: West Africa. Togo is bounded on the north by Upper Volta, on the east by Benin, on the south by the Gulf of Guinea, and on the west by Ghana **Features:** The country is cut in two from the northeast to the southwest by the Chaine du Togo hills. To the north is a large savanna, with a plain in the east and south **Chief Rivers:** Oti, Mono, Haho, Anié

Head of State and of Government: President: General Gnassingbé Eyadéma, born 1937, seized power in 1967, elected 1979 **Effective Date of Present Constitution:** Dec. 30, 1979 **Legislative Body:** National Assembly (unicameral), with 67 members elected for 7 years. The Assembly of the Togolese People (RPT) is the only party **Local Government:** 4 regions, headed by appointed inspectors

Ethnic Composition: Of the nation's 18 major ethnic groups, the dominant ones are the Ewe and Mina in the south and the Kabyé in the north **Population Distribution:** 15% urban **Density:** 113 inhabitants per sq. mi.

Largest Cities: (1970 census) Lomé 148,443, Sokodé 30,271

Per Capita Income: $328 (1978) **Gross National Product (GNP):** $790 million (1978) **Economic Statistics:** In 1973, 44% of GNP was from agriculture (coffee, cocoa, yams, cassava, corn, millet, sorghum, rice); 20% from trade and services; 18% from mining (phosphates) and manufacturing (food processing, cement, a brewery, textile mills) **Minerals and Mining:** Phosphates are abundant; there are also unexploited amounts of iron ore and limestone **Labor Force:** 730,000, with 78% in agriculture and 22% in industry. There were 44,000 wage earners **Foreign Trade:** Exports, mainly phosphates, cocoa, coffee, palm nuts, and cotton, totaled $258 million in 1978. Imports, chiefly cotton textiles, machinery, motor vehicles, tobacco, and petroleum products, totaled $437 million

Principal Trade Partners: France, Japan, Britain, West Germany, United States, Netherlands, Belgium

Vital Statistics: Birthrate, 50.6 per 1,000 of pop. (1975); death rate, 23.3 **Life Expectancy:** 40 years **Health Statistics:** 684 inhabitants per hospital bed; 23,500 per physician (1977) **Infant Mortality:** 127 per 1,000 births **Illiteracy:** 84% **Primary and Secondary School Enrollment:** 476,755 (1976) **Enrollment in Higher Education:** 2,353 (1975) **GNP Expended on Education:** 6.7% (1976)

Transportation: Paved roads total 764 mi. **Motor Vehicles:** 20,000 (1974) **Passenger Cars:** 13,000 **Railway Mileage:** 274 **Ports:** Lomé, Kpémé **Major Airlines:** Air Afrique maintains international services **Communications:** Government owned **Radio Transmitters:** 5 **Receivers:** 52,000 (1976) **Television Transmitters:** 3 **Telephones:** 10,000 (1976) **Newspapers:** 1 daily, 6 copies per 1,000 inhabitants (1975)

Weights and Measures: Metric system **Travel Requirements:** Passport, visa for a 3 months maximum, $2.39 fee for stay up to 15 days, $3.58 fee for stay up to 30 days, 3 photos

---

One of West Africa's smallest countries, Togo has had a disproportionate amount of trouble since it attained independence from France in 1960. The country's first president, Sylvanus Olympio, was assassinated. He was succeeded by his brother-in-law, the late Nicolas Grunitzky, the son of a Polish father and a Togolese mother.

The Grunitzky government became increasingly insecure, and on January 13, 1967 Grunitzky was ousted by then Lt. Col. Étienne Eyadéma (now Gen. Gnassingbé Eyadéma). Eyadéma admitted that he was responsible for the killing of President Olympio in the 1963 coup.

General Eyadéma has maintained firm control over the country. With political stability, the nation's economy—based on phosphates, cocoa, and coffee—has shown steady progress. The government also hopes to exploit the country's large limestone deposits. Largely because of improving economic conditions, an attempted coup in August 1970 was taken with relative calm by the Togolese. Nevertheless, President Eyadéma charged that a French mining company had plotted to kill him by causing the crash of an airplane in which he was a passenger in January 1974. Two weeks earlier, Eyadéma had announced a 15 percent increase in the government's controlling interest in the mining company. Shortly after making the charges, the Eyadéma government took over the mining facilities.

Liberal trade policies have strengthened an otherwise feeble Togolese economy. Following independence, Togo was the only former French African colony not to give preferential tariff treatment to French goods. As a result, imports from all countries enter Togo at the same relatively low rates. Togo's famous marketing women have consequently benefited from the lower prices generated by the competition in imports.

Although officially nonaligned, Togo has sought closer identification with the Third World, but maintains close ties with Western nations. France remains Togo's principal trading partner.

HISTORY: The Ewes, who now constitute the population of southern Togo, moved into the region from the Niger River Valley between the 12th and 14th centuries. Portuguese explorers and traders visited the coast of Togo in the 15th and 16th centuries. During the next two centuries, the coastal region was a major raiding ground for European traders in search of slaves, gaining Togo the name "Coast of Slaves." In 1884, Germany set up a small protectorate on the coast and later expanded inland

1914: Togoland is occupied by the French in the east and by the British in the west after the outbreak of World War I

1922: League of Nations confirms a French mandate in eastern Togoland and a British mandate in western Togoland

1946: United Nations changes the mandates to trusteeships

1956: British Togoland votes to join the Gold Coast; as the result of a plebiscite among the French-ruled Togolese, French Togoland is made an autonomous republic within the French Union, but the UN Trusteeship Council rejects this procedure

1958: In a UN-supervised election, the Committee for Togolese Unity party (CTU), wins control of Togo's legislature; its leader, Sylvanus Olympio, becomes premier

1960: French Togoland becomes the independent Republic of Togo, with Sylvanus Olympio as president

1963: Olympio, a southerner, is assassinated by a group of northern noncommissioned army officers; Nicolas Grunitzky, leader of the Togolese Party for Progress, is named president

1967: Army chief of staff Lt. Col. Étienne Eyadéma overthrows the Grunitzky government, names himself president, and institutes direct military rule; the constitution is suspended, the National Assembly dissolved, and all political activity prohibited

1968: Eyadéma announces indefinite postponement of a referendum for a new constitution and return to civilian government, which he promised upon taking over the government

1969: After carefully staged demonstrations demanding that he remain as president, Eyadéma announces he has "acceded to the popular will"

1970-77: Government thwarts three plots to overthrow Eyadéma

1979: Regime convicts 13 of conspiracies, including two sons of Sylvanus Olympio living in exile. Eyadéma is reelected to another seven-year term under new constitution which creates a parliament to replace the one he dissolved in 1967

1980: Forty of Eyadéma's opponents briefly occupy the Togolese embassy in Paris

---

TONGA

Area: 270 sq. mi. **Population:** 93,000 (1978 est.)

Official Name: Kingdom of Tonga **Capital:** Nuku'alofa **Nationality:** Tongan **Languages:** Tongan and English **Religion:** Christian, with 60% belonging to sects of the Wesleyan (Methodist) faith, and 20% to the Latter Day Saints (Mormons) **Flag:** A red field with a white rectangle in the upper left containing a red cross **Anthem:** National Anthem, beginning "O Almighty God above" **Currency:** Pa'anga (.87 per U.S. $1)

Location: Southwest Pacific Ocean. An archipelago of 150 islands (45 inhabited), covering 100,000 sq. mi. of sea (24°-15°S.,173°-180°W.), about 400 miles east of Fiji **Features:** There are 3 principal groups. Divided by a north-south line, the eastern chain (including the main island of Tongatapu) is low-lying coralline. The western chain (Ha'apai and Vava'u groups) is volcanic

Head of State and of Government: King Taufa'ahau Tupou IV, born 1918, ascended the throne in 1965. He is also president of the appointed Privy Council (cabinet) which includes the prime minister, Prince Fatafehi Tu'ipelehake, born 1922, appointed 1965 **Effective Date of Present Constitution:** 1875, revised 1970 **Legislative Body:** Parliament (unicameral Legislative Assembly), with 23 members, with the 7 cabinet ministers, 7 nobles elected by the 33 hereditary nobles, 7 elected by adult suffrage for 3 years, and the ex-officio governors of Ha'apai and Vava'u **Local Government:** 3 island districts, under appointed governors

Ethnic Composition: The Tongans are Polynesians, and make up 98% of the population, which also includes small groups of other Pacific islanders, Europeans and mixed **Population Distribution:** 60% is on Tongatapu **Density:** 344 inhabitants per sq. mi.

Largest Cities: (1976 census) Nuku'alofa 18,396; (1966 census) Neiafu 3,593, Mu'a 3,502

Per Capita Income: $400 (1975) **Gross National Product (GNP):** $39 million (1975) **Economic Statistics:** The economy is based on agriculture, (sweet potatoes, yams, taro, tapioca, cassava, corn, coconuts, bananas, pineapples, melons, fish, citrus fruits, livestock) and manufacturing (coconut and agricultural processing and canning, coir, tobacco, handicrafts, plastic products) **Minerals and Mining:** None **Labor Force:** 9,300 in agriculture, 9,000 in services and government, 400 in industry and commerce (1976) **Foreign Trade:** Exports, chiefly copra and bananas, totaled $7.2 million in 1975. Imports, mainly food, fuels and textiles, totaled $19.8 million **Principal Trade Partners:** Australia, New Zealand, Britain, Japan, Fiji, Netherlands

Vital Statistics: Birthrate 13.0 per 1,000 of pop.; death rate, 1.9 **Life Expectancy:** 56 years **Health Statistics:** 300 inhabitants per hospital bed; 3,000 per physician (1976) **Infant Mortality:** 20.5 per 1,000 births (1976) **Illiteracy:** Negligible **Primary and Secondary School Enrollment:** 30,825 (1976) **Enrollment in Higher Education:** 15 (1976), with 116 studying abroad (1974) **GNP Expended on Education:** 4.4% (1973)

Transportation: Surfaced roads total 121 mi. **Motor Vehicles:** 1,400 (1974) **Passenger Cars:** 1,000 **Railway Mileage:** None **Ports:** Nuku'alofa, Neiafu, Pangai **Major Airlines:** Air Pacific and Polynesian Airlines operate international services; South Pacific Islands Airways operates domestically **Communications:** Government owned **Radio Transmitters:** 2 **Receivers:** 15,000 (1976) **Television:** None **Telephones:** 1,090 (1974) **Newspapers:** 1 weekly, 49 copies per 1,000 inhabitants (1974)

Weights and Measures: British standards are used, but the metric system is being introduced **Travel Requirements:** Passport, no visa for 30 days, onward ticket

---

Though comprising 150 coral and volcanic islands, the Pacific kingdom of Tonga is considered to be one of the world's tiniest countries. For 70 years, it was a British protectorate, becoming an independent nation in the British Commonwealth in 1970. With independence, Tonga has moved to broaden the base of its economy, which has been based on the export of copra, bananas and coconuts.

There are two long-range hopes for broadening the economy. One is oil, the existence of which was discovered through seepage into water wells. An agreement with an international consortium provides that the country will get half the profits from possible oil production.

The other hope is to make Tonga a vacation paradise, with the kingdom looking for further economic development stemming from earnings from planned tourist hotels. Present air service to Tonga is only by small regional airlines that fly from Samoa and Fiji. The drive to independence from Britain was spurred by reported British reluctance to encourage the building of a jetport. In 1976 the Soviets agreed to upgrade the airport and Tonga's dockyard in return for the establishment of fisheries. Japan also expressed interest in Tonga through the signing of an agreement on hotel and fisheries development.

However, King Taufa'ahau Tupou IV has cautioned his countrymen, who wear *ta'ovalas*, or woven mats, around their waists, against basing their future on income from tourism, warning that "if too much tourism happens, we will become like Hawaii, where there are no more Hawaiians."

HISTORY: Tonga was at one time ruled by a line of sacred kings, one of whom eventually divested himself of his executive powers and delegated them to a temporal king. The system of dual kingship had become firmly established by the 17th century, when the first European contact was made by Dutch navigators. The peaceful conditions on the islands so impressed the 18th-century explorer Captain James Cook that he christened one of them the Friendly Island, a name later applied to the whole group. Within a few years of his departure, however, the islands were rent by civil war.

1845-93: Taufa'ahau, a leading chief, rules over a united Tonga as King George Tupou I after suppressing civil war. He makes treaties with France, Germany, the United States and Britain, all of which recognize his sovereignty, and introduces parliamentary government and a land system under which every male Tongan taxpayer is entitled to eight and one-quarter acres of land suitable for planting

1900: Tonga becomes a British protectorate

1918-65: Reign of Queen Salote, granddaughter of George Tupou I, sees the elimination of illiteracy and of Tonga's national debt

1970: Tonga gains independence from Britain

1978: Tonga's Bank of the South Pacific declared bankrupt after American bank president Jack Meier flees, defaulting on $600,000 contract to develop Fua'a'motu airport to handle jumbo jets

1979: King Taufa'ahau Tupou IV negotiates with Libyan strong man Col. Muammar Qaddafi for a $3-million loan to finish airport

---

TRINIDAD AND TOBAGO

Area: 1,980 sq. mi. **Population:** 1,133,000 (1978 est.)

Official Name: Republic of Trinidad and Tobago **Capital:** Port-of-Spain **Nationality:** Trinidadian, Tobagonian **Languages:** English is the official and predominant language; Hindi and other Indian languages are also spoken **Religion:** About 71% Christian, chiefly Roman Catholic and Anglican; 23% Hindu; 6% Moslem **Flag:** Red with a black diagonal stripe bordered in white running from upper left to lower right **Anthem:** National Anthem, beginning "Forged from the love of liberty" **Currency:** Trinidad/Tobago dollar (2.4 per U.S. $1)

Location: West Indies. Trinidad and Tobago are the most southerly of the Lesser Antilles. They lie 7 miles northeast of the Venezuelan coast and are separated from each other by a 19-mile channel **Features:** Three relatively low mountain ranges cross Trinidad from east to west. The land between the northern and central ranges is flat and well watered; south of the central range it is undulating. On Tobago, a main ridge of volcanic origin runs down the center of the island **Chief Rivers:** Ortoire, Caroni, Oropuche

Head of State: President Ellis Emmanuel Innocent Clarke, born 1917, elected by Parliament 1976 **Head of Government:** Prime Minister: Dr. Eric Eustace Williams, born 1911, reelected 1976 **Effective Date of Present Constitution:** August 1976 **Legislative Body:** Parliament (bicameral), consisting of a Senate with 31 appointed members, and a House of Representatives with 36 members elected for 5 years **Local Government:** 8 counties, 3 municipalities, and 1 ward (Tobago), governed by elected councils

Ethnic Composition: 43% of Trinidad's population is black, 40% East Indian, 14% of mixed ancestry, 2% Chinese, and 1% European. Tobago's population is largely black **Population Distribution:** 49% urban **Density:** 572 inhabitants per sq. mi.

Largest Cities: (1970 census) Port-of-Spain 62,680 (Metropolitan Area 250,000), San Fernando 36,879, Arima 11,636

Per Capita Income: $3,283 (1979) **Gross National Product (GNP):** $3.7 billion (1979) **Economic Statistics:** Trinidad is a major producer of crude oil and is also a major supplier of natural asphalt. Chief crops are sugar, fruits, bananas, coconuts, cocoa, and rice. Industries are oil refining and the manufacture of sugar, chemicals, fertilizers, molasses, rum, fruit juices, and cotton textiles. Tourism is important **Minerals and Mining:** Petroleum, lignite, asphalt, coal, gypsum, iron, clay, and natural gas **Labor Force:** 395,800 (1978), with 50% in manufacturing and construction, 19% in commerce and transportation and 13% in agriculture **Foreign Trade:** Exports, mainly mineral fuels, lubricants and related products, sugar, chemicals, fertilizers, fruits and vegetables, and coffee, totaled $2.3 billion in 1978. Imports, chiefly petroleum for refining, machinery and transportation equipment, foodstuffs, manufactured goods by material, and chemicals, totaled $1.8 billion **Principal Trade Partners:** United States, Britain, Saudi Arabia, Indonesia, Caribbean countries, Canada, Japan

Vital Statistics: Birthrate, 25.3 per 1,000 of pop. (1976); death rate, 6.9 **Life Expectancy:** 66 years **Health Statistics:** 224 inhabitants per hospital bed; 1,964 per physician (1975) **Infant Mortality:** 27.2 per 1,000 births (1977) **Illiteracy:** 5% **Primary and Secondary School Enrollment:** 183,238 (1975) **Enrollment in Higher Education:** 2,962 (1974) **GNP Expended on Education:** 4.1% (1973)

Transportation: Paved roads total 2,480 mi. **Motor Vehicles:** 149,700 (1977) **Passenger Cars:** 117,700 **Railway Mileage:** None **Ports:** Port-of-Spain, Pte-à-Pierre, Point Lisas **Major Airlines:** British West Indian Airways (BWIA) operates internationally **Communications:** Partly government controlled **Radio Transmitters:** 9 **Receivers:** 270,000 (1976) **Television Transmitters:** 3 **Receivers:** 110,000 (1976) **Telephones:** 70,000 (1976) **Newspapers:** 3 dailies, 92 copies per 1,000 inhabitants (1975)

Weights and Measures: British standards are used; the metric system is being introduced **Travel Requirements:** Passport, tourist card valid for 60 days

---

Trinidad's petroleum-fed industry has long been the most advanced in the former British West Indies. Offshore oil and gas finds have also contributed to the economy of Trinidad and its smaller sister island of Tobago, and have helped to make Trinidad a major oil exporter in the Western Hemisphere.

The economic problems are those of any developing country—lack of investment capital, shortage of jobs and lack of skilled personnel to fill those that are available, a small market for the products of light industry, and lack of administrative and technical capability below the top echelons of business and government. However, the democratic legislative and judicial structure inherited from the British makes meaningful political action in these areas possible without bringing down the government.

Trinidad's main problem is the lack of jobs, with the unemployment rate hovering around 15 percent and mainly affecting the islands' blacks—43 percent of the population. In an attempt to bolster the economy, the government of Prime Minister Eric Eustace Williams has emphasized a development program with large investment incentives for foreign capital and has imposed high import duties to give local products a competitive advantage. The government has also introduced a family-planning program—which has substantially reduced the rate of population growth—and is encouraging emigration to England and North America to relieve the labor-market pressure.

Domestically, race is the pivot of Trinidad's politics. Williams' People's National Movement claims the loyalties of most of Trinidad's blacks, while the principal opposition is the Democratic Labor party, the party of the less numerous East Indians. Complaints of discrimination in government jobs still come from the East Indians, but many of the highest officials are drawn from that bloc.

HISTORY: Trinidad and Tobago were discovered by Columbus in 1498 but were long ignored by the Spaniards because of the lack of precious metals in the islands. Spanish colonists began to establish plantations on Trinidad in the 17th century, importing African slaves to work them. The British captured the island in 1797 and in 1802 it was formally ceded to Britain. Tobago changed hands repeatedly during the 17th and 18th centuries, and in 1814 passed under the British crown

1834: Slavery is abolished in Trinidad

1845: Trinidad begins to import contract workers from India to replace the former slaves

1889: Trinidad and Tobago are amalgamated into a single colony

1958: Trinidad and Tobago joins the West Indies Federation

1962: Federation is dissolved; Trinidad and Tobago becomes independent

1970: Government restores order after island is rocked by black power demonstrations and mutiny in armed forces

1971: Elections result in complete victory for the People's National Movement under Prime Minister Dr. Eric Williams

1975: Strikes paralyze oil and sugar industries, causing worst government crisis since black power unrest in 1970

1976: Trinidad and Tobago becomes a republic, ending a 179-year link with the British monarchy. Governor General Sir Ellis Clarke becomes the first president. People's National Movement retains majority in Parliament following the general elections

1978: The nation's reserves of dry natural gas are put at 12 trillion cu. ft., and drilling continues. The government announces plans to build an aluminum smelter of 150,000-ton capacity. A government shipping company is set up jointly with Seatrain Lines

1979: A massive oil spill occurs when two fully-loaded supertankers, the Greek *Atlantic Empress* and the Liberian *Aegean Captain*, collide 19 miles off Tobago, but no oil washes onto the beaches. The *Atlantic Empress*, carrying two million gallons owned by Mobil Oil Co., is largely engulfed in flames from the outset, and is allowed to burn, thus limiting spillage

TUNISIA

Area: 63,170 sq. mi. **Population:** 6,367,000 (1979 est.)

Official Name: Republic of Tunisia **Capital:** Tunis **Nationality:** Tunisian **Languages:** Arabic is the official language, but French is widely used **Religion:** 98% are Moslems; and Islam is the official religion **Flag:** A red field with a white disc containing a red crescent and star in the center **Anthem:** National Anthem, beginning "Immortal and precious the blood we have shed" **Currency:** Tunisian dinar (0.40 per U.S. $1)

Location: North Africa. Tunisia is bounded on the north and east by the Mediterranean Sea, on the south by Libya, and on the west by Algeria **Features:** The country consists of a wooded and fertile region in the north, a central region comprising the coastal plains, and a southern region bordering the Sahara **Chief River:** Medjerda

Head of State and of Government: President Habib Bourguiba, born 1903, named president for life in 1975. He is assisted by a premier, Mohamed Mzali, appointed 1980 **Effective Date of Present Constitution:** 1959 **Legislative Body:** National Assembly (unicameral), consisting of 112 members elected by universal suffrage for 5 years **Local Government:** 18 governorates, under appointed governors

Ethnic Composition: The population is largely Arab, with a Berber minority; Europeans number about 50,000 **Population Distribution:** 49% urban **Density:** 101 inhabitants per sq. mi.

Largest Cities: (1975 census—Metropolitan Areas) Tunis 873,515, Sfax 256,739, Bizerte 109,879, Sousse 102,097, Kairouan 67,589

Per Capita Income: $1,071 (1979) **Gross National Product (GNP):** $6.8 billion (1979) **Economic Statistics:** 30% of the GNP is derived from services; 28% from industry including mining; 23% from commerce and finance; 19% from agriculture **Minerals and Mining:** There are large phosphate deposits and smaller amounts of oil, natural gas, lead, zinc **Labor Force:** 1,400,000, with 58% in agriculture, 23% in services and 19% in industry **Foreign Trade:** Exports, chiefly petroleum, phosphates, olive oil, wine, and cork, totaled $1.1 billion in 1978. Imports, mainly foodstuffs, industrial raw materials, machinery and equipment, and transportation equipment, totaled $2.1 billion **Principal Trade Partners:** EC countries, United States, Greece, Libya

Vital Statistics: Birthrate, 36.4 per 1,000 of pop. (1976); death rate, 13.8 **Life Expectancy:** 55 years **Health Statistics:** 428 inhabitants per hospital bed; 4,675 per physician (1976) **Infant Mortality:** 52.1 per 1,000 births (1974) **Illiteracy:** 45% **Primary and Secondary School Enrollment:** 1,222,776 (1977) **Enrollment in Higher Education:** 23,137 (1976) **GNP Expended on Education:** 4.9% (1975)

Transportation: Paved roads total 6,663 mi. **Motor Vehicles:** 169,800 (1975) **Passenger Cars:** 102,600 **Railway Mileage:** 1,256 **Ports:** Tunis, Sousse, Sfax, Bizerte, Skhirra **Major Airlines:** Tunis Air, a government-owned line, operates domestically and internationally **Communications:** Government owned **Radio Transmitters:** 8 **Receivers:** 280,000 (1975) **Television Transmitters:** 10 **Receivers:** 208,000 (1976) **Telephones:** 135,000 (1976) **Newspapers:** 4 dailies, 33 copies per 1,000 inhabitants (1975)

Weights and Measures: Metric system **Travel Requirements:** Passport, no visa for 4 months

Wedged in between Algeria and Libya—two larger and more militant neighbors—Tunisia has traditionally been one of the most stable and moderate Arab countries.

No Arab country has been more closely identified with one individual than Tunisia with Habib Bourguiba, its only president since the establishment of the republic in 1957. Bourguiba has long been one of the most magnetic and controversial figures in the Arab world. A professed "pragmatic idealist," he has befriended both the West and the Soviet Union and has not hesitated to quarrel publicly over the Arab struggle against Israel. His dovish views on that subject have infuriated many Arab leaders. However, Tunisia gained some prestige in the Arab world after the 1970 Jordanian civil war, which was mediated by an inter-Arab conciliation mission headed by Bourguiba's personal envoy. Moreover, Tunisia has condemned the peace treaty between Egypt and Israel.

The only Arab President outside of Lebanon without a military background, Bourguiba is a French-educated lawyer. He brought to Tunisia a benevolent despotism that has been comparatively free of corruption, and he has permitted relative individual freedom.

As part of a program to modernize the country, special attention was placed on the status of women, who enjoy few rights in much of the Arab world. Polygamy was outlawed; the marriageable age for girls was raised from 15 to 17; and divorce was made a matter of court discretion, rather than that of the husband.

The increase in Tunisia's literacy rate in the last decade was among the most rapid in the world, although some 45 percent of the population has had no schooling. In fact, Tunisia is turning out more educated people than the economy can absorb and they have much trouble in finding suitable jobs.

Economically, Tunisia is a significant producer of phosphates, oil, textiles and olives. The government has actively promoted foreign investment in all of these areas, although France remains Tunisia's principal trade partner. Since a 1976 trade agreement with the European Community, the first such pact signed with an Arab country, it is expected that large-scale investment will increase greatly.

Relations have deteriorated between Tunisia and neighboring Libya since a failed merger attempt in 1974, attributed to Tunisia's more moderate Arab-Israeli stance. A further erosion of relations occurred after a 1976 assassination plot against Bourguiba by Libyan commandos was uncovered. Subsequently, Tunisian workers were expelled from Libya, and diplomats were withdrawn from both countries. Relations have been restored.

Tunisia today is a nation poised, not always peacefully, on the brink of change. Many Tunisians contend that although a single party system was tolerable during the early years of nationhood, the time has come for full freedom of political expression. They are also concerned that a struggle for power could destroy Tunisian stability, following the aged Bourguiba's death. In fact, the struggle may already have begun. In January 1978 Tunisia was rocked by an outbreak of antigovernment violence, the nation's worst since gaining independence in 1956. The street fighting in Tunis and other cities left at least 100 dead and about 450 hurt. Although it began in peace—and legality—a general strike led by the nation's powerful labor unions (demanding more pay and attention to grievances) resulted in widespread vandalism, looting and arson, as the initial protests escalated into a direct challenge to Bourguiba's leadership. The government blamed the disorders on "extremist" labor leaders and "outside agitators." In January 1980, an attack on Gafsa by Tunisian expatriated workers caused 41 deaths. The government blamed the attack on Libya's leftist leaders.

HISTORY: Tunisia was settled by seafaring Phoenicians as far back as the 12th century B.C. In the 6th century B.C. the city of Carthage was founded near modern Tunis and became the center of a powerful city-state that lasted until 146 B.C., when it was destroyed by Rome. A new city of Carthage, built by Julius Caesar, was conquered by the Vandals in the 5th century A.D. and was later recovered for the Byzantine Empire. The Arabs conquered the region in the 7th century and during the Middle Ages transformed it into a major center of Arab power

1574: Turks add Tunisia to Ottoman Empire, but under its Turkish governors (beys) country enjoys virtual independence

1705: Hussein dynasty of hereditary beys is established

1881: Tunisia becomes a French protectorate

1934: Habib Bourguiba founds Neo-Destour (New Constitution) Party, which becomes spearhead of independence movement

1942-43: Tunisia becomes the site of World War II campaigns

1956: Tunisia wins independence

1957: Bey Sidi Lamine is deposed; Tunisia is proclaimed a republic; Bourguiba is elected as president

1963: France evacuates naval base at Bizerte

1968: Tunisia, at meeting of Arab League in Cairo, accuses Egypt of having provoked Six-Day War with Israel in 1967 and calls for Arab recognition of Israel; charges provoke uproar and Tunisian delegation walks out of meeting

1973: Tunisia sends token force to aid Arabs in Yom Kippur War

1974: Merger is proposed between Libya and Tunisia to form single nation, but the plan fails to materialize

1975: Bourguiba is named president for life

1976: Relations with Libya are strained by Libyan plot against Tunisian leaders

1977: Tunisian police arrest alleged Libyan agents suspected of plotting to assassinate Premier Hédi Nouira

1978: At least 100 die as general strike leads to worst antigovernment violence since nation gained independence

1980: Tunisia blames Libya for attack on Gafsa by Tunisia expatriated workers. Mohamed Mzali succeeds ailing Nouira as premier

---

TURKEY

Area: 300,946 sq. mi. **Population:** 44,375,000 (1979 est.)

Official Name: Republic of Turkey **Capital:** Ankara **Nationality:** Turkish **Languages:** Turkish is the official language and is spoken by 90% of the population; Kurdish (7%) and Arabic are spoken by the leading minorities **Religion:** 98% Sunni Moslem; the rest are Christians and Jews **Flag:** A white star and crescent on a red field **Anthem:** March of Independence **Currency:** Turkish lira (74.7 per U.S. $1)

Location: Asia Minor and Southeast Europe. Asiatic Turkey (Asia Minor) occupies 97% of the total area. Turkey is bounded on the north by the Black Sea, on the northeast by the USSR, on the east by Iran, on the south by Iraq, Syria, and the Mediterranean Sea, on the west by the Aegean Sea, and on the northwest by Greece and Bulgaria **Features:** European Turkey (Eastern Thrace) is separated from Asia Minor by the Dardanelles, the Sea of Marmara, and the Bosporus. The European part consists of rolling agricultural land. Asiatic Turkey has fertile coastal strips and is occupied in the center by the semiarid Anatolian plateau, surrounded by hills and mountains **Chief Rivers:** Kizilirmak, Yesilirmak, Seyhan, Menderes, Tigris (Dicle), Euphrates (Firat), Sakarya

Head of State and Government: Following the coup of Sept. 12, 1980, the country is governed by a six-man National Security Council headed by Gen. Kenan Evren, born 1918 **Effective Date of Present Constitution:** October 1961, abolished Sept. 1980. A new constitution is being prepared **Legislative Body:** Legislative and executive power is exercised by the National Security Council **Local Government:** 67 provinces, under governors

Ethnic Composition: Turks constitute 90% of the population; ethnic minorities include 7% Kurds and small groups of Greeks, Armenians, and Jews **Population Distribution:** 45% urban **Density:** 147 inhabitants per sq. mi.

Largest Cities (M.A. = Metropolitan Area): (1975 est.) Istanbul 2,534,839 (M.A. 3,864,493), Ankara 1,698,542 (M.A. 2,572,562), Izmir 636,078 (M.A. 1,660,529), Adana 467,122 (M.A. 1,234,735), Bursa 346,084 (M.A. 960,035)

Per Capita Income: $828 (1979) **Gross National Product (GNP):** $36.9 billion (1979) **Economic Statistics:** About 27% of the GNP is derived from agriculture (cereals, tobacco, grapes, fruits, and cotton) and animal husbandry and 21% from industry (steel, iron, sugar and cotton refining, tires, textiles, fertilizers) **Minerals and Mining:** Exploited minerals include copper, chrome (about 10% of the world's production), boracite, mercury, iron, manganese, coal, oil, natural gas **Labor Force:** 16,400,000 (1977), with 61% in agriculture, and 13% in industry **Foreign Trade:** Exports, mainly tobacco, cotton, hazelnuts, raisins, chrome, and citrus fruits, totaled $2.3 billion in 1978. Imports, chiefly machinery and transportation equipment, petroleum products, iron, steel and related products, fertilizers, and plastics, totaled $4.6 billion **Principal Trade Partners:** West Germany, France, Iraq, United States, Britain, Switzerland, Italy

Vital Statistics: Birthrate, 39.6 per 1,000 of pop. (1967); death rate, 14.6 **Life Expectancy:** 57 years **Health Statistics:** 456 inhabitants per hospital bed; 1,804 per physician (1975) **Infant Mortality:** 145 per 1,000 births (1970) **Illiteracy:** 38% **Primary and Secondary School Enrollment:** 5,689,506 (1974) **Enrollment in Higher Education:** 322,965 (1975) **GNP Expended on Education:** 4.6% (1976)

Transportation: Paved roads total 13,000 mi. **Motor Vehicles:** 702,300 (1976) **Passenger Cars:** 471,500 **Railway Mileage:** 5,700 **Ports:** Istanbul, Izmir, Mersin, Samsun, Iskenderun, Izmit, Trabzon **Major Airlines:** Turkish Airlines, government owned, operates domestically and internationally **Communications:** Government owned **Radio Transmitters:** 21 **Licenses:** 4,228,000 (1976) **Television Transmitters:** 38 **Receivers:** 1,769,000 (1976) **Telephones:** 1,131,000 (1976) **Newspapers:** 450 dailies

Weights and Measures: Metric system **Travel Requirements:** Passport, no visa for 3 months

---

In many ways, modern Turkey is the product of its first president, Mustafa Kemal, later surnamed Kemal Atatürk, or Father of the Turks. He was a dictator who believed that he had to be ruthless in bringing his country into the 20th century. Before his death in 1938, Atatürk cut as many ties with the past as possible. He had the Turkish alphabet transcribed from Arabic to Latin characters, outlawed the wearing in public of the traditional fez for men and the veil for women, and secularized the theocratic Moslem state of the former sultans. Islam is still a strong force among Turks, however; more people from Turkey make the holy pilgrimage to Mecca than from any other Moslem country.

Turkey is still plagued by a wide disparity between life in its more affluent cities and its backward rural areas in Asia Minor. There has been a rapid migration to the cities, causing crowding and a demand for goods and services on the part of the peasant who will wait no longer for the benefits of modernization to reach him.

The country's economy is still largely based on agriculture, but the government has been pushing industrial expansion at a rapid pace, causing a strain resulting in high inflation, a foreign exchange crisis marked by declining foreign reserves, and a huge balance-of-payments deficit.

Turkey, which under the sultans ruled virtually the entire Arab world, is the only Moslem country to maintain formal diplomatic relations with Israel. Its chief concern in foreign policy—other than the presence of the Soviet Union as a neighbor—is a recurring conflict with Greece over the nearby island republic of Cyprus. Turkey has maintained troops on the island since 1974 to protect the Turkish Cypriot community. Despite strong U.S. pressure Turkey's occupation of the northern part of the island continues.

In parliamentary by-elections of October 1979, public discontent with the worsening economy and with escalating political and religious sectarian violence led to the defeat of the coalition government headed by Bulent Ecevit, of the Republican People's party. A new government was formed by Suleyman Demirel, head of the conservative Justice party. The change of government had little effect on the rising terrorism by both rightist and leftist extremists which threatened to destroy Turkey's fragile democracy. The violent incidents included the murders of a U.S. soldier and three Americans working in Turkey by a left-wing terrorist group in an Istanbul suburb in December.

By February 1980, martial law had been extended to all major cities, but the political assassinations continued. It was estimated that about 2,000 persons had been killed from December 1978 to January 1980, and at least 2,000 more were murdered in the first seven months of 1980. In July political assassinations included such prominent Turks as a former premier, Nihat Erim, and a leftist labor leader, Kemal Turkler. Thousands of workers demonstrated against the political violence during the labor leader's funeral in Istanbul.

Amid public outcries that something be done to curb the violence, Premier Demirel and opposition leader Ecevit agreed to support legislation increasing the authority of the army and courts to deal with terrorists. There also were demands that the army take over the country in the crisis, as it had done during the past national emergencies. This came to pass when military leaders seized power in a bloodless coup on September 12. The constitution was abolished; Demirel, Ecevit and other political leaders were placed in protective custody, and government authority passed to a six-man National Security Council headed by Gen. Kenan Evren.

HISTORY: Asiatic Turkey is one of the oldest inhabited regions on Earth and for centuries served as a battleground for foreign conquerors. It was the site of the ancient states of Hatti, Urartu, Phrygia, Troy, Lydia, and Armenia. In the 7th century B.C., the Greeks founded the city of Byzantium on the site of present-day Istanbul. It was captured by the Romans in A.D. 196 and later rebuilt as Constantinople by the Christian Emperor Constantine. The Ottoman Empire was founded in 1299 by Turkish tribes from Central Asia on the remnants of the Byzantine and the Seljuk Turkish empires in Asia Minor. With its collapse in 1918, modern Turkey was born. The Turks had absorbed most of the major ethnic groups; the major exception were the Armenians, who were virtually exterminated by Ottoman attacks in the early 20th century

1920-23: Allied powers strip Ottoman Empire of its vast possessions, reducing it to a small state; Sultan Mohammed VI accepts Allied terms, but Turkish nationalists rally under Mustafa Kemal, later known as Kemal Atatürk, and organize resistance. Sultan is deposed and Turkey is declared a republic, with Atatürk as president

1924-38: A constitution is promulgated, providing for parliamentary government, but Atatürk rules as virtual dictator. He introduces sweeping reforms to westernize Turkey, which undergoes an unparalleled revolutionary transformation

1950-59: Celal Bayar, leader of the Democratic party, becomes president, with Adnan Menderes as premier. Turkey joins NATO in 1952. In 1955, Turkey and Iraq sign a mutual defense agreement, the Baghdad Pact. Marshall Plan aid leads to expansion of Turkish economy, but rapid industrialization results in economic crisis, forcing government to adopt restrictive measures to deal with discontent. Menderes is returned to office in 1957 elections; political controls tightened

1960: Army junta, led by General Cemal Gursel, stages coup, bans Democratic party, and puts Menderes, Bayar, and hundreds of other Democratic party members on trial for having violated the constitution. Most receive long prison sentences, but Menderes and several others are hanged

1961-62: A new constitution providing for a bicameral legislature and a strong executive is approved by referendum. Gursel is elected president and Ismet Inonu becomes premier. An attempted coup by army elements is crushed and many officers purged. Government amnesties most of imprisoned supporters of Menderes but keeps Bayar and a number of others in jail

1964: Relations between Turkey and Greece, long embroiled in dispute over Cyprus, become further strained as heavy fighting breaks out between Greek and Turkish Cypriots

1965: Suleyman Demirel, leader of Justice party, becomes premier following general elections

1966: Gursel falls ill; national assembly chooses General Cevdet Sunay, army chief of staff, to succeed him

1971: Following prolonged political and economic unrest, armed forces commanders demand resignation of Demirel government; Nihat Erim is named premier

1973: Bulent Ecevit elected premier. Retired Admiral Fahri Korutürk elected president

1974: Cypriot National Guard, under Greek officers, overthrows Cyprus President Archbishop Makarios. Turkish troops invade Cyprus and fight Greek Cypriots. Cease-fire arranged by UN representatives. Ecevit's coalition government collapses; interim government formed

1975: Citing "lack of progress" in Cyprus peace negotiations, U.S. Congress votes to cut off all military aid to Turkey. Turkey responds by seizing all American installations except the NATO base at Adana. Former Prime Minister Suleyman Demirel forms new coalition government

1976: Turkish exploration for oil in Aegean produces new tension with Greece. Earthquake in eastern Turkey kills thousands

1977: Ecevit's Republican People's party wins close to a majority of parliamentary seats in the general elections. Ecevit resigns the premiership 10 days later after his center-left government loses its first vote of confidence in parliament. Prime Minister Suleyman Demirel forms new government but his coalition soon dissolves. Economy continues serious decline

1978: Ecevit named premier. Turkey and Soviet Union sign nonaggression, trade and cultural pacts. U.S. Congress votes to allow President Carter to end embargo on arms sales to Turkey and provide substantial military aid. U.S. military bases reopen

1979: Ecevit's party loses local by-elections; Demirel forms new coalition government. Martial law extends to 19 provinces

1980: Political violence escalates, prominent leaders are assassinated; Premier Demirel and opposition leader Ecevit agree to increase authority of army and courts to combat terrorists. Military leaders, headed by Gen. Kenan Evren, seize power on Sept. 12

TUVALU

Area: 9.78 sq. mi. **Population:** 10,000 (1978 est.)

Official Name: Tuvalu **Capital:** Fongafale, on Funafuti **Nationality:** Tuvaluan **Languages:** Tuvaluan and English **Religion:** Christian, mostly Protestant **Flag:** A light blue field with the Union Jack in the upper left corner and nine yellow five-pointed stars in the right half **Anthem:** N.A. **Currency:** Australian dollar (0.90 per U.S. $1)

Location: Tuvalu is comprised of nine low-lying coral atolls, eight of which are inhabited; the islands form a chain approximately 360 miles long in the southwest Pacific Ocean (5°30'-11°S., 176°-180°E.). Tuvalu's nearest neighbors are Fiji and Kiribati **Features:** The islands have a tropical climate and are mostly covered with coconut palms

Head of State: Queen Elizabeth II through a governor-general, Sir Fiatau Penitala Teo, born 1912 **Head of Government:** Prime Minister Toalipi Lauti, born 1932, took office October 1, 1978 **Effective Date of Present Constitution:** October 1, 1978 **Legislative Body:** Unicameral Parliament, consisting of 12 members elected by universal suffrage **Local Government:** Island councils for the eight inhabited islands

Ethnic Composition: Almost entirely Polynesian **Population Distribution:** Non-urban **Density:** 1,022.5 inhabitants per sq. mi.

Largest center: (1973 census) Fongafale 871

Per Capita Income: Less than $50 annually **Gross National Product (GNP):** N.A. **Economic Statistics:** A large part of personal income in Tuvalu is derived from cash remittances from Tuvaluan men working as seamen and in the phosphate industries of Nauru and Banaba (Ocean Island) in Kiribati. Other income is derived from copra, the chief cash crop, the sale of postage stamps and coins, and handicrafts. Fishing is on a subsistence basis. Other agricultural crops are pulaka (taro), pandanus fruit, bananas and pawpaws **Minerals and Mining:** None **Labor Force:** N.A. **Foreign Trade:** Exports of copra (59 tons) totaled $4,277 in 1976. Copra exports usually average 120 tons per year. Imports include food and fuel **Principal Trade Partners:** N.A.

Vital Statistics: Birthrate, N.A; death rate, N.A. **Life Expectancy:** N.A. **Health Statistics:** 42 inhabitants per hospital bed (1978) **Infant Mortality:** N.A. **Illiteracy:** Over 50% **Primary and Secondary School Enrollment:** 1,788 (1976) **GNP Expended on Education:** N.A.

Transportation: Gravel roads total 5 mi. **Motor Vehicles** About 12 cars on Funafuti **Railway Mileage:** None **Port:** Funafuti **Major Airlines:** Air Pacific provides service to Fiji and Kiribati. See Bee Air operates domestic inter-island service with one 5-passenger seaplane **Communications:** Government owned **Radio Transmitters:** 1 **Receivers:** 4,000 **Television:** None **Telephones:** 300 **Newspapers:** 1 fortnightly

Weights and Measures: N.A. **Travel Requirements:** N.A.

On October 1, 1978, the nine atolls of the Ellice Islands (Tuvalu's name before 1975) became the independent nation of Tuvalu (Polynesian for "cluster of eight islands," after the eight inhabited atolls). The main post-independence aim of Tuvalu's people is for greater economic self-sufficiency. This goal, however, is not readily forthcoming. The climate makes these "paradise islands" beautiful to see; but the thin, alkaline soil makes them ill-suited for agriculture. The islands are dotted with coconut palms, and copra is the main export. Handicrafts and subsistence fishing are the chief occupations. The chief source of revenue is from remittances from overseas Tuvaluans, working as seamen or as phosphate workers on nearby Nauru and Banaba (Ocean Island). With phosphate production on Banaba scheduled to end in 1979, the economic impact of returning workers will exacerbate the present situation; per capita income is now less than 50 U.S. dollars annually.

Future development will probably center on the potentially rich fishing grounds to be found in Tuvalu's lagoons and ocean waters. The South Pacific Commission plans to open a tuna canning plant, and fisheries and other industrial projects may be forthcoming. Foreign aid will also be important in further development. Great Britain has been the islands' chief benefactor and has built up the new nation's administrative infrastructure, but independence is expected to attract aid and possible investment from Australia, New Zealand, the United States and Japan.

HISTORY: Tuvaluans consider Samoa as their ancestral home, with which they share a common Polynesian language and culture. Fishermen are thought to have drifted westward from the central Pacific and populated the islands, which were periodically raided by Micronesians from Tonga and the Gilberts. The Spaniard Mendaña is thought to have sighted Nui in 1568 and Niulakita in 1595. Permanent contact with Westerners came in the late 18th and early 19th centuries; the first European settlers were from the London Missionary Society, who arrived in 1865 and soon converted the islanders to Protestantism. During the "blackbirders" slave trade from 1850 to 1875, the islands' population was reduced from 20,000 to about 3,000.

1856: Guano Act of U.S. Congress establishes American claims to Funafuti, Nukefetau, Nukulaelae and Niulakita atolls

1877: Britain establishes the High Commission for the Western Pacific to stamp out "blackbird" raiders

1892: Britain proclaims a protectorate over Ellice Islands and neighboring Gilberts

1915: Protectorate reorganized as Gilbert and Ellice Islands Colony

1973: Britain appoints commissioner to study growing Polynesian demands for autonomy of the Ellice Islands

1974: August-September referendum, observed by UN, shows overwhelming support for separation from Gilbert Islands

1975: The islands are established as a separate dependency under British administration under the name *Tuvalu*

1977: U.S. announces its willingness to negotiate claims to four disputed islands

1978: Independence is declared October 1. Tuvalu becomes 38th member of the Commonwealth

1979: Prime Minister Toalipi Lauti signs Friendship Treaty with the United States; pact recognizes U.S. renunciation of claims over disputed islands and provides for continued consultations on security and marine reserves

---

UGANDA

Area: 91,076 sq. mi. **Population:** 13,225,000 (1979 est.)

Official Name: Republic of Uganda **Capital:** Kampala **Nationality:** Ugandan **Languages:** English is the official language and Swahili the national language; of the many local languages the most important is Luganda **Religion:** About half the population is Christian, 10% Moslem, and the rest animists **Flag:** 6 alternate horizontal stripes of black, yellow, and red, with the national emblem, a crested crane, in a white circle in the center **Anthem:** National Anthem, beginning "O Uganda! May God uphold thee" **Currency:** Ugandan shilling (7.4 per U.S. $1)

Location: East Africa. Landlocked Uganda is bordered on the north by Sudan, on the east by Kenya, on the south by Tanzania, Lake Victoria, and Rwanda, and on the west by Zaire **Features:** Most of the country consists of a plateau about 4,000 feet above sea level. About 18% of the total area consists of swamps and open water, including Lakes Victoria, George, Albert (Mobutu Sese Seko), Edward, and Kyoga. Thick forest covers parts of the south; the north is largely savanna with some semidesert areas in the northeast **Chief Rivers:** Victoria Nile, Albert Nile, Katonga

Head of State and of Government: Paulo Muwanga heads a 6-man Military Commission in power since the coup of May 12, 1980 **Effective Date of Present Constitution:** 1967, suspended 1971; a new constitution is being drafted **Legislative Body:** A new legislature is to be elected sometime in late 1980 **Local Government:** 10 provinces, divided into 26 districts

Ethnic Composition: About 98% of the population is African. The largest tribes include the Baganda, Iteso, Banyankore, and Basoga. Asians, mainly of Indian extraction, now number fewer than 500, and Europeans less than 3,500 **Population Distribution:** 7% urban **Density:** 145 inhabitants per sq. mi.

Largest Cities: (1973 est.) Kampala 380,000; (1969 census) Jinja 52,509, Mbale 23,544, Entebbe 21,096

Per Capita Income: $248 (1979) **Gross National Product (GNP):** $3.3 billion (1979) **Economic Statistics:** 52.7% of the GNP is derived from agriculture (coffee, cotton, tea, tobacco); 18.7% from commerce and finance; 15.7% from services; and 12.9% from industry (the manufacture of food products and textiles, cigarettes, brewing, enamel hollow ware, cement, wooden boxes, and soap) **Minerals and Mining:** There are substantial deposits of copper and smaller amounts of wolfram, beryl, and cassiterite **Labor Force:** 353,768 salaried workers (1974). 90% of the population is in agriculture, 4% in industry **Foreign Trade:** Exports, mainly coffee, copper, cotton, tea and feeds, totaled $376 million in 1978. Imports, chiefly machinery and transportation equipment, cotton and synthetic fabrics and petroleum products, totaled $308 million **Principal Trade Partners:** Britain, Kenya, United States, West Germany, Japan, Italy, Netherlands, Tanzania

Vital Statistics: Birthrate, 45.2 per 1,000 of pop. (1975); death rate, 15.9 **Life Expectancy:** 49 years **Health Statistics:** 636 inhabitants per hospital bed; 24,700 per physician (1975) **Infant Mortality:** 160 per 1,000 births **Illiteracy:** 65% **Primary and Secondary School Enrollment:** 1,103,906 (1976) **Enrollment in Higher Education:** 5,474 (1975) **GNP Expended on Education:** 3.0% (1975)

Transportation: Paved roads total 1,200 mi. **Motor Vehicles:** 35,900 (1975) **Passenger Cars:** 27,000 **Railway Mileage:** 756 **Ports:** None **Major Airlines:** Uganda Airlines operates both domestically and internationally **Communications:** Government owned **Radio Transmitters:** 7 **Receivers:** 250,000 (1976) **Television Transmitters:** 6 **Licenses:** 71,000 (1976) **Telephones:** 46,000 (1976) **Newspapers:** 1 daily, 5 copies per 1,000 inhabitants (1974)

Weights and Measures: Metric system **Travel Requirements:** Passport, visa, $3.15 fee, 1 photo

From the lushly green shores of Lake Victoria to the snow-capped Mountains of the Moon on its western border, Uganda's natural beauty is the fulfillment of a tourist's dream. Until recently elephant herds, great flocks of birds and other wildlife, vivid flowers, neat tea plantations, and farmlands rich in coffee and cotton delighted the visitor and gave support to the country's claim to being "the pearl of East Africa."

But Uganda changed drastically under the

harsh regime of Field Marshal Idi Amin Dada. The eight-year reign of terror claimed the lives of possibly as many as 300,000 Ugandans. An estimated 250,000 fled to neighboring Kenya, and many more lived in exile in Britain.

Hopes were bright at the outset of Ugandan independence from British rule in 1962, with Milton Obote, leader of the Uganda People's Congress (UPC), as prime minister. The country became a republic in 1963 and elected as president Mutesa II, the revered *Kabaka* (king) of Buganda, largest of the four old kingdoms. In 1966, Obote, a rival Lango tribesman, forced the *Kabaka* into exile. Under a new constitution adopted in 1967, the kingdoms were abolished and Obote assumed the presidency.

But in January 1971, Obote was ousted in a coup led by the Ugandan army commander, Maj. Gen. Idi Amin. Amin then declared himself president for life, abolished parliament and purged the judiciary and the civil service.

Amin, a Moslem, waged war against the predominantly Christian Acholi and Lango tribesmen. At least 3,000 of the tribesmen were killed when Amin came to power, and another 2,000 were killed in early 1977 after Amin uncovered an attempted coup which he linked to the two tribes.

From 1972 General Amin expelled 50,000 Ugandan Asians holding British passports and nationalized 41 chiefly British-owned businesses and tea estates. These actions spurred inflation and depressed exports. Overall, the economy deteriorated badly under the regime's inefficiency and lavish military spending.

Amin committed a fatal mistake in October 1978 when he sent troops into Tanzania and occupied more than 700 square miles of foreign soil. Tanzania quickly counterattacked, carried the war into Uganda the next month, and in April 1979 captured Kampala, whose residents greeted the invaders as liberators. Amin eluded capture and gained asylum in Libya.

Virtually the entire world welcomed Amin's ouster. The U.S. quickly lifted the trade embargo it had imposed against Uganda in 1978.

Yet problems remain. Yussufu Lule, the man chosen to succeed Amin, survived barely two months before political wrangling forced his resignation. He was replaced in June 1979 by Godfrey Binaisa, a former attorney general and longtime defender of human rights. A coup in May 1980 drove Binaisa out and a military commission took power.

HISTORY: Until the latter part of the 19th century, Uganda experienced a series of migrations extending over hundreds of years. As a result, a number of major chiefdoms grew up, the most powerful of which were the chiefdom of Bunyoro-Kitara and the rival state of Buganda. Britain established a protectorate over Buganda in 1894 and subsequently extended the protectorate to the rest of Uganda. However, the stubborn independence of Buganda's rulers, which continued well into the 20th century, hampered the development of national unity

1953: Kabaka (king) Mutesa II of Buganda is deposed and exiled to London when he refuses to help put down riots by local chiefs

1955: British restore Mutesa but stipulate he is to reign as constitutional monarch and that Buganda will participate in the central government of Uganda

1962: Uganda gains independence with a federal constitution that gives Buganda large measure of autonomy; Milton Obote becomes prime minister

1963: Post of governor-general is abolished; Mutesa is elected president by parliament

1966: Obote removes Mutesa, suspends constitution, abolishes federal system, and assumes full powers of government

1967: Uganda adopts republican constitution with a presidential form of government headed by Obote; traditional kingdoms are abolished

1971: Obote is ousted in coup led by Maj. Gen. Idi Amin, who assumes presidency; refusal of Tanzania to recognize his government results in minor warfare between the two countries

1972: Amin orders the expulsion of the estimated 50,000 Asians in Uganda holding British passports

1973: Lakes Albert and Edward, along Zaire border, renamed "Mobutu Sese Seko" and "Idi Amin Dada" (after Zairese and Ugandan presidents) in what is described as "another step in the decolonization of the minds of the people." U.S. severs ties with Uganda after repeated threats against U.S. Embassy officials and the detention of 100 American Peace Corps volunteers

1974: Amin suppresses military coup

1976: Israeli commandos rescue skyjacked hostages being held at Entebbe airport, crippling Amin's Soviet-equipped air force

1977: Anglican Archbishop Janani Luwum and two of Amin's cabinet ministers are arrested and murdered; the government claims the three were killed in an automobile accident after attempting to escape. Thirty-three Commonwealth nations, including 13 African nations, condemn Amin's regime for its repression. Twelve Ugandans are convicted of plotting a coup and are shot. Thirteen die in new anti-Christian purge; many arrested. Amin curtails travel, tightens security

1978: Ugandan forces invade Tanzania; general war ensues

1979: Ugandan rebels join Tanzanian forces in advance on Kampala, which falls on April 12 amid wild rejoicing and looting. Amin flees north and eventually to asylum in Libya. Yussufu Lule becomes provisional president; he is replaced in June by Godfrey Binaisa. Government tries to cope with near-anarchy and nationwide violence. A ban on Christianity is lifted

1980: Tanzanian troops remain in Uganda. Military takes over the government in May coup. Obote returns from exile; he appeals for unity, invites Asians to return, promises elections. Country suffers from drought, food shortages and political instability

---

UNION OF SOVIET SOCIALIST REPUBLICS

Area: 8,649,490 sq. mi. **Population:** 262,400,000 (1979 census) **Population of Union Republics:** (1979 census) Russian S.F.S.R. 137,551,000, Ukraine 49,755,000, Uzbek 15,391,000, Kazakh 14,681,000, Byelorussia (White Russia) 9,560,000, Azerbaidzhan 6,028,000, Georgia 5,015,000, Moldavia 3,947,000, Tadzhik 3,801,000, Kirgiz 3,529,000, Lithuania 3,398,000, Armenia 3,031,000, Turkmen 2,759,000, Latvia 2,521,000, Estonia 1,466,000

Official Name: Union of Soviet Socialist Republics **Capital:** Moscow **Nationality:** Soviet **Languages:** Russian, the official language, is the native tongue of about 60% of the population and is spoken as a second language by less than half of the rest; other languages are Ukrainian, Byelorussian, Lithuanian, Latvian, Estonian, Moldavian, Yiddish, Georgian, Armenian, Uzbek, Tatar, Kazakh, Azerbaijani, and over 100 other languages and dialects **Religion:** Atheism, officially propagated by the government, is followed by about 70% of the population; there are also 18% Russian Orthodox, 9% Moslems, and small groups of Roman Catholics, Protestants, Jews, and Buddhists **Flag:** Red field with a golden hammer and sickle (representing the industrial and farm workers) under a golden star in the upper left corner **Anthem:** Hymn of the Soviet Union **Currency:** Ruble (0.64 per U.S. $1)

Location: Northern Eurasia, from the Baltic Sea to the Pacific, with the Arctic Ocean on the north. The largest country in the world, the USSR is bordered on the northwest by Norway and Finland; on the west by Poland, Czechoslovakia, Hungary, and Romania; on the south by Turkey, Iran, and Afghanistan, and on the southeast by China, Mongolia, and North Korea **Features:** In the west, from the Pripet Marshes near the Polish frontier to the Ural Mountains, the land consists of a broad plain broken by occasional low hills and crossed by numerous rivers. Between the Black and Caspian seas lie the Caucasus Mountains. East of the Ural Mountains, which mark the traditional division between European and Asiatic Russia, are the Aral Sea, vast Siberian lowlands, steppes, and deserts of Central Asia. Beyond are the vast Siberian highlands and mountain ranges of the Soviet Far East. The highest ranges lie along the Chinese and Mongolian borders **Chief Rivers:** In Europe, the Dnieper, Dniester, Don, Volga; in Asia, the Ob, Yenisey, Lena, Amur, Kolyma, Amu Darya, Syr Darya

Political Leader and Head of State: Chairman of the Presidium of the Supreme Soviet (President) and General Secretary of the Central Committee of the Communist Party: Marshal Leonid Ilyich Brezhnev, born 1906, appointed general secretary in 1964 and president in 1977 **Head of Government:** Chairman of the Council of Ministers (Premier): Aleksey Nikolayevich Kosygin, born 1904, appointed 1964 **Effective Date of Present Constitution:** 1977 **Legislative Body:** Supreme Soviet (bicameral), consisting of the Soviet (Council) of the Union and the Soviet of Nationalities. The Soviet of the Union has 750 members elected on the basis of population; the

UNION OF SOVIET SOCIALIST REPUBLICS
(European Part)
CONIC PROJECTION
MILES
0 50 100 200 300
KILOMETRES
0 100 200 300
National Capitals
Capitals of Union Republics
International boundaries
Union Republic boundaries
Canals
ARCTIC OCEAN
KARA SEA
Novaya Zemlya
Yamal Pen.
Gulf of Ob'
North Cape
NORWAY
Varangerfjord
Kirkenes
Pechenga
Rybachiy Pen.
Polyarnyy
Murmansk
Monchegorsk
L. Imandra
Kirovsk
Kandalaksha
Kola Pen.
Iokan'ga
Shoyna
Kanin Pen.
Indiga
Nar'yan-Mar
Vorkuta
Amderma
Bovarata
Yugorskiy Pen.
Novyy Port
Salekhard
Ob'
Berezovo
Kondinskoye
Mezhdusharskiy I.
Kolguyev I.
Kem'jarvi
Kesten'ga
Kalevala
L. Top
White Sea
Ruch'i
Mezen'
Nizh. Pesha
Ust'-Tsil'ma
Kozhva
Izhma
Pechora
Ust'-Usa
Usa
Muzhi
Narodnaya 6,214
Troitsko-Pechorsk
Umea
FINLAND
Vaasa
Kuopio
Tampere
Sortavala
Petrozavodsk
Onets
Belomorsk
Severodvinsk
Onega Bay
Archangel (Arkhangel'sk)
Pinega
Leshukonskoye
Koslan
Ukhta
Yarensk
Ust'-Kulom
Syktyvkar
Krasnovishersk
Berezniki
Solikamsk
Severoural'sk
Serov
Turinsk
Tavda
Tura
SWEDEN
Gulf of Bothnia
Sundsvall
Helsinki
Turku
Vyborg
Olonets
L. Ladoga
G. of Finland
L. Onega
Medvezh'yegorsk
Pudozh
Kargopol'
Vel'sk
Velikiy Ustyug
Kotlas
Ob'yachevo
Kama
Kudymkar
Perm' (Molotov)
Nizhniy Tagil
Sverdlovsk
Kirovgrad
Alapayevsk
Stockholm
BALTIC SEA
Hiiumaa
Saaremaa
Gulf of Riga
Tallinn
ESTONIAN S.S.R.
Pushkin
LENINGRAD
Narva
Novgorod
Tikhvin
Babayevo
Belozersk
Cherepovets
Vologda
Sokol
Tot'ma
Soligalich
Nikol'sk
Murashi
Omutninsk
Kirov
Glazov
Votkinsk
Izhevsk
Kungur
Krasnoufimsk
Kyshtym
Chelyabinsk
Ventspils
Riga
LATVIAN S.S.R.
Valmiera
Tartu
L. Peipus
Pskov
Staraya Russa
Borovichi
Rybinsk Res.
Galich
Buy
Kostroma
Shar'ya
Kotel'nich
Nolinsk
Sovetsk
Yoshkar-Ola
Vyatka
Sarapul
Votkinsk
Zlatoust
Miass
Troitsk
Liepaja
Jelgava
Siauliai
Daugavpils
LITHUANIAN S.S.R.
Rezekne
Ostrov
Opochka
Velikiye Luki
Bologoye
Torzhok
Volochek
Yaroslavl
Kineshma
Ivanovo
Cheboksary
Kazan
Menzelinsk
Belaya
Birsk
Ufa
Klaipeda (Memel)
Sovetsk (Tilsit)
R.S.F.S.R.
Kaunas
Vilna
Polotsk
Vitebsk
Rzhev
Kalinin
Aleksandrov
Shuya
Vladimir
Gor'kiy
Semenov
Lyskovo
Kanash
Chistopol'
Ufa
Yamantau 5,374
Beloretsk
Magnitogorsk
Kaliningrad (Konigsberg)
WHITE RUSSIAN
Borisov
Orsha
Mogilev
Smolensk
Vyaz'ma
MOSCOW
Noginsk
Orekhovo-Zuevo
Dzerzhinsk
Murom
Vyksa
Arzamas
Alatyr
Volga
Ul'yanovsk
Inza
Kuybyshev Res.
Bugul'ma
Oktyabr'skiy
Abdulino
Sterlitamak
Ishimbay
South Ural Mts.
Bialystok
Grodno
Minsk
Roslavl
Kirov
Tula
Ryazan'
Kaluga
Serpukhov
Kolomna
Saransk
Penza
Kuznetsk
Melekess
Syzran'
Kuybyshev
Buzuluk
Orenburg (Chkalov)
Orsk
Mednogorsk
Baranovichi
Bobruysk
Brest
Pinsk
S.S.R.
Rechitsa
Zhlobin
Klintsy
Bryansk
Novomoskovsk
Ruzayevka
Morshansk
Kirsanov
Michurinsk
Tambov
Serdobsk
Vol'sk
Chapaevsk
Sorochinsk
Pugachev
Sol'-Iletsk
Aktyubinsk
Lublin
Kovel'
Korosten'
Mozyr'
Pripyat'
Gomel'
Orel
Yelets
Lipetsk
Yefremov
Voronezh
Balashov
Engel's
Ural'sk
POLAND
L'vov
Drogobych
Ternopol'
Shepetovka
Zhitomir
Nezhin
Sumy
Kursk
Staryy Oskol
Borisoglebsk
Saratov
Ural
Ivano-Frankovsk
Khmel'nitskiy
Vinnitsa
Berdichev
Kiev
Priluki
Akhtyrka
Belgorod
Liski
Buturlinovka
Uryupinsk
Kamyshin
Novouzensk
Uzhgorod
Kamenets-Podol'skiy
Cherkassy
Kremenchug
Poltava
Khar'kov
Izyum
Starobel'sk
Don
Frolovo
Kalmykovo
Chernovtsy
Bel'tsy
MOLDAVIAN S.S.R.
Kirovograd
Kadiyevka
Gorlovka
Donetsk
Voroshilovgrad
Volgograd (Stalingrad)
Petropavlovskiy
Urda
Cluj
Iasi
Kishinev
Tiraspol'
Nikolayev
Krivoy Rog
Zaporozh'ye
Makeyevka
Shakhty
Volga-Don Canal
Nikol'skoye
Kotel'nikovskiy
Gur'yev
ROMANIA
Bacau
Prut
Dniester
Melitopol'
Zhdanov
Novocherkassk
Elista
Ft. Shevchenko
Galati
Odessa
Kherson
Kakhovka
Taganrog
Rostov
Astrakhan
Ploiesti
Izmail
Yeysk
Sal'sk
Tikhoretsk
Divnoye
Kuma
CASPIAN SEA
Bucharest
Ruse
Constanta
Crimea
Kerch'
Simferopol'
Sevastopol'
Yalta
Novorossiysk
Krasnodar
Kuban
Armavir
Stavropol'
Prikumsk (Budennovsk)
Danube
BULGARIA
Varna
Burgas
Sea of Azov
Tuapse
Maykop
Cherkessk
Pyatigorsk
Kizlyar
Edirne
Istanbul
BLACK SEA
Sochi
Karachayevsk
Nal'chik
Groznyy
Makhachkala
Derbent
Sukhumi
El'brus 18,481
GEORGIAN S.S.R.
Ordzhonikidze
Kuba
Bursa
Sea of Marmara
Zonguldak
Sinop
Kutaisi
Poti
Chiatura
Tbilisi
Kazbek 16,558
Kuba
Baku
Izmir (Smyrna)
Bosporus
Cankiri
Samsun
Trabzon
Batumi
Leninakan
Karso
AZERBAIDZHAN S.S.R.
Dardanelles
Eskisehir
Ankara
Kizilirmak
Sivas
Erzurum
ARMENIAN S.S.R.
Erivan
Stepanakert
Nakhichevan
Lenkoran
Kayseri
TURKEY
L. Van
IRAN
Araks
RUSSIAN SOVIET FEDERATED SOCIALIST REPUBLIC
UKRAINIAN S.S.R.
The government of the United States does not recognize the incorporation of Estonia, Latvia and Lithuania into the Soviet Union. Post-war territorial changes shown on this map do not necessarily represent the final status of such boundaries. Only after the signing of peace treaties can changes be considered official and definite.
Copyright by C.S. HAMMOND & Co., N.Y.

Soviet of Nationalities has 750 elected on the basis of territorial units. Elections are called for every 5 years. Formal power is vested in the Presidium of the Supreme Soviet, which also appoints the Council of Ministers. Under Communist party direction, the council supervises all of the work of the government **Local Government:** 15 republics, each with its own Supreme Soviet and Council of Ministers, the latter headed by a premier. Ethnic divisions within the republics include 20 autonomous republics, 8 autonomous regions, and 10 national districts

Ethnic Composition: Russians constitute 53% of the population, Ukrainians 17%, Byelorussians 4%, Uzbeks 4%, and more than 150 other nationalities **Population Distribution:** 62% urban **Density:** 30 inhabitants per sq. mi.

Largest Cities: (1979 census) Moscow 8,011,000, Leningrad 4,588,000, Kiev 2,144,000; Tashkent 1,780,000, Baku 1,550,000, Khar'kov 1,444,000, Gor'kiy 1,344,000, Novosibirsk 1,312,000, Minsk 1,276,000, Kuybyshev 1,216,000, Sverdlovsk 1,211,000; Dnepropetrovsk 1,066,000, Tbilisi 1,066,000, Odessa 1,046,000

Per Capita Income: $4,387 (1979) **Gross National Product (GNP):** $1,156 billion (1979) **Economic Statistics:** 77.5% of the GNP is derived from industry (main industries include oil, steel, electricity, cement, pig iron, foodstuffs, textiles, and other heavy industry); 16.5% from agriculture (2 million square miles of arable land provide wheat, rye, corn, oats, potatoes, sugarbeets, linseed, sunflower seed, cotton, and flax; main livestock are cattle, sheep, and pigs) **Minerals and Mining:** Vast deposits of coal, iron, petroleum, natural gas, copper, nickel, bauxite, zinc, lead, gold, manganese, platinum, and tin **Labor Force:** Of 99,600,000 workers in 1974, there were 10,000,000 engaged in agricultural labor, 40,000,000 in industry and construction, 11,000,000 in transportation and communications, 13,000,000 in education, social security, and public health, and 25,000,000 in other sectors of the economy **Foreign Trade:** Exports, mainly machinery, iron and steel, crude oil, foodstuffs, lumber and paper products, and textiles, amounted to $52 billion in 1978. Imports, chiefly machinery, foodstuffs, and consumer goods, totaled $51 billion **Principal Trade Partners:** East Germany, Czechoslovakia, Poland, Hungary, Bulgaria, Romania, Cuba, Japan, West Germany, Finland, United States, Italy, France, Yugoslavia, Britain

Vital Statistics: Birthrate, 18.1 per 1,000 of pop. (1976); death rate, 9.6 **Life Expectancy:** 70 years **Health Statistics:** 83 inhabitants per hospital bed; 299 per physician (1976) **Infant Mortality:** 27.7 per 1,000 births (1974) **Illiteracy:** Negligible **Primary and Secondary School Enrollment:** 45,283,000 (1976) **Enrollment in Higher Education:** 4,853,958 **GNP Expended on Education:** 7.5% (1976)

Transportation: Paved roads total 200,000 mi. (1973) **Motor Vehicles:** 4,950,000 (1967) **Passenger Cars:** 1,100,000 **Railway Mileage:** 87,253 (1978) **Ports:** Main terminal ports on the Volga-Don system are Astrakhan, Rostov, Moscow, Perm; main transfer ports: Volgograd, Saratov, Kuybyshev, Kazan, Gorky, Yaroslavl; seaports: Leningrad, Odessa, Kaliningrad, Murmansk, Archangel, Riga, Vladivostok, Nakhodka **Major Airlines:** Aeroflot operates all international and domestic flights **Communications:** Government controlled **Radio Transmitters:** 3,034 **Receivers:** 122,477,000 (1975) **Television Transmitters:** 1,749 **Receivers:** 55,181,000 (1975) **Telephones:** 18,000,000 (1976) **Newspapers:** 691 dailies, 347 copies per 1,000 inhabitants (1975)

Weights and Measures: Metric system **Travel Requirements:** Passport, visa, valid 3 months, 3 photos. Make arrangements through travel agency that has a contract with Intourist

---

The Soviet Union, the world's largest country and one of the leading superpowers, has in recent years been experiencing alternating success and setbacks. Its policy of détente, the peaceful co-existence with non-Communist nations, has raised more ideological dilemmas than its original supporters could have imagined.

Leonid Brezhnev, General Secretary of the Communist party, the only political body in the Soviet Union, has now been in power longer than any of his predecessors since Stalin. Brezhnev's active role in the 25th Congress of the Communist Party of the Soviet Union dispelled rumors of possible illness or lack of support in the Soviet power structure. The Congress, which met in February-March 1976, endorsed the leadership of Secretary Brezhnev. In June 1977 Brezhnev was elected Chairman of the Presidium of the USSR and thus became the first leader in Soviet history to hold both the chief party and state post.

In the present five-year plan the party leaders have had to lower their targets for economic growth. In effect this was an admission of failure in the previous five-year plan to reach anticipated goals. For 1976-80 heavy industry receives strong emphasis at the expense of consumer goods. There is to be a retrenchment in the expansion of agriculture. The harvest failures before 1976 plagued Soviet planners hoping to achieve self-sufficiency in food needs.

Foreign trade, once a small part of the Russian economy, is now of great importance. Commerce with the West has reached an unprecedented level. Trade with the United States was over $2.8 billion in 1978 compared to $200 million in 1971. Purchases of much needed wheat in the United States and Canada have had substantial impact on world prices. Other Western nations, Japan, Britain, West Germany, have become involved with the USSR in trade pacts and long-range projects that require large investments in plant technology and resource development. The Soviets have been funding their trade deficits with the Western nations by selling gold or taking long-term loans.

The USSR built up its armed forces in the 1960s and 1970s, and sought influence in the Middle East and Africa. It transported Cuban soldiers to help pro-Soviet governments in Angola, Ethiopia, and Southern Yemen defeat domestic and foreign enemies. Enmity between China and the USSR continues to divide the Communist world, but the Soviets have maintained the solidarity of most East European Communist nations.

In late December 1979, the Soviet Army invaded Afghanistan to shore up its tottering Communist puppet regime. This was the first time the Soviets had used military force against a neutral country. Brezhnev declared the invasion was directed against "aggressive external forces of reaction" which were threatening Afghanistan, but the military move outraged the West and alarmed neutral countries. The U.S. government banned sales of grain and of high technology systems to the USSR, halted its efforts to have SALT II (strategic arms limitation treaty) ratified by the Senate, and called for a boycott of the 1980 summer Olympic Games in Moscow.

Although the UN General Assembly approved a resolution calling for the withdrawal of Soviet troops from Afghanistan, the USSR poured an estimated 90,000 soldiers into the country and seized major towns and highways. But Soviet forces met with stiff opposition from Afghan guerrillas in the mountainous areas and reportedly suffered about 8,000 casulaties by April 1980. Brezhnev said the USSR would withdraw its troops when the political situation in Afghanistan was stable, and in June the Soviet government withdrew a few army units (estimated at less than 10,000 soldiers) from the country—a move scorned as a token gesture by U.S. President Jimmy Carter. The Soviet government meantime launched an internal propaganda campaign to persuade its people that the invasion was necessary for the USSR's security.

HISTORY: About the 5th century A.D. the Russian steppes began to be peopled by the Slavs. By the 9th century, despite repeated invasions by other tribes, the Slavs constituted the majority of Russia's inhabitants

862-79: Rurik, a Scandinavian chieftain, establishes the first Russian city-state, at Novgorod. His successor, Oleg, expands his territory in 879 and makes Kiev his capital

1237-40: Mongol (Tatar) hordes overrun Russia, initiating two centuries of the "Tatar Yoke"

1547: Ivan IV (the Terrible), Prince of Moscow, is crowned tsar

1712: Peter the Great transfers capital from Moscow to St. Petersburg (now Leningrad)

1812: Napoleon invades Russia and occupies Moscow. Returning westward, he loses almost his entire army in the Russian snows

1861: Alexander II liberates the serfs

1914: Russia enters World War I

1917: Military setbacks lead to overthrow of Tsar Nicholas II. Succeeding Provisional Government is ousted by Bolsheviks, led by Lenin, who ends war by surrendering much territory

1922: Four Communist-ruled states—all formerly parts of Tsar's domain—form Union of Soviet Socialist Republics

1924-38: Lenin dies (1924). After a power struggle with Leon Trotsky, Stalin emerges as dictator. He institutes the forcible collectivization of agriculture, liquidating more than five million peasant families. In a great purge of his opponents, thousands of leading officials are executed

1941-45: Germany invades the USSR. After years of bitter warfare on Soviet soil, the Nazi armies are crushed. USSR regains most land surrendered in 1917 and becomes dominant in Eastern Europe

1953-56: Stalin dies (1953), causing another Kremlin power struggle. Nikita Khrushchev assumes leadership, denounces Stalin's "personality cult," and begins "de-Stalinization." Soviet forces invade Hungary and suppress anti-Communist revolution

1957: USSR launches world's first artificial satellite (Sputnik)

1961: Sino-Soviet split emerges over Khrushchev's policies of de-Stalinization and "peaceful coexistence" with the West

1962: USSR secretly installs missiles in Cuba; withdraws them after U.S. Navy quarantines island

1968: Soviet troops invade Czechoslovakia in move to halt liberalization of country's Communist regime

1974: Novelist Alexander Solzhenitsyn is arrested and deported for his criticisms of Soviet political repression

1975: Serious failure in grain crop; Soviet grain purchases abroad affect world food prices. In July, the joint U.S.-USSR Apollo/Soyuz space flight is successfully completed

1976: Leadership of Brezhnev is reaffirmed at 25th Communist Party Congress. New five-year plan calls for lowered economic goals

1977: Brezhnev chosen Chairman of the Presidium. Economic growth targets are significantly reduced

1979: Brezhnev and U.S. President Jimmy Carter sign treaty to limit strategic arms (SALT II). Soviet army invades Afghanistan to save tottering Communist regime

1980: Estimated 90,000 Soviet troops meet bitter resistance by Afghan rebels. UN condemns Soviet invasion; U.S. halts grain sales to USSR and refuses to ratify SALT treaty to protest Soviet military move; appeals for worldwide boycott of 1980 Olympic Games in Moscow

---

UNITED ARAB EMIRATES

Area: 32,278 sq. mi. **Population:** 862,000 (1978 est.)

Official Name: United Arab Emirates **Capital:** Abu Dhabi **Nationality:** Emiran **Languages:** Arabic is the official language; English is widely used **Religion:** 90% Sunni Moslem **Flag:** Equal green, white, and black horizontal stripes, with a red vertical stripe at the hoist **Anthem:** The National Anthem **Currency:** UAE Dirham (3.7 per U.S. $1)

Location: Southwest Asia on the Persian Gulf. The federation of seven emirates is bounded by Oman, Saudi Arabia, Qatar, and the Persian Gulf **Features:** A flat, barren island-dotted coastal plain gives way to extensive sand dunes in the interior. At the eastern end are the western Hajar Mountains

Head of State: President: Sheikh Zaid ibn Sultan al-Nahayan of Abu Dhabi, born 1918, reelected 1976, assisted by a Vice President, Sheikh Rashid ibn Said al-Maktum of Dubai, elected 1971, and a Supreme Council of the 7 rulers **Head of Government:** Premier: Sheikh Rashid ibn Said al-Maktum of Dubai, appointed 1979 **Effective Date of Present Constitution:** 1971 interim constitution amended 1976, and extended to 1981 **Legislative Body:** Federal National Council (unicameral), of 40 members in proportion to emirate population, appointed by the seven rulers **Local Government:** Each of the seven emirates (Abu Dhabi, Ajman, Dubai, Fujairah, Ras al-Khaimah, Sharjah, Umm al-Qaiwain) is self-governing, under a sheikh

Ethnic Composition: Arabs (42%), Iranians, Pakistanis, and Indians (50%); only about 25% are native-born **Population Distribution:** 90% urban **Density:** 27 inhabitants per sq. mi.

Largest Cities: (1977 est.) Abu Dhabi 210,000; (1972 est.) Dubai 60,000, Sharjah 25,000, Ras al-Khaimah 10,000, Ajman 4,000

Per Capita Income: $13,980 (1979) **Gross National Product (GNP):** $12.6 billion (1979) **Economic Statistics:** Oil production in 1978 was 1.8 million barrels per day, with Abu Dhabi producing 80%. Aside from the area's rich oil and natural gas deposits, the economy includes herding, date growing, fishing, and trading **Minerals and Mining:** There are rich oil and natural gas deposits, notably in Abu Dhabi, and copper, gypsum, and limestone exist **Labor Force:** 490,000 (1978), of which 87% is foreign **Foreign Trade:** Exports,

95% oil, totaled $8.6 billion in 1978. Imports, chiefly machinery, foods, and consumer goods, totaled $4.9 billion **Principal Trade Partners:** EC countries, United States, Japan, India

Vital Statistics: Birthrate, 50 per 1,000 of pop. (1974); death rate, 18 **Life Expectancy:** N.A. **Health Statistics:** 342 inhabitants per hospital bed; 230 per physician (1977) **Illiteracy:** 75% **Primary and Secondary School Enrollment:** 90,000 (1977) **Enrollment in Higher Education:** 2,100 (1976) **GNP Expended on Education:** 9.1% (1976)

Transportation: Paved roads total 500 mi. **Motor Vehicles:** 15,000 (1978) **Railway Mileage:** None **Ports:** Dubai, Abu Dhabi, Ruwais **Major Airlines:** Gulf Air **Communications:** Government controlled **Radio Transmitters:** 12 **Receivers:** 55,000 (1976) **Television Transmitters:** 3 **Receivers:** 26,065 **Telephones:** 95,000 **Newspapers:** 3 dailies

Weights and Measures: Metric, British and local standards **Travel Requirements:** Passport, visa, valid 3 months, $2.75 fee, 1 month stay, sponsorship required

---

The United Arab Emirates consists of seven emirates on the eastern Arabian Peninsula, extending from the southern base of the Qatar Peninsula to Fujairah on the Gulf of Oman. From west to east, they are Abu Dhabi, Dubai, Sharjah, Ajman, Umm al-Qaiwain, Ras al-Khaimah, and Fujairah. Before independence, the area was sometimes referred to as Trucial Oman, the Trucial Coast, or the Trucial Sheikdoms. Boundaries are vague and in many places disputed. The sheikdoms are largely desert, hot and dry.

The main economic link among the emirates is the desire to share in the vast oil wealth of one of them, Abu Dhabi, at least until reserves are found in their own areas, as has happened in Dubai.

British influence in the area was formalized by treaty with the principal sheiks of the coast as early as 1820. The Exclusive Agreement of 1892 provided for British control of foreign agreements and affairs. The agreement terminated, however, following the withdrawal of British troops. Independence was declared on December 2, 1971. The pending withdrawal, coupled with the possibility of border claims by Iran and Saudi Arabia, had led to a proposal for federation with Qatar and Bahrain. But in August 1971, Bahrain announced it would go it alone and Qatar followed suit.

The UAE supported the Arab states in their war against Israel in 1973, and ended diplomatic relations with Egypt after Egypt made peace with Israel in 1979.

HISTORY: European and Arab pirates roamed the Trucial Coast area from the 17th to the 19th centuries, hence the former label "Pirate Coast." Successful British expeditions against the pirates led to further campaigns against their headquarters at Ras al-Khaimah and other harbors along the southwest coast in 1819. In 1820 the sheiks signed a General Treaty of Peace with Britain

1853: Coastal sheiks sign treaty with the United Kingdom agreeing to a "perpetual maritime truce"

1892: UK and the Trucial States establish closer bonds in another treaty, similar to those entered into by the British and other Persian Gulf principalities

1955: UK effectively intervenes on the side of Abu Dhabi in the latter's dispute with Saudi Arabia over the Buraimi Oasis, resulting in control of the Oasis being shared between Abu Dhabi and the Sultanate of Oman

1958-60: Vast oil reserves are discovered in Abu Dhabi

1971: British protective treaty with the Trucial Sheikdoms ends. They become fully independent as the United Arab Emirates. Oil is discovered in Dubai

1975: UAE joins OPEC as its third largest contributor

1976: Supreme Defense Council unites the UAE's armed forces. Dubai officials announce plans for a $765-million port, a new airport and an oil refinery at Jebel Ali

1978: Dubai pulls forces from federal army and puts them on alert in dispute with Abu Dhabi over appointment of UAE armed forces commander

---

UNITED KINGDOM

Area: 94,399 sq. mi. **Population:** 55,883,100 (1979 est.)

Official Name: United Kingdom of Great Britain and Northern Ireland **Capital:** London **Nationality:** British **Languages:** English is the official and predominant language; Gaelic is spoken in parts of Scotland, while Welsh is the first language in western Wales and enjoys equal validity with English as an official language in Wales **Religion:** Although the Church of England and the Church of Scotland are established churches, there is complete religious freedom. About half the population belongs to the Church of England (Protestant Episcopal) and to its nonestablished branches in Scotland, Wales, and Northern Ireland. The Church of Scotland (Presbyterian) has about 1.3 million members. The other major Christian denominations are Roman Catholic (6 million); Methodist (900,000); Baptist (300,000); and Congregationalist (200,000). There are several hundred thousand Moslems, 410,000 Jews, and several thousand Buddhists **Flag:** Known as the Union Jack, the flag is a superimposition of the red cross of St. George of England, the white cross of St. Andrew of Scotland, and the red cross of St. Patrick of Ireland, all on a blue background **Anthem:** God Save the Queen **Currency:** Pound sterling (.44 per U.S. $1)

Location: Off the northwest coast of Europe. The island of Great Britain, containing England, Scotland, and Wales, is bordered by the Atlantic Ocean on the north and west, and is separated from the European continent by the North Sea, the Strait of Dover, and the English Channel on the east and south. The Irish Sea and the North Channel separate Great Britain from Ireland, the northern area of which constitutes Northern Ireland, bordered on the south by the Republic of Ireland **Features:** England is divided into hill districts in the north, west, and southwest, and the undulating downs and low-lying plains in the east and southeast. In the extreme north, the Cheviot Hills, running from east to west, separate England from Scotland. The Pennine Chain extends southward from the Cheviots into the Midlands, a plains region with low, rolling hills and valleys. Scotland has three natural topographic divisions: the Southern Uplands; the Central Lowlands; and the Northern Highlands, which contain the highest point in the British Isles. Wales is generally mountainous. Northern Ireland contains many plateaus and hills **Chief Rivers:** Severn, Thames, Trent, Aire, Great Ouse, Wye, Tay, Nene, Clyde, Spey, Tweed, Tyne

Head of State: Queen Elizabeth II, born 1926, ascended the throne 1952 **Head of Government:** Prime Minister Margaret Thatcher, born 1925, appointed May 4, 1979 **Effective Date of Present Constitution:** The British Constitution is formed partly by statute, partly by common law, and partly by "traditional rights" known as conventions. The rules of the constitution have never been codified, and can be adapted to changing conditions at any time by Act of Parliament or by the general acceptance of a new convention **Legislative Body:** Parliament (bicameral), consisting of the House of Lords and the House of Commons. The House of Commons, which is the ultimate authority for lawmaking, consists of 635 members elected by universal suffrage for a maximum term of 5 years. The House of Lords, which also functions as the highest court in the land, consists of some 1,200 members, including hereditary and life peers and peeresses, law lords appointed for life to carry out the judicial duties of the house, and the 2 archbishops and 24 senior bishops of the Church of England. The House of Lords has the power to delay, but not prevent, legislation **Local Government:** England is divided into 39 counties, 6 metropolitan counties, Greater London, and the Isles of Scilly; Wales is divided into 8 counties. Scotland is divided into 9 regions and 3 island areas. Northern Ireland is divided into 26 districts. Each local authority division throughout the United Kingdom is administered by its own elected council. In Northern Ireland the shape of the new institutions which will replace the former parliament had not been completely decided, although a 78-seat assembly and an executive or provincial cabinet which shares power between Roman Catholics and Protestants had been formed. A Constitutional Convention begun in 1975 was dissolved in 1976, having failed to agree on a system of government. Direct rule, first initiated in 1974, was therefore renewed. Northern Ireland continues to be represented in the U.K. House of Commons

Ethnic Composition: The contemporary Briton is descended from varied racial stocks that settled in the British Isles before the 12th century. Under the Normans, descendants of Scandinavian Vikings, pre-Celtic, Celtic, Roman, Anglo-Saxon, and Norse influences were blended into the Briton. The population includes some 1.9 million immigrant Pakistanis, Indians, West Indians and their British-born children **Population Distribution:** 78% urban **Density:** 592 inhabitants per sq. mi.

Largest Cities: (1976 est.) London 7,028,200, Birmingham 1,058,800, Glasgow 816,265, Leeds 744,500, Sheffield 558,000, Liverpool 539,700, Manchester 490,000, Bradford 458,900, Edinburgh 445,000, Bristol 416,300, Belfast 350,000

Per Capita Income: $4,972 (1979) **Gross National Product (GNP):** $278 billion (1979) **Economic Statistics:** About 32% of the GNP comes from manufacturing (iron and steel, engineering [vehicles and aircraft], textiles, chemicals, food products, and consumer goods); 12% from mining and quarrying (coal, petroleum, natural gas, iron ore, limestone, tin, gravel), construction, and public utilities; 9% from transportation and communications; 42% from trade and services; and 3% from agriculture **Minerals and Mining:** There are significant amounts of coal, small deposits of iron, limestone, tin, gravel and oilshale. There are large quantities of natural gas and oil in the North Sea **Labor Force:** 26.1 million (1977), with 28% in manufacturing and 2% in agriculture **Foreign Trade:** Exports, mainly manufactured goods including engineering products, motor vehicles, nonelectric and electric machinery, petroleum and nonmetallic mineral manufactures, totaled $92 billion in 1979. Imports, chiefly petroleum and petroleum products, machinery, nonferrous metals, meat and meat preparations, fruit and vegetables, amounted to $105 billion **Principal Trade Partners:** United States, West Germany, South Africa, Ireland, Canada, France, Netherlands, Switzerland

Vital Statistics: Birthrate, 11.8 per 1,000 of pop. (1977); death rate, 11.7 **Life Expectancy:** 72 years **Health Statistics:** 117 inhabitants per hospital bed; 761 per physician (1974) **Infant Mortality:** 14 per 1,000 births (1977) **Illiteracy:** Negligible **Primary and Secondary School Enrollment:** 10,801,957 (1974) **Enrollment in Higher Education:** 703,645 **GNP Expended on Education:** 6.2% (1974)

Transportation: Paved roads total 208,151 mi. **Motor Vehicles:** 16,460,000 (1976) **Passenger Cars:** 14,562,400 **Railway Mileage:** 11,467 **Ports:** London, Liverpool, Glasgow, Southampton, Belfast, Cardiff, Milford Haven, Manchester, Bristol, Hull, Swansea, Edinbugh, Newcastle **Major Airlines:** British Airways flies both domestically and internationally. There are some 30 independent air transport operations **Communications:** Government and privately owned **Radio Transmitters:** 364 **Receivers:** 39,500,000 (1976) **Television Transmitters:** 596 **Licenses:** 17,729,000 (1976) **Telephones:** 22,012,000 (1976) **Newspapers:** 111 dailies, 388 copies per 1,000 inhabitants (1975)

Weights and Measures: Metric system **Travel Requirements:** Passport, no visa

---

The basic problem for Great Britain has been that ever since losing an empire it has been unable to find a new role. When Britain dismantled the Empire, beginning in 1947, it also lost its captive markets and sources of supply. Britain was forced to compete in a changed world market with the disadvantages of aging industrial plants, war-depleted natural resources and an agricultural base that produced only half of the nation's food needs. In the postwar rebuilding, it did not do as well as its competitors, especially West Germany, France and Japan. Even the traditional British luxury goods—autos, liquor, and clothing, faced strong competition.

In economic terms Britain has suffered from slow growth, poor foreign trade results, low investment, weak currency, high inflation—in sum, a sluggish economy. No government has been able to arrest this decline. Entry into the Common Market in January 1973 was supposed to revitalize the British economy. It has not. Europe sells more to Britain than it buys. Trade balances improved only slightly.

But the economic picture is not all grim. The trickle of North Sea oil which began to flow from the British sector in 1974 has now grown to half a million barrels a day. By 1980 Britain was practically self-sufficient in oil and also able to earn enough in exports to put the country in the black for the first time since before World War II.

Although Britain has lost most of its 19th and early 20th century empire, troubles from former colonies as well as parts of the United Kingdom persisted, most notably in Northern Ireland, Zimbabwe (Rhodesia), Belize, Scotland, and Wales. The violent troubles in Northern Ireland, where some 14,000 troops are stationed, have resisted solution ever since the rioting between Protestant and Catholic communities broke out in Belfast and Londonderry in 1969. A definitive solution to the Ulster impasse has proved elusive, with violence continuing into 1980.

The Labour party, originally an outgrowth of the trade-union movement, has promoted social programs and nationalization of industry. It won a plurality, but not a majority, in the House of Commons in 1974 by promising a deal with the trade unions to end crippling strikes. Harold Wilson became prime minister in a Labour government and made the promised "social compact" with the unions. He retired in 1976 and was succeeded by a close ally, James Callaghan.

The Labour government fell in 1979 when it lost a no-confidence vote in Parliament on the issue of Scottish autonomy. The Conservatives won the ensuing elections in May with a solid majority and installed Margaret Roberts Thatcher, an outspoken free enterpriser, as the country's first woman prime minister. Mrs. Thatcher promised to set Britain on a different economic course by trying to establish a market-oriented, capital-owning economy that would free private business from extreme government regulation so that it might create new wealth.

After a year in office, the Thatcher government's conservative economic policies displayed mixed results. By the end of 1979, the inflation rate was nearly 22 percent and the nation's unemployment rate of 6.1 percent was the highest since World War II (7.8 percent in July 1980). For the first time in the postwar era, the government did not impose wage, price, dividend, or foreign exchange controls. It succeeded in stabilizing the money supply and revising the tax structure to encourage individual initiative. But economic experts say that it will require several years to determine whether the Conservative government can succeed in reshaping the British economy.

Mrs. Thatcher's government scored a notable diplomatic victory in late 1979 by helping to end the long civil war in the former white-ruled southern African country of Rhodesia, now Zimbabwe. The new British foreign minister, Lord Carrington, played a key role at the London conference which reconciled the conflicting forces in that country and established democratic rule under black majority rule.

HISTORY: The first known settlers of Britain were the Celts, who invaded the island from northern Europe before the 6th century B.C. A brief invasion by Julius Caesar in 55 B.C. paved the way for a long Roman occupation that began in the 1st century A.D. and lasted until the early 5th century. As the Roman army withdrew, waves of Anglo-Saxons and Jutes invaded Britain, forcing the Celts to retreat westward and into Brittany. The newcomers gradually established kingdoms of their own but were in turn invaded by the Danes, one of whom, Canute, became king of a united England in 1016

1066: William the Conqueror leads Norman army in the last successful invasion of England

1215: King John signs Magna Carta; the most important document of the British constitution, it establishes supremacy of law over the king and lays the foundation for parliamentary government

1337-1453: Hundred Years War rages as English kings seek to enforce claims to French territory; England is ultimately defeated and ceases to be a continental power

1455-85: Houses of York and Lancaster contend for English throne in Wars of the Roses, which end in victory for Henry Tudor, the Lancastrian claimant, and establishment of Tudor dynasty

1534: Breach with Rome, precipitated by pope's refusal to grant Henry VIII a divorce, is completed by Act of Supremacy declaring king head of the Church of England

1558-1603: Reign of Elizabeth I sees the rise of England as a leading European power, strengthened by the defeat of the Spanish Armada in 1588, and the flowering of the Renaissance in English literature; queen is succeeded by James VI of Scotland who, as James I of England, rules over both kingdoms

1642-49: Civil war rends England as Charles I and parliament struggle for power; war ends in defeat and execution of the king and establishment of a commonwealth dominated by Oliver Cromwell

1660: Monarchy is restored under Charles II

18th cent.: Britain undergoes marked transformation with development of parliamentary government and beginning of the Industrial Revolution; overseas, a huge empire is gained in Canada and India and another lost with the American Revolution, followed by war with Napoleonic France

1815: Duke of Wellington's army defeats Napoleon at Waterloo

1832: Enactment of Reform Bill extends franchise to middle class

1837-1901: Reign of Queen Victoria witnesses Britain's rise to world leadership in commerce and industry; reign closes with Britain industrially outstripped by United States and Germany, and fighting Boer War in South Africa

1902: Boers are defeated and accept British sovereignty

1914-18: Britain plays leading role in World War I, sharing in Allied victory over Germany but drained of wealth

1921: Southern Ireland is separated from United Kingdom

1924: Ramsay MacDonald forms Britain's first Labour Cabinet

1939-45: Britain again fights Germany in World War II; standing virtually alone after fall of France in 1940, British, under leadership of Winston Churchill, withstand intensive German bombing and defeat Luftwaffe in Battle of Britain; war ends with Britain again victorious but economically weakened; Labour party, under Clement Attlee, is swept into power

1956: Britain, under Conservative government of Anthony Eden, joins France and Israel in invasion of Egypt following nationalization of Suez Canal

1964: Labour party, led by Harold Wilson, is returned to power

1969: Troops are rushed to Northern Ireland after bloody riots break out between Protestants and Roman Catholics

1970: Wilson is defeated by Conservative leader Edward Heath

1971: Common Market approves Britain's bid for admission. New violence flares in Ulster

1972: Intensification of IRA terrorism in Ulster; Westminster assumes direct rule over the province

1973: Participation in Common Market (EC) begins

1974: National strike by coal miners threatens to halt industry. Conservative Prime Minister Edward Heath calls election for renewed mandate and loses. Harold Wilson becomes prime minister in minority Labour government, negotiates "social compact" with unions for labor peace

1975: Voters in referendum approve the government's recommendation to remain in EC under new terms

1976: Wilson resigns. He is succeeded by James Callaghan

1979: Unions call winter-time strikes despite social compact. Electorate in Wales rejects autonomy. Ambiguous results of autonomy referendum in Scotland lead to dispute between Callaghan and Scottish Nationalists. House of Commons votes no confidence in Callaghan and is dissolved. Conservatives win majority in new House; their leader, Margaret Thatcher, becomes Britain's first woman prime minister. Thatcher government sets new economic course by freeing economy of wage, price, and foreign exchange controls

1980: Unemployment reaches 7.8 % in July

UNITED STATES

Area: 3,615,123 sq. mi. **Population:** 220,099,000 (1979 est.)

Official Name: United States of America **Capital:** Washington, D.C. **Nationality:** American or United States **Languages:** English is the official and predominant language. Spanish is the preferred language of about 4 million, Italian of 400,000, French and Chinese of 300,000 each, and German, Greek, Japanese, Filipino, and Korean of 100,000 each. Other minority languages include Polish, Yiddish, Russian, and American Indian tongues **Religion:** About two-thirds of the population is Protestant, one-fourth Roman Catholic, 3% Jewish, and the rest of other or no affiliation **Flag:** Popularly known as the "Stars and Stripes" or "Old Glory," the flag consists of 13 horizontal, alternate red and white stripes, and a union of 50 five-pointed white stars arranged in alternate rows of 6 and of 5 on a blue field in the upper left corner **Anthem:** The Star-Spangled Banner

Location: The United States proper (excluding Hawaii and Alaska) stretches across North America from the Atlantic Ocean on the east to the Pacific Ocean on the west, from Canada on the north to Mexico and the Gulf of Mexico on the south **Features:** The United States proper (excluding Hawaii and Alaska) consists of the Atlantic coastal plain, the Appalachian highlands, a vast interior plains region, the Rocky Mountains belt, the intermontane basin and plateaus west of the Rockies, and the mountains and valleys of the Pacific borderland. Another division, part of the Laurentian Plain of Canada, dips into the United States in the Great Lakes region. Alaska's main physical divisions are the Pacific mountain system, the Central Plateau, the Arctic mountain system, and the Arctic Slope. Hawaii consists of a 1,610-mile-long chain of 122 islands, which represent mountain peaks of volcanic origin largely submerged in the Pacific **Chief Rivers:** Mississippi, Missouri, Rio Grande, Yukon, Arkansas, Colorado, Ohio-Allegheny, Red, Columbia, Snake, Pecos, Canadian

Head of State and of Government: President Jimmy Carter, born 1924, took office 1977 **Effective Date of Constitution:** March 4, 1789 **Legislative Body:** Congress (bicameral), consisting of the Senate and the House of Representatives. The Senate consists of

100 members—2 from each state—chosen by popular vote for a 6-year term; a third of its membership is renewed every 2 years. The House of Representatives has 435 members elected by popular vote every 2 years; each state is entitled to at least one Representative, with the total number determined periodically according to population **Local Government:** 50 states, each with a popularly elected governor and legislature. Below the state level, local self-government is usually conducted through municipalities, townships, and counties

Ethnic Composition: The nation's ethnic diversity is chiefly due to large-scale immigration, most of which took place before 1920. Whites comprise about 87% of the population, blacks 11.5%, and other races the remaining 1.5% **Population Distribution:** 74% urban **Density:** 60.9 inhabitants per sq. mi.

Largest Cities: (1976 est.; M.A. = Metropolitan Area—1977 est.) New York (1977) 7,312,200 (M.A. 9,386,700), Chicago 3,074,084 (M.A. 7,017,400), Los Angeles 2,743,994 (M.A. 7,031,000), Philadelphia (1977) 1,784,500 (M.A. 4,793,900), Houston (1978) 1,699,000 (M.A. 2,512,200), Detroit 1,314,206 (M.A. 4,370,200), Dallas 848,829 (M.A. 2,673,300), Baltimore (1977) 804,900 (M.A. 2,146,900), San Diego 789,059 (M.A. 1,683,000), San Antonio 783,765 (M.A. 1,024,900), Honolulu 723,400, Indianapolis 708,867 (M.A. 1,143,800), Washington (1977) 685,000 (M.A. 3,020,100)

Per Capita Income: $10,739 (1979) **Gross National Product (GNP):** $2,368.8 billion (1979) **Economic Statistics:** About 26% of the GNP is derived from manufacturing; 17% from wholesale and retail trade; 14% from finance, insurance, and real estate; 14% from services; 15% from government and government enterprises; 3% from agriculture, forestry, and fisheries; 5% from construction; 6% from transportation and communications; 2% from electric, gas, and sanitary services; and 2% from mining **Minerals and Mining:** The United States produces a great variety of minerals and consumes more than any other nation in the world. It is the world's leading producer of coal, copper, lead, natural gas, and molybdenum. Though no longer the leading producer, the United States ranks among the top group in petroleum and iron ore. Zinc, sulfur, vanadium, cadmium, uranium, phosphate rock, bauxite, gypsum, aluminum, nitrates, magnesium, potash, titanium, tungsten, feldspar and barite are among the other major minerals produced, and the nation is also rich in waterpower **Labor Force:** 104,996,000 (1979), of which 96% is engaged in nonagricultural industries **Foreign Trade:** Exports, chiefly machinery and transport equipment, food and live animals, crude materials (soybeans, textile fibers, ores and metal scrap), chemicals, other manufactured goods (metals and manufactures, scientific instruments, textiles, rubber, and paper), and mineral fuels, totaled $181.6 billion in 1979. Imports, mainly machinery and transport equipment, other manufactured goods (metals and manufactures, textiles, iron and steel-mill products, and nonferrous base metals), food and live animals, crude materials, and mineral fuels, totaled $206 billion **Principal Trade Partners:** Canada, Japan, Britain, West Germany, Saudi Arabia, Netherlands, Mexico, Nigeria, Italy, France, Venezuela, Brazil, Belgium and Luxembourg, China, South Korea

Vital Statistics: Birthrate, 15.3 per 1,000 of pop. (1978); death rate, 8.8 **Life Expectancy:** 74 years **Health Statistics:** 130 inhabitants per hospital bed; 621 per physician (1976) **Infant Mortality:** 13.6 per 1,000 births (1978) **Illiteracy:** Negligible **Primary and Secondary School Enrollment:** 47,000,000 (1978) **Enrollment in Higher Education:** 9,800,000 **GNP Expended on Education:** 7.1% (1978)

Transportation: Surfaced roads total 3,867,000 mi. (1977) **Motor Vehicles:** 149,100,000 (1978) **Passenger Cars:** 117,100,000 **Railway Mileage:** 190,000 (1977) **Ports:** New York, Philadelphia, Portland, Baltimore, Boston, Houston, Norfolk, Tampa, San Francisco, New Orleans, Los Angeles, Corpus Christi, Baton Rouge **Major Airlines:** Major international and domestic carriers are American Airlines, Braniff Airways, Eastern Airlines, Trans World Airlines, Pan American World Airways, Continental Air Lines, Delta Airlines, Northwest Orient Airlines, and United Air Lines **Communications:** Privately owned **Radio Transmitters:** 7,307 (1976) **Receivers:** 402,000,000 (1975) **Television Transmitters:** 3,853 (1974) **Receivers:** 121,100,000 (1974) **Telephones:** 162,072,000 (1977) **Newspapers:** 1,756 dailies (1978)

Weights and Measures: Avoirdupois units of weight and linear measures. Metric system gradually being introduced

For articles and statistics on the separate states, see **The Fifty States;** for important national events, see **'79/'80 Month-By-Month Chronology**

UPPER VOLTA

Area: 105,869 sq. mi. **Population:** 6,554,000 (1978 est.)
Official Name: Republic of Upper Volta **Capital:** Ouagadougou

Nationality: Upper Voltan **Languages:** The official language is French. Mossi is the main African language, others being Samo, Gourounsi, and Lobi, which belong to the Niger-Congo family of languages **Religion:** The majority of the population are animists. There are over 1 million Moslems, 130,000 Roman Catholics, and 9,000 Protestants **Flag:** Horizontal stripes of black, white, and red **Anthem:** The Volta **Currency:** CFA Franc (210.2 per U.S. $1)

Location: West Africa. Landlocked Upper Volta is bordered on the west and north by Mali, on the east by Niger, and on the south by Benin, Togo, Ghana, and Ivory Coast **Features:** The country consists for the most part of a vast plateau, slightly inclined toward the south and notched by valleys and formed by the three main rivers, with some savanna and semidesert **Chief Rivers:** Black, White, and Red Voltas, and their main tributaries

Head of State: President: Maj. Gen. Aboubacar Sangoulé Lamizana, born 1916, seized power in 1966, elected 1978 for 7-year term **Head of Government:** Premier: Joseph Conombo, appointed 1978 **Effective Date of Present Constitution:** 1977 **Legislative Body:** National Assembly (unicameral) with 57 members, serving 5-year terms **Local Government:** 10 departments

Ethnic Composition: The two main ethnic groups are the Voltaic people and the Mande (Mandingos). Among the Voltaic, 65% are Mossi and 15% Bobo; the Samo are the most numerous of the Mande group **Population Distribution:** 11% urban **Density:** 62 inhabitants per sq. mi.

Largest Cities: (1973 est.) Ouagadougou 105,000, Bobo-Dioulasso 90,000, Koudougou 40,000, Ouahigouya 20,000, Kaya 18,000, Fada N'Gourma 12,000, Banfora 7,000

Per Capita Income $114 (1978) **Gross National Product (GNP):** $740 million (1978) **Economic Statistics:** In 1976 about 67% of GNP was from agriculture (sorghum, millet, cotton, sesame, maize, rice, livestock products, peanuts); 6% from industry (textiles, bicycle assembly, maintenance and repairing of vehicles) **Minerals and Mining:** Manganese deposits are to be exploited; deposits of copper, gold, bauxite, and limestone exist **Labor Force:** 2,700,000 in 1976, with 87% engaged in subsistence agriculture **Foreign Trade:** Exports, chiefly livestock, cotton, and peanuts, totaled $57 million in 1978. Imports, mainly textiles, petroleum products, motor vehicles and parts, fruits and vegetables, and machinery, totaled $210 million **Principal Trade Partners:** EEC countries, Ivory Coast, Ghana

Vital Statistics: Birthrate, 48.5 per 1,000 of pop. (1975); death rate, 25.8 **Life Expectancy:** 38 years **Health Statistics:** 1,174 inhabitants per hospital bed; 59,595 per physician (1974) **Infant Mortality:** 260 per 1,000 births **Illiteracy:** 90% **Primary and Secondary School Enrollment:** 167,330 (1976) **Enrollment in Higher Education:** 1,067 (1975) **GNP Expended on Education:** 2.9% (1973)

Transportation: Improved roads total 4,000 mi. **Motor Vehicles:** 19,600 (1975) **Passenger Cars:** 9,500 **Railway Mileage:** 341 **Ports:** None **Major Airlines:** Air Afrique provides international services; Air Volta flies domestically **Communications:** Government owned **Radio Transmitters:** 5 **Receivers:** 105,000 (1976) **Television Transmitters:** 1 **Receivers:** 6,000 (1974) **Telephones:** 6,000 (1975) **Newspapers:** 3 dailies, 0.3 copies per 1,000 inhabitants (1975)

Weights and Measures: Metric system **Travel Requirements:** Passport, visa valid for 3 months, $2 fee, 2 photos

Upper Volta's name derives simply from the fact that its central region is watered by the upper tributaries of the Volta River, which flows southward through Ghana. Most of the country is a plateau where woodland and pasture contrast with a dry northern area seared by the desert wind.

Once the center of the ancient Mossi empire that provided a shield against Moslem conquest of the coastal regions, Upper Volta today is a land of hardworking farmers and cattle-raisers. Poor soil and variable rains, however, make the task of raising food and export crops, chiefly peanuts and cotton, a recurrent struggle. The nation's landlocked situation adds a further handicap.

Since independence from France in 1960, the country has faced the familiar trials of new African nations. Its first president, Maurice Yaméogo, proved an inept financial administrator. In 1966, with the country in virtual bankruptcy, his government was ousted by a military regime headed by army chief Lt. Col. Sangoulé Lamizana.

Elections were held in 1970, establishing a civilian parliament, but in 1974 Lamizana created a new cabinet composed largely of military officers. In 1976 another change occurred, when after two months of strife between the government and the unions, President Lamizana dismissed the military government and formed a new, largely civilian government. In May 1978, in an election marking the end of military rule, Lamizana was elected to the office he had assumed.

Meanwhile Upper Volta has received new aid from France, the Common Market, and the World Bank for further improvement of agriculture and transportation. At the same time, an even greater boost for the country's development is expected from the manganese deposits at Tambao, where tests indicate proven reserves of more than 10 million tons.

Offsetting these pluses in the early 1970s was the long siege of severe drought and famine that plagued Upper Volta and five other nations of the sub-Sahara (Chad, Mali, Mauritania, Niger, and Senegal); at least 150,000 persons were estimated to have died of starvation. Steps were taken in 1977 to deal with this problem through the adoption of an agricultural development program. The program, approved by Upper Volta and 8 other African nations of the drought-ridden Sahel region, would create food self-sufficiency within 20 years.

HISTORY: Upper Volta occupies the site of the former Mossi empire and its early history is mostly that of the Mossi people. According to legend, they entered the region as a warrior group between the 11th and 13th centuries and established three independent kingdoms, the most powerful of which was Ouagadougou. Between the 14th and 19th centuries, the Mossi engaged in recurrent wars with the neighboring empires of Mali and Songhai, and after severe defeats their power declined

1896: French subjugate territory and establish a protectorate

1904: Present-day Upper Volta is incorporated into a French colony called Upper Senegal and Niger

1919: Upper Volta is established as a separate French colony

1932: Upper Volta is divided among the colonies of French Sudan, Niger, and the Ivory Coast; is reunited in 1947

1958: Upper Volta becomes a self-governing state, called the Voltaic Republic, within the French Community

1959: Republic's name is changed to Upper Volta; in a general election, the pro-French African Democratic Rally wins a majority of seats in the national assembly and party's leader Maurice Yaméogo is elected premier

1960: Upper Volta becomes an independent republic; with Maurice Yaméogo as president

1966: Army chief of staff Lt. Col. Sangoulé Lamizana seizes control of the government, dismisses President Yaméogo and declares himself chief of state

1970-71: Elections and adoption of a new constitution mark return to constitutional rule the following year

1974: Lamizana suspends constitution, abolishes office of prime minister, and dissolves legislature

1976: President Lamizana dismisses military government and forms a new, largely civilian cabinet

1977: Government lifts three-and-one-half-year ban on political parties. Upper Voltans vote in favor of draft constitution aimed at restoring civilian rule after twelve years of military rule

1978: Military rule ends as Lamizana is elected president

1979: National Assembly institutes a three-party system

1980: Visiting Pope John Paul II appeals to world for aid to drought-stricken nations

---

URUGUAY

Area: 68,536 sq. mi. **Population:** 2,864,000 (1978 est.)

Official Name: Oriental Republic of Uruguay **Capital:** Montevideo **Nationality:** Uruguayan **Languages:** Spanish is the official and universal language **Religion:** 66% Roman Catholic, 2% Protestant, 2% Jewish, 30% other **Flag:** Four blue stripes and 5 white stripes, with a golden sun on a white field in the upper left corner **Anthem:** National Anthem, beginning "Easterners our country or death" **Currency:** Uruguayan peso (8.9 per U.S. $1)

Location: Southeast coast of South America. Uruguay is bounded on the north and northeast by Brazil, on the east by the Atlantic Ocean, on the south by the Rio de la Plata estuary, and on the west by Argentina **Features:** The country consists of rolling, grassy plains and low hills. There are scattered forest areas along the banks of the numerous streams, which provide natural irrigation for the soil **Chief Rivers:** Uruguay, Negro, Rio de la Plata, Cuareim, Yaguarón

Head of State and of Government: President Aparicio Méndez Manfredini, born 1904, took office in 1976 **Effective Date of Present Constitution:** 1967, nullified June 1973; a new one is planned **Legislative Body:** Congress dissolved 1973; a 25-member Council of State governs at present, while a new bicameral legislature is planned **Local Government:** 19 departments

Ethnic Composition: About 85% of the population is of European origin, mainly Spanish and Italian, with 10% mestizo, and 5% mulatto or black **Population Distribution:** 83% urban **Density:** 42 inhabitants per sq. mi.

Largest Cities: (1975 census) Montevideo 1,229,748; (1970 est.) Las Piedras 90,000, Salto 80,000

Per Capita Income: $1,513 (1979) **Gross National Product (GNP):** $4.4 billion (1979) **Economic Statistics:** In 1978 about 33% of GNP from manufacturing (meat packing, shoes, leather, textiles, construction and building materials, beverages, chemicals); 14% was from agriculture (livestock products, beef, wool, wheat, corn, rice) **Minerals and Mining:** Marble, building stone, gravel, and iron ore **Labor Force:** 1,174,376 (1975), with 34% in industry; 8% in agriculture; 40% in trade and services; 5% in construction; and 6% in transportation and communications **Foreign Trade:** Exports, chiefly wool, meat, and hides, totaled $681 million in 1978. Imports, mainly raw materials, fuels and lubricants, machinery and parts, automotive vehicles and parts, construction materials, and foodstuffs, totaled $774 million **Principal Trade Partners:** Brazil, United States, West Germany, Iraq, Nigeria, Argentina, Netherlands

Vital Statistics: Birthrate, 20.9 per 1,000 of pop. (1976); death rate, 10.2 **Life Expectancy:** 71 years **Health Statistics:** 235 inhabitants per hospital bed; 700 per physician (1976) **Infant Mortality:** 45.9 per 1,000 births (1976) **Illiteracy:** 9% **Primary and Secondary School Enrollment:** 453,781 (1977) **Enrollment in Higher Education:** 32,627 (1975) **GNP Expended on Education:** 3.6% (1970)

Transportation: Paved roads total 4,100 mi. **Motor Vehicles:** 231,300 (1976) **Passenger Cars:** 127,100 **Railway Mileage:** 1,736 **Ports:** Montevideo **Major Airlines:** Primeras Líneas Uruguayas de Navegación Aérea (PLUNA) operates domestically and internationally **Communications:** Government and privately controlled **Radio Transmitters:** 101 **Receivers:** 1,600,000 (1976) **Television Transmitters:** 27 **Receivers:** 355,000 (1976) **Telephones:** 258,000 (1976) **Newspapers:** 30 dailies, 140 copies per 1,000 inhabitants (1974)

Weights and Measures: Metric system **Travel Requirements:** Passport, no visa for 3 months

---

The Oriental Republic of Uruguay takes its name from the fact that it is situated on the east bank of the Uruguay River. Uruguay, the second smallest country in South America, is characterized by a high literacy rate and a large urban middle class.

Economic reverses and political repression have seriously affected Uruguayans in the last decade. Although politically stable since 1903, Uruguay began to experience problems in the late 1960s with a series of student riots, general strikes, and the rise of urban terrorism. A series of repressive government measures followed, then a 1973 coup against the presidency of Juan Bordaberry. The military group responsible for the coup retained Bordaberry as president and began tightening its already firm grip on the country. Political stability was not enhanced by Bordaberry's government, and dissidents were eliminated through a campaign of arrests, torture and murder. By June 1976 the military had ousted Bordaberry in a peaceful putsch because he planned to set up a corporate state structure with the participation of the armed forces written into law. The military preferred a gradual return to representative democracy. Bordaberry was replaced by Aparicio Méndez, who was named president by the conservative Council of the Nation.

Things were not always so sorrowful for Uruguay. Not long ago it could boast one of the highest per capita incomes in the hemisphere and a widely desired currency. The country was envied for its advanced laws, six-hour work day, retirement of workers at age 50 or 55, and incredibly rich soil. But the utopian social system, based on a growing population, became overburdened and began to fall behind in its payments. A 1963 census showed that the population had not grown, that, in fact, well-educated Uruguayans had been leaving for other lands in large numbers.

The economy has been marked by high inflation and, until recently, a high balance of payments deficit. In an effort to deal with the situation, the government has issued a series of mini-devaluations of the peso.

The political situation looks no brighter under Méndez. Upon taking office he immediately issued a decree suspending the political rights of the leaders of existing parties for 15 years. It has been reported that Uruguay, with a population of less than three million, has the highest proportion of political prisoners to total population. In 1978, the regime conceded that 2,511 persons accused of "crimes against state security" had served jail sentences and been released in the preceding six years. In 1979 it asserted that the number of political prisoners still being held was 1,600.

HISTORY: The eastern side of the Uruguay and La Plata rivers was occupied by warlike and seminomadic Indians, the Charrúa, until late in the colonial period when Europeans began to settle the area. The first settlers were the Spanish, who established a colony at Soriano in 1624. They were followed by the Portuguese, who were driven out in the 18th century by the Spanish, under whom Uruguay became part of a viceroyalty centered in Argentina. During the Napoleonic Wars, Uruguay was briefly occupied by the British, and the spread of revolutionary ideas during this period soon swept the country into the general Latin American fight for independence

1810-14: A war of independence, led by José Gervasio Artigas, begins; Uruguay, with aid from Argentina, ends Spanish rule

1820-28: Uruguay is occupied by Brazil. In 1825, a group of patriots known as the Thirty-Three Immortals declare Uruguay an independent republic; country throws off Brazilian rule and, in 1828, Uruguay is established as an independent buffer state between Brazil and Argentina

1865-70: Argentina, Brazil, and Uruguay unite in a victorious war against Paraguay

1911-15: President José Batlle y Ordóñez introduces wide range of social and economic reforms

1919-51: Fearful of the development of a dictatorship, nation adopts new constitution restricting president's power and vesting broad powers in Council of Administration; resulting conflict leads to restoration of strong executive powers to president in 1934. In 1951, office of president is abolished and executive power vested in nine-member national council

1958: The conservative Blancos (National party) win general elections, displacing liberal Colorado party which had governed for more than 90 years

1965: General strike paralyzes economic life of country

1966: Presidential form of government is restored in referendum; Colorados regain majority in general elections

1967-68: President Oscar D. Gestido dies and is succeeded by Vice-President Jorge Pacheco Areco; general strikes and student riots become widespread

1969: Pacheco decrees a limited state of siege in June following a new wave of disabling strikes; government closure of left-wing newspaper results in virtual shutdown of nation's press; move is made in Congress to impeach Pacheco

1971: Juan M. Bordaberry is elected president

1973: President Bordaberry's military-dominated civilian government suspends constitutional rule, replaces congress with a council of state, and curbs opposition press

1976: Bordaberry is ousted. Aparicio Méndez is named president

1977: U.S. moves to reduce aid to Uruguay because of human rights violations; Uruguay then rejects aid linked to human rights, claiming it is an internal matter

1978: OAS panel charges Uruguay with wholesale violations of human rights

1979: Elimination of duties on imported fertilizers and farm machinery leads to increased productivity of farmlands and herds

---

VANUATU

Area: 5,700 sq. mi. **Population:** 112,596 (1979 census)
Official Name: Republic of Vanuatu **Capital:** Vila **Nationality:** Vanuatuan **Languages:** Bislama, a pidgin dialect, is the national language. English, French and Bislama are official languages. There are many Melanesian languages throughout the islands **Religion:** Mostly Christian (Presbyterian, Roman Catholic, Anglican); some animists **Flag:** Two equal horizontal stripes of red over green with a black triangle at the hoist containing two crossed yellow mele leaves surrounded by a yellow hog tusk. The triangle is framed on two sides by borders of yellow and black which extend into a triple horizontal stripe of black-yellow-black running to the fly end of the flag **Anthem:** N.A. **Currency:** New Hebrides Franc (63 per U.S. $1)

Location: The Y-shaped chain of islands, located in the southwestern Pacific between 13°08' and 20°12'S., and 166°33' and 169°49'E., are 600 miles west of Fiji and 250 miles northeast of New Caledonia **Features:** The main islands are Espiritu Santo (the largest), Malekula, Epi, Pentecost and Efate. They are of coral and volcanic origin with active volcanoes on Ambryn, Lopevi and Tanna. Most islands are covered with dense forests

Head of State: President Ati George Sokomanu, born 1938, elected June 1980 **Head of Government:** Prime Minister: Rev. Walter Lini, born 1943, appointed July 1980 **Effective Date of Present Constitution:** Sept. 1979 **Legislative Body:** Representative Assembly (unicameral) with 39 members **Local Government:** 4 regions

Ethnic Composition: The population is 92% indigenous Melanesian. There are 5,000 French, 460 British and 1,500 Commonwealth citizens **Population Distribution:** 23% urban **Density:** 20 inhabitants per sq. mi.

Largest Cities: (1976 est.) Vila 17,367, Luganville 4,954

Per Capita Income: N.A. **Gross National Product (GNP):** N.A. **Economic Statistics:** Copra is the principal product, and cocoa and coffee are also grown. Yams, taro, manioc and bananas are produced for local consumption and there are a large number of cattle. Fishing is important, and tourism is growing **Minerals and Mining:** Manganese deposits are exploited **Labor Force:** The native population is mainly engaged in peasant farming **Foreign Trade:** Exports, chiefly copra, fish, prepared meats, and manganese, totaled $27 million in 1974. Imports, chiefly food, fuel, textiles and machinery, totaled $44 million **Principal Trade Partners:** Australia, France, United States, Japan

Vital Statistics: Birthrate, 45 per 1,000 of pop. (1966); death rate, 20 **Life Expectancy:** N.A. **Health Statistics:** 102 inhabitants per hospital bed; 3,200 per physician (1975) **Infant Mortality:** N.A. **Illiteracy:** 85% **Primary and Secondary School Enrollment:** 23,840 (1977) **Enrollment in Higher Education:** N.A. **GNP Expended on Higher Education:** N.A.

Transportation: Surfaced roads total 160 mi. **Motor Vehicles:** 3,400 (1974) **Passenger Cars:** 2,600 **Railway Mileage:** None **Ports:** Vila, Luganville **Major Airlines:** Air Melanesiae provides domestic service **Communications:** Government and privately owned **Radio Transmitters:** 2 **Receivers:** 15,000 (1976) **Television:** None **Telephones:** 2,400 **Newspapers:** 2 (fortnightly)

Weights and Measures: Metric system **Travel Requirements:** N.A.

A South-Sea islands paradise in so many ways—its main island of Espiritu Santo was the locale for James Michener's *Tales of the South Pacific*—the island nation of Vanuatu faces independence beset by internal divisions and outright rebellion that threaten to tear it apart at the seams.

This small Pacific archipelago situated west of the international date line—formerly known as the New Hebrides, and ruled since 1906 as a joint British-French Condominium—gained its independence July 30, 1980. Though its tropical climate makes it a potential haven for tourism, Vanuatu remains one of the more primitive and underdeveloped areas in the Pacific, with an economy dependent on subsistence agriculture and many tribal Melanesians still practicing various "cargo cult" religions.

In December 1978, a majority coalition government was formed to draft a new constitution and prepare the islands for independence. Father Gerard Lemyang—a French-educated Roman Catholic priest and moderate political leader—became chief minister and formed a Government of National Unity (GNU), with the pro-independence Vanuaaku Party (VP) sharing half the cabinet posts, and its leader, Rev. Walter Lini—an Anglican priest and nationalist spokesman—becoming deputy chief minister.

The constitution adopted in September 1979 provided for elections prior to independence, which was set for May-July 1980. It guaranteed French language rights, established a council of tribal chiefs to preserve traditional Melanesian customs, and set up regional assemblies for Santo and Tanna, in an attempt to mollify separatist sentiment there.

The VP won the November 14 elections to the Representative Assembly, beating the New Hebrides Federal party—a coalition including Lemyang, the Santo-based Na-Griamel separatists and pro-French groups—by two-to-one, with Lini becoming chief minister. The VP also won a majority in the two regional assemblies on Santo and Tanna, causing outbreaks of violence from separatist gangs claiming election fraud.

But on May 25 of 1980, Jimmy (Moli) Stevens and several hundred followers armed with bows and arrows—and backed up by 50 or more French-speaking planters armed with shotguns—stormed government offices in Luganville, took the British District Commissioner hostage, and declared Santo the independent nation of Vemarana. Stevens, a mixed-race plantation owner and hereditary tribal chief who founded the Na-Griamel movement in the 1960s, is seeking autonomy for Santo under French tutelage, and is supported by many French-speaking residents who fear the VP will nationalize their big plantations following independence. Stevens is allegedly advised by the Nevada-based Phoenix Foundation, a group of American businessmen who hope to establish a tax-free haven in the islands.

The insurrection died down when a joint 300-man Anglo-French military force arrived to restore order July 24, after clashes between insurgents and local police resulted in one rebel killed. But these troops were withdrawn soon after independence was declared, as rebel violence increased. Now prime minister of an independent state, Lini called on the United Nations for aid in maintaining Vanuatu's territorial integrity. Support came from other independent Pacific states, with Papua New Guinea sending 150 troops to replace the Anglo-French peacekeeping force. Authorities later arrested some 40 rebels on Santo August 19—including several French citizens now facing deportation—ending the latest round in the dispute. By the end of the month all resistance was crushed and Stevens was reported to be under arrest.

HISTORY: Little is known of the pre-history of the archipelago, though Melanesian settlement is thought to pre-date 400 B.C. The Spanish explorer de Quiros was the first European to sight the islands (1606). The islands were later visited by Bougainville in 1768 and by Captain Cook—who discovered, charted and named most of the southern islands—in 1774. Missionaries came to the islands in the 1820s, and were followed by settlers from Britain and France. The islands suffered during the 1860s from raids by "blackbirders" recruiting forced labor to work in Australia and Fiji

1887: Disputes between French and English-speaking settlers over control of the islands—and their possible annexation by either Australia or French New Caledonia—lead Britain and France to set up Joint Naval Commission to protect their subjects in the archipelago

1902: Resident Commissioners representing Britain and France are appointed to administer islands

1906: Anglo-French Condominium is established, with dual administration for British and French citizens, the terms of which are set officially in the Anglo-French Protocol of 1914

1940-45: French residency in Vila is one of first overseas departments to support Gen. de Gaulle's Free French government against Vichy. Islands become a major base for the Allied offensive in the South Pacific. John Frum "cargo cult" develops as anti-colonial movement among tribal people on Tanna Island; but near-rebellion is avoided with jailing of main leaders

1957: Advisory Council, partly elected and partly appointed by the Resident Commissioners, is established

1974: Nationalist agitation wins elected Representative Assembly, replacing Advisory Council; Luganville and Vila are granted municipal assemblies in move toward increased self-government

1975: August municipal elections in Vila and Luganville are won by pro-French and autonomist parties, but pro-independence Nationalist party wins majority in the Representative Assembly. Jimmy (Moli) Stevens, leader of the Na-Griamel movement on Santo, calls for unilateral independence for that island, demanding British withdrawal from the New Hebrides

1977: Pro-French "moderates" win uncontested Assembly elections in November; pro-independence Vanuaaku party, led by Rev. Walter Lini, boycotts elections and later forms "People's Provisional Government." George Kalsakau of Natatok party becomes chief minister

1978: French Secretary of State for Overseas Departments and Territories Paul Dijoud calls for coaliton government to end political crisis and move toward independence. Gerard Lemyang becomes chief minister and forms Government of National Unity; VP accepts five cabinet seats in GNU, with Lini becoming deputy chief minister

1979: New constitution is adopted, mandating pre-independence elections and regional legislatures for Espiritu Santo and Tanna. VP wins Nov. 14 elections, gaining 26 seats in the Assembly, with New Hebrides Federal party winning the other 13; Lini becomes chief minister. Violence flares as VP also wins majority in Santo and Tanna assemblies, but order is soon restored

1980: Jimmy Stevens stages revolt on Espiritu Santo May 25, proclaiming the island independent state of Vemarana; rebellion is joined by separatists on Tanna, but Anglo-French military force temporarily restores order July 24. New Hebrides becomes the independent nation of Vanuatu July 30; Walter Lini becomes nation's first prime minister. Secession continues as Lini calls for UN aid; Papua New Guinea sends 150-strong detachment Aug. 18 to replace Anglo-French force. All resistance crushed by Aug. 30; Stevens arrested

VATICAN CITY

Area: 0.17 sq. mi. (108.7 acres) **Population:** 728 (1978 est.)

Official Name: State of the Vatican City **Nationality:** The Papacy has a citizenship of its own, which is granted to those residing in the Vatican because of their work or rank **Languages:** Italian is the official language of the state; Latin is the official language of the Holy See, the administrative and legislative body for the Roman Catholic Church, and is used for most papal encyclicals and other formal pronouncements **Flag:** Yellow and white vertical bands, with the crossed keys of St. Peter under the triple papal tiara on the white band **Anthem:** Pontifical March (no words) **Currency:** Italian lira (847 per U.S. $1)

Location: Located in Rome, Vatican City is roughly a triangular area lying near the west bank of the Tiber River and to the west of Castel Sant' Angelo. On the west and south it is bounded by the Leonine Wall. The Vatican area comprises St. Peter's Square; St. Peter's Basilica, the largest Christian church in the world; a quadrangular area north of the square, containing the museums, library, and administrative buildings, and Belvedere Park; the Vatican Palace; and the Papal Gardens. Outside the Vatican City itself, extraterritoriality (but not sovereignty) is exercised over 12 churches and palaces in and near Rome, including St. John Lateran, St. Mary Major, and St. Paul Without the Walls Basilicas, and the papal villa at Castel Gandolfo

Government: Vatican City is the center of the worldwide organization of the Roman Catholic Church and the seat of the Pope, who is the absolute sovereign of the tiny state. The Supreme Pontiff is John Paul II (Karol Wojtyla), born 1920, elected Pope on October 16, 1978. He is assisted as temporal ruler by the Pontifical Commission, consisting of the cardinals, and the Administration of the Patrimony of the Apostolic See. Both of these organizations are presided over by a secretary of state (premier), at present held by Archbishop Agostino Casaroli, appointed 1979. Religious affairs are governed under the Pope's direction by a number of ecclesiastical bodies collectively known as the Roman Curia. The Pope rules from his election until death, at which time a successor is chosen by the College of Cardinals

Ethnic Composition: While the citizenry of the Vatican includes cardinals and other clergymen from all over the world, most of the inhabitants are Italian. The 75 members of the Swiss Guard are a notable exception

Economic Statistics: Vatican City does not engage in the economically productive activity common to other states. It is almost entirely dependent for income on the receipt of charitable contributions, the sale of Vatican stamps and tourist mementos, fees for admission to Vatican museums, and the sale of Vatican publications

Illiteracy: None **Enrollment in Higher Education:** 7,758 (1975)

Transportation: Vatican City is easily reached by the public transportation system of Rome. It has its own railroad station **Communi-**

cations: State controlled Radio Vatican, with 17 transmitters. There is no television **Newspapers:** 1 daily, the semiofficial *l'Osservatore Romano*

Weights and Measures: Metric system

For a long time after the unification of Italy in 1870, which stripped the popes of most of their temporal possessions, the status of the Vatican, the chief papal residence, was uncertain. Then, by the 1929 Lateran Treaty with Italy, the independent enclave of Vatican City came into being. In the treaty, the pontificate formally renounced all claims to the former Papal States.

Vatican City stands on the spot where Caligula constructed a circus and Nero had gardens. The ruler of Vatican City, the Pope, bears the title of Bishop of Rome, Vicar of Jesus Christ, Successor of the Prince of Apostles, Supreme Pontiff of the Universal Church, Patriarch of the West, Archbishop and Metropolitan of the Roman Province, and Sovereign of the State of the Vatican City. Currently he is Pope John Paul II. His .17-square-mile realm includes St. Peter's basilica, the largest church in Christendom; St. Peter's square, a roughly circular plaza set off by Giovanni Lorenzo Bernini's colonnade; and the pontifical palaces, or the Vatican proper, with magnificent chapels, museums, archives, a library, and a new hall for mass papal audiences.

Among the chapels are the Sistine, the ceiling and one wall of which are decorated with paintings by Michelangelo. The museums, galleries, and various interiors contain works by such masters as Raphael, Leonardo da Vinci, Fra Angelico, Titian, and Correggio, priceless sculpture that includes the Apollo Belvedere and Laocoön, and Egyptian, Etruscan, and other collections. The library, with its enormous wealth of books and manuscripts, is one of the world's great research institutions, and the archives house original material on such matters as the trial of Galileo and the request for annulment of the marriage of Henry VIII to Catherine of Aragon. Among other things, Vatican City also has gardens, courts, and quiet streets; its own daily newspaper and postal, telegraph, and broadcasting facilities; its own "armed forces," the colorfully garbed Swiss Guards; and its own railroad station, used almost exclusively as a freight terminal. Outside its confines but nonetheless enjoying extraterritoriality are a number of churches, palaces, and other structures in Rome and the papal villa at nearby Castel Gandolfo.

Vatican City is administered by a commission of cardinals, and a papal decree of 1968 established a body of 21 lay experts to advise them. A simultaneous decree reorganized the papal court, renaming it the papal household, abolishing hereditary offices, and putting an end to various picturesque anachronisms.

HISTORY: The State of the Vatican City and other places over which the Vatican retains control are the remnants of the old Papal States. For almost 1,000 years the papacy held vast temporal possessions, including large areas of Italy, and, until the French Revolution, parts of southern France. During the unification of the Italian peninsula in the 19th century, virtually all these possessions were absorbed by the House of Savoy, leaving only Rome and surrounding territory, protected by a French garrison, still under papal control

1870: French garrison withdraws and Rome is annexed by the Kingdom of Italy; Pope Pius IX refuses to recognize the loss of temporal power and initiates what becomes more than a half-century of self-imposed "imprisonment" of Popes

1929: Lateran Treaty is signed, by which Italy recognizes the sovereignty and independence of the new Vatican City state

1947: Italian Republic reaffirms Italy's adherence to Lateran Treaty

1962: Pope John XXIII convenes Second Vatican Council to promote Christian unity

1963: Archbishop Giovanni Montini of Milan is elected pope on death of John XXIII and reigns as Paul VI

1965: Pope Paul VI makes a historic journey to speak before the UN in New York "for the cause of peace in the world"

1978: Pope Paul VI dies on August 6 at age 80; during reign he sought to mediate between progressive and conservative forces within the Church. Conclave of cardinals convenes to elect Albino Cardinal Luciani, Patriarch of Venice, as the new Pope. The new pontiff, John Paul I, dies on September 28. Karol Cardinal Wojtyla, Archbishop of Krakow, Poland, succeeds as Pope John Paul II on October 16

1979: Pope John Paul II visits Mexico, Poland, Ireland, and U.S.

1980: The Pope visits Africa, France and Brazil

VENEZUELA

Area: 352,143 sq. mi. **Population:** 13,515,000 (1979 est.)

Official Name: Republic of Venezuela **Capital:** Caracas **Nationality:** Venezuelan **Languages:** Spanish is the official and universal language **Religion:** 96% Roman Catholic **Flag:** Horizontal stripes of yellow, blue, and red with an arc of 7 white stars in the center and the national coat of arms in the upper left **Anthem:** National Anthem, beginning "Glory to the brave people" **Currency:** Bollvar (4.3 per U.S. $1)

Location: North coast of South America. Venezuela is bounded on the north by the Caribbean Sea, on the east by Guyana, on the south by Brazil, and on the west by Colombia **Features:** The main regions are the Andes Mountains and outliers in the northwest; the northern coastal zone, the plains, or llanos, stretching from the mountains south and east to the Orinoco River; and the Guayana Highlands south and east of the Orinoco, consisting of high plateaus and rolling plains **Chief Rivers:** Orinoco, Caroni, Caura, Apure

Head of State and of Government: President Luis Herrera Campins, born 1925, inaugurated March 1979 for 5 years **Effective Date of Present Constitution:** January 1961 **Legislative Body:** Congress (bicameral), consisting of the Senate, with 47 members and the 199-man Chamber of Deputies, both elected by adult suffrage for 5-year terms **Local Government:** 20 states, 2 federal territories, a federal district, and the 72 islands of the federal dependencies. The governors of each are appointed by the president, and each, except the dependencies, has its own elected legislature

Ethnic Composition: About 70% of the population is mestizo (of mixed Indian and European ancestry), 17% of European (mainly Spanish) origin, 7% black, 1% Indian, and the rest mulattos of mixed Indian and black ancestry **Population Distribution:** 75% urban **Density:** 38 inhabitants per sq. mi.

Largest Cities: (1976 est.) Caracas 2,576,000, Maracaibo 792,000, Valencia 439,000, Barquisimeto 430,000, Maracay 301,000, Barcelona 242,000

Per Capita Income: $3,108 (1979) **Gross National Product (GNP):** $45.2 billion (1979) **Economic Statistics:** 27% is derived from services; 16% from industry (including oil refining, textiles, building materials, clothing, shoes, food, steel, and chemicals), 16% from commerce and finance; and 7% from agriculture **Minerals and Mining:** There are large deposits of oil, natural gas, bauxite, iron ore, salt, and smaller amounts of coal, gold, and diamonds **Labor Force:** 4.1 million (1977); 35% were in services, 15% in industry, and 10% in agriculture **Foreign Trade:** Exports, chiefly petroleum (95%) and products, and iron ore, totaled about $9.2 billion in 1978. Imports, mainly vehicles, iron and steel, wheat, mining and construction equipment, machinery and chemicals, totaled $11 billion **Principal Trade Partners:** United States, Canada, West Germany, Japan, Britain, Netherlands Antilles, Italy

Vital Statistics: Birthrate, 33.5 per 1,000 of pop.; death rate, 6.0 **Life Expectancy:** 67 years **Health Statistics:** 342 inhabitants per hospital bed; 870 per physician (1976) **Infant Mortality:** 40.4 per 1,000 births (1977) **Illiteracy:** 13% **Primary and Secondary School Enrollment:** 2,835,284 (1976) **Enrollment in Higher Education:** 247,518 **GNP Expended on Education:** 7% (1976)

Transportation: Paved roads total 12,400 mi. **Motor Vehicles:** 1,324,515 (1975) **Passenger Cars:** 955,151 **Railway Mileage:** 446 **Ports:** La Guaira, Maracaibo, Puerto Cabello, Puerto La Cruz **Major Airlines:** VIASA, a government-owned airline, flies internationally; Avensa, privately owned, and LAVA, government owned, fly domestically **Communications:** Government and privately controlled **Radio Transmitters:** 265 **Receivers:** 5,034,000 (1976) **Television Transmitters:** 43 **Receivers:** 1,431,000 (1976) **Telephones:** 847,000 **Newspapers:** 49 dailies, 93 copies per 1,000 inhabitants (1975)

Weights and Measures: Metric system **Travel Requirements:** Passport, tourist card valid 45 days, visa valid 1 year

---

Venezuela's prosperity has been based for years on petroleum, and this richest, most dynamic and most "American" country in Latin America is one of the world's largest petroleum exporters. In 1975-76 Venezuela nationalized the huge holdings of foreign petroleum and iron-ore mining companies, but did so peacefully, and the firms have been compensated. A government holding company, PETROVEN, controls and regulates the industry. Production was cut back from 2.35 to 2.2 million barrels per day in 1980, but revenues rose due to higher OPEC prices. Venezuela's proven oil reserves amount to about 18 billion barrels. No new fields have been discovered since 1958.

After the quadrupling of the price of oil in 1974, the government of President Carlos Andrés Pérez, with the largest and most sophisticated oil industry in Latin America, began pumping billions into development to promote the lagging agriculture industry, steel and petrochemicals production and construction. Rapid industrialization created an urban people, alleviating the problem of land hunger, but decreasing agricultural production. Government subsidies did little to stimulate agriculture and there were charges of government corruption and mismanagement, particularly following the severe food shortages in early 1977.

Venezuela's political stability—its last dictatorship was overthrown in 1958—was further demonstrated in 1978 when a new president was elected in what was basically a two-party race. Luis Herrera Campins, the candidate of the Social Christians, the "out" party, defeated Luis Piñerúa Ordaz, of the Democratic Action party. In a six-party contest, the two top parties polled 85% of the vote. In his inaugural speech in 1979, Herrera declared he had inherited "a mortgaged country." He promised to halt runaway public spending, and corruption, and give private business more flexibility in its operations.

Basic industries, such as steel and power, are owned and subsidized by the state. Venezuela's best hope for an industrial base to take the place of oil's proved reserves, which will last only through the year 2000, lies in Guayana, a region containing natural reserves of iron ore, sufficient for 75 years of production at current levels, and the hydroelectric potential of the Caroní River. Enough bauxite has been found to make the aluminum industry self-sufficient. The nation's oil riches are being used in a $12-billion industrialization program, in which the U.S. accounts for slightly more than half the foreign participation. However, a Spanish-Canadian group received the contracts for a national railroad grid, and the French for the $250-million Caracas subway.

HISTORY: Prior to the Spanish conquest in the 16th century, Venezuela was inhabited by 2 dominant Indian tribes—the Arawaks, who lived in agricultural communities, and the warlike Caribs. Charles I of Spain granted the Welsers, a German banking firm, the right to explore and colonize Venezuela but rescinded the right in 1546, after which the colony reverted to the Spanish crown

1811: Venezuela, under the leadership of Francisco de Miranda, declares its independence from Spain, but royalist forces maintain control

1812-21: Simón Bolívar leads a bloody war of independence against Spain, sets up Greater Colombia, encompassing the present territories of Venezuela, Colombia, Panama, and Ecuador, and is named president

1830-1900: Venezuela breaks away from Greater Colombia and becomes an independent republic; during the remainder of the century the nation is wracked by internal strife as dictator succeeds dictator. In 1895, Venezuela loses territory to British Guiana after a heated boundary dispute with Britain

1908-35: Gen. Juan Vicente Gómez becomes dictator; a tyrannical ruler, he succeeds in lifting the country to solvency by allotting oil concessions to foreign companies

1937-38: Gen. Eleázar López Contreras, Gómez' successor as president, exiles opposition political and labor leaders, declaring a moratorium on political and labor activities; he inaugurates a broad program of social and economic development

1945: A revolution breaks out and a liberal government headed by President Rómulo Betancourt takes power; he declares universal suffrage, and institutes social reforms

1947-48: A new constitution is adopted, providing for election of the president by direct popular vote. Rómulo Gallegos, of the Democratic Action party, is elected president but is ousted in 1948 by a military junta led by Colonels Marcos Pérez Jiménez and Carlos Delgado Chalbaud

1953-59: Pérez Jiménez takes power; he is overthrown in 1958 during a revolt supported by liberal elements of the armed forces. After brief interim government by a civilian-military junta, Betancourt is elected president

1962: Venezuela adopts new constitution limiting president to five-year term. Communists launch terrorist campaign to oust Betancourt because of his support for U.S. blockade of Cuba

1963-67: Raúl Leoni, leader of the liberal Democratic Action party, is elected president on a platform pledging economic and social reform; he suspends constitutional guarantees in drive against Castro-supported terrorists

1968: Rafael Caldera, the Social Christian candidate, is elected president; Democratic Action party retains control of Congress

1970: Venezuela and Guyana declare 12-year moratorium on border dispute

1973: Caldera government quadruples petroleum reference prices. Venezuela joins the Andean Pact, formed by Bolivia, Chile, Colombia, Ecuador and Peru. Carlos Andrés Pérez of Democratic Action party is elected president

1976: Oil industry is nationalized

1977: President Pérez announces a series of austerity measures aimed at controlling inflation and cutting government spending. Pérez visits President Carter; commonality of aims voiced

1978: Presidents Pérez and Carter sign agreements on maritime boundaries between Venezuela and U.S. and curbing flow of illicit drugs. Luis Herrera Campins of Social Christian party wins presidential election on Dec. 6

1979: Herrera is inaugurated on March 12. A U.S. businessman, William F. Niehous, is freed by police after being held prisoner 41 months by guerrillas. Foreign debt rises from $7.4 to $12.2 billion

1980: Former President Pérez is censured by Congress as "politically responsible" in a scandal involving the 1977 government purchase of a Norwegian refrigerated freighter, the *Sierra Nevada*. Venezuelan government obtains $1.8 billion Euromarket loan with a fluctuating interest rate

---

VIETNAM

Area: 128,405 sq. mi. **Population:** 47,870,000 (1978 est.)

Official Name: Socialist Republic of Vietnam **Capital:** Hanoi **Nationality:** Vietnamese **Languages:** Vietnamese, spoken by the majority of the people, is the official language; minorities speak Chinese, French, Khmer, Cham, and Montagnard (mountain tribal) languages **Religion:** The majority of the people nominally practice Buddhism and animism, although many combine these with elements of Taoism, Confucianism, and Christianity. However, organized religious activities have been discouraged in the North **Flag:** A yellow five-pointed star centered on a red field **Anthem:** Tien Quan Ca (Hymn of the Marching Army) **Currency:** Dong (2.15 per U.S. $1)

Location: Southeast Asia, occupying the eastern part of the Indochinese peninsula. It is bordered by China on the north, by the South China Sea on the east and south, and by Laos and Cambodia on the west **Features:** The jungle-covered hills in the north and northwest rise southeastward into the Annamese Cordillera and its outlying plateaus. East of the mountains are fertile coastal lowlands, with the deltas of the Mekong and Red rivers being the largest and most densely populated **Chief Rivers:** Red, Black, Lo, Ca, Mekong, Ba, Dong Nai

Political Leader: Le Duan, Secretary General of the Communist Party, born 1908, appointed 1960 **Head of State:** Vacant as of Aug. 1980 **Head of Government:** Premier Pham Van Dong, born 1906, elected 1976 **Effective Date of Present Constitution:** 1960 (North), currently being revised **Legislative Body:** National Assembly (unicameral), with 492 members. Its Presidium, or Standing Committee, under chairman Truong Chinh, born 1917, represents the ruling Communist party in the Assembly. The chief executive and legislative organ of government is the party's 17-man Politburo, the core of the 133-member Central Committee headed by Le Duan **Local Government:** 38 provinces, including 3 city provinces

Ethnic Composition: Vietnamese constitute about 85% of the population; Montagnards of both Malayo-Polynesian and Mon-Khmer ethnic groups make up about 8%, and the rest include Chinese, Khmer, and Cham minorities **Population Distribution:** North—14% urban; South—30% urban **Density:** 373 inhabitants per sq. mi.

Largest Cities: (1977 est.) Ho Chi Minh City (Saigon) 1,000,000; (1972 est.) Hanoi 643,000, Da Nang 438,000, Hue 200,000, Nha

Trang 195,000, Qui Nhon 189,000, Can Tho 154,000; (1970 est.) Haiphong 276,000, Nam Dinh 105,360

Per Capita Income: $143 (1979) **Gross National Product (GNP):** $7.5 billion (1979) **Economic Statistics:** Basically agricultural (rice, sugarcane, tea, maize, manioc, coffee, fish, rubber), rice, the staple food, still has to be imported. Light industry is confined to food processing, textiles, glass, paper, machinery, cement and, in the North, steel **Minerals and Mining:** Coal, iron ore, apatite, phosphates, chromite, tin, salt, granite, and limestone **Labor Force:** About 15 million with 70% in agriculture and 8% in industry **Foreign Trade:** Exports ($300 million, 1978) consist mainly of coal, rubber, ores, wood, tea, spices, and coffee. Imports ($900 million, 1978) include rice, heavy machinery, transportation equipment, vehicles, chemicals, and fuels **Principal Trade Partners:** USSR, Eastern Europe, Japan

Vital Statistics: Birthrate, 41.5 per 1,000 of pop. (1975); death rate, 20.5 **Life Expectancy:** 44 years **Health Statistics:** About 750 per hospital bed; 11,000 per physician **Infant Mortality:** North—N.A.; South—36.7 per 1,000 births **Illiteracy:** About 25% **Primary and Secondary School Enrollment:** 10,923,436 (1976) **Enrollment in Higher Education:** 100,027 **GNP Expended on Education:** N.A.

Transportation: Paved roads total 3,400 mi. **Motor Vehicles:** N.A. **Railway Mileage:** 1,718 **Ports:** Saigon, Haiphong, Da Nang, Qui Nhon, Cam Ranh, Ben Thuy, Hong Gai, Nha Trang **Major Airlines:** Air Vietnam **Communications:** Government controlled **Radio Transmitters:** North—3; South—27 **Receivers:** North—1,000,000 (1974); South—1,550,000 (1973) **Television Transmitters:** North—1; South—6 **Receivers:** North—N.A.; South—500,000 **Telephones:** North—N.A.; South—46,509 **Newspapers:** North—6 dailies

Weights and Measures: Metric system **Travel Requirements:** Traveler should consult U.S. Department of State

---

A unified Vietnam, from the China border to the Gulf of Siam, came into being on July 2, 1976. The formal reunification after 22 years of division came 16 months after the collapse and surrender of the South Vietnamese government in Saigon to its North Vietnamese conquerors. After 30 years of struggle against foreign powers and the regimes they fostered, revolutionary forces of Vietnam realized the goal of the late Ho Chi Minh. The Communists, with more than a little help from their friends, had all of Vietnam under one flag and one government. In the years since the fall of the Saigon Government the problems of peace have proved as hard to solve as those of war.

The split into North Vietnam and South Vietnam that marked the end of French presence and the beginnings of American involvement occurred in 1954. As a colonial war ended, a period of insurgency and war began. It was to last over two decades and leave a legacy of bomb craters, street rubble, bullet-pocked buildings, abandoned rice fields and patches of defoliated forest—in addition to the thousands of lost, maimed and dislocated Vietnamese people.

The long war that could not be won came to a close for U.S. troops in 1973. A peace accord that could not be enforced lasted only 20 months after the American withdrawal. The end to the tragic war came with unbelievable swiftness in April of 1975 as the Communist forces swept the coastal cities and took Saigon almost unopposed. The cost to the United States for its misadventure in Indochina was 57,000 lives and $150 billion.

For Vietnam, the process of rebuilding a shattered economy and restructuring society in the South left little time for looks backward. In the South a provisional government took over from the military and began the task of dealing with three million unemployed urban residents and reshaping the economy to fit a different ideology.

To achieve self-sufficiency in food the new unified government resettled millions of refugees from the cities into rural areas so they could resume food production. It is said that nearly 700,000 were moved from Saigon to work abandoned rice fields or develop new agricultural areas, and the population of Da Nang was reduced by half. For many, life in the "new economic zones" is tough, with former clerks, unaccustomed to manual labor, trying to coax crops from marginal lands.

The transfer of people also involves Northerners. Tens of thousands of civil servants, teachers and tax collectors have been moved to the South to provide a dependable cadre at lower echelons. Plans call for the eventual movement of millions from densely populated rural places in the North to the more agriculturally productive South.

To restore trade and industry the unified government has shown surprising flexibility and respect for private business. Factories that had not been abandoned by their owners were allowed to continue operating. However, inflation in Saigon (now called Ho Chi Minh City) has pushed up food prices while salaries have been cut.

Vietnam found itself involved in two wars in 1979, piling up further troubles for its wrecked economy and internal tumult—the latter attested to by an outflow of hundreds of thousands of refugees. The fighting in Cambodia seemingly ended on Jan. 7, when Vietnamese troops captured the enemy capital, Phnom Penh, but it turned into a guerrilla war, with Pol Pot's rebels controlling the countryside and the Vietnamese troops dominant around Phnom Penh. Then on Feb. 17, the Chinese, saying they wanted to "teach a lesson" to Vietnamese who allegedly crossed their border in hundreds of incidents, invaded northern Vietnam. The Chinese fought for four weeks, advanced no more than 20 miles, and then departed, calling their punitive invasion a victory. Vietnam's defenders obviously put up a strong fight, because months later China conceded that its own army suffered 20,000 killed and wounded. (China placed Vietnam's casulaties at 50,000.) The fighting did cause Vietnam to remove some veteran troops from Cambodia, China's ally, but Vietnam quickly sent great numbers of less-experienced troops to Cambodia.

The warfare and economic distress have made the Soviet Union a closer ally of the Vietnamese, who have a 2,000-year history of animosity toward the Chinese. Soviet warships have used the old U.S. naval base at Cam Ranh Bay. Vietnam and the Soviet Union signed a 25-year treaty of friendship and cooperation in November 1978. An ousted Politburo member, Hoang Van Hoan, an old comrade of Ho Chi Minh, fled to China in 1979, asserting that his country had become "subservient to a foreign power," meaning the USSR.

HISTORY: The Vietnamese are believed to have originated in North China, from where they were slowly driven southward by the Han Chinese. By the 3rd century B.C., the Vietnamese had become settled in the Red River Delta in northern Vietnam. China annexed the region in the 2nd century B.C. and ruled it until 938 A.D., when independence was reestablished by Ngo Quyen. The new state gradually expanded, occupying much of Cambodia and southern Vietnam

1858: French and Spanish forces intervene in Vietnam's southern region of Cochin China to halt persecution of native Catholics

1862-67: Vietnam is forced to yield Cochin China to the French

1884: France establishes a protectorate over Annam, in central Vietnam, and over Tonkin, in the north

1887: Cambodia, Cochin China, Annam, and Tonkin are incorporated into the Indo-Chinese Union

1940-45: Vietnam is occupied by Japanese forces during World War II; with defeat impending, Japan grants Vietnam independence under a puppet government headed by Bao Dai, emperor of Annam; following Japan's surrender to the Allies, Communist Viet Minh guerrillas, under leadership of Ho Chi Minh, set up Democratic Republic of Vietnam

1946-54: Viet Minh wages war against the French for eight years, culminating in the defeat of French forces at Dien Bien Phu; armistice is signed under a series of agreements concluded at Geneva, providing for the partition of Vietnam along the 17th parallel, with the north going to the government of Ho Chi Minh and the south placed under the control of Saigon. The agreements provided for the joining of North and South Vietnam into one country by holding elections in 1956. These were never held

NORTH VIETNAM

1955: Ho Chi Minh visits Communist China and USSR and signs aid agreements with both

1956: Peasant revolts break out in opposition to government's land collectivization program, but are crushed by troops

1959: North Vietnam, working through Viet Cong guerrillas, instigates campaign of terror and subversion in South Vietnam in attempt to annex state and unify Vietnam under Communist rule

1964-65: U.S. planes bomb North Vietnamese military targets following attacks on U.S. warships in Gulf of Tonkin in 1964; sustained U.S. air attacks are begun in 1965 to stem flow of equipment and North Vietnamese troops into the south

1968: United States orders halt to all bombing north of 20th parallel; move leads to an agreement between Hanoi and Washington to open peace talks in Paris

1969: Ho Chi Minh dies

1971: North Vietnamese troops drive South Vietnamese forces from Laos after the latter fail to cut Ho Chi Minh Trail

1973: Peace agreement signed in Paris officially ends Vietnam War, though fighting continues on a diminished scale

1974-75: Fighting escalates as both North and South repeatedly violate the cease-fire agreement. A stepped-up Communist offensive in early 1975 results in the abandonment by Saigon forces of the Central Highlands. The last resistance from the Saigon government ends on April 30 as Viet Cong and North Vietnamese troops enter Saigon

SOUTH VIETNAM

1955: Bao Dai is deposed and a republic established under the presidency of former Prime Minister Ngo Dinh Diem; a U.S. military advisory group is set up in South Vietnam

1959-63: South Vietnamese Communist guerrillas, known as Viet Cong, wage war against Diem government; harsh security measures introduced by Saigon regime incur wide resentment; Buddhist monks immolate themselves to protest what they charge is persecution by Diem. After violent demonstrations the government is overthrown and Diem is murdered

1965: New military regime is formed, with Gen. Nguyen Van Thieu as chief of state and Air Vice Marshal Nguyen Cao Ky as premier; U.S. planes begin systematic bombing of North Vietnam, while in the south U.S. troop strength mounts to 200,000 men by year's end

1967: In South Vietnam's first national elections, Nguyen Van Thieu becomes president and Nguyen Cao Ky vice-president

1968: President Johnson announces a halt of U.S. bombings over most of North Vietnam; peace talks between United States and North Vietnam open in Paris

1970: South Vietnamese and U.S. troops invade Cambodia in drive against Viet Cong and North Vietnamese forces; Saigon troops continue operations after U.S. withdrawal

1971: South Vietnamese forces attempting to cut Ho Chi Minh Trail in Laos are driven out by North Vietnamese. Enemy steps up attacks in South Vietnam on eve of elections. Thieu runs unopposed for president and is reelected

1973: Paris peace agreement formally ends Vietnam War in January, but fighting continues on reduced level. The first prisoner exchanges worked out at the conference table begin

1974: Fighting intensifies in the central highlands near the Cambodian border; the Saigon government suspends its participation with the Viet Cong in Paris reconciliation talks

1975: North Vietnamese and Viet Cong forces step up their offensive in the South, seizing major cities. President Ford orders U.S. naval ships to help evacuate refugees. President Thieu resigns but the Viet Cong refuse to negotiate with the new South Vietnamese leadership. Communist troops enter and occupy Saigon. War ends as the South Vietnamese government unconditionally surrenders to the Viet Cong on April 29, 1975. Provisional Revolutionary Government takes control on June 6

UNIFIED VIETNAM

1976: First countrywide assembly elections are held April 25. North and South are officially reunited July 2. Rail link between Hanoi and Saigon reopened

1977: Security Council approves Vietnam membership in the UN. Border fighting flares up between Vietnam and Cambodia. Vietnamese face serious food problem, with rice shortage estimated at 18% of need. Talks with U.S. on establishing relations recess after making little progress; behind impasse is Hanoi's insistence that promise of U.S. aid be made before ties are established, while U.S. rejects any preconditions

1978: Government introduces new national currency, cracks down on black-marketeers. Vietnamese-Cambodian border war intensifies. Refugees reportedly leaving Vietnam at highest rate since end of war in 1975. President Carter approves interim refugee policy permitting admission of Vietnamese "boat people" refused asylum elsewhere. In July, Vietnam is admitted to Soviet bloc's economic and trade group; in November, Vietnam and the Soviet Union sign a 25-year friendship treaty. China blames

Vietnam in first shooting incident along their mutual border, ends aid to Vietnam and closes Vietnamese consulates in southern China. Government inducts over 350,000 into armed forces "to defend country's territorial integrity against foreign aggressors" and to work at construction sites. The worst floods in 35 years destroy 500,000 homes and almost three million tons of rice. In December, Vietnamese troops advance steadily across Cambodia

1979: Vietnamese troops, together with Cambodian rebels, capture Phnom Penh on Jan. 7. But the deposed Cambodian premier, Pol Pot, escapes, and some 130,000 Vietnamese are tied down in Cambodia fighting guerrillas. On Feb. 7, China invades Vietnam with 100,000 troops that penetrate 15 or 20 miles in four weeks. The main fighting is at Lang Son, which is evacuated. The Chinese depart, with both sides claiming victory. By midyear, the number of ethnic Chinese fleeing Vietnam is estimated at 300,000 in a 12-month span

1980: More than 200,000 Vietnamese soldiers remain in Cambodia, and 50,000 are still stationed in Laos. At home, at least 20,000 former Vietnamese bureaucrats, military and professional men, and others are confined to "re-education" camps. For two days in June, Vietnamese troops cross the border into Thailand and attack two refugee camps—retaliation for the Thais' repatriation of Khmer soldiers to Cambodia

---

WESTERN SAMOA

Area: 1,133 sq. mi. **Population:** 154,000 (1978 est.)

Official Name: Independent State of Western Samoa **Capital:** Apia **Nationality:** Western Samoan **Languages:** Samoan, the predominant Polynesian language, and English are official **Religion:** The population is almost entirely Christian, with 50% Congregationalist, 20% Methodist, and 20% Roman Catholic **Flag:** A red field with a blue rectangle in the upper left corner bearing 5 white stars representing the Southern Cross **Anthem:** The Flag of Freedom Currency: Tala (0.74 per U.S. $1)

Location: South Pacific, forming part of an island group lying midway between Honolulu and Sydney, Australia. Western Samoa (14°S., 172°W.) consists of the islands of Savai'i and Upolu and seven smaller islands of which only Manono and Apolima are inhabited **Features:** The islands are formed mainly of volcanic rock, with coral reefs surrounding much of the coasts. Rugged mountain ranges form the core of the two main islands, and there are many dormant volcanoes and lava fields **Chief Rivers:** There are no large rivers

Head of State: Chief Malietoa Tanumafili II, born 1913, appointed in 1962; future holders of the office will be elected by the Legislative Assembly for 5-year terms **Head of Government:** Prime Minister Taisi Tupuola Efi, born 1948, reappointed 1979 **Effective Date of Present Constitution:** January 1962 **Legislative Body:** Legislative Assembly (unicameral), consisting of 47 members, 45 of whom are Samoans elected by family chiefs *(matai)*, and 2 are elected by universal suffrage, all for 3-year terms **Local Government:** 24 legislative districts *(faipule)*, grouped into 12 political districts. Local government is carried out by the village councils *(fono)*

Ethnic Composition: Samoans, who form the second-largest branch of the Polynesian race, constitute 88% of the population. Euronesians (of mixed Polynesian and European ancestry) make up 10%, and the rest consists of Europeans (700) and other Pacific Islanders **Population Distribution:** 21% urban **Density:** 136 inhabitants per sq. mi.

Largest City: (1974 est.) Apia 32,616

Per Capita Income: $450 (1978) **Gross National Product (GNP):** $70 million (1978) **Economic Statistics:** There are no detailed GNP statistics available; however, industries include handicrafts, foods, fruit processing, clothing, soap, and furniture; and agricultural products include taro, timber, fish, coconuts, cocoa, bananas, and pineapples **Minerals and Mining:** None **Labor Force:** There are 35,985 workers, with 90% in agriculture and fishing, and 10% in industry **Foreign Trade:** Exports, mainly copra, cocoa, bananas, timber, and taro, totaled $15 million in 1977. Imports, chiefly clothing and textiles, flour, canned fish and meat, motor vehicles, tobacco, sugar, and timber totaled $38 million **Principal Trade Partners:** New Zealand, Australia, Britain, West Germany, United States, Japan, Singapore

Vital Statistics: Birthrate, 21.4 per 1,000 of pop. (1977); death rate, 3.4 **Life Expectancy:** 67 years **Health Statistics:** 214 inhabitants per hospital bed; 2,884 per physician (1977) **Infant Mortality:** 17.8 per 1,000 births (1977) **Illiteracy:** 10% **Primary and Secondary School Enrollment:** 51,025 (1977) **Enrollment in Higher Education:** 180 **GNP Expended on Education:** 3% (1977)

Transportation: Paved roads total 230 mi. **Motor Vehicles:** 3,200 (1976) **Passenger Cars:** 1,300 **Railway Mileage:** None **Ports:** Apia, Asau **Major Airlines:** Polynesian Airlines, owned jointly by the government and private business, operates international and domestic flights **Communications:** Government controlled **Radio Transmitters:** 2 **Receivers:** 50,000 (1973) **Television Transmitters:** None; received from American Samoa **Receivers:** 1,800 **Telephones:** 3,800 **Newspapers:** 2 several times a week, 103 copies per 1,000 inhabitants

Weights and Measures: British standards are used **Travel Requirements:** Passport, no visa for stay up to 30 days

Western Samoa became, on January 1, 1962, the first fully independent Polynesian state. Until then, the country, along with Eastern Samoa, had been under foreign control or tutelage since the turn of the century. In 1899 the Samoan islands were apportioned between Germany, which got Western Samoa as a protectorate, and the United States, which obtained, and still holds, the eastern part as American Samoa. Western Samoa was held from 1914 to 1962 by New Zealand, which, after ousting the Germans in World War I, obtained a League of Nations mandate and then a UN trusteeship. Although independent, Western Samoa still has New Zealand handling its foreign relations.

Western Samoa is a nation in transition, struggling to preserve its traditional ways while grappling with a backward economy. The most striking of those ways, perhaps, is the social system, based on *aigas*, or extended family groups, which are headed by *matais*, or chiefs. The *matais* direct the use of *aiga* assets. Supported by most Western Samoans, the system is a conservative force that many observers feel hampers the country, but the government, now headed by younger men, points to the possibility of change.

Western Samoa's economy is predominantly agricultural but efforts are underway to develop its fishing industry and increase tourism.

HISTORY: Archaeological evidence indicates that Samoa may have been settled as far back as 1000 B.C., but little is known with certainty of its early history. The first Europeans to visit Samoa were the Dutch in 1722. Throughout the 19th century, the islands became pawns in a struggle for control by the United States, Germany, and Britain. After a brief attempt at tripartite control of Samoa, a treaty was signed in 1899 assigning Eastern Samoa to the United States and Western Samoa to Germany

1914-20: New Zealand occupies Western Samoa following outbreak of World War I and is later awarded mandate over islands by League of Nations

1927-36: Samoans and European settlers wage campaign of civil disobedience in opposition to the administration; campaign develops into movement for independence

1946: Western Samoa becomes United Nations trusteeship under continued supervision of New Zealand

1962: Western Samoa becomes independent, with Chief Tupua Tamasese Meaole and Chief Malietoa Tanumafili II as joint heads of state; New Zealand agrees to act as official channel with foreign governments and international organizations

1963: Tupua Tamasese Meaole dies, leaving Western Samoa with a single head of state

1970: Tamasese Lealofi IV is named prime minister as head of reform-minded government of younger men

1973: Fiame Mata'afa Mulinuu is elected prime minister

1975: Treaty is signed with EC. Mata'afa dies and is replaced by Tamasese Lealofi IV

1976: Taisi Tupuola Efi becomes prime minister. Western Samoa becomes a UN member

1979: Prime Minister Tupuola Efi barely retains post in 24-23 vote of the parliament following February 28 *matai* elections; criticized for seeking too rapid a rate of economic growth, Tupuola reshuffles cabinet, reflecting a shift toward a policy of consolidating past economic progress

YEMEN

Area: 77,220 sq. mi. **Population:** 7,080,000 (1978 est.)
Official Name: Yemen Arab Republic **Capital:** San'a **Nationality:**

Yemeni Languages: Arabic is the official and universal language **Religion:** Islam is the state religion, with the population almost equally divided between the Zaidi Shi'ite and Shafai Sunnite sects **Flag:** Horizontal stripes of red, white, and black with a green star in the center **Anthem:** National Anthem, beginning "Peace to the land" **Currency:** Yemeni rial (4.56 per U.S. $1)

Location: Southwest Arabia. Yemen is bounded on the north and east by Saudi Arabia, on the south by Southern Yemen, and on the west by the Red Sea **Features:** The country consists of a semidesert coastal plain (the Tihama) along the Red Sea and a mountainous area in the interior which receives abundant rainfall **Chief Rivers:** There are no permanent rivers

Head of State: President: Col. Ali Abdullah Saleh, born 1942, elected July 1978 **Head of Government:** Premier Abd al-Aziz Abd al-Ghani, appointed in January 1975 **Effective Date of Present Constitution:** 1971, suspended 1974 **Legislative Body:** Constituent People's Assembly of 159 members **Local Government:** 10 governorates under appointed emirs, divided into 40 districts

Ethnic Composition: The population is predominantly Arab. 10% are Afro-Arabs, residing in the Tihama **Population Distribution:** 11% urban **Density:** 92 inhabitants per sq. mi.

Largest Cities: (1975 census) San'a 134,588, Hodeida 80,314, Ta'izz 78,642, Dhamar 19,467, Ibb 19,066, Al Beida 5,975

Per Capita Income: $543 (1979) **Gross National Product (GNP):** $2.8 billion (1979) **Economic Statistics:** About 50% of GNP comes from agriculture (cotton, Mocha coffee, livestock, cereals, vegetables, fruit). There is some light industry (textiles, food products) **Minerals and Mining:** The only industrial mining enterprise is the extraction of salt. There are traces of copper, coal, sulfur, gypsum and quartz **Labor Force:** 800,000; 70% of the population is engaged in agriculture and animal husbandry, and 13% in trade. Many work abroad **Foreign Trade:** Exports, mainly cotton, coffee, hides and skins, salt, and qat, totaled $7.1 million in 1978. Imports, chiefly textiles, machinery, fuels, foods, totaled $834 million **Principal Trade Partners:** Southern Yemen, Saudi Arabia, Australia, EC countries, India, Japan

Vital Statistics: Birthrate, 49.6 per 1,000 of pop. (1975); death rate 20.6 **Life Expectancy:** 38 years **Health Statistics:** 1,443 inhabitants per hospital bed (1974); 17,175 per physician (1976) **Infant Mortality:** N.A. **Illiteracy:** 85% **Primary and Secondary School Enrollment:** 279,541 (1975) **Enrollment in Higher Education:** 2,408 **GNP Expended on Education:** 0.6% (1974)

Transportation: Paved roads total 300 mi. **Motor Vehicles:** 44,500 (1975) **Passenger Cars:** 14,000 **Railway Mileage:** None **Ports:** Hodeida, Mocha **Major Airlines:** Yemen Airways, government owned, operates domestic and international flights **Communications:** Government controlled **Radio Transmitters:** 4 **Receivers:** 90,000 (1976) **Television Transmitters:** 1 **Receivers:** N.A. **Telephones:** 5,000 (1975) **Newspapers:** 6 dailies, 10 copies per 1,000 inhabitants (1970)

Weights and Measures: Local units are used **Travel Requirements:** Passport, visa valid 3 months, $2 fee

Yemen is a land whose interior contains gauntly beautiful mountains and green, cultivated fields—a rarity in the Arabian peninsula—and whose crucially important location between the Gulf of Aden and the Red Sea, athwart the Arabian oil route to the West, has brought it a disproportionate degree of world attention.

Yemen remains a country that is difficult to govern, where tribal loyalties are stronger than national considerations. Those tendencies have been aggravated by a civil war (1962-1969), and by memories of ancient times when Yemen and Southern Yemen had common ties. The civil war began in 1962 as a revolt against Mohammed al-Badr, heir to a dynasty of Imams (religious rulers) who had become arbitrary and capricious. The rebels established a republic with Egyptian backing; the Imam continued resistance from the hills, with an army of tribesmen and mercenaries supported by Saudi Arabia. Egypt sent almost a third of its army to help the republic. Egypt and Saudi Arabia agreed to end their intervention in 1967, and the Imam's forces were defeated by those of the republic in 1969. But the republic was, and remained, unstable, plagued by a series of coups and countercoups.

In a 48-hour period in June 1978, the Presidents

of both Yemen and Southern Yemen were killed. The violence began in Sa'na just as Yemen's President Ahmed Hussein al-Ghashmi, a close ally of Saudi Arabia, was about to consider Southern Yemen's proposals for a merger of the Yemens. Yemen, blaming Soviet-backed Southern Yemen for the killing, severed their relations. Two days later, Southern Yemen President Salem Rubaye Ali, a moderate Marxist, lost a power struggle with the ultraleftist general secretary of the country's National Liberation Front party, Abdul Fattah Ismail, whom Western and Arab observers suspect may have been behind Ghashmi's murder. Ghashmi was succeed by Ali Abdullah Saleh, and tensions with Southern Yemen continued to build. Southern Yemeni soldiers—with Soviet, Cuban, and East German help—invaded Yemen in February 1979. Saudi Arabia and the United States rushed arms to Yemen, and U.S. ships showed the flag in nearby waters. In March, the League of Arab States arranged a cease-fire; and a special force, under the League's command, was established to patrol the border. President Saleh and President Ismail met in Kuwait and drew up a plan to merge their two countries, but Ismail's resignation as president of South Yemen in early 1980 left the plan in abeyance.

HISTORY: Yemen formed part of what was known as Arabia Felix in classical times and was the site of a series of rich mercantile kingdoms. One of these was Sheba, or Saba, which flourished from about 750 to 115 B.C. The Sabaeans were superseded by the Himyarites, under whom Judaism and Christianity took root. Himyarite rule was ended in 525 by an invading force of Christian Ethiopians, who in turn were driven out by the Persians in 575

7th cent.: Islam is introduced

9th cent.: Yemen comes under the control of the Rassite dynasty, religious leaders, called imams, of the Zaydi sect, who lay the foundations of a theocratic political structure lasting to 1962

1517-1918: Ottoman Empire exercises nominal sovereignty

1948: Imam Yahya is assassinated; his son, Crown Prince Ahmad, defeats forces of new government and succeeds as imam

1958: Yemen and United Arab Republic (union of Egypt and Syria) form confederation called United Arab States

1961: Following Syria's withdrawal from UAR, President Nasser dissolves the association with Yemen, denouncing Imam Ahmad as a reactionary

1962: Ahmad dies and is succeeded by Crown Prince Mohammad al-Badr, who favors a neutralist foreign policy; he is overthrown by pro-Nasser army officers who proclaim a republic under the leadership of Col. Abdullah al-Salal; civil war breaks out between republican and royalist forces, who win the respective backing of Egypt and Saudi Arabia

1963: Egypt sends 40,000 troops to Yemen to assist republicans

1967: Egypt withdraws troops from Yemen; riots in San'a force al-Salal to form new government free of Egyptian influence; he is deposed, however, while on a visit to Moscow and a new republican government is set up; royalist forces move on San'a

1968: Republicans, aided by Soviet-built aircraft, regain initiative; royalists retreat, reorganize their forces and in an effort to widen their political base fill top posts with officials not related to the Imam, who is deprived of all political power

1969: Republican government asserts that civil war has ended; Lt. Gen. Hassan al-Amri resigns as prime minister; a new cabinet is formed and Abdullah al-Karshumi becomes prime minister

1970: Amicable settlement is reached between republicans and royalists; Moshen al-Aini is named premier

1972: Yemen and Southern Yemen end hostilities after series of border clashes; they agree to future merger. Aini is replaced by Abdullah al-Hagri

1973: Border clashes resume between the two Yemens

1974: Hagri is replaced by Hassan Makki. Army ousts government in bloodless coup and establishes military junta headed by Col. Ibrahim al-Hamdi. Aini forms new government

1975: Premier Aini is replaced by Abd al-Aziz Ad al-Ghani

1977: Col. Ibrahim al-Hamdi is assassinated; new military rulers impose martial law, as Maj. Ahmed Hussein al-Ghashmi assumes leadership of government

1978: Constituent assembly formally elects Ghashmi president. Ghashmi is assassinated; Yemen blames Southern Yemen, severs relations. Ghashmi's murder is factor in overthrow two days later of Southern Yemen's President Rubaye Ali by colleagues in pro-Soviet National Front. Constituent People's Assembly elects Col. Ali Abdullah Saleh president

1979: Southern Yemen invades Yemen, which gets aid from United States and Saudi Arabia. Cease-fire agreement places Yemen-Southern Yemen border under patrol commanded by League of Arab States. Presidents Saleh and Ismail agree to merger plan

---

SOUTHERN YEMEN

Area: 111,101 sq. mi. **Population:** 1,853,000 (1978 est.)

Official Name: People's Democratic Republic of Yemen **Capital:** Aden **Nationality:** Southern Yemenite or Yemeni **Languages:** Arabic is the official language; Mahri is spoken in the east, and English is also widely understood **Religion:** 98% of the population are Sunni Moslems of the Shafai sect **Flag:** Horizontal stripes of red, white, and black with a red star on a blue triangle at the hoist **Anthem:** National Anthem (no words) **Currency:** Yemeni dinar (0.35 per U.S. $1)

Location: Southern part of the Arabian peninsula. Southern Yemen is bounded on the north by Saudi Arabia, on the east by Oman, on the south by the Gulf of Aden, and on the northwest by Yemen **Features:** A narrow, sandy plain along the coast gives way to mountainous terrain, interspersed with deep valleys. The land retains its mountainous character until it reaches the interior sands. Offshore islands include Socotra, Perim, and Kamaran **Chief Rivers:** There are no permanent rivers

Head of State and of Government: Chairman of the Presidium of the Supreme People's Council (President) and Prime Minister: Ali Nasir Mohammed, born 1938, appointed prime minister 1971, became head of state April 1980 **Effective Date of Present Constitution:** December 1, 1970 **Legislative Body:** Supreme People's Council (unicameral) of 111 elected members **Local Government:** 6 governorates under appointed governors, divided into 24 districts

Ethnic Composition: The population is mainly Arab; Indians, Pakistanis, and Somalis constitute small minorities **Population Distribution:** 33% urban **Density:** 17 inhabitants per sq. mi.

Largest Cities: (1977 est.) Aden 285,373; (1972 est.) Mukalla 45,000, Seiyun 20,000

Per Capita Income: $402 (1979) **Gross National Product (GNP):** $716 million (1979) **Economic Statistics:** The subsistence economy is based on agriculture (sorghum, millet, wheat) and fishing, though some cotton is grown for export. Aden, a leading oil bunkering port, is slowly recovering with the reopening of the Suez Canal. There is an oil refinery, and some light industry **Minerals and Mining:** Salt **Labor Force:** 395,568 (1977), with 62% in subsistence agriculture, and 18% in industry, with 72% of the latter in oil refining **Foreign Trade:** Exports, mainly petroleum products, raw cotton, hides and skins, and fuel oil, totaled $187 million in 1975. Imports, chiefly rice, wheat flour, tea, cotton and rayon piece goods, and petroleum products, totaled $312 million **Principal Trade Partners:** Kuwait, Britain, Japan, Yemen, India, Iraq

Vital Statistics: Birthrate, 49.6 per 1,000 of pop. (1975); death rate, 20.6 **Life Expectancy:** 45 years **Health Statistics:** 648 inhabitants per hospital bed; 8,750 per physician (1976) **Infant Mortality:** 79.9 per 1,000 births **Illiteracy:** 73% **Primary and Secondary School Enrollment:** 236,162 (1974) **Enrollment in Higher Education:** 934 **GNP Expended on Education:** 3.9% (1976)

Transportation: Paved roads total 200 mi. **Motor Vehicles:** 22,400 (1976) **Passenger Cars:** 11,900 **Railway Mileage:** None **Port:** Aden **Major Airlines:** Democratic Yemen Airlines, government owned **Communications:** Government controlled **Radio Transmitters:** 4 **Receivers:** 100,000 (1976) **Television Transmitters:** 5 **Receivers:** 32,000 (1976) **Telephones:** 10,000 (1973) **Newspapers:** 3 dailies, 1 copy per 1,000 inhabitants (1973)

Weights and Measures: British standards are generally used in Aden; local measures are used in the rest of the country **Travel Requirements:** Traveler should consult U.S. Department of State for travel information

---

One of the poorest member of the Arab League, Southern Yemen comprises the former colony of Aden, at the southwestern corner of the Arabian peninsula, and a forbidding hinterland with poorly defined borders. Under British rule, the country was known as "Aden," and later as the "Federation of South Arabia." It declared independence in 1967 as "People's Republic of Southern Yemen." In 1970, the official name was changed to the "People's Democratic Republic of Yemen." Hopes for union with the neighboring "Yemen Arab Republic" exist in both states, but each wants union on its own terms.

With its oppressively hot climate and barren terrain, Southern Yemen has few natural resources and little industry, and must rely heavily on foreign aid for its 1974-79 five-year development plan. About 62 percent of the population is engaged in primitive agriculture.

The departure of the British in 1967 and the closing of their naval base at Aden has further scarred the country's economy. Aden, once a flourishing port, now gripped by poverty, has not experienced the revitalization which was expected after the reopening of the Suez Canal in 1975.

In a two-day period in June 1978, as Yemen and Southern Yemen were about to work out details of a proposed merger, both Yemeni presidents were killed—the first in an unsolved assassination plot and the latter before a firing squad following a military coup led by Abdul Fattah Ismail, staunchly pro-Soviet general secretary of the country's National Liberation Front party. Assisted by the Soviet Union, East Germany, and Cuba, Southern Yemen invaded the Yemen Arab Republic in February 1979. Saudi Arabia and the United States supplied arms to the YAR. In March, both countries agreed to a resolution of the League of Arab States, under which their armies withdrew from the border, and soldiers under the League's command were stationed between them. The two Yemens agreed on a plan to merge their countries. But Ismail resigned as president in April 1980 and was replaced by the premier, Ali Nasir Mohammed, who reportedly opposed unification.

HISTORY: Southern Yemen formed part of the Minaean, Sabaean, and Himyarite kingdoms that flourished between 1200 B.C. and the 6th century A.D. The Himyarites were conquered in 525 by Christian Ethiopians, who were driven out by the Persians in 575. Islam was introduced in the 7th century and by the 9th century the highland regions of Southern Yemen had fallen under the rule of the Islamic religious leaders, or imams, of Yemen. The coastal area recognized the primacy of the Baghdad Caliphate and later fell under Egyptian and Turkish rule

19th cent.: Britain gains control of Aden and concludes treaties with southern Yemeni sheikhs to protect them from overland attack from Turkey

1914: Anglo-Turkish convention establishes demarcation line separating British-controlled Southern Yemen from Turkish-occupied Yemen

1959: Six of the states of Southern Yemen form Federation of Arab Emirates of the South, later renamed Federation of South Arabia

1963-66: Aden joins federation; revolt, led by National Liberation Front (NLF), breaks out against British rule; Britain promises to grant southern Yemen independence by 1968 but NLF refuses to negotiate; joined by other groups, it forms Front for the Liberation of Occupied South Yemen (FLOSY) but soon breaks away from new group

1967: NLF defeats FLOSY. Britain withdraws from Southern Yemen

1969: Qahtan al-Shaabi, Southern Yemen's first president, resigns and is replaced by a five-man Presidential Council

1970: Al-Shaabi is ousted from NLF

1971: Ali Nasir Mohammed al-Hassani is appointed prime minister, succeeding Mohammed Ali Haithem

1972: Southern Yemen and Yemen sign truce after brief border fighting; agreement provides for future merger

1973: Border clashes resume between the two Yemens

1974: U.S. charges Soviet military buildup in Red Sea-Indian Ocean area involves use of Aden as submarine base

1975: Perim Island, which controls southern entrance to Red Sea, is leased to Egypt, as agent for the Arab League, in return for financial aid. Discussion on unity with Yemen is revived

1976: A cease-fire between Southern Yemen and Oman, where Southern Yemen had supported left-wing rebel forces, comes into force

1978: Yemen blames Southern Yemen for assassination of Yemen president; two days later ultraleftist Abdul Fattah Ismail ousts President Salem Rubaye Ali, who is immediately tried and shot; five-man council headed by Prime Minister al-Hassani takes over government. Ismail is elected president

1979: Southern Yemen invades Yemen, withdraws after both sides agree to station between them a multinational patrol under command of League of Arab States. President Ismail and President Ali Abdullah Saleh of Yemen agree on merger plan

1980: Ismail resigns as president; succeeded by Ali Nasir Mohammed

YUGOSLAVIA

Area: 98,766 sq. mi. **Population:** 22,107,000 (1979 est.)

Official Name: Socialist Federal Republic of Yugoslavia **Capital:** Belgrade **Nationality:** Yugoslavia is officially made up of 6 "nations": Serbs, Croats, Slovenes, Macedonians, Montenegrins and Moslems. "Moslem" does not mean religion but nationality. Officially there exists no Yugoslav nation **Languages:** All "national" languages are official, with Serbo-Croatian serving as a lingua franca **Religion:** About 34% of the population belong to the Orthodox Church; 24% are Roman Catholics and 8% Moslems; 34% are of other or no affiliation **Flag:** Horizontal stripes of blue, white, and red with a red star edged in gold in the center **Anthem:** Fellow Slavs **Currency:** Yugoslav dinar (21 per U.S. $1)

Location: Southeast Europe. Yugoslavia, on the Balkan Peninsula, is bounded on the north by Austria and Hungary, on the east by Romania and Bulgaria, on the south by Greece and Albania, and on the west by the Adriatic Sea and Italy **Features:** The northern and eastern part consists of lowland hills and plains, with a few mountain ranges. The remaining two-thirds of the country is mountainous, culminating in the Dinaric Alps **Chief Rivers:** Danube, including its tributaries (Drava, Sava, Morava, Tisza), and Vardar

Head of State: President Cvijetin Mijatović, born 1913, succeeded to leadership of the 8-man collective presidency on May 15, 1980, for one-year term **Political Leader:** Stevan Doronjski, born 1919, selected Oct. 1979 for a one-year term as Chairman of the Presidium of the Central Committee of the League of Communists of Yugoslavia **Head of Government:** Premier Veselin Djuranović, born 1926, appointed president of 29-member Federal Executive Council in 1977 **Effective Date of Present Constitution:** February 1974 **Legislative Body:** Federal Assembly (bicameral), with a Federal Council of 220 proportionately elected delegates, and a Council of Republics and Provinces with 58 delegates **Local Government:** 6 republics and 2 autonomous provinces (within Serbia), each with its own locally elected executive council and assembly

Ethnic Composition: Serbs (40%), Croats (22%), Slovenes (8%), Bosnian Moslems (8%), Macedonians (6%), Albanians (6%), Montenegrins (2%), Hungarians (2%), Turks (1%) **Population Distribution:** 39% urban **Density:** 224 inhabitants per sq. mi.

Largest Cities: (Metropolitan Areas) (1976 est.) Belgrade 1,319,000; (1974 est.) Zagreb 700,000, Skopje 440,000, Sarajevo 400,000, Ljubljana 300,000; (1971 census) Novi Sad 216,358

Per Capita Income: $2,905 (1979) **Gross National Product (GNP):** $64 billion (1979) **Economic Statistics:** About 37% of the GNP is derived from mining and manufacturing (metals, woodworking, chemicals, textiles, food processing); 12% from agriculture (corn, wheat, fruits including wine grapes, sugar beets, tobacco, livestock, timber). Tourism is also an important source of revenue **Minerals and Mining:** Coal, copper, iron ore, lead, zinc, petroleum, bauxite, natural gas **Labor Force:** 10,700,000 (1977), with 35% in agriculture and 52% in industry **Foreign Trade:** Exports, chiefly fresh meat, ships, machinery, clothing, and hardwood, totaled $5.7 billion in 1978. Imports, mainly machinery and transport equipment, iron and steel, fuel raw materials, and chemicals, totaled $9.9 billion **Principal Trade Partners:** USSR, West Germany, Italy, United States, France, Poland, Iraq

Vital Statistics: Birthrate, 17.7 per 1,000 of pop. (1977); death rate, 8.4 **Life Expectancy:** 68 years **Health Statistics:** 167 inhabitants per hospital bed; 792 per physician (1975) **Infant Mortality:** 35.2 per 1,000 births (1977) **Illiteracy:** 15% **Primary and Secondary School Enrollment:** 3,772,937 (1976) **Enrollment in Higher Education:** 394,992 (1975) **GNP Expended on Education:** 5.4% (1976)

Transportation: Paved roads total 27,780 mi. **Motor Vehicles:** 2,123,100 (1977) **Passenger Cars:** 1,923,900 **Railway Mileage:** 6,190 **Ports:** Rijeka, Split, Dubrovnik, Kotor; on the Danube River: Novi Sad, Belgrade **Major Airlines:** Yugoslav Airlines operates domestically and internationally **Communications:** Government owned **Radio Transmitters:** 487 **Licenses:** 4,526,000 (1976) **Television Transmitters:** 430 **Licenses:** 3,463,000 (1976) **Telephones:** 1,431,000 (1976) **Newspapers:** 26 dailies (1975), 80 copies per 1,000 inhabitants (1976)

Weights and Measures: Metric system **Travel Requirements:** Passport, visa valid up to 1 year, no fee

---

A perennial subject of debate among orthodox Communists has been whether Yugoslavia is really Communist. The Yugoslavs insist they are. Others insist that they are not and that Yugoslavia's brand of political ideology is more Titoism than Communism. The question is now being asked after President Josip Broz Tito died in

1980: Can Titoism survive in Yugoslavia without Tito?

The Communist party of Yugoslavia was renamed the League of Communists of Yugoslavia in 1952. It has remained the dominant political force. But some scope for political activity is provided by the less disciplined Socialist Alliance of Working People of Yugoslavia, to which all League members and about half of the other adults belong. There are few state or collective farms; agriculture is dominated by private small holdings. Most businesses are managed by councils elected by the workers, and workers have been known to strike against their own councils. The worker-managed businesses compete vigorously against each other, and they are allowed to advertise. Individuals may own businesses with no more than five employees, and occupational licensure is almost unknown. More than half of Yugoslavia's trade is with non-Communist countries, and many Yugoslavs work in Western Europe, entering and leaving Yugoslavia across an open frontier. The press is not strictly controlled, and foreign publications are available to those who can read them.

The political system features a parliament with genuine independent power and a decentralization of authority among the nationality sub-republics. Yugoslavia is made up of many different peoples—notably the Serbs, Croats, Slovenes, and Macedonians—and their rivalry has not been diminished by the attempt to give each group a sense of political and cultural independence.

In 1974, Marshal Tito had himself proclaimed president for life and confirmed plans for Communist collective leadership of Yugoslavia after his death. In January 1980, Tito fell ill and had his leg amputated due to poor blood circulation. He grew steadily worse and died on May 4, at the age of 87. His funeral in Belgrade was attended by the heads of state or delegates from 115 nations.

As Tito lay dying, leadership of the Yugoslav presidency and Communist party began to rotate among the leaders of the country's six republics and two autonomous provinces. The goal was to avert ethnic rivalries for power while preserving Yugoslavia's independence and structure of a workers' state. Cvijetin Mijatovoć, a Serb, became president for a one-year term May 15th.

After 1948, when Yugoslavia was expelled from the world Communist movement, Marshal Tito moved closer to and received much aid from the United States, Britain, and France. After the reconciliation with the Soviet Union in 1955, Yugoslavia tended to follow the Soviet line on many world issues. Nevertheless, it sought a measure of independence in foreign policy by rallying African and Asian countries into a bloc of non-aligned nations. Yugoslavia's relations with the Soviet Union grew cool following the Russian invasion of Czechoslovakia in 1968, and again in 1979 after the Soviet invasion of Afghanistan.

HISTORY: In ancient times, what is now Yugoslavia was inhabited chiefly by Illyrian peoples who came under Roman rule in the 1st century B.C. In the 6th century A.D., Slavic immigrants settled in the country; their languages and cultures gradually became dominant. Most of the Yugoslav (Southern Slav) peoples were conquered by the Ottoman Empire in the 14th and 15th centuries. The House of Hapsburg pushed back the Turkish tide, and, by 1878, ruled Croatia, Slovenia, and Bosnia-Hercegovina. Montenegro had maintained a precarius independence, and Serbia had become independent in the 19th century, and had assumed the leadership of the movement for a Pan-Slav state

1914-15: Serbia and Montenegro are overrun by Central Powers in World War I, precipitated by assassination of Archduke Francis Ferdinand at Sarajevo, in Bosnia, by a Serbian nationalist

1918: Kingdom of Serbs, Croats, and Slovenes is proclaimed under the rule of King Peter I of Serbia

1929: Alexander I, Peter's successor, establishes dictatorship following moves toward separatism by Croatia; country's name is changed to Yugoslavia

1934: Alexander is assassinated in Marseilles by Croat terrorist; his son succeeds as Peter II under the regency of Prince Paul, Alexander's cousin

1941: Yugoslavia signs Berlin-Rome-Tokyo Pact; Prince Paul and his pro-German government are ousted in bloodless coup; new government signs nonaggression pact with USSR; Germany and Italy, joined by Hungary and Bulgaria, invade Yugoslavia, which collapses a week later

1943: Civil war breaks out between Chetniks, a Serbian resistance force headed by Draja Mikhailovich, and Communist partisans led by Josip Broz Tito

1944: Tito's forces expel Germans

1945: Monarchy is abolished and the People's Republic of Yugoslavia is proclaimed under Tito's leadership

1946: Tito launches vigorous program of socialization; political opposition is crushed and Mikhailovich executed; Roman Catholic Church comes under government attack, culminating in arrest and imprisonment of Archbishop Aloysius Stepinac

1948: Yugoslavia is expelled from Cominform after Tito resists Soviet attempts to control his regime; Tito begins to develop "national communism" and turns to West for aid

1955-60: Tito attempts to resume more cordial relations with USSR but new rift develops following the crushing of the 1956 Hungarian revolt by the Russians; in 1960 Yugoslavia again moves toward closer relations with Moscow

1968: Soviet-led invasion of Czechoslovakia draws warning from Yugoslav Communists that Yugoslavia stands ready to defend its independence

1972: Tito introduces presidency of Yugoslavia, a collective body designed to rule the country after he leaves

1973: Tito purges Serbian and Slovenian Communist party leaders accused of "liberalism;" new constitution calls for collective presidency of Yugoslavia

1976: Tito attends European Communist party meeting, ending Yugoslav boycott of such Communist conferences since 1957

1977: U.S. agrees to expand military ties with Yugoslavia. Government frees dissident author Mihajlo Mihajlov in amnesty affecting 723 prisoners

1978: Tito visits U.S. China's Hua Guofeng visits Yugoslavia

1980: Tito dies at the age of 87 after long illness. Vice President Lazar Kolisevski heads collective presidency, which is to rotate annually among Communist leaders of the republics and autonomous provinces; Cvijetin Mijatović takes office as president for one-year term on May 15

ZAIRE

Area: 918,962 sq. mi. **Population:** 27,936,000 (1979 est.)

Official Name: Republic of Zaire **Capital:** Kinshasa **Nationality:** Zairian **Languages:** French is the official and only common language; about 700 languages and dialects are spoken, the four serving as linguas franca being Lingala, Kingwana, Kikongo, and Tshiluba **Religion:** About 60% Christian (75% Roman Catholic); most of the remaining population practices traditional religions, especially animism **Flag:** A green field with yellow disc, in which a brown hand holds a red and brown torch **Anthem:** Song of Independence **Currency:** Zaire (2.9 per U.S. $1)

Location: South-central Africa. The Republic of Zaire is bordered on the west and north by the Congo, the Central African Republic, and Sudan; on the east by Uganda, Rwanda, Burundi, and Tanzania; and on the south by Angola and Zambia. Its only outlet to the ocean is a narrow strip of land on the north bank of the Congo (Zaire) estuary on the Atlantic **Features:** The huge Congo Basin, a low-lying, basin-shaped plateau sloping toward the west, is covered by tropical rain forest. Surrounding it are mountainous terraces on the west, plateaus merging into savannas to the south and southeast, and dense grasslands toward the northwest. High mountains lie to the east **Chief Rivers:** The Congo (Zaire) and its many tributaries, including the Ubangi, Aruwimi, Lindi, Lualaba, Lomami, Lomela, Momboyo, Kasai, Kwango, and Kwilu

Head of State and of Government: President: Lt. Gen. Mobutu Sese Seko, born 1930; seized power in a coup in 1965, reelected 1977 for a second seven-year term. He is assisted by the first state commissioner (premier), Nguza Karl-I-Bond, appointed Aug. 1980 **Effective Date of Present Constitution:** Feb. 1978 **Legislative Body:** National Legislative Council (unicameral), with 268 members, elected for 5 years. Actual power resides with the president, as head of the Political Bureau of the Popular Revolutionary Movement (MPR) **Local Government:** 8 regions, each with an appointed commissioner

Ethnic Composition: There are some 200 tribal groups, which can be divided into 3 main categories: the Negroes (Bantu [80%], Sudanese, and Nilotics); the Hamites; and the Pygmies **Population**

Distribution: 30% urban **Density:** 30 inhabitants per sq. mi.

Largest Cities: (1974 est.) Kinshasa 2,008,352, Kananga 601,239, Lubumbashi 403,623, Mbuji-Mayi 336,654, Kisangani 310,705, Bukavu 181,774, Kikwit 150,253, Matadi 143,598

Per Capita Income: $135 (1979) **Gross National Product (GNP):** $3.8 billion (1979) **Economic Statistics:** About 17% of GNP comes from industry (food processing, consumer durables, and construction materials); 15% from public administration; 15% from commerce and transportation; 15% from subsistence production; 13% from agriculture (coffee, rubber, and palm oil); 7% from mining **Minerals and Mining:** The country is the world's largest producer of industrial diamonds; copper provides one-half of export earnings. Other important minerals include cobalt, bauxite, gold, cassiterite, manganese, oil, and zinc **Labor Force:** 8.3 million, with about 75% in agriculture **Foreign Trade:** Exports, chiefly copper, cobalt, zinc, diamonds, coffee, palm oil and rubber totaled $1.4 billion in 1978. Imports, mainly machinery, transportation equipment, textiles, fuel, and foodstuffs, totaled $1.4 billion **Principal Trade Partners:** Belgium, United States, Italy, France, West Germany, Britain, Japan

Vital Statistics: Birthrate, 45.2 per 1,000 of pop. (1975); death rate, 20.5 **Life Expectancy:** 44 years **Health Statistics:** 327 inhabitants per hospital bed; 28,802 per physician (1973) **Infant Mortality:** 104 per 1,000 births **Illiteracy:** 70% **Primary and Secondary School Enrollment:** 3,875,143 (1974) **Enrollment in Higher Education:** 21,021 (1974) **GNP Expended on Education:** 4.2% (1970)

Transportation: Paved roads total about 1,650 mi. **Motor Vehicles:** 161,200 (1974) **Passenger Cars:** 84,800 **Railway Mileage:** 3,593 (1970) **Ports:** Matadi, Banana, Boma **Major Airlines:** Air Zaire provides domestic and international services **Communications:** Partly government owned **Radio Transmitters:** 22 **Receivers:** 2,448,000 (1974) **Television Transmitters:** 3 **Receivers:** 7,000 (1976) **Telephones:** 48,000 (1976) **Newspapers:** 11 dailies, 9 copies per 1,000 inhabitants (1974)

Weights and Measures: Metric system **Travel Requirements:** Passport, visa valid 1 to 3 months, $4 fee, 1 photo

---

Torn by bloody strife through more than half of its first decade of independence, Zaire's early name of Congo had been almost a synonym for disorder. For 85 years the big African country—its area equal to that of the United States east of the Mississippi—was the possession of Belgium. While Belgian administration checked tribal enmities, colonial monopolies reaped the wealth of ivory, gold, copper, and other minerals. Plantations used labor under conditions little different from slavery.

Although the colonial regime grew less harsh in the 20th century, with missionary schools and better economic treatment for Zairians (Congolese), Belgium administrators did little to prepare for self-government.

In 1960, spurred by rebellion in Zaire and the wave of decolonization elsewhere in Africa, the Belgian government reluctantly acceded to the independence demands of Zaire leaders headed by Joseph Kasavubu and Patrice Lumumba. The calm, conservative Kasavubu, who became the first president, and other leaders favored a loose federation, while the passionate, radical Lumumba, who became premier, wanted a strong central government. And with the formal grant of independence on June 30, 1960, the issue remained basically unresolved.

Peaceful independence lasted only five days. On July 5 the army mutinied, public authority broke down and on July 10 Belgian troops intervened to protect Belgian nationals caught in a wave of terror. On July 11 Moise Tshombe, governor of Katanga, declared his mineral-rich province an independent country.

With a UN force backing up the national army, there began the long struggle to quell the Katangan secession. The Katangan forces, with a hard core of white mercenaries—*les affreux* ("the frightful ones")—put up a stiff resistance and it was not until mid-1963 that Tshombe was defeated and forced into exile.

Meanwhile, breakaway governments arose in South Kasai and in Kivu Province. Following a quarrel between Kasavubu and Lumumba, the national army commander, Col. Joseph D. Mobutu, a tough, Israeli-trained paratrooper, took over the government on September 5, 1960 and expelled Soviet and Communist-bloc diplomats and technicians.

The following November, the deposed Lumumba was captured while trying to flee to Kivu Province. Lumumba was taken to Katanga and assassinated in February 1961, becoming a martyr for third-world radicals. That same month Mobutu returned the reins of government to Kasavubu and four groups then contended for power. The country was not unified until 1963.

In 1964 when Zaire seemed to be pulling itself together, Kasavubu, in a gesture of national reconciliation, recalled Tshombe from exile and made him premier. There followed renewed rebellion by former Lumumba followers. The rebels, however, were soon defeated in an attack by Belgian paratroopers brought in by U.S. planes.

But neither Tshombe nor his successor could end the country's malaise of disunity (Tshombe went into exile and died in Algeria in 1969.) Mobutu, now a general, seized power in November 1965. He reduced provincial authority and began building a strong central government to unify the country's 100 tribes into a true nation. By offering attractive incentives to foreign investment, he set out to make the Zaire an industrial country.

Elected president in 1970, Mobutu has proved an effective salesman in promoting investment through state visits to the United States, West Germany, Japan, and other countries. Early in 1974 the government created a state-owned company to take over all petroleum product distribution. Mobutu, in a campaign of "African authenticity," renamed the country Zaire and dropped his Christian names and called himself Mobutu Sese Seko.

Twice in a 14-month period, Zaire was invaded by Katangan soldiers who had fled the southern province of Shaba (formerly Katanga) after losing the secessionist war of the mid-1960s. In March 1977 President Mobutu's rule was threatened by the first invasion of Shaba, which contains copper mines that provide the bulk of the nation's annual revenues of $1.3 billion. Some 2,000 rebels, armed with Soviet-bloc weapons, had entered from bases in Angola; Zaire defeated them with the help of Moroccan troops and military aid from France and Belgium. (The U.S. supplied $13 million in "nonlethal" equipment.) In May 1978 the Katangans mounted another invasion of Shaba, this time with a force twice as large as before. French and Belgian paratroopers repulsed the attack, and an African peacekeeping force (mostly Moroccan and Senegalese) was sent in and later withdrawn. Belgian advisors set about to train Zairian army units to provide better security in Shaba. Meanwhile, guerrillas in Angola kept closed Zaire's shortest rail route to the sea at Benguela.

HISTORY: Pygmy tribes are believed to be among the earliest inhabitants of Zaire. Bantus from eastern Africa and Nilotes from the Nile region later entered the area. The Bantus established several kingdoms, including Bahuba, Baluba, and the Congo. When Portuguese explorers arrived at the mouth of the Zaire (Congo) River in the 15th century, the kingdom of the Congo included what is now Zaire and Angola

1879-84: Henry Stanley explores Zaire on behalf of Belgian king

1885: Leopold II sets up the Congo Free State and becomes its absolute monarch

1908: Congo Free State becomes Belgian Congo

1960: Colony is granted independence; within a week Congolese Army mutinies and Belgian troops intervene to protect Belgian nationals. Premier Moise Tshombe of Katanga, the Congo's richest region, proclaims his province an independent country; Albert Kalonji proclaims the independence of part of Kasai Province. At the request of the central government, UN troops are sent to the Congo to maintain order. Intense rivalry breaks out between Joseph Kasavubu, the head of state, and his premier, Patrice Lumumba; Col. Joseph Mobutu, commander of the Congo Army, seizes control of the government

1961: Mobutu returns reins of government to Kasavubu. Lumumba is killed under mysterious circumstances and his death plunges the Congo into further strife

1962-63: Heavy fighting takes place between UN troops and Katanga forces; secession of Katanga is ended

1964: Tshombe, who had gone into exile, is invited to return and is sworn in as Congo's new premier

1965: Tshombe is dismissed and goes into exile. Mobutu again stages military coup and overthrows Kasavubu government

1967: Mobutu announces new constitution providing for a federal system of government, with strong president and unicameral legislature. Central government takes over assets of Union Minière, the rich Belgian copper mining company in Katanga

1969: Kasavubu dies in March; Tshombe, captive in Algeria, in June

1971-73: In Africanization campaign, Democratic Republic of the Congo becomes Republic of Zaire, and Congo River becomes Zaire River. Many foreign-owned firms are nationalized

1974-75: World price of copper falls, earnings are cut

1976: Angolan war disrupts export of Zaire copper. Mobutu establishes relations with Agostinho Neto's victorious Marxist government in Angola after backing losing pro-Western faction

1977: Shaba Province invaded by former Katangan soldiers; Moroccan troops, and French, Belgian and U.S. aid end threat. Mobutu wins new seven-year term as president

1978: About 4,000 Angolan-based Katangan rebels capture towns in Shaba; France and Belgium drop in paratroopers to rout rebels; about 150 foreigners are found dead as rebels retreat. Zaire and Angola agree to establish full ties and reopen rail line from Kolwezi to Angolan coast

1979: A $150-million conditional credit from International Monetary Fund gives Zaire recovery plan a shot in the arm. Mpinga Kasenda is removed as prime minister on corruption charges and replaced by Boboliko Lokonga. Drought causes severe food shortages. Mobutu seeks to improve relations with neighbor states and Soviet bloc while keeping friendship with Western countries and China

1980: Currency is devalued 30%. Zaire fails to meet austere conditions for withdrawal of second part of IMF loan. Students boycott classes, then riot in protest against high transportation costs. Nine people are trampled to death in crowd at open-air Mass held by Pope Paul II in Kinshasa. Nguza Karl-I-Bond becomes prime minister

ZAMBIA

Area: 290,586 sq. mi. **Population:** 5,649,000 (1979 est.)

Official Name: Republic of Zambia **Capital:** Lusaka **Nationality:** Zambian **Languages:** The official language is English. Some 70 different Bantu languages and dialects are spoken, but 5 main languages are recognized for educational and administrative purposes: Nyanja, Bemba, Lozi, Luvale, and Tonga **Religion:** Most of the African population follow traditional religions. Christians number about 900,000, and the small Asian community practices Islam and Hinduism **Flag:** A green field with a swatch in the lower right corner of red, black, and orange vertical stripes topped by an orange flying eagle **Anthem:** National Anthem, beginning "Stand and sing of Zambia, proud and free" **Currency:** Zambian kwacha (.79 per U.S. $1)

Location: South-central Africa. Landlocked Zambia is bordered on the north by Zaire, on the east by Tanzania and Malawi, on the southeast by Mozambique, on the south by Zimbabwe, Botswana, and Namibia, and on the west by Angola **Features:** Most of the land mass is a high plateau lying between 3,500 and 4,000 feet above sea level. In the northeast the Muchinga Mountains exceed 7,000 feet in height. Elevations below 2,000 feet are encountered in the valleys of the major river systems. There are 3 large natural lakes: Bangweulu, Mweru, and Tanganyika, all in the northeast **Chief Rivers:** Zambezi, Luangwa, Chambeshi, Kafue, Luapula

Political Leader and Head of State: President: Dr. Kenneth David Kaunda, born 1924, head of the United National Independence party, reelected 1978 **Head of Government:** Prime Minister Daniel Lisulo **Effective Date of Present Constitution:** Aug. 1973 **Legislative Body:** National Assembly (unicameral), consisting of 125 members elected for 5 years, and 10 appointed members **Local Government:** 9 provinces, each administered by a cabinet member

Ethnic Composition: Over 98% of the population are Africans belonging chiefly to various Bantu-speaking tribes. There are approximately 40,000 Europeans and Asians **Population Distribution:** 40% urban **Density:** 19 inhabitants per sq. mi.

Largest Cities: (1978 est.) Lusaka 559,000, Kitwe 310,000, Ndola 291,000, Chingola 173,000, Mufulira 170,000, Luanshya 149,000, Kabwe 131,000

Per Capita Income: $470 (1978) **Gross National Product (GNP):** $2.5 billion (1978) **Economic Statistics:** Quarrying and mining account for 50% of the GNP. Agriculture (tobacco, corn, peanuts, cotton) accounts for 11%; indigenous manufacturing (food processing, textile, furniture and construction materials) for 8% **Minerals and Mining:** Zambia is a ranking producer of copper with an output of over 800,000 metric tons in 1977, cobalt, lead, zinc, and unexploited deposits of iron are also abundant **Labor Force:** 402,000 wage earners (1977); 23% in government, 15% in mining, 10% in manufacturing, 9% in agriculture, 9% in commerce and 6% in transportation **Foreign Trade:** Exports, mainly refined copper, lead, zinc, cobalt, and unmanufactured tobacco, totaled $779 million in 1978. Imports chiefly machinery and transportation equipment, petroleum products, manufactured articles, chemicals, and food totaled $640 million **Principal Trade Partners:** Britain, Japan, West Germany, United States, South Africa, China

Vital Statistics: Birthrate, 51.5 per 1,000 of pop. (1975); death rate, 20.3 **Life Expectancy:** 47 years **Health Statistics:** 250 inhabitants per hospital bed (1975); 8,159 per physician (1971) **Infant Mortality:** 160 per 1,000 births **Illiteracy:** 72% **Primary and Secondary School Enrollment:** 945,441 (1975) **Enrollment in Higher Education:** 8,403 (1975) **GNP Expended on Education:** 6.7% (1976)

Transportation: Paved roads total 3,355 mi. **Motor Vehicles:** 171,900 (1976) **Passenger Cars:** 93,500 **Railway Mileage:** 1,360 **Ports:** None **Major Airlines:** Zambia Airways operates domestically and internationally **Communications:** Government owned **Radio Transmitters:** 22 **Receivers:** 110,000 (1976) **Television Transmitters:** 4 **Receivers:** 25,000 (1976) **Telephones:** 55,000 (1976) **Newspapers:** 2 dailies, 22 copies per 1,000 inhabitants (1975)

Weights and Measures: Metric system **Travel Requirements:** Passport, visa, $3.50 fee

---

The land above the Zambezi River, Zambia was called a "rich pauper" when, as the former British protectorate of Northern Rhodesia, it adopted a new name and became independent in 1964. The designation was based on the fact that while the country produced great wealth in copper, most Zambians gained barely enough to eat from their meager agricultural economy. Since then President Kenneth D. Kaunda has taken forceful measures to end the paradox. By 1975 Zambia assumed full control of its copper industry.

The government has faced a costly adjustment in trade and transportation in line with black Africa's boycott of Rhodesia (now Zimbabwe). Zambian copper, which formerly had gone out through Rhodesia, was rerouted through Tanzania. The Tanzam railroad, constructed to link Zambian copper mines with Indian Ocean ports, was completed in 1976, but has proved inadequate in getting the product to market. Zambia has also been hard hit by a drop in the world price of copper.

Kaunda has committed Zambia to a form of socialism which he calls "humanism," designed to satisfy all Zambians' requirements through even distribution of the nation's wealth.

In December 1972 a bill went into effect making the governing United National Independence party (UNIP) Zambia's only legal political party. At the same time, President Kaunda ordered UNIP officials owning businesses to convert them into producers' cooperatives or relinquish their managing directorships.

After Kaunda allowed Patriotic Front guerrilla fighters from Rhodesia to establish bases in Zambia, those bases became subject to repeated air and ground attacks. Many Zambian civilians were killed, Lusaka's new rail link to Indian Ocean ports was broken, and the country's economy suffered severely. Kaunda mobilized the Zambian army and purchased weapons from Britain and China at the expense of sorely needed domestic programs in an effort to counter the threat from Rhodesia before it ended late in 1979.

HISTORY: The history of the territory constituting present-day Zambia before the coming of the white man is sparse. The first European to penetrate into the region was the Scottish missionary David Livingstone, who made extensive explorations of the area between 1851 and 1873. In 1891, the British South Africa Co., which was developing the local copper resources, took over administration of the territory, naming it Northern Rhodesia

1924: British South Africa Co. is relieved of the administration of Northern Rhodesia

1930-44: Discovery of large copper deposits brings rush of Europeans to Northern Rhodesia

1953-63: Northern Rhodesia is part of the Federation of Rhodesia and Nyasaland

1964: Northern Rhodesia becomes independent republic of Zambia; Kenneth Kaunda, leader of the ruling United National Independence party, becomes the nation's first president

1967: Zambia accepts offer by Communist China to finance 1,000-mile railroad linking Lusaka with Dar es Salaam

1968: Kaunda is reelected president

1969: Kaunda announces measures for government takeover of country's $1.2-billion copper industry from foreign owners

1973: New constitution is enacted to coincide with new one-party system of government. Kaunda is reelected for third term. Border with Rhodesia is closed

1976: Angolan MPLA government recognized and Rhodesian guerrillas aided; Tanzam Railway is completed

1978: Zambia undertakes austerity measures to meet International Monetary Fund terms for $390-million loan needed to bolster ailing economy. Rhodesia raids guerrilla camps in Zambia. Kaunda is reelected president without opposition

1979: Commonwealth heads of state, meeting in Lusaka, endorse proposals for holding elections in Zimbabwe Rhodesia under British supervision. Kaunda reportedly prevails upon Zimbabwe guerrillas to suspend border attacks during visit of Queen Elizabeth II

1980: Nine southern African nations meet in Lusaka April 1 to create a regional economic development plan aimed at decreasing dependence on white-ruled South Africa. Zambia purchases $85.4 million of arms from USSR

ZIMBABWE

Area: 150,803 sq. mi. **Population:** 7,140,000 (1979 est.)

Official Name: Republic of Zimbabwe **Capital:** Salisbury **Nationality:** Zimbabwean **Languages:** English, the official language, is spoken by the white population and a great number of Africans; the chief Bantu languages are Shona and Ndebele **Religion:** Over 50% practice a combination of animism and Christianity. There are also 24% Christians (mainly Anglicans) and some Moslems **Flag:** 7 equal horizontal stripes of green, yellow, red, black, red, yellow and green separated by a narrow black border from a white triangle at the hoist. The triangle contains a representation of the Great Zimbabwe bird superimposed on a red five-pointed star **Anthem:** Rise, O Voices of Zimbabwe **Currency:** Zimbabwe dollar (0:69 per U.S. $1)

Location: South-Central Africa. Landlocked Zimbabwe is bordered on the north by Zambia, on the east by Mozambique, on the south by the Republic of South Africa, and on the west by Botswana **Features:** Most of the country is a high, rolling plateau between 3,000 and 5,000 feet above sea level. The land is largely South African veld, or grassland, with scattered shrubs or trees **Chief Rivers:** Zambezi, Limpopo, Sabi, Gwaai, Shangani

Head of State: President: Rev. Canaan Banana, born 1935, took office April 18, 1980, for 6-year term **Head of Government:** Prime Minister Robert Gabriel Mugabe, born 1924, sworn in April 18, 1980 **Effective Date of Present Constitution:** April 18, 1980 **Legislative Body:** Parliament (bicameral), consists of (1) a House of Assembly with 100 members elected for 5 years from 80 black voters' roll constituencies and 20 white roll constituencies, (2) a 40-member Senate for 5 years consisting of 14 Senators elected by the 80 black members of the Assembly, 10 Senators chosen by the 20 white members of the Assembly, 10 Senators elected by traditional chiefs, and 6 appointed by the President **Local Government:** 7 provinces under appointed commissioners

Ethnic Composition: 95.2% are indigenous Bantus, principally Mashona and Matabele; 4.3% are of European descent, chiefly British **Population Distribution:** 20% urban **Density:** 47 inhabitants per sq. mi.

Largest Cities: (1975 est.—Metropolitan Areas) Salisbury 569,000, Bulawayo 340,000, Gwelo 64,000, Umtali 62,000, Que Que 41,000, Gatooma 32,000, Wankie 26,000

Per Capita Income: $460 (1979) **Gross National Product (GNP):** $3.3 billion (1979) **Economic Statistics:** In 1973 about 36% of GNP was derived from trade and services; 25% from manufacturing (metals and metal products, food processing, textiles, clothing and footwear, beverages, tobacco, chemicals); 17% from agriculture (Oriental tobacco, stock-raising, maize, groundnuts, cotton); and

6% from mineral wealth **Minerals and Mining:** There are deposits of asbestos, chrome ore, coal, copper, gold, iron ore, limestone, lithium, nickel, phosphate rock, and tin **Labor Force:** 991,600 (1978) **Foreign Trade:** Exports, mainly tobacco, asbestos, copper, apparel, meats, chrome, and sugar, totaled $652 million in 1973. Imports, chiefly machinery and transportation equipment, textiles, petroleum products, iron and steel products, fertilizers, and foodstuffs, totaled $541 million **Principal Trade Partner:** South Africa (pre-1980)

Vital Statistics: Birthrate, 47.9 per 1,000 of pop. (1975); death rate, 14.4 **Life Expectancy:** 52 years **Health Statistics:** 316 inhabitants per hospital bed; 5,700 per physician (1973) **Infant Mortality:** 17 per 1,000 births **Illiteracy:** 61% **Primary and Secondary School Enrollment:** 963,671 (1976) **Enrollment in Higher Education:** 1,076 (1972) **GNP Expended on Education:** 3.6% (1973)

Transportation: Paved roads total 4,964 mi. (1974) **Motor Vehicles:** 250,000 (1974) **Passenger Cars:** 180,000 **Railway Mileage:** 2,133 **Ports:** None **Major Airlines:** Air Zimbabwe operates domestic and international flights **Communications:** Government and privately controlled **Radio Transmitters:** 22 **Receivers:** 255,000 (1976) **Television Transmitters:** 5 **Receivers:** 72,000 (1976) **Telephones:** 190,000 (1976) **Newspapers:** 3 dailies, 18 copies per 1,000 inhabitants (1975)

Weights and Measures: British standards are being replaced by the metric system

---

At midnight April 17, 1980, with Britain's Prince Charles presiding and representatives of a hundred other countries looking on, the Union Jack was lowered for the last time in Salisbury and the striped flag of Zimbabwe went up in its place. The last but one (South Africa) of white-dominated, black-majority states of Africa had been recognized by the world as an independent country. Robert Mugabe, whose Zimbabwe African National Union party had won in free elections, was installed as prime minister. Soldiers of the former Rhodesian army, black and white, paraded side by side with guerrillas against whom they had so recently fought.

Lord Soames, the British governor who had ruled the country since the 1979 cease-fire, said, "This has been nothing less than a series of miracles." As it indeed had been. When, in 1964, Britain granted independence to Northern Rhodesia (now Zambia) and Nyasaland (Malawi), it denied such status to Southern Rhodesia until a government representative of the black majority as well as the whites was assured. A year later, Ian Smith, the white prime minister, unilaterally declared Rhodesia to be independent. Britain said the government was illegal, and the United Nations refused to recognize it.

With Smith's proclamation of a State of Rhodesia in March 1970, following a referendum the previous year in which white Rhodesians formally renounced their last British tie, loyalty to the Crown, there was an eventual withdrawal of all diplomatic missions except that of South Africa.

Despite diplomatic isolation, a total British trade blockade, UN economic sanctions, and its landlocked position in southern Africa, Rhodesia did manage to survive as an economic outcast.

Inspired by successful moves to black rule in the countries surrounding Rhodesia on three sides, nationalists organized the Patriotic Front to try to topple the Smith government by means of guerrilla warfare. Leading the estimated 12,000 guerrillas were Joshua Nkomo, patriarchal figure of Zimbabwe nationalism and Soviet-backed leader of the wing based in Zambia, and Robert Mugabe, whose Chinese-trained forces operated from bases in Mozambique and Tanzania.

Smith steadfastly refused to support equal voting rights as a step toward black rule. He relented only when escalating guerrilla warfare left him no alternative and not before safeguards had been built into an agreement to protect white interests. Finally, he gave in to a plan worked out with moderate black leaders for a black-majority government in which the white minority would retain much of the power. In May 1979, the name of the country was changed to Zimbabwe Rhodesia. Methodist Bishop Abel Muzorewa, who became the country's first black prime minister, faced insurmountable problems, notably the opposition of Patriotic Front leaders who regarded him as a puppet of white Rhodesians.

Bowing to the pressures, Muzorewa agreed late in 1979 to step down pending supervised elections in which all factions, including those of the Patriotic Front, could be represented. An uneasy truce with the guerrilla forces followed as Lord Soames became the interim governor. But after many threatened boycotts, the elections were held Feb. 27-29, 1980. The Zimbabwe African National Union (ZANU) won 57 of the 80 seats allotted to blacks in a 100-member House of Assembly, and Robert Mugabe, the revolutionary most feared by the white Rhodesians, became prime minister. "There is a place for everybody in this country," he said, seeking to reassure the whites and also the blacks who had supported candidates Nkomo and Muzorewa. "I urge you, whether you are black or white, to join me in a pledge to forget the grim past."

Mugabe included two prominent whites in his broad-based cabinet and offered the presidency to his rival, Nkomo, who refused the figurehead post but accepted appointment as Minister of Home Affairs. Lt. Gen. Peter Walls, a white, was kept as senior military commander but later resigned and was asked by Mugabe to leave Zimbabwe.

The new government faces many difficult problems—of achieving political and economic stability; of holding as many as possible of its experienced white workers, farmers and public servants, and of restoring diplomatic relations with the rest of the world.

HISTORY: The remains of Stone Age culture dating back 500,000 years have been found in Zimbabwe and it is thought that the Bushmen, who still survive, mostly in the Kalahari Desert of Botswana, are the last descendants of these original inhabitants. The first Bantu are thought to have reached Zimbabwe between the 5th and 10th centuries A.D., though southward migrations continued long after. The first Europeans to visit the region were 16th-century Portuguese explorers

1889-97: Cecil Rhodes forms the British South Africa Company; assisted by British troops, the company conquers the Mashona and Matabele; European colonists follow

1923: Southern Rhodesia becomes a self-governing colony within the British Commonwealth

1953: Britain establishes the Federation of Rhodesia and Nyasaland, linking Northern Rhodesia (now Zambia), Southern Rhodesia, and Nyasaland (now Malawi); the Federation remains dominated by the European settlers

1964: Federation of Rhodesia and Nyasaland is dissolved. Britain grants the two northern territories independence under African majority rule, but refuses independence to Southern Rhodesia unless representative government is assured.

1965: Prime Minister Ian Smith unilaterally declares Rhodesia's independence from Britain and promulgates a new constitution. Britain declares the Smith government an illegal, rebel regime

1966: UN Security Council calls on all member states to break off economic relations with Rhodesia; only Portugal and South Africa refuse to impose an embargo

1968: Smith government executes five black Africans convicted of murder, despite commutation of death sentences by Queen Elizabeth; act is viewed as most serious act of defiance against Britain by break-away Rhodesian regime

1969: Government publishes proposed constitution designed to perpetuate white minority rule. In a referendum in which 81,583 whites as against 6,634 blacks are eligible to vote, the Smith regime wins a mandate to place the proposed constitution before the Legislative Assembly and to proclaim Rhodesia a republic and cut formal remaining ties to British Crown

1970: Rhodesia proclaims a republic, severing ties with Britain; neither Britain nor the United Nations grant recognition

1974: Government suppression of black nationalists resumed as terrorism against white minority continues

1975: New 90-mile railway link with South Africa is opened

1976: John Wrathall is sworn in as Rhodesia's second president. Mozambique closes its 800-mile border with Rhodesia

1978: On March 3, Prime Minister Smith and three moderate nationalist leaders agree on plan for black-majority rule; while containing many guarantees for whites. Guerrilla leaders denounce pact as "sellout." Bush war turns bloodier as some 2,500 are killed in first four and a half months since March 3 accord. Rhodesian forces strike against guerrilla bases in Mozambique

1979: Blacks, voting in national elections for first time, elect Bishop Abel Muzorewa as first black prime minister. Zimbabwe Rhodesia is born May 31. Guerrilla war continues until Muzorewa agrees to turn over rule to a British governor pending all-party elections in 1980

1980: Robert Mugabe's Zimbabwe African National Union is victorious in elections; Canaan Banana, a Methodist minister, is chosen as president. Britain turns over reins of government of the new Republic of Zimbabwe to Mugabe, as prime minister, April 18. U.S. and Britain quickly offer aid. Several thousand whites emigrate. Zimbabwe severs diplomatic, but not trade, ties with South Africa. Cabinet minister Edgar Tekere is indicted for murdering a farmer

---

TERRITORIES AND DEPENDENCIES

Anguilla—*Status:* British Colony. *Population:* 6,600 (1977 est.). *Area:* 35 sq. mi. *Capital:* The Valley (760).

The island of Anguilla lies in the northern part of the Leeward group of the Lesser Antilles, in the eastern Caribbean. Anguilla is approximately 65 miles N.N.W. of St. Christopher and 9 miles from its nearest neighbor, St. Martin.

Anguilla is a flat, coralline island with its highest point at 213 feet above sea level. The island is covered with low scrub and fringed with white coral-sand beaches. Apart from sheep and goats, Anguilla's main product is salt. The majority of the population are African or of mixed descent, with a small white minority.

Anguilla unilaterally seceded from the associated state of St. Christopher-Nevis-Anguilla when it was formed in 1967. Britain took control of the island in 1969 after landing an "invasion" force, and in 1971 began direct administration of the island. On February 10, 1976, Anguilla was established as a self-governing British Colony with a new constitution (but it remains a legal part of the associated state). The charter created a seven-member House of Assembly and a chief minister, and gave the British Commissioner authority over defense, police and civil service, and foreign affairs. British engineers have installed a telephone system and improved the roads. At the outset of the 1980s, more hotels were built to support a bid for more tourism.

Antigua—*Status:* British Associated State. *Population:* 74,000 (1978 est.). *Area:* 171 sq. mi. *Capital:* St. John's (25,000).

Antigua, with its dependency of Barbuda and the small uninhabited island of Redonda, is in the Leeward Islands of the West Indies at the eastern edge of the Caribbean, 250 miles southeast of Puerto Rico. Its topography is rolling; its climate is tropical and subject to drought. Most of the people are of Negro-white descent. English is the formal language and everywhere understood, but a patois is commonly spoken.

Primarily agricultural, Antigua produces cotton and sugar. Bananas, citrus fruits, yams, and rice are also grown. Tourism is increasingly important.

There is a Crown-appointed governor, a premier, and a parliament consisting of an elected House of Representatives and an appointed Senate. Antigua's government is ruled by Prime Minister Vere Bird's Labour party, which was returned to power in April 1980, when it won 13 of 17 parliamentary seats. At the time of the vote, it was expected that Antigua would seek independence later in the year. Barbuda's desire for secession presents a difficulty, however.

Ashmore and Cartier Islands—*Status:* Australian External Territory. *Population:* Uninhabited. *Area:* 1.9 sq. mi.

These islands lie in the Indian Ocean, about 300 miles north of Broome in northwestern Australia (12°S.,123°E.). They are administered by the Northern Territory.

Australian Antarctic Territory—*Status:* External Territory of Australia. *Population:* Uninhabited. *Area:* 2,362,875 sq. mi. (of which 29,251 sq. mi. are ice shelf).

Australia claims all Antarctic islands and territories south of 60°S and between 45° and 160°E, except for French-claimed Adélie Land. (The United States does not recognize any Antarctic claims south of 60°S.)

Belize (formerly British Honduras)—*Status:* British Colony. *Population:* 153,000 (1978 est.). *Area:* 8,867 sq. mi. *Capital:* Belmopan (3,000).

The colony is on the east coast of Central America, bounded on the east by the Bay of Honduras of the Caribbean Sea, on the south and west by Guatemala, and on the northwest and north by Mexico. It has a swampy coast that rises gradually toward the interior, which is dominated by tropical jungle growth. The climate is subtropical and humid, with annual rainfall from 50 inches in the north to 175 inches in the far south. Forty percent of the people are of African descent, others are of Latin-Indian descent, and there are a few Europeans and East Indians. English is the official language.

Sugar, citrus, and clothing are the main exports. Fishing and cattle farming are being developed, as are the cultivation of bananas, cocoa, and vegetables. The discovery of large oil deposits in northern Belize was reported in 1978.

Belize is claimed by Guatemala on the grounds that it inherited Spanish sovereignty over the area and that British claims are void. In November 1975 Britain reinforced its army garrison in Belize because of an alleged threat of a Guatemalan invasion. In December the UN General Assembly passed a resolution supporting "the inalienable right of the people of Belize to self-determination and independence," and stated that the territorial integrity of the British colony "must be preserved." Britain again rushed troops to the colony in 1977 to counter the deployment of Guatemalan forces along the border.

The colony took its new name, Belize, in 1973. Its government consists of a bicameral national assembly, with an elected House of Representatives and an appointed senate, and a cabinet headed by a premier. The Crown-appointed governor is responsible for foreign affairs, defense, internal security, and civil service employment. The People's United party retained power by winning 13 of the 18 parliamentary seats in 1979. Its leader, Prime Minister George Price, reiterated then that total independence is the party's goal, but he added that, as a precondition, he would want security guarantees either from Britain or from the U.S.

Bermuda—*Status:* British Colony. *Population:* 58,000 (1978 est.). *Area:* 21 sq. mi. Capital: Hamilton (3,000).

The colony is in the western Atlantic (32°20′N.,64°40′W.), less than 600 miles east of Cape Hatteras, North Carolina. There are some 150 small islands, about 20 of which are inhabited. The main islands are close together, connected by bridges, and collectively called Bermuda. The islands are rocky, with lush vegetation. The climate, moderated by the Gulf Stream, is warm and pleasant. About two-thirds of the people are African or of mixed descent, the rest mostly British in origin. They are predominantly Protestant.

Tourism, largely from the United States, accounts for 70 percent of the economy. Also important is the provision of goods to British and American servicemen stationed on the islands. Almost all food is imported.

In 1968 a new constitution put most executive powers in the hands of the premier, who is the head of the majority party in the elected House of Assembly of the bicameral legislature (the oldest among British possessions). The Crown-appointed governor retains direct responsibility for external affairs, defense, internal security, and the police; otherwise, he acts only on the advice of the governor's (legislative) Council.

On March 10, 1973, the governor, Sir Richard Sharples, and his aide-de-camp were assassinated. The execution of the killer on December 2, 1977, resulted in a week of protest rioting, the declaration of a state of emergency, and the rushing of British troops to the colony. Property damage was great and tourism suffered for several years. A Royal Commission, meeting in London in 1978, recommended independence for the islands.

Bouvet Island—*Status:* Norwegian Dependency. *Population:* Uninhabited. *Area:* 23 sq. mi.

Situated between the extreme tip of South Africa and the Antarctic coast, Bouvet is in the South Atlantic Ocean at 54°26′S and 3°24′E. It is volcanic in origin and almost completely ice-covered. There are fur seals and seals of other varieties, penguins, and petrels.

British Antarctic Territory—*Status:* British Colony. *Population:* Uninhabited, except for personnel at scientific stations (76 in 1973). *Area:* 600,000 sq. mi. *Administrative Center:* Stanley, Falkland Islands.

The territory, created in 1962, extends below 60°S. from 20° to 80°W. and includes the South Orkney Islands, the South Shetland Islands, and the Antarctic Peninsula. Argentina claims the area and occupied one of the South Shetlands in 1976, resulting in a British protest.

British Indian Ocean Territory—*Status:* British Colony. *Population:* 2,000 (1978 est.) *Area:* 29 sq. mi. (land). *Administration Center:* London (U.K.).

The territory, made a separate colony in 1965, includes only the Chagos Archipelago at 7°20′S and 72°25′E, formerly a dependency of Mauritius; Diego Garcia (11 sq. mi.) is the largest island. The climate is tropical, with heavy rainfall.

The territory is administered from London by a commissioner. Diego Garcia is the site of a major U.S. air and naval base.

British Virgin Islands—*Status:* British Crown Colony. *Population:* 12,000 (1978 est.). *Area:* 59 sq. mi. *Capital:* Road Town (3,500) on Tortola.

These are in the eastern Caribbean, east of the U.S. Virgin Islands. They include 36 islands, 16 of which are inhabited, plus numerous rocks and *cays.* Tortola, Virgin Gorda, Anegada, and Jost Van Dyke are the largest islands. The climate is subtropical and pleasant; rainfall is light. Almost all the people are of African descent.

Cattle raising, farming, and fishing are the main activities. The shortage of water is a major problem. Tourism is an increasing factor in the economy.

The colony is governed by a Crown-appointed governor assisted by an appointed executive council and a chief minister. There is a partly elected legislative council.

Brunei—*Status:* British Protected State. *Population:* 213,000 (1978 est.). *Area:* 2,226 sq. mi. *Capital:* Bandar Seri Begawan, formerly Brunei Town (50,000).

This sultanate is on the north coast of Borneo, being two enclaves within the Malaysian state of Sarawak, washed by the South China Sea. The climate is tropical and humid, the rainfall heavy. The population is more than half Malay and is largely Moslem. Chinese are the second-largest element, and there are Dayak groups.

Oil and natural gas are the major factors in Brunei's economy, making it the richest state in Southeast Asia. Rice, cassava and bananas are grown.

Britain is responsible for Brunei's defense and foreign relations. A Crown-appointed high commissioner conducts relations between the two states. There is a council of ministers, presided over by the sultan. In 1967, after 17 years of rule, the Sultan, unwilling to bow to British demands for more representative government, abdicated and was succeeded by his son. In 1970, the new ruler dissolved the partly elected legislative council in favor of an entirely appointive body. Under a 1971 agreement with Britain, Brunei is fully self-governing in internal affairs. In 1978 it was announced in London that Brunei is to become independent in 1983.

Cayman Islands—*Status:* British Crown Colony. *Population:* 14,000 (1978 est.). *Area:* 100 sq. mi. *Capital:* George Town (3,975) on Grand Cayman.

Consisting mainly of three islands—Grand Cayman, Little Cayman, and Cayman Brac—this colony is in the Caribbean about 175 miles west of Jamaica. Grand Cayman is flat and rockbound, protected by coral reefs. The climate is tropical, hot and humid. About one-half of the people are of mixed Negro-white descent, about a third of European, and the rest of African ancestry.

Seafaring, commerce, and banking are the principal occupations. Tourism is important. Scuba divers are attracted to the Caymans—considered one of the world's best diving destinations—by the clear waters, wrecks, shallow reefs, walls, and caves.

There is a Crown-appointed governor, a partly elected legislative assembly and an executive council.

Ceuta and Melilla—*Status:* Under Spanish sovereignty. *Population:* Ceuta, 67,187; Melilla, 65,271 (1970 census). *Area:* Ceuta, 7.5 sq. mi.; Melilla, 4.8 sq. mi.

These two enclaves are on the Mediterranean coast of Morocco. Ceuta is opposite Gibraltar; Melilla, some 200 miles farther east, is on a rocky promontory. A good deal of fish are caught and exported from both towns. Ceuta, with a splendid climate, is increasingly visited by tourists. In 1975 Morocco laid formal claim.

Channel Islands—*Status:* British Crown Bailiwicks. *Population:* 130,000 (1978 est.). *Area:* 74 sq. mi.

These islands lie 80 miles south of the English coast, off the northwest coast of France. They consist of Jersey, Guernsey, and the latter's dependencies of Alderney, Brechou, Sark, Herm, Jethou, and Lihou. Ecrehou Rocks and Les Minquiers are dependencies of Jersey. The land is low and undulating and the climate mild with about 40 inches of annual rainfall. The people are mainly of Norman descent, with some of Breton ancestry. French is the official language of Jersey, English of Guernsey; in some country districts of Jersey and Guernsey and throughout Sark, a Norman-French dialect is spoken. English, however, is commonly used throughout the islands.

The main occupations are agriculture, dairying, and tourism. Agriculture is highly specialized, with Guernsey being noted for its hothouse tomatoes and cut flowers, Jersey for new potatoes and open-grown tomatoes. The farms of Jersey and Guernsey are, typically, tiny fields, the result of centuries of subdivision among heirs.

The Crown appoints the chief executives of Jersey and Guernsey, both of whom have the titles of lieutenant-governor and commander-in-chief. Jersey's partly elected legislature is called the States of Jersey, and St. Helier is the administrative center. The legislative body of Guernsey, partially elected, is the States of Deliberation. St. Peter Port is Guernsey's administrative center. Alderney and Sark have local legislative bodies subordinate to that of Guernsey. St. Anne is the administrative center of Alderney, Creux that of Sark. The head of Sark is *Le Seigneur de Sercq.*

Chilean Antarctica—*Status:* Chilean Dependency. *Population:* No permanent inhabitants. *Area:* 482,502 sq. mi.

Chile claims the Antarctic (or O'Higgins) Peninsula in the Antarctic, lying between 59° and 67°W. Parts of the area are also claimed by Great Britain and Argentina.

Christmas Island—*Status:* Australian External Territory. *Population:* 3,264 (1979). *Area:* 52 sq. mi. *Administrative Center:* Flying Fish Cove (1,300).

The island is in the Indian Ocean (10°30'S.,105°40'E.) some 1,630 miles northwest of Perth, Australia, and 225 miles south of the island of Java. It is hilly and rather barren. The climate is warm and dry. Over half the people are Chinese, with some Malayans and fewer Europeans.

Phosphate extraction, undertaken by the governments of Australia and New Zealand, is the island's only economic activity. Most of the deposits are expected to be exhausted at the end of this century.

Clipperton Island—*Status:* French Dependency. *Population:* Uninhabited. *Area:* 2 sq. mi.

This atoll is in the eastern Pacific (10°17'N.,109°13'W.), 700 miles southwest of Mexico. Formerly part of French Polynesia, it was placed in 1979 under the direct control of the French government in Paris.

Cocos (Keeling) Islands—*Status:* Australian External Territory. *Population:* 392 (1979). *Area:* 5.4 sq. mi. *Administrative Center:* West Island (92).

The territory, two separate atolls with 27 small coral islands, is in the Indian Ocean about 1,725 miles northwest of Perth, Australia, at 12°05'S and 96°53'E. The principal islands are West, Home, Direction, South, and Horsburgh. The climate is pleasant, with moderate rainfall. Three-quarters of the people are Cocos Islanders living on Home Island; the rest are of European descent, most of whom live on West Island, and Asians. Coconuts are the principal product.

Though the islands were placed under Australian authority in 1955, it was not until July 1978 that the Australian government purchased the Cocos from their owner, John Clunies Ross. His family had been granted title to the islands in 1886.

Cook Islands—*Status:* New Zealand Dependency. *Population:* 18,200 (1979 est.). *Area:* 91 sq. mi. *Administrative Center:* Avarua (4,429) on Rarotonga.

Situated in the South Pacific some 2,000 miles northeast of New Zealand, between 8° and 23°S and 156° and 167°W, the islands are in two groups—the Northern, with seven islands or atolls, and the Lower or Southern Group, with eight. The Northern islands are low and barren; the Lower ones, which are more elevated and fertile, support the greater part of the population. The climate is warm and humid, and the islands sometimes experience hurricanes. The people are Polynesian Christians, similar in language and traditions to the New Zealand Maori. Since 1971 the population has generally declined due to emigration, chiefly to New Zealand.

The economy is basically agricultural, with citrus fruits and juices, copra, and tomatoes, among other produce, being exported. Manufactured wearing apparel is also exported. The sale of postage stamps to collectors throughout the world is an important source of revenue.

The Cooks attained internal self-government in 1965, with New Zealand responsible for external affairs and defense. There is a prime minister and cabinet, and an elected legislative assembly. In 1978 Prime Minister Albert Henry was removed from office by the High Court for engaging in corrupt election practices.

Coral Sea Islands Territory—*Status:* Australian External Territory. *Population:* 3 (1971 census). *Area:* 8.5 sq. mi.

These islands, spread over 400,000 square miles, are situated east of Queensland, Australia, between the Great Barrier Reef and the 157°10'E meridian. One of the islands in the Willis Group has a meteorological station. The land consists mainly of scattered reefs and sand cays, many little more than sandbanks.

The Coral Sea Islands became an Australian External Territory on August 14, 1969, after having been acquired by acts of sovereignty over a number of years. The governor-general of Australia is empowered to make ordinances for the Territory. The Supreme Court and the Court of Petty Sessions of Norfolk Island have jurisdiction in the Territory.

Easter Island—*Status:* Chilean Dependency. *Population:* 1,598 (1970 census). *Area:* 63 sq. mi. *Settlement:* Hanga Roa (900).

Easter Island (*Rapa Nui* in Polynesian) lies in the Pacific Ocean some 2,300 miles west of Chile at 27°08'S. and 109°23'W. It is volcanic in origin, rising sharply from the sea. The climate is subtropical: warm, somewhat humid, and there is moderate rainfall. The island has no streams or lakes, and rainwater collects in the extinct volcanoes. The people, who are believed to be Polynesian in origin, speak Spanish. Easter Island is noted for its monolithic, stylized heads carved of volcanic rock.

Sheep raising is the most important activity. Despite the scarcity of fresh water, certain crops, including corn, wheat, taro, and tropical fruits, are grown. The island is administered as part of Valparaíso Province.

Faeroe Islands—*Status:* Integral part of the Danish Kingdom. *Population:* 42,000 (1977 est.). *Area:* 540 sq. mi. *Capital:* Tórshavn (10,726) on Streymoy.

These islands are in the Atlantic Ocean, north of Scotland, between 61°26' and 62°24'N and 6°15' and 7°41'W. Among the larger of the 18 islands (17 are inhabited) are Streymoy, Eysturoy and Váagar. They contain many lakes and peat bogs. The climate is mild, rainy, and foggy. Norse-descended, the inhabitants speak an old Norse dialect; Danish, however, is the official language. Most of the people are Lutherans.

The economy is based on fishing and sheep raising. Root vegetables, potatoes, and barley are grown.

A self-governing community within the Danish kingdom with a Crown commissioner, the Faeroes have their own elected parliament (*Lögting*) which chooses an administrative body (*Landsstyri*). The Faeroes send two representatives to the Danish parliament.

Falkland Islands—*Status:* British Crown Colony. *Population:* 1,950 (1977 est.). *Area:* 6,198 sq. mi. *Capital:* Stanley (1,079) on East Falkland.

Located in the South Atlantic some 500 miles northeast of Cape Horn, this group's major islands are East Falkland and West Falkland (4,618 sq. mi.), South Georgia (1,450 sq. mi.), and South Sandwich Islands (130 sq. mi.). East and West Falkland, which contain most of the population, consist largely of hilly moorland. The climate is cool and rainy, with persistently strong winds. The people are mostly of British origin.

Sheep farming is the main occupation, wool the main export. Offshore oil deposits are believed to exist.

The colony is administered by a Crown-appointed governor, assisted by partly elected councils. Argentina claims sovereignty over the islands, and refers to them as *Las Malvinas.* British and Argentine diplomats held discussions over the future sovereignty of the islands during 1977 and 1978.

French Guiana—*Status:* French Overseas Department. *Population:* 62,000 (1977 est.). *Area:* 35,135 sq. mi. *Capital:* Cayenne (29,405).

Situated on the northeast coast of South America, French Guiana is bounded by the Atlantic Ocean on the north, by Brazil on the east and south, and by Suriname on the west. Its coastline is 200 miles long, and Devil's Island (no longer used as a prison) is among its offshore islands. Extending almost 250 miles into the continent, French Guiana is divided into a low, swampy coastal area that ranges from 10 to 30 miles in width, and a plateau forming a series of low, steep hills inland. Most of the country is covered by rain forest. The climate is tropical, tempered by trade winds, and there is heavy rainfall from December to July. Ninety percent of the people live in the coastal areas; these are mostly a Negro-white mixture. In the interior are small groups of Indians (Carib, Arawak, Tupi-Guaraní) and descendants of escaped African slaves.

Forestry, including wood-veneer production, is a major element in the economy. Gold is mined, and bauxite and tantalite deposits are to be exploited. Arable land is scarce and limited to the coastal areas, where manioc, yams, sugarcane, and bananas are grown. The main source of income is French investment and contributions toward operating expenses and welfare. The French government maintains a space vehicle launching center at Kourou.

Guiana is administered by a Paris-appointed prefect, assisted by an elected general council. It elects a deputy and a senator to the French Parliament.

French Polynesia—*Status:* French Overseas Territory. *Population:* 137,382 (1977 census). *Area:* 1,544 sq. mi. *Capital:* Papeete (62,700) on Tahiti.

These widely scattered islands in the south central Pacific lie mainly between 7° and 27°S. and 134° and 155°W. The territory includes a number of island groups totaling 118 islands and atolls. The Society Islands (named after the Royal Society by their British discoverers) are the most important group and include Tahiti and Moorea; they contain about 70 percent of the Territory's population. Other groups are the Marquesas Islands, the Tuamotu Archipelago, the Gambier Islands, and the Tubuai or Austral Islands. All of these except the Tuamotus are volcanic in origin and mountainous, with fast-flowing streams, and are often circled by coral reefs and lagoons. The climate is hot and humid, tempered by steady winds. The people are predominantly Polynesians, with some Asians and a smaller number of Europeans, principally French. More than 60 percent of the people are Protestants.

The economy is based on agriculture. The main crops are copra, vanilla, and coffee. All common tropical plants and most European vegetables are grown. There has been extensive building in the islands to provide facilities for French nuclear tests, the first of which was held in 1966 on Mururoa Atoll, 800 miles southeast of Tahiti. In August 1968 the French exploded their first H-bomb nearby, at Fangataufa Atoll. In 1971 and 1973, French nuclear test activity in the Mururoa Atoll area met with worldwide protest. French nuclear testing has since continued. Vocal adherents of autonomy increased their representation in the assembly in 1976, and again in 1977.

The Territory is administered by a Paris-appointed governor, aided by a government council, with an elected territorial assembly, and elects two deputies and a senator to the French Parliament.

French Southern and Antarctic Territories—*Status:* French Overseas Territory. *Population:* 183 (1975). *Area:* 202,916 sq. mi. *Administrative Center:* Port-aux-Français (94) on Kerguélen.

These territories comprise a number of islands in the far southern Indian Ocean and Adélie Land on the Antarctic continent. The latter, with an area of 200,000 sq. mi., lies between 136° and 142°E. The Kerguélen Islands are between 48° and 50°S. and 68° and 70°E. The principal island, Kerguélen, has an area of 2,510 sq. mi. and is mostly mountainous. The Crozet Islands at 46°S. and between 50° and 52°E. are also mountainous, cold, windy, and inhospitable. Saint Paul Island is at 38°S. and 77°E. and its center is occupied by a large crater with volcanic hot springs. Amsterdam Island is at 37°S. and 70°E., and maintains a hospital.

The Territory, on which various research stations have been established, is under the authority of a high administrator assisted by a consultative council in Paris.

Gibraltar—*Status:* British Colony. *Population:* 29,000 (1978 est.). *Area:* 2.28 sq. mi. *Administrative Center:* Gibraltar.

Gibraltar is a tiny peninsula jutting into the western Mediterranean from Spain. It rises from a sandy plain to the 1,400-foot Rock, a cave-riddled, fortified limestone mass. The climate is temperate. The people are mostly of Genoese, Portuguese and Maltese descent. The language of the home is generally Spanish, with English the language of instruction in school. Most of the civilian population are Roman Catholics.

The colony has no natural resources other than its strategic position at the mouth of the Mediterranean, and is dependent on its naval and military bases, transshipments, dockyards, and tourist traffic.

Gibraltar is administered by a governor (also the commander of the fortress) appointed by the Crown, with the advice of the Gibraltar Council, the elected members of which compose a council of ministers presided over by a chief minister. There is also a partly elected House of Assembly.

Gibraltar was ceded in 1713 to Great Britain by Spain in the Treaty of Utrecht. Since 1964, Spain has been seeking its return, applying such pressures as the restriction of transit to and from the mainland. In a 1967 referendum, the people of Gibraltar voted overwhelmingly to retain the British connection. At the end of 1968, the UN General Assembly's Trusteeship Committee called on Britain to surrender control to Spain. Talks have been held between Britain and Spain on the Gibraltar question since 1972.

Greenland (Kalatdlit-Nunât)—*Status:* Semiautonomous state of the Danish Kingdom. *Population:* 49,000 (1978 est.). *Area:* 840,000 sq. mi. *Capital:* Nûk (Godthab) (8,995).

Greenland, the largest island in the world, lies northeast of Canada between the Arctic Ocean on the north and the Atlantic Ocean on the south. Its ice-free areas—the coastal strips plus the coastal islands—cover 132,000 sq. mi. The rest of Greenland is sheathed in ice at places 11,000 feet thick. The climate is arctic, with considerable variation in temperature between localities. The population, predominantly Eskimo, with some Europeans, lives mostly on the west coast. Danish and Greenlandic are the official languages. The principal occupations are fishing and hunting.

Home rule was established on May 1, 1979, with Denmark retaining control of defense and foreign affairs, and retaining mineral rights. A prime minister, the leader of the majority party in the 21-member parliament (*Landsting*) and four secretaries preside over the government (*Landsstyre*). Greenland sends two elected members to the Danish Parliament.

Guadeloupe—*Status:* French Overseas Department. *Population:* 319,000 (1979 est.). *Area:* 687 sq. mi. *Capital:* Basse-Terre (16,000) on the island of that name.

Guadeloupe lies in the Leeward Islands of the West Indies. In addition to Guadeloupe proper (584 sq. mi.), which a narrow channel divides into two islands, Basse-Terre and Grande-Terre, there are the nearby dependencies of Marie-Galante, La Désirade, Îles des Saintes, and Îsle de la Petite Terre. About 135 miles to the northwest are the dependencies of Saint Barthélemy and the French portion of Saint Martin.

Basse-Terre has a 4,000-foot active volcano, La Soufrière. Grande-Terre is low and encircled by coral reefs; it has the largest town in the department, Point-à-Pitre, twice the size of the capital. The climate is tropical, moderated by trade winds. Basse-Terre's mountains receive heavy rainfall, which feeds numerous streams. The people are blacks and, especially on the dependencies, descendants of Normans and Bretons who settled there in the 17th century, or a racial mixture.

The main crops are sugar and bananas, with cotton, sisal, coffee, vegetables and tropical fruits also grown. Fishing and rum production are significant activities.

Guadeloupe is administered by a Paris-appointed prefect and an elected general council; the department elects three deputies and two senators to the French Parliament.

There were serious riots in Guadeloupe in 1967, reportedly sparked by an organization advocating independence. French officials stated that Cuba was behind 1980 demonstrations on the island, later denied by Fidel Castro.

Heard and McDonald Islands—*Status:* Australian External Territory. *Population:* Uninhabited. *Area:* 113 sq. mi.

These islands lie in the south Indian Ocean, 2,575 miles southwest of Perth, Australia, at 53°S., 73°E. Heard Island is mountainous, the McDonald Islands, small and rocky.

Hong Kong—*Status:* British Colony. *Population:* 4,606,000 (1978 est.). *Area:* 403 sq. mi. *Capital:* Victoria (658,042) on the island of Hong Kong.

The colony is on the southern coast of China about 80 miles southeast of Canton, and surrounded by the Chinese province of Guangdong. It includes Hong Kong proper, an island of about 30 sq. mi., many other islands, and Kowloon and the New Territories on the mainland. The New Territories (370 sq. mi., including a number of small islands) are held under a 99-year lease from China, which expires in 1997. Most of the area is either swampy or rocky and hilly. The climate is subtropical, with hot, humid summers and heavy rainfall, but can be chilly January to April.

The population density of Hong Kong is very high, as more than 80 percent of the people live in the urban area. An overwhelming number of them are Chinese, including more than a million refugees. (English and Chinese are both official languages.)

Hong Kong is a major center for shipping, banking, commerce and industry, situated as it is at a crossroad of world trade. Light industries, particularly machinery, textiles and clothing, are important. Tourism is important and growing. Agriculture and fishing are intensively practiced, but much food must be imported, mostly from China. A large part of the water supply must also be brought in from China. A tunnel now links Hong Kong Island with the mainland.

Hong Kong is administered by a Crown-appointd governor, advised by executive and legislative councils. Communist China officially claims Hong Kong.

Isle of Man—*Status:* British Crown Fiefdom. *Population:* 63,000 (1978 est.). *Area:* 227 sq. mi. *Capital:* Douglas (20,262).

Situated in the Irish Sea, the Isle of Man is about 35 miles from Northern Ireland and the northwest coast of England. The central mass consists of treeless hills, extending in the north and south to low-lying agricultural land. The climate is pleasant, with mild winters and cool summers. Wesleyan Methodists predominate, but there are Roman Catholics and members of the Church of England.

By far the most important factor in the economy is the tourist trade. The major export is kippered herring, processed from fish landed by a Scottish fleet. Oats are the main crop, and there is sheep raising and dairying.

The Isle is administered under its own laws (Acts of Parliament do not apply unless they specifically so note). The ruling body is the Court of Tynwald, composed of the Crown-appointed governor, a legislative council, and the elected House of Keys.

Jan Mayen—*Status:* Norwegian Dependency. *Population:* Uninhabited. *Area:* 143 sq. mi.

This island 300 miles north-northeast of Iceland at 71°N.,8°30′W. is bleak and desolate. The Norwegian government operates radio, meteorological, and navigational stations at the South Lagoon, and since 1963 an airstrip has been maintained. In 1980 Norway and Iceland settled their dispute over the offshore area around Jan Mayen.

Juan Fernández—*Status:* Chilean Dependency. *Population:* 540. *Area:* 70 sq. mi. (the two main islands). *Administrative Center:* Juan Bautista, on Robinson Crusoe Island.

This island group is in the Pacific Ocean some 360 miles west of Valparaíso, Chile. Volcanic in origin, rugged and wooded, it was discovered in 1572 by Juan Fernández, a Spanish explorer. The two main islands, about 100 miles apart from east to west, are Robinson Crusoe (33°45′S.,79°W.) and Alejandro Selkirk (33°45′S.,80°45′W.). Lobster fishing is the main occupation.

Daniel Defoe's *Robinson Crusoe* is generally acknowledged to have been inspired by Alexander Selkirk's stay on Robinson Crusoe Island (1704-09).

Macao—*Status:* Portuguese Overseas Province. *Population:* 276,000 (1978 est.). *Area:* 6.2 sq. mi. *Capital:* Macao (226,880).

Macao or Macau (*Ao-men* in Chinese) is situated on a small peninsula of the south coast of China. It lies at the mouth of the Pearl (Canton) River and 40 miles west of Hong Kong; the province also includes two small islands. Macao proper is almost entirely urban, the islands forested. The climate is hot and humid, but sea breezes make the temperatures tolerable. Only about 10 percent of the population is Portuguese, the rest is Chinese.

Macao is almost completely dependent on imported food, mostly from China. Fishing, commerce, and, in recent years, light industry—textiles and clothing—are important. Macao is one of the few entirely free gold markets in the world, and trade in coin and bullion is a notable activity. There is a brisk tourist trade, some attracted by Macao's gambling houses—which accounted for one-third of total government income in 1977.

The province is administered by a Lisbon-appointed governor, a council, which serves as a cabinet, and a partially elected 18-member provincial council, the *Leal Senado*. China still officially claims dominion over Macao.

Martinique—*Status:* French Overseas Department. *Population:* 315,000 (1979 est.). *Area:* 425 sq. mi. *Capital:* Fort-de-France (98,561).

This island is in the West Indies some 130 miles south of Guadeloupe. It is largely mountainous, and its two highest peaks are active volcanoes. In 1902, Mount Pelée erupted and destroyed the city of St-Pierre. The climate is tropical, tempered by the trade winds. The people are descendants of blacks, Europeans, and Carib Indians.

Martinique's economy is agricultural, with sugarcane, pineapples and bananas being the principal crops. Rum is distilled, and there is livestock raising and fishing. Tourism is increasing. The economy is heavily dependent on direct and indirect French subsidies, and substantial emigration to France has not solved the island's stubborn unemployment problem. Efforts have been made for some time to broaden and diversify Martinique's economic base. Yet demand for Martinique's major export crops is leveling off at a time when the number of young persons coming into the labor market is increasing as a result of a higher birthrate since the 1940s.

Martinique's international airport is its primary link with principal cities in France, the United States, and elsewhere. The island also is visited by numerous oceangoing vessels and cruise ships.

Administration is in the hands of a Paris-appointed prefect with the aid of an elected general council of 36 members. Martinique elects three deputies and two senators to the French Parliament.

Strike violence in 1980 was blamed on Cuba; France flew in 225 elite police to assist in putting it down. Later France and Cuba concluded an economic agreement, and Cuba's Castro said he had not intervened and would not do so in Martinique.

Mayotte—*Status:* French Territorial Collectivity. *Population:* 47,300 (1978 census). *Area:* 144 sq. mi. *Capital:* Dzaoudzi.

The easternmost of the Comoro Islands in the Indian Ocean (13°S.,45°E.), Mayotte is a volcanic island surrounded by coral reefs and islets, with a tropical climate. The population is of African, Arab, and Malagasy origin, and the majority are Moslems. French, Arabic, and Swahili are spoken. Most of the people are engaged in the production of such agricultural products as vanilla, sisal, sugarcane, essential oils, and rum.

An Arab dynasty from Shiraz reigned from the 16th century to 1843, when a French colony was established. It was attached first to Réunion and later to Madagascar as a part of the Comoro Islands territory. When a future Comoro Islands referendum was first announced in 1974, Mayotte was the only island to vote against it, and after the unilateral declaration of independence in 1975, Mayotte refused to be considered a part of the new republic. In 1976 an island referendum resulted in 99.41 percent voting to remain French, and two months later the status as a French Territorial Collectivity was approved. The island sends one deputy to the French Parliament.

Montserrat—*Status:* British Crown Colony. *Population:* 11,000 (1978 est.). *Area:* 40 sq. mi. *Capital:* Plymouth (1,300).

Situated in the Leeward Islands of the West Indies, Montserrat is 260 miles southeast of Puerto Rico and north of Guadeloupe. In 1493, on his second voyage, Christopher Columbus reached the island and gave it its present name, after the mountaintop monastery in Spain. It has elevations of more than 3,000 feet, and the climate is tropical and humid. The people are mostly of Negro-white descent. English is the formal language and everywhere understood, but a patois is commonly spoken. As a result of an Irish settlement in the 1630s, many people on the island speak with a brogue.

The island is agricultural, sugar being the main export crop, and cotton and bananas also being grown. Yams, rice, breadfruit, and corn are raised for food. Tourism is of increasing economic importance.

There is a Crown-appointed governor, an executive council and a partly elected legislative council. In 1967, Montserrat elected to remain a British colony.

Namibia—*Status:* In dispute; administered by South Africa. *Population:* 1,000,000 (1979 est.). *Area:* 317,827 sq. mi. *Capital:* Windhoek (61,369).

Namibia (formerly South-West Africa) is bounded by Angola on the north, by Zambia on the northeast, by Botswana on the east, by South Africa on the east and south, and by the Atlantic Ocean on the west. The Namib Desert, stretching for 1,000 miles along the coast, is uninhabited except for three towns, including the South African enclave of Walvis Bay (434 sq. mi.), and the diamond workings at the mouth of the Orange River in the south. The Kalahari Desert of sand and limestone is on the east. The Caprivi Strip, 20 to 60 miles wide and some 300 miles long, extends from the northeast corner of the country and separates Botswana from Angola. The greater part of the country consists of a plateau, averaging 3,600 feet, with scattered mountains. The climate is generally hot and dry. There are only a few rivers and water must generally be obtained from boreholes. The people are largely African of various tribal groups, including Ovambo, Damara, Herero, Nama, and Bushmen. Whites are a minority of about 15 percent, mostly of South African and German descent. There is a smaller number of mixed descent, including the Rehoboth Bastards, of Nama-white ancestry. In general, the whites live in the Police Zone in the south, the native population in homelands in the north. Official languages are Afrikaans and English, but German is widely used, as are tribal languages.

Parts of the nonwhite population follow the traditional animist religions, although many Africans have been converted to Christianity. Missionary activity, which began in the 1800s, encompasses several denominations, including Lutheran, Roman Catholic, Methodist, Anglican, and Dutch Reformed.

Diamonds are Namibia's most valuable economic product, and copper, zinc, lead, uranium, cadmium, and manganese are also mined. Sheep, cattle, and goats are raised, and the production of karakul sheep pelts is increasingly important. The annual haul of fish has reached over three-quarters of a million tons.

South-West Africa had been mandated to South African administration by the League of Nations. When the UN Trusteeship System was established in 1945, South Africa refused to place South-West Africa under it (it was the only such case), claiming that the UN was not the legal successor to the League. In 1966 the UN General Assembly declared that the mandate was terminated; in 1967 it established a council to administer the area until independence; and in 1968 it proclaimed that the area be renamed Namibia. South Africa, however, declaring that the removal of the mandate was an "illegal act" because the UN charter makes no provision for such a move, announced its intention to continue administration, and has done so even after a 1971 ruling against its position by the International Court of Justice.

In January 1976, the UN Security Council voted to invoke mandatory sanctions against South Africa if it failed to accept a UN-supervised election leading to independence. In August the South African government announced plans for a multiracial Namibian government to bring about independence by December 31, 1978. Inasmuch as the South African proposal did not mention a specific date for elections, both the UN and the powerful guerrilla group, the South-West Africa People's Organization (SWAPO) rejected the plan. At a conference in the Turnhalle in Windhoek in August 1976, South Africa announced that it intended to set up an interim government. Sanctions against South Africa for not withdrawing were vetoed in the UN. In 1977 the United States, Britain, France, Canada and West Germany began diplomatic efforts to arrive at an independence plan acceptable to both South Africa and SWAPO. South Africa agreed to the Western plan in April, but SWAPO withheld its consent after a South African raid on its bases in Angola. Further efforts were made by the Western powers, and SWAPO's agreement was secured in July with the help of five black-ruled "front-line" states. Under the plan, all South African troops would be withdrawn except for 1,500 men who would be restricted to camps near the Angolan border. A United Nations force of 5,000 men would be sent into the territory to insure a free election, after which the territory would become independent. In the period leading up to the election, the territory would be administered jointly by a South African administrator and a UN representative. A dispute has arisen between South Africa and SWAPO over the Walvis Bay enclave, the future status of which was not determined in the Western powers' plan.

Negotiations between the UN and South Africa continued throughout 1978, 1979 and into 1980 without resolution of their differences regarding Namibian independence, originally scheduled for Dec. 31, 1978. A South African-sponsored election in Namibia in early Dec. 1978 elected a 50-member constituent assembly, with the Democratic Turnhalle Alliance winning 41 seats. SWAPO did not vote, and the UN Security Council declared the election null and void. The assembly, later known as the South-West African-Namibian National Assembly, met on May 21, with limited legislative powers, while South Africa retained ultimate powers over the territory. In May 1980 South Africa announced its willingness to cooperate in implementing the 1977 peace plan, but demanded assurances that the UN would not favor SWAPO.

Netherlands Antilles—*Status:* Autonomous Part of the Kingdom of the Netherlands. *Population:* 246,000 (1978 est.). *Area:* 390 sq. mi. *Capital:* Willemstad (95,000) on Curaçao.

The Netherlands Antilles, in the Caribbean, consists of two groups of three islands each: Curaçao, Aruba, and Bonaire, 15 to 38 miles off the northern coast of Venezuela; and Saba, St. Eustatius, and St. Maarten, which shares an island with the French St. Martin, more than 500 miles to the northeast. Curaçao and Aruba are by far the most populous and important. On these two islands, Dutch, English, Spanish, and Papiamento (a mixture of the three) are spoken.

The Leewards are semiarid and flat; the Windwards are mountainous, with enough rainfall for flourishing vegetation. The climate is warm and humid. The people are largely blacks, or Carib Indians, or either of these mixed with white strains. Dutch is the official language, and English is current in the Windwards. Papiamento is common. Catholicism predominates on the Leeward Islands, Protestantism on the Windward.

Curaçao and Aruba, with a higher per capita income than the Netherlands, owe their prosperity to oil refineries, which process crude oil from Venezuela. The refineries also stimulate other industries and commerce on the two islands. After oil refining, tourism is their most important economic factor. On Curaçao and Aruba little farming is possible because the land is so rocky. Most food is imported. On the other islands, small-scale agriculture and fishing are pursued.

In an effort to lessen dependence on the petroleum industry, the government has been attempting to attract new industries by offering tax holidays and customs exceptions to firms locating there and by creating free zones on Curaçao and Aruba.

Fully autonomous in internal affairs, the Netherlands Antilles are constitutionally equal with the Netherlands. There is a governor, who represents the sovereign, and a council of ministers—headed by a prime minister—which is responsible to an elected legislature (*Staten*). Aruba, Curaçao, Bonaire, and the Windward group each have autonomy in local affairs.

In 1974, Juancho Evertsz, premier of the Netherlands Antilles, met with the Dutch premier at The Hague to discuss the future status of the islands. It was decided that they would wait at least until 1980 to achieve independent status. In 1977, Aruba held its own referendum, with 57 percent voting for separate independence. In 1979, a two-day strike by police and firemen led the government of Premier Silvios Rosendal to resign. The New Antilles Movement, a coalition of trade unions, won the subsequent elections, both in the local council in Curaçao and throughout the islands, and its head, Don Martina, became the premier.

New Caledonia—*Status:* French Overseas Territory. *Population:* 137,000 (1979 est.). *Area:* 7,335 sq. mi. *Capital:* Nouméa (74,335).

This group of about 25 islands in the South Pacific is situated about 750 miles east of Australia. The territory takes its name from the main island, New Caledonia or Grande-Terre (22°S.,166°E.), which is 6,530 square miles in area and mountainous. The territory includes the dependencies of Île des Pins, Loyalty Islands, Île Huon, Îles Belep, Îles Chesterfield, and Île Walpole. The British explorer, James Cook, was the first European to visit New Caledonia (1774). Other Europeans followed. In 1853, France took over control and, eleven years later, turned it into a prison colony. The climate is mildly tropical, tempered by the trade winds. About half the people are Australo-Melanesian indigenes. Most of the rest are of French descent or are Polynesians.

Agriculture and mining are the basic economic activities. Coffee and copra are the commercial crops, while root plants, wheat, corn, fruits, and vegetables are also grown, but food must be imported. Nickel is mined on a large scale, and iron and chrome are also exploited.

Administration is in the hands of a Paris-appointed governor. In 1979 a new Territorial Assembly of 36 elected members was established. Independence cannot come before 1989. Two deputies and a senator are elected to the French Parliament.

Niue—*Status:* New Zealand Territory. *Population:* 4,000 (1979 est.). *Area:* 100 sq. mi. *Administrative Center:* Alofi (957).

Niue is in the South Pacific some 1,340 miles northeast of New Zealand (19°S.,170°W.); although geographically associated with the Cook Islands, its distance and cultural differences have led to separate administration. Niue is a coral island with fertile but sparse soil. The climate is hot and the islands suffer from hurricanes. The people are of Polynesian stock, speaking Samoan.

There is an appointed resident commissioner, a prime minister and cabinet, and an elected island assembly. Niue became self-governing on September 3, 1974.

Norfolk Island—*Status:* Australian External Territory. *Population:* 2,180 (1979 est.). *Area:* 13.3 sq. mi. *Administrative Center:* Kingston.

The island lies in the South Pacific 930 miles northeast of Sydney, Australia (29°S.,168°E.). Many of its inhabitants are descendants of H.M.S. *Bounty* mutineers, who were moved here in 1856 when they became too numerous for Pitcairn Island. Fruits and bean seed are grown and tourism is important. There is an Australian-appointed administrator and an elected Legislative Assembly.

Peter I Island—*Status:* Norwegian Dependency. *Population:* Uninhabited. *Area:* 96 sq. mi.

An Antarctic island, it is southwest of the South Shetland Islands, at 68°47'S and 90°35'W. It is of volcanic origin and almost entirely ice-covered.

Pitcairn Islands—*Status:* British Colony. *Population:* 65 (1979 est.). *Area:* 18 sq. mi. *Administrative Center:* Adamstown.

The colony is in the South Pacific, 4,000 miles southwest of the Panama Canal and 3,200 miles northeast of New Zealand. There are four islands: Pitcairn (1.75 sq. mi.), Henderson, Ducie, and Oeno, of which only Pitcairn (25°05'S.,130°05'W.) is inhabited. The climate is warm throughout the year. The people are descendants of H.M.S. *Bounty* mutineers and Polynesian women from Tahiti. The inhabitants were resettled on Norfolk Island in 1856 when their numbers grew too large for Pitcairn, but several families of them returned soon after.

Subsistence agriculture and fishing are the main occupations. Some fruits, vegetables, and handicrafts are sold to passing ships.

The colony is administered by the British High Commissioner in New Zealand with the assistance of a partly elected island council, presided over by an island magistrate.

Queen Maud Land—*Status:* Norwegian Dependency. *Population:* Uninhabited.

The portion of Antarctica between 20°W and 45°E, it is claimed by Norway.

Réunion—*Status:* French Overseas Department. *Population:* 489,000 (1979 est.). *Area:* 969 sq. mi. *Capital:* Saint-Denis (103,513).

An island in the Indian Ocean (21°S.,55°30'E.), it is about 400 miles east of Madagascar. Réunion is of volcanic origin and mountainous, the highest peak—Piton des Neiges—rising to more than 10,000 feet. One of its volcanoes is still active. There are many torrential rivers. The climate is essentially tropical, but varies greatly with altitude and exposure to the trade winds. Rainfall is heavy, and there are severe tropical storms. The people are of Malabar Indian, African, Malay, Vietnamese, Chinese, and French descent; the last make up about 20 percent of the population. Ninety-four percent of the population is Roman Catholic.

The cultivation of sugarcane is the main economic activity. Essential oils from geranium and vetiver plants are also important. Corn, potatoes and beans are grown for consumption, but food must be imported.

Réunion is administered by a Paris-appointed prefect and an elected general council; the island elects three deputies and two senators to the French Parliament.

Ross Dependency—*Status:* New Zealand Territory. *Population:* No permanent inhabitants. *Area:* 290,000 sq. mi. (of which 130,000 sq. mi. are ice shelf).

New Zealand claims that portion of Antarctica south of 60°S between 160°E and 150°W.

There are research and exploration activities in the area, and whaling in its territorial waters.

Saint Christopher-Nevis—*Status:* British Associated State. *Population:* 60,000 (1980 est.). *Area:* 120 sq. mi. *Capital:* Basseterre (12,771) on St. Christopher.

In the Leeward Islands of the West Indies, it includes St. Christopher (commonly called St. Kitts; 68 sq. mi.), Nevis (50 sq. mi.), and Sombrero (2 sq. mi.). The climate of the islands is tropical and humid. The people are largely of mixed black-white descent. English is the formal language, but a patois is commonly spoken.

Sugar, molasses, and cotton are the chief exports. Yams, rice, breadfruit, and corn are grown for food. Tourism is increasingly important.

There is a Crown-appointed governor, a prime minister, and a partially elected house of assembly. In 1975 separatist delegates from Nevis won their assembly seats. Although Anguilla became a self-governing British colony in 1976, it legally remains a part of the associated state of St. Christopher-Nevis-Anguilla. In talks in London in December 1979, it was decided that St. Kitts-Nevis should proceed toward independence in 1980. It was agreed that a referendum would be held 18 months after independence to determine whether Nevis wants to stay within the state.

Saint Helena—*Status:* British Colony. *Population:* 6,400 (1977 est.). *Area:* 162 sq. mi. *Capital:* Jamestown (1,601).

The island of Saint Helena (47 sq. mi.) is in the southeastern Atlantic about 1,200 miles from Africa, at 16°S. and 5°21'W. Its dependencies—Tristan da Cunha (38 sq.

mi.) and Ascension (34 sq. mi.)—are about 1,500 miles south-southwest and 750 miles northwest, respectively. Near Tristan da Cunha are the uninhabited islands of Gough, Nightingale, and Inaccessible. St. Helena is rocky, with a pleasant climate due to the trade winds. It was the place of Napoleon's exile from 1815 until his death in 1821. Tristan da Cunha suffered a volcanic eruption in 1961, and the tiny population of 248 was resettled in England. They suffered from respiratory diseases in that climate, however, and returned to their island in 1963. The people of the colony are of mixed origin, and their language is English.

St. Helena grows flax, fodder, and vegetables. Potatoes are the staple subsistence crop on Tristan da Cunha. Ascension is an important cable and missile tracking station.

The colony is administered by a Crown-appointed governor, assisted by an executive council and a partly elected legislative council.

Saint Kitts-Nevis: *See* Saint Christopher-Nevis.

Saint Pierre and Miquelon—*Status:* French Overseas Department. *Population:* 5,900 (1977 est.). *Area:* 93.5 sq. mi. *Capital:* Saint Pierre (5,232) on St. Pierre.

This archipelago lies some 15 miles south of Newfoundland in the North Atlantic. There are three main islands, Saint Pierre, Miquelon, and Langlade, the latter two connected by a low isthmus. Although volcanic in origin, the islands are low-lying. The climate is cool to cold, with seasons of strong winds and heavy fogs; there is a good deal of rain and snow. The people are mostly descendants of Breton, Norman, and Basque settlers.

The chief occupation is cod fishing, together with fish freezing and fish meal production.

The department is administered by a Paris-appointed prefect, aided by a privy council. There is an elected general council, and a deputy and a senator are elected to the French Parliament.

Sala y Gómez Island—*Status:* Chilean Dependency. *Population:* Uninhabited. *Area:* .05 sq. mi.

In the Pacific Ocean at 26°28'S.,105°28'W., some 2,100 miles west of Chile and 250 miles east of Easter Island, Sala y Gómez, an arid island of volcanic origin, is administered by Valparaíso Province.

San Ambrosio Island and San Félix Island—*Status:* Chilean Dependencies. *Population:* Uninhabited. *Area:* 1.29 sq. mi.

These two small islands—some 12 miles apart—are in the Pacific Ocean at 26°20'S.,80°W., about 600 miles west of Chile. They were discovered by the Spanish navigator, Juan Fernández, in 1574, and are administered by Atacama Province.

Svalbard—*Status:* Norwegian Dependency. *Population:* 3,431 (1975 est.). *Area:* 23,957 sq. mi. *Administrative Center:* Longyearbyen.

Svalbard is the name of an island territory in the Arctic Ocean between 74° and 81°N and 10° and 35°E. By far the most important of these islands is the Spitsbergen group, the largest of which are Spitsbergen, North East Land, Edge Island, and Barents Island. The islands are bleak and rugged, largely covered with ice running to the sea in glaciers. The climate is moderated, however, by winds from the Atlantic, and the Gulf Stream keeps open water for six months of the year. About two-thirds of the people are Russians who live in mining camps, the rest are Norwegians. Coal is the principal product.

Tokelau—*Status:* New Zealand Territory. *Population:* 1,625 (1977 est.). *Area:* 3.95 sq. mi. *Administrative Center:* Fenuafala (649) on Fakaofo.

These islands are in the South Pacific at 9°S.,172°W., 2,100 miles northeast of New Zealand, 300 miles north of Samoa. Geographically the group consists of four atolls—Atafu, Nukunono, Fakaofo, and Swains—but the last belongs to American Samoa. The people are of Polynesian origin. Their language, now dying, resembles Samoan, the official language.

Subsistence farming and copra production for export are the main occupations. Revenue is also derived from the sale of postage stamps.

The islands are administrated by the New Zealand Minister for Foreign Affairs. An islands' administrator exercises all executive and administrative functions.

Turks and Caicos Islands—*Status:* British Colony. *Population:* 6,000 (1978 est.). *Area:* 166 sq. mi. *Capital:* Cockburn Town (2,287), on Grand Turk.

Geographically part of the Bahamas, of which they form the southeastern groups, the Turks and Caicos lie in the Atlantic Ocean some 575 miles southeast of Florida. Of the 30 or so small islands, only six are inhabited, among them Grand Turk, Grand Caicos, and Salt Cay. The climate is hot, dry, and subject to hurricanes. The people are almost all of African descent.

Fishing and salt production are economic staples.

The administration of the islands is under a Crown-appointed governor and a partly elected state council.

Wallis and Futuna—*Status:* French Overseas Territory. *Population:* 9,162 (1976 census). *Area:* 106 sq. mi. *Capital:* Mata Utu (566) on Wallis.

These two small island groups are in the South Pacific,

Wallis (13°18′S.,176°10′W.) and its surrounding uninhabited islands being about 250 miles west of Samoa, while Futuna (14°19′S.,178°05′W.) and the uninhabited Alofi island are some 120 miles to the southwest. The islands are of volcanic origin. The climate is tropical, mitigated by sea breezes, with seasonal hurricanes. The people are mostly Polynesians. The principal crop is copra.

The territory is administered by a Paris-appointed high administrator, advised by a territorial council which includes the three traditional chiefs of the islands. A territorial assembly is elected, as are a deputy and a senator to the French Parliament.

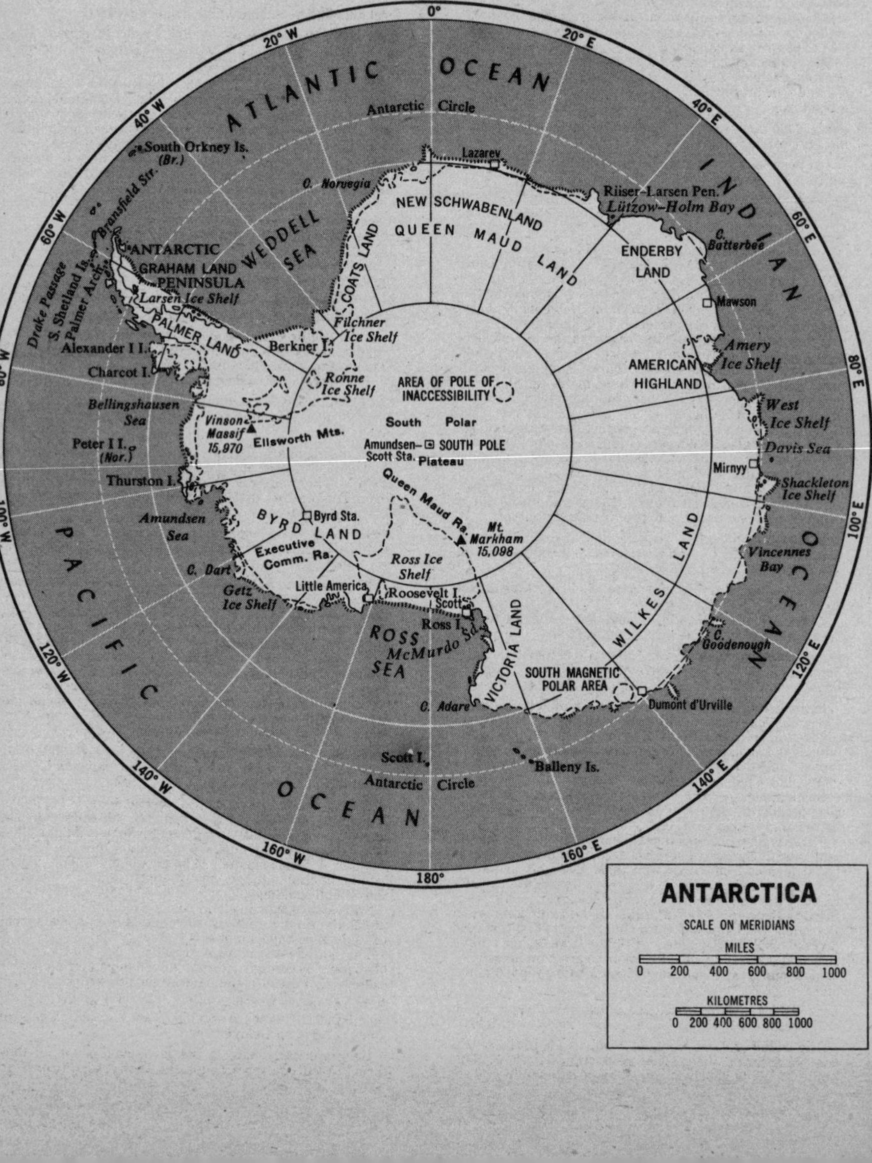

ANTARCTICA

SCALE ON MERIDIANS

MILES

0 200 400 600 800 1000

KILOMETRES

0 200 400 600 800 1000

DIPLOMATIC AFFAIRS

ROSTER OF THE UNITED NATIONS: 1980 (153 Members as of September 1)

Member Nation	Date of Admission		Member Nation	Date of Admission		Member Nation	Date of Admission	
Afghanistan	19 Nov.	1946	Germany (Fed. Rep.)	18 Sept.	1973	Pakistan	30 Sept.	1947
Albania	14 Dec.	1955	Ghana	8 Mar.	1957	Panama	13 Nov.	1945
Algeria	8 Oct.	1962	Greece	25 Oct.	1945	Papua New Guinea	10 Oct.	1975
Angola	1 Dec.	1976	Grenada	17 Sept.	1974	Paraguay	24 Oct.	1945
Argentina	24 Oct.	1945	Guatemala	21 Nov.	1945	Peru	31 Oct.	1945
Australia	1 Nov.	1945	Guinea	12 Dec.	1958	Philippines	24 Oct.	1945
Austria	14 Dec.	1955	Guinea-Bissau	17 Sept.	1974	Poland	24 Oct.	1945
Bahamas	18 Sept.	1973	Guyana	20 Sept.	1966	Portugal	14 Dec.	1955
Bahrain	21 Sept.	1971	Haiti	24 Oct.	1945	Qatar	21 Sept.	1971
Bangladesh	17 Sept.	1974	Honduras	17 Dec.	1945	Romania	14 Dec.	1955
Barbados	9 Dec.	1966	Hungary	14 Dec.	1955	Rwanda	18 Sept.	1962
Belgium	27 Dec.	1945	Iceland	19 Nov.	1946	Saint Lucia	18 Sept.	1979
Benin	20 Sept.	1960	India	30 Oct.	1945	São Tomé and Príncipe	16 Sept.	1965
Bhutan	21 Sept.	1971	Indonesia	28 Sept.	1950	Saudi Arabia	24 Oct.	1945
Bolivia	14 Nov.	1945	Iran	24 Oct.	1945	Senegal	28 Sept.	1960
Botswana	17 Oct.	1966	Iraq	21 Dec.	1945	Seychelles	21 Sept.	1976
Brazil	24 Oct.	1945	Ireland	14 Dec.	1955	Sierra Leone	27 Sept.	1961
Bulgaria	14 Dec.	1955	Israel	11 May	1949	Singapore	21 Sept.	1965
Burma	19 Apr.	1948	Italy	14 Dec.	1955	Solomon Islands	19 Sept.	1978
Burundi	18 Sept.	1962	Ivory Coast	20 Sept.	1960	Somalia	20 Sept.	1960
Byelorussian SSR	24 Oct.	1945	Jamaica	18 Sept.	1962	South Africa	7 Nov.	1945
Cambodia (Kampuchea)	14 Dec.	1955	Japan	18 Dec.	1956	Spain	14 Dec.	1955
Cameroon	20 Sept.	1960	Jordan	14 Dec.	1955	Sri Lanka	14 Dec.	1955
Canada	9 Nov.	1945	Kenya	16 Dec.	1963	Sudan	12 Nov.	1956
Cape Verde	16 Sept.	1975	Kuwait	14 May	1963	Suriname	4 Dec.	1975
Central African Republic	20 Sept.	1960	Laos	14 Dec.	1955	Swaziland	24 Sept.	1968
Chad	20 Sept.	1960	Lebanon	24 Oct.	1945	Sweden	19 Nov.	1946
Chile	24 Oct.	1945	Lesotho	17 Oct.	1966	Syria	24 Oct.	1945
China	24 Oct.	1945	Liberia	2 Nov.	1945	Tanzania	14 Dec.	1961
Colombia	5 Nov.	1945	Libya	14 Dec.	1955	Thailand	16 Dec.	1946
Comoros	12 Nov.	1975	Luxembourg	24 Oct.	1945	Togo	20 Sept.	1960
Congo	20 Sept.	1960	Madagascar	20 Sept.	1960	Trinidad and Tobago	18 Sept.	1962
Costa Rica	2 Nov.	1945	Malawi	1 Dec.	1964	Tunisia	12 Nov.	1956
Cuba	24 Oct.	1945	Malaysia	17 Sept.	1957	Turkey	24 Oct.	1945
Cyprus	20 Sept.	1960	Maldives	21 Sept.	1965	Uganda	25 Oct.	1962
Czechoslovakia	24 Oct.	1945	Mali	28 Sept.	1960	Ukrainian SSR	24 Oct.	1945
Denmark	24 Oct.	1945	Malta	1 Dec.	1964	USSR	24 Oct.	1945
Djibouti	20 Sept.	1977	Mauritania	27 Oct.	1961	United Arab Emirates	9 Dec.	1971
Dominica	18 Dec.	1978	Mauritius	24 Apr.	1968	United Kingdom	24 Oct.	1945
Dominican Republic	24 Oct.	1945	Mexico	7 Nov.	1945	United States	24 Oct.	1945
Ecuador	21 Dec.	1945	Mongolia	27 Oct.	1961	Upper Volta	20 Sept.	1960
Egypt	24 Oct.	1945	Morocco	12 Nov.	1956	Uruguay	18 Dec.	1945
El Salvador	24 Oct.	1945	Mozambique	16 Sept.	1975	Venezuela	15 Nov.	1945
Equatorial Guinea	12 Nov.	1968	Nepal	14 Dec.	1955	Vietnam	20 Sept.	1977
Ethiopia	13 Nov.	1945	Netherlands	10 Dec.	1945	Western Samoa	15 Dec.	1976
Fiji	13 Oct.	1970	New Zealand	24 Oct.	1945	Yemen	30 Sept.	1947
Finland	14 Dec.	1955	Nicaragua	24 Oct.	1945	Yemen (Southern Yemen)	14 Dec.	1967
France	24 Oct.	1945	Niger	20 Sept.	1960	Yugoslavia	20 Oct.	1945
Gabon	20 Sept.	1960	Nigeria	7 Oct.	1960	Zaïre	20 Sept.	1960
Gambia	21 Sept.	1965	Norway	27 Nov.	1945	Zambia	1 Dec.	1964
Germany (Dem. Rep.)	18 Sept.	1973	Oman	7 Oct.	1971	Zimbabwe	25 Aug.	1980

PRINCIPAL ORGANS OF THE UNITED NATIONS

There are six principal organs of the UN: the General Assembly, the Security Council, the Economic and Social Council, the Trusteeship Council, the International Court of Justice, and the Secretariat. The official languages in all these organs, other than the International Court of Justice, are Chinese, English, French, Russian, and Spanish. Working languages are English and French, with the addition of Russian, Spanish and Chinese in the General Assembly and the Security Council and Spanish in the Economic and Social Council. Arabic is an official and working language in the General Assembly. The official languages in the International Court of Justice are English and French.

General Assembly

The UN's main deliberative body, the General Assembly, consists of all member states, each of which has one vote. Any question may be discussed that is within the scope of the UN Charter or relates to the functions of any organ provided for in the Charter, as well as any questions on international peace and security that are brought up by a member, by the Security Council, or by a nonmember, if that state accepts in advance obligations of pacific settlement. The General Assembly may make recommendations to member states or to the Security Council with one exception: it may not make recommendations on any dispute under consideration by the Security Council unless the Council so requests.

Regular sessions of the Assembly convene once a year, commencing on the third Tuesday in September. There is provision for special and emergency special sessions. Voting is by simple majority of those present and voting, except on questions adjudged important, when a two-thirds majority is required. The Assembly controls the finances of the UN; it also elects the 10 nonpermanent members of the Security Council, all the members of the Economic and Social Council, and—with, but independently of, the Security Council—the International Court of Justice. On Security Council recommendations, the Secretary-General is appointed by the General Assembly.

The assembly elects its president and 17 vice-presidents for each session and adopts its own rules of procedure. It distributes most agenda items among its seven main committees (see list below). There is also a General Committee that organizes the work of each session, a Credentials Committee, an Advisory Committee on Administrative and Budgetary Questions, and a Committee on Contributions, which recommends the scale of members' payments to the UN. They may establish ad hoc and subsidiary bodies such as the Conference on Trade and Development (UNCTAD).

General Assembly Main Committee Chairmen, 34th Session:

First Committee (Political and Security) — Davidson L. Hepburn (Bahamas)

Special Political Committee — Hammoud El-Choufi (Syria)

Second Committee (Economic and Financial) — Constin Murgescu (Romania)

Third Committee (Social, Humanitarian and Cultural) — Samir I. Sobhy (Egypt)

Fourth Committee (Decolonization) — Thomas S. Boya (Benin)

Fifth Committee (Administrative and Budgetary) — André Xavier Pirson (Belgium)

Sixth Committee (Legal) — Pracha Guna-Kasem (Thailand)

Assembly Actions of the 34th Session:

The opening session of the UN General Assembly took place on September 18, 1979. Salem Ahmed Salem of Tanzania was elected president of the Assembly by acclamation. St. Lucia, a former British colony in the Caribbean, was admitted to the UN at that opening session. The membership of the world body was raised to 153 on August 25, 1980, when Zimbabwe was admitted to the UN.

SOUTHERN AFRICA — As in previous years the Assembly passed a number of resolutions condemning South Africa for apartheid and colonial policies in southern Africa. South Africa's raids against Angola and independence movements in Namibia (South-West Africa) were also subjects of the Assembly's deliberations.

MIDDLE EAST — The Assembly condemned Israeli actions in occupied Arab territories, and in November 1979, voted to reject the Egyptian-Israeli peace pact.

IRAN — When Iranian militants seized the U.S. embassy in Tehran in November 1979, the Assembly urged Iran to release the U.S. hostages. On December 17 the General Assembly adopted a convention, already in work before the crisis, to outlaw the taking of hostages.

AFGHANISTAN — The Soviet Union's invasion of Afghanistan in December 1979 was deplored in debate in the Assembly and although the Soviet Union was not named directly, the Assembly passed a resolution which demanded the exit of foreign troops from Afghanistan.

CAMBODIA — The Assembly allowed the ousted Cambodian government of Pol Pot to keep its Assembly seat, and voted on November 14, 1979 to demand the withdrawal of all Vietnamese troops in Cambodia. China supported the resolution while the USSR opposed it.

OTHER MATTERS — The General Assembly found itself unable to choose between Cuba and Colombia as the 15th member of the 1980 session of the Security Council. On January 7, 1980, the impasse was broken with the selection of Mexico to fill the vacant seat on the Council. Pope John Paul II addressed the General Assembly on October 2, 1979 and Cuban President Fidel Castro addressed the Assembly on October 12, 1979.

Security Council

There are 15 members on the Security Council, five of them permanent—The People's Republic of China, France, the USSR, the United Kingdom, and the United States—and 10 elected by the General Assembly for two-year terms and ineligible for immediate reelection. As of August 1980 the ten nonpermanent members were: Bangladesh, Germany (Dem. Rep.), Jamaica, Mexico, Niger, Norway, Philippines, Portugal, Tanzania and Zambia.

The council bears primary responsibility under the UN Charter for the maintenance of international peace and security. It may investigate any situation bearing the seeds of international friction. These may be brought to its attention by any UN member, by any nonmember accepting in advance the obligations of pacific settlement, by the General Assembly, or by the Secretary-General.

Having determined the existence of a threat to peace, the council may make recommendations, or may call on members to take such measures as economic sanctions or other steps short of armed force. Should these be inadequate, the council may take military action against an aggressor; all members agree under the charter to make available to the council, in accordance with agreements to be negotiated, armed forces necessary for maintaining international peace. The council also has responsibility for plans to regulate armaments.

On matters other than procedural, council decisions need an affirmative vote of nine, including all permanent members (hence the veto; abstentions do not in practice constitute a veto). On procedural matters, an affirmative vote of any nine members suffices. A UN member not on the council may take part in council discussion when it is considered that its interests are especially affected. The council presidency is held by members in monthly rotation in English alphabetical order. There is a *Committee of Experts* to advise the council on procedural and technical matters, a *Committee on Admission of New Members*, and a *Military Staff Committee*, which is composed of the chiefs of staff of the permanent members or their representatives, to advise on military matters.

Security Council Actions 1979 — mid-1980:
MIDDLE EAST — The Security Council extended for six-month periods the peacekeeping forces in Cyprus, Lebanon and the Golan Heights. However, the UN Emergency Force that had been serving in the Sinai was not extended by the Council. Egypt and Israel began jointly to police the Sinai truce areas with the help of strengthened U.S. "early warning" units. On March 1, 1980, the Security Council called on Israel to dismantle settlements on the West Bank occupied zone. The U.S. backed the resolution, then later disavowed its own vote as a "mistake." Israel was censured by the Council for the ouster of "problem" Arab mayors of West Bank cities and for making all Jerusalem its capital. In the first six months of 1980 there were 8 such Security Council censures against Israel.

IRAN — The Council voted on November 9, 1979, and again on November 27 in special session urging Iran to release the captives beseiged in the U.S. embassy in Tehran. Later it asked Secretary-General Waldheim to do what he could to free the hostages. A move for sanctions against Iran for its action was defeated by a Russian veto January 7, 1980.

SOUTHERN AFRICA — The Council condemned South Africa for its armed incursions into Angola against the South-West Africa People's Organization (SWAPO) bases. On December 21, 1979, the Council lifted its 13-year embargo against Zimbabwe-Rhodesia.

OTHER MATTERS — In Security Council deliberations on the Afghanistan invasion, the Soviet Union vetoed a resolution calling for a pullout of foreign troops. Action in the Council on the Vietnamese incursion into Cambodia was also stymied by Soviet veto power.

Economic and Social Council

The council makes studies and recommendations to the General Assembly on international social, economic, cultural, educational, health, and related matters. It negotiates agreements with the specialized agencies, defining their relationship with the UN, and coordinates their activities by means of consultation and recommendation.

It is composed of 54 members, 18 of whom are elected each year by the General Assembly to a three-year term. Each member has one vote, and a simple majority rules. The council works through committees, commissions, and various other subsidiary bodies. Its functional commissions include: the *Statistical Commission,* the *Population Commission,* the *Commission for Social Development,* the *Commission on Human Rights,* the *Commission on the Status of Women,* the *Commission on Narcotic Drugs* and the *Commission on Transnational Corporations.* There are also regional commissions for Europe, Asia and the Far East, Latin America, and Africa. There are a number of other related bodies, including the executive board of the children's fund (UNICEF) and the International Narcotics Control Board.

For list of members, see page 717: Membership of Principal United Nations Organizations.

Recent Developments: Resolutions in 1979 sessions dealt with human rights, advancement of women, crime prevention and racial discrimination.

Trusteeship Council

The council bears prime responsibility for supervision of territories placed under the UN Trusteeship System. It consists of member states administering trust territories and permanent members of the Security Council not administering territories. The present administering state is the United States (Trust Territory of the Pacific Islands). The nonadministering members are the People's Republic of China, France, the United Kingdom, and the USSR.

Voting is by simple majority. The Trusteeship Council meets once a year, usually in June.

Recent Developments: The Trusteeship Council moved ahead with its plans for a 1981 plebiscite under UN supervision on the future status of the Trust Territory of the Pacific Islands.

International Court of Justice

The principal judicial organ of the UN functions in accordance with its statute, which is an integral part of the UN Charter and is based on the Statute of the Permanent Court of International Justice of the League of Nations. The court is open to all UN members, plus nonmembers who become party to the statute (at present Switzerland, Liechtenstein, and San Marino), as well as other states fulfilling certain conditions. It is not open to private individuals. The court has jurisdiction over all cases that the parties refer to it and over all matters specifically provided for in the charter or in treaties or conventions in force, including treaties that refer to the Permanent Court of International Justice. In the event of a dispute as to whether the court has jurisdiction, it decides the issue itself.

The court is composed of 15 judges of different nationalities, who are elected independently by the General Assembly and the Security Council (election in the latter does not permit the veto). Terms are for nine years. All questions are decided by a majority of judges present, nine constituting a quorum. In case of a tie, the president of the court (elected by the court for a three-year term) casts the deciding vote. The court sits at The Hague, Netherlands.

Recent Developments: The United States filed suit on November 29, 1979 before the International Court for the seizure of the U.S. embassy and the taking of hostages in Tehran. The Court ruled on December 15 that Iran must free the American hostages. The Court, however, has no means for enforcing its decision.

Secretariat

The UN's administrative spine is composed of the Secretary-General, who is appointed by the General Assembly on the recommendation of the Security Council, and "such staff as the organization may require." As chief administrative officer, the Secretary-General acts in his capacity at all meetings of the General Assembly, the Security Council, the Economic and Social Council, and the Trusteeship Council. He makes an annual report to the General Assembly and appoints the Secretariat staff. The Secretary-General is also empowered to bring before the Security Council any matter that in his opinion threatens the maintenance of international peace.

The structure of the Secretariat includes the Offices of the Secretary-General (the Executive

Office of the Secretary-General, the Director-General for Economic Development, the Offices of the Under-Secretaries for Special Political Affairs, the Office of Legal Affairs, the Office of the Controller, and the Office of Personnel), the Department of Political and Security Council Affairs, the Department of Economic and Social Affairs, the Department of Trusteeship and Non-Self-Governing Territories, the Office of Public Information, the Office of Conference Services, the Office of General Services, and the UN Office in Geneva. There are also separate staffs serving subsidiary organs established by the General Assembly or the Economic and Social Council, including: the children's fund (UNICEF), the development program (UNDP), the office of the high commissioner for refugees (UNHCR), the relief and works agency for Palestine refugees (UNRWA), the institute for training and research (UNITAR), the industrial development organization (UNIDO) and trade and development (UNCTAD).

SPECIALIZED AGENCIES AND OTHER BODIES OF THE UNITED NATIONS

Specialized agencies are intergovernmental organizations linked to the UN by special agreement, working in partnership with it in social, scientific, and technical fields. The specialized agencies proper report annually to the Economic and Social Council. Although usually listed with them, the IAEA and GATT agencies are not, strictly speaking, specialized agencies. The former is an intergovernmental agency "established under the aegis of the UN" and reports to the General Assembly and, as appropriate, to the Security Council and the Economic and Social Council. The latter cooperates with the UN at the secretariat and intergovernmental levels.

Food and Agriculture Organization of the United Nations (FAO) *Function:* To help countries increase food production and improve distribution, to coordinate the Freedom from Hunger Campaign, and to help administer the World Food Program. *Members:* 147 countries. *Headquarters:* Rome. *Chief Officer:* Director-General Edouard Saouma (Lebanon).

General Agreement of Tariffs and Trade (GATT) *Function:* To establish and administer the code for orderly conduct of international trade; to assist governments to reduce customs tariffs and abolish other trade barriers; and to operate, jointly with the UN Conference on Trade and Development, the International Trade Center providing export promotion assistance for developing countries. (GATT rules govern as estimated 80 percent of international trade.) *Members:* 85 participating nations. *Headquarters:* Geneva. *Chief Officer:* Director-General Arthur Dunkel (Switzerland). *Recent Developments:* The Tokyo Round to negotiate industrial tariff reductions was concluded April 12, 1979. The reductions which average 35 percent over an eight-year period began January 1, 1980.

Inter-Governmental Maritime Consultative Organization (IMCO) *Function:* To promote cooperation on technical matters affecting shipping, to encourage the highest standards of maritime safety and efficient navigation, to convene international conferences highest standards of maritime safety and efficient navigation, to convene international conferences on shipping, and to draft international maritime conventions. *Members:* 113 countries plus one associate. *Headquarters:* London. *Chief Officer:* Secretary-General C.P. Srivastava (India). *Recent Developments:* The ninth session of the UN Law of the Sea Conference concluded its August meeting with approval of a draft treaty that has taken some six years of deliberations. The emerging treaty calls for a system of exploitation of mineral deposits of the sea bed which will benefit private companies who do the mining and the world community, chiefly have-not nations. It gives maritime countries exclusive mineral, oil and fishing rights out to 200 miles, reaffirms right of free passage on the high seas and in world straits, and calls for protection of the seas from pollution.

International Atomic Energy Agency (IAEA) *Function:* To promote the use of nuclear energy for peaceful purposes; to assist in nuclear research, development, and applications; and to apply safeguards against diversion of nuclear materials to military use. *Members:* 110 countries. *Headquarters:* Vienna. *Chief Officer:* Director-General Sigvard Eklund (Sweden).

International Bank for Reconstruction and Development (World Bank; IBRD) *Function:* To further members' economic development by loans (all loans made to or guaranteed by government) and technical advice. *Members:* 134 countries. *Headquarters:* Washington, DC *Chief Officer:* President Robert S. McNamara (United States).

International Civil Aviation Organization (ICAO) *Function:* To promote safety of international civil aviation, to provide statistical and economic information for governments and airlines, to work to reduce the red tape of customs formalities, and to help developing countries benefit from air transport. *Members:* 145 countries. *Headquarters:* Montreal. *Chief Officer:* Secretary-General Yves Lambert (France).

International Development Association (IDA) *Function:* To further economic development of members by providing finance on terms bearing less heavily on balance of payments than conventional loans. (Its credits have been for 50-year terms, interest free.) *Members:* 121 countries. *Headquarters:* Washington, DC (IDA is an affiliate of IBRD and has the same officers and staff.)

International Finance Corporation (IFC) *Function:* To assist less developed member countries by providing risk capital, without government guarantee, for the growth of productive private enterprise. *Members:* 111 countries. *Headquarters:* Washington, DC *Chief Officer:* Robert S. McNamara (United States). (IFC is an affiliate of IBRD.)

International Fund for Agricultural Development (IFAD) *Function:* To grant loans to promote agricultural improvement in developing countries. *Members:* 124 countries. *Headquarters:* Rome. President: Abelmuhsin al-Sudeary (Saudi Arabia).

International Labour Organization (ILO) *Function:* To bring together government, labor, and management on pressing international labor and manpower problems; to provide governments with technical assistance, and to develop world labor standards. *Members:* 140 countries. *Headquarters:* Geneva. *Chief Officer:* Director-General Francis Blanchard (France). *Recent Developments:* The U.S. rejoined the ILO on February 18, 1980. It had withdrawn its membership in 1977 in protest that the agency had become politicized. On May 12, 1980 the ILO criticized the Soviet Union and Czechoslavakia for their labor laws.

International Monetary Fund (IMF) *Function:* To promote international monetary cooperation and stabilization of currencies, to facilitate expansion of international trade, and to help members meet temporary difficulties in foreign payments. *Members:* 141 countries. *Headquarters:* Washington, DC *Chief Officer:* Managing Director Jacques de Larosière (France).

International Telecommunications Union (ITU) *Function:* To promote international cooperation in radio, telegraph, telephone, and space radio communications; to be instrumental in allocating radio frequencies, and to work to establish the lowest possible charges for telecommunications. *Members:* 154 countries. *Headquarters:* Geneva. *Chief Officer:* Secretary-General Mohammed Mili (Tunisia). *Recent Developments:* The second World Administration Radio Conference was held September 1979 (the last conference was in 1959). The U.S. proposed the expansion of the number of possible transmission frequencies and development of geosynchronous orbiting communications satellites. The proposals were opposed by third world representatives who anticipated added domination by developed countries.

United Nations Educational, Scientific and Cultural Organization (UNESCO) *Function:* To broaden the base of education in the world, to bring the benefits of science to all countries, and to encourage cultural exchange and appreciation. *Members:* 147 countries. *Headquarters:* Paris. *Chief Officer:* Director-General Amadou M'Bow (Senegal).

United Nations Children's Fund (UNICEF) *Function:* Established in 1946 to carry out post-war relief in Europe but now mainly concerned with the welfare of children in developing countries. *Headquarters:* New York. *Chief Officer:* Executive Director James P. Grant (United States). *Recent Developments:* Relief to the starving children in Cambodia and other areas of Southeast Asia was of prime concern.

United Nations Development Programme (UNDP) *Function:* To help developing countries increase the wealth-producing capabilities of their natural and human resources by providing experts or training of the local people. *Headquarters:* New York. *Chief Officer:* Administrator F. Bradford Morse (United States).

United Nations Environment Programme (UNEP) *Function:* Established in 1972 to provide machinery for international cooperation in matters relating to the human environment. *Members:* 55 countries. *Headquarters:* Nairobi. *Chief Officer:* Executive Director Mostafa K. Tolba (Egypt). *Recent Developments:* UNEP sponsored a pollution pact signed May 17, 1980, by most of the countries bordering the Mediterranean Sea.

United Nations High Commissioner for Refugees (UNHCR) *Function:* Set up in 1950, the office of the High Commissioner on Refugees aims chiefly to provide international protection for refugees and seek permanent solution to their problems through voluntary repatriation, migration to other countries or local integration. UNHCR also undertakes special humanitarian tasks. *Headquarters:* Geneva. *High Commissioner:* Poul Hartling (Denmark). *Recent Developments:* During 1979-80 the UNHCR was actively involved in aiding the "boat people" from Indochina, Afghan war refugees in Pakistan, Cambodian refugees in Thailand, and Zimbabwe refugees seeking return to now-independent Zimbabwe. It also aided thousands of homeless in Somalia.

United Nations Industrial Development Organization (UNIDO) *Function:* To encourage and extend assistance to developing countries for development, expansion and modernization of industry; to achieve full utilization of locally available natural and human resources; to provide a forum for consultation and negotiations among developing countries and between developing and industrialized countries. Administers UN Industrial Development Fund. *Headquarters:* Vienna. *Chief Officer:* Executive Director Dr. Abd-el Rahman Khane (Algeria). *Recent Developments:* Operates as an executing agency of the UN Development Programme (UNDP) until final ratification of autonomous specialized agency status. Consensus agreement and UNIDO Constitution were approved in April 1979. The UNIDO meeting at New Delhi in February 1980 ended in discord as industrialized nations blocked a proposal to set up a fund to assist developing nations. Disagreement came on who was to finance such a fund.

Universal Postal Union (UPU) *Function:* To assure the organization and improvement of the various postal services and to promote, in the sphere, the development of international cooperation. *Members:* 162. *Headquarters:* Bern. *Chief Officer:* Director-General Mohamed I. Sobhi (Egypt).

World Health Organization (WHO) *Function:* To direct and coordinate international health work, to help governments in public health programs, to set international drug and vaccine standards, and to promote medical research. *Members:* 152 countries. *Headquarters:* Geneva. *Chief Officer:* Director-General Dr. Halfdan Mahler (Denmark).

World Intellectual Property Organization (WIPO) *Function:* To promote and protect intellectual property, such as trademarks, industrial designs, literary and artistic works, throughout the world through new international treaties and harmonization of national legislation. *Members:* 88. *Headquarters:* Geneva. *Chief Officer:* Director-General Arpad Bogsch (United States).

World Meteorological Organization (WMO) *Function:* To promote international meteorological cooperation, especially in the establishment of a worldwide network of meteorological stations and rapid exchange of weather data, to promote standardization and publication of observations, and to further meteorological applications. *Members:* 150. *Headquarters:* Geneva. *Secretary-General:* Aksel Wiin-Nielson (Denmark).

UN SECRETARIES-GENERAL

Lie, Trygve Halvdan (1896-1968), Secretary-General from 1946 to 1953. Born in Oslo, Norway, the son of a carpenter, Lie earned a law degree from Oslo University in 1919 and later served as legal adviser to the Norwegian Trade Unions Federation. From 1935 to 1946 he held various Cabinet ministries, including justice, the department of shipping and supply, and foreign affairs. In the last capacity, he led the Norwegian delegation to the 1945 UN conference in San Francisco, where he headed the commission that drafted the security-council provisions of the Charter.

The rugged Norwegian was elected the first Secretary-General of the UN as a compromise candidate acceptable to both East and West. He immediately asserted himself and established the independence of the Secretary-General's office.

His strong stand on East-West issues alienated, at different times, both the United States and the Soviet Union. By endorsing UN membership for Communist China, he angered the Americans; his stand, however, against North Korean aggression so infuriated the Russians that they refused to deal with him during the remainder of his term. Lie's resignation in 1953 was partly due to Soviet ostracism, but was also brought on by McCarthy-era claims of subversives in the Secretariat.

Hammarskjöld, Dag Hjalmar Agne Carl (1905-1961), Secretary-General from 1953 to 1961. He was born in Jonkoping, Sweden, of an aristocratic family; his father, an eminent jurist, was Sweden's Prime Minister during World War I. Hammarskjöld earned a law degree from Uppsala University in 1930 and a Ph.D. in political economy from the University of Stockholm in 1934.

In 1949 he entered the foreign ministry, where he established his reputation as an international monetary expert. He became vice-chairman of Sweden's UN delegation in 1952 and was its chairman the following year, when he was elected Secretary-General. Hammarskjöld greatly extended the scope and influence of his office. His personal missions in the cause of peace began with his visit to Peking in 1955 to secure the release of captured American fliers and ended with his 1961 Congo mission on which he died in a plane crash near Ndola, Northern Rhodesia.

He created the international peace-keeping force sent to the Middle East after the 1956 Suez crisis. Hammarskjöld's most controversial action was his insistence, against strong Soviet opposition, on maintaining the UN peace force in the Congo. All these efforts won him the Nobel Peace Prize, awarded posthumously in 1961. Publicly, the bachelor Hammarskjöld was a cool, realistic diplomat, but his diary, published as Markings in 1964, revealed a profoundly mystical man.

U Thant (1909-1974), Secretary-General from 1961 to 1971. Born in Pantanaw, Burma, the son of a prosperous landowner, Thant graduated from the National High School in Pantanaw and attended University College in Rangoon. He taught English and modern history at his old high school where in 1931 he became headmaster. For many years he was also an active writer on politics.

He became a member of the Burmese UN delegation in 1952 and its chairman five years later. In 1959 he was chosen vice-president of the General Assembly. After Hammarskjöld's death in 1961, Thant, known as a moderate and neutralist, was elected acting Secretary-General, and a year later he was unanimously elected to office for a full five-year term, retroactive to 1961. Thant was widely praised for his role in calming international tensions during the 1962 Cuban missile crisis, for his part in healing the secessionist Katanga breach in the Congo, and for his handling of the 1964 UN financial crisis, when France and the Communist bloc refused to pay their share of peace-keeping operations.

On the other hand, he was criticized for precipitous speed in complying with Cairo's request in 1967 that the UN emergency force be withdrawn from the Sinai peninsula. It was also remarked that while he was an outspoken critic of American policy in Vietnam, he demonstrated marked restraint toward the 1968 Soviet invasion of Czechoslovakia. In 1971 he announced his December resignation.

Waldheim, Kurt (1918), Secretary-General since January 1972. Born in Lower Austria, the son of a teacher, Waldheim earned a law degree from the University of Vienna in 1944 and joined the Austrian foreign service the following year. He headed the ministry's personnel department for four years, then in 1955, when Austria was admitted to the UN, was appointed Austria's permanent observer at the UN. Since then he has been a member of Austria's delegation at all General Assembly sessions, while also active in other high-ranking foreign ministry appointments. After four years as head of the Austrian mission in Canada he returned to Vienna in 1960, directing the political affairs section there in 1962-1964. He was Austria's UN ambassador from 1964; he left his UN duties early in 1968 to become foreign minister, returning in 1970 to the UN. In April 1971, he contested unsuccessfully in Austria's presidential election.

After election as secretary-general, Waldheim, whose repute is that of a diplomat in the classic mold rather than an "activist," told the UN that he viewed admission of the divided countries as a move toward the goal of UN universality.

Waldheim was reelected for a second five-year term in December 1976. In the difficult Middle East negotiations Waldheim has often met with the national leaders involved and used his office to keep peace talks alive. He created somewhat of a political stir in Middle East affairs by publicly supporting the proposal to create a Palistinian state. Waldheim's special trip to Iran to seek release of the U.S. hostages did not achieve its goal.

UNITED STATES REPRESENTATIVES AND DELEGATES
TO THE UNITED NATIONS: 35th Session
(As of October 10, 1980)

Donald F. McHenry (Ambassador Extraordinary and Plenipotentiary) — Permanent United States Representative to the United Nations and Chairman of the Delegation to the General Assembly*

William J. vanden Heuvel (Ambassador) — Deputy Representative to the United Nations

Senator Jacob K. Javits—U.S. Delegate to the General Assembly

Senator Paul E. Tsongas—U.S. Delegate to the General Assembly

Hannah D. Atkins — U.S. Delegate to the General Assembly

Nathan Landow — Alternate U.S. Representative to the General Assembly

Barbara Newsom—Alternate U.S. Representative to the General Assembly

Richard W. Petree (Ambassador)—Deputy Representative on the Security Council

Joan E. Spero—Ambassador Representative on the Economic and Social Council

H. Carl McCall—Alternate Representative for Special Political Affairs

Dr. Ruth Morgenthau—Representative on the Commission for Social Development of the Economic and Social Council

Jerome Shestack—Representative on the Commission on Human Rights of the Economic and Social Council

Koryne Horbal—Representative on the Commission on the Status of Women of the Economic and Social Council

° The Secretary of State, Edmund S. Muskie, serves as *ex officio* Chairman when present at a session.

MEMBERSHIP OF PRINCIPAL UNITED NATIONS ORGANIZATIONS

SECURITY COUNCIL

Fifteen members: the 5 permanent members and 10 members are elected for two-year terms by the General Assembly.

Permanent members:	China	France	USSR	United Kingdom	United States
Elected members:					
Until December 1980:	Bangladesh	Jamaica	Norway	Portugal	Zambia
Until December 1981:	Germany (Dem. Rep.)	Mexico	Niger	Philippines	Tanzania

ECONOMIC AND SOCIAL COUNCIL

54 members: elected for 3-year terms by the General Assembly.

Aigeria	Central African Rep.	Germany (Dem. Rep.)	Japan	Nigeria	Turkey
Argentina	Chile	Germany (Fed. Rep.)	Jordan	Pakistan	USSR
Australia	China	Ghana	Lesotho	Romania	United Arab Emirates
Bahamas	Cyprus	Hungary	Libya	Senegal	United Kingdom
Barbados	Dominican Rep.	India	Malawi	Spain	United States
Belgium	Ecuador	Indonesia	Malta	Sweden	Venezuela
Brazil	Ethiopia	Iraq	Mexico	Tanzania	Yugoslavia
Bulgaria	Finland	Ireland	Morocco	Thailand	Zaire
Cameroon	France	Italy	Nepal	Trinidad & Tobago	Zambia

TRUSTEESHIP COUNCIL

5 members: one (*) an administering state, and four nonadministering permanent members of the Security Council.

China	France	USSR	United Kingdom	United States*

INTERNATIONAL COURT OF JUSTICE

15 members, elected by the General Assembly for 9-year terms that end on 5 February of the year indicated. Judges are listed in order of precedence.

Sir Humphrey Waldock (UK, 1982) president for 3 years	Nagendra Singh (India, 1982)	Salah el-Dine Tarazi (Syria, 1985)
Manfred Lachs (Poland, 1985)	José Maria Ruda (Argentina, 1982)	Roberto Ago (Italy, 1988)
Isaac Forster (Senegal, 1982)	Taslim Olawale Elias (Nigeria, 1985)	Richard Baxter (U.S., 1988)
André Gros (France, 1982)	Hermann Mosler (Germany, Fed. Rep., 1985)	Abdullah Ali El-Erian (Egypt, 1988)
Platon D. Morozov (USSR, 1988)	Shigeru Oda (Japan, 1985)	José Sette Câmara (Brazil, 1988)

HEADS OF MISSIONS TO THE UNITED NATIONS (as of September 1, 1980)

Country	Permanent Representative
Afghanistan	vacant
Albania	Abdi Baleta
Algeria	Mohamed Bedjaoui
Angola	Elisio de Figueiredo
Argentina	vacant
Australia	H.D. Anderson
Austria	Thomas Klestil
Bahamas	Davidson L. Hepburn
Bahrain	Salman Mohamed Al-Saffar
Bangladesh	Khwaja Mohammed Kaiser
Barbados	Ronald G. Mapp
Belgium	André Ernemann
Benin	Thomas Setondji Boya
Bhutan	Om Pradhan
Bolivia	Fernand Ortiz Sanz
Botswana	Legwaila Joseph Legwaila
Brazil	Sérgio Corréa da Costa
Bulgaria	vacant
Burma	Maung Maung Gyee
Burundi	Artémon Simbananiye
Byelorussian SSR	Anatoly Nikitich Sheldov
Cambodia (Kampuchea)	Thiounn Prasith
Cameroon	Ferdinand Léopold Oyono
Canada	Michel P. Dupuy
Cape Verde	Amaro Alexandre da Luz
Central African Republic	Simon Pierre Kibanda
Chad	vacant
Chile	Sergio Diez
China	Ling Qing
Colombia	Indalecio Lievano
Comoros	vacant
Congo	Nicolas Mondjo
Costa Rica	Rodolfo Piza Escalante
Cuba	Raúl Roa-Kouri
Cyprus	Andreas V. Mavrommatis
Czechoslovakia	Ilja Hulinský
Denmark	Wilhelm Ulrichsen
Djibouti	Saleh Haji Farah Dirir
Dominica	vacant
Dominican Republic	vacant
Ecuador	Migual A. Albornoz
Egypt	Ahmed Esmat Abdel Meguid
El Salvador	Mauricio Rosales-Rivera
Equatorial Guinea	Carmelo Nvono-Nca
Ethiopia	Mohamed Hamid Ibrahim
Fiji	Filipe Nagera Bole
Finland	Ilkka Olavi Pastinen
France	Jacques Leprette
Gabon	Léon N'Dong
Gambia	Ousman Ahmadou Sallah

Country	Permanent Representative
Germany (Dem. Rep.)	Peter Florin
Germany (Fed. Rep.)	Rüdiger von Wechmar
Ghana	vacant
Greece	Nicolas Katapodis
Grenada	Kendrick Bernard Radix
Guatemala	Eduardo Castillo Arriola
Guinea	Djebel Coumbassa
Guinea-Bissau	Gil Vicente Vaz Fernandes
Guyana	Noel G. Sinclair
Haiti	Jean Dominique Coradin
Honduras	Mario Carlas
Hungary	Pál Rácz
Iceland	Tómas A. Tómasson
India	Brajesh Chandra Mishra
Indonesia	Abdullah Kamil
Iran	vacant
Iraq	Salah Omar Al-Ali
Ireland	Paul J.G. Keating
Israel	Yehuda Z. Blum
Italy	Umberto La Rocca
Ivory Coast	Amoakon Thiemele
Jamaica	Donald O. Mills
Japan	Masahiro Nisibori
Jordan	Hazem Nuseibeh
Kenya	Charles Gatere Maina
Kuwait	Abdalla Yaccoub Bishara
Laos	Vithaya Sourinho
Lebanon	Ghassan Tuéni
Lesotho	Thabo Makeka
Liberia	Winston A. Tubman
Libya	Mansur Rashid Kikhia
Luxembourg	Paul Peters
Madagascar	Blaise Rabetafika
Malawi	T. Jacob X. Muwamba
Malaysia	Datuk Zainal
Maldives	Ahmed Zaki
Mali	Seydou Traore
Malta	Victor J. Gauci
Mauritania	vacant
Mauritius	Radha Krishna Ramphul
Mexico	Porfirio Muñoz Ledo
Mongolia	Buyzntyn Dashtseren
Morocco	Mehdi Mrani Zentar
Mozambique	José Carlos Lobo
Nepal	Uddhav Deo Bhatt
Netherlands	Hugo Scheltema
New Zealand	Harold Huyton Francis
Nicaragua	Victor Hugo Tinoco
Niger	Idé Oumarou
Nigeria	B. Akporode Clark
Norway	Ole Aalgaard
Oman	Mahmoud Aboul-Nasr
Pakistan	Niaz A. Naik
Panama	Jorge Enrique Illueca

Country	Permanent Representative
Papua New Guinea	Ilinome Tarua
Paraguay	Luis Gonzales Arias
Peru	Juan José Calle y Calle
Philippines	Alejandro D. Yango
Poland	Ryszard Frelek
Portugal	Vasco Futscher Pereira
Qatar	Jasim Yousif Jamal
Romania	Teodor Marinescu
Rwanda	Ignace Karuhije
Saint Lucia	Barry B.L. Auguste
São Tomé & Principe	vacant
Saudi Arabia	vacant
Senegal	Médoune Fall
Seychelles	vacant
Sierra Leone	George Gelaga-King
Singapore	T.T.B. Koh
Solomon Islands	vacant
Somalia	vacant
South Africa	Jacobus Adriaan Eksteen
Spain	Don Jaime de Piniés
Sri Lanka	vacant
Sudan	Abdel-Rahman Abdalla
Suriname	Henricus A.F. Heidweiller
Swaziland	Norman M. Malinga
Sweden	Anders I. Thunborg
Syria	vacant
Tanzania	Salim Ahmed Salim
Thailand	Birabhongse Kasemsri
Togo	vacant
Trinidad & Tobago	Frank Owen Abdulah
Tunisia	M'Hamed Essaafi
Turkey	A. Coşkun Kirca
Uganda	vacant
Ukrainian SSR	Vladimir Alekseyevich Kravets
USSR	Oleg Aleksandrovich Troyanovsky
United Arab Emirates	Ali Humaidan
United Kingdom	Anthony Parsons
United States	Donald F. McHenry
Upper Volta	Aïssé Mensah
Uruguay	Edmundo Narancio
Venezuela	Germán Nava-Carrillo
Vietnam	Ha Van Lau
Western Samoa	Maiava Iulai Toma
Yemen	Mohsin Ahmed Alaini
Yemen (Southern)	Abdalla Saleh Ashtal
Yugoslavia	Miljan Komatina
Zaire	Kamandawa Kamanda
Zambia	Paul J.F. Lusaka
Zimbabwe	Elleck Mashingaidze

UN GENERAL ASSEMBLY PRESIDENTS

Session	Year	President
1st	1946	Paul Henri Spaak
2nd	1947	Oswaldo Aranha
3rd	1948-49	Herbert V. Evatt
4th	1949	Carlos P. Romulo
5th	1950-51	Nasrollah Entezam
6th	1951-52	Luís Padilla Nervo
7th	1952-53	Lester B. Pearson
8th	1953-54	Mrs. Vijaya Lakshmi Pandit
9th	1954	Eelco N. van Kleffends
10th	1955	José Maza
11th	1956-57	Prince Wan Waithayakon
12th	1957	Sir Leslie Munro
13th	1958-59	Charles Malik
14th	1959	Victor Andrés Belaúnde
15th	1960-61	Frederick H. Boland
16th	1961-62	Mongi Slim
17th	1962	Muhammad Zafrulla Khan
18th	1963	Carlos Sosa Rodríguez
19th	1964-65	Alex Quaison-Sackey
20th	1965	Amintore Fanfani
21st	1966	Abdul Rahman Pazhwak
22nd	1967-68	Corneliu Manescu
23rd	1968	Emilio Arenales
24th	1969	Miss Angie Brooks
25th	1970	Edvard Isak Hambro
26th	1971	Adam Malik
27th	1972	Stanislaw Trepczynski
28th	1973	Leopoldo Benites
29th	1974	Abdelaziz Bouteflika
30th	1975	Gaston Thorn
31st	1976	Hamilton Shirley Amerasinghe
32nd	1977	Lazar Mojsov
33rd	1978	Indalecio Lievano Aguirre
34th	1979	Salim Ahmed Salim
35th	1980	Rudiger von Wechmar

REPRESENTATIVE INTERNATIONAL ORGANIZATIONS

Afro-Mauritian Common Organization (OCAM) *Formed:* 1965 *Members:* 10 African countries *Headquarters:* Bangui, Central African Empire *Secretary-General:* Sidney Moufia *Purpose:* To promote economic, technical, and cultural development of member French-speaking states within the framework of the OAU. *Recent Developments:* On September 7, 1976, Gabon withdrew from the Organization, and on February 9, 1977, Seychelles became a member.

Andean Group *Formed:* 1969 *Members:* Bolivia, Ecuador, Peru and Venezuela *Headquarters:* Lima, Peru *Director-Secretary:* Alberto Zelado Castedo *Purpose:* Regional association with the aim of closer economic and political cooperation among member countries. Venezuela joined in 1973. The Andean Reserve Fund (1977) and Andean Development Corporation (1968) are funding and planning arms for the Andean Group. *Recent Developments:* On September 3, 1980, Bolivia announced its intention to withdraw from the Andean Group.

ANZUS Council *Formed:* 1951 *Members:* Australia, New Zealand, and the United States *Headquarters:* Canberra, Australia *Purpose:* This loose military alliance is pledged to respond to aggression against any of its members. *Recent Developments:* In response to the Soviet invasion of Afghanistan, ANZUS leaders announced on February 28, 1980 a proposal to expand the military role of ANZUS partners in the Indian Ocean.

Arab League (AL) *Formed:* 1945 *Members:* Algeria, Bahrain, Djibouti, Egypt, Iraq, Jordan, Kuwait, Lebanon, Libya, Mauritania, Morocco, Oman, Qatar, Saudi Arabia, Somalia, Sudan, Syria, Tunisia, United Arab Emirates, Yemen, Southern Yemen, and the PLO government. *Headquarters:* Tunis *Secretary-General:* Chedli Klibi (Tunisia) *Purpose:* To strengthen member ties and further promote Arab aspirations. *Recent Developments:* The League moved its headquarters from Cairo to Tunis in 1979. All 20 members of the League have severed economic and political ties with Egypt because of the peace treaty signed with Israel. Syrian troop role in Lebanon was extended six months on January 23, 1980.

Association of Southeast Asian Nations (ASEAN) *Formed:* 1967 *Members:* Indonesia, Malaysia, the Philippines, Singapore and Thailand *Headquarters:* Jakarta, Indonesia *Secretary-General:* Datuk Ali bin Abdullah *Purpose:* To promote economic progress and political stability in Southeast Asia; it seeks to lower trade tariffs for intraregional trade, encourage exchange programs and sharing of scientific knowledge.

Benelux Economic Union *Formed:* 1958 *Members:* Belgium, Luxembourg, and the Netherlands *Headquarters:* Brussels *Secretary-General:* Egbert Kruijtbosch (Netherlands) *Purpose:* To achieve complete economic union of its members (as a subdivision of the EC).

Caribbean Community and Common Market (CARICOM) *Formed:* 1973 *Members:* Antigua, Barbados, Belize, Dominica, Grenada, Guyana, Jamaica, Montserrat, St. Kitts-Nevis-Anguilla, St. Lucia, St. Vincent & the Grenadines, and Trinidad and Tobago *Headquarters:* Georgetown, Guyana *Secretary-General:* Kurleigh D. King (Barbados) *Purpose:* To promote unity in the Caribbean through economic integration, a common external tariff and coordination of development plans.

Central African Economic and Customs Union (UDEAC) *Formed:* 1966 *Members:* Cameroon, Central African Republic, Congo, Gabon; Chad has had observer status since 1975 *Headquarters:* Bangui, Central African Republic *Secretary-General:* Pierre Tchanque (Cameroon) *Purpose:* To promote the gradual establishment of a Central African Common Market and see to the general improvement of living standards of the peoples of member states.

Central American Common Market (CACM) *Formed:* 1960 *Members:* Costa Rica, El Salvador, Guatemala, Honduras and Nicaragua. (Honduras withdrew from active membership in 1970) *Headquarters:* Guatemala City, Guatemala *Secretary-General:* Raúl Sierra Franco *Purpose:* To establish a free trade area and a customs union with joint planning for social and economic development of the region.

Colombo Plan for Cooperative Development in Asia and the Pacific *Formed:* 1950 *Members:* 26 countries *Headquarters:* Colombo, Sri Lanka *President:* Miss Ampha Bhadranawik (Thailand) *Purpose:* To aid developing countries through bilateral member agreements for the provision of capital, technical experts and training, and equipment.

Commonwealth, The (formerly British Commonwealth) *Formed:* 1931 *Members:* 43 *Headquarters:* London *Secretary-General:* Shridath Ramphal (Guyana) *Purpose:* A voluntary association of independent states and their dependencies who meet and consult of a regular basis to foster Commonwealth links and achieve a more equitable world society. All Commonwealth countries accept Queen Elizabeth II as the symbolic head of the association. *Recent Developments:* Peacekeeping forces dispatched to Zimbabwe (Rhodesia) in December 1979 helped monitor during the transition stages of the new nation and its election of a black government. Zimbabwe became the latest member of the Commonwealth April 18, 1980.

Council for Mutual Economic Assistance (COMECON) *Formed:* 1949 *Members:* Bulgaria, Cuba, Czechoslovakia, East Germany, Hungary, Mongolia, Poland, Romania, the Soviet Union and Vietnam; *Associate Member:* Yugoslavia *Headquarters:* Moscow *Secretary:* N.V. Faddeyev (Soviet Union) *Purpose:* To coordinate and integrate members' economies, under USSR leadership. *Recent Developments:* Fixed prices for purchasing Soviet raw materials are to continue until the mid-1980s. Experts noted an increase in 1979-80 in hard currency payments for scarce goods paid by COMECON nations.

Council of Europe *Formed:* 1949 *Members:* 21 countries, mostly in Western Europe but also includes Greece and Turkey *Headquarters:* Strasbourg, France *Secretary-General:* Franz Karasek (Austria) *Purpose:* To protect human rights, bring European countries closer together, and voice the views of the European public on the main political and economic questions of the day.

Eastern European Mutual Assistance Treaty (Warsaw Pact) *Formed:* 1955 *Members:* Bulgaria, Czechoslovakia, East Germany, Hungary, Poland, Romania, and the Soviet Union *Headquarters:* Moscow *Supreme Military Commander:* Marshal Viktor G. Kulikov (Soviet Union) *Purpose:* This major European military alliance is the Soviet bloc's equivalent of the North Atlantic Treaty Organization, and its forces, like NATO's, are composed of military elements from member countries. *Recent Developments:* The May 14-15, 1980, meeting of the Warsaw Pact countries celebrated the 25th anniversary of the Pact. The meeting, however, was a low-key affair with an emphasis on backing detente policy.

European Atomic Energy Community (Euratom) *Formed:* 1958 *Members:* Belgium, France, West Germany, Italy, Luxembourg, the Netherlands, Denmark, Ireland, and Britain *Headquarters:* Brussels *Purpose:* To promote the common development of nuclear energy for peaceful purposes.

European Coal and Steel Community (ECSC) *Formed:* 1952 *Members:* Belgium, France, West Germany, Italy, Luxembourg, Britain, Ireland, Denmark and the Netherlands *Headquarters:* Luxembourg *Purposes:* To maintain a common market for coal, iron ore, and steel, and harmonize external tariffs; to abolish discriminatory pricing systems and transport rates among members, while safe-guarding continuity of employment.

European Community (EC, the Common Market) *Formed:* 1958 *Members:* Belgium, France, West Germany, Italy, Luxembourg, the Netherlands, Britain, Denmark, and Ireland. *Headquarters:* Brussels *President:* Roy Jenkins (Britain) *Purpose:* To abolish all internal tariffs and other trade barriers and to align external tariffs, so that there can be free movement of goods, persons, services, and capital within the EC. *Recent Developments:* Plans for a tunnel between Britain and the continent received UK and EC backing in March, 1980. The summit meeting of EC leaders held March 27-28, 1980, failed to resolve the question of Britain's contribution to the EC budget. Spanish and Portuguese entry to EC seem to be delayed due to French opposition. On July 1, 1980, EC renewed Turkey's associate status in EC and provided a $840-million aid package.

European Free Trade Association (EFTA) *Formed:* 1960 *Members:* Austria, Iceland, Norway, Portugal, Sweden, and Switzerland; *Associate Member:* Finland *Headquarters:* Geneva *Secretary-General:* Charles Müller (Switzerland) *Purpose:* To maintain the elimination of internal tariffs on industrial goods (achieved at the end of 1966) and negotiate bilateral agreements on agricultural products. *Recent Developments:* Once called the Outer Seven, EFTA has aimed at a lesser degree of economic integration than the European Community. A customs union with the EC came into force July 1, 1977. The first stage of tariff reduction to give Spain access to EFTA markets began July 1, 1980.

International Bureau of Weights and Measures *Formed:* 1875 *Members:* 45 countries *Headquarters:* Paris (Sèvres) *Director:* Pierre Giacomo (France) *Purpose:* To ensure standardization of basic units of meausre throughout the world.

International Committee of the Red Cross (ICRC) *Formed:* 1863 *Members:* 370 Swiss citizens *Headquarters:* Geneva *President:* Alexandre Hay (Switzerland) *Purpose:* To organize care for the victims of war and enforce the various Conventions on wartime practices. The ICRC constitutes, with the League of Red Cross Societies, the International Red Cross.

International Criminal Police Organization (Interpol) *Formed:* 1956 *Members:* Official police bodies in 122 countries *Headquarters:* Paris (St. Cloud) *Secretary-General:* Jean Nepote (France) *Purpose:* To ensure maximum cooperation between police authorities, with the strict exclusion of political, military, religious, and racial matters. As successor to the International Criminal Police Commission, established in 1923, Interpol acts as a clearinghouse for information on international criminal activities.

International Energy Agency (IEA) *Formed:* 1974 *Members:* 20 countries including most western European nations with Greece and Turkey plus the U.S., Canada and Japan *Headquarters:* Paris *Chief Officer:* Chairman Niels Ersboll (Denmark) *Purpose:* To develop cooperation among major oil importing nations and to strengthen the security and stability of world energy markets. *Recent Developments:* Meeting at Venice summit in June 1980, the IEA endorsed oil import reductions of 4.2 million barrels a day by member states in the year 1985.

Latin American Free Trade Association (LAFTA) *Formed:* 1960 *Members:* Argentina, Bolivia, Brazil, Chile, Columbia, Ecuador, Mexico, Paraguay, Peru, Uruguay, and Venezuela *Headquarters:* Montevideo, Uruguay *Executive Secretary:* Daniel Mesa Bernal (Colombia) *Purpose:* To work toward the establishment of a Latin American common market.

Nordic Council *Formed:* 1953 *Members:* Denmark, Finland, Iceland, Norway, and Sweden *Headquarters:* Stockholm *Secretary of the Presidium:* Helge Lunde Seip (Norway) *Purpose:* To arrange cooperation among members in cultural, legal, social, and economic matters.

North Atlantic Treaty Organization (NATO) *Formed:* 1949 *Members:* Belgium, Canada, Denmark, France, West Germany, Great Britian, Greece, Iceland, Italy, Luxembourg, the Netherlands, Norway, Portugal, Turkey, and the United States *Headquarters:* Brussels *Secretary-General:* Dr. Joseph Luns (Netherlands) *Purpose:* This major Western military alliance, with prime responsibility for opposing Communist forces in Europe, is composed of elements from the armed forces of member nations. *Recent Developments:* NATO has committed itself to a modernization of its nuclear forces. In December 1979 NATO partners agreed, with some low voices of discontent, to accept U.S. medium range missiles in Europe by 1983. The plan would give Europe, for the first time, nuclear weapons capable of reaching Soviet soil. Gen. Bernard Rogers is the present NATO supreme commander.

Organization for Economic Cooperation and Development (OECD) *Formed:* 1961 *Members:* 24 countries, mostly in Western Europe, but also U.S., Australia, New Zealand and Japan *Headquarters:* Paris *Secretary-General:* Emile van Lennep (Netherlands) *Purpose:* To achieve economic growth and full employment and to further world economic development. As successor to the Organization for European Economic Cooperation (OEEC) that was established in 1948 to oversee Marshall Plan reconstruction, OECD has a broadened scope, having established an extensive aid program to developing countries.

Organization of African Unity (OAU) *Formed:* 1963 *Members:* All 50 independent African countries, except the white-dominated states and territories of the south *Headquarters:* Addis Ababa, Ethiopia *Secretary-General:* Edem Kodjo (Togo) *Purpose:* To promote African solidarity, coordinate policies, defend member sovereignty, and eliminate colonialism in Africa. *Recent Developments:* At the annual summit of OAU nations held in Sierra Leone July 1-4, 1980,

the conflict in Western Sahara was condemned, but sharp disagreements prevented any measures to ease the conflict or to give the Polisario support by admitting them to the OAU. The countries demanded the British-owned island of Diego Garcia (a U.S. Indian Ocean base) be ceded to Mauritius.

Organization of American States (OAS) *Formed:* 1948 *Members:* 28 American countries *Headquarters:* Washington, D.C. *Secretary-General:* Alejandro Orfila (Argentina) *Purpose:* To promote the solidarity and defend the sovereignty of members and provide through the Pan American Union—the OAS central organ and secretariat—social, political, economic, and technical services. *Recent Developments:* The ninth General Assembly meeting was held in La Paz, Oct. 22-31, 1979. Bolivia pressed its case for access to the Pacific, but the main theme of the meetings was human rights, with particular attention being called to conditions in Uruguay, Paraguay and Chile. An OAS report issued April 18, 1980, charged Argentina with massive violations of human rights.

Organization of Petroleum Exporting Countries (OPEC) *Formed:* 1960 *Members:* Algeria, Ecuador, Gabon, Indonesia, Iran, Iraq, Kuwait, Libya, Nigeria, Qatar, Saudi Arabia, United Arab Emirates and Venezuela *Headquarters:* Vienna *Secretary-General:* René G. Ortiz (Ecuador) *Purpose:* To coordinate policies and establish prices regarding petroleum exported to consumer nations. *Recent Developments:* Oil prices continued to soar in 1979-80. By January 1, 1980, the effective price was $25-30 a barrel for crude oil. In May 1980, OPEC set forth a plan for unified pricing with prices pegged to a basket of 10 currencies. At the OPEC meeting of Sept. 15-17, 1980, Saudi Arabia agreed to raise its crude price while other OPEC nations lowered their charges to the new reference price of $30 a barrel. A Saudia Arabian cut in production was part of the accord.

West African Economic Community (CEAO) *Formed:* 1973 *Members:* Ivory Coast, Mali, Mauritania, Niger, Senegal and Upper Volta (Observers: Benin and Togo) *Headquarters:* Ouagadougou, Upper Volta *Secretary-General:* Moussa N'gom (Senegal) *Purpose:* To establish an economic and customs union for West African states.

World Council of Churches (WCC) *Formed:* 1948 *Members:* 313 churches in over 90 countries, including most major Protestant and Eastern Orthodox denominations *Headquarters:* Geneva *General Secretary:* Dr. Philip A. Potter (British West Indies) *Purpose:* To promote cooperation and unity among the churches of the world. It is active in missionary work, aid to refugees, the sick and underprivileged and in helping promote education and the cause of world peace. *Recent Developments:* The annual conference held July 1979 stressed the need to reduce friction between science and religion.

U.S. CONTRIBUTIONS TO INTERNATIONAL ORGANIZATIONS

SOURCE: U.S. Department of State

FISCAL YEAR 1979 (In Millions of Dollars)

Organization	Estimated Amount
United Nations and Specialized Agencies:	
United Nations	$141.10
Food and Agricultural Organization	22.46
International Atomic Energy Agency	18.28
International Civil Aviation Organizations	4.43
Joint Financing Program	3.16
International Telecommunications Union	2.77
UNESCO	36.50
World Health Organization	49.20
World Meteorological Organization	4.27
Others	1.12
United Nations Peacekeeping Forces:	
United Nations Emergency Force	67.00
United Nations Force in Cyprus	8.70
Inter-American Organizations	
Organization of American States	34.73
Inte-American Institute of Agricultural Sciences	9.95
Pan American Health Organization	22.70
Inter-American Tropical Tuna Commission	1.61
Other	0.39
Regional Organizations:	
NATO Civilian Headquarters	12.61
Organization for Economic Cooperation and Development	12.94
Others	1.51
Other International Organizations:	
Customs Cooperation Council	1.41
General Agreement on Tariffs and Trade	3.33
Intergovernmental Committee for European Migration	2.60
International Institute for Cotton	2.10
Others	3.68
Special Voluntary Programs:	
Consultative Group on International Agricultural Research	24.80
Intergovernmental Committee for European Migration	53.28
International Atomic Energy Agency—Operational Program	12.00[1]
Organization of American States—Special Development Assistance Fund	6.00
Organization of American States—Special Multilateral Fund (Education and Science)	6.50
Organization of American States—Special Projects	2.60
Pan American Health Organization—Special Voluntary Program	3.00
United Nations Capital Development Fund	2.00
United Nations Children Fund	30.00
United Nations Decade for Women	2.00
United Nations Development Program	126.00
United Nations Educational and Training Program for South Africa	1.00
United Nations Environment Fund	10.00
UN/FAO World Food Program	95.10
United Nations Fund for Drug Abuse Control	3.00
United Nations Fund for Population Activities	30.00
United Nations High Commissioner for Refugees	34.97
Special Resettlement and Relief Programs	55.84
United Nations Relief and Works Agency	52.00
West African Rice Development Association	1.20
World Health Organization—Special Programs	6.91
World Meteorological Organization—Voluntary Assistance Program	2.00
Others	2.84
Total U.S. Contributions	**$1,031.65**

[1] Includes cash, commodities and services.

U.S. FOREIGN ECONOMIC ASSISTANCE

SOURCE: Program Data Services Division, Bureau for Program and Policy Coordination, Agency for International Development

The table below gives total U.S. foreign economic aid under the Foreign Assistance Act of 1961 and related precedent legislation—loans and grants—since 1946 and foreign aid data for fiscal year 1979.

The Agency for International Development (AID) has been the administering agency for foreign economic assistance under the Foreign Assistance Act since November 4, 1961. Agencies dealing with economic assistance programs prior to that date have been, successively: the Economic Cooperation Administration (Apr. 3, 1948-Oct. 31, 1951); the Mutual Security Agency (Nov. 1, 1951-July 31, 1953); the Foreign Operations Administration (Aug. 1, 1953-June 30, 1955); the International Cooperation Administration (July 1, 1955-Nov. 3, 1961); and the Development Loan Fund (Aug. 14, 1957-Nov. 3, 1961).

The latter two agencies operated concurrently for approximately four years until their functions were combined under the provisions of the Foreign Assistance Act of 1961.

Region and Country	Total 1946-1979 (Millions)	Fiscal Year 1979 (Millions)
GRAND TOTAL	$73,735.4	$3,848.5
Near East and South Asia	21,751.7	2,169.9
Afghanistan	340.4	3.1
Bahrain	1.2	—
Bangladesh	668.3	90.4
Cyprus	103.0	15.0
Egypt	3,600.3	835.0
Greece	1,126.3	—
India	3,939.8	90.7
Iran	600.2	—
Iraq	18.8	—
Israel	4,136.8	785.0
Jordan	1,151.9	93.0
Lebanon	97.7	0.4
Nepal	94.6	12.4
Pakistan	2,767.2	9.1
Saudi Arabia	27.4	—
Sri Lanka	125.4	29.0
Syria	442.8	90.0
Turkey	2,166.5	69.6
Yemen Arab Republic	84.8	16.6
Central Treaty Organization	55.8	0.1
Regional	202.7	30.6
Latin America	7,480.6	254.9
Argentina	137.3	—
Belize	1.0	—
Bolivia	597.2	28.9
Brazil	1,390.5	—
Chile	663.8	0.3
Colombia	919.4	0.3
Costa Rica	150.6	16.4
Cuba	2.8	—
Dominican Republic	379.9	26.4
Ecuador	170.4	0.5
El Salvador	116.7	6.9
Guatemala	283.3	17.4
Guyana	111.0	6.3
Haiti	149.9	9.1
Honduras	205.5	22.0
Jamaica	92.4	5.9
Mexico	77.6	—
Nicaragua	224.1	9.7
Panama	291.3	19.9
Paraguay	117.3	7.1
Peru	308.9	34.1
Suriname	4.0	—
Trinidad & Tobago	38.9	—
Uruguay	79.7	—
Venezuela	71.7	—
Regional Office for Central America & Panama	278.3	2.8
East Caribbean Regional	113.9	26.8
Regional	503.4	14.1
East Asia	15,059.5	172.6
Burma	60.0	—
Cambodia	549.7	—
China (Taiwan)	1,366.4	—
Indochina[a]	825.6	—
Indonesia	1,153.3	95.0
Japan	21.8	—
Korea	3,042.5	0.6
Laos	875.4	—
Malaysia	20.2	—
Philippines	720.3	43.7
Thailand	644.2	21.6
Vietnam	5,465.6	0.6
Regional	314.6	—
Africa	4,195.1	338.6
Algeria	3.8	—
Benin	7.8	0.2
Botswana	29.8	14.0
Burundi	1.6	0.1

Region and Country	Total 1946-1978 (Millions)	Fiscal Year 1978 (Millions)
Cameroon	$ 47.9	$ 7.7
Cape Verde	18.2	2.9
Central African Republic	7.0	0.1
Chad	32.4	3.1
Congo, People's Republic of	1.7	0.1
Djibouti, Democratic Republic of	1.3	1.2
Entente States	6.6	1.4
Ethiopia	269.5	3.3
Gabon	3.7	*
Gambia, The	7.3	4.5
Ghana	221.6	7.6
Guinea	50.4	2.7
Guinea-Bissau	6.0	2.2
Ivory Coast	13.7	0.1
Kenya	160.4	16.9
Lesotho	13.4	6.8
Liberia	224.9	14.9
Libya	137.3	—
Madagascar	9.8	—
Malawi	23.4	3.5
Mali, Republic of	71.6	16.6
Mauritania	20.6	6.3
Mauritius	0.8	0.1
Morocco	391.9	4.1
Mozambique	11.5	—
Niger	46.6	10.9
Nigeria	310.3	—
Rwanda	11.7	5.3
São Tomé and Príncipe	0.3	—
Senegal	47.5	15.0
Seychelles	0.7	0.6
Sierra Leone	19.7	3.9
Somali Republic	76.5	10.9
Sudan	109.9	16.7
Swaziland	19.4	6.0
Tanzania	118.0	21.4
Togo	9.7	1.2
Tunisia	381.3	14.8
Uganda	39.3	3.0
Upper Volta	47.8	15.9
Zaïre	353.2	12.0
Zambia	61.1	20.4
Zimbabwe	7.0	—
Portuguese Territories	3.2	—
Central & West Africa Regional	153.5	7.9
East Africa Regional	34.4	—
Southern Africa Regional	146.8	15.7
Regional	401.8	36.8
Europe	15,843.0	21.3
Austria	726.1	—
Belgium-Luxembourg	560.0	—
Denmark	280.8	—
France	3,190.3	—
Germany, West	1,472.4	—
West Berlin	119.0	—
Iceland	60.2	—
Ireland	146.5	—
Italy	1,699.5	3.6
Malta	74.6	—
Netherlands	991.6	—
Norway	276.8	—
Poland	61.0	—
Portugal	486.2	—
Romania	12.3	0.7
Spain	609.6	7.0
Sweden	106.9	—
United Kingdom	3,834.9	—
Yugoslavia	583.9	10.0
Regional	550.7	—
Other Oceania	1.8	1.3
Interregional	9,403.7	889.9

*Less than $50,000. —No economic assistance. [a]Prior to division into Vietnam, Cambodia, and Laos in 1955.

SELECTED FOREIGN EMBASSIES AND AMBASSADORS

Source: Department of State

Afghanistan: 2341 Wyoming Ave. NW, 20008
Chargé: A. Ghafar Farahi

Argentina: 1600 New Hampshire Ave. NW, 20009
Amb: Jorge A. Aja Espil

Australia: 1601 Massachusetts Ave. NW, 20036
Amb: Nicholas F. Parkinson

Austria: 2343 Massachusetts Ave. NW, 20008
Amb: Karl H. Schober

Bahamas: Suite 865, 600 New Hampshire Ave. NW, 20037
Amb.: Reginald L. Wood

Bangladesh: 3421 Massachusetts Ave. NW, 20007
Amb: Tabarak Husain

Belgium: 3330 Garfield St. NW, 20008
Amb: J. Raoul Schoumaker

Benin: 2737 Cathedral Ave. NW, 20008
Amb: Thomas S. Boya

Bolivia: 3014 Massachusetts Ave. NW, 20008
Amb: Roberto Arce A.

Brazil: 3006 Massachusetts Ave. NW, 20008
Amb: Antonio F.A. da Silveira

Bulgaria: 2100 16th St. NW, 20009
Amb: Konstantin N. Grigorov

Canada: 1746 Massachusetts Ave. NW, 20036
Amb: Peter M. Towe

Chad: Suite 410, 2600 Virginia Ave. NW, 20037
Chargé: Mahamat Ali Adoum

Chile: 1732 Massachusetts Ave. NW, 20036
Amb: Jose Miguel Barros

China (P.R.C.): 2300 Connecticut Ave. NW, 20008
Amb: Chai Zemin

Colombia: 2118 Leroy Pl. NW, 20008
Amb: Virgilio Barco

Costa Rica: 2112 S St. NW, 20008
Amb: Jose R. Echeverria

Cyprus: 2211 R St. NW, 20008
Amb: Andrew J. Jacovides

Czechoslovakia: 3900 Linnean Ave. NW, 20008
Amb: Dr. Jaromir Johanes

Denmark: 3200 Whitehaven St. NW, 20008
Amb: Otto R. Borch

Dominican Republic: 1715 22nd St. NW, 20008
Amb: Enriquillo A. del Rosario C.

Ecuador: 2535 15th St. NW, 20009
Amb: Ricardo Crespo-Zaldumbide

Egypt: 2310 Decatur Pl. NW, 20008
Amb: Dr. Ashraf A. Ghorbal

El Salvador: 2308 California St. NW, 20008
Amb.: Francisco Aquino

Ethiopia: 2134 Kalorama Rd. NW, 20008
Chargé: Tesfaye Demeke

Finland: 3216 New Mexico Ave. NW, 20016
Amb: Jaakko Iloniemi

France: 2535 Belmont Rd. NW, 20008
Amb: Francois de Laboulaye

Germany (Federal Rep.): 4645 Reservoir Rd. NW, 20007
Amb: Peter Hermes

German Democratic Rep.: 1717 Massachusetts Ave. NW, 20036
Amb: Dr. Horst Grunert

Ghana: 2460 16th St. NW, 20009
Amb: Dr. Alex Quaison-Sackey

Greece: 2221 Massachusetts Ave. NW, 20008
Amb: John A. Tzounis

Guatemala: 2220 R St. NW, 20008
Amb: Gen. Felipe D. Monterroso

Guinea: 2112 Leroy Pl. NW, 20008
Amb: Mamadi Lamine Conde

Guyana: 2490 Tracy Pl. NW, 20008
Amb: Laurence E. Mann

Honduras: Suite 100, 4301 Connecticut Ave. NW, 20008
Amb: Ricardo A. Midence

Hungary: 3910 Shoemaker St. NW, 20008
Amb: Ferenc Esztergalyos

India: 2107 Massachusetts Ave. NW, 20008
Chargé: Ashok B. Gokhale

Indonesia: 2020 Massachusetts Ave. NW, 20036
Amb: D. Ashari

Ireland: 2234 Massachusetts Ave. NW, 20008
Amb: Sean Donlon

Israel: 1621 22nd St. NW, 20008
Amb: Ephraim Evron

Italy: 1601 Fuller St. NW, 20009
Amb: Paolo Pansa Cedronio

Jamaica: 1666 Connecticut Ave. NW, 20009
Amb: Alfred A. Rattray

Japan: 2520 Massachusetts Ave. NW, 20008
Amb: Yoshio Okawara

Jordan: 2319 Wyoming Ave. NW, 20008
Amb: Al-Sharif Fawaz Sharif

Kenya: 2249 R St. NW, 20008
Amb: John P. Mbogua

Korea: 2370 Massachusetts Ave. NW, 20008
Amb: Yong Shik Kim

Laos: 2222 S St. NW, 20008
Chargé: Khamtan Ratanavong

Lebanon: 2560 28th St. NW, 20008
Amb: Khalil Itani

Liberia: 5201 16th St. NW, 20037
Amb: Herbert R.W. Brewer

Libya: 1118 22nd St. NW, 20037 Sec. of People's Com.: Dr. Ali A. Elhouderi

Luxembourg: 2200 Massachusetts Ave. NW, 20008
Amb: Adrien Meisch

Malawi: Bristol House, 1400 20th St. NW, 20036
Amb: Jacob T.X. Muwamba

Malaysia: 2401 Massachusetts Ave. NW, 20008
Amb: Zain Azraai

Malta: 2017 Connecticut Ave. NW, 20008
Chargé: Leslie N. Agius

Mexico: 2829 16th St. NW, 20009
Amb: Hugo B. Margain

Morocco: 1601 21st St. NW, 20009
Amb: Ali Bengelloun

Nepal: 2131 Leroy Pl. NW, 20008
Amb: Dr. Bekh Bahadur Thapa

Netherlands: 4200 Linnean Ave. NW, 20008
Amb: Age R. Tammenoms Bakker

New Zealand: 37 Observatory Cir. NW, 20008
Chargé: Hugo Judd

Nicaragua: 1627 New Hampshire Ave. NW, 20009
Amb: Dr. Rafael Solis

Nigeria: 2201 M St. NW, 20037
Amb: Olujimi Jolaoso

Norway: 2720 34th St. NW, 20008
Amb: Knut Hedemann

Pakistan: 2315 Massachusetts Ave. NW, 20008
Amb: Sultan Muhammad Khan

Panama: 2862 McGill Terr. NW, 20008
Amb: Juan Jose Amado

Paraguay: 2400 Massachusetts Ave. NW, 20008
Amb: Mario López Escobar

Peru: 1700 Massachusetts Ave. NW, 20036
Amb: Alfonso Arias-Schreiber

Philippines: 1617 Massachusetts Ave. NW, 20036
Amb: Eduardo Z. Romualdez

Poland: 2640 16th St. NW, 20009
Amb: Romauld Spasowski

Portugal: 2125 Kalorama Rd. NW, 20008
Amb: João Hall Themido

Romania: 1607 23rd St. NW, 20008
Amb: Nicolae Ionescu

Saudi Arabia: 1520 18th St. NW, 20036
Amb: Sheikh Faisal Alhegelan

Senegal: 2112 Wyoming Ave. NW, 20008
Amb: André Coulbary

Singapore: 1824 R St. NW, 20009
Amb: Punch Coomaraswamy

South Africa: 3051 Massachusetts Ave. NW, 20008
Amb: Donald B. Sole

Spain: 2700 15th St. NW, 20009
Amb: José Llado

Sri Lanka: 2148 Wyoming Ave. NW, 20008
Amb: Dr. W.S. Karunaratne

Sudan: Suite 400, 600 New Hampshire Ave. NW, 20037
Amb: Omer Salih Eissa

Sweden: Suite 1200, 600 New Hampshire Ave. NW, 20037
Amb: Count Wilhelm Wachtmeister

Switzerland: 2900 Cathedral Ave. NW, 20008
Amb: Raymond Probst

Syria: 2215 Wyoming Ave. NW, 20008
Amb: Dr. Sabah Kabbani

Tanzania: 2139 R St. NW, 20008
Amb: Paul Bomani

Thailand: 2300 Kalorama Rd. NW, 20008
Amb: Prok Amaranand

Trinidad and Tobago: 1708 Massachusetts Ave. NW, 20036
Amb: Victor C. McIntyre

Tunisia: 2408 Massachusetts Ave. NW, 20008
Amb: Ali Hedda

Turkey: 1606 23rd St. NW, 20008
Amb: Sukru Elekdag

Union of Soviet Socialist Republics: 1125 16th St. NW, 20036
Amb: Anatoliy F. Dobrynin

United Kingdom: 3100 Massachusetts Ave. NW, 20008
Amb: Sir Nicholas Henderson

Upper Volta: 5500 16th St. NW, 20011
Amb: Télesphore Yaguibou

Uruguay: 1918 F St. NW, 20006
Amb: Jorge Pacheco Areco

Venezuela: 2445 Massachusetts Ave. NW, 20008
Amb: Marcial Perez-Chiriboga

Yugoslavia: 2410 California St. NW, 20008
Amb: Budimir Loncar

Zaire: 1800 New Hampshire Ave. NW, 20009
Amb: Kasongo Mutuale

Zambia: 2419 Massachusetts Ave. NW, 20008
Amb: Putteho M. Ngonda

ACTION

As of July 1, 1971, a number of federal volunteer service programs—the Peace Corps and its domestic equivalent, VISTA, most prominent among them—were merged into a single agency, called ACTION. It is headed by Sam Brown, former state treasurer of Colorado.

The components of the organization and their volunteer strengths estimated in fiscal year 1980 are:

The Peace Corps, with 5,900 volunteers serving full-time in 64 developing countries. Its estimated fiscal year 1980 budget is $105 million.

Volunteers in Service to America (VISTA), with 5,475 volunteers at work full-time in programs throughout the United States. Its fiscal 1980 budget is $37 million.

The Retired Senior Volunteer Program (RSVP), which provides volunteer opportunities for elderly persons. It has 250,000 volunteers and a budget of $23 million.

Two other volunteer programs provide stipends to low-income senior citizens who devote 20 hours each week to institutionalized children or to the homebound elderly. With an estimated FY 1980 budget of $41 million, ACTION supports 16,640 volunteers in the Foster Grandparent Program. Approximately 3,300 elderly men and women serve as Senior Companions, a program that has a FY 1980 budget of $8 million.

ACTION's Urban Volunteer Programs include Technical Management Assistance, Fixed-Income Consumer Counseling, Helping Hand, and Good Neighborhood Fund, with a 1980 budget of $25 million and with an estimated 79,000 volunteers.

AMERICAN DIPLOMATS ABROAD

SOURCE: U.S. Department of State

*Chargé d'Affaires.

**Ambassador-nominated.

Country	Chief of Mission
Afghanistan	J. Bruce Amstutz*
Algeria	Ulric St. C. Haynes, Jr.
Argentina	Harry W. Salaudeman
Australia	Philip H. Alston, Jr.
Austria	Philip M. Kaiser
Bahamas	William B. Schwartz, Jr.
Bahrain	Peter A. Sutherland
Bangladesh	David T. Schneider
Barbados	Sally Angela Shelton
Belgium	Anne Cox Chambers
Benin	John S. Davidson*
Bolivia	Marvin Weissman
Botswana	Horace G. Dawson, Jr.
Brazil	Robert M. Sayre
Bulgaria	Jack R. Perry
Burma	Patricia M. Byrne
Burundi	Frances D. Cook
Cameroon	Hume A. Horan
Canada	Kenneth M. Curtis
Cape Verde	Peter deVos
Central African Republic	Arthur H. Woodruff
Chad	Donald R. Norland
Chile	George W. Landau
China (People's Rep.)	Leonard Woodcock
Colombia	Thomas D. Boyatt
Comoros	Fernando E. Rondon
Congo	William L. Swing
Costa Rica	Francis J. McNeil
Cyprus	Galen L. Stone
Czechoslovakia	Byron Morton, Jr.*
Denmark	Warren D. Manshel
Djibouti	Jerrold M. North
Dominica	Sally Angela Shelton
Dominican Rep.	Robert L. Yost
Ecuador	Raymond E. Gonzalez
Egypt	Alfred L. Atherton, Jr.
El Salvador	Robert E. White
Equatorial Guinea	Hume A. Horan
Ethiopia	Frederic L. Chapin
Fiji	William Bodde, Jr.
Finland	James E. Goodby
France	Arthur A. Hartman
Gabon	Arthur T. Tienken
The Gambia	Larry G. Piper
German Democratic Rep.	Herbert S. Okun
Germany, Fed. Rep. of	Walter J. Stoessel, Jr.
Ghana	Thomas W. M. Smith
Greece	Robert J. McCloskey
Grenada	Sally Angela Shelton
Guatemala	Frank V. Ortiz, Jr.
Guinea	Allen C. Davis
Guinea-Bissau	Peter deVos
Guyana	George B. Roberts, Jr.
Haiti	Henry L. Kimelman
Honduras	Jack R. Binns
Hungary	Harry E. Bergold, Jr.
Iceland	Richard A. Ericson, Jr.
India	Robert F. Goheen
Indonesia	Edward E. Masters
Ireland	William V. Shannon
Israel	Samuel W. Lewis
Italy	Richard N. Gardner
Ivory Coast	Nancy V. Rawis
Jamaica	Loren E. Lawrence
Japan	Michael J. Mansfield
Jordan	Nicholas A. Veliotes
Kenya	William C. Harrop
Kiribati	William Bodde, Jr.
Korea	William H. Gleysteen, Jr.
Kuwait	Francois M. Dickman
Laos	Leo J. Moser*
Lebanon	John G. Dean
Lesotho	John R. Clingerman
Liberia	Robert P. Smith
Libya	William L. Eagleton, Jr.*
Luxembourg	James G. Lowenstein
Madagascar	Fernando E. Rondon
Malawi	John A. Burroughs, Jr.
Malaysia	Barbara M. Watson
Maldives	Donald R. Toussaint
Mali	Anne F. Holloway
Malta	Joan M. Clark
Mauritania	Henry Precht
Mauritius	Robert C. F. Gordon
Mexico	Julian Nava
Morocco	Angier B. Duke
Mozambique	David E. Simcox
Nauru	Philip H. Alston, Jr.
Nepal	Philip R. Trimble
Netherlands	Geri M. Joseph
New Zealand	Anne C. Martindell
Nicaragua	Lawrence A. Pezzullo
Niger	James K. Bishop
Nigeria	Stephen Low
Norway	Sidney A. Rand
Oman	Marshall W. Wiley
Pakistan	Arthur W. Hummel, Jr.
Panama	Ambler H. Moss, Jr.
Papua New Guinea	Harvey J. Feldman
Paraguay	Lyle F. Lane
Peru	Edwin G. Corr
Philippines	Richard W. Murphy
Poland	Francis J. Meehan
Portugal	Richard J. Bloomfield
Qatar	Charles E. Marthinsen
Romania	O. Rudolph Aggrey
Rwanda	Harry R. Melone
Saint Lucia	Sally Angela Shelton
São Tomé & Principe	Arthur T. Tienken
Saudi Arabia	John C. West
Senegal	Walter C. Carrington
Seychelles	William C. Harrop
Sierra Leone	Theresa A. Healy
Singapore	Harry E.T. Thayer
Solomon Isls.	Harvey J. Feldman
Somalia	Donald K. Petterson
South Africa	William B. Edmundson
Spain	Terence A. Todman
Sri Lanka	Donald R. Toussaint
Sudan	C. William Kontos
Suriname	John P. Crowley, Jr.
Swaziland	Richard C. Matheron
Sweden	Rodney O. Kennedy-Minott
Switzerland	Richard D. Vine
Syria	Talcott W. Seelye
Tanzania	Richard N. Viets
Thailand	Morton I. Abramowitz
Togo	Marilyn P. Johnson
Tonga	Willaim Bodde, Jr.
Trinidad and Tobago	Irving G. Cheslaw
Tunisia	Stephen Warren Bosworth
Turkey	James W. Spain
Tuvalu	William Bodde, Jr.
Uganda	Gordon R. Beyer
U.S.S.R.	Thomas J. Watson, Jr.
United Arab Emirates	William D. Wolle
United Kingdom	Kingman Brewster, Jr.
Upper Volta	Larry Grahl*
Uruguay	Robert S. Gershenson**
Venezuela	William H. Luers
Western Samoa	Anne C. Martindell
Yemen	George M. Lane
Yugoslavia	Lawrence S. Eagleburger
Zaire	Robert B. Oakley
Zambia	Frank G. Wisner, II
Zimbabwe	Robert V. Keeley
Special Missions:	
United Nations	Donald F. McHenry
U.N. (European Office)	Gerald B. Helman
U.N.E.S.C.O.	Barbara W. Newell
O.A.S.	Gale W. McGee
N.A.T.O.	W. Tapley Bennett, Jr.
O.E.C.D.	Herbert Salzman
I.A.E.A.	Gerard C. Smith
U.S.E.C.	Thomas O. Enders
I.C.A.O.	John E. Downs
Ambassadors at Large	Elliot L. Richardson, Gerard C. Smith, Henry D. Owen, W. Beverly Carter, Jr., Robert Krueger, Victor H. Palmieri

BRITISH PRIME MINISTERS

Monarch and Prime Minister	Party	Served
George I, 1714–27		
Robert Walpole	Whig	1721–1727
George II, 1727–60		
Robert Walpole, Earl of Orford	Whig	1727–1742
Spencer Compton, Earl of Wilmington	Whig	1742–1743
Henry Pelham	Whig	1743–1754
Thomas Pelham-Holles,[1] Duke of Newcastle	Whig	1754–1756
William Cavendish, Duke of Devonshire	Whig	1756–1757
Thomas Pelham-Holles, Duke of Newcastle	Whig	1757–1760
George III, 1760–1820		
Thomas Pelham-Holles, Duke of Newcastle	Whig	1760–1762
John Stuart, Earl of Bute	Tory	1762–1763
George Grenville	Whig	1763–1765
Charles Watson-Wentworth, Marquis of Rockingham	Whig	1765–1766
William Pitt, Earl of Chatham	Coalition	1766–1767
Augustus Henry Fitzroy, Duke of Grafton	Whig	1767–1770
Frederick North, Lord North	Tory	1770–1782
Charles Watson-Wentworth, Marquis of Rockingham	Whig	1782
William Petty, Earl of Shelburne	Whig	1782–1783
William Henry Cavendish Bentinck, Duke of Portland	Coalition	1783
William Pitt (the Younger)	Tory	1783–1801
Henry Addington	Tory	1801–1804
William Pitt (the Younger)	Tory	1804–1806
William Wyndham Grenville,[2] Lord Grenville	Whig	1806–1807
William Henry Cavendish Bentinck, Duke of Portland	Tory	1807–1809
Spencer Perceval (assassinated)	Tory	1809–1812
Robert Banks Jenkinson, Earl of Liverpool	Tory	1812–1820
George IV, 1820–30		
Robert Banks Jenkinson, Earl of Liverpool	Tory	1820–1827
George Canning	Tory	1827
Frederick John Robinson, Viscount Goderich	Tory	1827–1828
Arthur Wellesley, Duke of Wellington	Tory	1828–1830
William IV, 1830–37		
Charles Grey, Earl Grey	Whig	1830–1834
William Lamb, Viscount Melbourne	Whig	1834
Sir Robert Peel	Tory	1834–1835
William Lamb, Viscount Melbourne	Whig	1835–1837
Victoria, 1837–1901		
William Lamb, Viscount Melbourne	Whig	1837–1841
Sir Robert Peel	Tory	1841–1846
John Russell,[3] Lord Russell	Whig	1846–1852
Edward George Geoffrey Smith Stanley, Earl of Derby	Tory	1852
George Hamilton Gordon, Earl of Aberdeen	Peelite[4]	1852–1855
Victoria, 1837–1901		
Henry John Temple, Viscount Palmerston	Liberal	1855–1858
Edward George Geoffrey Smith Stanley, Earl of Derby	Tory	1858–1859
Henry John Temple, Viscount Palmerston	Liberal	1859–1865
John Russell, Earl Russell	Liberal	1865–1866
Edward George Geoffrey Smith Stanley, Earl of Derby	Conservative	1866–1868
Benjamin Disraeli	Conservative	1868
William Ewart Gladstone	Liberal	1868–1874
Benjamin Disraeli, Earl of Beaconsfield	Conservative	1874–1880
William Ewart Gladstone	Liberal	1880–1885
Robert Arthur Talbot Gascoyne-Cecil, Marquis of Salisbury	Conservative	1885–1886
William Ewart Gladstone	Liberal	1886
Robert Arthur Talbot Gascoyne-Cecil, Marquis of Salisbury	Conservative	1886–1892
William Ewart Gladstone	Liberal	1892–1894
Archibald Philip Primrose, Earl of Rosebery	Liberal	1894–1895
Robert Arthur Talbot Gascoyne-Cecil, Marquis of Salisbury	Conservative	1895–1901
Edward VII, 1901–1910		
Robert Arthur Talbot Gascoyne-Cecil, Marquis of Salisbury	Conservative	1901–1902
Arthur James Balfour	Conservative	1902–1905
Sir Henry Campbell-Bannerman	Liberal	1905–1908
Herbert Henry Asquith	Liberal	1908–1910
George V, 1910–36		
Herbert Henry Asquith	Liberal	1910–1915
Herbert Henry Asquith	Coalition	1915–1916
David Lloyd George	Coalition	1916–1922
Andrew Bonar Law	Conservative	1922–1923
Stanley Baldwin	Conservative	1923–1924
James Ramsay MacDonald	Labour	1924
Stanley Baldwin	Conservative	1924–1929
James Ramsay MacDonald	Labour	1929–1931
James Ramsay MacDonald	Coalition	1931–1935
Stanley Baldwin	Coalition	1935–1936
Edward VIII, 1936 (abdicated)		
George VI, 1936–52		
Stanley Baldwin, Earl Baldwin of Bewdley	Coalition	1936–1937
(Arthur) Neville Chamberlain	Coalition	1937–1940
Winston Leonard Spencer Churchill	Coalition	1940–1945
Winston Leonard Spencer Churchill	Conservative	1945
Clement Richard Attlee	Labour	1945–1951
Winston Leonard Spencer Churchill	Conservative	1951–1952
Elizabeth II, 1952–		
Sir Winston Leonard Spencer Churchill	Conservative	1952–1955
Sir (Robert) Anthony Eden	Conservative	1955–1957
(Maurice) Harold Macmillan	Conservative	1957–1963
Sir Alec Douglas-Home	Conservative	1963–1964
(James) Harold Wilson	Labour	1964–1970
Edward Heath	Conservative	1970–1974
Harold Wilson	Labour	1974–1976
James Callaghan	Labour	1976–1979
Margaret Thatcher	Conservative	1979–

[1] Brother of Henry Pelham. [2] Son of George Grenville. [3] Lord Russell, later Earl Russell, sat in the House of Commons in his first ministry and in the House of Lords in his second. [4] On the sudden death of Sir Robert Peel in 1850, the Earl of Aberdeen became the leader of the Peelites, a coalition that supported the corn law and public reform policies of Sir Robert Peel.

THE COMMONWEALTH (September 1, 1980)

Formed in 1931, the Commonwealth is now a free association of 43 sovereign states and their dependencies.

State (date of entry)	Location	Administrative Center	Area (sq. mi.)	Population
UNITED KINGDOM* (12/31/31)	Europe	London	94,399	55,883,100
Brunei	Borneo	Bandar Seri Begawan	2,226	213,000
Dependencies				
Belize	Central America	Belmopan	8,867	153,000
Bermuda	Atlantic Ocean	Hamilton	21	57,000
British Antarctic Terr.	Antarctica	Stanley, Falkland Islands	600,000	uninhabited
British Indian Ocean Terr.	Indian Ocean	London, U.K.	29	2,000
British Virgin Islands	West Indies	Road Town	59	12,000
Cayman Islands	West Indies	George Town	100	14,000
Falkland Islands	Atlantic Ocean	Stanley	6,198	1,950
Gibraltar	Europe	Gibraltar	2.28	29,000
Hong Kong	Asia	Victoria	403	4,606,000
Montserrat	West Indies	Plymouth	40	11,000
Pitcairn Islands	Oceania	Adamstown	18	65
St. Helena	Atlantic Ocean	Jamestown	162	6,400
Turks and Caicos Islands	West Indies	Cockburn Town (on Grand Turk)	166	6,000
West Indies Associated States				
Antigua	West Indies	St. John's	171	74,000
St. Christopher-Nevis-Anguilla	West Indies	Basseterre	155	67,000
AUSTRALIA (12/31/31)	Oceania	Canberra	2,967,909	14,418,000
Dependencies				
Ashmore & Cartier Islands	Indian Ocean	—	1.9	uninhabited
Australian Antarctic Terr.	Antarctica	—	2,362,875	uninhabited
Christmas Island	Indian Ocean	Flying Fish Cove	52	3,264
Cocos Islands	Indian Ocean	West Island	5.4	392
Coral Sea Islands	Oceania	—	8.5	3
Heard and McDonald Islands	Indian Ocean	—	113	uninhabited
Norfolk Island	Oceania	Kingston	13.3	2,180
NEW ZEALAND (12/31/31)	Oceania	Wellington	103,736	3,096,000
Dependencies				
Cook Islands	Oceania	Avarua	91	18,200
Niue	Oceania	Alofi	100	4,000
Ross Dependency	Antarctica	—	290,000	uninhabited
Tokelau Islands	Oceania	Fenuafala	3.95	1,625
BAHAMAS (7/10/73)	Atlantic Ocean	Nassau	5,382	225,000
BANGLADESH (4/18/72)	Asia	Dacca	55,126	85,645,000
BARBADOS (11/30/66)	West Indies	Bridgetown	166	265,000
BOTSWANA (9/30/66)	Africa	Gaborone	224,764	791,000
CANADA (12/31/31)	North America	Ottawa	3,851,809	23,809,000
CYPRUS (3/13/61)	Mediterranean	Nicosia	3,572	621,000
DOMINICA (11/3/78)	West Indies	Roseau	291	81,000
FIJI (10/10/70)	Oceania	Suva	7,055	612,000
GAMBIA (2/18/65)	Africa	Banjul	4,127	585,000
GHANA (3/6/57)	Africa	Accra	92,099	10,969,000
GRENADA (2/7/74)	West Indies	St. George's	133	97,000
GUYANA (5/26/66)	South America	Georgetown	83,000	820,000
INDIA (8/15/47)	Asia	New Delhi	1,269,339	650,982,000
JAMAICA (8/6/62)	West Indies	Kingston	4,244	2,133,000
KENYA (12/12/63)	Africa	Nairobi	224,960	15,322,000
KIRIBATI (7/12/79)	Oceania	Bairiki (on Tarawa)	354	58,000
LESOTHO (10/4/66)	Africa	Maseru	11,720	1,279,000
MALAWI (7/6/64)	Africa	Lilongwe	45,747	5,817,000
MALAYSIA (9/16/63)	Asia	Kuala Lumpur	128,308	12,960,000
MALTA (9/21/64)	Mediterranean	Valletta	122	354,000
MAURITIUS (3/12/68)	Indian Ocean	Port Louis	790	940,000
NAURU (1/31/68)‡	Oceania	Yaren district	7.7	7,100
NIGERIA (10/1/60)	Africa	Lagos	379,628	84,500,000
PAPUA NEW GUINEA (9/16/75)	Oceania	Port Moresby	183,540	3,079,000
SAINT LUCIA (2/22/79)	West Indies	Castries	238	112,000
SAINT VINCENT & THE GRENADINES (10/27/79)	West Indies	Kingstown	150	104,000
SEYCHELLES (6/28/76)	Indian Ocean	Victoria	171	63,000
SIERRA LEONE (4/27/61)	Africa	Freetown	27,295	3,200,000
SINGAPORE (10/16/65)	Asia	Singapore	233	2,363,000
SOLOMON ISLANDS (7/7/78)	Oceania	Honiara	11,500	215,000
SRI LANKA (2/4/48)	Asia	Colombo	25,332	14,184,000
SWAZILAND (9/6/68)	Africa	Mbabane	6,705	544,000
TANZANIA (4/26/64)	Africa	Dar es Salaam	363,708	17,048,000
TONGA (6/4/70)	Oceania	Nuku'alofa	270	93,000
TRINIDAD AND TOBAGO (8/31/62)	West Indies	Port-of-Spain	1,980	1,133,000
TUVALU (10/1/78)‡	Oceania	Fongafale	9.78	10,000
UGANDA (10/9/62)	Africa	Kampala	91,076	13,225,000
WESTERN SAMOA (8/28/70)	South Pacific	Apia	1,133	154,000
ZAMBIA (10/24/64)	Africa	Lusaka	290,586	5,649,000
ZIMBABWE (4/18/80)	Africa	Salisbury	150,803	7,140,000

*As crown fiefdoms, the Isle of Man (227 sq. mi.; 63,000 pop.) and the Channel Islands (74 sq. mi.; 130,000 pop.) are included in the Commonwealth.
‡Special member

WORLD COMMUNIST PARTY STRENGTH

SOURCE: Richard F. Staar, (ed.), 1980 Yearbook on International Communist Affairs.
Hoover Institution Press, Stanford, CA 94305 © 1980

Country or Area	Communist Party Membership	Percent of vote; seats in legislature	Status	Sino-Soviet Dispute
Afghanistan	100,000	No elections scheduled	In power	Pro-Soviet
Albania	101,500	99.9 (1978); all 250 seats	In power	Independent
Algeria	400	– (1976)	Proscribed	Pro-Soviet
Argentina	70,000	No elections scheduled	Legal	Pro-Soviet
Australia	5,000	– (1977); no seats	Legal	Split
Austria	22,500	0.96 (1979); no seats	Legal	Pro-Soviet
Bangladesh	2,500	– (1979); 1 of 300 seats	Proscribed	Split
Belgium	10,000	3.3 (1978); 4 of 212 seats	Legal	Pro-Soviet
Berlin, West	7,500	1.1 (1979); no seats	Legal	Pro-Soviet
Bolivia	2,500	– (1979)	Proscribed	Split
Brazil	4,000	– (1978); no seats	Proscribed	Split
Bulgaria	817,000	99.9 (1976); 272 of 400 seats	In power	Pro-Soviet
Burma	7,000	– (1978)	Proscribed	Pro-Chinese
Cambodia	Unknown	No elections scheduled	In power	Pro-Soviet
Canada	2,500	0.2 (1979); no seats	Legal	Split
Chile	75,000	Elections promised	Proscribed	Split
China	37,000,000	Indirect elections	In power	—
Colombia	12,000	1.9 (1978); 3 of 311 seats	Legal	Split
Costa Rica	3,000	2.7 (1978); 2 of 57 seats	Legal	Pro-Soviet
Cuba	200,000	91.7 (1976); 441 of 481 seats	In power	Pro-Soviet
Cyprus	12,000	30.0 (1976); 9 of 35 Greek Cypriot seats	Legal	Pro-Soviet
Czechoslovakia	1,473,000	99.7 (1976); all 350 seats	In power	Pro-Soviet
Denmark	8,000	1.9 (1979)	Legal	Pro-Soviet
Dominican Republic	5,000	– (1978)	Legal	Factions
Ecuador	2,000	3.2 (1979); no seats	Legal	Split
Egypt	500	– (1979)	Proscribed	Pro-Soviet
El Salvador	225	– (1976); no seats	Legal	Pro-Soviet
Finland	45,000	17.9 (1979); 35 of 200 seats	Legal	Pro-Soviet
France	700,000	20.6 (1978); 86 of 491 seats	Legal	Pro-Soviet
Germany, East	2,107,981	99.9 (1976); 127 of 500 seats	In power	Pro-Soviet
Germany, West	42,000	0.3 (1976); no seats	Legal	Pro-Soviet
Greece	29,300	9.3 (1977); 11 of 300 seats	Legal	Split
Guadeloupe	3,000	– (1979); 7 of 36 seats	Legal	Pro-Soviet
Guatemala	750	– (1974); no seats	Proscribed	Pro-Soviet
Guyana	500	26.0 (1973); 14 of 53 seats	Legal	Pro-Soviet
Haiti	250	– (1973)	Proscribed	Pro-Soviet
Honduras	650	Elections scheduled 1979/80	Proscribed	Split
Hong Kong	2,000	—	Legal	Pro-Chinese
Hungary	797,000	99.6 (1975); all 352 seats	In power	Pro-Soviet
Iceland	3,000	19.7 (1979); 11 of 60 seats	Legal	Independent
India	100,000	4.3 (1977); 22 of 244 seats	Legal	Neutral
Indonesia	1,000	– (1977)	Proscribed	Split
Iran	1,500	– (1975)	Proscribed	Pro-Soviet
Iraq	2,000	No elections since 1958	Allowed	Pro-Soviet
Ireland	600	– (1977); no seats	Legal	Pro-Soviet
Israel	1,500	4.6 (1977); 5 of 120 seats	Legal	Pro-Soviet
Italy	1,790,450	30.4 (1979); 201 of 630 seats	Legal	Pro-Soviet
Jamaica	400	– (1976); no seats	Allowed	Pro-Soviet
Japan	400,000	10.4 (1979); 39 of 511 seats	Legal	Pro-Soviet
Jordan	500	– (1967)	Proscribed	Pro-Soviet
Korea, North	2,000,000	100.0 (1977); all 579 seats	In power	Neutral
Laos	15,000	No elections scheduled	In power	Pro-Soviet
Lebanon	2,500	– (1972); no seats	Legal	Pro-Soviet
Lesotho	negligible	—	Proscribed	Pro-Soviet
Luxembourg	600	4.8 (1979); 2 of 59 seats	Legal	Pro-Soviet
Malaysia	3,150	– (1978)	Proscribed	Split
Malta	100	– (1976); no seats	Legal	Pro-Soviet
Martinique	1,000	– (1979); 3 of 36 seats	Legal	Pro-Soviet
Mexico	25,000	5.0 (1979); 12 to 20 of 400 seats	Legal	Pro-Soviet
Mongolia	67,000	99.9 (1977); all 354 seats	In power	Pro-Soviet
Morocco	700	– (1977); no seats	Allowed	Pro-Soviet
Nepal	5,000	– (1959)	Proscribed	Split
Netherlands	15,000	1.7 (1977); 2 of 150 seats	Legal	Pro-Soviet
New Zealand	500	0.2 (1978); no seats	Legal	Neutral
Nicaragua	410	– (1974)	Proscribed	Split
Nigeria	unknown	– (1976)	Proscribed	Pro-Soviet
Norway	2,000	5.2 (1977); 2 of 155 seats	Legal	Independent
Pakistan	few hundred	– (1979); elections postponed	Proscribed	Split
Panama	500	– (1972); no seats	Allowed	Pro-Soviet
Paraguay	3,500	– (1973); no seats	Proscribed	Split
Peru	4,700	5.9 (1978); 6 of 100 seats	Legal	Split
Philippines	4,250	– (1978)	Proscribed	Split
Poland	3,080,000	99.4 (1976); 262 of 460 seats	In power	Pro-Soviet
Portugal	164,000	19.0 (1979); 47 of 263 seats	Legal	Pro-Soviet
Puerto Rico	125	– (1976); no seats	Legal	Pro-Soviet

Country or Area	Communist Party Membership	Percent of vote; seats in legislature	Status	Sino-Soviet Dispute
Réunion	2,000	32.8 (1978); none in Paris	Legal	Independent
Romania	2,930,000	99.9 (1975); all 349 seats	In power	Neutral
San Marino	300	21.1 (1978); 16 of 60 seats	Legal	Pro-Soviet
Saudi Arabia	negligible	—; no elections scheduled	Proscribed	Pro-Soviet
Senegal	2,000	0.32 (1978); no seats	Legal	Pro-Soviet
Singapore	500	— (1976)	Proscribed	Pro-Chinese
South Africa	Unknown	— (1977)	Proscribed	Pro-Soviet
Spain	200,000	10.5 (1979); 23 of 350 seats	Legal	Independent
Sri Lanka	6,000	1.9 (1977); no seats	Legal	Split
Sudan	3,500	— (1978); no parties	Proscribed	Pro-Soviet
Sweden	17,000	5.6 (1979); 20 of 349 seats	Legal	Independent
Switzerland	5,000	1.5 (1979); 3 of 200 seats	Legal	Pro-Soviet
Syria	5,000	— (1977); 6 of 195 seats	Allowed	Pro-Soviet
Thailand	1,200	— (1979)	Proscribed	Pro-Chinese
Tunisia	100	— (1974)	Proscribed	Pro-Soviet
Turkey	2,000	— (1977)	Proscribed	Pro-Soviet
USSR	16,630,000	99.9 (1979); all 1,500 seats CPSU-approved	In power	—
United Kingdom	20,599	0.5 (1979); no seats	Legal	Split
United States	18,000	0.2 (1976); no seats	Legal	Pro-Soviet
Uruguay	8,000	Elections promised by 1981	Proscribed	Pro-Soviet
Venezuela	10,000	9.0 (1978); 22 of 195 seats	Legal	Factions
Vietnam	1,533,500	99.0 (1976); all 492 seats	In power	Pro-Soviet
Yugoslavia	1,855,638	— (1978); all 308 seats	In power	Independent

SOVIET LEADERS: 1980   Source: U.S. Department of State

Brezhnev, Leonid I.
General Secretary, Soviet Communist party; b. 1906

POLITBURO
FULL MEMBERS

Brezhnev, Leonid I.
Chairman of the Presidium of the Supreme Soviet (President of the Soviet Union)

Kosygin, Aleksei N.
Chairman of the Council of Ministers; b. 1904

Suslov, Mikhail A.
A secretary, Soviet Communist party (ideology, foreign affairs); b. 1902

Kirilenko, Andrei P.
A secretary, Soviet Communist party (party affairs, industry); b. 1906

Pelshe, Arvid Y.
Chairman, Party Control Commission; b. 1899

Grishin, Viktor V.
First Secretary, Moscow city party organization; b. 1914

Kunayev, Dinmukhamed A.
First Secretary, Kazakhstan Communist party; b. 1912

Shcherbitsky, Vladimir V.
First Secretary, Ukrainian Communist party; b. 1918

Andropov, Yurly V.
KGB chief; b. 1914

Gromyko, Andrei A.
Minister of Foreign Affairs; b. 1909

Romanov, Grigory V.
First Secretary, Leningrad Oblast Party Committee; b. 1923

Ustinov, Dmitry F.
Minister of Defense; b. 1908

Chernenko, Konstantin U.
Head, General Department, Soviet Communist party Central Committee; b. 1911

Tikhonov, Nikolai A.
First Deputy Premier; b. 1905

CANDIDATE MEMBERS
Demichev, Pyotr N.
Minister of Culture; b. 1918

Masherov, Pyotr M.
First Secretary, Byelorussian Communist party; b. 1918

Solomentsev, Mikhail S.
Chairman of RSFSR Council of Ministers; b. 1913

Rashidov, Sharaf R.
First Secretary, Uzbek Communist party; b. 1917

Ponomaryov, Boris N.
A secretary (relations with nonruling parties); b. 1905

Aliyev, Geidar A.
First Secretary, Azerbaidzhan Communist party; b. 1923

Kuznetsov, Vasily V.
First Deputy Chairman, Presidium of the USSR Supreme Soviet; b. 1901

Shevardnadze, Eduard A.
Georgian Republic First Secretary; b. 1928

Gorbachev, Mikhail S.
A secretary (agriculture); b. 1931

COMMUNIST PARTY SECRETARIAT

Brezhnev, Leonid I.; Suslov, Mikhail A.; Kirilenko, Andrei P.; Chernenko, Konstantin U.

Ponomaryov, B. N.; Gorbachev, M. S.
(candidate members of Politburo)

Dolgikh, Vladimir I.
A secretary (heavy industry); b. 1924

Rusakov, Konstantin V.
A secretary (relations with ruling Communist parties); b. 1909

Kapitonov, Ivan V.
Head, Organizational Party Work Department, Soviet Communist Party Central Committee; b. 1915

Zimyanin, Mikhail V.
A secretary (culture, propaganda); b. 1914

RULERS OF CHINA: 1980   Source: Donald W. Klein, Department of Political Science, Tufts University

POLITBURO
FULL MEMBERS

*Hua Guofeng (Chairman), b.c. 1920
*Ye Jiangying (Vice-Chairman), b. 1898
*Deng Xiaoping (Vice-Chairman), b. 1904
*Li Xiannian (Vice-Chairman), b. 1907
*Chen Yun (Vice-Chairman), b.c. 1900
*Hu Yaobang, b. 1915
*Zhao Ziyang, b. 1919
Chen Yonggui, b.c. 1913
Deng Yingchao (Mrs. Zhou Enlai), b. 1903
*Also members of Politburo's Standing Committee.

Fang Yi, b. 1916
Geng Biao, b. 1909
Li Desheng, b. 1912
Liu Bocheng, b. 1892
Ni Zhifu
Nie Rongzhen, b. 1899
Peng Chong, b. 1915
Ulanhu, b. 1906
Wang Zhen, b. 1909
Wei Quoqing, b.c. 1914
Xu Shiyou, b.c. 1906
Xu Xiangqian, b. 1902
Yu Qiuli, b. 1914
Zhang Tingfa

STATE COUNCIL
Zhao Ziyang (Premier)
Bo Yibo (V.P.), b. 1907

Chen Muhua (V.P.)
Fang Yi (V.P.)
Geng Biao (V.P.)
Gu Mu, (V.P.), b. 1914
Huang Hua (V.P.) b.c. 1913
Ji Pengfei (V.P.)
Kang Shien (V.P.)
Wang Li (V.P.), b. 1916
Yang Jingren (V.P.)
Yao Yilin (V.P.), b. 1917
Zhang Aiping (V.P.), b.c. 1910

SECRETARIAT OF THE CHINESE COMMUNIST PARTY CENTRAL COMMITTEE
Hu Yaobang (General Secretary)
Fang Yi
Gu Mu

Hu Qiaomu, b. 1912
Hu Yaobang
Peng Chong
Song Renqiong, b. 1909
Wan Li
Wang Ronzhong
Yang Dezhi, b. 1910
Yao Yilin
Yu Qiuli

MILITARY AFFAIRS COMMITTEE
(of the Chinese Communist Party)
Hua Guofeng (Chairman)
Deng Xiaoping (V.C.)
Liu Bocheng (V.C.)
Nie Rongzhen (V.C.)
Xu Xiangqian (V.C.)
Ye Jiangying (V.C.)

MILITARY AFFAIRS

U.S. WARS AND CASUALTIES   Source: U.S. Department of Defense

Data prior to World War I are based, in many cases, on incomplete records. Casualty data are confined to dead and wounded personnel and therefore exclude personnel captured or missing in action who were subsequently returned to military control.

War	Branch of Service[†]	Number Serving	CASUALTIES Battle Deaths	CASUALTIES Other Deaths	Not Mortal Wounds
Revolutionary War (1775–1783)	Total	184,000–250,000 (estimated)	4,435	—	6,188
	Army		4,044	—	6,004
	Navy	—	342	—	114
	Marines	—	49	—	70
War of 1812 (1812–1815)	Total	286,730	2,260	—	4,505
	Army	—	1,950	—	4,000
	Navy	—	265	—	439
	Marines	—	45	—	66
Mexican War (1846–1848)	Total	78,718	1,733	11,550	4,152
	Army	—	1,721		4,102
	Navy	—	1	—	3
	Marines	—	11	—	47
Civil War (Union Forces only)[*] (1861–1865)	Total	2,213,363	140,414	224,097	281,881
	Army	2,128,948	138,154	221,374	280,040
	Navy	84,415	2,112	2,411	1,710
	Marines }		148	312	131
Spanish-American War (1898)	Total	306,760	385	2,061	1,662
	Army	280,564	369	2,061	1,594
	Navy	22,875	10	0	47
	Marines	3,321	6	0	21
World War I (6 April 1917– 11 November 1918)	Total	4,734,991	53,402	63,114	204,002
	Army	4,057,101	50,510	55,868	193,663
	Navy	599,051	431	6,856	819
	Marines	78,839	2,461	390	9,520
World War II (7 December 1941– 31 December 1946)[††]	Total	16,112,566	291,557	113,842	670,846
	Army	11,260,000	234,874	83,400	565,861
	Navy	4,183,466	36,950	25,664	37,778
	Marines	669,100	19,733	4,778	67,207
Korean War (25 June 1950– 27 July 1953)	Total	5,720,000	33,629	20,617	103,284
	Army	2,834,000	27,704	9,429	77,596
	Navy	1,177,000	458	4,043	1,576
	Marines	424,000	4,267	1,261	23,744
	Air Force	1,285,000	1,200	5,884	368
Vietnam War (1961—7 May 1975)	Total	3,300,000	47,072	10,390	303,706

[*] Authoritative statistics for the Confederate Forces are not available. Estimates of the number who served range from 600,000 to 1,500,000. Based upon incomplete information, 133,821 Confederates died (74,524 in battle and 59,297 otherwise). In addition, an estimated 26,000–31,000 Confederate personnel died in Union prisons. [†] U.S. Coast Guard data are excluded. [††] World War II hostilities declared terminated on December 31, 1946, by Presidential Proclamation.

U.S. VETERANS   Source: Veterans Administration

Veterans in civil life, end of month—

Total, September 1979	30,072,000
War Veterans—Total	26,310,000
Vietnam Era—Total	8,910,000
And service in Korean Conflict	547,000
No service in Korean Conflict	8,363,000
Korean Conflict—Total (includes line 4)	5,866,000
And service in WW II	1,187,000
No service in WW II	4,679,000
World War II (includes line 7)	12,674,000
World War I	594,000
Spanish-American War	209
Service between Korean Conflict (Jan. 31, 1955) and Vietnam (Aug. 5, 1964)	3,059,000

U.S. DEFENSE EXPENDITURES   Source: U.S. Office of Management and Budget

Fiscal Year	National defense[1] $ Billion	GNP $ Billion	Defense as % of GNP	Fiscal Year	National defense[1] $ Billion	GNP $ Billion	Defense as % of GNP
1960	45.2	497.3	9.1	1972	76.6	1,110.5	6.9
1961	46.6	508.3	9.2	1973	74.5	1,237.5	6.0
1962	50.4	546.9	9.2	1974	77.8	1,359.2	5.7
1963	51.5	576.3	8.9	1975	85.6	1,457.3	5.9
1964	52.7	616.2	8.6	1976	89.4	1,621.0	5.5
1965	48.6	657.1	7.4	TQ[2]	22.3	—	—
1966	55.9	721.1	7.8	1977	97.5	1,843.3	5.3
1967	69.1	774.4	8.9	1978	105.2	2,060.4	5.1
1968	79.4	829.9	9.6	1979	117.7	2,369.0	5.0
1969	79.4	903.7	8.8	1980 est.[3]	135.6	2,557.0	5.3
1970	78.6	959.0	8.2	1981 est.[3]	157.5	2,821.0	5.6
1971	75.8	1,019.3	7.4				

[1] Includes budget outlays for military activities of the Department of Defense, military assistance, atomic energy defense activities, and defense-related activities of civilian agencies. [2] See footnote 2, page 184. [3] Based on estimates of the 1981 Budget of the Mid-Session Review in July 1980.

NATIONAL GUARD 1979

Source: National Guard Bureau, U.S. Departments of the Army and the Air Force

State or Area	Units*	Personnel*	State or Area	Units*	Personnel*	State or Area	Units*	Personnel*	State or Area	Units*	Personnel*
TOTAL	4,500	49,096	Idaho	40	3,271	Missouri	102	10,476	Puerto Rico	67	10,756
Alabama	198	20,390	Illinois	103	9,834	Montana	38	2,933	Rhode Island	37	4,285
Alaska	57	3,012	Indiana	110	12,528	Nebraska	46	4,540	South Carolina	111	11,558
Arizona	60	5,691	Iowa	91	6,399	Nevada	23	1,771	South Dakota	58	4,344
Arkansas	100	10,896	Kansas	90	6,150	New Hampshire	31	2,716	Tennessee	126	14,469
California	203	20,030	Kentucky	64	7,069	New Jersey	119	13,029	Texas	198	18,745
Colorado	46	3,835	Louisiana	104	8,668	New Mexico	43	4,121	Utah	53	4,873
Connecticut	55	6,665	Maine	36	4,309	New York	197	18,981	Vermont	39	3,351
Delaware	24	2,954	Maryland	66	7,107	North Carolina	139	12,423	Virginia	82	7,238
Dist. of Columbia	24	3,547	Massachusetts	121	13,155	North Dakota	39	4,175	Virgin Islands	70	802
Florida	87	10,051	Michigan	105	11,654	Ohio	147	17,406	Washington	45	6,492
Georgia	105	12,733	Minnesota	99	9,349	Oklahoma	112	9,123	West Virginia	102	4,729
Hawaii	50	5,355	Mississippi	136	13,514	Oregon	75	7,216	Wisconsin	33	9,613
						Pennsylvania	170	18,462	Wyoming	24	2,303

*Army National Guard and Air National Guard.

U.S. MILITARY PAY SCALES BY GRADE: PER MONTH (Oct.) 1979

Public Law 96-343 effective October 1, 1980, increases military pay by 11.7 percent.

Pay Grade	2 years or less	Over 2	Over 3	Over 4	Over 6	Over 8	Over 10	Over 12	Over 14	Over 16	Over 18	Over 20	Over 22	Over 26
Commissioned Officers														
O–10[1]	$3,529.80	$3,654.00	$3,654.00	$3,654.00	$3,654.00	$3,794.10	$3,794.10	$4,084.80	$4,084.80	$4,377.00*	$4,377.00*	$4,669.80*	$4,669.80*	$4,961.10*
O–9	3,128.40	3,210.60	3,278.70	3,278.70	3,278.70	3,362.40	3,362.40	3,501.90	3,501.90	3,794.10	3,794.10	4,084.80	4,084.80	4,377.00*
O–8	2,833.50	2,918.40	2,987.70	2,987.90	2,987.70	3,210.60	3,210.60	3,362.40	3,362.40	3,501.90	3,654.00	3,794.10	3,946.20	3,946.20
O–7	2,354.40	2,514.60	2,514.60	2,514.60	2,627.10	2,627.10	2,779.80	2,779.80	2,918.40	3,210.60	3,431.10	3,431.10	3,431.10	3,431.10
O–6	1,745.10	1,917.60	2,042.70	2,042.70	2,042.70	2,042.70	2,042.70	2,042.70	2,112.00	2,446.50	2,571.60	2,627.10	2,779.80	3,014.70
O–5	1,395.90	1,639.20	1,752.30	1,752.30	1,752.30	1,752.30	1,805.70	1,902.30	2,029.50	2,181.60	2,307.00	2,376.60	2,459.70	2,459.70
O–4	1,176.60	1,432.20	1,528.20	1,528.20	1,556.10	1,625.40	1,736.10	1,833.90	1,917.60	2,001.30	2,057.10	2,057.10	2,057.10	2,057.10
O–3[2]	1,093.50	1,222.20	1,306.50	1,445.70	1,514.70	1,569.60	1,653.90	1,736.10	1,778.70	1,778.70	1,778.70	1,778.70	1,778.70	1,778.70
O–2[2]	953.10	1,041.30	1,250.70	1,293.00	1,319.70	1,319.70	1,319.70	1,319.70	1,319.70	1,319.70	1,319.70	1,319.70	1,319.70	1,319.70
O–1[2]	827.40	861.30	1,041.30	1,041.30	1,041.30	1,041.30	1,041.30	1,041.30	1,041.30	1,041.30	1,041.30	1,041.30	1,041.30	1,041.30
Commissioned Officers with over 4 years active service as enlisted members														
O–3	0.	0.	0.	1,445.70	1,514.70	1,569.60	1,653.90	1,736.10	1,805.70	1,805.70	1,805.70	1,805.70	1,805.70	1,805.70
O–2	0.	0.	0.	1,293.00	1,319.70	1,361.70	1,432.20	1,487.40	1,528.20	1,528.20	1,528.20	1,528.20	1,528.20	1,528.20
O–1	0.	0.	0.	1,041.30	1,112.10	1,153.20	1,194.90	1,236.60	1,293.00	1,293.00	1,293.00	1,293.00	1,293.00	1,293.00
Warrant Oficers														
W–4	1,113.90	1,194.90	1,194.90	1,222.20	1,278.00	1,334.40	1,390.20	1,487.40	1,556.10	1,611.30	1,653.90	1,707.90	1,765.20	1,902.30
W–3	1,012.50	1,098.30	1,098.30	1,112.10	1,125.30	1,207.50	1,278.00	1,319.70	1,361.70	1,402.50	1,445.70	1,501.50	1,556.10	1,611.30
W–2	886.30	959.10	959.10	987.00	1,041.30	1,098.30	1,139.70	1,181.40	1,222.20	1,265.10	1,306.50	1,347.90	1,402.50	1,402.50
W–1	738.90	847.20	847.20	917.70	959.10	1,000.50	1,041.30	1,084.20	1,125.30	1,166.70	1,207.50	1,250.70	1,250.70	1,250.70
Enlisted Members														
E–9[3]	0.	0.	0.	0.	0.	0.	1,265.40	1,294.20	1,323.60	1,354.20	1,384.20	1,411.20	1,485.60	1,629.60
E–8	0.	0.	0.	0.	0.	1,061.70	1,091.40	1,120.50	1,149.90	1,179.90	1,207.20	1,236.90	1,309.50	1,455.60
E–7	741.30	800.10	829.80	858.60	888.30	916.20	945.60	975.00	1,019.10	1,047.90	1,077.60	1,091.40	1,164.90	1,309.60
E–6	640.20	698.10	727.20	757.80	786.00	814.80	844.90	888.30	916.30	945.60	960.00	960.00	960.00	960.00
E–5	562.20	611.70	641.40	669.30	713.10	742.20	771.90	800.10*	814.80	814.80	814.80	814.80	814.80	814.80
E–4	540.30	570.60	603.90	651.00	676.80	676.80	676.80	676.80	676.80	676.80	676.80	676.80	676.80	676.80
E–3	519.60	548.10	570.30	592.80	592.80	592.80	592.80	592.80	592.80	592.80	592.80	592.80	592.80	592.80
E–2	500.10	500.10	500.10	500.10	500.10	500.10	500.10	500.10	500.10	500.10	500.10	500.10	500.10	500.10
E–1	448.80	448.80	448.80	448.80	448.80	448.80	448.80	448.80	448.80	448.80	448.80	448.80	448.80	448.80

[1]While serving as Chairman of the Joint Chiefs of Staff of the Army, Chief of Naval Operations, Chief of Staff of the Air Force, or Commandant of the Marine Corps, basic pay for this grade is $5,473.80 regardless of cumulative years of service. [2]Does not apply to commissioned officers who have been credited with over 4 years' active service as enlisted members.

*Basic pay is limited to $4,466.40 by Level V of the Executive Schedule. [3]Highest Enlisted Rank, while serving as Sergeant Major of the Army, Master Chief Petty Officer of the Navy, Chief Master Sergeant of the Air Force, or Sergeant Major of the Marine Corps, basic pay for this grade is $1,980.90 regardless of cumulative years of service.

U.S. MILITARY PAY GRADES

SOURCE: U.S. Department of Defense

COMMISSIONED OFFICERS

Pay Grade	Army	Navy	Marines	Air Force
O–1	Second Lieutenant	Ensign	Second Lieutenant	Second Lieutenant
O–2	First Lieutenant	Lieutenant Junior Grade	First Lieutenant	First Lieutenant
O–3	Captain	Lieutenant	Captain	Captain
O–4	Major	Lieutenant Commander	Major	Major
O–5	Lieutenant Colonel	Commander	Lieutenant Colonel	Lieutenant Colonel
O–6	Colonel	Captain	Colonel	Colonel
O–7	Brigadier General	Rear Admiral (lower half)	Brigadier General	Brigadier General
O–8	Major General	Rear Admiral (upper half)	Major General	Major General
O–9	Lieutenant General	Vice Admiral	Lieutenant General	Lieutenant General
O–10	General	Admiral	General	General

WARRANT OFFICERS (All Services)

W–1	Warrant Officer	W–3	Chief Warrant Officer
W–2	Chief Warrant Officer	W–4	Chief Warrant Officer

ENLISTED PERSONNEL

Pay Grade	Army	Navy	Marines	Air Force
E–1	Private	Seaman Recruit	Private	Airman Basic
E–2	Private	Seaman Apprentice	Private First Class	Airman
E–3	Private First Class	Seaman	Lance Corporal	Airman First Class
E–4	Corporal / Specialist 4	Petty Officer, Third Class	Corporal	Sergeant / Senior Airman
E–5	Sergeant / Specialist 5	Petty Officer, Second Class	Sergeant	Staff Sergeant
E–6	Staff Sergeant / Specialist 6	Petty Officer, First Class	Staff Sergeant	Technical Sergeant
E–7	Sergeant First Class / Specialist 7 / Platoon Sergeant	Chief Petty Officer	Gunnery Sergeant	Master Sergeant
E–8	First Sergeant / Master Sergeant	Senior Chief Petty Officer	First Sergeant / Master Sergeant	Senior Master Sergeant
E–9	Command Sergeant Major / Sergeant Major	Master Chief Petty Officer	Sergeant Major / Master Gunnery Sergeant	Chief Master Sergeant

AMERICAN MILITARY CEMETERIES ON FOREIGN SOIL

SOURCE: The American Battle Monuments Commission

The American Battle Monuments Commission, an agency of the U. S. Government, is responsible to the people of the United States for the construction and permanent maintenance of military cemeteries and memorials on foreign soil, as well as for certain memorials on American soil. Monuments are located in Audenarde, Belgium; Bellicourt, Aisne, France; Brest, Finistere, France; Cantigny, Somme, France; Chateau-Thierry, France; Gibraltar; Kemmel, Ypres, Belgium; Montfaucon, Meuse, France; Sommepy, Marne, France; Tours, France; Indre-et-Loire, France; and Pointe du Hoc, Calvados, France.

Cemetery	Location	Size (acres)	Burials Known	Burials Unknown	Missing Commemorated
Aisne-Marne	Belleau (Aisne), France	42.5	2,039	249	1,060
Ardennes	Neupre (Neuville-en-Condroz), Belgium	90	4,534	786	462
Brittany	St. James, France	28	4,313	97	497
Brookwood	Surrey, England	4.5	427	41	563
Cambridge	Cambridge, England	30.5	3,787	24	5,126
Corozal	Panama City, Panama	16	3,818	000	000
Epinal	Epinal, France	48	5,186	69	424
Flanders Field	Waregem, Belgium	6	347	21	43
Florence	Florence, Italy	70	4,189	213	1,409
Henri-Chapelle	Henri-Chapelle, Belgium	57	7,895	94	450
Lorraine	St. Avold, France	113.5	10,338	151	444
Luxembourg	Luxembourg City, Luxembourg	50.5	4,975	101	370
Manila	Fort Bonifacio, Philippines	152	13,462	3,744	36,279
Meuse-Argonne	Romagne, France	130.5	13,760	486	954
Mexico City	Mexico City, Mexico	1	813	750	000
Netherlands	Margraten, Holland	65.5	8,195	106	1,722
Normandy	St. Laurent, France	172.5	9,079	307	1,557
North Africa	Carthage, Tunisia	27	2,601	240	3,724
Oise-Aisne	Fere-en-Tardenois, France	36.5	5,415	597	241
Rhone	Draguignan, France	12	799	62	293
St. Mihiel	Thiaucourt, France	40.5	4,036	117	284
Sicily-Rome	Nettuno, Italy	77	7,372	490	3,094
Somme	Bony, France	14	1,707	137	333
Suresnes	Seine, France	7.5	1,535	30	974

THE JOINT CHIEFS OF STAFF

Source: Office of the Assistant Secretary of Defense

Chairman

	From	To
Gen. Omar N. Bradley, USA	Aug. 16, 1949	Aug. 14, 1953
Adm. Arthur W. Radford, USN	Aug. 15, 1953	Aug. 14, 1957
Gen. Nathan F. Twining, USAF	Aug. 15, 1957	Sept. 30, 1960
Gen. Lyman L. Lemnitzer, USA	Oct. 1, 1960	Sept. 30, 1962
Gen. Maxwell D. Taylor, USA	Oct. 1, 1962	July 3, 1964
Gen. Earle G. Wheeler, USA	July 3, 1964	July 2, 1970
Adm. Thomas H. Moorer, USN	July 2, 1970	June 30, 1974
Gen. George S. Brown, USAF	July 1, 1974	June 30, 1978
Gen. David C. Jones, USAF	July 1, 1978	To Date

Chief of Staff, U.S. Army

	From	To
Gen. of the Army Dwight D. Eisenhower	Nov. 19, 1945	Feb. 7, 1948
Gen. Omar N. Bradley	Feb. 17, 1948	Aug. 15, 1949
Gen. J. Lawton Collins	Aug. 16, 1949	Aug. 14, 1953
Gen. Matthew B. Ridgway	Aug. 15, 1953	June 30, 1955
Gen. Maxwell D. Taylor	June 30, 1955	June 30, 1959
Gen. Lyman L. Lemnitzer	July 1, 1959	Sept. 30, 1960
Gen. George H. Decker	Sept. 30, 1960	Sept. 30, 1962
Gen. Earle G. Wheeler	Oct. 1, 1962	July 3, 1964
Gen. Harold K. Johnson	July 3, 1964	July 3, 1968
Gen. William C. Westmoreland	July 3, 1968	July 1, 1972
Gen. Creighton W. Abrams	Oct. 16, 1972	Sept. 1974
Gen. Fred C. Weyand	Oct. 7, 1974	Oct. 1, 1976
Gen. Bernard W. Rogers	Oct. 1, 1976	July 1, 1979
Gen. Edward C. Meyer	July 1, 1979	To Date

Chief of Naval Operations

	From	To
Fleet Adm. Chester W. Nimitz	Dec. 5, 1945	Dec. 15, 1947
Adm. Louis E. Denfeld	Dec. 15, 1947	Nov. 2, 1949
Adm. Forrest P. Sherman	Nov. 2, 1949	July 22, 1951
Adm. William M. Fechteler	Aug. 16, 1951	Aug. 17, 1953
Adm. Robert B. Carney	Aug. 17, 1953	Aug. 16, 1955
Adm. Arleigh A. Burke	Aug. 17, 1955	Aug. 1, 1961
Adm. George W. Anderson	Aug. 1, 1961	July 31, 1963
Adm. David L. McDonald	Aug. 1, 1963	July 31, 1967
Adm. Thomas H. Moorer	Aug. 1, 1967	July 1, 1970
Adm. Elmo R. Zumwalt	July 1, 1970	June 30, 1974
Adm. James L. Holloway 3rd	July 1, 1974	June 30, 1978
Adm. Thomas C. Hayward	July 1, 1978	To Date

Chief of Staff, U.S. Air Force

	From	To
Gen. Carl Spaatz	Sept. 26, 1947	April 29, 1948
Gen. Hoyt S. Vandenberg	April 30, 1948	June 29, 1953
Gen. Nathan F. Twining	June 30, 1953	June 30, 1957
Gen. Thomas D. White	July 1, 1957	June 30, 1961
Gen. Curtis E. LeMay	June 30, 1961	Jan. 31, 1965
Gen. John P. McConnell	Feb. 1, 1965	Aug. 1, 1969
Gen. John D. Ryan	Aug. 1, 1969	July 31, 1973
Gen. George S. Brown	Aug. 1, 1973	June 30, 1974
Gen. David C. Jones	July 1, 1974	June 30, 1978
Gen. Lew Allen	July 1, 1978	To Date

Commandant, U.S. Marine Corps

	From	To
Gen. Lemuel C. Shepherd	Dec. 21, 1951	Dec. 31, 1955
Gen. Randolph McC. Pate	Jan. 1, 1956	Dec. 31, 1959
Gen. David M. Shoup	Jan. 1, 1960	Dec. 31, 1963
Gen. Wallace M. Greene, Jr.	Jan. 1, 1964	Dec. 31, 1967
Gen. Leonard F. Chapman, Jr.	Jan. 1, 1968	Dec. 31, 1971
Gen. Robert E. Cushman, Jr.	Jan. 1, 1972	July 1, 1975
Gen. Louis H. Wilson	July 1, 1975	July 1, 1979
Gen. Robert H. Barrow	July 1, 1979	To Date

U.S. CASUALTIES IN VIETNAM

Source: U.S. Department of Defense

47,072 U.S. military personnel were killed during the period 1961-1976 (June). Hospitalized wounded totaled 153,329. Casualties were highest during 1968, the year of the Tet offensive, with 14,589 killed and 46,796 wounded. Total casualties: 360,706.

TOTAL COST ESTIMATES OF AMERICAN WARS, BY RANK

Source: James L. Clayton, University of Utah. (Data in millions of dollars)

	Original Incremental Cost[1] Constant Dollars (1967)	Current dollars	Cost to Sept. 1, 1978[2]	SERVICE-CONNECTED VETERANS' BENEFITS Total Cost Under Present Programs	INTEREST PAYMENTS ON WAR LOANS % of Original Incremental Costs	Total Cost to 1979[3]	Estimated Current Cost (1979)
World War II	546,490	288,000	54,212	UKN	69	200,000	542,212
Vietnam Conflict	106,526	111,000	7,762	UKN	3	3,000	121,762
Korean Conflict	67,925	54,000	8,777	UKN	14	7,500	70,277
World War I	57,650	26,000	13,152	UKN	43	11,000	50,152
Civil War (Union only)	6,957	3,200[4]	3,289	3,300	60	1,200	7,689
Spanish-American War	1,600	400	2,089	2,500	15	60	2,549
American Revolution	UKN	100	28	28	20	20	148
War of 1812	182	93	20	20	15	14	127
Mexican War	270	73	26	26	14	10	109

[1]Except for Korean and Vietnam conflicts, original incremental costs are outlays for national security during war years minus avg. annual outlay for preceding five years. Vietnam conflict estimate is from Dept. of Defense and represents incremental costs from 1965-79. Korean conflict estimate uses running avg. of national security outlays from 1948-50 as a base, and then includes additional outlays over this base for 1951-52 and one-half increase for 1953 (because outlays for the Cold War increased at the same time outlays for Korean conflict declined). [2]For World War I and later wars, benefits are actual service-connected figures from 1978 Annual Report of the Veterans Admin. For earlier wars, service-connected veterans' benefits are estimated at 40% of total, the approximate ratio of service-connected to total benefits since World War I. [3]Interest costs use same formula as in footnote 1. Interest costs for wars since 1940 are rough approximations. [4]Data from Goldin and Lewis, "The Economic Cost of the American Civil War," Journal of Economic History, June 1975. Expenditures by Confederate Govt. are estimated by this study at $1.0 billion. UKN = Unknown.

VETERANS BENEFITS

SOURCE: Veterans Administration

Benefits: In order to qualify for most benefits, veterans must have been separated from the Armed Forces under conditions other than dishonorable.

Compensation for Service-Connected Disability: Veterans disabled by injury or disease incurred or aggravated during active service in the line of duty are entitled to monthly payments ranging from $48, for a 10 percent disability, to $889 for total disability. Loss of, or loss of use of, certain limbs and organs entitles the disabled veteran to additional compensation, up to a maximum monthly payment of $2,536. Certain veterans who are at least 30 percent disabled are entitled to additional allowances for dependents.

Pension: Wartime veterans, including those of Mexican Border Service, World Wars I and II, the Korean conflict, and the Vietnam era who served 90 days or more, or—if less than 90 days—were discharged for a service-connected disability, and who are permanently and totally disabled for reasons not traceable to service, may be eligible for pension benefits. A veteran 65 years of age or older is considered totally and permanently disabled. Maximum pension payment is $325 a month for a single veteran, depending upon other income. Veterans with dependents may be entitled to higher amounts.

Medical Care: Complete care in VA hospitals, other federal hospitals, and in some cases, private hospitals is authorized under a priority system for otherwise qualified veterans who require treatment of service-connected disabilities, have compensable disabilities but require treatment of nonservice-connected disabilities, and/or have no service-connected disabilities but require medical treatment (subject to financial need and availability of facilities). Other benefits authorized when certain conditions are met include domiciliary care; outpatient medical and dental treatment in VA field stations or, in some cases, by approved private physicians; fitting and training with prosthetic appliances; medical examinations; aid for the blind; and vocational rehabilitation.

Educational Assistance—G.I. Bill: Veterans who served on active duty for more than 180 continuous days, any part of which occurred after Jan. 31, 1955, but before Jan. 1, 1977, and who (a) were released under conditions other than dishonorable, (b) were discharged for a service-connected disability or (c) continue on active duty are eligible for educational assistance for a period of 1.5 months for each month served, up to 45 months. The full 45-month entitlement is earned after 18 months' service.

War orphans and surviving spouses are eligible for similar education benefits, and education benefits are also available to spouses and children of veterans who are permanently and totally disabled as the result of military service.

Educational institutions may include approved public and private secondary schools, junior or senior colleges, and vocational, scientific, or correspondence schools. Farm cooperative, on-the-job, and flight training are included. Eligibility ends ten years after release from active duty, but not later than Dec. 31, 1989.

Basic monthly payments to veterans enrolled in school courses: full time, no dependents, $311; one dependent, $370; two dependents, $422; and $26 for each additional.

A veteran who must complete elementary or high school training to qualify for higher education may receive this training without a charge against his basic entitlement.

Contributory Plan: Those who initially entered the service on or after Jan. 1, 1977, may participate by contributing $50 to $75 from their military pay, with a maximum contribution of $2,700. The VA then matches contributions at the rate of $2 for every $1 made by the participant. Payments from the fund may be received for school or training purposes for the number of months they contributed, or for 36 months, whichever is less.

Home Loans: The VA is authorized to guarantee home loans made to eligible veterans by private lenders. Such loans may be for the purpose of purchasing a conventionally constructed home or mobile home (with or without a lot), refinancing an existing home mortgage, purchasing a condominium unit, or buying a farm home. Loans may also be guaranteed for home improvement purposes, including the installation of a solar heating and/or cooling system or other weatherization improvements.

Eligibility requirements vary based on the period of service. For World War II, Korean Conflict and Vietnam veterans, active duty of at least 90 days' duration (unless discharged earlier for service-connected disability) and a discharge or separation under other than dishonorable conditions are required. Post-World War II, Post-Korean and Post-Vietnam veterans must have 181 days of active duty (unless discharged earlier for service-connected disability) and a discharge or separation under other than dishonorable conditions.

Service personnel who have served at least 181 continuous days in active duty status, though not discharged, are eligible while their service continues without a break.

Unmarried surviving spouses of veterans, including service personnel, who served during a period which occurred between September 16, 1940 and the present and who died as a result of service-connected disabilities are eligible for home loan purposes. Spouses of service personnel on active duty who are officially listed as missing in action or prisoners of war and have been in such status for more than 90 days are also eligible for home loan benefits. Spouses of POWs/MIAs are, however, limited to one loan.

Loan guaranty benefits are available to all eligible veterans and service personnel until used.

The VA may guarantee the lender against loss for up to 60 percent of the loan amount or $25,000, whichever is less, on all types of home loans, except for mobile home loans, for which the maximum guaranty is 50 percent of the loan amount, or $17,500, whichever is less.

There are no established loan maximums. However, no loan may exceed the property value established by VA.

Veterans who used their entitlement before October 1, 1978, may have additional entitlement available for GI home loan purposes. Veterans' maximum home loan entitlement was raised from $4,000 to $7,500 in 1950, to $12,500 in 1968, to $17,500 in 1974, and to $25,000 in 1978. The amount of such additional entitlement is the difference between $25,000 and the amount used on prior home loans.

Certain veterans may meet the requirements for having used GI entitlement restored. A veteran may qualify for restoration if VA has been relieved of liability on the GI loan which normally is accomplished by the loan being paid in full and if the property has been disposed of; or if an immediate veteran-transferee agrees to substitute his or her entitlement for that of the original veteran-borrower and meets all other requirements for substitution of entitlement.

Insurance: Members of the uniformed services including Ready Reservists, Army and Air National Guards, ROTC members, Reservists eligible for assignment to Retired Reserves who have not received their first increment of retired pay or reached their 61st birthday, whichever is earlier; and the full-time duty cadet or midshipman at a service academy are eligible for Servicemen's Group Life Insurance. Maximum coverage is for $20,000 and premiums are deducted from service pay, except Retired Reservists, who must pay direct. Coverage continues for 120 days after discharge, within which period veterans can apply for automatic conversion of SGLI to a non-renewable 5-year term policy under Veterans Group Life Insurance which may be converted at the end of the 5-year period to an individual policy with a commercial company. For a member totally disabled the 120-day period is extended to one year or to the end of total disability, whichever is earlier.

Dependency and Indemnity Compensation (DIC): Payments are authorized for widows, widowers, unmarried children under 18, helpless children, children between 18 and 23 who are attending an approved school, and certain parents of a serviceman or veteran who died on or after January 1, 1957, from a disease or injury incurred or aggravated in the line of duty while on active duty, active or inactive duty for training, or from a disability otherwise compensable under VA-administered laws.

Employment Preference and Reemployment Rights: Veterans are entitled to certain preference over nonveterans in obtaining federal civil service jobs, in referral to training programs and job openings by state employment offices, and in restoration to a former job in private employment or with the federal government. The Department of Labor has jurisdiction over veteran employment.

Burial: A payment of up to $300 is authorized for the person incurring burial expenses for a wartime veteran, or for a peacetime veteran who was receiving compensation or was discharged or retired for disability incurred in the line of duty. Up to $1,100 will be payable when death is due to service-connected causes.

Burial is allowed in a national cemetery (except Arlington, Va.) for veterans whose last period of service terminated honorably, and for reservists who die while performing active-duty training. The benefit applies to the deceased person's spouse, minor children, and certain unmarried adult children. Effective August 1, 1973, an interment allowance not exceeding $150, in addition to the $300 basic burial allowance, is payable when burial is in other than a national cemetery.

U.S. MILITARY AID: PROGRAM DELIVERIES: FISCAL YEARS 1950-1979

SOURCE: Department of Defense (figures in thousands of dollars)

	1950-79		1950-79		1950-79
Worldwide	48,331,207	Honduras	9,144	Oman	1,833
Argentina	164,463	Iceland	540	Pakistan	275,454
Australia	1,393,236	India	69,517	Panama	4,793
Austria	98,307	Indochina	8,542	Paraguay	689
Bahrain	124	Indonesia	58,490	Peru	141,962
Belgium	330,698	Iran	9,740,337	Philippines	128,022
Bolivia	1,938	Iraq	13,152	Portugal	14,494
Brazil	257,987	Ireland	635	Saudi Arabia	8,639,575
Brunei	10	Israel	5,747,243	Senegal	6
Burma	3,893	Italy	723,618	Singapore	132,618
Cameroon	237	Jamaica	157	South Africa	3,149
Canada	1,341,228	Japan	485,195	Spain	684,305
Chile	173,440	Jordan	602,343	Sri Lanka	4
China (Taiwan)	1,021,063	Kenya	62,239	Sudan	41,379
Colombia	29,438	Korea	1,261,914	Suriname	1
Costa Rica	1,348	Kuwait	469,289	Sweden	69,335
Cuba	4,510	Lebanon	26,278	Switzerland	554,950
Denmark	188,303	Liberia	3,892	Syria	1
Dominican Republic	2,150	Libya	29,594	Thailand	275,376
Ecuador	39,419	Luxembourg	3,039	Trinidad & Tobago	85
Egypt	282,212	Malaysia	60,545	Tunisia	50,802
El Salvador	3,127	Mali	154	Turkey	554,781
Ethiopia	91,238	Mexico	18,791	United Arab Emirates	2,694
Fiji	63	Morocco	307,127	United Kingdom	2,230,012
Finland	23	Nepal	72	Uruguay	17,732
France	367,783	Netherlands	373,049	Venezuela	203,491
Gabon	2,239	New Zealand	126,504	Vietnam	1,167
Germany	6,046,653	Nicaragua	5,218	Yemen	124,825
Ghana	354	Niger	8	Yugoslavia	13,958
Greece	1,198,498	Nigeria	23,385	Zaire	45,953
Guatemala	28,126	Norway	342,483	International Organizations	471,917
Haiti	1,243				

NUCLEAR ARMAMENTS: UNITED STATES AND SOVIET UNION

SOURCE: International Institute for Strategic Studies, London

United States

	Type[a]	Max. range (miles)[b]	Estimated Warhead yield[c]	Number deployed July 80
LAND-BASED MISSILES				
ICBM	Titan II	7,000	5-10 MT	54
	Minuteman II	7,000	1-2 MT	450
	Minuteman III	7,500	3 × 170 KT	550
SRBM	Pershing	450	KT-range	108[g]
	Lance	70	KT-range	36[g]
SEA-LAUNCHED MISSILES				
SLBM	Polaris A3	2,880	3 × 200 KT	160
	Poseidon C3	2,880	10 × 50 KT	448
	Trident C4	4,600	8 × 100 KT	48
AIR-LAUNCHED MISSILES				
ALCM	Hound Dog	600	KT range	400[h]
ALBM	SRAM	35-100	KT range	1,250

Soviet Union

	Type[a] [d]	Max. range (miles)[b]	Estimated Warhead yield[c]	Number deployed July 80
LAND-BASED MISSILES				
ICBM	SS-9 Scarp	7,500	18-25 MT[e]	[f]
	SS-11 Sego	6,500	1-2 MT[e]	580
	SS-13 Savage	5,000	1 MT	60
SS-17		6,500	5 MT[e]	158
SS-18		6,300+	18-25 MT[e]	308
	SS-19	6,300+	5 MT[e]	300
M/IRBM	SS-4 Sandal	1,200	1 MT	380
	SS-5 Skean	2,300	1 MT	60
	SS-20	3-4,000	3 × 150 KT	160
SRBM	SS-1b Scud A	90	KT range	
	SS-1c Scud B	100-190	MT range	
	FROG 7	10-45	KT range	
	SS-12 Scaleboard	300-600	[f]	1300
	SS-21	40-75	[f]	
	SS-22	330-600	[f]	
	SS-23	120-220	[f]	
LRCM	SS-N-3 Shaddock	280	[f]	
SEA-LAUNCHED MISSILES				
SLBN	SS-N-4 Sark	300	1-2 MT	9[h]
	SS-N-5 Serb	700	1-2 MT	60
	SS-N-6 Sawfly	1,500+	1-2 MT[e]	469
	SS-N-8	4,800	1-2 MT	302
	SS-NX-17	3,000+	1 MT[e]	12
	SS-N-18	5,000	3 × 1-2 MT	160
SLCM	SS-N-3 Shaddock	280	KT range	342
	SS-N-7 Siren	30	[f]	120
	SS-N-9	175	[f]	118
	SS-N-12	600-2,300	[f]	48
AIR-LAUNCHED MISSILES				
ALCM	AS-3 Kangaroo	370	MT range	[f]
	AS-4 Kitchen	450	KT range	800[h]
	AS-6 Kingfish	160	KT range	[f]

HISTORICAL CHANGES FOR STRENGTH, 1970-1980 (MID-YEARS)

		1970	1971	1972	1973	1974	1975	1976	1977	1978	1979	1980
USA	ICBM	1,054	1,054	1,054	1,054	1,054	1,054	1,054	1,054	1,054	1,054	1,054
	SLBM	656	656	656	656	656	656	656	656	656	656	656
	Long-range bombers [i]	400	360	390	397	397	397	387	373	366	365	338
USSR	ICBM	1,513	1,527	1,527	1,575	1,618	1,527	1,477	1,350	1,400	1,398	1,398
	SLBM	304	448	500	628	720	784	845	909	1,028	1,028	1,028
	Long-range bombers	140	140	140	140	140	135	135	135	135	156	156

[a] ICBM = inter-continental ballistic missile (range over 4,000 miles); M/IRBM = medium/intermediate-range ballistic missile (500-4,000 miles); SRBM = short-range ballistic missile (under 500 miles); LRCM = long-range cruise missile (over 350 miles); SLBM = submarine-launched ballistic missile; SLCM = submarine-launched cruise missile; ALCM = air-launched cruise missile; ALBM = air-launched ballistic missile. [b] Operational range depends upon payload carried; figures are given in statute miles. [c] MT = megaton = millions tons of TNT equivalent (MT range = 1 MT or over); KT = kiloton = thousands tons of TNT equivalent (KT range = less than 1 MT); 3 ×, 10 × = 3 warheads, 10 warheads. [d] Numerical designation of Soviet missiles are of U.S. origin; names are of NATO origin. [e] Also exists in multiple warhead mode with lesser yield per warhead. [f] Information not available. [g] Figures for systems in Europe only. [h] Estimate. [i] Reserves not included.

WARPLANES: UNITED STATES AND THE SOVIET UNION

United States

AIRCRAFT	Type	Max. range (statute miles)	Max. speed (Mach no.)	Max. weapons load (lb.)	Number deployed (July 1980)
Long-range bombers	B-52 D	6,000	0.95	60,000	338
	B-52 G/H	10,000	0.95	70,000	
Medium-range bombers	FB-111A	3,000	2.5	37,500	65
Strike aircraft (incl. short-range bombers): land-based	F-4 C/D/E	1,400	2.4	16,000	360
	F-111 A/E	2,925	2.2/2.5	28,000	
Strike aircraft: carrier-based	F-4 J/N	1,400	2.2	16,000	100
	A-6 E	2,000	0.9	18,000	
	A-7 E	1,750	0.9	20,000	

Soviet Union

Type	Max. range (statute miles)	Max. speed (Mach no.)	Max. weapons load (lb.)	Number deployed (July 1980)
Tu-95 Bear	8,000	0.78	40,000	113
Mya-4 Bison	7,000	0.87	20,000	43
Tu-22M/-26 Backfire	5,000	2.5	17,500	145
Tu-16 Badger	4,000	0.8	20,000	568
Su-7 Fitter A	900	1.7	5,500	165
Tu-22 Blinder	1,400	1.5	12,000	165
MiG-21 Fishbed J/K/L/N	700	2.2	2,000	1,000
Mig-27 Flogger D	900	1.7	7,500	400
Su-19/-24 Fencer	1,000	2.3	8,000	370
Su-17/-20 Fitter C/D	1,100	1.6	11,000	640

WARPLANES: NATO AND WARSAW PACT COUNTRIES

NATO

Aircraft[a]	Type[c]	Operated by[d]	Max. range[e] (statute miles)	Max. speed (Mach no.)[f]	Max. weapons load (lb)	No. deployed (July 1980)
Medium-range bombers	Vulcan B2[b]	BR	4,000	0.95	21,000	48
Strike aircraft (incl. short-range bombers)	F-104	[h]	1,500	2.2	4,000	318[j]
	F-4	BR, GE, GR	1,400	2.4	16,000	180[j]
	Buccaneer	BR	2,300	0.95	12,000	60[j]
	Mirage IVA	FR	2,000	2.2	16,000	33[j]
	Mirage III E	FR	1,500	1.8	19,000	30[j]
	Jaguar	BR, FR	1,000	1.4	10,000	80[j]
	Super Etendard	FR	900	1.0	16,000	36[j]

Warsaw Pact

Type[g]	Operated by[d]	Max. range[e] (statute miles)	Max. speed (Mach no.)[f]	Max. weapons load (lb)	No. deployed (July 1980)
Su-7 Fitter A[i]	CZ, PO	900	1.7	5,500	115
Su-20 Fitter C[i]	PO	1,100	1.6	4,000	35

[a] All aircraft listed are dual-capable and many would be more likely to carry conventional than nuclear weapons. [b] Medium-range bomber = maximum range 3,500-6,000 miles, primarily designed for bombing missions. [c] Vulcan and Buccaneer are of British origin; F-104 and F-4 are of American origin; Mirage is of French origin; Jaguar is Anglo-French. [d] BR = Britain, FR = France, CZ = Czechoslovakia; HU = Hungary, PO = Poland, RU = Rumania, GE = West Germany, GR = Greece. [e] Theoretical maximum range, with internal fuel only, at optimum altitude and speed. Ranges for strike aircraft assume no weapons load. Especially in the case of strike aircraft, therefore, range falls sharply for flights at lower altitudes, at higher speed or with full weapons load (e.g. combat radius of F-104, at operational height and speed, with typical weapons load, is approximately 420 miles). [f] Mach 1 (M = 1.0) = speed of sound. [g] Warsaw Pact aircraft of Soviet origin; names (e.g. Fitter) of NATO origin. [h] The dual-capable F-104 is operated by Belgium, West Germany, Greece, Italy, the Netherlands, Norway and Turkey. The warheads for all of these aircraft are held in American custody. [i] Nuclear warheads for these dual-capable aircraft are held in Soviet custody. [j] Uncertain as to how many of these nuclear-capable aircraft actually have a nuclear role.

ACTIVE U.S. MILITARY FORCES SOURCE: U.S. Office of Management and Budget

Description	Actual Sept. 30 1979	Estimated Sept. 30 1980	Estimated Sept. 30 1981
Military personnel (in thousands):			
End strength:			
Army	758	774	776
Navy	522	528	534
Marine Corps	185	185	185
Air Force	559	558	565
Total, Department of Defense	2,024	2,045	2,059
Average strength:			
Army	757	765	770
Navy	525	520	530
Marine Corps	186	183	184
Air Force	564	559	562
Total, Department of Defense	2,033	2,027	2,047
General purpose forces:			
Land forces:			
Army divisions	16	16	16
Marine Corps divisions	3	3	3
Tactical air forces:			
Air Force wings	26	26	26
Navy attack wings	12	12	12
Marine Corps wings	3	3	3
Naval forces:			
Attack and multipurpose carriers	13	13	12
Nuclear attack submarines	70	72	85
Other warships	172	184	198
Amphibious assault ships	65	63	60

BLACKS IN U.S. ARMED FORCES

SOURCE: U.S. Department of Defense (As of September 30, 1979)

	Officers		Enlisted		TOTAL	
ARMY	6,601	(6.8%)	211,553	(32.2%)	218,154	(28.9%)
NAVY	1,437	(2.3%)	48,620	(10.7%)	50,057	(97 %)
AIR FORCE	4,088	(4.3%)	72,659	(15.8%)	76,747	(13.8%)
MARINE CORPS	705	(3.9%)	35,435	(21.5%)	36,640	(19.8%)
TOTAL	12,831	(4.7%)	568,767	(21.2%)	581,598	(19.0%)

THE MILITARY-INDUSTRIAL COMPLEX SOURCE: Department of Defense

Companies doing more than $140,000,000 worth of business with the Department of Defense during the 1979 fiscal year, in thousands of dollars.

Rank	Company Name	1979 Contracts	% of Total	Rank	Company Name	1979 Contracts	% of Total
1.	General Dynamics Corp.	$3,492,140	5.52	33.	Ford Motor Co.	$337,758	0.53
2.	McDonnell Douglas Corp.	3,229,186	5.11	34.	Congoleum Corp.	336,233	0.53
3.	United Technologies Corp.	2,553,550	4.04	35.	Bendix Corp.	296,668	0.47
4.	General Electric Co.	2,042,476	3.23	36.	Hyun Dai Construction Co. Ltd.	290,486	0.46
5.	Lockheed Corp.	1,796,642	2.84	37.	International Tel. & Tel. Corp.	262,936	0.42
6.	Hughes Aircraft Co.	1,556,882	2.46	38.	American Motors Corp.	243,844	0.39
7.	Boeing Co.	1,514,502	2.39	39.	Standard Oil Co. of Calif.	241,451	0.38
8.	Grumman Corp.	1,364,153	2.16	40.	Amerada Hess Corp.	236,510	0.37
9.	Raytheon Co.	1,249,377	1.98	41.	General Tel. & Elec. Corp.	227,120	0.36
10.	Tenneco Inc.	1,092,607	1.73	42.	General Tire & Rubber Co.	219,995	0.35
11.	Litton Industries, Inc.	832,389	1.32	43.	Harsco Corp.	218,596	0.35
12.	Chrysler Corp.	808,944	1.28	44.	Goodyear Tire & Rubber Co.	217,982	0.34
13.	Northrop Corp.	800,279	1.27	45.	Al Huseini	205,622	0.33
14.	Sperry Rand Corp.	777,732	1.23	46.	North American Philips Corp.	204,994	0.32
15.	Rockwell International Corp.	683,892	1.08	47.	Hercules, Inc.	190,627	0.30
16.	Westinghouse Electric Corp.	659,747	1.04	48.	Kaiser Industries Corp.	186,025	0.29
17.	Honeywell Inc.	657,660	1.04	49.	Motorola Inc.	185,724	0.29
18.	American Tel. & Tel. Co.	569,607	0.90	50.	Motor Oil Hellas	184,287	0.29
19.	International Business Machines Co.	552,561	0.87	51.	Morris-Knudsen Co. Inc.	182.084	0.29
20.	Martin Marietta Corp.	518,608	0.82	52.	E. Systems, Inc.	178,552	0.28
21.	Fairchild Industries, Inc.	505,144	0.80	53.	Chin Heung International Inc.	178,440	0.28
22.	RCA Corp.	487,451	0.77	54.	Coastal Corp.	178,018	0.28
23.	Textron Inc.	476,621	0.75	55.	G. K. Technologies Inc.	176,809	0.28
24.	Todd Shipyards Corp.	449,332	0.71	56.	Harris Corp.	169,371	0.27
25.	General Motors Corp.	449,126	0.71	57.	Royal Dutch Shell Group	159,220	0.25
26.	LTV Corp.	447,591	0.71	58.	Emerson Electric Co.	158,663	0.25
27.	TRW Inc.	436,713	0.69	59.	Signal Companies Inc. (The)	156,795	0.25
28.	Teledyne Inc.	399,711	0.63	60.	Gould, Inc.	156,113	0.25
29.	Texas Instruments Inc.	373,631	0.59	61.	Johns Hopkins Univ. (N)	156,079	0.25
30.	FMC Corp.	352,135	0.56	62.	Summa Corp.	150,143	0.24
31.	Singer Co.	346,107	0.55	63.	Guam Oil & Refining Co. Inc.	149,716	0.24
32.	Exxon Corp.	341,462	0.54	64.	Mobil Corp.	144,355	0.23
				65.	Pan American World Airways Inc.	140,085	0.22

ARMED FORCES OF THE WORLD: 1978

SOURCE: U.S. Arms Control and Disarmament Agency (in thousands)

Country	Active-duty Military Personnel	Country	Active-duty Military Personnel	Country	Active-duty Military Personnel	Country	Active-duty Military Personnel
Afghanistan	110	El Salvador	10	Korea, Rep. of	600	Saudi Arabia	50
Albania	53	Equatorial Guinea	2	Kuwait	10	Senegal	13
Algeria	75	Ethiopia	233	Laos	N.A.	Singapore	64
Angola	47	Finland	39	Liberia	7	Somalia	54
Argentina	155	France	502	Libya	50	South Africa	78
Australia	70	German Dem. Rep.	228	Madagascar	20	Spain	321
Austria	40	Germany, Fed. Rep.	489	Malawi	5	Sri Lanka	13
Bangladesh	129	Ghana	19	Malaysia	82	Sudan	71
Belgium	90	Greece	184	Mali	8	Sweden	68
Bolivia	20	Guatemala	14	Malta	7	Switzerland	18
Brazil	450	Guinea	18	Mauritania	12	Syria	225
Bulgaria	164	Guinea-Bissau	6	Mexico	145	Tanzania	63
Burma	212	Guyana	7	Mongolia	36	Thailand	250
Burundi	8	Haiti	7	Morocco	115	Togo	5
Cambodia	N.A.	Honduras	13	Mozambique	13	Tunisia	20
Cameroon	11	Hungary	110	Nepal	32	Turkey	566
Canada	80	India	1,300	Netherlands	100	Uganda	6
Chad	N.A.	Indonesia	250	New Zealand	12	USSR	4,800
Chile	111	Iran	350	Nicaragua	N.A.	United Arab Emirates	25
China, People's Rep.	4,500	Iraq	140	Nigeria	204	United Kingdon	318
China, Rep. of	471	Ireland	13	Norway	39	UNITED STATES	2,100
Colombia	60	Israel	165	Oman	12	Upper Volta	6
Congo	11	Italy	365	Pakistan	518	Uruguay	28
Cuba	210	Ivory Coast	8	Panama	8	Venezuela	55
Cyprus	10	Japan	239	Paraguay	15	Vietnam	660
Czechoslovakia	212	Jordan	70	Peru	125	Yemen Arab Rep.	20
Denmark	34	Kenya	13	Philippines	156	Yemen, P.D.R.	40
Dominican Republic	19	Korea, Dem. People's Rep.	632	Poland	430	Yugoslavia	260
Ecuador	35			Portugal	58	Zaire	53
Egypt	350			Qatar	N.A.	Zambia	20
				Romania	218	Zimbabwe	24

EDUCATION: FACTS/FIGURES

EXPENDITURES FOR PUBLIC ELEMENTARY AND SECONDARY SCHOOL EDUCATION

SOURCE: National Center for Education Statistics

School year	Total	Total per pupil	School year	Total	Total per pupil
1929/1930	$ 2,316,790,000	$108	1963/1964	$21,324,993,000	$ 559
1939/1940	2,344,049,000	106	1965/1966	26,248,026,000	654
1949/1950	5,837,643,000	259	1967/1968	32,977,182,000	786
1953/1954	9,092,449,000	351	1969/1970	40,683,428,000	955
1955/1956	10,955,047,000	388	1971/1972	48,050,283,000	1,128
1957/1958	13,569,163,000	449	1973/1974	56,970,355,000	1,364
1959/1960	15,613,255,000	472	1975/1976	70,600,573,000	1,697
1961/1962	18,373,339,000	530	1977/1978	80,844,366,000	2,002
			1978/1979[1]	86,700,000,000	2,210

[1] Estimated.

HIGH SCHOOL GRADUATES   SOURCE: National Center for Education Statistics

School year	Population 17 years old	High school graduates Total	Boys	Girls	School year	Population 17 years old	High school graduates Total	Boys	Girls
1889/1890	1,259,177	43,731	18,549	25,182	1965/1966	3,515,000	2,632,000	1,308,000	1,324,000
1899/1900	1,489,146	94,883	38,075	56,808	1966/1967	3,518,000	2,679,000	1,331,000	1,348,000
1909/1910	1,786,240	156,429	63,676	92,753	1967/1968	3,521,000	2,702,000	1,341,000	1,361,000
1919/1920	1,855,173	311,266	123,684	187,582	1968/1969	3,622,000	2,839,000	1,408,000	1,431,000
1929/1930	2,295,822	666,904	300,376	366,528	1969/1970	3,825,343	2,896,000	1,433,000	1,463,000
1939/1940	2,403,074	1,221,475	578,718	642,757	1970/1971	3,859,000	3,036,000	1,506,000	1,530,000
1949/1950	2,034,450	1,199,700	570,700	629,000	1971/1972	3,957,000	3,006,000	1,490,000	1,516,000
1951/1952	2,040,800	1,196,500	569,200	627,300	1972/1973	4,024,000	3,037,000	1,501,000	1,536,000
1953/1954	2,128,600	1,276,100	612,500	663,600	1973/1974	4,096,000	3,080,000	1,515,000	1,565,000
1955/1956	2,270,000	1,414,800	679,500	735,300	1974/1975	4,210,000	3,140,000	1,541,000	1,599,000
1957/1958	2,324,000	1,505,900	725,500	780,400	1975/1976	4,215,000	3,155,000	1,554,000	1,601,000
1959/1960	2,862,005	1,864,000	898,000	966,000	1976/1977	4,206,000	3,161,000	1,550,000	1,611,000
1961/1962	2,768,000	1,925,000	941,000	984,000	1977/1978	4,208,000	3,147,000	1,541,000	1,606,000
1963/1964	3,001,000	2,290,000	1,121,000	1,169,000	1978/1979[1]	4,238,000	3,131,000	1,539,000	1,592,000

[1] Estimated.

COLLEGE AND UNIVERSITY GRADUATES   SOURCE: National Center for Education Statistics

School year	All degrees	Degrees conferred Bachelor's and First Professional	Master's	Doctor's	School year	All degrees	Degrees conferred Bachelor's and First Professional	Master's	Doctor's
1869/1870	9,372	9,371	0	1	1963/1964	614,194	498,654	101,050	14,490
1889/1890	16,703	15,539	1,015	149	1965/1966	709,832	551,040	140,555	18,237
1899/1900	29,375	27,410	1,583	382	1966/1967	768,871	590,548	157,706	20,617
1909/1910	39,755	37,199	2,113	443	1967/1968	866,548	666,710	176,749	23,089
1919/1920	53,516	48,622	4,279	615	1968/1969	984,129	764,185	193,756	26,188
1929/1930	139,752	122,484	14,969	2,299	1969/1970	1,065,391	827,234	208,291	29,866
1939/1940	216,521	186,500	26,731	3,290	1970/1971	1,140,292	877,676	230,509	32,107
1949/1950	496,661	432,058	58,183	6,420	1971/1972	1,215,680	930,684	251,633	33,363
1953/1954	356,608	290,825	56,788	8,995	1972/1973	1,270,528	972,380	263,371	34,777
1955/1956	376,973	308,812	59,258	8,903	1973/1974	1,310,441	999,592	277,033	33,816
1957/1958	436,979	362,554	65,487	8,938	1974/1975	1,305,382	978,849	292,450	34,083
1959/1960	476,704	392,440	74,435	9,829	1975/1976	1,334,230	988,395	311,771	34,064
1961/1962	514,323	417,846	84,855	11,622	1976/1977	1,334,304	983,908	317,164	33,232
					1977/1978	1,331,536	987,785	311,620	32,131
					1978/1979[1]	1,347,000	1,001,000	314,000	32,000

[1] Estimated.

EDUCATION AND INCOME   Source: U.S. Bureau of the Census (based on 1978 data)

Income Levels	Percent of Male Income Recipients**	School Years Completed*	Income Levels	Percent of Male Income Recipients**	School Years Completed*	Income Levels	Percent of Male Income Recipients**	School Years Completed*
$1 to $999 or less	1.6	12.4	$3,500 to $3,999	2.1	9.6	$ 9,000 to $9,999	3.7	12.2
$1,000 to $1,499	0.8	9.8	$4,000 to $4,999	4.0	10.6	$10,000 to $11,999	8.5	12.5
$1,500 to $1,999	1.0	9.1	$5,000 to $5,999	4.1	11.1	$12,000 to $14,999	11.8	12.6
$2,000 to $2,499	1.8	8.6	$6,000 to $6,999	4.0	11.7	$15,000 to $19,999	18.5	12.7
$2,500 to $2,999	1.9	8.7	$7,000 to $7,999	4.1	11.8	$20,000 to $24,999	11.8	12.9
$3,000 to $3,499	2.2	9.3	$8,000 to $8,999	4.0	12.3	$25,000 and over	14.1	16.0

* Median.   ** Males 25 years old and over

LEVEL OF EDUCATION: WHITE AND BLACK ADULTS Source: U.S. Bureau of the Census

	Persons 25 years old or older (1,000)	Elementary School			High School		College		Median School Years Completed
		Less than 5 years	5–7 years	8 years	1–3 years	4 years	1–3 years	4 years or more	
Race and Sex									
Total, all races, March 1979	125,295	3.5	6.2	8.6	14.0	36.6	14.7	16.4	12.5
Male	59,986	3.7	6.3	8.6	12.9	32.6	15.4	20.4	12.6
Female	66,309	3.2	6.1	8.6	15.0	40.2	14.0	12.9	12.4
White	110,798	2.7	5.6	8.7	13.3	37.6	15.0	17.2	12.5
Male	52,504	2.8	5.7	8.7	12.4	33.1	15.8	21.4	12.6
Female	58,294	2.6	5.5	8.6	14.1	41.6	14.3	13.3	12.5
Black	12,227	9.6	11.6	8.2	21.2	30.0	11.5	7.9	11.9
Male	5,393	11.9	12.8	7.5	18.6	29.5	11.3	8.3	11.9
Female	6,834	7.8	10.7	8.7	23.3	30.4	11.6	7.5	11.9

EDUCATION AND INCOME Source: U.S. Bureau of the Census

MEDIAN INCOME OF FULL-TIME YEAR-ROUND WORKERS, 25 YEARS OLD AND OVER, BY EDUCATIONAL ATTAINMENT

		Median Income, 1978	
		Male	Female
Elementary:	Total	$ 11,765	$ 7,079
	Less than 8 years	10,474	6,648
	8 years	12,965	7,489
High school:	Total	15,935	9,427
	1 to 3 years	14,199	7,996
	4 years	16,396	9,769
College:	1 or more years	20,078	12,115
	5 or more years	23,578	15,310

MEDIAN INCOME OF MEN 25 YEARS OLD AND OVER, BY EDUCATIONAL ATTAINMENT

		Median Income, 1978		
		Black	White	All Races
Elementary:	Total	$ 5,019	$ 6,839	$ 6,520
	Less than 8 years	4,403	5,936	5,641
	8 years	6,661	7,758	7,604
High school:	Total	10,110	13,594	13,174
	1 to 3 years	7,929	10,742	10,419
	4 years	11,049	14,744	14,341
College:	1 or more years	14,549	17,856	17,577
	5 or more years	17,501	21,699	21,428

COMPREHENSIVE EMPLOYMENT AND TRAINING ACT (CETA) Source: Dept. of Labor

The Comprehensive Employment and Training Act Amendments of 1978, approved by the President Oct. 27 (PL 95-524), extended public service employment (PSE) and job training and initiated several new program services through FY 1982. Its main provisions are:

Title I: Administrative Provisions: General provisions applicable to the act. Authorizes programs through FY 1982 except for three youth programs (Part A of Title IV) and the private sector initiatives (Title VII) which are authorized only through FY 1980. Directs the Secretary of Labor to establish an Office of Management Assistance to provide prime sponsors with management and technical services to help them improve program administration.

Title II: Training, education, work experience, upgrading, retraining, and other services (Parts A, B, and C), and counterstructural public service employment (Part D) to prepare jobless persons for unsubsidized employment. Participants in training programs and services (except upgrading and retraining) must have been economically disadvantaged and either unemployed, underemployed, or in school. PSE must be entry level and combined with training and supportive services, if available.

Title III: Programs for persons who have a particular disadvantage in the labor market, including Native Americans, migrants and other seasonal farmworkers, the handicapped, women, displaced homemakers, public assistance recipients, other special target groups, and for middle-aged and older workers.

Title IV: The Job Corps, Summer Youth Programs, and programs enacted in the Youth Employment and Demonstration Projects Act of 1977 (except the Young Adult Conservation Corps which is still Title VIII), namely, Youth Incentive Entitlement Pilot Projects, Youth Community Conservation and Improvement Projects, and Youth Employment and Training Programs.

Title V: National Commission for Employment Policy: Renames and reconstitutes the National Commission on Manpower Policy.

Title VI: Temporary public service employment opportunities during periods of high unemployment, in sufficient number to employ 20 percent of the unemployed in excess of 4 percent unemployment, and 25 percent of the excess when national unemployment is 7 percent or higher.

Persons not employed in projects must be hired at the entry level. Of the title's total funds, 2% must be reserved for programs for Native Americans.

Title VII: Authorizes a Private Sector Initiative Program (PSIP) to demonstrate the effectiveness of ways of increasing the involvment of the business community, including minority and small businesses, in employment and training activities supported by CETA, and increase private sector jobs for the economically disadvantaged.

Title VIII: Provides employment and experience in various occupational skills to out-of-school young people from all social and economic backgrounds through work on conservation and other projects on federal and non-federal public lands and waters. Participants may be hired for a maximum of 12 months. Operated under agreement by Departments of Labor, Agriculture, and Interior. Authorized for 4 years, through FY 1982.

CETA ENROLLMENT IN FISCAL 1979

Type of Program	Number Enrolled & Percent of Enrollment
Public Service Employment (Total)	924,503 (23%)
Title II ABC	10,461
Title II D	370,797
Title VI	543,245
Vocational Ed. (Classroom) (Total)	592,893 (15%)
Title II ABC	427,700
Title II D	14,500
Title VI	8,000
Title IV — Job Corps	85,000
Governor's Boc. Ed.	22,464
Title III — STIP	35,229
On-the-Job-Training (Total)	242,858 (6%)
Title II ABC	156,700
Title II D	2,400
Title VI	5,300
Title III — HIRE	37,093
— STIP	4,176
— Apprentice Outreach	14,189
— National Contracts	23,000

Type of Program	Number Enrolled & Percent of Enrollment
Work Experience (Total)	1,293,538 (33%)
Title II ABC	391,047
Title II D	9,591
Title IV	4,900
Title IV — Summer Jobs	888,000
Combination Programs (Total)	909,100 (23%)
Title II D, III, IV, & VI — Indians	105,000
Title III — Migrants/Seasonal Farmworkers	192,500
Title IV — YETP	440,000
— YIEPP	47,000
— YIEPP	53,400
— YCCIP	47,000
Title II — PSIP	4,000
Title III — YACC	67,200
TOTAL	3,962,892 (100%)

ELEMENTARY AND SECONDARY SCHOOLS

Source: National Center for Education Statistics

In the school year 1976-77, there were approximately 16,300 public school systems in the United States that included 62,600 public elementary schools and 25,400 public secondary schools. As the accompanying table indicates, the number of school districts and public elementary schools is declining, with a more rapid drop in the number of districts. However, since WWII, the number of pupils per school has risen substantially. In addition to the public schools, there are about 14,300 nonpublic elementary schools and 4,700 nonpublic secondary schools in the country.

School Year	Districts	PUBLIC SCHOOLS		NONPUBLIC SCHOOLS*	
		Elementary	Secondary	Elementary	Secondary
1945–46	101,382	160,227	24,314	9,863	3,294
1949–50	83,718	128,225	24,542	10,375	3,331
1955–56	54,859	104,427	26,046	12,372	3,887
1959–60	40,520	91,853	25,784	13,574	4,061
1965–66	26,983	73,216	26,597	15,340	4,606
1970–71	17,995	65,800	25,352	14,372	3,770
1972–73	16,960	64,945	25,922	NA	NA
1973–74	16,730	65,070	25,906	NA	NA
1974–75	16,570	63,619[1]	25,697[1]	NA	NA
1975–76	16,376	63,242[1]	25,330[1]	NA	NA
1976–77	16,271	62,644[1]	25,378[1]	14,323	4,723

* Data for most years are partly estimated.
[1] Excludes special education schools for the handicapped (not reported by level).

ESTIMATED U.S. EDUCATIONAL EXPENDITURES

Source: National Center for Education Statistics (amounts in billions of dollars)

Source of funds, by level of institution and type of control	1969-70 Amount	Percent	1975-76 Amount	Percent	1977-78 Amount	Percent	1979-80 Amount	Percent
All levels:	(Billions)		(Billions)		(Billions)		(Billions)	
Total public and nonpublic	$70.4	100.0	$121.6	100.0	$140.4	100.0	$166.2	100.0
Federal	7.5	10.7	12.8	10.5	14.6	10.4	17.2	10.3
State	22.2	31.5	44.4	36.5	51.1	36.4	61.3	36.9
Local	22.6	32.1	34.6	28.5	39.1	27.8	45.2	27.2
All other	18.1	25.7	29.8	24.5	35.6	25.4	42.5	25.6
Elementary and secondary schools:*								
Total public and nonpublic	45.7	100.0	78.9	100.0	90.9	100.0	197.1	100.0
Federal	3.4	7.4	6.3	8.0	7.7	8.5	9.1	8.5
State	15.8	34.6	31.6	40.1	36.0	39.7	42.9	40.1
Local	21.7	47.5	32.9	41.7	37.3	41.0	43.1	40.2
All other	4.8	10.5	8.1	10.3	9.8	10.8	12.0	11.2
Total public	41.0	100.0	70.9	100.0	81.2	100.0	95.4	100.0
Federal	3.4	8.2	6.3	8.9	7.7	9.5	9.1	9.5
State	15.8	38.6	31.6	44.6	36.0	44.3	42.9	45.0
Local	21.7	52.9	32.9	46.4	37.3	45.9	43.1	45.2
All other	.1	.3	.1	.1	.2	.3	.3	.3
Total nonpublic	4.7	100.0	8.0	100.0	9.6	100.0	11.7	100.0
Federal	—	—	—	—	—	—	—	—
State	—	—	—	—	—	—	—	—
Local	—	—	—	—	—	—	—	—
All other	4.7	100.0	8.0	100.0	9.6	100.0	11.7	100.0
Institutions of higher education:								
Total public and nonpublic	24.7	100.0	42.7	100.0	49.5	100.0	59.1	100.0
Federal	4.1	16.6	6.5	15.2	6.8	13.8	8.1	13.7
State	6.4	25.9	12.8	30.0	15.1	30.5	18.4	31.1
Local	.9	3.6	1.7	4.0	1.8	3.7	2.1	3.6
All other	13.3	53.9	21.7	50.8	25.8	52.0	30.5	51.6
Total public	15.8	100.0	29.1	100.0	33.4	100.0	39.9	100.0
Federal	2.4	14.9	4.0	13.8	4.0	11.9	4.7	11.8
State	6.3	39.7	12.5	43.0	14.8	44.2	18.0	45.2
Local	.8	5.1	1.6	5.4	1.7	5.1	2.0	5.0
All other	6.3	40.3	11.0	37.8	13.0	38.8	15.2	38.0
Total nonpublic	8.9	100.0	13.6	100.0	16.1	100.0	19.2	100.0
Federal	1.7	18.8	2.5	18.1	2.9	17.8	3.4	17.7
State	.1	1.6	.3	2.3	.3	2.0	.4	2.0
Local	.1	.7	.1	.8	.1	.7	.1	.6
All other	7.0	78.9	10.7	78.8	12.8	79.6	15.3	79.7

* In addition to regular schools, these figures include other elementary and secondary schools, such as residential schools for exceptional children, Federal schools for Indians, federally operated elementary and secondary schools on posts, and subcollegiate departments of colleges.

INDEX OF U.S. COLLEGES AND UNIVERSITIES: 1979-80

This list includes all regionally accredited four-year colleges and universities in the United States that grant baccalaureate degrees. Highly specialized institutions such as schools of mortuary science, optometry, and pharmacy are not included, nor are such professional colleges as law, medicine, or theology, which generally offer only post-baccalaureate work.

Institutions are listed in standard letter-by-letter alphabetical order. For example, University of Michigan will be found under U, not M; Marshall University comes before Mars Hill College.

The explanation of the data contained in each column is as follows. Column 1: **Est** shows the founding date of the institution. Column 2: **Type/Control** shows the student body makeup (C = coed, M = primarily men, W = primarily women) and the institutional control (Ind = independent, Pub = public, Cath = Catholic, Jewish, LDS = Latter-Day Saints, Prot = Protestant). Column 3: **UG Enroll** shows undergraduate enrollment as of fall 1979. Column 4: **% State Res** shows the percentage of the fall 1979 undergraduate enrollment that were state residents. Column 5: **Grad** shows whether graduate-level work is offered. Column 6: **Fac size** shows the number of total faculty teaching graduate and undergraduate programs as of fall 1979. Column 7: **Cmps** shows the campus setting (R = rural, S = suburban, T = college town, U = urban). Column 8: **ROTC** shows which ROTC branch has a program on campus (A = Army, N = Navy, AF = Air Force). Column 9: **Tuition** shows tuition per credit or per year for all students at private colleges or for in-state students at public colleges; X indicates campus room and board not available.

An asterisk appears where no information is available.

Name and Location	Est	Type/Control	UG Enroll	% of State Res	Grad	Fac Size	Cmps	ROTC	Tuition
Abilene Christian University, Abilene, TX 79699	1906	C/Prot	3800	65%	G	175	S	A	$2160
Abilene Christian University at Dallas, Garland, TX 75041	1971	C/Prot	600	80%	G	40	S		1584x
Academy of the New Church, Bryn Athyn, PA 19009	1876	C/Ind	149	42%		36	S		1005
Adams State College, Alamosa, CO 81102	1921	C/Pub	1679	87%	G	107	T		490
Adelphi University, Garden City, NY 11530	1896	C/Ind	5517	90%	G	800	S		3510
Adrian College, Adrian, MI 49221	1859	C/Ind	946	84%		95	T		3760
Agnes Scott College, Decatur, GA 30030	1889	W/Ind	544	50%		85	S		3900
Alabama A&M University, Normal, AL 35762	1875	C/Pub	3615	85%	G	500	S	A	530
Alabama Christian College, Montgomery, AL 36109	1942	C/Prot	1119	69%		93	S		1800
Alabama State University, Montgomery, AL 36101	1874	C/Pub	3653	86%	G	242	U	AF	525
Alaska Pacific University, Anchorage, AK 99504	1957	C/Prot	106	95%	G	38	U		2250
Albany State College, Albany, GA 31705	1903	C/Pub	4962	90%		128	U	A	699
Albertus Magnus College, New Haven, CT 06511	1925	W/Cath	561	82%		55	S		3600
Albion College, Albion, MI 49224	1835	C/Prot	1800	85%		119	T		4180
Albright College, Reading, PA 19604	1856	C/Prot	1275	60%		125	S		4180
Alcorn State University, Lorman, MS 39096	1871	C/Pub	2500	92%	G	150	R	A	744
Alderson-Broaddus College, Philippi, WV 26416	1871	C/Prot	878	43%		112	R		2835
Alfred University, Alfred, NY 14802	1836	C/Ind	1765	75%	G	176	R		4900
Alice Lloyd College, Pippa Passes, KY 41844	1923	C/Ind	231	93%		20	R		2000
Allegheny College, Meadville, PA 16335	1815	C/Prot	1850	50%	G	152	T		4300
Allentown Coll of St Francis de Sales, Center Valley, PA 18034	1965	C/Cath	600	70%		58	R		3330
Allen University, Columbia, SC 29204	1870	C/Prot	419	*		41	S		1800
Alliance College, Cambridge Springs, PA 16403	1912	C/Ind	251	53%		24	R		2200
Alma College, Alma, MI 48801	1886	C/Prot	1210	74%		99	T		4144
Alvernia College, Reading, PA 19607	1958	C/Cath	750	60%		80	S		1850
Alverno College, Milwaukee, WI 53215	1936	W/Cath	1340	95%		107	U		2950
Ambassador College, Pasadena, CA 91123	1947	C/Ind	331	18%	G	36	U		1350
American Baptist College, Nashville, TN 37207	1924	M/Prot	125	20%		16	S		920
American Conservatory of Music, Chicago, IL 60603	1886	C/Ind	311	90%	G	188	U		2400x
American International College, Springfield, MA 01109	1885	C/Ind	1463	60%	G	116	S		3060
American Technological University, Killeen, TX 76541	1973	C/Pub	401	*	G	29	S		1488
American University, Washington, DC 20016	1893	C/Prot	5717	27%	G	1173	S		4620
Amherst College, Amherst, MA 01002	1821	C/Ind	1541	18%		170	T		6250
Anderson College, Anderson, IN 46011	1917	C/Prot	1858	40%	G	132	S		3200
Andrews University, Berrien Springs, MI 49104	1874	C/Ind	2087	38%	G	272	T		3975
Angelo State University, San Angelo, TX 76909	1928	C/Pub	5292	95%	G	201	T	AF	344
Anna Maria College, Paxton, MA 01612	1946	C/Cath	580	75%	G	63	S		2950
Antioch College, Yellow Springs, OH 45387	1852	C/Ind	989	12%		83	T		5500
Antioch U-Maryland at Columbia, Columbia, MD 21044	1852	C/Ind	*	90%	G	*	*		*x
Appalachian Bible Institute, Bradley, WV 25818	1950	C/Ind	230	14%		20	T		1825
Appalachian State University, Boone, NC 28608	1899	C/Pub	8277	93%	G	554	T	A	620
Aquinas College, Grand Rapids, MI 49506	1886	C/Ind	1907	89%	G	122	S		3555
Arizona State University, Tempe, AZ 85281	1885	C/Pub	27,570	66%	G	1267	S	A,AF	600
Arkansas Baptist College, Little Rock, AR 72202	1884	C/Ind	534	*		*	*		*
Arkansas College, Batesville, AR 72501	1872	C/Prot	496	65%		52	T		1100
Arkansas State University, State University, AR 72467	1909	C/Pub	6641	88%	G	339	T	A	600
Arkansas Tech University, Russellville, AR 72801	1909	C/Pub	2846	85%	G	150	T	A	600
Armstrong College, Berkeley, CA 94704	1918	C/Ind	362	50%	G	48	U		2052x
Armstrong State College, Savannah, GA 31406	1935	C/Pub	2854	95%	G	160	S	A,N	627x
Art Center College of Design, Pasadena, CA 91103	1930	C/Ind	1057	50%	G	173	S		3250x
Asbury College, Wilmore, KY 40390	1890	C/Ind	1273	12%		101	T		2689
Ashland College, Ashland, OH 44805	1878	C/Prot	1901	75%	G	149	T		4205
Assumption College, Worcester, MA 01609	1904	C/Cath	1400	50%	G	151	S		3300
Athens State College, Athens, AL 35611	1822	C/Pub	1204	90%		70	T		675
Atlanta Christian College, East Point, GA 30344	1937	C/Ind	207	56%		17	S		1184
Atlanta College of Art, Atlanta, GA 30309	1928	C/Ind	260	40%		35	U		2950
Atlantic Christian College, Wilson, NC 27893	1902	C/Prot	1650	80%		112	S		2200
Atlantic Union College, South Lancaster, MA 01561	1882	C/Prot	640	38%		98	T		4048
Auburn University, Auburn, AL 36849	1856	C/Pub	16,336	68%	G	1123	T	A,N,AF	720
Auburn University at Montgomery, Montgomery, AL 36109	1856	C/Pub	3627	100%	G	350	U	A	555
Augsburg College, Minneapolis, MN 55454	1869	C/Ind	1625	88%		140	U	AF	3550
Augusta College, Augusta, GA 30904	1925	C/Pub	3378	90%	G	173	U	A	534x
Augustana College, Rock Island, IL 61201	1860	C/Prot	2220	80%	G	179	U		3540
Augustana College, Sioux Falls, SD 57102	1860	C/Prot	1874	55%	G	188	U		3650
Aurora College, Aurora, IL 60507	1893	C/Prot	1058	90%	G	99	S		3300
Austin College, Sherman, TX 75090	1849	C/Prot	1069	90%	G	107	S		3000
Austin Peay State University, Clarksville, TN 37040	1927	C/Pub	4407	88%	G	245	T	A	546
Averett College, Danville, VA 24541	1859	C/Prot	1077	78%	G	54	S		1525x
Avila College, Kansas City, MO 64145	1916	C/Cath	1980	31%	G	199	S		2550
Azusa Pacific College, Azusa, CA 91702	1899	C/Ind	1230	85%	G	128	S		3632
Babson College, Babson Park, MA 02157	1919	C/Ind	1335	75%	G	124	S		4512
Baker University, Baldwin City, KS 66006	1858	C/Prot	872	55%	G	89	T		2600

Name and Location	Est	Type/Control	UG Enroll	% of State Res	Grad	Fac Size	Cmps	ROTC	Tuition
Baldwin-Wallace College, Berea, OH 44017	1845	C/Prot	2656	80%	G	169	S		$4131
Ball State University, Muncie, IN 47306	1918	C/Pub	15,205	93%	G	963	S	A	975
Baltimore Hebrew College, Baltimore, MD 21215	1919	C/Ind	95	96%	G	17	S		1200x
Baptist Bible College of Pennsylvania, Clarks Summit, PA 18411	1932	C/Prot	780	8%		45	S		2176
Baptist College at Charleston, Charleston, SC 29411	1965	C/Prot	2420	85%		92	S	AF	2616
Barat College, Lake Forest, IL 60045	1858	W/Cath	737	88%		82	S		3650
Barber-Scotia College, Concord, NC 28025	1867	C/Prot	435	61%		38	T		1829
Bard College, Annandale, NY 12504	1860	C/Ind	700	43%		95	R		5440
Barnard College, New York, NY 10027	1889	W/Ind	2441	45%		225	U		5940
Barrington College, Barrington, RI 02806	1900	C/Ind	456	26%		47	S		3450
Barry College, Miami Shores, FL 33161	1940	C/Cath	1249	79%	G	171	S		2900
Bartlesville Wesleyan College, Bartlesville, OK 74003	1959	C/Prot	662	51%		53	S		2200
Bates College, Lewiston, ME 04240	1864	C/Ind	1450	11%		130	T		5720
Bayamon Central University, Bayamon, PR 00619	1961	C/Prot	2615	100%		66	U		600x
Baylor University, Waco, TX 76706	1845	C/Prot	8551	60%	G	476	U	AF	2100
Beacon College, Washington, DC 20009	1971	C/Ind	43	*	G	143	U		1950x
Beaver College, Glenside, PA 19038	1853	C/Prot	994	69%	G	130	S		4300
Belhaven College, Jackson, MS 39202	1883	C/Prot	886	85%		58	S		2215
Bellarmine College, Louisville, KY 40205	1950	C/Cath	1820	85%	G	96	S		2250
Bellevue College, Bellevue, NE 68005	1966	C/Ind	2272	99%		77	U		1050x
Belmont Abbey College, Belmont, NC 28012	1876	C/Cath	777	37%		57	S		2700
Belmont College, Nashville, TN 37203	1951	C/Prot	1483	75%		131	U		2050
Beloit College, Beloit, WI 53511	1846	C/Ind	1019	17%		120	T		5070
Bemidji State University, Bemidji, MN 56601	1919	C/Pub	4014	93%	G	247	R	A	585
Benedict College, Columbia, SC 29204	1870	C/Ind	1584	90%		107	U	A	2200
Benedictine College, Atchison, KS 66002	1971	C/Cath	1045	60%		75	T		2800
Bennett College, Greensboro, NC 27420	1873	W/Prot	645	35%		56	U		1950
Bennington College, Bennington, VT 05201	1932	C/Ind	655	1%	G	80	R		7380
Bentley College, Waltham, MA 02154	1917	C/Ind	4950	60%	G	190	S		3970
Berea College, Berea, KY 40403	1855	C/Ind	1438	38%		127	T		91
Berklee College of Music, Boston, MA 02215	1945	C/Ind	2583	20%		218	U		2880
Berkshire Christian College, Lenox, MA 01240	1897	C/Prot	136	33%		21	T		2200
Bernard M Baruch College, See City U of NY, Baruch College									
Berry College, Mount Berry, GA 30149	1902	C/Ind	1385	60%	G	98	S		2400
Bethany Bible College, Santa Cruz, CA 95066	1919	C/Prot	598	60%		33	R		1900
Bethany College, Lindsborg, KS 67465	1881	C/Prot	827	73%		67	T		2434
Bethany College, Bethany, WV 26032	1840	C/Prot	900	16%		77	R		3835
Bethany Nazarene College, Bethany, OK 73008	1899	C/Prot	1277	30%	G	85	S		1860
Bethel College, Mishawaka, IN 46544	1947	C/Prot	464	97%		37	U		2573
Bethel College, North Newton, KS 67117	1887	C/Prot	638	63%		63	T		2685
Bethel College, St Paul, MN 55112	1871	C/Prot	1989	59%		184	S		3400
Bethel College, McKenzie, TN 38201	1842	C/Prot	360	80%		36	T		1800
Bethune-Cookman College, Daytona Beach, FL 32015	1904	C/Prot	1736	84%		110	U		2425
Biola College, La Mirada, CA 90639	1908	C/Prot	2384	73%	G	170	S		3216
Birmingham-Southern College, Birmingham, AL 35204	1856	C/Prot	1402	75%		71	U	AF	2550
Biscayne College, Miami, FL 33054	1962	C/Cath	2109	65%	G	150	S		3050
Bishop College, Dallas, TX 75241	1881	C/Prot	926	38%		61	S	A	2100
Blackburn College, Carlinville, IL 62626	1837	C/Prot	531	85%		48	T		2250
Black Hills State College, Spearfish, SD 57783	1883	C/Pub	2056	91%	G	98	T	A	592
Bloomfield College, Bloomfield, NJ 07003	1868	C/Prot	2268	99%		141	S		3450
Bloomsburg State College, Bloomsburg, PA 17815	1839	C/Pub	5803	94%	G	325	T		1110
Bluefield College, Bluefield, VA 24605	1922	C/Prot	391	68%		29	S		1565
Bluefield State College, Bluefield, WV 24701	1895	C/Pub	2747	8%		100	U		380x
Blue Mountain College, Blue Mountain, MS 38610	1873	C/Prot	340	82%		32	T		1440
Bluffton College, Bluffton, OH 45817	1899	C/Prot	660	90%		56	T		3429
Boise State University, Boise, ID 83725	1932	C/Pub	8825	95%	G	457	U	A	475
Borromeo College of Ohio, Wickliffe, OH 44092	1953	M/Cath	80	90%		25	S		2375
Boston College, Chestnut Hill, MA 02167	1863	C/Cath	10,185	52%	G	674	S	AF	4530
Boston Conservatory of Music, Boston, MA 02215	1867	C/Ind	481	*	G	108	U		3400
Boston State College, Boston, MA 02115	1852	C/Pub	5241	90%	G	536	U		600x
Boston University, Boston, MA 02215	1869	C/Ind	11,279	25%	G	2449	U		5515
Bowdoin College, Brunswick, ME 04011	1794	C/Ind	1340	11%		115	T		5800
Bowie State College, Bowie, MD 20715	1865	C/Pub	2049	85%	G	159	S	A	655
Bowling Green State University, Bowling Green, OH 43403	1910	C/Pub	14,868	95%	G	791	T	A,AF	918
Bradford College, Bradford, MA 01830	1803	C/Ind	341	31%		41	S		4500
Bradley University, Peoria, IL 61625	1897	C/Ind	4780	78%	G	377	S	A	3626
Brandeis University, Waltham, MA 02154	1948	C/Ind	2798	22%	G	403	S		5835
Brenau College, Gainesville, GA 30501	1878	C/Ind	686	75%	G	78	T		2450
Brescia College, Owensboro, KY 42301	1950	C/Cath	832	91%		75	U		2100
Briar Cliff College, Sioux City, IA 51104	1930	C/Cath	1258	93%		70	U		2760
Bridgeport Engineering Institute, Bridgeport, CT 06606	1924	C/Ind	630	95%		80	S		1480x
Bridgewater College, Bridgewater, VA 22812	1880	C/Prot	914	71%		78	T		2670
Bridgewater State College, Bridgewater, MA 02324	1840	C/Pub	4358	96%	G	272	T		600
Brigham Young University, Provo, UT 84602	1875	C/Prot	24,107	31%	G	1315	T	A,AF	970
Brigham Young U-Hawaii Cmps, Laie, Oahu, HI 96762	1955	C/Prot	1053	34%		65	T	A	550x
Brooklyn College, See City U of NY, Brooklyn College									
Brooks Institute, Santa Barbara, CA 93108	1945	C/Ind	785	30%	G	32	U		3750x
Brown University, Providence, RI 02912	1764	C/Ind	5487	7%	G	527	U		6140
Bryan College, Dayton, TN 37321	1930	C/Ind	645	12%		45	R		2250
Bryant College, Smithfield, RI 02917	1863	C/Ind	2731	24%	G	145	S		3000
Bryn Mawr College, Bryn Mawr, PA 19010	1885	W/Ind	1026	12%	G	216	S		5950
Bucknell University, Lewisburg, PA 17837	1846	C/Ind	3084	35%	G	252	T	A	5500
Buena Vista College, Storm Lake, IA 50588	1891	C/Prot	899	94%		58	T		3710
Butler University, Indianapolis, IN 46208	1855	C/Ind	2516	75%	G	249	S		3400
Cabrini College, Radnor, PA 19087	1957	C/Cath	515	75%		58	S		3060
Caldwell College, Caldwell, NJ 07006	1939	W/Cath	723	85%		78	S		2700
California Baptist College, Riverside, CA 92504	1950	C/Prot	746	78%		58	S		2550
California College of Arts and Crafts, Oakland, CA 94618	1907	C/Ind	906	60%	G	145	U		3130

Name and Location	Est	Type/Control	UG Enroll	% of State Res	Grad	Fac Size	Cmps	ROTC	Tuition
California Institute of Technology, Pasadena, CA 91125	1891	C/Ind	817	45%	G	339	S	A,AF	$5229
California Institute of the Arts, Valencia, CA 91355	1961	C/Ind	543	54%	G	139	S		4500
California Lutheran College, Thousand Oaks, CA 91360	1959	C/Prot	1435	87%	G	256	S	A,AF	3500
California Maritime Academy, Vallejo, CA 94590	1929	M/Pub	485	85%		30	U		645
California Polytechnic State U, San Luis Obispo, CA 93407	1901	C/Pub	14,669	98%	G	*	T	A	324
California State College, California, PA 15419	1852	C/Pub	975	98%	G	305	T	A	1100
Calif State College, Bakersfield, Bakersfield, CA 93309	1970	C/Pub	2272	85%	G	200	R		180
Calif State College, San Bernardino, San Bernardino, CA 92407	1962	C/Pub	2752	93%	G	272	S		258
Calif State College, Stanislaus, Turlock, CA 95380	1957	C/Pub	2474	93%	G	227	T		212
California State Polytechnic U, Pomona, Pomona, CA 91768	1938	C/Pub	12,879	88%	G	813	S		180
Calif State U, Chico, Chico, CA 95929	1887	C/Pub	11,390	97%	G	704	T	A	225
Calif State U, Dominquez Hills, Carson, CA 90747	1960	C/Pub	6121	35%	G	307	U		189x
Calif State U, Fresno, Fresno, CA 93740	1911	C/Pub	11,954	90%	G	937	U	AF	240
Calif State U, Fullerton, Fullerton, CA 92634	1957	C/Pub	17,153	97%	G	1272	S		228x
Calif State U, Hayward, Hayward, CA 94542	1957	C/Pub	7970	98%	G	550	U		210x
Calif State U, Long Beach, Long Beach, CA 90840	1949	C/Pub	24,143	90%	G	1600	U		218
Calif State U, Los Angeles, Los Angeles, CA 90032	1947	C/Pub	15,420	95%	G	1200	U		200x
Calif State U, Northridge, Northridge, CA 91330	1958	C/Pub	22,302	98%	G	*	S		200x
Calif State U, Sacramento, Sacramento, CA 95819	1947	C/Pub	16,191	95%	G	1000	U	A,AF	200
Calumet College, Whiting, IN 46394	1951	C/Cath	1460	68%		75	U		1500x
Calvary Bible College, Kansas City, MO 64111	1932	C/Prot	454	33%	G	38	U		1600
Calvin College, Grand Rapids, MI 49506	1876	C/Prot	3900	57%	G	240	S		3000
Camden College of Arts and Sciences, See Rutgers University, Camden College of Arts and Sciences									
Cameron University, Lawton, OK 73501	1927	C/Pub	4712	99%		172	U	A	453
Campbellsville College, Campbellsville, KY 42718	1906	C/Prot	674	76%		60	T		2150
Campbell University, Buies Creek, NC 27506	1887	C/Prot	1790	75%	G	120	T	A	3020
Canisius College, Buffalo, NY 14208	1870	C/Pub	2422	95%	G	344	U	A	3050
Capital University, Columbus, OH 43209	1850	C/Prot	1825	87%	G	189	S	AF	4280
Capitol Institute of Technology, Kensington, MD 20795	1964	C/Ind	525	75%		26	S		2160x
Cardinal Glennon College, St Louis, MO 63119	1898	M/Cath	94	73%		29	S		1825
Cardinal Stritch College, Milwaukee, WI 53217	1937	C/Ind	597	65%	G	116	S	A	2900
Caribbean University College, Bayamon, PR 00619	1969	C/Ind	1600	100%		53	U		1350x
Carleton College, Northfield, MN 55057	1866	C/Ind	1850	25%		168	T		4855
Carlow College, Pittsburgh, PA 15213	1929	W/Cath	792	91%		81	U		3630
Carnegie-Mellon University, Pittsburgh, PA 15213	1900	C/Ind	3880	45%	G	552	U	A,AF	4700
Carroll College, Waukesha, WI 53186	1846	C/Prot	1168	77%		106	S		3760
Carroll College of Montana, Helena, MT 59601	1909	C/Cath	1342	74%		111	T		2160
Carson-Newman College, Jefferson City, TN 37760	1851	C/Prot	1649	52%		113	T	A	2200
Carthage College, Kenosha, WI 53141	1847	C/Prot	1134	45%	G	113	S		3650
Case Western Reserve University, Cleveland, OH 44106	1826	C/Ind	3158	60%	G	1465	U		4800
Castleton State College, Castleton, VT 05735	1787	C/Pub	1758	65%	G	123	R		970
Catawba College, Salisbury, NC 28144	1851	C/Prot	1000	50%		72	S		2850
Cathedral Coll of Immac Conception, Douglaston, NY 11362	1914	M/Cath	147	98%		30	U		2600
Catholic University of America, Washington, DC 20064	1887	C/Cath	2700	*	G	500	S		4250
Catholic University of Puerto Rico, Ponce, PR 00731	1948	C/Cath	8749	95%	G	534	U		*x
Cedar Crest College, Allentown, PA 18104	1867	W/Prot	1013	65%		81	S		4000
Cedarville College, Cedarville, OH 45314	1887	C/Prot	1185	50%		70	T		2376
Centenary College, Hackettstown, NJ 07840	1867	W/Ind	705	60%		67	T		3450
Centenary College of Louisiana, Shreveport, LA 71104	1825	C/Prot	808	63%	G	80	U	A	2400
Ctr for Creative Studies-Coll of Art & Design, Detroit, MI 48202	1926	C/Pub	756	92%		99	U		3200x
Central Baptist College, Conway, AR 72032	1952	C/Prot	231	60%		18	T		480
Central Bible College, Springfield, MO 65802	1922	C/Prot	1115	14%		60	S		1400
Central Connecticut State College, New Britain, CT 06050	1849	C/Pub	9886	97%	G	646	S		390
Central Methodist College, Fayette, MO 65248	1854	C/Prot	667	88%		62	R		3200
Central Michigan University, Mount Pleasant, MI 48858	1892	C/Pub	14,556	98%	G	855	T	A	1787
Central Missouri State University, Warrensburg, MO 64093	1871	C/Pub	8319	95%	G	530	T	A	465
Central New England College, Worcester, MA 01608	1905	C/Ind	*	60%		92	U		2400
Central State University, Wilberforce, OH 45384	1887	C/Pub	2380	75%		171	S		650
Central State University, Edmond, OK 73034	1890	C/Pub	8518	95%	G	430	S	A	413
Central University of Iowa, Pella, IA 50219	1853	C/Prot	1545	68%		90	T		3650
Central Washington University, Ellensburg, WA 98926	1890	C/Pub	5858	97%	G	332	T	AF	618
Central Wesleyan College, Central, SC 29630	1906	C/Prot	413	60%		30	T		2920
Centre College of Kentucky, Danville, KY 40422	1819	C/Ind	760	55%		64	T		3900
Chadron State College, Chadron, NE 69337	1911	C/Pub	1554	85%	G	104	T		570
Chaminade University of Honolulu, Honolulu, HI 96816	1955	C/Cath	1059	68%	G	162	S	A,AF	1900
Chapman College, Orange, CA 92666	1861	C/Prot	1259	70%	G	167	S		3790
Chatham College, Pittsburgh, PA 15232	1869	W/Ind	615	60%		86	U		4425
Chestnut Hill College, Philadelphia, PA 19118	1871	W/Cath	650	73%	G	102	U		2650
Cheyney State College, Cheyney, PA 19319	1837	C/Pub	2300	82%	G	198	R	A	1060
Chicago Conservatory College, Chicago, IL 60605	1932	C/Ind	121	98%	G	100	U		1550
Chicago State University, Chicago, IL 60628	1867	C/Pub	5165	99%	G	359	U		522x
Christian Brothers College, Memphis, TN 38104	1871	C/Cath	1330	79%		114	U		2690
Christopher Newport College, Newport News, VA 23606	1971	C/Pub	3918	90%		201	U	A	780x
Cincinnati Bible College, Cincinnati, OH 45204	1924	C/Prot	522	55%	G	40	U		1232
Circleville Bible College, Circleville, OH 43113	1948	C/Prot	226	65%		18	T		1392
Citadel, Charleston, SC 29409	1842	M/Pub	2378	65%		148	U	A,N,AF	125
City College, See City U of NY, City College									
City U of NY, Baruch College, New York, NY 10010	1968	C/Pub	12,425	95%	G	850	U		925x
City U of NY, Brooklyn College, Brooklyn, NY 11210	1930	C/Pub	14,651	98%	G	1318	U		925x
City U of NY, City College, New York, NY 10031	1847	C/Pub	11,510	96%	G	1183	U		925x
City U of NY, College of Staten Island, Staten Island, NY 10301	1955	C/Pub	10,500	99%	G	379	U		925x
City U of NY, Herbert H Lehman Coll, Bronx, NY 10468	1931	C/Pub	9076	99%	G	820	U		925x
City U of NY, Hunter College, New York, NY 10021	1870	C/Pub	14,872	98%	G	1234	U		925x
CUNY, JJ Col of Crim Justice, New York, NY 10019	1964	C/Pub	5223	97%	G	418	U	A	925x
City U of NY, Medgar Evers College, Brooklyn, NY 11225	1969	C/Pub	2894	97%		150	U		1425x
City U of NY, Queens College, Flushing, NY 11367	1937	C/Pub	13,000	99%	G	1400	U		925x
City U of NY, York College, Jamaica, NY 11451	1967	C/Pub	3889	95%		200	U		925x

Name and Location	Est	Type/Control	UG Enroll	% of State Res	Grad	Fac Size	Cmps	ROTC	Tuition
Claflin College, Orangeburg, SC 29115	1869	C/Prot	866	88%		65	T	A	$1850
Claremont Men's College, Claremont, CA 91711	1946	C/Ind	849	60%		99	S	A	5502
Clarion State College, Clarion, PA 16214	1867	C/Pub	4900	85%	G	360	T	A	1150
Clark College, Atlanta, GA 30314	1869	C/Prot	2031	60%		142	U		2080
Clarke College, Dubuque, IA 52001	1843	W/Cath	606	75%	G	72	S		3100
Clarkson College, Potsdam, NY 13676	1896	C/Ind	3304	84%	G	219	T	A	4400
Clark University, Worcester, MA 01610	1887	C/Ind	1810	25%	G	194	U		5400
Cleary College, Ypsilanti, MI 48197	1883	C/Ind	453	95%		46	U		2205x
Clemson University, Clemson, SC 29631	1889	C/Pub	9240	79%	G	671	T	A,AF	150
Cleveland College of Jewish Studies, Beachwood, OH 44122	1963	C/Jewish	84	100%	G	16	S		460x
Cleveland Institute of Art, Cleveland, OH 44106	1882	C/Ind	546	74%		71	U		3180
Cleveland Institute of Music, Cleveland, OH 44106	1920	C/Ind	179	25%	G	142	U		4450
Cleveland State University, Cleveland, OH 44115	1964	C/Pub	12,396	98%	G	700	U	A	984
Clinch Valley College of the U of Va, Wise, VA 24293	1954	C/Pub	942	91%		66	T		750
Coe College, Cedar Rapids, IA 52402	1851	C/Prot	1320	62%		104	U		3890
Cogswell College, San Francisco, CA 94108	1887	C/Pub	425	100%		54	U		2400x
Coker College, Hartsville, SC 29550	1908	C/Ind	321	88%		43	T		3030
Colby College, Waterville, ME 04901	1813	C/Ind	1677	18%		132	T		5390
Colby-Sawyer College, New London, NH 03257	1837	W/Ind	700	14%		69	T		4443
Colegio Cesar Chavez, Mount Angel, OR 97362	1882	C/Ind	81	*		*	*		*
Colgate University, Hamilton, NY 13346	1819	C/Ind	2600	50%	G	184	T		5400
College for Human Services, New York, NY 10014	1964	C/Ind	100	*		13	U		5016x
College Misericordia, Dallas, PA 18612	1924	W/Cath	1043	80%	G	97	S		2630
College of Charleston, Charleston, SC 29401	1770	C/Pub	4137	95%	G	220	U		850
College of Great Falls, Great Falls, MT 59405	1932	C/Cath	1200	80%		82	S		2550
College of Idaho, Caldwell, ID 83605	1891	C/Prot	482	52%	G	72	T		3465
College of Insurance, New York, NY 10038	1962	C/Ind	1825	45%	G	131	U		1700x
Coll of Mount St Joseph on-the-Ohio, Mt St Joseph, OH 45051	1920	W/Cath	1311	88%	G	122	S		2912
College of Mount Saint Vincent, Riverdale, NY 10471	1847	W/Ind	1308	90%		99	S		3200
College of New Rochelle, New Rochelle, NY 10801	1904	W/Ind	3669	75%	G	398	S		3150
College of Notre Dame, Belmont, CA 94002	1868	C/Cath	910	64%	G	114	S		3200
College of Notre Dame of Maryland, Baltimore, MD 21210	1896	W/Cath	540	75%		71	S		3150
College of Our Lady of the Elms, Chicopee, MA 01013	1928	W/Cath	425	65%		61	S		3000
College of Saint Benedict, Saint Joseph, MN 56374	1913	W/Cath	1620	88%		129	R		3350
College of St Catherine, St Paul, MN 55105	1905	W/Cath	2004	75%		120	U		3260
College of Saint Elizabeth, Convent Station, NJ 07961	1899	W/Cath	581	85%		83	S		3000
College of St Francis, Joliet, IL 60435	1925	C/Cath	745	90%	G	56	S		2870
College of St Joseph the Provider, Rutland, VT 05701	1954	C/Cath	212	70%		44	T		2825
College of Saint Mary, Omaha, NE 68124	1923	W/Cath	592	77%		78	U		3072
College of Saint Rose, Albany, NY 12203	1920	C/Ind	1627	95%	G	194	U		2850
College of St Scholastica, Duluth, MN 55811	1906	C/Cath	1082	72%	G	126	U		3219
College of Saint Teresa, Winona, MN 55987	1907	W/Cath	791	97%		100	T		3489
College of Saint Thomas, St Paul, MN 55105	1885	C/Cath	3183	89%	G	265	S	AF	3080
College of Santa Fe, Santa Fe, NM 87501	1947	C/Cath	1203	80%		90	U		2700
College of Staten Island, See City U of NY, College of Staten Island									
College of the Atlantic, Bar Harbor, ME 04609	1969	C/Ind	170	15%		25	T		3800
Coll of the Ctr for Early Education, Los Angeles, CA 90048	1939	C/Ind	7	100%	G	10	U		1932x
College of the Holy Cross, Worcester, MA 01610	1843	C/Cath	2500	47%	G	200	S	N,AF	4600
College of the Ozarks, Clarksville, AR 72830	1834	C/Prot	543	57%		40	T	A	1050
College of the Southwest, Hobbs, NM 88240	1956	C/Ind	156	87%		27	T		845
College of the Virgin Islands, St Thomas, St Thomas, VI 00801	1962	C/Pub	1784	70%	G	108	S		344x
College of William and Mary, Williamsburg, VA 23185	1693	C/Pub	4449	70%	G	454	T	A	1076
College of Wooster, Wooster, OH 44691	1866	C/Prot	1760	48%		155	T		5285
Colorado College, Colorado Springs, CO 80903	1874	C/Ind	1940	33%	G	205	U		4700
Colorado School of Mines, Golden, CO 80401	1874	C/Pub	2166	70%	G	195	T	A	1100
Colorado State University, Fort Collins, CO 80523	1870	C/Pub	15,346	75%	G	1158	U	A,AF	605
Colorado Women's College, Denver, CO 80220	1888	W/Ind	500	40%		44	U	A,AF	4350
Columbia Bible College, Columbia, SC 29203	1923	C/Ind	539	30%	G	32	S		2150
Columbia Christian College, Portland, OR 97220	1956	C/Prot	325	34%		33	U		2301
Columbia College, Chicago, IL 60605	1890	C/Ind	3200	90%		295	U		1350x
Columbia College, Columbia, MO 65201	1851	C/Ind	843	45%		72	T		3100
Columbia College, New York, NY 10027	1887	M/Ind	2800	*		560	U		5850
Columbia College, Columbia, SC 29203	1854	W/Prot	1103	90%		77	U		2800
Columbia Union College, Takoma Park, MD 20012	1904	C/Prot	956	40%		91	S		2990
Columbia University, See Barnard College and Columbia College, NY									
Columbus College, Columbus, GA 31907	1958	C/Pub	4070	88%	G	266	S	A	459x
Combs College of Music, Philadelphia, PA 19119	1885	C/Ind	91	70%	G	38	U		3420
Conception Seminary College, Conception, MO 64433	1891	M/Cath	94	43%		25	R		1450
Concord College, Athens, WV 24712	1872	C/Pub	2081	80%		97	T		368
Concordia College, River Forest, IL 60305	1864	C/Prot	984	55%	G	114	S		2400
Concordia College, Ann Arbor, MI 48105	1962	C/Prot	560	50%		52	T		2088
Concordia College, Moorhead, MN 56560	1891	C/Prot	2607	66%		191	S	A,AF	3635
Concordia College, St Paul, MN 55104	1893	C/Prot	664	60%		68	U		2790
Concordia College, Bronxville, NY 10708	1881	C/Prot	430	65%		56	U		2475
Concordia College, Portland, OR 97211	1905	C/Prot	313	40%		38	U		2400
Concordia Lutheran College, Austin, TX 78705	1926	C/Prot	334	87%		21	U	A	1750
Concordia Teachers College, Seward, NE 68434	1894	C/Prot	1137	25%	G	100	T	A	2500
Connecticut College, New London, CT 06320	1911	C/Ind	1627	25%	G	188	S		5900
Conservatory of Music, San Juan, PR 00936	1959	C/Pub	262	97%		38	U		*x
Converse College, Spartanburg, SC 29301	1889	W/Ind	732	40%	G	85	U		3650
Cook College, See Rutgers University, Cook College									
Cooper Union for Adv of Sci & Art, New York, NY 10003	1859	C/Ind	881	78%	G	132	U		300x
Coppin State College, Baltimore, MD 21216	1900	C/Pub	2638	97%	G	141	U		620x
Cornell College, Mount Vernon, IA 52314	1853	C/Prot	898	30%		104	T		4220
Cornell University, Ithaca, NY 14853	1865	C/Ind	11,945	55%	G	1848	T	A,N,AF	5860
Cornish Institute, Seattle, WA 98102	1914	C/Ind	422	84%		115	U		2700x
Corpus Christi State University, Corpus Christi, TX 78412	1925	C/Pub	1631	99%	G	144	U	A	100
Covenant College, Lookout Mountain, GA 37350	1955	C/Prot	494	15%		38	S		3380

Name and Location	Est	Type/Control	UG Enroll	% of State Res	Grad	Fac Size	Cmps	ROTC	Tuition
Cranbrook Academy of Art, Bloomfield Hills, MI 48013	1932	C/Ind	5	20%	G	9	S		$ *x
Creighton University, Omaha, NE 68178	1878	C/Cath	3520	38%	G	881	U	A	3300
Culver-Stockton College, Canton, MO 63435	1853	C/Ind	443	56%		46	T		2980
Cumberland College, Williamsburg, KY 40769	1889	C/Prot	2000	62%		107	T	A	1848
Curry College, Milton, MA 02186	1879	C/Ind	831	58%		69	S		4400
C W Post Center of Long Island U, Greenvale, NY 11548	1954	C/Ind	7229	93%	G	635	S		3380
Daemen College, Amherst, NY 14226	1947	C/Ind	1317	95%		120	S		3250
Dakota State College, Madison, SD 57042	1881	C/Pub	895	94%		61	T		555
Dakota Wesleyan University, Mitchell, SD 57301	1885	C/Prot	521	72%		56	T		2340
Dallas Baptist College, Dallas, TX 75211	1898	C/Prot	1008	85%		66	U	A	2100
Dallas Bible College, Dallas, TX 75228	1940	C/Ind	225	51%		20	U		1840
Dana College, Blair, NE 68008	1884	C/Ind	527	40%		45	T		3000
Daniel Hale Williams University, Chicago, IL 60644	1974	C/Ind	2195	*		*	*		2400
Daniel Payne College, Birmingham, AL 35214	1889	C/Prot	*	93%		*	U		*x
Daniel Webster College, Nashua, NH 03060	1965	C/Ind	500	25%		32	S	AF	3350
Dartmouth College, Hanover, NH 03755	1769	C/Ind	3200	6%	G	671	T		6075
David Lipscomb College, Nashville, TN 37203	1891	C/Prot	2293	51%		120	S		1920
Davidson College, Davidson, NC 28036	1837	C/Prot	1352	30%		115	T	A	4100
Davis and Elkins College, Elkins, WV 26241	1904	C/Prot	1098	25%		86	T		3600
Defiance College, Defiance, OH 43512	1850	C/Prot	800	82%		70	T		3520
Delaware State College, Dover, DE 19901	1891	C/Pub	2153	62%		144	R		515
Delaware Valley Coll of Science & Agr, Doylestown, PA 18901	1896	C/Ind	1428	65%		90	R		2457
Delta State University, Cleveland, MS 38733	1925	C/Pub	2521	97%	G	167	T	A	720
Denison University, Granville, OH 43023	1831	C/Ind	2080	26%		182	T		4880
DePaul University, Chicago, IL 60604	1898	C/Cath	8101	90%	G	671	U	A	3120
DePauw University, Greencastle, IN 46135	1837	C/Ind	2251	48%	G	185	T	A	4658
Detroit Bible College, Farmington Hills, MI 48018	1945	C/Ind	345	98%		20	S		1962
Detroit Institute of Technology, Detroit, MI 48201	1891	C/Ind	800	84%		59	U		2402x
DeVry Institute of Technology, Phoenix, AZ 85016	1967	C/Ind	2562	22%		*	U		2425x
DeVry Institute of Technology, Atlanta, GA 30341	1969	C/Ind	1019	18%		19	U		2425x
DeVry Institute of Technology, Chicago, IL 60618	1931	C/Ind	2497	84%		44	U		2425x
DeVry Institute of Technology, Dallas, TX 75235	1969	C/Ind	832	61%		30	U		2425x
Dickinson College, Carlisle, PA 17013	1773	C/Prot	1650	40%		125	T	A	4885
Dickinson State College, Dickinson, ND 58601	1918	C/Pub	1062	90%		*	T		477
Dillard University, New Orleans, LA 70122	1869	C/Prot	1217	60%		90	U	A,AF	2100
Divine Word College, Epworth, IA 52045	1912	M/Cath	92	21%		22	R		2600
Doane College, Crete, NE 68333	1858	C/Prot	689	76%		62	T	A	2995
Dr Martin Luther College, New Ulm, MN 56073	1884	C/Ind	849	15%		72	T		940
Dominican College, Orangeburg, NY 10962	1952	C/Ind	1230	74%		69	S	A	2100x
Dominican College of San Rafael, San Rafael, CA 94901	1890	C/Cath	451	81%	G	102	S		3300
Dominican School of Philos and Theol, Berkeley, CA 94709	1932	C/Cath	21	50%	G	18	U		1210x
Don Bosco College, Newton, NJ 07860	1928	M/Cath	83	30%		25	R		2600
Dordt College, Sioux Center, IA 51250	1955	C/Prot	1218	28%		75	R		2600
Douglass College, See Rutgers University, Douglass College									
Dowling College, Oakdale, NY 11769	1959	C/Ind	1500	98%	G	197	S		3350
Drake University, Des Moines, IA 50311	1881	C/Ind	4871	40%	G	340	S	AF	4060
Drew University, Madison, NJ 07940	1866	C/Prot	1510	50%	G	189	S		4700
Drexel University, Philadelphia, PA 19104	1891	C/Ind	6577	65%	Grad	292	U	A	3585
Drury College, Springfield, MO 65802	1873	C/Prot	1087	65%	Grad	104	U		2855
Duke University, Durham, NC 27710	1838	C/Ind	5700	16%	G	1256	S	N,AF	4740
Duns Scotus College, Southfield, MI 48075	1930	C/Cath	55	0%		13	S		1500
Duquesne University, Pittsburgh, PA 15219	1878	C/Cath	4530	85%	G	427	U	A	3510
Durham College, Durham, NC 27707	1947	C/Ind	275	40%		18	U		1580
Dyke College, Cleveland, OH 44114	1848	C/Ind	1375	98%		65	U		1800x
D'Youville College, Buffalo, NY 14201	1908	C/Ind	1550	98%		112	U		3100
Earlham College, Richmond, IN 47374	1847	C/Prot	1015	20%	G	103	S		4912
East Carolina University, Greenville, NC 27834	1907	C/Pub	10,824	89%	G	619	R	AF	310
East Central Oklahoma State U, Ada, OK 74820	1909	C/Pub	3517	91%	G	*	S	A	400
Eastern College, St Davids, PA 19087	1932	C/Prot	708	68%		71	S		3550
Eastern Connecticut State College, Willimantic, CT 06226	1889	C/Pub	2200	95%	G	200	T		390
Eastern Illinois University, Charleston, IL 61920	1895	C/Pub	8858	98%	G	494	T		606
Eastern Kentucky University, Richmond, KY 40475	1906	C/Pub	11,366	84%	G	784	T	A	580
Eastern Mennonite College, Harrisonburg, VA 22801	1917	C/Prot	1056	29%		64	T		3360
Eastern Michigan University, Ypsilanti, MI 48197	1849	C/Pub	14,502	96%	G	795	T	A	780
Eastern Montana College, Billings, MT 59101	1927	C/Pub	3103	95%	G	175	U		519
Eastern Nazarene College, Quincy, MA 02170	1918	C/Prot	771	32%	G	66	S		2520
Eastern New Mexico U, Portales Campus, Portales, NM 88130	1934	C/Pub	3100	85%	G	170	T	A	619
Eastern Oregon State College, La Grande, OR 97850	1929	C/Pub	1490	80%	G	100	T		930
Eastern Washington University, Cheney, WA 99004	1890	C/Pub	6069	95%	G	390	T	A	618
East Stroudsburg State College, East Stroudsburg, PA 18301	1893	C/Pub	3568	81%	G	269	T	A	1100
East Tennessee State University, Johnson City, TN 37601	1911	C/Pub	8487	86%	G	527	U	A	570
East Texas Baptist College, Marshall, TX 75670	1912	C/Prot	878	87%		90	S		1350
East Texas State University, Commerce, TX 75428	1889	C/Pub	5402	95%	G	456	T	AF	436
Eckerd College, St Petersburg, FL 33733	1958	C/Ind	1060	32%		79	S		4435
Edgecliff College, Cincinnati, OH 45206	1935	C/Cath	951	75%		98	U		2176
Edgewood College, Madison, WI 53711	1927	C/Cath	587	75%		60	U		2850
Edinboro State College, Edinboro, PA 16444	1857	C/Pub	4556	92%	G	396	T	A	1100
Edward Waters College, Jacksonville, FL 32209	1866	C/Ind	660	90%		43	U		1800
Eisenhower College of Rochester Inst of Tech, Seneca Falls, NY 13148	1965	C/Ind	550	70%		61	T		3879
Elizabeth City State University, Elizabeth City, NC 27909	1891	C/Pub	1600	90%		130	T		540
Elizabethtown College, Elizabethtown, PA 17022	1899	C/Prot	1466	68%		128	T		3825
Elmhurst College, Elmhurst, IL 60126	1871	C/Prot	3317	94%		129	S		3450
Elmira College, Elmira, NY 14901	1855	C/Ind	1913	52%	G	170	U		4100
Elon College, Elon College, NC 27244	1889	C/Prot	2501	64%		138	T	A	2230
Embry-Riddle Aeronautical University, Daytona Beach, FL 32014	1926	C/Ind	7115	10%	G	242	U	A,N,AF	2400
Emerson College, Boston, MA 02116	1880	C/Ind	1476	45%	G	134	U		4360
Emmanuel College, Boston, MA 02115	1919	W/Cath	542	65%	G	103	U		3920

Name and Location	Est	Type/ Control	UG Enroll	% of State Res	Grad	Fac Size	Cmps	ROTC	Tuition
Emory and Henry College, Emory, VA 24327	1836	C/Prot	825	78%		61	R		$2250
Emory University, Atlanta, GA 30322	1836	C/Ind	3041	25%	G	1305	S		4605
Emporia State University, Emporia, KS 66801	1863	C/Pub	4473	94%	G	283	T	A	600
Erskine College, Due West, SC 29639	1839	C/Prot	653	65%	G	60	T		2950
Eureka College, Eureka, IL 61530	1855	C/Prot	463	88%		37	T		3375
Evangel College, Springfield, MO 65802	1955	C/Prot	1612	21%		90	T	A	1940
Evergreen State College, Olympia, WA 98505	1967	C/Pub	2554	76%	G	155	S		456
Fairfield University, Fairfield, CT 06430	1942	C/Cath	2772	50%	G	326	S		3900
Fairleigh Dickinson U, Florham—Madison Cmps, Madison, NJ 07940	1958	C/Ind	3354	80%	G	303	S		3552
Fairleigh Dickinson U, Rutherford Campus, Rutherford, NJ 07070	1942	C/Ind	2787	85%	G	369	S		3552
Fairleigh Dickinson U, Teaneck-Hackensack Cmps, Teaneck, NJ 07666	1954	C/Ind	5532	85%	G	788	S		3552
Fairmont State College, Fairmont, WV 26554	1865	C/Pub	4848	94%		254	T	A,AF	360
Faith Baptist Bible College, Ankeny, IA 50021	1921	C/Prot	530	42%		28	T		1800
Fashion Institute of Technology, New York, NY 10001	1944	C/Pub	3468	71%		700	U		900
Fayetteville State University, Fayetteville, NC 28301	1877	C/Pub	2283	87%		160	U	AF	270
Felician College, Lodi, NJ 07644	1942	W/Cath	457	99%		77	T		2100x
Ferris State College, Big Rapids, MI 49307	1884	C/Pub	10,486	96%		673	T		891
Ferrum College, Ferrum, VA 24088	1913	C/Prot	1546	85%		81	R		2040
Findlay College, Findlay, OH 45840	1882	C/Prot	926	80%		100	S		3596
Fisk University, Nashville, TN 37203	1866	C/Ind	1063	10%	G	92	U		5985
Fitchburg State College, Fitchburg, MA 01420	1894	C/Pub	3719	97%	G	231	U	A	600
Flagler College, St Augustine, FL 32084	1968	C/Ind	745	40%		57	T		2200
Florida A&M University, Tallahassee, FL 32307	1887	C/Pub	5223	88%	G	527	T	A,N	675
Florida Atlantic University, Boca Raton, FL 33431	1961	C/Pub	5036	92%	G	317	S		780
Florida Institute of Technology, Melbourne, FL 32901	1958	C/Ind	2626	20%	G	332	S	A	3024
Florida International University, Miami, FL 33199	1965	C/Pub	6280	81%	G	630	U		750x
Florida Memorial College, Miami, FL 33054	1879	C/Prot	794	59%		88	U	A	2840
Florida Southern College, Lakeland, FL 33802	1885	C/Prot	1735	67%		135	T	A	2430
Florida State University, Tallahassee, FL 32306	1857	C/Pub	15,765	90%	G	1180	U	A,AF	735
Fontbonne College, St Louis, MO 63105	1917	C/Cath	757	90%	G	91	S		3200
Fordham University, Bronx, NY 10458	1841	C/Cath	7675	86%	G	930	U	A	3750
Fordham University at Lincoln Center, New York, NY 10023	1841	C/Cath	3042	90%	G	898	U	A	3296x
Fort Hays State University, Hays, KS 67601	1902	C/Pub	4050	92%	G	323	T	A	637
Fort Lauderdale College, Ft Lauderdale, FL 33301	1940	C/Ind	1087	85%		40	U		1225x
Fort Lewis College, Durango, CO 81301	1911	C/Pub	3028	70%		143	T		483
Fort Valley State College, Fort Valley, GA 31030	1895	C/Pub	1778	84%	G	156	T	A	729
Fort Wayne Bible College, Fort Wayne, IN 46807	1904	C/Prot	510	50%		56	S		2160
Fort Wright College, Spokane, WA 99204	1907	C/Cath	368	78%	G	59	S		3240
Framingham State College, Framingham, MA 01701	1839	C/Pub	3125	97%	G	170	S		600
Francis Marion College, Florence, SC 29501	1970	C/Pub	2392	99%	G	123	R	A	200
Franklin and Marshall College, Lancaster, PA 17604	1787	C/Ind	2094	30%		154	T		4950
Franklin College of Indiana, Franklin, IN 46131	1834	C/Ind	653	90%		51	T		3820
Franklin Pierce College, Rindge, NH 03461	1962	C/Ind	904	10%		57	R		4025
Franklin University, Columbus, OH 43215	1902	C/Ind	4214	100%		201	U		1470x
Freed-Hardeman College, Henderson, TN 38340	1869	C/Prot	1428	39%		82	T		2030
Free Will Baptist Bible College, Nashville, TN 37205	1942	C/Ind	528	16%		27	U		1440
Fresno Pacific College, Fresno, CA 93702	1944	C/Prot	450	84%	G	63	S		2955
Friends Bible College, Haviland, KS 67059	1917	C/Prot	167	37%		15	T		2600
Friends University, Wichita, KS 67213	1898	C/Prot	908	92%		79	S		2870
Friends World College, Huntington, NY 11743	1965	C/Ind	150	35%		23	S		3350
Frostburg State College, Frostburg, MD 21533	1898	C/Pub	3200	93%	G	185	T	A	620
Furman University, Greenville, SC 29613	1826	C/Prot	2698	47%	G	157	S	A	3008
Gallaudet College, Washington, DC 20002	1856	C/Ind	1063	*	G	200	U		618
Gannon University, Erie, PA 16541	1944	C/Cath	3200	89%	G	231	U	A	2400
Gardner-Webb College, Boiling Springs, NC 28017	1905	C/Prot	1354	10%	G	88	T		2650
General Motors Institute, Flint, MI 48502	1919	C/Ind	2241	42%		148	U		1200
Geneva College, Beaver Falls, PA 15010	1848	C/Prot	1500	64%		91	S		3230
George Fox College, Newberg, OR 97132	1891	C/Prot	734	70%		71	T		3600
George Mason University, Fairfax, VA 22030	1957	C/Pub	8984	89%	G	697	S		888
Georgetown College, Georgetown, KY 40324	1829	C/Prot	1031	57%	G	84	T		2640
Georgetown University, Washington, DC 20057	1789	C/Cath	5612	7%	G	1434	S	A	4970
George Washington University, Washington, DC 20052	1821	C/Ind	6123	20%	G	1512	U		3400
George Williams College, Downers Grove, IL 60515	1890	C/Ind	686	88%	G	128	S		3534
Georgia College, Milledgeville, GA 31061	1889	C/Pub	2810	95%	G	179	T		645
Georgia Institute of Technology, Atlanta, GA 30332	1885	C/Pub	9429	55%	G	770	U	A,N,AF	585
Georgian Court College, Lakewood, NJ 08701	1908	W/Cath	730	80%	G	110	S		2500
Georgia Southern College, Statesboro, GA 30458	1906	C/Pub	5735	91%	G	355	T	A	534
Georgia Southwestern College, Americus, GA 31709	1908	C/Pub	1784	97%	G	131	T		564
Georgia State University, Atlanta, GA 30303	1913	C/Pub	13,389	89%	G	968	U	A	585x
Gettysburg College, Gettysburg, PA 17325	1832	C/Prot	1900	30%		187	T	A	4720
Glassboro State College, Glassboro, NJ 08028	1923	C/Pub	9800	97%	G	534	T		903
Glenville State College, Glenville, WV 26351	1872	C/Pub	1845	92%		96	T		220
Goddard College, Plainfield, VT 05667	1938	C/Ind	1050	5%	G	55	R		5100x
Golden Gate University, San Francisco, CA 94105	1901	C/Ind	2847	80%	G	852	U		1740x
Gonzaga University, Spokane, WA 99258	1887	C/Cath	1937	45%	G	261	U	A	3490
Gordon College, Wenham, MA 01984	1889	C/Prot	1000	25%		64	S		3825
Goshen College, Goshen, IN 46526	1894	C/Prot	1209	37%		76	T		3325
Goucher College, Towson, MD 21204	1885	W/Ind	1000	39%	G	133	S		4650
Governors State University, Park Forest South, IL 60466	1969	C/Pub	1630	98%	G	309	S		558x
Grace Bible College, Grand Rapids, MI 49509	1945	C/Ind	210	25%		18	S		1220
Grace College, Winona Lake, IN 46590	1948	C/Prot	804	99%		44	T		2752
Grace College of the Bible, Omaha, NE 68108	1943	C/Ind	458	43%		33	U		1950
Graceland College, Lamoni, IA 50140	1895	C/Prot	1345	26%		101	T		3245
Grambling State University, Grambling, LA 71245	1901	C/Pub	3293	79%	G	200	T	AF	544
Grand Canyon College, Phoenix, AZ 85017	1949	C/Prot	1143	82%		67	S		1952
Grand Rapids Baptist College, Grand Rapids, MI 49505	1941	C/Prot	935	47%	G	76	S		2320
Grand Valley State Colleges, Allendale, MI 49401	1960	C/Pub	6170	97%	G	325	R		877

Name and Location	Est	Type/ Control	UG Enroll	% of State Res	Grad	Fac Size	Cmps	ROTC	Tuition
Grand View College, Des Moines, IA 50316	1896	C/Prot	1186	90%		84	U		$2390
Gratz College, Philadelphia, PA 19141	1895	C/Ind	142	95%	G	24	U		275x
Green Mountain College, Poultney, VT 05764	1834	C/Ind	475	10%		56	T		3700
Greensboro College, Greensboro, NC 27420	1838	C/Prot	664	60%		50	S		2500
Greenville College, Greenville, IL 62246	1892	C/Prot	879	62%		60	T		3168
Grinnell College, Grinnell, IA 50112	1846	C/Ind	1258	14%		117	T		5140
Grove City College, Grove City, PA 16127	1876	C/Prot	2211	72%		119	T	AF	*x
Guilford College, Greensboro, NC 27410	1837	C/Prot	1105	40%		107	S		3225
Gulf Coast Bible College, Houston, TX 77008	1953	C/Prot	341	98%		21	U		1890
Gustavus Adolphus College, St Peter, MN 56082	1862	C/Prot	2278	70%		255	T		4100
Gwynedd-Mercy College, Gwynedd Valley, PA 19437	1948	W/Cath	1573	90%		126	S		2600
Hamilton College, Clinton, NY 13323	1812	C/Ind	1600	50%		146	R		6150
Hamline University, St Paul, MN 55104	1854	C/Prot	1189	80%	G	170	U		4150
Hampden-Sydney College, Hampden-Sydney, VA 23943	1776	M/Ind	720	70%		58	R		4200
Hampshire College, Amherst, MA 01002	1965	C/Ind	1200	11%		101	R		6350
Hampton Institute, Hampton, VA 23668	1868	C/Ind	2700	39%	G	238	U	A	2290
Hannibal-LaGrange College, Hannibal, MO 63401	1858	C/Prot	450	60%		35	T		2000
Hanover College, Hanover, IN 47243	1827	C/Prot	1000	50%		73	R		2740
Harding University, Searcy, AR 72143	1924	C/Prot	2979	28%	G	154	T		2175
Hardin-Simmons University, Abilene, TX 79601	1891	C/Prot	1645	93%	G	121	U	A	1650
Harris-Stowe State College, St Louis, MO 63103	1857	C/Pub	1102	100%		66	U		350x
Hartwick College, Oneonta, NY 13820	1928	C/Ind	1418	52%		106	T		4900
Harvard and Radcliffe Colleges, Cambridge, MA 02138	1636	C/Ind	6557	21%	G	1579	U		5300
Harvard University, See Harvard and Radcliffe Colleges									
Harvey Mudd College, Claremont, CA 91711	1955	C/Ind	489	60%	G	63	S	A	5510
Hastings College, Hastings, NE 68901	1882	C/Prot	780	80%		66	T		2850
Haverford College, Haverford, PA 19041	1833	C/Ind	985	19%		97	S		5480
Hawaii Loa College, Kaneohe, HI 96744	1965	C/Prot	327	40%		29	S		2000
Hawaii Pacific College, Honolulu, HI 96813	1965	C/Ind	1463	70%		62	U		1700x
Hebrew College, Brookline, MA 02146	1921	C/Jewish	112	90%	G	7	U		600x
Hebrew Union Coll, Jewish Inst of Rel, New York, NY 10023	1948	C/Jewish	44	*		*	U		3300x
Heed University, Hollywood, FL 33020	1970	C/Ind	*	*	G	*	*		
Heidelberg College, Tiffin, OH 44883	1850	C/Prot	790	75%		92	T		4300
Hellenic College, Brookline, MA 02146	1937	C/Cath	78	5%		37	S		2200
Henderson State University, Arkadelphia, AR 71923	1890	C/Pub	2611	95%	G	180	T	A	600
Hendrix College, Conway, AR 72032	1876	C/Prot	980	85%		63	T		2400
Herbert H Lehman College, See City U of NY, Herbert H Lehman College									
High Point College, High Point, NC 27262	1924	C/Prot	1228	62%		61	S	A	2300
Hillsdale College, Hillsdale, MI 49242	1844	C/Ind	1025	48%		73	T		4140
Hillsdale Free Will Baptist College, Moore, OK 73160	1964	C/Prot	150	59%		20	S		2800
Hiram College, Hiram, OH 44234	1850	C/Prot	1150	66%		80	R		4487
Hobart College, Geneva, NY 14456	1822	M/Ind	1050	50%		121	U		5500
Hofstra University, Hempstead, NY 11550	1935	C/Ind	7049	80%	G	660	S	A	3400
Hollins College, Roanoke, VA 24020	1842	W/Ind	854	32%	G	91	S		4650
Holy Apostles College, Cromwell, CT 06416	1957	M/Cath	72	25%	G	20	S		1600
Holy Family College, Fremont, CA 94538	1946	W/Cath	143	*		98	U		1232
Holy Family College, Philadelphia, PA 19114	1954	W/Cath	1162	99%		112	S		2150x
Holy Names College, Oakland, CA 94619	1868	C/Cath	415	8%	G	101	U		3300
Holy Redeemer College, Waterford, WI 53185	1965	M/Cath	55	15%		22	R		1575
Hood College, Frederick, MD 21701	1893	W/Ind	1145	53%	G	154	S		4060
Hope College, Holland, MI 49423	1851	C/Prot	2371	67%		168	S		3920
Houghton College, Houghton, NY 14744	1883	C/Prot	1209	60%		80	R		3200
Houston Baptist University, Houston, TX 77074	1960	C/Prot	1757	88%	G	131	S		2475
Howard Payne University, Brownwood, TX 76801	1889	C/Prot	1173	95%		87	T		1650
Howard University, Washington, DC 20059	1867	C/Ind	7107	31%	G	1911	U	A,AF	1750
Humboldt State University, Arcata, CA 95521	1913	C/Pub	6677	98%	G	485	T		210
Hunter College, See City U of NY, Hunter College									
Huntingdon College, Montgomery, AL 36106	1854	C/Prot	693	70%		51	S	A,AF	2250
Huntington College, Huntington, IN 46750	1897	C/Prot	544	80%	G	60	T		3180
Huron College, Huron, SD 57350	1883	C/Prot	318	79%		41	T		2700
Husson College, Bangor, ME 04401	1898	C/Ind	812	65%	G	35	S		3350
Huston-Tillotson College, Austin, TX 78702	1875	C/Prot	634	56%		48	U		1400
Idaho State University, Pocatello, ID 83201	1901	C/Pub	5569	95%	G	505	T	A	460
Illinois Benedictine College, Lisle, IL 60532	1887	C/Cath	1669	98%	G	124	S		3200
Illinois College, Jacksonville, IL 62650	1829	C/Ind	760	88%		60	T		2550
Illinois Institute of Technology, Chicago, IL 60616	1892	C/Ind	4002	76%	G	692	U	N,AF	4290
Illinois State University, Normal, IL 61761	1857	C/Pub	17,605	98%	G	1091	T	A	596
Illinois Wesleyan University, Bloomington, IL 61701	1850	C/Ind	1638	94%		157	T		4380
Immaculata College, Immaculata, PA 19345	1920	W/Cath	581	90%		77	S		2500
Incarnate Word College, San Antonio, TX 78209	1881	C/Cath	1278	87%	G	108	U		2560
Indiana Central University, Indianapolis, IN 46227	1902	C/Prot	2892	96%	G	190	S		3200
Indiana Institute of Technology, Fort Wayne, IN 46803	1930	C/Ind	430	30%		41	U	A	1890
Indiana State University, Terre Haute, IN 47809	1865	C/Pub	9738	83%	G	728	U	A	1007
Indiana State University at Evansville, Evansville, IN 47712	1965	C/Pub	2863	95%		186	S		822x
Indiana University, Bloomington, IN 47405	1820	C/Pub	22,816	80%	G	1486	T		930
Indiana University at Kokomo, Kokomo, IN 46901	1945	C/Pub	1950	98%	G	145	U		900x
Indiana University at South Bend, South Bend, IN 46615	1922	C/Pub	4303	97%	G	330	U	A,N,AF	678x
Indiana University Northwest, Gary, IN 46408	1959	C/Pub	3364	99%	G	279	U		780x
Indiana University of Pennsylvania, Indiana, PA 15705	1871	C/Pub	10,866	97%	G	664	T	A	1100
Indiana U-Purdue U at Fort Wayne, Fort Wayne, IN 46805	1917	C/Pub	7781	97%	G	495	U	A	790x
Indiana U-Purdue U at Indianapolis, Indianapolis, IN 46202	1969	C/Pub	12,889	95%	G	2150	U	A	870
Indiana University Southeast, New Albany, IN 47150	1941	C/Pub	3868	97%	G	200	S	AF	780x
Inter Amer U of PR, San German Cmps, San German, PR 00753	1912	C/Ind	6188	100%	G	247	T		1290
Inter American U of PR, Hato Rey, PR 00919	1966	C/Prot	5908	*	G	270	U	A,N,AF	60cx
International College, Los Angeles, CA 90024	1970	C/Ind	60	85%	G	88	U		*x
Inupiat University of the Arctic, Barrow, AK 99723	1975	C/Ind	33	100%	G	12	R		
Iona College, New Rochelle, NY 10801	1940	C/Ind	3683	90%	G	246	S		3280

Name and Location	Est	Type/Control	UG Enroll	% of State Res	Grad	Fac Size	Cmps	ROTC	Tuition
Iowa State University, Ames, IA 50011	1858	C/Pub	18,558	79%	G	1992	T	A,N,AF	$816
Iowa Wesleyan College, Mount Pleasant, IA 52641	1842	C/Prot	730	72%		55	T		3560
Ithaca College, Ithaca, NY 14850	1892	C/Ind	4520	48%	G	442	T		4584
Jackson College, See Tufts University									
Jackson State University, Jackson, MS 39217	1877	C/Pub	6013	92%	G	375	U	A	750
Jacksonville State University, Jacksonville, AL 36265	1882	C/Pub	6208	80%	G	340	T	A	600
Jacksonville University, Jacksonville, FL 32211	1934	C/Ind	2141	51%	G	170	S		3000
James Madison University, Harrisonburg, VA 22807	1908	C/Pub	7198	81%	G	482	T	N	1026
Jamestown College, Jamestown, ND 58401	1883	C/Prot	540	55%		47	T		3235
Jarvis Christian College, Hawkins, TX 75765	1912	C/Prot	622	48%		55	R		1125
Jersey City State College, Jersey City, NJ 07305	1927	C/Pub	7700	95%		469	U		690
Jewish Theol Seminary of America, New York, NY 10027	1886	C/Jewish	158	26%	G	108	U		570
John Brown University, Siloam Springs, AR 72761	1919	C/Ind	742	25%		56	R		2100
John Carroll University, University Heights, OH 44118	1886	C/Cath	3133	60%	G	238	S	A	3300
John F Kennedy University, Orinda, CA 94563	1964	C/Ind	135	100%	G	199	S		1800x
John Jay College of Criminal Justice, See City U of NY, John Jay College of Criminal Justice									
Johns Hopkins University, Baltimore, MD 21218	1876	C/Ind	2156	32%	G	382	U	A	5075
Johnson and Wales College, Providence, RI 02903	1914	C/Ind	3000	20%		104	U		2985
Johnson Bible College, Knoxville, TN 37920	1893	C/Prot	396	29%		29	R		920
Johnson C Smith University, Charlotte, NC 28216	1867	C/Prot	1473	37%		85	U	A	1840
Johnson State College, Johnson, VT 05656	1828	C/Pub	904	72%	G	73	R		1070
Johnston College of the U of Redlands, Redlands, CA 92373	1969	C/Prot	1124	67%	G	173	T	A	5000
John Wesley College, Owosso, MI 48867	1909	C/Prot	80	60%		12	T		3000
Jones College, Jacksonville, FL 32211	1918	C/Ind	1088	92%		32	S		900x
Jones College, Orlando, FL 32803	1918	C/Ind	1350	96%		38	U		1093.50x
Judson Baptist College, Tha Dalles, OR 97058	1956	C/Prot	219	64%		28	T		2850
Judson College, Marion, AL 36756	1838	W/Prot	355	85%		42	R		1940
Judson College, Elgin, IL 60120	1963	C/Prot	486	60%		40	U		2640
Juilliard School, New York, NY 10023	1905	C/Ind	1000	40%	G	*	U		3500x
Juniata College, Huntingdon, PA 16652	1876	C/Ind	1250	73%		92	T		4065
Kalamazoo College, Kalamazoo, MI 49007	1833	C/Prot	1440	70%		91	S		4794
Kansas City Art Institute, Kansas City, MO 64111	1885	C/Ind	590	30%		54	U		4200
Kansas Newman College, Wichita, KS 67213	1933	C/Cath	660	91%		65	S		2400
Kansas State University, Manhattan, KS 66506	1863	C/Pub	14,525	85%	G	3000	T	A,AF	746
Kansas Wesleyan, Salina, KS 67401	1886	C/Prot	470	83%		41	S		2700
Kean College of New Jersey, Union, NJ 07083	1855	C/Pub	11,110	96%	G	716	S		690
Kearney State College, Kearney, NE 68847	1903	C/Pub	5865	*	G	300	T	A	570
Keene State College, Keene, NH 03431	1909	C/Pub	2700	65%	G	232	T		800
Kendall College, Evanston, IL 60201	1934	C/Prot	416	97%		34	S		3200
Kennesaw College, Marietta, GA 30061	1966	C/Pub	4132	95%		151	S	A	459x
Kent State University, Kent, OH 44242	1910	C/Pub	12,786	93%	G	774	T	A,AF	794
Kentucky Christian College, Grayson, KY 41143	1919	C/Prot	441	23%		27	R		1088
Kentucky State University, Frankfort, KY 40601	1886	C/Pub	2167	74%	G	165	S	A,AF	480
Kentucky Wesleyan College, Owensboro, KY 42301	1858	C/Prot	852	87%		73	S		2520
Kenyon College, Gambier, OH 43022	1824	C/Ind	1445	28%		120	R		5190
Keuka College, Keuka Park, NY 14478	1890	W/Ind	566	85%		49	R		4500
King College, Bristol, TN 37620	1867	C/Prot	238	36%		42	S		2925
King's College, Briarcliff Manor, NY 10510	1938	C/Ind	853	41%		70	S		3410
King's College, Wilkes-Barre, PA 18711	1946	C/Cath	1717	74%		126	U		3150
Knox College, Galesburg, IL 61401	1837	C/Ind	1042	80%		86	T	A	4850
Knoxville College, Knoxville, TN 37921	1875	C/Prot	699	21%		52	U	A,AF	2400
Kutztown State College, Kutztown, PA 19530	1866	C/Pub	4728	90%	G	303	T	A	1100
Ladycliff College, Highland Falls, NY 10928	1933	W/Ind	501	70%		78	T		3045x
Lafayette College, Easton, PA 18042	1826	C/Prot	2071	30%		167	S	A	5225
La Grange College, La Grange, GA 30240	1831	C/Prot	847	90%	G	51	T		1845
Lake Erie College, Painesville, OH 44077	1859	W/Ind	400	50%	G	90	S		4160
Lake Forest College, Lake Forest, IL 60045	1857	C/Ind	1067	41%		93	S		5240
Lake Land College, Mattoon, IL 61938	1966	C/Pub	3517	99%		285	R		1488x
Lakeland College, Sheboygan, WI 53081	1862	C/Prot	609	72%		47	R		3220
Lake Superior State College, Sault Ste Marie, MI 49783	1946	C/Pub	2309	90%		136	T	A	930
Lamar University, Beaumont, TX 77710	1923	C/Pub	12,213	91%	G	659	U	AF	150
Lambuth College, Jackson, TN 38301	1843	C/Prot	807	84%		72	U		2300
Lancaster Bible College, Lancaster, PA 17601	1933	C/Ind	437	82%		23	S		2220
Lander College, Greenwood, SC 29646	1872	C/Pub	1696	96%		109	T	A	850
Lane College, Jackson, TN 38301	1882	C/Prot	673	58%		47	U		1780
Langston University, Langston, OK 73050	1897	C/Pub	1087	60%		71	T		403
Laredo State University, Laredo, TX 78040	1969	C/Pub	458	95%	G	39	U		100x
La Roche College, Pittsburgh, PA 15237	1963	C/Cath	1122	*	G	103	S		2450
La Salle College, Philadelphia, PA 19141	1863	C/Cath	6318	80%	G	289	U	A	3320
Lawrence Institute of Technology, Southfield, MI 48075	1932	C/Ind	4991	90%		239	S		1530
Lawrence University, Appleton, WI 54911	1847	C/Ind	1156	45%		108	T		5256
Lebanon Valley College, Annville, PA 17003	1866	C/Prot	938	60%		90	T		4080
Lee College, Cleveland, TN 37311	1918	C/Prot	1442	30%		70	U		1800
Lehigh University, Bethlehem, PA 18015	1865	C/Ind	4400	43%	G	397	S	A,AF	5130
Le Moyne College, Syracuse, NY 13214	1946	C/Cath	1947	80%		136	S		3450
LeMoyne-Owen College, Memphis, TN 38126	1870	C/Ind	990	95%		62	U		2400x
Lenoir-Rhyne College, Hickory, NC 28601	1891	C/Prot	1291	70%	G	111	S		3000
Lesley College, Cambridge, MA 02138	1909	W/Ind	815	58%	G	334	U		4200
LeTourneau College, Longview, TX 75601	1946	M/Ind	962	15%		57	S		2650
Lewis and Clark College, Portland, OR 97219	1867	C/Ind	1887	42%	G	139	S		4498
Lewis-Clark State College, Lewiston, ID 83501	1893	C/Pub	1454	80%		100	T		400
Lewis University, Romeoville, IL 60441	1930	C/Cath	2437	99%	G	200	S		3360
Liberty Baptist College, Lynchburg, VA 24505	1971	C/Ind	2537	14%		130	S		1400
Limestone College, Gaffney, SC 29340	1845	C/Ind	1124	85%		77	T		3170
Lincoln Memorial University, Harrogate, TN 37752	1897	C/Ind	1067	60%		53	R		2100
Lincoln University, San Francisco, CA 94118	1919	C/Ind	216	0%	G	*	U		1750x
Lincoln University, Jefferson City, MO 65101	1866	C/Pub	2085	69%	G	189	T	A	400

Name and Location	Est	Type/Control	UG Enroll	% of State Res	Grad	Fac Size	Cmps	ROTC	Tuition
Lincoln University, Lincoln University, PA 19352	1854	C/Pub	1062	10%	G	88	T		$1430
Lindenwood Colleges, St Charles, MO 63301	1827	C/Prot	1403	21%	G	146	T		3400
Linfield College, McMinnville, OR 97128	1849	C/Ind	1072	50%	G	104	T		3940
Livingston College, See Rutgers University, Livingston College									
Livingstone College, Salisbury, NC 28144	1879	C/Prot	921	57%		55	T		1400
Livingston University, Livingston, AL 35470	1835	C/Pub	1055	86%	G	75	T		495
Lock Haven State College, Lock Haven, PA 17745	1870	C/Pub	2416	87%		168	T	A	1100
Loma Linda University, Loma Linda, CA 92354	1905	C/Prot	3108	58%	G	931	T		4125
Loma Linda University, La Sierra Cmps, Riverside, CA 92515	1922	C/Prot	2212	78%	G	174	S		4125
Long Island U, Brooklyn Center, Brooklyn, NY 11201	1926	C/Ind	4365	90%	G	481	U		3200
Long Island University, C W Post Center, See CW Post Center of Long Island U									
Long Island U, Southampton College, Southampton, NY 11968	1963	C/Ind	1298	70%	G	142	R		3720
Longwood College, Farmville, VA 23901	1839	C/Pub	2300	92%	G	158	T	A	1200
Loras College, Dubuque, IA 52001	1839	C/Cath	1700	60%	G	125	U		3050
Loretto Heights College, Denver, CO 80236	1918	C/Ind	850	65%		94	S		3900
Los Angeles Baptist College, Newhall, CA 91322	1927	C/Prot	393	75%		53	T		2700
Louisiana College, Pineville, LA 71360	1906	C/Prot	1314	90%		92	T	A	1088
Louisiana State U and A&M College, Baton Rouge, LA 70803	1860	C/Pub	21,504	88%	G	1187	S	A,AF	522
Louisiana State U in Shreveport, Shreveport, LA 71115	1965	C/Pub	3103	98%	G	146	S	A	480x
Louisiana Tech University, Ruston, LA 71272	1894	C/Pub	8476	85%	G	417	T	AF	651
Loyola College, Baltimore, MD 21210	1852	C/Cath	2111	75%	G	302	S	A	2775
Loyola Marymount University, Los Angeles, CA 90045	1911	C/Cath	3459	92%	G	298	S	AF	4020
Loyola University, New Orleans, LA 70118	1912	C/Cath	3216	75%	G	303	S	A	2500
Loyola University of Chicago, Chicago, IL 60611	1870	C/Cath	8593	95%	G	1370	U	A	3100
Lubbock Christian College, Lubbock, TX 79407	1957	C/Prot	1128	66%		97	S		2400
Lutheran Bible Institute of Seattle, Issaquah, WA 98027	1944	C/Prot	260	50%		18	R		1678
Luther College, Decorah, IA 52101	1861	C/Prot	1999	56%		148	T		4250
Lycoming College, Williamsport, PA 17701	1812	C/Prot	1159	58%		75	S		3720
Lynchburg College, Lynchburg, VA 24501	1903	C/Prot	1852	51%	G	148	S		3100
Lyndon State College, Lyndonville, VT 05851	1911	C/Pub	1037	48%	G	99	R		970
Macalester College, St Paul, MN 55105	1874	C/Prot	1763	35%		149	U		4725
MacMurray College, Jacksonville, IL 62650	1846	C/Prot	686	90%		67	T		3550
Madonna College, Livonia, MI 48150	1947	C/Ind	3011	98%		132	S		1500
Maharishi International University, Fairfield, IA 52556	1971	C/Ind	582	5%	G	55	T		3060
Maine Maritime Academy, Castine, ME 04421	1941	M/Pub	643	70%		60	T	N	1610
Malone College, Canton, OH 44709	1892	C/Prot	772	89%		50	S		3180
Manchester College, North Manchester, IN 46962	1889	C/Prot	1226	80%	G	98	T		3010
Manhattan College, Bronx, NY 10471	1853	C/Ind	4090	82%	G	329	S	AF	3200
Manhattan School of Music, New York, NY 10027	1917	C/Ind	427	55%	G	158	U		3350x
Manhattanville College, Purchase, NY 10577	1841	C/Ind	858	50%	G	168	S		4880
Mankato State University, Mankato, MN 56001	1867	C/Pub	9048	88%	G	640	U	A	586
Mannes College of Music, New York, NY 10021	1916	C/Ind	195	40%		110	U		3200x
Mansfield State College, Mansfield, PA 16933	1857	C/Pub	2501	90%	G	205	T		1100
Marian College, Indianapolis, IN 46222	1851	C/Cath	748	86%		77	S		2640
Marian College of Fond du Lac, Fond du Lac, WI 54935	1936	W/Cath	499	87%		60	T	A	2300
Marietta College, Marietta, OH 45750	1835	C/Ind	1488	45%	G	117	T		4500
Marion College, Marion, IN 46952	1920	C/Prot	1088	67%	G	78	S		2880
Marist College, Poughkeepsie, NY 12601	1949	C/Ind	1850	80%	G	120	S		3120
Marlboro College, Marlboro, VT 05344	1947	C/Ind	232	10%		35	R		4970
Marquette University, Milwaukee, WI 53233	1881	C/Cath	8818	54%	G	898	U	A,N	362c
Marshall University, Huntington, WV 25701	1837	C/Pub	8948	88%	G	514	U	A	196
Mars Hill College, Mars Hill, NC 28754	1856	C/Prot	1958	71%		127	T		2455
Mary Baldwin College, Staunton, VA 24401	1842	W/Prot	700	48%		62	T		3900
Mary College, Bismarck, ND 58501	1955	C/Cath	917	92%		76	R		2090
Marycrest College, Davenport, IA 52804	1939	C/Cath	708	54%	G	106	S		3225
Marygrove College, Detroit, MI 48221	1910	C/Cath	752	98%	G	56	U		3100
Maryland Institute College of Art, Baltimore, MD 21217	1826	C/Ind	780	55%	G	90	U		3750x
Marylhurst Education Center, Marylhurst, OR 97036	1893	C/Ind	526	97%		120	S		2100x
Marymount College, Tarrytown, NY 10591	1922	W/Cath	931	51%		132	S		3830
Marymount College of Kansas, Salina, KS 67401	1922	C/Cath	787	87%		70	T		2400
Marymount College of Virginia, Arlington, VA 22207	1950	W/Cath	852	34%	G	123	S		3100
Marymount Manhattan College, New York, NY 10021	1937	W/Ind	2252	94%		210	U		2790
Maryville College, Maryville, TN 37801	1819	C/Ind	634	45%		60	T	A	2803
Maryville College - Saint Louis, St Louis, Maryville College-Saint Louis 63141	1827	C/Cath	1355	85%	G	100	S		3230
Mary Washington College, Fredericksburg, VA 22401	1908	C/Pub	2471	78%		149	T		788
Marywood College, Scranton, PA 18509	1915	W/Cath	2100	55%	G	190	S		2250
Mason Gross School of the Arts, See Rutgers University, Mason Gross School of the Arts									
Massachusetts College of Art, Boston, MA 02215	1873	C/Pub	1050	85%	G	100	U		600x
Massachusetts Institute of Technology, Cambridge, MA 02139	1861	C/Ind	4232	17%	G	1700	U	A,N,AF	5300
Massachusetts Maritime Academy, Buzzards Bay, MA 02532	1891	M/Pub	850	85%		53	T		600
Mayville State College, Mayville, ND 58257	1889	C/Pub	746	80%		65	T		589
McKendree College, Lebanon, IL 62254	1828	C/Prot	805	81%		83	S		3200
McMurry College, Abilene, TX 79605	1923	C/Prot	1450	89%		84	S		2000
McNeese State University, Lake Charles, LA 70609	1939	C/Pub	4435	94%	G	302	S	A	452
McPherson College, McPherson, KS 67460	1887	C/Prot	493	56%		42	R		2660
Medaille College, Buffalo, NY 14214	1875	C/Ind	700	99%		64	U		2659x
Medgar Evers College, See City U of NY, Medgar Evers College									
Memphis Academy of Arts, Memphis, TN 38112	1936	C/Ind	217	62%		27	U		1900x
Memphis State University, Memphis, TN 38152	1912	C/Pub	15,770	93%	G	932	U	AF	556
Menlo College, Menlo Park, CA 94025	1927	C/Ind	681	56%		50	S		4530
Mercer University, Macon, GA 31207	1833	C/Prot	2070	50%	G	150	U	A	3117
Mercer University in Atlanta, Atlanta, GA 30341	1968	C/Prot	1177	95%	G	95	S		2250x
Mercy College, Dobbs Ferry, NY 10522	1951	C/Ind	10,500	92%		560	T		1950x
Mercy College of Detroit, Detroit, MI 48219	1941	C/Cath	2454	95%	G	236	U		2580
Mercyhurst College, Erie, PA 16501	1926	C/Ind	1300	79%	G	127	S	A	2975

Name and Location	Est	Type/Control	UG Enroll	% of State Res	Grad	Fac Size	Cmps	ROTC	Tuition
Meredith College, Raleigh, NC 27611	1891	W/Prot	1427	85%		120	U		$2500
Merrimack College, North Andover, MA 01845	1947	C/Cath	2196	74%		141	S		3700
Mesa College, Grand Junction, CO 81501	1925	C/Pub	4259	95%		155	T	A	494
Messiah College, Grantham, PA 17027	1909	C/Prot	1149	60%		108	T		3200
Methodist College, Fayetteville, NC 28301	1956	C/Prot	762	70%		57	S	A	2400
Metropolitan State College, Denver, CO 80204	1965	C/Pub	13,350	95%		584	U		262x
Metropolitan State University, St Paul, MN 55101	1971	C/Pub	1993	98%		372	U		750x
Miami Christian College, Miami, FL 33167	1949	C/Ind	190	81%		21	U		1900
Miami University, Oxford, OH 45056	1809	C/Pub	12,828	88%	G	800	T	N,AF	890
Michigan State University, East Lansing, MI 48824	1855	C/Pub	36,372	86%	G	2628	T	A,AF	1103
Michigan Technological University, Houghton, MI 49931	1885	C/Pub	7341	85%	G	508	T	A,AF	1059
Mid-America Nazarene College, Olathe, KS 66061	1966	C/Prot	1292	46%		78	S		1908
Middlebury College, Middlebury, VT 05753	1800	C/Ind	1870	7%	G	161	R		2400x
Middle Tennessee State University, Murfreesboro, TN 37132	1911	C/Pub	9144	95%	G	450	T	A	472
Midland Lutheran College, Fremont, NE 68025	1883	C/Prot	757	70%		65	T		3200
Midway College, Midway, KY 40347	1847	W/Ind	310	88%		57	T		2100
Midwest College of Engineering, Lombard, IL 60148	1967	C/Ind	179	95%	G	52	S		3600x
Midwestern State University, Wichita Falls, TX 76308	1922	C/Pub	3884	90%	G	195	S	A	120
Miles College, Birmingham, AL 35208	1907	C/Prot	1152			94	R	AF	2000
Millersville State College, Millersville, PA 17551	1854	C/Pub	5216	96%	G	360	T	A	1100
Milligan College, Milligan College, TN 37682	1866	C/Prot	772	27%		57	S		2072
Millikin University, Decatur, IL 62522	1901	C/Ind	1358	93%		121	S		3925
Millsaps College, Jackson, MS 39210	1890	C/Prot	972	74%	G	80	U		3000
Mills College, Oakland, CA 94613	1852	W/Ind	822	60%	G	104	U		4800
Milton College, Milton, WI 53563	1844	C/Ind	320	75%		38	R	A	3300
Milwaukee School of Engineering, Milwaukee, WI 53201	1903	M/Ind	1393	70%	G	80	U	A	3600
Minneapolis College of Art and Design, Minneapolis, MN 55404	1886	C/Ind	591	50%		60	U		3400
Minnesota Bible College, Rochester, MN 55901	1913	C/Prot	128	55%		13	U		1425
Minot State College, Minot, ND 58701	1913	C/Pub	2303	92%	G	138	T		568
Mississippi College, Clinton, MS 39058	1826	C/Ind	1871	90%	G	179	T		1920
Mississippi Industrial College, Holly Springs, MS 38635	1905	C/Prot	265	*					
Miss State University, Mississippi State, MS 39762	1878	C/Pub	9752	95%	G	802	T	A,AF	870
Mississippi University for Women, Columbus, MS 39701	1884	W/Pub	1970	75%	G	184	T		674
Mississippi Valley State University, Itta Bena, MS 38941	1946	C/Pub	2675	88%	G	175	T	A,AF	607
Missouri Baptist College, St Louis, MO 63141	1968	C/Prot	434	98%		37	S		1900
Missouri Institute of Technology, Kansas City, MO 64114	1931	C/Ind	740	40%		18	U		2425x
Missouri Southern State College, Joplin, MO 64801	1937	C/Pub	3790	95%		206	T	A	440
Missouri Valley College, Marshall, MO 65340	1889	C/Prot	376	62%		38	T		2644
Missouri Western State College, St Joseph, MO 64507	1915	C/Pub	3777	93%		175	S	A	470
Mobile College, Mobile, AL 36613	1961	C/Prot	1074	91%		66	S	A	1760
Molloy College, Rockville Centre, NY 11570	1955	W/Cath	1533	100%		176	S		3050x
Monmouth College, Monmouth, IL 61462	1853	C/Prot	700	86%		76	T	A	3675
Monmouth College, West Long Branch, NJ 07764	1933	C/Ind	2900	90%	G	214	S	A	3830
Montana Coll of Mineral Sci & Tech, Butte, MT 59701	1893	C/Pub	1283	80%	G	80	R		461
Montana State University, Bozeman, MT 59717	1893	C/Pub	9156	84%	G	743	T	A,AF	333
Montclair State College, Upper Montclair, NJ 07043	1908	C/Pub	11,695	95%	G	779	S		736
Monterey Institute of International Studies, Monterey, CA 93940	1955	C/Ind	92	61%	G	71	U		4590x
Moody Bible Institute, Chicago, IL 60610	1886	C/Ind	1363	25%		94	U		100
Moore College of Art, Philadelphia, PA 19103	1844	W/Ind	508	56%		84	U		3700
Moorhead State University, Moorhead, MN 56560	1885	C/Pub	6414	67%	G	320	S		700
Moravian College, Bethlehem, PA 18018	1742	C/Ind	1342	56%		118	T		3900
Morehead State University, Morehead, KY 40351	1922	C/Pub	5429	80%	G	306	U		270
Morehouse College, Atlanta, GA 30314	1867	M/Ind	1754	30%		141	U	A	2350
Morgan State University, Baltimore, MD 21239	1867	C/Pub	4779	63%	G	452	U	A	595
Morningside College, Sioux City, IA 51106	1894	C/Ind	1520	75%	G	105	S		3550
Morris Brown College, Atlanta, GA 30314	1881	C/Pub	1530	*	G	150	T	AF	2050
Morris College, Sumter, SC 29150	1908	C/Prot	727	95%		48	*		2025
Mount Angel Seminary, St Benedict, OR 97373	1887	M/Cath	41	70%	G	31	R		1650
Mount Holyoke College, South Hadley, MA 01075	1837	W/Ind	1850	20%	G	206	T		5430
Mount Marty College, Yankton, SD 57078	1936	C/Cath	590	46%		63	R		2500
Mount Mary College, Milwaukee, WI 53222	1913	W/Cath	1126	91%		124	S		2550
Mount Mercy College, Cedar Rapids, IA 52402	1928	C/Cath	1042	90%		74	U		3115
Mount Saint Mary College, Newburgh, NY 12550	1930	C/Ind	1046	80%		80	U		2700
Mount St Mary's College, Los Angeles, CA 90049	1925	W/Cath	944	86%	G	127	R		3450
Mount Saint Mary's College, Emmitsburg, MD 21727	1808	C/Cath	1400	38%	G	83	R		3200
Mount Senario College, Ladysmith, WI 54848	1962	C/Ind	474	80%		54	T		3260
Mount Union College, Alliance, OH 44601	1846	C/Prot	1020	82%		95	S		3825
Mount Vernon College, Washington, DC 20007	1875	W/Ind	462	14%		60	U		3700
Mount Vernon Nazarene College, Mt Vernon, OH 43050	1968	C/Prot	1005	75%		65	T		2200
Muhlenberg College, Allentown, PA 18104	1848	C/Prot	1530	35%		117	S		4575
Multnomah School of the Bible, Portland, OR 97220	1936	C/Ind	619	30%	G	43	U		2410
Mundelein College, Chicago, IL 60660	1929	W/Ind	1400	88%	G	145	U		3390
Murray State University, Murray, KY 42071	1922	C/Pub	6023	80%	G	381	T	A	480
Museum Art School, Portland, OR 97205	1909	C/Ind	175	60%		45	U		2650x
Muskingum College, New Concord, OH 43762	1837	C/Prot	883	80%		77	R		4337
Nasson College, Springvale, ME 04083	1912	C/Ind	643	16%		53	T	A	3490
Nathaniel Hawthorne College, Antrim, NH 03440	1962	C/Ind	500	5%		50	R	AF	3060
National College of Business, Rapid City, SD 57701	1941	C/Ind	1083	62%		55	U	A	2775
National College of Education, Evanston, IL 60201	1886	C/Ind	532	65%	G	118	S		4225
National Coll of Education, Urban Cmps, Chicago, IL 60603	1886	C/Ind	257	100%	G	50	U	N	3425x
National University, San Diego, CA 92106	1971	C/Ind	2687	*	G	391	U		3480x
Nazareth College, Nazareth, MI 49074	1924	C/Cath	540	97%		61	T	A	700
Nazareth College of Rochester, Rochester, NY 14610	1924	C/Ind	1678	92%	G	180	S		3400
Nebraska Wesleyan University, Lincoln, NE 68504	1887	C/Prot	1160	84%		100	S		3050
Newark College of Arts and Sciences, See Rutgers University, Newark College of Arts and Sciences									
Newberry College, Newberry, SC 29108	1856	C/Prot	883	75%		76	T		3265
New College of California, San Francisco, CA 94110	1971	C/Ind	200	40%	G	20	U		2700x

Name and Location	Est	Type/Control	UG Enroll	% of State Res	Grad	Fac Size	Cmps	ROTC	Tuition
New College of the University of South Florida, See University of South Florida, New College									
Newcomb College, See Tulane University, Newcomb College									
New England College, Henniker, NH 03242	1946	C/Ind	1249	15%		108	T		$4680
New England Conservatory of Music, Boston, MA 02115	1867	C/Ind	508	35%	G	165	U		4700
New Hampshire College, Manchester, NH 03104	1932	C/Ind	1475	30%	G	69	S		4234
New Jersey Institute of Technology, Newark, NJ 07102	1881	C/Pub	4531	95%	G	387	U	AF	832
New Mexico Highlands University, Las Vegas, NM 87701	1893	C/Pub	1680	85%	G	115	T		424
New Mexico Inst of Mining & Tech, Socorro, NM 87801	1889	C/Pub	904	86%	G	100	T		365
New Mexico State University, Las Cruces, NM 88003	1888	C/Pub	10,469	91%	G	800	S	A,AF	708
Newport College-Salve Regina, Newport, RI 02840	1934	C/Cath	1522	51%	G	152	T		3300
New School for Social Research, New York, NY 10011	1919	C/Ind	238	67%	G	125	U		3700
New School of Music, Philadelphia, PA 19103	1943	C/Ind	81	45%		46	U		3000x
NY Inst of Tech, Metropolitan Ctr, New York, NY 10023	1831	C/Ind	2387	59%	G	202	U		2816x
New York Inst of Tech, Old Westbury, Old Westbury, NY 11568	1910	C/Ind	10,443	95%	G	631	S		2816x
New York University, New York, NY 10006	1831	C/Ind	12,685	80%	G	5422	U		5062
Niagara University, Niagara University, NY 14109	1856	C/Cath	3328	88%	G	254	S	A	3300
Nicholls State University, Thibodaux, LA 70301	1948	C/Pub	5652	97%	G	233	T	A	530
Nichols College, Dudley, MA 01570	1815	C/Ind	776	50%	G	41	T		3490
Norfolk State University, Norfolk, VA 23504	1935	C/Pub	6550	80%	G	425	U	A	740
North Adams State College, North Adams, MA 01247	1894	C/Pub	2350	90%	G	190	T		600
North Carolina A&T State University, Greensboro, NC 27411	1891	C/Pub	4863	76%	G	347	T	A,AF	620
North Carolina Central University, Durham, NC 27707	1910	C/Pub	3922	90%	G	329	U	AF	310
North Carolina School of the Arts, Winston-Salem, NC 27107	1963	C/Pub	453	45%		105	U		568
N Carolina State U at Raleigh, Raleigh, NC 27650	1862	C/Pub	15,539	87%	G	1352	S	A,AF	364
North Carolina Wesleyan College, Rocky Mount, NC 27801	1956	C/Prot	743	74%		53	S		2760
North Central Bible College, Minneapolis, MN 55404	1930	C/Prot	587	*		*	*		*
North Central College, Naperville, IL 60540	1861	C/Prot	1111	96%		81	S		3729
North Dakota State University, Fargo, ND 58102	1890	C/Pub	6882	71%	G	570	U	A,AF	633
Northeastern Bible College, Essex Fells, NJ 07021	1950	C/Prot	337	74%		33	S		2592
Northeastern Illinois University, Chicago, IL 60625	1961	C/Pub	7752	99%	G	448	U	AF	558x
Northeastern Oklahoma State U, Tahlequah, OK 74464	1846	C/Pub	4323	96%	G	220	T	A	372
Northeastern University, Boston, MA 02115	1898	C/Ind	19,275	65%	G	2517	U	A,AF	3675
Northeast Louisiana University, Monroe, LA 71209	1931	C/Pub	8108	92%	G	400	U	A	450
Northeast Missouri State University, Kirksville, MO 63501	1867	C/Pub	5380	75%	G	312	T	A	340
Northern Arizona University, Flagstaff, AZ 86011	1899	C/Pub	*	75%	G	553	T	AF	600
Northern Illinois University, DeKalb, IL 60115	1895	C/Pub	17,411	99%	G	1268	T	A	548
Northern Kentucky University, Highland Heights, KY 41076	1968	C/Pub	6567	90%	G	408	S	A	540x
Northern Michigan University, Marquette, MI 49855	1899	C/Pub	7524	94%	G	396	U	A	1040
Northern Montana College, Havre, MT 59501	1929	C/Pub	1114	90%	G	81	T		453
Northern State College, Aberdeen, SD 57401	1901	C/Pub	2320	97%	G	110	T		592
North Georgia College, Dahlonega, GA 30533	1873	C/Pub	1609	95%	G	120	T	A	1815
Northland College, Ashland, WI 54806	1892	C/Prot	622	35%		46	T		3290
North Park College, Chicago, IL 60625	1891	C/Prot	1284	40%		98	U		3465
Northrop University, Inglewood, CA 90306	1942	C/Ind	1705	25%	G	43	S		2952
North Texas State University, Denton, TX 76203	1890	C/Pub	12,308	83%	G	1165	T	AF	420
Northwest Bible College, Minot, ND 58701	1934	C/Prot	150	32%		12	T		1275
Northwest Christian College, Eugene, OR 97401	1895	C/Prot	382	35%		23	U	A	2520
NW Coll of the Assemblies of God, Kirkland, WA 98033	1934	C/Prot	787	55%		46	S		1590
Northwestern College, Orange City, IA 51041	1882	C/Prot	861	65%		64	R		3220
Northwestern College, Roseville, MN 55113	1902	C/Ind	706	65%		60	S		3000
Northwestern Oklahoma State U, Alva, OK 73717	1897	C/Pub	1721	92%	G	71	T	A	400
Northwestern State University of Louisiana, Natchitoches, LA 71457	1884	C/Pub	4653	*	G	225	T	A	550
Northwestern University, Evanston, IL 60201	1851	C/Ind	6800	30%	G	1686	S	N	5985
Northwest Missouri State University, Maryville, MO 64468	1905	C/Pub	3860	65%	G	245	T		490
Northwest Nazarene College, Nampa, ID 83651	1913	C/Prot	1284	30%	G	82	T	A	2520
Northwood Institute-Midland Campus, Midland, MI 48640	1959	C/Ind	1770	50%		62	S		2640
Norwich University, Northfield, VT 05663	1819	M/Ind	1448	8%	G	166	R	A,AF	3190x
Notre Dame College, Manchester, NH 03104	1950	W/Cath	581	1%	G	69	S		2500
Notre Dame College of Ohio, Cleveland, OH 44121	1922	W/Cath	604	86%		57	S		2375
Nova University, Ft Lauderdale, FL 33314	1964	C/Ind	638	100%	G	403	S		2900x
Nyack College, Nyack, NY 10960	1882	C/Prot	602	50%	G	65	S		2768
Oakland City College, Oakland City, IN 47660	1885	C/Prot	545	71%		39	T		2403
Oakland University, Rochester, MI 48063	1957	C/Pub	9331	99%	G	527	S		872
Oakwood College, Huntsville, AL 35806	1896	C/Prot	1266	16%		92	R		3300
Oberlin College, Oberlin, OH 44074	1833	C/Ind	2724	14%	G	226	T		4725
Oblate College, Washington, DC 20017	1916	M/Cath	15	20%	G	15	U		1230x
Occidental College, Los Angeles, CA 90041	1887	C/Ind	1602	60%	G	157	U		5349
Oglethorpe University, Atlanta, GA 30319	1835	C/Ind	1030	51%	G	49	S		3100
Ohio Dominican College, Columbus, OH 43219	1911	C/Cath	849	84%		67	S	AF	3280
Ohio Institute of Technology, Columbus, OH 43219	1952	C/Ind	2327	40%		75	U		2425x
Ohio Northern University, Ada, OH 45810	1871	C/Prot	2174	80%		183	T		3651
Ohio State University, Columbus, OH 43210	1870	C/Pub	40,715	94%	G	3161	U	A,N,AF	1005
Ohio State University, Lima, OH 45804	1961	C/Pub	777	99%		56	T		960x
Ohio State University, Mansfield, OH 44906	1958	C/Pub	1081	99%		59	T		960x
Ohio University, Athens, OH 45701	1804	C/Pub	11,870	80%	G	826	T	A,AF	1071
Ohio University, Lancaster, OH 43130	1968	C/Pub	1450	97%	G	136	S	A	900x
Ohio Wesleyan University, Delaware, OH 43015	1841	C/Prot	2250	33%		180	T		4875
Oklahoma Baptist University, Shawnee, OK 74801	1909	C/Prot	1531	69%		127	T		1800
Oklahoma Christian College, Oklahoma City, OK 73111	1949	C/Prot	1522	44%		73	S		1570
Oklahoma City University, Oklahoma City, OK 73106	1904	C/Prot	1496	95%	G	171	U		1070
Oklahoma Panhandle State U, Goodwell, OK 73939	1909	C/Pub	1041	80%		60	R	A	422
Oklahoma State University, Stillwater, OK 74074	1890	C/Pub	18,714	90%	G	1041	T	A,AF	495
Old Dominion University, Norfolk, VA 23508	1930	C/Pub	10,768	86%	G	824	U	A	816
Olivet College, Olivet, MI 49076	1844	C/Prot	629	96%	G	51	T		3990
Olivet Nazarene College, Kankakee, IL 60901	1907	C/Prot	1905	40%	G	110	S		2448
Open Bible College, Des Moines, IA 50321	1930	C/Prot	117	70%		12	U		1600
Oral Roberts University, Tulsa, OK 74171	1963	C/Ind	3880	19%	G	300	S		2950

Name and Location	Est	Type/Control	UG Enroll	% of State Res	Grad	Fac Size	Cmps	ROTC	Tuition
Oregon College of Education, Monmouth, OR 97361	1856	C/Pub	2290	66%	G	200	T	AF	$921
Oregon Institute of Technology, Klamath Falls, OR 97601	1947	C/Pub	2195	87%		207	T		955
Oregon State University, Corvallis, OR 97331	1868	C/Pub	14,312	86%	G	1071	T	A,N,AF	924
Otis Art Inst of Parsons Sch of Design, Los Angeles, CA 90057	1918	C/Ind	143	6%	G	29	U		2900x
Ottawa University, Ottawa, KS 66067	1865	C/Prot	555	50%		47	T		2600
Otterbein College, Westerville, OH 43081	1847	C/Prot	1687	85%		110	S		4428
Ouachita Baptist University, Arkadelphia, AR 71923	1885	C/Prot	1438	81%	G	102	T	A	1910
Our Lady of Angeles College, Aston, PA 19014	1965	C/Cath	703	83%		65	S		2175x
Our Lady of Holy Cross College, New Orleans, LA 70114	1916	C/Cath	783	100%		93	S		1540x
Our Lady of the Lake U of San Antonio, San Antonio, TX 78285	1896	C/Cath	1150	90%	G	130	S		2400
Pace University, New York, NY 10038	1906	C/Ind	6143	91%	G	647	U		3264
Pace U, College of White Plains, White Plains, NY 10603	1923	C/Ind	1200	86%		90	S		3500
Pace U—Pleasantville/Briarcliff, Pleasantville, NY 10570	1963	C/Ind	4214	84%	G	536	S		3060
Pacific Christian College, Fullerton, CA 92631	1928	C/Prot	315	83%	G	42	U		2230
Pacific Lutheran University, Tacoma, WA 98447	1890	C/Prot	2878	72%	G	263	S		4064
Pacific Oaks College, Pasadena, CA 91105	1945	C/Ind	55	60%	G	31	U		2880x
Pacific Union College, Angwin, CA 94508	1882	C/Prot	2108	79%	G	162	R		4125
Pacific University, Forest Grove, OR 97116	1849	C/Ind	889	35%	G	106	T		4300
Paine College, Augusta, GA 30901	1882	C/Prot	828	82%		57	U		2175
Palm Beach Atlantic College, West Palm Beach, FL 33401	1968	C/Prot	580	76%		62	U		1700
Pan American University, Edinburg, TX 78539	1927	C/Pub	8351	95%	G	428	R	A	120
Park College, Parkville, MO 64152	1875	C/Prot	460	50%		40	S		2910
Parks Coll of St Louis Univ, Cahokia, IL 62206	1927	C/Cath	958	45%		56	S	AF	2560
Parsons School of Design, New York, NY 10011	1896	C/Ind	1400	27%	G	235	U		3980
Patten Bible College, Oakland, CA 94601	1944	C/Ind	125	95%		16	U		1638
Paul Quinn College, Waco, TX 76703	1872	C/Prot	421	71%		34	U	AF	1800
Peabody Cons of Johns Hopkins U, Baltimore, MD 21202	1857	C/Ind	260	35%	G	104	U		4575
Pembroke State University, Pembroke, NC 28372	1887	C/Pub	2102	97%	G	130	R		500
Penna State U-Behrend College, Erie, PA 16563	1926	C/Pub	1810	96%	G	102	S	A	1281
Penna State U-Capitol Campus, Middletown, PA 17057	1966	C/Pub	1604	97%	G	137	S		1440
Penna State U-Univ Park Campus, University Park, PA 16802	1855	C/Pub	27,131	91%	G	1640	T	A,N,AF	1485
Pepperdine University, Los Angeles, CA 90044	1937	C/Prot	532	*	G	184	U		3420x
Pepperdine University, Malibu, CA 90265	1937	C/Ind	2099	68%	G	136	S		5406
Peru State College, Peru, NE 68421	1867	C/Pub	718	75%		52	R		570
Pfeiffer College, Misenheimer, NC 28109	1885	C/Prot	844	70%		83	R		2345
Philadelphia College of Art, Philadelphia, PA 19104	1876	C/Ind	1131	57%	G	170	U		4500
Philadelphia College of Bible, Langhorne, PA 19047	1913	C/Ind	525	49%		45	S		2350
Philadelphia Coll of Textiles & Sci, Philadelphia, PA 19144	1884	C/Ind	1784	80%	G	168	S		3200
Phila College of the Performing Arts, Philadelphia, PA 19102	1870	C/Ind	355	69%	G	135	U		3800x
Philander Smith College, Little Rock, AR 72203	1877	C/Prot	600	75%		61	U		1413
Phillips University, Enid, OK 73701	1906	C/Prot	947	30%	G	121	T		2100
Piedmont Bible College, Winston-Salem, NC 27101	1947	C/Prot	470	48%		31	U		1570
Piedmont College, Demorest, GA 30535	1897	C/Prot	406	90%		26	R	A	1485
Pikeville College, Pikeville, KY 41501	1889	C/Prot	615	78%		52	T		2150
Pine Manor College, Chestnut Hill, MA 02167	1911	W/Ind	494	17%		48	S		4900
Pittsburg State University, Pittsburg, KS 66762	1903	C/Pub	3846	84%	G	324	T	A	440
Pitzer College, Claremont, CA 91711	1963	C/Ind	708	45%		103	S		5460
Plymouth State College, Plymouth, NH 03264	1871	C/Pub	2700	70%	G	150	T	A,AF	800
Point Loma College, San Diego, CA 92106	1902	C/Prot	1511	89%	G	84	U	AF	3120
Point Park College, Pittsburgh, PA 15222	1960	C/Ind	2072	77%		147	U		3500
Polytechnic Institute of New York, Brooklyn, NY 11201	1854	C/Ind	2455	90%	G	348	U	A	3850x
Pomona College, Claremont, CA 91711	1887	C/Ind	1362	58%		144	S		5320
Pontifical College Josephinum, Columbus, OH 43085	1888	M/Cath	80	56%	G	45	U		2063
Portland School of Art, Portland, ME 04101	1882	C/Ind	230	49%		24	U		2980x
Portland State University, Portland, OR 97207	1946	C/Pub	12,061	89%	G	824	U		693x
Post College, Waterbury, CT 06708	1890	C/Ind	1527	80%		86	S		3000
Prairie View A&M University, Prairie View, TX 77445	1876	C/Pub	3848	83%	G	305	T	A,N	144
Pratt Institute, Brooklyn, NY 11205	1887	C/Ind	3294	58%	G	490	U		4400
Presbyterian College, Clinton, SC 29325	1880	C/Prot	925	67%		67	T	A	3060
Princeton University, Princeton, NJ 08544	1746	C/Ind	4447	20%	G	777	S	A	6300
Principia College, Elsah, IL 62028	1910	C/Ind	866	11%		82	R		4426
Providence College, Providence, RI 02918	1917	C/Cath	3500	27%	G	235	U	A	3342
Purdue University, West Lafayette, IN 47907	1869	C/Pub	26,407	75%	G	3748	T	A,N,AF	1008
Purdue University-Calumet, Hammond, IN 46323	1951	C/Pub	5783	87%	G	377	U		960x
Purdue University-North Central Cmps, Westville, IN 46391	1967	C/Pub	1884	99%		*	R		883x
Queens College, See City U of NY, Queens College									
Queens College, Charlotte, NC 28274	1857	W/Prot	640	64%	G	70	S		3396
Quincy College, Quincy, IL 62301	1859	C/Cath	1715	83%		87	S		3200
Quinnipiac College, Hamden, CT 06518	1929	C/Ind	2936	50%	G	313	S		3800
Radcliffe College, See Harvard and Radcliffe Colleges									
Radford University, Radford, VA 24142	1913	C/Pub	4600	90%	G	290	R	A	945
Ramapo College of New Jersey, Mahwah, NJ 07430	1969	C/Pub	4318	96%		195	S		700
Randolph-Macon College, Ashland, VA 23005	1830	C/Prot	959	64%		72	T		3870
Randolph-Macon Woman's College, Lynchburg, VA 24503	1891	W/Prot	760	38%		83	S		4500
Reed College, Portland, OR 97202	1911	C/Ind	1139	20%	G	117	S		5560
Reformed Bible College, Grand Rapids, MI 49506	1940	C/Prot	230	50%		18	U		1800
Regis College, Denver, CO 80221	1877	C/Cath	1100	45%	G	95	S		3910
Regis College, Weston, MA 02193	1927	W/Cath	1099	80%	G	83	S		3395
Rensselaer Polytechnic Institute, Troy, NY 12181	1824	C/Ind	4155	43%	G	345	S	A,N,AF	5400
Rhode Island College, Providence, RI 02908	1854	C/Pub	6093	90%	G	393	S		625
Rhode Island School of Design, Providence, RI 02903	1877	C/Ind	1395	10%	G	159	U		5200
Rice University, Houston, TX 77001	1891	C/Ind	2430	60%	G	476	S	A,N	2900
Rider College, Lawrenceville, NJ 08648	1865	C/Ind	4984	76%	G	314	S	A	3250
Ringling School of Art, Sarasota, FL 33580	1931	C/Ind	465	30%		25	S		2000
Rio Grande Coll/Community Coll, Rio Grande, OH 45674	1876	C/Ind	1144	75%		66	R		2230
Ripon College, Ripon, WI 54971	1851	C/Ind	928	32%		91	T	A	4690
Rivier College, Nashua, NH 03060	1933	W/Cath	1083	43%	G	115	S		2750

Name and Location	Est	Type/ Control	UG Enroll	% of State Res	Grad	Fac Size	Cmps	ROTC	Tuition
Roanoke College, Salem, VA 24153	1842	C/Prot	1344	50%		86	T		$3500
Robert Morris College, Coraopolis, PA 15108	1921	C/Ind	4368	95%	G	179	S		2180
Roberts Wesleyan College, Rochester, NY 14624	1866	C/Prot	645	74%		89	S		3286
Rochester Institute of Technology, Rochester, NY 14623	1829	C/Ind	2108	60%	G	1125	S	A	3879
Rockford College, Rockford, IL 61101	1847	C/Ind	1600	75%	G	57	S		3490
Rockhurst College, Kansas City, MO 64110	1910	C/Cath	1315	73%	G	111	U		3000
Rockmont College, Denver, CO 80226	1914	C/Ind	311	61%		25	S		2312
Rocky Mountain College, Billings, MT 59102	1878	C/Prot	503	25%		56	S		2490
Roger Williams College, Bristol, RI 02809	1948	C/Ind	2000	15%		211	T		3460
Rollins College, Winter Park, FL 32789	1885	C/Ind	1350	30%	G	97	T		4350
Roosevelt University, Chicago, IL 60605	1945	C/Ind	4152	90%	G	505	U		3105
Rosary College, River Forest, IL 60305	1848	C/Cath	924	94%	G	136	S		3400
Rose-Hulman Institute of Technology, Terre Haute, IN 47803	1874	M/Ind	1221	61%	G	101	T	A	3600
Rosemont College, Rosemont, PA 19010	1921	W/Cath	585	40%		75	S		3800
Russell Sage College, Troy, NY 12180	1916	W/Ind	1400	62%	G	130	U		4100
Rust College, Holly Springs, MS 38635	1866	C/Prot	734	76%		40	R	A	2125
Rutgers U, Camden Coll of Arts and Sciences, Camden, NJ 08102	1950	C/Pub	3220	98%		167	U		940x
Rutgers University, College of Engineering, New Brunswick, NJ 08903	1864	C/Pub	2307	91%		98	S	A,AF	940
Rutgers University, College of Nursing, Newark, NJ 07102	1956	W/Pub	564	98%		47	U		940
Rutgers University, Cook College, New Brunswick, NJ 08903	1973	C/Pub	2943	90%		144	S	A,AF	940
Rutgers University, Douglass College, New Brunswick, NJ 08903	1918	W/Pub	3718	95%		266	S	A,AF	940
Rutgers U, Livingston College, New Brunswick, NJ 08903	1969	C/Pub	3717	90%		242	S	A,AF	940
Rutgers U, Mason Gross School of the Arts, New Brunswick, NJ 08903	1976	C/Pub	*	100%	G	16	S	A,AF	940
Rutgers U, Newark Coll of Arts and Sciences, Newark, NJ 07102	1892	C/Pub	4085	98%		254	U		940x
Rutgers University, Rutgers College, New Brunswick, NJ 08903	1766	C/Pub	8389	92%		578	S	A,AF	940
Sacred Heart College, Belmont, NC 28012	1892	W/Cath	475	76%		45	T	A	2354
Sacred Heart Seminary, Detroit, MI 48206	1919	M/Cath	50	100%		23	U		1150x
Sacred Heart University, Bridgeport, CT 06606	1963	C/Cath	1180	99%	G	168	S		2600x
Saginaw Valley State College, University Center, MI 48710	1963	C/Pub	3275	99%	G	213	S		840x
St Alphonsus College, Suffield, CT 06078	1963	M/Cath	55	92%		23	S		2700
St Ambrose College, Davenport, IA 52803	1882	C/Cath	1818	70%	G	126	U		3300
St Andrews Presbyterian College, Laurinburg, NC 28352	1958	C/Prot	601	52%		60	T		2850
St Anselm's College, Manchester, NH 03102	1889	C/Cath	1923	99%		145	S	A,AF	3600
Saint Augustine's College, Raleigh, NC 27611	1867	C/Prot	1709	61%		81	U	A	1550
St Bonaventure University, St Bonaventure, NY 14778	1854	C/Cath	2333	79%	G	181	R	A	3150
St Charles Borromeo Seminary, Philadelphia, PA 19151	1832	M/Cath	70	90%	G	*	S		1820x
St Cloud State University, St Cloud, MN 56301	1869	C/Pub	9970	98%	G	692	U	A	547
St Edward's University, Austin, TX 78704	1881	C/Cath	1893	80%	G	101	U		2428
Saint Francis College, Fort Wayne, IN 46808	1890	C/Cath	872	75%	G	85	S	A	2176
St Francis College, Brooklyn, NY 11201	1858	C/Cath	3356	97%		203	U		2480
Saint Francis College, Loretto, PA 15940	1847	C/Cath	1226	56%	G	89	R		2976
Saint Francis de Sales College, Milwaukee, WI 53207	1856	M/Cath	55	84%		24	S		1400
St Hyacinth College and Seminary, Granby, MA 01033	1927	M/Cath	51	30%		24	T		900
St John Fisher College, Rochester, NY 14618	1948	C/Ind	3007	53%		139	S		3753
St John's College, Camarillo, CA 93010	1927	M/Cath	112	95%		22	U		1750x
St John's College, Annapolis, MD 21404	1696	C/Ind	350	20%		56	T		5400
St John's College, Santa Fe, NM 87501	1964	C/Ind	270	5%	G	35	T		5400
Saint John's University, Collegeville, MN 56321	1857	M/Cath	1860	74%	G	146	R	A	3475
St John's University, Jamaica, NY 11439	1870	C/Cath	11,194	92%	G	824	U	A	2900x
St John Vianney College Seminary, Miami, FL 33165	1959	M/Cath	70	65%		22	U		2075x
Saint Joseph College, West Hartford, CT 06117	1932	W/Cath	771	74%	G	108	S		3100
Saint Joseph's College, Rensselaer, IN 47978	1889	C/Cath	1030	46%	G	75	T		2950
St Joseph's College, North Windham, ME 04062	1915	C/Cath	500	44%		54	R		2800
St Joseph's College, Brooklyn, NY 11205	1916	C/Ind	388	98%		70	U		2400x
St Joseph's Coll, Suffolk Campus, Patchogue, NY 11772	1916	C/Cath	500	100%		54	S		2400x
Saint Joseph Seminary College, St Benedict, LA 70457	1891	M/Cath	110	85%		30	T		1650
Saint Joseph's University, Philadelphia, PA 19131	1851	C/Cath	2220	70%	G	173	U	AF	3250
St Lawrence University, Canton, NY 13617	1856	C/Ind	2440	49%	G	175	T	A	4995
Saint Leo College, Saint Leo, FL 33574	1889	C/Cath	1053	50%		64	R	A	2670
Saint Louis Conservatory of Music, St Louis, MO 63130	1974	C/Ind	68	52%	G	44	U		3000x
Saint Louis University, St Louis, MO 63103	1818	C/Cath	6863	60%	G	2237	U	AF	3700
Saint Martin's College, Olympia, WA 98503	1895	C/Cath	515	77%		60	S		3422
Saint Mary College, Leavenworth, KS 66048	1923	W/Cath	798	74%		73	T		2400
Saint Mary of the Plains College, Dodge City, KS 67801	1952	C/Cath	616	60%		46	R		2550
Saint Mary-of-the-Woods College, St Mary-of-the-Woods, IN 47876	1846	W/Cath	625	44%		77	T		3145
Saint Mary's College, Notre Dame, IN 46556	1844	W/Cath	1817	16%		164	S		3950
Saint Mary's College, Orchard Lake, MI 48034	1885	C/Cath	225	85%		40	S		1800
Saint Mary's College, Winona, MN 55987	1912	C/Cath	1250	30%	G	95	T		3379
Saint Mary's College of California, Moraga, CA 94575	1863	C/Cath	1545	80%	G	137	S		3922
St Mary's College of Maryland, St Mary's City, MD 20686	1839	C/Pub	1318	93%		91	R		675
St Mary's Dominican College, New Orleans, LA 70118	1860	W/Cath	805	83%		77	U		2900
St Mary's of the Barrens Sem Coll, Perryville, MO 63775	1818	M/Cath	56	*		15	T		2500
St Mary's University of San Antonio, San Antonio, TX 78284	1852	C/Cath	2236	77%	G	221	S	A	2496
Saint Meinrad College, St Meinrad, IN 47577	1861	M/Cath	210	20%		40	R		1956
Saint Michael's College, Winooski, VT 05404	1904	C/Cath	1575	12%	G	101	S	AF	3660
St Norbert College, De Pere, WI 54178	1898	C/Cath	1642	45%		105	S	A	3425
St Olaf College, Northfield, MN 55057	1874	C/Cath	2971	60%		250	T		3925
St Patrick's College, Mountain View, CA 94042	1898	M/Cath	52	84%		22	S		1800
St Paul Bible College, Bible College, MN 55375	1916	C/Prot	656	54%		42	R		1792
Saint Paul's College, Lawrenceville, VA 23868	1888	C/Prot	615	73%		41	T	A	2040
Saint Peter's College, Englewood Cliffs, NJ 07632	1975	C/Ind	*	*	G	*	S	A	2574
Saint Peter's College, Jersey City, NJ 07306	1872	C/Cath	2790	95%		315	U	A	3069x
St Thomas Aquinas College, Sparkill, NY 10976	1958	C/Ind	1300	80%		67	S		2375
Saint Vincent College, Latrobe, PA 15650	1846	M/Cath	896	86%		93	R		3410
Saint Xavier College, Chicago, IL 60655	1847	C/Cath	1900	96%	G	160	U	AF	3200

Name and Location	Est	Type/Control	UG Enroll	% of State Res	Grad	Fac Size	Cmps	ROTC	Tuition
Salem College, Winston-Salem, NC 27108	1772	W/Prot	530	53%		66	U		$3400
Salem College, Salem, WV 26426	1888	C/Ind	1241	25%	G	92	R		2960
Salem State College, Salem, MA 01970	1854	C/Pub	5580	98%	G	297	S		600
Salisbury State College, Salisbury, MD 21801	1925	C/Pub	3644	86%	G	238	T		824
Samford University, Birmingham, AL 35209	1841	C/Prot	2860	67%	G	267	S	AF	2464
Sam Houston State University, Huntsville, TX 77340	1879	C/Pub	9326	96%	G	372	T	A	386
San Diego State University, San Diego, CA 92182	1897	C/Pub	24,787	96%	G	1935	U	A,AF	200
San Francisco Art Institute, San Francisco, CA 94133	1871	C/Ind	625	26%	G	63	U		3900x
San Francisco Conservatory of Music, San Francisco, CA 94122	1917	C/Ind	150	60%	G	*	U		4100x
San Francisco State University, San Francisco, CA 94132	1899	C/Pub	11,210	97%	G	1728	U	AF	284
Sangamon State University, Springfield, IL 62708	1969	C/Pub	1768	98%	G	211	R		596
San Jose Bible College, San Jose, CA 95108	1939	C/Prot	238	70%		21	U		1680
San Jose State University, San Jose, CA 95192	1857	C/Pub	21,426	90%	G	1685	U	A,AF	224
Sarah Lawrence College, Bronxville, NY 10708	1926	C/Ind	814	48%	G	126	S		6200
Savannah State College, Savannah, GA 31404	1890	C/Pub	2140	75%	G	150	U	N	608
School for International Training, Brattleboro, VT 05301	1962	C/Ind	48	2%	G	23	T		3968
School of the Art Inst of Chicago, Chicago, IL 60603	1866	C/Ind	934	75%	G	110	U		3180x
School of the Museum of Fine Arts, Boston, MA 02115	1948	C/Ind	*	*	G	*	U		3005
School of the Ozarks, Point Lookout, MO 65726	1906	C/Ind	1200	70%		82	T		2400
School of the Worcester Art Museum, Worcester, MA 01608	1898	C/Ind	112	95%		14	U		2575x
Scripps College, Claremont, CA 91711	1926	W/Ind	560	61%		68	S		5176
Seattle Pacific University, Seattle, WA 98119	1891	C/Prot	2185	64%	G	161	U		3525
Seattle University, Seattle, WA 98122	1891	C/Cath	2705	47%	G	276	U	A	3555
Seaver College, See Pepperdine University, Malibu									
Seton Hall University, South Orange, NJ 07079	1856	C/Cath	6555	90%	G	496	S	A	3270
Seton Hill College, Greensburg, PA 15601	1882	W/Cath	917	84%		97	T		3200
Shaw College at Detroit, Detroit, MI 48202	1936	C/Ind	603	99%		48	U		2700x
Shaw University, Raleigh, NC 27611	1865	C/Prot	1263	50%		83	U		1900
Sheldon Jackson College, Sitka, AK 99835	1878	C/Ind	170	85%		23	T		2500
Shenandoah Coll & Conserv of Music, Winchester, VA 22601	1875	C/Prot	875	55%	G	128	T		2700
Shepherd College, Shepherdstown, WV 25443	1871	C/Pub	2862	60%		136	T		370
Sherwood Music School, Chicago, IL 60605	1895	C/Ind	35	80%		24	U		2100x
Shimer College, Waukegan, IL 60085	1853	C/Ind	70	50%		14	U		3300
Shippensburg State College, Shippensburg, PA 17257	1871	C/Pub	4628	94%	G	304	T		1100
Shorter College, Rome, GA 30161	1873	C/Prot	840	78%		55	U		2150
Siena College, Loudonville, NY 12211	1938	C/Cath	3054	94%		180	S	A	3150
Siena Heights College, Adrian, MI 49221	1919	C/Cath	1039	87%	G	97	T		2520
Sierra Nevada College, Incline Village, NV 89450	1969	C/Ind	225	52%		30	R		2300x
Silver Lake College, Manitowoc, WI 54220	1869	C/Cath	320	98%		49	T		2900
Simmons College, Boston, MA 02115	1899	W/Ind	1797	51%	G	289	U		4928
Simon's Rock of Bard College, Great Barrington, MA 01230	1964	C/Ind	212	20%		34	T		5265
Simpson College, San Francisco, CA 94134	1921	C/Prot	220	60%	G	30	U		2000
Simpson College, Indianola, IA 50125	1860	C/Prot	850	75%		68	S		3985
Sinte Gleska College, Rosebud, SD 57570	1970	C/Pub	373	97%		110	R		396x
Sioux Falls College, Sioux Falls, SD 57101	1883	C/Prot	770	44%	G	52	U		2650
Skidmore College, Saratoga Springs, NY 12866	1922	C/Ind	2082	38%		185	T		5580
Slippery Rock State College, Slippery Rock, PA 16057	1889	C/Pub	5042	80%	G	350	R	AF	1100
Smith College, Northampton, MA 01063	1871	W/Ind	2651	23%	G	328	T		5900
Sonoma State University, Rohnert Park, CA 94928	1960	C/Pub	3982	97%	G	360	R		194
Southampton College, See Long Island U, Southampton College									
South Carolina State College, Orangeburg, SC 29117	1896	C/Pub	3201	97%	G	250	T	A	150
South Dakota School of Mines & Tech, Rapid City, SD 57701	1885	C/Pub	1552	80%	G	109	U	A	763
South Dakota State University, Brookings, SD 57007	1881	C/Pub	5992	88%	G	348	R	A,AF	624
Southeastern Baptist College, Laurel, MS 39440	1955	C/Prot	58	75%		12	U		720
Southeastern Bible College, Birmingham, AL 35205	1935	C/Ind	243	50%	G	26	U	·	1120
Southeastern College of the Assemblies of God, Lakeland, FL 33801	1935	C/Prot	1232	29%		50	S	A	1344
Southeastern Louisiana University, Hammond, LA 70402	1925	C/Pub	6346	95%	G	294	T	A	618
Southeastern Massachusetts University, North Dartmouth, MA 02747	1895	C/Pub	5063	96%	G	352	S		664
Southeastern Oklahoma State U, Durant, OK 74701	1909	C/Pub	3972	85%	G	180	T		448
Southeastern University, Washington, DC 20024	1879	C/Ind	650	66%	G	150	U		30
Southeast Missouri State University, Cape Girardeau, MO 63701	1873	C/Pub	7893	95%	G	432	T	AF	360
Southern Arkansas University, Magnolia, AR 71753	1909	C/Pub	1825	75%	G	112	T	A	600
Southern California College, Costa Mesa, CA 92626	1920	C/Prot	670	80%		62	S		2290
Southern Connecticut State College, New Haven, CT 06515	1893	C/Pub	6620	94%	G	639	U		768
Southern Illinois U at Carbondale, Carbondale, IL 62901	1869	C/Pub	18,836	89%	G	3304	R	A,AF	622
Southern Illinois U at Edwardsville, Edwardsville, IL 62026	1958	C/Pub	7895	90%	G	614	R	AF	615
Southern Methodist University, Dallas, TX 75275	1911	C/Prot	5802	45%	G	589	S		3840
Southern Missionary College, Collegedale, TN 37315	1892	C/Prot	2033	24%		130	T		3390
Southern Oregon State College, Ashland, OR 97520	1926	C/Pub	4177	90%	G	240	T		300
Southern Technical Institute, Marietta, GA 30060	1948	C/Pub	2380	85%		120	S	A	508.50
Southern U and A&M Coll, Baton Rouge, LA 70813	1880	C/Pub	7231	81%	G	486	S	A,N	450
Southern University in New Orleans, New Orleans, LA 70126	1959	C/Pub	2700	99%		111	U		494x
Southern Utah State College, Cedar City, UT 84720	1897	C/Pub	2048	81%		113	T		462
Southern Vermont College, Bennington, VT 05201	1926	C/Ind	364	39%		32	T		2550
Southwest Baptist College, Bolivar, MO 65613	1878	C/Prot	1383	75%		92	T		2250
Southwestern Assemblies of God Coll, Waxahachie, TX 75165	1927	C/Prot	809	44%		31	T		960
Southwestern at Memphis, Memphis, TN 38112	1848	C/Prot	1024	49%		104	U		4000
Southwestern Baptist Bible College, Phoenix, AZ 85032	1960	C/Prot	215	60%		21	S		1600
Southwestern College, Winfield, KS 67156	1885	C/Prot	656	74%		44	T		2400
Southwestern Oklahoma State U, Weatherford, OK 73096	1903	C/Pub	4143	87%	G	226	T	A	500
Southwestern Union College, Keene, TX 76059	1893	C/Prot	717	59%		70	T		3648
Southwestern University, Georgetown, TX 78626	1840	C/Pub	1001	92%		77	T		2500
Southwest Missouri State University, Springfield, MO 65802	1906	C/Pub	12,624	96%	G	640	S	A	420
Southwest State University, Marshall, MN 56258	1963	C/Pub	2040	79%		105	R		650
Southwest Texas State University, San Marcos, TX 78666	1899	C/Pub	14,018	98%	G	668	T	AF	120
Spalding College, Louisville, KY 40203	1920	C/Ind	664	88%	G	96	U		2400
Spelman College, Atlanta, GA 30314	1881	W/Ind	1257	29%		122	U		2350
Spertus College of Judaica, Chicago, IL 60605	1925	C/Jewish	337	95%	G	23	U		2700x

Name and Location	Est	Type/Control	UG Enroll	% of State Res	Grad	Fac Size	Cmps	ROTC	Tuition
Spring Arbor College, Spring Arbor, MI 49283	1873	C/Prot	847	87%		70	R		$3600
Springfield College, Springfield, MA 01109	1885	C/Ind	2146	38%	G	175	S		3360
Spring Garden College, Chestnut Hill, PA 19118	1851	C/Ind	1103	70%		80	S		3156x
Spring Hill College, Mobile, AL 36608	1830	C/Cath	904	32%		80	S	A	3300
Stanford University, Stanford, CA 94305	1891	C/Ind	6638	52%	G	1205	S		6285
State U of NY at Albany, Albany, NY 12222	1844	C/Pub	10,730	99%	G	840	S		900
State U of NY at Binghamton, Binghamton, NY 13901	1950	C/Pub	8100	97%	G	556	S		925
State U of NY at Buffalo, Buffalo, NY 14260	1846	C/Pub	16,960	95%	G	1917	S		900
State U of NY at Stony Brook, Stony Brook, NY 11794	1957	C/Pub	11,000	99%	G	1000	S		900
State U of NY at Stony Brook Health Sci Ctr, Stony Brook, NY 11794	1970	C/Pub	*	*	G	*	*		850
State U of NY College at Brockport, Brockport, NY 14420	1867	C/Pub	8201	99%	G	560	T		900
State U of NY College at Buffalo, Buffalo, NY 14222	1871	C/Pub	9291	98%	G	556	U		900
State U of NY College at Cortland, Cortland, NY 13045	1868	C/Pub	5274	98%	G	338	T		900
State U of NY College at Fredonia, Fredonia, NY 14063	1867	C/Pub	4776	97%	G	252	T	A	900
State U of NY College at Geneseo, Geneseo, NY 14454	1867	C/Pub	4886	99%	G	316	T		900
State U of NY College at New Paltz, New Paltz, NY 12561	1885	C/Pub	4980	95%	G	350	R		900
State U of NY College at Old Westbury, Old Westbury, NY 11568	1968	C/Pub	2854	96%		141	S		900
State U of NY College at Oneonta, Oneonta, NY 13820	1889	C/Pub	5702	98%	G	373	T		900
State U of NY College at Oswego, Oswego, NY 13126	1861	C/Pub	6500	90%	G	390	T	A	900
State U of NY College at Plattsburgh, Plattsburgh, NY 12901	1889	C/Pub	5183	98%	G	345	T		900
State U of NY College at Potsdam, Potsdam, NY 13676	1816	C/Pub	3927	98%	G	316	T		900
State U of NY College at Purchase, Purchase, NY 10577	1972	C/Pub	2100	75%		189	S		900
State U of NY Coll of Envr Sci & For, Syracuse, NY 13210	1911	C/Pub	1284	85%	G	125	U		900
SUNY College of Tech at Utica/Rome, Utica, NY 13502	1966	C/Pub	2600	98%	G	181	U		900x
State U of NY Health Science Ctr at Buffalo, Buffalo, NY 14214	1846	C/Pub	*	*	G	*	*		809
State U of NY Maritime College, Bronx, NY 10465	1874	C/Pub	970	80%	G	70	S	N	900
Steed College, Johnson City, TN 37601	1940	C/Ind	1150	85%		35	S		1440x
Stephen F Austin State University, Nacogdoches, TX 75961	1923	C/Pub	9200	97%	G	450	T	A	120
Stephens College, Columbia, MO 65215	1833	W/Ind	1402	23%		148	T		3800
Sterling College, Sterling, KS 67579	1887	C/Prot	534	45%		50	T		2770
Stern College for Women, New York, NY 10033	1886	W/Ind	523	34%		347	U		3550
Stetson University, Deland, FL 32720	1883	C/Ind	1950	60%	G	138	S	A	3345
Stevens Institute of Technology, Hoboken, NJ 07030	1870	C/Ind	1476	68%	G	230	U	AF	4800
Stillman College, Tuscaloosa, AL 35401	1876	C/Prot	645	69%		42	T	A	2972
Stockton State College, Pomona, NJ 08240	1971	C/Pub	4699	95%		213	R		736
Stonehill College, North Easton, MA 02356	1948	C/Cath	1687	60%		111	R	A	3725
Strayer College, Washington, DC 20005	1904	C/Ind	1807	55%		102	U		2160x
Suffolk University, Boston, MA 02114	1906	C/Ind	1954	98%	G	277	U		2900x
Sul Ross State University, Alpine, TX 79830	1917	C/Pub	1574	*	G	79	T		128
Susquehanna University, Selinsgrove, PA 17870	1858	C/Prot	1478	46%		126	T		4066
Swain School of Design, New Bedford, MA 02740	1881	C/Ind	167	71%		17	S		3150x
Swarthmore College, Swarthmore, PA 19081	1864	C/Ind	1280	25%		145	S		5400
Sweet Briar College, Sweet Briar, VA 24595	1901	W/Ind	685	19%		84	R		5200
Syracuse University, Syracuse, NY 13210	1870	C/Ind	11,044	50%	G	1233	U	A,AF	4950
Syracuse University, Utica College, Utica, NY 13502	1946	C/Ind	1312	84%		161	S		3940
Tabor College, Hillsboro, KS 67063	1908	C/Prot	434	58%		55	T		2416
Talladega College, Talladega, AL 35160	1867	C/Ind	647	50%		56	T		1740x
Tampa College, Tampa, FL 33607	1890	C/Ind	1413	90%		65	U		1620x
Tarkio College, Tarkio, MO 64491	1883	C/Prot	585	35%		35	R		2825
Tarleton State University, Stephenville, TX 76402	1899	C/Pub	2631	74%	G	156	T	A	128
Taylor University, Upland, IN 46989	1846	C/Prot	1540	30%		97	R		3618
Temple University, Philadelphia, PA 19122	1884	C/Pub	17,444	91%	G	2527	U	A	1810
Temple University, Ambler Campus, Ambler, PA 19002	1958	C/Pub	2455	95%	G	206	S	A	2086
Temple U Health Sciences Ctr, Philadelphia, PA 19140	1884	C/Pub	*	*	G	*	U		1300
Tennessee State University, Nashville, TN 37203	1909	C/Pub	8438	75%	G	517	U	AF	504
Tennessee Technological University, Cookeville, TN 38501	1915	C/Pub	5912	94%	G	376	T	A	483
Tennessee Wesleyan College, Athens, TN 37303	1857	C/Prot	453	78%		38	T		2160
Texas A&I University at Kingsville, Kingsville, TX 78363	1925	C/Pub	5004	90%	G	253	T	A	363
Texas A&M University, College Station, TX 77843	1876	C/Pub	25,947	89%	G	1879	T	A,N,AF	120
Texas Christian University, Fort Worth, TX 76129	1873	C/Prot	4493	70%	G	420	S	A,AF	3200
Texas College, Tyler, TX 75701	1894	C/Prot	531	57%		49	U	A	1800
Texas Lutheran College, Seguin, TX 78155	1891	C/Prot	1029	81%		77	T	A	2410
Texas Southern University, Houston, TX 77004	1947	C/Pub	7010	73%	G	499	U		120
Texas Tech University, Lubbock, TX 79409	1923	C/Pub	19,444	85%	G	864	U	A	120
Texas Wesleyan College, Fort Worth, TX 76105	1891	C/Prot	1555	91%	G	124	U		2300
Texas Woman's University, Denton, TX 76204	1901	W/Pub	4146	84%	G	554	T	AF	120
Thiel College, Greenville, PA 16125	1866	C/Prot	1042	77%		81	T		3793
Thomas College, Waterville, ME 04901	1894	C/Ind	962	72%	G	45	S		3560
Thomas Jefferson University, Philadelphia, PA 19107	1969	C/Ind	482	70%	G	55	U		4400
Thomas More College, Fort Mitchell, KY 41017	1921	C/Cath	1270	65%		130	S		2304
Tiffin University, Tiffin, OH 44883	1918	C/Ind	395	97%		20	T		1980
Tift College, Forsyth, GA 31029	1849	W/Prot	489	70%		43	T		1599
Toccoa Falls College, Toccoa Falls, GA 30577	1907	C/Ind	582	19%		38	T		1900
Tougaloo College, Tougaloo, MS 39174	1869	C/Prot	1031	73%		86	S	A	1930
Touro College, New York, NY 10036	1971	C/Ind	1957	85%		253	U		3105
Towson State University, Baltimore, MD 21204	1866	C/Pub	13,499	96%	G	926	U		620
Transylvania University, Lexington, KY 40508	1780	C/Ind	810	75%		84	U		4000
Trenton State College, Trenton, NJ 08625	1855	C/Pub	7500	97%	G	500	S		690
Trevecca Nazarene College, Nashville, TN 37210	1901	C/Prot	1225	65%		75	U		2265
Trinity Christian College, Palos Heights, IL 60463	1959	C/Prot	383	85%		53	S		2950
Trinity College, Hartford, CT 06106	1823	C/Ind	1840	22%	G	167	U		5350
Trinity College, Washington, DC 20017	1897	W/Cath	600	6%	G	103	S		4050x
Trinity College, Deerfield, IL 60015	1897	C/Prot	780	64%		64	S		3410
Trinity College, Burlington, VT 05401	1925	W/Cath	648	75%		52	T		3150
Trinity University, San Antonio, TX 78284	1869	C/Prot	2554	72%	G	290	U	A	3000
Tri-State University, Angola, IN 46703	1884	C/Ind	1298	39%		80	T		3015
Troy State University, Troy, AL 36081	1887	C/Pub	5394	95%	G	579	T	AF	630
Troy State U at Fort Rucker/Dothan, Dothan, AL 36301	1962	C/Pub	926	100%	G	71	U		630x

Name and Location	Est	Type/ Control	UG Enroll	% of State Res	Grad	Fac Size	Cmps	ROTC	Tuition
Troy State U at Montgomery, Montgomery, AL 36104	1965	C/Pub	1700	100%	G	154	U	AF	$630x
Tufts University, Medford, MA 02155	1852	C/Ind	4576	33%	G	448	S		5850
Tulane University, New Orleans, LA 70118	1834	C/Ind	5000	22%	G	804	U	A,N,AF	4500
Tulane University, Newcomb College, New Orleans, LA 70118	1886	W/Ind	1629	26%		133	U	A,N,AF	3940
Tusculum College, Greeneville, TN 37743	1794	C/Prot	376	36%		32	U		2700
Tuskegee Institute, Tuskegee, AL 36088	1881	C/Ind	2978	36%		289	T	A,AF	2000
Union College, Barbourville, KY 40906	1879	C/Ind	660	72%	G	46	T	A	2700
Union College, Lincoln, NE 68506	1891	C/Ind	909	25%		100	S		3454
Union College, Schenectady, NY 12308	1795	C/Ind	2062	71%	G	183	S		5520
Union for Experimenting Colleges and Universities, Cincinnati, OH 45201	1964	C/Ind	196	100%	G	37	U		2800x
Union University, Jackson, TN 38301	1825	C/Prot	1217	85%		76	T		1900
United States Air Force Academy, USAF Academy, CO 80840	1954	C/Pub	4400	5%		550	R		0x
United States Coast Guard Academy, New London, CT 06320	1876	C/Pub	831	7%		120	S		0x
U S International U, San Diego Campus, San Diego, CA 92131	1952	C/Ind	1565	52%	G	166	S		3690
United States Merchant Marine Academy, Kings Point, NY 10024	1936	C/Pub	1100	23%		80	S		0x
United States Military Academy, West Point, NY 10996	1802	C/Pub	4400	12%		639	T		0x
United States Naval Academy, Annapolis, MD 21402	1845	M/Pub	4300	2%		540	T		0x
United Wesleyan College, Allentown, PA 18103	1921	C/Prot	206	49%		19	U		2150
Unity College, Unity, ME 04988	1966	C/Ind	427	18%		40	R		3450
University of Akron, Akron, OH 44304	1870	C/Pub	19,090	98%	G	1875	U	A,AF	790
University of Alabama, University, AL 35486	1831	C/Pub	13,776	82%	G	952	T	A,AF	770
University of Alabama in Birmingham, Birmingham, AL 35294	1966	C/Pub	9794	94%	G	1472	U	A	891
University of Alabama in Huntsville, Huntsville, AL 35899	1950	C/Pub	4114	95%	G	294	S	A	768
University of Alaska, Anchorage, Anchorage, AK 99504	1970	C/Pub	3009	93%	G	174	U		177x
University of Alaska, Fairbanks, Fairbanks, AK 99701	1915	C/Pub	3153	80%	G	395	T	A	410
University of Alaska, Juneau, Juneau, AK 99803	1972	C/Pub	1700	98%	G	117	T		410
University of Albuquerque, Albuquerque, NM 87140	1920	C/Cath	2084	70%		148	S	N,AF	2640
University of Arizona, Tucson, AZ 85721	1885	C/Pub	24,155	74%	G	1689	U	A,AF	600
University of Arkansas, Fayetteville, AR 72701	1871	C/Pub	12,645	85%	G	750	T	A,AF	600
University of Arkansas at Little Rock, Little Rock, AR 72204	1927	C/Pub	8982	96%	G	450	U		600
University of Arkansas at Monticello, Monticello, AR 71655	1909	C/Pub	1800	89%		101	T		600
University of Arkansas at Pine Bluff, Pine Bluff, AR 71601	1873	C/Pub	2999	90%		174	U	A	600
University of Baltimore, Baltimore, MD 21201	1925	C/Pub	3087	94%	G	253	U		800x
University of Bridgeport, Bridgeport, CT 06602	1927	C/Ind	4837	69%	G	528	U		4500
University of California, Berkeley, Berkeley, CA 94720	1868	C/Pub	19,850	95%	G	3163	U	A,N,AF	730
University of California, Davis, Davis, CA 95616	1906	C/Pub	12,974	88%	G	1409	T	A	713
University of California, Irvine, Irvine, CA 92664	1960	C/Pub	7689	96%	G	731	S		768
University of California, Los Angeles, Los Angeles, CA 90024	1919	C/Pub	21,082	93%	G	2800	U	A,N,AF	759
University of California, Riverside, Riverside, CA 92521	1954	C/Pub	3199	97%	G	456	S	A	774
University of California, San Diego, La Jolla, CA 92093	1959	C/Pub	8818	90%	G	820	S		741x
U of Calif, Santa Barbara, Santa Barbara, CA 93106	1891	C/Pub	12,623	92%	G	890	S	A	860
University of California, Santa Cruz, Santa Cruz, CA 95064	1965	C/Pub	5695	90%	G	500	T		831
University of Central Arkansas, Conway, AR 72032	1907	C/Pub	4921	96%	G	311	T	A	600
University of Central Florida, Orlando, FL 32816	1963	C/Pub	9929	94%	G	455	S	A,AF	675
University of Charleston, Charleston, WV 25304	1888	C/Ind	1857	78%		101	U		2050
University of Chicago, Chicago, IL 60637	1890	C/Ind	2670	36%	G	1040	U		5100
University of Cincinnati, Cincinnati, OH 45221	1819	C/Pub	32,836	86%	G	2215	U	A,AF	1005
U of Cincinnati Ohio Coll of App Sci, Cincinnati, OH 45210	1870	C/Pub	818	*		*	U		780
U of Colorado at Boulder, Boulder, CO 80309	1876	C/Pub	17,965	66%	G	1162	S	A,N,AF	762
U of Colorado at Colorado Sprgs, Colorado Springs, CO 80907	1965	C/Pub	3263	90%	G	215	S	A	526x
U of Colorado at Denver, Denver, CO 80220	1912	C/Pub	5371	91%	G	507	U	A	522x
University of Connecticut, Stamford, CT 06903	1969	C/Pub	*	*	G	*	*		540
University of Connecticut, Storrs, CT 06268	1881	C/Pub	15,131	90%	G	1600	R	A,AF	1068
University of Dallas, Irving, TX 75061	1956	C/Cath	1111	49%	G	132	S		2730
University of Dayton, Dayton, OH 45469	1850	C/Cath	6158	59%	G	619	S	A	2874
University of Delaware, Newark, DE 19711	1743	C/Pub	13,525	52%	G	1025	T	A	940
University of Denver, Denver, CO 80208	1864	C/Ind	4522	39%	G	487	S		4530
University of Detroit, Detroit, MI 48221	1877	C/Cath	6005	80%	G	551	U	A	3840
University of Dubuque, Dubuque, IA 52001	1852	C/Prot	1034	63%	G	75	S	A	3100
University of Evansville, Evansville, IN 47702	1854	C/Prot	4206	75%	G	278	S		3249
University of Florida, Gainesville, FL 32611	1853	C/Pub	25,989	93%	G	2802	S	A,N,AF	450
University of Georgia, Athens, GA 30602	1785	C/Pub	17,730	82%	G	1916	T	A,AF	708
University of Guam, Agana, GU 96910	1952	C/Pub	2912	90%	G	236	R	A	360
University of Hartford, West Hartford, CT 06117	1877	C/Ind	7012	70%	G	707	S		4050
U of Hawaii at Hilo, Hilo, HI 96720	1970	C/Pub	2976	87%		212	T		150
University of Hawaii at Manoa, Honolulu, HI 96822	1907	C/Pub	15,173	87%	G	1581	U	A,AF	450
University of Houston, Houston, TX 77004	1927	C/Pub	21,665	87%	G	1863	U	A,N	354
U of Houston at Clear Lake City, Houston, TX 77058	1971	C/Pub	2036	93%	G	226	S		96x
U of Houston, Downtown Campus, Houston, TX 77002	1974	C/Pub	4612	87%		200	U		120x
University of Houston, Victoria Campus, Victoria, TX 77901	1973	C/Pub	300	99%	G	58	U		100x
University of Idaho, Moscow, ID 83843	1889	C/Pub	6662	83%	G	532	T	A,N	474
U of Illinois at Chicago Circle, Chicago, IL 60680	1946	C/Pub	17,036	*	G	1233	U	A	681x
U of Illinois at Urbana-Champaign, Urbana, IL 61801	1868	C/Pub	26,127	97%	G	2771	T	A,N,AF	682
University of Iowa, Iowa City, IA 52242	1847	C/Pub	15,449	79%	G	1555	U	A,AF	830
University of Judaism, Los Angeles, CA 90024	1947	C/Jewish	108	80%	G	50	U		2000x
University of Kansas, Lawrence, KS 66045	1865	C/Pub	16,898	74%	G	1027	T	A,N,AF	720
University of Kentucky, Lexington, KY 40506	1865	C/Pub	17,694	89%	G	1900	U	A,AF	682
University of La Verne, La Verne, CA 91750	1891	C/Ind	1557	98%	G	184	T		3900
University of Louisville, Louisville, KY 40208	1798	C/Pub	13,931	92%	G	2173	U	AF	670
University of Lowell, Lowell, MA 01854	1894	C/Pub	6866	93%	G	842	U	AF	700
University of Maine at Farmington, Farmington, ME 04938	1863	C/Pub	1590	85%		100	T	A	960
University of Maine at Fort Kent, Fort Kent, ME 04743	1878	C/Pub	325	63%		26	T		930
University of Maine at Machias, Machias, ME 04654	1909	C/Pub	698	80%		42	T		770
University of Maine at Orono, Orono, ME 04469	1865	C/Pub	10,566	77%	G	694	T	A	1080
University of Maine at Presque Isle, Presque Isle, ME 04769	1902	C/Pub	1027	88%		86	R		770
University of Mary Hardin-Baylor, Belton, TX 76513	1845	C/Prot	1050	81%		74	S	AF	*x
U of Maryland at College Park, College Park, MD 20742	1859	C/Pub	29,835	81%	G	2018	S	AF	884

Name and Location	Est	Type/ Control	UG Enroll	% of State Res	Grad	Fac Size	Cmps	ROTC	Tuition
University of Maryland, Baltimore, Baltimore, MD 21201	1807	C/Pub	1341	94%	G	1092	U		$705
U of Maryland Baltimore County, Catonsville, MD 21228	1966	C/Pub	5000	96%	G	330	S		1165
U of Maryland Eastern Shore, Princess Anne, MD 21853	1886	C/Pub	1069	63%	G	89	R		500
U of Massachusetts at Amherst, Amherst, MA 01003	1863	C/Pub	18,481	88%	G	1465	T	A,AF	750
U of Massachusetts at Boston, Boston, MA 02125	1965	C/Pub	7848	96%	G	594	U		750x
University of Miami, Coral Gables, FL 33124	1925	C/Ind	10,325	45%	G	1398	U	A,AF	4340
University of Michigan, Ann Arbor, MI 48109	1817	C/Pub	22,057	78%	G	2828	T	A,N,AF	1297
University of Michigan—Dearborn, Dearborn, MI 48128	1959	C/Pub	5913	99%	G	311	U		964
University of Michigan—Flint, Flint, MI 48503	1956	C/Pub	4054	99%	G	194	U		882x
University of Minnesota, Duluth, Duluth, MN 55812	1948	C/Pub	6507	87%	G	426	U	AF	918
U of Minnesota, Minneapolis-St Paul, Minneapolis, MN 55455	1851	C/Pub	31,404	88%	G	4419	U	A,N,AF	1135
University of Minnesota, Morris, Morris, MN 56267	1959	C/Pub	1450	95%		132	T		930
University of Mississippi, University, MS 38677	1844	C/Pub	7865	74%	G	574	T	A,N,AF	807
University of Missouri -Columbia, Columbia, MO 65211	1839	C/Pub	17,497	89%	G	1610	T	A,N,AF	822
University of Missouri -Kansas City, Kansas City, MO 64111	1933	C/Pub	6453	88%	G	1448	U		856
University of Missouri -Rolla, Rolla, MO 65401	1870	C/Pub	5117	84%	G	325	T	A	898
University of Missouri -St Louis, St Louis, MO 63121	1963	C/Pub	9409	98%	G	432	U		774x
University of Montana, Missoula, MT 59812	1893	C/Pub	6972	72%	G	447	T	A	625
University of Montevallo, Montevallo, AL 35115	1896	C/Pub	2526	90%	G	175	T		644
University of Nebraska -Lincoln, Lincoln, NE 68588	1869	C/Pub	19,903	93%	G	1259	U	A,N,AF	720
University of Nebraska at Omaha, Omaha, NE 68182	1968	C/Pub	12,815	94%	G	548	U	AF	860x
University of Nevada, Las Vegas, NV 89154	1957	C/Pub	6223	80%	G	380	U	A	720
University of Nevada, Reno, NV 89557	1874	C/Pub	5890	83%	G	398	U	A	368
University of New England, Biddeford, ME 04005	1939	C/Cath	406	18%	G	47	T		3600
University of New Hampshire, Durham, NH 03824	1866	C/Pub	8887	65%	G	625	T	A,AF	1150
University of New Haven, West Haven, CT 06516	1920	C/Ind	2399	75%	G	475	U		3496
University of New Mexico, Albuquerque, NM 87131	1889	C/Pub	17,980	92%	G	1265	U	N,AF	666
University of New Orleans, New Orleans, LA 70122	1958	C/Pub	12,452	96%	G	529	U	A,AF	524
University of North Alabama, Florence, AL 35630	1872	C/Pub	4592	88%	G	241	U	A	680
U of North Carolina at Asheville, Asheville, NC 28804	1927	C/Pub	1446	95%		106	S		270
U of North Carolina at Chapel Hill, Chapel Hill, NC 27514	1795	C/Pub	14,661	87%	G	1745	T	N,AF	364
U of North Carolina at Charlotte, Charlotte, NC 28223	1946	C/Pub	7703	91%	G	628	U		310
U of North Carolina at Greensboro, Greensboro, NC 27412	1891	C/Pub	7082	88%	G	637	U		364
U of North Carolina at Wilmington, Wilmington, NC 28401	1947	C/Pub	4132	94%	G	250	S		270
University of North Dakota, Grand Forks, ND 58201	1883	C/Pub	7729	80%	G	*	R		660
University of Northern Colorado, Greeley, CO 80639	1889	C/Pub	8500	80%	G	680	T	AF	606
University of Northern Iowa, Cedar Falls, IA 50613	1876	C/Pub	9169	97%	G	637	T		774
University of North Florida, Jacksonville, FL 32216	1965	C/Pub	3671	99%	G	155	S	A	742x
University of Notre Dame, Notre Dame, IN 46556	1842	C/Cath	6900	8%	G	798	U	A,N,AF	4700
University of Oklahoma, Norman, OK 73019	1890	C/Pub	16,252	85%	G	756	T	A,N,AF	488
University of Oregon, Eugene, OR 97403	1876	C/Pub	12,534	76%	G	1287	T	A	900
U of Oregon Health Sciences Center, Portland, OR 97201	1932	C/Pub	*	*	G	*	*		570
University of Pennsylvania, Philadelphia, PA 19104	1740	C/Ind	8730	28%	G	2500	U	A,N	6000
University of Pittsburgh, Pittsburgh, PA 15261	1787	C/Pub	17,815	95%	G	2267	U	A,AF	1590
University of Pittsburgh at Bradford, Bradford, PA 16701	1963	C/Pub	1100	93%		45	R	A,AF	1450
University of Pittsburgh at Johnstown, Johnstown, PA 15904	1927	C/Pub	3000	90%		161	S		1690
University of Portland, Portland, OR 97203	1901	C/Cath	2165	40%	G	175	U	AF	3300
U of PR, Cayey University Coll, Cayey, PR 00633	1966	C/Pub	2695	100%		139	U	A	170x
U of PR, Mayaguez, Mayaguez, PR 00708	1911	C/Pub	8081	98%	G	553	U	A,AF	120x
U of PR, Medical Science Cmps, San Juan, PR 00905	1950	C/Pub	*	*	G	*	*		*
U of PR, Rio Piedras, Rio Piedras, PR 00931	1903	C/Pub	20,819	*	G	1102	U	A,AF	200x
University of Puget Sound, Tacoma, WA 98416	1888	C/Prot	2744	52%	G	206	U	AF	4280
University of Redlands, Redlands, CA 92373	1909	C/Ind	1124	69%	G	174	T		5000
University of Rhode Island, Kingston, RI 02881	1892	C/Pub	9280	70%	G	830	T	A	3100
University of Richmond, University of Richmond, VA 23173	1830	C/Prot	2583	50%	G	318	S	A	4100
University of Rochester, Rochester, NY 14627	1850	C/Ind	4288	58%	G	1684	S	N	5300
University of St Thomas, Houston, TX 77006	1946	C/Cath	1637	90%	G	126	U		2250
University of San Diego, San Diego, CA 92110	1949	C/Cath	2636	65%	G	263	U		4050
University of San Francisco, San Francisco, CA 94117	1855	C/Cath	3272	63%	G	434	U	A	1925
University of Santa Clara, Santa Clara, CA 95053	1851	C/Cath	3600	78%	G	387	S	A	3990
U of Science and Arts of Oklahoma, Chickasha, OK 73018	1908	C/Pub	1289	90%		80	T		417
University of Scranton, Scranton, PA 18510	1888	C/Cath	3542	69%	G	227	U	A	2784
University of South Alabama, Mobile, AL 36688	1963	C/Pub	5996	75%	G	394	S	A	930
U of S Carolina at Columbia, Columbia, SC 29208	1801	C/Pub	18,636	84%	G	1456	U	N,AF	890
U of S Carolina at Spartanburg, Spartanburg, SC 29303	1967	C/Pub	2424	99%		176	U		710x
U of S Carolina, Coastal Carolina Coll, Conway, SC 29526	1959	C/Pub	1888	93%		136	R		710x
University of South Dakota, Vermillion, SD 57069	1862	C/Pub	4419	82%	G	399	T	A	624
University of South Dakota at Springfield, Springfield, SD 57062	1881	C/Pub	828	83%		64	T		686
University of Southern California, Los Angeles, CA 90007	1880	C/Ind	15,404	73%	G	2554	U	N,AF	5310
University of Southern Colorado, Pueblo, CO 81001	1933	C/Pub	4500	88%	G	230	S	A	720
U of Southern Maine, Gorham, ME 04038	1878	C/Pub	5084	89%	G	326	S	A	950
University of Southern Mississippi, Hattiesburg, MS 39401	1910	C/Pub	9560	88%	G	563	T	A,AF	776
U of South Florida, St Petersburg, FL 33701	1956	C/Pub	1700	94%	G	75	S		800
U of South Florida, Tampa, FL 33620	1956	C/Pub	17,214	91%	G	1059	S		690
University of South Florida, New College, Sarasota, FL 33580	1960	C/Pub	508	50%		*	S		800
University of Southwestern Louisiana, Lafayette, LA 70504	1898	C/Pub	12,070	87%	G	600	U	AF	543
University of Steubenville, Steubenville, OH 43952	1946	C/Cath	900	45%		65	T		2860
University of Tampa, Tampa, FL 33606	1931	C/Ind	1845	25%	G	142	U	A	3716
U of Tennessee at Chattanooga, Chattanooga, TN 37403	1886	C/Pub	6050	88%	G	288	U	A	546
U of Tennessee at Knoxville, Knoxville, TN 37916	1794	C/Pub	22,592	88%	G	1650	U	A,AF	483
U of Tennessee at Martin, Martin, TN 38238	1927	C/Pub	4686	92%	G	231	T	A	600
University of Texas at Arlington, Arlington, TX 76019	1895	C/Pub	16,322	87%	G	885	S	A	120
University of Texas at Austin, Austin, TX 78712	1876	C/Pub	34,617	75%	G	2000	S	A,N,AF	520
University of Texas at El Paso, El Paso, TX 79968	1913	C/Pub	13,907	90%	G	665	U	A	360
U of Texas at San Antonio, San Antonio, TX 78285	1969	C/Pub	7689	98%	G	383	U	A	375x
University of Texas at Tyler, Tyler, TX 75701	1972	C/Pub	1242	98%	G	120	U		120x
U of Texas of the Permian Basin, Odessa, TX 79762	1970	C/Pub	887	95%	G	92	U		300
U of the District of Columbia, Washington, DC 20004	1966	C/Pub	14,434	91%	G	905	U	AF	165x

Name and Location	Est	Type/Control	UG Enroll	% of State Res	Grad	Fac Size	Cmps	ROTC	Tuition
University of the Pacific, Stockton, CA 95211	1851	C/Ind	3654	70%	G	355	S		$5682
U of the Sacred Heart, Santurce, PR 00914	1935	C/Cath	6425	97%		275	U		1400
University of the South, Sewanee, TN 37375	1857	C/Prot	1000	22%	G	116	R		4480
University of Toledo, Toledo, OH 43606	1872	C/Pub	14,505	95%	G	1195	S	A	783
University of Tulsa, Tulsa, OK 74104	1894	C/Ind	4592	70%	G	409	U		2380
University of Utah, Salt Lake City, UT 84112	1850	C/Pub	17,446	86%	G	3564	U	A,N,AF	642
University of Vermont, Burlington, VT 05401	1791	C/Pub	7670	50%	G	990	S	A	1500
University of Virginia, Charlottesville, VA 22903	1819	C/Pub	10,838	64%	G	1579	S	A,N,AF	555
University of Washington, Seattle, WA 98195	1861	C/Pub	28,187	92%	G	2178	U	A,N,AF	687
University of West Florida, Pensacola, FL 32504	1963	C/Pub	4295	97%	G	342	S		743
University of West Los Angeles, Culver City, CA 90230	1966	C/Ind	45	95%		15	S		1755x
U of Wisconsin-Eau Claire, Eau Claire, WI 54701	1916	C/Pub	10,111	90%	G	516	U		830
U of Wisconsin-Green Bay, Green Bay, WI 54302	1968	C/Pub	3541	85%	G	166	U	A	810
U of Wisconsin-La Crosse, La Crosse, WI 54601	1909	C/Pub	7926	91%	G	777	U	A	955
U of Wisconsin-Madison, Madison, WI 53706	1849	C/Pub	26,428	82%	G	3400	U	A,N,AF	877
U of Wisconsin-Milwaukee, Milwaukee, WI 53201	1956	C/Pub	20,610	96%	G	1687	U	A	972
U of Wisconsin-Oshkosh, Oshkosh, WI 54901	1871	C/Pub	8500	97%	G	675	S	A	885
U of Wisconsin-Parkside, Kenosha, WI 53140	1965	C/Pub	5292	97%		280	S		865x
U of Wisconsin-Platteville, Platteville, WI 53818	1866	C/Pub	4510	89%	G	244	T	A	721
U of Wisconsin-River Falls, River Falls, WI 54022	1874	C/Pub	4733	61%	G	279	R		700
U of Wisconsin-Stevens Point, Stevens Point, WI 54481	1894	C/Pub	8363	91%	G	550	T	A	732
U of Wisconsin-Stout, Menomonie, WI 54751	1893	C/Pub	6528	70%	G	434	T		677
U of Wisconsin-Superior, Superior, WI 54880	1893	C/Pub	1706	71%	G	145	U	AF	885
U of Wisconsin-Whitewater, Whitewater, WI 53190	1868	C/Pub	7793	91%	G	626	T	A	920
University of Wyoming, Laramie, WY 82071	1886	C/Pub	7332	69%	G	868	T	A,AF	592
Upper Iowa University, Fayette, IA 52142	1850	C/Ind	580	70%		50	T	A	3250
Upsala College, East Orange, NJ 07019	1893	C/Prot	1801	85%	G	117	U		3794
Urbana College, Urbana, OH 43078	1850	C/Ind	750	95%		153	T		2631
Ursinus College, Collegeville, PA 19426	1869	C/Prot	1040	66%		91	T		4000
Ursuline College, Pepper Pike, OH 44124	1871	W/Cath	840	95%		70	S		2570
Utah State University, Logan, UT 84322	1888	C/Pub	7996	65%	G	1250	T	A	552
Utica College, See Syracuse University, Utica College									
Valdosta State College, Valdosta, GA 31601	1906	C/Pub	3903	87%	G	245	S	AF	579
Valley City State College, Valley City, ND 58072	1890	C/Pub	1145	93%		64	T	A	472
Valparaiso University, Valparaiso, IN 46383	1859	C/Prot	3678	29%	G	360	T		3600
Vanderbilt University, Nashville, TN 37212	1873	C/Ind	5860	21%	G	2021	U	A,N	4700
Vandercook College of Music, Chicago, IL 60616	1928	C/Ind	92	75%		19	U		2760
Vassar College, Poughkeepsie, NY 12601	1861	C/Ind	2295	41%	G	228	S		4525
Vennard College, University Park, IA 52595	1910	C/Ind	211	20%		19	T		1502
Vermont College, Montpelier, VT 05602	1834	W/Ind	447	50%	G	45	T	A,AF	*x
Vermont Institute of Community Involvement, South Burlington, VT 05401	1972	C/Ind	91	*		*	*		2127
Villa Maria College, Erie, PA 16505	1925	W/Cath	616	93%		76	S	A	3000
Villanova University, Villanova, PA 19085	1842	C/Cath	6000	44%	G	439	S	N	3900
Virginia Commonwealth University, Richmond, VA 23284	1838	C/Pub	10,407	93%	G	1727	U	A	820
Virginia Intermont College, Bristol, VA 24201	1884	C/Prot	631	38%		56	U		2750
Virginia Military Institute, Lexington, VA 24450	1839	M/Pub	1310	53%		98	T	A,N,AF	720
Virginia Polytechnic Inst & State U, Blacksburg, VA 24061	1872	C/Pub	17,847	80%	G	1743	T	A,AF	885
Virginia State College, Petersburg, VA 23803	1882	C/Pub	3998	78%	G	254	S	A	979
Virginia Union University, Richmond, VA 23220	1865	C/Ind	1112	58%	G	129	S		3610
Virginia Wesleyan College, Norfolk, VA 23502	1963	C/Prot	775	70%		55	S		3175
Viterbo College, La Crosse, WI 54601	1890	C/Cath	1012	80%		116	U		2970
Voorhees College, Denmark, SC 29042	1897	C/Prot	708	81%		49	T	A	2118
Wabash College, Crawfordsville, IN 47933	1832	M/Ind	803	80%		77	T		4100
Wadhams Hall Seminary-College, Ogdensburg, NY 13669	1924	M/Cath	63	87%		21	R		2000
Wagner College, Staten Island, NY 10301	1883	C/Prot	1947	80%	G	216	S		3828
Wake Forest University, Winston-Salem, NC 27109	1834	C/Prot	3160	47%	G	242	S	A	3600
Walla Walla College, College Place, WA 99324	1892	C/Prot	1813	40%	G	163	T		4125
Walsh College, North Canton, OH 44720	1958	C/Cath	690	90%		60	S		3000
Walsh Coll of Acc & Bus Admin, Troy, MI 48084	1922	C/Ind	1250	100%	G	75	S		1272x
Warner Pacific College, Portland, OR 97215	1937	C/Prot	409	49%	G	42	U	AF	2925
Warner Southern College, Lake Wales, FL 33853	1964	C/Prot	264	30%		39	S		2220
Warren Wilson College, Swannanoa, NC 28778	1893	C/Prot	527	30%		75	R		3000
Wartburg College, Waverly, IA 50677	1852	C/Prot	1086	65%		86	T		3500
Washburn University of Topeka, Topeka, KS 66621	1865	C/Pub	5049	97%	G	260	U	AF	720
Washington and Jefferson College, Washington, PA 15301	1781	C/Ind	1053	*		97	T	A	4508
Washington and Lee University, Lexington, VA 24450	1749	M/Ind	1364	25%		175	T	A	4050
Washington Bible College, Lanham, MD 20801	1938	C/Ind	506	45%		38	S		2016
Washington College, Chestertown, MD 21620	1782	C/Ind	783	44%	G	68	T		3350
Washington International College, Washington, DC 20005	1970	C/Ind	234	90%		*	U		2100x
Washington State University, Pullman, WA 99163	1892	C/Pub	13,751	84%	G	1064	R	A,AF	686
Washington University, St Louis, MO 63130	1853	C/Ind	5631	23%	G	2277	S	A,AF	5350
Wayland Baptist College, Plainview, TX 79072	1908	C/Prot	1268	87%		67	T		1700
Waynesburg College, Waynesburg, PA 15370	1849	C/Prot	820	70%		68	T	A	3700
Wayne State College, Wayne, NE 68787	1910	C/Pub	2143	85%	G	119	T		456
Wayne State University, Detroit, MI 48202	1868	C/Pub	23,883	99%	G	2200	U		1238
Webb Institute of Naval Architecture, Glen Cove, NY 11542	1889	M/Ind	78	39%		16	S		0
Weber State College, Ogden, UT 84408	1889	C/Pub	9568	93%	G	476	U	A,AF	588
Webster College, St Louis, MO 63119	1915	C/Ind	950	70%	G	621	S		3350
Wellesley College, Wellesley, MA 02181	1870	W/Ind	2147	26%		290	S		5400
Wells College, Aurora, NY 13026	1868	W/Ind	529	35%		54	T		5150
Wentworth Institute of Technology, Boston, MA 02115	1904	M/Ind	2300	75%		117	U		3050
Wesleyan College, Macon, GA 31297	1836	W/Prot	500	50%		61	S		3270
Wesleyan University, Middletown, CT 06457	1831	C/Ind	2400	20%	G	269	T		5600
Wesley College, Dover, DE 19901	1873	C/Prot	1345	95%		77	T		3500
Westbrook College, Portland, ME 04103	1831	C/Ind	500	58%		80	S		3825
West Chester State College, West Chester, PA 19380	1871	C/Pub	7016	89%	G	495	T	A	1100
West Coast University, Los Angeles, CA 90020	1909	C/Ind	734	80%	G	250	*		2820x

Name and Location	Est	Type/ Control	UG Enroll	% of State Res	Grad	Fac Size	Cmps	ROTC	Tuition
Western Baptist College, Salem, OR 97302	1936	C/Prot	394	33%		28	T		$2790
Western Bible College, Morrison, CO 80465	1948	C/Ind	214	64%		14	S		1920
Western Carolina University, Cullowhee, NC 28723	1889	C/Pub	5350	91%	G	363	R	A	648
Western Connecticut State College, Danbury, CT 06810	1903	C/Pub	2732	90%	G	220	U		540
Western Illinois University, Macomb, IL 61455	1889	C/Pub	10,514	98%	G	741	T	A	606
Western Kentucky University, Bowling Green, KY 42101	1906	C/Pub	8984	84%	G	757	T	A	580
Western Maryland College, Westminster, MD 21157	1868	C/Ind	1359	70%	G	150	T	A	3875
Western Michigan University, Kalamazoo, MI 49008	1903	C/Pub	17,070	91%	G	1043	S	A	892
Western Montana College, Dillon, MT 59725	1893	C/Pub	679	90%	G	45	R	A	474
Western New England College, Springfield, MA 01119	1919	C/Ind	2634	64%	G	285	S	A	2850
Western New Mexico University, Silver City, NM 88061	1893	C/Pub	1463	91%	G	75	T		220
Western State College of Colorado, Gunnison, CO 81230	1911	C/Pub	2843	80%	G	165	R		500
Western States Chiropractic College, Portland, OR 97230	1907	C/Ind	431	*		*	U		0
Western Washington University, Bellingham, WA 98225	1893	C/Pub	8598	87%	G	498	T		618
Westfield State College, Westfield, MA 01085	1838	C/Pub	2862	97%	G	180	S		600
West Georgia College, Carrollton, GA 30118	1933	C/Pub	3808	96%	G	281	T	A	612
West Liberty State College, West Liberty, WV 26074	1837	C/Pub	2679	65%		162	R		390
Westmar College, Le Mars, IA 51031	1890	C/Pub	646	76%		50	T		3170
Westminster Choir College, Princeton, NJ 08540	1926	C/Ind	376	36%	G	65	T		4100
Westminster College, Fulton, MO 65251	1851	C/Ind	664	45%		57	T	A	3700
Westminster College, New Wilmington, PA 16142	1852	C/Prot	1540	72%	G	140	T		3620
Westminster College, Salt Lake City, UT 84105	1875	C/Ind	1129	65%	G	105	S	A,N,AF	2850
Westmont College, Santa Barbara, CA 93108	1940	C/Prot	1021	75%		93	S	A	4250
West Texas State University, Canyon, TX 79016	1909	C/Pub	5259	93%	G	363	T	A	382
West Virginia Institute of Technology, Montgomery, WV 25136	1895	C/Pub	3005	80%		185	T	A	372
West Virginia State College, Institute, WV 25112	1891	C/Pub	3905	90%		210	S	A	50
West Virginia University, Morgantown, WV 26506	1867	C/Pub	14,479	59%	G	2071	T	A,AF	80
West Virginia Wesleyan College, Buckhannon, WV 26201	1890	C/Prot	1780	32%	G	128	T		2950
Wheaton College, Wheaton, IL 60187	1860	C/Prot	2044	25%	G	184	S	A	3534
Wheaton College, Norton, MA 02766	1834	W/Ind	1227	33%		125	T		6100
Wheeling College, Wheeling, WV 26003	1954	C/Cath	1031	40%	G	72	S		3240
Wheelock College, Boston, MA 02215	1888	W/Ind	600	41%	G	93	U		4240
Whitman College, Walla Walla, WA 99362	1859	C/Ind	1110	51%		90	T		4510
Whittier College, Whittier, CA 90608	1901	C/Ind	1340	62%	G	105	S		4200
Whitworth College, Spokane, WA 99251	1890	C/Prot	1533	46%	G	144	S		3950
Wichita State University, Wichita, KS 67208	1895	C/Pub	12,700	93%	G	588	U	A	558
Widener University, Chester, PA 19013	1821	C/Ind	1954	75%	G	131	S	A	3760
Wilberforce University, Wilberforce, OH 45384	1856	C/Prot	1112	31%		66	R	A	2360
Wiley College, Marshall, TX 75670	1873	C/Prot	603	52%		47	T		2220
Wilkes College, Wilkes-Barre, PA 18703	1933	C/Ind	2050	80%	G	152	U	AF	3750
Willamette University, Salem, OR 97301	1842	C/Prot	1281	49%	G	153	T		4110
William Carey College, Hattiesburg, MS 39401	1906	C/Prot	1460	65%	G	110	T		1800
William Jewell College, Liberty, MO 64068	1849	C/Prot	1410	70%		127	S		2720
William Paterson College of New Jersey, Wayne, NJ 07470	1855	C/Pub	10,732	97%	G	601	S	AF	850
William Penn College, Oskaloosa, IA 52577	1873	C/Prot	617	65%		52	T		3890
Williams College, Williamstown, MA 01267	1793	C/Ind	1987	17%	G	209	T		5950
William Smith College, Geneva, NY 14456	1906	W/Ind	700	50%		126	T		5500
William Woods College, Fulton, MO 65251	1870	W/Ind	1000	39%		94	T		*x
Wilmington College, New Castle, DE 19720	1967	C/Ind	683	63%	G	67	S	A	1920x
Wilmington College, Wilmington, OH 45177	1870	C/Prot	750	65%		75	R		3105
Wilson College, Chambersburg, PA 17201	1869	W/Prot	221	37%		50	T		4050
Wingate College, Wingate, NC 28174	1895	C/Prot	1501	88%		73	T		1570
Winona State University, Winona, MN 55987	1858	C/Pub	4000	75%	G	240	T	A	585
Winston-Salem State University, Winston-Salem, NC 27102	1892	C/Pub	2224	91%		145	U	A	270
Winthrop College, Rock Hill, SC 29733	1886	C/Pub	3913	89%	G	261	U	A	903
Wisconsin Conservatory of Music, Milwaukee, WI 53202	1899	C/Ind	160	90%	G	54	U		2900x
Wittenberg University, Springfield, OH 45501	1845	C/Prot	2270	60%	G	174	S		4494
Wofford College, Spartanburg, SC 29301	1854	C/Prot	1078	74%		73	U	A	3275
Woodbury University, Los Angeles, CA 90017	1884	C/Ind	1243	35%	G	67	U		3100x
Worcester Polytechnic Institute, Worcester, MA 01609	1865	C/Ind	2388	49%	G	224	U	A,AF	4950
Worcester State College, Worcester, MA 01602	1874	C/Pub	3125	98%	G	204	U		600
World College West, San Rafael, CA 94902	1971	C/Ind	51	60%		36	S		2700
World University, Hato Rey, PR 00917	1965	C/Ind	4187	96%	G	194	U		1700
Wright State University, Dayton, OH 45435	1967	C/Pub	11,218	97%	G	885	S	A	1005
Wright State University, Piqua Center, Piqua, OH 45356	1968	C/Pub	*	*	G	28	T		816x
Xavier University, Cincinnati, OH 45207	1831	C/Cath	3144	80%	G	280	S	A	2990
Xavier University of Louisiana, New Orleans, LA 70125	1915	C/Cath	1797	80%	G	161	U	A	2350
Yale University, New Haven, CT 06520	1701	C/Ind	5170	11%	G	2005	U		5550
Yankton College, Yankton, SD 57078	1881	C/Prot	289	38%		44	T	A	2820
Yeshiva College, New York, NY 10033	1886	M/Ind	809	54%		253	U		3550
Yeshiva University, See Stern College for Women and Yeshiva College									
York College, See City U of NY, York College									
York College of Pennsylvania, York, PA 17405	1941	C/Ind	3536	74%	G	195	S	A	2248
Youngstown State University, Youngstown, OH 44555	1908	C/Pub	13,736	91%	G	799	U	A	915

LARGE U.S. UNIVERSITY LIBRARIES

University	Number of Volumes
Harvard University	9,547,576
Yale University	6,884,604
University of Illinois (Urbana Campus)	5,494,786
University of Michigan, Ann Arbor	4,917,381
University of California at Berkeley	4,917,330
Columbia University (Main Division)	4,716,162
Stanford University	4,170,325
University of California, L.A.	3,908,053
University of Chicago	3,886,130
University of Texas at Austin	3,713,821
University of Minnesota, Minn.-St. Paul	3,363,576
Indiana University at Bloomington	3,242,300
University of Wisconsin, Madison	3,238,152
Cornell University	3,184,941
Ohio State University, Main Campus	3,126,131
Princeton University	2,910,461
University of Pennsylvania	2,784,260
Duke University	2,712,405
Northwestern University	2,544,896
University of Washington	2,381,642
University of No. Car. at Chapel Hill	2,274,173
New York University	2,251,948
Johns Hopkins University	2,091,315
University of Virginia, Main Campus	2,081,003
University of Iowa	2,055,581
University of Utah	1,944,566
University of Missouri, Columbia	1,882,394
University of Florida	1,852,841
University of Kansas, Main Campus	1,849,096
University of Southern California	1,784,192

THE REFERENCE SHELF

This list of reference books constitutes the nucleus of a reference shelf for small private, public, and organizational libraries.

Acronyms, Initialisms & Abbreviations Dictionary, ed. Ellen T. Crowley, 6th ed. (Gale Research, 1979).

American Authors, 1600-1900, ed. Stanley J. Kunitz and Howard Haycraft (H. W. Wilson Co., 1938).

American Heritage Dictionary of the English Language, ed. William Morris (American Heritage Publishing Co., Inc., and Houghton Mifflin Co., 1975).

American Men and Women of Science: The Physical and Biological Sciences, ed. The Jaques Cattell Press, 14th ed., 7 vols. plus index vol. (R. R. Bowker Co., 1979).

American Men and Women of Science: The Social and Behavioral Sciences, ed. The Jaques Cattell Press, 13th ed., 2 vols. (R. R. Bowker Co., 1977).

American Negro Reference Book, ed. John P. Davis (Prentice-Hall, Inc., 1966).

American Universities and Colleges, ed. W. Todd Furniss, 11th ed. (American Council on Education, 1973).

Amy Vanderbilt's Complete Book of Etiquette, Amy Vanderbilt, rev. ed. (Doubleday and Co., Inc., 197().

Baby and Child Care, Benjamin Spock, rev. ed. (Hawthorn, 1976).

Baker's Biographical Dictionary of Musicians, Theodore Baker, ed. Nicolas Slonimsky, 6th ed. (G. Schirmer, 1978).

Biographical Directory of the American Congress, 1774-1961, U.S. Congress (Government Printing Office, 1961).

Biographical Encyclopaedia and Who's Who of the American Theatre, ed. Walter Rigdon (Wm. Heineman, Ltd., 1966).

Biography Index: A Cumulative Index to Biographical Materials in Books and Magazines, annual (H. W. Wilson Co., 1946).

Black's Law Dictionary, Henry C. Black, rev. 4th ed. (West Publishing Co., 1968).

Book of the States, biennial, ed. Vincent Wilson, Jr., (American History Research Association, 1972).

Books in Print, annual, 2 vols. (R. R. Bowker Co., 1948).

Careful Writer: A Modern Guide to English Usage, Theodore M. Bernstein (Atheneum, 1965).

Chases' Calendar of Annual Events, annual, William D. Chase (Apple Tree, 1957).

Columbia Encyclopedia, ed. William H. Harris and Judith S. Levy, 4th ed. (Columbia University Press, 1975).

Columbia-Lippincott Gazetteer of the World, ed. Leon E. Seltzer et al. (Columbia University Press, 1952).

Commercial Atlas and Marketing Guide, annual (Rand McNally & Co., 1870).

Concise Dictionary of American Biography, ed. Joseph G. Hopkins (Charles Scribner's Sons, 1977).

Congress and The Nation, 1945-1964; vol. 2, 1965-1968, vol. 3, 1969-1972, vol. 4, 1972-1976, (Congressional Quarterly Service, 1965; 1969; 1973; 1977).

Congressional Directory, annual (Government Printing Office, 1935).

Contemporary Authors, ed. Clare Kinsman, semiannual (Gale Research, 1962).

Current Biography Yearbook, annual (H. W. Wilson Co., 1946).

Demographic Yearbook, annual (United Nations Statistical Office, 1949).

Dictionary of American Biography, 15 vols. and supplements. (Charles Scribner's Sons, 1927-77).

Dictionary of American History, ed. Michael Martin & Leonard Gelber, rev. ed., (Littlefield, Adams & Co., 1978).

Dictionary of Modern English Usage, Henry M. Fowler, 2nd ed., rev. by Sir Ernest Gowers (Oxford University Press, Inc., 1965).

Dictionary of Music and Musicians, George Grove, ed. Eric Blom, 5th ed., 10 vols. (St. Martin's Press, Inc., 1954; supplement, 1961).

Dictionary of National Biography, George Smith ed., 22 vols. including 1st supplement, plus 7 supplements (Oxford University Press, Inc.; 22 vols. reprinted, 1938); abridged: **Concise Dictionary of National Biography,** ed. Sir Sidney Lee, 2 vols. (Oxford University Press, Inc., 1975).

Dictionary of Quotations, Bergen Evans (Delacorte Press, 1968).

Dictionary of the Social Sciences, ed. H. F. Reading (Routledge & Kegan Paul, LTD, 1977).

Dictionary of Universal Biography, Albert M. Hyamson, 2nd rev. ed. (Routledge & Kegan Paul, LTD, 1976).

Directory of American Scholars, ed. The Jaques Cattell Press, 7th ed., 4 vols. (R. R. Bowker, 1978).

Documents of American History, 2 vols., ed. A. Commager, 9th ed. (Prentice-Hall, 1974).

Dorland's Illustrated Medical Dictionary, 25th ed. (W. B. Saunders Co., 1974).

Editor & Publisher International Yearbook, annual (Editor & Publisher, 1920).

Encyclopaedia Britannica, 30 vols. 15th ed. in (1978); 15th ed. in 30 vols. (Encyclopaedia Britannica, 1768).

Encyclopedia Americana, 30 vols. (Grolier Educational Corporation, 1979).

Encyclopedia of American Facts and Dates, ed. Gorton Carruth et al., 7th rev. ed. (Thomas Y. Crowell Co., 1979).

Encyclopedia of American History, ed. Richard B. Morris, 5th ed. (Harper & Row, Publishers, 1976).

Encyclopedia of Associations, 14th ed., 3 vols. (Gale Research, 1980).

Encyclopedia of Chemistry, The, ed. Clifford A. Hampel and Gessner G. Hawley, 3rd ed. (Van Nostrand Reinhold Co., 1973).

Encyclopedia of Philosophy, ed. Paul Edwards, 4 vols. (The Free Press, 1973).

Encylcopedia of Physics, The, ed. Robert M. Besancon (Van Nostrand Reinhold Co., 1974).

Encyclopedia of Sports, Frank G. Menke, 6th rev. ed. (A. S. Barnes & Co., Inc., 1978).

Encyclopedia of the Biological Sciences, Peter Gray, 2nd ed. (Van Nostrand Reinhold Co., 1970).

Encyclopedia of World Art, 15 vols. (McGraw-Hill, Inc., 1959-68).

Encyclopedia of World History, ed. William L. Langer, 5th ed. (Houghton Mifflin Co., 1972).

Europa Year Book, annual 2 vols. (International Publications Service, 1959).

European Authors, 1000-1900, ed. Stanley J. Kunitz and Vineta Colby (H. W. Wilson Co., 1967).

Facts about the Presidents, Joseph N. Kane, 3rd ed. (H. W. Wilson Co., 1974).

Facts on File, annual (Facts on File, Inc., 1940).

Familiar Quotations, John Bartlett, 15th ed., rev. and enl. (Citadel Press, 1971).

Famous First Facts, Joseph N. Kane, 3rd ed. (H. W. Wilson Co., 1964).

Foundation Directory, biannual, ed. Marianna O. Lewis, 6th ed. (Foundation Center, 1977).

Future: A Guide to Information Sources, The, (World Future Society, 1977).

Granger's Index to Poetry, Edith Granger, ed. William J. Smith, 6th rev. and enl. ed. (Columbia University Press, 1962; supplement to 6th ed., 1973).

Guide to Reference Books, Eugene P. Sheehy, 9th ed. (American Library Association, 1976).

Guinness Book of World Records, ed. Norris McWhirter (Sterling, 1980).

Hammond Medallion World Atlas (Hammond Inc., 1979).

Harper Bible Dictionary, Madeleine S. and John L. Miller, 8th ed. (Harper & Row, Publishers, 1973).

Harper Encyclopedia of Science, ed. James R. Newman, rev. ed. (Harper & Row, Publishers, 1967).

Harvard Guide to American History, 2 vols., rev. ed. F. Freidel and R. K. Showman (Harvard University Press, 1974).

Historical Statistics of the United States: 1790 to 1970, 2 vols. (University of Alabama Press, 1976).

Home Book of Quotations, Burton Stevenson, 10th ed. (Dodd, Mead & Co., 1967).

Home Book of Verse, Burton E. Stevenson, 9th ed., 2 vols. (Holt, Rinehart & Winston, 1953).

International Encyclopedia of the Social Sciences, ed. David E. Sills, 17 vols. (The Macmillan Co., 1968).

International Who's Who, annual (International Publications Service, 1935).

Keesing's Contemporary Archives, weekly (Keesing's, London, 1931).

Lincoln Library, see New Lincoln Library Encyclopedia

Literary Market Place, annual (R. R. Bowker Co., 1940).

McGraw-Hill Encyclopedia of Science and Technology, 3rd rev. ed., 15 vols. (McGraw-Hill, Inc., 1971).

Macmillan Book of Proverbs, Burton Stevenson (The Macmillan Co., 1965).

Manual of Style, Staff of the University of Chicago Press, rev. 12th ed. (University of Chicago Press, 1969).

Masterpieces of World Literature in Digest Form, ed. Frank N. Magill, 4 vols. (Harper & Row, Publishers, 1952-69).

Monthly Catalog of United States Government Publications, monthly (Government Printing Office, 1895).

Municipal Year Book, ed. International City Management Association (National Association of Counties, 1979).

National Geographic Atlas of the World, Melville B. Grovenor, 4th ed. (National Geographic Society, 1975).

Negro Almanac, ed. Harry A. Ploski and Warren Marr, rev. ed. (Bellwether Publishing, 1971).

The Reference Shelf, New Acronyms and Initialisms: supplement 1979 & 1980 to Acronyms and Initialisms Dictionary (Gale Research, 6th edition, 1976).

New Catholic Encyclopedia, prepared by Editorial Staff at Catholic University of America, 17 vols. (McGraw-Hill, Inc., 1967).

New Century Cyclopedia of Names, ed. Clarence L. Barnhart and William D. Halsey, 3 vols. (Prentice-Hall, Inc., 1954).

New Emily Post's Etiquette, Emily Post, rev. by Elizabeth L. Post, 12th rev. ed. (Funk & Wagnalls Co., Inc., 1975).

New Encyclopedia of the Opera, David Ewen (Hill and Wang, Inc., 1971).

New Lincoln Library Encyclopedia, ed by William H. Seibert, 2 vols. (Frontier Press, 1980).

New York Times Index, semimonthly and cumulated annually (The New York Times, 1851).

Oxford Classical Dictionary, ed. N. G. Hammond and H. H. Scullard, 2nd ed. (Oxford University Press, 1970).

Oxford Companion to American History, Thomas H. Johnson (Oxford University Press, Inc., 1966).

Oxford Companion to American Literature, James D. Hart, 4th ed. Oxford University Press, 1965).

Oxford Companion to Classical Literature, ed. Paul Harvey, 2nd ed. (Oxford University Press, 1937).

Oxford Companion to English Literature, ed. Paul Harvey and Dorothy Eagle, 4th ed. (Oxford University Press, Inc., 1967).

Oxford Companion to Film, ed. by Liz-Anne Bawden (Oxford University Press, Inc., 1976).

Oxford Companion to the Theatre, Phyllis Hartnoll, 3rd ed. (Oxford University Press, Inc., 1967)

Oxford Dictionary of Quotations, 3rd ed. (Oxford University Press, Inc., 1979).

Oxford English Dictionary, ed. James A. Murray et al., 13 vols. (Oxford University Press, Inc., 1933).

Peterson's Annual Guides to Graduate and Undergraduate Study, 13th ed., ed. Karen C. Hegener, 5 volumes (Peterson's Guides, 1980).

Political Handbook of the World 1980, ed. Arthur S. Banks (McGraw-Hill, 1980).

Random House Dictionary of the English Language, ed. Jess Stein (Random House, Inc., 1966).

Reader's Adviser, 12th ed., 3 vols. (R. R. Bowker Co., 1974-1977).

Reader's Encyclopedia, ed. William R. Benét, 2nd ed. (Thomas Y. Crowell Co., 1965).

Readers' Guide to Periodical Literature, 38 vols., annual (H. W. Wilson Co., 1900).

Roget's International Thesaurus, 4th ed., Peter M. Roget (Thomas Y. Crowell Co., 1977).

Shepherd's Historical Atlas, William R. Shepherd, 9th ed. (Barnes & Noble, Inc., 1964).

Statesman's Year-Book, annual (St. Martin's Press, Inc., 1864).

Statistical Abstract of the United States, annual (Government Printing Office, 1878).

The Reference Shelf, Statistical Yearbook, annual (United Nations Publishing Service, 1949).

Stedman's Medical Dictionary, Thomas L. Stedman, 23rd ed. (The William & Wilkins Co., 1976).

Times Atlas of the World, comprehensive ed. (London Times/Quadrangle, 1975).

Times Atlas of World History, ed. Geoffrey Barraclough (London Times/Hammond Inc., 1979).

Timetables of History, Bernard Grun (Simon & Schuster, Inc., 1979).

Twentieth Century Authors, ed. Stanley J. Kunitz and Howard Haycraft (H. W. Wilson Co., 1942).

Twentieth Century Authors: First Supplement, ed. Stanley J. Kunitz and Howard Haycraft (H. W. Wilson Co., 1955).

Ulrich's International Periodicals Directory, 18th ed. (R. R. Bowker Co., 1979).

United States Government Organization Manual, annual (Government Printing Office, 1935).

Universal Jewish Encyclopedia and Readers Guide, ed. Isaac Landman, 11 vols. (Ktav, 1944).

Van Nostrand's International Encyclopedia of Chemical Science (Van Nostrand Reinhold Co., Inc., 1964).

Van Nostrand's Scientific Encyclopedia, 5th ed. (Van Nostrand Reinhold Co., 1976).

Webster's New Geographical Dictionary, rev. ed. (G. and C. Merriam Co., 1977).

Webster's Third New International Dictionary of the English Language, unabridged (G. and C. Merriam Co., 1976).

Who Was Who, 6 vols. (St. Martin's Press, Inc., 1897-1961).

Who Was Who in America, 7 vols. (The A. N. Marquis Co., 1897-1976).

Who Was Who in America: Historical Volume, 1607-1896 (The A. N. Marquis Co., 1963).

Who's Who, annual (St. Martin's Press, Inc., 1849).

Who's Who in America, biennial (The A. N. Marquis Co., 1899).

Who's Who in American Politics, 1978-1979, compiled by Jaques Cattell Press, 7th ed. (R. R. Bowker Co., 1979).

Who's Who of American Women, 1979-1980, 11th ed. (The A. N. Marquis Co., 1979).

Worldmark Encyclopedia of the Nations, 5 vols., ed. Moshe Y. Sachs (J. Wiley & Sons, 1976).

World of Learning, annual (International Publications Service, 1947).

World Who's Who in Science, ed. Allen G. Debus (The A. N. Marquis Co., 1968).

Yearbook of International Organizations, biennial (Union of International Publications Service, 1948).

Yearbook of the United Nations, annual (International Publications Service, 1946/47).

COMMUNICATIONS/LANGUAGE

CURRENT WORDS AND PHRASES

The following list of words and phrases consists of terms and meanings that have only recently made an appearance in English or of terms that have had some restricted usage over a period of time but are now acquiring widespread usage. Many of these words have passed the test of time and have already entered the dictionaries. Some will prove to be fleeting, and will remain only as a curious reminder of some passing vogue. The list was prepared by the staff of Laurence Urdang Inc.

ABSCAM acronym for **Arab Scam,** an undercover operation conducted by the U.S. Department of Justice in which federal agents, posing as wealthy Arabs or their representatives, enticed government officials with offers of money in exchange for their favorable influence in a variety of schemes.

acid rain natural rainfall containing high concentrations of sulfuric and nitric acids, resulting from the ejection into the atmosphere of sulfur dioxide from the industrial burning of high-sulfur fuels and of nitrogen oxide from auto exhaust emissions. These compounds mix with water vapor and fall to earth as rain, often many miles from their source, raising the acid content of lakes and rivers to a level that is lethal to fish and other marine life. Compare **acid smog.**

acid smog smog containing high concentrations of sulfur and nitrogen oxides which, when combined with the moisture in the air, produce sulfuric and nitric acids. Acid smog differs from acid rain in that it does not fall to the ground as precipitation but is deposited in a more or less dry state, damaging structural materials, plastics and rubber, and plant life. Also called **acid dust.** Compare **acid rain.**

ADC abbreviation for **almost-developed country.**

Agent Orange a herbicide used as a defoliant in the Vietnam War, held by some to cause birth defects and cancer.

-aholic a suffix made up from a distortion of the last part of *alcoholic* with *-a-* usually substituted for *-o-*. It is used to mean 'addicted to' (in adjectival applications) and 'an addict of' (in noun applications), as in *workaholic, wordaholic,* etc.

Airbus a trade name for a wide-bodied airplane used chiefly as a domestic passenger carrier.

almost-developed country one of the more populous Third-World nations capable of supplying the workers for labor-intensive manufacturing developed by technologically advanced nations. Abbreviation: **ADC.**

angel dust *Slang.* phencyclidine, an addictive, halucinatory, narcotic drug. Also called **PCP.**

ayatollah *n. a* religious leader of the Shi'ite sect of Muslims.

bioclock *n. Informal.* **biological clock.**

biological clock the normal circadian rhythm of waking and sleeping within a given time zone as reflected by the habits of an individual.

bird *n. Slang.* any satellite.

blood reinfusion. See **reinfusion.** Also, *Informal.* **blood doping.**

boat people refugees who escape political unrest, oppression, etc., in their native countries by means of small boats which carry them, often under severe hardship, to nearby countries or to larger vessels of those nations willing to grant them asylum.

card *vb.* to check the identity cards of customers to determine their age and whether they are old enough to buy alcoholic beverages, attend movies with age-restricted ratings, etc.

chronotherapy *n.* a form of therapy in which the time during which a patient sleeps and remains awake is gradually shifted to adjust for jet-lag, a change in work shift, etc.

closet *n. used attributively.* secret; clandestine: *a closet homosexual; a closet novelist.*

COLA acronym for **cost-of-living adjustment.**

cost-of-living adjustment an adjustment (almost invariably an increase) in the salaries of workers whose wage contracts are tied to the cost-of-living index. Acronym: **COLA.**

CPR abbreviation of **cardiopulmonary resuscitation.** A method for administering first aid to a victim of a heart attack, esp. as taught to laymen.

DMSO abbreviation for **dimethyl sulfoxide.**

dimethyl sulfoxide a pharmaceutical being tested as a broad-spectrum analgesic. Abbreviation: **DMSO.**

downlink *n. Informal.* an earth station for receiving signals from a geostationary satellite. Compare **uplink.**

down-size *vb.* to reduce the scale of a product, esp. an automobile, in order to compete with lower-priced, more economical models manufactured by competitors.

Electronic Mail Service a proposed system for the rapid transmittal of mail in which businesses transmit a letter or document electronically to specially equipped post offices near the intended destination; the message is then transcribed onto paper, placed in an envelope, and delivered to the addressee along with the regular mail.

endorphin *n.* one of a group of chemicals, naturally produced in the human body and present in the brain, that act as pain suppressors.

footprint *n. Informal.* an area on the surface of the earth where the signal from a geostationary satellite can be received.

gasahol a mixture of 10% alcohol and 90% unleaded gasoline, slightly more expensive than premium unleaded gasoline, said to increase mileage per gallon of cars by 5%, used to reduce consumption of gasoline in internal combustion engines.

geostationary *adj.* (of an artificial satellite) orbiting around the earth at such velocity that it remains fixed at the zenith over a particular point on the equator of the earth.

GPM abbreviation for **graduated payment mortgage.** Also *Informal.* **Jeep.**

gridlock a deadlock in which the streets of a city become so congested with cars that it becomes impossible for traffic to move in any direction.

HBO abbreviation for **Home Box Office,** a subsidiary of Time, Inc. that broadcasts television programs over a channel that is scrambled for all viewers except subscribers with cable TV who pay an extra fee.

heavy oil a viscous, low-grade crude oil suitable for converting into gasoline by means of special processes.

Heimlich maneuver a technique for preventing someone from choking on food by applying pressure at specific places on the body.

Home Box Office. See **HBO.**

HVR abbreviation for **home video recorder,** a device by which television programs can be recorded on videotape for playback at another time. Also called **VCR.**

hyperinflation *n.* inflation at the upper end if the scale of superinflation (*q.v.*).

in-kind tax the payment of the tax on one's property by exchange of services.

innumerate *adj.* incapable of dealing with or understanding arithmetic, numerical relationships, etc. [Origin: modeled on *illiterate.*]

Jeep. See **GPM.**

junk phone call *Informal.* solicitation by telephone to purchase a product or service. [Origin: by analogy with *junk mail,* unsolicited advertising sent through the postal system.]

kneeling bus a public transport vehicle equipped with devices that allow the right front corner to be lowered so as to reduce the height of the entrance steps for elderly and handicapped passengers to board more easily.

mcte abbreviation for **million tons of coal equivalent** (used as a measure of saving of fossil fuels).

meltdown 1. physical disintegration of the core of a nuclear reactor 2. *Figurative.* any internal disintegration, as of the directorship of a company, etc.

membrane technology the industrial application of semipermeable membranes to filter, separate, and purify chemical fluids.

MFT abbreviation for **made for television.** See **vidpic.**

microsurgery *n.* a combination of surgical techniques used in the reattachment of severed limbs and other body parts. See also **replantation.**

MIS abbreviation for **manager of information services.**

mole *Informal.* an espionage agent who has infiltrated the spy network of another country.

mortgage out *Informal.* to take out a second mortgage on one's home in order to acquire equity in cash that can be spent for a child's education, investment in a business, etc.

mouse print the very small typeface used on food packages to describe the contents, showing the ingredients, weight, chemical constituents and potential harm to people, plants and animals, as required by the U.S. government.

mutagenicity *n.* the ability of a substance, esp. a chemical, to create genetic change and, consequently, to act as a carcinogenic.

narrowcast *vb.* to broadcast special-interest television programs, esp. via subscriber cable, to children, Spanish Americans, sports enthusiasts, etc.

ob/gyn (pronounced oh-bee, gee-why-en) the fields of *obstetrics* and *gynecology,* considered as a unit for some applications, as in clinical treatment.

palimony *Informal.* a suit brought by a person for a share in the property and money of a former lover to whom the individual was not wed.

Pinyin a system for transcribing Chinese into the Roman alphabet, in official use in China for communication with other countries and recently adopted by the United Nations, the U.S. Board on Geographic Names, and many Western newspapers, magazines, etc. It is considered a more accurate transcription of the sounds of Chinese than the Wade-Giles system, developed in the mid-19th century, which it replaces.

piperack *n. used attributively.* unadorned; produced with a low budget; lacking in decorative amenities: *piperack news broadcasts.* [Originally applied to stores equipped with "plain piperacks" instead of expensive fixtures for displaying men's clothing sold at reduced prices.]

Proposition 4 a legislative proposition, approved by the voters of California in 1979, requiring state and local governments to limit spending in fiscal 1979-80 to the levels of 1978-79, except for adjustments for population growth and inflation.

ragtop *n. Slang.* a convertible car with a cloth top that can be folded down.

reinfusion *n.* a technique of withdrawing some of an athlete's blood and reinfusing it into the body at a later date to improve athletic performance. Also called **blood reinfusion,** *Informal.* **blood doping.**

replantation *n.* the reattachment of severed limbs and other body parts by microsurgical techniques.

roboticist *n.* an expert in robotics.

robotics *n. pl., used as sing.* the technology of designing and manufacturing robots. — **robotic,** *adj.*

seismic gap an area of seismic inactivity around which earthquakes of high magnitude have taken place within 30 years.

shield law a law, within a state of the U.S., intended to protect the confidentiality of the notes and sources of a journalist.

slimnastics a system of calisthenics for those who wish to lose weight. [from *slim* and gym*nastics.*]

smart *adj.* (of an electronically controlled device) capable of simulating human judgments to a greater or lesser degree.

soft not involved in or directly to those functions of a business requiring expenditure unavoidable in producing a profit, as public relations, public affairs, and advertising staffs.

SPF abbreviation for **sun protection factor,** a numerical scale from 2 to 23 indicating the extent to which a substance can provide protection from the sun. A factor of 2 means twice as long as with no protection; a factor of 23 signifies a complete blockage.

static line ripcord hooked onto a fitting so as to release a parachute automatically when the parachutist jumps from an airplane.

Sunbelt a section of the United States in the southerly part, including Virginia, North Carolina, South Carolina, Georgia, Florida, Alabama, Louisiana, Tennessee, Mississippi, Arkansas, Oklahoma, Texas, New Mexico, Arizona, and southern California.

sun protection factor. See **SPF.**

sunrise law legislation that requires a governmental agency to describe in advance its goals for every new program and to provide for periodic reviews to determine whether those goals have been accomplished.

sunset law legislation that requires a governmental agency to justify its existence periodically.

superinflation *n.* inflation at a rate in excess of 25 percent per year. Compare **hyperinflation.**

superstation *n.* a local television station that transmits its signal to a geostationary satellite whence it can be received by receiving stations situated wthin the footprint of the satellite. See also **footprint.**

synfuel *n. Informal.* a synthetically produced fuel.

taggant *n.* a substance added to commercially produced chemical explosives in order to enable its identification as to source, date of manufacture, etc.

taphonomy *n.* the study of fossils, sediments, and other paleontological evidence in an effort to reconstruct the natural history and ecology of the past. — **taphonomist,** *n.*

technofix *n.* the application of technology to the control of disease, pollution, social unrest, etc.

telefeature *n.* See **vidpic.**

telefilm *n.* See **vidpic.**

ten the ultimate in any of a number of specified or implied qualities, on a scale of one to ten.

tetrahydrocannabinol *n.* an intoxicant compound found in marijuana.

THC abbreviation for **tetrahydrocannabinol.**

tofu a high-protein, cholesterol-free food made by solidifying soy milk. Also called **bean curd, soy cheese.**

Universal Product Code a pattern of lines and numbers by which information about a product may be encoded for automatic scanning by a device at the checkout counter in a supermarket that records its price for charging the consumer as well as for its stock numbers, inventory, etc.

unk-unk *n. Slang.* short for *unknown unknown,* a factor in technological development that creates unanticipated problems in the manufacture, performance, safety, etc., of the final product.

uplink *n. Informal.* an earth station for transmitting signals to a geostationary satellite. Compare **downlink.**

VCR abbreviation for **video cassette recorder.** Also called **HVR.**

videodisc *n.* a disc on which a visual scene has been recorded electronically for playback by a suitable device.

vidpic *n. Informal.* a movie made originally for television broadcast. Also called **telefeature, telefilm** and **MFT.**

wiseguy *Slang.* a person active in organized crime.

word processing a system for the application of automatic typewriters, simple display terminals, and other electronic equipment, esp. minicomputers, to the processing of correspondence and maintenance of files in a business office.

workfare *n.* a system under which able-bodied recipients of welfare stipends are required to work to qualify for payments.

MOST COMMON AMERICAN SURNAMES Source: U.S. Social Security Administration

This tabulation is based on the surnames that appear most frequently in social security records for the period of 1936 to 1973.

Rank	Surname	No. of Persons	Rank	Surname	No. of Persons	Rank	Surname	No. of Persons
1	Smith	2,382,509	21	Walker	486,498	41	Campbell	361,958
2	Johnson	1,807,263	22	Robins(on)	484,991	42	Gonzalex(ez)	360,994
3	Williams(on)	1,568,939	23	Peters(on)	479,249	43	Carter	349,950
4	Brown	1,362,910	24	Hall	471,479	44	Garcia	346,175
5	Jones	1,331,205	25	Allen	458,375	45	Evans	343,897
6	Miller	1,131,861	26	Young	455,416	46	Turner	329,752
7	Davis	1,047,848	27	Morris(on)	455,179	47	Stewart	329,581
8	Martin(ez), (son)	1,046,297	28	King	434,791	48	Collin(s)	324,680
9	Anders(on)	825,648	29	Wright	431,157	49	Parker	322,482
10	Wilson	787,825	30	Nelson	421-638	50	Edward	317,197
11	Harris(on)	754,083	31	Rodriguez	416,178	51	Murphy	311,337
12	Taylor	696,046	32	Hill	414,646	52	Cook	298,396
13	Moore	693,304	33	Baker	412,676	53	Rogers	298,288
14	Thomas	688,054	34	Richards(on)	409,262	54	Griffin, Griffith	291,862
15	White	636,185	35	Lee	409,068	55	Christian(son), Christopher	281,525
16	Thompson	635,426	36	Scott	408,439	56	Morgan	273,267
17	Jackson	630,003	37	Green	406,989	57	Cooper	269,560
18	Clark	549,107	38	Adams	406,841	58	Reed	267,589
19	Robert(s), (son)	524,688	39	Mitchell	371,434	59	Bell	267,026
20	Lewis	495,026	40	Phillips	362,013			

MAJOR WORLD LANGUAGES Source: Kenneth Katzner, author, The Languages of the World.

Language	Speakers*	Chief Location	Language	Speakers*	Chief Location	Language	Speakers*	Chief Location
Chinese	900	China	Nepali	10	Nepal	Lithuanian	2.5	USSR (Lithuania)
English	325	U.S., U.K., Canada, Ireland, Australia, New Zealand	Sinhalese	10	Sri Lanka	Moldavian	2.5	USSR (Moldavia)
Spanish	225	Spain, Latin America	Fulani	10	West Africa	Turkmen	2.5	USSR (Turkmen SSR), Iran
Russian	200	USSR	Assamese	9	India (Assam)	Karen	2.5	Burma
Hindi	200	India	Sindhi	9	Pakistan, India	Lao	2.5	Laos
Bengali	135	Bangladesh, India	Amharic	9	Ethiopia	Buginese	2.5	Indonesia (Celebes)
Portuguese	130	Portugal, Brazil	Swedish	8	Sweden	Tigrinya	2.5	Ethiopia
Arabic	130	Middle East, North Africa	Bulgarian	8	Bulgaria	Tswana	2.5	South Africa, Botswana
Japanese	115	Japan	Madurese	8	Indonesia (Java, Madura)	Makua	2.5	Mozambique
German	100	Germany, Austria, Switzerland	Ibo	8	Nigeria	Kirgiz	2	USSR (Kirgiz SSR)
Indonesian	100	Indonesia	Galla	8	Ethiopia	Gilaki	2	Iran
French	75	France, Belgium, Switzerland, Canada	Belorussian	7	USSR (Belorussia)	Bhili	2	India
Punjabi	65	India (Punjab), Pakistan	Kazakh	7	USSR (Kazakhstan)	Achinese	2	Indonesia (Sumatra)
Italian	60	Italy	Berber	7	Morocco, Algeria	Balinese	2	Indonesia (Bali)
Korean	55	Korea	Malagasy	7	Malagasy Republic	Bikol	2	Philippines (Luzon)
Telugu	50	India (Andhra Pradesh)	Quechua	7	Peru, Bolivia	Kikuyu	2	Kenya
Marathi	45	India (Maharashtra)	Catalan	6	Spain, France, Andorra	Malinke	2	West Africa
Tamil	45	India (Tamil Nadu), Sri Lanka	Uighur	6	China, USSR	Kanuri	2	Nigeria
Javanese	45	Indonesia (Java)	Malay	6	Malaysia, Singapore	Guarani	2	Paraguay
Turkish	40	Turkey	Danish	5	Denmark	Slovenian	1.5	Yugoslavia
Urdu	40	Pakistan, India	Finnish	5	Finland	Latvian	1.5	USSR (Latvia)
Vietnamese	40	Vietnam	Flemish	5	Belgium	Chuvash	1.5	USSR (Chuvash ASSR)
Polish	35	Poland	Tatar	5	USSR (Tatar ASSR)	Mazanderani	1.5	Iran
Ukrainian	35	USSR (Ukraine)	Kurdish	5	Iraq, Iran, Turkey, Syria, USSR	Baluchi	1.5	Pakistan, Iran
Thai	35	Thailand	Yi (Lolo)	5	China	Gondi	1.5	Central India
Persian	25	Iran, Afghanistan	Khmer	5	Cambodia	Puyi	1.5	China
Gujarati	25	India (Gujarat)	Somali	5	Somalia, Ethiopia	Shan	1.5	Burma
Kanarese	25	India (Karnataka)	Ruanda	5	Rwanda, Zaire	Batak	1.5	Indonesia (Sumatra)
Malayalam	25	India (Kerala)	Zulu	5	South Africa	Wolof	1.5	Senegal
Burmese	25	Burma	Xhosa	5	South Africa	Bambara	1.5	Mali
Tagalog	25	Philippines	Yiddish	4	U.S., USSR, Israel	Ewe	1.5	Ghana, Togo
Romanian	20	Romania	Norwegian	4	Norway	Fang	1.5	Cameroon, Gabon
Bihari	20	India (Bihar)	Slovak	4	Czechoslovakia	Dinka	1.5	Sudan
Oriya	20	India (Orissa)	Armenian	4	USSR (Armenia)	Lingala	1.5	Zaire, Congo
Hausa	20	Nigeria, Niger	Mongolian	4	Mongolia, China	Bemba	1.5	Zambia
Serbo-Croatian	15	Yugoslavia	Tibetan	4	Tibet	Tsonga	1.5	Mozambique
Pushtu	15	Afghanistan, Pakistan	Miao	4	China	Aymara	1.5	Bolivia, Peru
Rajasthani	15	India (Rajasthan)	Twi	4	Ghana	Breton	1	France (Brittany)
Swahili	15	East Africa	Sidamo	4	Ethiopia	Macedonian	1	Yugoslavia
Dutch	13	Netherlands	Rundi	4	Burundi	Estonian	1	USSR (Estonia)
Sundanese	13	Indonesia (Java)	Shona	4	Rhodesia	Mordvin	1	USSR (Mordovian ASSR)
Hungarian	12	Hungary, Romania	Nyanja	4	Malawi, Zambia			
Uzbek	12	USSR (Uzbekistan)	Sotho	4	South Africa, Lesotho	Bashkir	1	USSR (Bashkir ASSR)
Chuang	12	China	Afrikaans	4	South Africa	Tulu	1	India (Karnataka)
Visayan	12	Philippines	Albanian	3	Albania	Kurukh (Oraon)	1	Eastern India
Yoruba	12	Nigeria	Georgian	3	USSR (Georgia)	Tung	1	China
Czech	10	Czechoslovakia	Tadzhik	3	USSR (Tadzhikistan)	Yao	1	China
Greek	10	Greece	Hebrew	3	Israel	Mende	1	Sierra Leone
Azerbaijani	10	USSR (Azerbaijan), Iran	Kashmiri	3	Kashmir	Fon	1	Benin
			Santali	3	Eastern India	Tiv	1	Nigeria
			Minangkabau	3	Indonesia (Sumatra)	Ibibio	1	Nigeria
			Ilocano	3	Philippines (Luzon)	Luo	1	Kenya
			Mossi	3	Upper Volta	Kamba	1	Kenya
			Ganda	3	Uganda	Sukuma	1	Tanzania
			Luba	3	Zaire	Swazi	1	Swaziland, South Africa
			Kongo	3	Zaire, Congo, Angola			
			Mbundu	3	Angola	Nahuatl	1	Mexico
			Mayan	3	Mexico, Guatemala			

* In millions of speakers.

LEADING AMERICAN MAGAZINES

SOURCE: Magazine Publishers Association, Inc.

Based on average circulations per issue, 2nd six months of 1979

Rank	Magazine*	Circulation	Rank	Magazine*	Circulation
1	TV Guide	19,043,358	41	Farm Journal	1,337,873
2	Reader's Digest	17,888,680	42	Life	1,332,074
3	National Geographic	10,413,639	43	Ebony	1,262,619
4	Better Homes & Gardens	8,097,651	44	Nation's Business	1,256,270
5	Family Circle	7,753,604	45	Changing Times	1,233,718
6	Woman's Day	7,560,329	46	Sport	1,207,633
7	McCall's	6,526,745	47	New Woman	1,195,756
8	Ladies' Home Journal	5,502,149	48	Psychology Today	1,177,988
9	Good Housekeeping	5,271,172	49	Bon Appetit	1,144,718
10	Playboy	5,249,010	50	House & Garden	1,084,277
11	National Enquirer	5,024,180	51	'Teen	1,059,325
12	Penthouse	4,711,849	52	Book Digest	1,045,110
13	Redbook	4,303,951	53	Vogue	1,019,847
14	Time	4,272,888	54	Discovery	1,012,892
15	Star, The	3,292,106	55	Golf Digest	974,645
16	Newsweek	2,934,530	56	1,001 Decorating Ideas	967,379
17	Cosmopolitan	2,747,042	57	Mademoiselle	958,035
18	American Legion	2,592,065	58	Family Handyman	953,305
19	Sports Illustrated	2,274,819	59	Travel & Leisure	934,594
20	People Weekly	2,264,087	60	Progressive Farmer	932,685
21	U.S. News & World Report	2,042,910	61	Grit	899,515
22	Field & Stream	2,021,381	62	Hot Rod	896,927
23	Glamour	1,879,402	63	House Beautiful	867,096
24	Southern Living	1,862,667	64	Oui	861,979
25	V.F.W. Magazine	1,829,180	65	Money	860,843
26	Smithsonian	1,812,084	66	Scouting	845,193
27	Popular Science	1,800,319	67	Us Magazine	840,495
28	Outdoor Life	1,709,872	68	Apartment Life	833,950
29	Hustler	1,700,873	69	Yankee	833,553
30	Today's Education	1,694,024	70	Omni	829,909
31	Mechanix Illustrated	1,680,245	71	Popular Photography	824,213
32	Elks Magazine	1,644,618	72	Self	815,467
33	Popular Mechanics	1,642,570	73	Decorating & Craft Ideas	815,145
34	True Story	1,604,178	74	Junior Scholastic	811,772
35	Workbasket	1,569,788	75	Family Health	806,860
36	Midnight Globe	1,552,579	76	Michigan Living-AAA Motor News	806,612
37	Boys' Life	1,516,405	77	Co-Ed	802,396
38	Parents Magazine	1,456,311	78	Weight Watchers Magazine	800,842
39	Seventeen	1,450,625	79	Cuisine	800,387
40	Sunset	1,403,481	80	Business Week	793,519

*Includes general and farm magazine members of the Audit Bureau of Circulations. Groups and comics not included.

U.S. ADVERTISING VOLUME

SOURCE: Reprinted with permission from the December 31, 1979 issue of Advertising Age. Copyright 1979 by Crain Communications Inc.

Medium	1978		1979		% change
	Millions	% of total	Millions	% of total	
Newspapers					
Total	$12,707	28.9	$14,585	29.3	+14.8
National	1,787	4.1	2,085	4.2	+16.6
Local	10,920	24.8	12,500	25.1	+14.5
Magazines					
Total	2,597	5.9	2,930	5.9	+12.8
Weeklies	1,158	2.6	1,315	2.6	+13.4
Women's	672	1.5	735	1.5	+ 9.4
Monthlies	767	1.8	880	1.8	+ 4.5
Farm publications	104	0.2	120	0.2	+14.0
Television					
Total	8,979	20.4	10,195	20.5	+13.5
Network	3,975	9.0	4,540	9.1	+14.2
Spot	2,581	5.9	2,890	5.8	+12.0
Local	2,423	5.5	2,765	5.6	+14.0
Radio					
Total	3,052	6.9	3,385	6.8	+11.0
Network	147	0.3	170	0.3	+15.0
Spot	620	1.4	680	1.4	+ 9.8
Local	2,285	5.2	2,535	5.1	+11.0
Direct mail	5,987	13.6	6,650	13.3	+11.1
Business publications	1,400	3.2	1,595	3.2	+14.0
Outdoor					
Total	466	1.1	535	1.1	+14.8
National	307	0.7	350	0.7	+14.0
Local	159	0.4	185	0.4	+16.4
Miscellaneous					
Total	8,678	19.8	9,835	19.7	+13.4
National	4,485	10.2	5,060	10.2	+12.8
Local	4,193	9.6	4,775	9.5	+13.9
Total					
National	23,990	54.6	27,070	54.3	+12.8
Local	19,980	45.4	22,760	45.7	+13.9
U.S. Grand Total	43,970	100.0	49,830	100.0	+13.3

LARGEST U.S. SUNDAY NEWSPAPERS   Source: Audit Bureau of Circulations

Newspaper	Circulation*
New York News	2,202,601
New York Times	1,435,330
Los Angeles Times	1,276,195
Chicago Tribune	1,146,474
Philadelphia Inquirer	837,209
Washington Post	827,958
Detroit News	827,168
Boston Globe	710,731
Detroit Free Press	710,018
Chicago Sun-Times	700,315
San Francisco Chronicle-Examiner	669,665
Pittsburgh Press	659,998
Minneapolis Tribune	597,180
Miami Herald	576,261
Newark Star-Ledger†	574,966
Long Island Newsday	557,933
Philadelphia Bulletin	529,706
Milwaukee Journal	515,108
Atlanta Journal & Const.	501,867
Cleveland Plain Dealer	454,922
Houston Chronicle	436,940
St. Louis Post-Dispatch	436,419
Portland Oregonian	420,938
Kansas City Star	406,467
Phoenix Republic†	399,819
Houston Post	394,853
Des Moines Register	390,537
Baltimore Sun	374,989
Indianapolis Star†	357,694
Dallas News	353,677
Denver Post	351,149
Seattle Times	348,678
Dallas Times Herald	345,736
Columbus Dispatch	341,568
Louisville Courier-Journal & Times	331,103
Washington Star	326,512
New Orleans Times-Picayune†	323,302
San Diego Union†	321,792
Los Angeles Herald-Examiner	302,525
Cleveland Press	300,889
Cincinnati Enquirer	293,826
Denver Rocky Mountain News	293,004
Hartford Courant	289,124
St. Petersburg Times	288,775
Oklahoma City Sunday Oklahoman	287,371
Memphis Commercial Appeal	282,484
Omaha World-Herald	278,520
San Jose Mercury-News	269,821
Orange Co. (Calif.) Register	259,783
Fort Worth Star Telegram	256,664
Buffalo Courier Express	254,482
Nashville Tennesseean	246,031
Orlando Sentinel Star	243,704
St. Paul Pioneer Press	
Charlotte Observer	241,904
Tampa Tribune	239,399
Rochester Democrat & Chronicle	232,367
Syracuse Herald-American	231,470
Providence (R.I.) Journal	228,306

*Averages for 6 months ending March 31, 1980.   †Average for 3 months.

LARGEST U.S. DAILIES[1]   Source: Audit Bureau of Circulations

Newspaper	Circulation*
New York News	1,554,604
Los Angeles Times	1,024,322
New York Times	914,938
Chicago Tribune	789,767
Chicago Sun-Times	657,275
New York Post	654,314
Detroit News	630,573
Detroit Free Press	601,721
Washington Post	601,417
San Francisco Chronicle	506,600
Long Island Newsday	492,580
Boston Globe	491,682
Philadelphia Bulletin	458,849
Miami Herald	444,058
Philadelphia Inquirer	425,075
Newark Star-Ledger‡	407,844
Cleveland Plain Dealer	392,688
Baltimore Sun[2]	350,848
Houston Chronicle	348,601
Washington Star	345,641
Houston Post	330,203
Milwaukee Journal	323,932
Kansas City Times	314,007
Cleveland Press	300,889
Dallas News	286,955
Los Angeles Herald-Examiner	283,710
Kansas City Star	273,758
Pittsburgh Press	271,502
Denver Rocky Mountain News	271,153
Buffalo Evening News	269,474
St. Louis Globe-Democrat	264,609
Seattle Times	260,762
Denver Post	260,331
Phoenix Republic‡	260,090
Dallas Times Herald	249,890
Portland Oregonian	248,229
St. Louis Post-Dispatch	247,237
Fort Worth Star-Telegram[2]	240,579
Omaha World Herald[2]	235,313
Philadelphia Daily News	231,310
Minneapolis Tribune	230,815
Orange Co. (Calif.) Register	230,533
St. Petersburg Times	230,143
Atlanta Constitution	218,807
Indianapolis Star‡	215,858
New Orleans Times-Picayune‡	213,283
Hartford Courant	212,244
Atlanta Journal	211,081
Des Moines Register	210,577
Minneapolis Star	206,700
Memphis Commercial Appeal	203,847
Sacramento Bee	203,779
Columbus Dispatch	202,949
San Diego Union‡	201,798
Orlando Sentinel Star	201,383
Tampa Tribune	197,174
Seattle Post-Intelligencer	197,123
Louisville Courier-Journal	190,942
Cincinnati Enquirer	186,732
Pittsburgh Post Gazette-Sun Telegraph	185,215
Oklahoma City Daily Oklahoman	181,994

[1]Does not include Wall Street Journal, 1,798,416 circulation (National Edition).   [2]Combined morning and evening editions.
*Averages for 6 months ending March 31, 1980.   ‡Average for 3 months.

WORLD'S LARGEST DAILY NEWSPAPERS

Country and Newspaper	Daily Circulation
JAPAN	
Yomiurii Shimbun (A.M. & P.M. ed.)	13,469,725
Asahi Shimbun (A.M. & P.M. ed.)	11,000,000
Mainichi Shimbun (A.M. & P.M. ed.)	7,238,901
USSR	
Pravda	11,000,000
Izvestia	7,500,000
CHINA	
Cankao Xiaoxi (Reference News)	c. 10,000,000
CHINA, con't.	
Renmin Ribao (People's Daily)	c. 8,000,000
UNITED KINGDOM	
London Daily Sun[1]	3,851,719
London Daily Mirror[1]	3,650,106
London Daily Express[1]	2,358,993
UNITED STATES	
New York News	1,554,604
Los Angeles Times	1,024,322

[1]U.K. Audit Bureau of Circulation, Ltd.

LEADING TV ADVERTISERS   Source: Television Bureau of Advertising, Inc.

Company	Total TV Expenditure (1979)
Procter & Gamble Co.	$463,370,000
General Foods Corp.	296,694,100
American Home Products Corp.	165,053,200
General Mills, Inc.	156,847,200
General Motors Corp.	147,218,400
Bristol-Myers Co.	140,621,800
McDonalds Corp.	137,790,600
PepsiCo, Inc.	130,179,700
Ford Motor Co.	127,935,700
Lever Brothers Co.	112,112,000
Coca-Cola Co.	105,181,900
Philip Morris, Inc.	103,212,800
American Telephone & Telegraph Co.	97,828,600
Pillsbury Co.	93,004,100
Ralston Purina Co.	88,785,800
Johnson & Johnson	88,616,500
Warner-Lambert Pharmaceutical Co.	83,726,900
Chrysler Corp.	83,612,500
Sears Roebuck & Co.	83,008,800
Colgate-Palmolive Co.	81,350,800
Anheuser-Busch Companies, Inc.	78,816,200
Kellogg Co.	77,223,200
Nestle Co., Inc.	69,368,300
Sterling Drug, Inc.	69,037,400
The Gillette Co.	68,895,500
Kraftco Corp.	64,301,700
Nabisco, Inc.	63,789,500
Heublein, Inc.	55,808,700
Esmark, Inc.	54,827,800
Consolidated Foods Corp.	53,803,400
Mars, Inc.	51,224,400
William Wrigley, Jr. Co.	50,872,300
Richardson Merrell, Inc.	50,857,800
Quaker Oats Co.	48,927,400
Internat'l Telephone & Teleg. Corp.	47,211,600
Jos. Schlitz Brewing Co.	46,720,000
Toyota Motor Distributors, Inc.	46,629,100
Revlon, Inc.	46,086,800
Time, Inc.	43,602,500
Mobil Corp.	42,598,400
The Clorox Co.	42,284,900
Schering-Plough Corp.	42,182,700
Beecham Group, Ltd.	40,910,500
Chesebrough-Pond's, Inc.	39,736,400
Norton Simon, Inc.	39,658,900
Gulf & Western Industries, Inc.	38,524,000
J.C. Penney Co., Inc.	38,292,900
Miles Laboratories, Inc.	38,264,600
Eastman Kodak Co.	37,479,400
Morton-Norwich Products, Inc.	36,699,400
H.J. Heinz Co.	35,130,500
General Electric Co.	35,027,000

FORMS OF ADDRESS

Personage	Address	Social Correspondence	Salutation of Informal Letter*	Salutation of Formal Letter*
The President	The President The White House	The President and Mrs. Taylor	Dear Mr. President: or (if preferred) My dear Mr. President:[1]	Mr. President: or Sir:
The Vice-President	The Vice-President United States Senate	The Vice-President and Mrs. Taylor	Dear Mr. Vice-President: or (if preferred) My dear Mr. Vice-President:	Sir:
Chief Justice of the United States	The Chief Justice The Supreme Court	The Chief Justice and Mrs. Taylor	Dear Mr. Chief Justice: or (if preferred) My dear Mr. Chief Justice:	Sir:
Associate Justice, Supreme Court	Mr. Justice Taylor The Supreme Court	Mr. Justice Taylor and Mrs. Taylor	Dear Mr. Justice: or (if preferred) My dear Mr. Justice:	Sir:
Cabinet Member[2]	The Honorable Stephen Taylor Secretary of the Treasury (or applicable Cabinet-level department)	The Honorable The Secretary of the Treasury and Mrs. Taylor	Dear Mr. Secretary: or (if preferred) My dear Mr. Secretary:	Sir:
United States Senator[3]	The Honorable Stephen Taylor United States Senate	The Honorable Stephen Taylor and Mrs. Taylor (Dear Senator and Mrs. Taylor:) or (for a married woman senator) Mr. and Mrs. Stephen Taylor	Dear Senator Taylor: or (if preferred) My dear Senator:	Sir: or Madam:
Member, House of Representatives	The Honorable Stephen Taylor House of Representatives	The Honorable Stephen Taylor and Mrs. Taylor or (for a married woman member) Mr. and Mrs. Stephen Taylor	Dear Mr. [Mrs.] Taylor: or (if preferred) My dear Mr. [Mrs.] Taylor:	Sir: or Madam:
American Ambassador	The Honorable Stephen Taylor American Ambassador London	The Honorable The American Ambassador[4] and Mrs. Taylor (Dear Mr. Ambassador and Mrs. Taylor:) or (for a married woman ambassador) Mr. and Mrs. Stephen Taylor	Dear Mr. [Madam] Ambassador: or (if preferred) My dear Mr. [Madam] Ambassador:	Sir: or Madam:
American Chargé d'Affaires ad interim[5]	Stephen Taylor, Esquire[6] American Chargée d'Affaires ad interim (or other title)	Mr. and Mrs. Stephen Taylor	Dear Mr. Taylor: or (if preferred) My dear Mr. Taylor:	Sir:
Foreign Ambassador	His Excellency Dr.[7] Juan Luis Ortega Ambassador of Mexico	His Excellency The Ambassador of Mexico and Mrs. Ortega	Dear Mr. [Madam] Ambassador: or (if preferred) My dear Mr. [Madam] Ambassador:	Excellency:
Secretary-General, United Nations	His Excellency Juan Luis Ortega Secretary-General of the United Nations	The Secretary-General of the United Nations and Mrs. Ortega	Dear Mr. Secretary- General: or (if preferred) My dear Mr. Secretary-General:	Sir:
Governor of a State	The Honorable Stephen Taylor Governor of Idaho or His Excellency[8] Stephen Taylor Governor of the Commonwealth of Massachusetts	The Governor of Idaho and Mrs. Taylor	Dear Governor Taylor: or (if preferred) My dear Governor:	Sir:
Mayor of a Large City	The Honorable Stephen Taylor Mayor of Baltimore	The Honorable Stephen Taylor and Mrs. Taylor	Dear Mayor Taylor: or Dear Mr. Mayor:	Sir:
Mayor of a Town	Stephen Taylor, Esquire Mayor of Newtown	The Mayor of Newtown and Mrs. Taylor	Dear Mr. Taylor:	Sir:

*"Sincerely" or "Sincerely yours" is the acceptable mode of ending both informal and formal letters to distinguished personages. [1] In the United States, "My dear Mr. President:" or "My dear Mrs. Taylor:" is a more formal salutation than "Dear Mr. President:"; however, in Great Britain, the reverse is true. [2] All but two Cabinet members use the title "Secretary": The Attorney General and the Postmaster General. Their full titles are used (e.g., on envelope: The Attorney General). [3] State senators and representatives are referred to and addressed the same way as U.S. Senators and Representatives. [4] For an American ambassador on home leave, the proper form of social address on an envelope is: "The Honorable Stephen Taylor and Mrs. Taylor," plus home address. [5] "Chargé d'affaires ad interim" is the official title given to the individual who assumes responsibility for an embassy during an ambassador's absence or change of ambassadors. [6] "Esquire" is never used, if the individual is addressed by another title, even "Mr." [7] "His Excellency" is followed by the individual's personal title, if he has one (e.g., Dr., Prince, Baron). [8] "His Excellency" is acceptable for addressing the governors of the four Commonwealths: Massachusetts, Virginia, Kentucky, and Pennsylvania; however, the State Department prefers to address all U.S. governors as "The Honorable."

U.S. POSTAL INFORMATION AND REGULATIONS

SOURCE: U.S. Postal Service

First-Class Mail includes letters, postal cards, postcards, all matter wholly or partly in writing (except authorized additions to second-, third-, and fourth-class mail), as well as matter closed against inspection.

Kind of mail	Rate
All first-class mail weighing 12 ounces or less, except postal cards and postcards	15¢ 1st ounce & 13¢ each additional oz.
Single postal cards and postcards	10¢ each
Double postal cards and postcards (reply portion of double postcard does not have bear postage when originally mailed)	20¢ (10¢ each portion)
Business reply mail: Cards	12¢ each
With Advance Deposit Account:	3.5¢ surcharge
Without Advance Deposit Account:	12¢ surcharge

Second-Class Mail includes all newspapers, magazines, and other periodicals marked as second-class mail. Within the county, the bulk rate is 3.1¢ per pound or 1.6¢ per piece. Outside the county, the non-advertising portion is charged at a rate of 13.1¢ per pound, while the advertising portion is charged at a rate of from 17.5¢ to 31.8¢ per pound.

Charges for copies mailed by public vary with the level of pre-sorting. Consult local postmaster. For special rates available to nonprofit organizations, publishers, and news agents, consult local postmaster.

Third-Class Mail is mailable matter that is not sent or required to be mailed as first-class mail, not entered as second-class mail, and weighs less than 16 ounces. The single piece rate is 20¢ for the first two ounces or fraction, 20¢ for the next 2 oz., and 13¢ for each additional 2 oz.

Circulars and printed matter are considered third-class mail. Certain loose enclosures relating exclusively to the book or catalogue that they accompany may be enclosed and mailed at the third-class bulk rate. Third-class mail must be prepared so that it can be easily examined. For special bulk rates for nonprofit organizations, consult local postmaster.

Special Fourth-Class Rate. A rate of 59¢ up to 1 pound or fraction, and 22¢ for each additional pound or fraction through 7 lbs., 13¢ per lb. thereafter, is provided for the following: bound books with no advertising; 16 mm films; printed music; book mss, magazine articles, and music; sound recordings; and certain other matter. The maximum size is 84 inches combined length and girth. The identification statement: Special Fourth Class Rate—Books (or other appropriate notation) must be placed conspicuously.

Fourth-Class (Parcel Post) Mail includes merchandise, printed matter, mailable live animals, and all other matter not included in first-, second-, or third-class mail. Each addressed piece must weigh 16 ounces or more but not more than 40 pounds, if mailed from one first-class post office to another. When mailed to or from a second-, third-, or fourth-class post office, the weight limit is 70 pounds. The maximum size for this class is 84 inches combined length and girth. Fourth-class mail must be wrapped or packaged for easy examination. Consult local postmaster for specification on irregular or outsize parcels and their surcharge.

Library Rate. A special library rate applies to certain items that are conspicuously marked Library Rate and show nonprofit associations or organizations in the address or return address. The postage rate is 19¢ for the first pound, 7¢ for each additional pound through 7 pounds, and 5¢ per pound thereafter.

Priority Mail (heavy pieces) is carried by air and the fastest connecting surface carriers. It is given the most expeditious handling in dispatch and delivery. Priority mail may weigh over 9 ounces, surface mail first class may weigh over 12 ounces. The upper limit is 70 pounds. It is limited to 100 inches combined in length and girth.

Size Standards for Domestic Mail. Min. Height: 3-1⁄2"; Min. Length: 5"; Max. Length: 11-1⁄2"; Max. Thickness: 1⁄4" or less; Shape: rectangular. Letters & Postcards below these specifications will not be accepted; anything above and/or weighing less than an ounce will be charged an additional 7¢. Max. Weight: 70 lbs.

SPECIAL HANDLING

Third and fourth-class mail only. Special handling fees (fees in addition to postage):

Weight	Fee
Not more than 10 lbs.	70¢
More than 10 lbs.	$1.25

SPECIAL DELIVERY

Special delivery fees (fees in addition to postage):

Class of Mail	Not more than 2 lbs.	2 lbs. but not more than 10 lbs.	More than 10 lbs.
First class and priority	$2.00	$2.25	$2.85
All other classes	2.25	2.85	3.25

MONEY ORDERS

Amount of money order	Amount of fee Domestic
$ 0.01 to $ 10	$0.55
$10.01 to $ 50	0.80
$50.01 to $400	1.10

INSURANCE

Fees (in addition to postage):

Liability	Fee
$ 0.01 to $ 15	$.50
$ 15.01 to $ 50	.85
$ 50.01 to $100	1.10
$100.01 to $150	1.40
$150.01 to $200	1.75
$200.01 to $300	2.25
$300.01 to $400	2.75
Restricted delivery. (Not available for mail insured for $15 or less)	.80

C.O.D. MAIL

Consult postmaster for fees and conditions of mailing.

CERTIFIED MAIL

Fee (in addition to postage)	.80
Restricted delivery	.80

REGISTRY

Registry fees (in addition to postage):

Declared actual value	For mailers without insurance coverage	For mailers with insurance coverage
$ 0.00 to $ 100	3.00	3.00
$ 100.01 to $ 200	3.30	3.30
$ 200.01 to $ 400	3.70	3.70
$ 400.01 to $ 600	4.10	4.10
$ 600.01 to $ 800	4.50	4.50
$ 800.01 to $1,000	4.90	4.90
$1,000.01 to $2,000	5.30	4.90 + 35¢
For higher values and their fees consult local postmaster.		handling per $1000 or fraction thereof

RETURN RECEIPTS

Certified mail—numbered insured—registered

Requested at the time of mailing:

Showing to whom and when delivered	$ .45
Showing to whom, when and address where delivered	.55

Requested after mailing:

Showing to whom and when delivered	2.10

INTERNATIONAL POSTAL CHARGES

LETTERS AND LETTER PACKAGES:

Surface Mail: Canada and Mexico, 15¢ an ounce or fraction thereof; to all other countries, 20¢ for the first ounce, 36¢ for 1-2 ounces, 48¢ for 2-4 ounces, 96¢ for 4-8 ounces, $1.84 for 8-16 ounces, $3.20 for 1-2 lbs., $5.20 for 2-4 lbs. **Airmail:** Canada and Mexico, 15¢ an ounce or fraction thereof, 13¢ each additional ounce or fraction; to all other countries, 25¢-31¢ per half ounce through 2 ounces, with 21¢-26¢ for each additional 1⁄2 ounce. Consult local postmaster. **Aerogrammes:** To all countries, 22¢ each. Weight limit: 4 lbs., except to Canada, 60 lbs.

POSTCARDS:

Surface Mail: To Canada and Mexico, 10¢, to all other countries, 14¢. **Airmail:** to Canada and Mexico, 10¢; to all other countries, 21¢.

*On 4/21/80, it was announced that a postal rate proposal had been filed with the Postal Rate Commission for increases needed in 1981. If approved (the commission may consider measure for 10 mos.), 1st-Class rates would rise to 20¢ for 1 oz; other classes would be adjusted with proposed reductions in some categories of 2nd and 3rd Class mail.

PARCEL POST ZONE RATES

Weight 1 lb. and not exceeding	Local	Zone 1 & 2 Up to 150 mi.	Zone 3 150 to 300 mi.	Zone 4 300 to 600 mi.	Zone 5 600 to 1,000 mi.	Zone 6 1,000 to 1,400 mi.	Zone 7 1,400 to 1,800 mi.	Zone 8 Over 1,800 mi.
* 2	$1.15	$1.35	$1.39	$1.56	$1.72	$1.84	$1.98	$2.22
* 3	1.23	1.45	1.53	1.73	1.86	2.04	2.24	2.61
* 4	1.29	1.56	1.65	1.82	2.00	2.23	2.50	3.00
* 5	1.36	1.66	1.77	1.92	2.14	2.43	2.77	3.39
* 6	1.42	1.71	1.84	2.01	2.28	2.62	3.03	3.78
* 7	1.47	1.76	1.90	2.11	2.41	2.82	3.29	4.17
* 8	1.51	1.80	1.97	2.20	2.55	3.02	3.56	4.56
* 9	1.54	1.85	2.03	2.29	2.69	3.21	3.82	4.95
*10	1.57	1.89	2.10	2.39	2.83	3.41	4.08	5.34
*11	1.60	1.94	2.17	2.50	3.00	3.65	4.42	5.73
*12	1.64	1.98	2.22	2.56	3.09	3.77	4.57	6.12
*13	1.67	2.02	2.27	2.63	3.17	3.89	4.72	6.41
*14	1.70	2.05	2.32	2.69	3.25	3.99	4.86	6.62
15	1.73	2.09	2.36	2.74	3.33	4.09	4.99	6.80
16	1.76	2.13	2.41	2.80	3.40	4.19	5.11	6.98
17	1.79	2.16	2.45	2.85	3.47	4.28	5.23	7.15
18	1.82	2.20	2.49	2.91	3.54	4.37	5.34	7.31
19	1.86	2.23	2.53	2.96	3.61	4.46	5.45	7.47
20	1.89	2.27	2.58	3.01	3.67	4.54	5.55	7.62
21	1.92	2.30	2.62	3.06	3.74	4.62	5.66	7.76
22	1.95	2.34	2.66	3.14	3.85	4.78	5.80	7.90
23	1.98	2.37	2.72	3.25	3.99	4.96	6.02	8.03
24	2.01	2.44	2.80	3.35	4.12	5.13	6.24	8.16
25	2.04	2.51	2.89	3.46	4.26	5.31	6.46	8.28
26	2.07	2.58	2.97	3.56	4.39	5.48	6.68	8.40
27	2.11	2.65	3.06	3.67	4.53	5.66	6.90	8.52
28	2.14	2.72	3.14	3.77	4.66	5.83	7.12	8.63
29	2.17	2.79	3.23	3.88	4.80	6.01	7.34	8.75
30	2.20	2.86	3.31	3.98	4.93	6.18	7.56	8.85
31	2.68	3.09	3.46	4.09	5.07	6.36	7.78	9.41
32	2.71	3.12	3.49	4.19	5.20	6.53	8.00	9.51
33	2.74	3.16	3.57	4.30	5.34	6.71	8.22	9.61
34	2.77	3.19	3.65	4.40	5.47	6.88	8.44	9.80
35	2.80	3.22	3.74	4.51	5.61	7.06	8.66	10.06
36	2.83	3.28	3.82	4.61	5.74	7.23	8.88	10.32
37	2.86	3.35	3.91	4.72	5.88	7.41	9.10	10.58
38	2.89	3.42	3.99	4.82	6.01	7.58	9.32	10.84
39	2.93	3.49	4.08	4.93	6.15	7.76	9.54	11.10
40	2.96	3.56	4.16	5.03	6.28	7.93	9.76	11.36
41	2.99	3.63	4.25	5.14	6.42	8.11	9.98	11.62
42	3.02	3.70	4.33	5.24	6.55	8.28	10.20	11.88
43	3.05	3.77	4.42	5.35	6.69	8.46	10.42	12.14
44	3.08	3.84	4.50	5.45	6.82	8.63	10.64	12.40
45	3.11	3.91	4.59	5.56	6.96	8.81	10.86	12.66
46	3.14	3.98	4.67	5.66	7.09	8.98	11.08	12.92
47	3.17	4.05	4.76	5.77	7.23	9.16	11.30	13.18
48	3.20	4.12	4.84	5.87	7.36	9.33	11.52	13.44
49	3.23	4.19	4.93	5.98	7.50	9.51	11.74	13.70
50	3.27	4.26	5.01	6.08	7.63	9.68	11.96	13.96
51	3.30	4.33	5.10	6.19	7.77	9.86	12.18	14.22
52	3.33	4.40	5.18	6.29	7.90	10.03	12.40	14.48
53	3.36	4.47	5.27	6.40	8.04	10.21	12.62	14.74
54	3.39	4.54	5.35	6.50	8.17	10.38	12.84	15.00
55	3.42	4.61	5.44	6.61	8.31	10.56	13.06	15.26
56	3.45	4.68	5.52	6.71	8.44	10.73	13.28	15.52
57	3.48	4.75	5.61	6.82	8.58	10.91	13.50	15.78
58	3.51	4.82	5.69	6.92	8.71	11.08	13.72	16.04
59	3.54	4.89	5.78	7.03	8.85	11.26	13.94	16.30
60	3.57	4.96	5.86	7.13	8.98	11.43	14.16	16.56
61	3.60	5.03	5.95	7.24	9.12	11.61	14.38	16.82
62	3.64	5.10	6.03	7.34	9.25	11.78	14.60	17.08
63	3.67	5.17	6.12	7.45	9.39	11.96	14.82	17.34
64	3.70	5.24	6.20	7.55	9.52	12.13	15.04	17.60
65	3.73	5.31	6.29	7.66	9.66	12.31	15.26	17.86
66	3.76	5.38	6.37	7.76	9.79	12.48	15.48	18.12
67	3.79	5.45	6.46	7.87	9.93	12.66	15.70	18.38
68	3.82	5.52	6.54	7.97	10.06	12.83	15.92	18.64
69	3.85	5.59	6.63	8.08	10.20	13.01	16.14	18.90
70	3.88	5.66	6.71	8.18	10.33	13.18	16.36	19.16

*Parcels weighing less than 15 pounds, and measuring over 84 inches but not exceeding 100 inches in length and girth combined, are chargeable with a minimum rate equal to that for a 15-pound parcel for the zone to which addressed.

U.S. TOWNS AND CITIES: ZIP CODES AND 1970 POPULATIONS †

The following is a list of places with 6,200 or more inhabitants, according to revised final population counts of the 1970 U.S. Census. The ZIP code listed for each place is the five-digit national coding system that identifies each postal delivery area and is designed to expedite mail delivery. An asterisk indicates that there is more than one ZIP code for the town or city and that the code number applies to general delivery. To determine the exact ZIP code for a particular area within a place marked by an asterisk, consult the National Zip Code Directory or your nearest post office.

LOCATION	POPULATION	ZIP
ALABAMA		
Albertville	9,963	35950
Alexander City	12,358	35010
Andalusia	10,092	36420
Anniston	31,533	36201*
Athens	14,360	35611
Atmore	8,293	36503
Attalla	7,510	35954
Auburn	22,767	36830
Bay Minette	6,727	36507
Bessemer	33,663	35020
Birmingham	300,910	35203*
Bluff Park	12,431	35226
Brewton	6,747	36426
Center Point	15,675	35215
Chickasaw	8,447	36611
Cullman	12,601	35055
Decatur	38,044	35601*
Demopolis	7,651	36732
Dothan	36,733	36303*
Enterprise	15,591	36330
Eufaula	9,102	36027
Fairfield	14,369	35064
Florence	34,031	35630*
Fort Payne	8,435	35967
Gadsden	53,928	35901*
Gardendale	6,537	35071
Greenville	8,033	36037
Guntersville	6,491	35976
Hartselle	7,355	35640
Homewood	21,137	35209
Hueytown	8,174	35020
Huntsville	139,282	35804*
Jacksonville	7,715	36265
Jasper	10,798	35501
Lanett	6,908	36863
Leeds	6,991	35094
Midfield	6,340	35228
Mobile	190,026	36601*
Montgomery	133,386	36104*
Mountain Brook	19,509	35223
Muscle Shoals	6,907	35660
Northport	9,435	35476
Opelika	19,027	36801
Opp	6,493	36467
Ozark	13,555	36360
Phenix City	25,281	36867
Prattville	13,116	36067
Prichard	41,578	36610
Russellville	7,814	35653
Saraland	7,840	36571
Scottsboro	9,324	35768
Selma	27,379	36701
Sheffield	13,115	35660
Sylacauga	12,255	35150
Talladega	17,662	35160
Tarrant City	6,835	35217
Troy	11,482	36081
Tuscaloosa	65,773	35401*
Tuscumbia	8,828	35674
Tuskegee	11,028	36083
Vestavia Hills	8,311	35216
ALASKA		
Anchorage	49,126	99510*
Fairbanks	14,771	99701
Juneau	13,556	99801
Ketchikan	6,994	99901
Spenard	18,089	99503
ARIZONA		
Avondale	6,626	85323
Bisbee	8,329	85603
Casa Grande	10,536	85222
Chandler	13,763	85224
Douglas	12,462	85607
Flagstaff	26,117	86001
Glendale	36,228	85301*
Globe	7,333	85501
Kingman	7,312	86401
Mesa	62,853	85201*
Nogales	8,946	85621
Paradise Valley	7,155	85253
Phoenix	582,500	85026*
Prescott	13,134	86301
Scottsdale	67,823	85251*
Sierra Vista	6,689	85635
South Tucson	62,220	85713
Sun City	13,670	85351*
Tempe	63,550	85282*
Tucson	262,933	85702*
Winslow	8,066	86047
Yuma	29,007	85364
ARKANSAS		
Arkadelphia	9,841	71923
Batesville	7,209	72501
Benton	16,499	72015
Blytheville	24,752	72315
Camden	15,147	71701
Conway	15,510	72032
El Dorado	25,283	71730
Fayetteville	30,729	72701
Forrest City	12,521	72335
Fort Smith	62,802	72901*
Harrison	7,239	72601*
Helena	10,415	72342
Hope	8,830	71801
Hot Springs	35,631	71901
Jacksonville	19,832	72076
Jonesboro	27,050	72401
Little Rock	132,483	72201*
Magnolia	11,303	71753
Malvern	8,739	72104
Morrilton	6,814	72110
Newport	7,725	72112
North Little Rock	60,040	72114*
Osceola	7,204	72370
Paragould	11,840	72450
Pine Bluff	57,389	71601*
Rogers	11,050	72756
Russellville	11,750	72801
Searcy	9,040	72143
Springdale	16,783	72764
Stuttgart	10,477	72160
Texarkana	21,682	75501
Van Buren	8,373	72956
Warren	6,433	71671
West Helena	11,007	72390
West Memphis	26,070	72301
Wynne	6,696	72396
CALIFORNIA		
Alameda	70,968	94501
Alamo-Danville	14,059	94507
Albany	14,674	94706
Alhambra	62,125	91802*
Alondra Park	12,193	90249
Altadena	42,415	91001
Alum Rock	18,355	95116
Anaheim	166,408	92803*
Antioch	28,060	94509
Apple Valley	6,702	92307
Aptos	8,704	95003
Arcadia	45,138	91006
Arcata	8,985	95521
Arden-Arcade	82,492	95825
Arroyo Grande	7,454	93420
Artesia	14,757	90701
Ashland	14,810	94577
Atascadero	10,290	93422
Atherton	8,085	94025
Atwater	11,640	95301
Auburn	6,570	95603
Avocado Heights	9,810	91745
Azusa	25,217	91702
Bakersfield	69,515	93302*
Baldwin Park	47,285	91706
Banning	12,034	92220
Barstow	17,442	92311
Bell	21,836	90201
Bellflower	51,454	90706
Bell Gardens	29,308	90201
Belmont	23,538	94002
Benicia	7,349	94510
Berkeley	116,716	94701*
Beverly Hills	33,416	90213*
Bloomington	11,957	92316
Blythe	7,047	92225
Brawley	13,746	92227
Brea	18,447	92621
Broderick	9,781	95605
Buena Park	63,646	90622*
Burbank	88,871	91505*
Burlingame	27,320	94010
Calexico	10,625	92231
Camarillo	19,219	93010
Campbell	24,770	95008
Carlsbad	14,944	92008
Carmichael	37,625	95608
Carpinteria	6,982	93013
Carson	71,150	90745
Castro Valley	44,760	94546
Cerritos	15,856	90701
Cherryland	9,969	94521
Chico	19,580	95926
China Lake	11,105	93555
Chino	20,411	91710
Chula Vista	67,901	92010*
Citrus Heights	21,760	95610
Claremont	23,464	91711
Clovis	13,856	93612
Coachella	8,353	92236
Colton	20,016	92324
Commerce	10,536	90040
Compton	78,547	90220*
Concord	85,164	94520*
Corona	27,519	91720
Coronado	20,020	92118
Corte Madera	8,464	94925
Costa Mesa	72,660	92626*
Covina	30,395	91722*
Cudahy	16,998	90201
Culver City	34,451	90230
Cupertino	18,216	95014
Cypress	31,569	90630
Daly City	66,922	94015*
Davis	23,488	95616
Del Aire	11,930	90250
Delano	14,559	93215
Diamond Bar	10,576	91766
Dinuba	7,917	93618
Downey	88,442	90241*
Duarte	14,981	91010
Dublin	13,641	94566
East La Mirada	12,339	90638
East Los Angeles	105,033	90022
East Palo Alto	18,099	94303
El Cajon	52,273	92020*
El Centro	19,272	92243
El Cerrito	25,190	94530
El Encanto Hts.	6,225	93017
El Monte	69,892	91734*
El Segundo	15,620	90245
El Toro	8,654	92630
Enterprise	11,486	96001
Escondido	36,792	92025*
Eureka	24,337	95501
Fairfax	7,661	94930
Fairfield	44,146	94533
Fair Oaks	11,256	95628
Fallbrook	6,945	92028
Fillmore	6,285	93015
Florence-Graham	42,900	90001
Florin	9,646	95828
Fontana	20,673	92335
Foster City	9,522	94404
Fountain Valley	31,886	92708
Fremont	100,869	94538*
Fresno	165,972	93706*
Fullerton	85,987	92631*
Gardena	41,021	90247*

† 1980 Census population figures for selected cities will be found on pages 182 and 183.
* General Delivery—for all towns so marked there is more than one zip code.

LOCATION	POPULATION	ZIP
Garden Acres ..	7,870	95205
Garden Grove ..	121,357	92640*
Gilroy	12,665	95020
Glendale	132,664	91209*
Glendora	31,380	91740
Grossmont-Mt. Helix	8,723	92041
Hacienda Heights	35,969	91745
Hanford	15,179	93230
Hawaiian Gardens	9,052	90716
Hawthorne	53,304	90250
Hayward	93,058	94544*
Hemet	12,252	92343
Hermosa Beach	17,412	90254
Highland	12,669	92346
Hillsborough ..	8,753	94010
Hollister	7,663	95023
Huntington Bch.	115,960	92647*
Huntington Park	33,744	90255
Imperial Beach	20,244	92032
Indio	14,459	92201
Inglewood	89,985	90306*
Irvine	20,157	92713
Isla Vista	13,441	93017
La Canada-Flintridge ..	20,714	91011
La Crescenta-Montrose ...	19,620	91214
Ladera Heights .	6,535	90045
Lafayette	20,484	94549
Laguna Beach .	14,550	92652*
Laguna Hills ..	13,676	92653
La Habra	41,350	90631
Lakeside	11,991	92040
Lakewood	83,025	90714*
La Mesa	39,178	92041
La Mirada	30,808	90638
Lamont	7,007	93241
Lancaster	32,728	93534
La Palma	9,687	90620
La Puente	31,092	91747*
Larkspur	10,487	94939
La Verne	12,965	91750
Lawndale	24,825	90260
Lemon Grove ..	19,690	92045
Lennox	16,121	90304
Linda	7,731	95901
Live Oak	6,443	95073
Livermore	37,703	94550
Lodi	28,691	95240
Loma Linda ...	6,599	92354
Lomita	19,784	90717
Lompoc	25,284	93436
Long Beach ...	358,879	90801*
Los Alamitos ..	11,346	90720
Los Altos	24,726	94022
Los Altos Hills .	6,865	94022
Los Angeles ...	2,809,813	90053*
Los Banos	9,188	93635
Los Gatos	23,735	95030
Lynwood	43,354	90262
Madera	16,044	93637
Manhattan Beach	35,352	90266
Manteca	13,845	95336
Marina	8,343	93933
Martinez	16,506	94553
Marysville ...	9,353	95901
Maywood	16,996	90270
Menlo Park	26,826	94025
Merced	22,670	95340
Millbrae	20,792	94030
Mill Valley	12,942	94941
Milpitas	27,149	95035
Mira Loma	8,482	91752
Mission Viejo ...	11,933	92691
Modesto	61,712	95350*
Monrovia	30,562	91016
Montclair	22,546	91763
Montebello	42,807	90640
Monterey	26,302	93940
Monterey Park .	49,166	91754
Moraga	14,205	94556
Morgan Hill ...	6,485	95037
Morro Bay ...	7,109	93442
Mountain View.	54,304	94042*
Muscoy	7,091	92405
Napa	35,978	94558
National City ..	43,184	92050
Newark	27,153	94560
Newhall	9,651	91321
Newport Beach .	49,422	92660*
Norco	14,511	91760

LOCATION	POPULATION	ZIP
North Fair Oaks	9,740	94025
North Highlands	31,854	95660
Norwalk	91,827	90650
Novato	31,006	94947
Oakdale	6,594	95361
Oakland	361,561	94617*
Oceanside	40,494	92054
Oildale	20,879	93308
Olivehurst	8,100	95961
Ontario	64,118	91761*
Orange	77,365	92667*
Orangevale	16,493	95662
Orcutt	8,500	93454
Orinda	6,790	94563
Oroville	7,536	95965
Otay-Castle Park	15,445	92010
Oxnard	71,225	93030
Pacifica	36,020	94044
Pacific Grove ..	13,505	93950
Palmdale	8,511	93550
Palm Springs ..	20,936	92262
Palo Alto	55,835	94302*
Palos Verdes Estates	13,631	90274
Palos Verdes Pen.	38,914	90274
Paradise	14,539	95969
Paramount	34,734	90723
Pasadena	112,951	91109*
Paso Robles ...	7,168	93446
Petaluma	24,870	94952
Pico Rivera	54,170	90660
Piedmont	10,917	94611
Pinole	13,266	94564
Pittsburg	20,651	94565
Placentia	21,948	92670
Pleasant Hill ..	24,610	94523
Pleasanton	18,328	94566
Pomona	87,384	91766*
Porterville	12,602	93257
Port Hueneme .	14,295	93041
Poway	9,422	92064
Rancho Cordova	30,451	95670
Red Bluff	7,676	96080
Redding	16,659	96001
Redlands	36,355	92373
Redondo Beach.	57,451	90277*
Redwood City ..	55,686	94063*
Reedley	8,131	93654
Rialto	28,370	92376
Richmond	79,043	94802*
Ridgecrest	7,629	93555
Rio Linda	7,524	95673
Riverside	140,089	92502*
Rolling Hills Estates	6,735	90274
Rosemead	40,972	91770
Roseville	18,221	95678
Rossmoor	12,922	90720
Rowland Heights	16,881	91748
Rubidoux	13,969	92509
Sacramento ...	257,105	95814*
Salinas	58,896	93901*
San Anselmo ..	13,031	94960
San Bernardino	106,869	92403*
San Bruno	36,254	94066
San Carlos ...	26,053	94070
San Clemente ..	17,063	92672
San Diego	697,027	92101*
San Dimas	15,692	91773
San Fernando ..	16,571	91340*
San Francisco .	715,674	94101*
San Gabriel ...	29,336	91776*
Sanger	10,088	93657
San Jose	445,779	95113*
San Leandro ...	68,698	94577*
San Lorenzo ...	24,633	94580
San Luis Obispo	28,036	93401
San Marino ...	14,177	91108
San Mateo	78,991	94402*
San Pablo	21,461	94806
San Rafael ...	38,977	94902*
Santa Ana	155,762	92711*
Santa Barbara .	70,215	93102*
Santa Clara ...	87,717	95050*
Santa Cruz ...	32,076	95060*
Santa Fe Springs	14,750	90670
Santa Maria ..	32,749	93454
Santa Monica ..	88,289	90406*
Santa Paula ...	18,001	93060
Santa Rosa ...	50,006	95402*
Santee	21,107	92071

LOCATION	POPULATION	ZIP
Saratoga	27,110	95070
Seal Beach	24,441	90740
Seaside	35,935	93955
Selma	7,459	93662
Sierra Madre ..	12,140	91024
Simi Valley ...	59,832	93065*
South El Monte	13,443	91733
South Gate	56,909	90280
South Lake Tahoe	12,921	95705
South Modesto .	7,889	95350
South Pasadena	22,979	91030
South Sacramento	28,574	95823
South San Francisco ...	46,646	94080
South San Jose Hills	12,386	91744
South Whittier .	46,641	90605
Spring Valley ..	29,742	92077*
Stanford	8,691	94305
Stanton	18,186	90680
Stockton	109,963	95202*
Sunnymead	6,708	92388
Sunnyvale	95,408	94088*
Susanville	6,608	96130
Temple City ...	31,034	91780
Thousand Oaks	35,873	91360*
Tiburon	6,209	94920
Torrance	134,968	90510*
Tracy	14,724	95376
Tulare	16,235	93274
Turlock	13,992	95380
Tustin	21,180	92680
Tustin-Foothills	26,598	92705
Ukiah	10,095	95482
Union City	14,724	94587
Upland	32,551	91786
Vacaville	21,690	95688
Vallejo	71,710	94590
Ventura (San Buenaventura)	57,964	93001*
Victorville	10,845	92392
View Park—Windsor Hills	12,268	90043
Visalia	27,268	93277
Vista	24,688	92083
Walnut Creek ..	39,844	94596*
Walnut Park ...	8,925	90255
Wasco	8,269	93280
Watsonville ...	14,569	95076
West Athens ...	13,311	90044
West Carson ...	15,918	90745
West Covina ...	68,034	91793*
West Hollywood	34,622	90069
Westminster ...	59,874	92683
Westmont	29,310	90047
West Puente Val.	20,733	91746
West Sacramento	12,002	95691
West Whittier..	20,845	90606
Whittier	72,863	90605*
Willow Brook ..	32,328	90222
Woodland	20,677	95695
Yorba Linda ...	11,856	92686
Yuba City	13,986	95991
Yucaipa	19,284	92399

COLORADO

LOCATION	POPULATION	ZIP
Alamosa	6,985	81101
Applewood	8,214	80215
Arvada	49,083	80001*
Aurora	74,974	80010*
Boulder	66,870	80302*
Brighton	8,309	80601
Broomfield	7,261	80020
Canon City ...	9,206	81212
Colorado Springs	135,060	80901*
Commerce City	17,407	80022
Denver	514,678	80201*
Derby	10,206	80022
Durango	10,333	81301
Englewood	33,695	80110*
Fort Collins ...	43,337	80521
Fort Morgan ...	7,594	80701
Golden	9,817	80401
Grand Junction .	20,170	81501
Greeley	38,902	80631
La Junta	7,938	81050
Lakewood	92,743	80215
Lamar	7,797	81052
Littleton	26,466	80120*
Longmont	23,209	80501

LOCATION	POPULATION	ZIP
Loveland	16,220	80537
Montrose	6,496	81401
North Glenn	27,937	80233
Pueblo	97,453	81002*
Security-Widefield	15,297	80911
Sherrelwood	18,868	80221
Sterling	10,636	80751
Stratton Meadows	6,223	80906
Thornton	13,326	80229
Trinidad	9,901	81082
Welby	6,875	80229
Westminster	19,432	80030
Wheat Ridge	29,778	80033

CONNECTICUT

LOCATION	POPULATION	ZIP
Ansonia	21,160	06401
Avon	8,352	06001
Berlin	14,149	06037
Bethel	10,945	06801
Bloomfield	18,301	06002
Branford	20,444	06405
Bridgeport	156,542	06601*
Bristol	55,487	06010
Brookfield	9,688	06804
Canton	6,868	06019
Cheshire	19,051	06410
Clinton	10,267	06413
Colchester	6,603	06415
Conning Towers—Nautilus Park	9,791	06340
Coventry	8,140	06238
Cromwell	7,400	06416
Danbury	50,781	06810
Darien	20,336	06820
Derby	12,599	06418
East Hampton	7,078	06424
East Hartford	57,583	06108
East Haven	25,120	06512
East Lyme	11,399	06333
East Windsor	8,513	06088
Ellington	7,707	06029
Enfield	46,189	06082
Fairfield	56,487	06430
Farmington	14,390	06032
Glastonbury	20,651	06033
Granby	6,150	06035
Greenwich	59,755	06830
Griswold	7,763	06351
Groton	38,244	06340
Guilford	12,033	06437
Hamden	49,357	06514
Hartford	158,017	06101*
Killingly	13,573	06241
Ledyard	14,837	06339
Litchfield	7,399	06759
Madison	9,768	06443
Manchester	47,994	06040
Mansfield	19,994	06250
Meriden	55,959	06450
Middletown	36,924	06457
Milford	50,858	06460
Monroe	12,047	06468
Montville	15,662	06353
Naugatuck	23,034	06770
New Britain	83,441	06050*
New Canaan	17,451	06840
New Fairfield	6,991	06810
New Haven	137,707	06510*
Newington	26,037	06111
New London	31,630	06320
New Milford	14,601	06776
Newtown	16,942	06470
North Branford	10,778	06471
North Haven	22,194	06473
Norwalk	79,288	06856*
Norwich	41,739	06360
Old Saybrook	8,468	06475
Orange	13,524	06477
Plainfield	11,957	06374
Plainville	16,733	06062
Plymouth	10,321	06782
Portland	8,812	06480
Prospect	6,543	06712
Putnam	8,598	06260
Ridgefield	18,188	06877
Rocky Hill	11,103	06067
Seymour	12,776	06483
Shelton	27,165	06484
Simsbury	17,475	06070
Somers	6,893	06071
Southbury	7,852	06488
Southington	30,946	06489
South Windsor	15,553	06074
Stafford	8,680	06075
Stamford	108,798	06904*
Stonington	15,940	06378
Stratford	49,775	06497
Suffield	8,634	06078
Thomaston	6,233	06787
Thompson	7,580	06277
Tolland	7,857	06084
Torrington	31,952	06790
Trumbull	31,394	06611
Vernon	27,237	06066
Wallingford	35,714	06492
Waterbury	108,033	06720*
Waterford	17,227	06385
Watertown	18,610	06795
West Hartford	68,031	06107
West Haven	52,851	06516
Weston	7,417	06880
Westport	27,318	06880
Wethersfield	26,662	06109
Willimantic	14,402	06226
Wilton	13,572	06897
Winchester	11,106	06094
Windham	19,626	06280
Windsor	22,502	06095
Windsor Locks	15,080	06096
Winsted	8,954	06098
Wolcott	12,495	06716
Woodbridge	7,673	06515

DELAWARE

LOCATION	POPULATION	ZIP
Brookside Park	7,856	19713
Claymont	6,584	19703
Dover	17,488	19901
Elsmere	8,415	19804
Newark	21,298	19702*
Wilmington	80,386	19899*
Wilmington Manor	10,134	19720

DISTRICT OF COLUMBIA

LOCATION	POPULATION	ZIP
Washington	756,510	20013*

FLORIDA

LOCATION	POPULATION	ZIP
Atlantic Beach	7,106	32233
Avon Park	6,712	33825
Azalea Park	7,367	32807
Bartow	12,891	33830
Bayshore Gardens	9,255	33507
Belle Glade	15,949	33430
Boca Raton	29,538	33432*
Boynton Beach	18,115	33435*
Bradenton	21,040	33506*
Brandon	12,749	33511
Browardale	17,444	33311
Browns Village	23,442	33142
Cape Coral	11,470	33904
Carol City	27,361	33055
Casselberry	9,438	32707
Cedar Hammock	10,820	33505
Chattahoochee	7,944	32324
Clearwater	52,074	33515*
Cocoa	16,110	32922
Cocoa Beach	9,952	32931
Collier Manor	7,202	33064
Conway	8,642	32809
Coral Gables	42,494	33134
Crestview	7,952	32536
Cutler Ridge	17,441	33157
Dania	9,013	33004
Daytona Beach	45,327	32015*
Deerfield Beach	16,662	33441
De Land	11,641	32720
Delray Beach	19,915	33444*
Dunedin	17,639	33528
Egypt Lake	7,556	33614
Eustis	6,722	32726
Fernandina Beach	6,955	32034
Fort Lauderdale	139,590	33310*
Fort Myers	27,351	33902*
Fort Pierce	29,721	33450*
Fort Walton Beach	19,994	32548
Gainesville	64,510	32601*
Goulds	6,690	33170
Gulfport	9,976	33737
Haines City	8,956	33844
Hallandale	23,849	33009
Hialeah	102,452	33010*
Holly Hill	8,191	32017
Hollywood	106,873	33022*
Homestead	13,674	33030*
Jacksonville	528,865	32201*
Jacksonville Bch.	13,326	32250
Kendall	35,497	33156
Key West	29,312	33040
Kissimmee	7,119	32741
Lake City	10,575	32055
Lake Holloway	6,227	33801
Lakeland	41,550	33802*
Lake Magdalene	9,266	33612
Lake Park	6,993	33403
Lake Wales	8,240	33853
Lake Worth	23,714	33460*
Lantana	7,126	33462
Largo	22,031	33540*
Lauderdale Lakes	10,577	33313
Lauderhill	8,465	33313
Leesburg	11,869	32748
Leto	8,458	33614
Lighthouse Point	9,071	33064
Live Oak	6,830	32060
Maitland	7,157	32751
Margate	8,867	33063
Marianna	6,741	32446
Melbourne	40,236	32901*
Merritt Island	29,233	32952
Miami	334,859	33101*
Miami Beach	87,072	33139
Miami Shores	9,425	33153
Miami Springs	13,279	33166
Mims	8,309	32754
Miramar	24,906	33023
Myrtle Grove	16,186	32506
Naples	12,042	33940*
New Smyrna Bch.	10,580	32069
North Andrews Terrace	7,082	33308
North Fort Myers	8,798	33903
North Miami	34,767	33161
North Miami Bch.	30,544	33160
North Palm Bch.	9,035	33403
Norwood	14,973	33169
Oakland Park	16,261	33334
Ocala	22,583	32670*
Opa-Locka	11,902	33054
Orange Park	7,619	32073
Orlando	99,006	32802*
Ormond Beach	14,063	32074
Palatka	9,444	32077
Palm Bay	7,176	32905
Palm Beach	9,086	33480
Palmetto	7,422	33561
Palm River—Clair Mel	8,536	33619
Panama City	32,096	32401*
Pembroke Pines	15,496	33024
Pensacola	59,507	32502*
Perrine	10,257	33157
Perry	7,701	32347
Pine Hills	13,882	32808
Pinellas Park	22,287	33565
Plantation	23,523	33317
Plant City	15,451	33566
Pompano Beach	38,587	33060*
Port Charlotte	10,769	33952
Quincy	8,334	32351
Richmond Heights	6,663	33156
Riviera Beach	21,401	33404
Rockledge	10,523	32955
St. Augustine	12,352	32084
St. Petersburg	216,159	33733*
St. Petersburg Bch.	8,024	33736
Sanford	17,393	32771
Sarasota	40,237	33578*
Satellite Beach	6,558	32901
Sebring	7,223	33870
South Miami	11,780	33143
South Miami Hts.	10,395	33157
South Patrick Shores	10,313	32901
Sunrise Golf Vill.	7,403	33313
Sweetwater Creek	19,453	33614
Tallahassee	72,624	32301*
Tampa	277,753	33602*
Tarpon Springs	7,118	33589*
Temple Terrace	7,347	33617
Tice	7,254	33905
Titusville	30,515	32780

LOCATION	POPULATION	ZIP
University	10,039	33620
Valparaiso	6,504	32580
Venice	6,648	33595*
Vero Beach	11,908	32960
Warrington	15,848	32507
West Palm Beach	57,375	33401*
West Pensacola	20,924	32502
West Winter Haven	7,716	33880
Westwood Lakes	12,811	33165
Wilton Manors	10,948	33305
Winter Haven	16,136	33880
Winter Park	21,895	32789*
GEORGIA		
Albany	72,623	31706*
Americus	16,091	31709
Athens	44,342	30601*
Atlanta	497,421	30301*
Augusta	59,864	30903*
Bainbridge	10,887	31717
Brunswick	19,585	31520
Cairo	8,061	31728
Carrollton	13,520	30117
Cartersville	10,138	30120
Cedartown	9,253	30125
Chamblee	9,127	30341
College Park	18,203	30337
Columbus	167,377	31902*
Cordele	10,733	31015
Covington	10,267	30209
Dalton	18,872	30720
Decatur	21,943	30030*
Doraville	9,157	30340
Douglas	10,195	31533
Dublin	15,143	31021
East Point	39,315	30344
Elberton	6,438	30635
Fitzgerald	8,187	31750
Forest Park	19,994	30050
Fort Valley	9,251	31030
Gainesville	15,459	30501
Griffin	22,734	30223
Hapeville	9,567	30354
Hardwick	14,047	31034
Jesup	9,091	31545
La Grange	23,301	30240
Macon	122,423	31201*
Marietta	27,216	30060*
Milledgeville	11,601	31061
Monroe	8,071	30655
Moultrie	14,400	31768
Newnan	11,205	30263*
Perry	7,771	31069
Rome	30,759	30161
Savannah	118,349	31402*
Smyrna	19,157	30080
Statesboro	14,616	30458
Swainsboro	7,325	30401
Thomaston	10,024	30286
Thomasville	18,155	31792
Thomson	6,503	30824
Tifton	12,179	31794
Toccoa	6,971	30577
Valdosta	32,303	31601
Vidalia	9,507	30474
Warner Robins	33,491	31093
Waycross	18,996	31501
Winder	6,605	30680
Windsor Forest	7,288	31406
GUAM		
Tamuning	8,230	96911
HAWAII		
Aiea	12,560	96701
Ewa Beach	7,765	96706
Hickam Housing	7,352	96824
Hilo	26,353	96720
Honolulu	324,871	96819*
Kahului	8,280	96732
Kailua	33,783	96734
Kaneohe	29,903	96744
Mokapu	7,860	96734
Nanakuli	6,506	96792
Pacific Palisades	7,846	96782
Pearl City	19,552	96782
Schofield Barracks	13,516	96786
Wahiawa	17,598	96786
Wailuku	7,979	96793
Waipahu	24,150	96797

LOCATION	POPULATION	ZIP
IDAHO		
Blackfoot	8,716	83221
Boise	74,990	83701*
Burley	8,279	83318
Caldwell	14,219	83605
Coeur d'Alene	16,228	83814
Idaho Falls	35,776	83401
Lewiston	26,068	83501
Moscow	14,146	83843
Mountain Home	6,451	83647
Nampa	20,768	83651
Pocatello	40,036	83201
Rexburg	8,272	83440
Twin Falls	21,914	83301
ILLINOIS		
Addison	24,482	60101
Alsip	11,983	60658
Alton	39,700	62002
Arlington Hts.	64,884	60004*
Aurora	74,182	60507*
Barrington	8,674	60010
Bartonville	7,221	61607
Batavia	8,994	60510
Beardstown	6,222	62618
Belleville	41,699	62220*
Bellwood	22,096	60104
Belvidere	14,061	61008
Bensenville	13,396	60106
Benton	6,833	62812
Berwyn	52,502	60402
Bethalto	7,074	62010
Bloomington	39,992	61701
Blue Island	22,958	60406
Bolingbrook	8,504	60439
Bradley	9,881	60915
Bridgeview	12,522	60455
Broadview	9,623	60153
Brookfield	20,284	60513
Buffalo Grove	11,799	60090
Burbank	29,854	60459
Cahokia	20,649	62206
Calumet City	33,107	60409
Calumet Park	10,069	60643
Canton	14,217	61520
Carbondale	26,857	62901
Carpentersville	24,059	60110
Centralia	15,217	62801
Centreville	11,378	62206
Champaign	56,837	61820
Charleston	16,421	61920
Chicago	3,369,357	60607*
Chicago Heights	40,900	60411
Chicago Ridge	9,187	60415
Cicero	67,058	60650
Clarendon Hills	6,750	60514
Clinton	7,570	61727
Collinsville	19,567	62234
Country Club Hills	6,920	60477
Crest Hill	7,460	60431
Creve Coeur	6,440	61611
Crystal Lake	14,541	60014
Danville	42,570	61832
Darien	7,789	60559
Decatur	90,397	62521*
Deerfield	18,876	60015
De Kalb	32,949	60115
Des Plaines	57,239	60016*
Dixon	18,147	61021
Dolton	25,990	60419
Downers Grove	33,588	60515
Du Quoin	6,691	62832
East Alton	7,309	62024
East Moline	20,832	61244
East Peoria	20,226	61611
East St. Louis	69,996	62201*
Edwardsville	11,070	62025
Effingham	9,458	62401
Elgin	55,691	60120
Elk Grove Village	20,346	60007
Elmhurst	48,887	60126
Elmwood Park	26,160	60635
Evanston	80,113	60204*
Evergreen Park	25,921	60642
Fairview Heights	12,577	62232
Flossmoor	8,328	60422
Forest Park	15,472	60130
Franklin Park	20,348	60131
Freeport	27,736	61032
Galesburg	36,290	61401

LOCATION	POPULATION	ZIP
Geneva	9,115	60134
Glencoe	10,675	60022
Glendale Heights	11,406	60108
Glen Ellyn	21,909	60137
Glenview	29,159	60025
Glenwood	7,416	60425
Granite City	40,685	62040
Hanover Park	11,916	60103
Harrisburg	9,535	62946
Harvey	34,636	60426
Harwood Heights	9,060	60656
Hazel Crest	10,329	60429
Herrin	9,623	62948
Hickory Hills	13,176	60457
Highland Park	32,263	60035
Hillside	8,888	60162
Hinsdale	15,918	60521
Hoffman Estates	22,238	60195
Hometown	6,729	60456
Homewood	18,871	60430
Hoopeston	6,461	60942
Jacksonville	20,553	62650
Jerseyville	7,446	62052
Joliet	78,887	60431*
Justice	9,473	60458
Kankakee	30,944	60901
Kewanee	15,762	61443
La Grange	17,814	60525
La Grange Highlands	6,842	60525
La Grange Park	15,459	60525
Lake Forest	15,642	60045
Lansing	25,805	60438
La Salle	10,620	61301
Libertyville	11,684	60048
Lincoln	17,582	62656
Lincolnwood	12,929	60645
Litchfield	7,190	62056
Lockport	9,985	60441
Lombard	34,043	60148
Loves Park	12,390	61111
Lyons	11,124	60534
Macomb	19,643	61455
Madison	7,042	62060
Marion	11,724	62959
Markham	16,117	60426
Mattoon	19,681	61938
Maywood	29,019	60153
McHenry	6,772	60050
Melrose Park	22,716	60160*
Mendota	6,902	61342
Metropolis	6,940	62960
Midlothian	15,939	60445
Moline	46,237	61265
Monmouth	11,022	61462
Morris	8,194	60450
Morton	10,419	61550
Morton Grove	26,369	60053
Mount Carmel	8,096	62863
Mount Prospect	45,228	60056
Mount Vernon	16,382	62864
Mundelein	16,128	60060
Murphysboro	10,013	62966
Naperville	22,617	60540
Niles	31,432	60648
Normal	26,396	61761
Norridge	17,113	60656
Northbrook	27,297	60062
North Chicago	47,275	60064
Northlake	14,212	60164
North Park	15,679	61111
North Riverside	8,097	60546
Oak Forest	17,870	60452
Oak Lawn	60,305	60454*
Oak Park	62,511	60303*
O'Fallon	9,365	62269
Olney	9,159	62450
Orland Park	6,391	60462
Ottawa	18,716	61350
Palatine	26,050	60067
Palos Heights	9,915	60463
Palos Hills	6,629	60465
Pana	6,326	62557
Paris	9,971	61944
Park Forest	30,864	60466
Park Ridge	42,614	60068
Pekin	31,375	61554
Peoria	126,963	61601*
Peoria Heights	7,943	61614
Peru	11,772	61354
Pontiac	10,595	61764

LOCATION	POPULATION	ZIP
Princeton	6,959	61356
Prospect Heights	13,333	60070
Quincy	45,288	62301
Rantoul	25,562	61866
Riverdale	15,806	60627
River Forest	13,402	60305
River Grove	11,465	60171
Riverside	10,432	60546
Robbins	9,641	60472
Robinson	7,178	62454
Rochelle	8,594	61068
Rock Falls	10,287	61071
Rockford	147,370	61125*
Rock Island	50,166	61201
Rolling Meadows	19,178	60008
Romeoville	12,674	60441
Roselle	6,207	60172*
St. Charles	12,945	60174
Sauk Village	7,479	60411
Schaumburg	18,730	60194
Schiller Park	12,712	60176
Skokie	68,322	60076*
South Holland	23,931	60473
South Stickney	29,900	60459
Springfield	91,753	62708*
Steger	8,104	60475
Sterling	16,113	61081
Stickney	6,601	60402
Streamwood	18,176	60103
Streator	15,600	61364
Summit	11,569	60501
Sycamore	7,843	60178
Taylorville	10,927	62568
Tinley Park	12,382	60477
Urbana	33,739	61801
Villa Park	25,891	60181
Washington	7,722	61571
Washington Park	9,524	62204
Waukegan	65,134	60085
Westchester	20,033	60153
West Chicago	10,111	60185
West End	7,554	61102
Western Springs	13,029	60558
West Frankfort	8,854	62896
Westmont	8,920	60559
West Peoria	6,873	61604
Wheaton	31,138	60187
Wheeling	14,746	60090
Wilmette	32,134	60091
Winnetka	13,998	60093
Wood Dale	8,831	60191
Woodridge	11,028	60515
Wood River	13,186	62095
Woodstock	10,226	60098
Worth	11,999	60482
Zion	17,268	60099

INDIANA

LOCATION	POPULATION	ZIP
Anderson	70,787	46011*
Auburn	7,388	46706
Bedford	13,087	47421
Beech Grove	13,559	46107
Black Oak	9,624	46406
Bloomington	43,262	47401
Bluffton	8,297	46714
Brazil	8,163	47834
Carmel	6,568	46032
Cedar Lake	7,589	46303
Clarksville	13,806	47130
Columbus	26,457	47201
Connersville	17,604	47331
Crawfordsville	13,842	47933
Crown Point	10,931	46307
Decatur	8,445	46733
East Chicago	46,982	46312
East Gary	9,858	46405
Elkhart	43,152	46514
Elwood	11,196	46036
Evansville	138,764	47708*
Fort Wayne	178,021	46802*
Frankfort	14,956	46041
Franklin	11,477	46131
Gary	175,415	46401*
Goshen	17,871	46526
Greencastle	8,852	46135
Greenfield	9,986	46140
Greensburg	8,620	47240
Greenwood	11,408	46142
Griffith	18,168	46319
Hammond	107,885	46320*
Hartford City	8,207	47348

LOCATION	POPULATION	ZIP
Highland	24,947	46322
Hobart	21,485	46342
Huntington	16,217	46750
Indianapolis	746,302	46204*
Jasper	8,641	47546
Jeffersonville	20,008	47130
Kendallville	6,838	46755
Kokomo	44,042	46901
Lafayette	44,955	47902*
LaPorte	22,140	46350
Lawrence	16,917	46226
Lebanon	9,766	46052
Logansport	19,255	46947
Madison	13,081	47250
Marion	39,607	46952
Martinsville	9,723	46151
Merrillville	24,075	46410
Michigan City	39,369	46360
Mishawaka	35,517	46544
Mount Vernon	6,770	47620
Muncie	69,082	47302*
Munster	16,514	46321
New Albany	38,402	47150
New Castle	21,215	47362
Noblesville	7,548	46060
Peru	14,139	46970
Plainfield	8,211	46168
Plymouth	7,661	46563
Portage	19,127	46368
Portland	7,115	47371
Princeton	7,431	47670
Richmond	43,999	47374
Rushville	6,686	46173
Seymour	13,352	47274
Shelbyville	15,094	46176
South Bend	125,580	46624*
Speedway	14,649	46224
Tell City	7,933	47586
Terre Haute	70,335	47808*
Valparaiso	20,020	46383
Vincennes	19,867	47591
Wabash	13,379	46992
Warsaw	7,506	46580
Washington	11,358	47501
West Lafayette	19,157	47906
Whiting	7,152	46394

IOWA

LOCATION	POPULATION	ZIP
Ames	39,505	50010
Ankeny	9,151	50021
Atlantic	7,306	50022
Bettendorf	22,126	52722
Boone	12,468	50036
Burlington	32,366	52601
Carroll	8,716	51401
Cedar Falls	29,597	50613
Cedar Rapids	110,642	52401*
Centerville	6,531	52544
Charles City	9,268	50616
Cherokee	7,272	51012
Clear Lake	6,430	50428
Clinton	34,719	52732
Council Bluffs	60,348	51501
Creston	8,234	50801
Davenport	98,469	52802*
Decorah	7,458	52101
Denison	6,218	51442
Des Moines	201,404	50318*
Dubuque	62,309	52001
Estherville	8,108	51334
Fairfield	8,715	52556
Fort Dodge	31,263	50501
Fort Madison	13,996	52627
Grinnell	8,402	50112
Indianola	8,852	50125
Iowa City	46,850	52240
Iowa Falls	6,454	50126
Keokuk	14,631	52632
Knoxville	7,755	50138
Le Mars	8,159	51031
Marion	18,028	52302
Marshalltown	26,219	50158
Mason City	30,379	50401
Mount Pleasant	7,007	52641
Muscatine	22,405	52761
Newton	15,619	50208
Oelwein	7,735	50662
Oskaloosa	11,224	52577
Ottumwa	29,610	52501
Pella	6,668	50219

LOCATION	POPULATION	ZIP
Perry	6,906	50220
Red Oak	6,210	51566
Sioux City	85,925	51101*
Spencer	10,278	51301
Storm Lake	8,591	50588
Urbandale	14,434	50322
Waterloo	75,533	50701*
Waverly	7,205	50677
Webster City	8,488	50595
West Des Moines	16,441	50265
Windsor Heights	6,303	50311

KANSAS

LOCATION	POPULATION	ZIP
Abilene	6,661	67410
Arkansas City	13,216	67005
Atchison	12,565	66002
Chanute	10,341	66720
Coffeyville	15,116	67337
Concordia	7,221	66901
Derby	7,947	67037
Dodge City	14,127	67801
El Dorado	12,308	67042
Emporia	23,327	66801
Fort Leavenworth	8,060	66027
Fort Scott	8,967	66701
Garden City	14,790	67846
Great Bend	16,133	67530
Hays	15,396	67601
Haysville	6,483	67060
Hutchinson	36,885	67501
Independence	10,347	67301
Iola	6,493	66749
Junction City	19,018	66441
Kansas City	168,213	66110*
Lawrence	45,698	66044
Leavenworth	25,147	66048
Leawood	10,349	66206
Liberal	13,789	67901
Manhattan	27,575	66502
McPherson	10,851	67460
Merriam	10,851	66203
Mission	8,376	66205
Newton	15,439	67114
Olathe	17,917	66061
Ottawa	11,036	66067
Overland Park	79,034	66204
Parsons	13,015	67357
Pittsburg	20,171	66762
Prairie Village	28,138	66208
Pratt	6,736	67124
Roeland Park	9,974	66205
Salina	37,714	67401
Shawnee	20,482	66202*
Topeka	125,011	66601*
Wellington	8,072	67152
Wichita	276,554	67202*
Winfield	11,405	67156

KENTUCKY

LOCATION	POPULATION	ZIP
Ashland	29,245	41101
Bellevue	8,847	41073
Berea	6,956	40403
Bowling Green	36,705	42101
Campbellsville	7,598	42718
Corbin	7,317	40701
Covington	52,535	41011*
Cynthiana	6,356	41031
Danville	11,542	40422
Dayton	8,751	41074
Elizabethtown	11,748	42701
Erlanger	12,676	41018
Flatwoods	7,380	41139
Florence	11,661	41042
Fort Knox	37,608	40121
Fort Mitchell	6,982	41017
Fort Thomas	16,338	41075
Frankfort	21,902	40601
Franklin	6,553	42134
Georgetown	8,629	40324
Glasgow	11,301	42141
Harrodsburg	6,741	40330
Henderson	22,976	42420
Hopkinsville	21,250	42240
Jeffersontown	9,701	40299
Lexington	108,137	40507*
Louisville	361,706	40202*
Madisonville	15,332	42431
Mayfield	10,724	42066
Maysville	7,411	41056
Middlesborough	11,878	40965

LOCATION	POPULATION	ZIP
Morehead	7,191	40351
Murray	13,537	42071
Newport	25,998	41071*
Okolona	17,643	40219
Owensboro	50,329	42301
Paducah	31,627	42001
Paris	7,823	40361
Pleasure Ridge Pk.	28,566	40258
Princeton	6,292	42445
Radcliff	7,881	40160
Richmond	16,861	40475
Russellville	6,456	42276
St. Matthews	13,152	40207
Shively	19,139	40216
Somerset	10,436	42501
Valley Station	24,471	40272
Winchester	13,402	40391

LOUISIANA

LOCATION	POPULATION	ZIP
Abbeville	10,996	70510
Alexandria	41,557	71301
Baker	8,281	70714
Bastrop	14,713	71220
Baton Rouge	165,921	70821*
Bayou Cane	9,077	70360
Bogalusa	18,412	70427
Bossier City	41,595	71111*
Cooper Road	9,034	71107
Covington	7,170	70433
Crowley	16,104	70526
Denham Springs	6,752	70726
De Ridder	8,030	70634
Donaldsonville	7,367	70346
Eunice	11,390	70535
Franklin	9,325	70538
Gretna	24,875	70053
Hammond	12,487	70401
Harahan	13,037	70123
Harvey	6,347	70058
Houma	30,922	70360
Jeanerette	6,322	70544
Jefferson Heights	16,489	70121
Jennings	11,783	70546
Kenner	29,858	70062
Lafayette	68,908	70501*
Lake Charles	77,998	70601*
Leesville	8,928	71446
Little Farms	15,713	70123
Mansfield	6,432	71052
Marrero	29,015	70072
Metairie	136,477	70001*
Minden	13,996	71055
Monroe	56,374	71201*
Morgan City	16,586	70380
Natchitoches	15,974	71457
New Iberia	30,147	70560
New Orleans	593,471	70140*
Oakdale	7,301	71463
Opelousas	20,387	70570
Pineville	8,951	71360
Plaquemine	7,739	70764
Rayne	9,510	70578
Reserve	6,381	70084
Ruston	17,365	71270
St. Martinsville	7,153	70582
Scotlandville	22,599	70807
Shreveport	182,064	71102*
Slidell	16,101	70458
Springhill	6,496	71075
Sulphur	14,959	70663
Tallulah	9,643	71282
Terry Town	13,832	70053
Thibodaux	15,028	70301
Ville Platte	9,692	70586
West Monroe	14,868	71291
Westwego	11,402	70094
Winnfield	7,142	71483

MAINE

LOCATION	POPULATION	ZIP
Auburn	24,151	04210
Augusta	21,945	04330
Bangor	33,168	04401
Bath	9,679	04530
Biddeford	19,983	04005
Brewer	9,300	04412
Brunswick	16,195	04011
Cape Elizabeth	7,873	04107
Caribou	10,419	04736
Falmouth	6,291	04105
Gardiner	6,685	04345
Gorham	7,839	04038
Houlton	8,111	04730
Kittery	11,028	03904
Lewiston	41,779	04240
Limestone	10,360	04750
Lisbon	6,544	04250
Millinocket	7,742	04462
Old Town	9,057	04468
Orono	9,989	04473
Portland	65,116	04101*
Presque Isle	11,452	04769
Rockland	8,505	04841
Rumford	9,363	04276
Saco	11,678	04072
Sanford	15,812	04073
Scarborough	7,845	04074
Skowhegan	7,601	04976
South Portland	23,267	04106
Waterville	18,192	04901
Westbrook	14,444	04092
Windham	6,593	04082
Winslow	7,299	04901

MARYLAND

LOCATION	POPULATION	ZIP
Aberdeen	12,375	21001
Annapolis	30,095	21401*
Arbutus	22,745	21227
Aspen Hill	16,823	20906
Avenel-Hillandale	19,520	20903
Baltimore	905,787	21233*
Bel Aire	6,307	21014
Beltsville	8,912	20705
Bethesda	71,621	20014
Birchwood City	13,514	20021
Bladensburg	7,488	20710
Bowie	35,028	20715
Brooklyn	13,896	21225
Calverton	6,543	20705
Cambridge	11,595	21613
Camp Springs	22,776	20031
Carmody Hills	6,335	20028
Catonsville	54,812	21228
Cheverly	6,808	20785
Chevy Chase	16,424	20015
Chillum	35,656	20783
Colesville	9,455	20904
College Park	26,156	20740
Columbia	8,815	21045*
Coral Hills	9,058	20027
Cumberland	29,724	21502
Defense Heights	6,775	20710
District Heights	7,659	20028
Dundalk	85,377	21222
Easton	6,809	21601
Edgemere	10,352	21219
Edgewood	8,551	21040
Ellicott City	9,435	21043
Essex	38,193	21221
Ferndale	9,929	21061
Forestville	16,188	20028
Frederick	23,641	21701
Frostburg	7,327	21532
Gaithersburg	8,344	20760
Glen Burnie	38,608	21061
Good Luck	10,584	20715
Greenbelt	18,199	20770
Hagerstown	35,862	21740
Havre de Grace	9,791	21078
Hillcrest Heights	24,037	20031
Hyattsville	14,998	20781*
Joppatowne	9,092	21085
Kemp Mill	10,037	20902
Kentland	9,649	20785
Langley Park	11,564	20787
Lanham–Seabrook	13,244	20801
Lansdowne	17,770	21227
Laurel	10,525	20810*
Lexington Park	9,136	20653
Linthicum	9,775	21090
Lutherville	24,055	21093
Maryland City	7,102	20810
Middle River	19,935	21220
Mount Rainier	8,180	20822
New Carrollton	14,870	20784
North Potomac	12,784	20854
North Takoma Pk.	7,373	20012
Overlea	13,124	21201
Owings Mills	7,360	21117
Oxon Hill	11,974	20021
Palmer Park	8,172	20785
Parkville	33,589	21234
Pikesville	25,395	21208
Pumphrey	6,425	21090
Randallstown	33,683	21133
Randolph	13,215	20852
Reisterstown	12,568	21136
Riverside Hts.	8,941	20840
Riviera Beach	7,464	21061
Rockville	41,821	20850*
Rosedale	19,417	21237
Salisbury	15,252	21801
Seat Pleasant	7,217	20027
Severna Park	16,358	21146
Silver Spring	77,411	20907*
South Gate	9,356	21061
South Kensington	10,289	20795
South Laurel	13,345	20810
Suitland	30,355	20023
Takoma Park	18,507	20012
Towson	77,768	21204
Waldorf	7,368	20601
Walker Mill	7,103	20023
Westminster	7,207	21157
Wheaton	66,280	20902
White Oak	19,769	20904
Woodlawn	28,821	21207

MASSACHUSETTS

LOCATION	POPULATION	ZIP
Abington	12,334	02351
Acton	14,770	01720
Acushnet	7,767	02743
Adams	11,772	01220
Agawam	21,717	01001
Amesbury	11,388	01913
Amherst	26,331	01002
Andover	23,695	01810
Arlington	53,534	02174
Ashland	8,882	01721
Athol	11,185	01331
Attleboro	32,907	02703
Auburn	15,347	01501
Ayer	8,283	01432*
Barnstable	19,842	02630
Bedford	13,513	01730
Bellingham	13,967	02019
Belmont	28,285	02178
Beverly	38,348	01915
Billerica	31,648	01821
Blackstone	6,566	01504
Boston	641,071	02109*
Bourne	12,636	02532
Braintree	35,050	02184
Bridgewater	11,829	02324
Brockton	89,040	02403*
Brookline	58,689	02146
Burlington	21,980	01803
Cambridge	100,361	02138
Canton	17,100	02021
Chelmsford	31,432	01824
Chelsea	30,625	02150
Chicopee	66,676	01021*
Clinton	13,383	01510
Cohasset	6,954	02025
Concord	16,148	01742
Dalton	7,505	01226
Danvers	26,151	01923
Dartmouth	18,800	02714
Dedham	26,938	02026
Dennis	6,454	02638
Dracut	18,214	01826
Dudley	8,087	01570
Duxbury	7,636	02332
East Bridgewater	8,347	02333
Easthampton	13,012	01027
East Longmeadow	13,029	01028
Easton	12,157	02334
Everett	42,485	02149
Fairhaven	16,332	02719
Fall River	96,898	02722*
Falmouth	15,942	02540*
Fitchburg	43,343	01420
Foxboro	14,218	02035
Framingham	64,048	01701
Franklin	17,830	02038
Gardner	19,748	01440
Gloucester	27,941	01930
Grafton	11,659	01519
Great Barrington	7,537	01230
Greenfield	18,116	01301
Hamilton	6,373	01936
Hanover	10,107	02339
Hanson	7,148	02341

LOCATION	POPULATION	ZIP
Harvard	12,494	01451
Haverhill	46,120	01830
Hingham	18,845	02043
Holbrook	11,775	02343
Holden	12,564	01520
Holliston	12,069	01746
Holyoke	50,112	01040
Hudson	16,084	01749
Hull	9,961	02045
Hyannis	6,847	02601
Ipswich	10,750	01938
Lawrence	66,915	01842*
Lee	6,426	01238
Leicester	9,140	01524
Leominster	32,939	01453
Lexington	31,886	02173
Lincoln	7,567	01773
Littleton	6,380	01460
Longmeadow	15,630	01106
Lowell	94,239	01853*
Ludlow	17,580	01056
Lunenburg	7,419	01462
Lynn	90,294	01901*
Lynnfield	10,826	01940
Malden	56,127	02148
Mansfield	9,939	02048
Marblehead	21,295	01945
Marlborough	27,936	01752
Marshfield	15,223	02050
Maynard	9,710	01754
Medfield	9,821	02052
Medford	64,397	02155
Medway	7,938	02053
Melrose	33,180	02176
Methuen	35,456	01844
Middleboro	13,607	02346
Milford	19,352	01757
Millbury	11,987	01527
Milton	27,190	02186
Monson	7,355	01057
Montague	8,451	01351
Natick	31,057	01760
Needham	29,748	02192
New Bedford	101,777	02740*
Newburyport	15,807	01950
Newton	91,263	02158
North Adams	19,195	01247
Northampton	29,664	01060
North Andover	16,284	01845
North Attleboro	18,665	02760*
Northboro	9,218	01532
Northbridge	11,795	01534
North Reading	11,264	01864
Norton	9,487	02766
Norwell	7,796	02061
Norwood	30,815	02062
Oxford	10,345	01540
Palmer	11,680	01069
Peabody	48,080	01960
Pembroke	11,193	02359
Pittsfield	57,020	01201
Plymouth	18,606	02360
Quincy	87,966	02169
Randolph	27,035	02368
Raynham	6,705	02767
Reading	22,539	01867
Rehoboth	6,512	02769
Revere	43,159	02151
Rockland	15,674	02370
Salem	40,556	01970
Saugus	25,110	01906
Scituate	16,973	02066
Seekonk	11,116	02771
Sharon	12,367	02067
Shrewsbury	19,196	01545
Somerset	18,088	02725
Somerville	88,779	02143
Southbridge	17,057	01550
South Hadley	17,033	01075
Southwick	6,330	01077
Spencer	8,779	01562
Springfield	163,905	01101*
Stoneham	20,725	02180
Stoughton	23,459	02072
Sudbury	13,506	01776
Swampscott	13,578	01907
Swansea	12,640	02777
Taunton	43,756	02780
Tewksbury	22,755	01876
Uxbridge	8,253	01569
Wakefield	25,402	01880
Walpole	18,149	02081

LOCATION	POPULATION	ZIP
Waltham	61,582	02154
Ware	8,187	01082
Wareham	11,492	02571
Watertown	39,307	02172
Wayland	13,461	01778
Webster	14,917	01570
Wellesley	28,051	02181
Westboro	12,594	01581
West Bridgewater	7,152	02379
Westfield	31,433	01085
Westford	10,368	01886
Weston	10,870	02193
Westport	9,791	02790
West Springfield	28,461	01089
Westwood	12,750	02090
Weymouth	54,610	02188
Whitman	13,059	02382
Wilbraham	11,984	01095
Williamstown	8,454	01267
Wilmington	17,102	01887
Winchendon	6,635	01475
Winchester	22,269	01890
Winthrop	20,335	02152
Woburn	37,406	01801
Worcester	176,572	01613*
Wrentham	7,315	02093
Yarmouth	12,033	02675

MICHIGAN

LOCATION	POPULATION	ZIP
Adrian	20,382	49221
Albion	12,112	49224
Allen Park	40,747	48101
Alma	9,611	48801
Alpena	13,805	49707
Ann Arbor	99,797	48106*
Battle Creek	38,931	49016*
Bay City	49,449	48706
Benton Harbor	16,481	49022
Berkley	21,879	48072
Beverly Hills	13,598	48010
Big Rapids	11,995	49307
Birmingham	26,170	48012*
Cadillac	9,990	49601
Carrollton	7,300	48724
Center Line	10,379	48015
Charlotte	8,244	48813
Clawson	17,617	48017
Coldwater	9,155	49036
Cutlerville	6,267	49508
Dearborn	104,199	48120*
Dearborn Heights	80,069	48127
Detroit	1,513,601	48226*
Dowagiac	6,583	49047
Drayton Plains	16,462	48020
East Detroit	45,920	48021
East Grand Rapids	12,565	49506
East Lansing	47,540	48823
Eastwood	9,682	49001
Ecorse	17,515	48229
Escanaba	15,368	49829
Farmington	10,329	48018*
Farmington Hills	48,694	48024
Fenton	8,284	48430
Ferndale	30,850	48220
Flint	193,317	48502*
Flushing	7,190	48433
Fraser	11,868	48026
Garden City	41,864	48135
Grand Haven	11,844	49417
Grand Rapids	197,649	49501*
Grandville	10,764	49418
Greenville	7,493	48838
Grosse Ile	8,306	48138
Grosse Pointe	6,637	48236
Grosse Pte. Farms	11,701	48236
Grosse Pte. Pk.	15,641	48236
Grosse Pte. Woods	21,878	48236
Hamtramck	27,245	48212
Harper Woods	20,186	48225
Hastings	6,501	49058
Hazel Park	23,784	48030
Highland Park	35,444	48203
Hillsdale	7,728	49242
Holland	26,479	49423
Holt	6,980	48842
Huntington Woods	8,536	48070
Inkster	38,595	48141
Ionia	6,361	48846
Iron Mountain	8,702	49801
Ironwood	8,711	49938
Ishpeming	8,245	49849

LOCATION	POPULATION	ZIP
Jackson	45,484	49201*
Jenison	11,266	49428
Kalamazoo	85,555	49003*
Kentwood	20,310	49508
Lakeview	11,391	49015
Lansing	131,403	48924*
Lapeer	13,444	48446
Lincoln Park	52,984	48146
Livonia	110,109	48150*
Ludington	9,021	49431
Madison Heights	38,599	48071
Manistee	7,723	49660
Marquette	21,967	49855
Marshall	7,253	49068
Melvindale	13,862	48122
Menominee	10,748	49858
Midland	35,176	48640
Monroe	23,894	48161
Mount Clemens	20,476	48043*
Mount Pleasant	20,524	48858
Muskegon	44,631	49440*
Muskegon Heights	17,304	49444
Niles	12,988	49120
Norton Shores	22,271	49441
Novi	9,668	48050
Oak Park	36,762	48237
Okemos	7,770	48864
Owosso	17,179	48867
Petoskey	6,342	49770
Plymouth	11,758	48171*
Pontiac	85,279	48056*
Portage	33,590	49081
Port Huron	35,794	48060
River Rouge	15,947	48218
Riverview	11,342	48192
Rochester	7,054	48063
Romulus	22,879	48174
Roseville	60,529	48066
Royal Oak	86,238	48067*
Saginaw	91,849	48605*
St. Clair Shores	88,093	48083*
St. Johns	6,672	48879
St. Joseph	11,042	49085
Sault Ste. Marie	15,136	49783
Southfield	69,285	48034*
Southgate	33,909	48195
South Haven	6,471	49090
Sterling Heights	61,365	48077
Sturgis	9,295	49091
Taylor	70,020	48180
Tecumseh	7,120	49286
Three Rivers	7,355	49093
Traverse City	18,048	49684
Trenton	24,127	48183
Troy	39,419	48084*
Walker	11,492	49504
Warren	179,260	48089*
Wayne	21,054	48184
Westland	86,749	48185
Westwood	9,143	49007
Wurtsmith	6,932	48753
Wyandotte	41,061	48192
Wyoming	56,560	49509
Ypsilanti	29,538	48197

MINNESOTA

LOCATION	POPULATION	ZIP
Albert Lea	19,418	56007
Alexandria	6,973	56308
Anoka	13,295	55303
Apple Valley	8,502	55124
Austin	26,210	55912
Bemidji	11,490	56601
Blaine	20,625	55433
Bloomington	81,970	55420
Brainerd	11,667	56401
Brooklyn Center	35,173	55429
Brooklyn Park	26,230	55444
Burnsville	19,940	55378
Cloquet	8,699	55720
Columbia Heights	23,837	55421
Coon Rapids	30,505	55433
Cottage Grove	13,419	55016
Crookston	8,312	56716
Crystal	30,925	55428
Duluth	100,578	55806*
East Grand Forks	7,607	56721
Eden Prairie	6,938	55344
Edina	44,046	55424
Fairmont	10,751	56031

LOCATION	POPULATION	ZIP
Faribault	16,595	55021
Fergus Falls	12,443	56537
Fridley	29,233	55432
Golden Valley	24,246	55427
Grand Rapids	7,247	55744
Hastings	12,195	55033
Hibbing	16,104	55746
Hopkins	13,428	55343
Hutchinson	8,031	55350
Internat'l Falls	6,439	56649
Inver Grove Hts.	12,148	55075
Lakeville	7,556	55044
Little Falls	7,467	56345
Mankato	30,895	56001
Maple Grove	6,275	55369
Maplewood	25,222	55109
Marshall	9,886	56258
Minneapolis	434,400	55401*
Minnetonka	35,737	55343
Moorhead	29,687	56560
Mound	7,572	55364
Mounds View	10,641	55112
New Brighton	19,507	55112
New Hope	23,180	55428
New Ulm	13,051	56073
Northfield	10,235	55057
North Mankato	7,347	56001
North St. Paul	11,950	55109
Oakdale	7,304	55109
Orono	6,787	55323
Owatonna	15,341	55060
Plymouth	18,077	55441
Red Wing	12,834	55066
Richfield	47,231	55423
Robbinsdale	16,845	55422
Rochester	53,766	55901
Roseville	34,438	55113
St. Anthony Falls	9,239	55414
St. Cloud	39,691	56301
St. Louis Park	48,922	55426
St. Paul	309,714	55101*
St. Peter	8,339	56082
Shakopee	6,876	55379
Shoreview	10,995	55112
South St. Paul	25,016	55075
Spring Lake Pk.	6,417	55432
Stillwater	10,191	55082
Thief River Falls	8,618	56701
Virginia	12,450	55792
Waseca	6,789	56093
West St. Paul	18,799	55118
White Bear Lake	23,313	55110
Willmar	12,869	56201
Winona	26,438	55987
Worthington	9,916	56187

MISSISSIPPI

LOCATION	POPULATION	ZIP
Aberdeen	6,507	39730
Amory	7,236	38821
Bay St. Louis	6,752	39520
Biloxi	48,486	39530*
Brookhaven	10,700	39601
Canton	10,503	39046
Clarksdale	21,673	38614
Cleveland	13,327	38732
Clinton	7,289	39056
Columbia	7,587	39429
Columbus	25,795	39701
Corinth	11,581	38834
D'Iberville	7,288	39532
Greenville	39,648	38701
Greenwood	22,400	38930
Grenada	9,944	38901
Gulfport	40,791	39501*
Hattiesburg	38,277	39401
Indianola	8,947	38751
Jackson	153,968	39205*
Kosciusko	7,266	39090
Laurel	24,145	39440
Louisville	6,626	39339
McComb	11,969	39648
Meridian	45,083	39301
Moss Point	19,321	39563
Natchez	19,704	39120
New Albany	6,426	38652
Ocean Springs	9,580	39564
Oxford	13,846	38655
Pascagoula	27,264	39567
Pearl	12,165	39208
Petal	6,986	39465
Picayune	10,467	39466
Southaven	8,931	38671
Starkville	11,369	39759
Tupelo	20,471	38801
Vicksburg	25,478	39180
West Gulfport	6,996	39501
West Point	8,714	39773
Yazoo City	11,688	39194

MISSOURI

LOCATION	POPULATION	ZIP
Affton	24,264	63123
Arnold	17,381	63010
Ballwin	10,656	63011
Bellefontaine Neighbors	14,084	63137
Belton	12,179	64012
Berkeley	19,743	63134
Blue Springs	6,779	64015
Boonville	7,514	65233
Breckenridge Hills	7,011	63114
Brentwood	11,248	63144
Bridgeton	19,992	63044
Cape Girardeau	31,282	63701
Carthage	11,035	64836
Caruthersville	7,350	63830
Chillicothe	9,519	64601
Clayton	16,100	63105
Clinton	7,504	64735
Columbia	58,812	65201
Concord	21,217	63128
Crestwood	15,123	63126
Creve Coeur	8,967	63141
Dellwood	7,137	63135
Excelsior Springs	9,411	64024
Farmington	6,590	63640
Ferguson	28,759	63135
Festus	7,530	63028
Florissant	65,908	63033*
Fulton	12,248	65251
Gladstone	23,422	64118
Glendale	6,981	63122
Grandview	17,456	64030
Hannibal	18,698	63401
Hazelwood	14,082	63042*
Independence	111,630	64050*
Jefferson City	32,407	65101
Jennings	19,379	63136
Joplin	39,256	64801
Kansas City	507,330	64108*
Kennett	10,090	63857
Kirksville	15,560	63501
Kirkwood	31,679	63122
Ladue	10,359	64758
Lebanon	8,616	65536
Lee's Summit	16,230	64063
Lemay	40,516	63125
Liberty	13,704	64068
Maplewood	12,785	63143
Marshall	12,051	65340
Maryland Heights	8,805	63043
Maryville	9,970	64468
Mexico	11,807	65265
Moberly	12,988	65270
Neosho	7,517	64850
Nevada	9,736	64772
Normandy	6,236	63121
O'Fallon	7,018	63366
Olivette	9,156	63124
Overland	24,819	63114
Pine Lawn	6,517	63120
Poplar Bluff	16,653	63901
Raytown	33,306	64133
Richmond Hts.	13,802	63117
Rock Hill	6,815	63119
Rolla	13,571	65401
St. Ann	18,817	63074
St. Charles	31,834	63301
St. John	8,960	63114
St. Joseph	72,691	64501*
St. Louis	622,236	63166*
Sappington	10,603	63126
Sedalia	22,847	65301
Sikeston	14,699	63801
Spanish Lake	15,647	63138
Springfield	120,096	65801*
University City	47,527	63130
Warrensburg	13,125	64093
Washington	8,499	63090
Webb City	6,923	64870
Webster Groves	27,457	63119
Wellston	7,050	63112
West Plains	6,893	65775

MONTANA

LOCATION	POPULATION	ZIP
Anaconda	9,771	59711
Billings	61,581	59101*
Bozeman	18,670	59715
Butte	23,368	59701
Glendive	6,305	59330
Great Falls	60,091	59401*
Havre	10,558	59501
Helena	22,730	59601
Kalispell	10,526	59901
Lewistown	6,437	59457
Livingston	6,883	59047
Miles City	9,023	59301
Missoula	29,497	59801

NEBRASKA

LOCATION	POPULATION	ZIP
Alliance	6,862	69301
Beatrice	12,389	68310
Bellevue	21,953	68005
Columbus	15,471	68601
Fremont	22,962	68025
Grand Island	32,358	68801
Hastings	23,580	68901
Kearney	19,181	68847
Lincoln	149,518	68501*
McCook	8,285	69001
Millard	7,460	68137
Nebraska City	7,441	68410
Norfolk	16,607	68701
North Platte	19,447	69101
Omaha	346,929	68108*
Plattsmouth	6,371	68048
Scottsbluff	14,507	69361
Sidney	6,403	69162
South Sioux City	7,920	68776
York	6,778	68467

NEVADA

LOCATION	POPULATION	ZIP
Carson City	15,468	89701
East Las Vegas	6,501	89112
Elko	7,621	89801
Henderson	16,395	89015
Las Vegas	125,787	89114*
North Las Vegas	36,216	89030
Paradise Valley	24,477	89119
Reno	72,863	89501*
Sparks	24,187	89431
Sunrise Manor	10,886	89110
Vegas Creek	8,970	89121
Winchester	13,981	89109

NEW HAMPSHIRE

LOCATION	POPULATION	ZIP
Berlin	15,256	03570
Claremont	14,221	03743
Concord	30,022	03301
Derry	11,712	03038
Dover	20,850	03820
Durham	8,869	03824
Exeter	8,892	03833
Franklin	7,292	03235
Goffstown	9,284	03045
Hampton	8,011	03842
Hanover	8,494	03755
Hudson	10,638	03051
Keene	20,467	03431
Laconia	14,888	03246
Lebanon	9,725	03766
Manchester	87,754	03101*
Merrimack	8,595	03054
Milford	6,622	03055
Nashua	55,820	03060
Portsmouth	25,717	03801
Rochester	17,938	03867
Salem	20,142	03079
Somersworth	9,026	03878

NEW JERSEY

LOCATION	POPULATION	ZIP
Allendale	6,240	07401
Asbury Park	16,533	07712
Atlantic City	47,859	08401*
Audubon	10,802	08106
Barrington	8,409	08007
Bayonne	72,743	07002
Belleville	37,629	07109
Bellmawr	15,618	08031
Bergenfield	29,000	07621
Berkeley Hts. Twp.	13,078	07922

LOCATION	POPULATION	ZIP
Bernardsville	6,652	07924
Bloomfield	52,029	07003
Bloomingdale	7,797	07403
Bogota	8,960	07603
Boonton	9,261	07005
Bound Brook	10,450	08805
Brick	35,057	08723
Bridgeton	20,435	08302
Bridgewater Twp.	30,235	08807
Brigantine	6,741	08203
Browns Mills	7,144	08015
Burlington	12,010	08016
Butler	7,051	07405
Caldwell	8,677	07006
Camden	102,551	08101*
Carlstadt	6,724	07072
Carteret	23,137	07008
Cedar Grove Twp.	15,582	07009
Chatham	9,566	07928
Cherry Hill Twp.	64,395	08034*
Cinnaminson Twp.	16,962	08077
Clark Twp.	18,829	07066
Cliffside Park	18,891	07010
Cliffwood	7,056	07721
Clifton	82,437	07015*
Closter	8,604	07624
Collingswood	17,422	08108
Cranford Twp.	27,391	07016
Cresskill	8,298	07626
Delran Twp.	10,065	08075
Denville Twp.	14,045	07834
Deptford Twp.	24,232	08096
Dover	15,039	07801
Dumont	20,155	07628
Dunellen	7,072	08812
East Brunswick Twp.	34,166	08816
East Hanover Twp.	7,734	07936
East Orange	75,471	07019*
East Rutherford	8,536	07073
Eatontown	14,619	07724
Edison Twp.	67,120	08817
Elizabeth	112,654	07207*
Elmwood Park	20,511	07407
Emerson	8,428	07630
Englewood	24,985	07631*
Evesham Twp.	13,477	08053
Ewing Twp.	32,831	08618
Fairfield	6,884	07006
Fair Lawn	37,975	07410
Fairview	10,698	07022
Fanwood	8,920	07023
Florence-Roebling	7,551	08518
Florham Park	8,094	07932
Fort Lee	30,631	07024
Franklin Lakes	7,550	07417
Freehold	10,545	07728
Garfield	30,797	07026
Glassboro	12,938	08028
Glen Ridge	8,518	07028
Glen Rock	13,011	07452
Gloucester City	14,707	08030
Hackensack	36,008	07601*
Hackettstown	9,472	07840
Haddonfield	13,118	08033
Haddon Heights	9,365	08035
Haddon Twp.	18,192	08108
Haledon	6,767	07508
Hammonton	11,464	08037
Hanover Twp.	10,700	07981
Harrison	11,811	07029
Hasbrouck Hts.	13,651	07604
Hawthorne	19,173	07507
Hazlet Twp.	22,239	07730
Highland Park	14,385	08904
Hillsdale	11,768	07642
Hillside Twp.	21,636	07205
Hoboken	45,380	07030
Hopatcong	9,052	07843
Irvington	59,473	07111
Jackson Twp.	18,276	08527
Jersey City	260,350	07303*
Keansburg	9,720	07734
Kearny	37,585	07032
Kendall Park	7,412	08824
Kenilworth	9,165	07033
Keyport	7,205	07735
Kinnelon	7,600	07405
Lake Hiawatha	11,389	07034
Lake Mohawk	6,262	07871
Lake Parsippany	7,488	07054
Lakewood	17,874	08701
Laurence Harbor	6,715	08879
Leonia	8,847	07605
Lincoln Park	9,034	07035
Linden	41,409	07036
Lindenwold	12,199	08021
Little Falls Twp.	11,727	07424
Little Ferry	9,064	07643
Livingston Twp.	30,127	07039
Lodi	25,163	07644
Long Branch	31,774	07740
Lyndhurst Twp.	22,729	07071
Madison	16,710	07940
Mahwah Twp.	10,800	07430
Manville	13,029	08835
Maple Shade	16,464	08052
Maplewood Twp.	24,932	07040
Margate City	10,576	08402
Marlton	10,180	08053
Matawan	9,136	07747
Maywood	11,087	07607
Metuchen	16,031	08840
Middlesex	15,038	08846
Middletown Twp.	54,623	07748
Midland Park	8,159	07432
Millburn Twp.	21,089	07041
Milltown	6,470	08850
Millville	21,366	08332
Montclair	44,043	07042*
Montvale	7,327	07645
Montville Twp.	11,846	07045
Moorestown	14,179	08057
Morristown	17,662	07960
Mountainside	7,520	07092
Mount Holly Twp.	12,713	08060
Neptune Twp.	27,863	07753
Newark	381,930	07101*
New Brunswick	41,885	08901*
New Milford	19,149	07646
New Providence	13,796	07974
Newton	7,297	07860
North Arlington	18,096	07032
North Bergen Twp.	47,751	07047
North Brunswick Twp.	16,691	08902
North Caldwell	6,733	07006
Northfield	8,875	08225
North Haledon	7,614	07508
North Plainfield	21,796	07060
Nutley	31,913	07110
Oakland	14,420	07436
Ocean City	10,575	08226
Oceanport	7,503	07757
Old Bridge	25,176	08857
Oradell	8,903	07649
Orange	32,566	07050*
Palisades Park	13,351	07650
Palmyra	6,969	08065
Paramus	28,381	07652
Park Ridge	8,709	07656
Parsippany-Troy Hills Twp.	55,112	07054
Passaic	55,124	07055
Paterson	144,824	07510*
Paulsboro	8,084	08066
Pennsauken Twp.	36,394	08110
Pennsville	11,014	08070
Pequannock Twp.	14,350	07440
Perth Amboy	38,798	08861*
Phillipsburg	17,849	08865
Piscataway Twp.	36,418	08854
Pitman	10,257	08071
Plainfield	46,862	07061*
Pleasantville	13,778	08232
Point Pleasant	15,968	08742
Pompton Lakes	11,397	07442
Princeton	12,311	08540
Rahway	29,114	07065*
Ramsey	12,571	07446
Raritan	6,691	08869
Red Bank	12,847	07701
Ridgefield	11,308	07657
Ridgefield Park	13,990	07660
Ridgewood	27,547	07451*
Ringwood	10,393	07456
River Edge	12,850	07661
Riverside Twp.	8,591	08075
River Vale Twp.	8,883	07675
Rochelle Pk. Twp.	6,380	07662
Rockaway	6,383	07866
Roselle	22,585	07203
Roselle Park	14,277	07204
Rumson	7,421	07760
Runnemede	10,475	08078
Rutherford	20,802	07070*
Saddle Brook Twp.	15,975	07662
Salem	7,648	08079
Sayreville	32,508	08872
Scotch Plains Twp.	22,279	07076
Secaucus	13,228	07094
Somerdale	6,510	08083
Somers Point	7,919	08244
Somerville	13,652	08876
South Amboy	9,338	08879
South Orange	16,971	07079
South Plainfield	21,142	07080
South River	15,428	08882
Spotswood	7,891	08884
Springfield Twp.	15,740	07081
Stratford	9,801	08084
Strathmore	7,674	07747
Summit	23,620	07901
Teaneck Twp.	42,355	07666
Tenafly	14,827	07670
Tinton Falls	8,395	07724
Toms River	7,303	08753
Totowa	11,580	07512
Trenton	104,786	08608*
Union Beach	6,472	07735
Union City	57,305	07087
Union Twp.	53,077	07083
Upper Saddle River	7,949	07458
Ventnor City	10,385	08406
Verona	15,067	07044
Vineland	47,399	08360
Waldwick	12,313	07463
Wallington	10,284	07057
Wanaque	8,636	07465
Washington Twp.	10,577	07675
Wayne Twp.	49,141	07470
Weehawken Twp.	13,383	07087
West Caldwell	11,913	07006
Westfield	33,720	07091*
West Long Branch	6,845	07764
West Milford Twp.	17,304	07480
West New York	40,627	07093
West Orange	43,715	07052
West Paterson	11,692	07424
Westwood	11,105	07675
White Horse—Yardville	18,680	08620
White Meadow Lake	8,499	07866
Willingboro Twp.	43,386	08046
Woodbridge Twp.	98,944	07095
Woodbury	12,408	08096
Wood-Ridge	8,311	07075
Wyckoff Twp.	16,039	07481

NEW MEXICO

LOCATION	POPULATION	ZIP
Alamogordo	23,035	88310
Albuquerque	243,751	87101*
Artesia	10,315	88210
Carlsbad	21,297	88220
Clovis	28,495	88101
Deming	8,343	88030
Farmington	21,979	87401
Gallup	14,596	87301
Grants	8,768	87020
Hobbs	26,025	88240
Las Cruces	37,857	88001
Las Vegas	13,835	87701
Los Alamos	11,310	87544
Lovington	8,915	88260
North Valley	10,366	87114
Portales	10,554	88130
Raton	6,962	87740
Roswell	33,908	88201
Santa Fe	41,167	87501
Silver City	8,557	88061
South Valley	29,389	87105
Tucumcari	7,189	88401

NEW YORK

LOCATION	POPULATION	ZIP
Albany	115,781	12201*
Albertson	6,825	11507
Amherst Town	93,929	14226*
Amityville	9,794	11701
Amsterdam	25,524	12010
Arlington	11,203	12603

LOCATION	POPULATION	ZIP
Auburn	34,599	13021
Babylon	12,897	11702*
Baldwin	34,525	11510
Baldwinsville	6,298	13027
Batavia	17,338	14020
Bayport	8,232	11705
Bay Shore	11,119	11706
Beacon	13,255	12508
Bellmore	18,431	11710
Bethpage	18,555	11714
Binghamton	64,123	13902*
Bohemia	8,926	11716
Brentwood	28,327	11717
Briarcliff Manor	6,521	10510
Brighton Town	35,065	14610
Brockport	7,878	14420
Bronxville	6,674	10708
Buffalo	462,768	14240*
Canandaigua	10,488	14424
Canton	6,398	13617
Carle Place	6,326	11514
Cedarhurst	6,941	11516
Centereach	9,427	11720
Central Islip	36,391	11722
Cheektowaga Town	113,844	14225
Cohoes	18,653	12047
Colonie	8,701	12205
Commack	24,138	11725
Copiague	19,632	11726
Corning	15,792	14830
Cortland	19,621	13045
Croton-on-Hudson	7,523	10520
Deer Park	32,274	11729
Depew	22,158	14043
De Witt	10,032	13214
Dix Hills	10,050	11746
Dobbs Ferry	10,353	10522
Dunkirk	16,855	14048
East Aurora	7,033	14052
Eastchester	23,750	10709
East Half Hollow Hills	9,691	11746
East Hills	8,624	11576
East Islip	6,861	11730
East Massapequa	15,926	11758
East Meadow	46,290	11554
East Northport	12,392	11731
East Patchogue	8,092	11772
East Rochester	8,347	14445
East Rockaway	11,795	11518
East Vestal	10,472	13850
Elmira	39,945	14902*
Elmont	29,363	11003
Elwood	15,031	11731
Endicott	16,556	13760
Endwell	15,999	13760
Fairmount	15,317	13219
Fairport	6,474	14450
Fairview	8,517	12601
Farmingdale	9,297	11735
Floral Park	18,466	11002*
Franklin Square	32,156	11010
Fredonia	10,326	14063
Freeport	40,374	11520
Fulton	14,003	13069
Garden City	25,373	11530
Garden City Park	7,488	11530
Gates Town	26,442	14606
Geddes Town	21,032	13209
Geneva	16,793	14456
Glen Cove	25,770	11542
Glens Falls	17,222	12801
Gloversville	19,677	12078
Great Neck	10,798	11022*
Greece Town	75,136	14616
Greenburgh Town	85,746	10591
Greenlawn	8,493	11740
Half Hollow Hills	12,081	11746
Hamburg	10,215	14075
Harrison Town	21,509	10528
Hartsdale	12,226	10530
Hastings-on-Hudson	9,479	10706
Hauppauge	13,957	11787
Haverstraw	8,198	10927
Hempstead	39,411	11551*
Herkimer	8,960	13350
Herricks	9,112	11040
Hewlett	6,796	11557
Hicksville	49,820	11802*
Holbrook-Holtsville	12,103	11741
Hornell	12,144	14843
Horseheads	7,989	14845
Hudson	8,940	12534
Hudson Falls	7,917	12839
Huntington	12,601	11743
Huntington Sta.	28,817	11746
Ilion	9,808	13357
Inwood	8,433	11696
Irondequoit Town	63,675	14617
Islip	7,692	11751
Ithaca	26,226	14850
Jamestown	39,795	14701
Jefferson Valley–Yorktown	9,008	10535
Jericho	14,010	11753
Johnson City	18,025	13790
Johnstown	10,045	12095
Kenmore	20,980	14217
Kingston	25,544	12401
Lackawanna	28,657	14218
Lake Grove	8,133	11755
Lancaster	13,365	14086
Larchmont	7,203	10538
Latham	9,661	12110
Lawrence	6,566	11559
Levittown	65,440	11756
Lindenhurst	28,359	11757
Little Falls	7,629	13365
Lockport	25,399	14094
Locust Grove	11,626	11791
Long Beach	33,127	11561
Loudonville	9,299	12211
Lynbrook	23,151	11563
Malone	8,048	12953
Malverne	10,036	11565
Mamaroneck	18,909	10543
Manhasset	8,541	11030
Massapequa	26,821	11758
Massapequa Pk.	22,112	11762
Massena	14,042	13662
Mattydale	8,292	13211
Mechanicville	6,247	12118
Medina	6,415	14103
Melville	6,641	11747
Merrick	25,904	11566
Middletown	22,607	10940
Mineola	21,845	11501
Monsey	8,797	10952
Mount Kisco	8,172	10549
Mount Vernon	72,778	10551*
Nanuet	10,447	10954
Nesconset	10,048	11767
Newark	11,644	14513
Newburgh	26,219	12550
New Cassel	8,721	11590
New City	27,344	10956
New Hyde Park	10,116	11040
New Rochelle	75,385	10802*
New Windsor	8,803	12550
New York City	7,895,563	10001*
Niagara Falls	85,615	14302*
North Amityville	11,936	11701
North Babylon	39,526	11703
North Bellmore	22,893	11710
North Great River	12,080	11739
North Lindenhurst	11,117	11757
North Massapequa	23,123	11758
North Merrick	13,650	11566
North New Hyde Pk.	18,154	11040
Northport	7,494	17768
North Syracuse	8,687	13212
North Tarrytown	8,334	10591
North Tonawanda	36,012	14120
North Valley Str.	14,881	11580
North Wantagh	15,053	11793
Norwich	8,843	13815
Nyack	6,659	10960
Oakdale	7,334	11769
Oceanside	35,372	11572
Ogdensburg	14,554	13669
Old Bethpage	7,084	11804
Olean	19,169	14760
Oneida	11,658	13421
Oneonta	16,030	13820
Orangetown Town	53,533	10960
Ossining	21,659	10562
Oswego	20,913	13126
Oyster Bay	6,822	11771
Patchogue	11,582	11772
Pearl River	17,146	10965
Peekskill	19,283	10566
Pelham Manor	6,673	10803
Plainedge	10,759	11714
Plainview	31,695	11803
Plattsburgh	18,715	12901
Pleasantville	7,110	10570
Port Chester	25,803	10573
Port Jefferson Sta.	7,403	11776
Port Jervis	8,852	12771*
Port Washington	15,923	11050
Potsdam	10,303	13676
Poughkeepsie	32,029	12601*
Rensselaer	10,136	12144
Riverhead	7,585	11901
Rochester	296,233	14603*
Rockville Centre	27,444	11570
Rome	50,148	13440
Ronkonkoma	7,284	11779
Roosevelt	15,008	11575
Roslyn Heights	7,242	11577
Rotterdam	25,214	12303
Rye	15,869	10580
St. James	10,500	11780
Salamanca	7,877	14779
Salina Town	38,281	13208
San Remo	8,302	11754
Saranac Lake	6,086	12983
Saratoga Springs	18,845	12866
Sayville	11,680	11782
Scarsdale	19,229	10583
Schenectady	77,958	12305*
Scotia	7,370	12302
Seaford	17,379	11783
Selden	11,613	11784
Seneca Falls	7,794	13148
Setauket	6,857	11733
Shirley	6,280	11967
Solvay	8,280	13209
South Farmingdale	20,464	11735
South Holbrook	6,700	11741
South Huntington	9,115	11746
Southport	8,685	14904
South Stony Brk.	15,329	11790
South Valley Str.	6,595	11581
South Westbury	10,978	11590
Spring Valley	18,112	10977
Stony Brook	6,391	11790
Stony Point	8,270	10980
Suffern	8,273	10901
Syosset	10,084	11791
Syracuse	197,297	13201*
Tappan	7,424	10983
Tarrytown	11,115	10591
Thornwood	6,874	10594
Tonawanda	21,898	14150
Troy	62,918	12180*
Tuckahoe	6,236	10707
Uniondale	22,077	11553
Utica	91,340	13503*
Valley Stream	40,413	11580*
Vernon Valley	7,925	11768
Vestal	8,303	13850
Wantagh	21,873	11793
Watertown	30,787	13601
Watervliet	12,404	12189
West Amityville	6,424	11701
West Babylon	12,893	11704
Westbury	15,362	11590
West Haverstraw	8,558	10993
West Hempstead	20,375	11552
West Islip	17,374	11795
Westmere	6,364	12203
West Sayville	7,386	11796
West Seneca Town	48,404	14224
Westvale	7,253	13219
White Plains	50,346	10602*
Williamsville	6,835	14221
Williston Park	9,154	11596
Woodmere	19,831	11598
Wyandanch	15,716	11798
Yonkers	204,297	10701*
Yorktown Heights	6,805	10598

NORTH CAROLINA

LOCATION	POPULATION	ZIP
Albemarle	11,126	28001
Asheboro	10,797	27203
Asheville	57,681	28801*
Boone	8,754	28607
Burlington	35,930	27215
Cary	7,686	27511
Chapel Hill	25,537	27514

LOCATION	POPULATION	ZIP
Charlotte	241,178	28202*
Clinton	7,157	28328
Concord	18,464	28025
Dunn	8,302	28334
Durham	95,438	27701*
Eden	15,871	27288
Elizabeth City	14,381	27909
Fayetteville	53,510	28302*
Forest City	7,179	28043
Gastonia	47,142	28052
Goldsboro	26,810	27530
Graham	8,172	27253
Greensboro	144,076	27420*
Greenville	29,063	27834
Henderson	13,896	27536
Hendersonville	6,443	28739
Hickory	20,569	28601
High Point	63,259	27260*
Jacksonville	16,289	28540
Kannapolis	36,293	28081
Kings Mountain	8,465	28086
Kinston	23,020	28501
Laurinburg	8,859	28352
Lenoir	14,705	28645
Lexington	17,205	27292
Lumberton	16,961	28358
Monroe	11,282	28110
Mooresville	8,808	28115
Morganton	13,625	28655
Mount Airy	7,325	27030
New Bern	14,660	28560
New River-Gieger	8,699	28540
Newton	7,857	28658
North Belmont	10,672	28012
Oxford	7,178	27565
Raleigh	123,793	27611*
Reidsville	13,636	27320
Roanoke Rapids	13,508	27870
Rocky Mount	34,284	27801
Salisbury	22,515	28144
Sanford	11,716	27330
Shelby	16,328	28150
Smithfield	6,677	27577
Statesville	20,007	28677
Tarboro	9,425	27886
Thomasville	15,230	27360
Washington	8,961	27889
Waynesville	6,488	28786
Williamston	6,570	27892
Wilmington	46,169	28402*
Wilson	29,347	27893
Winston-Salem	133,683	27102*

NORTH DAKOTA

LOCATION	POPULATION	ZIP
Bismarck	34,703	58501
Devils Lake	7,078	58301
Dickinson	12,405	58601
Fargo	53,365	58102
Grand Forks	39,008	58201
Jamestown	15,385	58401
Mandan	11,093	58554
Minot	32,290	58701
Valley City	7,843	58072
Wahpeton	7,076	58075
Williston	11,280	58801

OHIO

LOCATION	POPULATION	ZIP
Akron	275,425	44309*
Alliance	26,547	44601
Amherst	9,902	44001
Ashland	19,872	44805
Ashtabula	24,313	44004
Athens	24,168	45701
Aurora	6,549	44202
Austintown	29,393	44515
Avon	7,214	44011
Avon Lake	12,261	44012
Barberton	33,052	44203
Bay Village	18,163	44140
Beachwood	9,631	44122
Bedford	17,552	44146
Bedford Heights	13,063	44146
Bellaire	9,655	43906
Bellefontaine	11,255	43311
Bellevue	8,604	44811
Belpre	7,189	45714
Berea	22,465	44017
Bexley	14,888	43209
Blacklick Estates	8,351	43004
Blue Ash	8,324	45242
Boardman	30,852	44512
Bowling Green	21,760	43402
Brecksville	9,137	44141
Bridgetown	13,352	45211
Broadview Heights	11,463	44141
Brooklyn	13,142	44144
Brook Park	30,774	44142
Brunswick	15,852	44212
Bryan	7,008	43506
Bucyrus	13,111	44820
Cambridge	13,656	43725
Campbell	12,577	44405
Canton	110,053	44711*
Celina	8,072	45822
Centerville	10,333	45459
Cheviot	11,135	45211
Chillicothe	24,842	45601
Churchill	7,457	44505
Cincinnati	451,455	45202*
Circleville	11,687	43113
Cleveland	750,879	44101*
Cleveland Heights	60,767	44118
Columbus	540,025	43216*
Conneaut	14,552	44030
Coshocton	13,747	43812
Covedale	6,639	45238
Cuyahoga Falls	49,678	44222*
Dayton	242,917	45401*
Deer Park	7,415	45236
Defiance	16,281	43512
Delaware	15,008	43015
Delphos	7,608	45833
Dover	11,516	44622
East Cleveland	39,600	44112
Eastlake	19,690	44094
East Liverpool	20,020	43920
Elyria	53,427	44035*
Englewood	7,885	45322
Euclid	71,552	44117
Fairborn	32,267	45324
Fairfield	14,680	45014
Fairview Park	21,681	44126
Findlay	35,800	45840
Forest Park	15,139	45405
Fort McKinley	11,536	45426
Fostoria	16,037	44830
Franklin	10,075	45005
Fremont	18,490	43420
Gahanna	12,400	43230
Galion	13,123	44833
Gallipolis	7,490	45631
Garfield Heights	41,417	44125
Geneva	6,449	44041
Girard	14,119	44420
Grandview Heights	8,460	43212
Greenville	12,380	45331
Grove City	13,911	43123
Hamilton	67,865	45012*
Heath	6,768	43055
Hilliard	8,369	43026
Hubbard	8,583	44425
Huber Heights	18,943	45424
Huron	6,896	44839
Independence	7,034	44131
Ironton	15,030	45638
Jackson	6,843	45640
Kent	28,183	44240
Kenton	8,315	43326
Kenwood	15,789	45236
Kettering	71,864	45429
Lakewood	70,173	44107
Lancaster	32,911	43130
Lebanon	7,934	45036
Lima	53,734	45801*
Lincoln Village	11,215	43228
Logan	6,269	43138
London	6,481	43140
Lorain	78,185	44052*
Louisville	6,298	44641
Loveland	7,144	45140
Lyndhurst	19,749	44124
Macedonia	6,375	44056
Madeira	6,713	45243
Mansfield	55,047	44901*
Maple Heights	34,093	44137
Marietta	16,861	45750
Marion	38,646	43302
Martins Ferry	10,757	43935
Massillon	32,539	44646
Maumee	15,937	43537
Mayfield Heights	22,139	44124
Medina	10,913	44256
Mentor	36,912	44060
Mentor-on-the-Lake	6,517	44060
Miamisburg	14,797	45342
Middleburg Hts.	12,367	44017
Middletown	48,767	45042
Mount Healthy	7,446	45231
Mount Vernon	13,373	43050
Napoleon	7,791	43545
Newark	41,836	43055
New Philadelphia	15,184	44663
Niles	21,581	44446
North Canton	15,228	44720
North College Hill	12,363	45239
North Madison	6,882	44057
North Olmsted	34,861	44070
Northridge	10,084	45414
North Ridgeville	13,152	44035
North Royalton	12,807	44133
Norton	12,308	44203
Norwalk	13,386	44857
Norwood	30,420	45212
Oakwood	10,095	45419
Oberlin	8,761	44074
Oregon	16,563	43616
Orrville	7,408	44667
Overlook-Page Manor	19,719	45431
Oxford	15,868	45056
Painesville	16,536	44077
Parma	100,216	44129
Parma Heights	27,192	44130
Perrysburg	7,693	43551
Piqua	20,741	45356
Port Clinton	7,202	43452
Portsmouth	27,633	45662
Ravenna	11,780	44266
Reading	14,617	45215
Reynoldsburg	13,921	43068
Richmond Hts.	9,220	44143
Rittman	6,308	44270
Rocky River	22,958	44116
St. Marys	7,699	45885
Salem	14,186	44460
Sandusky	32,674	44870
Seven Hills	12,700	44131
Shaker Heights	36,306	44120
Sharonville	11,393	45241
Sheffield Lake	8,734	44054
Shelby	9,847	44875
Shiloh	11,368	45426
Sidney	16,332	45365
Silverton	6,588	45201
Solon	11,519	44139
South Euclid	29,579	44121
Springdale	8,127	45246
Springfield	81,941	45501*
Steubenville	30,771	43952
Stow	19,847	44224
Streetsboro	7,966	44240
Strongsville	15,182	44136
Struthers	15,343	44471
Sylvania	12,031	43560
Tallmadge	15,274	44278
Tiffin	21,596	44883
Toledo	383,105	43601*
Toronto	7,705	43964
Trotwood	6,997	45426
Troy	17,186	45373
Twinsburg	6,432	44087
University Hts.	17,055	44118
Upper Arlington	38,727	43221
Urbana	11,237	43078
Vandalia	10,796	45377
Van Wert	11,320	45891
Vermilion	9,872	44089
Wadsworth	13,142	44281
Wapakoneta	7,324	45895
Warren	63,494	44482*
Warrensville Hts.	18,925	44128
Washington	12,495	43160
West Carrollton	10,748	45449
Westerville	12,530	43081
Westlake	15,689	44145
Whitehall	25,263	43213
Wickliffe	21,354	44092
Willoughby	18,634	44094
Willowick	21,237	44094
Wilmington	10,051	45177
Wooster	18,703	44691
Worthington	15,326	43085

LOCATION	POPULATION	ZIP
Wyoming	9,089	45215
Xenia	25,373	45385
Youngstown	140,909	44501*
Zanesville	33,045	43701

OKLAHOMA

LOCATION	POPULATION	ZIP
Ada	14,859	74820
Altus	23,302	73521
Alva	7,440	73717
Anadarko	6,682	73005
Ardmore	21,915	73401
Bartlesville	29,683	74003
Bethany	22,694	73008
Blackwell	8,645	74631
Broken Arrow	11,787	74012
Chickasha	14,194	73018
Claremore	9,084	74017
Clinton	8,513	73601
Cushing	7,529	74023
Del City	27,133	73115
Duncan	19,718	73533
Durant	11,118	74701
Edmond	16,633	73034
Elk City	7,323	73644
El Reno	14,510	73036
Enid	44,986	73701
Guthrie	9,575	73044
Guymon	7,674	73942
Henryetta	6,430	74437
Hugo	6,585	74743
Lawton	74,470	73501*
McAlester	18,802	74501
Miami	13,880	74354
Midwest City	48,212	73110
Moore	18,761	73160
Muskogee	37,331	74401
Norman	52,117	73069*
Oklahoma City	368,377	73125*
Okmulgee	15,180	74447
Ponca City	25,940	74601
Pryor	7,057	74361
Sand Springs	10,565	74063
Sapulpa	15,159	74066
Seminole	7,878	74868
Shawnee	25,075	74801
Stillwater	31,126	74074
Tahlequah	9,254	74464
The Village	13,695	73120
Tulsa	330,350	74101*
Warr Acres	9,887	73132
Weatherford	7,959	73096
Woodward	9,412	73801
Yukon	8,411	73099

OREGON

LOCATION	POPULATION	ZIP
Albany	18,181	97321
Altamont	15,746	97601
Ashland	12,342	97520
Astoria	10,244	97103
Baker	9,354	97814
Beaverton	18,577	97005
Bend	13,710	97701
Coos Bay	13,466	97420
Corvallis	35,056	97330
Dallas	6,361	97338
Eugene	79,028	97401*
Forest Grove	8,275	97116
Gladstone	6,254	97027
Grants Pass	12,455	97526
Gresham	10,030	97030
Hillsboro	14,675	97123
Keizer	11,405	97303
Klamath Falls	15,775	97601
La Grande	9,645	97850
Lake Oswego	14,615	97034
Lebanon	6,636	97355
McMinnville	10,125	97128
Medford	28,454	97501
Milwaukie	16,444	97222
Newberg	6,507	97132
North Bend	8,553	97459
Ontario	6,523	97914
Oregon City	9,176	97045
Pendleton	13,197	97801
Portland	379,967	97208*
Roseburg	14,461	97470
St. Helens	6,212	97051
Salem	68,480	97301*
Springfield	26,874	97477
The Dalles	10,423	97058

LOCATION	POPULATION	ZIP
West Linn	7,091	97068
Woodburn	7,495	97071

PENNSYLVANIA

LOCATION	POPULATION	ZIP
Abington Twp.	62,786	19001
Aliquippa	22,277	15001
Allentown	109,871	18105*
Altoona	63,115	16603*
Ambler	7,800	19002
Ambridge	11,324	15003
Arnold	8,174	15068
Avalon	7,010	15202
Bala Cynwyd	6,483	19004
Baldwin	26,729	15208
Beaver Falls	14,375	15010
Bellefonte	6,828	16823
Bellevue	11,586	15202
Berwick	12,274	18603
Bethel Park	34,791	15102
Bethlehem	72,686	18015*
Blakely	6,391	18447
Bloomsburg	11,652	17815
Braddock	8,795	15104
Bradford	12,672	16701
Brandywine Village	11,411	19406
Brentwood	13,732	15227
Bridgeville	6,717	15017
Bristol	12,085	19007
Brookhaven	7,370	19015
Butler	18,691	16001
California	6,635	15419
Camp Hill	9,931	17011
Canonsburg	11,439	15317
Carbondale	12,808	18407
Carlisle	18,079	17013
Carnegie	10,864	15106
Carnot–Moon	13,093	15108
Castle Shannon	11,899	15234
Cedarbrook	9,980	19095
Cedar Heights	6,326	19428
Chambersburg	17,315	17201
Charleroi	6,723	15022
Chatwood	7,168	19380
Chester	56,331	19013*
Clairton	15,051	15025
Clearfield	8,176	16830
Clifton Heights	8,348	19018
Coatesville	12,331	19320
Collingdale	10,605	19023
Columbia	11,237	17512
Connellsville	11,643	15425
Conshohocken	10,195	19428
Coraopolis	8,435	15108
Corry	7,435	16407
Crafton	8,233	15205
Darby	13,729	19023
Dickson City	7,698	18519
Donora	8,825	15033
Dormont	12,856	15216
Downingtown	7,437	19335
Doylestown	8,270	18901
DuBois	10,112	15801
Dunmore	17,300	18512
Duquesne	11,410	15110
Easton	29,450	18042
East Stroudsburg	7,894	18301
Economy	7,176	15005
Elizabethtown	8,072	17022
Ellwood City	10,857	16117
Emmaus	11,511	18049
Ephrata	9,662	17522
Erie	129,231	16501*
Farrell	11,022	16121
Flourtown	9,149	19031
Folcroft	9,610	19032
Forest Hills	9,561	15221
Franklin	8,629	16323
Fullerton	7,908	18052
Gettysburg	7,275	17325
Glassport	7,450	15045
Glenolden	8,697	19036
Glenside	17,353	19038
Greensburg	17,077	15601
Green Tree	6,441	15242
Greenville	8,704	16125
Grove City	8,312	16127
Hanover	15,623	17331
Harrisburg	68,061	17105*
Hatboro	8,880	19040
Hazleton	30,426	18201

LOCATION	POPULATION	ZIP
Hellertown	6,615	18055
Hershey	7,407	17033
Hollidaysburg	6,262	16648
Home Acre-Lyndora	8,415	16045
Homestead	6,309	15120
Huntingdon	6,987	16652
Indiana	16,100	15701
Jeannette	15,209	15644
Jefferson	8,512	15344
Jefferson-Trooper	13,022	19401
Johnstown	42,476	15901*
Kingston	18,325	18704
Kittanning	6,231	16201
Lafayette Hills-Plymouth Meeting	8,275	19444
Lancaster	57,690	17604*
Lansdale	18,451	19446
Lansdowne	14,090	19050
Latrobe	11,749	15650
Lebanon	28,572	17042
Lewisburg	6,376	17837
Lewistown	11,098	17044
Lititz	7,072	17543
Lock Haven	11,427	17745
Lower Burrell	13,654	15068
Mahanoy City	7,257	17948
McKeesport	37,977	15134*
McKees Rocks	11,901	15136
Meadville	16,573	16335
Mechanicsburg	9,385	17055
Media	6,444	19063*
Middletown	9,080	17057
Millersville	6,396	17551
Milton	7,723	17847
Monaca	7,486	15061
Monessen	15,216	15062
Monongahela	7,113	15063
Monroeville	29,011	15146
Morrisville	11,309	19067
Mount Carmel	9,317	17851
Munhall	16,574	15120
Nanticoke	14,632	18634
New Brighton	7,637	15066
New Castle	38,559	16101*
New Cumberland	9,803	17070
New Kensington	20,312	15068
Norristown	38,169	19401*
Northampton	8,389	18067
North Braddock	10,838	15104
North Hills	13,096	19038
Norwood	7,229	19074
Oakmont	7,550	15139
Oil City	15,033	16301
Old Forge	9,522	18518
Oreland	9,261	19075
Palmyra	7,615	17078
Pencoyd	6,650	19004
Penn Sq.–Plymouth Valley	7,020	19401
Philadelphia	1,949,996	19104*
Phoenixville	14,823	19460
Pittsburgh	520,117	15230*
Pittston	11,113	18640*
Plains	6,606	18701
Pleasant Hills	10,409	15236
Plum	21,922	15239
Plymouth	9,536	18651
Pottstown	25,355	19464
Pottsville	19,715	17901
Prospect Park	7,250	19076
Punxsutawney	7,792	15767
Quakertown	7,276	18951
Reading	87,643	19603*
Ridley Park	9,025	19078
Roslyn	18,380	19001
St. Marys	7,470	15857
Sayre	7,473	18840
Scranton	103,564	18501*
Shamokin	11,719	17872
Sharon	22,653	16146
Sharon Hill	7,464	19079
Shenandoah	8,287	17976
Shillington	6,249	19607
Shippensburg	6,536	17257
Somerset	6,269	15501
Souderton	6,366	18964
South Williamsport	7,153	17701
State College	33,778	16801
Steelton	8,556	17113
Sunbury	13,025	17801
Swissvale	13,819	15218

LOCATION	POPULATION	ZIP
Swoyersville	6,786	18704
Tamaqua	9,246	18252
Tarentum	7,379	15084
Taylor	6,977	18517
Titusville	7,331	16354
Turtle Creek	8,308	15145
Tyrone	7,072	16686
Uniontown	16,282	15401
Vandergrift	7,889	15690
Warren	12,998	16365
Washington	19,827	15301
Waynesboro	10,011	17268
West Chester	19,301	19380
West Mifflin	28,070	15122
Westmont	6,673	15905
West Pittston	7,074	18643
West View	8,312	15229
Whitehall	16,551	15234
White Oak	9,304	15131
Wilkes-Barre	58,856	18703*
Wilkinsburg	26,780	15221
Williamsport	37,918	17701
Willow Grove	16,494	19090
Wilson	8,406	15025
Wyomissing	7,136	19610
Yeadon	12,136	19050
York	50,335	17405*

PUERTO RICO

LOCATION	POPULATION	ZIP
Aguadilla	21,031	00603
Aibonito	7,582	00609
Arecibo	35,484	00612
Bayamón	147,552	00619
Cabo Rojo	7,181	00623
Caguas	63,215	00625
Carolina	94,271	00630
Cataño	26,459	00632
Cayey	21,562	00633
Cidra	6,306	00639
Coamo	12,077	00640
Comerío	6,297	00642
Fajardo	18,249	00648
Guánica	8,979	00653
Guayama	20,318	00654
Guaynabo	55,310	00657
Guarbo	6,290	00658
Hormigueros	6,531	00660
Humacao	12,411	00661
Isabela	9,515	00662
Juana Díaz	8,765	00665
Juncos	7,985	00666
Levittown	17,079	00632
Manatí	13,483	00701
Mayagüez	68,872	00708
Ponce	128,233	00731
San Germán	11,613	00753
San Juan	452,749	00936*
San Lorenzo	7,702	00754
San Sebastián	7,169	00755
Trujillo Alto	18,477	00760
Utuado	11,573	00761
Vega Alta	8,688	00762
Vega Baja	17,089	00763
Yauco	12,922	00768

RHODE ISLAND

LOCATION	POPULATION	ZIP
Barrington	17,554	02806
Bristol	17,860	02809
Burrillville	10,087	02830
Central Falls	18,716	02863
Coventry	22,947	02816
Cranston	74,287	02910
Cumberland	26,605	02864
East Greenwich	9,577	02818
East Providence	48,207	02914
Johnston	22,037	02919
Lincoln	16,182	02865
Middletown	29,290	02840
Narragansett	7,138	02882
Newport	34,562	02840
North Kingstown	29,793	02852
North Providence	24,337	02908
North Smithfield	9,349	02876
Pawtucket	76,984	02860*
Portsmouth	12,521	02871
Providence	179,116	02940*
Scituate	7,489	02857
Smithfield	13,468	02917
South Kingstown	16,913	02879

LOCATION	POPULATION	ZIP
Tiverton	12,559	02878
Wakefield	6,331	02880*
Warren	10,523	02885
Warwick	83,694	02887*
Westerly	17,248	02891
West Warwick	24,323	02893
Woonsocket	46,820	02895

SOUTH CAROLINA

LOCATION	POPULATION	ZIP
Aiken	13,436	29801
Anderson	27,556	29621*
Beaufort	9,434	29902
Bennettsville	7,468	29512
Berea	7,186	29611
Camden	8,532	29020
Cayce	9,967	29169
Charleston	66,945	29401*
Chester	7,045	29706
Clinton	8,138	29325
Columbia	113,542	29201*
Conway	8,151	29526
Darlington	6,990	29532
Dillon	6,391	29536
Easley	11,175	29640
Florence	25,997	29501
Forest Acres	6,808	29206
Gaffney	13,253	29340
Gantt	11,386	29609
Georgetown	10,449	29440
Greenville	61,436	29602*
Greenwood	21,069	29646
Greer	10,642	29651
Hanahan	9,118	29410
Hartsville	8,017	29550
Lake City	6,247	29560
Lancaster	9,186	29720
Laurens	10,298	29360
Marion	7,435	29571
Mount Pleasant	6,879	29464
Myrtle Beach	9,035	29577
Newberry	9,218	29108
North Augusta	12,883	29841
North Charleston	53,617	29406
Orangeburg	13,252	29115
Rock Hill	33,846	29730
St. Andrews	9,202	29407
Seneca	6,382	29678
Shannontown	7,491	29150
Spartanburg	44,546	29301*
Sumter	24,555	29150
Taylors	6,831	29687
Union	10,775	29379
Wade-Hampton	17,152	29607
Walterboro	6,257	29488
West Columbia	7,838	29169

SOUTH DAKOTA

LOCATION	POPULATION	ZIP
Aberdeen	26,476	57401
Brookings	13,717	57006
Huron	14,299	57350
Madison	6,315	57042
Mitchell	13,425	57301
Pierre	9,699	57501
Rapid City	43,836	57701
Sioux Falls	72,488	57101*
Vermillion	9,128	57069
Watertown	13,388	57201
Yankton	11,919	57078

TENNESSEE

LOCATION	POPULATION	ZIP
Alcoa	7,739	37701
Athens	11,790	37303
Bolivar	6,674	38008
Bristol	20,064	37620
Brownsville	7,011	38012
Chattanooga	119,923	37401*
Clarksville	31,719	37040
Cleveland	20,651	37311
Columbia	21,471	38401
Cookeville	14,270	38501
Dyersburg	14,523	38024
East Ridge	21,799	37412
Elizabethton	12,269	37643
Fayetteville	7,030	37334
Franklin	9,497	37064
Gallatin	13,271	37066
Greeneville	13,722	37743
Harriman	8,734	37748
Hendersonville	14,699	37075
Humboldt	10,066	38343

LOCATION	POPULATION	ZIP
Jackson	39,996	38301
Johnson City	33,770	37601
Kingsport	31,938	37662*
Knoxville	174,587	37901*
La Follette	6,902	37766
Lake Hills—Murray Hills	7,806	37401
Lawrenceburg	8,889	38464
Lebanon	12,492	37087
Lewisburg	7,207	37091
McMinnville	10,662	37110
Martin	7,781	38237
Maryville	13,808	37801
Memphis	623,530	38101*
Milan	7,313	38358
Millington	21,177	38053
Morristown	20,318	37814
Murfreesboro	26,360	37130
Nashville	447,877	37202*
Newport	7,328	37821
Oak Ridge	28,319	37830
Paris	9,892	38242
Pulaski	6,989	38478
Red Bank	12,715	37415
Shelbyville	12,262	37160
Soddy-Daisy	7,569	37319
Springfield	9,720	37172
Tullahoma	15,311	37388
Union City	11,925	38261

TEXAS

LOCATION	POPULATION	ZIP
Abilene	89,653	79604*
Alamo Heights	6,933	78209
Alice	20,121	78332
Alvin	10,671	77511
Amarillo	127,010	79105*
Andrews	8,625	79714
Angleton	9,770	77515
Arlington	90,032	76010*
Athens	9,582	75751
Austin	251,808	78767*
Balch Springs	10,464	75180
Bay City	13,445	77414
Baytown	43,980	77520*
Beaumont	117,548	77704*
Bedford	10,049	76021
Beeville	13,506	78102
Bellaire	19,009	77401
Bellmead	7,698	76704
Belton	8,696	76513
Benbrook	8,169	76126
Big Spring	28,735	79720
Bonham	7,698	75418
Borger	14,195	79007
Brenham	8,922	77833
Brownfield	9,647	79316
Brownsville	52,522	78520*
Brownwood	17,368	76801
Bryan	33,719	77801
Burkburnett	9,230	76354
Burleson	7,713	76028
Canyon	8,333	79015
Carrollton	13,855	75006*
Cleburne	16,015	76031
College Station	17,676	77840
Commerce	9,534	75428
Conroe	11,969	77301*
Copperas Cove	10,818	76522
Corpus Christi	204,525	78408*
Corsicana	19,972	75110
Crockett	6,616	75835
Crystal City	8,104	78839
Cuero	6,956	77954
Dallas	844,401	75221*
Deer Park	12,773	77536
Del Rio	21,330	78840
Denison	24,923	75020
Denton	39,874	76201
De Soto	6,617	75115
Dickinson	10,776	77539
Donna	7,365	78537
Dumas	9,771	79029
Duncanville	14,105	75116*
Eagle Pass	15,364	78852
Edinburg	17,163	78539
El Campo	9,332	77437
El Paso	322,261	79940*
Ennis	11,724	75119
Euless	19,316	76039
Falfurrias	6,375	78355

LOCATION	POPULATION	ZIP
Farmers Branch	27,492	75234
Forest Hill	8,236	76119
Fort Stockton	8,283	79735
Fort Worth	393,476	76101*
Freeport	11,997	77541
Gainesville	13,830	76240
Galena Park	10,479	77547
Galveston	61,809	77550*
Garland	81,437	75040*
Georgetown	6,395	78626
Graham	7,477	76046
Grand Prairie	50,904	75050*
Grapevine	7,023	76051
Greenville	22,043	75401
Groves	18,067	77619
Haltom City	28,127	76117
Harlingen	33,503	78550
Henderson	10,187	75652
Hereford	13,414	79045
Highland Park	10,133	75205
Hillsboro	7,224	76645
Houston	1,232,802	77052*
Huntsville	17,610	77340
Hurst	27,215	76053
Irving	97,260	75061*
Jacinto City	9,563	77029
Jacksonville	9,734	75766
Jasper	6,251	75951
Kermit	7,884	79745
Kerrville	12,672	78028
Kilgore	9,495	75662
Killeen	35,507	76541
Kingsville	28,915	78363
Lake Jackson	13,376	77566
La Marque	16,131	77568
Lamesa	11,559	79331
Lancaster	10,522	75146*
La Porte	7,149	77571
Laredo	69,024	78040*
League City	10,818	77573
Levelland	11,445	79336
Lewisville	9,264	75067*
Littlefield	6,738	79339
Lockhart	6,489	78644
Longview	45,547	75601*
Lubbock	149,101	79408*
Lufkin	23,049	75901
Marlin	6,351	76661
Marshall	22,937	75670
McAllen	37,636	78501
McKinney	15,193	75069
Mercedes	9,355	78570
Mesquite	55,131	75149*
Midland	59,463	79701*
Mineral Wells	18,411	76067
Mission	13,043	78572
Monahans	8,333	79756
Mount Pleasant	9,459	75455
Nacogdoches	22,544	75961
Nederland	16,810	77627
New Braunfels	17,859	78130
North Richland Hills	16,514	76118
Odessa	78,380	79760*
Orange	24,457	77630
Palestine	14,525	75801
Pampa	21,726	79065
Paris	23,441	75460
Pasadena	89,277	77501*
Pearland	6,444	77581
Pecos	12,682	79772
Perryton	7,810	79070
Pharr	15,829	78577
Plainview	19,096	79072
Plano	17,872	75074*
Port Arthur	57,371	77640
Portland	7,302	78374
Port Lavaca	10,491	77979
Port Neches	10,894	77651
Raymondville	7,987	78580
Richardson	48,582	75080*
Richland Hills	8,865	76118
River Oaks	8,193	77019
Robstown	11,217	78380
Rosenberg	12,098	77471
San Angelo	63,884	76901*
San Antonio	654,153	78205*
San Benito	15,176	78586
San Marcos	18,860	78666
Seguin	15,934	78155
Sherman	29,061	75090

LOCATION	POPULATION	ZIP
Silsbee	7,271	77656
Slaton	6,583	79364
Snyder	11,171	79549
South Houston	11,527	77587
Stephenville	9,277	76401
Sulphur Springs	10,642	75482
Sweetwater	12,020	79556
Taylor	9,616	76574
Temple	33,431	76501
Terrell	14,182	75160
Texarkana	30,497	75501*
Texas City	38,908	77590
Tyler	57,770	75701*
Universal City	7,613	78148
University Park	23,498	75205
Uvalde	10,764	78801
Vernon	11,454	76384
Victoria	41,349	77901
Vidor	9,738	77662
Waco	95,326	76703*
Waxahachie	13,452	75165
Weatherford	11,750	76086
Weslaco	15,313	78596
West University Pl.	13,317	77005
Wharton	7,881	77488
White Settlement	13,449	76108
Wichita Falls	96,265	76307*

UTAH

LOCATION	POPULATION	ZIP
American Fork	7,713	84003
Bountiful	27,751	84010
Brigham City	14,007	84302
Cedar City	8,946	84720
Clearfield	13,316	84015
Cottonwood	8,404	84121
East Millcreek	26,579	84109
Granite Park	9,573	84115
Holladay	23,014	84117
Hunter	9,029	84120
Kearns	17,247	84118
Layton	13,603	84041
Logan	22,333	84321
Midvale	7,840	84047
Murray	21,206	84107
Ogden	69,478	84401*
Orem	25,729	84057
Price	6,218	84501
Provo	53,131	84601
Roy	14,356	84067
St. George	7,097	84770
Salt Lake City	175,885	84101*
Sandy	6,438	84070
South Ogden	9,991	84403
South Salt Lake	7,810	84115
Spanish Fork	7,284	84660
Springville	8,790	84663
Sunset	6,268	84015
Tooele	12,539	84074
Washington Terr.	7,241	84403
White City	6,402	84070

VERMONT

LOCATION	POPULATION	ZIP
Barre	10,209	05641
Bennington	14,586	05201
Brattleboro	12,239	05301
Burlington	38,633	05401
Colchester	8,776	05446
Essex	10,951	05451
Essex Junction	6,511	05452
Hartford	6,477	05047
Middlebury	6,532	05753
Montpelier	8,609	05602
Rutland	19,293	05701
St. Albans	8,082	05478
St. Johnsbury	8,409	05819
South Burlington	10,032	05401
Springfield	10,063	05156
Winooski	7,309	05404

VIRGINIA

LOCATION	POPULATION	ZIP
Alexandria	110,927	22313*
Annandale	27,405	22003
Arlington	174,284	22210*
Bailey's Crossroads	7,295	22041
Belleview	8,299	22307
Blacksburg	9,384	24060
Bon Air	10,771	23235
Bristol	20,124	24201
Buena Vista	6,425	24416

LOCATION	POPULATION	ZIP
Charlottesville	38,880	22906*
Chesapeake	89,580	23320*
Christiansburg	7,857	24073
Colonial Heights	15,097	23834
Covington	10,060	24426
Dale City	13,857	22193
Danville	46,391	24541
Fairfax	22,009	22030
Falls Church	10,772	22046
Franklin	6,880	23851
Fredericksburg	14,450	22401
Front Royal	8,211	22630
Galax	6,278	24333
Groveton	11,761	22306
Hampton	120,779	23369*
Harrisonburg	14,605	22801
Highland Springs	7,345	23075
Hopewell	23,471	23860
Jefferson	25,432	22042
Lake Barcroft	11,605	22041
Lakeside	11,137	23228
Lexington	7,597	24450
Lincolnia	10,761	22313
Long Branch	21,634	22030
Lynchburg	54,083	24505*
Manassas	9,164	22110
Manassas Park	6,844	22110
Mantua	6,911	22030
Marion	8,158	24354
Martinsville	19,653	24112*
McLean	17,698	22101*
Newport News	138,177	23607*
Norfolk	307,951	23501*
North Springfield	8,631	22151
Petersburg	44,124	23803
Portsmouth	110,963	23705*
Pulaski	10,279	24301
Radford	11,596	24141
Richmond	249,431	23232*
Roanoke	92,115	24001*
Rose Hill	14,492	22310
Salem	21,982	24153
South Boston	6,889	24592
Springfield	11,613	22150*
Staunton	24,504	24401
Sterling Park	8,321	22170
Suffolk	45,024	23432*
Vienna	17,146	22180
Vinton	6,347	24179
Virginia Beach	172,106	23458*
Waynesboro	16,707	22980
West Springfield	14,143	22153
Williamsburg	9,069	23185
Winchester	19,429	22601
Woodbridge	25,412	22191*

VIRGIN ISLANDS

LOCATION	POPULATION	ZIP
Charlotte Amalie	12,220	00801

WASHINGTON

LOCATION	POPULATION	ZIP
Aberdeen	18,489	98520
Anacortes	7,701	98221
Auburn	21,653	98002
Bellevue	61,196	98009*
Bellingham	39,375	98225
Bremerton	35,307	98310
Centralia	10,054	98531
Cheney	6,358	99004
Clarkston	6,312	99403
Dishman	9,079	99213
Edmonds	23,998	98020
Ellensburg	13,568	98926
Everett	53,622	98201*
Hoquiam	10,466	98550
Kelso	10,296	98626
Kennewick	15,212	99336
Kent	16,596	98031
Kirkland	15,070	98033
Lacey	9,696	98503
Longview	28,373	98632
Lynnwood	16,919	98036
Mercer Island	19,819	98040
Moses Lake	10,310	98837
Mountlake Terr.	16,600	98043
Mount Vernon	8,804	98273
Oak Harbor	9,167	98277
Olympia	23,296	98501*
Opportunity	16,604	99214
Parkland	21,012	98444
Pasco	13,920	99301

LOCATION	POPULATION	ZIP
Port Angeles	16,367	98362
Pullman	20,509	99163
Puyallup	14,742	98371
Redmond	11,020	98052
Renton	25,878	98055
Richland	26,290	99352
Seattle	530,831	98101*
Shelton	6,515	98584
Spokane	170,516	99210*
Sunnyside	6,751	98944
Tacoma	154,407	98402*
Town and Country	6,484	99218
University Place	13,230	98416
Vancouver	41,859	98660*
Walla Walla	23,619	99362
Wenatchee	16,912	98801
Yakima	45,588	98901*

WEST VIRGINIA

LOCATION	POPULATION	ZIP
Beckley	19,884	25801
Bluefield	15,921	24701
Buckhannon	7,261	26201
Charleston	71,505	25301
Clarksburg	24,864	26301
Dunbar	9,151	25064
Elkins	8,287	26241
Fairmont	26,093	26554
Grafton	6,433	26354
Huntington	74,315	25701*
Keyser	6,586	26726
Martinsburg	14,626	25401
Morgantown	29,431	26505
Moundsville	13,560	26041
New Martinsville	6,528	26155
Nitro	8,019	25143
Parkersburg	44,208	26101
Princeton	7,253	24740
St. Albans	14,356	25177
South Charleston	16,333	25303
Vienna	11,549	26105
Weirton	27,131	26062
Weston	7,323	26452
Wheeling	48,188	26003

WISCONSIN

LOCATION	POPULATION	ZIP
Allouez	13,753	54301
Antigo	9,005	54409
Appleton	56,377	54911
Ashland	9,615	54806
Ashwaubenon	9,323	54304
Baraboo	7,931	53913
Beaver Dam	14,265	53916
Beloit	35,729	53511
Brookfield	32,140	53005
Brown Deer	12,582	53209
Burlington	7,479	53105
Cedarburg	7,697	53012
Chippewa Falls	12,351	54729
Cudahy	22,078	53110
De Pere	13,309	54115
Eau Claire	44,619	54701
Elm Grove	7,201	53122
Fond du Lac	35,515	54935
Fort Atkinson	9,164	53538
Fox Point	7,939	53201
Franklin	12,247	53132
Germantown	6,974	53022
Glendale	13,426	53209
Green Bay	87,809	54305*
Greendale	15,089	53129
Greenfield	24,424	53220
Hales Corners	7,771	53130
Janesville	46,426	53545
Kaukauna	11,308	54130
Kenosha	78,805	53141*
Kimberly	6,131	54136
La Crosse	51,153	54601
Madison	171,769	53703*
Manitowoc	33,430	54220
Marinette	12,696	54143
Marshfield	15,619	54449
Menasha	14,836	54952
Menomonee Falls	31,697	53051
Menomonie	11,112	54751
Mequon	12,150	53092
Merrill	9,502	54452
Middleton	8,286	53562
Milwaukee	717,372	53201*
Monona	10,420	53716
Monroe	8,654	53566
Muskego	11,573	53150
Neenah	22,902	54956
New Berlin	26,910	53151
Oak Creek	13,928	53154
Oconomowoc	8,741	53066
Oshkosh	53,082	54901
Platteville	9,599	53818
Portage	7,821	53901
Port Washington	8,752	53074
Racine	95,162	53401*
Rhinelander	8,218	54501
Rice Lake	7,278	54868
Ripon	7,053	54971
River Falls	7,238	54022
St. Francis	10,489	53207
Shawano	6,488	54166
Sheboygan	48,484	53081
Shorewood	15,576	53211
South Milwaukee	23,297	53172
Sparta	6,258	54656
Stevens Point	23,479	54481
Sturgeon Bay	6,776	54235
Sun Prairie	9,935	53590
Superior	32,237	54880
Two Rivers	13,553	54241
Watertown	15,683	53094
Waukesha	39,695	53186
Waupun	7,946	53963
Wausau	32,806	54401
Wauwatosa	58,676	53226
West Allis	71,649	53214
West Bend	16,555	53095
Whitefish Bay	17,402	53217
Whitewater	12,038	53190
Wisconsin Rapids	18,587	54494

WYOMING

LOCATION	POPULATION	ZIP
Casper	39,361	82601
Cheyenne	40,914	82001
Gillette	7,194	82716
Lander	7,125	82520
Laramie	23,143	82070
Rawlins	7,855	82301
Riverton	7,995	82501
Rock Springs	11,657	82901
Sheridan	10,856	82801

BIRTHSTONES

SOURCE: Jewelry Industry Council

Month	Stone	Month	Stone
January	Garnet	July	Ruby, star ruby
February	Amethyst	August	Peridot, sardonyx
March	Aquamarine, bloodstone	September	Sapphire, star sapphire
April	Diamond	October	Opal, tourmaline
May	Emerald	November	Topaz
June	Pearl, alexandrite, moonstone	December	Turquoise, zircon

FLOWERS OF THE MONTH

SOURCE: Society of American Florists, Alexandria, Va. in conjunction with Red Book Magazine 1977

Month	Flower	Month	Flower
January	Carnation	July	Larkspur (Delphinium)
February	Violet	August	Gladiolus
March	Daffodil	September	Aster
April	Sweet Pea	October	Calendula (Pot Marigold)
May	Lily of the Valley	November	Chrysanthemum
June	Rose	December	Narcissus

WEDDING ANNIVERSARY GIFTS

Anniversary	Traditional	Modern	Anniversary	Traditional	Modern
1	Paper / Plastics	Clocks	11	Steel	Fashion jewelry or accessories
2	Cotton / Calico / Straw	China	12	Silk or nylon / Linen	Pearl or colored gen
3	Leather or leatherlike items	Crystal or glass	13	Lace	Textiles / Furs
4	Fruit / Flowers / Books; also Linen / Silk or synthetic silks	Electrical appliance	14	Ivory / Agate	Gold jewelry
			15	Crystal or glass	Watch
5	Wood / Decorative home accessories	Silverware	20	China / Occasional furniture	Platinum
6	Candy or sugar / Iron	Wood	25	Silver	Silver
7	Wool / Copper, brass, or bronze	Desk set / Pen and pencil set	30	Pearl / Personal gifts	Diamond
			35	Coral / Jade	Jade
8	Bronze / Pottery / Rubber; also Electrical appliances	Linens / Lace	40	Ruby / Garnet	Ruby
			45	Sapphire	Sapphire
9	Pottery / Willow / China, glass, or crystal	Leather	50	Gold	Gold
			55	Emerald / Turquoise	Emerald
			60	Diamond / Gold	Diamond / Gold
10	Tin or aluminum	Diamond jewelry	75	Diamond / Gold	Diamond / Gold

HISTORY: ANCIENT/MODERN

PRESENT MONARCHS AND DYNASTIES

AFRICA

Lesotho—**Dynasty**: Before independence, the people of Lesotho accepted authority of the "Paramount Chief" of the House of Moshesh. With independence (October 1966), Moshoeshoe II of the Moshesh became head of state. **Monarch**: Moshoeshoe II ascended the throne in October 1966. In "voluntary exile" Feb.-Dec. 1970 **Born**: May 2, 1938 **Married**: Tabitha' Masentle Lerotholi Mojela **Children**: Two sons, one daughter **Heir**: Crown Prince David Letsie (b. 1963) **Religion**: Christian

Morocco—**Dynasty**: The Alaouite dynasty (Filali) has ruled Morocco since the 17th century. The country has been ruled by constitutional kings since independence (1956), and in 1957 King Mohammed V changed his title from "His Sherifian Majesty, the Sultan" to "His Majesty, the King of Morocco." **Monarch**: King Hassan II, son of Mohammed V, ascended the throne on March 3, 1961, following the death of his father on February 26, 1961. **Born**: July 9, 1929 **Married**: Lalla Latifa **Children**: One son and three daughters **Heir**: Crown Prince Sidi Mohammed (born 1963). **Religion**: Moslem (Sunni)

Swaziland—**Dynasty**: Descended from Sobhuza I, the present king succeeded as Ngwenyama (or lion) of the Swazi nation, after a 20-year regency of the Queen Mother, in 1921. The country gained independence on September 6, 1968. **Monarch**: King Sobhuza II was chosen to succeed his father upon the latter's death in December 1899, was installed as king of the Swazi nation in 1921, and was recognized as the country's king in 1967. He is the world's longest-reigning monarch. **Born**: 1899 **Married**: 100 wives **Children**: 500 **Heir**: By custom, the heir to the throne is not chosen until after the death of the monarch, when the eldest son of the favored wife is proclaimed king. **Religion**: Christian

ARABIA

Bahrain—**Dynasty**: The Emir of Bahrain, head of the powerful Bedouin Al Khalifa family, is the tenth of his family to rule in Bahrain. Succession is by primogeniture. **Monarch**: Sheikh Isa ibn Salman al Khalifa became ruler on the death of his father in 1961, and the first Emir of Bahrain on August 14, 1971, the date of Bahrain's independence. **Children**: Hamad, others **Heir**: Sheikh Hamad ibn Isa al Khalifa, defense minister, and the Emir's oldest son **Religion**: Moslem (Sunni)

Jordan—**Dynasty**: Hashemite cooperation with the British in World War I resulted in Abdullah Ibn Hussein's rule of British mandated Transjordan. By a 1946 treaty with Great Britain, Abdullah became the first king of the independent Hashemite Kingdom of Jordan. Assassinated in 1951, Abdullah was succeeded by his son, Talal, father of the present king. **Monarch**: King Hussein I (ibn Talal) ascended the throne on May 2, 1953, following the deposition of his sickly father, Talal, on August 11, 1952. **Born**: November 14, 1935 **Married**: Princess Dina Abdel Hamid (April 1955; divorced, 1957); Antoinette (Toni) Avril Gardiner (Muna al Hussein) (May 1961; divorced, 1972); Alia Toukan (1972; died 1977); Elizabeth Halaby (Nur al Hussein) (June 1978) **Children**: Four sons (Abdullah, born 1962; Faisal, born 1963; Ali, born 1976; Hamzah, born 1980) and four daughters (Alia, born 1956; Zein, born 1968; Ayeshia, born 1968; Haya, born 1974). Abir, an adopted daughter, was born in 1972. **Heir**: Prince Hassan, younger brother of the king **Religion**: Moslem (Sunni)

Kuwait—**Dynasty**: The Emir of Kuwait is the thirteenth ruler of the Al Sabah royal family. The nominated successor of the Emir must be approved by the National Assembly; succession usually alternates between the two branches of the royal family. **Monarch**: Sheikh Jabir al-Ahmad al-Jabir as-Sabah of the al-Jabir branch became Emir on the death of his cousin on Dec. 31, 1977. **Religion**: Moslem (Sunni)

Oman—**Dynasty**: The al Bu Said dynasty dates from 1741 when its founder, Ahmed Ibn Said, expelled the Turks from Muscat and Oman. **Monarch**: Sultan Qabus ibn Said al Bu Said ascended the throne in July 1970 after overthrowing his father, Said bin Taimur (1910-72), who had reigned since 1932. **Born**: November 18, 1940 **Married**: Kamilla (1976) **Heir**: Sahr bin Taimur, uncle to the Sultan **Religion**: Moslem (Ibadi)

Qatar—**Dynasty**: In the 19th century, the ruling Khalifa family deposed and forced to move to Bahrain, were succeeded by the Al Thani family. The present Emir, Khalifa ibn Hamad al-Thani, is the sixth ruler. In 1972 Khalifa assumed full power. Succession is designated by family consensus. **Monarch**: Sheikh Khalifa ibn Hamad al-Thani, Emir of Qatar, assumed power Feb. 22, 1972. **Born**: 1937 **Children**: Two sons—Hamad and Abd al Aziz, others **Heir**: Sheikh Hamad ibn Khalifa al-Thani **Religion**: Moslem (Wahhabi)

Saudi Arabia—**Dynasty**: The kingdoms of Nejd and Hejaz and their dependencies became the Kingdom of Saudi Arabia in 1932, under King Abdul-Aziz Ibn Abdur-Rahman Al-Faisal Al Saud. His son, King Saud, ruled from 1953 to 1964, when he was deposed, and succeeded by a brother, Faisal ibn Abdul-Aziz. **Monarch**: King Khalid ibn Abdul-Aziz Al Saud ascended the throne following the assassination of Faisal on March 25, 1975, by a nephew. **Born**: 1913 **Married**: one wife **Children**: five **Heir**: Prince Fahd ibn Abdul-Aziz, a younger brother **Religion**: Moslem (Sunni-Wahhabi sect)

ASIA

Bhutan—**Dynasty**: The present hereditary dynasty of Bhutan was founded in 1907 by Ugyen Dorji Wangchuk, a provincial governor, following the abolition of a dual system of government by spiritual and temporal rulers. The present king, installed in July 1972 after the death of his father, Jigme Dorji Wangchuk, is his great-grandson. **Monarch**: King Jigme Singhi Wangchuk (formally crowned on June 2, 1974) **Born**: 1955 **Children**: None **Heir**: To be selected from the royal family by the National Assembly **Religion**: Buddhist (Mahayana)

Japan—**Dynasty**: The Meiji Restoration (1867) placed Emperor Mutsuhito and his male descendants in command of a unified Japan. During the postwar American occupation of Japan, the Emperor, a grandson of Mutsuhito, renounced any claims to divinity, becoming a symbolic ruler. **Monarch**: Emperor Hirohito ascended the throne the throne on the death of his father, Yoshihito, on December 25, 1926; he was enthroned on November 10, 1928. **Born**: April 29, 1901 **Married**: Princess Nagako (1924) **Children**: Seven; two sons (Akihito, born 1933; Masahito, born 1935) and three daughters survive **Heir**: Crown Prince Akihito **Religion**: Shinto

Nepal—**Dynasty**: The Shah family has ruled the kingdom of Nepal since the middle of the 18th century; however, a hereditary prime minister from the Rana family held actual power from 1846 to 1951. The last prime minister resigned in November 1951, and King Tribhuvan assumed full control. **Monarch**: Maharajadhiraja Birendra Bir Bikram Shah Dev succeeded to the throne in January 1972 (crowned in 1975) at the death of his father, Mahendra Bir Bikram Shah Dev **Born**: 1946 **Married**: Aishwarya Rajya Lakshmi Shah Devi **Children**: Two sons, one daughter **Heir**: Crown Prince Dependra Bir Bikram Shah Dev (b. 1971) **Religion**: Hindu

Thailand—**Dynasty**: The present ruling family of Thailand began with Rama I in 1782. His great-grandson, Chulalongkorn, King Rama V, was responsible for accelerating the modernization of Thailand; his nephew is the current monarch. **Monarch**: King Bhumibol Adulyadej, or Phumiphol Aduldet (Rama IX) succeeded to the throne after the death of his elder brother, King Ananda Mahidol, on June 9, 1946; he was crowned on May 5, 1950 **Born:** December 5, 1927 **Married:** Princess Sirikit Kittiyakara (1950) **Children:** One son (Prince Vajiralongkorn, born 1952), and three daughters (Ubol Ratana, born 1951; Sirindhorn, born 1955; Chulabhorn, born 1957) **Heir:** Crown Prince Vajiralongkorn **Religion:** Buddhist (Hinayana)

EUROPE

Belgium—**Dynasty:** The ruling family of Belgium is of the Saxe-Coburg-Gotha line. After Belgian separation from the Netherlands (1830), Leopold, prince of Saxe-Coburg-Gotha, was elected hereditary King of the Belgians on June 4, 1831, as King Leopold I; he was enthroned on July 21, 1831. **Monarch:** King Baudouin I (Albert Charles Leopold Axel Marie Gustave) succeeded to the throne on July 17, 1951, on the abdication of his father, Leopold III, on the previous day. **Born:** September 7, 1930 **Married:** Fabiola de Mora y Aragón (1960) **Children:** None **Heir:** Albert, Prince of Liège, brother of the king (born 1934) **Religion:** Roman Catholic

Denmark—**Dynasty:** The House of Glücksburg has ruled Denmark since King Frederik VII of the House of Oldenburg died childless in November 1863. By a treaty (1852), King Frederik VII designated as heir Prince Christian X of Schleswig-Holstein-Sonderburg-Glücksburg, who became King Christian IX on Frederik's death. **Monarch:** Queen Margrethe II succeeded to the throne on the death of her father, King Frederik IX, on January 14, 1972. **Born:** April 16, 1940 **Married:** Count Henri de Laborde de Monpezat, now Prince Henrik of Denmark (1967) **Children:** Two sons: Frederik André Henrik Christian, born 1968; Joachim Holger Waldemar Christian, born 1969 **Heir:** Crown Prince Frederik **Religion:** Evangelical Lutheran

Liechtenstein—**Dynasty:** The ruling House of Liechtenstein is descended from Huc von Liechtenstein, who became hereditary ruler of the country in January 1719. **Royal Ruler:** Prince Franz Josef II succeeded at the death of his great-uncle, Prince Franz de Paula, on July 25, 1938. **Born:** August 16, 1906 **Married:** Countess Georgine von Wilczek (1943) **Children:** Four sons, one daughter: Prince Johannes Adam Ferdinand Alois Josef Maria Marko d'Aviano Pius (b. 1945), Prince Philipp Erasmus Alois Ferdinand Maria Sebaldus (b. 1946), Prince Nikolaus Ferdinand Maria Josef Raphael (b. 1947), Prince Franz-Josef Wenzel George Maria (b. 1962), and Princess Nora Elisabeth Maria Anunta Josefine Georgine Omnes Sancti (b. 1950) **Heir:** Crown Prince Johannes (Hans) Adam **Religion:** Roman Catholic

Luxembourg—**Dynasty:** Made a Grand Duchy in 1815, the country has been ruled by the Nassau-Braganza family, the elder line of the House of Nassau, since 1890. According to the succession agreement, Adolphe, Duke of Nassau, succeeded at the death of King William III of the Netherlands. The Grand Duchy is today ruled by the great-grandson of Adolphe. **Royal Ruler:** Grand Duke Jean succeeded to the throne on the abdication of his mother, the Grand Duchess Charlotte, on November 12, 1964. **Born:** January 5, 1921 **Married:** Princess Josephine-Charlotte of Belgium, daughter of King Leopold III (1953) **Children:** Three sons and two daughters: Prince Henri Albert Gabriel Félix Marie Guillaume (b. 1955), Prince Jean Félix Marie Guillaume (b. 1957), Prince Guillaume Marie Louis Christian (b. 1963), Princess Marie Astrid Charlotte Leopolding Wilhelmine Ingeborg Antonia Lilane Alberta Elisabeth Anne (b. 1954), and Princess Margaretha Antonia Maria Félicité (b. 1957) **Heir:** Prince Henri **Religion:** Roman Catholic

Monaco—**Dynasty:** The House of Grimaldi has controlled the principality of Monaco since 1297. **Royal Ruler:** Prince Rainier III (Louis Henri Maxence Bertrand) succeeded his grandfather, Prince Louis II, at his death on May 9, 1949. **Born:** May 31, 1923 **Married:** Grace Patricia Kelly of Philadelphia (1956) **Children:** One son and two daughters: Prince Albert Alexandre Louis Pierre (b. 1958), Princess Caroline Louise Marguerite (b. 1957), and Princess Stéphanie Marie Elisabeth (b. 1965) **Heir:** Prince Albert **Religion:** Roman Catholic

Netherlands—**Dynasty:** The Congress of Vienna, which settled the Napoleonic Wars, created the hereditary kingdom of the Netherlands under King William I in March 1815. The present sovereign is the sixth monarch of the dynasty. **Monarch:** Queen Beatrix Wilhelmina Armgard succeeded her mother, Queen Juliana, at the latter's abdication on April 30, 1980; she was invested on April 30, 1980. **Born:** January 31, 1938 **Married:** Prince Claus von Amsberg (1966) **Children:** Three sons: Prince Willem-Alexander Claus George Ferdinand (b. 1967), Johan Frisco Bernhard Christiaan David (b. 1968), Constantijn Christof Frederik Aschwin (b. 1969) **Heir:** Crown Prince Willem-Alexander **Religion:** Dutch Reformed Church

Norway—**Dynasty:** Norway was ruled by the kings of Denmark and Sweden from 1319 until its separation (1905), when Prince Carl of Denmark was elected King Haakon VII of an independent Norway. Married to Queen Maud, daughter of Edward VII of England, King Haakon VII was followed by his son, the present ruler. **Monarch:** King Olav V succeeded to the throne on the death of his father, King Haakon VII, on September 21, 1957. **Born:** July 2, 1903 **Married:** Princess Märtha, daughter of Prince Carl of Sweden (1929; d. 1954) **Children:** One son and two daughters: Prince Harald (b. 1937), Princess Ragnhild Alexandra (b. 1930), and Princess Astrid Maud Ingeborg (b. 1932) **Heir:** Crown Prince Harald **Religion:** Evangelical Lutheran

Spain—**Dynasty:** The 1947 law of succession recreated the Spanish Kingdom under the tutelage of Generalissimo Franco, who would select a successor from the royal family. The Bourbon dynasty had ruled from 1700-1808, 1814-1869, and again after 1875 until the abdication of Alfonso XIII in April 1931. In 1969 Franco named Juan Carlos, grandson of Alfonso, as heir, and after being approved by the Cortes he was entitled Prince of Spain on July 23, 1969. He was proclaimed king on November 22, 1975, following the death of Franco. **Monarch:** Juan Carlos I de BorboJAn y Borbón **Born:** January 5, 1938 **Married:** Princess Sofía of Greece (1962) **Children:** One son and two daughters: Prince of Asturias Felipe Juan Pablo Alfonso de Borbón y Sonderburg-Gluckberg (b. 1968), Princess Elena, Princess Cristina **Heir:** Prince Felipe **Religion:** Roman Catholic

Sweden—**Dynasty:** Jean-Baptiste-Jules Bernadotte was elected (1810) Prince Royal of Sweden and adopted by childless King Carl XIII. He ascended to the throne of Norway and Sweden in 1818 as King Carl XIV Johan. His descendant King Oscar II renounced the throne of Norway in 1905; however, the House of Bernadotte still reigns over Sweden. **Monarch:** King Carl XVI Gustav, succeeded to the throne on the death of his grandfather, King Gustav VI Adolf on September 16, 1973. King Carl's father died in 1947. **Born:** April 30, 1946 **Married:** Silvia Renate Sommerlath (1976) **Children:** Crown Princess Victoria Ingrid Alice Desiree (b. 1977), Prince Carl Philip Edmund Bertil (b. 1979) **Heir:** Crown Princess Victoria Ingrid Alice Desiree **Religion:** Lutheran

United Kingdom—**Dynasty:** The House of Windsor, a branch of the Saxe-Coburg and Brunswick-Lüneburg line, dates from the accession of King George V in 1910. Although of German heritage, George V abandoned the German name Wettin and adopted the surname Windsor during World War I. He was succeeded by his sons Edward VIII (the Duke of Windsor) and George VI, father of the present monarch. **Monarch:** Queen Elizabeth II succeeded her father, George VI, at his death on February 6, 1952. **Born:** April 21, 1926 **Married:** Philip Mountbatten (Duke of Edinburgh, Earl of Merioneth, Baron Greenwich, and Prince of Great Britain), the son of Prince Andrew of Greece and Denmark (1947) **Children:** Three sons and one daughter: Prince Charles Philip Arthur George (Prince of Wales and Duke of Cornwall) (b. 1948), Prince Andrew Albert Christian Edward (b. 1960), Prince Edward Antony Richard Louis (b. 1964), and Princess Anne Elizabeth Alice Louise (b. 1950) **Heir:** Prince Charles **Religion:** Anglican

OCEANIA

Tonga—**Dynasty:** Tonga was unified by Taufa'ahau Tupou (George I) in 1845. The kingdom is currently ruled by his descendants. **Monarch:** King Taufa'ahau Tupou IV succeeded to the throne at the death of his mother, Queen Salote, in December 1965; he was crowned on April 7, 1967 **Born:** July 4, 1918 **Married:** Princess Halaevalu Mata'aho 'Ahome'e (1947) **Children:** four **Heir:** Crown Prince Tupou To'a (Toufa'ahau Manumatuongo Tukuaho) (b. 1948) **Religion:** Christian

SELECTED PAST RULERS AND DYNASTIES

BRITISH RULERS

Victorious over his neighbors, Egbert of Wessex (d. 839) consolidated what was to become the first English kingdom. The British monarchy, although altered by Danish (1016) and Norman (1066) conquest, civil wars, and Cromwell's Commonwealth and weakened by constitutional restraints, still prevails.

Saxons and Danes	Reign Dates
Egbert	802–839
Ethelwulf	839–858
Ethelbald	858–860
Ethelbert	860–c. 866
Ethelred	c. 866–871
Alfred the Great	871–c. 899
Edward the Elder	c. 899–924
Athelstan	924–939
Edmund I	939–946
Edred	946–955
Edwy	955–959
Edgar	959–975
Edward the Martyr	975–978
Ethelred II	978–1016
Edmund Ironside	1016
Canute the Dane	1016–1035
Harold I	1035–1040
Hardicanute	1040–1042
Edward the Confessor	1042–1066
Harold II	1066

Norman	
William I (the Conqueror)	1066–1087
William II	1087–1100

	Reign Dates
Henry I	1100–1135
Stephen	1135–1154

Plantagenet	
Henry II	1154–1189
Richard I (Lion-Heart)	1189–1199
John	1199–1216
Henry III	1216–1272
Edward I	1272–1307
Edward II	1307–1327
Edward III	1327–1377
Richard II	1377–1399

Lancaster	
Henry IV (Bolingbroke)	1399–1413
Henry V	1413–1422
Henry VI	1422–1461
	1470–1471

York	
Edward IV	1461–1470
	1471–1483
Edward V	1483
Richard III	1483–1485

Tudor	
Henry VII	1485–1509
Henry VIII	1509–1547
Edward VI	1547–1553
Lady Jane Grey (nine days)	1553
Mary I	1553–1558
Elizabeth I	1558–1603

	Reign Dates
Stuart	
James I (VI of Scotland)	1603–1625
Charles I	1625–1649
Commonwealth	
Oliver Cromwell	1653–1658
Richard Cromwell	1658–1659
Military Rule	1659–1660
Stuart Restoration	
Charles II	1660–1685
James II	1685–1688
Interregnum	1688–1689
Orange	
William III	1689–1702
and Mary II	1689–1694
Stuart	
Anne	1702–1714
Hanover	
George I	1714–1727
George II	1727–1760
George III	1760–1820
George IV	1820–1830
William IV	1830–1837
Victoria	1837–1901
Saxe-Coburg	
Edward VII	1901–1910
Windsor (Wettin until 1917)	
George V	1910–1936
Edward VIII (325 days)	1936
George VI	1936–1952

CHINESE DYNASTIES

Hsia (legendary)	c. 1994 B.C.–c. 1523 B.C.
Shang	c. 1523 B.C.–c. 1027 B.C.
Chou	c. 1027 B.C.–256 B.C.
Western Chou	c. 1027 B.C.–771 B.C.
Eastern Chou	
Spring and Autumn Period	722 B.C.–481 B.C.
Warring States Period	403 B.C.–221 B.C.
Chin	221 B.C.–206 B.C.
Western Han	206 B.C.–9 A.D.
Hsin	9 A.D.–23 A.D.
Eastern Han	25–220

The Three Kingdoms	220–280
Shu	221–263
Wei	220–265
Wu	222–280
Western Tsin	266–316
Eastern Tsin	317–420
Southern and Northern Dynasties	420–581
Liu Sung	420–479
Southern Ch'i	479–502
Liang	502–557
Ch'en	557–589
Northern Wei and four minor dynasties	386–535

Sui	589–618
Tang	618–907
Five Dynasties	907–960
Later Liang	907–923
Later Tang	923–936
Later Chin	936–947
Later Han	947–951
Later Chou	951–960
Northern Sung	960–1127
Liao	916–1125
Southern Sung	1127–1279
Chin	1115–1234
Yuan	1271–1368
Ming	1368–1644
Ching (Manchu)	1644–1911

FRENCH RULERS

After the death (511) of Clovis I, the Merovingian founder of the Frankish monarchy, his kingdom was divided into Austrasia, Neustria, and Burgundy. These kingdoms were frequently at war. Dagobert I was the last active Merovingian ruler, and his descendants, called the idle kings, were completely subject to their mayors of the palace, the Carolingians, who became the actual rulers of France when Pepin the Short deposed (752) the last Merovingian king.

Carolingians	
*Pepin the Short	751–768
*Charlemagne (with Carloman up to 771)	768–814
*Louis I the Pious	814–840
Charles II the Bald	840–877
Louis II the Stammerer	877–879
Louis III and Carloman	879–882
Carloman	882–884
Charles the Fat, regent	884–887
Eudes (Capetian family)	888–898
Charles III the Simple	893–922
Robert I (Capetian)	922–923
Raoul of Burgundy	923–936
Louis IV d'Outremer	936–954
Lothaire	954–986
Louis V	986–987

* King of the Franks.

Capetians	
Hugh Capet	987–996
Robert II	996–1031
Henry I	1031–1060
Philip I	1060–1108
Louis VI	1108–1137
Louis VII	1137–1180
Philip II (Augustus)	1180–1223
Louis VIII	1223–1226
Louis IX (Saint)	1226–1270
Philip III	1270–1285
Philip IV	1285–1314
Louis X	1314–1316
John I (the Posthumous)	1316–1317
Philip V	1317–1321
Charles IV	1321–1328

Valois	
Philip VI	1328–1350
John II	1350–1364
Charles V	1364–1380
Charles VI	1380–1422
Charles VII	1422–1461
Louis XI	1461–1483
Charles VIII	1483–1498

Valois-Orléans	
Louis XII	1498–1515

Valois-Angoulême	
Francis I	1515–1547

Henry II	1547–1559
Francis II	1559–1560
Charles IX	1560–1574
Henry III	1574–1589
Bourbons	
Henry IV	1589–1610
Louis XIII	1610–1643
Louis XIV	1643–1715
Louis XV	1715–1774
Louis XVI	1774–1793
Louis XVII (titular)	1793–1795
First Republic	1792–1804
First Empire	
Napoleon I (Bonaparte)	1804–1814
Bourbon Restoration	
Louis XVIII	1814–1824
First Empire (100 days)	1815
Bourbons	
Charles X	1824–1830
Bourbon-Orleans	
Louis Philippe	1830–1848
Second Republic	
(Louis) Napoleon III	1848–1851
Second Empire	
(Louis) Napoleon III	1852–1870

GERMAN AND PRUSSIAN RULERS

House of Hohenzollern, Kings of Prussia

Frederick I	1701–1713
Frederick William I	1713–1740
Frederick II (the Great)	1740–1786
Frederick William II	1786–1797
Frederick William III	1797–1840
Frederick William IV	1840–1861
William I (German emperor after 1871)	1861–1888
*Frederick III	1888
*William II	1888–1918

* King of Prussia and Emperor of Germany.

ITALIAN RULERS

Guided by Camillo di Cavour, the House of Savoy undertook to liberate and unify the Italian peninsula, a movement known as the **Risorgimento**. Italy became a kingdom in 1861 and a republic in 1946.

House of Savoy

Emmanuel Philibert	1553–1580
Charles Emmanuel I	1580–1630
Victor Amadeus I	1630–1637
Charles Emmanuel II	1637–1675
Victor Amadeus II	1675–1730
Charles Emmanuel III	1730–1773
Victor Amadeus III	1773–1796
Charles Emmanuel IV	1796–1802
Victor Emmanuel I	1802–1821
Charles Felix	1821–1831

House of Savoy-Carignano

Charles Albert	1831–1849

Kings of Italy

Victor Emmanuel II (king after 1861)	1849–1878
Humbert I	1878–1900
Victor Emmanuel III	1900–1946
Humbert II	1946

ROMAN EMPERORS

Successor to Julius Caesar, Octavian (also known as Augustus), became the first Roman emperor in 27 B.C. His rule began a long period (200 years) of peace, called the **Pax Romana**. Stretching westward to the British Isles and eastward to the Caucasus, the vast Roman Empire was permanently divided into West and East Empires after the death (395) of Theodosius the Great. The Western Roman Empire came to an end in 476, when the German Odoacer deposed Romulus Augustulus. The Eastern Empire, with its capital at Constantinople, was gradually supplanted by the Byzantine Empire.

Emperor

Augustus	27 B.C.–14 A.D.
Tiberius	14–37
Caligula	37–41
Claudius	41–54
Nero	54–68
Galba	68–69
Otho	69
Vitellius	69
Vespasian	69–79
Titus	79–81
Domitian	81–96
Nerva	96–98
Trajan	98–117
Hadrian	117–138
Antoninus Pius	138–161
Marcus Aurelius	161–180
Commodus	180–192
Pertinax	193
Didius Julianus	193
Septimius Severus	193–211
Caracalla	211–217
Macrinus	217–218
Elagabalus (Heliogabalus)	218–222
Alexander Severus	222–235
Maximinus	235–238
Gordian I	238
Gordian II	238
Pupienus	238
Balbinus	238
Gordian III	238–244
Philip the Arab	244–249
Decius	249–251
Hostilianus	251
Gallus	251–253
Volusianus	c. 251–253
Valerian	253–260
Gallienus	253–268
Claudius II	268–270
Aurelian	270–275
Tacitus	275–276
Florianus	276
Probus	276–282
Carus	282–283
Carinus	283–285
Numerianus	283–284
Diocletian	284–305
Maximian	286–305
Constantius	305–306
Galerius	305–310
Maxentius	306–312
Constantine I the Great	306–337
Licinius	308–324
Constantine II	337–340
Constans	337–350
Constantius II	337–361
Magnentius	350–353
Julian the Apostate	361–363
Jovian	363–364
Valentinian I	364–375
Valens	364–378
Gratian	375–383
Valentinian II	375–392
Magnus Maximus	383–388
Eugenius	392–394
Theodosius I the Great	379–395

Emperors in the East

Arcadius	395–408
Theodosius II	408–450
Marcian	450–457
Leo I	457–474
Leo II	474

Emperors in the West

Honorius	395–423
Constantius III	421
Valentinian III	425–455
Petronius Maximus	455
Avitus	455–456
Majorian	457–461
Libius Severus	461–465
Anthemius	467–472
Olybrius	472
Glycerius	473
Julius Nepos	474–475
Romulus Augustulus	475–476

RUSSIAN RULERS

Grand Dukes of Moscow

Ivan I, Prince of Moscow	1328–1341
Ivan II, Ivanovich	1353–1359
Dmitry Donskoi	1359–1389
Vasily I Dmitrievich	1389–1425
Vasily II	1425–1462
Ivan III Vasilyevich	1462–1505
Vasily III Ivanovich	1505–1533
Ivan IV (the Terrible), tsar of Russia from 1547	1533–1584
Fyodor Ivanovich	1584–1598
Boris Godunov	1598–1605
Fyodor II	1605
False Dmitry I	1605–1606
Vasily Shuisky	1606–1610

Interregnum 1610–1613

House of Romanov

Tsar Mikhail	1613–1645
Tsar Alexei Mikhailovich	1645–1676
Fyodor Alexeyevich	1676–1682
Peter I, the Great (with Ivan V until 1689)	1682–1725
Catherine I	1725–1727
Peter II	1727–1730
Anna Ivanovna	1730–1740
Ivan VI	1740–1741
Elizabeth	1741–1761
Peter III	1761–1762
Catherine II (the Great)	1762–1796
Paul I	1796–1801
Alexander I	1801–1825
Nicholas I	1825–1855
Alexander II	1855–1881
Alexander III	1881–1894
Nicholas II	1894–1917

SPANISH RULERS

Spain was unified by the marriage of Ferdinand of Aragon and Isabella of Castile. Alfonso XIII was exiled in 1931, when Spain became a republic. The country came under the rule of Gen. Francisco Franco in 1939. The grandson of Alfonso XIII was proclaimed king, as Juan Carlos I, on the death of Franco in 1975.

Houses of Aragon and Castile

Ferdinand II of Aragon and Isabella of Castile	1474–1504
Ferdinand II and Philip I	1504–1506
Ferdinand II and Charles I	1506–1516

Spanish Hapsburgs

Charles I (V of Holy Roman Empire)	1516–1556
Philip II	1556–1598
Philip III	1598–1621
Philip IV	1621–1665
Charles II	1665–1700

Spanish Bourbons

Philip V	1700–1724
Louis I	1724
Philip V	1724–1746
Ferdinand VI	1746–1759
Charles III	1759–1788
Charles IV	1788–1808

French King of Spain

Joseph Bonaparte	1808–1813

Bourbon Restoration

Ferdinand VII	1814–1833
Isabella II	1833–1868

Provisional Government 1868–1870

House of Savoy

Amadeo I	1870–1873

First Spanish Republic 1873–1874

Bourbon Restoration

Alfonso XII	1875–1885
Alfonso XIII	1886–1931

FAMILY HISTORY IS FOR EVERYONE

Harriet Stryker Rodda, certified genealogist, lecturer and teacher; author of family histories and professional articles, including How to Climb Your Family Tree.

Everyone in America is descended from immigrant stock, no matter what the ethnic or cultural background. Even the "native American Indians" were immigrants. They just happened to arrive before the European sailors and settlers.

With the Bicentennial celebrations mostly behind us, we are facing the coming of our Tricentennial in the year 2076. By then, each of us could be an ancestor who could be a missing link to our descendants. Far too many people in this country are bemoaning the fact that they cannot complete their connections with their ancestral families because their folks left no records or they neglected to listen when stories were being told.

Families in the United States are the backbone of the nation, although they are not as stereotyped as they once were. No matter what the ethnic or cultural background, the family unit is still the core of our young, 202-year-old America. *Newsweek* declared in May 1978 "there is an underlying stability of family life that often goes unnoticed. Ninety-eight percent of all American children are raised in families, and last year 79 percent of those were living with their parents." These are the children, plus many more, who by 2076 will be asking "Who am I?", "Where did my family come from?", "When did they get here?", "How did they live?", "Why are we as we are?"

These very same questions are being asked today. The answers are not to be found easily for some, because the fore-parents left no private and often few public records of themselves. For the majority, however, most of the facts they need to answer the who, where, when, why and how are available. They can be found and the family history preserved to be passed along for years to come. "But how do I start?" is the first question.

Start with yourself. You are to be author of your family history. Your autobiography will not only inform others of the facts and facets of your life, but more importantly will reveal to you the debt you owe your family. It will show you what you would like to know about those earlier members of the family. *Who, when, where, how* and *why* will be your guides as you record yourself and your times. Add pictures to illustrate, and dig out the certificates of your birth, education, honors, marriage or anything else that will add documentation to your record. Even if you never go on to compile a family history, this autobiography may be of inestimable assistance to someone else who will take up the task where you left off.

Contact all older living members of your family. With tape recorder or pencil and notebook, get all the information on the family members they can supply. It will amaze you how much they know and how they will have contacts with relatives you have never heard of. Don't overlook the stories or traditions they may relate to you. There is a core of truth in most of them. Try not to antagonize, but tell them of your deep interest in preparing and preserving the family's history.

Check their possession of family or Bible records; ask about certificates, passports, naturalization records, pictures, letters, heirloom furniture or other items. You may want some of these, but don't be greedy. Take pictures of whatever you can and copy whatever you find in their records. But leave the original with the owner unless it is freely given to you.

Record your in-family findings. How you do this is for you to decide, but make the final record easily understandable by anyone who sees it. It should contain the time and place and from whom you received the statements so that later you won't have to wonder who told you that and where you heard it. For every statement you use in your final record, you should have some documentation to prove it. Birth, marriage, divorce, death and land ownership records are the basic public records that should be found to support your story.

Visit a good genealogical library and use their catalogs to determine whether someone in the past has written a family history or genealogy to which your family can relate. Read the local and general histories for a better understanding of where and how your people lived. See the vital records collected for researchers like you: church records, newspaper items, census records, maps, cemetery records, diaries, account books, and many, many more, including the work of genealogists whose notes on your family may have been deposited for safekeeping. Get acquainted with the publications of genealogical societies, especially those that publish genealogical records. Begin to took at some of the books on the shelves with a critical eye. Decide which of their features you like and what you would not want in your final record. Are they readable, interesting in form and format, well documented and illustrated; do they feel good in the hand; does the type of binding let them lie open readily for reading and research? Make note of those that please you so that you can refer to them when you are ready to prepare your final history.

Despite the wealth of recorded information to be found in the form of tax rolls, military records, probate, land, court and census records, not to mention church and cemetery records and the cemeteries themselves, with their informative gravestones, this information is not always easy to obtain. Help is available. Along the way you will have become acquainted with the many "how-to" books written by people who want to share their knowledge with you. You will hear and read of genealogical seminars, lectures and conferences at every level from the local historical society to the large university and the Federal Archives. Take advantage of as much of this as you can, for you will meet a vast number of people who are learning as you are, who are as eager to accomplish as you will be, and who are happy to share their knowledge with you.

Today, family history is recognized for its value in establishing a keen sense of identity. Such simple projects in elementary schools as collecting information about parents and grandparents are known to help children establish as sense of personal worth and dignity. Genealogy is no longer considered a snob hobby. It has come of age. Good hunting! Become an honored ancestor!

OUTLINE OF WORLD HISTORY

This capsule presentation of the history of the world covers the period from 4000 B.C. through 1979.

4000 B.C.—3000 B.C.

EUROPE

4000 B.C. Farmers living along **Danube River** in villages designed stone replicas of deities.

NEAR AND MIDDLE EAST

4000 B.C. Ubadians, who were settled in southern Mesopotamia, developed towns in the Tigris-Euphrates plain, laying foundation for future civilization of Ur. Semitic nomads from Syria and the Arabian peninsula invaded area and intermingled with Urbaidians.

3500 B.C. Sumerians, possibly from Asia, settled along the Euphrates and developed a civilization that flourished.

FAR EAST

4000 B.C. Farmers lived in villages in northern **China.**

AMERICAS

4000 B.C. Indians in North and South America, descendants of people who migrated from Asia over the Bering Strait many centuries earlier, obtained food by hunting and cultivating corn. The remains of extinct animals, such as the mastodon, as well as arrowheads and spear points found in caves at **Folsom** and **Clovis,** New Mexico, attest to the antiquity of Indians in the Americas.

AFRICA

4000 B.C. An early Negro civilization thrived in the **Sahara.** The **Tassili rock paintings** in southeast Algeria, which date from about 6000 B.C., portray an organized society of hunters and herders who had horses and cattle.

c. 3200 B.C. Upper and Lower Egypt were united by the legendary **Menes,** the first Pharaoh, who built his capital at Memphis.

3000 B.C.—2000 B.C.

EUROPE

2700–2000 B.C. Early Helladic culture existed on Greek mainland, and **Cycladic** culture in the Aegean islands; both noted for primitive figurines.

2500–1200 B.C. Barbarian **Celts,** who overran western Europe, rode horses, carried iron weapons, and were ruled by **Druids,** a priestly class.

2500–1100 B.C. Megalithic culture of western Europe was noted for its huge stone ceremonial constructions, such as **dolmens,** or chamber tombs, and **menhirs,** or monumental stone slabs, sometimes arranged in circles, as at **Stonehenge** in England; remains also exist at **Carnac,** Brittany.

NEAR AND MIDDLE EAST

c. 3000 B.C. Kish, which was situated near modern Baghdad, became leading Sumerian city in the reign of King Etana.

c. 2800 B.C. Meskiaggasher founded dynasty in **Erech,** which began to rival Kish.

2686–2181 B.C. Old Kingdom of Egypt: Egyptian art and architecture developed; great pyramid for Pharaoh **Khufu,** one of the Seven Wonders of the Ancient World, was completed (c. 2600 B.C.) at Gizeh.

c. 2650 B.C. Gilgamesh, hero of Sumerian legends, reigned as king of Erech.

2500 B.C. King Lugalannemundu of Adab briefly united Sumerian city-states; following his death, city-states fought each other for 200 years.

c. 2450 B.C. King Eannatum made the Sumerian city-state of Lagash supreme.

c. 2325 B.C. Sargon the Great ruled over vast empire in Mesopotamia and built capital at Agade in Akkad that had beautiful temples and palace.

2200 B.C. Gutians, barbarians from Iran, conquered Sumeria and destroyed Agade.

2133–1786 B.C. Middle Kingdom of Egypt: Egypt expanded territory southward and engaged in extensive foreign trade.

2100 B.C. Ur-Nammu founded last Sumerian dynasty and promulgated law code, the oldest in existence.

FAR EAST

3000–1500 B.C. Indus valley civilization of northern India: a sophisticated culture thrived and cities of **Harappa** and **Mohenjo-Daro** were built with courtyard houses and modern drainage systems.

c. 2205–c. 1766 B.C. Hsia dynasty of China: first historic Chinese dynasty thrived; horses were domesticated and rice and millet were cultivated.

AMERICAS

2500 B.C. Indians began to make pottery.

2000 B.C.—1500 B.C.

EUROPE

c. 2000–1700 B.C. Mycenaeans, Greek-speaking people, settled in Greece, established flourishing civilization, and traded with Crete.

c. 1900–1400 B.C. Stonehenge, a massive stone complex used for religious purposes, was erected on Salisbury Plain, England.

c. 1700–c. 1500 B.C. Minoan culture on Crete reached its zenith; magnificent Minoan palaces built at **Knossos** and **Phaistos** showed evidence of advanced engineering skills.

c. 1500 B.C. Linear B script existed in Crete, evidence of Mycenaean influence.

NEAR AND MIDDLE EAST

2000 B.C. Elamites destroyed Ur, marking end of Sumerian dominance in Mesopotamia.

c. 2000–c. 1900 B.C. Abraham, founder of Judaism, is said to have lived.

2000–1700 B.C. Hebrews lived as nomadic shepherds in Canaan.

1786–1567 B.C. Egypt ruled by **Hyksos kings,** who probably came from Canaan, introduced horse-drawn chariots.

1750–c. 1708 B.C. Hammurabi ruled Babylonia, brought most of Mesopotamia and Assyria under his control, and introduced his **law code.**

c. 1600 B.C. Babylonian dynasty destroyed by **Hittites** from Anatolia and Syria.

1567–1085 B.C. New Kingdom in Egypt: Hyksos kings ousted and Egyptian power and civilization reached its height.

FAR EAST

1523–1027 B.C. Shang dynasty ruled China, developing a high civilization characterized by specialized classes, writing, a medium of exchange, and ancestor worship.

AMERICAS

2000 B.C. By this time, Indians had permanent village settlements and were cultivating manioc, squash, maize, and beans and domesticating dogs.

1500 B.C.—1000 B.C.

EUROPE

1400 B.C. Mycenaeans gained supremacy of the Mediterranean, and Mycenae, in northern Peloponnesus, became major ancient city following collapse of Knossus.

c. 1200 B.C. Trojan Wars: Greece conquered Troy in Asia Minor.
Dorian barbarians from the north began to invade Greece, initiating Dark Ages of Greek history.

1150–1000 B.C. Greeks settled on Ionian coast of Asia Minor.

NEAR AND MIDDLE EAST

c. 1500 B.C. Mitanni kingdom of Hurrians (known as Horites in Old Testament) ruled much of Mesopotamia and Assyria.

1468 B.C. Battle of Megiddo: Egyptians, under **Thutmose III,** conquered Syria and part of Mesopotamia.

1292–1225 B.C. Ramses II ruled Egypt and completed temples at Karnak, Thebes, Luxor, and Abu-Simbel. Moses led Hebrews out of Egpt.

1250 B.C. Phoenicians flourished on coasts of Syria and Lebanon, establishing great city-states of **Tyre and Sidon** and beginning to colonize Mediterranean coast.

c. 1250 B.C. Hebrews entered **Canaan.**

1020–1004 B.C. Saul became the first king of the Hebrews.

FAR EAST

1500–500 B.C. Barbarian **Aryans**, Sanskrit-speaking people from central Asia, invaded **India** and destroyed Indus valley civilization; early *Vedas*, sacred Hindu texts, were composed.

1027–256 B.C. Chou dynasty of China superseded **Shang** dynasty and represented the Classical Age of China with the *Five Classics*, and teachings of **Confucius, Lao-tze,** and **Mencius.**

AMERICAS

c. 1250 B.C. **Olmecs** began to settle at **San Lorenzo, Mexico,** and developed civilization with widespread influence that was famous for gigantic sculptured heads (sometimes weighing over 20 tons) and austere figurines; ceremonial center was established at **La Venta** (fl. 800–c. 400 B.C.) for jaguar cult; Stele C found at **Tres Zapotes** has date equivalent to 31 B.C. carved in Mayan calendric system.

AFRICA

1200 B.C. Negroes in Nigeria developed **Nok culture,** which became advanced civilization, noted for expressive terra-cotta sculpture, but died out c. 200 B.C.

1000 B.C.—700 B.C.

EUROPE

1000 B.C. **Teutonic tribes** settled northern Europe.
Latin tribes began to settle in Italy.

900–400 B.C. **Etruscan** people, who had probably migrated from Lydia in Asia Minor, established a high civilization in **Italy** and became maritime power.

850–600 B.C. **Homeric Greece:** Greeks established colonies in Italy and along Mediterranean; the *Iliad* and the *Odyssey* were probably composed by **Homer, Hesiod** wrote poetry, and music developed.

776 B.C. Olympic games initiated.

753 B.C. Traditional date for founding of **Rome** by **Romulus** and **Remus.**

750 B.C. Romans seized **Sabine women** at public spectacle, taking them as wives.

747 B.C. **Rome** taken by **Sabines,** who united with Romans as one people.

736–630 B.C. **Sparta** became powerful on Greek mainland.

NEAR AND MIDDLE EAST

1000–774 B.C. **Phoenicians** dominated the seas, perhaps sailing to Cornwall, England, for tin and probably sailing down west coast of Africa.

910–606 B.C. **Assyrian Empire** controlled Mesopotamia.

774–625 B.C. Phoenicia came under **Assyrian** rule.

747–728 B.C. **Tiglath-Pilser III,** king of Assyria, subdued Aramaean tribes in Babylonia, conquered **Urartu** (Armenia), and established control over **Syria.**

721–705 B.C. **Sargon II,** king of Assyria, completed conquest of **Israel,** exiling most Israelites.

705–681 B.C. **Sennacherib,** king of Assyria, destroyed Babylon and built magnificent palace at **Nineveh.**

AMERICAS

c. 1000 B.C. **Chavin culture** in northern **Peru** began to flourish; elaborate stone ceremonial center with painted relief sculpture was erected at **Chavin de Huantar** for jaguar cult; and gold ornaments and ceramics were designed; this culture declined after 200 B.C.

AFRICA

c. 800–586 B.C. **Carthage,** founded in North Africa by **Phoenicians,** became a wealthy commercial center.

c. 750 B.C. **Kushites** settled in **Sudan** and developed high civilization, erecting palaces and pyramids; extensive archaeological remains of ironworks at **Meroë; Kush**ites used elephants and traded as far as Rome and India; their last king died in 320 A.D.

700 B.C.—500 B.C.

EUROPE

c. 700 B.C. Temple to Hera erected at **Olympia.**
Spartans, after a series of wars, annexed eastern part of Messenia.
Celts began to invade Spain and France.

c. 660 B.C. Byzantium founded by **Megara.**

c. 621 B.C. Draco codified harsh Athenian **law.**

600–300 B.C. **Teutonic tribes** invaded western Europe: the Alemanni settled on the upper Rhine, the **Franks** and **Saxons** between the Weser and the Elbe, and the Thuringians south of the Saxons.

594 B.C. Solon introduced constitutional and social reforms into **Athens,** establishing limited democracy.

c. 580 B.C. Thales, first Western philosopher, flourished.

566 B.C. First Roman **census** taken.

c. 560–510 B.C. **Athens** ruled by **tyrants** after Pisistratus seized power.

560 B.C. Croesus, wealthy king of Lydia, conquered Ionian cities and was defeated (546 B.C.) by **Cyrus the Great.**

c. 550 B.C. Temple of Artemis (Diana) erected at **Eph**esus.

c. 534–510 B.C. Reign of **Tarquinius Superbus,** Etruscan ruler; Etruscan supremacy ended soon after his death.

509 B.C. Traditional date for founding of the **Roman Republic.**
The **Temple of Jupiter,** on the Roman Capitol, was dedicated.

NEAR AND MIDDLE EAST

681–668 B.C. **Esarhaddon,** king of Assyria, reigned; at its peak Assyrian Empire extended from Iran to Egypt.

625–539 B.C. **Chaldean Empire** of Mesopotamia.

612 B.C. **Nineveh,** Assyrian capital, fell to Medes, Chaldeans, and Scythians.

606 B.C. Battle of **Carchemish** ended Assyrian Empire.

c. 605–562 B.C. Reign of **Nebuchadnezzar II,** king of Babylonia; **Babylon,** with its hanging gardens (one of Seven Wonders of Ancient World), was greatest city of its time during his reign; massive palaces, "Tower of Babel," and a temple to the god Marduk were also constructed.

586 B.C. Nebuchadnezzar took **Jerusalem,** destroying the temple of Solomon and carrying inhabitants back to Babylonia.

c. 550 B.C. **Persian Empire,** founded by **Cyrus the Great,** included vast areas of the Near and Middle East; Persian art and architecture flourished, and Zoroastrian religion spread.

538 B.C. **Cyrus the Great** conquered Babylon and returned Hebrews to Jerusalem.

525–404 B.C. Persians conquered and ruled **Egypt.**

521–486 B.C. **Darius I** (the Great), king of Persia, extended and strengthened the empire, warred with Greece, and unified Persian power in the East.

FAR EAST

c. 563–483 B.C. **Gautama Buddha** preached in **India.**

c. 551–479 B.C. **Confucius** taught in **China.**

AFRICA

c. 631 B.C. Greeks founded North African city of **Cyrene,** which became important commercial center.

500 B.C.—400 B.C.

EUROPE

500–449 B.C. **Greek-Persian Wars** were fought, caused by commercial rivalry between Athens and Persia; Athens became leading city-state of Greece.

500 B.C. **Classical Greek civilization** (drama, philosophy, and the arts) developed and flourished, declining after 300 B.C.

498 B.C. Earliest extant poem of **Pindar** was written.

490 B.C. Battle of **Marathon:** 30,000 Persians, who were sent by Darius I, landed at Marathon to march on Athens and were turned back by Athenian infantrymen under **Miltiades.**

460 B.C. Athens warred against **Peloponnesian cities,** which were allied with Sparta.

457–429 B.C. **Age of Pericles** or Golden Age of Athens: philosophy, sculpture, and painting flourished; **Par**thenon was built (447–432 B.C.) on the Acropolis.

c. 451 B.C. The Twelve Tablets: **Roman law** codified for the first time.

c. 435 B.C. Phidias completed his statue of Zeus (one of Seven Wonders of Ancient World) for temple of Olympia.

431–404 B.C. **Peloponnesian War** developed, growing out of Spartan-Athenian rivalry; Athens destroyed (430).

c. 411 Thucydides wrote *The Peloponnesian War.*

404–371 B.C. Sparta was leading Greek power.

NEAR AND MIDDLE EAST

490 B.C. First Persian expedition to Greece under Darius I was turned back at **Marathon.**

480–479 B.C. Second Persian expedition to Greece under **Xerxes I** was turned back at Plataea.

AMERICAS

c. 500 B.C. **Zapotecs** established ceremonial center at Monte Albán, Mexico, which showed Olmec influence.

AFRICA

c. 500 B.C. Kingdom of **Axum** in **Ethiopia** came into existence; palaces, temples, and carved stone obelisks were built and trade took place with Near East and India; this kingdom declined c. 700 A.D.

400 B.C.—300 B.C.

EUROPE

400–270 B.C. **Rome** conquered Italy, subduing Etruscans, Samnites, and Greek colonists.

399 B.C. **Socrates** was condemned to death and made to drink hemlock.

390 B.C. Rome sacked by **Gauls.**

c. 387 B.C. **Plato** founded his **Academy** in Athens, which is considered the first university of the Western world.

359–336 B.C. **Philip II** of **Macedon** conquered Thrace, Thebes, and Athens, and attempted to unite Greece during his reign; **Demosthenes**, greatest Greek orator, warned Athenians of Macedonian aims.

336–323 B.C. Reign of **Alexander the Great** of **Macedon** (son of Philip II), first of the great European conquerors; Alexander extended empire to include Egypt and the Near East and invaded India.

335 B.C. **Aristotle** founded a school in the Lyceum at Athens known as Peripatetic from his practice of lecturing in a covered portico (*peripatos*).

323 B.C. **Hellenistic Age** began, during which Greek influence spread throughout Mediterranean; this age ended in 31 B.C.

NEAR AND MIDDLE EAST

c. 352 B.C. **Mausoleum** at **Halicarnassus** in Asia Minor (one of Seven Wonders of Ancient World) was erected in memory of Mausolus of Caria.

334–330 B.C. **Alexander the Great** conquered Asia Minor, Phoenicia, Palestine, Egypt, and Persia and founded **Alexandria.**

323 B.C.–30 A.D. **Ptolemies,** a Greek dynasty, ruled **Egypt.**

FAR EAST

327–326 B.C. **Alexander the Great** and his Greek troops entered **India,** withdrawing after troops revolted.

325–298 B.C. Reign of **Chandragupta Maurya,** who founded Maurya dynasty and united **India.**

AFRICA

350 B.C. **Meroë,** Kushite capital, fell to **Ethiopians** and was abandoned.

300 B.C.—200 B.C.

EUROPE

300 B.C. City of **Rome** became a major power in Mediterranean world.

292–280 B.C. **Colossus of Rhodes** (one of Seven Wonders of Ancient World), a bronze statue, probably more than 100 feet tall, of the sun god, Helios, was constructed on promontory overlooking harbor.

282–272 B.C. **Pyrrhus,** king of **Epirus,** fought Romans and caused its ruin.

264–241 B.C. First **Punic War:** Carthage warred against Roman occupation of Sicily.

227 B.C. Rome annexed Sardinia and Corsica.

218–201 B.C. Second **Punic War:** Hannibal, the Carthaginian leader, crossed the Alps and invaded Italy; victorious Romans gained Spanish provinces and Carthaginian war fleet.

NEAR AND MIDDLE EAST

300 B.C. **Alexandria,** Egypt, became intellectual center of Hellenistic world until its influence ended in 50 B.C.

c. 280 B.C. Under Ptolemy II, a **lighthouse** (one of Seven Wonders of Ancient World) was constructed on Pharos, Alexandria.

250 B.C. **Parthian Empire,** which succeeded Persian Empire, ended in 226 A.D.

FAR EAST

269–232 B.C. **Emperor Asoka the Great** ruled **India,** making Buddhism state religion.

221–207 B.C. **Ch'in** dynasty of China: country was unified for first time, and construction of **Great Wall** was initiated.

202 B.C. **Han** dynasty of China established: during long peaceful rule, Chinese realized great artistic achievements, expanded territory, and introduced **Buddhism;** this dynasty collapsed in 220 A.D.

200 B.C.—100 B.C.

EUROPE

192–189 B.C. During **Syrian War** between Rome and Seleucid kingdom, Romans acquired territory in Asia Minor.

c. 150 B.C. **Polybius** completed six books of his *Universal History,* a political analysis of the rise of Rome.

149–146 B.C. Third **Punic War.**

146 B.C. **Macedonia** became a Roman province.

121 B.C. **Rome** conquered southeastern **Gaul,** modern Provence.

NEAR AND MIDDLE EAST

192–189 B.C. **Syrian War** between Rome and Seleucids: Antiochus III forced to give up Asia Minor.

167 B.C. Hebrew **Maccabees** revolted against Antiochus IV, king of Syria, who had tried to Hellenize Palestine.

FAR EAST

c. 200 B.C. *Mahabharata,* Sanskrit epic poem, began to be composed and was completed c. 200 A.D.

AFRICA

149–146 B.C. Third **Punic War:** Carthage destroyed by Romans, who established Roman province of Africa.

100 B.C.—A.D. 1

EUROPE

73–71 B.C. **Spartacus** led slave revolt in southern Italy; Pompey crushed revolt and crucified 6,000 slaves.

63 B.C. **Cicero,** greatest Roman orator, exposed **Catiline's** plot to seize consulship by force.

60–53 B.C. First Triumvirate: **Julius Caesar,** Pompey, and Marcus Licinius Crassus ruled Rome.

58–49 B.C. Gallic Wars: **Caesar's campaigns** brought Gaul under Roman rule.

48 B.C. Caesar met **Cleopatra** in Egypt.

46–44 B.C. **Caesar** ruled Rome, which included Gaul, Italy, part of Illyria, Macedonia, Greece, Asia Minor, Egypt, and part of North Africa.

44 B.C. Caesar stabbed to death in the Senate on **Ides of March.**

43–31 B.C. Second Triumvirate: **Marc Antony,** Lepidus, and **Octavian,** Caesar's grandnephew, ruled Rome.

c. 35 B.C. Roman poets **Vergil** and **Horace** flourished.

31 B.C. **Octavian** defeated **Antony** and **Cleopatra** at Actium, assuming title Augustus and becoming first Roman emperor; Augustus made Egypt a Roman province.

27 B.C. **Roman Empire** established.

14 B.C. **Pax Romana:** Roman Empire began 200 years of peace, which ended in 192 A.D.

NEAR AND MIDDLE EAST

74–63 B.C. Third **Mithridatic War** between King Mithridates VI of Pontus and Rome, which resulted in further Roman conquests in Near East.

48 B.C. **Cleopatra,** daughter of Ptolemy XI of Egypt, with the aid of **Julius Caesar,** became Queen of Egypt (47–30 B.C.).

37 B.C. **Rome** began to rule **Palestine;** this rule ended in 395 A.D.

36 B.C. Queen Cleopatra married **Marc Antony.**

30 B.C. **Egypt** annexed by Roman Empire, following the suicides of Antony and Cleopatra.

6 or 4 B.C. **Jesus** born in Bethlehem.

AMERICAS

100 B.C. **Paracus** culture, an offshoot of Chavin civilization in **Peru,** flourished.

A.D. 1—A.D. 100

EUROPE

1 **Christian era** began.

Gothic kingdom on the lower Vistula (Poland) developed.

5–40 **Cymbeline** reigned in Britain.

9 **Arminius** defeated Roman commander **Varus** at the Battle of Teutoburg Forest, ending Roman attempts to conquer Germany.

37 **Caligula** made emperor of Rome by army; his cruel regime ended (41) with his assassination.

41–54 Reign of Roman Emperor **Claudius I,** who disenfranchised many non-Italians, annexed Mauretania, expelled Jews from Rome, and initiated Roman rule of Britain.

43 Romans ruled **Britain** until 407.

54–69 Reign of **Emperor Nero,** last of Julio-Claudian line of Roman emperors; he blamed Christians for fire that almost destroyed (64) Rome and rebuilt city magnificently; Roman persecution of Christians was begun, which may have caused death of St. Peter and St. Paul; Nero committed suicide.

61–62 **Boadicea,** British queen of Iceni (Norfolk), led revolt against Romans at Fort Londinium; defeated, she took poison.

65 Seneca, philosopher and adviser to Nero, committed suicide after he was accused of conspiracy.

69–79 Reign of **Emperor Vespasian,** who founded Flavian dynasty and erected the **Colosseum** and **Forum** in Rome.

79 Mount **Vesuvius** erupted, destroying Pompeii and Herculaneum.

81–96 Reign of **Emperor Domitian,** son of Vespasian, was characterized by persecution of Christians; Domitian erected **Arch of Titus** to memorialize his brother's conquest of Jerusalem.

96–180 Reign of "the **Five Good Emperors**" of Rome: Nerva, Trajan, Hadrian, Antonius Pius, and Marcus Aurelius; the empire was enlarged and great public works undertaken.

c. 98 Tacitus, Roman historian, completed *Germania.*

NEAR AND MIDDLE EAST

c. 28 St. **John the Baptist** began preaching.

c. 30 Jesus crucified in Jerusalem.

c. 42–60 St. **Paul,** one of the apostles, conducted missionary work in Asia Minor and Greece and wrote his *Epistles.*

66 Jews revolted against Roman rule in Palestine; **Titus** suppressed rebellion and destroyed (70) Jerusalem.

FAR EAST

9 Emperor **Wang Mang** usurped Chinese throne, initiating agrarian reforms.

25 Han dynasty held Chinese throne until 220; Buddhism was introduced during reign of **Emperor Ming-ti** (58–76), and cultural ties with India were increased.

60 Kushan kings of Grandhara began to rule in West Pakistan, establishing an empire that extended from central Asia to India; a famous school of Buddhist sculpture was organized.

100—200

EUROPE

100 For the next 375 years, **Goths, Vandals,** and **Huns** raided Roman Empire.

117 Roman Empire reached its greatest extent after Emperor **Trajan** subdued Dacia (Rumania), Armenia, and Upper Mesopotamia; Trajan's Column was erected in Rome to honor his conquests.

117–138 Reign of **Emperor Hadrian;** he standardized Roman law throughout the empire, and constructed a 73-mile-long wall named after him in Britain.

130 **Pantheon** built at Rome and consecrated as Christian church in 609.

160–180 Marcus **Aurelius,** Stoic philosopher and author of *Meditations,* ruled Roman Empire and was forced to wage numerous wars.

192–284 Roman Empire ruled by army, "**Barracks Emperors.**"

196 Barbarians overran northern Britain.

NEAR AND MIDDLE EAST

132–135 Bar **Kokba** led Jewish revolt; defeated by Romans, Jews were barred from Jerusalem and further dispersed.

FAR EAST

100 Traditional date for beginning of **Japanese state.**

c. 100 **Funan Empire** established in Cambodia.

Champa kingdom founded in South Vietnam and parts of Cambodia.

c. 132 Indo-Scythians destroyed last traces of Hellenic rule in northern India.

c. 150 Kanishka reigned in India.

AMERICAS

100 Teotihuacán civilization, one of America's most splendid early civilizations, developed in central Mexico; Pyramid of the Sun was as tall as 20-story building, Temple of Quetzalcoátl erected to Feather Serpent deity, and agricultural techniques advanced enough to support large urban population around huge **pyramid complex;** influence ceased when city fell c. 700 to **Chichimecs.**

200—300

EUROPE

205 British revolt against Romans was suppressed in 211.

211–217 Reign of **Emperor Caracalla,** who constructed in Rome Baths named for him.

220–238 Goths invaded Balkans, Asia Minor, and eastern Roman Empire.

c. 240 Franks first appeared in Europe.

c. 252 Franks, Goths, and **Alemanni** broke through borders of Roman Empire.

268 Goths sacked Athens, Corinth, and Sparta.

270–275 Emperor **Aurelian** consolidated empire by retreating to Danubian borders, recovered Gaul, and overthrew Queen Zenobia of Palmyra (Syria).

276 Great wall around Rome erected against barbarian attacks.

284–305 Reign of **Emperor Diocletian,** who divided empire into western part (Italy and Africa), which was governed from Milan by **Maximian;** Diocletian ruled eastern part (Near and Middle East and Egypt) from Nicomedia (now Izmit, Turkey).

NEAR AND MIDDLE EAST

200–230 Clement and **Origen,** Christian theologians, taught in Alexandria.

226–240 Ardashir I (or Artaxerxes) overthrew Parthian Empire; founded Neo-Persian Empire under **Sassanid dynasty.**

232 Sassanian-Roman War established **Sassanians** as major Eastern power.

c. 242 Mani, founder of Manichaeism, began to preach in Persia; he was martyred c. 276.

260 Persians under **Shapur I** captured **Roman Emperor Valerian** and Roman territory in Near and Middle East.

268 Zenobia, queen of Palmyra, conquered Syria, Mesopotamia, and parts of Egypt; Zenobia was overthrown (273) by **Roman Emperor Aurelian.**

FAR EAST

205–225 Reign of **Fan Shih-man** in Cambodia extended empire to lower Mekong River.

220 Han dynasty came to an end; China was divided and invaded for next three centuries.

265 Western Tsin (Ch'in) dynasty began, uniting China until **White Huns** began to invade in 317.

300—400

EUROPE

303 Diocletian harshly persecuted **Christians.**

306–337 Reign of **Constantine I,** first Christian emperor.

313 Edict of Milan recognized Christianity as a legal religion in Roman Empire.

325 First ecumenical council, which was convened by Constantine at Nicaea, voted against Arianism.

330 Constantine made **Constantinople** (now Istanbul) **new** capital of Roman Empire.

337 Romans fought series of wars with Persians, which ended (363) with loss of parts of Armenia and Mesopotamia.

c. 340 Monasticism developed in the West.

341 Wulfila began Christianizing Visigoths and resettling them (c. 348) in Balkans.

c. 350 Huns, central Asian nomads, began to invade Europe, forcing Goths westward.

360–367 Picts, Irish, and Saxons invaded Britain.

361–363 Reign of **Julian the Apostate,** who tried unsuccessfully to revive paganism.

363 Emperor **Jovian** restored Christianity.

379–395 Theodosius, Roman emperor, resettled Goths in empire, many of whom became soldiers.

383–407 Roman legions evacuated **Britain.**

390 Massacre of 7,000 following anti-Roman rebellion at Thessalonica; Theodosius did public penance before Bishop Ambrose of Milan.

395 Alaric, former head of Visigothic troops under Theodosius, became king of **Visigoths** and pillaged Balkans and Greece.

Roman Empire permanently partitioned.

NEAR AND MIDDLE EAST

310–379 Reign of **Shapur II** of Persia, who recovered Armenia from Romans.

337 Persians fought series of wars with **Romans**, securing (363) territory in Armenia and Mesopotamia.

378 Battle of **Adrianople**: Roman defeat left Greece unprotected from barbarians.

381 First Council of Constantinople, **second ecumenical council** convened, formalized Nicene Creed, and outlawed paganism.

387 Armenia partitioned between Rome and Persia.

399–420 Reign of **Yazdegerd I** of Persia; Christianity was tolerated initially, but later persecutions were begun in Armenia and Persia.

FAR EAST

c. 300 Funan (**Cambodia**) ruled by an Indian Brahman, who introduced Hindu customs, Indian legal code, and alphabet of central India.

317 China was divided into Northern and Southern dynasties; reunited in 590. **Eastern Tsin dynasty** ruled southern China, and capital at Nanking was established.

c. 320–c. 380 Reign of **Chandragupta I,** who established Gupta Empire that ruled India until c. 544; his reign marked the Golden Age of Hindu art and literature.

386 Northern Wei dynasty gained control of northern China, ruled until 495.

AMERICAS

300 Mayan civilization in southern **Mexico** entered its Classical Age during which its influence spread into **Guatemala** and **Honduras;** Mayans, ruled by priests, had advanced arts and science: calendar, hieroglyphic writing, and major works of stone architecture; this civilization collapsed in 900.

AFRICA

300 Kingdom of **Ghana** developed in western Sudan.

320–350 Christianity introduced into kingdom of **Axum.**

400—500

EUROPE

400 Eastern Roman Empire superseded by **Byzantine Empire.**

400–450 Europe overrun by **Goths.**

402 Roman capital moved to **Ravenna.**

408–450 Reign of **Theodosius II,** Byzantine emperor, who systematized (438) Roman laws (*Codex Theodosianus*) and made separation of Eastern and Western sections of empire official.

410 Alaric and Visigoths sacked **Rome.**

413–426 St. Augustine wrote *The City of God.*

432 St. Patrick began missionary work among the **Irish.**

445–453 Attila, king of the Huns, ruled from Hungary over Russia, Poland, and Germany, extorting concessions from Theodosius II and ravaging Balkans.

449 Angles, Saxons, and **Jutes** began conquest of Britain.

451 Attila, defeated at Châlons in Champagne, then invaded northern Italy, but allegedly was stopped by **Pope Leo I.**

455–475 Rome ruled by series of puppet emperors; **Ricimer,** Suebi general from central Germany, was virtual ruler of western empire until 472.

466–484 Reign of **Euric,** who established kingdom in Spain, bringing Visigothic power to its peak.

476 Odoacer, Ostrogoth chieftain, deposed **Romulus Augustulus,** last Roman emperor of the West; Odoacer was recognized as head of western empire by Zeno, Byzantine emperor.

481–511 Reign of **Clovis I,** king of the Franks and founder of **Merovingian dynasty,** who defeated (486) Romans at Soissons, ending Roman rule in Gaul, and was converted (496) to Christianity.

493 Theodoric the Great, king of Ostrogoths, seized Ravenna, assassinated Odoacer, and established Ostrogothic kingdom in Italy.

NEAR AND MIDDLE EAST

428 Persians began to rule **Armenia;** their control ceased in 633.

491 Armenian Church separated from Byzantine and Roman churches.

FAR EAST

420 Liu Sung dynasty came to power in southern China and ruled until 479.

c. 450 Buddhism established in **Burma.**

465 By this time, **White Huns** had almost destroyed Gupta empire in India.

479 Chi dynasty began to rule southern China; its rule ceased in 502.

AFRICA

429 Vandal kingdom established in Africa by **Gaiseric,** who took his people out of Spain.

439 Gaiseric made **Carthage** Vandal capital.

476 Gaiseric concluded **treaty** with **Zeno,** who recognized Vandal rule over Roman Africa, Sicily, Sardinia, Corsica, and Balearic Islands.

500—600

EUROPE

500 Golden age of **Irish monastic scholarship** began, which died out c. 800.

506 Alaric II, king of Visigoths, issued *Lex Romana Visigothorum,* law code.

527–565 Reign of **Justinian,** Byzantine emperor, who was strongly influenced by his wife **Theodora;** Justinian issued *Corpus Juris Civilis* (also known as the **Justinian Code),** a comprehensive code of Roman law; erected public works; and recovered Africa from Vandals and Italy from Ostrogoths.

529 Benedict of Nursia founded Monte Cassino in Subiaco, Italy, first **Benedictine monastery.**

532–537 Cathedral of **Hagia Sophia** erected in Constantinople.

c. 537 Traditional date of **King Arthur's death** at the Battle of Camlan.

c. 560–616 Reign of **Ethelbert,** king of Kent, who received St. Augustine and was converted to Christianity; Ethelbert made Kent supreme in Britain and drew up first code of English laws.

563 St. Columba, an Irish missionary to Scotland, founded church and converted king of the Picts.

567 Frankish kingdom divided into Austrasia, Neustria, and Burgundy.

568 Lombards, ancient German tribe, invaded northern Italy and established a kingdom that lasted over 200 years.

584 Slavs in Balkan peninsula overran Greece and began to menace Byzantine Empire.

c. 585 Avars, conquering nomads from steppes of central Asia, reached Danube.

590–604 Papacy of **St. Gregory I (the Great)** laid basis for later papal claims to temporal authority and independence and codified church music; the Gregorian chant is named for him.

597 St. Augustine, a Roman monk, sent by Pope Gregory to convert English, founded a church at **Canterbury,** becoming (601) first Archbishop of Canterbury.

NEAR AND MIDDLE EAST

c. 500 Arabs invaded **Palestine.**

525 Yemen conquered by Abyssinians.

531–579 Reign of **Khosru I** (or Chosroes) of Persia marked political and cultural prime of Persia; Khosru fought Byzantines and overthrew Abyssinian control of Yemen.

c. 550 Migration of **Turks** began, which broke up (565) White Hun settlements in Western Turkestan.

570 Mohammed, prophet of Islam, born.

590–628 Reign of **Khosru II** of Persia, who conquered Jerusalem, Damascus, and Egypt and restored Persian boundaries to those at time of Darius I.

FAR EAST

c. 550 Khmers from Chen-la state to north began to overrun Funan and made **Cambodia** (about equal to Cambodia and Laos) dominant in Southeast Asia until c. 1400.

Japanese began to adopt **Chinese culture,** using Chinese script and introducing Buddhism.

590 Sui dynasty began to rule China; Great Wall of China was reconstructed as defense against Turks and Mongols, five million people were employed to construct complex water transport system, and **civil service examination** was introduced; this dynasty ended in 618.

600—700

EUROPE

610–641 Reign of **Heraclius,** Byzantine emperor, who recovered lands lost to Persia and then lost them to Moslem Arabs at end of his reign.

613–629 Reign of **Clotair** (Lothair) **II**, Merovingian king, who reunited Frankish realm and appointed **Pepin of Landen** and **Arnulf**, bishop of Metz, (ancestors of the Carolingians) to govern Austrasia.

617 Northumbria became dominant kingdom in Britain.

655 Saracens, Arab Moslems, destroyed Byzantine fleet.

664 Saracens began series of attacks on **Constantinople.**

c. 670 Caedmon, English poet, wrote early English version of *Old Testament.*

679 First Bulgarian **Empire** founded by **Khan Asparuhk.**

685–695 First part of reign of **Justinian II**, Byzantine emperor, who was defeated by Arabs at Sevastopol and later deposed and exiled to Crimea.

687 Pepin of Héristal became ruler of all Frankish kingdoms, except Aquitaine.

NEAR AND MIDDLE EAST

c. 610 Mohammed began his mission as prophet of Islam.

622 Traditional date of the **Hegira,** Mohammed's flight from Mecca to Medina, that marked beginning of **Moslem Era.**

630 Moslems conquered Mecca, which became spiritual center of Islam.

633 Islam began conquests by taking **Syria** and **Iraq.**

639 Moslems began to conquer **Egypt.**

640 Persia taken by Moslems.

651–652 First edition of the *Koran* issued.

661 Moawiya founded **Omayyad dynasty** (caliphs of Damascus), which held caliphate until 750.

FAR EAST

c. 606–647 Reign of **King Harsha,** ruler of Kanauj in northern India, which enjoyed **Hindu renaissance** of literature, arts, and theology; Harsha received Chinese pilgrim Hsuan-Tsang.

618 T'ang dynasty founded in China, which annexed Korea and led successful campaigns in Mongolia, Nepal, Tibet, and Turkestan; it marked the **Golden Age of medieval China** with notable advances in astronomy and mathematics, first historical encyclopedia (801), and the development of art of printing, painting, and poetry; this dynasty ended in 906.

664 Saracens attacked Afghanistan and India.

670 Silla kingdom established in **Korea;** Chinese helped Koreans unite peninsula, instituting a period of prosperity and artistic achievement that lasted until 935.

AMERICAS

600 Tiahuanaco became a major ceremonial center near Lake Titicaca; Tiahuanacans established first unified empire that included most of **Peru;** their rule ended c. 1000.

AFRICA

698 Carthage fell to **Saracens,** ending Byzantine rule in North Africa.

700—800

EUROPE

700–730 *Beowulf,* oldest extant English epic, was composed.

711 Tarik, Berber leader of Moslems, invaded Spain, initiating **Moorish rule** in Spain, which lasted until 1492.

715–741 Reign of **Charles Martel,** son of Pepin of Héristal and grandfather of Charlemagne; as Frankish ruler, he defeated (732) Saracens at battle of Tours, halting their advance into Europe.

c. 732 St. Bede (the Venerable Bede) wrote his *Ecclesiastical History of the English Nation.*

751–768 Pepin the Short, first Carolingian king of the Franks and son of Charles Martel, defended Rome from Lombards.

756 Papal states began when Pepin granted lands around Ravenna to pope.
Omayyad dynasty of Córdoba came to power in Moslem Spain and was to rule until 1031.

768–814 Reign of **Charlemagne** (son of Pepin the Short), who subdued Saxony, annexed Lombardy and Bavaria, and was crowned (800) emperor of the West by Pope Leo III at Rome; Charlemagne created Palace School at his capital, Aix-la-Chapelle, which helped preserve classical and early Christian scholarship.

NEAR AND MIDDLE EAST

749 Caliph Abul Abbas overthrew Omayyads and founded **Abbasid dynasty,** which ruled until 1258.

762 Baghdad founded by Caliph Al-Mansur.

786–809 Reign of **Caliph Harun al-Rashid,** during which Baghdad became major Islamic city; this glorious period is reflected in *The Thousands and One Nights.*

FAR EAST

712 Moslem Arabs devastated most of northwestern India.
Kojiki [= records of ancient matters], sacred book of the **Shinto,** was completed.

794 Heian period of Japan began; during this era, Japanese began to develop their own culture and established capital at **Kyoto;** this period ended 1185.

AMERICAS

700 Chichimec nomads from northern Mexico invaded **Teotihuacán** civilization.
Mayan temples built at **Tikal,** in jungles of Guatemala.

AFRICA

700 Moslem Arabs conquered northern **Africa,** which became base for invasions of Europe.
Kingdom of Ghana developed as first of Sudanese empires and became wealthy trading center, extending from Timbuktu to the Atlantic.

800—900

EUROPE

c. 800 Cynewulf, Old English religious poet, wrote *Fates of the Apostles.*

802 The **Vikings** raided **British Isles** and by 880 had permanent settlements in Ireland and England.

803–814 Reign of **Khan Krum,** Bulgarian ruler, who captured Sofia from Byzantines and besieged Constantinople.

813–820 Reign of **Leo V,** the Armenian, who ruled Byzantium and revived iconoclasm; he defeated Bulgars and concluded 30-year truce.

827–880 Moslems invaded Sicily, Palermo, Messina, Rome, and Malta.

835 Vikings began to raid **Continent.**

843 Treaty of **Verdun:** the **Carolingian kingdom** was divided into three separate states: the future **France, Italy,** and **Germany** with Charles the Bald, Emperor Lothair, and Louis the German as rulers of the respective territories.

847–c. 877 John Scotus Erigena headed court school at Paris for Charles the Bald and wrote translations and original philosophical works.

c. 850 Feudalism developed in western Europe.

858 Photius became patriarch of Constantinople, and a schism between eastern and western churches developed during his reign.

860–869 St. Cyril and St. Methodius performed missionary work among Slavs living near Black Sea and later in Moravia; Cyril developed early **Slavic alphabet.**

862 Rurik, a Varangian (Viking), settled **Novgorod,** Russia; house of Rurik ruled Grand Duchy of Moscow and later all Russia until 1598.

865 Boris I, ruler of Bulgaria, introduced Christianity of the Greek rite.

871–899 Reign of **Alfred the Great,** king of England, who made a treaty establishing Danish territory in England and began overseeing compilation of *Anglo-Saxon Chronicle.*

882 Oleg, Rurik's nephew, made **Kiev** capital of Russia.

893–927 Reign of **Simeon I** (Tsar of the Bulgars and autocrat of the Greeks), who drove Magyars into Hungary and conquered most of Serbia; Bulgarian Empire flourished during his reign, which is considered the Golden Age of **Church Slavonic literature.**

c. 895 Árpád, chief of Magyars, led his people into **Hungary.**

c. 899 Medical school in **Salerno** had been established, which merged Greek, Jewish, Arabic, and Latin influences.

FAR EAST

800 Feudalism developed in **Japan.**

889 Golden Age of **Khmer** civilization, which ruled modern Cambodia, Laos, Thailand, and South Vietnam, from capital at Angkor; the temple complex constructed at **Angkor Wat** is one of the largest religious centers in the world; this civilization declined after 1434.

AFRICA

800 Arabs colonized **Madagascar** and **Zanzibar,** making expeditions into African interior for slaves for the next 200 years.

Rulers of **Kanem** developed kingdom near caravan routes of eastern Sudan.

900—1000

EUROPE

900 **Danish kingdom** founded by **Gorm.**

904 **Saracens** sacked Salonika.

906 **Magyars** began invading Germany, and were defeated (955) at Augsburg.

911 **Rollo,** Norse chieftain, received in fief the future duchy of **Normandy** from King Charles III; he was baptized (912), and his descendants included William the Conqueror.

912–960 Omayyad rule in **Spain** at its zenith under Abdu-r-Rahman III; **Córdoba** became intellectual center of Europe.

919–936 Reign of **Henry I,** the Fowler, who was considered the founder of **German realm** and recovered Lorraine for Germany.

962 **Holy Roman Empire** founded after Otto I, German king, united Italy and Germany; it lasted until Francis II renounced the imperial title in 1806.

976–1025 Reign of **Basil II** (Bulgar slayer), Byzantine emperor, who annexed Syria and Bulgaria, bringing empire to greatest size since the time of Justinian I.

c. 980–1015 Reign of **Vladimir I** (Saint Vladimir), duke of Kiev, who made Christianity of the Greek rite the Russian religion.

c. 985 **Eric the Red** established a Viking colony in **Greenland.**

987 **Hugh Capet** became king of **France,** beginning of the Capetian line that ruled France until 1328.

992–1025 Reign of **Boleslaus I** (the Brave), founder of the **Polish kingdom,** who brought most of the western Slavs under his rule.

997–1038 Reign of **Stephen I** (Saint Stephen), called the Apostle of Hungary, first king of **Hungary.**

NEAR AND MIDDLE EAST

969 **Fatimite caliph** established in Egypt; Fatimites, who captured Palestine, parts of Syria, and west Arabia, ruled until 1171.

996 **Hakin,** sixth Fatimite caliph, persecutor of Jews and Christians and self-proclaimed (1020) reincarnation of God, a claim still maintained by **Druses** in Syria and Lebanon; Fatimite power declined rapidly after Hakin's assassination in 1021.

999 Sultan **Mahmud of Ghazni** founded Ghaznevid dynasty, which ruled Afghanistan until c. 1155; he annexed Punjab, India; forced conversions to Islam; destroyed Hindu temples; and built a mosque, the **Celestial Bride,** at Ghazni, his capital.

FAR EAST

907 **Khitan Mongols** began to rule northern China, holding sway until 1123. Kingdom of the **Five Dynasties and Ten States** in China: chaos existed in China until 960.

935 **Koryo kingdom** established in **Korea,** in which literature was cultivated and Confucianism replaced Buddhism; this kingdom ended in 1392.

960 **Sung dynasty** established in China; scholarly works were composed, and drama and picaresque novel flourished; gunpowder was used for first time, and trade was carried on with India and Persia; the dynasty ruled until 1279.

986 **Ghaznevids** from Afghanistan began to rule Punjab, remaining there until 1001.

AMERICAS

900 **Toltec** civilization developed in **Mexico;** capital was established (c. 950) at **Tula,** and warrior gods were worshiped; the Toltec Indians conquered most of Mexico, before influence died out c. 1200.

AFRICA

c. 912–1043 **Fatimite dynasty** dominated most of northwestern Africa and the Near East; fleets raided Mediterranean, capturing Malta, Sardinia, Corsica, and Balearics.

c. 990 **Great Zimbabwe** civilization, probably developed by Bantu people, flourished in **Southern Rhodesia;** huge stone buildings were constructed in about the 15th century; this civilization ended c. 1750.

1000—1100

EUROPE

1000 End of the world expected throughout Christendom.

c. 1000–1010 Early edition of *Chanson de Roland* probably composed, but not transcribed for many years.

1002 **Massacre of St. Brice:** Danes in England were murdered and, in retaliation, raided England regularly until 1014.

1014 **Knut** (Canute) **II,** king of **Denmark,** became (1017) king of England and later of **Norway;** his kingdom was divided after his death in 1035.

1019–1054 Reign of **Yaroslav,** duke of Kiev; he drew up Russian law code, encouraged learning, erected Cathedral of Sancta Sophia and monastery of Lavra, and consolidated power and prestige of Kiev.

1024 **Franconian house** began to rule **Germany;** great imperial age ended in 1125.

1039–1056 **Henry III,** king of Germany and Holy Roman Emperor (1046–1056); with authority over Hungary, Poland, and Bohemia, his empire was at its height.

1040 **Macbeth** became king of Scotland after murdering his predecessor, **Duncan;** Macbeth was killed (1057) by **Malcolm,** who became king until 1093.

Attempts were made to implement **Truce of God** in France, which would have prohibited war during certain seasons and times of the day.

1042–1066 Reign of **Edward the Confessor,** king of England; he began (c. 1050) construction of **Westminster Abbey.**

1054 **Reciprocal excommunication** of Roman and Greek Churches announced; it was **repealed** in 1965.

1063 Construction was begun on **Cathedral at Pisa,** an example of **Romanesque** style of architecture that flourished in 11th and 12th centuries.

1065–1109 **Alfonso VI of Leon,** king of Castile, reconquered Moorish lands, beginning with capture of Toledo in 1085.

1066 **William,** duke of Normandy, defeated Saxons under King Harold at the **Battle of Hastings,** ending Saxon rule in England; known as William I (the Conqueror) of England, he ordered (1086) all landed property surveyed for tax purposes and recorded in **Domesday Book.**

c. 1071 **Saint Mark's Church** in Venice was rebuilt in **Byzantine style.**

c. 1078 The **White Tower,** later named the **Tower of London,** was constructed.

1081 **The Cid** (Rodrigo Diaz) fought Moors and Spaniards; he founded and ruled Valencia until 1099.

1086 **Almoravides,** Berber Moslems from Morocco, took over control of Islam in Spain.

c. 1088 **University of Bologna** founded.

1093 **St. Anselm,** founder of Scholasticism, became Archbishop of Canterbury.

1095 **First Crusade** proclaimed by Pope Urban II, who urged battle cry to be *Deus vult* [God wills it]; he established (1099) **Latin Kingdom of Jerusalem** in Syria and Palestine that endured until 1291.

1097 Construction began on the **Houses of Parliament.**

NEAR AND MIDDLE EAST

c. 1000 **Avicenna,** Arabian philosopher and physician, wrote *Canon of Medicine.*

1055 **Seljuk Turks** conquered Baghdad.

1063–1072 **Alp Arslan,** ruler of Seljuks, conquered much of Near East and Asia Minor; he defeated Byzantine army at **Manzikert, Armenia.**

1072–1092 Reign of **Malik Shah** (son of Arslan), who was protector of **Omar Khayyam,** Persian poet and author of the *Rubáiyát.*

1096 **The First Crusade** began, and Crusaders captured Nicaea, Antioch, and Jerusalem, where they massacred the Moslems; Crusaders established (1099) **Latin Kingdom of Jerusalem** in Syria and Palestine, which endured until 1291.

FAR EAST

c. 1020 *The Tale of Genji,* said to be the world's first novel, written by Lady Murasaki Shikibu in Japan.

1044 **King Anawratha** made **Pagan,** Burma, the capital of his dynasty; it became known as the "city of a thousand temples."

AMERICAS

c. 1000 **Lief Ericsson** allegedly discovered part of North American coast and called it **Vinland.**

Chichén Itzá, ancient Mayan city in north-central Yucatán, became Toltec city and was occupied until 1194.

Mixtec people, who developed high culture in Oaxaca valley of Mexico, practised picture writing.

AFRICA

c. 1000 Kano, city in northern Nigeria, began to flourish; it became leading Moslem sultanate of Hausa States, which were vassals of Bornu after 1400.

1054 Almoravides, Moslem Berber tribes, began Islamic conquest of West Africa; they sacked Kumbi, capital of Ghana, in 1076.

1100—1200

EUROPE

1100–1135 Reign of Henry I of England; he gained control of Normandy; his attempts to have his daughter Matilda succeed him caused long civil strife.

1108–1137 Reign of Louis VI (the Fat) of France, who battled with Henry I and checked German invasion.

1113–1125 Reign of Vladimir Monomakh, grand duke of Kiev; state grew in power during his reign.

1118 Order of Knights Templar founded.

1120–1220 Aristotelian philosophy introduced into the West, especially through writings of Averroës, Spanish-Arabian philosopher, and Maimonides, Hebrew scholar.

1122–1152 Suger, abbot of Saint-Denis, was leading French statesman under Louis VI and Louis VII.

1128–1185 Reign of Alfonso I Henriques of Portugal; Portugal received (1144) papal consent to be independent kingdom.

1134–1150 Western facade of Chartres Cathedral was built.

c. 1135 Geoffrey of Monmouth completed History of the Kings of Britain, major source of Arthurian legends.

1147 Second Crusade preached by St. Bernard of Clairvaux after Turks captured (1144) Edessa; it was led by Conrad III of Germany and Louis VII of France.

c. 1150 University of Paris came into being; Peter Abelard is usually regarded as its founder.

1152 Frederick I (Barbarossa), became king of Germany, and was crowned (1155) Holy Roman Emperor; he acquired land in Italy, Germany, and Poland and was drowned (1190) in Asia Minor during Third Crusade.

Louis VII annulled his marriage to Eleanor of Aquitaine; Henry (Plantagenet) married Eleanor.

1154–1189 Reign of Henry II (Plantagenet) of England; he appointed Thomas à Becket his chancellor and centralized royal administration.

1154–1213 Georgian power reached its peak in Russia, a period known as Golden Age of Georgian literature.

1159 John of Salisbury dedicated Policraticus, his treatise on government, to Thomas à Becket.

Peter Lombard, bishop of Paris, began his theological text, Sentences.

1162 Becket became Archbishop of Canterbury; he opposed Henry's restrictions on ecclesiastical jurisdiction, but was formally reconciled after long quarrel in 1170, only to be murdered five months later by Norman knights.

1163–1235 Cathedral of Notre Dame constructed in Paris.

c. 1168 Oxford University founded.

1176 Construction of London Bridge was begun, and completed in 1209.

Lombard League of northern Italian states defeated Barbarossa at Legnano, representing the first major defeat of feudal cavalry by infantry.

c. 1180 Chrestien de Troyes composed the first literary works of Arthurian legend.

1182 Jews banished from France, but returned in 1189.

c. 1187 Igor's Campaign, first notable work of Russian literature, was based on true account of Prince Igor's defeat and release by Cumans.

1189–1193 Third Crusade led by Barbarossa, Richard I of England, and Philip II of France.

1189–1199 Reign of Richard I (the Lionhearted), king of England; returning from Crusades, he was captured by Leopold of Austria; after release two years later, he warred against Philip II.

1190–1199 Teutonic Knights, a German military religious order, was founded.

1191 The Nibelungenlied first appeared.

NEAR AND MIDDLE EAST

1144 Zengi, Turkish conqueror of Syria, seized Edessa.

1145–1174 Reign of Nureddin, Zengi's son and Sultan of Syria; he ousted Crusaders from northern Syria, made (1154) Damascus his capital, and conquered (1171) Egypt.

1147–1149 Second Crusade.

1157 Seljuk Empire fell to Khorezm shah.

1169–1193 Reign of Saladin, sultan of Egypt; he conquered Syria and Aleppo, defeated (1187) Christians at battle of Hattin (near Tiberias) and took Jerusalem, and signed treaty with Richard the Lionhearted that allowed Christians small strip of land along Jerusalem coast.

FAR EAST

1149 Rulers of Ghor took over Ghazni in Afghanistan, which became headquarters for campaigns into India; subjugation of Upper India was completed in 1203.

1186 Kamakura era began in Japan, establishing rule of military warriors; Yoritomo, first shogun, set up centralized feudal system; China and Korea were raided; Zen Buddhism was promoted; this era ended in 1333.

c. 1190 Temujin consolidated Mongol tribes in central Asia; he assumed (1206) title Jenghiz Khan and led Mongol hordes in conquests of eastern Europe and western Asia.

AFRICA

c. 1174 Almohades, fierce Berber Moslems, succeeded Almoravides in Morocco and conquered other parts of North Africa, ruling area until 1550.

1200—1300

EUROPE

1202–1204 The Fourth Crusade, was led by Venetian doge, Enrico Dandolo; Constantinople was captured and a Latin empire established.

1204 Philip II of France took English lands north of the Loire and established France as a leading European power.

1209 Franciscan order founded by Saint Francis of Assisi.

1211 Construction began on Rheims Cathedral.

1215 Magna Carta, signed by King John, became basis of modern English constitution with its principle that the king is subject to law.

1217–1221 Fifth Crusade led by Pelasius, papal legate, was directed against Moslems in Egypt and failed.

1218 Amiens Cathedral begun.

1223 Mongols invaded Russia.

1226–1270 Reign of Louis IX (Saint Louis), a period known as Golden Age of medieval France.

1226–1283 Teutonic Knights subjugated Prussia and achieved commercial power.

1227 Gothic Cathedral of Toledo, Spain, began to be constructed.

1228–1229 Sixth Crusade; led by Frederick II, it resulted in Sultan of Egypt signing treaty that restored Jerusalem, Nazareth, and Bethlehem to Christians.

c. 1230 Salamanca University founded in Spain.

c. 1231 Cambridge University founded.

1233 The Inquisition was established when Pope Gregory IX gave Dominicans authority to investigate Albigensian heresy in southern France.

1236–1263 Reign of Alexander Nevsky in Russia, under whom country was united; he defeated (1242) Teutonic Knights at Lake Peipus, and Mongols named him Grand Prince of Russia.

1237–1242 Batu Khan led Mongol invasions, taking Moscow and most of Russia, Hungary, and Poland, and invading Germany; his empire was known as the Golden Horde because of brillant tents.

1238 Kingdom of Granada became last refuge of the Moors until their expulsion from Spain in 1492.

1248–1254 Seventh Crusade; King Louis IX of France was its leader.

1270 Eighth Crusade; Tunis was attacked, and Louis IX died of plague.

1271 Marco Polo left Venice for China and other parts of the Far East; he returned in 1292 and informed Europeans of Oriental splendors.

1273 **Rudolph I** founded **Hapsburg** dynasty, which ruled **Austria** until 1918.

St. **Thomas Aquinas** completed *Summa Theologica*.

1272–1307 Reign of **Edward I** of **England**; he systematized laws and institutions and called (1295) his "**Model Parliament**," which represented all classes.

1285–1314 Reign of **Philip IV** (the Fair); he made **France** an absolute monarchy and called (1302) the first meeting of the Estates-General (clergy, nobility, and townsmen) to rally against Pope Boniface VIII's claims of papal supremacy.

1290 **Jews** were expelled from **England**; they returned c. 1650.

NEAR AND MIDDLE EAST

1202–1204 **Fourth Crusade:** Crusaders took Constantinople, sacked Byzantine territories, and established a Latin Empire.

1217–1221 **Fifth Crusade;** Crusaders failed in **Egypt.**

1218–1224 **Mongols** from central Asia conquered Turkestan, Afghanistan, and Persia.

1228–1229 **Sixth Crusade;** Sultan of Egypt signed a treaty with Crusaders allowing free access to Jerusalem.

1245–1253 Mesopotamia and Armenia ravaged by **Mongols.**

1248–1253 **Seventh Crusade;** Crusaders massacred in **Egypt.**

1250 **Mamelukes,** former slave-soldiers, began to rule **Egypt** and checked Mongol advances; their rule ended in 1517.

1258 Baghdad fell to **Hulagu Khan,** grandson of Jenghiz, who devastated surrounding lands.

1270 **Eighth Crusade;** Crusaders attacked **Tunis** and were turned back.

1288 **Osman I,** leader of Ottoman Turks, founded **Ottoman dynasty,** which endured until 1918.

FAR EAST

1206 **Delhi Sultanate** began, the first Moslem kingdom of India; Sultan Iltutmish (1210–1235) erected famous minaret, **Qutb Minar;** this dynasty ended in 1398.

1220–1227 **Jenghiz Khan** established his capital at Karakorum controlling most of Ch'in Empire of northern China; he conquered Turkestan, Afghanistan, Persia, and southern Russia.

1221–1241 **Ogotai Khan,** son of Jenghiz, captured Ghazni, Afghanistan.

1260 **Yüan,** Mongolian dynasty of China, founded by **Kublai Khan,** grandson of Jenghiz; Kublai's attempts to conquer Japan, Southeast Asia, and Indonesia failed; **Marco Polo** and other westerners visited capital at Peiping; during dynasty an advanced postal system and extensive network of roads and canals were created; gunpowder and printing were introduced into Europe from China at this time; this dynasty ended in 1368.

AMERICAS

1200 The **Incas** began to build empire centered at **Cuzco, Peru,** and established central control over local rulers; eventually empire extended from Quito, Ecuador, to Rio Maule, Chile, with population c. seven million people, who were linked by messenger system and common language; Incan civilization was noted for political organization and luxurious cities; stonework in **Machu Picchu,** fortress city in Andes, shows skillful engineering techniques; empire destroyed by **Francisco Pizarro** in 1533.

Aztecs entered the valley of Mexico, establishing powerful political and cultural civilization and capital (c. 1325) at **Tenochtitlán** (now **Mexico City**); Aztecs were noted for developed social organization and religion demanding human sacrifice; in 1519 their population numbered about five million; **Hernán Cortés** destroyed empire in 1521.

AFRICA

1200 **Mali Empire** developed in **western Sudan,** absorbing **Ghana** and neighboring lands; King **Mansa Musa's** pilgrimage (1324) to Mecca brought attention to empire's great wealth; **Timbuktu** grew into center of learning and culture; **Songhai** began to control region c. 1500.

1300—1400

EUROPE

1300 The **Renaissance** began, signaling end of Middle Ages and beginning of modern Europe; greatest cultural developments in European history occurred during next 300 years.

1305 "**Babylonian Captivity**" began; chaos in Italy forced Pope Clement V to desert (1309) Rome for Avignon, France, which was the papal seat until 1377.

c. 1306 **Giotto** completed Arena Chapel frescoes in Padua.

1321 Death of **Dante** following completion of *Divine Comedy.*

1325–1341 Reign of **Ivan I** (Money Bag), grand prince of Moscow and vassal of Mongols; Russian Orthodox Church became centered in Moscow during his reign.

1326 **Ottoman Turks** began invading eastern Europe.

1327–1377 Reign of **Edward III** of England, during which Parliament divided into two houses, later called **Lords** and **Commons.**

1337 **Hundred Years War,** which began after Edward III claimed French crown, ended in 1453; English defeated, but French devastated by famine, plague, and marauders who terrorized countryside.

1341 **Petrarch,** Italian humanist, crowned poet laureate at Rome.

1346–1355 Reign of **Stephen Dushan** over Serbs, Greeks, Bulgars, and Albanians; his rule marked height of Serbian power.

1347–1352 **Black Death,** an epidemic of plague that began (1334) in Constantinople, struck Europe; within 20 years, it killed up to three quarters of population of Europe and Asia.

1353 **Giovanni Boccaccio** completed the *Decameron.*

1358 French army suppressed the *Jacquerie,* a **peasant revolt** protesting war taxation.

1362 William Langland wrote *Piers the Plowman.*

1370 **Hanseatic League,** mercantile association of German towns, signed a treaty with Denmark giving League a virtual trade monopoly in Scandinavia.

1378 **Great Western Schism:** Rome and France began fight for control of papacy that lasted until 1417.

1379 After Parliament imposed poll tax, **Wat Tyler** led **peasant revolt** in England.

1382 **John Wycliffe** directed translation of the **Vulgate** Bible into English.

1386 **Heidelberg University** founded by Rupert I, Elector of Palatinate.

Lithuania and Poland united under Jagiello dynasty; **Golden Age of Polish culture** and power began; this dynasty came to an end in 1572.

1387 **Chaucer** began to compose his *Canterbury Tales.*

1389 **Turks** defeated **Serbs** at **Kossovo,** and Serbia became vassal state of Turks.

1391 **Ottoman Turks** began conquering Byzantine lands.

1399 **House of Lancaster** began reign in **England** that lasted until 1461.

NEAR AND MIDDLE EAST

1334 Epidemic of plague, **Black Death,** began in Constantinople, spreading throughout Europe and Asia and causing extremely large number of fatalities.

1354 **Ottoman Turks** expanded their empire and established capital at Adrianople; by end of century, Ottomans controlled most of Balkans and Byzantine possessions in Asia Minor.

1356–1363 **Sultan Hassan** mosque was constructed in Cairo.

1392 **Baghdad** sacked by **Tamerlane,** Mongol conqueror.

FAR EAST

1336 **Ashikaga** family began to dominate **Japan,** holding sway until 1558; Ashikaga period of warfare among feudal nobles was also a time of extraordinary economic and commercial growth.

1350 **Thais** from southern China established kingdom in modern **Thailand.**

1353 Lao kingdom of **Lan Xang** (Land of a Million Elephants) established by branch of Thais in **Laos.**

1368 **Ming dynasty** began to rule China after driving out Mongols; empire at its height extended from Burma to Korea; European settlements made at Macao and Canton; finest **Chinese porcelain** dates from this period, which ended in 1644.

1369–1405 Reign of **Tamerlane** (or Timur), Mongol leader and conqueror of Persia, Mesopotamia, and western India; Tamerlane ravaged Georgia and captured Angora from Ottomans.

1392 Yi dynasty began to rule **Korea** and established capital at Seoul; this dynasty ended in 1919.

AFRICA

1300 Kingdom of Ife flourished in Nigeria; Ife, a holy city noted for its fine **bronze sculpture**, probably died out c. 1500.

1350 Kingdom of Benin developed in **Nigeria**; within a century, Benin became famous commercial center and seat of royal court; bronze plaques on king's palace depict civilization of hunters, traders, and warriors; trade was established with Portugal c. 1486; Benin had disintegrated by 1897.

1400—1500

EUROPE

1409 Leipzig University founded by German émigrés from Prague.

1415 Henry V of England defeated French in Battle of Agincourt, making England first among European powers.

1415–1460 Reign of **Prince Henry the Navigator** of Portugal, who promoted explorations along the coast of Africa.

c. 1417 Donatello completed his statue of *St. George and the Dragon*.

1419–1436 Hussite religious wars that broke out following martyrdom of John Huss were fought in Bohemia.

c. 1427 Thomas à Kempis, German monk, wrote *The Imitation of Christ*.

1429 Joan of Arc liberated Orléans; she was burned at the stake in Rouen in 1431.

1432 Jan van Eyck completed his altarpiece with panels portraying the *Annunciation* and *Adoration of the Lamb*.

1434 Medicis began their domination of **Florence**, which lasted until 1494 and made Florence center of Italian Renaissance.

1450 Fra Angelico completed the *Annunciation*.
Vatican Library founded by Pope Nicholas V.

1453 Constantinople was lost to Turks, ending 1,000-year-old **Byzantine Empire.**
Hundred Years War came to an end, and English territory on Continent was limited to Calais.

1455–1485 Wars of the Roses: English Houses of Lancaster and York fought for throne.

1456 John Hunyadi, Hungarian ruler, defeated Turks at Belgrade, preventing their conquest of Hungary for 70 years.

c. 1456 Printing of **Mazarin Bible** was completed in Mainz, Germany; it is considered earliest book printed from movable type and attributed to **Gutenberg.**

1458–1490 Reign of **Matthias Corvinus** of Hungary (son of John Hunyadi), who took (1485) Vienna and made **Hungary** most important state of central Europe.

1461–1483 Reign of **Louis XI,** who made **France** a nation by annexing Burgundy, Provence, Maine, and Anjou.

1462–1505 Reign of Ivan III (the Great), first national sovereign of Russia; he subjugated Novgorod and almost all Russian principalities under Moscow's rule and repudiated "Tartar Yoke"; Ivan also adopted Byzantine court ceremonials and constructed great **Kremlin palaces** and cathedrals in Moscow.

1463 Turks and Venetians began major war, in which Venetians were defeated (1479) and had to pay Turks for trading privileges.

1466 Teutonic Knights ceded Pomerania and West Prussia to Poland.

1469 King Ferdinand of Aragon married Queen Isabella I of Castile, initiating unification of Spain.

1473 The Sistine Chapel in the Vatican was built under Pope Sixtus IV.

1478 Ferdinand and Isabella instituted the **Spanish Inquisition.**

1481 Botticelli began his Biblical frescoes in the Sistine Chapel.

1485 Henry VII of England founded the **House of Tudor,** increased power of the **Star Chamber,** developed English navy, sponsored explorations to New World, and ended feudalism by outlawing private armies.

1488 Bartolomeu Dias was the first European to round the Cape of Good Hope, thus opening sea route to India.

1490 Verrocchio's equestrian monument of *condottiere* Colleoni was cast.

1492 Ferdinand and Isabella conquered Moorish kingdom of **Granada,** expelled Jews who refused to accept Catholicism, and financed **Christopher Columbus** on his first voyage to America.

1494 Treaty of **Tordesillas:** Spain and Portugal divided the New World.
Italian Wars among Italian states and Spain began when Charles VIII of France invaded Italy; after 1559 Spain dominated Italy.

1497 Portugal expelled Jews who refused Catholic conversion.

1497–1498 John Cabot explored North American coast south of **Labrador.**

1497–1499 Vasco da Gama sailed from Lisbon to **India.**

1498 Savonarola, Dominican monk who preached against corruption in Florence, was burned at the stake.
Leonardo da Vinci, painter, engineer, and scientist, completed the *Last Supper* in Milan.

1499 Swiss independence acknowledged by Emperor Maximilian I.

NEAR AND MIDDLE EAST

1451–1481 Reign of **Mohammed II,** Ottoman sultan; he completed conquest of Byzantine Empire by taking (1453) **Constantinople** and making it his capital; conquering most of Balkans and several Venetian possessions in Aegean islands, he was stopped (1478) at Belgrade by John Hunyadi and in Albania by Scanderbeg.

FAR EAST

1412–1443 Reign of **Ahmad Shah,** king of Gujarat (India), who founded city of **Ahmedabad;** Gujarat became an independent, prosperous sultanate.

1495–1530 Reign of **Baber** (or Babar), remote descendant of Tamerlane; Baber founded **Mogul Empire** of India, captured (1504) Kabul and established a kingdom in **Afghanistan,** and conquered most of northern India.

1498 Portuguese explorer **Vasco da Gama** landed at Calicut, **India.**

AMERICAS

1492–1504 Christopher Columbus made four voyages to America; landed on Canary Islands, Bahamas, Cuba, Hispaniola, Jamaica, Virgin Islands, Trinidad, and Honduras.

1497 John Cabot arrived in North America; explored coast south of **Labrador.**

AFRICA

1400 Baluba Kingdom of the Congo first emerged and eventually controlled Katanga and Kivu provinces.

1415 Portuguese began to explore **West Africa,** gradually building up profitable trade.

1482 Diego Cão, Portuguese explorer, discovered mouth of Congo River.

1488 Bartolomeu Dias, Portuguese explorer, rounded Cape of Good Hope.

1491 Vasco da Gama rounded the Cape and sailed up East African coast en route to Asia.

1500—1600

1502 Cesare Borgia, son of Pope Alexander VI, completed conquest of neighboring states and added them to the Papal domain.

1503 Leonardo da Vinci began painting the *Mona Lisa.*
Alexander I, king of Poland and grand duke of Lithuania, ceded left bank of Dnieper to Ivan the Great.

1508 Michelangelo began to paint ceiling of **Sistine Chapel.**

1509 Erasmus, Dutch humanist, published *The Praise of Folly.*

1509–1547 Reign of Henry VIII of England; his first wife was **Katharine of Aragon** (m. 1509, div. 1533), mother of Mary I; second wife, **Anne Boleyn** (m. 1533, beheaded 1536), mother of Elizabeth I; third wife, **Jane Seymour** (m. 1536, d. 1537), mother of Edward VI; fourth wife, **Anne of Cleves** (m. 1540, div. 1540); fifth wife, **Katharine Howard** (m. 1540, beheaded 1542); sixth wife, **Katharine Parr** (m. 1543); Henry waged war against France and Scotland.

1513 Macchiavelli wrote *The Prince.*
Raphael painted the *Sistine Madonna.*

1515–47 Francis I ruled France; he fought Italian Wars and captured Milan at **Battle of Marignano.**

1515 Henry VIII appointed **Thomas Wolsey** cardinal and lord chancellor.

1516 Sir Thomas More, English statesman, wrote *Utopia.*

1517 Martin Luther began **Protestant Reformation** by posting his 95 theses against the sale of indulgences on door of Wittenberg Palace Church.

1518 Titian completed his altarpiece *Assumption of the Virgin.*

1519 Ulrich Zwingli began Reformation in Switzerland.

1519–1522 Ferdinand Magellan circumnavigated the globe.

1519–1556 Charles V, Holy Roman Emperor, ruled Spanish lands in Europe and America, as well as Hapsburg lands in central Europe; he sacked (1527) Rome and captured Pope Clement VII.

1520 Luther was declared a heretic by Pope Leo X and formally excommunicated (1521) by **Edict of Worms.**

1523–1560 Reign of **Gustavus I** (Vasa) of Sweden; he ended (1537) trade monopoly of Hanseatic League and promoted Reformation.

1524–1525 Peasants' War in Germany: revolt by south German peasants that was inspired by Lutheran religious ideas; however, Luther sided with princes.

1532 Rabelais wrote *Gargantua and Pantagruel.*

1533–1584 Reign of **Ivan IV** (the Terrible), first tsar of Russia; his conflicts with **boyars,** the powerful nobles who controlled regency, resulted in reign of terror; Ivan seized part of Livonia from Poles and concluded peace among Russia, Sweden, and Poland after much warfare.

1534 St. Ignatius Loyola founded **Jesuit order,** which became chief force in Roman Catholic Counter-Reformation.
Act of Supremacy: English Parliament made Henry VIII head of Church of England, initiating **English Reformation.**

1535 Sir Thomas More, former lord chancellor of England, was beheaded for refusing to subscribe to Act of Supremacy.

1536 Menno Simons, Dutch religious reformer, began preaching **Anabaptist doctrines.**
Hans Holbein, the younger, of Germany became court painter to Henry VIII.

1541–1564 John Calvin headed a theocratic state at Geneva.

1543 Nicholas Copernicus published his **astronomy** discoveries.

1545 Council of Trent was convened by Pope Paul III; it made internal reforms in Roman Catholic Church.

1553–1558 Reign of **Mary Tudor** (Bloody Mary) of England, who restored Catholicism and persecuted Protestants; she lost (1558) Calais, last English stronghold on Continent, to the French.

1555 Peace of Augsburg signed, which allowed German princes to choose Catholicism or Lutheranism, but not Calvinism, as religion of their states; Lutheranism prevailed in north; Catholicism, in south.

1556–1598 Reign of **Philip II** of Spain, during which Hapsburg power reached its zenith and **Golden Age of Spanish art** and **literature** was initiated.

1558–1603 Reign of **Elizabeth I** of England, who established (1563) **Church of England** and increased English power; **Elizabethan Age** was marked by great flowering of literature.

1559 Pope Paul IV established the **Index of Forbidden Books.**

1559–1567 Reign of **Mary Stuart, Queen of Scots,** who abdicated in favor of her son, James VI (later James I of England); she was imprisoned by Elizabeth I because of her claims to English throne.

1562 French began harsh persecution of **Huguenots,** French Protestants; Catherine de' Medici ordered (1572) **St. Bartholomew's Day Massacre;** religious wars ended in 1598.

1566 Netherlands, led by William the Silent of Orange, revolted against Spanish domination and gained independence in 1581.

1571 Battle of **Lepanto:** Ottoman Turks defeated in naval battle with Austrian and Holy League forces, the greatest naval battle since Actium.

1580 Montaigne began composing *Essays.*

1582 Gregorian calendar introduced.
Douay version of New Testament published.

1587 John Knox, founder of **Presbyterianism** in Scotland, wrote *History of the Reformation in Scotland.*

1588 Spanish Armada defeated by English fleet under Sir Francis Drake.

c. **1589 Christopher Marlowe** produced *Dr. Faustus.*

1589 Henry IV founded **House of Bourbon;** this dynasty ruled France until 1792.

1591–1613 William Shakespeare composed his plays and poems.

1597–1625 Francis Bacon wrote his *Essays.*

1598 Henry IV of France issued the **Edict of Nantes,** which granted religious toleration to Huguenots.
Boris Godunov became tsar of Russia and ruled until 1605.

NEAR AND MIDDLE EAST

1501 Safavid dynasty began rule of Iran that lasted until 1736.

1512–1520 Reign of **Selim I,** Ottoman sultan; he defeated Mamelukes in Syria and Egypt and assumed succession to Moslem Caliphate.

1520–1566 Reign of **Suleiman I** (the Magnificent), Ottoman sultan; he captured Belgrade, Rhodes, and Hungary during rule, which was marked by greatest flowering of **Turkish literature, art,** and **architecture.**

1571 Turks seized Cyprus and then suffered their first major defeat from Austrian and Holy League forces at **Lepanto,** the greatest naval battle since Actium.

1587–1628 Reign of **Abbas I,** shah of Iran, who erected palace and mosque at Isfahan.

FAR EAST

1510 Portuguese conquered **Goa, India.**

1526 Mogul Empire that was to endure until 1857 founded in India by **Baber.**

1549–1552 St. Francis Xavier introduced Christianity into **Japan.**

1557 Portuguese settled in **Macao** and began trade with China.

1560–1605 Reign of **Akbar the Great** (grandson of Baber), who enlarged domain and founded (1569) city of Fathpur Sikri, noted for Mogul architecture, especially **Jami Masjid** (the Great Mosque); Akbar also encouraged Persian arts and received European traders.

1568–1582 Nobunaga, who ruled Japan as military dictator, destroyed Buddhism as political force.

1571 Spanish founded **Manila** and began to colonize **Philippines.**

1582 Hideyoshi became military dictator of Japan; he initiated unification of country and unsuccessfully invaded Korea.

1590 Portuguese landed in Taiwan, calling it **Formosa.**

1595 Dutch began to colonize **East Indies.**

AMERICAS

1500 Cabral claimed **Brazil** for Portugal.

1501–1502 Amerigo Vespucci explored the coast of Brazil.

1511 Spanish took **Cuba** and **Puerto Rico,** founding San Juan and settling Jamaica.

1513 Ponce de Leon discovered **Florida.**
Balboa discovered the **Pacific.**

1519 Hernán Cortés of Spain landed in **Mexico;** Aztecs thought Cortés was **Quetzalcoatl,** their god who was supposed to appear at that period; Cortés, who met Montezuma II and later imprisoned him, captured (1521) Tenochtitlán and began harsh rule of Mexico.

1523–1524 Alvarado took **Guatemala** and **Salvador** for Spain.

1524 Verrazano explored the New England coast.

1530 Portuguese colonized **Brazil.**

1531–1535 Francisco Pizarro subjugated **Inca Empire** of Peru, executing Atahuallpa and installing Manco Capac as puppet ruler; Spanish founded (1535) Lima, which became capital of viceroyalty of Peru.

1534–1541 Jacques Cartier explored St. Lawrence River, stopping at sites of **Quebec** and **Montreal.**

1539–1542 De Soto made an expedition through Florida to the Mississippi.

1540–1542 Coronado explored the **Southwest**, reaching as far as Kansas.

1551 National University of Mexico founded. University of San Marcos founded in Lima, Peru.

1565 St. Augustine, Florida, oldest permanent settlement in the United States, was founded. Portuguese settled **Rio de Janeiro**.

1576–1577 Martin Frobisher searched for Northwest Passage.

1579 Sir Francis Drake claimed New Albion (California) for England.

1580 Buenos Aires, Argentina, founded by Juan de Garay for Spain.

AFRICA

1503–1507 Leo Africanus, Spanish Moslem of Morocco, explored Sudan; he issued (1526) book describing **Mali** and **Songhai** kingdoms.

1508 Portuguese began to colonize **Mozambique**.

1513 Songhai Empire conquered **Hausa States**.

1520 Portuguese visited **Ethiopian** court.

1529 Somali war in Ethiopia began; Moslems tried to conquer Ethiopia but were defeated (1543) when Portuguese aided Somalis.

1562 Sir John Hawkins of England began **slave trade** between Africa and the Americas.

1590 Moroccan invasions destroyed **Songhai Empire**.

1600—1700

EUROPE

1603 James VI of Scotland became **James I** of England, founding **house of Stuart**, which ruled England until 1688.

1605 Guy Fawkes executed for "Gunpowder Plot" to blow up Parliament.

1607 Jonson completed *Volpone*.

1609 Kepler published *Astronomia Nova*, laws of orbits of planets.

1609–1631 Newspapers were started on the Continent: *Avisa Relation oder Zeitung* (1609) in Germany; the *Nieuwe Tijdingen* (1616), Antwerp; the *Gazette*, later the *Gazette de France* (1631), Paris.

1609–1610 Douay version of Old Testament published.

1611 King James version of the Bible compiled by leading English scholars.

1613 Michael Romanov, tsar of Russia, founded **Romanov dynasty**, which ruled until 1917.

1614 The Estates General met for last time until the French Revolution.

1615 Cervantes published *Don Quixote*.

1618 Thirty Years War, final great religious war, broke out in Prague; this conflict between Catholic and Protestant Europe devastated Germany.

1624 Cardinal de Richelieu became chief minister of Louis XIII; he consolidated royal authority, strengthened army, built navy, and founded (1635) **French Academy**.

1625 Grotius published *De Jure Belli ac Pacis*, pioneer work in international law.

1625–1649 Reign of **Charles I** of England, who was involved with conflicts over supremacy of king or parliament and summoned (1640–1641) the **Long Parliament**, which abolished the courts of High Commission and the Star Chamber; Charles was beheaded for treason.

1628 William Harvey discovered principle of blood circulation. **Petition of Right** signed by Charles I; it prohibited arbitrary imprisonment, martial law, forced loans, and billeting of soldiers and sailors.

1632 Galileo published his work confirming Copernican theory of astronomy.

1640 Puritan revolution in England began; monarchists fought civil war that ended in 1649 against those who wanted republic.

1643–1715 Reign of **Louis XIV** (the Sun King) of France, during which royal absolutism reached a new peak; Louis allegedly said, *"L'état c'est moi"*; French art and culture flourished and **Versailles palace** was constructed.

1644 Milton wrote *Areopagitica*.

1645–1664 Venetian-Turkish wars caused further decline of Ottoman power.

1648 Peace of Westphalia, which ended Thirty Years War, recognized independence of Netherlands and of Swiss cantons and sovereignty of German states.

1649 King Charles I beheaded, and England had commonwealth form of government under **Oliver Cromwell** until 1660.

1651 Hobbes published *Leviathan*.

1652 England began series of wars with **French** and **Dutch** that lasted until 1678 over supremacy of the seas.

1659 Spanish power in Europe ended with **Peace of Pyrennes**.

1660 Monarchy restored by **Charles II** of England; Cavalier Parliament enacted repressive measures against Puritans.

1665 Great Plague hit **London**; the following year fire virtually destroyed city.

1675 Sir Christopher Wren began St. Paul's Cathedral, London.

1682–1725 Reign of **Peter the Great** of Russia; he tried to "Westernize" Russia and established schools and a newspaper.

1683 Turkish seige of Vienna repulsed.

1684 Newton published his theories of motion and gravitation.

1685 Edict of Nantes revoked by Louis XIV; Protestants fled abroad.

1688 "Glorious Revolution" occurred in England; this bloodless revolution against James II ended when William of Orange and Mary, his British wife, accepted crown. France began war against Grand Alliance of European powers that resulted in decline of French power.

1689 William and Mary began to rule England and signed **Bill of Rights**, limiting royal power; their rule ended in 1702.

1699 Peace of Karlowitz: Turkey ceded some of her conquered territories to Austria, Poland, and Venice.

NEAR AND MIDDLE EAST

1638 Turks won back **Baghdad** from Persians.

1656 Mohammed **Kuprili** became grand vizier to Mohammed IV and helped Ottoman empire regain some former power.

1699 Peace of Karlowitz: Turkey ceded Hungary, Croatia, and Slavonia to Austria; Podolia and Ukraine to Poland; and the Peloponnesus to Venice.

FAR EAST

1600 William Adams, an Englishman, arrived in Japan and imparted some technology to Japanese. **British East India Company** chartered for trade in India.

1603 Ieyasu Tokugawa came to power in Japan, and his dynasty ruled until 1867; it centralized feudalism, encouraged trade, and established capital at Tokyo; Kabuki theater was developed.

1611 British began to send envoys to Mogul Empire and later established settlements at Surat and factories in Bengal and Madras.

1615 Dutch seized Moluccas (Spice Islands) from Portuguese.

1616 Manchu Tartars from Manchuria began to invade China.

1619 Dutch founded **Batavia, Java**.

1627 Japan began to exclude foreigners, allowing one Dutch trading post to remain.

1628–1658 Reign of **Shah Jehan**, ruler of Mogul Empire; he erected **Taj Mahal**, one of the most beautiful buildings in the world.

1636 Dutch occupied **Ceylon**.

1641–1662 Dutch controlled **Formosa**.

1644 Ch'ing dynasty in China was founded by Manchus and ruled until 1912; **Korea** became vassal state known as the "Hermit Kingdom" because of its isolation.

1661–1722 Reign of **K'ang Hsi**, Chinese emperor who consolidated empire and issued edict of toleration after Jesuit missionaries appeared.

1668 Bombay became headquarters of East India Company.

1674 Mahratta State in west central India founded by Sivaji.

1675–1708 Guru Govind Singh ruled Sikhs and built up their military power.

AMERICAS

1607 English founded **Jamestown**, their first permanent settlement in America; **John Smith** became leader.

1608 Champlain founded **Quebec**.

Jesuit state in **Paraguay** founded.

1620 Pilgrims arrived at **Plymouth**, Massachusetts.

1630 Massachusetts Bay colony established by **Puritans**.

1671 Danes took St. Thomas.

British settled Barbados, and Leeward and Windward Islands.

1673 Jacques **Marquette** and Louis **Joliet** explored the Mississippi.

1682 After La Salle descended Mississippi River to its mouth, **French** began to rule colonial empire in North America that extended from Quebec to New Orleans.

AFRICA

1642 French established base on **Madagascar**.

c. 1650 Slave trade from **Gold Coast** thrived until early 19th century.

1652 Dutch founded **Capetown**; Jan van Riebeeck led settlers.

1680 Germans began to colonize West Africa.

1684 English lost **Tangier** to Morocco.

1687 Arguin, Guinea, established as Brandenburgian colony.

c. 1695 Osei Tutu founded **Ashanti** kingdom in western Africa and established capital at Kumasi; Ashanti, noted for high-quality **gold work**, grew wealthy from slave trade.

OCEANIA

1601 Australia began to be visited by Portuguese, Spanish, and Dutch.

1642 Abel **Tasman**, Dutch navigator, discovered **New Zealand** and **Tasmania**, which was named Van Diemen's Land.

1688 William **Dampier** of England landed on northwest coast of **Australia**.

1700—1800

EUROPE

1700 Great Northern War began: Russia, Poland, and Denmark fought Sweden for supremacy in the **Baltic**; when war ended in 1721, Russia emerged as a major European power with "window" on the Baltic. **Philip V** became first Bourbon king of **Spain**.

1701 Act of Settlement, which was passed by English parliament, provided that crown would pass to **house of Hanover**; king could not be Roman Catholic.

Hohenzollerns came to power in **Prussia** and Germany, ruling until 1918.

War of the **Spanish Succession** began; Treaty of Utrecht (1713) separated thrones of France and Spain and marked rise of British and decline of French.

1705 Moscow University founded by Peter the Great.

1707 Great Britain formed by union of **England** and Scotland.

1711 Joseph Addison and Richard Steele began publishing the *Spectator* in England.

1713–1740 Reign of **Frederick William I**, king of Prussia, who became known as the soldier king because he strengthened **Prussian army**.

1714 George I began the **Hanoverian** rule of England; house of Hanover was succeeded (1840) by house of Wettin when Queen Victoria married.

1715 The Age of Enlightenment began; also known as the Age of Reason; Europe experienced a rich period of **philosophy** that died out after 1789.

Louis XV began to rule France, but wars and financial policy weakened government.

1733 War of **Polish Succession** began: Russia and Austria defeated Spain and placed Augustus III on Polish throne two years later.

1738 John Wesley, founder of **Methodism**, began preaching in England.

1740 War of the **Austrian Succession**: a general European war broke out after **Maria Theresa** became Hapsburg ruler; it ended in 1748.

1740–1786 Reign of **Frederick the Great**, king of Prussia, who expanded territory and made Prussia leading European military power.

1747 Denis Diderot and other writers began editing the *Encyclopédie*.

1748 Montesquieu published *Spirit of the Laws*.

c. 1750 Industrial Revolution had begun in England; factory system, economic specialization, and urbanization changed social structure during next century.

1755 An earthquake devastated **Lisbon**, killing 30,000.

1756 Seven Years War began between **England** and France over colonial possessions in America and India; it ended in 1763; France lost Canada and India, England became world's major colonial power.

1758 Voltaire completed *Candide*.

1760 George III began his 60-year reign in England.

1762 Jean Jacques Rousseau completed *Social Contract*.

1762–1796 Reign of **Catherine II (the Great)** of Russia, who promoted education, the arts, and social reforms.

1768 Major **Russo-Turkish Wars**: Russia and Turkey waged a series of wars for over a century; in 1878 Turkey was finally ousted from Crimea and much of Slavic Europe.

1769 James Watt, Scottish inventor, patented his **steam engine**.

1772–1795 Poland was partitioned among Russia, Austria, and Prussia.

1773–1774 Pugachev led rebellion of Russian **peasants** and **Cossacks**, causing Catherine II to institute tighter control over serfs.

1774 Louis XVI and Marie Antoinette became king and queen of France.

1776 Adam Smith published *The Wealth of Nations*.

Edward Gibbon began *The Decline and Fall of the Roman Empire*.

1785 *The Times* of London was founded by John Walter.

1789 The French Revolution began when Paris mob stormed the **Bastille**; third estate drafted (1791) new constitution; Louis XVI and Marie Antoinette beheaded (1793).

1790 Edmund Burke wrote *Reflections on the French Revolution*.

1791 Thomas Paine wrote *The Rights of Man*, directed against critics of French Revolution.

1798 Robert Malthus published *Essay on the Principle of Population*.

1799 Napoleon Bonaparte staged a coup d'état in France; his conquests made France the most powerful country in Europe; Code Napoléon reformed legal system; Napoleon was exiled in 1815.

NEAR AND MIDDLE EAST

1736 Nadir Shah established Afshar dynasty in **Persia**; considered last of the great Asian conquerors, he conquered Afghanistan, sacked Delhi, and defeated Turks.

1768 Turkey and Russia began a century of wars, causing Turkey to lose Crimea and much of Slavic Europe to Russia.

1794 Kajar dynasty of Persia founded by **Aga Mohammed**; it remained in power until 1925.

1798 Napoleon Bonaparte attempted to occupy **Egypt** but was driven out (1801) by British and Turkish forces.

FAR EAST

1735–1796 Reign of **Emperor Ch'ien Lung**, during which Chinese empire reached its greatest territorial extent; Christian missionaries were persecuted.

1739 Nadir Shah of Persia sacked Delhi and conquered Punjab.

1757 Defeat of Nawab of Bengal by **Robert Clive** marked beginning of **British Empire in India**.

1758 Burma became an independent state with capital at Rangoon.

1782 Rama I founded **Chakri dynasty** in **Thailand** and established capital at Bangkok; this dynasty rules today.

1786 British East India Company leased the island of Penang in Malaya, first step in British domination of **Malay Peninsula**.

1798 Ceylon became British territory.

AMERICAS

1721 Revolts in **Paraguay** initiated a series of wars in Latin America for **independence from Spain**.

1754 French and Indian Wars started in North America; British general, **James Wolfe**, defeated (1759) French under Montcalm on the Plains of Abraham, Quebec, Canada, ending the wars; British dominated Canada thereafter.

1775 American Revolution began with battle of **Lexington** and **Concord**; it ended with British surrender at Yorktown in 1783.

1776 Declaration of Independence signed in Philadelphia.

1788 U.S. Constitution ratified.

1789 George Washington became first U.S. President.

1791 Canada Act: Canada was divided into Upper Canada (chiefly English) and Lower Canada (predominantly French).

AFRICA

1787 British abolitionists established colony at **Freetown,** which became center for British settlement of **Sierra Leone.**

1795–1796 Mungo Park, British explorer, explored Niger River.

1799 By this time Portuguese, French, Spanish, Danes, Dutch, and Swedes all held **trading posts** along West African coast and engaged in **slave trade.**

OCEANIA

1770 Captain James Cook claimed Cape York Peninsula, Australia, for Great Britain.

1777 Cook visited **Tasmania.**

1788 British established a penal colony in **Sydney, Australia.**

1800—1900

EUROPE

1800 Socialism developed in Europe in reaction to deplorable industrial conditions.

1801 United Kingdom was formed by union of **Great Britain and Ireland.**

1802 John Dalton introduced **atomic theory** into chemistry.
First **factory law** was introduced in England; it pertained to **child labor.**

1804 Napoleon I became emperor of France.

1806 Holy Roman Empire came to an end when **Francis II** renounced the imperial title.

1812 Napoleon invaded **Russia,** a disastrous campaign.

1814–1815 Congress of Vienna: Metternich of Austria, Talleyrand of France, Alexander I of Russia, Frederick William I of Prussia, and Castlereagh of England tried to restore European balance of power; the congress reestablished monarchies and organized German Confederation, which was dominated by Austria.

1815 Napoleon I returned from Elba and was later defeated by British and Prussian armies at **Waterloo.**

1821 Greeks began war with **Turkey,** achieving independence in 1830.

1830 July Revolution in France forced abdication of King Charles X; Louis Philippe became constitutional monarch.

1831 Russians suppressed **Polish insurrection,** marking beginning of "Russification" of Poland.

1837–1901 Reign of **Queen Victoria** of England, who married (1840) her cousin **Prince Albert of Saxe-Coburg;** English enjoyed era of prosperity due to industrial and colonial expansion.

1838 Chartist movement began, marking first attempt of British working classes to attain power.

1845 Friedrich Engels wrote *Situation of the Working Classes in England.*
Potato blight began in Ireland, which resulted by 1851 in death of about one million people from starvation and disease.

1848 Marx and Engels issued *Communist Manifesto.*
Revolutions broke out in France, Germany, Austria, Hungary, Bohemia, and Italy.

1848–1916 Reign of Francis Joseph, Emperor of Austria, who became (1867) ruler of **Austro-Hungarian Empire.**

1852–1870 Reign of Napoleon III, emperor of the Second French Empire.

1854–1856 Crimean War: Britain and France ended Russian domination of southeastern Europe.

1855–1881 Reign of **Alexander II,** tsar of Russia; he attempted to modernize government, emancipated (1861) serfs, and ceded (1867) Alaska to the United States; **Russian literature** began its most creative period.

1856 Bessemer invented process of converting iron into steel.

1859 De Lesseps began **Suez Canal,** which opened in 1869.
Darwin published *Origin of the Species.*

1859–1870 Risorgimento in Italy: a nationalist movement led by middle classes and nobility for political unification; its leaders included **Mazzini, Cavour,** and **Giuseppe Garibaldi.**

1861 Kingdom of Italy proclaimed, and Victor Emmanuel II of Sardinia became king.
Rumania formed by unification of Moldavia and Walachia.

1862 Otto von Bismarck became premier and chancellor of Germany and created German Empire.

1864 First International organized in London under leadership of **Karl Marx.**

1866 First permanent transatlantic cable laid by Cyrus Field.
Austro-Prussian War: Bismarck expelled Austrians from German Confederation; and established North German Confederation; Austria lost Venetia to Italy.
Nobel invented dynamite.

1867 Marx published first volume of *Das Kapital.*
Austro-Hungarian Empire founded: under pressure from Hungarian nationalists, Francis Joseph created dual monarchy; this empire collapsed in 1918.

1868–1894 British statesmen Benjamin Disraeli, an imperialist and Tory leader, and William Gladstone, an anti-imperialist and Liberal party leader, vied for control of prime ministry.

1870 Dogma of papal infallibility declared by Vatican Council.
Vladimir Lenin (V. I. Ulyanov), founder of modern Communism, was born.

1870–1871 Franco-Prussian War: Germans, directed by von Moltke, invaded and defeated France; French deposed Napoleon III and established **Third Republic of France,** which endured until 1940.
Italy incorporated **Papal States,** completing unification of the country.

1871 German Empire proclaimed at Versailles with William I as Emperor; north and south Germany became united into single *Reich.*
Paris Commune formed when Parisians refused to surrender to new regime; national troops suppressed revolutionaries.

1875 Charles Stewart Parnell, Irish nationalist leader, was elected to Parliament and began movement for Irish independence.

1878 Congress of Berlin: much of Ottoman Empire divided among Russia, Britain, and Austro-Hungarian Empire.

1881 Alexander II of Russia assassinated by member of revolutionary group called **People's Will.**

1882 Triple Alliance formed by Germany, Austria-Hungary, and Italy.

1885 Louis Pasteur used vaccine to prevent rabies in young boy.

1894–1906 Dreyfus Affair: Capt. Alfred Dreyfus, French Jewish military officer, was unjustly convicted of treason by a court-martial, sentenced to Devils Island, but eventually exonerated; his case divided France between left and right factions, causing (1905) separation of church and state.

1894–1917 Reign of Nicholas II, last tsar of Russia.

1895 Roentgen discovered X rays.
Marconi sent message over **wireless.**

1898 Zeppelin invented motor-driven **airship** and made first trial flight two years later.
The Curies discovered radium.

1899 First Peace Conference at The Hague established a permanent court of arbitration.

NEAR AND MIDDLE EAST

1811–1849 Reign of Mohammed Ali in Egypt extended Egyptian territory to Persian Gulf.

1854–1856 Crimean War: Britain and France backed Turkey in war with Russia that forced Russian concessions and guaranteed integrity of Ottoman Empire.

1859–1869 Suez Canal was built by De Lesseps.

c. 1870 Turkish government permitted European Jews to settle in Palestine.

1878 Congress of Berlin: Turks lost Cyprus to British, part of Asian lands to Russians, and Bosnia-Hercegovina to Austrians.

1888 European powers declared **neutrality of Suez Canal;** free passage was guaranteed to merchant and war vessels.

1892 British took over **Trucial Oman,** a region of eastern Arabia, and denied local sheiks treaty-making powers.

1894–1896 Sultan **Abdu-l-Hamid II** initiated extermination plan against Armenians; persecutions and massacres were resumed in 1915.

1896 **Young Turks,** a new national force, developed in Turkey, leading (1908) revolt against Sultan.

FAR EAST

1819 **Sir T. Stamford Raffles** secured transfer of **Singapore** to British East India Company.

1839–1842 **Opium War:** British provoked war with China and acquired commercial concessions and **Hong Kong.**

1848 **Taiping Rebellion** began in China, further weakening Ch'ing dynasty; with aid of Western powers, it was suppressed in 1865.

1853 **Commodore Perry,** an American, landed in isolationist **Japan;** the following year Japanese agreed to trade with West.

1857–1858 **Sepoy Rebellion,** or Great Mutiny: Indian soldiers revolted against British, representing first serious revolt of Indians against foreign rule.

1868 **Emperor Meiji Mutsuhito** began to rule **Japan;** he modernized country by abolishing feudalism, promoting foreign trade, and initiating industrialization and military conscription; Meiji period ended in 1912.

1887 France joined Vietnam and Cambodia as **Indo-China;** Laos was added to union in 1893.

1888 Britain completed annexation of **Burma,** making it a dependency of India.

1889 Meiji Mutsuhito issued modern **constitution** for **Japan.**

1894–1895 **Sino-Japanese War:** Japan became an imperial power by defeating Chinese in Korea and acquiring Formosa (Taiwan) and the Pescadores.

1898 Spain ceded Philippines to the United States.

1899 Western powers forced **Open Door** policy upon **China** by which equal trade rights for all nations were guaranteed.

AMERICAS

1801–1803 **Toussaint L'Ouverture,** martyred Haitian patriot, liberated **Santo Domingo** from the French and governed the island, thwarting Napoleon's colonial ambitions.

1803 United States purchased **Louisiana Territory** from France.

1806 **Henri Christophe,** Haitian revolutionary, elected president of Haitian republic.

1810 **Mexico** began to fight for independence from Spain.

1811 **Paraguay** achieved independence.

1811–1813 **Venezuela,** led by Francisco de Miranda, gained independence.

1812–1814 **War of 1812:** United States and Great Britain fought over neutrality of the seas and impressment of sailors; struggle strengthened American nationalist feelings.

1816 **Argentina** won independence.

1818 **Chile** gained independence under **José de San Martín.**

1818–1823 **Bernardo O'Higgins,** Chilean revolutionist, ruled **Chile.**

1819–1830 **Simón Bolívar,** the Liberator and greatest Latin American hero, defeated Spanish forces at Boyacá and was elected President of Greater Colombia (modern Colombia, Venezuela, Ecuador, and Panama).

1821 **Mexicans** achieved independence.

1822 Independence was won in **Brazil and Peru.**

1823 **Monroe Doctrine:** President James Monroe declared that the United States would neither interfere in European affairs nor tolerate European interference in American hemisphere.

1825 **Bolivia** became independent, the last Latin American country to win freedom from Spain.

1841 **Act of Union** joined Upper and Lower **Canada.**

1844 **Samuel Morse** transmitted message over **telegraph** from Washington to Baltimore.

1846 The **Mexican war** between United States (and Texas) and Mexico began; **Treaty of Guadalupe Hidalgo** established (1848) Rio Grande as Mexican-U.S. boundary and made New Mexico and California U.S. territory and Texas a possession.

1848 **Gold** discovered in **California.**

1861 **Civil War** (that ended in 1865) began in the United States.

1863 The **Emancipation Proclamation** ended slavery in the rebel states.

1864 **Maximilian,** Austrian archduke, became emperor of **Mexico;** he and his wife Carlotta retained power with aid of French troops; their rule was overthrown (1867) by **Benito Juárez,** an Indian, who became Mexican national hero.

1865 **War of the Triple Alliance** began: Paraguay fought against Argentina, Brazil, and Uruguay; it ended (1870) with devastation of Paraguay.

1867 **British North America Act:** Canada became a confederation.

United States purchased **Alaska** from Russia.

1868 **Cubans** fought **Ten Years War** for independence, being defeated by Spanish in 1878.

1876 **Porfirio Diaz** seized presidency of **Mexico** and ruled ruthlessly; he encouraged foreign capital, made Mexico prosperous but kept peasants in virtual bondage; deposed by **Madero revolution** in 1911.

1879–1884 **War of the Pacific:** Chile fought against Bolivia and Peru, securing territory from both countries; Bolivia lost sea access.

1889 Republic of **Brazil** established.

1895 Cuban poet, **José Martí,** led revolt against Spain.

1898 **Spanish-American War:** after U.S. battleship *Maine* was sunk in Havana harbor, the United States declared war on Spain and by Treaty of Paris (1898) acquired Puerto Rico, Guam, and the Philippines; the war dissolved Spanish control in Latin America.

1899 **Cuba** became an independent republic under U.S. protection.

AFRICA

1806 Britain annexed **Cape Province** in South Africa.

1807 Britain outlawed **slave trade** with France, Spain, and Portugal following suit.

1808 **Sierra Leone** became a British crown colony and administered **Gambia.**

1822 **Liberia** founded as haven for **freed American** slaves; it was declared an independent republic in 1847.

1830 French troops began conquest of **Algeria.**

1835 **Boers** began to leave Cape Province; the "**Great Trek**" established republics of Transvaal, Natal, and Orange Free State.

1841 **Dr. David Livingstone** began three decades of explorations in central Africa; he discovered (1855) Victoria Falls and his reports created interest in the "**Dark Continent**" and its natural resources.

1843 British annexed **Natal** after short war with Boers; it was made crown colony in 1856.

1848 British annexed **Orange Free State.**

1867–1871 **Diamonds** were discovered in South Africa, inciting diamond rush; **Kimberley** became center of diamond industry.

1874–1889 Henry Morton **Stanley** explored **Congo** River.

1876 **Leopold II,** with Stanley's aid, set up organization to exploit Congo; he founded (1885) **Congo Free State,** ruling as supreme monarch until 1908.

1878 Cetewayo led **Zulu revolt** against British that was defeated (1879) at Ulundi.

1880 **Brazzaville** founded in Congo by **French.**

1881 **Tunis** became French protectorate.

1884–1885 **Germans** proclaimed protectorates over **Tanganyika, Togoland, Cameroons, and South-West Africa.**

1886 **Gold** discovered in **Witwatersrand** in southern Transvaal.

1888 **Cecil Rhodes,** British diamond tycoon, gained monopoly of Kimberley diamond production; Rhodes became (1890) virtual dictator of Cape Province but resigned (1897) and thereafter developed **Rhodesia.**

1889 **Menelik II** of Ethiopia unwittingly signed Treaty of Uccialli that made Ethiopia an Italian protectorate; Italians invaded after he repudiated treaty; Menelik crushed (1896) Italians at **Aduwa.**

1891 British annexed **Nyasaland** and fought Arab slave traders.

1896 British, after a series of wars, defeated **Ashanti** kingdom and annexed it in 1901.

1899–1902 Boer War: British defeated Boers in South Africa and formed (1910) **Union of South Africa.**

OCEANIA

1803 British took possession of **Tasmania,** establishing a penal colony there.

1840 Treaty of **Waitangi** guaranteed Maoris in New Zealand that they would retain their land for surrendering sovereignty to British crown.

1900—1979

EUROPE

1903 Social Democrats held second party congress in London and split into **Mensheviks** and **Bolsheviks,** the nascent Communist party.

1904 France and England signed the **Entente Cordiale,** which became (1907) the **Triple Entente** when Russia joined.

1905 Einstein formulated theory of **relativity.**

1906 Britain launched the *Dreadnought,* first large **battleship,** signaling start of world naval buildup.

1908 Brief Balkan crisis erupted after **Austria** announced annexation of **Bosnia** and **Hercegovina.**

1910–1936 Reign of **George V,** king of Great Britain and Northern Ireland and emperor of India, was marked by **Home Rule for Ireland** (1914) and World War I.

1911 Italy declared war on **Turkey** and acquired Tripoli.

1912 First **Balkan War** began between Balkan countries and Turkey; a second broke out when Bulgaria attacked Serbia and Greece.

1913 European nations increased preparations for war.

1914 Assassination of **Archduke Francis Ferdinand** of Austria in Sarajevo by **Gavrilo Princip,** a member of Serbian terrorist society, sparked **World War I; Triple Entente** of France, Britain, and Russia and their allies Japan, Belgium, Serbia, and Montenegro fought **Central Powers** of Germany, Austria-Hungary, and Turkey; Italy, Portugal, Rumania, and the United States later sided with Triple Entente, which with its allies achieved **victory** in 1918, when an armistice was signed. At least 10,000,000 died during war.

1915 Cunard ship *Lusitania* sunk off the coast of Ireland after attack by German submarine; 1,198 were lost.

1916 President **Wilson** submitted his peace proposals to warring nations.

Gregory **Rasputin,** a hedonistic mystic who influenced Russian royal family, was murdered.

1917 Bolshevik Revolution broke out in Russia; **Alexander Kerensky,** a Menshevik, headed provisional government but was overthrown by Bolshevik leader, **Vladimir Lenin.**

Balfour Declaration: Great Britain announced that Palestine should become home for Jews.

1918 Treaty of **Brest-Litovsk:** Russians signed peace treaty with Germans, losing Poland, the Ukraine, and border areas inhabited by non-Russians.

Kaiser Wilhelm abdicated, and Germans adopted **Weimar Constitution** the following year.

Austro-Hungarian Empire ended, and Austria became a republic, while Poland and Hungary proclaimed their independence.

Czechoslovakia became independent; Thomas Masaryk served as president and Eduard Beneš as foreign minister.

"Kingdom of the Serbs, Croats, and Slovenes" was proclaimed under the regency of **Peter I** of Serbia; its name was changed to **Yugoslavia** (land of southern Slavs) in 1929.

Civil War began in **Russia** between Reds and Whites that was complicated by Allied interventions; by end of war in 1920, Russia had been devastated.

1919 Treaty of **Versailles** ending World War I was negotiated by Woodrow Wilson (United States), Georges Clemenceau (France), David Lloyd George (England), and Vittorio Orlando (Italy).

1920 League of Nations was established in Geneva; the United States refused to join.

Northern and Southern Ireland separated; Southern Ireland became (1921) **Irish Free State** with dominion status.

1922 Russia became the **Union of Soviet Socialist Republics,** the first Communist state in the world.

Benito Mussolini, founder of Fascism, became premier of **Italy,** gradually creating dictatorship.

Major powers agreed to limit size of **navies** at **Washington Disarmament Conference.**

1923 Adolf **Hitler,** leader of National Socialist (Nazi) Party, led unsuccessful **"Beer Hall Putsch"** in Munich; during imprisonment he wrote *Mein Kampf.*

1924 A power struggle began in Russia after Lenin's death; ultimately **Joseph Stalin** was victorious and became dictator.

1928 Stalin initiated **Five Year Plan** for rapid industrialization and collectivized farms; **peasants** who refused collectivization were either sent to Siberia to perform forced labor or killed; measures caused "liquidation" of more than five million peasants.

Kellogg-Briand Pact outlawing war was signed by the United States and 62 other nations in Paris.

1929 Lateran **Treaties** created independent state of **Vatican City** in Rome.

1930 Worldwide **economic depression** developed, pushing many countries into bankruptcy; this disaster encouraged rise of **extremist movements.**

1931 **British Commonwealth of Nations** established.

Spain became a republic.

1932 Antonio **Salazar** became prime minister of **Portugal,** ruling (1936–1968) as dictator.

1933 The democratic **Weimar Republic** fell in Germany. Hitler's Nazi party won majority in *Reichstag* and the government granted him dictatorial powers; Hitler built up war economy and began to rearm Germany; he withdrew from the League of Nations and set up **concentration camps,** where, in the years that followed, over six million people (mainly Jews and Poles) died.

1935 Nuremberg **Laws** deprived Jews of citizenship, barred them from certain professions, and prohibited marriage between Germans and Jews.

Ethiopia, in League of Nations, brought charges against Italy; League economic sanctions against Italy did not prevent annexation (1936) of Ethiopia.

1936 Hitler repudiated Locarno Pact and sent troops into **Rhineland.**

Rome-Berlin-Tokyo Axis formed.

Spanish Civil War began: Republicans were backed by Communist Russia, while Nazi Germany and Fascist Italy supported Falangists; liberals from many countries fought to save republic; Falangist forces, headed by **General Francisco Franco,** were victorious by 1939.

Stalin began liquidation of his enemies with series of **purge trials** that lasted until 1939.

George VI became king of England after Edward VIII abdicated.

1938 Germany annexed **Austria.**

Munich Pact: French and British, led by Neville Chamberlain, appeased Hitler and allowed Germany to occupy Sudetenland; Germans took remainder of Czechoslovakia in 1939.

1939 Germany signed nonaggression pact with Soviet Union.

Germans invaded Poland, beginning **World War II.** Russian troops invaded Poland, which was partitioned between Soviet Union and Germany.

Russians took **Lithuania, Latvia,** and **Estonia.**

Russians invaded **Finland,** defeating her the following year.

League of Nations performed its final act by expelling Soviet Union for invading Finland.

World War II broke out and developed into global conflict between Axis and Allies.

1940 Marshal Henri **Pétain** became head of French government and concluded peace treaty with Germany; Pétain set up government for unoccupied France in Vichy, which collaborated with Germans.

1940–1945 Winston **Churchill** was prime minister of England; his inspiring leadership helped British during dark days of war.

1941 Germany and Italy declared war on the **United States** on Dec. 11.

1942 Vidkun **Quisling** appointed by Germans to head puppet government in **Norway;** he was executed for collaboration in 1945.

1943 Mussolini's regime collapsed; **Marshal Pietro Badoglio** became prime minister, and Italy surrendered unconditionally to Allies and declared war on Germany.

President Roosevelt and Prime Minister Churchill held conferences at **Casablanca, Cairo,** and **Teheran** to coordinate war plans.

German defeat by Russian forces at **Stalingrad** (now Volgograd) marked turning point of war on the Eastern front.

1944 **D-Day:** Allied troops, commanded by **General Dwight D. Eisenhower,** invaded Fortress Europa at Normandy, France.

German generals staged unsuccessful attempt on Hitler's life.

U.S. and French troops liberated **Paris.**

General Charles de Gaulle established provisional government in France.

1945 **Yalta (Crimea) Conference:** Roosevelt, Churchill, and Stalin made postwar plans for German occupation and agreed to form a United Nations.

Josip Broz Tito, partisan leader, became head of Yugoslavia.

Mussolini captured and executed by Italian partisans. Hitler died in Berlin, reportedly a suicide.

Germany surrendered unconditionally to Allies; **Allied Control Council** set up to rule Germany and **Berlin,** both of which were divided among four powers. President Truman, Churchill, and Stalin met at **Potsdam, Germany,** to discuss control of Germany.

Clement Attlee, Labour party leader, became prime minister of England.

International War Crimes Tribunal began in **Nuremberg;** Nazi military and civilian leaders were tried for war crimes.

1946 **United Nations General Assembly** held its first session, in London; **Trygve Lie** of Norway became first secretary-general, holding office until 1951.

Civil war erupted in **Greece** between Communists and rightist government forces; Bulgaria, Albania, and Yugoslavia aided Communist guerrillas; conflict, which ended in 1949 with royalists retaining power, brought increased Western-Soviet hostility.

1946–1947 Bulgaria and Rumania proclaimed people's republics.

1947 **Cominform** was established in response to **Marshall Plan** when Communist leaders from nine countries met in Poland; it was dissolved in 1956.

1948 Communists came to power in **Hungary** and **Czechoslovakia;** Czech President Beneš resigned, and Foreign Minister Jan Masaryk was found dead. Yugoslavia withdrew from Cominform, proclaiming its independence of Soviet influence.

European Recovery Plan (the Marshall Plan) went into effect; ERP ended in 1951.

Berlin Blockade: Soviets barred road and rail travel between Berlin and West Germany; West airlifted supplies until ban was lifted in 1949.

1949 **North Atlantic Treaty Organization** set up by the United States, Canada, and 10 European countries for collective self-defense.

Soviet Union exploded atomic bomb, ending U.S. monopoly

Germany divided into **West Germany** (Federal Republic of Germany) and **East Germany** (German Democratic Republic).

1952 Reign of **Queen Elizabeth II** of England began.

1953 Joseph Stalin died; **Georgi Malenkov** became Soviet premier; **Nikita S. Khrushchev** elected first secretary of the Soviet Communist party's Central Committee.

Russians exploded their first **hydrogen bomb.**

Workers in East Germany staged riots that were suppressed by Soviet troops.

1954 Geneva settlement divided **Vietnam** into North and South Vietnam and recognized independence of **Cambodia** and **Laos.**

1955 **Warsaw Pact:** mutual defense treaty signed by Soviet Union, Albania, Czechoslovakia, Bulgaria, Hungary, Poland, Rumania, and East Germany.

1956 Premier Khrushchev denounced Stalin at 20th Communist Party Congress in Moscow, ushering in a period of **de-Stalinization** in Soviet Union and Eastern Europe. Workers rioted in **Poznan,** Poland. Hungarian rebellion against Communist regime ruthlessly put down by Soviet troops and tanks.

1957 **Common Market:** European Economic Community established by Belgium, Netherlands, Luxembourg, West Germany, France, and Italy; its ultimate aim was political union.

Sputnik: Soviet Union launched world's first artificial earth satellite, initiating Space Age.

1958 Nuclear test ban negotiations began in Geneva between Western and Soviet blocs.

De Gaulle elected president of France.

Russians provoked Berlin crisis that was limited to diplomatic confrontation.

1960 Cyprus gained independence with **Archbishop Makarios** as president.

European Free Trade Association established by "Outer Seven": Austria, United Kingdom, Denmark, Norway, Portugal, Sweden, and Switzerland; Finland joined in 1961.

American U-2 plane, on photoreconnaissance mission, was shot down over Russian territory; United States agreed to suspend flights.

1961 **Berlin Wall:** East Germans erected wall between East and West Berlin, causing war scare.

Yuri A. Gagarin, Russian astronaut, was first man to orbit earth.

1963 Pope John XXIII died; Giovanni Battista Cardinal Montini elected as **Pope Paul VI.**

The United States, Soviet Union, and Great Britain signed **treaty** banning **nuclear tests** above ground and under water.

Fighting broke out between **Greek** and **Turkish Cypriots;** UN force is still on island to maintain order.

1964 Soviet Presidium ousted **Khrushchev** and made **Aleksei N. Kosygin** premier and **Leonid I. Brezhnev** first secretary of Communist party.

1966 **De Gaulle** requested **NATO** troop removal from France.

1967 Military staged coup d'état in **Greece,** installing dictatorship and driving **King Constantine II** into exile.

Britain devalued the **pound** and instituted austerity program.

1968 International monetary crises developed because of faltering British pound and French franc, but both currencies were held.

Soviet troops invaded **Czechoslovakia;** President Ludvik Svodoba and Alexander Dubcek allowed to retain posts, but Czechs had to accept Soviet troop occupation for indefinite time.

Peace talks opened in Paris between representatives of Hanoi, National Liberation Front, Saigon, and Washington to discuss **Vietnam cease-fire.**

1969 **Charles de Gaulle** resigned as president of France and was replaced by Georges Pompidou.

1970 **West Germany** and USSR signed a nonaggression pact.

Conservative leader **Edward Heath** became prime minister in **England.**

Violent food price riots in **Poland** led to Wladyslav Gomulka's resignation. He was replaced by Edward Gierek as the first secretary of the Communist party. **Charles De Gaulle** died.

1972 **Great Britain, Ireland,** and **Denmark** joined the EEC.

Arab commandos disrupt the **XXth Olympic** games at Munich by taking 13 Israeli athletes hostage. The terrorists and hostages were later killed.

Terrorism rocked **Northern Ireland** in continued Protestant-Catholic conflict.

1973 **East** and **West Germany** established diplomatic relations, formally acknowledging their separation. Greece formally abolished the monarchy.

Western Europe was plunged into an energy crisis when the Arabs embargoed oil shipments to Europe, the U.S., and Japan.

1975 Western Europe experiences severe inflation and unemployment.
In Helsinki, Western and Eastern leaders signed pact at Conference on Security and Cooperation.
Francisco Franco dies; Juan Carlos is proclaimed Spanish king.

1978 Pope Paul VI died; Albino Cardinal Luciani elected as Pope John Paul I, but lives only 34 days. Karol Cardinal Wojtyla of Poland elected Pope John Paul II.

MIDDLE EAST

1900 Ibn Saud began to conquer Arabia, which became (1932) kingdom of Saudi Arabia.

1901 Persians discovered petroleum, causing increased rivalry in the area between Russia and England.

1914 British declared Egypt a protectorate, which it remained until 1922.

1916 British Colonel T. E. Lawrence (Lawrence of Arabia) led Arab military campaigns against Turks, hoping for independent Arab states.

1919 Kemal Ataturk organized Turkish Nationalist party and began to form army; he was elected (1923) president of newly founded Turkish republic and began "Westernization" of country, abolishing (1923) caliphate and ruling until 1938.

1920 Syria and Lebanon became French mandates; their independence was recognized when they were admitted to United Nations in 1945.
Palestine, including Jordan, became British mandate; three-way struggle among Jews, Arabs, and British developed, lasting until 1948.

1921 Reza Shah Pahlavi, who staged coup d'etat in Persia, eventually ruled as dictator; changed (1935) name of country to Iran; abdicated in 1941.

1936 Farouk became king of Egypt.

1941 Mohammed Reza Shah Pahlevi became shah of Iran.

1945 The Arab League, an association of Arab states, was formed for economic unity and as opposition to establishment of Jewish state in Palestine.

1946 Iran protested to UN Security Council the presence of Russian troops in Azerbaijan province; this incident, which ended the following year, was the first crisis of the Cold War.
Kingdom of Jordan proclaimed.

1948 State of Israel achieved independence after bitter struggle; David Ben-Gurion first prime minister.

1948–1949 Arab-Israeli war ended in defeat of Arab League forces.

1951–1953 Iran oil industry nationalized by Prime Minister Mohammed Mossadegh.

1952 Gamal Abdel Nasser led army coup against King Farouk; Nasser was elected (1956) president of Egypt and promoted Arab unity.

1956 Suez Crisis: when Nasser nationalized Suez Canal, Israel, Britain, and France attacked Egypt but withdrew after UN Emergency Task-Force entered conflict.

1958 United Arab Republic formed by unification of Egypt and Syria; Syria withdraws in 1961.
Lebanon accused U.A.R. of intervention; President Eisenhower dispatched troops to area.
Iraqi monarchy overthrown in bloody coup led by General Kassem.
British paratroopers landed in Jordan to prevent pro-Nasser take-over.

1960 U.A.R., with Russian aid, began construction of a new Aswan Dam.

1961 Kuwait achieved independence.

1962 Kurdish tribes in northern Iraq rebelled, demanding independent state. Revolt is crushed in 1975.
Adolf Eichmann, chief administrator of Nazi program for exterminating Jews, was tried and executed by Israel.
Yemen monarchy overthrown; civil war broke out between republicans, who were supported by Egyptians, and royalists, backed by Saudi Arabia.

1963 British protectorate of Federation of South Arabia formed by union of Aden and Aden Federation; terrorist groups worked for unification with Yemen; the area achieved independence in 1968 as Southern Yemen.

1967 Arab-Israeli war: six-day conflict broke out after Nasser closed Gulf of Aqaba to Israeli ships; Israelis defeated Arabs; Sinai and Jerusalem occupied.

1968 President Abdul Rahman Arif of Iraq was ousted in bloodless coup led by former premier Ahmed Hassan al-Bakr, who later assumed premiership.
Israel attacked Lebanese airport in Beirut in retaliation for Arab attack on El Al airplane at Athens.

1970 Nasser died in Cairo; succeeded by Anwar Sadat.
Palestinian commandos held 54 passengers of three hijacked planes as hostages in Jordan.
Civil war broke out between Jordanian army and Palestinian guerrilla groups.

1973 Large-scale fighting once again broke out between Israel and the Arab nations. The war ended in an inconclusive cease-fire.
The Arabs embargoed the shipment of oil to the U.S., Europe, and Japan, and boosted prices.

1974 The organization of petroleum exporting countries (OPEC) ended its oil embargo.

1975 Civil war raged in Lebanon between Christians and Moslems. Israel and Egypt signed Sinai disengagement pact. Suez Canal reopened.

1976 Cease-fire achieved in Lebanon.

1979 Israel and Egypt signed peace treaty calling for phased Israeli withdrawal from Sinai. Islamic Republic of Iran was proclaimed under the leadership of the Ayatollah Khomeini following the departure of the Shah and subsequent revolution. Militants seized U.S. Embassy in Tehran and held personnel hostage. Soviet troops occupied Afghanistan.

FAR EAST

1904–1905 Russo-Japanese War: Russia's fleet was destroyed, and Japan's victory gained her recognition as world power.

1907 Mohandas Gandhi organized his first campaign of civil disobedience in Africa; he returned (1915) to India and supported England during World War I, hoping to attain Indian independence.

1910 Japan annexed Korea.

1911 Chinese Revolution: Sun Yat-sen forced Manchu emperor to abdicate and served briefly as president of Chinese Republic.

1917 War developed in China between Kuomintang, Sun Yat-sen's party of the Republic, and "war lords" of the national government in the North; Kuomintang established capital in Canton.

1919 Amritsar Massacre: hundreds of Indian nationalists were fired upon and killed by British.

1921 Chinese Communist party founded and became allied (1923) with Kuomintang.

1926 Chiang Kai-shek led Nationalist army in capture of Hankow, Shanghai, and Nanking; he drove (1927) Chinese Communists from Shanghai, initiating long civil war between Kuomintang forces and Communists.

1927 Mao Tse-tung, one of the founders of the Chinese Communist party, led peasant uprising in Hunan province.

1931 Japanese invaded Manchuria and set up Manchukuo, a puppet state.
Mao Tse-tung elected chairman of Soviet Republic of China.

1934–1935 Mao Tse-tung led Red Army on Long March (6,000 miles) from Kiangsi province north to new headquarters at Yenan.

1937 Burma became independent of India.
Japanese invaded northern China and fought war that continued until 1945.
Gandhi's long fasts forced some Indian states to grant democratic reforms.

1940 Japanese established puppet government in Nanking and signed military alliance with Germany and Italy.

1941 Japan bombed Pearl Harbor, captured Singapore, Philippines, and other areas of the Pacific, initiating World War II in the Pacific and drawing United States into war.

1945 United States dropped atomic bombs on Hiroshima and Nagasaki, marking the beginning of the Nuclear Age; as a result, Japan surrendered, ending World War II.

Korea was divided into Russian and American occupation zones; partition was formalized in 1948 when country became North Korea (Democratic People's Republic of Korea) and South Korea (Republic of Korea), which were separated by 38th parallel.

Vietnamese nationalists began demands for independence from France; war broke out; **Ho Chi Minh,** founder of Communist party in Vietnam, led **Viet Minh** forces.

Indonesian nationalists led by **Sukarno** began to fight Dutch for independence.

1946 Philippines granted independence by the United States.

1947 India and Pakistan became separate independent dominions; Jawaharlal Nehru became prime minister of Hindu state of India and **Mahomed Ali Jinnah,** governor general of Moslem state of Pakistan; bloody rioting broke out after partition, causing the death of millions of Hindus and Moslems.

1948 Gandhi assassinated by Hindu fanatic.
Communists began guerrilla warfare in **Malaya** that lasted over a decade.

1949 Chinese People's Republic headed by Mao Tsetung established government at Peking, after defeating Chiang Kai-shek, whose **Nationalist government** was forced to **Taiwan** (Formosa).

1950 Sukarno elected president of the Republic of **Indonesia.**
Korean war broke out when North Koreans invaded South Korea; United Nations force under U.S. command intervened.
Chinese Communists invaded **Tibet** and sent troops to aid **North Koreans.**

1951 Armistice talks began at **Panmunjon** to end Korean war.

1954 Battle of Dienbienphu: Crushing French defeat ended her control in Indo-China; Vietnam divided at 17th parallel, with **Ho Chi Minh** as president of North Vietnam; Cambodia and Laos became independent.

1955 A U.S. military advisory group took over training of South Vietnamese army.
Premier Ngo Dinh Diem became president of **South Vietnam.**

1957 Federation of Malaya gained independence.

1959 Communist Chinese suppressed uprising in **Tibet.**
Communist Pathet Lao forces began civil war in Laos; a temporary cease-fire was secured (1961) in **Geneva. China** and **India** begun a series of border wars.

1961 India forcibly annexed Portuguese Goa, Damão, and Diu.
United States sent guerrilla warfare specialists to train South Vietnamese soldiers.

1962 Neutralist government set up in **Laos** under Prince **Souvanna Phouma,** but Pathet Lao continued sporadic fighting in North.

1963 Federation of Malaysia created by union of Federation of Malaya, Singapore, Sarawak, and North Borneo; the union suffered infiltration by Indonesian guerrillas until 1966; Singapore seceded (1965) and became independent.
Diem regime in South Vietnam overthrown; government changed hands frequently until military regime of **Nguyen Cao Ky** took over in 1965.

1964 China exploded her first atomic bomb.
France recognized Communist China.
Nehru died in India and was succeeded by Lal Bahadur Shastri.

1965 United States began bombing North Vietnam.
After an abortive Communist coup in Indonesia, the army slaughtered at least 100,000 Communists; Indonesia withdrew from United Nations.
India and Pakistan fought over **Kashmir.**

1966 Communist China initiated "cultural revolution" aimed at ideological conformity of party leaders.
Sukarno forced to yield power to **Suharto,** who outlawed Communist party.
Indira Gandhi, Nehru's daughter, became prime minister of India after Shastri's death.

1967 Communist China exploded first hydrogen bomb.
South Vietnam: first national election; Nguyen Van Thieu president and Nguyen Cao Ky vice-president.

1968 North Korea seized *Pueblo,* U.S. Navy intelligence ship, holding its officers and crew for 11 months. Peace talks for Vietnam cease-fire began in Paris. President Johnson ordered halt to bombing of North Vietnam.

1969 Soviet and Chinese forces fought on the Manchurian border over a disputed island in the Ussuri River.

1970 Prince Sihanouk was deposed as chief of state in Cambodia. He was replaced by Gen. Lon Nol. U.S. and South Vietnamese troops invaded Cambodia.

1971 Communist China admitted to U.N.; Nationalist Chinese (Taiwan) ousted.
East Pakistan became independent state of Bangladesh after bloody civil war.

1972 President Nixon visits Peking and Moscow.

1973 U.S. and South Vietnamese signed cease-fire agreement with North Vietnamese and Vietcong. Fighting continued through Indochina.

1975 The thirty year Indochina war ended with the military collapse of U.S.-backed **South Vietnam** and **Cambodia.**

1976 Communist Chinese leader Mao Tse-tung dies.

1978–79 Vietnam invaded **Cambodia** and drove Pol Pot regime from Phnom Penh.

1979 U.S. extended dipolmatic representation to the **People's Republic of China** (Communists) and broke relations with Taiwan.
China invaded **Vietnam;** withdrew after one month.

AMERICAS

1901 President **William McKinley** assassinated by anarchist; **Theodore Roosevelt** became President and held office until 1909.

1903 Panama, with U.S. assistance, revolted against Colombia and gained independence.
Orville and **Wilbur Wright** made their first airplane flight near Kitty Hawk, North Carolina.

1910 Francisco Madero led Mexican Revolution against President Diaz; after Madero's assassination, **Francisco (Pancho) Villa, Emiliano Zapata,** and **Venustiano Carranza** continued revolution; Mexico's constitution was enacted 1917.

1914 Panama Canal opened.

1916–1924 U.S. troops occupied **Dominican Republic.**

1917 United States entered **World War I** on side of Allies.

1929 Stock Market crash in the United States initiated the **Great Depression; during height of depression, 12** million people were unemployed.

1932–1935 Chaco War: Bolivia and **Paraguay** fought exhausting war over disputed Chaco plain.

1933 President **Franklin D. Roosevelt** was inaugurated; he enacted **New Deal** legislation aimed at improving social and economic conditions in the U.S.

1938 Mexico nationalized foreign oil companies.

1941–1945 United States in World War II: after Japanese bombed **Pearl Harbor,** December 7, 1941, the United States declared war; Nazi Germany and Fascist Italy declared war on the United States; war was terminated after defeat of German army and surrender of Japanese after atomic bombing of Hiroshima and Nagasaki.

1942 Enrico Fermi achieved first self-sustaining nuclear chain reaction.

1944 Bretton Woods (New Hampshire) Conference established the **International Bank for Reconstruction** and the **International Monetary Fund.**
Dumbarton Oaks, Washington, D.C., Conference: the United States, Great Britain, and Soviet Union laid plans for an international organization.

1945 Roosevelt died and was succeeded by Harry S Truman.
United Nations Charter signed at San Francisco.
United States made first atom bomb test at Los Alamos, New Mexico, warned Japan of her complete destruction unless she surrendered, and dropped atomic bombs on Hiroshima and Nagasaki.

1946 Juan Perón elected president of Argentina; he established totalitarian regime and an ultranationalistic program that ultimately ruined economy, and was deposed (1955) by miltary coup.
Churchill gave "iron curtain" speech at Fulton, Missouri, warning of Soviet expansionism.

1948 Truman won upset Presidential victory; he initiated overseas military and economic aid to contain Communism and became leader in NATO formation.
Organization of American States (OAS) founded for hemispheric unity and mutual defense.

1949 U.S. Senate ratified NATO treaty, establishing collective self-defense among Western powers.

1950 United States in UN Security Council charged North Korea with invading South Korea and initiated military intervention against aggressors with General MacArthur as UN Commander.

1952 Fulgencio Batista seized power in Cuba.
United States exploded its first hydrogen bomb.

1954 General Alfredo Stroessner staged coup in Paraguay; in spite of opposition, he remains in power.
Brown v. Board of Education: U.S. Supreme Court outlawed racial segregation in public schools, initiating civil rights movement.

1957 François Duvalier elected president of Haiti; his harsh rule included reign of terror.

1958 Explorer I: United States successfully launched her first artificial satellite.

1959 Fidel Castro came to power in Cuba; he gradually linked country with Soviet bloc and proclaimed (1961) loyalty to Communism.

1960 John F. Kennedy elected U.S. President.

1961 United States severed relations with Cuba.
Bay of Pigs: U.S.-trained Cuban exiles' invasion of Cuba ended disastrously.
Charter of the Alliance for Progress signed in Punta del Este, Uruguay; it was aimed at increasing economic and social development in Latin America with U.S. aid.

1962 The United States and Soviet Union appeared on the brink of war when Soviet missiles were discovered on Cuba; President Kennedy forced Khrushchev to have them dismantled.
John H. Glenn was first American to orbit earth.

1963 President Kennedy assassinated in Dallas, Texas, November 22; Lyndon Baines Johnson sworn in as President and defeated Barry M. Goldwater in 1964.

1964 Panamanians staged anti-U.S. riots.

1965 U.S. marines landed in Dominican Republic.
President Johnson signed Medicare and war on poverty legislation.
Race riots ravaged Los Angeles suburb of Watts.

1966 Guyana became independent.

1967 Race riots wasted Newark, Detroit, and other cities.

1968 Frank Borman, William A. Anders, and James A. Lovell, Jr., were first men to orbit the moon.
Dr. Martin Luther King, Jr. and Senator Robert Kennedy were assassinated in the United States.
Richard M. Nixon won U.S. Presidential contest.
Military coup deposed Peruvian President Fernando Belaúnde Terry.
Pierre Elliott Trudeau succeeded to Canadian premiership.

1969 U.S. astronaut Neil A. Armstrong became first man to walk on the Moon.

1970 U.S. student protests against the Viet Nam war resulted in the killing of four students by National Guard at Kent State, Ohio, and of two students by police at Jackson State, Miss.
Trudeau invoked the War Measures Act in Canada after the murder of Quebec Labor Minister Pierre Laporte by the Quebec Liberation Front.
Salvador Allende was elected president of Chile and Luis Echeverría Alvarez of Mexico.

1971 Wage-price freeze enacted by Nixon administration.

1972 Governor Wallace seriously injured in attempted assassination while campaigning in Maryland.
Watergate burglars apprehended in Democratic National Headquarters; "Watergate" begins.
Richard M. Nixon reelected president.

1973 Spiro T. Agnew resigned from the vice-presidency; Gerald R. Ford named to replace Agnew. "Watergate" dominates American political scene.
Salvador Allende Gossens, Marxist President of Chile, overthrown and reportedly committed suicide.
Juan Perón returned from exile to become Argentine president.

1974 Juan Perón died in Buenos Aires; His wife, Vice-President Isabel Perón assumes the presidency.
Richard M. Nixon resigned from the presidency; Gerald R. Ford succeeds to the office.

1975 Surinam and Grenada attained independence.
U.S. suffered severe economic recession.

1976 Argentine military junta deposed Mrs. Perón.
José López Portillo elected to Mexican presidency.
Jimmy Carter elected U.S. President.

1979 Somoza regime was toppled in Nicaragua by Sandinista rebels following 18-month civil war. Canal Zone was ceded to Panama by the U.S.

AFRICA

1906 Algeçiras Conference recognized predominance of French and Spanish interests in Morocco but also assured protection of German interests.

1908 Belgium annexed Congo Free State, calling it Belgian Congo.

1910 Union of South Africa formed from former British colonies of Cape of Good Hope and Natal, Orange Free State, and Transvaal.

1911 Germans sent gunboat *Panther* to Morocco as show of force.

1912 African partition among European powers was completed; only Ethiopia and Liberia remained independent.

1914 World War I in Africa: British and French troops occupied German colonies of Togoland and the Cameroons.

1920 Former German colonies became League mandates under Great Britain (Tanganyika, parts of Togoland and Cameroons), Belgium (Ruanda-Urundi), France (parts of Togoland and Cameroons), and Union of South Africa (South-West Africa).
Most of Kenya became British crown colony.
Abd-el-Krim, leader of Riff tribes of Morocco, began fight against Spanish and French rule in Africa; early successes followed by his defeat and deportation (1926) by combined Franco-Spanish troops.

1923 Rhodesia was divided into Southern and Northern Rhodesia and placed under British rule.

1930 Emperor Haile Selassie ascended Ethiopian throne.

1935 Italy invaded Ethiopia, causing Haile Selassie to flee country; League of Nations issued economic sanctions to no avail.

1946 India broke diplomatic relations with Union of South Africa because of her treatment of Indian minority.

1948 Apartheid: D. F. Malan made apartheid in Union of South Africa a political issue; the policy was aimed at perpetuating supremacy of white minority.

1951 Rising African nationalism achieved first victory with independence of Libya.

1952 Mau Mau, secret terrorist organization in Kenya, began bloody campaign to oust white settlers; British declared state of emergency that lasted until 1960.

1954 Algerian nationalists formed National Liberation Front and began terrorist campaign against French; war ended with Algeria gaining independence in 1962.

1956 Tunisia gained independence from France with Habib Bourguiba as premier.

1960 Immediately after Republic of the Congo achieved independence, civil war broke out; political struggle within central government developed between Patrice Lumumba, premier, and Joseph Kasavubu, head of state; UN peace-keeping force entered dispute; when Lumumba was seized by army and murdered (1961), Moise Tshombe became premier.
African nationalism reached peak of success when 16 nations gained freedom and African nations made up one third of UN membership.

1961 Dag Hammarskjöld, UN secretary-general, killed in plane crash on mission to **Congo.**
Union of South Africa became a republic; later left British Commonwealth.

1963 Jomo Kenyatta became Kenya's first premier.

1964 Tanzania formed by unification of Tanganyika and Zanzibar; Julius K. Nyerere became first president. Nyasaland became independent state of Malawi; Northern Rhodesia gained independence as Zambia.

1965 Mohammed Ben Bella, Algerian premier, overthrown by Col. Houari Boumédiene.
Rhodesia unilaterally declared independence from Great Britain.
President Kasavubu dismissed Tshombe and his government; General Mobutu, commander of Congolese National army, seized power.

1966 Kwame Nkrumah's government in **Ghana** toppled by military coup; Nkrumah went into exile.
United Nations terminated South Africa's mandate over South-West Africa and proclaimed UN administration over country.

1967 Tshombe held in custody in **Algeria** while Congo sought his extradition, in order to execute him; Congolese troops engaged rebel forces in Kisangani and Bukavu. Tshombe died (1969) in Algeria.
Republic of Biafra proclaimed when eastern province of Nigeria seceded; Nigerian government sent troops and blockaded province, causing widespread famine throughout 1968/69.
Dr. Christiaan Barnard performed first human **heart** transplant in Cape Town, South Africa.

1969 Pope Paul VI became the first pope to visit Africa when he flew to Kampala, Uganda to attend an African episcopal symposium meeting.
Portugal utilized 40% of her national budget and 120,000 troops to quell rebels in territories of Angola, Mozambique, and Portuguese Guinea.

1970 Surrender of secessionist Biafra on January 12 ended the 31-month civil war in **Nigeria.**

1973 A drought-induced famine cripples much of western Africa.

1975 Mozambique, Cape Verde, São Tomé and Príncipe, and Angola gained independence, ending centuries-old Portuguese colonial empire.

1976 Proponents of black majority rule wage guerrilla war against white regime in **Rhodesia.**

1977 Ethiopia and Somalia made war over disputed Ogaden region.

1978 Belgian and French paratroopers repelled Angola-based rebel invasion of Shaba province of **Zaire.**

1979 Amin regime was overthrown in Uganda following invasion by **Tanzania.**

OCEANIA

1901 **Commonwealth of Australia** formed by unification of Australia and Tasmania.

1907 New Zealand attained dominion status.

1959 Hawaii became a U.S. state.

1962 Western Samoa obtained independence.

1968 Nauru became an independent republic.

1970 Fiji and **Tonga** gained independence.

1975 Papua New Guinea achieved independence.

1978 Solomon Islands and **Tuvalu** gained independence.

1979 Kiribati became independent.

ARCTIC AND ANTARCTICA

1908–1909 E. H. Shackleton's expedition to **Antarctica** failed to reach South Pole.

1909 Robert E. Peary discovered North Pole.

1911 Roald Amundsen reached South Pole.

1926 Richard E. Byrd flew over North Pole.

1928 Byrd established Little America, in Antarctica.

1955–1958 Edmund Hillary and Vivian Fuchs from Great Britain led overland crossing of Antarctica.

1957–1958 During the International Geophysical Year, many nations participated in studies of Antarctica and the Arctic.

1958 *Nautilus*, U.S. nuclear submarine, was first ship to cross North Pole under ice pack.

1959–1960 Treaty accepted by 12 nations, including the United States, reserved Antarctica for scientific research and recognized no existing national claims to territory in area.

1967 Peter J. Barrett and geologists from New Zealand discovered bone fragment and plant fossils embedded beneath icy surface of Antarctica indicating that Antarctica formerly had warmer climate.

1968–1969 First overland crossing of the North Pole by foot and dog sled. Royal Geographic Society of Britain's 3,600-mile expedition, encompassing more than 15 months, reached Pole in April 1969.

SEVEN WONDERS OF THE ANCIENT WORLD

The Great Pyramid of Khufu (or Cheops)—the world's largest pyramid located at Gizeh near Cairo. Built of limestone blocks, it originally stood 756 feet square, 482 feet high and covered 13 acres.

The Hanging Gardens of Bablyon—luxurious gardens which added to the glamorous atmosphere of Mesopotamia's most important ancient city.

The Mausoleum at Halicarnassus—a magnificent sepulcher in Asia Minor constructed of white marble richly decorated with sculpture and erected (c. 352 B.C.) in memory of Mausolus of Caria.

The Artemision at Ephesus—great temple built (c. 550 B.C.) as a center of worship for the nature-goddess Artemis.

The Colossus of Rhodes—large bronze statue (height about 100 feet) of the sun god Helios situated in the harbor of Rhodes and thought to be built by Chares of Rhodes between 292 and 280 B.C.

The Olympian Zeus by Phidias—built for the temple of Olympia (c. 435 B.C.); it consisted of a majestic bearded figure wearing a mantle and seated upon a huge ornamented throne.

The Pharos at Alexandria—celebrated lighthouse (estimated height: 200–600 feet) built by Ptolemy II (c. 280 B.C.) on the peninsula of Pharos.

WORLD BIOGRAPHY

Abd-el-Krim, c. 1882-1963, Moroccan Rif leader and national hero.

Abdullah, 1882–1951, assassinated first Hashemite king of Jordan.

Abrams, Creighton W., Jr., 1914-1974, American general in Vietnam.

Abruzzi, Duca degli (Luigi Amedeo), 1873–1933, Italian explorer of the Arctic (1899–1900).

Acheson, Dean G., 1893-1971, U.S. Secretary of State (1949-52) who helped to establish NATO.

Adams, Samuel, 1722–1803, American patriot, signer of Declaration of Independence, and firebrand of Boston Tea Party.

Addams, Jane, 1860–1935, American social worker and co-founder of Hull House.

Adenauer, Konrad, 1876–1967, German statesman, postwar chancellor, and architect of West German recovery.

Aga Khan III, 1877-1957, fabulously wealthy Moslem leader and statesman.

Agnelli, Giovanni, 1921–   , Italian industrialist and chairman of FIAT.

Agrippina the Younger, A.D. c. 16-59, Nero's mother, who contrived his accession to the throne.

Aguinaldo, Emilio, c. 1869–1964, Filipino revolutionary against Spain and the United States.

Akbar, 1542–1605, greatest Mogul emperor of India.

Alanbrooke, Viscount (Alan F. Brooke), 1883-1963, British general, W.W. II chief of imperial general staff.

Alaric I, c. 370–410, Visigothic ruler who devastated southern Europe.

Albert, Prince, 1819–61, German-born consort of Victoria of England.

Albuquerque, Afonso de, 1453–1515, Portuguese admiral and founder of Portuguese empire in the East.

Alcibiades, c. 450–404 B.C., Athenian statesman and general in Peloponnesian War.

Alexander (III) the Great, 356–823 B.C., king of Macedon, Greek conqueror, and one of the greatest generals of all time.

Alexius I (Alexius Comnenus), 1048–1118, emperor who restored Byzantine military and political power.

Allen, Ethan, 1738–89, American Revolutionary hero, leader of Green Mountain Boys.

Allende (Gossens), Salvador, 1908–73, President of Chile (1970–73); advocated democratic socialism.

Altgeld, John P., 1847–1902, German-born American political leader and social reformer.

Amin Dada, Idi, 1925–   , Ugandan president (1971–79).

Amundsen, Roald, 1872–1928, Norwegian polar explorer, first to reach the South Pole (December 14, 1911).

Andrada e Silva, José Bonifácio de, 1763–1838, Brazilian statesman, chief founder of independent Brazil.

Andrassy, Julius (Count), 1823–90, Hungarian statesman and first constitutional premier (1867–71).

Andreotti, Giulio, 1919–   , Italian premier (1972-73, 1976–79).

Andropov, Yuri V., 1914–   , head of Soviet secret police, ambassador to Hungary during 1956 uprising.

Anthony, Susan B., 1820–1906, American reformer and suffragette leader.

Antonescu, Ion, 1882–1946, Rumanian dictator (1940–44), executed as a war criminal.

Antony, Mark, c. 83-80 B.C., Roman politician and soldier who allied himself with Cleopatra and defied Rome.

Arafat, Yasir, 1929–   , leader of the Palestine Liberation Organization.

Armstrong, Neil, 1930–   , American astronaut; first person to set foot on the moon (1969).

Arnold, Benedict, 1741–1801, American Revolutionary general and traitor.

Asoka, ?–232 B.C., first great Indian emperor; spreader of Buddhism.

al-Assad, Hafez, 1928–   , Syrian president (1971–   ).

Astor, John Jacob, 1763–1848, American merchant and fur trader, the richest man in America at his death.

Astor, Lady (Nancy W.), 1879–1964, American-born British political leader, first woman member of Parliament.

Astor, William W. (Viscount), 1848–1919, Anglo-American financier and philanthropist.

Atahualpa, d. 1533, Inca (ruling chief) of Peru, executed by Pizarro.

Ataturk, Kemal (b. Mustafa Kemal), 1881–1938, father of modern Turkey and president (1923–1938).

Attila, d. 453, Hun leader, conqueror of eastern Europe.

Attucks, Crispus, c. 1723–70, American Negro patriot killed by British in Boston Massacre.

Augustus (Octavius), 63 B.C.–14 A.D., first Roman emperor; he defeated Antony and returned Rome from military dictatorship to constitutional rule.

Aurangzeb, 1618–1707, Mogul Indian emperor who brought his empire to its greatest expanse.

Auriol, Vincent, 1884–1966, first president (1947–54) of French Fourth Republic.

Austin, Stephen F., 1793–1836, American leader of colonization in Texas.

Ayub Khan, Mohammad, 1907-74, Pakistani military leader who became (1958) president and resigned (1969).

Babar, c. 1482-1530, founder of Mogul empire in India.

Babeuf, François N., 1760–97, executed French revolutionary, philosophical forerunner of Marx.

Badoglio, Pietro, 1871–1956, Italian field marshal in Ethiopia, premier after fall of Mussolini.

Bakunin, Mikhail, 1814–76, militant Russian anarchist, expelled from First International by Marxists.

Balboa, Vasco Núñez de, c. 1475–1519, beheaded Spanish conquistador, discoverer of Pacific Ocean.

Bancroft, George, 1800–91, American statesman and historian, founder of U.S. Naval Academy.

Banneker, Benjamin, 1731–1806, American Negro colonial astronomer, mathematician, and inventor.

Barry, John, 1745-1803, Irish-born naval commander during the American Revolution; considered to be the "Father of the American Navy."

Barton, Clara, 1821–1912, American humanitarian, organizer of the American Red Cross.

Baruch, Bernard M., 1870–1965, American financier and government economic adviser.

Batista y Zaldívar, Fulgencio, 1901-73, Cuban dictator (president 1940-44, 1952-59), overthrown by Castro.

Batu Khan, d. 1255, Mongol leader of Golden Horde.

Beauregard, Pierre G. T., 1818–93, American Confederate general.

Beaverbrook, Lord (William Maxwell Aitken), 1879–1964, Canadian-born British statesman and publisher.

Begin, Menachem, 1913–   , Israeli prime minister.

Belisarius, c. 505-565, Byzantine general under Justinian.

Bellinghausen, Fabian von, 1778–1852, Russian admiral and discoverer (1819–21) of Antarctica.

Ben Bella, Ahmed, 1918–   , Algerian revolutionary, elected (1962) premier and deposed (1965) by Boumédienne.

Beneš, Eduard, 1884–1948, Czechoslovak president.

Ben-Gurion, David, 1886–1973, Israeli statesman, first prime minister (beginning in 1948).

Benjamin of Tudela, d. 1173, Jewish traveler and author of an itinerary of his trip (1159–73) to China.

Bennett, James Gordon, Jr., 1841-1918, American publisher who financed Stanley's trip to find Livingstone.

Bentinck, Lord William C., 1774–1839, British statesman, appointed (1833) first governor-general of British India.

Beria, Lavrenti P., 1899–1953, executed Soviet secret police chief under Stalin.

Bering, Vitus J., 1681–1741, Russian-backed Danish discoverer (1728) of Bering Strait.

Bernadotte, Count (Folke), 1895–1948, Swedish internationalist, UN mediator in Palestine until assassinated.

Betancourt, Romulo, 1908–   , progressive Venezuelan president (1945-48, 1959-64).

Bevan, Aneurin, 1897–1960, British political leader, developer of England's socialized medicine system.

Bevin, Ernest, 1881–1951, British labor leader and Labour government foreign minister (1945–51).

Bhave, Acharya Vinoba, 1895–   , foremost Indian advocate of nonviolent (Gandhian) social revolution.

Bhutto, Zulfikar Ali, 1928–79, Pakistani president (1971–73) and prime minister (1973–77). Overthrown (1977) and executed in 1979.

Biddle, Francis B., 1886–1968, American jurist, U.S. Attorney General (1941–45).

Bismarck, Otto von, 1815–98, German statesman who unified Germany under Prussian leadership.

Blackstone, Sir William, 1723–80, English jurist, first professor of English law at Oxford University.

Bloomer, Amelia J., 1818–94, American reformer, devoted to women's rights.

Blücher, Gebhard L. von, 1742–1819, Prussian field marshal who helped Wellington defeat Napoleon at Waterloo.

Blum, Léon, 1872–1950, French Socialist statesman, Popular Front organizer, and writer.

Boleyn, Anne, c. 1507–36, beheaded second wife of Henry VIII of England, mother of Elizabeth I.

Bolívar, Simón, 1783–1830, South American revolutionary who liberated much of the continent from Spanish rule.

Bonaparte, Joseph, 1768–1844, eldest brother of Napoleon I, ineffective king of Naples and Spain.

Bonaparte, Napoleon see **Napoleon Bonaparte.**

Booth, John Wilkes, 1838–65, egomaniacal American actor, assassin of Abraham Lincoln.

Booth, William, 1829–1912, English religious leader, founder and first general of Salvation Army.

Borgia, Caesar, c. 1475–1507, Italian Renaissance ecclesiastic and statesman; brother of Lucretia Borgia.

Borgia, Lucretia, 1480–1519, famous figure of Italian Renaissance, daughter of Pope Alexander VI.

Bormann, Martin L., 1900–1945, German Nazi leader.

Bosch, Juan, 1909–   , progressive Dominican leader.

Botha, Louis, 1862–1919, Boer soldier and first prime minister (1910–19) of Union of South Africa.

Bougainville, Louis Antoine de, 1729–1811, French navigator, leader of scientific expeditions in South Pacific.

Boumédiene, Houari, 1927–78, Algerian revolutionary, deposed (1965) Ben Bella.

Bourguiba, Habib, 1903–   , Tunisian independence leader and first premier (subsequently president).

Braddock, Edward, 1695–1755, British general in French and Indian Wars.

Bradley, Omar N., 1893–   , U.S. Army WW II general, later chairman of joint chiefs of staff.

Braille, Louis C., 1809–52, French inventor of Braille system of printing and writing for the blind.

Brandt, Willy, 1913–   , West German chancellor (1969-74), leader of Social Democratic party.

Brauchitsch, Walther von, 1881–1948, German WW II general.

Brezhnev, Leonid I., 1906–   , Soviet Communist party leader, successor to Khrushchev; Chairman of the Presidium of the Supreme Soviet (1977–   ).

Brian Boru, c. 940–1014, Irish king who broke Norse power in Ireland.

Briand, Aristide, 1862–1932, French statesman, chief architect of antiwar Kellogg-Briand Pact (1928).

Brown, John, 1800–59, hanged American abolitionist whose raid at Harpers Ferry stunned North and South.

Bryan, William Jennings, 1860–1925, American political leader, greatest orator of his day.

Brzezinski, Zbigniew, 1928–   , foreign affairs adviser to President Carter (1977–   ).

Bulganin, Nikolai A., 1895-1975, Soviet Communist leader and premier (1955–58).

Bullitt, William C., 1891–1967, American diplomat, first American ambassador to USSR (1933–36).

Bunche, Ralph J., 1904–1971, American Negro government official and UN mediator.

Bundy, McGeorge, 1919–   , American professor, Presidential adviser, and Ford Foundation head.

Bunker, Ellsworth, 1894–   , American business executive and diplomat.

Burghley, William Cecil (Baron), 1520–98, English statesman, influential adviser to Elizabeth I for 40 years.

Burgoyne, John, 1722–92, British statesman and general in American Revolution.

Burke, Edmund, 1729–97, English political writer and statesman, proponent of conservatism.

Burnside, Ambrose E., 1824–81, American Union general.

Burton, Sir Richard F., 1821–90, English writer, orientalist, and discoverer (1858) of Lake Tanganyika.

Byrd, Richard E., 1888–1957, American admiral and polar explorer, first to fly over the North Pole (1926).

Caesar, Julius, c. 102–44 B.C., Roman statesman and general who enlarged and pacified Rome's provinces.

Cagliostro, Alessandro (Giuseppe Balsamo), 1743–95, Italian adventurer.

Callaghan, James, 1912–   , Labour prime minister of Great Britain (1976–79).

Calles, Plutarco E., 1877–1945, Mexican Revolutionary statesman and president (1924–28).

Campesino, El (Valentín Gonzáles), c. 1909–   , Spanish Republican soldier in the civil war (1936–39).

Canaris, Wilhelm, 1887–1945, German WW II admiral and intelligence chief who opposed Hitler.

Cárdenas, Lázaro, 1895–1970, Mexican president (1934–40) and revolutionary general.

Cardigan, Earl of (James T. Brudenell), 1797–1868, British Crimean War general who led disastrous cavalry attack at Balaklava, immortalized in Tennyson's "The Charge of the Light Brigade."

Carnegie, Andrew, 1835–1919, Scottish-American iron and steel tycoon and philanthropist.

Carnot, Lazare, 1753–1823, French revolutionary general.

Carpini, Giovanni de Piano, c. 1180–1252, Italian monk who produced a full record of Mongol life from missionary experiences in Central Asia.

Carranza, Venustiano, 1859–1920, Mexican revolutionary leader who arranged Zapata's assassination.

Casanova de Seingalt, Giovanni G., 1725–98, Venetian adventurer and author.

Castelo Branco, Humberto, 1900–67, Brazilian revolutionary president.

Castiglione, Baldassare (Conte), 1478–1529, Italian Renaissance statesman and author.

Castlereagh, Robert S. (Viscount), 1769–1822, Irish-born British foreign secretary, and organizer of successful coalition against Napoleon I.

Castro, Fidel, 1927–   , Cuban Communist premier who wrested power from Fulgencio Batista in 1959.

Catherine de' Medici, 1519–89, queen of France who helped to plan (1572) French Protestant massacre on Saint Bartholomew's Day.

Catherine II, 1729–96, forceful German-born empress and tsarina of Russia, also known as Catherine the Great.

Cato the Elder (Cato the Censor), 234–149 B.C., Roman statesman and moralist.

Cavell, Edith, 1865–1915, English nurse executed by Germans during WW I.

Cavour, Camillo Benso (conte di), 1810–61, Italian statesman, leader in unifying Italy under house of Savoy.

Ceausescu, Nicolae, 1918–   , Romanian head of state.

Černik, Oldřich, 1921–   , liberal Czechoslovak Communist premier during 1968 Soviet invasion.

Chamberlain, (A.) Neville, 1869–1940, British prime minister who signed (1938) Munich Pact with Hitler.

Chang Tso-lin, 1873–1928, Chinese general, warlord of Manchuria.

Charcot, Jean B., 1867–1936, French neurologist and explorer in the Antarctic.

Charlemagne, 742–814, king of the Franks, (768–814) and Emperor of the West (800–814).

Chase, Salmon P., 1808–73, American abolitionist, statesman, and Secretary of the Treasury under Lincoln.

Cheops (or Khufu), fl. c. 2680 B.C., king of Egypt, builder of great pyramid at Gizeh.

Chiang Kai-shek, 1887–1975, Chinese Nationalist leader whose government was driven (1950) from mainland China to island of Taiwan.

Chiang Kai-shek, Madame (Soong Mai-ling), 1896–   , politically active wife of the Chinese Nationalist leader.

Ch'ien Lung (Hung-li), 1711–99, fourth emperor of Ching dynasty who greatly extended borders of China.

Chou En-lai see Zhou Enlai.

Christophe, Henri, 1767–1820, Haitian revolutionary and self-proclaimed king (Henri I).

Churchill, Sir Winston L. S., 1874–1965, British prime minister, soldier, author, and war leader.

Ciano, Galeazzo, 1903–44, Italian Fascist foreign minister who helped create Rome-Berlin Axis, executed by Mussolini—his father-in-law.

Cid, El, d. c. 1099, Spanish national hero, whose real name was Rodrigo (or Ruy) Díaz de Vivar.

Clarendon, Earl of (Edward Hyde), 1609–74, English statesman, historian, and adviser to Charles II.

Clark, Charles Joseph 1939–   , Conservative prime minister of Canada (1979–80).

Clay, Henry, 1777–1852, American statesman, author of Compromise of 1850.

Clemenceau, Georges, 1841–1929, French statesman (the "Tiger"), twice premier (1906–09, 1917–20).

Cleopatra, 69–30 B.C., Ptolemaic queen of Egypt, one of the great romantic figures of all time.

Clinton, De Witt, 1769–1828, American statesman, Presidential nominee (1812), sponsor of Erie Canal.

Cobden, Richard, 1804–65. British statesman, advocate (after 1849) of peace and international conferences.

Coen, Jan P., 1587–1629, Dutch colonial governor, founder of Dutch East Indian empire.

Coke, Sir Edward, 1552–1634, one of the most eminent English jurists in history.

Colbert, Jean B., 1619–83, French statesman under Louis XIV, successful practitioner of mercantilism.

Columbus, Christopher, 1451–1506, Italian-born discoverer of America for Spain (1492).

Constantine I (the Great), ?–337, first Christian Roman emperor (306–337).

Constantine V (Constantine Copronymus), 718–775, iconoclastic Byzantine emperor (741–775).

Constantine VI, b. c. 770, Byzantine emperor (780–797), blinded by Irene, his mother and successor.

Constantine XI (Constantine Palaeologus), d. 1453, last Byzantine emperor (1449–53).

Cook, James (Captain), 1728–79, English explorer along coasts of Australia and New Zealand.

Cooper, Peter, 1791–1883, American inventor, industrialist, and philanthropist.

Corday, Charlotte, 1768–93, aristocratic French Revolution sympathizer who assassinated Jean Paul Marat.

Cornwallis, Charles (Marquess), 1738–1805, English general in American Revolution.

Cortés, Hernán, 1485–1547, Spanish conquistador in Mexico who toppled Aztec empire of Montezuma.

Cossiga, Franceso, 1928–   , Italian premier (1979–   ).

Coty, René, 1882–1962, last president of French Fourth Republic.

Cox, James M., 1870–1957, American political leader, U.S. Presidential candidate (1920), and journalist.

Cranmer, Thomas, 1489–1556, English churchman, adviser to Henry VIII.

Croesus, d. c. 547 B.C., king of Lydia; his name has become synonym for wealth.

Cromwell, Oliver, 1599–1658, English general and statesman, lord protector of England (1653–58).

Cuauhtémoc, d. c. 1525, Aztec emperor executed by Cortés.

Cunard, Sir Samuel, 1787–1865, Canadian pioneer of regular transatlantic steam navigation (Cunard Line).

Curtis, Cyrus H. K., 1850–1933, American publisher and philanthropist.

Curzon, George N. (Marquess), 1859–1925, British statesman and viceroy of India.

Cyrano de Bergerac, Savinien, 1619–55, French poet and duelist romanticized by Edmond Rostand's drama.

Cyrus (the Great), ?–529 B.C., founder of the ancient Persian Empire.

Dalai Lama, 1935–   , theocratic ruler of Tibet, ousted (1959) by Chinese invasion of his country.

Danton, Georges J., 1759–94, French statesman and a leading figure of French Revolution.

Darius I (the Great), d. 486 B.C., king of Persia (521–486 B.C.) who consolidated Persian power in the East.

Darlan, Jean F., 1881–1942, assassinated French admiral, vice-premier of Vichy government.

Darnley, Lord (Henry S.), 1545–67, claimant to English throne, second husband of Mary Queen of Scots.

Davis, Angela, 1944–   , university lecturer and black political activist.

Davis, Jefferson, 1808–89, American statesman, president of Southern Confederacy.

Davitt, Michael, 1846–1906, Irish revolutionary and land reformer.

Dayan, Moshe, 1915–   , Israeli statesman, soldier, and hero of 1967 June War.

Debs, Eugene V., 1855–1926, American Socialist leader, Presidential candidate (1900, 1904, 1908, 1912, 1920).

De Gasperi, Alcide, 1881–1954, Italian premier (1945–53), organizer of Christian Democratic party.

de Gaulle, Charles, 1890–1970, French general and controversial nationalist president (1959–69).

Deng Xiaoping, 1904– , Chinese Communist Politburo vice-chairman (1977–).

Dassai, Morarji, 1895– , Indian prime minister (1977–79).

De Soto, Hernando, c. 1500–42, Spanish conquistador and explorer in what is now United States.

Dessalines, Jean J., c. 1758–1806, emperor of Haiti, born a slave.

De Valera, Eamon, 1882–1975, long-time Irish prime minister and president.

Dewey, George, 1837–1917, American admiral, hero of battle of Manila.

Dewey, Thomas E., 1902–71, governor of New York (1942–54), Republican Presidential candidate (1944, 1948).

Dias, Bartolomeu, d. 1500, Portuguese navigator, first European to round (1488) the Cape of Good Hope.

Díaz, Porfirio, 1830–1915, Mexican president (1876–1911), whose ruthless rule fostered revolution.

Díaz Ordaz, Gustavo, 1911-79, progressive Mexican president (1964-70) and lawyer.

Diefenbaker, John G., 1895–1979, Conservative prime minister of Canada (1957-63).

Diem, Ngo Dinh, 1901–63, assassinated South Vietnamese president.

Dimitrov, Georgi, 1882–1949, Bulgarian Communist premier (1946–49), acquitted of Reichstag fire.

Dirksen, Everett M., 1896–1969, U.S. Senator (Ill., first elected 1950) and Republican minority leader.

Disraeli, Benjamin (Earl of Beaconsfield), 1804–81, British prime minister (1868, 1874–80), founder of the Conservative party.

Dix, Dorothea L., 1802–87, American social reformer, champion of specialized treatment for the mentally ill.

Djilas, Milovan, 1911– , Yugoslavian political leader and intellectual, frequently imprisoned by Tito.

Dobrynin, Anatoly F., 1919– , Soviet ambassador to U.S.

Dollfuss, Engelbert, 1892–1934, Austrian chancellor assassinated by Austrian Nazis.

Douglas, Stephen A., 1813–61, American statesman who opposed (1860) Lincoln for Presidency.

Douglass, Frederick, c. 1817–95, American Negro abolitionist leader.

Drake, Sir Francis, c. 1540–96, first Englishman to circumnavigate the earth (1577–80).

Dreyfus, Alfred, 1859–1935, French soldier whose treason trial (and ultimate exoneration) was a *cause célèbre*.

Du Barry, Madame (Jeanne B.), 1743–93, mistress of Louis XV of France, guillotined during French Revolution.

Dubcek, Alexander, 1921– , liberal Czechoslovak Communist party secretary during 1968 Soviet invasion.

Du Bois, William E. B., 1868–1963, American Negro editor, author, exponent of equality for the Negro.

Duclos, Jacques, 1896–1975, French Communist leader.

Dulles, Allen W., 1893–1969, U.S. public official, director of CIA (1953–61).

Dulles, John Foster, 1888–1959, U.S. Secretary of State (1953–59), strong anti-Communist.

Duvalier, François, 1907–71, Haitian dictator.

Dzerzhinsky, Felix E., 1877–1926, Russian Bolshevik politician, organizer of Soviet secret police.

Earhart, Amelia, 1898–1937, pioneering American aviatrix who disappeared on a round-the-world flight.

Eban, Abba, 1915– , Israeli diplomat and statesman.

Ebert, Friedrich, 1871–1925, first president (1919–25) of the German republic.

Echeverría Álvarez, Luis, 1922– , President of Mexico (1970–76).

Eden, Sir Anthony (Earl of Avon), 1897–1977, British statesman, Conservative prime minister (1955–57).

Edinburgh, Duke of (Philip Mountbatten), 1921– , consort of Elizabeth II of Great Britain.

Eichmann, Adolf, 1906–62, German Nazi official executed by Israel for crimes against the Jewish people and humanity.

Elizabeth I, 1533–1603, queen of England during the great age of British expansion and exploration.

Ellsworth, Lincoln, 1880–1951, American explorer, the first man to fly over Antarctic (1935).

Emin Pasha (Eduard Schnitzer), 1840–92, German physician, colonial administrator, and explorer of Sudan.

Emmet, Robert, 1778–1803, executed Irish patriot.

Engels, Friedrich, 1820–95, German Socialist, co-founder with Karl Marx of modern Communism.

Enver Pasha, 1881–1922, Turkish general and political leader.

Erlander, Tage F., 1901– , Swedish Social Democratic premier (1946–69).

Ervin, Samuel J., Jr., 1896– , U.S. Senator from North Carolina (1954–1974).

Eshkol, Levi, 1895–1969, Israeli prime minister (1963-69)

Essex, Earl of (Robert Devereux), 1567–1601, favorite of Elizabeth I of England who signed his death warrant.

Fanfani, Amintore, 1908– , Italian statesman and premier (1958-59, 1960-63).

Farouk I, 1920–65, king of Egypt (1936–52), forced to abdicate (1952) by military coup.

Fawkes, Guy, 1570–1606, English Roman Catholic conspirator involved in scheme to blow up Parliament.

Fish, Hamilton, 1808–93, American statesman, one of the ablest of U.S. Secretaries of State.

Foch, Ferdinand, 1851–1929, French marshal, commander (1918) of British, French, and American armies.

Ford, Henry, 1863–1947, American industrialist, pioneer automobile manufacturer.

Forrestal, James V., 1892–1949, U.S. Secretary of the Navy (1944–47), first Secretary of Defense (1947–49).

Fox, Charles J., 1749–1806, British statesman, orator, and liberal reformer.

Francis (Franz) Ferdinand, 1863–1914, Austrian archduke whose assassination precipitated WW I.

Franco, Francisco, 1892–1975, leader of rebel forces in Spanish Civil War (1936–39) and dictator of Spain (1937–75).

Frank, Anne, 1929–45, Dutch Jewish girl killed by the Nazis; her diary made her posthumously famous.

Franklin, Benjamin, 1706–90, outstanding American statesman, also printer, scientist, and writer.

Fraser, John Malcolm, 1930– , Australian prime minister (1975–).

Frederick II (the Great), 1712–86, king of Prussia (1740–86) and military genius.

Frederick William, 1620–88, "Great Elector" of Brandenburg, who laid the base of the state of Prussia.

Frémont, John C., 1813–90, American explorer, soldier, and politician, a controversial figure of history.

Frobenius, Leo, 1873–1938, German archaeologist and authority on prehistoric African art and culture.

Fugger, Jacob (Jacob the Rich), 1459–1525, German merchant prince.

Fukuda, Takeo, 1905– , Japanese premier (1976–78).

Fulbright, J. William, 1905– , U.S. Senator (Ark., 1945-1974). chairman of Senate Foreign Relations Committee from 1959.

Gage, Thomas, 1721–87, English general in America whose orders led to battles of Lexington and Concord.

Gallatin, Albert, 1761–1849, American statesman and financier.

Gama, Vasco da, c. 1469–1524, Portuguese navigator, first European to journey to India by sea (1497–99).

Gambetta, Léon, 1838–82, French republican statesman.

Gamelin, Maurice G., 1872–1958, French general, leader of Allied forces at WW II's outbreak.

Gandhi, Indira, 1917– , Indian prime minister (1966–77, 1980–), daughter of Nehru, and first woman ever elected to head the government of a major power.

Gandhi, Mohandas K., 1869–1948, Indian ascetic who advocated nonviolent resistance to secure independence of India from Great Britain.

Garibaldi, Giuseppe, 1807–82, Italian patriot and soldier who fought for Italy's unification.

Garrison, William Lloyd, 1805–79, American abolitionist and social reformer.

Garvey, Marcus, 1887–1940, American Negro nationalist leader.

Genghis Khan see **Jenghiz Khan.**

Giap, Vo Nguyen, 1912– , North Vietnamese statesman and victor at Dienbienphu in 1954.

Giscard d'Estaing, Valéry, 1926– , French president since 1974.

Gladstone, William Ewart, 1809–98, British Liberal prime minister (1868–74, 1880–85, 1886, 1892–94).

Gneisenau, August (Graf Neithardt von), 1760–1831, Prussian field marshal in Napoleonic Wars.

Godfrey of Bouillon, c. 1058–1100, crusader, ruler of Jerusalem.

Godunov, Boris, c. 1551–1605, Russian tsar, advisor to Ivan the Terrible.

Goebbels, Paul J., 1897–1945, German Nazi propagandist, master of mass psychology.

Goering, Hermann W., 1893–1946, German Nazi leader, early supporter of Hitler, and head of Luftwaffe.

Goldwater, Barry M., 1909– , U.S. Senator (Ariz.), unsuccessful Republican Presidential candidate (1964).

Gompers, Samuel, 1850–1924, American labor leader, founder and president (1886–94, 1896–1924) of AFL.

Gomulka, Wladyslav, 1905– , Polish Communist Party leader.

Gordon, Charles G. (Chinese Gordon), 1833–85, British soldier and administrator killed by Moslems at Khartoum.

Gottwald, Klement, 1896–1953, Czechoslovak Communist leader, who ushered Communism into his country.

Gowon, Yakubu, 1934– , Nigerian head of state who opposed the unsuccessful secession of the late 1960s.

Greeley, Horace, 1811–72, American newspaper publisher (New York *Tribune*) and Presidential candidate (1872).

Grenville, Sir Richard, c. 1542–91, English naval hero against Spanish.

Grey, Lady Jane, 1537–54, queen of England for nine days, succeeded by Mary I.

Gromyko, Andrei A., 1909– , Soviet foreign minister and ambassador.

Grotius, Hugo, 1583–1645, Dutch jurist and humanist, considered the founder of international law.

Guevara, Che (Ernesto), 1928–67, Argentine-born Cuban guerrilla leader killed in Bolivia.

Gwyn, Nell (Eleanor), 1650–87, English actress, mistress of Charles II.

Haig, Alexander Meigs, Jr., 1924– , U.S. Army General; Chief of Staff of the White House (1973–74).

Haile Selassie, 1892–1975, emperor of Ethiopia (1930–74).

Hale, Nathan, 1755–76, American Revolutionary patriot, hanged by the British without trial as a spy.

Halsey, William F., 1882–1959, American WW II admiral in Pacific.

Hamilton, Alexander, 1755–1804, American Federalist statesman, first Secretary of the Treasury.

Hammurabi, fl. 1792–1750 B.C., king of Babylonia; his code of laws is one of the greatest of ancient codes.

Hannibal, 247–c. 182 B.C., Carthaginian general, great military opponent of Rome (Second Punic War).

Harriman, W. Averell, 1891– , American diplomat, U.S. representative (1968) at Vietnam peace talks.

Harun-al-Rashid, c. 764–809, famous caliph of Baghdad under whom the Abbasid empire reached its apogee.

Hastings, Warren, 1732–1818, controversial first governor-general of British India.

Hawkins, Sir John, 1532–95, Elizabethan sea dog, knighted for his actions in defeat of Spanish Armada.

Hay, John, 1838–1905, American author and statesman, who formulated the Open Door policy toward China.

Haya de la Torre, Victor Raúl, 1895–1979, Peruvian leader, advocate of Latin-American nationalist revolutions.

Hearst, William Randolph, 1863–1951, American journalist and publisher, innovator in mass-appeal newspapers.

Heath, Edward R. G., 1916– , British Conservative prime minister (1970–74).

Henry, Patrick, 1736–99, American orator and patriot, who worked to have Bill of Rights added to the Constitution.

Henry the Navigator, 1394–1460, Portuguese geographer and prince, who was the patron of the great age of Portuguese exploration.

Herodotus, c. 484–c. 425 B.C., Greek historian and traveler considered the father of history.

Herzl, Theodor, 1860–1904, Hungarian writer, founder of modern Zionism.

Hess, Rudolf, 1894– , erratic German Nazi leader, imprisoned (1946) for life as a war criminal.

Heydrich, Reinhard, 1904–42, German Nazi police official ("the Hangman") whose assassination by Czech patriots led to Lidice massacre.

Heyerdahl, Thor, 1914– , Norwegian explorer-ethnologist, substantiated the diffusionist theory of anthropology with his trans-pacific raft journeys.

Hidalgo y Costilla, Miguel, 1753–1811, executed Mexican national hero and priest.

Hillary, Sir Edmund P., 1919– , New Zealand mountain climber; first to reach summit of Mt. Everest (1953).

Hillel, fl. 30 B.C.–10 A.D., Jewish scholar; many of Christ's teachings resemble Hillel's sayings.

Hillman, Sidney, 1887–1946, Lithuanian-born American labor leader.

Himmler, Heinrich, 1900–45, terroristic Nazi chief of SS and Gestapo.

Hindenburg, Paul von, 1847–1934, German president (1925–34) who appointed Hitler as chancellor.

Hitler, Adolf, 1889–1945, founder of German Nazism and infamous tyrant who precipitated WW II.

Ho Chi Minh, c. 1890–1969, Vietnamese Communist leader and national hero; first president of North Vietnam.

Hoover, J. Edgar, 1895–1972, American administrator, director of FBI (1924–72).

Horthy de Nagybanya, Nicholas, 1868–1957, Hungarian admiral and political leader.

Houphouët-Boigny, Félix, 1905– , president of Ivory Coast, leader of former French Africa.

Houston, Samuel, 1793–1863, American frontier hero and Texan statesman.

Howe, Julia Ward, 1819–1910, American social reformer and writer of "The Battle Hymn of the Republic."

Howe, Richard (Earl), 1726–99, admiral and commander (1776–78) of British fleet in American Revolution.

Howe, William (Viscount), 1729–1814, English general in American Revolution.

Hoxha, Enver 1908– , Albanian Communist leader.

Hua Guofeng (Kuo-feng), 1921– , Chinese Communist premier (1976–80) and Politburo chairman (1976–).

Hull, Cordell, 1871–1955, U.S. Secretary of State (1933–44), recipient (1945) Nobel Peace Prize.

Hunyadi, John, c. 1385–1456, Hungarian national hero, resistance leader against Turks.

Ibn Saud, c. 1880–1953, founder (1932) and first king of Saudi Arabia.

Ikhnaton, d. c. 1354 B.C., pharaoh of Egypt who established perhaps the world's first monotheistic religion.

Iqbal, Mohammad, 1873–1938, Moslem leader, national hero of Pakistan.

Irene, 752–803, repressive Byzantine empress who had her son blinded.

Isabella I, 1451–1504, queen of Spain who supported the 1492 New World voyage of Columbus.

Jabotinsky, Vladimir, 1880–1940, Russian-born Zionist leader.

Jackson, Stonewall (Thomas J.), 1824–63, American Confederate general.

Jaurès, Jean, 1859–1914, assassinated French Socialist leader and historian.

Jenghiz (also Genghis) Khan, c. 1167–1227, brilliant Mongol conqueror, ruler of a vast Asian empire.

Jinnah, Mohammad Ali, 1876–1948, founder and first governor-general of Pakistan (1947–48).

Joan of Arc, c. 1412–31, French saint and national heroine, burned at the stake for heresy.

Joffre, Joseph J. C., 1852–1931, French WW I marshal.

John III (John Sobieski), 1620–96, king of Poland, champion of Christian Europe against Turks.

Jones, John Paul, 1747–92, Scottish-born American naval hero of American Revolution.

Jordan, Vernon E., Jr., 1935– , civil rights leader and executive director of the National Urban League.

Josephine, 1763–1814, empress of the French (1804–09), first wife of Napoleon I.

Juárez, Benito, 1806–72, Mexican Indian president, revered by Mexicans as great political figure.

Juin, Alphonse, 1888–1967, French soldier and marshal.

Justinian I, 483–565, Byzantine emperor (527–65) whose accomplishment was codification of Roman law.

Kadar, Janos, 1912– , Hungarian Communist premier who sided with Soviets in 1956 Hungarian revolt.

Kamenev, Lev B., 1883–1936, Soviet Communist leader executed during 1936 Moscow purges.

Karamanlis, Constantine, 1907– , twice Greek premier, president of Greece (1980–).

Kasavubu, Joseph, c. 1910–69, first president of the Congo.

Kassem, Abdul Karim, 1914–63, executed Iraqi general who overthrew (1958) monarchy and became premier.

Kaunda, Kenneth, 1924– , Zambian president, proponent of Gandhian principles.

Kefauver, (C.) Estes, 1903–63, U.S. Senator (Tenn., 1949–63), supporter of civil rights legislation.

Kekkonen, Urho K., 1900– , Finnish president (beginning 1956).

Kennedy, Edward M., 1932– , U. S. Senator (Mass., (1962–), brother of John F. and Robert F. Kennedy.

Kennedy, Robert F., 1925–68, assassinated U.S. Senator (N.Y., 1965–68), brother of slain President John F. Kennedy under whom he was U.S. Attorney General.

Kenyatta, Jomo, c. 1893–1978, first Kenyan president, an early African nationalist leader.

Kerensky, Aleksandr F., 1881–1970, exiled Russian revolutionary premier (1917), overthrown by Bolsheviks.

Keynes, John Maynard, 1883–1946, influential English economist and monetary authority.

Khomeini, Ayatollah Ruhollah, 1900– , Moslem religious leader who led Iranian Revolution of 1979.

Khrushchev, Nikita S., 1894–1971, Soviet Communist leader, deposed (1964) as premier.

Kidd, Captain (William), c. 1645–1701, British privateer hanged for murder and piracy.

Kiesinger, Kurt G., 1904– , West German chancellor (1966–69), advocate of reconciliation with Eastern Europe.

Kim Il Sung, 1912– , first premier of Communist North Korea.

King, Martin Luther, Jr., 1929–68, assassinated American Negro rights leader and Nobel Prize winner.

King, (W. L.) Mackenzie, 1874–1950, liberal Canadian prime minister (1921–30, 1935–48).

Kissinger, Henry A., 1923– , chief foreign affairs adviser to President Nixon, and leading authority on international relations and national defense policy. U.S. Secretary of State (1973–77).

Kitchener, Horatio H. (Earl), 1850–1916, British field marshal during the imperial era.

Kittikachorn, Thanom, 1911– , Thai premier and minister of defense (1963–73).

Knox, Henry, 1750–1806, American patriot and Revolutionary general, U.S. Secretary of War (1785–94).

Konev, Ivan S., 1897–1973, Soviet WW II field marshal, commander (1955–60) of Warsaw Pact military forces.

Konoye, Prince Fumimaro, 1891–1945, Japanese premier who allied Japan with Axis.

Koo, (V. K.) Wellington, 1887– , Chinese statesman elected (1957) to International Court of Justice at The Hague.

Kornilov, Lavr G., 1870–1918, Russian anti-Bolshevik general.

Kosciusko, Thaddeus, 1746–1817, Polish general who fought for patriot cause in American Revolution.

Kossuth, Louis, 1802–94, exiled Hungarian revolutionary leader.

Kosygin, Aleksei N., 1904– , Soviet Communist premier, successor to Khrushchev.

Kropotkin, Prince (Peter), 1842–1921, Russian anarchist who championed peasantry but opposed Bolshevism.

Kruger, S. J. Paulus (Paul Kruger), 1825–1904, South African pioneer, soldier, farmer, and statesman.

Krupp, Alfred, 1812–87, German armaments magnate known as the "Cannon King."

Krupp, Alfred (von Bohlen und Halbach), 1907–67, German industrialist and imprisoned war criminal.

Kublai Khan, c. 1215–94, Mongol emperor, founder of Yüan dynasty in China.

Kun, Bela, 1886–c. 1939, Hungarian Communist dictator.

Kutuzov, Mikhail I., 1745–1813, Russian field marshal, victor over Napoleon I.

Ky, Nguyen Cao, 1930– , South Vietnamese general and political leader.

Lafayette, Marquis de, 1757–1834, French statesman and general who served in American Revolution.

La Follette, Robert M., 1855–1925, U.S. Senator (Wis., 1906–25), Progressive Party Presidential candidate (1924).

LaFontaine, Sir Louis H., 1807–64, distinguished French-Canadian statesman.

LaGuardia, Fiorello H., 1882–1947, U.S. Congressman (1916, 1923–33) and reform mayor of New York City (1934–45), affectionately known as the "Little Flower."

Laing, Alexander G., 1793–1826, Scottish soldier and explorer who was murdered by Arabs near Timbuktu.

Langton, Stephen, c. 1155–1228, English archbishop who acted with barons to obtain Magna Carta's signing.

Largo Caballero, Francisco, 1869–1946, Spanish Socialist leader and premier (1936–37).

Laski, Harold J., 1893–1950, English political scientist, economist, author, and lecturer.

Lassalle, Ferdinand, 1825–64, a founder of German Socialist movement, killed in a duel over a love affair.

Lattre de Tassigny, Jean de, 1889–1952, French general who fought in Indo-China.

Laval, Pierre, 1883–1945, executed French politician and foreign minister of Vichy government.

Lawrence, Thomas E. (Lawrence of Arabia), 1888–1935, British scholar and Middle East soldier-adventurer.

Leahy, William D., 1875–1959, American diplomat and WW II admiral.

Leclerc, Jacques P. (comte de Hauteclocque), 1902–47, French WW II general who later served in Indo-China.

Lee, Henry, 1756–1818, American cavalry leader in the Revolution; known as Light-Horse Harry Lee.

Lee, Robert E., 1807–70, brilliant American Confederate commander in chief.

Lee Kuan Yew, 1923– , Singaporean Socialist prime minister.

Lehman, Herbert H., 1878–1963, liberal U.S. Senator (N.Y.), opponent of Senator Joseph R. McCarthy.

Lemnitzer, Lyman L., 1899– , American general, NATO commander (1963-1969).

Lenin, Vladimir I., 1870–1924, Russian revolutionary statesman, founder of Bolshevism and U.S.S.R.

Leo Africanus, c. 1465–1550, Moorish traveler in Africa and the Near East.

Lesseps, Ferdinand (Vicomte de), 1805–94, French diplomat and engineer who conceived idea of Suez Canal.

Lewis, John L., 1880–1969, important American labor spokesman, head of UMW and CIO.

Liaquat Ali Khan, 1895–1951, assassinated Moslem leader and first prime minister (1947–51) of Pakistan.

Liebknecht, Karl, 1871–1919, murdered German Communist leader.

Lindbergh, Charles A., 1902–74, American aviator, who made first solo transatlantic flight.

Lin Piao, 1907–1971, Chinese Communist leader and political heir to Mao.

Litvinov, Maxim M., 1876–1951, Soviet statesman, proponent of Soviet cooperation with Western powers.

Liu Shao-ch'i, c. 1898-1974, Chinese Communist leader who fell from grace in "cultural revolution" (1966-67).

Livingston, Edward, 1764–1836, American jurist and statesman, U.S. Secretary of State under Andrew Jackson.

Livingston, Robert R., 1746–1813, American Revolutionary political leader who negotiated Louisiana Purchase.

Livingstone, David, 1813–73, Scottish medical missionary, abolitionist, and African explorer.

Lodge, Henry Cabot, 1850–1924, conservative U.S. Senator (Mass., 1893–1924).

Lodge, Henry Cabot, Jr., 1902– , U.S. Senator, ambassador, and Vietnam peace negotiator.

Long, Huey P., 1893–1935, assassinated American political demagogue in Louisiana.

López Portillo, José, 1920- , Mexican president (1976-).

Low, Sir David, 1891–1963, British cartoonist, famous for caricatures.

Lübke, Heinrich, 1894–1972, West German administrator and president.

Luce, Henry R., 1898–1967, American publisher, founder of Time, Inc.

Luckner, Felix, Graf von, 1881-1966, German WW I naval commander, nicknamed "the Sea Devil."

Lumumba, Patrice E., 1925–61, murdered first prime minister (1960) of Republic of the Congo.

Luthuli, Albert J., 1898-1967, South African Zulu leader and Nobel Prize winner.

Luxemburg, Rosa, c. 1870–1919, Polish-born German Communist leader, murdered while being taken to prison.

MacArthur, Douglas, 1880–1964, distinguished American general in WW II, recalled (1951) from Korea for insubordination.

Maccabee, Judas, d. c. 161 B.C., Jewish military leader who opposed foreign rule in Judea.

McCarthy, Eugene J., 1916– , U.S. Senator (Minn.) who became nationally prominent for his opposition to American participation in Vietnam war.

McCarthy, Joseph R., 1908–57, U.S. Senator (Wis.) known for his charges of Communism in government.

McClellan, George B., 1826–85, American Union general.

McCormick, Robert R., 1880–1955, American publisher (Chicago Tribune), famous for his isolationist views.

McGill, James, 1744–1813, Scottish-born Canadian fur trader and university founder.

Machado, Gerardo, 1871–1939, repressive Cuban president (1925–33).

Machiavelli, Niccolò, 1469–1527, Florentine diplomat and political philosopher, an outstanding Renaissance figure.

Macmillan, M. Harold, 1894– , conservative British prime minister (1957–63).

McNamara, Robert S., 1916– , U.S. Secretary of Defense under Presidents Kennedy and Johnson.

Madero, Francisco I., 1873–1913, assassinated Mexican revolutionist and president (1911–13).

Magellan, Ferdinand, c. 1480–1521, Portuguese leader of first expedition to circumnavigate the earth (1519-22).

Magsaysay, Ramón, 1907–57, president of the Philippines (1953–57) who campaigned against the Huk rebels.

Mahan, Alfred T., 1840–1914, American naval officer and historian.

Mahdi, title claimed by **Mohammed Ahmed**, 1844–85, Moslem religious leader in Anglo-Egyptian Sudan.

Mahmud of Ghazni, c. 971–1030, Afghan emperor and conqueror.

Makarios III, 1913–77, Cypriot Greek Orthodox archbishop, first president (elected 1960) of Cyprus.

Malan, Daniel F., 1874–1959, Afrikaner prime minister of South Africa.

Malcolm X (b. Malcolm Little), 1925–65, assassinated American Negro separatist leader.

Malenkov, Georgi M., 1902– , Soviet Communist successor to Stalin (1953-55), expelled (1964) from party.

Malinovsky, Rodion Y., 1898–1967, Soviet marshal and minister of defense.

Malraux, André, 1901–76, French man of letters and political figure, minister of culture under de Gaulle.

Mannerheim, Baron Carl G. E., 1867–1951, Finnish field marshal, later president (1944–46).

Mansur, d. 775, Abbasid caliph (754–775), founder of Baghdad.

Mao Zedong (Tse-tung), 1893–1976, founder of Communist China, leader of radical wing of international Communism.

Marat, Jean Paul, 1743–93, French revolutionary stabbed to death in his bath by Charlotte Corday.

Marcos, Ferdinand E., 1917–   , Filipino president.

Maria Theresa, 1717–80, popular Hapsburg empress, queen of Bohemia and Hungary.

Marie Antoinette, 1755–93, guillotined queen of France, wife of Louis XVI.

Marion, Francis ("the Swamp Fox"), c. 1732–95, American guerrilla leader in the Revolution.

Marlborough, Duke of (John Churchill), 1650–1722, English general and statesman.

Martí, José, 1853–95, Cuban poet and patriot, leader of Cuban struggle for independence.

Marx, Karl H., 1818–83, German philosopher, proponent of modern Communism, author of *Das Kapital.*

Masaryk, Jan, 1886–1948, Czechoslovak statesman whose "suicide" mysteriously followed Communist coup.

Masaryk, Thomas G., 1850–1937, Czechoslovak statesman, founder and president (1918–35) of Czechoslovakia.

Massey, Vincent, 1887–1967, Canadian diplomat and governor-general.

Mata Hari (Margaretha G. Zelle), 1876–1917, Dutch dancer executed by the French as a WW I German spy.

Matteotti, Giacomo, 1885–1924, murdered Italian Socialist leader, opponent of Mussolini.

Matthias Corvinus, c. 1443–90, king of Hungary (1458–90) and of Bohemia (1478–90), crusader against Turks.

Mawson, Sir Douglas, 1882–1958, English-born Australian geologist who charted Antarctic coast.

Maximilian, 1832–67, Austrian archduke and emperor of Mexico (1864–67), executed by the forces of Juarez.

Mazarin, Jules, 1602–61, French statesman and Roman Catholic cardinal.

Mazzini, Giuseppe, 1805–72, Italian patriot and revolutionary who figured in Italy's unification.

Mboya, Tom (Thomas J.), 1930–69, Kenyan political leader, instrumental in securing independence for his country.

Medici, Cosimo de', 1389–1464, Florentine merchant prince and first Medici ruler of Florence.

Medici, Lorenzo de' (Lorenzo the Magnificent), 1449–92, Florentine statesman, Renaissance patron of the arts.

Meir, Golda, 1898–1978, Israeli prime minister (1969–74).

Mendès-France, Pierre, 1907–   , French premier (1954–55), who opposed Charles de Gaulle's return to power.

Menelik II, 1844–1913, emperor of Ethiopia after 1899, who expanded and modernized his country.

Metaxas, John, 1871–1941, Greek general and dictator.

Metternich, Clemens W. N. L., Fürst von, 1773–1859, Austrian foreign minister and arbiter of Europe.

Mikhailovich, Draja (Dragoliub), c. 1893–1946, executed Yugoslav soldier, foe of Tito.

Miki, Takeo, 1907–   , Japanese prime minister (1974-76).

Mikoyan, Anastas I., 1895–1978, Soviet Communist leader.

Mindszenty, Cardinal (Jozsef), 1892-1975, Hungarian Roman Catholic prelate who sought asylum in U.S. legation after Hungarian uprising (1956).

Minuit, Peter, c. 1580–1638, director general (1626–31) of New Netherland, who purchased Manhattan for $24.

Mirabeau, Honoré G. R., comte de, 1749–91, French revolutionary who favored a strong constitutional monarchy.

Mitchell, Billy (William), 1879–1936, American general, demoted for criticism of U.S. military leaders.

Mobuto Sese Seko, 1930–   , Zairean president who deposed (1960) Patrice Lumumba.

Mohammad Reza Pahlavi, 1919–80, shah of Iran (1941–1979).

Mohammed V, 1910–61, sultan of Morocco (1927–53), first king (1957–61) of independent Morocco.

Moi, Daniel arap, 1924–   , Kenyan president (1978–   ).

Molotov, Vyacheslav M., 1890–   , Soviet Communist leader whose political fortunes waned in post-Stalin era.

Moltke, Helmuth J. L., Graf von, 1800–91, Prussian field marshal, victor in Franco-Prussian War.

Mongkut (Rama IV), 1804–68, king of Siam, a main character in 1944 book, *Anna and the King of Siam.*

Monnet, Jean, 1888–1979, French political economist who conceived idea of the Common Market.

Montcalm, Louis de (Marquis de Saint-Véran), 1712–59, French general in French and Indian Wars, defeated and killed in Battle of Quebec.

Montezuma, c. 1480–1520, murdered Aztec emperor who defied Cortés.

Montgomery, Bernard L. (1st Viscount Montgomery of Alamein), 1887–1976, distinguished British WW II field marshal.

More, Sir Thomas, 1478–1535, English author (*Utopia*) and statesman, celebrated as a Roman Catholic martyr.

Morelos y Pavón, José M., 1765–1815, executed Mexican leader in revolution against Spain.

Morgan, Daniel, 1736–1802, American Revolutionary general, victor in the Carolina campaign.

Morgan, Sir Henry, c. 1635–88, English buccaneer, later acting governor of Jamaica.

Morgan, J. P. (John Pierpont), 1837–1913, American banker who built his family's fortunes into a financial colossus.

Morgenthau, Henry, Jr., 1891–1967, U.S. Secretary of the Treasury (1934–45).

Morris, Gouverneur, 1752–1816, American Revolutionary statesman who advocated centralized government.

Morris, Robert, 1734–1806, "financier of the American Revolution," signer of Declaration of Independence.

Mossadegh, Mohammed, 1880–1967, deposed and imprisoned Iranian premier (1951–53) who attempted to nationalize Iran's British-controlled oil industry.

Mountbatten, Lord Louis, 1900–79, British WW II admiral who commanded in both the Atlantic and Pacific.

Muñoz Marin, Luis, 1898–1980, long-time governor of Puerto Rico, supporter of its commonwealth status.

Mussolini, Benito ("Il Duce"), 1883–1945, Italian dictator 1922–45), founder of Fascism, ally of Adolf Hitler.

Mutsuhito (Meiji), 1852–1912, Japanese emperor (1867–1912) during whose reign feudalism came to an end.

Nadir Shah, 1688–1747, shah of Iran, perhaps the last great Asiatic conqueror.

Nagy, Imre, c. 1895–1958, Hungarian Communist premier (1953–55), executed after the 1956 uprising.

Nansen, Fridtjof, 1861–1930, Norwegian arctic explorer, statesman, and Nobel Peace Prize winner (1922).

Napoleon Bonaparte (Napoleon I), 1769–1821, Corsican-born emperor of the French (1804–15).

Napoleon III (Louis Napoleon Bonaparte), 1808–73, emperor of the French (nephew of Napoleon I).

Nasser, Gamal Abdel, 1918–70, Egyptian leader of Arab unification, became (1956) first president of Egypt.

Nebuchadnezzar, d. 562 B.C., king of Babylonia and destroyer of Jerusalem (586 B.C.).

Necker, Jacques, 1732–1804, Swiss-born French financier and statesman, father of Madame de Staël.

Negrin, Juan, 1891–1956, Spanish Socialist premier (1937–39), who fled from his country after the civil war.

Nehru, Jawaharlal, 1889–1964, first prime minister of India, guided country during early years of independence.

Nelson, Lord (Horatio), 1758–1805, English admiral in Napoleonic Wars, killed during victory at Trafalgar.

Nenni, Pietro, 1891–1980, Italian Socialist leader.

Ne Win, 1911–   , Burmese general and prime minister, leader of 1962 coup against U Nu.

Newman, Cardinal (John Henry), 1801–90, English prelate, a founder (1833) of Oxford Movement.

Ney, Michel, 1769–1815, executed marshal of France, commander at Waterloo.

Nightingale, Florence, 1820–1910, English nurse in Crimean War, founder of modern nursing.

Nimeiry, Jaafar Muhammad al, 1929–   , Sudanese president (1971–   ).

Nimitz, Chester W., 1885–1966, American admiral who headed Pacific naval forces throughout WW II.

Nkrumah, Kwame, 1909–1972, former dictatorial prime minister of Ghana, deposed in 1966.

Nobel, Alfred B., 1833–96, Swedish inventor of dynamite who established annual philanthropic prizes.

Nobile, Umberto, 1885–1978, Italian aeronautical engineer, arctic explorer, and pilot.

Norris, George W., 1861–1944, U.S. Senator (Neb.).

Norstad, Lauris, 1907–   , U.S. general, supreme commander (1956–63) of Allied Powers in Europe.

Nostradamus (Michel de Nostredame), 1503-66, French astrologer and physician.

Novotny, Antonin, 1904-1975, Czechoslovak leader eight months before 1968 Soviet invasion.

Nu, U, 1907–   , Burmese Socialist premier overthrown in 1962 coup.

Nyerere, Julius K., 1922–   , African statesman in Tanganyika, elected (1962) first president of Tanzania.

Oates, Titus, 1649–1705, English fabricator of Popish Plot (1678).

Obregón, Alvaro, 1880–1928, assassinated Mexican revolutionary general and president (1920–24).

Ochs, Adolph S., 1858–1935, American publisher of *The New York Times* and a director (1900–35) of the Associated Press.

O'Connell, Daniel (the Liberator), 1775–1847, Irish political leader whose nationalism affected Ireland's history.

O'Connor, Thomas P. (Tay Pay), 1848–1929, Irish journalist and nationalist who aided cause of Irish Home Rule.

O'Higgins, Bernardo, 1778-1842, Chilean revolutionary and dictator (1817–23) who died in exile in Peru.

Ohira, Masayoshi, 1910–80, Japanese premier (1978–80).

Ojukwu, C. Odumegwu, 1933–   , leader of Biafra's unsuccessful war of secession in the late 1960s.

Oppenheimer, J. Robert, 1904–67, American physicist who led research effort culminating in atom bomb.

Orlando, Vittorio Emanuele, 1860–1952, Italian jurist and premier (1917–19), one of the "Big Four" at WW I Paris Peace Conference.

Osman I, 1259–1326, founder of Ottoman dynasty who inaugurated a policy of religious toleration.

Oswald, Lee Harvey, 1939–63, President John F. Kennedy's assassin; murdered in Dallas jail by Jack Ruby.

Owen, Robert, 1771–1858, British social reformer, socialist, and cooperative-movement pioneer.

Paderewski, Ignace J., 1860–1941, Polish statesman, composer, and popular classical pianist.

Paley, William S., 1901– , American radio and television executive.

Palmer Nathaniel B., 1799–1877, American sea captain, ship designer and Antarctic explorer.

Pandit, Madame (Vijaya L.), 1900– , Indian diplomat and president of UN General Assembly (1953–54).

Pankhurst, Emmeline (née Goulden), 1858–1928, revered English woman suffragist.

Papadopoulos, George, 1919– , Greek premier, seized power in April 1967 and was overthrown in Nov. 1973.

Papandreou, George, 1888–1968, Greek premier, opponent of King Constantine and military junta.

Papen, Franz von, 1879–1969, German chancellor, diplomat under Hitler, acquitted by Nuremberg tribunal.

Park Chung Hee, 1917–79, South Korean president (1963–79).

Park, Mungo, 1771–1806, Scottish explorer of Niger River and western Africa.

Parnell, Charles S., 1846–91, magnetic Irish nationalist leader, "uncrowned king of Ireland."

La Pasionaria (Dolores Ibarruri), 1895– , Spanish revolutionist and a founder of Spain's Communist party.

Patiño, Simón I., 1868–1947, Bolivian tin king, reputed to have been one of world's wealthiest men.

Patterson, Joseph M., 1879–1946, American publisher of first successful U.S. tabloid, *Daily News.*

Patton, George S., Jr., 1885–1945, brilliant but controversial American WW II general ("Old Blood and Guts").

Paulus, Friedrich, 1890-1957, German field marshal who surrendered (1943) to Russians at Stalingrad.

Peabody, George, 1852-1938, American banker and philanthropist who fought for Negro education.

Pearson, Lester B., 1897–1972, Liberal prime minister of Canada (1963–68).

Peary, Robert E., 1856–1920, American rear admiral and first man to reach the North Pole (April 6, 1909).

Peel, Sir Robert, 1788–1850, British reformist statesman, organizer of London police force.

Pérez Jiménez, Marcos, 1914– , Venezuelan dictator and army officer.

Pericles, c. 495–429 B.C., democratic Athenian statesman, great patron of the arts.

Perkins, Frances, 1882–1965, U.S. Secretary of Labor during New Deal era, first woman cabinet member.

Perón, Juan D., 1895–1974, Argentine general and dictator (President 1946-55; 1973-74).

Perry, Oliver H., 1785–1819, American naval hero (Battle of Lake Erie) in War of 1812.

Pershing, John J. (Jack), 1860–1948, American WW I general, AEF commander in chief.

Pétain, Henri P., 1856–1951, French marshal, head of Vichy France (1940–42).

Peter I (the Great), 1672–1725, Russian czar (1682–1725), who westernized his country and made it a great power.

Pham Van Dong, 1906– , Vietnamese premier, a founder of the Vietminh.

Philby, Harold St. J. B., 1885–1960, British explorer, author and adviser to King Ibn Saud of Saudi Arabia.

Philip II, 382–336 B.C., father of Alexander the Great.

Pilsudski, Joseph, 1867–1935, Polish general and authoritarian premier (1926–28, 1930–35).

Pizarro, Francisco, c. 1476–1541, rapacious Spanish conquistador, conqueror of Peru.

Podgorny, Nikolai V., 1903– , Chairman of the Presidium of the Supreme Soviet (1965–77).

Poincaré, Raymond, 1860–1934, French president (1913–20) and advocate of harsh punishment for Germany after WW I.

Polo, Marco, c. 1254–c. 1324, Venetian traveler, favorite of Mongol Emperor Kublai Khan, and author of remarkably accurate Asian travelogue.

Pol Pot, 1928– , Communist leader in Cambodia whose regime is believed to be responsible for 2 million deaths in Cambodia after April 1975.

Pompadour, Madame, 1721–64, French mistress of Louis XV and his confidante until her death.

Pompey (the Great), 106–48 B.C., assassinated Roman general and statesman, rival of Caesar.

Pompidou, Georges J. R., 1911–74, French president (1969–1974).

Potemkin, Grigori A., 1739–91, eccentric Russian field marshal, a favorite of Catherine the Great.

Primo de Rivera, José A., 1903–36, Spanish founder of fascist Falange, executed by Loyalists after outbreak of Spanish Civil War.

Primo de Rivera, Miguel, 1870–1930, Spanish general and dictator (1923–30), father of José Primo de Rivera.

Princip, Gavrilo, 1895–1918, Serbian political agitator and hero, assassin (1914) of Archduke Francis Ferdinand.

Przhevalsky, Nikolai M., 1839–88, Russian geographer and explorer in central Asia and the Russian Far East.

Pugachev, Emelyan I., d. 1775, beheaded Russian leader who posed as Peter III in peasant rebellion (1773–75).

Pulaski, Casimir, c. 1748–79, Polish military commander in American Revolution, mortally wounded at Savannah.

Pulitzer, Joseph, 1847–1911, Hungarian-born publisher who established annual prizes for American letters.

Pu Yi, Henry, 1906–67, last emperor (1908–12) of China, later emperor of Japanese puppet state of Manchukuo.

el-Qaddafi, Muammar, 1938– , Libyan head of state since 1969.

Quezon, Manuel L., 1878–1944, first president of Philippines (1935–44), led it to independence.

Quisling, Vidkun, 1887–1945, executed Norwegian Fascist leader who helped Germany conquer his country.

Radek, Karl, 1885–1939?, Russian Communist leader and journalist, purged by Stalin.

Raeder, Erich, 1876–1960, German WW II admiral who disagreed with Hitler on strategy.

Raffles, Sir Thomas S. B., 1781–1826, British East Indian administrator, founder of Singapore.

Raglan, Lord (Fitzroy J. H. Somerset), 1788–1855, British general in Napoleonic and Crimean wars.

Rahman, Tunku Abdul, Prince, 1903-1973, first prime minister of Malaya (1957-1970).

Randolph, Edmund, 1753–1813, first U.S. Attorney General (1789–94), figure at Constitutional Convention (1787).

Rasmussen, Knud J. V., 1879–1933, Danish explorer of Greenland and the Arctic.

Rasputin, Grigori Y., 1872–1916, Russian libertine monk, a notorious influence on Nicholas II's court.

Rathenau, Walter, 1867–1922, assassinated German industrialist, idealistic social theorist, and statesman.

Rayburn, Sam (Samuel T.), 1882–1961, U.S. Congressman (Tex.), long-time Democratic House speaker.

Récamier, Madame (Juliette), 1777–1849, French beauty who presided over a salon of notables.

Reid, Ogden M., 1882–1947, American newspaper publisher.

Revere, Paul, 1735–1818, American Revolutionary patriot immortalized by Longfellow's poem.

Reza Shah Pahlavi, 1877-1944, shah of Iran (1925-41) who gained independence for his country.

Rhee, Syngman, 1875–1965, authoritarian president (1948–60) of Republic of (South) Korea.

Rhodes, Cecil J., 1853–1902, British statesman and business magnate in South Africa who set up Rhodes scholarship; Rhodesia (now Zimbabwe) was named for him.

Ribbentrop, Joachim von, 1893–1946, Anglophobic Nazi foreign minister (1938–45).

Ricci, Matteo, 1552–1610, Italian missionary and geographer in China, a favorite at the Chinese court.

Richelieu, Cardinal (Armand J.), duc de, 1585–1642, French prelate and statesman, founder of French Academy.

Riis, Jacob A., 1849–1914, Danish-American social reformer and journalist.

Rizal, José, 1861–96, Filipino patriot, author, poet, physician; his martyrdom inspired anti-Spanish revolt.

Robert I (Robert the Bruce), 1274–1329, king of Scotland who freed his country from England's grip.

Robert Guiscard, c. 1015–85, Norman conqueror of southern Italy.

Robespierre, Maximilien M. I., 1758–94, guillotined French revolutionary associated with the Reign of Terror.

Rob Roy (Robert MacGregor), 1671–1734, Scottish outlaw who figures in Scott's novel *Rob Roy.*

Rochambeau, Count (Jean B.), 1725–1807, French marshal in American Revolution.

Rockefeller, John D., 1839–1937, American oil tycoon and philanthropist, a founder of University of Chicago.

Rockefeller, Nelson A., 1908–79, governor of New York (1959–73), Vice-President of U.S. (1974–1977).

Rodino, Peter W., 1909– , chairman of the House Judiciary Committee which considered the impeachment of President Nixon in 1974.

Rokossovsky, Konstantin, 1896–1968, Soviet marshal, symbol of Russian influence in Poland (1949–56).

Rommel, Erwin, 1891–1944, German field marshal in Africa ("the Desert Fox") and France (1940–44).

Romulo, Carlos P., 1900– , Filipino statesman, president of UN General Assembly (1949).

Ronne Finn, 1899–1980, Norwegian-born American explorer and geographer.

Root, Elihu, 1845–1937, U.S. Secretary of State (1905–09), an architect of League of Nations; Nobel Peace Prize winner (1912).

Rosecrans, William S., 1818–98, American Union general.

Ross, James C., 1800–62, British rear admiral and polar explorer.

Rothschild, Guy, Baron de, 1909–   , descendant of the prominent French banking family and head of the Banque Rothschild.

Rothschild, Meyer A., 1743–1812, German founder (in Frankfurt) of international banking house of Rothschild.

Rundstedt, Karl R. G. von, 1875–1953, German WW II field marshal and supreme commander in West (1942–45).

Rusk, (D.) Dean, 1909–   , U.S. Secretary of State under Presidents Kennedy and Johnson.

Sadat, Anwar, 1918–   , Egyptian president since 1970.

Sage, Russell, 1816–1906, American tycoon whose widow established (1907) Russell Sage Foundation.

Saladin, c. 1137–93, Moslem warrior and sultan of Egypt, major opponent of Crusaders.

Salazar, Antonio de Oliveira, 1889–1970, long-time Portuguese dictator (beginning in 1932).

Salomon, Haym, 1740–85, American Revolutionary patriot and financier.

Sandracottus (Greek for Chandragupta), fl. c. 321–c. 298 B.C., Indian emperor, founder of the Maurya dynasty.

Sanger, Margaret, 1879–1966, American founder of the birth-control movement.

San Martín, José de, 1778–1850, South American revolutionary, protector of Peru (1821–22).

Santa Anna, Antonio L. de, 1794–1876, Mexican general at Alamo and in Mexican War, several times president.

Santander, Francisco de Paula, 1792–1840, Colombian revolutionary and political leader.

Sarnoff, David, 1891–1971; Russian-born American pioneer in radio and television.

Savonarola, Girolamo, 1452–98, executed Florentine religious reformer.

Saxe, Comte de (Maurice), 1696–1750, French marshal, one of the greatest generals of his era.

Scanderbeg (George Castriota), c. 1404–68, Albanian national hero who led his people against Turks.

Schacht, Hjalmar H. G., 1877–1970, German president of Reichsbank (1923–30, 1933–39), acquitted by Nuremberg tribunal.

Schlieffen, Alfred, Graf von, 1833–1913, German field marshal whose battle strategy was reflected in WWI.

Schliemann, Heinrich, 1822–90, German archaeologist, discovered ruins of Troy.

Schmidt, Helmut, 1918–   , West German chancellor since 1974.

Schuman, Robert, 1886–1963, French premier (1947–48) who worked to promote a European community.

Schurz, Carl, 1829–1906, German-born U.S. Secretary of the Interior (1877–81), newspaper editor, and author.

Schuschnigg, Kurt von, 1897–1977, Austrian chancellor (1934–38) imprisoned by Nazis until 1945.

Scipio Africanus Major, c. 234–183 B.C., Roman general, victor over Hannibal in Punic Wars.

Scott, Dred, c. 1795–1858, American slave and central figure in law case argued (1856–57) before U.S. Supreme Court.

Scott, Robert F., 1868–1912, British naval officer and antarctic explorer.

Scott, Winfield, 1786–1866, American army commander (1841–61), and Mexican War hero.

Scripps, Edward W., 1854–1926, American newspaper publisher.

Senghor, Léopold S., 1906–   , African statesman and poet, first president of independent Senegal.

Sennacherib, d. 681 B.C., king of Assyria (705–681 B.C.) and conqueror who was murdered by his sons.

Seward, William H., 1801–72, U.S. Secretary of State, purchaser (1867) of Alaska ("Seward's folly").

Sforza, Ludovico, c. 1451–1508, duke of Milan (1494–99), Renaissance prince, patron of Leonardo da Vinci.

Shackleton, Sir Ernest H., 1874–1922, Irish-born British explorer whose antarctic expedition (1907–09) crossed within 100 miles of the South Pole.

Shaftesbury, Earl of (Anthony A. Cooper), 1801–85, leading English social reformer who advocated government action to reduce misery caused by Industrial Revolution.

Sharett, Moshe, 1894–1965, Israeli prime minister (1953–55), Ben-Gurion's closest associate in promoting an independent Jewish state.

Shastri, Shri L. B., 1904–66, prime minister of India (1964–66), disciple of Gandhi.

Shays, Daniel, c. 1747–1825, American Revolutionary soldier, leader of Shays's Rebellion (1786–87) of financially depressed small farmers in Massachusetts.

Sheridan, Philip H., 1831–88, American Union general, observer with Prussian army in Franco-Prussian War.

Sherman, William Tecumseh, 1820–91, American Union general who practiced war of attrition in the South.

Smith, Ian Douglas, 1919–   , Rhodesian prime minister (1964–79).

Smith, John, c. 1580–1631, English adventurer and colonial leader; Pocahontas probably saved his life.

Smith, Walter Bedell, 1895–1961, U.S. WW II general, ambassador to USSR (1946–49), CIA head (1950–53).

Smuts, Jan C., 1870–1950, South African prime minister twice, WW II field marshal, and a UN organizer.

Snorri Sturluson, 1178–1241, Icelandic chieftain and historian, leading light in medieval Norse literature.

Somoza, Anastasio, 1896–1956, assassinated dictator of Nicaragua (1937–47, 1950–56).

Soong, T. V., 1894–1971, Harvard-educated Chinese statesman,

Sorge, Richard, 1895–1944, executed German spy for USSR in Japan.

Souphanouvong, Prince, 1902–   , Laotian politician, leader of leftist Pathet Lao forces. President since 1975.

Souvanna Phouma, Prince, 1901–   , Laotian neutralist prime minister (1962–75).

Spaak, Paul Henri, 1899–1972, Belgian statesman and Socialist leader, first president of UN general assembly (1946), and secretary-general of NATO (1957–61).

Spartacus, d. 71 B.C., Thracian gladiator and leader of Italian slave revolt, killed in battle.

Speke, John H., 1827–64, English explorer in Africa and discoverer (1858) of Lake Tanganyika.

Springer, Axel C., 1912–   , powerful German publisher.

De Staël, Germaine, 1766–1817, French-Swiss writer and intellectual leader.

Stalin, Joseph V. (b. J. V. Dzhugashvili), 1879–1953, Russian Communist dictator.

Stambuliski, Alexander, 1879–1923, murdered Bulgarian premier (1919–23) and agrarian reformer.

Stanley, Sir Henry M., 1841–1904, Anglo-American adventurer, journalist, and empire builder, who was commissioned (1871) by the *New York Herald* to find David Livingstone in Africa.

Stanton, Edwin M., 1814–69, U.S. Secretary of War under Presidents Lincoln and Andrew Johnson.

Stavisky, Serge A., 1886–1934, French swindler, chief figure in scandal that rocked France (1934).

Stefansson, Vilhjalmur, 1879–1962, Canadian-born Icelandic ethnologist and arctic explorer.

Stepinac, Cardinal (Aloysius), 1898–1960, Yugoslav Roman Catholic prelate convicted (1946) by Tito government of Nazi collaboration but released (1951).

Steuben, Baron von (Friedrich W.), 1730–94, Prussian general in American Revolution.

Stevens, Thaddeus, 1792–1868, U.S. Congressman (Pa., 1849–53, 1859–68) active during Civil War and Reconstruction, devoted to Negro betterment.

Stevenson, Adlai E., 1900–65, eloquent American lawyer, Presidential candidate (1952, 1956), and U.S. ambassador to UN (1961–65).

Stimson, Henry L., 1867–1950, U.S. Secretary of War (1911–13, 1940–45) and Secretary of State (1929–33).

Stolypin, Piotr A., 1862–1911, Russian premier and minister of interior (1906–11).

Stowe, Harriet Beecher, 1811–96, American humanitarian whose novel *Uncle Tom's Cabin* was a factor in bringing about the Civil War.

Strabo, b. c. 63 B.C., Greek geographer, historian, and traveler.

Stresemann, Gustav, 1878–1929, German foreign minister dedicated to regaining world friendship for post-WW I Germany, and sharer of 1926 Nobel Peace Prize.

Stroessner, Alfredo, 1913–   , repressive Paraguayan general and president.

Stuart, Charles Edward, 1720–88, claimant (Bonnie Prince Charlie) to English throne.

Stuyvesant, Peter, c. 1610–72, autocratic Dutch director general of New Netherland (beginning 1647).

Suárez González, Adolfo, 1932–   , Spanish premier (1976–).

Sucre, Antonio J. de, 1795–1830, South American revolutionary and military commander, associate of Bolívar.

Suharto, 1921–   , Indonesian general and chief executive who overthrew (1965) Sukarno.

Sukarno, 1902–70, independence leader and dictatorial first president of republic of Indonesia (1945–66).

Sukhe-Bator, 1893–1923, Mongolian political leader who helped set up Mongolian People's Revolutionary party.

Suleiman I (the Magnificent), 1494–1566, Ottoman sultan under whom Ottoman Empire reached its height.

Sulla, Lucius C., 138–78 B.C., notorious Roman general and dictator.

Sully, Maximilien de B., duc de, 1560–1641, French statesman and closest adviser to Henry IV of France.

Sun Yat-sen, 1866–1925, Chinese revolutionary founder of the Chinese republic and of the Kuomintang.

Suslov, Mikhail A., 1902–   , Soviet ideologist.

Suvarov, Aleksandr V., 1729–1800, revered Russian marshal in French Revolutionary Wars (1798–99).

Svoboda, Ludvík, 1895–1979, Communist president of Czechoslovakia during 1968 Soviet invasion.

Taft, Robert A., 1889–1953, conservative U.S. Senator who helped write Taft-Hartley Labor Act.

Talleyrand, Charles M. de, 1754–1838, French statesman and diplomat.

Tamerlane, c. 1336–1405, cruel Mongol conqueror of Asia, subject of a play by Christopher Marlowe.

Tanaka, Kakuei, 1918– , self-made businessman and premier of Japan (1972-74).

Tasman, Abel Janszoon, c. 1603–59, Dutch explorer who discovered (1642) Tasmania.

Teng Hsiao-ping see **Deng Xiaoping.**

Tetzel, Johann, c. 1465-1519, German Roman Catholic preacher who was attacked by Martin Luther.

Thatcher, Margaret, 1925– , British Conservative prime minister (1979–).

Themistocles, c. 525-c. 460 B.C., Athenian statesman and naval commander.

Theodora, d. 548, Byzantine empress, joint ruler with her husband, Justinian I.

Thiers, Adolphe, 1797–1877, French statesman, journalist, and historian of the Revolution and Bonaparte.

Thieu, Nguyen Van, 1923– , South Vietnamese president (1967–75), instrumental in 1963 overthrow of Diem.

Thomas, Norman M., 1884–1968, American Socialist leader, lecturer, and writer; frequent Socialist Party Presidential candidate after 1928.

Thomas à Becket, Saint, c. 1118–70, martyred English archbishop (Canterbury).

Thomson, Roy H., (1st Baron Thomson of Fleet), 1894–1976, Canadian-born British publisher.

Thorez, Maurice, 1900–64, French Communist leader, vice premier (1946–47).

Thurmond, (J.) Strom, 1902– , conservative U.S. Senator (S.C.), States' Rights Presidential candidate (1948).

Tilden, Samuel J., 1814–86, Democratic Presidential candidate (1876 against Rutherford B. Hayes).

Tirpitz, Alfred von, 1849–1930, German WW I admiral, advocate of unrestricted submarine warfare.

Tito, Josip B. (b. Josip Broz), 1892–1980, unorthodox Yugoslav Communist leader (1945–80).

Togliatti, Palmiro, 1893–1964, Italian Communist leader and party founder in his country.

Togo, Heihachiro, Count, 1847–1934, Japanese admiral and naval hero of Russo-Japanese War.

Tojo, Hideki, 1884–1948, Japanese general and prime minister (1941–44), executed by Allies as a war criminal.

Torquemada, Tomás de, 1420–98, severe Spanish Dominican who headed Spanish Inquisition.

Touré, Sékou, 1922– , African left-wing political leader, first president of Republic of Guinea.

Toussaint L'Ouverture, François D., c. 1744–1803, Haitian patriot and martyr who thwarted French colonial aims.

Trotsky, Leon, 1879–1940, exiled Soviet revolutionary and a principal founder of USSR.

Trudeau, Pierre E., 1919– , French-Canadian Liberal prime minister (1968–79, 1980–) and lawyer.

Trujillo Molina, Rafael L., 1891–1961, murdered president (1930–38, 1942–60) of Dominican Republic.

Trung Trac, fl. 39-43 A.D., Vietnamese national heroine who led a revolt against China.

Tshombe, Moise K., 1919–69, Congolese political leader of Katanga, which he proclaimed (1960) independent.

Tubman, Harriet, c. 1820–1913, slave-born American abolitionist and Underground Railroad "conductor."

Tubman, William V. S., 1895–1971, long-time Liberian president.

Tukhachevsky, Mikhail N., 1893–1937, Soviet marshal who helped to modernize and mechanize Red Army.

Tupac Amaru, c. 1742–81, Indian national hero of Peru, executed leader of antigovernment rebellion (1780).

Turner, Nat, 1800–31, executed American leader of slave rebellion (1831, Southampton Co., Va.).

Tutankhamen, fl. c. 1350 B.C., Egyptian pharaoh whose tomb revealed new knowledge of XVIII dynasty life.

Tweed, Boss (William M.), 1823–78, American politician and Tammany leader, who defrauded New York City.

Tyler, Wat, d. 1381, English leader of great peasant rebellion (1381) over labor conditions.

Tz'u Hsi, 1834–1908, dowager empress of China who encouraged Boxer Rebellion (1898–1900).

Ulbricht, Walter, 1893–1973, Communist who became (1960) East German head of state.

Vance, Cyrus R., 1917– , American lawyer, government official, and Secretary of State (1977–80).

Vanderbilt, Commodore (Cornelius), 1794–1877, American railroad magnate, founder of Vanderbilt University.

Vargas, Getúlio D., 1883–1954, Brazilian statesman and president (1930–45, 1951–54).

Venizelos, Eleutherios, 1864–1936, Cretan-born Greek statesman and reformer.

Verwoerd, Hendrik F., 1901–66, assassinated South African prime minister (1958–66), proponent of apartheid.

Victoria, 1819–1901, longest reigning English monarch in history (64 years), who ruled during the height of the British Empire's prestige.

Videla, Jorge Rafael, 1925– , Argentine general and president (1976–).

Villa, Pancho (b. Doroteo Arango), c. 1877–1923, assassinated Mexican bandit and revolutionary.

Visconti, Gian C., c. 1351–1402, Italian duke of Milan who reformed and centralized the government.

Vishinsky, Andrei Y., 1883–1954, Soviet jurist and diplomat, foreign minister (1949-53) of USSR.

Volstead, Andrew J., 1860–1947, American legislator, author (1919) of Volstead (alcohol prohibition) Act.

Voroshilov, Kliment Y., 1881-1969, Soviet general and statesman, close associate of Stalin.

Vorster, Balthazar J., 1915– , South African prime minister (1966–78) and lawyer.

Wainwright, Jonathan M., 1883–1953, American general who in World War II defended Bataan and Corregidor.

Waldheim, Kurt, 1918– , Austrian career diplomat and Secretary General of the United Nations (1972–).

Wallace, George C., 1919– , American conservative politician, third party Presidential candidate (1968).

Washington, Booker T., 1856-1915, Black American educator, organizer (1881) of Tuskegee Institute; author.

Wavell, Archibald P. (Earl), 1883–1950, British field marshal and viceroy of India (1943–47).

Webb, Beatrice (née Potter), 1858–1943, English Socialist economist; she and her husband, **Sidney J. Webb** (1859–1947), were leading figures in Fabian Society and building British Labour party.

Webster, Daniel, 1782–1852, American statesman, a leading political figure, noted orator, and Whig luminary.

Weizmann, Chaim, 1874–1952, Russian-born scientist, Zionist leader, and first president of Israel (1948–52).

Welles, Sumner, 1892–1961, American diplomat and statesman, specialist in Latin American affairs.

Westmoreland, William C., 1914– , American general in Vietnam.

White, William A., 1868–1944, American author and editor (1895–1944) of Emporia (Kans.) *Gazette.*

Wilkes, Charles, 1798–1877, American naval officer and discoverer of area in Antarctic named Wilkes Land.

William I (the Conqueror), 1027?–1087, Norman duke and English king (1066–87), who conquered England in 1066.

Willkie, Wendell L., 1892–1944, American industrialist and anti-isolationist political leader, Republican Presidential candidate (1940).

Wilson, J. Harold, 1916– , Labour prime minister (1964-1970, 1974–76), of Great Britain.

Wingate, Orde C., 1903–44, British WW II general, who demonstrated effectiveness of guerrilla warfare.

Wolfe, James, 1727–59, British victor against French in battle of Quebec (Plains of Abraham).

Wollstonecraft, Mary, 1759–97, English feminist whose writings inspired the American women's rights movement.

Wolsey, Cardinal (Thomas), c. 1473–1530, English prelate and favorite of Henry VIII.

Wrangel, Baron Ferdinand von, 1796–1870, Russian naval officer, arctic explorer, governor of Russian Alaska.

Wyszynski, Cardinal (Stefan), 1901– , Polish prelate often in conflict with Gomulka government.

Xenophon, c. 430 B.C.–c. 355 B.C., Greek historian who led retreat of "Ten Thousand" Greek mercenaries from Persia (401 B.C.).

Yamamoto, Isoroku, 1884–1943, Japanese admiral who masterminded (1941) attack on Pearl Harbor.

Yamani, Ahmed Zaki, 1930– , Saudi Arabian oil minister; leading figure in Arab and OPEC oil activities.

Yamashita, Tomoyuki, 1888–1946, Japanese general defeated (1945) by General MacArthur's invasion of Philippines, hanged in Manila as a war criminal.

Yoshida, Shigeru, 1878–1967, Japanese Liberal prime minister (1946–54).

Yüan Shih-kai, 1859–1916, dictatorial president of China (1912-16) who declared (1916) himself emperor.

Zaharoff, Sir Basil (b. Basileios Zacharias), 1850–1936, Turkish-born British financier and munitions manufacturer.

Zapata, Emiliano, c. 1879–1919, Mexican revolutionary.

Zenger, John Peter, 1697–1746, German-American journalist whose libel trial and acquittal furthered freedom of the press in America.

Zhdanov, Andrei A., 1896–1948, murdered Soviet Communist leader who fostered extreme nationalism.

Zhou Enlai, 1898–1976, Chinese Communist premier and foreign minister (1949–76).

Zhukov, Georgi K., 1896-1974, Soviet marshal who defeated Germans at Stalingrad and occupied Berlin.

Zinoviev, Grigori E., 1883–1936, Russian Communist leader executed by Stalin after the first spectacular purge trial.

SCIENTISTS AND MATHEMATICIANS

Ampère, André Marie, 1775–1836, French physicist, discovered, 1820, the left-hand and right-hand rules of the magnetic field about a current-carrying wire.

*****Archimedes,** c. 287–212 B.C., Greek mathematician.

Aston, Francis William, 1877–1945, English chemist and physicist, developed, 1919, the mass spectrograph.

Avogadro, Amedeo, 1776–1856, Italian physicist, put forth a hypothesis in which equal volumes of all gasses at the same temperature and pressure contain the same number of molecules.

Becquerel, Antoine Henri, 1852–1908, French physicist.

Bernoulli, Daniel, 1700–82, Dutch-Swiss mathematician, 1738, advanced the kinetic theory of gases and fluids.

Berzelius, Jons Jakob, 1779–1848, Swedish chemist, introduced chemical symbols and chemical radical theory.

Bethe, Hans Albrecht, 1906–   , German-born American physicist, proposed, 1938, the nuclear mechanism by which stars obtain their energy.

*****Bohr, Niels,** 1885–1962, Danish physicist.

Brahe, Tycho, 1546–1601, Danish astronomer.

Carnap, Rudolf, 1891–1970, German-born American philosopher of science, founded logical positivism.

Cavendish, Henry, 1731–1810, English chemist and physicist, discovered, 1766, hydrogen; devised, 1798, a gravitational method for weighing the Earth.

Charles, Jacques Alexandre César, 1746–1823, French physicist, discovered, 1787, the law governing the expansion and contraction of gases with changes in temperature.

Cockcroft, John Douglas, 1897–1967, English nuclear physicist, with E. T. S. Walton, constructed (c. 1932), the first atomic particle accelerator.

Compton, Arthur Holly, 1892–1962, American physicist, discovered, 1923, that X-rays scattered by diffraction in crystals have their wavelengths lengthened, the Compton effect; discovered, c. 1930, that cosmic rays consist of particles.

*****Copernicus (Mikolaj Kopernik),** 1473–1543, Polish astronomer.

Coulomb, Charles Augustin de, 1736–1806, French engineer and physicist, established the law describing the attraction and repulsion of electric charges.

*****Crick, Francis H. C.,** 1916–   , English biophysicist.

Ctesibius, 2d century B.C., Greek engineer, invented the water clock, force pump, and air as motive force.

Curie, Marie, 1867–1934, and **Pierre,** 1859–1906, French chemists, isolated, 1898, the first radioactive element —radium.

*****Darwin, Charles,** 1809–1882, English naturalist.

Davy, Humphry, 1778–1829, English chemist, established the electrical nature of chemical affinity.

*****Descartes, René,** 1596–1650, French mathematician.

Dewar, James, 1842–1923, British chemist and physicist, liquified, 1898, and solidified, 1899, hydrogen.

Dirac, Paul Adrien Maurice, 1902–   , English physicist, in 1920s, unified relativity and quantum theories, and unified wave mechanics and special relativity; proposed, 1930–31, antiparticles.

Dubos, René, 1901–   , French microbiologist and environmentallist in America.

Edison, Thomas Alva, 1847–1931, prolific American inventor. Discovered "Edison effect."

*****Einstein, Albert,** 1879–1955, American physicist (born Germany).

Euler, Leonhard, 1707–83, Swiss mathematician and physicist, produced work in astronomy, mechanics, hydrodynamics, and optics; founded higher mathematics.

Fahrenheit, Gabriel Daniel, 1686–1736, German physicist, developed temperature scale that bears his name.

*****Faraday, Michael,** 1791–1867, English chemist, physicist.

Fermat, Pierre de, 1601–65, French mathematician, discovered analytic geometry; founded modern theory of numbers and the calculus of probabilities.

Fermi, Enrico, 1901–54, Italian-born American physicist.

Fischer, Emil, 1852–1919, German chemist, especially noted for his work on structure of sugars.

Fourier, Jean Baptiste Joseph, 1768–1830, French mathematician, discovered, c. 1822, the theorem governing periodic oscillation.

Franklin, Benjamin, 1706–90, American statesman and scientist, discovered, 1752, the electrical nature ot lightning; proposed the one-fluid theory of electricity.

Gabor, Dennis, 1900–79, Hungarian-born British physicist known for the development of holography.

*****Galileo Galilei,** 1564–1642, Italian scientist.

*****Gauss, Karl F.,** 1777–1855, German mathematician.

Gay-Lussac, Joseph Louis, 1778–1850, French chemist, discovered, 1809, the law of combining volumes.

Gibbs, Josiah Willard, 1839–1903, American physicist, founded, 1876–78, chemical thermodynamics.

Grzimek, Bernhard, 1909–   , Polish zoologist and wildlife conservationist.

Guericke, Otto von, 1602–86, German physicist and engineer, invented the first vacuum pump and used it, (c. 1650) to demonstrate atmospheric pressure.

Haber, Fritz, 1868–1934, German chemist, developed, 1900–1911, a process for "fixing" atmospheric nitrogen in chemical compounds.

Hall, James, 1761–1832, British geologist and chemist, founded, c. 1797, experimental geology, geochemistry.

Halley, Edmund, 1656–1742, English astronomer, calculated orbits of many comets.

*****Heisenberg, Werner Karl,** 1901–1976, German physicist.

Helmont, Jan Baptista Van, 1577–1644, Flemish physician and alchemist, initiated quantitative biochemistry.

Hero of Alexandria, c. 1st century, Greek engineer, invented principle of the steam engine; extended Archimedes' principle of the lever.

*****Hertz, Heinrich,** 1857–94, German physicist.

Herzberg, Gerhard, 1904–   , Canadian physicist known for his work on electronic structure and molecular geometry.

Hilbert, David, 1862–1943, German mathematician, formulated, 1899, the first set of axioms for geometry.

Hubble, Edwin Powell, 1889–1953, American astronomer, discovered, 1929, the universal recession of galaxies.

Humboldt, Friedrich Wilhelm Heinrich Alexander von, 1769–1859, established, c. 1830–1859, geophysics.

Janssen (or Jansen), Zacharias, 1580–c. 1638, Dutch optician, invented, c. 1590, the microscope.

Jensen, Arthur Robert, 1923–   , educational psychologist. His view is that intelligence is primarily inherited.

Kamerlingh Onnes, Heike, 1853–1926, Dutch physicist, established, 1882, cryogenics.

Kapitza, Peter, 1894–   , Soviet physicist, research contributed to Soviet space achievements.

Kelvin, Lord (William Thompson), 1826–1907, British physicist, made advances in thermodynamics and thermometry.

*****Kepler, Johannes,** 1571–1630, German astronomer.

Khorana, Har Gobind, 1922–   , Indian organic chemist, synthesized functioning gene, 1976.

Landau, Lev Davidovich, 1908–68, Russian physicist, developed mathematical theory explaining behavior of superfluid helium at temperatures near absolute zero.

LaPlace, Pierre Simon, 1749–1827, French astronomer and mathematician, put forth, 1796, the nebular hypothesis of the origin of the solar system.

*****Lavoisier, Antoine,** 1743–94, French chemist.

Lawrence, Ernest Orlando, 1901–58, American physicist, constructed, 1930, the first cyclotron.

Leakey, Louis, 1903–72, **Mary,** 1913–   , and **Richard,** 1944–   , Anglo-Kenyan anthropologists, discovered important fossil remains of early hominids.

Lee, Tsung-Dao, 1926–   , Chinese-born American physicist, with Yang refuted the law of parity,

Leeuwenhoek, Anton van, 1632–1723, Dutch microscopist and the father of microbiology.

*****Leibniz, Gottfried,** 1646–1716, German mathematician, philosopher.

Levene, Phoebus Aaron Theodore, 1869–1940, Russian-born American chemist, discovered, 1909, the nucleic acids RNA and, 20 years later, DNA.

Lévi-Strauss, Claude, 1908–   , French anthropologist, leader of the structuralist school of ethnology.

Liebig, Justus von, 1803–73, German chemist, established, c. 1831, quantitative organic chemical analysis.

Lowell, Percival, 1855–1916, American astronomer, 1930, discovered Pluto.

Mach, Ernst, 1838–1916, Austrian physicist, psychologist, and philosopher of science, influential in the development of logical positivism.

Marshak, Robert E., 1916–   , American nuclear physicist who helped to develop the first atomic bomb.

*****Maxwell, James C.,** 1831–79, English physicist.

*****Mendel, Gregor Johann,** 1822–84, Austrian founder of genetics.

Mead, Margaret, 1901–78, American anthropologist noted for her studies in primitive and contemporary cultures.

---

* See listing in "Landmarks of Science," pp. 338-339.

*Mendeleyev, Dmitri Ivanovich, 1834–1907, Russian chemist.

Michelson, Albert Abraham, 1852–1931, German-born American physicist, developed the interferometer, which measured, 1881 and 1887, the velocity of light and proved the nonexistence of ether in space.

Mohorovicic, Andrija, 1857–1936, Croatian geophysicist, discovered, 1909, the ("Moho") discontinuity that marks the bottom of the Earth's crust.

Mössbauer, Rudolf Ludwig, 1929– , German-born American physicist, discovered, 1958, the recoilless emission and absorption of gamma rays by atoms in crystals.

*Napier, John, 1550–1617, Scottish mathematician.

*Newton, Isaac, 1642–1727, English mathematician.

Ochoa, Severo, 1905– , Spanish-born American biochemist, synthesized, 1955, ribonucleic acid (RNA).

Ostwald, Wilhelm, 1853–1932, German chemist, was chief founder, beginning in 1887, of physical chemistry.

Pascal, Blaise, 1623–62, French scientist, mathematician, and religious philosopher, founded the modern theory of probability and the law of hydrostatic pressure (Pascal's law).

Pauling, Linus Carl, 1901– , American chemist, developed, 1939, the theory of the chemical bond.

*Planck, Max, 1858–1947, German physicist.

Priestley, Joseph, 1733–1804, English theologian and scientist, discovered, 1774, oxygen.

Raman, Chandrasekhara Vankata, 1888–1970, Indian physicist, discovered, 1928, the change in wavelength and frequency of monochromatic light passing through a transparent medium.

Riemann, Georg F. B., 1826–66, German mathematician, developed non-Euclidian system of geometry representing elliptic space.

*Rutherford, Lord (Ernest), 1871–1937, British physicist, born in New Zealand.

*Schroedinger, Erwin, 1887–1961, Austrian physicist.

Seaborg, Glenn T., 1912– , American chemist, led, 1941–c. 1951, the group that discovered the transuranium elements americium, curium, berkelium, californium, einsteinium, fermium, plutonium, mendelevium and nobelium.

Stanley, Wendell Meredith, 1904–71, American biochemist, crystallized, 1935, the tobacco mosaic virus, thus demonstrating that matter may have both living and nonliving forms.

Steno, Nicolaus (Niels Stensen), 1638–86, Danish anatomist and Catholic prelate, recognized the nature of fossils.

Szilard, Leo, 1898–1964, Hungarian-born American physicist, proved, 1939, with Walter Zinn, the possibility of self-sustaining nuclear fission; worked, 1942, with Enrico Fermi, on development of first nuclear reaction.

Tsvett (or Tswett), Mikhail Semenovich, 1872–1919, Italian-born Russian botanist, discovered, 1906, chromatography.

Urey, Harold Clayton, 1893– , American chemist, discovered, 1931, heavy hydrogen (deuterium).

Volta, Alessandro, 1745–1827, Italian physicist, invented the first electric cell and electric battery.

Von Neumann, John, 1903–57, Hungarian-born American mathematician, was a founder of the mathematical theory of games and contributed to computer theory.

Walton, Ernest Thomas Sinton, 1903– , Irish physicist, constructed, 1929, the first atomic particle accelerator.

*Watson, James Dewey, 1928– , American biochemist.

Wegener, Alfred Lothar, 1880–1930, German meteorologist and geophysicist, postulated theory of continental drift.

Wiener, Norbert, 1894–1964, American mathematician, contributed to development of computers; founded cybernetics.

Wigner, Eugene Paul, 1902– , Hungarian-born American physicist, accomplished pioneering work in nuclear structure.

*Wilkins, Maurice H. F., 1916– , British biophysicist.

Yang, Chen Ning, 1922– , Chinese-born American physicist. See Lee.

Yukawa, Hideki, 1907– , Japanese physicist who predicted the existence of mesons.

PHILOSOPHERS, THEOLOGIANS, AND RELIGIONISTS

Abelard, Peter (1079–1142), French philosopher.

Abravanel, Isaac (1437–1508), Jewish theologian.

Adler, Felix (1851–1933), German-American Ethical Culture movement founder.

Alexander of Hales (d. 1245), English scholastic philosopher.

Ambrose, Saint (c. 340–397), bishop of Milan.

Anaxagoras (c. 500–c. 428 B.C.), Greek philosopher.

Anaximander (c. 611–c. 547 B.C.), Greek philosopher.

Anaximenes (6th cent. B.C.), Greek philosopher.

Anselm, Saint (c. 1033–1109), Italian founder of scholasticism.

Anthony, Saint (c. 251–c. 350), Egyptian father of Christian monasticism.

Antisthenes (c. 444 B.C.–after 371 B.C.), Greek philosopher.

Aristotle (384–322 B.C.), Greek philosopher.

Arius (c. 256–336), Libyan theologian.

Arminius, Jacobus (1560–1609), Dutch Reformed theologian.

Augustine, Saint (354–430), North African Doctor of the Church.

Averroës (1126–98), Spanish-Arabian philosopher.

Avicenna (980–1037), Arabian philosopher.

Ayer, Alfred Jules (1910–), British philosopher.

Baal-Shem-Tov (1700–60), Jewish founder of modern Hasidism.

Bacon, Francis (1561–1626), English philosopher.

Bacon, Roger (c. 1214–c. 1294), English philosopher.

Balthasar, Hans Urs von (1905–), German theologian.

Barth, Karl (1886–1968), Swiss Protestant theologian.

Bentham, Jeremy (1748–1832), English philosopher, founder of utilitarianism.

Berdyaev, Nicholas (1874–1948), Russian philosopher.

Berengar of Tours (c. 1000–c. 1088), French theologian.

Bergson, Henri (1859–1941), French philosopher.

Berkeley, George (1685–1753), Anglo-Irish philosopher.

Bernard of Clairvaux, Saint (c. 1090–1153), French mystic.

Bernard of Cluny (fl. 1150), Anglo-French monk.

Bernardine of Siena, Saint (1380–1444), Italian preacher.

Biddle, John (1615–62), English founder of Unitarianism.

Boehme, Jakob (1575–1624), German religious mystic.

Boethius (c. 475–525), Roman philosopher.

Bonaventure, Saint (1221–74), Italian scholastic theologian.

Bonhoeffer, Dietrich (1906–45), German theologian.

Brunner, Emil (1889–1966), Swiss Protestant theologian.

Bruno, Giordano (1548–1600), Italian philosopher.

Buber, Martin (1878–1965), German-Israeli philosopher.

Büchner, Ludwig (1824–99), German philosopher.

Bultmann, Rudolf (1884–1976), German existentialist theologian.

Cabrini, Mother Francesca (1850–1917), Italian-born American nun and first American saint.

Calvin, John (1509–64), French Protestant theologian.

Carnap, Rudolf (1891–1970), German-American philosopher.

Cassirer, Ernst (1874–1945), German philosopher.

Comte, Auguste (1798–1857), French positivist philosopher.

Cranmer, Thomas (1489–1556), English churchman.

Croce, Benedetto (1866–1952), Italian philosopher.

Democritus (c. 460–c. 370 B.C.), Greek philosopher.

Descartes, René (1596–1650), French philosopher.

Dewey, John (1859–1952), American philosopher.

Diderot, Denis (1713–84), French philosopher.

Diogenes (c. 412–323 B.C.), Greek Cynic philosopher.

Duns Scotus, John (c. 1266–1308), Scottish theologian.

Eckhart, Meister (c. 1260–c. 1328), German theologian.

Edwards, Jonathan (1703–58), American theologian.

Emerson, Ralph Waldo (1803–82), American transcendentalist.

Empedocles (c. 495–c. 435 B.C.), Greek philosopher.

Engels, Friedrich (1820–95), German social philosopher.

Enrique Tarancón, Vicente Cardinal (1907–), Spanish religious reformer.

Epictetus (c. 50–c. 138), Phrygian Stoic philosopher.

Epicurus (341–270 B.C.), Greek philosopher.

Erigena, John Scotus (c. 810–c. 877), Irish philosopher.

Fichte, Johann G. (1762–1814), German philosopher.

Fox, George (1624–91), English founder of Society of Friends.

George, Henry (1839–97), American economic theorist.

Ghazali, al (c. 1058–1111), Islamic philosopher.

Gilson, Etienne (1884–1978), French philosopher.

Gorton, Samuel (c. 1592–1677), Anglo-American religious founder.

Graham, Billy (1918–), American evangelist.

Groote, Gerard (1340–84), Dutch ecclesiastical reformer.

Guardini, Romano (1885–1968), Italian-born German Catholic theologian.

Hegel, Georg W. F. (1770–1831), German philosopher.

Heidegger, Martin (1889–1976), German philosopher.

---

* See listing in "Landmarks of Science"

Heraclitus (c. 535–c. 475 B.C.), Greek philosopher.
Hobbes, Thomas (1588–1679), English philosopher.
Hooker, Richard (c. 1554–1600), English theologian.
Hume, David (1711–76), Scottish philosopher.
Hus, Jan (c. 1369–1415), Czech religious reformer.
Husserl, Edmund (1859–1938), German philosopher, founder of phenomenology.
Huxley, Thomas H. (1825–95), English agnostic philosopher.
Ignatius of Loyola, Saint (1491–1556), Spanish founder of the Jesuits.
James, William (1842–1910), American philosopher.
Jansen, Cornelis (1585–1638), Dutch Roman Catholic theologian.
Jaspers, Karl (1883–1969), German philosopher and psychopathologist.
John of the Cross, Saint (1542–91), Spanish mystic.
Kant, Immanuel (1724–1804), German metaphysical philosopher.
Kierkegaard, Soren (1813–55), Danish philosopher.
Knox, John (c. 1514–72), Scottish founder of Presbyterianism.
Küng, Hans (1928–), Swiss Roman Catholic theologian.
Laing, R. D. (1927–), Scottish existentialist psychoanalyst, writer, and social critic.
Law, William (1686–1761), English churchman and mystic.
Leibniz, Gottfried W., Baron von (1646–1716), German philosopher.
Locke, John (1632–1704), English philosopher.
Lombard, Peter (c. 1100–c. 1160). Italian theologian.
Lonergan, Bernard J. F. (1904–), Canadian theologian and Thomist philosopher.
Lucretius (c. 99–c. 55 B.C.), Roman philosopher-poet.
Luther, Martin (1483–1546), German Protestant leader.
Mahesh Yogi, Maharishi (1911?–), Hindu guru.
Maimonides (1135–1204), Spanish-Jewish philosopher.
Malthus, Thomas R. (1766–1834), English economic and social philosopher.
Marcel, Gabriel (1889–1973), French philosopher.
Marcus Aurelius (121–180), Stoic philosopher.
Marías, Julián (1914–), Spanish philosopher.
Maritain Jacques (1882–1973), French Neo-Thomist philosopher.
Marx, Karl (1818–83), German social philosopher.
Mather, Cotton (1663–1728), American Puritan minister.
Mather, Increase (1639–1723), American Puritan minister.
May, Rollo (1909–), American humanistic psychoanalyst-philosopher.
Melanchthon, Philip (1497–1560), German theologian.
Mencius (c. 371–c. 288 B.C.), Chinese sage.
Mill, John Stuart (1806–73), English philosopher and economist.
Molina, Luis (1535–1600), Spanish Jesuit theologian.
Moore, George E. (1873–1958), English philosopher.
Murray, John (1741–1815), English founder of American Universalist denomination.
Nestorius (d. c. 451), Byzantine theologian.
Newman, John Henry, Cardinal (1801–90), English philosopher.
Nicholas of Cusa (c. 1401–46), German humanist.
Niebuhr, H. Richard (1894–1962), American theologian.
Niebuhr, Reinhold (1892–1971), American theologian.
Nietzsche, Friedrich W. (1844–1900), German philosopher.
Origen (c. 185–c. 254), Egyptian Christian philosopher.
Parmenides (b. c. 514 B.C.), Greek philosopher.
Pascal, Blaise (1623–62), French philosopher and mathematician.
Peirce, Charles S. (1839–1914), American philosopher.

Philo (c. 20 B.C.–A.D. c. 50), Alexandrian Jewish philosopher.
Plato (c. 427–c. 347 B.C.), Greek philosopher.
Plotinus (c. 205–270), Egyptian Neoplatonist philosopher.
Protagoras (c. 480–c. 410 B.C.), Greek Sophist.
Rapp, George (1757–1847), German-American Harmony Society founder.
Rousseau, Jean Jacques (1712–78), French philosopher.
Royce, Josiah (1855–1916), American philosopher.
Russell, Bertrand (1872–1970), British philosopher and mathematician.
Santayana, George (1863–1952), American philosopher.
Savonarola, Girolamo (1452–98), Italian religious reformer.
Schelling, Friedrich W. J. von (1775–1854), German philosopher.
Schopenhauer, Arthur (1788–1860), German philosopher.
Schweitzer, Albert (1875–1965), Alsatian philosopher and theologian.
Seneca (c. 3 B.C.–A.D. 65), Roman philosopher.
Seton, Elizabeth Ann Bayley (1774–1821), 1st U.S.-born canonized saint.
Shaftesbury, Anthony Ashley Cooper, 3d earl of (1671–1713), English philosopher.
Smith, Adam (1723–90), Scottish economist and philosopher.
Socrates (469–399 B.C.), Greek philosopher.
Spencer, Herbert (1820–1903), English philosopher of evolution.
Spinoza, Baruch (1632–77), Dutch philosopher.
Suso, Heinrich (c. 1295–1366), German mystic.
Suzuki, Daisetz Teitaro (1870–1966), Japanese Buddhist scholar.
Swedenborg, Emanuel (1688–1772), Swedish theologian and mystic.
Taylor, Jeremy (1613–67), English theologian.
Teilhard de Chardin, Pierre (1881–1955), French Jesuit scientist-theologian.
Thales (c. 636–c. 546 B.C.), Greek philosopher.
Theresa, Saint (1515–82), Spanish mystic.
Thomas Aquinas, Saint (1225–74), Italian philosopher and Doctor of the Church.
Tillich, Paul (1886–1965), German-born American theologian.
Tyndale, William (c. 1494–1536), English Bible translator.
Ussher, James (1581–1656), Irish prelate and scholar.
Veblen, Thorstein (1857–1929), American economic and social philosopher.
Vico, Giovanni B. (1668–1744), Italian philosopher and historian.
Watts, Isaac (1674–1748), English clergyman and hymn writer.
Wesley, John (1703–91), English founder of Methodism.
Whitehead, Alfred North (1861–1947), English philosopher and mathematician.
William of Occam (d. c. 1349), English philosopher.
Williams, Roger (c. 1603–83), Anglo-American clergyman.
Winebrenner, John (1797–1860), American founder of Churches of God in North America.
Wise, Stephen (1874–1949), American reform rabbi and Zionist leader.
Wittgenstein, Ludwig (1889–1951), Austrian philosopher.
Woodbridge, Frederick J. E. (1867–1940), American philosopher.
Wyclif, John (c. 1328–84), English reformer.
Zeno of Citium (c. 334–c. 262 B.C.), Greek philosopher, founder of Stoicism.
Zoroaster (628–551 B.C.), Persian prophet.
Zwingli, Huldreich (1484–1531), Swiss Protestant reformer.

MEN OF MEDICINE AND PHYSIOLOGY

Abulcasis, or Abu Khasim, fl. 11th century, Arabian physician, author of the *Tasrif* (collection), a detailed account of surgery and medicine of his day.
Addison, Thomas, 1793–1860, English physician, discoverer of the malady of the suprarenal cortex, known as Addison's disease.
Allbutt, Thomas Clifford, 1836–1925, English physician, invented, 1866, the clinical thermometer.
Avicenna, or Ibn Sina, A.D. 980–1037, Arabian physician and philosopher, wrote the *Canon of Medicine,* most famous textbook of medicine until the 17th century.
Baer, Karl Ernst von, 1792–1876, Estonian biologist, founded, 1827–37, embryology.
Banting, Frederick G., 1891–1941, Canadian physician, with Charles Best, discovered, 1921, the use of insulin in diabetic therapy.

Barnard, Christiaan N., 1923– , South African surgeon, performed, 1967, first transplant of a human heart.
Beaumont, William, 1785–1853, American physician, first to describe, 1822, the process of digestion.
Behring, Emil Adolf von, 1854–1917, German bacteriologist noted for work on diphtheria antitoxin.
Berger, Johannes (Hans), 1873–1941, German neurologist, invented, 1929, the electroencephalograph.
Bernard, Claude, 1813–78, French physiologist, considered founder of experimental medicine.
Best, Charles Herbert, 1899–1978, Canadian physiologist, with Frederick Banting discovered, 1921, the use of insulin in diabetic therapy.
Bichat, Marie François Xavier, 1771–1802, French physician, founded, 1800, histology, the study of living tissues.

Blalock, Alfred, 1899–1964, American surgeon, with Helen B. Taussig introduced, 1944, corrective heart surgery enabling survival of "blue babies."

Braun, Heinrich Friedrich Wilhelm, 1862–1934, German surgeon, introduced, 1905, procaine (Novocain) into clinical use.

Bright, Richard, 1789–1858, English physician, first to describe, 1827, the kidney disease known as Bright's disease.

Canano, Giovanni Battista, 1515–79, Italian anatomist, first to describe, c. 1547, venous valves.

Carrel, Alexis, 1873–1944, French-American surgeon, developed methods for transplanting blood vessels; invented, with Charles A. Lindbergh, a mechanical heart.

Cohn, Ferdinand Julius, 1828–98, German botanist, founded, c. 1872, science of bacteriology.

Cooley, Denton A., 1920–　, American surgeon, pioneer in cardiovascular surgery.

De Bakey, Michael Ellis, 1908–　, American surgeon, developed artificial heart.

De Forest, Lee, 1873–1961, American inventor, invented, 1907, the electrical high-frequency surgical knife.

Dick, George F., 1881–1967, and **Gladys H. Dick,** isolated, 1923, the scarlet fever toxin.

Domagk, Gerhard, 1895–1964, German chemist, used, c. 1932, the first sulfa drug (prontosil) in therapy.

Eberth, Karl Joseph, 1835–1926, German pathologist, discovered, 1880, the typhoid bacillus.

Edelman, Gerald M., 1929–　, American biochemist, deciphered, 1969, the structure of gamma globulin.

Ehrlich, Paul, 1854–1915, German bacteriologist and pathologist, developed, 1897, the differential blood count; established, 1892–94, serology and immunology; established, 1909, chemotherapy.

Eijkman, Christiaan, 1858–1930, Dutch bacteriologist, proved, 1896, that beriberi is a deficiency disease, thus leading to discovery of the first vitamin.

Einthoven, Willem, 1860–1927, Dutch physiologist, invented, 1903, the electrocardiograph.

Ermengem, Émile P. M. van, 1851–1932, Belgian bacteriologist, discovered, 1897, the food-poisoning bacillus.

Fabricius, Hieronymus, or Geronimo Fabrizio, 1537–1619, Italian anatomist, discovered, 1603, venous valves.

Fauchard, Pierre, 1678–1761, French dentist, founder of modern dentistry; described pyorrhea.

Finlay, Carlos Juan, 1833–1915, Cuban physician, first to suggest mosquitoes might be carriers of yellow fever.

Fleming, Alexander, 1881–1955, Scottish bacteriologist, discovered, 1928, penicillin.

Fleming, Lady Amalia, 1909–　, British bacteriologist, physician, civil libertarian.

Flourens, Marie J. P., 1794–1867, French physiologist, distinguished the three main parts of the brain.

Freud, Sigmund, 1856–1939, Austrian psychiatrist, founded, c. 1895, psychoanalysis.

Funk, Casimir, 1884–1967, Polish-American biochemist, discovered, 1912, the first vitamin.

Gaffky, Georg T. A., 1850–1918, German bacteriologist, proved, 1884, that *Bacillus typhosus,* discovered by Eberth, is cause of typhoid fever.

Galen, Claudius, c. A.D. 130–c. 200, Greco-Roman physician, systematized medical knowledge of his day; made first scientific dissections.

Goldberger, Joseph, 1874–1929, American public health physician, discovered, 1915, the cure for pellagra.

Golgi, Camillo, 1844–1926, Italian physician, established, 1870–1909, the science of neuroanatomy.

Good, Robert, 1922–　, American pediatrician; pioneer in fields of immunology and cancer research.

Gross, Robert E., 1905–　, performed, 1938, first surgery for congenital heart disease.

Hales, Stephen, 1677–1761, English physiologist and clergyman, first to demonstrate, c. 1705, blood pressure.

Haller, Albrecht von, 1708–77, Swiss physiologist and anatomist, established physiology as a branch of science.

Harvey, William, 1578–1657, English physician, discovered, 1628, the circulation of the blood.

Helmholtz, Hermann Ludwig Ferdinand von, 1821–94, German physicist and physiologist, invented, 1851, the modern type of ophthalmoscope.

Hench, Philip S., 1896–1965, American physician, introduced, 1949, the use of ACTH in the treatment of disease.

Herophilus, fl. 300 B.C., Egyptian-Greek physician and anatomist, distinguished sensory and motor nerves.

Hippocrates of Cos, c. B.C. 460–c. 370, Greek physician, "Father of Medicine," took medicine from the realm of superstition to that of disciplined observation.

Holmes, Oliver Wendell, 1809–94, American physician and author, recognized, 1843, contagious nature of puerperal fever and advocated antiseptic techniques.

Hunter, John, 1728–93, Scottish surgeon, raised surgery from a technical treatment mode to a branch of scientific medicine.

Ivanovski, Dmitri Iosifovich, 1864–1920, Russian botanist, discovered, 1892, filterable viruses, thus establishing virology.

Janssen, Zacharias, fl. late 16th–early 17th cent., Dutch spectacle maker, invented, c. 1590, the microscope.

Jenner, Edward, 1749–1823, English physician, introduced, 1796, the technique of vaccination against disease.

Kitasato, Shibasaburo, 1852–1931, Japanese bacteriologist, discovered, 1894, the bubonic plague causative bacillus.

Klebs, Edwin T. A., 1834–1913, German-American bacteriologist, discovered, 1875, pneumococcus, the bacillus causative of lobar pneumonia; discovered, 1883–84, the diphtheria causative bacillus.

Koch, Robert, 1843–1910, German bacteriologist, set forth criteria for establishing the etiology of a disease; introduced, 1877, staining of bacteria with aniline dyes; established, 1882, the identity of the tuberculosis causative cholera.

Laënnec, René T. H., 1781–1826, French physician, invented, 1816, the stethoscope.

Landsteiner, Karl, 1868–1943, Austrian-American pathologist, established, 1900, the basis for blood grouping; isolated, 1908, the poliomyelitis virus; discovered, 1940, the Rh factor.

Lister, Joseph, 1827–1912, English surgeon, introduced, 1865, antisepsis into surgical procedure.

Löffler, Friedrich A. J., 1852–1915, German pathologist, discovered, 1883–84, the diphtheria causative bacillus.

Long, Crawford Williamson, 1815–78, American surgeon, introduced, 1842, the use of ether in surgery.

Magnus-Levy, Adolf, 1865–1955, German physiologist, developed, 1893, the method for measuring the basal metabolic rate.

Malpighi, Marcello, 1628–94, Italian anatomist, discovered, 1661, that capillaries are vein-artery junctions.

Mesmer, Friedrich (or Franz) Anton, c. 1733–1815, Austrian physician, introduced, c. 1778, the use of hypnotism in medicine.

Metchnikoff, Élie, 1845–1916, Russian biologist, introduced theory of phagocytosis, i.e., the defensive nature of blood cells.

Minot, George Richards, 1885–1950, American physician, discovered, 1926, the liver extract treatment for anemia.

Morgan, Thomas Hunt, 1886–1945, American geneticist, discovered and demonstrated, c. 1907, the role of chromosomes in heredity.

Nitze, Max, 1848–1906, German surgeon and urologist, constructed, 1877, first cystoscope, with the aid of an instrument maker named Leiter.

Paracelsus (Theophrastus Bombastus von Hohenheim), c. 1493–1541, Swiss chemist, alchemist, and physician, established, 1526, chemotherapy.

Paré, Ambroise, 1510 or 1517–90, French surgeon, introduced modern surgery, including the tying-off of arteries to control bleeding.

Pasteur, Louis, 1822–95, French chemist and bacteriologist, discovered (1880–1885) methods for inoculation and vaccination against anthrax, rabies, and chicken cholera.

Perthes, Georg Clemens, 1869–1927, German surgeon, noted, 1903, effects of X rays on cancerous growths.

Plenciz, Marcus Antonius von, 1705–1786, Viennese physician, published, 1762, the germ theory of disease.

Pylarino, James, or Giacomo, 1659–1715, Italian physician, inoculated, 1701, three Turkish children with smallpox exudate in first attempt at immunization.

Reed, Walter, 1851–1902, American surgeon, studied the etiology of yellow fever and reported, 1901, that the disease was caused by a filterable virus transmitted by the mosquito.

Rhazes, or Rasis, c. A.D. 860–c. 925, Persian physician, first to differentiate, c. 910, measles and smallpox.

Roentgen, Wilhelm Conrad, 1845–1923, German physicist, discovered, 1895, X rays.

Roux, Pierre Paul Émile, 1853–1933, French physician and bacteriologist, with A. E. J. Yersin, demonstrated, 1888, that the diphtheria bacillus produces a toxin.

Rush, Benjamin, c. 1745–1813, American physician, established, 1786, first free dispensary in U.S.

Sabin, Albert Bruce, 1906–　, Russian-American bacteriologist, 1957, produced an oral vaccine for poliomyelitis.

Sakel, Manfred J., 1900–1957, Austro-American psychiatrist, introduced, 1929, insulin shock treatment of schizophrenia.

Salk, Jonas Edward, 1914– , American virologist, introduced, 1954, hypodermic vaccine for poliomyelitis.

Sanctorius, 1561–1636, Italian physician, described, c. 1626, the first use of the clinical thermometer in the diagnosis of disease.

Schick, Bela, 1877–1967, Hungarian-American pediatrician, developed, 1913, a test for determining susceptibility to diphtheria.

Schleiden, Matthias Jakob, 1804–1881, German botanist, founded, 1838, cytology.

Schwann, Theodor, 1810–1882, German anatomist, founder, 1839, of cell theory as applied to animals.

Semmelweis, Ignaz P., 1818–65, Hungarian physician, obstetrician, independently identified, c. 1850, puerperal (childbed) fever as an infectious disease.

Servetus, Michael, 1511–1553, Spanish physician and theologian, described, 1546, pulmonary circulation.

Sherrington, Charles Scott, 1857–1952, English physiologist, established, 1906–1940, neurophysiology.

Spallanzani, Lazzaro, 1729–99, Italian naturalist, performed, 1768, experiments that led to the discrediting of the doctrine of spontaneous generation.

Steptoe, Patrick C., 1913– , British gynecologist, performed first successful laboratory-conceived human birth (1978).

Swammerdam, Jan, 1637–80, Dutch naturalist, discovered, 1658, red blood cells.

Takamine, Jokichi, 1854–1922, Japanese chemist working in U.S., isolated, 1901, crystalline epinephrine (adrenalin), the first hormone known in pure form.

Taussig, Helen Brooke, 1898– , American physician, with Alfred Blalock, introduced, 1944, corrective heart surgery enabling survival of "blue babies."

Vesalius, Andreas, 1514–64, Flemish anatomist, published, 1543, first anatomical text based entirely on observation.

Virchow, Rudolf L. K., 1821–1902, German pathologist, founder, c. 1855, of cellular pathology.

Waksman, Selman Abraham, 1888–1973, Russian-American bacteriologist, discovered, 1943, streptomycin and its use in tuberculosis therapy.

Wassermann, August von, 1866–1925, German bacteriologist, developed, 1906, specific test for syphilis.

Wells, Horace, 1815–48, American dentist, first to use, 1844, nitrous oxide as an anesthetic in surgery.

Wiley, Harvey Washington, 1844–1930, American chemist, led fight for U.S. Pure Food Law of 1906.

Wundt, Wilhelm Max, 1832–1920, German psychologist, established, 1878, the first laboratory for experimental psychology, bringing mind into the realm of science.

Yersin, Alexandre Émile John, 1863–1943, French bacteriologist, discovered, 1888, the diphtheria toxin; discovered, 1894, *Pasteurella pestis,* the bubonic plague causative bacillus.

NOTABLES OF ART AND ARCHITECTURE

Aalto, Alvar (1898–1976), Finnish architect and designer.

Agostino di Duccio (1418–1498), Florentine sculptor.

Albers, Josef (1888–1976), German-American painter.

Alberti, Leone B. (1404–72), Italian architect and painter.

Alma-Tadema, Sir Lawrence (1836–1912), English painter.

Angelico, Fra (c. 1400–55), Florentine painter.

Antonello da Messina (c. 1430–79), Italian painter.

Apelles (fl. 330 B.C.), Greek painter.

Apollodorus (fl. 430–400 B.C.), Athenian painter.

Archipenko, Alexander (1887–1964), Ukrainian-American sculptor.

Arp, Jean (1887–1966), French sculptor and painter.

Asplund, Erik Gunnar (1885–1940), Swedish architect.

Audubon, John J. (d. 1851), American artist.

Avery, Milton (1893–1965), American painter.

Bacon, Francis (1910–), English painter.

Baldovinetti, Alessio, (c. 1425–99), Florentine painter.

Barlach, Ernst (1870–1938), German sculptor.

Barthé, Richmond (1901–), American sculptor.

Bartolomeo, Fra (1475–1517), Italian painter.

Baskin, Leonard (1922–), American sculptor.

Baziotes, William (1912–63), American painter.

Bearden, Romare (1914–), American realistic painter.

Beardsley, Aubrey (1872–98), English illustrator.

Beckmann, Max (1884–1950), German painter.

Bellini, Giovanni (c. 1430–1516), Venetian painter.

Bellows, George W. (1882–1925), American painter.

Benjamin, Asher (1773–1845), American architect.

Benton, Thomas Hart (1889–1975), American painter.

Berlage, Hendrik P. (1856–1934), Dutch architect.

Bernini, Giovanni Lorenzo (1598–1680), Italian architect.

Bertoia, Harry (1915–78), American sculptor and designer.

Beuys, Joseph (1921–), German artist.

Bierstadt, Albert (1830–1902), American Western painter.

Bingham, George Caleb (1811–79), American genre painter.

Boccioni, Umberto (1882–1916), Italian futurist painter.

Böcklin, Arnold (1827–1901), Swiss painter.

Bonheur, Rosa (1822–99), French painter.

Bonnard, Pierre (1867–1947), French painter.

Borromini, Francesco (1559–1677), Italian architect.

Bosch, Hieronymus (c. 1450–1516), Flemish painter.

Botero, Fernando (1932–), Colombian painter.

Botticelli, Sandro (c. 1444–1510), Florentine painter.

Boucher, François (1703–70), French painter.

Boudin, Eugène L. (1824–98), French painter.

Bouts, Dierick (c. 1420–75), Dutch painter.

Brady, Mathew B. (c. 1823–96), American photographer.

Bramante, Donato (1444–1514), Italian architect.

Brancusi, Constantin (1876–1957), Rumanian sculptor.

Braque, Georges (1882–1963), French painter.

Breuer, Marcel (1902–), Hungarian-born American architect and designer.

Bronzino, Il (1503–72), Florentine mannerist painter.

Brouwer, Adriaen (c. 1606–38), Flemish painter.

Bruegel, Pieter, the elder (c. 1525–69), Flemish genre painter.

Brunelleschi, Filippo (1377–1446), Florentine architect.

Bulfinch, Charles (1763–1844), American architect.

Burchfield, Charles E. (1893–1967), American painter.

Burne-Jones, Sir Edward (1833–98), English painter.

Calder, Alexander (1898–1976), American sculptor.

Canaletto (1697–1768), Venetian painter.

Candela, Felix (1910–), Mexican architect.

Caravaggio, Michelangelo M. da (1573–1610), Italian painter.

Carracci, Annibale (1560–1609), Bolognese painter.

Carracci, Lodovico (1555–1619), Bolognese painter.

Cartier-Bresson, Henri (1908–), French photographer.

Cassatt, Mary (1845–1926), American painter.

Castagno, Andrea del (c. 1423–57), Florentine painter.

Catlin, George (1796–1872), American painter.

Cellini, Benvenuto (1500–71), Italian sculptor and metalsmith.

Cézanne, Paul (1839–1906), French painter.

Chagall, Marc (1889–), Russian painter.

Chardin, Jean Baptiste (1699–1779), French painter.

Chippendale, Thomas (1718–79), English cabinetmaker.

Chirico, Giorgio de (1888–1978), Italian painter.

Christo (1935–), Bulgarian-born American artist.

Cimabue, Giovanni (d. c. 1302), Florentine painter.

Claude Lorrain (1600–82), French landscape painter.

Cole, Thomas (1801–48), English-born American painter.

Constable, John (1776–1837), English painter.

Copley, John Singleton (1738–1815), American painter.

Cornelius, Peter von (1783–1867), German painter.

Corot, Jean B. C. (1796–1875), French landscape painter.

Correggio, Antonio (1494–1534), Italian painter.

Costa, Lucio (1902–), Brazilian architect.

Courbet, Gustave (1819–77), French painter.

Cox, Kenyon (1856–1919), American painter and critic.

Cranach, Lucas, the elder (1472–1553), German painter.

Currier, Nathaniel (1813–88), American printmaker.

Curry, John S. (1897–1946), American painter.

Dali, Salvador (1904–), Spanish surrealist painter.

Daubigny, Charles F. (1817–78), French landscape painter.

Daumier, Honoré (1808–79), French painter.

David, Gerard (c. 1460–1523), Flemish painter.

David, Jacques L. (1748–1825), French painter.

Davis, Stuart (1894–1964), American painter.

Decamps, Alexandre G. (1803–60), French painter.

Degas, Edgar (1834–1917), French painter and sculptor.

de Kooning, Willem (1904–), Dutch-born American painter.

Delacroix, Ferdinand V. E. (1798–1863), French painter.

Delaunay, Robert (1885–1941), French painter.

Della Robbia, Luca (c. 1400–82), Florentine sculptor.

Demuth, Charles (1883–1935), American watercolorist.

Derain, André (1880–1954), French painter.

Dine, Jim (1935–), American neosurrealist artist.

Dix, Otto (1891–1969), German painter and draughtsman.

Doesburg, Theo van (1883–1931), Dutch painter.

Donatello (c. 1386–1466), Italian sculptor.
Dongen, Kees van (1877–1968), Dutch painter.
Dou, Gerard (1613–75), Dutch painter.
Dubuffet, Jean (1901–   ), French painter.
Duccio di Buoninsegna (fl. 1278–1319), Italian painter.
Duchamp, Marcel (1887–1968), French painter.
Dufy, Raoul (1877–1953), French painter and illustrator.
Dürer, Albecht (1471–1528), German painter and engraver.
Eakins, Thomas (1844–1916), American painter.
Eiffel, Alexandre G. (1832–1923), French engineer.
Elisofon, Eliot (1911–73), American photographer.
Ensor, James (1860–1949), Belgian painter and etcher.
Epstein, Sir Jacob (1880–1959), American-born English sculptor.
Ernst, Max (1891–1976), German painter.
Evergood, Philip (1901–1973), American painter.
Eyck, Hubert van (c. 1370–1426), Flemish painter.
Eyck, Jan van (c. 1390–1441), Flemish painter.
Fabritius, Carel (1622–54), Dutch painter.
Feininger, Lyonel (1871–1956), American painter and illustrator.
Flagg, Ernest (1857–1947), American architect.
Flandrin, Hippolyte J. (1809–64), French painter.
Fouquet, Jean (c. 1420–1480), French painter.
Fragonard, Jean-Honoré (1732–1806), French painter.
Frasconi, Antonio (1919–   ), South American-born woodcut artist in U.S.
Friesz, Othon (1879–1949), French painter.
Fuller, George (1822–84), American painter.
Fuller, (Richard) Buckminster (1895–   ), American architect and engineer.
Fuseli, Henry (1741–1825), Anglo-Swiss painter and draughtsman.
Gabo, Naum (1890–1977), Russian sculptor and architect.
Gainsborough, Thomas (1727–88), English painter.
Gaudi i Cornet, Antonio (1852–1926), Spanish architect.
Gauguin, Paul (1848–1903), French painter.
Gentile da Fabriano (c. 1370–1427), Italian painter.
Gentileschi, Orazio (c. 1562–1647), Tuscan painter.
Gérard, François P. S., Baron (1770–1837), French painter.
Géricault, Jean Louis A. T. (1791–1824), French painter.
Gérôme, Jean Léon (1824–1904), French painter.
Ghiberti, Lorenzo (c. 1378–1455), Florentine sculptor.
Ghirlandaio, Domenico (1449–94), Florentine painter.
Giacometti, Alberto (1901–66), Swiss sculptor and painter.
Gilbert, Cass (1859–1934), American architect.
Giordano, Luca (1632–1705), Italian painter.
Giorgio, Francesco di (1439–1502), Italian architect, painter, and sculptor.
Giorgione (c. 1478–1510), Venetian painter.
Giotto (c. 1266–c. 1337), Florentine painter.
Giovanni di Paulo (c. 1403–83), Italian painter.
Glackens, William J. (1870–1938), American painter.
Gleizes, Albert L. (1881–1953), French cubist painter.
Goes, Hugo van der (d. 1482), Flemish painter.
Gogh, Vincent van (1853–90), Dutch postimpressionist painter.
Gorky, Arshile (1904–48), Armenian-born American painter.
Goya y Lucientes, Francisco José de (1746–1828), Spanish painter and etcher.
Goyen, Jan van (1596–1656), Dutch landscape painter.
Greco, El (c. 1541–1614), Cretan painter in Spain.
Greuze, Jean Baptiste (1725–1805), French painter.
Gris, Juan (1887–1927), Spanish cubist painter.
Grooms, Red (1937–   ), American painter.
Gropius, Walter (1883–1969), German-American architect.
Gropper, William (1897–1977), American painter and cartoonist.
Grosz, George (1893–1959), German-American caricaturist and painter.
Grunewald, Mathias (c. 1475–1528), German painter.
Guardi, Francesco (1712–93), Venetian painter.
Guston, Philip (1913–1980), Canadian-born American painter.
Hals, Franz (c. 1580–1666), Dutch portrait painter.
Hartley, Marsden (1877–1943), American painter.
Harunobu, Suzuki (1725–70), Japanese color-print artist.
Hassam, Childe (1859–1935), American painter and etcher.
Hennebique, François (1842–1921), French architect.
Henri, Robert (1865–1929), American painter.
Hicks, Edward (1780–1849), American painter.
Hilliard, Nicholas (1537–1619), English miniaturist.
Hobbema, Meindert (1638–1709), Dutch landscape painter.
Hockney, David (1937–   ), English painter.
Hodler, Ferdinand (1853–1918), Swiss painter.
Hofmann, Hans (1880–1966), German-American painter.

Hogarth, William (1697–1764), English painter, satirist, and engraver.
Hokusai, Katsushika (1760–1849), Japanese wood engraver.
Holbein, Hans, the younger (c. 1497–1543), German-Swiss painter.
Homer, Winslow (1836–1910), American painter.
Hooch, Pieter de (c. 1629–after 1677), Dutch painter.
Hopper, Edward (1882–1967), American painter.
Houdon, Jean A. (1741–1828), French neoclassic sculptor.
Indiana, Robert (1928–   ), American pop artist.
Ingrès, Jean A. D. (1780–1867), French painter.
Inman, Henry (1801–46), American painter.
Inness, George (1825–1894), American landscape painter.
Ives, James Merritt (1824–95), American printmaker.
Jackson, William H. (1843–1942), American artist and pioneer photographer.
Jacobsen, Arne (1902–1971), Danish architect.
Jenney, William Le Baron (1832–1907), American architect.
John, Augustus Edwin (1879–1961), British painter.
Johns, Jasper (1930–   ), American pop artist.
Johnson, Philip C. (1906–   ), American architect.
Jones, Inigo (1573–1652), English architect.
Jordaens, Jacob (1593–1678), Flemish baroque painter.
Kandinsky, Wassily (1866–1944), Russian abstract painter.
Kano Motonobu (c. 1476–1559), Japanese artist.
Kaufmann, Angelica (1741–1807), Swiss painter and etcher.
Kepes, György (1906–   ), Hungarian-born artist.
Kirchner, Ernst L. (1880–1938), German painter and graphic artist.
Kiyonaga (1752–1815), Japanese woodcut designer.
Klee, Paul (1879–1940), Swiss painter and graphic artist.
Klimt, Gustav (1862–1918), Austrian painter.
Kokoschka, Oskar (1886–1980), Austrian expressionist painter.
Kollwitz, Käthe S. (1867–1945), German graphic artist and sculptor.
Kuhn, Walt (1880–1949), American painter.
Kuniyoshi, Yasuo (c. 1892–1953), Japanese-born American painter.
Kupka, Frank (1871–1957), Czech painter and illustrator.
Lachaise, Gaston (1882–1935), French-born American sculptor.
La Farge, John (1835–1910), American painter.
Lancret, Nicolas (1690–1743), French rococo painter.
Landseer, Sir Edwin H. (1802–73), English animal painter.
La Tour, Georges de (1593–1652), French painter.
Lawrence, Jacob (1917–   ), American painter.
Lawrence, Sir Thomas (1769–1830), English portrait painter.
Le Corbusier (1887–1965), Swiss-born French architect.
Ledoux, Claude N. (1736–1806), French architect.
Léger, Fernand (1881–1955), French painter.
Lehmbruck, Wilhelm (1881–1919), German sculptor.
L'Enfant, Pierre C. (1754–1825), French-American architect and engineer.
Leonardo da Vinci (1452–1519), Italian painter, sculptor, and architect.
Lescaze, William (1896–1969), Swiss-born American architect.
Leutze, Emanuel (1816–68), German-American painter.
Levine, Jack (1915–   ), American painter.
Lichtenstein, Roy (1923–   ), American pop artist.
Lipchitz, Jacques (1891–1973), Lithuanian-born French sculptor.
Lippi, Fra Filippo (c. 1406–69), Italian painter.
Lippo, Filippino (c. 1457–1504), Italian painter.
Lippold, Richard (1915–   ), American sculptor and engineer.
Lochner, Stephan (d. 1451), German religious painter.
Lombardo, Pietro (c. 1435–1515), Venetian architect.
Lorenzetti, Ambrogio (d. c. 1348), Sienese painter.
Lucas van Leyden (1494–1533), Dutch painter and engraver.
Luini, Bernardino (c. 1480–1532), Italian painter.
Luks, George B. (1867–1933), American painter.
Lysippus (4th cent. B.C.), Greek sculptor.
Mabuse, Jan de (c. 1478–c. 1533), Flemish painter.
Macke, August (1887–1914), German painter.
McKim, Charles F. (1847–1909), American architect.
Magritte, René (1898–1967), Belgian surrealist painter.
Maillol, Aristide (1861–1944), French sculptor and painter.
Manet, Edouard (1832–83), French painter.
Mansart, François (1598–1666), French architect.
Mansart, Jules H. (1646–1708), French architect.
Mantegna, Andrea (1431–1506), Italian painter of the Paduan school.
Marc, Franz (1880–1916), German painter.
Marisol (1930–   ), Venezuelan-American sculptor.

Marsh, Reginald (1898–1954), French-born American painter.

Martini, Simone (c. 1283–1344), Sienese painter.

Masaccio (1401–c. 1428), Florentine painter.

Massys, Quentin (c. 1466–1530), Flemish painter.

Matisse, Henri (1869–1954), French painter and sculptor.

Maurer, Alfred H. (1868–1932), American painter.

Meissonier, Jean L. E. (1815–91), French military painter.

Memling, Hans (c. 1430–94), German-born Flemish painter.

Mendelsohn, Eric (1887–1953), German architect.

Mestrovic, Ivan (1883–1962), Yugoslav sculptor.

Michelangelo Buonarroti (1475–1564), Italian sculptor, painter, and architect.

Mies van der Rohe, Ludwig (1886–1969), German-American architect.

Millais, Sir John E. (1829–96), English painter.

Millet, Jean F. (1814–75), French painter.

Miró, Joan (1893–   ), Spanish surrealist painter.

Modigliani, Amadeo (1884–1920), Italian painter.

Mondrian, Piet (1872–1944), Dutch painter.

Monet, Claude (1840–1926), French impressionist painter.

Moore, Henry (1898–   ), English sculptor.

Moreau, Gustave (1826–98), French painter.

Morisot, Berthe (1841–95), French impressionist painter.

Moronobu, Hishikawa (c. 1618–c. 1694), Japanese painter.

Morris, William (1834–96), English artist, printer, and poet.

Morse, Samuel F. B. (1791–1872), American artist and inventor.

Moses, Grandma (Anna Mary R. Moses) (1860–1961), American primitive painter.

Motherwell, Robert (1915–   ), American painter.

Munch, Edvard (1863–1944), Norwegian painter.

Murillo, Bartholomé E. (c. 1617–82), Spanish painter.

Muybridge, Eadweard (1830–1904), English photographer.

Myron (5th cent. B.C.), Greek sculptor.

Nash, John (1752–1835), English architect.

Nash, Paul (1889–1946), English painter and wood engraver.

Neel, Alice (1900–   ), American painter.

Nervi, Pier Luigi (1891–1979), Italian architect.

Neutra, Richard (1892–1970), American architect.

Nevelson, Louise (1900–   ), Russian-born American sculptor.

Nicholson, Ben (1894–   ), English abstract painter.

Niemeyer, Oscar (1907–   ), Brazilian architect.

Noguchi, Isamu (1904–   ), American sculptor.

Noland, Kenneth (1924–   ), American color-field painter.

Nolde, Emil (1867–1956), German expressionist painter.

O'Keeffe, Georgia (1887–   ), American painter.

Oldenburg, Claes (1929–   ), Swedish-born American pop artist.

Olmsted, Frederick L. (1822–1903), American landscape architect.

Orley, Bernard van (c. 1491–1542), Flemish painter.

Orozco, José C. (1883–1949), Mexican mural painter.

Ostade, Adriaen van (1610–85), Dutch genre painter.

Palladio, Andrea (1508–80), Italian architect.

Parks, Gordon (1912–   ), American photographer.

Parmigiano (1503–40), Italian mannerist painter.

Parrhasius (fl. c. 400 B.C.), Greek painter.

Parrish, Maxfield (1870–1966), American illustrator.

Patinir, Joachim de (d. 1524), Flemish landscape and religious painter.

Paxton, Sir Joseph (1803–65), English architect.

Peale, Charles Willson (1741–1827), American painter.

Peale, James (1749–1831), American portrait painter.

Peale, Raphaelle (1774–1825), American portrait painter.

Peale, Rembrandt (1778–1860), American portrait painter.

Pearlstein, Philip (1924–   ), American realist painter.

Pechstein, Max (1881–1955), German expressionist painter.

Pei, I(eoh) M(ing) (1917–   ), Chinese-born American architect.

Perrault, Claude (1613–88), French architect.

Perugino (c. 1445–c. 1523), Umbrian painter.

Pevsner, Antoine (1886–1962), Russian sculptor and painter.

Phidias (c. 500–c. 432 B.C.), Greek sculptor.

Phyfe, Duncan (c. 1768–1854), Scottish-born cabinetmaker.

Picasso, Pablo (1881–1973), Spanish painter and sculptor in France.

Piero della Francesca (c. 1420–92), Italian painter.

Piero di Cosimo (1462–1521), Florentine painter.

Pinturicchio (c. 1454–1513), Umbrian painter.

Piranesi, Giovanni B. (1720–78), Italian architect.

Pisanello (c. 1395–c. 1455), Italian medalist and painter.

Pisano, Andrea (c. 1290–c. 1348), Italian sculptor.

Pisano, Giovanni (c. 1250–after 1314), Italian architect.

Pisano, Nicola (c. 1220–between 1278 and 1287), Italian sculptor.

Pissarro, Camille (1830–1903), French impressionist painter.

Pollaiuolo, Antonio (c. 1429–98), Florentine goldsmith, painter, sculptor, and engraver.

Pollock, Jackson (1912–56), American painter.

Polyclitus the elder (fl. c. 450–c. 420 B.C.), Greek sculptor.

Polygnotus (fl. c. 460–447 B.C.), Greek painter.

Poussin, Nicolas (1594–1665), French painter.

Praxiteles (fl. c. 370–c. 330 B.C.), Greek sculptor.

Prendergast, Maurice B. (1859–1924), American painter.

Primaticcio, Francesco (1504–70), Italian painter.

Prud'hon, Pierre Paul (1758–1823), French painter.

Puvis de Chavannes, Pierre (1824–98), French mural painter.

Pyle, Howard (1853–1911), American painter, illustrator and writer.

Quercia, Jacopo della (c. 1374–1438), Italian sculptor.

Raeburn, Sir Henry (1756–1823), Scottish portrait painter.

Raphael Santi (1483–1520), Italian Renaissance painter.

Rauschenberg, Robert (1925–   ), American pop artist.

Ray, Man (1890–1976), American painter and photographer.

Redon, Odilon (1840–1916), French painter.

Reinhardt, Ad (1913–67), American painter.

Rembrandt Harmenszoon van Rijn (1606–69), Dutch painter and etcher.

Remington, Frederic (1861–1909), American painter and sculptor.

Renoir, Pierre A. (1841–1919), French impressionist painter.

Reynolds, Sir Joshua (1723–92), English portrait painter; first president of Royal Academy of Arts.

Ribera, Jusepe (c. 1590–1652), Spanish baroque painter.

Rivera, Diego (1886–1957), Mexican muralist.

Rivers, Larry (1923–   ), American pop artist.

Rodin, Auguste (1840–1917), French sculptor.

Romney, George (1734–1802), English portrait painter.

Rosa, Salvator (1615–73), Italian baroque painter.

Rosenquist, James (1933–   ), American pop artist.

Roszak, Theodore (1907–   ), Polish-born American sculptor.

Rothko, Mark (1903–70), Russian-born American abstract expressionist painter.

Rouault, Georges (1871–1958), French painter.

Rousseau, Henri (1844–1910), French primitive painter.

Rubens, Peter Paul (1577–1640), Flemish painter.

Rudolph, Paul (1918–   ), American architect.

Ruisdael, Jacob van (c. 1628–82), Dutch painter and etcher.

Ryder, Albert P. (1847–1917), American painter.

Saarinen, Eero (1910–61), Finnish-American architect.

Saarinen, Eliel (1873–1950), Finnish-American architect.

Saint-Gaudens, Augustus (1848–1907), Irish-born American sculptor.

Samaras, Lucas (1936–   ), Greek collage artist.

Sargent, John Singer (1856–1925), American painter.

Sarto, Andrea del (1486–1531), Florentine painter.

Sassetta (c. 1400–1450), Sienese painter.

Schongauer, Martin (1430–1491), German engraver and painter.

Scopas (fl. 4th cent. B.C.), Greek sculptor.

Scorel, Jan van (1495–1562), Dutch painter.

Segal, George (1924–   ), American sculptor.

Seurat, Georges (1859–91), French neoimpressionist painter.

Shahn, Ben (1898–1969), American painter and graphic artist.

Signac, Paul (1863–1935), French neoimpressionist painter.

Signorelli, Luca (c. 1441–1523), Italian painter of the Umbrian school.

Siqueiros, David A. (1898–1974), Mexican muralist.

Sisley, Alfred (1839–99), French landscape painter.

Sloan, John (1871–1951), American painter and etcher.

Sloane, Eric (1910–   ), American landscape painter.

Sluter, Claus (d. 1406), Flemish sculptor.

Smith, David (1906–65), American sculptor.

Soleri, Paolo (1919–   ), Italian architect.

Soutine, Chaim (1894–1943), Russian-born French painter.

Steen, Jan (1626–79), Dutch genre painter.

Steichen, Edward (1879–1973), Luxembourg-born American photographer.

Stella, Joseph (1877–1946), Italian-born American painter.

Stieglitz, Alfred (1864–1946), American photographer.

Stone, Edward Durell (1902–78), American architect.

Stoss, Veit (c. 1445–1533), German sculptor.

Stuart, Gilbert (1755–1828), American portrait painter.

Stuart, James (1713–88), English architect and painter.

Sullivan, Louis Henry (1856–1924), American architect.

Sutherland, Graham (1903–80), English painter.
Tamayo, Rufino (1899–   ), Mexican painter.
Tange, Kenzo (1913–   ), Japanese architect.
Tanguy, Yves (1900–55), French surrealist painter.
Tchelitchew, Pavel (1898–1957), Russian-American painter.
Teniers, David, the younger (1610–90), Flemish genre painter.
Ter Borch, Gerard (1617–81), Dutch painter.
Terbrugghen, Hendrick (1588–1629), Dutch painter.
Thoma, Hans (1839–1924), German painter and lithographer.
Thorvaldsen, Albert B. (1770–1844), Danish sculptor.
Tiepolo, Giovanni B. (1696–1770), Venetian painter.
Tiffany, Louis C. (1848–1933), American artist and decorative designer.
Tinguely, Jean (1925–   ), Swiss sculptor.
Tintoretto (1518–94), Venetian painter.
Titian (c. 1490–1576), Venetian painter.
Toulouse-Lautrec, Henri de (1864–1901), French painter and lithographer.
Trumbull, John (1756–1843), American painter.
Tura, Cosmé (c. 1430–95), Italian painter.
Turner, Joseph M. W. (1775–1851), English landscape painter.
Uccello, Paolo (c. 1396–1475), Florentine painter.
Utamaro, Kitagawa (1753–1806), Japanese color-print artist.
Utrillo, Maurice (1883–1955), French painter.
Utzon, Joern (1918–   ), Danish architect.
Van Dyck, Sir Anthony (1599–1641), Flemish portrait painter.
Vasari, Giorgio (1511–74), Italian architect, painter, and writer.

Vaux, Calvert (1824–95), English-born American landscape architect.
Velázquez, Diego R. de S. y (1599–1660), Spanish painter.
Velde, Henri van de (1863–1957), Belgian designer and architect.
Vermeer, Jan (1632–75), Dutch genre and landscape painter.
Veronese, Paolo (1528–88), Italian painter.
Verrocchio, Andrea del (1435–88), Florentine sculptor.
Vigée-Lebrun, Elisabeth (1755–1842), French painter.
Vignola, Giacomo da (1507–73), Italian architect.
Viollet-le-Duc, Eugène E. (1814–79), French architect.
Vlaminck, Maurice de (1876–1958), French painter.
Vos, Cornelis de (1584–1651), Flemish painter.
Vuillard, Edouard (1868–1940), French painter.
Warhol, Andy (1930?–   ), American pop artist.
Watteau, Antoine (1684–1721), French painter.
Wedgwood, Josiah (1730–95), English potter.
Wesselmann, Tom (1931–   ), American pop artist.
West, Benjamin (1738–1820), American historical painter.
Westermann, H. C. (1922–   ), American pop sculptor.
Weyden, Roger van der (c. 1400–64), Flemish painter.
Whistler, James A. McN. (1834–1903), American painter and etcher.
White, Stanford (c. 1853–1906), American architect.
Witz, Conrad (fl. c. 1434–c. 1447), German painter.
Wood, Grant (1891–1942), American painter.
Wren, Sir Christopher (1632–1723), English architect.
Wright, Frank Lloyd (1869–1959), American architect.
Wyeth, Andrew N. (1917–   ), American painter.
Wyeth, Newell Convers (1882–1945), American painter and illustrator.
Zorach, William (1887–1966), Lithuanian-born American sculptor.

NOVELISTS, DRAMATISTS, POETS, AND OTHER WRITERS

Adams, Henry (1838–1918), American biographer, historian, and novelist.
Addison, Joseph (1672–1719), English essayist and poet.
Aeschylus (525–456 B.C.), Athenian tragedian.
Aesop (c. 620–c. 560 B.C.), Greek fabulist.
Agee, James (1909–55), American essayist and journalist.
Agnon (b. Czaczkes), Shmuel Y. (1888–1970), Polish-born Israeli novelist.
Aiken, Conrad (1889–1973), American novelist and poet.
Alarcón, Pedro Antonio de (1833–91), Spanish novelist.
Albee, Edward (1928–   ), American dramatist.
Alcott, Louisa May (1832–88), American novelist.
Aldington, Richard (1892–1962), English poet and novelist.
Aleichem, Sholom (Solomon Rabinowitz) (1859–1916), Russian-born Yiddish writer.
Algren, Nelson (1909–   ), American novelist.
Amado, Jorge (1912–   ), Brazilian novelist.
Ambler, Eric (1909–   ), English suspense novelist.
Amis, Kingsley (1922–   ), English novelist.
Andersen, Hans Christian (1805–75), Danish poet and fairy tale writer.
Anderson, Maxwell (1888–1959), American dramatist.
Anderson, Robert (1917–   ), American dramatist.
Anderson, Sherwood (1876–1941), American novelist.
Andreyev, Leonid (1871–1919), Russian writer.
Andric, Ivo (1892–1975), Yugoslav novelist.
Anouilh, Jean (1910–   ), French dramatist.
Apollinaire, Guillaume (1880–1918), French poet.
Apuleius, Lucius (fl. 2d cent. A.D.), Latin romance writer.
Aragon, Louis (1897–   ), French novelist and poet.
Arden, John (1930–   ), English dramatist.
Ariosto, Ludovico (1474–1533), Italian epic and lyric poet.
Aristophanes (c. 448–after 388 B.C.), Athenian comic poet.
Arnold, Matthew (1822–88), English poet and critic.
Arrabel (Terán), Fernando (1932–   ), Spanish dramatist.
Asch, Sholem (1880–1957), Polish-born Yiddish novelist.
Auchincloss, Louis (1917–   ), American novelist.
Auden, W(ystan) H(ugh) (1907–73), Anglo-American poet.
Austen, Jane (1775–1817), English novelist.
Ayckbourn, Alan (1939–   ), English playwright.
Azuela, Mariano (1873–1952), Mexican novelist.
Bacon, Francis (1561–1626), English essayist.
Bagnold, Enid (1889–   ), English dramatist.
Baldwin, James (1924–   ), American novelist and essayist.
Balzac, Honoré de (1799–1850), French novelist.
Barrie, Sir James M. (1860–1937), British playwright.
Barth, John (1930–   ), American novelist.
Baudelaire, Charles (1821–67), French poet and critic.
Beaumarchais, Pierre A. C. de (1732–99), French dramatist.

Beaumont, Francis (c. 1584–1616), English dramatist.
Beauvoir, Simone de (1908–   ), French novelist and essayist.
Beckett, Samuel (1906–   ), Irish-French dramatist.
Bede (c. 673–735 A.D.), Old English historian.
Beerbohm, Sir Max (1872–1956), English parodist.
Behan, Brendan (1923–64), Irish dramatist.
Behn, Aphra (1640–89), English novelist and dramatist.
Behrman, S. N. (1893–1973), American playwright.
Belloc, Hilaire (1870–1953), British poet, essayist, satirist, and historian.
Bellow, Saul (1915–   ), Canadian-American novelist.
Benchley, Robert (1889–1945), American humorist.
Benét, Stephen Vincent (1898–1943), American poet, novelist, and short story writer.
Bennett, Arnold (1867–1931), English novelist.
Bernanos, Georges (1888–1948), French novelist.
Bernstein, Carl (1944–   ), American journalist and author.
Berryman, John (1914–72), American poet.
Betjeman, John (1906–   ), English poet.
Betti, Ugo (1892–1953), Italian poet and dramatist.
Bierce, Ambrose (1842–1914?), American short story writer and journalist.
Bishop, Elizabeth (1911–79), American poet.
Bjornson, Bjornstjerne (1832–1910), Norwegian novelist.
Blackmur, R(ichard) P. (1904–65), American critic and poet.
Blake, William (1757–1827), English poet.
Blasco-Ibáñez, Vicente (1867–1928), Spanish novelist.
Boccaccio, Giovanni (1313–75), Italian poet and storyteller.
Bodenheim, Maxwell (1893–1954), American poet.
Bogan, Louise (1897–1970), American poet.
Boileau-Despréaux, Nicolas (1636–1711), French literary critic and poet.
Böll, Heinrich (1917–   ), German novelist.
Bolt, Robert (1924–   ), English dramatist.
Borges, Jorge Luis (1899–   ), Argentine poet.
Boswell, James (1740–95), Scottish biographer and diarist.
Bowen, Elizabeth (1899–1973), Anglo-Irish novelist.
Bowles, Paul (1910–   ), American novelist.
Boyle, Kay (1903–   ), American novelist.
Bradbury, Ray (1920–   ), American science fiction writer.
Braine, John (1922–   ), English novelist.
Brecht, Bertolt (1898–1956), German dramatist and poet.
Breton, André (1896–1966), French surrealistic writer.
Bridges, Robert (1844–1930), English poet.
Brontë, Charlotte (1816–55), English novelist.
Brontë, Emily (1818–48), English novelist.
Brooke, Rupert (1887–1915), English poet.
Brooks, Van Wyck (1886–1963), American critic.

Brophy, Brigid (1929–   ), English novelist and critic.

Brown, John Mason (1900–69), American critic and biographer.

Browne, Sir Thomas (1605–82), English author and physician.

Browning, Elizabeth Barrett (1806–61), English poet.

Browning, Robert (1812–89), English poet.

Bryant, William Cullen (1794–1878), American poet.

Buchan, John (1875–1940), British novelist and historian.

Bullins, Ed (1935–   ), American dramatist.

Bunin, Ivan (1870–1953), Russian novelist.

Bunyan, John (1628–88), English allegorist.

Burgess, Anthony (1917–   ), English novelist and critic.

Burns, Robert (1759–96), Scottish poet.

Burroughs, Edgar Rice (1875–1950), American novelist.

Burroughs, William (1914–   ), American novelist.

Butler, Samuel (1835–1902), English novelist and essayist.

Byron, Lord (George Gordon) (1788–1824), English poet.

Cabell, James Branch (1879–1958), American novelist.

Caedmon (fl. 670 A.D.), Old English poet.

Calderón de la Barca, Pedro (1600–81), Spanish dramatist.

Calisher, Hortense (1911–   ), American novelist.

Callimachus (fl. c. 265 B.C.), Greek poet and critic.

Camoes, Luis de (1524?–80), Portuguese poet.

Camus, Albert (1913–60), French essayist, novelist, and dramatist.

Capek, Karel (1890–1938), Czech playwright.

Capote, Truman (1924–   ), American novelist.

Carew, Thomas (c. 1595–c. 1639), English poet.

Carlino, Lewis John (1932–   ), American dramatist.

Carlyle, Thomas (1795–1881), Anglo-Scottish essayist, critic, translator, and historian.

Carroll, Lewis (Charles Lutwidge Dodgson) (1832–98), English novelist.

Cary, Joyce (1888–1957), English novelist.

Cassill, R(onald) V(erlin) (1919–   ), American novelist, short story writer, and essayist.

Castiglione, Baldassare (1478–1529), Italian social critic.

Cather, Willa (1876–1947), American novelist.

Catton, Bruce (1899–1978), American historian.

Catullus, Caius Valerius (c. 84 B.C.–c. 54 B.C.), Roman poet.

Céline, Louis Ferdinand (1894–1961), French novelist.

Cervantes Saavedra, Miguel de (1547–1616), Spanish novelist.

Chandler, Raymond (1888–1959), American detective story writer.

Chateaubriand, François R. (1768–1848), French novelist.

Chaucer, Geoffrey (c. 1340–1400), English poet.

Chayefsky, Paddy (1923–   ), American dramatist.

Cheever, John (1912–   ), American novelist and short story writer.

Chekhov, Anton (1860–1904), Russian dramatist.

Chesterton, G(ilbert) K(eith) (1874–1936), English novelist, poet, biographer, and essayist.

Chikamatsu, Monzaemon (1653–1725), Japanese dramatist.

Christie, Agatha (1891–1976), English mystery writer.

Ciardi, John (1916–   ), American poet and critic.

Cicero, Marcus Tullius (106–43 B.C.), Roman essayist.

Claudel, Paul (1868–1955), French poet and dramatist.

Cocteau, Jean (1889?–1963). French novelist and filmmaker.

Coleridge, Samuel Taylor (1772–1834), English poet.

Colette (Sidonie Gabrielle Collette) (1873–1954), French novelist.

Collins, Wilkie (1824–89), English novelist.

Collins, William (1721–59), English poet.

Colum, Padraic (1881–1972), Irish-American poet, dramatist, and novelist.

Compton-Burnett, Ivy (1892–1969), English novelist.

Congreve, William (1670–1729), English dramatist.

Connolly, Cyril (1903–74), English critic and editor.

Conrad, Joseph (1857–1924), Polish-born English novelist.

Cooper, James Fenimore (1789–1851), American novelist.

Corneille, Pierre (1606–84), French dramatist.

Coward, Sir Noël (1899–1973), English dramatist, composer, lyricist, and autobiographer.

Cowley, Abraham (1618–67), English poet.

Cowper, William (1731–1800), English poet.

Cozzens, James Gould (1903–78), American novelist.

Crabbe, George (1754–1832), English poet.

Crane, Hart (1899–1932), American poet.

Crane, Stephen (1871–1900), American novelist.

Crashaw, Richard (c. 1612–49), English poet.

cummings, e. e. (1894–1962), American poet.

Cunha, Euclides da (1866–1909), Brazilian writer.

Cynewulf (fl. c. early 9th cent.), Old English poet.

D'Annunzio, Gabriele (1863–1938), Italian poet.

Dante (Alighieri) (1265–1321), Italian poet.

Daudet, Alphonse (1840–97), French novelist, poet, and short story writer.

Day Lewis, C(ecil) (1904–72), Anglo-Irish poet.

Defoe, Daniel (c. 1660–1731), English novelist.

Dekker, Thomas (1572?–1632?), English dramatist.

Delaney, Shelagh (1939–   ), English dramatist.

De la Mare, Walter (1873–1956), English novelist and poet.

De la Roche, Mazo (1885–1961), Canadian novelist.

Demosthenes (c. 384–322 B.C.), Greek orator.

De Quincey, Thomas (1785–1859), English essayist.

De Vries, Peter (1910–   ), American novelist.

Dickens, Charles (1812–70), English novelist.

Dickey, James (1923–   ), American poet and critic.

Dickinson, Emily (1830–86), American poet.

Diderot, Denis (1713–84), French encyclopedist, novelist, dramatist, satirist, and critic.

Didion, Joan (1934–   ), American novelist.

Dinesen, Isak (Karen Blixen) (1885–1962), Danish writer.

Donleavy, J(ames) P(atrick) (1926–   ), American-born, Irish novelist.

Donne, John (1572–1631), English poet and essayist.

Doolittle, Hilda ("H.D.") (1886–1961), American poet.

Dos Passos, John (1896–1970), American novelist.

Dostoyevsky, Feodor (1821–81), Russian novelist.

Doyle, Sir Arthur Conan (1859–1930), English detective story and romance writer.

Dreiser, Theodore (1871–1945), American novelist.

Drexler, Rosalyn (1926–   ), American dramatist.

Dryden, John (1631–1700), English poet and dramatist.

Dumas, Alexandre (fils) (1824–95), French dramatist.

Dumas, Alexandre (père) (1802–70), French novelist and dramatist.

Duras, Marguerite (1914–   ), French novelist.

Durrell, Lawrence (1912–   ), British novelist and poet.

Durrenmatt, Friedrich (1921–   ), Swiss dramatist.

Eberhart, Richard (1904–   ), American poet.

Ehrenburg, Ilya (1891–1967), Russian novelist.

Eliot, George (Mary Ann Evans) (1819–80), English novelist.

Eliot, T(homas) S(tearns) (1888–1965), American-born British poet, dramatist, and critic.

Ellison, Ralph (1914–   ), American novelist.

Emerson, Ralph Waldo (1803–82), American essayist and poet.

Erasmus, Desiderius (c. 1466–1536), Dutch humanist.

Euripides (c. 480–406 B.C.), Greek tragic poet.

Farrell, James T. (1904–79), American novelist.

Faulkner, William (1897–1962), American novelist.

Feuchtwanger, Lion (1884–1958), German novelist.

Fielding, Henry (1707–54), English novelist.

FitzGerald, Edward (1809–83), English translator.

Fitzgerald, F. Scott (1896–1940), American novelist.

Flaubert, Gustave (1821–80), French novelist.

Fleming, Ian (1908–64), English secret agent novelist.

Fletcher, John (1579–1625), English dramatist.

Ford, Ford Madox (Ford Madox Hueffer) (1873–1939), English poet, novelist, critic, and essayist.

Ford, John (1586–c. 1640), English dramatist.

Forster, E(dward) M(organ) (1879–1970), English novelist.

Foster, Paul (1931–   ), American dramatist.

France, Anatole (Jacques Anatole Thibault) (1844–1924), French novelist and satirist.

Friedman, Bruce Jay (1930–   ), American novelist.

Friel, Brian (1929–   ), Irish dramatist.

Frisch, Max (1911–   ), Swiss dramatist.

Froissart, Jean (c. 1337–1410?), French chronicler.

Frost, Robert (1874–1963), American poet.

Fry, Christopher (1907–   ), English dramatist.

Fuentes, Carlos (1928–   ), Mexican short story writer.

Galsworthy, John (1867–1933), English novelist.

Garcia Lorca, Federico (1898–1936), Spanish poet.

Garcià Márquez, Gabriel José (1928–   ), Colombian writer.

Gardner, Erle Stanley (1889–1970), American detective story writer.

Garland, Hamlin (1860–1940), American novelist.

Gaskell, Elizabeth (1810–65), English novelist and biographer.

Gay, John (1685–1732), English playwright and poet.

Gelber, Jack (1932–   ), American dramatist.

Genet, Jean (1910–   ), French novelist and dramatist.

George, Stefan (1868–1933), German poet.

Ghelderode, Michel de (1898–1962), Belgian dramatist.

Gibbon, Edward (1737–94), English historian.

Gide, André (1869–1951), French novelist.

Gilroy, Frank D. (1925–), American dramatist.
Ginsberg, Allen (1926–), American poet.
Giono, Jean (1895–1970), French novelist.
Giraudoux, Jean (1882–1944), French dramatist.
Gissing, George (1857–1903), English novelist.
Glasgow, Ellen (1873–1945), American novelist.
Godwin, William (1756–1836), English novelist and political philosopher.
Goethe, Johann Wolfgang von (1749–1832), German novelist.
Gogol, Nikolai (1809–52), Russian novelist.
Golding, William (1911–), English novelist.
Goldman, James (1927–), American dramatist.
Goldoni, Carlo (1707–93), Italian dramatist.
Goldsmith, Oliver (1730?–74), English essayist and dramatist.
Goodman, Paul (1911–1972), American writer and pacifist.
Gordimer, Nadine (1923–), South African novelist.
Gorey, Edward (1925–), American writer and artist.
Gorki, Maxim (Aleksey Maximovich Pyeshkov) (1868–1936), Russian novelist, dramatist, and short story writer.
Grass, Günter (1927–), German novelist.
Graves, Robert (1895–), English poet and novelist.
Gray, Thomas (1716–71), English poet.
Greene, Graham (1904–), English novelist.
Gregory, Lady Augusta (1859–1932), Irish dramatist.
Grimm, Jakob (1785–1863), German folklorist.
Grimm, Wilhelm (1786–1859), German folklorist.
Gunther, John (1901–70), American political writer.
Hafiz (Shams-ud-Din-Mohammed) (d. 1389?), Persian poet.
Haley, Alex (1921–), American historian.
Hammett, Dashiell (1894–1961), American novelist.
Hamsun, Knut (1859–1952), Norwegian novelist.
Hansberry, Lorraine (1930–65), American dramatist.
Hardy, Thomas (1840–1928), English novelist.
Harris, Joel Chandler (1848–1908), American short story writer.
Harte, Bret (1836–1902), American short story writer.
Hauptmann, Gerhart (1862–1946), German dramatist, novelist, and poet.
Hawthorne, Nathaniel (1804–64), American novelist.
Hazlitt, William (1778–1830), English essayist.
Hecht, Ben (1894–1964), American journalist and author.
Heine, Heinrich (1797–1856), German poet.
Heller, Joseph (1923–), American novelist.
Hellman, Lillian (1905–), American dramatist and author.
Hemingway, Ernest (1899–1961), American novelist.
Henry, O. (William Sydney Porter) (1862–1910), American short story writer.
Herbert, George (1593–1633), English poet.
Herder, Johann G. von (1744–1803), German poet.
Herodotus (c. 484–c. 425 B.C.), Greek historian.
Herrick, Robert (1591–1674), English poet.
Hersey, John (1914–), American novelist and journalist.
Hesiod (fl. c. 8th cent. B.C.), Greek poet.
Hesse, Hermann (1877–1962), German novelist.
Heyward, DuBose (1885–1940), American novelist.
Heywood, Thomas (1574?–1641), English dramatist.
Hochhuth, Rolf (1931–), German dramatist.
Hoffmann, E(rnst) T(heodor) A(madeus) (1776–1822), German novelist and short story writer.
Hölderlin, Johann C. F. (1770–1843), German poet.
Homer (before 700 B.C.), Greek epic poet.
Hopkins, Gerard Manley (1844–89), English poet.
Horace (65 B.C.–8 B.C.), Latin poet.
Horovitz, Israel (1939–), American dramatist.
Housman, A. E. (1859–1936), English poet.
Howard, Sidney (1891–1939), American dramatist.
Howe, Irving (1920–), American historian and critic.
Hughes, Langston (1902–67), American poet.
Hugo, Victor (1802–85), French novelist.
Huxley, Aldous (1894–1963), English novelist and essayist.
Huxtable, Ada Louise (1921–), American journalist and architecture critic.
Ibsen, Henrik (1828–1906), Norwegian dramatist.
Inge, William (1913–73), American dramatist.
Ionesco, Eugène (1912–), French dramatist.
Irving, Washington (1783–1859), American short story writer, historian, and biographer.
Isherwood, Christopher (1904–), Anglo-American novelist and dramatist.
Jackson, Shirley (1919–65), American novelist.
James, Henry (1843–1916), American novelist.
Jarrell, Randall (1914–65), American poet and novelist.

Jeffers, Robinson (1887–1962), American poet.
Jellicoe, Ann (1927–), English dramatist and director.
Jewett, Sarah Orne (1849–1909), American novelist.
Johnson, Samuel (1709–84), English critic, essayist, lexicographer, poet, and biographer.
Jones, James (1921–77), American novelist.
Jones, LeRoi (Imamu Baraka) (1934–), American dramatist.
Jonson, Ben (1572–1637), English dramatist and poet.
Joyce, James (1882–1941), Irish novelist.
Juvenal (1st–2d cent. A.D.), Roman satirical poet.
Kafka, Franz (1883–1924), German novelist.
Kawabata, Yasunari (1899–1972) Japanese novelist.
Kazantzakis, Nikos (c. 1883–1957), Greek novelist.
Keats, John (1795–1821), English poet.
Keller, Gottfried (1819–90), Swiss novelist.
Kempton, J. Murray (1918–), American journalist.
Kennedy, Adrienne (1932–), American dramatist.
Kerouac, Jack (1922–69), American novelist.
Kesey, Ken (1935–), American novelist.
Kingsley, Charles (1819–75), English novelist.
Kingsley, Sidney (1906–), American playwright.
Kipling, Rudyard (1865–1936), British poet and novelist.
Kleist, Heinrich von (1777–1811), German dramatic poet.
Knowles, John (1926–), American novelist.
Koestler, Arthur (1905–), Hungarian-born English novelist and essayist.
Kopit, Arthur (1937–), American dramatist.
Kyd, Thomas (1558–94), English dramatist.
La Fontaine, Jean de (1621–95), French fabulist and poet.
Lagerkvist, Pär (1891–1974), Swedish novelist.
Lagerlof, Selma (1858–1940), Swedish novelist.
Lamartine, Alphonse (1790–1869), French poet.
Lamb, Charles (1775–1834), English essayist.
Langland, William (c. 1332–c. 1440), English poet.
Lanier, Sidney (1842–81), American poet.
Lardner, Ring (1885–1933), American short story writer.
La Rochefoucauld, François, duc de (1613–80), French classical writer, maximist, and epigrammatist.
Lash, Joseph (1909–), American biographer.
Lawrence, D(avid) H(erbert) (1885–1930), English novelist.
Laxness, Halldor (1902–), Icelandic novelist.
Lear, Edward (1812–88), English humorist.
Leavis, F(rank) R(aymond) (1895–1978), English critic.
Le Carré, John (David J. M. Carnwell) (1931–), English spy novelist.
Lee, Robert E. (1918–), American playwright.
Leopardi, Giacomo (1798–1837), Italian poet.
Lermontov, Mikhail Y. (1814–41), Russian novelist.
Lessing, Doris (1919–), English novelist.
Lessing, Gotthold E. (1729–81), German dramatist.
Lewis, C(live) S(taples) (1898–1963), Anglo-Irish critic, spiritual writer, and novelist.
Lewis, Sinclair (1885–1951), American novelist.
Lewis, Wyndham (1886–1957), English novelist.
Lind, Jakov (1927–), Anglo-Austrian novelist.
Lindsay, Vachel (1879–1931), American poet.
Livy (59 B.C.–17 A.D.), Roman historian.
London, Jack (1876–1916), American novelist.
Longfellow, Henry Wadsworth (1807–82), American poet.
Lope de Vega Carpio, Félix (1562–1635), Spanish poet.
Lord, Walter (1917–), American historical novelist.
Lovelace, Richard (1618–57?), English poet.
Lowell, Amy (1874–1925), American poet and critic.
Lowell, James Russell (1819–91), American poet.
Lowell, Robert (1917–77), American poet and translator.
Lucian (c. 125–after 180), Greek satirist.
Lucretius (c. 99–c. 55 B.C.), Roman poet.
Macaulay, Thomas Babington (1800–59), English historian, essayist, and critic.
McCarthy, Mary (1912–), American novelist and literary critic.
McCullers, Carson (1917–67), American novelist.
Machiavelli, Niccoló (1469–1527), Italian political essayist.
MacLeish, Archibald (1892–), American poet.
McNally, Terrence (1939–), American dramatist.
Maeterlinck, Maurice (1862–1949), Belgian dramatist.
Mailer, Norman (1923–), American novelist and essayist.
Malamud, Bernard (1914–), American novelist.
Mallarmé, Stéphane (1842–98), French poet.
Malory, Sir Thomas (d. 1471), English Arthurian romance writer.
Malraux, André (1901–76), French man of letters.
Mann, Heinrich (1871–1950), German novelist.
Mann, Thomas (1875–1955), German novelist.
Mansfield, Katherine (1888–1923), British short story writer.

Manzoni, Alessandro (1785–1873), Italian novelist.
Marcus, Frank (1928–   ), English dramatist.
Marlowe, Christopher (1564–93), English dramatist.
Marquand, John P. (1893–1960), American novelist.
Marsh, Ngaio (1899–   ), New Zealand detective story writer.
Martial (c. 40–c. 104 A.D.), Roman epigrammatic poet.
Marvell, Andrew (1621–78), English poet.
Masefield, John (1878–1967), English poet.
Massinger, Philip (1583–1640), English dramatist.
Masters, Edgar Lee (1869–1950), American poet and biographer.
Maugham, W(illiam) Somerset (1874–1965), English novelist.
Maupassant, Guy de (1850–93), French novelist and short story writer.
Mauriac, François (1885–1970), French novelist.
Maurois, André (1885–1967), French biographer.
Melville, Herman (1819–91), American novelist.
Menander (c. 342 B.C.–c. 291 B.C.), Greek dramatist.
Mencken, H(enry) L(ouis) (1880–1956), American satirist, editor, critic, and philologist.
Meredith, George (1828–1909), English novelist and poet.
Mérimée, Prosper (1803–70), French novelist, dramatist, and poet.
Michener, James (1907–   ), American novelist.
Millay, Edna St. Vincent (1892–1950), American poet.
Miller, Arthur (1915–   ), American dramatist.
Miller, Henry (1891–1980), American novelist.
Milne, A(lan) A(lexander) (1882–1956), English poet, dramatist, and children's author.
Milton, John (1608–74), English poet.
Mistral, Frédéric (1830–1914), French Provençal poet.
Mistral, Gabriela (1889–1957), Chilean poet.
Molière, Jean Baptiste (Jean Baptiste Poquelin) (1622–73), French dramatist.
Molnar, Ferenc (1878–1952), Hungarian dramatist.
Montaigne, Michel Eyquem de (1533–92), French essayist.
Moore, George (1852–1933), Irish novelist.
Moore, Marianne (1887–1972), American poet.
Moore, Thomas (1779–1852), Irish poet.
Moravia, Alberto (1907–   ), Italian novelist.
More, Sir Thomas (1478–1535), English humanist.
Morison, Samuel Eliot (1887–1976), American historian.
Morley, Christopher (1890–1957), American novelist.
Morris, William (1834–96), English poet.
Murdoch, Iris (1919–   ), British novelist.
Musset, Alfred de (1810–57), French dramatist and poet.
Nabokov, Vladimir (1899–1977), Russian-American novelist.
Neruda, Pablo (1904–73), Chilean poet.
Nerval, Gérard de (Gérard Labrunie) (1808–55), French poet, translator, and short story writer.
Nevins, Allan (1890–1971), American historian.
Norris, Frank (1870–1902), American novelist.
Novalis (Friedrich von Hardenberg) (1772–1801), German poet.
Oates, Joyce Carol (1938–   ), American novelist.
O'Casey, Sean (1884–1964), Irish dramatist.
O'Connor, Flannery (1925–64), American novelist and short story writer.
O'Connor, Frank (Michael O'Donovan) (1903–66), Irish short story writer.
Odets, Clifford (1906–63), American dramatist.
O'Faoláin, Seán (1900–   ), Irish novelist.
O'Flaherty, Liam (1897–   ), Irish novelist.
O'Hara, John (1905–70), American novelist.
Omar Khayyam (fl. 11th cent.), Persian poet.
O'Neill, Eugene (1888–1953), American dramatist.
Orwell, George (Eric Blair) (1903–50), British novelist and essayist.
Osborne, John (1929–   ), English dramatist.
Ovid (43 B.C.–18 A.D.), Latin poet.
Parker, Dorothy (1893–1967), American poet, short story writer, satirist, and critic.
Pasternak, Boris (1890–1960), Russian poet and novelist.
Pater, Walter (1839–94), English essayist and critic.
Paton, Alan (1903–   ), South African novelist.
Pavese, Cesare (1908–50), Italian novelist.
Peacock, Thomas Love (1785–1866), English novelist.
Pepys, Samuel (1633–1703), English diarist.
Perelman, S(idney) J(oseph) (1904–79), American humorist.
Perse, St. John (Alexis St. Léger) (1887–1975), French poet.
Petrarch (1304–74), Italian poet and humanist.
Petronius (d. c. 66 A.D.), Roman satirist.
Peyrefitte, Roger (1907–   ), French novelist.
Pindar (c. 518–438 B.C.), Greek lyric poet.
Pinero, Sir Arthur Wing (1855–1934), English dramatist.

Pinter, Harold (1930–   ), English dramatist.
Pirandello, Luigi (1867–1936), Italian dramatist.
Plath, Sylvia (1932–63), American poet and novelist.
Plautus (c. 254 B.C.–184 B.C.), Roman comic poet.
Plutarch (c. 46–c. 120 A.D.), Greek biographer.
Poe, Edgar Allan (1809–49), American poet, short story writer, and critic.
Pope, Alexander (1688–1744), English poet.
Porter, Katherine Anne (1890–1980), American short story writer and novelist.
Pound, Ezra (1885–1972), American poet and critic.
Powell, Anthony (1905–   ), English novelist.
Priestley, J(ohn) B(oynton) (1894–   ), English novelist, dramatist, and critic.
Pritchett, V(ictor) S(awdon) (1900–   ), English novelist and critic.
Proust, Marcel (1871–1922), French novelist.
Purdy, James (1923–   ), American novelist.
Pushkin, Aleksandr (1799–1837), Russian poet.
Queneau, Raymond (1903–   ), French novelist.
Quintilian (c. 35–95 A.D.), Roman rhetorician.
Rabe, David (1940–   ), American playwright.
Rabelais, François (c. 1490–1553), French satirist.
Racine, Jean (1639–99), French dramatist.
Ransom, John Crowe (1888–1974), American poet and critic.
Rattigan, Terence (1911–77), English dramatist.
Reade, Charles (1814–84), English novelist and dramatist.
Remarque, Erich Maria (1897–1970), German-American novelist.
Rice, Elmer (1892–1967), American dramatist.
Richards, I. A. (1893–1979), British poet and critic.
Richardson, Jack (1935–   ), American dramatist.
Richardson, Samuel (1689–1761), English novelist.
Richler, Mordecai (1931–   ), Canadian novelist.
Richter, Conrad (1890–1968), American novelist.
Rilke, Rainer Maria (1875–1920), German poet.
Rimbaud, Arthur (1854–91), French poet.
Robinson, Edwin Arlington (1869–1935), American poet.
Roethke, Theodore (1908–63), American poet.
Rolland, Romain (1866–1944), French novelist.
Rolvaag, O(le) E(dvart) (1876–1931), Norwegian-American novelist.
Romains, Jules (1885–1972), French novelist.
Ronsard, Pierre de (c. 1524–85), French poet.
Rossetti, Christina (1830–94), English poet.
Rossetti, Dante G. (1828–82), English poet and translator.
Rostand, Edmond (1868–1918), French dramatist and poet.
Roth, Phillip (1933–   ), American novelist.
Ruskin, John (1819–1900), English critic and essayist.
Russell, George ("A.E.") (1867–1935), Irish poet.
Sachs, Nelly (1891–1970), German-born Swedish poet.
Sagan, Françoise (1935–   ), French novelist.
Sainte-Beuve, Charles A. (1804–69), French critic.
Saint-Exupéry, Antoine de (1900–44), French writer.
Saki (Hector H. Munro) (1870–1916), English short story writer.
Salinger, J(erome) D(avid) (1919–   ), American novelist.
Sand, George (Amandine A. L. Dupin, baronne Dudevant) (1804–76), French novelist.
Sandburg, Carl (1878–1967), American poet.
Santayana, George (1863–1952), American philosopher, poet, and essayist.
Sappho (fl. early 6th cent. B.C.), Greek lyric poet.
Saroyan, William (1908–   ), American novelist, dramatist, and short story writer.
Sartre, Jean Paul (1905–80), French philosopher, novelist, and dramatist.
Sayers, Dorothy L. (1893–1957), English novelist.
Schiller, Friedrich von (1759–1805), German dramatist.
Schisgal, Murray (1926–   ), American dramatist.
Schlegel, Friedrich von (1772–1829), German philosopher, critic, and writer.
Schnitzler, Arthur (1862–1931), Austrian dramatist and novelist.
Schwartz, Delmore (1913–66), American poet.
Scott, Sir Walter (1771–1832), Scottish novelist.
Seferis, George (1900–71), Greek poet.
Seneca, Lucius Annaeus (c. 3 B.C.–65 A.D.), Roman dramatist and philosopher.
Senghor, Léopold S. (1906–   ), Senegalese poet, essayist.
Shakespeare, William (1564–1616), English dramatist and poet.
Shange, Ntozake (1948–   ), American dramatist and poet.
Shapiro, Karl (1913–   ), American poet, critic, and editor.
Shaw, George Bernard (1856–1950), Irish dramatist.

Shaw, Irwin (1913–), American novelist.
Shelley, Mary Wollstonecraft (1797–1851), English novelist.
Shelley, Percy Bysshe (1792–1822), English poet.
Shepard, Sam (1943–), American playwright.
Sheridan, Richard Brinsley, (1751–1816), Irish-born dramatist.
Sherwood, Robert E. (1896–1955), American dramatist.
Sholokhov, Mikhail (1905–), Russian novelist.
Sidney, Sir Philip (1554–86), English poet and essayist.
Sienkiewicz, Henryk (1846–1916), Polish novelist.
Sillanpää, Frans E. (1888–1964), Finnish novelist.
Silone, Ignazio (1900–78), Italian novelist.
Simenon, Georges (1903–), Franco-Belgian novelist.
Simon, Neil (1927–), American playwright.
Sinclair, Upton (1878–1968), American novelist.
Singer, Isaac Bashevis (1904–), Polish-born Yiddish American novelist and short story writer.
Sitwell, Dame Edith (1887–1964), English poet and critic.
Sitwell, Sir Osbert (1892–1969), English poet and essayist.
Sitwell, Sacheverell (1897–), English poet and essayist.
Smollett, Tobias (1721–71), Scottish-born novelist.
Snow, C(harles) P(ercy) (1905–80), English critic and novelist.
Solzhenitsyn, Aleksandr I. (1918–), Russian novelist.
Sontag, Susan (1933–), American critic and novelist.
Sophocles (c. 496–406 B.C.), Greek tragic poet.
Southey, Robert (1774–1843), English poet.
Spark, Muriel (1918–), Scottish novelist, short story writer, poet, and biographer.
Spender, Stephen (1909–), English poet.
Spengler, Oswald (1880–1936), German historian.
Spenser, Edmund (1552?–99), English poet.
Spigelgass, Leonard (1908–), American playwright.
Steegmuller, Francis (1906–), American biographer.
Steele, Sir Richard (1672–1729), English essayist.
Stein, Gertrude (1874–1946), American poet, novelist, critic, and autobiographer.
Steinbeck, John (1902–68), American novelist.
Stendhal (Marie Henri Beyle) (1783–1842), French novelist.
Sterne, Laurence (1713–68), English novelist.
Stevens, Wallace (1879–1955), American poet.
Stevenson, Robert Louis (1850–94), Scottish-born English novelist.
Stoker, Bram (1847–1912), Irish-born novelist.
Stone, I. F. (1907–), American journalist and editor.
Stoppard, Tom (1937–), English dramatist.
Strindberg, August (1849–1912), Swedish dramatist.
Styron, William (1925–), American novelist.
Sudermann, Hermann (1857–1928), German dramatist.
Swados, Harvey (1920–1972), American novelist, short story writer, and essayist.
Swift, Jonathan (1667–1745), English satirist, poet, and essayist.
Swinburne, Algernon Charles (1837–1909), English poet.
Symonds, John Addington (1840–93), English cultural historian, critic, and translator.
Symons, Arthur (1865–1945), English poet and critic.
Synge, John Millington (1871–1909), Irish dramatist and poet.
Tacitus (c. 55–c. 117 A.D.), Roman historian.
Tagore, Sir Rabindranath (1861–1941), Indian poet, novelist, and essayist.
Taine, Hippolyte (1828–93), French critic and historian.
Tarkington, Booth (1869–1946), American novelist.
Tasso, Torquato (1544–95), Italian poet.
Tate, Allen (1899–1979), American poet and critic.
Taylor, Samuel (1912–), American playwright.
Teichmann, Howard (1916–), American dramatist.
Tennyson, Alfred (1809–92), English poet.
Thackeray, William Makepeace (1811–63), English novelist.
Theocritus (fl. c. 270 B.C.), Greek poet.
Thomas, Dylan (1914–53), Anglo-Welsh poet.
Thompson, Francis (1859–1907), English poet.
Thoreau, Henry David (1817–62), American essayist.

Thucydides (c. 460–c. 400 B.C.), Greek historian.
Thurber, James (1894–1961), American humorist.
Tolkien, J(ohn) R(onald) R(euel) (1892–1973), English novelist and critic.
Tolstoy, Leo (1828–1910), Russian novelist.
Toynbee, Arnold (1889–1975), English historian.
Traven, B. (Traven Torsvan) (1890–1969), American expatriate novelist.
Trollope, Anthony (1815–82), English novelist.
Trumbo, Dalton (1905–76), American screenwriter.
Turgenev, Ivan (1818–83), Russian novelist.
Tutuola, Amos (1920–), Nigerian writer.
Twain, Mark (Samuel L. Clemens) (1835–1910), American novelist and humorist.
Undset, Sigrid (1882–1949), Norwegian novelist.
Updike, John (1932–), American novelist and poet.
Valéry, Paul (1871–1945), French poet and critic.
van Itallie, Jean-Claude (1936–), Belgian-born American dramatist.
Van Doren, Mark (1894–1972), American poet and critic.
Vergil (70–19 B.C.), Roman poet.
Verne, Jules (1828–1905), French novelist.
Vidal, Gore (1925–), American novelist and critic.
Vigny, Alfred de (1797–1863), French dramatist.
Villon, François (1431–c. 1463), French poet.
Voltaire, François M. A. de (1694–1778), French novelist, dramatist, critic, and poet.
Vonnegut, Kurt, Jr. (1922–), American novelist.
Wain, John (1925–), English poet and novelist.
Waller, Edmund (1606–87), English poet.
Walpole, Horace (1717–97), English man of letters.
Walton, Izaak (1593–1683), English essayist.
Ward, Douglas Turner (1930–), American dramatist.
Warren, Robert Penn (1905–), American novelist, poet, and critic.
Wassermann, Jakob (1873–1934), Austrian novelist.
Waugh, Evelyn (1903–66), English novelist and satirist.
Webster, John (c. 1580–c. 1625), English dramatist.
Webster, Noah (1758–1843), American lexicographer.
Weidman, Jerome (1913–), American novelist.
Weiss, Peter (1916–), German-born Swedish dramatist.
Wells, H(erbert) G(eorge) (1866–1946), English novelist, essayist, and historian.
Werfel, Franz (1890–1945), Austrian novelist.
Wescott, Glenway (1901–), American novelist and critic.
Wesker, Arnold (1932–), English novelist.
West, Nathanael (Nathan Weinstein) (1903–40), American novelist.
Wharton, Edith (1862–1937), American novelist.
White, E(lwyn) B(rooks) (1899–), American essayist.
White, Patrick (1912–), Australian novelist.
Whitman, Walt (1819–92), American poet.
Whittier, John Greenleaf (1807–92), American poet.
Wilbur, Richard (1921–), American poet.
Wilde, Oscar (1854–1900), Irish dramatist.
Wilder, Thornton (1897–1975), American novelist and dramatist.
Williams, Tennessee (1914–), American dramatist.
Williams, William Carlos (1883–1963), American poet.
Wilson, Edmund (1895–1972), American writer and literary critic.
Wolfe, Thomas (1900–38), American novelist.
Woodward, Robert (1943–), American journalist.
Woolf, Virginia (1882–1941), English novelist.
Wordsworth, William (1770–1850), English poet and critic.
Wright, Richard (1908–60), American novelist.
Wyatt, Sir Thomas (1503–42), English poet.
Wylie, Elinor (1885–1928), American poet and novelist.
Xenophon (c. 430–c. 355 B.C.), Greek historian.
Yeats, William Butler (1865–1939), Irish poet.
Yevtushenko, Yevgeny (1933–), Russian poet.
Zola, Emile (1840–1902), French novelist.
Zweig, Stefan (1881–1942), Austrian novelist, poet, and biographer.

NOTABLES OF THE MUSICAL WORLD

Abbado, Claudio (1933–), Italian conductor.
Addinsell, Richard (1904–77), English film composer.
Adler, Kurt (1905–), American opera director.
Ailey, Alvin, Jr. (1931–), American choreographer.
Albanese, Licia (1913–), Italian-American soprano.
Albéniz, Isaac (1860–1909), Spanish pianist and composer.
Amara, Lucine (1927–), American soprano.
Amram, David (1930–), American composer.
Anderson, Marian (1902–), American contralto.

Ansermet, Ernest (1883–1969), Swiss conductor.
Antheil, George (1900–59), American composer.
Antonio (1921–), Spanish dancer.
Arnold, Malcolm (1921–), English composer.
Arpino, Gerald (1928–), American choreographer.
Arrau, Claudio (1903–), Chilean pianist.
Ashton, Sir Frederick (1906–), English choreographer.
Auber, Daniel F. E. (1782–1871), French operatic composer.

Auer, Leopold (1845–1930), Hungarian violinist-teacher.
Auric, Georges (1899–　), French composer.
Babbitt, Milton (1916–　), American composer.
Babin, Victor (1908–　), Russian-American pianist.
Bach, Carl P. E. (1714–88), German composer.
Bach, Johann C. (1735–82), German composer.
Bach, Johann Sebastian (1685–1750), German composer.
Bach, Wilhelm F. (1710–84), German composer.
Bachauer, Gina (1913–76), Greek pianist.
Bachaus, Wilhelm (1884–1969), German pianist.
Badura-Skoda, Paul (1927–　), Austrian pianist.
Baker, Janet (1933–　), British mezzo-soprano.
Balanchine, George (1904–　), American choreographer.
Balfe, Michael (1808–70), Irish operatic composer.
Barber, Samuel (1910–　), American composer.
Barbirolli, Sir John (1899–1970), English conductor.
Barenboim, Daniel (1942–　), Israeli pianist and conductor.
Bartók, Béla (1881–1945), Hungarian composer.
Baryshnikov, Mikhail (1948–　), Russian ballet dancer.
Bastianini, Ettore (1923–67), Italian operatic baritone.
Beecham, Sir Thomas (1879–1961), English conductor.
Beethoven, Ludwig van (1770–1827), German composer.
Bellini, Vincenzo (1801–35), Italian operatic composer.
Bennett, Robert Russell (1894–　), American composer.
Berg, Alban (1885–1935), Austrian composer.
Berganza, Teresa (1935–　), Spanish mezzo-soprano.
Berlin, Irving (1888–　), American popular composer.
Berlioz, Hector (1803–69), French composer.
Berman, Lazar (1930–　), Russian pianist.
Bernstein, Leonard (1918–　), American composer, conductor, and pianist.
Bettis, Valerie (1920–　), American choreographer.
Biggs, E. Power (1906–77), English-American organist.
Bing, Rudolf (1902–　), Austrian-English operatic manager.
Bizet, Georges (1838–75), French composer.
Björling, Jussi (1911–60), Swedish tenor.
Bliss, Sir Arthur (1891–1975), English composer.
Blitzstein, Marc (1905–64), American composer.
Bloch, Ernest (1880–1959), Swiss-American composer.
Boccherini, Luigi (1743–1805), Italian composer.
Boehm, Karl (1894–　), German conductor.
Boito, Arrigo (1842–1918), Italian composer and librettist.
Borkh, Inge (1921–　), German soprano.
Borodin, Aleksandr (1833–87), Russian composer.
Boulanger, Nadia (1887–1979), French pianist.
Boulez, Pierre (1925–　), French composer and conductor.
Boult, Sir Adrian (1889–　), English conductor.
Brahms, Johannes (1833–97), German composer.
Brailowsky, Alexander (1896–1976), Russian pianist.
Bream, Julian (1933–　), English guitarist and lutenist.
Britten, Benjamin (1913–76), English composer.
Browning, John (1933–　), American pianist.
Bruch, Max (1838–1920), German composer.
Bruckner, Anton (1824–96), Austrian composer.
Bülow, Hans von (1830–94), German pianist and conductor.
Bumbry, Grace (1937–　), American mezzo-soprano.
Butler, John (1920–　), American choreographer.
Buxtehude, Dietrich (1637–1707), Swedish composer.
Cage, John (1912–　), American composer.
Caldwell, Sarah (1928–　), American opera conductor.
Callas, Maria (1923–77), Greek-American soprano.
Carreras, José (1946–　), Spanish operatic tenor.
Caruso, Enrico (1873–1921), Italian operatic tenor.
Casadesus, Robert (1899–72), French pianist.
Casals, Pablo (1876–1973), Spanish cellist and conductor.
Chabrier, Alexis E. (1841–94), French composer.
Chaliapin, Feodor (1873–1938), Russian operatic bass.
Charpentier, Gustave (1860–1956), French composer.
Chausson, Ernest (1855–99), French composer.
Chávez, Carlos (1899–1978), Mexican composer.
Cherubini, Luigi (1760–1842), Italian composer.
Chopin, Frédéric (1810–49), Polish composer.
Christoff, Boris (1919–　), Bulgarian bass.
Cimarosa, Domenico (1749–1801), Italian composer.
Cleva, Fausto (1902–　), Italian-American conductor.
Cliburn, Van (1934–　), American pianist.
Clifford, John (1947–　), American dancer.
Copland, Aaron (1900–　), American composer.
Corelli, Arcangelo (1653–1713), Italian composer.
Corelli, Franco (1924–　), Italian dramatic tenor.
Couperin, François (1668–1733), French composer.
Crespin, Régine (1927–　), French dramatic soprano.
Creston, Paul (1906–　), American composer.
Cunningham, Merce (1922?–　), American choreographer.
Curtin, Phyllis (c. 1930–　), American operatic soprano.
Dallapiccola, Luigi (1904–75), Italian pianist and composer.

D'Amboise, Jacques (1934–　), American ballet dancer.
Damrosch, Leopold (1832–85), German conductor.
Damrosch, Walter (1862–1950), German-American conductor and composer.
Danilova, Alexandra (1906–　), Russian ballerina.
Debussy, Claude (1862–1918), French composer.
De Lavallade, Carmen (1931–　), American dancer.
Délibes, Léo (1836–91), French composer.
Delius, Frederick (1862–1934), English composer.
Della Casa, Lisa (1921–　), Swiss lyric soprano.
Dello Joio, Norman (1913–　), American composer.
Del Mar, Norman (1919–　), English conductor.
De Mille, Agnes (1908–　), American choreographer.
Del Monaco, Mario (1915–　), Italian dramatic tenor.
De los Angeles, Victoria (1923–　), Spanish lyric soprano.
Diaghilev, Sergei (1872–1929), Russian ballet impresario.
Di Stefano, Giuseppe (1921–　), Italian lyric tenor.
Dittersdorf, Karl D. von (1739–99), Austrian composer.
Dobbs, Mattiwilda (1925–　), American coloratura soprano.
Dohnanyi, Ernst von (1877–1960), Hungarian composer.
Dolin, Anton (1904–　), English ballet choreographer.
Domingo, Placido (1941–　), Spanish opera tenor.
Donizetti, Gaetano (1797–1848), Italian composer.
Dorati, Antal (1906–　), Hungarian-American conductor.
Dukas, Paul (1865–1935), French composer.
Duncan, Isadora (1878–1927), American dancer.
Dunham, Katherine (1910–　), American choreographer.
Dvorak, Antonin (1841–1904), Czech composer.
Eglevsky, André (1917–77), Russian-born American dancer.
Elgar, Sir Edward (1857–1934), English composer.
Ellington, Duke (1899–1974), American composer.
Elman, Mischa (1891–1967), Russian-American violinist.
Enesco, Georges (1881–1955), Rumanian composer.
Entremont, Philippe (1934–　), French pianist and conductor.
Falla, Manuel de (1876–1946), Spanish composer.
Farrar, Geraldine (1882–1967), American operatic soprano.
Farrell, Eileen (1920–　), American dramatic soprano.
Farrell, Suzanne (1945–　), American ballerina.
Fauré, Gabriel (1845–1924), French composer.
Feuermann, Emanuel (1902–42), Polish-American cellist.
Fiedler, Arthur (1894–1979), American conductor.
Fischer-Dieskau, Dietrich (1925–　), German baritone.
Flagstad, Kirsten (1895–1962), Norwegian soprano.
Flotow, Friedrich von (1812–83), German operatic composer.
Fokine, Michel (1880–1942), Russian-American dancer.
Fonteyn, Dame Margot (1919–　), English ballerina.
Foss, Lukas (1922–　), German-born American composer.
Foster, Stephen (1826–64), American song writer.
Francescatti, Zino (1905–　), French violinist.
Franck, César (1822–90), Belgian-French composer.
Frescobaldi, Girolamo (1583–1643), Italian composer.
Friml, Rudolf (1879–1972), Czech-American composer.
Furtwängler, Wilhelm (1886–1954), German conductor.
Gades, Antonio (1936–　), Spanish dancer.
Galli-Curci, Amelita (1882–1963), Italian-American soprano.
Galway, James (1939–　), Irish flutist.
Garden, Mary (1877–1967), Scottish-American soprano.
Gatti-Casazza, Giulio (1869–1940), Italian opera manager.
Gedda, Nicolai (1925–　), Swedish operatic tenor.
Gershwin, George (1898–1937), American composer.
Gieseking, Walter (1895–1956), German pianist.
Gigli, Beniamino (1890–1957), Italian tenor.
Gilbert, Sir William S. (1836–1911), English librettist.
Gilels, Emil (1916–　), Russian pianist.
Ginastera, Alberto (1916–　), Argentinian composer.
Glazunov, Aleksandr (1865–1936), Russian composer.
Glière, Reinhold (1875–1956), Russian composer.
Glinka, Mikhail (1804–57), Russian composer.
Gluck, Christoph W. von (1714–87), German composer.
Gobbi, Tito (1915–　), Italian operatic baritone.
Godowsky, Leopold (1870–1938), Polish pianist.
Goldmark, Karl (1830–1915), Hungarian composer.
Goldovsky, Boris (1908–　), Russian-American conductor.
Goldsand, Robert (1911–　), Austrian-American pianist.
Golschmann, Vladimir (1893–1972), French-American conductor.
Goossens, Sir Eugene (1893–1962), English conductor.
Gould, Glenn (1932–　), Canadian pianist.
Gould, Morton (1913–　), American conductor.
Gounod, Charles (1818–93), French composer.
Graham, Martha (1893?–　), American choreographer.
Grainger, Percy (1882–1961), Australian-American pianist and composer.
Greco, Jose (1918–　), Italian-born American dancer.
Gretchaninov, Aleksandr (1864–1956), Russian composer.

Grieg, Edvard (1843–1907), Norwegian composer.
Grofé, Ferde (1892–1972), American musician.
Gueden, Hilde (1917–   ), Austrian operatic lyric soprano.
Halévy, Jacques (1799–1862), French operatic composer.
Hammerstein, Oscar, II (1895–1960), American lyricist.
Handel, George Frideric (1685–1759), German composer.
Hanson, Howard (1896–   ), American composer.
Harris, Roy (1898–1979), American composer.
Hart, Lorenz (1895–1943), American lyricist.
Haydée, Marcia (1937–   ), Brazilian ballerina.
Haydn, Franz Joseph (1732–1809), Austrian composer.
Heifetz, Jascha (1901–   ), Russian-American violinist.
Helpmann, Robert (1909–   ), Australian choreographer.
Henze, Hans Werner (1926–   ), German composer.
Herbert, Victor (1859–1924), Irish-American musician.
Hess, Dame Myra (1890–1965), English pianist.
Hindemith, Paul (1895–1963), German-American composer.
Hines, Jerome (1921–   ), American operatic bass.
Hofmann, Joseph (1876–1957), Polish-American pianist.
Holst, Gustav (1874–1934), English composer.
Honegger, Arthur (1892–1955), Swiss-French composer.
Horne, Marilyn (1934–   ), American mezzo-soprano.
Horowitz, Vladimir (1904–   ), Russian-American pianist.
Humperdinck, Engelbert (1854–1921), German composer.
Humphrey, Doris (1895–1958), American choreographer.
Hurok, Sol (1888–1974), Russian-American impresario.
Ibert, Jacques (1890–1962), French composer.
Indy, Vincent d' (1851–1931), French composer.
Ippolitov-Ivanov, Mikhail (1859–1935), Russian composer.
Istomin, Eugene (1925–   ), American pianist.
Iturbi, José (1895–1980), Spanish-American pianist.
Ives, Charles (1874–1954), American composer.
Jamison, Judith (1944–   ), American dancer.
Jeritza, Maria (1887–   ), Austrian-American soprano.
Joffrey, Robert (1930–   ), American ballet director.
Kabalevsky, Dmitri (1904–   ), Russian composer.
Karajan, Herbert von (1908–   ), Austrian conductor.
Kempff, Wilhelm (1895–   ), German pianist.
Kern, Jerome (1885–1945), American popular composer.
Khachaturian, Aram (1903–1978), Russian composer.
Kidd, Michael (1919–   ), American choreographer.
Kiepura, Jan (1902–66), Polish tenor.
Kipnis, Alexander (1891–1978), Russian-American bass.
Kleiber, Erich (1890–1956), Austrian conductor.
Klemperer, Otto (1885–1973), German conductor.
Kodály, Zoltán (1882–1967), Hungarian composer.
Kogan, Leonid (1924–   ), Russian violinist.
Kondrashin, Kyril (1914–   ), Russian conductor.
Kostelanetz, André (1901–80), Russian-American conductor.
Koussevitzky, Serge (1874–1951), Russian-American conductor.
Kreisler, Fritz (1875–1962), Austrian-American violinst.
Krips, Josef (1902–1974), Austrian conductor.
Kubelik, Rafael (1914–   ), Czech conductor and composer.
Kunz, Erich (1909–   ), Austrian singer.
Lalo, Edouard (1823–92), French composer.
Lambert, Constant (1905–51), English composer.
Landowska, Wanda (1877–1959), Polish-French harpsichordist and pianist.
Lehár, Franz (1870–1948), Hungarian composer.
Lehmann, Lilli (1848–1929), German operatic soprano.
Lehmann, Lotte (1888–1976), German-American soprano.
Leinsdorf, Erich (1912–   ), Austrian-American conductor.
Leoncavallo, Ruggiero (1858–1919), Italian composer.
Lerner, Alan Jay (1918–   ), American lyricist.
Lewis, Henry (1932–   ), American conductor.
Lhevinne, Joseph (1874–1944), Russian-American pianist.
Lhevinne, Rosina (1880–1976), Russian-American pianist.
Limón, José (1908–72), Mexican-American choreographer.
Lind, Jenny (1820–87), Swedish soprano.
Liszt, Franz (1811–86), Hungarian composer.
Loewe, Frederick (1904–   ), American composer.
London, George (1920–   ), Canadian bass baritone.
Lorengar, Pilar (1931?–   ), Spanish lyric soprano.
Loring, Eugene (1914–   ), American choreographer.
Lully, Jean B. (1632–87), French operatic composer.
Lympany, Moura (1916–   ), English pianist.
Maazel, Lorin (1930–   ), American conductor.
McBride, Patricia (1942–   ), American ballerina.
McCormack, John (1884–1945), Irish-American tenor.
McCracken, James (1926–   ), American dramatic tenor.
MacDowell, Edward (1861–1908), American composer.
Mahler, Gustav (1860–1911), Austrian composer.
Makarova, Natalia (1940–   ), Russian ballerina.
Markevich, Igor (1912–   ), Russian-Swiss conductor.
Markova, Dame Alicia (1910–   ), English ballerina.

Martinelli, Giovanni (1885–1969), Italian-American tenor.
Martinon, Jean (1910–76), French conductor and composer.
Mascagni, Pietro (1863–1945), Italian operatic composer.
Massenet, Jules (1842–1912), French operatic composer.
Massine, Léonide (1896–1979), Russian-American choreographer.
Mehta, Zubin (1936–   ), Indian conductor.
Melba, Dame Nellie (c. 1859–1931), Australian soprano.
Melchior, Lauritz (1890–1973), Danish heroic tenor.
Mendelssohn, Felix (1809–47), German composer.
Mengelberg, Josef W. (1871–1951), Dutch conductor.
Mennin, Peter (1923–   ), American composer.
Menotti, Gian-Carlo (1911–   ), Italian-American composer.
Menuhin, Yehudi (1916–   ), American violinist.
Merrill, Robert (1919–   ), American operatic baritone.
Merriman, Nan (1920–   ), American mezzo-soprano.
Meyerbeer, Giacomo (1791–1864), German composer.
Milanov, Zinka (1906–   ), Yugoslavian operatic soprano.
Milhaud, Darius (1892–1974), French composer.
Milstein, Nathan (1904–   ), Russian violinist.
Mitchell, Arthur (1934–   ), American ballet dancer.
Mitropoulos, Dimitri (1896–1960), Greek-American conductor.
Moffo, Anna (c. 1935–   ), American soprano.
Moiseiwitsch, Benno (1890–1963), Russian-English pianist.
Moiseyev, Igor (1906–   ), Russian choreographer.
Monteux, Pierre (1875–1964), French-American conductor.
Monteverdi, Claudio (1567–1643), Italian composer.
Moore, Douglas (1893–1969), American operatic composer.
Moore, Grace (1901–47), American soprano.
Morini, Erica (c. 1905–   ), Austrian-American violinist.
Moussorgsky, Modest (1839–81), Russian composer.
Mozart, Wolfgang Amadeus (1756–91), Austrian composer.
Münch, Charles (1891–1968), French conductor.
Münchinger, Karl (1915–   ), German conductor.
Munsel, Patrice (1925–   ), American operatic soprano.
Muti, Riccardo (1941–   ), Italian conductor.
Muzio, Claudia (1889–1936), Italian operatic soprano.
Neway, Patricia (c. 1923–   ), American soprano.
Nicolai, Otto (1810–49), German composer.
Nielsen, Carl (1865–1931), Danish composer.
Nijinsky, Vaslav (1890–1950), Russian ballet dancer.
Nikolais, Alwin (1912–   ), American dancer.
Nilsson, Birgit (1918–   ), Swedish dramatic soprano.
Novaes, Guiomar (1895–1979), Brazilian pianist.
Nureyev, Rudolf (1938–   ), Russian ballet dancer.
Offenbach, Jacques (1819–80), French composer.
Oistrakh, David (1908–74), Russian violinist.
Olivero, Magda (1913–   ), Italian operatic soprano.
Orff, Carl (1895–   ), German composer.
Ormandy, Eugene (1899–   ), Hungarian-born American conductor.
Ozawa, Seiji (1935–   ), Japanese conductor.
Paderewski, Ignace J. (1860–1941), Polish pianist and composer.
Paganini, Niccolò (1782–1840), Italian violinist.
Palestrina, Giovanni P. da (c. 1525–94), Italian composer.
Pavarotti, Luciano (1935–   ), Italian opera singer.
Pavlova, Anna (c. 1882–1931), Russian ballerina.
Peerce, Jan (1904–   ), American tenor.
Pergolesi, Giovanni B. (1710–36), Italian composer.
Peters, Roberta (1930–   ), American coloratura soprano.
Petit, Roland (1924–   ), French choreographer and dancer.
Piatigorsky, Gregor (1903–76), Ukrainian-American cellist.
Pinza, Ezio (1892–1957), Italian-American basso.
Piston, Walter (1894–1976), American composer.
Pizzetti, Ildebrando (1880–1968), Italian composer.
Plisetskaya, Maya (1925–   ), Russian ballerina.
Ponchielli, Amilcare (1834–86), Italian composer.
Pons, Lily (1904–76), French-American coloratura soprano.
Ponselle, Rosa (1897–   ), American operatic soprano.
Porter, Cole (1893–1964), American composer and lyricist.
Poulenc, Francis (1899–1963), French composer.
Previn, André (1929–   ), German-American conductor.
Price, Leontyne (1927–   ), American dramatic soprano.
Primrose, William (1904–   ), Scottish-American violist.
Prokofiev, Sergei (1891–1953), Russian composer.
Puccini, Giacomo (1858–1924), Italian operatic composer.
Purcell, Henry (1659–95), English composer and organist.
Queler, Eve (1936–   ), American conductor.
Rabin, Michael (1936–1972), American violinist.
Rachmaninoff, Sergei (1873–1943), Russian composer.
Ravel, Maurice (1875–1937), French composer.
Reiner, Fritz (1888–1963), Hungarian-American conductor.
Reisenberg, Nadia (1905–   ), Russian-American pianist.
Resnik, Regina (1924–   ), American mezzo-soprano.

Respighi, Ottorino (1879–1936), Italian composer.
Reszke, Edouard de (1853–1917), Polish bass.
Reszke, Jan de (1850–1925), Polish tenor.
Ricci, Ruggiero (1918–   ), American violinist.
Richter, Sviatoslav (1914–   ), Russian pianist.
Rimsky-Korsakov, Nikolai (1844–1908), Russian composer.
Robbins, Jerome (1918–   ), American choreographer.
Robeson, Paul (1898–1976), American bass.
Rodgers, Richard (1902–79), American popular composer.
Rodzinski, Artur (1894–1958), Polish-American conductor.
Romberg, Sigmund (1887–1951), Hungarian-American operetta composer.
Rorem, Ned (1923–   ), American composer.
Rose, Leonard (1918–   ), American cellist.
Rosenthal, Moriz (1862–1946), Polish pianist.
Rossini, Gioacchino (1792–1868), Italian composer.
Rostropovitch, Mstislav (1927–   ), Russian cellist.
Roussel, Albert (1869–1937), French composer.
Rózsa, Miklos (1907–   ), Hungarian-American composer.
Rubinstein, Anton (1829–94), Russian pianist and composer.
Rubinstein, Artur (1886–   ), Polish-American pianist.
Rysanek, Leonie (1926–   ), Austrian dramatic soprano.
St. Denis, Ruth (1877?–1968), American dancer.
Saint-Saëns, Camille (1835–1921), French composer.
Sargent, Sir Malcolm (1895–1967), English conductor.
Satie, Erik (1866–1925), French composer.
Scarlatti, Alessandro (c. 1660–1725), Italian composer.
Scarlatti, Domenico (1685–1757), Italian composer.
Scherman, Thomas (1917–79), American conductor.
Schipa, Tito (1889–1965), Italian operatic tenor.
Schippers, Thomas (1930–77), American conductor.
Schmidt-Isserstedt, Hans (1900–1973), German conductor.
Schnabel, Artur (1882–1951), Austrian-American pianist.
Schneider, Alexander (1908–   ), Russian-American violinist.
Schoenberg, Arnold (1874–1951), Austrian composer.
Schubert, Franz (1797–1828), Austrian composer.
Schuller, Gunther (1925–   ), American composer.
Schuman, William (1910–   ), American composer.
Schumann, Clara (1819–96), German pianist and composer.
Schumann, Elisabeth (1885–1952), German soprano.
Schumann, Robert (1810–56), German composer.
Schumann-Heink, Ernestine (1861–1936), Austrian-American contralto.
Schwarzkopf, Elisabeth (1915–   ), German lyric soprano.
Scotti, Antonio (1866–1936), Italian operatic baritone.
Scotto, Renata (1936–   ), Italian soprano.
Scriabin, Aleksandr (1872–1915), Russian composer.
Seefried, Irmgard (1919–   ), German soprano.
Segovia, Andrés (1893–   ), Spanish guitarist.
Serkin, Rudolph (1903–   ), Czech-born American pianist.
Sessions, Roger (1896–   ), American composer.
Shaw, Robert (1916–   ), American choral conductor.
Shawn, Ted (1891–1972), American dancer.
Shostakovich, Dmitri (1906–1975), Russian composer.
Sibelius, Jean (1865–1957), Finnish composer.
Slepi, Cesare (1923–   ), Italian operatic bass.
Sills, Beverly (1929–   ), American coloratura soprano.
Slezak, Leo (1873–1946), Czech tenor.
Smallens, Alexander (1899–1972), Russian-born American conductor.
Smetana, Bedřich (1824–84), Czech composer.
Solomon (1902–   ), English pianist.
Solti, Georg (1912–   ), Hungarian conductor.
Somes, Michael (1917–   ), English ballet dancer.
Sousa, John Philip (1854–1932), American bandmaster and composer.
Sowerby, Leo (1895–1968), American organist.
Spivakovsky, Tossy (1907–   ), Russian-American violinist.
Steber, Eleanor (1916–   ), American operatic soprano.
Steinberg, William (1899–1978), German conductor.
Steiner, Max (1888?–1971), Austrian-American composer.
Stern, Isaac (1920–   ), Russian-born American violinist.
Stevens, Risë (1913–   ), American mezzo-soprano.
Stich-Randall, Teresa (c. 1928–   ), American soprano.

Stokowski, Leopold (1882–1977), English-born American conductor.
Stratas, Teresa (1938–   ), Canadian soprano.
Straus, Oscar (1870–1954), Austrian operetta composer.
Strauss, Johann (1804–49), Austrian composer.
Strauss, Johann, Jr. (1825–99), Austrian composer.
Strauss, Richard (1864–1949), German composer.
Stravinsky, Igor (1882–1971), Russian composer.
Sullivan, Sir Arthur (1842–1900), English composer.
Sutherland, Joan (1926–   ), Australian soprano.
Swarthout, Gladys (1904–69), American mezzo-soprano.
Szell, Georg (1897–1970), Hungarian-born American conductor.
Szigeti, Joseph (1892–1973), Hungarian violinist.
Tagliavini, Ferruccio (1913–   ), Italian lyric tenor.
Tallchief, Maria (1925–   ), American ballerina.
Tauber, Richard (1892–1948), Austrian tenor.
Taylor, Deems (1885–1966), American music critic.
Taylor, Paul (1930–   ), American choreographer.
Tchaikovsky, Piotr Ilich (1840–93), Russian composer.
Tebaldi, Renata (1922–   ), Italian lyric soprano.
Te Kanawa, Kiri (1946–   ), New Zealand mezzo-soprano.
Telemann, Georg P. (1681–1767), German composer.
Tetley, Glen (1926–   ), American choreographer.
Tetrazzini, Luisa (1871–1940), Italian coloratura soprano.
Tharp, Twyla (1941–   ), American choreographer.
Thebom, Blanche (1918–   ), American mezzo-soprano.
Theodorakis, Mikis (1925–   ), Greek composer.
Thomas, Ambroise (1811–96), French operatic composer.
Thomas, John Charles (1891–1960), American baritone.
Thomson, Virgil (1896–   ), American composer and critic.
Tibbett, Lawrence (1896–1960), American baritone.
Toscanini, Arturo (1867–1957), Italian conductor.
Tourel, Jennie (1910–73), Canadian operatic soprano.
Traubel, Helen (1899–1972), American soprano.
Troyanos, Tatiana (1938–   ), American mezzo-soprano.
Tucker, Richard (c. 1914–75), American dramatic tenor.
Tudor, Antony (1909–   ), English choreographer.
Tureck, Rosalyn (1914–   ), American pianist.
Ulanova, Galina (1910–   ), Russian ballerina.
Varèse, Edgard (1885–1965), French-American composer.
Varnay, Astrid (1918–   ), Swedish dramatic soprano.
Vaughan Williams, Ralph (1872–1958), English composer.
Verdi, Guiseppe (1813–1901), Italian composer.
Verrett, Shirley (c. 1933–   ), American mezzo-soprano.
Vickers, Jon (1926–   ), Canadian operatic tenor.
Villa-Lobos, Heitor (1887–1959), Brazilian composer.
Villella, Edward (1936–   ), American ballet dancer.
Vishnevskaya, Galina (1926–   ), Russian soprano.
Vivaldi, Antonio (c. 1675–1741), Italian composer.
von Stade, Frederica (1945–   ), American mezzo-soprano.
Wagner, Richard (1813–83), German composer.
Walter, Bruno (1876–1962), German-American conductor.
Walton, Sir William (1902–   ), English composer.
Warren, Leonard (1911–60), American baritone.
Watts, André (1946–   ), American pianist.
Weber, Carl M. von (1786–1826), German composer.
Webern, Anton von (1883–1945), Austrian composer.
Weidman, Charles (1901–75), American choreographer.
Weill, Kurt (1900–50), German-American composer.
Weingartner, Felix (1863–1942), Austrian conductor.
Weissenberg, Alexis (1929–   ), French pianist.
Welitsch, Ljuba (1913–   ), Bulgarian soprano.
Whiteman, Paul (1890–1967), American jazz conductor.
Wilde, Patricia (1928–   ), Canadian ballerina.
Wilder, Alec (1907–   ), American popular composer.
Wolf, Hugo (1860–1903), Austrian composer of lieder.
Wolf-Ferrari, Ermanno (1876–1948), German-Italian operatic composer.
Wunderlich, Fritz (1930–66), German lyric tenor.
Wuorinen, Charles (1938–   ), American composer.
Youmans, Vincent (1898–1946), American composer.
Youskevitch, Igor (1912–   ), Russian ballet dancer.
Zimbalist, Efrem (1889–   ), Russian-American violinist.
Zukerman, Pinchas (1948–   ), Israeli-American violinist.

FILM DIRECTORS

FRANCE

Allégret, Yves (1907–   ): *The Proud and the Beautiful, Oasis, Germinal.*

Becker, Jacques (1906–60): *Casque d'Or, Montparnasse 19, The Hole.*

Bresson, Robert (1901–   ): *Les Dames du Bois de Boulogne, Pickpocket, The Trial of Joan of Arc.*

Camus, Marcel (1912–   ): *Black Orpheus, Le Chant du Monde.*

Carné, Marcel (1909–   ): *Quai des Brumes, Les Enfants du Paradis, Terrain Vague.*

Cayatte, André (1909–   ): *Avant de Déluge, Le Passage du Rhin, La Vie Conjugale, La Raison d'état.*

Chabrol, Claude (1930–   ): *Les Cousins, A Double Tour, Landru, Une Partie de plaisir, Violette Nozière.*

Christian-Jaque (1904–   ): *La Chartreuse de Parme, Fanfan la Tulipe.*

Clair, René (1898–   ): *Sous les Toits de Paris, A Nous la Liberté, And Then There Were None.*

Clément, René (1913–   ): *Forbidden Games, Gervaise, Is Paris Burning?*

Clouzot, Henri-Georges (1907–77): *The Wages of Fear, Diabolique, La Vérité.*

Cocteau, Jean (1889–1963): *The Blood of a Poet, Beauty and the Beast, Orpheus.*

De Broca, Philippe (1933–   ): *Cartouche, That Man from Rio, King of Hearts.*

Delannoy, Jean (1908–   ): *La Symphonie Pastorale, La Princesse de Clèves.*

Demy, Jacques (1931–   ): *Lola, The Umbrellas of Cherbourg.*

Duvivier, Julien (1896–1967): *Poil de Carotte, Un Carnet de Bal, The Little World of Don Camillo.*

Godard, Jean-Luc (1930–   ): *Breathless, La Chinoise, Weekend.*

Guitry, Sacha (1885–1957): *La Poison, Désiré, Assassins et Voleurs.*

Malle, Louis (1932–   ): *Les Amants; Viva Maria!; Le Voleur; Lacombe, Lucien, Pretty Baby.*

Marker, Chris (1921–   ): *Cuba Si!, Joli Mai.*

Melville, Jean-Pierre (1917–73): *Les Enfants Terribles, Le Doulos.*

Ophuls, Max (1902–57): *La Ronde, Madame De, Lola Montès.*

Pagnol, Marcel (1895–1974): *César, Angèle, Topaze.*

Renoir, Jean (1894–1979): *The Crime of M. Lange, La Grande Illusion, The Diary of a Chambermaid.*

Resnais, Alain (1922–   ): *Hiroshima, Mon Amour; Last Year at Marienbad; La Guerre Est Finie; Providence.*

Tati, Jacques (1908–   ): *Jour de Fête, Mr. Hulot's Holiday, Mon Oncle. Traffic.*

Truffaut, François (1932–   ): *The 400 Blows, Stolen Kisses, Bed and Board, Jules et Jim, The Wild Child, Day for Night, The Story of Adele H., Small Change.*

Vadim, Roger (1928–   ): *And God Created Woman, Les Liaisons Dangereuses, Barbarella.*

Varda, Agnes (1928–   ): *Cléo from 5 to 7, Le Bonheur.*

Vigo, Jean (1905–34): *Zéro de Conduite, L'Atalante.*

GERMANY

Fassbinder, Rainer W. (1946–   ): *Fox and His Friends, Mother Küsters Goes to Heaven, The Marriage of Maria Braun.*

Harlan, Veit (1899–1964): *Kreutzer Sonata, Jew Süss.*

Herzog, Werner (1942–   ): *Aguirre: the Wrath of God, The Mystery of Kaspar Hauser, Stroszek, Woyzeck.*

Käutner, Helmut (1908–   ): *The Captain from Kopenick, The Wonderful Years, The Redhead.*

Murnau, Friedrich W. (1899–1931): *Nosferatu, Faust, Sunrise.*

Pabst, Georg W. (1885–1967): *The Joyless Street, Kameradschaft, The Threepenny Opera.*

Riefenstahl, Leni (1902–   ): *Triumph of the Will, Olympiad 1936.*

GREAT BRITAIN

Anderson, Michael (1920–   ): *The Naked Edge, The Quiller Memorandum.*

Asquith, Anthony (1902–68): *The Importance of Being Earnest, The Net, The Yellow Rolls-Royce.*

Clayton, Jack (1921–   ): *Room at the Top, The Innocents, The Great Gatsby.*

Cornelius, Henry (1913–58): *Passport to Pimlico; Genevieve; I Am a Camera.*

Crichton, Charles (1910–   ): *The Lavender Hill Mob, Battle of the Sexes, The Third Secret.*

Hamer, Robert (1911–63): *Kind Hearts and Coronets, The Scapegoat, School for Scoundrels.*

Lean, David (1908–   ): *Great Expectations, The Bridge on the River Kwai, Lawrence of Arabia, Dr. Zhivago, Ryan's Daughter.*

Lester, Richard (1932–   ): *A Hard Day's Night, Help! Mackendrick, Alexander* (1912–   ): *The Man in the White Suit, The Ladykillers, The Sweet Smell of Success.*

Olivier, Sir Laurence (1907–   ): *Henry V, Hamlet, Richard III, Othello.*

Powell, Michael (1905–   ): *One of Our Aircraft Is Missing, The Red Shoes, Tales of Hoffmann.*

Reed, Sir Carol (1906–76): *Odd Man Out, The Third Man, Oliver!*

Reisz, Karel (1926–   ): *Saturday Night and Sunday Morning, Morgan, Isadora, The Gambler.*

Richardson, Tony (1928–   ): *Look Back in Anger, The Entertainer, A Taste of Honey, Tom Jones.*

Schlesinger, John (1926–   ): *A Kind of Loving, Billy Liar, Darling, Midnight Cowboy, Sunday, Bloody Sunday.*

ITALY

Antonioni, Michelangelo (1912–   ): *L'Avventura, La Notte, Red Desert, Blow-Up, Zabriskie Point.*

Camerini, Mario (1895–   ): *I Promessi Sposi, Wife for a Night.*

Comencini, Luigi (1916–   ): *The Mill on the Po; Bread, Love, and Dreams; Mariti in Citta.*

De Santis, Giuseppe (1917–   ): *Bitter Rice, Rome Eleven O'Clock, Anna.*

De Sica, Vittorio (1902–74): *The Bicycle Thief, Umberto D, Two Women.*

Fellini, Federico (1920–   ): *La Strada, Nights of Cabiria, La Dolce Vita, 8½, Fellini Satyricon, Amarcord.*

Germi, Pietro (1914–74): *Divorce, Italian Style; Seduced and Abandoned.*

Monicelli, Mario (1915–   ): *The Organizer, Casanova 70.*

Pasolini, Pier Paolo (1922–75): *Accattone, Mamma Roma, The Gospel According to St. Matthew, Salo.*

Pontecorvo, Gillo (1919–   ): *Kapo, The Battle of Algiers.*

Rossellini, Roberto (1906–77): *Open City, Stromboli, Il Generale Della Rovere, The Rise of Louis XIV.*

Visconti, Luchino (1906–76): *Rocco and His Brothers, The Leopard, The Stranger, The Damned, Death in Venice, The Innocent.*

Wertmuller, Lina (1929–   ): *Swept Away, All Screwed Up, Seven Beauties.*

Zampa, Luigi (1905–   ): *City on Trial, The Woman of Rome.*

Zeffirelli, Franco (1922–   ): *The Taming of the Shrew, Romeo and Juliet, The Champ.*

SWEDEN

Bergman, Ingmar (1918–   ): *The Seventh Seal, Wild Strawberries, Virgin Spring, Persona, The Passion of Ànna, The Magic Flute, Face to Face, Cries and Whispers.*

Sjöberg, Alf (1903–   ): *Miss Julie, Barabbas, The Judge.*

Sjöström, Victor (1879–1960): *He Who Gets Slapped, The Scarlet Letter.*

Stiller, Mauritz (1883–1928): *The Story of Gösta Berling, Hotel Imperial, The Street of Sin.*

UNITED STATES

Allen, Woody, (1935–   ), *Annie Hall, Interiors, Manhattan.*

Altman, Robert (1925–   ): *M°A°S°H, Nashville, Buffalo Bill and the Indians, 3 Women, A Wedding.*

Bogdanovich, Peter (1939–   ): *Targets, The Last Picture Show, What's Up Doc?, Saint Jack.*

Brooks, Richard (1912–   ): *The Brothers Karamazov, Cat on a Hot Tin Roof, In Cold Blood, Looking for Mr. Goodbar.*

Capra, Frank (1897–   ): *It Happened One Night, You Can't Take It with You, A Hole in the Head.*

Cassavetes, John (1929–   ): *Shadows, A Child Is Waiting, Faces.*

Chaplin, Charles (1889–1977): *The Gold Rush, City Lights, Modern Times, The Great Dictator, Limelight.*

Coppola, Francis Ford (1939–   ): *The Godfather I & II, The Conversation, Apocalypse Now.*

Cukor, George (1899–   ): *Dinner at Eight, Camille, The Women, A Star Is Born, My Fair Lady.*

Curtiz, Michael (1888–1962): *Casablanca, Mildred Pierce.*

Dassin, Jules (1911–   ): *The Naked City, Rififi, He Who Must Die, Never on Sunday.*

De Mille, Cecil B. (1881–1959): *The King of Kings, Samson and Delilah, The Greatest Show on Earth.*

Donen, Stanley (1924–   ): *Seven Brides for Seven Brothers, Funny Face, Charade, Two for the Road.*

Flaherty, Robert (1884–1951): *Nanook of the North, Moana, Louisiana Story.*

Fleischer, Richard (1916–   ): *20,000 Leagues under the Sea, Compulsion, The Boston Strangler.*

Fleming, Victor (1883–1949): *Captains Courageous, The Wizard of Oz, Gone with the Wind.*

Ford, John (1895–1973): *Stagecoach, The Grapes of Wrath, The Quiet Man, Mogambo.*

Frankenheimer, John (1930–): *Birdman of Alcatraz, The Manchurian Candidate, Grand Prix, Black Sunday.*

Goulding, Edmund (1891–1959): *Grand Hotel, The Razor's Edge, Nightmare Alley.*

Griffith, D. W. (1875–1948): *The Birth of a Nation, Intolerance, Orphans of the Storm.*

Hawks, Howard (1896–1977): *Scarface, Twentieth Century, Bringing Up Baby, The Big Sleep.*

Hitchcock, Alfred (1899–1980): *The 39 Steps, Strangers on a Train, Rear Window, North by Northwest, Family Plot.*

Huston, John (1906–): *The Maltese Falcon, The Treasure of the Sierra Madre, The African Queen.*

Kazan, Elia (1909–): *A Streetcar Named Desire, Viva Zapata!, On the Waterfront, East of Eden.*

King, Henry (1891–): *Stella Dallas, State Fair, The Gunfighter.*

Kramer, Stanley (1913–): *Inherit the Wind, Judgment at Nuremberg, Guess Who's Coming to Dinner?*

Kubrick, Stanley (1928–): *Paths of Glory, Lolita, Dr. Strangelove, 2001, Clockwork Orange, Barry Lyndon.*

Le Roy, Mervyn (1900–): *I Am a Fugitive from a Chain Gang, Quo Vadis, Gypsy.*

Lubitsch, Ernst (1892–1947): *The Love Parade, Design for Living, Angel, Ninotchka.*

Lucas, George (1944–): *American Graffiti, Star Wars.*

Lumet, Sidney (1924–): *Long Day's Journey into Night, The Pawnbroker, The Seagull, Murder on the Orient Express, Network, Equus, The Wiz.*

McCarey, Leo (1898–1969): *The Awful Truth, Going My Way, An Affair to Remember.*

Mankiewicz, Joseph L. (1909–): *All About Eve, Julius Caesar, Suddenly Last Summer, Cleopatra.*

Milestone, Lewis (1895–1980): *All Quiet on the Western Front, Of Mice and Men, A Walk in the Sun.*

Nichols, Mike (1931–): *Who's Afraid of Virginia Woolf?, The Graduate, Catch 22, Carnal Knowledge.*

Peckinpah, Sam (1925–): *The Wild Bunch, Straw Dogs, Junior Bonner.*

Penn, Arthur (1922–): *The Miracle Worker, Mickey One, Bonnie and Clyde, Alice's Restaurant.*

Perry, Frank (1930–): *David and Lisa, Diary of a Mad Housewife, Last Summer.*

Preminger, Otto (1906–): *Laura, The Moon Is Blue, The Man with the Golden Arm, Anatomy of a Murder.*

Ray, Nicholas (1911–79): *Knock on Any Door, Rebel without a Cause, Johnny Guitar, In a Lonely Place.*

Ritt, Martin (1920–): *Edge of the City; The Long, Hot Summer; Hud; The Brotherhood; Sounder; The Front, Norma Rae.*

Rossen, Robert (1908–66): *Body and Soul, All the King's Men, The Hustler.*

Scorsese, Martin (1942–): *Mean Streets, Alice Doesn't Live Here Anymore, Taxi Driver, New York, New York, The Last Waltz.*

Silverstein, Elliot (1927–): *Cat Ballou, The Happening, A Man Called Horse.*

Siodmak, Robert (1900–73): *The Spiral Staircase, The Dark Mirror, The Killers.*

Spielberg, Steven (1947–): *The Sugarland Express, Jaws, Close Encounters of the Third Kind, 1941.*

Sternberg, Josef von (1894–1969): *The Blue Angel, Morocco, Shanghai Express.*

Stevens, George (1904–75): *A Place in the Sun, Shane, Giant, The Diary of Anne Frank.*

Stroheim, Erich von (1885–1957): *Merry Go Round, Greed, The Merry Widow.*

Sturges, Preston (1898–1959): *The Great McGinty, Sullivan's Travels, Hail the Conquering Hero.*

Vidor, King (1894–): *The Big Parade, Northwest Passage, Duel in the Sun, War and Peace.*

Walsh, Raoul (1892–): *Thief of Bagdad, They Drive by Night, The Naked and the Dead.*

Warhol, Andy (1927?–): *Chelsea Girls, Lonesome Cowboys, Blue Movie.*

Welles, Orson (1915–): *Citizen Kane, The Magnificent Ambersons, Touch of Evil, The Trial.*

Wellman, William (1896–1975): *Nothing Sacred, The Story of G. I. Joe, The High and the Mighty.*

Wilder, Billy (1906–): *The Lost Weekend, Sunset Boulevard, Stalag 17, Some Like It Hot.*

Wood, Sam (1883–1949): *A Night at the Opera; A Day at the Races; Goodbye, Mr. Chips; Our Town.*

Wyler, William (1902–): *Wuthering Heights, Mrs. Miniver, The Best Years of Our Lives, Ben Hur.*

Zinnemann, Fred (1907–): *High Noon, From Here to Eternity, The Nun's Story, A Man for All Seasons.*

USSR

Alexandrov, Grigori (1903–): *Jazz Comedy, Circus, Volga Volga.*

Bondarchuk, Sergei (1922–): *Destiny of a Man, War and Peace, The Steppe.*

Chukrai, Grigori (1921–): *The Forty-First, Ballad of a Soldier, Clear Sky.*

Donskoi, Mark (1897–): *The Maxim Gorki Trilogy, The Rainbow.*

Dovzhenko, Alexander (1894–1956): *Arsenal, Earth, Life in Blossom.*

Eisenstein, Sergei (1898–1948): *Potemkin, Alexander Nevsky, Ivan the Terrible.*

Gerasimov, Sergei (1906–): *Young Guard, And Quiet Flows the Don.*

Kalatosow, Mikhail (1903–1973): *The First Echelon, The Cranes Are Flying.*

Pudovkin, Vsevolod (1893–1953): *Mother, Storm over Asia, The Deserter.*

Pyryev, Ivan (1901–68): *The Wealthy Bride, The Idiot.*

Romm, Mikhail (1901–71): *Boule de Suif, Nine Days of One Year.*

OTHER COUNTRIES

Buñuel, Luis (1900–), Spain: *Evil Eden, Nazarin, Viridiana, Belle de Jour, Las Olvidados, Tristana, The Discrete Charm of the Bourgeoisie.*

Cacoyannis, Michael (1922–), Greece: *Stella, Electra, Zorba the Greek.*

Cavalcanti, Alberto (1897–), Brazil: *Dead of Night, Champagne Charlie, Monster.*

Costa-Gavras, Henri (1933–), Greece: *Z, The Confession, Claire de Femme.*

Dreyer, Carl Theodore (1889–1968), Denmark: *Joan of Arc, Vampyr, Day of Wrath, Gertrud.*

Fábri, Zoltán (1917–), Hungary: *Professor Hannibal, Twenty Hours, Late Season.*

Ford, Alexander (1908–), Poland: *The Young Chopin, Kings of the Teutonic Order.*

Forman, Milos (1932–), Czechoslovakia: *Loves of a Blonde, The Fireman's Ball, One Flew Over the Cuckoo's Nest, Hair.*

Ivens, Joris (1898–), Netherlands: *Zuyderzee, Spanish Earth.*

Jancso, Miklos (c. 1922–), Hungary: *The Round Up, The Red and the White.*

Kadar, Jan (1918–79), Czechoslovakia: *The Shop on Main Street, The Angel Levine, Adrift, Lies My Father Told Me.*

Kinugasa, Teinosuke (1898–), Japan: *Gate of Hell, The White Heron.*

Kurosawa, Akira (1910–), Japan: *Rashomon, Seven Samurai, Ikiru, The Lower Depths, Kagemushu.*

Lang, Fritz (1890–1976), Austria: *Metropolis, M, The 1,000 Eyes of Dr. Mabuse.*

Lindtberg, Leopold (1902–), Switzerland: *The Last Chance, Four in a Jeep, The Village.*

McLaren, Norman (1914–), Canada: *Blinkity-Blank; Dots, Loops.*

Menzel, Jiri (1938–), Czechoslovakia: *Closely Watched Trains, Capricious Summer, Those Wonderful Movie Cranks.*

Mizoguchi, Kenji (1898–1956), Japan: *Ugetsu, The Princess Yang, Street of Shame.*

Nemec, Jan (1936–), Czechoslovakia: *Diamonds of the Night, A Report on the Party and the Guests, The Martyrs of Love.*

Polanski, Roman (1933–), Poland: *Knife in the Water, Repulsion, Rosemary's Baby, Chinatown, The Tenant.*

Ray, Satyajit (1921–), India: *The Apu Trilogy, The Music Room, Devi, The Chess Players.*

Saura, Carlos (1932–), Spain: *The Hunt, Cousin Angelica, Cria!*

Teshigahara, Hiroshi (1927–), Japan: *Pitfall, Woman in the Dunes.*

Torre-Nilsson, Leopoldo (1924–78), Argentina: *The House of the Angel, The Hand in the Trap, Summer Skin.*

Wajda, Andrzej (1926–), Poland: *Kanal, Ashes and Diamonds, Fury is a Woman, Man of Marble.*

CELEBRITIES: PAST AND PRESENT

The Almanac celebrity list includes well-known personalities of stage, screen, radio, and television, as well as notables of other popular worlds. Entries indicate the celebrity's birthplace.

Aaron, Hank Mobile, Ala., 1934
Abbott, George Forestville, N.Y. 1887
Abel, Walter St. Paul, Minn., 1898
Abdul-Jabbar, Kareem New York, 1947
Ace, Goodman Kansas City, Mo., 1899
Acuff, Roy Maynardsville, Tenn., 1907
Adams, Don New York City, 1927
Adams, Edie Kingston, Pa., 1929
Adams, Joey New York City, 1911
Adams, Julie Waterloo, Iowa, 1928
Addams, Charles Westfield, N. J., 1912
Addams, Dawn Felixstowe, Eng., 1930
Adderley, Cannonball Tampa, 1928-75
Adjani, Isabelle Paris, 1956
Adler, Larry Baltimore, 1914
Adler, Luther New York City, 1903
Adler, Stella New York City, 1902
Alberghetti, Anna Maria Pesaro, Italy, 1936
Albert, Eddie Rock Island, Ill., 1908
Albertson, Jack Malden, Mass., 1910
Albright, Lola Akron, O., 1925
Alda, Alan New York City, 1936
Alda, Robert New York City, 1914
Alexander, Ben Goldfield, Nev., 1911-69
Alexander, Jane Boston, 1939
Allen, Fred Boston, 1894-1956
Allen, Gracie San Francisco, 1906-64
Allen, Mel Birmingham, Ala., 1913
Allen, Steve New York City, 1921
Allen, Woody New York City, 1935
Alllson, Fran La Porte City, Iowa, 1924?
Allyson, June New York City, 1923
Alpert, Herb Los Angeles, 1935
Ameche, Don Kenosha, Wis., 1908
Ames, Ed Boston, 1929
Ames, Leon Portland, Ind., 1903
Ames, Nancy Washington, D. C., 1937
Amory, Cleveland Nahant, Mass., 1917
Amsterdam, Morey Chicago, 1912
Anderson, Judith Adelaide, Austral., 1898
Anderson, Michael, Jr. London, 1943
Andersson, Bibi Stockholm, 1935
Andersson, Harriet Stockholm, 1932
Andress, Ursula, Berne, Switz., 1936
Andretti, Mario Trieste, 1940
Andrews, Dana Collins, Miss., 1912
Andrews, Julie Walton-on-Thames, Eng., 1935
Andrews, La Verne Minneapolis, 1915-67
Andrews, Maxine Minneapolis, 1918
Andrews, Patty Minneapolis, 1920
Angeli, Pier Sardinia, 1932-71
Anka, Paul Ottawa, Can., 1941
Annabella La Varenne-St. Hilaire, Fr., 1910
Ann-Margret Valsjobyn, Sweden, 1941
Arbuckle, "Fatty" Smith Center, Kans., 1887-1933
Arcaro, Eddie Newport, Ky., 1916
Arden, Elizabeth Ontario, 1891-1966
Arden, Eve Mill Valley, Cal., 1912
Arkin, Alan New York City, 1934
Armstrong, Louis New Orleans, 1900-71
Arnaz, Desi Santiago, Cuba, 1917
Arness, James Minneapolis, 1923
Arno, Peter New York, 1904-68
Arnold, Eddy Henderson, Tenn., 1918
Arnold, Edward New York, 1890-1956
Arquette, Cliff Toledo, O., 1905-74
Arthur, Beatrice New York, 1926
Arthur, Jean New York City, 1908
Ashcroft, Peggy London, 1907
Ashe, Arthur Richmond, Va., 1943
Ashley, Elizabeth Ocala, Fla., 1940
Asner, Edward Kansas City, Kans., 1929
Astaire, Adele Omaha, Neb., 1898
Astaire, Fred Omaha, Neb., 1899
Astor, Mary Quincy, Ill., 1906
Atkins, Chet Luttrell, Tenn., 1924
Attenborough, Richard Cambridge, Eng., 1923
Aumont, Jean-Pierre Paris, 1913
Austin, Tracy Palos Verdes, Cal., 1962
Autry, Gene Tioga, Tex., 1907
Avalon, Frankie Philadelphia, 1940
Avedon, Richard New York City, 1923

Ayres, Lew Minneapolis, 1908
Aznavour, Charles Paris, 1924
Bacall, Lauren New York City, 1924
Baccaloni, Salvatore Rome, 1900-69
Bacharach, Burt Kansas City, Mo., 1929
Backus, Jim Cleveland, 1913
Baer, Max Omaha, 1909-59
Baez, Joan New York City, 1941
Bailey, Mildred Washington, 1903-51
Bailey, Pearl Newport News, Va., 1918
Bainter, Fay Los Angeles, 1893-1963
Baird, Bil Grand Island, Neb., 1904
Baker, Carroll Johnstown, Pa., 1935
Baker, Diane Hollywood, Cal., 1940?
Baker, Josephine St. Louis, 1906-75
Baker, Kenny Monrovia, Cal., 1912
Balenciaga, Cristobal Guetaria, Sp., 1895-1972
Ball, Lucille Jamestown, N. Y., 1911
Ballard, Kaye Cleveland, 1926
Balmain, Pierre St.-Jean-de-Maurienne, Fr., 1914
Balsam, Martin New York City, 1919
Bancroft, Anne New York City, 1931
Bankhead, Tallulah Huntsville, Ala., 1903-68
Bara, Theda Cincinnati, 1890-1955
Barber, Red Columbus, Miss., 1908
Bardot, Brigitte Paris, 1934
Barker, Lex Rye, N. Y., 1919-73
Barnes, Binnie London, 1906
Barrault, Jean-Louis Vesinet, Fr., 1910
Barrie, Wendy London, 1913–78
Barry, Gene New York City, 1921
Barrymore, Diana New York, 1922-60
Barrymore, Ethel Phila., 1879-1959
Barrymore, John Phila., 1882-1942
Barrymore, John Blyth Beverly Hills, Cal., 1932
Barrymore, Lionel Phila. 1878-1954
Barthelmess, Richard New York, 1895-1963
Bartholomew, Freddie London, 1924
Bartok, Eva Budapest, 1926
Basehart, Richard Zanesville, O., 1914
Basie, Count Red Bank, N. J., 1904
Bassey, Shirley Cardiff, Wales, 1937
Bates, Alan Allestree, Eng., 1934
Baxter, Anne Michigan City, Ind., 1923
Baxter, Warner Columbus, O., 1893-1951
Bean, Orson Burlington, Vt., 1928
Beaton, Cecil London, 1904-80
Beatty, Clyde Bainbridge, O., 1905-65
Beatty, Warren Richmond, Va., 1938
Bechet, Sidney New Orleans, 1897-1959
Bee Gees see Gibb
Beene, Geoffrey Haynesville, La., 1927
Beery, Noah Kansas City, Mo., 1883-1946
Beery, Noah, Jr., New York City, 1916
Beery, Wallace Kansas City, Mo., 1886-1949
Begley, Ed Hartford, Conn., 1901-70
Belafonte, Harry New York City, 1927
Belasco, David San Francisco, 1854-1931
Bel Geddes, Barbara New York, 1922
Bel Geddes, Norman Adrian, Mich., 1893-1958
Bellamy, Ralph Chicago, 1904
Belmondo, Jean-Paul Neuilly-sur-Seine, Fr., 1933
Belushi, John Chicago, 1949
Benchley, Robert Worcester, Mass., 1889-1945
Bendix, William New York, 1906-64
Benjamin, Richard New York City, 1939
Bennett, Constance New York, 1914-65
Bennett, Joan Palisades, N. J., 1910
Bennett, Richard Indiana, 1873-1944
Bennett, Tony New York City, 1926
Benny, Jack Waukegan, Ill. 1894-1974
Benzell, Mimi Bridgeport, Conn., 1924-70
Berg, Gertrude New York, 1900-66
Bergen, Candice Beverly Hills, Cal., 1946

Bergen, Edgar Chicago, 1903-78
Bergen, Polly Knoxville, Tenn., 1930
Berger, Senta Vienna, 1941
Bergerac, Jacques Biarritz, Fr., 1927
Bergman, Ingrid Stockholm, 1917
Bergner, Elisabeth Vienna, 1900
Berkeley, Busby Los Angeles, 1895-1976
Berle, Milton New York City, 1908
Berlin, Irving Russia, 1888
Berman, Pandro S. Pittsburgh, 1905
Berman, Shelley Chicago, 1926
Bernardi, Herschel New York City, 1923
Bernhardt, Sarah Paris, 1844-1923
Bernie, Ben Bayonne, N.J., 1893-1943
Berra, Yogi St. Louis, 1925
Bickford, Charles Cambridge, Mass., 1889-1967
Bikel, Theodore Vienna, 1924
Birney, David Washington, 1940
Bishop, Joey New York City, 1918
Bisset, Jacqueline Weybridge, Eng., 1944
Black, Karen Park Ridge, Ill., 1942
Blackman, Honor London, 1929
Blackmer, Sidney Salisbury, N. C., 1898-1973
Blaine, Vivian Newark, N. J., 1924
Blair, Janet Altoona, Pa., 1921
Blair, Linda Westport, Conn., 1959
Blake, Robert Nutley, N.J., 1938
Blakeley, Ronee Idaho, 1946
Blass, Bill Fort Wayne, Ind., 1922
Blocker, Dan Bowie Co., Tex., 1929-72
Blondell, Joan New York City, 1912-79
Bloom, Claire London, 1931
Blue, Ben Montreal, 1901-75
Blue, Vida Mansfield, La., 1949
Blyth, Ann New York City, 1928
Bogarde, Dirk London, 1921
Bogart, Humphrey New York, 1899-1957
Boland, Mary Phila., 1885-1965
Bolger, Ray Dorchester, Mass., 1904
Bombeck, Erma Dayton, Ohio, 1927
Bond, Ward Den er, 1904-60
Bono, Sonny Detroit, 1940
Boone, Pat Jacksonville, Fla., 1934
Boone, Richard Los Angeles, 1917
Booth, Shirley New York City, 1909
Borg, Björn Södertalje, Sweden, 1956
Borge, Victor Copenhagen, 1909
Borgnine, Ernest Hamden, Conn., 1917
Bosley, Tom Chicago, 1927
Bourke-White, Margaret New York City, 1906-71
Bow, Clara New York, 1905-65
Bowes, "Major" San Francisco, 1874-1946
Bowie, David Brixton, Eng., 1947
Bowman, Lee Cincinnati, 1914-79
Boyd, Stephen Belfast, Northern Ireland, 1928-77
Boyd, William Cambridge, O., 1898-1972
Boyer, Charles Figeac Lot, Fr., 1899–1978
Bracken, Eddie New York City, 1920
Bradshaw, Terry Shreveport, La., 1948
Brady, Alice New York, 1892-1939
Brady, Scott New York City, 1924
Brand, Neville Kewanee, Ill., 1921
Brando, Marlon Omaha, Neb., 1924
Brasselle, Keefe Lorain, O., 1923
Brazzi, Rossano Bologna, Italy, 1916
Brel, Jacques Brussels, 1929-78
Brennan, Walter Lynn, Mass., 1894-1974
Brenner, David Philadelphia, 1945
Brent, George Dublin, 1904-79
Brewer, Teresa Toledo, O., 1931
Brice, Fanny New York, 1891-1951
Bridges, Lloyd San Leandro, Cal., 1913
Brinkley, David Wilmington, N. C., 1920
Brisson, Frederick Copenhagen, 1917
Britt, Mai Lidingo, Swed., 1936
Brock, Lou El Dorado, Ark., 1939
Broderick, Helen Phila., 1890-1959
Bronson, Charles Ehrenfeld, Pa., 1922
Brooks, Geraldine New York, 1925-77
Brooks, Mel New York City, 1926
Brothers, Joyce New York City, 1928

Broun, Heywood New York, 1888-1939
Broun, Heywood Hale New York, 1918
Brown, Helen Gurley Portland, Me., 1922
Brown, James Augusta, Ga., 1930?
Brown, Jim Manhasset, N. Y., 1936
Brown, Joe E. Holgate, O., 1892-1973
Brown, Vanessa Vienna, 1928
Brubeck, Dave Concord, Cal., 1920
Bruce, Carol Great Neck, N. Y., 1919
Bruce, Nigel Mexico, 1895-1953
Bruce, Virginia Minneapolis, 1910
Bryant, Anita Barnsdall, Okla., 1940
Brynner, Yul Sakhalin, 1917
Buchanan, Edgar Humansville, Mo., 1903-79
Buchanan, Jack Scotland, 1891-1957
Buchholz, Horst Berlin, 1933
Buchwald, Art Mount Vernon, N. Y., 1925
Buckley, William F. New York City, 1925
Bujold, Genevieve Montreal, 1942
Burke, Billie Washington, D.C., 1884-1970
Burnett, Carol Dallas, 1934
Burns, George New York City, 1896
Burr, Raymond New Westminster, Can., 1917
Burrows, Abe New York City, 1910
Burstyn, Ellen Detroit, Mich., 1932
Burton, Richard Pontrhydyfen, Wales, 1925
Busch, August A., Jr. St. Louis, 1899
Bushman, Francis X. Norfolk, 1883-1966
Butterworth, Charles South Bend, Ind., 1897-1946
Buttons, Red New York City, 1919
Buzzi, Ruth Westerly, R. I., 1936
Byington, Spring, Colorado Springs, 1893-1971
Byrd, Charlie Chuckatuck, Va., 1925
Caan, James New York City, 1939
Cabot, Susan Boston, 1927
Caen, Herb Sacramento, Cal., 1916
Caesar, Irving New York City, 1895
Caesar, Sid Yonkers, N. Y., 1922
Cagney, James New York City, 1904
Cahn, Sammy New York City, 1913
Caine, Michael London, 1933
Caldwell, Zoë Melbourne, Austral., 1933
Calhern, Louis New York, 1895-1956
Calhoun, Rory Los Angeles, 1923
Callan, Michael Philadelphia, 1935
Calloway, Cab Rochester, N. Y., 1907
Cambridge, Godfrey New York, 1933-76
Cameron, Rod Calgary, Can., 1912
Campbell, Glen near Delight, Ark., 1938
Campbell, Mrs. Patrick London, 1865-1940
Cannon, Dyan Tacoma, Wash., 1938?
Canova, Judy Jacksonville, Fla., 1916
Cantinflas Mexico City, 1911
Cantor, Eddie New York, 1892-1964
Cantrell, Lana Sydney, Austral., 1944
Capp, Al New Haven, Conn., 1909-79
Capucine Toulon, Fr., 1935?
Cardin, Pierre near Venice, 1922
Cardinale, Claudia Tunis, 1940
Carew, Rod Gatun, C.Z., 1945
Carey, Macdonald Sioux City, Iowa, 1913
Carlin, George New York City, 1938
Carlisle, Kitty New Orleans, 1914
Carmichael, Hoagy Bloomington, Ind., 1899
Carmines, Al Hampton, Va., 1937
Carne, Judy Northampton, Eng., 1939
Carney, Art Mt. Vernon, N. Y., 1918
Carnovsky, Morris St. Louis, 1897
Caron, Leslie Paris, 1931
Carr, Vikki El Paso, Tex., 1942
Carradine, John New York City, 1906
Carrillo, Leo Los Angeles, 1881-1961
Carroll, Diahann New York City, 1935
Carroll, Leo G. Weedon, Eng., 1892-1972
Carroll, Madeleine West Bromwich, Eng., 1906
Carroll, Nancy New York, 1906-65
Carroll, Pat Shreveport, La., 1927
Carson, Jack Carman, Can., 1910-63
Carson, Johnny Corning, Iowa, 1925
Carter, Billy Plains, Ga., 1937
Carter, Jack New York City, 1923

Cash, Johnny Kingsland, Ark., 1932
Cass, Peggy Boston, 1925
Cassavetes, John New York, 1929
Cassidy, Jack New York City, 1927-76
Cassini, Oleg Paris, 1913
Castle, Irene New Rochelle, N.Y., 1893-1969
Cauthen, Steve Covington, Ky., 1960
Cavett, Dick Gibbon, Neb., 1936
Cerf, Bennett New York City, 1898-1971
Chakiris, George Norwood, O., 1933
Chamberlain, Richard Beverly Hills, Cal., 1935
Chamberlain, Wilt Philadelphia, 1936
Champion, Gower Geneva, Ill., 1920-80
Champion, Marge Hollywood, Cal., 1925
Chancellor, John Chicago, 1927
Chandler, Jeff New York, 1918-61
Chanel, "Coco" Issoire, Fr., 1883-1971
Chaney, Lon Colorado Springs, 1883-1930
Chaney, Lon, Jr. Oklahoma City, 1915-73
Channing, Carol Seattle, 1921
Chaplin, Charles London, 1889—1977
Chaplin, Geraldine Santa Monica, Cal., 1944
Chaplin, Sydney Los Angeles, 1926
Charisse, Cyd Amarillo, Tex., 1923
Charles, Ray Albany, Ga., 1932
Chase, Chevy New York City, 1943
Chase, Ilka New York City, 1905—78
Chatterton, Ruth New York, 1893-1961
Cher El Centro, Cal., 1946
Chevalier, Maurice Paris, 1888-1972
Child, Julia Pasadena, Cal., 1912
Christian, Linda Tampico, Mexico, 1923
Christie, Julie Chukua, India, 1941
Christopher, Jordan Akron, O., 1941
Cilento, Diane Brisbane, Austral., 1933
Claire, Ina Washington, D. C., 1895
Clark, Bobby Springfield, O., 1888-1960
Clark, Dane New York City, 1915
Clark, Dick Mt. Vernon, N. Y., 1929
Clark, Fred Lincoln, Cal., 1914-68
Clark, Petula Ewell, Eng., 1932
Clark, Roy Meherrin, Va., 1933
Clayburgh, Jill New York City, 1944
Clift, Montgomery Omaha, 1920-66
Clooney, Rosemary Maysville, Ky., 1928
Cobb, Irvin S. Paducah, Ky., 1876-1944
Cobb, Lee J. New York City, 1911-76
Coburn, Charles Macon, Ga., 1877-1961
Coburn, James Laurel, Neb., 1928
Coca, Imogene Philadelphia, 1908
Coco, James New York City, 1929
Cohan, George M. Providence, R.I., 1878-1942
Cohen, Myron Grodno, Poland, 1902
Colbert, Claudette Paris, 1905
Colby, Anita Washington, D. C., 1914
Cole, Nat "King" Montgomery, Ala., 1919-65
Coleman, Ornette Fort Worth, Tex., 1930
Collingwood, Charles Three Rivers, Mich., 1917
Collins, Dorothy Windsor, Can., 1926
Collins, Joan London, 1933
Collins, Judy Seattle, 1939
Collyer, "Bud" New York, 1908-69
Colman, Ronald Richmond, Eng., 1891-1959
Colonna, Jerry Boston, 1905
Comaneci, Nadia Onesti, Romania, 1961
Comden, Betty New York City, 1919
Como, Perry Canonsburg, Pa., 1913
Condon, Eddie Goodland, Ind., 1905-73
Conklin, Peggy Dobbs Ferry, N. Y., 1912
Connelly, Marc McKeesport, Pa., 1890
Connery, Sean Edinburgh, 1930
Connolly, Walter Cincinnati, 1887-1940
Connors, Chuck New York City, 1921
Connors, Jimmy St. Louis, 1952
Connors, Mike Fresno, Cal., 1925
Conrad, William Louisville, Ky., 1920
Conried, Hans Baltimore, 1917
Conte, Richard New York City 1914-75
Conway, Tom Russia, 1904-67
Coogan, Jackie Los Angeles, 1914
Cook, Joe Chicago, 1890-1959

Cooke, Alistair Manchester, Eng., 1908
Cooney, Joan Ganz Phoenix, 1929
Cooper, Alice Phoenix, 1948
Cooper, Gary Helena, Mont., 1901-61
Cooper, Gladys Lewisham, Eng., 1888-1971
Cooper, Jackie Los Angeles, 1922
Coote, Robert London, 1909
Corey, Wendell Dracut, Mass., 1914-68
Corio, Ann Hartford, Conn., 1914?
Cornell, Katharine Berlin, 1898-1974
Cosby, Bill Philadelphia, 1937
Cosell, Howard Winston-Salem, N.C., 1920
Costello, Lou Paterson, N.J., 1906-59
Cotten, Joseph Petersburg, Va., 1905
Coulouris, George Manchester, Eng., 1903
Courrèges, André Pau, Fr., 1923
Courtenay, Tom Hull, Eng., 1937
Cousins, Norman Union Hill, N. J., 1912
Cousteau, Jacques Yves St. André-de-Cubzac, Fr., 1910
Cox, Wally Detroit, 1924-73
Crabbe, Buster Oakland, Cal., 1909
Crain, Jeanne Barstow, Cal., 1925
Craven, Frank Boston, 1878-1948
Crawford, Broderick Philadelphia, 1911
Crawford, Joan San Antonio, 1908-77
Cregar, Laird Phila., 1916-44
Crenna, Richard Los Angeles, 1927
Croce, Jim Philadelphia, Pa., 1943-73
Cronkite, Walter St. Joseph, Mo., 1916
Cronyn, Hume London, Can., 1911
Crosby, Bing Tacoma, Wash., 1904-77
Crosby, Bob Spokane, Wash., 1913
Crouse, Russel Findlay, O., 1893-1966
Csonka, Larry Stow, O., 1946
Cugat, Xavier Barcelona, 1900
Cukor, George New York City, 1899
Cullen, Bill Pittsburgh, 1920
Culp, Robert Berkeley, Cal., 1930
Cummings, Robert Joplin, Mo., 1910
Curtis, Tony New York City, 1925
Dahl, Arlene Minneapolis, 1927
Dailey, Dan New York City, 1915-78
Daly, John Johannesburg, South Africa, 1914
Damone, Vic New York City, 1928
Dana, Bill Quincy, Mass., 1924
Dandridge, Dorothy Cleveland, 1924-65
Daniels, Bebe Dallas, 1901-71
Daniels, Billy Jacksonville, Fla., 1914?
Danton, Ray New York City, 1931
Darcel, Denise Paris, 1925
Darin, Bobby New York City, 1936-73
Darnell, Linda Dallas, 1921-65
Darren, James Philadelphia, 1936
Darrieux, Danielle Bordeaux, Fr., 1917
Darwell, Jane Palmyra, Mo., 1880-1967
da Silva, Howard Cleveland, 1909
Dauphin, Claude Corbeil, Fr., 1903-78
Davenport, Harry New York 1866-1949
Davenport, Nigel Cambridge, Eng., 1928
Davidson, John Pittsburgh, Pa., 1941
Davies, Marion New York, 1897-1961
Davis, Bette Lowell, Mass., 1908
Davis, Joan St. Paul, Minn., 1908-61
Davis, Mac Lubbock, Tex., 1942
Davis, Meyer Ellicott City, Md., 1895-1976
Davis, Miles Alton, Ill., 1927
Davis, Ossie Cogdell, Ga., 1921
Davis, Sammy, Jr. New York City, 1925
Day, Dennis New York City, 1917
Day, Doris Cincinnati, 1924
Day, Laraine Roosevelt, Utah, 1920
Dean, Dizzy Lucas, Ark., 1911-74
Dean, James Fairmount, Ind., 1931-55
DeCamp, Rosemary Prescott, Ariz., 1914
De Carlo, Yvonne Vancouver, Can., 1924
Dee, Frances Los Angeles, 1907
Dee, Ruby Cleveland, 1923?
Dee, Sandra Bayonne, N. J., 1942
De Fore, Don Cedar Rapids, Iowa, 1916
De Haven, Gloria Los Angeles, 1925
de Havilland, Olivia Tokyo, 1916
Dekker, Albert New York, 1905-68
De Laurentiis, Dino Torre Annunziata, Italy, 1919
Delon, Alain Sceaux, Fr., 1935
Del Rio, Dolores Durango, Mex., 1905

DeLuise, Dom Brooklyn, N.Y., 1933
Demarest, William St. Paul, 1892
De Mille, Cecil B. Ashfield, Mass., 1881-1959
Dempsey, Jack Manassa, Colo., 1895
Deneuve, Catherine Paris, 1943
De Niro, Robert New York City, 1943
Dennis, Sandy Hastings, Neb., 1937
Denny, Reginald Richmond, Eng., 1891-1967
Denver, John Roswell, N.M., 1943
Derek, Bo Long Beach, Cal., 1956
Dern, Bruce Chicago, 1936
Desmond, Johnny Detroit, 1921
Devine, Andy Flagstaff, Ariz., 1905-77
Dewhurst, Colleen Montreal, 1926
de Wilde, Brandon New York, 1942-72
De Wolfe, Billy Wollaston, Mass. 1907-74
Diamond, Neil Brooklyn, N.Y., 1941
Dickinson, Angie Kulm, N. D., 1931
Dietrich, Marlene Berlin, 1904
Dietz, Howard New York City, 1896
Diller, Phyllis Lima, O., 1917
Dillman, Bradford San Francisco, 1930
Di Maggio, Joe San Francisco, 1914
Dior, Christian Granville, Fr., 1905-57
Disney, Walt Chicago, 1901-66
Dixon, Jeane Medford, Wis., 1918
Dolly, Jenny Hungary, 1892-1941
Dolly, Rosie Hungary, 1892-1970
Donahue, Phil Cleveland, 1935
Donahue, Troy New York City, 1937
Donat, Robert Manchester, Eng., 1905-59
Donlevy, Brian Portadown, Ire., 1899-1972
Donovan (Leitch) Glasgow, 1946
Dors, Diana Swindon, Eng., 1931
Dorsey, Jimmy Mahonoy Plane, Pa., 1904-57
Dorsey, Tommy Mahonoy Plane, Pa., 1905-56
Douglas, Kirk Amsterdam, N. Y., 1918?
Douglas, Melvyn Macon, Ga., 1901
Douglas, Michael New Brunswick, N.J., 1944
Douglas, Mike Chicago, 1925
Douglas, Paul Phila., 1907-59
Downs, Hugh Akron, O., 1921
Drake, Alfred New York City, 1914
Drake, Betsy Paris, 1923
Draper, Paul Florence, Italy, 1909
Draper, Ruth New York, 1884-1956
Dressler, Marie Canada, 1869-1933
Dreyfuss, Richard New York City, 1947
Dru, Joanne Logan, W. Va., 1923
Duchin, Eddy Boston, 1909-51
Duchin, Peter New York City, 1937
Duff, Howard Bremerton, Wash., 1917
Duke, Doris New York City, 1912
Duke, Patty New York City, 1946
Dullea, Keir Cleveland, 1939
Dunaway, Faye Tallahassee, Fla., 1941
Duncan, Sandy Henderson, Tex., 1946
Dunn, James New York, 1906-67
Dunne, Irene Louisville, Ky., 1904
Dunnock, Mildred Baltimore, 1906
Durante, Jimmy New York, 1893-1980
Durbin, Deanna Winnipeg, Can., 1922
Durocher, Leo West Springfield, Mass., 1906
Duryea, Dan White Plains, N.Y., 1907-68
Duse, Eleanora Italy, 1858-1924
Duvall, Robert San Diego, Cal., 1931
Dylan, Bob Duluth, Minn., 1941
Eagels, Jeanne Kansas City, Mo., 1894-1929
Eastwood, Clint San Francisco, 1933
Ebsen, Buddy Orlando, Fla., 1908
Eddy, Nelson Providence, R.I., 1901-67
Eden, Barbara San Francisco, 1936
Edwards, Ralph Merino, Colo., 1913
Edwards, Vince New York City, 1928
Egan, Richard San Francisco, 1923
Eggar, Samantha London, 1940
Ekberg, Anita Malmö, Swed., 1931
Eldridge, Florence New York City, 1901
Elliot, Cass Arlington, Va., 1943?-74
Elliott, Bob Boston, 1923
Elliott, Maxine Rockland, Me., 1868-1940

Emerson, Faye Elizabeth, N. J., 1917
Erickson, Leif Alameda, Cal., 1914
Erving, Julius Roosevelt, N.Y., 1950
Erwin, Stuart Squaw Valley, Cal., 1903-67
Esposito, Phil Sault Ste. Marie, Ont., 1942
Evans, Bergen Franklin, O., 1904-78
Evans, Dale Uvalde, Tex., 1912
Evans, Madge New York City, 1909
Evans, Maurice Dorchester, Eng., 1901
Evert-Lloyd, Chris Fort Lauderdale, Fla., 1954
Ewell, Tom Owensboro, Ky., 1909
Fabray, Nanette San Diego, Cal., 1920
Fadiman, Clifton New York City, 1904
Fairbanks, Douglas Denver, 1883-1939
Fairbanks, Douglas, Jr. New York, 1909
Faith, Percy Toronto, 1908-76
Falk, Peter New York City, 1927
Farber, Barry Baltimore, 1930
Farrell, Glenda Enid, Okla., 1904-71
Farrow, Mia Los Angeles, 1945
Faulk, John Henry Austin, Tex., 1913
Fawcett, Farrah Corpus Christi, Tex., 1947
Fay, Frank San Francisco, 1897-1961
Faye, Alice New York City, 1915
Feiffer, Jules New York City, 1929
Feldman, Marty London, 1933
Feldon, Barbara Pittsburgh, 1939
Feliciano, José Larez, P. R., 1945
Feller, Bob Van Meter, Iowa, 1918
Ferguson, Maynard Verdun, Can., 1928
Fernandel Marseilles, 1903-71
Ferrer, José Santurce, P. R., 1912
Ferrer, Mel Elberon, N. J., 1917
Field, Betty Boston, 1918-73
Field, Sally Pasadena, Cal., 1946
Fields, Dorothy Allenhurst, N. J., 1905
Fields, Gracie Rochdale, Eng., 1898-1979
Fields, Totie Hartford, Conn., 1931-78
Fields, W. C. Phila., 1879-1946
Finch, Peter London, 1916-77
Finney, Albert Salford, Eng., 1936
Fischer, Bobby Chicago, 1943
Fisher, Carrie Beverly Hills, 1956
Fisher, Eddie Philadelphia, 1928
Fitzgerald, Barry Dublin, 1888-1961
Fitzgerald, Ella Newport News, Va., 1918
Fitzgerald, Geraldine Dublin, 1914
Flack, Roberta Black Mountain, N. C., 1940
Fleming, Rhonda Los Angeles, 1923
Fletcher, Louise Birmingham, Ala., 1934
Flynn, Errol Tasmania, 1909-59
Foch, Nina Leyden, Neth., 1924
Fonda, Henry Grand Island, Neb., 1905
Fonda, Jane New York City, 1937
Fonda, Peter New York City, 1939
Fontaine, Frank Haverhill, Mass., 1920-78
Fontaine, Joan Tokyo, 1917
Fontanne, Lynn Woodford, Eng., 1887?
Ford, Glenn Quebec, 1916
Ford, Tennessee Ernie Bristol, Tenn., 1919
Forsythe, John Penns Grove, N. J., 1918
Fosse, Bob Chicago, 1927
Foster, Jodie Los Angeles, 1962
Foxx, Redd St. Louis, 1922
Foy, Eddie, Jr. New Rochelle, N.Y., 1910
Frampton, Peter Beckenham, Eng., 1950
Franciosa, Anthony New York City, 1928
Francis, Arlene Boston, 1908
Francis, Connie Newark, N. J., 1938
Francis, Kay Oklahoma City, 1905-68
Franklin, Aretha Memphis, Tenn., 1942
Frazier, Walt Atlanta, 1945
Freberg, Stan Pasadena, Cal., 1926
Freed, Arthur Charleston, S. C., 1894
Friedan, Betty Peoria, Ill., 1921
Friendly, Fred W. New York City, 1915
Fröbe, Gert Planitz, Ger., 1913
Froman, Jane St. Louis, 1908-80
Frost, David Tenterden, Eng., 1939
Funt, Allen New York City, 1914
Furness, Betty New York City, 1916
Gabel, Martin Philadelphia, 1912
Gable, Clark Cadiz, O., 1901-60
Gabor, Eva Budapest, 1926?

Gabor, Zsa Zsa Budapest, 1923?
Gallico, Paul New York City, 1897-1976
Gam, Rita Pittsburgh, 1928
Garagiola, Joe St. Louis, 1926
Garbo, Greta Stockholm, 1906
Gardiner, Reginald Wimbledon, Eng., 1903-80
Gardner, Ava Smithfield, N. C., 1922
Garfield, John New York, 1913-52
Garfunkel, Arthur New York City, 1941
Gargan, William New York City, 1905-79
Garland, Judy Grand Rapids, Minn., 1922-69
Garner, Erroll Pittsburgh, 1921-77
Garner, James Norman, Okla., 1928
Garner, Peggy Ann Canton, O., 1932
Garroway, Dave Schenectady, N.Y., 1913
Garson, Greer County Down, Northern Ireland, 1908
Gassman, Vittorio Genoa, Italy, 1922
Gavin, John Los Angeles, 1928
Gaxton, William San Francisco, 1893-1963
Gaynor, Janet Philadelphia, 1906
Gaynor, Mitzi Chicago, 1931
Gazzara, Ben New York City, 1930
Geer, Will Frankfort, Ind., 1902-78
Gehrig, Lou New York, 1903-41
Genn, Leo London, 1905-78
Gentry, Bobbie Chickasaw Co., Miss., 1944
George, Gladys Patten, Me., 1904-54
George, Grace New York, 1879-1961
Gere, Richard Philadelphia, 1950
Gernreich, Rudi Vienna, 1922
Gershwin, George New York, 1898-1937
Gershwin, Ira New York City, 1896
Gerulaitis, Vitas Brooklyn, 1954
Getty, J. Paul Minneapolis, 1892-1976
Getz, Stan Philadelphia, 1927
Ghostley, Alice Eve, Mo., 1926
Giannini, Giancarlo La Spezia, Italy, 1942
Gibb, Barry Manchester, Eng., 1946
Gibb, Maurice Manchester, Eng., 1949
Gibb, Robin Manchester, Eng., 1949
Gibbs, Georgia Worcester, Mass., 1923?
Gielgud, John London, 1904
Gilbert, Billy Louisville, Ky., 1894-1971
Gilbert, John Logan, Utah, 1895-1936
Gilford, Jack New York City, 1913?
Gillespie, Dizzy Cheraw, N. C., 1917
Gingold, Hermione London, 1897
Gish, Dorothy Massillon, O., 1898-1968
Gish, Lillian Springfield, O , 1899
Givenchy, Hubert Beauvais, Fr., 1927
Gleason, Jackie New York City, 1916
Gleason, James New York, 1886-1959
Gobel, George Chicago, 1920
Goddard, Paulette Great Neck, N. Y., 1911
Godfrey, Arthur New York City, 1903
Goldberg, Rube San Francisco, 1883-1970
Golden, Harry New York City, 1902
Goldwyn, Samuel Warsaw, 1882-1974
Gonzales, Pancho Los Angeles, 1928
Goodman, Benny Chicago, 1909
Goodman, Dody Columbus, O., 1929
Goodson, Mark Sacramento, Cal., 1915
Goolagong, Evonne Barellan, Australia, 1951
Gordon, Ruth Wollaston, Mass., 1896
Goren, Charles Philadelphia, 1901
Goring, Marius Isle of Wight, 1912
Gormé, Eydie New York City, 1932
Gould, Chester Pawnee, Okla., 1900
Gould, Elliott New York City, 1939
Goulding, Ray Lowell, Mass., 1922
Goulet, Robert Lawrence, Mass., 1933
Grable, Betty St. Louis, 1916-73
Graham, Sheilah London, 1905?
Graham, Virginia Chicago, 1912
Grahame, Gloria Los Angeles, 1929
Granger, Farley San José, Cal., 1925
Granger, Stewart London, 1913
Grant, Cary Bristol, Eng., 1904
Grant, Lee New York City, 1927
Gray, Barry Red Lion, N. J., 1916
Gray, Dolores Chicago, 1930
Grayson, Kathryn Winston-Salem, N.C., 1923

Graziano, Rocky New York City, 1922
Greco, Buddy Philadelphia, 1926
Green, Adolph New York City, 1915
Green, Johnny New York City, 1908
Green, Martyn London, 1899-1975
Greene, Lorne Ottawa, 1915
Greene, Richard Plymouth, Eng., 1918
Greenstreet, Sydney Sandwich, Eng., 1879-1954
Greenwood, Joan London, 1921
Greer, Jane Washington, D. C., 1924
Gregory, Dick St. Louis, 1932
Grey, Joel Cleveland, 1932
Griffin, Merv San Mateo, Cal., 1925
Griffith, Andy Mt. Airy, N. C., 1926
Griffith, Hugh Anglesey, Wales, 1912-80
Grimes, Tammy Lynn, Mass., 1934
Grizzard, George Roanoke Rapids, N. C., 1928
Guardino, Harry New York City, 1925
Guidry, Ron Lafayette, La., 1950
Guinness, Alec London, 1914
Gunn, Moses St. Louis, 1930?
Guthrie, Arlo New York City, 1947
Guthrie, Tyrone Tunbridge Wells, Eng., 1900-71
Guthrie, Woody Okemah, Okla., 1912-67
Gwenn, Edmund London, 1875-1959
Hackett, Buddy New York City, 1924
Hackman, Gene Danville, Ill., 1931
Hagen, Uta Göttingen, Ger., 1919
Hagman, Larry Weatherford, Tex., 1931
Hailey, Arthur Luton, Eng., 1920
Hale, Barbara De Kalb, Ill., 1922
Haley, Jack Boston, 1901-79
Hall, Gus Virginia, Minn., 1910
Hall, Juanita Keyport, N.J., 1901-68
Hall, Monty Winnipeg, Canada, 1923
Halston (Roy Halston Frowick) Des Moines, 1932
Hamill, Dorothy Riverside, Conn., 1956
Hamilton, George Memphis, Tenn., 1939
Hamilton, Margaret Cleveland, 1902
Hamlisch, Marvin New York, 1944
Hampden, Walter New York, 1879-1955
Hampton, Lionel Louisville, Ky., 1913
Handy, W. C. Florence, Ala., 1873-1958
Harburg, E. Y. New York City, 1896
Harding, Ann San Antonio, Tex., 1902
Hardwicke, Cedric Lye, Eng., 1893-1964
Hardy, Oliver Atlanta, 1892-1957
Harlow, Jean Kansas City, Mo., 1911-37
Harmon, Tom Rensselaer, Ind., 1919
Harper, Valerie Suffern, N.Y., 1940
Harrington, Michael St. Louis, 1928
Harris, Barbara Evanston, Ill., 1935
Harris, Jed Vienna, 1900-79
Harris, Julie Grosse Pointe, Mich., 1925
Harris, Phil Linton, Ind., 1906
Harris, Richard Limerick, Ireland, 1933
Harris, Rosemary Ashby, Eng., 1930
Harrison, George Liverpool, Eng., 1943
Harrison, Noel London, 1936
Harrison, Rex Huyton, Eng., 1908
Harry, Deborah Hawthorne, N.J., 1945
Hartford, Huntington New York, 1911
Hartman, David Pawtucket, R.I., 1935
Hartman, Elizabeth Youngstown, O., 1941
Hartman, Paul San Francisco, 1910-73
Harvey, Laurence Yonishkis, Lith., 1928-73
Hasso, Signë Stockholm, 1918
Hatfield, Hurd New York City, 1920
Haver, June Rock Island, Ill., 1926
Havoc, June Vancouver, Can., 1916
Hawkins, Jack London, 1910-73
Hawn, Goldie Washington, D. C., 1945
Haworth, Jill Sussex, Eng., 1945
Hayakawa, Sessue Chiba Prov., Japan, 1890-1973
Hayden, Melissa Toronto, 1928
Hayden, Sterling Montclair, N.J., 1916
Hayden, Tom Royal Oak, Mich., 1940
Hayes, "Gabby" Wellsville, N.Y., 1885-1969
Hayes, Helen Washington, D. C., 1900
Hayes, Isaac Covington, Ten., 1942
Hayes, Peter Lind San Francisco, 1915
Haymes, Dick Argentina, 1918-80
Hayward, Susan New York City, 1919-75

Hayworth, Rita New York City, 1919
Head, Edith Los Angeles, 1907
Healy, Mary New Orleans, 1918
Heatherton, Joey Rockville Centre, N. Y., 1944
Heckart, Eileen Columbus, O., 1919
Heflin, Van Waters, Okla., 1919-71
Hefner, Hugh Chicago, 1926
Heiden, Eric Madison, Wis., 1958
Hemingway, Margaux, Portland, Ore., 1955
Hemmings, David Surrey, Eng., 1941
Henderson, Florence Dale, Ind., 1934
Henderson, Skitch Halstad, Minn., 1918
Hendrix, Jimi Seattle, 1943-70
Henie, Sonja Oslo, 1913-69
Henning, Doug Ft. Garry, Can., 1947
Henreid, Paul Trieste, 1908
Henson, Jim Greenville, Miss., 1936
Hentoff, Nat Boston, 1925
Hepburn, Audrey Brussels, 1929
Hepburn, Katharine Hartford, 1909
Herman, Woody Milwaukee, 1913
Hershfield, Harry Cedar Rapids, Iowa, 1885-1974
Hersholt, Jean Copenhagen, 1886-1956
Heston, Charlton Evanston, Ill., 1923
Hickman, Darryl Los Angeles, 1931
Hickman, Dwayne Los Angeles, 1934
Hildegarde Adell, Wis., 1906
Hill, Arthur Melfort, Can., 1922
Hiller, Wendy Bramhall, Eng., 1912
Hines, Earl Fatha Duquesne, Pa., 1905
Hingle, Pat Denver, 1924
Hirsch, Judd New York, 1935
Hirschfeld, Al St. Louis, 1903
Hirt, Al New Orleans, 1922
Hodiak, John Pittsburgh, 1914-55
Hoffa, James R. Brazil, Ind., 1913-?
Hoffman, Dustin Los Angeles, 1937
Holbrook, Hal Cleveland, 1925
Holden, William O'Fallon, Ill., 1918
Holder, Geoffrey Port-of-Spain, 1930
Holiday, Billie Baltimore, 1915-59
Holliday, Judy New York, 1921-65
Holloway, Stanley London, 1890
Holm, Celeste New York City, 1919
Holman, Libby Cincinnati, 1906-71
Holt, Jack Winchester, Va., 1888-1951
Homeier, Skip Chicago, 1930
Homolka, Oscar Vienna, 1903-78
Hope, Bob Eltham, Eng., 1903
Hopkins, Anthony Port Talbot, Wales, 1937
Hopkins, Miriam Bainbridge, Ga., 1902-72
Hopper, Dennis Dodge City, Kans., 1936
Hopper, De Wolfe New York, 1858-1935
Hopper, Hedda Hollidaysburg, Pa., 1890-1966
Horne, Lena New York City, 1917
Hornung, Paul Louisville, Ky., 1935
Horton, Edward Everett New York, 1886-1970
Houdini, Harry Budapest, 1874-1926
Howard, Joe New York, 1867-1961
Howard, Leslie London, 1893-1943
Howard, Ron Duncan, Okla., 1954
Howard, Trevor Cliftonville, Eng., 1916
Howe, Gordie Floral, Sask., 1928
Howe, James Wong China, 1899-1976
Howes, Sally Ann London, 1934
Hudson, Rock Winnetka, Ill., 1925
Hughes, Howard Houston, Tex., 1905-76
Hull, Bobby Pt. Anne, Ont., 1939
Humperdinck, Engelbert Madras, India, 1940
Hunt, Marsha Chicago, 1917
Hunter, Alberta Memphis, 1895
Hunter, Jeffrey New Orleans, 1925-69
Hunter, Kim Detroit, 1922
Hunter, Tab New York City, 1931
Huntley, Chet Cardwell, Mont., 1911-74
Hussey, Ruth Providence, R. I., 1917
Huston, Walter Toronto, 1884-1950
Hutton, Barbara New York City, 1912-79
Hutton, Betty Battle Creek, Mich., 1921
Hutton, Lauren Tampa, Fla., 1948?
Hyde-White, Wilfrid Bourton-on-the-water, Eng., 1903
Ian, Janice New York City, 1951
Ingram, Rex Mississippi, 1895-1969
Ireland, John Victoria, Can., 1916

Ives, Burl Hunt City, Ill., 1909
Jackson, Anne Millvale, Pa., 1926
Jackson, Glenda Birkenhead, Eng., 1940
Jackson, Gordon Glasgow, 1923
Jackson, Jesse Greenville, N.C., 1941
Jackson, Kate Birmingham, Ala., 1949
Jackson, Mahalia New Orleans, 1911-72
Jackson, Michael Gary, Ind., 1958
Jackson, Reggie Philadelphia, 1946
Jacobi, Lou Toronto, 1913
Jaffe, Sam New York City, 1893
Jagger, Dean Lima, O., 1903
Jagger, Mick Dartford, Eng., 1944
Jamal, Ahmad Pittsburgh, 1930
James, Dennis Jersey City, N. J., 1917
James, Harry Albany, Ga., 1916
James, Joni Chicago, 1930
Janis, Elsie Columbus, O., 1889-1956
Jannings, Emil Switzerland, 1884?-1950
Janssen, David Naponee, Neb., 1930-80
Jeanmaire, Zizi Paris, 1924
Jeffreys, Anne Goldsboro, N. C., 1928
Jenkins, Allen New York City, 1900-74
Jenkins, Gordon Webster Groves, Mo., 1910
Jenner, Bruce Mt. Kisco, N.Y., 1949
Jens, Salome Milwaukee, 1935
Jessel, George New York City, 1898
Joel, Billy New York City, 1949
John, Elton Middlesex, Eng., 1947
Johns, Glynis Pretoria, South Africa, 1923
Johnson, Celia Richmond, Eng., 1908
Johnson, Van Newport, R. I., 1916
Jolson, Al Russia, 1880?-1950
Jones, Allan Scranton, Pa., 1908
Jones, Carolyn Amarillo, Tex., 1933
Jones, Dean Morgan Co., Ala., 1936
Jones, Jack Hollywood, Cal., 1938
Jones, James Earl Tate Co., Miss., 1931
Jones, Jennifer Tulsa, Okla., 1919
Jones, Shirley Smithton, Pa., 1934
Jones, "Spike" Long Beach, Cal., 1911-64
Jones, Tom Pontypridd, Wales, 1940
Jong, Erica New York City, 1942
Joplin, Janis Port Arthur, Tex., 1943-70
Jory, Victor Dawson City, Can., 1903
Jourdan, Louis Marseilles, 1920
Jurado, Katy Guadalajara, Mexico, 1927
Jurgens, Curt Munich, 1915
Kael, Pauline Petaluma, Calif., 1919
Kahn, Madeline Boston, 1942
Kaminska, Ida Odessa, Russ., 1899-1980
Kanin, Garson Rochester, N. Y., 1912
Kaplan, Gabe New York City, 1946
Karloff, Boris London, 1887-1969
Karpov, Anatoly Zlatoust, U.S.S.R., 1951
Karsh, Yousuf Mardin, Armenia, 1908
Kasznar, Kurt Vienna, 1913-79
Kaye, Danny New York City, 1913
Kaye, Sammy Lakewood, O., 1913
Kazan, Elia Constantinople, 1909
Kazan, Lainie New York City, 1940
Keach, Stacy Savannah, Ga., 1941
Keaton, Buster Piqua, Kans., 1895-1966
Keaton, Diane Los Angeles, Cal., 1946
Keel, Howard Gillespie, Ill., 1919
Keeler, Ruby Halifax, Nova Scotia, 1910
Keeshan, Bob Lynbrook, N.Y., 1927
Keith, Brian Bayonne, N. J., 1921
Keller, Helen Tuscumbia, Ala., 1880-1968
Kellerman, Sally Long Beach, Cal., 1938
Kelly, Gene Pittsburgh, 1912
Kelly, Grace Philadelphia, 1929
Kelly, Nancy Lowell, Mass., 1921
Kelly, Patsy Brooklyn, N. Y., 1910
Kendall, Kay Hull, Eng., 1927-59
Kennedy, Arthur Worcester, Mass., 1914
Kennedy, George New York City, 1925
Kenneth, Mr. (Batelle) Syracuse, 1927
Kenton, Stan Wichita, Kans., 1912-79
Kern, Jerome New York, 1885-1945
Kerr, Deborah Helensburgh, Scot., 1921
Kerr, Jean Scranton, Pa., 1923
Kerr, John New York City, 1931
Kibbee, Guy El Paso, Tex., 1882-1956
Kilbride, Percy San Francisco, 1888-1964

Kiley, Richard Chicago, 1922
Kilgallen, Dorothy Chicago, 1913-65
Killy, Jean-Claude St.-Cloud, Fr., 1943
King, Alan New York City, 1927
King, Billie Jean Long Beach, Cal., 1943
King, Carole New York City, 1941
King, Dennis Coventry, Eng., 1897-1971
Kirk, Lisa Brownsville, Pa., 1925
Kirsten, Dorothy Montclair, N.J., 1919
Kitt, Eartha North, S.C., 1928
Klein, Calvin New York City, 1942
Klein, Robert New York City, 1942
Klemperer, Werner Cologne, Ger., 1920
Klugman, Jack Philadelphia, 1922
Knievel, Evel Butte, Mont., 1938
Knight, Gladys Atlanta, 1944
Knotts, Don Morgantown, W. Va., 1924
Knox, Alexander Strathroy, Can., 1907
Korbut, Olga Grodno, Russia, 1956
Korda, Alexander Hungary, 1893-1956
Korman, Harvey Chicago, 1927
Koufax, Sandy New York City, 1935
Kovacs, Ernie Trenton, N.J., 1919-62
Kramer, Jack Las Vegas, Nev., 1921
Kramer, Stanley New York City, 1913
Kristofferson, Kris Brownsville, Tex., 1936
Krupa, Gene Chicago, 1909-73
Kuralt, Charles Wilmington, N.C., 1934
Kwan, Nancy Hong Kong, 1939
Ladd, Alan Hot Springs, Ark., 1913-64
Ladd, Cheryl Huron, S. Dak., 1951
Lahr, Bert New York, 1895-1967
Laine, Frankie Chicago, 1913
Lake, Veronica Lake Placid, N.Y., 1919-73
Laker, Freddie Canterbury, Eng., 1922
Lamarr, Hedy Vienna, 1915
Lamas, Fernando, Buenos Aires, 1920
Lamour, Dorothy New Orleans, 1914
Lancaster, Burt New York City, 1913
Lanchester, Elsa Lewisham, Eng., 1902
Landau, Martin New York City, 1925?
Landers, Ann Sioux City, Iowa, 1918
Landi, Elissa Venice, 1904-48
Landis, Carole Fairchild, Wis., 1919-48
Landon, Michael New York City, 1937
Lane, Abbe New York City, 1935
Langdon, Harry Council Bluffs, Iowa, 1884-1944
Lange, Hope Redding Ridge, Conn., 1933
Langella, Frank Bayonne, N. J., 1940
Langford, Frances Lakeland, Fla., 1914?
Langtry, Lily Jersey, Eng., 1852-1929
Lansbury, Angela London, 1925
Lanza, Mario Philadelphia, 1921-59
La Rosa, Julius New York City, 1930
Lasser, Louise New York, 1941
Lauder, Harry Scotland, 1870-1950
Laughton, Charles Scarborough, Eng., 1899-1962
Laurel, Stan Ulverson, Eng., 1890-1965
Laurents, Arthur New York City, 1918
Laurie, Piper Detroit, 1932
Lawford, Peter London, 1923
Lawrence, Carol Melrose Park, Ill., 1934
Lawrence, Gertrude London, 1898-1952
Lawrence, Mary Wells Youngstown, 1928
Lawrence, Vicki Los Angeles, 1949
Leachman, Cloris Des Moines, 1926
Learned, Michael Washington, 1939
Lederer, Francis Prague, 1906
Lee, Brenda Atlanta, 1944
Lee, Christopher London, 1922
Lee, Gypsy Rose Seattle, 1914-70
Lee, Peggy Jamestown, N. D., 1920
Le Gallienne, Eva London, 1899
Legrand, Michel Paris, 1932
Lehrer, Tom New York City, 1928
Leigh, Janet Merced, Cal., 1927
Leigh, Vivien India, 1913-67
Leighton, Margaret Barnt Green, Eng., 1922-76
Lembeck, Harvey New York City, 1923
Lemmon, Jack Boston, 1925
Lennon, John Liverpool, Eng., 1940
Lenya, Lotte Vienna, 1900
Leonard, Sheldon New York City, 1907
Leslie, Joan Detroit, 1925
Levant, Oscar Pittsburgh, 1906-72
Levene, Sam Russia, 1905

Levenson, Sam New York City, 1911-80
Levine, Joseph E. Boston, 1905
Lewis, Jerry Newark, N. J., 1926
Lewis, Joe E. New York City, 1902?-71
Lewis, Ramsey Chicago, 1935
Lewis, Robert Q. New York City, 1921
Lewis, Shari New York City, 1934
Lewis, Ted Circleville, O., 1891-1971
Liberace West Allis, Wis., 1919
Lightfoot, Gordon Orillia, Can., 1938
Lillie, Beatrice Toronto, 1898
Lindfors, Viveca Uppsala, Swed., 1920
Lindsay, Howard Saratoga, N.Y., 1889-1968
Lindsay, Margaret Dubuque, Iowa, 1910
Linkletter, Art Moose Jaw, Can., 1912
Lippmann, Walter New York, 1889-1974
Lisi, Virna Ancona, Italy, 1937
Little, Rich Ottawa, Can., 1938
Littlewood, Joan London, 1916
Litvak, Anatole Kiev, Russ., 1902
Livingstone, Mary Seattle, 1909
Lloyd, Harold Burchard, Neb., 1893-1971
Lockhart, Gene London, Can., 1891-1957
Lockhart, June New York City, 1925
Lockwood, Margaret Karachi, Pakistan, 1916
Loesser, Frank New York, 1910-69
Logan, Ella Glasgow, 1913-69
Lollobrigida, Gina Subiaco, Italy, 1928
Lom, Herbert Prague, 1917
Lombard, Carole Fort Wayne, Ind., 1908-42
Lombardi, Vince New York, 1913-70
Lombardo, Guy London, Can., 1902-77
London, Julie Santa Rosa, Cal., 1926
Loos, Anita Sissons, Cal., 1893
Lopez, Nancy Torrence, Cal., 1957
Lopez, Trini Dallas, 1937
Lopez, Vincent New York, 1895-1975
Lord, Jack New York City, 1930
Loren, Sophia Rome, 1934
Lorre, Peter Hungary, 1904-64
Louis, Joe near Lafayette, Ala., 1914
Louise, Anita New York, 1917-70
Louise, Tina New York City, 1937
Lovejoy, Frank New York, 1912-62
Lowe, Edmund San Jose, Cal., 1892-1971
Loy, Myrna Helena, Mont., 1905
Lubitsch, Ernst Berlin, 1892-1947
Luboff, Norman Chicago, 1917
Luce, Clare Boothe New York City, 1903
Lugosi, Bela Lugos, Hung., 1888-1956
Lukas, Paul Budapest, 1894-1971
Lulu Glasgow, 1948
Lumet, Sidney Philadelphia, 1924
Lund, Art Salt Lake City, 1920
Lund, John Rochester, N. Y., 1913
Lundigan, William Syracuse, 1914-75
Lunt, Alfred Milwaukee, 1892-1977
Lupino, Ida London, 1918
Lynde, Paul Mt. Vernon, O., 1926
Lynley, Carol New York City, 1942
Lynn, Diana Los Angeles, 1926-71
Lynn, Loretta Butcher Hollow, Ky., 1932?
Lyon, Sue Davenport, Iowa, 1946
Lyons, Leonard New York City, 1906-76
MacArthur, Charles Scranton, Pa., 1895-1956
MacArthur, James Los Angeles, 1937
McBride, Mary Margaret Paris, Mo., 1899-1976
McCallum, David Scotland, 1933
McCambridge, Mercedes Joliet, Ill., 1918
McCarey, Leo Los Angeles, 1898-1969
McCartney, Paul Allerton, Eng., 1942
McClure, Doug Glendale, Cal., 1938
McCormick, Myron Albany, Ind., 1907-62
McCrea, Joel Los Angeles, 1905
McDaniel, Hattie Wichita, 1895-1952
MacDonald, Jeanette Phila., 1906-65
McDowell, Malcolm Leeds, Eng., 1943
McDowell, Roddy London, 1928
McEnroe, John Wiesbaden, Ger., 1959
McGavin, Darren San Joaquin Valley, Cal., 1922
McGraw, Ali Westchester Co., N. Y., 1939
McGuire, Biff New Haven, Conn., 1927

McGuire, Dorothy Omaha, Neb. 1919
McHugh, Frank Homestead, Pa., 1898
McKelway, St. Clair Charlotte, N. C., 1905
McKenna, Siobhan Belfast, 1922
MacKenzie, Gisele Winnipeg, Can., 1927
McKuen, Rod Oakland, Calif. 1933
McLaglen, Victor Tunbridge Wells, Eng., 1886-1959
MacLaine, Shirley Richmond, Va., 1934
MacLane, Barton Columbia, S.C., 1902-68
McLean, Don New Rochelle, N.Y., 1945
McLuhan, Marshall Edmonton, Can., 1911
MacMahon, Aline McKeesport, Pa., 1899
McMahon, Ed Detroit, 1923
MacMurray, Fred Kankakee, Ill., 1908
McNair, Barbara Chicago, 1937?
MacNeil, Robert Montreal, 1931
McNeill, Don Galena, Ill., 1907
McQueen, Butterfly Tampa, Fla., 1911
McQueen, Steve Indianapolis, 1930
MacRae, Gordon East Orange, N. J., 1921
MacRae, Sheila London, 1923?
Madison, Guy Bakersfield, Cal., 1922
Magnani, Anna Rome, 1908-73
Maharis, George New York City, 1928
Main, Marjorie Acton, Ind., 1890-1975
Mainbocher Chicago, 1890-1976
Makeba, Miriam Prospect Township, South Africa, 1932
Malbin, Elaine New York City, 1932
Malden, Karl Chicago, 1914
Malina, Judith Kiel, Ger., 1926
Malone, Dorothy Chicago, 1930
Malone, Nancy New York City, 1935
Mamoulian, Rouben Tiflis, Russ., 1897
Mancini, Henry Cleveland, 1924
Mangano, Silvana Rome, 1930
Mangione, Chuck Rochester, N.Y., 1940
Manilow, Barry New York City, 1946
Mann, Herbie New York City, 1930
Mannes, Marya New York City, 1904
Mansfield, Jayne Bryn Mawr, Pa., 1933-67
Mantle, Mickey Spavinaw, Okla., 1931
Mantovani, Annunzio Venice, 1905-80
Marceau, Marcel Strasbourg, Fr., 1923
March, Fredric Racine, Wis., 1897-1975
March, Hal San Francisco, 1920-70
Marciano, Rocky Boston, 1924-69
Margo Mexico City, 1920
Marlowe, Hugh Philadelphia, 1911
Marsh, Jean London, 1934
Marshall, E. G. Owatonna, Minn., 1910
Marshall, Herbert London, 1890-1966
Marshall, Penny New York City, 1942
Martin, Dean Steubenville, O., 1917
Martin, Dick Battle Creek, Mich., 1927
Martin, Mary Weatherford, Tex., 1913
Martin, Steve Waco, Tex., 1945
Marvin, Lee New York City, 1924
Marx, Chico New York, 1891-1961
Marx, Groucho New York, 1895-1977
Marx, Harpo New York, 1893-1964
Masina, Giulietta Bologna, Italy, 1925?
Mason, Jackie Sheboygan, Wis., 1931
Mason, James Huddersfield, Eng., 1909
Mason, Marsha St. Louis, 1942
Mason, Pamela Westgate, Eng., 1918
Massey, Raymond Toronto, 1896
Mastroianni, Marcello Fontana Liri, Italy, 1924
Mathis, Johnny San Francisco, 1935
Matthau, Walter New York City, 1920
Mature, Victor Louisville, Ky., 1916
Mauldin, Bill Mountain Park, N. M., 1921
Maxwell, Elsa Keokuk, Iowa, 1883-1963
Maxwell, Marilyn Clarinda, Iowa, 1922-72
May, Elaine Philadelphia, 1932
Mayehoff, Eddie Baltimore, 1914
Mayer, Louis B. Minsk, Russ., 1885-1957
Mayo, Virginia St. Louis, 1928
Mays, Willie Westfield, Ala., 1931
Meadows, Audrey Wuchang, China, 1922?
Meadows, Jayne Wuchang, China, 1920?
Medford, Kay New York City, 1920-80
Meek, Donald Glasgow, 1880-1946

Radziwill, Lee New York City, 1933
Raft, George, New York City, 1903
Raines, Ella Snoqualmie Falls, Wash., 1921
Rains, Claude London, 1889-1967
Raitt, John Santa Ana, Cal., 1917
Rambeau, Marjorie San Francisco, 1889-1970
Rand, Sally Hickory, Mo., 1904?-79
Randall, Tony Tulsa, Okla., 1920
Rathbone, Basil South Africa, 1892-1967
Rather, Dan Wharton, Tex., 1931
Ratoff, Gregory Russia, 1893-1961
Ray, Aldo Pen Argyl, Pa., 1926
Ray, Johnny Dallas, Ore., 1927
Raye, Martha Butte, Mont., 1916
Raymond, Gene New York City, 1908
Reagan, Ronald, Tampico, Ill., 1911
Reasoner, Harry Dakota City, Iowa, 1923
Reddy, Helen Melbourne, Australia, 1941
Redford, Robert Santa Monica, Cal., 1937
Redgrave, Lynn London, 1943
Redgrave, Michael Bristol, Eng., 1908
Redgrave, Vanessa London, 1937
Reed, Donna Iowa, 1921
Reed, Rex Fort Worth, 1940?
Reed, Willis Hico, La., 1942
Reese, Della Detroit, 1932
Reeves, Steve Glasgow, Mont., 1926
Régine Etterbeck, Belgium, 1929
Reiner, Carl New York City, 1922
Reiner, Rob Beverly Hills, Calif., 1947
Reinhardt, Max Austria, 1873-1943
Remick, Lee Quincy, Mass., 1935
Rennie, Michael Bradford, Eng., 1909-71
Rey, Fernando La Coruña, Spain, 1917
Reynolds, Burt Waycross, Ga., 1936
Reynolds, Debbie El Paso, Tex., 1932
Rice, Jim Anderson, S.C., 1953
Rich, Buddy New York City, 1917
Rich, Irene Buffalo, N. Y., 1897
Richardson, Ralph Cheltenham, Eng., 1902
Rickles, Don New York City, 1926
Riddle, Nelson Hackensack, N. J., 1921
Rigg, Diana Doncaster, Eng., 1938
Ritchard, Cyril Sydney, Austral., 1897–1977
Ritter, John Burbank, Cal., 1948
Ritter, Tex Murvaul, Tex., 1907-74
Ritter, Thelma New York, 1905-69
Rivera, Chita Washington, D. C., 1933
Rivers, Joan New York City, 1937?
Roach, Hal Elmira, N. Y., 1892
Robards, Jason, Jr. Chicago, 1922
Robbins, Harold New York City, 1916
Robertson, Cliff La Jolla, Cal., 1925
Robertson, Dale Oklahoma City, 1923
Robeson, Paul, Princeton, N.J., 1898-1976
Robinson, "Bojangles" Richmond, Va., 1878-1949
Robinson, Edward G. Bucharest, 1893-1973
Robinson, Jackie Cairo, Ga., 1919-72
Robinson, Smokey Detroit, 1940
Robinson, Sugar Ray Detroit, 1921
Robson, Flora South Shields, Eng., 1902
Rockwell, Norman New York City, 1894-1978
Rogers, Buddy Olathe, Kans., 1904
Rogers, Ginger Independence, Mo., 1911
Rogers, Roy Cincinnati, 1912
Rogers, Will Oologah, Okla., 1879-1935
Roland, Gilbert Juarez, Mexico, 1905
Roman, Ruth Boston, 1924
Rome, Harold Hartford, Conn. 1908
Romero, Cesar New York City, 1907
Ronstadt, Linda Tucson, Ariz., 1946
Rooney, Mickey New York City, 1920
Rooney, Pat New York, 1880-1962
Rose, Billy New York, 1899-1966
Rose, David London, 1910
Rose, Pete Cincinnati, 1942
Ross, Diana Detroit, 1944
Ross, Katharine Hollywood, Cal., 1943
Ross, Lanny Seattle, 1906
Roth, Lillian Boston, 1910-80
Rowan, Dan Okla., 1926
Rowlands, Gena Cambria, Wis., 1936
Rozelle, Pete South Gate, Cal., 1914

Rudd, Paul Boston, 1940
Ruggles, Charles Los Angeles, 1892-1970
Rule, Janice Norwood, O., 1931
Runyon, Damon Manhattan, Kans., 1884-1946
Rush, Barbara Denver, 1929
Russell, Jane Lake Bemidji, Minn., 1921
Russell, Kurt Springfield, Mass., 1951
Russell, Lillian Clinton, Iowa, 1861-1922
Russell, Nipsey Atlanta, 1924?
Russell, "Pee Wee" St. Louis, 1906-69
Russell, Rosalind Waterbury, Conn., 1911-76
Ruth, "Babe" Baltimore, 1895-1948
Rutherford, Ann Toronto, 1924
Rutherford, Margaret London, 1892-1972
Ryan, Peggy Long Beach, Cal., 1924
Ryan, Robert Chicago, 1913-73
Rydell, Bobby Philadelphia, 1942
Sabu Mysore, India, 1924-63
Safer, Morley Toronto, 1931
Sahl, Mort Montreal, 1927
Saint, Eva Marie Newark, N. J., 1929
St. John, Jill Los Angeles, 1940
Saint Laurent, Yves Oran, Algeria, 1936
Saint-Subber, Arnold Washington, D. C., 1918
Sainte-Marie, Buffy Saskatchewan, 1942
Sakall, "Cuddles" Budapest, 1884-1955
Sales, Soupy Wake Forest, N. C., 1926?
Sanders, George St. Petersburg, Russ., 1906-72
Sanders, Col. Harland Henryville, Ind., 1890
Sarnoff, Dorothy New York City, 1919
Sarrazin, Michael Quebec, Can., 1940
Sassoon, Vidal London, 1928
Savalas, Telly Garden City, N. Y., 1924
Scali, John Canton, Ohio, 1918
Schary, Dore Newark, N.J., 1905-80
Scheider, Roy Orange, N.J., 1935
Schell, Maria Vienna, 1926
Schell, Maximilian Vienna, 1930
Schildkraut, Joseph Vienna, 1895-1964
Schiff, Dorothy New York, 1903
Schneider, Romy Vienna, 1938
Schulz, Charles Minneapolis, 1922
Schwarzenegger, Arnold Graz, Austria, 1947
Scofield, Paul King's Norton, Eng., 1922
Scott, George C. Wise, Va., 1927
Scott, Hazel Port of Spain, Trin., 1920
Scott, Lisbeth Scranton, Pa., 1922
Scott, Martha Jamesport, Mo., 1914
Scott, Randolph Orange Co., Va., 1903
Scott, Zachary, Austin, Tex., 1914-65
Scourby, Alexander New York City, 1913
Scruggs, Earl Flint Hill, N.C., 1924-79
Searle, Ronald Cambridge, Eng., 1920
Seaver, Tom Fresno, Cal., 1944
Seberg, Jean Marshalltown, Iowa, 1938-79
Sedaka, Neil Brooklyn, 1939
Seeger, Pete New York City, 1919
Segal, Erich Brooklyn, N.Y., 1937
Segal, George New York City, 1934
Sellers, Peter Southsea, Eng., 1925-80
Selznick, David O. Pittsburgh, 1902-65
Sennett, Mack Danville, Can., 1880-1960
Serban, Andrei Bucharest, 1943
Sevareid, Eric Velva, N. D., 1912
Seymour, Dan Chicago, 1915
Shankar, Ravi Benares, India, 1920
Sharif, Omar Cairo, 1933
Shatner, William Montreal, 1931
Shaw, Artie New York City, 1910
Shaw, Robert Westhoughton, Eng., 1927-78
Shawn, Dick Buffalo, N. Y., 1929?
Shearer, Moira Dunfermline, Scot., 1926
Shearer, Norma Montreal, 1905
Shearing, George London, 1919
Sheen, Martin Dayton, Ohio, 1940
Shepherd, Jean Chicago, 1923
Sheridan, Ann Denton, Tex., 1916?-67
Sherman, Allan Chicago, 1924-73
Shields, Brooke New York City, 1965
Shire, Talia Long Island, N.Y., 1947
Shoemaker, Willie El Paso, 1931

Shore, Dinah Winchester, Tenn., 1917
Short, Bobby Danville, Ill., 1936
Shrimpton, Jean High Wycombe, Eng., 1942
Shriner, Herb Toledo, O., 1918-70
Shubert, Lee Syracuse, N.Y., 1875-1953
Shulman, Max St. Paul, Minn., 1919
Shumlin, Herman Atwood, Colo., 1898-1979
Sidney, Sylvia New York City, 1910
Signoret, Simone Wiesbaden, Ger., 1921
Silverman, Fred New York City, 1937
Silvers, Phil New York City, 1911
Sim, Alastair Edinburgh, 1900-76
Simmons, Jean London, 1929
Simon, Carly, New York City, 1945
Simon, Paul Queens, N.Y., 1941
Simon, Simone Marseilles, 1914
Simpson, Adele New York City, 1903
Simpson, O. J., San Francisco, 1947
Sinatra, Frank Hoboken, N. J., 1915
Sinatra, Nancy Jersey City, N. J., 1940
Sissle, Noble Indianapolis, 1889-1975
Skelton, Red Vincennes, Ind., 1913
Skinner, Cornelia Otis Chicago, 1901-79
Skinner, Otis Cambridge, Mass., 1858-1943
Skulnik, Menasha Warsaw, 1898-1970
Slezak, Walter Vienna, 1902
Smith, Alexis Penticton, Can., 1921
Smith, Bessie Chattanooga, 1894-1937
Smith, C. Aubrey London, 1863-1948
Smith, Howard K. Ferriday, La., 1914
Smith, Kate Greenville, Va., 1909
Smith, Maggie Ilford, Eng., 1934
Smith, Roger South Gate, Cal., 1932
Smothers, Dick New York City, 1938
Smothers, Tommy New York City, 1937
Snodgress, Carrie Park Ridge, Ill., 1945
Snowdon, Lord (Antony Armstrong-Jones) London, 1930
Snyder, Tom Milwaukee, 1936
Somers, Suzanne San Bruno, Cal., 1946
Sommer, Elke Berlin, 1941
Sondergaard, Gale Litchfield, Minn., 1907
Sondheim, Stephen New York City, 1930
Sothern, Ann Valley City, N. D., 1909
Spacek, Sissy Quitman, Tex., 1949
Sparks, Ned Guelph, Can., 1884-1957
Spassky, Boris V. Leningrad, 1937
Spewack, Bella Bucharest, 1899
Spiegel, Sam Jaroslau, Poland, 1904?
Spitalney, Phil Russia, 1890-1970
Spitz, Mark Modesto, Calif., 1950
Spivak, Lawrence E. New York City, 1900
Spock, Benjamin N. Haven, Ct., 1903
Springsteen, Bruce Freehold, N. J., 1949
Stack, Robert Los Angeles, 1919
Stafford, Jo Coalinga, Cal., 1918
Stallone, Sylvester New York City, 1946
Stamp, Terence London, 1940
Stang, Arnold Chelsea, Mass., 1925
Stanislavsky, Konstantin Moscow, 1863-1938
Stanley, Kim Tularosa, N. M., 1925
Stanton, Frank Muskegon, Mich., 1908
Stanwyck, Barbara New York City, 1907
Stapleton, Jean New York City, 1923
Stapleton, Maureen Troy, N. Y., 1925?
Starr, Ringo Dingle, Eng., 1940
Staubach, Roger Cincinnati, 1942
Steele, Tommy London, 1936
Steiger, Rod Westhampton, N. Y., 1925
Stein, Jules C. South Bend, Ind., 1896
Steinberg, Saul Rumania, 1914
Steinem, Gloria Toledo, O., 1936
Stengel, Casey Kansas City, Mo., 1891-1975
Sterling, Jan New York City, 1923
Sternberg, Josef von Vienna, 1894-1969
Stevens, Connie New York City, 1938
Stevens, Kaye Pittsburgh, 1935
Stevens, Mark Cleveland, 1922
Stevens, Stella Yazoo City, Miss., 1938
Stevenson, McLean Bloomington, Ill., 1929
Stewart, James Indiana, Pa., 1908
Stewart, Rod London, 1945
Stickney, Dorothy Dickinson, N. D., 1900
Stigwood, Robert Adelaide, Australia, 1934
Stockwell, Dean Hollywood, Cal., 1936

ARTS: POPULAR/CLASSICAL

ALL-TIME MOVIE MONEYMAKERS

Source: *Variety*

The following list includes all feature films that have grossed $20 million or more domestically (U.S. and Canada), as of Jan. 1, 1980. The film title is followed by the name of the director, producer, production company, and release year.

Film	Gross
Star Wars (G. Lucas; G. Kurtz; 20th; 1977)	$175,849,013
Jaws (S. Spielberg; Zanuck/Brown; Universal; 1975)	133,429,000
Grease (R. Kleiser; R. Stigwood/A. Carr; Par; 1978)	93,292,000
The Exorcist (W. Friedkin; W.P. Blatty; WB; 1973)	88,100,000
The Godfather (F.F. Coppola; A. Ruddy; Par; 1972)	86,275,000
Superman (R. Donner; P. Spengler; WB; 1978)	81,000,000
The Sound of Music (R. Wise; 20th; 1965)	79,000,000
The Sting (G.R. Hill; T. Bill, M. & J. Phillips; Univ; 1973)	78,889,000
Close Encounters of the Third Kind (S. Spielberg; J. & M. Phillips; Col; 1977)	77,000,000
Gone With The Wind (V. Fleming; D. Selznick; MGM-UA; 1939)	76,700,000
Saturday Night Fever (J. Badham; R. Stigwood; Par; 1977)	73,522,000
National Lampoon's Animal House (J. Landis; M. Simmons/I. Reitman; Univ; 1978)	63,471,000
Smokey and the Bandit (H. Needham; M. Engelberg; Univ; 1977)	61,017,000
One Flew Over The Cuckoo's Nest (M. Forman; S. Zaentz/M. Douglas; UA; 1975)	59,000,000
American Graffiti (G. Lucas; F.F. Coppola; Univ; 1973)	55,886,000
Rocky (J. Avildsen; Chartoff/Winkler; UA; 1976)	54,000,000
Jaws II (J. Szwarc; Zanuck/Brown; Univ; 1978)	50,569,000
Love Story (A. Hiller; H. Minsky; Par; 1970)	50,000,000
Towering Inferno (J. Guillermin; I. Allen; 20th; 1975)	50,000,000
The Graduate (M. Nichols; L. Turman; Avco Embassy; 1968)	49,078,000
Every Which Way But Loose (J. Fargo; R. Daley; Warners; 1978)	48,000,000
Heaven Can Wait (W. Beatty; Par; 1978)	47,552,000
Doctor Zhivago (D. Lean; C. Ponti; MGM-UA; 1965)	46,550,000
Butch Cassidy and the Sundance Kid (G.R. Hill; J. Foreman; 20th; 1969)	46,039,000
Airport (G. Seaton; R. Hunter; Univ; 1970)	45,300,000
Blazing Saddles (M. Brooks; M. Hertzberg; WB; 1974)	45,200,000
Rocky II (S. Stallone; UA; 1979)	43,049,274
The Ten Commandments (C.B. DeMille; Par; 1956)	43,000,000
The Poseidon Adventure (R. Neame; I. Allen; 20th; 1972)	42,000,000
Mary Poppins (R. Stevenson; W. Disney; BV; 1964)	41,000,000
Goodbye Girl (H. Ross; R. Stark; MGM-WB; 1977)	41,000,000
Alien (R. Scott; G. Carroll/D. Giler/W. Hill; 20th; 1979)	40,086,573
Young Frankenstein (M. Brooks; M. Gruskoff; 20th; 1975)	38,523,000
A Star Is Born (F. Pierson; J. Peters; WB; 1976)	37,100,000
King Kong (J. Guillermin; D. DeLaurentiis; Par; 1976)	36,915,000
MASH (R. Altman; I. Preminger; 20th; 1970)	36,720,000
Ben-Hur (W. Wyler; S. Zimbalist; MGM-UA; 1959)	36,650,000
Fiddler On The Roof (N. Jewison; UA; 1971)	36,517,000
Earthquake (M. Robson; Univ; 1974)	36,250,000
Amityville Horror (S. Rosenberg; R. Saland/E. Geisinger; AIP; 1979)	35,000,000
Star Trek (R. Wise; G. Roddenberry; Par; 1979)	35,000,000
Hooper (H. Needham; B. Reynolds/L. Gordon; WB; 1978)	34,900,000
Moonraker (L. Gilbert; A. Broccoli; UA; 1979)	33,934,074
Billy Jack (T. Frank; M. Solti; WB; 1971)	32,500,000
The Muppet Movie (J. Frawley; J. Henson; AFD; 1979)	32,000,000
The Deep (P. Yates; P. Guber; Col; 1977)	31,300,000
Oh, God! (C. Reiner; J. Weintraub; WB; 1977)	31,000,000
Godfather, Part II (F.F. Coppola; Coppola/Frederickson/Roos; Par; 1974)	30,673,000
All The President's Men (A. Pakula; W. Coblenz; WB; 1976)	30,000,000
Silver Streak (A. Hiller; E.K. Milkis/T.L. Miller; 20th; 1976)	29,900,000
California Suite (H. Ross; R. Stark; Col; 1978)	29,200,000
Thunderball (T. Young; Eon; UA; 1965)	28,530,000
The Omen (R. Donner; H. Bernhard; 20th; 1976)	28,428,000
Patton (F. Schaffner; F. McCarthy; 20th; 1970)	28,100,000
What's Up Doc? (P. Bogdanovich; WB; 1972)	28,000,000
The Jungle Book (W. Reitherman; W. Disney; BV; 1967)	27,000,000
The Deer Hunter (M. Cimino; B. Spikings/M. Deeley/M. Cimino; Univ; 1978)	26,927,000
Up In Smoke (L. Adler; Adler/Lombardo; Par; 1978)	26,871,000
Snow White (animated; W. Disney; RKO/BV; 1937)	26,750,000
Wilderness Family (S. Raffill; A. Dubs; PIE; 1976)	26,649,000
Funny Girl (W. Wyler; R. Stark; Col; 1968)	26,325,000
The French Connection (W. Friedkin; P. D'Antoni/Schine-Moore; 20th; 1971)	26,315,000
Foul Play (C. Higgins; Miller/Milkis; Par; 1978)	26,269,000
Cleopatra (J. Mankiewicz; W. Wanger; 20th; 1963)	26,000,000
Main Event (H. Zieff; J. Peters/B. Streisand; Warners; 1979)	26,000,000
Airport 1975 (J. Smight; W. Fry; Univ; 1974)	25,805,000
Guess Who's Coming To Dinner? (S. Kramer; Col; 1968)	25,500,000
The China Syndrome (J. Bridges; M. Douglas; Col; 1979)	25,425,000
The Way We Were (S. Pollack; R. Stark; Col; 1973)	25,000,000
Revenge of the Pink Panther (B. Edwards; UA; 1978)	25,000,000
10 (B. Edwards; B. Edwards/T. Adams; Orion; 1979)	25,000,000
The Bad News Bears (M. Ritchie; S. Jaffe; Par; 1976)	24,888,000
2001: A Space Odyssey (S. Kubrick; MGM-UA; 1968)	24,100,000
Trial of Billy Jack (F. Laughlin; D. Cramer; T-L/WB; 1974)	24,000,000
The Enforcer (J. Fargo; R. Daley; WB; 1976)	24,000,000
In Search of Noah's Ark (J.L. Conway; C.E. Sellier, Jr.; Sunn; 1977)	24,000,000
Around the World in 80 Days (M. Anderson; M. Todd; UA; 1956)	23,120,000
The Love Bug (R. Stevenson; W. Walsh; BV; 1969)	23,050,000
The Longest Yard (R. Aldrich; A. Ruddy; Par; 1974)	23,017,000
Goldfinger (G. Hamilton; Eon; UA; 1964)	22,860,000
Apocalypse Now (F.F. Coppola; UA; 1979)	22,855,657
Semi-Tough (M. Ritchie; D. Merrick; UA; 1977)	22,786,000
Bonnie and Clyde (A. Penn; W. Beatty; WB; 1967)	22,700,000
Deliverance (J. Boorman; WB; 1972)	22,500,000
Papillon (F. Schaffner; R. Dorfmann; AA; 1973)	22,500,000
Dog Day Afternoon (S. Lumet; M. Bregman/M. Elfand; WB; 1975)	22,500,000
Midway (J. Smight; W. Mirisch; Univ; 1976)	22,329,000
Shampoo (H. Ashby; W. Beatty; Col; 1975)	22,000,000
Murder By Death (R. Moore; R. Stark; Col; 1976)	22,000,000
The Spy Who Loved Me (L. Gilbert; A. Broccoli; UA; 1977)	22,000,000
Jeremiah Johnson (S. Pollack; J. Wizan; WB; 1972)	21,800,000
101 Dalmatians (animated; W. Disney; BV; 1961)	21,375,000
Silent Movie (M. Brooks; M. Hertzberg; 20th; 1976)	21,178,000
Escape From Alcatraz (D. Siegel; Par; 1979)	21,014,000
A Bridge Too Far (R. Attenborough; J.E. Levine/R.P. Levine; UA; 1977)	21,000,000
It's A Mad, Mad, Mad, Mad World (S. Kramer; UA; 1963)	20,800,000
Summer of '42 (R. Mulligan; R. Roth; WB; 1971)	20,500,000
Midnight Cowboy (J. Schlesinger; J. Hellman; UA; 1969)	20,325,000
The Dirty Dozen (R. Aldrich; K. Hyman; MGM-UA; 1967)	20,300,000
Cabaret (B. Fosse; C. Feuer; AA; 1972)	20,250,000
Return of the Pink Panther (B. Edwards; UA; 1975)	20,122,000
Magnum Force (T. Post; R. Daley; WB; 1973)	20,100,000
Three Days of the Condor (S. Pollack; S. Schneider; Par; 1975)	20,014,000
Pink Panther Strikes Again (B. Edwards; UA; 1976)	20,003,000
The Valley of the Dolls (M. Robson; D. Weisbart; 20th; 1967)	20,000,000
The Odd Couple (G. Saks; H. Koch; Par; 1968)	20,000,000
The End (B. Reynolds; L. Gordon; UA; 1978)	20,000,000

LONGEST BROADWAY RUNS

SOURCE: *VARIETY*

Play	Perfor-mances
Grease	3,388
Fiddler on the Roof	3,242
Life with Father	3,224
Tobacco Road	3,182
Hello, Dolly!	2,844
My Fair Lady	2,717
Man of La Mancha	2,329
Abie's Irish Rose	2,327
Oklahoma!	2,212
A Chorus Line*	2,099
Pippin	1,944
South Pacific	1,925
Magic Show	1,920
Harvey	1,775
Hair	1,742
The Wiz	1,661
Oh! Calcutta!*	1,654
Born Yesterday	1,642
Mary, Mary	1,572
The Voice of the Turtle	1,557
Barefoot in the Park	1,532
Mame	1,503
Arsenic and Old Lace	1,444
Same Time, Next Year	1,444
The Sound of Music	1,443
How To Succeed in Business without Really Trying	1,417
Annie*	1,405
Hellzapoppin	1,404
The Music Man	1,375
Gemini*	1,365
Funny Girl	1,348
Mummenschanz	1,316
Angel Street	1,295
Lightnin'	1,291
Promises, Promises	1,281
The King and I	1,246
Cactus Flower	1,234
Sleuth	1,222
1776	1,217
Equus	1,209
Guys and Dolls	1,200
Cabaret	1,166
Mister Roberts	1,157
Annie Get Your Gun	1,147
The Seven Year Itch	1,141
Butterflies Are Free	1,128
Pins and Needles	1,108
Plaza Suite	1,097
Kiss Me Kate	1,071
Don't Bother Me I Can't Cope	1,065
Pajama Game	1,063
Deathtrap*	1,049
The Teahouse of the August Moon	1,027
Damn Yankees	1,019
Dancin'*	1,018
Never Too Late	1,007
Any Wednesday	984
Ain't Misbehavin'*	968
A Funny Thing Happened on the Way to the Forum	964
The Odd Couple	964
Kiss and Tell	962
Anna Lucasta	957
The Moon is Blue	924
Bells Are Ringing	924
The Best Little Whorehouse in Texas*	920
Beatlemania	914
Luv	902
Can-Can	895
Carousel	890
Hats Off to Ice	890
Fanny	888
Follow the Girls	882
The Bat	878
Camelot	873
My Sister Eileen	866
White Cargo	864
No, No, Nanette	861
Song of Norway	860
A Streetcar Named Desire	855
Comedy in Music	849
You Can't Take It with You	837
La Plume de Ma Tante	835
Three Men on a Horse	835

*As of August 31, 1980. Figures reflect consecutive performances.

MAJOR WORLD DANCE GROUPS

SOURCE: The Dance Collection, Library & Museum of the Performing Arts, Lincoln Center, New York

Dates in parentheses indicate the founding year.

AMSTERDAM: The Dutch National Ballet (1961); *Director:* Rudi van Dantzig.

BOSTON: Boston Ballet (1964); *Director:* E. Virginia Williams.

BRUSSELS: Ballets du Vingtième Siècle (1960); *Director:* Jorge Donn.

COPENHAGEN: Royal Danish Ballet (1771); *Director:* Henning Kronstam.

GLASGOW: Scottish Ballet (1969); *Dir.:* Peter Darrell.

THE HAGUE: Nederlands Dans Theater (1959); *Artistic Director:* Jiří Kylián.

HAMBURG: Hamburg State Opera Ballet (c. 1960); *Artistic Director:* John Neumeier.

HAVANA: Ballet Nacional de Cuba (1948); *Director:* Alicia Alonso.

HOUSTON: Houston Ballet (1968); *Artistic Director:* Ben Stevenson.

LENINGRAD: Kirov Ballet (1783); *Director:* Oleg Vinogradov.

LONDON:

Festival Ballet (1950); *Director:* John Field.

Royal Ballet, Covent Garden (formerly **Sadler's Wells Ballet**) (1931); *Director:* Norman Morrice.

Ballet Rambert (1926); *Directors:* Dame Marie Rambert, John Chesworth.

London Contemporary Dance Theatre (1969); *Director:* Robert Cohan.

MELBOURNE: Australian Ballet (1962); *Artistic Director:* Marilyn Jones.

MOSCOW: Bolshoi Ballet (c. 1820); *Director:* Stanislav Louchin; *Artistic Director:* Yuri Grigorovich.

NEW YORK CITY:

Nikolais Dance Theatre (1948); *Director:* Alwin Nikolais.

American Ballet Theatre (1939); *Director:* Mikhail Baryshnikov.

Alvin Ailey American Dance Theatre (1958); *Director:* Alvin Ailey.

The Joffrey Ballet (1954); *Artistic Director:* Robert Joffrey.

The Dance Theatre of Harlem (1969); *Directors:* Arthur Mitchell and Karel Shook.

Eliot Feld Ballet (1974); *Director:* Eliot Feld.

Martha Graham Dance Company (1930); *Director:* Martha Graham.

Merce Cunningham and Dance Group (1952); *Director:* Merce Cunningham.

New York City Ballet (1948); *Dance Masters:* George Balanchine, Jerome Robbins, John Taras.

Paul Taylor Dance Company (1954); *Director:* Paul Taylor.

Twyla Tharp Foundation (1965); *Artistic Director:* Twyla Tharp.

PARIS: Paris Opera Ballet (1671); *Director:* Raymond Franchetti.

PHILADELPHIA: Pennsylvania Ballet (1964); *Director:* Barbara Weisberger; *Artistic Director:* Benjamin Harkarvy.

PITTSBURGH: Pittsburgh Ballet Theatre (1970); *Artistic Director:* Patrick Frantz.

SAN FRANCISCO: San Francisco Ballet (1937); *Directors:* Lew Christensen and Michael Smuin.

STOCKHOLM: Royal Swedish Ballet (1773); *Artistic Director:* Ivo Cramer.

STUTTGART: Stuttgart Ballet (c. 1760); *Director:* Marcia Haydée.

TORONTO: National Ballet of Canada (1951); *Artistic Director:* Alexander Grant.

WASHINGTON (CONN.): Pilobolus Dance Theater (1971); *Manager:* Mark Ross.

WASHINGTON (D.C.): Washington Ballet (1962); *Director:* Mary Day.

WINNIPEG: Royal Winnipeg Ballet (1939); *Artistic Director:* Arnold Spohr.

POPULAR DISCOGRAPHY

Note: Numeral and hyphen preceding record label indicate multi-disc album, the numeral indicating the number of discs.

STANDARD POP

Herb Alpert & Tijuana Brass—You Smile/A&M 3620; **Paul Anka**—His Best/U. Artists LA922-H; **Frankie Avalon**—Venus/De-Lite 2020; **Burt Bacharach**—Greatest Hits/A&M 3661; **Tony Bennett**—Tony/Harmony KH 32171; **Glen Campbell**—Wichita Lineman/Capitol SM 103; **Captain & Tennille**—Love Will Keep Us Together/A&M SP4552; **Carpenters**—Singles/A&M 3601; **Nat "King" Cole**—Best/Capitol SKAO-2944; **Ray Conniff**—Harmony/Columbia KC-32553; **Bing Crosby**—Feels Good/London 679; **John Denver**—Greatest Hits/Victor CPL1-0374; **Neil Diamond**—September Morn/Columbia FC 36121; **José Feliciano**—Fireworks/RCA LSP 4370; **Four Seasons**—2nd Vault of Golden Hits/Philips PHS 600-221; **Bobbie Gentry**—Fancy/Capitol ST-428; **Tom Jones**—Greatest Hits/Paramount XPAS 71062; **Peggy Lee**/Arc. Folk. 294; **Henry Mancini**—Country Gentlemen/Victor APL1-0270; **Barry Manilow**—Greatest Hits/2-Arista 8601; **Mantovani**—Greatest Hits, Vol. 1/London XPS 906; **Johnny Mathis**—All-Time Greatest Hits/2-Columbia PG 31345; **Mabel Mercer (w. Bobby Short)**—At Town Hall/2-Atlantic S-604; **Olivia Newton-John**—Totally Hot/MCA 3067; **Tony Orlando & Dawn**—Prime Time/Bell 1317; **Donny & Marie Osmond**—Winning Combination/Polydor I-6127; **Pointer Sisters**—That's a Plenty/Blue Thumb 48; **Frank Sinatra**—Come Fly with Me/Capitol SY 4528; **Kate Smith**—At Carnegie Hall/Camden CAS-2587; **Barbra Streisand**—Wet/Columbia FC-36258; **Dionne Warwick**—Dionne/Arista 4230; **Andy Williams**—Solitaire/Columbia KC-32383; **Nancy Wilson**—Best/Capitol SKAO-2947.

ROCK 'N' ROLL

ABBA—Greatest Hits Vol. 2/Atlantic 16009; **The Band**—Best/Capitol ST-11553; **Beach Boys**—Good Vibrations/Reprise 2223; **Beatles**—Rubber Soul/Apple ST 2442; **Bee Gees**—Greatest Hits/2-RSO 4200; **Blondie**—Parallel Lines/Chrysalis 1192; **Boston**—Epic PE 34188; **David Bowie**—Space Oddity/RCA LSP-4813; **Cars**—Candy-O/Elektra 507; **Cheap Trick**—Dream Police/Epic FE-35773; **Chicago**—Hot Streets/Columbia FC-35512; **Joe Cocker**—Hits/A&M 4670; **Alice Cooper**—Welcome to My Nightmare/Atlantic SD 18130; **Cream**—Best of/Atco SD 33-291; **Crosby, Stills, Nash & Young**—Déjà Vu/Atlantic SD 7200; **Doors**—Elektra 74007; **Eagles**—The Long Run/Asylum 5E-508; **Earth, Wind & Fire**—Best of, Vol. 1/Columbia FC-35647; **Fleetwood Mac**—Tusk/2-Warner Bros. 2HS-3350; **Jimi Hendrix**—Are You Experienced?/Reprise S-6261; **Jefferson Starship**—Red Octopus/Grunt BFL1-0999; **Jethro Tull**—War Child/Chrysalis 1067; **Billy Joel**—52nd Street/Columbia FC-35609; **Elton John**—Greatest Hits/MCA 2128; **Carole King**—Tapestry/Ode 77009; **Kiss**—Alive/Casablanca NBLP 7020; **Led Zeppelin**—In Through the Out Door/Swan Song 16002; **Meat Loaf**—Bat Out of Hell/Epic PE-34974; **Bette Midler**—The Rose/Atlantic 16010; **Steve Miller**—Greatest Hits 1974-78/Capitol SOO-11872; **Mothers of Invention**—We're Only in it for the Money/Verve 65045; **Randy Newman**—Little Criminals/Warner Bros. 3079; **Pink Floyd**—The Wall/2-Columbia PC2-36183; **Elvis Presley**—Elvis/RCA APL1-0283; **Suzi Quatro**—If You Knew Suzi/RSO 3044; **Gerry Rafferty**—City to City/U. Artists LA840-H; **Rolling Stones**—Some Girls/Roll. Stones Rec. 39108; **Santana**—Abraxas/Columbia KC-30130; **Sex Pistols**—Never Mind the Bollocks/Warner Bros. K-3147; **Simon & Garfunkel**—Bridge Over Troubled Water/Columbia KCS-9914; **Southside Johnny & The Asbury Jukes**—Hearts of Stone/Epic JE-35488; **Rod Stewart**—Greatest Hits/Warner Bros. HS-3373; **Donna Summer**—On the Radio, Greatest Hits Vol. 1 & 2/2-Casablanca NBLP2-7191; **T. Rex**/Reprise 6440; **Village People**—Live & Sleazy/Casablanca 2-7183; **The Who**—Who Are You?/MCA 3050; **Wings**—Greatest/Capitol SOO-11905; **Neil Young & Crazy Horse**—Rust Never Sleeps/Warner Bros. HS 2295; **Warren Zevon**—Excitable Boy/Asylum 118.

FOLK AND FOLK-ROCK

Hoyt Axton—Free Sailin'/MCA 2319; **Joan Baez**—Blessed Are/2-Vanguard VSD 6570/1; **Jackson Browne**—For Everyman/Asylum 5067; **Leonard Cohen**—Songs of/Columbia CS 9533; **Judy Collins**—Whales & Nightingales/Elektra 75010; **Jim Croce**—Photographs & Memories/ABC 835; **Bob Dylan**—Blonde on Blonde/2-Columbia C2S-841, **Jack Elliott**/Vanguard 79151; **Kinky Friedman**—Sold American/Vanguard 79333; **Gathering at the Earl of Old Town**—Various/Mount. 670; **Bob Gibson**—Where I'm Bound/Elektra 7239; **Steve Goodman**—Somebody Else's Troubles/Buddah 5121; **Arlo Guthrie**—Washington County/Reprise 6411; **Woody Guthrie**—Dust Bowl Ballads/Folkways 5212; **Tim Hardin**—I/Verve Folk. FTS 3004; **George Harrison**—All Things Must Pass/3-Apple STCH 639; **Richie Havens**—Portfolio/Stormy Forest 6013; **Fred Holstein**—Chicago & Other Ports/Philo PH 1030; **Ian & Sylvia**—Best/2-Columbia CG-32516; **Michael Johnson**—Dialogue/EMI

SW-17010; **Bonnie Koloc**—Close-Up/Epic PE-34184; **Leo Kottke**—Ice Water/Capitol ST 11262; **Leadbelly**—Huddie Ledbetter/Fantasy 24715; **Gordon Lightfoot**—Gord's Gold/2-Reprise 2RS 2237; **Melanie**—Candles in the Rain/Buddah BDS-5060; **Joni Mitchell**—Court & Spark/Elek. Asylum 7E 1001; **Maria Muldaur**—Sweet Harmony/Reprise MS 2235; **Harry Nilsson**—Nilsson Schmilsson/RCA LSP-4515; **Oliver (Bill Swofford)**—Good Morning Starshine/Crewe CR 1333; **Jim Post**—Slow to 20/Fantasy 9408; **John Prine**—Bruised Orange/Asylum 139; **Linda Ronstadt**—Greatest Hits/Asylum 1092; **Rotary Connection**—Peace/Cadet-Concept LPS 318; **Leon Russell**—Will o' the Wisp/Shelter SR 2138; **Buffy Sainte-Marie**—It's My Way!/Vanguard VSD 79142; **Carly Simon**—Best/Elektra 7E-1048; **Skymonters (w. Hamid Hamilton Camp)**/Elektra 75073; **Bruce Springsteen**—Born to Run/Columbia PC-33795; **Cat Stevens**—Foreigner/A&M 4391; **James Taylor**—Mud Slide Slim/Warner Bros. BS-2561.

RHYTHM AND BLUES, SOUL, GOSPEL

Big Bill Broonzy—Blues/Encore 22017; **James Brown**—Jam 1980s/Polydor 6140(6); **Ray Charles**—Genius Sings the Blues/Atlantic SD 8052; **Sam Cooke**—You Send Me/Camden ACS1 0445; **Bo Diddley**—Greatest/Checker 8034; **Fats Domino**—Very Best/U. Artists LA 233-G; **Sleepy John Estes**—Broke & Hungry/Delmark 608; **Roberta Flack**—Killing Me Softly/Atlantic 7271; **Aretha Franklin**—With Everything I Feel in Me/Atlantic SD 18116; **B.B. King**—Best/ABC 724; **Gladys Knight & the Pips**—Knight Time/Soul 741; **Taj Mahal**—Mo Roots/Columbia KC 33051; **Curtis Mayfield**—Curtis in Chicago/Curtom 8018; **Mighty Clouds of Joy**—It's Time/Dunwich 50177; **Wilson Pickett**—Greatest Hits/2-Atlantic 2-501; **Lou Rawls**—Sit Down & Talk to Me/Philadelphia Intl. JZ-36304; **Otis Redding**—Tell the Truth/Atco SD 33-333; **Smokey Robinson & Miracles**—1957-72/2-Tamla 320; **Sly & Family Stone**—Fresh/Epic KE-32134; **Bessie Smith**—Empty Bed Blues/Columbia G 30450; **Supremes (w. Diana Ross)**—Where Did Our Love Go?/Motown 621; **Sweet Inspirations**—Sweet Sweet Soul/Atlantic SD 8253; **Temptations**—Greatest Hits, Vol. 2/Gordy 5 954; **Muddy Waters**—Live/Chess 50012; **Stevie Wonder**—Secret Life of Plants/Tamla T13-371C2.

JAZZ

Amanda Ambrose—Amanda/Dunwich 668; **George Benson**—Livin' Inside Your Love/2-Warner Bros. 3277; **Dave Brubeck**—Greatest Hits/Columbia CS-9284; **John Coltrane**—My Favorite Things/Atlantic 1361; **Miles Davis**—Kind of Blue/Columbia PC 8163; **Ella Fitzgerald**—Best/Reprise S 6354; **Erroll Garner**—Misty/Mercury 60662; **Stan Getz (w. Charlie Byrd)**—Jazz Samba/Verve 68432; **Dizzy Gillespie**—Groovin' High/Savoy 12020; **Benny Goodman**—1938 Carnegie Hall Jazz Concert/2-Columbia OSL-160; **Woody Herman**—Woody/Cadet 845; **Earl Hines**—Tea for Two/Black Lion BL-112; **Billie Holiday**—Lady Day/Columbia CL-637; **Scott Joplin**—Ragtime, Vol. 3/Biograph 1010Q; **Roland Kirk**—Gifts & Messages/Mercury S 90939; **Chuck Mangione**—Chase the Clouds Away/A&M 4518; **Charles Mingus**—Mingus Dynasty/Columbia CL 1440; **Modern Jazz Quartet**—Best/Atlantic 1546; **Wes Montgomery**—Best/Verve 68714; **Jelly Roll Morton**—King of New Orleans Jazz/Victor LPM 1649; **Oliver Nelson**—Blues & the Abstract Truth/Impulse A-5; **Charlie Parker**—Complete Savoy Sessions/5-Savoy 5500; **Joe Pass**—Virtuoso/Pablo 2310708; **Oscar Peterson**—Newport Years/Verve 8828; **Django Reinhardt**—Djangology/Victor LPM 2319; **Judy Roberts**—Inner City 1078; **Sonny Rollins (w. Max Roach)**—Freedom Suite/2-Milestone 47007; **Art Tatum**—Essential/Verve 68433; **Sarah Vaughan**—Golden Hits/Mercury 60645; **Fats Waller**—One Never Knows, Do One?/Victor LPM 1503; **Lester Young**—Essential/Verve 68398.

COUNTRY AND WESTERN

Bill Anderson—Bill/MCA 320; **Lynn Anderson**—Greatest Hits/Columbia KC 31641; **Eddy Arnold**—Best, Vol. 3/RCA LSP 4844; **Chet Atkins**—Mr. Atkins, Guitar Picker/Camden CASX 2464(e); **Jimmy Buffett**—Changes in Latitudes, Changes in Attitudes/ABC 990; **Johnny Cash**—Silver/Columbia JC-36086 **Jimmy Dean**—Favorite Son/Harmony 11270; **Flatt & Scruggs**—Greatest Hits/Columbia CS 9370; **Crystal Gayle**—Classic Crystal/U. Artists LOO 982; **Merle Haggard**—190Proof./MCA 3089; **Wanda Jackson**—Country Keepsakes/Capitol ST 11161; **Waylon Jennings**—Greatest Hits/RCA AHL 1-3378; **Loretta Lynn**—Greatest Hits, Vol. 2/MCA 420; **Jody Miller**—Country Girl/Epic KE-33349; **Willie Nelson**—Stardust/Columbia JC-35305; **Dolly Parton**—Here You Come Again/RCA AFL1-2544; **Charley Pride**—Pride of America/Victor APL1-0757; **Carl Smith**—Country on My Mind/Columbia CS-9688; **Statler Bros.**—Best/Mercury 1037; **Hank Williams**—Greatest Hits/2-MGM S-4755; **Bob Wills**—Anthology/Columbia KG 32416; **Tammy Wynette**—My Man/Epic KE 31717.

CLASSICAL DISCOGRAPHY

OPERA

Beethoven—Fidelio: Klemperer/3-Angel S-3625; **Bellini**—Norma: Serafin/3-Angel S-3615; **Berg**—Wozzeck: Böhm/2-DGG 2707023; **Bizet**—Carmen: Troyanos, Solti, London Phil./3-London 13115; **Debussy**—Pelléas et Mélisande: Ansermet/London 1379; **Donizetti**—Lucia di Lammermoor: Pritchard/London 25702; **Flotow**—Martha (highlights): Berlin Mun. Op./Angel S-36236; **Gilbert & Sullivan**—The Yeoman of the Guard: Gilbert & Sullivan Festival Orch./BSAF MIC BB 25l09; **Gluck**—Orfeo ed Euridice: Fasano/3-RCA LSC-6169; **Gounod**—Faust: Cluytens/4-Angel S-3622; **Leoncavallo**—Pagliacci: Gobbi/2-Angel S-3618; **Mascagni**—Cavalleria Rusticana: Serafin/3-London 1330; **Massenet**—Manon: Rudel/4-ABC ATS-20007; **Mozart**—Marriage of Figaro: Fricsay/3-DG 2728004; Don Giovanni: Klemperer/4-Angel S-3700; The Magic Flute: Böhm/3-DG-2709017; **Moussorgsky**—Boris Godunov: Cluytens/4-Angel S-3633; **Puccini**—La Bohème: Serafin/2-London 1208; Tosca: Karajan/2-London 1284; Madama Butterfly: Serafin/3-Angel S-3604; **Rossini**—The Barber of Seville: Leinsdorf/4-RCA 6143; **Schoenberg**—Moses and Aaron: Gielen/2-Philips 6700084; **R. Strauss**—Der Rosenkavalier: Solti/4-London 1435; **Verdi**—Aida: Leinsdorf/3-RCA LSC-6198; Falstaff: Karajan/3-Angel S-3552; La Forza del Destino: Previtali/3-London 13122; Otello: Karajan/3-London 1324; Rigoletto: Solti/2-Angel S-3718; La Traviata: Previtali/3-RCA LSC-6154; **Wagner**—GotterdAUmmerung: Solti/6-London 1604.

SYMPHONY

Beethoven—Complete Symphonies, 1-9: Karajan/8-DG 2721001; **Berlioz**—Symphonie Fantastique: Munch/RCA LSC-2608; **Bizet**—Symphony No. 1: Ansermet/London 6208; **Brahms**—Complete Symphonies 1-4: Szell/3-Columbia D3S-758; **Bruckner**—No. 4: Klemperer/Angel S-36245; No. 9: Mehta/London 6462; **Copland**—Symphony No. 3: Bernstein/Columbia MS-6954; **Dvořák**—Nos. 7-9: Szell/3-Columbia D3S-814; **Franck**—Symphony in D minor: Monteux/RCA LSC-2514; **Haydn**—Nos. 93-104: Dorati/3-London STS 15319-15324; **Mahler**—No. 1: Giulini/DG 2707097; No. 4: Reiner/RCA 2364; No. 9: Walter/2-Odyssey Y2-30308; **Mendelssohn**—Nos. 4-5: Munch/RCA LSC-2221; **Mozart**—Nos. 25,29: Marriner/Argo ZRG-706; Nos. 32, 35, 38: Boehm/DG 138112; Nos. 40,41: Klemperer/Angel S-36183; **Nielsen**—No. 5: Bernstein/Columbia MS-6414; **Prokofiev**—Classical Symphony, Lt. Kijé and "Three Oranges" Suites: Ormandy/Columbia MS-6545; **Saint-Saëns**—No. 3: Munch/RCA LSC-2341; **Schubert**—Nos. 5,8: Walter/Columbia MS-6218; No. 9: Szell/Angel S-36044; **Schumann**—Complete Symphonies, 1-4: Bernstein/3-Columbia D3S-725; **Shostakovich**—No. 2: Ormandy/Columbia MS-6124; **Sibelius**—No. 5: Bernstein/Columbia MS-6749; **Stravinsky**—Symphony in Three Movements: Ansermet/London MS-6190; **Tchaikovsky**—No. 4: Monteux/RCA 2369; No. 6: Ormandy/Columbia MS-6160; **Vaughan Williams**—No. 9: Boult/Everest 3006.

ORCHESTRAL AND CHORAL

Bach—Brandenburg Concertos: Harnoncourt/Telefunken S-9459/60; Cantatas 56 & 169: Saar Ch. Orch./Nonesuch 71142; Suites for Orchestra: Casals/2-Columbia M2S-755; **Bartók**—Concerto for Orchestra: Ormandy/Columbia MS-6626; Hungarian Sketches: Reiner/RCA VICS 1620; Music for Strings, Percussion and Celesta: Boulez/Columbia MS-7206; **Beethoven**—Overtures: Karajan/2-DG 2707046; **Copland**—Appalachian Spring; El Salon Mexico: Bernstein/Columbia MS-6355; Billy the Kid; Rodeo: Bernstein/Columbia MS-6175; **Debussy**—La Mer; Nocturnes: Giulini/Angel S-35977; Images pour Orchestre: Boulez/Columbia MS-7362; **Dvořák**—Slavonic Dances: Szell/Columbia MS-7208; **Elgar**—Enigma Variations; Cockaigne Overture: Barbirolli/Angel S-36120; **Falla**—Three Cornered Hat & La Vida Breve Dances: Reiner/RCA 2230; **Gershwin**—An American in Paris; Rhapsody in Blue: Bernstein/Columbia MS-6091; **Handel**—Concerti Grossi Op. 6: Leppard/Mercury 9124; Water Music and Royal Fireworks Suites: Szell/London 6236; **Hindemith**—Symphonic Metamorphoses of Themes by Weber: Mathis der Maler: Ormandy/Columbia MS-6562; **Kodály**—Háry János Suite; Dances from Galánta: Kertész/London 6417; **Liszt**—A Faust Symphony; Les Preludes: Bernstein/2-Columbia MG-699; **Mendelssohn**—A Midsummer Night's Dream: Klemperer/Angel S-3588l; **Mozart**—Eine Kleine Nachtmusik; Serenade No. 9: Szell/Columbia MS-7273; **Moussorgsky-Ravel**—Pictures at an Exhibition: Ansermet/London 6177; **Orff**—Carmina Burana: Thomas & Cleveland Orch. Chorus & Boys' Choir/Columbia M-33172; **Ravel**—Daphnis et Chloe: Ansermet/London 6456; La Valse; Menuet Antique; Ma Mère l'Oye: Boulez/Columbia M-32838Q; **Respighi**—The Pines of Rome; The Fountains of Rome: Reiner/RCA LSC-2436; **Rimsky-Korsakov**—Scheherazade: Rostropovich/Angel S-37061(Q); **Rossini**—Overtures: Toscanini/Victrola 1274; **Smetana**—Moldau; Bartered Bride Dances: Szell/Odyssey Y-30049; **J. Strauss**—Waltzes: Ormandy/Columbia MS-6217; **R. Strauss**—Also sprach Zarathustra, Don Juan & Till Eulenspiegel: Solti/London 6978; **Stravinsky**—The Firebird: Stokowski/London 21026; Le Sacre du Printemps: Bernstein/Columbia MS-6010; **Tchaikovsky**—The Nutcracker: Ansermet/London 2203; Romeo and Juliet; Francesca da Rimini: Munch/RCA VICS-1197; The Sleeping Beauty: Previn/3-Angel SX 3812(Q); **Wagner**—Siegfried Idyll; Overtures: Walter/Columbia MS-6507.

SOLOS WITH ORCHESTRA

Bach—Clavier Concertos Nos. 1,2: Kirkpatrick/DG ARC 198013; Violin Concertos Nos. 1, 2; Concerto for 2 Violins: David and Igor Oistrakh/DG 138820; **Bartók**—Piano Concertos Nos. 2,3: Anda/DG 138111; **Beethoven**—Piano Concertos Nos. 1-5: Ashkenazy/4-London 2404; Violin Concerto: Stern/Columbia MS-6093; **Berg**—Violin Concerto: Grumiaux/Philips 900194; **Berlioz**—Harold in Italy: Menuhin/Angel S-36123; **Brahms**—Piano Concerto No. 2: Dichter/Philips 9500414; Violin Concerto: Heifetz/RCA LSC-1903; Double Concerto: Oistrakh-Rostropovich/Angel S-36032; **Bruch**—Violin Concerto No. l: Stern/Columbia MS-7003; **Chopin**—Piano Concerto Nos. l,2; Andante: Rubinstein/2-RCA VCS-7091; **Dvořák**—Cello Concerto: Starker/Mercury 90303; **Grieg**—Piano Concerto: Rubinstein/RCA LSC-2566; **Lalo**—Symphonie Espagnole; **Liszt**—Piano Concertos Nos. 1,2: Richter/Philips 835474; **Mendelssohn**—Violin Concerto: Francescatti/Columbia MS-6758; **Mozart**—Horn Concertos Nos. 1-4; Rondo K.371: Civil/Philips 6500325; Piano Concertos Nos. 25,27: Gulda/DG 2530642; Violin Concertos Nos. 3,4: Francescatti/Columbia MS-6063; **Paganini**—Violin Concertos Nos. l,2: Gitlis/Turn. 34203; **Poulenc**—Organ Concerto: Duruflé (w. Gloria: Carteri)/Angel S-35953; **Prokofiev**—Piano Concertos Nos. 3,4: Browning/RCA 3019; **Rachmaninoff**—Piano Concerto No. 2: Ashkenazy/London 6390; **Saint-Saëns**—Cello Concertos Nos. 1,2, etc.: Walevska/Philips 6500459; **Schumann**—Cello Concerto: Rostropovich/DG 138674; Piano Concerto: Rubinstein/RCA LSC-2997; **Sibelius**—Violin Concerto: Heifetz/RCA LSC-2435; **Tchaikovsky**—Piano Concerto No. l: Cliburn/RCA LSC-2252; Violin Concerto: Zuckerman/Columbia MS-7313; **Vivaldi**—The Four Seasons: Virtuosi di Roma/Angel S-35877

CHAMBER MUSIC

Bartók—Quartets Nos. 1-6: Juilliard Quartet/3-Columbia D3S-717; **Beethoven**—Quartets (complete): Amadeus Quartet/4-DG 2721006; "Archduke" Trio: Stern-Rose-Istomin/Columbia MS-6819; Violin & Piano Sonatas (complete): Francescatti-Casadesus/4-Columbia D4S-724; **Berg**—Lyric Suite: RCA/Juilliard Quartet/RCA 2531; **Brahms**—Quintet Op. 34: Previn, Yale Quartet/Angel S-36928; Trio Op. 40: Tuckwell-Perlman-Ashkenazy/London 6628; Violin Sonatas: Szeryng, Rubinstein/2-RCA LSC-2619/20; **Debussy and Ravel**—Quartets: Juilliard Quartet/Columbia M-30650; **Dvořák**—Quartets Nos. 2,6: Janácek Quartet/London 6394; Piano Quintet: Curzon/Vienna Phil. Quartet/London 6357; **Haydn**—Quartets Op. 76, Nos. 2,5: Hungarian Quartet/Turnabout 34012; Quartets Op. 77, Nos. l,2: Amadeus Quartet/DG 138980; **Hindemith**—Kleine Kammermusik: Boston Symphony Players/RCA 3166; **Mendelssohn**—Octet: Laredo, et al/Columbia MS-6848; **Mozart**—Quartets Nos. 14-19: Italiano/3-Philips S-C 71AX301; Piano Quartets: Horszowski, Budapest/Columbia MS-6683; Quintets K. 515,516: Primrose, Griller/Vanguard S-158; Quintet, K. 581, Trio K. 498: De Peyer, Melos Ensemble/Angel S-36241; **Schubert**—Octet: Melos Ensemble/Angel S-36529; Quartets Nos. 12,14: Amadeus Quartet/DG 138048; "Trout" Quintet: Marlboro Players/Vanguard 71145; **Schumann**—Piano Quintet: Serkin, Budapest/2-Columbia M2S-734; **Stravinsky**—L'Histoire du Soldat: Cocteau, Markevitch/Philips 90046.

SOLO INSTRUMENTAL

Bach—Goldberg Variations: Leonhardt/Vanguard S-175; Welltempered Clavier, Bk. 1: Kirkpatrick/2-DG ARC 2708006; Sonatas and Partitas for Violin: Grumiaux/3-Philips 835198/200; Organ Music: Walcha/DG 198305; **Beethoven**—Piano Sonatas: 8,14,23: Kempff/DG 139300; 17,21: Brendel/Turnabout 34394; 28,31: Serkin/Columbia M 31239; 30,32: Backhaus/London CS-6246; **Chopin**—Ballades: Rubinstein/RCA LSC-2370; Mazurkas: Novaes/Vox 57920; Nocturnes: Rubinstein/RCA LSC-7050; Scherzos: Rubinstein/RCA LSC-2368; Sonatas Nos. 2,3: Rubinstein/RCA 3194; **Debussy**—Piano Music (complete): W. Haas/5-Philips 5-012; **Liszt**—Sonata in B minor; Piano Music: Curzon/London 6371; **Mendelssohn**—Songs without Words: Novaes/Turnabout 34245; **Mozart**—Piano Sonatas (complete): Eschenbach/-DG 2720031; **Rachmaninoff**—Preludes, etc.: Weissenberg/-RCA 7069; **Ravel**—Piano Music (complete): Simon/3-Vox SVBX-5473; **Scarlatti**—Sonatas: Kirkpatrick/DG ARC-2533072; **Schubert**—Sonata in A; Wanderer Fantasy: Richter/Angel S-36150; Sonata in D; Impromptus: Curzon/London 6416; Sonata in A, Op. Posth.; Serkin/Columbia MS-6849; **Schumann**—Carnaval; Fantasia, Op. 17: Arrau/Philips 802746; **Scriabin**—Piano Sonatas 3,4,5,9: Ashkenazy/London 6920.

LEADING OPERA COMPANIES
SOURCE: Central Opera Service

WORLD OPERA COMPANIES (exclusive of U.S.)

AMSTERDAM: Nederlandse Operastichting; *Manager:* J.H. de Roo

BARCELONA: Gran Teatro del Liceo; *General Director:* Juan A. Pamias

BAYREUTH: Bayreuther Festspiele; *Director:* Wolfgang Wagner

BELGRADE: Srpsko Narodno Pozoriste; *Director:* D. Djurdjevic

BERLIN: (West) **Deutsche Oper;** *Artistic Director:* Jesus Lopez-Lobos. (East) **Deutsche Staatsoper;** *General Director:* Goetz Friedrich. (East) **Komische Oper;** *Director:* Joachim Herz

BRUSSELS: Théâtre Royal de la Monnaie; *Director:* Maurice Huisman

BUCHAREST: Romanian Opera; *Director:* Petre Codreanu.

BUDAPEST: Magyar Allami Operahaz & Erkel Theater (Hungarian State Opera); *Director:* Miklos Lukacs

BUENOS AIRES: Teatro Colon

COLOGNE: Bühnen der Stadt Köln; *Director:* Michael Hampe, *Music Director:* John Pritchard

COPENHAGEN: Det kongelige Teater; *Manager:* Niels Moeller

DRESDEN: Staatsoper Dresden; *Director:* Horst Seeger

DUSSELDORF/DUISBURG: Deutsche Oper am Rhein; *Director:* Grischa Barfuss

EDINBURGH: Edinburgh Festival; *Director:* John Drummond

EDMONTON: Edmonton Opera Association: *Artistic Director:* Irving Guttman

FLORENCE: Teatro Comunale & Maggio Fiorentino; *Music Director:* Riccardo Muti

FRANKFURT: Stadtische Buhnen; *Director:* Michael Gielen

GENEVA: Grand Theatre de l'Opera; *General Director:* Jean-Claude Riber; *Director Designate:* Hugues Gall

GLASGOW: Scottish Opera; *General Director:* Peter Ebert

GLYNDEBOURNE: Festival Opera; *Chairman:* George W. Christie

HAMBURG: Staatsoper; *Dir. & Chief conductor:* Christoph von Dohnányi

HELSINKI: Finnish National Opera; *General Manager:* J. Raiskinen

LEIPZIG: Staedtische Theater; *Director Opera:* Karl Kayser

LENINGRAD: Kirov Opera & Ballet Theatre; *Director:* Yuri Temirkanov

LONDON: D'Oyly Carte Ltd.; *Musical Director:* Royston Nash. **Royal Opera, Covent Garden;** *General Administrator:* John Tooley. **English National Opera Ltd.;** *Managing Director:* Lord Harewood

MARSEILLE: Opera Municipal; *Director:* R. Giovaninetti

MILAN: Teatro alla Scala; *Music Director:* Francisco Siciliani

MONTE CARLO: L'Opera de Monte-Carlo; *Director:* Guy Grinda

MOSCOW: Bolshoi Theatre of the USSR; *Director:* Giorgy Ivanov

MUNICH: Bayerische Staatsoper; *Director:* August Everding. **Theater am Gartnerplatz;** *Director:* Kurt Pscherer

NAPLES: Teatro San Carlo; *Acting General Manager:* Adriano Falvo

OSLO: Den Norske Opera (The Norwegian Opera); *Director:* Aase Nordmo-Loevberg

OTTAWA: Ottawa Festival Opera; *General Director:* Donald MacSween

PARIS: Theatre National de l'Opera; *Administrator:* Bernard Lefort

PRAGUE: National Theatre & Smetana Theatre & Tyl Theatre; *Director:* Jiri Payer

RIO DE JANEIRO: Opera Estaveldo Teatro Municipal; *Director:* Edmundo Barreto Pintos

ROME: Teatro dell'Opera; *Gen. Mgr.:* Luca di Sciena

SALZBURG: Salzburg Festival; *Director:* Dr. Otto Sertl. **Easter Festival;** *Director:* Herbert von Karajan

SOFIA: Bulgarian National Opera; *Director:* Dimitar Petkov

STOCKHOLM: Kungliga Teatern; *General Manager:* Folke Abenius

STRASBOURG: L'Opera du Rhin; *Artistic Director:* René Terrasson

STUTTGART: Wurttembergisches Staatstheater; *Music Director:* Dennis Russell Davies

SYDNEY: Australian Opera; *General Manager:* Peter Hemmings

TEL AVIV: Israel National Opera; *Director:* Simha Evan Zohar

TORONTO: Canadian Opera Company; *General Director:* Lotfi Mansouri

VANCOUVER: Vancouver Opera Association; *General Manager:* Hamilton McClymont

VENICE: Teatro La Fenice; *General Manager:* Lamberto Trezzini

VERONA: Arena di Verona; *Artistic Director:* Luciano Chailly

VIENNA: Staatsoper; *Director:* Egon Seefehlner; *Director Designate:* Lorin Maazel. **Volksoper;** *Director:* Karl Doench

WARSAW: Teatr Wielki (Grand Theatre Warsaw); *Artistic Director:* Antoni Wicherek

ZURICH: Opernhaus Zurich; *General Manager:* Klaus Helmut Drese

AMERICAN OPERA COMPANIES

BALTIMORE: Baltimore Opera Company; *General Manager:* Robert Collinge

BOSTON: Opera Company of Boston; *Artistic Director:* Sarah Caldwell

CENTRAL CITY: Central City Opera House Association; *Artistic Director:* Robert Darling

CHARLESTON: Spoleto Festival USA; *General Manager:* James Kearney

CHARLOTTE: Charlotte Opera Association; *General Director:* Richard Marshall

CHICAGO: Lyric Opera of Chicago; *General Manager:* Carol Fox. **Chicago Opera Theatre;** *Artistic Director:* Alan Stone

CINCINNATI: Cincinnati Opera Association; *General Manager:* James de Blasis

CLEVELAND: Cleveland Opera; *Artistic Director:* David Bamberger

DALLAS: Dallas Civic Opera; *General Manager:* Plato Karayanis

DAYTON/TOLEDO: Dayton/Toledo Opera Associations; *General Director:* Lester Freedman

DETROIT: Michigan Opera Theater; *General Director:* David Di Chiera

DISTRICT OF COLUMBIA: Washington Opera, Inc.; *Executive Director:* Martin Feinstein

FORT WORTH: Fort Worth Opera Association; *General Manager:* Rudolf Kruger

GLENS FALLS: Lake George Opera Company; *General Director:* David Lloyd

HARTFORD: Connecticut Opera Association, Inc.; *General Manager:* George Osborne

HONOLULU: Hawaii Opera Theatre; *General Manager:* Robert C. Bickley

HOUSTON: Houston Grand Opera Association; *General Director:* R. David Gockley

KANSAS CITY (MO.): Lyric Opera of Kansas City; *General Manager:* Russell Patterson

LOUISVILLE: Kentucky Opera Association; *Artistic Director:* Moritz Bomhard

MEMPHIS: Opera Memphis; *General Director:* Kenneth Caswell

MIAMI: Greater Miami Opera Association; *General Manager:* Robert Herman

MILWAUKEE: Florentine Opera Company; *General Manager:* Robert Caulfield. **Skylight Opera;** *Managing Director:* Colin Cabot

NEW ORLEANS: New Orleans Opera; *General Director:* Arthur Cosenza

NEW YORK: Metropolitan Opera Association; *Executive Director:* Anthony A. Bliss. **New York City Opera;** *General Director:* Beverly Sills

NEWARK: New Jersey State Opera; *Artistic Director:* Alfredo Silipigni

NORFOLK: Virginia Opera Association; *Artistic Director:* Peter Mark

OMAHA: Opera/Omaha; *General Manager:* Martha Elsberry

PHILADELPHIA: Opera Company of Philadelphia; *Acting General Manager:* Margaret Everitt

PITTSBURGH: Pittsburgh Opera Company; *Manager:* Vincent Artz

PORTLAND (ORE.): Portland Opera Association; *General Director:* Stefan Minde

PROVIDENCE: Artists Internationale; *Manager:* Ken Russell Slade

ST. LOUIS: Opera Theater of St. Louis; *General Manager:* Richard Gaddes

ST. PAUL: Minnesota Opera Company; *Artistic Director:* H. Wesley Balk

SAN DIEGO: San Diego Opera Association; *Artistic Director:* Tito Copobianco

SAN FRANCISCO: San Francisco Opera Association; *General Director:* Kurt Herbert Adler. **Western Spring Opera;** *General Director:* Kurt Herbert Adler. **Western Opera Theatre;** *Manager:* Earl Jay Schub

SANTA FE: Santa Fe Opera; *General Director:* John O. Crosby

SEATTLE: Seattle Opera Association, Inc.; *General Director:* Glynn Ross

TUCSON: Arizona Opera Company; *General Director:* James Sullivan

TULSA: Tulsa Opera Company; *General Manager:* Edward Purrington

MAJOR SYMPHONY ORCHESTRAS OF THE UNITED STATES AND CANADA
1980-81 Season

SOURCE: American Symphony Orchestra League

Atlanta Symphony Orchestra
1280 Peachtree Street, NE, Atlanta, Georgia 30309
Mus. Dir.: Robert Shaw
Gen. Mgr.: Stephen Sell

Baltimore Symphony Orchestra
1313 St. Paul St., Baltimore, MD 21210
Mus. Dir.: Sergiu Commissiona
Gen. Mgr.: Joseph Leavitt

Boston Symphony Orchestra
301 Massachusetts Ave., Symphony Hall
Boston, Massachusetts 02115
Mus. Dir.: Seiji Ozawa
Exec. Dir.: Thomas W. Morris

Buffalo Philharmonic Orchestra
26 Richmond Avenue, Buffalo, New York 14222
Mus. Dir.: Julius Rudel
Co-Mgrs.: Michael Bielski & Ruth Spero

Chicago Symphony Orchestra
220 South Michigan Avenue, Chicago, Illinois 60604
Mus. Dir.: Sir Georg Solti
Exec. V. Pres. & Gen. Mgr.: John S. Edwards

Cincinnati Symphony Orchestra
1241 Elm Street, Cincinnati, Ohio 45210
Mus. Dir.: Michael Gilien
Gen. Mgr.: Steven I. Monder
Manager: Judith Arron

Cleveland Orchestra
11011 Euclid Avenue, Cleveland, Ohio 44106
Mus. Dir.: Lorin Maazel
Gen. Mgr.: Kenneth Haas

Dallas Symphony Orchestra
P.O. Box 26207, Dallas, Texas 75226
Mus. Dir.: Eduardo Mata
Mng. Dir.: Leonard D. Stone

Denver Symphony Orchestra
1615 California Street, Denver, Colorado 80202
Mus. Dir.: Gaetano Delogu
Exec. Dir.: Carlos Wilson

Detroit Symphony Orchestra
Ford Auditorium
20 Auditorium Drive, Detroit, Michigan 48226
Mus. Dir.: Antal Dorati
Exec. Dir.: Ralph O. Guthrie

Honolulu Symphony Orchestra
1000 Bishop Street, Suite 901
Honolulu, Hawaii 96813
Mus. Dir.: Donald Johanos
Exec Dir.: Robert C. Bickley

Houston Symphony Orchestra
15 Louisiana, Houston, TX 77002
Prin. Guest Cond.: Michael Palmer
Exec. Dir.: Michael J. Woolcock

Indianapolis Symphony Orchestra
P.O. Box 88207, Indianapolis, IN 46208
Mus. Dir.: John Nelson
Gen. Mgr.: Fritz Kumb

Kansas City Philharmonic Orchestra
200 W. 14th St., Kansas City, MO 64105
Mus. Dir.: Maurice Peress
Gen. Mgr.: David Kent

Los Angeles Philharmonic Orchestra
135 N. Grand Ave., Los Angeles, CA 90012
Mus. Dir.: Carlo Maria Giulini
Exec. Dir.: Ernest Fleischmann
Gen. Mgr. Robert Harth

Milwaukee Symphony Orchestra
Performing Arts Center
929 North Water St., Milwaukee, WI 53202
Mus. Dir.: Kenneth Schermerhorn
Exec. Dir.: Robert Caulfield
Gen. Mgr.: Richard Thomas

Minnesota Orchestra
1111 Nicollet Mall, Minneapolis, MN 55403
Mus. Dir.: Neville Marriner
President: Richard M. Cisek

Montreal Symphony Orchestra
200 Maisonneuve Blvd. W.
Montreal, Quebec H2X 1Y9 Canada
Mus. Dir.: Charles Dutoit
Mng. Dir.: Roger Larose

National Symphony Orchestra
J F. Kennedy Center for the Performing Arts
Washington, DC 20566
Mus. Dir.: Mstislav Rostropovich
Pres.: Martin Feinstein
Manager: Robert Noerr

New Jersey Symphony Orchestra
213 Washington St., 16th Floor
Newark, NJ 07101
Mus. Dir.: Thomas Michalak
Gen. Mgr.: John L. Hyer

New Orleans Philharmonic Symphony Orchestra
203 Carondelet St., Suite 903
New Orleans, LA 70130
Mus. Adv.: Philippe Entremont
V.P. & Exec. Dir.: James D. Hicks

New York Philharmonic Orchestra
Avery Fisher Hall
65th St. and Broadway
New York, NY 10023
Mus. Dir.: Zubin Mehta
Exec. V.P. & Mng. Dir.: Albert K. Webster

North Carolina Symphony Orchestra
Memorial Auditorium, P.O. Box 28026
Raleigh, NC 28026
Art. Dir.: John Gosling
Gen. Mgr.: Hiram Black

Philadelphia Orchestra
1420 Locust St., Philadelphia, PA 19102
Mus. Dir.: Ricardo Muti
Exec. Dir.: Seymour L. Rosen

Pittsburgh Symphony Orchestra
Heinz Hall for the Performing Arts
600 Penn Avenue, Pittsburgh, PA 15222
Mus. Dir.: André Previn
Mng. Dir.: Marshall W. Turkin

Rochester Philharmonic Orchestra
20 Grove Pl., Rochester, NY 14605
Mus. Dir.: David Zinman
Gen. Mgr.: Tony H. Dechario

Saint Louis Symphony Orchestra
718 N. Grand Blvd., St. Louis, MO 63103
Mus. Dir.: Leonard Slatkin
Exec. Dir.: David Hyslop
Manager: Joan Briccetti

San Antonio Symphony Orchestra
109 Lexington Ave., Suite 207
San Antonio, TX 78205
Mus. Dir.: Francois Huybrechts
Mng. Dir.: Nat Greenberg

San Francisco Symphony Orchestra
107 War Memorial Veterans' Bldg.
San Francisco, CA 94102
Mus. Dir.: Edo de Waart
Exec. Dir.: Peter Pastreich

Seattle Symphony Orchestra
305 Harrison St., Seattle, WA 98109
Mus. Dir.: Rainer Miedel
Gen. Mgr.: Lanham Deal

Syracuse Symphony Orchestra
Suite 40, Civic Center, 411 Montgomery St.
Syracuse, NY 13202
Mus. Dir.: Christopher Keene
Gen. Mgr.: Eleanor Shopiro

Toronto Symphony Orchestra
215 Victoria St.
Toronto, Ontario M5B 1V1 Canada
Mus. Dir.: Andrew Davis
Mng. Dir.: Walter Homburger

Utah Symphony Orchestra
123 West South Temple
Salt Lake City, UT 84101
Mus. Dir.: Varujan Kojian
Exec. Dir.: Herold L. Gregory

Vancouver Symphony Orchestra
873 Beatty St.
Vancouver, B.C. V6B 2M6 Canada
Mus. Dir.: Kazuyoshi Akiyama
Gen. Mgr.: Michael Allerton

PROFESSIONAL RESIDENT AND REPERTORY THEATERS

SOURCE: Actors' Equity Association. The following resident and repertory groups are member companies of the League of Resident Theatres or use the L.O.R.T. contract.

ABINGDON (VA): **Barter Theatre;** P.O. Box 250 Abingdon, VA 24210

ALBANY (NY): **The League of Theatre Artists;** P.O. Box 2114, Empire State Plaza, Albany, NY 12203

ALLENTOWN (PA): **Pennsylvania Stage Company;** J.I. Rodale Theatre, 837 Linden St.; Allentown, Pa 18101

ANCHORAGE (AK): **Alaska Repertory Theatre;** 523 W. 8th Ave., Suite 110, Anchorage, AK 99501

ARROW ROCK (MO): **Arrow Rock Lyceum Theatre;** Arrow Rock, MO 63520 (Summer)

ATLANTA (GA): **Alliance Theatre Company;** 1280 Peachtree St., N.E., Atlanta, GA 30309

BALTIMORE (MD): **Center Stage;** 700 N. Calvert St., Baltimore, MD 21202

BROOKLYN (NY): **Brooklyn Academy of Music;** 30 Lafayette Ave., Brooklyn, NY 11217

BUFFALO (NY): **Studio Arena Theatre;** 710 Main St., Buffalo, NY 14202

CAMBRIDGE (MA): **American Repertory;** 64 Brattle St., Cambridge, MA 02138

CHAPEL HILL (NC): **Playmakers Repertory Company;** 103 South Bldg., U. of N.C., Chapel Hill, NC 27514

CHICAGO (IL): **Goodman Theatre Company;** 200 S. Columbus Dr., Chicago, IL 60603

CINCINNATI (OH): **Playhouse in the Park;** P.O. Box 6537, Cincinnati, OH 45206

CLEVELAND (OH): **The Cleveland Playhouse;** 2040 E. 86th St., Cleveland, OH 44106 **Center Repertory Theatre;** 1630 Euclid Ave., Cleveland, OH 44115

COHOES (NY): **Cohoes Music Hall;** 58 Remsen St., Cohoes, NY 12047

COSTA MESA (CA): **South Coast Repertory Theatre;** 655 South Town Center Dr., Costa Mesa, CA 92626

DALLAS (TX): **Theatre 3;** 2800 Routh St., Dallas TX 75201

EVANSTON (IL): **The North Light Repertory Theatre, Inc,;** 927 Noyes, Evanston, IL 60201

GAMBIER (OH): **Kenyon Repertory Theatre & Festival, Inc.;** 202 West Brooklyn, Gambier, OH 43022

HARTFORD (CT): **Hartford Stage Company;** 50 Church St., Hartford, CT 06103

HORSE CAVE (KY): **Horse Cave Theatre;** P.O. Box 215, Horse Cave, KY 42749 (Summer)

HOUSTON (TX): **Alley Theatre;** 615 Texas Ave., Houston, TX 77002

HUNTINGTON STATION (NY): **The Performing Arts Foundation;** PAF Playhouse, 185 Second St., Huntington Station, NY 11746

INDIANAPOLIS (IN): **Indiana Repertory Theatre;** 411 E. Michigan St., Indianapolis, IN 46204

KANSAS CITY (MO): **Missouri Vanguard Theatre** (Spring); **Missouri Repertory Theatre** (Summer); U. of Missouri at Kansas City, 5100 Rockhill Rd., Kansas City, MO 64110

KNOXVILLE (TN): **Clarence Brown Theatre Company,** Department of Speech and Theatre; 206 Mc-Clung Tower, U. of Tennessee, Knoxville, TN 37916

LAKE PLACID (NY): **Center for Music, Drama, and Art;** Saranac Ave. at Fawn Ridge, Lake Placid, NY 12946

LAKEWOOD (OH): **Great Lakes Shakespeare Festival;** Lakewood Civic Auditorium, Franklin Blvd. & Bunts Rd., Lakewood, OH 44107 (Summer)

LENOX (MA): **Shakespeare and Company;** The Mount, Plunkett Street, Lenox, MA 01240 (Summer)

LEWISTON (ME): **Bates Summer Theatre;** Bates College, Lewiston, ME 04240 (Summer)

LOS ANGELES (CA): **Mark Taper Forum** (Center Theatre Group); 135 N. Grand Ave., Los Angeles, CA 90012

LOS GATOS (CA): **California Actors' Theatre;** P.O. Box 1355, Los Gatos, CA 95030

LOUISVILLE (KY): **Actors Theatre of Louisville;** 316-320 W. Main St., Louisville, KY 40202

LOWELL, (MA): **Merrimack Regional Theatre;** P.O. Box 228, Lowell, MA 01853

MADISON (NJ): **New Jersey Shakespeare Festival;** Drew U., Madison, NJ 07940 (Summer & Fall)

MIAMI (FL): **Players State Theatre;** Coconut Grove Playhouse, 3500 Main Hwy., Miami, FL 33133

MIDDLETOWN (VA): **The Wayside Theatre;** P.O. Box 260, Middletown, VA 22645

MILWAUKEE (WI): **Milwaukee Repertory Theatre;** Performing Arts Center, 929 N. Water St., Milwaukee, WI 53202

MINNEAPOLIS (MN): **Cricket Theatre;** 345 13th Ave. N.E., (University at 13th), Minneapolis, MN 55413 **The Guthrie Theater;** 725 Vineland Pl., Minneapolis, MN 55403

MISSOULA (MT): **Montana Repertory Theatre;** U. of Mont., Missoula, MT 59812

NEW BRUNSWICK (NJ): **George Street Playhouse;** 414 George St., New Brunswick, NJ 08901

NEW HAVEN (CT): **Long Wharf Theatre;** 222 Sargent Dr., New Haven, CT 06511

Yale Repertory Theatre; Yale School of Drama, New Haven, CT 06520

NEW YORK (NY): **The Acting Company;** 420 W. 42nd St., 3rd Fl., New York, NY 10036

Chelsea Theatre Center; 407 West 43rd St., New York, NY 10019

The Negro Ensemble Company; St. Mark's Playhouse, 133 Second Ave., New York, NY 10003

New York Shakespeare Festival; (Delacorte and Mobile Theatres),

The Public Theatre, 425 Lafayette St., New York, NY 10003 (Summer)

The Roundabout Theatre Company; 333 W. 23rd St., New York, NY 10011

NORFOLK (VA): **Virginia Stage Co.;** 142 West York St., Suite 902, Norfolk, VA 23510

PARK FOREST (IL): **Illinois Theatre Center;** 400 Lakewood Blvd., Park Forest, IL 60466

PHILADELPHIA (PA): **The Philadelphia Drama Guild;** 220 S. 16th St., Philadelphia, PA 19102

PITTSBURGH (PA): **Pittsburgh Public Theatre;** Suite 230, One Allegheny Square, Pittsburgh, PA 15212

PORTSMOUTH (NH): **Theatre By The Sea;** 125 Bow St., Portsmouth, NH 03801

PRINCETON (NJ): **McCarter Theatre Company, Inc.;** P.O. Box 526, Princeton U., Princeton, NJ 08540

PROVIDENCE (RI): **Trinity Square Repertory Company;** 201 Washington St., Providence, RI 02903

RICHMOND (VA): **Virginia Museum Theatre;** Boulevard & Grove Aves., Richmond, VA 22331 VA 22331

ROCHESTER (MI): **Meadow Brook Theatre;** Oakland U., Rochester, MI 48063

ROCHESTER (NY): **Genesee Valley Arts Foundation (GeVa);** 168 Clinton Ave. South, Rochester, NY 14604

ST. LOUIS (MO): **Loretto-Hilton Theatre;** 130 Edgar Rd., St. Louis, MO 63119

ST. PAUL (MN): **Actors Theatre of St. Paul;** 2115 Summit Ave., St. Paul, MN 55105

SAN DIEGO (CA): **Old Globe Theatre;** P.O. Box 2171, San Diego, CA 92112

SAN FRANCISCO (CA): **American Conservatory Theatre;** 450 Geary St., San Francisco, CA 94102

SARASOTA (FL): **Asolo Theatre Festival;** P.O. Box Drawer E, Sarasota, FL 33578

SEATTLE (WA): **Seattle Repertory Theatre;** P.O. Box B, Queen Anne Sta., Seattle Center, Seattle, WA 98109

A Contemporary Theatre; 709 First Ave. W., Seattle, WA 98119 **Intiman Theatre;** Box 4246, Seattle, WA 98104

STAMFORD (CT): **Hartman Theatre Company;** 61 Atlantic St., Stamford, CT 06901

STRATFORD (CT): **American Shakespeare Theatre;** 1850 Elm Street, Stratford, CT 06497

SYRACUSE (NY): **Syracuse Stage;** University Regent Theatre, 820 E. Genesee St., Syracuse, NY 13210

TUCSON (AZ): **Arizona Civic Theatre;** 120 W. Broadway, Tucson, AZ 85701

VISALIA (CA): **California Shakespeare Festival;** 417 North Locust St., Box 590, Visalia, CA 93277

WASHINGTON (DC): **Arena Stage;** Sixth and M Sts. S.W., Washington, DC 20024

The Folger Theatre Group; 201 E. Capitol St. S.E., Washington, DC 20003

WATERFORD (CT): **Eugene O'Neill Memorial Theatre Center;** P.O. Box 206, Waterford, CT 06385

WEST SPRINGFIELD (MA): **Stage West;** 1511 Memorial Ave., W. Springfield, MA 01089

ART MUSEUMS

WORLD

AMSTERDAM: Rijksmuseum (1808); *Collections:* 16th/17th-century Dutch paintings and drawings by Rembrandt, Hals, Vermeer, and others.
Stedelijk Museum (1895); *Collections:* Impressionist to modern paintings and sculpture, including works of van Gogh, Chagall, and Dubuffet.

ANTWERP: Koninklijk Museum voor Schone Kunsten (Royal Museum of Fine Arts) (1890); *Collections:* Dutch, Flemish, and French old masters, including Van Eyck, Van der Weyden, Memling, Rubens, Rembrandt, and Hals; 19th/20th-century Belgian art.

BERLIN: National-Galerie (1876); *Collections:* European paintings and sketches from the 18th century to the present.

BRUSSELS: Musée des Beaux-Arts (1892); *Collections:* Old and new masters, drawings, and sculpture.

BUDAPEST: Magyar Nemzeti Museum (Hungarian National Museum) (1802); *Collections:* Archaeological finds; medieval to contemporary art; coins and historical objects.
Szépmüveszéti Museum (Museum of Fine Arts) (1896); *Collections:* Egyptian and Greco-Roman antiquities; Hungarian and foreign old masters; sculpture, drawings, and engravings.

CAIRO: Coptic Museum (1908); *Collections:* Art treasures of early Christian culture in Egypt.
Museum of Islamic Art (1881); *Collections:* Islamic painting, sculpture, ceramics, and applied arts (7th to 19th century).

CALCUTTA: Indian Museum (1814); *Collections:* Indian art from prehistoric to Moslem times; Indian and Persian paintings; and Tibetan banners.

DRESDEN: National Gallery (1846); *Collections:* Italian, Dutch, Flemish, and German old and new masters, including Rembrandt, Correggio, Titian, Rubens, Van Dyck, Veronese, and del Sarto.

FLORENCE: Galleria dell'Accademia (1784); *Collections:* The most complete collection of Michelangelo's statues in Florence, as well as paintings by Tuscan masters of the 13th to 16th centuries.
Galleria degli Uffizi (16th century); *Collections:* The world's finest collection of Italian Renaissance painting.

THE HAGUE: Keninklijk Kabinet van Schilderijen (Mauritshuis) (Royal Picture Gallery) (1820); *Collections:* Dutch and German art; excellent Vermeers and Rembrandts.

ISTANBUL: Museum of the Seraglio of Topkapi (Built mid-15th century); *Collections:* Sultans' treasure; Chinese and Japanese porcelain; enamels, embroidery, miniatures, and precious stones.

JERUSALEM: Museum of Archaeology and Art (1965); *Collections:* Works concerning the Bible and Middle Eastern history; features the Billy Rose Art Garden and the Shrine of the Book.

LENINGRAD: Hermitage (1764); *Collections:* More than 2.5 million objets d'art, including gold artifacts from Helleno-Scythian times, jewelry of the tsars, French impressionist paintings, old and new masters.
State Russian Museum (1898); *Collections:* Exhibits numbering 250,000 of Russian art, sculpture, drawings, coins, and medals.

LONDON: The British Museum; *Collections:* Extensive collections spanning man's art and culture from neolithic age to present, including the Elgin Marbles.
National Gallery (1857); *Collections:* A superb collection from the 12th century to the present.
Tate Gallery (1897); *Collections:* British painting from the 16th century to the present, including works by Blake, Constable, Turner; French impressionists and modern sculpture.
Victoria and Albert Museum (1852); *Collections:* Fine and applied art of all countries, periods, and styles; ceramics, textile, sculpture, woodwork, paintings, prints, and drawings.

MADRID: El Prado (1819); *Collections:* Italian, Flemish, Dutch, and Spanish Renaissance paintings; classical, Renaissance, and baroque sculpture; includes a large collection of Murillo, Goya, El Greco, Rubens, Bosch, Van Dyck, da Vinci, and Tintoretto.

MEXICO CITY: Museo Nacional de Antropologia (1865); *Collections:* Anthropological, ethnological, and archaeological collections relating to Mexico.

MOSCOW: State Tretyakov Gallery (1856); *Collection* A rich collection of 40,000 Russian icons; Russian a Soviet sculpture, graphics and paintings, dating fro the 11th century to the present.

MUNICH: Alte Pinakothek (1836); *Collections:* Germa Dutch, Flemish, Italian, Spanish, and French maste

NEW DELHI: National Museum of India (1949); *Co lections:* Indian and Central Asian treasures that da from 3000 B.C. to the present; sculpture, painting manuscripts, miniatures, and crafts.

PARIS: Galerie du Jeu de Paume (1920); *Collection* Including examples by Monet, Cézanne, van Gog Renoir, Degas, Pissarro, and Gaugin.
Musée Guimet; *Collections:* The finest European co lection of oriental painting, sculpture, and applied art
Musée du Louvre (1793); *Collections:* Oriental, Egy tian, Roman, and Greek antiquities; medieval, Renai sance, and modern sculpture and painting.
Musee National d'Art Moderne (1943) **(Centre N tional d'Art et de Culture Georges Pompidou);** *Co lections:* 20th-century paintings and sculpture.
Musée de l'Orangerie (1853); *Collections:* A group Utrillos, Cézannes, Monets, and others, exhibited in th atmosphere of a collector's apartment.
Musée Rodin (1916); *Collections:* The sculptor's wor and collection are displayed in a home and garden.

ROME: Borghese Art Gallery (c. 1616); *Collection* Classical and baroque sculpture and painting.

ROTTERDAM: Museum Boymans-van Beuninge (1847); *Collections:* European art from the 15th cer tury to the present, including Van Eyck, Breughel th Elder, Hals, Rembrandt, van Ruisdael, Hobbema, Rι bens, Titian, Watteau, and Boucher.

SAO PAULO: Museu de Arte Contemporânea (1947 *Collections:* Nearly 1,700 works by such modern ma ters as Kandinsky, Léger, and the early cubists.
Museu de Arte de São Paulo (1947); *Collections:* panoramic view of Western art from gothic times to th present; paintings by Hals, Raphael, Renoir, Toulous Lautrec, and Rembrandt are included.

TAIPEI: National Palace Museum (1925); *Collection* Examples of Chinese art from the Shang to the Ch'ir dynasty that were brought to Taipei from the Mair land during the Communist revolution.

TORONTO: Royal Ontario Museum at Toronto (1912 *Collections:* Art and archaeological objects from th Americas, Africa, Polynesia, ancient Egypt, Rome an Greece; Chinese, Japanese, Islamic, and Indian ar European art from all ages.

VIENNA: Kunsthistorisches Museum (Museum of Fin Arts) (1891); *Collections:* Egyptian, Greek, Etruscar Roman, and Cyprian antiquities; excellent Breugh collection; French, Dutch, Italian, and German Renai sance and baroque art.

UNITED STATES

BALTIMORE: Baltimore Museum of Art (1914); *Collec tions:* Epstein and Jacobs collections of old maste and sculpture; 19th/20th-century French paintin; sculpture, graphics; Toulouse-Lautrec posters; cor temporary American art; Oriental art and mosaics.
Walters Art Gallery (1931); *Collections:* More tha 25,000 objects, of which the Byzantine and mediev examples are noteworthy; classical art of Greece, Rom Egypt, medieval to 19th-century European art.

BOSTON: Isabella Steward Gardner Museum (1900 *Collections:* American and European painting an sculpture, from classical times to the 20th century.
Museum of Fine Arts (1870); *Collections:* Excep tionally fine collection of prints, Oriental art, dec rative arts; Egyptian, Greek, and Roman art; old ma ters and 19th-century French paintings.

BUFFALO: Albright-Knox Art Gallery (1862); *Collec tions:* 18th-century English, 19th-century America and French and contemporary American and Europe an paintings; sculpture (3000 B.C. to the present).

CAMBRIDGE: Harvard University, Fogg Art Museu (1895); *Collections:* Oriental and Western art fro ancient times to the present; representative collection of painting, sculpture, prints, and drawings, includin Italian primitives and Chinese jades and bronzes.

CHICAGO: Art Institute of Chicago (1879); *Collection* Major periods of Western art and primitive and Or ental art.
University of Chicago, Oriental Institute Museum (1919); *Collections:* More than 70,000 objects tha

represent the art, religion, and daily life of ancient Egypt, Nubia, Assyria, Babylonia, Persia, Palestine, Syria, Anatolia, Libya, and Cyprus.

CINCINNATI: Cincinnati Art Museum (1881); *Collections:* Sculpture, painting, and ceramics of Egypt, Greece, Rome; Near Eastern and Far Eastern art; 19th/20th-century European and American art; primitive art from Oceania, Africa, and the Americas.

CLEVELAND: Cleveland Museum of Art (1913); *Collections:* Art from many cultures and periods, including old masters and modern paintings, sculpture, prints, drawings, porcelain, metalwork, and furniture.

COLUMBUS: Columbus Gallery of Fine Arts (1878); *Collections:* Schumacher Collection of old masters; Howald Collection of modern French and American painting; major collection of the art of George Bellows; South Pacific primitives.

DALLAS: Dallas Museum of Fine Arts (1903); *Collections:* Ancient, pre-Columbian, African sculpture, Japanese, European and American art.

DETROIT: Detroit Institute of Arts (1885); *Collections:* Art from many cultures, dating from prehistoric times to the present, including Italian medieval and Renaissance sculpture, 17th-century Dutch paintings, and French-Canadian art.

DISTRICT OF COLUMBIA: Corcoran Gallery of Art (1859); *Collections:* American painting, sculpture, and drawing from the 18th century to the present; Dutch, Flemish, French and English painting.
Hirshhorn Museum and Sculpture Garden (1974); *Collections:* Joseph Hirshhorn's private modern art collection valued at over $1 million.
National Gallery of Art (1937); *Collections:* Mellon, Kress, and Widener collections of old masters; Rosenwald Collection of prints and drawings; Garbisch Collection of American primitive paintings; East Building (1978) contains permanent and changing exhibits of painting and sculpture.
Phillips Collection (1918); *Collections:* Modern art, especially 19th/20th-century American and European works.
Smithsonian Institution, Freer Gallery of Art (1906); *Collections:* Near and Far Eastern art and artifacts, 19th/20th-century American art, including the Peacock Room entirely decorated by Whistler.

FORT WORTH: Amon Carter Museum of Western Art (1961); *Collections:* Western paintings and sculpture, includes Frederic Remington and Charles Russell.
Kimball Art Museum (1972); *Collections:* masterpieces from ancient times to cubism.
Fort Worth Art Museum (1961); *Collections:* 20th century paintings and sculpture.

HARTFORD: Wadsworth Atheneum (1842); *Collections:* European and American painting from 1400 to the present, including medieval and Renaissance European tapestries; early South and Central American art.

HOUSTON: Museum of Fine Arts of Houston (1900); *Collections:* Paintings, sculpture, and decorative arts covering most periods of history, including Renaissance painting, classical art and sculpture, and American art.

KANSAS CITY (MO.): William Rockhill Nelson Gallery and Atkins Museum of Fine Arts (1926); *Collections:* Oriental art, especially Chinese; classical, European, and American painting, sculpture, and decorative arts.

LOS ANGELES: Los Angeles County Museum of Art (1961); *Collections:* Major periods of European and American art; Oriental art.

MERION STATION (PA.): Barnes Foundation (1922); *Collections:* European Renaissance and 20th-century American painting; African sculpture and Chinese art.

MINNEAPOLIS: Minneapolis Institute of Arts (1914); *Collections:* Oriental and pre-Columbian art; American and European painting and sculpture.
Walker Art Center (1972); *Collections:* 20th century art, changing exhibits.

NEWARK: Newark Museum (1909); *Collections:* American painting and sculpture from all periods; Oriental art, emphasizing the expression of Tibet.

NEW HAVEN: Yale Center for British Art (1977); *Collections:* British paintings, prints and drawings.

NEW ORLEANS: Isaac Delgado Museum of Art (1910); *Collections:* Kress Collection of Renaissance painting; Hyams Collection of the Barbizon school; contemporary European and American painting, sculpture, and drawings; Howard Collection of Greek vases.

NEW YORK CITY: Brooklyn Museum (1893); *Collections:* Egyptian, Near and Far Eastern art; Renaissance and medieval painting; American painting from all periods and 19th/20th-century European art; primitive art and artifacts from Oceania, Africa, the Far East, and South America.
Frick Collection (1935); *Collections:* European painting, sculpture, prints, and drawings from the 14th century to the 1800s that constitute the former personal treasures of Henry Clay Frick; Limoges enamels, French and Chinese porcelains, and period furniture.
Jewish Museum (1904); *Collections:* This largest exhibit of Judaica in the Western Hemisphere is housed in the former Felix Warburg mansion.
Metropolitan Museum of Art (1870); *Collections:* Comprehensive collections that cover 5,000 years of history and represent the arts of Egypt, Babylonia, Assyria, Greece, Rome, Near and Far East, Europe, pre-Columbian culture, and the United States; Robert Lehman collection of European paintings and drawings; includes the Cloisters in Fort Tryon Park.
Museum of Modern Art (1929); *Collections:* One of the foremost collections of 19th/20th-century American and European painting, sculpture, prints, photographs, posters, and films.
Pierpont Morgan Library (1924); *Collections:* Old master drawings, Rembrandt etchings, and manuscripts.
Solomon R. Guggenheim Museum (1937); *Collections:* Impressionist to contemporary painting and sculpture, including the world's largest collection of Kandinsky's work; paintings and sculpture by Picasso, Chagall, Klee, Brancusi, and Modigliani.
Whitney Museum of American Art (1930); *Collections:* American paintings, sculpture, drawings, and prints; the 20th-century American art housed ranges from realism to abstract expressionism.

PASADENA (CALIF.): Norton Simon Museum of Art at Pasadena (1974); *Collections:* European paintings spanning six centuries; modern sculpture garden; Indian and South Asian bronzes and stone figures.

PHILADELPHIA: Philadelphia Museum of Art (1875); *Collections:* Dutch, Flemish, French, American, and Italian masters; cubist and postcubist art; Far Eastern and Near Eastern art; Pennsylvania Dutch folk art; tapestries, silver, china, and period rooms.
University of Pennsylvania, University Museum (1887); *Collections:* Archaeological finds of Near East, Egypt, the Mediterranean, and the Americas; ethnology of Africa, Oceania, and art of China, pre-1000 A.D.

PITTSBURGH: Carnegie Institute, Museum of Art (1896); *Collections:* American and European painting and sculpture, including old masters and impressionists; international collection of modern art.

SAN FRANCISCO: California Palace of the Legion of Honor (1924); *Collections:* European and American painting, sculpture, and decorative arts; Egyptian and Greek antiquities.
M. H. De Young Memorial Museum (1895); *Collections:* European and American art from ancient times to 1850; Oriental and South Pacific art, including the Avery Brundage Collection of Asian art; Kress Collection of European old masters, Flemish tapestries; art of pre-Columbian Central, South, and North American Indians.
San Francisco Museum of Modern Art (1921); *Collections:* Contemporary painting, sculpture, drawings, prints, photography, and decorative arts from Europe, the United States, and Latin America.

SAN MARINO (CALIF.): Henry E. Huntington Library and Art Gallery (1919); *Collections:* Eighteenth-century British portraits and French sculpture; 15th/16th-century Italian and Flemish paintings; 18th/19th-century French and British decorative arts, and Renaissance bronzes.

SEATTLE: Seattle Art Museum (1917); *Collections:* Chinese, Japanese, Indian, and Near Eastern art; Egyptian, Greek, Roman antiquities; European Renaissance painting, sculpture, and porcelain, including the Kress Collection; Northwest Indian and pre-Columbian primitive art.

TOLEDO: Toledo Museum of Art (1901); *Collections:* European art from classical times to the 20th century; American painting and decorative arts.

WORCESTER (MASS.): Worcester Art Museum (1896); *Collections:* American, European, and Oriental art—ancient through contemporary; painting, sculpture, prints, decorative arts; early American and Italian art.

THE REVIEWS: 1979/80
BOOKS

As the new decade crept in upon us, some writers were busy trying to puzzle out the past. Over a half dozen books published between August 1, 1979, and August 1, 1980, threw the '60s decade on the analyst's couch in an effort to understand what happened then to make us the people we were as the 1980s approached. Among the books looking behind us were: *White Kids: A Generation Revealed, Peace-Time Explored, Some Friends Made and Others Lost on a Long Trip Through a Strange Decade* by Michael Wolff, *Aquarian Odyssey: A 1960s Album* by Don Snyder, *Fire in the Streets: America in the 1960s* by Milton Viorst and *Of Kennedys and Kings: Making Sense of the Sixties* by Harris Wofford.

If these men showed us lessons to be learned from the past, there were still laughs to be had in the future. A group of wits pulled up a typewriter and hit out a satire of virtually the entire world. It was a wacky remembrance of things to come published in a large format paperback: *The '80s: A Look Back at the Tumultuous Decade* edited by Tony Hendra, Christopher Cerf and Peter Elbling. In case any of us weren't up to coping with the 1980s, we could live it by reading a history of the period before it began. Our dependable funny lady also fiddled with time, and Ms. Bombeck published *Aunt Erma's Cope Book: How to Get from Monday to Friday . . . in 12 Days.*

It was a full year of literary biographies. John Steinbeck was profiled by Thomas Kiernan, W. H. Auden by Charles Osborne, A. E. Housman by Richard Graves, Somerset Maugham by Ted Morgan, Katherine Mansfield by Antony Alpers and George Orwell by Peter Stansky and William Abrahams.

Sports figures were not ignored, particularly football stalwarts, and many recounted their own stories. *Terry Bradshaw: Man of Steel* was the modest title given to the Pittsburgh Steelers quarterback's autobiography written with Dave Diles. The owner of the Chicago Bears provided *Halas by Halas,* written by George Halas with Gwen Morgan and Arthur Veysey. Jack Tatum of the Oakland Raiders pulled few punches about the sport's violence in *They Call Me Assassin,* which he wrote with Bill Kuchner.

However, not everything was macho accented. The spate of women's books asserting itself in recent years was being met with increasing force from a shelf piled high with books about the many facets of men. This year we encountered *Men's Bodies, Men's Selves* by Sam Julty, *The New Male: From Self-Destruction to Self Care* by Herb Goldberg, *Real Men* by Frank Rose and *Of Men and Manhood* by Leonard Kriegel. The image of men in America as represented in the masculine figures we see in advertising and fashion was explored in *Male Model* by Charles Hix with Michael Taylor.

The woman's side of the camera was the focus of *How to Be a Top Model* by Naomi Sims, a black high fashion model herself. More black beauty was on display in *The Black Woman's Complete Guide to Great Looks* by La Verne Powlis, the beauty editor of *Bride's* magazine. Even songbird Marie Osmond sashayed into the spotlight with *Marie Osmond's Guide to Beauty, Health and Style,* which she wrote with Julie Davis.

There was evidence of a lot of style this year. One instance was the cool aplomb with which Bantam Books handed over $3.2 million, the most ever paid for the paperback rights to a book. The deal was with Judith Krantz for the honor of publishing the paperback edition of *Princess Daisy.* But when it came to acquisitions, one of the most riveting was when Doubleday shelled out $21.1 million and bought itself the New York Mets.

Happy endings weren't for everyone. Shockingly, violence darkened the world of books this year. Herman Tarnower, author of the astonishingly successful bestseller *The Complete Scarsdale Medical Diet,* was shot to death.

More jealousy and unhappines were to be found in *Little Gloria . . . Happy at Last* by Barbara Goldsmith, an ironically titled exploration of fashion designer and socialite Gloria Vanderbilt's tortured family past.

Another woman's life story retold was that of Mrs. Theodore Roosevelt. Sylvia Jukes Morris, wife of Edmund Morris, who had just won the Pulitzer Prize with his biography of Theodore Roosevelt, published a biography of his wife: *Edith Kermit Roosevelt: A Portrait of a First Lady.*

Henry Kissinger remembered his *White House Years* in a bestselling book, and former president Richard Nixon expostulated about our unresolved conflict with Russia in a cautionary book about *The Real War.* Other political titles were *With No Apologies: The Personal and Political Memoirs of Senator Barry Goldwater, Hubert: The Triumph and Tragedy of the Humphrey I Knew* by Edgar Berman (Humphrey's doctor) and *The Man Who Kept the Secrets: Richard Helms and the CIA* by Thomas Powers.

As usual, movie stars were reeled into numerous biographies. Fred L. Guiles wrote one about Tyrone Power. Charles Higham suggested that a swashbuckling hero was a secret Nazi agent in *Errol Flynn: The Untold Story.* Gary Cooper's life gave rise to no fewer than three biographies: *The Last Hero: A Biography of Gary Cooper* by Larry Swindell, *Coop* by Stuart Kaminsky and *Gary Cooper* by Hector Arce.

Heroes of another sort were aloft again in Tom Wolfe's portrayal of our early astronauts in *The Right Stuff.* The Supreme Court had some of its skeletons rattled in an indiscreet book called *The Brethren* by Bob Woodward and Scott Armstrong.

There were a pair of very successful, very naughty books on sex: *Men in Love* by Nancy Friday, which whispered a host of men's sexual fantasies in graphic detail, and *Thy Neighbor's Wife* by Gay Talese, a controversial look at the changing sexual mores in the United States.

The matter of dangerous waste stockpiles, such as those that so direly affected the residents of New York's Love Canal, became a heated subject. Books such as Michael Brown's *Laying Waste: The Poisoning of America by Toxic Chemicals* cried out warnings that some chemical companies didn't want heard.

Moving up as quickly as the inflation rate were sales of a book on economics by a Nobel Prize expert on the subject and his wife: *Free to Choose: A Personal Statement* by Milton and Rose Friedman.

In fiction, a number of writers returned to the bookstores with novels written after a long bsence. Perhaps the man who kept us waiting he longest, and who won the most critical hur-ahs with his first novel in eighteen years was William Maxwell. His was the brief but brilliant o Long, See You Tomorrow. William Golding, uthor of Lord of the Flies, offered his first novel n twelve years, Darkness Visible. John Barth's etters, an 864-page novel written in the style of he 18th-century epistolary novel, was his first n seven years.

Norman Mailer stretched out the meaning of ength still further with his Pulitzer Prize-win-ing fictional nonfiction about executed murderer ary Gilmore. The Executioner's Song went on or over 1,050 pages. Other well-received fiction ncluded Philip Roth's The Ghost Writer, Wright Morris' Plains Song, The Transit of Venus by hirley Hazzard and Jailbird by Kurt Vonnegut. A novel appeared from an unexpected source hen actor Dirk Bogarde wrote A Gentle Occu-ation, set in the Dutch East Indies after World War II.

With The Americans, John Jakes claimed he was concluding his Kent Family Chronicles, one of the most successful paperback series ever published. This was the eighth volume, and it brought the Kents into the 20th century, if not up to the present. P. D. James, a perennial darling of mystery reviewers, suddenly encoun-tered a great deal of affection in the book-buying public as well, who bought Innocent Blood in greater numbers than any of her earlier books. The Italian novelist, Alberto Moravia, sent us The Time of Desecration from across the Atlantic and said it was the last novel he would ever write.

Two writers, not best known for their verse, were published posthumously as poets. Eugene O'Neill's collection was Poems: 1912-1944. Er-nest Hemingway's was called simply 88 Poems.

Certainly not everything published during the year was worth saving, but if someone wanted to know how to put any of the above together in a properly bibliophilic fashion, one could turn to Collectible Books: Some New Paths edited by Jean Peters.

—Robert Dahlin

ELECTED BEST SELLERS: 1979-80

ICTION

Title	Author	Publisher
he Bourne Identity	Robert Ludlum	Richard Marek
miley's People	John le Carré	Knopf
ailbird	Kurt Vonnegut	Delacorte Press/ Seymour Lawrence
he Devil's Alternative	Frederick Forsyth	Viking
age of Angels	Sidney Sheldon	Morrow
andom Winds	Belva Plain	Delacorte Press
he Dead Zone	Stephen King	Viking
rincess Daisy	Judith Krantz	Crown
riple	Ken Follett	Arbor House
he Executioner's Song	Norman Mailer	Little, Brown
he Spike	Arnaud de Borchgrave and Robert Moss	Crown
The Establishment	Howard Fast	Houghton Mifflin
o Love Lost	Helen Van Slyke	Lippincott & Crowell
ane & Abel	Jeffrey Archer	Simon & Schuster
ortraits	Cynthia Freeman	Arbor House
he Last Enchantment	Mary Stewart	Morrow
nnocent Blood	P. D. James	Scribners
Vho's On First	William F. Buckley, Jr.	Doubleday
ins of the Fathers	Susan Howatch	Simon & Schuster
he Green Ripper	John D. MacDonald	Lippincott
he Bleeding Heart	Marilyn French	Summit Books
he Ninja	Eric Van Lustbader	M. Evans
Memories of Another Day	Harold Robbins	Simon & Schuster

ONFICTION

Title	Author	Publisher
ree to Choose: A Personal Statement	Milton and Rose Friedman	Harcourt Brace Jovanovich
he Brethren	Bob Woodward and Scott Armstrong	Simon & Schuster
hy Neighbor's Wife	Gay Talese	Doubleday
he Third Wave	Alvin Toffler	Morrow
en in Love	Nancy Friday	Delacorte Press
he Real War	Richard Nixon	Warner Books
unt Erma's Cope Book	Erma Bombeck	McGraw-Hill
ow to Become Financially Independent by Investing in Real Estate	Albert J. Lowry	Simon & Schuster
n a Clear Day You Can See General Motors	J. Patrick Wright	J. Patrick Wright Associates
onahue: My Own Story	Phil Donahue & Co.	Simon & Schuster
he Right Stuff	Tom Wolfe	Farrar, Strauss & Giroux
natomy of an Illness as Perceived by the Patient	Norman Cousins	Norton
ames Herriot's Yorkshire	James Herriot	St. Martin's Press
ll You Need to Know About the IRS	Paul N. Strassels with Robert Wool	Random House
estoring the American Dream	Robert Ringer	QED
lothing Down	Robert Allen	Simon & Schuster
rdeal	Linda Lovelace with Mike McGrady	Citadel Press
erpentine	Thomas Thompson	Doubleday
ill: The Autobiography of G. Gordon Liddy	G. Gordon Liddy	St. Martin's Press
ar Within and Without	Anne Morrow Lindbergh	Harcourt Brace Jovanovich
im Fixx's Second Book of Running	Jim Fixx	Random House
eartsounds	Martha Weinman Lear	Simon & Schuster

THEATRE

This season Broadway broke box office records, with total receipts of $143 million. Part of this figure was certainly attributable to rising ticket costs, but much of it could be traced to large profits from two new shows, "Evita" and "Sugar Babies," and to such holdover hits as "Annie" and "A Chorus Line." Although the musical scene improved toward the end of the season, and there were a few fine new plays, this was not an exceptionally creative year for Broadway.

Once again, the best plays came to Broadway from outside sources — Off Broadway, regional and London theatre. "Talley's Folly," Lanford Wilson's heartwarming romance, winner of both the Pulitzer Prize for drama and the New York Drama Critics Circle Award for best play, was developed within the Circle Repertory Company. Samm-Art Williams's "Home," a jubilant affirmation about a black man's odyssey, began at the Negro Ensemble Company, and came to Broadway, buoyed by the performance of Charles Brown in the central role. Michael Weller's "Loose Ends," a complementary work to the author's "Moonchildren" was first produced at Washington's Arena Stage. "Children of a Lesser God" by Mark Medoff, a Tony-award winning study of the world of the deaf, grew out of the Mark Taper Forum in Los Angeles. On Broadway, the play won three major Tonys — as best play, and for John Rubinstein and Phyllis Frelich as best actor and actress. The best new British play was Harold Pinter's "Betrayal," which told of adultery in reverse chronology. And Tom Stoppard sent Broadway "Night and Day," starring Maggie Smith.

As usual, a number of the season's most notable works were seen, and stayed, Off Broadway and Off-Off Broadway. "Tongues" was a two-part monologue about love and death, written by Sam Shepard and Joseph Chaikin and acted by Mr. Chaikin. "A Piece of Monologue" was a monologue by Samuel Beckett about death, acted by David Warrilow. Jean-Claude van Itallie made a comeback with an urban one-act piece called "Bag Lady." With great comic zeal, Wallace Shawn's "Marie and Bruce" showed us a modern marriage pulling itself apart. Two interesting new American playwrights made their debuts: Peter Parnell with the youthfully exuberant "Sorrows of Stephen," and David Hwang with "FOB," about the impact of America on Chinese immigrants.

Disappointments this season came from a number of our most significant playwrights — Tennessee Williams with "Clothes for a Summer Hotel," Edward Albee with "The Lady from Dubuque" and Howard Sackler with "Goodbye, Fidel." Comedy was represented by Bernard Slade ("Romantic Comedy") and Neil Simon ("I Ought to be in Pictures").

The most important dramatic event was the visit to America of Peter Brook's international company with a cycle of four plays, including the magical "Conference of the Birds," performed at La Mama. A powerful political play, Athol Fugard's "A Lesson from Aloes," had its U.S. premiere at the Yale Repertory Theatre, now under the artistic direction of Lloyd Richards.

"Evita," the Andrew Lloyd Webber-Tim Rice musical that traced the rise and fall of Eva Perón, received mixed reviews but went on to be named best musical by the New York Drama Critics and by the Tony voters; Patti LuPone also won a Tony as best musical actress for her performance as Evita. "Sugar Babies," a burlesque musical featuring Mickey Rooney in his Broadway debut also had its admirers, as did "Barnum," starring Jim Dale, a Tony winner, as the master bamboozler, P. T. Barnum. Late in the season there was "A Day in Hollywood/A Night in the Ukraine," a British spoof of the olden days of Hollywood musicals and Marx Brothers comedies headlined by the fantastic choreography of Tommy Tune. "Billy Bishop Goes to War" was a Kiplingesque tune of glory about Canada's greatest flying ace. Among Off-Broadway musicals were the nostalgic cavalcade, "Tintypes"; Elizabeth Swados's "The Haggadah," a loving theatricalization of the Passover seder and the Ten Commandments; and "Scrambled Feet," an irreverent look at the theatre itself.

Musical revivals continued to thrive — "Oklahoma!," "West Side Story," "Peter Pan," "The Music Man" and at season's end, Richard Burton returned as King Arthur in "Camelot."

The outstanding revival of the year was of Paul Osborn's "Morning's at Seven," an affectionate look at smalltown America in an eloquent production by Vivian Matalon, featuring four grand ladies of the theatre, Maureen O'Sullivan, Elizabeth Wilson, Nancy Marchand and Teresa Wright. Other exceptional performances were given by Pat Carroll in her one-woman show, "Gertrude Stein Gertrude Stein Gertrude Stein"; Anne Twomey making her broadway debut in Tom Topor's "Nuts"; Daniel Seltzer in Joseph Chaikin's production of Beckett's "Endgame"; Philip Bosco in "A Month in the Country" and "Major Barbara"; and Judd Hirsch in "Talley's Folly."

The New York theatre took a first, tentative step into repertory with the formation of the BAM Theatre Company under the direction of David Jones at the Brooklyn Academy of Music. It was an uneven season for the company, with only one unequivocal success, "The Purging," a one-act farce by Feydeau, starring Brian Murray, who proved to be BAM's most accomplished actor. The Vivian Beaumont Theatre at Lincoln Center remained dark as its producer, Richmond Crinkley, continued to map a 1980 season.

New York's other institutional theatres had varied success. The Public Theatre, the Circle Repertory Company, the Negro Ensemble Company, Chelsea Theatre Center and the Manhattan Theatre Club each had its share of worthy ventures, but the news was disappointing at the Phoenix Theatre, the American Place Theatre and the Hudson Guild. The Ensemble Studio Theatre provided a garland of one-act plays and Ellen Stewart's La Mama welcomed its usual United Nations of stimulating theatrical companies. The Mabou Mines company consolidated its position as the pivotal avant-garde troupe currently performing in New York.

This was the year that Off-Off Broadway, that rich environment of new work, was put in jeopardy by Actors Equity, as the union placed further restrictions on the participation of actors in showcase productions. One of the most encouraging signs in the New York theatre was the continuing activity at the Times Square Ticket Center, where Broadway tickets sell for half price.

— Mel Gussow

MUSIC

The classical audience is not large in the world of music but there were signs during the 1979-80 season that it may be the steadiest. While rock/pop concert and record sales plummeted amidst a shaky economy, classical sales with their dedicated following experienced little change. Even more positive, there were indications that the classical people were ready to do something to increase their tiny share of the total music audience, which in terms of record sales is about 5 percent. Recording executives were bullish in their assessment of the classical market's future. In New York, a new Association for Classical Music was formed to combat neglect of classics by record dealers and to encourage more classical programming on the air and more exposure to classical music for youngsters.

Performers and producers seemed to demonstrate a new aggressiveness in searching for wider audiences. Zubin Mehta led the New York Philharmonic on a nationwide television hookup from NBC's renovated Studio 8H where Toscanini had given so many memorable concerts. Joining Mehta in a tribute to Toscanini were violinist Itzhak Perlman and soprano Leontine Price. Leonard Bernstein returned to commercial television in his familiar role as conductor and commentator. In Boston, the Pops welcomed film composer John Williams as its new music director, and the new maestro's first program demonstrated the kind of popular appeal that made the late Arthur Fiedler's reign so successful. In Atlantic City, one of the casinos announced appearances by the Philadelphia Orchestra, Pittsburgh Symphony, New York Philharmonic and the Boston Pops along with established pop artists in an effort to elevate the tastes of the gambling crowd.

Among the more unusual debuts was that of Victor Borge, who turned serious to conduct opera for the first time with the New Cleveland Opera Company in a production of Mozart's "Magic Flute." A conductor of considerably greater stature, Eugene Ormandy, ended his 44-year tenure as the Philadelphia Orchestra's music director, but the 80-year-old maestro promised to remain active in guest appearances.

It was a season for anniversaries. Ruggiero Ricci marked the 50th anniversary of his New York debut by playing a sonata program, and William Primrose was honored by the International Viola Congress on his 75th birthday. The St. Louis Symphony celebrated its 100th anniversary under its new music director, Leonard Slatkin, by giving the New York premiere of Shostakovich's "Execution of Stepan Razin" (1964). Aaron Copland was honored in a Tanglewood Festival concert in July in anticipation of his 80th birthday later in the year, and Samuel Barber was honored on his 70th birthday by the Curtis Institute and the Chamber Music Society of Lincoln Center, which performed the composer's "Summer Music" for Wind Octet. The Metropolitan Opera's live radio broadcasts marked their 40th anniversary under Texaco's sponsorship, the longest continuous commercial underwriting of the same program by the same sponsor in radio history.

Among notable returns to the stages were that of pianist Magda Tagliafierro, who performed in Carnegie Hall after an absence of 37 years, and of soprano Victoria de los Angeles, who sang again in New York in opera and recital. Long anticipated was the return to the Metropolitan Opera of Birgit Nilsson who sung magnificently in a gala fall concert and in "Electra" three months later.

Pianists who gave impressive performances included Michel Block, Bella Davidovich, Jacob Lateiner and Krystian Zimerman, who made his debut with the New York Philharmonic in Chopin's F minor concerto.

The depth of the operatic literature continued to be revealed with the resurrection of such unfamiliar works as Kurt Weill's "Mahoggony" by the Metropolitan Opera and "Silverlake" by the New York City Opera, and Busoni's "Turandot" by the Berkeley (Calif.) Promenade Orchestra. The Tulsa Opera opened its season with a performance of Massenet's rarely-heard "La Navarraise," and the San Francisco Opera staged new productions of such offbeat fare as Rossini's "Tancredi," Donizetti's "Roberto Devereaux" and Poulenc's "La Voix Humaine," the last starring the veteran soprano Magda Olivero. Contemporary composers were represented in the New York Lyric Opera's premiere of Elie Siegmeister's "The Plough and the Stars" and in the Virginia Opera Association's presentation of Thea Musgrave's "A Christmas Carol" after the Dickens story.

One of music's nagging controversies, concerning contemporary music and its lack of popular appeal, surfaced again in a book by critic Samuel Lipman, who suggested that the time is at hand for a reexamination by composers and performers of the direction in which music is headed. Lipman outlined with new force the argument that music produced by contemporary composers is so lacking in appeal that performers dwell incessantly on the music of the past. When a performer or conductor comes along who champions the new music, he is likely to be dismissed, as was Pierre Boulez from the New York Philharmonic during the 1970s, or Francois Huybrects from the San Antonio Symphony during the '79-80 season.

Contemporary composers, however, continued to get a widespread hearing in premiere performances by major orchestras and artists. Among the more familiar names represented with new compositions were William Schuman, Ned Rorem, David del Tredici, George Rochberg, Lukas Foss, Donald Erb, Krzysztof Penderecki, Witold Lutoslawski, and George Crumb. Crumb's new work was "Makrokosmos IV" but his "Star Child," a work composed several years ago, was heard in a performance by the Philadelphia Orchestra in which 40 string players wore ear protectors against the intensity of its sound. Known more for his performances than for composing is Anthony Newman, the virtuoso harpsichordist-organist whose new violin concerto received its first performance by the Indianapolis Symphony Orchestra.

The music world mourned the deaths of conductors Andre Kostelanetz and Walter Susskind, composers Ben Weber and Roy Harris and composer-teacher Nadia Boulanger.

—Henry T. Wallhauser

TELEVISION

The biggest news in television in the 1979-1980 season was news.

It was a year when world events shaped the fortunes of much of the TV industry, and when news programs carried more significance than ever before in the history of the medium.

The crisis in Iran led to an unprecedented amount of television coverage of a foreign-based story, and the intense national interest in the coverage resulted in the first nightly expansion of network news coverage outside the evening newscast.

ABC news made its mark for the first time, principally through its Iran coverage. It reached a whole new audience for news, first through its nightly specials on Iran, under the title of "America Held Hostage," finally with its regular late-night report "Nightline," a completely new news program, 20 minutes of special coverage on one of the day's major events.

NBC's elaborate plans for 150 hours of coverage of the Moscow Olympics were wiped out by the American boycott of the games, called by President Carter to protest the Soviet aggression in Afghanistan. Though the boycott was extremely controversial, opposed by many athletes and not as widely supported by other Western nations as Mr. Carter expected, it was effective enough to cost NBC dearly both in profits and in exposure needed to help the network escape the prime-time ratings basement. (In 1979-1980 NBC landed there the fifth year in a row.)

NBC was insured for 90 percent of its Olympic investment of $87 million by Lloyd's of London, but it still lost considerably in unrealized advertising revenues. NBC filled in for the cancelled Olympic coverage with substitute programming and the ad money it made for those shows whittled down the revenue loss, first estimated at more than $50 million. But NBC executives openly admitted the real dollar loss was expected to be at least $15 million.

The whole Moscow fiasco cast a shadow on the future relationship between TV and the Olympics, but it did not come soon enough to diminish the wild escalation in dollars bid by the networks — and various other broadcast entities, including, for the first time, cable companies — for Olympic rights. ABC won both bidding wars for the 1984 games, with bids estimated at $90 million for the Winter Olympics in Sarajevo, Yugloslavia, and an astounding $225 million for the Summer Olympics in Los Angeles.

ABC was still bullish on the Olympics largely because it enjoyed ratings success with its heavy coverage of the 1980 winter games from Lake Placid. The network got all the mileage it could out of the startling upset gold medal by the American hockey team, despite the fact that the crucial victory over the Russians could not be carried live.

The dominance of news and news shows was further demonstrated by the emergence of "60 Minutes" as the top-rated show in all of television. Imitation "newsmagazines" from the other networks followed and soon a trend was born. They called it "reality programming," and it came to include the TV version of the "freak show" as exemplifed by "Real People" on NBC and "That's Incredible" on ABC.

A more serious news venture was undertaken in the suddenly exploding cable industry, which kicked off an all-news service, the Cable News Network. It began in June with all-day news of surprising quality; but it faced a tough financial road, with losses projected at $36 million in the first 18 months.

The big news in news personalities was CBS's naming of Dan Rather as successor to Walter Cronkite as the network's chief anchorman, following Cronkite's retirement next year. Rather's selection alienated the other man in line for the anchor job, Roger Mudd, who simply stopped working for CBS and wound up at NBC as a special Washington correspondent. His defection was part of a mass exodus from CBS news to NBC news; led by William Small, who became president of NBC news, and Marvin Kalb, the respected diplomatic correspondent.

TV also made news with its coverage of the presidential race. The medium's role in the election process was never before so all-consuming, much to the dismay of many political observers. The increased importance of the primaries and TV's incessant penchant for confirming frontrunners and dismissing slow-starters, served to turn the races for the nominations into TV-fulfilling prophecies. There was widespread complaint that the primary system and TV's coverage of it, served to disenfranchise a large section of the electorate.

The main news story TV itself made in 1979-1980 was the comeback of CBS and the comedown of ABC. After four years on top ABC lost the ratings race to CBS. CBS capitalized particularly in two programming areas: rural shows featuring auto accidents, and nighttime soap operas. In the latter category, one show, "Dallas," caused enormous excitement with a closing-episode whodunit that had many of America's viewers (and publicity agents) asking: "Who shot J.R.?"

The best news for NBC was the signing of Johnny Carson to a three-year contract, despite the fact it will cost NBC an estimated $7 million a year to have Johnny working 30 minutes less a night.

Also making news-and-money was that cable industry. You knew cable was having a big year when the networks began organized denouncements of it. Cable was growing, thanks partly to efforts of the FCC to deregulate the industry and open the marketplace to all the new technologies.

The videodisk industry was already benefitting from the new atmosphere. As was the pay-TV business, which had its finest hour in its participation in the big payday of the year's most exciting boxing match — the Duran-Leonard fight. That huge financial and artistic success had all the network sports moguls talking of future pay-TV inroads into major sports attractions.

As for public TV, it was fighting its familiar dollar demons, beset by inflation and fears of a shrinking market once the new technologies take hold. Even public TV got most noticed when it was making news. It stirred up a row by televising the controversial film, "Death of a Princess," despite censorship pressure inspired by the opposition of the Saudi Arabian government.

Nothing in the 1979-1980 TV season just happened; even when RCA announced a now-mundane event like the launching of a new communications satellite. Within a day, the news was out: The satellite was gone, lost in space.

             — **Bill Carter**

FILMS

Schizophrenia characterized the 1979-80 film season. At a time when Hollywood movie-making seemed doomed to emulate *Star Wars* or *Animal House,* such adult entertainments as *Kramer vs. Kramer, Apocalypse Now, 10, Manhattan* and *Being There* redeemed the late 1970s. By mid-1980, the casualties were piling up as fast as those on Omaha Beach in Sam Fuller's *The Big Red One.*

Kramer vs. Kramer demonstrated once again the superiority of solid writing, directing and acting over a recent trend, which relies largely on special effects, car crashes and disco album tie-ins. Writer-director Robert Benton's screenplay was so obviously favored, even at the screening room stage, to sweep the major Oscars that the Academy Awards became the most predictable in memory.

Even the most-anticipated picture of recent years, Francis Coppola's far over-budget and behind-schedule *Apocalypse Now,* was overshadowed, possibly because of the Academy's historic preference for "warm" films over "cold" ones, however brilliant—cf. *How Green Was My Valley* over *Citizen Kane* or *My Fair Lady* over *Dr. Strangelove*—or possibly backlash from the Iranian crisis. *Apocalypse* came close, particularly in a helicopter attack on an orphanage seen from the point of view of both victim and attacker, leaving the audience both exhilarated and gasping in horror at its own complicity in violence. Great scenes do not a great film make, however, and the last half hour collapsed like a wet sock.

The publicity over Bo Derek and the popularity of *10* nearly obscured Blake Edwards' achievement in coming closer than anyone in years to reviving the Ernst Lubitsch tradition of sophisticated sex comedy.

The most spectacular flop of the year, a $20,000,000 version of a Universal wartime "B" movie made by people too young to have any memory of the era, *1941* resembled nothing so much as the cast of "Saturday Night Live" turned loose in an antique clothing store and presented Spielberg at an artistic impasse: a wagonload of technical expertise and nothing much to say.

Star Trek—The Motion Picture, the work of Robert Wise, was another all-effect-and-no-story disappointment. Disney returned to big-time movie-making with *The Black Hole,* a conscious attempt to escape from the G-rated kiddie-and-animal ghetto. Oddly challenging Disney on its home ground was the Coppola-produced *The Black Stallion,* a bizarre mixture of 1940's Clarence Brown sentimentality à la *National Velvet* and *The Yearling* with high-tech cinematics aiming to out-Kubrick Kubrick.

Cruising, bitterly attacked during production by "gay rights" groups, ironically ended up playing to a heavily homosexual audience. If gays were stereotyped, so were police, Columbia music students, and the film's token woman.

Admissions fell off in the new year, refuting the cliché that movies were recession-proof. The disappointing returns and downright badness of the new pictures excited comment in the trade and general press. It was hardly a surprise that the inevitable *Animal House* imitations (*Gorp, Hollywood Knights*)were bad, but several seeming blue-chip investments also turned out otherwise. Clint Eastwood's pleasant but extremely slow-moving *Bronco Billy* disappointed his bloodthirstier fans and left theatre owners looking at figures they thought were misprints.

The most instructive relative failure was *Urban Cowboy,* a textbook example of contemporary commercial formulas. All the elements were there: location shooting reflecting the current preference for magazine articles and nonfiction over novels as script sources, a milieu with distinctive music (record tie-in) and a fashion "look" (to catch on in the streets and promote the picture), drop-dead cinematography, a star and subject of assured interest to the youth market. Vincent Canby praised *Urban Cowboy* for having the naïve directness of old "B" pictures, but they got their stories over within running times half of *Urban Cowboy's* 135 minutes.

Chasing after teen-aged taste, in fact, may have been the main cause of many bad pictures, especially *Blues Brothers, Can't Stop the Music,* and *Roadie.* Even *Blue Lagoon* emerged as a kind of soft-core teen-age sex/art film.

It was typical of the summer crop that a parody of bad movies, *Airplane,* should be a runaway hit. Much of the humor came from a cast featuring the same people (Lloyd Bridges, Robert Stack) who normally do this plot seriously.

But the real hero of the season was veteran action director Samuel Fuller, whose *The Big Red One* stood out amid packages conceived by agents and market researchers for having been made chiefly because its writer-director wanted it made. For film buffs who had kept Fuller's subterranean reputation alive, there was sweet revenge in seeing feature stories in such Establishment publications as *Life* Magazine and *The New York Times* Magazine hailing the 68-year-old director's first film in a decade.

It was "The End" for very famous Britishers who found success in Hollywood: Alfred Hitchcock, who died at age 80 (". . . apparently of natural causes") and comic actor Peter Sellers.

Horror à la Hitchcock may have been the surest formula left, as *The Shining* did business despite bad reviews and the disappointment of those who knew the book. The surer bet was more of *Star Wars. The Empire Strikes Back* produced appropriately gigantic grosses, apparently ensuring an institution like the James Bond or Pink Panther series.

Industry developments were more eventful than artistic ones. Instability at 20th Century-Fox apparently ended the movement to that company of Columbia's former management, including the industry's best-known woman executive, Sherry Lansing. The new Fox vice-chairman, Alan Hirschfeld, galled theatre owners by threatening to release videodiscs simultaneously with theatrical premieres. Four major companies dissatisfied with their share of Pay-TV revenues formed Premiere, financed by Getty Oil Co., which predictably provoked an anti-trust suit by the present leader in the field, Home Box Office. RCA scored a coup by acquiring United Artists' pictures for its videodisc system, while films on tape ranged from *The Godfather* to *Swing Parade of 1946.*

The theatres, who may soon be fighting for their lives, won a round by getting "Blind bidding" (putting up money for unseen—or unmade—pictures) struck down in the courts.

— **Stephen Handzo**

PRIZES/AWARDS

NOBEL PRIZE WINNERS

PHYSIOLOGY AND MEDICINE

Year	Winner and Life Dates	Nationality	Achievement
1901	Emil A. von Behring (1854–1917)	German	Serum therapy, especially for work on dipththeria antitoxin.
1902	Ronald Ross (1857–1932)	British	Discovery of the life cycle of the malaria parasite.
1903	Niels R. Finsen (1860–1904)	Danish	Treatment of skin diseases with concentrated light rays, especially **lupus vulgaris** (skin tuberculosis).
1904	Ivan P. Pavlov (1849–1936)	Russian	Work on the physiology of digestion.
1905	Robert Koch (1843–1910)	German	Work on tuberculosis and the scientific development of bacteriology.
1906	Camillo Golgi (c.1843–1926)	Italian	Their study of the nervous system and of cell distribution.
	Santiago Ramón y Cajal (1852–1934)	Spanish	
1907	Charles L. A. Laveran (1845–1922)	French	Study of protozoa-caused disease.
1908	Paul Ehrlich (1854–1915)	German	Their work on immunology including the introduction of quantitative methods.
	Élie Metchnikoff (1845–1916)	Russian	
1909	E. Theodor Kocher (1841–1917)	Swiss	Work on the physiology, pathology, and surgery of the thyroid gland.
1910	Albrecht Kossel (1853–1927)	German	Contributions to the knowledge of cell chemistry.
1911	Allvar Gullstrand (1862–1930)	Swedish	For his work on ocular dioptrics, the refraction of light through the eye.
1912	Alexis Carrel (1873–1944)	American (b. France)	Development of vascular suture and surgical transplantation of blood vessels and organs.
1913	Charles R. Richet (1850–1935)	French	Work on anaphylaxis.
1914	Robert Bárány (1876–1936)	Austrian	Study of physiology and pathology of the inner ear.
1919	Jules J. P. V. Bordet (1870–1961)	Belgian	Discoveries in the field of immunity.
1920	S. August Krogh (1874–1949)	Danish	Discovering the mechanism that regulates blood-capillary action.
1922	Archibald V. Hill (1886–1977)	English	Discoveries concerning heat produced by muscular activity.
	Otto F. Meyerhof (1884–1951)	American (b. Germany)	Establishing the correlation between oxygen and lactic acid in muscle.
1923	Frederick G. Banting (1891–1941)	Canadian	Their production of insulin and demonstration of its value in combating diabetes.
	John J. R. Macleod (1876–1935)	British	
1924	Willem Einthoven (1860–1927)	Dutch	Invention of the electrocardiograph.
1926	Johannes A. G. Fibiger (1867–1928)	Danish	Experimental work in cancer.
1927	Julius Wagner-Jauregg (1857–1940)	Austrian	Discovery of malarial therapy in paralysis.
1928	Charles J. H. Nicolle (1866–1936)	French	Work on typhus.
1929	Christiaan Eijkman (1858–1930)	Dutch	Discovering vitamin B.
	Frederick G. Hopkins (1861–1947)	English	Discovering vitamin A.
1930	Karl Landsteiner (1868–1943)	American (b. Austria)	Discovery of human blood groups.
1931	Otto H. Warburg (1883–1970)	German	Discovery of the character and action mode of the respiratory enzyme.
1932	Edgar C. Adrian (1889-1977)	English	Studies on the physiology of the nervous system, especially the function of neurons.
	Charles S. Sherrington (1857–1952)	English	
1933	Thomas H. Morgan (1866–1945)	American	Discovering the functions of chromosomes in heredity.
1934	George R. Minot (1885–1950)	American	Their discoveries that administering liver extract increases activity in the bone-marrow where red cells are formed.
	William P. Murphy (1892–)	American	
	George H. Whipple (1878–1976)	American	
1935	Hans Spemann (1869–1941)	German	Discovery of the organizer effect in embryonic development.
1936	Henry H. Dale (1875–1968)	English	Their discoveries of the chemical transmission of nerve impulses.
	Otto Loewi (1873–1961)	American (b. Germany)	
1937	Albert von Szent-Györgyi (1893–)	American (b. Hungary)	Studies of metabolism and the effects of vitamins A and C.
1938	Corneille J. F. Heymans (1892–1968)	Belgian	Discovery of the influence of the carotid sinus on respiration rate.
1939	Gerhard Domagk (1895–1964)	German	Discovering prontosil, the first sulfa drug.
1943	C. P. Henrik Dam (1895–1976)	Danish	Discovering vitamin K.
	Edward A. Doisy (1893–)	American	Discovery of the chemical nature of vitamin K.
1944	E. Joseph Erlanger (1874–1965)	American	Work on the highly differentiated functions of single nerve fibers.
	Herbert S. Gasser (1888–1963)	American	
1945	Alexander Fleming (1881–1955)	British	The discovery of penicillin and its curative properties in infections including those of the heart, syphilis, and certain types of pneumonia.
	Howard W. Florey (1898–1968)	British (b. Australia)	
	Ernst B. Chain (1906–1979)	British (b. Germany)	
1946	Hermann Joseph Muller (1890–1967)	American	Discovering the influence of X rays in genetics.
1947	Carl F. Cori (1896–)	American (b. Czechoslovakia)	Their research on carbohydrate metabolism and enzymes.
	Gerty T. Cori (1896–1957)	American (b. Czechoslovakia)	
	Bernardo A. Houssay (1887–1971)	Argentine	Discovery of the role of the pituitary hormone in sugar metabolism.

Year	Winner and Life Dates	Nationality	Achievement
1948	Paul H. Müller (1899–1965)	Swiss	Discovering the insect-killing properties of DDT.
1949	Walter R. Hess (1881–1973)	Swiss	Discovering how certain parts of the brain control body organs.
	Antonio de Egas Moniz (1874–1955)	Portuguese	Discovery of the therapeutic value in certain psychoses of prefrontal lobotomy.
1950	Philip S. Hench (1896–1965)	American	Their research in hormones including the discovery of cortisone and its antidisease effects.
	Edward C. Kendall (1886–1972)	American	
	Tadeus Reichstein (1897–)	Swiss (b. Poland)	
1951	Max Theiler (1899–1972)	American (b. South Africa)	Developing the yellow-fever vaccine.
1952	Selman A. Waksman (1888–1973)	American (b. Russia)	Work in the discovery of streptomycin and its value in treating tuberculosis.
1953	Fritz A. Lipmann (1899–)	American (b. Germany)	Their biochemical studies on cell metabolism, including the discovery of coenzyme A.
	Hans A. Krebs (1900–)	British (b. Germany)	
1954	John F. Enders (1897–)	American	Their successful growth of polio viruses in cultures of tissues and discovery of more effective methods of polio detection.
	Thomas H. Weller (1915–)	American	
	Frederick C. Robbins (1916–)	American	
1955	A. Hugo T. Theorell (1903–)	Swedish	Discoveries of the nature of oxidation enzymes.
1956	D. W. Richards (1895–1973)	American	Developing a technique of inserting a catheter through a vein into the heart to chart its interior and to diagnose circulatory ailments.
	André F. Cournand (1895–)	American (b. France)	
	Werner Forssmann (1904–1979)	German	
1957	Daniel Bovet (1907–)	Italian (b. Switzerland)	Developing muscle-relaxing drugs used in surgery.
1958	George W. Beadle (1903–)	American	Discovery that genes transmit hereditary traits.
	Edward L. Tatum (1909–1975)	American	
	Joshua Lederberg (1925–)	American	Experiments establishing that sexual recombination of bacteria results in exchange of genetic material.
1959	Severo Ochoa (1905–)	American (b. Spain)	Their synthesis of ribonucleic acid (RNA) and deoxyribonucleic acid (DNA), organic compounds that carry hereditary characteristics, in genetics.
	Arthur Kornberg (1918–)	American	
1960	F. Macfarlane Burnet (1899–)	Australian	Their discovery of acquired immunity, that is, that an animal can be made to accept foreign tissues.
	Peter B. Medawar (1915–)	British (b. Brazil)	
1961	Georg von Békésy (1899–1972)	American (b. Hungary)	Work on the mechanism of the inner ear.
1962	Francis H. C. Crick (1916–)	English	Their determining the molecular structure of deoxyribonucleic acid (DNA) and its significance for information transfer in living material.
	Maurice H. F. Wilkins (1916–)	British	
	James D. Watson (1928–)	American	
1963	Alan L. Hodgkin (1914–)	English	Their research on nerve cells and on how electrical charges pass through nerve membranes by means of a sodium-potassium exchange.
	Andrew F. Huxley (1917–)	English	
	John C. Eccles (1903–)	Australian	
1964	Konrad E. Bloch (1912–)	American (b. Germany)	Their discovery of the mechanism and control of cholesterol metabolism.
	Feodor Lynen (1911–1979)	German	
1965	François Jacob (1920–)	French	Their discovery of the regulatory processes in body cells that contribute to genetic control of enzymes and virus synthesis.
	Andre M. Lwoff (1902–)	French	
	Jacques L. Monod (1910–1976)	French	
1966	Charles B. Huggins (1901–)	American (b. Canada)	Discoveries concerning hormonal treatment of prostate-gland cancer.
	Francis P. Rous (1879–1970)	American	Discovery of a cancer virus.
1967	Haldan K. Hartline (1903–)	American	Their discoveries pertaining to the eye's primary chemical and physiological processes, including work on color reception.
	George Wald (1906–)	American	
	Ragnar A. Granit (1900–)	Swedish (b. Finland)	
1968	Robert W. Holley (1922–)	American	Their discovery of the process by which enzymes, consisting of a sequence of amino acids, determine a cell's function in genetic development.
	H. Gobind Khorana (c.1922–)	American (b. India)	
	Marshall W. Nirenberg (1927–)	American	
1969	Max Delbrück (1906–)	American (b. Germany)	Their discoveries concerning the replication mechanism and the genetic structure of viruses.
	Alfred D. Hershey (1908–)	American	
	Salvador E. Luria (1912–)	American (b. Italy)	
1970	Bernard Katz (1911–)	British (b. Germany)	Their discoveries on the nature of the substances found at the end of nerve fibers.
	Ulf von Euler (1905–)	Swedish	
	Julius Axelrod (1912–)	American	
1971	Earl W. Sutherland (1915–1974)	American	Discoveries concerning the mechanisms of the action of hormones.
1972	Gerald M. Edelman (1929–)	American	Research into the chemical structure of antibodies (Conducted independently).
	Rodney R. Porter (1917–)	English	
1973	Konrad Lorenz (1903–)	Austrian	Research into ethology.
	Nikolaas Tinbergen (1906–)	English (b. Netherlands)	
	Karl von Frisch (1886–)	German (b. Austria)	
1974	Albert Claude (1899–)	American	Research which helped create the science of cell biology.
	Christian Rene de Duve (1917–)	Belgian	
	George Emil Palade (1912–)	American	
1975	David Baltimore (1938–)	American	Discoveries concerning the interaction between tumor viruses and the genetic material of the cell.
	Renato Dulbecco (1914–)	American (b. Italy)	
	Howard M. Temin (1935–)	American	
1976	Baruch S. Blumberg (1925–)	American	Discoveries concerning new mechanisms for the origin and dissemination of infectious diseases.
	Daniel C. Gajdusek (1923–)	American	
1977	Rosalyn S. Yalow (1921–)	American	Developed analytic radioimmunoassay technique utilizing isotopes for diagnostic purposes.
	Roger C. L. Guillemin (1924–)	American (b. France)	Their use of radioimmunoassay in pituitary hormone research.
	Andrew V. Schally (1927–)	American (b. Poland)	
1978	Werner Arber (1929–)	Swiss	Discoveries and studies on the restriction enzymes' linkage control of genes on chromosomes.
	Daniel Nathans (1928–)	American	
	Hamilton Smith (1931–)	American	
1979	Allan MacLeod Cormack (1924–)	American (b. S. Africa)	Development of the CAT scan, a three dimensional X-ray diagnostic technique.
	Godfrey Newbold Hounsfield (1919–)	British	
1980	Baruj Benacerraf (1920–)	American (b. Venezuela)	Research in cell immunology and discovery of HLA antigens, which help fight disease and cause immune reactions to organ transplants.
	George D. Snell (1903–)	American	
	Jean Dausset (1915–)	French	

CHEMISTRY

Year	Winner and Life Dates	Nationality	Achievement
1901	Jacobus H. van't Hoff (1852–1911)	Dutch	Discovering laws of chemical dynamics and osmotic pressure in solutions.
1902	Emil H. Fischer (1852–1919)	German	Synthesizing sugars and purines.
1903	Svante A. Arrhenius (1859–1927)	Swedish	Originating the theory of ionization.
1904	William Ramsay (1852–1916)	British	Discovering helium, neon, xenon, and krypton.
1905	Adolf von Baeyer (1835–1917)	German	Research in organic dye stuffs, especially hydro-aromatic compounds.
1906	Henri Moissan (1852–1907)	French	Isolation of the element fluorine; development of the electric furnace.
1907	Eduard Buchner (1860–1917)	German	Discovering cell-free fermentation.
1908	Ernest Rutherford (1871–1937)	British	Artificial disintegration of elements; chemistry of radioactive elements.
1909	Wilhelm Ostwald (1853–1932)	German	Work on catalysts, chemical equilibria, and rate of chemical reactions.
1910	Otto Wallach (1847–1931)	German	Pioneer work in the field of alicyclic compounds.
1911	Marie S. Curie (1867–1934)	French (b. Poland)	Discovering radium and polonium.
1912	F. A. Victor Grignard (1871–1935)	French	Discovering the reagent that is named after him.
	Paul Sabatier (1854–1941)	French	Process of hydrogenating organic compounds.
1913	Alfred Werner (1866–1919)	Swiss (b. Germany)	Study of the linkage of atoms in molecules.
1914	Theodore W. Richards (1868–1928)	American	Determining the atomic weights of many elements.
1915	Richard M. Willstätter (1872–1942)	German	Research into plant pigments, especially chlorophyll.
1918	Fritz Haber (1868–1934)	German	Process of synthesizing ammonia from nitrogen and hydrogen.
1920	Walther Nernst (1864–1941)	German	Application of thermodynamics to chemistry.
1921	Frederick Soddy (1877–1956)	British	Research into radioactive substances and isotopes.
1922	Francis W. Aston (1877–1945)	British	Discovering many isotopes by use of the mass spectrograph.
1923	Fritz Pregl (1869–1930)	Austrian	Invention of methods of microanalysis of organic substances.
1925	Richard A. Zsigmondy (1865–1929)	German (b. Austria)	Clarifying the nature of colloid solutions.
1926	Theodor Svedberg (1884–1971)	Swedish	Work on colloids.
1927	Heinrich O. Wieland (1877–1957)	German	Studies of bile acids.
1928	Adolf O. R. Windaus (1876–1959)	German	Work defining a group of sterols (including cholesterol) and their connection to vitamins.
1929	Sir Arthur Harden (1865–1940)	British	Investigations into the fermentation of sugar and fermentative enzymes.
	Hans von Euler-Chelpin (1873–1964)	Swedish (b. Germany)	
1930	Hans Fischer (1881–1945)	German	Research into the constitution of hemin (coloring matter of blood) and chlorophyll.
1931	Carl Bosch (1874–1940)	German	Their invention and development of chemical high pressure methods.
	Friedrich Bergius (1884–1949)	German	
1932	Irving Langmuir (1881–1957)	American	Investigations of the fundamental properties of absorbed films and surface chemistry.
1934	Harold C. Urey (1893–)	American	Discovering heavy hydrogen, which he called deuterium.
1935	Frédéric Joliot-Curie (1900–58)	French	Their synthesizing of new radioactive elements, including radioactive nitrogen and phosphorus.
	Irène Joliot-Curie (1897–1956)	French	
1936	Peter J. W. Debye (1884–1966)	American (b. Netherlands)	Studies of the structure of molecules, dipole moments, and the diffraction of electrons and X rays in gases.
1937	Walter N. Haworth (1883–1950)	British	Research into carbohydrates and vitamin C.
	Paul Karrer (1889–1971)	Swiss (b. Russia)	Chemical anlysis of vitamins A and B$_2$.
1938	Richard Kuhn (1900–67)	Austrian	Work on carotinoids and vitamins.
1939	Adolf F. J. Butenandt (1903–)	German	Studying the chemistry of sex hormones, determining the chemical structure of the female hormone (progestin), and isolating the male hormone (androsterone).
	Leopold Ruzicka (1887–1976)	Swiss (b. Yugoslavia)	Work on polymethylenes and higher terpenes.
1943	Georg von Hevesy (1885–1966)	Hungarian	Using isotopes as tracer elements in chemistry.
1944	Otto Hahn (1879–1968)	German	Discovery of the fission of heavy atomic nuclei.
1945	Artturi I. Virtanen (1895–1973)	Finnish	Work on plant synthesis of nitrogen compounds; development of a new method of making silage.
1946	James B. Sumner (1887–1955)	American	Discovering the crystallizability of enzymes.
	John H. Northrop (1891–)	American	Their preparation of enzymes and virus proteins in pure form.
	Wendell M. Stanley (1904–1971)	American	
1947	Robert Robinson (1886–1975)	British	Research on plant substances, especially alkaloids.
1948	Arne W. K. Tiselius (1902–1971)	Swedish	Devising new methods of separating and detecting colloids and serum proteins.
1949	William F. Giauque (1895–)	American (b. Canada)	Studies of the properties of substances at extremely low temperatures.
1950	Otto P. H. Diels (1876–1954)	German	Developing a method of synthesizing organic compounds of the diene group.
	Kurt Alder (1902–58)	German	
1951	Edwin M. McMillan (1907–)	American	Their work in the field of synthetic transuranium elements.
	Glenn T. Seaborg (1912–)	American	
1952	Archer J. P. Martin (1910–)	British	Advancing the use of paper partition chromatography (a method of separating and identifying chemical substances).
	Richard L. M. Synge (1914–)	British	
1953	Hermann Staudinger (1881–1965)	German	Work in the nature of giant molecules.
1954	Linus C. Pauling (1901–)	American	Studies in molecular structure, especially the nature of the bonding of atoms in molecules.
1955	Vincent du Vigneaud (1901–1978)	American	Work on pituitary hormones and the first synthesis of a polypeptide hormone.
1956	Cyril N. Hinshelwood (1897–1967)	British	Parallel but independent research into the kinetics of certain chemical reactions.
	Nikolai N. Semenov (1896–)	Russian	
1957	Alexander R. Todd (1907–)	British	Studies of the compounds that are the components of nucleic acid.
1958	Frederick Sanger (1918–)	British	Isolating and identifying the amino acid components of the insulin molecule.
1959	Jaroslav Heyrovsky (1890–1967)	Czech	Developing polarography (an electrochemical method of analysis).

Year	Winner and Life Dates	Nationality	Achievement
1960	Willard F. Libby (1908–80)	American	Development of the "atomic time clock" (for determining geological age by measuring the amount of radioactive carbon-14 in organic objects).
1961	Melvin Calvin (1911–)	American	Establishing the chemical reactions that occur during photosynthesis.
1962	Max F. Perutz (1914–)	British (b. Austria)	Discovering the molecular structure of hemoglobin and myoglobin.
	John C. Kendrew (1917–)	British	
1963	Karl Ziegler (1898–1973)	German	Changing simple hydrocarbons into complex molecular substances.
	Giulio Natta (1903–1979)	Italian	
1964	Dorothy C. Hodgkin (1910–)	British	Discovery of the structure of biochemical substances, notably penicillin and vitamin B_{12}.
1965	Robert B. Woodward (1917–1979)	American	Development of fundamental techniques for synthesis of complicated organic compounds, notably chlorophyll and sterols.
1966	Robert S. Mulliken (1896–)	American	Fundamental work on chemical bonds and the electronic structure of molecules by the molecular orbital method.
1967	Manfred Eigen (1927–)	German	Studies of extremely fast chemical reactions effected by disturbing equilibrium by very short energy pulsations.
	Ronald G. W. Norrish (1897–1978)	English	
	George Porter (1920–)	English	
1968	Lars Onsager (1903–76)	American (b. Norway)	Discovery of the reciprocal relations between voltage and temperature that are fundamental for the thermodynamics of irreversible processes, such as those in living cells.
1969	Derek H. R. Barton (1918–)	British	Independent studies of conformation analysis: how certain compounds react when their three-dimensional molecular shape is known.
	Odd Hassel (1897–)	Norwegian	
1970	Luis F. Leloir (1906–)	Argentinian (b. France)	Discovery of sugar nucleotides and their role in the biosynthesis of carbohydrates.
1971	Gerhard Herzberg (1904–)	Canadian (b. Germany)	Study of electronic structure, geometry of molecules.
1972	Dr. Christian Boehmer Anfisen (1916–)	American	Research relating to the chemical structure of a complex protein known as ribonuclease.
	Dr. Stanford Moore (1913–)	American	
	Dr. William Howard Stein (1911–80)	American	
1973	Ernst Otto Fischer (1918–)	German	Research into how organic and metallic atoms can merge.
	Geoffrey Wilkinson (1921–)	British	
1974	Paul J. Flory (1910–)	American	For his work in macromolecules.
1975	John W. Cornforth (1917–)	English (b. Australia)	For contributions to stereochemistry — the study of how the properties of a chemical compound are affected by the exact arrangement of their atoms in three-dimension space.
	Vladimir Prelog (1906–)	Swiss (b. Yugoslavia)	
1976	William N. Lipscomb, Jr. (1920–)	American	For studies on the structure and bonding mechanisms of "boranes".
1977	Ilya Prigogine (1917–)	Belgian (b. Russia)	Theoretical work explaining contradictory biological process whereby increased growth and structural complexity on the molecular level are promoted while energy is dissipated.
1978	Peter Mitchell (1920–)	English	Study of energy reception of human cells.
1979	Herbert C. Brown (1912–)	American	Research on the basic molecular structures of boron and phosphorus.
	Georg Wittig (1897–)	German	
1980	Paul Berg (1926–)	American	Development of methods to map in detail the structure and function of DNA.
	Walter Gilbert (1932–)	American	
	Frederick Sanger (1918–)	British	

PHYSICS

Year	Winner and Life Dates	Nationality	Achievement
1901	Wilhelm C. Roentgen (1845–1923)	German	Discovering X rays.
1902	Hendrik A. Lorentz (1853–1928)	Dutch	Their research into the influence of magnetism upon radiation.
	Pieter Zeeman (1865–1943)	Dutch	
1903	Antoine H. Becquerel (1852–1908)	French	Discovery of spontaneous radioactivity.
	Pierre Curie (1859–1906)	French	Their study of the radiation phenomena that were discovered by Becquerel.
	Marie S. Curie (1867–1934)	French (b. Poland)	
1904	John W. S. Rayleigh (1842–1919)	British	Discovering argon.
1905	Philipp E. A. Lenard (1862–1947)	German (b. Hungary)	Experiments with cathode rays.
1906	Joseph J. Thomson (1856–1940)	British	Investigations on how gases conduct electricity.
1907	Albert A. Michelson (1852–1931)	American (b. Germany)	Developing optical measuring instruments; spectroscopic and meteorological investigations.
1908	Gabriel Lippmann (1845–1921)	French (b. Luxembourg)	Color photography.
1909	Guglielmo Marconi (1874–1937)	Italian	Their separate but parallel development of the wireless telegraph.
	Karl F. Braun (1850–1918)	German	
1910	Johannes D. van der Waals (1837–1923)	Dutch	Work on an equation relating gases and liquids.
1911	Wilhelm Wien (1864–1928)	German	Discoveries of the laws governing heat radiation.
1912	Nils G. Dalén (1869–1937)	Swedish	Their invention of automatic gas regulators, for turning acetylene buoys, beacons, and railway lights on and off.
1913	Heike Kamerlingh-Onnes (1853–1926)	Dutch	Experiments with the properties of matter at low temperatures, leading to helium liquefaction.
1914	Max von Laue (1879–1960)	German	Employing crystals to diffract X rays.
1915	William H. Bragg (1862–1942)	British	Their use of X rays to determine the structure of crystals.
	Lawrence Bragg (1890–1971)	British	
1917	Charles G. Barkla (1877–1944)	British	Discovery of X-ray radiation of elements.
1918	Max K. E. L. Planck (1858–1947)	German	Formulation of the quantum theory.
1919	Johannes Stark (1874–1957)	German	Discovery of the splitting of spectral lines in an electrical field.
1920	Charles É. Guillaume (1861–1938)	French (b. Switzerland)	Discovering anomalies in nickel-steel alloys.
1921	Albert Einstein (1879–1955)	American (b. Germany)	Contributing to theoretical physics: especially for the discovery of photoelectric-effect law.
1922	Niels H. D. Bohr (1885–1962)	Danish	Studies of the structure of atoms and their radiation.
1923	Robert A. Millikan (1868–1953)	American	Work on electrons and the photoelectric effect.
1924	Karl M. G. Siegbahn (1886–1978)	Swedish	Discoveries in X-ray spectroscopy.
1925	James Franck (1882–1964)	German	Their discovery of the laws governing the impact of an electron on an atom.
	Gustav Hertz (1887–1975)	German	

Year	Winner and Life Dates	Nationality	Achievement
1926	Jean B. Perrin (1870–1942)	French	Work on the discontinuous structure of matter; discovery of sedimentation equilibrium.
1927	Arthur H. Compton (1892–1962)	American	Discovering the Compton effect (the change in wavelength of X rays colliding with electrons).
	Charles T. R. Wilson (1869–1959)	British	Discovery of the cloud chamber method of tracking paths of electrically charged particles.
1928	Owen W. Richardson (1879–1959)	British	Study of electron emission from heated bodies; formulation of the law governing such emission.
1929	Louis-Victor de Broglie (1892–)	French	Discovering the wave nature of electrons.
1930	Chandrasekhara V. Raman (1888–1970)	Indian	Light diffusion research; discovery of Raman effect.
1932	Werner Heisenberg (1901–1976)	German	Creating a quantum mechanics; new discoveries in the study of hydrogen.
1933	Erwin Schrödinger (1887–1961)	Austrian	For their development of new useful forms of atomic theory.
	Paul A. M. Dirac (1902–)	British	
1935	James Chadwick (1891–1974)	British	Discovery of the neutron.
1936	Victor F. Hess (1883–1964)	American (b. Austria)	Discovering cosmic radiation.
	Carl D. Anderson (1905–)	American	Discovery of the positron.
1937	Clinton J. Davisson (1881–1958)	American	Their discovery of the diffraction of electrons by crystals.
	George P. Thomson (1892–1975)	British	
1938	Enrico Fermi (1901–54)	American (b. Italy)	Work on radioactive elements, including artificial ones produced by neutron bombardment.
1939	Ernest O. Lawrence (1901–58)	American	Inventing the cyclotron.
1943	Otto Stern (1888–1969)	American (b. Germany)	Studies related to the magnetic properties of atoms; discovery of the magnetic moment of the proton.
1944	Isidor Isaac Rabi (1898–)	American (b. Austrian)	Discovery of resonance method of recording the magnetic properties of atomic nuclei.
1945	Wolfgang Pauli (1900–58)	American (b. Austrian)	Discovering the exclusion principle governing the quantum state of electrons in an atom.
1946	Percy Williams Bridgman (1882–1961)	American	Work in the field of high-pressure physics.
1947	Edward V. Appleton (1892–1965)	British	Investigations of the physics of the upper atmosphere; discovery of the so-called Appleton layer.
1948	Patrick M. S. Blackett (1897–1974)	British	Improvement of the Wilson cloud chamber method and resulting discoveries in nuclear physics and cosmic rays.
1949	Hideki Yukawa (1907–)	Japanese	Theoretical deductions of the existence of mesons.
1950	Cecil F. Powell (1903–69)	British	Photographic method of tracking nuclear particles.
1951	Sir John D. Cockcroft (1897–1967)	British	Their pioneer work in transmuting atomic nuclei with artificially accelerated atomic particles.
	Ernest T. S. Walton (1903–)	Irish	
1952	Felix Bloch (1905–)	American (b. Switzerland)	Developing the nuclear resonance method for precision measurements of atomic nuclei magnetic fields.
	Edward M. Purcell (1912–)	American	
1953	Frits Zernike (1888–1966)	Dutch	Inventing the phase-contrast microscope.
1954	Max Born (1882–1970)	British (b. Germany)	Basic research in quantum mechanics and modern nuclear physics.
	Walther Bothe (1891–1957)	German	Development of the coincidence method for measuring time.
1955	Willis E. Lamb, Jr. (1913–)	American	Discoveries concerning the fine structure of the hydrogen spectrum.
	Polykarp Kusch (1911–)	American (b. Germany)	Precise measurement of the electron's electromagnetic properties.
1956	John Bardeen (1908–)	American	Their work on developing the transistor, a device which replaced electronic tubes in many applications.
	Walter H. Brattain (1902–)	American	
	William B. Shockley (1910–)	American (b. England)	
1957	Tsung-Dao Lee (1926–)	American (b. China)	Their disproving of the law of parity conservation in nuclear physics.
	Chen Ning Yang (1922–)	American (b. China)	
1958	Pavel A. Cherenkov (1904–)	Russian	Discovering the Cherenkov effect (radiated electrons accelerate in water to speeds greater than that of light in the same medium).
	Ilya M. Frank (1908–)	Russian	
	Igor Y. Tamm (1895–1971)	Russian	
1959	Emilio G. Segrè (1905–)	American (b. Italy)	Discovery of the antiproton, a particle of mass identical to the proton but of opposite charge.
	Owen Chamberlain (1920–)	American	
1960	Donald A. Glaser (1926–)	American	Inventing the bubble chamber to study subatomic particles.
1961	Robert Hofstadter (1915–)	American	Investigations of atomic nuclei; discoveries relating to the structure of nucleons.
	Rudolf L. Moessbauer (1929–)	German	The method named for him of producing and measuring recoil-free gamma rays.
1962	Lev D. Landau (1908–68)	Russian	Pioneering studies on condensed gases, especially liquid helium.
1963	Eugene P. Wigner (1902–)	American (b. Hungary)	Contributions to nuclear and theoretical physics.
	Maria Goeppert-Mayer (1906–1972)	American (b. Poland)	Their discoveries regarding atomic nucleus shell structure.
	J. Hans D. Jensen (1907–1973)	German	
1964	Charles H. Townes (1915–)	American	Their fundamental research in quantum electronics that led to development of the maser-laser principle.
	Nikolai G. Basov (1922–)	Russian	
	Aleksander M. Prokhorov (1916–)	Russian	
1965	Richard P. Feynman (1918–)	American	Research in quantum electrodynamics that contributed to the understanding of elementary particles in high-energy physics.
	Julian S. Schwinger (1918–)	American	
	Sin-itiro Tomonaga (1906–1979)	Japanese	
1966	Alfred Kastler (1902–)	French	Discovery and development of optical methods for studying Herzian resonances in atoms.
1967	Hans A. Bethe (1906–)	American (b. Germany)	Contributions to the theory of nuclear reaction; discoveries concerning the energy production of stars.
1968	Luis W. Alvarez (1911–)	American	Contributions to the physics of subatomic particles and techniques for their detection.
1969	Murray Gell-Mann (1929–)	American	Major theoretical insights into the interrelationships of elementary particles, including the theoretical model that he calls "The Eight-fold Way."
1970	Louis Néel (1904–)	French	Discoveries about ferromagnetism and antiferromagnetism; basic work in magneto-hydrodynamics.
	Hannes Alfvén (1908–)	Swedish	

Year	Winner and Life Dates	Nationality	Achievement
1971	Dennis Gabor (1900–1979)	British (b. Hungary)	Inventor of the three-dimensional, lensless system of photography known as holography.
1972	John Bardeen (1908–) Leon Cooper (1930–) John Robert Schrieffer (1931–)	American American American	Joint development of a theory explaining the phenomenon of superconductivity.
1973	Leo Esaki (1925–) Ivar Giaever (1929–) Brian D. Josephson (1940–)	Japanese American British	Research into how electrons tunnel through conductors to become superconductors.
1974	Sir Martin Ryle (1918–) Anthony Hewish (1924–)	British British	For their pioneering work in radio astrophysics.
1975	James Rainwater (1918–) Aage N. Bohr (1922–) Ben R. Mottelson (1926–)	American Danish Danish (b. U.S.)	Discovery of the connection between collective motion and particle motion in the atomic nucleus and the development of the theory of the structure of the atomic nucleus based on this connection.
1976	Burton Richter (1931–) Samuel C.C. Ting (1936–)	American American	For independent discovery of a new subatomic particle, known as "psi" or "J".
1977	John H. Van Vleck (1899–1980) Philip W. Anderson (1924–) Sir Nevill F. Mott (1905–)	American American British	For their contributions to the development of modern electronic solid state circuitry and basic theories of magnetism and conduction.
1978	Pyotr Kapitsa (1894–) Arno A. Penzias (1933–) Robert W. Wilson (1936–)	Russian American (b. Germany) American	Pioneer work in low-temperature physics. Discovery of cosmic microwave background radiation, further support for the Big Bang theory.
1979	Steven Weinberg (1933–) Sheldon L. Glashow (1933–) Abdus Salam (1926–)	American American Pakistani	Contributions to unified theory that electromagnetism and the "weak force" in subatomic particles are related phenomena.
1980	James W. Cronin (1931–) Val L. Fitch (1923–)	American American	Research into the symmetry of subatomic particles.

ECONOMIC SCIENCE

Year	Winner and Life Dates	Nationality	Achievement
1969	Ragnar Frisch (1895–1973) Jan Tinbergen (1903–)	Norwegian Dutch	Their development of econometrics: mathematical models in the analysis of economic processes.
1970	Paul Anthony Samuelson (1915–)	American	Deriving new theorems; devising new applications.
1971	Simon Kuznets (1901–)	American (b. Russia)	Development of concept of using GNP as measure of national economic growth.
1972	Kenneth J. Arrow (1921–) John R. Hicks (1904–)	American English	Contributions to equilibrium theory and welfare theory.
1973	Wassily Leontief (1906–)	American (b. Russia)	For the development of "input-output" analysis.
1974	Gunnar Myrdal (1898–) Friedrich A. von Hayek (1899–)	Swedish British (b. Austria)	Work on the theory of money and the interdependence of economic, social, and institutional phenomena.
1975	Leonid V. Kantorovich (1912–) Tjalling C. Koopmans (1910–)	Russian American (b. Netherlands)	Independent contributions to the theory of optimum allocation of resources.
1976	Milton Friedman (1912–)	American	For achievements in the fields of consumption analysis, monetary history and theory; demonstration of the complexity of stabilization policy.
1977	Bertil Ohlin (1899–1979) James Meade (1907–)	Swedish English	For their contribution to international trade theory.
1978	Herbert Simon (1916–)	American	Research in the decision-making process within economic organizations.
1979	Sir Arthur Lewis (1915–) Theodore W. Schultz (1902–)	British (b. West Indies) American	For their work on the economic problems of developing nations.
1980	Lawrence R. Klein (1920–)	American	For his creation of "econometric" models to forecast economic trends.

LITERATURE

1901	René F. A. Sully-Prudhomme (1839–1907), French
1902	Theodor Mommsen (1817–1903), German
1903	Björnstjerne Björnson (1832–1910), Norwegian
1904	Frédéric Mistral (1830–1914), French José Echegaray (1832–1916), Spanish
1905	Henryk Sienkiewicz (1846–1916), Polish
1906	Giosuè Carducci (1835–1907), Italian
1907	Rudyard Kipling (1865–1936), British
1908	Rudolf C. Eucken (1846–1926), German
1909	Selma Lagerlöf (1858–1940), Swedish
1910	Paul J. L. Heyse (1830–1914), German
1911	Maurice Maeterlinck (1862–1949), Belgian
1912	Gerhart Hauptmann (1862–1946), German
1913	Rabindranath Tagore (1861–1941), Indian
1915	Romain Rolland (1866–1944), French
1916	Verner von Heidenstam (1859–1940), Swedish
1917	Karl A. Gjellerup (1857–1919), Danish Henrik Pontoppidan (1857–1943), Danish
1919	Carl F. G. Spitteler (1845–1924), Swiss
1920	Knut Hamsun (1859–1952), Norwegian
1921	Anatole France (1844–1924), French
1922	Jacinto Benavente y Martínez (1866–1954), Spanish
1923	William Butler Yeats (1865–1939), Irish
1924	Wladyslaw S. Reymont (c. 1867–1925), Polish
1925	George Bernard Shaw (1856–1950), British (b. Ireland)
1926	Grazia Deledda (1875–1936), Italian
1927	Henri Bergson (1859–1941), French
1928	Sigrid Undset (1882–1949), Norwegian (b. Denmark)
1929	Thomas Mann (1875–1955), German
1930	Sinclair Lewis (1885–1951), American
1931	Erik A. Karlfeldt (1864–1931), Swedish
1932	John Galsworthy (1867–1933), English
1933	Ivan A. Bunin (1870–1953), Russian
1934	Luigi Pirandello (1867–1936), Italian
1936	Eugene O'Neill (1888–1953), American
1937	Roger Martin du Gard (1881–1958), French
1938	Pearl S. Buck (1892–1973), American
1939	Frans E. Sillanpää (1888–1964), Finnish
1944	Johannes V. Jensen (1873–1950), Danish
1945	Gabriela Mistral (1889–1957), Chilean
1946	Hermann Hesse (1877–1962), Swiss (b. Germany)
1947	André Gide (1869–1951), French
1948	T. S. Eliot (1888–1965), British (b. United States)
1949	William Faulkner (1897–1962), American
1950	Bertrand A. W. Russell (1872–1970), British
1951	Pär F. Lagerkvist (1891–1974), Swedish
1952	François Mauriac (1885–1970), French
1953	Sir Winston Churchill (1874–1965), British
1954	Ernest Hemingway (1899–1961), American
1955	Halldór K. Laxness (1902–), Icelandic
1956	Juan Ramón Jiménez (1881–1958), Spanish
1957	Albert Camus (1913–60), French
1958	Boris L. Pasternak (1890–1960), Russian
1959	Salvatore Quasimodo (1901–68), Italian
1960	Saint-John Perse (1887–1975), French
1961	Ivo Andrić (1892–1975), Yugoslav
1962	John Steinbeck (1902–68), American
1963	Giorgos Seferis (1900–71), Greek
1964	Jean Paul Sartre (1905–80), French
1965	Mikhail A. Sholokov (1905–), Russian
1966	Samuel Y. Agnon (1888–1970), Israeli (b. Poland) Nelly Sachs (1891–1970), Swedish (b. Germany)
1967	Miguel Angel Asturias (1899–1974), Guatemalan
1968	Yasunari Kawabata (1899–1972), Japanese
1969	Samuel Beckett (1906–), Irish (res. France)
1970	Aleksandr Solzhenitsyn (1918–), Russian
1971	Pablo Neruda (1904–1973), Chilean
1972	Heinrich Böll (1917–), German
1973	Patrick White (1912–), Australian
1974	Eyvind Johnson (1900–76), Swedish Edmund Martinson (1904–1978), Swedish
1975	Eugenio Montale (1896–), Italian
1976	Saul Bellow (1915–), American
1977	Vicente Aleixandre (1898–), Spanish
1978	Isaac Bashevis Singer (1904–), American (b. Poland)
1979	Odysseus Elytis (1911–), Greek
1980	Czeslaw Milosz (1911–), American (b. Poland)

PEACE

1901 Jean H. Dunant (1828–1910), Swiss
Frédéric Passy (1822–1912), French
1902 Élie Ducommun (1833–1906), Swiss
Charles A. Gobat (1843–1914), Swiss
1903 William R. Cremer (1828–1908), English
1904 Institute of International Law
1905 Bertha von Suttner (1843–1914), Austrian
1906 Theodore Roosevelt (1858–1919), American
1907 Ernesto T. Moneta (1833–1918), Italian
Louis Renault (1843–1918), French
1908 Klas P. Arnoldson (1844–1916), Swedish
1909 August M. F. Beernaert (1829–1912), Belgian
Paul H. Benjamin Estournelles de Constant (1852–1924), French
1910 International Peace Bureau
1911 Tobias M. C. Asser (1838–1913), Dutch
Alfred H. Fried (1864–1921), Austrian
1912 Elihu Root (1845–1937), American
1913 Henri La Fontaine (1854–1943), Belgian
1917 International Red Cross Committee
1919 Woodrow Wilson (1856–1924), American
1920 Léon Bourgeois (1851–1925), French
1921 Hjalmar Branting (1860–1925), Swedish
Christian L. Lange (1869–1938), Norwegian
1922 Fridtjof Nansen (1861–1930), Norwegian
1925 Sir J. Austen Chamberlain (1863–1937), British
Charles G. Dawes (1865–1951), American
1926 Aristide Briand (1862–1932), French
Gustav Stresemann (1878–1929), German
1927 Ferdinand E. Buisson (1841–1932), French
Ludwig Quidde (1858–1941), German
1929 Frank B. Kellogg (1856–1937), American
1930 Nathan Söderblom (1866–1931), Swedish
1931 Jane Addams (1860–1935), American
Nicholas Murray Butler (1862–1947), American
1933 Norman Angell (c. 1872–1967), British
1934 Arthur Henderson (1863–1935), British
1935 Carl von Ossietzky (1889–1938), German
1936 Carlos Saavedra Lamas (1880–1959), Argentine

1937 E. A. R. Cecil (1864–1958), British
1938 Nansen International Office for Refugees
1944 International Red Cross Committee
1945 Cordell Hull (1871–1955), American
1946 John R. Mott (1865–1955), American
Emily Balch (1867–1961), American
1947 Friends Service Council (British)
American Friends Service Committee (American)
1949 Sir John Boyd Orr (1880–1971), British
1950 Ralph J. Bunche (1904–71), American
1951 Léon Jouhaux (1879–1954), French
1952 Albert Schweitzer (1875–1965), Alsatian
1953 George C. Marshall (1880–1959), American
1954 Office of the UN High Commissioner for Refugees
1957 Lester B. Pearson (1897–1972), Canadian
1958 Father Georges H. Pire (1910–69), Belgian
1959 Philip J. Noel-Baker (1889–), British
1960 Albert J. Luthuli (1899–1967), South African
1961 Dag Hammarskjöld (1905–61), Swedish
1962 Linus C. Pauling (1901–), American
1963 International Red Cross Committee
League of Red Cross Societies
1964 Martin Luther King, Jr. (1929–68), American
1965 UNICEF (UN Children's Fund)
1968 René Cassin (1887–1976), French
1969 International Labor Organization
1970 Norman E. Borlaug (1914–), American
1971 Willy Brandt (1913–), German
1973 Henry A. Kissinger (1923–), American
Le Duc Tho (1910–), Vietnamese
1974 Eisaku Sato (1901–75), Japanese
Sean McBride (1904–), Irish
1975 Andrei D. Sakharov (1921–), Russian
1976 Mairead Corrigan (1944–), Northern Irish
Betty Williams (1943–), Northern Irish
1977 Amnesty International
1978 Menachem Begin (1913–), Israeli
Anwar el-Sadat (1918–), Egyptian
1979 Mother Teresa (1910–   ), Indian
1980 Adolfo Pérez Esquivel (1932–), Argentine

PULITZER PRIZES

LOCAL INVESTIGATIVE REPORTING

1953 Edward J. Mowery (*New York World-Telegram & Sun*)
1954 Alvin Scott McCoy (*Kansas City [Mo.] Star*)
1955 Roland Kenneth Towery (*Cuero [Tex.] Record*)
1956 Arthur Daley (*N.Y. Times*)
1957 Wallace Turner and William Lambert (*Portland Oregonian*)
1958 George Beveridge (*Evening Star, Washington, D.C.*)
1959 John Harold Brislin (*Scranton [Pa.] Tribune and Scrantonian*)
1960 Miriam Ottenberg (*Evening Star, Washington, D.C.*)
1961 Edgar May (*Buffalo [N.Y.] Evening News*)
1962 George Bliss (*Chicago [Ill.] Tribune*)
1963 Oscar O'Neal Griffin, Jr. (*Pecos [Tex.] Enterprise*)
1964 James V. Magee, Albert V. Gaudiosi, and Frederick A. Meyer (*Philadelphia [Pa.] Bulletin*)
1965 Gene Goltz (*Houston [Tex.] Post*)
1966 John A. Frasca (*Tampa [Fla.] Tribune*)
1967 Gene Miller (*Miami [Fla.] Herald*)
1968 J. Anthony Lukas (*New York Times*)
1969 Albert L. Delugach Denny Walsh (*St. Louis Globe-Democrat*)

1970 Harold Eugene Martin ([Montgomery] *Alabama Journal*)
1971 William Hugh Jones (*Chicago [Ill.] Tribune*)
1972 Richard Cooper and John Machacek (*Rochester [N.Y.] Times Union*)
1973 The Sun Newspapers, Omaha, Nebraska
1974 Arthur M. Petacque Hugh F. Hough (*The Chicago Sun-Times*)
1976 *The Chicago [Ill.] Tribune*
1977 Acel Moore and Wendell Rawls, Jr. (*The Philadelphia [Pa.] Inquirer*)
1978 Anthony R. Dolan (*Stamford [Conn.] Advocate*)
1979 Gilbert M. Gaul and Elliot G. Jaspin (*Pottsville [Pa.] Republican*)
1980 Stephen A. Kurkjian, Alexander B. Hawes, Jr., Nils J. Bruzelius, Joan Vennochi and Robert Porterfield (*The Boston [Mass.] Globe*)

GENERAL LOCAL REPORTING

1953 *Providence (R.I.) Journal and Evening Bulletin*
1954 *Vicksburg (Miss.) Sunday Post-Herald*
1955 Mrs. Caro Brown (*Alice [Tex.] Daily Echo*)
1956 Lee Hills (*Detroit [Mich.] Free Press*)
1957 *Salt Lake (Utah) Tribune*
1958 *Fargo (N.D.) Forum*
1959 Mary Lou Werner (*Evening Star, Washington, D.C.*)
1960 Jack Nelson (*Atlanta [Ga.] Constitution*)
1961 Sanche de Gramont (*New York Herald Tribune*)

1962 Robert D. Mullins (*Deseret News*, Salt Lake City, Utah)
1963 Sylvan Fox, Anthony Shannon, and William Longgood (*New York World-Telegram & Sun*)
1964 Norman C. Miller, Jr. (*Wall Street Journal*)
1965 Melvin H. Ruder (*Hungry Horse News*, Columbia Falls, Mont.)
1966 *Los Angeles (Calif.) Times* staff
1967 Robert V. Cox (*Chambersburg [Pa.] Public Opinion*)
1968 *Detroit (Mich.) Free Press*
1969 John Fetterman (*Louisville [Ky.] Times and Courier-Journal*)
1970 Thomas Fitzpatrick (*Chicago [Ill.] Sun-Times*)
1971 *Akron [Ohio] Beacon Journal*
1972 Timothy Leland, Gerald M. O'Neill, Stephen A. Kurjan, and Ann Desantis (*Boston Globe*)
1973 *Chicago Tribune*
1974 William Sherman (*New York Daily News*)
1976 Gene Miller (*Miami [Fla.] Herald*)
1977 Margo Huston (*The Milwaukee [Wis.] Journal*)
1978 Richard Whitt (*Louisville [Ky.] Courier-Journal*)
1979 *San Diego (Calif.) Evening Tribune*
1980 *Philadelphia (Pa.) Inquirer*

NATIONAL REPORTING

1948 Bert Andrews (*New York Herald Tribune*)
Nat S. Finney (*Minneapolis [Minn.] Tribune*)

1949 C. P. Trussel
(*New York Times*)
1950 Edwin O. Guthman
(*Seattle* [Wash.] *Times*)
1952 Anthony Leviero
(*New York Times*)
1953 **Don Whitehead (AP)**
1954 Richard Wilson
(Cowles Newspapers)
1955 Anthony Lewis
(*Washington* [D.C.] *Daily News*)
1956 Charles L. Bartlett
(*Chattanooga* [Tenn.] *Times*)
1957 James Reston
(*New York Times*)
1958 **Relman Morin (AP)**
Clark Mollenhoff
(*Des Moines* [Iowa] *Register & Tribune*)
1959 Howard Van Smith
(*Miami* [Fla.] *News*)
1960 Vance Trimble
(Scripps-Howard Newspaper Alliance)
1961 Edward R. Cony
(*Wall Street Journal*)
1962 Nathan G. Caldwell and Gene S. Graham
(*Nashville Tennessean*)
1963 Anthony Lewis
(*New York Times*)
1964 **Merriman Smith (UPI)**
1965 Louis M. Kohlmeier
(*Wall Street Journal*)
1966 Haynes Johnson
(*Evening Star*, Wash., D.C.)
1967 Monroe W. Karmin and Stanley W. Penn
(*Wall Street Journal*)
1968 Howard James
(*Christian Science Monitor*)
Nathan K. Kotz (*Des Moines* [Iowa] *Register*)
1969 Robert Cahn
(*Christian Science Monitor*, Boston, Mass.)
1970 William J. Eaton
(*Chicago* [Ill.] *Daily News*)
1971 Lucinda Franks and Thomas Powers (UPI)
1972 Jack Anderson (Columnist)
1973 Robert Boyd and Clark Hoyt (Knight Newspapers)
1974 James R. Polk
(*Washington Star News*)
Jack White
(*Providence Journal-Bulletin*)
1975 **Donald L. Barlett and James B. Steele** (*The Philadelphia Inquirer*)
1976 James Risser (*Des Moines* [Iowa] *Register*)
1977 Walter Mears (AP)
1978 Gaylord Shaw (*Los Angeles* [Calif.] *Times*)
1979 James Risser
(*Des Moines* [Iowa] *Register*)
1980 Bette Swenson Orsini and Charles Stafford
(*St. Petersburg* [Fla.] *Times*)

INTERNATIONAL CORRESPONDENCE
1948 Paul W. Ward
(*Sun*, Baltimore, Md.)
1949 Price Day
(*Sun*, Baltimore, Md.)
1950 Edmund Stevens
(*Christian Science Monitor*, Boston, Mass.)
1951 Keyes Beech
(*Chicago* [Ill.] *Daily News*)
Homer Bigart
Marguerite Higgins
(*New York Herald Tribune*)
Relman Morin (AP)

Fred Sparks
(*Chicago* [Ill.] *Daily News*)
Don Whitehead (AP)
1952 John M. Hightower (AP)
1953 Austin Wehrwein
(*Milwaukee* [Wis.] *Journal*)
1954 Jim G. Lucas
(Scripps-Howard Newspaper Alliance)
1955 Harrison E. Salisbury
(*New York Times*)
1956 William Randolph Hearst, Jr., Kingsbury Smith, and Frank Coniff
(International News Service)
1957 Russell Jones (UPI)
1958 *New York Times*
1959 Joseph Martin and Philip Santora (New York *Daily News*)
1960 A. M. Rosenthal
(*New York Times*)
1961 Lynn Heinzerling (AP)
1962 Walter Lippmann
(*New York Herald Tribune Syndicate*)
1963 Hal Hendrix
(*Miami* [Fla.] *News*)
1964 **Malcolm W. Browne (AP)**
David Halberstam
(*New York Times*)
1965 J. A. Livingston
(*Philadelphia Bulletin*)
1966 **Peter Arnett (AP)**
1967 R. John Hughes
(*Christian Science Monitor*, Boston, Mass.)
1968 Alfred Friendly
(*Washington* [D.C.] *Post*)
1969 William Tuohy
(*Los Angeles Times*)
1970 Seymour M. Hersh
(free-lance reporter)
1971 Jimmie Lee Hoagland
(*Washington* [D.C.] *Post*)
1972 Peter R. Kann
(*Wall Street Journal*)
1973 Max Frankel
(*New York Times*)
1974 Hedrick Smith
(*The New York Times*)
1975 **William Mullen and Ovie Carter** (*The Chicago Tribune*)
1976 Sydney H. Schanberg
(*The New York Times*)
1978 Henry Kamm (*The New York Times*)
1979 Richard Ben Cramer
(*Philadelphia* [Pa.] *Inquirer*)
1980 Joel Brinkley and Jay Mather
(*The Louisville* [Ky.] *Courier-Journal*)

EDITORIAL WRITING
1917 *New York Tribune*
1918 *Courier-Journal*, Louisville, Ky.
1920 Harvey E. Newbranch
(*Evening World-Herald*, Omaha, Nebr.)
1922 Frank M. O'Brien
(*New York Herald*)
1923 William Allen White
(*Emporia* [Kans.] *Gazette*)
1924 *Boston* (Mass.) *Herald*
Special prize: Frank I. Cobb
(*World*, New York, N.Y.)
1925 *Charleston* (S.C.) *News and Courier*
1926 Edward M. Kingsbury (*New York Times*)
1927 F. Lauriston Bullard (*Boston* [Mass.] *Herald*)

1928 Grover Cleveland Hall
(*Montgomery* [Ala.] *Advertiser*)
1929 Louis Isaac Jaffe
(*Norfolk Virginian-Pilot*)
1931 Charles S. Ryckman
(*Fremont* [Nebr.] *Tribune*)
1933 *Kansas City* (Mo.) *Star*
1934 E. P. Chase
(*Atlantic News Telegraph*)
1936 Felix Morley
(*Washington* [D.C.] *Post*)
George B. Parker
(Scripps-Howard Newspaper Alliance)
1937 John W. Owens
(*Sun*, Baltimore, Md.)
1938 W. W. Waymack
(*Register and Tribune*, Des Moines, Iowa)
1939 Ronald G. Callvert
(*Oregonian*, Portland, Ore.)
1940 Bart Howard
(*St. Louis Post-Dispatch*)
1941 Reuben Maury
(*Daily News*, N.Y.)
1942 Geoffrey Parsons
(*New York Herald Tribune*)
1943 Forrest W. Seymour
(*Register and Tribune*, Iowa)
1944 Henry J. Haskell
(*Kansas City* [Mo.] *Star*)
1945 George W. Potter
(*Providence* [R.I.] *Journal-Bulletin*)
1946 Hodding Carter
(*Delta Democrat-Times*, Greenville, Miss.)
1947 William H. Grimes
(*Wall Street Journal*)
1948 Virginius Dabney
(*Richmond* [Va.] *Times-Dispatch*)
1949 John H. Crider
(*Boston* [Mass.] *Herald*)
Herbert Elliston
(*Washington* [D.C.] *Post*)
1950 Carl M. Saunders
(*Jackson* [Mich.] *Citizen Patriot*)
1951 William Harry Fitzpatrick
(*New Orleans* [La.] *States*)
1952 Louis LaCoss
(*St. Louis Globe-Democrat*)
1953 Vermont C. Royster
(*Wall Street Journal*)
1954 Don Murray
(*Boston* [Mass.] *Herald*)
1955 Royce Howes
(*Detroit* [Mich.] *Free Press*)
1956 Lauren K. Soth
(*Des Moines* [Iowa] *Register and Tribune*)
1957 Buford Boone
(*Tuscaloosa* [Ala.] *News*)
1958 Harry S. Ashmore
(*Arkansas Gazette*)
1959 Ralph McGill
(*Atlanta* [Ga.] *Constitution*)
1960 Lenoir Chambers
(*Norfolk Virginian-Pilot*)
1961 William J. Dorvillier
(*San Juan* [P.R.] *Star*)
1962 Thomas M. Storke
(*Santa Barbara News-Press*)
1963 Ira B. Harkey, Jr.
(*Pascagoula* [Miss.] *Chronicle*)
1964 Hazel Brannon Smith
(*Lexington* [Miss.] *Advertiser*)
1965 John R. Harrison
(*Gainesville* [Fla.] *Sun*)
1966 Robert Lasch
(*St. Louis Post-Dispatch*)

1967 Eugene Patterson
(*Atlanta* [Ga.] *Constitution*)
1968 John S. Knight
(Knight Newspapers)
1969 Paul Greenberg
(*Pine Bluff* [Ark.] *Commercial*)
1970 Philip L. Geyelin
(*Washington* [D.C.] *Post*)
1971 Horance G. Davis, Jr.
(*Gainesville* [Fla.] *Sun*)
1972 John Strohmeyer (*Bethlehem* [Pa.] *Globe-Times*)
1973 Roger B. Linscott
(*Berkshire Eagle* [Pittsfield, Mass.])
1974 F. Gilman Spencer
(*Trenton Trentonian*)
1975 **John Daniell Maurice** (*Charleston Daily Mail*)
1976 Philip P. Kerby (*The Los Angeles* [Calif.] *Times*)
1977 Warren Lerude, Foster Church, Norman F. Cardoza (*The Reno* [Nev.] *Evening Gazette* and *Nevada State Journal*)
1978 Meg Greenfield (*The Washington* [D.C.] *Post*)
1979 Edwin M. Yoder, Jr. (*The Washington* [D.C.] *Star*)
1980 Robert L. Bartley (*The Wall Street Journal*)

CARTOONS
1922 Rollin Kirby
(*World*, New York, N.Y.)
1924 Jay Norwood Darling
(*New York Tribune*)
1925 Rollin Kirby
(*World*, New York, N.Y.)
1926 D. R. Fitzpatrick
(*St. Louis Post-Dispatch*)
1927 Nelson Harding
(*Brooklyn* [N.Y.] *Daily Eagle*)
1928 Nelson Harding
(*Brooklyn Daily Eagle*)
1929 Rollin Kirby
(*World*, New York, N.Y.)
1930 Charles R. Macauley
(*Brooklyn* [N.Y.] *Daily Eagle*)
1931 Edmund Duffy
(*Sun*, Baltimore, Md.)
1932 John T. McCutcheon
(*Chicago* [Ill.] *Tribune*)
1933 Harold M. Talburt
(*Washington* [D.C.] *Daily News*)
1934 Edmund Duffy
(*Sun*, Baltimore, Md.)
1935 Ross A. Lewis
(*Milwaukee* [Wis.] *Journal*)
1937 Clarence D. Batchelor
(*Daily News*, New York, N.Y.)
1938 Vaughn Shoemaker
(*Chicago* [Ill.] *Daily News*)
1939 Charles G. Werner
(*Daily Oklahoman*, Oklahoma City, Okla.)
1940 Edmund Duffy
(*Sun*, Baltimore, Md.)
1941 Jacob Burck
(*Times*, Chicago, Ill.)
1942 Herbert L. Block
(NEA Service)
1943 Jay Norwood Darling
(*New York Herald Tribune*)
1944 Clifford K. Berryman
(*Evening Star*, Washington, D.C.)
1945 William (Bill) Mauldin
(United Features Syndicate)
1946 Bruce Alexander Russell
(*Los Angeles* [Calif.] *Times*)

1947 Vaughn Shoemaker
(*Chicago* [Ill.] *Daily News*)
1948 Reuben L. (Rube) Goldberg
(*Sun*, New York, N.Y.)
1949 Lute Pease
(*Newark* [N.J.] *Evening News*)
1950 James T. Berryman
(*Evening Star*, Washington, D.C.)
1951 Reginald W. Manning
(*Arizona Republic*, Phoenix)
1952 Fred L. Packer
(*New York* [N.Y.] *Mirror*)
1953 Edward D. Kuekes
(*Cleveland Plain Dealer*)
1954 Herbert L. Block
(*Washington* [D.C.] *Post & Times-Herald*)
1955 Daniel R. Fitzpatrick
(*St. Louis Post-Dispatch*)
1956 Robert York
(*Louisville* [Ky.] *Times*)
1957 Tom Little
(*Nashville Tennessean*)
1958 Bruce M. Shanks
(*Buffalo Evening News*)
1959 William (Bill) Mauldin
(*St. Louis Post-Dispatch*)
1961 Carey Orr
(*Chicago* [Ill.] *Tribune*)
1962 Edmund S. Valtman
(*Hartford* [Conn.] *Times*)
1963 Frank Miller
(*Des Moines* [Iowa] *Register*)
1964 Paul Conrad
(*Denver* [Colo.] *Post*)
1966 Don Wright
(*Miami* [Fla.] *News*)
1967 Patrick B. Oliphant
(*Denver* [Colo.] *Post*)
1968 Eugene Gray Payne
(*Charlotte* [N.C.] *Observer*)
1969 John Fischetti
(*Chicago* [Ill.] *Daily News*)
1970 Thomas F. Darcy
(*Newsday*, Garden City, NY)
1971 Paul Conrad
(*Los Angeles* [Calif.] *Times*)
1972 Jeffrey K. MacNelly (*Richmond* [Va.] *News Leader*)
1974 Paul Szep
(*The Boston Globe*)
1975 **Garry Trudeau**
(Universal Press Syndicate)
1976 Tony Auth (*The Philadelphia* [Pa.] *Inquirer*)
1977 Paul Szep (*The Boston* [Mass.] *Globe*)
1978 Jeffrey K. MacNelly (*Richmond* [Va.] *News Leader*)
1979 Herbert L. Block
(*The Washington* [D.C.] *Post*)
1980 Don Wright
(*The Miami* [Fla.] *News*)

PHOTOGRAPHY
1942 Milton Brooks
(*Detroit* [Mich.] *News*)
1943 Frank Noel (AP)
1944 Frank Filan (AP)
Earle L. Bunker
(*World-Herald*, Omaha, Nebr.)
1945 Joe Rosenthal (AP)
1947 Arnold Hardy*
1948 Frank Cushing
(*Boston* [Mass.] *Traveler*)
1949 Nathaniel Fein
(*New York Herald Tribune*)
1950 Bill Crouch
(*Oakland* [Calif.] *Tribune*)
1951 **Max Desfor (AP)**
1952 John Robinson and Don Ultang (*Des Moines* [Iowa] *Register and Tribune*)
1953 William M. Gallagher
(*Flint* [Mich.] *Journal*)

1954 Mrs. Walter M. Schau*
1955 John L. Gaunt, Jr.
(*Los Angeles* [Calif.] *Times*)
1956 *Daily News*, New York, N.Y.
1957 Harry A. Trask
(*Boston* [Mass.] *Traveler*)
1958 William C. Beall
(*Washington* [D.C.] *Daily News*)
1959 William Seaman
(*Minneapolis* [Minn.] *Star*)
1960 **Andrew Lopez (UPI)**
1961 Yasushi Nagao
(*Mainichi Newspapers*, Tokyo, Japan)
1962 Paul Vathis (AP)
1963 Hector Rondon
(*La Republica*, Caracas, Venezuela)
1964 Robert H. Jackson
(*Dallas* [Tex.] *Times Herald*)
1965 **Horst Faas (AP)**
1966 Kyoichi Sawada (UPI)
1967 **Jack R. Thornell (AP)**
1968 Rocco Morabito
(*Jacksonville* [Fla.] *Journal*)
Toshio Sakai (UPI)
1969 **Edward T. Adams (AP)**
Moneta Sleet, Jr. (*Ebony*)
1970 **Steve Starr (AP)**
Dallas Kinney
(*Palm Beach* [Fla.] *Post*)
1971 John Paul Filo (Kent [Ohio] State University student)*
Jack Dykinga
(*Chicago* [Ill.] *Sun-Times*)
1972 Horst Fass and Michael Laurent (Associated Press) Dave Kenerly (United Press International)
1973 **Huynh Cong Ut (AP)**
Brian Lanker (*Topeka* [Kans.] *Capital-Journal*)
1974 **Slava Veder (AP)**
Anthony K. Roberts (AP)
1975 **Gerald H. Gay**
(*The Seattle Times*)
Matthew Lewis
(*Washington Post*)
1976 Stanley Forman (*The Boston* [Mass.] *Herald-American*); *Louisville* [Ky.] *Courier-Journal and Times*
1977 Stanley Forman (*The Boston* [Mass.] *Herald-American*); Neal Ulevich (AP); Robin Hood (*The Chattanooga* [Tenn.] *News-Free Press*)
1978 J. Ross Baughman (AP)
John W. Blair (free-lance, UPI Indianapolis [Ind.] bureau)
1979 Thomas J. Kelly 3d (*Pottstown* [Pa.] *Mercury*); the photographic staff of *The Boston* (Mass.) *Herald-American*
1980 Erwin H. Nagler
(*The Dallas* [Tex.] *Times Herald*)

MERITORIOUS PUBLIC SERVICE
1918 *New York Times*
1919 *Milwaukee* (Wis.) *Journal*
1921 *Boston* (Mass.) *Post*
1922 *World*, New York, N.Y.
1923 *Memphis* (Tenn.) *Commercial Appeal*
1924 *World* (New York, N.Y.)
1926 *Enquirer Sun* (Columbus, Ga.)
1927 *Canton* (Ohio) *Daily News*
1928 *Indianapolis* (Ind.) *Times*
1929 *Evening World*, New York, N.Y.
1931 *Atlanta* (Ga.) *Constitution*
1932 *Indianapolis* (Ind.) *News*
1933 *New York World-Telegram*

---

* Amateur photographer.

1934 *Medford (Ore.) Mail Tribune*
1935 *Sacramento (Calif.) Bee*
1936 *Cedar Rapids (Iowa) Gazette*
1937 *St. Louis (Mo.) Post-Dispatch*
1938 *Bismarck (N.D.) Tribune*
1939· *Miami (Fla.) Daily News*
1940 *Waterbury (Conn.) Republican and American*
1941 *St. Louis (Mo.) Post-Dispatch*
1942 *Los Angeles (Calif.) Times*
1943 *World-Herald, Omaha, Nebr.*
1944 *New York Times*
1945 *Detroit (Mich.) Free Press*
1946 *Scranton (Pa.) Times*
1947 *Sun, Baltimore, Md.*
1948 *St. Louis (Mo.) Post-Dispatch*
1949 *Nebraska State Journal*
1950 *Chicago (Ill.) Daily News* and *St. Louis Post-Dispatch*
1951 *Miami (Fla.) Herald* and *Brooklyn (N.Y.) Eagle*
1952 *St. Louis (Mo.) Post-Dispatch*
1953 *News Reporter (Whiteville, N.C.)* and *Tabor City (N.C.) Tribune*
1954 *Newsday,* Garden City, N.Y.
1955 *Columbus (Ga.) Ledger* and *Sunday Ledger-Enquirer*
1956 *Watsonville (Calif.) Register-Pajaronian*
1957 *Chicago (Ill.) Daily News*
1958 *Arkansas Gazette,* Little Rock
1959 *Utica (N.Y.) Observer-Dispatch* and *Utica Daily Press*
1960 *Los Angeles (Calif.) Times*
1961 *Amarillo (Tex.) Globe-Times*
1962 *Panama City (Fla.) News-Herald*
1963 *Chicago (Ill.) Daily News*
1964 *St. Petersburg (Fla.) Times*
1965 *Hutchinson (Kans.) News*
1966 *Boston (Mass.) Globe*
1967 *Courier Journal (Louisville, Ky.)* and *Milwaukee (Wis.) Journal*
1968 *Riverside (Calif.) Press-Enterprise*
1969 *Los Angeles (Calif.) Times*
1970 *Newsday,* Garden City, N.Y.
1971 *Winston-Salem [N.C.] Journal & Sentinel*
1972 *The New York Times*
1973 *The Washington Post*
1974 *Newsday,* Garden City, N.Y.
1975 *Boston (Mass.) Globe*
      The Xenia (Ohio) Daily Gazette
1976 *The Anchorage [Alaska] Daily News*
1977 *Lufkin (Tex.) News*
1978 *Philadelphia [Pa.] Inquirer*
1979 *Point Reyes (Calif.) Light*
1980 *The Gannett News Service*

FEATURE WRITING
1979 Jon D. Franklin (*The Baltimore [Md.] Evening Sun*)
1980 Madeleine Blais
      (*The Miami [Fla.] Herald*)

SPECIAL CITATIONS FOR JOURNALISM
1938 *Edmonton (Alberta) Journal,* for its editorial leadership in defense of the freedom of the press in the Province of Alberta, Canada.
1941 *New York Times,* for the public educational value of its foreign news reporting, exemplified by its scope, excellence of writing and presentation, and supplementary background information, illustration, and interpretation.

1944 Byron Price, Director of the Office of Censorship, for the creation and administration of the newspaper and radio codes during World War II.
1944 William Allen White, for his interest and service during his membership on the Advisory Board of Columbia University's School of Journalism.
1945 The cartographers of the American press, whose maps of the war fronts helped notably to clarify and increase public information on military progress.
1947 Columbia University and the Graduate School of Journalism, for their efforts to maintain and advance the high standards governing the Pulitzer Prize awards. The *St. Louis Post-Dispatch,* for its unswerving adherence to the public and professional ideals of its founder.
1948 Dr. Frank Diehl Fackenthal, a scroll indicating appreciation of his interest and service during the past years.
1951 Cyrus L. Sulzberger of the *New York Times* for his exclusive interview with Archbishop Stepinac.
1952 Max Kase of the *New York Journal-American* for his exclusive exposures of bribery and other forms of corruption in the popular American sport of basketball.
1952 *Kansas City (Mo.) Star* for coverage of the great regional floods of 1951 in Kansas and northwestern Missouri—a distinguished example of editing and reporting, as well as providing advance information that achieved maximum public protection.
1953 *New York Times,* for the section of its Sunday edition headed "Review of the Week," which for 17 years had been affording enlightenment and intelligent commentary.
1958 Walter Lippmann, nationally syndicated columnist of the *New York Herald Tribune,* for the wisdom, perception, and high sense of responsibility with which he commented for many years on national and international affairs.
1964 Gannett Newspapers, Rochester, N.Y.
1976 Professor John Hohenberg, expressing appreciation for his services for 22 years as Administrator of the Pulitzer Prizes and for his achievements as teacher and journalist
1978 Richard L. Strout, Washington, D.C. reporter for *The Christian Science Monitor* for 56 years and columnist for *The New Republic* since 1958, in recognition and appreciation of his thoughtful reporting and sharp analysis on events in the nation's capital.

BIOGRAPHY OR AUTOBIOGRAPHY
1917 *Julia Ward Howe,* by Laura E. Richards and Maude Howe Elliott, assisted by Florence Howe Hall
1918 *Benjamin Franklin, Self-Revealed,* by William Cabell Bruce
1919 *The Education of Henry Adams,* by Henry Adams
1920 *The Life of John Marshall* by Albert J. Beveridge
1921 *The Americanization of Edward Bok,* by Edward Bok
1922 *A Daughter of the Middle Border,* by Hamlin Garland
1923 *The Life and Letters of Walter H. Page,* by Burton J. Hendrick
1924 *From Immigrant to Inventor,* by Michael Idvorsky Pupin
1925 *Barrett Wendell and His Letters,* by M. A. DeWolfe Howe
1926 *The Life of Sir William Osler,* by Harvey Cushing
1927 *Whitman,* by Emory Holloway
1928 *The American Orchestra and Theodore Thomas,* by Charles Edward Russell
1929 *The Training of an American: The Earlier Life and Letters of Walter H. Page,* by Burton J. Hendrick
1930 *The Raven,* by Marquis James
1931 *Charles W. Eliot,* by Henry James
1932 *Theodore Roosevelt,* by Henry F. Pringle
1933 *Grover Cleveland,* by Allan Nevins
1934 *John Hay,* by Tyler Dennett
1935 *R. E. Lee,* by Douglas S. Freeman
1936 *The Thought and Character of William James,* by Ralph Barton Perry
1937 *Hamilton Fish,* by Allan Nevins
1938 *Pedlar's Progress,* by Odell Shepard, and *Andrew Jackson* (2 volumes), by Marquis James
1939 *Benjamin Franklin,* by Carl Van Doren
1940 *Woodrow Wilson, Life and Letters* (Volumes VII and VIII), by Ray Stannard Baker
1941 *Jonathan Edwards,* by Ola Elizabeth Winslow
1942 *Crusader in Crinoline,* by Forrest Wilson
1943 *Admiral of the Ocean Sea,* by Samuel Eliot Morison
1944 *The American Leonardo: The Life of Samuel F. B. Morse,* by Carleton Mabee
1945 *George Bancroft: Brahmin Rebel,* by Russell Blaine Nye
1946 *Son of the Wilderness,* by Linnie Marsh Wolfe
1947 *The Autobiography of William Allen White*
1948 *Forgotten First Citizen: John Bigelow,* by Margaret Clapp
1949 *Roosevelt and Hopkins,* by Robert E. Sherwood
1950 *John Quincy Adams and the Foundations of American Foreign Policy,* by Samuel Flagg Bemis

1951 *John C. Calhoun: American Portrait*, by Margaret Louise Coit

1952 *Charles Evans Hughes*, by Merlo J. Pusey

1953 *Edmund Pendleton 1721–1803*, by David J. Mays

1954 *The Spirit of St. Louis*, by Charles A. Lindbergh

1955 *The Taft Story*, by William S. White

1956 *Benjamin Henry Latrobe*, by Talbot Faulkner Hamlin

1957 *Profiles in Courage*, by John F. Kennedy

1958 *George Washington* (Volumes I–VI), by Douglas Southall Freeman; Volume VII, by Mary Wells Ashworth and John Alexander Carroll

1959 *Woodrow Wilson, American Prophet*, by Arthur Walworth

1960 *John Paul Jones*, by Samuel Eliot Morison

1961 *Charles Sumner and the Coming of the Civil War*, by David Donald

1963 *Henry James* (Volumes II and III), by Leon Edel

1964 *John Keats*, by Walter Jackson Bate

1965 *Henry Adams* (3 volumes), by Ernest Samuels

1966 *A Thousand Days*, by Arthur M. Schlesinger, Jr.

1967 *Mr. Clemens and Mark Twain*, by Justin Kaplan

1968 *Memoirs (1925–1950)*, by George F. Kennan

1969 *The Man from New York: John Quinn and His Friends*, by Benjamin Lawrence Reid

1970 *Huey Long*, by T.H. Williams

1971 *Robert Frost: The Years of Triumph*, by L. R. Thompson

1972 *Eleanor and Franklin*, by Joseph P. Lash

1973 *Luce and His Empire*, by W. A. Swanberg

1974 *O'Neill, Son and Artist*, by Louis Sheaffer

1975 *The Power Broker: Robert Moses and the Fall of New York*, by Robert A. Caro

1976 *Edith Wharton: A Biography*, by R.W.B. Lewis

1977 *A Prince of Our Disorder*, by John E. Mack

1978 *Samuel Johnson*, by Walter Jackson Bate

1979 *Days of Sorrow and Pain: Leo Baeck and the Berlin Jews*, by Leonard Baker

1980 *The Rise of Theodore Roosevelt*, by Edmund Morris

DRAMA

1918 *Why Marry?*, by Jesse Lynch Williams

1920 *Beyond the Horizon*, by Eugene O'Neill

1921 *Miss Lulu Bett*, by Zona Gale

1922 *Anna Christie*, by Eugene O'Neill

1923 *Icebound*, by Owen Davis

1924 *Hell-Bent for Heaven*, by Hatcher Hughes

1925 *They Knew What They Wanted*, by Sidney Howard

1926 *Craig's Wife*, by G. Kelly

1927 *In Abraham's Bosom*, by Paul Green

* Declined.

1928 *Strange Interlude*, by Eugene O'Neill

1929 *Street Scene*, by Elmer L. Rice

1930 *The Green Pastures*, by Marc Connelly

1931 *Alison's House*, by Susan Glaspell

1932 *Of Thee I Sing*, by George S. Kaufman, Morrie Ryskind, and Ira Gershwin (with music by George Gershwin)

1933 *Both Your Houses*, by Maxwell Anderson

1934 *Men in White*, by Sidney Kingsley

1935 *The Old Maid*, by Zoe Akins

1936 *Idiot's Delight*, by Robert E. Sherwood

1937 *You Can't Take It with You*, by Moss Hart and George S. Kaufman

1938 *Our Town*, by Thornton Wilder

1939 *Abe Lincoln in Illinois*, by Robert E. Sherwood

1940 *The Time of Your Life*, by William Saroyan*

1941 *There Shall Be No Night*, by Robert E. Sherwood

1943 *The Skin of Our Teeth*, by Thornton Wilder

1945 *Harvey*, by Mary Chase

1946 *State of the Union*, by Russel Crouse and Howard Lindsay

1948 *A Streetcar Named Desire*, by Tennessee Williams

1949 *Death of a Salesman*, by Arthur Miller

1950 *South Pacific*, by Richard Rodgers, Oscar Hammerstein II, and Joshua Logan

1952 *The Shrike*, by Joseph Kramm

1953 *Picnic*, by William Inge

1954 *The Teahouse of the August Moon*, by John Patrick

1955 *Cat on a Hot Tin Roof*, by Tennessee Williams

1956 *Diary of Anne Frank*, by Albert Hackett and Frances Goodrich

1957 *Long Day's Journey into Night*, by Eugene O'Neill

1958 *Look Homeward, Angel*, by Ketti Frings

1959 *J. B.*, by Archibald MacLeish

1960 *Fiorello!*, book by Jerome Weidman and George Abbott, music by Jerry Bock, and lyrics by Sheldon Harnick

1961 *All the Way Home*, by Tad Mosel

1962 *How to Succeed in Business Without Really Trying*, by F. Loesser and A. Burrows

1965 *The Subject Was Roses*, by Frank D. Gilroy

1967 *A Delicate Balance*, by Edward Albee

1969 *The Great White Hope*, by Howard Sackler

1970 *No Place to Be Somebody*, by Charles Gordone

1971 *The Effect of Gamma Rays on Man-in-the-Moon Marigolds*, by Paul Zindel

1973 *That Championship Season*, by Jason Miller

1975 *Seascape*, by Edward Albee

1976 *A Chorus Line*, conceived, choreographed and directed by Michael Bennett; book by James Kirkwood & Nicholas Dante; music by Marvin Hamlisch; lyrics by Edward Kleban.

1977 *The Shadow Box*, by Michael Cristofer

1978 *The Gin Game*, by Donald L. Coburn

1979 *Buried Child*, by Sam Shepard

1980 *Talley's Folly*, by Lanford Wilson

HISTORY

1917 *With Americans of Past and Present Days*, by His Excellency J. J. Jusserand, Ambassador of France to the U.S.

1918 *A History of the Civil War, 1861–1865*, by James Ford Rhodes

1920 *The War with Mexico* (2 volumes), by Justin H. Smith

1921 *The Victory at Sea*, by William Sowden Sims in collaboration with Burton J. Hendrick

1922 *The Founding of New England*, by James Truslow Adams

1923 *The Supreme Court in United States History*, by Charles Warren

1924 *The American Revolution—A Constitutional Interpretation*, by Charles Howard McIlwain

1925 *A History of the American Frontier*, by F. L. Paxson

1926 *The History of the United States* (Volume VI: *The War for Southern Independence*), by Edward Channing

1927 *Pinckney's Treaty*, by Samuel Flagg Bemis

1928 *Main Currents in American Thought*, 2 volumes, by Vernon Louis Parrington

1929 *The Organization and Administration of the Union Army, 1861–1865*, by Fred Albert Shannon

1930 *The War of Independence*, by Claude H. Van Tyne

1931 *The Coming of the War: 1914*, by Bernadotte E. Schmitt

1932 *My Experiences in the World War*, by John J. Pershing

1933 *The Significance of Sections in American History*, by Frederick J. Turner

1934 *The People's Choice*, by Herbert Agar

1935 *The Colonial Period of American History*, by Charles McLean Andrews

1936 *The Constitutional History of the United States*, by Andrew C. McLaughlin

1937 *The Flowering of New England*, by Van Wyck Brooks

1938 *The Road to Reunion, 1865–1900* by Paul Herman Buck

1939 *A History of American Magazines* by Frank Luther Mott

1940 *Abraham Lincoln: The War Years*, by Carl Sandburg

1941 *The Atlantic Migration, 1607–1860, by Marcus Lee Hansen*

1942 *Reveille in Washington*, by Margaret Leech

1943 *Paul Revere and the World He Lived In,* by Esther Forbes

1944 *The Growth of American Thought,* by Merle Curti

1945 *Unfinished Business,* by Stephen Bonsal

1946 *The Age of Jackson,* by Arthur M. Schlesinger, Jr.

1947 *Scientists Against Time,* by James Phinney Baxter III

1948 *Across the Wide Missouri,* by Bernard DeVoto

1949 *The Disruption of American Democracy,* by Roy Franklin Nichols

1950 *Art and Life in America,* by Oliver W. Larkin

1951 *The Old Northwest: Pioneer Period, 1815–1840,* by R. Carlyle Buley

1952 *The Uprooted,* by Oscar Handlin

1953 *The Era of Good Feelings,* by George Dangerfield

1954 *A Stillness at Appomattox,* by Bruce Catton

1955 *Great River: The Rio Grande in North American History,* by Paul Horgan

1956 *The Age of Reform,* by Richard Hofstadter

1957 *Russia Leaves the War: Soviet-American Relations, 1917–1920,* by George F. Kennan

1958 *Banks and Politics in America—From the Revolution to the Civil War,* by Bray Hammond

1959 *The Republican Era: 1869–1901,* by Leonard D. White, with the assistance of Jean Schneider

1960 *In the Days of McKinley,* by Margaret Leech

1961 *Between War and Peace: The Potsdam Conference,* by Herbert Feis

1962 *The Triumphant Empire: Thunder-Clouds Gather in the West 1763-1766,* by Lawrence H. Gipson

1963 *Washington: Village and Capital, 1800–1878,* by Constance McLaughlin Green

1964 *Puritan Village: The Formation of a New England Town,* by Sumner Chilton Powell

1965 *The Greenback Era,* by Irwin Unger

1966 *Life of the Mind in America. From the Revolution to the Civil War,* by Perry Miller

1967 *Exploration and Empire,* by William H. Goetzmann

1968 *The Ideological Origins of the American Revolution,* by Bernard Bailyn

1969 *Origins of the Fifth Amendment,* by Leonard W. Levy

1970 *Present at the Creation: My Years in the State Department,* by Dean Acheson

1971 *Roosevelt: The Soldier of Freedom,* by James Mac-Gregor Burns

1972 *Neither Black Nor White,* by Carl M. Degler

1973 *People of Paradox: An Inquiry Concerning the Origin of American Civilization,* by Michael Kammen

1974 *The Americans,* by Daniel J. Boorstin

1975 *Jefferson and His Time,* by Dumas Malone

1976 *Lamy of Santa Fe,* by Paul Horgan

1977 *The Impending Crisis,* by David M. Potter

1978 *The Invisible Hand: The Managerial Revolution in American Business,* by Alfred D. Chandler

1979 *The Dred Scott Case,* by Don E. Fehrenbacher

1980 *Been in the Storm So Long: The Aftermath of Slavery,* by Leon F. Litwack

PRIZES IN LETTERS

FICTION

1918 *His Family,* by Ernest Poole

1919 *The Magnificent Ambersons,* by Booth Tarkington

1921 *The Age of Innocence,* by Edith Wharton

1922 *Alice Adams,* by B. Tarkington

1923 *One of Ours,* by Willa Cather

1924 *The Able McLaughlins,* by Margaret Wilson

1925 *So Big,* by Edna Ferber

1926 *Arrowsmith,* by S. Lewis

1927 *Early Autumn,* by Louis Bromfield

1928 *The Bridge of San Luis Rey,* by Thornton Wilder

1929 *Scarlet Sister Mary,* by Julia Peterkin

1930 *Laughing Boy,* by Oliver LaFarge

1931 *Years of Grace,* by Margaret Ayer Barnes

1932 *The Good Earth,* by Pearl S. Buck

1933 *The Store,* by T. S. Stribling

1934 *Lamb in His Bosom,* by Caroline Miller

1935 *Now in November,* by Josephine Winslow Johnson

1936 *Honey in the Horn,* by Harold L. Davis

1937 *Gone With the Wind,* by Margaret Mitchell

1938 *The Late George Apley,* by John Phillips Marquand

1939 *The Yearling,* by Marjorie Kinnan Rawlings

1940 *The Grapes of Wrath,* by John Steinbeck

1942 *In This Our Life,* by Ellen Glasgow

1943 *Dragon's Teeth,* by Upton Sinclair

1944 *Journey in the Dark,* by Martin Flavin

1945 *A Bell for Adano,* by John Hersey

1947 *All the King's Men,* by Robert Penn Warren

1948 *Tales of the South Pacific,* by James A. Michener

1949 *Guard of Honor,* by James Gould Cozzens

1950 *The Way West,* by A. B. Guthrie, Jr.

1951 *The Town,* by Conrad Richter

1952 *The Caine Mutiny,* by Herman Wouk

1953 *The Old Man and the Sea,* by Ernest Hemingway

1955 *A Fable,* by Wm. Faulkner

1956 *Andersonville,* by MacKinlay Kantor

1958 *A Death in the Family,* by James Agee

1959 *The Travels of Jaimie McPheeters,* by Robert Lewis Taylor

1960 *Advise and Consent,* by Allen Drury

1961 *To Kill a Mockingbird,* by Harper Lee

1962 *The Edge of Sadness,* by Edwin O'Connor

1963 *The Reivers,* by Wm. Faulkner

1965 *The Keepers of the House,* by Shirley Ann Grau

1966 *Collected Short Stories,* by Katherine Ann Porter

1967 *The Fixer,* by Bernard Malamud

1968 *The Confessions of Nat Turner,* by William Styron

1969 *House Made of Dawn,* by M. Scott Momaday

1970 *Collected Stories,* by Jean Stafford

1972 *Angel of Repose,* by Wallace Stegner

1973 *The Optimist's Daughter,* by Eudora Welty

1975 *The Killer Angels,* by Michael Shaara

1976 *Humboldt's Gift,* by Saul Bellow

1978 *Elbow Room,* by James Allan McPherson

1979 *The Stories of John Cheever*

1980 *The Executioner's Song,* by Norman Mailer

POETRY

1918 *Love Songs,* by Sara Teasdale

1919 *Old Road to Paradise,* by Margaret Widdemer

1919 *Corn Huskers,* by Carl Sandburg

1922 *Collected Poems,* by Edwin Arlington Robinson

1923 *The Ballad of the Harp-Weaver; A Few Figs from Thistles; eight sonnets in American Poetry, 1922, A Miscellany,* by Edna St. Vincent Millay

1924 *New Hampshire: A Poem with Notes and Grace Notes,* by Robert Frost

1925 *The Man Who Died Twice,* by Edwin Arlington Robinson

1926 *What's O'Clock,* by Amy Lowell

1927 *Fiddler's Farewell,* by Leonora Speyer

1928 *Tristram,* by Edwin Arlington Robinson

1929 *John Brown's Body,* by Stephen Vincent Benét

1930 *Selected Poems,* by Conrad Aiken

1931 *Collected Poems,* by Robert Frost

1932 *The Flowering Stone,* by George Dillon

1933 *Conquistador,* by Archibald MacLeish

1934 *Collected Verse,* by Robert Hillyer

1935 *Bright Ambush,* by Audrey Wurdemann

1936 *Strange Holiness,* by Robert P. Tristram Coffin

1937 *A Further Range,* by Robert Frost

1938 *Cold Morning Sky,* by Marya Zaturenska

1939 *Selected Poems,* by John Gould Fletcher

1940 *Collected Poems*, by Mark Van Doren
1941 *Sunderland Capture*, by Leonard Bacon
1942 *The Dust Which Is God*, by William Rose Benét
1943 *A Witness Tree*, by Robert Frost
1944 *Western Star*, by Stephen Vincent Benét
1945 *V-Letter and Other Poems*, by Karl Shapiro
1947 *Lord Weary's Castle*, by Robert Lowell
1948 *The Age of Anxiety*, by W. H. Auden
1949 *Terror and Decorum*, by Peter Viereck
1950 *Annie Allen*, by Gwendolyn Brooks
1951 *Complete Poems*, by Carl Sandburg
1952 *Collected Poems*, by Marianne Moore
1953 *Collected Poems 1917–1952*, by Archibald MacLeish
1954 *The Waking, Poem 1933-1953*, by Theodore Roethke
1955 *Collected Poems*, by Wallace Stevens
1956 *Poems—North & South*, by Elizabeth Bishop
1957 *Things of This World*, by Richard Wilbur
1958 *Promises: Poems 1954–56*, by Robert Penn Warren
1959 *Selected Poems 1928–1958*, by Stanley Kunitz
1960 *Heart's Needle*, by W. D. Snodgrass
1961 *Times Three: Selected Verse from Three Decades*, by Phyllis McGinley
1962 *Poems*, by Alan Dugan
1963 *Pictures from Breughel*, by William Carlos Williams
1964 *At the End of the Open Road*, by Louis Simpson
1965 *77 Dream Songs*, by John Berryman
1966 *Selected Poems*, by Richard Eberhart
1967 *Live or Die*, by Anne Sexton
1968 *The Hard Hours*, by A. Hecht
1969 *Of Being Numerous*, by George Oppen
1970 *Untitled Subjects*, by Richard Howard
1971 *The Carrier of Ladders*, by William S. Merwin
1972 *Collected Poems*, by James Wright
1973 *Up Country*, by Maxine Winokur Kumin
1974 *The Dolphin*, by R. Lowell
1975 *Turtle Island*, by G. Snyder
1976 *Self-Portrait in a Convex Mirror*, by John Ashbery
1977 *Divine Comedies*, by James Merrill
1978 *Collected Poems*, by Howard Nemerov
1979 *Now and Then*, by Robert Penn Warren
1980 *Selected Poems*, by Donald Rodney Justice

GENERAL NONFICTION
1962 *The Making of the President 1960*, by Theodore H. White
1963 *The Guns of August*, by Barbara W. Tuchman
1964 *Anti-intellectualism in American Life*, by R. Hofstadter
1965 *O Strange New World*, by Howard Mumford Jones
1966 *Wandering Through Winter*, by Edwin Way Teale

1967 *The Problem of Slavery in Western Culture*, by David Brion Davis
1968 *The Story of Civilization* (Volume X), by Will and Ariel Durant
1969 *So Human An Animal*, by Rene Jules Dubos
     The Armies of the Night, by Norman Mailer
1970 *Gandhi's Truth*, by Erik H. Erikson
1971 *The Rising Sun*, by John Toland
1972 *Stilwell and the American Experience in China, 1911–1945*, by Barbara Tuchman
1973 *Fire in the Lake: The Vietnamese and the Americans in Vietnam*, by Frances Fitz-Gerald, and *Children of Crisis*, by Dr. Robert Coles
1974 *The Denial of Death*, by Ernest Becker
1975 *Pilgrim at Tinker Creek*, by Annie Dillard
1976 *Why Survive? Being Old in America*, by Robert N. Butler
1977 *Beautiful Swimmers: Watermen, Crabs and the Chesapeake Bay*, by William W. Warner
1978 *The Dragons of Eden*, by Carl Sagan
1979 *On Human Nature*, by Edward O. Wilson
1980 *Godel, Escher, Bach: An Eternal Golden Braid*, by Douglas R. Hofstadter

CRITICISM/COMMENTARY
1970 Ada Louise Huxtable of *The New York Times* for distinguished architecture criticism
     Marquis Childs of the *St. Louis (Mo.) Post-Dispatch* for distinguished commentary from Washington, D.C.
1971 Harold C. Schonberg, *The New York Times'* senior music critic
     William A. Caldwell, *The [Hackensack, N.J.] Record*, for "Simeon Stylites," a column on local affairs, written daily for more than 40 years.
1972 Frank Peters, Jr., *St. Louis (Mo.) Post Dispatch*
1973 Ronald Powers, *Chicago Sun-Times* and David S. Broder, *Washington Post*
1974 Emily Genauer, *Newday*
     Edwin A. Roberts, *National Observer*
1975 Mary McGrory, *The Washington Star* and Roger Ebert, *Chicago Sun Times*
1976 Alan M. Kriegsman, *The Washington [D.C.] Post*
     Walter W. (Red) Smith, *The New York Times*
1977 William McPherson, *The Washington Post*; George F. Will, Washington Post Writers Group
1978 Walter Kerr, *The New York Times*; William Safire, *The New York Times*
1979 Paul Gapp, *The Chicago Tribune*; Russell Baker, *The New York Times*
1980 William A. Henry III, *The Boston Globe*; Ellen H. Goodman, *The Boston Globe*

SPECIAL CITATIONS
1944 *Oklahoma!*, by Richard Rodgers and Oscar Hammerstein II

1957 Kenneth Roberts, a special citation for his historical novels which long contributed to the creation of greater interest in early American history
1960 Garrett Mattingly for *The Armada*
1961 *American Heritage Picture History of the Civil War*
1973 *George Washington*, by James Thomas Flexner
1976 Scott Joplin, for his contributions to American music
1977 Alex Haley for *Roots*
1978 E. B. White for his contributions to *The New Yorker* and his general enrichment of the American language

PRIZES IN MUSIC
1943 William Schuman: *Secular Cantata No. 2, A Free Song*
1944 Howard Hanson: *Symphony No. 4, Opus 34*
1945 Aaron Copland: *Appalachian Spring*
1946 Leo Sowerby: *The Canticle of the Sun*
1947 Charles Ives: *Symph. No. 3*
1948 Walter Piston: *Symph. No. 3*
1949 Virgil Thomson: *Louisiana Story*
1950 Gian-Carlo Menotti: *The Consul*
1951 Douglas S. Moore: *Giants in the Earth*
1952 Gail Kubik: *Symphony Concertante*
1954 Quincy Porter: *Concerto for Two Pianos and Orchestra*
1955 Gian-Carlo Menotti: *The Saint of Bleecker Street*
1956 Ernst Toch: *Symphony No. 3*
1957 Norman Dello Joio: *Meditations on Ecclesiastes*
1958 Samuel Barber: the score of *Vanessa*
1959 John La Montaine: *Concerto for Piano and Orchestra*
1960 Elliott Carter: *Second String Quartet*
1961 Walter Piston: *Symph. No. 7*
1962 Robert Ward: *The Crucible*
1963 Samuel Barber: *Piano Concerto No. 1*
1966 Leslie Bassett: *Variations for Orchestra*
1967 Leon Kirchner: *Quartet No. 3*
1968 George Crumb: *Echoes of Time and the River*
1969 Karel Husa: *String Quartet No. 3*
1970 Charles W. Wuorinen: *Time's Encomium*
1971 Mario Davidovsky: *Synchronisms No. 6 for Piano and Electronic Sound*
1972 Jacob Druckman: *Windows*
1973 Elliot Carter: *String Quartet No. 3*
1974 Donald Martino: *Notturno*
1975 Dominick Argento: *From the Diary of Virginia Wolff*
1976 Ned Rorem: *Air Music*
1977 Richard Wernick: *Visions of Terror and Wonder*
1978 Michael Colgrass: *Déja Vu for Percussion Quartet and Orchestra*
1979 Joseph Schwantner: *Aftertones of Infinity*
1980 David Del Tredici: *In Memory of a Summer Day*

OTHER PRIZES AND AWARDS

ACHIEVEMENT

ALL-AMERICA CITIES AWARD PROGRAM (1979-80) for Community Involvement Through Citizen Action, sponsored by the National Municipal League:
Bellingham, Washington; Gardena, California; Phoenix, Arizona; Portland, Oregon; Portsmouth, Ohio; Rockingham, North Carolina; Seminole, Oklahoma; Sherman, Texas; Shreveport, Louisiana.

WOMEN OF THE YEAR AWARDS (1979) for outstanding achievement by women in their fields, presented by *Ladies' Home Journal* magazine:

Women of the Decade (selected by *Journal* readers from past recipients): Marian Anderson; Joan Ganz Cooney; Betty Ford; Helen Hayes; Katherine Hepburn; Barbara Jordan; Elisabeth Kubler-Ross; Sylvia Porter; Beverly Sills; Barbara Walters; Margaret Mead (Posthumous award).

PUBLIC SERVICE

AMERICAN JEWISH COMMITTEE (1980):

Herbert H. Lehman Award in Human Relations: John H. Gutfreund

Institute of Human Relations Mass Media Award: Public Broadcasting Service

MEDALS OF FREEDOM awarded by the President of the United States, for exceptionally meritorious contributions to national security, world peace, or to cultural or other significant public or private endeavors. The most recent recipients are:
Ansel Adams, photographer
Rachel Carson (dec.), scientist and author
Lucia Chase, ballerina
Hubert Humphrey (dec.), United States Senator
Archbishop Iakovos, Primate of the Greek Orthodox Church in North and South America
Lyndon B. Johnson (dec.), President of the United States
Clarence M. Mitchell, Jr., retired director of the N.A.A.C.P.'s Washington bureau
Roger Tory Peterson, ornithologist
Adm. Hyman G. Rickover, Ret., known as father of the nuclear Navy
Beverly Sills, opera singer
Robert Penn Warren, writer
John Wayne (dec.), actor
Eudora Welty, author
Tennessee Williams, playwright

TEACHER OF THE YEAR (1980) awarded by the Chief State School Officers, the *Encyclopaedia Britannica*, and *Good Housekeeping* magazine: (Mrs.) Beverly Joyce Bimes, St. Louis, Missouri

SCIENCE

NATIONAL ACADEMY OF SCIENCES AWARDS (1980):
George P. Merrill Award: Robert N. Clayton
Award for Environmental Quality: Gilbert F. White
James Murray Luck Award: Conyers Herring
Public Welfare Medal: Walter Sullivan
U.S. Steel Foundation Award in Molecular Biology: Phillip A. Sharp
Waksman Award in Microbiology: Julius Adler
Henry Draper Medal: W.W. Morgan
Award in Chemical Sciences: Frank H. Westheimer
N.A.S. Award in Aeronautical Engineering: James S. McDonnell
N.A.S. Award in Applied Mathematics and Numerical Analysis: George F. Carrier
N.A.S. Staff Award for Distinguished Service: William C. Kelly

NATIONAL MEDAL OF SCIENCE, the highest award for outstanding achievement in science and engineering in the United States (1979):
Robert H. Burris, Madison, Wisconsin
Elizabeth Crosby, Ann Arbor, Michigan
Joseph L. Doob, Urbana, Illinois

Richard P. Feynman, Pasadena, California
Donald E. Knuth, Stanford, California
Arthur Kornberg, Stanford, California
Emmett Leith, Ann Arbor, Michigan
Herman F. Mark, Brooklyn, New York
Raymond D. Mindlin, New York, New York
Robert N. Noyce, Santa Clara, California
Severo Ochoa, Nutley, New Jersey
Earl R. Parker, Berkeley, California
Edward M. Purcell, Cambridge, Massachusetts
Simon Ramo, Cleveland, Ohio
John H. Sinfelt, Linden, New Jersey
Lyman Spitzer, Jr., Princeton, New Jersey
Earl R. Stadtman, Bethesda, Maryland
George L. Stebbins, Jr., Davis, California
Paul A. Weiss, New York, New York
Victor F. Weisskopf, Cambridge, Massachusetts

WESTINGHOUSE SCIENCE TALENT SEARCH (1980): high school student scholarship competition conducted by Science Service, Inc., sponsored by Westinghouse Educational Foundation and the Westinghouse Corporation:

$12,000:	Lisa Jay Randall, New York, N.Y.
	John Michael Andersland, East Lansing, Mich.
$10,000:	Michael Vincent Finn, Annandale, Va.
$ 7,500:	Craig Richard Bina, Arlington Heights, Ill.
	Melissa Willene Hull, New York, N.Y.
	Bryan Edward Penprase, San Marino, Calif.
$ 5,000:	Naomi Taylor, Bayside, N.Y.
	Paul Neil Feldman, Brooklyn, N.Y.
	Pamela Lynne Epstein, Merritt Island, Fla.
	David Chiang, New York, N.Y.

JOURNALISM

GEORGE POLK MEMORIAL AWARDS (1980) sponsored by Long Island University:
Foreign Reporting: John Kifner, *New York Times*
National Reporting: Brian Donovan, Bob Wyrick and Stuart Diamond, *Newsday*
Political Reporting: Jack Newfield, *Village Voice*
Television Reporting—National: Bob Currie, Lea Thompson, Jack Cloherty, WRC-TV, Washington, D.C.
Television Reporting—Foreign: Ed Bradley, CBS News

NIEMAN FELLOWSHIPS (1980-81) for working Journalists—(Harvard University):
Frank Adams; Carlos Aguilar; Peter Almond; Gerald Boyd; Robert J. Cox; Fleur De Villiers; Rose Economou; Mustafa Gursel; Michael Hill; Masayuki Ikeda; David Lamb; Douglas Marlette; Donald McNeill; Donald Semper; Laurel Shackelford; Howard Shapiro; James Stewart; Nancy Warnecke; Jing Lun Zhao

SIGMA DELTA CHI AWARDS (1979) for distinguished service in print and broadcast journalism:

Newspapers:
General Reporting: Gene Miller, Carl Hiaasen, Patrick Malone and William D. Montalbano, *Miami Herald*
Editorial Writing: Rick Sinding, *The* (Hackensack, N.J.) *Record*
Washington Correspondence: Gordon Eliot White, *Salt Lake City Deseret News*
Foreign Correspondence: Karen DeYoung, *Washington Post*
News Photography: Eddie Adams, The Associated Press
Editorial Cartoon: John P. Trever, Albuquerque *Journal*
Public Service: *Miami Herald*

Magazines:
Reporting: Michael W. Vargo, *Pennsylvania Illustrated*
Public Service: *National Geographic*

Radio:
Reporting: ABC Radio News, New York, N.Y.
Public Service: WJR Radio, Detroit, Mich.
Editorializing: WTLC Radio, Indianapolis, Ind.

Television:
Reporting: ABC TV News and Bob Dyk, New York, N.Y.
Public Service: KXAS-TV, Ft. Worth/Dallas, Tex.
Editorializing: KPIX-TV, San Francisco, Calif.
Research About Journalism: Lloyd Wendt, Sarasota, Fla.

ARTS

AMERICAN ACADEMY AND INSTITUTE OF ARTS AND LETTERS AWARDS (1980):

Academy-Institute Gold Medals: Peggy Bacon (Graphic Art), Edward Albee (Drama)

Howells Medal for Fiction: William Maxwell, for *So Long, See You Tomorrow*

ACADEMY-INSTITUTE AWARDS:

In Literature: Ann Beattie, William Dickey, Paul Fussell, Maxine Kumin, George Oppen, Robert Pinsky, Lewis Thomas, Larry Woiwode

In Art: Richard Anuszkiewicz, Edward Dugmore, Marion Lerner Levine, Howard Newman, Charmion von Wiegand

In Music: Donald Grantham, Eugene O'Brien, Malcolm Peyton, Lawrence Widdoes

SPECIAL AWARDS:

American Academy in Rome Fellowship in Creative Writing: Mary Morris

Arnold W. Brunner Memorial Prize in Architecture: Michael Graves

Witter Bynner Prize for Poetry: Pamela White Hadas

Charles Ives Scholarships: Thomas E. Barker, Laura Clayton, Lowell Lieberman, William Maiben, Mario J. Pelusi, George Tsontakis

Charles Ives Award: The Charles Ives Society

Sue Kaufman Prize for First Fiction: Jayne Anne Phillips

Goddard Lieberson Fellowships: David Chaitkin, Robert Xavier Rodriguez

The Award of Merit Medal for Poetry: Richard Howard

Richard and Hinda Rosenthal Foundation Awards: Fiction—Stanley Elkin; Painting—Dolores Milmoe

Harold D. Vursell Memorial Award: Tom Wolfe

Marjorie Peabody Waite Award: Sidney Laufman

Morton Dauwen Zabel Award: Donald Finkel

Art

NATIONAL ACADEMY OF DESIGN PRIZES (1980):

Benjamin Altman Prizes: Landscape—Ethel Magafan ($3,000); Charles H. Cecil ($1,500); Figure—Joe Lasker ($3,000); Anthony Toney ($1,500)

Emil and Dines Carlsen Award: John Heliker ($1,000)

Andrew Carnegie Prize: William Palmer ($1,000)

Adolph and Clara Obrig Prize: Paul Zimmerman ($600)

Aldro T. Hibbard Memorial Award: Harrison Groutage ($200)

Paul Puzinas Memorial Award: Jerome Witkin ($200)

Isaac N. Maynard Prize: Charles Pfahl ($150)

Salmagundi Club Prize: Martin Friedman ($100)

Joseph S. Isidor Gold Medal: Rudolf Baranik

Thomas B. Clarke Prize: Jeffrey Kronsnoble ($500)

S.J. Wallace Truman Prize: Marcia Mead Bailey ($850)

Julius Hallgarten Prizes: Masanobu Nihei ($400); Henry Ransom ($300)

Edwin Palmer Memorial Prize: Hans Moller ($2,000)

Saltus Gold Medal: Eric Isenburger

Gladys Emerson Cook Prize: Xavier Gonzalez ($100)

Certificates of Merit: Robert Angeloch; John A. Annus; Rose Naftulin; Priscilla Roberts

Sculpture Awards:

Artists Fund Prize: Albert Wein ($400)

Helen Foster Barnett Prize: Gerd Hesness ($500)

Dessie Greer Prize: Granville W. Carter ($100)

N.A.D. Gold Medal: Sidney Simon

Elizabeth N. Watrous Gold Medal: Charles Parks ($350)

Daniel Chester French Medal: Archimedes Giacomantonio

Thomas R. Proctor Prize: Philip Schrenker ($500)

Ellin P. Speyer Prize: Michael Lantz ($400)

Certificates of Merit: Zenos Frudakis; Philip Grausman; Susan Smyly

Graphic Art Awards:

Anonymous Prize: Julius Hubler ($100)

Cannon Prize: Gregory J. Paquette ($400)

Ralph Fabri Prize: Moishe Smith ($200)

William H. Leavin Prize: Jack Coughlin ($100)

Helen M. Loggie Prize: Joan A. Poole ($50)

Frank and Annie Shikler Prize: Dorothy Cochran ($250)

Leo Meissner Prize: Clare Romano ($200)

Certificates of Merit: Robert Kipniss; June Magaziner; Doel Reed

Watercolor Awards:

Walter Biggs Memorial Award: William Strohsahl

Adolph and Clara Obrig Prizes: Tom Nicholas ($450); Alexander Ross ($300)

William A. Paton Prize: William Thon ($1,000)

Leila Gardin Sawyer Prize: Serge Hollerbach ($50)

Certificates of Merit: Betty M. Bowes; Dale Meyers; Kathleen Zimmerman

Literature

AMERICAN BOOKSELLERS ASSOCIATION AWARD (1980):

Irita Van Doren Award: Studs Terkel

BANCROFT PRIZES (1980) presented by Columbia University for books of exceptional merit and distinction in American history (including biography) and diplomacy:

Robert Dallek, *Franklin D. Roosevelt and American Foreign Policy, 1932-1945*

Thomas Dublin, *Women at Work: The Transformation of Work and Community in Lowell, Massachusetts, 1826-1860*

Donald Worster, *Dust Bowl: The Southern Plains in the 1930s*

THE BOLLINGEN PRIZE IN POETRY (1977-78) an award of $5,000 given by Yale University Library: W.S. Merwin

THE AMERICAN BOOK AWARDS (1980) sponsored by the Association of American Publishers:

General Fiction: *Sophie's Choice*, William Styron

General Nonfiction: *The Right Stuff*, Tom Wolfe

Autobiography: *By Myself*, Lauren Bacall

Biography: *The Rise of Theodore Roosevelt*, Edmund Morris

History: *White House Years*, Henry Kissinger

First Novel: *Birdy*, William Wharton

Poetry: *Ashes*, Philip Levine (paperback)

Religion/Inspiration: *The Gnostic Gospels*, Elaine Pagels

Children's Books: *A Gathering of Days: A New England Girl's Journal, 1830-32*, Joan W. Blos

Translation: Osip E. Mandelstam's *The Complete Critical Prose and Letters*, translated by Jane Gary Harris and Constance Link

NEWBERY-CALDECOTT MEDALS (1980) presented by the American Library Association for the most distinguished American books in the children's field:

John Newbery Medal: *A Gathering of Days: A New England Girl's Journal, 1830-32*, Joan W. Blos

Randolph Caldecott Medal: *Ox-Cart Man*, Donald Hall

Laura Ingalls Wilder Medal (1980): Theodor S. Geisel (Dr. Seuss)

POETRY SOCIETY OF AMERICA PRIZES (1979-80):

Bernice Ames Memorial Award: Patricia Hooper

Gordon Barber Memorial Award: Myra Sklarew

Melville Cane Award: Richard Hugo

Gertrude B. Claytor Memorial Award: Marlene Rosen Fine

Gustav Davidson Memorial Award: Willis Barnstone

Mary Carolyn Davies Memorial Award: Ralph Robin

Alice Fay di Castagnola Award: Michael Heller; Diana O'Hehir, Charles Simic (shared)

Emily Dickinson Award: Virginia Linton

Consuelo Ford Award: Phyllis Janowitz

Cecil Hemley Memorial Award: L.L. Zeiger

Elias Lieberman Student Poetry Award: Laura B. Margolis

John Masefield Memorial Award: Ellery Akers

Alfred Kreymborg Memorial Award: L.L. Zeiger

Shelley Memorial Award: Julia Randall

Charles and Celia B. Wagner Award: Phyllis Janowitz

William Carlos Williams Award: David Ray; William Dickey (Honorable Mention)

Lucille Medwick Memorial Award: Florence Grossman and Gary Miranda (shared)

Witter Bynner Poetry Translation Prize: John and Bogdana Carpenter

Witter Bynner Grant-In-Aid: Charles Guenther and Anselm Hollo

Music

GRAMMY AWARDS (1979) given by the National Academy of Recording Arts and Sciences:

Record of the Year: "What a Fool Believes" (The Doobie Brothers)

Album of the Year: "52nd Street" (Billy Joel)

Song of the Year: "What a Fool Believes" (The Doobie Brothers)

Best New Artist of the Year: Rickie Lee Jones

Best Pop Vocal Performance, Female: "I'll Never Love This Way Again" (Dionne Warwick)

Best Pop Vocal Performance, Male: "52nd Street" (Billy Joel)

Best Pop Vocal Performance, Group: "Minute by Minute" (The Doobie Brothers)

Best Pop Instrumental Performance: "Rise" (Herb Alpert)

Best Rock Vocal Performance, Female: "Hot Stuff" (Donna Summer)

Best Rock Vocal Performance, Male: "Gotta Serve Somebody" (Bob Dylan)

Best Rock Vocal Performance, Group: "Heartache Tonight" (Eagles)

Best Disco Recording: "I Will Survive" (Gloria Gaynor)

Best Jazz Vocal Performance: "Fine and Mellow" (Ella Fitzgerald)

Best Jazz Instrumental Performance, Soloist: "Jousts" (Oscar Peterson)

Best Jazz Instrumental Performance, Group: "Duet" (Gary Burton and Chick Corea)

Best Jazz Instrumental Performance, Big Band: "At Fargo, 1940 Live" (Duke Ellington)

Best Rhythm & Blues Vocal Performance, Female: "Deja Vu" (Dionne Warwick)

Best Rhythm & Blues Vocal Performance, Male: "Don't Stop 'Til You Get Enough" (Michael Jackson)

Best Rhythm & Blues Instrumental Performance: "Boogie Wonderland" (Earth, Wind & Fire)

Best Rhythm & Blues Song: "After the Love Has Gone" (David Foster, Day Graydon, Bill Champlin, songwriters)

Best Gospel Performance, Contemporary or Inspirational: "Heed the Call" (Imperials)

Best Country Song: "You Decorated My Life" (Bob Morrison, Debbie Hupp, songwriters)

Best Country Vocal Performance, Female: "Blue Kentucky Girl" (Emmylou Harris)

Best Country Vocal Performance, Male: "The Gambler" (Kenny Rogers)

Best Country Vocal Performance, Group: "The Devil Went Down To Georgia" (Charlie Daniels Band)

Best Country Instrumental Performance: "Big Sandy/Leather Britches" (Doc and Merle Watson)

Best Recording for Children: "The Muppet Movie" (Jim Henson, creator; Paul Williams, producer)

Best Comedy Recording: "Reality...What A Concept" (Robin Williams)

Best Cast Show Album: "Sweeney Todd" (Stephen Sondheim, composer/lyricist; Thomas Z. Shepard, producer)

Best Classical Album: "Brahms: Symphonies Complete" (Sir Georg Solti, conductor; James Mallinson, producer)

Best Opera Recording: "Britten: Peter Grimes" (Colin Davis, conductor; Vittorio Negri, producer)

Television and Radio

EMMY AWARDS (1979-80): major awards presented by the Academy of Television Arts and Sciences:

Drama Series

Actor: Ed Asner, "Lou Grant"

Actress: Barbara Bel Geddes, "Dallas"

Supporting actor: Stuart Margolin, "The Rockford Files"

Supporting actress: Nancy Marchand, "Lou Grant"

Directing: Roger Grant, "Lou Grant"

Writing: Seth Freeman, "Lou Grant"

Best series: "Lou Grant"

Comedy Series

Actor: Richard Mulligan, "Soap"

Actress: Cathryn Damon, "Soap"

Supporting actor: Harry Morgan, "M*A*S*H"

Supporting actress: Loretta Swit, "M*A*S*H"

Directing: James Burrows, "Taxi"

Writing: Bob Colleary, "Barney Miller"

Best series: "Taxi"

Limited Series or Specials

Actor: Powers Boothe, "Guyana Tragedy: The Story of Jim Jones"

Actress: Patty Duke Astin, "The Miracle Worker"

Supporting actor: George Grizzard "The Oldest Living Graduate"

Supporting actress: Mare Winningham, "Amber Waves"

Best series: "Edward and Mrs. Simpson"

Special (Drama or Comedy): "The Miracle Worker"

1979 GEORGE FOSTER PEABODY
BROADCASTING AWARDS

Radio

WCBS Radio, New York City: "Follow That Cab: The Great Taxi Rip-Off"

WGBH Radio, Boston, Mass.: "Currer Bell, Esquire"

Children's Radio Theatre, Washington, D.C.: "Henny Penny Playwrighting Contest"

Canadian Broadcasting Corporation: "The Longest Journey"

KSJN/Minnesota Public Radio, St. Paul: "The Way to 8-A"

Television

KTVI, St. Louis, Mo.: "The Adventures of Whistling Sam"

WMAQ-TV, Chicago, Ill.: "Strip and Search"

CBS News, New York City: "CBS News Sunday Morning"

Sylvia Fine Kaye, Beverly Hills, Cal.: "Musical Comedy Tonight"

ABC-TV, New York City: "Valentine"

ABC-TV, New York City: "Friendly Fire"

CBS Entertainment, New York City: "Dummy"

NBC-TV, New York City: "When Hell Was In Session"

KOOL Television, Phoenix, Ariz.: "The Long Eyes of Kitt Peak"

NBC and the BBC, "Treasures of the British Crown"

ABC-TV, New York City: "A Special Gift"

KRON-TV, San Francisco, Cal.: "Politics of Poison"

WTTW-TV, Chicago, Ill.: "Miles to Go Before We Sleep"

WTTW-TV, Chicago, Ill.: "Little Rock Central High School"

KNXT, Hollywood, Cal.: "Down at the Dunbar"

WGBH-TV, Boston, Mass.: "World"

Roger Mudd, CBS News: "Teddy"

CBS News, New York City: "The Boston Goes to China"

Robert Trout, ABC News

ACADEMY AWARD WINNERS

Year	Best Picture	Best Actor	Supporting Actor	Best Actress	Supporting Actress	Best Director
1979	"Kramer vs. Kramer"	Dustin Hoffman "Kramer vs. Kramer"	Melvyn Douglas "Being There"	Sally Field "Norma Rae"	Meryl Streep "Kramer vs. Kramer"	Robert Benton "Kramer vs. Kramer"
1978	"The Deer Hunter"	Jon Voight "Coming Home"	Christopher Walken "The Deer Hunter"	Jane Fonda "Coming Home"	Maggie Smith "California Suite"	Michael Cimino "The Deer Hunter"
1977	"Annie Hall"	Richard Dreyfuss "The Goodbye Girl"	Jason Robards "Julia"	Diane Keaton "Annie Hall"	Vanessa Redgrave "Julia"	Woody Allen "Annie Hall"
1976	"Rocky"	Peter Finch "Network"	Jason Robards "All the President's Men"	Faye Dunaway "Network"	Beatrice Straight "Network"	John G. Avildsen "Rocky"
1975	"One Flew Over the Cuckoo's Nest"	Jack Nicholson "One Flew Over the Cuckoo's Nest"	George Burns "The Sunshine Boys"	Louise Fletcher "One Flew Over the Cuckoo's Nest	Lee Grant "Shampoo"	Milos Forman "One Flew Over the Cuckoo's Nest"
1974	"The Godfather, Part II"	Art Carney "Harry and Tonto"	Robert DeNiro "The Godfather, Part II"	Ellen Burstyn "Alice Doesn't Live Here Anymore"	Ingrid Bergman "Murder on the Orient Express"	Francis Ford Coppola "The Godfather, Part II"
1973	"The Sting"	Jack Lemmon "Save the Tiger"	John Houseman "The Paper Chase"	Glenda Jackson "A Touch of Class"	Tatum O'Neal "Paper Moon"	George Roy Hill "The Sting"
1972	"The Godfather"	Marlon Brando "The Godfather"	Joel Grey "Cabaret"	Liza Minnelli "Cabaret"	Eileen Heckart "Butterflies Are Free"	Bob Fosse "Cabaret"
1971	"The French Connection"	Gene Hackman "The French Connection"	Ben Johnson "The Last Picture Show"	Jane Fonda "Klute"	Cloris Leachman "The Last Picture Show"	William Friedkin "The French Connection"
1970	"Patton"	George C. Scott "Patton"	John Mills "Ryan's Daughter"	Glenda Jackson "Women in Love"	Helen Hayes "Airport"	Franklin Schaffner "Patton"
1969	"Midnight Cowboy"	John Wayne "True Grit"	Gig Young "They Shoot Horses, Don't They?"	Maggie Smith "The Prime of Miss Jean Brodie"	Goldie Hawn "Cactus Flower"	John Schlesinger "Midnight Cowboy"
1968	"Oliver!"	Cliff Robertson "Charly"	Jack Albertson "The Subject Was Roses"	Katharine Hepburn "The Lion in Winter" Barbra Streisand "Funny Girl"	Ruth Gordon "Rosemary's Baby"	Sir Carol Reed "Oliver!"
1967	"In the Heat of the Night"	Rod Steiger "In the Heat of the Night"	George Kennedy "Cool Hand Luke"	Katharine Hepburn "Guess Who's Coming to Dinner?"	Estelle Parsons "Bonnie and Clyde"	Mike Nichols "The Graduate"
1966	"A Man for All Seasons"	Paul Scofield "A Man for All Seasons"	Walter Matthau "The Fortune Cookie"	Elizabeth Taylor "Who's Afraid of Virginia Woolf?"	Sandy Dennis "Who's Afraid of Virginia Woolf?"	Fred Zinnemann "A Man for All Seasons"
1965	"The Sound of Music"	Lee Marvin "Cat Ballou"	Martin Balsam "A Thousand Clowns"	Julie Christie "Darling"	Shelley Winters "A Patch of Blue"	Robert Wise "The Sound of Music"
1964	"My Fair Lady"	Rex Harrison "My Fair Lady"	Peter Ustinov "Topkapi"	Julie Andrews "Mary Poppins"	Lila Kedrova "Zorba the Greek"	George Cukor "My Fair Lady"
1963	"Tom Jones"	Sidney Poitier "Lilies of the Field"	Melvyn Douglas "Hud"	Patricia Neal "Hud"	Margaret Rutherford "The V.I.P.s"	Tony Richardson "Tom Jones"
1962	"Lawrence of Arabia"	Gregory Peck "To Kill a Mockingbird"	Ed Begley "Sweet Bird of Youth"	Anne Bancroft "The Miracle Worker"	Patty Duke "The Miracle Worker"	David Lean "Lawrence of Arabia"
1961	"West Side Story"	Maximilian Schell "Judgment at Nuremberg"	George Chakiris "West Side Story"	Sophia Loren "Two Women"	Rita Moreno "West Side Story"	Jerome Robbins, Robert Wise "West Side Story"
1960	"The Apartment"	Burt Lancaster "Elmer Gantry"	Peter Ustinov "Spartacus"	Elizabeth Taylor "Butterfield 8"	Shirley Jones "Elmer Gantry"	Billy Wilder "The Apartment"
1959	"Ben-Hur"	Charlton Heston "Ben-Hur"	Hugh Griffith "Ben-Hur"	Simone Signoret "Room at the Top"	Shelley Winters "The Diary of Anne Frank"	William Wyler "Ben-Hur"
1958	"Gigi"	David Niven "Separate Tables"	Burl Ives "The Big Country"	Susan Hayward "I Want to Live"	Wendy Hiller "Separate Tables"	Vincente Minnelli "Gigi"
1957	"The Bridge on the River Kwai"	Alec Guiness "The Bridge on the River Kwai"	Red Buttons "Sayonara"	Joanne Woodward "The Three Faces of Eve"	Miyoshi Umeki "Sayonara"	David Lean "The Bridge on the River Kwai"
1956	"Around the World in 80 Days"	Yul Brynner "The King and I"	Anthony Quinn "Lust for Life"	Ingrid Bergman "Anastasia"	Dorothy Malone "Written on the Wind"	George Stevens "Giant"
1955	"Marty"	Ernest Borgnine "Marty"	Jack Lemmon "Mister Roberts"	Anna Magnani "The Rose Tattoo"	Jo Van Fleet "East of Eden"	Delbert Mann "Marty"
1954	"On the Waterfront"	Marlon Brando "On the Waterfront"	Edmond O'Brien "The Barefoot Contessa"	Grace Kelly "The Country Girl"	Eva Marie Saint "On the Waterfront"	Elia Kazan "On the Waterfront"

Year	Best Picture	Best Actor	Supporting Actor	Best Actress	Supporting Actress	Best Director
1953	"From Here to Eternity"	William Holden "Stalag 17"	Frank Sinatra "From Here to Eternity"	Audrey Hepburn "Roman Holiday"	Donna Reed "From Here to Eternity"	Fred Zinnemann "From Here to Eternity"
1952	"The Greatest Show on Earth"	Gary Cooper "High Noon"	Anthony Quinn "Viva Zapata!"	Shirley Booth "Come Back, Little Sheba"	Gloria Grahame "The Bad and The Beautiful"	John Ford "The Quiet Man"
1951	"An American in Paris"	Humphrey Bogart "The African Queen"	Karl Malden "A Streetcar Named Desire"	Vivian Leigh "A Streetcar Named Desire"	Kim Hunter "A Streecar Named Desire"	George Stevens "A Place in the Sun"
1950	"All About Eve"	Jose Ferrer "Cyrano de Bergerac"	George Sanders "All About Eve"	Judy Holliday "Born Yesterday"	Josephine Hull "Harvey"	Joseph L. Mankie-wicz "All About Eve"
1949	"All the King's Men"	Broderick Crawford "All the King's Men"	Dean Jagger "Twelve O'Clock High"	Olivia de Havilland "The Heiress"	Mercedes McCam-bridge "All the King's Men"	Joseph L. Mankie-wicz "A Letter to Three Wives"
1948	"Hamlet"	Laurence Olivier "Hamlet"	Walter Huston "The Treasure of the Sierra Madre"	Jane Wyman "Johnny Belinda"	Claire Trevor "Key Largo"	John Huston "The Treasure of the Sierra Madre"
1947	"Gentleman's Agreement"	Ronald Colman "A Double Life"	Edmund Gwenn "Miracle on 34th Street"	Loretta Young "The Farmer's Daughter"	Celeste Holm "Gentleman's Agreement"	Elia Kazan "Gentleman's Agreement"
1946	"The Best Years of Our Lives"	Fredric March "The Best Years of Our Lives"	Harold Russell "The Best Years of Our Lives"	Olivia de Havilland "To Each His Own"	Anne Baxter "The Razor's Edge"	William Wyler "The Best Years of Our Lives"
1945	"The Lost Week-end"	Ray Milland "The Lost Week-end"	James Dunn "A Tree Grows in Brooklyn"	Joan Crawford "Mildred Pierce"	Anne Revere "National Velvet"	Billy Wilder "The Lost Week-end"
1944	"Going My Way"	Bing Crosby "Going My Way"	Barry Fitzgerald "Going My Way"	Ingrid Bergman "Gaslight"	Ethel Barrymore "None But the Lonely Heart"	Leo McCarey "Going My Way"
1943	"Casablanca"	Paul Lukas "Watch on the Rhine"	Charles Coburn "The More the Merrier"	Jennifer Jones "The Song of Bernadette"	Katina Paxinou "For Whom the Bell Tolls"	Michael Curtiz "Casablanca"
1942	"Mrs. Miniver"	James Cagney "Yankee Doodle Dandy"	Van Heflin "Johnny Eager"	Greer Garson "Mrs. Miniver"	Teresa Wright "Mrs. Miniver"	William Wyler "Mrs. Miniver"
1941	"How Green Was My Valley"	Gary Cooper "Sergeant York"	Donald Crisp "How Green Was My Valley"	Joan Fontaine "Suspicion"	Mary Astor "The Great Lie"	John Ford "How Green Was My Valley"
1940	"Rebecca"	James Stewart "The Philadelphia Story"	Walter Brennan "The Westerner"	Ginger Rogers "Kitty Foyle"	Jane Darwell "The Grapes of Wrath"	John Ford "The Grapes of Wrath"
1939	"Gone with the Wind"	Robert Donat "Goodbye, Mr. Chips"	Thomas Mitchell "Stagecoach"	Vivien Leigh "Gone with the Wind"	Hattie McDaniel "Gone with the Wind"	Victor Fleming "Gone with the Wind"
1938	"You Can't Take It with You"	Spencer Tracy "Boys' Town"	Walter Brennan "Kentucky"	Bette Davis "Jezebel"	Fay Bainter "Jezebel"	Frank Capra "You Can't Take It with You"
1937	"The Life of Emile Zola"	Spencer Tracy "Captains Cou-rageous"	Joseph Schildkraut "The Life of Emile Zola"	Luise Rainer "The Good Earth"	Alice Brady "In Old Chicago"	Leo McCarey "The Awful Truth"
1936	"The Great Zieg-feld"	Paul Muni "The Story of Louis Pasteur"	Walter Brennan "Come and Get It"	Luise Rainer "The Great Zieg-feld"	Gale Sondergaard "Anthony Adverse"	Frank Capra "Mr. Deeds Goes to Town"
1935	"Mutiny on the Bounty"	Victor McLaglen "The Informer"	—	Bette Davis "Dangerous"	—	John Ford "The Informer"
1934	"It Happened One Night"	Clark Gable "It Happened One Night"	—	Claudette Colbert "It Happened One Night"	—	Frank Capra "It Happened One Night"
1932-33	"Cavalcade"	Charles Laughton "The Private Life of Henry VIII"	—	Katharine Hepburn "Morning Glory"		Frank Lloyd "Cavalcade"
1931-32	"Grand Hotel"	Wallace Beery "The Champ" Fredric March "Dr. Jekyll and Mr. Hyde"	—	Helen Hayes "The Sin of Made-lon Claudet"	—	Frank Borzage "Bad Girl"
1930-31	"Cimarron"	Lionel Barrymore "A Free Soul"	—	Marie Dressler "Min and Bill"	—	Norman Taurog "Skippy"
1929-30	"All Quiet on the Western Front"	George Arliss "Disraeli"	—	Norma Shearer "The Divorcee"	—	Lewis Milestone "All Quiet on the Western Front"
1928-29	"Broadway Melody"	Warner Baxter "In Old Arizona"	—	Mary Pickford "Coquette"	—	Frank Lloyd "The Divine Lady"
1927-28	"Wings"	Emil Jannings "The Last Com-mand" "The Way of All Flesh"	—	Janet Gaynor "Seventh Heaven" "Street Angel" "Sunrise"	—	Frank Borzage "Seventh Heaven" Lewis Milestone "Two Arabian Knights"

Theatre

ANTOINETTE PERRY (TONY) AWARDS (1979-80) presented by the League of New York Theatres and Producers and sponsored by the American Theatre Wing:

Best Play: "Children of a Lesser God"
Best Musical: "Evita"
Best Book of a Musical: Tim Rice, "Evita"
Best Score: Andrew Lloyd Webber and Tim Rice, "Evita"
Best Actor, Play: John Rubinstein, "Children of a Lesser God"
Best Actress, Play: Phyllis Frelich, "Children of a Lesser God"
Best Actor, Musical: Jim Dale, "Barnum"
Best Actress, Musical: Patti LuPone, "Evita"
Best Featured Actor, Play: David Rounds, "Morning's at Seven"
Best Featured Actress, Play: Dinah Manoff, "I Ought to Be in Pictures"
Best Featured Actor, Musical: Mandy Patinkin, "Evita"
Best Featured Actress, Musical: Priscilla Lopez, "A Day in Hollywood/A Night in the Ukraine"
Best Director, Play: Vivian Matalon, "Morning's at Seven"
Best Director, Musical: Harold Prince, "Evita"
Best Scenic Designer: John Lee Beatty, "Talley's Folly"; David Mitchell, "Barnum" (tie)
Best Costume Designer: Theoni V. Aldredge, "Barnum"
Best Lighting Designer: David Hersey, "Evita"
Best Choreographer: Tommy Tune and Thommie Walsh, "A Day in Hollywood/A Night in the Ukraine"
Revival of a Play or Musical: "Morning's at Seven"
Special Tony Awards: Mary Tyler Moore; Actors Theatre of Louisville; Goodspeed Opera House; Hobe Morrison, theatre editor, *Variety;* Richard Fitzgerald, Sound Associates
Lawrence Langner Award: Helen Hayes

OBIE (OFF BROADWAY AWARDS) (1979-80):

Sustained Achievement: Sam Shepard

Distinguished Performances: Michael Burrell, "Hess"; Michael Cristofer, "Chinchilla"; Lindsay Crouse, "Reunion"; Elizabeth Franz, "Sister Mary Ignatius Explains It All for You"; Morgan Freeman, "Mother Courage" and "Coriolanus"; John Heard, "Othello" and "Split"; Michael Higgins, "Reunion"; Madeleine Le Roux, "La Justice"; Jon Polito, for performances with Dodge Theatre Company and the BAM Theatre Company; Bill Raymond, "A Prelude to Death in Venice"; Dianne Wiest, "The Art of Dining"; Hattie Winston, "Mother Courage" and "The Michigan"
Distinguished Direction: A.J. Antoon, "The Art of Dining"; Edward Cornell, "Johnny on a Spot"; Elizabeth LeCompte, "Point Judith"
Design: Ruth Maleczech and Julie Archer, "Vanishing Pictures"; Sally Jacobs, "Conference of the Birds"; Beverly Emmons, Laura Crow, "Mary Stuart"
Playwriting: Lee Breuer, "A Prelude to Death in Venice"; Christopher Durang, "Sister Mary Ignatius Explains It All for You"; Romulus Linney, "Tennessee"; Roland Muldoon, "Full Confessions of a Socialist"; Jeff Weiss, "That's How the Rent Gets Paid (Part Three)"
Special Citations: The Flying Karamazov Brothers; The Actors of Le Centre International de Creations Theatrales; Ellen Stewart and La Mama E.T.C.; David Jones and Richard Nelson; Ntozake Shange

Films

CANNES INTERNATIONAL FILM FESTIVAL (1980):

Best Film: "Kagemusha," Akira Kurosawa, and "All That Jazz," Bob Fosse
Best Actress: Anouk Aimee, "Salto Nel Vuoto"
Best Actor: Michel Piccoli, "Salto Nel Vuoto"

NEW YORK FILM CRITICS CIRCLE AWARDS (1979):

Best Film: "Kramer vs. Kramer"
Best Director: Woody Allen, "Manhattan"
Best Actor: Dustin Hoffman, "Kramer vs. Kramer"
Best Actress: Sally Field, "Norma Rae"
Best Supporting Actor: Melvyn Douglas, "Being There"
Best Supporting Actress: Meryl Streep, "Kramer vs. Kramer"
Best Screenplay: "Breaking Away" by Steve Tesich
Best Foreign Film: "The Tree of Wooden Clogs"

MISS AMERICA

1921	Margaret Gorman, Washington, D.C.
1922-23	Mary Campbell, Columbus, Ohio
1924	Ruth Malcolmson, Philadelphia, Pennsylvania
1925	Fay Lamphier, Oakland, California
1926	Norma Smallwood, Tulsa, Oklahoma
1927	Lois Delaner, Joliet, Illinois
1933	Marion Bergeron, West Haven, Connecticut
1935	Henrietta Leaver, Pittsburgh, Pennsylvania
1936	Rose Coyle, Philadelphia, Pennsylvania
1937	Bette Cooper, Bertrand Island, New Jersey
1938	Marilyn Meseke, Marion, Ohio
1939	Patricia Donnelly, Detroit, Michigan
1940	Frances Marie Burke, Philadelphia, Pennsylvania
1941	Rosemary LaPlanche, Los Angeles, California
1942	Jo-Caroll Dennison, Tyler, Texas
1943	Jean Bartel, Los Angeles, California
1944	Venus Ramey, Washington, D.C.
1945	Bess Myerson, New York City, N.Y.
1946	Marilyn Buferd, Los Angeles, California
1947	Barbara Walker, Memphis, Tennesse
1948	BeBe Shopp, Hopkins, Minnesota
1949	Jacque Mercer, Litchfield, Arizona
1951	Yolande Betbeze, Mobile, Alabama
1952	Coleen Kay Hutchins, Salt Lake City, Utah
1953	Neva Jane Langley, Macon, Georgia
1954	Evelyn Margaret Ay, Ephrata, Pennsylvania
1955	Lee Meriwether, San Francisco, California
1956	Sharon Ritchie, Denver, Colorado
1957	Marian McKnight, Manning, South Carolina
1958	Marilyn Van Derbur, Denver, Colorado
1959	Mary Ann Mobley, Brandon, Mississippi
1960	Lynda Lee Mead, Natchez, Mississippi
1961	Nancy Fleming, Montague, Michigan
1962	Maria Fletcher, Asheville, North Carolina
1963	Jacquelyn Mayer, Sandusky, Ohio
1964	Donna Axum, El Dorado, Arkansas
1956	Vonda Kay Van Dyke, Phoenix, Arizona
1966	Deborah Irene Bryant, Overland Park, Kansas
1967	Jane Anne Jayroe, Laverne, Oklahoma
1968	Debra Dene Barnes, Moran, Kansas
1969	Judith Anne Ford, Belvidere, Illinois
1970	Pamela Anne Eldred, Birmingham, Michigan
1971	Pjyllis Ann George, Denton, Texas
1972	Laurie Lea Schaefer, Columbus, Ohio
1973	Terry Anne Meeuwsen, DePere, Wisconsin
1974	Rebecca Ann King, Denver, Colorado
1975	Shirley Cothran, Fort Worth, Texas
1976	Tawney Elaine Godin, Yonkers, N.Y.
1977	Dorothy Kathleen Benham, Edina, Minnesota
1978	Susan Perkins, Columbus, Ohio
1979	Kylene Baker, Galax, Virginia
1980	Cheryl Prewitt, Ackerman, Mississippi
1981	Susan Powell, Elk City, Oklahoma

THE DIRECTORY

SOCIETIES AND ASSOCIATIONS

Information abstracted from listings in the 1980 edition of the *Encyclopedia of Associations*, which includes details on more than 14,000 organizations. Used by permission of the publisher, Gale Research Company, Book Tower, Detroit, Michigan 48226

Academy of Applied Science, 65 India Wharf, Boston, MA 02110; **Membership:** 300

Academy of Motion Picture Arts and Science, 8949 Wilshire Blvd., Beverly Hills, CA 90211; **Membership:** 4,123

Academy of Political Science, 619 W. 114th St., Suite 500, New York, NY 10025; **Membership:** 11,000

Actors Equity Association, 1500 Broadway, New York, NY 10036; **Membership:** 27,000

Adult Education Association of the U.S.A., 810 18th St., NW, Washington, DC 20006; **Membership:** 400

Aerospace Industries Association of America, 1725 De Sales St., NW, Washington, DC 20036; **Membership:** 58 companies

African-American Institute, 833 United Nations Plaza, New York, NY 10017

AFS (American Field Service) International Exchange, 313 East 43rd St., New York, NY 10017; **Membership:** 100,000

Air Force Association, 1750 Pennsylvania Ave., NW, Washington, DC 20006; **Membership:** 148,000

Alcoholics Anonymous, 468 Park Ave. S., New York, NY 10016; **Membership:** 1,000,000

Alternatives to Abortion International, Hillcrest Hotel, Suite 511, 16th and Madison Sts., Toledo, OH 43699; **Membership:** 100,000

Amateur Athletic Union of the United States, 3400 West 86th St., Indianapolis, IN 46268; **Membership:** 331,000

America-Mideast Educational and Training Services (AMIDEAST), 1717 Massachusetts Ave., NW, Washington, DC 20036

American Academy of Arts and Letters, 633 West 155th St., New York, NY 10032; **Membership:** 250

American Academy of Arts and Sciences, 165 Allandale St., Boston, MA 02130; **Membership:** 2,300

American Academy of Political and Social Sciences, 3937 Chestnut St., Philadelphia, PA 19104; **Membership:** 14,000

American Alliance for Health, Physical Education, Recreation and Dance, 1201 16th St., NW, Washington, DC 20036; **Membership:** 50,000

American Anthropological Association, 1703 New Hampshire Ave., NW, Washington, DC 20009; **Membership:** 10,000

American Antiquarian Society, 185 Salisbury St., Worcester, MA 01609; **Membership:** 350

American Anti-Vivisection Society, 1903 Chestnut St., Philadelphia, PA 19103

American Arbitration Association, 140 West 51st St., New York, NY 10020

American Association for the Advancement of Science, 1515 Massachusetts Ave., NW, Washington, DC 20005; **Membership:** 133,000

American Association of Advertising Agencies, 200 Park Ave., New York, NY 10017; **Membership:** 450

American Association of Blood Banks, 1828 L St., NW, Washington, DC 20036; **Membership:** 8,000

American Association of Community and Junior Colleges, National Center for Higher Education, 1 Dupont Circle, NW, Washington, DC 20036; **Membership:** 1,507

American Association of Retired Persons, 1909 K St., NW, Washington, DC 20049; **Membership:** 12,000,000

American Association of University Professors, 1 Dupont Circle, NW, Washington, DC 20036; **Membership:** 68,100

American Assocation of University Women, 2401 Virginia Ave., NW, Washington, DC 20037; **Membership:** 190,885

American Astronomical Society, % Dr. Henry L. Shipman, Physics Dept., Univ. of Delaware, Sharp Labs, Newark, DE 19711; **Membership:** 3,500

American Automobile Association, 8111 Gatehouse Rd., Falls Church, VA 22042; **Membership:** 20,000,000

American Bankers Association, 1120 Connecticut Ave., NW, Washington, DC 20036; **Membership:** 13,486 banks and trust companies

American Bar Association, 1155 East 60th St., Chicago, IL 60637; **Membership:** 250,000

American Bible Society, 1865 Broadway, New York, NY 10023; **Membership:** 290,000

American Camping Association, Bradford Woods, Martinsville, IN 46151; **Membership:** 6,000

American Cancer Society, 777 Third Ave., New York, NY 10017; **Membership:** 2,500,000 with 58 divisions and 3,000 county units

American Chemical Society, 1155 16th St., NW, Washington, DC 20036; **Membership:** 776,000

American Civil Liberties Union, 22 E. 40th St., New York, NY 10016; **Membership:** 275,000

American Classical League, Miami University, Oxford, OH 45056; **Membership:** 3,000

American College of Hospital Administrators, 840 N. Lake Shore Dr., Chicago, IL 60611; **Membership:** 13,500

American College of Physicians, 4200 Pine St., Philadelphia, PA 19104; **Membership:** 41,000

American College of Surgeons, 55 E. Erie St., Chicago, IL 60611; **Membership:** 39,000

American Contract Bridge League, 2200 Democrat Rd., Memphis, TN 38132; **Membership:** 200,000 in 5,000 clubs

American Council for the Arts, 507 Seventh Ave., New York, NY 10018

American Council on Education, 1 Dupont Circle, NW, Washington, DC 20036; **Membership:** 1,492 and 234 affiliates

American Council for Judaism, 307 Fifth Ave., New York, NY 10016; **Membership:** 20,000

American Council of Learned Societies, 345 E. 46th St., New York, NY 10017; **Membership:** 42 organizations

American Council of Life Insurance, 1850 K St., NW, Washington, DC 20006; **Membership:** 480 companies

American Council on Schools and Colleges, P.O. Box 1252, York, PA 17405; **Membership:** 201 institutions

American Council on the Teaching of Foreign Languages, Two Park Ave., New York, NY 10016; **Membership:** 9,000

American Dental Association, 211 E. Chicago Ave., Chicago, IL 60611; **Membership:** 133,000 in 484 societies

American Diabetes Association, 600 Fifth Ave., New York, NY 10020; **Membership:** 125,000 in 68 state organizations

American Dietetic Association, 430 N. Michigan Ave., Chicago, IL 60611; **Membership:** 38,000 in 52 state groups

American Economic Foundation, 51 E. 42nd St., New York, NY 10017; **Membership:** 18,000

American Farm Bureau Federation, 225 Touhy Ave., Park Ridge, IL 60068; **Membership:** 3,076,867

American Federation of Arts, 41 E. 65th St., New York, NY 10021; **Membership:** 1,800

American Federation of Labor and Congress of Industrial Organizations, 815 16th St. NW, Washington, DC 20006; **Membership:** 13,600,000 in 105 organizations

American Federation of Teachers, 11 Dupont Circle, NW, Washington, DC 20036; **Membership:** 475,000

American Federation of Television and Radio Artists, 1350 Ave. of the Americas, New York, NY 10019; **Membership:** 38,600 in 39 locals

American Forestry Association, 1319 18th St., NW, Washington, DC 20036; **Membership:** 79,000

American Friends Service Committee, 1501 Cherry St., Philadelphia, PA 19102; **Membership:** 10 regional Offices

American Geographical Society, Broadway at 156th St., New York, NY 10032; **Membership:** 2,400

American Geological Institute, 5205 Leesburg Pike, Falls Church, VA 22041; **Membership:** 18 societies

American Geophysical Union, 2000 Florida Ave., NW, Washington, DC 20009; **Membership:** 12,000

American Geriatrics Society, 10 Columbus Circle, New York, NY 10019; **Membership:** 8,000

American Group Psychotherapy Association, 1995 Broadway, 14th Floor, New York, NY 10023; **Membership:** 3,000 in 22 societies

American Heart Association, 7320 Greenville Ave., Dallas, TX 75231; **Membership:** 123,000 in 55 affiliates and 110 chapters

American Historical Association, 400 A St., SE, Washington, DC 20003; **Membership:** 14,500

American Home Economics Association, 2010 Massachusetts Ave., NW, Washington, DC 20036; **Membership:** 50,000 in 52 associations

American Horse Shows Association, 598 Madison Ave., New York, NY 10022; **Membership:** 19,675

American Horticultural Society, Mt. Vernon, VA 22121; **Membership:** 33,000

American Hospital Association, 840 N. Lake Shore Dr., Chicago, IL 60611; **Membership:** 31,500

American Humane Association, 5351 Roslyn, Englewood, CO 80111; **Membership:** 2,000,000 in 1,500 societies

American Institute of Aeronautics and Astronautics, 1290 Ave. of the Americas, New York, NY 10019; **Membership:** 27,000 in 68 sections and 110 student branches

American Institute of Architects, 1735 New York Ave., NW, Washington, DC 20006; **Membership:** 32,000

American Institute of Biological Sciences, 1401 Wilson Blvd., Arlington, VA 22209; **Membership:** 9,000

American Institute of Certified Public Accountants, 1211 Ave. of the Americas, New York, NY 10036; **Membership:** 144,000

American Institute of Chemical Engineers, 345 E. 47th St., New York, NY 10017; **Membership:** 45,000

American Institute of Chemists, 7315 Wisconsin Ave., NW, Washington, DC 20014; **Membership:** 5,000 in 30 state groups

American Institute of Nutrition, 9650 Rockville Pike, Bethesda, MD 20014; **Membership:** 1,800

American Institute of Physics, 335 E. 45th St., New York, NY 10017; **Membership:** nine national societies

American Jewish Committee, % Institute of Human Relations, 165 E. 56th St., New York, NY 10022; **Membership:** 45,000 in 80 chapters

American Jewish Congress, 15 E. 84th St.; New York, NY 10028; **Membership:** 50,000 in 300 groups

American Kennel Club, 51 Madison Ave., New York, NY 10010; **Membership:** 406 associations

American Law Institute, 4025 Chestnut St., Philadelphia, PA 19104; **Membership:** 2,370

American Legion, 700 N. Pennsylvania St., Indianapolis, IN 46206; **Membership:** 2,700,000 in 58 state departments

American Legion Auxiliary, 777 N. Meridian St., Indianapolis, IN 46204; **Membership:** 1,000,000

American Library Association, 50 E. Huron St., Chicago, IL 60611; **Membership:** 35,000

American Lung Association, 1740 Broadway, New York, NY 10019; **Membership:** 7,500

American Management Associations, 135 W. 50th St., New York, NY 10020; **Membership:** 70,000

American Mathematical Society, P.O. Box 6248, Providence, RI 02940; **Membership:** 18,681

American Medical Assocation, 535 N. Dearborn St., Chicago, IL 60610; **Membership:** 213,940

American Ministerial Association, P.O. Box 1252, York, PA 17405; **Membership:** 58,700

American National Theatre and Academy, 245 W. 52nd St., New York, NY 10019

American Newspaper Publishers Association, 11600 Sunrise Valley Dr., Reston, VA 22091; **Membership:** 1,329 daily newspapers

American Numismatic Association, P.O. Box 2366, Colorado Springs, CO 80901; **Membership:** 34,000 individuals and 1,000 clubs

American Numismatic Society, 1814 Broadway betw. 155th and 156th St., New York, NY 10032; **Membership:** 1,842

American Nurses' Association, 2420 Pershing Rd., Kansas City, MO 64108; **Membership:** 200,000 in 53 state groups

American Optometric Association, 243 N. Lindbergh Blvd., St. Louis, MO 63141; **Membership:** 20,628

American Ornithologists' Union, National Museum of Natural History, Smithsonian Institution, Washington, DC 20560; **Membership:** 4,000

American Osteopathic Association, 212 E. Ohio St., Chicago, IL 60611; **Membership:** 13,002 in 54 state groups

American Personnel and Guidance Association, 2 Skyline Pl., Suite 400, 5203 Leesburg Pike, Falls Church, VA 22041; **Membership:** 41,000

American Pharmaceutical Association, 2215 Constitution Ave., NW, Washington, DC 20037; **Membership:** 56,000

American Philatelic Society, P.O. Box 800, State College, PA 16801; **Membership:** 46,800

American Philological Association, Dept. of Classics, University of Colorado, Boulder, CO 80309; **Membership:** 2,800

American Philosophical Society, University of Delaware, Newark, DE 19711; **Membership:** 6,000

American Physical Society, 335 E. 45th St., New York, NY 10017; **Membership:** 30,000

American Podiatry Association, 20 Chevy Chase Circle, NW, Washington, DC 20015; **Membership:** 7,200 in 52 state groups

American Political Science Association, 1527 New Hampshire Ave., NW, Washington, DC 20036; **Membership:** 15,000

American Power Boat Association, 17640 E. Nine Mile Rd., East Detroit, MI 48021; **Membership:** 6,000 in 300 clubs

American Psychiatric Association, 1700 18th St., NW, Washington, DC 20009; **Membership:** 25,000

American Psychoanalytic Association, 1 E. 57th St., New York, NY 10022; **Membership:** 2,613

American Psychological Association, 1200 17th St., NW, Washington, DC 20036; **Membership:** 48,000

American Public Health Assocation, 1015 18th St., NW, Washington, DC 20036; **Membership:** 30,021

American Radio Relay League, 225 Main St., Newington, CT 06111; **Membership:** 169,000 in 2,100 clubs

American Red Cross, 17th and D Sts., NW, Washington, DC 20006; **Membership:** 62 divisions and 3,124 chapters

American Social Health Association, 260 Sheridan Ave., Suite 307, Palo Alto, CA 94306; **Membership:** 2,000

American Society for the Prevention of Cruelty to Animals, 441 E. 92nd St., New York, NY 10028; **Membership:** 7,093

American Society of Civil Engineers, 345 E. 47th St., New York, NY 10017; **Membership:** 77,652

American Society of Composers, Authors, and Publishers, 1 Lincoln Plaza, New York, NY 10023; **Membership:** 23,000

American Society of Interior Designers, 730 Fifth Ave., New York, NY 10019; **Membership:** 10,000 in 45 chapters

American Society of Mechanical Engineers, 345 E. 47th St., New York, NY 10017; **Membership:** 80,000 in 177 local groups

American Society of Newspaper Editors, Box 551, 1350 Sullivan Trail, Easton, PA 18042; **Membership:** 800

American Society of Travel Agents, 711 Fifth Ave., New York, NY 10022; **Membership:** 16,000 worldwide

American Sociological Association, 1772 N St., NW, Washington, DC 20036; **Membership:** 14,000

American Speech-Language-Hearing Association, 10801 Rockville Pike, Rockville, MD 20852; **Membership:** 30,000

American Statistical Association, 806 15th St., NW, Washington, DC 20005; **Membership:** 13,000

American Thoracic Society, 1740 Broadway, New York, NY 10019; **Membership:** 8,000

American Trucking Associations, 1616 P St., NW, Washington, DC 20036; **Membership:** 51 organizations

American Veterans Committee, 1346 Connecticut Ave., NW, Washington, DC 20036; **Membership:** 25,000

American Veterinary Medical Association, 930 N. Meacham Rd., Schaumburg, IL 60196; **Membership:** 30,000

American Youth Hostels, Inc., National Campus, Delaplane, VA 22025; **Membership:** 70,000 in 30 local councils

Americans for Democratic Action, 1411 K St., NW, Washington, DC 20005; **Membership:** 65,000 in 20 state groups

Amnesty International, U.S. Affiliate, 304 W. 58th St., New York, NY 10017; **Membership:** 12,000

AMVETS, 1710 Rhode Island Ave., NW, Washington, DC 20036; **Membership:** 150,000

Ancient Order of Hibernians in America, Box 700, Riverdale Station, Bronx, NY 10471; **Membership:** 191,000

Anti-Defamation League of B'nai B'rith, 823 United Nations Plaza, New York, NY 10017

Appalachian Mountain Club, 5 Joy St., Boston, MA 02108; **Membership:** 23,000

Archaeological Institute of America, 53 Park Place, Eighth Fl.; New York, NY 10007; **Membership:** 7,500

Army and Navy Union, U.S.A., 1391 Main St., P.O. Box 537, Lakemore, OH 44250; **Membership:** 5,000

Arthritis Foundation, 3400 Peachtree Rd. NE, Atlanta, GA 30326; **Membership:** 73 chapters

Association for the Study of Afro-American Life and History, 1401 14th St., NW, Washington, DC 20005; **Membership:** 30,000

Association of American Colleges, 1818 R St., NW, Washington, DC 20009; **Membership:** 700 institutions

Association on American Indian Affairs, Inc., 432 Park Ave. S., New York, NY 10016

Association of American Railroads, American Railroads Bldg., 1920 L St., NW, Washington, DC 20036; **Membership:** 243

Association of American Universities, 1 Dupont Circle, NW, Suite 730, Washington, DC 20036; **Membership:** 50 university presidents

Association of Chairmen of Departments of Mechanics, c/o R.T. Shields, Dept. of Theoretical and Applied Mechanics, 216 Talbot Laboratory, Urbana, IL 61801; **Membership:** 98

Association of Computer Programmers and Analysts, P.O. Box 95, Kensington, MD 20975; **Membership:** 1,000

Association of Governing Boards of Universities and Colleges, 1 Dupont Circle, NW, Suite 720, Washington, DC 20036; **Membership:** 19,000

Association of Junior Leagues, 825 Third Ave., New York, NY 10022; **Membership:** 130,000 in 238 leagues

Audit Bureau of Circulations, 123 N. Wacker Dr., Chicago, IL 60606; **Membership:** 4,500

Authors League of America, 234 W. 44th St., New York, NY 10036; **Membership:** 8,000

Benevolent and Protective Order of Elks, 2750 Lake View Ave., Chicago, IL 60614; **Membership:** 1,640,000 in 2,237 lodges

Big Brothers/Big Sisters of America, 220 Suburban Station Bldg., Philadelphia, PA 19103; **Membership:** 387 local agencies

Blue Cross Association, 840 N. Lake Shore Dr., Chicago, IL 60611; **Membership:** 75 Blue Cross plans

B'nai B'rith International, 1640 Rhode Island Ave., NW, Washington, DC 20036; **Membership:** 500,000 in 3,500 groups

Boys' Clubs of America, 771 First Ave., New York, NY 10017; **Membership:** 1,071,000

Boy Scouts of America, P.O. Box 61030, Dallas/Ft. Worth Airport Sta., Dallas, TX 75261; **Membership:** 4,493,491 scouts and adult leaders

Brand Names Foundation, 477 Madison Ave., New York, NY 10022; **Membership:** 400

Brookings Institution, 1775 Massachusetts Ave., NW, Washington, DC 20036

Camp Fire Girls, 4601 Madison Ave., Kansas City, MO 64112; **Membership:** 750,000

CARE (Cooperative for American Relief Everywhere), 660 First Ave., New York, NY 10016; **Membership:** 25 agencies

Catholic Daughters of America, 10 W. 71st St., New York, NY 10023; **Membership:** 180,000 in 45 state groups

Catholic War Veterans of U.S.A., 2 Massachusetts Ave., NW, Washington, DC 20001; **Membership:** 50,000

CCCO, An Agency for Military and Draft Counseling, 2016 Walnut St., Rm. 300, Philadelphia, PA 19103

Chamber of Commerce of the United States, 1615 H St., NW, Washington, DC 20062; **Membership:** 3,800 chambers of commerce and trade associations, 77,000 business firms and individuals

Chautauqua Literary and Scientific Circle, Chautauqua, NY 14722; **Membership:** 1,100

Child Study Association of America, 853 Broadway, New York, NY 10003; **Membership:** 400

Child Welfare League of America, 67 Irving Pl, New York, NY 10003

College Entrance Examination Board, 888 Seventh Ave., New York, NY 10019; **Membership:** 2,480 colleges, universities, secondary schools, school systems and educational associations

Colonial Dames XVII Century, National Society, 1300 New Hampshire Ave., NW, Washington, DC 20036; **Membership:** 8,500

Committee for Economic Development, 477 Madison Ave., New York, NY 10022; **Membership:** 200 trustees

Common Cause, 2030 M St., NW, Washington, DC 20036; **Membership:** 225,000

The Conference Board, 845 Third Ave., New York, NY 10022; **Membership:** 4,000 organizations

Conference on Jewish Material Claims against Germany, 15 E. 26th St., New York, NY 10010; **Member Organizations:** 23

CORE (Congress of Racial Equality), 1916-38 Park Ave., New York, NY 10037

Cooperative League of the U.S.A., 1828 L St., NW, Washington, DC 20036; **Membership:** 178 organizations

Correspondance Chess League of America, P.O. Box 124, Algonquin, IL 60102; **Membership:** over 1,200

Council for the Advancement and Support of Education, 1 Dupont Circle, NW, Washington, DC 20036; **Membership:** 9,000

Council of Better Business Bureaus, 1150 17th St., NW, Washington, DC 20036; **Membership:** 1,000 in 150 member bureaus

Council on Foreign Relations, 58 E. 68th St., New York, NY 10021; **Membership:** 1,796 in 37 local groups

Council of Graduate Schools in the United States, 1 Dupont Circle, NW, Washington, DC 20036; **Membership:** 365

Council on International Educational Exchange, 205 E. 42nd St., New York, NY 10017; **Membership:** 174 North American institutions

Country Music Association, 7 Music Circle N., Nashville, TN 37203; **Membership:** 5,000

Credit Union National Association, Inc., P.O. Box 431, Madison, WI 53701; **Membership:** 22,272 credit unions

Daughters of the American Revolution, National Society, 1776 D St., NW, Washington, DC 20006; **Membership:** 208,000

Day Care and Child Development Council of America, 520 Southern Bldg., 805 15th St., NW, Washington, DC 20005; **Membership:** 6,000

Democratic National Committee, 1625 Massachusetts Ave., NW, Washington, DC 20036; **Membership:** 360

Disabled American Veterans, 3725 Alexandria Pike, Cold Spring, KY 41076; **Membership:** 600,000

Dramatists Guild, 234 W. 44th St., New York, NY 10036

Ecological Society of America, Library 3131, The Evergreen State College, Olympia, WA 98505; **Membership:** 5,700

English-Speaking Union of the United States, 16 E. 69th St., New York, NY 10021; **Membership:** 33,000 in 81 branches

Entomological Society of America, 4603 Calvert Rd., College Park, MD 20740; **Membership:** 7,500

Environmental Action, 1346 Connecticut Ave., NW, Suite 731, Washington, DC 20036; **Membership:** 20,000

Epilepsy Foundation of America, 1828 L St., NW, Suite 406, Washington, DC 20036; **Membership:** 161 affiliates in 50 states

Experiment in International Living, United States Headquarters, Brattleboro, VT 05301; **Membership:** national offices in 70 other countries and 10 regional U.S. offices

Eye-Bank for Sight Restoration, 210 E. 64th St., New York, NY 10021

Federation of American Scientists, 307 Massachusetts Ave., NE, Washington, DC 20002; **Membership:** 6,000

Fellowship of Reconciliation, Box 271, Nyack, NY 10960; **Membership:** 25,238 in 100 groups

Fleet Reserve Association, 1303 New Hampshire Ave., NW, Washington, DC 20036; **Membership:** 145,000

Foreign Policy Association, 205 Lexington Ave., New York, NY 10016

Foster Parents Plan, 155 Plan Way, Warwick, RI 02887

Fraternal Order of Eagles, 2401 W. Wisconsin Ave., Milwaukee, WI 53233; **Membership:** 750,000 in 50 state groups

Garden Club of America, 598 Madison Ave., New York, NY 10022; **Membership:** 13,500

General Federation of Women's Clubs, 1734 N St., NW, Washington, DC 20036; **Membership:** 10,000,000 in 45 countries

General Society of Mayflower Descendants, 4 Winslow St., Plymouth, MA 02360; **Membership:** 18,075 in 51 state groups

Gideons International, 2900 Lebanon Road, Nashville, TN 37214; **Membership:** 58,000 in 112 countries

Girl Scouts of the U.S.A., 830 Third Ave., New York, NY 10022; **Membership:** 3,084,000 in 348 local groups

Girls Clubs of America, 205 Lexington Ave., New York, NY 10016; **Membership:** 215,000

Group Health Association of America, 1717 Massachusetts Ave., NW, Washington, DC 20036; **Membership:** 1,000

Guide Dog Foundation for the Blind, Inc., 109-19 72nd Ave., Forest Hills, NY 11375

Hadassah, the Women's Zionist Organization of America, 50 W. 58th St., New York, NY 10019; **Membership:** 360,000 in 1,650 chapters and groups

Health Insurance Institute, 1850 K St., NW, Washington, DC 20006; **Membership:** 324 companies

Helicopter Association of America, 1156 15th St., NW, Suite 610, Washington, DC 20005; **Membership:** 700 firms

Humane Society of the United States, 2100 L St., NW, Washington, DC 20037; **Membership:** 70,000

Imperial Council of the Ancient Arabic Order of Nobles of the Mystic Shrine, 323 N. Michigan Ave., Chicago, IL 60601; **Membership:** 1,000,000

Independent Order of Odd Fellows, 5618 Wilson Blvd., Arlington, VA 22205; **Membership:** 1,200,000

Indian Rights Association, 1505 Race St., Philadelphia, PA 19102; **Membership:** 2,500

Information Industry Association, 316 Pennsylvania Ave., SE, Suite 502, Washington, DC 20003; **Membership:** 120 companies

Institute of International Education, 809 United Nations Plaza, New York, NY 10017

International Air Transport Association, P.O. Box 550, International Aviation Sq., 1000 Sherbrooke St. W, Montreal, PQ, Canada H3A 2R4; **Membership:** 103 airlines

International College of Surgeons, 1516 Lake Shore Dr., Chicago, IL 60610; **Membership:** 14,000

International Game Fish Association, 3000 E. Las Olas Blvd., Fort Lauderdale, FL 33316; **Membership:** 10,000

International Student Service, 291 Broadway, New York, NY 10007; **Membership:** 190 local groups

Italian-American War Veterans of the U.S., 115 S. Meridian Rd., Youngstown, OH 44509; **Membership:** 8,500 in 110 posts

Izaak Walton League of America, 1800 N. Kent St., Suite 806, Arlington, VA 22209; **Membership:** 53,000

Jewish War Veterans of the U.S.A., 1712 New Hampshire Ave., NW, Washington, DC 20009; **Membership:** 105,000

Junior Achievement, 550 Summer St., Stamford, CT 06901; **Membership:** 245,000

Kiwanis International, 101 E. Erie St., Chicago, IL 60611; **Membership:** 296,000 in 7,500 clubs

Knights of Columbus, Columbus Plaza, New Haven, CT 06507; **Membership:** 1,291,325

Knights of Pythias, Pythian Bldg., Rm. 201, 47 N. Grant St., Stockton, CA 95202; **Membership:** 200,000 in 55 domains

Knights Templar of the U.S.A., 14 E. Jackson Blvd., Suite 1700, Chicago, IL 60604; **Membership:** 365,000

League of Women Voters of the U.S., 1730 M St., NW, Washington, DC 20036; **Membership:** 131,000 in 1,340 leagues

Leukemia Society of America, Inc., 211 E. 43rd St., New York, NY 10017; **Membership:** 51 local groups

Lions Clubs International, 300 22nd, Oak Brook, IL 60521; **Membership:** 1,230,000

Little League Baseball, Williamsport, PA 17701; **Membership:** 10,951 leagues

Loyal Order of Moose, Mooseheart, IL 60539; **Membership:** 1,649,661 in 4,169 lodges and chapters

March of Dimes (The National Foundation), 1275 Mamaroneck Ave., White Plains, NY 10605

Marine Corps League, 933 N. Kenmore St., Suite 321, Arlington, VA 22201; **Membership:** 20,000

Masonic Service Association of the U.S., 8120 Fenton St., Silver Spring, MD 20910; **Membership:** 43 grand lodges

Mensa, American Mensa Ltd., 1701 W. 3d St., Brooklyn, NY 11223; **Membership:** 33,000 in 150 groups

Mental Health Association, 1800 N. Kent St., Rosslyn, VA 22209; **Membership:** 850 local, 47 state groups

Modern Language Association of America, 62 Fifth Ave., New York, NY 10011; **Membership:** 30,000

Modern Woodmen of America, 1701 First Ave., Rock Island, IL 61201; **Membership:** 510,000 in 1,000 local groups

Motor Vehicle Manufacturers Association of the United States, 300 New Center Bldg., Detroit, MI 48202; **Membership:** 11 manufacturers

Muscular Dystrophy Associations of America, Inc., 810 Seventh Ave., New York, NY 10019; **Membership:** 28,000 in 214 chapters

National Academy of Television Arts and Sciences, 110 W. 57th St., New York, NY 10019; **Membership:** 10,000

National Aeronautic Association, 821 15th St., NW, Washington, DC 20005; **Membership:** 160,000

National Amputation Foundation, 12-45 150th St., Whitestone, NY 11357; **Membership:** 5,200 veterans

National Association for Hearing and Speech Action, 6110 Executive Bldg., Suite 1000, Rockville, MD 20852; **Membership:** 2,000 in 180 groups

National Association for Retarded Citizens, 2709 Ave. E East, Arlington, TX 76011; **Membership:** 275,000 in 1,800 local groups

National Association for Stock Car Auto Racing, 1801 Volusia Ave., Daytona Beach, FL 32015; **Membership:** 18,000

National Association for the Advancement of Colored People, 1790 Broadway, New York, NY 10019; **Membership:** 450,673

National Association of Blue Shield Plans, 211 East Chicago Ave., Chicago, IL 60611; **Membership:** 72 medical care plans

National Association of Broadcasters, 1771 N St., NW, Washington, DC 20036; **Membership:** 6,000

National Association of Colored Women's Clubs, 5808 16th St., NW, Washington, DC 20011; **Membership:** 45,000

National Association of Intercollegiate Athletics, 1221 Baltimore, Kansas City, MO 64106; **Membership:** 515 members and 32 groups

National Association of Manufacturers, 1776 F St., NW, Washington, DC 20006; **Membership:** 13,000

National Association of Negro Business and Professional Women's Clubs, 1806 New Hampshire Ave., NW, Washington, DC 20009; **Membership:** 10,000 in 300 groups

National Association of Social Workers, 1425 H St., NW, Washington, DC 20005; **Membership:** 80,000

National Association of State Universities and Land Grant Colleges, 1 Dupont Circle, NW, Suite 710, Washington, DC 20036; **Membership:** 142 colleges and universities

National Association of Theatre Owners, 1500 Broadway, New York, NY 10036; **Membership:** 10,000

National Audubon Society, 950 Third Ave., New York, NY 10022; **Membership:** 400,000 plus 427 affiliated groups

National Automobile Dealers Association, 8400 Westpark Dr., McLean, VA 22101; **Membership:** 21,000

National Board of Review of Motion Pictures, P.O. Box 589, New York, NY 10021; **Membership:** 100

National Braille Association, Inc., 645A Godwin Ave., Midland Park, NJ 07432; **Membership:** 2,700

National Campers and Hikers Association, Inc., 7172 Transit Rd., Buffalo, NY 14221; **Membership:** 200,000

National Catholic Educational Association, 1 Dupont Circle, NW, Suite 350, Washington, DC 20036; **Membership:** 14,668

National Civil Service League, 5530 Wisconsin Ave., NW, Suite 1600, Washington, DC 20015; **Membership:** 3,000

National Collegiate Athletic Association, U.S. Hwy. 50 and Nall Ave., PO Box 1906, Shawnee Mission, KS 66222; **Membership:** 862 colleges and allied organizations

National Conference of Catholic Charities, 1346 Connecticut Ave., NW, Washington, DC 20036; **Membership:** 3,000

National Conference of Christians and Jews, 43 W. 57th St., New York, NY 10019; **Membership:** 70 regional groups

National Conference on Social Welfare, 22 W. Gay St., Columbus, OH 43215; **Membership:** 4,500

National Congress of American Indians, 1430 K St., NW, Washington, DC 20005; **Membership:** representing 600,000 Indians

National Council of Churches of Christ in the U.S.A., 475 Riverside Dr., New York, NY 10027; **Membership:** 40,286,104 in 32 denominations

National Council of Farmer Cooperatives, 1800 Massachusetts Ave., NW, Washington, DC 20036; **Membership:** 3,000,000 in 160 cooperative associations

National Council of Jewish Women, 15 E. 26th St., New York, NY 10010; **Membership:** 100,000

National Council of Negro Women, 1819 H St., NW, Washington, DC 20006; **Membership:** 4,000,000 in 200 local groups within 27 national affiliated organizations

National Council of State Garden Clubs, 824 N. Biltmore Ave., Clayton, MO 63105; **Membership:** 365,680

National Council of Women of the United States, 345 E. 46th St., New York, NY 10017

National Council on the Aging, 1828 L St., NW, Washington, DC 20036; **Membership:** 3,800

National Council on Crime and Delinquency, Continental Plaza, 411 Hackensack Ave., Hackensack, NJ 07601; **Membership:** 30,000

National Democratic Club, 52 E. 41st St., New York, NY 10017; **Membership:** 1,200

National Easter Seal Society for Crippled Children and Adults, 2023 W. Ogden Ave., Chicago, IL 60612

National Education Association, 1201 16th St., NW, Washington, DC 20036; **Membership:** 1,600,800; 53 state and 9,000 local affiliated groups

National Farmers Union (Farmers Educational and Cooperative Union of America), PO Box 39251, Denver, CO 80239; **Membership:** 300,000 farm families in 3,000 groups

National Federation of the Blind, 1800 Johnson St., Baltimore, MD 21230; **Membership:** 50,000

National Federation of Business and Professional Women's Clubs, Inc., 2012 Massachusetts Ave., NW, Washington, DC 20036; **Membership:** 170,000

National Federation of Music Clubs, 310 S. Michigan Ave., Suite 1936, Chicago, IL 60604; **Membership:** 500,000 in 4,500 clubs

National 4-H Council, 150 N. Wacker Dr., Chicago, IL 60606

National Genealogical Society, 1921 Sunderland Pl., NW, Washington, DC 20036; **Membership:** 4,500

National Geographic Society, 17th & M Sts. NW, Washington, DC 20036; **Membership:** 9,500,000

National Grange, 1616 H St., NW, Washington, DC 20006; **Membership:** 525,000 in 5,500 groups

National Hairdressers and Cosmetologists Assoc., Inc., 3510 Olive St., St. Louis, MO 63103; **Membership:** 71,000

National Health Council, Inc., 1740 Broadway, New York, NY 10019; **Membership:** 87 organizations

National Institute of Social Sciences, 150 Amsterdam Ave., New York, NY 10023; **Membership:** 1,000

National Jewish Welfare Board, 15 E. 26th St., New York, NY 10010; **Membership:** 370 Jewish community centers and YM-YWHAs

National League of Cities, 1620 Eye St., NW, Washington, DC 20006; **Membership:** 15,000 municipal governments in 49 states

National Legal Aid and Defender Association, 2100 M St., NW, Suite 601, Washington, DC 20037; **Membership:** 3200 offices and org., 6,000 attorneys, 2000 individuals

National Medical Association, Inc., 1720 Massachusetts Ave., NW, Washington, DC 20006; **Membership:** 8,000

National Multiple Sclerosis Society, 205 E. 42nd St., New York, NY 10017; **Membership:** 450,000 in 155 chapters

National Municipal League, 47 E. 68th St., New York, NY 10021; **Membership:** 6,500

National Newspaper Publishers Association, 770 National Press Bldg., Washington, DC 20004; **Membership:** 161 publishers

National Organization for Women (NOW), Suite 1048, 425 13th St., NW, Washington, DC 20004; **Membership:** 95,000

National Parks and Conservation Association, 1701 18th St., NW, Washington, DC 20009; **Membership:** 45,000

National Press Club, National Press Bldg., 529 14th St., NW, Room 1380, Washington, DC 20045; **Membership:** 4,734

National PTA, 700 N. Rush St., Chicago, IL 60611; **Membership:** 6,300,000

National Railway Historical Society, P.O. Box 2051, Philadelphia, PA 19103; **Membership:** 10,000

National Rifle Association of America, 1600 Rhode Island Ave., NW, Washington, DC 20036; **Membership:** 1,200,000

National Safety Council, 444 N. Michigan Ave., Chicago, IL 60611; **Membership:** 15,000

National Small Business Association, 1604 K St., NW, Washington, DC 20036; **Membership:** 40,000

National Society for the Prevention of Blindness, 79 Madison Ave., New York, NY 10016; **Membership:** 321

National Tax Association-Tax Institute of America, 21 E. State St., Columbus, OH 43215; **Membership:** 2,500

National Urban League, 500 E. 62nd St., New York, NY 10021; **Membership:** 50,000 in 115 local groups

National Wildlife Federation, 1412 16th St., NW, Washington, DC 20036; **Membership:** 4,100,000

National Woman's Christian Temperance Union, 1730 Chicago Ave., Evanston, IL 60201; **Membership:** 250,000

Newspaper Guild, The, 1125 15th St., NW, Washington, DC 20005; **Membership:** 33,500 in 80 locals

Optimist International, 4494 Lindell Blvd., St. Louis, MO 63108; **Membership:** 125,000

Order of AHEPA (American Hellenic Educational Progressive Association), 1422 K St., NW, Washington, DC 20005; **Membership:** 50,000 in 430 groups

Order of the Eastern Star, General Grand Chapter, 1618 New Hampshire Ave., NW, Washington, DC 20009; **Membership:** 3,000,000

Overseas Press Club of America, 55 E. 43rd St., New York, NY 10017; **Membership:** 1,600

Parkinson's Disease Foundation, William Black Medical Research Bldg., Columbia Presbyterian Medical Center, 640 W. 168th St., New York, NY 10032

P.E.N. American Center, 47 Fifth Ave., New York, NY 10010

Photographic Society of America, 2005 Walnut St., Philadelphia, PA 19103; **Membership:** 18,700

Planned Parenthood–World Population (Planned Parenthood Federation of America), 810 Seventh Ave., New York, NY 10019; **Membership:** 189 organizations

Polish Legion of American Veterans, U.S.A., 3024 N. Laramie Ave., Chicago, IL 60641; **Membership:** 15,000 in 114 posts

Public Relations Society of America, 845 Third Ave., New York, NY 10022; **Membership:** 9,000 executives

Puppeteers of America, 5 Cricklewood Path, Pasadena, CA 91107; **Membership:** 2,500 in 21 guilds

Republican National Committee, 310 First St., SE, Washington, DC 20003; **Membership:** 162

Rotary International, 1600 Ridge Ave., Evanston, IL 60201; **Membership:** 835,300

Screen Actors Guild, 7750 Sunset Blvd., Hollywood, CA 90046; **Membership:** 39,000

Sierra Club, 530 Bush St., San Francisco, CA 94108; **Membership:** 183,000

Society for the Advancement of Education, 1860 Broadway, New York, NY 10023; **Membership:** 3,000

Society of Automotive Engineers, 400 Commonwealth Dr., Warrendale, PA 15096; **Membership:** 30,000 in 52 groups

Society of the Cincinnati, 2118 Massachusetts Ave., NW, Washington, DC 20008; **Membership:** 2,800 in 14 groups

Sons of the American Revolution, National Society, 1000 S. Fourth St., Louisville, KY 40203; **Membership:** 22,000

Soroptimist International of the Americas, Inc., 1616 Walnut St., Philadelphia, PA 19103; **Membership:** 31,000 in 1,075 groups

Southern Christian Leadership Conference, 334 Auburn Ave. NE, Atlanta, GA 30303; **Membership:** 80 chapters

Speech Communication Association, 5205 Leesburg Pike, Falls Church, VA 22041; **Membership:** 9,000

Sports Car Club of America, Box 22476, Denver, CO 80222; **Membership:** 21,000

Supreme Council, Ancient Accepted Scottish Rite of Freemasonry, Northern Jurisdiction, 33 Marrett Rd., Lexington, MA 02173; **Membership:** 511,687 in 112 groups

Supreme Council 33°, Ancient Accepted Scottish Rite of Freemasonry, Southern Jurisdiction, 1733 16th St. NW, Washington DC 20009; **Membership:** 658,600

Transportation Association of America, 1100 17th St., NW, Washington, DC 20036; **Membership:** 1,000

UNICEF, 331 E. 38th St., New York, NY 10016; **Membership:** 90

United Cerebral Palsy Associations, 66 E. 34th St., New York, NY 10016; **Membership:** 291 affiliates

United Daughters of the Confederacy, 328 North Blvd., Richmond, VA 23220; **Membership:** 35,000

United Jewish Appeal, Inc., 1290 Ave. of the Americas, New York, NY 10019; **Membership:** 8 regional groups

United Nations Association of the United States of America, 300 E. 42nd St., New York, NY 10017; **Membership:** 26,000 in 200 chapters

United Negro College Fund, 500 E. 62nd St., New York, NY 10021; **Membership:** 39 private accredited four-year colleges; 2 graduate and professional schools

USO (United Service Organizations), 1146 19th St., NW, Washington, DC 20036

United States Catholic Conference, 1312 Massachusetts Ave., NW, Washington, DC 20005

United States Independent Telephone Association, 1801 K St., NW, Washington, DC 20006; **Membership:** 1,600

The United States Jaycees, 4 W. 21st St., P.O. Box 7, Tulsa, OK 74102; **Membership:** 380,000 in 51 state groups

United States Olympic Committee, 1750 E. Boulder St., Colorado Springs, CO 80909; **Membership:** 43

United States Power Squadrons, P.O. Box 30423, Raleigh, NC 27612; **Membership:** 67,000

United States Student Association, 1220 G St., SE, Washington, DC 20003; **Membership:** 400 colleges and universities

United Way of America, 801 N. Fairfax St., Alexandria, VA 22314; **Membership:** 2,322 local united funds, community chests and welfare councils.

Variety Clubs International, 58 W. 58th St., Suite 23-C, New York, NY 10019; **Membership:** 10,000 in 42 groups

Veterans of Foreign Wars of the U.S.A., V.F.W. Bldg., Kansas City MO 64111; **Membership:** 1,850,000 in 10,000 groups; ladies auxilliary numbers 610,000 in 6,855 groups

Volunteers of America, 340 W. 85th St., New York, NY 10024; **Membership:** 44 state groups

The Wilderness Society, 1901 Pennsylvania Ave., NW, Washington, DC 20006; **Membership:** 70,000

Wildlife Society, 7101 Wisconsin Ave., NW, Suite 611, Washington, DC 20014; **Membership:** 7,500

Women Strike for Peace, 145 S. 13th St., Philadelphia, PA 19107

Women's American ORT (Organization for Rehabilitation through Training), 1250 Broadway, New York, NY 10001; **Membership:** 137,000 in 1,131 chapters

Women's International League for Peace and Freedom, 1213 Race St., Philadelphia, PA 19107; **Membership:** 110 branches

Workmen's Benefit Fund of the U.S.A., 714 Seneca Ave., Brooklyn, NY 11227; **Membership:** 36,000 in 115 groups

Workmen's Circle, 45 E. 33rd St., New York, NY 10016; **Membership:** 60,000 in 310 groups

World Future Society, 4916 St. Elmo Ave., Washington, DC 20014; **Membership:** 50,000 in 60 groups

World Population Society, 1337 Connecticut Ave., NW, Suite 200, Washington, DC 20006; **Membership:** 1,100

Writers Guild of America, East, 22 W. 48th St., New York, NY 10036; **Membership:** 2,100

Writers Guild of America, West, 8955 Beverly Blvd., Los Angeles, CA 90048; **Membership:** 5,100

Young Democrats of America, % Democratic National Committee, 1625 Massachusetts Ave., NW, Washington, DC 20036; **Membership:** 115,000 in 1,400 groups

Young Men's and Young Women's Hebrew Association, 1395 Lexington Ave., New York, NY 10028; **Membership:** 9,600

Young Men's Christian Associations of the U.S.A., National Council, 291 Broadway, New York, NY 10017; **Membership:** 9,000,000 in 1,842 associations

Young Republican National Federation, 310 First St, SE, Washington, DC 20003; **Membership:** 300,000 in 4,000 groups

Young Women's Christian Association of the U.S.A., 600 Lexington Ave., New York, NY 10022; **Membership:** 2,434,000 in 4,771 local groups

Zionist Organization of America, 4 E. 34th St., New York, NY 10016; **Membership:** 150,000 in 600 groups

RELIGION: FAITHS/FOLLOWERS

MAJOR WORLD RELIGIONS

JUDAISM

The religion of the Jewish people is the world's oldest great monotheism and the parent religion of both Christianity and Islam. The name derives from the Latin *Judaeus* and the Hebrew *Yehudhi*, meaning *descendant of Judah*, who was the fourth son of Jacob.

The founder of Judaism was Abraham, who lived about 1500 B.C. and made a covenant with God that he and his descendants, as the Chosen People, would carry the message of one God to the world. The new nation was given structure by Moses, who in the 13th century B.C. led the Israelites out of slavery in Egypt, received the Ten Commandments from God on Mt. Horeb (Sinai), and brought his people to the edge of the land of Canaan, which had been promised to Abraham as part of the covenant.

Once in the Promised Land, the Israelites built a temple, established a priesthood, and began offering sacrifices in accordance with the teachings of Moses—practices that survived the 6th-century Babylonian Exile. But in A.D. 70, when the temple in Jerusalem was destroyed by the Roman army, sacrificial worship was supplanted by study and prayers in synagogues.

Although Judaism has no specific creeds, its sacred writings consist of laws, prophecies, and traditions that reflect 3,500 years of spiritual experience. The principal text is the Torah, or Pentateuch, which consists of the first five books of the Bible. The rest of the Hebrew Bible, known to Christians as the Old Testament, includes the Psalms and writings of the major and minor prophets.

Another authoritative work is the Talmud, a collection of laws that includes the Mishna, a Hebrew compilation of the Oral Law (in Hebrew), and the Gemara, a collection of comments (in Aramaic) on the Mishna by rabbis. There are actually two Talmuds, one that emanated from Palestine in the 5th century and one from Babylonia a century later.

The basis of Judaism is belief in the living God who is transcendent, omnipotent, and just, and who reveals himself to mankind. The faith rests on the words of Deuteronomy 6:4: "Hear, O Israel, the Lord our God, the Lord is One."

For Jews the oneness of God implies the brotherhood of men, and religious knowledge is considered inseparable from the ethical injunction "to do justly, and love mercy, and to walk humbly with thy God." Judaism's elaborate system of laws and rituals, such as dietary regulations, is designed to give sacred meaning to every aspect of daily life.

Jews have an ordained clergy and observe the Sabbath, which runs from sunset Friday to sunset Saturday and is observed with services of prayer and readings in local synagogues. Major festivals include Pesach (Passover, celebrating the Exodus), Shabuoth (Pentecost), Rosh Hashana (New Year), Yom Kippur (Day of Atonement), and Sukkoth (Feast of Tabernacles).

Judaism has generated numerous internal sects and movements, including the Sadduccees and Pharisees during the early Christian era. In the 12th century, Maimonides tried to relate Judaism to Western philosophy, especially that of Aristotle. Modern religious movements developed from Moses Mendelssohn, a rationalist of the 18th-century Enlightenment, and Hasidism, which preaches piety and mysticism.

Present-day American Judaism is divided among three major denominations. The Orthodox stresses strict adherence to the Torah. Reform Jews, in the tradition of Mendelssohn, have repudiated legalism and emphasize the compatibility of Judaism with secular liberal values. Conservative Judaism reflects a middle road—acceptance of the Torah but also a willingness to adapt it to modern conditions. In recent years a Reconstructionist movement, which was originated by Mordecai M. Kaplan and developed out of the Conservative wing, has stressed Judaism as an evolving religious civilization.

Since the destruction of their nation in A.D. 70, Jews have dreamed of once again having their own state. The first Zionist Congress was held (1897) in Basle and, in the wake of the Nazi holocaust that took the lives of six million Jews, the State of Israel came into being in 1948. Although the religious significance of the state's existence is not yet clear, the Six-Day War of 1967 nonetheless made many non-Israeli Jews realize how closely they are involved with Israel both in their cultural and religious lives.

MOSES (c. 1350–1250 B.C.)

According to Biblical accounts, the great lawgiver of Jewish monotheism was born probably in Egypt to slave parents, Amram and Jochebed, of the tribe of Levi. Because of an Egyptian law requiring newborn male Hebrew children to be killed, his mother is said to have hid him in a basket among the reeds of the Nile River. Found by one of Pharaoh's daughters, he was raised by her with Jochebed as his nurse.

As a young man Moses became interested in the cause of his people and had to flee to Midian after slaying an Egyptian whom he had discovered beating a Hebrew. Finding refuge as a shepherd for Jethro, a local priest, Moses married his daughter Zipporah.

While tending sheep one day at Mt. Horeb, Moses had a vision of God in a bush that burned but was not consumed, and he experienced a call to return to Egypt to liberate his people. With the aid of his brother Aaron, he aproached the Pharaoh (probably Ramses II: reigned c. 1292 to 1225 B.C.), who acceded to the Exodus of the Hebrews after a series of 10 plagues, the last of which took the life of his firstborn son. The Pharaoh subsequently changed his mind, pursued the Hebrews, and his army was drowned in the Red Sea, but the Israelites miraculously escaped.

Moses led his people across the Sinai desert to Mt. Horeb (Sinai), where he received the Ten Commandments from God in the form of two tablets, which he smashed on the ground when he discovered his Hebrews worshiping a Golden Calf. Later he prepared two new tablets and placed them in the most sacred section of the Tabernacle, a portable sanctuary that was set up according to divine instructions. He also taught the Hebrews a complete legal code, organized a judicial system, and spelled out sacrificial practices.

Moses spent 40 years leading his people in the wilderness, never entering the promised land of Canaan—a privilege that went to his chosen successor, Joshua. Moses' great achievement, however, was the development of a system of morality and law applicable to all aspects of daily life.

CHRISTIANITY

Christianity developed among first-century Jews out of the conviction that Jesus of Nazareth, who lived from about c. 4 B.C. to A.D. 29, was the long-awaited Hebrew *Messiah*. . . . The name Jesus is Greek for the Hebrew *Joshua*, a name meaning *Savior*, while Christ derives from the Greek *Christos*, meaning *Messiah*, or *Anointed*.

The Christian Bible includes the Hebrew Bible, which is called the Old Testament, and the New Testament, which contains 27 additional books and was formalized by the 4th century. Central are the four Gospels of Matthew, Mark, Luke, and John, which describe the life and teachings of Jesus. Some Christians also accept the 14-book appendix to the Authorized Version of the Old Testament, known as the Apocrypha, as canonical.

The essence of traditional Christian theology is that Jesus was the Son of God who came to save the world, was crucified, resurrected, and will come again to judge mankind. The core of the Christian ethic is the commandment: "Thou shalt love the Lord thy God with all thy heart and thy neighbor as thyself."

A turning point in Christian history occurred at the Council of Jerusalem in A.D. 49 when St. Paul convinced other church leaders to spread the faith to non-Jews. Early Christians endured severe persecution, but in

A.D. 313 Constantine I officially tolerated Christianity in the Roman Empire.

Fundamental theological issues such as the divinity of Jesus Christ were thrashed out at a series of ecumenical councils during the first eight centuries. Doctrinal statements emanated from these councils, such as the Nicene Creed and the teaching of the Trinity, which asserts that God has appeared to man as the Father, the Son, and the Holy Ghost.

In 1054 Christianity was split into a Western or Roman Catholic Church, which acknowledges the pope—the bishop of Rome—as Christ's supreme vicar on earth, and the Eastern Orthodox Churches, which recognize the patriarch of Constantinople as the preeminent ecclesiastical figure. In the 16th century the Roman Catholic Church was further divided by the Protestant Reformation. The ecumenical movement of this century has now shifted momentum toward a quest for unity among Christian churches. An important development was the founding in 1948 of the World Council of Churches, which has more than 220 Protestant and Orthodox churches as members.

ROMAN CATHOLICISM

Roman Catholicism is the form of Christianity practiced by those who recognize the authority of the pope—the bishop of Rome—as the successor of Peter and vicar of Christ on Earth. The great majority of Catholics follow the Western or Latin Rite, but there are also a number of Eastern or Uniate churches, including the Byzantine and Armenian rites, that exercise a considerable degree of autonomy.

The Roman Catholic Church claims to be the "One Holy, Catholic and Apostolic Church." Although it acknowledges the Old and New Testaments and the Apocrypha, it also asserts that teachings disclosed in only seminal form to the Apostles have subsequently germinated and flowered in the Christian Community and have been formulated by General Councils and/or the pope. Recent examples of articles of faith include the doctrines of papal infallibility (1870) and the Assumption of the Virgin Mary (1950).

The basis of the Church's claim to sanctity is its authority to offer the sacrifice of the Mass, the Eucharist, that reenacts and re-presents Christ's sacrifice in behalf of man's sins. There are six other recognized sacraments: baptism, confirmation, confession and penance, matrimony, ordination, and extreme unction.

The key figure in the church hierarchy is the bishop, who has the power to confirm and ordain. The members of the College of Cardinals serve as the pope's privy councillors and also have the responsibility of electing new popes. The central administrative body of the church is the Curia Romana, which is located in Rome and organized around a varying number of sacred "congregations."

Priests are divided into "secular," or diocesan, clergy and "regular" clergy, who belong to religious orders living under a "rule." Since the 12th century, celibacy has been required of both types of clergy.

Following the 16th-century Protestant Reformation, the Church entered a period of retrenchment that was characterized by sharply defined standards of orthodoxy. Since the First Vatican Council, which ended in 1870, the papacy has been exceptionally strong. The Second Vatican Council (1962–65), however, produced significant changes, and the Church is now undergoing a period of uncertainty and flux that is marked by demands for increased power for laymen and priests and serious questioning of such traditions as clerical celibacy and papal authority.

EASTERN ORTHODOXY

The term Eastern Orthodox refers to those churches and their offspring that, for a variety of cultural, political, and theological reasons, split with Rome in A.D. 1054. These churches regard themselves as the true heirs of the early Christian Church and define their theological unity by acceptance of the decrees of the first seven ecumenical (general) councils that were held from A.D. 325 to 787.

The Eastern communion is a fellowship of autonomous churches consisting of the ancient patriarchates of Constantinople, Alexandria, Antioch, and Jerusalem, as well as the Orthodox churches of Cyprus, Russia, Rumania, Yugoslavia, Greece, Bulgaria, Georgia, Albania, Finland, and Czechoslovakia. The leader is the Ecumenical Patriarch of Constantinople, who is regarded as "first among equals" but whose direct authority is limited to the affairs of his own church, whose members are for the most part located in Europe and the Americas.

Eastern Orthodox theology is grounded in Greek philosophy rather than Roman law, and its creeds are important more as acts of worship than as standards of belief. Great reverence is shown for the writings of the church fathers, including Saints Basil the Great, Gregory Nazianzen, and John Chrysostom.

In addition to rejecting the authority of the pope, Eastern Orthodoxy disagrees with the Roman Catholic Church by rejecting of the Nicene Creed's *Filioque*, which asserts that the Holy Spirit proceeds "from the Son" as well as from the Father. Orthodoxy also has no indulgences and pays honor to Mary as the mother of God but rejects the Roman dogma of Immaculate Conception. It reveres relics and icons but bans all "graven images," except the crucifix.

Orthodox priests may marry before but not after ordination, although monks must remain celibate and bishops are chosen from among the celibate clergy. The liturgy of Eastern Orthodox churches is sung, and great emphasis is placed on fasting. Eastern Orthodox church structures, which are normally square, feature a solid screen that separates the sanctuaries and the edifices' main bodies. They are often elaborately decorated with gilded icons and other works of art.

The fact that a majority of Orthodox believers now live in Communist-controlled areas has cut into the vitality of Orthodoxy, but nonetheless many of its churches—including the Russian one—are active in the World Council of Churches. Relations with Rome have greatly improved, and Ecumenical Patriarch Athenagoras I has had several dramatic meetings with Pope Paul VI, including one on the Mount of Olives in Jerusalem.

PROTESTANTISM

In a broad sense *Protestantism* is a generic term for most Western Christian churches that are not Roman Catholic or Eastern Orthodox. In a narrower connotation, it designates those churches and their heirs that came into being after the 16th-century Protestant Reformation.

The Reformation was sparked by Martin Luther, an Augustinian monk who challenged the papal practice of dispensing indulgences; with the support of German princes, he established a separate church. In addition to the Lutheran, there are at least three other Protestant traditions. The Reformed, or Calvinistic, tradition developed in Switzerland and led to the formation of Presbyterian and related churches. Anglicanism, which is represented in the United States by the Episcopal Church and originated in England, was the parent of Methodism. Numerous "free" or "independent" churches have also developed, including the Baptist and others that exercise a congregational system of government.

The fundamental philosophical characteristics of the reformers were the rejection of the authority of Rome, belief in the Bible as the only source of revelation, recognition of the "priesthood of all believers," and the assertion that salvation is the result of faith rather than good works or the dispensations of a church. Protestantism's characteristic individualism led to the development of religious liberty in many areas, but also contributed to denominational fragmentation.

Protestant churches permit ministers to marry, and even those that have bishops tend to concentrate governing powers in lay boards. Liturgies generally emphasize preaching and Bible reading rather than elaborate ritual; however, some traditions—notably the Anglo-Catholic wing of Anglicanism—are highly liturgical.

The modern ecumenical movement has developed out of Protestantism, and, except for fundamentalist churches (and thereby most Baptist churches), the major Protestant denominations tend to be involved in organizations such as the World Council of Churches. Mergers have been common in recent years, and nine major American denominations are in the process of negotiating a merger that would create a single, 25-million-member church.

JESUS (c. 4 B.C.–A.D. 29)

The founder of Christianity was born in Bethlehem to Mary, the wife of Joseph, who was a carpenter from Nazareth. Little is known about his early life. According to the Gospels, at the age of about 30 he was baptized by his cousin John the Baptist and began to preach, soon gathering a band of 12 disciples.

Jesus, who preached a message of repentance, made repeated attacks on Pharisees and scribes, the rulers of

Judaism. He couched his teachings in parables that could be understood by the masses and reinforced his words with extraordinary deeds that included healing the sick, raising the dead, and changing water into wine at the marriage feast of Cana.

After three years of preaching, Jesus set out for Jerusalem with his disciples for the celebration of Passover. He created a disturbance by throwing the money changers out of the Temple. Meanwhile, the Roman Governor Pontius Pilate, who was sensitive to Jewish nationalist threats, became alarmed. The authorities induced one of the disciples, Judas Iscariot, to betray Jesus. Following a Last Supper with his followers in which the Eucharist, or Lord's Supper, was symbolically enacted, Jesus was arrested in the Garden of Gethsemane.

He was tried for the treasonous charge of calling himself the Messiah and was crucified under a sign reading "Jesus of Nazareth, King of the Jews." The Gospels report, however, that three days later when Mary Magdalene went to the tomb she found it empty. An angel announced that Jesus had been resurrected; according to the Book of Acts, he appeared to his disciples, remained on earth 40 days, and then ascended into heaven.

Orthodox Christian theology asserts that Jesus was God made man and the second Person of the Trinity. The calendar of the Christian Church revolves around the events of his life, beginning with Advent—the preparation for his coming—and concluding with his Resurrection, Ascension, and the reception of the Holy Spirit by the church.

The discovery in 1947 of the Dead Sea Scrolls in a cave above the waters of the northwest Dead Sea in a section known as Qumran provided information about a pacifist and ascetic community generally identified with the Essene Jewish sect.

Some scholars attempted to link Jesus with the "Teacher of Righteousness," an Essene figure who would be "raised up" by God after death. A more general consensus now is that such ties are tenuous and that the scrolls are important primarily for their information about cultural conditions of the early Christian era, especially Palestinian Judaism and the background of John the Baptist.

ISLAM

Islam is the religion founded by the prophet Mohammed (c. A.D. 570–632) in 622 at Yathrib (now Medina) in Arabia. The Arabic word *Islam* means *submission to God,* and followers call themselves Moslems.

Mohammed was a caravan conductor and Mecca shopkeeper of the Koreish tribe who experienced a prophetic call at the age of 40. After founding his religion, he also acted as a governor, general, and judge. Mohammed is regarded as the "Seal of the Prophets"—the last in a series of messengers from God, consisting of Adam, Noah, Abraham, Moses, and Jesus.

The sacred text of Islam is the Koran (*Quran* in Arabic), which means *reading* and contains the revelations of Mohammed over a period of 20 years; it also deals with manners, religious laws, and morals. It has been supplemented by the Sunna, a collection of Traditions (moral sayings and anecdotes), and both are reinforced by the principle of Ijma, which states the belief that a majority of Moslems cannot agree in error. The Koran, the Sunna, and the Ijma are the three foundations of Islam.

Islam is radically theistic, and the essence of its creed is simply stated: "There is no God but Allah, and Mohammed is the messenger [or prophet] of Allah." Mohammed rejected the trinitarianism of Christianity, but he incorporated a number of Judeo-Christian concepts into his system. For example, the creed states: "I believe in God, his Angels, his Books and his Messengers, the Last Day, the Resurrection from the dead, Predestination by God, Good and Evil, the Judgment, the Balance, Paradise and Hell-fire."

There is no professional priesthood in Islam, and followers are expected to refrain from drinking wine. In addition to acceptance and recital of the creed, there are four duties required of the devout: prayer, fasting during the lunar month of Ramadan, giving alms, and a pilgrimage to the holy city of Mecca—if at all possible.

Moslems pray five times a day—at dawn, noon, midafternoon, dusk, and at night. The prayers, which consist primarily of thanksgiving and praise of Allah, are performed facing Mecca and involve traditional physical postures. The principal public service takes place at midday on Friday, usually in a mosque.

Early disputes over the "caliph," or successor of Mohammed, led to sectarian divisions within Islam. The most important were the Sunnites, Shiites, and Khawarij, who differed over matters of ceremony and law. Other modern movements have included the Babis and the Wahabis.

Islam is a missionary religion, though Moslems do not regard Jews and Christians as pagans and have normally permitted them to keep practicing their faiths after conquests. In centuries past, Moslem armies took over large sections of India and once came within 100 miles of Paris.

The principal areas of Islamic influence today are the Middle East, North Africa, and western Asia, and there are substantial communities in the Philippines, Indonesia, and Malaysia. It is currently increasing rapidly in African countries south of the Sahara.

Considerable theological activity has gone on during this century toward discrediting such Islamic practices as polygamy, slavery, and intolerance, thus making Islam more acceptable under modern conditions.

MOHAMMED (c. 570–A.D. 632)

The founder of Islam was born in Mecca in Arabia, the son of a poor merchant from the ruling tribe of Koreish. Both his parents died shortly after his birth, and he was raised by a grandfather and later an uncle. As a youth he was a shepherd and worked as a conductor of trading caravans.

Following his marriage at the age of 24 to the wealthy widow Khadija, who was 15 years his senior, Mohammed settled down in Mecca as a prosperous merchant and began devoting himself to the contemplative life. At the age of 40 in the cave of Mount Hira, north of Mecca, he had a vision, in which he was commanded to preach. This revelation and subsequent ones were recorded in the Koran, the sacred book of the Moslems.

Mohammed's first converts were his wife and children, and he began to collect other followers slowly and secretly, because of his many enemies. He taught belief in only one God, Allah, and preached heaven and hell and divine judgment.

When he began to operate openly, he aroused considerable hostility; some of his followers had to seek sanctuary in Abyssinia because of persecution. In 622 he himself barely escaped assassination and fled to Yathrib, which was later renamed Medina. Moslems regard this flight, the hegira, as the beginning of Islam and the start of their calendar.

Mohammed became the absolute ruler of Yathrib, where he founded his model theocratic state. He built the first mosque, changed the direction of prayers from Jerusalem to Mecca, and instituted the fast month of Ramadan and the practice of tithing. Relations with Christians and Jews deteriorated, but eventually he made treaties granting them freedom of worship in return for taxes. He initiated warfare with the Meccans, eventually gaining control of all of Arabia.

His private life has been the source of much attention, especially his frequent marriages—often politically inspired—and troubles with his harem. He basically led a simple and unpretentious life, however, and in 632 died in the arms of his last favorite wife, Ayesha.

HINDUISM

Known to its followers as *Santana Dharma* (the Eternal Religion), Hinduism is the religion of the majority of Indians today. It has developed gradually over a period of 5,000 years, making it possibly the world's oldest faith.

Hinduism has no ecclesiastical organization, and there are no beliefs or practices universal to all Hindus. It is polytheistic in the extreme, with literally hundreds of thousands of gods and some forms of animal life worshiped. The principal gods are Brahma, the unapproachable creative spirit, and the two popular gods, Siva and Vishnu—both of which have spawned innumerable cults.

Hindus emphasize the divinity of the soul and the harmony of all religions. Life is seen as a series of lives in which a man's position is determined by his *Karma,* or deeds, in previous lives. The social "caste" into which he is born is thus an indication of his spiritual status. The ultimate goal is to be released from the cycle of rebirths in various human and animal forms through absorption by the absolute. Asceticism and the discipline of Yoga are practiced to help achieve this release.

Hinduism has no fixed canon of sacred books. The principal text is the Veda (Vedic word meaning *divine knowledge*), a collection of 1,200 hymns and incantations addressed to various deities, including those of fire and wind. Some of this material is believed to date from the arrival of the Aryans in India c. 1500 B.C. More philosophical works that have also gained wide acceptance include the *Brahamanas*, the *Upanishads*, and the poem "Bhagavad-Gita" (Sanskrit for Song of the Lord).

For the ordinary man, Hinduism involves careful observance of food and marriage rules, pilgrimages to sacred rivers and shrines, participation in festivals, and worship in the temples and shrines that are found in every village. Entry to ultimate truth comes not from the acceptance of certain dogmas but from worship and religious experience.

Over the centuries Hinduism has produced numerous reform movements, including Buddhism and Sikhism. Modern social and cultural conditions are also bringing about modification of the caste system and other changes such as increased social status for women.

BUDDHISM

Buddhism is the way of life based on the teachings of Siddhartha Gautama, an Indian prince who lived in the sixth century B.C. and came to be known as the Buddha (Sanskrit for *enlightened one*).

Dissatisfied with the formalism of the Hinduism of his day and vowing to find an explanation for evil and human suffering, the prince left his family and wandered as a hermit for six years in search of a truth that would liberate mankind. He found it after seven weeks of meditation under a bo (pipal or sacred fig) tree (the tree of enlightenment) and began preaching and sending missionaries forth to spread his discovery.

The Buddha taught that the path beyond sorrow and suffering was the "middle way" between austerity and sensuality. He spoke of "four noble truths": existence involves suffering, suffering results from craving, craving can be destroyed, and such destruction of desire is obtainable by following the "noble eightfold path." The steps of this path are right views, right desires, right speech, right conduct, right livelihood, right endeavor, right mindfulness, and right meditation.

The Buddha did not speak of God, and his teachings constitute, in the ordinary Western sense, more of a philosophy and system of ethics than a religion. Buddhism affirms the law of Karma, by which a person's actions in life determine his status in future incarnations. The object of the Buddhist life is to achieve Nirvana, a condition of enlightenment and detachment from the world by which the cycle of successive rebirths comes to an end.

The simple life of the Buddha and his followers gave way after his death to the creation of monasteries, shrines, and temples; however, Buddhism eventually split into numerous branches. The two major ones today are Mahayana (greater vehicle) Buddhism, which is practiced in China, Korea, and Japan and has an elaborate theology in which the Buddha is regarded as a divine savior, and Hinayana (lesser vehicle) Buddhism, which is concentrated in Southeast Asia and preserves the earlier monastic traditions. Zen Buddhism, a Japanese variation of Mahayana Buddhism, stresses contemplation, while the Lamaism of Tibet represents a mixture of Buddhism with local demonolatry.

BUDDHA (c. 563–483 B.C.)

The founder of Buddhism, known as the Buddha or "Enlightened One," was born into a military caste in Lumbini, near the Himalayas in southern Nepal. Estimates of the precise year range from 624 to 466 B.C.

His original name was Siddhartha Gautama (or Gotama), and legend holds that his father, a rajah, had been warned at his birth that Siddhartha would become either a universal ruler or a universal teacher. Preferring the former course, the father took pains to prevent him from seeing any unpleasant aspects of life that might influence him to renounce the world.

Riding through the royal park one day when he was 29 years old, however, Siddhartha saw human misery for the first time in the form of an old man, a diseased man, a corpse, and a wandering religious mendicant. Resolving to solve the riddle of human suffering, he left his wife and newborn son and spent the next six years as a wandering hermit and ascetic.

His austere living failed to bring illumination, and he became an ordinary mendicant. One day he sat under a bo tree in the village of Buddh Gaya in northern India and resolved not to rise until he had found enlightenment. He stayed 49 days, resisting temptations by Mara, the Buddhist devil, and was finally rewarded with the "bliss of emancipation," or Nirvana. Suffering, he concluded, was caused by attachment to the world and could only be eliminated through mental discipline and correct living.

Two merchants heard his teachings and became his first lay disciples. Later he preached a sermon to five monks with whom he had shared his ascetic quest, and they were ordained as the first members of the Sangha, the Buddhist monastic order. He returned home briefly and converted his family, thereafter spending the rest of his life teaching among neighboring tribes and organizing monks to spread the message of life lived according to the "middle way" between the extremes of pleasure-seeking and self-mortification.

He died at the age of 80 in the lap of Ananda, his favorite disciple, and his last words were said to have been: "Decay is inherent in all component things. Work out your own salvation with diligence."

SHINTOISM

The ancestral religion of Japan, Shinto developed out of primitive nature and ancestor worship sometime before the sixth century, when written records first appeared. The term *Shinto* is the Chinese equivalent of *the way of the gods,* and came into use at that time to distinguish it from the Buddhism that was then being imported from the Chinese mainland.

Shinto is essentially a set of customs and rituals rather than an ethical or moral system. Followers participate in festivals and pilgrimages, and great emphasis is placed on ceremonial purity and bodily cleanliness. Many Shintoists are also practicing Buddhists.

The religion has a complex pantheon of *kami*, or deities, the most exalted of whom is the sun-goddess known as Ruler of Heaven. Other objects of veneration include deified emperors, guardian family spirits, national heroes, and the divinities of trees, rivers, villages, and water sources.

Shrines ranging from small wayside god-houses to great national sanctuaries have been constructed and dedicated to these deities. Each Shinto home also has a "god-shelf" on which is placed a miniature wooden shrine holding tablets bearing beloved ancestors' names.

TAOISM

The chief rival to Confucianism in influencing Chinese philosophy and culture, Taoism actually consists of two movements: a philosophy (Tao Chia) and a religion (Tao Chiao). Both derive from the philosopher Lao-tze, who, according to tradition, lived in the sixth century B.C.

The term *Tao* has been translated as *way, road,* and even *being*. The book *Tao-teh-king,* attributed to Lao-tze, states that "the eternal Tao cannot be put into words, nor can the unchanging name be given a definition."

Philosophical Taoism espoused a radical naturalism that urged the acceptance of "all things in their natural state" and deplored passion, unnecessary invention, artificial ceremonies, and government activities such as war and taxation. Virtue was cast in passive and feminine terms. "There is nothing softer and weaker than water, and yet there is nothing better for attacking hard and strong things," was one of its precepts.

Tao Chia declined by the fourth century, partly because of the excessive assimilation of Buddhism, but its spirit of simplicity and harmony has contributed to such Chinese customs as tea drinking.

Religious Taoism originated in the first century under the leadership of Chang Tao-lin, a popular religious leader who healed the sick and founded large numbers of monasteries, nunneries, and temples. His work was continued in the next four centuries by Wei Po-yang and Ko Hung, both philosophers, and by K'ou Ch'ien-chih, who organized elaborate ceremonies and fixed the names of its multifarious deities.

Taoism has been marked by a proliferation of sects and societies. Since a brief period of state patronage during the T'ang dynasty (618–907), it has been a religion of the semiliterate.

LAO-TZE OR LAO-TZU (b. c. 604 B.C.)

The reputed founder of Taoism is usually said to have been born in 604 B.C. in Honan province, China, though confusion about his historical identity and whether there even was such a person has existed since early times. The name means simply "the old philosopher."

According to Chinese tradition, he was born as Li Erh, lived as a recluse, and became an archivist in the Chou court. He was said to have met his younger contemporary Confucius in 517 and to have rebuked him for his pride and ambition. When he retired in his old age, Lao-tze supposedly journeyed westward and was never heard from again.

Legend says that as he was about to pass out of Honan the gatekeeper asked him to write down his views of the Tao and that in response he created the Tao-teh-king, the text of which became the basis of Taoist philosophy and religion.

Scholars now date the anthology in the mid-third century. It is a remarkable collection that is thought to have been built on Indian legends, especially those about Buddha; however, the work is Chinese in texture and emphasizes ethics and politics.

Living according to Tao (literally Way or Being) involved submission to natural actions and avoidance of all formality and artificiality. It emphasized the virtues of passivity and harmony in an effort to maintain "the original simplicity of human nature." Modern religious Taoism, however, has become highly institutionalized and marked by numerous gods, the use of magic and superstition, and an emphasis on earthly blessings such as wealth and long life.

CONFUCIANISM

More a religious philosophy or ethical system than a religion in the strict sense, Confucianism is known to the Chinese as *Ju Chaio* (teachings of the scholars) and was the dominant force in Chinese thought, education, and government for 2,000 years.

Its founder was Confucius (c. 551–c. 479 B.C.), who was not so much an original thinker as a teacher and compiler of wisdom from the past. His sayings, together with those of Mencius and other disciples, have been collected in the *Wu Ching (Five Classics)*, and the *Shih Shu (Four Books)*, the latter of which includes the *Analects*—the sayings of Confucius.

The central concept of Confucian ethics is *jen*, which originally signified benevolence on the part of rulers but was broadened to encompass the supreme virtue of love and goodness: "that by which a man is a man." Confucianism teaches that man is good and possesses free will and that virtue is its own reward.

There are no churches, clergy, or creeds in Confucianism, and its founder was far more interested in making this world more human than in contemplating the supernatural. Nevertheless, he believed in Heaven—although it was often interpreted in naturalistic terms—and encouraged the Chinese custom of ancestor-worship as a sign of gratitude and respect. Temples were built for this purpose and sacrificial rites performed in them.

From A.D. 125 to 1905 Confucianism dominated Chinese education, and members of the mandarin class of civil servants were appointed to government posts on the basis of examinations in the Confucian classics. This system had the effect of permitting many individuals from humble backgrounds to rise to prominence, and it placed a premium on the moral basis of the ruler and ruled. At the same time, its emphasis on book learning at the expense of natural science, for example, proved a liability in modern times.

Confucianism went into a period of decline following the elimination of the examination system (1905) and of the sacrificial rites (1911), but its ideas continued to play a part in the thought of some Chinese leaders, including Sun Yat-sen (1866–1925).

CONFUCIUS (551–479 B.C.)

The name of the founder of Confucianism and China's most prominent teacher and philosopher is a Latinized version of the Chinese K'ung Fu-tse.

Little reliable data is available about his life, although it is known that he was born in the feudal province of Lu, now Shantung, probably into an impoverished noble family. His father died when he was three, and he was evidently self-educated and as a young man earned his living keeping accounts.

Confucius became perhaps the most learned man of his day, but he was at heart a reformer rather than a scholar, a pragmatist rather than an intellectual. He was shocked by the constant warfare that went on between various states and by the suffering that aristocratic rulers brought upon the masses. He dedicated his life to relieving this suffering through governmental reforms, including the reduction of taxes, more humane punishments, and a system of statecraft that was based on mutual moral responsibilities between the ruler and the ruled.

His lifelong ambition was to occupy a governmental post from which he could implement his reforms, and for a short period he was apparently administrator of justice in his native province. Clashes with the nobility, however, forced him out of office and into voluntary exile.

At the age of 55, Confucius began touring neighboring states speaking to the feudal lords about his ideas. He was received as a scholar, but none of the rulers were willing to put his ideas into practice. He returned home to concentrate on teaching, in which he was successful; some of his students achieved positions of authority that Confucius himself had been unable to reach.

ESTIMATED MEMBERSHIP OF THE PRINCIPAL RELIGIONS OF THE WORLD

Source: Reprinted with permission from the 1980 BRITANNICA BOOK OF THE YEAR, copyright 1980, Encyclopaedia Britannica, Inc., Chicago, Ill.

Religions	No. Amer.[1]	So. Amer.	Europe[2]	Asia[3]	Africa	Oceania[4]	World
Total Christian	235,109,500	177,266,000	342,630,400	95,987,240	129,717,000	18,063,500	998,773,640
Roman Catholic	132,489,000	165,640,000	176,087,300	55,077,000	47,224,500	4,395,500	580,913,300
Eastern Orthodox	4,763,000	517,000	57,035,600	2,428,000	14,306,000[5]	414,000	79,463,600
Protestant[6]	97,857,500	11,109,000	109,507,500	38,482,240	68,186,500[7]	13,254,000	338,396,740
Jewish	6,155,340	635,800	4,061,620	3,212,860	176,400	76,000	14,318,020
Muslim[8]	371,200	251,500	14,145,000	427,266,000	145,214,700	87,000	587,335,400
Zoroastrian	250	2,100	7,000	254,000	650	—	264,000
Shinto[9]	60,000	92,000	—	57,003,000	200	—	57,155,200
Taoist	16,000	10,000	—	31,261,000	—	—	31,287,000
Confucian	97,100	70,150	—	157,887,500	1,500	80,300	158,136,550
Buddhist[10]	171,250	192,300	192,000	254,241,000	14,000	30,000	254,840,550
Hindu[11]	88,500	849,300	350,000	473,073,000	1,079,800	499,000	475,939,600
Totals	242,069,140	179,369,150	361,386,020	1,500,185,600	276,204,250	18,835,800	2,578,049,960

[1] Includes Central America and the West Indies. [2] Includes the U.S.S.R. and other countries with established Marxist ideology where religious adherence is difficult to estimate. [3] Includes areas in which persons have traditionally enrolled in several religions, as well as China with an official Marxist establishment. [4] Includes Australia and New Zealand as well as islands of the South Pacific. [5] Includes Coptic Christians. [6] Protestant statistics usually count "full members," that is adults, rather than all family members or baptized infants and are therefore not comparable with the statistics of ethnic religions or churches counting all constituents of all ages. [7] Including many new sects and cults among African Christians. [8] The chief base of Islam is still ethnic, although some missionary work is now carried on in Europe and America (viz. "Black Muslims"). In countries where Islam is established, minority religions are frequently persecuted and their statistics are hard to come by. [9] A Japanese ethnic religion, Shinto has declined since the Japanese emperor gave up his claim to divinity (1947). Neither does it survive well outside the homeland. [10] Buddhism has produced several modern renewal movements which have gained adherents in Europe and America and other areas not formerly ethnic-Buddhist. In Asia it has made rapid gains in recent years in some areas, and under persecution it has shown greater staying power than Taoism or Confucionism. It transplants better. [11] Hinduism's strength in India has been enhanced by nationalism, a phenomenon also observable in Islam. Modern Hinduism has also developed renewal movements that have won converts in Europe and America.

THE POPES

In the list below, the name of each pope is given, with, if known, his family name and birthplace, and the dates of his pontificate. The dates of the early popes are uncertain.

St. Peter (Simon, son of Jona); Bethsaida in Galilee; c.42–c.67
St. Linus; Tuscany; c.67–c.79
St. Anacletus or St. Cletus; Rome; c.79–c.92
St. Clement I (Clement of Rome); c.92–c.101
St. Evaristus; Asia Minor; c.99–c.107
St. Alexander I; Rome; c.107–c.116
St. Sixtus I; Rome; c.116–c.125
St. Telesphorus; Greece; c.125–c.138
St. Hyginus; Greece; 138–142
St. Pius I; Venetia; 142–155
St. Anicetus; Syria; 155–166
St. Soterus or St. Soter; Campania; c.166–c.174
St. Eleutherius or St. Eleuterius; Greece; c.174–c.189
St. Victor I; Africa; c.189–c.199
St. Zephyrinus; Rome; 199–217
St. Callistus I or St. Calixtus I; Rome; c.217–c.222
St. Urban I; Rome; 222–230
St. Pontianus or St. Pontian; Rome; 230–235
St. Anterus; Greece; c.235
St. Fabian; Rome; 236–250
St. Cornelius; Rome; 251–253
St. Lucius I; Rome; 253–254
St. Stephen I; Rome; 254–257
St. Sixtus II; Greece; 257–258
St. Dionysius; 259–268
St. Felix I; Rome; 269–274
St. Eutychian or St. Eutychianus; Tuscany; 275–283
St. Caius or St. Gaius; Dalmatia; 283–296
St. Marcellinus; Rome; 296–304
St. Marcellus I; Rome; 308–309
St. Eusebius; Greece; c.309–c.310
St. Melchiades or Meltiades cr Miltiades; Africa; 311–314
St. Sylvester I; Rome; 314–335
St. Marcus or St. Mark; Rome; 10 months, 336
St. Julius I; Rome; 337–352
Liberius; Rome; 352–366
St. Damascus I; Spain; 366–384
St. Siricius; Rome; 384–399
St. Anastasius I; Rome; 399–401
St. Innocent I; Latium; 401–417
St. Zozimus or St. Zosimus; Greece; 417–418
St. Boniface I; Rome; 418–422
St. Celestine I; Campania; 422–432
St. Sixtus III; Rome; 432–440
St. Leo I (the Great); Tuscany; 440–461
St. Hilary or St. Hilarius; Sardinia; 461–468
St. Simplicius; Latium; 468–483
St. Felix II; Rome; 483–492
St. Gelasius I; Africa; 492–496
Anastasius II; Rome; 496–498
St. Symmacus or St. Symmachus; Sardinia; 498–514
St. Hormisdas; Frosinone; 514–523
St. John I; Tuscany; 523–526
St. Felix III; Rome; 526–530
Boniface II; Rome; 530–532
John II; Rome; 533–535
St. Agapitus or St. Agapetus; Rome; 535–536
St. Silverius; Campania; 536–537
Vigilius; Rome; 537–555
Pelagius I; Rome; 556–561
John III; Rome; 561–574
Benedict I; Rome; 575–579
Pelagius II; Rome; 579–590
St. Gregory I (the Great); Rome; 590–604
Sabinianus or Sabinian; Tuscany; 604–606
Boniface III; Rome; 9 months, 607
St. Boniface IV; 608–615
St. Deusdedit I or St. Adeodatus I; Rome; 615–618
Boniface V; Naples; 619–c.625
Honorius I; Campania; 625–638
Severinus; Rome; 4 months, 640
John IV; Dalmatia; 640–642
Theodore I; Greece?; 642–649
St. Martin I; Umbria?; 649–655
St. Eugene I or St. Eugenius I; Rome; 654–657[a]
St. Vitalian; Latium; 657–672
Adeodatus II or Deusdedit II; Rome; 672–676
Donus I; Rome; 676–678
St. Agatho or St. Agathonus; Sicily; 678–681
St. Leo II; Sicily; 682–683
St. Benedict II; Rome; 684–685
John V; Syria; 685–686
Conon; 686–687
St. Sergius I; Palermo; 687–701
John VI; Greece; 701–705
John VII; Greece; 705–707
Sisinnius; Syria; 2 months, 708

Constantine; Syria; 708–715
St. Gregory II; Rome; 715–731
St. Gregory III; Syria; 731–741
St. Zachary or St. Zacharias; Greece; 741–752
Stephen II; Rome; 752–757
St. Paul I; Rome; 757–767
Stephen III; Sicily; 768–772
Adrian I or Hadrian I; Rome; 772–795
St. Leo III; Rome; 795–816
Stephen IV; Rome; 816–817
St. Paschal I or St. Pascal I; Rome; 817–824
Eugene II or Eugenius II; Rome; 824–827
Valentine; Rome; 2 months, 827
Gregory IV; Rome; 827–844
Sergius II; Rome; 844–847
St. Leo IV; Rome; 847–855
Benedict III; 855–858
St. Nicholas I (the Great); Rome; 858–867
Adrian II; Rome; 867–872
John VIII; Rome; 872–882
Marinus I or Martin II; Rome; 882–884
St. Adrian III; Rome; 884–885
Stephen V; Rome; 885–891
Formosus; Rome; 891–896
Boniface VI; Rome; one month, 896
Stephen VI; Rome; 896–897
Romanus; 4 months, 897
Theodore II; Rome; one month, 897
John IX; Tivoli; 898–900
Benedict IV; Rome; 900–903
Leo V; 3 months, 903
Sergius III; Rome; 904–911
Anastasius III; Rome; 911–913
Lando; Rome; 913–914
John X (John of Tossignano); Emilia-Romagna; 914–928
Leo VI; Rcme; 8 months, 928
Stephen VII; Rome; 928–931
John XI; 931–c.935
Leo VII; Rome; 936–939
Stephen VIII; Rome; 939–942
Marinus II or Martin III; Rome; 942–946
Agapitus II or Agapetus II; Rome; 946–955
John XII (Octavian); Latium; 955–964[b]
Leo VIII; Rome; 963–965[b]
Benedict V; Rome; 2 months; 964[b]
John XIII; Rome; 965–972
Benedict VI; Rome; 973–974
Benedict VII; Rome; 974–983
John XIV (Peter Canepanova); 983–984
John XV; Rome; 985–996
Gregory V (Bruno of Carinthia); Germany; 996–999
Sylvester II (Gerbert); France; 999–1003
John XVII (John Sicco); Rome; 7 months, 1003
John XVIII (Fasanus); Rome; 1003–09
Sergius IV (Peter Buccaporci); Rome; 1009–12
Benedict VIII (Theophylactus); 1012–24
John XIX (Romanus); Latium; 1024–c.32
Benedict IX (Theophylactus); 1032–44[c]
Sylvester III (John); Rome; 2 months, 1045
Benedict IX; 2 months, 1045
Gregory VI (John Gratian); Rome; 1045–46
Clement II (Suidger, Lord of Morsleben and Hornburg); Germany; 1046–47
Benedict IX; 1047–48
Damascus II (Poppo); Germany; 2 months, 1048
St. Leo IX (Bruno of Egisheim); Germany; 1048–54
Victor II (Gebhard); Germany; 1055–57
Stephen IX (Frederick); France; 1057–58
Nicholas II (Gerard); France; 1058–61
Alexander II (Anselmo da Baggio); Milan; 1061–73
St. Gregory VII (Hildebrand); Tuscany; 1073–85
Victor III (Dauferius; Desiderius); Campania; 1086–87
Urban II (Odo of Châtillon-sur-Marne); France; 1088–99
Paschal II or Pascal II (Rainerius); Latium; 1099–1118
Gelasius II (John of Gaeta); Latium; 1118–19
Callistus II or Calixtus II (Guido of Burgundy); France; 1119–24
Honorius II (Lambert Scannabecchi); Emilia-Romagna; 1124–30
Innocent II (Gregory Papareschi); Rome; 1130–43
Celestine II (Guido of Castellis); Ancona; 1143–44
Lucius II (Gerardo Caccianemici); Bologna; 1144–45
Eugene III (Bernard); Pisa; 1145–53
Anastasius IV (Conrad de Suburra); Rome; 1153–54
Adrian IV (Nicholas Breakspear); England; 1154–59
Alexander III (Roland Bandinelli); Siena; 1159–81
Lucius III (Ubaldus Allucingolus); Lucca; 1181–85
Urban III (Uberto Crivelli); Milan; 1185–87
Gregory VIII (Alberto de Morra); Benevento; 2 months, 1187
Clement III (Paolo Scolari); Rome; 1187–91
Celestine III (Giacinto Bobo); Rome; 1191–98
Innocent III (Lothar of Segni); Latium; 1198–1216
Honorius III (Cencio Savelli); Rome; 1216–27
Gregory IX (Hugo, Count of Segni); Latium; 1227–41

Celestine IV (Goffredo Castiglioni); Milan; 2 months, 1241
Innocent IV (Sinibaldo Fieschi); Genoa; 1243–54
Alexander IV (Rainaldo, Count of Segni); Latium; 1254–61
Urban IV (Jacques Pantaléon); France; 1261–64
Clement IV (Guy Fulcodi); France; 1265–68
Gregory X (Tedaldo Visconti); Emilia-Romagna; 1271–76
Innocent V (Peter of Tarentaise); Savoy; 5 months, 1276
Adrian V (Ottobono Fieschi); Genoa; 2 months, 1276
John XXI (Petrus Juliani or Petrus Hispanus); Portugal; 1276–77
Nicholas III (Giovanni Gaetano Orsini); Rome; 1277–80
Martin IV (Simon de Brie); France; 1281–85
Honorius IV (Jacobus Savelli); Rome; 1285–87
Nicholas IV (Girolamo Masci); Ascoli; 1288–92
St. Celestine V (Peter of Morrone); Abruzzi e Molise; 5 months, 1294
Boniface VIII (Benedetto Gaetani); Latium; 1294–1303
Benedict XI (Niccolo Boccasini); Venetia; 1303–04
Clement V (Bertrand de Got); France; 1305–14
John XXII (Jacques Duèse); France; 1316–34
Benedict XII (Jacques Fournier); France; 1334–42
Clement VI (Pierre Roger); France; 1342–52
Innocent VI (Étienne Aubert); France; 1352–62
Urban V (Guillaume de Grimoard); France; 1362–70
Gregory XI (Pierre Roger de Beaufort); France; 1370–78
Urban VI (Bartolomeo Prignano); Naples; 1378–89
Boniface IX (Pietro Tomacelli); Naples; 1389–1404
Innocent VII (Cosimo de' Migliorati); Abruzzi e Molise; 1404–06
Gregory XII (Angelo Correr); Venice; 1406–15
Martin V (Oddo Colonna); Abruzzi; 1417–31
Eugene IV (Gabriel Condulmaro); Venice; 1431–47
Nicholas V (Tommaso Parentucelli); Liguria; 1447–55
Callistus III or Calixtus III (Alfonso Borgia); Spain; 1455–58
Pius II (Enea Silvio Piccolomini); Siena; 1458–64
Paul II (Pietro Barbo); Venice; 1464–71
Sixtus IV (Francesco Della Rovere); Liguria; 1471–84
Innocent VIII (Giovanni Battista Cibo); Genoa; 1484–92
Alexander VI (Rodrigo Borgia); Spain; 1492–1503
Pius III (Francesco Todeschini Piccolomini); Siena; 2 months, 1503
Julius II (Giuliano Della Rovere); Liguria; 1503–13
Leo X (Giovanni de' Medici); Florence; 1513–21
Adrian VI (Adrian Florensz Dedal); Utrecht; 1522–23
Clement VII (Giulio de' Medici); Florence; 1523–34
Paul III (Alessandro Farnese); Rome; 1534–49
Julius III (Giovanni Maria Ciocchi del Monte); Rome; 1550–55
Marcellus II (Marcello Cervini); Siena; 2 months, 1555

Paul IV (Gian Pietro Carafa); Avellino; 1555–59
Pius IV (Giovanni Angelo de' Medici); Milan; 1559–65
St. Pius V (Antonio Ghislieri); Alessandria; 1556–72
Gregory XIII (Ugo Boncompagni); Bologna; 1572–85
Sixtus V (Felice Peretti); Astoli-Piceno; 1585–90
Urban VII (Giovanni Battista Castagna); Rome; one month, 1590
Gregory XIV (Niccolo Sfondrati); Milan; 1590–91
Innocent IX (Giovanni Antonio Facchinetti); Bologna; 2 months, 1591
Clement VIII (Ippolito Aldobrandini); Pesaro e Urbino, 1592–1605
Leo XI (Alessandro de' Medici); Florence; one month, 1605
Paul V (Camillo Borghese); Rome; 1605–21
Gregory XV (Alessandro Ludovisi); Bologna; 1621–23
Urban VIII (Maffeo Barberini); Florence; 1623–44
Innocent X (Giovanni Battista Pamphili); Rome; 1644–55
Alexander VII (Fabio Chigi); Siena; 1655–67
Clement IX (Giulio Rospigliosi); Tuscany; 1667–69
Clement X (Emilio Altieri); Rome; 1670–76
Innocent XI (Benedetto Odescalchi); Lombardy; 1676–89
Alexander VIII (Pietro Vito Ottoboni); Venice; 1689–91
Innocent XII (Antonio Pignatelli); Bari; 1691–1700
Clement XI (Giovanni Francesco Albani); Pesaro e Urbino; 1700–1721
Innocent XIII (Michelangelo dei Conti); Rome; 1721–24
Benedict XIII (Pietro Francesco Orsini); Bari; 1724–30
Clement XII (Lorenzo Corsini); Florence; 1730–40
Benedict XIV (Prospero Lambertini); Bologna; 1740–58
Clement XIII (Carlo Rezzonico); Venice; 1758–69
Clement XIV (Giovanni Vincenzo Antonio Ganganelli); Emilia-Romagna; 1769–74
Pius VI (Giovanni Angelo Braschi); Emilia-Romagna; 1775–99
Pius VII (Barnaba Chiaramonti); Emilia-Romagna; 1800–23
Leo XII (Annibale Della Genga); Spoleto; 1823–29
Pius VIII (Francesco Saverio Castiglioni); Ancona; 1829–30
Gregory XVI (Bartolomeo Alberto-Mauro-Cappellari); Venetia; 1831–46
Pius IX (Giovanni M. Mastai Ferretti); Ancona; 1846–78
Leo XIII (Gioacchino Pecci); Latium; 1878–1903
St. Pius X (Giuseppe Melchiorre Sarto); Treviso; 1903–14
Benedict XV (Giacomo Della Chiesa); Genoa; 1914–22
Pius XI (Achille Ratti); Milan; 1922–39
Pius XII (Eugenio Pacelli); Rome; 1939–58
John XXIII (Angelo Giuseppe Roncalli); Lombardy; 1958–63
Paul VI (Giovanni Battista Montini); Lombardy; 1963–1978
John Paul I (Albino Luciani), Venetia; 34 days, 1978
John Paul II (Karol Wojtyla); Wadowice, Poland; 1978–

---

[a] He was elected during the exile of St. Martin I, who had been banished to Crimea for his condemnation of the Monothelite heresy.
[b] There is confusion about the legitimacy of claims to the pontificate by Leo VIII and Benedict V. John XII was deposed on Dec. 4, 963. If his deposition was invalid, Leo was an antipope. If it was valid, Leo was the legitimate pope, and Benedict was an antipope.
[c] If the triple deposition of Benedict IX (in 1044, in 1046, and again in 1048) was illegitimate, Sylvester III, Gregory VI, and Clement II were antipopes.

CALENDAR OF RELIGIOUS HOLIDAYS: 1980-1981

SOURCE: Yearbook of American and Canadian Churches 1980. © copyright 1980, by the National Council of the Churches of Christ in the United States of America.

1st Sunday in Advent	Nov.	30, 1980
1st Day of Hanukkah	Dec.	3
Christmas	Dec.	25
New Year's Eve (Watch Night)	Dec.	31
New Year's Day	Jan.	1, 1981
Twelfth Night: Epiphany Eve	Jan.	5
Epiphany	Jan.	6
Week of Prayer for Christian Unity (Missionary Day)	Jan.	18 to 25
Presentation of Jesus in the Temple	Feb.	2
Brotherhood Week	Feb.	15 to 22
The Transfiguration	Mar.	1
Ash Wednesday	Mar.	4
1st Sunday in Lent	Mar.	8
Purim	Mar.	20
The Annunciation	Mar.	25
Holy Week	Apr.	12 to 18
Palm Sunday (Passion Sunday)	Apr.	12
Maundy Thursday	Apr.	16
Good Friday	Apr.	17
Easter Eve	Apr.	18
Easter (Latin)	Apr.	19
1st Day of Passover	Apr.	19
Easter (Orthodox)	Apr.	26
May Fellowship Day	May	1
National Family Week	May	3 to 10
Festival of the Christian Home (Mother's Day)	May	10
Rural Life Sunday (Rogation Sunday, 6th after Easter)	May	24
Ascension Day	May	28
Whitsunday (Pentecost)	Jun.	7
1st Day of Shavuot	Jun.	8
Trinity Sunday	Jun.	14
Children's Sunday	Jun.	14
Father's Day	Jun.	21
St-Jean Baptiste Day (Canada)	Jun.	24
The Transfiguration (also last Sunday after Epiphany)	Aug.	6
Labor Sunday	Sep.	6
1st Day of Rosh Hashanah	Sep.	29
World Communion Sunday	Oct.	4
Yom Kippur	Oct.	8
Thanksgiving Day (Canada)	Oct.	12
1st Day of Sukkot	Oct.	13
Shemini Atzeret	Oct.	20
Simhat Torah	Oct.	21
Reformation Sunday	Oct.	25
Reformation Day	Oct.	31
All Saints' Day	Nov.	1
All Souls' Day	Nov.	2
World Community Day	Nov.	6
Stewardship Day	Nov.	8
Bible Sunday	Nov.	15
Thanksgiving Sunday (U.S.)	Nov.	22
Thanksgiving Day (U.S.)	Nov.	26
1st Sunday in Advent	Nov.	29
1st Day of Hanukkah	Dec.	21
Christmas	Dec.	25
New Year's Eve (Watch Night)	Dec.	31

COLLEGE OF CARDINALS

SOURCE: 1981 Catholic Almanac. Data as of June 30, 1980.

The cardinals are bishops chosen by the pope to serve as his principal advisers in the central administration of church affairs; those under the age of 80 are electors of the pope. Collectively, they form the Sacred College of Cardinals.

The college evolved gradually during the first 11 centuries from the synods of Roman clergy. The first cardinals, in about the sixth century, were priests of the leading churches of Rome who assisted the Holy See in directing church affairs.

Name	Office or Dignity	Nationality	Created
Alfrink, Bernard	Former Archbishop of Utrecht	Dutch	1960
Antonelli, Ferdinando		Italian	1973
Aponte Martinez, Luis	Archbishop of San Juan	Puerto Rican	1973
Aramburu, Juan Carlos	Archbishop of Buenos Aires	Argentinian	1976
Arns, Paulo Evaristo	Archbishop of Sao Paolo	Brazilian	1973
Bafile, Corrado	Prefect of Sacred Congregation for Causes of Saints	Italian	1976
Baggio, Sebastiano	Prefect of Sacred Congregation for Bishops	Italian	1969
Ballestrero, Anastasio, O.C.D.	Archbishop of Turin	Italian	1979
Baum, William W.	Prefect of the Congregation for Catholic Education	American	1976
Benelli, Giovanni	Archbishop of Florence	Italian	1977
Beras Rojas, Octavio Antonio	Archbishop of Santo Domingo	Dominican	1976
Bertoli, Paolo	Chamberlain of Holy Roman Church	Italian	1969
Brandao Vilela, Avelar	Archbishop of Sao Salvador	Brazilian	1973
Bueno y Monreal, Jose M.	Archbishop of Seville	Spanish	1958
Caprio, Giuseppe	President of the Administration of the Patrimony of the Apostolic See	Italian	1979
Carberry, John	Former Archbishop of St. Louis	American	1969
Carpino, Francesco	Referendary of Sacred Congregation of Bishops	Italian	1967
Carter, Gerald Emmett	Archbishop of Toronto	Canadian	1979
Casariego, Mario	Archbishop of Guatemala	Guatamalan	1969
Casaroli, Agostino	Secretary of State	Italian	1979
Cé, Marco	Patriarch of Venice	Italian	1979
Ciappi, Mario Luigi	Pro-Theologian of the Pontifical Household	Italian	1977
Civardi, Ernesto	Secretary of the Sacred Congregation for Bishops	Italian	1977
Cody, John P.	Archbishop of Chicago	American	1967
Colombo, Giovanni	Archbishop of Milan	Italian	1965
Confalonieri, Carlo	Dean of College of Cardinals	Italian	1958
Cooke, Terence	Archbishop of New York	American	1969
Cooray, Thomas B.	Former Archbishop of Colombo	Sri Lankan	1965
Cordeiro, Joseph	Archbishop of Karachi	Pakistani	1973
Corripio Ahumada, Ernesto	Archbishop of Mexico City & Primate of Mexico	Mexican	1979
Darmojuwono, Justin	Archbishop of Semarang	Indonesian	1967
De Araujo Sales, Eugenio	Archbishop of Rio de Janeiro	Brazilian	1969
Dearden, John	Archbishop of Detroit	American	1969
de Furstenberg, Maximilien		Dutch	1967
Duval, Leon-Etienne	Archbishop of Algiers	Algerian	1965
Ekandem, Dominic	Bishop of Ikot Ekpene	Nigerian	1976
Enrique y Tarancon, Vicente	Archbishop of Madrid	Spanish	1969
Etchegaray, Roger	Archbishop of Marseilles	French	1979
Felici, Pericle	Prefect Supreme Tribunal of Apostolic Signatura	Italian	1967
Flahiff, George	Archbishop of Winnipeg	Canadian	1969
Florit, Ermenegildo	Former Archbishop of Florence	Italian	1965
Freeman, James Darcy	Archbishop of Sydney	Australian	1973
Gantin, Bernardin	President of Pontifical Commission for Justice and Peace	Beninese	1977
Garrone, Gabriele M.		French	1967
Gonzales Martin, Marcelo	Archbishop of Toledo	Spanish	1973
Gouyon, Paul	Archbishop of Rennes	French	1969
Gray, Gordon	Archbishop of St. Andrews and Edinburgh	Scottish	1969
Guerri, Sergio	Pro-President of the Pontifical Commission for the Vatican City State	Italian	1969
Guyot, Jean	Former Archbishop of Toulouse	French	1973
Hoeffner, Joseph	Archbishop of Cologne	German	1969
Hume, George Basil	Archbishop of Westminster	English	1976
Jubany Arnau, Narcisco	Archbishop of Barcelona	Spanish	1973
Kim Sou Hwan, Stephan	Archbishop of Seoul	Korean	1969
Knox, James	Prefect of Sacred Congregation for the Sacraments and Divine Worship	Australian	1973
Koenig, Franz	Archbishop of Vienna, President of Secretariat for Non-Believers	Austrian	1958
Krol, John	Archbishop of Philadelphia	American	1967
Landazuri Ricketts, Juan	Archbishop of Lima	Peruvian	1962
Leger, Paul	Former Archbishop of Montreal	Canadian	1953
Lekai, Laszlo	Archbishop of Esztergom	Hungarian	1976
Lorscheider, Aloisio	Archbishop of Fortaleza	Brazilian	1976
Macharski, Franciszek	Archbishop of Krakow	Polish	1979
Malula, Joseph	Archbishop of Kinshasa	Zairean	1969

Name	Office or Dignity	Nationality	Created
Manning, Timothy	Archbishop of Los Angeles	American	1973
Marella, Paolo	Sub-Dean of College of Cardinals; Arch-priest of Vatican Basilica	Italian	1959
Marty, François	Archbishop of Paris	French	1969
Maurer, Jose	Archbishop of Sucre	Bolivian	1967
McCann, Owan	Archbishop of Cape Town	South African	1965
Medeiros, Humberto	Archbishop of Boston	American	1973
Miranda y Gomez, Miguel	Former Archbishop of Mexico City	Mexican	1969
Motta, Carlos Carmelo de Vasconcellos	Archbishop of Aparecida	Brazilian	1946
Mozzoni, Umberto	President of Pontifical Commission for Sanctuaries of Pompei and Loreto	Italian	1973
Munoz Duque, Anibal	Archbishop of Bogota	Colombian	1973
Munoz Vega, Pablo	Archbishop of Quito	Ecuadorian	
Nasalli Rocca di Corneliano, Mario		Italian	1969
Nsubuga, Emmanuel	Archbishop of Kampala	Ugandan	1976
O'Boyle, Patrick	Former Archbishop of Washington	American	1967
Oddi, Silvio	Prefect of the Sacred Congregation for the Clergy	Italian	1969
O'Fiaich, Tomas	Archbishop of Armagh	Irish	1979
Otunga, Maurice	Archbishop of Nairobi	Kenyan	1973
Palazzini, Pietro		Italian	1973
Pappalardo, Salvatore	Archbishop of Palermo	Italian	1973
Parecattil, Joseph	Archbishop of Ernakulam	Indian	1969
Parente, Pietro		Italian	1967
Paupini, Giuseppe	Major Penitentiary	Italian	1969
Pellegrino, Michele	Former Archbishop of Turin	Italian	1967
Philippe, Paul	Prefect of Sacred Congregation for Oriental Churches	French	1973
Picachy, Lawrence Trevor	Archbishop of Calcutta	Indian	1976
Pironio, Eduardo	Prefect of Sacred Congregation for Religious and Secular Institutes	Argentinian	1976
Poletti, Ugo	Vicar General of Rome	Italian	1973
Poma, Antonio	Archbishop of Bologna	Italian	1969
Primatesta, Raul	Archbishop of Cordoba	Argentinian	1973
Quintero, Jose	Archbishop of Caracas	Venezuelan	1961
Ratzinger, Joseph	Archbishop of Munich and Freising	German	1977
Razafimahatrata, Victor	Archbishop of Tananarive	Madagascan	1976
Renard, Alexandre	Archbishop of Lyons	French	1967
Ribeiro, Antonio	Patriarch of Lisbon	Portuguese	1973
Righi-Lambertini, Egano		Italian	1979
Rosales, Julio	Archbishop of Cebu	Filipino	1969
Rossi, Agnelo	Prefect of the Sacred Congregation for the Evangelization of Peoples	Brazilian	1965
Rossi, Opilio	President of Pontifical Council for Laity and Committee for the Family	Italian	1976
Roy, Maurice	Archbishop of Québec	Canadian	1965
Rubin, Wladislaw		Polish	1979
Rugambwa, Laurean	Archbishop of Dar-es-Salaam	Tanzanian	1960
Salazar Lopez, Jose	Archbishop of Guadalajara	Mexican	1973
Samore, Antonio	Librarian and Archivist of Holy Roman Church	Italian	1967
Satowaki, Joseph Asajiro	Archbishop of Nagasaki	Japanese	1979
Scherer, Alfredo	Archbishop of Porto Alegre	Brazilian	1969
Schröffer, Joseph		German	1976
Sensi, Giuseppe M.		Italian	1976
Seper, Franjo	Prefect of Sacred Congregation for Doctrine of Faith	Yugoslavian	1965
Shehan, Lawrence	Former Archbishop of Baltimore	American	1965
Sidarouss, Stephanos	Coptic Patriarch of Alexandria	Egyptian	1965
Silva Henriquez, Raul	Archbishop of Santiago	Chilean	1962
Sin, Jaime L.	Archbishop of Manila	Filipino	1976
Siri, Giuseppe	Archbishop of Genoa	Italian	1953
Slipyj, Josyf	Archbishop of Lwow	Ukrainian	1965
Suenens, Leo	Former Archbishop of Mechelen-Brussels	Belgian	1962
Taofinu'u, Pius	Bishop of Samoa and Tokelau	Samoan	1973
Thiandoum, Hyacinthe	Archbishop of Dakar	Senegalese	1976
Tomasek, Frantisek	Archbishop of Prague	Czech	1976
Trinh-Van-Can, Joseph-Marie	Archbishop of Hanoi	Vietnamese	1979
Ursi, Corrado	Archbishop of Naples	Italian	1967
Vagnozzi, Egidio	President of the Prefecture of the Holy See's Economic Affairs	Italian	1967
Volk, Hermann	Bishop of Mainz	German	1973
Willebrands, Johannes	Archbishop of Utrecht, President of the Secretariat for the Union of Churches	Dutch	1969
Wyszynski, Stefan	Archbishop of Gniezno and Warsaw	Polish	1953
Zoungrana, Paul	Archbishop of Ouagadougou	Upper Voltese	1965

*Cardinal installed "in pectore" (in his breast only) by Pope John Paul II, 7/1/79.

U.S. RELIGIOUS BODIES

SOURCE: *Yearbook of American and Canadian Churches 1980*, edited by Constant H. Jacquet, Jr. Copyright © 1980, by the National Council of the Churches of Christ in the United States of America.

This directory of American religious denominations includes only those with a membership of 50,000 or more. Membership and other data are for 1978-79 unless otherwise noted.

African Methodist Episcopal Church This church began (1787) in Philadelphia when members of St. George's Methodist Episcopal Church withdrew as a protest against color segregation. In 1816 the denomination was started, led by Rev. Richard Allen. Membership: 1,970,000; Gen. Sec., Dr. Richard A. Chappelle, Sr., P.O. Box 183, St. Louis, MO 63166

African Methodist Episcopal Zion Church The A.M.E. Zion Church is an independent body, having withdrawn (1796) from the John Street Methodist Church of New York City. Membership: 1,093,001; Gen. Sec., Herman L. Anderson, P.O. Box 32843, Charlotte, NC 28232

American Baptist Association A fellowship of regular and independent missionary Baptist churches distributed throughout the United States, with their greatest strength in the South. Their national fellowship was formed in 1905. Membership: 1,500,000; Headquarters: 4605 N. State Line Ave., Texarkana, TX 75501

American Baptist Churches in the U.S.A. Formerly known as the Northern Baptist Convention, this body of Baptist churches changed the name to American Baptist Convention at the annual meeting in Boston, May 24, 1950. In 1972 the present name was adopted. Membership: 1,304,088 (1977); Headquarters: Valley Forge, PA 19481

The American Carpatho-Russian Orthodox Greek Catholic Church This body is a self-governing diocese that is in communion with the Ecumenical Patriarchate of Constantinople. In 1938 the late Patriarch Benjamin I canonized the Diocese in the name of the Orthodox Church of Christ. Membership: 100,000 (1976); Headquarters: Johnstown, PA 15906

The American Lutheran Church This body was organized during a constituting convention at Minneapolis, MN, April 22-24, 1960. It combined the following three church bodies: American Lutheran Church (ALC), the Evangelical Lutheran Church (ELC), and United Evangelical Lutheran Church (UELC). The union brought together major Lutheran church bodies of different national heritage–German (ALC), Norwegian (ELC), Danish (UELC). Headquarters of the new church were established (January 1, 1961) at Minneapolis. On Feb. 1, 1963, the Lutheran Free Church (LFC) merged with the American Lutheran Church. Membership: 2,377,235; Headquarters: 422 S. 5th St., Minneapolis, MN 55415

The Antiochian Orthodox Christian Archdiocese of North America In 1975 the Antiochian Orthodox Christian Archdiocèse of New York and All North America merged with the Antiochian Orthodox Archdiocese of Toledo, Ohio and Dependencies in N.A. under this name. Formerly the Syrian Antiochian Orthodox Archdiocese of New York and N.A., this body is a member of the Orthodox Church under the jurisdiction of the Patriarch of Antioch. Membership: 152,000 (1977); Headquarters: 358 Mountain Rd., Englewood, NJ 07631

Apostolic Overcoming Holy Church of God A black body incorporated (1919) in Alabama. It is evangelistic in purpose and emphasizes sanctification, holiness, and divine healing. Membership: 75,000 (1956); Sec., Mrs. Juanita Arrington, 909 Jasper Rd., West, Birmingham, AL 35204

Armenian Apostolic Church of America This church was under the jurisdiction of the Etchmiadzin See (now in Soviet Armenia) from 1887 to 1933, when a division occurred over the church's condition in Soviet Armenia. One group remained independent until 1957 when it came under the jurisdiction of the Holy See of Cilicia in Lebanon. Membership: 125,000 (1972); Headquarters: 138 E. 39th St., New York, NY 10016

Armenian Church of America, Diocese of the (Including Diocese of California) The American branch of the ancient Church of Armenia was established in America in 1889. Diocesan organization is under the jurisdiction of the Holy See of Etchmiadzin, Armenia, USSR. Membership: 326,500; Diocesan offices: 630 Second Ave., New York, NY 10016

Assemblies of God An evangelical missionary fellowship which grew out of the Pentecostal revivals at the turn of this century. The organization is composed of self-governing churches which constitute 55 districts and seven foreign language branches. The founding meetings of the denomination were held (1914) in Hot Springs, AR. Membership: 1,293,394; Headquarters: 1445 Boonville Ave., Springfield, MO 65802

Baptist General Conference This body has operated as a Conference since 1879; its first church was organized in 1852. It has a ministry through 752 churches and six boards of operation. Membership: 219,697; Headquarters: 1233 Central St., Evanston, IL 60201

Baptist Missionary Associaton of America A group of regular Baptist churches organized in associational capacity in Little Rock (1950) as North American Baptist Association. Name changed (1969) to Baptist Missionary Association of America. There are several state and numerous local associations of cooperating churches. In theology these churches are evangelical, missionary, fundamental, and in the main premillennial. Membership: 218,361; Rec. Sec.: Rev. Ralph Cottrell, P.O. Box 2866, Texarkana, AK 75501

Buddhist Churches of America Organized in 1914 as the Buddhist Mission of North America, this body was incorporated in 1942 under the present name and represents the Jodo Shinshu Sect of Buddhism in this country. Membership: 60,000 (1975); Headquarters: 1710 Octavia St., San Francisco, CA 94109

Bulgarian Eastern Orthodox Church (Diocese of N. & S. America and Australia) The Holy Synod of the Bulgarian Eastern Orthodox Church established for its Bulgarian Christians in North and South America and Australia a Bulgarian Orthodox church in 1907, which became (1938) Episcopate and was officially incorporated (1947) in New York State. Membership: 86,000 (1971); Headquarters: NY Diocese, 312 W. 101st St., New York, NY 10025

The Christian and Missionary Alliance An evangelical, evangelistic, and missionary movement, organized (1887) by Rev. A.B. Simpson, in New York. It stresses "the deeper Christian life and consecration to the Lord's service." Membership: 158,218; Headquarters: 350 N. Highland Ave., Nyack, NY 10960

Christian Church (Disciples of Christ) Started on the American frontier at the beginning of the 19th century as a movement to unify Christians, this body drew its major inspiration from Thomas and Alexander Campbell in western Pennsylvania and Barton W. Stone in Kentucky. Developing separately the "Disciples," under Alexander Campbell and the "Christians," led by Stone, merged in Lexington, Ky., in 1832. Membership: 1,231,817; Headquarters: 222 S. Downey Ave., Box 1986, Indianapolis, IN 46206

Christian Churches and Churches of Christ The fellowship has its origins in the American movement to "restore the New Testament church in doctrine, ordinances and life" initiated by Thomas and Alexander Campbell, Walter Scott and Barton W. Stone in the early 1800's. Membership: 1,054,266; no general organization.

The Christian Congregation, Inc. Original incorporation, March 10, 1887; revised incorporation, October 29, 1898. The New Commandment, John 13:34-35, is the bond of fellowship in creative ethical activism. Membership: 81,604; Gen. Supt.: Rev. Ora W. Eads, 804 W. Hemlock St., LaFollette, TN 37766

Christian Methodist Episcopal Church In 1870 the General Conference of the M.E. Church, South, approved the request of its colored membership for the formation of a separate ecclesiastical body, which became the Colored Methodist Episcopal Church. The Christian Methodist Episcopal Church became the official name on January 3, 1956. Membership: 466,718 (1965); Sec., Rev. N. Charles Thomas, P.O. Box 74, Memphis, TN 38101

Christian Reformed Church in North America A group of Dutch Calvinists that dissented (1857) from the Reformed Church in America and was strengthened by later accessions from the same source and by immigration. Doctrines: The Heidelberg Catechism (1563), the Canons of Dort (1618-19), and the Belgic Confession (1561). Membership: 211,302; Office Address: 2850 Kalamazoo Ave. S.E., Grand Rapids, MI 49560

The Church of Christ, Scientist (Christian Scientists) The Church of Christ, Scientist was founded in 1879 when Mrs. Mary Baker Eddy and 15 students met and voted to "organize a church designed to commemorate the word and works of our Master, which should reinstate primitive Christianity and its lost element of healing." Membership: not given; Headquarters: Christian Science Church Center, Boston, MA 02115

The Church of God This body was inaugurated by Bishop A.J. Tomlinson, who served (1903-43) as General Overseer, and many groups of the Pentecostal and Holiness Movement stem from it. It is episcopal in administration, evangelical in doctrines of justification by faith, sanctification as a second work of grace, and of the baptism of the Holy Ghost, speaking with other tongues, miracles of healing. Membership: 75,890; Headquarters: 2504 Arrow Wood Drive, S.E., Huntsville, AL 35803

Church of God (Anderson, IN) This body is one of the largest of the groups that have taken the name "Church of God." It originated about 1880 and emphasizes Christian unity. Membership: 175,753; Headquarters: Box 2420, Anderson, IN 46011

Church of God (Cleveland, TN) America's oldest Pentecostal church began (1886) as an outgrowth of the holiness revival under the name Christian Union. Reorganized (1902) as the Holiness Church, the church adopted (1907) the name Church of God. Its doctrine is fundamental and Pentecostal; it maintains a centralized form of government and a missionary program. Membership: 392,551; Headquarters: Keith St. at 25th NW, Cleveland, TN 37311

The Church of God in Christ Organized in Arkansas in 1895 by Charles Harrison Mason and incorporated in 1897. Membership: 425,000 (1965); Headquarters: 938 Mason St., Memphis, TN 38126

The Church of God in Christ, International Organized in 1969 in Kansas City, MO, by 14 bishops of the Church of God in Christ of Memphis, TN. The doctrine is the same, but the separation came because of a disagreement over polity and governmental authority. Membership: 501,000 (1971); Headquarters: 170 Adelphi St., Brooklyn, NY 11025

The Church of God of Prophecy Organized in 1886 at Barney Creek Meeting House, Monroe Co., TN, and reorganized in 1902 at Camp Creek, NC, this church formally adopted the name Church of God (1907), but since 1952 the name Church of God of Prophecy has been used for secular purposes and in order to avoid confusion with other similarly named organizations. Membership: 65,801 (1975); Headquarters: Bible Place, Cleveland, TN 37311

The Church of Jesus Christ of Latter-Day Saints (Mormons) was organized (April 6, 1830) at Fayette, NY, by Joseph Smith. Its members consider the Bible, Book of Mormon, Doctrine and Covenants, and the Pearl of Great Price to be the word of God. Their belief is summed up in 13 Articles of Faith written by Joseph Smith. Membership: 2,592,000; Headquarters: 50 East North Temple St., Salt Lake City, UT 84111

Church of the Brethren German pietists-anabaptists founded (1708) under Alexander Mack, Schwarzenau, Germany, entered the colonies in 1719 and settled at Germantown, PA. They have no creed other than the New Testament, hold to principles of nonviolence, temperance, and voluntarism, and emphasize religion in life. Membership: 175,335; Headquarters: Church of the Brethren General Offices, 1451 Dundee Ave., Elgin, IL 60120

Church of the Nazarene One of the larger holiness bodies, it was organized (1908) in Pilot Point, TX. It is in general accord with the early doctrines of Methodism and emphasizes entire sanctification as a second definite work of grace. Membership: 462,724; Headquarters: 6401 The Paseo, Kansas City, MO 64131

Churches of Christ This body is made up of a large group of churches, formerly reported with the Disciples of Christ but reported separately since the Religious Census (1906). They are strictly congregational and have no organization larger than the local congregation. Membership: 3,000,000

Community Churches, National Council of The result of a 1950 merger between the all-black Biennial Council of Community Churches and an association of white churches with the same name as the present body, the NCCC is a non-creedal fellowship of theologically ecumenical Protestant churches with congregational self-government. Membership: 190,000; National Office: 89 E. Wilson Bridge Rd., Worthington, OH 43085

Congregational Christian Churches, National Association of Organized (1955) in Detroit by delegates from Congregational Christian Churches committed to continuing the Congregational way of faith and order in church life. It has no doctrinal requirements. Participation by member churches is voluntary. Membership: 95,000; Headquarters: P.O. Box 1620, Oak Creek, WI 53154

Conservative Baptist Association of America Organized (May 17, 1947) at Atlantic City, N.J., the association regards the Old and New Testaments as the divinely inspired Word of God and as infallible and of supreme authority. Each local church is independent and autonomous. Membership: 300,000 (1977); Headquarters: Geneva Rd., P.O. Box 66, Wheaton, IL 60187

Cumberland Presbyterian Church An outgrowth of the Great Revival of 1800, the Cumberland Presbytery was organized on February 4, 1810, in Dickson County, Tenn., by three Presbyterian ministers, Revs. Finis Ewing, Samuel King, and Samuel McAdow. Membership: 93,268; Headquarters: Box 4149, Memphis, TN 38104

The Episcopal Church This body entered the colonies with the earliest settlers (Jamestown, Va., 1607) as the Church of England. It became autonomous and adopted its present name in 1789. It is an integral part of the Anglican Communion. In 1967 the General Convention adopted "The Episcopal Church" as an alternate name for the Protestant Episcopal Church in the United States. Membership: 2,815,359; Headquarters: 815 Second Ave., New York, NY 10017

ACTIVE EPISCOPAL BISHOPS IN THE U.S.

Note: MB, Missionary Bishop; Address: Right Reverend

Headquarters Staff: Presiding Bishop, John M. Allin; Exec. Vice-Pres., Milton L. Wood; Exec. for Mission and Ministry, Richard B. Martin; Suffragan Bishop for the Armed Forces, Charles L. Burgreen; 815 Second Ave., New York, NY 10017

Alabama: Furman C. Stough, 521 N. 20th St., Birmingham, AL 35203

Alaska: David E. Cochran, Box 441, Fairbanks, AK 99707

Albany: Wilbur E. Hogg, 62 S. Swan St., Albany, NY 12210

Arizona: Joseph T. Heistand, 110 W. Roosevelt St., Phoenix, AZ 85003

Arkansas: Christoph Keller, 300 W. 17th St., P.O. Box 6120, Little Rock, AR 72206

Atlanta: Bennett J. Sims, 2744 Peachtree Rd. NW, Atlanta, GA 30305

Bethlehem: Lloyd E. Gressle, 826 Delaware Ave., Bethlehem, PA 18015

California: C. Kilmer Myers, 1055 Taylor St., San Francisco, CA 94108

Central Florida: William H. Folwell, 324 N. Interlachen Ave., Box 790, Winter Park, FL 32789

Central Gulf Coast: George M. Murray, 3809 Old Shell Rd., P.O. Box 8395, Mobile, AL 36608

Central New York: Ned Cole, Jr., 310 Montgomery St., Syracuse, NY 13203

Central Pennsylvania: Dean T. Stevenson, 221 N. Front St., Harrisburg 17101, P.O. Box W, Harrisburg, PA 17108

Chicago: James W. Montgomery, 65 E. Huron St., Chicago, IL 60611

Colorado: William C. Frey, Box M, Capitol Hill Sta., Denver, CO 80218

Connecticut: Morgan Porteus, 1335 Asylum Ave., Hartford, CT 06105

Dallas: A. Donald Davies, 1630 Garrett St., Dallas, TX 75206

Delaware: William Hawley Clark, 2020 Tatnall St., Wilmington, DE 19802

East Carolina: Hunley A. Elebash, 305 S. 3rd St., Wilmington, NC 28401

Eastern Oregon: William B. Spofford, Jr., 1336 W. Glacier, Redmond, OR 97756

Easton: Moultrie Moore, Box 1027, Easton, MD 21601

Eau Claire: Stanley H. Atkins, 510 S. Farwell St., Eau Claire, WI 54701

Erie: Donald J. Davis, 145 W. 6th St., Erie, PA 16501

Florida: Frank S. Cerveny, 325 Market St., Jacksonville, FL 32202

Fond du Lac: William H. Brady, Box 149, Fond du Lac, WI 54935

Georgia: G. Paul Reeves, 611 E. Bay St., Savannah, GA 31401

Hawaii: Edmond L. Browning, Queen Emma Square, Honolulu, HI 96813

Idaho: Hanford L. King, Jr., Box 936, Boise, ID 83701

Indianapolis: Edward W. Jones, 1100 W. 42nd St., Indianapolis, IN 46208

Iowa: Walter C. Righter, 225 37th St., Des Moines, IA 50312

Kansas: Edward C. Turner, Bethany Pl., Topeka, KS 66612

Kentucky: David B. Reed, 421 S. 2nd St., Louisville, KY 40202

Lexington: Addison Hosea, 530 Sayre Ave., Lexington, KY 40508

Long Island: Robert Campbell Witcher, 36 Cathedral Ave., Garden City, NY 11530

Los Angeles: Robert C. Rusack, 1220 W. 4th St., Los Angeles, CA 90017

Louisiana: James Barrow Brown, P.O. Box 15719, New Orleans, LA 70175

Maine: Frederick B. Wolf, 143 State St., Portland, ME 04101

Maryland: David Leighton, Sr., 105 W. Monument St., Baltimore, MD 21230

Massachusetts: John B. Coburn, 1 Joy St., Boston, MA 02108

Michigan: H. Coleman McGehee, Jr., 4800 Woodward Ave., Detroit, MI 48201

Milwaukee: Charles T. Gaskell, 804 E. Juneau Ave., Milwaukee, WI 53202

Minnesota: Robert M. Anderson, 309 Clifton Ave., Minneapolis, MN 55403

Mississippi: Duncan M. Gray, Jr., P.O. Box 1636, Jackson, MS 39205

Missouri: William Augustus Jones, Jr., 1210 Locust St., St. Louis, MO 63103

Montana: Jackson E. Gilliam, 303 Horsky Block, Helena, MT 59601

Nebraska: James Daniel Warner, 200 N. 62nd St., Omaha, NB 68132

Nevada: Wesley Frensdorff, 2930 W. 7th St., Reno, NV 89503

Newark: John Shelby Spong, 24 Rector St., Newark, NJ 07102

New Hampshire: Philip A. Smith, 63 Green St., Concord, NH 03301

New Jersey: Albert W. Van Duzer, 808 W. State St., Trenton, NJ 08618

New York: Paul Moore, Jr., 1047 Amsterdam Ave., New York, NY 10025

North Carolina: Thomas A. Fraser, Jr., 20 St. Alban's, P.O. Box 17025, Raleigh, NC 27609

North Dakota: Harold A. Hopkins, Jr., 809 8th Ave., S., Fargo, ND 58102

Northern California: John L. Thompson III, 1322 27th St., P.O. Box 161268, Sacramento, CA 95816

Northern Indiana: William C.R. Sheridan, 117 N. Lafayette Blvd., South Bend, IN 46601

Northern Michigan: William Arthur Dimmick, 131 E. Ridge St., Marquette, MI 49855

Northwest Texas: Willis R. Henton, Texas Commerce Bank Bldg., Ste. 506, 1314 Ave. K, P.O. Box 1067, Lubbock, TX 79408

Ohio: John H. Burt, 2230 Euclid Ave., Cleveland, OH 44115

Oklahoma: Gerald N. McAllister, P.O. Box 1098, Oklahoma City, OK 73101

Olympia: Robert H. Cochrane, 1551 Tenth Ave., E., Seattle, WA 98102

Oregon: Matthew P. Bigliardi, 11800 S.W. Military La., Portland 97219, P.O. Box 467, Portland, OR 97034

Panama: Lemuel B. Shirley (MB), Box R, Balboa, Panama

Pennsylvania: Lyman C. Ogilby, 1700 Market St., Ste. 1600, Philadelphia, PA 19103

Pittsburgh: Robert B. Appleyard, 325 Oliver Ave., Pittsburgh, PA 15222

Puerto Rico: Francisco Reus-Froylán (MB), P.O. Box C, Saint Just, PR 00750

Quincy: Donald J. Parsons, 3601 N. North St., Peoria, IL 61604

Rhode Island: George Hunt, 275 N. Main St., Providence, RI 02903

Rio Grande: Richard M. Trelease, Jr., 120 Vassar S.E., Ste. 1-B, P.O. Box 4130, Albuquerque, NM 87106

Rochester: Robert R. Spears, Jr., 935 East Ave., Rochester, NY 14607

San Diego: Robert M. Wolterstorff, St. Paul's Church, 2728 6th Ave., San Diego, CA 92103

San Joaquin: Victor M. Rivera, 4159 East Dakota, Fresno, CA 93726

South Carolina: Gray Temple, 1020 King St., Drawer 2127, Charleston, SC 29403

South Dakota: Walter H. Jones, 200 W. 18th St., P.O. Box 517, Sioux Falls, SD 57101

Southeast Florida: Calvin O. Schofield, Jr., 525 NE 15th St., Miami, FL 33132

Southern Ohio: William G. Black, 412 Sycamore St., Cincinnati, OH 45202

Southern Virginia: Claude Charles Vaché, 600 Talbot Hill Rd., Norfolk, VA 23505

Southwest Florida: Emerson Paul Hayes, P.O. Box 20899, St. Petersburg, FL 33742

Southwestern Virginia: A. Heath Light, P.O. Box 2068, Roanoke, VA 24009

Spokane: Leigh Allen Wallace, Jr., 245 E. 13th Ave., Spokane, WA 99202

Springfield: Albert W. Hillestad, 821 S. 2nd St., Springfield, IL 62704

Tennessee: William E. Sanders, Box 3807, Knoxville, TN 37917

Texas: Milton Richardson, 520 San Jacinto St., Houston, TX 77002

Upper South Carolina: William A. Beckham, P.O. Box 1789, Columbia, SC 29202

Utah: E. Otis Charles, 231 E. First St. South, Salt Lake City, UT 84111

Vermont: Robert S. Kerr, Rock Point, Burlington, VT 05401

Virgin Islands: Edward M. Turner (MB), P.O. Box 1589, St. Thomas, U.S. VI 00801

Virginia: Robert B. Hall, 110 W. Franklin St., Richmond, VA 23220

Washington: John T. Walker, Mt. St. Alban, Washington, DC 20016

West Missouri: Arthur Vogel, 415 W. 13th St., P.O. Box 23216, Kansas City, MO 64141

West Texas: Scott Field Bailey, P.O. Box 6885, San Antonio, TX 78209

West Virginia: Robert P. Atkinson, 1608 Virginia St. E., Charleston, WV 25311

Western Kansas: William Davidson, 142 S. 8th St., P.O. Box 1383, Salina, KS 67401

Western Massachusetts: Alexander D. Stewart, 37 Chestnut St., Springfield, MA 01103

Western Michigan: Charles E. Bennison, 2600 Vincent Ave., Kalamazoo, MI 49001

Western New York: Harold B. Robinson, 1114 Delaware Ave., Buffalo, NY 14209

Western North Carolina: William G. Weinhauer, P.O. Box 368, Black Mountain, NC 28711

Wyoming: Bob Gordon Jones, 104 S. 4th St., Box 1007, Laramie, WY 82070

The Evangelical Covenant Church of America This church has its roots in historical Christianity. It emerged in the Protestant Reformation, the Biblical instruction of the Lutheran State Church of Sweden, and the spiritual awakenings of the 19th century. The denomination was organized (1885) in Chicago; prior to 1957 it was named the Evangelical Mission Covenant Church of America. Membership: 74,678; Headquarters: 5101 N. Francisco Ave., Chicago, IL 60625

The Evangelical Free Church of America Organized in Boone, Iowa, in the 1880s, as the Swedish Evangelical Free Mission. The Evangelical Free Church Association merged (June 1950) with this group, and the merged body is known as The Evangelical Free Church of America. Membership: 100,000 (1977); Headquarters: 1515 E. 66th St., Minneapolis, MN 55423

Evangelical Lutheran Churches, Association of Organized in Chicago at a December 3-4, 1976, meeting of regional synods of former affiliates to the Missouri Synod and several independent congregations, the AELC is doctrinally conservative and adheres to traditionalist Lutheran creeds and emphasizes Biblical fundamentalism and evangelical service. Membership: 106,684; Headquarters: 12015 Manchester Rd., St. Louis, MO 63131

Free Methodist Church of North America This body grew out of a movement in the Genesee Conference of the Methodist Epsicopal Church, about 1850, toward a more original Methodism. It was organized in 1860. Membership: 73,294; Headquarters: 901 College Ave., Winona Lake, IN 46590

Free Will Baptists This evangelical group of Arminian Baptists was organized (1727) by Paul Palmer in N.C. Another similar movement (teaching the same doctrines of free grace, free will, and free salvation) was organized (1780) in N.H. The northern line merged with the Northern Baptist Convention in 1911. It was reorganized (1935) as the National Association of Free Will Baptists in Nashville, Tenn. Membership: 216,831; National Offices: 1134 Murfreesboro Rd., Nashville, TN 37217

Friends United Meeting (The Five Years Meeting of Friends) This body was formed (1902) by 11 Yearly Meetings entering into a loose confederation. Since that time two of the original Yearly Meetings have withdrawn (Kansas and Oregon), and two American Yearly Meetings and three Yearly Meetings outside the United States have joined. It now consists of 15 Yearly Meetings. In 1965 the name was changed to Friends United Meeting. Membership: 62,080; Presiding Clerk, Walter Schutt, 101 Quaker Hill Dr., Richmond, IN 47374

General Association of Regular Baptist Churches Founded (May 1932) in Chicago by a group of churches that had withdrawn from the Northern Baptist Convention (now the American Baptist Churches in the U.S.A.) because of doctrinal differences. Its Confession of Faith, which it requires all churches to subscribe to, is the old, historic New Hampshire Confession of Faith with a premillennial ending applied to the last article. Membership: 240,000; Headquarters: 1300 N. Meacham Rd., Schaumburg, IL 60195

General Baptists (General Association of) An Arminian group of Baptists first organized (1607) by John Smyth and Thomas Helwys in England, and transplanted to the colonies in 1714. It died out along the seaboard, but was revived (1823) in the Midwest by Rev. Benoni Stinson. Membership: 72,030 (1977); Exec. Sec., Rev. Glen O. Spence, Box 537, Poplar Bluff, MO 63901

Greek Orthodox Archdiocese of North and South America Greek-speaking Orthodox Christians have parishes in the United States, Canada, and Central and South America, which are under the jurisdiction of the Ecumenical Patriarchate of Constantinople (Istanbul). Membership: 1,950,000 (1977); Headquarters: 8-10 E. 79th St., New York, NY 10021

Independent Fundamental Churches of America Organized (1930) at Cicero, Ill., by representatives of various independent churches. Membership: 87,582; Headquarters: 1860 Mannheim Rd., P.O. Box 250, Westchester, IL 60153

International Church of the Foursquare Gospel An evangelistic missionary body organized (1927) by Aimee Semple McPherson. The parent church is Angelus Temple in Los Angeles, organized (1923) with mission stations and meeting places in 30 foreign countries. Membership: 89,215 (1963); Headquarters: Angelus Temple, 1100 Glendale Blvd., Los Angeles, CA 90026

Jehovah's Witnesses It is the belief of Jehovah's Witnesses that they adhere to the oldest religion on earth: the worship of Almighty God revealed in his Bible as Jehovah. All of Jehovah's Witnesses are considered to be ministers of the gospel and have no human leader. Their Yearbook shows them active (1978) in 205 countries, where there are approximately 2,182,341 ministers preaching and teaching the people of all nations that God's word is true and that their only hope is in the Kingdom of Jehovah under Christ Jesus, which has been established to rule over earth and replace all governments. There are 7,526 churches and 519,218 ministers in the United States. Headquarters: 124 Columbia Heights, Brooklyn, NY 11201

Jewish Congregations Jews arrived in the colonies before 1650. The first congregation is recorded (1654) in New York City, the Shearith Israel (Remnant of Israel). Membership of Jewish congregations in the U.S.: 5,781,000

CONGREGATIONAL AND RABBINICAL ORGANIZATIONS

*Union of American Hebrew Congregations (Reform): 838 Fifth Ave., New York, NY 10021; Pres., Rabbi Alexander M. Schindler

*United Synagogue of America (Conservative): 155 Fifth Ave., New York, NY 10010; Pres., Simon Schwartz; Exec. Vice Pres., Rabbi Benjamin Kreitman

*Union of Orthodox Jewish Congregations of America: 116 E. 27th St., New York, NY 10016; Pres. Julius Berman; Exec. Vice Pres., Rabbi Pinchas Stolper

*Central Conference of American Rabbis (Reform): 790 Madison Ave., New York, NY 10021; Pres., Rabbi Jerome R. Malino; Exec. Vice-Pres., Rabbi Joseph B. Glaser

Rabbinical Alliance of America (Orthodox): 156 Fifth Ave., New York, NY 10011; Pres. Rabbi David B. Hollander

*The Rabbinical Assembly (Conservative): 3080 Broadway, New York, NY 10027; Pres., Saul I. Teplitz; Exec. Vice-Pres., Rabbi Wolfe Kelman

*Rabbinical Council of America, Inc. (Orthodox): 1250 Broadway, New York, NY 10003; Pres., Berard Rosenweig; Exec. Vice-Pres., Rabbi Israel Klavan

Union of Orthodox Rabbis of the United States and Canada: 235 E. Broadway, New York, NY 10002; Pres., Rabbi Moshe Feinstein, Chpsn., Rabbi Symcha Elberg

*Synagogue Council of America: 432 Park Ave., S., New York, NY 10016; Pres., Rabbi Arthur J. Lelyveld; Exec. Vice-Pres., Rabbi Bernard Mandelbaum

*Synagogue Council of America is the coordinating body of the organizations starred above

Lutheran Church in America This body was organized (1962) by consolidation of the American Evangelical Lutheran Church (1874); the Augustana Evangelical Lutheran Church (1860); the Finnish Evangelical Lutheran Church (1890); and the United Lutheran Church in America (1918). The new body began to function formally on January 1, 1963. Membership: 2,942,002; Headquarters: 231 Madison Ave., New York, NY 10016

The Lutheran Church—Missouri Synod This body, second largest Lutheran church in America, was organized (1847) and holds to an unwavering confessionalism coupled with a strong outreach in ministry. It is the leader in the conservative Lutheran group. Membership: 2,631,374; Headquarters: 500 N. Broadway, St. Louis, MO 63102

Mennonite Church The largest group of the Mennonites who began arriving in the U.S. as early as 1683, settled in Germantown, Pa., and derives their name from Menno Simons, their outstanding leader, b. 1496. Membership: 97,142; General Office: 528 E. Madison St., Lombard, IL 60148

Moravian Church in America (Unitas Fratrum) In 1735 Moravian missionaries of the pre-Reformation faith of John Hus came to Gerogia, in 1740 to Pennsylvania, and in 1753 to North Carolina. They established the Moravian Church, which is broadly evangelical, liturgical, with an episcopacy as a spiritual office and in form of government "conferential." NORTHERN PROVINCE: Headquarters: 69 W. Church St., P.O. Box 1245, Bethlehem, PA 18018; Membership: 32,519. SOUTHERN PROVINCE: Headquarters: 459 S. Church St., Winston-Salem, NC 27108; Membership: 21,002

National Baptist Convention of America This is the "unincorporated" body of National Baptists. Organized in 1880. Membership: 2,668,799 (1956); Corr. Sec., Albert E. Chew, 2823 N. Houston, Ft. Worth, TX 76106

National Baptist Convention, U.S.A., Inc. The older and parent convention of black Baptists, this body is to be distinguished from the National Baptist Convention of America, usually referred to as the "unincorporated" body. Membership: 5,500,000 (1958); Pres., Rev. J.H. Jackson, 405 E. 31st St., Chicago, IL 60616

National Primitive Baptist Convention, Inc. A group of Baptists having associations, state conventions, and a National Convention (organized 1907). Membership: 250,000 (1975); Headquarters: P.O. Box 2355, Tallahassee, FL 32304

North American Old Roman Catholic Church A body with the doctrine of the Old Catholics in right and succession of Catholic orders. Knott Missal used for Masses. Pontificale used for all Order Rights. Not under Papal jurisdiction. Membership: 67,314; Presiding Archbishop of the Americas and Canada: Most Rev. John E. Schweikert, 4200 N. Kedvale Ave., Chicago, IL 60641

Open Bible Standard Churches, Inc. An evangelical, full gospel denomination emphasizing evangelism, missions, and the message of the Open Bible. Originally composed of two separate groups, namely Bible Standard Churches and Open Bible Evangelistic Association, a merger took place July 26, 1935, and the name Open Bible Standard Churches, Inc., was adopted. Membership: 60,000; Headquarters: 2020 Bell Ave., Des Moines, IA 50315

The Orthodox Church in America The Russian Orthodox Greek Catholic Church of America entered Alaska in 1792 before its purchase by the United States in 1867. Its canonical status of independence (autocephaly) was granted by its Mother Church, the Russian Orthodox Church, on April 10, 1970. Membership: 1,000,000; Sec. to the Metropolitan: Serge Troubetzkoy, P.O. Box 675, Syosset, NY 11791

Pentecostal Church of God Organized (1919) at Chicago, the first convention was held in October, 1933. Membership: 110,670 (1977); Headquarters: Messenger Plaza, 211 Main St., Joplin, MO 64801

Pentecostal Holiness Church, International This body grew out of the holiness movement (1895-1900) in the South and Middle West. It is premillennial in belief, emphasizes Christian perfection as taught by John Wesley, and believes in the Pentecostal baptism with the Holy Spirit, accompanied by glossolalia. Membership: 86,103 (1977); Headquarters: P.O. Box 12609, Oklahoma City, OK 73157

Plymouth Brethren (Christian Brethren) An orthodox and evangelical movement to unite Christians from various denominations which began in the British Isles in the 1820's. In the 1840's the movement divided. The smaller "Exclusive branch" stresses the interdependency of congregations. The "Open Independence" branch stresses congregational independence. Membership: 74,000; No general organization.

Polish National Catholic Church of America After a long period of dissatisfaction with Roman Cathoic administration and ideology, accompanied by a strong desire for religious freedom, this body was organized in 1897. Membership: 282,411 (1960); Headquarters: 529 E. Locust St., Scranton, PA 18505

Presbyterian Church in America This body was formed December 4-7, 1973, in Birmingham, Ala., as the result of an act of separation from the Presbyterian Church in the U.S. The PCA has the intent of restoring purity of faith and practice and is committed to the Reformed Faith as set forth in the Westminster Confession and Catechisms. Membership: 82,095; Stated Clk., Rev. Morton H. Smith, P.O. Box 312, Brevard, NC 28712

Presbyterian Church in the U.S. This body is a branch of the Presbyterian Church established (1861) in separate existence. Membership: 862,416; Office of the General Assembly: 341 Ponce de Leon Ave. NE, Atlanta, GA 30308

Primitive Baptists A large group of Baptists, located mainly in the South, who are opposed to all centralization and to modern missionary societies. Membership: 72,000 (1960); Headquarters: Cayce Publ. Co., S. Second St., Thornton, AR 71766

Progressive National Baptist Convention, Inc. This body held its organizational meeting at Cincinnati (1961). The first annual session was held in Philadelphia (1962). Membership: 521,692 (1967); Gen. Sec., Dr. S.S. Hodges, 601 50th St. NE, Washington DC 20019

Reformed Church in America This body was established (1628) by the earliest Dutch settlers of New York as the Reformed Protestant Dutch Church. It is evangelical in theology, Presbyterian in government, and has 898 churches. Membership: 348,080; National Office: 475 Riverside Drive, New York, NY 10027

Reorganized Church of Jesus Christ of Latter Day Saints A division among the Latter-Day Saints occurred on the death (1844) of Joseph Smith, Jr. His son, Joseph Smith III, became presiding officer of this group, which has established headquarters at Independence, Mo. Membership: 185,636; Headquarters: The Auditorium, P.O. Box 1059, Independence, MO 64051

The Roman Catholic Church The largest single body of Christians in the United States, the Roman Catholic Church is under the spiritual leadership of His Holiness the Pope. Its establishment in America dates back to the priests who accompanied Columbus on his second voyage to the New World. A settlement, later discontinued, was made at St. Augustine, Fla. The continuous history of this Church began (1634) at St. Mary's, in Maryland. Membership: 49,812,178. The following information has been furnished by the editor of The Official Catholic Directory for 1979, published by P.J. Kenedy & Sons, P.O. Box 729, New York, NY 10150

VISIBLE HEAD OF THE CHURCH

His Holiness the Pope, Bishop of Rome, Vicar of Jesus Christ, Successor of St. Peter, Prince of the Apostles, Supreme Pontiff of the Universal Church, Patriarch of the West, Primate of Italy, Archbishop and Metropolitan of the Roman Province and Sovereign of Vatican City. ROMAN CATHOLIC HIERARCHY: Supreme Pontiff, His Holiness Pope John Paul II. APOSTOLIC DELEGATE IN THE UNITED STATES: Most Rev. Jean Jadot, 3339 Massachusetts Ave. NW, Washington, DC 20008

BISHOPS AND ARCHBISHOPS

Archdiocese of Anchorage, Alaska—Most Rev. Francis T. Hurley; Diocese of Fairbanks, Alaska—Most Rev. Robert L. Whelan; Diocese of Juneau, Alaska—Most Rev. Michael H. Kenny.

Archdiocese of Atlanta, GA—Most Rev. Thomas A. Donnellan; Diocese of Charlotte, NC—Most Rev. Michael J. Begley; Diocese of Charleston, SC—Most Rev. Ernest L. Unterkoefler; Diocese of Raleigh, NC—Most Rev. F. Joseph Gossman; Diocese of Savannah, GA—Most Rev. Raymond W. Lessard.

Archdiocese of Baltimore, MD—Most Rev. William D. Borders; Diocese of Arlington, VA—Most Rev. Thomas J. Welsh; Diocese of Richmond, VA—Most Rev. Walter F. Sullivan; Diocese of Wheeling-Charleston, WV—Most Rev. Joseph H. Hodges; Diocese of Wilmington, DE—Most Rev. Thomas J. Mardaga.

Archdiocese of Boston, MA—His Eminence Humberto Cardinal Medeiros; Diocese of Burlington, VT—Most Rev. John A. Marshall; Diocese of Fall River, MA—Most Rev. Daniel A. Cronin; Diocese of Manchester, NH—Most Rev. Odore J. Gendron; Diocese of Portland, ME—Most Rev. Edward C. O'Leary; Diocese of Springfield, MA—Most Rev. Joseph F. Maguire; Diocese of Worcester, MA—Most Rev. Bernard J. Flanagan.

Archdiocese of Chicago, IL—His Eminence John Cardinal Cody; Diocese of Belleville, IL—Most Rev. William M. Cosgrove; Diocese of Joliet, IL—Most Rev. Stanley G. Schlarman; Diocese of Peoria, IL—Most Rev. Edward W. O'Rourke; Diocese of Rockford, IL—Most Rev. Arthur J. O'Neill; Diocese of Springfield, IL—Most Rev. Joseph A. McNicholas.

Archdiocese of Cincinnati, OH—Most Rev. Joseph L. Bernadin; Diocese of Cleveland, OH—Vacant; Diocese of Columbus, OH—Most Rev. Edward J. Herrmann; Diocese of Steubenville, OH—Most Rev. Albert H. Ottenweller; Diocese of Toledo, OH—Most Rev. John A. Donovan; Diocese of Youngstown, OH—Most Rev. James W. Malone.

Archdiocese of Denver, CO—Most Rev. James V. Casey; Diocese of Cheyenne, WY—Most Rev. Joseph H. Hart; Diocese of Pueblo, CO—Vacant.

Archdiocese of Detroit, MI—Vacant; Diocese of Gaylord, MI—Most Rev. Edmund C. Szoka; Diocese of Grand Rapids, MI—Most Rev. Joseph M. Breitenbeck; Diocese of Kalamazoo, MI—Most Rev. Paul V. Donovan; Diocese of Lansing, MI—Most Rev. Kenneth J. Povish; Diocese of Marquette, MI—Most Rev. Mark F. Schmitt; Diocese of Saginaw, MI—Most Rev. Francis F. Reh.

Archdiocese of Dubuque, IA–Most Rev. James J. Byrne; Diocese of Davenport, IA–Most Rev. Gerald F. O'Keefe; Diocese of Des Moines, IA–Most Rev. Maurice J. Dingman; Diocese of Sioux City, IA–Most Rev. Frank H. Greteman.

Archdiocese of Hartford, CT–Most Rev. John F. Whealon; Diocese of Bridgeport, CT–Most Rev. Walter W. Curtis; Diocese of Norwich, CT–Most Rev. Daniel P. Reilly; Diocese of Providence, RI–Most Rev. Louis E. Gelineau.

Archdiocese of Indianapolis, IN–Most Rev. Edward T. O'Meara; Diocese of Evansville, IN–Most Rev. Francis R. Shea; Diocese of Fort Wayne-South Bend, IN–Most Rev. William E. McManus; Diocese of Gary, IN–Most Rev. Andrew G. Grutka; Diocese of Lafayette in Indiana, IN–Most Rev. Raymond J. Gallagher.

Archdiocese of Kansas City, KS–Most Rev. Ignatius J. Strecker; Diocese of Dodge City, KS–Most Rev. Eugene J. Gerber; Diocese of Salina, KS–Most Rev. Daniel Kucera; Diocese of Wichita, KS–Most Rev. David M. Maloney.

Archdiocese of Los Angeles, CA–His Eminence Timothy Cardinal Manning; Diocese of Fresno, CA–Most Rev. Hugh A. Donohoe; Diocese of Monterey, CA–Most Rev. Harry A. Clinch; Diocese of Orange, CA–Most Rev. William R. Johnson; Diocese of San Bernardino, CA–Most Rev. Phillip F. Stralina; Diocese of San Diego, CA–Most Rev. Leo T. Maher.

Archdiocese of Louisville, KY–Most Rev. Thomas J. McDonough; Diocese of Covington, KY–Most Rev. William A. Hughes; Diocese of Memphis, TN–Most Rev. Carroll T. Dozier; Diocese of Nashville, TN–Most Rev. James D. Niedergeses; Diocese of Owensboro, KY–Most Rev. Henry Soenneker.

Archdiocese of Miami, FL–Most Rev. Edward A. McCarthy; Diocese of Orlando, FL–Most Rev. Thomas J. Grady; Diocese of Pensacola-Tallahassee, FL–Most Rev. Rene H. Gracida; Diocese of St. Augustine, FL–Most Rev. John J. Snyder; Diocese of St. Petersburg, FL–Vacant

Archdiocese of Milwaukee, WI–Most Rev. Rembert G. Weakland, O.S.B.; Diocese of Green Bay, WI–Most Rev. Aloysius J. Wycislo; Diocese of La Crosse, WI–Most Rev. Frederick W. Freking; Diocese of Madison, WI–Most Rev. Cletus F. O'Donnell; Diocese of Superior, WI–Most Rev. George A. Hammes.

Archdiocese of Mobile, AL—Most Rev. Oscar Lipscomb; Diocese of Birmingham, AL–Most Rev. Joseph G. Vath; Diocese of Biloxi, MS–Most Rev. Joseph Lawson Howse; Diocese of Jackson, MS–Most Rev. Joseph B. Brunini.

Archdiocese of Newark, NJ–Most Rev. Peter L. Gerety; Diocese of Camden, NJ–Most Rev. George H. Guilfoyle; Diocese of Paterson, NJ–Most Rev. Frank J. Rodimer; Diocese of Trenton, NJ–Most Rev. John C. Reiss.

Archdiocese of New Orleans, LA–Most Rev. Philip M. Hannan; Diocese of Alexandria-Shreveport, LA–Most Rev. Lawrence P. Graves; Diocese of Baton Rouge, LA–Most Rev. Joseph V. Sullivan; Diocese of Houma-Thibodaux, LA–Most Rev. Warren L. Boudreaux; Diocese of Lafayette, LA–Most Rev. Gerard L. Frey.

Archdiocese of New York, NY–His Eminence Terence Cardinal Cooke; Diocese of Albany, NY–Most Rev. Howard J. Hubbard; Diocese of Brooklyn, NY–Most Rev. Francis J. Mugavero; Diocese of Buffalo, NY–Most Rev. Edward D. Head; Diocese of Ogdensburg, NY–Most Rev. Stanislaus J. Brzana; Diocese of Rochester, NY–Most Rev. Matthew H. Clark Diocese of Rockville Centre, NY–Most Rev. John R. McGann; Diocese of Syracuse, NY–Most Rev. Frank J. Harrison; Military Vicariate–His Eminence Terence Cardinal Cooke.

Archdiocese of Oklahoma City, OK–Most Rev. Charles A. Salatka; Diocese of Little Rock, AR–Most Rev. Andrew J. McDonald; Diocese of Tulsa, OK–Most Rev. Eusebius Beltran.

Archdiocese of Omaha, NB–Most Rev. Daniel E. Sheehan; Diocese of Grand Island, NB–Most Rev. Lawrence J. McNamara; Diocese of Lincoln, NB–Most Rev. Glennon P. Flavin.

Archdiocese of Philadelphia, PA–His Eminence John Cardinal Krol; Diocese of Allentown, PA–Most Rev. Joseph McShea; Diocese of Altoona-Johnstown, PA–Most Rev. James J. Hogan; Diocese of Erie, PA–Most Rev. Alfred M. Watson; Diocese of Greensburg, PA–Most Rev. William G. Connare; Diocese of Harrisburg, PA–Most Rev. Joseph T. Daley; Diocese of Pittsburgh, PA–Most Rev. Vincent M. Leonard; Diocese of Scranton, PA–Most Rev. J. Carroll McCormick.

Archdiocese of Portland, OR–Most Rev. Cornelius M. Power; Diocese of Baker, OR–Most Rev. Thomas J. Connolly; Diocese of Boise, ID–Most Rev. Sylvester W. Treinen; Diocese of Great Falls, MT–Most Rev. Thomas J. Murphy; Diocese of Helena, MT–Most Rev. Elden F. Curtiss.

Archdiocese of St. Louis, MO–Most Rev. John L. May; Diocese of Jefferson City, MO–Most Rev. Michael F. McAuliffe; Diocese of Kansas City-St. Joseph, MO–Most Rev. John J. Sullivan; Diocese of Springfield-Cape Girardeau, MO–Most Rev. Bernard F. Law.

Archdiocese of St. Paul and Minneapolis, MN–Most Rev. John R. Roach; Diocese of Bismarck, ND–Most Rev. Hilary B. Hacker; Diocese of Crookston, MN–Most Rev. Victor H. Balke; Diocese of Duluth, MN–Most Rev. Paul F. Anderson; Diocese of Fargo, ND–Most Rev. Justin A. Driscoll; Diocese of New Ulm, MN–Most Rev. Raymond A. Lucker; Diocese of Rapid City, SD–Most Rev. Harold J. Dimmerling; Diocese of St. Cloud, MN–Most Rev. George H. Speltz; Diocese of Sioux Falls, SD–Most Rev. Paul V. Dudley; Diocese of Winona, MN–Most Rev. Loras J. Watters.

Archdiocese of San Antonio, TX–Most Rev. Patrick F. Flores; Diocese of Amarillo, TX–Most Rev. Leroy T. Matthiesen; Diocese of Austin, TX–Most Rev. Vincent M. Harris; Diocese of Beaumont, TX–Most Rev. Bernard J. Ganter; Diocese of Brownsville, TX–Most Rev. John J. Fitzpatrick; Diocese of Corpus Christi, TX–Most Rev. Thomas J. Drury; Diocese of Dallas, TX–Most Rev. Thomas Tschoepe; Diocese of Fort Worth, TX–Most Rev. John J. Cassata; Diocese of Galveston-Houston, TX–Most Rev. John L. Morkovsky; Diocese of San Angelo, TX–Most Rev. Joseph A. Florenza.

Archdiocese of San Francisco, CA–Most Rev. John R. Quinn; Diocese of Agana, Guam–Most Rev. Felixberto C. Flores; Diocese of Honolulu, HI–Most Rev. John J. Scanlan; Diocese of Oakland, CA–Most Rev. John S. Cummins; Diocese of Reno-Las Vegas, NV–Most Rev. Norman F. McFarland; Diocese of Sacramento, CA–Most Rev. Francis A. Quinn; Diocese of Salt Lake City, UT–Most Rev. William K. Weigand; Diocese of Santa Rosa, CA–Most Rev. Mark J. Hurley; Diocese of Stockton, CA–Most Rev. Merlin J. Guilfoyle.

Archdiocese of Santa Fe, NM–Most Rev. Robert F. Sanchez; Diocese of El Paso, TX–Most Rev. Raymond J. Tena; Diocese of Gallup, NM–Most Rev. Jerome J. Hastrich; Diocese of Phoenix, AZ–Most Rev. James S. Rausch; Diocese of Tucson, AZ–Most Rev. Francis J. Green.

Archdiocese of Seattle, WA–Most Rev. Raymond G. Hunthausen; Diocese of Spokane, WA–Most Rev. Lawrence H. Welsh; Diocese of Yakima, WA–Most Rev. William S. Skylstad.

Archdiocese of Washington, DC–Most Rev. James A. Hickey; Prelature of the Virgin Islands–Most Rev. Edward J. Harper, C.SS.R.

Archeparchy (Byzantine) of Philadelphia, PA–Most Rev. Myroslav J. Lubachivsky; Eparchy of St. Nicholas in Chicago, IL–Most Rev. Jaroslav Gabro; Diocese of Stamford, CT–Vacant.

Archdiocese of Pittsburgh, PA–Most Rev. Stephen Kociske; Eparchy of Parma, OH–Most Rev. Emil Mihalik; Eparchy of Passaic, NJ–Most Rev. Michael J. Dudick.

MARONITES

Dioceses of St. Maron, Brooklyn, NY–Most Rev. Francis Zayek.

MELKITES

Exarchy for the Melkites, West Newton, MA–Most Rev. Joseph Tawil.

Russian Orthodox Church in the U.S.A., Patriarchal Parishes of the This autonomous body is the direct canonical successor of the Orthodox Catholic mission established (1793) in Alaska by the Russian Orthodox Church and is under the spiritual jurisdiction of the Patriarch of Moscow and All Russia. Membership: 51,500 (1975); Headquarters: St. Nicholas Patriarchal Cathedral, 15 E. 97th St., New York, NY 10029

The Russian Orthodox Church Outside Russia (Formerly The Russian Orthodox Church Abroad) This body was organized (1920) to unite the missions and parishes of

the Russian Orthodox Church outside of Russia. The governing body was set up in Constantinople; in November 1950, it came to the United States. This church emphasizes being true to the old traditions of the Russian Church, but it does not compromise with official church leaders in Moscow "since that would amount to being under the influence and direction of a godless State." Membership: 55,000 (1955); Headquarters: 75 E. 93rd St., New York, NY 10028

The Salvation Army An international religious & charitable organization with a military government, first set up (1865) by General William Booth in England and introduced (1880) into America. Membership: 414,035; National Headquarters: 120-130 W. 14th St., New York, NY 10011

Serbian Eastern Orthodox Church for the U.S.A. and Canada Membership: 65,000 (1967); Chancery: St. Sava Monastery, P.O. Box 519, Libertyville, IL 60048

Seventh-day Adventists This Protestant body developed out of an interdenomination movement that appeared in the early 19th century, stressing the imminence of the Second Advent of Christ. Seventh-day Adventists were not formally organized until 1863. Taking the Bible as their sole rule of faith and practice, they are evangelical, holding to the full inspiration of the Scriptures and the deity of Christ. They believe in the personal, imminent, and premillennial return of Christ, and in the observance of the seventh day as the Sabbath. Membership: 535,705; Headquarters: 6840 Eastern Ave. NW, Washington, DC 20012

Southern Baptist Convention Southern Baptists withdrew (1845) from the General Missionary Convention, when in 1845, Baptists in Northern states resolved to exclude slaveholders from missionary ranks, and formed the Southern Baptist Convention, the largest U.S. Protestant denomination. Membership: 13,191,394; Executive Committee Offices: 460 James Robertson Pkwy., Nashville, TN 37219

Triumph the Church and Kingdom of God in Christ (International) The Triumph Church, as this body is more commonly known, was founded in 1902. It was incorporated in Washington, DC, in 1918. Membership: 54,307 (1972); National Headquarters: 213 Farrington Ave., Atlanta, GA 30318

Ukrainian Orthodox Church in the U.S.A. This body was formally organized in the United States in 1919. Archbishop John Theodorovich arrived from Ukraine in 1924. Membership: 87,745 (1966); Headquarters: South Bound Brook, NJ 08880

Unitarian Universalist Association This association is the consolidated body of the former American Unitarian Association and the Universalist Church of America. The Unitarian movement arose in Congregationalism in the 18th century and produced (1825) the American Unitarian Association. In 1865 a national conference was organized. The philosophy of Universalism originated with the doctrine of universal salvation in the first century, and was brought to America in the 1700s. Universalists were first formally organized in 1793. In 1961 the Unitarian and Universalist bodies were consolidated to become the present association. The movement is non-creedal. Membership: 136,207; Pres., Dr. O. Eugene Pickett; Headquarters: 25 Beacon St., Boston, MA 02108

United Church of Christ This body results from a union (1957) of the Evangelical and Reformed Church and the General Council of the Congregational Christian Churches. The union was completed (1961) when the constitution was adopted in Philadelphia. Membership: 1,769,104; Headquarters: 105 Madison Ave., New York, NY 10016

The United Free Will Baptist Church A body that was organized in 1870. Membership: 100,000 (1952); Headquarters: Kinston College, 1000 University St., Kinston, NC 28501

The United Methodist Church The church was formed (1968) in Dallas by the union of The Methodist Church and The Evangelical United Brethren Church, which shared a common historical and spiritual heritage. The Methodist movement began in 18th-century England under John Wesley, but the Christmas Conference of 1784 in Baltimore is the date on which the organized Methodist Church was founded. It was there that Francis Asbury was elected the first bishop in this country. The Evangelical United Brethren Church was formed (1946) with the merger of the Evangelical Church and the Church of the United Brethren in Christ, both of which began in Pennsylvania in the evangelistic movement of the 18th and early 19th centuries. Membership: 9,731,779; Sec. of Gen. Conference, Dr. John B. Holt, Perkins School of Theology, Southern Methodist University, Dallas, TX 75222

METHODIST BISHOPS IN U.S.

Allen, L. Scott, Charlotte, NC; Alton, Ralph T., Indianapolis, IN; Ammons, Edsel A., Detroit, MI; Armstrong, A. James, Aberdeen, SD; Ault, James M., Valley Forge, PA; Blackburn, Robert M., Raleigh, NC; Bryan, Monk, Lincoln, NE; Cannon, William R., Atlanta, GA; Carleton, Alsie H., Albuquerque, NM; Carroll, Edward G., Boston, MA; Choy, Wilbur W.Y., Seattle, WA; Clymer, Wayne K., Minneapolis, MN; Crutchfield, Finis A., Houston, TX; DeWitt, Jesse R., Sun Prairie, WI; Dixon, Ernest T., Topeka, KS; Finger, H. Ellis, Jr., Knoxville, TN; Golden, Charles F., Los Angeles, CA; Goodrich, Robert E., Jr., St. Louis, MO; Goodson, W. Kenneth, Richmond, VA; Hicks, Kenneth W., Little Rock, AR; Hodapp, Leroy C., Springfield, IL; Hunt, Earl G., Jr., Nashville, TN; Loder, Dwight E., Columbus, OH; Lovern, J. Chess, San Antonio, TX; Mathews, James K., Washington, DC; McDavid, Joel D., Lakeland, FL; Milhouse, Paul W., Oklahoma City, OK; Nichols, Roy C., Pittsburgh, PA; Robertson, Frank L., Louisville, KY; Sanders, Carl J., Birmingham, AL; Shamblin, J. Kenneth, New Orleans, LA; Stokes, Mack B., Jackson, MS; Stowe, W. McFerrin, Dallas, TX; Stuart, R. Marvin, San Francisco, CA; Thomas, James S., Canton, OH; Tuell, Jack M., Portland, OR; Tullis, Edward L., Columbia, SC; Ward, W. Ralph, Rye, NY; Warman, John B., Harrisburg, PA; Washburn, Paul A., Chicago, IL; Webb, Lance, Des Moines, IA; Wertz, D. Frederick, Charleston, WV; Wheatley, Melvin E., Jr., Denver, CO; White, C. Dale, Princeton, NJ; Yeakel, Joseph H., Syracuse, NY

United Pentecostal Church International Pentecostal Church, Inc., and Pentecostal Assemblies of Jesus Christ merged (1945) at St. Louis. Membership: 450,000; Headquarters: 8855 Dunn Rd., Hazelwood, MO 63042

The United Presbyterian Church in the United States of America The United Presbyterian Church of North America and The Presbyterian Church in the U.S.A. united at a General Assembly in Pittsburgh, Pa. in 1958. The moderator is the presiding officer of the General Assembly, the supreme governing body. The Presbyterian Church in the United States of America dated from the first Presbytery organized (1706) in Philadelphia. The United Presbyterian Church of North America was formed (1858) when the Associate Reformed Presbyterian Church and the Associate Presbyterian Church united. Membership: 2,520,367; Headquarters: Office of the General Assembly: 475 Riverside Dr., Rm. 1201, New York, NY 10027

The Wesleyan Church This body orginated through the uniting of the Pilgrim Holiness Church (1897) and The Wesleyan Methodist Church of America (1943) at a merging conference held in June 1968. It emphasizes Scriptural truth concerning the new birth, the entire sanctification of believers, and the personal return of Christ. Membership: 99,016; Headquarters: P.O. Box 2000, Marion, IN 46952

Wisconsin Evangelical Lutheran Synod This body was organized (1850) in Wisconsin and subscribes to the confessional writings of the Lutheran Church. Membership: 402,972; Pres., Rev. Carl H. Mischke, 3512 W. North Ave., Milwaukee, WI 53208

DISASTERS/CATASTROPHES

MAJOR DISASTERS

This list encompasses both natural disasters and such "technological" catastrophes as rail and aircraft crashes (50 or more deaths), shipwrecks (200 or more deaths), and mine accidents (50 or more deaths). Some other calamities that resulted in fewer fatalities are also cited because of their recentness and/or significance. The list is worldwide in scope.

Year	Type of Disaster	Place	Remarks
64 A.D.	Fire	Rome	Fire destroyed most of Rome; Christians were blamed and executed as arsonists
79 A.D.	Volcanic eruption	Pompeii and Herculaneum, Italy	Mount Vesuvius erupted, destroying both cities; more than 2,000 dead
80 A.D.	Epidemic	Rome	Anthrax killed thousands
250–265	Epidemic	Roman Empire	Bubonic plague killed thousands
444	Epidemic	Great Britain	Bubonic plague claimed thousands
526	Earthquake	Antioch, Syria	Shock results killed 250,000 (?)
542	Epidemic	Roman Empire	Bubonic plague killed tens of thousands
558	Epidemic	Europe, Asia, and Africa	Bubonic plague and smallpox pandemic killed millions; 5,000–10,000 died daily in Constantinople
681	Earthquake	Tosa, Japan	Three-square-mile area submerged
740–744	Epidemic	Constantinople	Bubonic plague killed 200,000 (?)
772	Epidemic	Chichester, England	Disease killed 34,000 (?)
856	Earthquake	Corinth, Greece	Disaster killed 45,000 (?)
869	Earthquake	Sanriku coast, Japan	Shock followed by tidal wave; thousands killed
954	Epidemic	Scotland	Bubonic plague killed 40,000 (?)
1038	Earthquake	Shansi, China	Recorded deaths: 23,000
1057	Earthquake	Chihli, China	Earthquake killed 25,000 (?)
1228	Flood	Friesland, Holland	Killed 100,000 (?)
1290	Earthquake	Chihli, China	September 27; 100,000 (?) victims
1293	Earthquake	Kamakura, Japan	May 20; 30,000 (?) lives lost
1340s	Epidemic	Asia and Europe	"The Black Death," bubonic plague pandemic, is said to have killed 25 million
1361	Earthquake	Kotyi, Japan	Thousands killed by quakes
1382–85	Epidemic	Ireland	Bubonic plague claimed thousands
1407	Epidemic	London	Bubonic plague killed 30,000 (?)
1456	Earthquake	Naples	December 5; 30,000–40,000 killed
1491	Fire	Dresden	City almost destroyed
1499–1500	Epidemic	London	Bubonic plague and other scourges killed 30,000 (?)
1528	Epidemic	Italy	July; typhus killed 21,000 (?)
1531	Earthquake	Lisbon	January 26; 30,000 (?) killed
1545	Epidemic	Cuba	Typhus killed 250,000 (?)
1556	Earthquake	Shensi Province, China	January 24; quake killed more than 800,000, the largest number of fatalities from one earthquake in recorded history
1560	Epidemic	Brazil	Smallpox killed several million
1603	Epidemic	London	Bubonic plague killed more than 30,000
1618	Epidemic	Naples	Diphtheria fatal for 8,000 (?)
1624	Fire	Oslo	City destroyed
1625	Epidemic	London	Bubonic plague claimed 35,000
1628	Epidemic	Lyons, France	Typhus killed 60,000 (?)
1631	Volcanic eruption	southern Italy	Mount Vesuvius erupted, followed by earthquake and tidal wave; more than 4,000 dead
1642	Flood	China	Fatalities: 300,000 (?)
1665	Epidemic	London	Bubonic plague killed more than 70,000
1666	Fire	London	September 2–6; "The Great Fire" destroyed about 14,000 buildings, leaving 200,000 homeless
1669	Volcanic eruption	Catania, Italy	Mt. Etna erupted, killing 20,000 (?)
1672	Epidemic	Lyons, France	Bubonic plague killed 60,000 (?)
	Epidemic	Naples	In six months bubonic plague claimed 400,000 (?)
1693	Earthquake	Catania, Italy	January 11; 60,000 died
1694	Fire	Warwick, England	Destroyed more than half of city
1703	Storm	England	November 26–27; "Great Storm" killed 8,000 (?)
	Earthquake	Tokyo	December 30; earthquake killed 200,000 (?)
1711	Epidemic	Germany and Austria	Bubonic plague; more than 500,000 fatalities
	Marine	Egg Island, Labrador	August 23; 8 English transports wrecked; 900 (?) deaths
1716	Earthquake	Algiers	Earthquake killed 20,000 (?)
1720	Epidemic	Marseilles	Bubonic plague killed 50,000–60,000
1728	Fire	Copenhagen	City nearly destroyed
1737	Cyclone	Calcutta	October 7–11; earthquake followed tornado, killing 300,000 (?)
1741	Epidemic	Cadiz, Spain	Yellow fever fatal for 10,000 (?)
1752	Fire	Moscow	Destroyed about 18,000 houses
1755	Earthquake	Lisbon	November 1; quake, fire, and tidal waves killed 60,000 (?)
1759	Earthquake	Baalbek, Lebanon	October 30; death toll: 30,000
1783	Earthquake	southern Italy and Sicily	February 5–March 28; a series of six quakes claimed 50,000 (?)
	Volcanic eruption	Iceland	June 8; Mount Skaptar erupted, killing one fifth of the population
1787	Flood	eastern India	Storm drove seas 20 miles inland; 10,000 (?) fatalities
1792	Earthquake	Hizen, Japan	Earthquake killed 15,000 (?)
	Epidemic	Egypt	Bubonic plague; 800,000 (?) victims
1793	Epidemic	Philadelphia	Yellow fever killed 5,000 (?)
1797	Earthquake	Cuzco, Peru and Quito, Ecuador	February 4; quake killed 40,000 (?)

Year	Type of Disaster	Place	Remarks
1800	Epidemic	Spain	Yellow fever claimed 80,000 (?)
1802	Epidemic	Santo Domingo	Yellow fever killed 29,000 (?) of Napoleon's soldiers
1810	Epidemic	Cadiz and Barcelona, Spain	Yellow fever fatal for 25,000 (?)
1815	Volcanic eruption	Sumbawa Island, Indonesia	April 5; Tamboro erupted, followed by whirlwinds and tidal waves; 12,000 (?) fatalities
1816–19	Epidemic	Ireland	Typhus lessened population by one fourth
1822	Earthquake	Aleppo, Syria	September 5; quake claimed 22,000 (?) victims
1826–37	Epidemic	continental Europe	Cholera pandemic killed millions; 900,000 (?) Europeans died in 1831 alone
1828	Earthquake	Echigo, Japan	December 28; quake killed 30,000 (?)
1831	Marine	off Cape May, New Jersey	July 9; immigrant vessel **Lady Sherbrooke** sank; 263 dead
1833	Marine	in the Atlantic between England and Quebec	May 11; **Lady of the Lake** struck iceberg; 215 dead
1834	Fire	London	October 16; Houses of Parliament and part of city burned
1835	Fire	New York City	December 16; 700 buildings destroyed; damage: $20 million
1840–62	Epidemic	worldwide	Cholera pandemic claimed millions
1841	Earthquake	Shinano, Japan	Quake killed 12,000 (?)
1842	Fire	Hamburg, Germany	May 4–7; much of the city destroyed; damage: $35 million
1845–48	Famine	Ireland	Potato crop failure; over 750,000 died of starvation and hundreds of thousands left the country
1846	Fire	Quebec	June 12; theater burned; 200 (?) dead
1847–48	Epidemic	London	Influenza killed 15,000 (?)
1849	Fire	St. Louis	May 17; 15 blocks of the city destroyed; damage: $3.5 million
1850	Marine	off Margate, England	March 29; **Royal Adelaide** wrecked; 400 (?) lost
1851–55	Epidemic	England	Tuberculosis killed an average of 51,000 a year
1852	Marine	off South Africa	February 26; British troopship **Birkenhead** wrecked; 454 dead
1853	Marine	off Scotland	September 29; immigrant ship **Annie Jane** wrecked; 348 dead
1854	Marine	in the Atlantic between London and Philadelphia	March; **City of Glasgow** vanished; 450 lost
	Marine	in the Atlantic near Grand Banks	September 27; U.S.S. **Arctic** sank; 350 (?) dead
	Marine	off New Jersey coast	November 13; immigrant ship **New Era** wrecked; more than 300 dead
1855	Mine	Coalfield, Virginia	Coal mine exploded; 55 dead
1856	Rail	near Philadelphia	July 17; train wrecked; 66 fatalities
	Hurricane	Ile Dernière, Louisiana	August 10–11; tropical storm destroyed the island, killing more than 400
1857	Blizzard	U.S. eastern seaboard	January 17–19; this violent storm caused widespread damage
	Marine	in the Atlantic between New York and Havana	September 12; **Central America** sank; 400 (?) dead
1858	Marine	in the Atlantic between Hamburg and New York City	September 13; **Austria** burned; 471 dead
1859	Marine	off Ireland	April 27; **Pomona** wrecked; 400 (?) lost
	Marine	in the Irish Sea	October 25; **Royal Charter** wrecked; 450 (?) dead
1860	Marine	on Lake Michigan	September 8; excursion steamer **Lady Elgin** and lumbership **Augusta** collided; 300 (?) dead
1863	Epidemic	England	Scarlet fever killed more than 30,000
	Fire	Santiago, Chile	December 8; Church of Campania burned, killing over 2,000
1863–75	Epidemic	worldwide	Cholera pandemic; in 1866 Prussia lost 120,000 (?) and Austria, 110,000
1864	Rail	near St. Hilaire, Canada	June 29; train ran through open switch; 90 (?) dead
	Rail	near Shohola, Pennsylvania	July 15; two-train collision; 65 dead
	Cyclone	Calcutta	October 1; most of city destroyed by storm; 70,000 (?) dead
1865	Marine	Memphis, Tennessee	April 27; river streamer **Sultana** exploded and sank; 1,400 (?) dead
1866	Fire	Portland, Maine	July 4; city almost destroyed by fire; damage: $10 million
	Fire	Quebec	October 13; about 2,500 buildings destroyed
1867	Mine	Winterpock, Virginia	April 3; coal mines exploded, killing 69
	Marine	St. Thomas, West Indies	October 29; **Rhone, Wye,** and many small vessels wrecked in storm; 1,000 (?) dead
1868	Earthquake	Peru and Ecuador	August 13–15; quake killed 25,000 (?); damage: $300 million
1869	Mine	Plymouth, Pennsylvania	September 6; coal mine fire killed 110
1870	Marine	off Finistère, France	September 6; English warship **Captain** foundered; 472 fatalities
1871	Fire	Chicago	October 8–9; 3.5 sq. miles destroyed and 250 (?) dead from "Mrs. O'Leary's cow kicking over lantern"; damage $200 million
	Fire	Michigan and Wisconsin	October 8–14; more than 1 million acres of forest consumed; 1,000 (?) dead, mostly in Peshtigo, Wis.
1872	Fire	Boston	November 9–11; more than 600 buildings burned; damage: $75 million
	Marine	in the Atlantic	About November 25; Nova Scotian **Mary Celeste** abandoned; 10 lost
1873	Marine	off Nova Scotia	April 1; British steamer **Atlantic** wrecked; 481 dead
1875	Earthquake	Venezuela and Colombia	May 16; quake killed 16,000 (?)
1876	Cyclone	Bakarganj, India	October 31; storm and subsequent wave killed 200,000 (?)
	Fire	Brooklyn, New York	December 5; Conway's Theater burned; 300 (?) dead
	Rail	Ashtabula River, Ohio	December 29; train derailed as iron bridge collapsed in snowstorm; 91 dead
1877	Fire	St. John, New Brunswick, Canada	June 20; this Canadian fire killed 100; damage: $12.5 million
1878	Epidemic	southern United States	Yellow fever claimed 14,000 (?)
	Marine	on the Thames, London	September 3; British **Princess Alice** sank; 700 (?) dead
1881	Typhoon	China and Indo-China	October 8; violent storm plus tidal wave killed 300,000 (?)
	Fire	Vienna	December 8; Ring Theater burned; more than 600 dead
1882	Cyclone	Bombay	June 5; storm and subsequent tidal wave killed 100,000 (?)
	Rail	near Tchery, Russia	July 13; train derailed; more than 150 dead
1883	Fire	Berdichev, Russia	January 13; theater fire killed more than 150
	Mine	Braidwood, Illinois	February 16; coal mine flooded; 69 drowned
	Earthquakes	Ischia, Tyrrhenian Sea	July 28 and August 3; these two quakes killed 2,000 (?)

Year	Type of Disaster	Place	Remarks
1883	Volcanic eruption	Sunda Strait, Indonesia	August 26–28; Krakatoa erupted, destroying two thirds of the island; 36,419 dead and many missing after the greatest eruption of modern times.
1883–94	Epidemic	worldwide	Cholera pandemic killed millions
1884	Mine	Crested Butte, Colorado	January 24; coal mine exploded; 59 dead
	Tornado	central United States	February 18–19; series of tornadoes destroyed 10,000 (?) buildings and killed 800 (?)
	Mine	Pocahontas, Virginia	March 13; coal mine explosion killed 112
	Earthquake	Colchester, England	April 22; quake destroyed the city
1886	Blizzard	central United States	January 6–13; Kansas was hardest hit; 70 (?) dead
	Earthquake	Charleston, S.C.	August 31; quake caused severe damage and killed 60
1887	Flood	Honan, China	Yellow River overflowed; more than 900,000 dead
	Fire	Paris	May 25; Opéra Comique burned, killing 200 (?)
	Rail	Chatsworth, Illinois	August 10; train wrecked by collapse of burning bridge; 81 dead
	Fire	Exeter, England	September 4; theater burned; 200 (?) dead
1888	Blizzard	U.S. eastern seaboard	March 11–14; blizzard paralyzed major cities of Northeast, and killed more than 400; damage: several million dollars
	Rail	Mud Run, Pennsylvania	October 10; locomotive hit standing train; more than 50 dead
1889	Flood	Johnstown, Pennsylvania	May 31; this legendary American deluge killed more than 2,000
1889–90	Epidemic	worldwide	Influenza pandemic affected about 40 percent of the globe's population
1891	Mine	Mount Pleasant, Pennsylvania	January 27; coal mine exploded; 109 dead
	Marine	off Gibraltar	March 17; British steamer **Utopia** sank; 574 dead
	Rail	near Basel, Switzerland	June 14; trains collided; 100 (?) dead
	Earthquake	Mino-Owari, Japan	October 28; quake killed 10,000 (?)
1892	Mine	Krebs, Oklahoma	January 7; coal mine exploded; 100 dead
1893	Hurricane	southern United States and Caribbean	August 23–30; tropical storm devastated Charleston, S.C., and Savannah, Ga.; 1,000 (?) dead
1894	Fire	Hinckley, Minnesota	September 1; more than 160,000 acres of forest burned
1895	Marine	near Gibraltar	March 14; Spanish cruiser **Reina Regenta** foundered; 400 dead
	Mine	Red Canyon, Wyoming	March 20; coal mine exploded, killing 60
1896	Tornado	St. Louis	May; storm that devastated city killed 306; damage: $13 million
	Earthquake	Sanriku coast, Japan	June; quake and tidal wave killed 27,000 (?)
	Mine	Pittston, Pennsylvania	June 28; coal mine cave-in; 58 dead
	Rail	Atlantic City, New Jersey	July 30; train wrecked; 60 dead
1898	Marine	Havana	February 15; U.S. battleship **Maine** exploded; more than 260 dead
	Marine	near Sable Island, off Nova Scotia	July 4; French **La Bourgogne** and British **Cromartyshire** collided; 560 lost
	Marine	in the Atlantic off U.S. coast	November 26; **Portland** wrecked during storm; 200 (?) dead
1898–1908	Epidemic	China and India	Bubonic plague killed 3 (?) million
1900	Fire	Hull and Ottawa, Canada	April 26; conflagration damage: $10 million
	Mine	Scofield, Utah	May 1; coal mine exploded; 200 dead
	Fire	Hoboken, New Jersey	June 30; pier burned and 300 died; damage: over $4.6 million
	Hurricane	Texas	August 27–September 15; storm was followed by storm tide that inundated Galveston Island; 6,000 (?) dead
1901	Fire	Jacksonville, Florida	May 3; damage: $10 million
1902	Volcanic eruption	Martinique, West Indies	May 8; Mont Pelée erupted, totally destroying the city of St. Pierre and killing more than 30,000
	Mine	Coal Creek, Tennessee	May 19; coal mine exploded, killing 184
	Mine	Johnstown, Pennsylvania	July 10; coal mine exploded; 112 dead
	Fire	Birmingham, Alabama	September 20; church burned; 115 dead
1903	Flood	Heppner, Oregon	Flood destroyed this town and killed more than 250
	Mine	Hanna, Wyoming	June 30; coal mine explosion and fire killed 169
	Rail	Laurel Run, Pennsylvania	December 23; train crashed into fallen timber; 75 (?) dead
	Fire	Chicago	December 30; Iroquois Theater burned; 600 (?) victims
1904	Mine	Cheswick, Pennsylvania	January 25; coal mine exploded; 179 dead
	Fire	Baltimore	February 7–8; 75 city blocks burned; damage: $85 million
	Fire	Toronto	April 19; damage: $12 million
	Marine	New York City	June 15; steamer **General Slocum** burned in East River; more than 1,000 dead
	Marine	Rockall Reef, Scotland	June 28; **Norge** wrecked; more than 600 dead
	Rail	Eden, Colorado	August 7; train wreck killed 96
	Rail	New Market, Tennessee	September 24; train wrecked; 56 dead
1905	Mine	Virginia City, Alabama	February 26; coal mine exploded; 112 dead
1906	Mine	Courrières, France	March 10; explosion fatal for 1,060
	Earthquake	San Francisco	April 18; fire followed famous 'Frisco quake, which together killed 700 (?) and left more than 250,000 homeless; damage: $524 million
	Typhoon	Hong Kong	September 19; tropical cyclone claimed 50,000 (?)
	Rail	Washington, D.C.	December 30; train wrecked; 53 dead
1907	Mine	Stuart, West Virginia	January 29; coal mine exploded; 84 dead
	Mine	Monongah, West Virginia	December 6; coal mines exploded, killing 361
	Mine	Jacobs Creek, Pennsylvania	December 19; coal mine exploded; 239 dead
	Epidemic	India	Bubonic plague killed 1.3 million
1908	Fire	Boyertown, Pennsylvania	January 13; Rhoades Opera House burned; more than 100 dead
	Fire	Collinwood, Ohio	March 4; school burned, killing more than 160
	Mine	Hanna, Wyoming	March 28; coal mine exploded; 59 lost
	Fire	Chelsea, Massachusetts	April 12; city destroyed by fire; damage: $17 million
	Mine	Marianna, Pennsylvania	November 28; coal mines exploded; 154 killed
	Earthquake	southern Italy and Sicily	December 28; quake rendered one million (?) homeless and took lives of 100,000 (?)
	Mine	Switchback, West Virginia	December 29; coal mine exploded; 50 dead
1909	Mine	Switchback, West Virginia	January 12; coal mine exploded; 67 dead
	Fire	Acapulco	February 15; Flores Theater burned; 250 (?) dead
	Hurricane	Louisiana and Mississippi	September 14–21; this tropical storm killed 350
	Mine	Cherry, Illinois	November 13; coal mine fire killed 259
1909–18	Epidemic	China and India	Bubonic plague fatal for 1.5 million (?)
1910	Mine	Primero, Colorado	January 31; coal mine exploded; 75 dead

Year	Type of Disaster	Place	Remarks
	Rail	Wellington, Washington	March 1; avalanche swept two trains into canyon; 96 dead
	Rail	Green Mountain, Iowa	March 21; train wrecked; 55 dead
	Mine	Palos, Alabama	May 5; coal mine exploded; 90 dead
	Mine	Starkville, Colorado	October 8; coal mine exploded; 56 dead
	Mine	Delagua, Colorado	November 8; coal mine explosion and fire killed 79
1910–11	Epidemic	Manchuria	Pneumonic plague killed 60,000 (?)
1911	Flood	China	Yangtze River overflowed; 100,000 (?) dead
	Fire	New York City	March 25; Triangle Shirtwaist Factory holocaust claimed 145
	Mine	Throop, Pennsylvania	April 7; coal mine burned; 72 dead
	Mine	Littleton, Alabama	April 8; coal mine exploded; 128 dead
	Mine	Briceville, Tennessee	December 9; coal mine explosion killed 84
1912	Marine	off Spain	March 5; Spanish **Principe de Asturias** wrecked; 500 dead
	Mine	McCurtain, Oklahoma	March 20; coal mine exploded; 73 dead
	Mine	Jed, West Virginia	March 26; coal mine exploded; 83 dead
	Marine	in the North Atlantic	April 15; "unsinkable" British **Titanic** struck an iceberg and sank; 1,500 (?) dead
	Marine	off Japan	September 28; Japanese **Kichemaru** sank; 1,000 lost
1913	Tornado	Omaha	March 23; storm fatal for 100 (?); damage: $3.5 million
	Flood	Ohio and Indiana	March 25–27; Ohio and Indiana Rivers overflowed; 700 (?) dead
	Mine	Finleyville, Pennsylvania	April 23; coal mine exploded; 96 dead
	Mine	Dawson, New Mexico	October 22; coal mine exploded, killing 263
1914	Mine	Eccles, West Virginia	April 28; coal mines exploded; 183 dead
	Marine	St. Lawrence River	May 29; Canadian Pacific **Empress of Ireland** collided with collier and sank; 1,024 dead
	Fire	Salem, Massachusetts	June 25–26; conflagration destroyed 1,700 (?) buildings; damage: $14 million
	Mine	Royalton, Illinois	October 27; coal mine exploded; 52 dead
1915	Earthquake	central Italy	January 13; quake killed 30,000 (?)
	Mine	Layland, West Virginia	March 2; coal mine exploded; 112 dead
	Marine	off coast of Ireland	May 7; **Lusitania** sank after attack by German submarine; 1,198 dead
	Rail	near Gretna, Scotland	May 22; three trains crashed; 227 killed
	Marine	Chicago River, Chicago	July 24; excursion boat **Eastland** capsized in port; 800–900 dead
	Epidemic	Serbia	Summer; typhus claimed 150,000 (?)
	Hurricane	Texas and Louisiana	August 5–25; tropical storm followed by storm tide; 275 (?) dead
	Hurricane	Gulf Coast	September 22–October 1; in large area of Louisiana, 90 percent of the buildings were destroyed; more than 250 dead
1916	Marine	in the Mediterranean	February 26; French cruiser **Provence** sank; 3,100 (?) dead
	Fire	Paris, Texas	March 21; fire destroyed 1,440 structures; damage: $11 million
	Tornado	Arkansas	June 5; series of twisters claimed 100 (?)
	Explosion	Jersey City, New Jersey	July 30; German sabotage (explosion and fire) on Black Tom Island killed 4; damage: more than $14 million
	Marine	off China	August 29; **Hsin Yu** sank; 1,000 (?) dead
1917	Explosion	Chester, Pennsylvania	April 10; munitions-plant blast killed 125
	Mine	Hastings, Colorado	April 27; coal mine exploded; 121 dead
	Mine	Clay, Kentucky	August 4; coal mine exploded; 62 dead
	Fire	Halifax, Nova Scotia	December 6; S.S. **Mont Blanc** and Belgian relief ship **Imo** collided and exploded, with resulting fire consuming one square mile of the city; more than 1,400 dead
	Rail	near Modane, France	December 12; troop train derailed near entrance to Mont Cenis tunnel; 550 (?) dead
1917–19	Epidemic	worldwide	Influenza pandemic killed 20–30 million
1917–21	Epidemic	Russia	Typhus killed 2.5–3 million
1918	Marine	Barbados, West Indies	March 4; U.S.S. **Cyclops** lost at sea; 280 fatalities
	Rail	Ivanhoe, Indiana	June 22; two trains collided; 85 dead
	Rail	near Nashville, Tennessee	July 9; head-on collision killed 100 (?)
	Marine	Tokayama Bay, Japan	July 12; Japanese battleship **Kawachi** exploded; 500 (?) dead
	Earthquake	Puerto Rico	October 11; sea wave followed quake, causing severe damage; 116 dead
	Fire	Minnesota and Wisconsin	October 13–15; death toll: 1,000 (?); damages from the forest fires: $100 million
	Rail	Brooklyn, New York	November 1; derailment at Malbone St. tunnel; 100 (?) dead
1919	Marine	in the Strait of Messina	January 17; French **Chaonia** wrecked; 460 dead
	Mine	Wilkes-Barre, Pennsylvania	June 5; coal powder explosion killed 92
	Fire	San Juan, Puerto Rico	June 20; Mayaguez Theater burned, killing 150
	Tornado	Fergus Falls, Minnesota	June 22; storm killed 59; damages: $3.5 million
	Hurricane	Florida, Louisiana, and Texas	September 2–15; cyclone killed 287
1920s	Epidemic	India	Bubonic plague claimed 2 (?) million
1920	Blizzard	New England	March 5–6; this severe snowstorm considered comparable with "Blizzard of '88"
	Earthquake	Kansu, China	December 16; quake destroyed 10 cities and killed 180,000 (?)
1921	Epidemic	India	Cholera claimed 500,000 (?)
	Marine	off Swatow, South China Sea	March 18; **Hong Kong** wrecked on rocks; 1,000 (?) dead
	Aircraft	near Hull, England	August 24; British dirigible **ZR–2** broke in two; 62 dead
	Explosion	Oppau, Germany	September 21; ammonium nitrate blast killed 600 (?)
1922	Fire	Smyrna, Asia Minor	September 13; city almost destroyed; hundreds dead; damage: $100 million
	Mine	Spangler, Pennsylvania	November 6; coal mine exploded; 77 dead
	Mine	Dolomite, Alabama	November 22; coal mine explosion killed 90
1923	Mine	Dawson, New Mexico	February 8; coal mine exploded; 120 dead
	Mine	Kemmerer, Wyoming	August 14; coal mine exploded; 99 dead
	Earthquake	Tokyo and Yokohama	September 1; quake followed by fire destroyed most of both Japanese cities; 200,000 (?) dead
	Fire	Berkeley, California	September 17; fire destroyed more than 600 buildings; damage: $12.5 million
	Aircraft	in the Mediterranean or Sahara Desert	December 21; French dirigible **Dixmude** disappeared; 50 (?) lost
1924	Epidemic	India	Cholera death toll: 300,000 (?)
	Mine	Castle Gate, Utah	March 8; coal mine exploded; 171 dead

Year	Type of Disaster	Place	Remarks
1924	Mine	Benwood, West Virginia	April 28; coal mine explosion killed 119
	Tornado	Lorain and Sandusky, Ohio	June 28; twister killed 85; damage: $12 million
1925	Mine	Sullivan, Indiana	February 20; coal mine exploded; 52 dead
	Tornado	Missouri, Illinois, and Indiana	March 18; tornado killed 689; damage: $17 million
	Mine	Coal Glen, North Carolina	May 27; coal mine exploded; 53 dead
	Rail	Hackettstown, New Jersey	June 16; train derailed at highway crossing; 50 dead
	Mine	Acemar, Alabama	December 10; coal mine exploded; 53 dead
1926–30	Epidemic	India	Smallpox claimed 423,000 (?)
1926	Mine	Wilburton, Oklahoma	January 13; coal mine explosion killed 91
	Hurricane	Florida and Alabama	September 11–22; 243 dead
1927	Mine	Everettville, West Virginia	April 30; coal mine exploded; 97 dead
	Tornado	Arkansas and Missouri	May 9; 92 dead from storm
	Tornado	St. Louis	September 29; death toll: 90; damage: $40 million
1928	Flood	Santa Paula, California	March 13; St. Francis Dam collapsed; 450 dead
	Mine	Mather, Pennsylvania	May 19; coal mine explosion killed 195
	Flood	southern Florida	September 6–20; hurricane caused Lake Okeechobee to overflow; 1,836 lives lost
	Marine	off the Virginia Capes	November 12; British steamer **Vestris** sank; 110 (?) dead
1929	Fire	Cleveland	May 15; hospital burned; 125 suffocations from poisonous fumes
	Mine	McAlester, Oklahoma	December 17; coal mine exploded; 61 dead
1930	Fire	Columbus	April 21; Ohio State Penitentiary burned, killing 317 convicts
	Earthquake	Naples	July 23–25; shock results killed 1,883 and injured 10,000 (?)
	Hurricane	Dominican Republic	September 3; storm fatalities: 2,000 (?)
	Aircraft	Beauvais, France	October 5; British dirigible **R–101** crashed; 47 dead
	Mine	Millfield, Ohio	November 5; coal mine exploded; 82 dead
1931	Flood	Yangtze River, China	July–August; flood waters of Yangtze leave over 2 million homeless and 140,000 dead
1932	Tornado	southern United States	March 21–22; tornadoes hit five states; at least 362 dead
	Mine	Moweaqua, Illinois	December 23; coal mine exploded; 54 dead
	Earthquake	Kansu, China	December 26; quake killed 70,000 (?)
1933	Earthquake	Sanriku coast, Japan	March 3; quake killed more than 2,500
	Earthquake	Long Beach, California	March 10; quake claimed 115 lives; damage: $40 million
	Aircraft	New Jersey coast	April 4; U.S. dirigible **Akron II** crashed; 73 dead
1934	Fire	Hakodate, Japan	March 22; fire destroyed city; 1,500 dead (?)
	Marine	off New Jersey	September 8; luxury liner **Morro Castle** burned; 134 dead
	Typhoon	Honshu, Japan	September 21; storm killed 4,000 (?); damage: $50 million
	Mine	Wrexham, Wales	September 22; coal mine exploded; 265 dead
1935	Epidemic	Uganda	Bubonic plague killed 2,000 (?)
	Earthquake	India and Pakistan	May 31; quake killed more than 50,000
	Hurricane	southern Florida	August 29–September 10; storm killed 408; damage: up to $50 million
	Hurricane	Haiti	October 22; storm and flood fatalities: more than 2,000
1936	Tornado	southern United States	April 5–6; series of twisters, mostly in Mississippi and Georgia, killed 455; damage: $21 million
1937	Fire	Antung, Manchuria	February 13; theater burned, killing 658
	Explosion	New London, Texas	March 19; natural gas explosion destroyed school; more than 400 dead
	Aircraft	Lakehurst, New Jersey	May 6; German zeppelin **Hindenburg** exploded; 36 dead
	Rail	near Patna, India	July 16; Delhi-Calcutta express derailed; 107 dead
1938	Aircraft	Bogotá, Colombia	July 24; military stunt plane crashed into grandstand, killing 53
	Hurricane	Long Island and lower New England	September 10–22; this storm killed 600; damage: $50–500 million
	Rail	near Kishinev, Rumania	December 25; two-train collision killed 100 (?)
1939	Earthquake	Chile	January 24; quake killed 40,000 (?)
	Marine	off New Hampshire	May 23; U.S. submarine **Squalus** sank; 26 dead
	Marine	in the Irish Sea	June 1; British submarine **Thetis** sank; 99 lost
	Marine	off Indochina	June 15; French submarine **Phenix** sank; 63 dead
	Flood	Tientsin, China	July–August; millions rendered homeless and thousands dead
	Fire	Langunillas, Venezuela	November 14; oil town built over Lake Maracaibo destroyed
	Rail	near Magdeburg, Germany	December 22; two trains collided; 132 dead
	Rail	near Freidrichshafen, Germany	December 22; train wrecked; 99 dead
	Earthquake	Anatolia, Turkey	December 27; series of shocks and subsequent floods devastated about 60,000 square miles; more than 30,000 dead
1940	Mine	Bartley, West Virginia	January 10; coal mine exploded; 91 dead
	Rail	Osaka, Japan	January 29; two trains collided; 200 (?) dead
	Mine	St. Clairsville, Ohio	March 16; coal mine exploded; 72 dead
	Mine	Portage, Pennsylvania	July 15; coal mine explosion killed 63
	Blizzard	U.S. Northeast and Midwest	November 11–12; one of the most destructive snowstorms ever caused 144 deaths; damage: $6 million
1941	Marine	off Maine	June 16; U.S. submarine **O–9** sank in test dive; 33 fatalities
1942	Marine	New York City	February 9; French liner **Normandie** burned at pier; 1 dead
	Tornado	U.S. South and Midwest	March 17; twister killed 111
	Mine	Honkeiko Colliery, Manchuria	April 26; worst mine disaster in history; 1,549 dead
	Mine	Osage, West Virginia	May 12; coal mine exploded; 56 dead
	Marine	off England	October 2; British **Curacao** rammed and sunk by **Queen Mary**; more than 330 dead
	Cyclone	Bengal, India	October 16; storm fatalities: 40,000 (?)
	Fire	Boston	November 28; Cocoanut Grove night club burned; 492 dead
1943	Mine	Red Lodge, Montana	February 27; coal mine exploded; 74 dead
	Rail	Philadelphia	September 6; ''Congressional Limited'' derailed; 80 dead
	Rail	near Lumberton, North Carolina	December 16; two trains collided; 72 dead
1944	Earthquake	San Juan, Argentina	January 15; quake killed 5,000 (?)
	Rail	Leon Province, Spain	January 16; train wrecked inside tunnel; 500–800 dead
	Rail	near Salerno, Italy	March 2; train stalled in tunnel, suffocating 526
	Mine	Belmont, Ohio	July 5; coal mine fire claimed 66
	Fire	Hartford, Connecticut	July 6; circus ''big top'' burned, killing 168
	Marine	Port Chicago, California	July 18; two ammunition ships exploded; 322 dead
	Aircraft	Freckleton, England	August 23; U.S. bomber crashed into school; more than 70 dead

Year	Type of Disaster	Place	Remarks
	Hurricane	U.S. eastern seaboard	September 9–16; storm killed 46; damage: $50–500 million
	Fire	Cleveland	October 20; liquid gas tanks exploded, setting fire to 50-block area and killing 130; damage: $10 million
	Rail	near Ogden, Utah	December 31; two sections of "Pacific Limited" collided; 50 dead
1945	Marine	off Danzig	January 30; German passengership **Wilhelm Gustloff** loaded with refugees and hospital ship **General Steuben** sunk by Soviet submarine; 6,800 lives lost in world's largest marine disaster
	Rail	Cazadero, Mexico	February 1; train struck from rear by freight train; 100 (?) dead
	Marine	Bari, Italy	April 9; U.S.S. **Liberty** exploded in harbor; 360 dead
	Tornado	Oklahoma and Arkansas	April 12; twister killed 102; damage: $4 million
	Aircraft	New York City	July 28; U.S. bomber crashed into Empire State Building; 13 dead
1946	Rail	near Aracaju, Brazil	March 20; train wreck killed 185
	Earthquake	Dutch Harbor, Alaska	April 1; subterranean quake caused tidal waves that hit Hawaiian Islands, Aleutians, and the West Coast; 173 dead in Hawaii alone and damage there $25 million
	Fire	Atlanta	December 7; Winecoff Hotel burned; 119 dead
	Aircraft	near Shanghai	December 25; three China Air Transport planes crashed, separately, in fog; at least 71 dead
1947	Marine	off Athens	January 19; Greek ship **Himera** struck mine and sank; 392 lost
	Aircraft	Bogotá, Colombia	February 15; Avianca DC–4 crashed into Mount Tablazo; 53 fatalities
	Mine	Centralia, Illinois	March 25; coal mine exploded; 111 dead
	Tornado	Texas, Oklahoma, and Kansas	April 9; twister killed 167; damage: $10 million
	Explosion	Texas City, Texas	April 16; S.S. **Grandcamp** blew up, destroying most of city and killing 561; damage: $67 million
	Aircraft	Leesburg, Virginia	June 13; Pennsylvania Central DC–4 crashed; 50 dead
	Explosion	Cadiz, Spain	August 18; dockyard exploded; 147 dead
	Epidemic	Egypt	September–December; cholera killed 10,276
	Hurricane	Florida and Gulf coasts	September 4–21; storm fatalities: 51; damage: $50–500 million
	Typhoon	Honshu, Japan	September 15–19; storm plus floods killed 2,000 (?)
	Aircraft	Bryce Canyon, Utah	October 24; United DC–6 crashed into hillside; 52 dead
	Fire	Bar Harbor, Maine	October 25; forest fire on Mount Desert Island burned large part of famous summer resort; damage: $30 million
1948	Marine	in the Inland Sea, Japan	January 28; freighter **Joo Maru** struck mine and sank; 250 dead
	Earthquake	Fukui, Japan	June 28; quake destroyed most of city; more than 5,000 dead
	Explosion	Ludwigshafen, Germany	July 28; blast and fire at I. G. Farben chemical works killed more than 200; damage: $6 million
	Aircraft	French West Africa	August 1; Air France plane disappeared on flight from Martinique; 53 lost
	Explosion	Hong Kong	September 22; chemical warehouse blast and fire killed 135
1949	Marine	off southern China	January 27; Chinese **Taiping** and collier collided and sank; more than 600 dead
	Fire	Effingham, Illinois	April 5; St. Anthony's Hospital burned; 74 dead
	Aircraft	Puerto Rico	June 7; U.S. Strato Freight crashed into water ; 54 dead
	Earthquake	Ecuador	August 5; shock razed 50 towns; 100,000 (?) homeless and 6,000 (?) dead; damage: $20 million
	Marine	Toronto	September 17; Canadian **Noronic** burned at pier; 130 (?) dead
	Rail	Nowy Dwor, Poland	October 22; Danzig-Warsaw express derailed; 200 (?) dead
	Cyclone	southeastern India	October 27; storm fatalities: 1,000 (?)
	Typhoon	Philippine Islands	October 31–November 2; storm killed 1,000 (?)
	Aircraft	Washington, D.C.	November 1; Bolivian fighter plane and Eastern DC–4 collided over airport; 55 dead
1950	Marine	in the Thames estuary, England	January 12; British submarine **Truculent** rammed by Swedish tanker; more than 60 dead
	Aircraft	near Cardiff, Wales	March 12; British Avro Tudor V crashed; 80 dead
	Rail	near Tangua, Brazil	April 6; train plunged into Indios River; 108 dead
	Rail	near Jasidih, India	May 7; Punjab mail train crash killed 81
	Fire	Rimouski, Quebec	May 7; blaze left 2,000 homeless; damage: $12 million
	Trolley	Chicago	May 25; trolley and gas truck collided; 34 dead
	Aircraft	in Lake Michigan	June 24; Northwest DC–4 crash claimed 58
	Flood	Anhwei Province, China	August 14; cataclysm inundated more than five million acres, leaving 10 million homeless and killing 500
	Earthquake	Assam, India	August 15; quake killed 1,500 (?) and devastated area of about 30,000 miles
	Aircraft	Cairo	August 31; TWA Constellation crashed; 55 dead
	Hurricane	Florida	October 13–19; Miami struck and four dead; damage: $5–50 million
	Aircraft	Grenoble, France	November 13; Canadian Curtiss-Reid DC–4 crashed; 58 dead
	Rail	Richmond Hill, New York	November 22; commuter train rammed by another; 79 dead
	Blizzard	U.S. Northeast	November 25; this storm killed 100 (?)
1951	Tornado	Comoro Islands	January 4; more than 500 victims
	Rail	Woodbridge, New Jersey	February 6; commuter train plunged through overpass; 84 dead
	Aircraft	in the North Atlantic	March 23; U.S.A.F. plane wreckage found off Ireland; 53 lost
	Marine	off Isle of Wight	April 16; British submarine **Affray** sank; 75 dead
	Earthquake	Jacuapa, El Salvador	May 6; fatalities numbered more than 1,000
	Mine	Easington, England	May 29; coal mine explosion killed 81
	Rail	Nova Iguaca, Brazil	June 7; train and gasoline truck collided; 54 dead
	Aircraft	Rocky Mountain National Park, Colorado	June 30; United DC–6 crashed; 50 dead
	Flood	Kansas and Missouri	July 2–19; the most severe floods in American history killed 41 and left 200,000 homeless; damage: $1 billion
	Aircraft	near Decoto, California	August 24; United DC–6B crashed; 50 dead
	Flood	Manchuria	August 28; deluge caused extensive damage; 5,000 (?) dead or missing
	Typhoon	Philippine Islands	December 9–10; fatalities: 724
	Aircraft	Elizabeth, New Jersey	December 16; nonscheduled plane plunged into river after take-off from Newark Airport; 56 dead
	Mine	West Frankfort, Illinois	December 21; coal mine exploded; 119 dead

Year	Type of Disaster	Place	Remarks
1952	Rail	near Rio de Janeiro	March 4; two trains crashed; 119 dead
	Tornado	Mississippi Valley	March 21–22; twisters killed 229
	Aircraft	Moscow	March 27; two Soviet planes collided over Tula Airport; 70 dead
	Aircraft	San Juan, Puerto Rico	April 11; Pan Am DC–4 crashed; 52 dead
	Marine	in the Atlantic	April 26; U.S. destroyer-minesweeper **Hobson** and aircraft carrier **Wasp** collided; **Hobson** sank; 176 dead
	Aircraft	northern Brazil	April 29; Pan Am Stratocruiser crashed in jungle; 50 dead
	Rail	near Rzepin, Poland	July 9; train wrecked; 160 dead
	Earthquake	southern California	July 21; quake killed 14; damage: $60 million
	Bus	near Waco, Texas	August 4; two buses collided; 28 dead
	Rail	Harrow-Wealdstone, England	October 8; two trains collided with a third; 112 dead
	Typhoon	Luzon, Philippine Islands	October 22; this tropical cyclone left 1,000 (?) dead or missing; damage: $50 million
	Aircraft	near Elmendorf A.F.B., Alaska	November 23; U.S.A.F. plane crashed; 52 dead
	Aircraft	in Moses Lake, Washington	December 20; after takeoff, U.S.A.F. plane crashed and caught fire; 87 dead
1953	Marine	off Pusan, South Korea	January 9; South Korean liner sank in heavy seas; 249 dead
	Flood	northern Europe	January 31–February 1; floods devastated North Sea coastal areas; more than 2,000 dead
	Trolley	Mexico City	February 21; two trolley cars collided; more than 60 dead
	Earthquake	eastern Iran	February 22; town of Trud destroyed; 1,000 dead
	Earthquake	northwestern Turkey	March 18; quake killed 1,200 (?)
	Tornado	Waco, Texas	May 11; series of twisters killed 114
	Tornado	Michigan and Ohio	June 8; tornado series killed 142
	Tornado	central Massachusetts	June 9; storm killed 92; damage: $52 million
	Aircraft	near Tokyo	June 18; U.S.A.F. plane crashed; 129 fatalities
	Aircraft	off Wake Island	July 12; nonscheduled plane crashed in Pacific, killing 58
	Marine	near New Caledonia	August 1; French **Monique** vanished in South Pacific; 120 lost
	Tornado	Vicksburg, Mississippi	December 5; tornado killed 38; damage: $25 million
	Rail	near Waiouru, New Zealand	December 24; Wellington-Auckland express plunged into stream; 155 dead
1954	Rail	near Karachi, Pakistan	January 21; mail express wrecked; 60 dead
	Rail	near Seoul, South Korea	January 31; train wreck killed 56
	Marine	off Quonset Point, Rhode Island	May 26; U.S. aircraft carrier **Bennington** exploded and burned; 103 dead
	Flood	Kazvin District, Iran	August 1; flash flood killed 2,000 (?)
	Hurricane	U.S. eastern seaboard	August 25–31; storm fatalities numbered 60; damage: $50–500 million
	Rail	Negros Island, Philippines	September 2; train wrecked; 55 dead
	Earthquake	Orléansville, Algeria	September 9–12; quake killed 1,600 (?)
	Marine	in Tsugaru Strait, Japan	September 26; Japanese ferry **Toya Maru** sank; 1,172 dead
	Rail	east of Hyderabad, India	September 28; express train plunged from bridge; 137 dead
	Hurricane	U.S. eastern seaboard	October 5–18; this hurricane took 95 lives; damage: $50–500 million
1955	Fire	Yokohama, Japan	February 16–17; home for aged burned, killing 100 (?)
	Aircraft	Honolulu	March 22; U.S. Navy plane hit cliff; 66 dead
	Rail	near Guadalajara, Mexico	April 3; train plunged into canyon; 300 (?) dead
	Tornado	Kansas, Missouri, Oklahoma, and Texas	May 25; series of tornadoes killed 115
	Hurricane	U.S. eastern seaboard	August 7–21; storm and floods, by Hurricane Diane, took 184 lives, caused $1.75 million in damages
	Aircraft	near Edelweiler, West Germany	August 11; two U.S.A.F. planes collided in midair; 66 dead
	Hurricane	Mexico and West Indies	September 22–28; more than 750 lives lost; extensive damage
	Flood	Pakistan and India	October 4; claiming more than 1,700 lives, this deluge devastated about 5.6 million crop acres valued at $63 million
	Aircraft	near Laramie, Wyoming	October 6; United DC–4 crashed in mountains; 66 dead
1956	Aircraft	Malta	February 18; British Lancaster bomber crashed; 50 dead
	Aircraft	near Cairo	February 20; Transport Aeriens Intercontinentaux DC–6B crashed; 52 dead
	Earthquake	northern Afghanistan	June 10–17; series of shocks caused 2,000 (?) deaths
	Aircraft	in the Atlantic, south of New York City	June 20; Venezuelan Super-Constellation crashed; 74 dead
	Aircraft	Grand Canyon, Arizona	June 30; TWA Super-Constellation and United DC–7 collided in midair; 128 dead
	Marine	off Massachusetts	July 25; Italian **Andrea Doria** and Swedish **Stockholm** collided in fog, sinking the **Doria**; 50 (?) dead or missing
	Typhoon	Chekiang, China	August 1; storm and subsequent floods killed more than 2,000
	Explosion	Cali, Colombia	August 7; seven truckloads of dynamite exploded, killing more than 1,200 and destroying town; damage: $40 million
	Mine	Marcinelle, Belgium	August 8; coal mine fire claimed 263
	Rail	near Secunderabad, India	September 21; two trains plunged into river as bridge collapsed; 121 dead
	Aircraft	in the Atlantic, north of the Azores	October 10; U.S.A.F. plane disappeared; 59 lost
	Rail	Marudaiyar River, India	November 23; express train derailed; 143 dead
	Aircraft	near Vancouver, Canada	December 9; Trans-Canada North Star crashed; 62 dead
1957	Fire	Warrenton, Missouri	February 17; home for aged burned; 72 dead
	Aircraft	in the Pacific	March 21; U.S.A.F. transport disappeared; 67 lost
	Blizzard	Midwest	March 22–25; storm claimed 21 lives; damage: $5–6 million
	Tornado	Kansas and Missouri	May 18–21; twister killed 40 (?); damage: in the millions of dollars
	Hurricane	Texas to Alabama	June 25–28; storm killed 390; damage: $50–500 million
	Earthquake	Caspian Coast, Iran	July 2; quake killed more than 1,500 and rendered more than 10,000 homeless
	Marine	in the Caspian Sea	July 14; USSR **Eshghabad** ran aground in storm; 270 dead
	Aircraft	off Netherlands New Guinea	July 16; KLM Super-Constellation crashed in sea; 57 dead
	Aircraft	Quebec	August 11; Maritime Central DC–4 charter crashed; 79 dead
	Rail	near Kendal, Jamaica	September 1; train plunged into ravine; 175 (?) dead

Year	Type of Disaster	Place	Remarks
	Rail	near Montgomery, West Pakistan	September 29; express crashed into standing train; 250 dead
	Earthquake	Outer Mongolia	December 2; quake fatal for 1,200 (?)
	Rail	near London	December 4; two-train collision killed 92
	Aircraft	near Bolívar, Argentina	December 8; Aerolineas Argentina DC–4 crashed; 62 dead
	Earthquake	western Iran	December 13 and 15–17; quake killed 1,392
1958	Mine	near Asansoi, India	February 19; coal mine exploded; more than 180 dead
	Marine	near Istanbul	March 1; Turkish ferry **Uskudar** sank; 238 dead
	Rail	Santa Cruz, Brazil	March 7; two trains collided; 67 dead
	Rail	near Rio de Janeiro	May 8; two-train collision killed 128
	Aircraft	Casablanca	May 18; Sabena DC–6B crashed; 65 dead
	Aircraft	in the Atlantic, west of Ireland	August 14; KLM Super-Constellation crashed; 99 dead
	Typhoon	Tokyo	September 21; at least 681 killed
	Typhoon	Honshu, Japan	September 27–28; storm killed 679; many missing
	Aircraft	Kanash, USSR	October 17; Aeroflot TU–104 crashed; 65 dead
	Fire	Chicago	December 1; parochial school burned; 95 dead
	Fire	Bogotá, Colombia	December 16; department store conflagration caused 84 deaths
1959	Aircraft	New York City	February 3; American Electra crashed in the East River; 65 dead
	Rail	Java	May 28; train derailed, spilling into ravine and killing 92
	Rail	São Paulo, Brazil	June 5; two trains collided; 60 (?) dead
	Aircraft	near Milan	June 26; TWA Super-Constellation exploded in storm; 68 dead
	Typhoon	Fukien coast, China	August 20; storm claimed 2,334 lives
	Typhoon	Honshu, Japan	September 26–27; tropical cyclone killed more than 4,400
	Hurricane	Jalisco and Colima, Mexico	October 27–28; storm caused mudslides and floods; 1,000 (?) dead
	Flood	Frejus, France	December 2; Malpasset Dam collapsed; 412 victims
1960	Aircraft	near Wilmington, North Carolina	January 6; National DC–6B ''disintegrated'' in flight; 34 dead
	Aircraft	near Richmond, Virginia	January 18; Capitol Viscount crashed into ravine; 50 dead
	Mine	Coalbrook, South Africa	January 21; coal mine cave-in and explosion killed more than 400
	Aircraft	near La Paz, Bolivia	February 5; Lloyd Aereo Boliviano DC–4 crashed; 56 dead
	Mine	Zwickau, East Germany	February 22; explosion killed 123
	Aircraft	Rio de Janeiro	February 25; U.S. Navy plane and DC–3 collided; 61 dead
	Earthquake	Agadir, Morocco	February 29 and March 1; quakes followed by tidal waves destroyed city; 20,000 (?) dead
	Aircraft	near Tell City, Indiana	March 17; Northwest Electra exploded in flight; 63 dead
	Tornado	Oklahoma and Arkansas	May 5; tornadoes killed 29
	Rail	Leipzig, East Germany	May 15; two trains collided; 59 dead
	Earthquake	Chile, Japan, and Hawaii	May 22–29; series of earthquakes, volcanic eruptions, landslides, and tsunami caused widespread devastation; in Chile, more than 2,000 dead and damage: $550 million; in Hawaii, 61 dead and damage: $22 million; in Japan, 138 dead and damage: $50 million
	Fire	Guatemala City	July 14; hospital burned; 225 (?) dead
	Aircraft	near Dakar, Senegal	August 29; Air France Super-Constellation down at sea; 63 dead
	Hurricane	South and northeast United States	September 10; hurricane killed 30
	Aircraft	Agaña, Guam	September 18–19; World DC–6B exploded; 78 dead
	Aircraft	Boston	October 4; Eastern Electra crashed into harbor; 62 dead
	Cyclone	East Pakistan	October 10 and 31; fatalities from cyclones (6,000) and tidal waves (4,000)
	Fire	Amude, Syria	November 13; movie house burned; 152 deaths
	Rail	Pardubice, Czechoslovakia	November 14; two trains collided; 110 dead
	Aircraft	New York City	December 16; United DC–8 and TWA Super Constellation collided in mid-air over Staten Island, New York; 134 dead
	Fire	Brooklyn Navy Yard	December 19; fire swept aircraft carrier; 50 dead
1961	Aircraft	Berg, Belgium	February 15; Sabena Boeing 707 crashed; 73 dead, including 18 American figure skaters
	Aircraft	Nuremberg, West Germany	March 28; Czechoslovak Ilyushin–18 crashed; 52 dead
	Marine	in the Persian Gulf	April 8; British ship **Dara** burned; more than 200 dead
	Floods	Midwest United States	Early May; floods caused deaths of 25
	Typhoon	East Pakistan	May 9; cyclone plus tidal waves killed 2,000 (?)
	Aircraft	Ghadames, Libya	May 10; Air France Starliner crashed; 79 dead
	Marine	off Mozambique	July 8; Portuguese **Save** burned and exploded; 227 dead
	Mine	Dolna Suce, Czechoslovakia	July 8; coal gas explosion killed 108
	Aircraft	Casablanca	July 12; Czechoslovak Ilyushin–18 crashed; 72 dead
	Aircraft	near Chicago	September 1; TWA Constellation crashed in a field; 78 dead
	Aircraft	Shannon, Ireland	September 10; Presidential DC–6 charter crashed; 83 dead
	Hurricane	Southwest and Midwest United States	September 10–14; hurricane and associated tornadoes and floods caused deaths of 46
	Aircraft	Rabat, Morocco	September 12; Air France Caravelle crashed, killing 77
	Typhoon	Japan	September 16–17; storm killed 185; extensive damage
	Rail	west of Calcutta, India	October 20; express train derailed; more than 50 dead
	Hurricane	Belize, British Honduras	October 31; hurricane devastated city, causing 250 (?) deaths and damage: $150 million
	Aircraft	near Richmond, Virginia	November 8; charter Constellation crashed in woods; 77 dead
	Hurricane	southern Mexico	November 14; hurricane killed at least 330
	Fire	Niteroi, Brazil	December 17; circus tent burned, killing more than 320
	Rail	Catanzaro, Italy	December 23; train fell into gorge; 69 dead
1962	Rail	Woerden, Netherlands	January 8; two trains collided; 91 dead
	Avalanche	Mt. Huscaran, Peru	January 10; Andean avalanche buried more than 3,000
	Mine	Voelklingen, West Germany	February 7; coal mine exploded; 298 dead
	Aircraft	New York City	March 1; American 707 plunged into Jamaica Bay; 95 dead
	Aircraft	near Douala, Cameroon	March 4; British Caledonian DC–7C crashed in jungle; 111 dead
	Hurricane	eastern United States	March 6–7; windstorm and high tides caused 35 deaths
	Aircraft	in the western Pacific	March 16; Flying Tiger charter disappeared; 107 lost
	Rail	Tokyo	May 3; three trains collided; 163 dead

Year	Type of Disaster	Place	Remarks
	Rail	Voghera, Italy	May 31; two trains collided; 63 dead
	Aircraft	Paris	June 3; Air France Boeing 707 crashed; 130 killed
	Aircraft	Guadeloupe, West Indies	June 22; Air France Boeing 707 crashed; 113 dead
	Aircraft	Bombay	July 7; Alitalia DC–8 crashed; 94 dead
	Rail	Dumraon, India	July 21; two trains collided; 69 dead
	Earthquake	northwestern Iran	September 1; quake killed more than 10,000
	Flood	Barcelona	September 27; flash flood killed more than 470
	Hurricane	Pacific coast of United States	October 12–13; near-hurricane winds and floods killed 40
	Cyclone	Thailand	October 27; hurricane toll: 769 dead and 142 missing
	Aircraft	Lima, Peru	November 27; Varig Boeing 707 crashed; 97 dead
	Aircraft	in the Amazon jungle, Brazil	December 14; Panair Do Brasil Constellation crashed; 50 dead
	Flood	northern Europe	December 31; winter-storm floods caused over 300 deaths
1963	Aircraft	Ankara	February 1; Turkish Air Force plane and Lebanese Viscount collided; 95 dead
	Volcanic eruption	Bali	March 18; Mount Agung erupted, forcing 78,000 to flee homes; 1,584 deaths recorded
	Marine	in the Atlantic, east of Boston	April 10; **Thresher**, U.S. Navy nuclear submarine, sank; 129 dead in navy's worst peacetime submarine disaster
	Cyclone	Bay of Bengal, East Pakistan	May 28–29; hurricane and tidal waves took lives of 22,000 (?)
	Aircraft	in the Pacific, off Alaska	June 3; Northwest DC–7 charter crashed; 101 dead
	Earthquake	Skopje, Yugoslavia	July 26; quake killed 1,100 (?)
	Aircraft	near Bombay	July 28; wreckage found of United Arab Comet; 62 dead
	Aircraft	Zurich	September 4: Swissair Caravelle crashed; 80 dead
	Hurricane	Caribbean	October 1–9; cyclone killed 4,000 (?) in Cuba and Haiti
	Flood	near Belluno, Italy	October 9; landslides and flooding, near Vaiont Dam, resulted in death for more than 2,000
	Fire	Indianapolis, Indiana	October 31; explosion and fire at Coliseum; 74 dead
	Rail	near Yokohama	November 9; two Japanese trains hurtled into derailed freight train; at least 162 dead
	Mine	Omuta, Japan	November 9; coal mine exploded; 446 dead
	Flood	Haiti	November 14–15; deluges and landslides killed 500 (?)
	Fire	near Norwalk, Ohio	November 23; fire at nursing home for aged; 63 dead
	Aircraft	Montreal	November 29; Trans-Canada DC–8F crashed; 118 dead
	Aircraft	near Elkton, Maryland	December 8; Pan Am Boeing 707 crashed into a field; 81 dead
1964	Rail	Altamirano, Argentina	February 1; two trains collided; 70 dead
	Aircraft	near New Orleans, Louisiana	February 25; Eastern DC–8 crashed into Lake Pontchartrain; 58 dead
	Aircraft	near Innsbruck, Austria	February 29; British turboprop crashed, killing 83
	Aircraft	near Lake Tahoe, California	March 1; nonscheduled carrier plane crashed; 85 dead
	Earthquake	Alaska	March 27; earthquake was responsible for 114 deaths
	Aircraft	Clark A.F.B., Philippines	May 11; U.S. military transport crashed; 75 dead
	Floods	northern Montana	June 8–9; floods were responsible for 36 deaths
	Aircraft	near Fengyuan, Taiwan	June 20; Chinese Civil Air Patrol plane crashed; 57 dead
	Rail	near Oporto, Portugal	July 26; train wreck killed 94
	Bridge	near Caracas, Venezuela	August 23; 50 (?) killed in collapse of bridge over Caroni Falls
	Aircraft	near Granada, Spain	October 2; Union Transports Africains DC–6 crashed; 80 dead
	Hurricane	southern Louisiana	October 3; hurricane and associated tornadoes killed 36
	Floods	western United States	Late December; floods responsible for 45 deaths
1965	Aircraft	in the Andes, Chile	February 6; Chilean Airline DC–6B crashed; 87 dead
	Aircraft	near New York	February 8; Eastern DC–7B crashed in Atlantic; 84 dead
	Earthquake	near Santiago, Chile	March 28; quake killed 400 (?); damage: $200 million
	Aircraft	in the Strait of Gibraltar	March 31; Iberia Convair charter crashed; 50 dead
	Aircraft	near Damascus	April 10; Royal Jordanian plane crashed; 54 dead
	Tornadoes	Midwest United States	April 11; tornadoes killed 272
	Cyclone	Barisal, East Pakistan	May 12; storm killed 12,000 to 20,000; millions homeless
	Aircraft	near Cairo	May 20; Pakistan International Boeing 707 crashed; 119 dead
	Mine	Bihar State, India	May 28; coal mine accident; more than 400 dead
	Mine	Kyushu, Japan	June 1; accident killed 236
	Mine	Kakanj, Yugoslavia	June 7; gas explosion claimed 108
	Aircraft	near El Toro, California	June 25; military plane hit mountain; 84 dead
	Aircraft	British Columbia	July 8; Canadian Pacific DC–6B crashed; 52 dead
	Explosion	near Searcy, Arkansas	August 9; explosion and fire at missile site killed 53
	Hurricane	Florida and Louisiana	August 27–Sept. 12; Hurricane Betsy killed 75, injured 17,500
	Rail	near Durban, South Africa	October 4; train derailed; 81 dead
	Aircraft	near Cincinnati, Ohio	November 8; American Boeing 727 crashed into hill; 58 dead
	Marine	in the Caribbean	November 13; Panamanian cruise ship **Yarmouth Castle** caught fire and sank; 89 dead
	Rail	near Toungoo, Burma	December 9; two trains collided, killing 76
	Cyclone	Karachi, Pakistan	December 15; cyclone killed 10,000 (?)
1966	Flood	Rio de Janeiro	January 11–13; deluge and landslides killed more than 300
	Aircraft	in the French Alps	January 24; Air India 707 crashed into Mont Blanc; 117 dead
	Marine	Chandpur Port, East Pakistan	January 30; Pakistani launch and steamer collided; 80 dead
	Marine	near Belawan, Indonesia	February 2; Indonesian oil tanker sank; 89 lost
	Aircraft	Tokyo	February 4; Boeing 727 plunged into Tokyo Bay; 133 dead
	Tornadoes	Mississippi and Alabama	March 3; tornadoes killed 58
	Aircraft	Honshu, Japan	March 5; BOAC Boeing 707 caught fire and crashed into Mount Fujiyama; 124 dead
	Rail	Lumding Junction, India	April 20; train exploded, killing 55
	Aircraft	near Ardmore, Oklahoma	April 22; military charter plane crashed; 83 dead
	Rail	Bombay	June 13; two-train collision claimed 60
	Earthquake	eastern Turkey	August 19; quake killed 2,529, rendering 108,000 (?) homeless
	Aircraft	Belgrade	August 31; British Airways turboprop crashed; 96 dead
	Hurricane	Caribbean and Mexico	September 25–October 1; cyclone fatal for at least 200
	Marine	in the Gulf of Tonkin	October 26; U.S. aircraft carrier **Oriskany** caught fire; 43 lost
	Marine	in Kosi River, India	October 26; Indian vessel sank; more than 100 dead
	Flood	Arno Valley, Italy	November 3–4; overflow of Arno River, which killed 113, destroyed priceless art treasures in Florence and elsewhere
	Aircraft	Bratislava, Czechoslovakia	November 24; TABSO Bulgarian Ilyushin–18 crashed; 82 dead
	Marine	in the Sea of Crete	December 8; Greek ferry **Heraklion** sank in storm; 217 dead

Year	Type of Disaster	Place	Remarks
1967	Flood	southern Brazil	January–March; heavy rain floods killed more than 600
	Missile	Cape Kennedy, Florida	January 27; the three-man crew of Apollo 1 die in fire
	Fire	Tasmania	February 7–9; forest fire killed 52; damage: $11.2 million
	Aircraft	Nicosia, Cyprus	April 20; Swiss Globe Britannia turboprop charter crashed while landing; 126 dead
	Tornadoes	northeastern Illinois	April 21; tornadoes killed 55
	Fire	Brussels	May 22; Innovation department store burned; 322 lost their lives
	Aircraft	in the French Pyrenees	June 3; British Air Ferry Ltd. DC–6 charter crashed into Mont Canigou; 88 dead
	Aircraft	Stockport, England	June 4; British Midland charter DC–4 crashed; 72 dead
	Rail	Langenweddingen, East Germany	June 6; train collided with gasoline truck and exploded; 82 dead
	Aircraft	near Hendersonville, North Carolina	July 19; Piedmont Boeing 727 and private plane collided; 82 dead
	Marine	off Vietnam	July 25; U.S. aircraft carrier **Forrestal** crippled by fire; 134 dead
	Earthquake	Venezuela	July 30–31; quake, ranging from the Andes to Caribbean, killed 277; damage in Caracas alone: $15 million
	Fire	U.S. Northwest and British Columbia	August–September; millions of acres of forest consumed
	Aircraft	southern Turkey	October 12; BEA Comet crashed; 67 dead
	Rail	London	November 5; express train derailed; 53 dead
	Aircraft	near Cincinnati, Ohio	November 20; TWA Convair 880 crashed near airport; 70 dead
	Flood	Lisbon	November 26; fatality toll: 457
1968	Marine	in the eastern Mediterranean	January 26; Israeli submarine **Dakar** sank; 69 dead
	Marine	in the western Mediterranean	January 27; French submarine **Minerve** went down; 52 lost
	Aircraft	Guadeloupe, West Indies	March 5; Air France Boeing 707 crashed; 63 dead
	Aircraft	Atlantic Ocean off Wales	March 24; Irish International Viscount crashed; 61 dead
	Marine	Wellington Harbor	April 10; New Zealand ferry **Wahine** crashed and sank; 51 dead
	Aircraft	near Windhoek, South-West Africa	April 20; South African Boeing 707 crashed; 123 dead
	Aircraft	near Dawson, Texas	May 3; Braniff Electra crashed; 85 dead
	Tornadoes	Midwest United States	May 15; tornadoes killed 71
	Marine	in the Atlantic, southwest of the Azores	May 27; U.S. nuclear submarine **Scorpion** sank; 99 lost
	Flood	Gujarat, India	August 8–14; floods killed 1,000 (?)
	Earthquake	northeastern Iran	August 31; quake killed 12,000 (?)
	Aircraft	off the French Riviera	September 11; Air France Caravelle crashed; 95 dead
	Mine	near Mannington, West Virginia	November 20; coal mine exploded and caught fire; 78 dead
	Aircraft	off Caracas, Venezuela	December 12; Pan Am Boeing 707 crashed; 51 dead
1969	Floods	southern California	January 25–29; floods killed 95
	Aircraft	La Coruba, Venezuela	March 16; VIASA DC-9 crashed near Maracaibo; 154 dead
	Aircraft	Aswan Airport, Egypt	March 20; United Arab IL-18 crashed while landing; 91 dead
	Mine	Barroteran, Mexico	March 31; gas mine exploded; 156 dead
	Cyclone	Dacca, East Pakistan	April 15; storm killed 500 (?)
	Marine	in the South China Sea	June 2; U.S. destroyer **Frank E. Evans** sliced in two by the Australian carrier **Melbourne**; 74 assumed dead
	Aircraft	near Monterrey, Mexico	June 4; Mexican Airways Boeing 727 crashed; 79 dead
	Rail	near Benares, India	June 21; train plunged off tracks into river bed; 75 dead
	Rail	Jaipur, India	July 15; freight train rammed standing passenger train; 85 dead
	Hurricane	Mississippi and Louisiana	August 17; Hurricane Camille killed 256
	Floods	Virginia	August 23; floods killed 100 (?)
	Aircraft	near Indianapolis, Indiana	September 9; small plane and Allegheny DC–9 collided; 83 dead
	Aircraft	near Danang	September 20; Air Vietnam DC-4 crashed; 77 dead
	Aircraft	near La Paz, Bolivia	September 26; Lloyd Aereo Boliviano DC-6 crashed in the Andes; 74 dead
1970	Rail	near Buenos Aires	February 4; commuter train struck by express train; 236 killed
	Avalanche	Val d'Isère, France	February 10; worst snowslide in French history killed 42 at youth hostel
	Aircraft	in the Caribbean	February 15; Dominican DC–9 crashed, killing 102
	Marine	in the Mediterranean	March 4; French submarine **Eurydice** exploded, sank; 57 dead
	Earthquake	Kutahya, Turkey	March 28; quake toll: more than 1,000
	Aircraft	Casablanca, Morocco	April 1; Royal Air Maroc Caravelle jetliner crashed; 61 killed
	Explosion	Osaka, Japan	April 8; serial gas-main blasts killed 73; 300 injured
	Avalanche	Saint-Gervais, France	April 16; snowslide hit tuberculosis sanatorium, killing 72
	Flood	Oradea, Rumania	May 11–23; 200 (?) killed; more than 225 towns destroyed
	Earthquake	northern Peru	May 31; quake plus floods and landslides killed 30,000 (?)
	Aircraft	Barcelona	July 4; British charter Comet jet crashed; 112 dead
	Aircraft	Toronto	July 5; Air Canada DC-8 crashed; 108 killed
	Bus	New Delhi	July 22; 25 buses, 5 taxis, and an army vehicle swept into narrow gorge by floods; 600 dead
	Aircraft	near Cuzco, Peru	August 9; Peruvian Electra crashed; 100 dead
	Fire	Saint-Laurent-du-Pont, France	November 1; fire in a dance hall killed 146
	Cyclone	East Pakistan, delta region	November 12; storm and floods killed 500,000 (?)
	Aircraft	Huntington, West Virginia	November 14; Southern Airways DC-9 carrying the Marshall Univ. football team exploded while landing; 75 killed
1971	Aircraft	Moscow	January 1; Aeroflot II-18 crashed during takeoff; 90 killed
	Marine	near Dungeness, England	January 13; freighter hit submerged wreckage; 21 lost
	Earthquake	Los Angeles area	February 9; quake killed 64, of these, 43 were at V.A. hospital
	Tornado	Mississippi and Louisiana	February 21; storm killed 115
	Avalanche	Lima, Peru	February 19; Andean avalanche killed 600 (?)
	Earthquake	Bingol, Turkey	May 23; quake killed 800
	Aircraft	Belgrade	May 23; Yugoslav TU-134A crashed at Rijeka Airport; 78 killed
	Aircraft	Honshu, Japan	July 30; Japanese airliner struck by fighter plane over Japanese Alps; 162 dead
	Aircraft	Alaska	September 4; Alaska Airlines 727 crashed into a mountain in the Tongass National Forest; all 111 passengers killed

Year	Type of Disaster	Place	Remarks
	Fire	Seoul, S. Korea	December 25; explosion and fire at hotel; 163 dead
1972	Flood	Buffalo Creek, W. Virginia	February 26; coal mine waste waters caused a makeshift dam to collapse; 118 dead
	Aircraft	United Arab Emirates	March 14; Danish Sterling Airways charter crashed near Dubai; all 112 passengers killed
	Poisoning	Iraq	March–April; outbreak of mercury poisoning; over 100 dead
	Earthquake	Iran	April 10; 45 villages leveled; over 5,000 dead
	Mine	Kellogg, Idaho	May 2; fire in the Sunshine Silver Mine; 91 miners dead
	Aircraft	Palermo, Italy	May 6; Alitalia DC-8 struck a mountainside in bad weather; all 115 passengers killed
	Fire	Osaka, Japan	May 13; Sennichi department store gutted by flames; 115 killed
	Mine	Northwest Rhodesia	June 6; explosion in Wankie Colliery Co. coal mine; 427 dead
	Flood	Rapid City, S. Dakota	June 10; flash flooding caused over $120 million damage; 226 dead, 124 missing
	Hurricane	Eastern United States	June 10–20; Florida, Maryland, Pennsylvania, New York, and Virginia declared disaster areas; $1.7 billion damage; 134 dead
	Rail	Soissons, France	June 17; falling rocks in a tunnel cause derailment; 107 dead
	Aircraft	London	June 18; BEA Trident crashed on takeoff; 118 dead
	Flood	Luzon Island, Philippines	June-August; Typhoon Rita and six weeks of rain caused landslides and burst dams; 427 dead
	Aircraft	East Berlin	August 14; Interflug Ilyushin-62 crashed on takeoff; 156 dead
	Rail	Saltillo, Mexico	October 6; speeding passenger train jumped its tracks; 204 dead
	Aircraft	Krasnaya Polyana, USSR	October 14; Aeroflot Ilyushin-62 crashed; 176 dead
	Aircraft	Canary Islands	December 3; Spanish charter plane exploded; 155 dead
	Earthquake	Managua, Nicaragua	December 23; worst earthquake in Nicaraguan history; leveled 70% of the city; 10,000 dead
	Aircraft	near Miami	December 29; Eastern Airlines Tristar jetliner crashed into Everglades; 98 dead
1973	Aircraft	Kano, Nigeria	January 22; Boeing 707 jet carrying 200 Moslems from a pilgrimage to Mecca crashed in thick fog; 176 dead
	Epidemic	Bangladesh	Reported March 1; smallpox swept country, killing at least 1,000
	Flood	Western Tunisia	March 31; week-long rains flooded Mejerda River; 150 dead
	Aircraft	Basel, Switzerland	April 10; British charter flight crashed; 104 dead
	Marine	Dacca coast	May 5; two riverboats collided; 250 dead
	Storms	Indonesian Islands	Reported June 16; spring storms took 1,650 lives
	Aircraft	Paris	July 11; Brazilian Boeing 707 crashed in an emergency landing at Orly; 122 dead
	Aircraft	Boston	July 31; Delta jetliner crashed in fog; 88 dead
	Earthquake	central Mexico	August 28; earthquake and rains killed 527; 200,000 homeless
	Fire	Kumamoto, Japan	November 29; fire hit department store which had no fire escape chutes; 101 dead; 84 injured
	Marine	Ecuador coast	December 24; overloaded ferryboat capsized, killing 200
1974	Aircraft	Pago Pago, Samoa	January 31; Pan Am jet crashed on landing; 92 dead
	Fire	Sao Paulo, Brazil	February 1; a faulty air conditioner caused a flash fire to sweep a modern bank, killing 189 people in 25 minutes
	Famine	Sahel, West Africa	Reported March 3; 100,000 persons were estimated dead and millions starving due to drought in this sub-Sahara region
	Aircraft	Paris	March 3; Turkish DC-10 crashed on takeoff from Orly; 346 dead
	Aircraft	Leningrad	April 27; Soviet Ilyushin 18 crashed on takeoff; 108 killed
	Aircraft	Bali, Indonesia	April 27; Pan Am 707 crashed on landing; 107 dead
	Marine	Bangladesh coast	May 1; motor launch capsized; 250 dead
1975	Aircraft	Saigon, South Vietnam	April 4; U.S. Air Force C-5A transport jet carrying South Vietnamese orphans to U.S. crashed on takeoff; 155 dead
	Famine	East Africa	Reported May 25; drought since October 1974 in Ethiopia and Somalia; 40,000 dead
	Aircraft	New York	June 24; Eastern Airlines Boeing 727 crashed on landing at Kennedy International Airport; 113 dead
	Flood	northern India	July; month-long monsoon rains caused flooding; 300 dead
	Marine	near Canton, China	August 3; two ferries collided on Hsi River; 500 (?) drowned
	Aircraft	near Agadir, Morocco	August 3; charter Boeing 707 hit mountainside; 188 dead
	Aircraft	Damascus, Syria	August 20; Czechoslovak airliner crashed; 126 dead
	Flood	eastern India	August-September; monsoon rains cause flooding and spread of cholera; 450 (?) dead
	Earthquake	Lice, Turkey	September 6; earthquake leaves 2,312 dead, 3,372 injured
	Mine	near Dhanbad, India	December 27; coal mine explosion caused flooding of mine; 372 believed dead
1976	Aircraft	Saudi Arabia	January 1; Middle East Airlines Boeing 707 crashed; 82 dead
	Earthquake	Guatemala	February 4; earthquake toll estimated 22,419 dead, 74,105 injured and 1 million homeless
	Aircraft	Erivan, USSR	March 5; Soviet Il-18 crashed; 120 dead
	Earthquake	Friuli region of Italy	May 6; earthquake in northeast Italy; more than 1,000 dead
	Earthquake	Indonesia	June 26 and July 14; successive quakes, the first on West New Guinea caused mudslides, which left 443 dead, 3,000 missing; the second quake in Bali left 600 dead, 3,400 injured
	Earthquake	Tangshan area of China	July 28; two major quakes devastated industrial city of Tangshan; casualities estimated to be about 700,000, the second worst disaster in recorded history
	Flood	Big Thompson River, Colo.	July 31; vacationers and campers caught in flash flood in canyon; 138 dead, 5 missing
	Earthquake	southern Philippines	August 17; earthquake hit Mindanao and neighboring islands, 8,000 (?) dead or missing and 175,000 homeless
	Aircraft	near Zagreb, Yugoslavia	September 10; Yugoslav charter jet DC-10 and British Airlines Trident collided in world's worst midair collision; 176 dead
	Aircraft	near Isparta, Turkey	September 19; Turkish Boeing 727 hit mountain; 155 dead
	Flood	La Paz, Mexico	October 1; earthen dam broke after heavy rains; 630 dead
	Aircraft	Santa Cruz, Bolivia	October 15; Boeing 707 cargo plane crashed in downtown Santa Cruz; 100 dead
	Earthquake	Van Province, Turkey	November 24; earthquake; estimated 4,000 dead

Year	Type of Disaster	Place	Remarks
1977	Rail	Granville, Australia	January 18; Sydney-bound commuter train derailed; 82 dead
	Earthquake	Bucharest, Romania	March 4; earthquake leaves 1,541 dead, 11,275 injured and 80,000 homeless
	Aircraft	Tenerife, Canary Islands	March 27; Pan American 747 and KLM 747 jumbo jets collide on runway; 579 dead in worst disaster in aviation history
	Tornado	near Dacca, Bangladesh	April 1; tornado struck Madaripur district; about 900 dead
	Fire	Southgate, Kentucky	May 28; supper club fire; 161 dead, 129 injured
	Flood	Johnstown, Pennsylvania	July 19-20; nine-inch rainfall caused flash flood; over 70 dead
	Storm	Andhra Pradesh, India	November 19; cyclone caused tidal wave killing 20,000
	Aircraft	Funchal, Madeira	November 19; Portuguese 727 crashed on landing; 130 dead
	Aircraft	Johore Strait, Malaysia	December 4; Malaysian 737 exploded after hijacking; 100 dead
	Earthquake	Kerman Province, Iran	December 20; earthquake hit rural villages; over 520 dead
1978	Aircraft	near Bombay, India	January 1; Air India 747 exploded and crashed; 213 dead
	Aircraft	near Sofia, Bulgaria	March 16; Bulgarian airliner crashed; 73 dead
	Tornado	Orissa, India	April 16; storm killed 400 to 500 in six villages
	Construction	St. Marys, West Virginia	April 27; scaffolding on cooling tower collapsed; 51 dead
	Explosion	near Tarragona, Spain	July 11; propylene gas truck exploded at tourist camp; 200 dead
	Explosion	Beirut, Lebanon	August 13; blast destroyed building, killing 150 to 200
	Fire	Abadan, Iran	August 20; arsonist-set theater fire killed 430
	Earthquake	Tabas, Iran	September 16; major quake; estmated 25,000 dead
	Aircraft	San Diego, California	September 25; Pacific Southwest 727 jet and private plane collided in midair; 150 dead
	Marine	Bay of Bengal	April 4; fleet of cargo boats lost in storm; 1,000 dead
	Mass suicide	Jonestown, Guyana	November 18; mass poisoning and murder in American religious commune; over 900 dead
	Aircraft	Leh, India	November 19; Indian Air Force transport crashed; 78 killed
	Storm	Sri Lanka and India	November 23; cyclone leveled 500,000 buildings; over 1,500 dead
	Aircraft	Colombo, Sri Lanka	November 25; charter Icelandic DC-8 jet crashed in thunderstorm; 183 dead
	Aircraft	Tyrrhenian Sea	December 23; Alitalia DC-9 jet ditched at sea; 103 dead
1979	Earthquake	eastern Iran	January 16; quake killed 199
	Flood	southeast Brazil	early February; over 40 days of heavy rain caused severe flooding; over 600 dead, 350,000 homeless
	Volcanic eruption	central Java	February 21; 175 killed, 1,000 others injured by lava flow
	Aircraft	near Moscow	March 17; Tupolev 104 crashed after takeoff; 90 dead
	Poison	near Sverdlovsk, U.S.S.R.	April–May; anthrax epidemic reported, but experts suspect biological weapon mishap; toll put at more than 1,000 dead
	Tornado	Texas and Oklahoma	April 10; twisters struck border area; 60 dead, over 800 injured
	Earthquake	Yugoslavia and Albania	April 15; shocks hit coast; over 120 dead; 1,500 injured
	Cyclones	southeast India	May 12–13; storms killed over 600
	Aircraft	Chicago	May 25; American Airlines DC-10 crashed; 272 on board and 2 on ground dead in worst U.S. air disaster
	Aircraft	Sumatra, Indonesia	July 11; domestic airliner crashed into mountain; 61 dead
	Fire	Saragossa, Spain	July 13; hotel fire; 80 dead
	Bus	Lugezi, Tanzania	July 14; overcrowded bus fell into Lake Victoria; 60 dead
	Tidal wave	Lomblem, Indonesia	July 17; death toll estimated at 539
	Fire	Tuticorin, India	July 29; movie tent fire; 92 dead
	Flood	Morvi, India	August 11; dam collapsed; at least 5,000 dead
	Aircraft	over Ukraine	August 11; two Soviet jet liners collide; 173 dead
	Rail	Bangkok, Thailand	August 21; trains collided; 51 dead
	Hurricane	Caribbean and east coast of U.S.	Aug. 30–Sept. 7; Hurricane David took over 1,100 lives, left 150,000 homeless
	Rail	Stalac, Yugoslavia	Sept. 13; freight and passenger train collided; 80 dead
	Aircraft	Mexico City	October 31; Western Airlines DC-10 crashed while landing; 75 dead
	Marine	near Khulna, Bangladesh	early November; cargo ship and river launch collided, at least 200 dead
	Earthquake	northeastern Iran	November 14; quake took 248 lives
	Marine	Bo Hai Gulf, China	November 25; oil drilling rig collapsed during storm; 70 dead
	Aircraft	Taif, Saudi Arabia	November 26; Boeing 707 jetliner carrying pilgrims from Mecca crashed; 156 dead
	Aircraft	Mt. Erebus, Antarctica	November 28; New Zealand sightseeing DC-10 crashed into mountain; 257 dead
	Earthquake	Colombia-Ecuador border	December 12; quake and tidal waves took 200 lives
1980	Aircraft	near Tehran, Iran	January 21; Boeing 707 crashed; 128 dead
	Structural	Sincelejo, Colombia	January 21; bullring collapsed; 222 dead
	Aircraft	near Warsaw	March 14; Polish Ilyushin 62 crashed; 87 dead
	Marine	North Sea	March 27; Oil platform collapsed during storm; 137 dead
	Aircraft	Florianopolis, Brazil	April 12; Boeing 727 crashed; 57 dead
	Aircraft	Canary Islands	April 25; British Boeing 727 crashed; 146 dead
	Marine	Tampa Bay, Florida	May 9; Liberian freighter rammed bridge; bus and car thrown into water; 35 dead
	Volcanic eruption	Mt. St. Helens, Washington	May 18; volcano erupted devastating large area; 34 killed and 28 presumed dead
	Fire	Kingston, Jamaica	May 20; Fire involving arson, in home for elderly; 157 dead
	Aircraft	Alma Ata, U.S.S.R.	July 7; Soviet TU-142 jetliner crashed; 163 dead
	Hurricane	eastern Caribbean, Yucatan and Texas Gulf coast	August 4–11; Hurricane Allen demolished homes and crops; 272 dead
	Explosion	Bologna, Italy	August 6; bomb exploded in train station; 76 dead
	Flood	Uttar Pradesh, India	August 12; monsoon flooding of Ganges; over 600 dead
	Riot	Moradabad, India	August 13; riot in mosque caused 86 deaths
	Aircraft	Riyadh, Saudi Arabia	August 19; fire aboard Lockheed L-1011 jet liner; 301 dead
	Rail	near Torun, Poland	August 19; passenger and freight train collided; 62 dead, 50 hurt
	Marine	Ciudad del Carmen, Mexico	August 22; ferryboat sank; over 50 dead
	Flood	Ibadan, Nigeria	August 31; flooding from rainstorms; 240 dead
	Aircraft	near Medina, Saudi Arabia	Sept. 14; Saudi Air Force transport crashed; 89 killed
	Earthquake	Al Asnam, Algeria	October 10; earthquake toll over 6,000 dead
	Explosion	Ortuella, Spain	October 23; explosion destroyed school; 51 killed, mostly children

SPORTS

CONTENTS:

THE OLYMPICS

THE SUMMER OLYMPIC GAMES

Sites	Year	Total Events	Total Nations	Total Athletes	Sites	Year	Total Events	Total Nations	Total Athletes
I Athens	1896	42	13	285	XV Helsinki	1952	149	69	5,867
II Paris	1900	60	20	1,066	XVI Melbourne	1956	145	67	3,184
III St. Louis	1904	67	11	496	XVI Stockholm*	1956	3	29	154
IV London	1908	104	22	2,059	XVII Rome	1960	150	84	5,396
V Stockholm	1912	106	28	2,541	XVIII Tokyo	1964	163	94	5,565
VII Antwerp	1920	154	29	2,606	XIX Mexico City	1968	172	109	6,082
VIII Paris	1924	137	44	3,092	XX Munich	1972	194	121	8,500
IX Amsterdam	1928	120	46	3,015	XXI Montreal	1976	198	87	6,512
X Los Angeles	1932	124	37	1,408	XXII Moscow	1980	203	80	5,923
XI Berlin	1936	142	49	4,069	XXIII Los Angeles	1984			
XIV London	1948	138	59	4,468					

* Equestrian Games only.

1980 SUMMER OLYMPIC GAMES Moscow, U.S.S.R., July 19–August 3

Participating Nations

Afghanistan	Cuba	India	Mexico	Sierra Leone
Algeria	Cyprus	Iraq	Mongolia	Spain
Andorra	Czechoslovakia	Ireland	Mozambique	Sri Lanka
Angola	Denmark	Italy	Nepal	Sweden
Australia	Dominican Rep.	Jamaica	Netherlands	Switzerland
Austria	Ecuador	Jordan	New Zealand	Syria
Belgium	Ethiopia	Korea, North	Nicaragua	Tanzania
Benin	Finland	Kuwait	Nigeria	Trinidad & Tobago
Botswana	France	Laos	Peru	Uganda
Brazil	Germany, East	Lebanon	Poland	USSR
Bulgaria	Greece	Lesotho	Portugal	United Kingdom
Burma	Guatemala	Libya	Puerto Rico	Venezuela
Cameroon	Guinea	Luxembourg	Romania	Vietnam
Colombia	Guyana	Madagascar	San Marino	Yugoslavia
Congo	Hungary	Mali	Senegal	Zambia
Costa Rica	Iceland	Malta	Seychelles	Zimbabwe

Non-Participating Nations

Albania	Chile	Iran	Morocco	Sudan
Antigua	China	Israel	Neth. Antilles	Suriname
Argentina	China (Taiwan)	Ivory Coast	Nigeria	Swaziland
Bahamas	Egypt	Japan	Norway	Thailand
Bahrain	El Salvador	Kenya	Pakistan	Togo
Bangladesh	Fiji	Korea, South	Panama	Tunisia
Barbados	Gabon	Liberia	Papua New Guinea	Turkey
Belize	Gambia	Liechtenstein	Paraguay	United Arab Emirates
Bermuda	Germany, West	Malawi	Philippines	United States
Bolivia	Ghana	Malaysia	Qatar	Upper Volta
Canada	Haiti	Mauritania	Saudi Arabia	Uruguay
Cayman Is.	Honduras	Mauritius	Singapore	Virgin Islands
Central African Rep.	Hong Kong	Monaco	Somalia	Zaire
Chad	Indonesia			

1980 SUMMER OLYMPICS MEDAL TABLE

	Gold (1st)	Silver (2nd)	Bronze (3rd)	Total
USSR	80	69	46	195
East Germany	47	37	43	127
Bulgaria	8	16	17	41
Cuba	8	7	5	20
Italy	8	3	4	15
Hungary	7	10	15	32
Romania	6	6	13	25
France	6	5	3	14
Britain	5	7	9	21
Poland	3	14	15	32
Sweden	3	3	6	12
Finland	3	1	4	8
Czechoslovakia	2	3	8	13
Yugoslavia	2	3	4	9
Australia	2	2	5	9
Denmark	2	1	2	5
Brazil	2	0	2	4
Ethiopia	2	0	2	4
Switzerland	2	0	0	2
Spain	1	3	2	6
Austria	1	2	1	4
Greece	1	0	2	3
Belgium	1	0	0	1
India	1	0	0	1
Zimbabwe	1	0	0	1
North Korea	0	3	2	5
Mongolia	0	2	2	4
Mexico	0	1	3	4
Netherlands	0	1	2	3
Jamaica	0	0	3	3
Tanzania	0	2	0	2
Ireland	0	1	1	2
Venezuela	0	1	0	1
Uganda	0	1	0	1
Guyana	0	0	1	1
Lebanon	0	0	1	1

MEDALISTS AT MOSCOW: 1980

1st (gold), 2nd (silver), 3rd (bronze)

ARCHERY

Men—Tomi Poikolainen, Finland
2. USSR, 3. Italy

Women—Keto Losaberidze, USSR
2. USSR, 3. Finland

BASKETBALL

Men—Yugoslavia
2. Italy, 3. USSR

Women—USSR
2. Bulgaria, 3. Yugoslavia

BOXING

106 lb—Shamil Sabyrov, USSR
2. Cuba, 3. Bulgaria, N. Korea

112 lb—Petar Lessov, Bulgaria
2. USSR, 3. Hungary, Ireland

119 lb—Juan Hernandez, Cuba
2. Venezuela, 3. Guyana, Romania

126 lb—Rudi Fink, E. Germany
2. Cuba, 3. Poland, USSR

132 lb—Angel Herrera, Cuba
2. USSR, 3. E. Germany, Poland

140 lb—Patrizio Oliva, Italy
2. USSR, 3. Britain, Cuba

148 lb—Andres Aldama, Cuba
2. Uganda, 3. E. Germany, Poland

157 lb—Armando Martinez, Cuba
2. USSR, 3. Czechoslovakia, E. Germany

165 lb—Jose Gomez, Cuba
2. USSR, 3. Poland, Romania

179 lb—Slobodan Kacar, Yugoslavia
2. Poland, 3. Cuba, E. Germany

Hvywt—Teofilo Stevenson, Cuba
2. USSR, 3. E. Germany, Hungary

CANOEING—MEN

Single Canoe
500 m—Sergei Postrekhin, USSR
2. Bulgaria, 3. E. Germany

1000 m—Lubomir Lubenov, Bulgaria
2. USSR, 3. E. Germany

Double Canoe
500 m—Hungary (Foltan, Vaskuti)
2. Romania, 3. Bulgaria

1000 m—Romania (Potzaichin, Simionov)
2. E. Germany, 3. USSR

Single Kayak
500 m—Vladimir Parfenovich, USSR
2. Australia, 3. Romania

1000 m—Rudiger Helm, E. Germany
2. France, 3. Romania

Double Kayak
500 m—USSR (Parfenovich, Chukhrai)
2. Spain, 3. E. Germany

1000 m—USSR (Parfenovich, Chukhrai)
2. Hungary, 3. Spain

Four-Man Kayak
1000 m—East Germany
2. Romania, 3. Bulgaria

CANOEING—WOMEN

Single Kayak
500 m—Birgit Fischer, E. Germany
2. Bulgaria, 3. USSR

Double Kayak
500 m—E. Germany (Genauss, Bischof)
2. USSR, 3. Hungary

CYCLING

100 km Team Road Race—USSR
2. E. Germany, 3. Czechoslovakia

4000 m Team Pursuit—USSR
2. E. Germany, 3. Czechoslovakia

1000 m Time Trial—Lothar Thoms,
E. Germany, 2. USSR, 3. Jamaica

Individual Sprint—Lutz Hesslich,
E. Germany, 2. France, 3. USSR

Individual Pursuit—Robert Dill-Bundi,
Switzerland, 2. France, 3. Denmark

Individual Road Race—Sergei
Sukhoruchenkov, USSR
2. Poland, 3. USSR

DIVING

Springboard
Men—Aleksandr Portnov, USSR
2. Mexico, 3. Italy

Women—Irina Kalinina, USSR
2. E. Germany, 3. E. Germany

Platform
Men—Falk Hoffman, E. Germany
2. USSR, 3. USSR

Women—Martina Jaschke, E. Germany
2. USSR, 3. USSR

EQUESTRIAN

Three-Day Individual—Frederico
Euro Roman, Italy, 2. USSR, 3. USSR

Three-Day Team—USSR
2. Italy, 3. Mexico

Dressage Individual—Elisabeth Theurer,
Austria, 2. USSR, 3. USSR

Dressage Team—USSR
2. Bulgaria, 3. Romania

Jumping Individual—Jan Kowalczyk,
Poland, 2. USSR, 3. Mexico

Jumping Team—USSR
2. Poland, 3. Mexico

FENCING—MEN

Individual Foil—Vladimir Smirnov,
USSR, 2. France, 3. USSR

Team Foil—France
2. USSR, 3. Poland

Individual Epee—Johan Harmenberg,
Sweden, 2. Hungary, 3. France

Team Epee—France
2. Poland, 3. USSR

Individual Sabre—Viktor Krovopuskov,
USSR, 2. USSR, 3. Hungary

Team Sabre—USSR
2. Italy, 3. Hungary

FENCING—WOMEN

Individual Foil—Pascale Trinquet,
France, 2. Hungary, 3. Poland

Team Foil—France
2. USSR, 3. Hungary

FIELD HOCKEY

Men—India
2. Spain, 3. USSR

Women—Zimbabwe
2. Czechoslovakia, 3. USSR

GYMNASTICS—MEN

All-Around—Aleksandr Ditiatin, USSR
2. USSR, 3. Bulgaria

Parallel Bars—Aleksandr Tkachyov,
USSR, 2. USSR, 3. E. Germany

Vault—Nikolai Andrianov, USSR
2. USSR, 3. E. Germany

Pommel Horse—Zoltan Magyar, Hungary
2. USSR, 3. E. Germany

Rings—Aleksandr Ditiatin, USSR
2. USSR, 3. Czechoslovakia

Horizontal Bar—Stoyan Deltchev,
Bulgaria, 2. USSR, 3. USSR

Floor Exercise—Roland Bruckner,
E. Germany, 2. USSR, 3. USSR

Team Competition—USSR
2. E. Germany, 3. Hungary

GYMNASTICS—WOMEN

All-Around—Yelena Davydova, USSR
2. (tie) E. Germany, Romania

Balance Beam—Nadia Comaneci,
Romania, 2. USSR, 3. USSR

Uneven Bars—Maxi Gnauck, E. Germany
2. Romania, 3. (tie) Romania,
E. Germany, USSR

Vault—Natalia Shaposhnikova,
USSR, 2. E. Germany, 3. Romania

Floor Exercise—(tie) Nelli Kim, USSR-
Nadia Comaneci, Romania, 3. (tie)
USSR, E. Germany

Team Competition—USSR
2. Romania, 3. E. Germany

HANDBALL

Men—East Germany
2. USSR, 3. Romania

Women—USSR
2. Yugoslavia, 3. E. Germany

JUDO

132 lb—Thierry Rey, France
2. Cuba, 3. USSR, Hungary

143 lb—Nikolai Solodukhin, USSR
2. Mongolia, 3. Bulgaria, Poland

157 lb—Ezio Gamba, Italy
2. Britain, 3. Mongolia, E. Germany

172 lb—Shota Khabareli, USSR
2. Cuba, 3. E. Germany, France

190 lb—Juerg Roethlisberger, Switzerland
2. Cuba, 3. E. Germany, USSR

209 lb—Robert Van De Walle, Belgium
2. USSR, 3. E. Germany, Netherlands

Over 209 lb—Angelo Parisi, France
2. Bulgaria, 3. Czechoslovakia, Yugoslavia

Open Weight—Dietmar Lorenz, E. Germany
2. France, 3. Hungary, Britain

MODERN PENTATHLON

Individual—Anatoly Starostin, USSR
2. Hungary, 3. USSR

Team—USSR
2. Hungary, 3. Sweden

ROWING—MEN

Single Sculls—Pertti Karppinen,
Finland, 2. USSR, 3. E. Germany

Double Sculls—East Germany (Dreipke-
Kroppelein), 2. Yugoslavia,
3. Czechoslovakia

Pairs w/o Coxswain—E. Germany
(B. Landvoigt-J. Landvoigt)
2. USSR, 3. Britain

Pairs with Coxswain—East Germany
2. USSR, 3. Yugoslavia

Fours w/o Coxswain—East Germany
2. USSR, 3. Britain

Fours with Coxswain—East Germany
2. USSR, 3. Poland

Quadruple Sculls—East Germany
2. USSR, 3. Bulgaria

Eights—East Germany
2. Britain, 3. USSR

ROWING—WOMEN

Single Sculls—Sanda Toma, Romania
2. USSR, 3. E. Germany

Double Sculls—USSR (Khloptseva-
Popova), 2. E. Germany, 3. Romania

Pairs w/o Coxswain—East Germany
(Steindorf-Klier), 2. Poland 3. Bulgaria

Fours with Coxswain—East Germany
2. Bulgaria, 3. USSR

Quadruple Sculls—East Germany
2. USSR, 3. Bulgaria

Eights—East Germany
2. USSR, 3. Romania

SHOOTING

Free Pistol—Aleksandr Melentev,
USSR, 2. E. Germany, 3. Bulgaria

Rapid Fire Pistol—Corneliu Ion,
Romania, 2. E. Germany, 3. Austria

Rifle, Prone—Karoly Varga, Hungary
2. E. Germany, 3. Bulgaria

Rifle, 3-Position—Viktor Vlasov, USSR
2. E. Germany, 3. Sweden

Moving Target—Igor Sokolov, USSR
2. E. Germany, 3. USSR

Skeetshooting—Hans Kjeld Rasmussen,
Denmark, 2. Sweden, 3. Cuba

Trapshooting—Luciano Giovannetti,
Italy, 2. USSR, 3. E. Germany

SOCCER (FOOTBALL)

Team—Czechoslovakia
2. E. Germany, 3. USSR

SWIMMING—MEN
(*Olympic Record)

100 m Freestyle—Jorg Woithe, E. Germany
50.40, 2. Sweden, 3. Sweden

200 m Freestyle—Sergei Kopliakov, USSR
1:49.81*, 2. USSR, 3. Australia

400 m Freestyle—Vladimir Salnikov, USSR
3:51.31*, 2. USSR, 3. USSR

1500 m. Freestyle—Vladimir Salnikov, USSR
14:58.27*, 2. USSR, 3. Australia

100 m Backstroke—Bengt Baron, Sweden
56.53, 2. USSR, 3. USSR

200 m Backstroke—Sandor Wladar,
Hungary 2:01.93, 2. Hungary,
3. Australia

100 m Breaststroke—Duncan Goodhew,
Britain 1:03.34, 2. USSR, 3. Australia

200 m Breaststroke—Robertas Zulpa,
USSR 2:15.85, 2. Hungary, 3. USSR

100 m Butterfly—Par Arvidsson, Sweden
54.92, 2. E. Germany, 3. Spain

200 m Butterfly—Sergei Fesenko, USSR
1:59.76, 2. Britain, 3. E. Germany

400 m Indiv. Medley—Aleksandr
Sidorenko, USSR 4:22.89*, 2. USSR,
3. Hungary

400 m Medley Relay—Australia 3:45.70
2. USSR, 3. Britain

800 m Freestyle Relay—USSR 7:23.50
2. E. Germany, 3. Brazil

SWIMMING—WOMEN
(*Olympic Record)

100 m Freestyle—Barbara Krause,
E. Germany 54.79*, 2. E. Germany,
3. E. Germany

200 m Freestyle—Barbara Krause,
E. Germany 1:58.33*, 2. E. Germany,
3. E. Germany

400 m Freestyle—Ines Diers, E. Germany
4:08.76*, 2. E. Germany,
3. E. Germany

800 m Freestyle—Michelle Ford,
Australia 8:28.90*, 2. E. Germany,
3. E. Germany

100 m Backstroke—Rica Reinisch,
E. Germany 1:00.86*, 2. E. Germany
3. E. Germany

200 m Backstroke—Rica Reinisch,
E. Germany 2:11.77*, 2. E. Germany,
3. E. Germany

100 m Breaststroke—Ute Geweniger,
E. Germany 1:10.11*, 2. USSR,
3. Denmark

200 m Breaststroke—Lina Kachusite, USSR
2:29.54*, 2. USSR, 3. USSR

100 m Butterfly—Caren Metschuck,
E. Germany 1:00.42, 2. E. Germany,
3. E. Germany

200 m Butterfly—Ines Geissler,
  E. Germany 2:10.44*, 2. E. Germany,
  3. Australia

400 m Indiv. Medley—Petra Schneider,
  E. Germany 4:36.29*, 2. Britain,
  3. Poland

400 m Medley Relay—East Germany
  4:06.67*, 2. Britain, 3. USSR

400 m Freestyle Relay—East Germany
  3:42.71*, 2. Sweden, 3. Netherlands

TRACK AND FIELD—MEN
(*Olympic Record)

100 m Dash—Allan Wells, Britain 10.25
  2. Cuba, 3. Bulgaria

200 m Dash—Pietro Mennea, Italy
  20.19, 2. Britain, 3. Jamaica

400 m Dash—Viktor Markin, USSR 44.60
  2. Australia, 3. E. Germany

800 m Run—Steve Ovett, Britain
  1:45.4, 2. Britain, 3. USSR

1500 m Run—Sebastian Coe, Britain
  3:38.4, 2. E. Germany, 3. Britain

5000 m Run—Miruts Yifter, Ethiopia
  13:21.0*, 2. Tanzania, 3. Finland

10,000 m Run—Miruts Yifter, Ethiopia
  27:42.7, 2. Finland, 3. Ethiopia

Marathon—Waldemar Cierpinski,
  E. Germany 2:11:3, 2. Netherlands,
  3. USSR

110 m Hurdles—Thomas Munkelt,
  E. Germany 13.39, 2. Cuba, 3. USSR

400 m Hurdles—Volker Beck, E. Germany
  48.70, 2. USSR, 3. Britain

3000 m Steeplechase—
  Bronislaw Malinowski, Poland 8:09.7,
  2. Tanzania, 3. Ethiopia

400 m Relay—USSR 38.26
  2. Poland, 3. France

1600 m Relay—USSR 3:01.1
  2. E. Germany, 3. Italy

20 km Walk—Maurizio Damilano, Italy
  1:23:35.5*, 2. USSR, 3. E. Germany

50 km Walk—Hartwig Gauder, E. Germany
  3:49:24.0*, 2. Spain, 3. USSR

Long Jump—Lutz Dombrowski, E. Germany
  28' ¼", 2. E. Germany, 3. USSR

Triple Jump—Jaak Uudmae, USSR
  56' 11⅛", 2. USSR, 3. Brazil

High Jump—Gerd Wessig, E. Germany
  7' 8¾"*, 2. Poland, 3. E. Germany

Pole Vault—Wladyslaw Kozakiewicz, Poland
  18' 11½"*, 2. (tie) USSR, Poland

Shot Put—Vladimir Kiselyov, USSR
  70' ½"*, 2. USSR, 3. E. Germany

Discus Throw—Viktor Rashchupkin, USSR
  218' 8", 2. Czechoslovakia, 3. Cuba

Javelin Throw—Dainis Kula, USSR
  299' 2⅜", 2. USSR, 3. E. Germany

Hammer Throw—Yuri Sedykh, USSR
  268' 4½"*, 2. USSR, 3. USSR

Decathlon—Daley Thompson, Britain
  8,495 pts., 2. USSR, 3. USSR

TRACK AND FIELD—WOMEN
(*Olympic Record)

100 m Dash—Lyudmila Kondrateva, USSR
  11.06, 2. E. Germany, 3. E. Germany

200 m Dash—Barbel Wockel, E. Germany
  22.03*, 2. USSR, 3. Jamaica

400 m Dash—Marita Koch, E. Germany
  48.88*, 2. Czechoslovakia,
  3. E. Germany

800 m Run—Nadezhda Olizarenko, USSR
  1:53.5*, 2. USSR, 3. USSR

1500 m Run—Tatyana Kazankina, USSR
  3:56.6*, 2. E. Germany, 3. USSR

100 m Hurdles—Vera Komisova, USSR
  12.56*, 2. E. Germany, 3. Poland

400 m Relay—East Germany 41.60*
  2. USSR, 3. Britain

1600 m Relay—USSR 3:20.2
  2. E. Germany, 3. Britain

Long Jump—Tatiana Kolpakova, USSR
  23' 2"*, 2. E. Germany, 3. USSR

High Jump—Sara Simeoni, Italy
  6' 5½"*, 2. Poland, 3. E. Germany

Shot Put—Ilona Slupianek, E. Germany
  73' 6¼"*, 2. USSR, 3. E. Germany

Discus Throw—Evelin Jahl, E. Germany
  229' 6½"*, 2. Bulgaria, 3. USSR

Javelin Throw—Maria Colon, Cuba
  224' 5"*, 2. USSR, 3. E. Germany

Pentathlon—Nadezhda Tkachenko, USSR
  5083 pts.*, 2. USSR, 3. USSR

VOLLEYBALL

Men—USSR
  2. Bulgaria, 3. Romania

Women—USSR
  2. E. Germany, 3. Bulgaria

WATER POLO

Team—USSR
  2. Yugoslavia, 3. Hungary

WEIGHTLIFTING

115 lb—Kanybek Osmanoliev, USSR
  2. N. Korea, 3. N. Korea

123 lb—Daniel Nunez, Cuba
  2. USSR, 3. Poland

132 lb—Viktor Mazin, USSR
  2. Bulgaria, 3. Poland

149 lb—Yanko Roussev, Bulgaria
  2. E. Germany, 3. Bulgaria

165 lb—Assen Zlatev, Bulgaria
  2. USSR, 3. Bulgaria

182 lb—Yurik Vardanyan, USSR
  2. Bulgaria, 3. Czechoslovakia

198 lb—Peter Baczako, Hungary
  2. Bulgaria, 3. E. Germany

220 lb—Ota Zaremba, Czechoslovakia
  2. USSR, 3. Cuba

242 lb—Leonid Taranenko, USSR
  2. Bulgaria, 3. Hungary

Over 242 lb—Sultan Rakhmanov, USSR
  2. E. Germany, 3. Poland

WRESTLING, FREESTYLE

106 lb—Claudio Pollio, Italy
  2. N. Korea, 3. USSR

115 lb—Anatoly Beloglazov, USSR
  2. Poland, 3. Bulgaria

126 lb—Sergei Beloglazov, USSR
  2. N. Korea, 3. Mongolia

137 lb—Magomedgasan Abushev, USSR
  2. Bulgaria, 3. Greece

149 lb—Saipulla Absaidov, USSR
  2. Bulgaria, 3. Yugoslavia

165 lb—Valentin Raitchev, Bulgaria
  2. Mongolia, 3. Czechoslovakia

181 lb—Ismail Abilov, Bulgaria
  2. USSR, 3. Hungary

198 lb—Sanasar Oganesyan, USSR
  2. E. Germany, 3. Poland

220 lb—Ilya Mate, USSR
  2. Bulgaria, 3. Czechoslovakia

Over 220 lb—Soisan Andiev, USSR
  2. Hungary, 3. Poland

WRESTLING, GRECO-ROMAN

106 lb—Zaksylik Ushkempirov, USSR
  2. Romania, 3. Hungary

114 lb—Vakhtang Blagidze, USSR
  2. Hungary, 3. Bulgaria

125 lb—Shamil Serikov, USSR
  2. Poland, 3. Sweden

136 lb—Stilianos Migiakis, Greece
  2. Hungary, 3. USSR

150 lb—Stefan Rusu, Romania
  2. Poland, 3. Sweden

165 lb—Ferenc Kocsis, Hungary
  2. USSR, 3. Finland

180 lb—Gennady Korban, USSR
  2. Poland, 3. Bulgaria

198 lb—Norbert Nottny, Hungary
  2. USSR, 3. Romania

220 lb—Gheorghi Raikov, Bulgaria
  2. Poland, 3. Romania

Over 220 lb—Aleksandr Kolchinsky, USSR
  2. Bulgaria, 3. Lebanon

YACHTING

Tornado Class—Brazil
  2. Denmark, 3. Sweden

470 Class—Brazil
  2. E. Germany, 3. Finland

Flying Dutchman Class—Spain
  2. Ireland, 3. Hungary

Soling Class—Denmark
  2. USSR, 3. Greece

Finn Class—Finland
  2. Austria, 3. USSR

Star Class—USSR
  2. Austria, 3. Italy

1980 UNITED STATES OLYMPIC TEAM (Source: U.S. Olympic Committee)

The United States Olympic Team did not participate in the 1980 Moscow Olympics.

Archery

Judi Adams, Phoenix, Ariz.
Lynette Johnson, Glendale, Ariz.
Scott Kertson, Phoenix, Ariz.
Darrell Pace, Cincinnati, Ohio

Basketball—Men

Mark Aguirre, Chicago, Ill.
Rolando Blackman, Brooklyn, N.Y.
Sam Bowie, Lebanon, Pa.
Michael Brooks, Philadelphia, Pa.
Bill Hanzlick, Beloit, Wis.
Alton Lister, Dallas, Tex.
Rodney McCray, Mt. Vernon, N.Y.
Isaiah Thomas, Chicago, Ill.
Darnell Valentine, Wichita, Kans.
Danny Vranes, Salt L. City, Utah
Buck Williams, Rocky Mount, N.C.
Al Wood, Gray, Ga.

Basketball—Women

Carol Blazejowski, Elizabeth, N.J.
Denise Curry, Davis, Calif.
Anne Donovan, Ridgewood, N.J.
Tara Heiss, Bethesda, Md.
Kris Kirchner, Scotch Plains, N.J.
Debra Miller, Bronx, N.Y.
Cindy Noble, Clarksburg, Ohio
Lataunya Pollard, E. Chicago, Ind.
Jill Rankin, Phillips, Tex.
Rosie Walker, Emerson, Ark.
Holly Warlick, Knoxville, Tenn.
Lynette Woodard, Wichita, Kans.

Boxing

Jackie Beard, Jackson, Tenn.
Willie Broad, Wildwood, N.C.
Johnny Bumphus, Nashville, Tenn.
Willie Carter, Santa Monica, Calif.
Don Curry, Ft. Worth, Tex.
Joseph Manley, Ft. Bragg, N.C.
Lee Roy Murphy, Chicago, Ill.
Richard Sandoval, Pomona, Calif.
Robert Shannon, Edmonds, Wash.
James Shuler, Philadelphia, Pa.
Bernard Taylor, Knoxville, Tenn.

Canoeing—Men

Bruce Barton, Homer, Mich.
Gregory Barton, Homer, Mich.
David Gilman, Riverside, Calif.
Jay Kearney, Lexington, Ky.
Stephen Kelly, Bronx, N.Y.
Chuck Lyda, Olympic Valley, Calif.
Angus Morrison, Bryson, N.C.
Roland Muhlen, Cincinnati, Ohio
John Plankenhorn, Lombard, Ill.
Terry Streib, Bristol, Ind.
Jonathan Van Cleave,
    Laguna Beach, Calif.
Terry White, Arlington, Vt.
Andreas Weigand,
    Fountain Valley, Calif.

Canoeing—Women

Theresa DiMarino, Alexandria, Va.
Linda Dragan, Washington, D.C.
Leslie Klein, Concord, Mass.
Ann Turner, St. Charles, Ill.

Cycling

Leslie Barczewski, Milwaukee, Wis.
Robert Cook, Englewood, Colo.
Bruce Donaghy, Wescoville, Pa.
Thomas Doughty, Hobart, Ind.
Brent Emery, Milwaukee, Wis.
Mark Gorski, Itasca, Ill.
David Grylls, Grosse Pointe, Mich.
Greg LeMond, Carson City, Nev.
Leonard Nitz, Flushing, N.Y.
Thomas Schuler, Downers Grove, Ill.
Douglas Shapiro, Dix Hills, N.Y.
Dale Stetina, Indianapolis, Ind.
Wayne Stetina, Schererville, Ind.
Danny Van Haute, Chicago, Ill.
Andrew Weaver, Gainesville, Fla.

Diving—Men

Randolph Ableman, Cedar Rapids, Iowa
Brian Bungum, Austin, Tex.
Dave Burgering, Grand Rapids, Mich.
Gregory Louganis,
    Mission Viejo, Calif.
Kevin Machemer, Ann Arbor, Mich.

Diving—Women

Amy McGrath, Louisville, Ky.
Megan Neyer, Ashland, Ky.
Cynthia Potter, Dallas, Tex.
Chris Seufert, Ambler, Pa.
Barb Weinstein, Cincinnati, Ohio

Equestrian

Washington Bishop, Middleburg, Va.
Lendon Gray, Dixmont, Me.
Conrad Holmfeld, Pinehurst, N.C.
Norman Joio, South Salem, N.Y.
Katherine Monahan, Upperville, Va.
J. Michael Plumb, Chesapeake City,
    Md.
Teresa Rudd, New Hope, Pa.
Melanie Smith, Germantown, Tenn.
Karen Stives, Dover, Mass.
Gwen Stockebrand, Santa Rosa, Calif.
Torrance Watkins, Boyce, Va.
John Winnett, Tuxedo Park, N.Y.
James Wofford, Upperville, Va.
Linda Zang, Davidsonville, Md.

Fencing—Men

Timothy Glass, Houston, Tex.
Wayne Johnson, Vancouver, Wash.
Stanley Lekach, E. Moriches, N.Y.
Thomas Losonczy, New York, N.Y.
Michael Marx, Portland, Ore.
Gregory Massialas, Ann Arbor, Mich.
Robert Nieman, San Antonio, Tex.
John Nonna, Pleasantville, N.Y.
Alex Orban, Hackensack, N.J.
Paul Pesthy, San Antonio, Tex.
Phillip Reilly, New York, N.Y.
Mark Smith, Jamaica, N.Y.
Peter Westbrook, New York, N.Y.

Fencing—Women

Jana Angelakis, Peabody, Mass.
Gay D'Asaro, San Jose, Calif.
Nikki Franke, Philadelphia, Pa.
Elaine Ingram-Cheris, Denver, Colo.
Stacey Johnson, San Jose, Calif.

Field Hockey—Women

Elizabeth Anders, Norristown, Pa.
Elizabeth Beglin, Upper Saddle River,
    N.J.
Gwen Cheeseman, West Chester, Pa.
Denise Desautels, Hingham, Mass.
Jill Grant, Benton Harbor, Mich.
Sheryl Johnson, Cupertino, Calif.
Christine Larson, Glenolden, Pa.
Susan Marcellus, Somerset, Mass.
Anita Miller, Irvine, Calif.
Leslie Milne, Darien, Conn.
Charlene Morett, Aldan, Pa.
Diane Moyer, Laureldale, Pa.
Karen Shelton, Ocean View, N.J.
Julie Staver, Palmyra, Pa.
Judith Strong, Northampton, Pa.
Nancy White, McLean, Va.

Gymnastics—Men

Philip Cahoy, Omaha, Neb.
Bart Conner, Morton Grove, Ill.
Ron Galimore, Tallahassee, Fla.
Larry Gerard, Lincoln, Neb.
James Hartung, Omaha, Neb.
Peter Vidmar, Los Angeles, Calif.
Mike Wilson, Rowlett, Tex.

Gymnastics—Women

Luci Collins, Inglewood, Calif.
Marcia Frederick, North Haven, Conn.
Kathy Johnson, Doraville, Ga.
Beth Kline, Covina, Calif.
Amy Koopman, Arlington Hts., Ill.
Julianne McNamara, Danville, Calif.
Tracee Talavera, Walnut Creek, Calif.

Judo

Jesse Goldstein, Toms River, N.J.
Tommy Martin, Stockton, Calif.
Keith Nakasone, Cupertino, Calif.
Mitch Santa Maria, Roselle Park, N.J.
Steven Seck, Venice, Calif.
Michael Swain, Bridgewater, N.J.
Miguel Tudela, Alhambra, Calif.
Nicholas Yonezuka, Watchung, N.J.

Modern Pentathlon

Michael Burley, Barberton, Ohio
John Fitzgerald, San Antonio, Tex.
Dean Glenesk, San Antonio, Tex.
Robert Nieman, San Antonio, Tex.

Rowing—Men

Christopher Alsopp, Palo Alto, Calif.
Charles Alterkruse, Columbia, S.C.
William Belden, Paoli, Pa.
Frederick Borchelt, Arlington, Va.
Mark Borchelt, Arlington, Va.
John Carababas, Grosse Pte. Park,
    Mich.
Richard Cashin, Cambridge, Mass.
John Chatzky, Scarsdale, N.Y.
Steven Christensen, Dayton, Ohio
Sean Colgan, Ardmore, Pa.
Thomas Darling, Swampscott, Mass.
James Dietz, New Rochelle, N.Y.
Bruce Epke, Wilmington, Del.
Robert Espeseth, Champaign, Ill.
John Everett, South Easton, Mass.
Andy Fisher, Allston, Mass.
Thomas Hazeltine, Seattle, Wash.
Thomas Howes, Arlington, Mass.
Thomas Hull, Seattle, Wash.
Bruce Ibbetson, Tustin, Calif.
Robert Jaugstetter, Cambridge, Mass.
David Kehoe, Seattle, Wash.
Stephen Kiesling, New Haven, Conn.
Bradley Lewis, Corona del Mar,
    Calif.
Walter Lubsen, Arlington, Va.
Mark O'Brien, Mt. Clemens, Mich.
Paul Prioleau, Piedmont, Calif.
William Purdy, Liverpool, N.Y.
Daniel Sayner, Annapolis, Md.
Kurt Somerville, Wellesley, Mass.
Philip Stekl, Middletown, Conn.
John Terwilliger, Ben Lomond, Calif.
John Van Blom, Long Beach, Calif.
Christopher Wells, Alexandria, Va.
Christopher Wood, Allston, Mass.
Thomas Woodman, Beaverton, Ore.

Rowing—Women

Valerie Barber, West Dover, Vt.
Hope Barnes, Manchester, Mass.
Carol Bower, Manhattan Beach, Calif.
Carol Brown, Lake Forest, Ill.
Cristina Cruz, N. Fond du Lac, Wis.
Anita De Frantz, Philadelphia, Pa.
Karla Drewsen, Greenwich, Conn.
Jeanne Flanagan, Killingworth, Conn.
Charlotte Geer, W. Fairlee, Vt.
Julia Geer, W. Fairlee, Vt.
Virginia Gilder, New York, N.Y.
Carie Graves, Spring Green, Wis.
Janet Harville, Seattle, Wash.
Hollis Hatton, Philadelphia, Pa.
Elizabeth Hills, Hingham, Mass.
Kathryn Keeler, Chevy Chase, Md.
Elizabeth Kent, Philadelphia, Pa.
Joan Lind, Long Beach, Calif.
Anne Marden, Concord, Mass.
Peggy McCarthy, Madison, Wis.
Valerie McClain, Oakland, Calif.
Kristine Norelius, Bellevue, Wash.
Mary O'Connor, West Haven, Conn.
Jan Palchinoff, Santa Ana, Calif.
Kelly Rickon
Patricia Spratlen, Seattle, Wash.
Nancy Storrs, Philadelphia, Pa.
Cathleen Thaxton, San Diego, Calif.
Susan Tuttle, Middletown, Conn.
Nancy Vespoli, New Haven, Conn.
Anne Warner, Lexington, Mass.

Shooting

Terence Anderson, New Orleans, La.
Dean Clark, Ft. Benning, Ga.
Steven Collins, Sanborn, N.Y.
Matthew Dryke, Ft. Benning, Ga.
Martin Edmondson, Ft. Benning, Ga.
Roderick Fitz-Randolph, Palm Beach, Fla.
Boyd Goldsby, Little Rock, Ark.
Donald Hamilton, Kingston, Mass.
Terry Howard, Scott A.F.B., Ill.
David Kimes, Monterey Park, Calif.
Ernest Neel, Ft. Benning, Ga.
Steve Reiter, Daly City, Calif.
Randy Stewart, Columbus, Ga.
Lones Wigger, Ft. Benning, Ga.

Soccer (Football)

Peter Arnautoff, San Francisco, Calif.
Tony Bellinger
Timothy Clark, Burnsville, Minn.
Paul Coffee, Buffalo Grove, Ill.
Angelo DiBernardo, Woodbridge, N.J.
Donald Ebert
Darryl Gee, Columbia, Md.
John Hayes, Florissant, Mo.
Ty Keough
Adolphus Lawson
William McKeon, Florissant, Mo.
Joseph Morrone, Storrs, Conn.
Louis Nanchoff
Njego Pesa
Daniel Salvemini
Perry Van Der Beck, Tampa, Fla.
Greg Villa

Swimming—Men

Steve Barnicoat, Mission Viejo, Calif.
Bill Barrett, Alpharetta, Ga.
Craig Beardsley, Gainesville, Fla.
Mike Bottom, Walnut Creek, Calif.
Mike Bruner, Mesa, Ariz.
Rick Carey, Larchmont, N.Y.
Chris Cavanaugh, Cupertino, Calif.
Jeff Float, Carmichael, Calif.
Bill Forrester, Gainesville, Fla.
Rowdy Gaines, Gainesville, Fla.
Brian Goodell, Mission Viejo, Calif.
Matt Gribble
John Hencken, Santa Clara, Calif.
Bob Jackson, Tucson, Ariz.
Kris Kirchner, Austin, Tex.
David Larson, Gainesville, Fla.
Steve Lunquist, Jonesboro, Ga.
Glenn Mills, Cincinnati, Ohio
John Moffet, Fullerton, Calif.
Ron Neugent, Wichita, Kans.
William Paulus, Austin, Tex.
Peter Rocca, Pleasant Hill, Calif.
Brian Roney, City of Industry, Calif.
John Simons, Stanford, Calif.
Richard Thornton, Pleasant Hill, Calif.
Jesse Vassallo, Mission Viejo, Calif.

Swimming—Women

Terri Baxter, Menlo Park, Calif.
Lisa Buese, Cincinnati, Ohio
Kim Carlisle, Cincinnati, Ohio
Tracy Caulkins, Nashville, Tenn.
Stephanie Elkins, Cincinnati, Ohio
Nancy Hogshead, Gainesville, Fla.
Linda Jezek, Stanford, Calif.
Libby Kinkead, Newton Square, Pa.
Karin LaBerge, Ft. Washington, Pa.
Kim Linehan, Austin, Tex.
Marybeth Linzmeier, Mission Viejo, Calif.
Mary T. Meagher, Cincinnati, Ohio
Joan Pennington, Austin, Tex.
Susan Rapp, Fairfax, Va.
Jill Sterkel, Austin, Tex.
Susie Thayer, Bartow, Fla.
Sue Walsh, Lockport, N.Y.
Cynthia Woodhead, Cupertino, Calif.

Track and Field—Men

Colin Anderson, Golden Valley, Minn.
Duncan Atwood, Seattle, Wash.
Willie Banks, Los Angeles, Calif.
Andy Bessette, Vernon, Conn.
Douglas Brown, Eugene, Ore.
Richard Buerkle, Atlanta, Ga.
James Butler, Stillwater, Okla.
Gregory Caldwell, Los Angeles, Calif.
Anthony Campbell, Carson, Calif.
Matt Centrowitz, Eugene, Ore.
Bob Coffman, Houston, Tex.
Dedy Cooper, Richmond, Calif.
Fred Dixon, Placentia, Calif.
Boris Djerassi, Raynham, Mass.
Benji Durden, Stone Mountain, Ga.
Michael Durkin, Chicago, Ill.
Marco Evoniuk, Longmont, Colo.
Rod Ewaliko, Seattle, Wash.
Al Feuerbach, Los Gatos, Calif.
Benn Fields, Salisbury Mills, N.Y.
Stanley Floyd, Outney, Ga.
Herman Frazier, Tempe, Ariz.
Gregory Fredericks, Boalsburg, Pa.
Willie Gault, Griffin, Ga.
Harvey Glance, Phenix City, Ala.
Bill Green, Palo Alto, Calif.
John Gregorek, Northport, N.Y.
Kyle Heffner, Richardson, Tex.
James Heiring, San Bernardino, Calif.
Tomas Hintnaus, San Jose, Calif.
James Howard, Alvin, Tex.
Paul Jordan, Houston, Tex.
Bruce Kennedy, San Jose, Calif.
Stephen Lacy, Madison, Wis.
Mel Lattany, Brunswick, Ga.
David Lee, University City, Mo.
Carl Lewis, Willingboro, N.J.
John McArdle, Eugene, Ore.
William McChesney, Eugene, Ore.
Walter McCoy, Daytona Beach, Fla.
Henry Marsh, Eugene, Ore.
Edwin Moses, Mission Viejo, Calif.
Larry Myricks, Tallahassee, Fla.
Renaldo Nehemiah, Scotch Plains, N.J.
Daniel O'Connor, Westminster, Calif.
Nathaniel Page, Evanston, Ill.
Don Paige, Marcy, N.Y.
Lee Palles, Mobile, Ala.
Ben Plucknett, San Jose, Calif.
John Powell, Cupertino, Calif.
Dan Ripley, Bishop, Calif.
James Robinson, Oakland, Calif.
Alberto Salazar, Wayland, Mass.
Anthony Sandoval, Los Alamos, N.M.
Carl Schueler, Silver Spring, Md.
Steven Scott, Tempe, Ariz.
Todd Scully, Blacksburg, Va.
Peter Shmock, Cupertino, Calif.
Willie Smith, Auburn, Ala.
Frederick Taylor, Houston, Tex.
Michael Tully, Long Beach, Calif.
Craig Virgin, Lebanon, Ill.
James Walker, Atlanta, Ga.
Larry Walker, Canoga Park, Calif.
Clifford Wiley, Baltimore, Md.
Mac Wilkins, Soquel, Calif.
Barton Williams, Vallejo, Calif.
Randy Williams, Los Angeles, Calif.
Randy Wilson, Ankeny, Iowa

Track and Field—Women

Jodi Anderson, Los Angeles, Calif.
Lynne Winbigler-Anderson, Minneapolis, Minn.
Roberta Belle, Baltimore, Md.
Jeanette Bolden, Los Angeles, Calif.
Alice Brown, Altadena, Calif.
Julie Brown, Lake Arrowhead, Calif.
Robin Campbell, Palo Alto, Calif.
Chandra Cheeseborough, Jacksonville, Fla.
Sharon Dabney, Philadelphia, Pa.
Benita Fitzgerald, Woodbridge, Va.
Mary Decker, Eugene, Ore.
Gwen Gardner, Los Angeles, Calif.
Paula Girven, Dale City, Va.
Pamela Greene, Mesa, Ariz.
Lorna Griffin, Seattle, Wash.
Karen Hawkins, Houston, Tex.
Stephanie Hightower, Louisville, Ky.
Denean Howard, Granada Hills, Calif.
Sherri Howard, Granada Hills, Calif.
Francie Larrieu, Waco, Tex.
Carol Lewis, Willingboro, N.J.
Kathy McMillan, Raeford, N.C.
Madeline Manning, Tulsa, Okla.
Brenda Morehead, Toledo, Ohio
Mary Osborne, Billings, Mont.
Louise Ritter, Dallas, Tex.
Kate Schmidt, Coquitlam, B.C.
Maren Seidler, Los Gatos, Calif.
Karin Smith, Venice, Calif.
Pamela Spencer, Northridge, Calif.
Ann Turbyne, Waterville, Me.
Diane Williams, Chicago, Ill.
Canzetta Young, Beaver Falls, Pa.

Volleyball—Women

Janet Baier, Washington, Mo.
Carolyn Becker, Norwalk, Calif.
Laurel Brassey, San Diego, Calif.
Rita Crockett, Houston, Tex.
Patty Dowdell, Houston, Tex.
Laurie Flachmeier, Garland, Tex.
Debbie Green, Westminster, Calif.
Flo Hyman, Inglewood, Calif.
Debra Landreth, El Segundo, Calif.
Diane McCormick, Charleroi, Pa.
Terry Place, Redondo Beach, Calif.
Susan Woodstra, Sacramento, Calif.

Water Polo

Chris Dorst, Atherton, Calif.
Gary Figueroa, Costa Mesa, Calif.
Steve Hamann, San Jose, Calif.
Eric Lindroth, Costa Mesa, Calif.
Andrew McDonald, Orinda, Calif.
Kevin Robertson, Santa Ana, Calif.
Peter Schnugg, Orinda, Calif.
Terry Schroeder, Santa Barbara, Calif.
John Siman, Pasadena, Calif.
Jon Svendsen, Oakland, Calif.
Joseph Vargas, Hacienda Hts., Calif.

Weightlifting

Mark Cameron, Middletown, R.I.
Guy Carleton, Decatur, Ill.
Michael Cohen, Savannah, Ga.
James Curry, Berkeley, Calif.
Brian Derwin, Wharton, N.J.
Bob Giordano, Belleville, N.J.
Jerome Hannan, Levittown, N.Y.
Michael Karchut, Calumet City, Ill.
Luke Klaja, Jacksonville, Ore.
Joseph Puleo, Grosse Pte. Woods, Mich.
Cal Schake, Butler, Pa.
Kurt Setterberg, Masury, Ohio
Thomas Stock, Belleville, Ill.

Wrestling, Freestyle

John Azevedo, Patterson, Calif.
Christopher Campbell, Ames, Iowa
Russ Hellickson, Oregon, Wis.
Lee Kemp, Madison, Wis.
Randy Lewis, Rapid City, S.D.
Gene Mills, Pompton Lakes, N.J.
Ben Peterson, Watertown, Wis.
Bob Weaver, Easton, Pa.
Greg Wojciechowski, Toledo, Ohio
Chuck Yagla, Iowa City, Iowa

Wrestling, Greco-Roman

Jeffrey Blatnick, Schenectady, N.Y.
Daniel Chandler, Minneapolis, Minn.
Mark Fuller, Auburn, Calif.
Brian Gust, Lakeville, Minn.
Mark Johnson, Rock Island, Ill.
John Matthews, Mt. Pleasant, Mich.
Daniel Mello, Triangle, Va.
Thomas Minkel, Mt. Pleasant, Mich.
Brad Rheingans, Appleton, Minn.
Bruce Thompson, Rosemount, Minn.

Yachting

Ron Anderson, Sausalito, Calif.
Stephen Benjamin, Oyster Bay, N.Y.
Henry Bossett, Pt. Pleasant, N.J.
William Buchanan, Bellevue, Wash.
Rod Davis, Seal Beach, Calif.
John Duane, Delray Beach, Fla.
Neal Fowler, Easton, Conn.
Robert Haines, Coronado, Calif.
Jeff Kent, Weymouth, Mass.
Michael Loeb, New Haven, Conn.
Edward Trevelyan, Coronado, Calif.

SUMMER OLYMPIC CHAMPIONS: SWIMMING AND DIVING, TRACK AND FIELD, TEAM SPORTS

NOTE: An asterisk * denotes Olympic record.

SWIMMING AND DIVING (Men)

Year Champion and Country	Time

100 Meter Free Style — Min./Sec.

1896—Alfred Hajos, Hungary	1:22.2
1904—Zoltan de Halmay, Hungary (100 yds.)	1:02.8
1908—Charles Daniels, United States	1:05.6
1912—Duke Kahanamoku, United States	1:03.4
1920—Duke Kahanamoku, United States	1:01.4
1924—John Weissmuller, United States	59.0
1928—John Weissmuller, United States	58.6
1932—Yasuji Miyazaki, Japan	58.2
1936—Ferenc Csik, Hungary	57.6
1948—Walter Ris, United States	57.3
1952—Clarke Scholes, United States	57.4
1956—Jon Hendricks, Australia	55.4
1960—John Devitt, Australia	55.2
1964—Donald A. Schollander, United States	53.4
1968—Michael Wenden, Australia	52.2
1972—Mark Spitz, United States	51.2
1976—Jim Montgomery, United States	49.99*

200 Meter Free Style

1968—Michael Wenden, Australia	1:55.2
1972—Mark Spitz, United States	1:52.8
1976—Bruce Furniss, United States	1:50.29

400 Meter Free Style

1896—Paul Neumann, Austria (500 m.)	8:12.6
1904—Charles Daniels, United States (440 yds.)	6:16.2
1908—Henry Taylor, Great Britain	5:36.8
1912—George Hodgson, Canada	5:24.4
1920—Norman Ross, United States	5:26.8
1924—John Weissmuller, United States	5:04.2
1928—Albert Zorilla, Argentina	5:01.6
1932—Clarence Crabbe, United States	4:48.4
1936—Jack Medica, United States	4:44.5
1948—William Smith, United States	4:41.0
1952—Jean Boiteux, France	4:30.7
1956—Murray Rose, Australia	4:27.3
1960—Murray Rose, Australia	4:18.3
1964—Donald A. Schollander, United States	4:12.2
1968—Michael Burton, United States	4:09.0
1972—Bradford Cooper, Australia	4:00.3
1976—Brian Goodell, United States	3:51.93

1,500 Meter Free Style — Min./Sec.

1896—Alfred Hajos, Hungary (1,200 m.)	18:22.2
1900—John Jarvis, Great Britain (1,000 m.)	13:40.2
1904—Emil Rausch, Germany (1,609 m.)	27:18.2
1908—Henry Taylor, Great Britain	22:48.4
1912—George Hodgson, Canada	22:00.0
1920—Norman Ross, United States	22:23.2
1924—Andrew Charlton, Australia	20:06.6
1928—Arne Borg, Sweden	19:51.8
1932—Kusuo Kitamura, Japan	19:12.4
1936—Noboru Terada, Japan	19:13.7
1948—James P. McLane, United States	19:18.5
1952—Ford Konno, United States	18:30.0
1956—Murray Rose, Australia	17:58.9
1960—John Konrads, Australia	17:19.6
1964—Robert Windle, Australia	17:01.7
1968—Michael Burton, United States	16:38.9
1972—Michael Burton, United States	15:52.6
1976—Brian Goodell, United States	15:02.40

100 Meter Backstroke

1904—Walter Brack, Germany (100 yds.)	1:16.8
1908—Arno Bieberstein, Germany	1:24.6
1912—Harry Hebner, United States	1:21.2
1920—Warren Kealoha, United States	1:15.2
1924—Warren Kealoha, United States	1:13.2
1928—George Kojac, United States	1:08.2
1932—Masaji Kiyokawa, Japan	1:08.6
1936—Adolph Kiefer, United States	1:05.9
1948—Allen Stack, United States	1:06.4
1952—Yoshinobu Oyakawa, United States	1:05.4
1956—David Thiele, Australia	1:02.2
1960—David Thiele, Australia	1:01.9
1964—Not on Program	
1968—Roland Matthes, East Germany	58.7
1972—Roland Matthes, East Germany	56.6
1976—John Naber, United States	55.49*

200 Meter Backstroke

1900—Ernest Hoppenberg, Germany	2:47.0
1964—Jed R. Graef, United States	2:10.3
1968—Roland Matthes, East Germany	2:09.6
1972—Roland Matthes, East Germany	2:02.8
1976—John Naber, United States	1:59.19*

100 Meter Breaststroke

1968—Donald McKenzie, United States	1:07.7
1972—Nobutaka Taguchi, Japan	1:04.9
1976—John Hencken, United States	1:03.11

200 Meter Breaststroke

1908—Frederick Holman, Great Britain	3:09.2
1912—Walter Bathe, Germany	3:01.8
1920—Haken Malmroth, Sweden	3:04.4
1924—Robert Skelton, United States	2:56.6
1928—Yoshiyuki Tsuruta, Japan	2:48.8
1932—Yoshiyuki Tsuruta, Japan	2:45.4
1936—Tetsuo Hamuro, Japan	2:41.5
1948—Joseph Verdeur, United States	2:39.3
1952—John Davies, Australia	2:34.4
1956—Masura Furukawa, Japan	2:34.7
1960—William Mulliken, United States	2:37.4
1964—Ian O'Brien, Australia	2:27.8
1968—Felipe Muñoz, Mexico	2:28.7
1972—John Hencken, United States	2:21.5
1976—David Wilkie, Great Britain	2:15.1

100 Meter Butterfly

1968—Douglas Russell, United States	55.9
1972—Mark Spitz, United States	54.3*
1976—Matt Vogel, United States	54.35

200 Meter Butterfly

1956—William Yorzyk, United States	2:19.3
1960—Michael Troy, United States	2:12.8
1964—Kevin Berry, Australia	2:06.6
1968—Carl Robie, United States	2:08.7
1972—Mark Spitz, United States	2:00.7
1976—Michael Bruner, United States	1:59.23

200 Meter Individual Medley

1968—Charles Hickcox, United States	2:12.0
1972—Gunnar Larsson, Sweden	2:07.2*

400 Meter Individual Medley

1964—Richard W. Roth, United States	4:45.4
1968—Charles Hickcox, United States	4:48.4
1972—Gunnar Larsson, Sweden	4:32.0
1976—Rod Strachan, United States	4:23.6

400 Meter Free Style Relay

1964—United States	3:33.2
1968—United States	3:31.7
1972—United States	3:26.4*

400 Meter Medley Relay

1960—United States	4:05.4
1964—United States	3:58.4
1968—United States	3:54.9
1972—United States	3:48.2
1976—United States	3:42.22

800 Meter Free Style Relay

1908—Great Britain	10:55.6
1912—Australia	10:11.2
1920—United States	10:04.4
1924—United States	9:53.4
1928—United States	9:36.2
1932—Japan	8:58.2
1936—Japan	8:51.5
1948—United States	8:31.1
1952—United States	8:31.1
1956—Australia	8:23.6
1960—United States	8:10.2
1964—United States	7:52.1
1968—United States	7:52.3
1972—United States	7:38.8
1976—United States	7:23.2

Springboard Diving — Points

1908—Albert Zurner, Germany	85.50
1912—Paul Guenther, Germany	79.23
1920—Louis Kuehn, United States	675.00
1924—Albert C. White, United States	696.40
1928—Pete Desjardins, United States	185.04
1932—Michael Galitzen, United States	161.38
1936—Richard Degener, United States	163.57
1948—Bruce Harlan, United States	163.64
1952—David Browning, United States	205.29
1956—Robert L. Clotworthy, United States	159.56
1960—Gary Tobian, United States	170.00
1964—Kenneth R. Sitzberger, United States	159.90
1968—Bernard Wrightson, United States	170.15
1972—Vladimir Vasin, USSR	594.09
1976—Phil Boggs, United States	619.52

High Diving

1904—Dr. G. E. Sheldon, United States	12.75
1908—Hjalmar Johansson, Sweden	83.75

1912—Erik Adlerz, Sweden	73.94
1920—Clarence Pinkston, United States	100.67
1924—Albert C. White, United States	97.46
1928—Pete Desjardins, United States	98.74
1932—Harold Smith, United States	124.80
1936—Marshall Wayne, United States	113.58
1948—Dr. Samuel Lee, United States	130.05
1952—Dr. Samuel Lee, United States	156.28
1956—Joaquin Capilla, Mexico	152.44
1960—Robert Webster, United States	165.56
1964—Robert Webster, United States	148.58
1968—Klaus DiBiasi, Italy	164.18
1972—Klaus DiBiasi, Italy	504.12
1976—Klaus DiBiasi, Italy	600.51

SWIMMING AND DIVING (Women)

100 Meter Free Style — Min./Sec.

1912—Fanny Durack, Australia	1:22.2
1920—Ethelda Bleibtrey, United States	1:13.6
1924—Ethel Lackie, United States	1:12.4
1928—Albina Osipowich, United States	1:11.0
1932—Helene Madison, United States	1:06.8
1936—Hendrika Mastenbroek, Netherlands	1:05.9
1948—Greta Andersen, Denmark	1:06.3
1952—Katalin Szoke, Hungary	1:06.8
1956—Dawn Fraser, Australia	1:02.0
1960—Dawn Fraser, Australia	1:01.2
1964—Dawn Fraser, Australia	59.5
1968—Margo Jan Henne, United States	1:00.0
1972—Sandra Neilson, United States	58.6
1976—Kornelia Ender, East Germany	55.65

200 Meter Free Style

1968—Deborah Meyer, United States	2:10.5
1972—Shane Gould, Australia	2:03.6
1976—Kornelia Ender, East Germany	1:59.26

400 Meter Free Style

1920—Ethelda Bleibtrey, United States (300 m.)	4:34.0
1924—Martha Norelius, United States	6:02.2
1928—Martha Norelius, United States	5:42.4
1932—Helene Madison, United States	5:28.5
1936—Hendrika Mastenbroek, Netherlands	5:26.4
1948—Ann Curtis, United States	5:17.8
1952—Valeria Gyenge, Hungary	5:12.1
1956—Lorraine Crapp, Australia	4:54.6
1960—S. Chris Von Saltza, United States	4:50.6
1964—Virginia Duenkel, United States	4:43.3
1968—Deborah Meyer, United States	4:31.8
1972—Shane Gould, Australia	4:19.0
1976—Petra Thuemer, East Germany	4:09.89

800 Meter Free Style

1968—Deborah Meyer, United States	9:24.0
1972—Keena Rothhammer, United States	8:53.7
1976—Petra Thuemer, East Germany	8:37.14

100 Meter Backstroke

1924—Sybil Bauer, United States	1:23.2
1928—Marie Braun, Netherlands	1:22.0
1932—Eleanor Holm, United States	1:19.4
1936—Dina Senff, Netherlands	1:18.9
1948—Karen Harup, Denmark	1:14.4
1952—Joan Harrison, South Africa	1:14.3
1956—Judy Grinham, Great Britain	1:12.9
1960—Lynn Burke, United States	1:09.3
1964—Cathy Ferguson, United States	1:07.7
1968—Kaye Hall, United States	1:06.2
1972—Melissa Belote, United States	1:05.8
1976—Ulrike Richter, East Germany	1:01.83

200 Meter Backstroke

1968—Lillian (Pokey) Watson, United States	2:24.8
1972—Melissa Belote, United States	2:19.2
1976—Ulrike Richter, East Germany	2:13.43

100 Meter Butterfly

1956—Shelley Mann, United States	1:11.0
1960—Carolyn Schuler, United States	1:09.5
1964—Sharon Stouder, United States	1:04.7
1968—Lynn McClements, Australia	1:05.5
1972—Mayumi Aoki, Japan	1:03.3
1976—Kornelia Ender, East Germany	1:00.13*

200 Meter Butterfly

1968—Ada Kok, Netherlands	2:24.7
1972—Karen Moe, United States	2:15.6
1976—Andrea Pollack, East Germany	2:11.41

100 Meter Breaststroke

1968—Djurdjica Bjedov, Yugoslavia	1:15.8
1972—Cathy Carr, United States	1:13.6
1976—Hannelore Anke, East Germany	1:11.16

200 Meter Breaststroke

1924—Lucy Morton, Great Britain	3:33.2
1928—Hilde Schrader, Germany	3:12.6
1932—Clare Dennis, Australia	3:06.3
1936—Hideko Maehata, Japan	3:03.6
1948—Nelly Van Vliet, Netherlands	2:57.2
1952—Eva Szekely, Hungary	2:51.7
1956—Ursula Happe, Germany	2:53.1
1960—Anita Lonsbrough, Great Britain	2:49.5
1964—Galina Prozumenshikova, USSR	2:46.4
1968—Sharon Wichman, United States	2:44.4
1972—Beverly Whitfield, Australia	2:41.7
1976—Marina Koshevaya, USSR	2:33.35

400 Meter Free Style Relay

1912—Great Britain	5:52.8
1920—United States	5:11.6
1924—United States	4:58.8
1928—United States	4:47.6
1932—United States	4:38.0
1936—Netherlands	4:36.0
1948—United States	4:29.2
1952—Hungary	4:24.4
1956—Australia	4:17.1
1960—United States	4:08.9
1964—United States	4:03.8
1968—United States	4:02.5
1972—United States	3:55.2
1976—United States	3:44.82

400 Meter Medley Relay

1960—United States	4:41.1
1964—United States	4:33.9
1968—United States	4:28.3
1972—United States	4:20.7
1976—East Germany	4:07.95

200 Meter Individual Medley

1968—Claudia Kolb, United States	2:24.7
1972—Shane Gould, Australia	2:23.1*

400 Meter Individual Medley

1964—Donna de Varona, United States	5:18.7
1968—Claudia Kolb, United States	5:08.5
1972—Gail Neall, Australia	5:03.0
1976—Ulrike Tauber, East Germany	4:42.77

Springboard Diving — Points

1920—Aileen Riggin, United States	539.90
1924—Elizabeth Becker, United States	474.50
1928—Helen Meany, United States	78.62
1932—Georgia Coleman, United States	87.52
1936—Marjorie Gestring, United States	89.27
1948—Victoria Draves, United States	108.74
1952—Patricia McCormick, United States	147.30
1956—Patricia McCormick, United States	142.36
1960—Ingrid Kramer, Germany	155.81
1964—Ingrid Engle-Kramer, Germany	145.00
1968—Sue Gossick, United States	150.77
1972—Micki King, United States	450.03
1976—Jennifer Chandler, United States	506.19

High Diving

1912—Greta Johansson, Sweden	39.90
1920—Stefani Fryland-Clausen, Denmark	34.60
1924—Caroline Smith, United States	33.20
1928—Elizabeth Pinkston, United States	31.60
1932—Dorothy Poynton, United States	40.26
1936—Dorothy Poynton Hill, United States	33.93
1948—Victoria Draves, United States	68.87
1952—Patricia McCormick, United States	79.37
1956—Patricia McCormick, United States	84.85
1960—Ingrid Kramer, Germany	91.28
1964—Lesley Bush, United States	99.80
1968—Milena Duchkova, Czechoslovakia	109.59
1972—Ulrika Knape, Sweden	390.00
1976—Yelena Vaitsekhovskaya, USSR	406.49

TRACK AND FIELD (Men)

100 Meter Dash — Sec.

1896—Thomas E. Burke, United States	12.0
1900—Francis W. Jarvis, United States	10.8
1904—Archie Hahn, United States	11.0
1908—Reginald E. Walker, South Africa	10.8
1912—Ralph C. Craig, United States	10.8
1920—Charles W. Paddock, United States	10.8
1924—Harold M. Abrahams, Great Britain	10.6
1928—Percy Williams, Canada	10.8
1932—Eddie Tolan, United States	10.3
1936—Jesse Owens, United States	10.3
1948—Harrison Dillard, United States	10.3
1952—Lindy J. Remigino, United States	10.4
1956—Bobby J. Morrow, United States	10.5
1960—Armin Hary, Germany	10.2
1964—Robert L. Hayes, United States	10.0
1968—James Hines, United States	9.9*
1972—Valery Borzov, USSR	10.1
1976—Hasely Crawford, Trinidad & Tobago	10.06

200 Meter Dash

Year	Athlete	Time
1900	John W. B. Tewksbury, United States	22.2
1904	Archie Hahn, United States	21.6
1908	Robert Kerr, Canada	22.6
1912	Ralph C. Craig, United States	21.7
1920	Allan Woodring, United States	22.0
1924	Jackson V. Scholz, United States	21.6
1928	Percy Williams, Canada	21.8
1932	Eddie Tolan, United States	21.2
1936	Jesse Owens, United States	20.7
1948	Melvin Patton, United States	21.1
1952	Andrew W. Stanfield, United States	20.7
1956	Bobby J. Morrow, United States	20.6
1960	Livio Berruti, Italy	20.5
1964	Henry Carr, United States	20.3
1968	Tommie Smith, United States	19.8*
1972	Valery Borzov, USSR	20.0
1976	Donald Quarrie, Jamaica	20.23

400 Meter Dash

Year	Athlete	Time
1896	Thomas E. Burke, United States	54.2
1900	Maxwell W. Long, United States	49.4
1904	Harry I. Hillman, United States	49.2
1908	Wyndham Halswelle, Great Britain	50.0
1912	Charles D. Reidpath, United States	48.2
1920	Bevil G. D. Rudd, South Africa	49.6
1924	Eric H. Liddel, Great Britain	47.6
1928	Ray Barbuti, United States	47.8
1932	William A. Carr, United States	46.2
1936	Archie Williams, United States	46.5
1948	Arthur Wint, Jamaica	46.2
1952	George Rhoden, Jamaica	45.9
1956	Charles L. Jenkins, United States	46.7
1960	Otis Davis, United States	44.9
1964	Michael D. Larrabee, United States	45.1
1968	Lee Evans, United States	43.8*
1972	Vince Matthews, United States	44.7
1976	Alberto Juantorena, Cuba	44.26

800 Meter Run

Year	Athlete	Min./Sec.
1896	Edwin H. Flack, Australia	2:11.0
1900	Alfred E. Tysoe, Great Britain	2:01.4
1904	James D. Lightbody, United States	1:56.0
1908	Melvin W. Sheppard, United States	1:52.8
1912	James E. Meredith, United States	1:51.9
1920	Albert G. Hill, Great Britain	1:53.4
1924	Douglas G. A. Lowe, Great Britain	1:52.4
1928	Douglas G. A. Lowe, Great Britain	1:51.8
1932	Thomas Hampson, Great Britain	1:49.8
1936	John Woodruff, United States	1:52.9
1948	Malvin Whitfield, United States	1:49.2
1952	Malvin Whitfield, United States	1:49.2
1956	Thomas W. Courtney, United States	1:47.7
1960	Peter Snell, New Zealand	1:46.3
1964	Peter Snell, New Zealand	1:45.1
1968	Ralph Doubell, Australia	1:44.3
1972	Dave Wottle, United States	1:45.9
1976	Alberto Juantorena, Cuba	1:43.50*

1,500 Meter Run

Year	Athlete	Min./Sec.
1896	Edwin H. Flack, Great Britain	4:33.2
1900	Charles Bennett, Great Britain	4:06.2
1904	James D. Lightbody, United States	4:05.4
1908	Melvin W. Sheppard, United States	4:03.4
1912	Arnold N. S. Jackson, Great Britain	3:56.8
1920	Albert G. Hill, Great Britain	4:01.8
1924	Paavo Nurmi, Finland	3:53.6
1928	Harry E. Larva, Finland	3:53.2
1932	Luigi Beccali, Italy	3:51.2
1936	Jack E. Lovelock, New Zealand	3:47.8
1948	Henry Eriksson, Sweden	3:49.8
1952	Joseph Barthel, Luxembourg	3:45.2
1956	Ronald Delany, Ireland	3:41.2
1960	Herbert Elliott, Australia	3:35.6
1964	Peter Snell, New Zealand	3:38.1
1968	Kipchoge Keino, Kenya	3:34.9*
1972	Pekka Vasala, Finland	3:36.3
1976	John Walker, New Zealand	3:39.17

5,000 Meter Run

Year	Athlete	Time
1912	Hannes Kolehmainen, Finland	14:36.6
1920	Joseph Guillemot, France	14:55.6
1924	Paavo Nurmi, Finland	14:31.2
1928	Willie Ritola, Finland	14:38.0
1932	Lauri Lehtinen, Finland	14.30.0
1936	Gunnar Hockert, Finland	14:22.2
1948	Gaston Reiff, Belgium	14:17.6
1952	Emil Zatopek, Czechoslovakia	14:06.6
1956	Vladimir Kuts, USSR	13.39.6
1960	Murray Halberg, New Zealand	13:43.4
1964	Robert K. Schul, United States	13:48.8
1968	Mohamed Gammoudi, Tunisia	14:05.0
1972	Lasse Viren, Finland	13:26.4
1976	Lasse Viren, Finland	13:24.76

10,000 Meter Run

Year	Athlete	Time
1912	Hannes Kolehmainen, Finland	31:20.8
1920	Paavo Nurmi, Finland	31:45.8
1924	Willie Ritola, Finland	30:23.2
1928	Paavo Nurmi, Finland	30:18.8
1932	Janusz Kusocinski, Poland	30:11.4
1936	Ilmari Salminen, Finland	30:15.4
1948	Emil Zatopek, Czechoslovakia	29:59.6
1952	Emil Zatopek, Czechoslovakia	29:17.0
1956	Vladimir Kuts, USSR	28:45.6
1960	Petr Bolotnikov, USSR	28:32.2
1964	William Mills, United States	28:24.4
1968	Naftali Temu, Kenya	29:27.4
1972	Lasse Viren, Finland	27:38.4*
1976	Lasse Viren, Finland	27:40.38

Marathon

Year	Athlete	Hr./Min./Sec.
1896	Spyros Loues, Greece	2:58:50.0
1900	Michel Theato, France	2:59:45.0
1904	Thomas J. Hicks, United States	3:28:53.0
1908	John J. Hayes, United States	2:55:18.4
1912	Kenneth McArthur, South Africa	2:36:54.8
1920	Hannes Kolehmainen, Finland	2:32:35.8
1924	Albin Stenroos, Finland	2:41:22.6
1928	A. B. El Ouafi, France	2:32:57.0
1932	Juan Zabala, Argentina	2:31:36.0
1936	Kitei Son, Japan	2:29:19.2
1948	Delfo Cabrera, Argentina	2:34:51.6
1952	Emil Zatopek, Czechoslovakia	2:23:03.2
1956	Alain Mimoun, France	2:25:00.0
1960	Abebe Bikila, Ethiopia	2:15:16.2
1964	Abebe Bikila, Ethiopia	2:12:11.2
1968	Mamo Wolde, Ethiopia	2:20:26.4
1972	Frank Shorter, United States	2:12:19.7
1976	Waldemar Cierpinski, East Germany	2:09:55.0*

110 Meter Hurdles

Year	Athlete	Sec.
1896	Thomas P. Curtis, United States	17.6
1900	Alvin E. Kraenzlein, United States	15.4
1904	Frederick W. Schule, United States	16.0
1908	Forrest Smithson, United States	15.0
1912	Frederick W. Kelley, United States	15.1
1920	Earl J. Thomson, Canada	14.8
1924	Daniel C. Kinsey, United States	15.0
1928	Sydney Atkinson, South Africa	14.8
1932	George Saling, United States	14.6
1936	Forrest Towns, United States	14.2
1948	William Porter, United States	13.9
1952	Harrison Dillard, United States	13.7
1956	Lee Q. Calhoun, United States	13.5
1960	Lee Q. Calhoun, United States	13.8
1964	Hayes W. Jones, United States	13.6
1968	Willie Davenport, United States	13.3
1972	Rod Milburn, United States	13.2*
1976	Guy Drut, France	13.30

400 Meter Hurdles

Year	Athlete	Sec.
1900	John W. B. Tewksbury, United States	57.6
1904	Harry L. Hillman, United States	53.0
1908	Charles J. Bacon, United States	55.0
1920	Frank F. Loomis, United States	54.0
1924	F. Morgan Taylor, United States	52.6
1928	Lord David Burghley, Great Britain	53.4
1932	Robert Tisdall, Ireland	51.8
1936	Glenn Hardin, United States	52.4
1948	Roy Cochran, United States	51.1
1952	Charles Moore, United States	50.8
1956	Glenn A. Davis, United States	50.1
1960	Glenn A. Davis, United States	49.3
1964	Warren (Rex) Cawley, United States	49.6
1968	David Hemery, Great Britain	48.1
1972	John Akii-Bua, Uganda	47.8
1976	Edwin Moses, United States	47.64*

3,000 Meter Steeplechase

Year	Athlete	Min./Sec.
1920	Percy Hodge, Great Britain	10:00.4
1924	Willie Ritola, Finland	9:33.6
1928	Toivo A. Loukola, Finland	9:21.8
1932	Volmari Iso-Hollo, Finland	10:33.4
	(3,460 meters—extra lap by official error)	
1936	Volmari Iso-Hollo, Finland	9:03.8
1948	Thore Sjostrand, Sweden	9:04.6
1952	Horace Ashenfelter, United States	8:45.4
1956	Chris Brasher, Great Britain	8:41.2
1960	Zdzislaw Krzyszkowiak, Poland	8:34.2
1964	Gaston Roelants, Belgium	8:30.8
1968	Amos Biwott, Kenya	8:51.0
1972	Kipchoge Keino, Kenya	8:23.6
1976	Anders Gärderud, Sweden	8:08.20*

20,000 Meter Walk

Year	Athlete	Hr./Min./Sec.
1956	Leonid Spirine, USSR	1:31:27.4
1960	Vladimir Golubnichy, USSR	1:34:07.2
1964	Kenneth Matthews, Great Britain	1:29:34.0
1968	Vladimir Golubnichy, USSR	1:33:58.4

1972—Peter Frenkel, East Germany		1:26:42.4
1976—Daniel Bautista, Mexico		1:24:40.6

50,000 Meter Walk

1932—Thomas W. Green, Great Britain	4:50:10.0
1936—Harold Whitlock, Great Britain	4:30:41.4
1948—John A. Ljunggren, Sweden	4:41:52.0
1952—Giuseppe Dordoni, Italy	4:28:07.8
1956—Norman Read, New Zealand	4:30:42.8
1960—Donald Thompson, Great Britain	4:25:30.0
1964—Abdon Pamich, Italy	4:11:12.4
1968—Christoph Kohne, East Germany	4:20:13.6
1972—Bernd Kannenberg, West Germany	3:56:11.6

400 Meter Relay

	Sec.
1912—Great Britain	42.4
1920—United States	42.2
1924—United States	41.0
1928—United States	41.0
1932—United States	40.0
1936—United States	40.0
1948—United States	40.3
1952—United States	40.1
1956—United States	39.5
1960—Germany	39.5
1964—United States	39.0
1968—United States	38.2
1972—United States	38.2*
1976—United States	38.33

1,600 Meter Relay

	Min./Sec.
1908—United States	3:29.4
1912—United States	3:16.6
1920—Great Britain	3:22.2
1924—United States	3:16.0
1928—United States	3:14.2
1932—United States	3:08.2
1936—Great Britain	3:09.0
1948—United States	3:10.4
1952—Jamaica	3:03.9
1956—United States	3:04.8
1960—United States	3:02.2
1964—United States	3:00.7
1968—United States	2:56.1*
1972—Kenya	2:59.8
1976—United States	2:58.65

Pole Vault

	Height
1896—William W. Hoyt, United States	10' 9¾"
1900—Irving K. Baxter, United States	10' 9 9/10"
1904—Charles E. Dvorak, United States	11' 6"
1908—Albert C. Gilbert, United States Edward T. Cook, Jr., United States	12' 2"
1912—Harry S. Babcock, United States	12' 11½"
1920—Frank K. Foss, United States	12' 5 9/16"
1924—Lee S. Barnes, United States	12' 11½"
1928—Sabin W. Carr, United States	13' 9⅜"
1932—William Miller, United States	14' 1⅞"
1936—Earle Meadows, United States	14' 3¼"
1948—O. Guinn Smith, United States	14' 1¼"
1952—Robert Richards, United States	14' 11¼"
1956—Robert Richards, United States	14' 11½"
1960—Donald Bragg, United States	15' 5⅛"
1964—Fred M. Hansen, United States	16' 8¾"
1968—Robert Seagren, United States	17' 8½"
1972—Wolfgang Nordwig, East Germany	18' ½"
1976—Tadeusz Slusarki, Poland	18' ½"

High Jump

1896—Ellery Clark, United States	5' 11¼"
1900—Irving K. Baxter, United States	6' 2⅘"
1904—Samuel Jones, United States	5' 11"
1908—Harry Porter, United States	6' 3"
1912—Almer Richards, United States	6' 4"
1920—Richmond Landon, United States	6' 4¼"
1924—Harold Osborn, United States	6' 5 15/16"
1928—Robert W. King, United States	6' 4⅜"
1932—Duncan McNaughton, Canada	6' 5⅝"
1936—Cornelius Johnson, United States	6' 7 15/16"
1948—John Winter, Australia	6' 6"
1952—Walter Davis, United States	6' 8¼"
1956—Charles E. Dumas, United States	6' 11¼"
1960—Robert Shavlakadze, USSR	7' 1"
1964—Valery Brumel, USSR	7' 1¾"
1968—Richard Fosbury, United States	7' 4¼"
1972—Juri Tarmak, USSR	7' 3¾"
1976—Jacek Wszola, Poland	7' 4½"

Long Jump

	Distance
1896—Ellery Clark, United States	20' 10"
1900—Alvin Kraenzlein, United States	23' 6⅞"
1904—Myer Prinstein, United States	24' 1"
1908—Francis Irons, United States	24' 6½"
1912—Albert Gutterson, United States	24' 11¼"
1920—William Pettersson, Sweden	23' 5½"
1924—DeHart Hubbard, United States	24' 5⅛"
1928—Edward Hamm, United States	25' 4¾"
1932—Edward Gordon, United States	25' ¾"
1936—Jesse Owens, United States	26' 5⅜"
1948—Willie Steel, United States	25' 8"
1952—Jerome Biffle, United States	24' 10"
1956—Gregory C. Bell, United States	25' 8¼"
1960—Ralph H. Boston, United States	26' 7¾"
1964—Lynn Davies, Great Britain	26' 5¾"
1968—Robert Beamon, United States	29' 2½"*
1972—Randy Williams, United States	27' ½"
1976—Arnie Robinson, United States	27' 4¾"

Triple Jump

1896—James B. Connolly, United States	45' 0"
1900—Myer Prinstein, United States	47' 4¼"
1904—Myer Prinstein, United States	47' 0"
1908—Timothy Ahearne, Great Britain	48' 11¼"
1912—Gustaf Lindblom, Sweden	48' 5⅛"
1920—Vilho Tuulos, Finland	47' 6⅞"
1924—Archibald Winter, Australia	50' 11⅛"
1928—Mikio Oda, Japan	49' 10 13/16"
1932—Chuhei Nambu, Japan	51' 7"
1936—Naoto Tajima, Japan	52' 5⅞"
1948—Arne Ahman, Sweden	50' 6¼"
1952—Adhemar Ferreira da Silva, Brazil	53' 2½"
1956—Adhemar Ferreira da Silva, Brazil	53' 7½"
1960—Jozef Schmidt, Poland	55' 1¾"
1964—Jozef Schmidt, Poland	55' 3¼"
1968—Viktor Saneyev, USSR	57' ¾"*
1972—Viktor Saneyev, USSR	56' 11"
1976—Viktor Saneyev, USSR	56' 8¾"

16-Pound Shot Put

1896—Robert Garrett, United States	36' 9¾"
1900—Richard Sheldon, United States	46' 3⅛"
1904—Ralph Rose, United States	48' 7"
1908—Ralph Rose, United States	46' 7½"
1912—Patrick McDonald, United States	50' 4"
1920—Ville Porhola, Finland	48' 7⅛"
1924—Clarence Houser, United States	49' 2½"
1928—John Kuck, United States	52' 13/16"
1932—Leo Sexton, United States	52' 6 3/16"
1936—Hans Woellke, Germany	53' 1¾"
1948—Wilbur Thompson, United States	56' 2"
1952—Wm. Parry O'Brien, Jr., United States	57' 1½"
1956—Wm. Parry O'Brien, Jr., United States	60' 11"
1960—William Nieder, United States	64' 6¾"
1964—Dallas C. Long, United States	66' 8¼"
1968—James Randel Matson, United States	67' 4¾"
1972—Wladyslaw Komar, Poland	69' 6"
1976—Udo Beyer, East Germany	69' 6.7"

Discus Throw

1896—Robert Garrett, United States	95' 7½"
1900—Rudolf Bauer, Hungary	118' 2 9/10"
1904—Martin Sheridan, United States	128' 10½"
1908—Martin Sheridan, United States	134' 2"
1912—Armas Taipale, Finland	145' 9/16"
1920—Elmer Niklander, Finland	146' 7"
1924—Clarence Houser, United States	151' 5¼"
1928—Clarence Houser, United States	155' 2⅖"
1932—John Anderson, United States	162' 4⅞"
1936—Kenneth Carpenter, United States	165' 7½"
1948—Adolfo Consolini, Italy	173' 2"
1952—Sim Iness, United States	180' 6½"
1956—Alfred A. Oerter, United States	184' 10½"
1960—Alfred A. Oerter, United States	194' 2"
1964—Alfred A. Oerter, United States	200' 1½"
1968—Alfred A. Oerter, United States	212' 6½"
1972—Ludwick Danek, Czechoslovakia	211' 3½"
1976—Mac Wilkins, United States	221' 5.4"*

16-Pound Hammer Throw

1900—John Flanagan, United States	167' 4"
1904—John Flanagan, United States	168' 1"
1908—John Flanagan, United States	170' 4¼"
1912—Matthew McGrath, United States	179' 7⅛"
1920—Patrick Ryan, United States	173' 5⅝"
1924—Frederick Tootell, United States	174' 10¼"
1928—Patrick O'Callaghan, Ireland	168' 7½"
1932—Patrick O'Callaghan, Ireland	176' 11⅛"
1936—Karl Hein, Germany	185' 4¼"
1948—Imre Nemeth, Hungary	183' 11½"
1952—Jozsef Csermak, Hungary	197' 11¾"
1956—Harold V. Connolly, United States	207' 3½"
1960—Vasiliy Rudenkov, USSR	220' 1⅝"
1964—Romuald Klim, USSR	228' 9½"
1968—Gyula Zsivotzky, Hungary	240' 8"
1972—Anatol Bondarchuk, USSR	247' 8"
1976—Yuri Sedykh, USSR	254' 4"

Javelin Throw

1908—Erik Lemming, Sweden	179' 10½"
1912—Erik Lemming, Sweden	198' 11¼"
1920—Jonni Myyra, Finland	215' 9¾"
1924—Jonni Myyra, Finland	206' 6¾"

1928—Erik Lundquist, Sweden	218' 6⅛"	
1932—Matti Jarvinen, Finland	238' 7"	
1936—Gerhard Stock, Germany	235' 8 5/16"	
1948—Tapio Rautavaara, Finland	228' 10½"	
1952—Cyrus Young, United States	242' ¾"	
1956—Egil Danielson, Norway	281' 2¼"	
1960—Viktor Tsibulenko, USSR	277' 8⅜"	
1964—Pauli Nevala, Finland	271' 2¼"	
1968—Janis Lusis, USSR	295' 7¼"	
1972—Klaus Wolfermann, West Germany	296' 10"	
1976—Miklos Nemeth, Hungary	310' 4½"*	

Decathlon — Points

1912—Hugo Wieslander, Sweden	7724.49
1920—Helge Lovland, Norway	6804.35
1924—Harold Osborn, United States	7710.77
1928—Paavo Yrjola, Finland	8053.29
1932—James Bausch, United States	8462.23
(Old point system, 1912 through 1932)	
1936—Glenn Morris, United States	7900.00
1948—Robert Mathias, United States	7139.00
1952—Robert Mathias, United States	7887.00
1956—Milton G. Campbell, United States	7937.00
1960—Rafer Johnson, United States	8392.00
(Revised point system, 1936 through 1960)	
1964—Willi Holdorf, Germany	7887.00
(New scoring system)	
1968—William Toomey, United States	8193.00
1972—Nikolai Avilov, USSR	8454.00
1976—Bruce Jenner, United States	8618.00*

TRACK AND FIELD (Women)

100 Meter Dash — Sec.

1928—Elizabeth Robinson, United States	12.2
1932—Stanislawa Walasiewicz, Poland	11.9
1936—Helen Stephens, United States	11.5
1948—Francina Blankers-Koen, Netherlands	11.9
1952—Marjorie Jackson, Australia	11.5
1956—Betty Cuthbert, Australia	11.5
1960—Wilma Rudolph, United States	11.0
1964—Wyomia Tyus, United States	11.4
1968—Wyomia Tyus, United States	11.0
1972—Renate Stecher, East Germany	11.1
1976—Annegret Richter, West Germany	11.01*

200 Meter Dash

1948—Francina Blankers-Koen, Netherlands	24.4
1952—Marjorie Jackson, Australia	23.7
1956—Betty Cuthbert, Australia	23.4
1960—Wilma Rudolph, United States	24.0
1964—Edith McGuire, United States	23.0
1968—Irena Kirszenstein Szewinska, Poland	22.5
1972—Renate Stecher, East Germany	22.4
1976—Baerbel Eckert, East Germany	22.37

400 Meter Dash

1964—Betty Cuthbert, Australia	52.0
1968—Colette Besson, France	52.0
1972—Monika Zehrt, East Germany	51.1
1976—Irena Szewinska, Poland	49.29

800 Meter Run — Min./Sec.

1928—Linda Radke-Batschauer, Germany	2:16.8
1960—Ljudmila Shevcova-Lysenko, USSR	2:04.3
1964—Ann Packer, Great Britain	2:01.1
1968—Madeline Manning, United States	2:00.9
1972—Hildegard Falck, West Germany	1:58.6
1976—Tatyana Kazankina, USSR	1:54.94

1,500 Meter Run

1972—Ludmila Bragina, USSR	4:01.4
1976—Tatyana Kazankina, USSR	4:05.48

400 Meter Relay — Sec.

1928—Canada	48.4
1932—United States	47.0
1936—United States	46.9
1948—Netherlands	47.5
1952—United States	45.9
1956—Australia	44.5
1960—United States	44.5
1964—Poland	43.6
1968—United States	42.8

1972—West Germany	42.8	
1976—East Germany	42.55	

1,600 Meter Relay — Min./Sec.

1972—East Germany	3:23.0
1976—East Germany	3:19.23*

80 Meter Hurdles — Sec.

1932—Mildred Didrikson, United States	11.7
1936—Trebisonda Valla, Italy	11.7
1948—Francina Blankers-Koen, Netherlands	11.2
1952—Shirley Strickland de la Hunty, Australia	10.9
1956—Shirley Strickland de la Hunty, Australia	10.7
1960—Irina Press, USSR	10.8
1964—Karin Balzer, Germany	10.5
1968—Maureen Caird, Australia	10.3*

100 Meter Hurdles

1972—Annelie Erhardt, East Germany	12.6
1976—Johanna Schaller, East Germany	12.77

High Jump — Height

1928—Ethel Catherwood, Canada	5' 3"
1932—Jean Shiley, United States	5' 5¼"
1936—Ibolya Csak, Hungary	5' 3"
1948—Alice Coachman, United States	5' 6⅛"
1952—Esther Brand, South Africa	5' 5¾"
1956—Mildred McDaniel, United States	5' 9¼"
1960—Iolanda Balas, Rumania	6' ¼"
1964—Iolanda Balas, Rumania	6' 2¾"
1968—Miloslava Rezkova, Czechoslovakia	5' 11¾"
1972—Ulrika Meyfarth, West Germany	6' 3½"
1976—Rosemarie Ackermann, East Germany	6' 4"

Long Jump — Distance

1948—Olga Gyarmati, Hungary	18' 8¼"
1952—Yvette Williams, New Zealand	20' 5¾"
1956—Elizbieta Krzeskinska, Poland	20' 9¾"
1960—Vyera Krepkina, USSR	20' 10¾"
1964—Mary Rand, Great Britain	22' 2"
1968—Viorica Viscopoleanu, Rumania	22' 4½"
1972—Heidemarie Rosendahl, West Germany	22' 3"
1976—Angela Voigt, East Germany	22' 2½"

Discus Throw

1928—Helena Konopacka, Poland	129' 11⅞"
1932—Lillian Copeland, Unted States	133' 2"
1936—Gisela Mauermayer, Germany	156' 3 3/16"
1948—Micheline Ostermeyer, France	137' 6½"
1952—Nina Romaschkova, USSR	168' 8½"
1956—Olga Fikotova, Czechoslovakia	176' 1½"
1960—Nina Ponomareva, USSR	180' 8¼"
1964—Tamara Press, USSR	187' 10¾"
1968—Lia Manoliu, Rumania	191' 2½"
1972—Faina Melnik, USSR	218' 7"
1976—Evelin Schlaak, East Germany	226' 4½"

8-Lb./13-Oz. Shot Put

1948—Micheline Ostermeyer, France	45' 1½"
1952—Galina Zybina, USSR	50' 1½"
1956—Tamara Tishkyevich, USSR	54' 5"
1960—Tamara Press, USSR	56' 9¾"
1964—Tamara Press, USSR	59' 6"
1968—Margitta Gummel, East Germany	64' 4"
1972—Nadezhda Chizhova, USSR	69'
1976—Ivanka Khristova, Bulgaria	69' 5"

Javelin Throw

1932—Mildred Didrikson, United States	143' 4"
1936—Tilly Fleischer, Germany	148' 2¾"
1948—Herma Bauma, Austria	149' 6"
1952—Dana Zatopekova, Czechoslovakia	165' 7"
1956—Inessa Janzeme, USSR	176' 8"
1960—Elvira Ozolina, USSR	183' 8"
1964—Mihaela Penes, Rumania	198' 7½"
1968—Angela Nemeth, Hungary	198' ½"
1972—Ruth Fuchs, East Germany	209' 7"
1976—Ruth Fuchs, East Germany	216' 4"

Pentathlon — Points

1964—Irina Press, USSR	5,246
1968—Ingrid Becker, West Germany	5,098
1972—Mary Peters, Britain	4,801
1976—Siegrun Siegl, East Germany	4,745

TEAM SPORTS (since 1948)

Basketball—Men

1948—United States	
1952—United States	
1956—United States	
1960—United States	
1964—United States	
1968—United States	
1972—USSR	
1976—United States	

Basketball—Women

1976—USSR

Field Hockey

1948—India	
1952—India	
1956—India	
1960—Pakistan	
1964—India	
1968—Pakistan	
1972—West Germany	
1976—New Zealand	

Handball—Men

1972—Yugoslavia	
1976—USSR	

Handball—Women

1976—USSR

Soccer (Football)

1948—Sweden	
1952—Hungary	
1956—USSR	
1960—Yugoslavia	
1964—Hungary	
1968—Hungary	
1972—Poland	
1976—East Germany	

Volleyball—Men

1964—USSR	
1968—USSR	
1972—Japan	
1976—Poland	

Volleyball—Women

1964—Japan	
1968—USSR	
1972—USSR	
1976—Japan	

Water Polo

1948—Italy	
1952—Hungary	
1956—Hungary	
1960—Italy	
1964—Hungary	
1968—Yugoslavia	
1972—USSR	
1976—Hungary	

THE WINTER OLYMPIC GAMES

Sites	Year	Sites	Year
I Chamonix, France	1924	VIII Squaw Valley, California	1960
II St. Moritz, Switzerland	1928	IX Innsbruck, Austria	1964
III Lake Placid, New York	1932	X Grenoble, France	1968
IV Garmisch-Partenkirchen, Germany	1936	XI Sapporo, Japan	1972
V St. Moritz, Switzerland	1948	XII Innsbruck, Austria	1976
VI Oslo, Norway	1952	XIII Lake Placid, New York	1980
VII Cortina, Italy	1956	XIV Sarajevo, Yugoslavia	1984

1980 WINTER OLYMPICS MEDAL STANDINGS

	Gold (1st)	Silver (2d)	Bronze (3d)	Total		Gold (1st)	Silver (2d)	Bronze (3d)	Total
East Germany	9	7	7	23	Netherlands	1	2	1	4
U.S.S.R.	10	6	6	22	Italy	0	2	0	2
U.S.A.	6	4	2	12	Canada	0	1	1	2
Norway	1	3	6	10	United Kingdom	1	0	0	1
Finland	1	5	3	9	Hungary	0	1	0	1
Austria	3	2	2	7	Japan	0	1	0	1
Switzerland	1	1	3	5	Bulgaria	0	0	1	1
West Germany	0	2	3	5	Czechoslovakia	0	0	1	1
Sweden	3	0	1	4	France	0	0	1	1
Liechtenstein	2	2	0	4					

LAKE PLACID MEDALISTS: 1980 (*Olympic Record, ** World Record)

ALPINE SKIING (Men)

Downhill
1. Leonhard Stock, Austria
2. Peter Wirnsberger, Austria
3. Steve Podborski, Canada

Giant Slalom
1. Ingemar Stenmark, Sweden
2. Andreas Wenzel, Liechtenstein
3. Hans Enn, Austria

Slalom
1. Ingemar Stemark, Sweden
2. Phil Mahre, U.S.A.
3. Jacques Luethy, Switzerland

ALPINE SKIING (Women)

Downhill
1. Annemarie Moser-Proell, Austria
2. Hanni Wenzel, Liechtenstein
3. Marie-Theres Nadig, Switzerland

Giant Slalom
1. Hanni Wenzel, Liechtenstein
2. Irene Epple, West Germany
3. Perrine Pelen, France

Slalom
1. Hanni Wenzel, Liechtenstein
2. Christa Kinshofer, West Germany
3. Erika Hess, Switzerland

NORDIC SKIING (Men)

15-kilometer cross-country
1. Thomas Wassberg, Sweden
2. Juha Mieto, Finland
3. Ove Aunli, Norway

30-kilometer cross-country
1. Nikolai Zimyatov, U.S.S.R.
2. Vasili Rochev, U.S.S.R.
3. Ivan Lebanov, Bulgaria

50-kilometer cross-country
1. Nikolai Zimyatov, U.S.S.R.
2. Juha Mieto, Finland
3. Aleksandr Zavjalov, U.S.S.R.

4 x 10-kilometer cross-country relay
1. U.S.S.R. (Rochev, Bazhukov, Beliaev, Zimyatov)
2. Norway
3. Finland

70-meter jump
1. Anton Innauer, Austria
2. (tie) Manfred Deckert, East Germany– Hirokazu Yagi, Japan

90-meter special jump
1. Jouko Tormanen, Finland
2. Hubert Neuper, Austria
3. Jari Puikkonen, Finland

Nordic combined (jumping and cross-country)
1. Ulrich Wehling, East Germany
2. Jouko Karjalainen, Finland
3. Konrad Winkler, East Germany

NORDIC SKIING (Women)

5-kilometer cross-country
1. Raisa Smetanina, U.S.S.R.
2. Hilkka Riihivuori, Finland
3. Kveta Jeriova, Czechoslovakia

10-kilometer cross-country
1. Barbara Petzold, East Germany
2. Hilkka Riihivuori, Finland
3. Helena Takalo, Finland

4 x 5-kilometer cross-country relay
1. East Germany (Rostock, Anding, Hesse, Petzold)
2. U.S.S.R.
3. Norway

BIATHLON

10-kilometer individual
1. Frank Ullrich, East Germany
2. Vladimir Alikin, U.S.S.R.
3. Anatoli Alabyev, U.S.S.R.

20-kilometer individual
1. Anatoli Alabyev, U.S.S.R.
2. Frank Ullrich, East Germany
3. Eberhard Rosch, East Germany

4 x 7.5-kilometer relay
1. U.S.S.R. (Alikin, Tikhonov, Barnaschov, Alabyev)
2. East Germany
3. West Germany

HOCKEY
1. U.S.A.
2. U.S.S.R.
3. Sweden

BOBSLED

Two-man
1. Switzerland II (Erich Schaerer-Josef Benz)
2. East Germany II
3. East Germany I

Four-man
1. East Germany I (Nehmer, Musiol, Germeshausen, Gerhardt)
2. Switzerland I
3. East Germany II

LUGE

Singles (Men)
1. Bernhard Glass, East Germany
2. Paul Hildgartner, Italy
3. Anton Winkler, East Germany

Doubles (Men)
1. Hans Rinn-Norbert Hahn, East Germany
2. Peter Gschnitzer-Karl Brunner, Italy
3. Georg Fluckinger-Karl Schrott, Austria

Singles (Women)
1. Vera Zozulya, U.S.S.R.
2. Melitta Sollmann, East Germany
3. Ingrida Amantova, U.S.S.R.

FIGURE SKATING

Men
1. Robin Cousins, United Kingdom
2. Jan Hoffmann, East Germany
3. Charles Tickner, U.S.A.

Women
1. Anett Poetzsch, East Germany
2. Linda Fratianne, U.S.A.
3. Dagmar Lurz, West Germany

Pairs
1. Irina Rodnina-Aleksandr Zaitsev, U.S.S.R.
2. Marina Chereskova-Sergei Shakrai, U.S.S.R.
3. Manuela Mager-Uwe Bewersdorf, East Germany

Ice Dancing
1. Natalia Linichuk-Gennadi Karponosov, U.S.S.R.
2. Krisztina Regoczy-Andras Sallay, Hungary
3. Irina Moiseeva-Andrei Minenkov, U.S.S.R.

SPEED SKATING (Men)

500-meter
1. Eric Heiden, U.S.A., 38.03*
2. Evgeni Kulikov, U.S.S.R.
3. Lieuwe DeBoer, Netherlands

1,000-meter
1. Eric Heiden, U.S.A., 1:15.18*
2. Gaetan Boucher, Canada
3. (tie) Frode Roenning, Norway– Vladimir Lobanov, U.S.S.R.

1,500-meter
1. Eric Heiden, U.S.A., 1:55.44*
2. Kai Arne Stenshjemmet, Norway
3. Terje Andersen, Norway

5,000-meter
1. Eric Heiden, U.S.A., 7:2.29*
2. Kai Arne Stenshjemmet, Norway
3. Tom Erik Oxholm, Norway

10,000-meter
1. Eric Heiden, U.S.A. 14:28.13**
2. Piet Kleine, Netherlands
3. Tom Erik Oxholm, Norway

SPEED SKATING (Women)

500-meter
1. Karin Enke, East Germany, 41.78*
2. Leah Poulos Mueller, U.S.A.
3. Natalia Petruseva, U.S.S.R.

1,000-meter
1. Natalia Petruseva, U.S.S.R., 24.1*
2. Leah Poulos Mueller, U.S.A.
3. Silvia Albrecht, East Germany

1,500-meter
1. Annie Borckink, Netherlands, 2:10.95*
2. Ria Visser, Netherlands
3. Sabine Becker, East Germany

3,000-meter
1. Bjoerg Eva Jensen, Norway, 4:32.13*
2. Sabine Becker, East Germany
3. Beth Heiden, U.S.A.

WINTER OLYMPIC CHAMPIONS

ALPINE SKIING (Men)

Downhill

1948—Henri Oreiller, France
1952—Zeno Colo, Italy
1956—Toni Sailer, Austria
1960—Jean Vuarnet, France
1964—Egon Zimmermann, Austria
1968—Jean Claude Killy, France
1972—Bernhard Russi, Switzerland
1976—Franz Klammer, Austria

Giant Slalom

1952—Stein Eriksen, Norway
1956—Toni Sailer, Austria
1960—Roger Staub, Switzerland
1964—Francois Bonlieu, France
1968—Jean Claude Killy, France
1972—Gustavo Thoeni, Italy
1976—Heini Hemmi, Switzerland

Slalom

1948—Edi Reinalter, Switzerland
1952—Othmar Schneider, Austria
1956—Toni Sailer, Austria
1960—Ernst Hinterseer, Austria
1964—Josef Stiegler, Austria
1968—Jean Claude Killy, France
1972—Francisco Fernandez Ochoa, Spain
1976—Piero Gros, Italy

ALPINE SKIING (Women)

Downhill

1948—Hedi Schlunegger, Switzerland
1952—Trude Jochum-Beiser, Austria
1956—Madeleine Berthod, Switzerland
1960—Heidi Biebl, Germany
1964—Christl Haas, Austria
1968—Olga Pall, Austria
1972—Marie-Theres Nadig, Switzerland
1976—Rosi Mittermaier, West Germany

Giant Slalom

1952—Andrea Mead Lawrence, United States
1956—Ossi Reichert, Germany
1960—Yvonne Ruegg, Switzerland
1964—Marielle Goitschel, France
1968—Nancy Greene, Canada
1972—Marie-Theres Nadig, Switzerland
1976—Kathy Kreiner, Canada

Slalom

1948—Gretchen Fraser, United States
1952—Andrea Mead Lawrence, United States
1956—Renee Colliard, Switzerland
1960—Anne Heggtveigt, Canada
1964—Christine Goitschel, France
1968—Marielle Goitschel, France
1972—Barbara Cochran, United States
1976—Rosi Mittermaier, West Germany

NORDIC SKIING AND JUMPING (Men)

15-Kilometer Cross-Country

1924—Thorleif Haug, Norway
1928—Johan Grottumsbraaten, Norway
1932—Sven Utterstrom, Sweden
1936—Erik-August Larsson, Sweden
1948—Martin Lundstrom, Sweden
1952—Hallgeir Brenden, Norway
1956—Hallgeir Brenden, Norway
1960—Hakon Brusveen, Norway
1964—Eero Mantyranta, Finland
1968—Harald Groenningen, Norway
1972—Sven-Ake Lundback, Sweden
1976—Nikolai Bajukov, USSR

30-Kilometer Cross-Country

1956—Veikko Hakulinen, Finland
1960—Sixten Jernberg, Sweden
1964—Eero Mantyranta, Finland
1968—Franco Nones, Italy
1972—Vyacheslav Vedenin, USSR
1976—Sergei Saveliev, USSR

50-Kilometer Cross-Country

1924—Thorleif Haug, Norway
1928—Per Erik Hedlund, Sweden
1932—Veli Saarinen, Finland
1936—Elis Viklund, Sweden
1948—Nils Karlsson, Sweden

1952—Veikko Hakulinen, Finland
1956—Sixten Jernberg, Sweden
1960—Kalevi Hamalainen, Finland
1964—Sixten Jernberg, Sweden
1968—Ole Ellefsaeter, Norway
1972—Paal Tyldum, Norway
1976—Ivar Formo, Norway

4 x 10-Kilometer Cross-Country Relay

1936—Finland
1948—Sweden
1952—Finland
1956—USSR
1960—Finland
1964—Sweden
1968—Norway
1972—USSR
1976—Finland

70-Meter Special Jump

1964—Veikko Kankkonen, Finland
1968—Jiri Raska, Czechoslovakia
1972—Yukio Kasaya, Japan
1976—Hans-Georg Aschenbach, East Germany

90-Meter Special Jump

1924—Jacob T. Thambs, Norway
1928—Alfred Andersen, Norway
1932—Birger Ruud, Norway
1936—Birger Ruud, Norway
1948—Petter Hugsted, Norway
1952—Arnfinn Bergmann, Norway
1956—Antti Hyvarinen, Finland
1960—Helmut Recknagel, Germany
1964—Toralf Engan, Norway
1968—Vladimir Beloussov, USSR
1972—Wojiech Fortuna, Poland
1976—Karl Schnabl, Austria

Nordic Combined

1924—Thorleif Haug, Norway
1928—Johan Grottumsbraaten, Norway
1932—Johan Grottumsbraaten, Norway
1936—Oddbjorn Hagen, Norway
1948—Heikki Hasu, Finland
1952—Simon Slattvik, Norway
1956—Sverre Stenersen, Norway
1960—Georg Thoma, Germany
1964—Tormod Knutsen, Norway
1968—Franz Keller, West Germany
1972—Ulrich Wehling, East Germany
1976—Ulrich Wehling, East Germany

NORDIC SKIING (Women)

5-Kilometer Cross-Country

1964—Claudia Boyarskikh, USSR
1968—Toini Gustafsson, Sweden
1972—Galina Koulacova, USSR
1976—Helena Takalo, Finland

10-Kilometer Cross-Country

1952—Lydia Wideman, Finland
1956—Lyubov Kozyreva, USSR
1960—Marija Gusakova, USSR
1964—Claudia Boyarskikh, USSR
1968—Toini Gustafsson, Sweden
1972—Galina Koulacova, USSR
1976—Raisa Smetanina, USSR

15-Kilometer Relay

1956—Finland
1960—Sweden
1964—USSR
1968—Norway
1972—USSR
1976 (20 km.)—USSR

BIATHLON

20-Kilometer Individual

1960—Klas Lestander, Sweden
1964—Vladimir Melanin, USSR
1968—Magnar Solberg, Norway
1972—Magnar Solberg, Norway
1976—Nikolai Kruglov, USSR

40-Kilometer Relay

1968—USSR
1972—USSR
1976—USSR

HOCKEY

1920—Canada
1924—Canada
1928—Canada
1932—Canada
1936—Great Britain
1948—Canada
1952—Canada
1956—USSR
1960—United States
1964—USSR
1968—USSR
1972—USSR
1976—USSR

BOBSLEDDING

Two-Man

1932—United States	1964—Great Britain
1936—United States	1968—Italy
1948—Switzerland	1972—West Germany
1952—Germany	1976—East Germany
1956—Italy	

Four-Man

1924—Switzerland	1956—Switzerland
1928—United States (5-Man)	1964—Canada
1932—United States	1968—Italy
1936—Switzerland	1972—Switzerland
1948—United States	1976—East Germany
1952—Germany	

LUGE

Singles (Men)

1964—Thomas Kohler, Germany
1968—Manfred Schmid, Austria
1972—Wolfgang Scheidel, East Germany
1976—Detlef Guenther, East Germany

Doubles (Men)

1964—Austria
1968—East Germany
1972—Italy, East Germany (tie)
1976—East Germany

Singles (Women)

1964—Ortrun Enderlein, Germany
1968—Erica Lechner, Italy
1972—Anna M. Muller, East Germany
1976—Margit Schumann, East Germany

FIGURE SKATING

Men

1908—Ulrich Salchow, Sweden
1920—Gillis Grafstrom, Sweden
1924—Gillis Grafstrom, Sweden
1928—Gillis Grafstrom, Sweden
1932—Karl Schafer, Austria
1936—Karl Schafer, Austria
1948—Richard Button, United States
1952—Richard Button, United States
1956—Hayes Alan Jenkins, United States
1960—David W. Jenkins, United States
1964—Manfred Schnelldorfer, Germany
1968—Wolfgang Schwartz, Austria
1972—Ondrej Nepela. Czechoslovakia
1976—John Curry, United Kingdom

Women

1908—Madge Syers, Great Britain
1920—Magda Julin-Mauroy, Sweden
1924—Heima von Szabo-Planck, Austria
1928—Sonja Henie, Norway
1932—Sonja Henie, Norway
1936—Sonja Henie, Norway
1948—Barbara Ann Scott, Canada
1952—Jeanette Altwegg, Great Britain
1956—Tenley Albright, United States
1960—Carol Heiss, United States
1964—Sjoukje Dijkstra, Netherlands
1968—Peggy Fleming, United States
1972—Beatrix Schuba, Austria
1976—Dorothy Hamill, United States

Pairs

1908—Germany-Anna Hubler, Heinrich Burger
1920—Finland-Ludovika & Walter Jakobsson
1924—Austria-Helene Engelman, Alfred Berger
1928—France-Andree Joly, Pierre Brunet
1932—France-Andree & Pierre Brunet
1936—Germany-Maxie Herber, Ernst Baier
1948—Belgium-Micheline Lannoy, Pierre Baugniet
1952—Germany-Ria & Paul Falk
1956—Austria-Elisabeth Schwartz, Kurt Oppelt
1960—Canada-Barbara Wagner, Robert Paul
1964—USSR-Ludmila Beloussova, Oleg Protopopov
1968—USSR-Ludmila Beloussova, Oleg Protopopov
1972—USSR-Irina Rodnina, Alexei Ulanov
1976—USSR-Irina Rodnina, Aleksandr Zaitsev

Ice Dancing

1976—USSR-Lyudmila Pakhomova, Aleksandr Gorshkov

SPEED SKATING (Men)

500-Meters

1924—Charles Jewtraw, United States, 44.0
1928—Clas Thunberg, Finland and
    Bernt Evensen, Norway (tie), 43.4
1932—John A. Shea, United States, 43.4
1936—Ivar Ballangrud, Norway, 43.4
1948—Finn Helgesen, Norway, 43.1
1952—Ken Henry, United States, 43.2
1956—Yevgeni Grishin, USSR, 40.2
1960—Yevgeni Grishin, USSR, 40.2
1964—Terry McDermott, United States, 40.1
1968—Erhard Keller, West Germany, 40.3
1972—Erhard Keller, West Germany, 39.4
1976—Evgeni Kulikov, USSR, 39.17

1,000 Meters

1976—Peter Mueller, United States, 1:19.32

1,500-Meters

1924—Clas Thunberg, Finland, 2:20.8
1928—Clas Thunberg, Finland, 2:21.1
1932—John A. Shea, United States, 2:57.5
1936—Charles Mathisen, Norway, 2:19.2
1948—Sverre Farstad, Norway, 2:17.6
1952—Hjalmar Andersen, Norway, 2:20.4
1956—Yevgeni Grishin and Yuri
    Mikhailov, USSR (tie), 2:08.6
1960—Roald Aas, Norway and
    Yevgeni Grishin, USSR (tie), 2:10.4
1964—Ants Anston, USSR, 2:10.3
1968—Cornelis Verkerk, Netherlands, 2:03.4
1972—Ard Schenk, Netherlands, 2:02.9
1976—Jan Egil Storholt, Norway, 1:59.38

5.000-Meters

1924—Clas Thunberg, Finland, 8:39
1928—Ivar Ballangrud, Norway, 8:50.5
1932—Irving Jaffee, United States, 9:40.8
1936—Ivar Ballangrund, Norway, 8:19.6
1948—Reidar Liaklev, Norway, 8:29.4
1952—Hjalmar Andersen, Norway, 8:10.6
1956—Boris Shilkov, USSR, 7:48.7
1960—Viktor Kosichkin, USSR, 7:51.3
1964—Knut Johannesen, Norway, 7:38.4
1968—F. Anton Maier, Norway, 7:22.4*
1972—Ard Schenk, Netherlands, 7:23.6
1976—Sten Stensen, Norway, 7:24.48

10,000-Meters

1924—Julien Skutnabb, Finland, 18:04.8
1928—(ice thawed, event cancelled)
1932—Irving Jaffee, United States, 19:13.6
1936—Ivar Ballangrud, Norway, 17:24.3
1948—Ake Seyffarth, Sweden, 17:26.3
1952—Hjalmar Andersen, Norway, 16:45.8
1956—Sigvard Ericsson, Sweden, 16:35
1960—Knut Johannessen, Norway, 15:46.6
1964—Jonny Nilsson, Sweden, 15:50.1
1968—Johnny Hoeglin, Sweden, 15:23.6
1972—Ard Schenk, Netherlands, 15:01.3
1976—Piet Kleine, Netherlands, 14:50.59

SPEED SKATING (Women)

500-Meters

1960—Helga Haase, Germany, 45.9
1964—Lydia Skoblikova, USSR, 45.0
1968—Ludmila Titova, USSR, 46.1
1972—Anne Henning, United States, 43.3
1976—Sheila Young, United States, 42.76

1,000-Meters

1960—Klara Guseva, USSR, 1:34.1
1964—Lydia Skoblikova, USSR, 1:33.2
1968—Carolina Geijssen, Netherlands, 1:32.6
1972—Monika Pflug, West Germany, 1:31.4
1976—Tatiana Averina, USSR, 1:28.43

1,500-Meters

1960—Lydia Skoblikova, USSR, 2:25.2
1964—Lydia Skoblikova, USSR, 2:22.6
1968—Kaija Mustonen, Finland, 2:22.4
1972—Dianne Holum, United States, 2:20.8
1976—Galina Stepanskaya, USSR, 2:16.58

3,000-Meters

1960—Lydia Skoblikova, USSR, 5:14.3
1964—Lydia Skoblikova, USSR, 5:14.9
1968—Johanna Schut, Netherlands, 4:56.2
1972—Stien Kaiser-Baas, Netherlands, 4:52.1
1976—Tatiana Averina, USSR, 4:45.19

BASEBALL

BASEBALL GOVERNMENT

Office of the Commissioner: 75 Rockefeller Plaza, New York City 10019

Prior to 1920, major league baseball was governed by a three-man commission. However, in that year, following the "Black Sox" scandal of the 1919 World Series, the office of baseball commissioner was created. The first commissioner was Kenesaw M. Landis (1921–44); he was succeeded by Albert B. Chandler (1945–51), Ford C. Frick (1951–65), William D. Eckert (1965–69), and the current commissioner, Bowie Kuhn (1969–   ).

THE NATIONAL LEAGUE: One Rockefeller Plaza, Suite 1602, New York City 10020. Organized in 1876.

President: **Charles S. Feeney** Vice-President: **John J. McHale**

Club	President	1980 Manager
Atlanta Braves	R. E. (Ted) Turner	Bobby Cox
Chicago Cubs	William J. Hagenah, Jr.	Preston Gomez, Joe Amalfitano
Cincinnati Reds	Richard Wagner	John McNamara
Houston Astros	Talbot M. Smith	Bill Virdon
Los Angeles Dodgers	Peter O'Malley	Tom Lasorda
Montreal Expos	J. J. McHale	Dick Williams
New York Mets	Fred Wilpon	Joe Torre
Philadelphia Phillies	R. R. M. Carpenter, III	Dallas Green
Pittsburgh Pirates	Daniel M. Galbreath	Chuck Tanner
St. Louis Cardinals	August A. Busch, Jr.	Ken Boyer, Whitey Herzog, Red Schoendienst
San Diego Padres	Ballard Smith	Jerry Coleman
San Francisco Giants	Robert A. Lurie	Dave Bristol

THE AMERICAN LEAGUE: 280 Park Ave., New York City 10017 Founded in 1900.

Chairman: **Joseph E. Cronin** President: **Leland S. MacPhail, Jr.** Vice-Pres.: **Calvin R. Griffith**

Club	President	1980 Manager
Baltimore Orioles	Jerry C. Hoffberger	Earl Weaver
Boston Red Sox	Mrs. Jean Yawkey	Don Zimmer
California Angels	Gene Autry	Jim Fregosi
Chicago White Sox	Bill Veeck	Tony LaRussa
Cleveland Indians	Gabe Paul	Dave Garcia
Detroit Tigers	J. E. Fetzer	Sparky Anderson
Kansas City Royals	Ewing Kauffman	Jim Frey
Milwaukee Brewers	Allan Selig	George Bamberger, Bob Rodgers
Minnesota Twins	Calvin Griffith	Gene Mauch, John Goryl
New York Yankees	George Steinbrenner	Dick Howser
Oakland Athletics	Charles O. Finley	Billy Martin
Seattle Mariners	Daniel O'Brien	Darrell Johnson, Maury Wills
Texas Rangers	Bradford G. Corbett	Pat Corrales
Toronto Blue Jays	Peter Bavasi	Bobby Mattick

MAJOR LEAGUE RECORDS: 1900–1980

BATTING

Highest Batting Average, Lifetime: .367, Ty Cobb (AL), 1905–1928; .358, Rogers Hornsby (NL), 1915–1937.

Highest Batting Average, Season: .424, Rogers Hornsby, St. Louis (NL), 1924; .420, George Sisler, St. Louis (AL), 1922.

Most Years Led League in Batting: 12, Ty Cobb, Detroit (AL), 1907–1915, 1917–1919; 8, Honus Wagner, Pittsburgh (NL), 1900, 1903–1904, 1906–1909, 1911.

Most Years Batting .300 or More: 23, Ty Cobb, Detroit and Philadelphia (AL), 1906–1928; 17, Honus Wagner, Louisville and Pittsburgh (NL), 1897–1913; 17, Stan Musial, St. Louis (NL), 1942–1944, 1946–1958, 1962.

Most Hits: 4,191, Ty Cobb (AL), 1905–1928; 3,630, Stan Musial (NL), 1941–1944, 1946–1963.

Most Hits, Season: 257, George Sisler, St. Louis (AL), 1920; 254, Lefty O'Doul, Philadelphia (NL), 1929; 254, Bill Terry, New York (NL), 1930.

Most Consecutive Games Batted Safely: 56, Joe DiMaggio, New York (AL), 1941; 44, Pete Rose, Cincinnati (NL), 1978

Most Consecutive Games Played: 2,130, Lou Gehrig, New York (AL), 1925-39; 1,117, Billy Williams, Chicago (NL), 1963-70.

Most Runs: 2,244, Ty Cobb (AL), 1905–1928; 2,174, Babe Ruth, Boston (AL), New York (AL), Boston (NL), 1914–1935.

Most Runs, Season: 177, Babe Ruth, New York (AL), 1921; 158, Chuck Klein, Philadelphia (NL), 1930.

Most Consecutive Years 100 or More Runs: 13, Lou Gehrig, New York (AL), 1926–1938; 13, Hank Aaron, Milwaukee and Atlanta (NL), 1955–1967.

Most Runs Batted In, Lifetime: 2,297, Hank Aaron, 1954–1976; 2,204, Babe Ruth, 1914–1935.

Most Runs Batted In, Season: 190, Hack Wilson, Chicago (NL), 1930; 184, Lou Gehrig, New York (AL), 1931.

Highest Slugging Percentage, Lifetime: .690, Babe Ruth, Boston and New York (AL), Boston (NL); .634, Ted Williams, Boston (AL).

Most Home Runs, Lifetime: 755, Hank Aaron, Milwaukee and Atlanta (NL), Milwaukee (AL), 1954–1976; 714, Babe Ruth, Boston and New York (AL), Boston (NL).

Most Home Runs, Season: 61, Roger Maris, New York (AL), 1961, 162-game schedule; 60, Babe Ruth, New York (AL), 1927, 154-game schedule.

Most Years League Home-Run Leader: 12, Babe Ruth (AL), 1918–1919, 1920–1921, 1923–1924, 1926–1931; 7, Ralph Kiner, Pittsburgh (NL), 1946–1952.

Most Years 20 or More Home Runs: 19, Henry Aaron (NL); 17, Willie Mays (NL); 16, Babe Ruth (AL).

Most Grand Slam Home Runs, Lifetime: 23, Lou Gehrig, New York (AL); 18, Willie McCovey, San Francisco, San Diego (NL).

Most Grand Slam Home Runs, Season: 5, Ernie Banks, Chicago (NL), 1955; 5, Jim Gentile, Baltimore (AL), 1961.

Most Bases on Balls, Season: 170, Babe Ruth, New York (AL), 1923; 162, Ted Williams, Boston (AL), 1947, 1949.

Fewest Strikeouts, Lifetime (7,000 or More At Bats): 114, Joe Sewell (AL); 173, Lloyd Waner (NL).

Most Consecutive Games without Strikeouts: 98, Nelson Fox, Chicago (AL), 1958; 77, Lloyd Waner (NL), 1941.

Most Pinch Hits, Lifetime: 150, Manny Mota (NL).

Most Stolen Bases, Lifetime: 938, Lou Brock (NL); 892, Ty Cobb (AL).

Most Stolen Bases, Season: 118, Lou Brock, St. Louis (NL), 1974, 162-game schedule; 96, Ty Cobb, Detroit (AL), 1915, 154-game schedule.

PITCHING

Most Games Won, Lifetime: 511, Cy Young (NL–AL); 416, Walter Johnson (AL).

Most Games Won, Season: 41, Jack Chesbro, New York (AL), 1904; 39, Ed Walsh, Chicago (AL), 1908.

Most Years 20-or-More-Game Winner: 16, Cy Young (NL–AL), 1891–1904, 1907–1908; 13, Christy Mathewson (NL), 1901, 1903–1914; 13, Warren Spahn (NL), 1947, 1949–1951, 1953–1954, 1956–1961, 1963; 12, Walter Johnson (AL), 1910–1919, 1924–1925.

Most Consecutive Games Won, Lifetime: 24, Carl Hubbell, New York (NL), 16 in 1936, 8 in 1937; 17, John Allen, Cleveland (AL), 2 in 1936, 15 in 1937; 17, Dave McNally, Baltimore (AL), 2 in 1968, 15 in 1969.

Most Consecutive Games Won, Season: 19, Rube Marquard, New York (NL), 1912; 17, ElRoy Face, Pittsburgh (NL), 1959.

Most Shutout Games, Lifetime: 113, Walter Johnson (AL); 90, Grover Alexander (NL).

Most Shutout Games, Season: 16, Grover Alexander, Philadelphia (NL), 1916; 13, Jack Coombs, Philadelphia (AL), 1910; 13, Bob Gibson, St. Louis, 1968.

Most Consecutive Shutout Games, Season: 6, Don Drysdale, Los Angeles (NL), 1968; 5, Harris White, Chicago (AL), 1904.

Most Consecutive Shutout Innings, Season: 58, Don Drysdale, Los Angeles (NL), 1968; 56, Walter Johnson, Washington (AL), 1913; 46⅓, Carl Hubbell, New York (NL), 1933.

Lowest Earned Run Average, Season: 1.01, Hubert Leonard, Boston (AL), 1914; 1.04, Three Finger Brown, Chicago (NL), 1906.

Most Consecutive Years Lowest Earned Run Average: 5, Sandy Koufax, Los Angeles (NL), 1962–1966; 4, Lefty Grove, Philadelphia (AL), 1929–1932.

Highest Won-Lost Percentage, Lifetime (100 or More Decisions): .690, Whitey Ford, New York (AL), 1950–1967.

Highest Won-Lost Percentage, Season (15 or More Decisions): .947, ElRoy Face, Pittsburgh (NL), 1959.

Most Strikeouts, Lifetime: 3,508, Walter Johnson (AL); 3,117, Bob Gibson, St. Louis (NL).

Most Strikeouts, Season: 383, Nolan Ryan, California (AL), 1973; 382, Sandy Koufax, Los Angeles (NL), 1965.

Most Strikeouts in 9-Inning Game: 19, Steve Carlton, St. Louis (NL), 1969; 19, Tom Seaver, New York (NL), 1970; 19, Nolan Ryan, California (AL), 1974, 1977.

Most Games Won, Relief Pitcher, Lifetime: 123, Hoyt Wilhelm (NL-AL), 1952-70; 114, Lindy McDaniel (NL-AL), 1955-73.

MAJOR LEAGUE BASEBALL ALL-TIME LEADERS[1]

BATTING

SEASONS
James McGuire	26
Eddie Collins	25
Bobby Wallace	25
Ty Cobb	24
Hank Aaron	23
Brooks Robinson	23
Rabbit Maranville	23
Rogers Hornsby	23
Stan Musial	22
Tris Speaker, Mel Ott	22
Babe Ruth	22
Bill Dahlen	22
Jimmie Dykes	22
Cap Anson	22
Phil Cavarretta	22
Harry Davis	22
Willie Mays, Al Kaline	22
Harmon Killebrew	22
Willie McCovey	22

GAMES
Hank Aaron	3,298
Ty Cobb	3,033
Stan Musial	3,026
Willie Mays	2,992
Carl Yastrzemski	2,967
Brooks Robinson	2,896
Al Kaline	2,834
Pete Rose	2,830
Eddie Collins	2,826
Frank Robinson	2,808
Tris Speaker	2,789
Honus Wagner	2,785
Mel Ott	2,730
Rabbit Maranville	2,670
Lou Brock	2,616
Luis Aparicio	2,599
Willie McCovey	2,588
Paul Waner	2,549
Rusty Staub	2,533

BATTING AVERAGE
Ty Cobb	.367
Rogers Hornsby	.358
Joe Jackson	.356
Ed Delahanty	.346
Willie Keeler	.345
Ted Williams	.344
Tris Speaker	.344
Billy Hamilton	.344
Dan Brouthers	.342
Babe Ruth	.342
Harry Heilmann	.342
Pete Browning	.341
Bill Terry	.341
George Sisler	.340
Lou Gehrig	.340
Jesse Burkett	.340
Nap Lajoie	.339

AT BATS
Hank Aaron	12,364
Pete Rose	11,479
Ty Cobb	11,429
Stan Musial	10,972
Willie Mays	10,881
Carl Yastrzemski	10,811
Brooks Robinson	10,654
Honus Wagner	10,427
Lou Brock	10,332
Luis Aparicio	10,230
Tris Speaker	10,208
Al Kaline	10,116
Rabbit Maranville	10,078
Frank Robinson	10,006
Eddie Collins	9,949
Vada Pinson	9,645
Nap Lajoie	9,589
Sam Crawford	9,579
Jake Beckley	9,476

RUNS
Ty Cobb	2,244
Babe Ruth	2,174
Hank Aaron	2,174
Willie Mays	2,062
Stan Musial	1,949
Lou Gehrig	1,888
Tris Speaker	1,881
Mel Ott	1,859
Pete Rose	1,840
Frank Robinson	1,829
Eddie Collins	1,818
Ted Williams	1,798

HITS
Ty Cobb	4,191
Hank Aaron	3,771
Stan Musial	3,630
Pete Rose	3,557
Tris Speaker	3,515
Honus Wagner	3,430
Eddie Collins	3,311
Willie Mays	3,283
Nap Lajoie	3,251
Paul Waner	3,152
Carl Yastrzemski	3,109
Cap Anson	3,081

DOUBLES
Tris Speaker	793
Stan Musial	725
Ty Cobb	724
Pete Rose	654
Honus Wagner	651
Nap Lajoie	650
Hank Aaron	624
Paul Waner	603
Carl Yastrzemski	586
Charlie Gehringer	574
Harry Heilmann	542
Rogers Hornsby	541

TRIPLES
Sam Crawford	312
Ty Cobb	297
Honus Wagner	252
Jake Beckley	246
Roger Connor	227
Tris Speaker	224
Fred Clarke	219
Dan Brouthers	212
Paul Waner	190
Joe Kelley	189
Bid McPhee	189
Eddie Collins	186

HOME RUNS
Hank Aaron	755
Babe Ruth	714
Willie Mays	660
Frank Robinson	586
Harmon Killebrew	573
Mickey Mantle	536
Jimmie Foxx	534
Ted Willams	521
Willie McCovey	521
Eddie Mathews	512
Ernie Banks	512
Mel Ott	511
Lou Gehrig	493
Stan Musial	475
Willie Stargell	472
Billy Williams	426
Carl Yastrzemski	419
Reggie Jackson	410
Duke Snider	407
Al Kaline	399
Frank Howard	382
Orlando Cepeda	379
Norm Cash	377
Rocky Colavito	374
Gil Hodges	370
Ralph Kiner	369

TOTAL BASES
Hank Aaron	6,838
Stan Musial	6,134
Willie Mays	6,066
Ty Cobb	5,863
Babe Ruth	5,793
Frank Robinson	5,373
Tris Speaker	5,101
Carl Yastrzemski	5,066
Lou Gehrig	5,059
Mel Ott	5,041
Jimmie Foxx	4,956
Pete Rose	4,910

EXTRA BASE HITS
Hank Aaron	1,477
Stan Musial	1,377
Babe Ruth	1,356
Willie Mays	1,323
Lou Gehrig	1,190
Frank Robinson	1,186
Ty Cobb	1,139
Tris Speaker	1,132
Jimmie Foxx	1,117
Ted Williams	1,117
Mel Ott	1,071
Carl Yastrzemski	1,062

BASES ON BALLS
Babe Ruth	2,056
Ted Williams	2,018
Mickey Mantle	1,734
Mel Ott	1,708
Carl Yastrzemski	1,683
Eddie Yost	1,614
Stan Musial	1,599
Harmon Killebrew	1,559
Joe Morgan	1,559
Lou Gehrig	1,508
Eddie Collins	1,503
Willie Mays	1,464

STOLEN BASES
Lou Brock	938
Ty Cobb	892
Eddie Collins	743
Max Carey	738
Bert Campaneris	728
Honus Wagner	720
Joe Morgan	625
Maury Wills	586
Luis Aparicio	506
Clyde Milan	494
Cesar Cedeno	475
Jimmy Sheckard	460

RUNS BATTED IN
Hank Aaron	2,297
Babe Ruth	2,204
Lou Gehrig	1,990
Ty Cobb	1,954
Stan Musial	1,951
Jimmie Foxx	1,921
Willie Mays	1,903
Mel Ott	1,860
Ted Williams	1,839
Al Simmons	1,827
Frank Robinson	1,812
Honus Wagner	1,732

STRIKEOUTS
Willie Stargell	1,903
Lou Brock	1,730
Reggie Jackson	1,728
Bobby Bonds	1,714
Mickey Mantle	1,710
Harmon Killebrew	1,699
Dick Allen	1,556
Willie McCovey	1,550
Frank Robinson	1,532
Willie Mays	1,526
Eddie Mathews	1,487
Frank Howard	1,460

PITCHING

SEASONS
Early Wynn	23
Jack Quinn	23
Cy Young	22
Sad Sam Jones	22
Red Ruffing	22
Herb Pennock, Jim Kaat	22
Hoyt Wilhelm	21
Walter Johnson	21
Warren Spahn	21
Eppa Rixey	21
Waite Hoyt	21
Ted Lyons	21

WINS
Cy Young	511
Walter Johnson	416
Christy Mathewson	373
Grover Alexander	373
Warren Spahn	363
Pud Galvin	361
Kid Nichols	360
Tim Keefe	343
John Clarkson	327
Eddie Plank	327
Mickey Welch	311

COMPLETE GAMES
Cy Young	751
Pud Galvin	639
Tim Keefe	554
Walter Johnson	531
Kid Nichols	531
Mickey Welch	525
John Clarkson	488
Old Hoss Radbourn	479
Tony Mullane	464
Jim McCormick	462
Gus Weyhing	448

INNINGS PITCHED
Cy Young	7,377
Pud Galvin	5,959
Walter Johnson	5,924
Warren Spahn	5,246
Grover Alexander	5,189
Kid Nichols	5,067
Tim Keefe	5,043
Gaylord Perry	4,798
Christy Mathewson	4,781
Mickey Welch	4,784
Robin Roberts	4,689

SHUTOUTS
Walter Johnson	113
Grover Alexander	90
Christy Mathewson	83
Cy Young	77
Eddie Plank	64
Warren Spahn	63
Ed Walsh	58
Three Finger Brown	58
Pud Galvin	57

STRIKEOUTS
Walter Johnson	3,508
Gaylord Perry	3,276
Bob Gibson	3,117
Nolan Ryan	3,109
Tom Seaver	2,988
Steve Carlton	2,969
Ferguson Jenkins	2,899
Jim Bunning	2,855
Cy Young	2,819

BASES ON BALLS
Early Wynn	1,775
Bob Feller	1,764
Nolan Ryan	1,744
Bobo Newsom	1,732
Amos Rusie	1,637
Gus Weyhing	1,569
Red Ruffing	1,541
Bump Hadley	1,442
Warren Spahn	1,434

EARNED RUN AVERAGE
Ed Walsh	1.82
Addie Joss	1.88
Three Finger Brown	2.06
Monte Ward	2.10
Christy Mathewson	2.13
Rube Waddell	2.16
Walter Johnson	2.17
Orval Overall	2.24
Tommy Bond	2.25

[1]At start of 1981 season.

HALL OF FAME

ELECTED FOR MERITORIOUS SERVICE

Barrow, Edward, manager and executive
Bulkeley, Morgan G., first National League president
Cartwright, Alexander J., formulated first baseball rules
Chadwick, Henry, first reporter and keeper of records
Comiskey, Charles A., player, manager, and executive
Conlan, Jocko, National League umpire
Connolly, Thomas, American League umpire
Cummings, William A., early pitcher, said to have invented the curve ball
Evans, William, American League Umpire
Frick, Ford C., National League president and commissioner
Giles, Warren G., general manager and National League pres.
Griffith, Clark C., player, manager, and executive
Harridge, William, American League president
Harris, Stanley (Bucky), player, manager, executive
Hubbard, Robert C. (Cal), American League umpire
Huggins, Miller J., manager
Johnson, Byron Bancroft, first American League president
Klem, William, National League umpire
Landis, Kenesaw M., first commissioner of baseball
Lopez, Alfonso R., manager
Mack, Connie, manager and executive
Mac Phail, Larry, executive
McCarthy, Joseph, manager
McGraw, John J., player and manager
McKechnie, William B., manager
Rickey, W. Branch, manager and executive
Robinson, Wilbert, player and manager
Spalding, Albert G., early pitcher and organizer of the National League
Stengel, Charles D., player and manager
Weiss, George, general manager
Wright, George, early player
Wright, Harry, early player and manager
Yawkey, Tom, executive

PITCHERS

	Years	Won	Lost
Alexander, Grover Cleveland	1911–1930	373	208
Bender, Charles (Chief)	1903–1925	212	128
Brown, Mordecai (Three-Finger)	1903–1916	239	130
Chesbro, John	1899–1909	199	128
Clarkson, John	1882–1894	328	175
Coveleski, Stanley	1912–1928	215	141
Dean, Jerome (Dizzy)	1930–1947	150	83
Faber, Urban (Red)	1914–1933	254	212
Feller, Robert	1936–1956	266	162
Ford, Edward (Whitey)	1950–1967	236	106
Galvin, James (Pud)	1879–1892	361	309
Gomez, Vernon (Lefty)	1930–1943	189	102
Grimes, Burleigh	1916–1934	270	212
Grove, Robert (Lefty)	1925–1941	300	141
Haines, Jesse	1918–1937	210	158
Hoyt, Waite	1918–1938	237	182
Hubbell, Carl	1928–1943	253	154
Johnson, Walter (Big Train)	1907–1927	416	279
Joss, Adrian (Addie)	1902–1910	160	97
Keefe, Timothy	1880–1893	346	225
Koufax, Sanford	1955–1966	165	87
Lemon, Robert	1941–1958	207	128
Lyons, Theodore	1923–1946	260	230
Marquard, Richard (Rube)	1908–1925	201	177
Mathewson, Christopher	1900–1916	373	188
McGinnity, Joseph (Iron Man)	1899–1908	247	142
Nichols, Charles (Kid)	1890–1906	360	202
Pennock, Herbert	1912–1934	240	162
Plank, Edward	1901–1917	325	190
Radbourne, Charles (Old Hoss)	1880–1891	308	191
Rixey, Eppa	1912–1933	266	251
Roberts, Robin	1948–1966	286	245
Ruffing, Charles (Red)	1924–1947	273	225
Rusie, Amos	1889–1901	246	174
Spahn, Warren	1942–1965	363	245
Vance, Arthur (Dazzy)	1915–1935	197	140
Waddell, George (Rube)	1897–1910	193	140
Walsh, Edward (Big Ed)	1904–1917	195	126
Welch, Mickey	1880–1892	308	209
Wynn, Early	1939–1963	300	244
Young, Denton (Cy)	1890–1911	511	315

ELECTED FROM NEGRO LEAGUES

Bell, James (Cool Page)
Charleston, Oscar
Dihigo, Martin
Gibson, Joshua
Irvin, Monte
Johnson, William (Judy)
Leonard, Walter (Buck)
Lloyd, John Henry (Pop)
Paige, Leroy (Satchel)

BATTERS

	Years	Average
Anson, Adrian (Cap)	1876–1897	.339
Appling, Lucius B. (Luke)	1930–1950	.310
Averill, H. Earl	1929–1941	.318
Baker, J. Frank (Home Run)	1908–1922	.307
Bancroft, Dave	1915–1930	.279
Banks, Ernest	1953–1971	.274
Beckley, Jake	1888–1907	.309
Berra, Lawrence (Yogi)	1946–1965	.285
Bottomley, James	1922–1937	.310
Boudreau, Louis	1938–1952	.295
Bresnahan, Roger	1897–1915	.279
Brouthers, Dennis (Dan)	1879–1904	.349
Burkett, Jesse	1890–1905	.342
Campanella, Roy	1948–1957	.276
Carey, Max	1910–1929	.285
Chance, Frank	1898–1914	.297
Clarke, Fred	1894–1915	.315
Clemente, Roberto	1955–1972	.317
Cobb, Tyrus	1905–1928	.367
Cochrane, Gordon (Mickey)	1925–1937	.320
Collins, Edward	1906–1930	.333
Collins, James	1895–1908	.294
Combs, Earle	1924–1935	.325
Connor, Roger	1880–1897	.325
Crawford, Samuel (Wahoo)	1899–1917	.309
Cronin, Joseph	1926–1945	.302
Cuyler, Hazen (Kiki)	1921–1938	.321
Delahanty, Edward	1888–1903	.346
Dickey, William	1928–1946	.313
DiMaggio, Joseph	1936–1951	.325
Duffy, Hugh	1888–1906	.330
Evers, John	1902–1929	.270
Ewing, William (Buck)	1880–1897	.311
Flick, Elmer	1898–1910	.315
Foxx, James	1925–1945	.325
Frisch, Frank	1919–1937	.316
Gehrig, Henry (Lou)	1923–1939	.340
Gehringer, Charles	1924–1942	.320
Goslin, Leon (Goose)	1921–1938	.316
Greenberg, Henry	1930–1947	.313
Hafey, Charles (Chick)	1924–1937	.317
Hamilton, William	1888–1901	.344
Hartnett, Charles (Gabby)	1922–1941	.297
Heilmann, Harry	1914–1932	.342
Herman, William	1931–1947	.304
Hooper, Harry	1909–1925	.281
Hornsby, Rogers (Rajah)	1915–1937	.358
Jennings, Hugh	1891–1918	.314
Kaline, Al	1953–1974	.297
Keeler, William (Wee Willie)	1892–1910	.345
Kelley, Joe	1891–1908	.321
Kelly, George	1915–1932	.297
Kelly, Michael (King)	1878–1893	.313
Kiner, Ralph	1946–1955	.279
Klein, Charles (Chuck)	1928–1944	.320
Lajoie, Napoleon	1896–1916	.339
Lindstrom, Fred	1924–1939	.311
McCarthy, Thomas	1884–1896	.294
Manush, Henry (Heinie)	1923–1939	.330
Mantle, Mickey	1951–1968	.298
Maranville, Walter (Rabbit)	1912–1935	.258
Mathews, Eddie	1952–1968	.271
Mays, Willie	1951–1973	.302
Medwick, Joseph (Ducky)	1932–1948	.324
Musial, Stan	1941–1963	.331
O'Rourke, James	1876–1904	.314
Ott, Melvin	1926–1947	.304
Rice, Edgar (Sam)	1915–1934	.322
Robinson, Jack	1947–1956	.311
Roush, Edd	1913–1931	.323
Ruth, George (Babe)	1914–1935	.342
Schalk, Raymond	1912–1929	.253
Sewell, Joseph	1920–1933	.312
Simmons, Al	1924–1944	.334
Sisler, George	1915–1930	.340
Snider, Edwin (Duke)	1947–1964	.295
Speaker, Tris	1907–1928	.344
Terry, William	1923–1936	.341
Thompson, Samuel L.	1885–1906	.336
Tinker, Joseph	1902–1916	.264
Traynor, Harold (Pie)	1920–1937	.320
Wagner, John (Honus)	1897–1917	.329
Wallace, Roderick (Bobby)	1894–1918	.267
Waner, Lloyd (Little Poison)	1927–1945	.316
Waner, Paul (Big Poison)	1926–1945	.333
Ward, John Montgomery	1878–1894	.283
Wheat, Zachary	1909–1927	.317
Williams, Theodore	1939–1960	.344
Wilson, Hack	1923–1934	.307
Youngs, Ross (Pep)	1917–1926	.322

1980 MAJOR LEAGUE STANDINGS

NATIONAL LEAGUE

Eastern Division	W	L	Pct.	GB
Philadelphia	91	71	.562	—
Montreal	90	72	.556	1
Pittsburgh	83	79	.512	8
St. Louis	74	88	.457	17
New York	67	95	.414	24
Chicago	64	98	.395	27

Western Division	W	L	Pct.	GB
Houston	93	70	.571	..
Los Angeles	92	71	.564	1
Cincinnati	89	73	.549	3½
Atlanta	81	80	.503	11
San Francisco	75	86	.466	17
San Diego	73	89	.451	19½

AMERICAN LEAGUE

Eastern Division	W	L	Pct.	GB
New York	103	59	.636	—
Baltimore	100	62	.617	3
Milwaukee	86	76	.531	17
Boston	83	77	.519	19
Detroit	84	78	.519	19
Cleveland	79	81	.494	23
Toronto	67	95	.414	36

Western Division	W	L	Pct.	GB
Kansas City	97	65	.599	—
Oakland	83	79	.512	14
Minnesota	77	84	.478	19½
Texas	76	85	.472	20½
Chicago	70	90	.438	26
California	65	95	.406	31
Seattle	59	103	.364	38

1980 ALL-STAR GAME Los Angeles, July 8

AMERICAN LEAGUE	ab	r	h	bi
Randolph, 2b	4	0	2	0
Stieb, p	0	0	0	0
Gossage, p	0	0	0	0
Carew, 1b	2	1	2	0
Cooper, 1b	1	0	0	0
Lynn, cf	3	1	1	2
Bumbry, cf	1	0	0	0
Jackson, rf	2	0	1	0
Landreaux, rf	1	0	0	0
Oglivie, lf	2	0	0	0
Oliver, lf	1	0	0	0
Trammell, ss	0	0	0	0
Fisk, c	2	0	0	0
Porter, c	1	0	0	0
Henderson, lf	1	0	0	0
Nettles, 3b	2	0	0	0
Bell, 3b	2	0	0	0
Dent, ss	2	0	1	0
John, p	1	0	0	0
Farmer, p	0	0	0	0
Grich, 2b	0	0	0	0
Stone, p	1	0	0	0
Yount, ss	2	0	0	0
Parrish, c	1	0	0	0
Total	**32**	**2**	**7**	**2**

NATIONAL LEAGUE	ab	r	h	bi
Lopes, 2b	1	0	0	0
Garner, 2b	2	1	1	0
Smith, cf	2	0	0	0
Hendrick, cf	2	0	1	1
Sutter, p	0	0	0	0
Parker, rf	2	0	0	0
Winfield, rf	2	0	0	0
Garvey, 1b	2	0	0	0
Hernandez, 1b	2	0	2	0
Bench, c	1	0	0	0
Stearns, c	1	0	0	0
Rose, ph	1	0	0	0
Bibby, p	0	0	0	0
Murphy, cf	1	0	0	0
Kingman, lf	1	0	0	0
Griffey, lf	3	1	2	1
Reitz, 3b	2	0	0	0
Reuss, p	0	0	0	0
Concepcion, ss	1	1	0	0
Russell, ss	2	0	0	0
Carter, c	1	0	0	0
Richard, p	0	0	0	0
Welch, p	1	0	0	0
Knight, 3b	1	1	1	0
Total	**31**	**4**	**7**	**2**

```
American League .......  0 0 0 0 2 0 0 0 0 — 2
National League .......  0 0 0 0 1 2 1 0 x — 4
```

E—Randolph 2. DP—American 1. National 1. LOB—American 7, National 5. 2B—Carew. HR—Lynn, Griffey. SB—Carew, Knight, Garner.

American	IP	H	R	ER	BB	SO
Stone	3	0	0	0	0	3
John (L)	2⅓	4	3	3	0	1
Farmer	⅔	1	0	0	0	0
Stieb	1	1	1	1	2	0
Gossage	1	1	0	0	0	0

National	IP	H	R	ER	BB	SO
Richard	2	1	0	0	2	3
Welch	3	5	2	2	1	4
Reuss (W)	1	0	0	0	0	3
Bibby	1	1	0	0	0	0
Sutter (S)	2	0	0	0	1	1

WP—Welch, Stieb. PB—Porter. T—2:33. A—56,088.

1980 PLAYOFF RESULTS

NATIONAL LEAGUE

	Game No.				
	One	Two	Three	Four	Five
Philadelphia	3	4	0	5	8
Houston	1	7	1	3	7

AMERICAN LEAGUE

	Game No.				
	One	Two	Three	Four	Five
Kansas City	7	3	4	—	—
New York	2	2	2	—	—

1980 WORLD SERIES BOX SCORES

FIRST GAME: Veterans Stadium, October 14

KANSAS CITY (AL)	ab	r	h	bi
Wilson, lf	5	0	0	0
McRae, dh	3	1	1	0
G. Brett, 3b	4	1	1	0
Aikens, 1b	4	2	2	4
Porter, c	2	1	0	0
Otis, cf	4	1	3	2
Hurdle, rf	3	0	1	0
Wathan, rf	1	0	0	0
White, 2b	4	0	1	0
Washington, ss	4	0	0	0
Total	**34**	**6**	**9**	**6**

PHILADELPHIA (NL)	ab	r	h	bi
Smith, lf	4	0	2	0
Gross, lf	1	0	0	0
Rose, 1b	3	1	0	0
Schmidt, 3b	2	2	1	0
McBride, rf	4	1	3	3
Luzinski, dh	3	0	0	0
Maddox, cf	3	0	0	1
Trillo, 2b	4	1	1	0
Bowa, ss	4	1	1	0
Boone, c	4	1	3	2
Total	**32**	**7**	**11**	**6**

```
Kansas City ........  0 2 2 0 0 0 0 2 0 — 6
Philadelphia .......  0 0 5 1 1 0 0 0 x — 7
```

E—Leonard. DP—Philadelphia 1. LOB—Kansas City 4, Philadelphia 6. 2B—Boone 2, G. Brett. HR—Otis, Aikens 2, McBride. SB—Bowa, White. SF—Maddox.

	IP	H	R	ER	BB	SO
Kansas City—Leonard (L, 0-1)	3⅔	6	6	6	1	3
Martin	4	5	1	1	1	1
Quisenberry	⅓	0	0	0	0	0
Philadelphia—Walk (W, 1-0)	7*	8	6	6	3	3
McGraw (S, 1)	2	1	0	0	0	2

*Pitched to two batters in the eighth.

HBP—by Leonard (Rose) by Martin (Luzinski). WP—Walk. Time—3:01. Attendance—65,791.

SECOND GAME: Veterans Stadium, October 15

KANSAS CITY (AL)	ab	r	h	bi
Wilson, lf	4	1	1	0
Washington, ss	4	0	1	0
G. Brett, 3b	2	0	2	0
Chalk, 3b	0	1	0	0
Porter, ph	1	0	0	0
McRae, dh	4	1	3	0
Otis, cf	5	1	2	2
Wathan, c	3	0	0	1
Aikens, 1b	3	0	1	0
LaCock, 1b	0	0	0	0
Cardenal, rf	4	0	0	0
White, 2b	4	0	1	0
Total	**34**	**4**	**11**	**3**

PHILADELPHIA (NL)	ab	r	h	bi
Smith, lf	3	0	0	0
Unser, cf	1	1	1	1
Rose, 1b	4	0	0	0
McBride, rf	3	1	1	1
Schmidt, 3b	4	1	2	1
Moreland, dh	4	1	2	1
Maddox, cf	3	1	1	0
Gross, lf	1	0	0	0
Trillo, 2b	2	0	0	1
Bowa, ss	3	0	1	1
Boone, c	1	1	0	0
Total	**29**	**6**	**8**	**6**

```
Kansas City ........  0 0 0 0 0 1 3 0 0 — 4
Philadelphia .......  0 0 0 0 2 0 0 4 x — 6
```

E—Trillo. DP—Kansas City 2, Philadelphia 4. LOB—Kansas City 11, Philadelphia 3. 2b—Maddox, Otis, Unser, Schmidt. SB—Wilson, Chalk. S—Washington. SF—Trillo, Wathan.

	IP	H	R	ER	BB	SO
Kansas City—Gura	6	4	2	2	2	2
Quisenberry (L, 0-1)	2	4	4	4	1	0
Philadelphia—Carlton (W, 1-0)	8	10	4	3	6	10
Reed (S, 1)	1	1	0	0	0	2

WP—Carlton. Time—3:01. Attendance—65,775.

THIRD GAME: Royals Stadium, October 17

PHILADELPHIA (NL)	ab	r	h	bi		KANSAS CITY (AL)	ab	r	h	bi
Smith, lf	4	0	2	1		Wilson, lf	4	1	0	0
Gross, lf	0	0	0	0		White, 2b	5	0	0	0
Rose, 1b	4	0	1	1		G. Brett, 3b	4	1	2	1
Schmidt, 3b	5	1	1	1		Aikens, 1b	5	1	2	1
McBride, rf	5	0	2	0		McRae, dh	4	0	2	1
Moreland, dh	5	0	1	0		Otis, cf	4	1	2	1
Maddox, cf	4	0	1	0		Hurdle, rf	4	0	2	0
Trillo, 2b	5	1	2	0		Concepcion, pr	0	0	0	0
Bowa, ss	5	1	3	0		Cardenal, rf	0	0	0	0
Boone, c	4	0	1	0		Porter, c	4	0	0	0
						Washington, ss	4	0	1	0
Total	41	3	14	3		Total	38	4	11	4

```
Philadelphia ........ 0 1 0 0 1 0 0 1 0 0 — 3
Kansas City  ........ 1 0 0 1 0 0 1 0 0 1 — 4
```

DP—Philadelphia 1, Kansas City 2. LOB—Philadelphia 15, Kansas City 7. 2B—Trillo, G. Brett. 3B—Aikens. HR—G. Brett, Schmidt, Otis. SB—Hurdle, Bowa, Wilson. S—Gross.

	IP	H	R	ER	BB	SO
Philadelphia—Ruthven	9	9	3	3	0	7
McGraw (L, 0-1)	2/3*	2	1	1	2	1
Kansas City—Gale	4 1/3	7	2	2	3	3
Martin	3 1/3	5	1	1	1	1
Quisenberry (W, 1-1)	2 1/3	2	0	0	2	0

* Two out when winning run scored.
Time—3:19. Attendance—42,380.

FOURTH GAME: Royals Stadium, October 18

PHILADELPHIA (NL)	ab	r	h	bi		KANSAS CITY (AL)	ab	r	h	bi
Smith, dh	4	0	0	0		Wilson, lf	4	1	1	0
Rose, 1b	4	1	2	0		White, 2b	5	0	0	0
McBride, rf	3	0	1	0		G. Brett, 3b	5	1	1	1
Schmidt, 3b	3	0	1	1		Aikens, 1b	3	2	2	3
Unser, lf	4	0	1	0		McRae, dh	4	1	2	0
Maddox, cf	4	0	1	0		Otis, cf	4	0	2	1
Trillo, 2b	4	2	1	0		Hurdle, rf	2	0	1	0
Bowa, ss	4	0	2	1		Porter, c	3	0	0	0
Boone, c	3	0	1	1		Washington, ss	4	0	1	0
Total	33	3	10	3		Total	34	5	10	5

```
Philadelphia .......... 0 1 0 0 0 0 1 1 0 — 3
Kansas City  .......... 4 1 0 0 0 0 0 0 x — 5
```

E—White, Christenson, Washington. DP—Kansas City 1. LOB—Philadelphia 5, Kansas City 10. 2B—McRae 2, Otis, Hurdle, McBride, Trillo, Rose. 3B—G. Brett. HR—Aikens 2. SB—Bowa. SF—Schmidt.

	IP	H	R	ER	BB	SO
Philadelphia—Christenson (L, 0-1)	1/3	5	4	4	0	0
Noles	4 2/3	5	1	1	2	6
Saucier	2/3	0	0	0	2	0
Brusstar	2 1/3	0	0	0	1	0
Kansas City—Leonard (W, 1-1)	7*	9	3	2	1	2
Quisenberry (S, 1)	2	1	0	0	0	0

* Pitched to one batter in the eighth.
WP—Leonard, Saucier. Time—2:37. Attendance—42,363.

FIFTH GAME: Royals Stadium, October 19

PHILADELPHIA (NL)	ab	r	h	bi		KANSAS CITY (AL)	ab	r	h	bi
Rose, 1b	4	0	0	0		Wilson, lf	5	0	2	0
McBride, rf	4	1	0	0		White, 2b	3	0	0	0
Schmidt, 3b	4	2	2	2		G. Brett, 3b	5	0	1	1
Luzinski, lf	2	0	0	0		Aikens, 1b	3	0	1	0
Smith, lf	0	0	0	0		Concepcion, pr	0	0	0	0
Unser, lf	1	1	1	1		McRae, dh	5	0	1	0
Moreland, dh	3	0	1	0		Otis, cf	3	1	2	1
Maddox, cf	4	0	0	0		Hurdle, rf	3	1	1	0
Trillo, 2b	4	0	1	1		Cardenal, rf	2	0	0	0
Bowa, ss	4	0	1	0		Porter, c	4	0	2	0
Boone, c	3	0	1	0		Washington, ss	3	1	2	1
Total	33	4	7	4		Total	36	3	12	3

```
Philadelphia ........... 0 0 0 2 0 0 0 0 2 — 4
Kansas City  ........... 0 0 0 0 1 2 0 0 0 — 3
```

E—Aikens, G. Brett. DP—Kansas City 2. LOB—Philadelphia 4, Kansas City 13. 2B—Wilson, McRae, Unser. HR—Schmidt, Otis. SB—G. Brett. S—White, Moreland. SF—Washington.

	IP	H	R	ER	BB	SO
Philadelphia—Bystrom	5*	10	3	3	1	4
Reed	1	1	0	0	0	0
McGraw (W, 1-1)	3	1	0	0	4	5
Kansas City—Gura	6 1/3	4	2	1	1	2
Quisenberry (L, 1-2)	2 2/3	3	2	2	0	0

*Pitched to three batters in the sixth.
Time—2:51. Attendance—42,369.

SIXTH GAME: Veterans Stadium, October 21

KANSAS CITY (AL)	ab	r	h	bi		PHILADELPHIA (NL)	ab	r	h	bi
Wilson, lf	4	0	0	0		Smith, lf	4	2	1	0
Washington, ss	3	0	1	1		Gross, lf	0	0	0	0
G. Brett, 3b	4	0	2	0		Rose, 1b	4	0	3	0
McRae, dh	4	0	0	0		Schmidt, 3b	3	0	1	2
Otis, cf	3	0	0	0		McBride, rf	4	0	0	1
Aikens, 1b	2	0	0	0		Luzinski, dh	4	0	0	0
Concepcion, pr	0	0	0	0		Maddox, cf	4	0	2	0
Wathan, c	3	1	2	0		Trillo, 2b	4	0	0	0
Cardenal, rf	4	0	2	0		Bowa, ss	4	1	1	0
White, 2b	4	0	0	0		Boone, c	2	1	1	1
Total	31	1	7	1		Total	33	4	9	4

```
Kansas City  ............ 0 0 0 0 0 0 0 1 0 — 1
Philadelphia ............ 0 0 2 0 1 1 0 0 x — 4
```

E—White, Aikens. DP—Kansas City 1, Philadelphia 2. LOB—Kansas City 9, Philadelphia 7. 2B—Maddox, Smith, Bowa. SF—Washington.

	IP	H	R	ER	BB	SO
Kansas City—Gale (L, 0-1)	2*	4	2	1	1	1
Martin	2 1/3	1	1	1	1	0
Splittorff	1 2/3**	4	1	1	0	0
Pattin	1	0	0	0	0	2
Quisenberry	1	0	0	0	0	0
Philadelphia—Carlton (W, 2-0)	7†	4	1	1	3	7
McGraw (S, 2)	2	3	0	0	2	2

*Pitched to four batters in the third. **Pitched to one batter in the seventh. †Pitched to two batters in the eighth. Time—3:00. Attendance—65,838.

WORLD SERIES—MOST VALUABLE PLAYERS

Year	Player	Position	Team
1955	Johnny Podres	pitcher	Brooklyn Dodgers
1956	Don Larsen	pitcher	New York Yankees
1957	Lew Burdette	pitcher	Milwaukee Braves
1958	Bob Turley	pitcher	New York Yankees
1959	Larry Sherry	pitcher	Los Angeles Dodgers
1960	Bobby Richardson	second base	New York Yankees
1961	Whitey Ford	pitcher	New York Yankees
1962	Ralph Terry	pitcher	New York Yankees
1963	Sandy Koufax	pitcher	Los Angeles Dodgers
1964	Bob Gibson	pitcher	St. Louis Cardinals
1965	Sandy Koufax	pitcher	Los Angeles Dodgers
1966	Frank Robinson	right field	Baltimore Orioles
1967	Bob Gibson	pitcher	St. Louis Cardinals
1968	Mickey Lolich	pitcher	Detroit Tigers
1969	Donn Clendenon	first base	New York Mets
1970	Brooks Robinson	third base	Baltimore Orioles
1971	Roberto Clemente	right field	Pittsburgh Pirates
1972	Gene Tenace	catcher	Oakland Athletics
1973	Reggie Jackson	outfield	Oakland Athletics
1974	Rollie Fingers	pitcher	Oakland Athletics
1975	Pete Rose	third base	Cincinnati Reds
1976	Johnny Bench	catcher	Cincinnati Reds
1977	Reggie Jackson	right field	New York Yankees
1978	Bucky Dent	shortstop	New York Yankees
1979	Willie Stargell	first base	Pittsburgh Pirates
1980	Mike Schmidt	third base	Philadelphia Phillies

1980 CLUB AND INDIVIDUAL RECORDS

NATIONAL LEAGUE

CLUB BATTING

CLUB BATTING	Pct.	R	H	HR
St. Louis	.275	738	1,541	101
Philadelphia	.270	728	1,517	117
Pittsburgh	.266	666	1,469	116
Los Angeles	.263	663	1,462	148
Cincinnati	.262	707	1,445	113
Houston	.261	637	1,455	75
Montreal	.257	694	1,407	114
New York	.257	611	1,407	61
San Diego	.255	591	1,410	67
Chicago	.251	614	1,411	107
Atlanta	.250	630	1,352	144
San Francisco	.244	573	1,310	80

INDIVIDUAL BATTING

INDIVIDUAL BATTING	Avg.	R	H	HR
Buckner, Chicago	.324	69	187	10
Hernandez, St. Louis	.321	111	191	16
Templeton, St. Louis	.319	83	161	4
McBride, Philadelphia	.309	68	171	9
Cedeno, Houston	.309	71	154	10
Dawson, Montreal	.308	96	178	17
Garvey, Los Angeles	.304	77	200	26
Collins, Cincinnati	.303	94	167	3
Simmons, St. Louis	.303	84	150	21
Hendrick, St. Louis	.302	73	173	25

Runs — Hernandez (St. L.) 111, Schmidt (Phila.) 104, Murphy (Atl.) 98, Dawson (Mont.)-Rose (Phila.) 96.

Hits — Garvey, (L.A.) 200, Richards (S.D.) 193, Hernandez (St. L.) 191, Buckner (Chi.) 187.

Doubles — Rose (Phila.) 42, Buckner (Chi.)-Dawson (Mont.) 41, Hernandez (St. L.)-Knight (Cin.) 39.

Triples — Moreno (Pitt.)-Scott (Mont.) 13, Herndon (S.F.)-LeFlore (Mont.) 11.

Home Runs — Schmidt (Phila.) 48, Horner (Atl.) 35, Murphy (Atl.) 33, Baker (L.A.)-Carter (Mont.) 29.

Runs Batted In — Schmidt (Phila.) 121, Hendrick (St. L.) 109, Garvey (L.A.) 106, Carter (Mont.) 101.

Stolen Bases — LeFlore (Mont.) 97, Moreno (Pitt.) 96, Collins (Cin.) 79, Scott (Mont.) 63.

CLUB PITCHING

CLUB PITCHING	ERA	H	BB	SO
Houston	3.10	1,367	466	929
Los Angeles	3.24	1,358	480	835
Philadelphia	3.43	1,419	530	889
San Francisco	3.46	1,446	492	811
Montreal	3.48	1,447	460	823
Pittsburgh	3.58	1,422	451	832
San Diego	3.65	1,474	536	728
Atlanta	3.77	1,397	454	696
Cincinnati	3.85	1,404	506	833
New York	3.85	1,473	510	886
Chicago	3.89	1,525	589	923
St. Louis	3.93	1,454	495	664

INDIVIDUAL PITCHING

INDIVIDUAL PITCHING	IP	W	L	ERA
Sutton, Los Angeles	212	13	5	2.21
Carlton, Philadelphia	304	24	9	2.34
Reuss, Los Angeles	229	18	6	2.52
Blue, San Francisco	224	14	10	2.97
Rogers, Montreal	281	16	11	2.98
Zachry, New York	165	6	10	3.00
Soto, Cincinnati	190	10	8	3.08
Whitson, San Francisco	212	11	13	3.10
Sanderson, Montreal	211	16	11	3.11
Forsch, Houston	222	12	13	3.20

Innings Pitched — Carlton (Phila.) 304, Rogers (Mont.) 281, P. Niekro (Atl.) 275, Reuschel (Chi.) 257.

Complete Games — Rogers (Mont.) 14, Carlton (Phila.) 13, P. Niekro (Atl.)-J. Niekro (Hou.) 11.

Wins — Carlton (Phila.) 24, J. Niekro (Hou.) 20, Bibby (Pitt.) 19, Reuss (L.A.) 18.

Shutouts — Reuss (L.A.) 6, Richard (Hou.)-Rogers (Mont.) 4, 10 tied with 3.

Strikeouts — Carlton (Phila.) 286, Ryan (Hou.) 200, Soto (Cin.) 182, P. Niekro (Atl.) 176.

Saves — Sutter (Chi.) 28, Hume (Cin.) 25, Fingers (S.D.) 23, Allen (N.Y.)-Camp (Atl.) 22.

AMERICAN LEAGUE

CLUB BATTING

CLUB BATTING	Pct.	R	H	HR
Kansas City	.286	809	1,633	115
Texas	.284	756	1,616	124
Boston	.283	757	1,588	162
Cleveland	.277	738	1,517	89
Milwaukee	.275	811	1,555	203
Detroit	.273	830	1,543	143
Baltimore	.273	805	1,523	156
New York	.267	820	1,484	189
Minnesota	.265	670	1,468	99
California	.265	698	1,442	106
Oakland	.259	686	1,424	137
Chicago	.259	587	1,408	91
Toronto	.251	624	1,398	126
Seattle	.248	610	1,359	104

INDIVIDUAL BATTING

INDIVIDUAL BATTING	Avg.	R	H	HR
Brett, Kansas City	.390	87	175	24
Cooper, Milwaukee	.352	96	219	25
Dilone, Cleveland	.341	82	180	0
Rivers, Texas	.333	96	210	7
Carew, California	.331	74	179	3
Bell, Texas	.329	76	161	17
Wilson, Kansas City	.326	133	230	3
Stapleton, Boston	.321	61	144	7
Oliver, Texas	.319	96	209	19
Bumbry, Baltimore	.318	118	205	9

Runs — Wilson (K.C.) 133, Yount (Milw.) 121, Bumbry (Balt.) 118, Henderson (Oak.) 111.

Hits — Wilson (K.C.) 230, Cooper (Milw.) 219, Rivers (Tex.) 210, Oliver (Tex.) 209.

Doubles — Yount (Milw.) 49, Oliver (Tex.) 43, Morrison (Chi.) 40, McRae (K.C.) 39.

Triples — Wilson (K.C.)-Griffin (Tor.) 15, Washington (K.C.)-Landreaux (Minn.) 11.

Home Runs — Jackson (N.Y.)-Oglivie (Milw.) 41, Thomas (Milw.) 38, Armas (Oak.) 35.

Runs Batted In — Cooper (Milw.) 122, Brett (K.C.)-Oglivie (Milw.) 118, Oliver (Tex.) 117.

Stolen Bases — Henderson (Oak.) 100, Wilson (K.C.) 79, Dilone (Clev.) 61, Cruz (Sea.) 45.

CLUB PITCHING

CLUB PITCHING	ERA	H	BB	SO
Oakland	3.46	1,347	521	769
New York	3.59	1,433	463	845
Baltimore	3.64	1,438	507	789
Milwaukee	3.71	1,530	420	575
Kansas City	3.83	1,496	465	614
Chicago	3.92	1,434	563	724
Minnesota	3.93	1,502	468	744
Texas	4.02	1,561	519	890
Toronto	4.19	1,523	635	705
Detroit	4.25	1,505	558	741
Boston	4.38	1,557	481	696
Seattle	4.38	1,565	540	703
California	4.52	1,548	529	725
Cleveland	4.68	1,519	552	843

INDIVIDUAL PITCHING

INDIVIDUAL PITCHING	IP	W	L	ERA
May, New York	175	15	5	2.47
Norris, Oakland	284	22	9	2.54
Burns, Chicago	238	15	13	2.84
Keough, Oakland	250	16	13	2.92
Gura, Kansas City	283	18	10	2.96
Haas, Milwaukee	252	16	15	3.11
Stone, Baltimore	251	25	7	3.23
Erickson, Minnesota	191	7	13	3.25
Langford, Oakland	290	19	12	3.26
Clancy, Toronto	251	13	16	3.30

Innings Pitched — Langford (Oak.) 290, Norris (Oak.) 284, Gura (K.C.) 283, Leonard (K.C.) 280.

Complete Games — Langford (Oak.) 28, Norris (Oak.) 24, Keough (Oak.) 20, Gura (K.C.)-John (N.Y.) 16.

Wins — Stone (Balt.) 25, John (N.Y.)-Norris (Oak.) 22, Leonard (K.C.)-McGregor (Balt.) 20.

Shutouts — John (N.Y.) 6, Zahn (Minn.) 5, Gura (K.C.)-Stieb (Tor.)-McGregor (Balt.) 4.

Strikeouts — Barker (Clev.) 187, Norris (Oak.) 180, Guidry (N.Y.) 166, Leonard (K.C.)-Bannister (Sea.) 155.

Saves — Quisenberry (K.C.)-Gossage (N.Y.) 33, Farmer (Chi.) 30, Stoddard (Balt.) 26.

ALL-TIME WORLD SERIES RESULTS

Year	Winner	Games Won	Lost	Loser	Year	Winner	Games Won	Lost	Loser
1903	Boston (AL)	5	3	Pittsburgh (NL)	1942	St. Louis (NL)	4	1	New York (AL)
1905	New York (NL)	4	1	Philadelphia (AL)	1943	New York (AL)	4	1	St. Louis (NL)
1906	Chicago (AL)	4	2	Chicago (NL)	1944	St. Louis (NL)	4	2	St. Louis (AL)
1907	Chicago (NL)	4	0	Detroit (AL)	1945	Detroit (AL)	4	3	Chicago (NL)
1908	Chicago (NL)	4	1	Detroit (AL)	1946	St. Louis (NL)	4	3	Boston (AL)
1909	Pittsburgh (NL)	4	3	Detroit (AL)	1947	New York (AL)	4	3	Brooklyn (NL)
1910	Philadelphia (AL)	4	1	Chicago (NL)	1948	Cleveland (AL)	4	2	Boston (NL)
1911	Philadelphia (AL)	4	2	New York (NL)	1949	New York (AL)	4	1	Brooklyn (NL)
1912	Boston (AL)	4	3	New York (NL)	1950	New York (AL)	4	0	Philadelphia (NL)
1913	Philadelphia (AL)	4	1	New York (NL)	1951	New York (AL)	4	2	New York (NL)
1914	Boston (NL)	4	0	Philadelphia (AL)	1952	New York (AL)	4	3	Brooklyn (NL)
1915	Boston (AL)	4	1	Philadelphia (NL)	1953	New York (AL)	4	2	Brooklyn (NL)
1916	Boston (AL)	4	1	Brooklyn (NL)	1954	New York (NL)	4	0	Cleveland (AL)
1917	Chicago (AL)	4	2	New York (NL)	1955	Brooklyn (NL)	4	3	New York (AL)
1918	Boston (AL)	4	2	Chicago (NL)	1956	New York (AL)	4	3	Brooklyn (NL)
1919	Cincinnati (NL)	5	3	Chicago (AL)	1957	Milwaukee (NL)	4	3	New York (AL)
1920	Cleveland (AL)	5	2	Brooklyn (NL)	1958	New York (AL)	4	3	Milwaukee (NL)
1921	New York (NL)	5	3	New York (AL)	1959	Los Angeles (NL)	4	2	Chicago (AL)
1922	New York (NL)	4	0	New York (AL)	1960	Pittsburgh (NL)	4	3	New York (AL)
1923	New York (AL)	4	2	New York (NL)	1961	New York (AL)	4	1	Cincinnati (NL)
1924	Washington (AL)	4	3	New York (NL)	1962	New York (AL)	4	3	San Francisco (NL)
1925	Pittsburgh (NL)	4	3	Washington (AL)	1963	Los Angeles (NL)	4	0	New York (AL)
1926	St. Louis (NL)	4	3	New York (AL)	1964	St. Louis (NL)	4	3	New York (AL)
1927	New York (AL)	4	0	Pittsburgh (NL)	1965	Los Angeles (NL)	4	3	Minnesota (AL)
1928	New York (AL)	4	0	St. Louis (NL)	1966	Baltimore (AL)	4	0	Los Angeles (NL)
1929	Philadelphia (AL)	4	1	Chicago (NL)	1967	St. Loius (NL)	4	3	Boston (AL)
1930	Philadelphia (AL)	4	2	St. Louis (NL)	1968	Detroit (AL)	4	3	St. Louis (NL)
1931	St. Louis (NL)	4	3	Philadelphia (AL)	1969	New York (NL)	4	1	Baltimore (AL)
1932	New York (AL)	4	0	Chicago (NL)	1970	Baltimore (AL)	4	1	Cincinnati (NL)
1933	New York (NL)	4	1	Washington (AL)	1971	Pittsburgh (NL)	4	3	Baltimore (AL)
1934	St. Louis (NL)	4	3	Detroit (AL)	1972	Oakland (AL)	4	3	Cincinnati (NL)
1935	Detroit (AL)	4	2	Chicago (NL)	1973	Oakland (AL)	4	3	New York (NL)
1936	New York (AL)	4	2	New York (NL)	1974	Oakland (AL)	4	1	Los Angeles (NL)
1937	New York (AL)	4	1	New York (NL)	1975	Cincinnati (NL)	4	3	Boston (AL)
1938	New York (AL)	4	0	Chicago (NL)	1976	Cincinnati (NL)	4	0	New York (AL)
1939	New York (AL)	4	0	Cincinnati (NL)	1977	New York (AL)	4	2	Los Angeles (NL)
1940	Cincinnati (NL)	4	3	Detroit (AL)	1978	New York (AL)	4	2	Los Angeles (NL)
1941	New York (AL)	4	1	Brooklyn (NL)	1979	Pittsburgh (NL)	4	3	Baltimore (AL)
					1980	Philadelphia (NL)	4	2	Kansas City (AL)

THE ALL-STAR GAMES

Year	Site	Winner	Score	Year	Site	Winner	Score
1933	Comiskey Park, Chicago	American	4-2	1959	Forbes Field, Pittsburgh	National	5-4
1934	Polo Grounds, New York	American	9-7		Memorial Coliseum, L.A.	American	5-3
1935	Municipal Stadium, Cleveland	American	4-1	1960	Municipal Stadium, Kansas City	National	5-3
1936	Braves Field, Boston	National	4-3		Yankee Stadium, New York	National	6-0
1937	Griffith Stadium, Washington	American	8-3	1961	Candlestick Park, San Francisco[4]	National	5-4
1938	Crosley Field, Cincinnati	National	4-1		Fenway Park, Boston[5]	Tie	1-1
1939	Yankee Stadium, New York	American	3-1	1962	D.C. Stadium, Washington	National	3-1
1940	Sportsman's Park, St. Louis	National	4-0		Wrigley Field, Chicago	American	9-4
1941	Briggs Stadium, Detroit	American	7-5	1963	Municipal Stadium, Cleveland	National	5-3
1942	Polo Grounds, New York	American	3-1	1964	Shea Stadium, New York	National	7-4
1943	Shibe Park, Philadelphia*	American	5-3	1965	Metropolitan Stadium, Bloomington, Minnesota	National	6-5
1944	Forbes Field, Pittsburgh*	National	7-1	1966	Busch Stadium, St. Louis[6]	National	2-1
1945	Not played	—	—	1967	Anaheim Stadium, California[7]	National	2-1
1946	Fenway Park, Boston	American	12-0	1968	Houston Astrodome[8]	National	1-0
1947	Wrigley Field, Chicago	American	2-1	1969	R. F. Kennedy Stadium, Wash.	National	9-3
1948	Sportsman's Park, St. Louis	American	5-2	1970	Riverfront Stadium, Cincinnati[8]	National	5-4
1949	Ebbets Field, Brooklyn	American	11-7	1971	Tiger Stadium, Detroit	American	6-4
1950	Comiskey Park, Chicago[1]	National	4-3	1972	Atlanta, Georgia[6]	National	4-3
1951	Briggs Stadium, Detroit	National	8-3	1973	Kansas City, Missouri	National	7-1
1952	Shibe Park, Philadelphia[2]	National	3-2	1974	Pittsburgh, Pennsylvania	National	7-2
1953	Crosley Field, Cincinnati	National	5-1	1975	Milwaukee, Wis.	National	6-3
1954	Municipal Stadium, Cleveland	American	11-9	1976	Veterans Stadium, Philadelphia	National	7-1
1955	Milwaukee County Stadium[3]	National	6-5	1977	Yankee Stadium, New York	National	7-5
1956	Griffith Stadium, Washington	National	7-3	1978	San Diego Stadium	National	7-3
1957	Busch Stadium, St. Louis	American	6-5	1979	Seattle Kingdome	National	7-6
1958	Memorial Stadium, Baltimore	American	4-3	1980	Dodger Stadium, Los Angeles	National	4-2

* A night game. [1] Fourteen-inning game. [2] Game called at the end of the fifth inning because of rain. [3] Twelve-inning game. [4] Ten-inning game. [5] Game called in the ninth inning because of rain. [6] Ten-inning game. [7] Fifteen-inning game. [8] First All-Star game played indoors.

MODERN FRANCHISE CHANGES IN MAJOR LEAGUES

NATIONAL LEAGUE

Year	New Team	How Created
1953	Milwaukee Braves	Formerly, Boston Braves
1958	Los Angeles Dodgers	Formerly, Brooklyn Dodgers
1958	San Francisco Giants	Formerly, New York Giants
1962	New York Mets	Expansion team
1962	Houston Astros†	Expansion team
1966	Atlanta Braves	Formerly, Milwaukee Braves
1969	Montreal Expos	Expansion team
1969	San Diego Padres	Expansion team

AMERICAN LEAGUE

Year	New Team	How Created
1954	Baltimore Orioles	Formerly, St. Louis Browns
1955	Kansas City Athletics	Formerly, Philadelphia Athletics
1961	Minnesota Twins	Formerly, Washington Senators
1961	Washington Senators*	Expansion team
1961	Los Angeles Angels	Expansion team
1965	California Angels	Formerly, Los Angeles Angels
1968	Oakland Athletics	Formerly, Kansas City Athletics
1969	Kansas City Royals	Expansion team
1969	Seattle Pilots	Expansion team
1970	Milwaukee Brewers	Formerly, Seattle Pilots
1972	Texas Rangers	Formerly, Washington Senators
1977	Seattle Mariners	Expansion team
1977	Toronto Blue Jays	Expansion team

† Originally Colts, then Colt-45's. * New Washington Senators.

AMERICAN LEAGUE PENNANT WINNERS

Year	Club	Won	Lost	%	Manager
1901	Chicago	83	53	.610	Clark Griffith
1902	Philadelphia	83	53	.610	Connie Mack
1903	Boston	91	47	.659	James Collins
1904	Boston	95	59	.617	James Collins
1905	Philadelphia	92	56	.622	Connie Mack
1906	Chicago	93	58	.616	Fielder Jones
1907	Detroit	92	58	.613	Hugh Jennings
1908	Detroit	90	63	.588	Hugh Jennings
1909	Detroit	98	54	.645	Hugh Jennings
1910	Philadelphia	102	48	.680	Connie Mack
1911	Philadelphia	101	50	.669	Connie Mack
1912	Boston	105	47	.691	J. Garland Stahl
1913	Philadelphia	96	57	.627	Connie Mack
1914	Philadelphia	99	53	.651	Connie Mack
1915	Boston	101	50	.669	William Carrigan
1916	Boston	91	63	.591	William Carrigan
1917	Chicago	100	54	.649	Clarence Rowland
1918	Boston	75	51	.595	Edward Barrow
1919	Chicago	88	52	.629	William Gleason
1920	Cleveland	98	56	.636	Tris Speaker
1921	New York	98	55	.641	Miller Huggins
1922	New York	94	60	.610	Miller Huggins
1923	New York	98	54	.645	Miller Huggins
1924	Washington	92	62	.597	Stanley Harris
1925	Washington	96	55	.636	Stanley Harris
1926	New York	91	63	.591	Miller Huggins
1927	New York	110	44	.714	Miller Huggins
1928	New York	101	53	.656	Miller Huggins
1929	Philadelphia	104	46	.693	Connie Mack
1930	Philadelphia	102	52	.662	Connie Mack
1931	Philadelphia	107	45	.704	Connie Mack
1932	New York	107	47	.695	Joseph McCarthy
1933	Washington	99	53	.651	Joseph Cronin
1934	Detroit	101	53	.656	Gordon Cochrane
1935	Detroit	93	58	.616	Gordon Cochrane
1936	New York	102	51	.667	Joseph McCarthy
1937	New York	102	52	.662	Joseph McCarthy
1938	New York	99	53	.651	Joseph McCarthy
1939	New York	106	45	.702	Joseph McCarthy
1940	Detroit	90	64	.584	Delmar Baker
1941	New York	101	53	.656	Joseph McCarthy
1942	New York	103	51	.669	Joseph McCarthy
1943	New York	98	56	.636	Joseph McCarthy
1944	St. Louis	89	65	.578	James Sewell
1945	Detroit	88	65	.575	Stephen O'Neill
1946	Boston	104	50	.675	Joseph Cronin
1947	New York	97	57	.630	Stanley Harris
1948	Cleveland	97	58	.626	Louis Boudreau
1949	New York	97	57	.630	Charles Stengel
1950	New York	98	56	.636	Charles Stengel
1951	New York	98	56	.636	Charles Stengel
1952	New York	95	59	.617	Charles Stengel
1953	New York	99	52	.656	Charles Stengel
1954	Cleveland	111	43	.721	Alfonso Lopez
1955	New York	96	58	.623	Charles Stengel
1956	New York	97	57	.630	Charles Stengel
1957	New York	98	56	.636	Charles Stengel
1958	New York	92	62	.597	Charles Stengel
1959	Chicago	94	60	.610	Alfonso Lopez
1960	New York	97	57	.630	Charles Stengel
1961	New York	109	53	.673	Ralph Houk
1962	New York	96	66	.593	Ralph Houk
1963	New York	104	57	.646	Ralph Houk
1964	New York	99	63	.611	Lawrence Berra
1965	Minnesota	102	60	.630	Sabath Mele
1966	Baltimore	97	63	.606	Henry Bauer
1967	Boston	92	70	.568	Richard Williams
1968	Detroit	103	59	.636	Mayo Smith
1969	Baltimore	109	53	.673	Earl Weaver
1970	Baltimore	108	54	.667	Earl Weaver
1971	Baltimore	101	57	.639	Earl Weaver
1972	Oakland	93	62	.600	Dick Williams
1973	Oakland	94	68	.580	Dick Williams
1974	Oakland	90	72	.556	Alvin Dark
1975	Boston	95	65	.594	Darrell Johnson
1976	New York	97	62	.610	Billy Martin
1977	New York	100	62	.617	Billy Martin
1978	New York	100	63	.613	Bob Lemon
1979	Baltimore	102	57	.642	Earl Weaver
1980	Kansas City	97	65	.599	Jim Frey

NATIONAL LEAGUE PENNANT WINNERS

Year	Club	Won	Lost	%	Manager
1880	Chicago	67	17	.798	Adrian C. Anson
1881	Chicago	56	28	.667	Adrian C. Anson
1882	Chicago	55	29	.655	Adrian C. Anson
1883	Boston	63	35	.643	John F. Morrill
1884	Providence	84	28	.750	Frank C. Bancroft
1885	Chicago	87	25	.777	Adrian C. Anson
1886	Chicago	90	34	.726	Adrian C. Anson
1887	Detroit	79	45	.637	W. H. Watkins
1888	New York	84	47	.641	James J. Mutrie
1889	New York	83	43	.659	James J. Mutrie
1890	Brooklyn	86	43	.667	Wm. H. McGunnigle
1891	Boston	87	51	.630	Frank G. Selee
1892	Boston	102	48	.680	Frank G. Selee
1893	Boston	86	43	.667	Frank G. Selee
1894	Baltimore	89	39	.695	Edward H. Hanlon
1895	Baltimore	87	43	.669	Edward H. Hanlon
1896	Baltimore	90	39	.698	Edward H. Hanlon
1897	Boston	93	39	.705	Frank G. Selee
1898	Boston	102	47	.685	Frank G. Selee
1899	Brooklyn	88	42	.677	Edward H. Hanlon
1900	Brooklyn	82	54	.603	Edward H. Hanlon
1901	Pittsburgh	90	49	.647	Fred C. Clarke
1902	Pittsburgh	103	36	.741	Fred C. Clarke
1903	Pittsburgh	91	49	.650	Fred Clarke
1904	New York	106	47	.693	John McGraw
1905	New York	105	48	.686	John McGraw
1906	Chicago	116	36	.763	Frank Chance
1907	Chicago	107	45	.704	Frank Chance
1908	Chicago	99	55	.643	Frank Chance
1909	Pittsburgh	110	42	.724	Fred Clarke
1910	Chicago	104	50	.675	Frank Chance
1911	New York	99	54	.647	John McGraw
1912	New York	103	48	.682	John McGraw
1913	New York	101	51	.664	John McGraw
1914	Boston	94	59	.614	George Stallings
1915	Philadelphia	90	62	.592	Patrick Moran
1916	Brooklyn	94	60	.610	Wilbert Robinson
1917	New York	98	56	.636	John McGraw
1918	Chicago	84	45	.651	Fred Mitchell
1919	Cincinnati	96	44	.686	Patrick Moran
1920	Brooklyn	93	61	.604	Wilbert Robinson
1921	New York	94	59	.614	John McGraw
1922	New York	93	61	.604	John McGraw
1923	New York	95	58	.621	John McGraw
1924	New York	93	60	.608	John McGraw
1925	Pittsburgh	95	58	.621	William McKechnie
1926	St. Louis	89	65	.578	Rogers Hornsby
1927	Pittsburgh	94	60	.610	Owen Bush
1928	St. Louis	95	59	.617	William McKechnie
1929	Chicago	98	54	.645	Joseph McCarthy
1930	St. Louis	92	62	.597	Charles Street
1931	St. Louis	101	53	.656	Charles Street
1932	Chicago	90	64	.584	Charles Grimm
1933	New York	91	61	.599	William Terry
1934	St. Louis	95	58	.621	Frank Frisch
1935	Chicago	100	54	.649	Charles Grimm
1936	New York	92	62	.597	William Terry
1937	New York	95	57	.625	William Terry
1938	Chicago	89	63	.586	Charles Hartnett
1939	Cincinnati	97	57	.630	William McKechnie
1940	Cincinnati	100	53	.654	William McKechnie
1941	Brooklyn	100	54	.649	Leo Durocher
1942	St. Louis	106	48	.688	William Southworth
1943	St. Louis	105	49	.682	William Southworth
1944	St. Louis	105	49	.682	William Southworth
1945	Chicago	98	56	.636	Charles Grimm
1946	St. Louis	98	58	.628	Edwin Dyer
1947	Brooklyn	94	60	.610	Burton Shotton
1948	Boston	91	62	.595	William Southworth
1949	Brooklyn	97	57	.630	Burton Shotton
1950	Philadelphia	91	63	.591	Edwin Sawyer
1951	New York	98	59	.624	Leo Durocher
1952	Brooklyn	96	57	.627	Charles Dressen
1953	Brooklyn	105	49	.682	Charles Dressen
1954	New York	97	57	.630	Leo Durocher
1955	Brooklyn	98	55	.641	Walter Alston
1956	Brooklyn	93	61	.604	Walter Alston
1957	Milwaukee	95	59	.617	Fred Haney
1958	Milwaukee	92	62	.597	Fred Haney
1959	Los Angeles	88	68	.564	Walter Alston
1960	Pittsburgh	95	59	.617	Daniel Murtaugh
1961	Cincinnati	93	61	.604	Fred Hutchinson
1962	San Francisco	103	62	.624	Alvin Dark
1963	Los Angeles	99	63	.611	Walter Alston
1964	St. Louis	93	69	.574	John Keane
1965	Los Angeles	97	65	.599	Walter Alston
1966	Los Angeles	95	67	.586	Walter Alston
1967	St. Louis	101	60	.627	Albert Schoendienst
1968	St. Louis	97	65	.599	Albert Schoendienst
1969	New York	100	62	.617	Gil Hodges
1970	Cincinnati	102	60	.630	Sparky Anderson
1971	Pittsburgh	97	65	.599	Danny Murtaugh
1972	Cincinnati	95	59	.617	Sparky Anderson
1973	New York	82	79	.509	Lawrence Berra
1974	Los Angeles	102	60	.630	Walter Alston
1975	Cincinnati	108	54	.667	Sparky Anderson
1976	Cincinnati	102	60	.630	Sparky Anderson
1977	Los Angeles	98	64	.605	Tom Lasorda
1978	Los Angeles	95	67	.586	Tom Lasorda
1979	Pittsburgh	98	64	.605	Chuck Tanner
1980	Philadelphia	91	71	.562	Dallas Green

NATIONAL LEAGUE BATTING CHAMPIONS

Year	Player and Club	Percent
1876	Roscoe Barnes, Chicago	.404
1877	Jim White, Boston	.385
1878	Abner Dalrymple, Milwaukee	.356
1879	Cap Anson, Chicago	.407
1880	George Gore, Chicago	.365
1881	Cap Anson, Chicago	.399
1882	Dan Brouthers, Buffalo	.367
1883	Dan Brouthers, Buffalo	.371
1884	James O'Rourke, Buffalo	.350
1885	Roger Connor, N.Y.	.371
1886	King Kelly, Chicago	.388
1887	Cap Anson, Chicago	.421
1888	Cap Anson, Chicago	.343
1889	Dan Brouthers, Boston	.373
1890	John Glasscock, N.Y.	.336
1891	Wm. Hamilton, Philadelphia	.338
1892	Dan Brouthers, Brooklyn, and Clarence Childs, Cleveland	.335
1893	Hugh Duffy, Boston	.378
1894	Hugh Duffy, Boston	.438
1895	Jesse Burkett, Cleveland	.423
1896	Jesse Burkett, Cleveland	.410
1897	Willie Keeler, Baltimore	.432
1898	Willie Keeler, Baltimore	.379
1899	Ed Delahanty, Philadelphia	.408
1900	Honus Wagner, Pittsburgh	.381
1901	Jesse Burkett, St. Louis	.382
1902	Clarence Beaumont, Pittsburgh	.357
1903	Honus Wagner, Pittsburgh	.355
1904	Honus Wagner, Pittsburgh	.349
1905	Cy Seymour, Cincinnati	.377
1906	Honus Wagner, Pittsburgh	.339
1907	Honus Wagner, Pittsburgh	.350
1908	Honus Wagner, Pittsburgh	.354
1909	Honus Wagner, Pittsburgh	.339
1910	Sherwood Magee, Philadelphia	.331
1911	Honus Wagner, Pittsburgh	.334
1912	Henry Zimmerman, Chicago	.372
1913	Jake Daubert, Brooklyn	.350
1914	Jake Daubert, Brooklyn	.329
1915	Larry Doyle, New York	.320
1916	Hal Chase, Cincinnati	.339
1917	Edd Roush, Cincinnati	.341
1918	Zack Wheat, Brooklyn	.335
1919	Edd Roush, Cincinnati	.321
1920	Rogers Hornsby, St. Louis	.370
1921	Rogers Hornsby, St. Louis	.397
1922	Rogers Hornsby, St. Louis	.401
1923	Rogers Hornsby, St. Louis	.384
1924	Rogers Hornsby, St. Louis	.424
1925	Rogers Hornsby, St. Louis	.403
1926	Gene Hargrave, Cincinnati	.353
1927	Paul Waner, Pittsburgh	.380
1928	Rogers Hornsby, Boston	.387
1929	Lefty O'Doul, Philadelphia	.398
1930	Bill Terry, New York	.401
1931	Chick Hafey, St. Louis	.349
1932	Lefty O'Doul, Brooklyn	.368
1933	Chuck Klein, Philadelphia	.368
1934	Paul Waner, Pittsburgh	.362
1935	Arky Vaughan, Pittsburgh	.385
1936	Paul Waner, Pittsburgh	.373
1937	Joe Medwick, St. Louis	.374
1938	Ernie Lombardi, Cincinnati	.342
1939	Johnny Mize, St. Louis	.349
1940	Debs Garms, Pittsburgh	.355
1941	Pete Reiser, Brooklyn	.343
1942	Ernie Lombardi, Boston	.330
1943	Stan Musial, St. Louis	.357
1944	Dixie Walker, Brooklyn	.357
1945	Phil Cavaretta, Chicago	.355
1946	Stan Musial, St. Louis	.365
1947	Harry Walker, St. Louis-Philadelphia	.363
1948	Stan Musial, St. Louis	.376
1949	Jackie Robinson, Brooklyn	.342
1950	Stan Musial, St. Louis	.346
1951	Stan Musial, St. Louis	.355
1952	Stan Musial, St. Louis	.336
1953	Carl Furillo, Brooklyn	.344
1954	Willie Mays, New York	.345
1955	Richie Ashburn, Philadelphia	.338
1956	Hank Aaron, Milwaukee	.328
1957	Stan Musial, St. Louis	.351
1958	Richie Ashburn, Philadelphia	.350
1959	Hank Aaron, Milwaukee	.355
1960	Dick Groat, Pittsburgh	.325
1961	Roberto Clemente, Pittsburgh	.351
1962	Tommy Davis, Los Angeles	.346
1963	Tommy Davis, Los Angeles	.326
1964	Roberto Clemente, Pittsburgh	.339
1965	Roberto Clemente, Pittsburgh	.329
1966	Matty Alou, Pittsburgh	.342
1967	Roberto Clemente, Pittsburgh	.357
1968	Pete Rose, Cincinnati	.335
1969	Pete Rose, Cincinnati	.348
1970	Rico Carty, Atlanta	.366
1971	Joe Torre, St. Louis	.363
1972	Billy Williams, Chicago	.333
1973	Pete Rose, Cincinnati	.338
1974	Ralph Garr, Atlanta	.353
1975	Bill Madlock, Chicago	.354
1976	Bill Madlock, Chicago	.339
1977	Dave Parker, Pittsburgh	.338
1978	Dave Parker, Pittsburgh	.334
1979	Keith Hernandez, St. Louis	.344
1980	Bill Buckner, Chicago	.324

NATIONAL LEAGUE HOME RUN CHAMPIONS

Year	Player and Club	Home Runs
1876	George Hall, Phila. Athletics	5
1877	George Shaffer, Louisville	3
1878	Paul Hines, Providence	4
1879	Charles Jones, Boston	9
1880	James O'Rourke, Boston	6
	Harry Stovey, Worcester	6
1881	Dan Brouthers, Buffalo	8
1882	George Wood, Detroit	7
1883	William Ewing, New York	10
1884	Ed Williamson, Chicago	27
1885	Abner Dalrymple, Chicago	11
1886	Arthur Richardson, Detroit	11
1887	Roger Connor, New York	17
	Wm. O'Brien, Washington	17
1888	Roger Connor, New York	14
1889	Sam Thompson, Philadelphia	20
1890	Tom Burns, Brooklyn	13
	Mike Tiernan, New York	13
1891	Harry Stovey, Boston	16
	Mike Tiernan, New York	16
1892	Jim Holliday, Cincinnati	13
1893	Ed Delahanty, Philadelphia	19
1894	Hugh Duffy, Boston	18
	Robert Lowe, Boston	18
1895	Bill Joyce, Washington	17
1896	Ed Delahanty, Philadelphia	13
	Sam Thompson, Philadelphia	13
1897	Nap Lajoie, Philadelphia	10
1898	James Collins, Boston	14
1899	John Freeman, Washington	25
1900	Herman Long, Boston	12
1901	Sam Crawford, Cincinnati	16
1902	Tom Leach, Pittsburgh	6
1903	James Sheckard, Brooklyn	9
1904	Harry Lumley, Brooklyn	9
1905	Fred Odwell, Cincinnati	9
1906	Tim Jordan, Brooklyn	12
1907	David Brain, Boston	10
1908	Tim Jordan, Brooklyn	12
1909	John Murray, New York	7
1910	Fred Beck, Boston	10
	Frank Schulte, Chicago	10
1911	Frank Schulte, Chicago	21
1912	Henry Zimmerman, Chicago	14
1913	Cliff Cravath, Philadelphia	19
1914	Cliff Cravath, Philadelphia	19
1915	Cliff Cravath, Philadelphia	24
1916	Davis Robertson, New York	12
	Cy Williams, Chicago	12
1917	Davis Robertson, New York	12
	Gavvy Cravath, Philadelphia	12
1918	Gavvy Cravath, Philadelphia	8
1919	Gavvy Cravath, Philadelphia	12
1920	Cy Williams, Philadelphia	15
1921	George Kelly, New York	23
1922	Rogers Hornsby, St. Louis	42
1923	Cy Williams, Philadelphia	41
1924	Jack Fournier, Brooklyn	27
1925	Rogers Hornsby, St. Louis	39
1926	Hack Wilson, Chicago	21
1927	Hack Wilson, Chicago	30
	Cy Williams, Philadelphia	30
1928	Hack Wilson, Chicago	31
	Jim Bottomley, St. Louis	31
1929	Chuck Klein, Philadelphia	43
1930	Hack Wilson, Chicago	56
1931	Chuck Klein, Philadelphia	31

NATIONAL LEAGUE HOME RUN CHAMPIONS (Cont.)

Year	Player and Club	Home Runs	Year	Player and Club	Home Runs
1932	Chuck Klein, Philadelphia	38	1954	Ted Kluszewski, Cincinnati	49
	Mel Ott, New York	38	1955	Willie Mays, New York	51
1933	Chuck Klein, Philadelphia	28	1956	Duke Snider, Brooklyn	43
1934	Mel Ott, New York	35	1957	Hank Aaron, Milwaukee	44
	Rip Collins, St. Louis	35	1958	Ernie Banks, Chicago	47
1935	Wally Berger, Boston	34	1959	Eddie Mathews, Milwaukee	46
1936	Mel Ott, New York	33	1960	Ernie Banks, Chicago	41
1937	Mel Ott, New York	31	1961	Orlando Cepeda, San Francisco	46
	Joe Medwick, St. Louis	31	1962	Willie Mays, San Francisco	49
1938	Mel Ott, New York	36	1963	Hank Aaron, Milwaukee	44
1939	Johnny Mize, St. Louis	28		Willie McCovey, San Francisco	44
1940	Johnny Mize, St. Louis	43	1964	Willie Mays, San Francisco	47
1941	Dolph Camilli, Brooklyn	34	1965	Willie Mays, San Francisco	52
1942	Mell Ott, New York	30	1966	Hank Aaron, Atlanta	44
1943	Bill Nicholson, Chicago	29	1967	Hank Aaron, Atlanta	39
1944	Bill Nicholson, Chicago	33	1968	Willie McCovey, San Francisco	36
1945	Tommy Holmes, Boston	28	1969	Willie McCovey, San Francisco	45
1946	Ralph Kiner, Pittsburgh	23	1970	Johnny Bench, Cincinnati	45
1947	Ralph Kiner, Pittsburgh	51	1971	Willie Stargell, Pittsburgh	48
	Johnny Mize, New York	51	1972	Johnny Bench, Cincinnati	40
1948	Ralph Kiner, Pittsburgh	40	1973	Willie Stargell, Pittsburgh	44
	Johnny Mize, New York	40	1974	Mike Schmidt, Philadelphia	36
1949	Ralph Kiner, Pittsburgh	54	1975	Mike Schmidt, Philadelphia	38
1950	Ralph Kiner, Pittsburgh	47	1976	Mike Schmidt, Philadelphia	38
1951	Ralph Kiner, Pittsburgh	42	1977	George Foster, Cincinnati	52
1952	Ralph Kiner, Pittsburgh	37	1978	George Foster, Cincinnati	40
	Hank Sauer, Chicago	37	1979	Dave Kingman, Chicago	48
1953	Eddie Mathews, Milwaukee	47	1980	Mike Schmidt, Philadelphia	48

NATIONAL LEAGUE RUNS BATTED IN CHAMPIONS

Year	Player and Club	RBI	Year	Player and Club	RBI
1920	Rogers Hornsby, St. Louis	94	1950	Del Ennis, Philadelphia	126
	George Kelly, New York	94	1951	Monte Irvin, New York	121
1921	Rogers Hornsby, St. Louis	126	1952	Hank Sauer, Chicago	121
1922	Rogers Hornsby, St. Louis	152	1953	Roy Campanella, Brooklyn	142
1923	Irish Meusel, New York	125	1954	Ted Kluszewski, Cincinnati	141
1924	George Kelly, New York	136	1955	Duke Snider, Brooklyn	136
1925	Rogers Hornsby, St. Louis	143	1956	Stan Musial, St. Louis	109
1926	Jim Bottomley, St. Louis	120	1957	Hank Aaron, Milwaukee	132
1927	Paul Waner, Pittsburgh	131	1958	Ernie Banks, Chicago	129
1928	Jim Bottomley, St. Louis	136	1959	Ernie Banks, Chicago	143
1929	Hack Wilson, Chicago	159	1960	Hank Aaron, Milwaukee	126
1930	Hack Wilson, Chicago	190	1961	Orlando Cepeda, San Francisco	142
1931	Chuck Klein, Philadelphia	121	1962	Tommy Davis, Los Angeles	153
1932	Don Hurst, Philadelphia	143	1963	Hank Aaron, Milwaukee	130
1933	Chuck Klein, Philadelphia	120	1964	Ken Boyer, St. Louis	119
1934	Mel Ott, New York	135	1965	Deron Johnson, Cincinnati	130
1935	Wally Berger, Boston	130	1966	Hank Aaron, Atlanta	127
1936	Joe Medwick, St. Louis	138	1967	Orlando Cepeda, St. Louis	111
1937	Joe Medwick, St. Louis	154	1968	Willie McCovey, San Francisco	105
1938	Joe Medwick, St. Louis	122	1969	Willie McCovey, San Francisco	126
1939	Frank McCormick, Cincinnati	128	1970	Johnny Bench, Cincinnati	148
1940	Johnny Mize, St. Louis	137	1971	Joe Torre, St. Louis	137
1941	Dolf Camilli, Brooklyn	120	1972	Johnny Bench, Cincinnati	125
1942	Johnny Mize, New York	110	1973	Willie Stargell, Pittsburgh	119
1943	Bill Nicholson, Chicago	128	1974	Johnny Bench, Cincinnati	129
1944	Bill Nicholson, Chicago	122	1975	Greg Luzinski, Philadelphia	120
1945	Dixie Walker, Brooklyn	124	1976	George Foster, Cincinnati	121
1946	Enos Slaughter, St. Louis	130	1977	George Foster, Cincinnati	149
1947	Johnny Mize, New York	138	1978	George Foster, Cincinnati	120
1948	Stan Musial, St. Louis	131	1979	Dave Winfield, San Diego	118
1949	Ralph Kiner, Pittsburgh	127	1980	Mike Schmidt, Philadelphia	121

AMERICAN LEAGUE BATTING CHAMPIONS

Year	Player and Club	Percent	Year	Player and Club	Percent
1901	Nap Lajoie, Phila	.422	1923	Harry Heilmann, Detroit	.403
1902	Ed Delahanty, Wash.	.376	1924	Babe Ruth, New York	.378
1903	Nap Lajoie, Cleve.	.355	1925	Harry Heilmann, Detroit	.393
1904	Nap Lajoie, Cleve.	.381	1926	Henry Manush, Detroit	.378
1905	Elmer Flick, Cleve.	.306	1927	Harry Heilmann, Detroit	.398
1906	George Stone, St. Louis	.358	1928	Goose Goslin, Washington	.379
1907	Ty Cobb, Det.	.350	1929	Lew Fonseca, Cleveland	.369
1908	Ty Cobb, Det.	.324	1930	Al Simmons, Philadelphia	.381
1909	Ty Cobb, Det.	.377	1931	Al Simmons, Philadelphia	.390
1910	Ty Cobb, Detroit	.385	1932	Dale Alexander, Detroit-Boston	.367
1911	Ty Cobb, Detroit	.420	1933	Jimmy Foxx, Philadelphia	.356
1912	Ty Cobb, Detroit	.410	1934	Lou Gehrig, New York	.363
1913	Ty Cobb, Detroit	.390	1935	Buddy Myer, Washington	.349
1914	Ty Cobb, Detroit	.368	1936	Luke Appling, Chicago	.388
1915	Ty Cobb, Detroit	.369	1937	Charley Gehringer, Detroit	.371
1916	Tris Speaker, Cleveland	.386	1938	Jimmy Foxx, Boston	.349
1917	Ty Cobb, Detroit	.383	1939	Joe DiMaggio, New York	.381
1918	Ty Cobb, Detroit	.382	1940	Joe DiMaggio, New York	.352
1919	Ty Cobb, Detroit	.384	1941	Ted Williams, Boston	.406
1920	George Sisler, St. Louis	.407	1942	Ted Williams, Boston	.356
1921	Harry Heilmann, Detroit	.394	1943	Luke Appling, Chicago	.328
1922	George Sisler, St. Louis	.420	1944	Lou Boudreau, Cleveland	.327

AMERICAN LEAGUE BATTING CHAMPIONS (Cont.)

Year	Player and Club	Percent	Year	Player and Club	Percent
1945	George Sternweiss, New York	.309	1963	Carl Yastrzemski, Boston	.321
1946	Mickey Vernon, Washington	.353	1964	Tony Oliva, Minnesota	.323
1947	Ted Williams, Boston	.343	1965	Tony Oliva, Minnesota	.321
1948	Ted Williams, Boston	.369	1966	Frank Robinson, Baltimore	.316
1949	George Kell, Detroit[1]	.343	1967	Carl Yastrzemski, Boston	.326
1950	Billy Goodman, Boston	.354	1968	Carl Yastrzemski, Boston	.301
1951	Ferris Fain, Philadelphia	.344	1969	Rod Carew, Minnesota	.332
1952	Ferris Fain, Philadelphia	.327	1970	Alex Johnson, California[2]	.329
1953	Mickey Vernon, Washington	.337	1971	Tony Oliva, Minnesota	.337
1954	Bobby Avila, Cleveland	.341	1972	Rod Carew, Minnesota	.318
1955	Al Kaline, Detroit	.340	1973	Rod Carew, Minnesota	.350
1956	Mickey Mantle, New York	.353	1974	Rod Carew, Minnesota	.364
1957	Ted Williams, Boston	.388	1975	Rod Carew, Minnesota	.359
1958	Ted Williams, Boston	.328	1976	George Brett, Kansas City	.333
1959	Harvey Kuenn, Detroit	.353	1977	Rod Carew, Minnesota	.388
1960	Pete Runnels, Boston	.320	1978	Rod Carew, Minnesota	.333
1961	Norm Cash, Detroit	.361	1979	Fred Lynn, Boston	.333
1962	Pete Runnels, Boston	.326	1980	George Brett, Kansas City	.390

[1] Kell .3429; Ted Williams, Boston .3427. [2] Johnson .3289; Carl Yastrzemski, Boston .3286.

AMERICAN LEAGUE HOME RUN CHAMPIONS

Year	Player and Club	Home Runs	Year	Player and Club	Home Runs
1901	Nap Lajoie, Philadelphia	13	1941	Ted Williams, Boston	37
1902	Ralph Seybold, Philadelphia	16	1942	Ted Williams, Boston	36
1903	Buck Freeman, Boston	13	1943	Rudy York, Detroit	34
1904	Harry Davis, Philadelphia	10	1944	Nick Etten, New York	22
1905	Harry Davis, Philadelphia	8	1945	Vern Stephens, St. Louis	24
1906	Harry Davis, Philadelphia	12	1946	Hank Greenberg, Detroit	44
1907	Harry Davis, Philadelphia	8	1947	Ted Williams, Boston	32
1908	Sam Crawford, Detroit	7	1948	Joe DiMaggio, New York	39
1909	Ty Cobb, Detroit	9	1949	Ted Williams, Boston	43
1910	J. Garland Stahl, Boston	10	1950	Al Rosen, Cleveland	37
1911	Franklin Baker, Philadelphia	9	1951	Gus Zernial, Chicago-Philadelphia	33
1912	Franklin Baker, Philadelphia	10	1952	Larry Doby, Cleveland	32
1913	Franklin Baker, Philadelphia	12	1953	Al Rosen, Cleveland	43
1914	Franklin Baker, Philadelphia	8	1954	Larry Doby, Cleveland	32
	Sam Crawford, Detroit	8	1955	Mickey Mantle, New York	37
1915	Robert Roth, Chi.-Cleve.	7	1956	Mickey Mantle, New York	52
1916	Wally Pipp, New York	12	1957	Roy Sievers, Washington	42
1917	Wally Pipp, New York	9	1958	Mickey Mantle, New York	42
1918	Clarence Walker, Philadelphia	11	1959	Rocky Colavito, Cleveland	42
	Babe Ruth, Boston	11		Harmon Killebrew, Washington	42
1919	Babe Ruth, Boston	29	1960	Mickey Mantle, New York	40
1920	Babe Ruth, New York	54	1961	Roger Maris, New York	61
1921	Babe Ruth, New York	59	1962	Harmon Killebrew, Minnesota	48
1922	Ken Williams, St. Louis	39	1963	Harmon Killebrew, Minnesota	45
1923	Babe Ruth, New York	41	1964	Harmon Killebrew, Minnesota	49
1924	Babe Ruth, New York	46	1965	Tony Conigliaro, Boston	32
1925	Bob Meusel, New York	33	1966	Frank Robinson, Baltimore	49
1926	Babe Ruth, New York	47	1967	Harmon Killebrew, Minnesota	44
1927	Babe Ruth, New York	60		Carl Yastrzemski, Boston	44
1928	Babe Ruth, New York	54	1968	Frank Howard, Washington	44
1929	Babe Ruth, New York	46	1969	Harmon Killebrew, Minnesota	49
1930	Babe Ruth, New York	49	1970	Frank Howard, Washington	44
1931	Babe Ruth, New York	46	1971	Bill Melton, Chicago	33
	Lou Gehrig, New York	46	1972	Dick Allen, Chicago	37
1932	Jimmy Foxx, Philadelphia	58	1973	Reggie Jackson, Oakland	32
1933	Jimmy Foxx, Philadelphia	48	1974	Dick Allen, Chicago	32
1934	Lou Gehrig, New York	49	1975	Reggie Jackson, Oakland	36
1935	Jimmy Foxx, Philadelphia	36		George Scott, Milwaukee	36
	Hank Greenberg, Detroit	36	1976	Graig Nettles, New York	32
1936	Lou Gehrig, New York	49	1977	Jim Rice, Boston	39
1937	Joe DiMaggio, New York	46	1978	Jim Rice, Boston	46
1938	Hank Greenberg, Detroit	58	1979	Gorman Thomas, Milwaukee	45
1939	Jimmy Foxx, Boston	35	1980	Reggie Jackson, New York	41
1940	Hank Greenberg, Detroit	41		Ben Oglivie, Milwaukee	41

AMERICAN LEAGUE RUNS BATTED IN CHAMPIONS

Year	Player and Club	RBI	Year	Player and Club	RBI
1920	Babe Ruth, New York	137	1936	Hal Trosky, Cleveland	162
1921	Babe Ruth, New York	171	1937	Hank Greenberg, Detroit	183
1922	Ken Williams, St. Louis	155	1938	Jimmie Foxx, Boston	175
1923	Babe Ruth, New York	131	1939	Ted Williams, Boston	145
1924	Goose Goslin, Washington	129	1940	Hank Greenberg, Detroit	150
1925	Bob Meusel, New York	138	1941	Joe DiMaggio, New York	125
1926	Babe Ruth, New York	145	1942	Ted Williams, Boston	137
1927	Lou Gehrig, New York	175	1943	Rudy York, Detroit	118
1928	Lou Gehrig, New York	142	1944	Vern Stephens, St. Louis	109
	Babe Ruth, New York	142	1945	Nick Etten, New York	111
1929	Al Simmons, Philadelphia	157	1946	Hank Greenberg, Detroit	127
1930	Lou Gehrig, New York	174	1947	Ted Williams, Boston	114
1931	Lou Gehrig, New York	184	1948	Joe DiMaggio, New York	155
1932	Jimmie Foxx, Philadelphia	169	1949	Ted Williams, Boston	159
1933	Jimmie Foxx, Philadelphia	163		Vern Stephens, Boston	159
1934	Lou Gehrig, New York	165	1950	Vern Stephens, Boston	144
1935	Hank Greenberg, Detroit	170		Walt Dropo, Boston	144

AMERICAN LEAGUE RUNS BATTED IN CHAMPIONS (Cont.)

Year	Player and Club	RBI	Year	Player and Club	RBI
1951	Gus Zernial, Chicago-Phliadelphia	129	1965	Rocky Colavito, Cleveland	108
1952	Al Rosen, Cleveland	105	1966	Frank Robinson, Baltimore	122
1953	Al Rosen, Cleveland	145	1967	Carl Yastrzemski, Boston	121
1954	Larry Doby, Cleveland	126	1968	Ken Harrelson, Boston	109
1955	Ray Boone, Detroit	116	1969	Harmon Killebrew, Minnesota	140
	Jackie Jensen, Boston	116	1970	Frank Howard, Washington	126
1956	Mickey Mantle, New York	130	1971	Harmon Killebrew, Minnesota	119
1957	Roy Sievers, Washington	114	1972	Richie Allen, Chicago	113
1958	Jackie Jensen, Boston	122	1973	Reggie Jackson, Oakland	117
1959	Jackie Jensen, Boston	112	1974	Jeff Burroughs, Texas	118
1960	Roger Maris, New York	112	1975	George Scott, Boston	109
1961	Roger Maris, New York	142	1976	Lee May, Baltimore	109
1962	Harmon Killebrew, Minnesota	126	1977	Larry Hisle, Minnesota	119
1963	Dick Stuart, Boston	118	1978	Jim Rice, Boston	139
1964	Brooks Robinson, Baltimore	118	1979	Don Baylor, California	139
			1980	Cecil Cooper, Milwaukee	122

MOST NO-HITTERS IN A LIFETIME

4, Sandy Koufax, Los Angeles (NL), 1962, 1963, 1964, 1965.
4, Nolan Ryan, California (AL), 1973, 1973, 1974, 1975.
3, Cy Young, Boston (NL–AL), 1897, 1904, 1908.
3, Bob Feller, Cleveland (AL), 1940, 1946, 1951.
3, Jim Maloney, Cincinnati (NL), 1965 (2), 1969

NO-HITTERS OF TEN OR MORE INNINGS

Year	Pitcher	Clubs Playing	Score
1884	Samuel Kimber	Brooklyn–Toledo (AA)	0–0
1906	Harry McIntire	Brooklyn–Pittsburgh (NL)	0–1
1908	George Wiltse	New York–Philadelphia (NL)	1–0
1917	Fred Toney	Cincinnati–Chicago (NL)	1–0
1959	Harvey Haddix	Pittsburgh–Milwaukee (NL)*	0–1
1965	Jim Maloney	Cincinnati–New York (NL)	0–1
1965	Jim Maloney	Cincinnati–Chicago (NL)	1–0

* Perfect game for 12 innings. Lost in 13th.

PERFECT GAMES

Year	Pitcher	Clubs Playing	Score
1880	John Richmond	Worcester–Cleveland (NL)	1–0
1880	John Ward	Providence–Buffalo (NL)	5–0
1904	Cy Young	Boston–Philadelphia (AL)	3–0
1908	Addie Joss	Cleveland–Chicago (AL)	1–0
1917	Ernie Shore*	Boston–Washington (AL)	4–0
1922	Charles Robertson	Chicago–Detroit (AL)	2–0
1956	Don Larsen†	New York (AL)–Brooklyn (NL)	2–0
1964	Jim Bunning	Philadelphia–New York (NL)	6–0
1965	Sandy Koufax	Los Angeles–Chicago (NL)	1–0
1968	Jim Hunter	Oakland–Minnesota (AL)	4–0

* Babe Ruth, the starting pitcher. was ejected from the game by the umpire after walking the first batter. Ernie Shore relieved him, the base-runner was thrown out trying to steal second base, and Shore retired the next 26 batters to complete a perfect game. † The only World Series perfect game.

CY YOUNG AWARD

Year	Pitcher
BOTH MAJOR LEAGUES	
1956	Don Newcombe, Dodgers (NL)
1957	Warren Spahn, Boston (NL)
1958	Bob Turley, New York (AL)
1959	Early Wynn, Chicago (AL)
1960	Vernon Law, Pittsburgh (NL)
1961	Whitey Ford, New York (AL)
1962	Don Drysdale, Los Angeles (NL)
1963	Sandy Koufax, Los Angeles (NL)
1964	Dean Chance, Los Angeles (AL)
1965	Sandy Koufax, Los Angeles (NL)
1966	Sandy Koufax, Los Angeles (NL)
NATIONAL LEAGUE	
1967	Mike McCormick, San Francisco
1968	Bob Gibson, St. Louis
1969	Tom Seaver, New York
1970	Bob Gibson, St. Louis
1971	Ferguson Jenkins, Chicago
1972	Steve Carlton, Philadelphia
1973	Tom Seaver, New York
1974	Mike Marshall, Los Angeles
1975	Tom Seaver, New York
1976	Randy Jones, San Diego
1977	Steve Carlton, Philadelphia
1978	Gaylord Perry, San Diego
1979	Bruce Sutter, Chicago
AMERICAN LEAGUE	
1967	Jim Lonborg, Boston
1968	Denny McLain, Detroit
1969	Denny McLain, Detroit
	Mike Cuellar, Baltimore
1970	Jim Perry, Minnesota
1971	Vida Blue, Oakland
1972	Gaylord Perry, Cleveland
1973	Jim Palmer, Baltimore
1974	James Hunter, Oakland
1975	Jim Palmer, Baltimore
1976	Jim Palmer, Baltimore
1977	Sparky Lyle, New York
1978	Ron Guidry, New York
1979	Mike Flanagan, Baltimore

MAJOR LEAGUE NO-HIT GAMES SINCE 1969

Year	Pitcher	Clubs Playing	Score
1969	Bill Stoneman	Montreal–Philadelphia (NL)	6–0
1969	Jim Maloney	Cincinnati–Houston (NL)	10–0
1969	Don Wilson	Houston–Cincinnati (NL)	4–0
1969	Jim Palmer	Baltimore–Oakland (AL)	8–0
1969	Ken Holtzman	Chicago–Atlanta (NL)	3–0
1969	Bob Moose	Pittsburgh–New York (NL)	4–0
1970	Dock Ellis	Pittsburgh–San Diego (NL)	2–0
1970	Clyde Wright	California–Oakland (AL)	4–0
1970	Bill Singer	Los Angeles–Philadelphia (NL)	5–0
1970	Vida Blue	Oakland–Minnesota (AL)	6–0
1971	Ken Holtzman	Chicago–Cincinnati (NL)	1–0
1971	Rick Wise	Philadelphia–Cincinnati (NL)	4–0
1971	Bob Gibson	St. Louis–Pittsburgh (NL)	11–0
1972	Burt Hooton	Chicago–Philadelphia (NL)	4–0
1972	Milt Pappas	Chicago–San Diego (NL)	8–0
1972	Bill Stoneman	Montreal–New York (NL)	7–0
1973	Steve Busby	Kansas City–Detroit (AL)	3–0
1973	Nolan Ryan	California–Kansas City (AL)	3–0
1973	Nolan Ryan	California–Detroit (AL)	6–0
1973	Jim Bibby	Texas–Oakland (AL)	6–0

Year	Pitcher	Clubs Playing	Score
1973	Phil Niekro	Atlanta–San Diego (NL)	9–0
1974	Steve Busby	Kansas City–Milwaukee (AL)	2–0
1974	Dick Bosman	Cleveland–Oakland (AL)	4–0
1974	Nolan Ryan	California–Minnesota (AL)	4–0
1975	Nolan Ryan	California–Baltimore (AL)	1–0
1975	Ed Halicki	San Francisco–New York (NL)	6–0
1975	Vida Blue, Glenn Abbott, Paul Lindblad, Rollie Fingers	Oakland–California (AL)	5–0
1976	Larry Dierker	Houston–Montreal (NL)	6–0
1976	John Odom, Francisco Barrios	Chicago–California (AL)	2–1
1976	John Candelaria	Pittsburgh-Los Angeles (NL)	2–0
1976	John Montefusco	San Francisco–Atlanta (AL)	9–0
1977	Jim Colborn	Kansas City–Texas (AL)	6–0
1977	Dennis Eckersley	Cleveland–California (AL)	1–0
1977	Bert Blyleven	Texas–California (AL)	6–0
1978	Bob Forsch	St. Louis–Philadelphia (NL)	5–0
	Tom Seaver	Cincinnati–St. Louis (NL)	4–0
1979	Ken Forsch	Houston–Atlanta (NL)	6–0
1980	Jerry Reuss	Los Angeles–San Francisco (NL)	8–0

PITCHERS WITH BEST WON-AND-LOST PERCENTAGES (162 or More Innings)

NATIONAL LEAGUE Year Pitcher and Club	Won	Lost	Per-cent	AMERICAN LEAGUE Year Pitcher and Club	Won	Lost	Per-cent
1941—Elmer Riddle, Cincinnati	19	4	.826	1941—Lefty Gomez, New York	15	5	.750
1942—Larry French, Brooklyn	15	4	.789	1942—Ernie Bonham, New York	21	5	.808
1943—Mort Cooper, St. Louis	21	8	.724	1943—Spud Chandler, New York	20	4	.833
1944—Ted Wilkes, St. Louis	17	4	.810	1944—Tex Hughson, Boston	18	5	.783
1945—Harry Brecheen, St. Louis	15	4	.789	1945—Hal Newhouser, Detroit	25	9	.735
1946—Murry Dickson, St. Louis	15	6	.714	1946—Dave Ferriss, Boston	25	6	.806
1947—Larry Jansen, New York	21	5	.808	1947—Allie Reynolds, New York	19	8	.704
1948—Harry Brecheen, St. Louis	20	7	.741	1948—Jack Kramer, Boston	18	5	.783
1949—Preacher Roe, Brooklyn	15	6	.714	1949—Ellis Kinder, Boston	23	6	.793
1950—Sal Maglie, New York	18	4	.818	1950—Vic Raschi, New York	21	8	.724
1951—Preacher Roe, Brooklyn	22	3	.880	1951—Bob Feller, Cleveland	22	8	.733
1952—Hoyt Wilhelm, New York	15	3	.833	1952—Bobby Shantz, Philadelphia	24	7	.774
1953—Carl Erskine, Brooklyn	20	6	.769	1953—Ed Lopat, New York	16	4	.800
1954—Johnny Antonelli, New York	21	7	.750	1954—Sandy Consuegra, Chicago	16	3	.842
1955—Don Newcombe, Brooklyn	20	5	.800	1955—Tommy Byrne, New York	16	5	.762
1956—Don Newcombe, Brooklyn	27	7	.794	1956—Whitey Ford, New York	19	6	.760
1957—Bob Ruhl, Milwaukee	18	7	.720	1957—Dick Donovan, Chicago	16	6	.727
1958—Warren Spahn, Milwaukee	22	11	.667	Tom Sturdivant, New York	16	6	.727
Lew Burdette, Milwaukee	20	10	.667	1958—Bob Turley, New York	21	7	.750
1959—El Roy Face, Pittsburgh	18	1	.947	1959—Bob Shaw, Chicago	18	6	.750
1960—Ernie Broglio, St. Louis	21	9	.700	1960—Jim Perry, Cleveland	18	10	.643
1961—Johnny Podres, Los Angeles	18	5	.783	1961—Whitey Ford, New York	25	4	.862
1962—Bob Purkey, Cincinnati	23	5	.821	1962—Ray Herbert, Chicago	20	9	.690
1963—Ron Perranoski, Los Angeles	16	3	.842	1963—Whitey Ford, New York	24	7	.774
1964—Sandy Koufax, Los Angeles	19	5	.792	1964—Wally Bunker, Baltimore	19	5	.792
1965—Sandy Koufax, Los Angeles	26	8	.765	1965—Jim Grant, Minnesota	21	7	.750
1966—Juan Marichal, San Francisco	25	6	.806	1966—Sonny Seibert, Cleveland	16	8	.667
1967—Dick Hughes, St. Louis	16	6	.727	1967—Joel Horlen, Chicago	19	7	.731
1968—Steve Blass, Pittsburgh	18	6	.750	1968—Denny McLain, Detroit	31	6	.836
1969—Tom Seaver, New York	25	7	.781	1969—Jim Palmer, Baltimore	16	4	.800
1970—Bob Gibson, St. Louis	23	7	.767	1970—Mike Cuellar, Baltimore	24	8	.750
1971—Tug McGraw, New York	11	4	.733	1971—Daye McNally, Baltimore	21	5	.807
1972—Steve Carlton, Philadelphia	27	10	.730	1972—James Hunter, Oakland	21	7	.750
1973—Tommy John, Los Angeles	16	7	.696	1973—James Hunter, Oakland	21	5	.808
1974—Tommy John, Los Angeles	13	3	.813	1974—Mike Cuellar, Baltimore	22	10	.688
1975—Al Hrabosky, St. Louis	13	3	.813	1975—Roger Moret, Boston	14	3	.824
1976—Steve Carlton, Philadelphia	20	7	.741	1976—Wayne Garland, Baltimore	20	7	.741
1977—John Candelaria, Pittsburgh	20	5	.800	1977—Paul Splittorff, Kansas City	16	6	.727
1978—Gaylord Perry, San Diego	21	6	.778	1978—Ron Guidry, New York	25	3	.893
1979—Tom Seaver, Cincinnati	16	6	.727	1979—Mike Caldwell, Milwaukee	16	6	.727
1980—Jim Bibby, Pittsburgh	19	6	.760	1980—Steve Stone, Baltimore	25	7	.781

PITCHERS WITH LOWEST-EARNED-RUN AVERAGES (162 or More Innings)

NATIONAL LEAGUE Year Pitcher and Club	Innings Pitched	ERA	AMERICAN LEAGUE Year Pitcher and Club	Innings Pitched	ERA
1945 .... Hank Borowy, Chicago	122	2.14	1945 .... Hal Newhouser, Detroit	313	1.81
1946 .... Howie Pollet, St. Louis	266	2.10	1946 .... Hal Newhouser, Detroit	293	1.94
1947 .... Warren Spahn, Boston	290	2.33	1947 .... Spud Chandler, New York	128	2.46
1948 .... Harry Brecheen, St. Louis	233	2.24	1948 .... Gene Bearden, Cleveland	230	2.43
1949 .... Dave Koslo, New York	212	2.50	1949 .... Mel Parnell, Boston	295	2.78
1950 .... Jim Hearn, St. Louis-New York	134	2.49	1950 .... Early Wynn, Cleveland	214	3.20
1951 .... Chet Nichols, Boston	156	2.88	1951 .... Saul Rogovin, Detroit-Chicago	217	2.78
1952 .... Hoyt Wilhelm, New York	159	2.43	1952 .... Allie Reynolds, New York	244	2.07
1953 .... Warren Spahn, Milwaukee	266	2.10	1953 .... Eddie Lopat, New York	178	2.43
1954 .... John Antonelli, New York	259	2.29	1954 .... Mike Garcia, Cleveland	259	2.64
1955 .... Bob Friend, Pittsburgh	200	2.84	1955 .... Billy Pierce, Chicago	206	1.97
1956 .... Lew Burdette, Milwaukee	256	2.71	1956 .... Whitey Ford, New York	226	2.47
1957 .... John Podres, Brooklyn	196	2.66	1957 .... Bobby Shantz, New York	173	2.45
1958 .... Stu Miller, San Francisco	182	2.47	1958 .... Whitey Ford, New York	219	2.01
1959 .... Sam Jones, San Francisco	271	2.82	1959 .... Hoyt Wilhelm, Baltimore	226	2.19
1960 .... Mike McCormick, San Francisco	253	2.70	1960 .... Frank Baumann, Chicago	185	2.68
1961 .... Warren Spahn, Milwaukee	263	3.01	1961 .... Dick Donovan, Washington	169	2.40
1962 .... Sandy Koufax, Los Angeles	184	2.54	1962 .... Hank Aguirre, Detroit	216	2.21
1963 .... Sandy Koufax, Los Angeles	311	1.88	1963 .... Gary Peters, Chicago	243	2.33
1964 .... Sandy Koufax, Los Angeles	223	1.74	1964 .... Dean Chance, Los Angeles	278	1.65
1965 .... Sandy Koufax, Los Angeles	336	2.04	1965 .... Sam McDowell, Cleveland	273	2.18
1966 .... Sandy Koufax, Los Angeles	323	1.73	1966 .... Gary Peters, Chicago	205	1.98
1967 .... Phil Niekro, Atlanta	207	1.87	1967 .... Joel Horlen, Chicago	258	2.06
1968 .... Bob Gibson, St. Louis	305	1.12	1968 .... Luis Tiant, Cleveland	258	1.60
1969 .... Juan Marichal, San Francisco	300	2.10	1969 .... Dick Bosman, Washington	193	2.19
1970 .... Tom Seaver, New York	291	2.81	1970 .... Diego Segui, Oakland	162	2.56
1971 .... Tom Seaver, New York	286	1.76	1971 .... Vida Blue, Oakland	312	1.82
1972 .... Steve Carlton, Philadelphia	346	1.98	1972 .... Luis Tiant, Boston	179	1.91
1973 .... Tom Seaver, New York	290	2.08	1973 .... Jim Palmer, Baltimore	296	2.40
1974 .... Buzz Capra, Atlanta	217	2.28	1974 .... James Hunter, Oakland	318	2.49
1975 .... Randy Jones, San Diego	288	2.24	1975 .... Jim Palmer, Baltimore	323	2.09
1976 .... John Denny, St. Louis	207	2.52	1976 .... Mark Fidrych, Detroit	250	2.34
1977 .... John Candelaria, Pittsburgh	231	2.34	1977 .... Frank Tanana, California	241	2.54
1978 .... Craig Swan, New York	207	2.43	1978 .... Ron Guidry, New York	274	1.74
1979 .... J. Rodney Richard, Houston	292	2.71	1979 .... Ron Guidry, New York	236	2.78
1980 .... Don Sutton, Los Angeles	212	2.21	1980 .... Rudy May, New York	175	2.47

LONGEST GAMES IN THE MAJOR LEAGUES

Innings	Teams	Date	Innings	Teams	Date
26	Brooklyn 1, Boston 1, NL	May 1, 1920	24	Houston 1, New York 0, NL	April 15, 1968
25	St. Louis 4, New York 3, NL	Sept. 11, 1974	23	Brooklyn 2, Boston 2, NL	June 27, 1939
24	Philadelphia 4, Boston 1, AL	Sept. 1, 1906	23	San Francisco 8, New York 6, NL	May 31, 1964
24	Detroit 1, Philadelphia 1, AL	July 21, 1945			

MOST-VALUABLE-PLAYER AWARD Source: Baseball Writers' Association of America

NATIONAL LEAGUE

Year	Player	Club
1931	Frank Frisch	St. Louis
1932	Chuck Klein	Philadelphia
1933	Carl Hubbell	New York
1934	Dizzy Dean	St. Louis
1935	Gabby Hartnett	Chicago
1936	Carl Hubbell	New York
1937	Joe Medwick	St. Louis
1938	Ernie Lombardi	Cincinnati
1939	Bucky Walters	Cincinnati
1940	Frank McCormick	Cincinnati
1941	Dolph Camilli	Brooklyn
1942	Mort Cooper	St. Louis
1943	Stan Musial	St. Louis
1944	Marty Marion	St. Louis
1945	Phil Cavarretta	Chicago
1946	Stan Musial	St. Louis
1947	Bob Elliott	Boston
1948	Stan Musial	St. Louis
1949	Jackie Robinson	Brooklyn
1950	Jim Konstanty	Philadelphia
1951	Roy Campanella	Brooklyn
1952	Hank Sauer	Chicago
1953	Roy Campanella	Brooklyn
1954	Willie Mays	New York
1955	Roy Campanella	Brooklyn
1956	Don Newcombe	Brooklyn
1957	Hank Aaron	Milwaukee
1958	Ernie Banks	Chicago
1959	Ernie Banks	Chicago
1960	Dick Groat	Pittsburgh
1961	Frank Robinson	Cincinnati
1962	Maury Wills	Los Angeles
1963	Sandy Koufax	Los Angeles
1964	Ken Boyer	St. Louis
1965	Willie Mays	San Francisco
1966	Roberto Clemente	Pittsburgh
1967	Orlando Cepeda	St. Louis
1968	Bob Gibson	St. Louis
1969	Willie McCovey	San Francisco
1970	Johnny Bench	Cincinnati
1971	Joe Torre	St. Louis
1972	Johnny Bench	Cincinnati
1973	Pete Rose	Cincinnati
1974	Steve Garvey	Los Angeles
1975	Joe Morgan	Cincinnati
1976	Joe Morgan	Cincinnati
1977	George Foster	Cincinnati
1978	Dave Parker	Pittsburgh
1979	Willie Stargell	Pittsburgh
	Keith Hernandez	St. Louis

AMERICAN LEAGUE

Year	Player	Club
1931	Lefty Grove	Philadelphia
1932	Jimmy Foxx	Philadelphia
1933	Jimmy Foxx	Philadelphia
1934	Mickey Cochrane	Detroit
1935	Hank Greenberg	Detroit
1936	Lou Gehrig	New York
1937	Charley Gehringer	Detroit
1938	Jimmy Foxx	Boston
1939	Joe DiMaggio	New York
1940	Hank Greenberg	Detroit
1941	Joe DiMaggio	New York
1942	Joe Gordon	New York
1943	Spud Chandler	New York
1944	Hal Newhouser	Detroit
1945	Hal Newhouser	Detroit
1946	Ted Williams	Boston
1947	Joe DiMaggio	New York
1948	Lou Boudreau	Cleveland
1949	Ted Williams	Boston
1950	Phil Rizzuto	New York
1951	Yogi Berra	New York
1952	Bobby Shantz	Philadelphia
1953	Al Rosen	Cleveland
1954	Yogi Berra	New York
1955	Yogi Berra	New York
1956	Mickey Mantle	New York
1957	Mickey Mantle	New York
1958	Jackie Jensen	Boston
1959	Nelson Fox	Chicago
1960	Roger Maris	New York
1961	Roger Maris	New York
1962	Mickey Mantle	New York
1963	Elston Howard	New York
1964	Brooks Robinson	Baltimore
1965	Zoilo Versalles	Minnesota
1966	Frank Robinson	Baltimore
1967	Carl Yastrzemski	Boston
1968	Denny McLain	Detroit
1969	Harmon Killebrew	Minnesota
1970	John (Boog) Powell	Baltimore
1971	Vida Blue	Oakland
1972	Dick Allen	Chicago
1973	Reggie Jackson	Oakland
1974	Jeff Burroughs	Texas
1975	Fred Lynn	Boston
1976	Thurman Munson	New York
1977	Rod Carew	Minnesota
1978	Jim Rice	Boston
1979	Don Baylor	California

ROOKIE-OF-THE-YEAR AWARD

NATIONAL LEAGUE

Year	Player and Position	Club
1949	Don Newcombe, pitcher	Brooklyn
1950	Sam Jethroe, outfielder	Boston
1951	Willie Mays, outfielder	New York
1952	Joe Black, pitcher	Brooklyn
1953	Jim Gilliam, second baseman	Brooklyn
1954	Wally Moon, outfielder	St. Louis
1955	Bill Virdon, outfielder	St. Louis
1956	Frank Robinson, outfielder	Cincinnati
1957	Jack Sanford, pitcher	Philadelphia
1958	Orlando Cepeda, first baseman	San Francisco
1959	Willie McCovey, first baseman	San Francisco
1960	Frank Howard, outfielder	Los Angeles
1961	Billy Williams, outfielder	Chicago
1962	Ken Hubbs, second baseman	Chicago
1963	Pete Rose, second baseman	Cincinnati
1964	Richie Allen, third baseman	Philadelphia
1965	Jim Lefebvre, second baseman	Los Angeles
1966	Tommy Helms, third baseman	Cincinnati
1967	Tom Seaver, pitcher	New York
1968	Johnny Bench, catcher	Cincinnati
1969	Ted Sizemore, second baseman	Los Angeles
1970	Carl Morton, pitcher	Montreal
1971	Earl Williams, catcher	Atlanta
1972	Jon Matlack, pitcher	New York
1973	Gary Mathews, outfielder	San Francisco
1974	Bake McBride, outfielder	St. Louis
1975	John Montefusco, pitcher	San Francisco
1976	Pat Zachry, pitcher	Cincinnati
	Butch Metzger, pitcher	San Diego
1977	Andre Dawson, outfielder	Montreal
1978	Bob Horner, third baseman	Atlanta
1979	Rick Sutcliffe, pitcher	Los Angeles

AMERICAN LEAGUE

Year	Player and Position	Club
1949	Roy Sievers, outfielder	St. Louis
1950	Walt Dropo, first baseman	Boston
1951	Gil McDougald, third baseman	New York
1952	Harry Byrd, pitcher	Philadelphia
1953	Harvey Kuenn, shortstop	Detroit
1954	Bob Grim, pitcher	New York
1955	Herb Score, pitcher	Cleveland
1956	Luis Aparicio, shortstop	Chicago
1957	Tony Kubek, infielder-outfielder	New York
1958	Albie Pearson, outfielder	Washington
1959	Bob Allison, outfielder	Washington
1960	Ron Hansen, shortstop	Baltimore
1961	Don Schwall, pitcher	Boston
1962	Tom Tresh, infielder-outfielder	New York
1963	Gary Peters, pitcher	Chicago
1964	Tony Oliva, outfielder	Minnesota
1965	Curt Blefary, outfielder	Baltimore
1966	Tommie Agee, outfielder	Chicago
1967	Rod Carew, second baseman	Minnesota
1968	Stan Bahnsen, pitcher	New York
1969	Lou Piniella, outfielder	Kansas City
1970	Thurman Munson, catcher	New York
1971	Chris Chambliss, infielder	Cleveland
1972	Carlton Fisk, catcher	Boston
1973	Al Bumbry, outfielder	Baltimore
1974	Mike Hargrove, first baseman	Texas
1975	Fred Lynn, outfielder	Boston
1976	Mark Fidrych, pitcher	Detroit
1977	Eddie Murray, first baseman	Baltimore
1978	Lou Whitaker, second baseman	Detroit
1979	John Castino, third baseman	Minnesota
	Alfredo Griffin, shortstop	Toronto

ROBERTO CLEMENTE AWARD

Ability, sportsmanship, character, community involvement, humanitarianism, contribution to team and baseball

1971	Willie Mays, San Francisco	1974	Willie Stargell, Pittsburgh	1977	Rod Carew, Minnesota
1972	Brooks Robinson, Baltimore	1975	Lou Brock, St. Louis	1978	Greg Luzinski, Philadelphia
1973	Al Kaline, Detroit	1976	Pete Rose, Cincinnati	1979	Andre Thornton, Cleveland
				1980	Phil Niekro, Atlanta

BASEBALL STADIUMS

AMERICAN LEAGUE

	Seating	Field Distances			Wall Heights		
		LF	CF	RF	LF	CF	RF
Baltimore (Memorial Stadium)	52,860	309'	405'	309'	14'	7'	14'
Boston (Fenway Park)	33,538	315'	390'	302'	37'	17'	3–5'
California (Anaheim Stadium)	43,250	333'	404'	333'	8'	8'	8'
Chicago (Comiskey Park)	44,492	352'	445'	352'	9'	17'	9'
Cleveland (Municipal Stadium)	76,713	320'	400'	320'	9'	8'	9'
Detroit (Tiger Stadium)	53,676	340'	440'	325'	9'	9'	9'
Kansas City (Royals Stadium)	40,760	330'	410'	330'	12'	12'	12'
Milwaukee (County Stadium)	54,192	320'	402'	315'	8'	10'	10'
Minnesota (Metropolitan Stadium)	45,919	343'	402'	330'	12'	8'	8'
New York (Yankee Stadium)	57,545	312'	417'	310'	7'	7'	8'
Oakland (Oakland Coliseum)	50,000	330'	400'	330'	8'	8'	8'
Seattle (Kingdome)	59,438	316'	410'	316'	11½'	11½'	11½'
Texas (Arlington Stadium)	41,097	330'	400'	330'	11'	11'	11'
Toronto (Exhibition Stadium)	43,737	330'	400'	330'	12'	12'	12'

NATIONAL LEAGUE

	Seating	Field Distances			Wall Heights		
		LF	CF	RF	LF	CF	RF
Atlanta (Atlanta Stadium)	52,194	330'	402'	330'	6'	6'	6'
Chicago (Wrigley Field)	37,741	355'	400'	353'	11½'	11½'	11½'
Cincinnati (Riverfront Stadium)	51,880	330'	404'	330'	12'	12'	12'
Houston (Astrodome)	45,000	340'	406'	340'	10'	10'	10'
Los Angeles (Dodger Stadium)	56,000	330'	395'	330'	8'	8'	8'
Montreal (Olympic Stadium)	60,476	325'	404'	325'	12'	12'	12'
New York (Shea Stadium)	55,300	341'	410'	341'	8'	8'	8'
Philadelphia (Veterans Stadium)	60,515	330'	408'	330'	12'	12'	12'
Pittsburgh (Three Rivers Stadium)	50,230	335'	400'	335'	10'	10'	10'
San Diego (San Diego Stadium)	51,362	330'	420'	330'	17'	17'	17'
San Francisco (Candlestick Park)	58,000	335'	410'	335'	12'	12'	12'
St. Louis (Busch Memorial Stadium)	50,222	330'	414'	330'	10½'	10½'	10½'

MINOR LEAGUE BASEBALL AFFILIATIONS: 1980

American League	Class AAA	Class AA	National League	Class AAA	Class AA
Baltimore	Rochester (IL)	Charlotte (SL)	Atlanta	Richmond (IL)	Savannah (SL)
Boston	Pawtucket (IL)	Bristol (EL)	Chicago	Wichita (AA)	Midland (TL)
California	Salt Lake City (PCL)	El Paso (TL)	Cincinnati	Indianapolis (AA)	Waterbury (EL)
Chicago	Iowa (AA)	Knoxville (SL)	Houston	Charleston (IL)	Columbus (SL)
Cleveland	Tacoma (PCL)	Chattanooga (SL)	Los Angeles	Albuquerque (PCL)	San Antonio (TL)
Detroit	Evansville (AA)	Montgomery (SL)	Montreal	Denver (AA)	Memphis (SL)
Kansas City	Omaha (AA)	Jacksonville (SL)	New York	Tidewater (IL)	Jackson (TL)
Milwaukee	Vancouver (PCL)	Holyoke (EL)	Philadelphia	Oklahoma City (AA)	Reading (EL)
Minnesota	Toledo (IL)	Orlando (SL)	Pittsburgh	Portland (PCL)	Buffalo (EL)
New York	Columbus (IL)	Nashville (SL)	St. Louis	Springfield (AA)	Arkansas (TL)
Oakland	Ogden (PCL)		San Diego	Hawaii (PCL)	Amarillo (TL)
Seattle	Spokane (PCL)	West Haven (EL)	San Francisco	Phoenix (PCL)	Shreveport (TL)
Texas	Tucson (PCL)	Tulsa (TL)			
Toronto	Syracuse (IL)				

(AA) American Association, (IL) International League, (PCL) Pacific Coast League, (EL) Eastern League, (SL) Southern League, (TL) Texas League.

NATIONAL COLLEGIATE BASEBALL CHAMPIONSHIPS Source: NCAA

Year	Champion	Coach	Runner-up	Outstanding Player
1970	Southern California	Rod Dedeaux	Florida State	Gene Ammann (Florida State)
1971	Southern California	Rod Dedeaux	Southern Illinois	Jerry Tabb (Tulsa)
1972	Southern California	Rod Dedeaux	Arizona State	Russ McQueen (USC)
1973	Southern California	Rod Dedeaux	Arizona State	Dave Winfield (Minnesota)
1974	Southern California	Rod Dedeaux	Miami (Fla.)	George Mike (USC)
1975	Texas	Cliff Gustafson	South Carolina	Mickey Reichenbach (Texas)
1976	Arizona	Jerry Kindall	Eastern Michigan	Steve Powers (Arizona)
1977	Arizona State	Jim Brock	South Carolina	Bob Horner (Arizona State)
1978	Southern California	Rod Dedeaux	Arizona State	Rod Boxberger (USC)
1979	Cal. State-Fullerton	Augie Garrido	Arkansas	Tony Hudson (Cal. State)
1980	Arizona	Jerry Kindall	Hawaii	Terry Francona (Arizona)

BASKETBALL

PROFESSIONAL BASKETBALL GOVERNMENT

National Basketball Association (NBA): Olympic Tower, 645 5th Ave., New York City 10022. **Commissioner:** Lawrence F. O'Brien. Founded in 1946, the NBA today consists of 23 teams.

ATLANTIC DIVISION	Governor	Coach
Boston Celtics	Harry Mangurian	Bill Fitch
New York Knicks	Michael Burke	Red Holzman
New Jersey Nets	Joseph Taub	Kevin Loughery
Philadelphia 76ers	F. Eugene Dixon	Billy Cunningham
Washington Bullets	Abe Pollin	Gene Shue

CENTRAL DIVISION	Governor	Coach
Atlanta Hawks	Mike Gearon	Hubie Brown
Chicago Bulls	William Wirtz	Jerry Sloan
Cleveland Cavaliers	Ted Stepien	Bill Musselman
Detroit Pistons	William Davidson	Scotty Robertson
Indiana Pacers	Sam Nassi	Jack McKinney
Milwaukee Bucks	James Fitzgerald	Don Nelson

MIDWEST DIVISION	Governor	Coach
Dallas Mavericks	Donald Carter	Dick Motta
Denver Nuggets	Carl Scheer	Donnie Walsh
Houston Rockets	George Maloof	Del Harris
Kansas City Kings	Paul Rosenberg	Cotton Fitzsimmons
San Antonio Spurs	Angelo Drossos	Stan Albeck
Utah Jazz	Sam Battistone	Tom Nissalke

PACIFIC DIVISION	Governor	Coach
Golden State Warriors	Franklin Mieuli	Al Attles
Los Angeles Lakers	Jerry Buss	Paul Westhead
Phoenix Suns	Richard Bloch	John MacLeod
Portland Trail Blazers	Lawrence Weinberg	Jack Ramsay
San Diego Clippers	Irving Levin	Paul Silas
Seattle SuperSonics	Samuel Schulman	Lenny Wilkens

THE NBA CHAMPIONS

Season	Eastern Conference (W–L)	Western Conference (W–L)	Playoff Champions (W–L)
1957/58	Boston Celtics (49–23)	St. Louis Hawks (41–31)	St. Louis Hawks (4–2) over Boston
1958/59	Boston Celtics (52–20)	St. Louis Hawks (49–23)	Boston Celtics (4–0) over Minneapolis
1959/60	Boston Celtics (59–16)	St. Louis Hawks (46–29)	Boston Celtics (4–3) over St. Louis
1960/61	Boston Celtics (57–22)	St. Louis Hawks (51–28)	Boston Celtics (4–1) over St. Louis
1961/62	Boston Celtics (60–20)	Los Angeles Lakers (54–26)	Boston Celtics (4–3) over Los Angeles
1962/63	Boston Celtics (58–22)	Los Angeles Lakers (53–27)	Boston Celtics (4–2) over Los Angeles
1963/64	Boston Celtics (59–21)	San Francisco Warriors (48–32)	Boston Celtics (4–1) over San Francisco
1964/65	Boston Celtics (62–18)	Los Angeles Lakers (49–31)	Boston Celtics (4–1) over Los Angeles
1965/66	Philadelphia 76ers (55–25)	Los Angeles Lakers (45–35)	Boston Celtics (4–3) over Los Angeles
1966/67	Philadelphia 76ers (68–13)	San Francisco Warriors (44–37)	Philadelphia 76ers (4–2) over San Francisco
1967/68	Philadelphia 76ers (62–20)	St. Louis Hawks (56–26)	Boston Celtics (4–2) over Los Angeles
1968/69	Baltimore Bullets (57–25)	Los Angeles Lakers (55–27)	Boston Celtics (4–3) over Los Angeles
1969/70	New York Knickerbockers (60–22)	Los Angeles Lakers (46–36)	New York Knicks (4–3) over Los Angeles
1970/71	Baltimore Bullets (42–40)	Milwaukee Bucks (66–16)	Milwaukee Bucks (4–0) over Baltimore
1971/72	New York Knickerbockers (48–34)	Los Angeles Lakers (69–13)	Los Angeles Lakers (4–1) over New York
1972/73	New York Knickerbockers (57–25)	Los Angeles Lakers (60–22)	New York (4–1) over Los Angeles
1973/74	Boston Celtics (56–26)	Milwaukee Bucks (59–23)	Boston (4–3) over Milwaukee
1974/75	Washington Bullets (60–22)	Golden State Warriors (48–34)	Golden State (4–0) over Washington
1975/76	Boston Celtics (54–28)	Phoenix Suns (42–40)	Boston Celtics (4–2) over Phoenix
1976/77	Philadelphia 76ers (50–32)	Los Angeles Lakers (53–29)	Portland Trail Blazers (4–2) over Phila.
1977/78	Philadelphia 76ers (55–27)	Portland Trail Blazers (58–24)	Washington Bullets (4–3) over Seattle
1978/79	Washington Bullets (54–28)	Seattle SuperSonics (52–30)	Seattle (4–1) over Washington
1979/80	Boston Celtics (61–21)	Los Angeles Lakers (60–22)	Los Angeles (4–2) over Philadelphia

TOP NBA SCORERS

Season	Player and Team	Points	Game Avg.
1957/58	George Yardley, Detroit	2,001	27.8
1958/59	Bob Pettit, St. Louis	2,105	29.2
1959/60	Wilt Chamberlain, Philadelphia	2,707	37.6
1960/61	Wilt Chamberlain, Philadelphia	3,033	38.4
1961/62	Wilt Chamberlain, Philadelphia	4,029	50.4
1962/63	Wilt Chamberlain, San Francisco	3,586	44.8
1963/64	Wilt Chamberlain, San Francisco	2,948	36.5
1964/65	Wilt Chamberlain, Philadelphia	2,534	34.7
1965/66	Wilt Chamberlain, Philadelphia	2,649	33.5
1966/67	Rick Barry, San Francisco	2,775	35.6
1967/68	Dave Bing, Detroit	2,142	27.1
1968/69	Elvin Hayes, San Diego	2,327	28.4
1969/70	Jerry West, Los Angeles	2,309	31.2
1970/71	Lew Alcindor, Milwaukee	2,596	31.7
1971/72	Kareem Abdul-Jabbar, Milwaukee	2,822	34.8
1972/73	Nate Archibald, Kansas City-Omaha	2,719	34.0
1973/74	Bob McAdoo, Buffalo	2,261	30.6
1974/75	Bob McAdoo, Buffalo	2,831	34.5
1975/76	Bob McAdoo, Buffalo	2,427	31.1
1976/77	Pete Maravich, New Orleans	2,273	31.1
1977/78	George Gervin, San Antonio	2,232	27.2
1978/79	George Gervin, San Antonio	2,365	29.6
1979/80	George Gervin, San Antonio	2,585	33.1

TOP NBA FIELD GOAL PERCENTAGE

Season	Pct.	Player and Team
1957/58	.452	Jack Twyman, Cincinnati
1958/59	.490	Ken Sears, New York
1959/60	.477	Ken Sears, New York
1960/61	.509	Wilt Chamberlain, Philadelphia
1961/62	.519	Walt Bellamy, Chicago
1962/63	.528	Wilt Chamberlain, San Francisco
1963/64	.527	Jerry Lucas, Cincinnati
1964/65	.510	Wilt Chamberlain, Philadelphia
1965/66	.540	Wilt Chamberlain, Philadelphia
1966/67	.683	Wilt Chamberlain, Philadelphia
1967/68	.595	Wilt Chamberlain, Philadelphia
1968/69	.583	Wilt Chamberlain, Los Angeles
1969/70	.559	Johnny Green, Cincinnati
1970/71	.587	Johnny Green, Cincinnati
1971/72	.649	Wilt Chamberlain, Los Angeles
1972/73	.727	Wilt Chamberlain, Los Angeles
1973/74	.547	Bob McAdoo, Buffalo
1974/75	.539	Don Nelson, Boston
1975/76	.561	Wes Unseld, Washington
1976/77	.579	Kareem Abdul-Jabbar, Los Angeles
1977/78	.578	Bobby Jones, Denver
1978/79	.584	Cedric Maxwell, Boston
1979/80	.609	Cedric Maxwell, Boston

TOP NBA FREE THROW PERCENTAGE

Season	Pct.	Player and Team	Season	Pct.	Player and Team
1957/58	.904	Dolph Schayes, Syracuse	1968/69	.864	Larry Siegfried, Boston
1958/59	.932	Bill Sharman, Boston	1969/70	.898	Flynn Robinson, Milwaukee
1959/60	.892	Dolph Schayes, Syracuse	1970/71	.859	Chet Walker, Chicago
1960/61	.921	Dolph Schayes, Syracuse	1971/72	.894	Jack Marin, Baltimore
1961/62	.896	Bill Sharman, Boston	1972/73	.902	Rick Barry, Golden State
1962/63	.881	Larry Costello, Syracuse	1973/74	.902	Ernie DiGregorio, Buffalo
1963/64	.853	Oscar Robertson, Cincinnati	1974/75	.904	Rick Barry, Golden State
1964/65	.877	Larry Costello, Philadelphia	1975/76	.923	Rick Barry, Golden State
1965/66	.881	Larry Siegfried, Boston	1976/77	.945	Ernie DiGregorio, Buffalo
1966/67	.903	Adrian Smith, Cincinnati	1977/78	.924	Rick Barry, Golden State
1967/68	.873	Oscar Robertson, Cincinnati	1978/79	.947	Rick Barry, Houston
			1979/80	.935	Rick Barry, Houston

NBA REBOUND LEADERS

Season	Rebs.	Player and Team	Season	Rebs.	Player and Team
1957/58	1564	Bill Russell, Boston	1968/69	1712	Wilt Chamberlain, Los Angeles
1958/59	1612	Bill Russell, Boston	1969/70	1386	Elvin Hayes, San Diego
1959/60	1941	Wilt Chamberlain, Philadelphia	1970/71	1493	Wilt Chamberlain, Los Angeles
1960/61	2149	Wilt Chamberlain, Philadelphia	1971/72	1572	Wilt Chamberlain, Los Angeles
1961/62	2052	Wilt Chamberlain, Philadelphia	1972/73	1526	Wilt Chamberlain, Los Angeles
1962/63	1946	Wilt Chamberlain, San Francisco	1973/74	1463	Elvin Hayes, Capital
1963/64	1930	Bill Russell, Boston	1974/75	1077	Wes Unseld, Washington
1964/65	1878	Bill Russell, Boston	1975/76	1383	Kareem Abdul-Jabbar, Los Angeles
1965/66	1943	Wilt Chamberlain, Philadelphia	1976/77	1090	Kareem Abdul-Jabbar, Los Angeles
1966/67	1957	Wilt Chamberlain, Philadelphia	1977/78	1288	Truck Robinson, New Orleans
1967/68	1952	Wilt Chamberlain, Philadelphia	1978/79	1444	Moses Malone, Houston
			1979/80	1216	Swen Nater, San Diego

NBA ASSIST LEADERS

Season	Asst.	Player and Team	Season	Asst.	Player and Team
1957/58	463	Bob Cousy, Boston	1968/69	772	Oscar Robertson, Cincinnati
1958/59	557	Bob Cousy, Boston	1969/70	683	Len Wilkens, Seattle
1959/60	715	Bob Cousy, Boston	1970/71	832	Norm Van Lier, Cincinnati
1960/61	690	Oscar Robertson, Cincinnati	1971/72	747	Jerry West, Los Angeles
1961/62	899	Oscar Robertson, Cincinnati	1972/73	910	Nate Archibald, Kansas City-Omaha
1962/63	825	Guy Rodgers, San Francisco	1973/74	663	Ernie DiGregorio, Buffalo
1963/64	868	Oscar Robertson, Cincinnati	1974/75	650	Kevin Porter, Washington
1964/65	861	Oscar Robertson, Cincinnati	1975/76	661	Don Watts, Seattle
1965/66	847	Oscar Robertson, Cincinnati	1976/77	685	Don Buse, Indiana
1966/67	908	Guy Rodgers, Chicago	1977/78	837	Kevin Porter, New Jersey
1967/68	702	Wilt Chamberlain, Philadelphia	1978/79	1099	Kevin Porter, Detroit
			1979/80	832	Mike Richardson, New York

NBA FINAL STANDINGS: 1979-80

EASTERN CONFERENCE

ATLANTIC DIVISION	Won	Lost	Pct.	G.B.
Boston Celtics	61	21	.744	—
Philadelphia 76ers	59	23	.720	2
Washington Bullets	39	43	.476	22
New York Knicks	39	43	.476	22
New Jersey Nets	34	48	.415	27

CENTRAL DIVISION	Won	Lost	Pct.	G.B.
Atlanta Hawks	50	32	.610	—
San Antonio Spurs	41	41	.500	9
Houston Rockets	41	41	.500	9
Indiana Pacers	37	45	.451	13
Cleveland Cavaliers	37	45	.451	13
Detroit Pistons	16	66	.195	34

WESTERN CONFERENCE

MIDWEST DIVISION	Won	Lost	Pct.	G.B.
Milwaukee Bucks	49	33	.598	—
Kansas City Kings	47	35	.573	2
Chicago Bulls	30	52	.366	19
Denver Nuggets	30	52	.366	19
Utah Jazz	24	58	.293	25

PACIFIC DIVISION	Won	Lost	Pct.	G.B.
Los Angeles Lakers	60	22	.732	—
Seattle SuperSonics	56	26	.683	4
Phoenix Suns	55	27	.671	5
Portland Trail Blazers	38	44	.463	22
San Diego Clippers	35	47	.427	25
Golden State Warriors	24	58	.293	36

NBA PLAYOFFS: 1980

EASTERN CONFERENCE

FIRST ROUND: Philadelphia over Washington (2–0)
  Houston over San Antonio (2–1)
SEMIFINALS: Philadelphia over Atlanta (4–1)
  Boston over Houston (4–0)
FINALS: Philadelphia over Boston (4–1)

WESTERN CONFERENCE

FIRST ROUND: Phoenix over Kansas City (2–1)
  Seattle over Portland (2–1)
SEMIFINALS: Los Angeles over Phoenix (4–1)
  Seattle over Milwaukee (4–3)
FINALS: Los Angeles over Seattle (4–1)

CHAMPIONSHIP SERIES

Los Angeles 4   Philadelphia 2

(Most Valuable Player—Earvin Johnson, Los Angeles)

May 4 — Los Angeles 109, Philadelphia 102
May 7 — Philadelphia 107, Los Angeles 104
May 10 — Los Angeles 111, Philadelphia 101
May 11 — Philadelphia 105, Los Angeles 102
May 14 — Los Angeles 108, Philadelphia 103
May 16 — Los Angeles 123, Philadelphia 107

Scoring Leader: Abdul-Jabbar, Los Angeles .... 167 pts.
Scoring Average: Abdul-Jabbar 33.4
Rebounds: Abdul-Jabbar 68
Assists: Hollins, Philadelphia 53
Field Goals Made: Abdul-Jabbar 73
Free Throws Made: Johnson, Los Angeles 35

NBA INDIVIDUAL LEADERS: 1979-80

SCORING

Minimum: 70 games played or 1400 points

	Games	FG	FT	Pts.	Avg.		Games	FG	FT	Pts.	Avg.
Gervin, San Ant.	78	1024	505	2585	33.1	Williams, Seattle ...	82	739	331	1816	22.1
Free, San Diego	68	737	572	2055	30.2	Westphal, Phoenix ...	82	692	382	1792	21.9
Dantley, Utah	68	730	443	1903	28.0	Cartwright, N.Y.	82	665	451	1781	21.7
Erving, Phila.	78	838	420	2100	26.9	Johnson, Milw.	77	689	291	1671	21.7
Malone, Houston	82	778	563	2119	25.8	Davis, Phoenix	75	657	299	1613	21.5
Abdul-Jabbar, L.A. ..	82	835	364	2034	24.8	Bird, Boston	82	693	301	1745	21.3
Issel, Denver	82	715	517	1951	23.8	Newlin, N.J.	78	611	367	1634	20.9
Hayes, Wash.	81	761	334	1859	23.0	R. Williams, N.Y. ..	82	687	333	1714	20.9
Birdsong, K.C.	82	781	286	1858	22.7	Theus, Chicago	82	566	500	1660	20.2
Mitchell, Cleve.	82	775	270	1820	22.2	Kenon, San Ant. ...	78	647	270	1565	20.1

FIELD GOAL PERCENTAGE

Minimum: 300 FG made

	FG	Attempted	Pct.
Maxwell, Boston	457	750	.609
Abdul-Jabbar, Los Angeles	835	1383	.604
Gilmore, Chicago	305	513	.595
Dantley, Utah	730	1267	.576
Boswell, Utah	346	613	.564

FREE THROW PERCENTAGE

Minimum: 125 FT made

	FT	Attempted	Pct.
Barry, Houston	143	153	.935
Murphy, Houston	271	302	.897
Boone, Utah	175	196	.893
Silas, San Antonio	339	382	.887
Newlin, New Jersey	367	415	.884

REBOUNDS

Minimum: 70 games or 800 rebounds

	G	Off.	Def.	Total	Avg.
Nater, San Diego	81	352	864	1216	15.0
Malone, Houston	82	573	617	1190	14.5
Unseld, Washington	82	334	760	1094	13.3
C. Jones, Philadelphia	80	219	731	950	11.9
Sikma, Seattle	82	198	710	908	11.1

ASSISTS

Minimum: 70 games or 400 assists

	G	No.	Avg.
Richardson, New York	82	832	10.1
Archibald, Boston	80	671	8.4
Walker, Cleveland	76	607	8.0
Nixon, Los Angeles	82	642	7.8
Lucas, Golden State	80	602	7.5

STEALS

Minimum: 70 games or 125 steals

	G	No.	Avg.
Richardson, New York	82	265	3.23
Jordan, New Jersey	82	223	2.72
Bradley, Indiana	82	211	2.57
Williams, Seattle	82	200	2.44
Johnson, Los Angeles	77	187	2.43

BLOCKED SHOTS

Minimum: 70 games or 100 blocked shots

	G	No.	Avg.
Abdul-Jabbar, Los Angeles	82	280	3.41
Johnson, New Jersey	81	258	3.19
Rollins, Atlanta	82	244	2.98
Tyler, Detroit	82	220	2.68
Hayes, Washington	81	189	2.33

NBA ALL-STAR TEAMS: 1979-80

First Team		Second Team	
Player, Club	**Position**	**Player, Club**	**Position**
Julius Erving Philadelphia	F	Dan Roundfield, Atlanta	F
Larry Bird, Boston	F	Marques Johnson, Milwaukee	F
Kareem Abdul-Jabbar, Los Angeles	C	Moses Malone, Houston	C
George Gervin, San Antonio	G	Dennis Johnson, Seattle	G
Paul Westphal, Phoenix	G	Gus Williams, Seattle	G

NBA ALL-ROOKIE TEAM: 1979-80

First Team
Player, Club, Votes
Larry Bird, Boston (22)
Earvin Johnson, Los Angeles (22)
Bill Cartwright, New York (22)
Calvin Natt, Portland (20)
David Greenwood, Chicago (13)

Others Receiving Votes
Player, Club, Votes
Cliff Robinson, New Jersey (3)
Allen Leavell, Houston (2)
Reggie King, Kansas City (2)
Johnny High, Phoenix (1)
Greg Kelser, Detroit (1)

Sidney Moncrief, Milwaukee (1)
Clint Richardson, Philadelphia (1)

NBA ROOKIE OF THE YEAR

Year	Player	Year	Player
1952–53	Don Meineke, Fort Wayne	1966–67	Dave Bing, Detroit
1953–54	Ray Felix, Baltimore	1967–68	Earl Monroe, Baltimore
1954–55	Bob Pettit, Milwaukee	1968–69	Wes Unseld, Baltimore
1955–56	Maurice Stokes, Rochester	1969–70	Lew Alcindor, Milwaukee
1956–57	Tom Heinsohn, Boston	1970–71	Dave Cowens, Boston, and
1957–58	Woody Sauldsberry, Philadelphia		Geoff Petrie, Portland
1958–59	Elgin Baylor, Minneapolis	1971–72	Sidney Wicks, Portland
1959–60	Wilt Chamberlain, Philadelphia	1972–73	Bob McAdoo, Buffalo
1960–61	Oscar Robertson, Cincinnati	1973–74	Ernie DiGregorio, Buffalo
1961–62	Walt Bellamy, Chicago	1974–75	Keith Wilkes, Golden State
1962–63	Terry Dischinger, Chicago	1975–76	Alvan Adams, Phoenix
1963–64	Jerry Lucas, Cincinnati	1976–77	Adrian Dantley, Buffalo
1964–65	Willis Reed, New York	1977–78	Walter Davis, Phoenix
1965–66	Rick Barry, San Francisco	1978–79	Phil Ford, Kansas City
		1979–80	Larry Bird, Boston

NBA COACH OF THE YEAR

Year	Coach, Team	Year	Coach, Team
1962–63	Harry Gallatin, St. Louis	1971–72	Bill Sharman, Los Angeles
1963–64	Alex Hannum, San Francisco	1972–73	Tom Heinsohn, Boston
1964–65	Red Auerbach, Boston	1973–74	Ray Scott, Detroit
1965–66	Dolph Schayes, Philadelphia	1974–75	Phil Johnson, Kansas City–Omaha
1966–67	Johnny Kerr, Chicago	1975–76	Bill Fitch, Cleveland
1967–68	Richie Guerin, St. Louis	1976–77	Tom Nissalke, Houston
1968–69	Gene Shue, Baltimore	1977–78	Hubie Brown, Atlanta
1969–70	Red Holzman, New York	1978–79	Cotton Fitzsimmons, Kansas City
1970–71	Dick Motta, Chicago	1979–80	Bill Fitch, Boston

NBA PODOLOFF TROPHY WINNERS (Most Valuable Player)

Year	Player, Team	Year	Player, Team
1956–57	Bob Cousy, Boston	1968–69	Wes Unseld, Baltimore
1957–58	Bill Russell, Boston	1969–70	Willis Reed, New York
1958–59	Bob Pettit, St. Louis	1970–71	Lew Alcindor, Milwaukee
1959–60	Wilt Chamberlain, Philadelphia	1971–72	Kareem Abdul-Jabbar, Milwaukee
1960–61	Bill Russell, Boston	1972–73	Dave Cowens, Boston
1961–62	Bill Russell, Boston	1973–74	Kareem Abdul-Jabbar, Milwaukee
1962–63	Bill Russell, Boston	1974–75	Bob McAdoo, Buffalo
1963–64	Oscar Robertson, Cincinnati	1975–76	Kareem Abdul-Jabbar, Los Angeles
1964–65	Bill Russell, Boston	1976–77	Kareem Abdul-Jabbar, Los Angeles
1965–66	Wilt Chamberlain, Philadelphia	1977–78	Bill Walton, Portland
1966–67	Wilt Chamberlain, Philadelphia	1978–79	Moses Malone, Houston
1967–68	Wilt Chamberlain, Philadelphia	1979–80	Kareem Abdul-Jabbar, Los Angeles

1980 NBA FIRST ROUND COLLEGE DRAFT

	Team	Player	College		Team	Player	College
1.	Golden State	Joe Barry Carroll	Purdue	13.	Golden State	Rickey Brown	Mississippi State
2.	Utah	Darrell Griffith	Louisville	14.	Washington	Wes Matthews	Wisconsin
3.	Boston	Kevin McHale	Minnesota	15.	San Antonio	Reggie Johnson	Tennessee
4.	Chicago	Kelvin Ransey	Ohio State	16.	Kansas City	Charles Whitney	North Carolina State
5.	Denver	James Ray	Jacksonville	17.	Detroit	Larry Drew	Missouri
6.	New Jersey	Mike O'Koren	North Carolina	18.	Atlanta	Don Collins	Washington State
7.	New Jersey	Mike Gminski	Duke	19.	Utah	John Duren	Georgetown
8.	Philadelphia	Andrew Toney	S. W. Louisiana	20.	Seattle	Bill Hanzlik	Notre Dame
9.	San Diego	Michael Brooks	LaSalle	21.	Philadelphia	Monti Davis	Tennessee State
10.	Portland	Ronnie Lester	Iowa	22.	Cleveland	Chad Kinch	N. Carolina–Charlotte
11.	Dallas	Kiki Vandeweghe	U.C.L.A.	23.	Denver	Carl Nicks	Indiana State
12.	New York	Mike Woodson	Indiana				

BASKETBALL HALL OF FAME

Springfield, Massachusetts

Player	Year Elected
Paul Arizin	1977
Elgin Baylor	1976
John Beckman	1972
Bennie Borgmann	1961
Joseph Brennan	1974
Wilt Chamberlain	1979
Charles (Tarzan) Cooper	1976
Bob Cousy	1970
Bob Davies	1969
Forrest DeBernardi	1961
H. G. (Dutch) Dehnert	1968
Paul Endacott	1971
Harold (Bud) Foster	1964
Max (Marty) Friedman	1971
Joe Fulks	1977
Lauren (Laddie) Gale	1976
Tom Gola	1975
Robert (Ace) Gruenig	1963
Cliff Hagan	1977
Victor Hanson	1960
Nat Holman	1964
Chuck Hyatt	1959
William Johnson	1976
Edward (Moose) Krause	1975
Bob Kurland	1961
Joe Lapchick	1966
Jerry Lucas	1980
Hank Luisetti	1959
Branch McCracken	1960
Jack McCracken	1962
Ed Macauley	1960
George Mikan	1959
Charles (Stretch) Murphy	1960
H. O. (Pat) Page	1962
Bob Pettit	1970
Andy Phillip	1961
Jim Pollard	1977
Oscar Robertson	1980
Col. John Roosma	1961
John (Honey) Russell	1964
Bill Russell	1974
Dolph Schayes	1972
Ernest Schmidt	1973
John Schommer	1959
Barney Sedran	1962
Bill Sharman	1975
Christian Steinmetz	1961
John (Cat) Thompson	1962
Robert (Fuzzy) Vandivier	1974
Edward Wachter	1961
Jerry West	1980
John Wooden	1960

Coach	Year Elected
A. J. (Red) Auerbach	1968
Sam Barry	1979
Ernest Blood	1960
Howard Cann	1967
Dr. H. Clifford Carlson	1959
Ben Carnevale	1969
Everett Dean	1966
Edgar Diddle	1971
Bruce Drake	1972
Amory (Slats) Gill	1967
Ed Hickey	1979
Howard Hobson	1965
Hank Iba	1968
A. F. (Doggie) Julian	1967
Frank Keaney	1960
George Keogan	1961
Ward Lambert	1960
Harry Litwack	1975
Ken Loeffler	1964
A. C. (Dutch) Lonborg	1972
John McLendon	1979
Frank McGuire	1976
Dr. Walter Meanwell	1959
Ray Meyer	1979
Pete Newell	1979
Adolph Rupp	1968
Leonard Sachs	1961
Everett Shelton	1980
John Wooden	1972

Referee	Year Elected
George Hepbron	1960
George Hoyt	1961
Matthew Kennedy	1959
John Nucatola	1977
Ernest Quigley	1961
J. Dallas Shirley	1980
David Tobey	1961
David Walsh	1961

Contributor	Year Elected
Dr. Forrest (Phog) Allen	1959
Clair Bee	1967
Walter Brown	1965
John Bunn	1964
Bob Douglas	1971
Jim Enright	1979
Harry Fisher	1973
Edward Gottlieb	1971
Dr. Luther Gulick	1959
Les Harrison	1980
Edward Hickox	1959
Paul (Tony) Hinkle	1965
Ned Irish	1964
William Jones	1964
Emil Liston	1974
Bill Mokray	1965
Ralph Morgan	1959
Frank Morgenweck	1962
Dr. James Naismith	1959
John O'Brien	1961
Harold Olsen	1959
Maurice Podoloff	1973
H. V. Porter	1960
William Reid	1963
Elmer Ripley	1972
Lynn St. John	1962
Abe Saperstein	1970
Arthur Schabinger	1961
Amos Alonzo Stagg	1959
Chuck Taylor	1968
Oswald Tower	1959
Arthur Trester	1961
Clifford Wells	1971

NBA ALL-STAR GAMES

Year	Result	Site	Year	Result	Site	Year	Result	Site
1951	East 111, West 94	Boston	1961	West 153, East 131	Syracuse	1971	West 108, East 107	San Diego
1952	East 108, West 91	Boston	1962	West 150, East 130	St. Louis	1972	West 112, East 110	Los Angeles
1953	West 79, East 75	Ft. Wayne	1963	East 115, West 108	Los Angeles	1973	East 104, West 84	Chicago
1954	East 98, West 93	New York	1964	East 111, West 107	Boston	1974	West 134, East 123	Seattle
1955	East 100, West 91	New York	1965	East 124, West 123	St. Louis	1975	East 108, West 102	Phoenix
1956	West 108, East 94	Rochester	1966	East 137, West 94	Cincinnati	1976	East 123, West 109	Philadelphia
1957	East 109, West 97	Boston	1967	West 135, East 120	San Francisco	1977	West 125, East 124	Milwaukee
1958	East 130, West 118	St. Louis	1968	East 144, West 124	New York	1978	East 133, West 125	Atlanta
1959	West 124, East 108	Detroit	1969	East 123, West 112	Baltimore	1979	West 134, East 129	Detroit
1960	East 125, West 115	Philadelphia	1970	East 142, West 135	Philadelphia	1980	East 144, West 136	Washington

ALL-TIME NBA LEADERS

SOURCE: National Basketball Association

At start of 1980/81 season

Top Scorers

Player	Years	Games	Points	Avg.
Wilt Chamberlain	14	1,045	31,419	30.1
Oscar Robertson	14	1,040	26,710	25.7
John Havlicek	16	1,270	26,395	20.8
Jerry West	14	932	25,192	27.0
Kareem Abdul-Jabbar	11	855	24,175	28.3
Elgin Baylor	14	846	23,149	27.4
Elvin Hayes	12	978	23,108	23.6
Hal Greer	15	1,122	21,586	19.2
Walt Bellamy	14	1,043	20,941	20.1
Bob Pettit	11	792	20,880	26.4
Dolph Schayes	16	1,059	19,249	18.2
Gail Goodrich	14	1,031	19,181	18.6
Chet Walker	13	1,032	18,831	18.2
Rick Barry	10	794	18,395	23.2
Dave Bing	12	901	18,327	20.3
Lou Hudson	13	890	17,940	20.2
Len Wilkens	15	1,077	17,772	16.5
Bailey Howell	12	950	17,770	18.7
Earl Monroe	13	926	17,454	18.8
Bob Cousy	14	924	16,960	18.4
Paul Arizin	10	713	16,266	22.8
Pete Maravich	10	658	15,948	24.2
Bob Lanier	10	707	15,896	22.5
Jack Twyman	11	823	15,840	19.2
Bob McAdoo	8	583	15,627	26.8
Walt Frazier	13	825	15,581	18.9
Sam Jones	12	871	15,411	17.7
Dick Barnett	14	971	15,358	15.8
Bob Dandridge	11	805	15,248	18.9
Calvin Murphy	10	798	15,212	19.1
Dick Van Arsdale	12	921	15,079	16.4
Richie Guerin	13	848	14,676	17.3
Bill Russell	13	963	14,522	15.1
Nate Thurmond	14	964	14,437	15.0
Jo Jo White	11	824	14,316	17.4
Tom Van Arsdale	12	929	14,232	15.3
Dave DeBusschere	12	875	14,053	16.1
Jerry Lucas	11	829	14,053	17.0
Bob Love	11	789	13,895	17.6
Billy Cunningham	9	654	13,626	20.8

Most Games Played

John Havlicek	1,270
Paul Silas	1,254
Hal Greer	1,122
Len Wilkens	1,077
Dolph Schayes	1,059
Johnny Green	1,057
Don Nelson	1,053
Leroy Ellis	1,048
Wilt Chamberlain	1,045
Walt Bellamy	1,043

Most Field Goals Made

Wilt Chamberlain	12,681
John Havlicek	10,513
Kareem Abdul-Jabbar	9,979
Oscar Robertson	9,508
Elvin Hayes	9,291
Jerry West	9,016
Elgin Baylor	8,693
Hal Greer	8,504
Walt Bellamy	7,914
Gail Goodrich	7,431

Most Field Goals Attempted

John Havlicek	23,900
Wilt Chamberlain	23,497
Elvin Hayes	20,597
Elgin Baylor	20,171
Oscar Robertson	19,620
Jerry West	19,032
Hal Greer	18,811
Kareem Abdul-Jabbar	17,983
Bob Pettit	16,872
Bob Cousy	16,468

Most Assists

Oscar Robertson	9,887
Len Wilkens	7,211
Bob Cousy	6,955
Guy Rodgers	6,917
Jerry West	6,238
John Havlicek	6,114
Dave Bing	5,397
Norm Van Lier	5,217
Walter Frazier	5,040
Gail Goodrich	4,805

Highest Scoring Average (400 Games Minimum)

Player	G.	FG	FTM	Pts.	Avg.
Wilt Chamberlain	1,045	12,681	6,057	31,419	30.1
Kareem Abdul-Jabbar	855	9,979	4,217	24,175	28.3
Elgin Baylor	846	8,693	5,763	23,149	27.4
Jerry West	932	9,016	7,160	25,192	27.0
Bob McAdoo	583	6,157	3,310	15,627	26.8
Bob Pettit	792	7,349	6,182	20,880	26.4
Oscar Robertson	1,040	9,508	7,694	26,710	25.7
Pete Maravich	658	6,187	3,564	15,948	24.2
Elvin Hayes	978	9,291	4,523	23,108	23.6
Rick Barry	794	7,252	3,818	18,395	23.2

Most Minutes Played

Wilt Chamberlain	47,859
John Havlicek	46,471
Oscar Robertson	43,886
Elvin Hayes	40,741
Bill Russell	40,726
Hal Greer	39,789
Walt Bellamy	38,940
Len Wilkens	38,064
Jerry West	36,571
Nate Thurmond	35,875

Highest Field Goal Percentage (2000 FG Minimum)

Player	FGA	FGM	Pct.
Artis Gilmore	4,174	2,332	.559
Kareem Abdul-Jabbar	17,983	9,979	.555
Walter Davis	4,022	2,207	.549
Wilt Chamberlain	23,497	12,681	.540
Marques Johnson	3,962	2,137	.539
George Gervin	6,635	3,561	.537
Adrian Dantley	4,174	2,226	.533
Clifford Ray	4,298	2,269	.528
Walt Bellamy	15,340	7,914	.516
Paul Westphal	8,384	4,310	.514

Highest Free Throw Percentage (1200 FTM Minimum)

Player	FTA	FTM	Pct.
Rick Barry	4,243	3,818	.900
Calvin Murphy	3,389	3,001	.886
Bill Sharman	3,557	3,143	.884
Mike Newlin	2,843	2,465	.867
Fred Brown	1,716	1,477	.861
Larry Siegfried	1,945	1,662	.854
Flynn Robinson	1,881	1,597	.849
Dolph Schayes	8,273	6,979	.844
Jack Marin	2,852	2,405	.843
Rickey Sobers	1,458	1,229	.843

Most Free Throws Made

Oscar Robertson	7,694
Jerry West	7,160
Dolph Schayes	6,979
Bob Pettit	6,182
Wilt Chamberlain	6,057
Elgin Baylor	5,763
Len Wilkens	5,394
John Havlicek	5,369
Walt Bellamy	5,113
Chet Walker	5,079

Most Free Throws Attempted

Wilt Chamberlain	11,862
Oscar Robertson	9,185
Jerry West	8,801
Dolph Schayes	8,273
Bob Pettit	8,119
Walt Bellamy	8,088
Elgin Baylor	7,391
Len Wilkens	6,973
Elvin Hayes	6,719
John Havlicek	6,589

Most Rebounds

Wilt Chamberlain	23,924
Bill Russell	21,620
Nate Thurmond	14,464
Walt Bellamy	14,241
Elvin Hayes	13,867
Wes Unseld	13,096
Jerry Lucas	12,942
Bob Pettit	12,849
Paul Silas	12,357
Kareem Abdul-Jabbar	12,346

Most Personal Fouls

Hal Greer	3,855
Dolph Schayes	3,664
Walt Bellamy	3,536
Bailey Howell	3,498
Bill Bridges	3,375
Len Wilkens	3,285
John Havlicek	3,281
Elvin Hayes	3,251
Paul Silas	3,105
Tom Sanders	3,044

NCAA CONFERENCE CHAMPIONS: 1979-80 (Record of all games shown in parenthesis)

Conference	Champion	Conf. Won	Conf. Lost	Conf. Runner Up	Tournament Winner
Atlantic Coast	Maryland (23-6)	11	3	North Carolina (21-7) No. Carolina State (20-7)	Duke (22-8)
Big East	Syracuse (25-3)	5	1	—	Georgetown
	St. John's (24-4)	5	1		
	Georgetown (24-5)	5	1		
Big Eight	Missouri (23-5)	11	3	Kansas State (21-8) Nebraska (18-12)	Kansas State
Big Sky	Weber State (26-2)	13	1	Idaho (17-10)	Weber State
Big Ten	Indiana (20-7)	13	5	Ohio State (20-7)	—
East Coast (East)	St. Joseph's (20-8)	10	1	Temple (14-12)	
East Coast (West)	Lafayette (21-7)	13	3	—	LaSalle (21-8)
	Bucknell (20-7)	13	3		
E.C.A.C. (Metro)	Iona (28-4)	—		St. Peter's (20-8)	Iona
E.C.A.C. (North)	Boston University (21-8)	—		Northeastern (19-8)	Holy Cross (20-9)
E.C.A.C. (South)	Old Dominion (25-4)	—		James Madison (18-8)	Old Dominion
Eastern Eight	Villanova (22-7)	7	3	—	Villanova
	Duquesne (17-9)	7	3		
	Rutgers (14-14)	7	3		
Ivy League	Pennsylvania (16-11)	12	3	Princeton (15-15)	—
Metro 7	Louisville (28-3)	12	0	Florida State (21-8) Virginia Tech (20-7)	Louisville
Mid-American	Toledo (23-5)	14	2	Bowling Green (20-9)	Toledo
Mid-Eastern Athletic	Howard (21-7)	—		Delaware State (15-12)	Howard
Midwestern City	Loyola (Chicago) (19-9)	5	0	Oral Roberts (18-10)	Oral Roberts
Missouri Valley	Bradley (23-9)	13	3	West Texas St. (19-10) Wichita State (17-11) Creighton (16-12)	Bradley
Ohio Valley	Murray State (21-7)	10	2	—	Western Kentucky
	Western Kentucky (21-7)	10	2		
Pacific Coast Athletic	Utah State (19-7)	11	2	Long Beach St. (20-11)	San Jose State (17-11)
Pacific 10	Oregon State (26-3)	16	2	Arizona State (21-6)	—
Southeastern	Kentucky (28-5)	15	3	Louisiana State (24-5)	Louisiana State
Southern	Furman (23-6)	14	1	Marshall (18-12)	Furman
Southland	Lamar (20-10)	8	2	S.W. Louisiana (19-8) McNeese State (15-12) Arkansas State (15-12)	—
Southwest	Texas A & M (24-7)	14	2	Arkansas (21-7)	Texas A & M
Southwestern Athletic	Alcorn State (27-1)	12	0	Grambling State (22-7)	Alcorn State
Sun Belt	South Alabama (23-5)	12	2	Ala.-Birmingham (18-11) Jacksonville (20-8)	Va. Commonwealth (18-11)
Trans-America	N.E. Louisiana (18-10)	6	0	Pan American (19-9)	Centenary (15-14)
West Coast Athletic	San Francisco (22-7)	11	5	Loyola Marymount (14-13)	Loyola Marymount
Western	Brigham Young (24-4)	13	1	Texas-El Paso (19-7) Utah (13-15)	—

MAJOR INDEPENDENTS (NCAA DIV. I)

Team	Won	Lost	Team	Won	Lost	Team	Won	Lost
DePaul	26	1	Cleveland State	18	8	Southern Mississippi	17	10
Notre Dame	22	5	Marquette	18	8	Arkansas-Little Rock	16	10
Tennessee State	20	6	Denver	18	8	East Carolina	16	11
Nevada-Las Vegas	20	7	Penn State	18	9	South Carolina	15	11
Illinois State	19	8	UNC-Wilmington	19	10			

NATIONAL COLLEGE TOURNAMENT CHAMPIONS

NCAA (Division I)

Year	Champion	Year	Champion
1951	Kentucky	1966	Texas Western
1952	Kansas	1967	UCLA
1953	Indiana	1968	UCLA
1954	LaSalle	1969	UCLA
1955	San Francisco	1970	UCLA
1956	San Francisco	1971	UCLA
1957	North Carolina	1972	UCLA
1958	Kentucky	1973	UCLA
1959	California	1974	N.C. State
1960	Ohio State	1975	UCLA
1961	Cincinnati	1976	Indiana
1962	Cincinnati	1977	Marquette
1963	Loyola (Chicago)	1978	Kentucky
1964	UCLA	1979	Michigan State
1965	UCLA	1980	Louisville

NIT

Year	Champion	Year	Champion
1951	Brigham Young	1966	Brigham Young
1952	LaSalle	1967	Southern Illinois
1953	Seton Hall	1968	Dayton
1954	Holy Cross	1969	Temple
1955	Duquesne	1970	Marquette
1956	Louisville	1971	North Carolina
1957	Bradley	1972	Maryland
1958	Xavier of Ohio	1973	Virginia Tech
1959	St. John's	1974	Purdue
1960	Bradley	1975	Princeton
1961	Providence College	1976	Kentucky
1962	Dayton	1977	St. Bonaventure
1963	Providence College	1978	Texas
1964	Bradley	1979	Indiana
1965	St. John's	1980	Virginia

NCAA (Division II)

Year	Champion	Year	Champion
1975	Old Dominion	1978	Cheyney St. (Pa.)
1976	Puget Sound	1979	North Alabama
1977	Tenn.-Chattanooga	1980	Virginia Union

NCAA (Division III)

Year	Champion	Year	Champion
1975	LeMoyne Owen	1978	North Park (Chicago)
1976	Scranton	1979	North Park (Chicago)
1977	Wittenberg	1980	North Park (Chicago)

1980 COLLEGE ALL-AMERICA SELECTIONS

Associated Press (AP), United Press (UPI), Sporting News (SN)

Player	Height	School	Class	Selected by	NBA Draft by
Joe Barry Carroll	7'1"	Purdue	Senior	AP, UPI, SN	Golden State
Mark Aguirre	6'7"	DePaul	Sophomore	AP, UPI, SN	—
Darrell Griffith	6'3"	Louisville	Senior	AP, UPI, SN	Utah
Kyle Macy	6'3"	Kentucky	Senior	AP, UPI, SN	Phoenix
Michael Brooks	6'7"	LaSalle	Senior	UPI, SN	San Diego
Albert King	6'6"	Maryland	Junior	AP	—

NCAA DIVISION I BASKETBALL RECORDS

SOURCE: N.C.A.A.

INDIVIDUAL

Scoring Average (Career) : 44.2, Maravich, LSU, 1968–70
Scoring Average (Season) : 44.5, Maravich, LSU, 1970
Scoring (Game) : 100 points, Selvy, Furman, 1954
Field Goals Attempted (Season) : 1168, Maravich, LSU, 1970
Field Goal Percentage (Season) : .710, Steve Johnson, Oregon State, 1980
Free Throws Attempted (Season) : 444, Selvy, Furman, 1954
Free Throw Percentage (Season) : .944, Gibson, Marshall, 1978
Rebounds (Season) : 734, Dukes, Seton Hall, 1953
Rebounds Per Game (Season) : 25.6, Slack, Marshall, 1955

TEAM

Points Per Game (Season) : 110.5, Nevada-Las Vegas, 1976
Field Goals Per Game (Season) : 46.3, Nevada-Las Vegas, 1976
Field Goal Percentage (Season) : .572, Missouri, 1980
Free Throw Percentage (Season) : .809, Ohio State, 1970
Least Points Allowed Per Game (Season) : 32.5, Oklahoma State, 1948

WOMEN'S BASKETBALL

WOMEN'S PROFESSIONAL LEAGUE (WBL) — 1979-80 FINAL STANDINGS

EASTERN DIVISION	Won	Lost	Pct.	G.B.
New York Stars	28	7	.800	—
New Orleans Pride	22	13	.629	6
New Jersey Gems	19	17	.528	9½
St. Louis Streak	15	21	.417	13½

WESTERN DIVISION	Won	Lost	Pct.	G.B.
Houston Angels	19	14	.576	—
San Francisco Pioneers	18	18	.500	2½
California Dreams	11	17	.393	5½
Dallas Diamonds	7	28	.200	13

MIDWEST DIVISION	Won	Lost	Pct.	G.B.
Iowa Cornets	24	12	.667	—
Minnesota Fillies	22	12	.647	1
Chicago Hustle	17	19	.472	7
Milwaukee Does	10	24	.294	13

Playoffs: San Francisco over Houston (2-1)
Minnesota over New Orleans (2-1)
Iowa over Minnesota (2-1)
New York over San Francisco (2-0)

Championship: New York over Iowa (3-1)

The Washington Metros (3-7) and Philadelphia Fox (2-8) withdrew from the league in December 1979.

WBL ALL-STARS

Alfreda Abernathy, Dallas
*Molly Bolin, Iowa
Doris Draving, Iowa
Rita Easterling, Chicago
Sharon Farrah, New York

Bertha Hardy, New Orleans
Marie Kocurek, Minnesota
Pat Mayo, San Francisco
Paula Mayo, Houston
Charlene McWhorter, Chicago

*Ann Meyers, New Jersey
Adrian Mitchell, St. Louis
Heidi Nestor, Milwaukee
Anita Ortega, San Francisco
Janice Thomas, New York

* Co-winners of the league's Most Valuable Player award.

A.I.A.W. COLLEGIATE CHAMPIONS — 1980

SOURCE: Association for Intercollegiate Athletics for Women

DIVISION I

Eastern Final: Tennessee 93, Maryland 76

Central Final: South Carolina 63, S.F. Austin 56

Southern Final: Old Dominion 84, Rutgers 62

Western Final: Louisian Tech 96, Long Beach State 78

Semifinals: Tennessee 75, South Carolina 72; Old Dominion 73, Louisiana Tech 59

National Championship: Old Dominion 68, Tennessee 53

Consolation: South Carolina 77, Louisiana Tech 69

DIVISION II

National Championship: Dayton 83, Charleston 53

Consolation: William Penn 77, Louisiana College 71

DIVISION III

National Championship: Worcester State 76, Wisconsin-LaCrosse 73

Consolation: Scranton 78, Mount Mercy 68

OTHER 1980 BASKETBALL CHAMPIONS

N.A.I.A. Tournament: Cameron University (Oklahoma)
National AAU: Men—Iowa City Airliner
        Women — 20th Century Blazers (Philadelphia)

PROFESSIONAL FOOTBALL

NATIONAL FOOTBALL LEAGUE
410 Park Avenue, New York City 10022.   Commissioner: Pete Rozelle.

NATIONAL FOOTBALL CONFERENCE (George Halas, Pres.)

Eastern Division	Chief Executive	Coach
Dallas Cowboys	Clint W. Murchison, Jr.	Tom Landry
New York Giants	Wellington T. Mara	Ray Perkins
Philadelphia Eagles	Leonard H. Tose	Dick Vermeil
St. Louis Cardinals	William V. Bidwill	Jim Hanifan
Washington Redskins	Edward B. Williams	Jack Pardee

Central Division		
Chicago Bears	George Halas, Sr.	Neill Armstrong
Detroit Lions	William Clay Ford	Monte Clark
Green Bay Packers	Dominic Olejniczak	Bart Starr
Minnesota Vikings	Max Winter	Bud Grant
Tampa Bay Buccaneers	Hugh Culverhouse	John McKay

Western Division		
Atlanta Falcons	Rankin M. Smith, Jr.	Leeman Bennett
Los Angeles Rams	Steve Rosenbloom	Ray Malavasi
New Orleans Saints	John W. Mecom, Jr.	Dick Nolan
San Francisco 49ers	Edward J. DeBartolo, Jr.	Bill Walsh

AMERICAN FOOTBALL CONFERENCE (Lamar Hunt, Pres.)

Eastern Division	Chief Executive	Coach
Baltimore Colts	Robert Irsay	Mike McCormack
Buffalo Bills	Ralph C. Wilson, Jr.	Chuck Knox
Miami Dolphins	Joseph Robbie	Don Shula
New England Patriots	William H. Sullivan	Ron Erhardt
New York Jets	James Kensil	Walt Michaels

Central Division		
Cincinnati Bengals	John Sawyer	Forrest Gregg
Cleveland Browns	Arthur B. Modell	Sam Rutigliano
Houston Oilers	K. S. Adams, Jr.	O. A. Phillips
Pittsburgh Steelers	Art Rooney	Chuck Noll

Western Division		
Denver Broncos	Gerald Phipps	Bob Miller
Kansas City Chiefs	Lamar Hunt	Marv Levy
Oakland Raiders	Al Davis	Tom Flores
San Diego Chargers	Eugene V. Klein	Don Coryell
Seattle Seahawks	Elmer Nordstrom	Jack Patera

PROFESSIONAL FOOTBALL HALL OF FAME (Canton, Ohio)

MEMBERS

Herb Adderly, Defensive Back, Green Bay Packers, 1961–69, Dallas Cowboys, 1970–72.

Lance Alworth, Wide Receiver, San Diego Chargers, 1962–70.

Cliff Battles, Back, 1932, Boston Braves; 1933–36, Boston Redskins; 1937, Washington Redskins.

Sammy Baugh, Quarterback, Washington Redskins, 1937–52.

Chuck Bednarik, Center and Linebacker, Philadelphia Eagles, 1949–62.

Bert Bell, Founder, Philadelphia Eagles, 1933, and Head Coach; Commissioner, National Football League, 1946–59.

Raymond Berry, End, Baltimore Colts, 1955–67.

Charles W. Bidwill, Founder, Chicago Cardinals, 1933–47

Jim Brown, Fullback, Cleveland Browns, 1957–65.

Paul E. Brown, Head Coach, Cleveland Browns, 1946–62; Cincinnati Bengals, 1968–75.

Roosevelt Brown, Tackle, N.Y. Giants, 1953–65.

Dick Butkus, Linebacker, Chicago Bears, 1965–73.

Tony Canadeo, Backfield, Green Bay Packers, 1940–52.

Joe Carr, Founder, Columbus Panhandles, 1904; Organizer, National Football League, 1920; President of League, 1921–39.

Guy Chamberlin, Head Coach, Halfback, End, Canton Bulldogs, Decatur Staleys, Cleveland Bulldogs, Frankford Yellowjackets, Chicago Cardinals, 1918–28.

Jack Christiansen, Defensive Back, Detroit Lions, 1951–58.

Dutch Clark, Quarterback and Head Coach, Portsmouth (O.) Spartans, Detroit Lions, Cleveland Rams, 1931–42.

George Connor, Tackle, Defensive Tackle, Linebacker, Chicago Bears, 1948–55.

Jimmy Conzelman, Head Coach, Halfback, Executive, Decatur Staleys, Rock Island Independents, Milwaukee Badgers, Detroit Panthers, Providence Steam Rollers, Chicago Cardinals, 1920–48.

Art Donovan, Tackle, 1950, Baltimore Colts; 1951, New York Yanks; 1952, Dallas Texans; 1953–61, Baltimore Colts.

Paddy Driscoll, Halfback and Head Coach, Chicago Cardinals and Chicago Bears, 1919–31, 1941–68.

Bill Dudley, Halfback, Pittsburgh Steelers, Detroit Lions, Washington Redskins, 1942, 1945–53.

Turk Edwards, Tackle, Washington Redskins, 1932–40.

Weeb Ewbank, Head Coach, 1954–62 Baltimore Colts; 1963–73, New York Jets

Tom Fears, End, Los Angeles Rams, 1948–56.

Ray Flaherty, End and Head Coach, New York Giants, New York Yankees, Boston & Washington Redskins, Chicago Hornets, 1928–49.

Len Ford, Defensive End, Los Angeles Dons, Cleveland Browns, Green Bay Packers, 1948–58.

Daniel J. Fortmann, M.D., Guard, Chicago Bears, 1936–46.

Bill George, Middle Linebacker, Chicago Bears, 1952–65.

Frank Gifford, Halfback, New York Giants, 1952–60, 1962–64.

Otto Graham, Quarterback, Cleveland Browns, 1946–55.

Red Grange, Halfback, Chicago Bears, New York Yankees, 1925–37.

Forrest Gregg, Tackle, 1956, 1958–70, Green Bay Packers; 1971, Dallas Cowboys.

Lou Groza, Tackle, Kicker, Cleveland Browns, 1946–67.

Joe Guyon, Halfback, Canton Bulldogs, Cleveland Indians, Oorang Indians, Rock Island Independents, Kansas City Cowboys, New York Giants, 1919–27.

George Halas, Founder, Head Coach, End, Decatur Staleys (1920) which became the Chicago Bears; retired as Bears' head coach in 1968.

Ed Healey, Tackle, Rock Island Independents, Chicago Bears, 1920–27.

Mel Hein, Center, New York Giants, 1931–45.

Pete Henry, Tackle, Canton Bulldogs, Akron, New York Giants, Pottsville Maroons, Staten Island Stapletons, 1920–30.

Arnie Herber, Halfback, Green Bay Packers, New York Giants, 1930–41, 1944–45.

Bill Hewitt, End, 1932–36, Chicago Bears; 1936–39, Philadelphia Eagles; 1943, Philadelphia-Pittsburgh.

Clarke Hinkle, Fullback, Green Bay Packers, 1932–41.

Elroy Hirsch, End, 1946–48, Chicago Rockets (AAFC); 1949–57, Los Angeles Rams; Rams' club executive, 1960–68.

Cal Hubbard, Tackle, New York Giants, Green Bay Packers, Pittsburgh Pirates, 1927–36.

Lamar Hunt, Founder, American Football League, 1959. Owner, Dallas Texans, 1960–1962, Kansas City Chiefs, 1963 to present.

Don Hutson, End, Green Bay Packers, 1935–45.

Deacon Jones, Defensive End, Los Angeles Rams, 1961–71, San Diego Chargers, 1972–73, Washington Redskins, 1974.

Walt Kiesling, Player-Coach, Duluth Eskimos, Pottsville Maroons, Boston Braves, Chicago Cardinals, Chicago Bears, Green Bay Packers, Pittsburgh Steelers, Philadelphia-Pittsburgh, Chicago-Pittsburgh, 1926–61.

Frank (Bruiser) Kinard, Tackle, 1938–43, Brooklyn Dodgers; 1944, Brooklyn Tigers; 1946–47, New York Yankees.

Curly Lambeau, Founder, Head Coach, Halfback, Green Bay Packers, 1919–49; also Head Coach of Chicago Cardinals and Washington Redskins, 1950–54.

Dick Lane, Defensive Back, Los Angeles Rams, Chicago Cardinals, Detroit Lions, 1952–65.

Yale Lary, Defensive Back, Detroit Lions, 1952–53, 1956–64.

Dante Lavelli, End, Cleveland Browns, 1946–56.

Bobby Layne, Quarterback, Chicago Bears, New York Bulldogs, Detroit Lions, Pittsburgh Steelers, 1948–62.

Alphonse (Tuffy) Leemans, Fullback, New York Giants, 1937–43

Bob Lilly, Defensive Tackle, Dallas Cowboys, 1961–74.

Vince Lombardi, Head Coach, 1959–67, Green Bay Packers; 1969, Washington Redskins.

Sid Luckman, Quarterback, Chicago Bears, 1939–50.

Link Lyman, Tackle, Canton Bulldogs, Cleveland Bulldogs, Chicago Bears, 1922–34.

Tim Mara, Founder, New York Giants, 1925.

Gino Marchetti, Defensive End, Dallas Texans, 1952; Baltimore Colts, 1953–1964–1966.

George P. Marshall, Founder, Washington Redskins (as Boston Braves) in 1932.

Ollie Matson, Halfback, Chicago Cardinals, 1952, 1954–1958, Los Angeles Rams, 1959–1962, Detroit Lions, 1963, Philadelphia Eagles, 1964–1966.

George McAfee, Halfback, Chicago Bears, 1940–41, 1945–50.

Hugh McElhenny, Halfback, San Francisco 49ers, Minnesota Vikings, New York Giants, Detroit Lions, 1952–64.

John Blood McNally, Halfback, Milwaukee Badgers, Duluth Eskimos, Pottsville Maroons, Green Bay Packers, Pittsburgh Steelers, 1925–39.

Mike Michalske, Guard, New York Yankees, Green Bay Packers, 1926–37.

Wayne Millner, End, 1936, Boston Redskins; 1937–41, 1945 Washington Redskins.

Ron Mix, Tackle, Los Angeles-San Diego Chargers, 1960–69, Oakland Raiders, 1971.

Lenny Moore, Running Back, Baltimore Colts, 1956–67.

Marlon Motley, Fullback, 1946–53, Cleveland Browns; 1955, Pittsburgh Steelers.

Bronko Nagurski, Fullback and Tackle, Chicago Bears, 1930–37, 1943.

Earl (Greasy) Neale, Head Coach, Philadelphia Eagles, 1941–50.

Ernie Nevers, Fullback and Head Coach, Duluth Eskimos, Chicago Cardinals, 1926–31, 1939.

Ray Nitschke, Linebacker, Green Bay Packers, 1958–72.

Leo Nomellini, Defensive Tackle, San Francisco 49ers, 1950–63.

Jim Otto, Center, Oakland Raiders, 1960–74.

Steve Owen, Player-Coach, Kansas City Cowboys, New York Giants, 1924–53.

Ace Parker, Quarterback, Brooklyn Dodgers, 1937–1941, Boston Yanks, 1945, New York Yankees (AAFC), 1946.

Jim Parker, Tackle, Baltimore Colts, 1957–67.

Joe Perry, Fullback, San Francisco 49ers, Baltimore Colts, 1949–63.

Pete Pihos, End, Philadelphia Eagles, 1947–55.

Hugh (Shorty) Ray, National Football League technical adviser and supervisor of officials, 1938–56.

Dan Reeves, Founder, Cleveland Rams, 1941 (moved to Los Angeles in 1946).

Andy Robustelli, Defensive End, 1951–55, Los Angeles Rams; 1956–64, New York Giants.

Art Rooney, Founder, Pittsburgh Steelers, 1933.

Gale Sayers, Running Back, 1965–1971, Chicago Bears.

Joe Schmidt, Linebacker, Detroit Lions, 1953–65.

Bart Starr, Quarterback, Green Bay Packers, 1956–71.

Ernie Stautner, Defensive End, Pittsburgh Steelers, 1950–63.

Ken Strong, Halfback, Staten Island Stapletons, New York Giants, New York Yankees, 1929–37, 1939, 1944–47.

Joe Stydahar, Tackle, Chicago Bears, 1936–42, 1945–46. Head Coach of Los Angeles Rams, 1950–51; Head Coach of Chicago Cardinals, 1953–54.

Jim Taylor, Fullback, Green Bay Packers, New Orleans Saints, 1958–67.

Jim Thorpe, Halfback, Canton Bulldogs, Pine Village (Ind.) A. A., Oorang Indians, Toledo Maroons, Rock Island Independents, New York Giants, 1915–26; President of American Professional Football Association, forerunner of N.F.L., 1920.

Y. A. Tittle, Quarterback, 1948–50, Baltimore Colts; 1951–60, San Francisco 49ers; 1961–64, New York Giants.

George Trafton, Center, Chicago Bears, 1920–32.

Charley Trippi, Halfback-Quarterback, 1947–55, Chicago Cardinals.

Emlen Tunnell, Halfback, New York Giants, Green Bay Packers, 1946–61.

Clyde (Bulldog) Turner, Center, Chicago Bears, 1940–52.

Johnny Unitas, Quarterback, Baltimore Colts, 1956–72, San Diego Chargers, 1973.

Norm Van Brocklin, Quarterback, 1949–57, Los Angeles Rams; 1958–60, Philadelphia Eagles.

Steve Van Buren, Halfback, Philadelphia Eagles, 1944–51.

Bob Waterfield, Quarterback, Cleveland and Los Angeles Rams, 1945–52; Head Coach of Rams, 1960–62.

Bill Willis, Guard, 1946–53, Cleveland Browns.

Larry Wilson, Defensive Back, St. Louis Cardinals, 1960–72

Alex Wojciechowicz, Center and Linebacker, 1938–46, Detroit Lions; 1946–50, Philadelphia Eagles.

NATIONAL FOOTBALL LEAGUE RECORDS   Source: Elias Sports Bureau and N.F.L.

Through 1979 season; includes all performonces in American Football League (1960–69)

Most Points, Lifetime: 2,002, George Blanda, Chicago Bears, Baltimore, Houston, Oakland

Most Points, Season: 176, Paul Hornung, Green Bay, 1960

Most Points, Game: 40, Ernie Nevers, Chicago Cards vs. Chicago Bears, November 28, 1929

Most Touchdowns, Lifetime: 126, Jim Brown, Cleveland

Most Touchdowns, Season: 23, O. J. Simpson, Buffalo, 1975.

Most Yards Gained Rushing, Lifetime: 12,312, Jim Brown, Cleveland, 1957–65

Most Yards Gained Rushing, Season: 2,003, O. J. Simpson, Buffalo, 1973

Most Yards Gained Rushing, Game: 275, Walter Payton, Chicago vs. Minnesota, Nov. 20, 1977

Highest Average Gain Rushing, Lifetime: 5.22, Jim Brown, Cleveland

Highest Average Gain Rushing, Season: 9.94, Beattie Feathers, Chicago, 1934; 6.87, Bobby Douglass, Chicago, 1972

Most Touchdowns Rushing, Lifetime: 106, Jim Brown, Cleveland

Most Touchdowns Rushing, Season: 19, Jim Taylor, Green Bay, 1962

Most Passes Completed, Lifetime: 3,686, Fran Tarkenton, Minnesota, New York Giants, Minnesota

Most Passes Completed, Season: 347, Steve DeBerg, San Francisco, 1979

Most Passes Completed, Game: 37, George Blanda, Houston, 1964

Passing Percent (Attempts-Completions), Lifetime: 59.61, Ken Stabler, Oakland

Passing Percent (Attempts-Completions), Season: 70.33, Sammy Baugh, Washington, 1945

Most Yards Gained Passing, Lifetime: 47,003, Fran Tarkenton, Minnesota, New York Giants, Minnesota

Most Yards Gained Passing, Season: 4,082, Dan Fouts, San Diego, 1979

Most Yards Gained Passing, Game: 554, Norm Van Brocklin, Los Angeles, 1951

Most Touchdown Passes, Lifetime: 342, Fran Tarkenton, Minnesota, New York Giants, Minnesota

Lowest Interception Percent, Lifetime: 3.31, Roman Gabriel, Los Angeles, Philadelphia

Receptions, Most Yards Gained, Lifetime: 11,834, Don Maynard, New York Giants, New York Jets, St. Louis

Receptions, Most Yards Gained, Season: 1,746, Charlie Hennigan, Houston, 1961

Receptions, Most Touchdowns, Lifetime: 99, Don Hutson, Green Bay

Receptions, Most Touchdowns, Season: 17, Don Hutson, Green Bay, 1942; 17, Elroy Hirsch, Los Angeles, 1951; 17, Bill Groman, Houston, 1961

Most Receptions, Lifetime: 649, Charley Taylor, Washington

Interceptions, Most Touchdowns from, Lifetime: 9, Ken Houston, Washington

Most Points After Touchdown, Lifetime: 943, George Blanda, Chicago Bears, Baltimore, Houston, Oakland

Most Points After Touchdown, Season: 64, George Blanda, Houston, 1961

Most Consecutive Points After Touchdown: 234, Tommy Davis, San Francisco, 1959–65

Most Field Goals, Lifetime: 335, George Blanda, Chicago Bears, Baltimore, Houston, Oakland

Most Field Goals, Season: 34, Jim Turner, New York Jets, 1968

Most Field Goals, Game: 7, Jim Bakken, St. Louis vs. Pittsburgh, September 24, 1967

Longest Field Goal: 63 yards, Tom Dempsey, New Orleans vs. Detroit, November 8, 1970

Most Consecutive Field Goals: 20, Garo Yepremian, Miami, 1978; New Orleans, 1979

Longest Punt: 98, Steve O'Neal, New York Jets, 1969

Highest Punting Average, Lifetime: 45.10, Sammy Baugh, Washington; 44.68, Tommy Davis, San Francisco

Most Punt Returns, Lifetime: 258, Em Tunnell, New York Giants and Green Bay

Punt Returns, Most Yardage Gained, Lifetime: 2,298, Rick Upchurch, Denver, 1975–79

Punt Returns, Highest Average, Season: 23.00, Herb Rich, Baltimore, 1950

Kickoff Returns, Most Yards Gained, Lifetime: 6,922, Ron Smith, Chicago, Atlanta, Los Angeles, San Diego, Oakland

Kickoff Returns, Highest Average Yardage Gained, Lifetime: 30.56, Gale Sayers, Chicago

Kickoff Returns, Highest Average Yardage Gained, Season: 41.06, Travis Williams, Green Bay, 1967

Most Seasons, Active Player: 26, George Blanda, Chicago Bears, Baltimore, Houston, Oakland

Most Games Played, Lifetime: 340, George Blanda, Chicago Bears, Baltimore, Houston, Oakland

Most Seasons NFL Champion Team: 11, Green Bay, 1929-1931, 1936, 1939, 1944, 1961-1962, 1965-1967.

Team, Most Consecutive Victories, Regular Season: 17, Chicago Bears, 1933-1934

Most Fumbles, Season: 17, Dan Pastorini, Houston, 1973

Most Fumbles, Game: 7, Len Dawson, Kansas City, 1964

NATIONAL FOOTBALL LEAGUE ALL-TIME LEADERS

Rushing Yardage		Pass Receptions		Points		Interceptions	
12,312	Jim Brown	649	Charley Taylor	2,002	George Blanda	79	Emlen Tunnell
11,236	O. J. Simpson	633	Don Maynard	1,439	Jim Turner	78	Paul Krause
8,597	Jim Taylor	631	Raymond Berry	1,380	Jim Bakken	68	Night Train Lane

NFL FINAL 1979 STANDINGS

AMERICAN FOOTBALL CONFERENCE

EASTERN DIVISION

	W	L	T	Pct.	Pts.	OP
Miami	10	6	0	.625	341	257
New England	9	7	0	.563	411	326
N.Y. Jets	8	8	0	.500	337	383
Buffalo	7	9	0	.438	268	279
Baltimore	5	11	0	.313	271	351

CENTRAL DIVISION

	W	L	T	Pct.	Pts.	OP
Pittsburgh	12	4	0	.750	416	262
*Houston	11	5	0	.688	362	331
Cleveland	9	7	0	.563	359	352
Cincinnati	4	12	0	.250	337	421

WESTERN DIVISION

	W	L	T	Pct.	Pts.	OP
San Diego	12	4	0	.750	411	246
*Denver	10	6	0	.625	289	262
Oakland	9	7	0	.563	365	337
Seattle	9	7	0	.563	378	372
Kansas City	7	9	0	.438	238	262

NATIONAL FOOTBALL CONFERENCE

EASTERN DIVISION

	W	L	T	Pct.	Pts.	OP
Dallas	11	5	0	.688	371	313
*Philadelphia	11	5	0	.688	339	282
Washington	10	6	0	.625	348	295
N.Y. Giants	6	10	0	.375	237	323
St. Louis	5	11	0	.313	307	358

CENTRAL DIVISION

	W	L	T	Pct.	Pts.	OP
Tampa Bay	10	6	0	.625	273	237
*Chicago	10	6	0	.625	306	249
Minnesota	7	9	0	.438	259	337
Green Bay	5	11	0	.313	246	316
Detroit	2	14	0	.125	219	365

WESTERN DIVISION

	W	L	T	Pct.	Pts.	OP
Los Angeles	9	7	0	.563	323	309
New Orleans	8	8	0	.500	370	360
Atlanta	6	10	0	.375	300	388
San Francisco	2	14	0	.125	308	416

*Wild card qualifiers

POST-SEASON GAMES

	AMERICAN CONFERENCE	NATIONAL CONFERENCE
WILD CARD TEAMS	Houston 13, Denver 7	Philadelphia 27, Chicago 17
DIVISION PLAYOFFS	Houston 17, San Diego 14 Pittsburgh 34, Miami 14	Tampa Bay 24, Philadelphia 17 Los Angeles 21, Dallas 19
CONFERENCE CHAMPIONSHIP	Pittsburgh 27, Houston 13	Los Angeles 9, Tampa Bay 0
LEAGUE CHAMPIONSHIP (SUPER BOWL)		Pittsburgh 31, Los Angeles 19

1979 INDIVIDUAL LEADERS

RUSHING-AFC

	Att.	Yds.	Avg.	TDs.
Campbell, Houston	368	1697	4.6	19
M. Pruitt, CLeveland	264	1294	4.9	9
Harris, Pittsburgh	267	1186	4.4	11
Gaines, New York	186	905	4.9	0
Washington, Baltimore	242	884	3.7	4

RUSHING-NFC

	Att.	Yds.	Avg.	TDs.
Payton, Chicago	369	1610	4.4	14
Anderson, St. Louis	331	1605	4.8	8
Montgomery, Philadelphia	338	1512	4.5	9
Bell, Tampa Bay	283	1263	4.5	7
Muncie, New Orleans	238	1198	5.0	11

PASSING-AFC

	Att.	Comp.	Yds.	Int.	TDs.
Fouts, San Diego	530	332	4082	24	24
Stabler, Oakland	498	304	3615	22	26
Anderson, Cincinnati	339	189	2340	10	16
Zorn, Seattle	505	285	3661	18	20
Grogan, New England	423	206	3286	20	28

PASSING-NFC

	Att.	Comp.	Yds.	Int.	TDs.
Staubach, Dallas	461	267	3586	11	27
Theisman, Washington	395	233	2797	13	20
Jaworski, Philadelphia	374	190	2669	12	18
Manning, New Orleans	420	252	3169	20	15
DeBerg, San Francisco	578	347	3652	21	17

RECEIVING-AFC

	No.	Yds.	Avg.	Tds.
Washington, Baltimore	82	750	9.1	3
Joiner, San Diego	72	1008	14.0	4
Stallworth, Pittsburgh	70	1183	16.9	8
Largent, Seattle	66	1237	18.7	9
Upchurch, Denver	64	937	14.6	7

RECEIVING-NFC

	No.	Yds.	Avg.	Tds.
Rashad, Minnesota	80	1156	14.5	9
Francis, Atlanta	74	1013	13.7	8
Young, Minnesota	72	519	7.2	4
Chandler, New Orleans	65	1069	16.4	6
Scott, Detroit	62	929	15.0	5

INTERCEPTIONS-AFC

	No.	Yds.	Long	TDs.
Reinfeldt, Houston	12	205	39	0

INTERCEPTIONS-NFC

	No.	Yds.	Long	TDs.
Parrish, Washington	9	65	23	0

PUNTING-AFC

	No.	Yds.	Avg.	Long
Grupp, Kansas City	89	3883	43.6	74

PUNTING-NFC

	No.	Yds.	Avg.	Long
Jennings, New York	104	4445	42.7	72

SCORING-KICKING

	XP	FG	Pts.
Smith, New England	46	23	115

SCORING-KICKING

	XP	FG	Pts.
Moseley, Washington	39	25	114

ALL-PRO SELECTIONS (AP) Associated Press, (UPI) United Press International

Offense

Quarterback	—Dan Fouts, San Diego (AP, UPI)
Running backs	—Earl Campbell, Houston (AP, UPI)
	—Ottis Anderson, St. Louis (AP)
	—Mike Pruitt, Cleveland (UPI)
Wide receivers	—John Stallworth, Pittsburgh (AP, UPI)
	—John Jefferson, San Diego (AP, UPI)
Tight end	—Dave Casper, Oakland (AP)
	—Ozzie Newsome, Cleveland (UPI)
Center	—Mike Webster, Pittsburgh (AP, UPI)
Guards	—John Hannah, New England (AP, UPI)
	—Bob Young, St. Louis (AP)
	—Joe DeLamielleure, Buffalo (UPI)
Tackles	—Marvin Powell, New York Jets (AP, UPI)
	—Leon Gray, Houston (AP, UPI)
Place kicker	—Toni Fritsch, Houston (AP, UPI)
Punter	—Dave Jennings, New York Giants (AP)
	—Bob Grupp, Kansas City (UPI)

Defense

Ends	—Lee Roy Selmon, Tampa Bay (AP)
	—Jack Youngblood, Los Angeles (AP)
	—L.C. Greenwood, Pittsburgh (UPI)
	—Fred Dean, San Diego (UPI)
Tackles	—Randy White, Dallas (AP)
	—Larry Brooks, Los Angeles (AP)
	—Joe Greene, Pittsburgh (UPI)
	—Wilbur Young, San Diego (UPI)
Middle linebacker	—Jack Lambert, Pittsburgh (AP, UPI)
Outside linebackers	—Robert Brazile, Houston (AP, UPI)
	—Jack Ham, Pittsburgh (AP, UPI)
Cornerbacks	—Louis Wright, Denver (AP, UPI)
	—Lemar Parrish, Washington (AP)
	—Mike Haynes, New England (UPI)
Free safety	—Mike Reinfeldt, Houston (AP, UPI)
Strong safety	—Donnie Shell, Pittsburgh (AP)
	—Bill Thompson, Denver (UPI)

CHAMPIONSHIP GAMES

NATIONAL FOOTBALL LEAGUE

1933 Dec. Chicago Bears 23, New York Giants 21
1934 Dec. New York Giants 30, Chicago Bears 13
1935 Dec. Detroit Lions 26, New York Giants 7
1936 Dec. Green Bay Packers 21, Washington Redskins 6
1937 Dec. Washington Redskins 28, Chicago Bears 21
1938 Dec. New York Giants 23, Green Bay Packers 17
1939 Dec. Green Bay Packers 27, New York Giants 0
1940 Dec. Chicago Bears 73, Washington Redskins 0
1941 Dec. Chicago Bears 37, New York Giants 9
1942 Dec. Washington Redskins 14, Chicago Bears 6
1943 Dec. Chicago Bears 41, Washington Redskins 21
1944 Dec. Green Bay Packers 14, New York Giants 7
1945 Dec. Cleveland Rams 15, Washington Redskins 14
1946 Dec. Chicago Bears 24, New York Giants 14
1947 Dec. Chicago Cardinals 28, Philadelphia Eagles 21
1948 Dec. Philadelphia Eagles 7, Chicago Cardinals 0
1949 Dec. Philadelphia Eagles 14, Los Angeles Rams 0
1950 Dec. Cleveland Browns 30, Los Angeles Rams 28
1951 Dec. Los Angeles Rams 24, Cleveland Browns 17
1952 Dec. Detroit Lions 17, Cleveland Browns 7
1953 Dec. Detroit Lions 17, Cleveland Browns 16
1954 Dec. Cleveland Browns 56, Detroit Lions 10
1955 Dec. Cleveland Browns 38, Los Angeles Rams 14
1956 Dec. New York Giants 47, Chicago Bears 7
1957 Dec. Detroit Lions 59, Cleveland Browns 14
1958 Dec. Baltimore Colts 23, New York Giants 17
1959 Dec. Baltimore Colts 31, New York Giants 16
1960 Dec. Philadelphia Eagles 17, Green Bay Packers 13
1961 Dec. Green Bay Packers 37, New York Giants 0
1962 Dec. Green Bay Packers 16, New York Giants 7
1963 Dec. Chicago Bears 14, New York Giants 10
1964 Dec. Cleveland Browns 27, Baltimore Colts 0
1966 Jan. Green Bay Packers 23, Cleveland Browns 12
1967 Jan. Green Bay Packers 34, Dallas Cowboys 27
1967 Dec. Green Bay Packers 21, Dallas Cowboys 17
1968 Dec. Baltimore Colts 34, Cleveland Browns 0
1970 Jan. Minnesota Vikings 27, Cleveland Browns 7

NATIONAL FOOTBALL CONFERENCE

1971 Jan. Dallas Cowboys 17, San Francisco 49ers 10
1972 Jan. Dallas Cowboys 14, San Francisco 49ers 3
1972 Dec. Washington Redskins 26, Dallas Cowboys 3
1973 Dec. Minnesota Vikings 27, Dallas Cowboys 10
1974 Dec. Dallas Cowboys 37, Los Angeles Rams 7
1976 Jan. Minnesota Vikings 14, Los Angeles Rams 10
1976 Dec. Minnesota Vikings 24, Los Angeles Rams 13
1978 Jan. Dallas Cowboys 23, Minnesota Vikings 6
1979 Jan. Dallas Cowboys 28, Los Angeles Rams 0
1980 Jan. Los Angeles Rams 9, Tampa Bay Buccaneers 0

AMERICAN FOOTBALL LEAGUE

1961 Jan. Houston Oilers 24, San Diego Chargers 16
1961 Dec. Houston Oilers 10, San Diego Chargers 3
1962 Dec. Kansas City Chiefs 20, Houston Oilers 17
1964 Jan. San Diego Chargers 51, Boston Patriots 10
1964 Dec. Buffalo Bills 20, San Diego Chargers 7
1965 Dec. Buffalo Bills 23, San Diego Chargers 0
1967 Jan. Kansas City Chiefs 31, Buffalo Bills 7
1967 Dec. Oakland Raiders 40, Houston Oilers 7
1968 Dec. New York Jets 27, Oakland Raiders 23
1970 Jan. Kansas City Chiefs 17, Oakland Raiders 7

AMERICAN FOOTBALL CONFERENCE

1971 Jan. Baltimore Colts 27, Oakland Raiders 17
1972 Jan. Miami Dolphins 21, Baltimore Colts 0
1972 Dec. Miami Dolphins 21, Pittsburgh Steelers 17
1973 Dec. Miami Dolphins 27, Oakland Raiders 10
1974 Dec. Pittsburgh Steelers 24, Oakland Raiders 13
1976 Jan. Pittsburgh Steelers 16, Oakland Raiders 10
1976 Dec. Oakland Raiders 24, Pittsburgh Steelers 7
1978 Jan. Denver Broncos 20, Oakland Raiders 17
1979 Jan. Pittsburgh Steelers 34, Houston Oilers 5
1980 Jan. Pittsburgh Steelers 27, Houston Oilers 13

SUPER BOWL GAMES

I Jan. 15, 1967—Memorial Coliseum, Los Angeles

Green Bay Packers (NFL)	7	7	14	7–35
Kansas City Chiefs (AFL)	0	10	0	0–10

II Jan. 14, 1968—Orange Bowl, Miami

Green Bay Packers (NFL)	3	13	10	7–33
Oakland Raiders (AFL)	0	7	0	7–14

III Jan. 12, 1969—Orange Bowl, Miami

New York Jets (AFL)	0	7	6	3–16
Baltimore Colts (NFL)	0	0	0	7–7

IV Jan. 11, 1970—Tulane Stadium, New Orleans

Kansas City Chiefs (AFL)	3	13	7	0–23
Minnesota Vikings (NFL)	0	0	7	0–7

V Jan. 17, 1971—Orange Bowl, Miami

Baltimore Colts (AFC)	0	6	0	10–16
Dallas Cowboys (NFC)	3	10	0	0–13

VI Jan. 16, 1972—Tulane Stadium, New Orleans

Dallas Cowboys (NFC)	3	7	7	7–24
Miami Dolphins (AFC)	0	3	0	0–3

VII Jan. 14, 1973—Memorial Coliseum, Los Angeles

Miami Dolphins (AFC)	7	7	0	0–14
Washington Redskins (NFC)	0	0	0	7–7

VIII Jan. 13, 1974—Rice Stadium, Houston

Miami Dolphins (AFC)	14	3	7	0–24
Minnesota Vikings (NFC)	0	0	0	7–7

IX Jan. 12, 1975—Tulane Stadium, New Orleans

Pittsburgh Steelers (AFC)	0	2	7	7–16
Minnesota Vikings (NFC)	0	0	0	6–6

X Jan. 18, 1976—Orange Bowl, Miami

Pittsburgh Steelers (AFC)	7	0	0	14–21
Dallas Cowboys (NFC)	7	3	0	7–17

XI Jan. 9, 1977—Rose Bowl, Pasadena

Oakland Raiders (AFC)	0	16	3	13–32
Minnesota Vikings (NFC)	0	0	7	7–14

XII Jan. 15, 1978—Superdome, New Orleans

Dallas Cowboys (NFC)	10	3	7	7–27
Denver Broncos (AFC)	0	0	10	0–10

XIII Jan. 21, 1979—Orange Bowl, Miami

Pittsburgh Steelers (AFC)	7	14	0	14–35
Dallas Cowboys (NFC)	7	7	3	14–31

XIV Jan. 20, 1980—Rose Bowl, Pasadena

Pittsburgh Steelers (AFC)	3	7	7	14–31
Los Angeles Rams (NFC)	7	6	6	0–19

Pitt—FG, Bahr, 41
LA—Bryant, 1, run (Corral kick)
Pitt—Harris, 1, run (Bahr kick)
LA—FG, Corral, 31
LA—FG, Corral, 45
Pitt—Swann, 47, pass from Bradshaw (Bahr kick)
LA—R. Smith, 24, pass from McCutcheon (kick failed)
Pitt—Stallworth, 73, pass from Bradshaw (Bahr kick)
Pitt—Harris, 1, run (Bahr kick)

TEAM DEPARTMENTAL CHAMPIONS

Total Yards Gained		Yards Rushing		Yards Passing		Points Scored	
1979–Pittsburgh (AFC)	6,258	1979–New York (AFC)	2,646	1979–San Diego (AFC)	3,915	1979–Pittsburgh (AFC)	416
1978–New England (AFC)	5,965	1978–New England (AFC)	3,165	1978–San Diego (AFC)	3,375	1978–Dallas (NFC)	384
1977–Dallas (NFC)	4,812	1977–Chicago (NFC)	2,811	1977–Buffalo (AFC)	2,530	1977–Oakland (AFC)	351
1976–Baltimore (AFC)	5,236	1976–Pittsburgh (AFC)	2,971	1976–Baltimore (AFC)	2,933	1976–Baltimore (AFC)	417
1975–Buffalo (AFC)	5,467	1975–Buffalo (AFC)	2,974	1975–Cincinnati (AFC)	3,241	1975–Buffalo (AFC)	420
1974–Dallas (NFC)	4,983	1974–Pittsburgh (AFC)	2,417	1974–Washington (NFC)	2,978	1974–Oakland (AFC)	355
1973–Los Angeles (NFC)	4,906	1973–Buffalo (AFC)	3,088	1973–Philadelphia (NFC)	3,236	1973–Dallas (AFC)	388
1972–Miami	5,036	1972–Miami (AFC)	2,960	1972–New York Jets (AFC)	2,777	1972–Miami (AFC)	385
1971–Dallas (NFC)	5,035	1971–Miami (AFC)	2,429	1971–San Diego (AFC)	3,134	1971–Dallas (NFC)	406
1970–Oakland (AFC)	4,829	1970–Dallas (NFC)	2,300	1970–San Francisco (NFC)	2,923	1970–San Francisco (NFC)	352
1969–Dallas (NFL)	5,122	1969–Dallas (NFL)	2,276	1969–Oakland (AFL)	3,271	1969–Minnesota (NFL)	379
1968–Oakland (AFL)	5,696	1968–Chicago (NFL)	2,377	1968–San Diego (AFL)	3,623	1968–Oakland (AFL)	453
1967–New York (AFL)	5,152	1967–Cleveland (NFL)	2,139	1967–New York (AFL)	3,845	1967–Oakland (AFL)	468
1966–Dallas (NFL)	5,145	1966–Kansas City (AFL)	2,274	1966–New York (AFL)	3,464	1966–Kansas City (AFL)	448
1965–San Francisco (NFL)	5,270	1965–Cleveland (NFL)	2,331	1965–San Francisco (NFL)	3,487	1965–San Francisco (NFL)	421
1964–Buffalo (AFL)	5,206	1964–Green Bay (NFL)	2,276	1964–Houston (AFL)	3,527	1964–Baltimore (NFL)	428
1963–San Diego (AFL)	5,153	1963–Cleveland (NFL)	2,639	1963–Baltimore (NFL)	3,296	1963–New York (NFL)	448
1962–New York (NFL)	5,005	1962–Buffalo (AFL)	2,480	1962–Denver (AFL)	3,404	1962–Green Bay (NFL)	415
1961–Houston (AFL)	6,288	1961–Green Bay (NFL)	2,350	1961–Houston (AFL)	4,392	1961–Houston (AFL)	513
1960–Houston (AFL)	4,936	1960–St. Louis (NFL)	2,356	1960–Houston (AFL)	3,203	1960–New York (AFL)	382
1959–Baltimore	4,458	1959–Cleveland	2,149	1959–Baltimore	2,753	1959–Baltimore	374
1958–Baltimore	4,539	1958–Cleveland	2,526	1958–Pittsburgh	2,752	1958–Baltimore	381
1957–Los Angeles	4,143	1957–Los Angeles	2,142	1957–Baltimore	2,388	1957–Los Angeles	307
1956–Chicago Bears	4,537	1956–Chicago Bears	2,468	1956–Los Angeles	2,419	1956–Chicago Bears	363
1955–Chicago Bears	4,316	1955–Chicago Bears	2,388	1955–Philadelphia	2,472	1955–Cleveland	349
1954–Los Angeles	5,187	1954–San Francisco	2,498	1954–Chicago Bears	3,104	1954–Detroit	337
1953–Philadelphia	4,811	1953–San Francisco	2,230	1953–Philadelphia	3,089	1953–San Francisco	372
1952–Cleveland	4,352	1952–San Francisco	1,905	1952–Cleveland	2,566	1952–Los Angeles	349
1951–Los Angeles	5,506	1951–Chicago Bears	2,408	1951–Los Angeles	3,296	1951–Los Angeles	392
1950–Los Angeles	5,420	1950–New York Giants	2,336	1950–Los Angeles	3,709	1950–Los Angeles	466
1949–Chicago Bears	4,873	1949–Philadelphia	2,607	1949–Chicago Bears	3,055	1949–Philadelphia	364
1948–Chicago Cards	4,705	1948–Chicago Cards	2,560	1948–Washington	2,861	1948–Chicago Cards	395
1947–Chicago Bears	5,053	1947–Los Angeles	2,171	1947–Washington	3,336	1947–Chicago Bears	363
1946–Los Angeles	3,793	1946–Green Bay	1,765	1946–Los Angeles	2,080	1946–Chicago Bears	289
1945–Washington	3,549	1945–Cleveland Rams	1,714	1945–Chicago Bears	1,857	1945–Philadelphia	272
1944–Chicago Bears	3,239	1944–Philadelphia	1,661	1944–Washington	2,021	1944–Philadelphia	267
1943–Chicago Bears	4,045	1943–Phil-Pitt	1,730	1943–Chicago Bears	2,310	1943–Chicago Bears	303
1942–Chicago Bears	3,900	1942–Chicago Bears	1,881	1942–Green Bay	2,407	1942–Chicago Bears	376
1941–Chicago Bears	4,265	1941–Chicago Bears	2,263	1941–Chicago Bears	2,002	1941–Chicago Bears	396
1940–Green Bay	3,400	1940–Chicago Bears	1,818	1940–Washington	1,887	1940–Washington	245
1939–Chicago Bears	3,988	1939–Chicago Bears	2,043	1939–Chicago Bears	1,965	1939–Chicago Bears	298
1938–Green Bay	3,037	1938–Detroit	1,893	1938–Washington	1,536	1938–Green Bay	223
1937–Green Bay	3,201	1937–Detroit	2,074	1937–Green Bay	1,398	1937–Green Bay	220
1936–Detroit	3,703	1936–Detroit	2,885	1936–Green Bay	1,629	1936–Green Bay	248
1935–Chicago Bears	3,454	1935–Chicago Bears	2,096	1935–Green Bay	1,449	1935–Chicago Bears	192
1934–Chicago Bears	3,750	1934–Chicago Bears	2,847	1934–Green Bay	1,165	1934–Chicago Bears	286
1933–New York Giants	2,970	1933–Boston Redskins	2,260	1933–New York	1,348	1933–New York Giants	244
1932–Chicago Bears	2,755	1932–Chicago Bears	1,770	1932–Chicago Bears	1,013	1932–Green Bay	152

Since 1952 based on net yards.

NATIONAL FOOTBALL LEAGUE STARS: BY YEARS

PASSERS

PASSERS	Passes	Comp	Yards	Tds	Inter.
1979—Roger Staubach, Dallas (NFC)	461	267	3,586	27	11
1978—Roger Staubach, Dallas (NFC)	413	231	3,190	25	16
1977—Bob Griese, Miami (AFC)	307	180	2,252	22	13
1976—Ken Stabler, Oakland (AFC)	291	194	2,737	27	17
1975—Ken Anderson, Cincinnati (AFC)	377	228	3,169	21	11
1974—Ken Anderson, Cincinnati (AFC)	328	213	2,667	18	10
1973—Roger Staubach, Dallas Cowboys (NFC)	286	179	2,428	23	15
1972—Norm Snead, New York Giants (NFC)	325	196	2,307	17	12
1971—Bob Griese, Miami (AFC)	263	145	2,089	19	9
1970—John Brodie, San Francisco (NFC)	378	223	2,941	24	10
1969—C. A. (Sonny) Jurgensen, Wash. (NFL)	442	274	3,102	22	15
1968—Earl Morrall, Baltimore (NFL)	317	182	2,909	26	17
1967—C. A. (Sonny) Jurgensen, Wash. (NFL)	508	288	3,747	31	16
1966—Len Dawson, Kansas City (AFL)	284	159	2,527	26	10
1965—John Hadl, San Diego (AFL)	348	174	2,798	20	21
1964—Len Dawson, Kansas City (AFL)	354	199	2,879	30	18
1963—Y. A. Tittle, New York (NFL)	367	221	3,145	36	14
1962—Len Dawson, Dallas (AFL)	310	189	2,759	29	17
1961—George Blanda, Houston (AFL)	362	187	3,330	36	22
1960—Jack Kemp, Los Angeles (AFL)	406	211	3,018	20	25
1959—Charles Conerly, N.Y.	194	113	1,706	14	4
1958—Eddie LeBaron, Wash.	145	79	1,365	11	10
1957—Tommy O'Connell, Cleveland	110	63	1,229	9	8
1956—Eddie Brown, Chicago	168	96	1,667	11	12
1955—Otto Graham, Cleveland	185	98	1,721	15	8
1954—Norman Van Brocklin, L.A.	260	139	2,637	13	21
1953—Otto Graham, Clev.	258	167	2,722	11	9
1952—Norman Van Brocklin, L.A.	205	113	1,736	14	17
1951—Bob Waterfield, L.A.	176	88	1,566	13	10
1950—Norman Van Brocklin, L.A.	233	127	2,061	18	14
1949—Sammy Baugh, Wash.	255	145	1,903	18	14
1948—Tommy Thompson, Phila.	246	141	1,965	25	11
1947—Sammy Baugh, Wash.	354	210	2,938	25	15
1946—Bob Waterfield, L.A.	251	127	1,747	18	17
1945—Sid Luckman, Chicago	217	117	1,725	14	10
1944—Frank Filchock, Washington	147	84	1,139	13	9
1943—Sammy Baugh, Wash.	239	133	1,754	23	19
1942—Cecil Isbell, Green Bay	268	146	2,021	24	14
1941—Cecil Isbell, Green Bay	206	117	1,479	15	11
1940—Sammy Baugh, Washington	177	111	1,367	12	10
1939—Parker Hall, Clev.*	208	106	1,227	9	13
1938—Ed Danowski, N.Y.	129	70	848	8	8
1937—Sammy Baugh, Washington*	171	81	1,127	7	14

* First year in League

RUSHERS

	Yards	Att.	TDs
1979—Earl Campbell, Houston (AFC)	1,697	368	19
1978—Earl Campbell, Houston (AFC)*	1,450	302	13
1977—Walter Payton, Chicago (NFC)	1,852	339	14
1976—O. J. Simpson, Buffalo (AFC)	1,503	290	8
1975—O. J. Simpson, Buffalo (AFC)	1,817	329	16
1974—Otis Armstrong, Denver (AFC)	1,407	263	9
1973—O. J. Simpson, Buffalo (AFC)	2,003	332	12
1972—O. J. Simpson, Buffalo (AFC)	1,251	292	6
1971—Floyd Little, Denver (AFC)	1,133	284	6
1970—Larry Brown, Washington (NFC)	1,125	237	5
1969—Gale Sayers, Chicago (NFL)	1,032	236	8
1968—Leroy Kelly, Cleveland (NFL)	1,239	248	16
1967—Jim Nance, Boston (AFL)	1,216	269	7
1966—Jim Nance, Boston (AFL)	1,458	299	11
1965—Jim Brown, Cleveland (NFL)	1,544	289	17
1964—Jim Brown, Cleveland (NFL)	1,446	280	7
1963—Jim Brown, Cleveland (NFL)	1,863	291	12
1962—Jim Taylor, Green Bay (NFL)	1,474	272	19
1961—Jim Brown, Cleveland (NFL)	1,408	305	8
1960—Jim Brown, Cleveland (NFL)	1,257	215	9
1959—Jim Brown, Cleveland	1,329	290	14
1958—Jim Brown, Cleveland	1,527	257	17
1957—Jim Brown, Cleveland*	942	202	9
1956—Rick Casares, Chicago Bears	1,126	234	12
1955—Alan Ameche, Baltimore*	961	213	9
1954—Joe Perry, San Francisco	1,049	173	8
1953—Joe Perry, San Francisco	1,018	192	10
1952—Dan Towler, Los Angeles	894	156	10
1951—Eddie Price, New York Giants	971	271	7
1950—Marion Motley, Cleveland*	810	140	3
1949—Steve Van Buren, Philadelphia	1,146	263	11
1948—Steve Van Buren, Philadelphia	945	201	10
1947—Steve Van Buren, Philadelphia	1,008	217	13
1946—Bill Dudley, Pittsburgh	604	146	3
1945—Steve Van Buren, Philadelphia	832	143	15
1944—Bill Paschal, New York	737	196	9
1943—Bill Paschal, New York*	572	147	10
1942—Bill Dudley, Pittsburgh*	696	162	5
1941—Clarence Manders, Brooklyn	486	111	6
1940—Byron White, Detroit	514	146	5
1939—Bill Osmanski, Chicago Bears*	699	121	7
1938—Byron White, Pittsburgh*	567	152	4
1937—Cliff Battles, Washington	874	216	6

*First year in League

RECEIVERS

	No.	Yards	TDs
1979—Joe Washington, Baltimore (AFC)	82	750	3
1978—Rickey Young, Minnesota (NFC)	88	704	5
1977—Lydell Mitchell, Baltimore (AFC)	71	620	4
1976—MacArthur Lane, Kansas City (AFC)	66	686	1
1975—Chuck Foreman, Minnesota (NFC)	73	691	9
1974—Lydell Mitchell, Baltimore (AFC)	72	544	2
1973—Harold Carmichael, Philadelphia (NFC)	67	1,116	9
1972—Harold Jackson, Philadelphia (NFC)	62	1,048	4
1971—Fred Biletnikoff, Oakland (AFC)	61	929	9
1970—Dick Gordon, Chicago (NFC)	71	1,026	13
1969—Dan Abramowicz, New Orleans (NFL)	73	1,015	7
1968—Lance Alworth, San Diego (AFL)	68	1,312	10
1967—George Sauer, New York (AFL)	75	1,189	6
1966—Lance Alworth, San Diego (AFL)	73	1,383	13
1965—Dave Parks, San Francisco (NFL)	80	1,344	12
1964—Charley Hennigan, Houston (AFL)	101	1,546	8
1963—Lionel Taylor, Denver (AFL)	78	1,101	10
1962—Bobby Mitchell, Washington (NFL)	72	1,384	11
1961—Lionel Taylor, Denver (AFL)	100	1,176	4
1960—Raymond Berry, Baltimore, (NFL)	74	1,298	10
1959—Raymond Berry, Baltimore	66	959	14
1958—Raymond Berry, Baltimore	56	794	9
1957—Billy Wilson, San Francisco	52	757	6
1956—Billy Wilson, San Francisco	60	889	5
1955—Pete Pihos, Philadelphia	62	864	7
1954—Pete Pihos, Philadelphia	60	872	10
1953—Pete Pihos, Philadelphia	63	1,049	10
1952—Mac Speedie, Cleveland	62	911	5
1951—Elroy Hirsch, Los Angeles	66	1,495	17
1950—Tom Fears, Los Angeles	84	1,116	7
1949—Tom Fears, Los Angeles	77	1,013	9
1948—Tom Fears, Los Angeles*	51	698	4
1947—Jim Keane, Chicago Bears	64	910	10
1946—Jim Benton, Los Angeles	63	981	6
1945—Don Hutson, Green Bay	47	834	9
1944—Don Hutson, Green Bay	58	866	9
1943—Don Hutson, Green Bay	47	776	11
1942—Don Hutson, Green Bay	74	1,211	17
1941—Don Hutson, Green Bay	58	738	10
1940—Don Looney, Philadelphia*	58	707	4
1939—Don Hutson, Green Bay	34	846	6
1938—Gaynell Tinsley, Chi. Cards	41	516	1
1937—Don Hutson, Green Bay	41	552	7

PUNTERS

	Att.	Avg.
1979—Bob Grupp, Kansas City (AFC)	89	43.6
1978—Pat McInally, Cincinnati (AFC)	91	43.1
1977—Ray Guy, Oakland (AFC)	59	43.3
1976—Marv Bateman, Buffalo (AFC)	86	42.8
1975—Ray Guy, Oakland (AFC)	68	43.8
1974—Ray Guy, Oakland (AFC)	74	42.2
1973—Jerrel Wilson, Kansas City (AFC)	80	45.5
1972—Jerrel Wilson, Kansas City (ACF)	66	44.8
1971—Dave Lewis, Cincinnati (AFC)	72	44.8
1970—Dave Lewis, Cincinnati (AFC)*	79	46.2
1969—David Lee, Baltimore (NFL)	57	45.3
1968—Jerrel Wilson, Kansas City (AFL)	63	45.1
1967—Bob Scarpitto, Denver (AFL)	105	44.9
1966—Bob Scarpitto, Denver (AFL)	76	45.8
1965—Gary Collins, Cleveland (NFL)	65	46.7
1964—Bobby Walden, Minnesota (NFL)	72	46.4
1963—Yale Lary, Detroit (NFL)	35	48.9
1962—Tommy Davis, San Francisco (NFL)	48	45.6
1961—Yale Lary, Detroit (NFL)	52	48.4
1960—Jerry Norton, St. Louis (NFL)	39	45.6
1959—Yale Lary, Detroit	45	47.1
1958—Sam Baker, Washington	48	45.4
1957—Don Chandler, New York	60	44.6
1956—Norm Van Brocklin, Los Angeles	48	43.1
1955—Norm Van Brocklin, Los Angeles	60	44.6
1954—Pat Brady, Pittsburgh	66	43.2
1953—Pat Brady, Pittsburgh	80	46.9
1952—Horace Gillom, Cleveland Browns	61	45.7
1951—Horace Gillom, Cleveland Browns	73	45.5
1950—Fred Morrison, Chicago Bears*	57	43.3
1949—Mike Boyda, N.Y. Bulldogs*	56	44.2
1948—Joe Muha, Philadelphia	57	47.3
1947—Jack Jacobs, Green Bay	57	43.5
1946—Roy McKay, Green Bay	64	42.7
1945—Roy McKay, Green Bay	44	41.2
1944—Frank Sinkwich, Detroit	45	41.0
1943—Sammy Baugh, Washington	50	45.9
1942—Sammy Baugh, Washington	37	48.2
1941—Sammy Baugh, Washington	30	48.7
1940—Sammy Baugh, Washington	35	51.4

TOTAL POINTS

	TDs	XP	FG	Points
1979—John Smith, New England (AFC)	0	46	23	115
1978—Frank Corral, Los Angeles (NFC)	0	31	29	118
1977—Errol Mann, Oakland (AFC)	0	39	20	99
1976—Tony Linhart, Baltimore (AFC)	0	49	20	109
1975—O. J. Simpson, Buffalo (AFC)	23	0	0	138
1974—Chester Marcol, Green Bay (NFC)	0	19	25	94
1973—David Ray, Los Angeles (NFC)	0	40	30	130
1972—Chester Marcol, Green Bay (NCF)*	0	29	33	128
1971—Garo Yepremian, Miami (ACF)	0	33	18	117
1970—Fred Cox, Minnesota (NFC)	0	35	30	125
1969—Jim Turner, New York (AFL)	0	33	32	129
1968—Jim Turner, New York (AFL)	0	43	34	145
1967—Jim Bakken, St. Louis (NFL)	0	36	27	117
1966—Gino Cappelletti, Boston (AFL)	6	35	16	119
1965—Gale Sayers, Chicago (NFL)*	22	0	0	132
—Gino Cappelletti, Boston (AFL)	9	27	17	132
1964—Gino Cappelletti, Boston (AFL)	7	36	25	155
1963—Gino Cappelletti, Boston (AFL)	2	35	22	113
1962—Gene Mingo, Denver (AFL)	4	32	27	137
1961—Gino Cappelletti, Boston (AFL)	8	48	17	147
1960—Paul Hornung, Green Bay (NFL)	15	41	15	176
1959—Paul Hornung, Green Bay	7	31	7	94
1958—Jim Brown, Cleveland Browns	18	0	0	108
1957—Sam Baker, Washington	1	29	14	77
—Lou Groza, Cleveland Browns	0	32	15	77
1956—Bobby Layne, Detroit	5	33	12	99
1955—Doak Walker, Detroit	7	27	9	96
1954—Robert Walston, Philadelphia	11	36	4	114
1953—Gordon Soltau, San Francisco	6	48	10	114
1952—Gordon Soltau, San Francisco	7	34	6	94
1951—Elroy Hirsch, Los Angeles	17	0	0	102
1950—Doak Walker, Detroit*	11	38	8	128
1949—Pat Harder, Chicago Cardinals	8	45	3	102
—Gene Roberts, New York Giants	17	0	0	102
1948—Pat Harder, Chicago Cardinals	6	53	7	110
1947—Pat Harder, Chicago Cardinals	7	39	7	102
1946—Ted Fritsch, Green Bay	10	13	9	100
1945—Steve Van Buren, Philadelphia	18	2	0	110
1944—Don Hutson, Green Bay	9	31	0	85
1943—Don Hutson, Green Bay	12	36	3	117
1942—Don Hutson, Green Bay	17	33	1	138
1941—Don Hutson, Green Bay	17	20	1	95
1940—Don Hutson, Green Bay	7	15	0	57
1939—Andy Farkas, Washington	11	2	0	68
1938—Clarke Hinkle, Green Bay	7	7	3	58
1937—Jack Manders, Chicago Bears	5	15	8	69

1979 NFL ALL-ROOKIE TEAM   (Selected by United Press International)

Offense

Running Backs	—Ottis Anderson, St. Louis
	—William Andrews, Atlanta
Wide Receivers	—Jerry Butler, Buffalo
	—Earnest Gray, N.Y. Giants
Quarterback	—Phil Simms, N.Y. Giants
Tight End	—Dan Ross, Cincinnati
Tackles	—Keith Dorney, Detroit
	—Dave Studdard, Denver
Guards	—Greg Roberts, Tampa Bay
	—Cody Risien, Cleveland
Center	—Mark Dennard, Miami
Place Kicker	—Matt Bahr, Pittsburgh

Defense

Ends	—Jesse Baker, Houston
	—Dan Hampton, Chicago
Tackles	—Fred Smerlas, Buffalo
	—Manu Tuiasosopo, Seattle
Middle Linebacker	—Stan Blinka, N.Y. Jets
Outside Linebackers	—Jim Haslett, Buffalo
	—Jerry Robinson, Philadelphia
Cornerbacks	—Henry Williams, Oakland
	—Aaron Mitchell, Dallas
Free Safety	—Bernard Wilson, Philadelphia
Strong Safety	—Vernon Perry, Houston
Punter	—Bob Grupp, Kansas City

1980 NATIONAL FOOTBALL LEAGUE DRAFT

First Two Choices of Each Team; Position Played, School and Order of Selection

Atlanta	Junior Miller, te, Nebraska (7)
	Buddy Curry, lb, North Carolina (36)
Baltimore	Curtis Dickey, rb, Texas A & M (5)
	Derrick Hatchett, db, Texas (24)
Buffalo	Jim Ritcher, c, N. Carolina State (17)
	Joe Cribbs, rb, Auburn (29)
Chicago	Otis Wilson, lb, Louisville (19)
	Matt Suhey, rb, Penn State (46)
Cincinnati	Anthony Munoz, t, USC (3)
	Kirby Criswell, lb, Kansas (31)
Cleveland	Charles White, rb, USC (27)
	Cleveland Crosby, de, Arizona (54)
Dallas	Bill Roe, lb, Colorado (78)
	James Jones, rb, Mississippi State (81)
Denver	Rulon Jones, de, Utah State (42)
	Larry Carter, db, Kentucky (74)
Detroit	Billy Sims, rb, Oklahoma (1)
	Tom Turnure, c, Washington (57)
Green Bay	Bruce Clark, dt, Penn State (4)
	George Cumby, lb, Oklahoma (26)
Houston	Angelo Fields, t, Michigan State (38)
	Daryle Skaugstad, dt, California (52)
Kansas City	Brad Budde, g, USC (11)
	James Hadnot, rb, Texas Tech (65)
Los Angeles	Johnnie Johnson, db, Texas (15)
	Irv Pankey, t, Penn State (50)
Miami	Don McNeal, db, Alabama (21)
	Dwight Stephenson, c, Alabama (48)
Minnesota	Doug Martin, de, Washington (9)
	Willie Teal, db, Louisiana State (30)
New England	Roland James, db, Tennessee (14)
	Vagas Ferguson, rb, Notre Dame (25)
New Orleans	Stan Brock, t, Colorado (12)
	Dave Waymer, db, Notre Dame (41)
N.Y. Giants	Mark Haynes, db, Colorado (8)
	Myron Lapka, dt, USC (64)
N.Y. Jets	Johnny (Lam) Jones, wr, Texas (2)
	Darrol Ray, db, Oklahoma (40)
Oakland	Marc Wilson, qb, Brigham Young (16)
	Matt Millen, lb, Penn State (43)
Philadelphia	Roynell Young, db, Alcorn State (23)
	Perry Harrington, rb, Jackson State (53)
Pittsburgh	Mark Malone, qb, Arizona State (28)
	Bob Kohrs, lb, Arizona State (35)
St. Louis	Curtis Greer, de, Michigan (6)
	Doug Marsh, te, Michigan (33)
San Diego	Ed Luther, qb, San Jose State (103)
	Bob Gregor, db, Washington State (110)
San Francisco	Earl Cooper, rb, Rice (13)
	Jim Stuckey, de, Clemson (20)
Seattle	Jacob Green, de, Texas A & M (10)
	Andre Hines, t, Stanford (44)
Tampa Bay	Ray Snell, g, Wisconsin (22)
	Kevin House, wr, Southern Illinois (49)
Washington	Art Monk, wr, Syracuse (8)
	Mat Mendenhall, de, Brigham Young (55)

NATIONAL FOOTBALL LEAGUE STADIUMS

AMERICAN FOOTBALL CONFERENCE

Team	Stadium	Capacity
Baltimore	Memorial Stadium	60,020
Buffalo	Rich Stadium	80,020
Cincinnati	Riverfront Stadium	56,200
Cleveland	Cleveland Stadium	79,891
Denver	Mile High Stadium	76,000
Houston	Astrodome	50,000
Kansas City	Arrowhead Stadium	78,198
Miami	Orange Bowl	76,000
New England	Schaefer Stadium (Foxboro, Mass.)	61,279
N.Y. Jets	Shea Stadium	60,000
Oakland	Oakland-Alameda Co. Coliseum	54,615
Pittsburgh	Three Rivers Stadium	50,350
San Diego	San Diego Stadium	53,000
Seattle	Kingdome	64,752

NATIONAL FOOTBALL CONFERENCE

Team	Stadium	Capacity
Atlanta	Atlanta-Fulton Co. Stadium	60,498
Chicago	Soldier Field	57,359
Dallas	Texas Stadium	65,100
Detroit	Pontiac Silverdome	80,638
Green Bay	Lambeau Field	56,267
	Milwaukee Co. Stadium	55,896
Los Angeles	Anaheim Stadium	69,000
Minnesota	QL Metropolitan Stadium	48,446
New Orleans	Louisiana Superdome	71,300
N.Y. Giants	Giants Stadium (E. Rutherford, N.J.)	76,500
Philadelphia	Veterans Stadium	66,000
St. Louis	Busch Memorial Stadium	51,392
San Francisco	Candlestick Park	61,246
Tampa Bay	Tampa Stadium	71,600
Washington	Robert F. Kennedy Stadium	55,004

1979 CANADIAN FOOTBALL LEAGUE FINAL STANDINGS

EASTERN CONFERENCE	W	L	T	PF	PA	Pts.
Montreal Alouettes	11	4	1	351	284	23
Ottawa Rough Riders	8	6	2	349	315	18
Hamilton Tiger-Cats	6	10	0	280	338	12
Toronto Argonauts	5	11	0	234	352	10

WESTERN CONFERENCE	W	L	T	PF	PA	Pts.
Edmonton Eskimos	12	2	2	495	219	26
Calgary Stampeders	12	4	0	382	278	24
B.C. Lions	9	6	1	328	333	19
Winnipeg Blue Bombers	4	12	0	283	340	8
Saskatchewan Roughriders	2	14	0	194	437	4

Conference Semifinals: Ottawa 29–Hamilton 26, Calgary 37–B.C. 2
Conference Finals: Montreal 17–Ottawa 6, Edmonton 19–Calgary 7
Championship (Grey Cup): Edmonton 17–Montreal 9

CANADIAN FOOTBALL LEAGUE CHAMPIONS (GREY CUP)

Year	Champion	Year	Champion	Year	Champion	Year	Champion
1952	Toronto	1959	Winnipeg	1966	Saskatchewan	1973	Ottawa
1953	Hamilton	1960	Ottawa	1967	Hamilton	1974	Montreal
1954	Edmonton	1961	Winnipeg	1968	Ottawa	1975	Edmonton
1955	Edmonton	1962	Winnipeg	1969	Ottawa	1976	Ottowa
1956	Edmonton	1963	Hamilton	1970	Montreal	1977	Montreal
1957	Hamilton	1964	British Columbia	1971	Calgary	1978	Edmonton
1958	Winnipeg	1965	Hamilton	1972	Hamilton	1979	Edmonton

COLLEGE FOOTBALL

RECORD OF THE MAJOR COLLEGE BOWL GAMES

ROSE BOWL   Pasedena, California (January)

Year	Result	Year	Result	Year	Result
1902	Michigan 49, Stanford 0	1936	Stanford 7, Southern Methodist 0	1959	Iowa 38, California 12
1916	Washington State 14, Brown 0	1937	Pittsburgh 21, Washington 0	1960	Washington 44, Wisconsin 8
1917	Oregon 14, Pennsylvania 0	1938	California 13, Alabama 0	1961	Washington 17, Minnesota 7
1918	Mare Island Marines 19, Camp Lewis 7	1939	So. California 7, Duke 3	1962	Minnesota 21, UCLA 3
1919	Great Lakes 17, Mare Island Marines 0	1940	So. California 14, Tennessee 0	1963	So. California 42, Wisconsin 37
1920	Harvard 7, Oregon 6	1941	Stanford 21, Nebraska 13	1964	Illinois 17, Washington 7
1921	California 28, Ohio State 0	1942*	Oregon State 20, Duke 16	1965	Michigan 34, Oregon State 7
1922	Washington and Jefferson 0, California 0	1943	Georgia 9, UCLA 0	1966	UCLA 14, Michigan State 12
1923	So. California 14, Penn State 3	1944	So. California 29, Washington 0	1967	Purdue 14, So. California 13
1924	Navy 14, Washington 14	1945	So. California 25, Tennessee 0	1968	So. California 14, Indiana 3
1925	Notre Dame 27, Stanford 10	1946	Alabama 34, So. California 14	1969	Ohio State 27, Southern California 16
1926	Alabama 20, Washington 19	1947	Illinois 45, UCLA 14	1970	So. California 10, Michigan 3
1927	Alabama 7, Stanford 7	1948	Michigan 49, Southern California 0	1971	Stanford 27, Ohio State 17
1928	Stanford 7, Pittsburgh 6	1949	Northwestern 20, California 14	1972	Stanford 13, Michigan 12
1929	Georgia Tech 8, California 7	1950	Ohio State 17, California 14	1973	So. California 42, Ohio State 17
1930	So. California 47, Pittsburgh 14	1951	Michigan 14, California 6	1974	Ohio State 42, So. California 21
1931	Alabama 24, Washington State 0	1952	Illinois 40, Stanford 7	1975	So. California 18, Ohio State 17
1932	So. California 21, Tulane 12	1953	So. California 7, Wisconsin 0	1976	UCLA 23, Ohio State 10
1933	So. California 35, Pittsburgh 0	1954	Michigan State 28, UCLA 20	1977	So. California 14, Michigan 6
1934	Columbia 7, Stanford 0	1955	Ohio State 20, So. California 7	1978	Washington 27, Michigan 20
1935	Alabama 29, Stanford 13	1956	Michigan State 17, UCLA 14	1979	So. California 17, Michigan 10
		1957	Iowa 35, Oregon State 19	1980	So. California 17, Ohio State 16
		1958	Ohio State 10, Oregon 7		

* Played at Durham, North Carolina.

ORANGE BOWL   Miami, Florida (January)

Year	Result	Year	Result	Year	Result
1933	Miami (Fla.) 7, Manhattan 0	1948	Georgia Tech 20, Kansas 14	1964	Nebraska 13, Auburn 7
1934	Duquesne 33, Miami (Fla.) 7	1949	Texas 41, Georgia 28	1965	Texas 21, Alabama 17
1935	Bucknell 26, Miami (Fla.) 0	1950	Santa Clara 21, Kentucky 13	1966	Alabama 39, Nebraska 28
1936	Catholic Univ. 20, Mississippi 19	1951	Clemson 15, Miami (Fla.) 14	1967	Florida 27, Georgia Tech 12
1937	Duquesne 13, Miss. State 12	1952	Georgia Tech 17, Baylor 14	1968	Oklahoma 26, Tennessee 24
1938	Auburn 6, Michigan State 0	1953	Alabama 61, Syracuse 6	1969	Penn State 15, Kansas 14
1939	Tennessee 17, Oklahoma 0	1954	Oklahoma 7, Maryland 0	1970	Penn State 10, Missouri 3
1940	Georgia Tech 21, Missouri 7	1955	Duke 34, Nebraska 7	1971	Nebraska 17, Louisiana State 12
1941	Miss. State 14, Georgetown 7	1956	Oklahoma 20, Maryland 6	1972	Nebraska 38, Alabama 6
1942	Georgia 40, Texas Christian 26	1957	Colorado 27, Clemson 21	1973	Nebraska 40, Notre Dame 6
1943	Alabama 37, Boston College 21	1958	Oklahoma 48, Duke 21	1974	Penn State 16, Louisiana State 9
1944	LSU 19, Texas A&M 14	1959	Oklahoma 21, Syracuse 6	1975	Notre Dame 13, Alabama 11
1945	Tulsa 26, Georgia Tech 12	1960	Georgia 14, Missouri 0	1976	Oklahoma 14, Michigan 6
1946	Miami (Fla.) 13, Holy Cross 6	1961	Missouri 21, Navy 14	1977	Ohio State 27, Colorado 10
1947	Rice 8, Tennessee 0	1962	Louisiana State 25, Colorado 7	1978	Arkansas 31, Oklahoma 6
		1963	Alabama 17, Oklahoma 0	1979	Oklahoma 31, Nebraska 24
				1980	Oklahoma 24, Florida State 7

SUGAR BOWL   New Orleans, Louisiana (January)

Year	Result	Year	Result	Year	Result
1935	Tulane 20, Temple 14	1949	Oklahoma 14, North Carolina 6	1965	Louisiana State 13, Syracuse 10
1936	TCU 3, Louisiana State 2	1950	Oklahoma 35, Louisiana State 0	1966	Missouri 20, Florida 18
1937	Santa Clara 21, Louisiana State 14	1951	Kentucky 13, Oklahoma 7	1967	Alabama 34, Nebraska 7
1938	Santa Clara 6, Louisiana State 0	1952	Maryland 28, Tennessee 13	1968	Louisiana State 20, Wyoming 13
1939	TCU 15, Carnegie Tech 7	1953	Georgia Tech 24, Mississippi 7	1969	Arkansas 16, Georgia 2
1940	Texas A&M 14, Tulane 13	1954	Georgia Tech 42, West Va. 19	1970	Mississippi 27, Arkansas 22
1941	Boston College 19, Tennessee 13	1955	Navy 21, Mississippi 0	1971	Tennessee 34, Air Force 13
1942	Fordham 2, Missouri 0	1956	Georgia Tech 7, Pittsburgh 0	1972	Oklahoma 40, Auburn 22
1943	Tennessee 14, Tulsa 7	1957	Baylor 13, Tennessee 7	1972 (Dec.)	Oklahoma 14, Penn State 0
1944	Georgia Tech 20, Tulsa 18	1958	Mississippi 39, Texas 7	1973 (Dec.)	Notre Dame 24, Alabama 23
1945	Duke 29, Alabama 26	1959	Louisiana State 7, Clemson 0	1974 (Dec.)	Nebraska 13, Florida 10
1946	Oklahoma A & M 33, St. Mary's (Calif.) 13	1960	Mississippi 21, Louisiana State 0	1975 (Dec.)	Alabama 13, Penn State 6
1947	Georgia 20, North Carolina 10	1961	Mississippi 14, Rice 6	1977	Pittsburgh 27, Georgia 3
1948	Texas 27, Alabama 7	1962	Alabama 10, Arkansas 3	1978	Alabama 35, Ohio State 6
		1963	Mississippi 17, Arkansas 13	1979	Alabama 14, Penn State 7
		1964	Alabama 12, Mississippi 7	1980	Alabama 24, Arkansas 9

COTTON BOWL   Dallas, Texas (January)

Year	Result	Year	Result	Year	Result
1937	Texas Christian 16, Marquette 6	1951	Tennessee 20, Texas 14	1966	Louisiana State 14, Arkansas 7
1938	Rice 28, Colorado 14	1952	Kentucky 20, Texas Christian 7	1966 (Dec.)	Georgia 24, SMU 9
1939	St. Mary's (Calif.) 20, Texas Tech 13	1953	Texas 16, Tennessee 0	1968	Texas A&M 20, Alabama 16
1940	Clemson 6, Boston College 3	1954	Rice 28, Alabama 6	1969	Texas 36, Tennessee 13
1941	Texas A&M 13, Fordham 12	1955	Georgia Tech 14, Arkansas 6	1970	Texas 21, Notre Dame 17
1942	Alabama 29, Texas A&M 21	1956	Mississippi 14, TCU 13	1971	Notre Dame 24, Texas 11
1943	Texas 14, Georgia Tech 7	1957	Texas Christian 28, Syracuse 27	1972	Penn State 30, Texas 6
1944	Randolph Field 7, Texas 7	1958	Navy 20, Rice 7	1973	Texas 17, Alabama 13
1945	Oklahoma A & M 34, TCU 0	1959	Air Force 0, Texas Christian 0	1974	Nebraska 19, Texas 3
1946	Texas 40, Missouri 27	1960	Syracuse 23, Texas 14	1975	Penn State 41, Baylor 20
1947	Louisiana State 0, Arkansas 0	1961	Duke 7, Arkansas 6	1976	Arkansas 31, Georgia 10
1948	So. Methodist 13, Penn St. 13	1962	Texas 12, Mississippi 7	1977	Houston 30, Maryland 21
1949	So. Methodist 21, Oregon 13	1963	Louisiana State 13, Texas 0	1978	Notre Dame 38, Texas 10
1950	Rice 27, North Carolina 13	1964	Texas 28, Navy 6	1979	Notre Dame 35, Houston 34
		1965	Arkansas 10, Nebraska 7	1980	Houston 17, Nebraska 14

SUN BOWL
El Paso, Texas (J = January, D = December)

Year	Result	Year	Result	Year	Result
1936J	H.-Simmons 14, N.M. State 14	1951J	W. Tex. St. 14, Cincinnati 13	1965D	Texas Western 13, TCU 12
1937J	H.-Simmons 34, Tex. Mines 6	1952J	Texas Tech 25, Col. Pacific 14	1966D	Wyoming 28, Florida State 20
1938J	West Virginia 7, Texas Tech 6	1953J	Col. Pacific 26, Miss. Southern 7	1967D	Texas-El Paso 14, Miss. 7
1939J	Utah 26, New Mexico 0	1954J	Tex. Western 37, Miss. So. 14	1968D	Auburn 34, Arizona 10
1940J	Catholic U. 0, Arizona St. 0	1955J	Tex. Western 47, Florida St. 20	1969D	Nebraska 45, Georgia 6
1941J	W. Reserve 26, Arizona St. 13	1956J	Wyoming 21, Texas Tech 14	1970D	Georgia Tech 17, Texas Tech 9
1942J	Tulsa 6, Texas Tech 0	1957J	George Wash. 13, Texas W. 0	1971D	LSU 33, Iowa State 15
1943J	2nd Air Force 13, H.-Simmons 7	1958J	Louisville 34, Drake 20	1972D	N. Carolina 32, Texas Tech 28
1944J	Southwestern 7, New Mexico 0	1958D	Wyoming 14, H.-Simmons 6	1973D	Missouri 34, Auburn 17
1945J	Southwestern 35, U. Mexico 0	1959D	N.M. State 28, N. Tex. State 8	1974D	Miss. State 26, N. Carolina 24
1946J	New Mexico 34, Denver 24	1960D	N.M. State 20, Utah State 13	1975D	Pittsburgh 33, Kansas 19
1947J	Cincinnati 18, Virginia Tech 6	1961D	Villanova 17, Wichita 9	1977J	Texas A & M 37, Florida 14
1948J	Miami (Ohio) 13, Texas Tech 12	1962D	W. Texas St. 15, Ohio U. 14	1977D	Stanford 24, LSU 14
1949J	W. Virginia 21, Texas Mines 12	1963D	Oregon 21, SMU 14	1978D	Texas 42, Maryland 0
1950J	Tex. Western 33, Georgetown 20	1964D	Georgia 7, Texas Tech 0	1979D	Washington 14, Texas 7

GATOR BOWL
Jacksonville, Florida (J = January, D = December)

Year	Result	Year	Result	Year	Result
1946J	Wake Forest 26, S. Carolina 14	1956D	Georgia Tech 21, Pittsburgh 14	1968D	Missouri 35, Alabama 10
1947J	Oklahoma 34, N.C. State 13	1957D	Tennessee 3, Texas A & M 0	1969D	Florida 14, Tennessee 13
1948J	Maryland 20, Georgia 20	1958D	Mississippi 7, Florida 3	1971J	Auburn 35, Mississippi 28
1949J	Clemson 24, Missouri 23	1960J	Arkansas 14, Georgia Tech 7	1971D	Georgia 7, N. Carolina 3
1950J	Maryland 20, Missouri 7	1960D	Florida 13, Baylor 12	1972D	Auburn 24, Colorado 3
1951J	Wyoming 20, Wash. & Lee 7	1961D	Penn State 30, Georgia Tech 15	1973D	Texas Tech 28, Tennessee 19
1952J	Miami (Fla.) 14, Clemson 0	1962D	Florida 17, Penn State 7	1974D	Auburn 27, Texas 3
1953J	Florida 14, Tulsa 13	1963D	N. Carolina 35, Air Force 0	1975D	Maryland 13, Florida 0
1954J	Texas Tech 35, Auburn 13	1965J	Florida St. 36, Oklahoma 19	1976D	Notre Dame 20, Penn State 9
1954D	Auburn 33, Baylor 13	1965D	Georgia Tech 31, Texas Tech 21	1977D	Pittsburgh 34, Clemson 3
1955D	Vanderbilt 25, Auburn 13	1966D	Tennessee 18, Syracuse 12	1978D	Clemson 17, Ohio State 15
		1967D	Penn State 17, Florida St. 17	1979D	N. Carolina 17, Michigan 15

TANGERINE BOWL
Orlando, Florida (J = January, D = December)

Year	Result	Year	Result	Year	Result
1947J	Catawba 31, Maryville 6	1958J	E. Texas St. 10, So. Miss. 9	1968D	Richmond 49, Ohio U. 42
1948J	Catawba 7, Marshall 0	1958D	E. Texas St. 26, Missouri Va. 7	1969D	Toledo 56, Davidson 33
1949J	Murray St. 21, Sul Ross St. 21	1960J	Middle Tenn. 21, Presbyterian 12	1970D	Toledo 40, William & Mary 12
1950J	St. Vincent 7, Emory & Henry 6	1960D	Citadel 27, Tennessee Tech 0	1971D	Toledo 28, Richmond 3
1951J	Mor. Harvey 35, Emory & Henry 14	1961D	Lamar 21, Middle Tennessee 14	1972D	Tampa 21, Kent State 18
1952J	Stetson 35, Arkansas St. 20	1962D	Houston 49, Miami (Ohio) 21	1973D	Miami (Ohio) 16, Florida 7
1953J	E. Texas St. 33, Tenn. Tech 0	1963D	W. Kentucky 27, Coast Guard 0	1974D	Miami (Ohio) 21, Georgia 10
1954J	E. Texas St. 7, Arkansas St. 7	1964D	E. Carolina 14, Massachusetts 13	1975D	Miami (Ohio) 20, S. Carolina 7
1955J	Nebraska (Omaha) 7, E. Ken. 6	1965D	E. Carolina 31, Maine 0	1976D	Okla. State 49, Brigham Young 21
1956J	Juniata 6, Missouri Valley 6	1966D	Morgan St. 14, West Chester 6	1977D	Florida St. 40, Texas Tech 17
1957J	W. Texas St. 20, So. Miss. 13	1967D	Tenn. (Martin) 25, West Chester 8	1978D	N. Carolina St. 30, Pittsburgh 17
				1979D	LSU 34, Wake Forest 10

BLUEBONNET BOWL
Houston, Texas (December)

Year	Result	Year	Result	Year	Result
1959	Clemson 23, TCU 7	1966	Texas 19, Mississippi 0	1973	Houston 47, Tulane 7
1960	Texas 3, Alabama 3	1967	Colorado 31, Miami (Fla.) 21	1974	N.C. State 31, Houston 31
1961	Kansas 33, Rice 0	1968	SMU 28, Oklahoma 27	1975	Texas 38, Colorado 21
1962	Missouri 14, Georgia Tech 10	1969	Houston 36, Auburn 7	1976	Nebraska 27, Texas Tech 24
1963	Baylor 14, LSU 7	1970	Alabama 24, Oklahoma 24	1977	USC 47, Texas A & M 28
1964	Tulsa 14, Mississippi 7	1971	Colorado 29, Houston 17	1978	Stanford 25, Georgia 22
1965	Tennessee 27, Tulsa 6	1972	Tennessee 24, LSU 17	1979	Purdue 27, Tennessee 22

LIBERTY BOWL
Memphis, Tennessee* (December)

Year	Result	Year	Result	Year	Result
1959	Penn State 7, Alabama 0	1966	Miami (Fla.) 14, Virginia Tech 7	1973	N.C. State 31, Kansas 18
1960	Penn State 41, Oregon 12	1967	N.C. State 14, Georgia 7	1974	Tennessee 7, Maryland 3
1961	Syracuse 15, Miami (Fla.) 14	1968	Mississippi 34, Virginia Tech 17	1975	USC 20, Texas A & M 0
1962	Oregon St. 6, Villanova 0	1969	Colorado 47, Alabama 33	1976	Alabama 36, UCLA 6
1963	Mississippi St. 16, N.C. State 12	1970	Tulane 17, Colorado 3	1977	Nebraska 21, N. Carolina 17
1964	Utah 32, West Virginia 6	1971	Tennessee 14, Arkansas 13	1978	Missouri 20, LSU 15
1965	Mississippi 13, Auburn 7	1972	Georgia Tech 31, Iowa State 30	1979	Penn State 9, Tulane 6

*Philadelphia 1960-1964, Atlantic City 1965

PEACH BOWL
Atlanta, Georgia (December)

Year	Result	Year	Result	Year	Result
1968	LSU 31, Florida State 27	1972	N.C. State 49, W. Virginia 13	1976	Kentucky 21, N. Carolina 0
1969	W. Virginia 14, S. Carolina 3	1973	Georgia 17, Maryland 16	1977	N.C. State 24, Iowa State 14
1970	Arizona St. 48, N. Carolina 26	1974	Vanderbilt 6, Texas Tech 6	1978	Purdue 41, Georgia Tech 21
1971	Mississippi 41, Georgia Tech 18	1975	W. Virginia 13, N.C. State 10	1979	Baylor 24, Clemson 18

FIESTA BOWL
Tempe, Arizona (December)

Year	Result	Year	Result	Year	Result
1971	Arizona St. 45, Florida St. 38	1974	Okla. St. 16, Brigham Young 6	1977	Penn State 42, Arizona St. 30
1972	Arizona St. 49, Missouri 35	1975	Arizona St. 17, Nebraska 14	1978	Arkansas 10, UCLA 10
1973	Arizona St. 28, Pittsburgh 7	1976	Oklahoma 41, Wyoming 7	1979	Pittsburgh 16, Arizona 10

NATIONAL COLLEGE FOOTBALL CHAMPIONS

The college football team selected each year by The Associated Press poll of sportswriters and the United Press International poll of football coaches is unofficially recognized as national champion. Where the polls disagree, both teams are given.

Year	Champion	Year	Champion	Year	Champion	Year	Champion
1924	Notre Dame	1938	Texas Christian	1952	Michigan State	1966	Notre Dame
1925	Dartmouth	1939	Texas A & M	1953	Maryland	1967	Southern California
1926	Stanford	1940	Minnesota	1954	Ohio State-UCLA	1968	Ohio State
1927	Illinois	1941	Minnesota	1955	Oklahoma	1969	Texas
1928	Southern California	1942	Ohio State	1956	Oklahoma	1970	Texas-Nebraska
1929	Notre Dame	1943	Notre Dame	1957	Auburn-Ohio State	1971	Nebraska
1930	Notre Dame	1944	Army	1958	Louisiana State	1972	Southern California
1931	Southern California	1945	Army	1959	Syracuse	1973	Notre Dame
1932	Michigan	1946	Notre Dame	1960	Minnesota	1974	Oklahoma-USC
1933	Michigan	1947	Notre Dame	1961	Alabama	1975	Oklahoma
1934	Minnesota	1948	Michigan	1962	Southern California	1976	Pittsburgh
1935	Southern Methodist	1949	Notre Dame	1963	Texas	1977	Notre Dame
1936	Minnesota	1950	Oklahoma	1964	Alabama	1978	Alabama-USC
1937	Pittsburgh	1951	Tennessee	1965	Alabama	1979	Alabama

COLLEGE FOOTBALL CONFERENCE CHAMPIONS

ATLANTIC COAST

Year	Champion
1962	Duke
1963	No. Carolina State
1964	No. Carolina State
1965	Duke
1966	Clemson
1967	Clemson
1968	No. Carolina State
1969	South Carolina
1970	Wake Forest
1971	North Carolina
1972	North Carolina
1973	No. Carolina State
1974	Maryland
1975	Maryland
1976	Maryland
1977	North Carolina
1978	Clemson
1979	No. Carolina State

BIG EIGHT

Year	Champion
1962	Oklahoma
1963	Nebraska
1964	Nebraska
1965	Nebraska
1966	Nebraska
1967	Oklahoma
1968	Kansas-Oklahoma
1969	Missouri-Nebraska
1970	Nebraska
1971	Nebraska
1972	Oklahoma
1973	Oklahoma
1974	Oklahoma
1975	Nebraska-Oklahoma
1976	Colorado-Oklahoma-Oklahoma State
1977	Oklahoma
1978	Nebraska-Oklahoma
1979	Oklahoma

BIG TEN

Year	Champion
1962	Wisconsin
1963	Illinois
1964	Michigan
1965	Michigan State
1966	Michigan State
1967	Indiana-Purdue-Minnesota
1968	Ohio State
1969	Ohio State-Michigan
1970	Ohio State
1971	Michigan
1972	Ohio State-Michigan
1973	Michigan-Ohio State
1974	Michigan-Ohio State
1975	Ohio State
1976	Michigan-Ohio State
1977	Michigan-Ohio State
1978	Michigan St.-Michigan
1979	Ohio State

IVY LEAGUE

Year	Champion
1962	Dartmouth
1963	Dartmouth-Princeton
1964	Princeton
1965	Dartmouth
1966	Dartmouth-Harvard-Princeton
1967	Yale
1968	Yale-Harvard
1969	Princeton-Yale-Dartmouth
1970	Dartmouth
1971	Cornell-Dartmouth
1972	Dartmouth
1973	Dartmouth
1974	Yale-Harvard
1975	Harvard
1976	Yale-Brown
1977	Yale
1978	Dartmouth
1979	Yale

MISSOURI VALLEY

Year	Champion
1962	Tulsa
1963	Cincinnati-Wichita
1964	Cincinnati
1965	Tulsa
1966	North Texas-Tulsa
1967	North Texas
1968	Memphis State
1969	Memphis State
1970	Louisville
1971	North Texas
1972	Louisville-Drake-West Texas
1973	North Texas-Tulsa
1974	Tulsa
1975	Tulsa
1976	Tulsa-N. Mexico State
1977	West Texas State
1978	New Mexico State
1979	West Texas State

PACIFIC TEN

Year	Champion
1962	Southern California
1963	Washington
1964	Oregon State-Southern California
1965	UCLA
1966	Southern California
1967	Southern California
1968	Southern California
1969	Southern California
1970	Stanford
1971	Stanford
1972	Southern California
1973	Southern California
1974	Southern California
1975	UCLA-California
1976	Southern California
1977	Washington
1978	Southern California
1979	Southern California

SOUTHEASTERN

Year	Champion
1962	Mississippi
1963	Mississippi
1964	Alabama
1965	Alabama
1966	Georgia-Alabama
1967	Tennessee
1968	Georgia
1969	Tennessee
1970	Louisiana State
1971	Alabama
1972	Alabama
1973	Alabama
1974	Alabama
1975	Alabama
1976	Georgia
1977	Alabama
1978	Alabama
1979	Alabama

SOUTHERN

Year	Champion
1962	VMI
1963	Virginia Tech
1964	West Virginia
1965	West Virginia
1966	William & Mary-East Carolina
1967	West Virginia
1968	Richmond
1969	Richmond-Davidson
1970	William & Mary
1971	Richmond
1972	East Carolina
1973	East Carolina
1974	VMI
1975	Richmond
1976	East Carolina
1977	VMI-Tenn.-Chattanooga
1978	Tenn.-Chattanooga-Furman
1979	Tenn.-Chattanooga

MID-AMERICAN

Year	Champion
1962	Bowling Green
1963	Ohio University
1964	Bowling Green
1965	Miami (Ohio)-Bowling Green
1966	Miami (Ohio)-Western Michigan
1967	Toledo-Ohio U.
1968	Ohio University
1969	Toledo
1970	Toledo
1971	Toledo
1972	Kent State
1973	Miami (Ohio)
1974	Miami (Ohio)
1975	Miami (Ohio)
1976	Ball State
1977	Miami (Ohio)
1978	Ball State
1979	Central Michigan

SOUTHWEST

Year	Champion
1962	Texas
1963	Texas
1964	Arkansas
1965	Arkansas
1966	Southern Methodist
1967	Texas A & M
1968	Texas-Arkansas
1969	Texas
1970	Texas
1971	Texas
1972	Texas
1973	Texas
1974	Baylor
1975	Texas-Texas A & M-Arkansas
1976	Houston-Texas Tech
1977	Texas
1978	Houston
1979	Arkansas

WESTERN

Year	Champion
1963	New Mexico
1964	New Mexico-Utah-Arizona
1965	Brigham Young
1966	Wyoming
1967	Wyoming
1968	Wyoming
1969	Arizona State
1970	Arizona State
1971	Arizona State
1972	Arizona State
1973	Arizona-Ariz. St.
1974	Brigham Young
1975	Arizona State
1976	Wyoming-Brigham Young
1977	Arizona State-Brigham Young
1978	Brigham Young
1979	Brigham Young

PACIFIC COAST

Year	Champion
1969	San Diego State
1970	Long Beach State
1971	Long Beach State
1972	San Diego State
1973	San Diego State
1974	San Diego State
1975	San Jose State
1976	San Jose State
1977	Fresno State
1978	Utah State-San Jose State
1979	Utah State-San Jose State

1979 REGULAR SEASON RECORDS OF MAJOR COLLEGE FOOTBALL TEAMS

Team	W	L	T	Team	W	L	T	Team	W	L	T
Air Force	2	9	0	Kansas	3	8	0	Richmond	0	11	0
Alabama	11	0	0	Kansas State	3	8	0	Rutgers	8	3	0
Arizona	6	4	1	Kentucky	5	6	0	San Diego State	8	3	0
Arizona State	1	11	0	Louisiana State	6	5	0	San Jose State	6	4	1
Arkansas	10	1	0	Louisville	4	5	1	South Carolina	8	3	0
Army	2	8	1	Maryland	7	4	0	Southern California	10	0	1
Auburn	8	3	0	Memphis State	4	6	0	Southern Methodist	5	6	0
Baylor	7	4	0	Miami (Fla.)	5	6	0	Southern Mississippi	6	4	1
Boston College	5	6	0	Michigan	8	3	0	Stanford	5	5	1
Brigham Young	11	0	0	Michigan State	5	6	0	Syracuse	6	5	0
Brown	6	3	0	Minnesota	4	6	1	Temple	9	2	0
California	6	5	0	Mississippi	4	7	0	Tennessee	7	4	0
Cincinnati	2	9	0	Mississippi State	3	8	0	Texas	9	2	0
Citadel	6	5	0	Missouri	6	5	0	Texas A & M	6	5	0
Clemson	8	3	0	Navy	7	4	0	Texas Christian	2	8	1
Colgate	5	4	1	Nebraska	10	1	0	Texas-El Paso	2	9	0
Colorado	3	8	0	Nevada-Las Vegas	8	1	2	Texas Tech	3	6	2
Colorado State	4	7	1	New Mexico	6	6	0	Tulane	9	2	0
Columbia	1	8	0	New Mexico State	2	9	0	Tulsa	6	5	0
Cornell	5	4	0	North Carolina	7	3	1	UCLA	5	6	0
Dartmouth	4	4	1	North Carolina State	7	4	0	Utah	6	6	0
Duke	2	8	1	North Texas State	5	6	0	Utah State	7	3	1
East Carolina	7	3	1	Northwestern	1	10	0	Vanderbilt	1	10	0
Florida	0	10	1	Notre Dame	7	4	0	Villanova	5	6	0
Florida State	11	0	0	Ohio State	11	0	0	Virginia	6	5	0
Furman	5	6	0	Oklahoma	10	1	0	Virginia Military	6	4	1
Georgia	6	5	0	Oklahoma State	7	4	0	Virginia Tech	5	6	0
Georgia Tech	4	6	1	Oregon	6	5	0	Wake Forest	8	3	0
Harvard	3	6	0	Oregon State	2	9	0	Washington	9	2	0
Hawaii	6	5	0	Pacific	3	7	0	Washington State	4	7	0
Holy Cross	5	6	0	Pennsylvania	0	9	0	West Virginia	5	6	0
Houston	10	1	0	Pennsylvania State	7	4	0	Wichita State	1	10	0
Illinois	2	8	1	Pittsburgh	10	1	0	William & Mary	4	7	0
Indiana	7	4	0	Princeton	5	4	0	Wisconsin	4	7	0
Iowa	5	6	0	Purdue	9	2	0	Wyoming	4	8	0
Iowa State	3	8	0	Rice	1	10	0	Yale	8	1	0

1979 FINAL COLLEGE FOOTBALL RANKINGS

ASSOCIATED PRESS

1. Alabama
2. Southern California
3. Oklahoma
4. Ohio State
5. Houston
6. Florida State
7. Pittsburgh
8. Arkansas
9. Nebraska
10. Purdue
11. Washington
12. Texas
13. Brigham Young
14. Baylor
15. North Carolina
16. Auburn
17. Temple
18. Michigan
19. Indiana
20. Penn State

UNITED PRESS INTERNATIONAL

1. Alabama
2. Southern California
3. Oklahoma
4. Ohio State
5. Houston
6. Pittsburgh
7. Nebraska
8. Florida State
9. Arkansas
10. Purdue
11. Washington
12. Brigham Young
13. Texas
14. North Carolina
15. Baylor
16. Indiana
17. Temple
18. Penn State
19. Michigan
20. Missouri

MAJOR COLLEGE FOOTBALL STADIUMS (40,000 or more seats)

Team (Stadium) Location	Capacity
Air Force (Falcon) A.F. Academy, Colo.	46,600
Alabama (Denny) University, Ala.	59,000
Arizona (Arizona) Tucson, Ariz.	57,000
Arizona State (Sun Devil) Tempe, Ariz.	70,000
Arkansas (Razorback) Fayetteville, Ark.	43,000
Army (Michie) West Point, N.Y.	41,600
Auburn (Jordan Hare) Auburn, Ala.	61,200
Baylor (Baylor) Waco, Tex.	48,000
California (Memorial) Berkeley, Cal.	76,700
Clemson (Memorial) Clemson, S.C.	53,000
Colorado (Folsom) Boulder, Colo.	52,000
Duke (Wallace Wade) Durham, N.C.	44,000
Florida (Florida Field) Gainesville, Fla.	62,000
Florida State (Campbell) Tallahassee, Fla.	40,500
Georgia (Sanford) Athens, Ga.	59,200
Georgia Tech (Grant Field) Atlanta, Ga.	58,100
Hawaii (Aloha) Honolulu, Hawaii	50,000
Illinois (Memorial) Champaign, Ill.	71,200
Indiana (Memorial) Bloomington, Ind.	52,300
Iowa (Kinnick) Iowa City, Iowa	60,000
Iowa State (Cyclone) Ames, Iowa	50,000
Jackson State (Miss. Memorial) Jackson, Miss.	46,000
Kansas (Memorial) Lawrence, Kans.	51,500
Kansas State (KSU) Manhattan, Kans.	42,000
Kentucky (Commonwealth) Lexington, Ky.	58,000
Louisiana State (Tiger) Baton Rouge, La.	75,000
Maryland (Byrd) College Park, Md.	45,000
Memphis State (Liberty Bowl) Memphis, Tenn.	50,100
Michigan (Michigan) Ann Arbor, Mich.	101,700
Michigan State (Spartan) East Lansing, Mich.	76,000
Minnesota (Memorial) Minneapolis, Minn.	56,700
Missouri (Faurot Field) Columbia, Mo.	60,000
Nebraska (Memorial) Lincoln, Neb.	76,400
North Carolina (Kenan) Chapel Hill, N.C.	47,000
North Carolina State (Carter) Raleigh, N.C.	44,000
Northwestern (Dyche) Evanston, Ill.	48,500
Notre Dame (Notre Dame) South Bend, Ind.	59,000
Ohio State (Ohio) Columbus, Ohio	83,100
Oklahoma (Owen Field) Norman, Okla.	71,000
Oklahoma State (Lewis) Stillwater, Okla.	50,500
Oregon (Autzen) Eugene, Ore.	42,000
Oregon State (Parker) Corvallis, Ore.	41,000
Pennsylvania (Franklin Field) Philadelphia, Pa.	60,500
Pennsylvania State (Beaver) University Park, Pa.	76,000
Pittsburgh (Pitt) Pittsburgh, Pa.	56,500
Princeton (Palmer) Princeton, N.J.	45,700
Purdue (Ross-Ade) West Lafayette, Ind.	69,200
Rice (Rice) Houston, Tex.	70,000
San Diego State (San Diego) San Diego, Cal.	53,000
South Carolina (Williams-Brice) Columbia, S.C.	54,400
Stanford (Stanford) Stanford, Cal.	86,300
Tennessee (Neyland) Knoxville, Tenn.	80,200
Texas (Memorial) Austin, Tex.	80,000
Texas A & M (Kyle Field) College Station, Tex.	54,000
Texas Christian (TCU-Amon Carter) Fort Worth, Tex.	46,000
Texas Tech (Jones) Lubbock, Tex.	47,000
Tulsa (Skelly) Tulsa, Okla.	40,200
Va. Polytechnic Inst. (Lane) Blacksburg, Va.	40,000
Washington (Husky) Seattle, Wash.	58,900
Wisconsin (Camp Randall) Madison, Wis.	77,200
Yale (Yale Bowl) New Haven, Conn.	70,800

OTHER STADIUMS USED BY MAJOR COLLEGE TEAMS

	Capacity
Astrodome, Houston (Houston, Texas Southern)	50,000
Cotton Bowl, Dallas	72,000
Los Angeles Memorial Coliseum (USC, UCLA)	93,000
Louisiana Superdome, New Orleans (Tulane)	71,300
Orange Bowl, Miami (Miami, Fla.)	76,000
Texas Stadium, Irving (Southern Methodist)	65,100
Veterans Stadium, Philadelphia (Temple)	66,000

THE HEISMAN MEMORIAL TROPHY: Awarded annually to the nation's outstanding college football player.

Year	Player and College	Year	Player and College	Year	Player and College
1941	Bruce Smith, Minnesota	1954	Alan Ameche, Wisconsin	1967	Gary Beban, UCLA
1942	Frank Sinkwich, Georgia	1955	Howard Cassady, Ohio State	1968	O. J. Simpson, USC
1943	Angelo Bertelli, Notre Dame	1956	Paul Hornung, Notre Dame	1969	Steve Owens, Oklahoma
1944	Les Horvath, Ohio State	1957	John Crow, Texas A&M	1970	Jim Plunkett, Stanford
1945	Felix Blanchard, Army	1958	Pete Dawkins, Army	1971	Pat Sullivan, Auburn
1946	Glenn Davis, Army	1959	Billy Cannon, Louisiana State	1972	Johnny Rogers, Nebraska
1947	John Lujack, Notre Dame	1960	Joe Bellino, Navy	1973	John Capelletti, Penn State
1948	Doak Walker, Southern Methodist	1961	Ernie Davis, Syracuse	1974	Archie Griffin, Ohio State
1949	Leon Hart, Notre Dame	1962	Terry Baker, Oregon State	1975	Archie Griffin, Ohio State
1950	Vic Janowicz, Ohio State	1963	Roger Staubach, Navy	1976	Tony Dorsett, Pittsburgh
1951	Dick Kazmaier, Princeton	1964	John Huarte, Notre Dame	1977	Earl Campbell, Texas
1952	Billy Vessels, Oklahoma	1965	Mike Garrett, Southern California	1978	Billy Sims, Oklahoma
1953	John Lattner, Notre Dame	1966	Steve Spurrier, Florida	1979	Charles White, USC

COLLEGE FOOTBALL COACH OF THE YEAR (American Football Coaches Ass'n)

Year	Coach and College	Year	Coach and College	Year	Coach and College
1942	Bill Alexander, Georgia Tech	1955	Duffy Daugherty, Michigan State	1968	Joe Paterno, Penn State
1943	Amos Alonzo Stagg, Pacific	1956	Bowden Wyatt, Tennessee	1969	Bo Schembechler, Michigan
1944	Carroll Widdoes, Ohio State	1957	Woody Hayes, Ohio State	1970	Darrell Royal, Texas
1945	Bo McMillin, Indiana	1958	Paul Dietzel, Louisiana State		Charlie McLendon, La. State
1946	Earl H. Blaik, Army	1959	Ben Schwartzwalder, Syracuse	1971	Paul Bryant, Alabama
1947	Fritz Crisler, Michigan	1960	Murray Warmath, Minnesota	1972	John McKay, Southern California
1948	Bennie Oosterbaan, Michigan	1961	Paul Bryant, Alabama	1973	Paul Bryant, Alabama
1949	Bud Wilkinson, Oklahoma	1962	John McKay, Southern California	1974	Grant Teaff, Baylor
1950	Charlie Caldwell, Princeton	1963	Darrell Royal, Texas	1975	Frank Kush, Arizona State
1951	Chuck Taylor, Stanford	1964	Ara Parseghian, Notre Dame	1976	Johnny Majors, Pittsburgh
1952	Biggie Munn, Michigan State	1965	Tommy Prothro, UCLA	1977	Don James, Washington
1953	Jim Tatum, Maryland	1966	Tom Cahill, Army	1978	Joe Paterno, Penn State
1954	Red Sanders, UCLA	1967	John Pont, Indiana	1979	Earl Bruce, Ohio State

OUTLAND AWARDS: Awarded annually to the nation's leading college football lineman.

Year	Player, College, Pos.	Year	Player, College, Pos.	Year	Player, College, Pos.
1946	George Connor, Notre Dame, T	1957	Alex Karras, Iowa, T	1968	Bill Stanfill, Georgia, T
1947	Joe Steffy, Army, G	1958	Zeke Smith, Auburn, G	1969	Mike Reid, Penn State, DT
1948	Bill Fischer, Notre Dame, G	1959	Mike McGee, Duke, T	1970	Jim Stillwagon, Ohio State, LB
1949	Ed Bagdon, Michigan St., G	1960	Tom Brown, Minnesota, G	1971	Larry Jacobson, Nebraska, DT
1950	Bob Gain, Kentucky, T	1961	Merlin Olsen, Utah State, T	1972	Rich Glover, Nebraska, MG
1951	Jim Weatherall, Oklahoma, T	1962	Bobby Bell, Minnesota, T	1973	John Hicks, Ohio State, T
1952	Dick Modzelewski, Maryland, T	1963	Scott Appleton, Texas, T	1974	Randy White, Maryland, DT
1953	J. D. Roberts, Oklahoma, G.	1964	Steve DeLong, Tennessee, T	1975	Leroy Selmon, Oklahoma, DT
1954	Bill Brooks, Arkansas, G	1965	Tommy Nobis, Texas, G	1976	Ross Browner, Notre Dame, DT
1955	Calvin Jones, Iowa, G	1966	Lloyd Phillips, Arkansas, T	1977	Brad Shearer, Texas, DT
1956	Jim Parker, Ohio State, G	1967	Ron Yary, Southern Cal, T	1978	Greg Roberts, Oklahoma, G
				1979	Jim Richter, N. Carolina St., C

1979 COLLEGE ALL-AMERICA SELECTIONS

OFFENSIVE TEAM

Receivers	Junior Miller, Nebraska (AP) (UPI) (SN) (FW)
	Ken Margerum, Stanford (AP) (UPI) (SN)
	Johnny Lam Jones, Texas (SN)
	Art Monk, Syracuse (FW)
Tackles	Greg Kolenda, Arkansas (AP) (UPI) (FW)
	Tim Foley, Notre Dame (UPI) (SN)
	Jim Bunch, Alabama (AP) (FW)
	Stan Brock, Colorado (SN)
Guards	Brad Budde, USC (AP) (UPI) (SN) (FW)
	Ken Fritz, Ohio State (AP) (UPI) (FW)
	Ray Snell, Wisconsin (SN)
Center	Jim Richter, N. Carolina State (AP) (UPI) (SN) (FW)
Quarterbacks	Marc Wilson, Brigham Young (AP) (UPI) (FW)
	Art Schlichter, Ohio State (SN)
Running backs	Billy Sims, Oklahoma (AP) (UPI) (SN) (FW)
	Charles White, USC (AP) (UPI) (SN) (FW)
	Vagas Ferguson, Notre Dame (UPI) (FW)
	George Rogers, South Carolina (AP)
Kicker	Dale Castro, Maryland (UPI) (SN) (FW)

DEFENSIVE TEAM

Linemen	Hugh Green, Pittsburgh (AP) (UPI) (SN) (FW)
	Jim Stuckey, Clemson (AP) (UPI) (SN) (FW)
	Steve McMichael, Texas (AP) (UPI) (FW)
	Bruce Clark, Penn State (UPI) (SN) (FW)
	Ron Simmons, Florida State (AP) (UPI)
	Jacob Green, Texas A & M (AP)
	Rulon Jones, Utah State (SN)
	Curt Greer, Michigan (FW)
Linebackers	George Cumby, Oklahoma (AP) (UPI) (SN) (FW)
	Ron Simpkins, Michigan (AP) (UPI) (FW)
	Dennis Johnson, USC (UPI) (SN)
	Mike Singletary, Baylor (AP) (FW)
	Otis Wilson, Louisville (SN)
Defensive backs	Kenny Easley, UCLA (AP) (UPI) (SN) (FW)
	Johnny Johnson, Texas (AP) (UPI) (SN) (FW)
	Roland James, Tennessee (UPI) (SN) (FW)
	Mark Haynes, Colorado (AP)
	Don McNeal, Alabama (SN)
Punter	Jim Miller, Mississippi (UPI) (SN) (FW)

Selections by (AP) Associated Press, (UPI) United Press International, (SN) The Sporting News, (FW) Football Writers Association of America

NATIONAL CHAMPIONSHIP GAMES

Year	NCAA Division I-AA
1978	Florida A&M 35, Massachusetts 28
1979	Eastern Kentucky 30, Lehigh 7

Year	NCAA Division II
1975	Northern Michigan 16, Western Kentucky 14
1976	Montana State 24, Akron 13
1977	Lehigh 33, Jacksonville (Ala.) State 0
1978	Eastern Illinois 10, Delaware 9
1979	Delaware 38, Youngstown State 21

Year	NCAA Division III
1975	Wittenberg 28, Ithaca 0
1976	St. Johns (Minn.) 31, Towson State 28
1977	Widener 39, Wabash 36
1978	Baldwin-Wallace 24, Wittenberg 10
1979	Ithaca (N.Y.) 14, Wittenberg 10

Year	NAIA Division I
1975	Texas A & I 37, Salem (W. Va.) 0
1976	Texas A & I 26, Central Arkansas 0
1977	Abilene Christian 24, Southwestern Oklahoma State 7
1978	Angelo State (Tex.) 34, Elon (N.C.) 14
1979	Texas A & I 20, Central State Okla. 14

Year	NAIA Division II
1975	Texas Lutheran 34, California Lutheran 8
1976	Westminster (Pa.) 20, Redlands 13
1977	Westminster (Pa.) 17, California Lutheran 9
1978	Concordia (Minn.) 7, Findlay (Ohio) 0
1979	Findlay (Ohio) 51, Northwestern (Iowa) 6

HOCKEY

HOCKEY GOVERNMENT

The National Hockey League (NHL): 960 Sun Life Building, Montreal, Quebec. President: John A. Ziegler, Jr. Chairman of the Board: William W. Wirtz. Organized in 1917. The NHL expanded to 21 teams in 1979 with the Edmonton Oilers, Hartford Whalers, Quebec Nordiques and Winnipeg Jets joining the league.

PRINCE OF WALES CONFERENCE

JAMES NORRIS DIVISION

	Pres./Owner	Coach
Detroit Red Wings	Bruce A. Norris	Ted Lindsay
Los Angeles Kings	Lou Baumeister	Bob Berry
Hartford Whalers	Howard L. Baldwin	Don Blackburn
Montreal Canadiens	Morgan McCammon	Claude Ruel
Pittsburgh Penguins	Vincent J. Bartimo	Ed Johnston

CHARLES F. ADAMS DIVISION

Boston Bruins	Paul A. Mooney	Gerry Cheevers
Buffalo Sabres	Seymour H. Knox III	Roger Neilson
Minnesota North Stars	George Gund III	Glen Sonmor
Quebec Nordiques	Marcel Aubut	Maurice Filion
Toronto Maple Leafs	Harold E. Ballard	Punch Imlach

CLARENCE CAMPBELL CONFERENCE

CONN SMYTHE DIVISION

	Pres./Owner	Coach
Chicago Black Hawks	William W. Wirtz	Keith Magnuson
Colorado Rockies	Armand Pohan	Billy MacMillan
Edmonton Oilers	Peter Pocklington	Bryan Watson
St. Louis Blues	Emile Francis	Red Berenson
Vancouver Canucks	Frank A. Griffiths	Harry Neale
Winnipeg Jets	Michael Gobuty	Tom McVie

LESTER PATRICK DIVISION

Calgary Flames	Nelson Skalbania	Al MacNeil
New York Islanders	John O. Pickett, Jr.	Al Arbour
New York Rangers	William M. Jennings	Fred Shero
Philadelphia Flyers	Edward M. Snider	Pat Quinn
Washington Capitals	Abe Pollin	Gary Green

NATIONAL HOCKEY LEAGUE RECORDS   At start of 1980-81 season

Most Goals, Lifetime: 801, Gordie Howe, Detroit Red Wings, Hartford Whalers.

Most Goals, One Season: 76, Phil Esposito, Boston Bruins, 1970/71.

Most Assists, One Season: 102, Bobby Orr, Boston Bruins, 1970/71.

Most Points, One Game: 10, Darryl Sittler, Toronto Maple Leafs, February 7, 1976.

Most Victories, One Season: 60, Montreal Canadiens, 1976/77.

Longest Winning Streak: 14 games, Boston Bruins, 1929/30.

Most Goals, One Season: 399, Boston Bruins, 1970/71.

Most Shutouts by a Goaltender: 103, Terry Sawchuk, Detroit, Boston, Toronto, Los Angeles, N.Y. Rangers.

Most Penalty Minutes, One Season: 472, Dave Schultz, Philadelphia Flyers, 1974/75.

Most Seasons: 26, Gordie Howe, Detroit Red Wings, 1946/47 through 1970/71, Hartford Whalers, 1979/80.

Most Games, Including Playoffs, Lifetime: 1,924, Gordie Howe, Detroit Red Wings, Hartford Whalers.

Most Goals, Including Playoffs, Lifetime: 869, Gordie Howe, Detroit Red Wings, Hartford Whalers.

Most Assists, Including Playoffs, Lifetime: 1,141, Gordie Howe, Detroit Red Wings, Hartford Whalers.

Most Points, Including Playoffs, Lifetime: 2,010, Gordie Howe, Detroit Red Wings, Hartford Whalers.

Most Penalty Minutes, Including Playoffs, Lifetime: 2,706, Dave Schultz, Philadelphia Flyers, Los Angeles Kings, Pittsburgh Penguins, Buffalo Sabres.

Most Consecutive Games: 914, Garry Unger, Toronto Maple Leafs, Detroit Red Wings, St. Louis Blues, Atlanta Flames, 1967/68–1979/80.

Most Consecutive Complete Games by Goaltender: 502, Glenn Hall, Detroit Red Wings and Chicago Black Hawks, 1955/56 through 1962/63.

Most Shutouts by a Goaltender, One Season: 22, George Hainsworth, Montreal Canadiens, 1928/29.

Longest Shutout Sequence by a Goaltender: 461 Minutes 29 Seconds, Alex Connell, Ottawa Senators, 1927/28.

Most Goals, One Game: 7, Joe Malone, Quebec Bulldogs, January 31, 1920.

Most Assists, One Game: 7, Billy Taylor, Detroit Red Wings, March 16, 1947; Wayne Gretzky, Edmonton Oilers, February 15, 1980.

Most Penalties, One Game: 9, Jim Dorey, Toronto Maple Leafs, October 16, 1968; Dave Schultz, Pittsburgh Penguins, April 6, 1978; Russ Anderson, Pittsburgh Penguins, January 19, 1980.

Most Penalty Minutes, One Game: 67, Randy Holt, Los Angeles Kings, March 11, 1979.

Most Goals in One Period: 4, Harvey (Busher) Jackson, Toronto Maple Leafs, November 20, 1934; Max Bentley, Chicago Black Hawks, January 28, 1943; Clint Smith, Chicago Black Hawks, March 4, 1945; Gordon (Red) Berenson, St. Louis Blues, November 7, 1968.

Fastest Opening Goal: 6 seconds, Henry Boucha, Detroit Red Wings, January 28, 1973; Jean Pronovost, Pittsburgh Penguins, March 25, 1976.

Fastest Two Goals: 4 seconds, Nels Stewart, Montreal Maroons, January 3, 1931.

Fastest Three Goals: 21 seconds, Bill Mosienko, Chicago Black Hawks, March 23, 1952.

NHL CHAMPIONS

Season	Regular Season	Stanley Cup
1954/55	Detroit Red Wings	Detroit Red Wings
1955/56	Montreal Canadiens	Montreal Canadiens
1956/57	Detroit Red Wings	Montreal Canadiens
1957/58	Montreal Canadiens	Montreal Canadiens
1958/59	Montreal Canadiens	Montreal Canadiens
1959/60	Montreal Canadiens	Montreal Canadiens
1960/61	Montreal Canadiens	Chicago Black Hawks
1961/62	Montreal Canadiens	Toronto Maple Leafs
1962/63	Toronto Maple Leafs	Toronto Maple Leafs
1963/64	Montreal Canadiens	Toronto Maple Leafs
1964/65	Detroit Red Wings	Montreal Canadiens
1965/66	Montreal Canadiens	Montreal Canadiens
1966/67	Chicago Black Hawks	Toronto Maple Leafs
1967/68	Montreal Canadiens* Philadelphia Flyers†	Montreal Canadiens
1968/69	Montreal Canadiens* St. Louis Blues†	Montreal Canadiens
1969/70	Chicago Black Hawks* St. Louis Blues†	Boston Bruins
1970/71	Boston Bruins* Chicago Black Hawks†	Montreal Canadiens
1971/72	Boston Bruins* Chicago Black Hawks†	Boston Bruins
1972/73	Montreal Canadiens* Chicago Black Hawks†	Montreal Canadiens
1973/74	Boston Bruins* Philadelphia Flyers†	Philadelphia Flyers
1974/75	Montreal Canadiens Buffalo Sabres Philadelphia Flyers Vancouver Canucks	Philadelphia Flyers
1975/76	Montreal Canadiens Boston Bruins Philadelphia Flyers Chicago Black Hawks	Montreal Canadiens
1976/77	Montreal Canadiens Boston Bruins Philadelphia Flyers St. Louis Blues	Montreal Canadiens
1977/78	Montreal Canadiens Boston Bruins New York Islanders Chicago Black Hawks	Montreal Canadiens
1978/79	Montreal Canadiens Boston Bruins New York Islanders Chicago Black Hawks	Montreal Canadiens
1979/80	Montreal Canadiens Buffalo Sabres Philadelphia Flyers Chicago Black Hawks	New York Islanders

* East Division. † West Division.

NHL FINAL STANDINGS: 1979-80

CAMPBELL CONFERENCE

PATRICK DIVISION	W	L	T	Pts.	GF	GA
Philadelphia	48	12	20	116	327	254
NY Islanders	39	28	13	91	281	247
NY Rangers	38	32	10	86	308	284
Atlanta	35	32	13	83	282	269
Washington	27	40	13	67	261	293
SMYTHE DIVISION						
Chicago	34	27	19	87	241	250
St. Louis	34	34	12	80	266	278
Vancouver	27	37	16	70	256	281
Edmonton	28	39	13	69	301	322
Winnipeg	20	49	11	51	214	314
Colorado	19	48	13	51	234	308

WALES CONFERENCE

ADAMS DIVISION	W	L	T	Pts.	GF	GA
Buffalo	47	17	16	110	318	201
Boston	42	21	13	105	310	234
Minnesota	36	28	16	88	311	253
Toronto	35	40	5	75	304	327
Quebec	25	44	11	61	248	313
NORRIS DIVISION						
Montreal	47	20	13	107	328	240
Los Angeles	30	36	14	74	290	313
Pittsburgh	30	37	13	73	251	303
Hartford	27	34	19	73	303	312
Detroit	26	43	11	63	268	306

STANLEY CUP PLAYOFFS: 1980 Top 16 Teams (Total Points) Qualify

Preliminary Round (Best-of-five series)
- Philadelphia over Edmonton: 3-0
- Buffalo over Vancouver: 3-1
- Montreal over Hartford: 3-0
- Boston over Pittsburgh: 3-2
- NY Islanders over Los Angeles: 3-1
- Minnesota over Toronto: 3-0
- Chicago over St. Louis: 3-0
- NY Rangers over Atlanta: 3-1

Quarter Finals (Best-of-seven series)
- Philadelphia over NY Rangers: 4-1
- Buffalo over Chicago: 4-0
- Minnesota over Montreal: 4-3
- NY Islanders over Boston: 4-1

Semi-Finals (Best-of-seven series)
- Philadelphia over Minnesota: 4-1
- NY Islanders over Buffalo: 4-2

Finals (Best-of-seven series)
1. NY Islanders 4, Philadelphia 3
2. Philadelphia 8, NY Islanders 3
3. NY Islanders 6, Philadelphia 2
4. NY Islanders 5, Philadelphia 2
5. Philadelphia 6, NY Islanders 3
6. NY Islanders 5, Philadelphia 4

STANLEY CUP CHAMPIONS

Season	Champions	Manager
1919-20	Ottawa Senators	Tommy Gorman
1920-21	Ottawa Senators	Tommy Gorman
1921-22	Toronto St. Pats	Charlie Querrie
1922-23	Ottawa Senators	Tommy Gorman
1923-24	Montreal Canadiens	Leo Dandurand
1924-25	Victoria Cougars	Lester Patrick
1925-26	Montreal Maroons	Eddie Gerard
1926-27	Ottawa Senators	Dave Gill
1927-28	New York Rangers	Lester Patrick
1928-29	Boston Bruins	Art Ross
1929-30	Montreal Canadiens	Cecil Hart
1930-31	Montreal Canadiens	Cecil Hart
1931-32	Toronto Maple Leafs	Conn Smythe
1932-33	New York Rangers	Lester Patrick
1933-34	Chicago Black Hawks	Tommy Gorman
1934-35	Montreal Maroons	Tommy Gorman
1935-36	Detroit Red Wings	Jack Adams
1936-37	Detroit Red Wings	Jack Adams
1937-38	Chicago Black Hawks	Bill Stewart
1938-39	Boston Bruins	Art Ross
1939-40	New York Rangers	Lester Patrick
1940-41	Boston Bruins	Art Ross
1941-42	Toronto Maple Leafs	Conn Smythe
1942-43	Detroit Red Wings	Jack Adams
1943-44	Montreal Canadiens	Tommy Gorman
1944-45	Toronto Maple Leafs	Conn Smythe
1945-46	Montreal Canadiens	Tommy Gorman
1946-47	Toronto Maple Leafs	Conn Smythe
1947-48	Toronto Maple Leafs	Conn Smythe
1948-49	Toronto Maple Leafs	Conn Smythe
1949-50	Detroit Red Wings	Jack Adams
1950-51	Toronto Maple Leafs	Conn Smythe
1951-52	Detroit Red Wings	Jack Adams
1952-53	Montreal Canadiens	Frank Selke
1953-54	Detroit Red Wings	Jack Adams
1954-55	Detroit Red Wings	Jack Adams
1955-56	Montreal Canadiens	Frank Selke
1956-57	Montreal Canadiens	Frank Selke
1957-58	Montreal Canadiens	Frank Selke
1958-59	Montreal Canadiens	Frank Selke
1959-60	Montreal Canadiens	Frank Selke
1960-61	Chicago Black Hawks	Tommy Ivan
1961-62	Toronto Maple Leafs	Punch Imlach
1962-63	Toronto Maple Leafs	Punch Imlach
1963-64	Toronto Maple Leafs	Punch Imlach
1964-65	Montreal Canadiens	Sam Pollock
1965-66	Montreal Canadiens	Sam Pollock
1966-67	Toronto Maple Leafs	Punch Imlach
1967-68	Montreal Canadiens	Sam Pollock
1968-69	Montreal Canadiens	Sam Pollock
1969-70	Boston Bruins	Milt Schmidt
1970-71	Montreal Canadiens	Sam Pollock
1971-72	Boston Bruins	Milt Schmidt
1972-73	Montreal Canadiens	Hector Blake
1973-74	Philadelphia Flyers	Keith Allen
1974-75	Philadelphia Flyers	Keith Allen
1975-76	Montreal Canadiens	Sam Pollock
1976-77	Montreal Canadiens	Sam Pollock
1977-78	Montreal Canadiens	Sam Pollock
1978-79	Montreal Canadiens	Irving Grundman
1979-80	New York Islanders	Bill Torrey

NHL SCORING LEADERS

Season	Player and Team	Points
1947-48	Elmer Lach, Montreal	61
1948-49	Roy Conacher, Chicago	68
1949-50	Ted Lindsay, Detroit	78
1950-51	Gordie Howe, Detroit	86
1951-52	Gordie Howe, Detroit	86
1952-53	Gordie Howe, Detroit	95
1953-54	Gordie Howe, Detroit	81
1954-55	Bernie Geoffrion, Montreal	75
1955-56	Jean Beliveau, Montreal	88
1956-57	Gordie Howe, Detroit	89
1957-58	Dickie Moore, Montreal	84
1958-59	Dickie Moore, Montreal	96
1959-60	Bobby Hull, Chicago	81
1960-61	Bernie Geoffrion, Montreal	95
1961-62	Bobby Hull, Chicago	84
1962-63	Gordie Howe, Detroit	86
1963-64	Stan Mikita, Chicago	89
1964-65	Stan Mikita, Chicago	87
1965-66	Bobby Hull, Chicago	97
1966-67	Stan Mikita, Chicago	97
1967-68	Stan Mikita, Chicago	87
1968-69	Phil Esposito, Boston	126
1969-70	Bobby Orr, Boston	120
1970-71	Phil Esposito, Boston	152
1971-72	Phil Esposito, Boston	133
1972-73	Phil Esposito, Boston	130
1973-74	Phil Esposito, Boston	145
1974-75	Bobby Orr, Boston	135
1975-76	Guy Lafleur, Montreal	125
1976-77	Guy Lafleur, Montreal	136
1977-78	Guy Lafleur, Montreal	132
1978-79	Brian Trottier, NY Islanders	134
1979-80	Marcel Dionne, Los Angeles	137
	Wayne Gretzky, Edmonton	137

NHL SCORING LEADERS: 1979/80

Player	Team	G	A	Pts.	Player	Team	G	A	Pts.
Marcel Dionne	Los Angeles	53	84	137	Darryl Sittler	Toronto	40	57	97
Wayne Gretzky	Edmonton	51	86	137	Blair MacDonald	Edmonton	46	48	94
Guy Lafleur	Montreal	50	75	125	Bernie Federko	St. Louis	38	56	94
Gilbert Perreault	Buffalo	40	66	106	Al MacAdam	Minnesota	42	51	93
Mike Rogers	Hartford	44	61	105	Kent Nilsson	Atlanta	40	53	93
Bryan Trottier	N.Y. Islanders	42	62	104	Mike Bossy	N.Y. Islanders	41	51	92
Charlie Simmer	Los Angeles	56	44	100	Rick Middleton	Boston	40	52	92
Blaine Stoughton	Hartford	56	44	100	Dave Taylor	Los Angeles	38	53	91

NHL ALL-TIME SCORING LEADERS   At start of 1980/81 season.

Player (Team)	Seasons	Games	Goals	Assists	Points	Scoring Percentage
Gordie Howe (Detroit, Hartford)	26	1,767	801	1,049	1,850	1.047
Phil Esposito (Chicago, Boston, N.Y. Rangers)	17	1,241	710	860	1,570	1.265
Stan Mikita (Chicago)	22	1,394	541	926	1,467	1.052
Johnny Bucyk (Detroit, Boston)	23	1,540	556	813	1,369	.889
Alex Delvecchio (Detroit)	24	1,549	456	825	1,281	.827
Jean Ratelle (N.Y. Rangers, Boston)	20	1,234	480	750	1,230	.997
Norm Ullman (Detroit, Toronto)	20	1,410	490	739	1,229	.872
Jean Beliveau (Mtl. Canadiens)	20	1,125	507	712	1,219	1.084
Bobby Hull (Chicago, Winnipeg, Hartford)	16	1,063	610	560	1,170	1.100
Frank Mahovlich (Toronto, Detroit, Mtl. Canadiens)	18	1,181	533	570	1,103	.934
Henri Richard (Mtl. Canadiens)	20	1,256	358	688	1,046	.833
Rod Gilbert (N.Y. Rangers)	18	1,065	406	615	1,021	.959
Andy Bathgate (N.Y. Rangers, Toronto, Detroit, Pittsburgh Penguins)	17	1,069	349	624	973	.910
Maurice Richard (Mtl. Canadiens)	18	978	544	421	965	.987
Guy Lafleur (Mtl. Canadiens)	9	667	405	536	941	1.390
Bobby Clarke (Philadelphia Flyers)	11	849	282	655	937	1.103
Marcel Dionne (Detroit, Los Angeles)	9	699	380	548	928	1.328
Dave Keon (Toronto, Hartford)	16	1,138	375	545	920	.808
Bobby Orr (Boston, Chicago)	12	657	270	645	915	1.393
Gilbert Perreault (Buffalo)	10	753	340	529	869	1.154
Yvan Cournoyer (Mtl. Canadiens)	16	968	428	435	863	.892
Dean Prentice (N.Y. Rangers, Boston, Detroit, Pittsburgh Penguins, Minnesota)	22	1,378	391	469	860	.624
Ted Lindsay (Detroit, Chicago)	17	1,068	379	472	851	.797
Jacques Lemaire (Montreal Canadiens)	12	853	366	469	835	.978
Red Kelly (Detroit, Toronto)	20	1,316	281	542	823	.625
Bernie Geoffrion (Mtl. Canadiens, N.Y. Rangers)	16	883	393	464	791	1.278
Pit Martin (Detroit, Boston, Chicago, Vancouver)	17	1,101	324	485	809	.735
Ken Hodge (Chicago, Boston, N.Y. Rangers)	14	881	328	472	800	.908
Darryl Sittler (Toronto)	10	726	328	454	782	1.077
Pete Mahovlich (Detroit, Mtl. Canadiens, Pittsburgh Penguins)	15	860	287	481	768	.893
Garry Unger (Toronto, Detroit, St. Louis, Atlanta)	13	972	394	368	762	.784
Murray Oliver (Detroit, Boston, Toronto, Minnesota)	17	1,127	274	454	728	.646
Bob Nevin (Toronto, N.Y. Rangers, Minnesota, Los Angeles)	18	1,128	307	419	726	.644
Jean Pronovost (Pittsburgh, Atlanta)	12	908	368	345	713	.785
George Armstrong (Toronto)	21	1,187	296	417	713	.601
Vic Hadfield (N.Y. Rangers, Pittsburgh Penguins)	16	1,002	323	389	712	.711
Doug Mohns (Boston, Chicago, Minnesota, Atlanta, Washington)	22	1,390	248	462	710	.511
Bobby Rousseau (Mtl. Canadiens, Minnesota, N.Y. Rangers)	15	942	245	458	703	.736
Wayne Cashman (Boston)	14	821	236	439	675	.822
Richard Martin (Buffalo)	9	658	375	299	674	1.024
Phil Goyette (Mtl. Canadiens, N.Y. Rangers, St. Louis Blues, Buffalo)	16	941	207	467	674	.716
Butch Goring (Los Angeles, N.Y. Islanders)	11	748	281	389	670	.896
Red Berenson (Mtl. Canadiens, NY Rangers, St. Louis, Detroit)	14	821	236	439	675	.822

NATIONAL HOCKEY LEAGUE TROPHY WINNERS

HART TROPHY For Most Valuable Player

1956/57	Gordie Howe, Detroit	1964/65	Bobby Hull, Chicago	1972/73	Bobby Clarke, Philadelphia
1957/58	Gordie Howe, Detroit	1965/66	Bobby Hull, Chicago	1973/74	Phil Esposito, Boston
1958/59	Andy Bathgate, New York	1966/67	Stan Mikita, Chicago	1974/75	Bobby Clarke, Philadelphia
1959/60	Gordie Howe, Detroit	1967/68	Stan Mikita, Chicago	1975/76	Bobby Clarke, Philadelphia
1960/61	Bernie Geoffrion, Montreal	1968/69	Phil Esposito, Boston	1976/77	Guy Lafleur, Montreal
1961/62	Jacques Plante, Montreal	1969/70	Bobby Orr, Boston	1977/78	Guy Lafleur, Montreal
1962/63	Gordie Howe, Detroit	1970/71	Bobby Orr, Boston	1978/79	Bryan Trottier, N.Y. Islanders
1963/64	Jean Beliveau, Montreal	1971/72	Bobby Orr, Boston	1979/80	Wayne Gretzky, Edmonton

VENZINA TROPHY For Best Goalie Record

1962/63	Glenn Hall, Chicago	1968/69	Glenn Hall and Jacques Plante, St Louis	1974/75	Bernie Parent, Philadelphia
1963/64	Charlie Hodge, Montreal			1975/76	Ken Dryden, Montreal
1964/65	Terry Sawchuk and Johnny Bower, Toronto	1969/70	Tony Esposito, Chicago	1976/77	Ken Dryden and Michel Larocque, Montreal
1965/66	Lorne Worsley and Charlie Hodge, Montreal	1970/71	Ed Giacomin and Gilles Villemure, New York	1977/78	Ken Dryden and Michel Larocque, Montreal
1966/67	Denis DeJordy and Glenn Hall, Chicago	1971/72	Tony Esposito and Gary Smith, Chicago	1978/79	Ken Dryden and Michel Larocque, Montreal
1967/68	Lorne Worsley and Rogatien Vachon, Montreal	1972/73	Ken Oryden, Montreal		
		1973/74	Bernie Parent, Philadelphia and Tony Esposito, Chicago	1979/80	Don Edwards and Bob Sauve, Buffalo

JAMES NORRIS TROPHY For Best Defenseman

1956/57 Doug Harvey, Montreal	1964/65 Pierre Pilote, Chicago	1972/73 Bobby Orr, Boston
1957/58 Doug Harvey, Montreal	1965/66 J. Laperriere, Montreal	1973/74 Bobby Orr, Boston
1958/59 Tom Johnson, Montreal	1966/67 Harry Howell, New York	1974/75 Bobby Orr, Boston
1959/60 Doug Harvey, Montreal	1967/68 Bobby Orr, Boston	1975/76 Denis Potvin, N.Y. Islanders
1960/61 Doug Harvey, Montreal	1968/69 Bobby Orr, Boston	1976/77 Larry Robinson, Montreal
1961/62 Doug Harvey, New York	1969/70 Bobby Orr, Boston	1977/78 Denis Potvin, N.Y. Islanders
1962/63 Pierre Pilote, Chicago	1970/71 Bobby Orr, Boston	1978/79 Denis Potvin, N.Y. Islanders
1963/64 Pierre Pilote, Chicago	1971/72 Bobby Orr, Boston	1979/80 Larry Robinson, Montreal

FRANK J. SELKE TROPHY For Best Defensive Forward

1977/78 Bob Gainey, Montreal	1978/79 Bob Gainey, Montreal	1979/80 Bob Gainey, Montreal

CALDER TROPHY For Best Rookie

1953/54 Camille Henry, New York	1962/63 Kent Douglas, Toronto	1971/72 Ken Dryden, Montreal
1954/55 Ed Litzenberger, Chicago	1963/64 Jacques Laperriere, Montreal	1972/73 Steve Vickers, N. Y. Rangers
1955/56 Glenn Hall, Detroit	1964/65 Roger Crozier, Detroit	1973/74 Denis Potvin, N. Y. Islanders
1956/57 Larry Regan, Boston	1965/66 Brit Selby, Toronto	1974/75 Eric Vail, Atlanta
1957/58 Frank Mahovlich, Toronto	1966/67 Bobby Orr, Boston	1975/76 Bryan Trottier, N.Y. Islanders
1958/59 Ralph Backstrom, Montreal	1967/68 Derek Sanderson, Boston	1976/77 Willie Plett, Atlanta
1959/60 Billy Hay, Chicago	1968/69 Danny Grant, Minnesota	1977/78 Mike Bossy, N. Y. Islanders
1960/61 Dave Keon, Toronto	1969/70 Tony Esposito, Chicago	1978/79 Bobby Smith, Minnesota
1961/62 Bobby Rousseau, Montreal	1970/71 Gil Perreault, Buffalo	1979/80 Ray Bourque, Boston

LADY BYNG TROPHY For Sportsmanship

1953/54 Red Kelly, Detroit	1962/63 Dave Keon, Toronto	1971/72 Jean Ratelle, New York
1954/55 Sid Smith, Toronto	1963/64 Ken Wharram, Chicago	1972/73 Gil Perreault, Buffalo
1955/56 Earl Reibel, Detroit	1964/65 Bobby Hull, Chicago	1973/74 John Bucyk, Boston
1956/57 Andy Hebenton, New York	1965/66 Alex Delvecchio, Detroit	1974/75 Marcel Dionne, Detroit
1957/58 Camille Henry, New York	1966/67 Stan Mikita, Chicago	1975/76 Jean Ratelle, Boston
1958/59 Alex Delvecchio, Detroit	1967/68 Stan Mikita, Chicago	1976/77 Marcel Dionne, Los Angeles
1959/60 Don McKenney, Boston	1968/69 Alex Delvecchio, Detroit	1977/78 Butch Goring, Los Angeles
1960/61 Red Kelly, Toronto	1969/70 Phil Goyette, St. Louis	1978/79 Bob MacMillan, Atlanta
1961/62 Dave Keon, Toronto	1970/71 Johnny Bucyk, Boston	1979/80 Wayne Gretzky, Edmonton

CONN SMYTHE TROPHY For Most Valuable Player in Stanley Cup Playoffs

1965 Jean Beliveau, Montreal	1970 Bobby Orr, Boston	1975 Bernie Parent, Philadelphia
1966 Roger Crozier, Detroit	1971 Ken Dryden, Montreal	1976 Reggie Leach, Philadelphia
1967 Dave Keon, Toronto	1972 Bobby Orr, Boston	1977 Guy Lafleur, Montreal
1968 Glenn Hall, St. Louis	1973 Yvan Cournoyer, Montreal	1978 Larry Robinson, Montreal
1969 Serge Savard, Montreal	1974 Bernie Parent, Philadelphia	1979 Bob Gainey, Montreal
		1980 Bryan Trottier, N.Y. Islanders

1980 NHL ALL-STARS

Results of voting by members of the Professional Hockey Writers Association

Goal	Tony Esposito, Chicago	Don Edwards, Buffalo	Mike Liut, St. Louis
Defense	Larry Robinson, Montreal	Borje Salming, Toronto	Mark Howe, Hartford
	Ray Bourque, Boston	Jim Schoenfeld, Buffalo	Barry Beck, N.Y. Rangers
Center	Marcel Dionne, Los Angeles	Wayne Gretzky, Edmonton	Gil Perreault, Buffalo
Right Wing	Guy Lafleur, Montreal	Danny Gare, Buffalo	Mike Bossy, N.Y. Islanders
Left Wing	Charlie Simmer, Los Angeles	Steve Shutt, Montreal	Steve Payne, Minnesota

NHL ALL-STAR GAME RESULTS

Prior to 1969 the All-Star Game between the chosen team and the holder of the Stanley Cup.

Year	Score	Location	Year	Score	Location
1947	All-Stars 4, Toronto 3	Toronto	1967	Montreal 3, All-Stars 0	Montreal
1948	All-Stars 3, Toronto 1	Chicago	1968	Toronto 4, All-Stars 3	Toronto
1949	All-Stars 3, Toronto 1	Toronto	1969	East 3, West 3	Montreal
1950	Detroit 7, All-Stars 1	Detroit	1970	East 4, West 1	St. Louis
1951	1st Team 2, 2nd Team 2	Toronto	1971	West 2, East 1	Boston
1952	1st Team 1, 2nd Team 1	Detroit	1972	East 3, West 2	Minnesota
1953	All-Stars 3, Montreal 1	Montreal	1973	East 5, West 4	New York
1954	All-Stars 2, Detroit 2	Detroit	1974	West 6, East 4	Chicago
1955	Detroit 3, All-Stars 1	Detroit	1975	Prince of Wales 7, Campbell 1	Montreal
1956	All-Stars 1, Montreal 1	Montreal	1976	Prince of Wales 7, Campbell 5	Philadelphia
1957	All-Stars 5, Montreal 3	Montreal	1977	Prince of Wales 4, Campbell 3	Vancouver
1958	Montreal 6, All-Stars 3	Montreal	1978	Prince of Wales 3, Campbell 2	Buffalo
1959	Montreal 6, All-Stars 1	Montreal	1979	no game played	
1960	All-Stars 2, Montreal 1	Montreal	1980	Prince of Wales 6, Campbell 3	Detroit
1961	All-Stars 3, Chicago 1	Chicago			
1962	Toronto 4, All-Stars 1	Toronto			
1963	All-Stars 3, Toronto 3	Toronto			
1964	All-Stars 3, Toronto 2	Toronto			
1965	All-Stars 5, Montreal 2	Montreal			

HOCKEY HALL OF FAME

Source: N.H.L.

Players
Sidney Abel
John Adams
C. J. "Syl" Apps
George Armstrong
I. W. "Ace" Bailey
Donald Bain
Hobart Baker
Martin Barry
Andrew Bathgate
Jean Beliveau
Clinton Benedict
Douglas Bentley
Maxwell Bentley
Hector "Toe" Blake
Richard Boon
Emile "Butch" Bouchard
Frank Boucher
George "Buck" Boucher
John Bower
Russell Bowie
Francis Brimsek
H. L. "Punch" Broadbent
W. E. "Turk" Broda
Billy Burch
Harold Cameron
F. M. "King" Clancy
Aubrey "Dit" Clapper
Sprague Cleghorn
Neil Colville
Charles Conacher
Alex Connell
William Cook
Arthur Coulter
William Cowley
S. R. "Rusty" Crawford
John Darragh
A. M. "Scotty" Davidson
Clarence "Hap" Day
Alex Delvecchio
Cyril Denneny
Gordon Drillon
Charles Drinkwater
Thomas Dunderdale
William Durnan
M. A. "Red" Dutton
C. H. "Babe" Dye
Arthur Farrell
Frank Foyston
Frank Frederickson
William Gadsby
Charles Gardiner
Herbert Gardiner
James Gardner
J. A. Bernard Geoffrion
Eddie Gerard
H. L. "Billy" Gilmour
F. X. "Moose" Goheen

Players
Ebenezer Goodfellow
Michael Grant
W. "Shorty" Green
Silas Griffis
George Hainsworth
Glenn Hall
Joseph Hall
Douglas Harvey
George Hay
W. M. "Riley" Hern
Bryan Hextall
Harry Holmes
C. Thomas Hooper
G. R. "Red" Horner
M. G. "Tim" Horton
Gordon Howe
Sydney Howe
Harry Howell
J. B. "Bouse" Hutton
Harry Hyland
J. D. "Dick" Irvin
H. "Busher" Jackson
E. "Moose" Johnson
Ivan "Ching" Johnson
Thomas Johnson
Aurel Joliat
G. "Duke" Keats
L. P. "Red" Kelly
T. S. "Teeder" Kennedy
Elmer Lach
E. C. "Newsy" Lalonde
Jean Laviolette
Hugh Lehman
Percy LeSeur
Robert "Ted" Lindsay
Harry Lumley
D. "Mickey" MacKay
Joseph Malone
Sylvio Mantha
John Marshall
Fred "Steamer" Maxwell
Frank McGee
William McGimsie
George McNamara
Richard Moore
Patrick Moran
Howie Morenz
William Mosienko
Frank Nighbor
E. Reginald Noble
Harry Oliver
Bobby Orr
Lester Patrick
Lynn Patrick
Tommy Phillips
J. A. Pierre Pilote
Didier "Pit" Pitre
J. Jacques Plante
Walter "Babe" Pratt

Players
A. Joseph Primeau
J. R. Marcel Pronovost
Harvey Pulford
H. G. "Bill" Quackenbush
Frank Rankin
C. E. "Chuck" Rayner
Kenneth Reardon
Henri Richard
J. H. Maurice Richard
George Richardson
Gordon Roberts
Arthur Ross
Blair Russel
J. D. "Jack" Ruttan
Terrance Sawchuk
Fred Scanlan
Milton Schmidt
D. "Sweeney" Schriner
Earl Seibert
Oliver Seibert
Edward Shore
A. C. "Babe" Siebert
Harold Simpson
Alfred Smith
R. "Hooley" Smith
Thomas Smith
R. "Barney" Stanley
John Stewart
Nelson Stewart
Bruce Stuart
Hod Stuart
F. "Cyclone" Taylor
C. R. "Tiny" Thompson
Col. Harry J. Trihey
Georges Vezina
John Walker
Martin Walsh
Harry Watson
Ralph "Cooney" Weiland
Harry Westwick
Fred Whitcroft
Gordon Wilson
Lorne "Gump" Worsley
Roy Worters

Referees
William Chadwick
Chaucer Elliott
Robert Hewitson
Fred "Mickey" Ion
Michael Rodden
J. Cooper Smeaton
R. A. "Red" Storey
Frank Udvari

Builders
Charles Adams
Weston Adams

Builders
Thomas "Frank" Ahearn
John "Bunny" Ahearne
Sir Montague Allen
Harold Ballard
John Bickell
George Brown
Walter Brown
Frank Buckland
Jack Butterfield
Frank Calder
Angus Campbell
Clarence Campbell
Joseph Cattarinich
Joseph "Leo" Dandurand
Francis Dilio
George Dudley
James Dunn
Dr. John Gibson
Thomas Gorman
Charles Hay
James Hendy
Foster Hewitt
William Hewitt
Fred Hume
Thomas Ivan
William Jennings
Gen. John Kilpatrick
George Leader
Robert LeBel
Thomas Lockhart
Paul Loicq
Maj. Frederic McLaughlin
Hon. Hartland Molson
Francis Nelson
Bruce Norris
James Norris, Sr.
James D. Norris
William Northey
John O'Brien
Frank Patrick
Allan Pickard
Samuel Pollock
Sen. Donat Raymond
John Robertson
Claude Robinson
Philip Ross
Frank Selke
Frank Smith
Conn Smythe
Lord Stanley of Preston
Capt. James Sutherland
Anatoli Tarasov
Lloyd Turner
William Tutt
Carl Voss
Fred Waghorne
Arthur Wirtz
William Writz

NATIONAL COLLEGIATE HOCKEY CHAMPIONSHIPS

DIVISION I

1957	Colorado College 13, Michigan 6
1958	Denver 6, North Dakota 2
1959	North Dakota 4, Michigan State 3
1960	Denver 5, Michigan Tech 3
1961	Denver 12, St. Lawrence 2
1962	Michigan Tech 7, Clarkson 1
1963	North Dakota 6, Denver 5
1964	Michigan 6, Denver 3
1965	Michigan Tech 8, Boston College 2
1966	Michigan State 6, Clarkson 1
1967	Cornell 4, Boston University 1
1968	Denver 4, North Dakota 0
1969	Denver 4, Cornell 3
1970	Cornell 6, Clarkson 4
1971	Boston University 4, Minnesota 2
1972	Boston University 4, Cornell 0
1973	Wisconsin 4, Denver 2
1974	Minnesota 4, Michigan Tech 2
1975	Michigan Tech 6, Minnesota 1
1976	Minnesota 6, Michigan Tech 4
1977	Wisconsin 6, Michigan 5
1978	Boston University 5, Boston College 3
1979	Minnesota 4, North Dakota 3
1980	North Dakota 5, Northern Michigan 2

DIVISION II

1978	Merrimack 12, Lake Forest 2
1979	Lowell 6, Mankato State 4
1980	Mankato State 5, Elmira 2

SOCCER

NORTH AMERICAN SOCCER LEAGUE: 1980 FINAL STANDINGS

NATIONAL CONFERENCE

Eastern Division	Won	Lost	Pts.	Goals For	Ag'st
New York Cosmos	24	8	213	87	41
Washington Diplomats	17	15	159	72	61
Toronto Metros	14	18	128	49	65
Rochester Lancers	12	20	109	42	67
Central Division					
Dallas Tornado	18	14	157	57	58
Minnesota Kicks	16	16	147	66	56
Tulsa Roughnecks	15	17	139	56	62
Atlanta Chiefs	7	25	74	34	84
Western Division					
Seattle Sounders	25	7	207	74	31
Los Angeles Aztecs	20	12	174	61	52
Vancouver Whitecaps	16	16	139	52	47
Portland Timbers	15	17	133	50	53

AMERICAN CONFERENCE

Eastern Division	Won	Lost	Pts.	Goals For	Ag'st
Tampa Bay Rowdies	19	13	168	61	50
Ft. Lauderdale Strikers	18	14	163	61	55
New England Tea Men	18	14	154	54	56
Philadelphia Fury	10	22	98	42	68
Central Division					
Chicago Sting	21	11	187	80	50
Houston Hurricane	14	18	130	56	69
Detroit Express	14	18	129	51	52
Memphis Rogues	14	18	126	49	57
Western Division					
Edmonton Drillers	17	15	149	58	51
California Surf	15	17	144	61	67
San Diego Sockers	16	16	140	53	51
San Jose Earthquake	9	23	95	45	68

LEADING SCORERS

	Games	Goals	Assists	Pts.
Giorgio Chinaglia, New York	32	32	13	77
Karl-Heinz Granitza, Chicago	31	19	26	64
Roger Davies, Seattle	29	25	11	61
Luis Fernando, Los Angeles	28	28	4	60
Alan Green, Washington	31	25	9	59
Laurie Abrahams, California	28	17	15	49

LEADING SCORERS

	Games	Goals	Assists	Pts.
Julio Romero, New York	32	14	19	47
Arno Steffenhagen, Chicago	28	15	15	45
Ace Ntsoelengoe, Minnesota	32	13	17	43
Edi Kirschner, Edmonton	31	15	12	42
Teofilo Cubillas, Ft. Lauderdale	27	14	14	42

LEADING GOALKEEPERS

	Games	Saves	Goals Ag'st	Avg.
Jack Brand, Seattle	32	169	30	0.91
Hubert Birkenmeier, New York	32	213	38	1.14
Bruce Grobbelaar, Vancouver	23	117	28	1.19
Alfredo Anhielo, Los Angeles	31	156	40	1.32
Volkmar Gross, San Diego	31	176	43	1.38

LEADING GOALKEEPERS

	Games	Saves	Goals Ag'st	Avg.
Phil Parkes, Chicago	30	181	43	1.39
Jim Brown, Detroit	32	162	47	1.407
Tino Lettieri, Minnesota	31	191	44	1.411
Winston DuBose, Tampa Bay	31	176	47	1.49
Bob Stetler, Memphis	27	113	42	1.52

AWARD WINNERS

Most Valuable Player — Roger Davies, Seattle
Coach of the Year — Alan Hinton, Seattle
PSRA Star of the Year — Johan Cruyff, Washington
North American Player of the Year — Jack Brand, Seattle

Rookie of the Year — Jeff Durgan, New York
Top Scorer — Giorgio Chinaglia, New York
Top Goalkeeper — Jack Brand, Seattle
Goal of the Year — Johan Cruyff, Washington

NASL PLAYOFFS

National Conference
New York over Tulsa
Dallas over Minnesota
Los Angeles over Washington
Seattle over Vancouver
New York over Dallas
Los Angeles over Seattle
New York over Los Angeles

American Conference
Ft. Lauderdale over California
Edmonton over Houston
San Diego over Chicago
Tampa Bay over New England
Ft. Lauderdale over Edmonton
San Diego over Tampa Bay
Ft. Lauderdale over San Diego

CHAMPIONSHIP (SOCCER BOWL 1980) — New York 3, Ft. Lauderdale 0

NASL ALL-STAR TEAMS: 1980

Position	First Team	Second Team	Honorable Mention
Goalkeeper	Phil Parkes, Chicago	Jack Brand, Seattle	Jan Van Beveren, Ft. Lauderdale
Defender	Carlos Alberto, New York	Mihalj Keri, Los Angeles	Edskandarian, New York
Defender	Mike Connell, Tampa Bay	Peter Nogly, Edmonton	John Gorman, Tampa Bay
Defender	Rudi Krol, Vancouver	Wim Rijsbergen, New York	Frantz Mathieu, Chicago
Defender	Bruce Rioch, Seattle	John Ryan, Seattle	David Nish, Seattle
Midfielder	Franz Beckenbauer, New York	Alan Hudson, Seattle	Ray Hudson, Ft. Lauderdale
Midfielder	Vladislav Bogicevic, New York	Johan Neeskens, New York	Ace Ntsoelengoe, Minnesota
Midfielder	Teofilo Cubillas, Ft. Lauderdale	Arno Steffenhagen, Chicago	Jomo Sono, Toronto
Forward	Giorgio Chinaglia, New York	Luis Fernando, Los Angeles	Alan Green, Washington
Forward	Johan Cruyff, Washington	Karl-Heinz Granitza, Chicago	Tommy Hutchison, Seattle
Forward	Roger Davies, Seattle	Steve Wegerle, Tampa Bay	Julio Romero, New York

1978 WORLD CUP CHAMPIONSHIP

Games played in Argentina, June 1 – June 25
Qualified for First Round: Argentina, Austria, Brazil, France, Germany (West), Hungary, Iran, Italy, Mexico, Netherlands, Peru, Poland, Scotland, Spain, Sweden, Tunisia.
Advanced to Second Round: Argentina, Austria, Brazil, Germany (West), Italy, Netherlands, Peru, Poland.
Third Place Game: Brazil 2, Italy 1   **Championship Game:** Argentina 3, Netherlands 1

OTHER CHAMPIONSHIPS (1980)

American Soccer League	Pennsylvania Stoners
Major Indoor League	New York Arrows
NCAA Division I (1979)	So. Illinois (Edwardsville)
NCAA Division II (1979)	Alabama A & M
NCAA Division III (1979)	Babson (Mass.)
NAIA (1979)	Quincy
English Association Cup	West Ham
Scottish Cup	Glasgow Celtic
European Cup	Nottingham Forest, England
European Championship	West Germany

GOLF

TOTAL MONEY-WINNING LEADERS: 1979   Source: PGA

Official Money shall be awarded to individual prize winners in major tournaments and such other events as the Tournament Policy Board may designate, even if part of the tournament is canceled provided; however, that Official Money shall not be awarded, in any team competition or a pro-am tournament (but Official Money will be awarded in a major tournament for individuals even if held concurrently with a pro-am tournament). The scale of Official Money will be determined from time to time by the Tournament Policy Board.

Rank	Name	Winnings
1.	Tom Watson	462,636
2.	Larry Nelson	281,022
3.	Lon Hinkle	247,693
4.	Lee Trevino	238,732
5.	Ben Crenshaw	236,770
6.	Bill Rogers	230,500
7.	Andy Bean	208,253
8.	Bruce Lietzke	198,439
9.	Fuzzy Zoeller	196,951
10.	Lanny Wadkins	195,710
11.	Jerry Pate	193,707
12.	Lou Graham	190,827
13.	Hubert Green	183,111
14.	Jack Renner	182,808
15.	Howard Twitty	179,619
16.	David Graham	177,684
17.	Tom Kite	166,878
18.	Jerry McGee	166,735
19.	Hale Irwin	154,168
20.	Wayne Levi	141,612
21.	Curtis Strange	138,368
22.	Bob Gilder	134,428
23.	Mark Hayes	130,878
24.	J. C. Snead	129,585
25.	Ed Sneed	123,606
26.	Ray Floyd	122,872
27.	Calvin Peete	122,481
28.	Bobby Wadkins	121,373
29.	Gil Morgan	115,857
30.	Tom Purtzer	113,270
31.	Grier Jones	111,501
32.	John Fought	108,427
33.	George Burns	107,830
34.	Jay Haas	102,515
35.	Bill Kratzert	101,628
36.	Rex Caldwell	98,168
37.	Keith Fergus	97,045
38.	Rod Curl	95,460
39.	Bob Byman	94,243
40.	Jim Colbert	91,139
41.	Leonard Thompson	90,465
42.	Alan Tapie	88,113
43.	Doug Tewell	84,500
44.	Victor Regalado	82,964
45.	John Mahaffey	81,993
46.	Don January	79,720
47.	John Schroeder	78,510
48.	Tom Weiskopf	76,999
49.	Gibby Gilbert	76,807
50.	Jim Simons	76,350

THE BRITISH OPEN

Year	Winner	Score
1860	Willie Park	174
1861	Tom Morris	163
1862	Tom Morris	163
1863	Willie Park	168
1864	Tom Morris	160
1865	Andrew Strath	162
1866	Willie Park	169
1867	Tom Morris	170
1868	Tom Morris, Jr.	154
1869	Tom Morris, Jr.	157
1870	Tom Marris, Jr.	149
1871	No championship played	
1872	Tom Morris, Jr.	166
1873	Tom Kipp	179
1874	Mungo Park	159
1875	Willie Park	166
1876	Robert Martin	176
1877	Jamie Anderson	160
1878	Jamie Anderson	157
1879	Jamie Anderson	169
1880	Robert Ferguson	162
1881	Robert Ferguson	170
1882	Robert Ferguson	171
1883	*Willie Fernie	159
1884	Jack Simpson	160
1885	Bob Martin	171
1886	David Brown	157
1887	Willie Park, Jr.	161
1888	Jack Burns	171
1889	*Willie Park, Jr.	155 (158)
1890	John Ball	164
1891	Hugh Kirkaldy	166
	(Championship extended from 36 to 72 holes)	
1892	Harold H. Hilton	305
1893	William Auchterlonie	322
1894	John H. Taylor	326
1895	John H. Taylor	322
1896	*Harry Vardon	316 (157)
1897	Harold H. Hilton	314
1898	Harry Vardon	307
1899	Harry Vardon	310
1900	John H. Taylor	309
1901	James Braid	309
1902	Alexander Herd	307
1903	Harry Vardon	300
1904	Jack White	296
1905	James Braid	318
1906	James Braid	300
1907	Arnaud Massy	312
1908	James Braid	291
1909	John H. Taylor	295
1910	James Braid	299
1911	Harry Vardon	303
1912	Edward (Ted) Ray	295
1913	John H. Taylor	304
1914	Harry Vardon	306
1915–1919 No championships played		
1920	George Duncan	303
1921	*Jock Hutchison	296 (150)
1922	Walter Hagen	300
1923	Arthur G. Havers	295
1924	Walter Hagen	301
1925	James M. Barnes	300
1926	Robert T. Jones, Jr.	291
1927	Robert T. Jones, Jr.	285
1928	Walter Hagen	292
1929	Walter Hagen	292
1930	Robert T. Jones, Jr.	291
1931	Tommy D. Armour	296
1932	Gene Sarazen	283
1933	*Denny Shute	292 (149)
1934	Henry Cotton	283
1935	Alfred Perry	283
1936	Alfred Padgham	287
1937	Henry Cotton	290
1938	R. A. Whitcombe	295
1939	Richard Burton	290
1940–1945 No championships played		
1946	Sam Snead	290
1947	Fred Daly	293
1948	Henry Cotton	294
1949	*Bobby Locke	283 (135)
1950	Bobby Locke	279
1951	Max Faulkner	285
1952	Bobby Locke	287
1953	Ben Hogan	282
1954	Peter Thomson	283
1955	Peter Thomson	281
1956	Peter Thomson	286
1957	Bobby Locke	279
1958	Peter Thomson	278 (139)
1959	Gary Player	284
1960	Kel Nagle	278
1961	Arnold Palmer	284
1962	Arnold Palmer	276
1963	*Bob Charles	277
1964	Tony Lema	279
1965	Peter Thomson	285
1966	Jack Nicklaus	282
1967	Roberto De Vicenzo	278
1968	Gary Player	289
1969	Tony Jacklin	280
1970	*Jack Nicklaus	283 (72)
1971	Lee Trevino	278
1972	Lee Trevino	278
1973	Tom Weiskopf	276
1974	Gary Player	282
1975	*Tom Watson	279 (71)
1976	Johnny Miller	279
1977	Tom Watson	268
1978	Jack Nicklaus	281
1979	Severiano Ballesteros	283
1980	Tom Watson	271

* Winner in playoff, figures in parentheses indicate playoff scores.

THE MASTERS

Year	Winner	Score
1936	Horton Smith	285
1937	Byron Nelson	283
1938	Henry Picard	285
1939	Ralph Guldahl	279
1940	Jimmy Demaret	280
1941	Craig Wood	280
1942	Byron Nelson*	280
1946	Herman Keiser	282
1947	Jimmy Demaret	281
1948	Claude Harmon	279
1949	Sam Snead	282
1950	Jimmy Demaret	283
1951	Ben Hogan	280
1952	Sam Snead	286
1953	Ben Hogan	274
1954	Sam Snead*	289
1955	Cary Middlecoff	279
1956	Jack Burke	289
1957	Doug Ford	283
1958	Arnold Palmer	284
1959	Art Wall	284
1960	Arnold Palmer	282
1961	Gary Player	280
1962	Arnold Palmer*	280
1963	Jack Nicklaus	286
1964	Arnold Palmer	276
1965	Jack Nicklaus	271
1966	Jack Nicklaus*	288
1967	Gay Brewer	280
1968	Bob Goalby	277
1969	George Archer	281
1970	Billy Casper*	279
1971	Charles Coody	279
1972	Jack Nicklaus	286
1973	Tommy Aaron	283
1974	Gary Player	278
1975	Jack Nicklaus	276
1976	Ray Floyd	271
1977	Tom Watson	276
1978	Gary Player	277
1979	Fuzzy Zoeller*	280
1980	Severiano Ballesteros	275

* Won in playoff.

THE UNITED STATES OPEN — SOURCE: U.S. Golf Association

Year	Site	Winner	Score
1895	Newport, R.I.	Horace Rawlins	173
1896	Southampton, N.Y.	James Foulis	152
1897	Wheaton, Ill.	Joe Lloyd	162
1898	S. Hamilton, Mass.	Fred Herd	328
1899	Baltimore, Md.	Willie Smith	315
1900	Wheaton, Ill.	Harry Vardon	313
1901	S. Hamilton, Mass.	Willie Anderson	331*
1902	Garden City, N.Y.	Lawrence Auchterlonie	307
1903	Springfield, N.J.	Willie Anderson	307*
1904	Golf, Ill.	Willie Anderson	303
1905	S. Hamilton, Mass.	Willie Anderson	314
1906	Lake Forest, Ill.	Alex Smith	295
1907	Philadelphia, Pa.	Alex Ross	302
1908	S. Hamilton, Mass.	Fred McLeod	322*
1909	Englewood, N.J.	George Sargent	290
1910	St. Martins, Pa.	Alex Smith	298*
1911	Wheaton, Ill.	John J. McDermott	307*
1912	Buffalo, N.Y.	John J. McDermott	294
1913	Brookline, Mass.	Walter Hagen	290
1914	Blue Island, Ill.	Francis Ouimet (A)	304*
1915	Springfield, N.J.	Jerome D. Travers (A)	297
1916	Minneapolis, Minn.	Charles Evans, Jr. (A)	286
1917–1918 No Competion Held			
1919	West Newton, Mass.	Water Hagen	301*
1920	Toledo, Ohio	Edward Ray	295
1921	Chevy Chase, Md.	James M. Barnes	289
1922	Glencoe, Ill.	Gene Sarazen	288
1923	Inwood, N.Y.	Robert T. Jones, Jr. (A)	296*
1924	Birmingham, Mich.	Cyril Walker	297
1925	Worcester, Mass.	William Macfarlane	291*
1926	Columbus, Ohio	Robert T. Jones, Jr. (A)	293
1927	Oakmont, Pa.	Tommy Armour	301*
1928	Mateson, Ill.	Johnny Farrell	294*
1929	Mamaroneck, N.Y.	Robert T. Jones, Jr. (A)	294*
1930	Minneapolis, Minn.	Robert T. Jones, Jr. (A)	287
1931	Toledo, Ohio	Billy Burke	292*
1932	Flushing, N.Y.	Gene Sarazen	286
1933	Glen View, Ill.	John G. Goodman (A)	287
1934	Ardmore, Pa.	Olin Dutra	293
1935	Oakmont, Pa.	Sam Parks, Jr.	299
1936	Springfield, N.J.	Tony Manero	282
1937	Birmingham, Mich.	Ralph Guldahl	281
1938	Denver, Colo.	Ralph Guldahl	284
1939	W. Conshohocken, Pa.	Byron Nelson	284*
1940	Cleveland, Ohio	Lawson Little	287*
1941	Ft. Worth, Texas	Craig Wood	284
1942–1945 No Competition Held			
1946	Cleveland, Ohio	Lloyd Mangrum	284*
1947	Clayton, Mo.	Lew Worsham	282*
1948	Los Angeles, Calif.	Ben Hogan	276
1949	Medinah, Ill.	Cary Middlecoff	286
1950	Ardmore, Pa.	Ben Hogan	287*
1951	Birmingham, Mich.	Ben Hogan	287
1952	Dallas, Texas	Julius Boros	281
1953	Oakmont, Pa.	Ben Hogan	283
1954	Springfield, N.J.	Ed Furgol	284
1955	San Francisco, Calif.	Jack Fleck	287*
1956	Rochester, N.Y.	Cary Middlecoff	281
1957	Toledo, Ohio	Dick Mayer	282*
1958	Tulsa, Okla.	Tommy Bolt	283
1959	Mamaroneck, N.Y.	Bill Casper, Jr.	282
1960	Englewood, Colo.	Arnold Palmer	280
1961	Birmingham, Mich.	Gene Littler	281
1962	Oakmont, Pa.	Jack Nicklaus	283*
1963	Brookline, Mass.	Julius Boros	293*
1964	Washington, D.C.	Ken Venturi	278
1965	St. Louis, Mo.	Gary Player	282*
1966	San Francisco, Calif.	Bill Casper, Jr.	278*
1967	Springfield, N.J.	Jack Nicklaus	275
1968	Rochester, N.Y.	Lee Trevino	275
1969	Houston, Texas	Orville Moody	281
1970	Chaska, Minn.	Tony Jacklin	281
1971	Ardmore, Pa.	Lee Trevino	280*
1972	Pebble Beach, Calif.	Jack Nicklaus	290
1973	Oakmont, Pa.	John Miller	279
1974	Mamaroneck, N.Y.	Hale Irwin	287
1975	Medinah, Ill.	Lou Graham	287*
1976	Duluth, Ga.	Jerry Pate	277
1977	Tulsa, Okla.	Hubert Green	278
1978	Denver, Colo.	Andy North	285
1979	Toledo, Ohio	Hale Irwin	284
1980	Springfield, N.J.	Jack Nicklaus	272

(A) Amateur.   *Won Playoff

PGA CHAMPIONSHIP — SOURCE: P.G.A.

Year	Winner	Score
1916	James M. Barnes	1 up
1917–1918 No Competition Held		
1919	James M. Barnes	6 & 5
1920	Jock Hutchison	1 up
1921	Walter Hagen	3 & 2
1922	Gene Sarazen	4 & 3
1923	Gene Sarazen	1 up
1924	Walter Hagen	2 up
1925	Walter Hagen	6 & 5
1926	Walter Hagen	5 & 3
1927	Walter Hagen	1 up
1928	Leo Diegel	6 & 5
1929	Leo Diegel	6 & 4
1930	Tommy Armour	1 up
1931	Tom Creavy	2 & 1
1932	Olin Dutra	4 & 3
1933	Gene Sarazen	5 & 4
1934	Paul Runyan	1 up
1935	Johnny Revolta	5 & 4
1936	Denny Shute	3 & 2
1937	Denny Shute	1 up
1938	Paul Runyan	8 & 7
1939	Henry Picard	1 up
1940	Byron Nelson	1 up
1941	Vic Ghezzi	1 up
1942	Sam Snead	2 & 1
1943	No Competition Held	
1944	Bob Hamilton	1 up
1945	Byron Nelson	4 & 3
1946	Ben Hogan	6 & 4
1947	Jim Ferrier	2 & 1
1948	Ben Hogan	7 & 6
1949	Sam Snead	3 & 2
1950	Chandler Harper	4 & 3
1951	Sam Snead	7 & 6
1952	Jim Turnesa	1 up
1953	Walter Burkemo	2 & 1
1954	Chick Harbert	4 & 3
1955	Doug Ford	4 & 3
1956	Jack Burke	3 & 2
1957	Lionel Hebert	2 & 1
1958	Dow Finsterwald	276
1959	Bob Rosburg	277
1960	Jay Hebert	281
1961	Jerry Barber	277*
1962	Gary Player	278
1963	Jack Nicklaus	279
1963	Bobby Nichols	271
1965	Dave Marr	280
1966	Al Geiberger	280
1967	Don January	281*
1968	Julius Boros	281
1969	Ray Floyd	276
1970	Dave Stockton	279
1971	Jack Nicklaus	281
1972	Gary Player	281
1973	Jack Nicklaus	277
1974	Lee Trevino	276
1975	Jack Nicklaus	276
1976	Dave Stockton	281
1977	Lanny Wadkins	282*
1978	John Mahaffey	276*
1979	Dave Graham	272*
1980	Jack Nicklaus	274

*Won Playoff

THE CANADIAN OPEN

Year	Winner	Score
1950	Jim Ferrier	271
1951	Jim Ferrier	273
1952	John Palmer	263
1953	Dave Douglas	273
1954	Pat Fletcher	280
1955	Arnold Palmer	265
1956	Doug Sanders (A)	273
1957	George Bayer	271
1958	Wesley Ellis, Jr.	267
1959	Doug Ford	276
1960	Art Wall, Jr.	269
1961	Jacky Cupit	270
1962	Ted Kroll	278
1963	Doug Ford	280
1964	Kel Nagle	277
1965	Gene Littler	273
1966	Don Massengale	280
1967	Bill Casper	279*
1968	Bob Charles	274
1969	Tommy Aaron	275*
1970	Kermit Zarley	279
1971	Lee Trevino	275*
1972	Gay Brewer	275
1973	Tom Weiskopf	278
1974	Bobby Nichols	270
1975	Tom Weiskopf	274*
1976	Jerry Pate	267
1977	Lee Trevino	280
1978	Bruce Lietzke	283
1979	Lee Trevino	281
1980	Bob Gilder	274

(A) Amateur.   *Won Playoff

PROFESSIONAL GOLF'S LEADING MONEY WINNERS, 1935–1979

Year	Player	Winnings	Year	Player	Winnings	Year	Player	Winnings
1935	Johnny Revolta	$ 9,543.00	1950	Sam Snead	$35,758.83	1965	Jack Nicklaus	$140,752.14
1936	Horton Smith	7,682.00	1951	Lloyd Mangrum	26,088.83	1966	Billy Casper	121,944.92
1937	Harry Cooper	14,138.69	1952	Julius Boros	37,032.97	1967	Jack Nicklaus	188,998.08
1938	Sam Snead	19,534.49	1953	Lew Worsham	34,002.00	1968	Billy Casper	205,168.67
1939	Henry Picard	10,303.00	1954	Bob Toski	65,819.81	1969	Frank Beard	175,223.93
1940	Ben Hogan	10,655.00	1955	Julius Boros	63,121.55	1970	Lee Trevino	157,037.00
1941	Ben Hogan	18,358.00	1956	Ted Kroll	72,835.83	1971	Jack Nicklaus	244,490.50
1942	Ben Hogan	13,143.00	1957	Dick Mayer	65,835.00	1972	Jack Nicklaus	320,542.26
1943	No statistics compiled		1958	Arnold Palmer	42,607.50	1973	Jack Nicklaus	308,362.00
1944	Byron Nelson	37,967.69	1959	Art Wall, Jr.	52,167.60	1974	Johnny Miller	353,021.00
1945	Byron Nelson	63,335.66	1960	Arnold Palmer	75,262.85	1975	Jack Nicklaus	298,149.00
1946	Ben Hogan	42,556.16	1961	Gary Player	64,540.45	1976	Jack Nicklaus	266,426.00
1947	Jimmy Demaret	27,936.83	1962	Arnold Palmer	81,448.33	1977	Tom Watson	310,653.00
1948	Ben Hogan	32,112.00	1963	Arnold Palmer	128,230.00	1978	Tom Watson	362,429.00
1949	Sam Snead	31,593.83	1964	Jack Nicklaus	113,284.50	1979	Tom Watson	462,636.00

RYDER CUP MATCHES (PROFESSIONALS)

Year	Played at	Results	Year	Played at	Results
1927	Worcester C.C., Worcester, Mass.	U.S. 9½–Britain 2½	1959	Eldorado C.C., Palm Desert, Calif.	U.S. 8½–Britain 3½
1929	Moortown, England	Britain 7 –U.S. 5	1961	Royal Lytham and St. Anne's Golf Club, St. Anne's-On-The-Sea, England	U.S. 14½–Britain 9½
1931	Scioto C.C., Columbus, Ohio	U.S. 9 –Britain 3			
1933	Southport & Ainsdale Courses, England	Britain 6½–U.S. 5½	1963	East Lake C.C., Atlanta, Georgia	U.S. 23 –Britain 9
1935	Ridgewood C.C., Ridgewood, N.J.	U.S. 9 –Britain 3	1965	Royal Birkdale Golf Club, Southport, England	U.S. 19½–Britain 12½
1937	Southport & Ainsdale Courses, England	U.S. 8 –Britain 4	1967	Champions Golf Club, Houston	U.S. 23½–Britain 8½
	Ryder Cup Matches not held during World War II years.				
1947	Portland Golf Club, Portland, Oregon	U.S. 11 –Britain 1	1969	Royal Birkdale Golf Club, Southport, England	U.S. 16–Tie –Britain 16
1949	Ganton Golf Course, Scarborough, England	U.S. 7 –Britain 5	1971	Old Warson Country Club, St. Louis, Mo.	U.S. 18½–Britain 13½
1951	Pinehurst C.C., Pinehurst, N.C.	U.S. 9½–Britain 2½	1973	Muirfield, Scotland	U.S. 18 –Britain 13
1953	Wentworth, England	U.S. 6½–Britain 5½	1975	Laurel Valley Golf Club, Ligonier, Pa.	U.S. 21 –Britain 11
1955	Thunderbird Ranch and C.C., Palm Springs, Calif.	U.S. 8 –Britain 4	1977	Royal Lytham and St. Annes Golf Club, England	U.S. 12½–Britain 7½
1957	Lindrick Golf Club, Yorkshire, England	Britain 7½–U.S. 4½	1979	Greenbrier Hotel Resort, White Sulphur Sprs., W.Va.	U.S. 17 –Europe 11

PGA HALL OF FAME
SOURCE: P.G.A.

Member	Year Elected	Member	Year Elected	Member	Year Elected
Willie Anderson	1940	Johnny Farrell	1961	Byron Nelson	1953
Tommy Armour	1940	Doug Ford	1975	Francis Ouimet	1940
Jim Barnes	1940	Vic Ghezzi	1965	Arnold Palmer	1980
Patty Berg	1977	Ralph Guldahl	1963	Henry Picard	1961
Julius Boros	1974	Walter Hagen	1940	Johnny Revolta	1963
Mike Brady	1960	Chick Harbert	1968	Paul Runyan	1959
Billy Burke	1966	Chandler Harper	1969	Gene Sarazen	1940
Jack Burke, Jr.	1975	Dutch Harrison	1962	Denny Shute	1957
Harry Cooper	1959	Ben Hogan	1953	Alex Smith	1940
Bobby Cruickshank	1967	Jock Hutchison, Sr.	1959	Horton Smih	1958
Jimmy Demaret	1960	Bobby Jones	1940	MacDonald Smith	1954
Roberto De Vicenzo	1978	Lawson Little	1961	Sam Snead	1953
Leo Diegel	1955	Lloyd Mangrum	1964	Jerry Travers	1940
Ed Dudley	1964	John McDermott	1940	Walter Travis	1940
Olin Dutra	1962	Fred McLeod	1960	Craig Wood	1956
Chick Evans	1940	Cary Middlecoff	1974	Babe Zaharias	1977

WORLD AMATEUR TEAM CHAMPIONSHIPS
SOURCE: U. S. Golf Association

Year	Men's Champion	Women's Champion	Site
1958	Australia	—	St. Andrews, Scotland
1960	United States	—	Ardmore, Pa.
1962	United States	—	Kanawa, Japan
1964	Great Britain & Ireland	—	Rome, Italy
		France	St. Germain, France
1966	Australia	United States	Mexico City, Mexico
1968	United States	United States	Melbourne, Australia
1970	United States	United States	Madrid, Spain
1972	United States	United States	Buenos Aires, Argentina
1974	United States	United States	LaRomana, Dominican Rep.
1976	Great Britain & Ireland	United States	Algarve, Portugal
1978	United States	Australia	Pacific Harbour, Fiji
1980	United States	United States	Pinehurst, North Carolina

LPGA TOTAL MONEY WINNERS: 1979
SOURCE: L.P.G.A.

Rank	Name	Amount	Rank	Name	Amount	Rank	Name	Amount
1.	Nancy Lopez	$197,488	18.	Vicki Fergon	$57,205	34.	Lori Garbacz	$32,457
2.	Sandra Post	178,750	19.	Betsy King	53,900	35.	Janet Coles	31,218
3.	Amy Alcott	144,838	20.	Penny Pulz	51,142	36.	Kathy Postlewait	29,004
4.	Pat Bradley	132,428	21.	Sandra Palmer	50,892	37.	Jo Ann Prentice	27,395
5.	Donna C. Young	125,493	22.	Joyce Kazmierski	47,395	38.	Barbara Moxness	27,273
6.	Sally Little	119,501	23.	Laura Baugh	44,361	39.	Cathy Sherk	26,924
7.	Jane Blalock	115,226	24.	Marlene Floyd	43,976	40.	Marlene Hagge	26,812
8.	Judy Rankin	108,511	25.	Dot Germain	43,847	41.	Murle Breer	26,492
9.	Joanne Carner	98,218	26.	Shelley Hamlin	41,739	42.	Susie McAllister	26,400
10.	Beth Daniel	97,026	27.	at Meyers	38,234	43.	Sue Berning	25,534
11.	Hollis Stacy	81,265	28.	Mary Dwyer	36,679	44.	Kathy Ahern	25,320
12.	Jo Ann Washam	77,303	29.	Sandra Spuzich	36,633	45.	Bonnie Bryant	25,137
13.	Silvia Bertolaccini	76,244	30.	Kathy Whitworth	36,246	46.	Lynn Adams	24,987
14.	Donna H. White	70,796	31.	Peggy Conley	35,217	47.	Alice Ritzman	24,647
15.	Jan Stephenson	69,519	32.	Kathy McMullen	33,757	48.	Judy Clark	24,561
16.	Jerilyn Britz	68,131	33.	Debbie Austin	32,597	49.	Barbara Barrow	23,833
17.	Debbie Massey	57,778				50.	Gloria Ehret	22,852

LEADING LPGA MONEY WINNERS BY YEAR, 1948–1979

Year	Player	Amount	Year	Player	Amount	Year	Player	Amount
1948	Babe Zaharias	$ 3,400.00*	1959	Betsy Rawls	$26,774.39	1969	Carol Mann	$49,152.50
1949	Babe Zaharias	4,650.00*	1960	Louise Suggs	16,892.12	1970	Kathy Whitworth	30,235.01
1950	Babe Zaharias	14,800.00*	1961	Mickey Wright	22,236.21	1971	Kathy Whitworth	41,181.75
1951	Babe Zaharias	15,087.00*	1962	Mickey Wright	21,641.99	1972	Kathy Whitworth	65,063.99
1952	Betsy Rawls	14,505.00	1963	Mickey Wright	31,269.50	1973	Kathy Whitworth	82,864.25
1953	Louise Suggs	19,816.25	1964	Mickey Wright	29,800.00	1974	JoAnne Carner	87,094.04
1954	Patty Berg	16,011.00	1965	Kathy Whitworth	28,658.00	1975	Sandra Palmer	76,374.51
1955	Patty Berg	16,492.34	1966	Kathy Whitworth	33,517.50	1976	Judy Rankin	150,734.28
1956	Marlene Hagge	20,235.50	1967	Kathy Whitworth	32,937.50	1977	Judy Rankin	122,890.44
1957	Patty Berg	16,272.00	1968	Kathy Whitworth	48,379.50	1978	Nancy Lopez	189,813.83
1958	Beverly Hanson	12,639.55				1979	Nancy Lopez	197,488.61

* Approximate Figure

WOMEN'S OPEN CHAMPIONSHIP
SOURCE: U.S. Golf Association

Year	Site	Winner	Score	Year	Site	Winner	Score
1946	Spokane, Wash.	Patty Berg	5 & 4	1963	Cincinnati, Ohio	Mary Mills	289
1947	Greensboro, N.C.	Betty Jameson	295*	1964	Chula Vista, Calif.	Mickey Wright	290*
1948	Northfield, N.J.	Babe Zaharias	300	1965	Northfield, N.J.	Carol Mann	290
1949	Landover, Md.	Louise Suggs	291	1966	Minneapolis, Minn.	Sandra Spuzich	297
1950	Wichita, Kans.	Mildred Zaharias	291	1967	Hot Springs, Va.	Catherine Lacoste (A)	294
1951	Atlanta, Ga.	Betsy Rawls	293	1968	Fleetwood, Pa.	Susie Berning	289
1952	Philadelphia, Pa.	Louise Suggs	284	1969	Pensacola, Fla.	Donna Caponi	294
1953	Rochester, N.Y.	Betsy Rawls	302*	1970	Muskogee, Okla.	Donna Caponi	287
1954	Peabody, Mass.	Babe Zaharias	291	1971	Erie, Pa.	JoAnne Carner	288
1955	Wichita, Kans.	Fay Crocker	299	1972	Mamaroneck, N.Y.	Susie Berning	299
1956	Duluth, Minn.	Kathy Cornelius	302*	1973	Rochester, N.Y.	Susie Berning	290
1957	Mamaroneck, N.Y.	Betsy Rawls	299	1974	LaGrange, Ill.	Sandra Haynie	295
1958	Bloomfield Hills, Mich.	Mickey Wright	290	1975	Northfield, N.J.	Sandra Palmer	295
1959	Pittsburg, Pa.	Mickey Wright	287	1976	Springfield, Pa.	JoAnne Carner	292*
1960	Worcester, Mass.	Betsy Rawls	292	1977	Chaska, Minn.	Hollis Stacy	292
1961	Springfield, N.J.	Mickey Wright	293	1978	Indianapolis, Ind.	Hollis Stacy	289
1962	Myrtle Beach, S.C.	Murle Lindstrom	301	1979	Fairfield, Conn.	Jerilyn Britz	284
				1980	Nashville, Tenn	Amy Alcott	280

(A) Amateur. *Won Playoff

LPGA CHAMPIONSHIP
SOURCE: L.P.G.A.

Year	Winner	Score	Year	Winner	Score	Year	Winner	Score
1955	Beverly Hanson	4 & 3	1963	Mickey Wright	294	1972	Kathy Ahern	293
1956	Marlene Hagge	291*	1964	Mary Mills	278	1973	Mary Mills	288
1957	Louise Suggs	285	1965	Sandra Haynie	279	1974	Sanda Haynie	288
1958	Mickey Wright	288	1966	Gloria Ehret	282	1975	Kathy Whitworth	288
1959	Betsy Rawls	288	1967	Kathy Whitworth	284	1976	Betty Burfeindt	287
1960	Mickey Wright	292	1968	Sandra Post	294*	1977	Chako Higuchi	279
1961	Mickey Wright	287	1969	Betsy Rawls	293	1978	Nancy Lopez	275
1962	Judy Kimball	282	1970	Shirley Englehorn	285*	1979	Donna Caponi Young	279
			1971	Kathy Whitworth	288	1980	Sally Litle	285

*Won Playoff

LPGA HALL OF FAME
SOURCE: L.P.G.A.

Member	Year Elected	Member	Year Elected	Member	Year Elected
Patty Berg	1951	Babe Zaharias	1951	Kathy Whitworth	1975
Betty Jameson	1951	Betsy Rawls	1960	Sandra Haynie	1977
Louise Suggs	1951	Mickey Wright	1964	Carol Mann	1977

U.S. AMATEUR CHAMPIONSHIP WINNERS

SOURCE: U.S. Golf Association

Year	Winner	Year	Winner	Year	Winner	Year	Winner
1895	Charles B. Macdonald	1915	Robert A. Gardner	1936	John W. Fischer	1960	Deane R. Beman
1896	H. J. Whigham	1916	Charles Evans, Jr.	1937	John Goodman	1961	Jack Nicklaus
1897	H. J. Whigham	1917–1918	No Competition	1938	William P. Turnesa	1962	Labron Harris, Jr.
1898	Findlay S. Douglas	1919	S. Davidson Herron	1939	Marvin H. Ward	1963	Deane R. Beman
1899	H. M. Harriman	1920	Charles Evans, Jr.	1940	Richard D. Chapman	1964	William C. Campbell
1900	Walter J. Travis	1921	Jesse P. Guilford	1941	Marvin H. Ward	1965	Robert J. Murphy, Jr.
1901	Walter J. Travis	1922	Jess W. Sweetser	1942–1945	No Competition	1966	Gary Cowan
1902	Louis N. James	1923	Max R. Marston	1946	S. E. (Ted) Bishop	1967	Robert B. Dickson
1903	Walter J. Travis	1924	Robert T. Jones, Jr.	1947	R. H. (Skee) Riegel	1968	Bruce Fleisher
1904	H. Chandler Egan	1924	Robert T. Jones, Jr.	1948	William P. Turnesa	1969	Steven Melnyk
1905	H. Chandler Egan	1926	George Von Elm	1949	Charles R. Coe	1970	Lanny Wadkins
1906	Eben M. Byers	1927	Robert T. Jones, Jr.	1950	Sam Urzetta	1971	Gary Cowan
1907	Jerome D. Travers	1928	Robert T. Jones, Jr.	1951	Billy Maxwell	1972	Marvin Giles
1908	Jerome D. Travers	1929	Harrison R. Johnston	1952	Jack Westland	1973	Craig Stadler
1909	Robert A. Gardner	1930	Robert T. Jones, Jr.	1953	Gene Littler	1974	Jerome Pate
1910	William C. Fownes, Jr.	1931	Francis Ouimet	1954	Arnold Palmer	1975	Fred Ridley
1911	Harold H. Hilton	1932	C. Ross Somerville	1955	E. Harvie Ward, Jr.	1976	Bill Sander
1912	Jerome D. Travers	1933	George T. Dunlap, Jr.	1956	E. Harvie Ward, Jr.	1977	John Fought
1913	Jerome D. Travers	1934	Lawson Little	1957	Hillman Robbins, Jr.	1978	John Cook
1914	Francis Ouimet	1935	Lawson Little	1958	Charles R. Coe	1979	Mark O'Meara
				1959	Jack Nicklaus	1980	Hal Sutton

WOMEN'S AMATEUR CHAMPIONSHIP WINNERS

SOURCE: U.S. Golf Association

Year	Winner	Year	Winner	Year	Winner	Year	Winner
1951	Dorothy Kirby	1958	Anne Quast	1965	Jean Ashley	1973	Carol Semple
1952	Jacqueline Pung	1959	Barbara McIntire	1966	JoAnne Carner	1974	Cynthia Hill
1953	Mary Faulk	1960	JoAnne Gunderson	1967	Mary Lou Dill	1975	Beth Daniel
1954	Barbara Romack	1961	Anne Quast Decker	1968	JoAnne Carner	1976	Donna Horton
1955	Patricia Lesser	1962	JoAnne Gunderson	1969	Catherine Lacoste	1977	Beth Daniel
1956	Marlene Stewart	1963	Anne Quast Welts	1970	Martha Wilkinson	1978	Cathy Sherk
1957	JoAnne Gunderson	1964	Barbara McIntire	1971	Laura Baugh	1979	Carolyn Hill
				1972	Mary Budke	1980	Julie Inkster

THE WALKER CUP (Men Amateur Golfers)

SOURCE: U.S. Golf Association

Year	Results	Site	Year	Results	Site
1922	U.S. 8, Great Britain 4	Southampton, N.Y.	1953	U.S. 9, Great Britain 3	Marion, Mass.
1923	U.S. 6, Great Britain 5	St. Andrews, Scotland	1955	U.S. 10, Great Britain 2	St. Andrews, Scotland
1924	U.S. 9, Great Britain 3	Garden City, N.Y.	1957	U.S. 8, Great Britain 3	Minneapolis, Minn.
1926	U.S. 6, Great Britain 5	St. Andrews, Scotland	1959	U.S. 9, Great Britain 3	Muirfield, Scotland
1928	U.S. 11, Great Britain 1	Wheaton, Ill.	1961	U.S. 11, Great Britain 1	Seattle, Wash.
1930	U.S. 10, Great Britain 2	Sandwich, England	1963	U.S. 12, Great Britain 8	Turnberry, Scotland
1932	U.S. 8, Great Britain 1	Brookline, Mass.	1965	U.S. 11, Great Britain 11	Baltimore, Md.
1934	U.S. 9, Great Britain 2	St. Andrews, Scotland	1967	U.S. 13, Great Britain 7	Sandwich, England
1936	U.S. 9, Great Britain 0	Clementon, N.J.	1969	U.S. 10, Great Britain 8	Milwaukee, Wis.
1938	Great Britain 7, U.S. 4	St. Andrews, Scotland	1971	Great Britain 13, U.S. 11	St. Andrews, Scotland
1947	U.S. 8, Great Britain 4	St. Andrews, Scotland	1973	U.S. 14, Great Britain 10	Brookline, Mass.
1949	U.S. 10, Great Britain 2	Mamaroneck, N.Y.	1975	U.S. 15½, Great Britain 8½	St. Andrews, Scotland
1951	U.S. 6, Great Britain 3	Southport, England	1977	U.S. 16, Great Britain 8	Southampton, N.Y.
			1979	U.S. 15½, Great Britain 8½	Muirfield, Scotland

THE CURTIS CUP (Women Amateur Golfers)

SOURCE: U.S. Golf Association

Year	Results	Site	Year	Results	Site
1932	U.S. 5½, British Isles 3½	Wentworth, England	1960	U.S. 6½, British Isles 2½	Worksop, England
1934	U.S. 6½, British Isles 7½	Chevy Chase, Md.	1962	U.S. 8, British Isles 1	Colorado Sprs., Colo.
1936	U.S. 4½, British Isles 4½	Gleneagles, Scotland	1964	U.S. 10½, British Isles 7½	Porthcawl, South Wales
1938	U.S. 5½, British Isles 3½	Manchester, Mass.	1966	U.S. 13, British Isles 5	Hot Springs, Va.
1948	U.S. 6½, British Isles 2½	Southport, England	1968	U.S. 10½, British Isles 7½	Newcastle, No. Ireland
1950	U.S. 7½, British Isles 1½	Williamsville, N.Y.	1970	U.S. 11½, British Isles 6½	West Newton, Mass.
1952	British Isles 5, U.S. 4	Muirfield, Scotland	1972	U.S. 10, British Isles 8	Western Gailes, Scotland
1954	U.S. 6, British Isles 3	Ardmore, Pa.	1974	U.S. 13, British Isles 5	San Francisco, Calif.
1956	British Isles 5, U.S. 4	Sandwich Bay, England	1976	U.S. 11½, British Isles 6½	St. Annes-On-Sea, Eng.
1958	British Isles 4½, U.S. 4½	West Newton, Mass.	1978	U.S. 12, British Isles 6	Rye, N.Y.
			1979	U.S. 13, British Isles 5	Chepstow, Wales

OTHER GOLF CHAMPIONS

Year	NCAA Team	NCAA Individual	Women's Intercollegiate
1968	Florida	Grier Jones, Oklahoma State	Gail Sykes, Odessa (Texas)
1969	Houston	Bob Clark, California (L.A.) State	Jane Bastanchury, Arizona State
1970	Houston	John Mahaffey, Houston	Cathy Gaughan, Arizona State
1971	Texas	Ben Crenshaw, Texas	Shelley Hamlin, Stanford
1972	Texas	Ben Crenshaw & Tom Kite, Texas	Ann Laughlin, Miami (Florida)
1973	Florida	Ben Chrenshaw, Texas	Bonnie Lauer, Michigan State
1974	Wake Forest	Curtis Strange, Wake Forest	Mary Budke, Oregon State
1975	Wake Forest	Jay Haas, Wake Forest	Barbara Barrow, San Diego State
1976	Oklahoma State	Scott Simpson, Southern California	Nancy Lopez, Tulsa
1977	Houston	Scott Simpson, Southern California	Cathy Morse, Miami (Florida)
1978	Oklahoma State	David Edwards, Oklahoma State	Deborah Petrizzi, Texas-Austin
1979	Ohio State	Gary Hallberg, Wake Forest	Kyle O'Brien, Southern Methodist
1980	Oklahoma State	Jay Don Blake, Utah State	Patty Sheehan, San Jose State

TENNIS

United States Tennis Association (USTA); 51 East 42nd Street, New York 10017. President: W. E. Hester Jr. Executive Secretary: Michael J. Burns.

USTA NATIONAL CHAMPIONS (U.S. Open since 1968)

Men's Singles

1925	Bill Tilden (U.S.A.)	1939	Bobby Riggs (U.S.A.)	1953	Tony Trabert (U.S.A.)	1967	John Newcombe (Australia)
1926	Rene Lacoste (France)	1940	Don McNeill (U.S.A.)	1954	Vic Seixas (U.S.A.)	1968	Arthur Ashe (U.S.A.)
1927	Rene Lacoste (France)	1941	Bobby Riggs (U.S.A.)	1955	Tony Trabert (U.S.A.)	1969	Rod Laver (Australia)
1928	Henri Cochet (France)	1942	Ted Schroeder (U.S.A.)	1956	Ken Rosewall (Australia)	1970	Ken Rosewall (Australia)
1929	Bill Tilden (U.S.A.)	1943	Joe Hunt (U.S.A.)	1957	Mal Anderson (Australia)	1971	Stan Smith (U.S.A.)
1930	John Doeg (U.S.A.)	1944	Frank Parker (U.S.A.)	1958	Ashley Cooper (Australia)	1972	Ilie Nastase (Romania)
1931	Ellsworth Vines (U.S.A.)	1945	Frank Parker (U.S.A.)	1959	Neale Fraser (Australia)	1973	John Newcombe (Australia)
1932	Ellsworth Vines (U.S.A.)	1946	Jack Kramer (U.S.A.)	1960	Neale Fraser (Australia)	1974	Jimmy Connors (U.S.A.)
1933	Fred Perry (England)	1947	Jack Kramer (U.S.A.)	1961	Roy Emerson (Australia)	1975	Manuel Orantes (Spain)
1934	Fred Perry (England)	1948	Pancho Gonzales (U.S.)	1962	Rod Laver (Australia)	1976	Jimmy Connors (U.S.A.)
1935	Wilmer Allison (U.S.A.)	1949	Pancho Gonzalez (U.S.A.)	1963	Rafael Osuna (Mexico)	1977	Guillermo Vilas (Argentina)
1936	Fred Perry (England)	1950	Art Larsen (U.S.A.)	1964	Roy Emerson (Australia)	1978	Jimmy Connors (U.S.A.)
1937	Don Budge (U.S.A.)	1951	Frank Sedgman (Australia)	1965	Manuel Santana (Spain)	1979	John McEnroe (U.S.A.)
1938	Don Budge (U.S.A.)	1952	Frank Sedgman (Australia)	1966	Fred Stolle (Australia)	1980	John McEnroe (U.S.A.)

Men's Doubles

1925	Vinnie Richards–R. Norris Williams	1944	Don McNeill–Bob Falkenburg	1963	Chuck McKinley–Dennis Ralston
1926	Vinnie Richards–R. Norris Williams	1945	Gardnar Mulloy–Bill Talbert	1964	Chuck McKinley–Dennis Ralston
1927	Bill Tilden–Frank Hunter	1946	Gardnar Mulloy–Bill Talbert	1965	Roy Emerson–Fred Stolle
1928	George Lott–John Hennessey	1947	Jack Kramer–Ted Schroeder	1966	Roy Emerson–Fred Stolle
1929	George Lott–John Doeg	1948	Gardnar Mulloy–Bill Talbert	1967	John Newcombe–Tony Roche
1930	George Lott–John Doeg	1949	Jack Bromwich–William Sidwell	1968	Stan Smith–Bob Lutz
1931	Wilmer Allison–John Van Ryn	1950	Jack Bromwich–Frank Sedgman	1969	Ken Rosewall–Fred Stolle
1932	Ellsworth Vines–Keith Gledhill	1951	Frank Sedgman–Ken McGregor	1970	Nikki Pilic–Pierre Barthes
1933	George Lott–Lester Stoefen	1952	Vic Seixas–Mervyn Rose	1971	John Newcombe–Roger Taylor
1934	George Lott–Lester Stoefen	1953	Rex Hartwig–Mervyn Rose	1972	Cliff Drysdale–Roger Taylor
1935	Wilmer Allison–John Van Ryn	1954	Vic Seixas–Tony Trabert	1973	Owen Davidson–John Newcombe
1936	Don Budge–Gene Mako	1955	Kosei Kamo–Atsushi Miyagi	1974	Bob Lutz–Stan Smith
1937	Gottfried von Cramm–Henner Henkel	1956	Lew Hoad–Ken Rosewall	1975	Jimmy Connors–Ilie Nastase
1938	Don Budge–Gene Mako	1957	Ashley Cooper–Neale Fraser	1976	Marty Riessen–Tom Okker
1939	Adrian Quist–Jack Bromwich	1958	Alex Olmedo–Ham Richardson	1977	Bob Hewitt–Frew McMillan
1940	Jack Kramer–Ted Schroeder	1959	Neale Fraser–Roy Emerson	1978	Stan Smith–Bob Lutz
1941	Jack Kramer–Ted Schroeder	1960	Neale Fraser–Roy Emerson	1979	John McEnroe–Peter Fleming
1942	Gardnar Mulloy–Bill Talbert	1961	Chuck McKinley–Dennis Ralston	1980	Stan Smith–Bob Lutz
1943	Jack Kramer–Frank Parker	1962	Rafael Osuna–Antonio Palafox		

Women's Singles

1925	Helen Wills (U.S.A.)	1944	Pauline Betz (U.S.A.)	1963	Maria Bueno (Brazil)
1926	Molla Bjurstedt Mallory (U.S.A.)	1945	Sarah Palfrey Cooke (U.S.A.)	1964	Maria Bueno (Brazil)
1927	Helen Wills (U.S.A.)	1946	Pauline Betz (U.S.A.)	1965	Margaret Smith (Australia)
1928	Helen Wills (U.S.A.)	1947	Louise Brough (U.S.A.)	1966	Maria Bueno (Brazil)
1929	Helen Wills (U.S.A.)	1948	Margaret Osborne du Pont (U.S.A.)	1967	Billie Jean King (U.S.A.)
1930	Betty Nuthall (England)	1949	Margaret Osborne du Pont (U.S.A.)	1968	Virginia Wade (England)
1931	Helen Wills Moody (U.S.A.)	1950	Margaret Osborne du Pont (U.S.A.)	1969	Margaret Smith Court (Australia)
1932	Helen Hull Jacobs (U.S.A.)	1951	Maureen Connolly (U.S.A.)	1970	Margaret Court (Australia)
1933	Helen Hull Jacobs (U.S.A.)	1952	Maureen Connolly (U.S.A.)	1971	Billie Jean King (U.S.A.)
1934	Helen Hull Jacobs (U.S.A.)	1953	Maureen Connolly (U.S.A.)	1972	Billie Jean King (U.S.A.)
1935	Helen Hull Jacobs (U.S.A.)	1954	Doris Hart (U.S.A.)	1973	Margaret Court (Australia)
1936	Alice Marble (U.S.A.)	1955	Doris Hart (U.S.A.)	1974	Billie Jean King (U.S.A.)
1937	Anita Lizana (Chile)	1956	Shirley Fry (U.S.A.)	1975	Chris Evert (U.S.A.)
1938	Alice Marble (U.S.A.)	1957	Althea Gibson (U.S.A.)	1976	Chris Evert (U.S.A.)
1939	Alice Marble (U.S.A.)	1958	Althea Gibson (U.S.A.)	1977	Chris Evert (U.S.A.)
1940	Alice Marble (U.S.A.)	1959	Maria Bueno (Brazil)	1978	Chris Evert (U.S.A.)
1941	Sarah Palfrey Cooke (U.S.A.)	1960	Darlene Hard (U.S.A.)	1979	Tracy Austin (U.S.A.)
1942	Pauline Betz (U.S.A.)	1961	Darlene Hard (U.S.A.)	1980	Chris Evert Lloyd (U.S.A.)
1943	Pauline Betz (U.S.A.)	1962	Margaret Smith (Australia)		

Women's Doubles

1925	Mary K. Browne–Helen Wills	1953	Shirley Fry–Doris Hart
1926	Elizabeth Ryan–Eleanor Goss	1954	Shirley Fry–Doris Hart
1927	Mrs. Kathleen McKane Godfree–Ermyntrude Harvey	1955	Louise Brough–Mrs. Margaret Osborne duPont
1928	Mrs. Hazel Wightman–Helen Wills	1956	Louise Brough–Mrs. Margaret Osborne duPont
1929	Mrs. Phoebe Watson–Mrs. L. R. C. Michell	1957	Louise Brough–Mrs. Margaret Osborne duPont
1930	Betty Nuthall–Sarah Palfrey	1958	Jeanne Arth–Darlene Hard
1931	Betty Nuthall–Mrs. Eileen Whittingstall	1959	Jeanne Arth–Darlene Hard
1932	Helen Jacobs–Sarah Palfrey	1960	Maria Bueno–Darlene Hard
1933	Betty Nuthall–Freda James	1961	Darlene Hard–Lesley Turner
1934	Helen Jacobs–Sarah Palfrey	1962	Darlene Hard–Maria Bueno
1935	Helen Jacobs–Mrs. Sarah Palfrey Fabyan	1963	Robyn Ebbern–Margaret Smith
1936	Mrs. Marjorie Van Ryn–Carolin Babcock	1964	Billie Jean Moffitt–Mrs. Karen Susman
1937	Mrs. Sarah Palfrey Fabyan–Alice Marble	1965	Carole Graebner–Nancy Richey
1938	Mrs. Sarah Palfrey Fabyan–Alice Marble	1966	Maria Bueno–Nancy Richey
1939	Mrs. Sarah Palfrey Fabyan–Alice Marble	1967	Mrs. Billie Jean King–Rosemary Casals
1940	Mrs. Sarah Palfrey Fabyan–Alice Marble	1968	Maria Bueno–Margaret Smith Court
1941	Mrs. Sarah Palfrey Cooke–Margaret Osborne	1969	Darlene Hard–Françoise Durr
1942	Louise Brough–Margaret Osborne	1970	Margaret Smith Court–Judy Tegart Dalton
1943	Louise Brough–Margaret Osborne	1971	Rosemary Casals–Judy Tegart Dalton
1944	Louise Brough–Margaret Osborne	1972	Françoise Durr–Betty Stove
1945	Louise Brough–Margaret Osborne	1973	Mrs. Margaret Smith Court–Virginia Wade
1946	Louise Brough–Margaret Osborne	1974	Billie Jean King–Rosemary Casals
1947	Louise Brough–Margaret Osborne	1975	Mrs. Margaret Smith Court–Virginia Wade
1948	Louise Brough–Mrs. Margaret Osborne duPont	1976	Linky Boshoff–Ilana Kloss
1949	Louise Brough–Mrs. Margaret Osborne duPont	1977	Betty Stove–Martina Navratilova
1950	Louise Brough–Mrs. Margaret Osborne duPont	1978	Billie Jean King–Martina Navratilova
1951	Shirley Fry–Doris Hart	1979	Betty Stove–Wendy Turnbull
1952	Shirley Fry–Doris Hart	1980	Billie Jean King–Martina Navratilova

ALL-ENGLAND CHAMPIONS, WIMBLEDON (Open competition since 1968)

Men's Singles

1929	Henri Cochet (France)	1950	Budge Patty (U.S.A.)	1965	Roy Emerson (Australia)
1930	Bill Tilden (U.S.A.)	1951	Dick Savitt (U.S.A.)	1966	Manuel Santana (Spain)
1931	Sid Wood (U.S.A.)	1952	Frank Sedgman (Australia)	1967	John Newcombe (Australia)
1932	Ellsworth Vines (U.S.A.)	1953	Vic Seixas (U.S.A.)	1968	Rod Laver (Australia)
1933	John Crawford (Australia)	1954	Jaroslav Drobny (Egypt)	1969	Rod Laver (Australia)
1934	Fred Perry (England)	1955	Tony Trabert (U.S.A.)	1970	John Newcombe (Australia)
1935	Fred Perry (England)	1956	Lew Hoad (Australia)	1971	John Newcombe (Australia)
1936	Fred Perry (England)	1957	Lew Hoad (Australia)	1972	Stan Smith (U.S.A.)
1937	Don Budge (U.S.A.)	1958	Ashley Cooper (Australia)	1973	Jan Kodes (Czechoslovakia)
1938	Don Budge (U.S.A.)	1959	Alex Olmedo (U.S.A.)	1974	Jimmy Connors (U.S.A.)
1939	Bobby Riggs (U.S.A.)	1960	Neale Fraser (Australia)	1975	Arthur Ashe (U.S.A.)
1946	Yvon Petra (France)	1961	Rod Laver (Australia)	1976	Bjorn Borg (Sweden)
1947	Jack Kramer (U.S.A.)	1962	Rod Laver (Australia)	1977	Bjorn Borg (Sweden)
1948	Bob Falkenburg (U.S.A.)	1963	Chuck McKinley (U.S.A.)	1978	Bjorn Borg (Sweden)
1949	Ted Schroeder (U.S.A.)	1964	Roy Emerson (Australia)	1979	Bjorn Borg (Sweden)
				1980	Bjorn Borg (Sweden)

Men's Doubles

1929	Wilmer Allison–John Van Ryn	1951	Ken McGregor–Frank Sedgman	1966	Ken Fletcher–John Newcombe
1930	Wilmer Allison–John Van Ryn	1952	Ken McGregor–Frank Sedgman	1967	Bob Hewitt–Frew McMillan
1931	John Van Ryn–George Lott	1953	Lew Hoad–Ken Rosewall	1968	John Newcombe–Tony Roche
1932	Jean Borotra–Jacques Brugnon	1954	Rex Hartwig–Mervyn Rose	1969	John Newcombe–Tony Roche
1933	Jean Borotra–Jacques Brugnon	1955	Rex Hartwig–Lew Hoad	1970	John Newcombe–Tony Roche
1934	George Lott–Lester Stoefen	1956	Lew Hoad–Ken Rosewall	1971	Rod Laver–Roy Emerson
1935	John Crawford–Adrian Quist	1957	Gardnar Mulloy–Budge Patty	1972	Bob Hewitt–Frew McMillan
1936	George Hughes–Charles Tuckey	1958	Sven Davidson–Ulf Schmidt	1973	Jim Connors–Illie Nastase
1937	Don Budge–Gene Mako	1959	Neale Fraser–Roy Emerson	1974	John Newcombe–Tony Roche
1938	Don Budge–Gene Mako	1960	Rafael Osuna–Dennis Ralston	1975	Vitas Gerulatis–Sandy Mayer
1939	Bobby Riggs–Elwood Cooke	1961	Neale Fraser–Roy Emerson	1976	Brian Gottfried–Raul Ramirez
1946	Jack Kramer–Tom Brown	1962	Fred Stolle–Bob Hewitt	1977	Ross Case–Geoff Masters
1947	Jack Kramer–Bob Falkenburg	1963	Rafael Osuna–Antonio Palafox	1978	Bob Hewitt–Frew McMillan
1948	Jack Bromwich–Frank Sedgman	1964	Bob Hewitt–Fred Stolle	1979	John McEnroe–Peter Fleming
1949	Pancho Gonzalez–Frank Parker	1965	John Newcombe–Tony Roche	1980	Peter McNamara–Paul McNamee
1950	Jack Bromwich–Adrian Quist				

Women's Singles

1929	Helen Wills (U.S.A.)	1951	Doris Hart (U.S.A.)	1967	Billie Jean King (U.S.A.)
1930	Helen Wills Moody (U.S.A.)	1952	Maureen Connolly (U.S.A.)	1968	Billie Jean King (U.S.A.)
1931	Cecile Aussem (Germany)	1953	Maureen Connolly (U.S.A.)	1969	Ann Haydon Jones (England)
1932	Helen Wills Moody (U.S.A.)	1954	Maureen Connolly (U.S.A.)	1970	Margaret S. Court (Australia)
1933	Helen Wills Moody (U.S.A.)	1955	Louise Brough (U.S.A.)	1971	Evonne Goolagong (Australia)
1934	Dorothy Round (England)	1956	Shirley Fry (U.S.A.)	1972	Billie Jean King (U.S.A.)
1935	Helen Wills Moody (U.S.A.)	1957	Althea Gibson (U.S.A.)	1973	Billie Jean King (U.S.A.)
1936	Helen Hull Jacobs (U.S.A.)	1958	Althea Gibson (U.S.A.)	1974	Chris Evert (U.S.A.)
1937	Dorothy Round (England)	1959	Maria Bueno (Brazil)	1975	Billie Jean King (U.S.A.)
1938	Helen Wills Moody (U.S.A.)	1960	Maria Bueno (Brazil)	1976	Chris Evert (U.S.A.)
1939	Alice Marble (U.S.A.)	1961	Angela Mortimer (England)	1977	Virginia Wade (England)
1946	Pauline Betz (U.S.A.)	1962	Karen Hantze Susman (U.S.A.)	1978	Martina Navratilova (U.S.A.)
1947	Margaret Osborne (U.S.A.)	1963	Margaret Smith (Australia)	1979	Martina Navratilova (U.S.A.)
1948	Louise Brough (U.S.A.)	1964	Maria Bueno (Brazil)	1980	Evonne Goolagong Cawley (Australia)
1949	Louise Brough (U.S.A.)	1965	Margaret Smith (Australia)		
1950	Louise Brough (U.S.A.)	1966	Billie Jean King (U.S.A.)		

Women's Doubles

1929	Phoebe Watson–Peggy Saunders Mitchel	1949	Louise Brough–Margaret Osborne duPont	1964	Margaret Smith–Lesley Turner
1930	Elizabeth Ryan–Helen Wills Moody	1950	Louise Brough–Margaret Osborne duPont	1965	Maria Bueno–Billie Jean Moffitt
1931	Mrs. D. C. Shepherd–Baron–Phyllis Mudford King	1951	Shirley Fry–Doris Hart	1966	Maria Bueno–Nancy Richey
1932	D. Metaxa–J. Sigart	1952	Shirley Fry–Doris Hart	1967	Billie Jean King–Rosemary Casals
1933	Elizabeth Ryan–Rene Mathieu	1953	Shirley Fry–Doris Hart	1968	Billie Jean King–Rosemary Casals
1934	Elizabeth Ryan–Rene Mathieu	1954	Louise Brough–Margaret Osborne duPont	1969	Margaret S. Court–Judy Tegart
1935	Kay Stammers–Freda James	1955	Angela Mortimer–Anne Shilcock	1970	Billie Jean King–Rosemary Casals
1936	Kay Stammers–Freda James	1956	Angela Buxton–Althea Gibson	1971	Billie Jean King–Rosemary Casals
1937	Rene Mathieu–A. M. Yorke	1957	Althea Gibson–Darlene Hard	1972	Billie Jean King–Betty Stove
1938	Alice Marble–Sarah Palfrey Fabyan	1958	Maria Bueno–Althea Gibson	1973	Billie Jean King–Rosemary Casals
1939	Alice Marble–Sarah Palfrey Fabyan	1959	Jeanne Arth–Darlene Hard	1974	Peggy Michel–Evonne Goolagong
1946	Louise Brough–Margaret Osborne	1960	Maria Bueno–Darlene Hard	1975	Kazuko Sawamatsu–Ann Kiyomura
1947	Doris Hart–Patricia Canning Todd	1961	Karen Hantze–Billie Jean Moffitt	1976	Chris Evert–Martina Navratilova
1948	Louise Brough–Margaret Osborne duPont	1962	Karen Hantze Susman–Billie Jean Moffitt	1977	Helen G. Cawley–Joanne Russell
		1963	Maria Bueno–Darlene Hard	1978	Wendy Turnbull–Kerry Reid
				1979	Billie Jean King–Martina Navratilova
				1980	Kathy Jordan–Anne Smith

WIGHTMAN CUP

Year	Result	Year	Result	Year	Result
1929	United States 4, Great Britain 3	1950	United States 7, Great Britain 0	1965	United States 5, Great Britain 2
1930	Great Britain 4, United States 3	1951	United States 6, Great Britain 1	1966	United States 4, Great Britain 3
1931	United States 5, Great Britain 2	1952	United States 7, Great Britain 0	1967	United States 6, Great Britain 1
1932	United States 4, Great Britain 3	1953	United States 7, Great Britain 0	1968	Great Britain 4, United States 3
1933	United States 4, Great Britain 3	1954	United States 6, Great Britain 0	1969	United States 5, Great Britain 2
1934	United States 5, Great Britain 2	1955	United States 6, Great Britain 1	1970	United States 4, Great Britain 3
1935	United States 4, Great Britain 3	1956	United States 5, Great Britain 2	1971	United States 4, Great Britain 3
1936	United States 4, Great Britain 3	1957	United States 6, Great Britain 1	1972	United States 5, Great Britain 2
1937	United States 6, Great Britain 1	1958	Great Britain 4, United States 3	1973	United States 5, Great Britain 2
1938	United States 5, Great Britain 2	1959	United States 4, Great Britain 3	1974	Great Britain 6, United States 1
1939	United States 5, Great Britain 2	1960	Great Britain 4, United States 3	1975	Great Britain 5, United States 2
1946	United Sisters 7, Great Britain 0	1961	United States 6, Great Britain 1	1976	United States 5, Great Britain 2
1947	United States 7, Great Britain 0	1962	United States 4, Great Britain 3	1977	United States 7, Great Britain 0
1948	United States 6, Great Britain 1	1963	United States 6, Great Britain 1	1978	Great Britain 4, United States 3
1949	United States 7, Great Britain 0	1964	United States 5, Great Britain 2	1979	United States 7, Great Britain 0

DAVIS CUP CHALLENGE ROUND (No matches in 1910, 1915–18, and 1940–45)

Year	Result	Year	Result	Year	Result
1906	British Isles 5, United States 0	1932	France 3, United States 2	1959	Australia 3, United States 2
1907	Australasia 3, British Isles 2	1933	Great Britain 3, France 2	1960	Australia 4, Italy 1
1908	Australasia 3, United States 2	1934	Great Britain 4, United States 1	1961	Australia 5, Italy 0
1909	Australasia 5, United States 0	1935	Great Britain 5, United States 0	1962	Australia 5, Mexico 0
1911	Australasia 5, United States 0	1936	Great Britain 3, Australia 2	1963	United States 3, Australia 2
1912	British Isles 3, Australasia 2	1937	United States 4, Great Britain 1	1964	Australia 3, United States 2
1913	United States 3, British Isles 2	1938	United States 3, Australia 2	1965	Australia 4, Spain 1
1914	Australasia 3, United States 2	1939	Australia 3, United States 2	1966	Australia 4, India 1
1919	Australasia 4, British Isles 1	1946	United States 5, Australia 0	1967	Australia 4, Spain 1
1920	United States 5, Australasia 0	1947	United States 4, Australia 1	1968	United States 4, Australia 1
1921	United States 5, Japan 0	1948	United States 5, Australia 0	1969	United States 5, Rumania 0
1922	United States 4, Australasia 1	1949	United States 4, Australia 1	1970	U.S. 5, W. Germany 0
1923	United States 4, Australasia 1	1950	Australia 4, United States 1	1971	United States 3, Rumania 2
1924	United States 5, Australia 0	1951	Australia 3, United States 2	1972	United States 3, Rumania 2
1925	United States 5, France 0	1952	Australia 4, United States 1	1973	Australia 5, United States 0
1926	United States 4, France 1	1953	Australia 3, United States 2	1974	South Africa defeated India, by default
1927	France 3, United States 2	1954	United States 3, Australia 2	1975	Sweden 3, Czechoslovakia 2
1928	France 4, United States 1	1955	Australia 5, United States 0	1976	Italy 4, Chile 1
1929	France 3, United States 2	1956	Australia 5, United States 0	1977	Australia 3, Italy 1
1930	France 4, United States 1	1957	Australia 3, United States 2	1978	U.S. 4, Great Britain 1
1931	France 3, Great Britain 2	1958	United States 3, Australia 2	1979	U.S. 5, Italy 0

OTHER FOREIGN CHAMPIONSHIPS (Open competition since 1969)

Men's Singles

Year	AUSTRALIAN	CANADIAN	FRENCH	ITALIAN
1967	Roy Emerson	Manuel Santana	Roy Emerson	Martin Mulligan
1968	Bill Bowrey	Ramanathan Krishnan	Ken Rosewall	Tom Okker
1969	Rod Laver	Cliff Richey	Rod Laver	John Newcombe
1970	Arthur Ashe	Rod Laver	Jan Kodes	Ilie Nastase
1971	Ken Rosewall	John Newcombe	Jan Kodes	Rod Laver
1972	Ken Rosewall	Ilie Nastase	Andres Gimeno	Manuel Orantes
1973	John Newcombe	Tom Okker	Ilie Nastase	Ilie Nastase
1974	Jimmy Connors	Guillermo Vilas	Bjorn Borg	Bjorn Borg
1975	John Newcombe	Manuel Orantes	Bjorn Borg	Raul Ramirez
1976	Mark Edmondson	Guillermo Vilas	Adriano Panatta	Adriano Panatta
1977	Roscoe Tanner	Jeff Borowiak	Guillermo Vilas	Vitas Gerulaitis
1978	Vitas Gerulaitis	Eddie Dibbs	Bjorn Borg	Bjorn Borg
1979	Guillermo Vilas	Bjorn Borg	Bjorn Borg	Vitas Gerulaitis
1980	Guillermo Vilas	Ivan Lendl	Bjorn Borg	Guillermo Vilas

Women's Singles

Year	AUSTRALIAN	CANADIAN	FRENCH	ITALIAN
1967	Nancy Richey	Kathy Harter	Françoise Durr	Lesley Turner
1968	Billie Jean King	Peaches Bartkowicz	Nancy Richey	Lesley Turner Bowrey
1969	Margaret Smith Court	Faye Urban	Margaret Smith Court	Julie Heldman
1970	Margaret Smith Court	Margaret Smith Court	Margaret Smith Court	Billie Jean King
1971	Margaret Smith Court	Françoise Durr	Evonne Goolagong	Virginia Wade
1972	Virginia Wade	Evonne Goolagong	Billie Jean King	Linda Tuero
1973	Margaret Court	Evonne Goolagong	Margaret Court	Evonne Goolagong
1974	Evonne Goolagong	Chris Evert	Chris Evert	Chris Evert
1975	Evonne Goolagong	Marcie Louie	Chris Evert	Chris Evert
1976	Evonne Goolagong	Mima Jausovec	Sue Barker	Mima Jausovec
1977	Kerry Reid	Regina Marsikova	Mima Jausovec	Janet Newberry
1978	Evonne Goolagong	Regina Marsikova	Virginia Ruzici	Regina Marsikova
1979	Chris O'Neill	Laura DuPont	Chris Evert Lloyd	Tracy Austin
1980	Barbara Jordan	Chris Evert Lloyd	Chris Evert Lloyd	Chris Evert Lloyd

THE GRAND SLAM OF TENNIS
Winners of the Australian, French, British and United States Championships in the same season.

Year	Champions	Country	Event
1938	Don Budge	United States	Men's Singles
1951	Frank Sedgman–Ken McGregor	Australia	Men's Doubles
1953	Maureen Connolly	United States	Women's Singles
1960	Maria Bueno	Brazil	Women's Doubles*
1962	Rod Laver	Australia	Men's Singles
1963	Margaret Smith–Ken Fletcher	Australia	Mixed Doubles
1967	Owen Davidson	Australia	Mixed Doubles*
1969	Rod Laver	Australia	Men's Singles
1970	Margaret Smith Court	Australia	Women's Singles

*Won in Australia with a different doubles partner.

COLLEGIATE SINGLES CHAMPIONS

Year	Man	School	Woman	School
1966	Charles Pasarell	U.C.L.A.	Cecilia Martinez	San Francisco State
1967	Bob Lutz	Southern California	Patsy Rippy	Odessa Jr. College
1968	Stan Smith	Southern California	Emilie Burrer	Trinity
1969	Joaquin Loyo-Mayo	Southern California	Emilie Burrer	Trinity
1970	Jeff Borowiak	U.C.L.A.	Laura DuPont	North Carolina
1971	Jimmy Connors	U.C.L.A.	Pam Richmond	Arizona State
1972	Dick Stockton	Trinity	Janice Metcalf	Redlands
1973	Alex Mayer	Stanford	Janice Metcalf	Redlands
1974	John Whitlinger	Stanford	Carrier Meyer	Marymount
1975	Bill Martin	U.C.L.A.	Stephanie Tolleson	Trinity
1976	Bill Scanlon	Trinity	Barbara Hallquist	Southern California
1977	Matt Mitchell	Stanford	Barbara Hallquist	Southern California
1978	John McEnroe	Stanford	Jeanne DuVall	U.C.L.A.
1979	Kevin Curran	Texas	Kathy Jordan	Stanford
1980	Robert Van't Hof	Southern California	Wendy White	Rollins College

FEDERATION CUP
Women's International Team Competition
SOURCE: U.S.T.A.

Year	Final Round Results	Year	Final Round Results
1963	United States, 2, Australia 1	1972	South Africa 2, Great Britain 1
1964	Australia 2, United States 1	1973	Australia 3, South Africa 0
1965	Australia 2, United States 1	1974	Australia 2, United States 1
1966	United States 3, West Germany 0	1975	Czechoslovakia 3, Australia 0
1967	United States 2, Great Britain 0	1976	United States 2, Australia 1
1968	Australia 3, Netherlands 0	1977	United States 2, Australia 1
1969	United States 2, Australia 1	1978	United States 2, Australia 1
1970	Australia 3, West Germany 0	1979	United States 3, Australia 0
1971	Australia 3, Great Britain 0	1980	United States 3, Australia 0

1980 TOP MONEY WINNERS (to Oct. 4)

MEN
1.	Bjorn Borg, Sweden	$472,200
2.	John McEnroe, United States	423,345
3.	Jimmy Connors, United States	347,647
4.	Vitas Gerulaitis, United States	271,606
5.	Guillermo Vilas, Argentina	198,886
6.	Brian Gottfried, United States	198,082
7.	Gene Mayer, United States	191,644
8.	Ivan Lendl, Czechoslovakia	187,631
9.	Vijay Amritraj, India	158,156
10.	Harold Solomon, United States	155,643

WOMEN
1.	Martina Navratilova, United States	$478,050
2.	Tracy Austin, United States	442,737
3.	Billie Jean King, United States	301,541
4.	Chris Evert Lloyd, United States	265,038
5.	Evonne Goolagong Cawley, Australia	177,880
6.	Wendy Turnbull, Australia	172,648
7.	Hana Mandlikova, Czechoslovakia	148,380
8.	Andrea Jaeger, United States	140,564
9.	Kathy Jordan, United States	138,026
10.	Virginia Ruzici, Romania	116,213

WORLD CHAMPIONSHIP TENNIS (WCT) FINALS: 1980

Singles—Jimmy Connors   **Doubles**—Brian Gottfried · Raul Ramirez   **Challenge Cup** (Dec. 1979) — Bjorn Borg

1980 COLLEGIATE TENNIS CHAMPIONS

NCAA DIVISION I
Singles — Robert Van't Hof, Southern California
Doubles — Mel Purcell · Rodney Harmon, Tennessee
Team — Stanford

NCAA DIVISION II
Singles — Juan Farrow, Southern Illinois (Edwardsville)
Doubles — Juan Farrow-Hugo Nunez, Southern Illinois (Edwardsville))
Team — Southern Illinois (Edwardsville)

NCAA DIVISION III
Singles — Chris Burns, Kalamazoo
Doubles — John Mattke · Paul Holbach, Gustavus Adolphus
Team — Gustavus Adolphus (Minn.)

AIAW DIVISION I
Singles — Wendy White, Rollins College
Doubles — Trey Lewis · Anne White, Southern California
Team — Southern California

AIAW DIVISION II
Singles — Helen Park, Calif. State-Los Angeles
Doubles — Joan Kreider · Sue Overvold, Stetson
Team — Calif. State Poly.-Pomona

AIAW DIVISION III
Singles — Kim Schmidt, Drew
Doubles — Carrie Zarranonandia · Diane Demartini, Calif.-Davis
Team — California-Davis

NAIA Team — Redlands (Calif.)

JUNIOR COLLEGES — Team
Men — Tyler J.C. (Texas)
Women — Palm Beach J.C. (Fla.)

JAMES E. SULLIVAN MEMORIAL TROPHY
Sportsmanship — Outstanding Amateur Athlete

Year	Athlete	Sport	Year	Athlete	Sport
1930	Bobby Jones	Golf	1955	Harrison Dillard	Track & Field
1931	Bernard Berlinger	Track & Field	1956	Patricia McCormick	Diving
1932	James Bausch	Track & Field	1957	Bobby Morrow	Track & Field
1933	Glenn Cunningham	Track & Field	1958	Glenn Davis	Track & Field
1934	Bill Bonthron	Track & Field	1959	Parry O'Brien	Track & Field
1935	Lawson Little	Golf	1960	Rafer Johnson	Track & Field
1936	Glen Morris	Track & Field	1961	Wilma Rudolph Ward	Track & Field
1937	Don Budge	Tennis	1962	Jim Beatty	Track & Field
1938	Donald Lash	Track & Field	1963	John Pennel	Track & Field
1939	Joe Burk	Rowing	1964	Don Schollander	Swimming
1940	Greg Rice	Track & Field	1965	Bill Bradley	Basketball
1941	Leslie MacMitchell	Track & Field	1966	Jim Ryun	Track & Field
1942	Cornelius Warmerdam	Track & Field	1967	Randy Matson	Track & Field
1943	Gilbert Dodds	Track & Field	1968	Debbie Meyer	Swimming
1944	Ann Curtis	Swimming	1969	Bill Toomey	Track & Field
1945	Doc Blanchard	Football	1970	John Kinsella	Swimming
1946	Arnold Tucker	Football	1971	Mark Spitz	Swimming
1947	John Kelly, Jr.	Rowing	1972	Frank Shorter	Track & Field
1948	Robert Mathias	Track & Field	1973	Bill Walton	Basketball
1949	Richard Button	Skating	1974	Rick Wohlhuter	Track & Field
1950	Fred Wilt	Track & Field	1975	Tim Shaw	Swimming
1951	Bob Richards	Track & Field	1976	Bruce Jenner	Track & Field
1952	Horace Ashenfelter	Track & Field	1977	John Naber	Swimming
1953	Sammy Lee	Diving	1978	Tracy Caulkins	Swimming
1954	Mal Whitfield	Track & Field	1979	Kurt Thomas	Gymnastics

AUTO RACING

THE HISTORY OF THE MILE RECORD

DATE	DRIVER	CAR	AMERICAN TIME	AVG.	WORLD'S TIME	AVG.
12/18/98	Chasseloup-Laubat	Jeantaud			57.000	39.24
1/17/99	Camille Jenatzy	Jamais Contente Jeantzy			54.000	41.42
1/17/99	Chasseloup-Laubat	Jeantaud			51.500	43.69
1/27/99	Camille Jenatzy	Jamais Contente Jeantzy			44.800	49.40
3/4/99	Chasseloup-Laubat	Jeantaud			38.400	58.25
4/29/99	Camille Jenatzy	Jamais Contente Jeantzy			34.400	65.79
4/13/02	Serpollet	Serpollet			29.800	76.06
8/5/02	W. K. Vanderbilt	Mors			29.400	76.08
11/5/02	H. Fournier	Mors			29.200	76.60
11/17/02	Augieres	Mors			29.000	77.13
3/17/03	Rigolly	Gorbron-Brillie			26.800	83.46
11/5/03	A. Duray	Gobron-Brillie			26.400	84.73
1/12/04	Henry Ford	Ford "999"	39.40	91.370		
1/22/04	W. K. Vanderbilt	Mercedes	39.00	92.307		
3/31/04	Rigolly	Gobbron-Brillie			23.600	94.78
5/12/04	De Caters	Mercedes			23.000	97.26
7/21/04	Rigolly	Gobron-Brillie			21.600	103.56
11/13/04	Victor Hemery	Darracq			21.400	104.53
12/30/04	Barras	Darracq			20.400	109.65
1/24/05	Arthur MacDonald	Napier	34.40	104.65		
1/25/05	H. L. Bowden	Mercedes	32.80	109.75		
1/26/06	Fred Marriott	Stanley (Steam)	28.20	127.659		
11/8/09*	Victor Hemery	Benz			17.761	125.914*
3/16/10	Barney Oldfield	Benz	27.33	131.724		
4/23/11	Bob Burman	Benz	25.40	141.732		
6/24/14	L. G. Hornsted	Benz			29.01	124.095
2/12/19	Ralph DePalma	Packard	24.02	149.875		
4/27/20	Tom Milton	Duesenberg	23.07	156.046		
5/17/22	K. Lee Guinness	Sunbeam			27.87	129.171
6/26/24	J. G. Parry-Thomas	Leyland-Thomas			27.75	129.730
7/6/24	Rene Thomas	Delage			25.12	143.312
7/12/24	E. A. D. Eldridge	Fiat			24.675	145.897
9/25/24	Capt. M. Campbell	Sunbeam			24.630	146.163
7/21/25	Capt. M. Campbell	Sunbeam			23.878	150.766
4/27/26	J. G. Parry-Thomas	Thomas Special			21.419	168.075
4/28/26	J. G. Parry-Thomas	Thomas Special			21.099	170.624
2/4/27	Capt. M. Campbell	Napier-Campbell			20.663	174.224
3/29/27	Maj. H. O. D. Seagrave	Sunbeam	17.665	203.790	17.665	203.790
2/19/28	Capt. M. Campbell	Napier-Campbell	17.395	206.956	17.395	206.956
4/22/28	Ray Keech	White Triplex	17.345	207.552	17.345	207.552
3/11/29	Maj. H. O. D. Seagrave	Irving-Napier	15.56	231.446	15.56	231.446
2/5/31	Sir Malcolm Campbell	Napier-Campbell	14.65	245.086	14.65	246.086
2/24/32	Sir Malcolm Campbell	Napier-Campbell	14.175	253.96	14.175	253.96
2/22/33	Sir Malcolm Campbell	Napier-Campbell	13.23	272.109	13.23	272.109
3/7/35	Sir Malcolm Campbell	Bluebird Special	13.01	276.82	13.01	276.82
9/3/35	Sir Malcolm Campbell	Bluebird Special	11.96	301.13	11.96	301.13
11/19/37	Capt. G. E. T. Eyston	Thunderbolt No. 1	11.56	311.42	11.56	311.42
8/27/38	Capt. G. E. T. Eyston	Thunderbolt No. 1	10.42	345.5	10.42	345.5
9/15/38	John Cobb	Railton	10.28	350.2	10.28	350.2
9/16/38	Capt. G. E. T. Eyston	Thunderbolt No. 1	10.07	357.5	10.07	357.5
8/23/39	John Cobb	Railton	9.76	368.9	9.76	368.9
9/16/47	John Cobb	Railton-Mobil Special	9.1325	394.2	9.1325	394.2
8/5/63	Craig Breedlove	Spirit of America	8.8355	407.45	8.8355	407.45
10/2/64	Tom Green	Wingfoot Express	8.7125	413.20	8.7125	413.20
10/5/64	Art Arfons	Art Arfons Green Monster	8.2945	434.02	8.2945	434.02
10/13/64	Craig Breedlove	Spirit of America	7.6805	468.719	7.6805	468.719
10/15/64	Craig Breedlove	Spirit of America	6.8405	526.277	6.8405	526.277
10/27/64	Art Arfons	Art Arfons Green Monster	6.7075	536.71	6.7075	536.71
11/2/65	Craig Breedlove	Spirit of America—Sonic I	6.485	555.127	6.485	555.127
11/7/65	Art Arfons	Art Arfons Green Monster	6.244	576.553	6.244	576.553
11/15/65	Craig Breedlove	Spirit of America—Sonic I	5.994	600.601	5.994	600.601
10/23/70	Gary Gabelich	Blue Flame	5.784	622.407	5.784	622.407
9/9/79**	Stan Barrett	The Budweiser Rocket	5.637	638.637	5.637	638.637

* Records above this point for World's Time were made over the flying kilometer, the recognized distance in the early years.
NOTE: The above records are the average of two runs made in opposite directions within one hour. ** Run made in one direction. Record not officially sanctioned.

FORMULA 1 GRAND PRIX CHAMPIONS   Source: Sports Car Club of America

Year	Champion	Car	Country
1950	Giuseppe Farina	Alfa Romeo	Italy
1951	Juan Manuel Fangio	Alfa Romeo	Argentina
1952	Alberto Ascari	Ferrari	Italy
1953	Alberto Ascari	Ferrari	Italy
1954	Juan Manuel Fangio	Mercedes & Maserati	Argentina
1955	Juan Manuel Fangio	Mercedes	Argentina
1956	Juan Manuel Fangio	Lancia	Argentina
1957	Juan Manuel Fangio	Maserati	Argentina
1958	Mike Hawthorn	Ferrari	Great Britain
1959	Jack Brabham	Cooper	Australia
1960	Jack Brabham	Cooper	Australia
1961	Phil Hill	Ferrari	USA
1962	Graham Hill	BRM	Great Britain
1963	Jim Clark	Lotus	Great Britain
1964	John Surtees	Ferrari	Great Britain
1965	Jim Clark	Lotus	Great Britain
1966	Jack Brabham	Brabham	Australia
1967	Denis Hulme	Brabham	New Zealand
1968	Graham Hill	Lotus	Great Britain
1969	Jackie Stewart	Matra	Great Britain
1970	Jochen Rindt	Lotus	Austria
1971	Jackie Stewart	Tyrrell	Great Britain
1972	Emerson Fittipaldi	Lotus	Brazil
1973	Jackie Stewart	Tyrrell	Great Britain
1974	Emerson Fittipaldi	McLaren	Brazil
1975	Niki Lauda	Ferrari	Austria
1976	James Hunt	McLaren	Great Britain
1977	Niki Lauda	Ferrari	Austria
1978	Mario Andretti	Lotus	USA
1979	Jody Scheckter	Ferrari	South Africa
1980	Alan Jones	Williams	Australia

UNITED STATES GRAND PRIX, WATKINS GLEN, N.Y.   Source: Sports Car Club of America

Year	Winner	Car	Year	Winner	Car
1959*	Bruce McLaren	Cooper	1970	Emerson Fittipaldi	Lotus
1960**	Stirling Moss	Lotus	1971	Francois Cevert	Tyrrell
1961	Ines Ireland	Lotus	1972	Jackie Stewart	Tyrrell
1962	Jim Clark	Lotus	1973	Ronnie Peterson	Lotus
1963	Graham Hill	BRM	1974	Carlos Reutemann	Brabham
1964	Graham Hill	BRM	1975	Niki Lauda	Ferrari
1965	Graham Hill	BRM	1976	James Hunt	McLaren
1966	Jim Clark	Lotus	1977	James Hunt	McLaren
1967	Jim Clark	Lotus	1978	Carlos Reutemann	Ferrari
1968	Jackie Stewart	Matra	1979	Gilles Villeneuve	Ferrari
1969	Jochen Rindt	Lotus	1980	Alan Jones	Williams

* Held at Sebring   ** Held at Riverside

UNITED STATES GRAND PRIX WEST, LONG BEACH, CALIF.   Source: Sports Car Club of America

Year	Winner	Car	Year	Winner	Car
1976	Clay Regazzoni	Ferrari	1978	Carlos Reutemann	Ferrari
1977	Mario Andretti	Lotus	1979	Gilles Villeneuve	Ferrari
			1980	Nelson Piquet	Brabham

SPORTS CAR CLUB OF AMERICA SERIES CHAMPIONS   Source: Sports Car Club of America

Year	Champion	Car	Year	Champion	Car
Citicorp Can-Am® Challenge			**Trans-Am® Championship**		
1966	John Surtees	Lola	1972	George Follmer	Javelin
1967	Bruce McLaren	McLaren M6A	1973	Peter Gregg	Chevrolet
1968	Denis Hulme	McLaren M6A	1974	Peter Gregg	Porsche
1969	Bruce McLaren	McLaren M8B	1975	John Greenwood	Chevrolet
1970	Denis Hulme	McLaren M8D	1976	George Follmer	Porsche
1971	Peter Revson	McLaren M8F	1977	Category I Bob Tullius	Jaguar
1972	George Follmer	Porsche 917/10		Category II Ludwig Heimrath	Porsche
1974	Mark Donohue	Porsche 917/30	1978	Category I Bob Tullius	Jaguar
1973	Jackie Oliver	Shadow		Category II Greg Pickett	Corvette
1975–1976	(no series)		1979	Category I Gene Bothello	Corvette
1977	Patrick Tambay	Lola T-333CS		Category II John Paul	Porsche
1978	Alan Jones	Lola T-333CS			
1979	Jacky Ickx	Lola T-333CS			
1980	Patrick Tambay	Lola T530	**Pro Rally Series**		
			1973	Scott Harvey/Wayne Zitkus	Dodge Colt
			1974	Gene Henderson/Ken Pogue	Jeep Cherokee
			1975	John Buffum/Vicki Dykema	Ford Escort
Robert Bosch/VW Gold Cup			1976	Hendrik Blok/Erick Hauge	Dodge Colt
1971	Bill Scott	Royale	1977	John Buffum/"Vicki"	TR-7
1972	Bill Scott	Royale	1978	John Buffum/Doug Shepherd	TR-7
1973	Bertil Roos	Tui BH3	1979	John Buffum/Doug Shepherd	TR-8
1974	Elliott Forbes-Robinson	Lynn			
1975	Eddie Miller	Lola T-324	**Rabbit/Bilstein Cup**		
1976	Tom Bagley	Zink Z-11	1976	Paul Hacker	Scirocco
1977	Bob Lazier	Lola T-324	1977	Bill Deters	Scirocco
1978	Bill Alsup	Argo	1978	Gary Benson	Rabbit
1979	Geoff Brabham	Ralt RT-1	1979	Gary Benson	Rabbit

INDIANAPOLIS 500

SOURCE: Jack C. Fox, *The Indianapolis 500* (1967), and other sources

Year	Winner	Chassis	Engine	Cylinders	Mph	Gross	Second Place
1920	Gaston Chevrolet	Frontenac	Frontenac	4	88.16	$ 93,550	Rene Thomas
1921	Tommy Milton	Frontenac	Frontenac	8	89.62	$ 86,650	Roscoe Sarles
1922	Jimmy Murphy	Duesenberg	Miller	8	94.48	$ 70,575	Harry Hartz
1923	Tommy Milton	Miller	Miller	8	90.95	$ 83,425	Harry Hartz
1924	L. L. Corum, Joe Boyer	Duesenberg	Duesenberg	8	98.23	$ 86,850	Earl Cooper
1925	Peter DePaolo	Duesenberg	Duesenberg*	8	101.13	$ 87,750	Dave Lewis
1926	Frank Lockhart	Miller	Miller*	8	95.885[1]	$ 88,100	Harry Hartz
1927	George Souders	Duesenberg	Duesenberg*	8	97.545	$ 89,850	Earl DeVore
1928	Lou Meyer	Miller	Miller*	8	99.482	$ 90,750	Lou Moore
1929	Ray Keech	Miller	Miller*	8	97.585	$ 95,150	Lou Meyer
1930	Billy Arnold	Summers	Miller†	8	100.448	$ 97,600	Shorty Cantlon
1931	Lou Schneider	Stevens	Miller	8	96.629	$ 81,800	Fred Frame
1932	Fred Frame	Wetteroth	Miller†	8	104.144	$ 93,900	Howdy Wilcox 2d
1933	Lou Meyer	Miller	Miller	8	104.162	$ 54,450	Wilbur Shaw
1934	Bill Cummings	Miller	Miller†	4	104.863	$ 83,775	Mauri Rose
1935	Kelly Petillo	Wetteroth	Offenhauser	4	106.240	$ 78,575	Wilbur Shaw
1936	Lou Meyer	Stevens	Miller	4	109.069	$ 82,525	Ted Horn
1937	Wilbur Shaw	Shaw	Offenhauser	4	113.580	$ 92,135	Ralph Hepburn
1938	Floyd Roberts	Wetteroth	Miller	4	117.200	$ 91,075	Wilbur Shaw
1939	Wilbur Shaw	Maserati	Maserati*	8	115.035	$ 87,050	Jimmy Snyder
1940	Wilbur Shaw	Maserati	Maserati*	8	114.277	$ 85,525	Rex Mays
1941	Floyd Davis, Mauri Rose	Wetteroth	Offenhauser	4	115.117	$ 90,925	Rex Mays
1946	George Robson	Adams	Sparks*	6	114.820	$115,450	Jimmy Jackson
1947	Mauri Rose	Deidt	Offenhauser†	4	116.338	$137,425	Bill Holland
1948	Mauri Rose	Deidt	Offenhauser†	4	119.814	$171,075	Bill Holland
1949	Bill Holland	Deidt	Offenhauser†	4	121.327	$179,050	Johnnie Parsons
1950	Johnnie Parsons	Kurtis Kraft	Offenhauser	4	124.002[2]	$201,135	Bill Holland
1951	Lee Wallard	Kurtis Kraft	Offenhauser	4	126.244	$207,650	Mike Nazaruk
1952	Troy Ruttman	Kuzma	Offenhauser	4	128.922	$230,100	Jim Rathmann
1953	Bill Vukovich	Kurtis Kraft 500A	Offenhauser	4	128.740	$246,300	Art Cross
1954	Bill Vukovich	Kurtis Kraft 500A	Offenhauser	4	130.840	$269,375	Jimmy Bryan
1955	Bob Sweikert	Kurtis Kraft 500C	Offenhauser	4	128.209	$270,400	Tony Bettenhausen
1956	Pat Flaherty	Watson	Offenhauser	4	128.490	$282,052	Sam Hanks
1957	Sam Hanks	Epperly	Offenhauser	4	135.601	$300,252	Jim Rathmann
1958	Jimmy Bryan	Epperly	Offenhauser	4	133.791	$305,217	George Amick
1959	Rodger Ward	Watson	Offenhauser	4	135.857	$338,100	Jim Rathmann
1960	Jim Rathmann	Watson	Offenhauser	4	138.767	$369,150	Rodger Ward
1961	A. J. Foyt	Watson	Offenhauser	4	139.130	$400,000	Eddie Sachs
1962	Rodger Ward	Watson	Offenhauser	4	140.293	$426,152	Len Sutton
1963	Parnelli Jones	Watson	Offenhauser	4	143.137	$494,031	Jim Clark
1964	A. J. Foyt	Watson	Offenhauser	4	147.350	$506,625	Rodger Ward
1965	Jim Clark	Lotus	Ford‡	8	151.388	$628,399	Parnelli Jones
1966	Graham Hill	Lola	Ford‡	8	144.317	$691,809	Jim Clark
1967	A. J. Foyt	Coyote	Ford‡	8	151.207	$737,109	Al Unser
1968	Bobby Unser	Eagle	Ford‡**	8	152.882	$809,627	Dan Gurney
1969	Mario Andretti	Hawk	Ford‡**	8	156.867	$805,127	Dan Gurney
1970	Al Unser	P. J. Colt	Ford‡**	8	155.749	$1,000,002	Mark Donohue
1971	Al Unser	P. J. Colt	Ford‡**	8	157.735	$1,001,604	Peter Revson
1972	Mark Donohue	McLaren	Offenhauser	8	162.962	$1,011,846	Al Unser
1973	Gordon Johncock	Eagle	Offenhauser	4	159.014	$1,006,105	Billy Vukovich
1974	Johnny Rutherford	McLaren	Offenhauser	4	158.589	$1,015,686	Bobby Unser
1975	Bobby Unser	Eagle	Offenhauser	4	149.213[3]	$1,001,322	Johnny Rutherford
1976	Johnny Rutherford	McLaren	Drake-Offennauser	4	148.7[4]	$1,038,776	A. J. Foyt
1977	A. J. Foyt	Coyote	Foyt	8	161.331	$1,116,807	Tom Sneva
1978	Al Unser	Lola	Cosworth	8	161.363	$1,145,255	Tom Sneva
1979	Rick Mears	Penske	Cosworth	8	155.899	$1,271,954	A. J. Foyt
1980	Johnny Rutherford	Chaparral	Cosworth	8	142.862	$1,502,425	Tom Sneva

*Supercharged. **Turbocharged. †Front drive. ‡Rear engine. [1]400 miles. [2]345 miles; all other races at 500 miles. [3]Race stopped at 435 miles due to rain. [4]Race stopped at 255 miles due to rain.

NATIONAL RACING CHAMPIONS—USAC*

Year	Champion	Year	Champion	Year	Champion	Year	Champion
1902	Harry Harkness	1920	Gaston Chevrolet	1939	Wilbur Shaw	1962	Rodger Ward
1903	Barney Oldfield	1921	Thomas Milton	1940	Rex Mays	1963	A. J. Foyt
1904	George Heath	1922	James Murphy	1941	Rex Mays	1964	A. J. Foyt
1905	Victor Hemery	1923	Eddie Hearne	1946	Ted Horn	1965	Mario Andretti
1906	Joe Tracy	1924	James Murphy	1947	Ted Horn	1966	Mario Andretti
1907	Eddie Bald	1925	Peter DePaolo	1948	Ted Horn	1967	A. J. Foyt
1908	Louis Strang	1926	Harry Hartz	1949	Johnnie Parsons	1968	Bobby Unser
1909	George Robertson	1927	Peter DePaolo	1950	Henry Banks	1969	Mario Andretti
1910	Ray Harroun	1928	Louis Meyer	1951	Tony Bettenhausen	1970	Al Unser
1911	Ralph Mulford	1929	Louis Meyer	1952	Chuck Stevenson	1971	Joe Leonard
1912	Ralph DePalma	1930	Billy Arnold	1953	Sam Hanks	1972	Joe Leonard
1913	Earl Cooper	1931	Louis Schneider	1954	Jimmy Bryan	1973	Roger McCluskey
1914	Ralph DePalma	1932	Bob Carey	1955	Bob Sweikert	1974	Bobby Unser
1915	Earl Cooper	1933	Louis Meyer	1956	Jimmy Bryan	1975	A. J. Foyt
1916	Dario Resta	1934	Bill Cummings	1957	Jimmy Bryan	1976	Gordon Johncock
1917	Earl Cooper	1935	Kelly Petillo	1958	Tony Bettenhausen	1977	Tom Sneva
1918	Ralph Mulford	1936	Mauri Rose	1959	Rodger Ward	1978	Tom Sneva
1919	Howard Wilcox	1937	Wilbur Shaw	1960	A. J. Foyt	1979	A. J. Foyt
		1938	Floyd Roberts	1961	A. J. Foyt	1980	Johnny Rutherford

* USAC founded 1956.

1979 USAC NATIONAL CHAMPIONSHIP SERIES DRIVER STANDINGS

(SOURCE: United States Auto Club)

Pos.	Driver/Hometown	Pts.	Pos.	Driver/Hometown	Pts.
1.	A. J. Foyt, Houston, Tex.	3,320	17.	Tony Bettenhausen, Indianapolis, Ind.	185
2.	Billy Vukovich, Coarsegold, Calif.	1,770	18.	Dana Carter, Huntington Beach, Calif.	165
3.	Tom Bigelow, Whitewater, Wis.	1,305	19.	Phil Threshie, Tucson, Ariz.	153
4.	Larry Dickson, Marietta, Ohio	1,225	20.	Al Loquasto, Easton, Pa.	150
5.	Gary Bettenhausen, Monrovia, Ind.	1,008	21.	Todd Gibson, Richwood, Ohio	130
6.	Jim McElreath, Arlington, Tex.	975	22.	Jerry Karl, Manchester, Pa.	113
7.	Jerry Sneva, Spokane, Wash.	851	23.	Herm Johnson, Eau Claire, Wis.	100
8.	Dick Simon, San Juan Capistrano, Calif.	766	24.	Eldon Rasmussen, Calgary, Alberta, Canada	85
9.	Roger McCluskey, Tucson, Ariz.	716	25.	Jerry Miller, Albuquerque, N.M.	80
10.	Sheldon Kinser, Bloomington, Ind.	673	26.	Roger Rager, Mound, Minn.	65
11.	Cliff Hucul, Prince George, B.C., Canada	653	27.	Dick Ferguson, Glendale, Calif.	48
12.	Howdy Holmes, Ann Arbor, Mich.	600	28.	John Martin, Irvine, Calif.	30
13.	Johnny Parsons, Indianapolis, Ind.	598	29.	Bob Harkey, Indianapolis, Ind.	23
14.	George Snider, Bakersfield, Calif.	361	30.	Ken Nichols, San Carlos, Calif.	10
15.	Janet Guthrie, New York, N.Y.	225		Bill Puterbaugh, Indianapolis, Ind.	10
16.	Frank Weiss, Calgary, Alberta, Canada	218	32.	Jan Sneva, Spokane, Wash.	8

1979 USAC TOP MONEY WINNERS

	Driver	Total		Driver	Total
1.	A. J. Foyt, Houston, Tex.	$345,659	11.	Roger McCluskey, Tucson, Ariz.	$54,828
2.	Rick Mears, Bakersfield, Calif.	252,420	12.	Gary Bettenhausen, Monrovia, Ind.	51,855
3.	Tom Bigelow, Whitewater, Wis.	105,231	13.	Jerry Sneva, Spokane, Wash.	46,948
4.	Billy Vukovich, Coarsegold, Calif.	83,057	14.	Larry Rice, Brownsburg, Ind.	46,484
5.	Sheldon Kinser, Bloomington, Ind.	70,734	15.	Howdy Holmes, Ann Arbor, Mich.	45,466
6.	Jim McElreath, Arlington, Tex.	67,147	16.	Cliff Hucul, Prince George, B.C., Canada	43,668
7.	Larry Dickson, Marietta, Ohio	66,215	17.	Danny Ongais, Costa Mesa, Calif.	43,429
8.	Mike Mosley, Fallbrook, Calif.	59,828	18.	Pancho Carter, Brownsburg, Ind.	43,312
9.	Bobby Unser, Albuquerque, N.M.	59,353	19.	Dick Simon, San Juan Capistrano, Calif.	41,914
10.	Johnny Parsons, Indianapolis, Ind.	59,049	20.	Al Unser, Albuquerque, N.M.	38,195

USAC NATIONAL CHAMPIONSHIP ALL-TIME RACE WINNERS (1956-1979)

Driver	Wins	Driver	Wins	Driver	Wins	Driver	Wins
A. J. Foyt	66	Gordon Johncock	19	Lloyd Ruby	7	Danny Ongais	6
Al Unser	35	Johnny Rutherford	17	Johnny Thomson	6	Jud Larson	5
Mario Andretti	33	Eddie Sachs	8	Parnelli Jones	6	Jim McElreath	5
Rodger Ward	24	Jimmy Bryan	7	Don Branson	6	Wally Dallenbach	5
Bobby Unser	24	Dan Gurney	7	Joe Leonard	6	Roger McCluskey	5

USAC ROOKIE OF THE YEAR

Year	Name	Year	Name	Year	Name
1971	George Eaton	1974	Duane Carter, Jr.	1977	Danny Ongais
1972	Mike Hiss	1975	Spike Gehlhausen	1978	Tom Bagley
1973	Tom Sneva	1976	Rick Mears	1979	Tony Bettenhausen, Jr.

1980 DAYTONA-LE MANS 24-HOUR ENDURANCE RACES

	Drivers	Laps	Car	Avg. Speed (Mph)
DAYTONA:	1. Rolf Stommelen, Reinhold Jost and Volkert Merl (West Germany)	715 (2,745 mi.)	Porsche	114.4
	2. Preston Henn, John Paul and Al Holbert (U.S.)	682	Porsche	
LE MANS:	1. Jean-Pierre Jaussaud and Jean Rondeau (France)	388 (2,859 mi.)	Rondeau	119.17
	2. Jacky Ickx (Belgium) and Reinhold Jost (West Germany)	336	Porsche	

STOCK CAR RACING

SOURCE: The National Association for Stock Car Auto Racing, Inc.

RESULTS OF 1979 WINSTON CUP GRAND NATIONAL SEASON

EVENT-LOCATION	DATE	FIRST	SECOND
WINSTON WESTERN 500, Riverside, Calif.	Jan. 14	Darrell Waltrip, Chevrolet	David Pearson, Mercury
DAYTONA 500, Daytona Beach, Fla.	Feb. 18	Richard Petty, Oldsmobile	Darrell Waltrip, Oldsmobile
CAROLINA 500, Rockingham, N.C.	Mar. 4	Bobby Allison, Ford	Joe Millikan, Chevrolet
RICHMOND 400, Richmond, Va.	Mar. 11	Cale Yarborough, Oldsmobile	Bobby Allison, Ford
ATLANTA 500, Atlanta, Ga.	Mar. 18	Buddy Baker, Oldsmobile	Bobby Allison, Ford
NORTHWESTERN BANK 400, N. Wilkesboro, N.C.	Mar. 25	Bobby Allison, Ford	Richard Petty, Chevrolet
SOUTHEASTERN 500, Bristol, Tenn	Apr. 1	Dale Earnhardt, Chevrolet	Bobby Allison, Ford
CRC CHEMICALS REBEL 500, Darlington, S.C.	Apr. 8	Darrell Waltrip, Chevrolet	Richard Petty, Chevrolet
VIRGINIA 500, Martinsville, Va.	Apr. 22	Richard Petty, Chevrolet	Buddy Baker, Chevrolet
WINSTON 500, Talladega, Ala.	May 6	Bobby Allison, Ford	Darrell Waltrip, Oldsmobile
SUN-DROP MUSIC CITY USA 420, Nashville, Tenn.	May 12	Cale Yarborough, Oldsmobile	Richard Petty, Chevrolet
MASON-DIXON 500, Dover, Del.	May 20	Neil Bonnett, Mercury	Cale Yarborough, Chevrolet
WORLD 600, Charlotte, N.C.	May 27	Darrell Waltrip, Chevrolet	Richard Petty, Chevrolet
TEXAS 400, College Sta., Tex.	June 3	Darrell Waltrip, Chevrolet	Bobby Allison, Ford
NAPA RIVERSIDE 400, Riverside, Calif.	June 10	Bobby Allison, Ford	Darrell Waltrip, Chevrolet
GABRIEL 400, Brooklyn, Mich.	June 17	Buddy Baker, Chevrolet	Donnie Allison, Chevrolet
FIRECRACKER 400, Daytona Beach, Fla.	July 4	Neil Bonnett, Mercury	Benny Parsons, Oldsmobile
BUSCH NASHVILLE 420, Nashville, Tenn.	July 14	Darrell Waltrip, Chevrolet	Cale Yarborough, Chevrolet
COCA-COLA 500, Pocono, Pa.	July 30	Cale Yarborough, Chevrolet	Richard Petty, Chevrolet
TALLADEGA 500, Talladega, Ala.	Aug. 5	Darrell Waltrip, Oldsmobile	David Pearson, Oldsmobile
CHAMPION SPARK PLUG 400, Brooklyn, Mich.	Aug. 19	Richard Petty, Chevrolet	Buddy Baker, Chevrolet
VOLUNTEER 500, Bristol, Tenn.	Aug. 25	Darrell Waltrip, Chevrolet	Richard Petty, Chevrolet
SOUTHERN 500, Darlington, S.C.	Sept. 3	David Pearson, Chevrolet	Bill Elliott, Mercury
CAPITAL CITY 400, Richmond, Va.	Sept. 9	Bobby Allison, Ford	Darrell Waltrip, Chevrolet
CRC CHEMICALS 500, Dover, Del.	Sept. 16	Richard Petty, Chevrolet	Donnie Allison, Chevrolet
OLD DOMINION 500, Martinsville, Va.	Sept. 23	Buddy Baker, Chevrolet	Richard Petty, Chevrolet
NAPA NATIONAL 500, Charlotte, N.C.	Oct. 7	Cale Yarborough, Chevrolet	Bobby Allison, Ford
HOLLY FARMS 400, N. Wilkesboro, N.C.	Oct. 14	Benny Parsons, Chevrolet	Bobby Allison, Ford
AMERICAN 500, Rockingham, N.C.	Oct. 21	Richard Petty, Chevrolet	Benny Parsons, Chevrolet
DIXIE 500, Atlanta, Ga.	Nov. 4	Neil Bonnett, Mercury	Dale Earnhardt, Chevrolet
LOS ANGELES TIMES 500, Ontario, Calif.	Nov. 18	Benny Parsons, Chevrolet	Bobby Allison, Ford

NASCAR CHAMPIONS

WINSTON CUP GRAND NATIONAL

1964—Richard Petty, Randleman, N.C. (Plymouth)
1965—Ned Jarrett, Camden, S.C. (Ford)
1966—David Pearson, Spartanburg, S.C. (Dodge)
1967—Richard Petty, Randleman, N.C. (Plymouth)
1968—David Pearson, Spartanburg, S.C. (Ford)
1969—David Pearson, Spartanburg, S.C. (Ford)
1970—Bobby Isaac, Catawba, N.C. (Dodge)
1971—Richard Petty, Randleman, N.C. (Plymouth)
1972—Richard Petty, Randleman, N.C. (Plymouth-Dodge)
1973—Benny Parsons, Ellerbe, N.C. (Chevrolet)
1974—Richard Petty, Randleman, N.C. (Dodge)
1975—Richard Petty, Randleman, N.C. (Dodge)
1976—Cale Yarborough, Timmonsville, S.C. (Chevrolet)
1977—Cale Yarborough, Timmonsville, S.C. (Chevrolet)
1978—Cale Yarborough, Timmonsville, S.C. (Oldsmobile)
1979—Richard Petty, Randleman, N.C. (Chevrolet)

1979 WINSTON CUP GRAND NATIONAL STANDINGS

	Driver	Points	Starts	Wins	Top 5	Top 10	Money Won
1.	Richard Petty	4830	31	5	23	27	$531,292
2.	Darrell Waltrip	4819	31	7	19	22	523,691
3.	Bobby Allison	4633	31	5	18	22	403,014
4.	Cale Yarborough	4604	31	4	19	22	413,872
5.	Benny Parsons	4256	31	2	16	21	241,205
6.	Joe Millikan	4014	31	0	5	20	222,053
7.	Dale Earnhardt	3749	27	1	11	17	264,086
8.	Richard Childress	3735	31	0	1	11	132,922
9.	Ricky Rudd	3642	28	0	4	17	146,302
10.	Terry Labonte	3615	31	0	2	13	130,057
11.	Buddy Arrington	3589	31	0	1	7	131,833
12.	D. K. Ulrich	3508	31	0	0	5	108,862
13.	J. D. McDuffie	3473	31	0	1	7	103,478
14.	James Hylton	3405	30	0	0	5	97,428
15.	Buddy Baker	3249	26	3	12	15	287,552
16.	Frank Warren	3199	31	0	0	3	94,539

1980 WINSTON CUP GRAND NATIONAL (to Sept. 22)

EVENT	DATE	WINNER	EVENT	DATE	WINNER
WINSTON WESTERN 500	Jan. 19	Darrell Waltrip	NASCAR 400	June 1	Cale Yarborough
DAYTONA 500	Feb. 17	Buddy Baker	WARNER W. HODGON 400	June 8	Darrell Waltrip
RICHMOND 400	Feb. 24	Darrell Waltrip	GABRIEL 400	June 15	Benny Parsons
CAROLINA 500	Mar. 9	Cale Yarborough	FIRECRACKER 400	July 4	Bobby Allison
ATLANTA 500	Mar. 16	Dale Earnhardt	BUSCH NASHVILLE 420	July 12	Dale Earnhardt
VALLEYDALE S.E. 500	Mar. 30	Dale Earnhardt	COCA-COLA 500	July 27	Neil Bonnett
CRC CHEMICALS REBEL 500	Apr. 13	David Pearson	TALLADEGA 500	Aug. 3	Neil Bonnett
NORTHWESTERN BANK 400	Apr. 20	Richard Petty	CHAMPION SPARK PLUG 400	Aug. 17	Cale Yarborough
VIRGINIA 500	Apr. 27	Darrell Waltrip	BUSCH VOLUNTEER 400	Aug. 23	Cale Yarborough
WINSTON 500	May 4	Buddy Baker	SOUTHERN 500	Sept. 1	Terry Labonte
MUSIC CITY 420	May 10	Richard Petty	CAPITAL CITY 400	Sept. 7	Bobby Allison
MASON-DIXON 500	May 18	Bobby Allison	CRC CHEMICALS 500	Sept. 14	Darrell Waltrip
WORLD 600	May 25	Benny Parsons	HOLLY FARMS 400	Sept. 21	Bobby Allison

THOROUGHBRED RACING

SOURCE: *American Racing Manual*, 1980 ed. Reproduced with permission of the copyright owner, Daily Racing Form, Inc.

HIGHEST ANNUAL PAYOFF ODDS

Date	Winner	Track	Payoff Odds	Date	Winner	Track	Payoff Odds
1948 Sept. 30	Buddie Bones	Rockingham Park	192–1	1963 Aug. 12	Ivalinda	Arlington Park	190–1
1949 Sept. 20	Luxuriant	Narragansett Park	282–1	1964 Dec. 11	Wilson Hill Doll	Bay Meadows	279–1
1950 Oct. 30	Minnix	Lincoln Downs	253–1	1965 June 5	Blunt Edge	Cahokia Downs	142–1
1951 Sept. 27	Royal Marvel	Rockingham Park	183–1	1966 Oct. 7	Dutch Wrackateer	Narragansett Park	186–1
1952 Sept. 16	Rock House	Woodbine Park	214–1	1967 May 26	Mambo Rhythm	Seminole Downs	214–1
1953 Aug. 28	Can It Yes	Exhibition Park	253–1	1968 June 24	Waverley Steps	Woodbine	396–1
1954 Nov. 10	Ruff Mate	Pimlico Race Course	209–1	1969 Sept. 24	Judes Song	Latonia	241–1
1955 May 27	Gold Champ	Suffolk Downs	144–1	1970 May 7	Corpus Delicti	Fort Erie	175–1
1956 July 24	Buster Bell	Charles Town	203–1	1971 Apr. 1	Moonlight City	Portland Meadows	169–1
1957 Aug. 27	Miss Profit	Detroit Race Course	172–1	1972 Nov. 16	Norton	Churchill Downs	190–1
1958 Mar. 22	Whisk Tru	Bowie Race Course	231–1	1973 Sept. 28	Cedars Crown	Detroit Race Course	256–1
1959 June 5	Janie Brown	Thistledown	168–1	1974 Mar. 17	Campus Bright	Yakima Meadows	156–1
1960 Nov. 4	Kamal Bey	Laurel Race Course	175–1	1975 Sept. 1	Second Ticking	Narragansett Park	147–1
1961 Sept. 29	Djebonita	Bay Meadows	259–1	1976 Sept. 21	Tiger Red K	Columbus	188–1
1962 July 20	Wee Highway	Delaware Park	170–1	1977 Mar. 10	Black Ticket	Fonner Park	259–1
1963 Sept. 13	Confiancita	El Comandante	201–1	1978 Nov. 21	Golden Rubies	Churchill Downs	246–1
				1978 Mar. 14	Young Migrant	Portland Meadows	228–1

STRAIGHT MUTUEL PAYOFFS RECORD

Tabulation based on a $2 straight mutuel ticket

Horse — Track and Date	Payoff	Horse — Track and Date	Payoff
Wishing Ring, Latonia, June 17, 1912	$1,885.50	Nanamay, Tanforan, April 14, 1932	$602.20
Augeas, Agua Caliente, February 14, 1933	840.00	Zombro, Charles Town, December 5, 1933	590.00
Muzetta W., Lexington, May 7, 1910	830.70	Cadeau, Pimlico, May 7, 1913	577.10
King Jack, Agua Caliente, January 8, 1933	820.00	Escohigh, Tropical Park, December 29, 1937	571.00
Trycook, Hagerstown, May 19, 1934	810.00	Luxuriant, Narragansett Park, September 20, 1949	566.80
Fincastle, Havana, December 19, 1923	702.60	Welga, Douglas Park, May 29, 1916	560.40
Lt. Wm. J. Murray, Havana, February 11, 1923	696.00	Wilson Hill Doll, Bay Meadows, December 11, 1964	559.80
Miss Fountain, Havana, February 9, 1930	685.60	Mad Scramble, Bay Meadows, April 22, 1941	530.80
Playmay, Santa Anita Park, February 4, 1938	673.40	Djebonita, Bay Meadows, September 29, 1961	520.80
Fleetglow, Green Mountain, May 9, 1968	658.80	Black Ticket, Fonner Park, March 10, 1977	520.50
Meadow Money, Lincoln Fields, June 5, 1941	652.40	Cedars Crown, Detroit Race Course, September 28, 1973	514.20
		Minnix, Lincoln Downs, October 30, 1950	508.80

THE TRIPLE CROWN

Only eleven three-year-olds have managed to win the celebrated Triple Crown of American Racing—the Kentucky Derby, the Preakness Stakes, and the Belmont Stakes:

1919—Sir Barton	1943—Count Fleet
1930—Gallant Fox	1946—Assault
1935—Omaha	1948—Citation
1937—War Admiral	1973—Secretariat
1941—Whirlaway	1977—Seattle Slew
	1978—Affirmed

The following horses won two of the three great races: Cloverbrook (1877), Duke of Magenta (1878), Grenada (1880), Saunterer (1881), Belmar (1895), Man o' War (1920), Pillory (1922), Zev (1923), Twenty Grand (1931), Burgoo King (1932), Bold Venture (1936), Johnstown (1939), Bimelech (1940), Shut Out (1942), Pensive (1944), Capot (1949), Middleground (1950), Native Dancer (1953), Nashua (1955), Needles (1956), Tim Tam (1958), Carry Back (1961), Chateaugay (1963), Northern Dancer (1964), Kauai King (1966), Damascus (1967), Forward Pass (1968), Majestic Prince (1969), Canonero II (1971), Riva Ridge (1972), Little Current (1974), Spectacular Bid (1979).

LEADING MONEY-WINNING THOROUGHBRED HORSES

Year	Horse	Age	Starts	1st	2d	3d	Amount Won	Year	Horse	Age	Starts	1st	2d	3d	Amount Won
1924	Sarazen	3	12	8	1	1	$ 95,640	1952	Crafty Admiral	4	16	9	4	1	277,225
1925	Pompey	2	10	7	2	0	121,630	1953	Native Dancer	3	10	9	1	0	513,425
1926	Crusader	3	15	9	4	0	166,033	1954	Determine	3	15	10	3	2	328,700
1927	Anita Peabody	2	7	6	0	1	111,905	1955	Nashua	3	12	10	1	1	752,550
1928	High Strung	2	6	5	0	0	153,590	1956	Needles	3	8	4	2	0	440,850
1929	Blue Larkspur	3	6	4	1	0	153,450	1957	Round Table	3	22	15	1	3	600,383
1930	Gallant Fox	3	10	9	1	0	308,275	1958	Round Table	4	20	14	4	0	662,780
1931	Top Flight	2	7	7	0	0	219,000	1959	Sword Dancer	3	13	8	4	0	537,004
1932	Gusto	3	16	4	3	2	145,940	1960	Bally Ache	3	15	10	3	1	455,045
1933	Singing Wood	2	9	3	2	2	88,050	1961	Carry Back	3	16	9	1	3	565,349
1934	Cavalcade	3	7	6	1	0	111,235	1962	Never Bend	2	10	7	1	2	402,969
1935	Omaha	3	9	6	1	2	142,255	1963	Candy Spots	3	12	7	2	1	604,481
1936	Granville	3	11	7	3	0	110,295	1964	Gun Bow	4	16	8	4	2	580,100
1937	Seabiscuit	4	15	11	2	2	168,580	1965	Buckpasser	2	11	9	1	0	568,096
1938	Stagehand	3	15	8	2	3	189,710	1966	Buckpasser	3	14	13	1	0	669,078
1939	Challedon	3	15	9	2	3	184,535	1967	Damascus	3	16	12	3	1	817,941
1940	Bimelech	3	7	4	2	1	110,005	1968	Forward Pass	3	13	7	2	0	546,674
1941	Whirlaway	3	20	13	5	2	272,386	1969	Arts and Letters	3	14	8	5	1	555,604
1942	Shut Out	3	12	8	2	0	238,872	1970	Personality	3	18	8	2	1	444,049
1943	Count Fleet	3	6	6	0	0	174,055	1971	Riva Ridge	2	9	7	0	0	503,263
1944	Pavot	2	8	8	0	0	179,040	1972	Droll Role	4	19	7	3	4	471,633
1945	Busher	3	13	10	2	1	273,735	1973	Secretariat	3	12	9	2	1	860,404
1946	Assault	3	15	8	2	3	424,195	1974	Chris Evert	3	8	5	1	2	551,063
1947	Armed	6	17	11	4	1	376,325	1975	Foolish Pleasure	3	11	5	4	1	716,278
1948	Citation	3	20	19	1	0	709,470	1976	Forego	6	8	6	1	1	491,701
1949	Ponder	3	21	9	5	2	321,825	1977	Seattle Slew	3	7	6	0	0	641,370
1950	Noor	5	12	7	4	1	346,940	1978	Affirmed	3	11	8	2	0	901,541
1951	Counterpoint	3	15	7	2	1	250,525	1979	Spectacular Bid	3	12	10	1	1	1,279,333

THE KENTUCKY DERBY (THREE-YEAR-OLDS) Distance: 1¼ miles (Churchill Downs, Ky.)

Year	Winner	Jockey	Net to Winner	Time	Second
1938	Lawrin	E. Arcaro	47,050	2:04⅘	Dauber
1939	Johnstown	J. Stout	46,350	2:03⅗	Challedon
1940	Gallahadion	C. Bierman	60,150	2:05	Bimelech
1941	Whirlaway	E. Arcaro	61,275	2:01⅖	Staretor
1942	Shut Out	W. D. Wright	64,225	2:04⅖	Alsab
1943	Count Fleet	J. Longden	60,275	2:04	Blue Swords
1944	Pensive	C McCreary	64,675	2:04⅕	Broadcloth
1945	Hoop Jr.	E. Arcaro	64,850	2:07	Pot o' Luck
1946	Assault	W. Mehrtens	96,400	2:06⅗	Spy Song
1947	Jet Pilot	E. Guerin	92,160	2:06¾	Phalanx
1948	Citation	E. Arcaro	83,400	2:05⅖	Coaltown
1949	Ponder	S. Brooks	91,600	2:04⅕	Capot
1950	Middleground	W. Boland	92,650	2:01⅗	Hill Prince
1951	Count Turf	C. McCreary	98,050	2:02⅗	Royal Mustang
1952	Hill Gail	E. Arcaro	96,300	2:01⅗	Sub Fleet
1953	Dark Star	H. Moreno	90,050	2:02	Native Dancer
1954	Determine	R. York	102,050	2:03	Hasty Road
1955	Swaps	W. Shoemaker	108,400	2:01⅘	Nashua
1956	Needles	D. Erb	123,450	2:03⅘	Fabius
1957	Iron Liege	W. Hartack	107,950	2:02⅕	Gallant Man
1958	Tim Tam	I. Valenzuela	116,400	2:05	Lincoln Road
1959	Tomy Lee	W. Shoemaker	119,650	2:02⅕	Sword Dancer
1960	Venetian Way	W. Hartack	114,850	2:02⅖	Bally Ache
1961	Carry Back	J. Sellers	120,500	2:04	Crozier
1962	Decidedly	W. Hartack	119,650	2:00⅖	Roman Line
1963	Chateaugay	B. Baeza	108,900	2:01⅘	Never Bend
1964	Northern Dancer	W. Hartack	114,300	2:00	Hill Rise
1965	Lucky Debonair	W. Shoemaker	112,000	2:01⅕	Dapper Dan
1966	Kauai King	D. Brumfield	120,500	2:02	Advocator
1966	Proud Clarion	R. Ussery	119,700	2:00⅗	Barbs Delight
1967	Forward Pass	I. Valenzuela	122,600	2:02⅕	Francie's Hat
1968	Majestic Prince	W. Hartack	113,200	2:01⅘	Arts & Letters
1969	Dust Commander	M. Manganello	127,800	2:03⅖	My Dad George
1970	Canonero II	G. Avila	145,500	2:03⅕	Jim French
1971	Riva Ridge	Ron Turcotte	140,300	2:01.8	No Le Hace
1972	Secretariat	Ron Turcotte	155,050	1:59⅖	Sham
1973	Cannonade	Angel Cordero, Jr.	274,000	2:04	Hudson County
1974	Foolish Pleasure	Jacinto Vasquez	209,600	2:02	Avatar
1975	Bold Forbes	Angel Cordero, Jr.	217,700	2:01⅗	Honest Pleasure
1976	Seattle Slew	Jean Cruguet	214,700	2:02⅕	Run Dusty Run
1977	Affirmed	Steve Cauthen	186,900	2:01⅕	Alydar
1978	Spectacular Bid	Ron Franklin	228,650	2:02⅖	General Assembly
1979	Genuine Risk	Jacinto Vasquez	250,550	2:02	Rumbo

THE PREAKNESS STAKES (THREE-YEAR-OLDS) Distance 1-3/16 miles (Pimlico, Md.)

Year	Winner	Jockey	Net to Winner	Time	Second
1938	Dauber	M. Peters	51,875	1:59⅘	Cravat
1939	Challedon	G. Seabo	53,710	1:59⅘	Gilded Knight
1940	Bimelech	F. A. Smith	53,230	1:58⅗	Mioland
1941	Whirlaway	E. Arcaro	49,365	1:58⅘	King Cole
1942	Alsab	B. James	58,175	1:57	tie
1943	Count Fleet	J. Longden	43,190	1:57⅖	Blue Swords
1944	Pensive	C. McCreary	60,075	1:59⅕	Platter
1945	Polynesian	W. D. Wright	66,170	1:58⅖	Hoop Jr.
1946	Assault	W. Mehrtens	96,620	2:01⅖	Lord Boswell
1947	Faultless	D. Dodson	98,005	1:59	On Trust
1948	Citation	E. Arcaro	91,870	2:02⅖	Vulcan's Forge
1949	Capot	T. Atkinson	79,985	1:56	Palestinian
1950	Hill Prince	E. Arcaro	56,115	1:59⅕	Middleground
1951	Bold	E. Arcaro	83,110	1:56⅗	Counterpoint
1952	Blue Man	C. McCreary	86,135	1:57⅖	Jampol
1953	Native Dancer	E. Guerin	65,200	1:57⅘	Jamie K.
1954	Hasty Road	J. Adams	91,600	1:57⅖	Correlation
1955	Nashua	E. Arcaro	67,550	1:54⅘	Saratoga
1956	Fabius	W. Hartack	84,250	1:58⅖	Needles
1957	Bold Ruler	E. Arcaro	65,250	1:56⅕	Iron Liege
1958	Tim Tam	I. Valenzuela	97,900	1:57⅕	Lincoln Road
1959	Royal Orbit	W. Harmatz	136,200	1:57	Sword Dancer
1960	Bally Ache	R. Ussery	121,000	1:57⅗	Victoria Park
1961	Carry Back	J. Sellers	126,200	1:57⅗	Globemaster
1962	Greek Money	J. L. Rotz	135,800	1:56⅕	Ridan
1963	Candy Spots	W. Shoemaker	127,500	1:56⅕	Chateaugay
1964	Northern Dancer	W. Hartack	124,200	1:56⅘	The Scoundrel
1965	Tom Rolfe	R. Turcotte	128,100	1:56⅕	Dapper Dan
1966	Kauai King	D. Brumfield	129,000	1:55⅗	Stupendous
1967	Damascus	W. Shoemaker	141,500	1:55⅕	In Reality
1968	Forward Pass	I. Valenzuela	142,700	1:56⅘	Out of the Way
1969	Majestic Prince	W. Hartack	129,500	1:55⅗	Arts & Letters
1970	Personality	E. Belmonte	151,300	1:56⅕	My Dad George
1971	Canonero II	G. Avila	137,400	1:54	Eastern Fleet
1972	Bee Bee Bee	Eldon Nelson	135,000	1:55.4	No Le Hace
1973	Secretariat	Ron Turcotte	129,900	1:54⅖	Sham
1974	Little Current	Miguel Rivera	156,500	1:54⅗	Neopolitan Way
1975	Master Derby	Darrel McHarque	158,100	1:56⅖	Foolish Pleasure
1976	Elocutionist	John Lively	129,700	1:55	Play the Red
1977	Seattle Slew	Jean Cruguet	138,600	1:54⅖	Iron Constitution
1978	Affirmed	Steve Cauthen	136,200	1:54⅖	Alydar
1979	Spectacular Bid	Ron Franklin	165,300	1:54⅕	Golden Act
1980	Codex	Angel Cordero	180,600	1:54⅕	Genuine Risk

THE BELMONT STAKES (THREE-YEAR-OLDS) Distance: 1½ miles. (Elmont, N.Y.)

Year	Winner	Jockey	Net to Winner	Time	Second
1938	Pasteurized	J. Stout	34,530	2:29⅗	Dauber
1939	Johnstown	J. Stout	37,020	2:29⅗	Belay
1940	Bimelech	F. A. Smith	35,030	2:29⅗	Your Chance
1941	Whirlaway	E. Arcaro	39,770	2:31	Robert Morris
1942	Shut Out	E. Arcaro	44,520	2:29⅕	Alsab
1943	Count Fleet	J. Longden	35,340	2:28⅕	Fairy Manhurst
1944	Bounding Home	G. L. Smith	55,000	2:32⅕	Pensive
1945	Pavot	E. Arcaro	52,675	2:30⅕	Wildlife
1946	Assault	W. Mehrtens	75,400	2:30⅘	Natchez
1947	Phalanx	R. Donoso	78,900	2:29⅖	Tide Rips
1948	Citation	E. Arcaro	77,700	2:28⅕	Better Self
1949	Capot	T. Atkinson	60,900	2:30⅕	Ponder
1950	Middleground	W. Boland	61,350	2:28⅗	Lights Up
1951	Counterpoint	D. Gorman	82,000	2:29	Battlefield
1952	One Count	E. Arcaro	82,400	2:30⅕	Blue Man
1953	Native Dancer	E. Guerin	82,500	2:28⅗	Jamie K.
1954	High Gun	E. Guerin	89,000	2:30⅘	Fisherman
1955	Nashua	E. Arcaro	83,700	2:29	Blazing Count
1956	Needles	D. Erb	83,600	2:29⅘	Career Boy
1957	Gallant Man	W. Shoemaker	77,300	2:26⅗	Inside Tract
1958	Cavan	P. Anderson	73,440	2:30⅕	Tim Tam
1959	Sword Dancer	W. Shoemaker	93,525	2:28⅖	Bagdad
1960	Celtic Ash	W. Hartack	96,785	2:29⅗	Venetian Way
1961	Sherluck	B. Baeza	104,900	2:29⅕	Globemaster
1962	Jaipur	W. Shoemaker	109,550	2:28⅘	Admiral's Voyag
1963	Chateaugay	B. Baeza	101,700	2:30⅕	Candy Spots
1964	Quadrangle	M. Ycaza	110,850	2:28⅖	Roman Brother
1965	Hail to All	J. Sellers	104,150	2:28⅖	Tom Rolfe
1966	Amberoid	W. Boland	117,700	2:29⅗	Buffle
1967	Damascus	W. Shoemaker	104,950	2:28⅘	Cool Reception
1968	Stage Door Johnny	H. Gustines	117,700	2:27⅕	Forward Pass
1969	Arts and Letters	B. Baeza	104,050	2:28⅘	Majestic Prince
1970	High Echelon	J. L. Rotz	115,000	2:34	Needles n Pens
1971	Pass Catcher	W. Blum	97,710	2:30⅖	Jim French
1972	Riva Ridge	Ron Turcotte	93,540	2:28	Ruritania
1973	Secretariat	Ron Turcotte	90,720	2:24	Twice a Prince
1974	Little Current	Miguel Rivera	101,970	2:29⅕	Jolly Johu
1975	Avatar	W. Shoemaker	116,160	2:28	Foolish Pleasure
1976	Bold Forbes	Angel Cordero, Jr.	117,000	2:29	McKenzie Bridge
1977	Seattle Slew	Jean Cruguet	109,080	2:29⅗	Run Dusty Run
1978	Affirmed	Steve Cauthen	110,580	2:26⅘	Alydar
1979	Coastal	Ruben Hernandez	161,400	2:28⅗	Golden Act
1980	Temperence Hill	Eddie Maple	176,220	2:29⅘	Genuine Risk

WORLD THOROUGHBRED RACING RECORDS

Distance	Horse, age, weight	Track	Date	Time
¼ mi.	Big Racket, 4, 114	Hipodromo de las Americas, Mexico City	Feb. 5, 1945	:20⅘
2½ f.	Tie Score, 5, 115	Hipodromo de las Americas, Mexico City	Feb. 5, 1946	:26⅘
⅜ mi.	Atoka, 6, 105	Butte, Mont.	Sept. 7, 1906	:33½
3½ f.	Tango King, 6, 116	Northlands Park, Canada	April 22, 1978	:38⅘
½ mi.	Norgor, 9, 118	Ruidoso Downs, Ruidoso, N.M.	Aug. 14, 1976	:44¾
4½ f.	Kathryn's Doll, 2, 111	Turf Paradise, Phoenix, Ariz.	April 9, 1967	:50⅖
	Dear Ethel, 2, 114	Miles Park, Louisville, Ky.	July 4, 1967	:50⅖
	Scott's Poppy, 2, 118	Turf Paradise, Phoenix, Ariz.	Feb. 22, 1976	:50⅖
⅝ mi.	Zip Pocket, 3, 122	Turf Paradise, Phoenix, Ariz.	April 22, 1967	:55⅖
5½ f.	Zip Pocket, 3, 129	Turf Paradise, Phoenix, Ariz.	Nov. 19, 1967	1:01⅗
5¾ f.	Last Freeby, 4, 116	Timonium, Md.	July 20, 1974	1:07⅕
¾ mi	Grey Papa, 6, 112	Longacres, Seattle, Wash.	Sept. 4, 1972	1.07⅕
6½ f.	Best Hitter, 4, 114	Longacres, Seattle, Wash.	Aug. 24, 1973	1:13⅘
⅞ mi.	Rich Cream, 5, 118	Hollywood Park, Inglewood, Calif.	May 28, 1980	1:19⅖
1 mi.	Dr. Fager, 4, 134	Arlington Park, Arlington Heights, Ill.	Aug. 24, 1968	1:32⅕
1 mi. 70 yd.	Aborigine, 6, 119	Penn National, Pa.	Aug. 20, 1978	1:37⅕
1 1/16 mi.	Swaps, 4, 130	Hollywood Park, Inglewood, Calif.	June 23, 1956	1:39
1⅛ mi.	Tentam, 4, 118	Saratoga, Saratoga Springs, N.Y.	Aug. 10, 1973	1:45⅖
	Secretariat, 3, 124	Belmont Park, Elmont, N.Y.	Sept. 15, 1973	1:45⅖
1⅜ mi	Toonerville, 5, 120	Hialeah Park, Hialeah, Fla.	Feb. 7, 1976	1:51⅖
1¼ mi.	Double Discount, 4, 116	Santa Anita, Arcadia, Calif.	Oct. 9, 1977	1:57⅖
1 5/16 mi.	Roberto, 3, 122	York, England	Aug. 15, 1972	2:07
1⅜ mi.	Cougar II, 6, 126	Hollywood Park, Inglewood, Calif.	April 29, 1972	2:11
1½ mi.	Fiddle Isle, 5, 124	Santa Anita Park, Arcadia, Calif.	Mar. 21, 1970	2:23
	John Henry, 5, 126	Santa Anita, Arcadia, Calif.	Mar. 16, 1980	2:23
1 9/16 mi.	Lone Wolf, 5, 115	Keeneland, Lexington, Ky.	Oct. 31, 1961	2:37⅗
1⅝ mi.	Red Reality, 6, 113	Saratoga, Saratoga Springs, N.Y.	Aug. 23, 1972	2:37⅘
	Malwak, 5, 110	Saratoga, Saratoga Springs, N.Y.	Aug. 22, 1973	2:37⅘
1¾ mi.	Noor, 5, 117	Santa Anita Park, Arcadia, Calif.	March 4, 1950	2:52⅘
1⅞ mi.	El Moro, 8, 116	Delaware Park, Wilmington, Del.	July 22, 1963	3:11⅘
2 mi.	Polazel, 3, 142	Salisbury, England	July 8, 1924	3:15
2 1/16 mi.	Midafternoon, 4, 126	Jamaica, Jamaica, N.Y.	Nov. 15, 1956	3:29⅗
2⅛ mi.	Ceinturion, 5, 119	Newbury, England	Sept. 29, 1923	3:35
2 3/16 mi.	Santiago, 5, 112	Narragansett Park, Pawtucket, R.I.	Sept. 27, 1941	3:51⅕
2¼ mi.	Dakota, 4, 116	Lingfield, England	May 27, 1927	3:37⅗
2⅜ mi.	Pamroy, 4, 120	Goodwood Park, Sussex, England	Aug. 1, 1973	4:10⅗
2½ mi.	Miss Grillo, 6, 118	Pimlico, Baltimore, Md.	Nov. 12, 1948	4:14⅗
2⅝ mi.	Girandole, 4, 126	Goodwood Park, Sussex, England	July 31, 1975	4:38⅘
2¾ mi.	Shot Put, 4, 126	Washington Park, Homewood, Ill.	Aug. 14, 1940	4:48⅘
2⅞ mi.	Bosh, 5, 100	Tijuana, Mexico	Mar. 8, 1925	5:23
3 mi.	Farragut, 5, 113	Agua Caliente, Mexico	Mar. 9, 1941	5:15

HARNESS RACING Source: The U.S. Trotting Association
LEADING MONEY-WINNERS

TROTTERS

Year	Horse	Amount Won
1949	Bangaway	$74,438.81
1950	Proximity	87,175.00
1951	Pronto Don	80,850.44
1952	Sharp Note	101,625.70
1953	Newport Dream	94,933.31
1954	Katie Key	84,867.50
1955	Scott Frost	186,101.00
1956	Scott Frost	85,851.00
1957	Hoot Song	114,877.00
1958	Emily's Pride	118,830.00
1959	Diller Hanover	149,897.00
1960	Su Mac Lad	159,662.00
1961	Su Mac Lad	245,750.00
1962	Duke Rodney	206,113.00
1963	Speedy Scot	244,403.00
1964	Speedy Scot	235,710.00
1965	Dartmouth	252,348.00
1966	Noble Victory	210,696.00
1967	Carlisle	231,243.00
1968	Nevele Pride	427,440.00
1969	Lindy's Pride	323,997.00
1970	Fresh Yankee	359,002.00
1971	Fresh Yankee	293,950.00
1972	Super Bowl	436,258.00
1973	Spartan Hanover	262,023.00
1974	Delmonica Hanover	252,165.00
1975	Savoir	351,385.00
1976	Steve Lobell	357,005.00
1977	Green Speed	584,405.00
1978	Speedy Somolli	362,404.00
1979	Chiola Hanover	553,058.00

PACERS

Year	Horse	Amount Won
1949	Good Time	$88,766.17
1950	Scottish Pence	73,387.00
1951	Tar Heel	66,629.58
1952	Good Time	110,299.10
1953	Keystoner	59,131.23
1954	Red Sails	66,615.00
1955	Adios Harry	98,900.00
1956	Adios Harry	129,912.00
1957	Torpid	113,982.00
1958	Belle Acton	167,887.00
1959	Bye Bye Byrd	199,933.00
1960	Bye Bye Byrd	187,612.00
1961	Adios Butler	180,250.00
1962	Henry T. Adios	220,302.00
1963	Overtrick	208,833.00
1964	Race Time	199,292.00
1965	Bret Hanover	341,784.00
1966	Bret Hanover	407,534.00
1967	Romulus Hanover	277,636.00
1968	Rum Customer	355,618.00
1969	Overcall	373,150.00
1970	Most Happy Fella	387,239.00
1971	Albatross	558,009.00
1972	Albatross	459,921.00
1973	Sir Dalrae	307,354.00
1974	Armbro Omaha	357,146.00
1975	Silk Stockings	336,312.00
1976	Keystone Ore	539,759.00
1977	Governor Skipper	522,148.00
1978	Abercrombie	703,260.00
1979	Hot Hitter	826,542.00

HARNESS HORSE OF THE YEAR

Year	Horse	Gait	Year	Horse	Gait
1951	Pronto Don	trotter	1965	Bret Hanover	pacer
1952	Good Time	pacer	1966	Bret Hanover	pacer
1953	Hi-Lo's Forbes	pacer	1967	Nevele Pride	trotter
1954	Stenographer	trotter	1968	Nevele Pride	trotter
1955	Scott Frost	trotter	1969	Nevele Pride	trotter
1956	Scott Frost	trotter	1970	Fresh Yankee	trotter
1957	Torpid	pacer	1971	Albatross	pacer
1958	Emily's Pride	trotter	1972	Albatross	pacer
1959	Bye Bye Byrd	pacer	1973	Sir Dalrae	pacer
1960	Adios Butler	pacer	1974	Delmonica Hanover	trotter
1961	Adios Butler	pacer	1975	Savoir	trotter
1962	Su Mac Lad	trotter	1976	Keystone Ore	pacer
1963	Speedy Scot	trotter	1977	Green Speed	trotter
1964	Bret Hanover	pacer	1978	Abercrombie	pacer
			1979	Niatross	pacer

THE HAMBLETONIAN (THREE-YEAR-OLD TROTTERS)

Year	Purse	Winner	Second	Winning Driver	Fastest Heat
1949	69,791.08	Miss Tilly	Volume	Fred Egan	2:01⅖
1950	75,209.12	Lusty Song	Star's Pride	Delvin Miller	2:02
1951	95,263.93	Mainliner	Spennib	Guy Crippen	2:02⅗
1952	87,637.55	Sharp Note	Hit Song	Bion Shively	2:02⅗
1953	117,117.98	Helicopter	Morse Hanover	Harry M. Harvey	2:01⅗ (a)
1954	106,830.68	Newport Dream	Princess Rodney	Adelbert Cameron	2:02⅘
1955	86,863.32	Scott Frost	(1)	Joe O'Brien	2:00⅗
1956	100,603.99	The Intruder	Valiant Rodney	Ned F. Bower	2:01⅖
1957	111,126.25	Hickory Smoke	Hoot Song	John F. Simpson, Sr.	2:00⅕
1958	106,719.24	Emily's Pride	Little Rocky	Flave T. Nipe	1:59⅘
1959	125,283.98	Diller Hanover	Tie Silk	Frank Ervin	2:01⅕
1960	147,481.94	Blaze Hanover	Quick Song	Joe O'Brien	1:59⅗ (b)
1961	131,573.01	Harlan Dean	Caleb	James W. Arthur	1:58⅖
1962	116,612.78	A. C.'s Viking	Isaac	Sanders Russell	1:59⅗
1963	115,549.28	Speedy Scot	Florlis	Ralph N. Baldwin	1:57⅗ (c)
1964	115,281.40	Ayres	Big John	John F. Simpson	1:56⅘ (R)
1965	122,245.56	Egyptian Candor	Armbro Flight	Adelbert Cameron	2:03⅘ (d)
1966	122,540.00	Kerry Way	Polaris	Frank Ervin	1:58⅘
1967	122,650.00	Speedy Streak	Keystone Pride	Adelbert Cameron	2:00
1968	116,190.00	Nevele Pride	Keystone Spartan	Stanley Dancer	1:59⅖
1969	124,910.00	Lindy's Pride	The Prophet	Howard Beissinger	1:57⅗
1970	143,630.00	Timothy T.	Formal Notice	John F. Simpson, Jr.	1:58⅖ (e)
1971	129,770.00	Speedy Crown	Savoir	Howard Beissinger	1:57⅖
1972	119,090.00	Super Bowl	Delmonica Hanover	Stanley Dancer	1:56⅖ (R)
1973	144,710.00	Flirth	Florinda	Ralph Baldwin	1:57⅕
1974	160,150.00	Christopher T.	Nevele Diamond	Wm. Haughton	1:58⅗
1975	232,192.00	Bonefish	Yankee Bambino	Stanley Dancer	1:59
1976	263,524.00	Steve Lobell	Zoot Suit	Wm. Haughton	1:56⅖ (R)
1977	284,000.00	Green Speed	Texas	Wm. Haughton	1:55⅗ (R)
1978	241,000.00	Speedy Somolli	Briscoe Hanover	Howard Beissinger	1:55 (R)
1979	300,000.00	Legend Hanover	Chiola Hanover	George Sholty	1:56⅕
1980	293,570.00	Burgomeister	Devil Hanover	Wm. Haughton	1:56⅗

(1) Galophone and Leopold Hanover divided second and third monies. (a) By Morse Hanover. (b) By Quick Song and Hoot Frost. (c) By Floris. (d) By Armbro Flight. (e) By Formal Notice. (R) Record.

THE KENTUCKY FUTURITY (THREE-YEAR-OLD TROTTERS)

Year	Purse	Winner	Second	Winning Driver	Fastest Heat
1951	66,659.57	Ford Hanover	Candy Man	John F. Simpson, Sr.	2:01 2/5
1952	66,231.89	Sharp Note	Duke of Lullwater	Bion Shively	2:00
1953	67,485.05	Kimberly Kid	Faber Hanover	Thomas S. Berry	2:00 3/5
1954	63,121.84	Harlan	Pronto Boy	Delvin Miller	2:01
1955	62,702.60	Scott Frost	Home Free	Joe O'Brien	2:00 3/5
1956	53,731.74	Nimble Colby	Barlow Hanover	Ralph N. Baldwin	2:02
1957	50,460.00	Cassin Hanover	Storm Cloud	Fred Egan	2:02 1/5
1958	53,330.00	Emily's Pride	Senator Frost	Flave T. Nipe	1:59 1/5 (a)
1959	53,810.00	Diller Hanover	Tie Silk	Ralph N. Baldwin	2:01 1/5
1960	64,040.00	Elaine Rodney	Quick Song	Clint T. Hodgins	1:58 3/5
1961	59,330.00	Duke Rodney	Caleb	Eddie T. Wheeler	1:58 1/5 (b)
1962	55,230.00	Safe Mission	Impish	Joe O'Brien	1:59 1/5
1963	61,128.82	Speedy Scot	Florlis	Ralph N. Baldwin	1:57 1/5
1964	57,096.21	Ayres	Dashing Rodney	John F. Simpson, Sr.	1:58 1/5
1965	65,133.93	Armbro Flight	Noble Victory	Joe O'Brien	1:59 3/5
1966	61,602.18	Governor Armbro	Gay Sam	Joe O'Brien	2:00 2/5
1967	58,642.36	Speed Model	Rocket Speed	Arthur L. Hult	1:59 3/5 (c)
1968	57,397.00	Nevele Pride	Snow Speed	Stanley F. Dancer	1:57 (R)
1969	64,757.00	Lindy's Pride	Nevele Major	Howard Beissinger	1:59
1970	76,351.00	Timothy T.	Paris Air	John F. Simpson, Jr.	1:59 4/5
1971	63,415.00	Savoir	Keystone Hilliard	James Arthur	1:58 1/5
1972	56,210.00	Super Bowl	Spartan Hanover	Stanley Dancer	1:59
1973	64,174.00	Arnie Almahurst	Knightly Way	Joe O'Brien	1:59 1/5
1974	100,000.00	Waymaker	Dancing Party	John Simpson, Jr.	1:58 1/5
1975	100,000.00	Noble Rogue	Exclusive Way	William Herman	1:59 (d)
1976	100,000.00	Quick Pay	Steve Lobell	Peter Haughton	1:59
1977	100,000.00	Texas	Cold Comfort	William Herman	1:57 3/5
1978	100,000.00	Doublemint	Way to Gain	Peter Haughton	1:58 3/5
1979	100,000.00	Classical Way	Chiola Hanover	John Simpson, Jr.	1:57 4/5

(a) By Senator Frost. (b) By Caleb. (c) By Rocket Speed (d) By Exclusive Way. (R) Record.

WORLD HARNESS RACING RECORDS

Age	Record		Horse	Driver	Track	Year
TROTTERS: MILE TRACK						
All Ages	1:54 4/5		Nevele Pride	Stanley Dancer	Indianapolis, Ind.	1969
2-year-old	1:57	(r)	Briscoe Hanover	James Miller	Du Quoin, Ill.	1977
3-year-old	1:55	(r)	Speedy Somolli	Howard Beissinger	DuQuoin, Ill.	1978
	1:55	(r)	Florida Pro	George Sholty	DuQuoin, Ill.	1978
4-year-old	1:54 4/5		Nevele Pride	Stanley Dancer	Indianapolis, Ind.	1969
TROTTERS: FIVE-EIGHTHS MILE						
All Ages	1:57 1/5	(r)	Lindy's Crown	Howard Beissinger	Wilmington, Del.	1980
2-year-old	2:00 2/5	(r)	Smokin Yankee	Stanley Dancer	Meadow Lands, Pa.	1980
3-year-old	1:58 1/5	(r)	Speedy Somolli	Howard Beissinger	Meadow Lands, Pa.	1978
	1:58 1/5	(r)	Florida Pro	George Sholty	Philadelphia, Pa.	1978
4-year-old	1:57 1/5	(r)	Lindy's Crown	Howard Beissinger	Wilmington, Del.	1980
TROTTERS: HALF-MILE TRACK						
All Ages	1:56 4/5	(r)	Nevele Pride	Stanley Dancer	Saratoga Springs, N.Y.	1969
2-year-old	2:00 1/5	(r)	Ayres	John Simpson, Sr.	Delaware, Ohio	1963
3-year-old	1:58 3/5	(r)	Songcan	George Sholty	Delaware, Ohio	1972
4-year-old	1:56 4/5	(r)	Nevele Pride	Stanley Dancer	Saratoga Springs, N.Y.	1969
PACERS: MILE TRACK						
All Ages	1:52		Steady Star	Joe O'Brien	Lexington, Ky.	1971
2-year-old	1:54 1/5	(r)	Jade Prince	Jack Kopas	Lexington, Ky.	1976
	1:54 1/5		Fulla Strikes	Joe O'Brien	Inglewood, Calif.	1976
3-year-old	1:52 2/5		Falcon Almahurst	Wm. Haughton	Lexington, Ky.	1978
4-year-old	1:52		Steady Star	Joe O'Brien	Lexington, Ky.	1971
PACERS: FIVE-EIGHTHS MILE						
All Ages	1:53 2/5	(r)	Storm Damage	Joe O'Brien	Meadow Lands, Pa.	1980
2-year-old	1:57	(r)	Wellwood Hanover	Peter Haughton	Philadelphia, Pa.	1977
3-year-old	1:53 2/5	(r)	Storm Damage	Joe O'Brien	Meadow Lands, Pa.	1980
4-year-old	1:54 2/5	(r)	Direct Scooter	Warren Cameron	Windsor, Ont.	1980
PACERS: HALF-MILE TRACK						
All Ages	1:55 2/5	(r)	Falcon Almahurst	Wm. Haughton	Delaware, Ohio	1978
2-year-old	1:57 4/5	(r)	Whamo	Charles Clark	Louisville, Ky.	1979
3-year-old	1:55 2/5	(r)	Falcon Almahurst	Wm. Haughton	Delaware, Ohio	1978
4-year-old	1:55 3/5	(r)	Albatross	Stanley Dancer	Delaware, Ohio	1972

(r) Record made in race. Other records were set in time trials.

HARNESS RACING DOLLAR EARNINGS (through August 15, 1980)

Pacers, All-Time			Trotters, All-Time			Drivers, All-Time		
Rank	Horse	Winnings	Rank	Horse	Winnings	Rank	Driver	Winnings
1.	Rambling Willie	$1,699,647	1.	Bellino II	$1,960,945*	1.	Herve Filion	$31,360,975
2.	Niatross	1,478,254	2.	Un De Mai	1,660,627*	2.	William Haughton	29,571,536
3.	Albatross	1,201,470	3.	Ideal du Gazeau	1,445,958*	3.	Carmine Abbatiello	24,740,334
4.	Governor Skipper	1,039,756	4.	Savoir	1,365,145	4.	Del Insko	24,238,228
5.	Land Grant	1,026,510	5.	Fresh Yankee	1,294,252	5.	John Chapman	21,350,861
6.	Rum Customer	1,001,548	6.	Eleazar	1,290,194*	6.	Stanley Dancer	21,305,277
7.	Cardigan Bay	1,000,837	7.	Hadol du Vivier	1,214,554*	7.	Joe O'Brien	18,562,548
8.	Abercrombie	984,391	8.	Keystone Pioneer	1,071,927	8.	Lucien Fontaine	17,174,384
9.	Hot Hitter	964,574	9.	Green Speed	953,013	9.	William Gilmour	17,009,851
10.	Bret Hanover	922,616	10.	Cold Comfort	913,386	10.	Ben Webster	16,523,690

* compiled by French authorities

BOXING

AMATEUR BOXING CHAMPIONS

1979 WORLD CUP

Tony Tubbs, United States
Tony Tucker, United States
Vladimir Shin, U.S.S.R.
James Shuler, United States
Eddie Green, United States
Serik Konakbayev, U.S.S.R.
Viktor Demyanenko, U.S.S.R.
Bernard Taylor, United States
Jackie Beard, United States
Albert Mercado, Puerto Rico
Richard Sandoval, United States

CLASS

Heavyweight (over 178 lbs.)
Light Heavyweight (178 lbs.)
Middleweight (165 lbs.)
Light Middleweight (156 lbs.)
Welterweight (147 lbs.)
Light Welterweight (139 lbs.)
Lightweight (132 lbs.)
Featherweight (125 lbs.)
Bantamweight (119 lbs.)
Flyweight (112 lbs.)
Light Flyweight (106 lbs.)

1980 NATIONAL AAU

Marvis Frazier, Philadelphia, Pa.
Jeff Lampkin, Youngstown, Ohio
Martin Pierce, Flint, Mich.
Don Bowers, Jackson, Tenn.
Ronald Hatcher, Ft. Worth, Tex.
Johnny Bumphus, Houston, Tex.
Melvin Paul, New Orleans, La.
Clifford Gray, Boynton Beach, Fla.
Jackie Beard, Jackson, Tenn.
Richard Sandoval, Pomona, Calif.
Robert Shannon, Edmonds, Wash.

PROFESSIONAL BOXING CHAMPIONS

To October 6, 1980

DIVISION	WORLD BOXING ASSOCIATION (WBA)	WORLD BOXING COUNCIL (WBC)
Heavyweight	Mike Weaver, Los Angeles, Calif.	Larry Holmes, Easton, Pa.
Cruiserweight		Marvin Camel, Missoula, Mont.
Light Heavyweight	Mustafa Muhammad, Brooklyn, N.Y.	Matthew Saad Muhammad, Phila., Pa.
Middleweight	Marvin Hagler, Brockton, Mass.	Marvin Hagler
Jr. Middleweight	Ayub Kalule, Uganda	Maurice Hope, United Kingdom
Welterweight	Thomas Hearns, Detroit, Mich.	Roberto Duran, Panama
Jr. Welterweight	Aaron Pryor, Cincinnati, Ohio	Saoul Mamby, New York, N.Y.
Lightweight	Hilmer Kenty, Detroit, Mich.	Jim Watt, Scotland
Jr. Lightweight	Yasutsune Uehara, Japan	Alexis Arguello, Nicaragua
Featherweight	Eusebio Pedroza, Panama	Salvador Sanchez, Mexico
Jr. Featherweight	Sergio Palma, Argentina	Wilfredo Gomez, Panama
Bantamweight	Julian Solis, Puerto Rico	Lupe Pintor, Mexico
Flyweight	Kim Tae-Shik, South Korea	Shoji Oguma, Japan
Jr. Flyweight	Yoko Gushiken, Japan	Hilario Zapata, Panama

HEAVYWEIGHT CHAMPIONSHIP FIGHTS IN WHICH TITLE CHANGED HANDS

Date	Site	Winner	Weight (age)	Citizen	Loser	Weight (age)	Rounds	Referee
July 8, 1889[a]	Richburg, Miss.	John L. Sullivan, 198 (30)		U.S.	Jake Kilrain, 185 (30)		75	John Fitzpatrick
Sept. 7, 1892	New Orleans	James J. Corbett, 178 (26)		U.S.	John L. Sullivan, 212 (33)		21	Prof. John Duffy
Mar. 17, 1897	Carson City, Nev.	Bob Fitzsimmons, 167 (34)		England	James J. Corbett, 183 (30)		KO 14	George Siler
June 9, 1899	Coney Island	[b]James J. Jeffries, 206 (24)		U.S.	Bob Fitzsimmons, 167 (37)		KO 11	George Siler
Feb. 23, 1906	Los Angeles	[c]Tommy Burns, 180 (24)		Canada	Marvin Hart, 188 (29)		20	James J. Jeffries
Dec. 26, 1908	Sydney, Australia	Jack Johnson, 196 (30)		U.S.	Tommy Burns, 176 (27)		KO 14	Hugh McIntosh
April 5, 1915	Havana, Cuba	Jess Willard, 230 (33)		U.S.	Jack Johnson, 205½ (37)		KO 26	Jack Welch
July 4, 1919	Toledo	Jack Dempsey, 187 (24)		U.S.	Jess Willard, 245 (37)		KO 3	Ollie Pecord
Sept. 23, 1926	Philadelphia	[d]Gene Tunney, 189 (28)		U.S.	Jack Dempsey, 190 (31)		10	Pop Reilly
June 12, 1930	New York	[h]Max Schmeling, 188 (24)		Germany	Jack Sharkey, 197 (27)		4	Jim Crowley
June 21, 1932	Long Island City	Jack Sharkey, 205 (29)		U.S.	Max Schmeling, 188 (26)		15	Gunboat Smith
June 29, 1933	Long Island City	Primo Carnera, 260½ (26)		Italy	Jack Sharkey, 201 (30)		KO 6	Arthur Donovan
June 14, 1934	Long Island City	Max Baer, 209½ (25)		U.S.	Primo Carnera, 263¼ (27)		KO 11	Arthur Donovan
June 13, 1935	Long Island City	Jim Braddock, 193¾ (29)		U.S.	Max Baer, 209½ (26)		15	Jack McAvoy
June 22, 1937	Chicago	Joe Louis, 197¼ (23)		U.S.	Jim Braddock, 197 (31)		KO 8	Tommy Thomas
June 22, 1949	Chicago	[e]Ezzard Charles, 181¾ (27)		U.S.	Joe Walcott, 195½ (35)		15	Davey Miller
Sept. 27, 1950	New York	[f]Ezzard Charles, 184½ (29)		U.S.	Joe Louis, 218 (36)		15	Mark Conn
July 18, 1951	Pittsburgh	Joe Walcott, 194 (37)		U.S.	Ezzard Charles, 182 (30)		KO 7	Buck McTiernan
Sept. 23, 1952	Philadelphia	[g]Rocky Marciano, 184 (29)		U.S.	Joe Walcott, 196 (38)		KO 13	Charley Daggert
Nov. 30, 1956	Chicago	Floyd Patterson, 182¼ (21)		U.S.	Archie Moore, 187¾ (42)		KO 5	Frank Sikora
June 26, 1959	New York	Ingemar Johansson, 196 (26)		Sweden	Floyd Patterson, 182 (24)		KO 3	Ruby Goldstein
June 20, 1960	New York	Floyd Patterson, 190 (25)		U.S.	Ingemar Johansson, 193¾ (27)		KO 5	Arthur Mercante
Sept. 25, 1962	Chicago	Sonny Liston, 214 (28)		U.S.	Floyd Patterson, 189 (27)		KO 1	Frank Sikora
Feb. 25, 1964	Miami Beach	Cassius Clay, 210 (22)		U.S.	Sonny Liston, 218 (30)		KO 7	Barney Felix
March 4, 1968	New York	[i]Joe Frazier, 204½ (24)		U.S.	Buster Mathis, 243½ (23)		KO 11	Arthur Mercante
April 27, 1968	Oakland, Calif.	[i]Jimmy Ellis, 197 (28)		U.S.	Jerry Quarry, 195 (22)		15	Elmer Costa
Feb. 16, 1970	New York	[i]Joe Frazier, 205 (26)		U.S.	Jimmy Ellis, 201 (29)		KO 5	Tony Perez
Jan. 22, 1973	Kingston, Jamaica	George Foreman, 217½ (25)		U.S.	Joe Frazier, 214 (29)		TKO 2	Arthur Mercante
Oct. 30, 1974	Zaire, Africa	Muhammad Ali, 216 (32)		U.S.	George Foreman, 220 (25)		KO 8	Zach Clayton
Feb. 15, 1978	Las Vegas	Leon Spinks, 197½ (24)		U.S.	Muhammad Ali, 224½ (36)		15	David Pearl
Sept. 15, 1978	New Orleans	Muhammad Ali, 221 (36)		U.S.	Leon Spinks, 201 (25)		15	Locien Joubert

[a] Last bareknuckle heavyweight title fight. [b] Jim Jeffries retired in March 1905 for lack of opposition. He named Marvin Hart and Jack Root as the leading contenders; they fought on July 3, 1905, and Hart knocked out Root in the 12th round. [c] Burns claimed title after beating Hart. [d] Tunney retired in July 1928. [e] On March 1, 1949, Joe Louis retired; the NBA named Charles champion after he defeated Walcott. [f] Charles became undisputed champion by beating Louis, who had come out of retirement. [g] Marciano retired as champion in April 1956. [h] Won on a foul. [i] Immediately after a Federal Grand Jury had indicted Clay (also known as Muhammad Ali) on May 9, 1967, for refusing to accept induction into the Army, his title was vacated by the World Boxing Association and the New York State Athletic Commission. The WBA then staged an eight-man tournament, won by Ellis, to crown a successor. Frazier eventually earned recognition in New York and several other states and later defeated Ellis.

BOXING CHAMPIONS SOURCE: World Boxing Association

LIGHT HEAVYWEIGHT DIVISION

1903–05	Bob Fitzsimmons
1905–12	"Philadelphia" Jack O'Brien
1912–16	Jack Dillon
1916–20	Battling Levinsky
1920–22	Georges Carpentier
1922–23	Battling Siki
1923–25	Mike McTigue
1925–26	Paul Berlenbach
1926–27	Jack Delaney
1927	Mike McTigue
1927–29	Tommy Loughran
1930	Jimmy Slattery
1930–34	Maxie Rosenbloom
1934–35	Bob Olin
1935–39	John Henry Lewis
1939	Melio Bettina
1939–41	Billy Conn
1941	Anton Christoforidis (NBA)
1941–48	Gus Lesnevich
1948–50	Freddie Mills
1950–52	Joey Maxim
1952–61	Archie Moore
1961–63	Harold Johnson
1963–65	Willie Pastrano
1965–66	Jose Torres
1966–68	Dick Tiger
1968–71	Bob Foster
1971–72	Vicente Rondon
1972–73	Bob Foster
1973–78	Victor Galindez
1978–79	Mike Rossman (WBA)
1979	Victor Galindez (WBA)
1979–80	Marvin Johnson (WBA)
1980	Mustafa Muhammad (WBA)

MIDDLEWEIGHT DIVISION

1891–97	Bob Fitzsimmons
1897–1907	Tommy Ryan
1908	Stanley Ketchel
1908	Billy Papke
1908–10	Stanley Ketchel
1913	Frank Klaus
1913–14	George Chip
1914–17	Al McCoy
1917–20	Mike O'Dowd
1920–23	Johnny Wilson
1923–26	Harry Greb
1926	Tiger Flowers
1926–31	Mickey Walker
1931–41	Title in dispute
1941–47	Tony Zale
1947–48	Rocky Graziano
1948	Tony Zale
1948–49	Marcel Cerdan
1949–51	Jake LaMotta
1951	Ray Robinson, Randy Turpin
1951–52	Ray Robinson
1953–55	Bobo Olson
1955–57	Ray Robinson
1957	Gene Fullmer, Ray Robinson
1957–58	Carmen Basilio
1958–60	Ray Robinson
1959–62	Gene Fullmer (NBA)
1960–61	Paul Pender
1961–62	Terry Downes
1962	Paul Pender
1962–63	Dick Tiger
1963–65	Joey Giardello
1965–66	Dick Tiger
1966–67	Emile Griffith
1967	Nino Benvenuti
1967–68	Emile Griffith
1968–70	Nino Benvenuti
1970–77	Carlos Monzon
1977–78	Rodrigo Valdes
1978–79	Hugo Corro
1979–80	Vito Antuofermo
1980	Alan Minter
1980–	Marvin Hagler

WELTERWEIGHT DIVISION

1901	Rube Ferns
1901–04	Joe Walcott
1904	Dixie Kid
1904–06	Joe Walcott
1906–07	Honey Mollody
1907–15	Mike (Twin) Sullivan
1915–19	Ted Lewis
1919–22	Jack Britton
1922–26	Mickey Walker
1926–27	Pete Latzo
1927–29	Joe Dundee
1929–30	Jackie Fields
1930	Young Jack Thompson
1930–31	Tommy Freeman
1931	Young Jack Thompson
1931–32	Lou Brouillard
1932–33	Jackie Fields
1933	Young Corbett 3d
1933–34	Jimmy McLarnin
1934	Barney Ross
1934–35	Jimmy McLarnin
1935–38	Barney Ross
1938–40	Henry Armstrong
1940–41	Fritzie Zivic
1941–46	Freddie Cochrane
1946	Marty Servo
1946–51	Ray Robinson
1951	Johnny Bratton (NBA)
1951–54	Kid Gavilan
1954–55	Johnny Saxton
1955	Tony DeMarco
1955–56	Carmen Basilio
1956	Johnny Saxton
1956–57	Carmen Basilio
1958	Virgil Akins
1958–60	Don Jordan
1960–61	Benny (Kid) Paret
1961	Emile Griffith
1961–62	Benny (Kid) Paret
1962–63	Emile Griffith
1963	Luis Rodriguez
1963–66	Emile Griffith
1966–69	Curtis Cokes
1969–70	Jose Napoles
1970–71	Billy Backus
1971–72	Jose Napoles
1972–76	Angel Espada
1976–80	Jose Cuevas (WBA)
1980	Thomas Hearns (WBA)

LIGHTWEIGHT DIVISION

1901–08	Joe Gans
1908–10	Battling Nelson
1910–12	Ad Wolgast
1912–14	Willie Ritchie
1914–17	Freddie Welsh
1917–25	Benny Leonard
1925	Jimmy Goodrich
1925–26	Rocky Kansas
1926–30	Sammy Mandell
1930	Al Singer
1930–33	Tony Canzoneri
1933–35	Barney Ross
1935–36	Tony Canzoneri
1936–38	Lou Ambers
1938–39	Henry Armstrong
1939–40	Lou Ambers
1940–41	Lew Jenkins
1941–42	Sammy Angott
1943–47	Title holders, according to the N.Y. Commission, were Beau Jack and Bob Montgomery, and according to the NBA, Sammy Angott, Juan Zurita, and Ike Williams.
1947–51	Ike Williams
1951–52	Jimmy Carter
1952	Lauro Salas
1952–54	Jimmy Carter
1954	Paddy DeMarco
1954–55	Jimmy Carter
1955–56	Wallace (Bud) Smith
1956–62	Joe Brown
1962–65	Carlos Ortiz
1965	Ismael Laguna
1965–68	Carlos Ortiz
1968–69	Carlos (Teo) Cruz
1969–70	Mando Ramos
1970	Ismael Laguna
1970–71	Ken Buchanan
1971–72	Mando Ramos
1972–73	Chango Carmona
1973–78	Roberto Duran
1979–80	Ernesto Espana (WBA)
1980	Hilmer Kenty (WBA)

FEATHERWEIGHT DIVISION

1904	Abe Attell
1904–08	"Brooklyn" Tommy Sullivan
1908–12	Abe Attell
1912–23	Johnny Kilbane
1923	Eugene Criqui
1923–25	Johnny Dundee
1926–27	Louis (Kid) Kaplan
1927–28	Benny Bass
1928	Tony Canzoneri
1928–29	Andre Routis
1929–32	Battling Battalino
1932	Tommy Paul (NBA)
1932	Kid Chocolate (NY)
1933–36	Freddie Miller
1936–37	Petey Sarron
1937–38	Henry Armstrong
1938–40	Joey Archibald
1940–41	Harry Jeffra
1941	Joey Archibald
1941–42	Chalky Wright
1942–48	Willie Pep
1948–49	Sandy Saddler
1949–50	Willie Pep
1950–57	Sandy Saddler
1957–59	Kid Bassey
1959–63	Davey Moore
1963–64	Sugar Ramos
1964–67	Vicente Saldivar
1968	Raul Rojas
1968	Sho Saijyo
1969	Johnny Famechon
1969–70	Vicente Saldivar
1970–71	Kuniaki Shibata
1971–72	Clemente Sanchez
1972–74	Ernesto Marcell
1974–77	Alexis Arguello
1977	Rafael Ortega
1977–78	Celio Lastra
1978–	Eusebio Pedroza (WBA)

BANTAMWEIGHT DIVISION

1936	Tony Marino
1936–37	Sixto Escobar
1937–38	Harry Jeffra
1938–40	Sixto Escobar
1940–42	Lou Salica
1942–47	Manuel Ortiz
1947	Harold Dade
1947–50	Manuel Ortiz
1950–52	Vic Toweel
1952–54	Jimmy Carruthers
1954–56	Robert Cohen
1956–57	Mario D'Agata
1957–59	Alphonse Halimi
1959–60	Joe Becerra
1961–65	Eder Jofre
1965–68	Masahiko (Fighting) Harada
1968–69	Lionel Rose
1969–70	Ruben Olivares
1970–71	Chucho Castillo
1971–72	Ruben Olivares
1972–73	Enrique Pinder
1973–74	Arnold Taylor
1974–77	Alfonso Zamora
1977–80	Jorge Lujan (WBA)
1980	Julian Solis (WBA)

FLYWEIGHT DIVISION

1938–43	Peter Kane
1943–48	Jackie Paterson
1948–50	Rinty Monaghan
1950	Terry Allen
1950–52	Dado Marino
1952–54	Yoshio Shirai
1954–60	Pascual Perez
1960–62	Pone Kingpetch
1962–63	Masahiko (Fighting) Harada
1963	Pone Kingpetch
1963–64	Hiroyuki Ebihara
1964–65	Pone Kingpetch
1965–66	Salvatore Burruni
1966	Horacio Accavallo
1966	Walter McGowan
1966–69	Chartchai Choinoi
1969	Hiroyuki Ebihara
1969–70	Bernabe Villacampo
1970	Berkrek Chartvanchai
1970–71	Masao Ohba
1971–72	Bertulio Gonzales
1972–73	Masao Ohba
1973–74	Chatchai Chionoi
1974–75	Erbito Salavarria
1976	Alfonso Lopez
1976–78	Gutty Espadas
1978–79	Betulio Gonzalez (WBA)
1979–80	Luis Ibarra (WBA)
1980	Kim Tae-Shik (WBA)

TRACK AND FIELD

1980 NCAA INDOOR CHAMPIONS

60-Yard Dash—	Curtis Dickey, Texas A & M, 6.12
440-Yard Dash—	(tie) Anthony Blair, Tennessee & Bert Cameron, Texas-El Paso, 48.7
600-Yard Run—	Mike Ricks, Kansas, 1:10.06
880-Yard Run—	Evans White, Prairie View, 1:52.32
1,000-Yard Run—	Don Paige, Villanova, 2:05.80
One-Mile Run—	Suleiman Nyambui, Texas-El Paso, 4:05.26
Two-Mile Run—	Suleiman Nyambui, Texas-El Paso, 8:36.82
Three-Mile Run—	Solomon Chebor, Fairleigh Dickinson, 13:20.94
60-Yard Hurdles—	Rodney Wilson, Villanova, 7.15
One-Mile Relay—	Florida State, 3:16.64
Two-Mile Relay—	Oklahoma, 7:32.68
Distance Medley Relay—	Villanova, 9:42.22
High Jump—	Franklin Jacobs, Fairleigh Dickinson, 7'4¼"
Long Jump—	Carl Lewis, Houston, 26'4½"
Triple Jump—	Sanya Owalabi, Kansas, 54'3½"
Pole Vault—	Randy Hall, Texas A & M, 17'9½"
35 lb.-Weight Throw—	David Pellegrini, Princeton, 69'3¼"
Shot Put—	Michael Carter, Southern Methodist, 67'7½"
Team—	Texas-El Paso

1980 AIAW INDOOR CHAMPIONS

60-Meter Dash—	Lelith Hodges, Texas Woman's Univ., 7.38
300-Meter Dash—	Merlene Ottey, Nebraska, 37.13
600-Meter Run—	Chris Mullen, Georgetown, 1:28.77
1,000-Meter Run—	Chris Mullen, Georgetown, 2:43.83
2,000-Meter Run—	Deborah Pearson, Texas-El Paso, 6:04.79
5,000-Meter Run—	Eileen Hornberger, West Chester State, 16:28.58
60-Meter Hurdles—	Stephanie Hightower, Ohio State, 8.19
880-Yard Relay—	Morgan State, 1:38.92
One-Mile Relay—	Texas-El Paso, 3:44.99
Distance-Medley Relay—	Villanova, 11:29.30
High Jump—	Paula Girven, Maryland, 6'2"
Long Jump—	Pat Johnson, Wisconsin, 20'10"
Shot Put—	Jill Stenwell, Kearney State, 51'1"
Pentathlon—	Themis Zambrzycki, Brigham Young, 4014 pts.
Team—	Texas-El Paso

1980 NAIA INDOOR CHAMPIONS

60-Yard Dash—	Alvin Matthias, Adams State, 6.1
440-Yard Dash—	Kenneth Brown, Jackson State, 48.79
600-Yard Run—	Joe Johnson, Prairie View A & M, 1:12.23
880-Yard Run—	Evans White, Prairie View A & M, 1:51.34
1,000-Yard Run—	Michael Watson, Jackson State, 2:11.17
One-Mile Run—	John Esquibel, Adams State, 4:11.60
Two-Mile Run—	Kregg Einspahr, Concordia, 9:01.64
Three-Mile Run—	Tim Terrill, Adams State, 14:03.33
Two-Mile Walk—	Jeff Ellis, Wisconsin-Stevens Pt., 13:53.35
60-Yard Hurdles—	Steve Parker, Abilene Christian, 7.2
One-Mile Relay—	Prairie View A & M, 3:17.09
Two-Mile Relay—	Prairie View A & M, 7:42.02
Distance Medley Relay—	Jackson State, 10:12.48
High Jump—	Vic White, Eastern Washington, 7'2"
Long Jump—	Ricky Smith, Alabama State, 23'11"
Triple Jump—	Larry Perkins, Jackson State, 49'7¾"
Pole Vault—	Billy Olson, Abilene Christian, 17'6½"
Shot Put—	Harold Ledet, Angelo State, 59'8½"
Team—	Jackson State

1980 U.S. INDOOR CHAMPIONS

MEN'S EVENTS

60-Yard Dash—	Curtis Dickey, Texas A & M, 6.09
600-Yard Run—	Mark Enyeart, Logan, Utah, 1:09.2
1,000-Yard Run—	Billy Martin, Iona College, 2.07.7
One-Mile Run—	Craig Masback, N.Y. Pioneer Club, 4:02.2
Three-Mile Run—	Eamonn Coghlan, New York A.C., 13:02.8
60-Yard Hurdles—	Rod Milburn, Houston T.C., 7:09
One-Mile Relay—	Philadelphia Pioneer Club, 3:10.9
Two-Mile Relay—	Virginia Tech, 7:29.2
Sprint Medley Relay—	Philadelphia Pioneer Club, 2:01.0
Two-Mile Walk—	Todd Scully, Shore A.C., 12:35.1
High Jump—	Franklin Jacobs, Fairleigh Dickinson, 7'4½"
Long Jump—	Larry Myricks, Athletic Attic, 26'11¼"
Triple Jump—	Ron Livers, Phila. Pioneer Club, 55'1½"
Pole Vault—	Earl Bell, unattached, 18'2¼"
35 lb.-Weight Throw—	Ed Kania, unattached, 72'8"
Shot Put—	Jesse Stuart, Univ. of Chicago T.C., 66'5"

WOMEN'S EVENTS

60-Yard Dash—	Evelyn Ashford, Amer. Council of Athletics 6.76
220-Yard Dash—	Wanda Hooker, Memphis State, 24.0
440-Yard Dash—	Rosalyn Bryant, Muhammad Ali T.C., 53.92
880-Yard Run—	Madeline Manning, Oral Roberts T.C., 2:04.5
One-Mile Run—	Maggie Keyes, Maccabi Union T.C., 4:39.3
Two-Mile Run—	Cindy Bremser, Wisconsin United T.C., 9:45.0
60-Yard Hurdles—	Stephanie Hightower, Ohio State, 7.4
640-Yard Relay—	D.C. International, 1:09.5
One-Mile Relay—	Muhammad Ali T.C., 3:41.0
Sprint Medley Relay—	Los Angeles Mercurettes, 1:45.0
One-Mile Walk—	Susan Brodock, So. Calif. Roadrunners, 7:06.9
High Jump—	Louise Ritter, Texas Woman's Univ. 6'3"
Long Jump—	Pat Johnson, Wisconsin, 20'11½"
Shot Put—	Maren Seidler, San Jose Stars, 57'¾"

1980 NCAA OUTDOOR CHAMPIONS

100-Meter Dash—	Stanley Floyd, Auburn, 10.10
200-Meter Dash—	Mike Roberson, Florida State, 19.96
400-Meter Dash—	Bert Cameron, Texas-El Paso, 45.23
800-Meter Run—	Don Paige, Villanova, 1:45.81
1,500-Meter Run—	Sydney Maree, Villanova, 3:38.64
5,000-Meter Run—	Suleiman Nyambui, Texas-El Paso, 13:44.43
10,000-Meter Run—	Suleiman Nyambui, Texas-El Paso, 29:21.85
3,000-Meter Steeplechase—	Randy Jackson, Wisconsin, 8:22.81
110-Meter Hurdles—	Greg Foster, UCLA, 13.43
400-Meter Hurdles—	David Lee, Southern Illinois, 48.87
400-Meter Relay—	Southern California, 39.16
1,600-Meter Relay—	Tennessee, 3:03.94
High Jump—	Jeff Woodard, Alabama, 7'7¼"
Long Jump—	Carl Lewis, Houston, 27'4¾"
Triple Jump—	Steve Hanna, Texas-El Paso, 55'1"
Pole Vault—	Randy Hall, Texas A & M, 18'2"
Discus Throw—	Goran Svensson, Brigham Young, 202'6"
Hammer Throw—	Thommie Sjoholm, Texas-El Paso, 225'
Javelin Throw—	Curt Ransford, San Jose State, 269'3"
Shot Put—	Michael Carter, Southern Methodist, 66'11¼"
Team—	Texas-El Paso

1980 AIAW OUTDOOR CHAMPIONS

100-Meter Dash—	Alice Brown, Calif. State-Northridge, 11.27
200-Meter Dash—	Merlene Ottey, Nebraska, 22.86
400-Meter Dash—	Yolanda Rich, Calif. State-Los Angeles, 52.7
800-Meter Run—	Delisa Walton, Tennessee, 2:04.88
1,500-Meter Run—	Maggie Keyes, Calif. Poly. State, 4:15.85
3,000-Meter Run—	Julie Shea, N. Carolina State, 9:13.15
5,000-Meter Run—	Julie Shea, N. Carolina State, 15:41.28
10,000-Meter Run—	Julie Shea, N. Carolina State, 33:02.32
100-Meter Hurdles—	Stephanie Hightower, Ohio State, 13.07
400-Meter Hurdles—	Sandra Myers, Calif. State-Northridge, 56.40
400-Meter Relay—	California State-Northridge, 44.79
800-Meter Medley Relay—	California State-Los Angeles, 1:38.4
One-Mile Relay—	Oregon, 3:37.44
Two-Mile Relay—	UCLA, 8:41.64
High Jump—	Coleen Rienstra, Arizona State, 6'1¼"
Long Jump—	Sandra Myers, Calif. State-Northridge, 20'7¾"
Discus Throw—	Meg Ritchie, Arizona, 211'11"
Javelin Throw—	Jacqueline Nelson, Calif. State-Long Branch, 173'
Shot Put—	Meg Ritchie, Arizona, 54'2"
Pentathlon—	Themis Zambrzycki, Brigham Young, 4180 pts.
Team—	California State-Northridge

1980 NAIA OUTDOOR CHAMPIONS

100-Meter Dash—	Ellison Portis, Angelo State, 10.15
200-Meter Dash—	Charles Pickens, Miss. Valley, 20.77
400-Meter Dash—	Kevin Jones, Northwood Inst., 45.74
800-Meter Run—	Herman Sanders, Miss. Valley, 1:48.53
1,500-Meter Run—	Michael Watson, Jackson State, 3:46.86
5,000-Meter Run—	Sammy Maritim, Azusa Pacific, 14:34.19
10,000-Meter Run—	Tim Schmid, William Jewell, 30:05.86
Marathon—	Bill Langhout, Wisconsin-Eau Claire, 2:30:33.30
3,000-Meter Steeplechase—	Kregg Einspahr, Concordia, 8:58.4
10,000-Meter Walk—	Jeff Ellis, Wisconsin-Stevens Pt., 47:35.1
110-Meter Hurdles—	Steve Parker, Abilene Christian, 13.84
400-Meter Hurdles—	James Baldwin, Texas Southern, 50.48
440-Yard Relay—	Mississippi Valley State, 40.22
One-Mile Relay—	Texas Southern, 3:07.2
High Jump—	Bruce Beckel, Wisconsin-River Falls, 7'2"
Long Jump—	Carl Hanns, Cumberland, 25'3½"
Triple Jump—	Vic White, Eastern Washington, 52'8"
Pole Vault—	Billy Olson, Abilene Christian, 18'2"
Discus Throw—	Martin Guerrero, Abilene Christian, 195'7"
Hammer Throw—	Harold Willers, Simon Fraser (Can.), 195'5"
Javelin Throw—	Mike Barnett, Azusa Pacific, 242'5"
Shot Put—	Harold Ledet, Angelo State, 60'11½"
Decathlon—	Gary Wise, Azusa Pacific, 7331 pts.
Team—	Mississippi Valley State

1980 U.S. OUTDOOR CHAMPIONS

MEN'S EVENTS

100-Meter Dash—	Stanley Floyd, Auburn T.C., 10.19
200-Meter Dash—	LaMonte King, Stars & Stripes T.C., 20.08
400-Meter Dash—	Willie Smith, Auburn T.C., 46.35
800-Meter Run—	James Robinson, Inner City A.C., 1:46.2
1,500-Meter Run—	Steve Lacy, So. Calif. Striders, 3:40.86
5,000-Meter Run—	Matt Centrowitz, Oregon T.C., 13:33.61
10,000-Meter Run—	Rodolfo Gomez, Mexico, 28:44.0
3,000-Meter Steeplechase—	Doug Brown, Athletics West, 8:26.2
5,000-Meter Walk—	Ray Sharp, unattached, 20:27.8
110-Meter Hurdles—	Renaldo Nehemiah, D.C. International, 13.49
400-Meter Hurdles—	David Lee, Southern Illinois, 49.38
High Jump—	Franklin Jacobs, Athletic Attic, 7'4¼"
Long Jump—	Larry Myricks, Athletic Attic, 27'1¼"
Triple Jump—	Willie Banks, Amer. Council of Athletics, 56'11½"
Pole Vault—	Tom Hintnaus, So. Calif. Striders, 18'2½"
Discus Throw—	Mac Wilkins, Athletics West, 224'3"
Hammer Throw—	Gian Paolo Urlando, Italy, 251'3"
Javelin Throw—	Duncan Atwood, Athletics West, 273'10"
Shot Put—	Brian Oldfield, Univ. of Chicago T.C., 71'7"

WOMEN'S EVENTS

100-Meter Dash—	Alice Brown, L.A. Naturite T.C., 11.21
200-Meter Dash—	Karen Hawkins, Texas Southern, 22.80
400-Meter Dash—	Sherri Howard, Muhammad Ali T.C., 51.51
800-Meter Run—	Madeline Manning, Oral Roberts T.C., 1:58.75
1,500-Meter Run—	Francie Larrieu, Pacific Coast Club, 4:12.72
3,000-Meter Run—	Julie Brown, L.A. Naturite T.C., 9:07.90
10,000-Meter Run—	Judi St. Hilaire, Liberty A.C., 33:31.02
5,000-Meter Walk—	Sue Brodock, So. Calif. Roadrunners, 23:19.1
10,000-Meter Walk—	Sue Brodock, So. Calif. Roadrunners, 51:01.0
100-Meter Hurdles—	Stephanie Hightower, Ohio State, 13.14
400-Meter Hurdles—	Esther Mahr, KCBQ T.C., 56.3
400-Meter Relay—	Los Angeles Naturite T.C., 43.81
1,600-Meter Relay—	Muhammad Ali T.C., 3:34.16
3,200-Meter Relay—	Los Angeles Naturite T.C., 8:32.3
800-Meter Medley Relay—	Muhammad Ali T.C., 1:37.40
High Jump—	Coleen Rienstra, Sun Devil Sports, 6'4"
Long Jump—	Jodi Anderson, L.A. Naturite T.C., 21'9¾"
Discus Throw—	Lorna Griffin, Amer. Council of Athletics, 191'9"
Javelin Throw—	Karin Smith, Amer. Council of Athletics, 199'1"
Shot Put—	Maren Seidler, San Jose Stars, 59'1"

1980 U.S. OLYMPIC TRIALS

MEN'S EVENTS

100-Meter Dash
1. Stanley Floyd, Auburn A.A., 10.26
2. Harvey Glance, Auburn A.A.
3. Mel Lattany, Georgia

200-Meter Dash
1. James Butler, Oklahoma State, 20.49
2. Cliff Wiley, D.C. International
3. Fred Taylor, Philadelphia Pioneer Club

400-Meter Dash
1. Bill Green, Palo Alto, California, 45.85
2. Willie Smith, Auburn A.A.
3. Walter McCoy, Athletic Attic

800-Meter Run
1. Don Paige, Athletic Attic, 1:44.53
2. James Robinson, Inner City A.C.
3. Randy Wilson, Ankeny, Iowa

1,500-Meter Run
1. Steve Scott, Sub-4 T.C., 3:35.15
2. Steve Lacy, So. Calif. Striders
3. Mike Durkin, Univ. of Chicago T.C.

5,000-Meter Run
1. Matt Centrowitz, Oregon T.C., 13:30.62
2. Dick Buerkle, New York A.C.
3. Bill McChesney, Oregon

10,000-Meter Run
1. Craig Virgin, Front Runner Inc. T.C., 27:45.61
2. Greg Fredericks, Brooks T.C.
3. Alberto Salazar, Greater Boston T.C.

Marathon
1. Anthony Sandoval, Athletics West, 2:10:18.6
2. Benji Durden, Atlanta T.C.
3. Kyle Heffner, Adidas U.S.A.

3,000-Meter Steeplechase
1. Henry Marsh, Athletics West, 8:15.68
2. Doug Brown, Athletics West
3. John Gregorek, New York A.C.

20-Kilometer Walk
1. (tie) Marco Evoniuk, Frank Shorter Racing Team
   and Jim Heiring, So. Calif. Roadrunners, 1:27:12.0
3. Dan O'Connor, New York A.C.

50-Kilometer Walk
1. Carl Schueler, Silver Spring, Md., 3:59:33.2
2. Marco Evoniuk, Longmont, Colo.
3. Dan O'Connor, Westminster, Calif.

110-Meter Hurdles
1. Renaldo Nehemiah, D.C. International, 13.26
2. Dedy Cooper, Bay Area Striders
3. Anthony Campbell, Muhammad Ali T.C.

400-Meter Hurdles
1. Edwin Moses, Utopian International, 47.90
2. James Walker, Auburn T.C.
3. (tie) David Lee, Southern Illinois
   and Bart Williams, Stars & Stripes T.C.

High Jump
1. Benn Fields, Philadelphia Pioneer Club, 7'5" (2.26m)
2. Nat Page, Evanston, Ill.
3. Jim Howard, Texas A & M

Long Jump
1. Larry Myricks, Athletic Attic, 27'2" (8.28m)
2. Carlton Lewis, Houston
3. Randy Williams, Maccabi T.C.

Triple Jump
1. Willie Banks, Amer. Council of Athletics, 55'1½" (16.80m)
2. Paul Jordan, Houston A.C.
3. Greg Caldwell, Stars & Stripes T.C.

Pole Vault
1. Tom Hintnaus, Oregon, 18'4½" (5.60m)
2. (tie) Dan Ripley, Pacific Coast Club
   and Mike Tully, New York A.C.

Discus Throw
1. Mac Wilkins, Athletics West, 225'4" (68.68m)
2. John Powell, San Jose, California
3. Ben Plucknett, South Central T.C.

Hammer Throw
1. Andy Bessette, New York A.C., 232'10" (70.98m)
2. John McArdle, Oregon T.C.
3. Boris Djerassi, New York A.C.

Javelin Throw
1. Rod Ewaliko, Athletics West, 291' (88.70m)
2. Bruce Kennedy, San Jose Stars
3. Duncan Atwood, Athletics West

Shot Put
1. Pete Shmock, So. Calif. Striders, 68'4" (20.83m)
2. Al Feuerbach, Athletics West
3. Colin Anderson, Univ. of Chicago T.C.

Decathlon
1. Bob Coffman, Houston A.C., 8184 pts
2. Lee Palles, Athletic Attic
3. Fred Dixon, So. Calif. Striders

WOMEN'S EVENTS

100-Meter Dash
1. Alice Brown, Los Angeles Naturite T.C., 11.32
2. Brenda Morehead, Tennessee State
3. Chandra Cheeseborough, Tennessee State

200-Meter Dash
1. Chandra Cheeseborough, Tennessee State, 22.70
2. Karen Hawkins, Texas Southern
3. Pamela Greene, Mesa, Arizona

400-Meter Dash
1. Sherri Howard, Muhammad Ali T.C., 51.48
2. Gwen Gardner, Los Angeles Mercurettes
3. Denean Howard, Muhammad Ali T.C.

800-Meter Run
1. Madeline Manning, Oral Roberts T.C., 1:58.30
2. Julie Brown, Los Angeles Naturite T.C.
3. Robin Campbell, Stanford T.C.

1,500-Meter Run
1. Mary Decker, Athletics West, 4:04.91
2. Julie Brown, Los Angeles Naturite T.C.
3. Leann Warren, Oregon

5,000-Meter Run (exhibition)
1. Julie Shea, North Carolina State, 15:44.12
2. Mary Shea, North Carolina State
3. Rocky Racette, Minnesota

10,000-Meter Run (exhibition)
1. Kristen Bankes, Reading A.A., 33:45.6
2. Judi St. Hilaire, Liberty A.C.
3. Ellen Hart, Liberty A.C.

100-Meter Hurdles
1. Stephanie Hightower, Ohio State, 12.90
2. Benita Fitzgerald, Tennessee
3. Candy Young, Ryan's Angels

400-Meter Hurdles (exhibition)
1. Esther Mahr, KCBQ T.C., 57.46
2. Kim Whitehead, Iowa State
3. Debra Melrose, Prairie View

High Jump
1. Louise Ritter, Texas Woman's Univ., 6'1'¼" (1.86m)
2. Paula Girven, Maryland
3. Pam Spences, Los Angeles Naturite T.C.

Long Jump
1. Jodi Anderson, Los Angeles Naturite T.C., 22'11½"
2. Kathy McMillan, Tennessee State
3. Carol Lewis, Willingboro T.C.

Discus Throw
1. Lorna Griffin, Amer. Council of Athletics, 197'6" (60.20m)
2. Lynn Winbigler-Anderson, Oregon T.C.
3. Lisa Vogelsang, Amer. Council of Athletics

Javelin Throw
1. Karin Smith, Amer. Council of Athletics 208'5" (63.54m)
2. Kate Schmidt, Pacific Coast Club
3. Mary Osborne, Stanford T.C.

Shot Put
1. Maren Seidler, San Jose Stars, 58'9½"
2. Ann Turbyne, Gilly's Gym
3. Lorna Griffin, Amer. Council of Athletics

Pentathlon
1. Jodi Anderson, Los Angeles Naturite T.C., 4697 pts.
2. Marilyn King, Millbrae Lions
3. Linda Waltman, Texas T.C.

AMERICAN TRACK AND FIELD RECORDS

SOURCE: Track & Field News

Men's Event	Time/Distance	Name/Site	Date
100-Meter Dash	9.95 sec.	Jim Hines, Mexico City	Oct. 1968
200-Meter Dash	19.83 sec.	Tommie Smith, Mexico City	Oct. 1968
400-Meter Dash	43.86 sec.	Lee Evans, Mexico City	Oct. 1968
800-Meter Run	1 min., 43.9 sec.	Rick Wohlhuter, Los Angeles, Calif.	June 1974
1,000-Meter Run	2 min., 13.9 sec.	Rick Wohlhuter, Oslo, Norway	July 1974
1,500-Meter Run	3 min., 33.1 sec.	Jim Ryun, Los Angeles, Calif.	July 1967
One-Mile Run	3 min., 51.1 sec.	Jim Ryun, Bakersfield, Calif.	June 1967
2,000-Meter Run	5 min., 1.4 sec.	Steve Prefontaine, Coos Bay, Ore.	May 1975
3,000-Meter Run	7 min., 37.7 sec.	Rudy Chapa, Eugene, Ore.	May 1979
5,000-Meter Run	13 min., 15.1 sec.	Marty Liquori, Dusseldorf, W. Ger.	Sept. 1977
10,000-Meter Run	27 min., 29.16 sec.	Craig Virgin, Paris, France	July 1980
20,000-Meter Run	58 min., 15.0 sec.	Bill Rodgers, Boston, Mass.	Aug. 1977
25,000-Meter Run	1 hr., 14 min., 12 sec.	Bill Rodgers, Saratoga, Calif.	Feb. 1979
30,000-Meter Run	1 hr., 31 min., 50 sec.	Bill Rodgers, Saratoga, Calif.	Feb. 1979
Marathon	2 hr., 9 min., 55 sec.	Bill Rodgers, Boston, Mass.	Apr. 1975
20-Kilometer Walk	1 hr., 30 min., 10 sec.	Larry Young, Columbia, Mo.	May 1972
30-Kilometer Walk	2 hr., 23 min., 14 sec.	Goetz Klopfer, Seattle, Wash.	Nov. 1970
50-Kilometer Walk	4 hr., 13 min., 36 sec.	Bob Kitchen, San Francisco, Calif	Feb. 1972
110-Meter Hurdles	13.00 sec.	Renaldo Nehemiah, Westwood, Calif.	May 1979
400-Meter Hurdles	47.13 sec.	Edwin Moses, Milan, Italy	July 1980
3000-Meter Steeplechase	8 min., 15.68 sec.	Henry Marsh, Eugene, Ore.	June 1980
4 X 100-Meter Relay	38.03 sec.	World Cup Team, Dusseldorf, W. Ger.	Sept. 1977
4 X 200-Meter Relay	1 min., 20.26 sec.	Southern California, Tempe, Ariz.	May 1978
4 X 400-Meter Relay	2 min., 56.16 sec.	Olympic Team, Mexico City	Oct. 1968
4 X 800-Meter Relay	7 min., 10.4 sec.	Univ. of Chicago T.C., Durham, N.C.	May 1973
4 X 1,500-Meter Relay	14 min., 46.3 sec.	National Team, Bourges, France	June 1979
Sprint Medley Relay (Mile)	3 min., 15.2 sec.	Kansas, Austin, Tex.	Mar. 1967
Distance Medley Relay (2½ Mi.)	9 min., 31.8 sec.	Kansas State, Des Moines, Iowa	Apr. 1972
High Jump	2.32 m (7'7¼")	Dwight Stones, Philadelphia, Pa.	Aug. 1976
		Jeff Woodard, Austin, Tex.	June 1980
Long Jump	8.90 m (29'2½")	Bob Beamon, Mexico City	Oct. 1968
Triple Jump	17.24 m (56'6¾")	James Butts, Helsinki, Finland.	June 1978
Pole Vault	5.70 m (18'8¼")	Dave Roberts, Eugene, Ore.	June 1976
Shot Put	21.85 m (71'8½")	Terry Albritton, Honolulu, Hawaii	Feb. 1976
Discus Throw	70.98 m (232'10")	Mac Wilkins, Helsinki, Finland	July 1980
Hammer Throw	71.90 m (235'11")	Ed Burke, Bakersfield, Calif.	June 1967
Javelin Throw	91.44 m (300')	Mark Murro, Tempe, Ariz.	Mar. 1970
Decathlon	8,617 points	Bruce Jenner, Montreal, Canada	July 1976

Women's Event	Time/Distance	Name/Site	Date
100-Meter Dash	10.97 sec.	Evelyn Ashford, Walnut, Calif.	June 1979
200-Meter Dash	21.83 sec.	Evelyn Ashford, Montreal, Canada	Aug. 1979
400-Meter Dash	50.62 sec.	Rosalyn Bryant, Montreal, Canada	July 1976
800-Meter Run	1 min., 57.90 sec.	Madeline Jackson, College Park, Md.	Aug. 1976
1,500-Meter Run	4 min., 0.9 sec.	Mary Decker, Philadelphia, Pa.	July 1980
One-Mile Run	4 min., 21.7 sec.	Mary Decker, Auckland, N.Z.	Jan. 1980
3,000-Meter Run	8 min., 38.73 sec.	Mary Decker, Oslo, Norway	July 1980
5,000-Meter Run	15 min., 30.6 sec.	Jan Merrill, Stanford, Calif.	Mar. 1980
10,000-Meter Run	33 min., 15.1 sec.	Peg Neppel, Westwood, Calif.	June 1977
Marathon	2 hr., 30 min., 57 sec.	Patti Lyons-Catalano, Montreal, Canada	Sept. 1980
10-Kilometer Walk	50 min., 32.6 sec.	Sue Brodock, Walnut, Calif.	June 1979
100-Meter Hurdles	12.86 sec.	Deby LaPlante, Walnut, Calif.	June 1979
400-Meter Hurdles	56.16 sec.	Esther Mahr, Sittard, Neth.	Aug. 1980
4 X 100-Meter Relay	42.87 sec.	Olympic Team, Mexico City	Oct. 1968
4 X 200-Meter Relay	1 min., 32.6 sec.	National Team, Bourges, France	June 1979
4 X 400-Meter Relay	3 min., 22.8 sec.	Olympic Team, Montreal, Canada	July 1976
4 X 800-Meter Relay	8 min., 19.9 sec.	National Team, Bourges, France	June 1979
High Jump	1.95 m (6'4¾")	Louise Ritter, Wichita, Kans.	May 1980
Long Jump	7.00 m (22'11½")	Jodi Anderson, Eugene, Ore.	June 1980
Shot Put	19.09 m (62'7¾")	Maren Seidler, Walnut, Calif.	June 1979
Discus Throw	63.22 m (207'5")	Lorna Griffin, Long Beach, Calif.	May 1980
Javelin Throw	69.32 m (227'5")	Kate Schmidt, Fuerth, W. Ger.	Sept. 1977
Pentathlon	4,708 points	Jane Frederick, Gotzis, Austria	May 1979

WORLD TRACK AND FIELD RECORDS

SOURCE: Track & Field News

Men's Event	Time/Distance	Name (Country)	Date
100–Meter Dash	9.95 sec.	Jim Hines (United States)	Oct. 1968
200–Meter Dash	19.83 sec.	Tommie Smith (United States)	Oct. 1968
400–Meter Dash	43.86 sec.	Lee Evans (United States)	Oct. 1968
800–Meter Run	1 min., 42.33 sec.	Sebastian Coe (United Kingdom)	July 1979
1,000–Meter Run	2 min., 13.40 sec.	Sebastian Coe (United Kingdom)	July 1980
1,500–Meter Run	3 min., 31.36 sec.	Steve Ovett (United Kingdom)	Aug. 1980
One–Mile Run	3 min., 48.8 sec.	Steve Ovett (United Kingdom)	July 1980
2,000–Meter Run	4 min., 51.4 sec.	John Walker (New Zealand)	June 1976
3,000–Meter Run	7 min., 32.1 sec.	Henry Rono (Kenya)	June 1978
5,000–Meter Run	13 min., 8.4 sec.	Henry Rono (Kenya)	May 1978
10,000–Meter Run	27 min., 22.4 sec.	Henry Rono (Kenya)	June 1978
20,000–Meter Run	57 min., 24.2 sec.	Jos Hermens (Netherlands)	May 1976
25,000–Meter Run	1 hr., 14 min., 12 sec.	Bill Rodgers (United States)	Feb. 1979
30,000–Meter Run	1 hr., 31 min., 30.4 sec.	Jim Adler (United Kingdom)	Sept. 1970
Marathon	2 hr., 8 min., 34 sec.	Derek Clayton (Australia)	May 1969
One–Hour Run	13 miles, 24 yards	Jos Hermens (Netherlands)	May 1976
20–Kilometer Walk	1 hr., 20 min., 7 sec.	Daniel Bautista (Mexico)	Oct. 1979
30–Kilometer Walk	1 hr., 49 min., 54 sec.	Raul Gonzalez (Mexico)	May 1978
50–Kilometer Walk	3 hr., 52 min., 24 sec.	Raul Gonzalez (Mexico)	May 1978
Two–Hour Walk	16 miles, 1637 yards	Raul Gonzalez (Mexico)	May 1978
110–Meter Hurdles	13.00 sec.	Renaldo Nehemiah (United States)	May 1979
400–Meter Hurdles	47.13 sec.	Edwin Moses (United States)	July 1980
3,000–Meter Steeplechase	8 min., 5.4 sec.	Henry Rono (Kenya)	April 1978
4 X 100–Meter Relay	38.03 sec.	United States	Sept. 1977
4 X 200–Meter Relay	1 min., 20.26 sec.	United States	May 1977
4 X 400–Meter Relay	2 min., 56.16 sec.	United States	Oct. 1968
4 X 800–Meter Relay	7 min., 8.6 sec.	West Germany	Aug. 1966
4 X 1,500–Meter Relay	14 min., 38.8 sec.	West Germany	Aug. 1977
High Jump	2.36m (7'8¾")	Gerd Wessig (East Germany)	Aug. 1980
Long Jump	8.90m (29'2½")	Bob Beaman (United States)	Oct. 1968
Triple Jump	17.89m (58'8¼")	Joao Oliveira (Brazil)	Oct. 1975
Pole Vault	5.78m (18'11½")	Wladyslaw Kozakiewicz (Poland)	July 1980
Shot Put	22.15m (72'8")	Udo Beyer (East Germany)	July 1978
Discus Throw	71.16m (233'5")	Wolfgang Schmidt (East Germany)	Aug. 1978
Hammer Throw	81.80m (268'4")	Yuri Sedykh (U.S.S.R.)	July 1980
Javelin Throw	96.72m (317'4")	Ferenc Paragi (Hungary)	April 1980
Decathlon	8649 points	Guido Kratschmer (West Germany)	June 1980

Women's Event	Time/Distance	Name (Country)	Date
100–Meter Dash	10.88 sec.	Marlies Gohr (East Germany)	July 1977
200–Meter Dash	21.71 sec.	Marita Koch (East Germany)	June 1979
400–Meter Dash	48.60 sec.	Marita Koch (East Germany)	Aug. 1979
800–Meter Run	1 min., 53.42 sec.	Nadezhde Olizarenko (U.S.S.R.)	July 1980
1,000–Meter Run	2 min., 30.6 sec.	Tatyana Providokhina (U.S.S.R.)	Aug. 1978
1,500–Meter Run	3 min., 52.47 sec.	Tatyana Kazankina (U.S.S.R.)	July 1980
One–Mile Run	4 min., 21.7 sec.	Mary Decker (United States)	Jan. 1980
2,000–Meter Run	5 min., 25.5 sec.	Maricica Puica (Romania)	May 1979
3,000–Meter Run	8 min., 27.12 sec.	Lyudmila Bragina (U.S.S.R.)	Aug. 1976
5,000–Meter Run	15 min., 8.8 sec.	Loa Olafsson (Denmark)	May 1978
10,000–Meter Run	31 min., 45.4 sec.	Loa Olafsson (Denmark)	April 1978
Marathon	2 hr., 27 min., 33 sec.	Greta Waitz (Norway)	Oct. 1979
100–Meter Hurdles	12.36 sec.	Grazyna Rabsztyn (Poland)	June 1980
400–Meter Hurdles	54.28 sec	Karin Rossley (East Germany)	May 1980
4 X 100–Meter Relay	41.60 sec.	East Germany	Aug. 1980
4 X 200–Meter Relay	1 min., 28.15 sec.	East Germany	Aug. 1980
4 X 400–Meter Relay	3 min., 19.23 sec.	East Germany	July 1976
4 X 800–Meter Relay	7 min., 52.3 sec.	U.S.S.R.	Aug. 1976
High Jump	2.01m (6'7")	Sara Simeoni (Italy)	Aug. 1978
Long Jump	7.09m (23'3¼")	Vilma Bardauskiene (U.S.S.R.)	Aug. 1978
Shot Put	22.45m (73'8")	Ilona Slupianek (East Germany)	May 1980
Discus Throw	71.80m (235'7")	Maria Vergova-Petkova (Bulgaria)	July 1980
Javelin Throw	70.08m (229'11")	Tatyana Biryulina (U.S.S.R.)	July 1980
Pentathlon	5083 points	Nadyezhda Tkachenko (U.S.S.R.)	July 1980

BOWLING

1980 LEADING MONEY WINNERS (to Aug. 20)
Source: PBA

	Bowler	Tournaments	Amount		Bowler	Tournaments	Amount
1.	Wayne Webb, Rehoboth, Mass.	26	$85,830	11.	Ernie Schlegel, Vancouver, U.S.A.	25	49,555
2.	Mark Roth, Little Silver, N.J.	21	84,350	12.	Joe Hutchinson, Scranton, Pa.	18	48,910
3.	Mike Aulby, Indianapolis	27	71,735	13.	Tommy Hudson, Akron	21	46,540
4.	Gary Dickinson, Ft. Worth	17	61,422	14.	Alvin Lou, El Cajon, Calif.	25	46,380
5.	Steve Martin, Kingsport, Tenn.	25	58,100	15.	Johnny Petraglia, Staten Island, N.Y.	15	42,183
6.	Nelson Burton, Jr., St. Louis	18	55,366	16.	Pete Couture, Windsor Locks, Conn.	26	40,748
7.	Earl Anthony, Dublin, Calif.	16	53,241	17.	Marshall Holman, Medford, Ore.	15	40,640
8.	Tom Baker, Buffalo	21	53,150	18.	Guppy Troup, Jacksonville, Fla.	23	37,820
9.	Palmer Fallgren, Sacramento	22	51,007	19.	Kyle Shedd, Downey, Calif.	20	36,201
10.	George Pappas, Charlotte, N.C.	23	50,150	20.	Bill Spigner, Chicago	24	32,477

PBA TOP-MONEY WINNERS, 1959–1979

Year	Bowler	Winnings	Year	Bowler	Winnings
1959	Dick Weber	$ 7,672	1969	Billy Hardwick	64,160
1960	Don Carter	22,525	1970	Mike McGrath	52,049
1961	Dick Weber	26,280	1971	John Petraglia	85,065
1962	Don Carter	49,972	1972	Don Johnson	56,648
1963	Dick Weber	46,333	1973	Don McCune	69,000
1964	Bob Strampe	33,592	1974	Earl Anthony	99,585
1965	Dick Weber	47,675	1975	Earl Anthony	107,585
1966	Wayne Zahn	54,720	1976	Earl Anthony	110,883
1967	Dave Davis	54,165	1977	Mark Roth	105,583
1968	Jim Stefanich	$67,375	1978	Mark Roth	134,500
			1979	Mark Roth	124,517

BOWLING CHAMPIONS

BPAA U.S. Open (Formerly All-Star)	ABC Masters		PBA National Championship	ABC All-Events
1962 .... Dick Weber	1962 .... Billy Golembiewski	1962 .... Carmen Salvino	1962 .... Jack Winters
1963 .... Dick Weber	1963 .... Harry Smith	1963 .... Billy Hardwick	1963 .... Tom Hennessey
1964 .... Bob Strampe	1964 .... Billy Welu	1964 .... Bob Strampe	1964 .... Billy Hardwick
1965 .... Dick Weber	1965 .... Billy Welu	1965 .... Dave Davis	1965 .... Tom Hennessey
1966 .... Dick Weber	1966 .... Bob Strampe	1966 .... Wayne Zahn	1966 .... Les Schissler
1967 .... Les Schissler	1967 .... Lou Scalia	1967 .... Dave Davis	1967 .... Bob Strampe
1968 .... Jim Stefanich	1968 .... Pete Tountas	1968 .... Wayne Zahn	1968 .... Jim Stefanich
1969 .... Billy Hardwick	1969 .... Jim Chestney	1969 .... Mike McGrath	1969 .... Larry Lichstein
1970 .... Bobby Cooper	1970 .... Don Glover	1970 .... Mike McGrath	1970 .... Bob Strampe
1971 .... Mike Lemongello	1971 .... Jim Godman	1971 .... Mike Lemongello	1971 .... Gary Dickinson
1972 .... Don Johnson	1972 .... Bill Beach	1972 .... John Guenther	1972 .... Teata Semiz
1973 .... Mike McGrath	1973 .... Dave Soutar	1973 .... Earl Anthony	1973 .... Jimmy Mack
1974 .... Larry Laub	1974 .... Paul Colwell	1974 .... Earl Anthony	1974 .... Jim Godman
1975 .... Steve Neff	1975 .... Ed Ressler	1975 .... Earl Anthony	1975 .... Bobby Meadows
1976 .... Paul Moser	1976 .... Nelson Burton, Jr.	1976 .... Paul Colwell	1976 .... Gary Fust
1977 .... John Petraglia	1977 .... Earl Anthony	1977 .... Tommy Hudson	1977 .... Dick Ritger
1978 .... Nelson Burton, Jr.	1978 .... Frank Ellenburg	1978 .... Warren Nelson	1978 .... Bill Beach
1979 .... Joe Berardi	1979 .... Doug Myers	1979 .... Mike Aulby	1979 .... Nelson Burton, Jr.
1980 .... Steve Martin	1980 .... Neil Burton	1980 .... Johnny Petraglia	1980 .... Steve Fehr

BOWLER OF THE YEAR
Selected by Bowling Writers Associaton of America

MEN		WOMEN	
1956	Bill Lillard, Chicago, Ill.	1956	Anita Cantaline, Detroit, Mich.
1957	Don Carter, St. Louis, Mo.	1957	Marion Ladewig, Grand Rapids, Mich.
1958	Don Carter, St. Louis, Mo.	1958	Marion Ladewig, Grand Rapids, Mich.
1959	Ed Lubanski, Detroit, Mich.	1959	Marion Ladewig, Grand Rapids, Mich.
1960	Don Carter, St. Louis, Mo.	1960	Sylvia Wene, Philadelphia, Pa.
1961	Dick Weber, St. Louis, Mo.	1961	Shirley Garms, Palatine, Ill.
1962	Don Carter, St. Louis, Mo.	1962	Shirley Garms, Palatine, Ill.
1963	Dick Weber, St. Louis, Mo.	1963	Marion Ladewig, Grand Rapids, Mich.
1964	Billy Hardwick, San Mateo, Calif.	1964	LaVerne Carter, St. Louis, Mo.
1965	Dick Weber, St. Louis, Mo.	1965	Betty Kuczynski, Chicago, Ill.
1966	Wayne Zahn, Atlanta, Ga.	1966	Joy Abel, Chicago, Ill.
1967	Dave Davis, Phoenix, Ariz.	1967	Mildred Martorella, Rochester, N.Y.
1968	Jim Stefanich, Joliet, Ill.	1968	Dotty Fothergill, N. Attleboro, Mass.
1969	Billy Hardwick, Louisville, Ky.	1969	Dotty Fothergill, N. Attleboro, Mass.
1970	Nelson Burton, Jr., St. Louis, Mo.	1970	Mary Baker, Central Islip, N.Y.
1971	Don Johnson, Akron, Ohio	1971	Paula Sperber, Miami, Fla.
1972	Don Johnson, Akron, Ohio	1972	Patty Costello, New Carrollton, Md.
1973	Don McCune, Munster, Ind.	1973	Judy Soutar, Kansas City, Mo.
1974	Earl Anthony, Tacoma, Wash.	1974	Betty Morris, Stockton, Calif.
1975	Earl Anthony, Tacoma, Wash.	1975	Judy Soutar, Kansas City, Mo.
1976	Earl Anthony, Tacoma, Wash.	1976	Patty Costello, Scranton, Pa.
1977	Mark Roth, Staten Island, N.Y.	1977	Betty Morris, Stockton, Calif.
1978	Mark Roth, N. Arlington, N.J.	1978	Donna Adamek, Monrovia, Calif.
1979	Mark Roth, Little Silver, N.J.	1979	Donna Adamek, Duarte, Calif.

1980 LEADING WOMEN'S MONEY WINNERS SOURCE: W.P.B.A.
(to Sept. 1) — WPBA Events, WIBC Queen's Tournament and U.S. Open

Bowler	Amount	Bowler	Amount
1. Pat Costello, Union City, Calif.	$19,795	6. Vesma Grinfelds, San Francisco, Calif.	$8,545
2. Donna Adamek, Duarte, Calif.	19,107	7. Cheryl Robinson, Van Nuys, Calif.	7,935
3. Shinobu Saitoh, Tokyo, Japan	10,500	8. Betty Morris, Stockton, Calif.	6,947
4. Nikki Gianulias, Vallejo, Calif.	9,055	9. Robin Romeo, Beverly Hills, Calif.	6,687
5. Pam Buckner, Reno, Nev.	8,855	10. Patty Ann, Arlington Heights, Ill.	6,395

WOMEN'S BOWLING CHAMPIONS

	U.S. Open (Formerly All-Star)	WIBC Queen's Tournament	WPBA National Championship
1961	Phyllis Notaro	Janet Harman	Shirley Garms
1962	Shirley Garms	Dorothy Wilkinson	Stevie Balogh
1963	Marion Ladewig	Irene Monterosso	Janet Harman
1964	LaVerne Carter	D.D. Jacobson	Betty Kuczynski
1965	Ann Slattery	Betty Kuczynski	Helen Duval
1966	Joy Abel	Judy Lee	Judy Lee
1967	Gloria Bouvia	Mildred Martorella	Betty Mivalez
1968	Dotty Fothergill	Phyllis Massey	Dotty Fothergill
1969	Dotty Fothergill	Ann Feigel	Dotty Fothergill
1970	Mary Baker	Mildred Martorella	Bobbe North
1971	Paula Sperber	Mildred Martorella	Patty Costello
1972	Lorrie Koch	Dotty Fothergill	Patty Costello
1973	Mildred Martorella	Dotty Fothergill	Betty Morris
1974	Pat Costello	Judy Soutar	Pat Costello
1975	Paula Sperber	Cindy Powell	Pam Rutherford
1976	Patty Costello	Pam Rutherford	Patty Costello
1977	Betty Morris	Dana Stewart	Vesma Grinfelds
1978	Donna Adamek	Loa Boxberger	Toni Gillard
1979	Diana Silva	Donna Adamek	Cindy Coburn
1980	Pat Costello	Donna Adamek	

1979 LEADING MONEY WINNERS — WOMEN SOURCE: W.P.B.A.

Bowler	Amount	Bowler	Amount
1. Pat Costello, Union City, Calif.	$25,060	8. Lorrie Nichols, Island Lake, Ill.	$13,605
2. Donna Adamek, Duarte, Calif.	21,280	9. Vesma Grinfelds, San Francisco, Calif.	13,380
3. Nikki Gianulias, Vallejo, Calif.	18,293	10. Patty Costello, Scranton, Pa.	11,230
4. Pam Buckner, Reno, Nev.	18,170	11. Bev Ortner, Tucson, Ariz.	10,757
5. Betty Morris, Stockton, Calif.	17,095	12. Cindy Coburn, Buffalo, N.Y.	10,325
6. Virginia Norton, South Gate, Calif.	14,357	13. Sherry Yohn, Pottstown, Pa.	9,210
7. Kathy Wodka, New London, Conn.	14,005	14. Judy Soutar, Leawood, Kans.	8,365
		15. Diana Silva, Albuquerque, N.M.	8,000

CHESS SOURCE: U.S. Chess Federation

WORLD CHAMPIONSHIPS

Year	Winner, Country	Year	Winner, Country	Year	Winner, Country
1886	Wilhelm Steinitz, Austria	1921	Jose Capablanca, Cuba	1958	Mikhail Botvinnik, USSR
1889	Wilhelm Steinitz, Austria	1927	Alexander Alekhine, France	1960	Mikhail Tal, USSR
1891	Wilhelm Steinitz, Austria	1929	Alexander Alekhine, France	1961	Mikhail Botvinnik, USSR
1892	Wilhelm Steinitz, Austria	1934	Alexander Alekhine, France	1963	Tigran Petrosian, USSR
1894	Emanuel Lasker, Germany	1935	Max Euwe, Netherlands	1966	Tigran Petrosian, USSR
1897	Emanuel Lasker, Germany	1937	Alexander Alekhine, France	1969	Boris Spassky, USSR
1907	Emanuel Lasker, Germany	1948	Mikhail Botvinnik, USSR	1972	Bobby Fischer, US
1908	Emanuel Lasker, Germany	1951	Mikhail Botvinnik, USSR	1975	Anatoly Karpov, USSR
1909	Emanuel Lasker, Germany	1954	Mikhail Botvinnik, USSR	1978	Anatoly Karpov, USSR
1910*	Emanuel Lasker, Germany	1957	Vassily Smyslov, USSR		

* Two championship matches held in 1910. Lasker won both.

U.S. NATIONAL CHAMPIONSHIPS

UNOFFICIAL CHAMPIONS

Year	Winner	Year	Winner	Year	Winner	Year	Winner
1857-71	Paul Morphy	1894	Albert Hodges	1946	Arnold Denker	1966	Bobby Fischer
1871-76	George Mackenzie	1895	Jackson Showalter	1946	Samuel Reshevsky	1968	Larry Evans
1876-80	James Mason	1896	Jackson Showalter	1948	Herman Steiner	1969	Samuel Reshevsky
1880-89	George Mackenzie	1896	Jackson Showalter	1951	Larry Evans	1972	Robert Byrne
1889-90	S. Lipschutz	1897	Harry Pillsbury	1952	Larry Evans	1973	Lubomir Kavalek
1890	Jackson Showalter	1898	Harry Pillsbury	1954	Arthur Bisguier		and John Grefe
1890-91	Max Judd	1909	Frank Marshall	1958	Bobby Fischer	1974	Walter Browne
1891	Jackson Showalter	1923	Frank Marshall	1959	Bobby Fischer	1975	Walter Browne
		1936	Samuel Reshevsky	1960	Bobby Fischer	1977	Walter Browne
		1938	Samuel Reshevsky	1961	Bobby Fischer	1978	Lubomir Kavalek
CHAMPIONS		1940	Samuel Reshevsky	1962	Larry Evans	1980	Walter Browne
1892	Jackson Showalter	1941	Samuel Reshevsky	1963	Bobby Fischer		Larry Christiansen
1892	S. Lipschutz	1942	Samuel Reshevsky	1964	Bobby Fischer		Larry Evans
1894	Jackson Showalter	1944	Arnold Denker	1965	Bobby Fischer		

SWIMMING AND DIVING

1980 NCAA CHAMPIONS

DIVISION I

50 yd. Freestyle	Andy Coan, Tennessee
100 yd. Freestyle	Rowdy Gaines, Auburn
200 yd. Freestyle	Rowdy Gaines, Auburn
500 yd. Freestyle	Brian Goodell, UCLA
1,650 yd. Freestyle	Brian Goodell, UCLA
100 yd. Backstroke	Clay Britt, Texas
200 yd. Backstroke	James Fowler, USC
100 yd. Breaststroke	Steve Lundquist, SMU
200 yd. Breaststroke	Bill Barrett, UCLA
100 yd. Butterfly	Par Arvidsson, California
200 yd. Butterfly	Par Arvidsson, California
200 yd. Indiv. Medley	Bill Barrett, UCLA
400 yd. Indiv. Medley	Brian Goodell, UCLA
400 yd. Freestyle Relay	Auburn
800 yd. Freestyle Relay	Auburn
400 yd. Medley Relay	Texas
One Meter Dive	Gary Louganis, Miami (Fla.)
Three Meter Dive	Gary Louganis, Miami (Fla.)
Team	California
Division II Team	Oakland (Michigan)
Division III Team	Kenyon (Ohio)

1980 AIAW CHAMPIONS

DIVISION I

50 yd. Freestyle	Jill Sterkel, Texas
100 yd. Freestyle	Jill Sterkel, Texas
200 yd. Freestyle	Nancy Garapick, USC
500 yd. Freestyle	Maura Walsh, USC
1,650 yd. Freestyle	Kimberly Black, Texas
50 yd. Backstroke	Kim Carlisle, Stanford
100 yd. Backstroke	Linda Jezek, Stanford
200 yd. Backstroke	Linda Jezek, Stanford
50 yd. Breaststroke	Anette Fredericksson, USC
100 yd. Breaststroke	Anne Gagnon, Arizona State
200 yd. Breaststroke	Anne Gagnon, Arizona State
50 yd. Butterfly	Jill Sterkel, Texas
100 yd. Butterfly	Jill Sterkel, Texas
200 yd. Butterfly	Diane Johannigman, Houston
100 yd. Indiv. Medley	Joan Pennington, Texas
200 yd. Indiv. Medley	Nancy Garapick, USC
400 yd. Indiv. Medley	Janet Buchan, Stanford
200 yd. Freestyle Relay	Stanford
400 yd. Freestyle Relay	Texas
800 yd. Freestyle Relay	Arizona State
200 yd. Medley Relay	Stanford
400 yd. Medley Relay	Texas
One Meter Dive	Amy McGrath, Indiana
Three Meter Dive	Denise Christensen, Texas
Team	Stanford
Division II Team	Clarion State (Pa.)
Division III Team	Hamline (Minn.)

1980 NAIA CHAMPIONS

50 yd. Freestyle	James Harmon, Wisconsin-Eau Claire
100 yd. Freestyle	James Harmon, Wisconsin-Eau Claire
200 yd. Freestyle	James Yount, Drury (Mo.)
500 yd. Freestyle	Gary Davis, Simon Fraser (Can.)
1,650 yd. Freestyle	Robert Barton, Simon Fraser (Can.)
100 yd. Backstroke	Mike Wagnon, Drury (Mo.)
200 yd. Backstroke	Nick Borrelly, Simon Fraser (Can.)
100 yd. Breaststroke	John McMahon, Fairmount St. (W. Va.)
200 yd. Breaststroke	John McMahon, Fairmount St. (W. Va.)
100 yd. Butterfly	Mark Hahto, Simon Fraser (Can.)
200 yd. Butterfly	Mark Hahto, Simon Fraser (Can.)
200 yd. Indiv. Medley	Mike Wagnon, Drury (Mo.)
400 yd. Indiv. Medley	Robert Barton, Simon Fraser (Can.)
400 yd. Freestyle Relay	Drury (Mo.)
800 yd. Freestyle Relay	Wisconsin-Eau Claire
400 yd. Medley Relay	Wisconsin-Eau Claire
One Meter Dive	Jim Martin, Southwest St. (Minn.)
Three Meter Dive	Tony Perriello, Clarion St. (Pa.)
Team	Simon Fraser (Canada)

1980 U.S. OUTDOOR SWIMMING CHAMPIONS

MEN

50 m. Freestyle	Joe Bottom, Walnut Creek, Calif.
100 m. Freestyle	Rowdy Gaines, Gainesville, Fla.
200 m. Freestyle	Rowdy Gaines, Gainesville, Fla.
400 m. Freestyle	Mike Bruner, Mesa, Ariz.
800 m. Freestyle	Brian Goodell, Mission Viejo, Calif.
1500 m. Freestyle	Mike Bruner, Mesa, Ariz.
100 m. Backstroke	Peter Rocca, Pleasant Hill, Calif.
200 m. Backstroke	Steve Barnicoat, Mission Viejo, Calif.
100 m. Breaststroke	Steve Lundquist, Jonesboro, Ga.
200 m. Breaststroke	Glenn Mills, Cincinnati, Ohio
100 m. Butterfly	William Paulus, Austin, Tex.
200 m. Butterfly	Craig Beardsley, Gainesville, Fla.
200 m. Indiv. Medley	Bill Barrett, Alpharetta, Ga.
400 m. Indiv. Medley	Jesse Vassallo, Mission Viejo, Calif.
400 m. Freestyle Relay	Florida Aquatic
800 m. Freestyle Relay	Florida Aquatic
400 m. Medley Relay	Dr. Pepper

WOMEN

50 m. Freestyle	Jill Sterkel, Austin, Tex.
100 m. Freestyle	Cynthia Woodhead, Cupertino, Calif.
200 m. Freestyle	Cynthia Woodhead, Cupertino, Calif.
400 m. Freestyle	Kim Linehan, Austin, Tex.
800 m. Freestyle	Kim Linehan, Austin, Tex.
1500 m. Freestyle	Kim Linehan, Austin, Tex.
100 m. Backstroke	Linda Jezek, Stanford, Calif.
200 m. Backstroke	Linda Jezek, Stanford, Calif.
100 m. Breaststroke	Tracy Caulkins, Nashville, Tenn.
200 m. Breaststroke	(tie) Tracy Caulkins, Nashville, Tenn. and Terri Baxter, Menlo Park, Calif.
100 m. Butterfly	Mary T. Meagher, Cincinnati, Ohio
200 m. Butterfly	Mary T. Meagher, Cincinnati, Ohio
200 m. Indiv. Medley	Tracy Caulkins, Nashville, Tenn.
400 m. Indiv. Medley	Tracy Caulkins, Nashville, Tenn.
400 m. Freestyle Relay	Cincinnati Pepsi Marlins
800 m. Freestyle Relay	Cincinnati Pepsi Marlins
400 m. Medley Relay	Cincinnati Pepsi Marlins

1980 AAU INDOOR DIVING CHAMPIONS

MEN

One Meter	Greg Louganis, Mission Viejo, Calif.
Three Meter	Greg Louganis, Mission Viejo, Calif.
Platform	Bruce Kimball

WOMEN

One Meter	Karen Gorham, Fayetteville, Ark.
Three Meter	Carrie Finneran, Columbus, Ohio
Platform	Christine Loock, Dallas, Tex.

1980 U.S. OLYMPIC TRIALS DIVING CHAMPIONS

MEN

Three Meter	Greg Louganis, Mission Viejo, Calif.
Platform	Greg Louganis, Mission Viejo, Calif.

WOMEN

Three Meter	Megan Neyer, Ashland, Ky.
Platform	Megan Neyer, Ashland, Ky.

1980 AIAW SYNCHRONIZED SWIMMING CHAMPIONS

Senior Figures . . . . Michele Beaulieu, Arizona
Solo Routine . . . . Pamela Tryon, Arizona
Duet Routine . . . . Tara Cameron-Karen Callaghan
                                                                    Ohio State

Trio Routine . . . . Tara Cameron-Karen Callaghan-
                                                              Janet Tope, Ohio State
Team Routine . . . . Ohio State
Team . . . . (tie) Ohio State, Arizona

WORLD SWIMMING RECORDS (September 1980)

MEN'S EVENTS

Event	Time	Name	Country	Date	
100 meter freestyle	0:49.44	Jonty Skinner	South Africa	August	1976
200 meter freestyle	1:49.16	Rowdy Gaines	United States	April	1980
400 meter freestyle	3:50.49	Peter Szmidt	Canada	July	1980
800 meter freestyle	7:56.49	Vladimir Salnikov	USSR	March	1979
1500 meter freestyle	14:58.27	Vladimir Salnikov	USSR	July	1980
400 meter freestyle relay	3:19.74	Babashoff, Gaines McCagg, Montgomery	United States	August	1978
800 meter freestyle relay	7:20.82	Furniss, Forrester, Gaines, Hackett	United States	August	1978
100 meter breaststroke	1:02.86	Gerald Mörken	West Germany	August	1977
200 meter breaststroke	2:15.11	David Wilkie	United Kingdom	July	1976
100 meter butterfly	0:54.15	Par Arvidsson	Sweden	April	1980
200 meter butterfly	1:58.21	Craig Beardsley	United States	July	1980
100 meter backstroke	0:55.49	John Naber	United States	July	1976
200 meter backstroke	1:59.19	John Naber	United States	July	1976
200 meter individual medley	2:03.24	Bill Barrett	United States	August	1980
400 meter individual medley	4:20.05	Jesse Vassallo	United States	August	1978
400 meter medley relay	3:42.22	Naber, Hencken, Vogel, Montgomery	United States	July	1976

WOMEN'S EVENTS

Event	Time	Name	Country	Date	
100 meter freestyle	54.79	Barbara Krause	East Germany	July	1980
200 meter freestyle	1:58.23	Cynthia Woodhead	United States	Sept.	1979
400 meter freestyle	4:06.28	Tracey Wickham	Australia	August	1978
800 meter freestyle	8:18.77	Cynthia Woodhead	United States	February	1980
1500 meter freestyle	16:04.49	Kim Linehan	United States	August	1979
400 meter freestyle relay	3:42.71	Krause, Metschuck, Diers, Hulsenbeck	East Germany	July	1980
100 meter breaststroke	1:10.11	Ute Geweniger	East Germany	July	1980
200 meter breaststroke	2:28.36	Lina Kachushite	USSR	April	1979
100 meter butterfly	59.26	Mary T. Meagher	United States	April	1980
200 meter butterfly	2:06.37	Mary T. Meagher	United States	August	1980
100 meter backstroke	1:00.86	Rica Reinisch	East Germany	July	1980
200 meter backstroke	2:11.93	Rica Reinisch	East Germany	May	1980
200 meter individual medley	2:13.00	Petra Schneider	East Germany	May	1980
400 meter individual medley	4:38.44	Petra Schneider	East Germany	May	1980
400 meter medley relay	4:07.95	Richter, Anke, Pollack, Ender	East Germany	July	1976

SPORTS FIGURES OF THE CENTURY

Results of a 1980 international poll of twenty leading newspapers of the world.

1. **Pele**, Brazil, soccer
2. **Jesse Owens**, U.S., track and field
3. **Eddy Merckx**, Belgium, cycling
4. **Paavo Nurmi**, Finland, track and field
5. **Bjorn Borg**, Sweden, tennis, and **Mark Spitz**, U.S., swimming
7. **Emil Zatopek**, Czechoslovakia, track and field
8. **Fauto Coppi**, Italy, cycling
9. **Muhammad Ali**, U.S., boxing
10. **Sugar Ray Robinson**, U.S., boxing
11. **Jack Nicklaus**, U.S., golf
12. **Joe Louis**, U.S., boxing
13. **Babe Ruth**, U.S., baseball
14. **Juan Manuel Fangio**, Argentina, auto racing
15. **Jean-Claude Killy**, France, skiing, and **Eric Heiden**, U.S., speed skating
17. **Dawn Fraser**, Australia, swimming, and **Irena Szewinska**, Poland, track and field
19. **Vasily Alexeyev**, USSR, weightlifting, and **Nadia Comaneci**, Romania, gymnastics

WORLD FRESHWATER FISHING RECORDS

Source: International Game Fish Association (All tackle records, as of August 1, 1980)

Species	Weight	Where Caught	Date	Angler
Bass, Largemouth	22 lbs. 4 oz.	Montgomery Lake, Ga.	June 2, 1932	George W. Perry
Bass, Redeye	8 lbs. 3 oz.	Flint River, Ga.	Oct. 23, 1977	David A. Hubbard
Bass, Rock	3 lbs.	York River, Ontario	Aug. 1, 1974	Peter Gulgin
Bass, Smallmouth	11 lbs. 15 oz.	Dale Hollow Lake, Ky.	July 9, 1955	David L. Hayes
Bass, Spotted	8 lbs. 15 oz.	Smith Lake, Ala.	Mar. 18, 1978	Philip C. Terry, Jr.
Bass, White	5 lbs. 6 oz.	Grenada Lake, Miss.	Apr. 21, 1979	William C. Mulvihill
Bass, Whiterock	20 lbs.	Savannah R., Ga.	May 5, 1977	Don Raley
Bass, Yellow	2 lbs. 4 oz.	Lake Monroe, Ind.	Mar. 27, 1977	Donald L. Stalker
Bluegill	4 lbs. 12 oz.	Ketona Lake, Ala.	Apr. 9, 1950	T. S. Hudson
Bowfin	21 lbs. 8 oz.	Florence, N.C.	Jan. 29, 1980	Robert L. Harmon
Buffalo, Bigmouth	56 lbs.	Lock Loma L., Mo.	Aug. 19, 1976	M. R. Webster
Buffalo, Smallmouth	51 lbs.	Lawrence, Kansas	May 2, 1979	Scott Butler
Bullhead, Black	8 lbs.	Lake Waccabuc, N.Y.	Aug. 1, 1951	Eddie O'Daniel
Carp	55 lbs. 5 oz.	Clearwater Lake, Minn.	July 10, 1952	Kani Evans
Catfish, Blue	97 lbs.	Missouri River, S.D.	Sept. 16, 1959	Frank J. Ledwein
Catfish, Channel	58 lbs.	Santee-Cooper Res., S.C.	July 7, 1964	Edward B. Elliott
Catfish, Flathead	79 lbs. 8 oz.	White Riv., Ind.	Aug. 13, 1966	W. B. Whaley
Catfish, White	10 lbs. 5 oz.	Raritan R., N.J.	June 23, 1976	Glenn T. Simpson
Char, Arctic	29 lbs. 11 oz.	Arctic River, N.W.T.	Aug. 21, 1968	Lewis W. Lomerson
Crappie, Black	5 lbs.	Santee-Cooper Res., S.C.	Mar. 15, 1957	Jeanne P. Branson
Crappie, White	5 lbs. 3 oz.	Enid Dam, Miss.	July 31, 1957	Paul E. Foust
Dolly Varden	32 lbs.	L. Pend Oreille, Idaho	Oct. 27, 1949	Fred L. Bright
Drum, Freshwater	54 lbs. 8 oz.	Nickajack Lake, Tenn.	Apr. 20, 1972	N. L. Higgins
Gar, Alligator	279 lbs.	Rio Grande, Texas	Dec. 2, 1951	Benny E. Hull
Gar, Longnose	50 lbs. 5 oz.	Trinity River, Texas	July 30, 1954	Bill Valverde
Grayling, American	5 lbs. 15 oz.	Katseyedie R., N.W.T.	Aug. 16, 1967	Townsend Miller
Kokanee	6 lbs. 9¾ oz.	Priest L., Idaho	June 9, 1975	Jeanne P. Branson
Muskellunge	69 lbs. 15 oz.	St. Lawrence R., N.Y.	Sept. 22, 1957	Jerry Verge
Perch, White	4 lbs. 12 oz.	Messalonskee Lake, Me.	June 4, 1949	Arthur Lawton
Perch, Yellow	4 lbs. 3½ oz.	Bordentown, N.J.	May 1865	Mrs. Earl Small
Pickerel, Chain	9 lbs. 6 oz.	Homerville, Ga.	Feb. 17, 1961	Dr. C. C. Abbot
Pike, Northern	46 lbs. 2 oz.	Sacandaga Res., N.Y.	Sept. 15, 1940	Baxley McQuaig, Jr.
Redhorse, Silver	4 lbs. 2 oz.	Gasconade Riv., Mo.	Oct. 5, 1974	Peter Dubuc
Salmon, Atlantic	79 lbs. 2 oz.	Tana River, Norway	1928	C. Larry McKinney
Salmon, Chinook	93 lbs.	Kelp Bay, Alaska	June 24, 1977	Henrik Henriksen
Salmon, Chum	27 lbs. 3 oz.	Raymond Cove, Alaska	June 11, 1977	Howard C. Rider
Salmon, Coho or Silver	31 lbs.	Cowichan Bay, B.C.	Oct. 11, 1947	Robert A. Jahnke
Salmon, Landlocked	22 lbs. 8 oz.	Sebago Lake, Maine	Aug. 1, 1907	Mrs. Lee Hallberg
Sauger	8 lbs. 12 oz.	Lake Sakakawea, N.D.	Oct. 6, 1971	Edward Blakely
Shad, American	9 lbs. 4 oz.	Delaware River, Pa.	Apr. 26, 1979	J. Edward Whitman
Sturgeon, White	360 lbs.	Snake River, Idaho	Apr. 24, 1956	Willard Cravens
Sunfish, Green	2 lbs. 2 oz.	Stockton Lake, Mo.	June 18, 1971	Paul M. Dilley
Sunfish, Redbreast	1 lb. 8½ oz.	Suwanee R., Fla.	Apr. 30, 1977	Tommy D. Cason, Jr.
Sunfish, Redear	4 lbs. 8 oz.	Chase City, Va.	June 19, 1970	Maurice E. Ball
Trout, Brook	14 lbs. 8 oz.	Nipigon River, Ontario	July 1916	Dr. W. J. Cook
Trout, Brown	35 lbs. 15 oz.	Nahuel Huapi, Arg.	Dec. 16, 1952	Eugenio Cavaglia
Trout, Cutthroat	41 lbs.	Pyramid Lake, Nev.	Dec. 1925	John Skimmerhorn
Trout, Golden	11 lbs.	Cook's Lake, Wyo.	Aug. 5, 1948	Chas. S. Reed
Trout, Lake	65 lbs.	Great Bear Lake, N.W.T.	Aug. 8, 1970	Larry Daunis
Trout, Rainbow, Stlhd. or Kamloops	42 lbs. 2 oz.	Bell Island, Alaska	June 22, 1970	David R. White
Trout, Sunapee	11 lbs. 8 oz.	Lake Sunapee, N.H.	Aug. 1, 1954	Ernest Theoharis
Trout, Tiger	17 lbs.	L. Michigan, Wis.	Aug. 2, 1977	Edward Rudnicki
Walleye	25 lbs.	Old Hickory L., Tenn.	Aug. 1, 1960	Mabry Harper
Warmouth	2 lbs.	Sylvania, Ga.	May 4, 1974	Carlton Robbins
Whitefish, Lake	13 lbs.	Great Bear L., N.W.T.	July 14, 1974	Robert L. Stintsman
Whitefish, Mountain	5 lbs.	Athabasca R., Alberta	June 3, 1963	Orville Welch

WORLD SALTWATER FISHING RECORDS

Source: International Game Fish Association (All tackle records, as of August 1, 1980)

Species	Weight	Where Caught	Date	Angler
Albacore	88 lbs. 2 oz.	Morgan Port, Canary Islands	11/19/77	Siegfried Dickemann
Amberjack (Greater)	149 lbs.	Bermuda	6/21/64	Peter Simons
Barracuda (Great)	83 lbs.	Lagos, Nigeria	1/13/52	K. J. W. Hackett
Bass (Black Sea)	8 lbs. 12 oz.	Oregon Inlet, N.C.	4/21/79	Joe W. Mizelle, Sr.
Bass (Giant Sea)	563 lbs. 8 oz.	Anacapa Island, Calif.	8/20/68	James D. McAdam, Jr.
Bass (Striped)	72 lbs.	Cuttyhunk, Mass.	10/10/69	Edward J. Kirker
Bluefish	31 lbs. 12 oz.	Hatteras Inlet, N.C.	1/30/72	James M. Hussey
Bonefish	19 lbs.	Zululand, South Africa	5/26/62	Brian W. Batchelor
Bonito (Atlantic)	13 lbs. 3 oz.	Canary Islands	8/22/79	Renate Reichel
Bonito (Pacific)	23 lbs. 8 oz.	Victoria, Seychelles	2/19/75	Mrs. Anne Cochain
Cobia	110 lbs. 5 oz.	Mombasa, Kenya	9/8/64	Eric Tinworth
Cod	98 lbs. 12 oz.	Isles of Shoals, N.H.	6/8/69	Alphonse J. Bielevich
Dolphin	87 lbs.	Papagayo Gulf, Costa Rica	9/25/76	Manuel Salazar
Drum (Black)	113 lbs. 1 oz.	Lewes, Del.	9/15/75	Gerald M. Townsend
Drum (Red)	90 lbs.	Rodanthe, N.C.	11/7/73	Elvin Hooper
Flounder (Summer)	22 lbs. 7 oz.	Montauk, N.Y.	9/15/75	Charles Nappi
Halibut (California)	37 lbs. 8 oz.	San Diego, Calif.	7/22/79	William E. Williams
Jack (Crevalle)	51 lbs.	Lake Worth, Fla.	6/20/78	Stephen V. Schwenk
Jack (Horse-Eye)	21 lbs. 5 oz.	Arcus Bank, Bermuda	6/24/79	Tom Smith
Jewfish	680 lbs.	Fernandina Beach, Fla.	5/20/61	Lynn Joyner
Kawakawa	26 lbs.	Merimbula, N.S.W., Australia	1/26/80	Wally Elfring
Mackerel (King)	90 lbs.	Key West, Fla.	2/16/76	Norton I. Thomton
Marlin (Atlantic Blue)	1282 lbs.	St. Thomas, Virgin Is.	8/6/77	Larry Martin
Marlin (Black)	1560 lbs.	Cabo Blanco, Peru	8/4/53	Alfred C. Glassell, Jr.
Marlin (Pacific Blue)	1153 lbs.	Ritidian Point, Guam	8/21/69	Greg D. Perez
Marlin (Striped)	417 lbs. 8 oz.	Cavalli Is., New Zealand	1/14/77	Phillip Bryers

SALTWATER FISHING RECORDS (Continued)

Species	Weight	Where Caught	Date	Angler
Marlin (White)	181 lbs. 14 oz.	Vitoria, Brazil	12/8/79	Evandro Luiz Coser
Permit	51 lbs. 8 oz.	Lake Worth, Fla.	4/28/78	William M. Kenney
Pollock	46 lbs. 7 oz.	Brielle, N.J.	5/26/75	John Tomes Holton
Pompano (African)	41 lbs. 8 oz.	Fort Lauderdale, Fla.	2/15/78	Wayne Sommers
Roosterfish	114 lbs.	LaPaz, Mexico	6/1/60	Abe Sackheim
Runner (Rainbow)	33 lbs. 10 oz.	Clarion Island, Mexico	3/14/76	Ralph A. Mikkelsen
Sailfish (Atlantic)	128 lbs. 1 oz.	Luanda, Angola	3/27/74	Harm Steyn
Sailfish (Pacific)	221 lbs.	Santa Cruz Island, Galapagos Is.	2/12/47	C. W. Stewart
Seabass (White)	83 lbs. 12 oz.	San Felipe, Mexico	3/31/53	L. C. Baumgardner
Seatrout (Spotted)	16 lbs.	Mason's Beach, Va.	5/28/77	William Katko
Shark (Blue)	437 lbs.	Catherine Bay, Australia	10/2/76	Peter Hyde
Shark (Hammerhead)	703 lbs.	Jacksonville Beach, Fla.	7/5/75	H. B. "Blackie" Reasor
Shark (Porbeagle)	465 lbs.	Padstow, Cornwall, England	7/23/76	Jorge Potier
Shark (Shortfin Mako)	1080 lbs.	Montauk, N.Y.	8/26/79	James L. Melanson
Shark (Thresher)	739 lbs.	Tutukaka, New Zealand	2/17/75	Brian Galvin
Shark (Tiger)	1780 lbs.	Cherry Grove, S.C.	6/14/64	Walter Maxwell
Shark (White)	2664 lbs.	Ceduna, Australia	4/21/59	Alfred Dean
Skipjack (Black)	14 lbs. 8 oz.	Cabo San Lucas, Mexico	5/24/77	Lorraine Carlton
Snook	53 lbs. 10 oz.	Rio de Parasmina, Costa Rica	10/18/78	Gilbert Ponzi
Spearfish	79 lbs. 5 oz.	Madeira Islands	5/25/79	Ronald Eckert
Swordfish	1182 lbs.	Iquique, Chile	5/7/53	L. Marron
Tanguigue	85 lbs. 6 oz.	Rottnest I., West Australia	5/5/78	Barry Wrightson
Tarpon	283 lbs.	Lake Maracaibo, Venezuela	3/19/56	M. Salazar
Tautog	21 lbs. 6 oz.	Cape May, New Jersey	6/12/54	R. N. Sheafer
Trevally (Giant)	116 lbs.	Pago Pago, Amer. Samoa	2/20/78	William G. Foster
Tuna (Atlantic Bigeye)	375 lbs. 8 oz.	Ocean City, Md.	8/26/77	Cecil Browne
Tuna (Blackfin)	42 lbs.	Bermuda	6/2/78	Alan J. Card
Tuna (Bluefin)	1496 lbs.	Aulds Cove, Nova Scotia, Canada	10/26/79	Ken Fraser
Tuna (Dog-tooth)	189 lbs. 2 oz.	Dar es Salaam, Tanzania	11/12/78	L. J. Samaras
Tuna (Longtail)	65 lbs.	Port Stephens, N.S.W., Australia	4/20/78	Michael James
Tuna (Pacific Bigeye)	435 lbs.	Cabo Blanco, Peru	4/17/57	Dr. Russel V. A. Lee
Tuna (Skipjack)	40 lbs.	Baie du Tambeau, Mauritius	4/19/71	Joseph R. P. Caboche, Jr.
Tuna (Southern Bluefin)	256 lbs. 13 oz.	Hippolyte Rock, Tasmania, Austr.	5/29/79	Rodney J. Beard
Tuna (Yellowfin)	388 lbs. 12 oz.	San Benedicto I., Mexico	4/1/77	Curt Wiesenhutter
Tunny (Little)	27 lbs.	Key Largo, Fla.	4/20/76	William E. Allison
Wahoo	149 lbs.	Cat Cay, Bahamas	6/15/62	John Pirovano
Weakfish	19 lbs. 8 oz.	Trinidad, West Indies	4/13/62	Dennis B. Hall
Yellowtail (California)	71 lbs. 15 oz.	Alijos Rocks, Mexico	6/24/79	Michael Carpenter
Yellowtail (Southern)	111 lbs.	Bay of Islands, New Zealand	6/11/61	A. F. Plim

WRESTLING

1980 NAT'L AAU FREESTYLE CHAMPIONS

105.5 lbs.—Bob Weaver, New York A.C.
114.5 lbs.—Joe Gonzales, Sunkist Kids
125.5 lbs.—Joe Corso, Hawkeye W.C.
136.5 lbs.—Ricky Dellagatta, New York A.C.
149.5 lbs.—Jim Humphrey, Oklahoma Underdogs
163 lbs.—Bruce Kinseth, Hawkeye W.C.
180.5 lbs.—Chris Campbell, Cyclone W.C.
198 lbs.—Ben Peterson, Wisconsin W.C.
220 lbs.—Russ Hellickson, Wisconsin W.C.
Heavyweight—Bruce Baumgartner, New York A.C.
Outstanding Wrestler—Jim Humphrey
Team—New York Athletic Club

1980 NAT'L AAU GRECO-ROMAN CHAMPIONS

105.5 lbs.—Mark Fuller, San Francisco Grapplers
114.5 lbs.—John Hartupee, Michigan W.C.
125.5 lbs.—Bruce Thompson, Land of Lakes
136.5 lbs.—Abdurrahim Kuzu, Nebraska Olympic Club
149.5 lbs.—Doug Yeats, Canada
163 lbs.—John Matthews, Michigan W.C.
180.5 lbs.—Louis Santere, Canada
198 lbs.—Laurent Soucie, Wisconsin W.C.
220 lbs.—Brad Rheingans, Minnesota W.C.
Heavyweight—Jeff Blatnick, Adirondack 3-style W.C.
Outstanding Wrestler—Laurent Soucie
Team—U.S. Marine Corps

1980 NCAA CHAMPIONS

DIVISION I
118 lbs.—Joe Gonzales, Bakersfield State
126 lbs.—John Azevedo, Bakersfield State
134 lbs.—Randy Lewis, Iowa
142 lbs.—Lee Roy Smith, Oklahoma State
150 lbs.—Andy Rein, Wisconsin
158 lbs.—Rickey Stewart, Oklahoma State
167 lbs.—Matt Reiss, North Carolina State
177 lbs.—Ed Banach, Iowa
190 lbs.—Noel Loban, Clemson
Heavyweight—Howard Harris, Oregon State
Team—Iowa
Division II Team—Bakersfield State
Division III Team—Brockport State

1980 WORLD CUP FREESTYLE CHAMPIONS

105.5 lbs.—Bob Weaver, U.S.A.
114.5 lbs.—Gene Mills, U.S.A.
125.5 lbs.—Sergi Beloglasov, U.S.S.R.
136.5 lbs.—Victor Alexiev, U.S.S.R.
149.5 lbs.—Dave Shultz, U.S.A.
163 lbs.—Leroy Kemp, U.S.A.
180.5 lbs.—John Peterson, U.S.A.
198 lbs.—Ben Peterson, U.S.A.
220 lbs.—Ivan Yarygin, U.S.S.R.
Heavyweight—Jimmy Jackson, U.S.A.
Teams—1. U.S.A., 2. U.S.S.R., 3. Canada, 4. Japan, 5. Africa

OTHER SPORTS

ARCHERY (1980)

PROFESSIONAL DIVISION
Freestyle—Michael Leiter, Maryland
Women—Liz Colombo, California
Bowhunter—Jim Brown, Maryland
Bowhunter Freestyle—Steve Lash, Illinois

OPEN DIVISION
Freestyle—George Gorman, Texas
Women—Becky Lawrence, Arizona
Barebow—David Hughes, Texas
Women—Gloria Shelley, Connecticut
Bowhunter—Cal Vogt, California
Women—Cay McManus, Virginia
Bowhunter Freestyle—Jean Lamoureux, Rhode Island
Women—Sandy Hildreth, New York

AMATEUR DIVISION
Freestyle—Russell Coulson, Pennsylvania
Women—Connie Wise, Pennsylvania
Barebow—Donald Morehead, Illinois
Women—Pat Colson, Connecticut
Bowhunter—Robert Kedding, Minnesota
Women—Betty Snider, Illinois
Bowhunter Freestyle—John Legates, Delaware

BADMINTON (1980)

U.S. National Champions
Men's Singles—Gary Higgins, Alhambra, Calif.
Women's Singles—Cheryl Carton, San Diego, Calif.
Men's Doubles—Matt Fogarty, Duxbury, Mass.-Mike Walker, Manhattan Beach, Calif.
Women's Doubles—Judianne Kelly, Costa Mesa, Calif.-Pam Brady, Flint, Mich.
Mixed Doubles—Mike Walker-Judianne Kelly

AIAW Champions
Singles—Heather Ross, Ariz. State
Doubles—Heather Ross-Regina Rubin, Arizona State
Team—Arizona State

World Champions
Men's Singles—Rudy Hartono, Indonesia
Women's Singles—Wiharjo Verawaty, Indonesia
Men's Doubles—Ade Chandra-Christian Hadinata, Indonesia
Women's Doubles—Nora Perry-Jane Webster, England

BIATHLON (1979)
20km—Klaus Seibert, E. Germany
10km—Frank Ullrich, E. Germany
U.S. Nat'l Champion
(20 km)—Ken Alligood, Anchorage, Alaska
(10 km)—Lyle Nelson, Olympic Valley, Calif.

BILLIARDS
1980 PPPA World Open Pocket—Men: Nick Varner, Owensboro, Ky.; Women: Jean Balukas, Brooklyn, N.Y.
1980 World 3-Cushion—Raymond Ceulemans, Belgium
1979 BCA National 8-Ball—Men: Jimmy Reid; Women: Gloria Walker
1980 BCA All-American Team 8-Ball—Colorado Springs Tam O'Shanters

BOBSLEDDING (1980)
AAU 2-Man—Brent Rushlaw, Joe Tyler
AAU 4-Man—Bob Hickey, Jeff Jordan, Ron Smith, Jeff Hadley

CANOEING
1980 U.S. Slalom and Wildwater Champions
Canoe Slalom—David Hearn, Garret Park, Md.
Canoe Slalom Doubles—Paul Grabow, College Park, Md.-Jefry Huey, Chevy Chase, Md.
Canoe Slalom Mixed Doubles—Barbara McKee, Rochester, N.Y.-John Sweet, State College, Pa.
Canoe Wildwater—David Hearn
Canoe Wildwater Doubles—Paul Grabow-Jefry Huey

Kayak Slalom—Chuck Stanley, Portland, Ore.
Women—Linda Harrison, Newark, Del.
Kayak Wildwater—Dan Schnurrenberger, Silver Spring, Md.
Women—Cathy Hearn, Garrett Park, Md.
1979 U. S. Champions — KAYAK
Singles (500m.)—Terry White, Amherst, Mass.
Women—Linda Dragan, Washington, D.C.
Singles (100m.)—Terry White
Women's Singles (5000m.)—Ann Turner, St. Charles, Ill.
Singles (10,000m.)—Brent Turner, St. Charles, Ill.
Tandem (500m.)—Steve Kelly, Inwood (N.Y.) C.C.-Brent Turner
Women's Tandem—Leslie Klein, Amherst, Mass.-Ann Turner
Tandem (1000m.)—S. Kelley-B. Turner
Women's Tandem (5000m.)—Sue Turner, St. Charles, Ill.-Jean Campbell, Webster Groves, Mo.
13 miles—Brent Turner
Tandem—Turner-Kelly
Women—A. Turner
Women's Tandem—A. Turner-L. Klein
1979 U.S. Champions — CANOE
Singles (500m)—Roland Muhlen, Cincinnati, Ohio
Singles (1000m.)—R. Muhlen
Singles (10,000m.)—Kurt Doberstein, Lombard, Ill.
Tandem (500m.)—Jay Kearney, Lexington, Ky.-Jay Batlick, Seattle, Wash.
Tandem (1000m.)—Blaise Staneck, New York-Kurt Doberstein
Tandem (10,000m.)—Bruce and Berry Merritt, Washington, D.C.

CROSS-COUNTRY (1979)
National AAU Champions
Men—Alberto Salazar, Greater Boston T.C.
Women—Margaret Gross, Charlottesville T.C.
Men's Team—Greater Boston Track Club
Women's Team—Liberty A.C.
National Collegiate Champions
NCAA Div. I—Henry Rono, Washington St.
Team—Texas-El Paso
NCAA Div. II—James Schankel, Calif. Poly-San Luis Obispo
Team—Calif. Poly-San Luis Obispo
NCAA Div. III—Steve Hunt, Boston State
Team—North Central (Ill.)
NAIA—Sam Montoya, Adams State
Team—Adams State
AIAW Div. I—Julie Shea, N. Carolina St.
Team—North Carolina State
AIAW Div. II—Joan Corbin, Seattle Pacific
Team—U.S. Air Force Academy
AIAW Div. III—Joan Benoit, Bowdoin Coll.
Team—California State-Hayward
1980 World Champions
Men—Craig Virgin, Lebanon, Ill.
Women—Grete Waitz, Norway

CYCLING
1980 World Road Champion (Professional)
Bernard Hinault, France
1980 Tour de France
Joop Zoetemelk, Netherlands
1979 U.S. Champions—ROAD RACING
Senior—Steve Wood, Albuquerque, N.M.
Women—Connie Carpenter, Berkeley, Calif.
1979 U.S. Champions—TRACK RACING
Sprint—Leigh Barczewski, W. Allis, Wis.
Women—Sue Novara, Flint, Mich.
Pursuit—Dave Grylls, Grosse Pte., Mich.
Women—Connie Carpenter, Berkeley, Calif.
Point Race—Gus Pipenhagen, Northhbrook, Ill.
Women—Mary Jane Reoch, Philadelphia, Pa.
1979 World Champions (Amateur)
Sprint—Lutz Hesslich, E. Ger.
Women—Galina Tsareva, USSR
Pursuit—Nikolai Makarov, USSR

Time Trials—Lothar Thoms, E. Ger.
Road—Gianni Giacomini
Women—Petra de Bruin
Point Race—Jiry Slama, Czech.

DOGS
Best-in-Show Winners
1980 Westminster (N.Y.)—Ch. Innisfree's Sierra Cinnar (Siberian husky); Kathleen Kanzler, Accokeek, Md.; 2,769 entries
1980 International (Chicago)—Ch. Thrumpton's Lord Brady (Norwich terrier); Ruth Cooper, Glenview, Ill.; 2,704 entries
1979 Boardwalk (Atlantic City)—Ch. Sporting Fields Clansman (whippet); Dionne and James Butt; 2,902 entries
1980 Westchester (Tarrytown, N.Y.)—Ch. Beaucrest Ruffian (Bouvier des Flandres); Pat and Roy Schiller, Ijamsville, Md.; 3,122 entries
1979 Philadelphia—Ch. Kamp's Kaptain Kool (parti-colored cocker spaniel); Mr. and Mrs. Byron Covey and Mai Wilson; 2,093 entries

FENCING (1980)
U.S. Champions
Foil—Greg Massiales, Salle D'Asaro, San Jose, Calif.
Epee—Leonid Dervbinsky, New York A.C.
Sabre—Peter Westbrook, N.Y. Fencers Club
Women's Foil—Nikki Franke, Salle Csiszar Philadelphia, Pa.
Foil Team—N.Y. Fencers Club
Epee Team—U.S. Mod. Pentathlon Training Center
Sabre Team—N.Y. Athletic Club
Women's Foil Team—Salle Csiszar
NCAA Champions
Foil—Andy Bonk, Notre Dame, Ernie Simon, Wayne State
Epee—Carlo Sangini, Cleveland State, Gil Pezza, Wayne State
Sabre—Yuri Rabinovich, Wayne State, Paul Friedberg, Pennsylvania
Team—Wayne State
Nat'l Intercollegiate Fencing Association Champions — MEN
Foil—Joe Wolfson, Pennsylvania
Team—M.I.T.
Epee—Geoff Pingree, M.I.T.
Team—M.I.T.
Sabre—Paul Friedberg, Pennsylvania
Team—Pennsylvania
Overall Team—Pennsylvania

FIELD HOCKEY
U.S. Collegiate Champions
Div. I—California State-Long Beach
Div. II—Southwest Missouri State
Div. III—Shippensburg State (Pa.)

GYMNASTICS (1980)
U.S. National Champions
All Around—Peter Vidmar, California
Floor Exercise—Ron Galimore, Iowa State
Pommel Horse—Jim Hartung, Nebraska
Rings—Jim Hartung
Vault—Ron Galimore
Parallel Bars—Phil Cahoy, Nebraska
Horizontal Bar—Peter Vidmar
Nat'l AAU Champions—MEN
All Around—Scott Barclay, Athletes in Action
Floor Exercise—Steve Elliott, Nebraska
Pommel Horse—Robert Stanley, unattached
Rings—Gary Handler, Arizona
Vault—Mike Silverstein, Gymnastics of Ohio
Parallel Bars—Mike Naddor, Athletes in Action
Horizontal Bar—Dan MacWilliam, Arizona
Team—Athletes in Action
Nat'l AAU Champions—WOMEN
All-Around—Shari Mann, M. G. Gymnastics
Floor Exercise—Barrie Muzbeck, Acronauts
Vault—Jackie Cassello, M. G. Gymnastics

OTHER SPORTS (Cont.)

Balance Beam—Shari Mann
Uneven Parallel Bars—Shari Mann
Team—M. G. Gymnastics
NCAA Champions
Division I
All Around—Jim Hartung, Nebraska
Floor Exercise—Steve Elliott, Nebraska
Pommel Horse—Dave Stoldt, Illinois
Rings—Jim Hartung
Vault—Ron Galimore, Iowa State
Parallel Bars—Phil Cahoy, Nebraska
High Bar—Phil Cahoy
Team—Nebraska
Div. II Team—Wisconsin-Oshkosh
AIAW (Women's) Nat'l Champions
Floor Exercise—Sharon Shapiro, U.C.L.A.
Vault—Sharon Shapiro
Balance Beam—Sharon Shapiro
Uneven Parallel Bars—Sharon Shapiro
All Around—Sharon Shapiro
Team—Penn State
U.S. Federation Women's Champions
Overall—Julianne McNamara
Floor Exercise—Beth Kline
Vault—Julianne McNamara-Beth Kline
Balance Beam—Kelly Garrison
Uneven Parallel Bars—Marcia Frederick
NAIA Team—Wisconsin-Oshkosh

HANDBALL
1980 U.S. Handball Ass'n Champions
Singles—Naty Alvarado, Hisperia, Calif.
Doubles—Skip McDowell-Harry Robertson,
   Long Beach, Calif.
1980 National Team Champions
Men—Blick's All-Stars, Colorado Springs,
   Colo.
Women—Midwest Orange
Collegiate—U.S. Military Academy

HORSESHOE PITCHING
1980 National AAU Champions
Hunter Dorman, Jasonville, Ind.
Class B—Richard Anderson, Martinsville,
   Ind.

HORSE SHOWS (1980)
National Horse Show Champions
Working Hunter Champion—Ruxton,
   August A. Busch, Jr. and Cismont Manor
   Farm
Conformation Hunter Champion—There'll
   Be Times, Lysa Burke and Meadow
   Bluffs Farm
Grand Hunter Champion—Harvard Square,
   Betty F. McGuire
National Horse Show Equitation Champions
Saddle Seat (Good Hands)—Schauna
   Schoonmaker, Denver, Colo.
ASPCA Trophy (Maclay)—Gary Young,
   Pittsford, N.Y.
The Nations Cup—U.S. Equestrian Team

ICE SKATING (1980)
World Figure Skating Champions
Men—Jan Hoffmann, E. Germany
Women—Anett Poetzsch, E. Germany
Pairs—Marina Chersekova—Sergei
   Shakhrai, USSR
Dance—Krisztina Regoeczy-Andras Sallay,
   Hungary
U.S. Figure Skating Champions
Men—Charles Tickner, Littleton, Colo.
Women—Linda Fratianne, Northridge, Cal.
Pairs—Tai Babilonia, Mission Hills, Cal.-
   Randy Gardner, Los Angeles, Cal.
Dance—Stacey Smith-John Summers,
   Wilmington, Del.
World Speed Skating Champions
Men—Herbert van der Duim, Netherlands
Women—Natalya Petruseva, USSR
Sprint—Eric Heiden, Madison, Wis.
Women's Sprint—Karin Enke, E. Germany
U.S. Speed Skating Champions
Outdoor—Greg Oly, Minneapolis, Minn.
Women—Shari Miller, Butte, Mont.
Indoor—Barth Levy, Lakewood, Ohio
Women—(tie) Pam Mercer, Wyandotte,
   Mich. and Debbie Carlstrom,
   Des Plaines, Ill.

**North American Speed Skating
   Championships**
Outdoor—Barth Levy, Lakewood, Ohio
Women—Shari Miller, Butte, Mont.
Indoor—Gaetan Boucher, Quebec, Canada
Women—Cathy Turnbull, Saskatchewan,
   Canada

JUDO (1980)
National AAU Champions—MEN
132 Lbs.—Maurice DeLaTorriente, Arlington Hts., Ill.
143 Lbs.—Fred Glock, Minnesota
156 Lbs.—Steven Seck, Los Angeles, Calif.
172 Lbs.—Brett Barron, San Mateo, Calif.
189 Lbs.—Tommy Martin, Stockton, Calif.
Under 209 Lbs.—Miguel Tudela, Los
   Angeles, Calif.
Over 209 Lbs.—John Saylor, Westfield,
   N.Y.
Open Division—Dewey Mitchell, Seven
   Springs, Fla.
National AAU Champions—WOMEN
106 Lbs.—Jan Zakarzecki, E. Lansing,
   Mich.
114 Lbs.—Eve Aronoff
123 Lbs.—Geri Bindell, New Milford, N.J.
134 Lbs.—Sandra Coons, Rochelle, Ill.
145 Lbs.—Christine Penick, Los Angeles,
   Calif.
Under 158 Lbs.—Amy Kublin, Boston,
   Mass.
Over 158 Lbs.—Margaret Castro, New
   York City

JUNIOR COLLEGES (1979-80)
Nat'l J.C. Champions — Men's Div.
Baseball—Middle Georgia Coll.
Basketball—Western Texas Coll.
Bowling—Vincennes (Ind.) Univ.
Cross-Country—New Mexico J.C.
Decathlon—Craig Branham, Pima (Ariz.)
   C.C.
Football—Ranger J.C. (Tex.)
Golf—Miami-Dade J.C. North (Fla.)
Gymnastics—Long Beach City Coll.
Ice Hockey—Coll. of DuPage (Ill.)
Lacrosse—Nassau C.C. (N.Y.)
Marathon—Joe Broze, Golden Valley
   Lutheran Coll. (Minn.)
Rifle—New Mexico Military Inst.
Skiing (Alpine)—Vermont Tech. C.C.
Skiing (Nordic)—SUNY at Morrisville
   (N.Y.)
Skiing (Combined)—Vermont Tech C.C.
Soccer—Miami-Dade South C.C. (Fla.)
Swimming—Indian River C.C. (Fla.)
Tennis—Tyler (Tex.) J.C.
Track & Field (Indoor)—New Mexico J.C.
Track & Field (Outdoor)—Mesa (Ariz.)
   C.C.
Wrestling—Lakeland (Ohio) C.C.
Nat'l J.C. Champions—Women's Div.
Basketball—Truett-McConnell Coll. (Ga.)
Bowling—Suffolk C.C. (N.Y.)
Cross-Country—Lane (Ore.) C.C.
Field Hockey—Mitchell Coll. (Ct.)
Golf—Miami-Dade J.C. North (Fla.)
Gymnastics—Spokane C.C.
Skiing (Alpine)—North Country C.C.
   (N.Y.)
Skiing (Nordic)—Adirondack C.C. (N.Y.)
Skiing (Combined)—North Country C.C.
   (N.Y.)
Softball (Fast Pitch)—Erie C.C. (N.Y.)
Swimming—Daytona Beach C.C.
Tennis—Palm Beach (Fla.) J.C.
Track & Field (Indoor and Outdoor)—
   Barton County C.C. (Kans.)
Volleyball—Kellogg (Mich.) C.C.

KARATE
1980 Nat'l AAU Champions
MEN (18-34) KATA
Nov.—Ian Neelan, Ore.
Int.—Neil Eichlebaum, Fla.
Adv.—Domingo Llanos, N.Y.
MEN (18-34) KUMITE
Nov.—Marvin Coleman, Ohio
Int.—Dann Deere, Ohio

Open—Tokey Hill, Ohio
WOMEN (18-34) KATA
Nov.—Sue Gristy, Ill.
Int.—Ann Bouman, N.J.
Adv.—Tilly Garcia, Utah
WOMEN (18-34) KUMITE
Nov.—Elaine Stevens, Ohio
Int.—Ann Bouman, N.J.
Hvwt.—Julia Beal

LACROSSE (1980)
NCAA Div. I—Johns Hopkins
NCAA Div. II—Maryland (Baltimore Co.)
NCAA Div. III—Hobart

LUGE (1980)
World Champions
Singles—Erich Graber, Italy
Women—Delia Vaudan, Italy
Doubles—Pornbacher-Pigneter, Italy
World Cup Champions
Singles—Ernst Haspinger, Italy
Women—Angelika Schafferer, Austria
Doubles—Guenther Lemmerer-Reinhold
   Sulzbacher, Austria
Nat'l AAU Champions
Singles—Jeff Tucker, Westport, Conn.
Women—Donna Burke, Amherst, Mass.
Doubles—Frank Masley, Newark, Del.-
   Ray Bateman, Somerville, N.J.

MARATHON
1980 Boston Marathon—Bill Rodgers,
   Melrose, Mass.
Women—Jacqueline Gareau, Montreal,
   Canada
1980 N.Y. City Marathon—Alberto Salazar,
   Eugene, Ore.
Women—Grete Waitz, Norway
1980 Chicago Marathon—Frank Richard-
   son, Ames, Iowa
1980 Atlantic City Pro Marathon—
Men—Ron Nabers, San Francisco, Calif.
Women—Katie McDonald, New York, N.Y.
1980 U.S. Champions
Men—Frank Richardson
Women—Sue Munday

MODERN PENTATHLON
   (1979)
World Champion—Robert Nieman,
   Hinsdale, Ill.
World Team Champion—United States
U.S. Champion—Lt. Michael Burley,
   Beria, Ohio
Women—Kimberly Dunlop, Tallahassee,
   Fla.

MOTORCYCLING (1980)
AMA National Champions
125 cc Motocross—Mark Barnett, Bridge-
   view, Ill. (Suzuki)
250 cc Motocross—Ken Howerton, San
   Antonio, Tex. (Suzuki)
500 cc Motocross—Chuck Sun, Sherwood,
   Ore. (Honda)
AMA Supercross—Mike Bell, Lakewood,
   Calif. (Yamaha)
U.S. Road Racing—Formula I (750 cc)—
   Richard Schlachter, Old Lyme, Ct.
   Superbike (1979)—Wes Cooley,
   Mission Viejo, Calif.
   Lightweight—Eddie Lawson, Ontario,
   Calif.
   Novice—Thad Wolff, Thousand Oaks,
   Calif.
   Sidecar—Peter Essaff-Ken Harrold, Mill-
   brae, Calif.
Grand National (1979)—Steve Eklund, San
   Jose, Calif.

PADDLEBALL (1979)
Nat'l Four-Wall Champions
Singles—Marty Hogan, San Diego, Calif.
Women—Grace Louwsma, Ann Arbor, Mich.
Doubles—R. P. Valenciano, Flint, Mich.-
   Dick Jury, Lansing, Mich.
Women—Judy Shirley, Ann Arbor, Mich.-
   Grace Louwsma

OTHER SPORTS (Cont.)

PADDLE TENNIS (1980)

U.S. National Champions
...gles—Nels Van Patten, Santa Monica, Calif.
Doubles—Sol Hauptman-Jeff Fleitman, Brooklyn, N.Y.
Women (1979)—Annabel Rogan, Pacific Palisades, Calif.-Nena Perez, Venice, Calif.
Mixed Doubles (1979)—Annabel Rogan, Pacific Palisades, Calif.-Rick Beckendorf, Los Angeles, Calif.

U.S. National Clay Court Champions
Doubles—Sol Hauptman-Jeff Fleitman, Brooklyn, N.Y.
Women—Jeannie Hall, Los Angeles, Calif.-Donna Sweeny, St. Augustine, Fla.
Mixed Doubles—Joanne Glasper-Jeff Fleitman, Brooklyn, N.Y.

PARACHUTING

1980 U.S. Chanmpions
Men's Accuracy—Matt O'Gwynn
Men's Style—Maurice Fernandez
Men's Overall—Matt O'Gwynn
Women's Accuracy—Cheryl Stearns
Women's Style—Cheryl Stearns
Women's Combined—Cheryl Stearns
Four-way Relative Work—Desert Heat
Eight-way Relative Work—Visions.
Ten-way Relative Work—Visions

PENTATHLON (1980)

U.S. Women's Champion—
Themis Zambrzycki, Athletes International/Brazil

PLATFORM TENNIS
(1979-80)

U.S. National Doubles Champions
Men—Steve Baird, Rye, N.Y.—Richard Maier, Allendale, N.J.
Women—Yvonne Hackenberg, Kalamazoo, Mich.-Hilary Hilton, Glen Ellyn, Ill.
Mixed—Hilary Hilton, Glen Ellyn, Ill.-Doug Russell, New York, N.Y.

POLO

1980 Champions
North American Cup—Kingsville
America Cup—Macondo
Silver Cup—Retama
Delegate's Cup—Tennessee
Michelob World Cup—Hallal (Nigeria)
Cup of the Americas—Argentina
Women's Collegiate—Calif.-Davis
1979 Champions
U.S. Open—Retama
Gold Cup—Retama
Intercollegiate—Calif.-Davis

POWERBOATING

1980 U.S. National Champion—Dean Chenoweth, Tallahassee, Fla.
1980 Championship Boat—Miss Budweiser
1979 U.S. Offshore Champion—Betty Cook, Newport Beach, Calif.

POWERLIFTING (1979)

Nat'l AAU Champions
52 kilos—Chuck Dunbar
56 kilos—Robert Lech
60 kilos—George Hummel
67.5 kilos—Clyde Wright
75 kilos—Mike Bridges
82.5 kilos—Walter Thomas
90 kilos—Roger Estep
100 kilos—Larry Pacifico
110 kilos—John Kuc
125 kilos—Larry Kidney
Superheavyweight—Paul Wrenn

QUARTER HORSE RACING
(1980)

Race—Winner and Jockey
All American Futurity—Higheasterjet, Billy Hunt
All American Derby—Native Gambler, Billy Hunt
Rainbow Derby—Rocket Jet Bug, Larry Byers

Kansas Futurity—Clever Bug, Nicky Wilson
Rainbow Futurity—Mighty Deck Three, Jerry Burgess
Kindergarten Futurity—Ettago Chickie, Steve Treasure

RODEO (1979)

World Champions
All-Around—Tom Ferguson, Miami, Okla.
Saddle Bronc Riding—Bobby Berger, Lexington, Okla.
Bareback Bronc Riding—Bruce Ford, Kersey, Colo.
Bull Riding—Don Gay, Mesquite, Tex.
Steer Wrestling—Stan Williamson, Kellyville, Okla.
Calf Roping—Paul Tierney, Rapid City, S.D.
Steer Roping—Gary Good, Elida, N.M.
Team Roping—Allen Bach, Queen Creek, Ariz.
Women's Barrel Racing—Carol Goostree, Verdon, Okla.

ROLLER SKATING

World Champions (1979)
Singles—Michael Butzke, W. Germany
Women—Natalie Dunn, Bakersfield, Cal.
Dance—Fleurette Arsenault-Dan Littel, East Meadow, N.Y.
Mixed Pairs—Ray Chappatta-Karen Mejia, Chicago, Ill.
U.S. Champions (1980)
Singles—Michael Glatz, San Diego, Calif.
Women—Kathleen O'Brien DiFelice, Delanco, N.J.
Figures—Tony St. Jacques, Virginia Beach, Va.
Women—Anna Conklin, Bakersfield, Calif.
Dance—Charles Kirchner-Linda Todd, Cherry Hill, N.J.
Mixed Pairs—Tina Kneisley-Paul Price, Brighton, Mich.

ROWING

1980 U.S. Champions
Singles—Harvard (Tiff Wood)
Dash—N.Y.A.C. (Jim Dietz)
Doubles—N.Y.A.C. (Belden, Dietz)
Pairs without Coxswain—N.Y.A.C. (Houlihan, Brisson)
Pairs with Coxswain—Vesper (Teti, Leeds, Meck)
4s without Coxswain—Pennsylvania/Harvard
4s with Coxswain—Pennsylvania/M.I.T.
Quadruple Sculls—N.Y.A.C.
8s—National Lightweight Camp
1980 Intercollegiate Champions
IRA Varsity—Navy
IRA Freshman—Orange Coast
IRA Second Varsity—Cornell
IRA Jim Ten Eyck Trophy—Wisconsin
Eastern Women's—Pennsylvania
Eastern Regional Sprint—Harvard
Pac-10—Washington
Western Sprint—U.C.L.A.
1980 The Boat Race (Cambridge-Oxford)—Oxford; series: Cam: 68, Oxf: 57, 1 tie
1980 Grand Challenge Cup (Henley)—Charles River Rowing Assn. (U.S. Olympic Eight)
1979 Nile Int'l Festival—Univ. of Washington

RUGBY

1979 Five Nations Tournament—England
1979 South Africa Currie Cup—(tie) Northern Transvaal, Western Provinces
1980 U.S. Nat'l Club Champion—Old Blue R.F.C., Oakland, Calif.
U.S. vs Canada
(1977) Canada 17, U.S. 6
(1978) U.S. 12, Canada 7
(1979) Canada 19, U.S. 12
(1980) Canada 16, U.S. 0

SHOOTING (1980)

U.S. National Outdoor Champions
Men's Pistol—SFC Joseph Pascarella, Las Cruces, N.M.

Women's Pistol—SP4 Ruby E. Fox, Parker, Ariz.
Smallbore Rifle (Prone)—Capt. Ernest Vande Zande, Ft. Benning, Ga.
Smallbore Rifle (Position)—Lt. Col. Lones W. Wigger, Ft. Benning, Ga.
High Power Rifle—Carl R. Bernosky, Gordon, Pa.
U.S. National Indoor Champions
Conv. Rifle—Karen Monez, Ft. Benning, Ga.
Int'l Rifle—Ronald Butterman, Ft. Benning, Ga.
Women—Karen Monez
Conv. Pistol—Donald Hamilton, Kingston, Mass.
Int'l Std. Pistol—Erich Buljung, Ft. Benning, Ga.
Women—Patricia Olsowsky, York, N.Y.
Int'l Free Pistol—Jack Elliott, Dothan, Ala.
Women—Patricia Olsowsky, York, N.Y.
NRA Int'l Clay Pigeon Champions
Men—Earnest Neal, Ft. Benning, Ga.
Women—Connie Hoyle, San Diego, Calif.
Junior—Billy Cole, McMinnville, Ore.
NRA Int'l Skeet Champions
Men—Dean Clark, Ft. Benning, Ga.
Women—Ila Hill, Birmingham, Mich.
Junior—Jeff Sizemore, Corpus Christi, Tex.
NCAA Rifle
Smallbore—Rod Fitz-Randolph, Tennessee Tech
Air Rifle—Rod Fitz-Randolph, Tennessee Tech
Team—Tennessee Tech

SKIING

1979-80 World Cup Champions
Overall—Andreas Wenzel, Liechtenstein
Women—Hanni Wenzel, Liechtenstein
Downhill—Peter Mueller, Switzerland
Women—Marie-Theres Nadig, Switzerland
Slalom—Ingemar Stenmark, Sweden
Women—Perrine Pelen, France
Giant Slalom—Ingemar Stenmark
Women—Hanni Wenzel
1980 U.S. Alpine Champions
Downhill—Dale Irwin, Canada
Women—Cindy Nelson, Lutsen, Minn.
Slalom—Steve Mahre, White Pass, Wash.
Women—Christin Cooper, Sun Valley, Ida.
Giant Slalom—Peter Monod, Canada
Women—Christin Cooper
1980 U.S. Nordic Champions
Combined—Walter Malmquist, Post Mills, Vt.
Jumping—Walter Malmquist
Men's Cross-Country
15km.—Bill Koch, Putney, Vt.
30km.—Stan Dunklee, Barton, Vt.
50km.—Jim Galanes, Brattleboro, Vt.
Women's Cross-Country
7.5km.—Alison Owen-Spencer, McCall, Idaho
10km.—Alison Owen-Spencer
20km.—Betsy Haines, Anchorage, Alaska
1980 NCAA Champions
Slalom—Bret Williams, N. Michigan
Giant Slalom—John Teague, Vermont
Jumping—Jorn Stromberg, Wyoming
Cross-Country—Pal Sjulstad, Vermont
Team—Vermont
1980 AIAW (Women's) Nat'l Champions
Slalom—Mary Seaton, Vermont
Giant Slalom—Rebecca Smith, Wyoming
Alpine Combined—Mary Seaton
Cross-Country (7.5 km.)—Sissel Bjerkewas, Wyoming
Cross-Country Relay—Middlebury
Team—Middlebury

SOFTBALL

1980 Amateur Softball Ass'n Champions
Men's Fast Pitch—Peterbilt Western, Seattle, Wash.
Women—Raybestos Brakettes, Stratford, Conn.
Men's Slow Pitch—Campbell's Carpets, Concord, Calif.
Women—Howard Rubi-otts, Graham, N.C.

OTHER SPORTS (Cont.)

Industrial Slow Pitch—Sikorsky, Stamford, Ct.
Women—Provident Vets, Chattanooga, Tenn.
16" Slow Pitch—Whips, Chicago, Ill.
Men's Class A Fast Pitch—S. H. Good, Narvon, Pa.
Women—Astros, San Diego, Calif.
Men's Class A Slow Pitch—Houston Wreckers, Houston, Tex.
Women—Encore, Brandywine, Md.
Men's Class A Industrial Slow Pitch—Local 761, Louisville, Ky.
Men's Church Slow Pitch—West End Baptist, Houston, Tex.
Women—Rock Creek Methodist, Snow Camp, N.C.
Modified Fast Pitch—Cadillacs, Atlanta, Ga.
1980 AIAW Div. I—Utah State
Div. II—Emporia State (Kans.)
Div. III—Calif. State-Chico

SQUASH RACQUETS (1980)
U.S. Association Champions
Men's Singles—Michael Desaulniers, Montreal, Que.
Women's Singles—Barbara Maltby, Philadelphia, Pa.
Men's Doubles—John Bottger, Philadelphia, Pa.-Gilbert Mateer, Cleveland, Ohio
Women's Doubles—Joyce Davenport, King of Prussia, Pa.-Carol Thesieres, Broomall, Pa.
Mixed Doubles—Ralph Howe, Cold Spring Harbor, N.Y.-Joyce Davenport
Intercollegiate—Michael Desaulniers, Harvard
North American Open—Sharif Khan, Toronto, Ont.
U.S. Pro Singles—Sharif Khan

TABLE TENNIS
1979 World Champions
Singles—Seiji Ono, Japan
Women—Ge Xinai, P.R. China
Doubles—Dragutin Surbek-Anton Stipancic, Yugoslavia
Women—Zhang Li-Zhang Deying, P.R. China
Mixed Doubles—Ge Xinai-Liang Geliang, P.R. China
Men's Team—Hungary
Women's Team—P.R. China
1979 U.S. National Champions
Singles—Attila Malek, Las Vegas, Nev.
Women—He-Ja Lee, Las Vegas, Nev.
Doubles—Danny and Ricky Seemiller, Pittsburgh, Pa.
Women—Angelita Sistrunk, Cardiff, Calif.-He-Ja Lee
Mixed Doubles—Eric Boggan, Merrick, N.Y.-Kasia Dawidowicz, Aurora, Colo.
1980 U.S. Open Champions
Singles—Mikael Appelgren, Sweden
Women—Kayoko Kawahigashi, Japan
Doubles—Danny and Ricky Seemiller, Pittsburgh, Pa.

Women—Kyung-Ja Kim—Soo-Ja Lee, South Korea
Mixed Doubles—Si-Hung Yoo—Soo-Ja Lee, South Korea
Men's Team—United States
Women's Team—South Korea

TRAMPOLINE & TUMBLING
1979 Nat'l AAU Champions
MEN
Trampoline—Stuart Ransom, Lafayette, La.
Tumbling—Dickie Bivins, Newark, N.J.
Double Mini-Tramp—Stuart Ransom
Synchronized Trampoline—Ron Seibert, Geneva, Ohio and Stuart Ransom
WOMEN
Trampoline—Karen Kernan, Livingston, N.J.
Tumbling—Nancy Quattrocki, Chicago
Double Mini-Tramp—Karen Kernan
Synchronized Trampoline—Mary Rugheimer, Bozeman, Mont. and Karen Kernan

VOLLEYBALL (1980)
U.S. Volleyball Ass'n Champions
Men's Open—Olympic Club, San Francisco, Calif.
Women's Open—ANVA, Fountain Valley, Calif.
Men's Senior—Outrigger Canoe Club, Honolulu, Hawaii
Women's Senior—South Bay Spoilers, Hermosa Beach, Calif.
NCAA—Southern California
AIAW Div. I—Hawaii (1979)
Div II—Hawaii-Hilo (1979)
Div. III—Azusa Pacific (1979)

WATER POLO (1979)
World Cup—Hungary
Women—United States
NCAA Champion—California-Santa Barbara
Nat'l AAU Outdoor Champions
Men—Newport (Calif.)
Women—Seal Beach (Calif.)
Nat'l AAU Indoor Champions
Women—Long Beach, California

WATER SKIING (1980)
U.S. Open Champions
Overall—Carl Roberge, Orlando, Fla.
Women—Karin Roberge, Orlando, Fla.
Slalom—Carl Roberge
Women—Cyndi Benzel, Newberry Springs, Calif.
Tricks—Cory Pickos, Eagle Lake, Fla.
Women—Karin Roberge
Jumping—Bob La Point, Castro Valley, Calif.
Women—Linda Giddens, Eastman, Ga.
Masters Tournament
Overall—Mike Hazelwood, London, England
Women—Karin Roberge, Orlando, Fla.
Slalom—Bob La Point, Castro Valley, Calif.

Women—Karin Roberge
Tricks—Cory Pickos, Eagle Lake, Fla.
Women—Ana Marie Carrasco, Venezuela
Jumping—Sammy Duvall, Greenville, S.C.
Women—Linda Giddens, Eastman, Ga.

WEIGHTLIFTING
1979 World Champions
52 kilos—Kanybek Osmonoliev, USSR
56 kilos—Anton Kodjabasev, Bulgaria
60 kilos—Marek Seweryn, Poland
67½ kilos—Yanko Roussev, Bulgaria
75 kilos—Roberto Urrutia, Cuba
82½ kilos—Yurik Vardanian, USSR
90 kilos—Gennadi Bessonov, USSR
100 kilos—Pavel Sirchin
110 kilos—Sergei Arakelov, USSR
Over 110 kilos—Sultan Rakhmanov, USSR
1980 Nat'l AAU Champions
52 kilos—Leslie Sewall
56 kilos—Joe Widdel
60 kilos—Phil Sanderson
67½ kilos—Carl Schake
75 kilos—Myron Davis
82½ kilos—Michael Karchut
90 kilos—Jim Curry, Jr.
100 kilos—Brian Derwin
110 kilos—Mark Cameron
Over 110 kilos—Tom Stock
1980 Collegiate Champions
60 kilos—Jon Schrott, NYU-Dentistry
67½ kilos—Mark Level, DeVry Inst. of Tech.
75 kilos—Frank Pinheiro, Santa Clara
82½ kilos—Rod Shirley, Auburn
90 kilos—Steve Abo, Eastern Illinois
100 kilos—Bud Charnigo, Wayne St.
110 kilos—Herb Bohm, Georgetown
Over 110 kilos—Bob Crist, Old Dominion
Team—Penn State

YACHTING
1980 America's Cup—US (Freedom; Dennis Conner, skipper) over Australia (Australia; Jim Hardy, skipper) 4-1
1979 Yachtsman of the Year—Ted Turner, Atlanta, Ga.
1979 Yachtswoman of the Year—Nell Taylor, San Francisco, Calif.
1980 U.S. Yacht Racing Union Champions
Mallory Cup—David Ullman, Newport Beach, Calif.
Adams Trophy—Judy McKinney, Bay St. Louis, Miss.
Sears Cup—John Shadden, Long Beach, Calif.
O'Day Trophy—Shawn Kempton, Ocean Gate, N.J.
Prince of Wales Trophy—Jonathan McKee, Seattle, Wash.
Bemis Cup—Mike Funsch, St. Petersburg, Fla.
Smythe Cup—Brian Ledbetter, San Diego, Calif.
1980 Little America's Cup—United States (Patient Lady V)
North American Intercollegiate Sailing Champion—Boston University

POPULARITY OF DOG BREEDS

SOURCE: American Kennel Club

1979 Rank	Breed	1979 Registrations	1978 Rank	1979 Rank	Breed	1979 Registrations	1978 Rank
1.	Poodle	94,950	1	16.	Siberian Husky	19,876	15
2.	Doberman Pinscher	80,363	2	17.	Pekingese	17,992	17
3.	Cocker Spaniel	65,658	4	18.	Brittany Spaniel	17,038	18
4.	German Shepherd	57,683	3	19.	Pomeranian	16,184	20
5.	Labrador Retriever	46,077	5	20.	Shih Tzu	16,042	22
6.	Golden Retriever	38,060	7	21.	Chihuahua	15,512	21
7.	Beagle	35,374	6	22.	Great Dane	15,322	19
8.	Dachshund	32,777	8	23.	Basset Hound	14,930	23
9.	Miniature Schnauzer	32,666	9	24.	Boxer	13,250	24
10.	Shetland Sheepdog	25,943	11	25.	Old English Sheepdog	12,018	25
11.	Lhasa Apso	22,714	12	26.	Chow Chow	11,739	29
12.	Yorkshire Terrier	22,458	14	27.	Boston Terrier	11,125	27
13.	Collie	21,210	13	28.	German Shorthaired Pointer	10,579	26
14.	Irish Setter	20,912	10	29.	Samoyed	8,653	30
15.	English Springer Spaniel	20,071	16	30.	St. Bernard	7,444	28

OBITUARIES

Abrams, Harry N., 74, publisher and pioneer in the popularizing of quality art books; in New York City, November 25, 1979.

Adamson, Joy, 69, Austrian-born naturalist, artist, and internationally known African wildlife conservationist and acclaimed author of *Born Free*, the story of Elsa, the orphaned lioness cub; killed in the bush in northern Kenya, January 3, 1980.

Allon, Yigal, 61, respected Israeli military and political leader and a hero of the 1948 struggle for independence; near Kfar Tabor (Afula), Israel, February 29, 1980.

Amin, Hafizullah, 54?, President of Afghanistan, a position he assumed after he overthrew Pres. Noor Mohammed Taraki in September 1979; executed after a coup toppled him from power with the aid of Soviet troops; in Kabul, Afghanistan, December 27, 1979.

Ardrey, Robert, 71, author best known for his controversial books on anthropology and the evolution of human behavior *(African Genesis, The Territorial Imperative, The Social Contract,* and *The Hunting Hypothesis)* in which he argued that man resembles a "risen ape" whose aggressive and territorial drives lead to conflict and war; in Kalk Bay, near Capetown, South Africa, January 14, 1980.

Arzner, Dorothy, 82, Hollywood's lone woman film director in the 1930s and 40s, noted for her treatment of women in unconventional roles; in La Quinta, Calif., October 1, 1979.

Barthes, Roland, 64, French writer, social critic and philosopher and one of the most influential French intellectuals of the postwar era, whose varied interests were reflected by his works on popular cultural phenomena, classical literary figures and the science of semiology — the study of signs and symbols; in Paris, France, March 25, 1980.

Bateson, Gregory, 76, English-born anthropologist, author and philosopher. He was noted for his studies of primitive cultures in collaboration with the late Margaret Mead, his first wife, and for his contributions to psychological theory, especially his "double-bind" hypothesis explaining schizophrenia; in San Francisco, Calif., July 4, 1980.

Beaton, Cecil, 76, distinguished British designer and portrait photographer of notables in the worlds of art, fashion and film; he won acclaim for his costume and set design for stage and screen and Academy Awards for his work in "Gigi" (1959) and "My Fair Lady" (1965); near Salisbury, England, January 18, 1980.

Belmont, Eleanor Robson, 100, wife of millionaire financier August Belmont and *grand dame* of New York's high society and patron of the arts; in New York City, October 24, 1979.

Bishop, Elizabeth, 68, Pulitzer Prize-winning American poet (for *North and South* and *A Cold Spring,* 1956) best known for her evocations of the natural world; in Boston, Mass., October 6, 1979.

Blondell, Joan, 70, Hollywood and television actress known for playing the brash, wisecracking blonde in the 1930s and 40s; in Santa Monica, Calif., December 25, 1979.

Boulanger, Nadia, 92, French pianist and conductor considered one of the most influential teachers of musical composition of the 20th century; in Paris, France, October 22, 1979.

Bowman, Lee, 64, veteran stage and screen actor who starred with Jean Arthur in "The Impatient Years" and with Rita Hayworth in "Cover Girl," and played the writer-detective Ellery Queen on television in the 1950s; in Brentwood, Calif., December 25, 1979.

Britton, Barbara, 59, film and television actress of the 1940s and 50s ("Till We Meet Again," "Champagne for Caesar" and "The Virginian"), who starred as the better half of the amateur detective team in the TV series "Mr. and Mrs. North"; in New York City, January 17, 1980.

Bullard, Sir Edward, 72, British geophysicist who pioneered the study of continental drift, the theory that the continents were once part of one giant landmass that broke up and drifted apart over the ages; in La Jolla, Calif., April 3, 1980.

Burpee, David, 87, horticulturalist and seed merchant who ran the world's largest mail-order seed company. As head of W. Atlee Burpee Company, he developed hundreds of varieties of flowers and vegetables; in Doylestown, Pa., June 24, 1980.

Capp, Al (Alfred Gerald Caplin), 70, cartoonist and creator of the satirical comic strip *Li'l Abner,* whose characters lampooned the foibles of the high and mighty for 43 years; in Cambridge, Mass., November 5, 1979.

Champion, Gower, 61, Broadway stage choreographer and musical director of such hits as *Hello, Dolly!, Carnival* and *Bye, Bye Birdie.* He died just hours before the Broadway opening of his latest show, *42nd Street;* in New York City, August 25, 1980.

Clurman, Harold, 78, theatre director, producer and one of the preeminent figures of the American stage. As founder of the Group Theater in 1931, he trained such actors as Lee Strasberg, Stella Adler, Franchot Tone and John Garfield, first produced young playwrights like Clifford Odets, Irwin Shaw and William Saroyan, and introduced Stanislavsky's Method acting to this country. He was drama critic for *New Republic* and *The Nation* magazines; his books include *Fervent Years* and *The Divine Pastime,* perhaps the most authoritative volume on the American theatre; in New York City, September 9, 1980.

Cochran, Jacqueline, 70 or 74, pioneer aviatrix and businesswoman who was the first woman to fly faster than the speed of sound, setting more than 200 aviation records in her career, also serving as director of the Women's Air Force Service Pilots during World War II; in Indio, Calif., August 10, 1980.

Coughlin, Rev. Charles E., 88, the "radio priest" who, in his weekly radio sermons during the 1930s, preached against what he saw as the multiple evils of Communism, Wall Street, labor unions, Jews and the New Deal. His public pronouncements were finally halted by the Roman Catholic hierarchy in 1942; in Bloomfield Hills, Mich., October 27, 1979.

Crittenberger, Lt. Gen. (ret.) Willis D., 89, commander of Allied troops in Italy during World War II who led his IV Corps in 326 days of continuous fighting, and accepted the surrender of the German Ligurian Army on April 29, 1945, signaling the collapse of Nazi resistance; in Chevy Chase, Md., August 4, 1980.

Davis, Benny, 84, popular vaudeville performer and songwriter who wrote or collaborated on hundreds of popular songs, including "Carolina Moon," "Margie," and "Baby Face"; in North Miami, Fla., December 20, 1979.

de Gaulle, Yvonne, 79, widow of French President Charles de Gaulle, known as "Aunt Yvonne" to an entire generation and respected for her modest, retiring demeanor; in Paris, November 8, 1979.

Delaunay, Sonia, 94, French artist considered a major influence on fashion design during the 1920s, and one of the last survivors of the pre-World War I Paris art world; in Paris, France, December 5, 1979.

Deutsch, Adolph, 82, Hollywood film composer who won Academy Awards for the scores of "Annie Get Your Gun," "Seven Brides for Seven Brothers," and "Oklahoma!"; in Palm Desert, Calif., January 1, 1980.

Devers, Gen. Jacob L., 92, combat commander during World War II who helped develop American armored units into an effective, modernized fighting force, and helped to direct the North African and Italian campaigns and to plan the Normandy invasion; in Washington, D.C., October 15, 1979.

Dionne, Oliva, 76, father of the world-famous Dionne quintuplets, five identical sisters who were the first-known survivors of such a multiple birth. Dionne and his wife, Elzire, shunned most of the publicity surrounding the quints, who became a tourist attraction following their birth in 1934; in North Bay, Ontario, November 15, 1979.

Dornberger, Walter, 84, German missile expert who headed the Nazi V-2 rocket bomb project during World War II, directing the firing of over 1,000 V-weapons on London and its suburbs in the last years of the war. He later became an advisor to the U.S. Air Force and worked for military industries in the United States; in West Germany, June 28 or 29, 1980.

Douglas, Helen Gahagan, 79, actress, concert singer and Democratic Representative from California (1944-50) known for her support of liberal causes. Her unsuccessful 1950 Senate campaign against Republican challenger Richard Nixon — who charged her with alleged Communist sympathies — brought Nixon to national prominence and ended her political career; in New York City, June 28, 1980.

Douglas, William O., 81, colorful and controversial Associate Justice of the U.S. Supreme Court for over 36 years; he was its most consistent champion of individual liberties and the right to dissent, surviving two unsuccessful impeachment efforts; in Washington, D.C., January 19, 1980.

Durante, Jimmy, 86, comedian whose trademarks included his bulbous nose, raspy voice, battered hat, and fractured diction, which along with his honky-tonk-style piano playing, won him fame as part of the song-and-dance team of Clayton, Jackson and Durante in the 1920s. He later appeared on Broadway, movies, radio and television; in Santa Monica, Calif., January 29, 1980.

Dutschke, Rudi, 39, German leader of radical student revolts in Western Europe during the 1960s, known as "Red Rudi," for his fiery oratory; in Aarhus, Denmark, December 24, 1979.

Dvorak, Anne, 67, film actress known for her somber beauty and dramatic intensity; acclaimed for her 1932 debut opposite Paul Muni in "Scarface," she was often cast as the hard-luck victim of circumstances; in Honolulu, Hawaii, December 10, 1979.

Eisenhower, Mamie Doud, 82, widow of Dwight D. Eisenhower, 34th President of the United States and Supreme Allied Commander in Europe during World War II. One of the nation's most consistently admired women, she was a self-effacing helpmate to "Ike"; in Washington, D.C., November 11, 1979.

Farb, Peter, 50, naturalist, linguist, anthropologist and author of over 20 books on popular studies of the natural and human sciences, including *Man's Rise to Civilization, Humankind* and *Wordplay: What Happens When People Talk;* in Boston, Mass., April 18, 1980.

Finletter, Thomas K., 86, former Secretary of the Air Force (1950-53) who later served as U.S. envoy to NATO (1961-65); he was chief author of a 1948 government report, "Survival in the Air Age," which led to expansion of U.S. military air power; in New York City, April 24, 1980.

Fitzsimmons, Freddie, 78, knuckleball pitcher with the New York Giants and Brooklyn Dodgers whose major league career spanned 19 years; in Yucca Valley, Calif., November 18, 1979.

Fogarty, Anne, 60, award-winning fashion designer who helped create, and later became identified with, a distinctively American look in the 1950s; in New York City, January 15, 1980.

Frank, Otto, 91, father of Anne Frank, the teenage girl whose recollections of two years of hiding from the Nazis. *The Diary of Anne Frank,* became a world-renowned document of the Holocaust. He was the only member of that Dutch Jewish family of four to survive; in Basel, Switzerland, August 19, 1980.

Froman, Jane, 72, big band singer and film actress of the 1930s and 1940s whose dramatic comeback from injuries suffered in a 1943 plane crash was portrayed in the 1952 film "With a Song in My Heart"; in Columbia, Mo., April 22, 1980.

Fromm, Erich, 79, German-born psychoanalyst, social philosopher, humanist, and author *(Escape From Freedom,* 1941, *The Sane Society,* 1955, and *The Art of Loving,* 1956). Trained as a Freudian analyst, he later developed his own theories on human behavior stressing economic and social factors as well as unconscious drives; in Muralto, Switzerland, March 18, 1980.

Gandhi, Sanjay, 33, son of India's Prime Minister Indira Gandhi, considered by many her heir apparent. He played a controversial role in Madame Gandhi's 1977 administration, subsequently facing numerous criminal charges for abuse of power, but with her return to power in 1979 he won a seat in Parliament; in a small-plane crash near New Delhi, India, June 23, 1980.

Gardiner, Reginald, 77, British-born character actor who appeared in nearly 100 feature films, including "The Great Dictator" — with Charlie Chaplin — "The Man Who Came to Dinner" and "Mr. Hobbs Takes a Vacation"; in Westwood, Calif., July 7, 1980.

Gottlieb, Eddie, 81, basketball Hall of Fame member and a founder of the National Basketball Association; he was coach and owner of the Philadelphia Warriors when that team won the first NBA championship in the 1946-47 season; in Philadelphia, Pa., December 7, 1979.

Grenfell, Joyce, 69, lanky, toothy British actress-comedienne known for her hilarious one-woman shows and film roles as dotty, English spinsters, best remembered for her role in "The Belles of St. Trinian's"; in London, England, November 30, 1979.

Griffith, Hugh, 67, Welsh character actor of stage and screen, acclaimed for playing Shakespeare and modern drama alike; he was nominated for a Tony Award in 1957 for his acting in *Look Homeward, Angel,* and won an Oscar for his supporting role in "Ben-Hur" in 1959, though he is remembered best for his portrayal of the lusty Squire Western in the 1963 film, "Tom Jones"; in London, England, May 14, 1980.

Guggenheim, Peggy, 81, expatriate American millionairesse and art patron who owned one of the foremost private collections of modern art; she was also known for her Bohemian lifestyle and her numerous romantic liaisons with such luminaries as playwright Samuel Beckett and surrealist painter Max Ernst; near Venice, Italy, December 23, 1979.

Guston, Philip, 68, leading American painter of the Abstract Expressionist school whose light, gestural paintings of the 1950s influenced a generation of younger painters; in Woodstock, N.Y., June 7, 1980.

Hall, Jon, 66, actor best known for his he-man roles in romantic films with exotic locales. He first won fame in the 1937 South Seas epic, "The Hurricane," opposite Dorothy Lamour, and later starred in the popular television series "Ramar of the Jungle" in the 1950s; in North Hollywood, Calif., December 13, 1979.

Hall, Paul, 65, a vice-president of the AFL-CIO, founder and former president of the Seafarers International Union, remembered for his battle against Communists in the maritime unions in the 1930s and the growth of organized crime on the docks in the 1940s and 50s; in New York City, June 22, 1980.

Harris, Jed, 79, Broadway producer and director with a reputation as a flamboyant theatrical genius, who during his 30-year career directed some of Broadway's most distinguished plays, including *Our Town, The Front Page, The Royal Family* and *The Heiress;* in New York City, November 15, 1979.

Harris, Roy, 81, distinguished American composer often called the Walt Whitman of American music. A prolific composer, he wrote sixteen symphonies and over 185 other major works; in Santa Monica, Calif., October 1, 1979.

Hatta, Mohammed, 78, a leader of Indonesia's struggle for independence from Dutch colonial rule, who with Sukarno, declared that nation a republic in 1945, later serving as vice-president (1945-56) and premier until he split with Sukarno over the latter's increasing leftism; in Jakarta, Indonesia, March 14, 1980.

Haymes, Dick, 61, popular singer of the big band era and film star of the 1940s. Known as a soloist with the Tommy Dorsey, Harry James and Benny Goodman bands, he also appeared in the films "One Touch of Venus" and "State Fair"; in Los Angeles, Calif., March 28, 1980.

Hébert F. Edward, 78, Democratic Congressman from Louisiana (1941-77) and chairman of the House Armed Services Committee (1971-75), known for his support of military spending and opposition to civil rights and welfare programs; in New Orleans, La., December 29, 1979.

Heindorf, Ray, 71, Hollywood film score composer and head of Warner Bros. studio music department who won three Academy Awards for his music for "Yankee Doodle Dandy," "This Is the Army," and "The Music Man"; in Los Angeles, Calif., February 2, 1980.

Hitchcock, Alfred, 80, British-born film director and a master of cinematic technique and screen suspense. Hitchcock's *forte* was the psychological thriller. His early British career included "The Man Who Knew Too Much," "The 39 Steps," and "The Lady Vanishes." He moved to Hollywood in 1939, winning an Academy Award for "Rebecca" in 1940. His best-remembered films include "Suspicion," "Notorious," "Rear Window," "North by Northwest," "The Birds" and "Psycho"; in Los Angeles, Calif., April 29, 1980.

Hoge, Gen. William M., 85, director of Army engineers who built the 1,500-mile Alaska Highway in 1942, and commander of the combat unit that captured the Remagen bridge over the Rhine River in 1945; in Fort Leavenworth, Kansas, October 30, 1979.

Iturbi, José, 84, Spanish-born concert pianist, conductor and actor who popularized classical music in his many appearances in Hollywood musicals of the 1940s, including "A Song to Remember," "Music for the Millions" and "Anchors Away"; in Los Angeles, Calif., June 28, 1980.

Jackson, Eddie, 84, gravel-voiced vaudeville singer, dancer and comedian and Jimmy Durante's sidekick, known for his rendition of such old favorites as "Bill Bailey, Won't You Please Come Home," and his high-stepping performance of the Strut; in Los Angeles, Calif., July 16, 1980.

Janssen, David, 49, television and film actor best known for his role as Dr. Richard Kimble in "The Fugitive" (1963-67), the tough-but-decent "Richard Diamond, Private Detective" (1957-60) and the middle-aged, sarcastic detective in the 1974 series "Harry O"; in Malibu, Calif., February 13, 1980.

Jones, Howard Mumford, 88, Pulitzer Prize-winning historian of American culture and professor of English and humanities at Harvard University (1932-62), who wrote over 30 books, including *O Strange New World* (1965) and *The Age of Energy* (1971); in Cambridge, Mass., May 11, 1980.

Kaminska, Ida, 80, Polish actress, director and producer who headed Poland's Jewish State Theatre until her emigration to the U.S. in 1968. She was acclaimed for her performance as the elderly Jewish shopkeeper during the Nazi occupation in Jan Kadar's 1966 Czech film, "The Shop on Main Street"; in New York City, May 21, 1980.

Khama, Sir Seretse, 59, President of Botswana since that south-central African nation won its independence in 1966. A hereditary tribal chief, he was exiled in 1950 for marrying a white British woman, but later led his moderate Bechuanaland Democratic party to power. A racial moderate, he sought to conciliate in the Rhodesian conflict; in Gaborone, Botswana, July 13, 1980.

Kim Jae Kyu, 54, former director of Korea's Central Intelligence Agency convicted of assassinating South Korean President Park Chung Hee on October 26, 1979; executed along with four convicted co-conspirators; in Seoul, South Korea, May 24, 1980.

Kokoschka, Oscar, 93, Austrian painter and a leading figure in the Expressionist movement in pre-World War I Vienna; in Montreux, Switzerland, February 22, 1980.

Kostelanetz, Andre, 78, conductor of popular and symphonic music and one of the best-known conductors of his time, bringing classical and modern composers to a mass audience; in Port-au-Prince, Haiti, January 13, 1980.

Kronenberger, Louis, 75, drama critic for *Time* magazine (1938-61), essayist and author of several books on 18th-century England *(Kings and Desperate Men, Marlborough's Duchess,* and *The Extraordinary Mr. Wilkes);* in Brookline, Mass., April 30, 1980.

Kuter, Gen. Lawrence S., 74, architect of the U.S. Air Force who was instrumental in planning the strategic use of air power in World War II, serving as staff officer and field commander in both North Africa and the South Pacific and becoming commander-in-chief of the North American Defense Command in 1959; in Naples, Fla., November 30, 1980.

Larabee, Leonard W., 82, professor emeritus of history at Yale University, authority on American colonial history and editor of *The Papers of Benjamin Franklin;* in Northford, Conn., May 5, 1980.

Lauck, Chester A., 78, radio personality who portrayed Lum on "Lum 'n' Abner," the long-running series (1931-55) about the hillbilly proprietors of Pine Ridge, Ark.; in Hot Springs, Ark., February 21, 1980.

Lesser, Sol, 90, prolific film pioneer who produced the 1930s "Tarzan" series and won an Academy Award for the documentary "Kon-Tiki"; a theatre owner, in the 1950s he also introduced the idea of a ratings system for movies which later developed into the system of *G, PG, R* and *X* ratings of today; in Hollywood, Calif., September 19, 1980.

Levenson, Sam, 68, author and television humorist who won fame in the 1940s and 1950s for his poignant and shrewd stories of immigrant family life on New York's Lower East Side; in Brooklyn, N.Y., August 27, 1980.

Libby, William F., 71, chemist who won the Nobel Prize in 1960 for developing the carbon-14 dating method, an "atomic calendar" to measure radiation levels in archaeological artifacts or geological material, proving the age of an object accurately to within 120 years; in Los Angeles, Calif., September 8, 1980.

Loden, Barbara, 48, actress of stage and screen who won a Tony Award for her 1964 role as the ill-fated wife in Arthur Miller's *After the Fall,* directed by Elia Kazan — whom she later married — and was one of the first women to write, direct and star in her own feature film, the critically acclaimed 1970 movie, "Wanda"; in New York City, September 5, 1980.

Longworth, Alice Roosevelt, 96, eldest daughter and last surviving child of Theodore Roosevelt. Widow of Nicholas Longworth, Republican Speaker of the House (1925-31), "Washington's other Monument" was the reigning queen of Washington society for nearly 80 years, renowned for her charm, beauty, sharp wit and influential political connections; in Washington, D.C., February 20, 1980.

Lowenstein, Allard K., 51, former U.S. Representative from New York (1968-70) who led the "Dump Johnson" movement within the Democratic party in 1968 and was a leading civil rights attorney and anti-war activist; shot dead in his New York City law office, March 14, 1980.

Malik, Yakov A., 73, Soviet diplomat, deputy Foreign Minister and envoy to the United Nations (1948-52, 1968-76). As Soviet delegate on the Security Council in 1950, his absence at the outbreak of the Korean War allowed the UN to send troops to South Korea, while his later proposal for a Korean truce helped lead to a cease-fire in 1953; he also played a key role in negotiating the end of the Berlin Blockade in 1949; in Moscow, USSR, February 11, 1980.

Mantovani, Annunzio Paolo, 74, Italian-born conductor who achieved fame in the 1950s with his arrangements of light, string-filled popular music; in Tunbridge Wells, Kent, England, March 29, 1980.

Marquand, Richard ("Rube"), 90, major league pitcher who set a modern baseball record by winning 19 consecutive games for the New York Giants, and was elected to the Hall of Fame in 1971; in Baltimore, Md., June 1, 1980.

Martin, Strother, 61, veteran character actor who played the grizzled sourdough in Hollywood Westerns for over 30 years, best remembered as the prison warden in the 1967 film, "Cool Hand Luke"; in Thousand Oaks, Calif., August 1, 1980.

Marx, Herbert ("Zeppo"), 78, last surviving member of the madcap Marx Brothers clan. The youngest and considered the best looking of the comedy team, he was cast as the straight man in their first five films, but left the group in 1933; in Palm Springs, Calif., November 30, 1979.

Mauchly, John W., 72, co-inventor in 1946 with J. Pesper Eckert, Jr., of the Electronic Numerical Integrator and Computer (ENIAC), the first electronic brain, later developing the BINAC and UNIVAC I computers in 1949 and 1950; near his home in Ambler, Pa., January 8, 1980.

McDonnell, James S., Jr., 81, chairman of McDonnell Douglas Corp., and a pioneer in the aviation industry who built that company into the world's largest aerospace manufacturer; in Ladue, Mo., near St. Louis, August 22, 1980.

Meany, George, 85, president of the AFL-CIO (1955-79) and principal spokesman for organized labor for over 25 years. He was the main architect of the 1955 merger of the craft-oriented AFL with Walter Reuther's Congress of Industrial Organizations, becoming its first president, a post he held until his retirement in November 1979; in Washington, D.C., January 10, 1980.

Milestone, Lewis, 84, Hollywood film director who made the tough transition from silent to "talkie" movies (winning an Academy Award in both mediums— for "Two Arabian Knights" in 1929 and "All Quiet on the Western Front" in 1930) and went on to make "Rain," "The Front Page," "The General Died at Dawn," "Of Mice and Men" and "A Walk in the Sun"; in Los Angeles, Calif., September 25, 1980.

Miller, Henry, 88, American novelist famed for his often controversial works, including the acclaimed 1934 *Tropic of Cancer,* which was banned from the United States until 1964. An advocate of absolute individualism who thumbed his nose at established conventions, his works include *Tropic of Capricorn,* the *Sexus* trilogy, *The Colossus of Maroussi* and *The Air-Conditioned Nightmare;* in Pacific Palisades, Calif., June 7, 1980.

Monroney, A. S. Mike, 77, former Democratic Representative and Senator from Oklahoma (1939-50, 1950-68) who spearheaded reform measures to streamline Congressional operations and introduced the measure creating the Federal Aviation Administration in 1956; in Rockville, Md., February 13, 1980.

Morgenthau, Hans J., 76, author, teacher and political scientist and one of the nation's most respected foreign policy analysts, who stressed in his many books *(Scientific Man Vs. Power Politics, Politics Among Nations: The Struggle for Power and Peace,* and *A New Foreign Policy for the United States)* national interest rather than world opinion in policy-making; in New York City, July 19, 1980.

Muñoz Marin, Luis, 82, first elected governor of Puerto Rico (1948-64) and architect of the island's modern economic development; an advocate of economic association with the U.S., he helped found the Popular Democratic party in 1938; his Operation Bootstrap is credited with developing backward rural areas and diversifying the island's economy; in San Juan, Puerto Rico, April 30, 1980.

Muse, Charles, 89, pioneer black film and stage actor; he appeared in the second talking picture ever made in 1929, and was the first black actor to star in a film ("Way Down South" in 1932); he is best remembered for his role as Jim in the 1931 "Huckleberry Finn"; in Perris, Calif., October 13, 1979.

Mussolini, Rachele Guidi, 89, widow of Italian dictator Benito Mussolini, *"Donna Rachele"* shunned the limelight during her husband's reign, earning her a popularity which outlasted his fall and subsequent assassination; at her home near Forli, Italy, October 30, 1979.

Narayan, Jaya Prakash ("J. P."), 76, India's elder statesman and disciple of Mohandas K. Gandhi and played a leading role in India's struggle for independence in the 1930s and 1940s. He also led the opposition against Prime Minister Indira Gandhi's authoritarian rule in 1977; in Patna, India, October 8, 1979.

Nenni, Pietro, 88, Italian Socialist leader whose political career spanned seven decades. An unrelenting foe of Fascism, he headed the Socialist party for 20 years (1949-69), helped to found the postwar Italian Republic, and served as its first deputy prime minister and foreign minister. Reversing his pro-Communist views after the Soviet invasion of Hungary in 1956, he allied his party with the Christian Democrats in a coalition that ruled Italy until 1976; in Rome, Italy, January 1, 1980.

Nielsen, Arthur C., 83, founder and chairman of A. C. Nielsen Co., the world's largest marketing research company who developed the Nielsen rating system for radio and television in 1950; in Chicago, Ill., June 1, 1980.

Nugent, Elliott, 83, Broadway stage and Hollywood film actor, writer and producer. His best-known works include *The Male Animal,* co-authored with James Thurber; *The Voice of the Turtle,* in which he starred; and *The Seven Year Itch,* which he co-produced, and two books, *Of Cheat and Charmer* and *Events Leading Up to the Comedy;* in New York City, August 9, 1980.

Oberon, Merle, 68, film actress known for her striking beauty remembered for her portrayal of Cathy in the classic "Wuthering Heights." She rose to fame with her 1932 portrayal of Anne Boleyn in "The Private Life of Henry VIII" and went on to star in over 30 films; in Malibu, Calif., November 22, 1979.

Ohira, Masayoshi, 70, Prime Minister of Japan since 1978 and leader of the ruling Liberal Democratic party who served in previous administrations as Foregin Minister (1972-74) and Finance Minister (1976-78); in Tokyo, Japan, June 12, 1980.

Okun, Arthur, 51, economist and member of the Council of Economic Advisers during the Kennedy and Johnson Administrations (1961-62, 1964-68). Respected for his contributions to economic forecasting, analysis and policy making, he is best known for "Okun's Law," his formulation of the inverse relation between a society's economic growth and the level of employment; in Washington, D.C., March 23, 1980.

Owens, Jesse, 66, black American track and field star; considered among the greatest athletes in the history of track competition, he won four gold medals at Berlin's 1936 Summer Olympic Games in the face of Adolph Hitler's boasts of "Aryan superiority"; in Tucson, Ariz., March 31, 1980.

Pahlavi, Mohammed Reza, 60, the deposed Shah of Iran, who ruled for nearly 40 years until he was overthrown by a rebellion led by the Ayatollah Khomeini; in a military hospital outside of Cairo, Egypt, July 27, 1980.

Pal, George, 72, Hungarian-born film director and producer considered the father of the science-fiction movies of the 1950s, who directed such classics as "Destination Moon," "When Worlds Collide," "The Time Machine," and "The War of the Worlds" — which all won Academy Awards for special effects; in Beverly Hills, Calif., May 2, 1980.

Park Chung Hee, 62, President of South Korea for over 18 years; his rule was marked by controversy and had become increasingly dictatorial since constitutional changes he promulgated in 1972 gave him vast powers; assassinated by Korean C.I.A. chief Kim Jae Kyu in an abortive coup attempt; in Seoul, South Korea, October 26, 1979.

Patrick, Gail, 69, film actress of the 1930s and 1940s ("My Man Godfrey," "Death Takes a Holiday") who gave up that career to become a televison producer; her most notable success was as producer of the popular courtroom drama series, "Perry Mason"; in Hollywood, Calif., July 6, 1980.

Patterson, William A., 80, pioneer in commercial aviation and president of United Airlines (1938-66) who built United into the world's largest commercial airline. He is credited with introducing female flight attendants and a guaranteed monthly salary for pilots; in Glenview, Ill., June 13, 1980.

Payne-Gaposhkin, Dr. Cecelia, 79, one of the foremost women in modern astronomy and the first woman to receive tenured professorship at Harvard University; she and her Russian-born husband, Sergei I. Gaposhkin, became interna-

tionally known in the 1930s for their studies of novae; in Cambridge, Mass., December 6, 1979.

Perelman, Sidney Joseph (S.J.), 75, one of America's leading humorists whose dazzling wordplay, spoofery and zaniness in his books (*Westward Ha!*), plays (*One Touch of Venus*), and screenplays ("Monkey Business," "Horsefeathers" and the Oscar-winning "Around the World in Eighty Days"), helped to shape American humor for 40 years; in New York City, October 17, 1979.

Piaget, Jean, 84, Swiss psychologist known for his pioneering studies of child development (*Six Psychological Studies, The Psychology of the Child);* Piaget's main thesis posited the idea that children learn by discrete stages related to age, and that each child is a significant agent in that process, relating the interaction of biological functions and the structure of childhood environment; in Geneva, Switzerland, September 17, 1980.

Porter, Katherine Anne, 90, author acclaimed for her short stories and novelettes (*Noon Wine, Pale Horse, Pale Rider* and *Flowering Judas*) and her immensely popular 1962 novel, *Ship of Fools;* her 1965 anthology, *The Collected Short Stories of Katherine Anne Porter,* won both the Pulitzer Prize and The National Book Award; in Silver Springs, Md., September 18, 1980.

Powers, Lt. Col. John A. ("Shorty"), 57, NASA spokesman and "voice of the astronauts" who recounted the early U.S. space flights over radio and television during the 1960s, coining the expression "everything is A-O.K."; in Phoenix, Ariz., January 1, 1980.

Reed, Stanley Forman, 95, retired Justice of the U.S. Supreme Court (1938-57) and the longest-lived member of the Court in history; he was noted for his support of New Deal legislation and civil rights; in Huntington (L.I.), N.Y., April 3, 1980.

Renaldo, Duncan, 76, Romanian-born actor who appeared in many of Hollywood's early films ("The Bridge at San Luis Rey," "Trader Horn") but was best known for his portrayal of the Cisco Kid in that popular 1950s television series; in Santa Barbara, Calif., September 3, 1980.

Rhine, Dr. Joseph B., 84, psychologist and pioneer in the field of psychical research whose experiments in clairvoyance, mental telepathy and other phenomena at Duke University helped to open the entirely new field of parapsychological research, and led to his theory of extrasensory perception; his published works include *Extra-Sensory Perception* and *New Frontiers of the Mind;* in Hillsborough, N.C., February 20, 1980.

Rodgers, Richard, 77, composer and lyricist of Broadway musicals for more than 60 years; with his two principal lyricists, Lorenz Hart and Oscar Hammerstein II, helped to make the American musical into an art form of stature, combining music, dance and drama into an integrated plot, with many of the 39 musicals he wrote—including *Pal Joey, Oklahoma!, Carousel, South Pacific, The King and I, Flower Drum Song* and *The Sound of Music*—becoming hallmarks of the American musical theatre; in New York City, December 30, 1979.

Romero, Archbishop Oscar Arnulfo, 62, Roman Catholic cleric of El Salvador who was the main spokesman for human rights in his nation; assassinated by an unknown gunman while officiating at a memorial mass; in San Salvador, El Salvador, March 24, 1980.

Ronne, Finne, 80, Norwegian-born polar explorer who accompanied Adm. Richard E. Byrd on his second Antarctic expedition in 1923 and traveled a record 3,600 miles by dogsled and skis to chart the South Pole; in Bethesda, Md., January 12, 1980.

Roosevelt, Archibald B., 85, last surviving son of President Theodore Roosevelt, a decorated soldier in both World Wars who was also a leading conservationist and a Wall Street investment banker; in Hobe Sound, Fla., October 13, 1979.

Roth, Lillian, 69, actress and singer who wrote of her struggle against alcoholism and mental illness in her 1954 autobiography, *I'll Cry Tomorrow* (which became a successful motion picture) and later made a dramatic comeback in musicals and nightclubs; in New York City, May 12, 1980.

Rovere, Richard H., 64, author and political correspondent for *New Yorker* magazine for 30 years and one of the nation's most respected political commentators, acclaimed for his books *Senator Joe McCarthy* (1959) and *Affairs of State: The Eisenhower Years* (1956); in Poughkeepsie, N.Y., November 23, 1979.

Rukeyser, Muriel, 66, poet of social protest for over four decades; her *Collected Poems* (1979) demonstrated her talents as a dramatic and lyric poet whose verse displayed rare originality and power; in New York City, February 12, 1980.

Sartre, Jean-Paul, 74, French Existentialist philosopher and writer whose work profoundly influenced the social consciousness of the post-World War II generation; in his over 20 major published works *(No Exit, Nausea, Being and Nothingness, The Words* and *Situations)* he expressed the widespread disillusionment in postwar Europe, influencing the development of the anti-novel, New Wave Cinema and the philosophical notion of modern man's anguished consciousness and moral doubt; he was awarded the Nobel Prize in literature in 1964, which he declined; in Paris, France, April 15, 1980.

Schary, Dore, 74, Hollywood screenwriter and film producer. He produced or oversaw production of over 250 films for the MGM and RKO studios ("An American in Paris," "The Blackboard Jungle," "Tea and Sympathy," "Seven Brides for Seven Brothers") and wrote over 40 screenplays, winning the Academy Award in 1938 for "Boys' Town," and won a Tony Award in 1958 for his Broadway play, *Sunrise at Campobello;* in New York City, July 7, 1980.

Sellers, Peter, 54, British comedian famous for his zany film roles, farcical humor and masterful impersonations; best known for his portrayal of Inspector Jacques Clouseau, the bumbling French detective in "The Pink Panther" and four movie sequels and received an Academy Award nomination for best actor in 1979 as Chance in "Being There"; in London, England, July 24, 1980.

Sheen, Archbishop Fulton A., 84, Roman Catholic clergyman, radio and television evangelist and author who became one of the best-known religious figures in America. The first regular radio preacher with his program "The Catholic Hour" in the 1930s, he repeated his success on television in the 1950s with his popular "Life is Worth Living" series; in New York City, December 9, 1979.

Sherrill, Bishop Henry Knox, 89, Presiding Bishop of the Episcopal Church (1948-58) and one of the most influential church leaders of the postwar era who helped turn American Protestantism toward a more ecumenical outlook; in Boxford, Mass., May 11, 1980.

Short, Dewey, 82, Republican Congressman from Missouri (1928-30, 1935-57) and Assistant Secretary of the Army (1957-61); a conservative legislator, he opposed lend-lease aid to Britain and all New Deal programs except Social Security; in Washington, D.C., November 19, 1979.

Silverheels, Jay, 62, Mohawk Indian actor who portrayed Tonto in "The Lone Ranger" television series (1949-57); he appeared in over 20 feature films, including "Broken Arrow," "Battle at Apache Pass" and "Walk the Proud Land," and founded the Indian Actors Institute; in Woodland Hills, Calif., March 5, 1980.

Simpson, Gen. William H., 92, World War II commander who led the Ninth Army during its thrust into the heart of Germany in 1944-45, and was known for his unusual tactical knowledge and sound military judgment; in San Antonio, Tex., August 15, 1980.

Smith, Charlie, 137?, reportedly the oldest U.S. citizen. Born in what is present-day Liberia, he claimed to have been kidnapped into slavery in 1854 and sold in New Orleans to a Texas rancher, Charles Smith (who gave him his name), and to have ridden with Jesse James; in Bartow, Fla., October 5, 1979.

Snow, C. P. (Charles Percy), 74, British novelist, playwright, social critic and scientist best known for his examination of power and conscience in a managerial society and the artificial gap between the arts and science, symbolizing what he termed "the two cultures"; his best-known work is the 11-part series of novels, *Strangers and Brothers,* which traced the social and political changes in English society since 1920; in London, England, July 1, 1980.

Somoza, Anastasio Debayle, 54, former ruler of Nicaragua until his overthrow in July 1979 by popular revolutionary forces led by the Sandinist National Liberation Front. He was the American-educated scion of the U.S.-installed family dynasty that ruled the Central American country since 1936; assassinated in Asunción, Paraguay, September 17, 1980.

Spaulding, William E., 81, former president and chairman of Houghton Mifflin Company, who joined the firm as a salesman in 1919 and rose to head that prestigious Boston publishing house from 1957 until his retirement in 1966; in Woburn, Mass., December 19, 1979.

Stein, Dr. William H., 68, biochemist at New York's Rockefeller University who shared the 1972 Nobel Prize in Chemistry for his studies on the chemical structure of a pancreatic enzyme; in New York City, February 2, 1980.

Stewart, Donald O., 85, American parodist and screenwriter who won the Academy Award for co-writing the 1940 classic, "Philadelphia Story." Blacklisted by Hollywood in 1950, he later moved to London; his other film credits include "The Prisoner of Zenda," "Keeper of the Flame," "The Barretts of Wimpole Street," and "Dinner at Eight"; in London, England, August 2, 1980.

Still, Clyfford, 75, painter considered to be one of the foremost American artists of the 20th century. A founder of the Abstract Expressionist school of painting, he believed in the development of a unique American art form free of European artistic traditions; in Baltimore, Md., June 23, 1980.

Stone, Millburn, 75, veteran character actor who played supporting roles in over 250 Hollywood features, but was best known for his portrayal of Doc Adams in the long-running TV series "Gunsmoke" from 1955 until 1975; in La Jolla, Calif., June 12, 1980.

Sutherland, Graham, 76, British neo-Romantic landscapist and portrait painter best known for his penetrating portraits of such great personages as W. Somerset Maugham, Helena Rubinstein and Winston Churchill; in London, England, February 17, 1980.

Taraki, Noor Mohammed, 62, former President of Afghanistan and leader of the pro-Moscow People's Democratic party before resigning for "health" reasons September 17; reported shot in a power struggle, his death from an 'unspecified illness' was later confirmed; in Kabul, Afghanistan, October 9, 1979.

Tarnower, Dr. Herman, 69, physician and author of the best-selling diet book *The Complete Scarsdale Medical Diet* who founded the Scarsdale Medical Group, where he developed the high-protein, low-fat diet promising weight loss through chemical interactions between foods rather than reduced quantities; shot in his secluded Purchase, N.Y., home, March 10, 1980.

Templer, Field Marshall Sir Gerald W. R., 81, British army officer who as High Commissioner of Malaya directed the defeat of Communist guerrillas in the early 1950s; in London, England, October 25, 1979.

Tiomkin, Dimitri, 85, Russian-born composer of over 160 Hollywood film scores, four of which — "High Noon," "The Alamo," "The Old Man and the Sea," and "The High and the Mighty" — won him Academy Awards; his work was characterized by soaring Tchaikovskian melodies evocative of his native Russia; in London, England, November 11, 1979.

Tito, Josip Broz, 87, President of Yugoslavia since 1946; leader of Partisan resistance to Nazi occupation during World War II, Marshall Tito shook the foundations of the Communist world in 1948 when he broke with Stalin and pursued his own independent policies, later helping to found the nonaligned movement; in the Slovenian city of Ljubljana, Yugoslavia, May 4, 1980.

Tynan, Kenneth, 53, one of Britain's foremost drama critics known for his erudite and often controversial opinions; as critic for the London *Observer* and manager of Britain's National Theatre, he exerted a lasting influence on the English stage, championing the new realism in drama of the 1950s and early 1960s, and was well known in America for his reviews and show business profiles for *New Yorker* magazine, and as the co-author of the erotic Broadway hit, *Oh, Calcutta!;* in Santa Monica, Calif., July 26, 1980.

Van, Bobby (Robert King), 47, actor, comedian and song-and-dance man; he starred in nine films, including "The Affairs of Dobie Gillis," "Small Town Girl" and "Kiss Me Kate," and appeared in a dozen Broadway musicals, including the 1971 revival of *No, No, Nanette;* in Los Angeles, Calif., July 31, 1980.

Vance, Nina, 65, founder of Houston's Alley Theatre, and who as manager and producing director since 1947 turned that intially modest playhouse into one of the nation's foremost resident repertory theatres; in Houston, Tex., February 18, 1980.

Velikovsky, Immanuel, 84, Russian-born psychoanalyst and author of *Worlds in Collision;* his iconoclastic theories of cosmic evolution combined Freudian psychology with a vast knowledge of biblical and mythic lore to develop the hypothesis that cataclysmic changes in the solar system were caused by colliding planets; in Princeton, N.J., November 17, 1979.

Wagner, Winifred, 82, British-born daughter-in-law of German composer Richard Wagner who directed the Bayreuth Opera Festival of Wagner's works (1930-44), and was an outspoken admirer of Adolph Hitler; at Ueberlingen, on Lake Constance, West Germany, March 5, 1980.

Wright, James, 52, Pulitzer Prize-winning poet (*The Branch Will Not Break,* 1963, *Collected Poems,* 1971) whose simple, lyrical verse about poverty and growing up in his native Middle West achieved a sustained intensity that won him acclaim as one of the finest contemporary poets in the English language; in New York City, March 25, 1980.

Yahya Khan, Agha Mohammed, 63, military ruler of Pakistan (1969-71). A protégé of then-Pres. Mohammed Ayub Khan who abdicated in 1969 due to political unrest, he quelled rioting and instituted reforms, including the nation's first free elections, but was ousted after East Pakistan seceded to become Bangladesh in 1971; in Rawalpindi, Pakistan, August 8, 1980.

Zanuck, Darryl F., 77, film producer and studio executive with 20th Century-Fox and one of the most influential figures in the motion picture industry; the last of the flamboyant movie moguls, he created screen stars and produced many film classics, and won Academy Awards for "How Green Was My Valley" (1941) and "Gentlemen's Agreement" (1947), with some of his best-remembered films including "Forty-Second Street," "Little Caesar," "The Grapes of Wrath," "All About Eve," and "The Longest Day"; in Palm Springs, Calif., December 22, 1979.

A